7

8

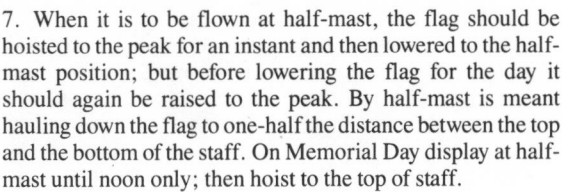

7. When it is to be flown at half-mast, the flag should be hoisted to the peak for an instant and then lowered to the half-mast position; but before lowering the flag for the day it should again be raised to the peak. By half-mast is meant hauling down the flag to one-half the distance between the top and the bottom of the staff. On Memorial Day display at half-mast until noon only; then hoist to the top of staff.

8. When the flag is displayed in a manner other than by being flown from a staff, it should be displayed flat, whether indoors or out. When displayed either horizontally or vertically against a wall, the union should be uppermost and to the flag's own right, that is, to the observer's left. When displayed in a window it should be displayed in the same way, that is, with the union or blue field to the left of the observer in the street. When festoons, rosettes or drapings are desired, bunting of blue, white and red should be used, but never the flag.

9

9. When carried in a procession with another flag or flags, the Stars and Stripes should be either on the marching right, or when there is a line of other flags, in front of the center of that line.

10

11

10. When a number of flags of states or cities or pennants of societies are grouped and displayed from staffs with our National flag, the latter should be at the center and at the highest point of the group.

11. When the flags of two or more nations are displayed they should be flown from separate staffs of the same height, and the flags should be of approximately equal size. International usage forbids the display of the flag of one nation above that of another nation in time of peace.

WEBSTER'S ⊕⊕⊕⊕⊕⊕ NEW REFERENCE LIBRARY

1989 Edition

A NELSON/REGENCY PUBLICATION

THOMAS NELSON PUBLISHERS

Nashville

Published in Nashville, Tennessee by Thomas Nelson, Inc. and distributed in canada by Lawson Falle, Ltd., Cambridge, Ontario.

Printed in the United States of America.

Library of Congress Cataloging-in-Publication Data

Webster's new reference library.

   Collection of reprints from various dictionaries and encyclopedias.
   1. Encyclopedias and dictionaries. I. Thomas Nelson Publishers.
AE6.W43   1988   030   88-9942
ISBN 0-8407-5067-6

2 3 4 5 - 91 90 89

CONTENTS

Quick Reference to Essential Information

CREDITS

Webster's Dictionary of Modern English
- Copyright © 1987 Atlantic Book Publishing. No part of this book may be reproduced or transmitted in any form or by any means, electronic or mechanical, including photocopying and recording, or by any information storage or retrieval system, except as may be expressly permitted by the 1979 Copyright Act, or with prior written permission from both Atlantic Book Publishing and Thomas Nelson, Inc.

Words that are believed to be registered trademarks have been checked with authoritative sources. No investigation has been made of common-law trademark rights in any word, because such investigation is impracticable. Words that are known to have current registrations are shown with an initial capital and are also identified as trademarks. The inclusion of any word in this Dictionary is not, however, an expression of the publishers' opinion as to whether or not it is subject to proprietary rights. Indeed, no definition in this Dictionary is to be regarded as affecting the validity of any trademark.

Word Division Dictionary
- based on *Word Division: Supplement to Government Printing Office Style Manual.* Washington, D.C.: U.S. Government Printing Office, 1976.

German/English Dictionary
- based on *German: A Guide to the Spoken Language.* Washington, D.C.: U.S. Government Printing Office, 1975.

Spanish/English Dictionary
- based on *Spanish: A Guide to the Spoken Language.* Washington, D.C.: U.S. Government Printing Office, 1975.

French/English Dictionary
- based on *French: A Guide to the Spoken Language.* Washington, D.C.: U.S. Government Printing Office, 1974.

Medical Dictionary
- based on *Nelson's New Compact Medical Dictionary,* copyright 1978 Thomas Nelson Inc., Publishers.
- illustrations from the *Quick Reference Handbook Set—Basic Health Care and Emergency Aid,* copyright 1984 Thomas Nelson Inc., Publishers and *Medical Aid Encyclopedia for the Home,* copyright 1965, 1972 Stravon Publishers, Inc.

Heart Terms Dictionary
- based on *A Handbook of Heart Terms,* U.S. Department of Health, Education, and Welfare. Washington, D.C.: U.S. Government Printing Office, 1978.

Bible Dictionary
- based on *Nelson's New Compact Illustrated Bible Dictionary,* copyright 1978 Thomas Nelson Inc., Publishers, copyright 1964 Nelson-National.

Roget's Thesaurus
- based on *Nelson's New Compact Roget's Thesaurus,* copyright 1978 Thomas Nelson Inc., Publishers.

Dictionary of Occupational Titles
- based on *Dictionary of Occupational Titles,* U.S. Department of Labor. Washington, D.C.: U.S. Government Printing Office, 1982.

Where to Write for Vital Records
- based on *Where to Write for Vital Records: Births, Deaths, Marriages, and Divorces,* U.S. Department of Health and Human Services. Washington, D.C.: U.S. Government Printing Office, 1982.

World History
- based on *World History Made Simple* copyrighted by Doubleday & Company, Inc., and used by special permission.

The Shuttle Era
- based on *NASA Facts–(100),* National Aeronautics and Space Administration. Washington, D.C.: U.S. Government Printing Office, 1980; *NASA Facts–(127),* National Aeronautics and Space Administration. Washington, D.C.: U.S. Government Printing Office, 1981.

Business Terms Dictionary

Biographical Dictionary

Communication Through Language

Special Compositions

Reading Skills

American History

States and Countries

Math Formulas/Equivalent Measures

Metric Conversions

Four-Year Public Colleges and Universities

Computer Science

Computer Glossary

Music Glossary

Space Glossary
- based on the *Quick Reference Handbook Set—Basic Knowledge and Modern Technology,* copyright 1984 Thomas Nelson, Inc., Publishers; *The Complete Reference Handbook,* copyright 1964 Stravon Publishers; the *Quick Reference Encyclopedia,* copyright 1976 Thomas Nelson, Inc., Publishers; and *The Quick Reference Handbook of Basic Knowledge,* copyright 1979, revised 1982 by Thomas Nelson, Inc., Publishers.

Endsheets (front)
- based on *How To Respect and Display OUR FLAG.* Washington, D.C.: U.S. Government Printing Office, 1973.

Endsheets (back)
- based on *The Great Seal of the United States.* Washington, D.C.: U.S. Government Printing Office, 1980.

PICTURE ACKNOWLEDGMENTS

Air France, 1188; Alaska Travel Division, 1137; American Airlines, 1138(t), 1139, 1146, 1151(t), 1159, 1162, 1172; Arab Information Center, 1207, 1229, 1262; Argosy Gallery, 761, 774, 782; Austrian News and Information Bureau, 1190; Bahamas News Bureau, 1191; BOAC, 988, 989, 990, 1210, 1211, 1217, 1227, 1231, 1232, 1239, 1256, 1258; Brazilian Government Trade Bureau, 1194; British European Airways, 995, 1214, 1222, 1261; Canadian Consulate General, 1197(b), 1198; Chamber of Commerce, 1165; Civic Promotion Division of Commerce of South Bend, 1147; Colorado Department of Public Relations, 1140; Connecticut Development Committee, 1141; Consul General of Chile, 1201; Cram, George F., Co., Inc., maps following page 886; Delaware State Development Department, 1142; Irish Tourist Office, 1005; Italian Tourist Office, 1001, Japan Air Lines, 997; Japan Tourist Association, 1224; Library of Congress, 756, 1088, 1090, Miami Bureau, 1143; Montana Highway Commission, 1157(t); NASA, 1108(t), 1109, 1110; National Park Service, 1138(b), 1144(t), 1144(b), 1145, 1149, 1151(b), 1153, 1155, 1164, 1166, 1171, 1175; Nebraska Game Commission, 1157(b); Netherlands Information Service, 1235; New York-Historical Society, 1084, 1085(t), 1085(b), North Carolina Department of Conservation and Development, 1163; Northwest Orient Airlines, 1169(r); Ontario Department Travel and Publicity, 1197(t); Oregon State Highway Department, 1167; Philippine Tourist and Travel Association, 1240; Rhode Island Development Council, 1169(l); Scandinavian Travel Commission, 1206; "Sni-Yan," 1241; Spanish Ministry of Tourism, 1007; Standard Oil Company, (N.J.), 1150; TWA Airlines, 1152, 1158, 1161; Union Pacific Railroad, 1178; United Nations, 1208, 1219, 1228, 1276(t), 1276(b), 1278, 1279, 1280, 1281, 1283; United Press International, 751, 753, 759, 760, 763, 771, 773, 775, 776, 788, 790, 795, 801, 804, 1108(b.r.), 1113, 1202, 1263, 1264, 1265; U.S. Army, 1096, 1097(t), 1097(b); U.S. Department of State, endsheets (back), 1098, 1099, 1101, 1102, 1103, 1105, 1106, 1107, 1112(t), 1112(b)U.S. Marine Corps, endsheets (front); U.S. Navy, 1083, 1094(b), 1094(t), 1100; Utah Tourist and Publicity Council, 1173(t); Vermont Development Department, 1173(b); Venezuela Ministry of Tourism, 1259; Vilko Zuber, 1003; Virginia Department of Conservation and Economic Development, 1174; West Virginia Department of Commerce, 1176; Wisconsin Conservation Department, 1177

The letters in the parentheses next to the page numbers stand for the following: t = top of page; m = middle of page; b = bottom of page; r = right side of page; l = left side of page; b.l. = bottom left of page; b.r. = bottom right of page; m.l. = middle left of page; m.r. = middle right of page; t.l. = top left of page; t.r. = top right of page.

CONTRIBUTORS AND EDITORS

Titles given below are as of the time of the author's contributions to the book.

Elvin Abeles
Former Associate Editor
Collier's Encyclopedia

Frank Alweis
Director, Honor School
James Monroe High School

Roy O. Billett
Professor of Education, Emeritus
Boston University

Lawrence D. Brennan
Professor, Business Writing and
Speaking
New York University

Oscar Cargill
Head, Department of English
Graduate School of Arts and Science
New York University

Bradford Chambers
Author, Editor, *Home Library Press*

Allan Danzig
Assistant Professor,
Department of English
Lafayette College

Mary F. Doherty
Librarian
The Metropolitan Museum of Art

John R. Dugan
Professor of Law
New York Law School

David Ebner
Author, *Elementary Algebra*

Willard Hutcheon
Lecturer, Philosophy
The City University of New York

William Jaber
Geographer

Steele M. Kennedy
Former Education Editor and
Director of Information Services
New Jersey State
Department of Education

Jerome E. Leavitt
Professor of Education
Portland State College

Paul B. Panes
Director, The Reading Institute
New York University

Thomas N. Pappas
Dean of Academic Administration
Warner Pacific College

Ernest D. Partridge, Jr.
Assistant Professor of Philosophy
and Education
Paterson State College

Mario Pel
Professor, Romance Languages,
Emeritus
Columbia University

Louis M. Pell
Chairman, Department of English
Columbia Grammar School

Gary Ruse
Vice-President, First National Bank
Gordon, Nebraska

Robert M. Segal
Editor
Stravon Educational Press

Clem Stein, Jr.
Merchandising Supervisor
Sears, Roebuck and Co.

Mitchell Weiner
Director
College Entrance Tutoring Service

Consulting Editors
Calvin D. Linton, Ph.D
Dean, Columbian College
The George Washington University

Edward H. Litchfield, Ph.D.
Chancellor
University of Pittsburgh

Editor
Stephen Hines

Editorial Assistants
Teri Keas Mitchell

Updating Editors
Alice C. Ewing
John A. Fribley
Ramona Richards
Peggy Guy

v

DICTIONARY SECTION

- Webster's Dictionary of Modern English
- Word Division Dictionary
- German/English Dictionary
- Spanish/English Dictionary
- French/English Dictionary
- Medical Dictionary
- Heart Terms Dictionary
- Bible Dictionary
- Business Terms Dictionary
- Biographical Dictionary
- Roget's Thesaurus
- Dictionary of Occupational Titles

WEBSTER'S DICTIONARY OF MODERN ENGLISH

About the Dictionary

This Dictionary has been specially prepared to provide concise but wide-ranging coverage of the contemporary American language in a format that is convenient to handle and easy to use. The coverage is up-to-date and the emphasis is on today's written and spoken language. With 50,000 entries and over 61,000 definitions, it is a compact all-purpose dictionary that will serve the everyday needs of most people.

All main entries are given in a single alphabetical listing that includes abbreviations, foreign words, and prefixes and suffixes (combining forms). These last enable the reader to construct for himself the meanings of hundreds of additional terms.

Within each main entry different meanings are clearly marked off from ea other by bold numbers. After the meanings of the main headword co *derived words* as subentries in smaller bold type, in alphabetical order. Th in turn are followed by *compounds* (if any) and then by *phrases*, again alphabetical order within the paragraph.

Words that can function as more than one part of speech are printed out o once, the change of function being shown by a second (or subsequent) part-speech label, thus: **advance** (əd'väns) *vt.* **1.** bring forward ... —*vi.* **5.** forward ... —*n.* **7.** forward movement ... —*a.* **11.** (*with* of) ahead in time ... the case of very short, simple entries, two parts of speech may be combin thus: **agape** (ə'gāp) *a./adv.* open-mouthed ... Spelling of verb part indicated as necessary in brackets after the definition of the verb, thus: **jab** stab abruptly (-**bb**-).

Pronunciation Key

Stress is shown by placing a mark, ', *before* the syllable that carries the main stress in a word.

Most of the letters used in the phonetic respelling are pronounced in the usual way; but the following special symbols are also used.

ə   as in *above* (ə'buv), *butter* ('butər), *nation* ('nāshən), *bird* (bərd)

ä   as in *calm* (käm), *father* ('fädhər), *farm* (färm)

ā   as in *fate* (fāt), *neigh* (nā), *explain* (ik'splān)

ē   as in *keep* (kēp), *deceive* (di'sēv), *machine* (mə'shēn)

ī   as in *thigh* (thī), *dive* (dīv), *guy* (gī)

ö   as in *all* (öl), *crawl* (kröl), *drawer* ('dröər)

ō   as in *code* (kōd), *road* (rōd), *beau* (bō)

ŏŏ   as in *book* (bŏŏk), *woman* ('wŏŏmən), *should* (shŏŏd)

ōō   as in *food* (fōōd), *queue* (kyōō), *you* (yōō)

ow   as in *bow* (bow), *out* (owt), *bough* (bow)

oi   as in *boy* (boi), *oil* (oil), *employment* (im'ploimənt)

zh   as in *pleasure* ('plezhər), *invasion* (in'vāzhən)

dh   as in *those* (dhōz), *bathe* (bādh), *lather* ('ladhər)

Foreign Sounds

ü   as in French *tu* (tü)

œ   as in French *deux* (dœ)

˜   is placed over a nasal vowel, as in French *bon* (bõ), *vin* (vĕ), *sans* (sã), *un* (œ̃)

kh   as in Scots *loch* (lokh), German *Buch* (bōōkh)

Note: Though the pronunciaton of words like *where, why, whe* shown with a simple 'w' sound, many speakers use 'hw' in such wor Both versions are equally acceptable and such variation is to assumed in these cases.

Abbreviations used in the Dictionary

a.	adjective	*conj.*	conjunction	It.	Italian	*pers.*	person	*sing.*	singular
abbrev.	abbreviation	cu.	cubic	k	kilogram(s)	pert.	pertaining	*sl.*	slang
Acc.	Accounting	*dial.*	dialect	km	kilometer(s)	*Philos.*	Philosophy	*Sociol.*	Sociology
adv.	adverb	*dim.*	diminutive	l	liter(s)	*Phonet.*	Phonetics	Sp.	Spanish
Aeron.	Aeronautics	E	East	Lat.	Latin	*Photog.*	Photography	sq.	square
Afr.	Africa(n)	*Eccles.*	Ecclesiastical	*Linguis.*	Linguistics	*Phys.*	Physics	*St.Ex.*	Stock Exchang
Amer.	America(n)	*Ecol.*	Ecology	lit.	literally	*Phys. Ed.*	Physical Education	*sup.*	superlative
Anat.	Anatomy	*Econ.*	Economics	*Lit.*	Literary, Literature	*Physiol.*	Physiology	*Surg.*	Surgery
Archaeol.	Archaeology	*Educ.*	Education	m	meter(s)	*pl.*	plural	*Surv.*	Surveying
Archit.	Architecture	*eg*	for example	*masc.*	masculine	*pl.n.*	plural noun	*Theat.*	Theater
Arith.	Arithmetic	*Elec.*	Electricity	*Math.*	Mathematics	*Poet.*	Poetic, Poetry	*Trig.*	Trigonometry
Astrol.	Astrology	*Electron.*	Electronics	*Mech.*	Mechanics	*Pol.*	Politics	*T.V.*	Television
Astron.	Astronomy	*esp.*	especially	*Med.*	Medicine	*poss.*	possessive	*usu.*	usually
Aust.	Australia(n)	*fem.*	feminine	*Met.*	Meteorology	*pp.*	past participle	*v.*	verb
Biochem.	Biochemistry	*fig.*	figuratively	*Mil.*	Military	*prep.*	preposition	*v.aux.*	auxiliary verb
Biol.	Biology	*Fin.*	Finance	*Min.*	Mineralogy	*pres.t.*	present tense	*Vet.*	Veterinary Medi
Bot.	Botany	Fr.	French	mm	millimeter(s)	*Print.*	Printing	*vi.*	intransitive ver
Brit.	Britain, British	g	gram(s)	*Mus.*	Music	*pron.*	pronoun	*vt.*	transitive verb
Bus.	Business	*Geog.*	Geography	*Myth.*	Mythology	*pr.p.*	present participle	W	West
Canad.	Canada, Canadian	Ger.	German	*n.*	noun	*Psych.*	Psychiatry	*Zool.*	Zoology
cent.	century	Gr.	Greek	N	North	*Psychoanal.*	Psychoanalysis		
Ch.	Church	*Gram.*	Grammar	*Naut.*	Nautical	*Psychol.*	Psychology		
Chem.	Chemistry	*Her.*	Heraldry	*N.T.*	New Testament	*pt.*	past tense		
Cine.	Cinema	*Hist.*	History	N.Z.	New Zealand	*Rad.*	Radio		
Class. lit.	Classical literature	*Hort.*	Horticulture	*obs.*	obsolete, obsolescent	*R.C.*	Roman Catholic		
Class. myth.	Classical mythology	*ie*	that is	*offens.*	offensive	*refl.*	reflexive	**A**	**Australian**
cm.	centimeter(s)	*impers.*	impersonal	oft.	often	*Rel.*	Religion	**C**	**Canadian**
Comm.	Commerce	*ind.*	indicative	orig.	originally	S	South	**NZ**	**New Zealand**
comp.	comparative	*inf.*	informal	*O.T.*	Old Testament	*Sc.*	Science	**SA**	**South African**
Comp.	Computers	*interj.*	interjection	*Pathol.*	Pathology	*Scot.*	Scottish	**UK**	**United Kingdom**

Aa

a *or* **A** (ā) *n.* **1.** first letter of English alphabet **2.** any of several speech sounds represented by this letter, as in *take, calm* **3.** first in series, *esp.* grade rating student as superior (*pl.* **a's, A's,** *or* **As**) **—from A to Z** from start to finish

a (ə; *emphatic* ā) *a.* the indefinite article meaning one; *an* is used before vowel sounds, and sometimes before unaccented syllables beginning with *h* aspirate

a. **1.** absent **2.** acceleration **3.** acre **4.** adult **5.** alto **6.** ampere **7.** anode **8.** answer **9.** ante **10.** anterior **11.** are **12.** area **13.** author

A 1. *Mus.* sixth note of scale of C major; major or minor key having this note as its tonic **2.** human blood type of ABO group **3.** ampere **4.** absolute (temperature) **5.** area **6.** alto **7.** (*comb. form*) atomic, as in *A-bomb, A-plant*

Å angstrom unit

a-¹ *or before vowel* **an-** (*comb. form*) not; without; opposite to, as in *atonal, asocial, anesthetic*

a-² (*comb. form*) **1.** on; in; toward, as in *aground, aback* **2.** in state of, as in *afloat, asleep*

A1, A-1, *or* **A-one** ('ā'wun) *a.* **1.** physically fit **2.** *inf.* first-class; excellent **3.** (of vessel) in first-class condition

AA 1. Alcoholics Anonymous **2.** anti-aircraft **3.** associate in arts

A.A.A. American Automobile Association

aardvark

A and M agricultural and mechanical

aardvark ('ärdvärk) *n.* nocturnal Afr. mammal which feeds on termites

Aaron ('arən) *n.* in O.T., brother and helper of Moses **—Aaron's beard** popular name for many wild plants including rose of Sharon, ivy-leaved toadflax, meadowsweet *etc.* **—Aaron's rod** popular name for goldenrod, great mullein

AAU Amateur Athletic Union of the United States

ab about

AB Alberta

A.B. 1. able-bodied seaman **2.** bachelor of arts

ab-¹ (*comb. form*) away from; opposite to, as in *abnormal*

ab-² (*comb. form*) cgs unit of measurement in electromagnetic system, as in *abampere, abvolt*

ABA American Bar Association

aback (ə'bak) *adv.* **—taken aback** startled

abacus ('abəkəs) *n.* **1.** counting device of frame holding rods designating place value on which counters are free to slide **2.** flat tablet at top of column

abaft (ə'baft) *Naut. adv./a.* **1.** toward rear of vessel **—prep. 2.** behind; aft of

abalone (abə'lōni) *n.* edible gastropod, yielding mother-of-pearl

abandon (ə'bandən) *vt.* **1.** desert **2.** give up altogether **—n. 3.** freedom from inhibitions *etc.* **—a'bandoned** *a.* **1.** deserted, forsaken **2.** uninhibited **3.** wicked **—a'bandonment** *n.*

abase (ə'bās) *vt.* humiliate, degrade **—a'basement** *n.*

abash (ə'bash) *vt.* (*usu. passive*) confuse, make ashamed **—a'bashment** *n.*

abate (ə'bāt) *v.* make or become less, diminish **—a'batement** *n.*

abattoir ('abətwär) *n.* slaughterhouse

abbé ('abā) *n.* **1.** French abbot **2.** title used in addressing any French cleric

abbess ('abis) *n.* head of convent

abbey ('abi) *n.* **1.** dwelling place of community of monks or nuns **2.** church of an abbey

abbot ('abət) *n.* head of abbey or monastery **—'abbacy** *n.* office, rights of abbot

abbr. *or* **abbrev.** abbreviation

abbreviate (ə'brēviāt) *vt.* shorten, abridge **—abbrevi'ation** *n.* shortened form of word or phrase

ABC¹ *n.* **1.** (*oft. pl.*) the alphabet **2.** (*pl.*) rudiments of subject

ABC² **1.** American Bowling Congress **2.** American Broadcasting Company

Abdias (ab'dīəs) *n. Bible* Obadiah in the Douay Version of the O.T.

abdicate ('abdikāt) *v.* formally give up (throne *etc.*) **—abdi'cation** *n.*

abdomen ('abdəmən) *n.* **1.** in mammals, cavity of the body between chest and pelvis **2.** in arthropods, the hindmost part of the body **—abdominal** (ab'dominəl) *a.*

abduct (ab'dukt) *vt.* carry off, kidnap **—ab'duction** *n.*

abeam (ə'bēm) *adv.* abreast, in line

Abel ('ābəl) *n.* in O.T., son of Adam and Eve, murdered by his brother Cain

abele (ə'bēl, 'ābəl) *n.* white poplar

Aberdeen Angus ('abərdēn 'anggəs) breed of cattle, *orig.* Scottish

aberration (abə'rāshən) *n.* **1.** failure of lens or mirror to form exact image **2.** deviation from what is normal **3.** flaw **4.** lapse **—a'berrant** *a.*

abet (ə'bet) *vt.* assist, encourage, *esp.* in doing wrong (-tt-) **—a'bettor** *or* **a'better** *n.*

abeyance (ə'bāəns) *n.* condition of not being in use or action

abhor (əb'hör) *vt.* dislike strongly, loathe **—ab'horrence** *n.* **—ab'horrent** *a.* hateful

abide (ə'bīd) *vt.* **1.** endure, put up with **—vi. 2.** *obs.* stay, reside (a'**bode** *or* a'**bided** *pt./pp.,* a'**biding** *pr.p.*) **—abide by** obey

ability (ə'biliti) *n.* **1.** competence, power **2.** talent

ab initio (ab i'nishiō) *Lat.* from the start

abject ('abjekt) *a.* **1.** humiliated, wretched **2.** despicable **—ab'jection** *or* **'abjectness** *n.*

abjure (əb'jōōr) *vt.* give up by oath, renounce **—abju'ration** *n.*

ablation (ab'lāshən) *n.* **1.** surgical removal of organ or part **2.** *Astrophysics* melting or wearing away of part **3.** wearing away of rock or glacier

ablative ('ablətiv) *n.* case in (*esp.* Latin) nouns indicating source, agent, instrument of action

ablaut ('ablowt) *n.* vowel change within word, indicating modification of use, *eg sink, sank, sunk*

ablaze (ə'blāz) *a.* burning

able ('ābəl) *a.* capable, competent **—'ably** *adv.* **—able-bodied** *a.* **—able-bodied seaman** seaman, *esp.* one in merchant navy, trained in certain skills (*also* **able seaman**)

-able (*a. comb. form*) **1.** capable of or deserving of (being acted upon as indicated), as in *enjoyable, washable* **2.** inclined to; able to; causing, as in *comfortable, variable* **—-ably** (*adv. comb. form*) **—-ability** (*n. comb. form*)

ablution (ə'blōōshən) *n.* (*usu. pl.*) act of washing (oneself)

ABM antiballistic missile

Abnaki (ab'näki) *n.* confederacy of more than 20 Amerindian tribes of Maine, New Brunswick and southern Quebec, including Penobscots, Malacites and Passamaquoddies

abnegate ('abnigāt) *vt.* give up, renounce **—abne'gation** *n.*

abnormal (ab'nörməl) *a.* **1.** irregular **2.** not usual or typical **3.** freakish, odd **—abnor'mality** *n.* **—ab'normally** *adv.*

aboard (ə'börd) *adv.* on board, on ship, train or aircraft

abode (ə'bōd) *n.* **1.** home **2.** dwelling **—v. 3.** *pt./pp. of* ABIDE

ABO group the classification of human blood into the groups A, B, AB and O according to the reactions to each other

abolish (ə'bolish) *vt.* do away with **—abo'lition** *n.* **—abo'litionist** *n.* one who wishes to do away with something, *esp.* slavery

A-bomb *n.* atomic bomb

abominate (ə'bomināt) *vt.* detest **—a'bominable** *a.* **—a'bominably** *adv.* **—abomi'nation** *n.* **1.** loathing **2.** the object loathed **—abominable snowman** large legendary apelike creature said to inhabit the Himalayas (*also* **yeti**)

aborigine (abə'rijini) *n.* **1.** original inhabitant of region **2.** Australian aborigine **—pl. 3.** native flora and fauna **—abo'riginal** *a.* **1.** of, relating to the aborigines of Aust. **2.** indigenous, earliest

abort (ə'börт) *v.* **1.** (cause to) end prematurely (*esp.* pregnancy) **—vi. 2.** give birth to dead fetus **3.** fail **—aborti'facient** *n./a.* (drug or agent) inducing abortion **—a'bortion** *n.* **1.** operation to terminate pregnancy **2.** something deformed **—a'bortionist** *n.* one who performs abortion, *esp.* illegally **—a'bortive** *a.* unsuccessful **—a'bortively** *adv.*

abound (ə'bownd) vi. **1.** be plentiful **2.** overflow —**a'bounding** a.

about (ə'bowt) adv. **1.** on all sides **2.** nearly **3.** up and down **4.** out, astir —prep. **5.** round **6.** near **7.** concerning —**about** to ready to —**about-turn** n. reversal, complete change

above (ə'buv) adv. **1.** higher up —prep. **2.** over **3.** higher than, more than **4.** beyond

abracadabra (abrəkə'dabrə) n. supposedly magic word

abrade (ə'brād) vt. rub off, scrape away

Abraham ('ābrəham) n. in O.T., founder of the nation of Israel, and its first patriarch —**Abraham's bosom** repose of the happy in death —**Abraham's covenant 1.** covenant made by God with Abraham that Messiah should spring from his seed **2.** rite of circumcision

abrasion (ə'brāzhən) n. **1.** place scraped or worn by rubbing (eg on skin) **2.** scraping, rubbing —**a'brasive** n. **1.** substance for grinding, polishing etc. —a. **2.** causing abrasion **3.** grating

abreast (ə'brest) adv. side by side —**abreast** of keeping up with

abridge (ə'brij) vt. cut short, abbreviate —**a'bridgment** or **a'bridgement** n.

abroad (ə'brôd) adv. **1.** to or in a foreign country **2.** at large

abrogate ('ābrōgāt) vt. cancel, repeal —**abro'gation** n.

abrupt (ə'brupt) a. **1.** sudden **2.** blunt **3.** hasty **4.** steep —**a'bruptly** adv. —**a'bruptness** n.

abscess ('abses) n. gathering of pus in any part of the body

abscissa (ab'sisə) n. Math. distance of point from the axis of coordinates (pl. **-s**, **-sae** (-sē))

abscond (əb'skond) vi. leave secretly, esp. having stolen something

abseil ('absīl) vi. descend vertical slope by means of rope

absent ('absənt) a. **1.** away **2.** not attentive —vt. (ab'sent) **3.** keep away —'**absence** n. —**absen'tee** n. one who stays away, esp. habitually —**absen'teeism** n. persistent absence from work etc. —'**absently** adv. —**absentee ballot** ballot submitted in advance of election by voter unable to be present at the polls —**absent-minded** a.

absinthe or **absinth** ('absinth) n. potent aniseed-flavored liqueur

absolute ('absəlōōt) a. **1.** complete **2.** not limited, unconditional **3.** pure (as **absolute alcohol**) —n. **4.** something that is absolute —'**absolutely** adv. **1.** completely —interj. **2.** certainly —'**absoluteness** n. —'**absolutism** n. political system in which unrestricted power is vested in dictator etc.; despotism —'**absolutist** n. —**absolute pitch** ability to identify immediately a musical sound by name or to sing any tone at will —**absolute zero** lowest temperature theoretically attainable

absolve (əb'zolv) vt. free, pardon, acquit —**absolution** (absə'lōōshən) n.

absorb (əb'sôrb) vt. **1.** suck up, drink in **2.** engage, occupy (attention etc.) **3.** receive (impact) —**ab'sorbent** a. —**ab'sorption** n. —**ab'sorptive** a.

abstain (əb'stān) vi. (usu. with from) keep (from), refrain (from drinking alcohol, voting etc.) —**ab'stainer** n. —**abstention** (əb'stenchən) n. —**abstinence** ('abstinəns) n. —**abstinent** ('abstinənt) a.

abstemious (əb'stēmiəs) a. sparing in food or esp. drink, temperate —**ab'stemiously** adv. —**ab'stemiousness** n.

abstract ('abstrakt) a. **1.** existing only in the mind **2.** not concrete **3.** not representational

—n. **4.** summary, abridgment —vt. (ab'strakt) **5.** draw (from), remove **6.** deduct —**ab'stracted** a. preoccupied —**ab'straction** n. —'**abstractly** adv. —**abstract expressionism** direction in abstract art of 1940s and 1950s of which the essence was the spontaneous assertion of the artist in a nonobjective visual expression

abstruse (əb'strōōs) a. obscure, difficult to understand, profound —**ab'strusely** adv.

absurd (əb'sərd) a. contrary to reason —**ab'surdity** n. —**ab'surdly** adv.

abundance (ə'bundəns) n. great amount —**a'bundant** a. plentiful —**a'bundantly** adv.

abuse (ə'byōōz) vt. **1.** misuse **2.** address rudely —n. (ə'byōōs) **3.** improper use **4.** insulting speech —**a'busive** a. —**a'busively** adv. —**a'busiveness** n.

abut (ə'but) vi. adjoin, border (on) (**-tt-**) —**a'butment** n. support, esp. of bridge or arch

abuzz (ə'buz) a. noisy, busy with activity etc.

abysmal (ə'bizməl) a. **1.** immeasurable, very great **2.** inf. extremely bad —**a'bysmally** adv.

abyss (ə'bis) n. very deep gulf or pit

Abyssinian (abi'siniən) n. purebred short-haired domestic cat with slender body and brownish coat marked with darker-color bands

ac 1. account **2.** money of account

Ac Chem. actinium

AC 1. air-conditioning **2.** alternating current **3.** athletic club **4.** (on prescription) before meals **5.** area code **6.** ante Christum: before Christ

acacia (ə'kāshə) n. **1.** genus of deciduous or evergreen shrubs or trees of the pea family grown in warm regions (also **wattle**) **2.** see **gum arabic** at GUM[2]

academy (ə'kadəmi) n. **1.** society to advance arts or sciences **2.** institution for specialized training **3.** secondary school **4.** (**A-**) Greek school of philosophy founded by Plato —**academic** (akə'demik) a. **1.** of academy **2.** belonging to University etc. **3.** theoretical —**academically** (akə'demikəli) adv. —**academician** (akədə'mishən) n.

Acadia (ə'kādiə) n. former name for Nova Scotia

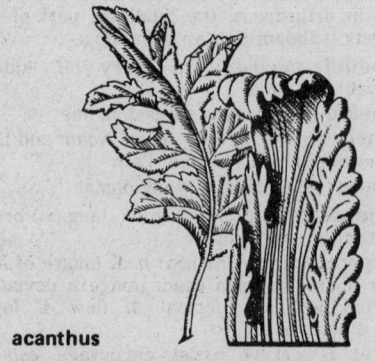
acanthus

acanthus (ə'kanthəs) n. **1.** prickly plant **2.** architectural ornament like leaf of acanthus plant (pl. **-es**, **-thi** (-thī))

a cappella (ä kə'pelə) (of choral music) without instrumental accompaniment

acc. accusative

accede (ak'sēd) vi. (usu. with to) **1.** agree, consent **2.** attain (office, right etc.)

accelerando (akselə'rando) a./adv. Mus. becoming faster

accelerate (ak'selərāt) v. (cause to) increase speed, hasten —**accele'ration** n. —**ac'celerative** a. —**ac'celerator** n. mechanism to increase speed, esp. in motor vehicle

accent ('aksent) n. **1.** stress or pitch in speaking **2.** mark to show such stress **3.** local or national style of pronunciation **4.** particular attention or emphasis **5.** Mus. stress on one tone or chord —vt. **6.** stress **7.** mark with accent

accentor (ak'sentər) n. member of family of sparrowlike songbirds found in Europe and north Asia

accentuate (ak'senchōōāt) vt. stress, emphasize —**ac'centual** a. —**accentu'ation** n.

accept (ək'sept) vt. **1.** take, receive **2.** admit, believe **3.** agree to —**accepta'bility** n. —**ac'ceptable** a. —**ac'ceptably** adv. —**ac'ceptance** n. —**accep'tation** n. common or accepted meaning of word etc. —**ac'cepter** n. —**ac'ceptor** n. **1.** Comm. person or organization on which bill of exchange is drawn **2.** Electron. impurity added to semiconductor to increase its p-type conductivity

access ('akses) n. **1.** act, right or means of entry —vt. Comp. **2.** obtain or retrieve (information) from storage device **3.** place (information) in storage device —**accessi'bility** n. —**ac'cessible** a. easy to approach —**ac'cessibly** adv. —**access time** Comp. time required to retrieve stored information

accessary (ək'sesəri) see ACCESSORY

accession (ək'seshən) n. **1.** attaining of office, right etc. **2.** increase, addition

accessory (ək'sesəri) n. **1.** additional or supplementary part of car, woman's dress etc. **2.** person inciting or assisting in crime —a. **3.** contributory, assisting

accidence ('aksidəns) n. the part of grammar dealing with changes in the form of words

accident ('aksidənt) n. **1.** event happening by chance **2.** misfortune or mishap, esp. causing injury **3.** nonessential quality —**acci'dental** a. **1.** happening by chance —n. **2.** Mus. sign used in notation to indicate chromatic alterations or to cancel them —**acci'dentally** adv.

acclaim (ə'klām) vt. **1.** applaud, praise —n. **2.** applause —**acclamation** (aklə'māshən) n. —**acclamatory** (ə'klamətôri) a.

acclimatize (ə'klīmətīz) vt. accustom to new climate or environment —**acclimati'zation** n.

accolade ('akəlād) n. **1.** praise, public approval **2.** award, honor **3.** token of award of knighthood

accommodate (ə'komədāt) vt. **1.** supply, esp. with board and lodging **2.** oblige **3.** harmonize, adapt —**ac'commodating** a. obliging —**accommo'dation** n. **1.** lodging **2.** agreement **3.** adjustment of lens of eye **4.** loan

accompany (ə'kumpəni) vt. **1.** go with **2.** supplement **3.** occur with **4.** provide a musical accompaniment for (**-panied,** **-panying**) —**ac'companiment** n. that which accompanies, esp. in music, part which goes with solos etc. —**ac'companist** n.

accomplice (ə'komplis, ə'kum-) n. one assisting another in criminal deed

accomplish (ə'komplish, ə'kum-) vt. **1.** carry out **2.** finish —**ac'complished** a. **1.** complete, perfect **2.** proficient —**ac'complishment** n. **1.** completion **2.** personal ability

accord (ə'kôrd) n. **1.** agreement, harmony (esp. in **in accord with**) —v. **2.** (cause to) be in accord —vt. **3.** grant —**ac'cordance** n. —**ac'cordant** a. —**ac'cordingly** adv. **1.** as the circumstances suggest 2. therefore —**according to** 1. in proportion to 2. as stated by 3. in conformity with

accordion (ə'kördiən) *n*. portable musical instrument with keys, metal reeds and a bellows. The right hand plays piano-like keyboard —**ac'cordionist** *n*.

accost (ə'kost) *vt*. approach and speak to, ask question *etc*.

account (ə'kownt) *n*. 1. report, description 2. importance, value 3. statement of moneys received, paid or owed 4. person's money held in bank 5. credit available to person at store *etc*. —*vt*. 6. reckon 7. judge —*vi*. 8. give reason, answer (for) —**accounta'bility** *n*. —**ac'countable** *a*. responsible —**ac'countancy** *n*. keeping, preparation of business accounts, financial records *etc*. —**ac'countant** *n*. one practicing accountancy —**ac'counting** *n*. skill or practice of keeping and preparing business accounts

accouter (ə'kōōtər) *vt*. equip —**ac'couterments** *pl.n*. 1. equipment, *esp*. military 2. trappings

accredit (ə'kredit) *vt*. 1. ascribe, attribute 2. give official recognition to 3. certify as meeting required standards 4. (*oft. with* at, to) send (envoy *etc*.) with official credentials; appoint as envoy *etc*. 5. believe —**ac'credited** *a*.

accretion (ə'krēshən) *n*. 1. growth 2. something added on

accrue (ə'krōō) *vi*. 1. be added 2. result

acct. 1. account 2. accountant

acculturate (ə'kulchərāt) *vi*. assimilate traits of another cultural group —**accultur'ation** *n*.

accumulate (ə'kyōōmyōōlāt) *v*. 1. gather, become gathered in increasing quantity 2. collect —**accumu'lation** *n*. —**ac'cumulator** *n*. (in computer) part where numbers are totaled or stored

accurate ('akyərit) *a*. exact, correct, without errors —'**accuracy** *n*. —'**accurately** *adv*.

accursed (ə'kərsid, ə'kərst) *or* **accurst** (ə'kərst) *a*. 1. under a curse 2. hateful, detestable

accuse (ə'kyōōz) *vt*. 1. charge with wrongdoing 2. blame —**accu'sation** *n*. —**ac'cusative** *n*. grammatical case indicating the direct object —**ac'cusatory** *a*. —**ac'cuser** *n*.

accustom (ə'kustəm) *vt*. make used (to), familiarize —**ac'customed** *a*. 1. usual 2. used (to) 3. in the habit (of)

ace (ās) *n*. 1. the one at dice, cards, dominoes 2. *Tennis* winning serve, *esp*. one untouched by opponent 3. *Golf* hole made in one shot 4. very successful fighter pilot 5. *inf*. person expert at anything —*a*. 6. *inf*. excellent —**ace up one's sleeve** something effective kept secretly in reserve

-aceous (*comb. form*) relating to, having the nature of, or resembling, as in *herbaceous*

acerbate ('asərbāt) *vt*. 1. make worse 2. make sour, bitter —**a'cerbity** *n*. 1. severity, sharpness 2. sourness, bitterness

acetate ('asitāt) *n*. 1. fiber made from cellulose 2. salt of acetic acid

acetic (ə'sētik) *a*. derived from or having the nature of vinegar —**acetic acid** acid which gives vinegar its characteristic taste, also important industrial chemical

aceto- *or before vowel* **acet-** (*comb. form*) containing acetyl group or derived from acetic acid, as in *acetone*

acetone ('asitōn) *n*. colorless liquid used as solvent

acetylcholine (asətil'kōlēn) *n*. derivative of choline involved in transmission of nerve impulses

acetylene (ə'setilēn) *n*. colorless, flammable gas used *esp*. in welding metals

acetylsalicylic acid (ə'setilsalisilik) aspirin

Acey Deucy ('āsi 'dyōōsi, -'dōōsi) variation of backgammon

ache (āk) *n*. 1. continuous pain —*vi*. 2. be painful 3. be in pain —'**aching** *a*.

achieve (ə'chēv) *vt*. 1. accomplish, perform successfully 2. gain —**a'chievement** *n*. something accomplished

Achilles (ə'kilēz) *n*. greatest warrior among the Greeks at the siege of Troy, and slayer of Hector —**Achilles' heel** vulnerable point —**Achilles tendon** fibrous cord connecting muscles of calf to heelbone

achlorhydria (āklör'hidriə) *n*. lack of production of hydrochloric acid in the stomach

achromatic (akrə'matik) *a*. 1. free from or not showing color, as of a lens 2. colorless 3. (of musical scale) without accidentals or modulations

acid ('asid) *a*. 1. sharp, sour —*n*. 2. sour substance 3. *Chem*. one of a class of compounds which combines with bases (alkalis, oxides *etc*.) to form salts —**a'cidic** *a*. —**a'cidify** *v*. (**-fied, -fying**) —**a'cidity** *n*. —**aci'dosis** *n*. condition when the ability of the blood to neutralize acidic substances decreases —**a'cidulate** *vt*. make slightly acid —**a'cidulous** *a*. —'**acidhead** *n*. person who uses LSD —**acid rain** rain acidified by atmospheric pollution —**acid test** conclusive test of value

acidophilus milk (asi'dofiləs) milk fermented by bacteria used therapeutically to modify intestinal flora

ack-ack ('akak) *n*. anti-aircraft guns or gunfire

acknowledge (ək'nolij) *vt*. 1. admit, own, recognize 2. say one has received —**ac'knowledgment** *or* **ac'knowledgement** *n*.

aclinic (ā'klinik) *a*. without inclination, said of the magnetic equator, on which the magnetic needle has no dip

ACLU American Civil Liberties Union

acme ('akmi) *n*. highest point

acne ('akni) *n*. pimply skin disease

acolyte ('akəlīt) *n*. follower or attendant, *esp*. of priest

aconite ('akənīt) *n*. 1. genus of plants related to the buttercup, including monkshood 2. drug, poison obtained from such

acorn ('ākörn) *n*. nut or fruit of the oak tree —**acorn squash** acorn-shaped dark green winter squash with sweet yellowish-to-orange flesh

acoustic (ə'kōōstik) *or* **acoustical** *a*. pert. to sound and to hearing —**a'coustics** *pl.n*. 1. (*with sing. v*.) science of sound 2. features of room or building as regards sounds heard within it —**acoustic guitar** ordinary guitar, not amplified

acquaint (ə'kwānt) *vt*. make familiar, inform —**ac'quaintance** *n*. 1. person known 2. personal knowledge —**ac'quaintanceship** *n*.

acquiesce (akwi'es) *vi*. agree, consent without complaint —**acqui'escence** *n*. —**acqui'escent** *a*.

acquire (ə'kwīər) *vt*. gain, get —**ac'quirement** *n*. —**acquisition** (akwi'zishən) *n*. 1. act of getting 2. material gain —**acquisitive** (ə'kwizitiv) *a*. desirous of gaining —**acquisitiveness** (ə'kwizitivnis) *n*. —**acquired immuno-deficiency syndrome** disease that breaks down the body's natural immunity, oft. resulting in fatal infection (*also* **AIDS**)

acquit (ə'kwit) *vt*. 1. declare innocent 2. settle, discharge, as a debt 3. behave

(oneself) (**-tt-**) —**ac'quittal** *n*. declaration of innocence in court —**ac'quittance** *n*. discharge of debts

acre ('ākər) *n*. 1. measure of land, 4840 square yards, 4047 square meters —*pl*. 2. lands, estates 3. *inf*. large area or plenty —'**acreage** *n*. extent of land in acres

acrid ('akrid) *a*. 1. pungent, sharp 2. irritating —**a'cridity** *n*.

acrimony ('akrimōni) *n*. bitterness of feeling or language —**acri'monious** *a*.

acrobat ('akrəbat) *n*. one skilled in gymnastic feats, *esp*. as entertainer in circus *etc*. —**acro'batic** *a*. —**acro'batics** *pl.n*. (*with sing. v*.) any activity requiring agility

acromegaly (akrō'megəli) *n*. rare disease of adult life in which enlargement of many parts of the body occurs

acronym ('akrənim) *n*. word formed from initial letters of other words, *eg* UNESCO, ANZUS, NATO

acrophobia (akrə'fōbiə) *n*. abnormal fear of being at great height —**acro'phobic** *a*.

acropolis (ə'kropəlis) *n*. citadel, *esp*. in ancient Greece

across (ə'kros) *adv./prep*. 1. crosswise 2. from side to side 3. on or to the other side —**get** (*or* **put**) **something across** explain something, make something understood

acrostic (ə'krostik) *n*. word puzzle in which the first, middle, or last letters of each line spell a word or words

acrylic (ə'krilik) *n*. variety of synthetic materials, *esp*. textiles, derived from an organic acid —**acrylic resin** any of group of polymers of acrylic acid, its esters or amides, used as paints, plastics *etc*.

act (akt) *n*. 1. thing done, deed 2. doing 3. law, decree 4. section of a play —*v*. 5. perform, as in a play —*vi*. 6. exert force, work, as mechanism 7. behave —'**acting** *n*. 1. performance of a part —*a*. 2. temporarily performing the duties of another —'**action** *n*. 1. operation 2. deed 3. gesture 4. expenditure of energy 5. battle 6. lawsuit —'**actionable** *a*. subject to lawsuit —'**activate** *vt*. 1. make active, put into operation 2. make radioactive 3. make chemically active —**acti'vation** *n*. —'**activator** *n*. —'**active** *a*. 1. moving, working 2. brisk, energetic —'**actively** *adv*. —'**activism** *n*. —'**activist** *n*. one who takes (direct) action to achieve political or social ends —**ac'tivity** *n*. —'**actor** *n*. person who acts in a play, motion picture *etc*. (**-tress** *fem*.) —**action painting** type of abstract painting characterized by smeared or spattered paint (*also* '**tachism**) —**activated sludge** aerated sewage added to untreated sewage to hasten bacterial decomposition —**active service** full-time service in the armed forces —**Act of God** *Law* unavoidable occurrence, such as earthquake, caused by natural forces

A.C.T. Australian Capital Territory

ACTH adrenocorticotrophic hormone: protein hormone of pituitary gland

actinide series ('aktinīd) series of 15 radioactive elements with increasing atomic numbers from actinium to lawrencium

actinism ('aktinizəm) *n*. chemical action of sun's rays —**ac'tinic** *a*.

actinium (ak'tiniəm) *n*. *Chem*. radioactive element discovered in 1899 in pitchblende *Symbol* Ac, at. wt. 227, at. no. 89

actinomycetes (aktinō'mīsēts) *pl.n*. moldlike bacteria sometimes called ray fungi, some of which excrete antibiotic substances

Acts (akts) *pl.n*. (*with sing. v*.) *Bible* 5th book of the N.T., written by Luke in about 63 A.D., describing the beginnings of the early Church

actual ('akchŏŏəl) *a.* **1.** existing in the present **2.** real —**actu'ality** *n.* —**'actually** *adv.* really, indeed

actuary ('akchŏŏeri) *n.* statistician who calculates insurance risks, premiums *etc.* —**actu'arial** *a.*

actuate ('akchŏŏāt) *vt.* **1.** activate **2.** motivate —**actu'ation** *n.*

acuity (ə'kyŏŏiti) *n.* keenness, *esp.* in vision or thought

acumen (ə'kyŏŏmən) *n.* sharpness of wit, perception, penetration

acupuncture ('akyŏŏpungkchər) *n. orig.* Chinese treatment involving insertion of needles at various points on the body to cure disease or relieve pain —**'acupuncturist** *n.*

acute (ə'kyŏŏt) *a.* **1.** keen, shrewd **2.** sharp **3.** severe **4.** less than 90° —*n.* **5.** accent (´) over a letter to indicate the quality or length of its sound, *eg* abbé —**a'cutely** *adv.* —**a'cuteness** *n.*

ad (ad) *n.* advertisement —**'adman** *n. inf.* man who works in advertising

A.D. anno Domini

ad- (*comb. form*) **1.** to; toward, as in *adverb* **2.** near; next to, as in *adrenal*

ADA **1.** average daily attendance **2.** Americans for Democratic Action **3.** American Dental Association

adage ('adij) *n.* much-used wise saying, proverb

adagio (ə'däjiō) *a./adv./n. Mus.* **1.** slow (tempo), between andante and largo —*n.* **2.** composition in this tempo, often second movement of sonata (*pl.* **-s**)

Adam[1] ('adəm) *n.* in O.T., the first man —**Adam's ale** water —**Adam's apple** projecting part at front of the throat, the thyroid cartilage —**Adam's needle** popular name for plant furnishing needle-like leaves, *eg* yucca

Adam[2] ('adəm) *a.* in neoclassical style made popular by Robert Adam (1728-92), Scottish architect and furniture designer

adamant ('adəmənt) *a.* very hard, unyielding —**ada'mantine** *a.*

Adams[1] ('adəmz) *n.* **John.** the 2nd President of the U.S. (1797-1801)

Adams[2] ('adəmz) *n.* **John Quincy.** the 6th President of the U.S. (1825-29)

adapt (ə'dapt) *v.* **1.** alter for new use **2.** fit, modify **3.** change —**adapta'bility** *n.* —**a'daptable** *a.* —**adap'tation** *n.* —**a'dapter** *or* **a'daptor** *n. esp.* appliance for connecting two parts (*eg* electrical)

A.D.C. **1.** aide-de-camp **2.** analog-digital converter **3.** Aid to Dependent Children **4.** Air Defense Command **5.** assistant division commander

add (ad) *v.* **1.** join **2.** increase by **3.** say further —**ad'dition** *n.* —**ad'ditional** *a.*

addax ('adaks) *n.* large light-colored antelope of N Afr., Arabia and Syria

addendum (ə'dendəm) *n.* thing to be added (*pl.* **-da** (-də)) —**'addend** *n.* any of set of numbers that form sum

adder ('adər) *n.* small poisonous snake

addict ('adikt) *n.* **1.** one who has become dependent on something, *eg* drugs (*drug addict*) —*vt.* (ə'dikt) **2.** (*usu. passive*) cause to become dependent (on something, *esp.* drug) —**ad'dicted** *a.* —**ad'diction** *n.* —**ad'dictive** *a.* causing addiction

Addison's disease ('adisənz) disease characterized by deep bronzing of skin, anemia and extreme weakness, caused by underactivity of adrenal glands

additive ('aditiv) *n.* **1.** something added to another substance, *esp.* food, to improve it or

to suppress unwanted properties —*a.* **2.** of, relating to or characterized by addition

addle ('adəl) *v.* make or become rotten or muddled

address (ə'dres) *n.* **1.** direction on letter **2.** place where one lives **3.** speech —*pl.* **4.** courtship —*vt.* **5.** mark destination on **6.** speak to **7.** direct **8.** dispatch —**addressee** (adre'sē) *n.* person addressed

adduce (ə'dyŏŏs, -'dŏŏs) *vt.* **1.** offer as proof **2.** cite —**ad'ducible** *a.* —**adduction** (ə'dukshən) *n.*

-ade (*comb. form*) sweetened drink made of fruit, as in *lemonade*

adenoids ('adinoidz) *pl.n.* tissue at back of nose —**ade'noidal** *a.*

adept (ə'dept) *a.* **1.** skilled —*n.* ('adept) **2.** expert

adequate ('adikwit) *a.* **1.** sufficient, enough, suitable **2.** not outstanding —**'adequacy** *n.* —**'adequately** *adv.*

à deux (a 'dœ) *Fr.* of or for two persons

adhere (əd'hēər) *vi.* **1.** stick **2.** be firm in opinion *etc.* —**ad'herent** *n./a.* —**ad'hesion** *n.* band of scar tissue formed within the body in response to inflammation or injury —**ad'hesive** *a./n.* (substance) capable of holding materials together by surface attachment

ad hoc (ad 'hok) **1.** for a particular occasion only **2.** improvised

ad hominem (ad 'hominem) *Lat.* directed against person rather than his arguments

adieu (ə'dyŏŏ, -'dŏŏ) *interj.* **1.** farewell —*n.* **2.** act of taking leave (*pl.* **-s, adieux** (ə'dyŏŏz, -'dŏŏz))

ad infinitum (ad infi'nītəm) *Lat.* endlessly

ad interim (ad 'intərim) *Lat.* for the meantime

adipose ('adipōs) *a.* of fat, fatty

adit ('adit) *n.* almost horizontal entrance into a mine

adj. **1.** adjective **2.** adjourned **3.** adjutant

adjacent (ə'jāsənt) *a.* lying near, next (to) —**ad'jacency** *n.*

adjective ('ajiktiv) *n.* word which qualifies or limits a noun —**adjectival** (ajik'tīvəl) *a.* of adjective

adjoin (ə'join) *v.* **1.** be next (to) **2.** join —**ad'joining** *a.* next (to), near

adjourn (ə'jərn) *vt.* **1.** postpone temporarily, as meeting —*vi.* **2.** *inf.* move elsewhere —**ad'journment** *n.*

adjudge (ə'juj) *vt.* **1.** declare **2.** decide **3.** award —**ad'judgment** *or* **ad'judgement** *n.*

adjudicate (ə'jŏŏdikāt) *v.* **1.** try, judge —*vi.* **2.** sit in judgment —**adjudi'cation** *n.* —**ad'judicator** *n.*

adjunct ('ajungkt) *a.* **1.** joined, added —*n.* **2.** person or thing added or subordinate —**ad'junctive** *a.* —**adjunct professor** temporary or honorary professor at college or university

adjure (ə'jŏŏər) *vt.* beg, entreat earnestly —**adju'ration** *n.*

adjust (ə'just) *v.* **1.** make suitable, adapt **2.** alter slightly, regulate —**ad'justable** *a.* —**ad'juster** *or* **ad'justor** *n.* one that adjusts, *esp.* insurance agent assessing damage —**ad'justment** *n.*

adjutant ('ajətənt) *n.* military officer who assists superiors —**'adjutancy** *n.* his office, rank

ad-lib (ad'lib) *v.* **1.** improvise, speak *etc.* without previous preparation (**-bb-**) —*n.* **2.** such speech *etc.* —*a.* **3.** improvised —**ad lib** without preparation; freely

ad libitum (ad 'libitəm) *Mus.* at performer's discretion

Adm. Admiral

admin ('admin) *n. inf.* administration

administer (əd'ministər) *vt.* **1.** manage, look after **2.** dispense, as justice *etc.* **3.** apply —**ad'ministrate** *v.* manage (business, institution, government department *etc.*) —**admini'stration** *n.* —**ad'ministrative** *a.* —**ad'ministrator** *n.* (**admini'stratrix** *fem.*)

admiral ('admərəl) *n.* **1.** commissioned officer in navy or coastguard ranking above vice admiral and whose insignia is four stars **2.** any of several brightly colored butterflies

admire (əd'mīər) *vt.* **1.** look on with wonder and pleasure **2.** respect highly —**admirable** ('admərəbl) *a.* —**admirably** ('admərəbli) *adv.* —**admiration** (admə'rāshən) *n.* —**ad'mirer** *n.* —**ad'miringly** *adv.*

admit (əd'mit) *vt.* **1.** confess **2.** accept as true **3.** allow **4.** let in (**-tt-**) —**ad'missible** *a.* —**ad'missibly** *adv.* —**ad'mission** *n.* **1.** permission to enter **2.** entrance fee **3.** confession —**ad'mittance** *n.* permission to enter —**ad'mittedly** *adv.* willingly conceded

admixture (ad'mikschər) *n.* **1.** mixture **2.** ingredient —**ad'mix** *vt.*

admonish (əd'monish) *vt.* **1.** reprove **2.** advise **3.** warn **4.** exhort —**admo'nition** *n.* —**ad'monitory** *a.*

ad nauseam (ad 'nōziəm) *Lat.* to a boring or disgusting extent

ado (ə'dŏŏ) *n.* fuss

adobe (ə'dōbi) *n.* sun-dried brick

adolescence (adə'lesəns) *n.* period of life just before maturity —**ado'lescent** *n.* **1.** a youth —*a.* **2.** of adolescence **3.** immature

Adonis (ə'dōnis) *n.* a beautiful youth beloved by Aphrodite

adopt (ə'dopt) *vt.* **1.** take into relationship, *esp.* as one's child **2.** take up, as belief, principle, resolution —**a'doption** *n.* —**a'doptive** *a.* due to adoption

adore (ə'dör) *vt.* **1.** love intensely —*v.* **2.** worship —**a'dorable** *a.* —**ado'ration** *n.* —**a'dorer** *n.* lover

adorn (ə'dörn) *vt.* beautify, embellish, deck —**a'dornment** *n.* ornament, decoration

A.D.P. automatic data processing

ad rem (ad 'rem) *Lat.* to the point

adrenal (ə'drēnəl) *a.* near the kidney —**adrenal gland** either of pair of thumbnail-sized glands above the kidneys secreting sex hormones and hormones affecting metabolism —**Adrenalin** (ə'drenəlin) *n.* trade name for preparation of adrenaline —**adrenaline** (ə'drenəlin) *n.* epinephrine

Adriatic (ādri'atik) *n.* arm of the Mediterranean Sea, between Italy and Yugoslavia (*also* **Adriatic Sea**)

adrift (ə'drift) *a./adv.* **1.** drifting free **2.** *inf.* detached **3.** *inf.* off course

adroit (ə'droit) *a.* **1.** skilful, expert **2.** clever —**a'droitly** *adv.* —**a'droitness** *n.* dexterity

adsorb (əd'sörb) *v.* (of gas, vapor) condense and form thin film on surface —**ad'sorbent** *a./n.* —**ad'sorption** *n.*

adulation (ajə'lāshən) *n.* flattery —**'adulate** *vt.* flatter —**'adulator** *n.* —**'adulatory** *a.*

adult ('adult, ə'dult) *a.* **1.** grown-up, mature —*n.* **2.** grown-up person **3.** full-grown animal or plant

adulterate (ə'dultərāt) *vt.* make impure by addition —**a'dulterant** *n./a.* —**a'dulterated** *a.* —**adulter'ation** *n.* —**a'dulterator** *n.*

adultery (ə'dultəri) *n.* sexual unfaithfulness of a husband or wife —**a'dulterer** *n.* (**a'dulteress** *fem.*) —**a'dulterous** *a.*

adumbrate ('adumbrāt) *vt.* **1.** outline **2.** give indication of —**a'dumbrant** *or* **a'dumbrative** *a.* —**adum'bration** *n.*

adv. **1.** adverb(ial) **2.** advertisement

ad valorem (ad vəˈlörəm) *Lat.* in proportion to the value of goods in question

advance (ədˈväns) *vt.* **1.** bring forward **2.** suggest **3.** encourage **4.** pay beforehand —*vi.* **5.** go forward **6.** improve in position or value —*n.* **7.** forward movement **8.** improvement **9.** loan —*pl.* **10.** personal approach(es) to gain favor *etc.* —*a.* **11.** (*with* of) ahead in time or position —**adˈvanced** *a.* **1.** at a late stage **2.** not elementary **3.** ahead of the times —**adˈvancement** *n.* promotion

advantage (ədˈväntij) *n.* **1.** superiority **2.** more favorable position or state **3.** benefit —**advanˈtageous** *a.* —**advanˈtageously** *adv.*

advent (ˈadvent) *n.* **1.** a coming, arrival **2.** (A-) the four weeks before Christmas **3.** (A-) the coming of Christ —**Adˈventist** *n.* one of number of Christian sects believing in imminent return of Christ and the end of the world

adventitious (advenˈtishəs) *a.* **1.** added, artificial **2.** accidental, occurring by chance

adventure (ədˈvenchər) *n.* **1.** risk **2.** bold exploit **3.** remarkable happening **4.** enterprise **5.** commercial speculation —*v.* **6.** (take) risk —**adˈventurer** *n.* **1.** one who seeks adventures **2.** one who lives on his wits (**adˈventuress** *fem.*) —**adˈventurism** *n.* recklessness, *esp.* in politics and finance —**adˈventurous** *a.* —**adˈventurously** *adv.* —**adˈventurousness** *n.*

adverb (ˈadvərb) *n.* word added to verb, adjective or other adverb to modify meaning —**adˈverbial** *a.* —**adˈverbially** *adv.*

adverse (adˈvərs, ˈadvərs) *a.* **1.** opposed **2.** hostile **3.** unfavorable, bringing harm —ˈ**adversary** *n.* enemy —**adˈversative** *a.* —**adˈversely** *adv.* —**adˈversity** *n.* distress, misfortune

advert (ədˈvərt) *vi.* **1.** turn the mind or attention **2.** refer —**adˈvertence** *n.* —**adˈvertently** *adv.*

advertise (ˈadvərtīz) *vt.* **1.** publicize **2.** make known **3.** give notice of, *esp.* in newspapers *etc.* —*vi.* **4.** make public request (for) —**adverˈtisement** *n.* —ˈ**advertiser** *n.* —ˈ**advertising** *a./n.*

advice (ədˈvīs) *n.* **1.** opinion given **2.** counsel **3.** information **4.** (formal) notification

advise (ədˈvīz) *vt.* **1.** offer advice **2.** recommend a line of conduct **3.** give notice (of) —**adˈvisable** *a.* expedient —**adˈvised** *a.* considered, as in *well-advised* —**adˈvisedly** (ədˈvīzidli) *adv.* —**adˈviser** *or* **adˈvisor** *n.* —**adˈvisory** *a.*

advocaat (ˈadvōkä) *n.* liqueur made with egg yolk and brandy

advocate (ˈadvəkit) *n.* **1.** one who pleads the cause of another, *esp.* in court of law —*vt.* (ˈadvəkāt) **2.** uphold, recommend —ˈ**advocacy** *n.* —**advoˈcation** *n.*

adz *or* **adze** (adz) *n.* carpenter's tool, like ax, but with arched blade set at right angles to handle

AEC Atomic Energy Commission

AEF American Expeditionary Force

aegis (ˈejis) *n.* sponsorship, protection (*orig.* shield of Zeus)

Aeolian (ēˈōliən) *a.* acted on by the wind, as **Aeolian harp** open narrow box with strings tuned in unison

aerate (ˈāərāt) *vt.* **1.** charge liquid with gas, as effervescent drink **2.** expose to air —**aerˈation** *n.* —ˈ**aerator** *n.* apparatus for charging liquid with gas

aerial (ˈāəriəl) *a.* **1.** of the air **2.** operating in the air **3.** pertaining to aircraft —*n.* **4.** antenna —ˈ**aerialist** *n.* trapeze artist

aerie *or* **aery** (ˈāəri) *n.* **1.** nest of bird of prey, *esp.* eagle **2.** high dwelling place

aero-, aeri-, *or before vowel* **aer-** (*comb. form*) air or aircraft, as in *aero engine*

aerobatics (āərōˈbatiks) *pl.n.* stunt flying

aerobic (āəˈrōbik) *a.* **1.** taking place in the presence of oxygen —*pl.n.* **2.** (*with sing. or pl.v.*) system of exercises designed to improve respiratory and circulatory functions of body

aerodynamics (āərōdīˈnamiks) *pl.n.* (*with sing. v.*) study of air flow, *esp.* round moving solid bodies

aero engine engine for powering aircraft

aerofoil (ˈāərōfoil) *n.* surfaces of wing *etc.* of aircraft designed to give lift

aerolite (ˈāərəlīt) *n.* meteoric stone

aerometry (āəˈromitri) *n.* measurement of weight or density of gases

aeronaut (ˈāərənöt) *n.* pilot or navigator of lighter-than-air craft —**aeroˈnautical** *a.* —**aeroˈnautics** *pl.n.* (*with sing. v.*) science of air navigation and flying in general

aerosol (ˈāərəsol) *n.* (substance dispensed as fine spray from) pressurized can

aerospace (ˈāərəspās) *n.* **1.** earth's atmosphere and space beyond —*a.* **2.** of missiles, space vehicles *etc.*

aerostatics (āərəˈstatiks) *pl.n.* (*with sing. v.*) **1.** study of gases in equilibrium and bodies held in equilibrium in gases **2.** study of lighter-than-air craft

aesthetic (esˈthetik, is-) *or* **aesthetical** *a.* relating to principles of beauty, taste and art —**aesthete** (ˈesthēt) *n.* one who affects extravagant love of art —**aesˈthetically** *adv.* —**aesˈtheticism** *n.* —**aesˈthetics** *pl.n.* (*with sing. v.*) study of art, taste *etc.*

AF 1. air force **2.** audio frequency

afar (əˈfär) *adv.* from, at, or to, a great distance

AFB air force base

A.F.C. 1. American Football Conference **2.** automatic frequency control

affable (ˈafəbəl) *a.* easy to speak to, polite and friendly —**affaˈbility** *n.* —ˈ**affably** *adv.*

affair (əˈfâr) *n.* **1.** thing done or attended to **2.** business **3.** happening **4.** sexual liaison —*pl.* **5.** personal or business interests **6.** matters of public interest

affect (əˈfekt) *vt.* **1.** act on, influence **2.** move feelings of **3.** make show, pretense of **4.** assume **5.** have liking for —**affecˈtation** *n.* show, pretense —**afˈfected** *a.* **1.** making a pretense **2.** moved **3.** acted upon —**afˈfectedly** *adv.* —**afˈfecting** *a.* moving the feelings of —**afˈfectingly** *adv.* —**afˈfection** *n.* fondness, love —**afˈfectionate** *a.* —**afˈfectionately** *adv.*

affenpinscher (ˈafənpinchər) *n.* purebred toy dog with hard wiry black coat, pointed ears, bushy eyebrows, chin tuft and mustache

afferent (ˈafərənt) *a.* bringing to, *esp.* describing nerves which carry sensation to the brain

affiance (əˈfīəns) *vt.* betroth —**afˈfianced** *a./n.* (one) promised in marriage

affidavit (afiˈdāvit) *n.* written statement on oath

affiliate (əˈfiliāt) *vt.* (*with* to *or* with) **1.** connect, attach (with larger body, organization) **2.** adopt —**affiliˈation** *n.*

affinity (əˈfiniti) *n.* **1.** natural liking **2.** resemblance **3.** relationship by marriage **4.** chemical attraction —**afˈfinitive** *a.*

affirm (əˈfərm) *v.* **1.** assert positively, declare **2.** maintain (statement) —*vi.* **3.** make solemn declaration —**affirˈmation** *n.* —**afˈfirmative** *a.* **1.** asserting —*n.* **2.** word of assent —**afˈfirmatively** *adv.*

affix (əˈfiks) *vt.* **1.** fasten **2.** attach, append —*n.* (ˈafiks) **3.** addition, *esp.* to word, as suffix, prefix

afflatus (əˈflātəs) *n.* impulse of creative power or inspiration

afflict (əˈflikt) *vt.* **1.** give pain or grief to, distress **2.** trouble, vex —**afˈfliction** *n.* —**afˈflictive** *a.*

affluent (ˈaflōōənt) *a.* **1.** wealthy **2.** abundant —*n.* **3.** tributary stream —ˈ**affluence** *n.* wealth, abundance

afford (əˈförd) *vt.* **1.** be able to buy **2.** be able to spare (the time *etc.*) **3.** produce, yield, furnish

afforest (əˈforist) *vt.* turn into forest, plant trees on —**afforesˈtation** *n.*

affray (əˈfrā) *n.* fight, brawl

affront (əˈfrunt) *vt.* **1.** insult openly —*n.* **2.** insult **3.** offense

Afghanistan (afˈganistan) *n.* country in southern Asia, bounded north by the U.S.S.R., east and south by Pakistan and west by Iran —ˈ**Afghan** *n.* **1.** native or inhabitant of Afghanistan **2.** Pashto **3.** (a-) knitted or crocheted blanket or shawl made up of squares or stripes **4.** (a-) large Turkoman carpet with long pile woven in geometric designs —**Afghan hound** purebred dog with long narrow head with topknot and long thick silky coat

aficionado (əfishiəˈnädō) *n.* **1.** ardent supporter or devotee **2.** devotee of bullfighting (*pl.* **-s**)

afield (əˈfēld) *adv.* **1.** away from home **2.** in or on the field

afire (əˈfīr) *adv.* on fire

aflame (əˈflām) *adv.* burning

AFL-CIO American Federation of Labor and Congress of Industrial Organizations

afloat (əˈflōt) *adv.* **1.** floating **2.** at sea **3.** in circulation

afoot (əˈfŏŏt) *adv.* **1.** astir **2.** on foot

afore (əˈför) *prep./adv.* before, usu. in compounds —**aˈforeˈmentioned** *a.* chiefly in legal documents, stated or mentioned before —**aˈforethought** *a.* premeditated (*esp. in malice aforethought*)

a fortiori (ā förtiˈörī) *adv.* for a stronger reason

afoul (əˈfowl) *a./adv.* into difficulty

Afr. Africa(n)

afraid (əˈfrād) *a.* **1.** frightened **2.** sorry

A-frame (ˈāfrām) *n.* a building with steeply angled sides meeting at the top like the shape of the letter A

afresh (əˈfresh) *adv.* again, anew

Africa (ˈafrikə) *n.* continent in eastern hemisphere south of Europe, between the Atlantic and Indian oceans —ˈ**African** *a.* **1.** belonging to Africa —*n.* **2.** native of Africa —**Afriˈcana** *pl.n.* objects of cultural or historical interest of southern Afr. origin —**African lily** S Afr. plant with funnel-shaped flowers —**African violet** house plant with pink, white or purple flowers and hairy leaves

Africander (afriˈkandər) *n.* breed of humpbacked S Afr. cattle

Afrikaans (afriˈkäns, -ˈkänz) *n.* language used in S Afr., derived from 17th-cent. Dutch —**Afriˈkaner** *n.* White native of S Afr. with Afrikaans as mother tongue

Afro (ˈafrō) *n.* fuzzy, bushy hairstyle

Afro- (*comb. form*) Africa or African, as in *Afro-Asiatic*

Afro-American *n./a.* American of African and *esp.* of Negroid descent

Afro-Asian *n.* language phylum comprising Semitic, Berber, Cushitic and Chadic families

afrormosia (afrörˈmōzhiə) *n.* hard teaklike wood obtained from tropical Afr. tree

aft (äft) *adv.* toward rear of ship

after ('äftər) *adv.* 1. later 2. behind —*prep.* 3. behind 4. later than 5. on the model of 6. pursuing —*conj.* 7. at a later time than that at which —*a.* 8. nearer ship's rear —'**afterward** *or* '**afterwards** *adv.* later

afterbirth ('äftərbərth) *n.* membrane expelled after a birth (*also* **placenta**)

aftercare ('äftərkåər) *n.* care, *esp.* medical, bestowed on person after period of treatment, and *esp.* after childbirth

aftereffect ('äftərifekt) *n.* subsequent effect of deed, event *etc.*

afterglow ('äftərglō) *n.* light after sunset

afterlife ('äftərlif) *n.* life after death or at later time in person's lifetime

aftermath ('äftərmath) *n.* result, consequence, *esp.* difficult one

afternoon (äftər'nōon) *n.* time from noon to evening

afterpains ('äftərpānz) *pl.n.* pains caused by contraction of uterus after childbirth

aftershave (lotion) ('äftərshåv) *n.* lotion applied to face after shaving

afterthought ('äftərthöt) *n.* idea occurring later

Ag *Chem.* silver

AG 1. adjutant general 2. attorney general

Agada (ə'gädə) *n.* fables, folklore and anecdotes in the Talmud

again (ə'gen, ə'gin) *adv.* 1. once more 2. in addition 3. back, in return 4. besides

against (ə'genst, ə'ginst) *prep.* 1. in opposition to 2. in contact with 3. opposite 4. in readiness for

Aga Khan ('ägə 'kän) the spiritual leader of Ismaili Muslims

Agamemnon (agə'memnon) *n.* in Greek legend, the King of Mycenae and leader of the Greeks at the siege of Troy

agape (ə'gāp) *a./adv.* open-mouthed as in wonder *etc.*

agar ('ägär) *n.* gelatinous carbohydrate obtained from seaweeds, used as culture medium for bacteria in food *etc.* (*also* **agar-agar**)

agaric ('agərik) *n.* 1. any of various fungi, *eg* mushroom —*a.* 2. fungoid

agate ('agit) *n.* 1. colored, semiprecious, decorative form of quartz 2. playing marble of agate 3. size of type approximately 5½ point —**agate line** unit of measurement used in classified advertising

agave (ə'gävi) *n.* any of genus of plants native to tropical Amer., with spiny-margined leaves cultivated for fiber or for ornament

age (āj) *n.* 1. length of time person or thing has existed 2. time of life 3. period of history 4. maturity 5. long time —*v.* 6. make or grow old —**aged** ('ājid) *a.* 1. old —*pl.n.* 2. old people —'**ageism** *n.* discrimination against the old —'**ageless** *a.* —**age-old** *a.*

-age (*comb. form*) 1. collection, set or group, as in *baggage* 2. process or action or result of action, as in *breakage* 3. state or relationship, as in *bondage* 4. house or place, as in *orphanage* 5. charge or fee, as in *postage* 6. rate, as in *dosage*

agenda (ə'jendə) *pl.n.* (*with sing. v.*) 1. things to be done 2. program of business meeting

agent ('ājənt) *n.* 1. one authorized to carry on business or affairs for another 2. person or thing producing effect 3. cause 4. natural force —'**agency** *n.* 1. instrumentality 2. business, place of business of agent

agent provocateur (a'zhä provoka'tœr) *Fr.* police spy who tries to provoke persons to act illegally

Aggeus (a'gēəs) *n. Bible* Haggai in the Douay Version of the O.T.

agglomerate (ə'glomərāt) *v.* 1. gather into a mass —*n.* (ə'glomərit, -rāt) 2. confused mass 3. rock consisting of volcanic fragments —*a.* (ə'glomərit, -rāt) 4. formed into a mass —**agglomer'ation** *n.* —**ag'glomerative** *a.*

agglutinate (ə'glōōtināt) *vt.* 1. unite with glue *etc.* 2. form (words) into compounds —*a.* (ə'glōōtinit, -nāt) 3. united, as by glue —**aggluti'nation** *n.* —**ag'glutinative** *a.*

aggrandize (ə'grandiz) *vt.* make greater in size, power or rank —**aggrandizement** (ə'grandizmənt) *n.*

aggravate ('agrəvāt) *vt.* 1. make worse or more severe 2. *inf.* annoy —'**aggravating** *a.* —**aggra'vation** *n.*

aggregate ('agrigāt) *vt.* 1. gather into mass —*a.* ('agrigit) 2. gathered thus —*n.* ('agrigit, -gāt) 3. mass, sum total 4. rock consisting of mixture of minerals 5. mixture of gravel *etc.* for concrete —**aggre'gation** *n.*

aggression (ə'greshən) *n.* 1. unprovoked attack 2. hostile activity —**ag'gress** *vi.* —**ag'gressive** *a.* —**ag'gressiveness** *n.* —**ag'gressor** *n.*

aggrieve (ə'grēv) *vt.* inflict pain on, injure —**ag'grieved** *a.*

aghast (ə'gäst) *a.* overcome with horror or amazement

agile ('ajil) *a.* 1. nimble 2. active 3. quick —'**agilely** *adv.* —**a'gility** *n.*

Agilon ('ajilon) *n.* trade name for stretch yarn

agin (ə'gin) *prep. inf., dial.* against

agitate ('ajitāt) *vt.* 1. disturb, excite 2. keep in motion, stir, shake up 3. trouble —*vi.* 4. stir up public opinion (for or against something) —**agi'tation** *n.* —'**agitator** *n.*

agitprop ('ajitprop) *n.* political agitation and propaganda, *esp.* of Communist nature

agley (ə'glā, ə'glē, ə'glī) *a. Scot.* awry

aglitter (ə'glitər) *a.* sparkling; glittering

aglow (ə'glō) *a.* glowing

agnostic (ag'nostik) *n.* 1. one who holds that we know nothing of things outside the material world —*a.* 2. of this theory —**ag'nosticism** *n.*

Agnus Dei ('agnōōs 'dāi) 1. figure of a lamb emblematic of Christ 2. part of Mass beginning with these words

ago (ə'gō) *adv.* in the past

agog (ə'gog) *a.* eager, astir

agony ('agəni) *n.* extreme suffering of mind or body, violent struggle —'**agonize** *vi.* 1. suffer agony 2. worry greatly —'**agonizing** *a.* —**agony column** newspaper column containing personal advertisements relating to lost relatives, pets *etc.*

agoraphobia (agərə'fōbiə) *n.* fear of open spaces —**agora'phobic** *a.*

agouti (ə'gōōti) *n.* 1. rabbit-sized tropical American rodent 2. barred pattern as result of alternating light and dark bands of fur 3. animal with fur of this pattern

agrarian (ə'greriən, -'grar-) *a.* of agriculture, land, or its management —**a'grarianism** *n.*

agree (ə'grē) *v.* 1. be of same opinion 2. consent 3. harmonize 4. determine, settle 5. suit (a'greed, a'greeing) —**agreea'bility** *n.* —**a'greeable** *a.* 1. willing 2. pleasant —**a'greeableness** *n.* —**a'greeably** *adv.* —**a'greement** *n.* 1. concord 2. contract

agriculture ('agrikulchər) *n.* art, practice of cultivating land —**agri'cultural** *a.* —**agri'culturist** *n.*

agrimony ('agrimōni) *n.* yellow-flowered plant with bitter taste

agronomy (ə'gronəmi) *n.* study of manage-

ment of land and scientific cultivation of crops —a'**gronomist** *n.*

aground (ə'grownd) *adv./a.* (of boat) touching bottom

agt. agent

ague ('āgyōō) *n. obs.* 1. malarial fever with periodic attacks of chills and sweating 2. fit of shivering

ah (ä) *interj.* exclamation of pleasure, pain *etc.*

A.H. 1. (indicating years in Muslim system of dating, numbered from Hegira (622 A.D.)) anno hegirae 2. ampere-hour 3. arts and humanities

aha (ä'hä) *interj.* exclamation of triumph, surprise *etc.*

Ahab ('ahab) *n.* in O.T., king of Israel whose name is a byword for wickedness

ahead (ə'hed) *adv.* 1. in front 2. onward

ahem (ə'hem) *interj.* clearing of throat to attract attention *etc.*

ahoy (ə'hoi) *interj.* shout used at sea for hailing

A.I. 1. artificial insemination 2. artificial intelligence 3. ad interim

aid (ād) *vt.* 1. to help —*n.* 2. help, support, assistance

AID Agency for International Development

A.I.D. artificial insemination by donor

aide (ād) *or* **aide-de-camp** ('āddə'kamp) *n.* military officer personally assisting superior (*pl.* **aides(-de-camp)**)

AIDS (ādz) acquired immuno-deficiency syndrome

aigrette (ā'gret, 'agret) *n.* 1. long plume worn on hats or as headdress, *esp.* one of egret feathers 2. ornament in imitation of plume of feathers

aiguille (ā'gwēl) *n.* 1. sharp, slender peak 2. blasting drill

A.I.H. artificial insemination by husband

ail (āl) *vt.* 1. trouble, afflict, disturb —*vi.* 2. be ill —'**ailing** *a.* sickly —'**ailment** *n.* illness

aileron ('aləron) *n.* movable section of wing of aircraft which gives lateral control

aim (ām) *v.* 1. give direction to (weapon *etc.*) 2. direct effort (toward) —*n.* 3. direction 4. object, purpose —'**aimless** *a.* without purpose

A.I.M. American Indian Movement

ain't (ānt) *nonstandard* 1. am not 2. is not 3. are not 4. has not 5. have not

Ainu ('īnōō) *n.* 1. member of indigenous Caucasoid people of Japan (*pl.* **Ainu** *or* **-s**) 2. their language

air (åər) *n.* 1. mixture of gases we breathe, the atmosphere 2. breeze 3. tune 4. manner —*pl.* 5. affected manners —*vt.* 6. expose to air to dry or ventilate —'**airily** *adv.* —'**airiness** *n.* —'**airing** *n.* 1. exposure to open air or heat for drying or freshening 2. exercise in open air 3. exposure to public view 4. radio or television broadcast —'**airy** *a.* 1. of or relating to air 2. unreal, illusory 3. open to air circulation 4. carelessly condescending —**air bag** automatically inflating bag in front of automobile passengers to protect them from impact in case of accident —**air base** military airfield —**air bladder** sac containing gas and air, *esp.* present in most fishes serving as accessory to respiration —'**airborne** *a.* flying in the air —**air brake** 1. brake operated by compressed air 2. structure for lowering speed of airplane —'**airbrush** *n.* 1. atomizer, *esp.* for applying paint —*vt.* 2. paint with airbrush —**air-condition** *vt.* —**air conditioner** —**air-conditioning** *n.* apparatus for controlling temperature and humidity of air —**air-cool**

vt. cool (engine) by flow of air —**'aircraft** *n.* 1. collective name for flying machines 2. airplane —**aircraft carrier** warship with flight deck on which airplanes can be launched and landed —**air cushion** pocket of air supporting hovercraft —**air-cushion vehicle** *see* **ground-effect machine** *at* GROUND¹ —**'airfield** *n.* 1. landing field for aircraft 2. airport —**air force** 1. military organization of nation for air warfare 2. unit of U.S. Air Force higher than division and lower than command —**air gun** 1. gun from which projectile is propelled by compressed air 2. hand tool operated by compressed air —**air lane** path usu. followed by airplanes —**air letter** airmail letter —**'airlift** *n.* system of transporting goods and persons by aircraft to or from otherwise inaccessible area —**'airline** *n.* air transportation system including equipment, routes and personnel —**'airliner** *n.* large passenger aircraft —**air lock** 1. intermediate chamber between places of unequal atmospheric pressure or temperature 2. stoppage of flow caused by air being in a part where water ought to circulate —**'airmail** *n.* 1. system of transporting mail by aircraft 2. mail so transported —**'airman** *n.* 1. pilot, aviator or aviation technician 2. enlisted man in U.S. Air Force ranking above airman basic and below airman first class —**airman basic** enlisted man of lowest rank in U.S. Air Force —**airman first class** enlisted man above airman and below sergeant —**airplane** *n.* fixed-wing aircraft heavier than air, driven by propeller or by high-velocity jet, supported by the dynamic reaction of the air against its wings —**air plant** 1. epiphyte 2. bryophyllum —**air pocket** condition of local atmosphere causing airplane to drop suddenly —**air pollution** waste products in the form of extraneous gases and small suspended particles in the atmosphere —**'airport** *n.* place maintained for landing and take-off of aircraft and receiving and discharging passengers and cargo, with facilities for shelter, supply and repair of aircraft —**air pump** machine to extract, compress or supply air —**air raid** attack by armed aircraft —**air rifle** rifle whose projectile is propelled by compressed air or carbon dioxide —**air sac** 1. air-filled space in body of bird, connected to lungs 2. air cell of the lungs of mammals —**air screw** 1. screw propeller designed to operate in air 2. **UK** airplane propeller —**air shaft** well-like ventilating passage —**'airship** *n.* lighter-than-air aircraft with propulsion and steering control —**'airsickness** *n. see* **motion sickness** *at* MOTION —**'airspace** *n.* space above the earth, *esp.* that lying above a country and under its jurisdiction —**'airspeed** *n.* speed of aircraft relative to air —**'airstrip** *n.* runway lacking airport facilities —**'airtight** *a.* 1. impermeable to air or nearly so 2. (of argument) without weakness or loophole —**air-to-air** *a.* relating to aircraft in flight —**air trap** device to prevent escape of foul gases —**air valve** —**'airwave** *n.* 1. medium of radio and television transmission 2. channel of designated radio frequency for communication —**'airway** *n.* 1. passage for current of air 2. designated route for aircraft —**'airworthiness** *n.* —**'airworthy** *a.* fit for operation in the air

Airedale ('ăərdāl) *n.* purebred large rough-coated terrier

aisle (īl) *n.* passageway separating seating areas in church, theater *etc.*

aitch (āch) *n.* letter *h* or sound represented by it

aitchbone ('āchbōn) *n.* 1. hip bone in cattle 2. cut of beef containing this bone

ajar¹ (ə'jär) *a./adv.* partly open

ajar² (ə'jär) *a.* (*with* with) in contradiction (to), at variance (with)

AK Alaska

AKA *or* **a.k.a.** also known as

AKC American Kennel Club

akialoa (äkiə'lōə) *n.* Hawaiian honeycreeper: songbird found only in Hawaiian Islands, having long thin beak and tubular tongue with brushlike tip

akimbo (ə'kimbō) *adv.* with hands on hips and elbows outward

akin (ə'kin) *a.* 1. related by blood 2. alike, having like qualities

akita (ə'kētə) *n.* purebred working dog resembling a spitz, orig. from Japan

Al *Chem.* aluminum

AL 1. Alabama 2. American League 3. American Legion

-al¹ (*a. comb. form*) of; related to, as in *functional, sectional*

-al² (*n. comb. form*) act or process of, as in *renewal*

-al³ (*n. comb. form*) 1. aldehyde, as in *salicylal* 2. pharmaceutical product, as in *phenobarbital*

à la (ä lä) 1. in the manner of 2. as prepared in, by or for

ALA 1. American Legal Association 2. American Library Association

Ala. Alabama

Alabama (alə'bamə) *n.* East South Central state of the U.S., admitted to the Union in 1819. Abbrev.: **Ala., AL** (with ZIP code)

alabaster ('aləbăstər) *n.* soft, white, semi-transparent stone —**ala'bastrine** *a.* of, like this

à la carte (ä lä 'kärt) (of menu) pricing each item separately

alack (ə'lak) *or* **alackaday** (ə'lakədā) *interj. obs., poet.* cry of sorrow

alacrity (ə'lakriti) *n.* quickness, briskness, readiness

à la mode *or* **a la mode** (ä lä 'mōd) 1. in fashion 2. topped with ice cream

alarm (ə'lärm) *n.* 1. sudden fright 2. apprehension 3. notice of danger 4. bell, buzzer 5. call to arms 6. frighten 7. warn of danger —**a'larming** *a.* —**a'larmist** *n.* one given to prophesying danger or exciting alarm *esp.* needlessly —**alarm clock** clock which sounds a buzzer or bell at a set time —**alarm reaction** initial response (as increased hormonal activity) of an organism to stress

alas (ə'las) *interj.* cry of grief

Alaska (ə'laskə) *n.* Pacific state of the U.S., admitted to the Union in 1959. Abbrev.: **AK** (with ZIP code) —**Alaskan malamute** purebred working dog with heavy coat, erect ears, heavily cushioned feet and plumy tail

alate ('ālāt) *a.* having wings

alb (alb) *n.* long white priestly vestment, worn at Mass

albacore ('albəkōr) *n.* any of several tunas

Albania (al'bāniə) *n.* country of eastern Europe bounded north and east by Yugoslavia, south by Greece and west by Adriatic Sea —**Al'banian** *n./a.* 1. (native or inhabitant) of Albania —*n.* 2. language of Albania, which is the only member of its branch

albatross

albatross ('albətrös) *n.* member of family of sea-living birds found from the Antarctic to the tropics, about the size of a goose or swan, except for the wandering albatross with an 11-12ft. wingspan

albeit (öl'bēit) *conj.* although

Alberta (al'bərtə) *n.* western province of Canada, bounded south by the U.S., west by British Columbia, north by Northwest Territory and east by Saskatchewan

albino (al'bīnō) *n.* person or animal with white skin and hair, and pinkish eyes, due to lack of coloring matter (*pl.* -s) —**albinism** ('albinizəm) *n.*

Albion ('albiən) *n. obs., poet.* 1. Britain 2. England

album ('albəm) *n.* 1. book of blank leaves, for photographs, stamps, autographs *etc.* 2. one or more long-playing records released as single item

albumen *or* **albumin** (al'byōōmin) *n.* egg white

albumin (al'byōōmin) *n.* constituent of animal and vegetable matter, found nearly pure in white of egg —**al'buminous** *a.*

alchemy ('alkəmi) *n.* medieval chemistry, *esp.* attempts to turn base metals into gold and find elixir of life —**'alchemist** *n.*

alcohol ('alkəhöl) *n.* 1. intoxicating fermented liquor 2. class of organic chemical substances —**alco'holic** *a.* 1. of alcohol —*n.* 2. one addicted to alcoholic drink —**'alcoholism** *n.* (disease caused by) habitual heavy consumption of alcoholic drink

alcove ('alkōv) *n.* recess

aldehyde ('aldihīd) *n.* one of the class of chemical compounds with the general formula RCHO, where R is an organic group, the simplest aldehyde being formaldehyde

alder ('öldər) *n.* tree related to the birch

alderman ('öldərmən) *n.* member of governing body of a municipality —**alder'manic** *a.*

ale (āl) *n.* fermented malt liquor, type of beer, orig. without hops —**'alehouse** *n. obs.* public house

aleatory ('āliətöri) *or* **aleatoric** (āliə'törik) *a.* 1. dependent on chance 2. *Mus.* involving elements chosen at random

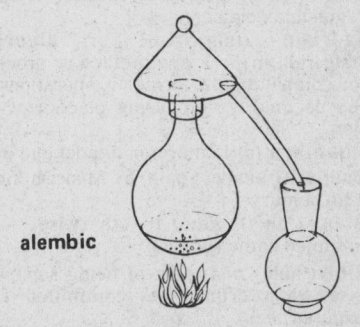

alembic

alembic (ə'lembik) *n.* 1. formerly, retort used for distillation 2. anything that distills or purifies

alert (ə'lərt) a. 1. watchful 2. brisk, active —n. 3. warning of sudden attack or surprise —vt. 4. warn, esp. of danger 5. draw (someone's) attention to something —a'lertness n. —on the alert watchful

Aleut (ali'ōōt) n. 1. member of Amerindian people inhabiting Kenai and Alaska peninsula and the Aleutian Islands 2. language of this people —**Aleutian Islands** (ə'lōōshən) archipelago extending southwest from the Alaska peninsula in the north Pacific Ocean (also **Aleutians**)

Alexander the Great (alig'zandər) (356-323 B.C.) conqueror of the civilized world who extended Greek civilization to the East

Alexandrine (alig'zandrin) n. 1. verse of six iambic feet 2. verse of 12 syllables containing four accents

alexandrite (alig'zandrit) n. variety of chrysoberyl, green by daylight and red-violet by artificial light, used as gemstone

alexia (ə'leksiə) n. impaired ability to read

Alfa ('alfə) n. word used in communications for the letter a

alfalfa (al'falfə) n. plant of Europe and Asia used as fodder (also **lu'cerne**)

alfresco (al'freskō) adv./a. in the open air

alg. algebra

alga ('algə) n. lower plant classified according to color: blue-green, green, brown or red, which may be microscopic unicellular organisms, sometimes colonial, to multicellular seaweed (pl. **algae** ('aljē)) —**al'gologist** n. specialist in study of algae

algebra ('aljibrə) n. 1. branch of mathematics dealing with the properties and relations of numbers 2. the generalization and extension of arithmetic —**algebraic(al)** (alji'brāik(əl)) a. —**algebraist** (alji'brāist) n.

Algeria (al'jēəriə) n. country in north Africa, bounded west by Morocco and Western Sahara, southwest by Mauritania and Mali, southeast by Niger, east by Libya and Tunisia, and north by the Mediterranean Sea —**Al'gerian** a./n.

-algia (n. comb. form) pain in part specified, as in neuralgia —**-algic** (a. comb. form)

algid ('aljid) a. Med. chilly, cold

ALGOL ('algol) computer programming language designed for mathematical and scientific purposes

Algonkin (al'gongkin) n. 1. Algonquian 2. Geol. period of Precambrian era, about 600 000 000 to about 1 000 000 000 years ago, marked by appearance of bacteria and marine algae

Algonquian (al'gongkwiən), **Algonquin** (al'gonkwin), or **Algonkin** n. 1. Amerindian language group formerly spoken from Labrador south to the Carolinas and westward to the Rockies 2. a people of Ottawa River Valley 3. speaker of any of Algonquian dialects

algorism ('algərizəm) or **algorithm** ('algəridhəm) n. 1. any method or procedure for computation 2. formerly, operations with the decimal system using placement notation

Alhambra (al'hambrə) n. citadel and palace built at Granada, Spain, by Moorish kings in 13th century

alias ('āliəs) adv. 1. otherwise —n. 2. assumed name (pl. **-es**)

alibi ('alibī) n. 1. plea of being somewhere else when crime was committed 2. inf. excuse (pl. **-s**)

alien ('āliən) a. 1. foreign 2. different in nature 3. repugnant —n. 4. foreigner —**aliena'bility** n. —**'alienable** a. able to be transferred to another owner —**'alienate** vt.

1. estrange 2. transfer —**alie'nation** n. —**'alienist** n. psychiatrist, esp. one who specializes in legal aspects of mental illness

alight¹ (ə'līt) vi. 1. get down 2. land, settle

alight² (ə'līt) a. 1. burning 2. lit up

align (ə'līn) vt. 1. bring into line or agreement —vi. 2. be in or come into correct relative position —**a'lignment** n.

alike (ə'līk) a. 1. like, similar —adv. 2. in the same way

aliment ('alimənt) n. something that nourishes or sustains body or mind —**ali'mentary** a. of food —**alimentary canal** tubular passage extending from mouth to anus, whose function is to ingest food and eliminate residual waste

alimony ('alimōni) n. allowance paid under court order to separated or divorced spouse

A-line ('ālīn) a. (of garments) flaring out slightly from waist or shoulders

aliped ('aliped) a. 1. wing-footed —n. 2. animal, like the bat, whose toes are joined by membrane that serves as wing

aliphatic (ali'fatik) a. Chem. of any organic compound having open chain structure

aliquant ('alikwənt) a. Math. (of quantity or number) that is not exact divisor of given quantity or number

aliquot ('alikwot) a. Math. of or signifying an exact divisor of a quantity or number

alive (ə'līv) a. 1. living 2. active 3. aware 4. swarming

aliyah or **aliya** (ä'lēyä) n. the immigration of Jews to Israel

alizarin (ə'lizərin) n. red dye formerly obtained from madder

alkali ('alkəlī) n. one of a class of substances that neutralize or are neutralized by acids and form corrosive solutions in water, eg caustic soda, ammonia (pl. **-s**, **-es**) —**alkaline** ('alkəlin) a. —**alka'linity** n. —**'alkalize** vt. —**'alkaloid** n./a. —**alka'losis** n. condition caused by excess of alkaline substances or shortage of acidic substances in the body fluids —**alkali metal** Chem. any of group of elements comprising lithium, sodium, potassium, rubidium, cesium and francium (so-called because their hydroxides are strongly alkaline)

Alkoran or **Alcoran** (alko'ran) n. see KORAN

all (ōl) a. 1. the whole of, every one of —adv. 2. wholly, entirely —n. 3. the whole 4. everything, everyone —**all-American** a. 1. comprising wholly American elements 2. typical of the U.S. 3. (esp. of athlete) selected as one of the best in U.S. in category at particular time —n. 4. such a person —**all around** 1. competent in many fields 2. having general usefulness or merit —**all fours** 1. all limbs of quadruped 2. legs and arms of person when crawling —**all get-out** utmost conceivable degree —**all in** tired —**all in all** on the whole —**all out** with enthusiasm —**all over** 1. over whole extent 2. everywhere 3. thoroughly —**all-over** a. covering whole surface —**'allover** a. consisting of repeated pattern —**all right** a. 1. adequate; satisfactory 2. unharmed; safe —adv. 3. very well 4. satisfactorily 5. without doubt (also (nonstandard) **al'right**) —**All Saints' Day** Christian festival celebrated on Nov. 1st to honor all saints —**all set** ready to begin —**All Souls' Day** R.C. day of prayer (Nov. 2nd) for the dead —**all there** mentally alert

alla breve ('alə brēv) Mus. a./adv. 1. in quick duple time with half note rather than quarter note as the beat, ie 2/2 instead of 4/4 —n. 2. mark indicating this

Allah ('alə, ä'lä) n. Muslim name for the Supreme Deity

allay (ə'lā) vt. lighten, relieve, calm, soothe

allege (ə'lej) vt. 1. state without or before proof 2. produce as argument —**allegation** (ali'gāshən) n. —**al'leged** a. —**allegedly** (ə'lejidli) adv.

Allegheny (ali'gāni) n. river flowing south from southwest New York through western Pennsylvania, joining Monongahela at Pittsburgh to form Ohio River —**Allegheny Mountains** mountain range in Pennsylvania, Maryland, West Virginia and Virginia: part of the Appalachian Mountains —**Allegheny spurge** (spərj) low perennial of the box family widely grown as ground cover

allegiance (ə'lējəns) n. duty of a subject to his sovereign or state, loyalty

allegory ('aligōri) n. 1. story with a meaning other than literal one 2. description of one thing under image of another —**alle'goric(al)** a. —**alle'gorically** adv. —**'allegorist** n. —**'allegorize** vt.

allegretto (ali'gretō) Mus. adv./a./n. 1. (in) tempo between allegro and andante —n. 2. short piece in lively tempo (pl. **-s**)

allegro (ə'lagrō, -'leg-) Mus. adv./a./n. 1. (in) fast tempo —n. 2. title for movement or composition in fast tempo (pl. **-s**)

alleluia (ali'lōōyə) interj. praise the Lord (also **hallelujah**)

allemande ('alimand) n. Mus. 1. first dance movement in suites of pre-18th-cent. composers 2. in late 18th cent., quick waltzlike dance in 3/4 or 3/8 time

allentando (alen'tandō) a./adv. Mus. slowing down

allergy ('alərji) n. abnormal sensitivity to some food or substance innocuous to most people —**'allergen** n. substance capable of inducing an allergy —**aller'genic** a. —**al'lergic** a. 1. having or caused by an allergy 2. inf. having an aversion (to)

alleviate (ə'lēviāt) vt. 1. ease, lessen, mitigate 2. make light —**allevi'ation** n. —**al'leviator** n.

alley ('ali) n. 1. narrow street, esp. through middle of block giving rear access to buildings 2. walk, path 3. enclosure for skittles 4. hardwood lane for bowling 5. building housing group of such lanes 6. playing marble (pl. **-s**)

alliance (ə'līəns) n. 1. state of being allied 2. union between families by marriage, and states by treaty 3. confederation

alligator ('aligātər) n. 1. reptile of crocodile family of southern U.S. and northern Central America —a. 2. (of article) made from skin of alligator —**alligator clip** spring-loaded clip with jaws resembling alligator's, used for temporary electrical connections —**alligator pear** avocado

alliteration (əlitə'rāshən) n. beginning two or more words in close succession with same sound, eg Sing a Song of Sixpence —**al'literate** v. —**al'literative** a.

allo- (comb. form) other, as in allogamy, allopathy

allocate ('aləkāt) vt. 1. assign as a share 2. place —**allo'cation** n.

allocution (alə'kyōōshən) n. formal address

allogamy (ə'logəmi) n. cross-fertilization

allomorphism (alə'mörfizəm) n. 1. variation of form without change in essential nature 2. variation of crystalline form of chemical compound

allopathy (ə'lopəthi) n. orthodox practice of medicine: opposite of homeopathy

allot (ə'lot) vt. 1. distribute as shares 2. give out (**-tt-**) —**al'lotment** n. 1. distribution 2. portion of land rented for cultivation 3. portion allotted

allotropy (ə'lotrəpi) *or* **allotropism** *n.* property of some elements of existing in more than one form, *eg* carbon in the form of diamond and graphite —'**allotrope** *n.* —**allo**'**tropic** *a.*

allow (ə'low) *vt.* 1. permit 2. acknowledge 3. set aside —*vi.* (*usu. with* for) 4. take into account —**al**'**lowable** *a.* —**al**'**lowably** *adv.* —**al**'**lowance** *n.* —**allowedly** (ə'lowidli) *adv.* 1. by general agreement 2. admittedly

alloy ('aloi, ə'loi) *n.* 1. mixture of two or more metals —*vt.* (ə'loi) 2. mix (metals) to form an alloy 3. debase by mixing with something inferior

allspice ('ölspīs) *n.* 1. (berry of) W Indian tree 2. spice made from this berry

allude (ə'lōōd) *vi.* 1. mention lightly, hint (at), make indirect reference (to) 2. refer (to) —**al**'**lusion** *n.* —**al**'**lusive** *a.* —**al**'**lusively** *adv.*

allure (ə'lōōr) *vt.* 1. entice, win over, fascinate —*n.* 2. attractiveness —**al**'**lurement** *n.* —**al**'**luring** *a.* charming, seductive —**al**'**luringly** *adv.*

alluvial (ə'lōōviəl) *a.* deposited by rivers —**al**'**luvion** *n.* land formed by washed-up deposit —**al**'**luvium** *n.* water-borne matter deposited by rivers, floods *etc.* (*pl.* **-s, -via** (-viə))

ally (ə'lī) *vt.* 1. join in relationship by treaty, marriage or friendship *etc.* (**al**'**lied, al**'**lying**) —*n.* ('alī) 2. state or sovereign bound to another by treaty 3. confederate (*pl.* '**allies**) —**allied** (ə'līd, 'alīd) *a.* —'**Allies** *pl.n.* 1. (in World War I) powers of the Triple Entente (France, Russia and Britain) together with nations allied with them 2. (in World War II) countries that fought against the Axis, *esp.* Britain and Commonwealth countries, U.S., Soviet Union and France

alma mater ('almə 'mätər) *Lat.* 1. one's school, university or college 2. song or hymn of school, university or college

almanac ('ölmənak) *n.* 1. yearly calendar with detailed information on year's tides, events *etc.* 2. annual publication containing astronomical or meteorological data 3. compendium of useful facts

almighty (öl'mīti) *a.* 1. having all power, omnipotent 2. *inf.* very great —**the Almighty** God

almond ('ämənd) *n.* 1. edible kernel of the fruit of a tree related to the peach 2. tree bearing this fruit —**almond paste** edible paste made from ground almonds

almost ('ölmōst) *adv.* very nearly, all but

alms (ämz) *pl.n.* gifts to the poor

aloe ('alō) *n.* 1. genus of succulent plants of the lily family, with basal leaves and spikelike flowers grown for ornament —*pl.n.* (*with sing. v.*) 2. bitter drug made from plant

aloft (ə'loft) *adv.* 1. on high 2. overhead 3. in ship's rigging

alone (ə'lōn) *a.* 1. single, solitary —*adv.* 2. separately, only

along (ə'long) *adv.* 1. in a line 2. together with one 3. forward —*prep.* 4. over the length of —**a**'**long**'**side** *adv./prep.* beside (something)

aloof (ə'lōōf) *a.* 1. withdrawn 2. distant 3. uninvolved —**a**'**loofness** *n.*

alopecia (alə'pēshiə) *n.* baldness

aloud (ə'lowd) *adv.* 1. loudly 2. audibly

alp (alp) *n.* high mountain —**alpine** ('alpīn) *a.* 1. of the Alps 2. of high mountains —*n.* 3. mountain plant —**alpinist** ('alpinist) *n.* mountain climber —'**alpenstock** *n.* iron-shod staff used by climbers —**alpine horn** primitive wind instrument used by herdsmen in the Alps for calling cattle and rendering simple melodies —**the Alps** high mountain range in S central Europe

alpaca

alpaca (al'pakə) *n.* 1. Peruvian llama 2. its wool 3. cloth made from this

alpha ('alfə) *n.* 1. first letter in Greek alphabet (A, α) —*a.* 2. involving helium nuclei; denoting isomeric or allotropic form of substance —**alpha particle** helium nucleus emitted during some radioactive transformations —**alpha ray** ionizing radiation consisting of stream of alpha particles —**alpha and omega** the first and last

alphabet ('alfəbet) *n.* 1. the set of letters used in writing a language 2. system of signs or signals substituting for alphabet —**alpha**'**betic(al)** *a.* in the standard order of the letters —**alpha**'**betically** *adv.* —'**alphabetize** *vt.* 1. arrange in alphabetical order 2. express by alphabet

alphanumeric (alfənyōō'merik, -nōō-) *or* **alphanumerical** *a.* consisting of alphabetical and numerical symbols

already (öl'redi) *adv.* 1. before, previously 2. sooner than expected

alright (öl'rīt) *adv.* nonstandard *see* **all right** *at* **ALL**

Alsatian (al'sāshən) *n. see* **German shepherd** *at* **GERMAN**

also ('ölsō) *adv.* 1. as well, too 2. besides, moreover —**also-ran** *n.* 1. contestant *etc.* failing to finish among first three 2. *inf.* loser

alt. 1. alternate 2. altitude 3. alto

Alta. Alberta

altar ('öltər) *n.* 1. raised place, stone *etc.*, on which sacrifices are offered 2. in Christian church, table on which priest consecrates the Eucharist —**altar boy** boy serving as an acolyte —'**altarcloth** *n.* —'**altarpiece** *n.*

alter ('öltər) *v.* change, make or become different —**altera**'**bility** *n.* —'**alterable** *a.* —'**alterably** *adv.* —**alte**'**ration** *n.* —'**alterative** *a.*

altercation (öltər'kāshən) *n.* dispute, wrangling, controversy —'**altercate** *vi.*

alter ego ('öltər 'ēgō, 'egō) *Lat.* 1. second self 2. close friend

alternate ('öltərnāt) *v.* 1. occur or cause to occur by turns —*a.* ('öltərnit) 2. one after the other, by turns —*n.* ('öltərnit) 3. one that substitutes for another —'**alternately** *adv.* —**alter**'**nation** *n.* 1. in algebra and geometry, one of the properties of proportion 2. in symbolic logic, one of several names given to the relation 'either-or-both' —**al**'**ternative** *n.* 1. one of two choices —*a.* 2. presenting choice, *esp.* between two possibilities only 3. (of two things) mutually exclusive 4. denoting life style *etc.* regarded as preferable to that of contemporary society because it is less conventional, materialistic or institutionalized —**al**'**ternatively** *adv.* —'**alternator** *n.* electric generator for producing alternating current —**alternating current** electric current that reverses direction with a frequency independent of characteristics of circuit —**alternative society** group of people who agree in rejecting traditional values of society around them

althaea *or* **althea** (al'thēə) *n.* hollyhock

althorn ('alt-hörn) *n.* alto saxhorn

although (öl'dhō) *conj.* despite the fact that

altimeter (al'timitər, 'altimētər) *n.* instrument for measuring height

altitude ('altityōōd, -tōōd) *n.* height, eminence, elevation, loftiness

alto ('altō) *n. Mus.* 1. contralto 2. male singing voice or instrument above tenor (*pl.* **-s**) —*a.* 3. of an alto —**alto clef** clef that establishes middle C as being on third line of staff

altogether (öltə'gedhər) *adv.* 1. entirely 2. on the whole 3. in total —*n.* 4. (*with* the) nude

altruism ('altrōōizəm) *n.* principle of living and acting for good of others —**altru**'**istic** *a.* —**altru**'**istically** *adv.*

alum ('aləm) *n.* mineral salt, double sulfate of aluminum and potassium, used as astringent and styptic —**aluminous** (ə'lōōminəs) *a.*

aluminum (ə'lōōminəm) *n. Chem.* metallic element noted for its lightness and resistance to oxidation *Symbol* Al, at. wt. 27.0, at. no. 13 —**a**'**lumina** *n.* oxide of aluminum —**a**'**luminize** *vt.* coat with aluminum —**a**'**luminous** *a.*

alumnus (ə'lumnəs) *or* (*fem.*) **alumna** (ə'lumnə) *n.* one who has attended or graduated from a particular school, college or university (*pl.* **-ni** (-nī) *or* **-nae** (-nē))

alumroot ('aləmrōōt) *n.* heuchera with an astringent root

always ('ölwāz) *adv.* 1. at all times 2. for ever

alyssum (ə'lisəm) *n.* genus of hardy annuals, herbaceous perennials and evergreen subshrubs of the cabbage family, widely grown as ornamentals

Alzheimer's disease ('älts-hīmərz) disease characterized by loss of memory for recent events and inability to store new memories

am (am; *unstressed* əm) *first person sing. pres. ind. of* BE

Am 1. *Chem.* americium 2. America(n)

AM *or* **am** amplitude modulation

a.m. *or* **A.M.** ante meridiem

AMA American Medical Association

amah ('ämä) *n.* Chinese nursemaid or maidservant

amain (ə'mān) *adv. obs., poet.* with great strength or haste

amalgam (ə'malgəm) *n.* 1. compound of mercury and another metal 2. soft, plastic mixture 3. combination of elements

amalgamate (ə'malgəmāt) *v.* mix, combine or cause to combine —**amalga**'**mation** *n.*

amanuensis (əmanyōō'ensis) *n.* 1. person employed to take dictation 2. copyist 3. secretary (*pl.* **-ses** (-sēz))

amaranth ('aməranth) *n.* 1. imaginary purple everlasting flower 2. genus of flowering plants —**ama**'**ranthine** *a.* never fading

amaryllis (amə'rilis) *n.* 1. genus comprising single bulbous species of lily family (*also* **belladonna lily**) 2. hippeastrum 3. (A-) rustic sweetheart

amass (ə'mas) *vt.* collect in quantity —**a**'**massable** *a.*

amateur ('amətər) *n.* 1. one who carries on an art, study, game *etc.* for pleasure rather than for financial gain 2. unskilled practitioner —*a.* 3. not professional or expert —**ama**'**teurish** *a.* imperfect, untrained —**ama**'**teurishly** *adv.* —'**amateurism** *n.*

Amati (ə'mäti) *n.* member of family of violin-makers of Cremona from about 1535 to 1684 who brought the art of violin-making to its peak, and teachers of Stradivarius and Guarnerius (*pl.* **-s**)

amatol ('amətöl) *n.* high explosive consisting of ammonium nitrate and trinitrotoluene (TNT)

amatory ('amətöri) *or* **amatorial** (amə'töriəl) *a.* relating to love

amaze (ə'māz) *vt.* surprise greatly, astound —**a'mazement** *n.* —**a'mazing** *a.* —**a'mazingly** *adv.*

Amazon ('aməzən) *n.* 1. female warrior of legend 2. tall, strong woman —**Ama'zonian** *a.*

ambassador (am'basədər) *n.* 1. official envoy, *esp.* person accredited to a foreign state as representative of own country 2. authorized representative 3. unofficial representative —**ambassa'dorial** *a.* —**am'bassadorship** *n.* —**ambassador-at-large** *n.* person performing same duties as ambassador, but not accredited to a particular state

amber ('ambər) *n.* 1. yellowish, translucent fossil resin —*a.* 2. made of, colored like amber

ambergris ('ambərgrēs, -gris) *n.* waxy substance secreted by the sperm whale, used in making perfumes

ambi- (*comb. form*) both, as in *ambidextrous, ambivalence*

ambidextrous (ambi'dekstrəs) *a.* able to use both hands with equal ease —**ambidex'terity** *n.*

ambience *or* **ambiance** ('ambiəns) *n.* atmosphere of a place

ambient ('ambiənt) *a.* surrounding

ambiguous (am'bigyōōs) *a.* 1. having more than one meaning 2. obscure —**ambi'guity** *n.* —**am'biguously** *adv.*

ambit ('ambit) *n.* 1. circuit 2. compass

ambition (am'bishən) *n.* 1. desire for power, fame, honor *etc.* 2. the object of that desire —**am'bitious** *a.* —**am'bitiously** *adv.* —**am'bitiousness** *n.*

ambivalence (am'bivələns) *n.* simultaneous existence of two conflicting desires, opinions *etc.* —**am'bivalent** *a.*

amble ('ambəl) *vi.* 1. move along easily and gently 2. move at an easy pace —*n.* 3. this movement or pace —**'ambler** *n.*

ambrosia (am'brōzhiə) *n.* 1. *Myth.* food of the gods 2. anything smelling or tasting particularly good

ambulance ('ambyōōləns) *n.* conveyance for sick or injured —**ambulance chaser** lawyer or agent who incites accident victim to sue for damages

ambulatory ('ambyōōlətöri) *a.* 1. of or for walking 2. not fixed 3. able to walk (*also* **'ambulant**) —*n.* 4. place for walking, such as cloister

ambuscade (ambə'skād) *n.* 1. act of hiding to launch surprise attack 2. ambush

ambush ('ambōōsh) *n.* 1. act of lying in wait —*vt.* 2. waylay, attack from hiding, lie in wait for

ameliorate (ə'mēlyərāt) *v.* make better, improve—**amelio'ration** *n.*—**a'meliorative** *a.*

amen (ā'men, ä'men) *interj.* 1. surely 2. so let it be

amenable (ə'mēnəbəl) *a.* easy to be led or controlled —**amena'bility** *or* **a'menableness** *n.*—**a'menably** *adv.* —**amenable to 1.** likely to respond to **2.** answerable to

amend (ə'mend) *vt.* 1. correct 2. improve 3. alter in detail, as bill in parliament *etc.* —**a'mendment** *n.* —**a'mends** *pl.n.* reparation

amenity (ə'meniti, -'mē-) *n.* (*oft. pl.*) useful or pleasant facility or service

amenorrhea (āmenə'rēə, ä-) *n.* abnormal absence of menstruation

Amer. America(n)

America (ə'merikə) *n.* 1. continent in western hemisphere between the Atlantic and Pacific Oceans 2. the U.S. —**A'merican** *n./a.* (native or inhabitant) of the American continent or the U.S. —**Ameri'cana** *pl.n.* 1. artifacts typical of American civilization 2. American culture —**A'mericanism** *n.* characteristic of American English, *esp.* in contrast to British English —**A'mericanist** *n.* 1. anthropologist specializing in Amerindian languages or cultures 2. specialist in American culture or history —**Americani'zation** *n.* —**A'mericanize** *v.* 1. make or become American in character —*vt.* 2. naturalize as an American —**American Civil War** war (1861-65) between the U.S. and 11 Southern states which seceded from the Union and formed the Confederate States of America (*also* **War Between the States**) —**American English** native language of most U.S. inhabitants, distinguishable from British English in vocabulary and syntax but not sufficiently so as to make it a separate language —**American foxhound** purebred hound smaller than English foxhound but with longer ears and a dense hard glossy coat, usu. black, tan and white —**American Indian** Amerindian —**American Legion** organization of veterans of U.S. wars, founded in 1919 —**American leopard** jaguar —**American plan** hotel plan in which rates cover the cost of meals —**American Revolution** war (1775-83) for independence, waged by the 13 American colonies against Great Britain —**American saddle horse** 3- or 5-gaited horse of breed developed from thoroughbreds and native stock, mainly in Kentucky —**American shorthair** purebred domestic cat with short plushy coat —**American water spaniel** purebred medium-sized sporting dog of Amer. origin with curly chocolate- or liver-colored coat —**American wirehair** purebred domestic cat with short-haired woolly coat —**America's Cup** an international yachting trophy first won by the schooner *America* in 1851 —**the Americas** North and South America considered together

americium (amə'risiəm) *n. Chem.* transuranic element *Symbol* Am, at. wt. 243, at. no. 95

Amerindian (amə'rindiən) *n./a.* (of) member of any of the aboriginal peoples of the western hemisphere (*also* **American Indian**) —**'Amerind** *n.*

amethyst ('amithist) *n.* bluish-violet semiprecious stone

Amharic (am'harik) *n.* 1. official language of Ethiopia —*a.* 2. denoting this language

amiable ('āmiəbəl) *a.* friendly, kindly —**amia'bility** *or* **'amiableness** *n.* —**'amiably** *adv.*

amicable ('amikəbəl) *a.* friendly —**amica'bility** *n.* —**'amicably** *adv.*

amid (ə'mid) *or* **amidst** *prep.* in the middle of, among

amidships (ə'midships) *adv.* near, toward middle of ship

amino acid (ə'mēnō) any of group of nitrogen-containing organic compounds that form the proteins from which plants and animals are made

Amish ('āmish) *n./a.* (of or relating to) strict sect of Mennonites that settled in eastern Pennsylvania in 18th century

amiss (ə'mis) *a.* 1. wrong —*adv.* 2. faultily, badly —**take amiss** be offended by

amity ('amiti) *n.* friendship

ammeter ('amētər) *n.* instrument for measuring electric current

ammo ('amō) *n. inf.* ammunition

ammonia (ə'mōnyə) *n.* 1. pungent alkaline gas containing hydrogen and nitrogen 2. its solution in water —**am'moniac** *or* **ammoniacal** (amə'nīəkəl) *a.* —**am'moniated** *a.* —**am'monium** *n.*

ammonite ('amənīt) *n.* whorled fossil shell like ram's horn

ammunition (amyōō'nishən) *n.* 1. any projectiles (bullets, rockets *etc.*) that can be discharged from a weapon 2. any means of defense or attack, as in argument

amnesia (am'nēzhə) *n.* loss of memory

amnestic confabulatory syndrome (am'nestik kən'fabyələtöri) Korsakoff's psychosis

amnesty ('amnisti) *n.* 1. general pardon —*vt.* 2. grant amnesty to

amnion ('amniən) *n.* innermost of two membranes enclosing embryonic reptile, bird or mammal (*pl.* **-s, amnia** ('amniə)) —**amni'otic** *a.* —**amniotic fluid** fluid surrounding baby in womb

amoeba (ə'mēbə) *n.* one-celled microorganism found in water, damp soil, and digestive tracts of animals (*pl.* **-s, -bae** (-bē)) —**a'moebic** *a.* —**amoebic dysentery** destruction of the intestinal lining by amoeba

amok *or* **amuck** (ə'muk) *adv.* possessed with murderous frenzy

among (ə'mung) *or* **amongst** *prep.* mixed with, in the midst of, of the number of, between

amoral (ā'mörəl) *a.* nonmoral, having no moral qualities —**amo'rality** *n.*

amorous ('amərəs) *a.* 1. inclined to love 2. in love —**'amorously** *adv.* —**'amorousness** *n.*

amorphous (ə'mörfəs) *a.* without distinct shape —**a'morphism** *n.*

amortize (ə'mörtīz) *vt.* pay off (a debt) by a sinking fund

Amos ('āmos) *n.* 1. *Bible* 30th book of the O.T. 2. author of this book, 8th-cent. B.C. prophet, who pled for social justice

amount (ə'mount) *vi.* 1. come (to), be equal (to) —*n.* 2. quantity 3. sum total

amour (ə'mōōr) *n.* (illicit) love affair

amour-propre (amōōr'propr) *Fr.* self-respect

amp ampere

ampere ('ampēər) *n.* unit of electric current —**amperage** ('ampərij) *n.* strength of electric current measured in amperes —**ampere-hour** *n.* practical unit of quantity of electricity

ampersand ('ampərsand) *n.* the sign & (and)

amphetamine (am'fetəmēn) *n.* synthetic liquid used medicinally mainly for its stimulant action on central nervous system

amphi- (*comb. form*) 1. on both sides; at both ends; of both kinds, as in *amphipod, amphibious* 2. around, as in *amphibole*

amphibious (am'fibiəs) *a.* living or operating both on land and in water —**am'phibian** *n.* 1. cold-blooded egg-laying vertebrate with soft skin, gills at tadpole stage when aquatic, replaced by lungs as land-living adults, *eg* frogs, salamanders, toads 2. vehicle able to travel on land or water 3. aircraft that can alight on land or water

amphitheater ('amfithēətər) *n.* building with tiers of seats rising round an arena

amphora ('amfərə) *n.* two-handled jar of ancient Greece and Rome (*pl.* **-rae** (-rē), **-s**)

amp hr ampere-hour

ampicillin (ampi'silin) *n.* form of penicillin used to treat infections of respiratory, intestinal and urinary tracts

ample ('ampəl) *a.* **1.** big enough **2.** large, spacious —'**amply** *adv.*

amplify ('amplifī) *vt.* **1.** increase **2.** make bigger, louder *etc.* (**-fied, -fying**) —**amplifi-**'**cation** *n.* —'**amplifier** *n.*

amplitude ('amplityōōd, -tōōd) *n.* spaciousness, width, magnitude —**amplitude modulation** *Rad.* method of transmitting information in which amplitude of carrier wave is varied

ampoule, ampule, *or* **ampul** ('ampyōōl, -pōōl) *n.* container for hypodermic dose

ampulla (am'pōōlə) *n.* **1.** *Anat.* dilated end part of duct or canal **2.** *Christianity* vessel for wine and water used at the Eucharist; small flask for consecrated oil **3.** Roman two-handled bottle (*pl.* **ampullae** (-'pōōlē))

amputate ('ampyōōtāt) *v.* cut off (limb *etc.*) —**ampu**'**tation** *n.*

amt amount

Amtrak ('amtrak) *n.* railroad system in U.S.

amuck (ə'muk) *adv. see* AMOK

amulet ('amyōōlit) *n.* something carried or worn as a charm

amuse (ə'myōōz) *vt.* **1.** divert **2.** occupy pleasantly **3.** cause to laugh or smile —a'**musement** *n.* entertainment, pastime —a'**musing** *a.* —a'**musingly** *adv.*

AMVETS ('amvets) American Veterans of World War II

amylase ('amilās, -lāz) *n.* enzyme that hydrolyzes starch and glycogen to simple sugar

amylum ('amiləm) *n. see* STARCH

an (an; *unstressed* ən) *see* A

an- *or before consonant* **a-** (*comb. form*) not; without, as in *anaphrodisiac*

-an, -ean, *or* **-ian** (*comb. form*) **1.** belonging to; coming from; typical of; adhering to, as in *European, Elizabethan, Christian* **2.** person who specializes or is expert in, as in *dietician*

Anabaptist (anə'baptist) *n.* member of Protestant movement that rejected infant baptism and insisted adults be rebaptized

anabolism (ə'nabəlizəm) *n.* metabolic process in which complex molecules are synthesized from simpler ones with storage of energy —ana'**bolic** *a.* —**anabolic steroid** any of various hormones that encourage muscle and bone growth

anabranch ('anəbränch) *n.* stream that leaves a river and re-enters it further downstream

anachronism (ə'nakrənizəm) *n.* **1.** mistake of time, by which something is put in wrong historical period **2.** something out of date —anachro'**nistic** *a.*

anacoluthon (anəkə'lōōthon) *n.* a sentence or words faulty in grammatical sequence (*pl.* **-tha** (-thə))

anaconda (anə'kondə) *n.* large snake which kills by constriction

anadromous (ə'nadrəməs) *a.* (of salmon *etc.*) migrating up rivers to breed

anaerobe (an'āərōb) *n.* organism that can live without oxygen —anaer'**obic** *a.*

anaesthetic (anis'thetik) *n./a. see* ANESTHETIC

anagram ('anəgram) *n.* word or words made by arranging in different order the letters of another word or words, *eg* **ant** from *tan* —**anagram**'**matical** *a.* —ana'**grammatist** *n.*

anal ('ānəl) *a. see* ANUS

analects ('anəlekts) *or* **analecta** (anə'lektə) *pl.n.* selected literary passages from one or more works, usu. by one author

analgesia (anəl'jēzə) *n.* absence of pain —anal'**gesic** *a./n.* pain-relieving (agent)

analog ('anəlog) *n.* **1.** something analogous to something else **2.** *Biol.* analogous part or organ —*a.* **3.** using analog (such as dial and pointer) to represent data or information —**analog computer** computer that uses voltages to represent numbers of physical quantities

analogy (ə'naləji) *n.* **1.** agreement or likeness in certain respects **2.** correspondence —ana'**logical** *a.* —ana'**logically** *adv.* —a'**nalogist** *n.* —a'**nalogize** *v.* explain by analogy —**analogous** (ə'naləgəs) *a.* **1.** similar **2.** parallel —**analogously** (ə'naləgəsli) *adv.*

analysis (ə'nalisis) *n.* separation of something into its elements or components (*pl.* **-yses** (-isēz)) —a'**nalysand** *n.* person undergoing psychoanalysis —'**analyst** *n.* one skilled in analysis, *esp.* chemical or psychiatric analysis —ana'**lytic(al)** *a.* **1.** relating to analysis **2.** capable of or given to analyzing —ana'**lytically** *adv.* —'**analyze** *vt.* **1.** examine critically **2.** determine the constituent parts of —**analytic geometry** technique of using algebra to deal with geometry

anapest ('anəpest) *n.* metrical foot of two short syllables followed by one long syllable or two unstressed syllables followed by one stressed syllable

anaphora (ə'nafərə) *n.* **1.** *Rhetoric* repetition of word or phrase at beginning of successive clauses **2.** *Gram.* use of word such as pronoun to avoid repetition

anaphylaxis (anəfi'laksis) *n.* phenomenon of severe allergic reaction —anaphy'**lactic** *a.* —**anaphylactic shock** shock produced by ingesting allergen

anarchy ('anərki) *n.* **1.** lawlessness **2.** lack of government in a state **3.** confusion —an'**archic(al)** *a.* —an'**archically** *adv.* —'**anarchism** *n.* —'**anarchist** *n.* one who opposes all forms of government

anastigmat (a'nastigmat, anə'stigmat) *n.* lens corrected for astigmatism —anastig-'**matic** *a.* (of lens) not astigmatic

anastomosis (anastə'mōsis) *n.* interconnection of branches (streams, blood vessels, leaf veins) (*pl.* **-ses** (-sēz))

anat. **1.** anatomical **2.** anatomy

anathema (ə'nathəmə) *n.* **1.** anything detested, hateful **2.** ban of the church **3.** curse —a'**nathematize** *v.*

anatomy (ə'natəmi) *n.* **1.** science of structure of organisms **2.** detailed analysis **3.** the body —ana'**tomical** *a.* —ana'**tomically** *adv.* —a'**natomist** *n.* —a'**natomize** *vt.*

-ance *or* **-ancy** (*comb. form*) action, state or condition, or quality, as in *utterance, resemblance*

ancestor ('ansestər) *n.* **1.** person from whom another is descended **2.** early type of later form or product —an'**cestral** *a.* —'**ancestry** *n.*

anchor ('angkər) *n.* **1.** heavy (*usu.* hooked) implement dropped on cable, chain *etc.* to bottom of sea to secure vessel **2.** source of stability or security —*vt.* **3.** fasten by or as by anchor —'**anchorage** *n.* act of, place of anchoring —**anchor man 1.** *Sport* last competitor in relay team **2.** broadcaster who usu. introduces other reporters and reads the news **3.** one with lowest standing in a graduating class —**weigh anchor** haul up anchor and set sail

anchorite ('angkərīt) *n.* hermit, recluse ('**anchoress** *fem.*)

anchovy ('anchōvi) *n.* small savory fish of herring family

anchusa (ang'kyōōsə) *n.* plant with hairy leaves and blue flowers

ancien régime (äsyē rā'zhēm) **1.** *Fr.* political and social system of France before the Revolution of 1789 **2.** the old order of things (*pl.* **anciens régimes** (äsyē rā'zhēm))

ancient ('ānshənt) *a.* **1.** belonging to former age **2.** old **3.** timeworn —*n.* **4.** (*oft. pl.*) one who lived in an earlier age —'**anciently** *adv.* —**ancient history 1.** history of ancient times **2.** common knowledge

ancillary (an'siləri) *a.* subordinate, subservient, auxiliary

-ancy (*comb. form*) condition or quality, as in *poignancy* (*see also* -ANCE)

and (and; *unstressed* ənd, ən) *conj.* connecting word, used to join words and sentences, to introduce a consequence *etc.* —**and/or** *conj.* used to join terms when either one or other or both is indicated

andante (an'danti) *Mus. a./adv.* **1.** at moderately slow tempo, between allegretto and adagio —*n.* **2.** passage or piece performed in this manner

andantino (andan'tēnō) *a./adv. Mus.* slightly faster than andante

Andean ('andiən) *a.* of the Andes, range of mountains in western S Amer. —**andesine** ('andizēn) *n.* mineral of feldspar group having play of colors, usu. found as crystals in igneous rock —**andesite** ('andizīt) *n.* volcanic rock, usu. dark gray

andiron ('andīərn) *n.* iron bar or bracket for supporting logs in fireplace

Andorra (an'dörə) *n.* country in southern Europe, situated in eastern Pyrenees on the French-Spanish border —An'**dorran** *a./n.*

andro- *or before vowel* **andr-** (*comb. form*) **1.** male; masculine **2.** in botany, stamen or anther

androgen ('andrəjən) *n.* steroid that promotes development of male sexual characteristics

androgynous (an'drojinəs) *a.* **1.** *Bot.* having male and female flowers in same inflorescence **2.** hermaphrodite

android ('android) *n.* **1.** in science fiction, robot resembling human being —*a.* **2.** resembling human being

Andromeda (an'dromədə) *n.* **1.** in Greek legend, princess rescued from monster by her future husband Perseus **2.** northern constellation directly south of Cassiopeia, between Pegasus and Perseus

anecdote ('anikdōt) *n.* very short story dealing with single incident —**anec'dotal** *or* **anec'dotic** *a.*

anemia (ə'nēmiə) *n.* deficiency in number of red blood cells —a'**nemic** *a.* **1.** suffering from anemia **2.** pale, sickly, lacking vitality

anemograph (ə'neməgraf) *n.* recording anemometer

anemometer (ani'momitər) *n.* instrument for recording force and direction of wind —anemo'**metric** *or* **anemo'metrical** *a.* —ane'**mometry** *n.*

anemone (ə'neməni) *n.* flower related to buttercup —**sea anemone** plantlike sea animal

anent (ə'nent) *prep. obs.* concerning

aneroid ('anəroid) *a.* without liquid —**aneroid barometer** barometer in which pointer is actuated by atmospheric pressure bending a metallic surface

anesthetic (anis'thetik) *n./a.* (agent) causing loss of sensation —**anesthesia** (anis'thēzhə) *n.* loss of sensation —**anes'thetically** *adv.* —**anesthetist** (ə'nesthətist) *n.* expert in use of anesthetics —**anesthetize** (ə'nesthətīz) *vt.*

aneurysm ('anyərizəm) n. swelling out of a part of an artery

anew (ə'nyōō, -'nōō) adv. afresh, again

angel ('ānjəl) n. 1. divine messenger 2. ministering or attendant spirit 3. person with the qualities of such a spirit, as gentleness, purity etc. 4. financial backer, esp. of theatrical production —**angelic** (an'jelik) a. —**angelically** (an'jelikəli) adv. —**angel dust** drug used illicitly as hallucinogen —**'angelfish** n. 1. small tropical marine fish which has brightly colored body 2. S Amer. freshwater fish which has large dorsal and anal fins 3. shark with flattened pectoral fins (pl. **-fish, -fishes**) —**angel food cake** light sponge cake made without egg yolks

Angeleno (anjə'lēnō) n. inhabitant or native of Los Angeles, California (pl. **-s**)

angelica (an'jelikə) n. 1. aromatic plant 2. the candied stalks of this plant used in cookery 3. (**A-**) white dessert wine of Californian origin

Angelus ('anjiləs) n. devotional service in R.C. Church in memory of the Incarnation, said at morning, noon and sunset

anger ('anggər) n. 1. strong emotion excited by a real or supposed injury 2. wrath 3. rage —vt. 4. excite to wrath 5. enrage —**'angrily** adv. —**'angry** a. 1. full of anger 2. inflamed

angina pectoris (an'jīnə 'pektəris) severe pain accompanying heart disease

angiosperm ('anjiəspərm) n. a flowering plant

angle¹ ('anggəl) vi. fish with hook and line —**'angler** n. 1. fisherman 2. sea fish with spiny dorsal fin (also **angler fish**) —**'angling** n.

angle² ('anggəl) n. 1. meeting of two lines or surfaces 2. sharp corner 3. point of view 4. inf. devious motive —vt. 5. bend at an angle —**angle of incidence** 1. angle of line or beam of radiation to line perpendicular to surface at point of incidence 2. angle between chord line of aircraft wing or tailplane and longitudinal axis

Anglican ('angglikən) a./n. (member) of the Church of England —**'Anglicanism** n.

anglicize ('angglisīz) vt. express in English, turn into English form —**'Anglicism** n. English idiom or peculiarity

Anglo ('angglō) n. 1. (among Hispanics and Indians) person of Caucasian descent 2. C English-speaking Canadian (pl. **-s**)

Anglo- (comb. form) English, as in Anglo-American

Anglo-French a. 1. of England and France 2. of Anglo-French —n. 3. Norman-French language of medieval England

Anglo-Norman a. 1. relating to Norman conquerors of England or their language —n. 2. Norman inhabitant of England after 1066 3. Anglo-French language

Anglophile ('angglōfīl) or **Anglophil** n. person having admiration for England or the English

Anglophobia (angglō'fōbiə) n. dislike of England etc.

Anglo-Saxon n. 1. member of West Germanic tribes that settled in Britain from 5th cent. A.D. 2. language of these tribes (see **Old English** at OLD) 3. White person whose native language is English 4. inf. plain blunt English —a. 5. forming part of Germanic element in Modern English 6. of Anglo-Saxons or Old English language 7. of White Protestant culture of Britain and Amer.

Angola (ang'gōlə) n. country in west Africa, bounded by Congo on the north, Zaïre on the north and northeast, Zambia on the east, Namibia on the south and the Atlantic Ocean on the west —**An'golan** a./n.

angora (ang'gōrə) n. (sometimes **A-**) 1. goat with long white silky hair which is used in the making of mohair 2. cloth or wool made from this hair —**angora cat** or **rabbit** purebred varieties of cat and rabbit with long, silky fur

angostura bitters (anggə'styōōərə, -'stōōə-) (oft. **A-**) trade name for bitter tonic used as flavoring in alcoholic drinks

angstrom ('angstrəm) n. unit of length equal to one ten-billionth of a meter for measuring wavelengths of light

Anguilla (ang'gwilə) n. country comprising the most northerly of the Leeward Islands in the Caribbean Sea

anguish ('anggwish) n. great mental or physical pain

angular ('anggyōōlər) a. 1. (of people) bony, awkward 2. having angles 3. measured by an angle —**angu'larity** n.

anhydrous (an'hīdrəs) a. (of chemical substances) free from water

anil ('anil) n. leguminous West Indian shrub (also **'indigo**)

aniline ('anilin) n. product of coal tar or indigo, which yields dyes

animadvert (animad'vərt) vi. (usu. with on or upon) criticize, pass censure —**animad'version** n. criticism, censure

animal ('animəl) n. 1. living creature, having sensation and power of voluntary motion 2. beast —a. 3. of, pert. to animals 4. sensual —**ani'malcular** a. —**ani'malcule** n. very small animal, esp. one which cannot be seen by naked eye —**'animalism** n. —**'animally** adv. —**animal husbandry** science of breeding and rearing farm animals —**animal kingdom** the animal species of the world collectively —**animal magnetism** 1. quality of being attractive, esp. to opposite sex 2. obs. hypnotism

animate ('animāt) vt. 1. give life to 2. enliven 3. inspire 4. actuate 5. make cartoon film of —**'animated** a. 1. lively 2. in form of cartoons —**ani'mation** n. 1. life, vigor 2. cartoon film —**'animator** n.

animato (ani'mätō) a./adv. Mus. lively; animated

animism ('animizəm) n. belief that natural effects are due to spirits or that inanimate things have spirits —**'animist** n. —**ani'mistic** a.

animosity (ani'mositi) n. hostility, enmity

animus ('animəs) n. 1. intense dislike; hatred 2. animosity

anion ('anīən) n. ion with negative charge

anise ('anis) n. annual herb related to carrot, with licorice-flavored seeds ('aniseed) —**ani'sette** n. sweet liqueur flavored with aniseed

ankh (ängk) n. cross with loop for its upper vertical arm, serving as an emblem of life

ankle ('angkəl) n. joint between foot and leg —**'anklet** n. ornamental chain etc. worn around ankle

ankylosis (angki'lōsis) n. abnormal adhesion or immobility of bones in joint, by disease or by surgery

anna ('anə) n. 1. formerly, monetary unit of Burma, India and Pakistan 2. coin representing one anna

annals ('anəlz) pl.n. historical records of events —**'annalist** n.

Annapolis (ə'napolis) n. U.S. Naval Academy

anneal (ə'nēl) vt. 1. toughen (metal or glass) by heating and slow cooling 2. temper (determination, will etc.) —**an'nealing** n.

annelid ('anəlid) n. any member of a phylum of invertebrate animals with segmented cylindrical bodies, including earthworms, lugworms and leeches

annex (a'neks) vt. 1. add, append, attach 2. take possession of (esp. territory) —n. ('aneks) 3. supplementary building 4. something added —**annex'ation** n.

Annie Oakley ('ani 'ōkli) a free ticket

annihilate (ə'nīəlāt) vt. reduce to nothing, destroy utterly —**annihi'lation** n. —**an'nihilative** a. —**an'nihilator** n.

anniversary (ani'vərsəri) n. 1. yearly recurrence of a date of notable event 2. celebration of this

anno Domini ('anō 'dominī, -nē) Lat. in the year of our Lord

annotate ('anōtāt, 'anə-) vt. provide notes for (literary work etc.), comment —**anno'tation** n. —**'annotator** n.

announce (ə'nowns) vt. make known, proclaim —**an'nouncement** n. —**an'nouncer** n. broadcaster who announces items in program, introduces speakers etc.

annoy (ə'noi) vt. 1. vex 2. make slightly angry 3. tease —**an'noyance** n.

annual ('anyōōl) a. 1. yearly 2. of, for a year —n. 3. plant which completes its life cycle in a year 4. book published each year —**'annually** adv.

annuity (ə'nyōōiti, -'nōō-) n. sum or grant paid every year —**an'nuitant** n. holder of annuity

annul (ə'nul) vt. make void, cancel, abolish (-ll-) —**an'nulment** n.

annular ('anyələr) a. ring-shaped —**'annulate** a. having or marked with rings —**'annulated** a. formed in rings —**annu'lation** n. —**'annulet** n. small ring or fillet —**'annulus** n. Math. the area between two circles when one is inside the other

Annunciation (ənunsi'āshən) n. 1. angel's announcement to the Virgin Mary, commemorated on March 25th as a church festival 2. (**a-**) announcing —**an'nunciate** vt. proclaim, announce

anode ('anōd) n. Elec. the positive pole, or point of entry of current —**'anodize** vt. cover (metal object) with protective film by using it for anode in electrolysis

anodyne ('anədīn) a. 1. relieving pain, soothing —n. 2. pain-relieving drug

anoint (ə'noint) vt. 1. smear with oil or ointment 2. consecrate with oil —**a'nointment** n. —**the Anointed** the Messiah

anomalous (ə'nomələs) a. irregular, abnormal —**a'nomaly** n. 1. irregularity 2. deviation from rule

anomie or **anomy** ('anəmi) n. Sociol. lack of social or moral standards of person or group

anon (ə'non) adv. obs. 1. in a short time, soon 2. now and then

anon. anonymous(ly)

anonymous (ə'noniməs) a. nameless, esp. without an author's name —**ano'nymity** n. —**a'nonymously** adv.

anopheles (ə'nofilēz) n. genus including all mosquitoes which transmit malaria to man

anorexia (anə'reksiə) n. loss of appetite —**anorexia nervosa** (nər'vōsə) psychological condition characterized by refusal to eat

another (ə'nudhər) pron./a. 1. one other 2. a different (one) 3. one more

anoxia (an'oksiə) n. decrease in supply of oxygen to the tissues of the body

anserine ('ansərīn) a. 1. of or like goose 2. silly

answer ('ansər) v. 1. reply (to) 2. be accountable (for, to) —vt. 3. solve; reply correctly 4. meet 5. match 6. satisfy, suit —n.

7. reply **8.** solution —**'answerable** *a.* accountable

ant (ant) *n.* small social insect, proverbial for industry —**ant bear** *see* AARDVARK —**ant hill** mound raised by ants

Ant. Antarctica

-ant (*comb. form*) causing or performing action or existing in certain condition, as in *pleasant, deodorant, servant*

Antabuse ('antəbyōōs) *n.* trade name for disulfiram: used to treat alcoholism

antacid (ant'asid) *n.* **1.** substance used to treat acidity, *esp.* in stomach —*a.* **2.** having properties of this substance

antagonist (an'tagənist) *n.* opponent, adversary —**an'tagonism** *n.* —**antago'nistic** *a.* —**antago'nistically** *adv.* —**an'tagonize** *vt.* arouse hostility in

Antarctic (ant'ärktik) *a.* **1.** of south polar regions —*n.* **2.** region round South Pole —**An'tarctica** *n.* continent surrounding South Pole —**Antarctic Circle** imaginary circle around earth at latitude 66° 32′ S —**Antarctic Ocean** seas surrounding Antarctica, comprising southernmost parts of Pacific, Atlantic and Indian Oceans

ante ('anti) *n.* **1.** player's stake in poker —*v.* **2.** place stake

ante- (*comb. form*) before, as in *antechamber.* Such words are not given here where the meaning may easily be inferred from the simple word

anteater ('antētər) *n.* any of several mammals that feed entirely on ants or termites, *eg* aardvark, echidna

antebellum (anti'beləm) *a.* existing before a war, *esp.* the American Civil War

antecedent (anti'sēdənt) *a./n.* (event, person or thing) going before

antedate ('antidāt) *vt.* **1.** be or occur at earlier date than **2.** affix or assign date to (document *etc.*) earlier than actual date **3.** cause to occur sooner —*n.* **4.** earlier date

antediluvian (antidi'lōōviən) *a.* **1.** before the Flood **2.** ancient

antelope ('antilōp) *n.* deerlike ruminant animal, remarkable for grace and speed

ante meridiem (mə'ridiəm) *Lat.* before noon

antenatal (anti'nātəl) *a.* prenatal

antenna (an'tenə) *n.* **1.** movable segmented organ of sensation on head of insects, myriapods and crustaceans **2.** part of radio *etc.* receiving or sending radio waves (*pl.* **-ae** (-ē))

antepenultimate (antipi'nultimit) *a.* **1.** third last —*n.* **2.** anything third last

anterior (an'tēəriər) *a.* **1.** to the front **2.** earlier

anteroom ('antirōōm, -rŏŏm) *n.* room giving entrance to larger room, oft. used as waiting room

anthem ('anthəm) *n.* **1.** song of loyalty, *esp.* to a country **2.** Scripture passage set to music **3.** piece of sacred music, *orig.* sung in alternate parts by two choirs

anther ('anthər) *n.* sac in flower, containing pollen, at top of stamen —**'antheral** *a.*

anthology (an'tholəji) *n.* collection of poems, literary extracts *etc.* —**an'thologist** *n.* maker of such —**an'thologize** *vt.* include (poem *etc.*) in anthology

anthracite ('anthrəsīt) *n.* hard coal that burns slowly almost without flame or smoke

anthrax ('anthraks) *n.* **1.** bacterial disease of sheep and cattle, communicable to man **2.** sore caused by this

anthropo- (*comb. form*) man, human, as in *anthropology*

anthropocentric (anthrəpō'sentrik) *a.* regarding man as central factor in universe

anthropoid ('anthrəpoid) *a.* **1.** like man —*n.* **2.** ape resembling man

anthropology (anthrə'poləji) *n.* **1.** science of human beings, their origins, distribution, physical attributes and culture **2.** aspect of Christian teaching dealing with the origin, nature and destiny of human beings —**anthropo'logical** *a.* —**anthro'pologist** *n.*

anthropomorphize (anthrəpə'môrfīz) *vt.* ascribe human attributes to (God or an animal) —**anthropo'morphic** *a.* —**anthropo'morphism** *n.* —**anthropo'morphous** *a.* shaped like human being

anti ('antī, 'anti) *inf. a.* **1.** opposed to party *etc.* —*n.* **2.** opponent

anti- (*comb. form*) against, as in *anti-aircraft, antispasmodic.* Such words are not given here where meaning may easily be inferred from simple word

antibiosis (antibī'ōsis, antī-) *n.* association between two organisms that is harmful to one of them

antibiotic (antibī'otik, antī-) *n.* **1.** any of various chemical, fungal or synthetic substances, *esp.* penicillin, used against bacterial or fungal infection —*a.* **2.** of antibiotics

antibody ('antibodi) *n.* substance produced by the body in response to the presence of antigens

Antichrist ('antikrīst) *n.* **1.** *Bible* the antagonist of Christ **2.** (*sometimes* a-) an enemy of Christ or Christianity

anticipate (an'tisipāt) *vt.* **1.** expect **2.** take or consider beforehand **3.** foresee **4.** enjoy in advance —**antici'pation** *n.* —**an'ticipative** *or* **an'ticipatory** *a.*

anticlerical (anti'klerikəl, antī-) *a.* **1.** opposed to influence of clergy, *esp.* in politics —*n.* **2.** supporter of anticlerical party

anticlimax (anti'klīmaks) *n.* **1.** disappointing conclusion to series of events *etc.* **2.** sudden descent to the trivial or ludicrous

anticline ('antiklīn) *n.* formation of stratified rock folded into broad arch so that strata slope down on both sides from common crest

anticoagulant (antikō'agyələnt, antī-) *n.* substance that inhibits blood clotting

antics ('antiks) *pl.n.* absurd or grotesque movements or acts

anticyclone (anti'sīklōn) *n.* system of winds moving round center of high barometric pressure

antidote ('antidōt) *n.* counteracting remedy

antifreeze ('antifrēz) *n.* liquid added to water to lower its freezing point, as in automobile radiators

antigen ('antijən) *n.* substance stimulating production of antibodies in the blood

Antigone (an'tigəni) *n.* in Greek legend, daughter of Oedipus by his mother Jocasta, famed for her heroic attachment to her father and brothers

Antigua and Barbuda (an'tēgə; bär'bōōdə) country comprising three islands of the Lesser Antilles in the eastern Caribbean

antihero ('antihēərō, 'antī-) *n.* central character in novel *etc.*, who lacks traditional heroic virtues

antihistamine (anti'histəmēn, antī-; -min) *n.* drug used *esp.* to treat allergies

antiknock (anti'nok) *n.* compound added to gasoline to reduce knocking in engine

antilogarithm (anti'logəridhəm, antī-) *n.* number whose logarithm is the given number (*also* **'antilog**)

antimacassar (antimə'kasər) *n.* cover to protect back or arms of furniture

antimatter ('antimatər) *n.* hypothetical form of matter composed of antiparticles

antimony ('antimōni) *n. Chem.* metallic element used in alloys, drugs and dyes *Symbol* Sb, at. wt. 121.8, at. no. 51

antinomy (an'tinəmi) *n.* **1.** opposition of one law *etc.* to another **2.** *Philos.* contradiction between two conclusions correctly derived from two laws both assumed to be correct

antinovel ('antinovəl, 'antī-) *n.* prose fiction in which conventional novelistic elements are rejected

antiparticle ('antipärtikəl, 'antī-) *n.* any of group of elementary particles that have same mass as corresponding particle but have charge of equal magnitude but opposite sign

antipasto (anti'pastō, -'päs-) *n.* course of hors d'œuvres in Italian meal (*pl.* **-s**)

antipathy (an'tipəthi) *n.* dislike, aversion —**antipa'thetic** *a.*

antiperspirant (anti'pərspərənt) *n.* substance used to reduce sweating

antiphon ('antifən) *n.* **1.** composition in which verses, lines are sung alternately by two choirs **2.** anthem —**an'tiphonal** *a.*

antipodes (an'tipədēz) *pl.n.* countries, peoples on opposite side of the globe (oft. refers to Aust. and N.Z.) —**an'tipodal** *or* **antipo'dean** *a.*

antipope ('antipōp) *n.* pope elected in opposition to the one regularly chosen

antipyretic (antipī'retik, antī-) *n./a.* (remedy) effective against fever

antique (an'tēk) *n.* **1.** relic of former times, usu. piece of furniture *etc.* that is collected —*a.* **2.** ancient **3.** old-fashioned —**antiquary** ('antikweri) *or* **antiquarian** (anti'kweriən) *n.* student or collector of old things —**antiquated** ('antikwātid) *a.* out-of-date —**antiquity** (an'tikwiti) *n.* **1.** former times **2.** age of Greek and Roman civilization ending with fall of Roman Empire in 5th cent. A.D.

antirrhinum (anti'rīnəm) *n.* genus of plants including snapdragon

antiscorbutic (antiskôr'byōōtik, antī-) *n./a.* (agent) preventing or curing scurvy

anti-Semitic *a.* discriminating against Jews —**anti-Semitism** (-'semitizəm) *n.*

antiseptic (anti'septik) *n./a.* **1.** (substance) destroying or preventing the growth of disease-producing microorganisms —*a.* **2.** free from infection

antisocial (anti'sōshəl, antī-) *a.* **1.** avoiding company of other people; unsociable **2.** contrary to interests of society in general

antistatic (anti'statik, antī-) *a.* (of textile *etc.*) retaining sufficient moisture to provide conducting path, thus avoiding effects of static electricity

antithesis (an'tithisis) *n.* **1.** direct opposite **2.** contrast **3.** opposition of ideas (*pl.* **-eses** (-isēz)) —**anti'thetical** *a.* —**anti'thetically** *adv.*

antitoxin (anti'toksin) *n.* serum used to neutralize bacterial poisons

antitrades ('antitrādz, 'antī-) *pl.n.* winds blowing in opposite direction from and above trade winds

antitrust (anti'trust, antī-) *a.* regulating or opposing trusts or similar organizations

antitype ('antitīp) *n.* **1.** person or thing foreshadowed or represented by type or symbol **2.** opposite type

antivenin (anti'venin, antī-) *n.* antitoxin to a venom

antler ('antlər) *n.* branching horn of certain deer —**'antlered** *a.*

antonym ('antənim) *n.* word of opposite meaning to another, *eg cold* is an antonym of *hot*

Antron ('antron) *n.* trade name for a type of nylon

antrum ('antrəm) *n. Anat.* natural cavity or sinus, *esp.* in bone (*pl.* **-tra** (-trə))

anuresis (anyŏŏ'rēsis) *n.* inability to urinate

anus ('ānəs) *n.* the posterior opening of the alimentary canal —**'anal** *a.* of or near the anus

anvil ('anvil) *n.* heavy iron block on which a smith hammers metal into shape

anxious ('angkshəs, 'angshəs) *a.* 1. troubled, uneasy 2. concerned —**anxiety** (ang'zīiti) *n. Psych.* emotional reaction of fear to indiscernible source of danger —**'anxiously** *adv.*

any ('eni) *a./pron.* 1. one indefinitely 2. some 3. whatever, whichever —**'anybody** *pron.* any person —**'anyhow** *adv.* in any manner —**any'more** *adv.* any longer; still; nowadays —**'anyone** *pron.* any person at all —**'anything** *pron.* any thing whatever —**'anyway** *adv.* —**'anywhere** *adv.* in or to any place

Anzac ('anzak) *a.* 1. of Australian-New Zealand Army Corps in WWI —*n.* 2. soldier of that corps, Gallipoli veteran

ANZUS ('anzəs) Aust., N.Z. and U.S., with reference to security alliance between them

AO 1. account of 2. and others

aorist ('āərist) *n. Gram.* tense of verb, *esp.* in classical Greek, indicating past action without reference to whether action involved was momentary or continuous

aorta (ā'örtə) *n.* main artery of the body —**a'ortal** *a.* —**aor'titis** *n.* inflammation of the aorta

aoudad ('owdad, 'āŏŏdad) *n.* a wild sheep of N Afr.

AP 1. additional premium 2. Associated Press

apace (ə'pās) *adv.* swiftly

Apache (ə'pachi) *n.* 1. group or member of Amerindian peoples of SW U.S. (*pl.* **A'pache**, **-s**) 2. language of these peoples 3. (ə'pash) (**a-**) member of gang of criminals in Paris

apart (ə'pärt) *adv.* 1. separately, aside 2. in pieces

apartheid (ə'pärtīt, -āt) *n. esp.* in S Afr., official government policy of racial segregation

apartment (ə'pärtmənt) *n.* room or rooms, furnished with housekeeping equipment and usu. leased —**apartment building** *or* **house** building containing separate apartments —**apartment hotel** hotel containing apartments as well as accommodation for transients

apathy ('apəthi) *n.* 1. indifference 2. lack of emotion —**apa'thetic** *a.* —**apa'thetically** *adv.*

apatite ('apətīt) *n.* common mineral consisting basically of calcium fluorophosphate

APB all points bulletin

ape (āp) *n.* 1. tailless primate (*eg* chimpanzee, gorilla) 2. coarse, clumsy person 3. imitator —*vt.* 4. imitate —**'apish** *a.* —**'apishly** *adv.* —**'apeman** *n.* apelike primate thought to have been forerunner of modern man

aperient (ə'pēəriənt) *a.* 1. mildly laxative —*n.* 2. any mild laxative

aperiodic (āpēəri'odik) *a. Elec.* having no natural period or frequency

apéritif (əperi'tēf) *n.* alcoholic appetizer

aperture ('apərchər) *n.* opening, hole

apex ('āpeks) *n.* 1. top, peak 2. vertex (*pl.* **-es**, **'apices**) —**'apical** *a.* of, at, or being apex

aphasia (ə'fāzhiə) *n.* dumbness or loss of speech control, due to disease of brain

aphelion (a'fēlyən) *n.* point of planet's orbit farthest from sun (*pl.* **-lia** (-lyə))

aphis ('āfis) *n.* any of various sap-sucking insects (*pl.* **aphides** ('āfidēz)) —**'aphid** *n.* an aphis

aphorism ('afərizəm) *n.* maxim, pithy saying —**'aphorist** *n.* —**apho'ristic** *a.*

aphrodisiac (afrə'diziak) *a.* 1. exciting sexual desire —*n.* 2. substance believed to excite sexual desire

apiary ('āpieri) *n.* place where bees are kept —**api'arian** *or* **'apian** *a.* —**'apiarist** *n.* beekeeper —**'apiculture** *n.* breeding and care of bees

apices ('āpisēz, 'a-) *n., pl. of* APEX

apiece (ə'pēs) *adv.* for each

APL computer-programming language designed for the concise representation of algorisms

aplastic anemia (ā'plastik) anemia characterized by defective function of blood-forming organs, caused by toxic agents or arising spontaneously

aplomb (ə'plom) *n.* self-possession, coolness, assurance

APO army post office

apo- *or* **ap-** (*comb. form*) 1. away from; off, as in *apogee* 2. separation of, as in *apocarpous*

apocalypse (ə'pokəlips) *n.* 1. prophetic revelation, of Jewish and Christian writing of 200 B.C. to 150 A.D. 2. (**A-**) *Bible* Revelation in the Douay Version of the N.T. —**apoca'lyptic** *a.* —**apoca'lyptically** *adv.* —**Apocalypse of Baruch** noncanonical apocalyptic sacred scripture

apocrypha (ə'pokrifə) *n.* religious writing of doubtful authenticity —**a'pocryphal** *a.* spurious —**the Apocrypha** collective name for 14 books orig. in Old Testament

apodosis (ə'podəsis) *n.* consequent clause in conditional sentence, as distinct from protasis or *if* clause (*pl.* **-oses** (-ōsēz))

apogee ('apəjē) *n.* 1. point of moon's or satellite's orbit farthest from the earth 2. climax

apolitical (āpə'litikəl) *a.* politically neutral

apologia (apə'lōjiə) *n.* written defense of one's beliefs, conduct *etc.*

apologue ('apəlog) *n.* allegory, moral fable

apology (ə'poləji) *n.* 1. acknowledgment of offense and expression of regret 2. written or spoken defense 3. (*with* for) poor substitute —**apolo'getic** *a.* —**apolo'getically** *adv.* —**apolo'getics** *pl.n.* (*with sing. v.*) branch of theology charged with defense of Christianity —**a'pologist** *n.* —**a'pologize** *vi.*

apoplexy ('apəpleksi) *n.* loss of sense and oft. paralysis caused by broken or blocked blood vessel in brain —**apo'plectic** *a.*

apostasy (ə'postəsi) *n.* abandonment of one's religious or other faith —**a'postate** *n./a.*

a posteriori (ā postēəri'ôrī, ǎ; -rē) 1. denoting form of inductive reasoning which arrives at causes from effects 2. empirical

apostle (ə'posəl) *n.* 1. (*oft.* **A-**) one sent to preach the Gospel, *esp.* one of the first disciples of Jesus 2. founder of Christian church in a country 3. leader of reform —**a'postleship** *n.* —**apostolic(al)** (apə'stolik-(əl)) *a.* —**Apostles' Creed** concise statement of Christian beliefs —**Apostolic See** see of pope

apostrophe (ə'postrəfi) *n.* 1. mark (') showing omission of letter or letters in word 2. digression to appeal to someone dead or absent —**a'postrophize** *v.*

apothecary (ə'pothikeri) *n.* 1. one who prepares and sells drugs for medical purposes 2. pharmacy —**apothecaries' measure** system of measurement in which the pound equals 12 ounces (0.373 kilogram)

apothegm ('apəthem) *n.* startling or paradoxical aphorism —**apothegmatic** (apətheg-'matik) *a.*

apothem ('apəthem) *n.* perpendicular from center of regular polygon to any of its sides

apotheosis (əpothi'ōsis) *n.* deification, act of raising any person or thing to status of a god (*pl.* **-ses** (-sēz)) —**apo'theosize** *vt.* 1. deify 2. glorify, idealize

Appalachian (apə'lāchən) *a.* 1. of mountain range extending from southern Quebec to northern Alabama —*n.* 2. Caucasian native or resident of this mountain area —**Appalachian trail** hiking trail through these mountains from central Maine to northern Georgia

appall (ə'pöl) *vt.* dismay, terrify —**ap'palling** *a.* dreadful, terrible

Appaloosa (apə'lōōsə) *n.* rugged saddle horse bred in western N Amer. with a mottled hide, striped hoofs and patches of white hair over the rump and loins

appanage *or* **apanage** ('apənij) *n.* 1. land or other provision granted by king for support of *esp.* younger son 2. customary perquisite

apparatus (apə'ratəs, -'rātəs) *n.* 1. equipment, instruments, for performing any experiment, operation *etc.* 2. means by which something operates

apparel (ə'parəl) *n.* 1. clothing —*vt.* 2. clothe

apparent (ə'parənt) *a.* 1. seeming 2. obvious 3. acknowledged, as in *heir apparent* —**ap'parently** *adv.*

apparition (apə'rishən) *n.* unexpected appearance, *esp.* of ghost

appeal (ə'pēl) *vi.* 1. make earnest request 2. be attractive 3. refer, have recourse 4. apply to higher court —*n.* 5. request 6. reference 7. supplication —**ap'pealable** *a.* —**ap'pealing** *a.* 1. making appeal 2. pleasant, attractive —**ap'pealingly** *adv.* —**ap'pellant** *n.* one who appeals to higher court —**appellate** (ə'pelit) *a.* of appeals

appear (ə'pēər) *vi.* 1. become visible or present 2. seem, be plain 3. be seen in public —**ap'pearance** *n.* 1. an appearing 2. aspect 3. pretense

appease (ə'pēz) *vt.* pacify, quiet, allay, satisfy —**ap'peasable** *a.* —**ap'peasement** *n.*

appellant (ə'pelənt) *n. see* APPEAL

appellation (api'lāshən) *n.* name or title —**ap'pellative** *a./n.*

append (ə'pend) *vt.* join on, add —**ap'pendage** *n.*

appendix (ə'pendiks) *n.* 1. subsidiary addition to book *etc.* 2. *Anat.* projection, *esp.* small worm-shaped part of intestine (*pl.* **-dices** (-disēz), **-es**) —**appen'dectomy** *n.* surgical removal of any appendage, *esp.* vermiform appendix —**appendi'citis** *n.* inflammation of vermiform appendix

apperception (apər'sepshən) *n.* 1. perception 2. apprehension 3. the mind's perception of itself as a conscious agent —**apper'ceive** *vt.*

appertain (apər'tān) *vi.* belong, relate, be appropriate

appetence ('apitəns) *or* **appetency** *n.* 1. desire, craving 2. sexual appetite —**'appetent** *a.*

appetite ('apitīt) *n.* desire, inclination, *esp.* desire for food —**ap'petitive** *a.* —**'appetizer** *n.* something stimulating to appetite —**'appetizing** *a.* —**'appetizingly** *adv.*

applaud (ə'plöd) *v.* **1.** express approval (of) by hand-clapping —*vt.* **2.** praise; approve —**ap'plauder** *n.* —**ap'plause** *n.* loud approval

apple ('apəl) *n.* **1.** round, firm, fleshy fruit **2.** tree bearing it —**'applejack** *n.* liquor distilled from fermented cider —**apple-pie order** *inf.* perfect order —**apple of one's eye** person or thing very much loved

appliance (ə'plīəns) *n.* piece of equipment, *esp.* electrical

appliqué

appliqué ('aplikā) *n.* **1.** ornaments, embroidery *etc.*, secured to surface of material —*vt.* **2.** ornament thus

apply (ə'plī) *vt.* **1.** utilize, employ **2.** lay or place on **3.** administer, devote —*vi.* **4.** have reference (to) **5.** make request (to) (**-lied, -lying**) —**applicability** (aplikə'biliti) *n.* —**applicable** ('aplikəbl, ə'plikə-) *a.* relevant —**applicably** ('aplikəbli, ə'plikə-) *adv.* —**applicant** ('aplikənt) *n.* —**application** (apli'kāshən) *n.* **1.** applying something for a particular use **2.** relevance **3.** request for job *etc.* **4.** concentration, diligence —**applicator** ('aplikātər) *n.* device, such as spatula, for applying medicine, glue *etc.* —**ap'plied** *a.* (of skill, science *etc.*) put to practical use

appoint (ə'point) *vt.* **1.** name for, assign to job or position **2.** fix, settle **3.** equip —**ap'pointment** *n.* **1.** engagement to meet **2.** (selection for a) job —*pl.* **3.** fittings

apportion (ə'pörshən) *vt.* divide out in shares —**ap'portionment** *n.*

appose (ə'pōz) *vt.* **1.** place side by side **2.** place (something) near or against another thing

apposite ('apəzit) *a.* suitable, apt —**'appositely** *adv.* —**'appositeness** *n.* —**appo'sition** *n.* **1.** proximity **2.** the placing of one word beside another

appraise (ə'prāz) *vt.* set price on, estimate value of —**ap'praisable** *a.* —**ap'praisal** *or* **ap'praisement** *n.* —**ap'praiser** *n.*

appreciate (ə'prēshiāt) *vt.* **1.** value at true worth **2.** be grateful for **3.** understand **4.** enjoy —*vi.* **5.** rise in value —**ap'preciable** *a.* **1.** estimable **2.** substantial —**ap'preciably** *adv.* —**appreci'ation** *n.* —**ap'preciative** *or* **ap'preciatory** *a.* capable of expressing pleasurable recognition —**ap'preciator** *n.*

apprehend (apri'hend) *vt.* **1.** seize by authority **2.** take hold of **3.** recognize, understand **4.** dread —**apprehensi'bility** *n.* —**appre'hensible** *a.* —**appre'hension** *n.* **1.** dread, anxiety **2.** arrest **3.** conception **4.** ability to understand —**appre'hensive** *a.*

apprentice (ə'prentis) *n.* **1.** person learning a trade under specified conditions **2.** novice —*vt.* **3.** bind as apprentice —**ap'prenticeship** *n.*

apprise (ə'prīz) *vt.* inform

approach (ə'prōch) *v.* **1.** draw near (to) —*vt.* **2.** set about **3.** address request to **4.** approximate to —*n.* **5.** a drawing near **6.** means of reaching or doing **7.** approximation **8.** (*oft. pl.*) friendly overture(s) —**approach-a'bility** *n.* —**ap'proachable** *a.*

approbation (aprə'bāshən) *n.* approval

appropriate (ə'prōpriāt) *vt.* **1.** take for oneself **2.** put aside for particular purpose —*a.* (ə'prōpriit) **3.** suitable, fitting —**ap'propriately** *adv.* —**ap'propriateness** *n.* —**appropri'ation** *n.* **1.** act of setting apart for purpose **2.** money set aside by formal action for particular use —**ap'propriative** *a.* —**ap'propriator** *n.*

approve (ə'prōōv) *vt.* **1.** think well of, commend **2.** authorize, agree to —*vi.* **3.** (*usu.* with of) take favorable view —**ap'proval** *n.* —**ap'prover** *n.* —**ap'provingly** *adv.*

approx. approximate(ly)

approximate (ə'proksimit) *a.* **1.** very near, nearly correct **2.** inexact, imprecise —*vt.* (ə'proksimāt) **3.** bring close **4.** be almost the same as —*vi.* (ə'proksimāt) **5.** come near —**ap'proximately** *adv.* —**approxi'mation** *n.* —**ap'proximative** *a.*

appurtenance (ə'pərtinəns) *n.* **1.** less significant thing or part **2.** accessory

Apr. April

après-ski (aprä'skē) *n.* social activities after day's skiing

apricot ('aprikot, 'āpri-) *n.* **1.** orange-colored stone-fruit related to plum —*a.* **2.** of the color of the fruit

April ('āprəl) *n.* fourth month —**April fool** victim of practical joke performed on Apr. 1st (**April Fools' Day** *or* **All Fools' Day**)

a priori (ā prī'ōrī, ä pri'ōri) **1.** denoting deductive reasoning from general principle to expected facts or effects **2.** denoting knowledge gained independently of experience

apron ('āprən) *n.* **1.** cloth, piece of leather *etc.*, worn in front of body to protect clothes, or as part of official dress **2.** in theater, strip of stage before curtain **3.** on airfield, tarmac area where aircraft stand, are loaded *etc.* **4.** *fig.* any of a variety of things resembling these —**apron strings** symbol of dominance or complete control

apropos (aprə'pō) *adv.* **1.** to the purpose **2.** by the way —*a.* **3.** apt, appropriate —**apropos of** concerning

apse (aps) *n.* arched recess, *esp.* in church —**'apsidal** *a.*

apsis ('apsis) *n.* either of two points lying at extremities of eccentric orbit of satellite *etc.* (*pl.* **apsides** ('apsidēz)) (*also* **apse**)

apso ('apsō) *n. see* LHASA APSO (*pl.* **-s**)

apt (apt) *a.* **1.** suitable **2.** likely **3.** prompt, quick-witted **4.** dexterous —**'aptitude** *n.* capacity, fitness —**'aptly** *adv.* —**'aptness** *n.*

apteryx ('aptəriks) *n. see* KIWI (sense 1)

aqua ('akwə) *n.* **1.** water (*pl.* **aquae** ('akwē), **-s**) —*a.* **2.** *see* AQUAMARINE (sense 2) —**aqua regia** ('rējiə) mixture of nitric and hydrochloric acids that dissolves gold and platinum

aquaculture ('akwəkulchər) *n.* hydroponics

Aqualung ('akwəlung) *n.* trade name for apparatus enabling swimmer to breathe underwater

aquamarine (akwəmə'rēn) *n.* **1.** variety of beryl used as gemstone —*a.* **2.** greenish-blue, sea-colored

aquanaut ('akwənöt) *n.* person who works or swims underwater

aquaplane ('akwəplān) *n.* **1.** plank or boat towed by fast motorboat —*vi.* **2.** ride on aquaplane **3.** (of automobile) be in contact with water on road, not with road surface —**'aquaplaning** *n.*

aquarelle (akwə'rel) *n.* picture executed with transparent watercolors

aquarium (ə'kwariəm, -'kwer-) *n.* tank or pond for keeping aquatic animals or plants (*pl.* **-s, -ria** (-riə))

Aquarius (ə'kwariəs, -'kwer-) *n.* (the water-bearer) 11th sign of zodiac, operative c. Jan. 20th–Feb. 18th

aquatic (ə'kwotik, -'kwat-) *a.* living, growing, done in or on water —**a'quatics** *pl.n.* water sports

aquatint ('akwətint) *n.* etching, engraving imitating drawings *etc.*

aqua vitae ('vītē) *Lat. obs.* brandy

aqueduct ('akwidukt) *n.* **1.** artificial channel for water, *esp.* one like bridge **2.** conduit

aqueous ('ākwiəs) *a.* of, like, containing water —**aqueous humor** *Physiol.* fluid between cornea and lens of eye

aquilegia (akwi'lējiə) *n.* columbine

aquiline ('akwilīn) *a.* **1.** relating to eagle **2.** hooked like eagle's beak

Ar *Chem.* argon

AR Arkansas

ar. 1. arrival **2.** arrive(s)

Ar. 1. Arabic **2.** Aramaic

Arab ('arəb) *n.* **1.** native of Arabia **2.** general term for inhabitants of Middle Eastern countries **3.** Arabian horse (small breed used for riding) —**Arabia** (ə'rābiə) *n.* peninsula in southwest Asia, including Saudi Arabia, Yemen, Oman and Aden —**A'rabian** *a.* **1.** of Arabia **2.** Arab —**'Arabic** *n.* **1.** language of Arabs —*a.* **2.** of Arabia or Arabs —**Arabian Sea** northwest arm of Indian Ocean, between India and Arabia —**Arabic numeral** one of numbers 1,2,3,4,5,6,7,8,9,0 —**Arab League** regional organization of sovereign states within framework of United Nations

arabesque (arə'besk) *n.* **1.** classical ballet position **2.** fanciful painted or carved ornament of Arabian origin —*a.* **3.** (in style) of arabesque

arabis ('arəbis) *n.* genus of low-growing annual or evergreen perennial garden plants of the cabbage family, with white or pink flowers

arable ('arəbəl) *a.* suitable for plowing or planting crops

Araby ('arəbi) *n. obs., poet.* Arabia

arachnid (ə'raknid) *n.* land-living arthropod with four pairs of legs, *eg* scorpion, spider, mite and tick —**a'rachnoid** *a.* —**arach'nology** *n.*

Aramaic (arə'māik) *n.* **1.** ancient Semitic language of Middle East —*a.* **2.** of, relating to or using this language

Aran ('arən) *a.* (of sweaters *etc.*) made with naturally oily, unbleached wool, oft. with complicated pattern

Arapaho (ə'rapəhō) *n.* member of Amerindian people of Algonquian linguistic stock, orig. of Plains, now living in Montana and Wyoming (*pl.* **Arapaho, -s**)

Araucanian (arow'käniən) *n.* **1.** American Indian of central Chile and Argentina **2.** language of Araucanians, which constitutes a language family

Arawak ('arəwäk) *n.* **1.** member of American Indian people of Arawakan group now living chiefly along the coast of Guyana **2.** their language —**Ara'wakan** *n.* **1.** member of group of American Indian people of S Amer. and the W Indies **2.** their language, which constitutes a language family

arbiter ('ärbitər) *n.* judge, umpire —**ar'bitrament** *n.* —**arbi'trarily** *adv.* —**'arbitrary** *a.* **1.** not bound by rules, despotic **2.** random —**'arbitrate** *vt.* **1.** decide (dispute) **2.** submit to, settle by arbitration —*vi.* **3.** act as umpire —**arbi'tration** *n.* hearing, settling of disputes, *esp.* industrial and legal, by impartial referee(s) —**'arbitrator** *n.*

arbor[1] ('ärbər) *n.* **1.** rotating shaft in machine on which grinding wheel is fitted **2.** rotating shaft

arbor[2] ('ärbər) *n.* leafy glade *etc.*, sheltered by trees —**Arbor Day** day designated for planting trees

arboreal (är'bōriəl) *a.* relating to trees —**arbo'rescent** *a.* having characteristics of tree —**arbo'retum** *n.* place for cultivating specimens of trees (*pl.* **-s**, **-ta** (-tə)) —**'arboriculture** *n.* forestry, cultivation of trees

arbutus (är'byōōtəs) *n.* genus of half-hardy and hardy shrubs or trees of the heather family, with edible fruits (*pl.* **-es**)

arc (ärk) *n.* **1.** part of circumference of circle or similar curve **2.** luminous electric discharge between two conductors —*vi.* **3.** form an arc —**arc lamp** —**arc light**

ARC American Red Cross

arcade (är'kād) *n.* **1.** row of arches on pillars **2.** covered walk or avenue, *esp.* lined by shops

Arcadian (är'kādiən) *a.* **1.** of idealized Arcadia of pastoral poetry **2.** rustic, bucolic —*n.* **3.** person who leads simple rural life

arcane (är'kān) *a.* **1.** mysterious **2.** esoteric

arch[1] (ärch) *n.* **1.** curved structure in building, supporting itself over open space by pressure of stones one against the other **2.** any similar structure **3.** curved shape **4.** curved part of sole of foot —*v.* **5.** form, make into, an arch —**arched** *a.* —**'archway** *n.*

arch[2] (ärch) *a.* **1.** chief **2.** experienced, expert **3.** superior, knowing; coyly playful —**'archly** *adv.* —**'archness** *n.*

arch. 1. archaic **2.** architecture

arch- *or* **archi-** (*comb. form*) chief, as in *archenemy*. Such words are not given here where the meaning may easily be inferred from the simple word

-arch (*comb. form*) leader; ruler; chief, as in *patriarch, monarch, matriarch*

archaeology *or* **archeology** (ärki'oləji) *n.* study of ancient times from remains of art, implements *etc.* —**archaeo'logical** *or* **archeo'logical** *a.* —**archae'ologist** *or* **arche'ologist** *n.*

archaeopteryx (ärki'optəriks) *n.* extinct bird of Jurassic times, with teeth, long tail and well-developed wings

archaic (är'kāik) *a.* old, primitive —**ar'chaically** *adv.* —**'archaism** *n.* the use of obsolete words or syntax for deliberate effect

archangel ('ärkānjəl) *n.* **1.** chief angel, in Christianity Michael, in Islam Gabriel, Michael, Azrael and Israfel **2.** in celestial hierarchy, order higher than angel, lower than principality

archduke (ärch'dyōōk, -'dōōk) *n.* **1.** sovereign prince **2.** prince of imperial family of Austria (**arch'duchess** *fem.*) —**arch'ducal** *a.* —**arch'duchy** *n.*

archery ('ärchəri) *n.* skill, sport of shooting with bow and arrow (*also* **tox'ophily**) —**'archer** *n.*

archetype ('ärkitīp) *n.* **1.** prototype **2.** perfect specimen —**arche'typal** *a.*

archfiend (ärch'fēnd) *n.* (*oft.* **A-**) the devil; Satan

archiepiscopal (ärkii'piskəpəl) *a.* of archbishop —**archie'piscopate** *n.*

archimandrite (ärki'mandrīt) *n.* dignitary in Eastern Catholic Church ranking below bishop, *esp.* head of monastery or group of monasteries

Archimedes (ärki'mēdēz) *n.* Sicilian mathematician and physical scientist (287-212 B.C.) who made many discoveries, *esp.* the principle of the lever —**Archi'medean** *a.* —**Archimedean solid** polyhedron whose faces are all regular polygons not congruent to one another —**Archimedes' screw** device used to raise water

archipelago (ärki'peləgō) *n.* **1.** group of islands **2.** sea full of small islands, *esp.* Aegean (*pl.* **-es**, **-s**) —**archipelagic** (ärkipə'lajik) *a.*

architect ('ärkitekt) *n.* **1.** one qualified to design and supervise construction of buildings **2.** contriver —**architec'tonic** *a.* of or resembling architecture —**archi'tectural** *a.* —**'architecture** *n.*

architrave ('ärkitrāv) *n. Archit.* **1.** lowest division of entablature **2.** ornamental band round door or window opening

archives ('ärkīvz) *pl.n.* **1.** collection of records, documents *etc.* about institution, family *etc.* **2.** place where these are kept —**ar'chival** *a.* —**archivist** ('ärkivist) *n.*

archpriest (ärch'prēst) *n.* **1.** formerly, chief assistant to bishop **2.** senior priest

Arctic ('ärktik) *a.* **1.** of northern polar regions **2.** (**a-**) very cold —*n.* **3.** region round North Pole —**Arctic Circle** imaginary circle around earth at latitude 66° 32′ N

ardent ('ärdənt) *a.* **1.** fiery **2.** passionate —**'ardency** *n.* —**'ardently** *adv.* —**'ardor** *n.* **1.** enthusiasm **2.** zeal

arduous ('ärjōōs) *a.* **1.** hard to accomplish, difficult **2.** strenuous; laborious —**'arduously** *adv.* —**'arduousness** *n.*

are[1] (är; *unstressed* ər) *pres. ind. pl. of* BE

are[2] (ãər, är) *n.* unit of measure, 100 square meters

area ('ãəriə) *n.* **1.** extent, expanse of any surface **2.** two-dimensional expanse enclosed by boundary (area of square, circle *etc.*) **3.** region **4.** part, section **5.** subject, field of activity **6.** small sunken yard —**area code** 3-digit number identifying telephone service area in a country

areca ('arikə, ə'rēkə) *n.* genus of palms, including betel palm

arena (ə'rēnə) *n.* **1.** enclosure for sports events *etc.* **2.** space in middle of amphitheater or stadium **3.** sphere, scene of conflict

arenaceous (ari'nāshəs) *a.* **1.** composed of sand **2.** growing in sandy soil

aren't (ärnt) **1.** *contraction of* are not **2.** *inf.*, *chiefly* UK (used in interrogative sentences) *contraction of* am not

areola (ə'rēələ) *n.* **1.** *Biol.* space outlined on surface, such as area between veins on leaf **2.** *Anat.* any small circular area, such as pigmented ring around human nipple (*pl.* **-lae** (-lē), **-s**)

arête (ə'rāt) *n.* sharp ridge that separates glacial valleys

argent ('ärjənt) *n.* **1.** silver —*a.* **2.** silver, silvery-white, *esp.* in heraldry

Argentina (ärjən'tēnə) *n.* country in South America bounded north by Bolivia, northeast by Paraguay, east by Brazil, Uruguay and the Atlantic Ocean, and west by Chile —**Argentinian** (ärjən'tiniən) *a./n.*

argon ('ärgon) *n. Chem.* noble gas used for filling fluorescent and incandescent lamps *Symbol* Ar, at. wt. 39.944, at. no. 18

argosy ('ärgəsi) *n. Poet.* large richly-laden merchant ship

argot ('ärgət, -gō) *n.* special vocabulary of any set of persons

argue ('ärgyōō) *vi.* **1.** quarrel, dispute **2.** offer reasons —*vt.* **3.** prove by reasoning **4.** discuss —**'arguable** *a.* —**'arguably** *adv.* as can be argued —**'arguer** *n.* —**'argument** *n.* **1.** quarrel **2.** reasoning **3.** discussion **4.** theme —**argumen'tation** *n.* —**argu'mentative** *a.*

Argus ('ärgəs) *n.* fabulous being with a hundred eyes —**Argus-eyed** *a.* watchful

aria ('äriə) *n.* composition for solo voice with instrumental accompaniment in opera, oratorio or cantata

arid ('arid) *a.* **1.** parched with heat, dry **2.** dull —**a'ridity** *n.*

Aries ('ariēz, 'er-) *n.* (the ram) 1st sign of zodiac, operative c. Mar. 21st–Apr. 21st

aright (ə'rīt) *adv.* rightly

arise (ə'rīz) *vi.* **1.** come about **2.** get up **3.** rise (up), ascend (**a'rose, arisen** (ə'rizən), **a'rising**)

aristocracy (ari'stokrəsi) *n.* **1.** nobility **2.** upper classes **3.** government by the best in birth or fortune —**a'ristocrat** *n.* —**aristo'cratic** *a.* **1.** noble **2.** elegant —**aristo'cratically** *adv.*

Aristotle ('aristotəl) *n.* Greek philosopher (384-322 B.C.), master of every field of learning known, pupil of Plato and tutor to Alexander the Great —**Aristotelian** *or* **Aristotelean** (aristə'tēlyən) *a./n.* —**Aristotelian elements** fire, air, earth and water —**Aristotelian theory** notion that these elements formed all matter in the world

arithmetic (ə'rithmətik) *n.* **1.** science of numbers **2.** art of reckoning by figures —**arith'metic(al)** *a.* —**arith'metically** *adv.* —**arithme'tician** *n.* —**arithmetic mean** average value of set of terms or quantities, expressed as their sum divided by their number (*also* **'average**) —**arithmetic progression** sequence, each term of which differs from succeeding term by constant amount

Arizona (ari'zōnə) *n.* Mountain state of the U.S., admitted to the Union in 1912. Abbrev.: **Ariz., AZ** (with ZIP code)

ark (ärk) *n.* **1.** Noah's vessel **2.** structure giving protection and safety

Ark (ärk) *n. Judaism* **1.** most sacred symbol of God's presence among Hebrew people, carried in their journey from Sinai to Promised Land (*also* **Ark of the Covenant**) **2.** receptacle for the scrolls of the Law (*also* **Holy Ark**)

Arkansas ('ärkənsö) *n.* West South Central state of the U.S., admitted to the Union in 1836. Abbrev.: **Ark., AR** (with ZIP code)

arm[1] (ärm) *n.* **1.** limb extending from shoulder to wrist **2.** anything projecting from main body, as branch of sea, supporting rail of chair *etc.* **3.** sleeve —**'armlet** *n.* band worn round arm —**armchair** *n.* —**'armful** *n.* —**'armhole** *n.* —**'armpit** *n.* hollow under arm at shoulder

arm[2] (ärm) *vt.* **1.** supply with weapons, furnish **2.** prepare (bomb *etc.*) for use —*vi.* **3.** take up arms —*n.* **4.** weapon **5.** branch of army **6.** power, *esp.* of law —*pl.* **7.** weapons **8.** war, military exploits **9.** official heraldic symbols —**'armament** *n.* —**armed forces** military, naval and air forces of a nation —**arms race** competition among nations in accumulating weapons

armada (är'mädə) *n.* large number of ships or aircraft

armadillo (ärmə'dilō) *n.* any of several small Amer. nocturnal burrowing mammals protected by bands of bony plates (*pl.* **-s**)

Armageddon (ärmə'gedən) *n.* **1.** *Bible* place designated as scene of final battle at end of world **2.** catastrophic and extremely destructive conflict

armature ('ärməchōōr) *n.* **1.** part of electric machine, *esp.* revolving structure in electric motor, generator **2.** rigid framework used by sculptor as foundation for moldable substance

Armenia (är'mēniə) *n.* 1. ancient country in west Asia 2. popular name for Armenian Soviet Socialist Republic —**Ar'menian** *a.* 1. of, relating to Armenia, its inhabitants or language —*n.* 2. native or inhabitant of Armenia 3. the Indo-European language of Armenians, which is the only member of its branch

armistice ('ärmistis) *n.* truce, suspension of fighting —**Armistice Day** anniversary of signing of armistice that ended World War I (Nov. 11th)

armoire (ärm'wär) *n.* large cabinet, orig. used for storing weapons

armor ('ärmər) *n.* 1. defensive covering or dress 2. plating of tanks, warships *etc.* 3. armored fighting vehicles, as tanks —**'ar-morer** *n.* —**ar'morial** *a.* relating to heraldic arms —**'armory** *n.* —**armor plate** tough heavy steel oft. hardened on surface, used for protecting warships *etc.*

army ('ärmi) *n.* 1. large body of men armed for warfare and under military command 2. host, great number —**army corps** military unit of U.S. Army comprising at least two divisions and commanded by a lieutenant general

arnica ('ärnikə) *n. Bot.* genus of hardy perennials. A tincture of *Arnica montana* is used for sprains and bruises

aroma (ə'rōmə) *n.* 1. sweet smell, fragrance 2. peculiar charm —**aro'matic** *a. Chem.* of the class of cyclic organic compounds derived from or having similar properties to benzene —**a'romatize** *vt.*

arose (ə'rōz) *pt. of* ARISE

around (ə'rownd) *prep.* 1. on all sides of 2. somewhere in or near 3. approximately (of time) —*adv.* 4. on every side 5. in a circle 6. here and there, nowhere in particular 7. *inf.* present in or at some place

arouse (ə'rowz) *vt.* 1. awaken 2. stimulate

arpeggio (är'pejiō) *n. Mus.* playing of a chord with its notes sounded in succession (*pl.* -s)

arquebus ('ärkwibəs) *n. see* HARQUEBUS

arr. 1. arranged 2. arrival 3. arrive(d)

arrack ('arək) *n.* coarse spirit distilled from rice *etc.*

arraign (ə'rān) *vt.* accuse, indict, put on trial —**ar'raigner** *n.* —**ar'raignment** *n.*

arrange (ə'rānj) *vt.* 1. set in order 2. arrive at agreement about 3. plan 4. adapt, as music 5. settle, as dispute —**ar'rangement** *n.*

arrant ('arənt) *a.* downright, notorious —**'arrantly** *adv.*

arras ('arəs) *n.* tapestry

array (ə'rā) *n.* 1. order, *esp.* military order 2. dress 3. imposing show, splendor —*vt.* 4. set in order 5. dress, equip, adorn

arrears (ə'rēərz) *pl.n.* amount unpaid or undone

arrest (ə'rest) *vt.* 1. detain by legal authority 2. stop 3. catch (attention) —*n.* 4. seizure by warrant 5. making prisoner —**ar'resting** *a.* attracting attention, striking —**ar'restor** *n.* 1. person who arrests 2. mechanism to stop or slow moving object

arrière-pensée (aryerpä'sā) *Fr.* hidden meaning or purpose

arris ('aris) *n.* sharp ridge or edge

arrive (ə'rīv) *vi.* 1. reach destination 2. (*with* at) reach, attain 3. *inf.* succeed —**ar'rival** *n.*

arriviste (arē'vēst) *n.* person who is a new and uncertain arrival

arrogance ('arəgəns) *n.* aggressive conceit —**'arrogant** *a.* 1. proud 2. overbearing —**'arrogantly** *adv.*

arrogate ('arəgāt) *vt.* 1. claim for oneself without justification 2. attribute to another without justification

arrow ('arō) *n.* pointed shaft shot from bow —**'arrowhead** *n.* 1. head of arrow 2. any triangular shape

arrowroot ('arōrōōt) *n.* nutritious starch from W Indian plant, used as a food

arroyo (ə'roiō) *n.* 1. watercourse in arid region 2. water-carved channel (*pl.*-s)

ARS Agricultural Research Service

arsenal ('ärsnəl) *n.* magazine of stores for warfare, guns, ammunition

arsenic ('ärsnik) *n. Chem.* metalloid element, solid, brittle, and highly poisonous *Symbol* As, at. wt. 74.9, at. no. 33 —**arsenical** (är'senikəl) *a.* —**arsenious** (är'sēniəs) *a.*

arson ('ärsən) *n.* crime of intentionally setting property on fire

art (ärt) *n.* 1. skill 2. human skill as opposed to nature 3. creative skill in painting, poetry, music *etc.* 4. any of the works produced thus 5. profession, craft 6. knack 7. contrivance, cunning, trick 8. system of rules —*pl.* 9. certain branches of learning, languages, history *etc.*, as distinct from natural science 10. wiles —**'artful** *a.* wily —**'artfully** *adv.* —**'artfulness** *n.* —**'artist** *n.* 1. one who practices fine art, *esp.* painting 2. one who makes his craft a fine art —**ar'tiste** *n.* professional entertainer, singer, dancer *etc.* —**ar'tistic** *a.* —**ar'tistically** *adv.* —**'artistry** *n.* —**'artless** *a.* natural, frank —**'artlessly** *adv.* —**'artlessness** *n.* —**'arty** *a.* ostentatiously artistic —**art therapy** practice of painting, modeling, craftwork *etc.* as curative activity of patients

art. 1. article 2. artificial

arteriosclerosis (ärtē əriōskli'rōsis) *n.* hardening of the arteries (*pl.* -ses (-sēz))

artery ('ärtəri) *n.* 1. one of tubes carrying blood from heart 2. any main channel of communications —**ar'terial** *a.* 1. pert. to an artery 2. of or relating to through-traffic facilities

artesian well (är'tēzhən) 1. deep well in which water rises by internal pressure 2. deep-bored well

arthritis (är'thrītis) *n.* painful inflammation of joint(s) —**arthritic** (är'thritik) *a./n.*

arthropod ('ärthrəpod) *n.* any member of a phylum of invertebrate animals with segmented bodies and paired jointed legs such as insects, spiders and centipedes

Arthur[1] ('ärthər) *n.* 1. hero of a great cycle of medieval romance 2. 6th-cent. Welsh chieftain —**Arthurian** (är'thyōōəriən, -'thōō-) *a.* —**Arthurian legend** body of literature from 6th cent. to present, based on the combined mythical and historical Arthur

Arthur[2] ('ärthər) *n.* **Chester Alan.** the 21st President of the U.S. (1881-85)

artichoke ('ärtichōk) *n.* 1. thistlelike perennial 2. its edible flower —**Jerusalem artichoke** sunflower with edible tubers like potato

article ('ärtikəl) *n.* 1. item, object 2. short written piece 3. paragraph, section 4. *Gram.* words *the, a, an* 5. clause in contract 6. rule, condition —*vt.* 7. bind as apprentice

articular (är'tikyələr) *a.* of joints or structural components in joint

articulate (är'tikyəlit) *a.* 1. able to express oneself fluently 2. jointed 3. (of speech) clear, distinct —*vt.* (är'tikyəlāt) 4. joint 5. utter distinctly —*vi.* (är'tikyəlāt) 6. speak —**ar'ticulated** *a.* jointed —**ar'ticulately** *adv.* —**ar'ticulateness** *n.* —**articu'lation** *n.*

artifact ('ärtifakt) *n.* something made by man, *esp.* by hand

artifice ('ärtifis) *n.* 1. contrivance 2. trick 3. cunning; skill —**ar'tificer** *n.* craftsman —**arti'ficial** *a.* 1. manufactured, synthetic 2. insincere —**artifici'ality** *n.* —**arti'ficially** *adv.* —**artificial respiration** method of restarting person's breathing after it has stopped

artillery (är'tiləri) *n.* 1. large guns on wheels 2. troops who use them

artisan ('ärtizən) *n.* craftsman; skilled mechanic; manual worker

artiste (är'tēst) *n. see* ART

Art Nouveau ('är nōō'vō; *Fr.* ar nōō'vō) style of art and architecture of 1890s, characterized by sinuous outlines and stylized natural forms

arum lily ('arəm, 'er-) plant with large white flower

ARV *Bible* American Revised Version

-ary (*comb. form*) 1. of; related to; belonging to, as in *cautionary* 2. person or thing connected with, as in *missionary, aviary*

Aryan ('ariən, 'er-) *a.* 1. relating to Indo-European family of languages 2. non-Jewish and Caucasian, *esp.* Nordic —*n.* 3. member or descendant of prehistoric people who spoke Indo-European 4. (in Nazi doctrine) non-Jewish Caucasian, *esp.* of Nordic stock

as (az; əz) *adv./conj.* denoting 1. comparison 2. similarity 3. equality 4. identity 5. concurrence 6. reason

As *Chem.* arsenic

AS 1. Anglo-Saxon (*also* **A.S.**) 2. antisubmarine

A.S.A. American Standards Association

asafetida *or* **asafoetida** (asə'fetidə) *n.* bitter resin with unpleasant smell, obtained from roots of some umbelliferous plants, formerly used medicinally

asap as soon as possible

asbestos (as'bestəs) *n.* fibrous mineral which does not burn —**asbestosis** (asbes'tōsis) *n.* lung disease caused by inhalation of asbestos fiber

ASCAP ('askap) American Society of Composers, Authors and Publishers

ascariasis (askə'rīəsis) *n.* infestation with the giant intestinal roundworm

ascend (ə'send) *vi.* 1. climb, rise —*vt.* 2. walk up, climb, mount —**as'cendancy** *or* **as'cendency** *n.* control, dominance —**as'cendant** *or* **as'cendent** *a.* rising —**as'cension** *n.* —**as'cent** *n.* rise

Ascension Day (ə'senchən) 40th day after Easter, when Ascension of Christ into heaven is celebrated

ascertain (asər'tān) *vt.* get to know, find out, determine —**ascer'tainable** *a.* —**ascer'tainment** *n.*

ascetic (ə'setik) *n.* 1. one who practices severe self-denial —*a.* 2. rigidly abstinent, austere —**as'cetically** *adv.* —**as'ceticism** *n.*

ascites (ə'sītēz) *n.* accumulation of large amounts of fluid in the abdomen (*pl.* **ascites**)

ascorbic acid (ə'skörbik) vitamin C

ascot ('askət) *n.* 1. broad neck scarf looped under the chin —*n./a.* 2. (**A-**) (of the) racecourse and horse races at Ascot Heath in Berkshire, England

ascribe (ə'skrīb) *vt.* attribute, impute, assign —**as'cribable** *a.* —**ascription** (ə'skripshən) *n.*

aseptic (ā'septik, ə-) *a.* germ-free —**a'sepsis** *n.*

asexual (ā'sekshōōəl) *a.* without sex

ash[1] (ash) *n.* 1. dust or remains of anything burnt —*pl.* 2. ruins 3. remains, *eg* of cremated body —**'ashen** *a.* 1. like ashes 2. pale —**'ashy** *a.* —**ash can** metal receptacle for refuse (*also* **garbage can, trash can**) —**Ashcan school** early 20th-century group of American realist painters whose subject was urban life —**'ashtray** *n.* receptacle for tobacco ash, cigarette butts *etc.* —**Ash Wednesday** first day of Lent —**the Ashes** symbol of victory in cricket test-match series between England and Australia

ash² (ash) *n.* **1.** any of a genus (*Fraxinus*) of deciduous trees of the olive family with opposite compound leaves, catkin-like flowers and winged seeds in drooping clusters **2.** its tough fine-grained elastic wood

ashamed (ə'shāmd) *a.* affected with shame, abashed

Ashkenazi (ashkə'nazi) *n.* **1.** Jew in or from central eastern Europe (*pl.* **-zim** (-zim)) —*a.* **2.** of Ashkenazim

ashlar ('ashlər) *n.* hewn or squared building stone

ashore (ə'shör) *adv.* to or on shore

ashram ('äshrəm) *n.* religious retreat or community where Hindu holy man lives

Asia ('āzhə) *n.* continent in eastern hemisphere bounded by Europe and the Arctic, Pacific and Indian oceans —**'Asian** *a.* **1.** of Asia —*n.* **2.** native of Asia or descendant of one **3.** UK person orig. from Bangladesh, India or Pakistan —**Asi'atic** *a.* —**Asia Minor** the peninsula in west Asia between the Black and Mediterranean Seas

aside (ə'sīd) *adv.* **1.** to or on one side **2.** privately —*n.* **3.** words spoken in an undertone not to be heard by some person present

asinine ('asinīn) *a.* of or like an ass, silly —**asininity** (asi'niniti) *n.*

ask (äsk) *vt.* **1.** request, require, question, invite —*vi.* **2.** make inquiry or request

askance (ə'skans) *or* **askant** (ə'skant) *adv.* **1.** sideways, awry **2.** with a side look or meaning —**look askance** view with suspicion

askew (ə'skyōō) *adv.* awry

aslant (ə'slänt) *adv.* on the slant, obliquely, athwart

asleep (ə'slēp) *a.* sleeping, at rest

asocial (ā'sōshəl) *a.* **1.** avoiding contact **2.** unconcerned about welfare of others **3.** hostile to society

asp (asp) *n.* small venomous snake of Egypt

asparagus (ə'sparəgəs) *n.* perennial plant of lily family, cultivated for edible shoot (*also* **sparrow grass**)

aspect ('aspekt) *n.* **1.** look **2.** view **3.** appearance **4.** expression

aspen ('aspən) *n.* any of several N Amer. poplars with leaves that flutter in the slightest breeze

aspergillosis (aspərji'lōsis) *n.* fungus disease attacking the skin, ear, nose, lungs and other parts of body

asperity (a'speriti) *n.* **1.** roughness **2.** harshness **3.** coldness

aspersion (ə'spərzhən, -shən) *n.* **1.** (*usu. in pl.*) malicious remarks **2.** slanderous attack

asphalt ('asfölt) *n.* **1.** brown-to-black bituminous substance found in natural beds and also obtained as residue in refining petroleum **2.** asphaltic composition used for pavements and as waterproof coating —**as'phaltic** *a.* —**asphalt jungle** big city

asphodel ('asfədel) *n.* plant with clusters of yellow or white flowers

asphyxia (as'fiksiə) *n.* suffocation —**as'phyxiate** *v.* —**as'phyxiated** *a.* —**asphyxi'ation** *n.*

aspic ('aspik) *n.* **1.** jelly used to coat meat, eggs, fish *etc.* **2.** *Bot.* species of lavender

aspidistra (aspi'distrə) *n.* plant with broad tapered leaves (*also* **cast-iron plant**)

aspire (ə'spīər) *vi.* **1.** desire eagerly **2.** rise to great height —**aspirant** ('aspirənt) *n.* **1.** one who aspires **2.** candidate —**aspirate** ('aspirāt) *vt.* pronounce with full breathing, as 'h' —**aspiration** (aspi'rāshən) *n.* —**aspirator** ('aspirātər) *n.* device employing suction, such as jet pump or one for removing fluids from body cavity —**as'piring** *a.* —**as'piringly** *adv.*

aspirin ('asprin) *n.* (a tablet of) drug used to allay pain and fever

ass¹ (as) *n.* **1.** quadruped of horse family **2.** contemptible person

ass² (as) *n. offens.* **1.** buttocks **2.** anus **3.** sexual intercourse —**smart ass** *see* **smart aleck** *at* SMART

assagai ('asəgī) *n. see* ASSEGAI

assail (ə'sāl) *vt.* attack, assault —**as'sailable** *a.* —**as'sailant** *n.*

Assamese (asə'mēz) *n./a.* **1.** (native or inhabitant) of Assam, India (*pl.* **-ese**) —*n.* **2.** the Indic language of the Assamese, one of the languages of the constitution of India

assassin (ə'sasin) *n.* **1.** one who kills, *esp.* prominent person, by treacherous violence **2.** murderer —**as'sassinate** *vt.* —**assassi'nation** *n.*

assault (ə'sölt) *n.* **1.** attack, *esp.* sudden —*vt.* **2.** attack —**assault and battery** *Law* threat of attack to person followed by actual attack

assay (ə'sā, 'asā) *v.* **1.** test (*esp.* proportions of metals) in alloy or ore —*n.* ('asā, ə'sā) **2.** analysis, *esp.* of metals **3.** trial, test —**as'sayer** *n.*

assegai *or* **assagai** ('asəgī) *n.* slender spear of S Afr. tribes

assemble (ə'sembəl) *v.* **1.** meet, bring together **2.** collect —*vt.* **3.** put together (of machinery *etc.*) —**as'semblage** *n.* —**as'sembly** *n.* **1.** gathering, meeting **2.** assembling —**assembly line** sequence of machines, workers in factory assembling product

assent (ə'sent) *vi.* **1.** concur, agree —*n.* **2.** acquiescence, agreement, compliance

assert (ə'sərt) *vt.* **1.** declare strongly **2.** insist upon —**as'sertion** *n.* —**as'sertive** *a.* —**as'sertively** *adv.*

assess (ə'ses) *vt.* **1.** fix value of **2.** evaluate, estimate, *esp.* for taxation **3.** fix amount of (tax or fine) **4.** impose tax or fine on (a person *etc.*) —**as'sessable** *a.* —**as'sessment** *n.* —**as'sessor** *n.*

asset ('aset) *n.* **1.** valuable or useful person, thing —*pl.* **2.** property available to pay debts, *esp.* of insolvent debtor

asseverate (ə'sevərāt) *vt.* assert solemnly —**asseve'ration** *n.*

assiduous (ə'sijōōs) *a.* persevering, attentive, diligent —**assiduity** (asi'dyōōiti, -'dōō-) *n.* —**as'siduously** *adv.*

assign (ə'sīn) *vt.* **1.** appoint to job *etc.* **2.** allot, apportion, fix **3.** ascribe **4.** transfer —*n.* **5.** assignee —**as'signable** *a.* —**assignation** (asig'nāshən) *n.* **1.** secret meeting **2.** appointment to meet —**assignee** (asi'nē) *n. Law* person to whom property *etc.* is transferred —**as'signment** *n.* **1.** act of assigning **2.** allotted duty —**assignor** (asi'nör) *n.*

assimilate (ə'similāt) *vt.* **1.** learn and understand **2.** make similar **3.** absorb into the system —**as'similable** *a.* —**assimi'lation** *n.* —**as'similative** *a.*

assist (ə'sist) *v.* **1.** give help **2.** work as assistant (to) —**as'sistance** *n.* —**as'sistant** *n.* helper —**assistant professor** member of college or university faculty who ranks above instructor and below associate professor

assize (ə'sīz) *n.* **1.** enactment made by legislature **2.** statute regulating weights and

measures **3.** fixed or customary standard **4.** judicial inquest

assn. association

assoc. **1.** associate **2.** associated **3.** association

associate (ə'sōshiāt, -si-) *vt.* **1.** link, connect, *esp.* as ideas in mind **2.** join —*vi.* **3.** keep company **4.** combine, unite —*n.* (ə'sōshiit, -si-) **5.** companion, partner **6.** friend, ally **7.** subordinate member of association —*a.* (ə'sōshiit, -si-) **8.** affiliated —**associ'ation** *n.* society, club —**associate professor** member of college or university faculty who ranks above assistant professor and below professor —**association football** soccer

assonance ('asənəns) *n.* **1.** likeness in sound **2.** rhyming of vowels only —**'assonant** *a.*

assort (ə'sört) *vt.* **1.** classify, arrange —*vi.* **2.** match, agree, harmonize —**as'sorted** *a.* mixed —**as'sortment** *n.*

ASSR Autonomous Soviet Socialist Republic

asst. assistant

assuage (ə'swāj) *vt.* **1.** soften, pacify **2.** soothe —**as'suagement** *n.*

assume (ə'sōōm) *vt.* **1.** take for granted **2.** pretend to **3.** take upon oneself **4.** claim —**assumption** (ə'sumpshən) *n.* —**assumptive** (ə'sumptiv) *a.* —**Assumption of Moses** noncanonical apocalyptic sacred scripture

assure (ə'shōōər) *vt.* **1.** tell positively, promise **2.** make sure **3.** insure against loss **4.** affirm —**as'surance** *n.* —**as'sured** *a.* sure —**assuredly** (ə'shōōəridli) *adv.*

A.S.T. Atlantic Standard Time

astatic (ā'statik) *a. Phys.* having no tendency to take fixed position

astatine ('astətēn) *n. Chem.* highly unstable radioactive element of the halogen group *Symbol* At, at. wt. 210, at. no. 85

aster ('astər) *n.* **1.** any of various fall-blooming perennials of the daisy family with showy radiated flowers **2.** structure formed in cell radiating around centrosome during meiosis or mitosis

asterisk ('astərisk) *n.* **1.** star (*) used in printing —*vt.* **2.** mark thus —**'asterism** *n.*

astern (ə'stərn) *adv.* **1.** in or toward the rear of ship **2.** backward

asteroid ('astəroid) *n.* **1.** small planet —*a.* **2.** star-shaped

asthma ('azmə) *n.* condition in which bronchial tubes go into spasm resulting in labored breathing and wheezing —**asth'matic** *a./n.* —**asth'matically** *adv.*

astigmatism (ə'stigmətizəm) *n.* inability of lens to focus clearly all portions of horizontal, diagonal or vertical lines —**astig'matic** *a.*

astilbe (ə'stilbi) *n.* genus of herbaceous perennials of the saxifrage family with spirelike clusters of white, pink or red flowers

astir (ə'stər) *a.* **1.** on the move **2.** out of bed **3.** in excitement

astonish (ə'stonish) *vt.* amaze, surprise —**a'stonishing** *a.* —**a'stonishment** *n.*

astound (ə'stownd) *vt.* **1.** astonish greatly **2.** stun with amazement —**a'stounding** *a.* startling

astraddle (ə'stradəl) *a.* **1.** with a leg on either side of something —*prep.* **2.** astride

astrakhan ('astrəkən) *n.* **1.** karakul **2.** cloth imitating this

astral ('astrəl) *a.* of the stars or spirit world —**astral body**

astray (ə'strā) *adv.* **1.** off the right path **2.** in error

astride (ə'strīd) *adv.* **1.** with the legs apart —*prep.* **2.** straddling

astringent (ə'strinjənt) *a.* **1.** severe, harsh **2.** sharp **3.** constricting (body tissues, blood vessels *etc.*) —*n.* **4.** astringent substance —**as'tringency** *n.*

astro- (*comb. form*) indicating star or star-shaped structure

astrol. astrology

astrolabe ('astrəlāb) *n.* instrument used by early astronomers to measure altitude of stars *etc.*

astrology (ə'stroləji) *n.* **1.** foretelling of events by stars **2.** medieval astronomy —**as'trologer** *n.* —**astro'logical** *a.*

astrometry (ə'stromitri) *n.* determination of apparent magnitudes of fixed stars

astron. astronomy

astronaut ('astrənöt) *n.* one trained for travel in space —**astro'nautics** *pl.n.* (*with sing. v.*) science and technology of space flight

astronomy (ə'stronəmi) *n.* scientific study of heavenly bodies —**as'tronomer** *n.* —**astro-'nomical** *a.* **1.** very large **2.** of astronomy —**astronomical unit** unit of distance used in astronomy equal to the mean distance between the earth and the sun

astrophysics (astrō'fiziks) *n.* the science of the chemical and physical characteristics of heavenly bodies —**astro'physical** *a.* —**astro-'physicist** *n.*

astute (ə'styōōt, -'stōōt) *a.* perceptive, shrewd —**as'tutely** *adv.* —**as'tuteness** *n.*

asunder (ə'sundər) *adv.* **1.** apart **2.** in pieces

ASV *Bible* American Standard Version (published 1901)

asylum (ə'sīləm) *n.* **1.** refuge, sanctuary, place of safety **2.** home for care of the unfortunate, *esp.* of mentally ill

asymmetry (ā'simitri) *n.* **1.** lack of symmetry **2.** *Chem.* condition of not being superimposable on a mirror image —**asym-'metric(al)** *a.*

asymptote ('asimtōt) *n.* straight line that continually approaches a curve, but never meets it

asyndeton (ə'sinditon) *n.* omission of conjunctions between parts of sentence (*pl.* **-deta** (-ditə)) —**asyn'detic** *a.* without conjunctions or cross-references

at (at) *prep./adv. denoting* **1.** location in space or time **2.** rate **3.** condition or state **4.** amount **5.** direction **6.** cause

At *Chem.* astatine

at. **1.** atmosphere **2.** atomic

Atabrine ('atəbrin) *n.* trade name for yellow dye used in the treatment of malaria

ataractic (atə'raktik) *or* **ataraxic** (atə'raksik) *n.* drug that induces calmness or emotional tranquillity

atavism ('atəvizəm) *n.* appearance of ancestral, not parental, characteristics in human beings, animals or plants —**ata'vistic** *a.*

ataxia (ə'taksiə) *or* **ataxy** (ə'taksi) *n.* lack of muscular coordination

ate (āt) *pt. of* EAT

-ate¹ (*comb. form*) **1.** having appearance or characteristics of, as in *fortunate* **2.** chemical compound, *esp.* salt or ester of acid, as in *carbonate* **3.** product of process, as in *condensate* **4.** forming verbs from nouns and adjectives, as in *hyphenate*

-ate² (*comb. form*) office, rank or group having certain function, as in *episcopate*

atelier (atəl'yā) *n.* **1.** artist's studio **2.** workshop

Athabaskan (athə'baskən) *n./a.* (of) Amerindian people inhabiting central Alaska, closely related to Navaho, Apache and Hupas of southwest U.S.

Athapaskan (athə'paskən) *n.* Amerindian language family found in Pacific Northwest and Alaska and in southwest U.S.

atheism ('āthiizəm) *n.* belief that there is no God —**'atheist** *n.* —**athe'istic(al)** *a.*

athenaeum *or* **atheneum** (athi'nēəm) *n.* **1.** institution for promotion of learning **2.** building containing reading room or library

atherosclerosis (athərōskli'rōsis) *n.* degenerative disease of arteries characterized by thickening of arterial walls, caused by deposits of fatty material (*pl.* **-oses** (-ōsēz))

athlete ('athlēt) *n.* **1.** one trained for physical exercises, feats or contests of strength **2.** one good at sports —**athletic** (ath'letik) *a.* —**athletically** (ath'letikəli) *adv.* —**athleti-cism** (ath'letisizəm) *n.* —**athletics** (ath'letiks) *pl.n.* (*with sing. v.*) term for all competitive individual and team games and sports depending upon feats of physical strength or skill —**athlete's foot** fungal infection of skin of foot, *esp.* between toes and on soles —**athletic supporter** jockstrap

at-home *n.* **1.** social gathering in person's home —*a.* **2.** suitable for one's home

athwart (ə'thwört) *prep.* **1.** across —*adv.* **2.** across, *esp.* obliquely

Atlantic (ət'lantik) *n.* **1.** (*short for* **Atlantic Ocean**) world's second largest ocean —*a.* **2.** of or bordering Atlantic Ocean **3.** of Atlas or Atlas Mountains

Atlantis (ət'lantis) *n.* in ancient legend, continent said to have sunk beneath Atlantic west of Gibraltar

atlas ('atləs) *n.* **1.** bound volume of maps **2.** bound collection of tables, charts or plates **3.** (**A-**) titan condemned to support sky on his shoulders **4.** (**A-**) mountains in northwest Africa ranging through Morocco, Algeria and Tunisia

atm. **1.** atmosphere **2.** atmospheric

atmosphere ('atməsfēər) *n.* **1.** mass of gas surrounding heavenly body, *esp.* the earth **2.** prevailing tone or mood (of place *etc.*) **3.** unit of pressure in cgs system —**atmospher-ic** (atməs'ferik) *a.* —**atmospherics** (atməs-'feriks) *pl.n.* noises in radio reception due to electrical disturbance in the atmosphere —**atmospheric perspective** effect of distance in a painting, created by using color (*also* **aerial perspective, color perspective**)

at. no. atomic number

atoll ('atöl) *n.* ring-shaped coral island enclosing lagoon

atom ('atəm) *n.* **1.** smallest unit of an element which can enter into chemical combination **2.** any very small particle —**a'tomic** *a.* of, arising from atoms —**ato-'micity** *n.* number of atoms in molecule of an element —'**atomize** *vt.* reduce to atoms or small particles —'**atomizer** *n.* instrument for discharging liquids in fine spray —**atom bomb** *or* **atomic bomb** bomb whose immense power derives from nuclear fission or fusion, nuclear bomb —**atomic energy** nuclear energy —**atomic number** the number of protons in the nucleus of an atom —**atomic pile** *see* **nuclear reactor** *at* REACT —**atomic theory** **1.** any theory in which matter is regarded as consisting of atoms **2.** current concept of atom as entity with definite structure —**atomic weight** the weight of an atom of an element relative to that of carbon 12 —**atom smasher** *see* **particle accelerator** *at* PARTICLE

atonality (ātō'naliti) *n.* **1.** absence of or disregard for established musical key in composition **2.** principles of composition embodying this

atone (ə'tōn) *vi.* **1.** make reparation, amends **2.** give satisfaction —**a'tonement** *n.*

atonic (ā'tonik, a-) *a.* unaccented

atop (ə'top) *adv.* **1.** at or on the top —*prep.* **2.** above

atracurium (atrə'kyōōriəm) *n.* drug used as muscle relaxant during surgery

atrium ('ātriəm) *n.* open central court in Greek and Roman dwellings (*pl.* **'atria, -s**) —**atrium house** house built around a courtyard

atrocious (ə'trōshəs) *a.* **1.** extremely cruel or wicked **2.** horrifying **3.** *inf.* very bad —**a'trociously** *adv.* —**atrocity** (ə'trositi) *n.* wickedness

atrophy ('atrəfi) *n.* **1.** wasting away, emaciation —*vi.* **2.** waste away, become useless

atropine ('atrəpēn) *n.* poisonous alkaloid obtained from deadly nightshade, used medicinally: main ingredient of belladonna

att. **1.** attached **2.** attention **3.** attorney

attach (ə'tach) *v.* **1.** join, fasten **2.** unite **3.** be connected **4.** attribute **5.** appoint **6.** seize by law —**at'tached** *a.* (*with* to) fond (of) —**at'tachment** *n.*

attaché (atə'shā) *n.* specialist attached to diplomatic mission —**attaché case** (ə'tashā) small thin suitcase for papers

attack (ə'tak) *vt.* **1.** take action against (in war, sport *etc.*) **2.** criticize **3.** set about with vigor **4.** affect adversely —*n.* **5.** attacking action **6.** bout

attain (ə'tān) *vt.* **1.** arrive at **2.** reach, gain by effort, accomplish —**attaina'bility** *n.* —**at-'tainable** *a.* —**at'tainment** *n.* *esp.* personal accomplishment

attainder (ə'tāndər) *n. Hist.* loss of rights through conviction of high treason

attar ('atər) *n.* fragrant oil made *esp.* from rose petals

attempt (ə'tempt) *vt.* **1.** try, endeavor —*n.* **2.** trial, effort

attend (ə'tend) *vt.* **1.** be present at **2.** accompany —*vi.* (*with* to) **3.** take care (of) **4.** give the mind (to), pay attention (to) —**at'tendance** *n.* **1.** an attending **2.** presence **3.** persons attending —**at'tendant** *n./a.* —**at'tention** *n.* **1.** notice **2.** heed **3.** act of attending **4.** care **5.** courtesy **6.** alert position in military drill —**at'tentive** *a.* —**at'tentive-ly** *adv.* —**at'tentiveness** *n.*

attenuate (ə'tenyōōāt) *v.* **1.** weaken or become weak **2.** make or become thin —**at'tenuated** *a.* —**attenu'ation** *n.* reduction of intensity

attest (ə'test) *vt.* bear witness to, certify —**atte'station** *n.* formal confirmation by oath *etc.*

attic ('atik) *n.* space within roof where ceiling follows line of roof

Attic ('atik) *a.* **1.** of Athens **2.** classically pure —*n.* **3.** literary language of the Greek-speaking world

Attila (ə'tilə) *n.* king of the Huns (died 453), noted for his cruelty and vandalism

attire (ə'tīər) *vt.* **1.** dress, array —*n.* **2.** dress, clothing

attitude ('atityōōd, -tōōd) *n.* **1.** mental view, opinion **2.** posture, pose **3.** disposition, behavior —**atti'tudinize** *vi.* assume affected attitudes

attorney (ə'tərni) *n.* one legally appointed to act for another, *esp.* a lawyer (*pl.* **-s**) —**attorney-at-law** *n.* legally qualified practitioner who may act for clients in court —**attorney general** the chief law officer of the U.S. or State who represents the government in litigation and is chief legal adviser to the State

attract (ə'trakt) *vt.* **1.** draw (attention *etc.*) **2.** arouse interest of **3.** cause to come closer (as magnet *etc.*) —**at'traction** *n.* **1.** power to attract **2.** something offered so as to interest, please —**at'tractive** *a.* —**at'tractively** *adv.* —**at'tractiveness** *n.*

attribute (ə'tribyət) *vt.* **1.** (*usu.* *with* to) regard as belonging (to) or produced (by) —*n.* ('atribyōōt) **2.** quality, property or characteristic of anything —**at'tributable** *a.* —**attri'bution** *n.* —**at'tributive** *a./n.* (of) word or phrase used as adjective —**at'tributively** *adv.*

attrition (ə'trishən) *n.* **1.** wearing away of strength *etc.* **2.** rubbing away, friction

attune (ə'tyōōn, -'tōōn) *vt.* **1.** tune, harmonize **2.** make accordant

at. wt. atomic weight

atypical (ā'tipikəl) *a.* not typical

Au *Chem.* gold

aubergine ('ōbərzhēn) *n.* UK eggplant

aubrietia (ō'brēshə) *n.* genus of low-growing or trailing evergreen perennials of the cabbage family grown in rock and wall gardens

auburn ('ōbərn) *a.* **1.** reddish-brown —*n.* **2.** this color

au courant (ō kōō'rā) *Fr.* **1.** up-to-date **2.** acquainted

auction ('ōkshən) *n.* **1.** public sale in which bidder offers increase of price over another and what is sold goes to one who bids highest —*vt.* **2.** (*oft.* *with* off) sell by auction —**auctio'neer** *n.* —**auction bridge** *see* BRIDGE²

audacious (ō'dāshəs) *a.* **1.** bold **2.** daring, impudent —**audacity** (ō'dasiti) *n.*

audible ('ōdibəl) *a.* able to be heard —**audi'bility** *n.* —**'audibly** *adv.*

audience ('ōdiəns) *n.* **1.** assembly of hearers **2.** act of hearing **3.** judicial hearing **4.** formal interview

audio ('ōdiō) *n.* frequency in audible range of 50 hertz to 20 000 hertz

audio- (*comb. form*) relating to sound or hearing

audiometer (ōdi'omitər) *n.* instrument for testing hearing

audiotape ('ōdiōtāp) *n.* tape recording of sound

audiovisual (ōdiō'vizhōōəl) *a.* (*esp.* of teaching aids) involving, directed at, both sight and hearing, as film *etc.*

audit ('ōdit) *n.* **1.** formal examination or settlement of accounts —*vt.* **2.** examine (accounts) —**'auditor** *n.*

audition (ō'dishən) *n.* **1.** screen or other test of prospective performer **2.** hearing —*v.* **3.** conduct or be tested in such a test —**audi'torium** *n.* **1.** place where audience sits **2.** hall (*pl.* **-s, -ia** (-iə)) —**'auditory** *a.* pert. to sense of hearing

Audubon Society ('ōdəbon) society founded in 1905 for the preservation of wildlife, *esp.* birds

au fait (ō 'fā) *Fr.* **1.** fully informed **2.** expert

auf Wiedersehen (owf 'vēdərzāən) *Ger.* goodbye

Aug. August

Augean stable (ō'jēən) extremely dirty place

auger ('ōgər) *n.* carpenter's tool for boring holes, large gimlet

aught (ōt) *n.* **1.** *Lit., obs.* anything **2.** zero, cipher

augment (ōg'ment) *v.* increase, enlarge —**augmen'tation** *n.* —**aug'mentative** *a.* increasing in force

au gratin (ō gra'tē) *Fr.* covered with breadcrumbs or grated cheese and browned under broiler

augur ('ōgər) *n.* **1.** among the Romans, soothsayer —*v.* **2.** be a sign of future events, foretell —**augural** ('ōgyərəl) *a.* —**augury** ('ōgyəri) *n.*

august (ō'gust) *a.* majestic, dignified

August ('ōgəst) *n.* eighth month

Augustan (ō'gustən) *a.* **1.** of Augustus, the Roman Emperor **2.** classic, distinguished, as applied to a period of literature, *esp.* in 18th-century England

auk (ōk) *n.* family of black-and-white diving marine birds found from Arctic southward to California, western Europe and Japan

au lait (ō 'lā) with milk

auld lang syne (ōld lang 'zīn) times past, *esp.* those remembered with nostalgia

au naturel (ō natü'rel) *Fr.* **1.** naked; nude **2.** uncooked or plainly cooked

aunt (änt) *n.* **1.** father's or mother's sister **2.** uncle's wife —**'auntie** *or* **'aunty** *n. inf.* aunt

au pair (ō 'pāər) young foreigner who receives free board and lodging in return for housework *etc.*

aura ('ōrə) *n.* **1.** quality, air, atmosphere considered distinctive of person or thing **2.** medical symptom warning of impending epileptic fit *etc.*

aural ('ōrəl) *a.* of, by ear —**'aurally** *adv.*

aureate ('ōriit) *a.* **1.** covered with gold; gilded **2.** (of style of writing or speaking) excessively elaborate

aureole ('ōriōl) *or* **aureola** (ō'rēələ) *n.* **1.** gold disk round head in sacred pictures **2.** halo

au revoir (ō rə'vwär) *Fr.* goodbye

auricle ('ōrikəl) *n.* **1.** outside ear **2.** upper cavity of heart —**au'ricular** *a.* **1.** of the auricle **2.** aural

auricula (ō'rikyələ) *n.* **1.** UK alpine primrose with leaves shaped like bear's ear **2.** *Biol.* ear-shaped part (*also* **'auricle**) (*pl.* **-lae** (-lē), **-s**)

auriferous (ō'rifərəs) *a.* gold-bearing

aurochs ('owroks) *n.* species of wild ox, now extinct (*also* **wisent**)

aurora (ō'rōrə) *n.* **1.** lights in the atmosphere seen radiating from regions of the poles. The northern is called **aurora borealis** and the southern **aurora australis 2.** *Poet.* dawn

AUS Army of the United States

auscultation (ōskəl'tāshən) *n.* listening to movement of heart and lungs with stethoscope —**'auscultator** *n.* —**aus'cultatory** *a.*

auspice ('ōspis) *n.* **1.** omen, augury —*pl.* **2.** patronage —**aus'picious** *a.* of good omen, favorable —**aus'piciously** *adv.*

Aussie ('ōsi) *n./a. inf.* Australian

austere (o'stēər) *a.* **1.** harsh, strict, severe **2.** without luxury —**aus'terely** *adv.* —**austerity** (o'steriti) *n.*

austral ('ōstrəl) *a.* southern

Australasia (ōstrə'lāzhə) *n.* Australia, New Zealand and adjacent islands —**Austral'asian** *a./n.*

Australia (ō'strālyə) *n.* **1.** continent in eastern hemisphere, southeast of Asia, between the Indian and Pacific oceans **2.** (*also* **Commonwealth of Australia**) federation of former British colonies of New South Wales, Victoria, Queensland, South Australia, Western Australia and Tasmania —**Aus'tralian** *n./a.* —**Australian Rules** game resembling rugby football, played in Aust. between teams of 18 men on oval pitch with oval ball

Austria ('ōstriə) *n.* country in central Europe bounded north by Germany and Czechoslovakia, east by Hungary, south by Yugoslavia and Italy, and west by Switzerland —**'Austrian** *a./n.*

Austro-¹ (*comb. form*) southern, as in *Austro-Asiatic*

Austro-² (*comb. form*) Austrian, as in *Austro-Hungarian*

autarchy ('ōtärki) *n.* **1.** absolute sovereignty **2.** absolute or autocratic rule **3.** autarky

autarky ('ōtärki) *n.* (*esp.* of political unit) policy of economic self-sufficiency

auth. 1. author **2.** authentic **3.** authorized

authentic (ō'thentik) *a.* **1.** real, genuine, true **2.** trustworthy —**au'thentically** *adv.* —**au'thenticate** *vt.* **1.** make valid, confirm **2.** establish truth, authorship *etc.* of —**authenti'cation** *or* **authenticity** (ōthen'tisiti) *n.*

author ('ōthər) *n.* **1.** writer of book **2.** originator, constructor (**-ess** *fem.*) —**'authorship** *n.*

authority (ō'thoriti) *n.* **1.** legal power or right **2.** delegated power **3.** influence **4.** permission **5.** expert **6.** (*oft. pl.*) body or board in control —**authori'tarian** *a.* **1.** favoring or characterized by strict obedience to authority or government by small elite **2.** dictatorial —*n.* **3.** person who favors or practices authoritarian policies —**au'thoritative** *a.* —**au'thoritatively** *adv.* —**authori'zation** *n.* —**'authorize** *vt.* **1.** empower **2.** permit, sanction —**Authorized Version** English translation of the Bible published in 1611 under James I (*also* **King James Version**)

autism ('ōtizəm) *n.* tendency to see world in terms of one's own needs and wishes —**au'tistic** *a.*

auto- *or sometimes before vowel* **aut-** (*comb. form*) self, as in *autograph, autosuggestion.* Such words are not given here where the meaning may easily be inferred from the simple word

autobahn ('ōtōbän) *n.* German motorway

autobiography (ōtōbī'ogrəfi) *n.* life story of person written by himself —**autobi'ographer** *n.* —**autobio'graphical** *a.* —**autobio'graphically** *adv.*

autochthon (ō'tokthon) *n.* original inhabitant (person, plant or animal) —**au'tochthonous** *a.*

autocrat ('ōtəkrat) *n.* **1.** absolute ruler **2.** despotic person —**au'tocracy** *n.* —**auto'cratic** *a.* —**auto'cratically** *adv.*

autocross ('ōtōkros) *n.* motor-racing sport over rough course

auto-da-fé (ōtōdə'fā) *n.* **1.** *Hist.* ceremony of Spanish Inquisition including pronouncement and execution of sentences passed on heretics **2.** burning to death of people condemned as heretics by Inquisition (*pl.* **autos-da-fé**)

autoeroticism (ōtōi'rotisizəm) *or* **autoerotism** (ōtō'erətizəm) *n.* self-produced sexual arousal

autogamy (ō'togəmi) *n.* self-fertilization

autogenous (ō'tojinəs) *a.* self-generated

autogiro *or* **autogyro** (ōtō'jīrō) *n.* aircraft like helicopter using horizontal airscrew for vertical ascent and descent

autograph ('ōtəgraf) *n.* **1.** handwritten signature **2.** person's handwriting —*vt.* **3.** sign —**auto'graphic** *a.*

autogyro (ōtō'jīrō) *n. see* AUTOGIRO

Autoharp ('ōtōhärp) *n.* trade name for zither with button-controlled dampers

autointoxication (ōtōintoksi'kāshən) *n.* poisoning of tissues of the body as a result of internally produced toxic substances

Automat ('ōtəmat) *n.* trade name for cafeteria in which food is usu. dispensed from vending machines

automate ('ōtəmāt) *vt.* make (manufacturing process *etc.*) automatic

automatic (ötə'matik) *a.* **1.** operated or controlled mechanically **2.** done without conscious thought —*a./n.* **3.** self-loading (weapon) —**auto'matically** *adv.* —**automation** (ötə'māshən) *n.* use of automatic devices in industrial production —**au'tomatism** *n.* involuntary action —**au'tomaton** *n.* self-acting machine, *esp.* simulating a human being (*pl.* **-ata** (-ətə)) —**automatic transmission** transmission system in motor vehicle, in which gears change automatically

automobile (ötəmō'bēl) *n.* self-propelling (*usu.* by internal-combustion engine) vehicle for passenger transportation on streets and roadways —**automo'bilist** *n.* motorist —**automobile racing 1.** speed competition among racing cars **2.** racing against clock for individual performance records

automotive (ötə'mōtiv) *a.* **1.** relating to motor vehicles **2.** self-propelling

autonomy (ö'tonəmi) *n.* self-government —**au'tonomous** *a.*

autopsy ('ötopsi, -təp-) *n.* **1.** post-mortem examination to determine cause of death **2.** critical analysis —**au'toptic(al)** *a.*

autoroute ('ötōrōōt) *n.* French motorway

autostrada ('ötöströdə) *n.* Italian motorway

autosuggestion (ötösə'jeschən) *n.* process of influencing the mind (toward health *etc.*), conducted by the subject himself

autumn ('ötəm) *n./a.* (typical of) the season after summer —**autumnal** (ö'tumnəl) *a.* typical of the onset of winter —**autumnally** (ö'tumnəli) *adv.*

aux. auxiliary

auxiliary (ög'zilyəri, -'zilə-) *a.* **1.** helping, subsidiary —*n.* **2.** helper **3.** something subsidiary, as troops **4.** verb used to form tenses of others

av 1. avenue **2.** average **3.** avoirdupois

AV 1. *Bible* Authorized Version (King James) **2.** ad valorem **3.** audiovisual

avail (ə'vāl) *v.* **1.** be of use, advantage, value (to) —*n.* **2.** benefit (*esp.* **in of no avail, to little avail**) —**availa'bility** *n.* —**a'vailable** *a.* **1.** obtainable **2.** accessible —**avail oneself of** make use of

avalanche ('avəlänch) *n.* **1.** mass of snow, ice, sliding down mountain **2.** sudden overwhelming quantity of anything

avant-garde (ävänt'gärd) *a.* markedly experimental or in advance, *esp.* in the arts

avarice ('avəris) *n.* greed for wealth —**ava'ricious** *a.* —**ava'riciously** *adv.*

avast (ə'väst) *interj. Naut.* stop

avatar ('avətär) *n.* **1.** *Hinduism* manifestation of deity in human or animal form **2.** visible manifestation of abstract concept

avaunt (ə'vönt) *interj. obs.* go away, depart

avdp. avoirdupois

Ave. *or* **ave.** Avenue

Ave Maria ('ävä mə'rēə) *see* **Hail Mary** at HAIL²

avenge (ə'venj) *vt.* take vengeance on behalf of (person) or on account of (thing) —**a'venger** *n.*

avenue ('avinyōō, -nōō) *n.* **1.** wide street, oft. lined with trees **2.** approach **3.** double row of trees

aver (ə'vər) *vt.* affirm, assert (**-rr-**) —**a'verment** *n.*

average ('avərij, 'avrij) *n.* **1.** the mean value or quantity of a number of values or quantities —*a.* **2.** calculated as an average **3.** medium, ordinary —*vt.* **4.** fix or calculate an average of —*vi.* **5.** exist in or form a mean

averse (ə'vərs) *a.* disinclined, unwilling —**a'version** *n.* (*usu.* **with** to *or* **for**) dislike, person or thing disliked —**aversion therapy** *Psych.* way of suppressing undesirable habit by associating unpleasant effect, such as electric shock, with it

avert (ə'vərt) *vt.* **1.** turn away **2.** ward off

avg average

aviary ('āvieri) *n.* enclosure for birds —**'aviarist** *n.*

aviation (āvi'āshən) *n.* **1.** art of flying aircraft **2.** design, production and maintenance of aircraft —**'aviator** *n.*

avid ('avid) *a.* **1.** keen, enthusiastic **2.** (*oft.* **with** for) greedy —**a'vidity** *n.*

avn aviation

avocado (avə'kädō) *n.* **1.** tropical tree **2.** its green-skinned edible fruit

avocation (avə'kāshən) *n.* **1.** vocation **2.** employment, business

avocet ('avəset) *n.* wading bird of snipe family with upward-curving bill

Avogadro number (avə'gädrō) number of atoms in one gram-atom —**Avogadro's law** law stating that gases at the same temperature and pressure have same number of molecules per unit volume

avoid (ə'void) *vt.* **1.** keep away from **2.** refrain from **3.** not allow to happen —**a'voidable** *a.* —**a'voidance** *n.*

avoirdupois *or* **avoirdupois weight** (avərdə'poiz) *n./a.* (of) system of weights based on 16 ounces to pound and 16 drams to ounce

avouch (ə'vowch) *vt. obs.* affirm, maintain, attest, own —**a'vouchment** *n.*

avow (ə'vow) *vt.* **1.** declare **2.** admit —**a'vowable** *a.* —**a'vowal** *n.* —**a'vowed** *a.* —**avowedly** (ə'vowidli) *adv.*

avuncular (ə'vungkyələr) *a.* of or resembling an uncle, genial

await (ə'wāt) *vt.* **1.** wait or stay for **2.** be in store for

awake (ə'wāk) *v.* **1.** emerge or rouse from sleep **2.** become or cause to become alert (**a'woke** *or* **a'waked**, **a'woken** *or* **a'waked**, **a'waking**) —*a.* **3.** not sleeping **4.** alert —**a'wakening** *n.*

award (ə'wörd) *vt.* **1.** give formally (*esp.* prize or punishment) —*n.* **2.** prize **3.** judicial decision

aware (ə'wāər) *a.* informed, conscious —**a'wareness** *n.*

awash (ə'wosh) *a.* **1.** level with surface of water **2.** filled or overflowing with water

away (ə'wā) *a.* **1.** absent, apart, at a distance, out of the way —*n.* **2.** *Sport* game played on opponent's ground

awe (ö) *n.* dread mingled with reverence —**'awesome** *a.*

aweigh (ə'wā) *a. Naut.* (of anchor) no longer hooked into bottom; hanging by its rope or chain

awful ('öfəl) *a.* **1.** very bad, unpleasant **2.** *obs.* impressive **3.** *inf.* very great —**'awfully** *adv.* **1.** in an unpleasant way **2.** *inf.* very much

awhile (ə'wīl) *adv.* for a time

awkward ('ökwərd) *a.* **1.** clumsy, ungainly **2.** difficult **3.** inconvenient **4.** embarrassed —**'awkwardly** *adv.* —**'awkwardness** *n.*

awl (öl) *n.* pointed tool for boring wood, leather *etc.*

awn (ön) *n.* any of bristles growing from flowering parts of certain grasses and cereals

awning ('öning) *n.* (canvas) roof or shelter, to protect from weather

awoke (ə'wōk) *pt.* of AWAKE —**a'woken** *pp.* of AWAKE

A.W.O.L. *or* **AWOL** (*when acronym* 'āwöl) absent without leave

awry (ə'rī) *adv.* **1.** crookedly **2.** amiss **3.** at a slant —*a.* **4.** crooked, distorted **5.** wrong

ax *or* **axe** (aks) *n.* **1.** tool with sharp blade for chopping **2.** *inf.* dismissal from employment *etc.* —*vt.* **3.** remove (from job, budget, agenda *etc.*)

axel ('aksəl) *n. Skating* jump of one and a half turns, taking off from forward outside edge of one skate and landing on backward outside edge of other

axes¹ ('aksēz) *n., pl.* of AXIS

axes² ('aksiz) *n., pl.* of AX

axil ('aksil) *n.* upper angle between branch or leaf stalk and stem

axiom ('aksiəm) *n.* **1.** received or accepted principle from which secondary ones are derived **2.** self-evident truth —**axio'matic** *a.*

axis ('aksis) *n.* **1.** (imaginary) line round which body spins **2.** line or column around which parts of thing, system *etc.* are arranged (*pl.* **'axes**) —**'axial** *a.* —**'axially** *adv.* —**'Axis** *n.* coalition of Germany, Italy and Japan, 1936-45

axle ('aksəl) *n.* rod on which wheel turns

axolotl ('aksəlotəl) *n.* aquatic salamander of N Amer. capable of breeding in larval state

ay *or* **aye** (ā) *adv. Poet., obs.* always

ayah ('īə) *n.* Indian maidservant or nursemaid

ayatollah (īə'tolə) *n.* one of class of Islamic religious leaders

aye *or* **ay** (ī) *adv.* **1.** yes —*n.* **2.** affirmative answer or vote —*pl.* **3.** those voting for motion

AYH American Youth Hostels

Aymara (īmə'rä) *n.* Amerindian language spoken in Bolivia and Peru

AZ Arizona

azalea (ə'zālyə) *n.* gardening term for genus (*Azalea*) of rhododendron

Azazel (ə'zāzəl) *n. Judaism* evil spirit living in the wilderness, associated with scapegoat

azimuth ('aziməth) *n.* **1.** vertical arc from zenith to horizon **2.** angular distance of this from meridian

Azores ('āzörz, ə'zörz) *pl.n.* autonomous division of Portugal situated in the Atlantic at 40° N latitude and 30° E latitude

Azrael ('azrāl) *n. Islam* the angel of death

Aztec ('aztek) *a./n.* **1.** (member) of Indian race ruling Mexico before Spanish conquest —*n.* **2.** language of this people

azure ('azhər) *n.* **1.** sky-blue color **2.** sky —*a.* **3.** sky-blue

Bb

b *or* **B** (bē) *n.* **1.** second letter of English alphabet **2.** speech sound represented by this letter, as in *bell* **3.** second in series, class or rank (*also* **'beta**) (*pl.* **b's, B's,** *or* **Bs**)

b 1. bachelor **2.** bass(o) **3.** bishop **4.** book **5.** born

B 1. *Mus.* seventh note of scale of C major; major or minor key having this note as its tonic **2.** less important of two things **3.** human blood type of ABO group **4.** rating of student's work as better than average **5.** *Chem.* boron **6.** magnetic flux density **7.** (of pencils) softness of graphite **8.** *Phys.* bel (*also* **b**) **9.** *Phys.* baryon number

b. *or* **B. 1.** (on maps *etc.*) bay **2.** (**B.**) Bible **3.** (**b.**) *Cricket* bowled; bye **4.** breadth **5.** black

Ba *Chem.* barium

B.A. 1. Bachelor of Arts **2.** batting averages **3.** Buenos Aires

baa (bä) *vi.* **1.** make cry of sheep; bleat (**'baaing, baaed**) —*n.* **2.** cry made by sheep

baas (bäs) *n.* SA boss

baba (**'bäbä**) *n.* small cake, usu. soaked in rum

babble (**'babəl**) *vi.* **1.** speak foolishly, incoherently, or childishly —*n.* **2.** foolish, confused talk —**'babbler** *n.* **1.** one who babbles **2.** tropical bird with incessant song —**'babbling** *n./a.*

babe (bāb) *n.* **1.** *old-fashioned* baby **2.** guileless person

babel (**'bābəl**) *n.* confused noise or scene, uproar

baboon (ba'bōōn) *n.* any of several large African or Asian terrestrial monkeys with cheek pouches, doglike muzzles and usu. short tails —**ba'boonish** *a.*

baby (**'bābi**) *n.* very young child, infant —**'babyhood** *n.* —**'babyish** *a.* —**baby carriage** cotlike four-wheeled carriage for baby (*also* **baby buggy**) —**baby grand** small grand piano —**baby-sit** *vi.* —**baby-sitter** *n.* one who cares for children when parents are out

baccarat (**bäkə'rä**) *n.* gambling card game in which object is to hold a combination of cards totaling 9, differing from chemin de fer in that players bet against the house

bacchanal (**'bakənəl**) *n.* **1.** follower of Bacchus **2.** (participant in) drunken, riotous celebration

bacchanalia (bakə'nälyə) *pl.n.* **1.** (*oft.* **B-**) orgiastic rites associated with Bacchus **2.** drunken revelry —**baccha'nalian** *a./n.*

bacchant (**'bakənt**) *or* (*fem.*) **bacchante** (bə'kanti) *n.* **1.** priest or priestess of Bacchus **2.** drunken reveler

bachelor (**'bachələr, 'bachlər**) *n.* **1.** unmarried man **2.** holder of university degree **3.** *Hist.* young knight —**'bachelorhood** *or* **'bachelorship** *n.* —**bachelor girl** young unmarried woman, *esp.* one who is self-supporting

bacillus (bə'siləs) *n.* any rod-shaped bacterium (*pl.* **-cilli** (-'silī)) —**ba'cilliform** *a.*

back (bak) *n.* **1.** hinder part of anything, *eg* human body **2.** part opposite front **3.** part or side of something further away or less used **4.** (position of) player in ball games behind other (forward) players —*a.* **5.** situated behind **6.** earlier —*adv.* **7.** at, to the back **8.** in, into the past **9.** in return —*vi.* **10.** move backwards —*vt.* **11.** support **12.** put wager on **13.** provide with back or backing —**'backer** *n.* **1.** one supporting another, *esp.* in contest **2.** one betting on horse *etc.* in race —**'backing** *n.* **1.** support **2.** material to protect the back of something **3.** musical accompaniment, *esp.* for pop singer —**'backward** *a.* **1.** directed toward the rear **2.** behind in education **3.** reluctant, bashful —*adv.* **4.** backwards —**'backwardness** *n.* —**'backwards** *adv.* **1.** to the rear **2.** to the past **3.** into a worse state (*also* **'backward**) —**'backache** *n.* lumbago —**'back'bencher** *n.* member of parliament not holding office in government or opposition —**'backbite** *v.* slander (absent person) —**'backbiter** *n.* —**'backbiting** *n.* —**'backboard** *n.* **1.** board that is placed behind something to form or support its back **2.** board worn to support back, as after surgery **3.** *Basketball* flat upright surface under which basket is attached —**'backbone** *n.* **1.** spinal column **2.** strength of character —**'backbreaking** *a.* exhausting —**'backcomb** *v.* comb under layers of (hair) toward roots to add bulk to hairstyle (*also* **tease**) —**back'date** *vt.* make effective from earlier date —**back door 1.** door at rear or side of building **2.** means of entry to job *etc.* that is secret or obtained through influence —**'backdrop** *n.* painted cloth at back of stage —**back'fire** *vi.* **1.** ignite at wrong time, as fuel in cylinder of internal-combustion engine **2.** (of plan, scheme *etc.*) fail to work, *esp.* to the cost of the instigator **3.** ignite wrongly, as gas burner *etc.* —*n.* **4.** explosion in exhaust of internal-combustion engine —**'backgammon** *n.* game for two players played on a board with pieces called stones or men whose moves toward 'home' are governed by throwing dice —**'background** *n.* **1.** space behind chief figures of picture *etc.* **2.** past history of person —**'backhand** *n. Tennis etc.* stroke with hand turned backwards —**back'handed** *a.* (of compliment) with second, uncomplimentary meaning —**'backhander** *n.* **1.** blow with back of hand **2.** *inf.* a bribe —**'backlash** *n.* sudden and adverse reaction —**'backlog** *n.* **1.** large log at back of hearth **2.** accumulation of work *etc.* to be dealt with —**back number 1.** issue of newspaper *etc.* that appeared on a previous date **2.** *inf.* person or thing considered old-fashioned —**back pack** *n.* **1.** type of knapsack —*vi.* **2.** travel with knapsack —**back-pedal** *vi.* **1.** turn pedals backward **2.** retract previous opinion *etc.* —**back room** place where important and usu. secret research is done —**back seat 1.** seat at back, *esp.* of vehicle **2.** *inf.* subordinate or inconspicuous position (*esp.* **in take a back seat**) —**back-seat driver** *inf.* **1.** passenger who offers unwanted advice to driver **2.** person who offers advice on matters that are not his concern —**back'side** *n.* rump —**'backslide** *vi.* fall back in faith or morals —**back'stage** *adv.* **1.** behind part of theater in view of audience —*a.* **2.** situated backstage —**'back'stairs** *pl.n.* **1.** secondary staircase in house —*a.* **2.** underhand (*also* **'back'stair**) —**'backstroke** *n. Swimming* stroke performed on the back —**'backtrack** *vi.* **1.** return by same route by which one has come **2.** retract or reverse one's opinion *etc.* —**'backup** *n.* **1.** support; reinforcement **2.** reserve; substitute —**'backwash** *n.* **1.** water thrown back by ship's propellers *etc.* **2.** a backward current **3.** a reaction —**'backwater** *n.* **1.** remote place **2.** still water fed by back flow of stream —**'backwoods** *pl.n.* remote forest areas —**back yard** yard at back of house *etc.* —**back up 1.** support **2.** (of water) accumulate **3.** *Comp.* make copy of (data file) —**in one's own back yard** close at hand

bacon (**'bākən**) *n.* cured pig's flesh

Baconian (bā'kōniən) *a.* **1.** pert. to English philosopher Francis Bacon (1561–1626) or his inductive method of reasoning —*n.* **2.** follower of Bacon's philosophy **3.** person believing that Bacon is the author of the works of Shakespeare

bacteria (bak'tēəriə) *pl.n.* microscopic unicellular organisms (*sing.* **-rium** (-riəm)) —**bacter'emia** *n.* invasion of blood by bacteria without giving rise to symptoms of disease, but resulting in boils or sore throats —**bac'terial** *a.* —**bacteri'ologist** *n.* —**bacteri'ology** *n.* study of bacteria —**bacteriophage** (bak'tēəriəfāj) *n.* virus that infects bacteria —**bacterial endocarditis** bacterial infection of the lining of the heart, *esp.* the valves

Bactrian camel (**'baktriən**) two-humped camel, used in deserts of central Asia

bad (bad) *a.* **1.** of poor quality **2.** faulty **3.** evil **4.** immoral **5.** offensive **6.** severe **7.** rotten, decayed (**worse** *comp.*, **worst** *sup.*) —**'badly** *adv.* —**'badness** *n.* —**bad blood** feeling of intense hatred or hostility; enmity —**bad debt** debt which is not collectable

bade *or* **bad** (bad) *pt. of* BID

badge (baj) *n.* distinguishing emblem or sign

badger (**'bajər**) *n.* **1.** any of various carnivorous burrowing mammals —*vt.* **2.** pester, worry —**badger game** method of extortion in which the victim is lured into a compromising sexual situation and then threatened with exposure unless money is paid

badinage (badi'näzh) *n.* playful talk, banter

badminton (**'badmintən**) *n.* court game for two or four players played with light rackets and a shuttlecock volleyed over a net

baffle (**'bafəl**) *vt.* **1.** check **2.** frustrate **3.** bewilder —**'baffler** *n.* —**'baffling** *a.* —**baffle plate** device to regulate or divert flow of liquid, gas, sound waves *etc.*

bag (bag) *n.* **1.** sack, pouch **2.** measure of quantity **3.** woman's handbag **4.** *offens.* unattractive woman —*pl.* **5.** *inf.* lots (of) —*vi.* **6.** swell out **7.** bulge **8.** sag —*vt.* **9.** put in bag **10.** kill as game *etc.* (**-gg-**) —**'bagging** *n.* cloth —**'baggy** *a.* loose, drooping —**'bagman** *n.* agent who collects bribe, extortion or kidnaping money

bagasse (bə'gas) *n.* sugar cane refuse

bagatelle (bagə'tel) n. 1. trifle 2. game like pinball played with nine balls and cue on a board

bagel ('bāgəl) n. ring-shaped bread roll, hard and glazed on the outside, soft in the center

baggage ('bagij) n. 1. suitcases etc., packed for journey 2. portable equipment

bagpipe ('bagpīp) n. musical instrument comprising reed pipes and a windbag, the chanter pipes producing the melody and the drone pipes the one-tone accompaniment —'**bagpiper** n.

bah (bä, ba) interj. expression of contempt or disgust

Bahaism (bä'häizəm) n. religious movement founded in 1863 stressing unity of all faiths, education, sexual equality, monogamy and the attainment of world peace —**Ba'ha'i** a. —**Ba'haist** n.

Bahamas (bə'häməz) pl.n. country in Atlantic Ocean consisting of 700 islands and more than 1000 cays off the southeastern coast of Florida —**Bahamian** (bə'hāmiən, -'hä-) or **Bahaman** (bə'hāmən, -'hä-) n./a.

Bahrain or **Bahrein** (bä'rān) n. country comprising an archipelago in the Arabian Gulf between the Qatar peninsula and the mainland of Saudi Arabia —**Bah'raini** or **Bah'reini** n./a.

bail[1] (bāl) n. 1. Law security given for person's reappearance in court 2. one giving such security —vt. 3. release, or obtain release of, on security —**bail out** inf. help (person, firm etc.) out of trouble

bail[2] (bāl) n. 1. Cricket crosspiece on wicket 2. bar separating horses in stable

bail[3] (bāl) vt. empty out (water) from boat —**bail out** leave aircraft by parachute

bailey ('bāli) n. outermost wall of castle

Bailey bridge ('bāli) bridge composed of prefabricated sections

bailiff ('bālif) n. 1. land steward, agent 2. sheriff's officer

bailiwick ('bāliwik) n. jurisdiction of bailiff

bain-marie (bēma'rē) Fr. vessel for holding hot water, in which sauces etc. are gently cooked or kept warm (pl. **bains-marie** (bēma'rē))

bairn (bāərn) n. Scot. infant, child

bait (bāt) n. 1. food to entice fish 2. any lure or enticement —vt. 3. set a lure for 4. annoy, persecute

baize (bāz) n. smooth woolen or cotton cloth resembling felt

bake (bāk) vt. 1. cook or harden by dry heat —vi. 2. make bread, cakes etc. 3. be scorched or tanned —'**baker** n. —'**bakery** or '**bakehouse** n. —'**baking** n. —**baked beans** navy beans, baked in tomato sauce —**baker's dozen** thirteen —**baking powder** raising agent containing sodium bicarbonate and cream of tartar used in baking —**baking soda** common name for sodium hydrogen carbonate (also **sodium bicarbonate**)

Bakelite ('bākəlīt) n. trade name for hard nonflammable synthetic resin, used for dishes, trays, electrical insulators etc.

baksheesh or **backsheesh** ('bakshēsh) n. in some Eastern countries, esp. formerly, money given as tip

bal. balance

Balaclava helmet (balə'klävə) close-fitting woolen helmet covering head and neck

balalaika (balə'līkə) n. Russian guitar of variable size with triangular body, long neck with frets, and usu. three gut strings tuned in fourths

balance ('baləns) n. 1. pair of scales 2. equilibrium 3. surplus 4. sum due on an account 5. difference between two sums —vt. 6. weigh 7. bring to equilibrium —**balance of payments** difference over given time between total payments to and receipts from foreign nations —**balance of power** distribution of power among countries so that no nation can seriously threaten another —**balance sheet** tabular statement of assets and liabilities —**balance wheel** regulating wheel of watch

balcony ('balkəni) n. 1. railed platform outside window 2. upper seats in theater

bald (böld) a. 1. hairless 2. plain 3. bare —'**balding** a. becoming bald —'**baldly** adv. —'**baldness** n.

balderdash ('böldərdash) n. idle, senseless talk

baldric ('böldrik) n. shoulder belt for sword etc.

bale (bāl) n. 1. bundle or package —vt. 2. make into bundles or pack into cartons —'**baler** n. machine which makes bales of hay etc.

baleen (bə'lēn) n. whalebone

baleful ('bālfəl) a. menacing —'**balefully** adv.

balk (bök) vi. 1. swerve, pull up —vt. 2. thwart, hinder —n. 3. hindrance 4. square timber, beam 5. Baseball illegal pitching motion while one or more runners are on base —**balk at** 1. recoil from 2. stop short at

Balkan ('bölkən) a. of or denoting large peninsula in SE Europe, its inhabitants, countries etc. —'**Balkanize** vt. divide (region, territory) into small, ineffective countries

ball[1] (böl) n. 1. anything round 2. globe, sphere, esp. as used in games 3. Baseball ball as delivered 4. bullet —vi. 5. clog, gather into a mass —**ball-and-socket joint** Anat. joint in which rounded head fits into rounded cavity —**ball bearings** steel balls used to lessen friction on bearings —**ball boy** esp. in tennis, person who retrieves balls that go out of play —**ball cock** device for regulating flow of liquid into cistern etc., consisting of floating ball and a valve —**ball game** 1. any game played with a ball 2. game of baseball 3. inf. any activity —**ball-park figure** rough estimate; guess —'**ballpoint** or **ballpoint pen** n. pen with tiny ball bearing as nib

ball[2] (böl) n. assembly for dancing —'**ballroom** n.

ballad ('baləd) n. 1. narrative poem 2. simple song

ballade (ba'läd) n. 1. short poem with refrain and envoy 2. piece of music

ballast ('baləst) n. 1. heavy material put in ship to give steadiness 2. that which renders anything steady —vt. 3. load with ballast, steady

ballet ('balā, ba'lā) n. theatrical presentation of dancing and miming —**balle'rina** n. female ballet dancer

balletomania (baletō'māniə) n. enthusiasm for ballet —**bal'letomane** n.

ballista (bə'listə) n. ancient catapult for hurling stones etc. (pl. **-tae** (-tē)) —**bal'listic** a. moving as, or pertaining to motion of a projectile —**bal'listics** pl.n. (with sing. v.) scientific study of ballistic motion —**ballistic missile** missile that follows ballistic trajectory when propulsive power is discontinued

balloon (bə'lōōn) n. 1. large, airtight bag that rises when filled with air or gas —vi. 2. puff out —**bal'looning** n. —**bal'loonist** n.

ballot ('balət) n. 1. method of voting secretly, usu. by marking ballot paper and putting it into box —v. 2. vote or elicit a vote from —**ballot box** 1. sealed receptacle for completed ballot papers 2. fig. the democratic process

ballyhoo ('balihōō) n. 1. noisy confusion or uproar 2. vulgar, exaggerated publicity or advertisement

balm (bäm) n. 1. aromatic substance obtained from certain trees, used for healing or soothing 2. anything soothing —'**balminess** n. —'**balmy** a. 1. mild 2. silly

baloney (bə'lōni) n. inf. foolish talk; nonsense

balsa ('bölsə) n. tropical Amer. tree with light but strong wood

balsam ('bölsəm) n. 1. resinous aromatic substance obtained from various trees and shrubs 2. soothing ointment —**bal'samic** a.

Baltic ('böltik) a. 1. denoting or relating to the Baltic Sea or the states bordering it 2. of or relating to group of Indo-European languages comprising Lithuanian and Latvian —**Baltic Sea** sea in northern Europe bounded by Sweden, Finland, U.S.S.R., Poland, East Germany, West Germany and Denmark

Balto-Slavic (böltō'slavik, -'släv-) n. branch of Indo-European languages spoken from eastern Europe to the Pacific comprising the Baltic and Slavic groups

baluster ('baləstər) n. short pillar used as support to rail of staircase etc. —'**balustrade** n. row of short pillars surmounted by rail

bamboo (bam'bōō) n. any of various usu. tropical woody grasses ranging in size from a foot to that of a tall tree —**bamboo curtain** barrier of secrecy in Asian countries —**bamboo shoot** edible rhizome of certain bamboos

bamboozle (bam'bōōzəl) vt. 1. mystify 2. hoax

ban (ban) vt. 1. prohibit, forbid, outlaw (**-nn-**) —n. 2. prohibition 3. proclamation

banal (bə'näl) a. commonplace, trivial, trite —**ba'nality** n.

banana (bə'nanə) n. 1. tropical treelike plant 2. its fruit —**banana republic** inf. small country, esp. in Central Amer., that is politically unstable and has economy dominated by foreign interest

band[1] (band) n. 1. strip used to bind 2. range of values, frequencies etc., between two limits —'**bandage** n. strip of cloth for binding wound —**band saw** power-operated saw consisting of endless toothed metal band running over two wheels

band[2] (band) n. 1. company, group 2. company of musicians —v. 3. (with together) bind together —'**bandmaster** n. —'**bandsman** n. —'**bandstand** n.

bandanna or **bandana** (ban'danə) n. large figured colored silk or cotton handkerchief

B and B bed-and-breakfast

bandbox ('bandboks) n. light box of cardboard for hats etc.

B and E breaking and entering

bandeau (ban'dō) n. 1. band, ribbon for the hair 2. lightweight brassiere (pl. **-deaux** (-'dōz))

bandicoot ('bandikōōt) n. ratlike Aust. marsupial

bandit ('bandit) n. 1. outlaw 2. robber, brigand (pl. **-s, banditti** (ban'diti))

bandolier or **bandoleer** (bandə'lēər) n. 1. shoulder belt for cartridges 2. band worn for ornament or part of ceremonial dress

b and w black-and-white

bandwagon ('bandwagən) n. —**climb, jump, get on the bandwagon** join something that seems assured of success

bandy ('bandi) vt. 1. beat to and fro 2. toss from one to another ('**bandied, 'bandying**)

—**'bandy** *or* **bandy-legged** *a.* having legs curving outward (*also* **bow-legged**)

bane (bān) *n.* person or thing causing misery or distress —**'baneful** *a.* —**'banefully** *adv.*

bang[1] (bang) *n.* **1.** sudden loud noise, explosion **2.** heavy blow —*vi.* **3.** make loud noise —*vt.* **4.** beat, strike violently **5.** slam

bang[2] (bang) *n.* (*usu. pl.*) fringe of hair cut straight across forehead

Bangladesh (bänggla'desh) *n.* country in Asia bounded west, northwest and north by India, east by India and Burma and south by the Bay of Bengal —**Bangla'deshi** *n./a.*

bangle ('banggal) *n.* ring worn on arm or leg

banish ('banish) *vt.* **1.** condemn to exile **2.** drive away **3.** dismiss —**'banishment** *n.* exile

banister *or* **bannister** ('banistar) *n.* railing and supporting balusters on staircase

banjo ('banjō) *n.* stringed musical instrument with body like shallow drum, long fretted neck and usu. six strings (*pl.* **-s, -es**) —**'banjoist** *n.*

bank[1] (bangk) *n.* **1.** establishment for keeping, lending, exchanging *etc.* money **2.** any supply or store for future use, as blood bank —*vt.* **3.** put in bank —*vi.* **4.** transact business with bank —**'banker** *n.* —**'banking** *n.* —**bank account** account created by deposit of money at bank by customer —**'bankbook** *n.* book held by depositor, in which bank enters record of deposits, withdrawals *etc.* (*also* **'passbook**) —**bank note** written promise of payment —**bank on** rely on

bank[2] (bangk) *n.* **1.** mound or ridge of earth **2.** edge of river, lake *etc.* **3.** rising ground in sea —*vt.* **4.** enclose with ridge —*v.* **5.** pile up **6.** (of aircraft) tilt inward in turning

bank[3] (bangk) *n.* **1.** tier **2.** row of oars

bankrupt ('bangkrupt, -rapt) *n.* **1.** one who fails in business, insolvent debtor —*a.* **2.** financially ruined —*vt.* **3.** make, cause to be, bankrupt —**'bankruptcy** *n.*

banksia ('bangksia) *n.* genus of Aust. shrubs with dense, usu. yellow, cylindrical heads of flowers

Banlon ('banlon) *n.* trade name for method of stretching and bulking thermoplastic fibers

banner ('banar) *n.* **1.** long strip with slogan *etc.* **2.** placard **3.** flag used as ensign

bannister ('banistar) *n. see* BANISTER

banns (banz) *pl.n.* announcement, usu. in church, of intention to marry

banquet ('bangkwit) *n.* **1.** feast —*vi.* **2.** hold or take part in banquet —*vt.* **3.** treat with feast —**'banqueter** *n.*

banquette (bang'ket) *n.* **1.** raised firing step behind parapet **2.** upholstered bench

banshee ('banshē, ban'shē) *n.* Irish fairy with a wail portending death

bantam ('bantam) *n.* dwarf variety of domestic fowl —**'bantamweight** *n.* **1.** professional boxer weighing 112-118 lbs. (51-53.5 kg); amateur boxer weighing 112-119 lbs. (51-54 kg) **2.** wrestler weighing usu. 115-126 lbs. (52-57 kg)

banter ('bantar) *v.* **1.** speak or tease lightly or jokingly —*n.* **2.** light, teasing language

Bantu ('bantōō) *n.* **1.** member of a group of Negroid peoples in equatorial and southern Africa (*pl.* **-tu, -s**) **2.** (*also* **'Bantic**) group of languages of the Niger-Congo group of which Swahili has the largest number of speakers —*a.* **3.** of the Bantu

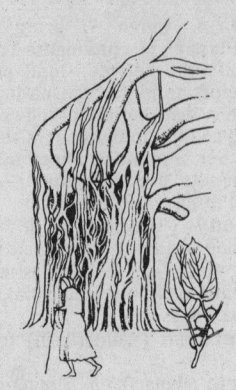

banyan

banyan ('banyan) *n.* Indian fig tree with spreading branches which take root

baobab ('bāōbab) *n.* Afr. tree with thick trunk and angular branches

Bap *or* **Bapt** Baptist

baptize (bap'tīz) *vt.* **1.** immerse in, sprinkle with water ceremoniously **2.** christen —**'baptism** *n.* —**bap'tismal** *a.* —**bap'tismally** *adv.* —**'Baptist** *n.* member of Protestant Christian denomination holding that true church is of believers only, who are all equal, and the only authority the Bible —**'baptistery** *or* **'baptistry** *n.* place where baptism is performed —**baptism of fire 1.** soldier's first experience of battle; any initiating ordeal **2.** spiritual baptism

bar[1] (bär) *n.* **1.** rod or block of any substance **2.** obstacle **3.** bank of sand at mouth of river **4.** rail in law court **5.** body of lawyers **6.** counter where drinks are served, *esp.* in hotel *etc.* **7.** unit of music —*vt.* **8.** fasten **9.** obstruct **10.** exclude (**-rr-**) —*prep.* **11.** except —**'barring** *prep.* excepting —**bar code** arrangement of parallel lines, readable by computer, printed on, and giving details of, merchandise in shop *etc.* —**bar graph** graph consisting of bars whose lengths are proportional to quantities —**'barmaid** *n.* —**bar sinister 1.** erroneous term for bend sinister or baton sinister **2.** condition of being of illegitimate birth —**'bartender** *n.*

bar[2] (bär) *n.* unit of pressure

bar. 1. barometer **2.** barrel

barathea (bara'thēa) *n.* **1.** fine woolen cloth, usu. black **2.** imitation of this in cotton and rayon

barb (bärb) *n.* **1.** sharp point curving backwards behind main point of spear, fish hook *etc.* **2.** cutting remark —**barbed** *a.* —**barbed wire** fencing wire with barbs at close intervals

Barbados (bär'bādas) *n.* country in the Windward Islands of the Caribbean Sea —**Bar'badian** *n./a.*

barbarous ('bärbaras) *a.* **1.** savage, brutal **2.** uncivilized —**barbarian** (bär'berian, -'bar-) *n.* —**barbaric** (bär'barik) *a.* —**'barbarism** *n.* —**barbarity** (bär'bariti) *n.* —**'barbarously** *adv.*

Barbary ape ('bärbari) tailless macaque that inhabits NW Afr. and Gibraltar

barbecue ('bärbikyōō) *n.* **1.** meal cooked outdoors over open fire **2.** fireplace or grill used for this —*vt.* **3.** cook (meat *etc.*) in this manner (**-cued, -cuing**)

barbel ('bärbal) *n.* **1.** spine or bristle that hangs from jaws of certain fishes **2.** any of several European fishes resembling carp

barbell ('bärbel) *n.* metal rod to which heavy disks are attached at each end used for weightlifting exercises

barber ('bärbar) *n.* one who shaves beards and cuts hair

Barbera (bär'bera) *n.* **1.** red table wine **2.** grape used to make this wine

barberry ('bärberi) *n.* any spiny Asian shrub, having yellow flowers and orange or red berries

barbican ('bärbikan) *n.* **1.** outwork of fortified place, *esp.* to defend drawbridge **2.** watchtower projecting from fortification

barbital ('bärbitöl) *n. see* BARBITURATE

barbiturate (bär'bityōōrit, -rāt) *n.* derivative of barbituric acid used as sedative, anesthetic, and to induce sleep, *eg* barbital, Veronal —**barbi'turic** *a.* —**barbituric acid** crystalline solid used in preparation of barbiturate drugs

barcarole *or* **barcarolle** ('bärkaröl) *n.* **1.** gondolier's song **2.** composition imitating gondolier's song, written in 6/8 or 12/8 meter

bard (bärd) *n.* **1.** formerly, Celtic poet **2.** wandering minstrel —**'bardic** *a.* —**the Bard** Shakespeare

bare (bâar) *a.* **1.** uncovered **2.** naked **3.** plain **4.** scanty —*vt.* **5.** make bare —**'barely** *adv.* only just, scarcely —**'bareness** *n.* —**bare-backed** *a.* on unsaddled horse —**barefaced** *a.* shameless

bargain ('bärgin) *n.* **1.** something bought at price favorable to purchaser **2.** contract, agreement —*vi.* **3.** haggle, negotiate **4.** make bargain

barge (bärj) *n.* **1.** flat-bottomed freight boat **2.** state or pleasure boat —*vi. inf.* **3.** (with into *or* in) interrupt **4.** (with into) bump (into), push —**'bargeman** *n.* —**'bargepole** *n.* long pole used to propel barge

baritone ('baritōn) *n.* **1.** (singer with) second lowest adult male voice **2.** musical instrument larger than cornet with the bell pointing upwards, used in a brass band —*a.* **3.** written for or possessing baritone voice

barium ('bâariam) *n. Chem.* metallic element *Symbol* Ba, at. wt. 137.3, at. no. 56 —**barium meal** preparation of barium sulfate —**barium sulfate** white insoluble fine heavy powder which is opaque to x-rays; swallowed by patient before x-ray of alimentary canal

bark[1] (bärk) *n.* **1.** sharp loud cry of dog *etc.* —*v.* **2.** make, utter with such sound —**'barker** *n.* crier outside fair booth *etc.*

bark[2] (bärk) *n.* **1.** outer layer of trunk, branches of tree —*vt.* **2.** strip bark from **3.** rub off (skin), graze (shins *etc.*)

bark[3] (bärk) *n.* **1.** sailing ship, *esp.* large, three-masted one (*also* **barque, 'barkentine, 'barquentine**) **2.** craft propelled by sails or oars

barley ('bärli) *n.* grain used for food and in making malt —**'barleycorn** *n.* **1.** (grain of) barley **2.** *obs.* unit of length equal to a third of an inch

barm (bärm) *n.* **1.** yeast **2.** froth —**'barmy** *a. see* **balmy** (sense 2) *at* BALM

bar mitzvah (bär 'mitsva) (*sometimes* B-M-) *Judaism* **1.** ceremony marking 13th birthday of boy, who then assumes full religious obligations **2.** the boy himself

barn (bärn) *n.* farm building, used to store grain, hay *etc.* —**barn dance** (party with) country dancing —**barn owl** owl with pale brown-and-white plumage —**'barnstorm** *vi.* tour rural districts putting on shows or making speeches in political campaign —**'barnstormer** *n.* —**'barnyard** *n.* farmyard

barnacle ('bärnakal) *n.* marine crustacean which adheres to rocks and ships' bottoms —**barnacle goose** N European goose that has black-and-white head and body

barograph ('barəgraf) *n*. recording barometer

barometer (bə'romitər) *n*. instrument to measure pressure of atmosphere —**baro-'metric** *a*. —**ba'rometry** *n*.

baron ('barən) *n*. 1. member of lowest rank of British peerage 2. powerful businessman 3. indeterminate rank of European nobleman —**'baronage** *n*. —**'baroness** *n*. 1. wife, ex-wife or widow of baron 2. woman holding baronial rank in own right —**ba'ronial** *a*. —**'barony** *n*.

baronet ('barənit) *n*. lowest British hereditary title, below baron but above knight —**'baronetage** *n*. —**'baronetcy** *n*.

baroque (bə'rok, bə'rōk) *a*. extravagantly ornamented, *esp*. in architecture and art

baroscope ('barəskōp) *n*. any instrument for measuring atmospheric pressure —**baroscopic** (barə'skopik) *a*.

barouche (bə'rōōsh) *n*. four-wheeled carriage with folding top over rear seat

barrack ('barək) *n*. 1. (*usu. pl.*) building for lodging soldiers 2. huge bare building

barracouta (barə'kōōtə) *n*. marine food fish of southern hemisphere

barracuda (barə'kōōdə) *n*. any of several voracious, pikelike marine fishes, some caught as food, others dangerous or poisonous

barrage (bə'räzh) *n*. 1. heavy artillery fire 2. continuous and heavy delivery, *esp*. of questions *etc*. 3. ('bärij) dam across river —**barrage balloon** one of number of tethered balloons with cables or net suspended from them, used to deter low-flying air attack

barratry ('barətri) *n*. 1. fraudulent breach of duty by master of ship 2. stirring up of law suits —**'barrator** *n*. —**'barratrous** *a*.

barre (bar) *Fr*. rail used for ballet practice

barrel ('barəl) *n*. 1. round wooden vessel, made of curved staves bound with hoops 2. amount that barrel can hold (*also* **'barrelful**) 3. anything long and hollow, as tube of gun *etc*. —*vt*. 4. put in barrel —**'barreled** *a*. —**barrel organ** instrument consisting of cylinder turned by handle, having pins that interrupt air flow to certain pipes or pluck strings, thereby playing tunes —**barrel vault** *Archit*. vault in form of half cylinder

barren ('barən) *a*. 1. unfruitful, sterile 2. unprofitable 3. dull —**'barrenness** *n*. —**Barren Lands** *or* **Grounds** sparsely inhabited tundra region in N Canada

barricade (bari'kād, 'barikād) *n*. 1. improvised fortification, barrier —*vt*. 2. protect by building barrier 3. block

barrier ('bariər) *n*. fence, obstruction, obstacle, boundary —**barrier cream** cream to protect skin —**barrier reef** coral reef lying parallel to shore

barrister ('baristər) *n*. advocate in the higher law courts of England

barrow[1] ('barō) *n*. 1. small wheeled handcart 2. wheelbarrow

barrow[2] ('barō) *n*. 1. burial mound 2. tumulus

Bart. Baronet

barter ('bärtər) *v*. 1. trade by exchange of goods —*n*. 2. practice of bartering

Baruch (bə'rōōk, 'bärōōk) *n*. *Bible* 30th book in the Douay Version of the O.T.

baryon ('barion) *n*. *Phys*. elementary particle of matter

baryta (bə'rītə) *n*. 1. barium oxide 2. barium hydroxide

barytes (bə'rītēz) *n*. barium sulfate

basalt (bə'sölt) *n*. dark-colored, hard, compact, igneous rock —**ba'saltic** *a*.

bascule ('baskyōōl) *n*. 1. lever apparatus 2. drawbridge on counterpoise principle

base[1] (bās) *n*. 1. bottom, foundation 2. starting point 3. center of operations 4. fixed point 5. *Chem*. compound that combines with an acid to form a salt 6. medium into which other substances are mixed 7. *Math*. in arithmetic, the number which raised to various powers, forms the main counting unit of a system; in logarithms, the number which when raised to a certain power will produce a certain number —*vt*. 8. found, establish —**basal** *a*. of base —**'baseless** *a*. —**basal metabolism rate** measure of body energy output at rest and in the fasting state —**'baseline** *n*. 1. *Surv*. measured line through survey area from which triangulations are made 2. line at each end of games court that marks limit of play —**'basement** *n*. lowest level of building

base[2] (bās) *a*. 1. low, mean 2. despicable —**'basely** *adv*. —**'baseness** *n*. —**'baseborn** *a*. illegitimate

baseball ('bāsböl) *n*. 1. outdoor game played with bat and ball by two teams with nine players each on a field with four bases arranged in a diamond in which the object is to score runs 2. the ball used in this game

bases ('bāsēz) *n*., *pl. of* BASIS

bash (bash) *inf. vt*. 1. strike violently —*n*. 2. blow 3. attempt

bashful ('bashfəl) *a*. shy, modest —**'bashfully** *adv*. —**'bashfulness** *n*.

basic ('bāsik) *a*. 1. relating to, serving as base 2. fundamental 3. necessary —**basic slag** slag produced in steel-making, containing calcium phosphate

BASIC ('bāsik) *Comp*. Beginners' All-purpose Symbolic Instruction Code

basil ('bazəl) *n*. annual plant of the mint family, the leaves of which are used in cooking

basilica (bə'silikə, -'zil-) *n*. type of church with long hall and pillars —**ba'silican** *a*.

basilisk ('bazilisk) *n*. legendary small fire-breathing dragon

basin ('bāsin) *n*. 1. deep circular dish 2. harbor 3. land drained by river

basis ('bāsis) *n*. 1. foundation 2. principal constituent (*pl.* **'bases**)

bask (bäsk) *vi*. lie in warmth and sunshine —**basking shark** large plankton-eating shark

basket ('bäskit) *n*. vessel made of woven cane, straw *etc*. —**'basketry** *or* **'basketwork** *n*. —**'basketball** *n*. indoor or outdoor game played by two teams of five players each whose object is to score points by tossing a ball into the opposing team's basket —**basket chair** wickerwork chair —**basket weave** weave where two or more warp or weft threads are interlaced

basque (bask) *n*. tight-fitting bodice for women

Basque (bask) *n*. 1. one of race from W Pyrenees 2. their language which is a relic of a non-Indo-European language

bas-relief (bäri'lēf) *n*. sculpture with figures standing out slightly from background

bass[1] (bās) *n*. 1. lowest part in music 2. bass singer or voice —*a*. 3. relating to or denoting the bass —**bass clef** clef that establishes F a fifth below middle C on fourth line of staff

bass[2] (bas) *n*. any of numerous freshwater food and game fishes of N Amer.

basset (basit) *n*. type of smooth-haired dog

basset horn forerunner of clarinet

bassinet (basi'net) *n*. wickerwork or wooden cradle, usu. hooded

bassoon (bə'sōōn) *n*. orchestral woodwind instrument of the oboe family pitched two octaves below the oboe with a tube bent

back on account of its great length —**bas'soonist** *n*. —**double bassoon** instrument with range an octave lower than bassoon, with a tube doubled on itself four times

bast (bast) *n*. fibrous material obtained from phloem of jute, flax *etc*. used for making rope *etc*.

bastard ('bastəd) *n*. 1. child born of unmarried parents 2. *inf*. person, as in *lucky bastard* —*a*. 3. illegitimate 4. spurious —**'bastardize** *vt*. 1. debase 2. declare illegitimate —**'bastardy** *n*.

baste[1] (bāst) *vt*. 1. moisten (meat) during cooking with hot fat 2. beat with stick —**'basting** *n*.

baste[2] (bāst) *vt*. sew loosely, tack

bastinado (basti'nādō) *n*. 1. beating with stick, *esp*. on soles of feet (*pl.* **-es**) —*vt*. 2. inflict a bastinado on (**-doing**, **-doed**)

bastion

bastion ('baschən) *n*. 1. projecting part of fortification, tower 2. strong defense or bulwark

bat[1] (bat) *n*. 1. any of various types of club used to hit ball in certain sports, *eg* cricket, baseball —*v*. 2. strike with bat or use bat in sport (**-tt-**) —**'batting** *n*. performance with bat —**'batsman** *n*.

bat[2] (bat) *n*. nocturnal mouselike flying animal

bat[3] (bat) *vt*. flutter (one's eyelids) (**-tt-**)

batch (bach) *n*. group or set of similar objects, *esp*. cakes *etc*. baked together

bated ('bātid) *a*. —**with bated breath** anxiously

bath (bäth) *n*. 1. vessel or place to bathe in 2. water for bathing 3. act of bathing —**bath cube** cube of soluble scented material for use in bath —**'bathrobe** *n*. loose-fitting garment of toweling, for wear before or after bath or swimming —**'bathroom** *n*. 1. room containing bath and usu. washbowl and toilet 2. toilet —**bath salts** soluble scented salts for use in bath

Bath chair (bäth) UK invalid chair

bathe (bādh) *vi*. 1. swim —*vt*. 2. apply liquid to —*v*. 3. wash 4. immerse or be immersed in water (**bathed**, **'bathing**) —*n*. 5. a swim or paddle —**'bather** *n*.

bathometer (bə'thomitər) *n*. instrument for measuring depth of water —**batho'metric** *a*.

bathos ('bāthos) *n*. ludicrous descent from the elevated to the ordinary in writing or speech

bathyscaphe ('bathiskāf, -skaf) *or* **bathyscaph** ('bathiskaf) *n*. vessel for deep-sea observation

bathysphere ('bathisfēər) *n*. strong steel deep-sea diving sphere, lowered by cable

batik (bə'tēk, 'batik) *n*. dyeing process using wax to cover parts not to be dyed

batiste (ba'tēst) *n*. 1. fine sheer cotton or linen fabric 2. imitation made of rayon or wool

baton (bə'ton) *n*. 1. slender stick used by conductor of an orchestra 2. policeman's truncheon 3. staff serving as symbol of office

batrachian (bə'trākiən) *n.* any vertebrate amphibian, *esp.* frog or toad

battalion (bə'talyən) *n.* **1.** U.S. Army unit consisting of four or more companies usu. commanded by a lieutenant colonel **2.** large group

batten[1] ('batən) *n.* **1.** narrow piece of board, strip of wood —*vt.* **2.** (*esp. with* down) fasten, make secure

batten[2] ('batən) *vi.* (*usu. with* on) thrive, *esp.* at someone else's expense

batter ('batər) *vt.* **1.** strike continuously —*n.* **2.** mixture of flour, eggs, milk, used in cooking —**battered baby** young child who has sustained serious injuries through violence of parent or other adult —**battering ram** *esp.* formerly, large beam used to break down fortifications

battery ('batəri) *n.* **1.** connected group of electrical cells **2.** any electrical cell or accumulator **3.** number of similar things occurring together **4.** *Law* assault by beating **5.** number of guns **6.** place where they are mounted **7.** unit of artillery **8.** pitcher and catcher of baseball team

batting ('bating) *n.* fiber, used as stuffing

battle ('batəl) *n.* **1.** fight between armies, combat —*vi.* **2.** fight **3.** struggle —**'battlement** *n.* wall, parapet on fortification with openings or embrasures —**battle-ax** *n. inf.* domineering woman —**battle cruiser** high-speed heavily armed warship of battleship size but with light armor —**battle dress** ordinary uniform of soldier —**'battlefield** *or* **'battleground** *n.* place where battle is fought —**battle royal 1.** fight involving more than two combatants **2.** long violent argument —**'battleship** *n.* heavily armed and armored fighting ship

battledore ('batəldör) *n.* **1.** ancient racket game (*also* **battledore and shuttlecock**) **2.** light racket used in this game

batty ('bati) *a. inf.* crazy, silly

bauble ('böbəl) *n.* showy trinket

Bauhaus ('bowhows) *n.* center for research and teaching architecture, art and industrial design whose practitioners created the prevailing international style in architecture

bauxite ('böksīt) *n.* chief ore of aluminum

bawd (böd) *n.* **1.** prostitute **2.** brothel keeper —**'bawdy** *a.* obscene, lewd

bawl (böl) *v.* **1.** cry **2.** shout —*n.* **3.** loud cry or shout

bay[1] (bā) *n.* **1.** wide inlet of sea **2.** space between two columns **3.** recess —**bay window 1.** window projecting to exterior thus forming recess in room **2.** potbelly

bay[2] (bā) *n.* **1.** bark **2.** cry of hounds in pursuit —*vi.* **3.** bark —**at bay 1.** cornered **2.** at a distance

bay[3] (bā) *n.* **1.** laurel tree —*pl.* **2.** honorary crown of victory —**'bayberry** *n.* tropical Amer. tree that yields oil —**bay rum** aromatic liquid, used in medicines *etc.*, orig. obtained by distilling leaves of bayberry tree with rum

bay[4] (bā) *a.* (of horse) reddish-brown

bayonet ('bāənit) *n.* **1.** stabbing weapon fixed to rifle —*vt.* **2.** stab with this ('bayoneted, 'bayoneting)

bazaar (bə'zär) *n.* **1.** market, *esp.* in Orient **2.** department store **3.** sale of goods for charity

bazooka (bə'zōōkə) *n.* antitank rocket launcher

B.B. 1. ball bearing **2.** base on balls **3.** B'nai Brith

BBB Better Business Bureau

B.B.C. British Broadcasting Corporation

bbl barrel(s)

BC British Columbia

B.C. before Christ

BCD binary code decimal

B.C.E. *Judaism* before Common Era

BCG Bacillus Calmette-Guérin (antituberculosis vaccine)

B.Com. *or* **B.Comm.** Bachelor of Commerce

bd 1. barrels per day **2.** bound **3.** bundle

BD 1. Bachelor of Divinity **2.** bills discounted **3.** bomb disposal

bd ft board foot

bdrm bedroom

be (bē; *unstressed* bi) *vi.* **1.** live **2.** exist **3.** have a state or quality (**I am, he is**; **we, you, they are,** *pr. ind.* —**was,** *pl.* **were,** *pt.* —**been** *pp.* —**'being** *pr.p.*)

Be *Chem.* beryllium

be- (*comb. form*) **1.** surround; cover, as in *befog* **2.** affect completely, as in *bedazzle* **3.** consider as; cause to be, as in *befriend* **4.** at, for, against, on, or over, as in *bewail, berate*

B.E. 1. bill of exchange **2.** Bachelor of Engineering

beach (bēch) *n.* **1.** shore of sea —*vt.* **2.** run (boat) on shore —**'beachcomber** *n.* **1.** loafer who lives on casual earnings, *esp.* in S Pacific **2.** one who habitually searches shore debris for items of value —**'beachhead** *n.* **1.** area on beach captured from enemy **2.** base for operations

beacon ('bēkən) *n.* **1.** signal fire **2.** lighthouse, buoy **3.** (radio) signal used for navigation

bead (bēd) *n.* **1.** little ball pierced for threading on string of necklace, rosary *etc.* **2.** drop of liquid **3.** narrow molding —**'beaded** *a.* —**'beading** *n.* —**'beady** *a.* small and bright

beadle ('bēdəl) *n. Hist.* church or parish officer

beagle ('bēgəl) *n.* small short-legged smooth-coated hound

beak (bēk) *n.* **1.** projecting horny jaws of bird **2.** anything pointed or projecting

beaker ('bēkər) *n.* **1.** large drinking cup **2.** glass vessel used by chemists and pharmacists

beam (bēm) *n.* **1.** long squared piece of wood **2.** ship's cross timber, side or width **3.** ray of light *etc.* **4.** broad smile **5.** bar of a balance —*vt.* **6.** aim (light, radio waves *etc.*) in a certain direction —*vi.* **7.** shine **8.** smile benignly —**on her beam-ends** (of vessel) heeled over through angle of 90°

bean (bēn) *n.* any of various leguminous plants and their seeds —**'beanery** *n.* restaurant —**'beanbag** *n.* **1.** small cloth bag filled with dried beans and thrown in games **2.** pellet-filled cushion used as furniture —**bean-ball** *n.* baseball pitched at batter's head —**bean curd** soft cheese made from soybean milk (*also* **tofu**) —**bean-eater** *n.* inhabitant of Boston, Massachusetts —**bean pole** tall, skinny person —**bean sprout** shoot of mung bean, eaten raw or cooked —**know one's beans** be informed in or be skillful in one's field of endeavor

bear[1] (bāər) *vt.* **1.** carry **2.** support **3.** produce **4.** endure —*vi.* **5.** (*with* upon) press (upon) (**bore** *pt.*, **born** *or* **borne** *pp.*, **'bearing** *pr.p.*) —**'bearable** *a.* endurable; tolerable —**'bearer** *n.*

bear[2] (bāər) *n.* **1.** any of a family of massive mammals with coarse fur, short legs, plantigrade feet and rudimentary tail and feeding mainly on fruit and insects **2.** any of various other bearlike animals, *eg* ant bear, koala bear **3.** gruff, shambling person **4.** *Fin.* someone who believes the market will decline —**bear garden** scene of tumult —**bear hug 1.** wrestling hold in which arms are locked round opponent's chest and arms

2. any similar tight embrace —**'bearskin** *n.* Guards' tall fur helmet

beard (bēərd) *n.* **1.** hair on chin —*vt.* **2.** oppose boldly

bearing ('bāəring) *n.* **1.** support or guide for mechanical part, *esp.* one reducing friction **2.** relevance **3.** behavior **4.** direction **5.** relative position **6.** device on shield

beast (bēst) *n.* **1.** animal **2.** four-footed animal **3.** brutal man —**'beastliness** *n.* —**'beastly** *a.*

beat (bēt) *vt.* **1.** strike repeatedly **2.** overcome **3.** surpass **4.** stir vigorously with striking action **5.** flap (wings) **6.** make, wear (path) —*vi.* **7.** throb **8.** sail against wind (**beat** *pt.*, **'beaten, beat** *pp.*) —*n.* **9.** stroke **10.** pulsation **11.** appointed course **12.** basic rhythmic unit in piece of music —*a.* **13.** *sl.* exhausted —**'beater** *n.* **1.** instrument for beating **2.** one who rouses game for shooters

beatify (bi'atifī) *vt.* **1.** make happy **2.** *R.C.Ch.* pronounce in eternal happiness (first step in canonization) (**-fied, -fying**) —**bea'tific** *a.* —**beatifi'cation** *n.* —**be'atitude** *n.* blessedness

beatnik ('bētnik) *n.* **1.** member of Beat Generation of 1950s, rebelling against conventional attitudes **2.** *inf.* person with long hair and shabby clothes

beau (bō) *n.* suitor (*pl.* **-s, beaux** (bōz))

Beaufort scale ('bōfərt) system of indicating wind strength (from 0, calm, to 12, hurricane)

beaujolais (bōzhō'lā) *n.* (*sometimes* **B**-) red or white wine from southern Burgundy, France

beauty ('byōōti) *n.* **1.** loveliness, grace **2.** beautiful person or thing —**'beauteous** *a.* —**beau'tician** *n.* one who works in beauty parlor —**'beautiful** *a.* —**'beautifully** *adv.* —**'beautify** *vt.* —**beauty parlor** *or* **salon** establishment offering hairdressing, manicure *etc.* —**beauty sleep** *inf.* sleep, *esp.* before midnight —**beauty spot 1.** small dark-colored patch worn on lady's face as adornment **2.** mole or similar natural mark on skin **3.** place of outstanding beauty

beaver ('bēvər) *n.* **1.** any of two semiaquatic rodents with webbed hind feet and broad flat tail **2.** fur or pelt of the beaver **3.** hat with plush finish **4.** beard **5.** *offens.* female genitalia —**beaver away** work hard

bebop ('bēbop) *n. see* BOP (sense 1)

becalmed (bi'kämd, -'kälmd) *a.* (of ship) motionless through lack of wind

became (bi'kām) *pt. of* BECOME

because (bi'koz, -'kəz) *conj.* since —**because of** on account of

béchamel sauce (bāshə'mel) thick white sauce

bêche-de-mer (beshdə'māər) *n.* edible sea slug

beck (bek) *n.* —**at someone's beck and call** subject to someone's slightest whim

beckon ('bekən) *v.* (*sometimes with* to) summon or lure by silent signal

become (bi'kum) *vi.* **1.** come to be —*vt.* **2.** suit (**be'came** *pt.*, **be'come** *pp.*, **be'coming** *pr.p.*) —**be'coming** *a.* **1.** suitable **2.** proper

bed (bed) *n.* **1.** piece of furniture for sleeping on **2.** garden plot **3.** place in which anything rests **4.** bottom of river **5.** layer, stratum —*vt.* **6.** lay in a bed **7.** plant (**-dd-**) —**'bedding** *n.* —**bed-and-breakfast** *a.* offering overnight accommodation and breakfast —**'bedbug** *n.* blood-sucking small wingless insect with flattened body and characteristic unpleasant odor living in mattresses or cracks of furniture or houses —**'bedclothes** *pl.n.* sheets, blankets and other bed coverings —**bed linen** sheets, pillowcases *etc.* —**'bed-**

pan *n.* container used as toilet by bedridden people —'**bedridden** *a.* confined to bed by age or sickness —'**bedrock** *n.* —'**bedroom** *n.* —'**bedsitter** *n.* one-roomed apartment —'**bedsore** *n.* chronic ulcer on skin of bedridden person, caused by prolonged pressure —'**bedspread** *n.* top cover on bed —'**bedstead** *n.* —**bed-wetting** *n. see* ENURESIS

B.Ed. Bachelor of Education

bedaub (bi'döb) *vt.* 1. smear with something thick, sticky or dirty 2. ornament in gaudy or vulgar fashion

bedeck (bi'dek) *vt.* cover with decorations; adorn

bedevil (bi'devəl) *vt.* 1. confuse 2. torment —**be'devilment** *n.*

bedew (bi'dyōō, -'dōō) *vt.* wet as with dew

Bedford cord ('bedfərd) very strong fabric with prominent rib weave made of cotton, wool or rayon

bedizen (bi'dīzən, -'dizən) *vt. obs.* dress gaudily or tastelessly —**be'dizenment** *n.*

bedlam ('bedləm) *n.* noisy confused scene

Bedlington terrier ('bedlingtən) woolly-coated terrier with convex head profile

bedouin *or* **beduin** ('bedōōin) *n.* 1. member of nomadic Arab race —*a.* 2. nomadic

bedraggle (bi'dragəl) *vt.* dirty by trailing in wet or mud —**be'draggled** *a.*

bee¹ (bē) *n.* social insect that makes honey from nectar gathered from flowers —**bee-eater** *n.* insect-eating bird found in warm regions of Europe, Asia, Afr. and Aust. —'**beehive** *n.* —'**beeline** *n.* shortest route —'**beeswax** *n.* wax secreted by bees —'**beeswing** *n.* filmy crust of tartar that forms in some wines after long keeping in bottle

bee² (bē) *n.* social gathering for specific purpose —**spelling bee** competition to test proficiency in spelling

beech (bēch) *n.* 1. any of family of N Amer. woodland trees common east of the Mississippi with smooth gray bark and triangular nuts eaten by birds and mammals 2. its wood 3. any of several European varieties, *eg* copper beech and weeping beech grown as ornamentals —'**beechen** *a.*

beef (bēf) *n.* 1. flesh of cattle raised and killed for eating 2. *inf.* complaint —*vi.* 3. *inf.* complain —'**beefy** *a.* fleshy, stolid —**beeves** *pl.n.* cattle —'**beefburger** *n.* hamburger —'**beefcake** *n.* photographs, usu. in magazines, displaying muscle development of male physique —'**beefeater** *n.* 1. yeoman of the guard 2. warder of Tower of London —**beef tea** drink made by boiling pieces of lean beef

Beelzebub (bi'elzibub) *n.* Satan or any devil

been (bēn, bin) *pp. of* BE

beep (bēp) *n.* 1. short, loud sound of automobile horn *etc.* —*vi.* 2. make this sound

beer (bēər) *n.* fermented alcoholic drink made from hops and malt —'**beery** *a.* —**beer parlor** C licensed place where beer is sold to the public —**beer and skittles** *inf.* enjoyment or pleasure

beestings ('bēstingz) *pl.n.* (*with sing. v.*) first milk secreted by cow

beet (bēt) *n.* any of various plants with root used for food or extraction of sugar

beetle¹ ('bētəl) *n.* class of insect with hard upper-wing cases closed over the back for protection —**beetle-browed** *a.* with prominent brows

beetle² ('bētəl) *vi.* 1. overhang; jut —*a.* 2. overhanging; prominent

bef before

befall (bi'föl) *v.* happen (to) (**be'fell, be'fallen**)

befit (bi'fit) *vt.* be suitable to (**-tt-**) —**be'fittingly** *adv.*

befog (bi'fog) *vt.* perplex, confuse (**-gg-**)

before (bi'för) *prep.* 1. in front of 2. in presence of 3. in preference to 4. earlier than —*adv.* 5. earlier 6. in front —*conj.* 7. sooner than —**be'forehand** *adv.* previously

befoul (bi'fowl) *vt.* make filthy

befriend (bi'frend) *vt.* make friend of

befuddle (bi'fudəl) *vt.* 1. confuse 2. make stupid with drink —**be'fuddlement** *n.*

beg¹ (beg) *vt.* 1. ask earnestly, beseech —*vi.* 2. ask for or live on alms (**-gg-**) —'**beggar** *n.* —'**beggarly** *a.*

beg² begin(ning)

began (bi'gan) *pt. of* BEGIN

beget (bi'get) *vt.* produce, generate (**be'got, be'gat** *pt.*, **be'gotten, be'got** *pp.*, **be'getting** *pr.p.*) —**be'getter** *n.*

begin (bi'gin) *v.* 1. (cause to) start —*vt.* 2. originate 3. initiate (**be'gan, be'gun, be'ginning**) —**be'ginner** *n.* novice —**be'ginning** *n.*

begone (bi'gon) *interj.* go away

begonia (bi'gōnyə) *n.* any of a large genus of tender perennial evergreen and deciduous plants grown for their flowers and foliage

begot (bi'got) *pt./pp. of* BEGET

begrudge (bi'gruj) *vt.* grudge, envy (someone) the possession of

beguile (bi'gīl) *vt.* 1. charm, fascinate 2. amuse 3. deceive —**be'guiler** *n.*

beguine (bi'gēn) *n.* 1. dance of S Amer. origin 2. music in rhythm of this dance

begum ('bāgəm) *n. esp.* in India, Muslim woman of high rank

begun (bi'gun) *pp. of* BEGIN

behalf (bi'häf) *n.* favor, benefit, interest (*esp. in* **in behalf of**)

behave (bi'hāv) *vi.* act, function in particular way —**be'havior** *n.* conduct —**be'haviorism** *n.* school of psychology that regards observable behavior as the only valid subject for study —**behave oneself** conduct oneself (well)

behead (bi'hed) *vt.* cut off head of

beheld (bi'held) *pt./pp. of* BEHOLD

behemoth (bi'hēməth) *n.* 1. *Bible* gigantic beast described in Job 2. huge person or thing

behest (bi'hest) *n.* charge, command

behind (bi'hīnd) *prep.* 1. further back or earlier than 2. in support of —*adv.* 3. in the rear —**be'hindhand** *a./adv.* 1. in arrears 2. tardy

behold (bi'hōld) *vt.* watch, see (**be'held** *pt.*, **be'held, be'holden** *pp.*) —**be'holder** *n.*

beholden (bi'hōldən) *a.* bound in gratitude

behove (bi'hōv) *vt.* (*only impers.*) be fit, necessary for

beige (bāzh) *n.* 1. undyed woolen cloth 2. its color

being ('bēing) *n.* 1. existence 2. that which exists 3. creature —*v.* 4. *pr.p. of* BE

bejewel (bi'jōōəl) *vt.* decorate as with jewels

bel (bel) *n.* ten decibels

belabor (bi'lābər) *vt.* beat soundly

belated (bi'lātid) *a.* 1. late 2. too late

belay (bi'lā) *vt.* fasten (rope) to peg, pin *etc.*

belch (belch) *vi.* 1. void wind by mouth —*vt.* 2. eject violently 3. cast up —*n.* 4. emission of wind *etc.*

beldam *or* **beldame** ('beldəm) *n. obs.* old woman

beleaguer (bi'lēgər) *vt.* besiege

belfry ('belfri) *n.* bell tower

Belgium ('beljəm) *n.* country in Europe bounded north by the Netherlands, northwest by the North Sea, west and south by

France, east by Federal Republic of Germany and Luxembourg —'**Belgian** *n./a.*

Belial ('bēliəl) *n.* the devil, Satan

belie (bi'lī) *vt.* 1. contradict 2. misrepresent (**be'lied** *pt./pp.*, **be'lying** *pr.p.*)

believe (bi'lēv) *vt.* 1. regard as true or real —*vi.* 2. have faith —**be'lief** *n.* —**be'lievable** *a.* credible —**be'liever** *n. esp.* one of same religious faith

belittle (bi'litəl) *vt.* regard, speak of, as having little worth or value —**be'littlement** *n.*

Belize (bə'lēz) *n.* country in Central America bounded north by Mexico, west by Guatemala and south and east by the Caribbean Sea —**Be'lizean** *n./a.*

bell (bel) *n.* 1. hollow metal instrument giving ringing sound when struck 2. electrical device emitting ring or buzz as signal 3. the sound of this, *esp.* as a signal on a ship to mark the passing of the half hour of each watch: thus eight bells marks the end of each watch —**bell-bottomed** *a.* —**bell-bottoms** *pl.n.* pants that flare from knee —'**bellboy** *n.* page boy in hotel —**bell jar** bell-shaped glass cover to protect flower arrangements *etc.* or to cover apparatus in experiments (*also* **bell glass**) —**bell metal** alloy of copper and tin, used in casting bells —'**bellwether** *n.* 1. sheep that leads flock, oft. bearing bell 2. leader, *esp.* one followed blindly

belladonna (belə'donə) *n.* deadly nightshade —**belladonna lily** *see* AMARYLLIS (sense 1)

belle (bel) *n.* beautiful woman, reigning beauty

belles-lettres (Fr. bel'letr) *pl.n.* (with *sing. v.*) literary works, *esp.* essays and poetry —**bel'letrist** *n.*

bellicose ('belikōs) *a.* warlike

belligerent (bi'lijərənt) *a.* 1. hostile, aggressive 2. making war —*n.* 3. warring person or nation —**bel'ligerence** *n.*

bellow ('belō) *v.* 1. roar like bull 2. shout —*n.* 3. roar of bull 4. any deep cry or shout

bellows ('belōz) *pl.n.* instrument for creating stream of air

Bell's palsy (belz) paralysis of one side of the face produced by degeneration of the nerve that supplies the muscles of the face

belly ('beli) *n.* 1. part of body which contains intestines 2. stomach —*v.* 3. swell out (**'bellied, 'bellying**) —**belly ache** *inf.* ache in stomach —'**bellyache** *vi. sl.* complain repeatedly —'**bellybutton** *n. inf.* navel —**belly dance** sensuous dance performed by women, with undulating movements of abdomen —**belly-dance** *vi.* perform belly dance —**belly flop** dive into water in which body lands horizontally —**belly-flop** *vi.* perform belly flop —'**bellyful** *n.* 1. as much as one wants or can eat 2. *sl.* more than one can tolerate —**belly laugh** *inf.* hearty laugh

belong (bi'long) *vi.* 1. (*with to*) be the property or attribute (of) 2. (*with to*) be a member or inhabitant (of) 3. have an allotted place 4. pertain —**be'longings** *pl.n.* personal possessions

beloved (bi'luvid, -'luvd) *a.* 1. much loved —*n.* 2. dear one

below (bi'lō) *adv.* 1. beneath —*prep.* 2. lower than

Bel Paese (bel pä'āzi) semihard, mold-ripened, rich, creamy cheese with a mild flavor, orig. made in Italy

belt (belt) *n.* 1. band 2. girdle 3. zone or district —*vt.* 4. surround, fasten with belt 5. mark with band 6. *inf.* thrash

beluga (bi'lōōgə) *n.* large white sturgeon

belvedere ('belvidēər) *n.* building, such as summerhouse, sited to command fine view

Bemberg ('bembərg) *n.* trade name for rayon cloth

bemoan (bi'mōn) *vt.* grieve over (loss *etc.*)

bemuse (bi'myōōz) *vt.* confuse, bewilder

ben (ben) *n. Scot., Irish* mountain peak

bench (bench) *n.* 1. long seat 2. seat or body of judges *etc.* —*vt.* 3. provide with benches —**bench mark** fixed point, criterion

bend (bend) *v.* 1. (cause to) form a curve (**bent** *pt./pp.*) —*n.* 2. curve —*pl.* 3. decompression sickness —**'bender** *n. inf.* drinking bout —**bend sinister** *Her.* diagonal line on shield, typically indicating bastard line

beneath (bi'nēth) *prep.* 1. under, lower than —*adv.* 2. below

Benedictine (beni'diktin, -tēn) *n.* 1. monk or nun of order of Saint Benedict 2. liqueur first made at Benedictine monastery

benediction (beni'dikshən) *n.* invocation of divine blessing

benefit ('benifit) *n.* 1. advantage, favor, profit, good 2. fund-raising event, usu. entertainment, for a person or cause —*vt.* 3. do good to —*vi.* 4. receive good (**'benefited, 'benefiting**) —**bene'faction** *n.* —**'benefactor** *n.* 1. one who helps or does good to others 2. patron (**'benefactress** *fem.*) —**'benefice** *n.* an ecclesiastical living —**be'neficence** *n.* —**be'neficent** *a.* 1. doing good 2. kind —**be'neficently** *adv.* —**bene'ficial** *a.* advantageous, helpful —**bene'ficially** *adv.* —**bene'ficiary** *n.* —**benefit society** association of persons to create a fund for the assistance of its members in case of sudden need

Benelux nations ('beniluks) Belgium, Netherlands and Luxembourg

benevolent (bi'nevələnt) *a.* 1. kindly 2. charitable —**be'nevolence** *n.* —**be'nevolently** *adv.*

Bengali (ben'göli, beng-) *n.* 1. member of people living chiefly in Bangladesh and West Bengal in India 2. their language —*a.* 3. of Bengal, Bengalis or their language —**bengaline** ('benggəlēn) *n.* crosswise-ribbed fabric made of rayon, silk, wool or cotton

benighted (bi'nītid) *a.* ignorant, uncultured

benign (bi'nīn) *a.* 1. kindly 2. mild 3. favorable 4. (of tumor *etc.*) not malignant —**benignancy** (bi'nignənsi) *n.* —**benignant** (bi'nignənt) *a.* —**benignantly** (bi'nignəntli) *adv.* —**benignity** (bi'nigniti) *n.* —**be'nignly** *adv.*

Benin (bə'nin, -'nēn, 'benin) *n.* country in Africa bounded east by Nigeria, north by Niger and Burkina-Faso, west by Togo and south by the Gulf of Guinea —**Benin'ese** *n./a.*

benison ('benizən, -sən) *n. obs.* blessing

bent (bent) *v.* 1. *pt./pp. of* BEND —*a.* 2. curved 3. resolved (on) 4. *inf.* corrupt 5. *inf.* deviant 6. *inf.* crazy —*n.* 7. inclination, personal propensity —**'bentwood** *a.* of furniture permanently bent into various forms by heat, moisture and pressure

bentwood chair

bent grass low-growing perennial grass which spreads by rhizomes and is used widely as a fine lawn grass

benumb (bi'num) *vt.* make numb, deaden

Benzedrine ('benzidrēn) *n.* trade name for amphetamine

benzene ('benzēn) *n.* volatile, flammable, carcinogenic cyclic hydrocarbon, the simplest member of the class of aromatic compounds —**benzene ring** planar ring of six carbon atoms arranged in a regular hexagon

benzoin ('benzoin, -zōin) *n.* gum resin obtained from various tropical Asian trees, used in ointments, perfume *etc.*

bequeath (bi'kwēdh, -'kwēth) *vt.* leave (property *etc.*) by will —**bequest** (bi'kwest) *n.* 1. bequeathing 2. legacy

berate (bi'rāt) *vt.* scold harshly

Berber ('bərbər) *n.* 1. member of various Caucasoid peoples of N Afr. 2. any of the 24 languages of the Afro-Asiatic group of these peoples —*a.* 3. of these peoples or their languages

berceuse (*Fr.* ber'sœz) *n.* 1. lullaby 2. instrumental piece suggestive of this

berdache (bər'dash) *n.* (in some Amerindian tribes) man adopting dress and social role of woman

bereave (bi'rēv) *vt.* (*usu. with* of) deprive (of), *esp.* by death (-'reaved, -'reft *pt./pp.*) —**be'reavement** *n.* loss, *esp.* by death

beret (bə'rā) *n.* round, close-fitting hat

berg (bərg) *n.* 1. large mass of ice 2. SA mountain

bergamot ('bərgəmot) *n.* 1. ornamental plant of the mint family the leaves of which are dried and used for flavoring and to make Oswego tea 2. pear-shaped orange cultivated for oil of bergamot obtained from its rind which is also used in confectionery and cooking 3. type of English pear

beriberi (beri'beri) *n.* disease caused by vitamin B deficiency

berk (bərk) *n. sl.* stupid person

berkelium ('bərkliəm) *n. Chem.* transuranic element *Symbol* Bk, at. wt. 249, at. no. 97

Bermuda (bər'myōōdə) *n.* country consisting of about 150 small islands in the western Atlantic Ocean, 570 miles from Cape Hatteras, North Carolina, and 690 miles from New York —**Ber'mudian** *or* **Ber'mudan** *n./a.* —**Bermuda shorts** close-fitting shorts that come down to knees

berry ('beri) *n.* 1. small juicy stoneless fruit 2. *Bot.* fruit in which seeds are imbedded in pulp, *eg* tomato, melon, orange, grape —*vi.* 3. look for or pick berries

berserk (bər'zərk, -'sərk) *a.* frenzied

berth (bərth) *n.* 1. ship's mooring place 2. place to sleep in ship or train —*vt.* 3. moor

beryl ('beril) *n.* variety of crystalline mineral including aquamarine and emerald

beryllium (be'riliəm) *n. Chem.* metallic element *Symbol* Be, at. wt. 9.0, at. no. 4 —**beryli'osis** *n.* beryllium poisoning

beseech (bi'sēch) *vt.* entreat, implore (**be'sought** *pt./pp.*)

beset (bi'set) *vt.* assail, surround with danger, problems (**be'set, be'setting**)

beside (bi'sīd) *prep.* 1. by the side of, near 2. distinct from —**be'sides** *adv./prep.* in addition (to)

besiege (bi'sēj) *vt.* surround (with armed forces *etc.*)

besmirch (bi'smərch) *vt.* 1. make dirty; soil 2. reduce brightness of 3. sully

besom ('bēzəm) *n.* broom, *esp.* one made of bundle of twigs tied to handle

besotted (bi'sotid) *a.* 1. drunk 2. foolish 3. infatuated

besought (bi'söt) *pt./pp. of* BESEECH

bespangle (bi'spanggəl) *vt.* cover with or as if with spangles

bespatter (bi'spatər) *vt.* 1. splash, as with dirty water 2. defile; besmirch

bespeak (bi'spēk) *vt.* engage beforehand (**be'spoke** *pt.*, **be'spoke, be'spoken** *pp.*) —**be'spoke** *a.* 1. (of garments) made to order 2. selling such garments

Bessemer process ('besimər) process for producing steel by blowing air through molten pig iron in refractory-lined furnace to remove impurities

best (best) *a./adv.* 1. *sup. of* GOOD *and* WELL —*vt.* 2. defeat —**best man** (male) attendant of bridegroom at wedding —**best seller** 1. book or other product that has sold in great numbers 2. author of one or more such books *etc.*

bestial ('beschəl) *a.* like a beast, brutish —**besti'ality** *n.*

bestiary ('beschəri) *n.* moralizing medieval collection of descriptions of real and/or mythical animals

bestir (bi'stər) *vt.* rouse to activity

bestow (bi'stō) *vt.* give, confer —**be'stowal** *n.*

bestrew (bi'strōō) *vt.* scatter over (surface)

bestride (bi'strīd) *vt.* 1. sit or stand over with legs apart 2. mount (horse) (**be'strode, be'stridden, be'striding**)

bet (bet) *v.* 1. agree to pay (money *etc.*) if wrong (or win if right) in guessing result of contest *etc.* (**bet** *or* **'betted** *pt./pp.*, **'betting** *pr.p.*) —*n.* 2. money risked in this way

bet² between

beta ('bātə) *n.* 1. second letter in Gr. alphabet (B or β) 2. second in group or series

betake (bi'tāk) *vt.* —**betake oneself** go; move

beta particle electron or positron emitted by nucleus during radioactive decay

betatron ('bātətron) *n.* particle accelerator for producing high-energy beams of electrons by magnetic induction

betel ('bētəl) *n.* pepper whose leaves are chewed in parts of Asia as a narcotic —**betel nut** the nut of the areca palm

bête noire (bet 'nwar) *Fr.* pet aversion

bethink (bi'thingk) *obs., dial. v.* 1. cause (oneself) to consider or meditate —*vt.* 2. (*oft. with* of) remind (oneself)

betide (bi'tīd) *v.* happen (to)

betimes (bi'tīmz) *adv. obs.* 1. in good time; early 2. soon

betoken (bi'tōkən) *vt.* be a sign of

betony ('betəni) *n.* garden perennial grown for its white, silky leaves and reddish-purple flower spike

betray (bi'trā) *vt.* 1. be disloyal to, *esp.* by assisting an enemy 2. reveal, divulge 3. show signs of —**be'trayal** *n.* —**be'trayer** *n.*

betroth (bi'trōdh) *vt.* promise to marry —**be'trothal** *n.* —**be'trothed** *n./a.*

better ('betər) *a./adv.* 1. *comp. of* GOOD *and* WELL —*v.* 2. improve —**'betterment** *n.*

between (bi'twēn) *prep./adv.* 1. in the intermediate part, in space or time 2. indicating reciprocal relation or comparison

betwixt (bi'twikst) *prep./adv. obs.* between

bevel ('bevəl) *n.* 1. surface not at right angle to another 2. slant —*vi.* 3. slope, slant —*vt.* 4. cut on slant —*a.* 5. slanted —**bevel gear** gear having teeth cut into conical surface

beverage ('bevərij, 'bevrij) *n.* drink

bevy ('bevi) *n.* flock or group

bewail (bi'wāl) *vt.* lament

beware (bi'wâər) *v.* be on one's guard (against), be wary (of)

bewilder (bi'wildər) vt. puzzle, confuse —be'wildering a. —be'wilderingly adv. —be'wilderment n.

bewitch (bi'wich) vt. 1. cast spell over 2. charm, fascinate —be'witching a. —be'witchingly adv.

bey (bā) n. 1. in Ottoman Empire, title given to provincial governors 2. in modern Turkey, title of address, corresponding to *Mr.* (also **beg**)

beyond (bi'yond) adv. 1. farther away 2. besides —prep. 3. on the farther side of 4. later than 5. surpassing, out of reach of

bezel ('bezəl) n. 1. sloping face adjacent to working edge of cutting tool 2. oblique faces of cut gem 3. grooved ring or part holding watch crystal *etc.*

bezique (bi'zēk) n. 1. card game for two players played with a 64-card deck made up of two standard decks with sixes and cards below that rank omitted. The object is to score points by melding and taking tricks 2. meld of queen of spades and jack of diamonds

b.f. *Print.* boldface

BF 1. board foot 2. brought forward 3. *inf.* boyfriend

BG or **B. Gen** brigadier general

Bhagavad Gita ('bägəväd 'gētə) 'The Song of the Lord', the most popular book of Hindu scripture which conveys the message that there are many ways to salvation

bhang (bang) n. preparation of leaves and flower tops of Indian hemp, much used as narcotic in India

b.h.p. brake horsepower

Bhutan (bōō'tän, -'tän) n. country in Asia situated in the eastern Himalaya Mountains bordered on the north and east by Tibet and India, on the west by Sikkim and on the south by India —**Bhutan'ese** n./a.

Bi *Chem.* bismuth

bi- or sometimes before vowel **bin-** (comb. form) 1. two; having two, as in *bifocal* 2. occurring every two, as in *biennial* 3. on both sides *etc.*, as in *bilateral* 4. occurring twice during, as in *biweekly* 5. indicating acid salt of dibasic acid, as in *sodium bicarbonate*

B.I.A. 1. Bureau of Indian Affairs 2. Braille Institute of America

biannual (bī'anyōōl) a. occurring twice a year —**bi'annually** adv.

bias ('bīəs) n. 1. slant 2. personal inclination or preference 3. one-sided inclination (pl. **-es**) —vt. 4. influence, affect (**-s-, -ss-**) —'**biased** a. prejudiced —**bias binding** strip of material cut on bias, used for binding hems or for decoration

biathlon (bī'athlən, -lon) n. athletic event comprising skiing and rifle shooting

biaxial (bī'aksiəl) a. (esp. of crystal) having two axes

bib (bib) n. 1. cloth put under child's chin to protect clothes when eating 2. top of apron or overalls —**best bib and tucker** best clothes

Bibb lettuce (bib) variety of lettuce with small head and dark green leaves

bibcock ('bibkok) n. faucet with nozzle bent downward

bibelot ('bēbəlō) n. attractive or curious trinket

bibl. 1. bibliographical 2. bibliography

Bibl. Biblical

Bible ('bībəl) n. the sacred writings of the Christian religion —**biblical** ('biblikəl) a. —**biblicist** ('biblisist) n.

biblio- (comb. form) book or books, as in *bibliography*

bibliography (bibli'ogrəfi) n. 1. list of books on a subject 2. history and description of books —**bibli'ographer** n. —**biblio'graphical** a.

bibliomania (bibliō'māniə) n. extreme fondness for books —**biblio'maniac** n./a.

bibliophile ('bibliəfīl) or **bibliophil** ('bibliəfil) n. lover, collector of books —**bibli'ophily** n.

bibliotherapy (bibliō'therəpi) n. the treatment of illness by using books and other reading materials

bibulous ('bibyōōləs) a. given to drinking

bicameral (bī'kamərəl) a. (of legislature) consisting of two chambers —**bi'cameralism** n.

bicarbonate (bī'kärbənit, -nāt) n. chemical compound releasing carbon dioxide when mixed with acid —**bicarbonate of soda** sodium bicarbonate

bicentennial (bīsen'teniəl) or **bicentenary** (bīsen'tēnəri) n. 1. two hundredth anniversary 2. its celebration

biceps ('bīseps) n. two-headed muscle, *esp.* muscle of upper arm

bicker ('bikər) vi./n. quarrel over petty things —'**bickering** n.

bicolor ('bīkulər) or **bicolored** ('bīkulərd) a. two-colored

bicuspid (bī'kuspid) a. 1. having two points —n. 2. bicuspid tooth; premolar

bicycle ('bīsikəl) n. vehicle with two wheels, one in front of other, pedaled by rider —'**bicyclist** n.

bid (bid) vt. 1. offer 2. say 3. command 4. invite (**bade** or **bid, 'bidden**) —n. 5. offer, *esp.* of price 6. try 7. *Cards* call —'**biddable** a. 1. having sufficient value to be bid on 2. docile; obedient —'**biddableness** n. —'**bidder** n. —'**bidding** n.

biddy ('bidi) n. dial. young chicken or hen

bide (bīd) vi. 1. remain 2. dwell —vt. 3. await ('**bided** or **bode, 'bided**) —'**biding** n.

bidet (bē'dā) n. low basin for washing genital area and posterior of body

Biedermeier ('bēdərmīər) a. of German and Austrian form of empire style ca. 1815-48, *esp.* in furniture

biennial (bī'eniəl) a. 1. happening every two years 2. lasting two years —n. 3. plant living two years —**bi'ennially** adv.

bier (bēər) n. 1. coffin and its stand 2. frame for bearing dead to grave

biff (bif) sl. n. 1. blow with fist —vt. 2. give (someone) such a blow

bifid ('bīfid) a. divided into two lobes by median cleft —**bi'fidity** n.

bifocal (bī'fōkəl) a. having two different focal lengths —**bi'focals** pl.n. eyeglasses having bifocal lenses for near and distant vision

bifurcate ('bīfərkāt) vi. 1. divide into two branches —a. ('bīfərkāt, -kit) 2. forked or divided into two branches —**bifur'cation** n.

big (big) a. of great or considerable size, height, number, power *etc.* ('**bigger** comp., '**biggest** sup.) —'**bigness** n. —**Big Board** the New York Stock Exchange —**Big Brother** person or organization that exercises total dictatorial control —**big deal!** sl. you can't impress me! —**Big Dipper** the seven main stars in the constellation of Ursa Major which are arranged in the form of a dipper —**big league** 1. league of highest division in baseball 2. highest level of enterprise —**big name** famous person —**big shot** sl. important person —**big stick** inf. force or threat of force —**big time** sl. highest level of profession, *esp.* entertainment —**big-timer**

n. —**big top** inf. 1. main tent of circus 2. circus itself —'**bigwig** n. sl. important person

bigamy ('bigəmi) n. crime of marrying a person while one is still legally married to someone else —'**bigamist** n. —'**bigamous** a.

bight (bīt) n. 1. curve or loop in rope 2. long curved shoreline or water bounded by it

bigot ('bigət) n. person intolerant or not receptive to ideas of others, *esp.* on religion *etc.* —'**bigoted** a. —'**bigotry** n.

bijou ('bēzhōō) n. 1. something small and delicately worked (pl. **-joux** (-zhōōz)) —a. 2. small but tasteful

bike (bīk) n. 1. bicycle 2. motorbike

bikini (bi'kēni) n. 1. woman's brief two-piece bathing suit 2. man or woman's low-cut briefs

bilateral (bī'latərəl) a. two-sided

bile (bīl) n. 1. fluid secreted by the liver 2. anger, ill temper —**biliary** ('bilieri) a. of bile, ducts that convey bile, or gall bladder —**bilious** ('bilyəs) a. nauseous, nauseating —**biliousness** ('bilyəsnis) n. —**biliary calculus** gallstone

bilge (bilj) n. 1. bottom of ship's hull 2. dirty water that collects in vessel's bilge (also **bilge water**) 3. inf. nonsense —vi. 4. spring a leak

bilharzia (bil'härziə) n. schistosomiasis

bilingual (bī'linggwəl) a. speaking, or written in, two languages —**bi'lingualism** n. equal competence in two languages

bilk (bilk) vt. 1. balk; thwart 2. (oft. with of) cheat, deceive 3. escape from; elude —n. 4. swindle, cheat 5. person who swindles or cheats —'**bilker** n.

bill[1] (bil) n. 1. written account of charges 2. draft of law presented for enactment by legislative assembly 3. poster 4. commercial document 5. piece of paper money —vt. 6. present account of charges to 7. announce by advertisement —'**billing** n. degree of importance, *esp.* in theater *etc.* —'**billboard** n. 1. large board for displaying advertisements 2. ledge on vessel on which anchor rests —**bill of exchange** written order to pay designated sum to a nominated person —**bill of fare** menu, program —**bill of health** 1. certificate of freedom from disease, usu. of ship's company 2. favorable account of person's or company's financial position —**bill of indictment** indictment before it is presented to a grand jury —**bill of lading** list giving details of ship's cargo —**Bill of Rights** statement of people's rights and privileges as guaranteed in the first 10 amendments to U.S. Constitution —**bill of sale** document transferring ownership of personal property

bill[2] (bil) n. 1. bird's beak —vi. 2. touch bills, as doves 3. caress

billhook

bill[3] (bil) n. 1. tool for pruning 2. hooked weapon —'**billhook** n. hatchet with hook at end of cutting edge

billabong ('biləbong) n. A pool in intermittent stream

billet[1] ('bilit) n. 1. civilian quarters for troops 2. resting place —vt. 3. quarter, as troops

billet[2] ('bilit) n. 1. chunk of wood, *esp.* for fuel 2. small bar of iron or steel

billet-doux (bilə'dōō) Fr. love letter

billiards ('bilyərdz) pl.n. (with sing. v.) 1. indoor game played with ivory or composition balls and a cue on felt-covered rectangular table whose object is to propel the cue ball to hit the two object balls in succession (*also* **carom billiards**) 2. game played on billiard table with pockets when the object is to drive a number of colored balls into pockets (*also* **pocket billiards, pool**)

billion ('bilyən) *n.* in U.S. and France, the numeral 1 followed by 9 zeros, a thousand millions; in U.K. and Germany, the numeral 1 followed by 12 zeros, a million millions

billow ('bilō) *n.* 1. great swelling wave —*pl.* 2. the sea —*vi.* 3. surge 4. swell out

billy ('bili) *n.* policeman's club

billy goat male goat

Biloxi (bi'loksi) *n.* (member of) Siouan-speaking Amerindian people of Mississippi (*pl.* **Biloxi, -s**)

biltong ('biltong) *n.* **SA** thin strips of meat dried in sun

bimetallism (bī'metəlizəm) *n.* use of two metals, *esp.* gold and silver, in fixed relative values as standard of value and currency

bimonthly (bī'munthli) *adv./a.* 1. every two months 2. twice a month

bin (bin) *n.* 1. receptacle for corn, refuse *etc.* 2. one particular bottling of wine

binary ('bīnəri) *a.* 1. composed of, characterized by, two 2. dual —**binary star** double star system containing two associated stars revolving around common center of gravity

bind (bīnd) *vt.* 1. tie fast 2. tie round, gird 3. tie together 4. oblige 5. seal 6. constrain 7. bandage 8. unite 9. put (book) into cover —*v.* 10. (cause to) cohere (**bound** *pt./pp.*) —**binder** *n.* one who, or that which, binds —**bindery** *n.* —**binding** *n.* 1. cover of book 2. tape for hem *etc.* —**bindweed** *n.* convolvulus

bine (bīn) *n.* climbing or twining stem of any of various plants, such as woodbine

binge (binj) *n. inf.* 1. excessive indulgence in eating or drinking 2. spree

bingo ('binggō) *n.* game of chance in which numbers drawn are matched with those on a card

binnacle ('binəkəl) *n.* box holding ship's compass

binocular (bi'nokyōōlər, bī-) *a.* seeing with, made for both eyes —**binoculars** *pl.n.* telescope made for both eyes

binomial (bī'nōmiəl) *a./n.* (denoting) mathematical expression consisting of two terms connected by a plus sign or a minus sign —**binomial nomenclature** system for naming plants and animals giving every species an official scientific name accepted internationally —**binomial theorem** general formula that expresses any power of binomial

bio- or before vowel **bi-** (*comb. form*) life, living, as in *biochemistry*. Such words are not given here where the meaning may easily be inferred from the simple word

bioastronautics (bīōastrə'nōtiks) *pl.n.* (*with sing. v.*) study of effects of space flight on living organisms

biocenosis (bīōsi'nōsis) *n.* relationships between animals and plants subsisting together

biochemistry (bīō'kemistri) *n.* science concerned with the chemistry of plants and animals

biodegradable (bīōdi'grādəbəl) *a.* capable of decomposition by natural means

bioengineering (bīōenji'nēəring) *n.* 1. design and manufacture of aids to rectify defective body functions 2. design, manufacture and maintenance of engineering equip-

ment used in biosynthetic processes —**bioengi'neer** *n.*

biofeedback (bīō'fēdbak) *n.* the mechanical monitoring of bodily functions for the purpose of gaining control over the functions monitored

biog. 1. biographer 2. biographical 3. biography

biogenesis (bīō'jenisis) *n.* principle that living organism must originate from similar parent organism —**bioge'netic(al)** *a.*

biography (bī'ogrəfi) *n.* story of one person's life —**bi'ographer** *n.* —**bio'graphical** *a.* —**bio'graphically** *adv.*

biol. 1. biological 2. biology

biology (bī'oləji) *n.* study of living organisms —**bio'logical** *a.* —**bio'logically** *adv.* —**bi'ologist** *n.* —**biological clock** means by which living organisms can time their rhythmic periods without external cues —**biological control** control of destructive organisms by nonchemical means —**biological warfare** use of living organisms or their toxic products as weapon of war

biomass ('bīōmas) *n.* the various forms of plant and animal life on the earth

biomedicine (bīō'medisin) *n.* medical and biological study of effects of unusual environmental stress

bionics (bī'oniks) *pl.n.* (*with sing. v.*) study of relation of biological and electronic processes —**bi'onic** *a.* having physical functions augmented by electronic equipment

biophysics (bīō'fiziks) *pl.n.* (*with sing. v.*) physics of biological processes and application of methods used in physics to biology —**bio'physical** *a.* —**biophysicist** (bīō'fizisist) *n.*

biopolymer (bīō'polimər) *n.* polymeric substance found in living organisms, *esp.* proteins, carbohydrates and nucleic acids

biopsy ('bīopsi) *n.* examination of tissue removed surgically from a living body

biorhythm ('bīōridhəm) *n.* complex repeated pattern of physiological states, believed to affect physical, emotional, or mental states

bioscope ('bīəskōp) *n.* **SA** cinema

bioscopy (bī'oskəpi) *n.* examination of body to determine whether it is alive

biosphere ('bīəsfēər) *n.* part of earth's surface and atmosphere inhabited by living things

biosynthesis (bīō'sinthisis) *n.* formation of chemical compounds by living organisms —**biosynthetic** (bīōsin'thetik) *a.*

biotin ('bīətin) *n.* vitamin of B complex, abundant in egg yolk and liver

bipartisan (bī'pärtizən) *a.* consisting of or supported by two political parties

bipartite (bī'pärtīt) *a.* consisting of two parts or parties

biped ('bīped) *n.* two-footed animal —**bi'pedal** *a.*

biplane ('bīplān) *n.* airplane with two pairs of wings

bipolar (bī'pōlər) *a.* 1. having two poles 2. of North and South Poles 3. having two opposed opinions *etc.*—**bipo'larity** *n.*

birch (bərch) *n.* 1. tree with silvery bark —*vt.* 2. flog —**birchen** *a.* —**birchbark** *n.* canoe made of birch bark —**birch beer** carbonated or fermented drink flavored with extract of birch bark

bird (bərd) *n.* 1. warm-blooded egg-laying vertebrate with a feathered body, scaly legs, and forelimbs modified to form wings 2. *inf.* a person 3. shuttlecock —**birder** *n.* 1. birdwatcher 2. one who catches or hunts birds to sell —**birdbrain** *n.* 1. stupid person 2. scatterbrain —**birdlime** *n.* 1. sticky

substance smeared on twigs to catch birds —*vt.* 2. smear with birdlime —**bird of paradise** 1. any of various brilliantly plumed birds of the New Guinea area 2. perennial house plant with flower resembling bird's head —**bird of passage** 1. transient person 2. migratory bird —**bird's eye** fabric or wood marked with spots resembling bird's eye —**bird's-eye** *a.* seen from above, summarizing (*esp. in* **bird's-eye view**) —**birdwatcher** *n.* person who observes or identifies birds in their natural habitat —**get the bird** *sl.* be rejected —**strictly for the birds** *sl.* trivial, to be regarded with contempt

birdie ('bərdi) *n.* 1. *Golf* score of one stroke under par for hole 2. *inf.* bird, *esp.* small bird

biretta (bi'retə) *n.* square cap worn by Catholic clergy

birth (bərth) *n.* 1. bearing, or the being born, of offspring 2. parentage, origin 3. noble descent —**birth control** limitation of child bearing usu. by artificial means —**birthday** *n.* —**birthday suit** state of nakedness —**birthmark** *n.* blemish, usu. dark, formed on skin before birth —**birth rate** ratio of live births in specified area *etc.* to population, usu. expressed per 1000 population per year —**birthright** *n.* 1. privileges that person is entitled to as soon as he is born 2. privileges of first-born son 3. inheritance —**birthstone** *n.* precious or semiprecious stone associated with month or sign of zodiac and thought to bring luck if worn by person born in that month

biscuit ('biskit) *n.* 1. dry, small, thin variety of bread 2. unglazed porcelain or pottery

bisect (bi'sekt) *vt.* divide into two equal parts —**bi'sector** *n.*

bisexual (bī'sekshōōəl) *a.* 1. sexually attracted to both men and women 2. of both sexes

bishop ('bishəp) *n.* 1. clergyman governing diocese 2. chessman —**bishopric** *n.* diocese or office of a bishop

bismuth ('bizməth) *n. Chem.* metallic element *Symbol* Bi, at. wt. 209.0, at. no. 83

bison ('bīsən) *n.* 1. large wild ox 2. Amer. buffalo

bisque[1] (bisk) *n.* thick rich soup made from shellfish

bisque[2] (bisk) *n.* 1. pink to yellowish tan color 2. earthenware or porcelain that has been fired but not glazed

bister or **bistre** ('bistər) *n.* 1. transparent water-soluble brownish-yellow pigment made by boiling soot of wood 2. yellowish-brown to dark brown color

bistro ('bēstrō) *n.* small restaurant

bit[1] (bit) *n.* 1. fragment, piece 2. biting, cutting part of tool 3. mouthpiece of horse's bridle —**bitty** *a.* 1. lacking unity; disjointed 2. containing bits, sediment *etc.*

bit[2] (bit) *pt./pp. of* BITE

bit[3] (bit) *n. Comp.* smallest unit of information

bitch (bich) *n.* 1. female dog, fox or wolf 2. *offens. sl.* spiteful woman 3. *inf.* complaint —*vi.* 4. *inf.* complain —**bitchy** *a.*

bite (bīt) *vt.* 1. cut into, *esp.* with teeth 2. grip —*vi.* 3. rise to bait —*v.* 4. (of corrosive material) eat away or into (**bit** *pt.*, **bit**, **bitten** *pp.*, **biting** *pr.p.*) —*n.* 5. act of biting 6. wound so made 7. mouthful —**biter** *n.* —**biting** *a.* 1. piercing; keen 2. sarcastic; incisive —**bitingly** *adv.*

bitter ('bitər) *a.* 1. sharp, sour-tasting 2. unpleasant 3. (of person) angry or resentful 4. sarcastic —**bitterly** *adv.* —**bitterness** *n.* —**bitters** *pl.n.* essence of bitter herbs —**bitter end** final extremity —**bittersweet** *n.* 1. N Amer. climbing plant 2. woody nightshade —*a.* **3.** being a mixture of bitterness and sweetness **4.** pleasant but tinged with sadness

bittern ('bitərn) *n.* any of various nocturnal herons noted for their booming cry

bitumen (bi'tyōōmin, -'tōō-) *n.* viscous substance occurring in asphalt, tar *etc.* —**bi'tuminous** *a.*

bivalent (bi'vālənt) *a.* **1.** *Chem. see* DIVALENT **2.** (of homologous chromosomes) associated together in pairs —**bi'valency** *n.*

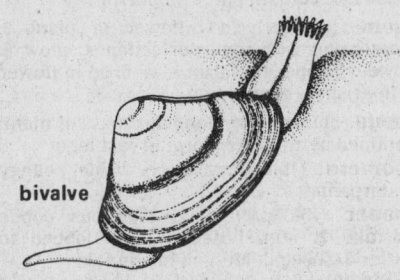

bivalve

bivalve ('bivalv) *a.* **1.** having a double shell —*n.* **2.** mollusk with such shell

bivouac ('bivŏŏak, 'bivwak) *n.* **1.** temporary encampment of soldiers, hikers *etc.* —*vi.* **2.** pass the night in temporary camp ('**bivou-acked,** '**bivouacking**)

bizarre (bi'zär) *a.* unusual, weird

bk 1. bank **2.** book **3.** brook

Bk berkelium

bkgd background

bks barracks

bl 1. bale **2.** barrel **3.** black **4.** block **5.** blue

blab (blab) *v.* **1.** reveal (secrets) —*vi.* **2.** chatter idly (-bb-) —*n.* **3.** telltale **4.** gossip —'**blabber** *n.* **1.** person who blabs **2.** idle chatter —*vi.* **3.** talk without thinking; chatter

black (blak) *a.* **1.** of the darkest color **2.** without light **3.** dark **4.** evil **5.** somber **6.** dishonorable —*n.* **7.** darkest color **8.** black dye, clothing *etc.* **9.** (B-) person of dark-skinned race —*vt.* **10.** boycott (specified goods *etc.*) in industrial dispute —'**blacken** *v.* —'**blacking** *n.* substance used for blacking and cleaning leather *etc.* —'**blackamoor** *n. obs.* Negro or other person with dark skin —**black-and-blue** *a.* **1.** (of skin) discolored, as from bruise **2.** feeling pain, as from beating —**black-and-white** *n.* photograph *etc.* in black, white, and shades of gray rather than in color —**black art** black magic —'**black-ball** *vt.* vote against, exclude —**black belt 1.** (*oft.* **B- B-**) region or area occupied by Blacks **2.** highest ranking in judo and karate; person of this rank —'**blackberry** *n.* plant with thorny stems and dark juicy berries, bramble —'**blackbird** *n.* common European and Asian songbird —'**blackboard** *n.* dark-colored surface for writing on with chalk —**black book** book containing names of people to be punished, blacklisted *etc.* —**black box** *inf.* flight recorder —'**blackcap** *n.* European warbler —'**blackcock** *n.* male of the black grouse —**black'currant** *n.* **1.** N temperate shrub having edible black berries **2.** its fruit —**black eye** *inf.* bruising round eye —**black gum** woodland tree of eastern N Amer. of the dogwood family characterized by sharp horizontal twigs and branches (*also* **sour gum, pepperidge,** '**tupelo**) —'**black-head** *n.* dark, fatty plug blocking pore in skin —**black hole** *Astron.* region of space resulting from collapse of star, and surrounded by gravitational field that neither matter nor radiation could escape from —'**black-jack** *n.* **1.** flexible loaded club **2.** card game in which the object is to hold a combination of

cards higher than dealer but totaling less than 21 (*also* **twenty-one**) —'**blackleg** *n.* **1.** swindling gambler **2.** disease of cattle —'**blacklist** *n.* **1.** list of people, organizations considered suspicious, untrustworthy *etc.* —*vt.* **2.** put on blacklist —**black magic** magic used for evil purposes —'**blackmail** *vt.* **1.** extort money from (a person) by threats —*n.* **2.** act of blackmailing **3.** money extorted thus —'**blackmailer** *n.* —**Black Maria** (mə'rīə) patrol wagon —**black mark** indication of disapproval *etc.* —**black market** illegal buying and selling of goods —**black mass** travesty of Christian Mass performed by practitioners of black magic —**Black Muslim** member of Amer. Muslim sect advocating establishment of separate Black nation in U.S. —'**blackout** *n.* **1.** complete failure of electricity supply **2.** sudden cutting off of all stage lights **3.** state of temporary unconsciousness **4.** obscuring of all lights as precaution against night air attack —**Black Power** social, economic, and political movement of Black people to obtain equality with Whites —**black sheep** person regarded as disgrace or failure by his family or group —'**Blackshirt** *n.* member of fascist organization, *esp.* It. Fascist party before and during World War II —'**blacksmith** *n.* smith who works in iron —**black spot** any of several plant diseases —'**blackthorn** *n.* shrub with black twigs —**black tie 1.** black bow tie worn with dinner jacket —*a.* **2.** denoting occasion when dinner jacket should be worn —**black widow** poisonous spider, female having red hourglass spot on abdomen —**black out 1.** obliterate or extinguish (lights) **2.** create a blackout in (a city *etc.*) **3.** lose consciousness, vision or memory temporarily —**in black and white** in print or writing; in extremes —**the Black Death** name given to bubonic plague pandemic in Europe during 14th cent.

Blackfoot ('blakfŏŏt) *n.* **1.** confederacy of Amerindians of Montana, Alberta and Saskatchewan **2.** member of the Blackfoot (*pl.* **Blackfoot,** '**Blackfeet**) **3.** the Algonquian language of the Blackfoot

blackguard ('blagärd, -gərd) *n.* **1.** scoundrel —*a.* **2.** unprincipled, wicked —*vt.* **3.** revile —'**blackguardism** *n.* —'**blackguardly** *a.*

bladder ('bladər) *n.* membranous bag to contain liquid, *esp.* urinary bladder

blade (blād) *n.* **1.** edge, cutting part of knife or tool **2.** leaf of grass *etc.* **3.** sword **4.** *obs.* dashing fellow **5.** flat of oar

blain (blān) *n.* **1.** inflamed swelling **2.** pimple, blister

blame (blām) *n.* **1.** censure **2.** culpability —*vt.* **3.** find fault with **4.** censure —'**blamable** *or* '**blameable** *a.* —'**blameless** *a.* —'**blame-worthy** *a.*

blanch (blanch) *vt.* **1.** whiten, bleach, take color out of **2.** (of foodstuffs) briefly boil or fry —*v.* **3.** turn pale

blancmange (blə'monzh) *n.* Jello-like dessert made with milk

bland (bland) *a.* **1.** devoid of distinctive characteristics **2.** smooth in manner

blandish ('blandish) *vt.* **1.** coax **2.** flatter —'**blandishments** *pl.n.*

blank (blangk) *a.* **1.** without marks or writing **2.** empty **3.** vacant, confused **4.** (of verse) without rhyme —*n.* **5.** empty space **6.** void **7.** cartridge containing no bullet —'**blankly** *adv.* —**blank check 1.** check that has been signed but on which amount payable has not been specified **2.** complete freedom of action —**blank verse** unrhymed verse, *esp.* in iambic pentameters

blanket ('blangkit) *n.* **1.** thick (woolen) covering for bed **2.** concealing cover —*vt.* **3.** cover with blanket **4.** cover, stifle —**blanket stitch** strong reinforcing stitch for edges of blankets and other thick material

blare (blâr) *v.* **1.** sound loudly and harshly —*n.* **2.** such sound

blarney ('blärni) *n.* flattering talk —**Blarney stone** stone at Blarney Castle in Ireland said to confer a skillful tongue on those who kiss it

blasé (blä'zā) *a.* **1.** indifferent through familiarity **2.** bored

blaspheme (blas'fēm) *v.* show contempt for (God or sacred things, *esp.* in speech) —**blas'phemer** *n.* —**blasphemous** ('blasfiməs) *a.* —**blasphemously** ('blasfiməsli) *adv.* —**blasphemy** ('blasfimi) *n.*

blast (blast) *n.* **1.** explosion **2.** high-pressure wave of air coming from an explosion **3.** current of air **4.** gust of wind or air **5.** loud sound **6.** *sl.* reprimand —*vt.* **7.** blow up **8.** remove, open *etc.* by explosion **9.** blight **10.** ruin —'**blasted** *a.* **1.** blighted, withered **2.** damned —**blast furnace** furnace for smelting ore, using preheated blast of air —'**blastoff** *n.* **1.** launching of rocket **2.** time at which this occurs —**blast off** be launched

blastomycosis (blastōmī'kōsis) *n.* fungus disease, apparently limited to N Amer. continent affecting the skin and internal organs (*also* **Gilchrist's disease**)

blatant ('blātənt) *a.* obvious —'**blatancy** *n.*

blather ('bladhər) *vi.* **1.** speak foolishly —*n.* **2.** foolish talk; nonsense

Blaue Reiter ('blowə 'rītər) *Ger.* —**der Blaue Reiter** (dər). group of Munich-based artists formed in 1911 to attest to liveliness of modern art

blaze[1] (blāz) *n.* **1.** strong fire or flame **2.** brightness **3.** outburst —*vi.* **4.** burn strongly **5.** be very angry

blaze[2] (blāz) *v.* **1.** mark (trees) to establish trail —*n.* **2.** mark on tree **3.** white mark on horse's face

blaze[3] (blāz) *vt.* **1.** proclaim, publish (as with trumpet) —*n.* **2.** wide publicity

blazer ('blāzər) *n.* type of jacket, worn *esp.* for sports

blazon ('blāzən) *vt.* **1.** make public, proclaim **2.** describe, depict (arms) —*n.* **3.** coat of arms

bldg building

bleach (blēch) *v.* **1.** make or become white —*n.* **2.** bleaching substance

bleak[1] (blēk) *a.* **1.** cold and cheerless **2.** exposed —'**bleakly** *adv.*

bleak[2] (blēk) *n.* European river fish of the carp family

bleary ('blēəri) *a.* with eyes dimmed, as by tears or tiredness —**bleary-eyed** *or* **bleary-eyed** *a.* having bleary eyes

bleat (blēt) *vi.* **1.** cry, as sheep —*v.* **2.** say, speak plaintively —*n.* **3.** sheep's cry

bleed (blēd) *vi.* **1.** lose blood —*vt.* **2.** draw blood or liquid from **3.** extort money from (**bled** *pt./pp.*)

bleep (blēp) *n.* short high-pitched sound —'**bleeper** *n.* small portable electronic signaling device

blemish ('blemish) *n.* **1.** defect **2.** stain —*vt.* **3.** make (something) defective, dirty *etc.* —'**blemished** *a.*

blench (blench) *vi.* start back, flinch

blend (blend) *vt.* **1.** mix —*n.* **2.** mixture —'**blender** *n.* one who, that which blends, *esp.* electrical kitchen appliance for mixing food (*also* **liquidizer**)

blende (blend) *n.* 1. a zinc ore 2. any of several sulfide ores

blenny ('bleni) *n.* any of several small fishes of rocky shores, with tapering scaleless body

blesbok ('blesbok) *n.* S Afr. antelope

bless (bles) *vt.* 1. consecrate 2. give thanks to 3. ask God's favor for 4. (*usu. pass.*) endow (with) 5. glorify 6. make happy (**blessed, blest** *pp.*) —**blessed** ('blesid) *a.* 1. made holy 2. worthy of deep reverence 3. *R.C.Ch.* (of person) beatified by pope 4. characterized by happiness 5. bringing great happiness 6. damned —**blessedness** ('blesidnis) *n.* —'**blessing** *n.* 1. (ceremony asking for) God's protection, aid 2. short prayer 3. approval 4. welcome event, benefit

Bleu cheese (bloo) *see* **blue cheese** *at* BLUE

blew (bloo) *pt. of* BLOW[1]

blight (blit) *n.* 1. plant disease 2. harmful influence —*vt.* 3. injure as with blight

blimp (blimp) *n.* small, nonrigid airship used for observing

blind (blind) *a.* 1. unable to see 2. heedless, random 3. dim 4. closed at one end 5. *sl.* very drunk —*vt.* 6. deprive of sight —*n.* 7. something cutting off light 8. window screen 9. pretext —'**blindly** *adv.* —'**blindness** *n.* —**blind alley** 1. alley open at one end only; cul-de-sac 2. *inf.* situation in which no further progress can be made —**blind date** *inf.* social meeting between man and woman who have not met before —**blindfold** *vt.* 1. cover the eyes of, so as to prevent vision —*n.* 2. piece of cloth *etc.* used to cover eyes —**blindman's buff** game in which one player is blindfolded —**blind spot** 1. small area of retina, where optic nerve enters, in which vision is not experienced 2. area where vision is obscured 3. subject about which person is ignorant or prejudiced —**blind trust** arrangement made by person, usu. politician, to relinquish control of his financial affairs by placing it in the hands of an agent during his period of office

blink (blingk) *vi.* 1. wink 2. twinkle 3. shine intermittently —*n.* 4. gleam —'**blinkers** *pl.n.* leather flaps to prevent horse from seeing to the side —**blink at** see, know about, but ignore —**on the blink** *inf.* not working (properly)

blintz (blints) *n.* pancake folded around a filling of cottage cheese or fruit and covered with sour cream

blip (blip) *n.* repetitive sound or visible pulse, *eg* on radar screen

bliss (blis) *n.* perfect happiness —'**blissful** *a.* —'**blissfully** *adv.* —'**blissfulness** *n.*

blister ('blistər) *n.* 1. bubble on skin 2. surface swelling, *eg* on paint —*v.* 3. form blisters (on) —'**blistering** *a.* (of verbal attack) bitter —**blister pack** package for goods with hard, raised, transparent cover

blithe (blidh) *a.* happy, gay —'**blithely** *adv.* —'**blitheness** *n.*

blithering ('blidhəring) *a.* 1. talking foolishly; jabbering 2. *inf.* stupid; foolish

blitz (blits) *n.* sudden, concentrated attack —**blitzkrieg** ('blitskrēg) *n.* intensive military attack designed to defeat opposition quickly

blizzard ('blizərd) *n.* blinding storm of wind and snow

blk 1. black 2. block 3. bulk

bloat (blōt) *v.* 1. puff or swell out —*n.* 2. distension of stomach of cow *etc.* by gas —'**bloated** *a.* swollen —'**bloater** *n.* smoked herring

blob (blob) *n.* 1. soft mass, *esp.* drop of liquid 2. shapeless form

bloc (blok) *n.* (political) grouping of people or countries

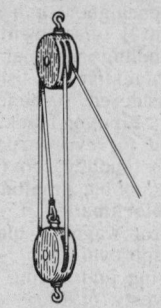

block and tackle

block (blok) *n.* 1. solid (rectangular) piece of wood, stone *etc., esp. Hist.* that on which people were beheaded 2. obstacle 3. stoppage 4. pulley with frame 5. main part of internal-combustion engine, *ie* the cylinders and valves 6. large portion of shares, seats *etc.* as a unit 7. area enclosed by intersecting streets —*vt.* 8. obstruct, stop up 9. shape on block —'**blockage** *n.* obstruction —**block and tackle** hoisting device in which rope or chain is passed around pair of blocks containing one or more pulleys —'**blockbuster** *n. inf.* 1. large bomb used to demolish extensive areas 2. very forceful person, thing *etc.* —'**blockbusting** *n.* inducing owners to sell their homes at a low price by the threat of a fall in value as the result of predicted change in neighborhood racial pattern —'**blockflute** *n. see* **recorder** (sense 2) *at* RECORD —'**blockhead** *n.* derogatory fool, simpleton —'**blockhouse** *n.* 1. formerly, wooden fortification with ports for defensive fire *etc.* 2. concrete structure strengthened for protection against enemy fire, with apertures for defensive gunfire 3. building constructed of logs or squared timber —**block letters** written capital letters —**block in** sketch in

blockade (blo'kād) *n.* 1. physical prevention of access, *esp.* to port *etc.* —*vt.* 2. subject to blockade

blond (blond) *a.* 1. (of hair) light-colored —*n.* 2. someone with blond hair (**blonde** *fem.*)

blood (blud) *n.* 1. red body fluid 2. race 3. kindred 4. parental heritage 5. temperament 6. passion —*vt.* 7. initiate (into hunting, war *etc.*) —'**bloodily** *adv.* —'**bloodless** *a.* —'**bloody** *a.* 1. covered in blood 2. slaughterous —*a./adv.* 3. *sl.* common intensifier —*vt.* 4. make bloody —**blood bank** (institution managing) store of human blood preserved for transfusion —**blood bath** indiscriminate slaughter; massacre —**blood count** determination of number of red and white blood corpuscles in sample of blood —'**bloodcurdling** *a.* terrifying; horrifying —**blood group** any of various groups into which human blood is classified (*also* **blood type**) —'**bloodhound** *n.* breed of large hound noted for its keen powers of scent —'**bloodletting** *n.* 1. therapeutic removal of blood (*also* **phlebotomy**) 2. bloodshed, *esp.* in feud —**blood money** 1. compensation paid to relatives of murdered person 2. money paid to hired murderer —**blood poisoning** condition in which blood is invaded by bacteria leading to bacteremia or septicemia —**blood pressure** pressure exerted by blood on inner walls of arteries —**blood relation** *or* **relative** person related by birth —'**bloodshed** *n.* slaughter, killing —'**bloodshot** *a.* (of eyes) inflamed —**blood sport** sport in which animals are killed —'**bloodstone** *n.* green variety of chalcedony spotted or streaked with red, used as a gem —'**bloodstream** *n.* flow of blood through vessels of living body —'**bloodsucker** *n.* 1. parasite (*eg* mosquito)

living on host's blood 2. parasitic person —**blood test** examination of sample of blood —'**bloodthirsty** *a.* murderous, cruel —**blood transfusion** replacement of blood loss —**blood vessel** artery, capillary or vein —**Bloody Mary** ('māəri) cocktail consisting of vodka and tomato juice —**bloody-minded** *a. inf.* deliberately obstructive and unhelpful —**in cold blood** cruelly and ruthlessly; deliberately and calmly —**make one's blood boil** cause one to be angry —**make one's blood run cold** fill one with horror

bloom[1] (bloom) *n.* 1. flower of plant 2. blossoming 3. prime, perfection 4. glow 5. powdery deposit on fruit —*vi.* 6. be in flower 7. flourish —'**blooming** *a.*

bloom[2] (bloom) *n.* rectangular mass of metal obtained by rolling or forging cast ingot

bloomers ('bloomərz) *pl.n.* wide, baggy underpants

blooper ('bloopər) *n.* 1. ludicrous public mistake 2. high baseball pitch lobbed to batter 3. baseball hit high into infield

blossom ('blosəm) *n.* 1. flower 2. flower bud —*vi.* 3. flower 4. develop

blot (blot) *n.* 1. spot, stain 2. disgrace 3. backgammon counter exposed to capture —*vt.* 4. spot, stain 5. obliterate 6. detract from 7. soak up (ink *etc.*) from (**-tt-**) —**blotting paper** absorbent paper, used *esp.* for soaking up surplus ink

blotch (bloch) *n.* 1. dark spot on skin —*vt.* 2. make spotted —'**blotchy** *a.*

blotto ('blotō) *a. sl.* drunk

blouse (blows) *n.* light, loose upper garment

blouson ('bloozon) *n.* loosely fitting but tight-waisted jacket

blow[1] (blō) *vi.* 1. make a current of air 2. pant 3. make sound by blowing 4. (of whale) spout —*vt.* 5. drive air upon or into 6. drive by current of air 7. sound 8. fan 9. *sl.* squander (**blew, blown**) —*n.* 10. blast 11. gale —'**blower** *n.* —'**blowy** *a.* windy —**blow-by-blow** *a.* explained in great detail —**blow-dry** *vt.* 1. style (hair) after washing, using hand-held hair dryer —*n.* 2. this method of drying hair —'**blowfly** *n.* fly which infects food *etc.* (*also* '**bluebottle**) —'**blowhole** *n.* 1. nostril of whales, situated far back on skull 2. hole in ice through which seals *etc.* breathe 3. vent for air or gas —**blow-out** *n.* 1. sudden puncture in tire 2. uncontrolled escape of oil or gas from well —'**blowpipe** *n.* 1. small tubular device used for directing jet of air on to flame to intensify and to concentrate the heat 2. dart tube —**blow torch** small burner with very hot flame, for removing paint *etc.* —**blow out** 1. extinguish 2. (of tire) puncture suddenly 3. (of fuse) melt —**blow hot and cold** be for and then against something or someone —**blow one's mind** 1. astound one 2. induce hallucinations in one with drugs —**blow one's own trumpet** praise oneself —**blow the whistle on** reveal —**blow up** 1. explode 2. inflate 3. enlarge (photograph) 4. *inf.* lose one's temper

blow[2] (blō) *n.* 1. stroke, knock 2. sudden misfortune, loss

blown (blōn) *pp. of* BLOW[1]

blowsy *or* **blowzy** ('blowzi) *a.* 1. slovenly, sluttish 2. red-faced

BLS Bureau of Labor Statistics

BLT bacon, lettuce and tomato (sandwich)

blubber ('blubər) *vi.* 1. weep —*n.* 2. fat of whales 3. weeping

bludgeon ('blujən) *n.* 1. short thick club —*vt.* 2. strike (as) with bludgeon 3. coerce

blue (bloo) *a.* 1. of color of sky or shades of that color 2. depressed 3. indecent —*n.* 4. the color 5. dye or pigment 6. clothing, *esp.* of police force —*vt.* **7.** make blue **8.** dip in blue liquid (**blued** *pt./pp.*) —**blues** *pl.n. inf.* (*oft. with sing. v.*) **1.** depression **2.** form of Amer. Negro folk song in slow tempo, employed in jazz music —'**bluish** *a.* —**blue baby** baby born with bluish skin caused by heart defect —'**bluebell** *n.* wild spring flower —'**blueberry** *n.* N Amer. shrub with blue-black edible berries —'**bluebird** *n.* common songbird related to robin of eastern N Amer. —**blue blood** royal or aristocratic descent —'**bluebook** *n.* **1.** volume of specialized information, *esp.* that published by government **2.** directory of socially prominent persons **3.** booklet in which students write examination papers **4.** the examination itself —'**bluebottle** *n.* blowfly —**blue cheese** any of various semihard cheeses with blue veins —**blue chip** *Fin.* reliable stock —**blue-collar** *a.* denoting manual industrial workers —**Blue Cross Plans** U.S. and Canad. nonprofit organizations providing hospital care to subscribers —**Blue Dorset** Dorset vinny —**blue nose** *sl.* puritanical person —**bluepencil** *vt.* alter, delete parts of, *esp.* to censor —**blue peter** signal flag of blue with white square at center, displayed by vessel about to leave port —'**bluepoint** *n.* edible oyster —'**blueprint** *n.* **1.** copy of drawing **2.** original plan —**blue ribbon 1.** honor or award for excellence **2.** badge awarded as first prize in competition —**Blue Shield Plans** U.S. and Canad. nonprofit organizations providing medical and surgical care to subscribers —'**bluestocking** *n.* scholarly, intellectual woman —**Blue vinny** Dorset vinny —**blue whale** largest living mammal: bluish-gray whalebone whale —**blue in the face** furious —**once in a blue moon** very rarely —**out of the blue** unexpectedly —**true blue** loyal

bluff¹ (bluf) *n.* **1.** cliff, steep bank **2.** C clump of trees —*a.* **3.** hearty **4.** blunt **5.** steep **6.** abrupt

bluff² (bluf) *v.* **1.** deceive (someone) by pretense of strength —*n.* **2.** pretense

blunder ('blundər) *n.* **1.** clumsy mistake —*vi.* **2.** make stupid mistake **3.** act clumsily

blunderbuss ('blundərbus) *n.* obsolete short gun with wide bore

blunt (blunt) *a.* **1.** not sharp **2.** (of speech) abrupt —*vt.* **3.** make blunt —'**bluntly** *adv.* —'**bluntness** *n.*

blur (blər) *v.* **1.** make, become less distinct (**-rr-**) —*n.* **2.** something vague, indistinct —'**blurry** *a.*

blurb (blərb) *n.* statement, advertising or recommending book *etc.*

blurt (blərt) *vt.* (*oft. with* out) utter suddenly or unadvisedly

blush (blush) *vi.* **1.** become red in face **2.** be ashamed **3.** redden —*n.* **4.** this effect —'**blusher** *n.* cosmetic applied to cheeks to give rosy color

bluster ('blustər) *vi./n.* (indulge in) noisy, aggressive behavior —'**blustering** *or* '**blustery** *a.* (of wind *etc.*) noisy and gusty

blvd boulevard

bm beam

BM 1. basal metabolism **2.** bill of material **3.** board measure **4.** bowel movement

BMOC big man on campus

BMR basal metabolism rate

BNDD Bureau of Narcotics and Dangerous Drugs

B.O. 1. back order **2.** body odor **3.** box office

boa ('bōə) *n.* **1.** any of family of nonvenomous snakes ranging in size from 15 inches to 33 feet that kill prey by crushing **2.** long scarf of fur or feathers —**boa constrictor** boa native

to tropical S Amer. that reaches 15 feet in length

boar (bör) *n.* **1.** male pig **2.** wild pig

board (börd) *n.* **1.** broad, flat piece of wood **2.** sheet of rigid material for specific purpose **3.** table **4.** meals **5.** group of people who administer company **6.** governing body **7.** thick, stiff paper —*pl.* **8.** theater, stage **9.** C wooden enclosure where ice hockey, box lacrosse is played —*vt.* **10.** cover with planks **11.** supply with regular meals **12.** enter (ship *etc.*) —*vi.* **13.** take daily meals —'**boarder** *n.* —**boarding house** lodging house where meals may be had —**boarding school** school providing living accommodation for pupils —'**boardroom** *n.* room where board of company meets —**above board** beyond suspicion —**board up** cover with boards —**on board** in or into ship

boast (bōst) *vi.* **1.** speak too much in praise of oneself, one's possessions *etc.* —*n.* **2.** something boasted (of) —'**boaster** *n.* —'**boastful** *a.* —'**boastfully** *adv.* —'**boastfulness** *n.* —**boast of 1.** brag of **2.** have to show

boat (bōt) *n.* **1.** small open vessel **2.** ship —*vi.* **3.** sail about in boat —'**boater** *n.* flat straw hat —'**boating** *n.* —'**boathook** *n.* —'**boathouse** *n.* —'**boatman** *n.* —**boatswain** ('bōsən) *n.* ship's officer in charge of boats, sails *etc.* —**in the same boat** having identical troubles

bob (bob) *vi.* **1.** move up and down —*vt.* **2.** move jerkily **3.** cut (hair) short (**-bb-**) —*n.* **4.** short, jerking motion **5.** short hair style **6.** weight on pendulum *etc.* **7.** *inf.* formerly, shilling —**bobbed** *a.*

bobbin ('bobin) *n.* cylinder on which thread is wound

bobble ('bobəl) *n.* small, tufted ball for decoration

bobby ('bobi) *n.* UK *inf.* policeman

bobcat ('bobkat) *n.* medium-sized feline with black-spotted reddish-brown coat of eastern N Amer. (*also* **wildcat**)

bobolink ('bobəlingk) *n.* Amer. songbird

bobsled ('bobsled) *n.* large four-runner sled with steering wheel and hand brake capable of carrying two to four persons —'**bobsledding** *n.* competitive downhill racing in a bobsled over specially constructed course covered with ice or snow

bobtail ('bobtāl) *n.* **1.** docked or diminutive tail **2.** animal with such tail —*a.* **3.** having tail cut short (*also* '**bobtailed**) —*vt.* **4.** dock tail of **5.** cut short; curtail

boccie, bocci, *or* **bocce** ('bochē) *n.* grass court game played by two players or teams of two to four players in which the object is to bowl eight wooden balls close to the jack ball

bock beer (bok) special brew of beer, usu. strong, dark and sweet, brewed in winter for use in spring

bode¹ (bōd) *vt.* be an omen of

bode² (bōd) *pt. of* BIDE

bodega (bō'dāgə) *n.* shop selling wine, *esp.* in Spanish-speaking country

bodge (boj) *vt. inf.* make mess of; botch

bodice ('bodis) *n.* upper part of woman's dress

bodkin ('bodkin) *n.* **1.** large blunt needle **2.** tool for piercing holes

body ('bodi) *n.* **1.** whole frame of man or animal **2.** main part of such frame **3.** corpse **4.** main part of anything **5.** substance **6.** mass **7.** person **8.** number of persons united or organized **9.** matter, opposed to spirit —'**bodiless** *a.* —'**bodily** *a./adv.* —**body colors** pigments with opacity in contrast to transparent pigments —'**bodyguard** *n.* escort to protect important person —**body**

politic people of nation or nation itself considered as political entity —**body stocking** one-piece undergarment, usu. of nylon, covering torso —**body types** categories of human physique based on major anatomical characteristics developed by theories relating body type and personality —'**bodywork** *n.* shell of motor vehicle

Boer (bōōr) *n.* a S Afr. of Dutch or Huguenot descent

bog (bog) *n.* wet, soft ground —'**boggy** *a.* marshy —**bog down** stick as in a bog

bogan ('bōgən) *n.* C sluggish side stream

bogey *or* **bogy** ('bōgi) *n.* **1.** evil or mischievous spirit **2.** *Golf* par, popularly one stroke above par —'**bogeyman** *n.*

boggle ('bogəl) *vi.* stare, be surprised

bogie *or* **bogy** ('bōgi) *n.* **1.** low truck on four wheels **2.** pivoted undercarriage, as on railway rolling stock

bogus ('bōgəs) *a.* sham, false

Bohemian (bō'hēmiən) *a.* **1.** unconventional —*n.* **2.** (*oft.* **b-**) one who leads an unsettled life —**Bo'hemianism** *n.*

boil¹ (boil) *vi.* **1.** change from liquid to gas, *esp.* by heating **2.** become cooked by boiling **3.** bubble **4.** be agitated **5.** seethe **6.** *inf.* be hot **7.** *inf.* be angry —*vt.* **8.** cause to boil **9.** cook by boiling —*n.* **10.** boiling state —'**boiler** *n.* vessel for boiling —**boiler suit** garment covering whole body —**boiling point** temperature at which boiling occurs (212°F, 100°C for water)

boil² (boil) *n.* inflamed suppurating swelling on skin

boisterous ('boistərəs, -strəs) *a.* **1.** wild **2.** noisy **3.** turbulent —'**boisterously** *adv.* —'**boisterousness** *n.*

bola ('bōlə) *or* **bolas** ('bōləs) *n.* weapon used for hunting consisting of weights joined by cords or thongs

bold (bōld) *a.* **1.** daring, fearless **2.** presumptuous **3.** striking, prominent —'**boldly** *adv.* —'**boldness** *n.* —'**boldface** *a.* —**bold face** *Print.* type with thick heavy lines

bole (bōl) *n.* trunk of tree

bolero (bə'lārō) *n.* **1.** Spanish dance **2.** short loose jacket

Bolivia (bə'liviə) *n.* country in South America landlocked by Brazil to the north and east, Paraguay to the southeast, Argentina to the south, and Chile and Peru to the west —**Bo'livian** *n./a.*

boll (bōl) *n.* seed capsule of cotton, flax *etc.*

bollard ('bolərd) *n.* **1.** post on quay or ship to secure mooring lines **2.** short post in road or footpath as barrier or marker

Bolshevik ('bolshivik) *n.* member of Russian Social Democratic Party that seized power in the revolution of November 1917

bolster ('bōlstər) *vt.* **1.** support, uphold —*n.* **2.** long pillow **3.** pad, support

bolt¹ (bōlt) *n.* **1.** bar or pin, *esp.* with thread for nut **2.** rush **3.** discharge of lightning **4.** roll of cloth —*vt.* **5.** fasten with bolt **6.** swallow hastily —*vi.* **7.** rush away **8.** break from control

bolt² (bōlt) *vt.* **1.** pass (flour *etc.*) through sieve **2.** examine and separate —'**bolter** *n.*

bomb (bom) *n.* **1.** explosive projectile **2.** any explosive device **3.** small pressurized dispenser (*also* **aerosol**) —*vt.* **4.** attack with bombs —**bom'bard** *vt.* **1.** shell **2.** attack (verbally) —**bombardier** (bombər'dēər) *n.* artillery noncommissioned officer —**bom'bardment** *n.* —'**bomber** *n.* aircraft capable of carrying bombs —'**bombshell** *n.* **1.** shell of bomb **2.** surprise —**the bomb** nuclear bomb

bombast ('bombast) *n.* **1.** pompous language **2.** pomposity —**bom'bastic** *a.*

Bombay duck (bom'bă) salty dried fish eaten with curry dishes (also 'bummalo)

bombazine (bombə'zēn) n. twilled fabric, esp. one of silk and worsted

bona fide ('bōnə fīd, 'bōnə 'fīdi) Lat. 1. genuine(ly) 2. sincere(ly) —**bona fides** ('fīdēz) good faith, sincerity

bonanza (bə'nanzə) n. sudden good luck or wealth

bonbon ('bonbon) n. candy with chocolate or fondant coating and with any of various fillings

bond (bond) n. 1. that which binds 2. link, union 3. written promise to pay money or carry out contract —vt. 4. bind 5. store (goods) until duty is paid on them —'**bonded** a. 1. placed in bond 2. mortgaged —'**bonds-man** n. 1. Law person bound by bond to act as surety for another 2. serf, slave (also 'bondservant)

bondage ('bondij) n. slavery

bone (bōn) n. 1. hard substance forming animal's skeleton 2. piece of this —pl. 3. essentials —vt. 4. remove bones from —vi. 5. inf. (with up) study hard —'**boneless** a. —'**bony** a. —**bone china** porcelain containing bone ash —**bone-dry** a. inf. completely dry —**bone graft** section of bone used to repair injured or diseased bone —'**bonehead** n. inf. stupid person —'**bonemeal** n. dried and ground animal bones, used as fertilizer —'**boneshaker** n. 1. early type of bicycle having solid tires 2. sl. any rickety vehicle

bonfire ('bonfīər) n. large outdoor fire

bongo ('bonggō) n. small drum, usu. one of pair, played with fingers (pl. -s, -es)

bonhomie (bonə'mē) Fr. good humor, geniality

bonkers ('bongkərz) a. sl. crazy

bon mot (Fr. bō 'mō) clever and fitting remark (pl. bons mots (bō 'mō))

bonnet ('bonit) n. 1. hat with strings 2. cap

bonny ('boni) a. beautiful, handsome —'**bon-nily** adv.

bonsai (bon'sī) n. (art of growing) dwarf trees, shrubs

bontebok ('bontibuk) n. S Afr. antelope

bonus ('bōnəs) n. extra (unexpected) payment or gift

bon vivant (bō vē'vä) Fr. person who enjoys luxuries, esp. good food and drink (pl. bons vivants (bō vē'vä))

bon voyage (Fr. bō vwa'yazh) phrase used to wish traveler pleasant journey

bonze (bonz) n. Buddhist monk

boo (bōō) interj. 1. expression of disapproval or contempt 2. exclamation to surprise esp. child —v. 3. make this sound (at)

boob (bōōb) n. sl. 1. awkward person 2. simpleton 3. female breast

booby ('bōōbi) n. 1. fool 2. tropical marine bird —**booby prize** mock prize for poor performance —**booby trap** 1. harmless-looking object which explodes when disturbed 2. trap for the unwary

boodle ('bōōdəl) n. sl. money

boogie-woogie ('bōōgi'wōōgi, 'bōōgi'wōōgi) n. kind of jazz piano playing, emphasizing a rolling bass in syncopated eighth notes

book (bōōk) n. 1. collection of sheets of paper bound together 2. literary work 3. main division of this —v. 4. reserve (room, ticket etc.) —vt. 5. charge with legal offense 6. enter name in book —'**booking** n. reservation —'**bookish** a. studious, fond of reading —'**booklet** n. —'**bookbinder** n. —'**bookcase** n. —**book club** club that sells books at low prices to members —**book end** one of pair of ornamental supports for holding row of books upright —**book-keeping** n. systematic recording of business transactions —'**book-maker** n. person whose work is taking bets (also (inf.) 'bookie) —'**bookmark** or 'book-marker** n. strip of material put between pages of book to mark place —**book of hours** late medieval book of prayers for private devotions often sumptuously decorated —'**bookplate** n. label bearing owner's name and design, pasted into book —**book value** 1. value of asset of business according to its books 2. net capital value of enterprise as shown by excess of book assets over book liabilities —'**bookworm** n. 1. insect that eats holes in books 2. great reader

boom[1] (bōōm) n. 1. sudden commercial activity 2. prosperity —vi. 3. become active, prosperous

boom[2] (bōōm) vi./n. (make) loud, deep sound

boom[3] (bōōm) n. 1. long spar, as for stretching the bottom of a sail 2. barrier across harbor 3. pole carrying overhead microphone etc.

boomerang ('bōōmərang) n. 1. curved wooden missile of Aust. Aborigines, which returns to the thrower —vi. 2. recoil 3. return unexpectedly 4. backfire

boon (bōōn) n. something helpful, favor

boor (bōōər) n. rude person —'**boorish** a.

boost (bōōst) n. 1. encouragement, help 2. upward push 3. increase —vt. 4. encourage, assist or improve —'**booster** n. person or thing that supports, increases power etc. —**booster shot** inf. supplementary injection of vaccine given to maintain immunization

boot[1] (bōōt) n. 1. shoe covering the foot and ankle or leg 2. inf. kick —vt. 3. inf. kick —'**booted** a. —'**bootee** n. baby's soft shoe —**boot camp** training base for recruits to U.S. Navy or Marine Corps

boot[2] (bōōt) n. profit, use —'**bootless** a. fruitless, vain —**to boot** in addition

booth (bōōth) n. 1. stall 2. cubicle

bootleg ('bōōtleg) v. 1. make, carry, sell (illicit goods, esp. liquor) (-gg-) —a. 2. produced, distributed or sold illicitly —'**boot-legger** n.

booty ('bōōti) n. plunder, spoil

booze (bōōz) n./vi. inf. (consume) alcoholic drink —'**boozer** n. inf. person fond of drinking —'**boozy** a. inf. inclined to or involving excessive consumption of alcohol —**booze-up** n. inf. drinking spree

bop (bop) n. 1. form of jazz characterized by rhythmic and harmonic complexity (also bebop) —vi. 2. inf. dance to pop music (-pp-) —'**bopper** n.

BOQ bachelor officers' quarters

bor borough

borage ('borij) n. hardy annual culinary herb with flavor resembling cucumber

borax ('bōraks) n. white soluble substance, compound of boron used to make glass, enamels and detergents

Bordeaux (bôr'dō) n. any of several red, white or rosé wines produced around Bordeaux in SW France

border ('bôrdər) n. 1. margin 2. frontier 3. limit 4. flower bed —vt. 5. provide with border 6. adjoin —'**borderline** n. 1. border; dividing line 2. indeterminate position between two conditions —a. 3. on edge of one category and verging on another

bore[1] (bôr) vt. 1. pierce —vi. 2. make a hole —n. 3. hole 4. caliber of gun —'**borer** n. 1. instrument for making holes 2. insect which bores holes

bore[2] (bôr) vt. 1. make weary by repetition etc. —n. 2. tiresome person or thing —'**boredom** n. —'**boring** a.

bore[3] (bôr) n. tidal wave which rushes up river estuary

bore[4] (bôr) pt. of BEAR[1]

born (bôrn) pp. of BEAR[1] —**born again** Christian person having undergone a conversion to Christianity —**not born yesterday** difficult to deceive

borne (bôrn) pp. of BEAR[1] —**be borne in on** or **upon** (of fact etc.) be realized by

boron ('bôron) n. Chem. metalloid element Symbol B, at. wt. 10.8, at. no. 5 —'**boric** a. of or containing boron (also bo'racic) —**boric acid** white crystalline boron compound formerly in wide use as antiseptic, before the discovery of its poisonous properties

borough ('burə) n. town

borrow ('borō) vt. 1. obtain on loan or trust 2. appropriate —'**borrower** n.

borscht (bôrsht) or **borsch** (bôrsh) n. soup made from beets and served hot or cold with or without sour cream —**borscht belt** or **circuit** resort area in the Catskill Mountains of New York

borzoi ('bôrzoi) n. breed of tall hound with long, silky coat and narrow head (also **Russian wolfhound**)

bosh (bosh) n. inf. nonsense

bo's'n ('bōsən) n. Naut. see **boatswain** at BOAT

bosom ('bōōzəm) n. 1. human breast 2. seat of passions and feelings

boss[1] (bos) n. 1. person in charge of or employing others —vt. 2. be in charge of 3. be domineering over —'**bossy** a. overbearing

boss[2] (bos) n. 1. knob or stud 2. raised ornament —vt. 3. emboss

bosun ('bōsən) n. Naut. see **boatswain** at BOAT

bot. 1. botanical 2. botany 3. bottle

botany[1] ('botəni) n. branch of biology concerned with plant life —bo'**tanic(al)** a. —'**botanist** n. —**botanical garden** garden, usu. public, where plants are grown for scientific study

botany[2] ('botəni) a. of fine wool from merino sheep

botch (boch) vt. (oft. with up) spoil by clumsiness

botfly ('botflī) n. fly, larvae of which are parasites of man, sheep and horses

both (bōth) a./pron. 1. the two —adv./conj. 2. as well

bother ('bodhər) vt. 1. pester 2. perplex —vi./n. 3. fuss, trouble —bothe'**ration** n. 1. state of worry, trouble or confusion —interj. 2. exclamation of slight annoyance —'**bothersome** a. causing bother; troublesome

Bothnia ('bothniə) n. —**Gulf of Bothnia** arm of the Baltic Sea separating Sweden and Finland

bo tree (bō) Indian fig tree sacred to Buddhists

Botswana (bot'swänə) n. country in Africa lying between the Molopo River on the south and the Zambesi on the north, extending from the Transvaal Province and Zimbabwe on the east to Namibia on the west

Botticelli (boti'cheli) n. parlor game in which players attempt to discover the identity selected by person who is 'it'

bottle ('botəl) n. 1. vessel for holding liquid 2. its contents —vt. 3. put into bottle —'**bottler** n. —'**bottlebrush** n. 1. cylindrical brush for cleaning bottle 2. any of various Aust. shrubs with brushlike flowers —**bottled gas** pressurized gas in portable cylinders —'**bottleneck** n. narrow outlet which impedes smooth flow of traffic or production of goods —**bottle party** party to which guests bring drink

—**bottle up** 1. restrain (powerful emotion) 2. *inf.* keep (army or other force) contained or trapped

bottom ('botəm) *n.* 1. lowest part of anything 2. bed of sea, river *etc.* 3. buttocks —*vt.* 4. put bottom to 5. base 6. get to bottom of —'**bottomless** *a.* —**bottom line** last line of financial statement that shows net profit or loss of company *etc.* —**bottom out** reach lowest point

botulism ('botyōōlizəm) *n.* food poisoning caused by contamination by anaerobic soil bacillus

bouclé (bōō'klā) *n.* looped yarn giving knobbly effect

boudoir ('bōōdwär) *n.* 1. lady's private sitting room 2. bedroom

bouffant (bōō'fänt) *a.* 1. (of hairstyle) having extra height through backcombing 2. (of skirts *etc.*) puffed out

bougainvillea (bōōgən'vilyə) *n.* (sub)tropical climbing plant with red or purple bracts

bough (bow) *n.* branch of tree

bought (böt) *pt./pp. of* BUY

bouillabaisse (bōōyə'bäs) *n.* rich stew or soup of fish and vegetables

bouillon ('bōōyon) *n.* plain unclarified broth or stock

boulder ('bōldər) *n.* large weatherworn rounded stone —**boulder clay** unstratified glacial deposit consisting of fine clay, boulders and pebbles

boulevard ('bōōləvärd) *n.* broad street or promenade

boulle (bōōl) *n.* ornamental furniture inlay of silver, brass, mother-of-pearl, tortoiseshell *etc.* (*also* **buhl**)

bounce (bowns) *v.* 1. (cause to) rebound (repeatedly) on impact, as a ball —*n.* 2. rebounding 3. quality in object causing this 4. *inf.* vitality, vigor —'**bouncer** *n. sl.* man, *esp.* one employed at club *etc.* to evict undesirables (forcibly) —'**bouncing** *a.* vigorous, robust —'**bouncy** *a.* lively

bound¹ (bownd) *n./vt.* limit —'**boundary** *n.* —'**bounded** *a.* —'**boundless** *a.*

bound² (bownd) *vi./n.* spring, leap

bound³ (bownd) *a.* on a specified course, as *outward bound*

bound⁴ (bownd) *v.* 1. *pt./pp. of* BIND —*a.* 2. committed 3. certain 4. tied

bounden ('bowndən) *a.* morally obligatory (*obs. except in* **bounden duty**)

bounty ('bownti) *n.* 1. liberality 2. gift 3. premium —'**bounteous** *or* '**bountiful** *a.* liberal, generous

bouquet (bō'kā, bōō-) *n.* 1. bunch of flowers 2. fragrance of wine 3. compliment —**bouquet garni** (gär'nē) bunch of herbs tied together and used for flavoring stews *etc.* (*pl.* **bouquets garnis** (gär'nē))

bourbon ('bərbən) *n.* whiskey made from corn mash

bourgeois ('bōōərzhwä) *n./a. oft. disparaging* 1. middle class 2. smugly conventional (person) —**bourgeoi'sie** *n.* 1. middle classes 2. in Marxist thought, capitalist ruling class

bourn *or* **bourne** (börn) *n. obs.* 1. destination; goal 2. boundary

Bourse (bōōərs) *n.* stock exchange of continental Europe, *esp.* Paris

bout (bowt) *n.* 1. period of time spent doing something 2. contest, fight

boutique (bōō'tēk) *n.* small shop, *esp.* one selling clothes

bouzouki (bōō'zōōki) *n.* Greek stringed musical instrument resembling mandolin

bovine ('bōvīn) *a.* 1. of the ox or cow 2. oxlike 3. stolid, dull

bow¹ (bō) *n.* 1. weapon for shooting arrows 2.

implement for playing violin *etc.* 3. ornamental knot of ribbon *etc.* 4. bend, bent line 5. rainbow —*v.* 6. bend —**bow-legged** *a.* bandy —**bow tie** tie tied in bow —**bow window** window with outward curve

bow² (bow) *vi.* 1. bend body in respect, assent *etc.* 2. submit —*vt.* 3. bend downward 4. cause to stoop 5. crush —*n.* 6. bowing of head or body

bow³ (bow) *n.* 1. fore end of ship, prow 2. rower nearest bow —**bowline** ('bōlin) *n. Naut.* 1. line for controlling weather leech of square sail when vessel is close-hauled 2. knot for securing loop —**bowsprit** ('bōsprit) *n.* spar projecting from ship's bow

bowdlerize ('bowdlərīz) *vt.* expurgate

bowel ('bowəl) *n.* (*oft. pl.*) 1. part of intestine (*esp.* with reference to defecation) 2. inside of anything

bower ('bowər) *n.* 1. shady retreat 2. inner room —'**bowerbird** *n. Aust.* bird that hoards decorative but useless things

bowie knife ('bōōi, 'bōi) stout hunting knife with short hilt and guard for hand

bowl¹ (bōl) *n.* 1. round vessel, deep basin 2. drinking cup 3. hollow

bowl² (bōl) *n.* 1. composition or wooden ball —*pl.* 2. game for two, three, or four players in which such balls are rolled toward a smaller ball called a jack in which the object is to get as close as possible to the jack —*v.* 3. roll or throw (ball) in various ways —'**bowler** *n.* —'**bowling** *n.* 1. indoor game in which players roll solid composition balls down wooden alleys toward groups of ten wooden pins trying to knock all of the pins down in one or two attempts 2. game of bowls —**bowling alley** —**bowling green**

bowler ('bōlər) *n.* UK man's low-crowned stiff felt hat; derby

bowser ('bowzər) *n.* fuel tanker

box¹ (boks) *n.* 1. (wooden) container, usu. rectangular with lid 2. its contents 3. small enclosure 4. any boxlike cubicle, shelter or receptacle, *eg* letter box —*vt.* 5. put in box 6. confine —**box girder** girder that is hollow and square or rectangular in shape —**Boxing Day** UK first weekday after Christmas —**box lacrosse** C indoor lacrosse —**box lunch** packed lunch —**box number** number given to newspaper advertisements to which replies may be sent —**box office** 1. office at theater *etc.* where tickets are sold 2. public appeal of actor or production —**box pleat** double pleat made by folding under fabric on either side of it —**box score** printed score of baseball or basketball game recording names of players, their positions and activity for each phase of the game —**box seat** 1. seat in the box of a theater or grandstand 2. any favorable position for viewing something —**box social** fund-raising event at which box lunches are auctioned —**box turtle** *or* **tortoise** any of several N Amer. land turtles with ability to withdraw completely into shell —**box the compass** 1. name 32 points of compass in order 2. make complete turn

box² (boks) *v.* 1. fight with fists, *esp.* wearing padded gloves —*vt.* 2. strike —*n.* 3. blow —'**boxer** *n.* 1. one who boxes 2. breed of large dog resembling bulldog —'**boxing** *n.* art or profession of fighting with fists

box³ (boks) *n.* evergreen shrub used for hedges

boy (boi) *n.* 1. male child 2. young man —*interj.* 3. exclamation of surprise —'**boy-hood** *n.* —'**boyfriend** *n.* male friend with whom person is romantically or sexually involved —**Boy Scout** member of Boy Scouts

of America, an organization for boys aged 11 to 17, whose aim is to develop character, self-reliance and usefulness to others

boycott ('boikot) *vt.* 1. refuse to deal with or participate in —*n.* 2. act of boycotting

boysenberry ('boizənberi) *n.* 1. type of bramble, cross of loganberry, various blackberries and raspberries 2. edible fruit of this plant

BP 1. beautiful people 2. before the present 3. blood pressure 4. boiling point

BPD barrels per day

bpi 1. bits per inch 2. bytes per inch

BPOE Benevolent and Protective Order of Elks

BPW 1. Board of Public Works 2. Business and Professional Women's Clubs

Br *Chem.* bromine

br. 1. branch 2. bronze 3. brother

Br. 1. Britain 2. British

bra (brä) *n. short for* BRASSIERE

brace (brās) *n.* 1. tool for boring 2. clasp, clamp 3. pair, couple 4. strut, support —*pl.* 5. straps worn over shoulders to hold up trousers 6. dental appliance for straightening teeth —*vt.* 7. steady (oneself), as before a blow 8. support, make firm —'**bracelet** *n.* 1. ornament for the arm —*pl.* 2. *sl.* handcuffs —'**bracing** *a.* invigorating

brachiopod ('brākiəpod) *n.* any marine invertebrate animal having ciliated feeding organ and shell consisting of dorsal and ventral valves

bracken ('brakən) *n.* large fern

bracket ('brakit) *n.* 1. support for shelf *etc.* 2. group —*pl.* 3. marks [ ], ( ) used to enclose words *etc.* —*vt.* 4. enclose in brackets 5. connect

brackish ('brakish) *a.* (of water) slightly salty

bract (brakt) *n.* leaflike structure at base of flower stalk which may be large and brightly colored as in the poinsettia

brad (brad) *n.* small nail —'**bradawl** *n.* small boring tool

brae (brā) *n. Scot.* hill(side); slope

brag (brag) *vi.* 1. boast (-gg-) —*n.* 2. boastful talk —'**braggart** *n.*

braggadocio (bragə'dōshiō) *n.* 1. vain empty boasting 2. braggart (*pl.* -s)

Brahma ('brämə) *n.* 1. Hindu god, the Creator 2. *Hinduism* ultimate and impersonal divine reality of universe (*also* '**Brahman**)

Brahman ('brämən) *n.* 1. member of priestly Hindu caste (*also esp. (formerly)* '**Brahmin**) 2. breed of beef cattle

braid (brād) *vt.* 1. interweave 2. trim with braid —*n.* 3. length of anything interwoven or plaited 4. ornamental tape

Braille (brāl) *n.* system of printing for the blind, with arrangements of raised dots instead of letters

brain (brān) *n.* 1. mass of nerve tissue in head 2. intellect —*vt.* 3. kill by hitting on head —'**brainless** *a.* —'**brainy** *a.* —'**brain-child** *n.* invention —**brain death** irreversible cessation of respiration due to irreparable brain damage —'**brainpicking** *n.* act of getting information from another person —'**brainstorm** *vi.* 1. engage in conference with aim of problem-solving through spontaneous contribution of participants resulting in bright idea(s) —*n.* 2. the bright idea(s) so generated —**brain trust** unofficial and sometimes unacknowledged panel of experts and advisers, *esp.* to president —'**brainwash** *vt.* change, distort ideas or beliefs of —**brain wave** sudden, clever idea

braise (brāz) *vt.* cook slowly in small amount of fat and water usu. in covered pan

brake[1] (brāk) *n.* **1.** instrument for retarding motion of wheel on vehicle —*vt.* **2.** apply brake to —**brake horsepower** rate at which engine does work, expressed in horsepower, measured by a dynamometer —**brake shoe** curved metal casting to which brake lining is riveted in drum brake

brake[2] (brāk) *n.* **1.** fern **2.** bracken **3.** thicket **4.** brushwood

bramble ('brambəl) *n.* **1.** prickly shrub **2.** blackberry —**'brambly** *a.*

brambling ('brambling) *n.* an Old World finch

bran (bran) *n.* sifted husks of cereal grain

branch (brănch) *n.* **1.** limb of tree **2.** offshoot or subsidiary part of something larger or primary —*vi.* **3.** bear branches **4.** diverge **5.** spread —**branched** *a.* —**'branchy** *a.*

brand (brand) *n.* **1.** trademark **2.** class of goods **3.** particular kind, sort **4.** mark made by hot iron **5.** burning piece of wood **6.** sword **7.** mark of infamy —*vt.* **8.** burn with iron **9.** mark **10.** stigmatize —**brand-new** *a.* absolutely new

brandish ('brandish) *vt.* flourish, wave (weapon *etc.*)

brandy ('brandi) *n.* spirit distilled from wine —**brandy snap** crisp, sweet cookie

brant (brant) *n.* small goose of eastern N Amer. with black head, neck and breast which flies in irregular formation

brash (brash) *a.* bold, impudent

brass (bräs) *n.* **1.** alloy of copper and zinc **2.** group of brass wind instruments forming part of orchestra or band **3.** *inf.* money **4.** *inf.* (army) officers —*a.* **5.** made of brass —**'brassy** *a.* **1.** showy **2.** harsh —**brass hat** *inf.* top-ranking official, *esp.* military officer —**brass tacks** *inf.* basic realities; hard facts (*esp. in* **get down to brass tacks**)

brasserie (brasə'rē) *n.* restaurant specializing in food and beer

brassica ('brasikə) *n.* plant of cabbage family

brassiere (brə'zēər) *n.* woman's undergarment for supporting the breasts

brat (brat) *n. disparaging* child

bravado (brə'vädō) *n.* showy display of boldness

brave (brāv) *a.* **1.** bold, courageous **2.** splendid, fine —*n.* **3.** warrior, *esp.* Amerindian —*vt.* **4.** defy, meet boldly —**'bravely** *adv.* —**'bravery** *n.*

bravo (brä'vō) *interj.* well done

Bravo ('brävō) *n.* word used in communications for the letter b

bravura (brə'vyŏŏərə, -'vŏŏərə) *n.* **1.** display of boldness or daring **2.** *Mus.* passage requiring great spirit and skill by performer

brawl (brôl) *vi.* **1.** fight noisily —*n.* **2.** noisy disagreement or fight —**'brawler** *n.*

brawn (brôn) *n.* **1.** muscle **2.** strength —**'brawny** *a.* muscular

bray (brā) *n.* **1.** donkey's cry —*vi.* **2.** utter this sound **3.** give out harsh or loud sounds

braze[1] (brāz) *vt.* decorate with or make of brass

braze[2] (brāz) *vt.* make joint between (two metal surfaces) by fusing layer of high-melting solder between them —**'brazer** *n.*

brazen ('brāzən) *a.* **1.** of, like brass **2.** impudent, shameless —*vt.* **3.** (*usu. with* out) face, carry through with impudence —**'brazenness** *n.* effrontery

brazier[1] *or* **brasier** ('brāzhər) *n.* brass worker

brazier[2] *or* **brasier** ('brāzhər) *n.* pan for burning charcoal or coals

Brazil (brə'zil) *n.* country in South America

bounded east by the Atlantic and on its northwest and southern borders by all the countries of South America except Chile and Ecuador —**Bra'zilian** *n./a.* —**brazil nut 1.** tropical S Amer. tree producing globular capsules, each containing several triangular nuts **2.** its nut

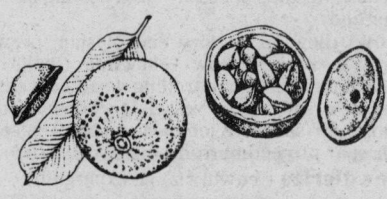

brazil nut

breach (brēch) *n.* **1.** break, opening **2.** breaking of rule, duty *etc.* **3.** quarrel —*vt.* **4.** make a gap in

bread (bred) *n.* **1.** food made of flour or meal and then baked **2.** food **3.** *sl.* money —**'breaded** *a.* coated with bread crumbs —**'breadbasket** *n.* **1.** stomach **2.** important cereal-producing region —**'breadfruit** *n.* breadlike fruit found in Pacific Islands —**'breadwinner** *n.* person supporting dependants by his earnings —**bread and butter** *inf.* means of support or subsistence; livelihood —**bread and circuses** palliative for the masses —**cast one's bread upon the waters** perform charitable deeds without expectation of return —**on the breadline** *inf.* living at subsistence level

breadth (bredth, bretth) *n.* **1.** extent across, width **2.** largeness of view, mind

break (brāk) *vt.* **1.** part by force **2.** shatter **3.** burst, destroy **4.** fail to observe **5.** disclose **6.** interrupt **7.** surpass **8.** make bankrupt **9.** relax **10.** mitigate **11.** accustom (horse) to being ridden **12.** decipher (code) —*vi.* **13.** become broken, shattered, divided **14.** open, appear **15.** come suddenly **16.** crack, give way **17.** part, fall out **18.** (of voice) change in tone, pitch (**broke**, **'broken**) —*n.* **19.** fracture **20.** gap **21.** opening **22.** separation **23.** interruption **24.** respite **25.** interval **26.** *inf.* opportunity **27.** dawn **28.** *Billiards* consecutive series of successful strokes **29.** *Boxing* separation after a clinch —**'breakable** *a.* —**'breakage** *n.* —**'breaker** *n.* **1.** one that breaks, *eg* electrical circuit breaker **2.** wave beating on rocks or shore —**'breakaway** *n.* loss or withdrawal of group of members from association, club *etc.* —**breakbone fever** dengue fever —**'breakdown** *n.* **1.** collapse, as nervous breakdown **2.** failure to function effectively **3.** analysis —**break-even point** when sales have covered costs in an enterprise —**breakfast** ('brekfəst) *n.* first meal of the day —**break-in** *n.* illegal entering of building, *esp.* by thieves —**'breakneck** *a.* dangerous —**break-out** *n.* escape, *esp.* from prison —**'breakthrough** *n.* important advance —**break-up** *n.* **1.** separation or disintegration **2.** in Canad. north, breaking up of ice on body of water that marks beginning of spring **3.** this season —**'breakwater** *n.* barrier to break force of waves —**break a leg** good luck expression made to performer —**break away** (*oft. with* from) **1.** leave hastily; escape **2.** withdraw, secede —**break camp** pack up camp site —**break (new) ground** pioneer —**break out 1.** begin suddenly **2.** make escape, *esp.* from prison **3.** (*with* in) (of skin) erupt (in rash *etc.*) —**break up 1.** (cause to) separate **2.** put an end to (a relationship) or (of a relationship) to come to an end **3.** dissolve or

cause to dissolve **4.** *sl.* lose control of emotions —**break wind** expel gas from anus

bream (brim, brēm) *n.* **1.** small game fish of eastern N Amer. ponds and streams **2.** European or Aust. marine food fish

breast (brest) *n.* **1.** human chest **2.** milk-secreting gland on chest of human female **3.** seat of the affections **4.** any protuberance —*vt.* **5.** face, oppose **6.** reach summit of —**'breastbone** *n.* thin flat structure of bone to which most of ribs are attached in front of chest (*also* **'sternum**) —**breast-feed** *v.* feed (baby) with milk from breast —**'breastplate** *n.* piece of armor covering chest —**'breaststroke** *n.* stroke in swimming —**'breastwork** *n.* temporary defensive work, usu. breast-high

breath (breth) *n.* **1.** air used by lungs **2.** life **3.** respiration **4.** slight breeze —**breathe** (brēth) *vi.* **1.** inhale and exhale air from lungs **2.** live **3.** pause, rest —*vt.* **4.** inhale and exhale **5.** utter softly, whisper —**'breather** ('brēðər) *n.* short rest —**'breathing** ('brēðing) *n.* —**'breathless** *a.* —**'breathtaking** *a.* causing awe or excitement

bred (bred) *pt./pp. of* BREED

breech (brēch) *n.* **1.** buttocks **2.** hinder part of anything, *esp.* gun —**breeches** ('brichiz, 'brē-) *pl.n.* trousers —**breech delivery** birth of baby with feet or buttocks appearing first —**breeches buoy** ring-shaped life buoy with support in form of pair of breeches —**'breechloader** *n.*

breed (brēd) *vt.* **1.** generate, bring forth, give rise to **2.** rear —*vi.* **3.** be produced **4.** be with young (**bred** *pt./pp.*) —*n.* **5.** offspring produced **6.** race, kind —**'breeder** *n.* —**'breeding** *n.* **1.** producing **2.** manners **3.** ancestry —**breeder reactor** nuclear reactor that produces more fissionable material than it consumes

breeze (brēz) *n.* gentle wind —**'breezily** *adv.* —**'breezy** *a.* **1.** windy **2.** jovial, lively **3.** casual

Bren gun (bren) air-cooled gas-operated sub-machine gun, used by Brit. in World War II

brethren ('bredhrin) *n., pl. of* BROTHER, *obs.* except in religious contexts

Breton ('bretən) *a.* **1.** of Brittany, its people or their Celtic language —*n.* **2.** native or inhabitant of Brittany

breviary ('brēvyəri) *n.* book of daily prayers of R.C. Church

brevity ('breviti) *n.* **1.** conciseness of expression **2.** short duration

brew (brŏŏ) *vt.* **1.** prepare (liquor, as beer) from malt *etc.* **2.** make (drink, as tea) by infusion **3.** plot, contrive —*vi.* **4.** be in preparation —*n.* **5.** beverage produced by brewing —**'brewer** *n.* —**'brewery** *n.* —**'brewing** *n.*

briar ('brīər) *n.* tobacco pipe made from root of brier

bribe (brīb) *n.* **1.** anything offered or given to someone to gain favor, influence —*vt.* **2.** influence by bribe —**'briber** *n.* —**'bribery** *n.*

bric-a-brac ('brikəbrak) *n.* miscellaneous small objects, used for ornament

brick (brik) *n.* **1.** oblong mass of hardened clay used in building —*vt.* **2.** build, block *etc.* with bricks —**'brickbat** *n.* **1.** piece of brick *etc.*, *esp.* used as weapon **2.** *inf.* blunt criticism —**brick cheese** semihard, whole-milk cheese produced in brick form with a yellowish-brown surface originating in Amer. —**'bricklayer** *n.*

bride (brīd) *n.* woman about to be, or just, married —**'bridal** *a.* of, relating to, a bride or wedding —**'bridegroom** *n.* man about to be, or just, married —**'bridesmaid** *n.*

bridge¹ (brij) n. 1. structure for crossing river etc. 2. something joining or supporting other parts 3. raised narrow platform on ship 4. upper part of nose 5. part of violin etc. supporting strings —vt. 6. make bridge over, span —**'bridgehead** n. advanced position established on enemy territory

bridge² (brij) n. card game of whist family in which winner of the auction (declarer) nominates the trump suit or no-trump and plays his partner's hand —**auction bridge** form of bridge in which tricks made are scored toward game —**Chicago bridge** four-deal contract bridge —**contract bridge** form of bridge in which only tricks bid are scored toward game (also **rubber bridge**) —**duplicate bridge** contract bridge played in competition

bridle ('brīd'l) n. 1. headgear of horse harness 2. curb —vt. 3. put bridle on 4. restrain —vi. 5. show resentment —**bridle path** path suitable for riding horses

Brie (brē) n. flat, round cheese with an edible crust made from fermented, mold-inoculated whole milk, originally from France

brief (brēf) a. 1. short in duration 2. concise 3. scanty —n. 4. summary of case for counsel's use 5. papal letter 6. instructions —pl. 7. underpants 8. panties —vt. 9. give instructions —**'briefly** adv. —**'briefness** n. —**'briefcase** n. hand case for carrying papers

brier ('brīər) n. plant, esp. rose, with prickly stem

brig (brig) n. two-masted, square-rigged ship

brigade (bri'gād) n. 1. U.S. army unit consisting of three or more battalions and usu. commanded by a colonel 2. organized band —**brigadier general** (brigə'dēər) commissioned officer in the army, air force or marine corps ranking above a colonel and below a major general whose insignia is one star

brigand ('brigənd) n. bandit, esp. member of gang in mountainous areas

brigantine ('brigəntēn) n. two-masted vessel with square-rigged foremast and fore-and-aft mainmast

bright (brīt) a. 1. shining 2. full of light 3. cheerful 4. clever —**'brighten** v. —**'brightly** adv. —**'brightness** n.

Bright's disease (brīts) chronic inflammation of kidneys; chronic nephritis

brill (bril) n. European food fish

brilliant ('brilyənt) a. 1. shining 2. sparkling 3. splendid 4. very clever 5. distinguished —**'brilliance** or **'brilliancy** n. —**'brilliantly** adv.

brilliantine ('brilyəntēn) n. 1. perfumed hair oil 2. light lustrous fabric resembling alpaca and with a cotton warp and worsted weft

brim (brim) n. margin, edge, esp. of river, cup, hat —**brim'ful** a. —**'brimless** a. —**'brimming** a.

brimstone ('brimstōn) n. sulfur

brindled ('brind'ld) a. spotted and streaked

brine (brīn) n. 1. salt water 2. pickle —**'briny** a. 1. very salty —n. 2. inf. the sea

bring (bring) vt. 1. fetch 2. carry with one 3. cause to come (**brought** pt./pp.)

brink (bringk) n. 1. edge of steep place 2. verge, margin —**'brinkmanship** n. practice of pressing dangerous situation, esp. in international affairs, to limit of safety in order to win advantage

briquette or **briquet** (bri'ket) n. block of compressed coal dust

bris (bris) or **brith** (brith) n. Judaism ceremony of circumcision

brisk (brisk) a. active, vigorous —**'briskly** adv. —**'briskness** n.

brisket ('briskit) n. meat from breast or lower chest of animal

brisling or **bristling** ('brizling, 'bris-) n. see SPRAT

bristle ('bris'l) n. 1. short stiff hair —vi. 2. stand erect 3. show temper —**'bristliness** n. —**'bristly** a.

Brit (brit) n. inf. British person

Brit. 1. Britain 2. British

Britannia (bri'taniə) n. 1. female warrior carrying trident, personifying Great Britain or British Empire 2. in ancient Roman Empire, southern part of Great Britain —**Britannia metal** alloy of tin with antimony and copper, used for decorative purposes and for bearings

Britannic (bri'tanik) a. of Britain; British (esp. in His or Her Britannic Majesty)

britches ('brichiz) pl.n. inf. trousers

British ('british) a. 1. of Great Britain or the British Commonwealth 2. relating to English language as spoken in Britain —n. 3. natives or inhabitants of Britain —**Briticism** ('britisizəm) n. word or idiom used in Great Britain but not in the U.S. —**'Briton** n. native or inhabitant of Britain —**British Antarctic Territory** colony consisting of the Graham Land peninsula, certain parts of the Antarctic mainland and the archipelagoes, the South Shetland Islands and South Orkney Islands —**British Indian Ocean Territory** colony comprising the Chagos Archipelago, lying 1180 miles (1899 km) northwest of Mauritius —**British thermal unit** amount of heat required to raise the temperature of one pound of water through one degree Fahrenheit (1055 joules)

brittle ('brit'l) a. 1. easily broken, fragile 2. curt, irritable —**'brittleness** n.

broach (brōch) vt. 1. pierce (cask) 2. open, begin —vi. 3. Naut. turn beam-on to wind and waves

broad (brôd) a. 1. wide, spacious, open 2. plain, obvious 3. coarse 4. general 5. tolerant 6. (of pronunciation) dialectal —**'broaden** v. —**'broadly** adv. —**'broadness** n. —**broad bean** 1. Eurasian plant cultivated for its large edible seeds 2. its seed —**'broadcast** v. 1. transmit (broadcast) by radio or television —vt. 2. make widely known 3. scatter, as seed —n. 4. radio or television program —**'broadcaster** n. —**'broadcloth** n. 1. fabric woven on wide loom 2. closely woven fabric of wool etc. with lustrous finish —**broad-minded** a. 1. tolerant 2. generous —**'broadsheet** n. 1. newspaper with large format 2. ballad or popular song printed on one side of sheet of paper, esp. in 16th-cent. England (also **broadside (ballad)**) —**'broadside** n. 1. discharge of all guns on one side of ship 2. strong (verbal) attack —**'broadsword** n. broad-bladed sword for cutting rather than stabbing

brocade (brō'kād) n. rich woven fabric with raised design

broccoli ('brokəli) n. type of cauliflower with densely packed green florets

brochure (brō'shōōr) n. pamphlet, booklet

brogue (brōg) n. 1. stout shoe with perforated wingtip band at toe 2. dialect, esp. Irish accent

broil¹ (broil) n. noisy quarrel

broil² (broil) vt. 1. cook over hot coals 2. cook under direct heat —vi. 3. be heated —**'broiler** n.

broke (brōk) v. 1. pt. of BREAK —a. 2. inf. penniless —**'broken** pp. of BREAK —**broken chord** arpeggio —**broken-down** a. 1. worn out, as by age; dilapidated 2. not in working order —**broken'hearted** a. overwhelmed by grief or disappointment

broker ('brōkər) n. 1. one employed to buy and sell for others 2. dealer —**'brokerage** n. payment to broker

bromeliad (brō'mēliad) n. any of various plants of the pineapple family, which have many forms and mainly warm habitats. Terrestrial forms are widely grown as house plants for their decorative flowers and leaves

bromide ('brōmīd) n. 1. chemical compound used in medicine and photography 2. commonplace or soothing remark —**bromide paper** fast-printing photographic printing paper

bromine ('brōmēn) n. Chem. nonmetallic element Symbol Br, at. wt. 79.9, at. no. 35 —**'bromic** a.

bronchus ('brongkəs) n. either of two main branches of trachea (pl. **bronchi** ('brongkī)) —**'bronchial** a. —**bronchiectasis** (brongki-'ektəsis) n. disease of the air passages marked by weakening and stretching of the walls of the bronchi —**bron'chitis** n. inflammation of bronchi —**'bronchoscope** n. tube with light at one end used to inspect the bronchi

bronco or **broncho** ('brongkō) n. half-tamed horse (pl. **-s**)

brontosaurus (brontə'sôrəs) or **brontosaur** ('brontəsôr) n. very large herbivorous dinosaur

Bronx (brongks) n. —**Bronx cheer** inf. rude sound made with lips, raspberry —**the Bronx** borough of New York City

bronze (bronz) n. 1. alloy of copper and tin —a. 2. made of, or colored like, bronze —vt. 3. give appearance of bronze to —**bronzed** a. 1. coated with bronze 2. sunburnt —**Bronze Age** era of bronze implements beginning in Europe from about 2000 B.C. to 500 B.C. ending with the coming of iron

brooch (brōch) n. ornamental pin or fastening

brood (brōōd) n. 1. family of young, esp. of birds 2. tribe, race —vi. 3. sit, as hen on eggs 4. meditate, fret —**'broody** a. moody, sullen

brook¹ (brōōk) n. small stream —**'brooklet** n.

brook² (brōōk) vt. put up with, endure, tolerate

Brooklyn ('brōōklin) n. borough of New York City

broom (brōōm, brŏŏm) n. 1. brush for sweeping 2. any shrub of the pea family with long slender branches, small leaves and usu. showy yellow or cream flowers —**'broomstick** n. handle of a broom

bros. or **Bros.** brothers

broth (broth) n. thick soup

brothel ('brothəl) n. house of prostitution

brother ('brudhər) n. 1. son of same parents as another person 2. one closely united with another —**'brotherhood** n. 1. relationship 2. fraternity, company —**'brotherliness** n. —**'brotherly** a. —**brother-in-law** n. 1. brother of husband or wife 2. husband of sister

brougham ('brōōəm, brŏŏm) n. 1. four-wheeled horse-drawn closed carriage having raised open driver's seat in front 2. obs. early electric automobile

brought (brôt) pt./pp. of BRING

brouhaha (brōō'hähä) n. loud confused noise; uproar

brow (brow) n. 1. ridge over eyes 2. forehead 3. eyebrow 4. edge of hill —**'browbeat** vt. bully

brown (brown) a. 1. of dark color inclining to red or yellow —n. 2. brown color, pigment or dye —v. **3.** make, become brown —**'brownie** n. **1.** in folklore, elf said to do helpful work at night, *esp.* household chores **2.** flat, nutty chocolate cake **3.** (B-) junior Girl Scout —**brown bagging 1.** bringing lunch to work from home **2.** carrying alcoholic drink to club or restaurant —**Brownie points** credit, *esp.* with superior —**brown rice** unpolished rice —**brown study** mood of deep absorption; reverie —**brown sugar** unrefined or partially refined sugar

browse (browz) *vi.* **1.** look (through book, articles for sale *etc.*) in a casual manner **2.** feed on shoots and leaves

brucellosis (broōsi'lōsis) *n.* bacterial disease occurring in goats, cattle, hogs and man (*also* **Malta fever, undulant fever, Mediterranean fever**)

Brücke ('brükə) *Ger.* —**die Brücke** (dē). group of German expressionist painters in Dresden about 1905

bruin ('broōin) *n.* name for a bear, used in children's tales *etc.*

bruise (broōz) *vt.* **1.** injure without breaking skin —*n.* **2.** contusion, discoloration caused by blow —**'bruiser** *n.* strong, tough person

brumby ('brumbi) *n.* Aust. wild horse

brunch (brunch) *n. inf.* breakfast and lunch combined

Brunei ('broōnī) *n.* country in the Indian Ocean on the northwest coast of Borneo bounded on all sides by Sarawak territory

brunette (broō'net) *n.* **1.** woman of dark complexion and hair —*a.* **2.** dark brown

brunt (brunt) *n.* **1.** shock of attack, chief stress **2.** first blow

brush (brush) *n.* **1.** device with bristles, hairs, wires *etc.* used for cleaning, painting *etc.* **2.** act, instance of brushing **3.** brief contact **4.** skirmish, fight **5.** bushy tail **6.** brushwood **7.** (carbon) device taking electric current from moving to stationary parts of generator *etc.* —*vt.* **8.** apply, remove, clean, with brush —*v.* **9.** touch lightly —**'brushoff** *n. inf.* **1.** dismissal **2.** refusal **3.** snub **4.** rebuff —**'brushwood** *n.* **1.** broken-off branches **2.** land covered with scrub —**brush up** *inf.* **1.** (*oft. with* on) refresh one's knowledge, memory of (subject) **2.** make person or oneself clean or neat as after journey

brusque (brusk) *a.* rough in manner, curt, blunt

Brussels sprout ('brusəlz) **1.** variety of cabbage, having stem with heads resembling tiny cabbages **2.** head of this plant, eaten as vegetable

brute (broōt) *n.* **1.** any animal except man **2.** crude, vicious person —*a.* **3.** animal **4.** sensual, stupid **5.** physical —**'brutal** *a.* —**bru'tality** *n.* —**'brutalize** *vt.* —**'brutally** *adv.* —**'brutish** *a.* bestial, gross

bryony ('brīəni) *n.* wild climbing hedge plant

bryophyllum (brīō'filəm) *n.* any of various kalanchoes grown as foliage plants that propagate new plants from leaves

bryophyte ('brīəfīt) *n.* plant phylum comprising mosses and liverworts —**bryophytic** (brīə'fitik) *a.*

B.Sc. Bachelor of Science

BSI British Standards Institution

Bt. Baronet

B.t.u. British thermal unit

bubble ('bubəl) *n.* **1.** hollow globe of liquid, blown out with air **2.** something insubstantial, not serious **3.** transparent dome —*vi.* **4.** rise in bubbles **5.** make gurgling sound —**'bubbly** *a.* —**bubble and squeak** UK dish of cabbage and potatoes fried together —**bubble gum** chewing gum that can be blown into bubbles

bubonic plague (byoō'bonik) acute infectious disease characterized by swellings and fever

buccaneer (bukə'nēər) *n.* pirate, sea rover —**bucca'neering** *n.*

Buchanan (byoō'kanən) *n.* **James.** the 15th President of the U.S. (1857-61)

buck¹ (buk) *n.* **1.** male deer, or other male animal **2.** act of bucking **3.** *sl.* dollar —*vt.* **4.** (of horse) attempt to throw rider by jumping upward *etc.* **5.** resist, oppose —**'buckshot** *n.* lead shot in shotgun shell —**'buckskin** *n.* **1.** skin of male deer **2.** strong grayish-yellow leather —*pl.* **3.** buckskin breeches —**'buckteeth** *pl.n.* projecting upper teeth

buck² (buk) *n. Poker* marker in jackpot to remind winner of some obligation when his turn to deal —**pass the buck** *inf.* shift blame or responsibility

buck³ (buk) *n.* small vaulting horse used in gymnastics

buckboard ('bukbōrd) *n.* open four-wheeled horse-drawn carriage with seat attached to flexible board between front and rear axles

bucket ('bukit) *n.* **1.** vessel, round with arched handle, for water *etc.* **2.** anything resembling this —*vt.* **3.** put, carry, in bucket —**'bucketful** *n.* —**bucket seat** seat with back shaped to occupier's figure

buckle ('bukəl) *n.* **1.** metal clasp for fastening belt, strap *etc.* —*vt.* **2.** fasten with buckle —*vi.* **3.** warp, bend —**'buckler** *n.* shield —**buckle down** start work

buckram ('bukrəm) *n.* coarse cloth stiffened with size

bucolic (byoō'kolik) *a.* rustic

bud (bud) *n.* **1.** embryo shoot, flower or flower cluster of plant —*vi.* **2.** begin to grow —*vt.* **3.** graft (-**dd**-)

Buddha

Buddha ('boōdə) *n.* **1.** the state of perfect enlightenment **2.** image of Siddhartha Gautama (about 563-483 B.C.), founder of Buddhism —**'Buddhism** *n.* system of ethics and philosophy based on belief that purpose of life is to attain enlightenment, which has manifestations in many forms, *eg* Lamaism, Zen *etc.* —**'Buddhist** *n./a.* —**Bud'dhistic** *a.*

buddleia ('budliə) *n.* shrub with mauve flower spikes

buddy ('budi) *n.* companion, friend —**buddy system** arrangement where two persons are mutually responsible for each other, *esp.* in potentially dangerous situations

budge (buj) *v.* move, stir

budgerigar ('bujərigär) *n.* small Aust. parakeet (*also* **'budgie**)

budget ('bujit) *n.* **1.** annual financial statement **2.** plan of systematic spending —*vi.* **3.** prepare financial statement —*v.* **4.** plan financially

Buerger's disease ('bərgərz) circulatory disease of unknown cause which gradually closes off blood vessels in the arms and legs (*also* **thromboangiitis obliterans**)

buff¹ (buf) *n.* **1.** leather made from buffalo or ox hide **2.** light yellow color **3.** bare skin **4.** polishing pad —*vt.* **5.** polish

buff² (buf) *n. inf.* expert on some subject

buffalo ('bufəlō) *n.* **1.** type of ox found in Asia and S Afr. **2.** domesticated ox of Asia (*also* **water buffalo**) **3.** N Amer. bison (*pl.* **-es, -s, -lo**) —*vt. sl.* **4.** intimidate **5.** mystify (-**loed, -loing**)

buffer ('bufər) *n.* contrivance to lessen shock of concussion —**buffer state** small, usu. neutral state between two rival powers —**buffer zone** neutral territory between two hostile powers

buffet¹ (bu'fā, boō-) *n.* **1.** refreshment bar **2.** meal at which guests serve themselves **3.** sideboard

buffet² ('bufit) *n.* **1.** blow, slap **2.** misfortune —*vt.* **3.** strike with blows **4.** contend against —**'buffeting** *n.*

buffoon (bə'foōn) *n.* **1.** clown **2.** fool —**buf'foonery** *n.* clowning

bug (bug) *n.* **1.** any small insect **2.** *inf.* germ or virus infection **3.** *inf.* concealed listening device —*vt. inf.* **4.** install secret microphone *etc.* in **5.** irritate (-**gg**-)

bugbear ('bugbāər) *n.* **1.** object of needless terror **2.** nuisance

buggy ('bugi) *n.* **1.** light horse-drawn carriage having two or four wheels **2.** *see* **baby carriage** at BABY

bugle ('byoōgəl) *n.* brass military musical instrument shaped like a trumpet without valves —**'bugler** *n.*

buhl (boōl) *n. see* BOULLE

build (bild) *v.* **1.** make, construct, by putting together parts or materials (**built** *pt./pp.*) —*n.* **2.** make, form —**'builder** *n.* —**'building** *n.* —**build-up** *n.* **1.** progressive increase in number *etc.* **2.** extravagant publicity or praise **3.** *Mil.* process of attaining required strength of forces and equipment —**built-in** *a.* **1.** made as integral part **2.** essential; inherent —**built-up** *a.* having many buildings —**build up 1.** construct gradually **2.** increase, *esp.* by degrees **3.** improve health of **4.** prepare for climax, as in story

bulb (bulb) *n.* **1.** modified bud with fleshy scales usu. formed underground sometimes used as food **2.** any plant with fleshy rootstock *eg* corms, tubers and rhizomes **3.** globe surrounding filament of electric light —**'bulbous** *a.*

bulbul ('boōlboōl) *n.* any of several songbirds of Afr. and southern Asia

Bulgaria (bul'gariə, -'ger-) *n.* country in Europe bounded in the north by Romania, east by the Black Sea, south by Turkey and Greece and west by Yugoslavia —**Bul'garian** *n./a.* **1.** (native or inhabitant) of Bulgaria —*n.* **2.** language of Bulgaria which is a Balto-Slavic language and is written in the Cyrillic alphabet

Bulgaria

bulge (bulj) *n.* **1.** swelling, protuberance **2.** temporary increase —*vi.* **3.** swell out —**'bulginess** *n.* —**'bulgy** *a.*

bulk (bulk) *n.* **1.** size, volume **2.** greater part **3.** cargo —*vi.* **4.** be of weight or importance —**'bulkiness** *n.* —**'bulking** *n.* process for fluffing up surface of man-made yarns to give extra absorbency, lightness and springiness —**'bulky** *a.*

bulkhead ('bulk-hed) *n.* **1.** interior partition in ship, aircraft or vehicle **2.** retaining wall at harbor **3.** frame with sloping doors giving outside access to cellar —**bulkhead door** such a door opening on to a stairway

bull[1] (bool) *n.* **1.** male of cattle **2.** male of various other animals **3.** *Fin.* someone who believes the market will rise —**'bullock** *n.* castrated bull —**'bulldog** *n.* thickset breed of dog —**'bulldoze** *vt.* —**'bulldozer** *n.* powerful tractor with blade for excavating *etc.* —**'bullfight** *n.* spectacle pitting matador against the bull in an arena for the diversion of an audience —**'bullfighter** *n.* —**'bullfighting** *n.* —**'bullfinch** *n.* **1.** European finch, male of which has bright red throat and breast **2.** any of similar finches —**bullheaded** *a.* blindly obstinate; stupid —**'bullpen** *n.* *Baseball* area where pitchers warm up before game —**'bullring** *n.* arena for bullfighting —**bull's-eye** *n.* middle part of target —**bull terrier** breed of terrier developed by crossing bulldog with English terrier

bull[2] (bool) *n.* papal edict

bull[3] (bool) *n.* *sl.* nonsense

bull[4] bulletin

bullet ('boolit) *n.* projectile discharged from rifle, pistol *etc.*

bulletin ('boolitin) *n.* official report

bullion ('boolyən) *n.* **1.** gold or silver in bars or ingots **2.** garment decoration in gold or silver threads

bully ('booli) *n.* **1.** one who hurts, persecutes or intimidates weaker people —*vt.* **2.** intimidate, overawe **3.** ill-treat ('bullied, 'bullying) —**bully beef** corned beef

bully-off *n.* *Hockey* method of starting play, in which two players strike sticks together and against ground three times before trying to hit ball (*also* 'bully) —**bully off** *Hockey* start play with bully-off (*also* 'bully)

bulrush ('boolrush) *n.* tall reedlike marsh plant with brown velvety spike

bulwark ('boolwərk) *n.* **1.** rampart **2.** any defense or means of security **3.** raised side of ship **4.** breakwater

bum (bum) *sl.* *n.* **1.** loafer, scrounger —*vt.* **2.** get by scrounging (-mm-) —*a.* **3.** useless

bumble ('bumbəl) *vi.* speak or proceed clumsily —**'bumbler** *n.*

bumblebee ('bumbəlbē) *n.* large hairy social bee

bump (bump) *n.* **1.** heavy blow, dull in sound **2.** swelling caused by blow **3.** protuberance **4.** sudden movement —*vt.* **5.** strike or push against —**'bumper** *n.* **1.** horizontal bar at front and rear of automobile to protect against damage **2.** full glass —*a.* **3.** full, abundant —**bump off** *sl.* murder

bumpkin ('bumpkin) *n.* rustic

bumptious ('bumpshəs) *a.* offensively self-assertive

bun (bun) *n.* **1.** small, round cake **2.** round knot of hair

bunch (bunch) *n.* **1.** number of things tied or growing together **2.** cluster **3.** tuft, knot **4.** group, party —*vt.* **5.** put together in bunch —*vi.* **6.** gather together —**'bunchy** *a.* —**like (someone** *or* **something) a bunch** be enthusiastic about (someone *or* something)

bundle ('bundəl) *n.* **1.** package **2.** number of things tied together **3.** *sl.* lot of money —*vt.* **4.** tie in bundle **5.** send (off) without ceremony

bung (bung) *n.* **1.** stopper for cask, large cork —*vt.* **2.** stop up, seal, close **3.** *inf.* throw, sling —**'bunghole** *n.*

bungalow ('bunggəlō) *n.* one-storied house

bungle ('bunggəl) *vt.* **1.** do badly from lack of skill, botch —*vi.* **2.** act clumsily, awkwardly —*n.* **3.** blunder, muddle —**'bungled** *a.* —**'bungler** *n.* —**'bungling** *a./n.*

bunion ('bunyən) *n.* deformity of the great toe

bunk[1] (bungk) *n.* narrow, shelflike bed —**bunk bed** one of pair of beds constructed one above the other

bunk[2] (bungk) *n.* bunkum

bunker ('bungkər) *n.* **1.** large storage container for oil, coal *etc.* **2.** sandy hollow on golf course **3.** (military) underground defensive position

bunkum *or* **buncombe** ('bungkəm) *n.* nonsensical talk

bunny ('buni) *n.* *inf.* rabbit

Bunsen burner ('bunsən) gas burner, producing great heat, used for chemical experiments

bunt (bunt) *v.* attempt to hit (baseball) with shortened grip so that infielder cannot reach it in time

bunting[1] ('bunting) *n.* material for flags

bunting[2] ('bunting) *n.* bird with short, stout bill

buoy (booi) *n.* **1.** floating marker anchored in sea **2.** lifebuoy —*vt.* **3.** mark with buoy **4.** keep from sinking **5.** support —**buoyancy** ('boiənsi) *n.* —**buoyant** ('boiənt) *a.*

bur[1] (bər) *n.* **1.** rough prickly envelope of fruit **2.** plant bearing burs

bur[2] bureau

Burberry ('bərbəri) *n.* **1.** trade name for a light raincoat made of water-resistant fabric (*pl.* **-ries**) **2.** plaid pattern used for lining, scarves, hats and luggage

burble ('bərbəl) *vi.* **1.** gurgle, as stream or baby **2.** talk idly

burden[1] ('bərdən) *n.* **1.** load, weight **2.** cargo **3.** anything difficult to bear —*vt.* **4.** load, encumber —**'burdensome** *a.*

burden[2] ('bərdən) *n.* **1.** chorus of a song **2.** chief theme

burdock ('bərdok) *n.* plant with prickly burs

bureau ('byŏŏrō) *n.* **1.** writing desk **2.** office **3.** government department (*pl.* **-s, -reaux** (-rōz)) —**bureaucracy** (byŏŏ'rokrəsi) *n.* **1.** government by officials **2.** body of officials —**'bureaucrat** *n.* —**bureau'cratic** *a.*

burette *or* **buret** (byŏŏ'ret) *n.* graduated glass tube with stopcock on one end, for dispensing known volumes of fluids

burgee (bər'jē, 'bərjē) *n.* small nautical flag

burgeon ('bərjən) *vi.* **1.** bud **2.** develop rapidly

burgess ('bərjis) *n.* inhabitant of borough, *esp.* citizen with full municipal rights

burgh ('bərō) *n.* Scottish borough —**burgher** ('bərgər) *n.* citizen

burglar ('bərglər) *n.* one who enters building to commit crime, *esp.* theft —**'burglary** *n.* —**'burgle** *or* **'burglarize** *vt.*

burgundy ('bərgəndi) *n.* name of various red or white wines produced in the Burgundy region of France

burin ('byŏŏrin) *n.* chisel of tempered steel used for engraving metal, wood or marble

Burkina-Faso (bər'kēnə'fasō) *n.* country in Africa bounded north and west by Mali, east by Niger and south by Benin, Togo, Ghana and the Ivory Coast

burlap ('bərlap) *n.* coarse plain-weave fabric of jute or hemp

burlesque (bər'lesk) *n.* **1.** (artistic) caricature **2.** ludicrous imitation —*vt.* **3.** caricature

burly ('bərli) *a.* sturdy, stout, robust —**'burliness** *n.*

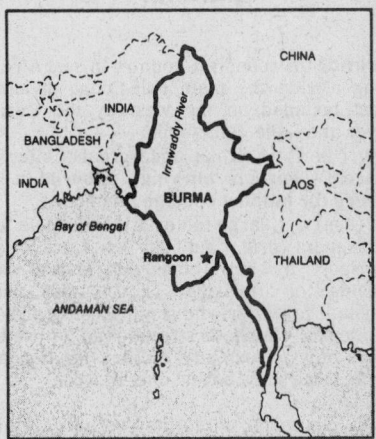

Burma

Burma ('bərmə) *n.* country in Asia bounded east by China, Laos and Thailand, west by the Indian Ocean, Bangladesh and India —**'Burman** *n./a.* (denoting) native or inhabitant of Burma —**Bur'mese** *n.* the language of Burma which is a member of the Sino-Tibetan family

burn (bərn) *vt.* **1.** destroy or injure by fire —*vi.* **2.** be on fire (*lit.* or *fig.*) **3.** be consumed by fire (**burned** *or* **burnt** *pt./pp.*) —*n.* **4.** wound caused by action of heat, caustic chemicals or electricity —**'burner** *n.* **1.** part of stove *etc.* that produces flame **2.** apparatus for burning fuel, refuse *etc.* —**'burning** *a.* —**burning glass** convex lens for concentrating sun's rays to produce fire

burnish ('bərnish) *vt.* **1.** make bright by rubbing, polish —*n.* **2.** gloss, luster —**'burnisher** *n.*

burnoose *or* **burnous** (bər'nŏŏs) *n.* long circular cloak with hood, worn *esp.* by Arabs

burnt (bərnt) *v.* **1.** *pt./pp.* of BURN —*a.* **2.** affected as if by burning; charred

burp (bərp) *n./v.* *inf.* (*esp.* of baby) belch

burr[1] (bər) *n.* soft trilling sound given to letter *r* in some dialects

burr[2] (bər) *n.* rough edge left after cutting, drilling *etc.*

burro ('bŏŏrō) *n.* donkey (*pl.* **-s**)

burrow ('burō) *n.* **1.** hole dug by rabbit *etc.* —*v.* **2.** make holes in (ground) —*vt.* **3.** bore **4.** conceal

bursar ('bərsər) *n.* official managing finances of college, school *etc.*

burst (bərst) *vi.* **1.** fly asunder **2.** break into pieces **3.** rend **4.** break suddenly into some expression of feeling —*vt.* **5.** shatter, break violently (**burst** *pt./pp.*) —*n.* **6.** bursting **7.** explosion **8.** outbreak **9.** spurt

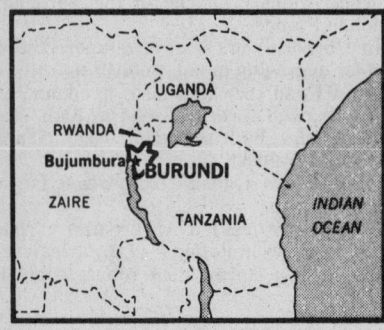

Burundi

Burundi (bə'rōōndi) *n.* country in east Africa lying astride the main Nile-Congo dividing crest bounded on the west by the Ruzizi River and Lake Tanganyika

bury ('beri) *vt.* **1.** put underground, inter **2.** conceal (**buried, 'burying**) —'**burial** *n./a.* —**bury the hatchet** become reconciled

bus (bus) *n.* **1.** large motor-driven vehicle for passengers (*orig.* omnibus) —*v.* **2.** travel or transport by bus (**bused** *or* **bussed** *pt.,* '**busing** *or* '**bussing** *pr.p.*) —**bus boy** assistant to waiter who removes dirty dishes to kitchen —**bus lane** strip of road for use by buses only —**busman's holiday** *inf.* holiday spent doing same as one does at work

bus. business

busby ('buzbi) *n.* tall fur hat worn by certain soldiers

bush[1] (bŏŏsh) *n.* **1.** shrub **2.** woodland, thicket **3. A, SA** *etc.* uncleared country, backwoods, interior —**bushed** *a.* **1.** tired out **2. A** lost, bewildered —'**bushy** *a.* shaggy —'**bushbaby** *n.* tree-living, nocturnal Afr. animal —**bush fire** widespread destructive fire in the bush —**bush-league** *a.* mediocre of its kind —**bush line C** airline operating in bush country —'**Bushman** *n.* member of hunting and gathering people of southern Afr. —**bush pilot** —**bush telegraph** *inf.* means of spreading rumor *etc.*

bush[2] (bŏŏsh) *n.* **1.** thin metal sleeve or tubular lining serving as bearing —*v.* **2.** fit bush to (casing *etc.*)

bushel ('bŏŏshəl) *n.* unit of dry capacity equal to 4 pecks: 2150.42 cubic inches or 35.239 liters

business ('biznis) *n.* **1.** profession, occupation **2.** commercial or industrial establishment **3.** commerce, trade **4.** responsibility, affair, matter **5.** work —'**businesslike** *a.* —'**businessman** *n.* person engaged in business, *esp.* as owner or executive ('**businesswoman** *fem.*)

busker ('buskər) *n.* one who makes money by singing, dancing *etc.* in the street —**busk** *vi.*

buskin ('buskin) *n.* **1.** formerly, sandal-like covering for foot and leg, reaching calf **2.** thick-soled laced half boot worn *esp.* by actors of ancient Greece **3.** (*usu. with* the) tragic drama

bust[1] (bust) *n.* **1.** sculpture of head and shoulders of human body **2.** woman's breasts

bust[2] (bust) *inf. v.* **1.** burst **2.** make, become bankrupt —*vt.* **3.** raid **4.** arrest —*a.* **5.** broken **6.** bankrupt —*n.* **7.** police raid or arrest

bustard ('bustərd) *n.* any of several swift-running birds of Afr. related to cranes

bustle[1] ('busəl) *vi.* **1.** be noisily busy, active —*n.* **2.** fuss, commotion

bustle[2] ('busəl) *n. Hist.* pad worn by ladies to support back of skirt

busy ('bizi) *a.* **1.** actively employed **2.** full of activity —*vt.* **3.** occupy ('**busied, 'busying**) —'**busily** *adv.* —'**busybody** *n.* meddler —'**busywork** *n.* inessential activity performed to keep one occupied

but (but; *unstressed* bət) *prep./conj.* **1.** without **2.** except **3.** only **4.** yet **5.** still **6.** besides

butane ('byōōtān) *n.* gas used for fuel

butch (bŏŏch) *a./n. sl.* **1.** markedly or aggressively masculine (person) **2.** (woman) assuming male role in lesbian relationship

butcher ('bŏŏchər) *n.* **1.** one who kills animals for food, or sells meat **2.** ruthless or brutal murderer —*vt.* **3.** slaughter, murder **4.** spoil (work) —'**butchery** *n.*

butler ('butlər) *n.* chief male servant

butt[1] (but) *n.* **1.** the thick end **2.** target **3.** object of ridicule **4.** bottom or unused end of anything —*v.* **5.** lie, be placed end-on to

butt[2] (but) *vt.* **1.** strike with head **2.** push —*n.* **3.** blow with head, as of sheep —**butt in** interfere, meddle

butt[3] (but) *n.* large cask

butter ('butər) *n.* **1.** fatty substance made from cream by churning —*vt.* **2.** spread with butter —**butter bean** lima bean with large pale edible seeds —'**butterfingered** *a.* —'**butterfingers** *n. inf.* person who drops things inadvertently —'**buttermilk** *n.* milk that remains after churning —'**butterscotch** *n.* kind of hard, brittle toffee or flavoring —**butter up** *inf.* flatter

buttercup ('butərkup) *n.* wild plant with glossy, yellow flowers

butterfly ('butərflī) *n.* **1.** insect with large wings **2.** inconstant person **3.** stroke in swimming —**have butterflies in the stomach** feel nervous

buttock ('butək) *n.* (*usu. pl.*) rump, protruding hinder part

button ('butən) *n.* **1.** knob, stud for fastening —*vt.* **2.** fasten with buttons —'**buttonhole** *n.* **1.** slit in garment to pass button through as fastening —*vt.* **2.** detain (reluctant listener) in conversation

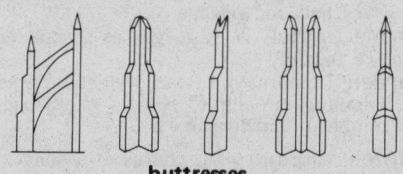

buttresses

buttress ('butris) *n.* **1.** structure to support wall **2.** prop —*vt.* **3.** support (wall) with buttress

buxom ('buksəm) *a.* **1.** full of health, plump, gay **2.** large-breasted

buy (bī) *vt.* **1.** get by payment, purchase **2.** bribe (**bought** *pt./pp.*) —'**buyer** *n.*

buzz (buz) *vi.* **1.** make humming sound —*n.* **2.** humming sound of bees **3.** *inf.* telephone call —'**buzzer** *n.* any apparatus that makes buzzing sound —**buzz saw** circular saw —'**buzzword** *n.* catch phrase used to impress —**buzz off** *sl.* go away

buzzard ('buzərd) *n.* bird of prey of hawk family

BV Blessed Virgin

BW 1. bacteriological warfare **2.** biological warfare **3.** black-and-white **4.** bread and water

bwana ('bwänə) *n.* in E Afr., master, oft. used as form of address corresponding to *sir*

B.W.I. British West Indies

BWOC big woman on campus

bx box

BX base exchange

by[1] (bī) *prep.* **1.** near **2.** along **3.** across **4.** past **5.** during **6.** not later than **7.** through use or agency of **8.** in units of —*adv.* **9.** near **10.** away, aside **11.** past —**by and by** soon, in the future —**by and large 1.** on the whole **2.** speaking generally —**come by** obtain

by[2] billion years

by- *or* **bye-** (*comb. form*) subsidiary, incidental, out-of-the-way, near, as in *bypath, by-product, bystander*

bye (bī) *n. Sport* situation where player, team advances in a tournament without playing a given round

bygone ('bīgon) *a.* **1.** past, former —*n.* **2.** (*oft. pl.*) past occurrence **3.** small antique

bylaw *or* **bye-law** ('bīlō) *n.* standing rule adopted by organization to govern its internal affairs

by-line *n.* line under title of newspaper or magazine article giving author's name

BYO bring your own

BYOB bring your own bottle

byp bypass

bypass ('bīpäs) *n.* **1.** road around a town **2.** secondary channel connected to a main passage —**bypass surgery** operation on blood vessels of heart

by-play *n.* diversion, action apart from main action of play

byre (bīər) *n.* cowshed

bystander ('bīstandər) *n.* person present but not involved; spectator

byte (bīt) *n. Comp.* sequence of bits processed as single unit of information

byway ('bīwā) *n.* **1.** seldom-traveled side road **2.** area, field of study *etc.* that is of secondary importance

byword ('bīwərd) *n.* well-known name, saying

Byzantine ('bizəntēn, 'bī-; -tīn; bi'zan-, bī-) *a.* **1.** of the eastern Roman Empire at Byzantium (later Constantinople, now Istanbul) **2.** (*oft.* **b-**) complicated, devious, underhand **3.** of style of art and architecture of which high points were in early 6th cent. and 9th cent. **4.** of the eastern Catholic churches in communion with the Patriarch of Constantinople

Cc

c *or* **C** (sē) *n.* **1.** third letter of English alphabet **2.** speech sound represented by this letter, usu. either as in *cigar* or as in *case* **3.** third in series, *esp.* third highest grade in examination **4.** something shaped like C (*pl.* **c's, C's** *or* **Cs**)

C 1. *Mus.* first degree of major scale containing no sharps or flats (**C major**); major or minor key having this note as tonic; time signature denoting four quarter notes to bar (*see also* ALLA BREVE (sense 2), **common time** *at* COMMON) **2.** *Chem.* carbon **3.** capacitance **4.** heat capacity **5.** cold (water) **6.** *Phys.* compliance **7.** Celsius **8.** centigrade **9.** Conservative **10.** century, as in *C20* **11.** Roman numeral, 100

c. 1. carat **2.** cent **3.** circa **4.** copyright

Ca *Chem.* calcium

CA California

ca. circa

C.A. chartered accountant

cab (kab) *n.* **1.** taxi **2.** driver's enclosed compartment on locomotive, truck *etc.* —**'cabman** *or* **'cabby** *n.* taxi driver

CAB Civil Aeronautics Board

cabal (kə'bal) *n.* **1.** small group of intriguers **2.** secret plot

cabala, cabbala, *or* **cabbalah** (kə'bälə) *n.* **1.** ancient Jewish mystical tradition **2.** any secret or occult doctrine —**'cabalist** *n.* —**caba'listic** *a.*

cabaret (kabə'rā, 'kabərā) *n.* floor show at nightclub or restaurant

cabbage ('kabij) *n.* vegetable with large head of green or reddish leaves

caber ('kābər) *n.* heavy wooden pole tossed as trial of strength at Highland games

Cabernet ('kabərnā) *n.* red table wine

cabin ('kabin) *n.* **1.** hut, shed **2.** small room, *esp.* in ship —*vt.* **3.** cramp, confine —**cabin boy** boy who waits on officers and passengers of ship —**cabin cruiser** power boat with cabin, bunks *etc.*

cabinet ('kabinit) *n.* **1.** piece of furniture with drawers or shelves **2.** outer case of television, radio *etc.* **3.** (*oft.* **C-**) body of advisers to a head of state **4.** in parliamentary system, committee of politicians governing country **5.** *obs.* small room —**cabinetmaker** *n.* craftsman who makes fine furniture

cable ('kābəl) *n.* **1.** strong rope **2.** wire or bundle of wires conveying electric power, telegraph signals *etc.* **3.** message sent by this **4.** nautical unit of measurement (100-120 fathoms) —*v.* **5.** telegraph by cable —**cable car** passenger car on cable railway, drawn by strong cable operated by motor —**'cablegram** *n.* cabled message

cabochon ('kabəshon) *n.* **1.** convex oval or round decoration used on furniture and articles made in metal **2.** unfaceted, highly polished gemstone in this form

caboodle (kə'bōōdəl) *n. inf.* entity, group or lot —**the whole (kit and) caboodle** the whole lot

caboose (kə'bōōs) *n.* **1.** ship's galley **2.** freight-train car for use of train crew **3.** one that brings up the rear

cabriolet (kabriō'lā) *n.* early type of hansom cab

cacao (kə'kow, -'kāō) *n.* tropical tree from the seeds of which chocolate and cocoa are made

Cacciocavallo (kachiŏkə'valō) *n.* a hard, whole-cream cheese with a salty, smoky flavor orig. from Italy

cachalot ('kashəlot) *n.* sperm whale

cache (kash) *n.* **1.** secret hiding place **2.** store of food *etc.*

cachet (ka'shā) *n.* **1.** mark, stamp **2.** mark of authenticity **3.** prestige, distinction

cachinnate ('kakināt) *vi.* laugh loudly —**cachin'nation** *n.*

cachou ('kashōō, ka'shōō) *n.* **1.** lozenge eaten to sweeten breath **2.** substance obtained from certain tropical plants and used in medicine *etc.* (*also* **'catechu, cutch**)

cackle ('kakəl) *vi.* **1.** make chattering noise, as hen —*n.* **2.** cackling noise or laughter **3.** empty chatter —**'cackler** *n.*

caco- (*comb. form*) bad, unpleasant, incorrect, as in *cacophony*

cacophony (kə'kofəni) *n.* **1.** disagreeable sound **2.** discord of sounds —**ca'cophonous** *a.*

cactus ('kaktəs) *n.* spiny succulent plant (*pl.* **-es, cacti** ('kaktī))

cad (kad) *n.* dishonorable, unchivalrous person —**'caddish** *a.*

cadaver (kə'davər) *n.* corpse —**ca'daverous** *a.* **1.** corpselike **2.** sickly-looking **3.** gaunt

caddie *or* **caddy** ('kadı) *n.* **1.** golfer's attendant **2.** small cart used by golfers to carry clubs (*also* **caddie cart**) —*vi.* **3.** act as caddie

caddis fly ('kadis) small mothlike insect having two pairs of hairy wings —**caddis worm** *or* **'caddis** *n.* aquatic larva of caddis fly, which constructs protective case around itself made of silk *etc.* (*also* **'caseworm, 'strawworm**)

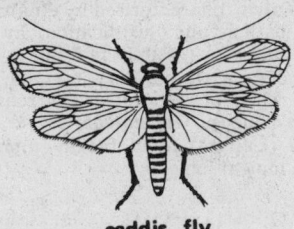

caddis fly

caddy ('kadi) *n.* small box for tea

cadence ('kādəns) *or* **cadency** *n.* fall or modulation of voice in music or verse

cadenza (kə'denzə) *n. Mus.* elaborate passage for solo instrument or singer

cadet (kə'det) *n.* youth in training, *esp.* for officer status in armed forces

cadge (kaj) *v.* get (food, money *etc.*) by sponging or begging —**'cadger** *n.* sponger

cadi *or* **kadi** ('kādi, 'kädi) *n.* judge in Muslim community (*pl.* **-s**)

cadmium ('kadmiəm) *n. Chem.* metallic element *Symbol* Cd, at. wt. 112.4, at. no. 48

cadre ('kadri) *n.* **1.** nucleus or framework, *esp.* of indoctrinated personnel **2.** member of a cadre, *esp.* in China

caduceus (kə'dyōōsiəs, -'dōō-) *n.* **1.** *Class. myth.* winged staff entwined with two serpents carried by Hermes (Mercury) **2.** insignia resembling this, used as emblem of medical profession (*pl.* **-cei** (-siī))

Caenozoic (sēnō'zōik) *see* CENOZOIC

Caerphilly (kär'fili) *n.* creamy white mild-flavored cheese

caesura *or* **cesura** (si'zhōōrə) *n.* **1.** in modern prosody, pause, *esp.* for sense, usu. near middle of verse line **2.** in classical prosody, break between words within metrical foot (*pl.* **-s, -rae** (-rē))

café (ka'fā) *n.* small or inexpensive restaurant serving light refreshments —**cafe'teria** *n.* restaurant designed for self-service

caff (kaf) *n. sl.* café

caffeine ('kafēn) *n.* naturally occurring chemical found in the coffee bean, tea leaf, cocoa bean and kola nut used in high dose to stimulate the nervous system

caftan ('kaftan) *n.* ankle-length garment with long loose sleeves based on open-sleeved overtunic worn since Biblical times in the Levant

cage (kāj) *n.* **1.** enclosure, box with bars or wires, *esp.* for keeping animals or birds **2.** place of confinement **3.** enclosed platform of lift, *esp.* in mine —*vt.* **4.** put in cage, confine —**'cagey** *or* **'cagy** *a.* wary, not communicative

cahoots (kə'hōōts) *pl.n. sl.* partnership (*esp. in* **in cahoots with**)

caiman *or* **cayman** ('kāmən) *n.* any of several tropical Amer. crocodilians related to alligator

cairn (kāərn) *n.* heap of stones, *esp.* as monument or landmark —**cairn terrier** small rough-haired terrier orig. from Scotland

cairngorm ('kāərngörm) *n.* yellow or brownish-colored gem

caisson ('kāson) *n.* **1.** chamber for working under water **2.** apparatus for lifting vessel out of water **3.** ammunition wagon

caitiff ('kātif) *obs. n.* **1.** mean, despicable fellow —*a.* **2.** base, mean

cajole (kə'jōl) *vt.* persuade by flattery, wheedle —**ca'jolement** *n.* —**ca'joler** *n.* —**ca'jolery** *n.*

Cajun *or* **Cajan** ('kājən) *n.* **1.** inhabitant of Louisiana descended from 18th-cent. French-Canadian immigrants **2.** the dialect spoken by Cajuns

cake (kāk) *n.* **1.** baked, sweetened, breadlike food **2.** compact mass —*vt.* **3.** make into cake —*vi.* **4.** harden (as of mud) —**'cakewalk** *n.* **1.** dance orig. performed by Amer. Negroes for prize of cake **2.** piece of music for this dance

cal. 1. calendar **2.** caliber **3.** (small) calorie

Cal. (large) Calorie

calabash ('kaləbash) *n.* **1.** tree with large hard-shelled fruit **2.** this fruit **3.** drinking, cooking vessel made from gourd

calaboose ('kaləbōōs) *n. inf.* prison

calamine ('kaləmīn) *n.* mixture of zinc oxide

and ferric oxide used in soothing lotion or ointment

calamity (kə'lamiti) n. 1. great misfortune 2. deep distress, disaster —**ca'lamitous** a.

calceolaria (kalsiə'leriə) n. Amer. plant with speckled, slipper-shaped flowers (also **slipperwort**)

calces ('kalsēz) n., pl. of CALX

calcicole ('kalsikōl) n. plant requiring a chalky soil

calciferol (kal'sifərol) n. fat-soluble steroid, found esp. in fish-liver oils and used in treatment of rickets (also **vitamin D₂**)

calcifuge ('kalsifyōōj) n. plant requiring an acid soil

calcium ('kalsiəm) n. Chem. metallic element Symbol Ca, at. wt. 40.1, at. no. 20 —**calcareous** (kal'kariəs, -'ker-) a. containing lime —**cal'ciferous** a. producing salts of calcium, esp. calcium carbonate —**calcify** v. convert, be converted, to lime —**calcine** vt. 1. reduce to quicklime 2. burn to ashes —**calcite** n. crystalline calcium carbonate —**calcium carbonate** white crystalline salt occurring in limestone, chalk etc.

calculate ('kalkyōōlāt) vt. 1. estimate 2. compute —vi. 3. make reckonings —**calculable** a. —**calculated** a. 1. undertaken after considering likelihood of success 2. premeditated —**calculating** a. 1. able to perform calculations 2. shrewd, designing, scheming —**calcu'lation** n. —**calculator** n. electronic device for making calculations —**calculus** n. 1. Math. any system of operations involving the use of symbols, esp. infinitesimal calculus, a system of mathematical analysis 2. stone in body formed by mineral deposit around an organic core (pl. **calculi** ('kalkyōōlī))

caldron ('köldrən) n. kettle or pot used for boiling

calèche (Fr. ka'lesh) n. C horse-drawn carriage for taking tourists around

Caledonian (kali'dōniən) a. 1. relating to Scotland —n. 2. Lit. native of Scotland

calendar ('kalindər) n. 1. table of months and days in the year 2. list of events, documents, register —vt. 3. enter in list 4. index

calender ('kalindər) n. 1. machine in which paper or cloth is smoothed by passing between rollers —vt. 2. subject to such process

calends ('kalindz) pl.n. first day of each month in ancient Roman calendar

calendula (ka'lenjələ) n. marigold

calf¹ (käf) n. 1. young of cow and of other animals 2. leather made of calf's skin (pl. **calves**) —**calve** vi. give birth to calf —**calf love** infatuation of adolescent for member of opposite sex

calf² (käf) n. fleshy back part of leg below knee (pl. **calves**)

caliber ('kalibər) n. 1. size of bore of gun 2. capacity, character —**calibrate** vt. mark (scale of measuring instrument) so that readings can be made in appropriate units —**cali'bration** n.

calices ('kalisēz) n., pl. of CALIX

calico ('kalikō) n. cheap cotton cloth

California (kali'förniə) n. Pacific state of the U.S., admitted to the Union in 1850. Abbrev.: **Calif., CA** (with ZIP code)

californium (kali'förniəm) n. Chem. transuranic element Symbol Cf, at. wt. 251, at. no. 98

caliper ('kalipər) n. 1. metal or plastic splint for leg —pl. 2. measuring implement with two adjustable legs used to determine distance on a surface 3. instrument for measuring diameters

caliph, calif or **khalif** ('kālif, 'kal-) n. Islam title of successors of Mohammed as rulers of Islamic world —**'caliphate, 'califate** or **'khalifate** n. office or reign of caliph

calix ('kāliks, 'ka-) n. cup; chalice (pl. **'calices**)

calk¹ (kök) vt. see CAULK

calk² (kök) or **calkin** ('kökin) n. 1. metal projection on horse's shoe to prevent slipping —vt. 2. provide with calks

call (köl) vt. 1. speak loudly to attract attention of 2. summon 3. (oft. with up) telephone 4. name —vi. 5. shout 6. pay visit —n. 7. shout 8. animal's cry 9. visit 10. inner urge, summons, as to be priest etc. 11. need, demand —**'caller** n. —**'calling** n. vocation, profession —**call box** kiosk for public telephone—**call girl** prostitute with whom appointments are made by telephone —**call up** 1. summon to serve in army 2. imagine

calligraphy (kə'ligrəfi) n. handwriting, penmanship —**calli'graphic** a.

callisthenics or **calisthenics** (kalis'theniks) pl.n. light gymnastic exercises —**callis'thenic** or **calis'thenic** a.

callosity (kə'lositi) n. 1. hardheartedness 2. callus

callous ('kaləs) a. hardened, unfeeling —**'callously** adv. —**'callousness** n.

callow ('kalō) a. inexperienced, immature

callus ('kaləs) n. area of thick, hardened skin

calm (käm, kälm) a. 1. still 2. quiet 3. tranquil —n. 4. stillness 5. tranquillity 6. absence of wind —v. 7. become, make, still or quiet —**'calmly** adv. —**'calmness** n.

calomel ('kaləmel, -məl) n. colorless, tasteless powder used medicinally, esp. as cathartic

calorie or **calory** ('kaləri) n. 1. unit of heat 2. unit of energy obtained from foods —**ca'loric** a. 1. of heat or calories —n. 2. obs. hypothetical elastic fluid, embodiment of heat —**calo'rific** a. heat-making —**calo'rimeter** n.

calumet ('kalyōōmet) n. long, ornamented tobacco pipe of Amerindians used at ceremonies, esp. as token of peace

calumny ('kaləmni) n. slander, false accusation —**ca'lumniate** vt. —**columni'ation** n. —**ca'lumniator** n. —**ca'lumnious** a.

Calvary ('kalvəri) n. place outside walls of Jerusalem where Jesus was crucified (also **Gol'gotha**)

calves (kävz) n., pl. of CALF¹, CALF²

Calvinism ('kalvinizəm) n. theological system of Calvin, characterized by emphasis on predestination and justification by faith —**'Calvinist** n./a. —**Calvin'istic(al)** a.

calx (kalks) n. 1. powdery metallic oxide formed when ore or mineral is roasted 2. calcium oxide (pl. **-es, 'calces**)

calypso (kə'lipsō) n. W Indian improvised song on topical subject

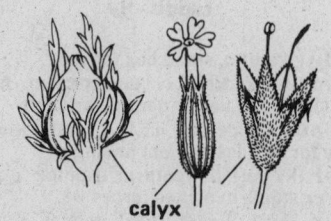

calyx

calyx ('kāliks, 'kaliks) n. covering of bud (pl. **-es, calyces** ('kalisēz, 'kāli-))

cam (kam) n. device to change rotary to reciprocating motion —**'camshaft** n. in

motoring, rotating shaft to which cams are fixed to lift valves

camaraderie (kamə'rädəri) n. spirit of comradeship, trust

camber ('kambər) n. 1. convexity on upper surface of road, bridge etc. 2. curvature of aircraft wing

cambium ('kambiəm) n. layer of cells between the xylem and phloem that retains the power of growth

Cambodia (kam'bōdiə) n. former name of KAMPUCHEA

Cambrian ('kambriən) a. 1. of first 100 million years of Paleozoic era 2. of Wales —n. 3. Cambrian period or rock system 4. Welshman

cambric ('kāmbrik) n. fine white linen or cotton cloth

came (kām) pt. of COME

camel ('kaməl) n. animal of Asia and Afr., with humped back, used as beast of burden —**camel's hair** or **'camelhair** n. 1. hair of camel, used in rugs etc. 2. soft cloth made of this hair, usu. tan in color —a. 3. (of painter's brush) made from tail hairs of squirrels

camellia (kə'mēlyə) n. ornamental shrub

camelopard (kə'meləpärd) n. obs. giraffe

Camembert ('kaməmbãor) n. a rich, soft cheese from cow's milk with an edible crust, orig. from France

cameo ('kamiō) n. 1. medallion, brooch etc. with profile head or design carved in relief 2. single brief scene or appearance in film etc. by (well-known) actor

camera ('kamərə) n. apparatus used to take photographs —**'cameraman** n. photographer, esp. for television or cinema —**camera obscura** (əb'skyōōrə) darkened chamber in which views of surrounding country are shown on sheet by means of lenses —**in camera** (of legal proceedings etc.) conducted in private

Cameroon (kamə'rōōn) n. country in Africa bounded west by the Gulf of Guinea, northwest by Nigeria, east by Chad and the Central African Republic, and south by Congo, Gabon and Equatorial Guinea

camisole ('kamisōl) n. underbodice

camomile ('kaməmīl) n. see CHAMOMILE

camouflage ('kaməfläzh) n. 1. disguise, means of deceiving enemy observation, eg by paint, screen —vt. 2. disguise

camp (kamp) n. 1. (place for) tents of hikers, army etc. 2. cabins etc. for temporary accommodation 3. group supporting political party etc. 4. SA field, pasture —a. inf. 5. homosexual 6. consciously artificial —vi. 7. form or lodge in camp —**'camper** n. 1. person who lives or temporarily stays in tent etc. 2. vehicle equipped for camping out —**'camping** n. —**Camp Fire Girl** member of national organization for girls aged 7 to 18 —**camp follower** 1. civilian, esp. prostitute, who unofficially provides services to military personnel 2. nonmember who is sympathetic to group etc.

campaign (kam'pān) n. 1. series of coordinated activities for some purpose, eg political or military campaign —vi. 2. serve in campaign —**cam'paigner** n.

campanile (kampə'nēli) n. esp. in Italy, bell tower, not usu. attached to another building

campanology (kampə'noləji) n. art of ringing bells

campanula (kam'panyōōlə) n. plant with blue or white bell-shaped flowers

camphor ('kamfər) n. crystalline highly odorous substance from the wood and bark of the camphor tree used as antiseptic and irritant —**camphorated oil** liniment consisting of camphor and peanut oil, used as irritant —**camphorated opium tincture** paregoric —**camphor tree** evergreen Asian tree which yields camphor

campion ('kampiən) *n.* white or pink wild flower

campus ('kampəs) *n.* grounds and buildings of school, college or university

can[1] (kan; *unstressed* kən) *vi.* **1.** be able to **2.** have the power to **3.** be allowed to (**could** *pt.*)

can[2] (kan) *n.* **1.** container, usu. metal, for liquids, foods —*vt.* **2.** put in can (**-nn-**) —**canned** *a.* **1.** preserved in can **2.** (of music, programs *etc.*) previously recorded —'**cannery** *n.* factory where food is canned

Can. 1. Canada **2.** Canadian

Canada ('kanədə) *n.* country in N Amer. bounded south by U.S., west by Pacific Ocean, north by Arctic Ocean and east by Atlantic Ocean —**Canadian** (kə'nādiən) *n./a.* (native) of Canada —**Ca'nadianize** *v.* make or become Canadian —**Canada balsam 1.** yellow transparent resin obtained from balsam fir **2.** balsam fir —**Canada Day** Jul. 1st, anniversary of day in 1867 when Canad. received dominion status —**Canada goose** large grayish-brown N Amer. goose —**Canada lynx** medium-sized feline of northern N Amer. with long, loose, mottled gray body —**Canadian Shield** wide area of rock extending over most of E and Central Canad.: rich in minerals (*also* **Laurentian Shield**)

canaille (kə'nī) *Fr.* masses; mob; rabble

canal (kə'nal) *n.* **1.** artificial watercourse **2.** duct in body —**canali'zation** *n.* —'**canalize** *vt.* **1.** convert into canal **2.** direct (thoughts, energies *etc.*) into one channel

canapé ('kanəpi, -pā) *n.* small piece of toast *etc.* with savory topping

canard (kə'närd) *n.* **1.** false report; rumor, hoax **2.** aircraft in which tailplane is mounted in front of wing

canary (kə'nāəri) *n.* small usu. yellow finch, noted for singing

canasta (kə'nastə) *n.* form of rummy played with two standard 52-card decks and four jokers for four players (two partnerships) with variations for two players, three players and six players using three decks and six jokers

cancan ('kankan) *n.* high-kicking (orig. Fr. music-hall) dance

cancel ('kansəl) *vt.* **1.** cross out **2.** annul **3.** call off —**cancel'lation** *n.*

cancer ('kansər) *n.* abnormal and uncontrolled growth of the cells of living organisms —'**cancerous** *a.*

Cancer ('kansər) *n.* **1.** (crab) 4th sign of zodiac, operative c. Jun. 21st–Jul. 21st **2.** constellation —**tropic of Cancer** parallel of latitude 23½° N of the equator

candela (kan'dēlə, -'delə) *n.* basic SI unit of luminous intensity

candid ('kandid) *a.* **1.** frank, open **2.** impartial —'**candidly** *adv.* —'**candidness** *or* '**candor** *n.* frankness —**candid camera** small camera used to take informal photographs of people

candidate ('kandidāt) *n.* **1.** one who seeks office, appointment *etc.* **2.** person taking examination or test —'**candidacy** *or* '**candidature** *n.*

candle ('kandəl) *n.* **1.** stick of wax with wick **2.** light —**candelabrum** (kandi'labrəm) *n.* large, branched candle holder (*pl.* **-bra** (-brə)) —'**candlepower** *n.* unit for measuring light —'**candlestick** *n.* —'**candlewick** *n.* cotton fabric with tufted surface

Candlemas ('kandəlməs) *n. Christianity* Feb. 2nd, Feast of Purification of Virgin Mary and presentation of Christ in Temple

candy ('kandi) *n.* **1.** crystallized sugar **2.** confectionery in general —*vt.* **3.** preserve with sugar —*vi.* **4.** become encrusted with sugar ('**candied**, '**candying**) —'**candied** *a.*

candytuft ('kandituft) *n.* garden plant with clusters of white, pink or purple flowers

cane (kān) *n.* **1.** stem of small palm or large grass **2.** walking stick —*vt.* **3.** beat with cane —**cane sugar 1.** sucrose obtained from sugar cane **2.** *see* SUCROSE

canine ('kānīn) *a.* like, pert. to, dog —**canine tooth** one of four sharp, pointed teeth, two in each jaw

canister ('kanistər) *n.* container, *usu.* of metal, *esp.* for storing dry food

canker ('kangkər) *n.* **1.** eating sore **2.** thing that eats away, destroys, corrupts —*vt.* **3.** infect, corrupt —*vi.* **4.** decay —'**cankered** *or* '**cankerous** *a.* —'**cankerworm** *n.*

canna ('kanə) *n.* tropical flowering plant

cannabis ('kanəbis) *n.* **1.** hemp plant **2.** drug derived from this

cannel coal ('kanəl) dull coal burning with smoky luminous flame

cannelloni (kani'lōni) *pl.n.* tubular pieces of pasta filled with meat *etc.*

cannibal ('kanibəl) *n.* **1.** one who eats human flesh —*a.* **2.** relating to this practice —'**cannibalism** *n.* —**cannibal'istic** *a.* —'**cannibalize** *vt.* use parts from (one machine *etc.*) to repair another

cannon[1] ('kanən) *n.* large gun (*pl.* **-s,** '**cannon**) —**canno'nade** *n./vt.* attack with cannon —'**cannonball** *n.* —**cannon bone** horse's leg bone —**cannon fodder** men regarded as expendable in war because they are part of huge army

cannon[2] ('kanən) *n.* **1.** billiard stroke, hitting both object balls with one's own —*vi.* **2.** make this stroke **3.** rebound, collide

cannot ('kanot, ka'not) *negative form of* CAN[1]

canoe (kə'nōō) *n.* **1.** light narrow boat with pointed ends propelled by paddling —*vi.* **2.** travel in canoe —*vt.* **3.** transport in canoe —**ca'noeist** *n.*

canon[1] ('kanən) *n.* **1.** law or rule, *esp.* of church **2.** standard **3.** body of books accepted as genuine **4.** list of saints —**canoni'zation** *n.* —'**canonize** *vt.* enroll in list of saints

canon[2] ('kanən) *n.* church dignitary, member of cathedral chapter —**ca'nonical** *a.* —**ca'nonicals** *pl.n.* vestments worn by clergy when officiating —**canon'istic** *a.* —**canonical hour 1.** *R.C.Ch.* one of seven prayer times appointed for each day by canon law **2.** *Ch. of England* any time at which marriages may lawfully be celebrated —**canon law** body of laws enacted by supreme authorities of Christian Church

canopy ('kanəpi) *n.* **1.** covering over throne, bed *etc.* **2.** any overhanging shelter —*vt.* **3.** cover with canopy (**-opied, -opying**)

can't (känt) *v.* cannot

cant[1] (kant) *n.* **1.** hypocritical speech **2.** whining **3.** language of a sect **4.** technical jargon **5.** slang, *esp.* of thieves —*vi.* **6.** use cant

cant[2] (kant) *vt.* **1.** tilt, slope **2.** bevel —*n.* **3.** inclination from vertical or horizontal plane

Cant. *Bible* Canticle of Canticles

cantabile (kan'tabili) *Mus. a./adv.* **1.** singing —*n.* **2.** piece or passage performed in this way

cantaloupe *or* **cantaloup** ('kantəlōp) *n.* variety of muskmelon with netted rind and orange flesh

cantankerous (kan'tangkərəs) *a.* ill-natured, quarrelsome

cantata (kan'tätə) *n.* choral work like, but shorter than, oratorio

canteen (kan'tēn) *n.* **1.** flask for carrying liquid used by hikers *etc.* **2.** small shop in military camp

canter ('kantər) *n.* **1.** 3-beat gait slower than gallop —*v.* **2.** move at, make to canter —**at a canter** with ease

Canterbury bell ('kantərberi) cultivated campanula

cantharides (kan'tharidēz) *pl.n.* diuretic and urogenital stimulant prepared from dried bodies of Spanish fly (*sing.* '**cantharis**) (*also* **Spanish fly**)

canticle ('kantikəl) *n.* short hymn —**Canticle of Canticles** *Bible* Song of Solomon in the Douay Version of the O.T.

cantilever ('kantilēvər, -levər) *n.* beam, girder *etc.* fixed at one end only

canto ('kantō) *n.* division of poem (*pl.* **-s**)

canton ('kantən, -ton) *n.* division of country, *esp.* Swiss federal state

Cantonese (kantə'nēz) *n.* **1.** dialect of Chinese spoken in Canton **2.** native or inhabitant of Canton (*pl.* **-ese**) —*a.* **3.** of Canton or Chinese language spoken there

cantonment (kən'tōnmənt) *n.* quarters for troops

cantor ('kantər) *n.* **1.** *Judaism* leading singer in synagogue liturgy **2.** *Christianity* leader of singing in church choir

Cantrece (kan'trēs) *n.* trade name for self-crimping nylon yarn used for stockings and panty hose

Canuck (kə'nuk) *n./a.* C *inf.* Canadian

canvas ('kanvəs) *n.* **1.** coarse cloth used for sails, painting on *etc.* **2.** sails of ship **3.** picture —**under canvas** in tents

canvass ('kanvəs) *vt.* **1.** solicit votes, contributions *etc.* from **2.** discuss, examine —*n.* **3.** solicitation

canyon ('kanyən) *n.* deep gorge

caoutchouc ('kowchōōk) *n. see* RUBBER[1] (sense 1)

cap (kap) *n.* **1.** covering for head **2.** lid, top or other covering —*vt.* **3.** put cap on **4.** outdo **5.** select for a team (**-pp-**)

CAP Civil Air Patrol

cap. 1. capacity **2.** capital **3.** capitalize **4.** capital letter

capable ('kāpəbəl) *a.* **1.** able, gifted, competent **2.** having the capacity, power —**capa'bility** *n.*

capacity (kə'pasiti) *n.* **1.** power of holding or grasping **2.** room **3.** volume **4.** character **5.** ability, power of mind —**capacious** (kə'pāshəs) *a.* roomy —**ca'pacitance** *n.* (measure of) ability of system to store electric charge —**ca'pacitor** *n.*

caparison (kə'parisən) *n.* **1.** ornamental covering, equipment for horse —*vt.* **2.** adorn thus

CAPD continuous ambulatory peritoneal dialysis

cape[1] (kāp) *n.* covering for shoulders

cape[2] (kāp) *n.* point of land running into sea, headland —**Cape Colored SA** *see* **Colored** (sense 2) *at* COLOR —**Cape pigeon** pied petrel of southern oceans —**Cape salmon SA** geelbek —**Cape sparrow** common S Afr. bird

caper[1] ('kāpər) *n.* **1.** skip **2.** frolic **3.** escapade —*vi.* **4.** skip, dance

caper[2] ('kāpər) *n.* pickled flower bud of Sicilian shrub

capercaillie *or* **capercailzie** (kapər'kālyi) *n.* large black old world grouse

Cape Verde (vərd) country in the Atlantic Ocean 385 miles west-northwest of Senegal consisting of 10 islands and 5 islets

capillary ('kapileri) *a.* **1.** hairlike **2.** of capillarity —*n.* **3.** extremely small blood vessel connecting arteries with veins and the point of interaction between the blood and body tissues —**capil'larity** n. phenomenon caused by surface tension and resulting in elevation or depression of surface of liquid in contact with solid (*also* **capillary action**)

capital ('kapitəl) n. **1.** chief town **2.** money, stock, funds **3.** large-sized letter **4.** headpiece of column —a. **5.** involving or punishable by death **6.** serious **7.** chief, leading **8.** excellent —'**capitalism** n. economic system which is based on private ownership of industry —'**capitalist** n. **1.** owner of capital **2.** supporter of capitalism —a. **3.** run by, possessing, capital —'**capitalize** vt. **1.** convert into capital —vi. **2.** (*with* on) turn to advantage —'**capitally** adv. —**capital gain** amount by which selling price of financial asset exceeds cost —**capital levy** tax on capital or property as contrasted with tax on income —**capital punishment** punishment of death for crime; death penalty —**capital stock 1.** par value of total share capital a company is authorized to issue **2.** total physical capital existing in economy at any time

capitation (kapi'tāshən) n. **1.** tax or grant per head **2.** census

Capitol Hill ('kapitəl) the legislative branch of the U.S. government

capitulate (kə'pichəlāt) vi. surrender on terms, give in —**capitu'lation** n.

capo ('kapō) n. device fitted across all strings of guitar etc. to raise pitch of each string simultaneously (pl. -**s**) (*also* **capo tasto** ('tastō))

capon ('kāpən) n. castrated cock fowl fattened for eating —'**caponize** vt.

cappuccino (kapōō'chēnō) n. coffee with steamed milk

caprice (kə'prēs) n. whim —**capricious** (kə'prishəs) a. —**capriciousness** (kə'prishəs-nis) n.

Capricorn ('kaprikörn) n. **1.** (sea-goat) 10th sign of zodiac, operative c. Dec. 21st–Jan. 19th **2.** constellation —**tropic of Capricorn** parallel of latitude 23½° S of the equator

capriole ('kapriōl) *Dressage* n. **1.** upward but not forward leap made by horse with all four feet off ground —vi. **2.** perform capriole

caps. **1.** capital letters **2.** capsule

capsicum ('kapsikəm) n. tropical vegetable with mild peppery flavor, sweet pepper

capsize (kap'sīz) vt. **1.** (of boat) upset —vi. **2.** be overturned —**cap'sizal** n.

capstan ('kapstən) n. machine to wind cable, *esp.* to hoist anchor

capsule ('kapsyəl, -sōōl) n. **1.** gelatin case for dose of medicine or drug **2.** any small enclosed area or container **3.** seed vessel of plant —'**capsulize** vt. **1.** state in highly condensed form **2.** enclose in capsule

capsules

Capt. Captain

captain ('kaptin) n. **1.** commander of vessel or company of soldiers **2.** leader, chief —vt. **3.** be captain of

caption ('kapshən) n. heading, title of article, picture etc.

captious ('kapshəs) a. ready to find fault, critical, peevish —'**captiously** adv. —'**captiousness** n.

captive ('kaptiv) n. **1.** prisoner —a. **2.** taken, imprisoned **3.** unable to avoid speeches etc. —'**captivate** vt. fascinate —'**captivating** a. delightful —**cap'tivity** n.

capture ('kapchər) vt. **1.** seize, make prisoner —n. **2.** seizure, taking —'**captor** n.

Capuchin ('kapyəshin, 'kapə-) n. friar belonging to branch of Franciscan Order

capybara (kapi'barə) n. largest rodent, found in S Amer.

car (kär) n. **1.** self-propelled road vehicle **2.** passenger compartment, as in cable car **3.** railroad carriage of specified type —**car park** esp. UK area, building where vehicles may be left for a time —'**carport** n. shelter for automobile usu. consisting of roof supported by posts —'**carsickness** n. see **motion sickness** at MOTION

carabineer or **carabinier** (karəbi'nēər) n. see **carbineer** at CARBINE

caracal ('karəkal) n. **1.** lynxlike feline mammal inhabiting deserts of N Afr. and S Asia, having smooth coat of reddish fur **2.** this fur

caracole ('karəkōl) or **caracol** ('karəkol) *Dressage* n. **1.** half turn to right or left —vi. **2.** execute half turn

caracul ('karəkul) n. see KARAKUL

carafe (kə'raf, -'räf) n. glass water bottle for table, decanter

caramel ('karəməl) n. **1.** burnt sugar for cooking **2.** type of confectionery

carapace ('karəpās) n. thick hard shield that covers part of body of tortoise etc.

carat ('karət) n. see KARAT

caravan ('karəvan) n. group of vehicles traveling together in single file —**caravanserai** (karə'vansərī) or **caravansary** (karə-'vansərī) n. in some Eastern countries, large inn enclosing courtyard, providing accommodation for caravans

caravel ('karəvel) n. two- or three-masted sailing ship in 15th and 16th centuries

caraway ('karəwā) n. plant of which the seeds are used as spice in cakes etc.

carbide ('kärbīd) n. compound of carbon with an element, esp. calcium carbide

carbine ('kärbēn, -bīn) n. short rifle —**carbineer** (kärbi'nēər), **carabi'neer** or **carabi'nier** n. formerly, soldier equipped with carbine

carbo- or before vowel **carb-** (comb. form) carbon, as in carbohydrate, carbonate

carbohydrate (kärbō'hīdrāt) n. any of large group of compounds containing carbon, hydrogen and oxygen, esp. sugars and starches as components of food

carbolic acid (kär'bolik) disinfectant derived from coal tar —**carbolated** a. containing carbolic acid

carbon ('kärbən) n. *Chem.* nonmetallic element occurring in nature as diamond and graphite and a constituent of all organic matter *Symbol* C, at. wt. 12.0, at. no. 6 —**carbo'naceous** a. of, resembling or containing carbon —'**carbonate** n. salt of carbonic acid —**car'bonic** a. —**carbo'niferous** a. —'**carbonize** v. —**carbon black** finely divided carbon produced by incomplete combustion of natural gas or petroleum: used in pigments and ink —**carbon dating** technique for determining age of wood etc., based on its content of radioisotope ^{14}C acquired from atmosphere when it formed part of living plant —**carbon dioxide** colorless gas exhaled in respiration of animals —**carbonic acid 1.** carbon dioxide **2.** compound formed by carbon dioxide and water —**carbon monoxide** colorless, odorless poisonous gas formed when carbon com-

pounds burn in insufficient air —**carbon paper** paper coated with a dark, waxy pigment, used for duplicating written or typed matter, producing **carbon copy** —**carbon tetrachloride** colorless volatile nonflammable liquid made from chlorine and used as solvent etc.

Carboniferous (kärbə'nifərəs) a. **1.** of fifth period of Paleozoic era during which coal measures were formed —n. **2.** Carboniferous period or rock system divided into **Upper Carboniferous** and **Lower Carboniferous** periods

Carborundum (kärbə'rundəm) n. trade name for various abrasives

carboy ('kärboi) n. glass, plastic or metal container for liquids of about 5 to 15 gallons in capacity usu. in protective cushion

carbuncle ('kärbungkəl) n. **1.** inflamed ulcer, boil or tumor **2.** fiery-red precious stone

carburetor ('kärbyərātər, -bə-) n. device for vaporizing and mixing fuel with air in internal-combustion engine

carcass ('kärkəs) n. **1.** dead animal body **2.** skeleton **3.** basic structure of object

carcinoma (kärsi'nōmə) n. a malignant tumor —**car'cinogen** n. substance producing cancer —'**carcinoid** a. —**carcinoid syndrome** disease caused by cancerous tumor of glandular tissue

card[1] (kärd) n. **1.** thick, stiff paper **2.** piece of this giving identification etc. **3.** illustrated card sending greetings etc. **4.** one of the 52 playing cards making up a deck **5.** inf. a character, eccentric —pl. **6.** any card game —'**cardboard** n. thin, stiff board made of paper pulp —**card index** index in which each entry is made on separate card —'**cardsharp** or '**cardsharper** n. professional card player who cheats

card[2] (kärd) n. **1.** instrument for combing wool etc. —vt. **2.** comb —'**carder** n.

cardamom ('kärdəməm) n. **1.** tropical Asian plant with large hairy leaves **2.** seeds of this plant, used esp. as spice or condiment

cardiac ('kärdiak) a. **1.** pert. to the heart —n. **2.** person with heart disorder —'**cardiogram** n. tracing made by cardiograph —'**cardiograph** n. instrument which records movements of the heart —**cardioid** a. heart-shaped —**cardi'ologist** n. —**cardi'ology** n. branch of medical science concerned with heart and its diseases

cardigan ('kärdigən) n. knitted jacket

cardinal ('kärdinəl) a. **1.** chief, principal —n. **2.** highest rank, next to the Pope in R.C. Church **3.** bright red N Amer. bunting (*also* '**redbird**) —'**cardinalate** n. —**cardinal numbers** 1, 2, 3, etc. —**cardinal points** north, south, east and west

cardio- or before vowel **cardi-** (comb. form) heart, as in cardiogram

cardiolipin test (kärdiō'lipin) Wassermann test

care (kāər) vi. **1.** be anxious —n. **2.** attention **3.** pains, heed **4.** charge, protection **5.** anxiety **6.** caution —'**carefree** a. —'**careful** a. —'**carefully** adv. —'**carefulness** n. —'**careless** a. —'**carelessness** n. —'**caretaker** n. **1.** person in charge of premises —a. **2.** temporary, interim —'**careworn** a. showing signs of care, stress etc. —**care for 1.** have regard or liking for **2.** look after **3.** be disposed to

careen (kə'rēn) vt. **1.** lay (ship) over on her side for cleaning and repair —vi. **2.** keel over **3.** sway dangerously

career (kə'rēər) n. **1.** course through life **2.** profession **3.** rapid• motion —vi. **4.** run or move at full speed —ca'**reerist** *n*. person who seeks to advance his career by any possible means

caress (kə'res) *vt*. 1. fondle, embrace, treat with affection —*n*. 2. act or expression of affection

caret ('karit) *n*. mark (∧) showing where to insert something omitted

cargo ('kärgō) *n*. load, freight, carried by ship, plane *etc*. (*pl*. **-es**)

Carib ('karib) *n*. 1. member of group of Amer. Indian peoples of NE South Amer. and Lesser Antilles (*pl*. **-s**, '**Carib**) 2. family of languages spoken by these peoples

caribou ('karibōō) *n*. any of several large deer of N Amer. and Siberia with palmate antlers in both sexes and grouped with reindeer in one species

caricature ('karikətyōōər, -tōōər) *n*. 1. likeness exaggerated or distorted to appear ridiculous —*vt*. 2. portray in this way

caries ('kâərēz) *n*. decay of tooth or bone —'**carious** *a*. (of teeth or bone) affected with caries; decayed

carillon ('karilon) *n*. 1. set of bells *usu*. hung in tower and played by means of a keyboard or other mechanism 2. the orchestral glockenspiel —**carillonneur** (karilə'nər) *n*.

Carmelite ('kärməlīt) *n*. *R.C.Ch*. 1. member of order of mendicant friars 2. member of corresponding order of nuns

carminative (kär'minətiv) *n*. 1. medicine to remedy flatulence —*a*. 2. acting as this

carmine ('kärmīn) *n*. 1. brilliant red color (prepared from cochineal) —*a*. 2. of this color

carnage ('kärnij) *n*. slaughter

carnal ('kärnəl) *a*. 1. fleshly, sensual 2. worldly —'**carnalism** *n*. —**car'nality** *n*. —'**carnally** *adv*. —**carnal knowledge** *chiefly law* sexual intercourse

carnation (kär'nāshən) *n*. 1. cultivated flower 2. flesh color

carnelian (kär'nēlyən) *n*. reddish-yellow translucent chalcedony, used as gemstone

carnival ('kärnivəl) *n*. 1. festive occasion 2. traveling fair 3. show or display for amusement

carnivorous (kär'nivərəs) *a*. flesh-eating —'**carnivore** *n*.

carob ('karəb) *n*. 1. evergreen Mediterranean tree with edible pods 2. long blackish sugary pod of this tree, used for fodder and sometimes human food

carol ('karəl) *n*. 1. song or hymn of joy or praise (*esp*. Christmas carol) —*vi*. 2. sing carols

Caroline ('karəlīn) *or* **Carolean** (karə'lēən) *a*. of Charles I or Charles II (kings of England, Scotland and Ireland), society over which they ruled or their government (*also* **Caro'linian**)

Carolingian (karə'linjiən) *Hist. a*. 1. of Frankish dynasty founded by Pepin the Short —*n*. 2. member of dynasty of Carolingian Franks (*also* **Carlo'vingian, Caro'linian**) —**Carolingian art** European art from end of 8th cent. to beginning of 10th cent.

carom billiards ('karəm) *see* BILLIARDS

carotid (kə'rotid) *n*. 1. either of two principal arteries that supply blood to head and neck —*a*. 2. of either of these arteries

carouse (kə'rowz) *vi*. 1. have merry drinking spree —*n*. 2. merry drinking party (*also* **ca'rousal**) —**ca'rouser** *n*.

carousel ('karə'sel, -'zel) *n*. merry-go-round

carp¹ (kärp) *n*. freshwater fish

carp² (kärp) *vi*. complain about small faults or errors; nag —'**carper** *n*. —'**carping** *a*. —'**carpingly** *adv*.

carpal ('kärpəl) *n*. any bone of wrist

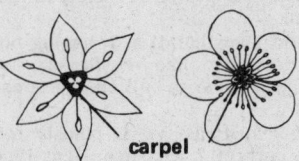
carpel

carpel ('kärpəl) *n*. female reproductive organ of flowering plants, consisting of ovary, style and stigma

carpenter ('kärpəntər) *n*. person who builds or repairs wooden structures or their constituent parts —'**carpentry** *n*. art of carpenter —**carpenter ant** ant that gnaws tunnels in dead wood —**carpenter bee** solitary bee that gnaws galleries in sound wood

carpet ('kärpit) *n*. 1. heavy fabric for covering floor —*vt*. 2. cover (floor) with carpet 3. *inf*. call up for censure —'**carpetbag** *n*. traveling bag —'**carpetbagger** *n*. political adventurer, *esp*. Northerner in southern states after Civil War —**carpet slipper** slipper orig. made with woolen upper resembling carpeting

carpus ('kärpəs) *n*. 1. wrist 2. eight small bones of human wrist (*pl*. **carpi** ('kärpī))

carrageen *or* **carragheen** ('karəgēn) *n*. edible red seaweed of N Amer. and N Europe, used to make jelly *etc*. (*also* **Irish moss**)

carriage ('karij) *n*. 1. railway coach 2. bearing, conduct 3. horse-drawn vehicle 4. act, cost, of carrying —**carriage clock** portable clock, usu. in rectangular case, orig. used by travelers —**carriage forward** charge for conveying, to be paid by receiver —**carriage paid** charge for conveying, to be paid by sender —'**carriageway** *n*. part of road along which traffic passes in single line

carrion ('kariən) *n*. rotting dead flesh —**carrion crow** scavenging European crow

carrot ('karət) *n*. 1. plant with orange-red edible root 2. inducement —'**carroty** *a*. red, reddish

carry ('kari) *vt*. 1. convey, transport 2. capture, win 3. effect 4. conduct (oneself) in specified manner —*vi*. 5. (of projectile, sound) reach or penetrate to distance ('**carried, 'carrying**) —*n*. 6. range —'**carrier** *n*. 1. one that carries goods 2. one who, himself immune, communicates a disease to others 3. aircraft carrier —**carrier pigeon** homing pigeon, *esp*. for carrying messages —**carrier wave** *Rad*. wave of fixed amplitude and frequency, modulated to carry signal in radio transmission *etc*. (*also* '**carrier**) —**carry-out** *n*. *chiefly Scot*. 1. alcohol bought at liquor store *etc*. for consumption elsewhere 2. shop which sells hot cooked food for consumption away from premises —**carry on** 1. continue 2. *inf*. fuss unnecessarily 3. *inf*. have an affair —**carry out** 1. perform; cause to be implemented 2. accomplish

cart (kärt) *n*. 1. open (two-wheeled) vehicle, *esp*. pulled by horse —*vt*. 2. convey in cart 3. carry with effort —'**cartage** *n*. —'**carter** *n*. —'**carthorse** *n*. —'**cartwheel** *n*. 1. large, spoked wheel 2. sideways somersault —'**cartwright** *n*. maker of carts

carte blanche (kärt 'blänch) *Fr*. complete discretion or authority

cartel (kär'tel) *n*. 1. industrial combination for the purpose of fixing prices, output *etc*. 2. alliance of political parties *etc*. to further common aims

Carter ('kärtər) *n*. **James Earl**. the 39th President of the U.S. (1977-81)

Cartesian (kär'tēzhən) *a*. 1. pert. to French philosopher René Descartes (1596-1650) or his system of coordinates —*n*. 2. adherent of his philosophy —**Cartesian coordinates** system of coordinates that defines location of point in terms of perpendicular distance from each of set of mutually perpendicular axes

Carthusian (kär'thyōōzhən, -'thōō-) *n*. *R.C.Ch*. member of monastic order founded by Saint Bruno

cartilage ('kärtilij) *n*. 1. firm elastic tissue in the body lacking blood vessels and nerves 2. gristle —**cartilaginous** (kärti'lajinəs) *a*.

cartogram ('kärtəgram) *n*. map showing statistical information in diagrammatic form

cartography (kär'togrəfi) *n*. mapmaking —**car'tographer** *n*. —**carto'graphic(al)** *a*.

carton ('kärtən) *n*. cardboard or plastic container

cartoon (kär'tōōn) *n*. 1. drawing, *esp*. humorous or satirical 2. sequence of drawings telling story 3. preliminary design for painting —**car'toonist** *n*.

cartouche *or* **cartouch** (kär'tōōsh) *n*. 1. carved or cast ornamental tablet or panel in form of scroll 2. oblong figure enclosing characters expressing royal or divine names in Egyptian hieroglyphics

cartridge ('kärtrij) *n*. 1. case containing charge for gun 2. container for film, magnetic tape *etc*. 3. unit in head of phonograph pick-up —**cartridge paper** strong, thick paper

carve (kärv) *vt*. 1. cut, hew 2. sculpture 3. engrave 4. cut (meat) in pieces or slices —'**carver** *n*. —'**carving** *n*.

caryatid (kari'atid) *n*. supporting column in shape of female figure

Casanova (kasə'nōvə) *n*. any man noted for amorous adventures

casbah ('kazbä) *n*. (*sometimes* C-) 1. citadel of various N Afr. cities 2. quarter where casbah is located (*also* '**kasbah**)

cascade (kas'kād) *n*. 1. waterfall 2. anything resembling this —*vi*. 3. fall in cascades

cascara (kas'kärə) *n*. 1. dried bark of cascara buckthorn, used as laxative and stimulant (*also* **cascara sagrada**) 2. shrub or small tree of NW North Amer. (*also* **cascara buckthorn**)

case¹ (kās) *n*. 1. instance 2. event, circumstance 3. question at issue 4. state of affairs, condition 5. arguments supporting particular action *etc*. 6. *Med*. patient under treatment 7. lawsuit 8. grounds for suit 9. grammatical relation of words in sentence —**case history** record of person's background, medical history *etc*. —**case law** law established by following judicial decisions given in earlier cases

case² (kās) *n*. 1. box, sheath, covering 2. receptacle 3. box and contents —*vt*. 4. put in a case —'**casing** *n*. 1. protective cover 2. material for cover 3. frame containing door or window (*also* **case**) —**case-harden** *vt*. 1. harden by carbonizing the surface of (iron) by converting into steel 2. make hard, callous

casein (kā'sēn, 'kāsiin) *n*. protein in milk and its products —'**caseous** *a*. like cheese —**casein paint** alkaline paint based on casein producing effects ranging from transparency to thick-textured opacity

casement ('kāsmənt) *n*. window opening on hinges

cash (kash) *n*. 1. money, bank notes and coins —*vt*. 2. turn into or exchange for money —**ca'shier** *n.* one in charge of receiving and paying of money —**cash-and-carry** *a./adv.* sold on basis of cash payment for merchandise that is taken away by buyer —**'cashbook** *n.* —**cash crop** crop grown for sale rather than subsistence —**cash flow** movement of money into and out of a business —**cash register** till that records amount of money put in —**cash on delivery** service entailing cash payment to carrier on delivery of merchandise

cashew ('kashōō, kə'shōō) *n.* 1. tropical tree bearing kidney-shaped nuts 2. nut of this tree (*also* **cashew nut**)

cashier (ka'shēər) *vt.* dismiss from office or service

cashmere ('kazhmēər, 'kash-) *n.* 1. fine soft fabric 2. shawl made from goat's wool

casino (kə'sēnō) *n.* building, institution for gambling (*pl.* **-s**)

cask (kask) *n.* 1. barrel 2. container for wine

casket ('kaskit) *n.* 1. small case for jewels *etc.* 2. coffin

casque (kask) *n. Zool.* helmet or helmetlike structure, as on bill of most hornbills

Cassandra (kə'sandrə) *n.* 1. *Gr. myth.* daughter of Priam and Hecuba, endowed with gift of prophecy but fated never to be believed 2. anyone whose prophecies of doom are unheeded

cassata (kə'sätə) *n.* ice cream, *esp.* containing fruit and nuts

cassava (kə'sävə) *n.* 1. any of various tropical plants, *esp.* Amer. species (**bitter cassava, sweet cassava**) (*also* **'manioc**) 2. starch derived from root of this plant: source of tapioca

casserole ('kasərōl) *n.* 1. fireproof cooking and serving dish 2. kind of stew cooked in this dish —*v.* 3. cook or be cooked in casserole

cassette (ka'set) *n.* plastic container for film, magnetic tape *etc.*

cassia ('kashə) *n.* 1. tropical plant whose pods yield **cassia pulp**, mild laxative (*see also* SENNA) 2. lauraceous tree of tropical Asia —**cassia bark** cinnamonlike bark of this tree, used as spice

cassis (kä'sēs) *n.* blackcurrant cordial

cassock ('kasək) *n.* long tunic worn by clergymen

cassowary ('kasəweri) *n.* large flightless bird of NE Aust., New Guinea and adjacent islands

cast (kast) *v.* 1. throw, fling 2. shed 3. throw down 4. deposit (a vote) 5. allot, as parts in play 6. mold, as metal (**cast** *pt./pp.*) —*n.* 7. throw 8. distance thrown 9. squint 10. mold 11. that which is shed or ejected 12. set of actors 13. type, quality —**'caster** *n.* machine that casts type —**'casting** *n.* —**'castaway** *n./a.* shipwrecked (person) —**casting vote** decisive vote —**cast iron** iron containing so much carbon that it must be cast into shape —**cast-iron** *a.* 1. made of cast iron 2. rigid, unyielding —**cast-off** *a.* abandoned —**'cast-off** *n.* 1. person or thing discarded or abandoned 2. *Print.* estimate of amount of space a piece of copy will occupy —**cast steel** steel containing varying amounts of carbon *etc.*, that is cast into shape —**cast off** 1. remove (mooring lines) that hold (vessel) to dock 2. knot (row of stitches, *esp.* final row) in finishing off knitted or woven material 3. *Print.* estimate amount of space that will be taken up by (book *etc.*)

castanets (kastə'nets) *pl.n.* 1. percussion instrument consisting of two shell-shaped pieces of hard wood hinged together used by Spanish dancers 2. orchestral castanets with springs and handles

caste (kast) *n.* 1. section of society in India 2. social rank

castellated ('kastilātid) *a.* 1. having turrets and battlements, like castle 2. having indentations similar to battlements —**castel'lation** *n.*

castigate ('kastigāt) *vt.* 1. punish, rebuke severely, correct 2. chastise —**casti'gation** *n.* —**'castigator** *n.* —**'castigatory** *a.*

castle ('kasəl) *n.* 1. fortress 2. country mansion 3. chessman (*also* **rook**) —**castle in the air** *or* **in Spain** hope or desire unlikely to be realized; daydream

castor ('kastər) *n.* 1. bottle with perforated top 2. small swiveled wheel on table leg *etc.*

castor oil vegetable medicinal oil

castrate (ka'strāt) *vt.* 1. remove testicles of, deprive of power of generation 2. deprive of vigor, masculinity *etc.* —**cas'tration** *n.*

casual ('kazhōōl) *a.* 1. accidental 2. unforeseen 3. occasional 4. unconcerned 5. informal —**'casually** *adv.* —**'casualty** *n.* 1. person killed or injured in accident, war *etc.* 2. thing lost, destroyed, in accident *etc.*

casuarina (kashōōə'rēnə) *n.* tree of Aust. and E Indies, having jointed leafless branches

casuist ('kazhōōist) *n.* 1. one who studies and solves moral problems 2. quibbler —**casu'istical** *a.* —**'casuistry** *n.*

cat (kat) *n.* any of various feline animals, including small domesticated furred animal, and lions, tigers *etc.* —**'catkin** *n.* drooping flower spike —**'catty** *a.* spiteful —**'catcall** *n.* derisive cry —**'catfish** *n.* mainly freshwater fish with catlike whiskers —**'catgut** *n.* strong cord made from dried intestines of sheep *etc.*, used for stringing musical instruments and sports rackets —**'catmint** *n.* scented plant —**'catnap** *vi./n.* doze —**cat-o'-nine-tails** *n.* whip consisting of nine knotted thongs, used formerly to flog prisoners (*pl.* **-tails**) (*also* **cat**) —**cat's cradle** game played by making patterns with loop of string between fingers —**cat's-paw** *n.* 1. person used by another as tool; dupe 2. pattern of ripples on surface of water caused by light wind —**'catwalk** *n.* narrow, raised path or plank

catabolism (kə'tabəlizəm) *n.* breaking down of complex molecules, destructive metabolism

cataclysm ('katəklizəm) *n.* 1. (disastrous) upheaval 2. deluge —**cata'clysmal** *a.*

catacomb ('katəkōm) *n.* 1. underground gallery for burial —*pl.* 2. series of underground tunnels and caves

catafalque ('katəfalk) *n.* temporary raised platform on which body lies in state before or during funeral

Catalan ('katələn) *n.* 1. language of Catalonia, closely related to Provençal 2. native of Catalonia —*a.* 3. of Catalonia

catalepsy ('katəlepsi) *n.* condition of unconsciousness with rigidity of muscles —**cata'leptic** *a.*

catalog *or* **catalogue** ('katəlog) *n.* 1. descriptive list —*vt.* 2. make such list of 3. enter in catalog

catalyst ('katəlist) *n.* substance causing or assisting a chemical reaction without taking part in it —**ca'talysis** *n.* —**'catalyze** *vt.*

catamaran (katəmə'ran) *n.* 1. type of sailing boat with twin hulls 2. raft of logs

cataplexy ('katəpleksi) *n.* 1. sudden loss of muscle tone causing victim to collapse 2. state assumed by animals shamming death —**cata'plectic** *a.*

catapult ('katəpult) *n.* 1. small forked stick with elastic sling used for throwing stones 2. *Hist.* engine of war for hurling arrows, stones *etc.* 3. launching device —*vt.* 4. shoot forth (as) from catapult —*v.* 5. move precipitately

cataract ('katərakt) *n.* 1. waterfall 2. downpour 3. disease of eye marked by opacity of the lens

catarrh (kə'tär) *n.* inflammation of a mucous membrane —**ca'tarrhal** *a.*

catastrophe (kə'tastrəfi) *n.* 1. great disaster, calamity 2. culmination of a tragedy —**cata'strophic** *a.*

catatonia (katə'tōniə) *n.* form of schizophrenia characterized by stupor, with outbreaks of excitement —**catatonic** (katə'tonik) *a./n.*

Catawba (kə'töbə) *n.* 1. (member of) Siouan-speaking Amerindian people of South Carolina (*pl.* **-ba, -s**) 2. dry or semisweet white table wine

catch (kach) *vt.* 1. take hold of, seize 2. understand 3. hear 4. contract (disease) 5. be in time for 6. surprise, detect —*vi.* 7. be contagious 8. get entangled 9. begin to burn (**caught** *pt./pp.*) —*n.* 10. seizure 11. thing that holds, stops *etc.* 12. what is caught 13. *inf.* snag, disadvantage 14. form of musical composition 15. thing, person worth catching —**'catcher** *n.* —**'catching** *a.* —**'catchy** *a.* 1. pleasant, memorable 2. tricky —**catchment area** 1. area in which rainfall collects to form the supply of river *etc.* 2. area from which people are allocated to a particular school, hospital *etc.* —**'catchpenny** *a.* 1. worthless 2. made to sell quickly —**catch phrase** frequently used phrase, *esp.* associated with particular group *etc.* —**'catchword** *n.* popular phrase or idea

catechize ('katikīz) *vt.* 1. instruct by question and answer 2. question —**cate'chetical** *a.* —**'catechism** *n.* —**'catechist** *n.* —**cate'chumen** *n.* one under instruction in Christianity

catechu ('katichōō) *n.* astringent resinous substance obtained from certain tropical plants, and used in dyeing *etc.*

category ('katigöri) *n.* class, order, division —**cate'gorical** *a.* 1. positive 2. of category —**cate'gorically** *adv.* —**'categorize** *vt.*

catenary ('katəneri) *n.* 1. curve formed by heavy flexible cord hanging from two points 2. hanging cable between pylons along railway track, from which trolley wire is suspended —*a.* 3. of catenary or suspended chain

catenation (kati'nāshən) *n.* chain, or series as links of chain

cater ('kātər) *vi.* provide what is required or desired, *esp.* food *etc.* —**'caterer** *n.*

caterpillar ('katərpilər) *n.* 1. hairy grub of moth or butterfly 2. type of tractor fitted with caterpillar wheels —**caterpillar wheel** articulated belt revolving round two or more wheels to propel heavy vehicle over difficult ground

caterwaul ('katərwöl) *vi.* wail, howl

catharsis (kə'thärsis) *n.* 1. purging of emotions through evocation of pity and fear, as in tragedy 2. *Psychoanal.* bringing repressed ideas or experiences to consciousness, by means of free association *etc.* 3. purgation, *esp.* of bowels (*pl.* **catharses** (kə'thärsēz)) —**ca'thartic** *a.* 1. purgative 2. effecting catharsis —*n.* 3. purgative drug or agent

Cathay (ka'thā) *n. Lit., obs.* China

cathedral (kə'thēdrəl) *n.* 1. principal church of diocese —*a.* 2. pert. to, containing cathedral

catherine wheel ('kathrin) wheel with spikes around rim

catheter ('kathitər) *n. Med.* long slender flexible tube for inserting into bodily cavity for introducing or withdrawing fluid

cathode ('kathōd) *n.* negative electrode —**cathode rays** stream of electrons —**cathode-ray tube** vacuum tube in which beam of electrons is focused on to fluorescent screen to give visible spot of light

catholic ('kathəlik, 'kathlik) *a.* 1. universal 2. including whole body of Christians 3. (C-) relating to R.C. Church —*n.* 4. (C-) adherent of R.C. Church —**Ca'tholicism** *n.* —**catho'licity** *n.* —**ca'tholicize** *v.*

cation ('katīən) *n.* positively charged ion; ion attracted to cathode during electrolysis —**cati'onic** *a.*

catsup ('kechəp, 'kach-, 'katsəp) *or* **ketchup** *n.* tomato purée seasoned with vinegar and spices

cattle ('katəl) *pl.n.* beasts of pasture, *esp.* oxen, cows —**cattle-grid** *n.* heavy grid over ditch in road to prevent passage of livestock —**'cattleman** *n.*

Caucasian (kö'kāzhən) *a.* 1. of or pert. to White racial group of mankind 2. of Caucasus in SW U.S.S.R. —*n.* 3. member of Caucasian race; White person 4. native of Caucasus —**'Caucasoid** *a./n.* Caucasian

caucus ('kökəs) *n.* group, meeting, *esp.* of members of political party, with power to decide policy *etc.*

caudal ('ködəl) *a.* 1. *Anat.* of posterior part of body 2. *Zool.* resembling or in position of tail —**'caudate** *or* **'caudated** *a.* having tail

caudle ('ködəl) *n.* hot spiced wine drink made with gruel, formerly used medicinally

caught (köt) *pt./pp. of* CATCH

caul (köl) *n. Anat.* portion of amniotic sac sometimes covering child's head at birth

cauliflower ('koliflowər) *n.* variety of cabbage with flowering head —**cauliflower ear** permanent distortion of ear

caulk *or* **calk** (kök) *vt.* stop up (cracks) with waterproof filler —**'caulker** *n.* —**'caulking** *n.*

cause (köz) *n.* 1. that which produces an effect 2. reason, origin 3. motive, purpose 4. charity, movement 5. lawsuit —*vt.* 6. bring about, make happen —**'causal** *a.* —**cau'sality** *n.* —**cau'sation** *n.* —**'causative** *a.* 1. *Gram.* relating to form or class of verbs that express causation 2. (*oft. with* of) producing effect —*n.* 3. causative form or class of verbs —**'causeless** *a.* groundless

cause célèbre (köz sə'lebrə) *Fr.* famous case

causerie (kōzə'rē) *n.* 1. informal talk 2. conversational piece of writing

causeway ('közwā) *n.* 1. raised way over marsh *etc.* 2. paved street

caustic ('köstik) *a.* 1. burning 2. bitter, severe —*n.* 3. corrosive substance —**'caustically** *adv.* —**caustic soda** *see* **sodium hydroxide** *at* SODIUM

cauterize ('kötərīz) *vt.* burn with caustic or hot iron —**cauteri'zation** *n.* —**'cautery** *n.*

caution ('köshən) *n.* 1. heedfulness, care 2. warning —*vt.* 3. warn —**'cautionary** *a.* containing warning or precept —**'cautious** *a.* —**'cautiously** *adv.* —**'cautiousness** *n.*

cavalcade (kavəl'kād) *n.* column or procession of riders

cavalier (kavə'lēər) *a.* 1. careless, disdainful —*n.* 2. courtly gentleman 3. *obs.* horseman 4. (C-) adherent of Charles I in English Civil War —**cava'lierly** *adv.*

cavalry ('kavəlri) *n.* mounted troops

cave (kāv) *n.* 1. hollow place in the earth 2. den —**cavern** ('kavərn) *n.* deep cave —**cavernous** ('kavərnəs) *a.* —**cavernously** ('kavərnəsli) *adv.* —**'caving** *n.* sport of exploring caves —**cavity** ('kaviti) *n.* hollow —**'caveman** *n.* prehistoric cave dweller —**cave in** 1. fall in 2. submit, give in

caveat ('kaviät, 'kāv-) *n.* 1. *Law* formal notice requesting court not to take action without warning person lodging caveat 2. a caution

caviar *or* **caviare** ('kaviär) *n.* salted sturgeon roe

cavil ('kavil) *vi.* find fault without sufficient reason, make trifling objections —**'caviler** *n.* —**'caviling** *a./n.*

cavort (kə'vört) *vi.* prance, frisk

cavy ('kāvi) *n.* small S Amer. rodent

caw (kö) *n.* 1. crow's cry —*vi.* 2. cry so

cay (kē, kā) *n.* low island or bank composed of sand and coral fragments (*also* **key**)

cayenne pepper (kī'en, kā-) pungent red pepper

cayman ('kāmən) *n. see* CAIMAN

Cayman Islands country in the Caribbean Sea comprising three islands about 200 miles northwest of Jamaica

Cayuga (kē'ōōgə, 'kyōō-) *n.* (member of) Iroquoian-speaking Amerindian people of upper New York state (*pl.* **-ga, -s**)

Cb *Chem.* columbium

CB citizens band

CBC Canadian Broadcasting Corporation

cc *or* **c.c.** 1. carbon copy or copies 2. cubic centimeter

cc. chapters

C.C. 1. City Council 2. County Council 3. Cricket Club

CCC Commodity Credit Corporation

cd candela

Cd *Chem.* cadmium

C.D. 1. Civil Defense (Corps) 2. Corps Diplomatic (Diplomatic Corps)

CDMB Civil and Defense Mobilization Board

Cdr. *Mil.* Commander

Ce *Chem.* cerium

C.E. *Judaism* Common Era

CEA Council of Economic Advisers

cease (sēs) *v.* bring or come to an end —**'ceaseless** *a.* —**'ceaselessly** *adv.*

cecum ('sēkəm) *n. Anat.* pouch, *esp.* at beginning of large intestine (*pl.* **-ca** (-kə))

cedar ('sēdər) *n.* 1. large evergreen tree 2. its wood

cede (sēd) *v.* yield, give up, transfer, *esp.* of territory

cedilla (si'dilə) *n.* hooklike mark (¸) placed under a letter *c* to show the sound of *s*

ceiling ('sēling) *n.* 1. inner, upper surface of a room 2. maximum price, wage *etc.* 3. *Met.* lower level of clouds 4. *Aviation* limit of height to which aircraft can climb —**ceil** *vt.* line (room), *esp.* with plaster

celadon ('selədon) *n.* Chinese or Japanese porcelain ware with a grayish or greenish glaze

celandine ('seləndīn) *n.* yellow wild flower

Celanese (selə'nēz) *n.* trade name for viscose rayon

celebrate ('selibrāt) *v.* 1. rejoice or have festivities to mark (happy day, event *etc.*) —*vt.* 2. observe (birthday *etc.*) 3. perform (religious ceremony *etc.*) 4. praise publicly —**'celebrant** *n.* —**'celebrated** *a.* famous —**cele'bration** *n.* —**ce'lebrity** *n.* 1. famous person 2. fame

celeriac (si'leriak) *n.* variety of celery with large turniplike root, used as vegetable

celerity (si'leriti) *n.* swiftness

celery ('seləri) *n.* vegetable with long juicy edible stalks

celesta (sə'lestə) *n.* orchestral percussion instrument resembling a small piano, with its hammers operating on steel bars

celestial (si'leschəl) *a.* 1. heavenly, divine 2. of the sky —**celestial equator** great circle lying on celestial sphere, plane of which is perpendicular to line joining north and south celestial poles (*also* **equi'noctial, equinoctial circle**) —**celestial sphere** imaginary sphere of infinitely large radius enclosing universe

celiac ('sēliak) *a.* pertaining to abdominal cavity —**celiac disease** chronic disease of young children marked by inability to digest fats

celibacy ('selibəsi) *n.* single life, unmarried state —**'celibate** *n./a.*

cell (sel) *n.* 1. small room, *esp.* in prison 2. small cavity 3. minute, basic unit of living matter 4. device converting chemical energy into electrical energy 5. small local group operating as nucleus of larger political or religious organization —**'cellular** *a.* —**'cellule** *n.* small cell

cellar ('selər) *n.* 1. underground room for storage 2. stock of wine —**'cellarage** *n.* —**'cellarer** *n.* monastic official responsible for food *etc.* —**cella'ret** *n.* cabinet for wine

cello ('chelō) *n.* popular name for violoncello, musical instrument of the violin family larger (thus lower in pitch) than the viola and smaller than the double bass

cellophane ('seləfān) *n.* regenerated cellulose in thin transparent sheets used *esp.* in packing and making adhesive tape

cellulite ('selyōōlīt) *n.* subcutaneous fat alleged to resist dieting

celluloid ('selyōōloid) *n.* 1. synthetic plastic substance with wide range of uses 2. coating of photographic film 3. a motion-picture film

cellulose ('selyōōlōs, -lōz) *n.* 1. substance of vegetable cell wall 2. group of carbohydrates 3. varnish

Celsius ('selsiəs) *a./n.* (of) scale of temperature from 0° (melting point of ice) to 100° (boiling point of water) divided into 100 equal degrees

Celtic ('keltik, 'sel-) *or* **Keltic** ('keltik) *n.* 1. branch of languages including Gaelic and Welsh —*a.* 2. of Celtic peoples or languages —**Celt** *or* **Kelt** *n.* 1. person who speaks a Celtic language 2. member of Indo-European people who in pre-Roman times inhabited Brit., Gaul and Spain

cement (si'ment) *n.* 1. fine mortar 2. adhesive, glue —*vt.* 3. unite with cement 4. join firmly

cemetery ('semiteri) *n.* burial ground, *esp.* other than churchyard

cenotaph ('senətaf) *n.* monument to person buried elsewhere

Cenozoic (sēnō'zōik) *a.* 1. of most recent geological era characterized by appearance of hominids —*n.* 2. this era

censer ('sensər) *n.* pan in which incense is burned

censor ('sensər) *n.* 1. one authorized to examine films, books *etc.* and suppress all or part if considered morally or otherwise unacceptable —*vt.* 2. ban or cut portions of (film *etc.*) 3. act as censor of (behavior *etc.*) —**cen'sorial** *a.* of censor —**cen'sorious** *a.* fault-finding —**cen'soriousness** *n.* —**'censorship** *n.*

censure ('senchər) *n.* 1. blame; harsh criticism —*vt.* 2. blame; criticize harshly

census ('sensəs) *n.* official counting of people, things *etc.*

cent (sent) *n.* 1. monetary unit equal to ⅟₁₀₀ of a basic unit 2. piece of metal or paper money representing this 3. the fen of the People's Republic of China

cent. 1. centigrade 2. central 3. century

centaur ('sentôr) *n.* mythical creature, half man, half horse

centenary (sen'tenəri) *n.* 1. 100 years 2. celebration of hundredth anniversary —*a.* 3. pert. to a hundred —**cente'narian** *n.* one a hundred years old —**cen'tennial** *a.* lasting, happening every hundred years

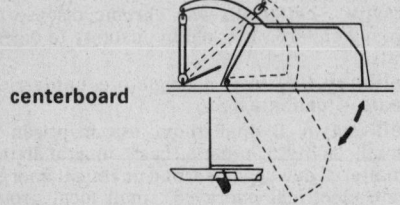

centerboard

center ('sentər) *n.* 1. midpoint 2. pivot, axis 3. point to or from which things move or are drawn 4. place for specific organization or activity —**'central** *a.* —**cen'trality** *n.* —**centrali'zation** *n.* —**'centralize** *vt.* 1. bring to a center 2. concentrate under one control —**'centrally** *adv.* —**'centric** *a.* —**cen'trifugal** *a.* tending from center —**'centrifuge** *n.* 1. rotating machine that separates liquids from solids or other liquids by centrifugal force 2. rotating device for subjecting human beings or animals to varying accelerations —*vt.* 3. subject to action of centrifuge —**cen'tripetal** *a.* tending toward center —**'centrist** *n.* person holding moderate political views —**'centerboard** *n.* supplementary keel for sailing vessel —**'centerfold** *n.* large colored illustration folded to form central spread of magazine —**center forward** *Soccer, hockey etc.* central forward in attack —**center half** *Soccer* defender in middle of defense —**center of gravity** point through which resultant of gravitational forces on body always acts —**'centerpiece** *n.* object used as center of something, *esp.* for decoration —**central bank** national bank that does business mainly with government and other banks —**central heating** method of heating building from one central source —**central processing unit** part of computer that performs logical and arithmetical operations on data —**Central Standard Time** time reckoned from the 90th to 105th meridians west of Greenwich

centi- or before vowel **cent-** (*comb. form*) 1. one hundredth, as in *centimeter* 2. rare hundred, as in *centipede*

centigrade ('sentigrād) *a.* 1. Celsius 2. having one hundred degrees

centigram ('sentigram) *n.* hundredth part of gram

centiliter ('sentilētər) *n.* hundredth part of liter

centime ('sontēm; *Fr.* sä'tēm) *n.* monetary unit of France *etc.*, worth one hundredth of standard unit of currency

centimeter ('sentimētər) *n.* hundredth part of meter —**centimeter-gram-second** *n. see* CGS UNITS

centipede ('sentipēd) *n.* small segmented animal with many legs

CENTO ('sentō) Central Treaty Organization

Central African Republic country in Africa bounded north by Chad, east by Sudan, south by Zaïre and Congo, and west by Cameroon

centrosome ('sentrəsōm) *n.* minute, protoplasmic body regarded as active center of cell division in mitosis

centuplicate (sen'tyōoplikāt, -'tōo-) *vt.* 1. increase 100 times —*a.* (sen'tyōoplikit, -'tōo-) 2. increased hundredfold —*n.* (sen'tyōoplikit, -'tōo-) 3. one hundredfold (*also* '**centuple**)

centurion (sen'tyōoriən, -'tōo-) *n.* Roman commander of 100 men

century ('senchəri) *n.* 1. 100 years 2. any set of 100

cephalic (si'falik) *a.* 1. of head 2. situated in, on or near head

cephalopod ('sefələpod) *n.* any of various marine mollusks characterized by well-developed head and eyes and ring of sucker-bearing tentacles, including octopus

ceramic (si'ramik) *n.* 1. hard brittle material of baked clay 2. object made of this —*pl.* 3. (*with sing. v.*) art, techniques of making ceramic objects 4. such objects —*a.* 5. of ceramic or ceramics

cere (sēər) *n.* soft waxy swelling, containing nostrils, at base of upper beak, as in parrot

cereal ('sēəriəl) *n.* 1. any edible grain, *eg* wheat, rice *etc.* 2. (breakfast) food made from grain —*a.* 3. of cereal

cerebellum (seri'beləm) *n.* one of major divisions of vertebrate brain whose function is coordination of voluntary movements (*pl.* -**s**, -**la** (-lə))

cerebrum (sə'rēbrəm) *n.* 1. anterior portion of brain of vertebrates: dominant part of brain in man, associated with intellectual function *etc.* 2. brain as whole (*pl.* -**s**, -**bra** (-brə)) —**ce'rebral** *a.* pert. to brain —**cerebrate** ('seribrāt) *vi. usu. jocular* use the mind; think; ponder; consider —**cerebration** (seri'brāshən) *n.* —**cerebro'spinal** *a.* of brain and spinal cord —**cerebro'vascular** *a.* of blood vessels and blood supply of brain —**cerebral atherosclerosis** hardening of the arteries of the brain —**cerebral embolism** *or* **hemorrhage** *see* STROKE —**cerebral palsy** impairment of muscular function and weakness of limbs, caused by damage to brain —**cerebral thrombosis** *see* STROKE

cerecloth ('sēərkloth) *n.* waxed waterproof cloth formerly used for shrouds

ceremony ('serimōni) *n.* 1. formal observance 2. sacred rite 3. courteous act —**cere'monial** *a./n.* —**cere'monially** *adv.* —**cere'monious** *a.* —**cere'moniously** *adv.* —**cere'moniousness** *n.*

cerise (sə'rēs, -'rēz) *n./a.* clear, pinkish red

cerium ('sēəriəm) *n. Chem.* metallic element *Symbol* Ce, at. wt. 140.1, at. no. 58

CERN (sərn) Conseil Européen pour la Recherche Nucléaire; organization of European states with center in Geneva, for research in high-energy particle physics

cert (sərt) *n. inf.* something certain (*esp. in a dead cert*)

cert. 1. certificate 2. certification 3. certified

certain ('sərtən) *a.* 1. sure 2. settled, inevitable 3. some, one 4. of moderate (quantity, degree *etc.*) —**'certainly** *adv.* —**'certainty** *n.* —**'certitude** *n.* confidence

certes ('sərtiz) *adv. obs.* with certainty; truly

certify ('sərtifi) *vt.* 1. declare formally 2. endorse, guarantee 3. declare legally insane (-**fied**, -**fying**) —**certificate** (sər'tifikit) *n.* 1. written declaration —*vt.* (sər'tifikāt) 2. authorize by or present with official document —**certifi'cation** *n.* —**'certified** *a.* 1. holding or guaranteed by certificate 2. endorsed, guaranteed 3. (of person) declared legally insane —**'certifier** *n.*

cerulean (si'rōoliən) *a.* sky-blue

cervix ('sərviks) *n.* neck, *esp.* of womb —**'cervical** *a.* —**cervical smear** *Med.* smear taken from neck of uterus for detection of cancer (*see also* PAP SMEAR)

Cesarean *or* **Cesarian** (si'zariən, -'zer-) *a.* 1. of any of Caesars, *esp.* Julius Caesar —*n.* 2. (*sometimes* **c-**) *Surg.* Cesarean section —**Cesarean section** surgical incision through abdominal wall to deliver baby

cesium ('sēziəm) *n. Chem.* metallic element *Symbol* Cs, at. wt. 132.9, at. no. 55

cessation (se'sāshən) *n.* ceasing, stopping; pause

cession ('seshən) *n.* yielding up

cesspool ('sespōol) *or* **cesspit** ('sespit) *n.* pit in which filthy water collects, receptacle for sewage

cestus[1] ('sestəs) *n.* woman's belt, *esp.* that worn by bride

cestus[2] ('sestəs) *n.* in classical Roman boxing, pugilist's gauntlet of bull's hide studded with metal (*pl.* -**tus**, -**es**)

cesura (si'zhōorə) *n. Prosody see* CAESURA

cetacean (si'tāshən) *a.* 1. of order of aquatic mammals having no hind limbs and blowhole for breathing: includes toothed and whalebone whales (*also* ce'**taceous**) —*n.* 2. whale

cetane ('sētān) *n.* colorless liquid hydrocarbon used in determination of cetane number of diesel fuel (*also* '**hexadecane**) —**cetane number** measure of quality of diesel fuel expressed as percentage of cetane (*also* **cetane rating**)

ceteris paribus ('kātəris 'paribəs) *Lat.* all things being equal

Ceylon (si'lon) *n. former name of* SRI LANKA

Cf *Chem.* californium

cf. confer (*Lat.*, compare)

c/f carried forward

CFL Canadian Football League

cg centigram

cgs units metric system of units based on *centimeter, gram, second*

ch. 1. chapter 2. church

Chablis (sha'blē) *n.* dry white table wine

cha-cha ('chächä) *n.* 1. fast ballroom dance from Latin Amer. 2. music composed for this dance —*vi.* 3. perform this dance

Chad (chad) *n.* country in central Africa bounded west by Cameroon, Nigeria and Niger, north by Libya, east by Sudan and south by Central African Republic

chafe (chāf) *vt.* 1. make sore or worn by rubbing 2. make warm by rubbing 3. vex, irritate —**chafing dish** vessel with heating apparatus beneath it, for cooking or keeping food warm at table

chafer ('chāfər) *n.* any of various beetles, such as cockchafer

chaff (chaf) *n.* 1. husks of grain 2. worthless matter 3. banter —*vt.* 4. tease good-naturedly

chaffer ('chafər) *vi.* 1. haggle, bargain —*n.* 2. bargaining

chaffinch ('chafinch) *n.* small songbird

Chagas' disease ('shägəs) tropical infection with a parasite transmitted by insects, *esp.* bedbugs

chagrin (shə'grin) *n.* 1. vexation, disappointment —*vt.* 2. embarrass 3. annoy 4. disappoint

chain (chān) *n.* 1. series of connected links or rings 2. thing that binds 3. connected series of things or events 4. surveyor's measure —*vt.* 5. fasten with chain 6. confine 7. restrain —**chain armor** —**chain gang** group of prisoners chained together —**chain**

mail —**chain reaction** —**chain smoker** one who smokes cigarettes *etc.* continuously, *esp.* lighting one from preceding one —**chain stitch** —**chain store**

chair (chãər) *n.* 1. movable seat, with back, for one person 2. seat of authority 3. professorship 4. iron support for rail on railway —*vt.* 5. preside over 6. carry in triumph —**'chairlift** *n.* series of chairs fixed to cable for conveying people (*esp.* skiers) up mountain —**'chairman** *n.* one who presides over meeting —**'chairmanship** *n.*

chaise (shãz) *n.* light horse-drawn carriage —**chaise longue** (long) sofa

chalcedony (kal'sedəni) *n.* translucent variety of quartz, often milky or grayish, used as gem

chalet (sha'lã) *n.* Swiss wooden house

chalice ('chalis) *n.* 1. *Poet.* cup; bowl 2. communion cup

chalk (chök) *n.* 1. white substance, carbonate of lime 2. crayon —*v.* 3. rub, draw, mark with chalk —**'chalkiness** *n.* —**'chalky** *a.*

challa ('hälə) *n.* braided white bread glazed with egg white

challenge ('chalinj) *vt.* 1. call to fight or account 2. dispute 3. stimulate 4. object to 5. claim —*n.* 6. call to engage in fight *etc.* 7. questioning of statement *etc.* 8. demanding situation *etc.* 9. demand by sentry *etc.* for identification or password —**'challenger** *n.* —**'challenging** *a.* difficult but stimulating

challis ('shali) *n.* soft lightweight woven fabric made of worsted wool

chamber ('chãmbər) *n.* 1. room for assembly 2. assembly, body of men 3. compartment 4. cavity 5. *obs.* room —**chamberlain** ('chãmbərlin) *n.* official at court of a monarch having charge of domestic and ceremonial affairs —**'chambermaid** *n.* servant with care of bedrooms —**chamber music** music for performance by a few instruments —**chamber of commerce** organization composed mainly of local businessmen to promote and protect their interests —**chamber pot** vessel for urine

chambray ('shãmbrã) *n.* fine-quality cotton fabric made with white weft threads and colored warp threads

chameleon (kə'mēlyən) *n.* 1. small lizard famous for its power of changing color 2. changeable person

chamfer ('chamfər) *vt.* 1. groove 2. bevel 3. flute —*n.* 4. groove

chamois ('shami) *n.* 1. goatlike mountain antelope 2. soft pliable leather

chamomile *or* **camomile** ('kaməmīl) *n.* aromatic creeping plant of the daisy family, used medicinally

champ[1] (champ) *v.* 1. munch (food) noisily, as horse 2. be nervous, impatient

champ[2] (champ) *n. inf.* champion

champagne (sham'pãn) *n.* 1. light, sparkling white wine made in a strictly defined area in France 2. wine resembling this made elsewhere 3. a pale yellowish-brown color

champion ('champiən) *n.* 1. one that excels all others 2. defender of a cause 3. one who fights for another 4. hero —*vt.* 5. fight for, maintain —**'championship** *n.*

chance (chans) *n.* 1. unpredictable course of events 2. fortune, luck 3. opportunity 4. possibility 5. risk 6. probability —*vt.* 7. risk —*vi.* 8. happen —*a.* 9. casual, unexpected —**'chancy** *a.* risky

chancel ('chansəl) *n.* part of church where altar is

chancellor ('chansələr) *n.* 1. high officer of state 2. chief officer of university or state

college system —**'chancellery** *or* **'chancellory** *n.* —**'chancellorship** *n.* —**Chancellor of the Exchequer** UK cabinet minister responsible for finance

chancery ('chansəri) *n.* the office of an embassy

chancre ('shangkər) *n.* small hard growth: first sign of syphilis —**'chancrous** *a.*

chandelier (shandi'lēər) *n.* hanging frame with branches for holding lights

chandler ('chandlər) *n.* dealer in ropes, ships' supplies *etc.*

Chanel-line (sha'nel-) *a.* of loose cardigan-type jacket worn with straight or slightly flared skirt, usu. worn with mass of necklaces in gold

change (chãnj) *v.* 1. alter, make or become different 2. put on (different clothes, fresh coverings) —*vt.* 3. put or give for another 4. exchange, interchange —*n.* 5. alteration, variation 6. variety 7. conversion of money 8. small money, coins 9. balance received on payment —**changea'bility** *n.* —**'changeable** *a.* —**'changeably** *adv.* —**'changeful** *a.* —**'changeless** *a.* —**'changeling** *n.* child believed substituted for another by fairies —**change of life** menopause

channel ('chanəl) *n.* 1. bed of stream 2. strait 3. deeper part of strait, bay, harbor 4. groove 5. means of passing or conveying 6. band of radio frequencies 7. television broadcasting station —*vt.* 8. groove, furrow 9. guide, convey

chant (chant) *n.* 1. simple song or melody 2. rhythmic or repetitious slogan —*vi.* 3. sing or utter chant 4. speak monotonously or repetitiously

Chantelle (shan'tel) *n.* a red-coated semi-hard cheese with open texture and a mild flavor

chanticleer (chanti'klēər) *n.* rooster

chantry ('chantri) *n. Christianity* 1. endowment for singing of Masses for soul of founder 2. chapel or altar so endowed

chanty ('shanti, 'chan-) *n. see* SHANTY[2]

Chanuka, Channuka, *or* **Hanuka** ('hänəkə) *n. Judaism* the Feast of Lights, an eight-day holiday in December memorializing the successful rebellion against Greco-Syrian despots

chaos ('kãos) *n.* 1. disorder, confusion 2. state of universe before Creation —**cha'otic** *a.*

chap[1] (chap) *v.* (of skin) become dry, raw and cracked, *esp.* by exposure to cold and wind (-**pp**-) —**chapped** *a.*

chap[2] (chap) *n. inf.* fellow, man

chapatti *or* **chapati** (chə'pati, -'päti) *n.* in Indian cookery, flat unleavened bread resembling pancake (*pl.* -**ti,** -**s,** -**es**)

chapel ('chapəl) *n.* 1. private church 2. subordinate place of worship 3. division of church with its own altar 4. organization of the union printers in a printing house

chaperon *or* **chaperone** ('shapərõn) *n.* 1. one who attends young unmarried lady in public as protector —*vt.* 2. attend in this way

chaplain ('chaplin) *n.* clergyman attached to chapel, regiment, warship, institution *etc.* —**'chaplaincy** *n.* his office

chaplet ('chaplit) *n.* 1. ornamental wreath of flowers worn on head 2. string of beads 3. *R.C.Ch.* string of prayer beads constituting one third of rosary; prayers counted on this string 4. narrow molding in form of string of beads

chapman ('chapmən) *n. obs.* trader, *esp.* itinerant peddler

chappie ('chapi) *n. inf. see* CHAP[2]

chaps (chaps, shaps) *pl.n.* cowboy's leggings of thick leather

chapter ('chaptər) *n.* 1. division of book 2. section, heading 3. assembly of clergy, bishop's council *etc.* 4. organized branch of society, fraternity, sorority —**'chapterhouse** *n.*

char[1] (chär) *vt.* scorch, burn to charcoal (-**rr**-) —**charred** *a.*

char[2] *or* **charr** (chär) *n.* troutlike small fish

character ('kariktər) *n.* 1. nature 2. total of qualities making up individuality 3. moral qualities 4. reputation, *esp.* good one 5. statement of qualities of person 6. an eccentric 7. personality in play or novel 8. letter, sign or any distinctive mark 9. essential feature —**character'istic** *n./a.* —**character'istically** *adv.* —**characteri'zation** *n.* —**'characterize** *vt.* 1. mark out, distinguish 2. describe by peculiar qualities —**'characterless** *a.*

charade (shə'rãd) *n.* 1. absurd act 2. travesty —*pl.* 3. word-guessing parlor game with syllables of word acted

charcoal ('chärkõl) *n.* 1. black residue of wood, bones *etc.*, produced by smothered burning 2. charred wood —**charcoal-burner** *n.*

chard (chärd) *n.* beet with large succulent leaves and thick stalks, used as vegetable (*also* **Swiss chard**)

charge (chärj) *vt.* 1. ask as price 2. bring accusation against 3. lay task on 4. command 5. attack 6. deliver injunction against 7. fill with electricity 8. fill, load —*vi.* 9. make onrush, attack —*n.* 10. cost, price 11. accusation 12. attack, onrush 13. command, exhortation 14. accumulation of electricity —*pl.* 15. expenses —**'chargeable** *a.* —**'charger** *n.* 1. strong, fast battle horse 2. that which charges, *esp.* electrically

chargé d'affaires ('shärzhã da'fãər) 1. temporary head of diplomatic mission in absence of ambassador or minister 2. head of diplomatic mission of lowest level (*pl.* **chargés d'affaires** ('shärzhã, -zhãz))

chariot ('chariət) *n.* 1. two-wheeled car used in ancient fighting 2. state carriage —**chario'teer** *n.*

charisma (kə'rizmə) *or* **charism** ('karizəm) *n.* special power of individual to inspire fascination, loyalty *etc.* (*pl.* **cha'rismata**) —**charis'matic** *a.*

charity ('chariti) *n.* 1. the giving of help, money *etc.* to those in need 2. organization for doing this 3. the money *etc.* given 4. love, kindness 5. disposition to think kindly of others —**'charitable** *a.* —**'charitably** *adv.*

charlatan ('shärlətən) *n.* quack, impostor —**'charlatanry** *n.*

charleston ('chärlstən) *n.* fast, rhythmic dance of 1920s

Charlie ('chärli) *n.* word used in communications for the letter *c*

charlock ('chärlok) *n.* weedy Eurasian plant with yellow flowers (*also* **wild mustard**)

charlotte ('shärlət) *n.* 1. dessert made with fruit and bread or cake crumbs, sponge cake *etc.* 2. cold dessert made with sponge fingers, cream *etc.* (*also* **charlotte russe**)

charm (chärm) *n.* 1. attractiveness 2. anything that fascinates 3. amulet 4. magic spell —*vt.* 5. bewitch 6. delight, attract —**charmed** *a.* —**'charmer** *n.* —**'charming** *a.*

charnel house ('chärnəl) *esp.* formerly, vault for bones of the dead

chart (chärt) *n.* 1. map of sea 2. diagram or tabulated statement —*vt.* 3. map 4. represent on chart —**the charts** *inf.* lists produced weekly of best-selling pop records

charter ('chärtər) n. 1. document granting privileges etc. 2. patent —vt. 3. let or hire 4. establish by charter

chartreuse (shär'trōōz; Fr. shar'trœz) n. 1. either of two liqueurs, green or yellow, made from herbs 2. yellowish-green color

chary ('châəri) a. cautious, sparing —'**charily** adv. —'**chariness** n. caution

Charybdis (kə'ribdis) n. ship-devouring monster in classical mythology, identified with whirlpool off coast of Sicily

chase[1] (chās) vt. 1. hunt, pursue 2. drive (from, away, into etc.) —n. 3. pursuit, hunting 4. the hunted 5. hunting ground —'**chaser** n. drink of beer, soda etc. taken after spirit

chase[2] (chās) vt. engrave —'**chaser** n. —'**chasing** n.

chase[3] (chās) n. 1. Letterpress print. rectangular steel frame into which metal type and blocks are locked for printing 2. part of cannon enclosing bore 3. groove or channel, esp. to take pipe etc. —vt. 4. cut groove, furrow or flute in (surface etc.) (also '**chamfer**)

chasm ('kazəm) n. 1. deep cleft, fissure 2. abyss

chassé (sha'sā) n. 1. rapid gliding step used in dancing —vi. 2. perform the step

chassis ('chasi) n. 1. framework, wheels and machinery of motor vehicle excluding body and coachwork 2. underframe of aircraft (pl. -**sis** (-siz))

chaste (chāst) a. 1. virginal 2. pure 3. modest 4. virtuous —'**chastely** adv. —**chastity** ('chastiti) n.

chasten ('chāsən) vt. 1. correct by punishment 2. restrain, subdue —'**chastened** a. —**chastise** (chas'tīz) vt. inflict punishment on —**chastisement** (chas'tīzmənt) n.

chasuble ('chazhŏŏbəl) n. priest's long sleeveless outer vestment

chat[1] (chat) vi. 1. talk idly or familiarly (-**tt**-) —n. 2. familiar idle talk —'**chattily** adv. —'**chatty** a.

chat[2] (chat) n. any of various European songbirds, Amer. warblers, Aust. wrens

château (sha'tō) n. esp. in France, castle, country house (pl. -**teaux** (-'tō, -'tōz), -**s**)

chateaubriand (shatōbrē'än) n. broiled tenderloin steak served with a sauce

chatelaine ('shatəlān; Fr. shat'len) n. 1. esp. formerly, mistress of castle or large household 2. chain or clasp worn at waist by women in 16th to 19th century, with handkerchief etc. attached

chattel ('chatəl) n. (usu. pl.) any movable property

chatter ('chatər) vi. 1. talk idly or rapidly 2. (of teeth) click rapidly —n. 3. idle talk —'**chatterer** n. —'**chattering** n. —'**chatterbox** n. one who chatters incessantly

chauffeur ('shōfər, shō'fər) n. paid driver motor vehicle (**chauf'feuse** fem.)

chauvinism ('shōvinizəm) n. 1. assertive patriotism 2. smug sense of superiority —'**chauvinist** or **chauvin'istic** a.

cheap (chēp) a. 1. low in price, inexpensive 2. easily obtained 3. of little value or estimation 4. mean, inferior —'**cheapen** vt. —'**cheaply** adv. —'**cheapness** n. —'**cheapjack** inf. n. 1. person who sells cheap and shoddy goods —a. 2. shoddy, inferior —'**cheapskate** n. inf. miserly person

cheat (chēt) vt. 1. deceive, defraud, swindle, impose upon —vi. 2. practice deceit to gain advantage —n. 3. fraud

check[1] (check) n. 1. written order to banker to pay money from one's account 2. printed slip of paper used for this —'**checkbook** n. book of blank checks

check[2] (chek) vt. 1. stop 2. restrain 3. hinder 4. repress 5. control 6. examine for accuracy, quality etc. 7. leave or receive for temporary safekeeping —n. 8. repulse 9. stoppage 10. restraint 11. brief examination for correctness or accuracy 12. pattern of squares on fabric 13. threat to king at chess —'**checker** n. 1. person who examines for accuracy 2. person who receives coats, parcels etc. for temporary safekeeping 3. cashier at supermarket or restaurant —'**checkmate** n. 1. Chess final winning move 2. any overthrow, defeat —vt. 3. Chess place (opponent's king) in checkmate 4. defeat —'**checkout** n. counter in supermarket where customers pay —'**checkroom** n. room where items may be temporarily stored, esp. in restaurant —'**checkup** n. examination (esp. medical) to see if all is in order

checked (chekt) a. having pattern of small squares

checker ('chekər) n. man in checkers

checkers ('chekərz) pl.n. (with sing. v.) board game for two players played with 12 thick disks called checkers or men —'**checkerboard** n. board with 64 squares of alternating colors for playing checkers —**Chinese checkers** board game for two or three players in which the player who first succeeds in moving his pieces across the board wins

Cheddar ('chedər) n. a hard cheese made from cow's milk with a mild-to-sharp flavor depending on age, orig. from England

cheek (chēk) n. 1. side of face below eye 2. inf. impudence —vt. 3. inf. address impudently —'**cheeky** a.

cheep (chēp) vi./n. (utter) high-pitched cry, as of young bird

cheer (chēar) vt. 1. comfort 2. gladden 3. encourage by shouts —vi. 4. shout applause —n. 5. shout of approval 6. happiness, good spirits 7. mood 8. obs. rich food —'**cheerful** a. —'**cheerfully** adv. —'**cheerfulness** n. —'**cheerily** adv. —'**cheerless** a. —'**cheerlessness** n. —**cheers** interj. inf., chiefly UK 1. drinking toast 2. goodbye, cheerio 3. thanks —'**cheery** a.

cheerio (chēəri'ō) inf. interj. 1. chiefly UK farewell greeting 2. chiefly UK drinking toast —n. 3. NZ small sausage

cheese (chēz) n. food derived from milk, usu. made by separating curd from whey by mechanical means or by action of rennet, and then ripened and molded —'**cheesiness** n. —'**cheesy** a. —'**cheeseburger** n. hamburger cooked with cheese on top —'**cheesecake** n. 1. pastry shell filled with cheese, esp. cream cheese, cream, sugar etc. 2. sl. women displayed for their sex appeal, as in photographs or films —'**cheesecloth** n. loosely woven cotton cloth —'**cheeseparing** a. stingy

cheetah ('chētə) n. large, swift, spotted feline animal

chef (shef) n. head cook, esp. in restaurant

chef-d'œuvre (she'dœvr) Fr. masterpiece

chem. 1. chemical 2. chemistry

chemin de fer (shə'man də 'fâər) gambling game, variation of baccarat

chemise (shə'mēz) n. loose-fitting dress hanging straight from shoulders; loose shirtlike undergarment (also **shift**)

chemistry ('kemistri) n. science concerned with composition, properties and reactions of matter —'**chemical** n./a. —'**chemically** adv. —'**chemist** n. person trained in chemistry —**chemical engineer** —**chemical engineering** engineering concerned with design and manufacture of plant used in industrial chemical processes —**chemical reaction** process in which substances are converted to other substances with different sets of properties —**chemical warfare** warfare using asphyxiating gases, poisons etc.

chemotherapy (kēmō'therəpi) n. treatment of disease by chemical agent

chemurgy ('kemərji) n. branch of applied chemistry devoted to the development of agricultural products —**che'murgic(al)** a.

chenille (shə'nēl) n. woven fabric with tufted pile —**chenille yarn** yarn with soft fluffy finish

cheongsam ('chōngsäm) n. tight dress with mandarin collar and slits at each side of skirt

cherish ('cherish) vt. 1. treat with affection 2. protect 3. foster

Cherokee ('cherəkē) n. 1. member of Amerindian people orig. of Tennessee and North Carolina (pl. -**kee**, -**s**) 2. Iroquoian language of this people

cheroot (shə'rōōt) n. cigar with both ends open

cherry ('cheri) n. 1. small red or yellow fruit with stone 2. tree bearing it —a. 3. ruddy, bright red

cherub ('cherəb) n. 1. winged creature with human face 2. angel (pl. '**cherubim**, -**s**) —**che'rubic** a.

chervil ('chərvil) n. a herb

Cheshire ('cheshər) n. a hard cheese made from cow's milk, blue-veined, with a mild-to-rich flavor, orig. from England where it is the oldest cheese known

chess (ches) n. universal game for two players played on board with 16 pieces each: king, queen, two rooks or castles, two bishops, two knights and eight pawns —'**chessboard** n. board with 64 squares of alternating colors for playing chess —'**chessman** n. one of the pieces for playing chess

chest (chest) n. 1. upper part of trunk of body 2. large, strong box —**chest of drawers** piece of furniture containing drawers

chesterfield ('chestərfēld) n. overcoat

chestnut ('chesnut) n. 1. large reddish-brown nut growing in prickly husk 2. tree bearing it 3. inf. old joke 4. horse of golden-brown color —a. 5. reddish-brown

cheval glass (shə'val) full-length mirror mounted to swivel within frame

chevalier (shevə'lēər) n. 1. member of order of merit, such as French Legion of Honor 2. lowest title of rank in old French nobility 3. obs. knight 4. chivalrous man; gallant

Cheviot ('sheviət) n. 1. Brit. sheep reared for its wool 2. (oft. **c**-) rough woolen fabric

chevron ('shevrən) n. Mil. V-shaped band of braid worn on sleeve to designate rank

chew (chōō) v. 1. grind with teeth —n. 2. act of chewing 3. something that is chewed —'**chewy** a. firm, sticky when chewed —**chewing gum** —**chew the fat** sl. 1. argue over a point 2. talk idly; gossip

Cheyenne (shī'an) n. 1. member of Amerindian people of western plains (pl. -**enne**, -**s**) 2. Algonquian language of this people

chi (kī) n. 22nd letter in Gr. alphabet (χ, X)

chianti (ki'anti) n. It. wine

chiaroscuro (kiärə'skyōōərō, -'skōō-) n. 1. treatment of light and shade in a painting 2. formerly, line-block woodcut printed in several colors (pl. -**s**)

chic (shēk) a. 1. stylish, elegant —n. 2. stylishness, esp. in dress

chicane (shɪ'kān) n. 1. bridge or whist hand without trumps 2. *Motor racing* barrier placed before dangerous corner to reduce speeds 3. *rare* chicanery —vt. 4. deceive or trick by chicanery —vi. 5. use chicanery —**chi'canery** n. 1. quibbling 2. trick, artifice

chicano (chi'käno) n. American of Mexican descent (pl. **-s**)

chick (chik) n. 1. young of birds, *esp.* of hen 2. *sl.* girl, young woman —'**chicken** n. 1. domestic fowl bred for flesh or eggs 2. its flesh as food 3. *sl.* cowardly person —a. 4. *sl.* easily scared; cowardly; timid —**chicken feed** trifling amount (of money) —**chickenhearted** a. cowardly —'**chickenpox** n. highly contagious virus disease (*also* **varicella**) —'**chickpea** n. dwarf pea —'**chickweed** n. weed with small white flowers

Chickahominy (chikə'homini) n. (member of) Amerindian people of Virginia (pl. **-ny, -nies**)

chicle ('chikəl) n. substance obtained from sapodilla; main ingredient of chewing gum

chicory ('chikəri) n. salad plant of which the root is ground and used with, or instead of, coffee

chide (chīd) vt. scold, reprove, censure (**chid** pt., **'chidden, chid** pp., **'chiding** pr.p.)

chief (chēf) n. 1. head or principal person —a. 2. principal, foremost, leading —**'chiefly** adv. —**'chieftain** ('chēftən, -tin) n. leader, chief of clan or tribe —**chief petty officer** senior naval rank for personnel without commissioned or warrant rank

chiffchaff ('chifchaf) n. common European warbler

chiffon (shi'fon, 'shifon) n. thin gauzy material —**chiffo'nier** n. ornamental cupboard

chigger ('chigər) n. any of various small mites in their larval stage which attack man

chignon ('shēnyon) n. roll, knot of hair worn at back of head

chigoe ('chigō) n. tropical flea, female of which burrows into skin of man *etc.* (*also* **'chigger**)

Chihuahua (chi'wäwä, -wə) n. breed of tiny dog, *orig.* from Mexico

chilblain ('chilblān) n. inflamed sore on hands, legs *etc.*, due to cold (*also* **pernio**)

child (chīld) n. 1. young human being 2. offspring (pl. **children** ('childrən)) —'**childhood** n. period between birth and puberty —'**childish** a. 1. of or like a child 2. silly 3. trifling —'**childishly** adv. —'**childless** a. —'**childlike** a. 1. of or like a child 2. innocent 3. frank 4. docile —'**childbed** n. state of giving birth to child —'**childbirth** n. act of giving birth: in humans, takes place about 280 days after the last menstrual period —**child's play** very easy task

Chile ('chili) n. country in South America bounded north by Peru, east by Bolivia and Argentina, and south and west by the Pacific Ocean

chili ('chili) n. 1. small red hot-tasting seed pod 2. plant producing it

chiliad ('kiliad) n. 1. group of one thousand 2. thousand years —**chili'astic** a.

chill (chil) n. 1. coldness 2. cold with shivering 3. anything that damps, discourages —v. 4. make, become cold (*esp.* food, drink) —**chilled** a. —'**chilliness** n. —'**chilly** a.

chime (chīm) n. 1. sound of bell 2. harmonious, ringing sound —pl. 3. orchestral percussion instrument consisting of a set of about eighteen metal tubes suspended from a frame and struck with a hammer —vi. 4. ring harmoniously 5. agree —vt. 6. strike (bells) —**chime in** come into conversation with agreement

chimera *or* **chimaera** (kī'mēərə, ki-) n. 1. fabled monster, made up of parts of various animals 2. wild fancy 3. living organism in which two separate kinds of tissue exist —**chimeric(al)** (kī'merik(əl), ki-) a. fanciful

chimney ('chimni) n. 1. a passage for smoke 2. narrow vertical cleft in rock (pl. **-s**)

chimp (chimp) n. *inf.* chimpanzee

chimpanzee (chimpan'zē) n. gregarious, intelligent ape of Afr.

chin (chin) n. part of face below mouth

china ('chīnə) n. 1. fine earthenware, porcelain 2. cups, saucers *etc.* collectively —**china clay** kaolin

China ('chīnə) n. 1. **People's Republic of China.** country in Asia bounded north by the U.S.S.R. and Mongolia, east by Korea, the Yellow Sea and the East China Sea, with Hong Kong and Macao as enclaves on the southeast coast, south by Vietnam, Laos, Burma, India, Bhutan and Nepal, west by India, Pakistan, Afghanistan and the U.S.S.R. 2. **Republic of China.** see TAIWAN

chincherinchee (chinchərin'chē) n. S Afr. plant with white or yellow flower spikes

chinchilla (chin'chilə) n. S Amer. rodent with soft, gray fur —**chinchilla cloth** durable fabric with small balls and loops on surface —**chinchilla rabbit** breed of rabbit with bluish-white black-tipped pelt

chine (chīn) n. 1. backbone 2. joint of meat 3. ridge or crest of land 4. intersection of bottom and sides of flat-bottom boat

Chinese (chī'nēz) a. 1. of China, its people or their languages —n. 2. native of China or descendant of one (pl. **-ese**) 3. any of languages of China —**Chinese checkers** see CHECKERS —**Chinese lantern** Asian plant cultivated for its orange-red inflated calyx

chink[1] (chingk) n. cleft, crack

chink[2] (chingk) n. 1. light metallic sound —v. 2. (cause to) make this sound

chino ('chēnō) n. tan-colored cotton fabric used for men's trousers and summer army uniforms

chinoiserie (shēnwäzə'rē, -'wäzəri) n. 1. style of decorative art based on imitations of Chinese motifs 2. object or objects in this style

Chinook (shi'nŏŏk, -'nōōk) n. 1. member of Amerindian people of Oregon (pl. **-nook, -s**) 2. (c-) warm moist SW wind of W coast of U.S.A. from Oregon northward or warm dry wind descending eastern slopes of the Rocky Mountains —**Chi'nookan** n. language of the Chinook —**Chinook salmon** large red-fleshed salmon occurring in N Pacific Ocean

chintz (chints) n. cotton cloth printed in colored designs with glazed finish

chip (chip) n. 1. splinter 2. place where piece has been broken off 3. thin strip of potato, fried 4. tiny wafer of silicon or other semiconductor forming integrated circuit in computer *etc.* —vt. 5. chop into small pieces 6. break small pieces from 7. shape by cutting off pieces —vi. 8. break off (**-pp-**) —**chip-based** a. using microchips in electronic equipment —'**chipboard** n. paperboard made from waste paper —**chip in** 1. interrupt 2. contribute

chipmunk ('chipmungk) n. small, striped N Amer. squirrel

Chippendale ('chipəndāl) a. (of furniture) in style of Thomas Chippendale (1718–79), characterized by use of Chinese and Gothic motifs *etc.*

Chippewa ('chipiwŏ, -wä) n. see OJIBWA (pl. **-wa, -s**)

Chippendale

chirography (kī'rogrəfi) n. penmanship

chiromancy ('kīrəmansi) n. palmistry —'**chiromancer** n.

chiropodist (ki'ropədist) n. one who treats disorders of feet —**chi'ropody** n. podiatry

chiropractor ('kīrəpraktər) n. one skilled in treating bodily disorders by manipulation, massage *etc.* —**chiro'practic** n. the principle and method of drugless healing

chirp (chərp) n. 1. short, sharp cry of bird —vi. 2. make this sound —'**chirpy** a. *inf.* happy

chisel ('chizəl) n. 1. cutting tool, usu. bar of steel with edge across main axis —vt. 2. cut, carve with chisel 3. *sl.* cheat

chit[1] (chit) n. informal note, memorandum

chit[2] (chit) n. child, young girl

chitchat ('chitchat) n. 1. gossip —vi. 2. gossip

chitin ('kītin) n. polysaccharide that is principal component of outer coverings of arthropods *etc.* —'**chitinous** a.

chivalry ('shivəlri) n. 1. bravery and courtesy 2. medieval system of knighthood —'**chivalrous** a. —'**chivalrously** adv.

chive (chīv) n. herb with mild onion flavor

chivy, chivvy ('chivi), *or* **chevy** ('chevi) UK vt. 1. harass; nag 2. hunt —vi. 3. run about ('**chivied, 'chivying, 'chivvied, 'chivvying** *or* '**chevied, 'chevying**) —n. 4. hunt 5. *obs.* hunting cry

chloral hydrate ('klōrəl) colorless crystalline soluble solid produced by reaction of chloral with water and used as sedative

chloramphenicol (klōram'fenikol) n. broad-spectrum antibiotic derived from a soil microorganism or prepared synthetically

chlorine ('klōrēn) n. *Chem.* nonmetallic element *Symbol* Cl, at. wt. 35.5, at. no. 17 —'**chlorate** n. salt of chloric acid —'**chloric** a. —'**chloride** n. 1. compound of chlorine 2. bleaching agent —'**chlorinate** vt. 1. disinfect 2. purify with chlorine

chloroform ('klōrəförm) n. 1. compound of carbon, hydrogen and chlorine used as anesthetic, liniment, cleansing agent, solvent for fats and oils, and antifreeze —vt. 2. render insensible with it

Chloromycetin (klōrōmī'sētin) n. trade name for chloramphenicol

chlorophyll ('klōrəfil) n. green coloring matter in plants

Chloroquine ('klōrōkwēn) n. antimalarial drug

chlorpromazine (klōr'proməzēn) n. tranquilizing drug used to treat anxiety, as pain reliever, antiemetic and treatment for hiccups (trade name Thorazine)

chlorpropamide (klōr'propəmīd) n. drug taken by mouth as pill to control diabetes

chock (chok) n. block or wedge to prevent heavy object rolling or sliding —**chock-full** *or* **chock-a-block** a. packed full

chocolate ('chokəlit, 'choklit, -lət) *n.* **1.** paste from ground cacao seeds **2.** confectionery, drink made from this —*a.* **3.** dark brown —**choc-ice** *n.* chocolate-covered slice of ice cream —**chocolate-box** *a. inf.* sentimentally pretty or appealing

Choctaw ('choktö) *n.* **1.** member of Amerindian people of Mississippi, Alabama and Louisiana (*pl.* **-taw, -s**) **2.** the Muskogean language of the Choctaw people

choice (chois) *n.* **1.** act or power of choosing **2.** alternative **3.** thing or person chosen —*a.* **4.** select, fine, worthy of being chosen —**'choicely** *adv.*

choir ('kwīər) *n.* **1.** band of singers, *esp.* in church **2.** part of church set aside for them

choke (chōk) *vt.* **1.** hinder, stop the breathing of **2.** smother, stifle **3.** obstruct —*vi.* **4.** suffer choking —*n.* **5.** act, noise of choking **6.** device in carburetor to increase richness of fuel-air mixture —**choked** *a.* —**'choker** *n.* **1.** woman's high collar **2.** neckband or necklace worn tightly around throat **3.** high clerical collar; stock **4.** person or thing that chokes —**'chokebore** *n.* gun with bore narrowed toward muzzle —**'chokedamp** *n.* carbon dioxide gas in coal mines

cholecystectomy (kolisis'tektəmi) *n.* surgical removal of the gall bladder

choler ('kolər) *n.* bile, anger —**'choleric** *a.* bad-tempered

cholera ('kolərə) *n.* acute bacterial infection of the gastrointestinal tract caused by contaminated water

cholesterol (kə'lestərol) *n.* organic compound found in all tissues of the human body *esp.* the brain and spinal cord

chomp (chomp) *v.* chew noisily

choose (chōōz) *vt.* **1.** pick out, select **2.** take by preference —*vi.* **3.** decide, think fit (**chose, 'chosen, 'choosing**) —**'chooser** *n.* —**'choosy** *a.* fussy

chop[1] (chop) *vt.* **1.** cut with blow **2.** hack (**-pp-**) —*n.* **3.** hewing blow **4.** slice of meat containing rib or other bone —**'chopper** *n.* **1.** short ax **2.** *inf.* helicopter **3.** *inf.* customized motorcycle **4.** high-bouncing batted baseball —**'choppy** *a.* (of sea) having short, broken waves

chop[2] (chop) *vt.* exchange, bandy (*esp. in* **chop logic, chop and change**) (**-pp-**)

chops (chops) *pl.n. inf.* jaws, cheeks

chopsticks ('chopstiks) *pl.n.* implements used for eating food, orig. Chinese

chop suey ('sōōi) dish of stir-fried vegetables and meat or fish served with rice

choral ('körəl) *a.* of, for, sung by, a choir

chorale *or* **choral** (kə'ral) *n.* slow, stately hymn tune

chord (körd) *n.* **1.** emotional response, *esp.* of sympathy **2.** simultaneous sounding of musical notes **3.** straight line joining ends of arc

chordotomy (kör'dotəmi) *n.* surgical severance of pain-carrying nerve fibers in the spinal cord

chore (chör) *n.* **1.** (unpleasant) task **2.** odd job

chorea (kə'rēə) *n.* disorder of central nervous system characterized by uncontrollable jerky movements (*also* **Saint Vitus's dance, Sydenham's chorea**)

choreography (köri'ogrəfi) *n.* art of arranging dances, *esp.* ballet —**chore'ographer** *n.* —**choreo'graphic** *a.*

choreology (köri'oləji) *n.* notation of ballet dancing

chorography (kə'rogrəfi) *n.* art of describing and making maps of particular regions —**choro'graphic** *a.*

choroid ('köroid) *or* **chorioid** ('körioid) *n.*

vascular membrane of eyeball between sclera and retina

chorology (kə'roləji) *n.* science of geographical distribution of plants and animals —**cho'rologist** *n.*

chortle ('chörtəl) *vi.* **1.** chuckle happily —*n.* **2.** gleeful chuckle

chorus ('körəs) *n.* **1.** band of singers **2.** combination of voices singing together **3.** refrain —*vt.* **4.** sing or say together —**choric** ('korik) *a.* —**chorister** ('koristər) *n.*

chose (chōz) *pt. of* CHOOSE —**'chosen** *pp. of* CHOOSE

chough (chuf) *n.* black passerine bird of Europe, Asia and Afr., with red bill

choux pastry (shōō) very light pastry made with eggs

chow (chow) *n. inf.* food

chow-chow *n.* thick-coated dog with curled tail, *orig.* from China (*also* **chow**)

chowder ('chowdər) *n.* thick soup or stew containing clams or fish

chow mein (mān) Chinese dish consisting of sliced vegetables and meat, poultry or shellfish on a noodle base

chrism ('krizəm) *n.* mixture of olive oil and balsam used for sacramental anointing

Christ (krīst) *n.* **1.** Jesus of Nazareth, regarded by Christians as fulfilling Old Testament prophecies of Messiah **2.** Messiah as subject of Old Testament prophecies **3.** image of Christ —*interj.* **4.** *offens. sl.* oath expressing annoyance *etc.* (*see also* JESUS)

Christian ('krischən) *n.* **1.** follower of Christ —*a.* **2.** following Christ **3.** relating to Christ or his religion **4.** exhibiting kindness or goodness —**christen** ('krisən) *vt.* baptize, give name to —**Christendom** ('krisəndəm) *n.* all the Christian world —**Christi'anity** *n.* religion of Christ —**'christianize** *vt.* —**Christian name** name given at baptism —**Christian Science** religious system of Church of Christ, Scientist, emphasizing spiritual healing and unreality of matter

christie *or* **christy** ('kristi) *n. Skiing* turn in which body is swung sharply round with skis parallel

Christmas ('krisməs) *n.* festival of birth of Christ —**'Christmassy** *a.* —**Christmas card** —**Christmas Day** Dec. 25th, U.S. national holiday —**Christmas rose** evergreen plant of S Europe and W Asia, with white or pinkish winter-blooming flowers (*also* **'hellebore, winter rose**) —**Christmas tree**

chromatic (krə'matik) *a.* **1.** of color **2.** *Mus.* of raised or lowered notes instead of normal degrees of the scale

chromatin ('krōmətin) *n.* part of protoplasmic substance in nucleus of cells which takes color in staining tests

chromatography (krōmə'togrəfi) *n.* technique of separating and analyzing components of mixture by selective adsorption in column of powder or on strip of paper

chrome (krōm) *n.* metal used in alloys and for plating

chromium ('krōmiəm) *n. Chem.* metallic element *Symbol* Cr, at. wt. 52.0, at. no. 24

chromosome ('krōməsōm) *n.* body found in the nucleus of all plant and animal cells, always occurring in pairs and incorporating genes

chromosphere ('krōməsfēr) *n.* layer of incandescent gas surrounding the sun

Chron. Chronicles

chronic ('kronik) *a.* **1.** lasting a long time **2.** habitual **3.** *inf.* serious **4.** *inf.* of bad quality

chronicle ('kronikəl) *n.* **1.** record of events

in order of time **2.** account —*vt.* **3.** record —**'chronicler** *n.*

Chronicles ('kronikəlz) *pl.n.* (*with sing. v.*) *Bible* 13th and 14th books of the O.T., which record the genealogies of Adam, Saul's life and David's victory over Philistines, reign of Solomon, kings of Judah

chronology (krə'noləji) *n.* **1.** determination of sequence of past events **2.** arrangement in order of occurrence —**chrono'logical** *a.* arranged in order of time —**chrono'logically** *adv.* —**chro'nologist** *n.*

chronometer (krə'nomitər) *n.* **1.** instrument for measuring time exactly **2.** watch —**chrono'metrical** *a.* —**chro'nometry** *n.*

chrysalis ('krisəlis) *n.* **1.** resting state of insect between grub and butterfly *etc.* **2.** case enclosing it (*pl.* **-es, chrysalides** (kri'salidēz))

chrysanthemum (kri'santhəməm) *n.* garden flower of various colors

chrysoberyl ('krisəberil) *n.* yellowish mineral consisting of an aluminum-iron compound used as a gem

chrysolite ('krisəlīt) *n.* an olive-green semiprecious stone

chub (chub) *n.* **1.** European freshwater fish **2.** any of various N Amer. fishes, *esp.* whitefishes and minnows

chubby ('chubi) *a.* plump

chuck[1] (chuk) *vt.* **1.** *inf.* throw **2.** pat affectionately (under chin) **3.** *inf.* give up, reject

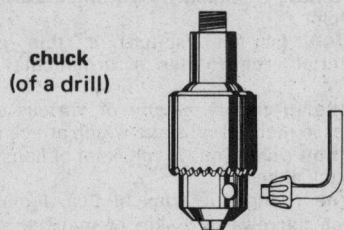

chuck
(of a drill)

chuck[2] (chuk) *n.* **1.** cut of beef **2.** device for gripping, adjusting bit in power drill *etc.*

chuckle ('chukəl) *vi.* **1.** laugh softly —*n.* **2.** such laugh —**'chucklehead** *n. inf.* stupid person; blockhead; dolt

chuff (chuf) *n.* **1.** puffing sound as of steam engine —*vi.* **2.** move while emitting such sounds

chug (chug) *n.* **1.** short dull sound, such as that made by engine —*vi.* **2.** (of engine *etc.*) operate while making such sounds (**-gg-**)

chukker, chukkar ('chukər), *or* **chukka** ('chukə) *n.* period of play in game of polo

chum (chum) *n. inf.* close friend —**'chummy** *a.*

chump (chump) *n.* **1.** *inf.* stupid person **2.** heavy block of wood **3.** thick blunt end of anything, *esp.* meat

chunk (chungk) *n.* thick, solid piece —**'chunky** *a.*

church (chərch) *n.* **1.** building for Christian worship **2.** (C-) whole body or sect of Christians **3.** clergy —**'churchman** *n.* —**Church of Christ** Protestant Christian denomination whose doctrine is based on basic New Testament faith and is highly tolerant in doctrinal and religious matters —**Church of England** reformed state Church in England, with Sovereign as temporal head —**'churchwarden** *n.* **1.** officer who represents interests of parish **2.** long clay pipe —**'churchyard** *n.*

churl (chərl) *n.* **1.** rustic **2.** ill-bred fellow —**'churlish** *a.* —**'churlishly** *adv.* —**'churlishness** *n.*

churn (chɔrn) n. 1. large container for milk 2. vessel for making butter —v. 3. shake up, stir (liquid) violently

chute (shōōt) n. 1. slide for sending down parcels, coal etc. 2. channel 3. slide into swimming pool 4. narrow passageway, eg for spraying, counting cattle, sheep etc. 5. inf. parachute

chutney ('chutni) n. pickle of fruit, spices etc.

chutzpa or **chutzpah** ('hŏŏtspə) n. shameless audacity, presumption or gall

chyle (kīl) n. milky fluid composed of lymph and emulsified fat globules, formed in small intestine during digestion

chyme (kīm) n. thick fluid mass of partially digested food that leaves stomach

C.I.A. Central Intelligence Agency

cicada (si'kādə) or **cicala** (si'kälə) n. cricketlike insect

cicatrix ('sikətriks) n. scar of healed wound —**cicatri'zation** n. —'**cicatrize** v. heal

cicely ('sisəli) n. perennial plant similar to chervil, used as herb (also **sweet cicely**)

cicerone (sisə'rōni, chēch-) n. person who conducts and informs sightseers (pl. **-s, -ni** (-ni))

C.I.D. Criminal Investigation Department

-cide (n. comb. form) 1. person or thing that kills, as in insecticide 2. killing; murder, as in homicide —**-cidal** (a. comb. form)

cider ('sīdər) n. drink made from apples

c.i.f. or **C.I.F.** cost, insurance and freight (included in price quoted)

cigar (si'gär) n. roll of tobacco leaves for smoking —**ciga'rette** n. finely-cut tobacco rolled in paper for smoking

cilium ('siliəm) n. 1. short thread projecting from surface of cell etc., whose rhythmic beating causes movement 2. eyelash (pl. **cilia** ('siliə)) —'**ciliary** a. of cilia —'**ciliate** or '**ciliated** a. —**ciliary body** part of eye that joins choroid to iris

C in C or **C.-in-C.** Commander-in-Chief

cinch (sinch) n. inf. easy task, certainty

cinchona (sing'kōnə) n. 1. tree or shrub of S Amer. having medicinal bark 2. dried bark of this tree, which yields quinine 3. any of drugs derived from cinchona bark

cincture ('singkchər) n. something that encircles, esp. belt or girdle

cinder ('sindər) n. remains of burned coal

Cinderella (sində'relə) n. 1. girl who achieves fame after being obscure 2. poor, neglected or unsuccessful person or thing

cine- (comb. form) relating to motion pictures

cinema ('sinimə) n. 1. motion picture 2. motion-picture theater 3. motion pictures generally or collectively —**cine'matograph** n. combined camera, printer and projector —**cinema'tography** n.

cineraria (sinə'reriə, -'rar-) n. garden plant with daisylike flowers

cinerarium (sinə'reriəm, -'rar-) n. place for keeping ashes of dead after cremation (pl. **-ria** (-riə))

cinerary ('sinəreri) a. pert. to ashes

cinnabar ('sinəbär) n. 1. heavy red mineral consisting of mercuric sulfide: chief ore of mercury 2. red form of mercuric sulfide, esp. when used as pigment 3. bright red; vermilion 4. large red-and-black European moth

cinnamon ('sinəmən) n. 1. spice got from bark of Asian tree 2. the tree —a. 3. of light-brown color

cinque (singk) n. number five in cards, dice

etc. —**cinquecento** (chingkwi'chentō) n. the 16th cent. esp. when referring to Italian art and literature —'**cinquefoil** n. plant with five-lobed leaves

cipher ('sīfər) n. 1. secret writing 2. arithmetical symbol 3. person of no importance 4. monogram —vt. 5. write in cipher

circa ('sɜrkə) Lat. about, approximately

circadian (sɜr'kādiən) a. of biological processes that occur at 24-hour intervals

circle ('sɜrkəl) n. 1. perfectly round plane figure 2. line enclosing it with every point on the line the same distance from the center 3. ring 4. group, society with common interest 5. spiritualist seance 6. class of society —vt. 7. surround —vi. 8. move round —'**circular** a. 1. round 2. moving round —n. 3. letter sent to several persons —**circulari'zation** n. —'**circularize** vt. 1. distribute circulars to 2. canvass or petition, as for votes etc. by distributing letters etc. 3. make circular —'**circulate** vi. 1. move round 2. pass from hand to hand or place to place —vt. 3. send round —**circu'lation** n. 1. flow of blood from, and back to, heart 2. act of moving round 3. extent of sale of periodical —'**circulatory** a. —**circular saw** saw in which circular disk with toothed edge is rotated at high speed —**circulating library** lending library —**circulatory system** system of blood vessels, heart etc. involved in the circulation of blood and lymph

circuit ('sɜrkit) n. 1. complete round or course 2. area 3. path of electric current 4. round of visitation, esp. of judges 5. series of sporting events 6. district —**circuitous** (sɜr'kyōōitəs) a. roundabout, indirect —**circuitously** (sɜr'kyōōitəsli) adv. —'**circuitry** n. electrical circuit(s) —**circuit breaker** device that under abnormal conditions stops flow of current in electrical circuit

circum- (comb. form) around; surrounding; on all sides, as in circumlocution, circumpolar. Such compounds are not given here where the meaning may easily be found from the simple word

circumambient (sɜrkəm'ambiənt) a. surrounding

circumcise ('sɜrkəmsīz) vt. cut off foreskin of —**circum'cision** n.

circumference (sɜr'kumfərəns) n. boundary line, esp. of circle

circumflex ('sɜrkəmfleks) n. 1. mark (ˆ) placed over vowel to show it is pronounced with rising and falling pitch or as long vowel —a. 2. (of nerves etc.) bending or curving around

circumlocution (sɜrkəmlə'kyōōshən) n. roundabout speech

circumnavigate (sɜrkəm'navigāt) vt. sail or fly right round —**circumnavi'gation** n. —**circum'navigator** n.

circumscribe ('sɜrkəmskrīb) vt. confine, bound, limit, hamper

circumspect ('sɜrkəmspekt) a. watchful, cautious, prudent —**circum'spection** n. —'**circumspectly** adv.

circumstance ('sɜrkəmstans) n. 1. detail 2. event 3. matter of fact —pl. 4. state of affairs 5. condition in life, esp. financial 6. surroundings or things accompanying an action —**circum'stantial** a. 1. depending on detail or circumstances 2. detailed, minute 3. incidental —**circumstanti'ality** n. —**circum'stantially** adv. —**circum'stantiate** vt. 1. prove by details 2. describe exactly —**circumstantial evidence** indirect evidence that tends to establish conclusion by inference

circumvent (sɜrkəm'vent) vt. outwit, evade, get round —**circum'vention** n.

circus ('sɜrkəs) n. 1. (performance of) traveling group of acrobats, clowns, performing animals etc. 2. circular structure for public shows

ciré ('sērā) n. 1. any supple fabric with highly lustrous and smooth finish 2. satin treated with surface wax

cirque (sɜrk) n. steep-sided semicircular depression found in mountainous regions

cirrhosis (si'rōsis) n. any of various chronic progressive diseases of liver —**cirrhotic** (si'rotik) a.

cirrus ('sirəs) n. high wispy cloud (pl. **cirri** ('sirī)) —**cirro'cumulus** n. high cloud of ice crystals grouped into small separate globular masses (pl. **-li** (-lī)) —**cirro'stratus** n. uniform layer of cloud above about 6000 meters (pl. **-tai** (-tī))

cisco ('siskō) n. N Amer. whitefish (pl. **-s, -es**)

cist (sist) n. neolithic burial chamber made from stone slabs

Cistercian (si'stɜrshən) n. member of Christian order of monks and nuns, which follows strict form of Benedictine rule (also **White Monk**)

cistern ('sistərn) n. water tank

cistus ('sistəs) n. any of various shrubs or herbaceous plants cultivated for yellow-white or reddish roselike flowers (also '**rockrose**)

citadel ('sitədəl, -del) n. fortress in, near or commanding a city

cite (sīt) vt. 1. quote 2. bring forward as proof 3. commend (soldier etc.) for outstanding bravery etc. 4. summon to appear before court of law —**ci'tation** n. 1. quoting 2. commendation for bravery etc.

cithara ('sithərə, 'kith-) n. see KITHARA

citizen ('sitizən) n. 1. native, naturalized member of state, nation etc. 2. inhabitant of city —'**citizenry** n. citizens collectively —'**citizenship** n. —**citizens band** range of radio frequencies assigned officially for use by public for private communication

citron ('sitrən) n. 1. fruit like a lemon 2. the tree —'**citric** a. of the acid of lemon or citron —**citric acid cycle** see KREBS CYCLE —**citrus fruit** fruit covered by leathery rind with acidic juicy pulp divided into segments by a membrane

citronella (sitrə'nelə) n. 1. tropical Asian grass with bluish-green lemon-scented leaves 2. aromatic oil obtained from this grass, used in perfumes etc. (also **citronella oil**)

cittern ('sitərn), **cither** ('sidhər), or **cithern** ('sidhərn) n. medieval stringed instrument resembling lute but having wire strings and flat back

city ('siti) n. large town —**city editor** (on newspaper) editor in charge of local news —**city father** person who is prominent in public affairs of city —**the City 1.** area in central London where United Kingdom's major financial business is transacted **2.** financial institutions located in this area

civet ('sivit) n. strong, musky perfume —**civet-cat** n. catlike animal producing it

civic ('sivik) a. pert. to city or citizen —'**civics** pl.n. (with sing. v.) study of the rights and responsibilities of citizenship

civil ('sivəl) a. 1. relating to citizens of state 2. not military 3. refined, polite 4. Law not criminal —**ci'vilian** n. nonmilitary person —**ci'vility** n. —'**civilly** adv. —**civil defense** organizing of civilians to deal with enemy attacks —**civil disobedience** refusal to obey laws, pay taxes etc.: nonviolent means of protesting —**civil engineer** person qualified to design and construct roads, bridges *etc.* —**civil engineering** —**civil law** 1. law of state relating to private affairs 2. body of law in ancient Rome, *esp.* as applicable to private citizens 3. law based on Roman system —**civil liberty** right of individual to freedom of speech and action —**civil marriage** *Law* marriage performed by official other than clergyman —**civil rights** *pl.n.* 1. personal rights of individual citizen —*a.* 2. of equality in social, economic and political rights —**civil service** service responsible for public administration of government of a country —**civil war** war between factions within same nation

civilize ('sivilīz) *vt.* 1. bring out of barbarism 2. refine —**civili'zation** *n.* —**'civilized** *a.*

civvy ('sivi) *sl. n.* 1. civilian —*pl.* 2. civilian clothing —**civvy street** civilian life

cl centiliter

Cl *Chem.* chlorine

clack (klak) *n.* 1. sound, as of two pieces of wood striking together —*v.* 2. make such sound 3. jabber

clad (klad) *pt./pp. of* **clothe** (*see* CLOTH)

cladding ('klading) *n.* material used for outside facing of building *etc.*

claim (klām) *vt.* 1. demand as right 2. assert 3. call for —*n.* 4. demand for thing supposed due 5. right 6. thing claimed 7. plot of mining land marked out by stakes as required by law —**'claimant** *n.*

clairvoyance (klāər'voiəns) *n.* power of seeing things not present to senses, second sight —**clair'voyant** *n./a.*

clam (klam) *n.* edible mollusk

clamber ('klambər) *vi.* climb with difficulty or awkwardly

clammy ('klami) *a.* moist and sticky —**'clamminess** *n.*

clamor ('klamər) *n.* 1. loud shouting, outcry, noise —*vi.* 2. shout, call noisily —**'clamorous** *a.* —**'clamorously** *adv.*

clamp[1] (klamp) *n.* 1. tool for holding or compressing —*vt.* 2. fasten, strengthen with or as with clamp

clamp[2] (klamp) *n.* 1. mound of harvested root crop, covered with straw and earth to protect it from winter weather —*vt.* 2. enclose in mound

clan (klan) *n.* 1. tribe or collection of families under chief and of common ancestry 2. faction, group —**'clannish** *a.* —**'clannishly** *adv.* —**'clannishness** *n.*

clandestine (klan'destin) *a.* 1. secret 2. sly

clang (klang) *v.* 1. (cause to) make loud ringing sound —*n.* 2. loud ringing sound —**'clanger** *n.* 1. *inf.* conspicuous mistake 2. that which clangs

clangor ('klangər, 'klanggər) *n.* 1. loud resonant noise 2. uproar —*vi.* 3. make loud resonant noise —**'clangorous** *a.*

clank (klangk) *n.* 1. short sound as of pieces of metal struck together —*v.* 2. cause, move with, such sound

clap[1] (klap) *v.* 1. (cause to) strike with noise 2. strike (hands) together 3. applaud —*vt.* 4. pat 5. place or put quickly (**-pp-**) —*n.* 6. hard, explosive sound 7. slap —**'clapper** *n.* —**'clapping** *n.* —**'claptrap** *n. inf.* empty words

clap[2] (klap) *n. sl.* gonorrhea

claque (klak) *n.* 1. group of people hired to applaud 2. group of fawning admirers

claret ('klarət) *n.* a dry dark red wine of Bordeaux

clarify ('klarifī) *v.* make or become clear, pure or more easily understood (**-fied, -fying**) —**clarifi'cation** *n.* —**'clarity** *n.* clearness

clarinet (klari'net) *n.* orchestral woodwind musical instrument formed like a cylindrical pipe with holes closed by keys ending in a bell, with a mouthpiece which has a single reed fixed to its back, available in many sizes and types

clarion ('klariən) *n.* 1. clear-sounding trumpet 2. rousing sound

clary ('klāri) *n.* herb

clash (klash) *n.* 1. loud noise, as of weapons striking 2. conflict, collision —*vi.* 3. make clash 4. come into conflict 5. (of events) coincide 6. (of colors) look ugly together —*vt.* 7. strike together to make clash

clasp (klasp) *n.* 1. hook or other means of fastening 2. embrace —*vt.* 3. fasten 4. embrace, grasp —**clasp knife** large knife with one or more blades or other devices folding into handle

class (klas) *n.* 1. any division, order, kind, sort 2. rank 3. group of persons taught together 4. persons graduating in same year 5. *Biol.* taxonomic category of plants and animals below phylum and above order 6. division by merit 7. quality 8. *inf.* excellence; elegance —*vt.* 9. assign to proper division —**classifi'cation** *n.* —**'classified** *a.* 1. arranged in classes 2. secret 3. (of advertisements) arranged under headings in newspapers —**'classify** *vt.* arrange methodically in classes (**-fied, -fying**) —**'classy** *a. inf.* stylish, elegant —**class-conscious** *a.* aware of belonging to particular social rank —**class-consciousness** *n.*

classic ('klasik) *a.* 1. of first rank 2. of highest rank generally, but *esp.* of art 3. (of clothing) in simple style based on excellence of cut, proportion and color 4. refined 5. typical 6. famous —*n.* 7. (literary) work of recognized excellence —*pl.* 8. ancient Latin and Greek literature —**'classical** *a.* 1. of Greek and Roman literature, art, culture 2. of classic quality 3. *Mus.* of established standards of form, complexity *etc.* —**'classically** *adv.* —**'classicism** *n.* —**'classicist** *n.*

clatter ('klatər) *n.* 1. rattling noise 2. noisy conversation —*v.* 3. (cause to) make clatter

clause (klöz) *n.* 1. part of sentence, containing verb 2. article in formal document as treaty, contract *etc.*

claustrophobia (klöstrə'fōbiə) *n.* abnormal fear of confined spaces

clavichord ('klavikörd) *n.* earliest type of stringed keyboard musical instrument made of small rectangular wooden box with keyboard of three octaves and strings running parallel to keyboard

clavicle ('klavikəl) *n.* collarbone —**cla'vicular** *a.* pert. to this

clavier (klə'vēər, 'klavēər) *n.* generic name for the stringed keyboard instruments: clavichord, harpsichord and pianoforte

claw (klö) *n.* 1. sharp hooked nail of bird or beast 2. foot of bird of prey 3. clawlike article —*vt.* 4. tear with claws 5. grip

clay (klā) *n.* 1. fine-grained earth, plastic when wet, hardening when baked 2. earth —**'clayey** *a.* —**clay pigeon** disk of baked clay hurled into air as target to be shot at

claymore ('klāmör) *n.* ancient Highland two-edged sword

CLC Canadian Labor Congress

clean (klēn) *a.* 1. free from dirt, stain or defilement 2. pure 3. guiltless 4. trim, shapely —*adv.* 5. so as to leave no dirt 6. entirely —*vt.* 7. free from dirt —**'cleaner** *n.* —**cleanliness** ('klenlinis) *n.* —**cleanly** ('klēnli) *adv.* 1. in a clean manner —*a.* ('klenli) 2. clean —**'cleanness** *n.* —**cleanse** (klenz) *vt.* make clean —**cleanser** ('klenzər)

n. preparation used for cleaning —**clean-cut** *a.* 1. clearly outlined; neat 2. definite —**come clean** *inf.* confess

clear (klēər) *a.* 1. pure, undimmed, bright 2. free from cloud 3. transparent 4. plain, distinct 5. without defect or drawback 6. unimpeded —*adv.* 7. brightly 8. wholly, quite —*vt.* 9. make clear 10. acquit 11. pass over or through 12. make as profit 13. free from obstruction, difficulty 14. free by payment of dues —*vi.* 15. become clear, bright, free, transparent —**'clearance** *n.* 1. making clear 2. removal of obstructions, surplus stock *etc.* 3. certificate that ship has been cleared at customhouse 4. space for moving part, vehicle, to pass within, through or past something —**'clearing** *n.* land cleared of trees —**'clearly** *adv.* —**'clearness** *n.* —**clear-cut** *a.* 1. definite; not vague 2. clearly outlined —**clearing house** 1. *Banking* institution where checks *etc.* drawn on member banks are canceled against each other 2. central agency for collection and distribution of information —**clear-sighted** *a.* discerning

clearstory ('klēərstöri) *n. see* CLERESTORY

cleat (klēt) *n.* 1. wedge 2. piece of wood or iron with two projecting ends around which ropes are made fast

cleave[1] (klēv) *vt.* 1. split asunder —*vi.* 2. crack, part asunder (**clove, cleft** *pt.*, **'cloven, cleft** *pp.*, **'cleaving** *pr.p.*) —**'cleavage** *n.* 1. separation between woman's breasts, *esp.* as revealed by low-cut dress 2. division, split —**'cleaver** *n.* short chopper

cleave[2] (klēv) *vi.* 1. stick, adhere 2. be loyal (**cleaved, 'cleaving**)

clef (klef) *n. Mus.* mark to show pitch of staff

cleft (kleft) *n.* 1. crack, fissure, chasm 2. opening made by cleaving —*v.* 3. *pt./pp. of* CLEAVE[1] —**cleft lip** *see* **harelip** *at* HARE —**cleft palate** congenital fissure in midline of hard palate, oft. associated with harelip —**cleft stick** situation involving choice between two equally unsatisfactory alternatives

cleg (kleg) *n.* horsefly

clematis ('klemətis) *n.* flowering climbing perennial plant

clement ('klemənt) *a.* 1. merciful 2. gentle 3. mild —**'clemency** *n.* —**'clemently** *adv.*

clench (klench) *vt.* 1. set firmly together 2. grasp, close (fist)

clerestory *or* **clearstory** ('klēərstöri) *n.* 1. outside wall of room or building that rises above an adjoining roof and contains windows 2. row of windows in upper part of church above the nave —**'clerestoried** *or* **'clearstoried** *a.*

clergy ('klərji) *n.* body of appointed ministers of Christian Church —**'clergyman** *n.*

clerical ('klerikəl) *a.* 1. of clergy 2. of, connected with, office work —**'cleric** *n.* clergyman —**'clericalism** *n.*

clerk (klərk) *n.* 1. subordinate who keeps files *etc.* in an office 2. officer in charge of records, correspondence *etc.*, of department or corporation 3. salesperson —**'clerkly** *a.* —**'clerkship** *n.* —**clerk of the works** employee who supervises building work

Cleveland ('klēvlənd) *n.* **Grover.** the 22nd and 24th President of the U.S. (1885-89 and 1893-97)

clever ('klevər) *a.* 1. intelligent 2. able, skillful, adroit —**'cleverly** *adv.* —**'cleverness** *n.*

clew (kloō) *n.* 1. ball of thread or yarn 2. *Naut.* lower corner of sail —*vt.* 3. coil into ball

cliché (klē'sha) *n.* hackneyed phrase

click¹ (klik) *n*. **1.** short, sharp sound, as of latch in door **2.** catch —*v*. **3.** (cause to) make short, sharp sound

click² (klik) *vi*. **1.** *sl*. be a success **2.** *inf*. become clear **3.** *inf*. strike up friendship

client ('klīənt) *n*. **1.** customer **2.** one who employs professional person —**clientele** (klīən'tel) *n*. body of clients

cliff (klif) *n*. steep rock face —**'cliffhanger** *n*. tense situation, *esp*. in film *etc*.

climacteric (klī'maktərik, klīmak'terik) *n*. **1.** critical event or period **2.** *see* MENOPAUSE **3.** period in life of man corresponding to menopause, characterized by diminished sexual activity —*a*. (*also* **climac'terical**) **4.** involving crucial event or period

climate ('klīmit) *n*. **1.** condition of country with regard to weather **2.** prevailing feeling, atmosphere —**cli'matic** *a*. of climate

climax ('klīmaks) *n*. **1.** highest point, culmination **2.** point of greatest excitement, tension in story *etc*. —**cli'mactic** *a*.

climb (klīm) *v*. **1.** go up or ascend **2.** progress with difficulty **3.** creep up, mount **4.** slope upward —**'climber** *n*. —**'climbing** *n*.

clime (klīm) *n*. **1.** region, country **2.** climate

clinch (klinch) *vt*. **1.** *see* CLENCH **2.** settle, conclude (an agreement) —**'clincher** *n*. *inf*. something decisive

cling (kling) *vi*. **1.** adhere **2.** be firmly attached **3.** be dependent (on) (**clung** *pt./pp.*)

clinic ('klinik) *n*. place for medical examination, advice or treatment —**'clinical** *a*. **1.** relating to clinic, care of sick *etc*. **2.** objective, unemotional **3.** bare, plain —**'clinically** *adv*. —**clinical thermometer** thermometer used for taking body temperature

clink¹ (klingk) *n*. sharp metallic sound —*v*. **2.** (cause to) make this sound

clink² (klingk) *n*. *sl*. prison

clinker ('klingkər) *n*. **1.** fused coal residues from fire or furnace **2.** hard brick

clinker-built *a*. (of boat) with outer boards or plates overlapping

Clio ('klīō, 'klēō) *n*. statuette awarded annually for notable achievements in radio and television by a professional organization (*pl*. **-s**)

clip¹ (klip) *vt*. **1.** cut with scissors **2.** cut short (**-pp-**) —*n*. **3.** *inf*. sharp blow —**'clipper** *n*. —**'clipping** *n*. something cut out, *esp*. article from newspaper; cutting —**clip joint** *sl*. nightclub *etc*. in which customers are overcharged

clip² (klip) *n*. device for gripping or holding together, *esp*. hair, clothing *etc*. —**'clipboard** *n*. portable writing board with clip at top for holding paper

clipper ('klipər) *n*. fast sailing ship

clippie ('klipi) *n*. UK *inf*. bus conductress

clique (klēk, klik) *n*. **1.** small exclusive set **2.** faction, group of people —**'cliquish** *a*.

clitoris ('klitəris, kli'tōris) *n*. small erectile part of female genitals

cloak (klōk) *n*. **1.** loose outer garment **2.** disguise, pretext —*vt*. **3.** cover with cloak **4.** disguise, conceal —**cloak-and-dagger** *a*. concerned with intrigue and espionage —**'cloakroom** *n*. place for keeping coats, hats, luggage

clobber ('klobər) *vt*. *inf*. **1.** beat, batter **2.** defeat utterly

cloche (klōsh) *n*. woman's close-fitting hat

clock (klok) *n*. **1.** instrument for measuring time **2.** device with dial for recording or measuring —**'clockwise** *adv./a*. in the direction that the hands of a clock rotate —**'clockwork** *n*. mechanism similar to that of a clock, as in a wind-up toy —**clock in** *or*

on, out *or* **off** record arrival or departure on automatic time recorder

clod (klod) *n*. **1.** lump of earth **2.** blockhead —**'cloddish** *a*. —**'clodhopper** *n*. *inf*. **1.** clumsy person; lout **2.** (*usu. pl.*) large heavy shoe

clog (klog) *vt*. **1.** hamper, impede, choke up (**-gg-**) —*n*. **2.** obstruction, impediment **3.** wooden-soled shoe —**clog dance**

cloisonné (kloizə'nā) *n*. **1.** enamel decoration in compartments formed by small fillets of metal —*a*. **2.** of cloisonné

cloister ('kloistər) *n*. **1.** covered pillared arcade **2.** monastery or convent —**'cloistered** *a*. confined, secluded, sheltered

clomp (klomp) *see* CLUMP²

clone (klōn) *n*. **1.** any living organism produced by division from one parent with the result being genetically identical —*v*. **2.** (cause to) produce clone

clop (klop) *vi*. move, sound, as horse's hooves (**-pp-**)

cloqué (klō'kā) *n*. fabric with a blistered finish

close¹ (klōs) *a*. **1.** adjacent, near **2.** compact **3.** crowded **4.** affectionate, intimate **5.** almost equal **6.** careful, searching **7.** confined **8.** secret **9.** unventilated, stifling **10.** reticent **11.** niggardly **12.** strict, restricted —*adv*. **13.** nearly **14.** tightly —*n*. **15.** shut-in place **16.** precinct of cathedral —**'closely** *adv*. —**'closeness** *n*. —**close-fisted** *a*. mean; avaricious —**close harmony** singing in which all parts except bass lie close together —**close quarters** cramped space or position —**close season** time when it is illegal to kill certain kinds of game and fish —**close shave** *inf*. narrow escape —**'closeup** *n*. close view, *esp*. portion of motion picture —**at close quarters** engaged in hand-to-hand combat; in close proximity; very near together

close² (klōz) *vt*. **1.** shut **2.** stop up **3.** prevent access to **4.** finish —*vi*. **5.** come together **6.** grapple —*n*. **7.** end —**closed circuit** complete electrical circuit through which current can flow —**closed shop** place of work in which all workers must belong to a union

closet ('klozit) *n*. **1.** cupboard **2.** small private room **3.** water closet, toilet —*a*. **4.** private, secret —*vt*. **5.** shut up in private room, *esp*. for conference **6.** conceal

closure ('klōzhər) *n*. **1.** act of closing **2.** ending of debate by majority vote or other authority

clot (klot) *n*. **1.** mass or lump **2.** *inf*. fool **3.** *Med*. coagulated mass of blood —*vt*. **4.** form into lumps —*vi*. **5.** coagulate (**-tt-**)

cloth (kloth) *n*. fabric made by weaving, knitting, netting or compressing filaments —**clothe** (klōdh) *vt*. put clothes on (**clothed** *or* **clad** *pt./pp.*) —**clothes** (klōdhz) *pl.n*. **1.** dress **2.** bed coverings —**clothier** ('klōdhiər) *n*. —**clothing** ('klōdhing) *n*. —**clotheshorse** ('klōdhz-hôrs) *n*. **1.** frame on which to hang laundry for drying or airing **2.** *inf*. excessively fashionable person

cloud (klowd) *n*. **1.** condensed water vapor floating in air **2.** state of gloom **3.** multitude —*vt*. **4.** overshadow, dim, darken —*vi*. **5.** become cloudy —**'cloudless** *a*. —**'cloudy** *a*. —**'cloudburst** *n*. heavy downpour

clout (klowt) *n*. **1.** *inf*. blow **2.** influence, power —*vt*. **3.** *inf*. strike

clove¹ (klōv) *n*. **1.** dried flower bud of tropical tree, used as spice **2.** one of small bulbs making up compound bulb

clove² (klōv) *pt. of* CLEAVE¹ —**'cloven** *pp. of* CLEAVE¹ —**cloven hoof** *or* **foot** **1.** divided hoof of cow, deer *etc*. **2.** symbol of Satan

clove hitch knot for securing rope to spar, post or larger rope

clover ('klōvər) *n*. low-growing forage plant, trefoil —**'cloverleaf** *n*. **1.** arrangement of connecting roads, resembling four-leaf clover, that joins two intersecting main roads —*a*. **2.** in shape of leaf of clover —**be in clover** be in luxury

clown (klown) *n*. **1.** comic entertainer in circus **2.** jester, fool —*vi*. **3.** play jokes or tricks **4.** act foolishly —**'clownish** *a*.

cloy (kloi) *vt*. weary by sweetness, sameness *etc*.

CLU chartered life underwriter

club (klub) *n*. **1.** thick stick **2.** bat, stick used in some games **3.** association for pursuance of common interest **4.** building used by such association **5.** one of the suits at cards —*vt*. **6.** strike with club —*vi*. **7.** join for a common object (**-bb-**) —**club foot** deformed foot —**club moss** any primitive plant with trailing, branching stems at free ends —**club root** fungal disease of cabbages *etc*., in which roots become thickened and distorted

cluck (kluk) *vi./n*. (make) noise of hen

clue *or* **clew** (kloo) *n*. **1.** indication, *esp*. of solution of mystery or puzzle —*vt*. **2.** (*usu. with* up) provide with helpful information

clump¹ (klump) *n*. **1.** cluster of trees or plants **2.** compact mass

clump² (klump) *vi*. **1.** walk, tread heavily —*n*. **2.** dull, heavy tread or similar sound

clumsy ('klumzi) *a*. **1.** awkward, unwieldy, ungainly **2.** badly made or arranged —**'clumsily** *adv*. —**'clumsiness** *n*.

clung (klung) *pt./pp. of* CLING

clunk (klungk) *n*. (sound of) blow or something falling

cluster ('klustər) *n*. **1.** group, bunch —*v*. **2.** gather, grow in cluster

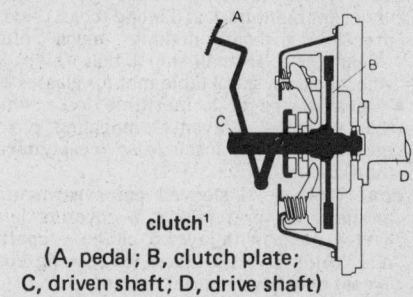

clutch¹
(A, pedal; B, clutch plate;
C, driven shaft; D, drive shaft)

clutch¹ (kluch) *v*. **1.** grasp eagerly **2.** snatch (at) —*n*. **3.** grasp, tight grip **4.** device enabling two revolving shafts to be connected and disconnected at will

clutch² (kluch) *n*. **1.** set of eggs hatched at one time **2.** brood of chickens

clutter ('klutər) *v*. **1.** strew **2.** crowd together in disorder —*n*. **3.** disordered, obstructive mass of objects

Clydesdale ('klīdzdāl) *n*. heavy powerful carthorse, orig. from Scotland

cm *or* **cm.** centimeter

Cm *Chem*. curium

Cmdr. *Mil*. Commander

cml commercial

CN credit note

C.N.D. UK Campaign for Nuclear Disarmament

Co *Chem*. cobalt

CO **1.** Colorado **2.** cash order

Co. *or* **co.** Company

Co. County

C.O. **1.** Commanding Officer **2.** conscientious objector

co- (*comb. form*) **1.** together, as in *coproduction* **2.** partnership or equality, as in *costar, copilot* **3.** to similar degree, as in *coextend* **4.** *Math., astron.* of complement of angle, as in *cosecant*

c/o care of

coach (kōch) *n.* **1.** long-distance or touring bus **2.** large four-wheeled carriage **3.** railroad carriage **4.** tutor, instructor —*vt.* **5.** instruct —**coach-builder** *n.* —**'coachman** *n.*

coadjutor (kō'ajōōtər) *n.* **1.** bishop appointed as assistant to diocesan bishop **2.** *rare* assistant

coagulate (kō'agyŏŏlāt) *v.* **1.** curdle, clot, form into a mass **2.** congeal, solidify —**coagu'lation** *n.*

coal (kōl) *n.* **1.** rock consisting of carbonized vegetable matter, used as fuel **2.** glowing ember —*v.* **3.** supply with or take in coal —**'coalface** *n.* exposed seam of coal in mine —**'coalfield** *n.* district in which coal is found —**coal gas** mixture of gases produced by distillation of bituminous coal and used for heating and lighting —**coal tar** black tar, produced by distillation of bituminous coal, that can be further distilled to yield benzene *etc.* —**coal tit** small songbird having black head with white patch on nape

coalesce (kōə'les) *vi.* unite, merge —**coa'lescence** *n.*

coalfish ('kōlfish) *n.* food fish with dark-colored skin

coalition (kōə'lishən) *n.* alliance, *esp.* of political parties

coaming ('kōming) *n.* raised frame round ship's hatchway for keeping out water

coarse (körs) *a.* **1.** rough, harsh **2.** unrefined **3.** indecent —**'coarsely** *adv.* —**'coarsen** *v.* make or become coarse —**'coarseness** *n.* —**coarse fish** freshwater fish not of salmon family —**coarse fishing**

coast (kōst) *n.* **1.** sea shore —*v.* **2.** move under momentum **3.** sail along (coast) —*vi.* **4.** proceed without making much effort —**'coaster** *n.* **1.** small ship **2.** that which, one who, coasts **3.** small table mat for glasses *etc.* —**'coastguard** *n.* **1.** maritime force which aids shipping, prevents smuggling *etc.* **2.** member of such force (*also* **'coastguardsman**)

coat (kōt) *n.* **1.** sleeved outer garment **2.** animal's fur or feathers **3.** covering layer —*vt.* **4.** cover with layer **5.** clothe —**'coating** *n.* **1.** outer layer **2.** fabric for making coats —**coat of arms** armorial bearings

coax (kōks) *vt.* wheedle, cajole, persuade, force gently

coaxial (kō'aksiəl) *a.* having the same axis —**coaxial cable** high-frequency cable with outer conductor tube surrounding insulated central conductor (*also* **coaxial line**)

cob (kob) *n.* **1.** short-legged stout horse **2.** male swan **3.** corncob

cobalt ('kōbölt) *n.* **1.** *Chem.* metallic element Symbol Co, at. wt. 58.9, at. no. 27 **2.** blue pigment from it —**cobalt bomb 1.** cobalt-60 device used in radiotherapy **2.** nuclear weapon consisting of hydrogen bomb encased in cobalt

cobber ('kobər) *n.* **A, NZ** friend: used as term of address to males

cobble ('kobəl) *vt.* **1.** patch roughly **2.** mend (shoes) —*n.* **3.** round stone —**'cobbler** *n.* shoe mender —**'cobblestone** *n.* rounded stone used for paving (*also* **'cobble**)

cobbler ('koblər) *n.* **1.** sweetened iced drink, usu. made from fruit and wine **2.** deep-dish fruit pie

COBOL ('kōböl) computer-programming language for general commercial use

cobra ('kōbrə) *n.* venomous, hooded snake of Asia and Afr.

cobweb ('kobweb) *n.* spider's web

coca ('kōkə) *n.* either of two shrubs, native to Andes, whose dried leaves contain cocaine

cocaine (kō'kān) *n.* addictive narcotic drug obtained from leaves of certain S Amer. trees

coccidioidomycosis (koksidioidōmī'kōsis) *n.* fungus disease found principally in southern U.S.

coccus ('kokəs) *n.* spherical or nearly spherical bacterium, such as staphylococcus (*pl.* **-ci** (-sī))

coccyx ('koksiks) *n.* small triangular bone at end of spinal column (*pl.* **coccyges** ('koksijēz))

cochineal ('kochinēl) *n.* scarlet dye from Mexican insect

cochlea ('kōkliə) *n.* spiral tube that forms part of internal ear, converting sound vibrations into nerve impulses (*pl.* **-leae** (-liē))

cock (kok) *n.* **1.** male bird, *esp.* of domestic fowl **2.** tap for liquids **3.** hammer of gun **4.** its position drawn back —*vt.* **5.** draw back (gun hammer) to firing position **6.** raise, turn in alert or jaunty manner —**cockerel** *n.* young rooster —**cock-a-hoop** *a.* **1.** in ˹very high spirits **2.** boastful **3.** askew; confused —**cock-and-bull story** *inf.* obviously improbable story, *esp.* one used as excuse —**'cockcrow** *or* **'cockcrowing** *n.* daybreak —**cocked hat** hat with brims turned up and caught together to give two or three points —**'cockeyed** *a.* **1.** cross-eyed **2.** with a squint **3.** askew —**'cockfight** *n.* —**'cockfighting** *n.* sport, illegal in U.S. and many other countries, in which two gamecocks fight until one is acknowledged winner —**'cockscomb** *or* **'coxcomb** *n.* **1.** comb of domestic cock **2.** garden plant with flowers in broad spike resembling comb of cock **3.** *inf.* conceited dandy —**cock'sure** *a.* overconfident; arrogant —**knock into a cocked hat** *sl.* outdo, defeat

cockade (ko'kād) *n.* rosette, badge for hat

cockatoo ('kokətōō) *n.* **Aust., New Guinea,** crested parrot

cockatrice ('kokətris, -trīs) *n.* fabulous animal similar to basilisk

cockchafer ('kokchāfər) *n.* large, flying beetle

cocker spaniel ('kokər) small compact spaniel

cockle[1] ('kokəl) *n.* shellfish —**'cockleshell** *n.* **1.** shell of cockle **2.** shell of certain other mollusks **3.** small light boat

cockle[2] ('kokəl) *v.* wrinkle, pucker

cockney ('kokni) *n.* (*oft.* **C-**) native of London, *esp.* of East End (*pl.* **-s**)

cockpit ('kokpit) *n.* **1.** pilot's seat, compartment in small aircraft **2.** driver's seat in racing car **3.** orig. enclosure for cockfights

cockroach ('kokrōch) *n.* kind of insect, household pest

cocktail ('koktāl) *n.* **1.** short drink of spirits with flavorings *etc.* **2.** appetizer

cocky ('koki) *a.* conceited, pert

cocoa ('kōkō) *n.* **1.** powder made from seed of cacao (tropical) tree **2.** drink made from the powder

coconut ('kōkənut) *n.* **1.** tropical palm **2.** very large, hard nut from this palm —**coconut matting** coarse matting made from fibrous husk of coconut —**coconut milk** liquid extracted from grated flesh of fresh mature coconut or from reconstituted dried shredded coconut

cocoon (kə'kōōn) *n.* **1.** sheath of insect in chrysalis stage **2.** any protective covering

cocotte (ko'kot) *n.* **1.** small fireproof dish in which individual portions of food are cooked and served **2.** prostitute; promiscuous woman

cod (kod) *n.* food fish of northern Atlantic (*also* **'codfish**) —**cod-liver oil** oil extracted from fresh codfish livers, rich in vitamins A and D

C.O.D. cash on delivery

coda ('kōdə) *n. Mus.* final part of musical composition

coddle ('kodəl) *vt.* overprotect, pamper

code (kōd) *n.* **1.** system of letters, symbols and rules for their association to transmit messages secretly or briefly **2.** scheme of conduct **3.** collection of laws —**codifi'cation** *n.* —**'codify** *vt.*

codeine ('kōdēn) *n.* narcotic derived from opium used to relieve pain and to control coughing

codex ('kōdeks) *n.* ancient manuscript volume, *esp.* of Bible *etc.* (*pl.* **codices** ('kōdisēz, 'kodi-))

codger ('kojər) *n. inf.* odd old man

codicil ('kodisil) *n.* addition to will —**codi'cillary** *a.*

codpiece ('kodpēs) *n.* bag covering male genitals, attached to breeches: worn in 15th and 16th centuries

coeducation (kōeju'kāshən) *n.* instruction in schools *etc.* attended by both sexes —**co-ed** *n.* **1.** female student in such an institution —*a.* **2.** coeducational —**coedu'cational** *a.* of education of boys and girls together in mixed classes

coefficient (kōi'fishənt) *n. Math.* numerical or constant factor

coelenterate (si'lentərāt, -rit) *n.* any member of a phylum (*Coelenterata*) of invertebrate animals including the corals, sea anemones, jellyfishes and hydroids

coequal (kō'ēkwəl) *a.* **1.** of same size, rank *etc.* —*n.* **2.** person or thing equal with another —**coe'quality** *n.*

coerce (kō'ərs) *vt.* compel, force —**co'ercion** *n.* forcible compulsion or restraint —**co'ercive** *or* **co'ercible** *a.*

coeval (kō'ēvəl) *a.* of same age or generation

coexist (kōig'zist) *vi.* exist together —**coex'istence** *n.* —**coex'istent** *a.*

coextend (kōik'stend) *v.* extend or cause to extend equally in space or time —**coex'tension** *n.* —**coex'tensive** *a.*

coffee ('kofi) *n.* **1.** seeds of tropical shrub **2.** drink made from roasting and grinding these —**coffee mill** machine for grinding roasted coffee beans —**coffee shop** informal restaurant —**coffee table** low table on which coffee may be served

coffer ('kofər) *n.* **1.** chest for valuables **2.** treasury, funds

cofferdam ('kofərdam) *n.* watertight structure enabling construction work to be done under water

coffin ('kofin) *n.* box in which corpse is buried or cremated

cog (kog) *n.* **1.** one of series of teeth on rim of wheel **2.** person, thing forming small part of big process, organization *etc.* —**'cogwheel** *n.*

cogent ('kōjənt) *a.* convincing, compelling, persuasive —**'cogency** *n.* —**'cogently** *adv.*

cogitate ('kojitāt) *vi.* think, reflect, ponder —**cogi'tation** *n.* —**'cogitative** *a.*

Cognac ('konyak) *n.* French brandy

cognate ('kognāt) *a.* of same stock, related, kindred —**cog'nation** *n.*

cognition (kog'nishən) *n.* act or faculty of knowing —**cog'nitional** *a.*

cognizance ('kognizəns) *n.* knowledge, perception —**'cognizable** *a.* —**'cognizant** *a.*

cognomen (kog'nōmən) *n.* surname, nickname (*pl.* **-s, -nomina** (-'nomina, -'nō-))

cognoscenti (konyō'shenti, kognə-) *or* **conoscenti** (konō'shenti) *pl.n.* people with knowledge in particular field, *esp.* arts (*sing.* **-te** (-tē))

cohabit (kō'habit) *vi.* live together as husband and wife

coheir (kō'âər) *n.* a joint heir (**co'heiress** *fem.*)

cohere (kō'hēər) *vi.* stick together, be consistent —**co'herence** *n.* —**co'herent** *a.* 1. capable of logical thought 2. connected, making sense 3. sticking together —**co'herently** *adv.* —**co'hesion** *n.* cohering —**co'hesive** *a.*

cohort ('kōhört) *n.* 1. troop 2. associate

coif (koif) *n.* 1. close-fitting cap worn under veil in Middle Ages 2. leather cap worn under chainmail hood 3. (kwäf) *rare* coiffure —*vt.* 4. cover with or as if with coif 5. (kwäf) arrange (hair) (**-ff-**)

coiffure (kwä'fyōōr) *n.* hairstyle —**coiffeur** (kwä'fər) *n.* hairdresser

coign of vantage (koin) advantageous position for observation or action

coil (koil) *vt.* 1. lay in rings 2. twist into winding shape —*vi.* 3. twist, take up a winding shape or spiral —*n.* 4. series of rings 5. device in vehicle *etc.* to transform low-tension current to higher voltage for ignition purposes 6. contraceptive device inserted in womb

coin (koin) *n.* 1. piece of money 2. money —*vt.* 3. make into money, stamp 4. invent —'**coinage** *n.* 1. coining 2. coins collectively —'**coiner** *n.* maker of counterfeit money —**coin silver** silver alloy containing about 900 parts silver and 100 parts base metal

coincide (kōin'sīd) *vi.* 1. happen together 2. agree exactly —**co'incidence** *n.* —**co'incident** *a.* coinciding —**coinci'dental** *a.*

Cointreau ('kwäntrō) *n.* trade name for colorless liqueur with orange flavoring

coir ('koiər) *n.* fiber of coconut husk

coitus ('kōitəs) *or* **coition** (kō'ishən) *n.* sexual intercourse

coke[1] (kōk) *n.* residue left from distillation of coal, used as fuel

coke[2] (kōk) *n. sl.* cocaine

Coke (kōk) *n.* trade name for a carbonated cola drink

col (kol) *n.* high mountain pass

Col. 1. Colonel 2. Colossians

cola ('kōlə) *n.* 1. tropical tree 2. its nut, used to flavor drink

colander ('kuləndər, 'kol-) *n.* culinary strainer perforated with small holes

cold (kōld) *a.* 1. lacking heat 2. indifferent, unmoved, apathetic 3. dispiriting 4. reserved or unfriendly 5. (of colors) giving an impression of coldness —*n.* 6. lack of heat 7. illness, marked by runny nose *etc.* —'**coldly** *adv.* —'**coldness** *n.* —**cold-blooded** *a.* 1. lacking pity, mercy 2. having body temperature that varies with that of the surroundings —**cold chisel** toughened steel chisel —**cold cream** emulsion of water and fat for softening and cleansing skin —**cold feet** *sl.* loss of confidence —**cold frame** unheated wooden frame with glass top, used to protect young plants —**cold front** *Met.* boundary line between warm air mass and cold air pushing it —**cold-hearted** *a.* lacking in feeling or warmth; unkind —**cold-heartedness** *n.* —**cold shoulder** *inf.* show of indifference; slight —**cold-shoulder** *vt. inf.* treat with indifference —**cold sore** cluster of blisters caused by virus infection which may appear anywhere in the body (*also* **fever blisters**)

—**cold storage** 1. method of preserving perishable foods *etc.* by keeping them at artificially reduced temperature 2. *inf.* state of temporary suspension —**cold sweat** *inf.* bodily reaction to fear or nervousness, characterized by chill and moist skin —**cold war** economic, diplomatic but nonmilitary hostility —(**out**) **in the cold** *inf.* neglected; ignored

cole (kōl) *n.* any of various plants such as cabbage and rape (*also* '**colewort**)

coleopteran (kōli'optərən) *n.* 1. any of order of insects, including beetles, in which forewings form shell-like protective elytra (*also* **cole'opteron**) —*a.* 2. of this order (*also* **cole'opterous**)

coleslaw ('kōlslö) *n.* salad dish based on shredded cabbage

coleus ('kōliəs) *n.* plant of the mint family cultivated for its variegated leaves

colic ('kolik) *n.* severe pains in the intestines —**co'litis** *n.* inflammation of the colon

coliseum (koli'sēəm) *or* **colosseum** (kolə'sēəm) *n.* large building, such as stadium, used for entertainments *etc.*

collaborate (kə'labərāt) *vi.* work with another on a project —**collabo'ration** *n.* —**col'laborator** *n.* one who works with another, *esp.* one who aids an enemy in occupation of his own country

collage (kə'läzh, kö-) *n.* picture or design made up of flat everyday materials *esp.* paper, fixed to a background

collagen ('koləjən) *n.* fibrous protein of connective tissue and bones that yields gelatin on boiling —**collagen diseases** group of ailments characterized by inflammation of the collagen tissue, *eg* rheumatoid arthritis

collapse (kə'laps) *vi.* 1. fall 2. give way 3. lose strength, fail —*n.* 4. act of collapsing 5. breakdown —**col'lapsible** *or* **col'lapsable** *a.*

collar ('kolər) *n.* 1. band, part of garment, worn round neck —*vt.* 2. seize by collar 3. *inf.* capture, seize —'**collarbone** *n.* bone from shoulder to breastbone

collate (ko'lāt, kə-) *vt.* 1. compare carefully 2. place in order (as printed sheets for binding) —**col'lation** *n.* 1. collating 2. light meal

collateral (kə'latərəl) *n.* 1. security pledged for repayment of loan —*a.* 2. accompanying 3. side by side 4. of same stock but different line 5. subordinate

colleague ('kolēg) *n.* associate, companion in office or employment, fellow worker

collect[1] (kə'lekt) *vt.* 1. gather, bring together —*vi.* 2. come together 3. *inf.* receive money —*adv./a.* 4. (of telephone calls *etc.*) paid for by the receiver —**col'lected** *a.* 1. calm 2. gathered —**col'lection** *n.* —**col'lective** *n.* 1. factory, farm *etc.*, run on principles of collectivism —*a.* 2. formed or assembled by collection 3. forming whole or aggregate 4. of individuals acting in cooperation —**col'lectively** *adv.* —**col'lectivism** *n.* theory that the state should own all means of production —**col'lector** *n.* —**collective bargaining** negotiation between labor union and employer or employers' organization on incomes and working conditions of employees —**collector's item** any rare or beautiful object thought worthy of collection

collect[2] ('kolekt) *n.* short prayer

colleen (ko'lēn, 'kolēn) *n. Irish name for* girl

college ('kolij) *n.* 1. place of higher education 2. society of scholars 3. association —**collegi'ality** *n.* participation of bishops in governance of R.C. Church —**col'legian** *n.* student —**col'legiate** *a.* —**college boards** set

of examinations taken by aspirants to certain colleges

collide (kə'līd) *vi.* 1. strike or dash together 2. come into conflict —**collision** (kə'lizhən) *n.* colliding

collie ('koli) *n.* any of several breeds of dog orig. bred to herd sheep

collier ('kolyər) *n.* 1. coal miner 2. coal ship —'**colliery** *n.* coal mine

collimate ('kolimāt) *vt.* 1. adjust line of sight of (optical instrument) 2. make parallel or bring into line —**colli'mation** *n.*

collocate ('koləkāt) *vt.* group, place together —**collo'cation** *n.*

collodion (kə'lōdiən) *n.* chemical solution used in photography and medicine

colloid ('koloid) *n.* suspension of particles in a solution

collop ('koləp) *n.* 1. slice of meat 2. small piece of anything

colloquial (kə'lōkwiəl) *a.* pert. to, or used in, informal conversation —**col'loquialism** *n.* —'**colloquy** *n.* 1. conversation 2. dialogue

colloquium (kə'lōkwiəm) *n.* 1. gathering for discussion 2. academic seminar (*pl.* **-s, -quia** (-kwiə))

collotype ('kolōtīp) *n.* printing process used for fine illustration work (*also* **photogelatin**)

collusion (kə'lōōzhən) *n.* secret agreement for a fraudulent purpose, *esp.* in legal proceedings —**col'lusive** *a.*

Colo. Colorado

cologne (kə'lōn) *n.* perfumed liquid (*also* **eau de cologne**)

Colombia (kə'lumbiə) *n.* country in South America bounded north by the Caribbean Sea, northwest by Panama, west by the Pacific Ocean, southwest by Ecuador and Peru, northwest by Venezuela and southeast by Brazil

colon[1] ('kōlən) *n.* mark (:) indicating break in sentence

colon[2] ('kōlən) *n.* part of large intestine from cecum to rectum

colonel ('kərnəl) *n.* commander of regiment or battalion —'**colonelcy** *n.*

colonnade (kolə'nād) *n.* row of columns

colony ('koləni) *n.* 1. body of people who settle in new country but remain subject to parent state 2. country so settled 3. distinctive group living together —**co'lonial** *a.* of colony —**co'lonialism** *n.* policy and practice of extending control over weaker peoples or areas (*also* **im'perialism**) —**co'lonialist** *n./a.* —**co'lonist** *n.* —**coloni'zation** *n.* —'**colonize** *v.*

colophon ('koləfən, -fon) *n.* publisher's imprint or device

color ('kulər) *n.* 1. hue, tint 2. complexion 3. paint 4. pigment 5. *fig.* semblance, pretext 6. *fig.* timber, quality 7. *fig.* mood —*pl.* 8. flag 9. *Sport* distinguishing badge, symbol —*vt.* 10. stain, dye, paint, give color to 11. *fig.* disguise 12. *fig.* influence or distort —*vi.* 13. become colored 14. blush —'**colorable** *a.* 1. capable of being colored 2. appearing to be true; plausible 3. pretended; feigned —**colo'ration** *n.* —'**colored** *a.* 1. possessing color 2. having strong element of fiction or fantasy; distorted (*esp. in* **highly colored**) —'**Colored** *a.* 1. non-White 2. in S Afr., of mixed descent —'**colorful** *a.* 1. with bright or varied colors 2. distinctive —'**coloring** *n.* 1. process or art of applying color 2. anything used to give color, such as paint 3. appearance with regard to shade and color 4. arrangements of colors, as in markings of birds 5. color of complexion 6. false appearance —'**colorless** *a.* 1. without color 2. lacking interest 3. gray;

pallid **4.** without prejudice; neutral —**color bar** discrimination against people of different race, *esp.* as practiced by Whites against Blacks —**color blindness 1.** inability to distinguish one or more colors **2.** nonrecognition of racial differences —**'colorfast** *a.* (of fabric) having colors that are able to resist fading —**color perspective** *see* **atmospheric perspective** *at* ATMOSPHERE

Colorado (kolə'radō) *n.* Mountain state of the U.S., admitted to the Union in 1876. Abbrev.: **Colo., CO** (with ZIP code) —**Colorado beetle** black-and-yellow beetle that is serious pest of potatoes

coloratura (kolərə'työŏərə, -'töŏərə) *n. Mus.* **1.** florid virtuoso passage **2.** soprano who specializes in such music (*also* **coloratura soprano**)

Colossians (kə'losiənz) *pl.n.* (*with sing. v.*) *Bible* 12th book of the N.T., epistle written by St. Paul to Christians of Colossae and Laodicea

colossus (kə'losəs) *n.* **1.** huge statue **2.** something, somebody very large (*pl.* **colossi** (kə'losī), **-es**) —**co'lossal** *a.* huge, gigantic

colostomy (kə'lostəmi) *n.* surgical formation of opening from colon on to surface of body, which functions as anus

colostrum (kə'lostrəm) *n.* thin milky secretion from nipples that precedes and follows true lactation

colt (kōlt) *n.* young male horse —**'coltish** *a.* **1.** inexperienced; unruly **2.** playful and lively

coltsfoot ('kōltsfŏŏt) *n.* wild plant with heart-shaped leaves and yellow flowers (*pl.* **-s**)

columbine ('koləmbīn) *n.* flower with five spurred petals

columbium (kə'lumbiəm) *n. see* NIOBIUM

Columbus Day (kə'lumbəs) Oct. 12th, legal holiday in most U.S. states: date of Columbus's landing in West Indies in 1492 (*also* **Discovery Day**)

column ('koləm) *n.* **1.** long vertical cylinder, pillar **2.** support **3.** division of page **4.** *Journalism* regular feature in paper **5.** body of troops —**columnar** (kə'lumnər) *a.* —**'columnist** *n.* journalist writing regular feature for newspaper

colza oil ('kolzə, 'kōl-) *see* RAPE²

com- *or* **con-** (*comb. form*) together; with; jointly, as in *commingle*

coma ('kōmə) *n.* state of unconsciousness —**'comatose** *a.*

Comanche (kə'manchi) *n.* **1.** member of Amerindian people ranging from Wyoming and Nebraska into New Mexico and Texas (*pl.* **-che, -s**) **2.** the Uto-Aztecan language of the Comanche

comb (kōm) *n.* **1.** toothed instrument for tidying, arranging, ornamenting hair **2.** cock's crest **3.** mass of honey cells —*vt.* **4.** use comb on **5.** search with great care —**'comber** *n.* **1.** person, tool or machine that combs wool, flax *etc.* **2.** long curling wave; roller —**'combing** *n.* method of separating long from short fibers

combat ('kombat) *vt./n.* fight, contest —**'combatant** *n.* —**'combative** *a.* —**combat fatigue** form of nervous breakdown that appears under stress of battle (*also* **combat neurosis, combat exhaustion, shell shock**)

combine (kəm'bīn) *v.* **1.** join together **2.** ally —*n.* ('kombīn) **3.** trust, syndicate, *esp.* of businesses, trade organizations *etc.* —**combination** (kombi'nāshən) *n.* —**combinative** ('kombinātiv) *a.* —**combination lock** lock that can only be opened when set of dials is turned to show specific sequence of numbers —**combine harvester** machine to harvest

and thresh grain in one operation —**combining form** linguistic element that occurs only as part of compound word, such as *anthropo-* in *anthropology*

combo ('kombō) *n.* **1.** small group of jazz musicians **2.** *inf.* any combination (*pl.* **-s**)

combustion (kəm'buschən) *n.* process of burning —**combusti'bility** *n.* —**com'bustible** *a.*

come (kum) *vi.* **1.** approach, arrive, move toward something or someone nearer **2.** reach **3.** happen as a result **4.** occur **5.** be available **6.** originate **7.** become, turn out to be (**came, come, 'coming**) —**'coming** *a.* **1.** (of time *etc.*) approaching; next **2.** promising (*esp. in* **up and coming**) —*n.* **3.** arrival; approach —**'comeback** *n. inf.* **1.** return to active life after retirement **2.** retort —**'comedown** *n.* **1.** setback **2.** descent in social status —**come-hither** *a. inf.* alluring; seductive —**come-on** *n. inf.* anything that serves as lure —**come'uppance** *n. sl.* just retribution —**come on 1.** (of power *etc.*) start functioning **2.** progress **3.** advance, *esp.* in battle **4.** begin **5.** make entrance on stage —**come on strong** make forceful or exaggerated impression —**have it coming to one** *inf.* deserve what one is about to suffer

Comecon ('komikon) *n.* association of Soviet-oriented Communist nations, founded in 1949 to coordinate economic development *etc.*

comedy ('komidi) *n.* **1.** dramatic or other work of light, amusing character **2.** humor **3.** *Class. lit.* play in which main characters triumph over adversity —**co'median** *n.* **1.** entertainer who tells jokes *etc.* **2.** actor in comedy (**comedi'enne** *fem.*)

comely ('kumli) *a.* fair, pretty, good-looking —**'comeliness** *n.*

comestible (kə'mestibəl) *n.* (*usu. pl.*) food

comet ('komit) *n.* luminous heavenly body consisting of diffuse head, nucleus and long tail —**'cometary** *a.*

comfit ('kumfit, 'kom-) *n.* candy

comfort ('kumfərt) *n.* **1.** wellbeing **2.** ease **3.** consolation **4.** means of consolation or satisfaction —*vt.* **5.** soothe **6.** cheer, gladden, console —**comfortable** ('kumftəbəl) *a.* **1.** free from pain *etc.* **2.** *inf.* well-off financially —**comfortably** ('kumftəbli) *adv.* —**comforter** *n.* **1.** one who comforts **2.** long narrow knitted scarf —**'comfy** *a. inf.* comfortable

comfrey ('kumfri) *n.* wild plant with hairy leaves

comic ('komik) *a.* **1.** relating to comedy **2.** funny, laughable —*n.* **3.** comedian **4.** magazine consisting of strip cartoons —**'comical** *a.* —**'comically** *adv.* —**comic strip** sequence of drawings in newspaper *etc.*, relating comic or adventurous situation

comity ('komiti) *n.* **1.** mutual civility; courtesy **2.** friendly recognition accorded by nation to laws and usages of another (*also* **comity of nations**)

comm. 1. commonwealth **2.** communist

comma ('komə) *n.* punctuation mark (,) separating parts of sentence

command (kə'mand) *vt.* **1.** order **2.** rule **3.** compel **4.** have in one's power **5.** overlook, dominate **6.** receive as due —*vi.* **7.** exercise rule —*n.* **8.** order **9.** power of controlling, ruling, dominating, overlooking **10.** knowledge, mastery **11.** post of one commanding **12.** district commanded, jurisdiction —**'commandant** *n.* —**comman'deer** *vt.* seize for military use, appropriate —**com'mander** *n.* —**com'manding** *a.* **1.** in command **2.** with air of authority —**com'mandment** *n.*

commando (kə'mandō) *n.* (member of)

special military unit trained for airborne, amphibious attack (*pl.* **-s**)

commedia dell'arte (kom'medya dāl'lartā) *It.* form of improvised comedy in Italy in 16th to 18th cent., with stock characters such as Punchinello, Harlequin *etc.*

commemorate (kə'memərāt) *vt.* **1.** celebrate, keep in memory by ceremony **2.** be a memorial of —**commemo'ration** *n.* —**com'memorative** *a.*

commence (kə'mens) *v.* begin —**com'mencement** *n.*

commend (kə'mend) *vt.* **1.** praise **2.** commit, entrust —**com'mendable** *a.* —**com'mendably** *adv.* —**commen'dation** *n.* —**com'mendatory** *a.*

commensurate (kə'mensərit, -chə-) *a.* **1.** equal in size or length of time **2.** in proportion, adequate —**com'mensurable** *a.* **1.** *Math.* having common factor; having units of same dimensions and being related by whole numbers **2.** proportionate

comment ('koment) *n.* **1.** remark, criticism **2.** gossip **3.** note, explanation —*vi.* **4.** remark, note **5.** write notes explaining or criticizing a text —**'commentary** *n.* **1.** explanatory notes or comments **2.** spoken accompaniment to film *etc.* —**'commentate** *vi.* —**'commentator** *n.* author, speaker of commentary

commerce ('komərs) *n.* **1.** buying and selling **2.** dealings **3.** trade —**com'mercial** *a.* **1.** of, concerning, business, trade, profit *etc.* —*n.* **2.** advertisement, *esp.* on radio or television —**com'mercialize** *vt.* **1.** make commercial **2.** exploit for profit, *esp.* at expense of quality

commie ('komi) *n./a. inf., offens.* communist

commination (komi'nāshən) *n.* act of threatening punishment or vengeance —**'comminatory** *a.*

commingle (ko'minggəl) *v.* mix or be mixed

comminute ('kominyŏŏt, -nŏŏt) *vt.* **1.** break (bone) into small fragments **2.** divide (property) into small lots —**commi'nution** *n.*

commiserate (kə'mizərāt) *vi.* (*usu. with* with) pity, condole, sympathize —**commiser'ation** *n.*

commissar ('komisär) *n.* official of Communist Party responsible for political education

commissariat (komi'seriət, -'sar-) *n.* military department of food supplies and transport

commissary ('komiseri) *n.* **1.** shop supplying food or equipment, as in military camp **2.** army officer responsible for supplies **3.** restaurant in film studio **4.** representative or deputy, *esp.* of bishop

commission (kə'mishən) *n.* **1.** something entrusted to be done **2.** delegated authority **3.** body entrusted with some special duty **4.** payment by percentage for doing something **5.** warrant giving authority **6.** document appointing soldier, sailor or airman to officer's rank **7.** doing, committing —*vt.* **8.** charge with duty or task **9.** *Mil.* confer a rank on **10.** give order for —**com'missioner** *n.* **1.** one empowered to act by commission or warrant **2.** member of commission or government board —**commissioned officer** officer in armed forces holding commission, such as second lieutenant in air force, army or marine corps or ensign in coastguard or navy, or officer senior to these ranks

commit (kə'mit) *vt.* **1.** entrust, give in charge **2.** perpetrate, be guilty of **3.** pledge, promise **4.** compromise, entangle **5.** send for trial (**-tt-**) —**com'mitment** *n.* —**com'mittal** *n.*

committee (kə'miti) *n.* body appointed, elected for special business *usu.* from larger body

commode (kə'mōd) *n*. **1.** chest of drawers **2.** stool containing chamber pot

commodious (kə'mōdiəs) *a*. roomy

commodity (kə'moditi) *n*. **1.** article of trade **2.** anything useful

commodore ('komədör) *n*. **1.** presiding officer of yacht club or boating society **2.** ranking officer in convoy of merchant ships

common ('komən) *a*. **1.** shared by or belonging to all, or to several **2.** public, general **3.** ordinary, usual, frequent **4.** inferior **5.** vulgar —*n*. **6.** land belonging to community —*pl*. **7.** ordinary people **8.** (C-) lower House of British Parliament, House of Commons —**commo'nality** *n*. **1.** fact of being common **2.** commonalty —**'commonalty** *n*. general body of people —**'commoner** *n*. one of the common people, *ie* not of the nobility —**'commonly** *adv*. —**common fraction** fraction whose numerator and denominator are both whole numbers —**common law** body of law based on judicial decisions and custom —**common-law marriage** state of marriage deemed to exist between man and woman after years of cohabitation —**Common Market** European Economic Community —**'commonplace** *a*. **1.** ordinary, everyday —*n*. **2.** trite remark **3.** anything occurring frequently —**common room** sitting room in schools *etc*. —**common sense** sound, practical understanding —**common time** *Mus*. time signature indicating four quarter notes to bar; 4/4 time —**'commonwealth** *n*. **1.** republic **2.** (C-) federation of self-governing states

commotion (kə'mōshən) *n*. stir, disturbance, tumult

commune¹ (kə'myōōn) *vi*. converse together intimately —**com'munion** *n*. **1.** sharing of thoughts, feelings *etc*. **2.** fellowship **3.** body with common faith **4.** (C-) participation in sacrament of the Lord's Supper **5.** (C-) that sacrament, Eucharist

commune² ('komyōōn) *n*. group of families, individuals living together and sharing property, responsibility *etc*. —**'communal** *a*. for common use

communicate (kə'myōōnikāt) *vt*. **1.** impart, convey **2.** reveal —*vi*. **3.** give or exchange information **4.** have connecting passage, door **5.** receive Communion —**com'municable** *a*. —**com'municant** *n*. one who receives Communion —**communi'cation** *n*. **1.** act of giving, *esp*. information **2.** information, message **3.** (*usu. pl.*) passage (road, railroad *etc*.) or means of exchanging messages (radio, mail *etc*.) between places —*pl*. **4.** connections between military base and front —**com'municative** *a*. free with information

communiqué (kə'myōōnikā) *n*. official announcement

communism ('komyōōnizəm) *n*. **1.** doctrine that all goods, means of production *etc*. should be property of community and each member should work for common benefit **2.** (C-) political movement seeking to overthrow capitalism and to establish form of communism dominated by totalitarian bureaucracy —**'communist** *n./a*. —**commu'nistic** *a*.

community (kə'myōōniti) *n*. **1.** body of people with something in common, *eg* district of residence, religion *etc*. **2.** society, the public **3.** joint ownership **4.** similarity, agreement —**community center** place for community to participate in recreational and educational activities —**community chest** (*oft*. **C- C-**) fund of individual contributions distributed by community —**community college** tax-supported nonresi-dential two-year college —**community property** assets held jointly by husband and wife —**community sing** concert by large crowd singing in unison

commute (kə'myōōt) *vi*. **1.** travel daily some distance to work —*vt*. **2.** exchange **3.** change (punishment *etc*.) into something less severe **4.** change (duty *etc*.) for money payment —**commu'tation** *n*. —**com'mutative** *a*. relating to or involving substitution —**'commutator** *n*. —**commutative law** *Math*. principle in addition and multiplication of numbers that the end product is not affected by the order in which the terms are manipulated

Comoros ('komərōz) *pl.n.* country in the Indian Ocean consisting of three islands between the Afr. mainland and Madagascar

compact¹ (kəm'pakt) *a*. **1.** neatly arranged or packed **2.** solid, concentrated **3.** terse —*v*. **4.** make, become compact —*vt*. **5.** compress —**com'pactly** *adv*. —**com'pactness** *n*. —**compact disk** small audio disk read by optical laser system

compact² ('kompakt) *n*. small case to hold face powder, powder puff and mirror

compact³ ('kompakt) *n*. agreement, covenant, treaty, contract

companion¹ (kəm'panyən) *n*. **1.** fellow, comrade, associate **2.** person employed to live with another —**com'panionable** *a*. —**com'panionship** *n*.

companion² (kəm'panyən) *n*. **1.** raised cover over staircase from deck to cabin of ship **2.** deck skylight —**com'panionway** *n*. staircase from deck to cabin

company ('kumpəni) *n*. **1.** gathering of persons **2.** companionship, fellowship **3.** guests **4.** business firm **5.** subdivision of military battalion **6.** crew of ship **7.** actors in play —**company man** person identifying completely with firm he works for —**company town** town whose residents are completely dependent on one company for employment, housing *etc*.

compare (kəm'pāər) *vt*. **1.** notice or point out likenesses and differences of **2.** liken **3.** make comparative and superlative of (adjective or adverb) —*vi*. **4.** compete —**comparability** (kompərə'biliti) *n*. —**comparable** ('kompərəbəl) *a*. —**comparative** (kəm'parətiv) *a*. **1.** that may be compared **2.** not absolute **3.** relative, partial **4.** *Gram*. denoting form of adjective, adverb, indicating 'more' —*n*. **5.** comparative form of adjective or adverb —**comparatively** (kəm'parətivli) *adv*. —**comparison** (kəm'parisən) *n*. act of comparing —**compare with** be like

compartment (kəm'pärtmənt) *n*. **1.** division or part divided off, *eg* in railway carriage **2.** section —**compart'mentalize** *vt*. put into categories *etc*., *esp*. to excessive degree

compass ('kumpəs) *n*. **1.** instrument for showing the north **2.** (*usu. pl.*) instrument for drawing circles **3.** circumference, measurement round **4.** space, area **5.** scope, reach —*vt*. **6.** surround **7.** comprehend **8.** attain, accomplish

compassion (kəm'pashən) *n*. pity, sympathy —**com'passionate** *a*. —**com'passionately** *adv*.

compatible (kəm'patəbəl) *a*. **1.** capable of harmonious existence **2.** consistent, agreeing —**compati'bility** *n*. —**com'patibly** *adv*.

compatriot (kəm'pātriət) *n*. fellow countryman

compel (kəm'pel) *vt*. **1.** force, oblige **2.** bring about by force (**-ll-**)

compendium (kəm'pendiəm) *n*. **1.** collection of different games **2.** abridgment, summary (*pl.* **-s, -ia** (-iə)) —**com'pendious** *a*. brief but inclusive —**com'pendiously** *adv*.

compensate ('kompənsāt) *vt*. **1.** make up for **2.** recompense suitably **3.** reward —*vi*. **4.** (*with* for) supply an equivalent —**compen'sation** *n*. **1.** act or process of compensating **2.** *Psych., psychol*. psychological mechanism whereby deficiency in one area is counter-balanced by achievement in another —**com'pensatory** *a*.

compete (kəm'pēt) *vi*. (*oft. with* with) strive in rivalry, contend, vie —**competition** (kompi'tishən) *n*. —**competitive** (kəm'petitiv) *a*. —**competitor** (kəm'petitər) *n*.

competent ('kompitənt) *a*. **1.** able, skillful **2.** properly qualified **3.** proper, due, legitimate **4.** suitable, sufficient —**'competence** *n*. efficiency —**'competently** *adv*.

compile (kəm'pīl) *vt*. **1.** make up (*eg* book) from various sources or materials **2.** gather, put together —**compilation** (kompi'lāshən) *n*. —**com'piler** *n*.

complacent (kəm'plāsənt) *a*. **1.** self-satisfied **2.** pleased, gratified —**com'placence** *or* **com'placency** *n*. —**com'placently** *adv*.

complain (kəm'plān) *vi*. **1.** protest **2.** bring charge, make known a grievance **3.** (*with* of) make known that one is suffering (from) —**com'plainant** *n*. —**com'plaint** *n*. **1.** statement of a wrong, grievance **2.** ailment, illness

complaisant (kəm'plāzənt) *a*. obliging, willing to please, compliant —**com'plaisance** *n*. **1.** act of pleasing **2.** affability

complement ('komplimənt) *n*. **1.** person or thing that completes something **2.** full allowance, equipment *etc*. —*vt*. (-ment) **3.** add to, make complete —**comple'mentary** *a./n*. —**complementary color** color with maximum contrast to another color. Complementary of a primary color is the mixture of the other 2 primary colors, *eg* green (blue and yellow mixed) is the complementary of red

complete (kəm'plēt) *a*. **1.** full, perfect **2.** finished, ended **3.** entire **4.** thorough —*vt*. **5.** make whole, perfect **6.** finish —**com'pletely** *adv*. —**com'pleteness** *n*. —**com'pletion** *n*.

complex ('kompleks) *a*. **1.** intricate, compound, involved —*n*. **2.** complicated whole **3.** group of related buildings **4.** psychological abnormality, obsession —**com'plexity** *n*. —**complex fraction** *Math*. fraction in which numerator or denominator or both contain fractions (*also* **compound fraction**) —**complex number** number of form $a + bi$, where a and b are real numbers and $i = \sqrt{-1}$

complexion (kəm'plekshən) *n*. **1.** look, color, of skin, *esp*. of face, appearance **2.** aspect, character **3.** disposition

compliant (kəm'plīənt) *a*. *see* COMPLY

complicate ('komplikāt) *vt*. make intricate, involved, difficult, mix up —**compli'cation** *n*.

complicity (kəm'plisiti) *n*. partnership in wrongdoing

compliment ('komplimənt) *n*. **1.** expression of regard, praise **2.** flattering speech —*pl*. **3.** expression of courtesy, formal greetings —*vt*. ('kompliment) **4.** praise, congratulate —**compli'mentary** *a*. **1.** expressing praise **2.** free of charge

compline ('komplin, -plīn) *n*. *Eccles*. last service of day

comply (kəm'plī) *vi*. consent, yield, do as asked (**com'plied, com'plying**) —**com'pliance** *n*. —**com'pliant** *a*.

component (kəm'pōnənt) *n*. **1.** part, element, constituent of whole —*a*. **2.** composing, making up

comport (kəm'pört) *vi*. **1.** agree —*vt*. **2.** behave

compose (kəm'pōz) vt. 1. arrange, put in order 2. write, invent 3. make up 4. calm 5. settle, adjust —**com'posed** a. calm —**com'poser** n. one who composes, esp. music —'**composite** a. 1. made up of distinct parts —n. 2. any member of the daisy family in which many small individual flowers are united in one head —**compo'sition** n. —**compositor** (kəm'pozitər) n. typesetter, one who arranges type for printing —**com'posure** n. calmness —**composite school** C school offering both academic and nonacademic courses

compos mentis ('kompəs 'mentis) Lat. of sound mind

compost ('kompōst) n. fertilizing mixture of decayed vegetable matter for soil

compote ('kompōt) n. 1. fruit stewed or preserved in syrup 2. bowl with stem and base

compound[1] ('kompownd) n. 1. mixture, joining 2. substance, word, made up of parts 3. Chem. substance that can be decomposed into simpler substances —a. 4. not simple 5. composite, mixed —vt. (kom'pownd) 6. mix, make up, put together 7. intensify, make worse 8. Law agree not to prosecute in return for a consideration —v. 9. compromise, settle (debt) by partial payment —**compound eye** convex eye of insects and some crustaceans, consisting of numerous separate units —**compound fracture** fracture in which broken bone pierces skin —**compound interest** interest calculated on both principal and its accrued interest —**compound sentence** sentence containing at least two coordinate clauses —**compound time** Mus. time in which number of beats per bar is multiple of three

compound[2] ('kompownd) n. (fenced or walled) enclosure containing houses etc.

comprehend (kompri'hend) vt. 1. understand, take in 2. include, comprise —**compre'hensible** a. —**compre'hension** n. —**compre'hensive** a. 1. wide, full 2. taking in much —**compre'hensively** adv. —**compre'hensiveness** n.

compress (kəm'pres) vt. 1. squeeze together 2. make smaller in size, bulk —n. ('kompres) 3. pad of lint applied to wound, inflamed part etc. —**com'pressible** a. —**com'pression** n. in internal-combustion engine, squeezing of explosive charge before ignition, to give additional force —**com'pressor** n. esp. machine to compress air, gas

comprise (kəm'prīz) vt. include, contain —**com'prisable** a.

compromise ('komprəmīz) n. 1. meeting halfway, coming to terms by giving up part of claim 2. middle course —v. 3. settle (dispute) by making concessions —vt. 4. expose to risk or suspicion

Comptometer (komp'tomitər) n. trade name for office machine used for arithmetical calculations

comptroller (kən'trōlər) n. controller (in some titles)

compulsion (kəm'pulshən) n. 1. act of compelling 2. irresistible impulse —**com'pulsive** a. —**com'pulsorily** adv. —**com'pulsory** a. not optional

compunction (kəm'pungkshən) n. regret for wrongdoing

compute (kəm'pyōōt) v. reckon, calculate, esp. using computer —**compu'tation** n. reckoning, estimate —**com'puter** n. electronic machine for storing, retrieving information and performing calculations —**com'puterize** v. equip with, perform by computer

comrade ('komrad, -rid) n. companion, friend —'**comradeship** n.

con[1] (kon) vt. inf. swindle, defraud after winning victim's confidence (-nn-) —**con game** sl. see **confidence game** at CONFIDE —**con man** person who swindles another by means of confidence game

con[2] (kon) n. argument against —**pros and cons** arguments for and against

con[3] (kon) see CONN (-nn-)

con[4] (kon) vt. commit (something) to memory, study (-nn-)

con[5] (kon) n. sl. convict

concatenate (kon'katināt) vt. link together —**concate'nation** n. connected chain (as of circumstances)

concave (kon'kāv, 'konkāv) a. hollow, rounded inward —**concavity** (kon'kaviti) n.

conceal (kən'sēl) vt. hide, keep secret —**con'cealment** n.

concede (kən'sēd) vt. 1. admit, admit truth of 2. grant, allow —vi. 3. yield

conceit (kən'sēt) n. 1. vanity, overweening opinion of oneself 2. far-fetched comparison —**con'ceited** a.

conceive (kən'sēv) vt. 1. believe 2. form conception of 3. become pregnant with —vi. 4. become pregnant —**con'ceivable** a. —**con'ceivably** adv. —**conceive of** have an idea of; imagine; think of

concentrate ('konsəntrāt) vt. 1. focus (one's efforts etc.) 2. increase in strength 3. reduce to small space —vi. 4. devote all attention 5. come together —n. 6. concentrated material or solution —**concen'tration** n. —**concentration camp** detention camp where civilian political prisoners are confined

concentric (kən'sentrik) a. having the same center, as of circles or spheres one inside another

concept ('konsept) n. 1. abstract idea 2. mental expression —**con'ceptual** a. —**con'ceptualize** v.

conception (kən'sepshən) n. 1. idea, notion 2. act of conceiving

concern (kən'sərn) vt. 1. relate or apply to 2. interest, affect, trouble 3. (with in or with) involve (oneself) —n. 4. affair 5. regard, worry 6. importance 7. business enterprise —**con'cerned** a. 1. connected 2. interested 3. worried 4. involved —**con'cerning** prep. respecting, about

concert ('konsərt) n. 1. musical entertainment 2. harmony, agreement —v. (kən'sərt) 3. arrange, plan together —**con'certed** a. 1. mutually arranged, planned 2. determined —**concert grand** the largest-size grand piano, adapted to concert use —**concer'tina** n. 1. musical instrument of hexagonal shape, resembling accordion —vi. 2. fold, collapse, as bellows —'**concertmaster** n. the first violinist of an orchestra, who sits closest to the conductor and occasionally substitutes for him —**concerto** (kən'chertō) n. musical composition for solo instrument and orchestra (pl. -s) —**concert pitch** 1. international pitch 2. inf. state of extreme readiness

concession (kən'seshən) n. 1. act of conceding 2. thing conceded 3. grant 4. special privilege 5. C land division in township survey —**concession'aire** or **con'cessioner** n. someone who holds or operates concession —**con'cessive** a.

conch (kongk, konch) n. large spiral-shelled gastropod —**conchology** (kong'koləji) n. branch of zoology concerned with shells

concierge (kōn'syerzh) n. in France, caretaker, doorkeeper

conciliate (kən'siliāt) vt. pacify, win over

from hostility —**concili'ation** n. —**con'ciliator** n. —**con'ciliatory** a.

concise (kən'sīs) a. brief, terse —**con'cisely** adv. —**con'ciseness** n. —**concision** (kən'sizhən) n.

conclave ('konklāv) n. 1. private meeting 2. assembly for election of Pope

conclude (kən'klōōd) vt. 1. end, finish 2. deduce 3. settle 4. decide —vi. 5. come to an end —**con'clusion** n. —**con'clusive** a. decisive, convincing —**con'clusively** adv.

concoct (kən'kokt) vt. 1. make (mixture), with various ingredients 2. make up 3. contrive, plan —**con'coction** n.

concomitant (kən'komitənt) a. accompanying —**con'comitance** n. existence

concord ('konkörd) n. 1. agreement 2. harmony —**con'cordance** n. 1. agreement 2. index to words of book (esp. Bible) —**con'cordant** a. —**con'cordat** n. pact or treaty, esp. between Vatican and another state concerning interests of religion in that state

concourse ('konkörs) n. 1. crowd 2. large, open place in public area

concrete ('konkrēt) n. 1. mixture of sand, cement etc., used in building —a. 2. made of concrete 3. particular, specific 4. perceptible, actual 5. solid —'**concretely** adv. —**con'cretion** n. 1. mass of compressed particles 2. stonelike growth in body

concubine ('kongkjōōbīn) n. 1. woman living as secondary wife in society where polygamy is sanctioned 2. (also mistress) woman living with man as his wife, but not married to him —**concubinage** (kon'kyōōbinij) n.

concupiscence (kən'kyōōpisəns) n. lust

concur (kən'kər) vi. 1. agree, express agreement 2. happen together 3. coincide (-rr-) —**con'currence** n. —**con'current** a. —**con'currently** adv. at the same time

concuss (kən'kus) vt. injure (brain) by blow, fall etc. —**con'cussion** n. temporary paralysis of brain function occurring immediately after injury to brain

condemn (kən'dem) vt. 1. blame 2. find guilty 3. doom 4. find, declare unfit for use —**condemnation** (kondem'nāshən) n. —**condemnatory** (kon'demnətöri) a.

condense (kən'dens) vt. 1. concentrate, make more solid 2. turn from gas into liquid 3. pack into few words —vi. 4. turn from gas to liquid —**conden'sation** n. —**con'denser** n. 1. Elec. apparatus for storing electrical energy, a capacitor 2. apparatus for reducing vapors to liquid form 3. a lens or mirror for focusing light —**condensed milk** milk reduced by evaporation to thick concentration, with sugar added

condescend (kondi'send) vi. 1. treat graciously one regarded as inferior 2. do something below one's dignity —**conde'scending** a. —**conde'scension** n.

condign (kən'dīn) a. (esp. of punishment) fitting; deserved

condiment ('kondimənt) n. relish, seasoning for food

condition (kən'dishən) n. 1. state or circumstances of anything 2. thing on which statement or happening or existing depends 3. stipulation, prerequisite 4. health, physical fitness 5. rank —vt. 6. accustom 7. regulate 8. make fit, healthy 9. be essential to happening or existence of —**con'ditional** a. 1. dependent on circumstances or events —n. 2. Gram. conditional verb form, clause etc. —**conditioned reflex** in psychology and physiology, automatic response induced by stimulus

condo ('kondō) n. see CONDOMINIUM (senses 1, 2)

condole (kən'dōl) vi. **1.** grieve (with), offer sympathy **2.** commiserate (with) —**con'dolence** n.

condom ('kondəm) n. sheathlike rubber contraceptive device worn by man

condominium (kondə'miniəm) n. **1.** building in which apartments are individually owned **2.** an apartment in such a building **3.** sovereignty over a territory by at least two states **4.** a territory so administered

condone (kən'dōn) vt. overlook, forgive, treat as not existing

condor

condor ('kondər) n. large vulture found in the Andes

conduce (kən'dyŏŏs, -'dŏŏs) vi. (with to) **1.** help, promote **2.** tend (toward) —**con'ducive** a.

conduct ('kondukt) n. **1.** behavior **2.** management —vt. (kən'dukt) **3.** escort, guide **4.** lead, direct **5.** manage **6.** transmit (heat, electricity) —**con'ductance** n. ability of system to conduct electricity —**con'duction** n. —**con'ductive** a. —**conduc'tivity** n. —**con'ductor** n. **1.** director of orchestra **2.** one who leads, guides **3.** substance capable of transmitting heat, electricity etc. **4.** person who collects fares in a public conveyance

conduit ('kondyŏŏit, -dŏŏit) n. channel or pipe for conveying water, electric cables etc.

cone (kōn) n. **1.** solid figure with circular base, tapering to a point **2.** fruit of pine, fir etc. —**'conic(al)** a. of or like cone —**conic section** one of group of curves formed by intersection of plane and right circular cone

Conestoga (koni'stōgə) n. covered wagon used by settlers of Amer. traveling across prairies

confabulate (kən'fabyŏŏlāt) vi. chat —'**confab** n. inf. shortened form of **confabu'lation** n. confidential conversation

confection (kən'fekshən) n. prepared delicacy, esp. something sweet —**con'fectioner** n. manufacturer of or dealer in confectionery —**con'fectionery** n. sweet foods, eg candy, pastry

confederate (kən'fedərit) n. **1.** ally **2.** accomplice —v. (kən'fedərāt) **3.** unite —**con'federacy** n. —**confede'ration** n. alliance of political units

confer (kən'fər) vt. **1.** grant, give **2.** bestow **3.** award —vi. **4.** consult together (-rr-) —'**conference** n. meeting for consultation or deliberation —**con'ferment** n.

confess (kən'fes) vt. **1.** admit, own **2.** (of priest) hear sins of —vi. **3.** acknowledge **4.** declare one's sins orally to priest —**con'fession** n. —**con'fessional** n. confessor's stall or box —**con'fessor** n. priest who hears confessions

confetti (kən'feti) n. small bits of colored paper for throwing esp. at weddings

confide (kən'fīd) vi. **1.** (with in) tell secrets, trust —vt. **2.** entrust —**confidant** ('konfidant) n. one entrusted with secrets (-e fem.) —**confidence** ('konfidəns) n. **1.** trust **2.** boldness, assurance **3.** intimacy **4.** something confided, secret —**confident** ('konfidənt) a. **1.** having or showing certainty; sure **2.** sure of oneself **3.** presumptuous —**confidential** (konfi'denchəl) a. **1.** private **2.** secret **3.** entrusted with another's confidences —**confidentially** (konfi'denchəli) adv. —**confidently** ('konfidəntli) adv. —**con'fiding** a. unsuspicious; trustful —**confidence game** swindle in which victim entrusts money etc. to thief, believing him honest

configuration (kənfigyə'rāshən, -figə-) n. shape, aspect, conformation, arrangement

confine (kən'fīn) vt. **1.** keep within bounds **2.** keep in house, bed etc. **3.** shut up, imprison —**con'finement** n. **1.** act of confining or state of being confined **2.** period of birth of child —'**confines** pl.n. boundaries, limits

confirm (kən'fərm) vt. **1.** make certain of, verify **2.** strengthen, settle **3.** make valid, ratify **4.** administer confirmation to —**confir'mation** n. **1.** making strong, certain **2.** rite administered by bishop to confirm vows made at baptism —**con'firmatory** a. tending to confirm or establish, corroborative —**con'firmed** a. (of habit etc.) long-established

confiscate ('konfiskāt) vt. seize by authority —**confis'cation** n. —**con'fiscatory** a.

conflagration (konflə'grāshən) n. great destructive fire

conflate (kən'flāt) vt. combine, blend to form whole

conflict ('konflikt) n. **1.** struggle, trial of strength **2.** disagreement —vi. (kən'flikt) **3.** be at odds (with), be inconsistent (with) **4.** clash

confluence ('konflŏŏəns) or **conflux** ('konfluks) n. **1.** union of streams **2.** meeting place —'**confluent** a.

conform (kən'fôrm) vi. **1.** comply with accepted standards, conventions etc. —v. **2.** adapt to rule, pattern, custom etc. —**con'formable** a. —**con'formably** adv. —**confor'mation** n. structure, adaptation —**con'formist** n. one who conforms, esp. excessively —**con'formity** n. compliance

confound (kən'fownd) vt. **1.** baffle, perplex **2.** confuse **3.** defeat —**con'founded** a. esp. inf. damned

confrère ('konfrāər) n. fellow member of profession etc.

confront (kən'frunt) vt. **1.** face **2.** bring face to face (with) —**confron'tation** n.

Confucianism (kən'fyŏŏshənizəm) n. ethical system of Confucius (551-479 B.C.), Chinese philosopher, emphasizing devotion to family, peace and justice

confuse (kən'fyŏŏz) vt. **1.** bewilder **2.** jumble **3.** make unclear **4.** mistake (one thing) for another **5.** disconcert —**con'fusion** n.

confute (kən'fyŏŏt) vt. prove wrong; disprove —**confu'tation** n.

conga ('konggə) n. Latin American dance performed by number of people in single file

congé (kōn'zhā) n. **1.** permission to depart or dismissal, esp. when formal **2.** farewell

congeal (kən'jēl) v. solidify by cooling or freezing —**conge'lation** n.

congener ('konjinər, kən'jēnər) n. member of same genus as another plant or animal

congenial (kən'jēnyəl) a. **1.** pleasant, to one's liking **2.** of similar disposition, tastes etc. —**congeni'ality** n. —**con'genially** adv.

congenital (kən'jenitəl) a. **1.** existing at birth **2.** dating from birth

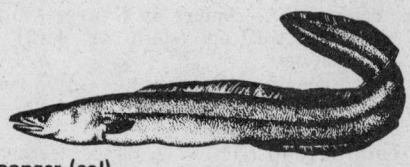

conger (eel)

conger ('konggər) n. large, voracious sea eel, important as food fish

congeries ('konjərēz) n. sing. and pl. collection or mass of small bodies, conglomeration

congest (kən'jest) v. overcrowd or clog —**con'gested** a. —**con'gestion** n. abnormal accumulation, overcrowding

conglomerate (kən'glomərit) n. **1.** thing, substance (esp. rock) composed of mixture of other, smaller elements or pieces **2.** business organization comprising many companies —v. (kən'glomərāt) **3.** gather together —a. **4.** made up of heterogeneous elements **5.** (of sedimentary rocks) consisting of rounded fragments within finer matrix —**conglomer'ation** n.

Congo ('konggō) n. **1.** country in Africa bounded by Cameroon and the Central African Republic to the north, Zaïre to the east and south, Angola and the Atlantic Ocean to the southwest and Gabon to the west **2.** former name of ZAÏRE

congratulate (kən'grachəlāt, -'graj-) vt. express pleasure at good fortune, success etc. —**congratu'lation** n. —**con'gratulatory** a.

congregate ('konggrigāt) v. **1.** assemble **2.** collect, flock together —**congre'gation** n. assembly, esp. for worship —**congre'gational** a. —**Congre'gationalism** n. system in which each separate church is self-governing —**Congre'gationalist** n.

congress ('konggris) n. **1.** meeting **2.** formal assembly for discussion **3.** legislative body —**con'gressional** a. —'**congressman** n. member of the U.S. House of Representatives

congruent ('konggrŏŏənt) a. **1.** suitable, accordant **2.** fitting together, esp. triangles —'**congruence** n. —**con'gruity** n. —'**congruous** a.

conic(al) ('konik(əl)) a. see CONE

conifer ('konifər, 'kōn-) n. **1.** order of mainly evergreen trees and shrubs including pine, fir, spruce and also yews and related species **2.** cone-bearing plant or other plant producing pollen in cones —**co'niferous** a.

conjecture (kən'jekchər) n. **1.** guess, guesswork —v. **2.** guess, surmise —**con'jectural** a.

conjoin (kən'join) vt. **1.** combine —vi. **2.** come, or act, together —**con'joint** a. concerted, united —**con'jointly** adv.

conjugal ('konjŏŏgəl) a. **1.** relating to marriage **2.** between married persons —**conju'gality** n.

conjugate ('konjŏŏgāt) vt. inflect (verb) in its various forms (past, present etc.) —**conju'gation** n.

conjunction (kən'jungkshən) n. **1.** union **2.** simultaneous happening **3.** part of speech joining words, phrases etc. —**con'junctive** a. —**con'juncture** n.

conjunctiva (konjungk'tīvə) n. mucous membrane lining eyelid —**conjuncti'vitis** n. inflammation of this

conjure ('konjər) vi. **1.** produce magic effects **2.** perform tricks by jugglery etc. **3.** invoke devils —vt. (kən'jŏŏr) **4.** implore earnestly —**conju'ration** n. —'**conjurer** or '**conjuror** *n.* —**conjure up 1.** present to the mind **2.** call up (spirit or devil) by incantation

conk (kongk) *inf. vt.* **1.** strike (*esp.* on head) —*n.* **2.** nose —**conk out** *inf.* **1.** break down **2.** tire suddenly; collapse

conn *or* **con** (kon) *vt.* **1.** direct steering of (ship) —*n.* **2.** the control of one who conns

Conn. Connecticut

connect (kə'nekt) *v.* **1.** join together, unite —*vt.* **2.** associate in the mind —**con'nection** *n.* **1.** association **2.** train *etc.* timed to enable passengers to transfer from another **3.** family relation —**con'nective** *a.* —**connecting rod** that part of engine which transfers motion from piston to crankshaft

Connecticut (kə'netikət) *n.* New England state of the U.S.: ratified the Constitution in 1788. Abbrev.: **Conn., CT** (with ZIP code)

conning tower ('koning) armored control position in submarine, battleship *etc.* (*see also* CONN)

connive (kə'nīv) *vi.* **1.** plot, conspire **2.** assent, refrain from preventing or forbidding —**con'nivance** *n.*

connoisseur (koni'sər) *n.* **1.** critical expert in matters of taste, *esp.* fine arts **2.** competent judge

connote (ko'nōt) *vt.* imply, mean in addition to primary meaning —**conno'tation** *n.*

connubial (kə'nyoobiəl, -'noo-) *a.* of marriage

conquer ('kongkər) *vt.* **1.** win by force of arms, overcome **2.** defeat —*vi.* **3.** be victorious —'**conqueror** *n.* —'**conquest** *n.*

conquistador (kon'kwistədör) *n.* adventurer or conqueror, *esp.* one of Sp. conquerors of New World in 16th cent. (*pl.* **-s, -dores** (-dörəs))

consanguinity (konsan'gwiniti) *n.* kinship —**consan'guineous** *a.*

conscience ('konchəns) *n.* sense of right or wrong governing person's words and actions —**consci'entious** *a.* **1.** scrupulous **2.** obedient to the dictates of conscience —**consci'entiously** *adv.* —**conscience money** money paid voluntarily to compensate for dishonesty, *esp.* for taxes formerly evaded —**conscience-stricken** *a.* feeling anxious or guilty (*also* **conscience-smitten**) —**conscientious objector** one who refuses military service on moral or religious grounds

conscious ('konchəs) *a.* **1.** aware **2.** awake to one's surroundings and identity **3.** deliberate, intentional —'**consciously** *adv.* —'**consciousness** *n.* being conscious

conscript ('konskript) *n.* **1.** one compulsorily enlisted for military service —*vt.* (kən'skript) **2.** enroll for compulsory military service —**con'scription** *n.*

consecrate ('konsikrāt) *vt.* make sacred —**conse'cration** *n.*

consecutive (kən'sekyətiv, -kə-) *a.* in unbroken succession —**con'secutively** *adv.*

consensus (kən'sensəs) *n.* widespread agreement, unanimity

consent (kən'sent) *vi.* **1.** agree, comply —*n.* **2.** acquiescence **3.** permission **4.** agreement —**con'sentient** *a.*

consequence ('konsikwəns) *n.* **1.** result, effect, outcome **2.** that which naturally follows **3.** significance, importance —'**consequent** *a.* —**conse'quential** *a.* important —'**consequently** *adv.* therefore, as a result

conservatoire (kən'sərvətwär) *n.* *see at* CONSERVE

conserve (kən'sərv) *vt.* **1.** keep from change or decay **2.** preserve **3.** maintain —*n.* ('konsərv) **4.** jam, preserved fruit *etc.*

—**conser'vation** *n.* protection, careful management of natural resources and environment —**conser'vationist** *n./a.* —**con'servatism** *n.* —**con'servative** *a.* **1.** tending or wishing to conserve **2.** moderate —*n.* **3.** *Pol.* one who desires to preserve institutions of his country against change and innovation **4.** one opposed to hasty changes or innovations —**conservatoire** (kən'sərvətwär) *n.* an institution or school for instruction in music —**con'servatory** *n.* **1.** greenhouse **2.** conservatoire —**conservation of energy** principle that total energy of isolated system is constant and independent of changes occurring within system —**conservation of mass** principle that total mass of isolated system is constant and independent of chemical and physical changes taking place within system

consider (kən'sidər) *vt.* **1.** think over **2.** examine **3.** make allowance for **4.** have as opinion **5.** discuss —**con'siderable** *a.* **1.** important **2.** somewhat large —**con'siderably** *adv.* —**con'siderate** *a.* thoughtful for others' feelings, careful —**con'siderately** *adv.* —**conside'ration** *n.* **1.** deliberation **2.** point of importance **3.** thoughtfulness **4.** bribe, recompense —**con'sidered** *a.* **1.** presented or thought out with care **2.** esteemed —**con'sidering** *prep.* **1.** in view of —*adv.* **2.** *inf.* all in all; taking circumstances into account —*conj.* **3.** in view of the fact (that)

consign (kən'sīn) *vt.* **1.** commit, hand over **2.** entrust to carrier —**consign'ee** *n.* —**con'signment** *n.* goods consigned —**con'signor** *n.*

consist (kən'sist) *vi.* **1.** be composed (of) **2.** (*with* in) have as basis **3.** agree (with), be compatible (with) —**con'sistency** *or* **con'sistence** *n.* **1.** agreement **2.** harmony **3.** degree of firmness —**con'sistent** *a.* **1.** unchanging, constant **2.** agreeing (with) —**con'sistently** *adv.*

consistory (kən'sistəri) *n.* ecclesiastical court or council, *esp.* of Pope and Cardinals

console[1] (kən'sōl) *vt.* comfort, cheer in distress —**conso'lation** *n.* —**con'solatory** *a.*

console[2] ('konsōl) *n.* **1.** bracket supporting shelf **2.** keyboard, stops *etc.,* of organ **3.** cabinet for television, radio *etc.*

consolidate (kən'solidāt) *vt.* **1.** combine into connected whole **2.** make firm, secure —**consoli'dation** *n.*

consommé (konsə'mā) *n.* clear soup made from concentrated stock —**jellied consommé** consommé which has been chilled

consonant ('konsənənt) *n.* **1.** sound making a syllable only with vowel **2.** nonvowel —*a.* **3.** agreeing, in accord —'**consonance** *n.*

consort (kən'sört) *vi.* **1.** associate, keep company —*n.* ('konsört) **2.** husband, wife, *esp.* of ruler **3.** ship sailing with another —**con'sortium** *n.* association of banks, companies *etc.*

conspectus (kən'spektəs) *n.* **1.** a comprehensive view or survey of subject **2.** synopsis

conspicuous (kən'spikyooəs) *a.* **1.** striking, noticeable, outstanding **2.** prominent **3.** eminent —**con'spicuously** *adv.*

conspire (kən'spīr) *vi.* **1.** combine for evil purpose **2.** plot, devise —**conspiracy** (kən'spirəsi) *n.* —**conspirator** (kən'spirətər) *n.* —**conspiratorial** (konspirə'töriəl) *a.*

constable ('kunstəbəl, 'kon-) *n. Hist.* officer of the peace —**con'stabulary** *n.* police force

constant ('konstənt) *a.* **1.** fixed, unchanging **2.** steadfast **3.** always duly happening or continuing —*n.* **4.** quantity that does not vary —'**constancy** *n.* **1.** steadfastness **2.** loyalty —'**constantly** *adv.*

constellation (konsti'lāshən) *n.* **1.** any of 88 designated configurations of stars **2.** assembly of related persons or things

consternation (konstər'nāshən) *n.* alarm, dismay, panic —'**consternate** *vt.*

constipation (konsti'pāshən) *n.* difficulty in emptying bowels —'**constipate** *vt.* affect with this disorder

constituent (kən'stichooənt) *a.* **1.** going toward making up whole **2.** having power to make, alter constitution of state **3.** electing representative —*n.* **4.** component part **5.** element **6.** elector —**con'stituency** *n.* **1.** residents of electoral district **2.** electoral district

constitute ('konstityoot, -toot) *vt.* **1.** compose, set up, establish, form **2.** make into, found, give form to —**consti'tution** *n.* **1.** structure, composition **2.** health **3.** character, disposition **4.** principles on which state is governed —**consti'tutional** *a.* **1.** pert. to constitution **2.** in harmony with political constitution —*n.* **3.** walk taken for health's sake —**consti'tutionally** *adv.* —'**constitutive** *a.* **1.** having power to enact or establish **2.** *see* CONSTITUENT (sense 1)

constrain (kən'strān) *vt.* force, compel —**con'straint** *n.* **1.** compulsion **2.** restraint **3.** embarrassment, tension

constriction (kən'strikshən) *n.* compression, squeezing together —**con'strict** *vt.* —**con'strictive** *a.* —**con'strictor** *n.* that which constricts (*see also* BOA)

construct (kən'strukt) *vt.* **1.** make, build, form **2.** put together **3.** compose —*n.* ('konstrukt) **4.** something formulated systematically —**con'struction** *n.* —**con'structive** *a.* **1.** serving to improve **2.** positive —**con'structively** *adv.*

construe (kən'stroo) *vt.* **1.** interpret **2.** deduce **3.** analyze grammatically

consul ('konsəl) *n.* **1.** officer appointed by a government to represent it in a foreign country **2.** in ancient Rome, one of the chief magistrates —'**consular** *a.* —'**consulate** *n.* —'**consulship** *n.*

consult (kən'sult) *vt.* seek counsel, advice, information from —**con'sultant** *n.* **1.** specialist **2.** expert —**consul'tation** *n.* **1.** consulting **2.** appointment to seek professional advice, *esp.* of doctor, lawyer —**con'sultative** *a.* **1.** having privilege of consulting, but not of voting **2.** advisory

consume (kən'soom) *vt.* **1.** eat or drink **2.** engross, possess **3.** use up **4.** destroy —**con'sumer** *n.* **1.** buyer or user of commodity **2.** one who consumes —**con'sumerism** *n.* **1.** protection of interests of consumers **2.** advocacy of high rate of consumption as basis for sound economy —**consumption** (kən'sumpshən) *n.* **1.** using up **2.** destruction **3.** tuberculosis —**consumptive** (kən'sumptiv) *a./n.* —**consumptiveness** (kən'sumptivnis) *n.*

consummate ('konsəmāt) *vt.* **1.** perfect **2.** fulfill **3.** complete (*esp.* marriage by sexual intercourse) —*a.* (kən'sumit, 'konsəmit) **4.** of greatest perfection or completeness —**con'summately** *adv.* —**consum'mation** *n.*

cont. continued

contact ('kontakt) *n.* **1.** touching **2.** being in touch **3.** junction of two or more electrical conductors **4.** useful acquaintance —*vt.* ('kontakt, kən'takt) **5.** put, come or be in touch (with) —**contact lens** lens fitting over eyeball to correct defect of vision

contagion (kən'tājən) *n.* **1.** passing on of disease by touch, contact **2.** contagious disease **3.** harmful physical or moral influence —**con'tagious** a. communicable by contact, catching

contain (kən'tān) vt. 1. hold 2. have room for 3. include, comprise 4. restrain —**con'tainer** n. 1. box etc. for holding 2. large cargo-carrying standard-sized receptacle for different modes of transport —**containeri'zation** n. —**con'tainerize** vt. 1. convey in standard-sized containers 2. adapt to use of standard-sized containers —**con'tainment** n. act of containing, esp. of restraining power of hostile country or operations of hostile military force

contaminate (kən'tamināt) vt. 1. stain, pollute, infect 2. make radioactive —**con-tami'nation** n. pollution

contemn (kən'tem) vt. regard with contempt; scorn

contemplate ('kontəmplāt) vt. 1. reflect, meditate on 2. gaze upon 3. intend —**contem-'plation** n. 1. thoughtful consideration 2. spiritual meditation —**con'templative** a./n. (one) given to contemplation

contemporary (kən'tempəreri) a. 1. existing or lasting at same time 2. of same age 3. present-day —n. 4. one existing at same time as another —**contempo'raneous** a.

contempt (kən'tempt) n. 1. feeling that something is worthless, despicable etc. 2. expression of this feeling 3. state of being despised, disregarded 4. willful disrespect of authority

contend (kən'tend) vi. 1. strive, fight —v. 2. dispute —vt. 3. maintain —**con'tention** n. 1. strife 2. debate 3. subject matter of dispute —**con'tentious** a. 1. quarrelsome 2. causing dispute —**con'tentiously** adv.

content¹ ('kontent) n. 1. that contained 2. holding capacity —pl. 3. that contained 4. index of topics in book

content² (kən'tent) a. 1. satisfied 2. willing —vt. 3. satisfy —n. 4. satisfaction —**con'tent-ed** a. —**con'tentment** n.

conterminous (kən'tərminəs) a. 1. of the same extent (in time etc.) 2. meeting along a common boundary 3. meeting end to end

contest ('kontest) n. 1. competition 2. conflict —vt. (kən'test) 3. dispute, debate 4. fight or compete for —**con'testable** a. —**con'testant** n. —**contes'tation** n.

context ('kontekst) n. 1. words coming before, after a word or passage 2. conditions and circumstances of event, fact etc. —**con'textual** a.

contiguous (kən'tigyōōs) a. touching, near —**conti'guity** n.

continent¹ ('kontinənt) n. large continuous mass of land —**conti'nental** a. —**continental breakfast** light breakfast of coffee and rolls —**continental code** the International Morse Code —**continental drift** Geol. theory that earth's continents move gradually over surface of planet on substratum of magma —**continental shelf** submarine plain bordering continent and sloping eventually to a deep abyss

continent² ('kontinənt) a. 1. able to control one's urination and defecation 2. sexually chaste —**'continence** n.

contingent (kən'tinjənt) a. 1. depending 2. possible 3. accidental —n. 4. group (of troops, sportsmen etc.) part of or representative of a larger group —**con'tingency** n. —**con'tin-gently** adv.

continue (kən'tinyōō) v. 1. remain, keep in existence 2. carry on, last, go on 3. resume 4. prolong —**con'tinual** a. recurring frequently, esp. at regular intervals —**con'tinually** adv. —**con'tinuance** n. 1. act of continuing 2. duration of action etc. 3. adjournment of legal proceeding —**continu'ation** n. 1. extension, extra part 2. resumption 3. constant succession, prolongation —**conti-'nuity** n. 1. logical sequence 2. state of being continuous —**con'tinuo** n. Mus. representation of keyboard part by bass notes only (pl. -s) (also **basso continuo, thorough bass**) —**con'tinuous** a. unceasing —**con'tinuously** adv. —**con'tinuum** n. continuous series or whole with no part perceptibly different from adjacent parts (pl. -'tinua, -s)

contort (kən'tört) vt. twist out of normal shape —**con'tortion** n. —**con'tortionist** n. one who contorts his body to entertain

contour ('kontōōər) n. outline, shape, esp. mountains, coast etc. —**contour line** line on map drawn through places of same height —**contour map**

contra- (comb. form) against, as in contraposition. Such words are omitted where the meaning may easily be inferred from the simple word

contraband ('kontrəband) n. 1. smuggled goods 2. illegal traffic in such goods —a. 3. prohibited by law

contrabassoon (kontrəbə'sōōn) n. see **double bassoon** at BASSOON

contraception (kontrə'sepshən) n. prevention of conception usu. by artificial means, birth control —**contra'ceptive** a./n.

contract (kən'trakt) v. 1. make or become smaller, shorter —vi. ('kontrakt) 2. make a contract —vt. 3. become affected by 4. incur 5. undertake by contract —n. ('kontrakt) 6. bargain, agreement 7. formal document recording agreement 8. agreement enforceable by law —**con'tracted** a. drawn together —**con'tractile** a. tending to contract —**con-'traction** n. —**con'tractor** n. one making contract, esp. builder —**con'tractual** a. —**contract bridge** see BRIDGE²

contradict (kontrə'dikt) vt. 1. deny 2. be at variance or inconsistent with —**contra'dic-tion** n. —**contra'dictious** a. —**contra'dictor** n. —**contra'dictory** a.

contradistinction (kontrədi'stingkshən) n. distinction made by contrasting different qualities

contralto (kən'traltō) n. 1. singing voice with range between mezzosoprano and tenor 2. person having this voice 3. the part sung by a contralto (pl. -s)

contraption (kən'trapshən) n. 1. gadget 2. device 3. construction, device oft. overelaborate or eccentric

contrapuntal (kontrə'puntəl) a. Mus. pert. to counterpoint

contrary ('kontreri) a. 1. opposed 2. opposite, other 3. (kən'trāəri) perverse, obstinate —n. 4. something the exact opposite of another —adv. 5. in opposition —**contra'riety** n. —**'contrarily** adv. —**'con-trariwise** adv. conversely

contrast (kən'träst) vt. 1. distinguish by comparison of unlike or opposite qualities —vi. 2. show great difference —n. ('konträst) 3. striking difference 4. T.V. sharpness of image

contravene (kontrə'vēn) vt. 1. transgress, infringe 2. conflict with 3. contradict —**contra'vention** n.

contretemps ('kontrətän) n. unexpected and embarrassing situation or mishap

contribute (kən'tribyōōt) v. 1. give, pay to common fund 2. write (articles etc.) for the press —vi. 3. help to occur —**contri'bution** n. —**con'tributive** a. —**con'tributor** n. one who writes articles for newspapers etc. 2. one who donates —**con'tributory** a. 1. partly responsible 2. giving to pension fund etc.

contrite ('kontrīt, kən'trīt) a. remorseful for wrongdoing, penitent —**'contritely** adv. —**contrition** (kən'trishən) n.

contrive (kən'trīv) vt. 1. manage 2. devise, invent, design —v. 3. plot, scheme —**con-'trivance** n. artifice or device —**con'trived** a. obviously planned, artificial —**con'triver** n.

control (kən'trōl) vt. 1. command, dominate 2. regulate 3. direct, check, test (-ll-) —n. 4. power to direct or determine 5. curb, check 6. standard of comparison in experiment —pl. 7. system of instruments to control car, aircraft etc. —**con'trollable** a. —**con'troller** n. 1. one who controls 2. official controlling expenditure —**control tower** tower in airfield from which take-offs and landings are directed

controversy ('kontrəvərsi) n. dispute, debate, esp. over public issues —**contro'versial** a. —**contro'versialist** n. —**'controvert** vt. 1. deny 2. argue about —**contro'vertible** a.

contumacy (kən'tyōōməsi, -'tōō-) n. stubborn disobedience —**contu'macious** a.

contumely (kən'tyōōmili, -'tōō-) n. insulting language or treatment —**contumelious** (kontyə'mēliəs, -tə-) a. abusive, insolent

contusion (kən'tyōōzhən, -'tōō-) n. bruise —**con'tuse** vt. bruise

conundrum (kə'nundrəm) n. riddle, esp. with punning answer

conurbation (konər'bāshən) n. densely populated urban sprawl formed by spreading of towns

convalesce (konvə'les) vi. recover health after illness, operation etc. —**conva'les-cence** n. —**conva'lescent** a./n.

convection (kən'vekshən) n. transmission, esp. of heat, by currents in liquids or gases —**con'vector** n.

convene (kən'vēn) vt. call together, assemble, convoke —**convention** (kən'venchən) n. 1. assembly 2. treaty, agreement 3. rule 4. practice based on agreement 5. accepted usage —**conventional** (kən'venchənəl) a. 1. (slavishly) observing customs of society 2. customary 3. (of weapons, war etc.) not nuclear —**conventionality** (kənvenchə'nali-ti) n. —**conventionally** (kən'venchənəli) adv.

convenient (kən'vēnyənt) a. 1. handy 2. favorable to needs, comfort 3. well-adapted to one's purpose —**con'venience** n. 1. ease, comfort, suitability 2. toilet —a. 3. (of food) quick to prepare —**con'veniently** adv.

convent ('konvənt) n. 1. religious community, esp. of nuns 2. their building 3. school in which teachers are nuns (also **convent school**) —**con'ventual** a.

conventicle (kən'ventikəl) n. 1. secret or unauthorized assembly for worship 2. small meeting house or chapel, esp. of Dissenters

converge (kən'vərj) vi. 1. move toward same point 2. meet, join 3. Math. (of infinite series) approach finite limit as number of terms increases —**con'vergence** or **con'vergency** n. —**con'vergent** a.

conversant (kən'vərsənt) a. acquainted, familiar, versed (in)

converse¹ (kən'vərs) vi. 1. talk —n. ('konvərs) 2. talk —**conver'sation** n. —**con-ver'sational** a. —**conver'sationalist** n.

converse² (kən'vərs, 'konvərs) a. 1. opposite, turned round, reversed —n. 2. the opposite, contrary

convert (kən'vərt) vt. 1. apply to another purpose 2. change 3. transform 4. cause to adopt (another) religion, opinion —vi. 5. make successful try for point or free throw —n. ('konvərt) 6. converted person —**con-'version** n. 1. change of state 2. unauthorized appropriation **3.** change of opinion, religion or party —**con'verter** *n.* **1.** one who, that which converts **2.** electrical device for changing alternating current into direct current **3.** vessel in which molten metal is refined —**con'vertible** *n.* **1.** automobile with folding roof —*a.* **2.** capable of being converted **3.** (of automobile) having folding or removable roof

convex (kon'veks, 'konveks) *a.* **1.** curved outward **2.** of a rounded form —**con'vexity** *n.*

convey (kən'vā) *vt.* **1.** carry, transport **2.** impart, communicate **3.** *Law* make over, transfer —**con'veyance** *n.* **1.** carrying **2.** vehicle **3.** act by which title to property is transferred —**con'veyancer** *n.* one skilled in legal forms of transferring property —**con'veyancing** *n.* this work —**conveyor belt** continuous moving belt for transporting things, *esp.* in factory

convict (kən'vikt) *vt.* **1.** prove or declare guilty —*n.* ('konvikt) **2.** person found guilty of crime **3.** criminal serving prison sentence —**con'viction** *n.* **1.** verdict of guilty **2.** being convinced, firm belief, state of being sure

convince (kən'vins) *vt.* firmly persuade, satisfy by evidence or argument —**con'vincing** *a.* capable of compelling belief, effective

convivial (kən'viviəl) *a.* sociable, festive, jovial —**convivi'ality** *n.*

convoke (kən'vōk) *vt.* call together —**convo'cation** *n.* calling together, assembly, *esp.* of clergy, university graduates *etc.*

convolute ('konvəlōōt) *vt.* twist, coil, tangle —**'convoluted** *a.* —**convo'lution** *n.*

convolvulus (kən'volvyōōləs) *n.* genus of plants with twining stems of the morning-glory family

convoy ('konvoi) *n.* **1.** party of ships, troops, trucks *etc.* traveling together for protection —*vt.* **2.** escort for protection

convulse (kən'vuls) *vt.* **1.** shake violently **2.** affect with violent involuntary contractions of muscles —**con'vulsion** *n.* **1.** violent upheaval —*pl.* **2.** spasms **3.** fits of laughter or hysteria —**con'vulsive** *a.* —**con'vulsively** *adv.*

cony *or* **coney** ('kōni) *n.* rabbit

coo (kōō) *n.* **1.** cry of doves —*vi.* **2.** make such cry (**cooed, 'cooing**)

cook (kŏŏk) *vt.* **1.** prepare (food) for table, *esp.* by heat **2.** *inf.* falsify (accounts *etc.*) —*vi.* **3.** undergo cooking **4.** act as cook —*n.* **5.** one who prepares food for table —**'cooker** *n.* cooking apparatus —**'cookery** *n.* —**'cookie** *n.* **1.** small flat dry cake of sweet dough **2.** attractive woman **3.** *sl.* person —**'cookbook** *n.* **1.** book of recipes and cooking directions **2.** book of detailed instructions —**cook one's goose** ruin one's chances —**cook up 1.** *inf.* invent, plan **2.** prepare (meal)

cool (kōōl) *a.* **1.** moderately cold **2.** unexcited, calm **3.** lacking friendliness or interest **4.** *inf.* calmly insolent **5.** *inf.* sophisticated, elegant —*v.* **6.** make, become cool —*n.* **7.** cool time, place *etc.* **8.** *inf.* calmness, composure —**'coolant** *n.* fluid used for cooling tool, machinery *etc.* —**'cooler** *n.* **1.** vessel in which liquids are cooled **2.** *sl.* prison **3.** tall iced alcoholic drink —**'coolly** *adv.* —**cooling tower** structure used in industrial processes to cool hot water for reuse —**cool it** calm down

Coolidge ('kōōlij) *n.* **Calvin.** the 30th President of the U.S. (1925-29)

coolie ('kōōli) *n.* cheaply hired oriental unskilled laborer

coon (kōōn) *n. sl. offens.* Black person

coop (kōōp) *n.* **1.** cage or pen for fowls —*vt.* (*oft. with* up) **2.** shut up in a coop **3.** confine

co-op ('kōop) *n.* cooperative society or shop run by one

cooper ('kōōpər) *n.* one who makes casks

cooperate (kō'opərāt) *vi.* work together —**coope'ration** *n.* —**co'operative** *a.* **1.** willing to cooperate **2.** (of an enterprise) owned collectively and managed for joint economic benefit —*n.* **3.** cooperative organization, such as farm —**co'operator** *n.*

co-opt (kō'opt) *vt.* bring on (committee *etc.*) as member, colleague, without election by larger body choosing first members

coordinate (kō'ördināt) *vt.* **1.** bring into order as parts of whole **2.** place in same rank **3.** put into harmony —*n.* (kō'ördinit) **4.** *Math.* any of set of numbers defining location of point —*pl.* **5.** clothes of matching or harmonious colors and design, suitable for wearing together —*a.* (kō'ördinit) **6.** equal in degree, status *etc.* —**coordi'nation** *n.* —**co'ordinative** *a.* —**coordinate geometry** *see* **analytic geometry** *at* ANALYSIS

coot (kōōt) *n.* **1.** small black water fowl **2.** *sl.* silly (old) person

cop (kop) *sl. vt.* **1.** catch **2.** (*usu. with* it) be punished (**-pp-**) —*n.* **3.** policeman **4.** a capture —**cop-out** *n. sl.* act of copping out —**cop out** *sl.* fail to assume responsibility, fail to perform

copal ('kōpəl, -pal) *n.* resin used in varnishes

copartner (kō'pärtnər) *n.* joint partner —**co'partnership** *n.*

cope¹ (kōp) *vi.* deal successfully

cope² (kōp) *n.* ecclesiastical vestment like long cloak

Copernican (kə'pərnikən) *a.* pert. to Copernicus, Polish astronomer (1473-1543), or to his system —**Copernican system** theory published by Copernicus, which stated that earth and planets rotated around sun

copestone ('kōpstōn) *n.* **1.** stone used to form coping **2.** stone at top of wall *etc.*

copier ('kopiər) *n. see* COPY

copilot ('kōpīlət) *n.* second or relief pilot of aircraft

coping ('kōping) *n.* top course of wall, usu. sloping to throw off rain

coping saw handsaw with U-shaped frame for cutting curves in wood

copious ('kōpiəs) *a.* **1.** abundant **2.** plentiful **3.** full, ample —**'copiously** *adv.* —**'copiousness** *n.*

copper¹ ('kopər) *n.* **1.** *Chem.* metallic element *Symbol* Cu, at. wt. 63.5, at. no. 29 **2.** bronze money, coin **3.** large washing vessel —*vt.* **4.** cover with copper —**copper-bottomed** *a.* reliable, *esp.* financially —**'copperplate** *n.* **1.** plate of copper for engraving, etching **2.** print from this **3.** copybook writing **4.** fine handwriting based upon that used on copperplate engravings —**'coppersmith** *n.* one who works with copper

copper² ('kopər) *n. sl.* policeman

coppice ('kopis) *n.* wood of small trees

copra ('kōprə) *n.* dried coconut kernels

Copt (kopt) *n.* **1.** member of Coptic Church **2.** Egyptian descended from ancient Egyptians —**'Coptic** *n.* **1.** Afro-Asiatic language, written in Greek alphabet but descended from ancient Egyptian —*a.* **2.** of this language **3.** of Copts —**Coptic art** Christian art in Egypt from the 3rd to 9th centuries

copula ('kopyōōlə) *n.* **1.** word, *esp.* verb acting as connecting link in sentence **2.** connection, tie

copulate ('kopyōōlāt) *vi.* unite sexually —**copu'lation** *n.* —**'copulative** *a.*

copy ('kopi) *n.* **1.** imitation **2.** single specimen of book **3.** matter for printing **4.** *Journalism inf.* suitable material for an article —*vt.* **5.** make copy of, imitate **6.** transcribe **7.** follow example of ('copied, 'copying) —**'copier** *n.* person or device that copies —**'copyist** *n.* —**'copybook** *n.* **1.** book of specimens, *esp.* of penmanship, for imitation —*a.* **2.** trite, unoriginal —**'copycat** *n. inf.* person, *esp.* child, who imitates another —**copy editor 1.** editor who prepares copy for the printer **2.** person who edits and headlines newspaper copy —**'copyhold** *n. Law* formerly, tenure less than freehold of land in England evidenced by copy of Court roll —**'copyright** *n.* **1.** legal exclusive right to print and publish book, article, work of art *etc.* —*vt.* **2.** protect by copyright (*see also* **Universal Copyright Convention** *at* UNIVERSE) —**'copywriter** *n.* one who composes advertisements —**blot one's copybook** *inf.* sully one's reputation

coquette (kō'ket) *n.* woman who flirts —**'coquetry** *n.* —**co'quettish** *a.*

coracle ('korəkəl) *n.* boat of wicker covered with skins

coral ('korəl) *n.* **1.** hard substance made by sea polyps and forming growths, islands, reefs **2.** ornament of coral —*a.* **3.** made of coral **4.** of deep pink color —**'coralline** *a.*

cor anglais ('kör 'änggla) UK English horn

corbel ('körbəl) *n.* stone or timber projection from wall to support something

corbie ('körbi) *n. Scot.* **1.** raven **2.** crow

cord (körd) *n.* **1.** thin rope or thick string **2.** rib on cloth **3.** ribbed fabric —*vt.* **4.** fasten with cord —**'cordage** *n.*

cordate ('kördāt) *a.* (of leaf) heart-shaped

cordial ('körjəl) *a.* **1.** hearty, sincere, warm —*n.* **2.** sweet, fruit-flavored drink —**cordi'ality** *n.* —**'cordially** *adv.*

cordite ('kördīt) *n.* explosive compound

cordon ('kördən) *n.* **1.** chain of troops or police **2.** fruit tree grown as single stem —*vt.* **3.** (*oft. with* off) form cordon around

cordon bleu (*Fr.* kordō 'blœ) (*esp.* of food preparation) of highest standard

cordovan ('kördəvən) *n.* fine leather now made principally from horsehide

corduroy ('kördəroi) *n.* cotton fabric with velvety, ribbed surface

cordwainer ('kördwānər) *n. obs.* shoemaker or worker in leather

core (kör) *n.* **1.** horny seed case of apple and other fruits **2.** central or innermost part of anything —*vt.* **3.** take out the core of

corespondent (kōri'spondənt) *n.* one cited in divorce case, alleged to have committed adultery with the respondent

corgi ('körgi) *n.* a small Welsh dog

coriaceous (kori'āshəs) *a.* of, like leather

coriander ('koriandər) *n.* type of herb

Corinthian (kə'rinthiən) *a.* **1.** of Corinth **2.** of Corinthian order of architecture, ornate Greek

Corinthians (kə'rinthiənz) *pl.n.* (*with sing. v.*) *Bible* 7th and 8th books of the N.T., epistles written to Christians at Corinth by St. Paul probably in 55 and 56 A.D.

cork (körk) *n.* **1.** bark of an evergreen Mediterranean oak tree **2.** piece of it or other material, *esp.* used as stopper for bottle *etc.* —*vt.* **3.** stop up with cork —**'corkage** *n.* charge for opening wine bottles in restaurant —**corked** *a.* tainted through having cork containing excess tannin —**'corker** *n. sl.* something, someone outstanding —**'corkscrew** *n.* tool for pulling out corks

corm (körm) *n.* storage organ of plant, a

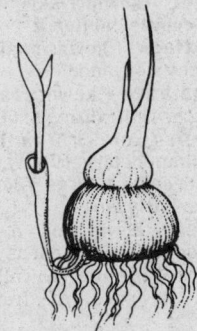

corm

compact thickened stem resembling a bulb but without the separate scales

cormorant ('körmərənt) *n.* large voracious sea bird

corn¹ (körn) *n.* **1.** grain, fruit of cereals **2.** grain of all kinds **3.** maize **4.** oversentimental, trite quality in play, film *etc.* —*vt.* **5.** preserve (meat) with salt —'**corny** *a. inf.* trite, oversentimental, hackneyed —'**corncob** *n.* core of ear of Indian corn, to which kernels are attached —'**corncrake** *n.* brown bird with harsh call, land rail —'**cornflakes** *pl.n.* toasted flakes of corn meal eaten for breakfast —'**cornflower** *n.* bachelor's button —**corn snow** granular snow formed by alternate freezing and thawing —'**cornstarch** *n.* starch made from corn, used as thickening agent in food and in many industrial processes —**corn syrup** sweetener obtained by partial hydrolysis of cornstarch

corn² (körn) *n.* painful horny growth on foot or toe

cornea ('körniə) *n.* transparent membrane covering front of eye —'**corneal** *a.* —**corneal transplant** cornea usu. obtained from deceased person used to replace diseased or deformed cornea of a blind or partially blind person —**corneal ulcer** patch of destroyed cornea resulting from injury or infection

cornel ('körnəl) *n.* any small tree with very hard wood, as the dogwood *etc.*

cornelian (kör'nēlyən) *n.* precious stone, kind of chalcedony

corner ('körnər) *n.* **1.** part of room where two sides meet **2.** remote or humble place **3.** point where two walls, streets *etc.* meet **4.** angle, projection **5.** *Business* buying up of whole existing stock of commodity **6.** *Sport* free kick or shot from corner of field —*vt.* **7.** drive into position of difficulty, or leaving no escape **8.** acquire enough of (commodity) to attain control of the market **9.** attain control of (market) in such a manner (*also* en'**gross**) —*vi.* **10.** move round corner —'**cornered** *a.* —'**cornerstone** *n.* indispensable part, basis

cornet (kör'net) *n.* musical instrument shorter than the trumpet usu. played in a brass band

cornice ('körnis) *n.* **1.** projection near top of wall **2.** ornamental, carved molding below ceiling

Cornish ('körnish) *a.* **1.** of Cornwall or its inhabitants —*n.* **2.** Celtic language of Cornwall: extinct by 1800 —*pl.* **3.** natives of Cornwall —'**Cornishman** *n.*

cornucopia (környə'kōpiə, -nə-) *n.* symbol of plenty, consisting of goat's horn, overflowing with fruit and flowers

corolla (kə'rolə) *n.* flower's inner envelope of petals

corollary ('korəleri) *n.* **1.** inference from a preceding statement **2.** deduction **3.** result

corona (kə'rōnə) *n.* **I.** halo around heavenly body **2.** flat projecting part of cornice **3.** top or crown (*pl.* **-s, -nae** (-nē)) —'**coronal** *a.*

coronary ('korəneri) *a.* **1.** of blood vessels surrounding heart —*n.* **2.** coronary thrombosis —**coronary thrombosis** formation of obstructing clot in coronary artery

coronation (korə'nāshən) *n.* ceremony of crowning a sovereign

coroner ('korənər) *n.* officer who holds inquests on bodies of persons supposed killed by violence, accident *etc.* —'**coronership** *n.*

coronet (korə'net) *n.* small crown

corporal¹ ('körpərəl) *a.* **1.** of the body **2.** material, not spiritual —**corporal punishment** punishment (flogging *etc.*) of physical nature

corporal² ('körpərəl, 'körprəl) *n.* noncommissioned officer in army ranking above private first class and below sergeant; in marine corps above lance corporal and below sergeant

corporation (körpə'rāshən) *n.* **1.** association, body of persons legally authorized to act as an individual **2.** authorities of town or city —'**corporate** *a.*

corporeal (kör'pöriəl) *a.* **1.** of the body, material **2.** tangible

corps (kör) *n.* **1.** military force, body of troops **2.** any organized body of persons (*pl.* **corps** (körz)) —**corps de ballet** members of ballet company who dance together in group —**corps diplomatique** (diplōma'tēk) body of diplomats accredited to state (*also* **diplomatic corps**)

corpse (körps) *n.* dead body

corpulent ('körpyōōlənt) *a.* fat —'**corpulence** *n.*

corpus ('körpəs) *n.* **1.** collection or body of works, *esp.* by single author **2.** main part or body of something (*pl.* **-pora** (-pərə))

corpuscle ('körpusəl) *n.* minute organism or particle, *esp.* red and white corpuscles of blood

corral (ko'ral) *n.* enclosure for cattle, or for defense

correct (kə'rekt) *vt.* **1.** set right **2.** indicate errors in **3.** rebuke, punish **4.** counteract, rectify —*a.* **5.** right, exact, accurate **6.** in accordance with facts or standards —**cor'rection** *n.* —**cor'rective** *n./a.* —**cor'rectly** *adv.* —**cor'rectness** *n.*

correlate ('korilāt) *vt.* **1.** bring into reciprocal relation —*n.* **2.** either of two things or words necessarily implying the other —**corre'lation** *n.* —**cor'relative** *a./n.*

correspond (kori'spond) *vi.* **1.** be in agreement, be consistent (with) **2.** be similar (to) **3.** exchange letters —**corre'spondence** *n.* **1.** agreement, corresponding **2.** similarity **3.** exchange of letters **4.** letters received —**corre'spondent** *n.* **1.** writer of letters **2.** one employed by newspaper *etc.* to report on particular topic, country *etc.* —**correspondence school** educational institution that offers tuition by mail

corridor ('koridər) *n.* **1.** passage in building, railroad passenger car *etc.* **2.** strip of territory (or air route) not under control of state through which it passes

corrie ('kori) *n.* **1.** *Scot.* circular hollow on hillside **2.** *Geol.* cirque

corrigendum (kori'jendəm) *n.* thing to be corrected (*pl.* **-da** (-də))

corrigible ('korijibəl) *a.* **1.** capable of being corrected **2.** submissive

corroborate (kə'robərāt) *vt.* confirm, support (statement *etc.*) —**corrobo'ration** *n.* —**cor'roborative** *a.*

corroboree (kə'robəri) *n.* **A 1.** native assembly of sacred, festive or warlike character **2.** any noisy gathering

corrode (kə'rōd) *vt.* eat, wear away, eat into (by chemical action, disease *etc.*) —**cor'rosion** *n.* —**cor'rosive** *a.*

corrugate ('korəgāt) *v.* wrinkle, bend into wavy ridges —'**corrugated** *a.* —**corru'gation** *n.*

corrupt (kə'rupt) *a.* **1.** lacking integrity **2.** open to, or involving, bribery **3.** wicked **4.** spoilt by mistakes, altered for the worse (of words, literary passages *etc.*) —*vt.* **5.** make evil, pervert **6.** bribe **7.** make rotten —**corrupti'bility** *n.* —**cor'ruptible** *a.* —**cor'ruption** *n.* —**cor'ruptly** *adv.*

corsage (kör'säzh) *n.* (flower, spray, worn on) bodice of woman's dress

corsair ('körsâər) *n.* pirate

corselet ('körslit) *n.* **1.** piece of armor to cover the trunk **2.** (körsə'let) one-piece foundation garment

corset ('körsit) *n.* close-fitting undergarment stiffened to give support or shape to the body

cortege *or* **cortège** (kör'tezh) *n.* formal (funeral) procession

cortex ('körteks) *n.* **1.** *Anat.* outer layer **2.** bark **3.** sheath (*pl.* **cortices** ('körtisēz)) —'**cortical** *a.*

corticosteroid (körtikō'stēəroid) *n.* any of various adrenal cortex steroids (corticosterone, cortisone, aldosterone)

cortisone ('körtisōn, -zōn) *n.* product of the adrenal cortex or its synthesized equivalent used in medical treatment

corundum (kə'rundəm) *n.* native crystalline aluminum oxide, used as abrasive

coruscate ('korəskāt) *vi.* emit flashes of light; sparkle —**corus'cation** *n.*

corvette (kör'vet) *n.* lightly armed warship for escort and antisubmarine duties

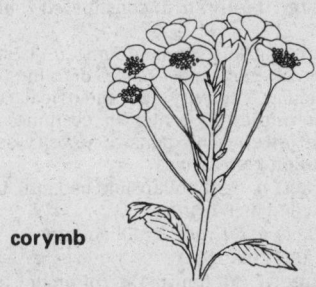

corymb

corymb ('korimb, -rim) *n.* inflorescence in form of flat-topped flower cluster with oldest flowers at periphery

coryza (kə'rīzə) *n.* acute inflammation of mucous membrane of nose, with discharge of mucus; head cold

cos (koz) cosine

cosec ('kōsek) cosecant

cosecant (kō'sēkant) *n.* (of angle) trigonometric function that in right triangle is ratio of length of hypotenuse to that of opposite side

cosh (kosh) *n.* **1.** blunt weapon —*vt.* **2.** strike with one

cosignatory (kō'signətöri) *n.* **1.** person, country *etc.* that signs document jointly with others —*a.* **2.** signing jointly

cosine ('kōsīn) *n.* in a right triangle, the ratio of a side adjacent to a given angle and the hypotenuse

cos lettuce (kos) romaine

cosmetic (koz'metik) *n.* **1.** preparation to beautify or improve skin, hair *etc.* —*a.* **2.** designed to improve appearance only

cosmic ('kozmik) *a.* 1. relating to the universe 2. of the vastness of the universe —**cosmic rays** high-energy electromagnetic rays from space

cosmo- *or before vowel* **cosm-** (*comb. form*) world; universe, as in *cosmology, cosmonaut*

cosmopolitan (kozmə'politən) *n.* 1. person who has lived and traveled in many countries —*a.* 2. familiar with many countries 3. sophisticated 4. free from national prejudice —**cosmo'politanism** *n.* —**cos'mopolite** *n.*

cosmos[1] ('kozməs) *n.* the world or universe considered as an ordered system —**cos'mogony** *n.* study of origin and development of universe or system in universe —**cos'mographer** *n.* —**cosmo'graphic** *a.* —**cos'mography** *n.* description or mapping of the universe —**cosmo'logical** *a.* —**cos'mology** *n.* the science or study of the universe —**'cosmonaut** *n.* Soviet astronaut

cosmos[2] ('kozməs) *n.* plant cultivated for brightly colored flowers (*pl.* -**mos, -es**)

Cossack ('kosak) *n.* member of tribe in SE Russia

cosset ('kosit) *vt.* pamper, pet

cost (kost) *n.* 1. price 2. expenditure of time, labor *etc.* —*pl.* 3. expenses of lawsuit —*vt.* 4. have as price 5. entail payment, loss or sacrifice of (**cost** *pt./pp.*) —**'costing** *n.* system of calculating cost of production —**'costliness** *n.* —**'costly** *a.* 1. valuable 2. expensive —**cost of living** basic cost of food, clothing and shelter necessary to maintain life —**cost price** price at which article is bought by one intending to resell it

costal ('kostəl) *a.* pert. to side of body or ribs —**'costate** *a.* ribbed

Costa Rica (kostə 'rēkə) country in Central America bounded north by Nicaragua, east by the Caribbean Sea, southeast by Panama, and south and west by the Pacific Ocean

costive ('kostiv) *a.* 1. constipated 2. niggardly

costume ('kostyōōm, -tōōm) *n.* 1. style of dress of particular place or time, or for particular activity 2. theatrical clothes —**cos'tumier** *n.* dealer in costumes —**costume jewelry** inexpensive jewelry set with imitation gemstones

cot[1] (kot) *n.* light collapsible bed, usu. canvas, stretched on a frame

cot[2] (kot) *n. Lit., obs.* small cottage

cot[3] (kot) cotangent

cotangent (kō'tanjənt) *n.* (of angle) trigonometric function that in right triangle is ratio of length of adjacent side to that of opposite side

cote (kōt) *n.* shelter, shed for animals or birds, *eg* dovecote

coterie ('kōtərē) *n.* 1. exclusive group of people with common interests 2. social clique

coterminous (kō'tərminəs) *a. see* CONTERMINOUS (sense 2)

cotillion (kō'tilyən) *n.* 1. ballroom dance resembling quadrille 2. formal ball

cotoneaster (kət'ōniastər) *n.* garden shrub with red berries

cottage ('kotij) *n.* small house —**cottage cheese** a soft cheese made by coagulating skim milk with a lactic acid culture, frequently flavored with fruit, spices *etc.* —**cottage industry** industry in which workers work in their own homes —**cottage pudding** plain cake covered with hot sauce

cotter ('kotər) *n.* pin, wedge *etc.* to prevent relative motion of two parts of machine *etc.*

cotton ('kotən) *n.* 1. plant 2. white downy fibrous covering of its seeds 3. thread or

cloth made of this —**cotton candy** candy made from spun sugar —**cotton gin** machine that separates debris from cotton —**'cottonmouth** *n.* water moccasin —**cotton-picking** *a.* damned —**cottonseed oil** oil obtained from seed of cotton plant —**'cottontail** *n.* any of several small sandy-brown N Amer. rabbits with white tufted tail —**cotton to** *or* **on to** understand (idea *etc.*)

cotyledon (koti'lēdən) *n.* seed leaf

couch (kowch) *n.* 1. piece of furniture for reclining on by day, sofa —*vt.* 2. express in a particular style of language 3. cause to lie down —**'couchant** *a. Her.* lying down

couch grass *see* QUACK GRASS

cougar ('kōōgər) *n.* large tawny feline found throughout the New World (*also* **puma, painter, mountain lion**)

cough (kof) *vi.* 1. expel air from lungs with sudden effort and noise, oft. to remove obstruction —*n.* 2. act of coughing —**cough drop** lozenge to relieve cough —**cough syrup** medicine that relieves coughing

could (kŏŏd) *pt. of* CAN[1]

coulomb ('kōōlom) *n.* derived SI unit of electric charge; quantity of electricity transported in one second by current of one ampere

coulter ('kōltər) *n.* sharp blade or disk at front of plow

council ('kownsəl) *n.* 1. deliberative or administrative body 2. one of its meetings 3. local governing authority of town *etc.* —**'councillor** *or* **'councilor** *n.* member of council

counsel ('kownsəl) *n.* 1. advice, deliberation, debate 2. lawyer; lawyers 3. plan, policy —*vt.* 4. advise, recommend —**'counselor** *or* **'counsellor** *n.* 1. lawyer that manages cases for clients 2. adviser 3. person with supervisory duties at summer camp —**keep one's counsel** keep a secret

count[1] (kownt) *vt.* 1. reckon, calculate, number 2. include 3. consider to be —*vi.* 4. depend (on) 5. be of importance —*n.* 6. reckoning 7. total number reached by counting 8. item in list of charges or indictment 9. act of counting —**'countless** *a.* too many to be counted —**'countdown** *n.* act of counting backwards to time critical operation exactly, such as launching of rocket —**counting house** room or building for book-keeping —**count down** count backwards to time critical operation exactly —**count out** 1. *inf.* leave out; exclude 2. (of boxing referee) judge (floored boxer) to have failed to recover within specified time

count[2] (kownt) *n.* nobleman corresponding to British earl —**'countess** *n.* wife, ex-wife or widow of count or earl

countenance ('kowntinəns) *n.* 1. face or its expression 2. support, approval 3. composure; self-control —*vt.* 4. give support to, approve

counter[1] ('kowntər) *n.* 1. horizontal surface in bank, shop *etc.*, over which business is transacted 2. disk, token used for counting or scoring

counter[2] ('kowntər) *adv.* 1. in opposite direction 2. contrary —*vt.* 3. oppose, contradict 4. *Fencing* parry —*n.* 5. parry

counter- (*comb. form*) reversed, opposite, rival, retaliatory, as in *counterclaim, counterclockwise, counterirritant, countermarch, countermeasure, countermine, counterrevolution.* Such words are not given here where the meaning may be inferred from the simple word

counteract (kowntər'akt) *vt.* neutralize, hinder —**counter'action** *n.*

counterattack ('kowntərətak) *v./n.* attack after enemy's advance

counterbalance ('kowntərbaləns) *n.* weight balancing or neutralizing another

counterfeit ('kowntərfit) *a.* 1. sham, forged —*n.* 2. imitation, forgery —*vt.* 3. imitate with intent to deceive 4. forge —**'counterfeiter** *n.* —**'counterfeitly** *adv.*

counterfoil ('kowntərfoil) *n.* part of check, receipt, money order, kept as record

counterintelligence (kowntərin'telijəns) *n.* activities designed to frustrate enemy espionage

countermand ('kowntərmand) *vt.* cancel (previous order)

counterpane ('kowntərpān) *n.* bedspread

counterpart ('kowntərpärt) *n.* 1. thing so like another as to be mistaken for it 2. something complementary to or correlative of another

counterpoint ('kowntərpoint) *n.* 1. melody added as accompaniment to given melody 2. art of so adding melodies

counterpoise ('kowntərpoiz) *n.* 1. force, influence *etc.* that counterbalances another 2. state of balance; equilibrium 3. weight that balances another —*vt.* 4. oppose with something of equal effect, weight or force; offset 5. bring into equilibrium

counterproductive (kowntərprə'duktiv) *a.* tending to hinder achievement of aim; having effects contrary to those intended

Counter-Reformation (kowntərrefər'māshən) *n.* reform movement in Catholic Church in 16th and early 17th centuries

countersign ('kowntərsɪn) *vt.* sign (document already signed by another), ratify

countersink ('kowntərsingk) *vt.* enlarge (upper part of hole drilled in timber *etc.*) to take head of screw, bolt *etc.* below surface

countertenor ('kowntərtenər) *n.* 1. adult male voice with alto range 2. singer with such voice

countervail (kowntər'vāl) *v.* 1. act or act against with equal power or force —*vt.* 2. make up for; compensate; offset

counterweight ('kowntərwāt) *n.* counterbalancing weight, influence or force

countess ('kowntis) *n. see* COUNT[2]

country ('kuntri) *n.* 1. region, district 2. territory of nation 3. land of birth, residence *etc.* 4. rural districts as opposed to town 5. nation —**'countrified** *a.* rural in manner or appearance —**country-and-western** *n.* urban 20th-century White folk music of SE Amer. —**country club** club in the country, having sporting and social facilities —**country dance** folk dance in which couples face one another in line —**'countryman** *n.* 1. rustic 2. compatriot —**'countryside** *n.* 1. rural district 2. its inhabitants

county ('kownti) *n.* 1. largest local government division within a state of the U.S. 2. chief administrative division of most of the United Kingdom —*a.* 3. UK *inf.* upper-class; of or like landed gentry

coup (kōō) *n.* 1. successful stroke, move or gamble 2. (*short for* **coup d'état**) sudden, violent seizure of government

coup de grâce (kōō də 'gräs) *Fr.* 1. mortal or finishing blow, *esp.* delivered as act of mercy to sufferer 2. final or decisive stroke (*pl.* **coups de grâce** (kōō də 'gräs))

coupé (kōō'pā) *or* **coupe** (kōō'pā, kōōp) *n.* closed 2-door automobile usu. for two persons

couple ('kupəl) *n.* 1. two, pair 2. indefinite small number 3. two people who regularly associate with each other or live together **4.** any two persons —*vt.* **5.** connect, fasten together **6.** associate, connect in the mind —*vi.* **7.** join —'**coupler** *n.* —'**couplet** *n.* two lines of verse, *esp.* rhyming and of equal length —'**coupling** *n.* act of coming together

coupon ('kyŏ͞opon, 'kŏ͞o-) *n.* **1.** ticket or voucher entitling holder to discount, gift *etc.* **2.** detachable slip used as order form **3.** (in betting *etc.*) printed form on which to forecast results

courage ('kurij) *n.* bravery, boldness —**cou-'rageous** *a.* —**cou'rageously** *adv.*

courgette (kŏ͞or'zhet) *n.* UK zucchini

courier ('kŏ͞oriər) *n.* **1.** express messenger **2.** person who looks after, guides travelers

course (körs) *n.* **1.** movement in space or time **2.** direction of movement **3.** successive development, sequence **4.** line of conduct or action **5.** series of lectures, exercises *etc.* **6.** any of successive parts of meal **7.** continuous line of masonry at particular level in building **8.** area where golf is played **9.** track or ground on which a race is run —*vt.* **10.** hunt —*vi.* **11.** run swiftly, gallop about **12.** (of blood) circulate —'**courser** *n. Poet.* swift horse —'**coursing** *n.* **1.** (of hounds or dogs) hunting by sight **2.** sport in which hounds are matched against one another in pairs for hunting of hares by sight

court (kört) *n.* **1.** space enclosed by buildings, yard **2.** area marked off or enclosed for playing various games **3.** retinue and establishment of sovereign **4.** body with judicial powers, place where it meets, one of its sittings **5.** attention, homage, flattery —*vt.* **6.** woo, try to win or attract **7.** seek, invite —'**courtier** *n.* one who frequents royal court —'**courtliness** *n.* —'**courtly** *a.* **1.** ceremoniously polite **2.** characteristic of a court —'**courtship** *n.* wooing —'**courthouse** *n.* public building in which courts of law are held —**court martial** court of naval or military officers for trying naval or military offenses (*pl.* **court martials, courts martial**) —**court plaster** plaster, composed of isinglass on silk, formerly used as beauty spots —**court tennis** ancient form of tennis played in four-walled indoor court —'**courtyard** *n.* paved space enclosed by buildings or walls

courtesan ('körtizən) *n. obs.* **1.** court mistress **2.** high-class prostitute

courtesy ('kərtisi) *n.* **1.** politeness, good manners **2.** act of civility —'**courteous** *a.* polite —'**courteously** *adv.* —**courtesy title** title accorded by usage usu. to heir of peer

cousin ('kuzən) *n.* **1.** son or daughter of uncle or aunt **2.** formerly, any kinsman —'**cousinly** *a.*

couture (kŏ͞o'tŏ͞or) *n.* high-fashion designing and dressmaking —**couturier** (kŏ͞o'tŏ͞oriər) *n.* person who designs, makes and sells fashion clothes for women (**couturière** (kŏ͞o'tŏ͞oriər) *fem.*)

cove[1] (kōv) *n.* small inlet of coast, sheltered bay

cove[2] (kōv) *vt.* make in concave form

coven ('kuvən) *n.* gathering of witches

covenant ('kuvənənt) *n.* **1.** contract, mutual agreement **2.** compact —*v.* **3.** agree to a covenant (concerning) —**Covenanter** ('kuvə-nəntər, kuvə'nantər) *n. Scot. hist.* person upholding either of two 17th-cent. Presbyterian covenants

Coventry ('kuvəntri) *n.* —**send to Coventry** ostracize; ignore

cover ('kuvər) *vt.* **1.** place or spread over **2.** extend over, spread over **3.** bring upon (oneself) **4.** screen, protect **5.** travel over **6.** include **7.** be sufficient to meet **8.** *Journalism*

report on **9.** point a gun at —*n.* **10.** lid, wrapper, envelope, binding, screen, anything which covers —'**coverage** *n.* amount, extent covered —'**coverlet** *n.* bedspread —**cover charge** fixed charge added to cost of food in restaurant *etc.* —**covering letter** accompanying letter sent as explanation, introduction or record —**cover-up** *n.* concealment or attempted concealment of crime *etc.* —**cover up 1.** cover completely **2.** attempt to conceal (mistake or crime)

covert ('kuvərt) *a.* **1.** secret, veiled, concealed, sly —*n.* **2.** thicket, place sheltering game **3.** worsted twill cloth once used for hunting clothes —'**covertly** *adv.*

covet ('kuvit) *vt.* long to possess, *esp.* what belongs to another —'**covetous** *a.* avaricious —'**covetousness** *n.*

covey ('kuvi) *n.* brood of partridges or quail (*pl.* **-s**)

cow[1] (kow) *n.* **1.** the female of the bovine and of certain other animals, *eg* elephant, whale **2.** *inf.* disagreeable woman —'**cowboy** *n.* **1.** herdsman in charge of cattle on western plains of U.S. **2.** *inf.* ruthless or unscrupulous operator in business *etc.* —**cow parsley** Eurasian umbelliferous hedgerow plant —'**cowpox** *n.* viral disease of cows. Same infection in man protects against smallpox

cow[2] (kow) *vt.* frighten into submission, overawe, subdue

coward ('kowərd) *n.* one who lacks courage, shrinks from danger —'**cowardice** *n.* —'**cowardly** *a.*

cower ('kowər) *vi.* crouch, shrink in fear

cowl (kowl) *n.* **1.** monk's hooded cloak **2.** its hood **3.** hooded top for chimney, ship's funnel *etc.*

cowling ('kowling) *n.* covering for aircraft engine

co-worker *n.* fellow worker; associate

cowrie *or* **cowry** ('kowri) *n.* brightly-marked glossy marine gastropod of warm seas

cowslip ('kowslip) *n.* wild species of primrose

coxcomb ('kokskōm) *n. obs.* one given to showing off

Coxsackie virus (kok'saki) any of several virus infections principally affecting children in late summer and fall

coxswain ('koksən, -swān) *n.* steersman of boat —**cox** *n.* **1.** coxswain —*v.* **2.** command or steer

coy (koi) *a.* (pretending to be) shy, modest —'**coyly** *adv.* —'**coyness** *n.*

coyote (kI'ōti) *n.* N Amer. prairie wolf

coypu ('koipŏ͞o) *n.* aquatic rodent, orig. from S Amer., yielding nutria fur

cozen ('kuzən) *vt.* flatter in order to cheat, beguile

cozy ('kōzi) *a.* **1.** snug, comfortable, sheltered —*n.* **2.** covering to keep teapot hot —'**cozily** *adv.*

cp. compare

C.P. 1. Canadian Pacific **2.** Cape Province **3.** Communist Party

cpd. compound

Cpl. Corporal

C.P.U. central processing unit

CQ symbol transmitted by amateur radio operator requesting communication with any other amateur radio operator

Cr *Chem.* chromium

crab[1] (krab) *n.* **1.** edible crustacean with ten legs, noted for sidelong and backward walk **2.** type of louse —*vi.* **3.** catch crabs **4.** move sideways (**-bb-**) —**crabbed** ('krabid) *a.* (of handwriting) hard to read —'**crabby** *a.* bad-

tempered —**crab louse** parasitic louse that infests pubic region in man —**catch a crab** *Rowing* dig oar too deeply for clean retrieval

crab[2] (krab) *inf. vi.* **1.** find fault; grumble (**-bb-**) —*n.* **2.** irritable person

crab apple wild sour apple

crack (krak) *vt.* **1.** break, split partially **2.** break with sharp noise **3.** cause to make sharp noise, as of whip, rifle *etc.* **4.** yield **5.** *inf.* tell (joke) **6.** solve, decipher —*vi.* **7.** make sharp noise **8.** split, fissure **9.** (of the voice) lose clearness when changing from boy's to man's —*n.* **10.** sharp explosive noise **11.** split, fissure **12.** flaw **13.** *inf.* joke, *esp.* sarcastic **14.** *dial.* chat **15.** a pure form of cocaine —*a.* **16.** *inf.* special, smart, of great reputation for skill *etc.* —**cracked** *a.* **1.** damaged by cracking **2.** *sl.* crazy —'**cracker** *n.* **1.** *see* **snapper** (sense 2) *at* SNAP **2.** explosive firework **3.** thin dry biscuit —'**cracking** *a.* **1.** *inf.* fast; vigorous —*n.* **2.** process of breaking down hydrocarbons by heat and pressure —'**crackle** *n.* **1.** sound of repeated small cracks **2.** network of fine cracks on the glaze of fine porcelain —*vi.* **3.** make crackling sound —'**crackling** *n.* **1.** crackle **2.** crisp skin of roast pork —'**crackbrained** *a.* insane, idiotic, crazy —'**crackerbarrel** *a.* of or suggesting rustic directness —'**crackerjack** *n./a.* (of) person or thing of exceptional merit —**Cracker Jack** trade name for candied popcorn and peanuts —'**crackpot** *inf. n.* **1.** eccentric person; crank —*a.* **2.** eccentric; crazy —'**cracksman** *n.* burglar, *esp.* safe-breaker —**crack-up** *n.* **1.** collision **2.** *inf.* nervous breakdown —**crack of dawn** daybreak —**crack the whip** *n.* **1.** game in which players in a line run, roller-skate or ice-skate until the leader suddenly changes direction, causing those at the tail of the line to fall or let go —*vi.* **2.** demand obedience from another —**crack up 1.** (cause to) laugh out loud **2.** smash up (vehicle) by losing control —**get cracking** *inf.* start doing something quickly or with increased speed

cradle ('krādəl) *n.* **1.** infant's bed (on rockers) **2.** *fig.* earliest resting-place or home **3.** supporting framework —*vt.* **4.** hold or rock as in a cradle **5.** cherish —'**cradling** *n.*

craft[1] (kraft) *n.* **1.** skill, ability, *esp.* manual ability **2.** cunning **3.** skilled trade **4.** members of a trade —'**craftily** *adv.* —'**craftsman** *n.* —'**craftsmanship** *n.* —'**crafty** *a.* cunning, shrewd

craft[2] (kraft) *n.* vessel, ship (*pl.* **craft**)

crag (krag) *n.* steep rugged rock —'**craggy** *a.* rugged

crake (krāk) *n.* any of various birds of rail family

cram (kram) *vt.* **1.** fill quite full **2.** stuff, force **3.** pack tightly **4.** feed to excess **5.** prepare quickly for examination —*vi.* **6.** study, *esp.* for examination, by hastily memorizing (**-mm-**) —*n.* **7.** act or condition of cramming **8.** crush

cramp (kramp) *n.* **1.** painful muscular contraction **2.** clamp for holding masonry, timber *etc.* together —*vt.* **3.** restrict, hamper **4.** hem in, keep within too narrow limits

crampon ('krampon) *n.* spike in shoe for mountain climbing, *esp.* on ice

cranberry ('kranberi, -bəri) *n.* edible red berry of dwarf evergreen shrub

crane (krān) *n.* **1.** wading bird with long legs, neck and bill **2.** machine for moving heavy weights —*v.* **3.** stretch (neck) to see

crane fly insect with long spindly legs (*also* **daddy longlegs**)

cranesbill ('krānzbil) *n.* plant with pink or purple flowers and beaked fruits

craniometry (krăni'omitri) *n.* the study of the measurements of the human head

cranium ('krăniəm) *n.* skull (*pl.* **-s, -nia** (-niə)) —**'cranial** *a.* —**cranio'logical** *a.* —**crani'ologist** *n.* —**crani'ology** *n.* branch of science concerned with shape and size of human skull —**cranial capacity** measurement of internal capacity or brain volume of the skull —**cranial nerves** nerves arising directly from brain of vertebrates that communicate with head and neck but do not pass through the spinal cord

crank (krangk) *n.* **1.** arm at right angles to axis, for turning main shaft, changing reciprocal into rotary motion *etc.* **2.** *inf.* eccentric person, faddist —*v.* **3.** start (engine) by turning crank —**'cranky** *a.* **1.** eccentric **2.** bad-tempered **3.** shaky —**'crankpin** *n.* short cylindrical surface fitted between two arms of crank parallel to main shaft of crankshaft —**'crankshaft** *n.* principal shaft of engine

cranny ('krani) *n.* small opening, chink —**'crannied** *a.*

crap[1] (krap) *n.* gambling game played with two dice (*also* **craps**)

crap[2] (krap) *n.* **1.** *sl.* nonsense, lies **2.** *offens.* excrement **3.** anything inferior

crape (krăp) *n.* crepe, *esp.* when used for mourning clothes

crapulous ('krapyələs) *a.* **1.** given to or resulting from intemperance **2.** suffering from intemperance; drunken

crash[1] (krash) *v.* **1.** (cause to) make loud noise **2.** (cause to) fall with crash **3.** cause (aircraft) to hit land or water or (of aircraft) land in this way **4.** (cause to) collide **5.** move noisily or violently —*vi.* **6.** break, smash **7.** collapse, fail, *esp.* financially —*n.* **8.** loud, violent fall or impact **9.** collision, wrecking **10.** sudden, uncontrolled descent of aircraft to land **11.** sudden collapse or downfall **12.** bankruptcy —*a.* **13.** requiring, using, great effort to achieve results quickly —**'crashing** *a. inf.* thorough (*esp. in* **crashing bore**) —**crash helmet** helmet worn by motorcyclists *etc.* to protect head —**crash-land** *v.* land (aircraft) in emergency, *esp.* with damage to craft

crash[2] (krash) *n.* fabric, usu. linen, with rough texture and coarse uneven yarns

crass (kras) *a.* grossly stupid —**'crassly** *adv.* —**'crassness** *n.*

crate (krăt) *n.* large (*usu.* wooden) container for packing goods

crater ('krător) *n.* **1.** mouth of volcano **2.** bowl-shaped cavity, *esp.* one made by explosion of large shell, bomb, mine *etc.*

cravat (krə'vat) *n.* man's neckcloth

crave (krăv) *v.* **1.** have very strong desire (for), long (for) —*vt.* **2.** ask humbly **3.** beg —**'craving** *n.*

craven ('krăvən) *a.* **1.** cowardly, abject, spineless —*n.* **2.** coward

Cravenette (krăvə'net) *n.* trade name for rainproofing process applied to woolens and worsteds for making outer garments

craw (krö) *n.* **1.** bird's or animal's stomach **2.** bird's crop

crawfish ('kröfish) *n. see* CRAYFISH

crawl (kröl) *vi.* **1.** move on belly or on hands and knees **2.** move very slowly **3.** ingratiate oneself, cringe **4.** swim with crawl-stroke **5.** be overrun (with) —*n.* **6.** crawling motion **7.** very slow pace or motion **8.** racing stroke at swimming —**'crawler** *n.*

crayfish ('krăfish) *or* **crawfish** *n.* edible freshwater crustacean like lobster

crayon ('krăon, -ən) *n.* stick or pencil of colored chalk, wax *etc.*

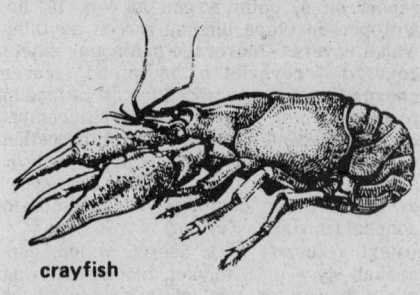

crayfish

craze (krăz) *n.* **1.** short-lived current fashion **2.** strong desire or passion, mania **3.** madness —**crazed** *a.* **1.** demented **2.** (of porcelain) having fine cracks —**'crazy** *a.* **1.** insane **2.** very foolish **3.** (*with* about *or* over) madly eager (for)

CRC Civil Rights Commission

creak (krĕk) *n.* **1.** harsh grating noise —*vi.* **2.** make creaking sound

cream (krĕm) *n.* **1.** fatty part of milk **2.** various foods, dishes, resembling cream **3.** cosmetic *etc.* with creamlike consistency **4.** yellowish-white color **5.** best part of anything —*vt.* **6.** take cream from **7.** take best part from **8.** beat to creamy consistency —**'creamer** *n.* **1.** vessel or device for separating cream from milk **2.** powdered milk substitute for coffee —**'creamery** *n.* **1.** establishment where milk and cream are made into butter and cheese **2.** place where dairy products are sold —**'creamy** *a.* —**cream cheese** soft cheese made by draining superfluous moisture from whole milk —**cream of tartar** potassium hydrogen tartrate, used in baking powders

crease (krĕs) *n.* **1.** line made by folding **2.** wrinkle **3.** superficial bullet wound —*v.* **4.** make, develop creases

create (krĕ'ăt) *vt.* **1.** bring into being **2.** give rise to **3.** make —*vi.* **4.** *inf.* make a fuss —**cre'ation** *n.* —**cre'ative** *a.* —**cre'ator** *n.*

creatine ('krĕətĕn) *n.* nitrogenous substance found in muscles of vertebrates where it stores energy

creature ('krĕchər) *n.* **1.** living being **2.** thing created **3.** dependant —**creature comforts** bodily comforts

crèche (kresh, krăsh) *n.* **1.** day nursery for very young children **2.** foundling home **3.** Nativity scene

credence ('krĕdəns) *n.* **1.** belief, credit **2.** side-table for elements of the Eucharist before consecration

credentials (kri'denshəlz) *pl.n.* **1.** testimonials **2.** letters of introduction, *esp.* those given to ambassador

credible ('kredibəl) *a.* **1.** worthy of belief **2.** trustworthy —**credi'bility** *n.* —**'credibly** *adv.* —**credibility gap** disparity between claims or statements and facts

credit ('kredit) *n.* **1.** commendation, approval **2.** source, cause, of honor **3.** belief, trust **4.** good name **5.** influence, honor or power based on trust of others **6.** system of allowing customers to take goods for later payment **7.** money at one's disposal in bank *etc.* **8.** side of book on which such sums are entered **9.** reputation for financial reliability —*pl.* **10.** list of those responsible for production of film —*vt.* **11.** (*with* with) attribute **12.** believe **13.** put on credit side of account —**'creditable** *a.* bringing honor —**'creditably** *adv.* —**'creditor** *n.* one to whom debt is due —**credit card** card issued by banks *etc.* enabling holder to obtain goods and services on credit —**credit union** nonprofit organiza-

tion, regulated by law, owned by its members, whose function is to make low-interest loans exclusively to members

credo ('krĕdō, 'krā-) *n.* formal statement of beliefs, principles or opinions (*pl.* **-s**)

credulous ('krejələs) *a.* too easy of belief, easily deceived or imposed on, gullible —**cre'dulity** *n.* —**'credulousness** *n.*

Cree (krĕ) *n.* **1.** member of Amerindian people of Manitoba and Saskatchewan (*pl.* **Cree, -s**) **2.** the Algonquian language of this people

creed (krĕd) *n.* **1.** formal statement of Christian beliefs **2.** statement, system of beliefs or principles

creek (krĕk) *n.* natural stream of water smaller than a river —**up the creek** in a difficult situation

Creek (krĕk) *n.* **1.** confederacy of Amerindian peoples of Alabama, Georgia and Florida **2.** member of any of these peoples **3.** Muskogean language of the Creek nation

creel (krĕl) *n.* angler's fishing basket

creep (krĕp) *vi.* **1.** make way along ground, as snake **2.** move with stealthy, slow movements **3.** crawl **4.** act in servile way **5.** (of skin or flesh) feel shrinking, shivering sensation, due to fear or repugnance (**crept** *pt./pp.*) —*n.* **6.** creeping **7.** *sl.* repulsive person —*pl.* **8.** *sl.* feeling of fear or repugnance —**'creeper** *n.* **1.** creeping or climbing plant, *eg* ivy **2.** one-piece garment for child at crawling stage —**'creepy** *a. inf.* **1.** uncanny, unpleasant **2.** causing flesh to creep

cremation (kri'măshən) *n.* burning as means of disposing of corpses —**cre'mate** *vt.* —**crema'torium** *n.* place for cremation

crème de la crème (krem də la 'krem) *n. Fr.* the very best

crème de menthe (krĕm də 'mint, 'menth; krem də 'mänt) *n.* liqueur flavored with peppermint

crenate ('krĕnăt) *or* **crenated** *a.* having scalloped margin, as certain leaves —**cre'nation** *n.*

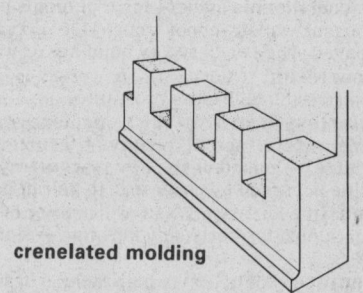

crenelated molding

crenelated ('krenilătid) *a.* having battlements

creole ('krĕōl) *n.* **1.** hybrid language **2.** (**C-**) native-born W Indian, Latin American, of European descent

creosote ('krĕəsōt) *n.* **1.** oily antiseptic liquid distilled from coal or wood tar, used for preserving wood —*vt.* **2.** coat or impregnate with creosote

crepe *or* **crêpe** (krăp) *n.* **1.** fabric with crimped surface **2.** very thin pancake, oft. folded round filling —**crepe de Chine** (də 'shĕn) very thin crepe of silk or similar light fabric —**crepe paper** thin crinkled paper resembling crepe —**crepe rubber** rough-surfaced rubber used for soles of shoes

crepitate ('krepităt) *vi.* make rattling or crackling sound

crepitus ('krepitəs) *n.* **1.** crackling chest sound heard in pneumonia *etc.* **2.** grating sound of two ends of broken bone rubbing together

crepon ('krāpon) *n.* crinkle-weave fabric heavier than crepe

crept (krept) *pt./pp. of* CREEP

crepuscular (kri'puskyŏōlər) *a.* **1.** of or like twilight; dim **2.** (of creatures) active at twilight

Cres. Crescent

crescendo (kri'shendō) *n.* **1.** gradual increase of loudness, *esp.* in music —*adv.* **2.** with a crescendo

crescent ('kresənt) *n.* **1.** (shape of) moon as seen in first or last quarter **2.** any figure of this shape

cress (kres) *n.* any of various plants with edible pungent leaves

crest (krest) *n.* **1.** comb or tuft on bird's or animal's head **2.** plume on top of helmet **3.** top of mountain, ridge, wave *etc.* **4.** badge above shield of coat of arms, also used separately on seal, plate *etc.* —*vt.* **5.** crown **6.** reach top of —**'crestfallen** *a.* cast down by failure, dejected

cretaceous (kri'tāshəs) *a.* chalky

Cretaceous (kri'tāshəs) *a.* **1.** of last period of Mesozoic era, during which chalk deposits were formed —*n.* **2.** Cretaceous period or rock system

cretin ('krētin) *n.* **1.** person afflicted with cretinism **2.** *inf.* stupid person —**'cretinism** *n.* deficiency in thyroid gland causing physical and mental retardation

cretonne ('krēton, kri'ton) *n.* unglazed cotton cloth printed in colored patterns

crevasse (kri'vas) *n.* deep open chasm, *esp.* in glacier

crevice ('krevis) *n.* cleft, fissure, chink

crew (krōō) *n.* **1.** ship's, boat's or aircraft's company, excluding passengers **2.** *inf.* gang, set —*v.* **3.** serve as crew (on) —**crew cut** man's closely cropped haircut —**crew neck** round collarless neckline

crewel ('krōōil) *n.* fine worsted yarn, used in fancy work and embroidery

crib (krib) *n.* **1.** child's bed with enclosing sides **2.** barred rack used for fodder **3.** plagiarism **4.** something used to cheat in examination —*vt.* **5.** confine in small space **6.** copy unfairly (**-bb-**) —**crib death** unexplained death of healthy baby while asleep (*also* **sudden infant death syndrome**)

cribbage ('kribij) *n.* card game for 2 to 4 persons, in which players try to win a set number of points before their opponents

crick (krik) *n.* spasm or cramp in muscles, *esp.* in neck or back

cricket¹ ('krikit) *n.* chirping insect

cricket² ('krikit) *n.* outdoor game played with bats, ball and wickets by two teams of 11 players on a large grassy field in which object is to score runs —**'cricketer** *n.*

cri de coeur (krē də 'kœr) *Fr.* heartfelt or impassioned appeal (*pl.* **cris de coeur** (krē də 'kœr))

cried (krīd) *pt./pp. of* CRY

crier ('krīər) *n.* **1.** person or animal that cries **2.** formerly, official who made public announcements, *esp.* in town or court

crime (krīm) *n.* **1.** violation of law (usu. a serious offense) **2.** wicked or forbidden act **3.** *inf.* something to be regretted —**criminal** ('kriminəl) *a./n.* —**criminality** (krimi'naliti) *n.* —**criminally** ('kriminəli) *adv.* —**criminology** (krimi'nolɔji) *n.* study of crime and criminals

crimp (krimp) *vt.* **1.** make wavy or pleated **2.** pinch together to form seal, *esp.* pie crust

—*n.* **3.** artificially waved hair **4.** curl in synthetic fiber —**'crimpy** *a.* frizzy

crimson ('krimzən) *a./n.* **1.** (of) rich deep red —*v.* **2.** turn crimson

cringe (krinj) *vi.* **1.** shrink, cower **2.** behave obsequiously

crinkle ('kringkəl) *v./n.* wrinkle

crinoline ('krinəlin) *n.* **1.** hooped petticoat or skirt **2.** stiff-sized fabric

cripple ('kripəl) *n.* **1.** one not having normal use of limbs, disabled or deformed person —*vt.* **2.** maim, disable, impair **3.** weaken, lessen efficiency of

crisis ('krīsis) *n.* **1.** turning point or decisive moment, *esp.* in illness **2.** time of acute danger or difficulty (*pl.* **crises** ('krīsēz))

crisp (krisp) *a.* **1.** brittle but firm **2.** brisk, decided **3.** clear-cut **4.** fresh, invigorating **5.** (of hair) curly —**'crisper** *n.* refrigerator compartment for storing salads *etc.* —**'crispy** *a.*

crisscross ('kriskros) *v.* **1.** (cause to) move in crosswise pattern **2.** mark with or consist of pattern of crossing lines —*a.* **3.** (*esp.* of lines) crossing one another in different directions —*n.* **4.** pattern made of crossing lines —*adv.* **5.** in crosswise manner or pattern

criterion (krī'tēəriən) *n.* standard of judgment (*pl.* **-ria** (-riə))

critical ('kritikəl) *a.* **1.** fault-finding **2.** discerning **3.** skilled in or given to judging **4.** of great importance, crucial, decisive —**'critic** *n.* **1.** one who passes judgment **2.** writer expert in judging works of literature, art *etc.* —**'critically** *adv.* —**'criticism** *n.* —**'criticize** *v.* —**critique** (kri'tēk) *n.* critical essay, carefully written criticism —**critical path analysis** technique for planning projects with reference to critical path, which is sequence of stages requiring longest time

croak (krōk) *vi.* **1.** utter deep hoarse cry, as raven, frog **2.** talk dismally **3.** *sl.* die —*n.* **4.** deep hoarse cry —**'croaker** *n.* —**'croaky** *a.* hoarse

Croatian (krō'āshən) *a.* **1.** of Croatia in Yugoslavia, its people or their dialect of Serbo-Croatian —*n.* **2.** dialect of Croatia **3.** native or inhabitant of Croatia

crochet (krō'shā) *n.* **1.** handicraft in which item or fabric is formed by interlocking a single thread with a hooked needle —*vi.* **2.** do such work —*vt.* **3.** make (garment *etc.*) by such work

crock (krok) *n.* **1.** earthenware jar or pot **2.** broken piece of earthenware **3.** dye rubbed off from suede **4.** *inf.* cripple —**crocked** *a. sl.* drunk —**'crockery** *n.* earthenware dishes, utensils *etc.*

Crockpot ('krokpot) *n.* trade name for electric pot used for slow cooking

crocodile ('krokədīl) *n.* **1.** large amphibious reptile **2.** skin or hide of a crocodile —**crocodilian** (krokə'diliən) *n.* **1.** large predatory reptile, such as crocodile, alligator *etc.* —*a.* **2.** of crocodiles or crocodilians —**crocodile tears** insincere grief

crocus ('krōkəs) *n.* small bulbous plant with yellow, white or purple flowers

Croesus ('krēsəs) *n.* very rich man

croft (kroft) *n. Scot.* small piece of arable land, smallholding —**'crofter** *n.* one who works croft

Crohn's disease (krōnz) inflammatory disease of the small intestine giving rise to a wide range of symptoms

croissant (krɔwä'sän, kwä-) *n.* crescent-shaped roll of rich flaky pastry

Cro-Magnon man (krō'magnən, -'manyən)

early type of modern man who lived in Europe during late Paleolithic times

cromlech ('kromlek) *n.* **1.** prehistoric structure, monument of flat stone resting on two upright ones (*also* **dolmen**) **2.** circle of stones enclosing such a structure

crone (krōn) *n.* witchlike old woman

crony ('krōni) *n.* intimate friend

crook (krŏŏk) *n.* **1.** hooked staff **2.** any hook, bend, sharp turn **3.** *inf.* swindler, criminal —**crooked** ('krŏŏkid) *a.* **1.** bent, twisted **2.** deformed **3.** *inf.* dishonest

croon (krōōn) *v.* hum, sing in soft, low tone —**'crooner** *n.*

crop (krop) *n.* **1.** produce of cultivation of any plant or plants **2.** harvest (*lit. or fig.*) **3.** pouch in bird's gullet **4.** stock of whip **5.** hunting whip **6.** short haircut —*vt.* **7.** cut short **8.** poll, clip **9.** (of animals) bite, eat down —*vi.* **10.** raise, produce or occupy land with crop (**-pp-**) —**'cropper** *n. inf.* **1.** heavy fall **2.** disastrous failure —**crop-dusting** *n.* spreading fungicide *etc.* on crops from aircraft —**crop up** *inf.* happen unexpectedly

croquet (krō'kā) *n.* lawn game played with balls, wooden mallets and hoops where the object is to propel the ball through the hoops in a prescribed sequence

croquette (krō'ket) *n.* fried ball of minced meat, fish *etc.* in bread crumbs

crosier *or* **crozier** ('krōzhər) *n.* bishop's or abbot's staff

cross (kros) *n.* **1.** structure or symbol of two intersecting lines or pieces (at right angles) **2.** such a structure of wood as means of execution by tying or nailing victim to it **3.** symbol of Christian faith **4.** any thing or mark in the shape of cross **5.** misfortune, annoyance, affliction **6.** intermixture of breeds, hybrid —*v.* **7.** move or go across (something) **8.** intersect —*vi.* **9.** meet and pass —*vt.* **10.** mark with lines across **11.** (*with out*) delete **12.** place or put in form of cross **13.** make sign of cross on or over **14.** modify breed of animals or plants by intermixture **15.** thwart **16.** oppose —*a.* **17.** out of temper, angry **18.** peevish, perverse **19.** transverse **20.** intersecting **21.** contrary **22.** adverse —**'crossing** *n.* **1.** intersection of roads, rails *etc.* **2.** place or structure where pedestrians and vehicles cross —**'crossly** *adv.* —**'crosswise** *adv./a.* —**'crossbar** *n.* **1.** horizontal bar, line, stripe *etc.* **2.** horizontal beam across pair of goal posts **3.** horizontal bar on man's bicycle —**'crossbill** *n.* bird whose mandibles cross when closed —**'crossbow** *n.* bow fixed across wooden shoulder stock —**'crossbreed** *n.* breed produced from parents of different breeds —**cross'check** *v.* **1.** verify (report *etc.*) by consulting other sources —*n.* **2.** act of crosschecking —**cross-country** *n.* long race held over open ground —**cross-examination** *n.* —**cross-examine** *vt.* examine (witness already examined by other side) —**cross-eyed** *a.* having eye(s) turning inward —**cross-fertilization** *n.* fertilization of one plant by pollen of another —**'crossfire** *n.* **1.** *Mil.* converging fire from one or more positions **2.** lively exchange of ideas, opinions *etc.* —**cross-grained** *a.* perverse —**'crosspatch** *n. inf.* bad-tempered person —**cross-ply** *a.* (of tire) having fabric cords in outer casing running diagonally —**cross-purpose** *n.* contrary aim or purpose —**cross-question** *vt.* **1.** cross-examine —*n.* **2.** question asked in cross-examination —**cross-refer** *v.* refer from one part to another —**cross-reference** *n.* reference within text to another part of text —**'crossroads** *n.* —**cross section 1.** transverse section **2.** group of people fully representative of a nation, community etc. —**cross-stitch** n. 1. embroidery stitch made by two stitches forming cross —v. 2. embroider (piece of needlework) with cross-stitch —**cross-talk** n. Rad., telephony unwanted sounds picked up on receiving channel —**'crosswalk** n. place marked where pedestrians may cross road —**crossword (puzzle)** puzzle built up of intersecting words, of which some letters are common, the words being indicated by clues —**at cross-purposes** conflicting; opposed; disagreeing —**the Cross** 1. cross on which Jesus Christ was executed 2. model or picture of this

crosse (kros) n. light staff with triangular frame to which network is attached, used in playing lacrosse

crotch (kroch) n. 1. angle between two legs, branches or members 2. forked pole used as prop

crotchet ('krochit) n. whimsical notion —'**crotchety** a. peevish; irritable

croton ('krōtən) n. any chiefly tropical shrub or tree, seeds of which yield croton oil, formerly used as purgative

crouch (krowch) vi. 1. bend low 2. huddle down close to ground 3. stoop servilely, cringe —n. 4. act of stooping or bending

croup[1] (krōōp) n. group of symptoms esp. spasm of the larynx, hoarseness, cough esp. in infants

croup[2] (krōōp) n. 1. hindquarters of horse 2. place behind saddle

croupier ('krōōpiər) n. person dealing cards, collecting money etc. at gambling table

crouton ('krōōton, krōō'ton) n. small piece of fried or toasted bread, usu. served in soup

crow[1] (krō) n. large black carrion-eating bird —'**crowfoot** n. any of several plants that have yellow or white flowers and leaves resembling foot of crow (pl. -s) —**crow's-foot** n. wrinkle at corner of eye —**crow's-nest** n. lookout platform high on ship's mast

crow[2] (krō) vi. 1. utter cock's cry 2. boast one's happiness or superiority —n. 3. cock's cry

Crow (krō) n. 1. member of Amerindian people of Montana 2. the Siouan language of this people

crowbar ('krōbär) n. iron bar, usu. flattened at working end for levering

crowd (krowd) n. 1. throng, mass —vi. 2. flock together —vt. 3. cram, force, thrust, pack 4. fill with people —**crowd out** exclude by excess already in

crown (krown) n. 1. monarch's headdress 2. wreath for head 3. monarch 4. monarchy 5. royal power 6. formerly, British coin of five shillings 7. any of various foreign coins 8. top of head 9. summit, top 10. completion or perfection of thing —vt. 11. put crown on 12. confer title upon 13. occur as culmination of (series of events) 14. inf. hit on head —**crown jewels** jewelry, including regalia, used by sovereign on state occasion —**crown prince** heir to throne

crozier ('krōzhər) n. see CROSIER

CRT cathode-ray tube

crucial ('krōōshəl) a. 1. decisive, critical 2. inf. very important

cruciate ('krōōshiāt) a. cross-shaped

crucible ('krōōsibəl) n. small melting pot

crucify ('krōōsifī) vt. 1. put to death on cross 2. treat cruelly 3. inf. ridicule (**crucified**, **'crucifying**) —**'crucifix** n. cross 2. image of (Christ on the) Cross —**cruci'fixion** n. —'**cruciform** a.

crude (krōōd) a. 1. lacking taste, vulgar 2. in natural or raw state, unrefined 3. rough, unfinished —'**crudely** adv. —'**crudity** n.

cruel ('krōōəl) a. 1. delighting in others' pain 2. causing pain or suffering —'**cruelly** adv. —'**cruelty** n.

cruet ('krōōit) n. 1. small container for salt, pepper, vinegar, oil etc. 2. stand holding such containers 3. vessel to hold wine and water for the Eucharist

cruise (krōōz) vi. 1. travel about in a ship for pleasure etc. 2. (of vehicle, aircraft) travel at safe, average speed —n. 3. cruising voyage, esp. organized for holiday purposes —'**cruiser** n. 1. ship that cruises 2. warship lighter and faster than battleship —'**cruiserweight** n. Boxing light-heavyweight

crumb (krum) n. 1. small particle, fragment, esp. of bread —vt. 2. reduce to, break into, cover with crumbs

crumble ('krumbəl) v. 1. break into small fragments, disintegrate, crush 2. perish, decay —vi. 3. fall apart or away —n. 4. pudding covered with crumbly mixture —'**crumbly** a.

crummy ('krumi) a. sl. inferior, contemptible

crump (krump) vi. 1. thud, explode with dull sound —n. 2. crunching sound 3. inf. shell, bomb

crumpet ('krumpit) n. flat round bread baked on griddle usu. toasted before eating

crumple ('krumpəl) v. 1. (cause to) collapse 2. make or become crushed, wrinkled, creased —'**crumpled** a.

crunch (krunch) n. 1. sound made by chewing crisp food, treading on gravel, hard snow etc. 2. inf. critical moment or situation —v. 3. (cause to) make crunching sound

crupper ('krupər) n. 1. strap holding back saddle in place by passing round horse's tail 2. horse's hindquarters

crusade (krōō'sād) n. 1. medieval Christian war to recover Holy Land 2. campaign against something believed to be evil 3. concerted action to further a cause —vi. 4. campaign vigorously for something 5. go on crusade —**cru'sader** n.

cruse (krōōz) n. small earthenware jug or pot

crush[1] (krush) vt. 1. compress so as to break, bruise, crumple 2. break to small pieces 3. defeat utterly, overthrow —n. 4. act of crushing 5. crowd of people etc. 6. drink prepared by or as if by crushing fruit

crush[2] (krush) n. inf. infatuation

crust (krust) n. 1. hard outer part of bread 2. similar hard outer casing on anything —v. 3. cover with, form, crust —'**crustily** adv. —'**crusty** a. 1. having, or like, crust 2. short-tempered

crustacean (kru'stāshən) n. hard-shelled animal, eg crab, lobster —**crus'taceous** a.

crutch (kruch) n. 1. staff with crosspiece to go under armpit of lame person 2. support 3. groin, crotch

crux (kruks) n. 1. that on which a decision turns 2. anything that puzzles very much (pl. -es, **cruces** ('krōōsēz))

cry (krī) vi. 1. weep 2. wail 3. utter call 4. shout 5. clamor or beg (for) —vt. 6. utter loudly, proclaim (**cried**, '**crying**) —n. 7. loud utterance 8. scream, wail, shout 9. call of animal 10. fit of weeping 11. watchword —'**crying** a. notorious; lamentable (esp. in **crying shame**)

cryogenics (krīə'jeniks) n. branch of physics concerned with phenomena at very low temperatures —**cryo'genic** a.

crypt (kript) n. vault, esp. under church —'**cryptic** a. secret, mysterious —'**cryptically** adv. —'**cryptogram** n. piece of writing

in code —**cryp'tography** n. art of writing, decoding ciphers

cryptococcosis (kriptōko'kōsis) n. fungus infection usu. attacking brain and meninges

cryptogam ('kriptōgam) n. nonflowering plant, eg fern, moss etc.

crystal ('kristəl) n. 1. clear transparent mineral 2. very clear glass 3. cut-glass ware 4. characteristic form assumed by many substances, with definite internal structure and external shape of symmetrically arranged plane surfaces —'**crystalline** or '**crystalloid** a. —**crystalli'zation** or -ali'zation n. —'**crystallize** or -alize v. 1. (cause to) form into crystals 2. (cause to) become definite —**crystal'lographer** n. —**crystal'lography** n. science of the structure, forms and properties of crystals —**crystal gazer** —**crystal gazing** 1. act of staring into crystal ball supposedly to arouse visual perceptions of future etc. 2. act of trying to foresee or predict

Cs Chem. cesium

CS gas gas causing tears, salivation and painful breathing, used in chemical warfare and civil disturbances

CST Central Standard Time

CT Connecticut

ct. 1. cent 2. carat 3. court

ctenophore ('tenəför) n. marine invertebrate whose body bears eight rows of fused cilia for locomotion

CTV Canadian Television (Network Ltd.)

cu or **cu.** cubic

Cu Chem. copper

cub (kub) n. 1. young of fox and other animals 2. (C-) Cub Scout —v. 3. give birth to (cubs) (-**bb**-) —**Cub Scout** 8- to 10-year-old member of Boy Scouts of America

Cuba ('kyōōbə) n. country in Caribbean comprising islands of the Greater Antilles group lying 135 miles south of the tip of Florida

cubbyhole ('kubihōl) n. small, enclosed space or room

cube (kyōōb) n. 1. regular solid figure contained by six equal square sides 2. cube-shaped block 3. the third power of a quantity, the product of three equal factors —vt. 4. multiply to produce this —'**cubic(al)** a. —'**cubism** n. movement of modern art led by Pablo Picasso and Georges Braque as reaction to impressionism flourishing between 1907 and 1915 —'**cubist** n./a. —**cube root** a number which taken 3 times as a factor produces the cube of the given factor, eg 3 is the cube root of 27 —**cubic measure** system of units for measurement of volumes

cubicle ('kyōōbikəl) n. partially or totally enclosed section of room, as in dormitory

cubit ('kyōōbit) n. old measure of length, about 18 inches

cuckold ('kukəld) n. 1. man whose wife has committed adultery —vt. 2. make cuckold of

cuckoo ('kōōkōō) n. 1. migratory bird which deposits its eggs in nests of other birds 2. its call —a. 3. sl. crazy —**cuckoopint** ('kōōkōōpint) n. European plant with arrow-shaped leaves, pale purple spadix and scarlet berries (also **lords-and-ladies**) —**cuckoo spit** white frothy mass on plants, produced by froghopper larvae

cucumber ('kyōōkumbər) n. 1. plant with long fleshy green fruit 2. the fruit, used in salad

cud (kud) n. food which ruminant animal brings back into mouth to chew again —**chew the cud** reflect, meditate

cuddle ('kudəl) vt. **1.** hug —vi. **2.** lie close and snug, nestle —n. **3.** close embrace, esp. when prolonged

cuddy ('kudi) n. small cabin in boat

cudgel ('kujəl) n. **1.** short thick stick —vt. **2.** beat with cudgel

cue[1] (kyoo) n. **1.** last words of actor's speech etc. as signal to another to act or speak **2.** signal, hint, example for action

cue[2] (kyoo) n. long tapering rod used in billiards etc. —**cue ball** ball struck by cue in billiards or pool

cuff[1] (kuf) n. **1.** ending of sleeve **2.** wristband —**cuff link** one pair of linked buttons to join buttonholes on shirt cuffs —**off the cuff** inf. without preparation

cuff[2] (kuf) vt. **1.** strike with·open hand —n. **2.** blow of this kind

cuirass (kwi'ras) n. metal or leather armor of breastplate and backplate

Cuisenaire rod (kwizə'nãər) trade name for any of set of rods of various colors and lengths representing different numbers, used to teach arithmetic

cuisine (kwi'zēn) n. **1.** style of cooking **2.** menu, food offered by restaurant etc.

cul-de-sac (kuldə'sak, kool-) n. **1.** street, lane open only at one end **2.** blind pouch (pl. **culs-de-sac**)

culinary ('kulineri, 'kyoo-) a. of, for, suitable for, cooking or kitchen

cull (kul) vt. **1.** gather, select **2.** take out (selected animals) from herd —n. **3.** act of culling

culminate ('kulmināt) vi. **1.** reach highest point **2.** come to climax, to a head —**culmi'nation** n.

culottes ('koolots, 'kyoo-; koo'lots, kyoo-) pl.n. divided skirt

culpable ('kulpəbəl) a. blameworthy —**cul-pa'bility** n. —**'culpably** adv.

culprit ('kulprit) n. one guilty of usu. minor offense

cult (kult) n. **1.** system of religious worship **2.** pursuit of, devotion to, some person, thing, or activity

cultivate ('kultivāt) vt. **1.** till and prepare (ground) to raise crops **2.** develop, improve, refine **3.** devote attention to, cherish **4.** practice **5.** foster —**'cultivable** or **'cultivat-able** a. (of land) capable of being cultivated —**culti'vation** n. —**'cultivator** n.

culture ('kulchər) n. **1.** state of manners, taste and intellectual development at a time or place **2.** cultivating **3.** artificial rearing **4.** set of bacteria so reared —**'cultural** a. —**'cultured** a. refined, showing culture —**cultured pearl** pearl artificially induced to grow in oyster shell

culvert ('kulvərt) n. tunneled drain for passage of water under road, railroad etc.

cum (koom, kum) Lat. with —**cum laude** (koom 'lowdə) with distinction, esp. of college or university degree

cumbersome ('kumbərsəm) or **cumbrous** ('kumbrəs) a. awkward, unwieldy —**'cumber** vt. **1.** obstruct; hinder **2.** obs. inconvenience —**'cumbrance** n. **1.** burden; obstacle; hindrance **2.** trouble; bother

cumin ('kumin) n. herb cultivated for aromatic seed used as spice

cummerbund ('kumərbund) n. broad sash worn round waist

cumulative ('kyoomyoolətiv) a. **1.** becoming greater by successive additions **2.** representing the sum of many items

cumulus ('kyoomyooləs) n. cloud shaped in rounded white woolly masses (pl. **cumuli** ('koomyoolī))

cuneiform (kyoo'nēiförm, 'kyooni-) a. wedge-shaped, esp. of ancient Babylonian writing

cunnilingus (kuni'linggəs) n. sexual activity in which female genitalia are stimulated by partner's lips and tongue

cunning ('kuning) a. **1.** crafty, sly **2.** ingenious —n. **3.** skill in deceit or evasion **4.** skill, ingenuity —**'cunningly** adv.

cup (kup) n. **1.** small drinking vessel with handle at one side **2.** any small drinking vessel **3.** contents of cup **4.** any of various cup-shaped formations, cavities, sockets etc. **5.** cup-shaped trophy as prize **6.** portion, lot **7.** iced drink of wine and other ingredients **8.** either of two cup-shaped parts of brassiere etc. —vt. **9.** shape as cup (hands etc.) (-pp-) —**'cupful** n. (pl. **'cupfuls, 'cupsful**) —**'cupping** n. Med. formerly, use of evacuated glass cup to draw blood to surface of skin for bloodletting —**cupboard** ('kubərd) n. recess in room, with door, for storage —**'cupcake** n. small cake baked in cuplike mold —**in one's cups** drunk

cupel (kyoo'pel, 'kyoopəl) n. small vessel used in refining metals

Cupid ('kyoopid) n. god of love

cupidity (kyoo'piditi) n. **1.** greed for possessions **2.** covetousness

cupola ('kyoopələ) n. dome

cupreous ('kyooprias, 'koo-) a. of, containing, copper

cupronickel (kyooprō'nikəl, koo-) n. copper alloy containing up to 40 per cent nickel

cur (kər) n. **1.** dog of mixed breed **2.** surly, contemptible or mean person

curaçao (kyooərə'sō, kooə-) n. liqueur flavored with bitter orange peel

curare (kyoo'räri, koo-) n. poisonous resin of S Amer. tree, now used as muscle relaxant in medicine

curate ('kyooərit) n. **1.** clergyman in charge of parish **2.** clergyman serving as assistant to rector —**'curacy** n. curate's office

curative ('kyooərətiv) a. **1.** tending to cure disease —n. **2.** anything able to heal or cure

curator (kyooə'rātər) n. custodian, esp. of museum, library etc. —**cura'torial** a. —**cu-'ratorship** n.

curb (kərb) n. **1.** check, restraint **2.** chain or strap passing under horse's lower jaw and giving powerful control with reins **3.** stone edging along paved street —vt. **4.** restrain, apply curb to

curd (kərd) n. coagulated milk —**'curdle** v. turn into curd, coagulate —**'curdy** a.

cure (kyooər) vt. **1.** heal, restore to health **2.** remedy **3.** preserve (fish, skins etc.) —n. **4.** remedy **5.** course of medical treatment **6.** successful treatment, restoration to health —**cura'bility** n. —**'curable** a. —**cure of souls** care of parish or congregation

curette (kyoo'ret) n. spoon-shaped surgical instrument for removing dead tissue etc. from some body cavities —**curettage** (kyooəri'täzh) n. technique or act of using curette

curfew ('kərfyoo) n. **1.** official regulation restricting or prohibiting movement of people, esp. at night **2.** time set as deadline by such regulation

curia ('kyooəria, 'koo-) n. **1.** papal court and government of Roman Catholic Church **2.** (in Middle Ages) court held in king's name (pl. **curiae** ('kyooərie, 'koo-))

curie ('kyooəri, -rē; 'kooə-) n. standard unit of radium emanation

curio ('kyooəriō) n. rare or curious thing of the kind sought for collections (pl. **-s**)

curious ('kyooəriəs) a. **1.** eager to know, inquisitive **2.** prying **3.** puzzling, strange, odd —**curi'osity** n. **1.** eagerness to know **2.** inquisitiveness **3.** strange or rare thing —**'curiously** adv.

curium ('kyooəriəm) n. Chem. transuranic element Symbol Cm, at. wt. 248, at. no. 96

curl (kərl) vi. **1.** take spiral or curved shape or path —vt. **2.** bend into spiral or curved shape —n. **3.** spiral lock of hair **4.** spiral, curved state, form or motion —**'curler** n. **1.** pin, clasp etc. for curling hair **2.** person or thing that curls **3.** person who plays curling —**'curling** n. game like bowls, played with large rounded stones on ice by teams of four players each —**'curly** a. —**curling tongs** heated, metal, scissor-like device for curling hair

curlew ('kərlyoo, -loo) n. large long-billed wading bird

curlicue ('kərlikyoo) n. intricate ornamental curl or twist

curmudgeon (kər'mujən) n. surly or miserly person

curragh or **currach** ('kurəkh, 'kurə) n. coracle with a keel

currant ('kurənt) n. **1.** dried type of grape **2.** fruit of various plants allied to gooseberry **3.** any of these plants

current ('kurənt) a. **1.** of immediate present, going on **2.** up-to-date, not yet superseded **3.** in circulation or general use —n. **4.** body of water or air in motion **5.** tendency, drift **6.** transmission of electricity through conductor —**'currency** n. **1.** money in use **2.** state of being in use **3.** time during which thing is current —**'currently** adv.

curricle ('kurikəl) n. two-wheeled open carriage drawn by two horses side by side

curriculum (kə'rikyələm) n. specified course of study (pl. **-s, -la** (-lə)) —**curriculum vitae** ('vītē) outline of person's educational and professional history, usu. for job applications (pl. **curricula vitae**)

curry[1] ('kuri) n. **1.** food or dish flavored with curry powder **2.** curry powder —vt. **3.** prepare, flavor dish with curry powder (**'curried, 'currying**) —**curry powder** condiment consisting of combination of various pungent aromatic ground spices

curry[2] ('kuri) vt. **1.** groom (horse) with comb **2.** dress (leather) (**'curried, 'currying**) —**curry comb** metal comb for grooming horse —**curry favor** try to win favor, ingratiate oneself

curse (kərs) n. **1.** profane or obscene expression of anger etc. **2.** utterance expressing extreme ill will towards some person or thing **3.** affliction, misfortune, scourge —v. **4.** utter curse, swear (at) —vt. **5.** afflict —**cursed** ('kərsid, kərst) a. **1.** hateful **2.** wicked **3.** deserving of, or under, a curse —**cursedly** ('kərsidli) adv. —**cursedness** ('kərsidnis) n.

cursive ('kərsiv) a. written in running script, with letters joined

cursor ('kərsər) n. **1.** sliding part of measuring instrument **2.** movable point of light etc. that identifies specific position on visual display unit

cursory ('kərsəri) a. rapid, hasty, not detailed, superficial —**'cursorily** adv.

curt (kərt) a. short, rudely brief, abrupt —**'curtly** adv. —**'curtness** n.

curtail (kər'tāl) vt. cut short, diminish —**cur'tailment** n.

curtain ('kərtən) *n.* **1.** hanging drapery at window *etc.* **2.** cloth hung as screen **3.** screen separating audience and stage in theater **4.** end to act or scene *etc.* —*pl.* **5.** *inf.* death or ruin; the end —*vt.* **6.** provide, cover with curtain —**curtain call** return to stage by performers to acknowledge applause —**curtain-raiser** *n.* **1.** short play coming before main one **2.** any preliminary event —**curtain wall** wall that divides space but does not bear structural weight

curtsy *or* **curtsey** ('kərtsi) *n.* **1.** woman's bow or respectful gesture made by bending knees and lowering body —*vi.* **2.** make a curtsy

curve (kərv) *n.* **1.** line of which no part is straight **2.** bent line or part —*v.* **3.** bend into curve —**cur'vaceous** *a. inf.* shapely —**'curvature** *n.* **1.** a bending **2.** bent shape —**curvi'linear** *a.* of bent lines

curvet (kər'vet) *n.* **1.** leap of horse in which forelegs touch the ground first —*vi.* **2.** prance or frisk about (**-tt-**)

Cushing's disease ('kŏŏshingz) tumor of the pituitary gland —**Cushing's syndrome** disease of the adrenal gland marked by excessive secretions from the gland

cushion ('kŏŏshən) *n.* **1.** bag filled with soft stuffing or air, to support or ease body **2.** any soft pad or support **3.** resilient rim of billiard table —*vt.* **4.** provide, protect with cushion **5.** lessen effects of

cushy ('kŏŏshi) *a. inf.* soft, comfortable, pleasant, light, well-paid

cusp (kusp) *n.* **1.** either end of crescent moon **2.** point on grinding surface of tooth **3.** point of transition from one astrological sign to another —**'cuspid** *n.* pointed tooth —**'cuspidal** *a.* ending in point **2.** of or like cusp

cuspidor ('kuspidôr) *n.* spittoon

cuss (kus) *inf. n.* **1.** curse; oath **2.** person or animal, *esp.* annoying one —*v.* **3.** *see* CURSE (sense 4) —**cussed** ('kusid) *a. inf.* **1.** *see* **cursed** *at* CURSE **2.** obstinate **3.** annoying —**'cussedness** *n.*

custard ('kustərd) *n.* dish made of eggs and milk

custody ('kustədi) *n.* safekeeping, guardianship, imprisonment —**cus'todian** *n.* keeper, caretaker, curator

custom ('kustəm) *n.* **1.** habit **2.** practice **3.** fashion, usage **4.** business patronage **5.** toll, tax —*pl.* **6.** duties levied on imports **7.** government department which collects these **8.** area in airport *etc.* where customs officials examine luggage for dutiable goods —**custom'arily** *adv.* —**'customary** *a.* usual, habitual —**'customer** *n.* **1.** one who enters shop to buy, *esp.* regularly **2.** purchaser —**custom-built** *a.* (of automobiles, houses *etc.*) made to specifications of buyer —**'customhouse** *n.* building where customs are collected —**custom-made** *a.* (of suits *etc.*) made to specifications of buyer —**customs duties** taxes laid on imported or exported goods

cut (kut) *vt.* **1.** sever, penetrate, wound, divide, or separate with pressure of edge or edged instrument **2.** pare, detach, trim, or shape by cutting **3.** divide **4.** intersect **5.** reduce, decrease **6.** abridge **7.** *inf.* refuse to recognize (person) **8.** strike (with whip *etc.*) **9.** divide (deck of cards), *esp.* to decide dealer —*vi. Cine.* **10.** call a halt to shooting sequence **11.** (*with* to) move quickly to another scene (**cut, 'cutting**) —*n.* **12.** act of cutting **13.** stroke **14.** blow, wound (of knife, whip *etc.*) **15.** reduction, decrease **16.** fashion, shape **17.** incision **18.** engraving **19.** piece cut off **20.** division **21.** *inf.* share, *esp.* of profits

—**'cutter** *n.* **1.** one who, that which, cuts **2.** warship's rowing and sailing boat **3.** small sloop-rigged vessel with straight running bowsprit —**'cutting** *n.* **1.** act of cutting, thing cut off or out, *esp.* excavation (for road, canal *etc.*) through high ground **2.** shoot, twig of plant **3.** *esp.* **UK** piece cut from newspaper *etc.;* clipping —*a.* **4.** sarcastic, unkind —**'cutaway** *n.* **1.** man's coat cut diagonally from front waist to back of knees **2.** drawing or model of machine *etc.* in which part of casing is omitted to reveal workings —**'cutback** *n.* decrease; reduction —**cut glass** glass, *esp.* vases *etc.,* decorated by facet cutting or grinding —**cut-rate** *a.* **1.** available at prices or rates below standard price or rate **2.** offering goods or services at prices below standard price —**'cutthroat** *a.* **1.** merciless **2.** (of partnership card games) characterized by players changing partners in order to attain highest personal scores —*n.* **3.** murderous person —**cut back 1.** shorten by cutting off end; prune **2.** reduce or make reduction (in) —**cut in 1.** intrude **2.** interrupt (in conversation) **3.** interrupt dancing couple and take one as one's partner **4.** mix (dried food ingredients) with chopping motion

cutaneous (kyŏŏ'tāniəs) *a.* of skin

cute (kyŏŏt) *a.* appealing, attractive, pretty

cuticle ('kyŏŏtikəl) *n.* **1.** the skin **2.** dead skin at edges of fingernail or toenail **3.** thin fatty film covering surface of many higher plants

cutis ('kyŏŏtis) *n. Anat.* skin (*pl.* **-tes** (-tēz), **-es**)

cutlass ('kutləs) *n.* short broad-bladed sword

cutlery ('kutləri) *n.* implements for cutting food —**'cutler** *n.* one who makes, repairs, deals in knives and cutting implements

cutlet ('kutlit) *n.* small piece of meat broiled or fried

cuttlefish ('kutəlfish) *n.* marine mollusk resembling squid but with calcified internal shell (*also* **'cuttle**) —**'cuttlebone** *n.* internal shell of cuttlefish, used as mineral supplement to diet of cagebirds and as polishing agent

C.V. curriculum vitae

Cwlth. Commonwealth

cwm (kŏŏm) *n.* **1.** in Wales, valley **2.** *Geol. see* CIRQUE

c.w.o. *or* **C.W.O.** cash with order

cwt. hundredweight

-cy (*comb. form*) **1.** state, quality, condition, as in *plutocracy, lunacy* **2.** rank, office, as in *captaincy*

cyan ('sīan, 'sīən) *n.* **1.** green-blue color —*a.* **2.** of this color

cyanide ('sīənīd) *n.* extremely poisonous organic compound, used for fumigating buildings and soil —**cy'anogen** *n.* poisonous gas composed of nitrogen and carbon

cyanosis (sīə'nōsis) *n.* blueness of the skin

cybernetics (sībər'netiks) *pl.n.* (*with sing. v.*) comparative study of control mechanisms of electronic and biological systems

cyclamate ('sīkləmāt) *n.* compound formerly used as food additive and sugar substitute

cyclamen ('sīkləmən, 'sik-) *n.* plant with flowers having turned-back petals

cycle ('sīkəl) *n.* **1.** recurrent series or period **2.** rotation of events **3.** complete series or period **4.** development following course of stages **5.** series of poems *etc.* **6.** bicycle, tricycle or motorcycle —*vi.* **7.** move in cycles **8.** ride cycle —**'cyclic(al)** *a.* **1.** recurring or revolving in a cycle **2.** *Chem.* (of compound) having atoms which form a ring —**'cyclist** *n.* cycle rider —**cy'clometer**

n. instrument for measuring circles or recording distance traveled by wheel, *esp.* of bicycle

cyclo- *or before vowel* **cycl-** (*comb. form*) **1.** indicating circle or ring, as in *cyclotron* **2.** denoting cyclic compound, as in *cyclopropane*

cyclone ('sīklōn) *n.* **1.** system of winds moving round centre of low pressure **2.** circular storm —**cyclonic** (sī'klonik) *a.*

cyclopedia *or* **cyclopaedia** (sīklō'pēdiə) *n. see* ENCYCLOPEDIA

cyclopropane (sīklō'prōpān) *n.* colorless gaseous hydrocarbon, used as anesthetic

Cyclops ('sīklops) *n. Class. myth.* one of race of giants having single eye in middle of forehead (*pl.* **Cyclopes** (sī'klōpēz), **-es**)

cyclorama (sīklō'rämə) *n.* **1.** picture on interior wall of cylindrical room, designed to appear in natural perspective to spectator **2.** *Theat.* curtain or wall curving along back of stage —**cycloramic** (sīklō'ramik) *a.*

cyclostyle ('sīkləstīl) *vt.* **1.** produce (pamphlets *etc.*) in large numbers for distribution —*a./n.* **2.** (of) machine, method for doing this

cyclotron ('sīklətron) *n.* powerful apparatus which accelerates the circular movement of subatomic particles in a magnetic field, used for work in nuclear disintegration *etc.*

cygnet ('signit) *n.* young swan

cylinder ('silindər) *n.* **1.** solid or hollow object with straight sides and circular ends **2.** piston chamber of engine —**cy'lindrical** *a.*

cymbal ('simbəl) *n.* one of pair of two brass plates struck together to produce ringing or clashing sound in orchestra

cyme (sīm) *n.* inflorescence in which first flower is terminal bud of main stem and subsequent flowers develop as terminal buds of lateral stems —**cy'miferous** *a.*

Cymric *or* **Kymric** ('kimrik) *a.* Welsh

cynic ('sinik) *n.* one who expects, believes, the worst about people, their motives, or outcome of events —**'cynical** *a.* —**'cynicism** *n.* being cynical

cynosure ('sīnəshŏŏər, 'sin-) *n.* center of attraction

cypress ('sīprəs) *n.* any of genus of mainly evergreen trees of pine family with overlapping leaves resembling scales

Cyprus ('sīprəs) *n.* country in eastern Mediterranean comprising one island lying 50 miles off the south coast of Turkey and 65 miles off the coast of Syria —**Cypriot** ('sipriət) *or* **Cypriote** ('sipriōt) *n.* **1.** native of Cyprus **2.** dialect of Greek spoken in Cyprus —*a.* **3.** relating to Cyprus

Cyrillic (si'rilik) *a.* **1.** relating to alphabet devised supposedly by Saint Cyril, for Slavonic languages —*n.* **2.** this alphabet

cyst (sist) *n.* **1.** abnormal sac formed in the body **2.** resistant cover surrounding a parasite produced by the parasite or host —**'cystic** *a.* **1.** of cysts **2.** of the bladder —**cys'titis** *n.* inflammation of bladder —**cystic fibrosis** congenital disease, usu. affecting children, characterized by chronic infection of respiratory tract and pancreatic insufficiency

cystocele ('sistōsēl) *n.* the protrusion of the urinary bladder into the vagina

cytochrome ('sītōkrōm) *n.* pigment found in plant and animal tissue enabling air-breathing organisms to utilize atmospheric oxygen

cytology (sī'toləji) *n.* branch of biology concerned with all aspects of plant or animal cells

cytoplasm ('sītōplazəm) *n.* protoplasm of cell excluding nucleus

cytoscope ('sītəskōp) *n.* slender tubular medical instrument for examining interior of urethra and urinary bladder —**cy'toscopy** *n.* visual examination of the urinary bladder with cytoscope

czar, tsar, *or* **tzar** (zär) *n.* 1. emperor, king, *esp.* of Russia 1547-1917 2. one having great power —**cza'rina, cza'ritsa, tsa'ritsa** *or* **tza'ritsa** *n.* wife of czar

czardas ('chärdash) *n.* 1. Hungarian national dance of alternating slow and fast sections 2. music for this dance

Czechoslovakia (chekōslō'vakiə) *n.* country in central Europe bounded north by the German Democratic Republic and Poland, south by Hungary and Austria, and west by the Federal Republic of Germany —**Czech** *n.* member of western branch of Slavs —**Czecho'slovak** *or* **Czechoslo'vakian** *a.* 1. of Czechoslovakia, its peoples or languages —*n.* 2. (loosely) either of two languages of Czechoslovakia: Czech or Slovak

Czechoslovakia

Dd

d *or* **D** (dē) *n.* 1. fourth letter of English alphabet 2. speech sound represented by this letter (*pl.* **d's, D's** *or* **Ds**)

d *Phys.* density

D 1. *Mus.* second note of scale of C major; major or minor key having this note as its tonic 2. *Chem.* deuterium 3. Roman numeral, 500

d. 1. day 2. denarius (*Lat.,* penny) 3. departs 4. diameter 5. died

D. Democratic

dab[1] (dab) *vt.* 1. apply with momentary pressure (*esp.* anything wet and soft) 2. strike feebly (**-bb-**) —*n.* 3. smear 4. slight blow or tap 5. small mass —**'dabchick** *n.* small grebe —**dab hand** *inf.* someone good at something

dab[2] (dab) *n.* any of various small flatfishes, *esp.* flounder

dabble ('dabəl) *vi.* 1. splash about 2. be desultory student or amateur —**'dabbler** *n.*

da capo (dä 'käpō) *Mus.* repeat from beginning

dace (dās) *n.* any of various small European or N Amer. freshwater fishes (*pl.* **dace, -s**)

dachshund ('däks-hōōnt) *n.* short-legged long-bodied dog

Dacron ('dākron, 'dak-) *n.* trade name for polyester fiber

dactyl ('daktil) *n.* metrical foot of one long followed by two short syllables

dad (dad) *or* **daddy** ('dadi) *n. inf.* father —**daddy longlegs** ('longlegz) *inf.* any of various insects or spiders with long slender legs

Dada ('dädä) *or* **Dadaism** ('dädäizəm) *n.* artistic movement of early 20th century, founded on principles of incongruity and irreverence toward accepted aesthetic criteria —**'Dadaist** *n./a.*

dado ('dādō) *n.* lower part of room wall when lined or painted separately (*pl.* **-es, -s**)

daemon ('dēmən) *or* **daimon** ('dīmon) *n.* 1. demigod 2. guardian spirit of place or person

daff (daf) *inf.* daffodil

daffodil ('dafədil) *n.* spring flower, yellow narcissus (*also* **Lent lily**)

daft (daft) *a.* foolish, crazy

dag (dag) *n.* 1. daglock 2. **A, NZ** *sl.* eccentric character —**'daglock** *n.* dung-caked locks of wool around hindquarters of sheep

dagga ('dakhə, 'dägə) *n.* **SA** hemp, smoked as narcotic

dagger ('dagər) *n.* short, edged stabbing weapon

dago ('dāgō) *n. offens.* person of Italian descent (*pl.* **-s, -es**)

daguerreotype (də'gerōtīp) *n.* 1. early photographic process 2. photograph formed by this process

dahlia ('dalyə) *n.* garden plant of various colors

Dáil Éireann ('doil 'aərən) *or* **Dáil** *n.* lower chamber of parliament in the Irish Republic

daily ('dāli) *a.* 1. done, occurring, published every day —*adv.* 2. every day —*n.* 3. daily newspaper

dainty ('dānti) *a.* 1. delicate 2. elegant, choice 3. pretty and neat 4. fastidious —*n.* 5. delicacy —**'daintily** *adv.* —**'daintiness** *n.*

daiquiri ('dīkiri, 'dak-) *n.* iced drink containing rum, lime juice and sugar (*pl.* **-s**)

dairy ('dāəri) *n.* place for processing milk and its products —**'dairying** *n.* —**dairy cattle** cows raised mainly for milk —**dairy farm** farm specializing in producing milk—**'dairymaid** *n.* —**'dairyman** *n.* —**dairy products** milk, cheese, butter *etc.*

dais ('dāis, 'dīis) *n.* raised platform, usu. at end of hall

daisy ('dāzi) *n.* flower with yellow center and white petals —**daisy-wheel** *n.* flat, wheel-shaped device with printing characters at end of spokes

Dakota (də'kōtə) *n.* 1. member of Amerindian people of northern Mississippi Valley (*pl.* **-s, Dakota**) 2. the Siouan language of this people (*also* **Sioux**)

Dalai Lama ('dälī 'lämə) head of Tibetan Buddhism

dale (dāl) *n.* valley —**'dalesman** *n.* native of dale, *esp.* of N England

dalles (dalz) *pl.n.* **C** river rapids flowing between high rock walls

dally ('dali) *vi.* 1. trifle, spend time in idleness or amusement 2. loiter (**'dallied, 'dallying**) —**'dalliance** *n.*

Dalmatian (dal'māshən) *n.* large dog, white with black spots

dal segno ('däl 'sānyō) *Mus.* repeat from point marked with sign to word *fine*

dam[1] (dam) *n.* 1. barrier to hold back flow of waters 2. water so collected —*vt.* 3. hold with or as with dam (**-mm-**)

dam[2] (dam) *n.* female parent (used of animals)

damage ('damij) *n.* 1. injury, harm, loss —*pl.* 2. sum claimed or adjudged in compensation for injury —*vt.* 3. harm

Dalmatian

damascene ('daməsēn) *n.* 1. technique of decorating iron and steel with inlaid patterns of gold and silver —*vt.* 2. decorate (iron and steel) thus

damask ('daməsk) *n.* 1. figured woven material of silk or linen, *esp.* white table linen with design shown up by light 2. color of damask rose, velvety red —**damask rose** fragrant rose used to make the perfume attar

dame (dām) *n.* 1. *obs.* lady 2. (**D-**) title of lady in Order of the British Empire 3. *sl.* woman

damn (dam) *vt.* 1. condemn to hell 2. be the ruin of 3. give hostile reception to —*vi.* 4. curse (**damned, 'damning**) —*interj.* 5. expression of annoyance, impatience *etc.* —**damnable** ('damnǝbǝl) *a.* 1. deserving damnation 2. hateful, annoying —**dam'nation** *n.* —**damnatory** ('damnǝtöri) *a.*

damp (damp) *a.* 1. moist 2. slightly moist —*n.* 3. diffused moisture 4. in coal mines, dangerous gas —*vt.* 5. make damp 6. (*oft. with* down) deaden, discourage —**'dampen** *v.* 1. make, become damp —*vt.* 2. stifle, deaden —**'damper** *n.* 1. anything that discourages or depresses 2. plate in flue to control draft

damsel ('damzǝl) *n. obs.* girl

damson ('damzǝn) *n.* 1. small dark purple plum 2. tree bearing it 3. its color

dan (dan) *n.* any one of 12 grades of proficiency in judo

Dan. *Bible* Daniel

dance (dans) *vi.* 1. move with measured rhythmic steps, usu. to music 2. be in lively movement 3. bob up and down —*vt.* 4. perform (dance) 5. cause to dance —*n.* 6. lively, rhythmical movement 7. arrangement of such movements 8. tune for them 9. social gathering for the purpose of dancing —**'dancer** *n.*

D and C dilation and curettage (of womb)

dandelion ('dandiliǝn) *n.* yellow-flowered wild plant

dander ('dandǝr) *n. inf.* temper, fighting spirit

dandle ('dandǝl) *vt.* 1. move (young child) up and down (on knee or in arms) 2. pet; fondle

dandruff ('dandrǝf) *n.* dead skin in small scales among the hair

dandy ('dandi) *n.* 1. man excessively concerned with smartness of dress —*a.* 2. *inf.* excellent —**'dandify** *vt.* dress like or cause to resemble a dandy —**'dandyism** *n.*

Dane (dān) *n. see* DENMARK

danger ('dānjǝr) *n.* 1. liability or exposure to harm 2. risk, peril —**'dangerous** *a.* —**'dangerously** *adv.*

dangle ('danggǝl) *vi.* 1. hang loosely and swaying —*vt.* 2. hold suspended 3. tempt with

Daniel ('danyǝl) *n. Bible* 27th book of the O.T., written by the prophet Daniel, presenting Jerusalem under Gentile control

Danish ('dānish) *see* DENMARK

dank (dangk) *a.* unpleasantly damp and chilly —**'dankness** *n.*

danseuse (dã'sœz) *n.* female dancer

daphne ('dafni) *n.* ornamental shrub with bell-shaped flowers

dapper ('dapǝr) *a.* neat and precise, *esp.* in dress, spruce

dapple ('dapǝl) *v.* mark or become marked with spots —**'dappled** *a.* spotted, mottled, variegated —**dapple-gray** *a.* (of horse) gray marked with darker spots

DAR Daughters of the American Revolution

dare (dāǝr) *v.* 1. venture, have courage (to) —*vt.* 2. challenge —*n.* 3. challenge —**'daring** *a.* 1. bold —*n.* 2. adventurous courage —**'daredevil** *a./n.* reckless (person)

dark (därk) *a.* 1. without light 2. gloomy 3. deep in tint 4. secret 5. unenlightened 6. wicked —*n.* 7. absence of light, color or knowledge —**'darken** *v.* —**'darkly** *adv.* —**'darkness** *n.* —**Dark Ages** *Hist.* period from about late 5th cent. A.D. to about 1000 A.D. —**Dark Continent** Africa when relatively unexplored —**dark horse** somebody, *esp.* competitor in race, about whom little is known —**'darkroom** *n.* darkened room for processing film

darling ('därling) *a./n.* much loved or very lovable (person)

darn¹ (därn) *vt.* 1. mend by filling (hole) with interwoven yarn —*n.* 2. place so mended —**'darning** *n.*

darn² (därn) *interj.* mild expletive

darnel ('därnǝl) *n.* grass that grows as weed in grain fields

dart (därt) *n.* 1. small light pointed missile 2. darting motion 3. tapering seam in garment —*pl.* 4. indoor game played with numbered target and miniature darts —*vt.* 5. cast, throw rapidly (glance *etc.*) —*vi.* 6. go rapidly or abruptly —**'dartboard** *n.* circular piece of wood *etc.* used as target in darts

Darwinian (där'winiǝn) *a.* pert. to Charles Darwin (1809-82) or his theory of evolution

dash (dash) *vt.* 1. smash, throw, thrust, send with violence 2. cast down 3. tinge, flavor, mix —*vi.* 4. move, go with great speed or violence —*n.* 5. rush 6. vigor 7. smartness 8. small quantity, tinge 9. stroke (-) between words —**'dasher** *n.* C ledge along top of boards at ice-hockey rink —**'dashing** *a.* spirited, showy —**'dashboard** *n.* in vehicle, instrument panel in front of driver

dastard ('dastǝrd) *n. obs.* contemptible, sneaking coward —**'dastardly** *a.*

data ('dātǝ, 'dätǝ) *pl.n.* (*oft.* with *sing. v.*) 1. series of observations, measurements or facts 2. information —**data bank** *or* **base** store of information, *esp.* in form that can be handled by computer —**data processing** sequence of operations performed on data, *esp.* by computer, to extract information *etc.*

DATA Defense Air Transportation Administration

date¹ (dāt) *n.* 1. day of the month 2. statement on document of its time of writing 3. time of occurrence 4. period of work of art *etc.* 5. engagement, appointment —*vt.* 6. mark with date 7. refer to date of 8. reveal age of 9. *inf.* accompany on social outing —*vi.* 10. exist (from) 11. betray time or period of origin, become old-fashioned —**'dateless** *a.* 1. without date 2. immemorial —**'dateline** *n. Journalism* date and location of story, placed at top of article —**date line** (*oft.* D- L-) line (180° meridian) E of which is one day earlier than W of it —**date stamp** 1. adjustable rubber stamp for recording date 2. inked impression made by this

date² (dāt) *n.* 1. sweet, single-stone fruit of palm 2. the palm

dative ('dātiv) *n.* noun case indicating indirect object

datum ('dātǝm, 'dätǝm) *n.* thing given, known or assumed as basis for reckoning, reasoning *etc.* (*pl.* **'data**)

daub (döb) *vt.* 1. coat, plaster, paint coarsely or roughly —*n.* 2. rough picture 3. smear —**'dauber** *n.*

daughter ('dötǝr) *n.* 1. one's female child —*a.* 2. *Biol.* of cell or unicellular organism produced by division of one of its own kind. 3. *Phys.* (of nuclide) formed from another nuclide by radioactive decay —**'daughterly** *a.* —**daughter-in-law** *n.* son's wife

daunt (dönt) *vt.* frighten, *esp.* into giving up purpose —**'dauntless** *a.* intrepid, fearless

dauphin ('döfin; *Fr.* dō'fɛ̃) *n.* formerly, eldest son of French king

davenport ('davǝnpört) *n.* 1. small writing table with drawers 2. large couch or settee

davit ('dāvit, 'da-) *n.* crane, usu. one of pair, at ship's side for lowering and hoisting boats

Davy Jones's locker ('dāvi 'jōnziz) bottom of the sea; ships' or sailors' graveyard

daw (dö) *n. obs.* jackdaw

dawdle ('dödǝl) *vi.* idle, waste time, loiter —**'dawdler** *n.*

dawn (dön) *n.* 1. first light 2. first gleam or beginning of anything —*vi.* 3. begin to grow light 4. appear, begin 5. (begin to) be understood —**'dawning** *n.* —**dawn chorus** singing of birds at dawn

day (dā) *n.* 1. period of 24 hours 2. time when sun is above horizon 3. point or unit of time 4. daylight 5. part of day occupied by certain activity, time period 6. special or designated day —**day bed** couch intended for use as seat and as bed —**'daybook** *n.* diary —**'daybreak** *n.* dawn —**'daydream** *n.* 1. idle fancy —*vi.* 2. indulge in idle fantasy —**'daylight** *n.* 1. natural light 2. dawn —*pl.* 3. consciousness, wits —**daylight robbery** *inf.* blatant overcharging —**daylight saving time** time set one hour ahead of local standard time (*also* **daylight time**) —**day room** communal living room in residential institution —**'dayspring** *n.* dawn —**'daystar** *n.* morning star —**'daytime** *n.* time between sunrise and sunset —**day-to-day** *a.* routine; everyday —**see daylight** begin to apprehend the solution to a problem or the end of a task

Dayak *or* **Dyak** ('dīak) *n.* 1. member of any of the Indonesian peoples of Borneo 2. the language of these peoples

Day-Glo ('dāglō) *n.* trade name for luminous printing ink

daze (dāz) *vt.* 1. stupefy, stun, bewilder —*n.* 2. stupefied or bewildered state —**dazed** *a.*

dazzle ('dazǝl) *vt.* 1. blind, confuse or overpower with brightness, light, brilliant display or prospects —*n.* 2. brightness that dazzles the vision —**'dazzlement** *n.*

dB *or* **db** decibel(s)

DC 1. District of Columbia 2. direct current 3. *Mus.* da capo

DD Doctor of Divinity

D-day *n.* day selected for start of something, *esp.* Allied invasion of Europe in 1944

DDT dichlorodiphenyltrichloroethane, hydrocarbon compound used as an insecticide

DE Delaware

de- (*comb. form*) removal of, from, reversal of, as in *delouse, desegregate.* Such words are not given here where the meaning may be inferred from the simple word

deacon ('dēkǝn) *n.* 1. clergyman ranking below priest in certain Christian denominations 2. layman in charge of business matters in certain churches 3. Mormon in lowest grade of priesthood (**'deaconess** *fem.*)

deactivate (dē'aktivāt) *vt.* 1. make (bomb *etc.*) harmless or inoperative 2. make less radioactive

dead (ded) *a.* 1. no longer alive 2. obsolete 3. numb, without sensation 4. no longer functioning, extinguished 5. lacking luster, movement or vigor 6. sure, complete —*pl.* 7. dead persons —*adv.* 8. utterly —**'deaden** *vt.* —**'deadly** *a.* 1. fatal 2. deathlike —*adv.* 3. as if dead —**dead-and-alive** *a.* dull —**'deadbeat** *a./n. inf.* lazy, useless (person) —**dead duck** *sl.* person or thing doomed to death, failure *etc., esp.* because of mistake —**dead end** 1. cul-de-sac 2. situation in which further progress is impossible —**'deadhead** *n.* 1. one who has not paid for a ticket or contributed to the pot in a poker game. 2. log sticking out of water as hindrance to navigation —**dead heat** race in which competitors finish exactly even —**dead letter** 1. law no longer observed 2. letter which post office cannot deliver —**'deadline** *n.* limit of time allowed —**'deadlock** *n.* standstill —**dead loss** 1. complete loss for which no compensation is paid 2. *inf.* useless person or thing —**deadly nightshade** belladonna —**dead man's handle** *or* **pedal** safety switch on piece of machinery that allows operation only while depressed by operator —**dead march** solemn funeral music to accompany procession —**'deadpan** a. expressionless —**dead reckoning** calculation of ship's position from log and compass, when observations cannot be taken —**dead set** adv. 1. absolutely —n. 2. resolute attack —**dead weight** 1. heavy weight or load 2. oppressive burden 3. difference between loaded and unloaded weights of ship 4. intrinsic invariable weight of structure —**'deadwood** n. 1. dead trees or branches 2. inf. useless person; encumbrance —**dead of night** time of greatest stillness and darkness

deaf (def) a. 1. wholly or partly without hearing 2. unwilling to listen —**'deafen** vt. make deaf —**'deafness** n. —**deaf aid** hearing aid —**deaf-and-dumb** a. 1. unable to hear or speak 2. for use of deaf-mutes —**deaf-mute** n. 1. person unable to hear or speak —a. 2. unable to hear or speak

deal¹ (dēl) vt. 1. distribute, give out 2. inflict —vi. 3. act 4. treat 5. do business (with, in) (dealt pt./pp.) —n. 6. agreement 7. treatment 8. share 9. business transaction —**'dealer** n. 1. one who deals (esp. cards) 2. trader —**'dealings** pl.n. transactions or relations with others —**deal with** handle, act toward

deal² (dēl) n. (plank of) fir or pine wood

dealt (delt) pt./pp. of DEAL¹

dean (dēn) n. 1. university or college official 2. head of cathedral chapter 3. secondary-school administrator in charge of discipline —**'deanery** n. cathedral dean's house or appointment

dear (dēər) a. 1. beloved; precious 2. costly, expensive —n. 3. beloved one —adv. 4. at a high price —**'dearly** adv. —**'dearness** n.

dearth (dərth) n. scarcity

death (deth) n. 1. dying 2. end of life 3. end, extinction 4. annihilation 5. (D-) personification of death, as skeleton —**'deathless** a. immortal —**'deathly** a./adv. like death —**'deathbed** n. bed in which person is about to die —**'deathblow** n. thing or event that destroys life or hope, esp. suddenly —**death cap** kind of toadstool —**death certificate** legal document issued by doctor, certifying death of person and stating cause if known —**death mask** cast of person's face taken after death —**death penalty** capital punishment —**death rate** ratio of deaths in specified area etc. to population of that area etc. (also **mortality rate**) —**death's-head** n. human skull or representation of one —**death tax** tax on property left at death —**death trap** building etc. considered unsafe —**death warrant** official authorization for carrying out sentence of death —**death-watch beetle** beetle that bores into wood —**sign one's (own) death warrant** cause one's own destruction

debacle (di'bäkəl) n. utter collapse, rout, disaster

debar (di'bär) vt. 1. shut out 2. stop 3. prohibit 4. preclude (**-rr-**)

debark (di'bärk) v. disembark

debase (di'bās) vt. 1. lower in value, quality or character 2. adulterate —**de'basement** n.

debate (di'bāt) v. 1. argue, discuss, esp. in a formal assembly 2. consider (something) —n. 3. discussion 4. controversy —**de'batable** a. —**de'bater** n.

debauch (di'böch) vt. 1. lead into a life of depraved self-indulgence —n. 2. bout of sensual indulgence —**debau'chee** n. dissipated person —**de'bauchery** n.

debenture (di'benchər) n. bond of company or corporation secured by its general assets

debility (di'biliti) n. 1. feebleness, esp. of

health 2. languor —**de'bilitate** vt. weaken, enervate

debit ('debit) Accounting n. 1. entry in account of sum owed 2. side of book in which such sums are entered —vt. 3. charge, enter as due

debonair (debə'nāər) a. 1. suave 2. genial 3. affable

debouch (di'bowch) vi. move out from narrow place to wider one —**de'bouchment** n.

debrief (dē'brēf) vt. interrogate (pilot, agent) to obtain results of mission

debris (də'brē, dā-; 'dābrē) n. fragments of unwanted material

debt (det) n. 1. what is owed 2. state of owing —**'debtor** n. —**debt of honor** debt that is morally but not legally binding

debug (dē'bug) vt. inf. 1. remove concealed microphones from (room etc.) 2. remove defects in (device etc.) 3. remove insects from (**-gg-**)

debunk (dē'bungk) vt. expose falseness, pretentiousness of, esp. by ridicule

debut ('dābyōō, dā'byōō) n. first appearance in public —**debutante** ('debyōōtänt) n. girl making official debut into society

Dec. December

deca-, deka- or before vowel **dec-, dek-** (comb. form) ten, as in decaliter

decade ('dekäd, de'käd) n. 1. period of ten years 2. set of ten

decadent ('dekədənt) a. 1. declining, deteriorating 2. morally corrupt —**'decadence** or **'decadency** n.

decaffeinated (dē'kafinātid) a. (of coffee or tea) with caffeine removed

decagon ('dekəgon) n. figure of 10 angles —**de'cagonal** a.

decagram ('dekəgram) n. see DEKAGRAM

decahedron (dekə'hēdrən) n. solid of 10 faces —**deca'hedral** a.

decalcify (dē'kalsifī) vt. deprive of lime, as bones or teeth of their calcareous matter (**-fied, -fying**)

decaliter ('dekəlētər) n. see DEKALITER

Decalogue ('dekəlog) n. the Ten Commandments

decameter ('dekəmētər) n. see DEKAMETER

decamp (di'kamp) vi. 1. make off 2. break camp 3. abscond

decanal (di'kānəl) a. of dean, deanery

decant (di'kant) vt. pour off (liquid, as wine) without disturbing sediment —**de'canter** n. stoppered bottle for wine or spirits

decapitate (di'kapitāt) vt. behead —**decapi-'tation** n. —**de'capitator** n.

decapod

decapod ('dekəpod) n. 1. crustacean having five pairs of walking limbs, as crab etc. 2. cephalopod mollusk having eight short tentacles and two longer ones, as squid etc.

decarbonize (dē'kärbənīz) vt. remove (deposit of carbon) from, as from motor cylinder (also **decoke**) —**decarboni'zation** n.

decasyllable ('dekəsiləbəl) n. ten-syllabled line —**decasyl'labic** a.

decathlon (di'kathlən, -lon) n. athletic contest with ten events

decay (di'kā) v. 1. rot, decompose 2. (cause to) fall off, decline —n. 3. rotting 4. a falling away, break-up

decease (di'sēs) n. 1. death —vi. 2. die —**de'ceased** n./a.

deceive (di'sēv) vt. 1. mislead 2. delude 3. cheat —**de'ceit** n. 1. fraud 2. duplicity —**de'ceitful** a. —**de'ceiver** n.

decelerate (dē'selərāt) vi. slow down

December (di'sembər) n. twelfth and last month of year

decennial (di'seniəl) a. of period of ten years —**de'cennially** adv.

decent ('dēsənt) a. 1. respectable 2. fitting, seemly 3. not obscene 4. adequate 5. inf. kind —**'decency** n. —**'decently** adv.

decentralize (dē'sentrəlīz) vt. divide (government, organization) among local centers

deception (di'sepshən) n. 1. deceiving 2. illusion 3. fraud 4. trick —**de'ceptive** a. 1. misleading 2. apt to mislead

deci- (comb. form) one tenth, as in decimeter

decibel ('desibel) n. unit for measuring intensity of a sound

decide (di'sīd) vt. 1. settle, determine, bring to resolution 2. give judgment on —vi. 3. come to a decision, conclusion —**de'cided** a. 1. unmistakable 2. settled 3. resolute —**de'cidedly** adv. certainly, undoubtedly —**decision** (di'sizhən) n. —**de'cisive** a. —**de'cisively** adv.

deciduous (di'sijōōəs) a. 1. (of trees) losing leaves annually 2. (of antlers, teeth etc.) being shed at the end of a period of growth

decigram ('desigram) n. tenth of gram

deciliter ('desilētər) n. tenth of liter

decimal ('desiməl) a. 1. relating to tenths 2. proceeding by tens —n. 3. decimal fraction —**decimali'zation** n. —**'decimalize** vt. convert into decimal fractions or system —**decimal number system** the ordinary system in use which denotes real numbers according to place values for multiples of 10 (plus the digits 0 through 9)

decimate ('desimāt) vt. kill a tenth or large proportion of —**deci'mation** n. —**'decimator** n.

decimeter ('desimētər) n. tenth of meter

decipher (di'sīfər) vt. 1. make out meaning of 2. decode —**de'cipherable** a.

deck (dek) n. 1. platform or floor, esp. one covering whole or part of ship's hull 2. turntable of record-player 3. part of tape recorder supporting tapes —vt. 4. array, decorate —**deck chair** folding chair made of canvas suspended in wooden frame —**deck hand** 1. seaman assigned duties on deck of ship 2. helper aboard yacht

deckle edge ('dekəl) 1. rough edge of paper oft. left as ornamentation 2. imitation of this

declaim (di'klām) vi. 1. speak dramatically, rhetorically or passionately 2. protest loudly —**declamation** (deklə'māshən) n. —**declamatory** (di'klamətöri) a.

declare (di'klāər) vt. 1. announce formally 2. state emphatically 3. show 4. name (as liable to customs duty) —vi. 5. take sides (for) —**declaration** (deklə'rāshən) n. —**declarative** (di'klarətiv) or **declaratory** (di'klarətöri) a. —**de'clarer** n. Bridge person who plays the hand

declassify (dē'klasifī) vt. release (document etc.) from security list (**-fying, -fied**) —**declassifi'cation** n.

decline (di'klīn) v. 1. refuse 2. list case endings of (nouns) —vi. 3. slope, bend or sink downward 4. deteriorate gradually 5. grow smaller, diminish —*n.* **6.** gradual deterioration **7.** movement downward **8.** diminution **9.** downward slope —**declension** (di'klenshən)' *n.* **1.** group of nouns **2.** falling off **3.** declining —**de'clinable** *a.* —**declination** (dekli-'nāshən) *n.* **1.** sloping away, deviation **2.** angle

declivity (di'kliviti) *n.* downward slope

declutch (di'kluch) *vi.* disengage clutch of car *etc.*

decoction (di'kokshən) *n.* **1.** extraction of essence by boiling down **2.** such essence —**de'coct** *vt.* boil down

decode (dē'kōd) *vt.* convert from code into intelligible language

decoke (dē'kōk) *vt.* decarbonize

décollage (dākə'läzh, -ko-) *n.* the tearing away of parts of posters *etc.* that have been applied in layers so that sections of the underlayers create the composition; the reverse of collage

décolleté (dākolə'tā) *a.* (of women's garment) having a low-cut neckline —**décolletage** (dākolə'täzh) *n.* low-cut dress or neckline

decommission (dēkə'mishən) *vt.* dismantle (industrial plant or nuclear reactor) to an extent such that it can be safely abandoned

decompose (dēkəm'pōz) *v.* **1.** separate into elements **2.** rot —**decompo'sition** *n.* decay

decompress (dēkəm'pres) *vt.* **1.** free from pressure **2.** return to condition of normal atmospheric pressure —**decom'pression** *n.* —**decompression sickness** or **illness** disorder characterized by severe pain *etc.*, caused by sudden change in atmospheric pressure

decongestant (dēkən'jestənt) *a./n.* (drug) relieving (*esp.* nasal) congestion

decontaminate (dēkən'tamināt) *vt.* free from contamination, *eg* from poisons, radioactive substances *etc.* —**decontami'nation** *n.*

decontrol (dēkən'trōl) *vt.* release from state control (**-ll-**)

decor or **décor** (dā'kör) *n.* **1.** decorative scheme of room *etc.* **2.** stage decoration, scenery

decorate ('dekərāt) *vt.* **1.** beautify by additions **2.** paint or wallpaper (room *etc.*) **3.** invest (with an order, medal *etc.*) —**deco'ration** *n.* —**'decorative** *a.* —**'decorator** *n.* —**Decorated style** 14th-century style of English architecture characterized by geometrical tracery *etc.*

decorum (di'körəm) *n.* seemly behavior, propriety, decency —**'decorous** *a.* —**'decorously** *adv.*

decoy ('dēkoi, di'koi) *n.* **1.** something used to entrap others or to distract their attention **2.** bait, lure —*v.* (di'koi) **3.** lure, be lured as with decoy

decrease (di'krēs) *v.* **1.** diminish, lessen —*n.* ('dēkrēs, di'krēs) **2.** lessening

decree (di'krē) *n.* **1.** order having the force of law **2.** edict —*vt.* **3.** determine judicially **4.** order

decrement ('dekrimənt) *n.* **1.** act or state of decreasing **2.** quantity lost by decrease

decrepit (di'krepit) *a.* **1.** old and feeble **2.** broken-down, worn-out —**de'crepitude** *n.*

decrescendo (dākri'shendō) *a.* diminuendo

decretal (di'krētəl) *n.* **1.** *R.C.Ch.* papal decree; edict on doctrine or church law —*a.* **2.** of decree

decry (di'krī) *vt.* disparage (**de'cried, de'crying**)

dedicate ('dedikāt) *vt.* **1.** commit wholly to special purpose or cause **2.** inscribe or address (book *etc.*) **3.** devote to God's service —**'dedicated** *a.* **1.** devoted to particular

purpose or cause **2.** *Comp.* designed to fulfill one function **3.** manufactured for specific purpose —**dedi'cation** *n.* —**'dedicator** *n.* —**'dedicatory** *a.*

deduce (di'dyōōs, -'dōōs) *vt.* draw as conclusion from facts —**de'duct** *vt.* take away, subtract —**de'ductible** *a.* capable of being deducted, *esp.* against income tax —**de'duction** *n.* **1.** deducting **2.** amount subtracted **3.** conclusion deduced **4.** inference from general to particular —**de'ductive** *a.* —**de'ductively** *adv.*

deed (dēd) *n.* **1.** action **2.** exploit **3.** legal document

deejay ('dē'jā) *inf.* disc jockey

deem (dēm) *vt.* judge, consider, regard —**'deemster** *n.* title of either of two justices in Isle of Man (*also* **'dempster**)

deep (dēp) *a.* **1.** extending far down, in or back **2.** at, of given depth **3.** profound **4.** heartfelt **5.** hard to fathom **6.** cunning **7.** engrossed, immersed **8.** (of color) dark and rich **9.** (of sound) low and full —*n.* **10.** deep place **11.** the sea —*adv.* **12.** far down *etc.* —**'deepen** *v.* —**'deeply** *adv.* —**deep-freeze** *vt.* quick-freeze —**deep-laid** *a.* (of plot or plan) carefully worked out and kept secret —**deep-rooted** or **deep-seated** *a.* (of ideas *etc.*) firmly fixed or held; ingrained

deer (dēər) *n.* family of ruminant animals typically with antlers in male (*pl.* **deer, -s**) —**'deerhound** *n.* large rough-coated dog —**'deerskin** *n.* hide of deer —**'deerstalker** *n.* **1.** one who stalks deer **2.** kind of cloth hat with peaks

deface (di'fās) *vt.* **1.** spoil or mar surface of **2.** disfigure —**de'facement** *n.*

de facto (dā 'faktō) *Lat.* existing in fact, whether legally recognized or not

defalcate (di'falkāt) *vi.* *Law* misuse or misappropriate property or funds entrusted to one

defame (di'fām) *vt.* speak ill of, dishonor by slander or rumor —**defamation** (defə-'māshən) *n.* —**defamatory** (di'famətöri) *a.*

default (di'fölt) *n.* **1.** failure to act, appear or pay —*vi.* **2.** fail (to pay) —**de'faulter** *n.* *esp.* soldier guilty of military offense —**in default of** in the absence of

defeat (di'fēt) *vt.* **1.** overcome, vanquish **2.** thwart —*n.* **3.** overthrow **4.** lost battle or encounter **5.** frustration —**de'featism** *n.* attitude tending to accept defeat —**de'featist** *n./a.*

defecate ('defikāt) *vi.* **1.** empty the bowels —*vt.* **2.** clear of impurities —**defe'cation** *n.*

defect ('dēfekt, di'fekt) *n.* **1.** lack **2.** blemish, failing —*vi.* (di'fekt) **3.** desert one's country, cause *etc.*, *esp.* to join opponents —**de'fection** *n.* abandonment of duty or allegiance —**de'fective** *a.* **1.** incomplete **2.** faulty

defend (di'fend) *vt.* **1.** protect **2.** support by argument, evidence **3.** (try to) maintain (title *etc.*) against challenger —**de'fendant** *n.* person accused in court —**de'fender** *n.* —**de'fense** *n.* —**defensi'bility** *n.* —**de'fensible** *a.* —**de'fensive** *a.* **1.** serving for defense —*n.* **2.** position or attitude of defense

defer¹ (di'fər) *vt.* put off, postpone (**-rr-**) —**de'ferment** *n.*

defer² (di'fər) *vi.* submit to opinion or judgment of another (**-rr-**) —**deference** ('defərəns) *n.* respect for another inclining one to accept his views *etc.* —**deferential** (defə'renchəl) *a.* —**deferentially** (defə'renchəli) *adv.*

defiance (di'fīəns) *n.* see DEFY

deficient (di'fishənt) *a.* lacking or falling short in something, insufficient —**de'ficiency** *n.* —**deficit** ('defisit) *n.* amount by which

sum of money is too small —**deficiency disease** any condition, such as pellagra, produced by lack of vitamins and minerals

defile¹ (di'fīl) *vt.* **1.** make dirty, pollute, soil **2.** sully **3.** desecrate —**de'filement** *n.*

defile² (di'fīl, 'dēfīl) *n.* **1.** narrow pass or valley —*vi.* **2.** march in file

define (di'fīn) *vt.* **1.** state contents or meaning of **2.** show clearly the form or outline of **3.** lay down clearly, fix **4.** mark out —**de'finable** *a.* —**definite** ('definit) *a.* **1.** exact, defined **2.** clear, specific **3.** certain, sure —**definitely** ('definitli) *adv.* —**definition** (defi'nishən) *n.* —**definitive** (di'finitiv) *a.* conclusive, to be looked on as final —**definitively** (di'finitivli) *adv.*

deflate (dē'flāt) *v.* **1.** (cause to) collapse by release of gas **2.** *Econ.* cause deflation of (an economy *etc.*) —*vt.* **3.** take away self-esteem from —**de'flation** *n.* **1.** deflating **2.** *Econ.* reduction of economic and industrial activity —**de'flationary** *a.*

deflect (di'flekt) *v.* (cause to) turn from straight course —**de'flection** *n.*

deflower (dē'flowər) *vt.* deprive of virginity, innocence *etc.* —**defloration** (dēflö'rāshən) *n.*

defoliate (dē'fōliāt) *v.* (cause to) lose leaves, *esp.* by action of chemicals —**de'foliant** *n.* —**defoli'ation** *n.*

deforest (dē'forist) *vt.* clear of trees —**deforest'ation** *n.*

deform (di'förm) *vt.* **1.** spoil shape of **2.** make ugly **3.** disfigure —**defor'mation** *n.* —**de'formed** *a.* —**de'formity** *n.*

defraud (di'fröd) *vt.* cheat, swindle

defray (di'frā) *vt.* provide money for (expenses *etc.*)

defrock (dē'frok) *vt.* deprive (priest, minister) of ecclesiastical status

defrost (dē'frost) *v.* **1.** make, become free of frost, ice **2.** thaw

deft (deft) *a.* skillful, adroit —**'deftly** *adv.* —**'deftness** *n.*

defunct (di'fungkt) *a.* **1.** dead **2.** obsolete

defuse (dē'fyōōz) *vt.* **1.** remove fuse of (bomb *etc.*) **2.** remove tension from (situation *etc.*)

defy (di'fī) *vt.* **1.** challenge, resist successfully **2.** disregard (**de'fied, de'fying**) —**de'fiance** *n.* resistance —**de'fiant** *a.* **1.** openly and aggressively hostile **2.** insolent —**de'fiantly** *adv.*

degauss (dē'gows) *vt.* equip (ship) with apparatus which prevents it detonating magnetic mines

degenerate (di'jenərāt) *vi.* **1.** deteriorate to lower mental, moral or physical level —*a.* (di'jenərit) **2.** fallen away in quality —*n.* (di'jenərit) **3.** degenerate person —**de'generacy** *n.* —**degene'ration** *n.* —**de'generative** *a.*

degrade (di'grād) *vt.* **1.** dishonor **2.** debase **3.** reduce to lower rank —*vi.* **4.** decompose chemically —**de'gradable** *a.* capable of chemical, biological decomposition —**degradation** (degrə'dāshən) *n.* —**de'graded** *a.* shamed, humiliated

degree (di'grē) *n.* **1.** step, stage in process, scale, relative rank, order, condition, manner, way **2.** university award **3.** unit of measurement of temperature or angle —**third degree** severe, lengthy examination, *esp.* of accused person by police, to extract information, confession

dehiscent (di'hisənt) *a.* opening, as capsule of plant —**de'hisce** *vi.* burst open —**de'hiscence** *n.*

dehumanize (dē'hyōōmənīz) *vt.* **1.** deprive

of human qualities **2.** render mechanical, artificial or routine

dehumidify (dēhyōō'midifī) *vt.* extract moisture from

dehydrate (dē'hīdrāt) *vt.* remove moisture from —**dehy'dration** *n.* excessive loss of body fluid

de-ice (dē'īs) *vt.* dislodge ice from (*eg* windshield) or prevent its forming

deify ('dēifī, 'dā-) *vt.* make god of, treat, worship as god (**'deified, 'deifying**) —**deifi'cation** *n.* —**'deiform** *a.* godlike in form

deign (dān) *vi.* **1.** condescend, stoop **2.** think fit

deism ('dēizəm, 'dā-) *n.* belief in god but not in revelation —**'deist** *n.* —**de'istic** *a.* —**'deity** *n.* **1.** divine status or attributes **2.** a god

déjà vu ('dāzhä 'vōō, 'vyōō) *Fr.* experience of perceiving new situation as if it had occurred before

deject (di'jekt) *vt.* dishearten, cast down, depress —**de'jected** *a.* —**de'jection** *n.*

de jure (dā 'yōōərə) *Lat.* in law, by right

deka- *or before vowel* **dek-** *see* DECA-

dekagram *or* **decagram** ('dekəgram) *n.* measure of weight equal to 10 grams

dekaliter *or* **decaliter** ('dekəlētər) *n.* 10 liters

dekameter *or* **decameter** ('dekəmētər) *n.* 10 meters

Delaware[1] ('deləwāər) *n.* South Atlantic state of the U.S.: ratified the Constitution in 1787. Abbrev.: **Del., DE** (with ZIP code)

Delaware[2] ('deləwāər) *n.* **1.** member of Amerindian people orig. of Delaware Valley (*pl.* **-ware, -s**) **2.** Algonquian language of this people

Delaware[3] ('deləwāər) *n.* **1.** dry white table wine **2.** grape used to make this wine

delay (di'lā) *vt.* **1.** postpone, hold back —*vi.* **2.** be tardy, linger (**de'layed, de'laying**) —*n.* **3.** act or instance of delaying **4.** interval of time between events

delectable (di'lektəbəl) *a.* delightful —**delec'tation** *n.* pleasure

delegate ('deligit, -gāt) *n.* **1.** person chosen to represent another —*vt.* ('deligāt) **2.** send as deputy **3.** commit (authority, business *etc.*) to a deputy —**'delegacy** *n.* —**dele'gation** *n.*

delete (di'lēt) *vt.* remove, cancel, erase —**de'letion** *n.*

deleterious (deli'tēəriəs) *a.* harmful, injurious

Delft (delft) *n.* **1.** town in Netherlands **2.** tin-glazed earthenware orig. from Delft, usu. with blue decoration on white ground (*also* **'delftware**)

deliberate (di'libərit) *a.* **1.** intentional **2.** well-considered **3.** without haste, slow —*vt.* (di'libərāt) **4.** consider, debate —**de'liberately** *adv.* —**delibe'ration** *n.* —**de'liberative** *a.*

delicate ('delikit) *a.* **1.** exquisite **2.** not robust, fragile **3.** sensitive **4.** requiring tact **5.** deft —**'delicacy** *n.* —**'delicately** *adv.*

delicatessen (delikə'tesən) *n.* shop selling *esp.* imported or unusual foods

delicious (di'lishəs) *a.* delightful, pleasing to senses, *esp.* taste —**de'liciously** *adv.*

delight (di'līt) *vt.* **1.** please greatly —*vi.* **2.** take great pleasure (in) —*n.* **3.** great pleasure —**de'lightful** *a.* charming

delimitation (dēlimi'tāshən) *n.* assigning of boundaries —**de'limit** *vt.*

delineate (di'liniāt) *vt.* portray by drawing or description —**deline'ation** *n.* —**de'lineator** *n.*

delinquent (di'lingkwənt) *n.* someone, *esp.*

young person, guilty of delinquency —**de'linquency** *n.* (minor) offense or misdeed

deliquesce (deli'kwes) *vi.* become liquid —**deli'quescence** *n.* —**deli'quescent** *a.*

delirium (di'liriəm) *n.* **1.** disorder of the mind, *esp.* in feverish illness **2.** violent excitement (*pl.* **-s, -liria** (-'liriə)) —**de'lirious** *a.* **1.** raving **2.** light-headed, wildly excited —**delirium tremens** ('tremenz, 'trē-) disordered mental state produced by advanced alcoholism (*also* **D.T.s**)

deliver (di'livər) *vt.* **1.** carry (goods *etc.*) to destination **2.** hand over **3.** release **4.** give birth (to) or assist in birth (of) **5.** utter or present (speech *etc.*) —**de'liverance** *n.* rescue —**de'liverer** *n.* —**de'livery** *n.*

dell (del) *n.* wooded hollow

Delphic ('delfik) *a.* pert. to Delphi or to the oracle of Apollo

delphinium (del'finiəm) *n.* garden plant with tall spikes of usu. blue flowers (*pl.* **-s, -ia** (-iə))

delta ('deltə) *n.* **1.** alluvial tract where river at mouth breaks into several streams **2.** fourth letter in Gr. alphabet (Δ or δ) **3.** shape of this letter —**delta wing** triangular swept-back aircraft wing —**'deltoid** *or* **deltoid muscle** triangular muscle covering front, side and rear portions of the shoulder joint

Delta ('deltə) *n.* word used in communications for the letter *d*

delude (di'lōōd) *vt.* **1.** deceive **2.** mislead —**de'lusion** *n.* —**de'lusive** *a.*

deluge ('delyōōj) *n.* **1.** flood, great flow **2.** rush **3.** downpour, cloudburst —*vt.* **4.** flood **5.** overwhelm

de luxe (də 'lōōks, 'luks) **1.** rich, sumptuous **2.** superior in quality

delve (delv) *v.* **1.** (*with* into) search intensively **2.** dig

demagnetize (dē'magnətīz) *vt.* deprive of magnetic polarity

demagogue *or* **demagog** ('deməgog) *n.* mob leader or agitator —**demagogic** (demə'gogik) *a.* —**'demagogy** ('deməgogi) *n.*

demand (di'mand) *vt.* **1.** ask as giving an order **2.** ask as by right **3.** call for as due, right or necessary —*n.* **4.** urgent request, claim, requirement **5.** call (for specific commodity) —**de'manding** *a.* requiring great skill, patience *etc.*

demarcate (di'märkāt) *vt.* mark boundaries or limits of —**demar'cation** *or* **demar'kation** *n.*

demean (di'mēn) *vt.* degrade, lower, humiliate

demeanor (di'mēnər) *n.* **1.** conduct, behavior **2.** bearing

demented (di'mentid) *a.* **1.** mad, crazy **2.** beside oneself —**dementia** (di'menchə) *n.* deterioration of mental faculties

demerge (di'mərj) *v.* **1.** split (business concern) into two or more independent companies —*vi.* **2.** (of companies) be so split **3.** undo previous merger —**de'merger** *n.*

demerit (di'merit) *n.* **1.** bad point **2.** undesirable quality

Demerol ('demərōl) *n.* trade name for meperidine

demesne (di'mān, -'mēn) *n.* **1.** estate, territory **2.** sphere of action —**hold in demesne** have unrestricted possession of

demi- (*comb. form*) half, as in *demigod.* Such words are not given here where the meaning may be inferred from the simple word

demijohn ('demijon) *n.* narrow-necked bottle holding from one to 10 gallons

demilitarize (dē'militərīz) *vt.* prohibit military presence or function in (an area) —**demilitari'zation** *n.*

demimonde ('demimond) *n.* class of women of doubtful reputation

demise (di'mīz) *n.* **1.** death **2.** conveyance by will or lease **3.** transfer of sovereignty on death or abdication —*vt.* **4.** convey to another by will **5.** lease

demist (dē'mist) *v.* free or become free of condensation —**de'mister** *n.*

demiurge ('demiərj) *n.* name given in some philosophies (*esp.* Platonic) to the creator of the world and man

demo ('demō) *inf.* demonstration

demobilize (dē'mōbilīz) *vt.* **1.** disband (troops) **2.** discharge (soldier) —**demobili'zation** *n.*

democracy (di'mokrəsi) *n.* **1.** government by the people or their elected representatives **2.** state so governed —**'democrat** *n.* advocate of democracy —**demo'cratic** *a.* **1.** connected with democracy **2.** favoring popular rights —**demo'cratically** *adv.* —**democrati'zation** *n.* —**de'mocratize** *vt.*

demodulation (dēmojə'lāshən) *n. Electron.* process by which output wave or signal is obtained having characteristics of original modulating wave or signal

demography (di'mogrəfi) *n.* study of population statistics, as births, deaths, diseases —**de'mographer** *n.* —**demo'graphic** *a.*

demolish (di'molish) *vt.* **1.** knock down (buildings *etc.*) **2.** destroy utterly **3.** overthrow —**demo'lition** *n.*

demon ('dēmən) *n.* **1.** devil, evil spirit **2.** very cruel or malignant person **3.** person very good at or devoted to a given activity —**demoniac** (di'mōniak) *n.* one possessed with a devil —**demo'niacal** *a.* —**de'monic** *a.* of the nature of a devil —**demo'nology** *n.* study of demons

demonetize (dē'monitīz, -'mun-) *vt.* **1.** deprive (metal) of its capacity as monetary standard **2.** withdraw from use as currency —**demoneti'zation** *n.*

demonstrate ('demənstrāt) *vt.* **1.** show by reasoning, prove **2.** describe, explain by specimens or experiments —*vi.* **3.** make exhibition of support, protest *etc.* by public parade, rally **4.** make show of armed force —**de'monstrable** *a.* —**de'monstrably** *adv.* —**demon'stration** *n.* **1.** making clear, proving by evidence **2.** exhibition and description **3.** organized expression of public opinion **4.** display of armed force —**de'monstrative** *a.* **1.** expressing feelings, emotions easily and unreservedly **2.** pointing out **3.** conclusive —**'demonstrator** *n.* **1.** one who demonstrates equipment, products *etc.* **2.** one who takes part in a public demonstration

demoralize (di'morəlīz) *vt.* **1.** deprive of courage and discipline **2.** undermine morally —**demorali'zation** *n.*

demote (di'mōt) *vt.* reduce in status or rank —**de'motion** *n.*

demotic (di'motik) *a.* **1.** of common people; popular **2.** of simplified form of hieroglyphics used in ancient Egypt —*n.* **3.** demotic script of ancient Egypt

demur (di'mər) *vi.* **1.** make difficulties, object (**-rr-**) —*n.* **2.** raising of objection **3.** objection raised —**de'murrer** *n. Law* exception taken to opponent's point

demure (di'myōōr) *a.* reserved, quiet —**de'murely** *adv.*

demurrage (di'murij) *n.* charge for keeping ship *etc.* beyond time agreed for unloading

demystify (dē'mistifī) *vt.* remove mystery from; make clear —**demystifi'cation** *n.*

den (den) *n.* **1.** cave or hole of wild beast **2.** lair **3.** small room, *esp.* study **4.** site, haunt

denarius (di'narias, -'ner-) *n.* **1.** ancient Roman silver coin, oft. called penny in translation **2.** gold coin worth 25 silver denarii (*pl.* **-narii** (-'narii, -'ner-))

denary ('dēnəri) *a.* **1.** calculated by tens; decimal **2.** containing ten parts; tenfold

denationalize (dē'nashənəlīz) *vt.* return (an industry) from public to private ownership —**denationali'zation** *n.*

denature ('dē'nāchər) *or* **denaturize** (dē'nāchərīz) *vt.* deprive of essential qualities, adulterate —**denatured alcohol** alcohol made undrinkable

denazify (dē'nätsifī) *vt.* obliterate Nazi influence from (**-ified, -ifying**)

dendrology (den'drolǝji) *n.* natural history of trees

dengue fever ('denggi, -gā) virus disease of subtropical and tropical regions transmitted by the mosquito (*also* **breakbone fever**)

denial (di'nīəl) *n. see* DENY

denier ('denyǝr) *n.* gauge of yarn used for stockings and panty hose

denigrate ('denigrāt) *vt.* belittle or disparage character of

denim ('denim) *n.* strong cotton drill for trousers, overalls *etc.*

denizen ('denizǝn) *n.* inhabitant

Denmark ('denmärk) *n.* country in Europe occupying a peninsula between the North Sea to the west and the Baltic Sea to the east and bounded south by the Federal Republic of Germany —**Dane** *n.* native of Denmark —'**Danish** *a.* **1.** of Denmark —*n.* **2.** language of Denmark which is a Scandinavian language

denominate (di'nomināt) *vt.* give name to —**denomi'nation** *n.* **1.** distinctly named church or sect **2.** name, *esp.* of class or group —**denomi'national** *a.* —**de'nominator** *n.* divisor in common fraction

denote (di'nōt) *vt.* **1.** stand for, be the name of **2.** mark, indicate, show —**deno'tation** *n.*

denouement (dānōō'män) *or* **dénouement** (*Fr.* dānōō'mä) *n.* **1.** unraveling of dramatic plot **2.** final solution of mystery

denounce (di'nowns) *vt.* **1.** speak violently against **2.** accuse **3.** terminate (treaty) —**denunci'ation** *n.* denouncing —**denunciatory** (di'nunsiǝtöri) *a.*

dense (dens) *a.* **1.** thick, compact **2.** stupid —'**densely** *adv.* —'**density** *n.* mass per unit of volume

dent (dent) *n.* **1.** hollow or mark left by blow or pressure —*vt.* **2.** make dent in **3.** mark with dent

dental ('dentǝl) *a.* **1.** of, pert. to teeth or dentistry **2.** pronounced by applying tongue to teeth —'**dentate** *a.* toothed —**dentifrice** ('dentifris) *n.* powder, paste or wash for cleaning teeth —'**dentist** *n.* surgeon who attends to teeth —'**dentistry** *n.* science concerned with diseases of teeth and mouth, *esp.* gums —**den'tition** *n.* **1.** teething **2.** arrangement of teeth —'**denture** *n.* (*usu. pl.*) set of false teeth —**dental floss** waxed thread for cleaning between teeth

dentin ('dentin) *or* **dentine** ('dentēn) *n.* the hard bonelike part of a tooth

denude (di'nyōōd, -'nōōd) *vt.* **1.** strip, make bare **2.** expose (rock) by erosion of plants, soil *etc.* —**denudation** (dēnyōō'dāshǝn, -nōō-) *n.*

denumerable (di'nyōōmǝrǝbǝl, -'nōō-) *a. Math.* capable of being counted by correspondence with positive integers; countable

denunciation (dinunsi'āshǝn) *n. see* DE-NOUNCE

deny (di'nī) *vt.* **1.** declare untrue **2.** contradict **3.** reject, disown **4.** refuse to give

5. refuse **6.** (*refl.*) abstain from (**de'nied, de'nying**) —**de'niable** *a.* —**de'nial** *n.*

deodar ('dēǝdär) *n.* **1.** Himalayan cedar with drooping branches **2.** fragrant wood of this tree

deodorize (dē'ōdǝrīz) *vt.* rid of smell or mask smell of —**de'odorant** *n.* —**deodori'zation** *n.* —**de'odorizer** *n.*

deontology (dēon'tolǝji) *n.* science of ethics and moral obligations —**deon'tologist** *n.*

Deo volente ('dāō vǝ'lenti) *Lat.* God willing

deoxidize (dē'oksidīz) *vt.* deprive of oxygen —**deoxidi'zation** *n.*

dep. 1. depart(s) **2.** departure **3.** deposed **4.** deposit **5.** deputy

depart (di'pärt) *vi.* **1.** go away **2.** start out, set forth **3.** deviate, vary **4.** die —**de'parture** *n.*

department (di'pärtmǝnt) *n.* **1.** division **2.** branch **3.** province —**depart'mental** *a.* —**depart'mentally** *adv.* —**department store** store selling all kinds of goods

depend (di'pend) *vi.* **1.** (*usu. with* on) rely entirely **2.** be contingent, await settlement or decision —**de'pendable** *a.* reliable —**de'pendant** *n.* one for whose maintenance another is responsible —**de'pendence** *n.* —**de'pendency** *n.* subject territory —**de'pendent** *a.* depending

depict (di'pikt) *vt.* **1.** give picture of **2.** describe in words —**de'piction** *n.* —**de'pictor** *n.*

depilatory (di'pilǝtöri) *n.* **1.** substance that removes hair —*a.* **2.** serving to remove hair

deplete (di'plēt) *vt.* **1.** empty **2.** reduce **3.** exhaust —**de'pletion** *n.*

deplore (di'plör) *vt.* **1.** lament, regret **2.** deprecate, complain of —**de'plorable** *a.* **1.** lamentable **2.** disgraceful

deploy (di'ploi) *v.* **1.** (of troops, ships) (cause to) adopt battle formation —*vt.* **2.** arrange —**de'ployment** *n.*

depolarize (dē'pōlǝrīz) *vt.* deprive of polarity —**depolari'zation** *n.*

deponent (di'pōnǝnt) *a.* **1.** (of verb) having passive form but active meaning —*n.* **2.** deponent verb **3.** one who makes statement on oath **4.** deposition

depopulate (dē'popyōōlāt) *v.* (cause to) be reduced in population —**depopu'lation** *n.*

deport (di'pört) *vt.* expel from a country, banish —**depor'tation** *n.*

deportment (di'pörtmǝnt) *n.* behavior, conduct, bearing —**de'port** *vt.* behave, carry (oneself)

depose (di'pōz) *vt.* **1.** remove from office, *esp.* of sovereign —*vi.* **2.** make statement on oath, give evidence —**de'posable** *a.* —**de'posal** *n.* **1.** removal from office **2.** statement made on oath

deposit (di'pozit) *vt.* **1.** set down, *esp.* carefully **2.** give into safekeeping, *esp.* in bank. **3.** let fall (as sediment) —*n.* **4.** thing deposited **5.** money given in part payment or as security **6.** sediment —**de'positary** *n.* person with whom thing is deposited —**deposition** (depǝ'zishǝn) *n.* **1.** statement written and attested **2.** act of deposing or depositing —**de'positor** *n.* —**de'pository** *n.* place for safekeeping

depot ('depō, 'dēpō) *n.* **1.** storehouse **2.** building for storage and servicing of buses, railway engines *etc.* **3.** railroad station

deprave (di'prāv) *vt.* make bad, corrupt, pervert —**depravity** (di'praviti) *n.* wickedness, viciousness

deprecate ('deprikāt) *vt.* **1.** express disapproval of **2.** advise against —**depre'cation** *n.* —'**deprecatory** *a.*

depreciate (di'prēshiāt) *vt.* **1.** lower price, value or purchasing power of **2.** belittle —*vi.*

3. fall in value —**depreci'ation** *n.* —**de'preciator** *n.* —**de'preciatory** *a.*

depredation (depri'dāshǝn) *n.* plundering, pillage —'**depredate** *vt.* plunder, despoil —'**depredator** *n.*

depress (di'pres) *vt.* **1.** affect with low spirits **2.** lower in level or activity —**de'pressant** *n.* —**de'pressed** *a.* **1.** low in spirits; downcast **2.** lower than surrounding surface **3.** pressed down; flattened **4.** characterized by economic hardship **5.** lowered in force *etc.* **6.** *Bot., zool.* flattened —**de'pression** *n.* **1.** hollow **2.** low spirits, dejection, despondency **3.** low state of trade, slump —**de'pressive** *a.*

deprive (di'prīv) *vt.* strip, dispossess —**deprivation** (depri'vāshǝn) *n.* —**de'prived** *a.* lacking adequate food, care, amenities *etc.*

dept. department

depth (depth) *n.* **1.** (degree of) deepness **2.** deep place, abyss **3.** intensity (of color, feeling) **4.** profundity (of mind) —**depth charge** bomb for use against submarines

depute (di'pyōōt) *vt.* **1.** allot **2.** appoint as agent or substitute —**depu'tation** *n.* persons sent to speak for others —'**deputize** *vi.* **1.** act for another —*vt.* **2.** depute —'**deputy** *n.* **1.** assistant **2.** substitute, delegate

derail (di'rāl) *v.* (cause to) go off the rails, as train *etc.* —**de'railment** *n.*

derailleur (di'rālǝr) *a./n.* (of) gearshift mechanism for bicycles

derange (di'rānj) *vt.* **1.** put out of place, out of order **2.** upset **3.** make insane —**de'rangement** *n.*

derby ('dǝrbi) *n.* **1.** annual horse race at Churchill Downs, Kentucky and at Epsom, England **2.** contest of any kind open to all **3.** man's stiff felt hat with dome-shaped crown

deregulate (dē'regyǝlāt) *v.* **1.** cancel regulations (concerning an activity or process) —*vt.* **2.** exempt (an activity) from regulations —**deregu'lation** *n.*

derelict ('derilikt) *a.* **1.** abandoned, forsaken **2.** falling into ruins, dilapidated —*n.* **3.** social outcast, vagrant **4.** abandoned property, ship *etc.* —**dere'liction** *n.* **1.** neglect (of duty) **2.** abandoning

derestrict (dēri'strikt) *vt.* render or leave free from restriction, *esp.* road from speed limits

deride (di'rīd) *vt.* speak of or treat with contempt, ridicule —**derision** (di'rizhǝn) *n.* ridicule —**de'risive** *a.* —**de'risory** *a.* mocking, ridiculing

de rigueur (dǝ rē'gœr) *Fr.* required by etiquette or fashion

derive (di'rīv) *vt.* **1.** deduce, get (from) **2.** show origin of —*vi.* **3.** issue, be descended (from) —**derivation** (deri'vāshǝn) *n.* —**derivative** (di'rivǝtiv) *a./n.*

dermatitis (dǝrmǝ'tītis) *n.* inflammation of skin

dermato-, derma- *or before vowel* **dermat-, derm-** (*comb. form*) skin, as in *dermatitis*

dermatology (dǝrmǝ'tolǝji) *n.* science of skin —**derma'tologist** *n.* physician specializing in skin diseases

dermatomyositis (dǝrmǝtōmīō'sītis) *n.* disease of unknown origin marked by inflammation and degeneration of muscles of the limbs and trunk

dermis ('dǝrmis) *n.* the fine skin, below the epidermis, containing blood vessels

derogate ('derǝgāt) *vi.* **1.** (*with* from) cause to seem inferior; detract **2.** (*with* from) deviate in standard or quality —*vt.* **3.** cause to seem inferior *etc.;* disparage —**dero'gation** *n.*

derogatory (di'rogətöri) *a.* disparaging, belittling, intentionally offensive

derrick ('derik) *n.* 1. hoisting machine 2. framework over oil well *etc.*

derring-do (dering'dōō) *n.* (act of) spirited bravery, boldness

derringer ('derinjər) *n.* small pistol with large bore

dervish ('dərvish) *n.* member of Muslim ascetic order, noted for frenzied, whirling dance

desalination (dēsali'nāshən) *or* **desalinization** *n.* process of removing salt, *esp.* from sea water

descant ('deskant) *n.* 1. *Mus.* decorative variation sung as accompaniment to basic melody —*vi.* (*with* on *or* upon) 2. talk in detail (about) 3. dwell (on) at length

descend (di'send) *vi.* 1. come or go down 2. slope down 3. stoop, condescend 4. spring (from ancestor *etc.*) 5. pass to heir, be transmitted 6. swoop on, attack —*vt.* 7. go or come down —**des'cendant** *n.* person descended from an ancestor —**des'cendent** *a.* 1. descending —*n.* 2. descendant —**des'cent** *n.*

describe (di'skrīb) *vt.* 1. give detailed account of 2. pronounce, label 3. trace out (geometrical figure *etc.*) —**description** (di'skripshən) *n.* 1. detailed account 2. marking out 3. kind, sort, species —**descriptive** (di'skriptiv) *a.*

descry (di'skrī) *vt.* make out, catch sight of, *esp.* at a distance, espy (**de'scried, de'scrying**)

desecrate ('desikrāt) *vt.* 1. violate sanctity of 2. profane 3. convert to evil use —**dese'cration** *n.*

desert[1] ('dezərt) *n.* 1. uninhabited and barren region —*a.* 2. barren, uninhabited, desolate

desert[2] (di'zərt) *vt.* 1. abandon, forsake, leave —*vi.* 2. (*esp.* of soldiers) run away from service —**de'serter** *n.* —**de'sertion** *n.*

desert[3] (di'zərt) *n.* 1. (*usu. pl.*) what is due as reward or punishment 2. merit, virtue

deserve (di'zərv) *vt.* 1. show oneself worthy of 2. have by conduct a claim to —**de'served** *a.* rightfully earned; justified; warranted —**deservedly** (di'zərvidli) *adv.* —**deservedness** (di'zərvidnis) *n.* —**de'serving** *a.* worthy (of reward *etc.*)

deshabille (desə'bēl) *n. see* DISHABILLE

desiccate ('desikāt) *vt.* 1. dry 2. dry up —**'desiccant** *n.* drying agent —**desic'cation** *n.*

desideratum (disidə'rātəm, -zid-) *n.* something lacked and wanted (*pl.* **-ta** (-tə))

design (di'zīn) *vt.* 1. make working drawings for 2. sketch 3. plan out 4. intend, select for —*n.* 5. outline sketch 6. working plan 7. art of making decorative patterns *etc.* 8. project, purpose, mental plan —**designedly** (di'zīnidli) *adv.* on purpose —**de'signer** *n. esp.* one who draws designs for manufacturers —**de'signing** *a.* crafty, scheming

designate ('dezignāt) *vt.* 1. name 2. pick out 3. appoint to office —*a.* ('dezignāt, -nit) 4. appointed but not yet installed —**desig'nation** *n.* name, appellation

desire (di'zīər) *vt.* 1. wish, long for 2. ask for, entreat —*n.* 3. longing, craving 4. expressed wish, request 5. sexual appetite 6. something wished for or requested —**desira'bility** *n.* —**de'sirable** *a.* worth desiring —**de'sirous** *a.* filled with desire

desist (di'zist) *vi.* cease, stop

desk (desk) *n.* 1. table or other piece of furniture designed for reading or writing at 2. counter 3. section of organization covering specific subject

desolate ('desəlit, 'dez-) *a.* 1. uninhabited 2. neglected, barren, ruinous 3. solitary 4. dreary, dismal, forlorn —*vt.* ('desəlāt, 'dez-) 5. depopulate, lay waste 6. overwhelm with grief —**deso'lation** *n.*

despair (di'spāər) *vi.* 1. (*oft. with* of) lose hope —*n.* 2. loss of all hope 3. cause of this 4. despondency

despatch (di'spach) *see* DISPATCH

desperate ('despərit, -prit) *a.* 1. reckless from despair 2. difficult; dangerous 3. frantic 4. hopelessly bad 5. leaving no room for hope —**desperado** (despə'rädō) *n.* reckless, lawless person (*pl.* **-es, -s**) —**'desperately** *adv.* —**despe'ration** *n.*

despise (di'spīz) *vt.* look down on as contemptible, inferior —**despicable** (di'spikəbəl, 'despik-) *a.* base, contemptible, vile —**despicably** (di'spikəbli, 'despik-) *adv.*

despite (di'spīt) *prep.* in spite of

despoil (di'spoil) *vt.* plunder, rob, strip —**despoliation** (dispōli'āshən) *n.*

despondent (di'spondənt) *a.* dejected, depressed —**de'spond** *vi.* —**de'spondency** *n.* —**de'spondently** *adv.*

despot ('despət, -pot) *n.* tyrant, oppressor —**des'potic** *a.* —**des'potically** *adv.* —**'despotism** *n.* autocratic government, tyranny

despumate (di'spyōōmāt, 'despyōōmāt) *vi.* 1. throw off impurities 2. form scum

desquamate ('deskwəmāt) *vi.* (of skin) come off in scales —**desqua'mation** *n.*

dessert (di'zərt) *n.* sweet course, or fruit, served at end of meal

destination (desti'nāshən) *n.* 1. place a person or thing is bound for 2. goal 3. purpose

destine ('destin) *vt.* 1. ordain or fix beforehand 2. set apart, devote

destiny ('destini) *n.* 1. course of events; person's fate 2. the power which foreordains

destitute ('destityōōt, -tōōt) *a.* 1. in absolute want 2. in great need, devoid (of) 3. penniless —**desti'tution** *n.*

destroy (di'stroi) *vt.* 1. ruin 2. pull to pieces 3. undo 4. put an end to 5. demolish 6. annihilate —**de'stroyer** *n.* 1. one who destroys 2. small, swift, heavily armed warship —**de'struct** *vt.* destroy (one's own missile *etc.*) for safety —**de'structible** *a.* —**de'struction** *n.* 1. ruin, overthrow 2. death —**de'structive** *a.* 1. destroying 2. negative, not constructive —**de'structively** *adv.* —**de'structor** *n.* that which destroys, *esp.* incinerator

desuetude ('deswityōōd, di'sōōityōōd, -tōōd) *n.* disuse, discontinuance

desultory ('desəltöri, 'dez-) *a.* 1. passing, changing fitfully from one thing to another 2. aimless 3. unmethodical

detach (di'tach) *vt.* unfasten, disconnect, separate —**de'tachable** *a.* —**de'tached** *a.* 1. standing apart, isolated 2. impersonal, disinterested —**de'tachment** *n.* 1. aloofness 2. detaching 3. a body of troops detached for special duty

detail (di'tāl, 'dētāl) *n.* 1. particular 2. small or unimportant part 3. treatment of anything item by item 4. party or man assigned for duty in army —*vt.* 5. relate in full 6. appoint for duty

detain (di'tān) *vt.* 1. keep under restraint 2. hinder 3. keep waiting —**de'tention** *n.* 1. confinement 2. arrest 3. detaining

detect (di'tekt) *vt.* find out or discover existence, presence, nature or identity of —**de'tection** *n.* —**de'tective** *n.* 1. policeman or private agent employed in detecting crime —*a.* 2. employed in detection —**de-**'**tector** *n. esp.* mechanical sensing device or device for detecting radio signals

détente (dā'tänt; *Fr.* dā'tāt) *n.* lessening of tension in political or international affairs

detention (di'tenchən) *n. see* DETAIN

deter (di'tər) *vt.* 1. discourage, frighten 2. hinder, prevent (**-rr-**) —**de'terrent** *a./n.*

detergent (di'tərjənt) *n.* 1. cleansing, purifying substance —*a.* 2. having cleansing power —**de'terge** *vt.*

deteriorate (di'tēəriərāt) *v.* become or make worse —**deterio'ration** *n.*

determine (di'tərmin) *vt.* 1. make up one's mind on, decide 2. fix as known 3. bring to a decision 4. be deciding factor in 5. *Law* end —*vi.* 6. come to an end 7. come to decision —**de'terminable** *a.* —**de'terminant** *a./n.* —**de'terminate** *a.* fixed in scope or nature —**determi'nation** *n.* 1. determining 2. firm or resolute conduct or purpose 3. resolve —**de'termined** *a.* resolute —**de'terminism** *n.* theory that human action is settled by forces independent of will —**de'terminist** *n./a.*

detest (di'test) *vt.* hate, loathe —**de'testable** *a.* —**de'testably** *adv.* —**detes'tation** *n.*

dethrone (di'thrōn) *vt.* remove from throne, depose —**de'thronement** *n.*

detonate ('detənāt) *vt.* 1. cause (bomb, mine *etc.*) to explode —*vi.* 2. (of bomb, mine *etc.*) explode —**deto'nation** *n.* —**'detonator** *n.* mechanical, electrical device, or small amount of explosive, used to set off main explosive charge

detour ('dētōōər) *n.* 1. course which leaves main route to rejoin it later 2. roundabout way —*vi.* 3. make detour

detoxify (dē'toksifī) *vt.* remove poison from (**-fying, -fied**) —**detoxifi'cation** *n.*

detract (di'trakt) *v.* take away (a part) from, diminish —**de'traction** *n.* —**de'tractive** *a.* —**de'tractor** *n.*

detriment ('detrimənt) *n.* harm done, loss, damage —**detri'mental** *a.* damaging, injurious —**detri'mentally** *adv.*

detritus (di'trītəs) *n.* worn-down matter, such as gravel or rock debris —**de'trital** *a.* —**detrition** (di'trishən) *n.* wearing away from solid bodies by friction

de trop (də 'trō) *Fr.* not wanted, superfluous

detrude (di'trōōd) *vt.* thrust down —**de'trusion** *n.*

detumescence (detyōō'mesəns, -tōō-) *n.* subsidence of swelling

deuce (dyōōs, dōōs) *n.* 1. two 2. card with two spots 3. *Tennis* forty all 4. in exclamatory phrases, the devil —**deuced** ('dyōōsid, 'dōōsid) *a. inf.* excessive

Deut. Deuteronomy

deuterium (dyōō'tēəriəm, dōō-) *n.* form of hydrogen twice as heavy as normal gas —'**deuteron** *n.* nucleus of this gas

Deuteronomy (dyōōtə'ronəmi, dōō-) *n. Bible* 5th book of the O.T., last of the five books written by Moses, reinterpreting the law for the new generation

deutsch mark (doich) monetary unit of West Germany

deutzia ('dyōōtsiə, 'dōōtsiə) *n.* shrub with white or pink flower clusters

devalue (dē'valyōō) *or* **devaluate** (dē'valyōōāt) *v.* 1. (of currency) reduce or be reduced in value —*vt.* 2. reduce the value or worth of —**devalu'ation** *n.*

devastate ('devəstāt) *vt.* 1. lay waste 2. ravage 3. *inf.* overwhelm —**devas'tation** *n.*

develop (di'veləp) *vt.* 1. bring to maturity 2. elaborate 3. bring forth, bring out 4. evolve 5. treat (photographic plate or film) to bring out image 6. improve value or change use of (land) by building *etc.* —*vi.* **7.** grow to maturer state (**de'veloped, de'veloping**) —**de'veloper** *n.* **1.** one who develops land **2.** chemical for developing film —**de'velopment** *n.* —**developing country** poor country seeking to develop its resources by industrialization

deviate ('dēviāt) *vi.* leave the way, turn aside, diverge —**'deviant** *n./a.* (person) deviating from normal, *esp.* in sexual practices —**devi'ation** *n.* —**'deviator** *n.* —**'devious** *a.* **1.** deceitful, underhand **2.** roundabout, rambling **3.** erring —**deviated septum** abnormal displacement of the bone and cartilage partition dividing the nasal cavity into two halves

device (di'vīs) *n.* **1.** contrivance, invention **2.** apparatus **3.** stratagem **4.** scheme, plot **5.** heraldic or emblematic figure or design

devil ('devəl) *n.* **1.** personified spirit of evil **2.** superhuman evil being **3.** person of great wickedness, cruelty *etc.* **4.** *inf.* fellow **5.** *inf.* something difficult or annoying **6.** energy, dash, unconquerable spirit **7.** *inf.* rogue, rascal —*vi.* **8.** do work that passes for employer's, as for lawyer or author —*vt.* **9.** season with hot condiments —**'devilish** *a.* **1.** like, of the devil **2.** evil —*adv.* **3.** *inf.* very, extremely —**'devilment** *n.* **1.** wickedness **2.** wild and reckless mischief, revelry, high spirits —**'devilry** *n.* —**devil-may-care** *a.* happy-go-lucky —**devil's advocate** one who advocates opposing, unpopular view, *usu.* for sake of argument —**devil to pay** trouble to be faced

devious ('dēviəs) *a. see* DEVIATE

devise (di'vīz) *vt.* **1.** plan, contrive **2.** invent **3.** plot **4.** leave by will —**devi'see** *n.* —**de'visor** *n.*

devitrification (dēvitrifi'kāshən) *n.* loss of glassy or vitreous condition —**de'vitrify** *vt.* deprive of character or appearance of glass (**-fied, -fying**)

devoid (di'void) *a.* (*usu. with* of) empty, lacking, free (from)

devolve (di'volv) *vi.* **1.** pass or fall (to, upon) —*vt.* **2.** throw (duty *etc.*) on to another —**devo'lution** *n.* devolving, *esp.* transfer of authority from central to regional government

Devonian (də'vōniən) *a.* **1.** of fourth period of Paleozoic era, between Silurian and Carboniferous periods **2.** of Devon, England —*n.* **3.** Devonian period or rock system

devote (di'vōt) *vt.* set apart, give up exclusively (to person, purpose *etc.*) —**de'voted** *a.* loving, attached —**devotee** (devə'tē) *n.* **1.** ardent enthusiast **2.** zealous worshipper —**de'votion** *n.* **1.** deep affection, loyalty **2.** dedication **3.** religious earnestness —*pl.* **4.** prayers, religious exercises —**de'votional** *a.*

devour (di'vowər) *vt.* **1.** eat greedily **2.** consume, destroy **3.** read, gaze at eagerly —**de'vourer** *n.*

devout (di'vowt) *a.* **1.** earnestly religious, pious **2.** sincere, heartfelt —**de'voutly** *adv.*

dew (dyōō, dōō) *n.* **1.** moisture from air deposited as small drops on cool surface between nightfall and morning **2.** any beaded moisture —*vt.* **3.** wet with or as with dew —**'dewiness** *n.* —**'dewy** *a.* —**'dewclaw** *n.* partly developed inner toe of dogs —**'dewlap** *n.* fold of loose skin hanging from neck —**dew point** temperature at which dew begins to form —**dew pond** small natural pond —**dew-worm** *n.* C large earthworm used as bait —**dewy-eyed** *a.* naive, innocent

dewberry ('dyōōberi, 'dōō-) *n.* bramble with blue-black fruits

Dewey Decimal System ('dyōōi, 'dōōi) system of library book classification with ten main subject classes (*also* **decimal classification**)

DEW line (dyōō, dōō) distant early warning line, network of sensors situated in Arctic regions of N Amer.

Dexedrine ('deksədrēn) *n.* trade name for preparation of amphetamine

dexterity (dek'steriti) *n.* **1.** manual skill **2.** neatness **3.** deftness **4.** adroitness —**'dexter** *a. Her.* on the bearer's right-hand side of a shield —**'dexterous** *a.* showing dexterity, skillful

dextran ('dekstrən) *n.* gummy polysaccharide produced by certain bacteria from sucrose used as partial substitute for blood plasma

dextrin ('dekstrin) *or* **dextrine** ('dekstrēn, -trin) *n.* sticky substance obtained from starch, used as thickening agent in foods and as gum

dextrose ('dekstrōs, -trōz) *n.* white, soluble, sweet-tasting crystalline solid, occurring naturally in fruit, honey, animal tissue

D.F. Defender of the Faith

D.F.C. Distinguished Flying Cross

D.F.M. Distinguished Flying Medal

dg *or* **dg.** decigram

dharma ('därmə) *n.* **1.** *Hinduism* social custom regarded as religious and moral duty **2.** *Hinduism* essential principle of cosmos; natural law; conduct that conforms with this **3.** *Buddhism* ideal truth

dhow (dow) *n.* lateen-rigged Arab sailing vessel

di-¹ (*comb. form*) **1.** twice; two; double, as in *dicotyledon* **2.** containing two specified atoms or groups of atoms, as in *carbon dioxide*

di-² (*comb. form*) *see* DIA-

dia- *or before vowel* **di-** (*comb. form*) through

diabetes (dīə'bētēz, -tis) *n.* disorder characterized by excretion of abnormal amount of urine —**diabetes insipidus** (in'sipidəs) condition marked by discharge of large quantities of dilute urine —**diabetes mellitus** (mə'lītəs) disease marked by inability of the body to burn sugar as a fuel —**diabetic** (dīə'betik) *n./a.*

diabolic (dīə'bolik) *a.* devilish —**dia'bolical** *a. inf.* very bad —**dia'bolically** *adv.* —**di'abolism** *n.* devil-worship

diabolo (di'abəlō) *n.* game in which top is spun into air from string attached to two sticks

diaconal (dī'akənəl) *a.* pert. to deacon —**di'aconate** *n.* **1.** office, rank of deacon **2.** body of deacons

diacritic (dīə'kritik) *n.* **1.** sign above letter or character indicating special phonetic value *etc.* —*a.* **2.** diacritical —**dia'critical** *a.* **1.** of a diacritic **2.** showing a distinction (*also* **dia'critic**)

diadem ('dīədem) *n.* a crown

diaeresis *or* **dieresis** (dī'erisis) *n.* mark (¨) placed over vowel to show that it is sounded separately from preceding one, as in *Noël* (*pl.* **-ses** (-sēz))

diagnosis (dīəg'nōsis) *n.* identification of disease from symptoms (*pl.* **-ses** (-sēz)) —**'diagnose** *v.* —**diag'nostic** *a.*

diagonal (dī'agənəl) *a.* **1.** from corner to corner **2.** oblique —*n.* **3.** line from corner to corner —**di'agonally** *adv.*

diagram ('dīəgram) *n.* drawing, figure in lines, to illustrate something being expound-

ed —**diagram'matic** *a.* —**diagram'matically** *adv.*

dial ('dīəl) *n.* **1.** face of clock *etc.* **2.** plate marked with graduations on which pointer moves (as on meter, weighing machine *etc.*) **3.** numbered disk on front of telephone **4.** *sl.* face —*vt.* **5.** operate (telephone) **6.** indicate on dial —**dial tone** continuous purring heard over telephone indicating that number can be dialed

dialect ('dīəlekt) *n.* **1.** characteristic speech of district **2.** local variety of a language —**dia'lectal** *a.*

dialectic (dīə'lektik) *n.* discovery of truth by systematic reasoning —**dia'lectical** *a.* —**dia'lectically** *adv.* —**dialec'tician** *n.* **1.** logician **2.** reasoner

dialogue ('dīəlog) *n.* **1.** conversation between two or more (persons) **2.** representation of such conversation in drama, novel *etc.* **3.** discussion between representatives of two states, countries *etc.*

dialysis (dī'alisis) *n. Med.* filtering of blood through membrane to remove waste products

diamagnetism (dīə'magnitizəm) *n.* phenomenon exhibited by substances that are repelled by both poles of magnet

diamanté (dēəmän'tā) *n.* (fabric covered with) glittering particles —**diamantine** (dīəman'tīn) *a.* like diamond

diameter (dī'amitər) *n.* **1.** (length of) straight line from side to side of figure or body (*esp.* circle) through center **2.** thickness —**dia'metrical** *a.* opposite —**dia'metrically** *adv.*

diamond ('dīəmənd) *n.* **1.** precious stone, usu. bluish-white, crystallized pure carbon, the hardest known substance, poorer grades of which are used as abrasives **2.** rhomboid figure **3.** suit at cards **4.** playing field in baseball —**diamond jubilee** *or* **wedding** 60th (sometimes 75th) anniversary

dianthus (dī'anthōs) *n.* genus of herbaceous flowers, *eg* pinks and carnations

diapason (dīə'pāzən) *n.* **1.** fundamental organ stop **2.** compass of voice or instrument

diaper ('dīəpər) *n.* **1.** absorbent material worn by infant to retain excreta **2.** fabric with small diamond pattern **3.** pattern of that kind —**'diapered** *a.* —**diaper rash** redness, maceration and erosion of the skin of the diaper area in infants

diaphanous (dī'afənəs) *a.* transparent

diaphoretic (dīəfə'retik) *n.* **1.** diaphoretic drug —*a.* **2.** relating to or causing perspiration

diaphragm ('dīəfram) *n.* **1.** muscular partition dividing two cavities of body, midriff **2.** plate or disk wholly or partly closing tube or opening **3.** any thin dividing or separating membrane **4.** contraceptive cap covering neck of womb —**diaphragmatic** (dīəfrag'matik) *a.*

diapositive (dīə'pozitiv) *n.* positive transparency; slide

diarrhea (dīə'rēə) *n.* excessive looseness of the bowels

diary ('dīəri) *n.* **1.** daily record of events, engagements, thoughts *etc.* **2.** book for this —**'diarist** *n.* writer of diary

Diaspora (dī'aspərə) *n.* **1.** dispersion of Jews from Palestine after Babylonian captivity; Jewish communities that arose after this **2.** (*oft.* **d-**) dispersion, as of people orig. of one nation

diastase ('dīəstās, -stāz) *n.* enzyme that converts starch into sugar

diastole (dī'astəli) *n.* dilation of chambers of heart

diathermy ('dīəthərmi) *n.* heating of body tissues with electric current for medical treatment

diatom ('dīətom) *n.* one of order of microscopic algae —**dia'tomic** *a.* of two atoms

diatonic (dīə'tonik) *a. Mus.* 1. pert. to regular major and minor scales 2. (of melody) composed in such a scale

diatribe ('dīətrīb) *n.* violently bitter verbal attack, invective, denunciation

dibble ('dibəl) *n.* 1. small tool used to make holes in ground for bulbs *etc.* (*also* '**dibber**) —*v.* 2. make hole in (ground) with dibble 3. plant (seeds *etc.*) with dibble

dice (dīs) *pl.n.* 1. (*also functions as sing., orig. sing.* **die**) cubes each with six sides marked one to six for games of chance —*vi.* 2. gamble with dice —*vt.* 3. cut into small cubes —'**dicer** *n.* —'**dicey** *a. inf.* dangerous, risky

dicephalous (dī'sefələs) *a.* two-headed

dichotomy (dī'kotəmi) *n.* division into two parts

dichroism ('dīkrōizəm) *n.* property possessed by some crystals of exhibiting different colors when viewed from different directions —**di'chroic** *a.*

dichromatic (dīkrō'matik) *a.* 1. having two colors (*also* **di'chroic**) 2. (of animal species) having two different color varieties 3. able to perceive only two colors

dick (dik) *n. sl.* 1. fellow, person 2. detective

Dickensian (di'kenziən) *a.* 1. of Charles Dickens (1820–70), English novelist, or his novels 2. denoting poverty, distress and exploitation as depicted in Dickens's novels 3. grotesquely comic, as some Dickens characters

dicker ('dikər) *v.* 1. trade (goods) by bargaining; barter —*n.* 2. petty bargain or barter

dickey *or* **dicky** ('diki) *n.* detachable false shirt front (*pl.* '**dickeys**, '**dickies**) —'**dicky-bird** *n. inf.* child's word for small bird

dicotyledon (dīkoti'lēdən) *n.* flowering plant having two embryonic seed leaves

Dictaphone ('diktəfōn) *n.* trade name for machine that records and plays back dictation

dictate (dik'tāt) *v.* 1. say or read for another to transcribe —*vt.* 2. prescribe, lay down —*vi.* 3. seek to impose one's will on others —*n.* ('diktāt) 4. bidding —**dic'tation** *n.* —**dic'tator** *n.* absolute ruler —**dicta'torial** *a.* 1. despotic 2. overbearing —**dicta'torially** *adv.* —**dic'tatorship** *n.*

diction ('dikshən) *n.* 1. choice and use of words 2. enunciation

dictionary ('dikshəneri) *n.* 1. book setting forth, alphabetically, words of language with meanings *etc.* 2. reference book with items in alphabetical order

dictum ('diktəm) *n.* 1. pronouncement 2. saying, maxim (*pl.* **-s, -ta** (-tə))

dicumarol (dī'kyōōmərōl, -'kōō-; -rōl) *n.* drug used to prevent formation of blood clots in arteries and veins

did (did) *pt. of* DO[1]

didactic (dī'daktik, di-) *a.* 1. designed to instruct 2. (of people) opinionated, dictatorial —**di'dacticism** *n.*

diddle ('didəl) *vt. inf.* cheat

didgeridoo (dijəri'dōō) *n. Mus.* native Aust. wind instrument

die[1] (dī) *vi.* 1. cease to live 2. come to an end 3. stop functioning 4. *inf.* be nearly overcome (with laughter *etc.*) (**died, 'dying**) —'**diehard** *n.* one who resists (reform *etc.*) to the end —**be dying for** be looking eagerly forward to

die[2] (dī) *n. see* DICE

die[3] (dī) *n.* 1. shaped block of hard material to form metal in forge, press *etc.* 2. tool for cutting thread on pipe *etc.* —**die-cast** *vt.* shape or form (object) by introducing molten metal or plastic into reusable mold —**die-casting** *n.*

dieldrin ('dēldrin) *n.* highly toxic crystalline insecticide

dielectric (dīi'lektrik) *n.* 1. substance through or across which electric induction takes place 2. nonconductor 3. insulator

dieresis (dī'erisis) *n. see* DIAERESIS

diesel ('dēzəl) *a.* 1. pert. to internal-combustion engine using oil as fuel —*n.* 2. this engine 3. diesel oil —**diesel-electric** *n.* 1. locomotive fitted with diesel engine driving electric generator —*a.* 2. of such locomotive or system —**diesel oil** fuel, distilled from petroleum, used in diesel engines

diet[1] ('dīət) *n.* 1. restricted or regulated course of feeding 2. kind of food lived on 3. food —*vi.* 4. follow a dietary regimen, as to lose weight —'**dietary** *a.* 1. relating to diet —*n.* 2. a regulated diet 3. system of dieting —**die'tetic** *a.* —**die'tetics** *pl.n.* (*with sing. v.*) science of diet —**die'titian** *or* **die'tician** *n.* one skilled in dietetics

diet[2] ('dīət) *n.* 1. legislature of some provinces or nations 2. formal assembly

differ ('difər) *vi.* 1. be unlike 2. disagree —'**difference** *n.* 1. unlikeness 2. degree or point of unlikeness 3. disagreement 4. remainder left after subtraction —'**different** *a.* unlike —'**differently** *adv.*

differentia (difə'renchiə) *n. Logic* feature by which subclasses of same class of named objects can be distinguished (*pl.* **-tiae** (-chiē))

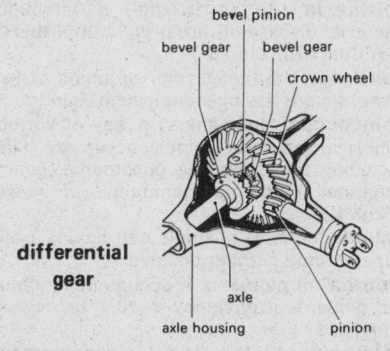

bevel pinion
bevel gear   bevel gear
crown wheel

differential gear

axle
axle housing   pinion

differential (difə'renchəl) *a.* 1. varying with circumstances 2. special 3. *Math.* pert. to an infinitesimal change in variable quantity 4. *Phys. etc.* relating to difference between sets of motions acting in the same direction or between pressures *etc.* —*n.* 5. *Math.* infinitesimal difference between two consecutive states of variable quantity 6. differential gear 7. difference between rates of pay for different types of labor —**differ'entially** *adv.* —**differ'entiate** *vt.* 1. serve to distinguish between, make different —*vi.* 2. discriminate —**differenti'ation** *n.* —**differential calculus** method of calculating relative rate of change for continuously varying quantities —**differential gear** epicyclic gear mounted in driving axle of vehicle, that permits one driving wheel to rotate faster than the other, as when cornering

difficult ('difikəlt) *a.* 1. requiring effort, skill *etc.* to do or understand, not easy 2. obscure —'**difficulty** *n.* 1. being difficult 2. difficult task, problem 3. embarrassment 4. hindrance 5. obscurity 6. trouble

diffident ('difidənt) *a.* lacking confidence, timid, shy —'**diffidence** *n.* shyness —'**diffidently** *adv.*

diffract (di'frakt) *vi.* break up, *esp.* of rays of light, sound waves —**dif'fraction** *n.* deflection of ray of light, electromagnetic wave caused by obstacle

diffuse (di'fyōōz) *vt.* 1. spread abroad —*a.* (di'fyōōs) 2. widely spread 3. loose, verbose, wordy —**diffusely** (di'fyōōsli) *adv.* 1. loosely 2. wordily —**dif'fusible** *a.* —**dif'fusion** *n.* process by which one substance mixes with another through the motion of its particles —**diffusive** (di'fyōōsiv, -ziv) *a.* —**diffusively** (di'fyōōsivli, -zivli) *adv.*

dig (dig) *vi.* 1. work with spade 2. search, investigate —*vt.* 3. turn up with spade 4. hollow out, make hole in 5. excavate 6. thrust 7. (*oft. with* out *or* up) discover by searching (**dug, 'digging**) —*n.* 8. piece of digging 9. archaeological excavation 10. thrust 11. jibe, taunt —*pl.* 12. *inf.* lodgings —'**digger** *n.* 1. one who digs 2. gold miner 3. Aust. or N.Z. soldier

digest (dī'jest, di-) *vt.* 1. prepare (food) in stomach *etc.* for assimilation 2. bring into handy form by sorting, tabulating, summarizing 3. reflect on 4. absorb —*vi.* 5. (of food) undergo digestion —*n.* ('dījest) 6. methodical summary, *esp.* of laws 7. magazine containing condensed version of articles *etc.* already published elsewhere —**di'gestible** *a.* —**di'gestion** *n.* digesting —**di'gestive** *a.* 1. relating to digestion —*n.* 2. substance that aids digestion

digit ('dijit) *n.* 1. finger or toe 2. any of the numbers 0 to 9 —'**digital** *a.* 1. of, resembling digits 2. performed with fingers 3. displaying information (time *etc.*) by numbers rather than by pointer on dial —'**digitate** *a.* having separate fingers, toes —**digital clock** *or* **watch** clock or watch in which time is indicated by digits rather than by hands on dial —**digital computer** electronic computer consisting of numbers, letters *etc.* that are represented internally in binary notation

digitalis (diji'talis, -'tā-) *n.* group of chemically related drugs obtained from dried leaves of certain flowering plants, *esp.* foxgloves: used to treat heart disease

dignity ('digniti) *n.* 1. stateliness, gravity 2. worthiness, excellence, repute 3. honorable office or title —'**dignified** *a.* stately, majestic —'**dignify** *vt.* give dignity to (**-fied, -fying**) —'**dignitary** *n.* holder of high office

digraph ('dīgraf) *n.* combination of two letters used to represent single sound such as *gh* in *tough*

digress (dī'gres, di-) *vi.* turn from main course, *esp.* to deviate from subject in speaking or writing —**di'gression** *n.* —**di'gressive** *a.*

dihedral (dī'hēdrəl) *a.* having two plane faces or sides

dik-dik ('dikdik) *n.* small Afr. antelope

dike *or* **dyke** (dīk) *n.* 1. embankment to prevent flooding 2. ditch

diktat (dik'tät) *n.* arbitrary decree

dilapidate (di'lapidāt) *v.* (cause to) fall into ruin —**di'lapidated** *a.* 1. in ruins 2. decayed —**dilapi'dation** *n.*

dilate (dī'lāt, 'dīlāt) *vt.* 1. widen, expand —*vi.* 2. expand 3. talk or write at length (on) —**di'lation** *or* **dilatation** (dilə'tāshən, dī-) *n.*

dilatory ('dilətōri) *a.* tardy, slow, belated —'**dilatorily** *adv.* —'**dilatoriness** *n.* delay

dilemma (di'lemə, dī-) *n.* 1. position in fact or argument offering choice only between unwelcome alternatives 2. predicament

dilettante ('dilitänt) *n.* 1. person with taste and knowledge of fine arts as pastime 2.

dabbler (*pl.* **dilettanti** (dili'tänti)) —*a.* **3.** amateur, desultory —**'dilettantism** *n.*

diligent ('dilijənt) *a.* unremitting in effort, industrious, hard-working —**'diligence** *n.*

dill (dil) *n.* yellow-flowered herb with medicinal seeds

dilly ('dili) *n. sl.* remarkable person or thing

dilly-dally ('dilidali) *vi. inf.* **1.** loiter **2.** vacillate

dilute (dɪ'lōōt, di-) *vt.* **1.** reduce (liquid) in strength, *esp.* by adding water **2.** thin **3.** reduce in force, effect *etc.* —*a.* **4.** weakened thus —**diluent** ('dilyōōənt) *a./n.* —**di'lution** *n.*

diluvial (di'lōōviəl, dɪ-) *or* **diluvian** *a.* of, connected with, a deluge or flood, *esp.* the Flood of the book of Genesis

dim (dim) *a.* **1.** indistinct, faint, not bright **2.** mentally dull **3.** unfavorable (**'dimmer** *comp.,* **'dimmest** *sup.*) —*v.* **4.** make, grow dim (-**mm**-) —**'dimly** *adv.* —**'dimmer** *n.* device for dimming electric lights —**'dimness** *n.* —**'dimwit** *n. inf.* stupid or silly person —**dim-witted** *a.*

dime (dɪm) *n.* 10-cent piece, coin of U.S. and Canad.

dimenhydrinate (dɪmen'hɪdrināt) *n. see* DRAMAMINE

dimension (di'menchən, dɪ-) *n.* **1.** measurement, size **2.** aspect —**di'mensional** *a.* —**dimension'ality** *n.* —**fourth dimension 1.** *Phys.* time **2.** supranatural, fictional dimension additional to those of length, breadth, thickness

diminish (di'minish) *v.* lessen —**dimi'nution** *n.* —**di'minutive** *a.* **1.** very small —*n.* **2.** derivative word, affix implying smallness

diminuendo (diminyōō'endō) *a. Mus.* (oï sound) dying away

dimity ('dimiti) *n.* strong cotton fabric

dimple ('dimpəl) *n.* **1.** small hollow in surface of skin, *esp.* of cheek **2.** any small hollow —*v.* **3.** mark with, show dimples

din (din) *n.* continuous roar of confused noises —**din into** instill into by constant repetition (-**nn**-)

dinar (di'när, 'dēnär) *n.* **1.** standard monetary unit of Iraq, Jordan, Libya, Yugoslavia *etc.* **2.** an Iranian monetary unit

dine (dɪn) *vi.* **1.** eat dinner —*vt.* **2.** give dinner to —**'diner** *n.* **1.** one who dines **2.** small cheap restaurant —**dining car** railroad coach in which meals are served (*also* **restaurant car**) —**dining room** room where meals are eaten

ding (ding) *v.* **1.** ring (*esp.* with tedious repetition) —*vi.* **2.** make (imitation of) sound of bell —*n.* **3.** this sound —**ding-dong** *n.* **1.** sound of bell **2.** imitation of sound of bell **3.** violent exchange of blows or words —*a.* **4.** sounding or ringing repeatedly

dinghy ('dingi, 'dinggi) *n.* **1.** small open boat **2.** collapsible rubber boat

dingle ('dinggəl) *n.* dell

dingo ('dinggō) *n.* Aust. wild dog

dingy ('dinji) *a.* dirty-looking, dull —**'dinginess** *n.*

dinkum ('dingkəm) *a.* **A, NZ** *inf.* genuine; right —**dinkum oil** truth

dinky ('dingki) *a. inf.* inconsequential; insignificant

dinner ('dinər) *n.* **1.** chief meal of the day **2.** official banquet —**dinner jacket** tuxedo

dinosaur ('dɪnəsör) *n.* extinct reptile, oft. of gigantic size —**dino'saurian** *a.*

dint (dint) *n.* dent, mark —**by dint of** by means of

diocese ('dɪəsis, -sēz, -sēs) *n.* district, jurisdiction of bishop —**diocesan** (dɪ'osisən) *a.* **1.** of diocese —*n.* **2.** bishop of diocese

diode ('dɪōd) *n.* **1.** semiconductor device for converting alternating current to direct current **2.** electronic valve having two electrodes between which current can flow in only one direction

dioecious (dɪ'ēshəs) *a.* (of plants) having male and female reproductive organs on separate plants

Dionysian (dɪə'nizian) *a.* **1.** of Dionysus, Gr. god of wine and revelry **2.** (*oft.* **d-**) wild; orgiastic

diopter (dɪ'optər) *n.* unit for measuring refractive power of lens —**di'optrics** *pl.n.* (*with sing. v.*) that part of the science of optics which deals with refraction of light

diorama (dɪə'rämə) *n.* **1.** miniature three-dimensional scene, *esp.* as museum exhibit **2.** device for producing changing effects in a partly translucent painting by manipulating direction, color and intensity of light

dioxide (dɪ'oksɪd) *n.* oxide with two parts of oxygen to one of the other constituents

dioxin (dɪ'oksin) *n.* any of various by-products of manufacture of certain herbicides and bactericides

dip (dip) *vt.* **1.** put partly or briefly into liquid, *esp.* to coat **2.** immerse **3.** lower and raise again **4.** take up in ladle, bucket *etc.* **5.** direct (headlights of vehicle) downwards —*vi.* **6.** plunge partially or temporarily **7.** go down, sink **8.** slope downwards (-**pp**-) —*n.* **9.** act of dipping **10.** bathe **11.** liquid chemical in which livestock are immersed to treat insect pests *etc.* **12.** downward slope **13.** hollow **14.** creamy (savory) mixture in which crackers *etc.* are dipped before being eaten **15.** lottery —**'dipstick** *n.* graduated rod dipped into container to indicate fluid level —**dip switch** device for dipping car headlights —**dip into 1.** glance at **2.** make inroads into for funds

diphtheria (dif'thēriə, dip-) *n.* infectious bacterial disease of throat *etc.* —**diphtheritic** (difthə'ritik, dip-) *a.*

diphthong ('difthong, 'dip-) *n.* union of two vowel sounds in single compound sound

diplococcus (diplō'kokəs) *n.* any of various spherical bacteria which occur in pairs including those causing pneumonia, gonorrhea and epidemic meningitis (*pl.* -**cocci** (-'koksɪ))

diploid ('diploid) *n.* single cell having basic chromosome number doubled

diploma (di'plōmə) *n.* **1.** document vouching for person's proficiency **2.** title to degree, honor *etc.*

diplomacy (di'plōməsi) *n.* **1.** management of international relations **2.** skill in negotiation **3.** tactful, adroit dealing —**'diplomat** *n.* one engaged in official diplomacy —**diplo'matic** *a.* —**diplo'matically** *adv.* —**di'plomatist** *n.* **1.** diplomat **2.** tactful person —**diplomatic corps** *see* **corps diplomatique** *at* CORPS —**diplomatic immunity** immunity from local jurisdiction *etc.* afforded to diplomatic staff abroad

diplopia (di'plōpiə) *n.* double vision

dipolar ('dɪpōlar, di'pōlar) *a.* having two poles

dipole ('dɪpōl) *n.* type of radio and television antenna

dipper ('dipər) *n.* **1.** ladle, bucket, scoop **2.** (*also* **water ouzel**) N Amer. swimming and diving songbird

dipsomania (dipsō'māniə) *n.* uncontrollable craving for alcohol —**dipso'maniac** *n.* victim of this

dipterous ('diptərəs) *a.* **1.** of order of insects having single pair of wings and sucking or piercing mouthparts (*also* **'dipteran**) **2.** *Bot.* having two winglike parts

diptych ('diptik) *n.* **1.** ancient tablet hinged in center, folding together like a book **2.** painting, carving on two hinged panels

dire ('dɪər) *a.* **1.** terrible **2.** urgent

direct (di'rekt, dɪ-) *vt.* **1.** control, manage, order **2.** tell or show the way **3.** aim, point, turn **4.** address (letter *etc.*) **5.** supervise (actors *etc.*) in (play or motion picture) —*a.* **6.** frank, straightforward **7.** straight **8.** going straight to the point **9.** immediate **10.** lineal —**di'rection** *n.* **1.** directing **2.** aim, course of movement **3.** address, instruction —**di'rectional** *a.* **1.** of or relating to spatial direction **2.** *Electron.* having or relating to increased sensitivity to radio waves *etc.* coming from particular direction; (of antenna) transmitting or receiving radio waves more effectively in some directions than in others **3.** *Phys., electron.* concentrated in, following or producing motion in particular direction —**di'rective** *a./n.* —**di'rectly** *adv.* —**di'rectness** *n.* —**di'rector** *n.* **1.** one who directs, *esp.* a motion picture **2.** member of board managing company (**di'rectress** *fem.*) —**di'rectorate** *n.* **1.** body of directors **2.** office of director —**di'rectorship** *n.* —**di'rectory** *n.* **1.** alphabetical book of names, addresses, streets *etc.* **2.** (**D-**) French revolutionary government 1795-99 —**direct current** continuous electric current that flows in one direction —**direct election** election decided by voters, not by representatives —**direction finder** radio receiver that determines the direction of incoming waves —**direct mail** advertisements, requests for donations *etc.* addressed directly to individuals —**direct object** *Gram.* noun, pronoun or noun phrase whose referent receives direct action of verb

dirge (dərj) *n.* poem or song of mourning

dirigible ('dirijibəl, di'rij-) *a.* **1.** steerable —*n.* **2.** balloon; airship

dirk (dərk) *n.* short dagger orig. carried by Scottish clansmen

dirndl ('dərndəl) *n.* full, gathered skirt

dirt (dərt) *n.* **1.** filth **2.** soil, earth **3.** obscene or pornographic material **4.** contamination —**'dirtiness** *n.* —**'dirty** *a.* **1.** unclean, filthy **2.** obscene **3.** unfair **4.** dishonest —**dirt-cheap** *a./adv. inf.* at extremely low price —**dirt track** loose-surfaced track, *eg* for motorcycle racing

dis- (*comb. form*) negation, opposition, deprivation; in many verbs indicates undoing of the action of simple verb. See the list below

disable (dis'äbəl) *vt.* **1.** make unable **2.** cripple, maim —**disa'bility** *n.* **1.** incapacity **2.** drawback

disabuse (disə'byōōz) *vt.* **1.** undeceive, disillusion **2.** free from error

disadvantage (disəd'vantij) *n.* **1.** drawback **2.** hindrance **3.** detriment —*vt.* **4.** handicap —**disad'vantaged** *a.* deprived, discriminated against, underprivileged —**disadvan'tageous** *a.*

disaffected (disə'fektid) *a.* ill-disposed, alienated, estranged —**disaf'fection** *n.*

disagree (disə'grē) *vi.* (*oft. with* with) **1.** be at variance **2.** conflict **3.** (of food *etc.*) have bad effect (on) —**disa'greeable** *a.* unpleasant —**disa'greement** *n.* **1.** difference of opinion **2.** discord **3.** discrepancy

disallow (disə'low) *vt.* reject as untrue or invalid —**disal'lowance** *n.*

disappear (disə'pēər) *vi.* **1.** vanish **2.** cease to exist **3.** be lost —**disap'pearance** *n.*

disappoint (disə'point) *vt.* fail to fulfill (hope), frustrate —**disap'pointment** *n.*

disarm (dis'ärm) *vt.* **1.** deprive of arms or

weapons **2.** reduce war weapons of (a country) **3.** win over —**dis'armament** *n.* —**dis'arming** *a.* removing hostility, suspicion

disarray (disə'rā) *vt.* **1.** throw into disorder, derange —*n.* **2.** disorderliness, *esp.* of clothing

disassociate (disə'sōshiāt) *v. see* DISSOCIATE

disaster (di'zastər) *n.* calamity, sudden or great misfortune —**dis'astrous** *a.* calamitous

disbar (dis'bär) *vt.* expel from the legal profession

disbud (dis'bud) *vt.* remove superfluous buds, shoots from (plants, cattle)

disburse (dis'bərs) *vt.* pay out —**dis'burse-ment** *n.*

disc (disk) *n. see* DISK —**disc brake** brake in which two pads rub against flat disc attached to wheel hub when brake is applied —**disc jockey** announcer playing records, oft. on radio

discard (dis'kärd) *vt.* **1.** reject **2.** give up **3.** cast off, dismiss

discern (di'sərn) *vt.* **1.** make out **2.** distinguish —**dis'cernible** *a.* —**dis'cerning** *a.* **1.** discriminating **2.** penetrating —**dis'cern-ment** *n.* insight

discharge (dis'chärj) *vt.* **1.** release **2.** dismiss **3.** emit **4.** perform (duties), fulfill (obligations) **5.** let go **6.** fire off **7.** unload **8.** pay —*n.* ('dischärj, dis'chärj) **9.** discharging **10.** being discharged **11.** release **12.** matter emitted **13.** document certifying release, payment *etc.*

disciple (di'sīpəl) *n.* follower, one who takes another as teacher and model —**dis'ciple-ship** *n.*

discipline ('disiplin) *n.* **1.** training that produces orderliness, obedience, self-control **2.** result of such training in order, conduct *etc.* **3.** system of rules *etc.* **4.** instrument of self-mortification, *eg* hair shirt —*vt.* **5.** train **6.** punish —**discipli'narian** *n.* one who enforces rigid discipline —'**disciplinary** *a.*

disclaim (dis'klām) *vt.* deny, renounce —**dis'claimer** *n.* repudiation, denial

disclose (dis'klōz) *vt.* **1.** allow to be seen **2.** make known —**dis'closure** *n.* revelation

disco ('diskō) discotheque

discobolus

discobolus (dis'kobələs) *n.* discus thrower (*pl.* **-li** (-lī))

discolor (dis'kulər) *vt.* alter color of, stain —**discolor'ation** *n.*

discomfit (dis'kumfit) *vt.* embarrass, disconcert, baffle —**dis'comfiture** *n.*

discomfort (dis'kumfort) *n.* **1.** inconvenience, distress or mild pain **2.** something that disturbs or deprives of ease —*vt.* **3.** make uncomfortable or uneasy

discommode (diskə'mōd) *vt.* **1.** put to inconvenience **2.** disturb —**discom'modious** *a.*

disconcert (diskən'sərt) *vt.* **1.** ruffle, confuse **2.** upset, embarrass

disconsolate (dis'konsəlit) *a.* unhappy, downcast, forlorn

discord ('diskörd) *n.* **1.** strife **2.** difference, dissension **3.** disagreement of sounds —**dis-'cordance** *n.* —**dis'cordant** *a.* —**dis'cordant-ly** *adv.*

discotheque ('diskətek) *n.* **1.** club *etc.* for dancing to recorded music **2.** mobile equipment for providing music for dancing

discount (dis'kownt, 'diskownt) *vt.* **1.** consider as possibility but reject as unsuitable, inappropriate *etc.* **2.** deduct (amount, percentage) from usual price **3.** sell at reduced price —*n.* ('diskownt) **4.** amount deducted from cost, expressed as cash amount or percentage

discountenance (dis'kowntinəns) *vt.* **1.** abash **2.** discourage **3.** frown upon

discourage (dis'kurij) *vt.* **1.** reduce confidence of **2.** deter **3.** show disapproval of —**dis'couragement** *n.*

discourse ('diskörs, dis'körs) *n.* **1.** conversation **2.** speech, treatise, sermon —*vi.* (dis'körs) **3.** speak, converse, lecture

discover (di'skuvər) *vt.* **1.** (be the first to) find out, light upon **2.** make known —**dis'coverable** *a.* —**dis'coverer** *n.* —**dis-'covery** *n.* —**Discovery Day** *see* COLUMBUS DAY

discredit (dis'kredit) *vt.* **1.** damage reputation of **2.** cast doubt on **3.** reject as untrue —*n.* **4.** disgrace **5.** doubt —**dis'creditable** *a.*

discreet (di'skrēt) *a.* prudent, circumspect —**dis'creetly** *adv.* —**dis'creetness** *n.*

discrepancy (di'skrepənsi) *n.* conflict, variation, as between figures —**dis'crepant** *a.*

discrete (dis'krēt, 'diskrēt) *a.* separate, disunited, discontinuous

discretion (di'skreshən) *n.* **1.** quality of being discreet **2.** prudence **3.** freedom to act as one chooses —**dis'cretionary** *or* **dis'cre-tional** *a.*

discriminate (di'skrimināt) *vi.* **1.** single out particular person, group *etc.* for special favor or disfavor **2.** distinguish (between) **3.** be discerning —**discrimi'nation** *n.* —**dis-'criminatory** *or* **dis'criminative** *a.* **1.** based on prejudice; biased **2.** capable of making fine distinctions

discursive (di'skərsiv) *a.* passing from subject to subject, rambling

discus ('diskəs) *n.* disk-shaped object thrown in athletic competition (*pl.* **-es, disci** ('diskī))

discuss (di'skus) *vt.* **1.** exchange opinions about **2.** debate —**dis'cussion** *n.*

disdain (dis'dān) *n.* **1.** scorn, contempt —*vt.* **2.** scorn —**dis'dainful** *a.* —**dis'dainfully** *adv.*

disease (di'zēz) *n.* illness, disorder of health —**dis'eased** *a.* —**disease vector** insect or other animal carrying infectious organism from infected to noninfected individual

disembodied (disim'bodid) *a.* (of spirit) released from bodily form

disembowel (disim'bowəl) *vt.* take out entrails of

disenchanted (disin'chantid) *a.* disillusioned

disengage (disin'gāj) *v.* **1.** release or become released from connection *etc.* **2.** *Mil.* withdraw (forces) from close action **3.** *Fencing* move (one's blade) from one side of opponent's blade to another in circular motion —**disen'gaged** *a.* —**disen'gagement** *n.*

disfavor (dis'fāvər) *n.* **1.** disapproval; dislike **2.** state of being disapproved of or disliked **3.** unkind act —*vt.* **4.** treat with disapproval or dislike

disfigure (dis'figyər) *vt.* mar appearance of —**disfigu'ration** *n.* —**dis'figurement** *n.* blemish, defect

disgorge (dis'görj) *vt.* **1.** vomit **2.** give up —**dis'gorgement** *n.*

disgrace (dis'grās) *n.* **1.** shame, loss of reputation, dishonor —*vt.* **2.** bring shame or discredit upon —**dis'graceful** *a.* shameful —**dis'gracefully** *adv.*

disgruntled (dis'gruntəld) *a.* vexed, put out

disguise (dis'gīz) *vt.* **1.** change appearance of, make unrecognizable **2.** conceal, cloak **3.** misrepresent —*n.* **4.** false appearance **5.** costume, mask *etc.* to conceal identity

disgust (dis'gust) *n.* **1.** violent distaste, loathing, repugnance —*vt.* **2.** affect with loathing

dish (dish) *n.* **1.** shallow vessel for food **2.** portion or variety of food **3.** contents of dish **4.** *sl.* attractive person —*vt.* **5.** put in dish —'**dishcloth** *n.* cloth for washing dishes —**dish out** *inf.* give generously —**dish up 1.** serve (meal *etc.*) **2.** *inf.* prepare or present, *esp.* attractively

dishabille (disa'bēl) *or* **deshabille** *n.* state of being partly or carelessly dressed

disheveled *or* **dishevelled** (di'shevəld) *a.* **1.** with disordered hair **2.** ruffled, untidy, unkempt

dishonor (dis'onər) *vt.* **1.** treat with disrespect **2.** fail or refuse to pay **3.** cause disgrace of (woman) by seduction or rape —*n.* **4.** lack of honor or respect **5.** state of shame or disgrace **6.** person or thing that causes loss of honor **7.** insult; affront **8.** refusal or failure to accept or pay a commercial paper —**dis'honorable** *a.* **1.** characterized by or causing dishonor or discredit **2.** having little or no integrity; unprincipled

disillusion (disi'lōōzhən) *vt.* **1.** destroy ideals, illusions, or false ideas of —*n.* **2.** act of

---

disappro'bation	discon'nect	disen'cumber	dis'honest	dis'organize	dis'similar
disap'proval	discon'tent	disen'tangle	dis'honesty	dispro'portion	dissimi'larity
disap'rove	discon'tented	disen'tanglement	disin'ter	dispro'portionate	dis'symmetry
disar'range	discon'tentment	disequi'librium	disin'terment	disre'gard	dis'trust
disa'vow	discon'tinue	dises'tablish	dis'join	dis'reputable	dis'trustful
dis'band	discon'tinuous	dises'tablishment	dis'loyal	disre'pute	disu'nite
disbe'lief	dis'courteous	dis'franchise	dis'loyalty	disre'spect	
disbe'lieve	dis'courtesy	dis'harmony	dis'mast	disre'spectful	
discom'pose	disem'bark	dis'hearten	dis'mount	dissatis'faction	
discom'posure	disen'chant	dis'heartenment	disorgani'zation	dis'satisfy	

disillusioning or being disillusioned (*also* **disil'lusionment**)

disincentive (disin'sentiv) *n*. 1. something that acts as deterrent —*a*. 2. acting as deterrent

disincline (disin'klīn) *v*. make or be unwilling, reluctant or averse —**disinclination** (disinkli'nāshən) *n*.

disinfectant (disin'fektənt) *n*. agent which kills disease-producing organisms —**disin'fect** *vt*.

disinformation (disinfər'māshən) *n*. deliberately leaked false information intended to mislead foreign agents

disingenuous (disin'jenyoŏəs) *a*. not sincere or frank

disinherit (disin'herit) *vt*. deprive of inheritance

disintegrate (dis'intigrāt) *vi*. break up, fall to pieces —**disinte'gration** *n*.

disinterest (dis'intrist) *n*. freedom from bias or involvement —**dis'interested** *a*.

disjoint (dis'joint) *vt*. 1. put out of joint 2. break the natural order or logical arrangement of —**dis'jointed** *a*. 1. (of discourse) incoherent 2. disconnected

disjunctive (dis'jungktiv) *a*. 1. serving to disconnect or separate 2. *Gram.* denoting word, *esp.* conjunction, that serves to express opposition or contrast 3. *Logic* characterizing, containing or included in disjunction —*n*. 4. *Gram.* disjunctive word, *esp.* conjunction 5. *Logic* disjunctive proposition

disk *or* **disc** (disk) *n*. 1. thin, flat, circular object like a coin 2. phonograph record

dislike (dis'līk) *vt*. 1. consider unpleasant or disagreeable —*n*. 2. aversion; antipathy —**dis'likable** *or* **dis'likeable** *a*.

dislocate (dis'ləkāt) *vt*. 1. put out of joint 2. disrupt, displace —**dislo'cation** *n*.

dislodge (dis'loj) *vt*. drive out or remove from hiding place or previous position —**dis'lodgement** *or* **dis'lodgment** *n*.

dismal (diz'məl) *a*. 1. depressing 2. depressed 3. cheerless, dreary, gloomy —**dis'mally** *adv*.

dismantle (dis'mantəl) *vt*. take apart —**dis'mantlement** *n*.

dismay (dis'mā) *vt*. 1. dishearten, daunt —*n*. 2. consternation, horrified amazement 3. apprehension

dismember (dis'membər) *vt*. 1. remove limbs or members of 2. divide, partition —**dis'memberment** *n*.

dismiss (dis'mis) *vt*. 1. remove, discharge from employment 2. send away 3. reject —**dis'missal** *n*.

disobey (disə'bā) *v*. refuse or fail to obey —**disobedience** (disə'bēdiəns) *n*. —**disobedient** (disə'bēdiənt) *a*.

disoblige (disə'blīj) *vt*. disregard the wishes, preferences of

disorder (dis'ōrdər) *n*. 1. disarray, confusion, disturbance 2. upset of health, ailment —*vt*. 3. upset order of 4. disturb health of —**dis'orderly** *a*. 1. untidy 2. unruly

disorient (dis'ōrient) *or* **disorientate** *vt*. cause (someone) to lose his bearings, confuse

disown (dis'ōn) *vt*. refuse to acknowledge

disparage (di'sparij) *vt*. 1. speak slightingly of 2. belittle —**dis'paragement** *n*.

disparate (dis'parit, 'dispərit) *a*. essentially different, unrelated —**dis'parity** *n*. 1. inequality 2. incongruity

dispassionate (dis'pashənit) *a*. 1. unswayed by passion 2. calm, impartial

dispatch *or* **despatch** (di'spach) *vt*. 1. send off to destination or on an errand 2. send off 3. finish off, get done with speed 4. *inf.* eat up 5. kill —*n*. 6. sending off 7. efficient speed 8. official message, report —**dispatch case** container for carrying official documents —**dispatch rider** horseman or motorcyclist who carries dispatches

dispel (di'spel) *vt*. clear, drive away, scatter (-ll-)

dispense (di'spens) *vt*. 1. deal out 2. make up (medicine) 3. administer (justice) 4. grant exemption from —**dis'pensable** *a*. —**dis'pensary** *n*. place where medicine is made up —**dispen'sation** *n*. 1. act of dispensing 2. license; exemption 3. provision of nature or providence —**dis'penser** *n*. —**dispense with** 1. do away with 2. manage without

disperse (di'spərs) *v*. scatter —**dis'persal** *or* **dis'persion** *n*. —**dis'persed** *a*. 1. scattered 2. placed here and there

dispirited (di'spiritid) *a*. dejected, disheartened —**dis'piritedly** *adv*. —**dis'piriting** *a*.

displace (dis'plās) *vt*. 1. move from the usual place 2. remove from office 3. take place of —**dis'placement** *n*. 1. displacing 2. weight of liquid displaced by a solid in a fluid —**displaced person** person forced from his home country, *esp.* by war *etc*.

display (di'splā) *vt*. 1. spread out for show 2. show, expose to view 3. (of visual display unit *etc*.) represent (data) visually, as on cathode-ray tube screen —*n*. 4. displaying 5. parade 6. show, exhibition 7. ostentation 8. *Electron.* device capable of representing data visually, as on cathode-ray tube screen

displease (dis'plēz) *v*. offend; annoy —**displeasure** (dis'plezhər) *n*. anger, vexation

disport (di'spōrt) *v.refl.* 1. amuse oneself —*vi*. 2. frolic, gambol

dispose (di'spōz) *vt*. 1. arrange 2. distribute 3. incline 4. adjust —*vi*. 5. determine —**dis'posable** *a*. designed to be thrown away after use —**dis'posal** *n*. —**dis'posed** *a*. having inclination as specified (toward something) —**dispo'sition** *n*. 1. inclination 2. temperament 3. arrangement 4. plan —**dispose of** 1. sell, get rid of 2. have authority over 3. deal with

dispossess (dispə'zes) *vt*. cause to give up possession (of)

disprove (dis'proŏv) *vt*. to show (assertion, claim *etc*.) to be incorrect

dispute (di'spyoŏt) *vi*. 1. debate, discuss —*vt*. 2. call in question 3. debate, argue 4. oppose, contest —**dis'putable** *a*. —**dis'putant** *n*. —**dispu'tation** *n*. —**dispu'tatious** *a*. argumentative, quarrelsome

disqualify (dis'kwolifī) *vt*. make ineligible, unfit for some special purpose

disquiet (dis'kwīət) *n*. 1. anxiety, uneasiness —*vt*. 2. cause (someone) to feel this —**dis'quietude** *n*. feeling of anxiety

disquisition (diskwi'zishən) *n*. learned or elaborate treatise, discourse or essay

disrepair (disri'pāər) *n*. state of bad repair, neglect

disrobe (dis'rōb) *v*. 1. undress —*vt*. 2. divest of robes

disrupt (dis'rupt) *vt*. 1. interrupt 2. throw into turmoil or disorder —**dis'ruption** *n*. —**dis'ruptive** *a*.

dissect (di'sekt, dī-) *vt*. 1. cut up (body, organism) for detailed examination 2. examine or criticize in detail —**dis'section** *n*. —**dis'sector** *n*. anatomist

dissemble (di'sembəl) *v*. 1. conceal, disguise (feelings *etc*.) —*vt*. 2. simulate —**dis'sembler** *n*.

disseminate (di'semināt) *vt*. spread abroad, scatter —**dissemi'nation** *n*. —**dis'seminator** *n*.

dissent (di'sent) *vi*. 1. differ in opinion 2. express such difference 3. disagree with doctrine *etc*. of established church —*n*. 4. such disagreement —**dis'sension** *n*. —**dis'senter** *n*. —**dis'sentient** *a./n*.

dissertation (disər'tāshən) *n*. 1. written thesis 2. formal discourse —**'dissertate** *vi*. hold forth

disservice (dis'sərvis) *n*. ill turn, wrong, injury

dissident ('disidənt) *n./a*. (one) not in agreement, *esp.* with government —**'dissidence** *n*. dissent; disagreement

dissimulate (di'simyoŏlāt) *v*. dissemble, practice deceit —**dissimu'lation** *n*. —**dis'simulator** *n*.

dissipate ('disipāt) *vt*. 1. scatter 2. waste, squander —**'dissipated** *a*. 1. indulging in pleasure without restraint, dissolute 2. scattered, wasted —**dissi'pation** *n*. 1. scattering 2. frivolous, dissolute way of life

dissociate (di'sōshiāt, -si-) *v*. 1. separate —*vt*. 2. disconnect, sever —**dissoci'ation** *n*.

dissolute ('disəloŏt) *a*. lax in morals

dissolution (disə'loŏshən) *n*. 1. break-up 2. termination of parliament, meeting or legal relationship 3. destruction 4. death

dissolve (di'zolv) *vt*. 1. absorb or melt in fluid 2. break up, put an end to, annul —*vi*. 3. melt in fluid 4. disappear, vanish 5. break up, scatter —**dis'solvable** *a*. capable of being dissolved —**dis'solvent** *n*. thing with power to dissolve

dissonant ('disənənt) *a*. jarring, discordant —**'dissonance** *n*.

dissuade (di'swād) *vt*. advise to refrain, persuade not to do something —**dis'suasion** *n*. —**dis'suasive** *a*.

distaff ('distaf) *n*. cleft stick to hold wool *etc*. for spinning —**distaff side** maternal side, female line of family

distance ('distəns) *n*. 1. amount of space between two things 2. remoteness 3. aloofness, reserve —*vt*. 4. hold or place at distance —**'distant** *a*. 1. far off, remote 2. haughty, cold —**'distantly** *adv*.

distaste (dis'tāst) *n*. 1. dislike of food or drink 2. aversion, disgust —**dis'tasteful** *a*. unpleasant, displeasing to feelings —**dis'tastefully** *adv*. —**dis'tastefulness** *n*.

distemper (dis'tempər) *n*. 1. disease of dogs 2. method of painting on plaster without oil 3. paint used for this —*vt*. 4. paint with distemper

distend (di'stend) *v*. swell out by pressure from within, inflate —**dis'tensible** *a*. —**dis'tension** *n*.

distich ('distik) *n*. couplet

distill (dis'til) *vt*. 1. vaporize and recondense (a liquid) 2. purify, separate, concentrate (liquids) by this method 3. *fig.* extract quality of —*vi*. 4. trickle down —**'distillate** *n*. distilled liquid, *esp.* as fuel for some engines —**distil'lation** *n*. 1. distilling 2. process of evaporating or boiling liquid and condensing its vapor 3. purification or separation of mixture by using different evaporation rates or boiling points of their components 4. process of obtaining essence or extract of substance, usu. by heating in solvent 5. distillate 6. concentrated essence —**dis'tiller** *n*. one who distills, *esp.* manufacturer of alcoholic spirits —**dis'tillery** *n*.

distinct (di'stingkt) *a*. 1. clear, easily seen 2. definite 3. separate, different —**dis'tinction** *n*. 1. point of difference 2. act of distinguishing 3. eminence, repute, high honor, high quality —**dis'tinctive** a. characteristic —**dis'tinctly** adv. —**dis'tinctness** n.

distingué (dĕstĕ'gä) Fr. distinguished; noble

distinguish (di'stinggwish) vt. **1.** make difference in **2.** recognize, make out **3.** honor **4.** make prominent or honored (usu. refl.) **5.** class —vi. **6.** (usu. with between or among) draw distinction, grasp difference —**dis'tinguishable** a. —**dis'tinguished** a. **1.** noble, dignified **2.** famous, eminent

distort (di'stört) vt. **1.** put out of shape, deform **2.** misrepresent **3.** garble, falsify —**dis'tortion** n.

distract (di'strakt) vt. **1.** draw attention of (someone) away from work etc. **2.** divert **3.** perplex, bewilder **4.** drive mad —**dis'traction** n.

distraint (di'strānt) n. legal seizure of goods to enforce payment —**dis'train** vt. —**dis'trainment** n.

distrait (di'strā; Fr. dē'stre) a. **1.** absentminded **2.** abstracted

distraught (di'ströt) a. **1.** bewildered, crazed with grief **2.** frantic, distracted

distress (di'stres) n. **1.** severe trouble, mental pain **2.** severe pressure of hunger, fatigue or want **3.** Law distraint —vt. **4.** afflict, give mental pain —**dis'tressed** a. **1.** much troubled; upset; afflicted **2.** in financial straits; poor —**dis'tressful** a.

distribute (di'stribyət) vt. **1.** deal out, dispense **2.** spread, dispose at intervals **3.** classify —**distri'bution** n. —**dis'tributive** a. —**dis'tributor** n. rotary switch distributing electricity in engine —**distributive law 1.** in arithmetic, the rule that permits the multiplier to be applied separately to each term **2.** the rule that conjunction ('and') can be applied separately to each of the 2 members of a disjunction ('either-or')

district ('distrikt) n. **1.** region, locality **2.** portion of territory —**District of Columbia** (kə'lumbiə) postal district of Washington, the U.S. capital. Abbrev.: **DC** (with ZIP code)

disturb (di'stərb) vt. trouble, agitate, unsettle, derange —**dis'turbance** n. —**dis'turbed** a. Psych. emotionally or mentally unstable —**dis'turber** n.

disuse (dis'yōōs) n. state of being no longer used —**disused** (dis'yōōzd) a.

disyllable ('dīsiləbəl) n. word of two syllables —**disyl'labic** a.

ditch (dich) n. **1.** long narrow hollow dug in ground for drainage etc. —v. **2.** make ditch in **3.** run (car etc.) into ditch —vt. **4.** sl. abandon, discard

dither ('didhər) vi. **1.** be uncertain or indecisive —n. **2.** this state

dithyramb ('dithiram, -ramb) n. ancient Gr. hymn sung in honor of Dionysus —**dithy'rambic** a.

dittany ('ditəni) n. aromatic plant native to Greece

ditto ('ditō) n. **1.** the aforementioned; the above; the same: used in lists etc. to avoid repetition, and symbolized by two small marks („) placed under thing to be repeated **2.** inf. duplicate (pl. -s) —adv. **3.** in same way —interj. **4.** inf. used to avoid repeating or confirm agreement with preceding sentence —vt. **5.** copy; repeat (-**toing**, -**toed**)

ditty ('diti) n. simple song

diuretic (dīyə'retik) a. **1.** increasing the discharge of urine —n. **2.** substance with this property

diurnal (dī'ərnəl) a. **1.** daily **2.** in or of daytime **3.** taking a day

divalent (dī'vālənt) a. capable of combining with two atoms of hydrogen or their equivalent —**di'valency** n.

divan (di'van) n. **1.** bed, couch without back or head **2.** backless low cushioned seat

dive (dīv) vi. **1.** plunge under surface of water **2.** descend suddenly **3.** disappear **4.** go deep down **5.** rush or go quickly (**dove, dived, 'diving**) —n. **6.** act of diving **7.** sl. disreputable bar or club —**'diver** n. **1.** one who descends into deep water **2.** any of various kinds of diving bird —**dive bomber** aircraft which attacks after diving steeply —**diving bell** early diving submersible having open bottom and being supplied with compressed air —**diving board** platform or springboard from which swimmers may dive —**diving suit** waterproof suit used by divers, having heavy detachable helmet and air supply

diverge (di'vərj, dī-) vi. **1.** get farther apart **2.** separate —**di'vergence** or **di'vergency** n. —**di'vergent** a.

divers ('dīvərz) a. obs. some, various

diverse (dī'vərs, di-; 'dīvərs) a. different, varied —**di'versely** adv. —**diversifi'cation** n. —**di'versify** vt. **1.** make diverse or varied **2.** give variety to (-**ified, -ifying**) —**di'versity** n.

divert (di'vərt, dī-) vt. **1.** turn aside, ward off **2.** amuse, entertain —**di'version** n. **1.** a diverting **2.** official detour for traffic when main route is closed **3.** amusement —**di'verting** a.

diverticulosis (dīvərtikyoo'lōsis) n. the presence of pouches in the walls of the gastrointestinal tract

divertissement (di'vərtismənt) n. brief entertainment or diversion, usu. between acts of play

divest (dī'vest, di-) vt. **1.** unclothe, strip **2.** dispossess, deprive

divide (di'vīd) vt. **1.** make into two or more parts, split up, separate **2.** distribute, share **3.** classify —v. **4.** diverge in opinion —vi. **5.** become separated **6.** part into two groups for voting —n. **7.** watershed —**dividend** ('dividend) n. **1.** share of profits, of money divided among creditors etc. **2.** number to be divided by another —**di'viders** pl.n. measuring compasses

divine (di'vīn) a. **1.** of, pert. to, proceeding from, God **2.** sacred **3.** heavenly —n. **4.** theologian **5.** clergyman —vt. **6.** guess **7.** predict, foresee, tell by inspiration or magic —**divination** (divi'nāshən) n. divining —**di'vinely** adv. —**di'viner** n. —**divinity** (di'viniti) n. **1.** quality of being divine **2.** god **3.** theology —**divining rod** forked stick said to move when held over ground where water is present (also **dowsing rod**)

division (di'vizhən) n. **1.** act of dividing **2.** part of whole **3.** barrier **4.** section **5.** political constituency **6.** difference in opinion etc. **7.** Math. method of finding how many times one number is contained in another **8.** army unit **9.** separation, disunion —**di'visible** a. capable of division —**di'visional** a. —**divisive** (di'vīsiv) a. causing disagreement —**divisor** (di'vīzər) n. Math. number which divides dividend —**division sign** symbol ÷, placed between dividend and divisor to indicate division, as in 12 ÷ 6 = 2

divorce (di'vörs) n. **1.** legal dissolution of marriage **2.** complete separation, disunion —v. **3.** separate or be separated by divorce —vt. **4.** separate **5.** sunder —**divorcée** or (masc.) **divorcé** (divör'sā) n.

divot ('divət) n. piece of turf

divulge (di'vulj, dī-) vt. reveal, let out (secret) —**di'vulgence** n.

divvy ('divi) vt. inf. (esp. with up) divide and share

dixie ('diksi) n. **1.** inf. (military) cooking utensil or mess tin **2.** (D-) southern states of U.S.A. (also **'Dixieland**) —**'Dixieland** n. **1.** jazz derived from New Orleans tradition of playing, but with more emphasis on melody, regular rhythms etc. **2.** Dixie

D.I.Y. or **d.i.y.** do-it-yourself

dizzy ('dizi) a. **1.** feeling dazed, unsteady, as if about to fall **2.** causing or fit to cause dizziness, as speed etc. **3.** inf. silly —vt. **4.** make dizzy (**'dizzied, 'dizzying**) —**'dizzily** adv. —**'dizziness** n.

D.J. or **d.j.** disc jockey

djellaba or **djellabah** (jə'läbə) n. loose cloak with full sleeves and hood

Djibouti (ji'bōōti) n. country in Africa bounded northeast by the Gulf of Aden, southeast by Somalia and on all other sides by Ethiopia

djinni ('jēni), **djinn,** or **djin** (jin) n. see JINNI (pl. **djinn, djinns**)

dl deciliter

D.Litt. or **D.Lit. 1.** Doctor of Letters **2.** Doctor of Literature

dm decimeter

D.Mus. or **DMus** Doctor of Music

DNA deoxyribonucleic acids, nucleic acids responsible for preserving the information which guides the synthesis of proteins

do[1] (dōō; unstressed dŏŏ, də) vt. **1.** perform, effect, transact, bring about, finish **2.** work at **3.** work out, solve **4.** suit **5.** cover (distance) **6.** provide, prepare **7.** sl. cheat, swindle **8.** frustrate —vi. **9.** (oft. with for) look after **10.** act **11.** manage **12.** work **13.** fare **14.** serve, suffice **15.** happen —v. aux. **16.** makes negative and interrogative sentences and expresses emphasis (**did, done, 'doing**) —n. **17.** inf. celebration, festivity —**'doer** n. active or energetic person —**do-gooder** n. inf. well-intentioned person, esp. naive or impractical one —**do-it-yourself** n. hobby of constructing and repairing things oneself —**do away with** destroy —**do up 1.** fasten **2.** renovate —**do with 1.** need **2.** make use of —**do without** deny oneself

do[2] (dō) n. Mus. **1.** in fixed system of solmization, the note C **2.** in movable do system, the first note of a major scale

do. ditto (It., the same)

dobbin ('dobin) n. name for horse, esp. workhorse

Doberman pinscher ('dōbərmən 'pinchər) breed of working dog with glossy black-and-tan coat

doc (dok) n. inf. doctor

docile ('dosil) a. willing to obey, submissive —**do'cility** n.

dock[1] (dok) n. **1.** artificial enclosure near harbor for loading or repairing ships —v. **2.** (of vessel) put or go into dock **3.** (of spacecraft) link or be linked together in space —**'docker** n. one who works at docks, esp. loading etc. cargoes —**'dockyard** n. enclosure with docks, for building or repairing ships

dock[2] (dok) n. **1.** solid part of tail **2.** cut end, stump —vt. **3.** cut short (esp. tail) **4.** curtail, deduct (an amount) from

dock[3] (dok) n. enclosure in criminal court for prisoner

dock[4] (dok) n. coarse weed with broad leaves and long taproot used in folk medicine

docket ('dokit) n. **1.** piece of paper sent with package etc. with details of contents, delivery instructions etc. —vt. **2.** fix docket to

doctor ('doktər) n. **1.** medical practitioner **2.** one holding university's highest degree in any faculty —vt. **3.** treat medically **4.** repair, mend **5.** falsify (accounts *etc.*) **6.** *inf.* castrate, spay —**'doctoral** *a.* —**'doctorate** *n.*

doctrine ('doktrin) *n.* **1.** what is taught **2.** teaching of church, school or person **3.** belief, opinion, dogma —**doctri'naire** *n.* **1.** person who stubbornly applies theory without regard for circumstances —*a.* **2.** adhering to a doctrine in a stubborn, dogmatic way —**'doctrinal** *a.*

document ('dokyəmənt) *n.* **1.** piece of paper *etc.* providing information or evidence —*vt.* ('dokyəment) **2.** furnish with proofs, illustrations, certificates —**docu'mentary** *a./n. esp.* (of) type of film dealing with real life, not fiction —**documen'tation** *n.*

dodder[1] ('dodər) *vi.* totter or tremble, as with age —**'dodderer** *n.* feeble or inefficient person

dodder[2] ('dodər) *n.* any of genus of parasitic plants

dodecagon (dō'dekəgon) *n.* polygon having twelve sides

dodecahedron (dōdekə'hēdrən) *n.* solid figure having twelve plane faces

dodge (doj) *v.* **1.** avoid or attempt to avoid (blow, discovery *etc.*) as by moving quickly **2.** evade (questions) by cleverness —*n.* **3.** trick, artifice **4.** ingenious method **5.** act of dodging —**'dodger** *n.* shifty person —**'dodgy** *a. inf.* **1.** dangerous **2.** unreliable **3.** tricky

dodo ('dōdō) *n.* **1.** large extinct bird **2.** stupid or inept person (*pl.* **-s, -es**)

doe (dəu) *n.* female of deer, hare, rabbit —**'doeskin** *n.* **1.** skin of deer, lamb or sheep **2.** very supple leather made from this. **3.** heavy smooth cloth

doer ('dōōər) *n. see* DO[1]

does (duz) *third pers. sing., pres. ind. active of* DO[1]

doff (dof) *vt.* **1.** take off (hat, clothing) **2.** discard, lay aside

dog (dog) *n.* **1.** domestic mammal closely related to wolf with great differences in form **2.** male of wolf, fox and other animals **3.** person (in contempt, abuse or playfully) **4.** name given to various mechanical contrivances acting as holdfasts **5.** device with tooth which penetrates or grips object and detains it **6.** firedog —*vt.* **7.** follow steadily or closely (**-gg-**) —**dogged** ('dogid) *a.* persistent, resolute, tenacious —**'doggy** *a.* —**'doglike** *a.* —**'dogcart** *n.* open vehicle with crosswise back-to-back seats —**dog collar 1.** collar for dog **2.** *inf.* clerical collar **3.** *inf.* tight-fitting necklace —**dog days 1.** hot season of the rising of Dog Star **2.** period of inactivity —**dog-ear** *n.* **1.** turned-down corner of page in book —*vt.* **2.** turn down corners of (pages) —**'dogfight** *n.* **1.** skirmish between fighter planes **2.** savage contest characterized by disregard of rules —**'dogfish** *n.* very small species of shark —**'doghouse** *n.* **1.** kennel **2.** *inf.* disfavor (*esp. in* **in the doghouse**) —**dog in the manger** person who refuses to give up something that is of no use to him —**'dogleg** *n.* sharp bend or angle —**dog paddle** swimming stroke in which swimmer paddles his hands in imitation of swimming dog —**dog-paddle** *vi.* swim using dog paddle —**dog rose** European wild rose —**Dog Star** bright star in Sirius or Procyon —**dog tag** identification tag worn around neck by serviceperson —**dog-tired** *a. inf.* exhausted —**dog train C** sleigh drawn by dog team —**'dogwatch** *n.* in ships, short half-watch, 4-6, 6-8 p.m. —**'dogwood** *n.* any of various shrubs and trees —**go to the dogs** degenerate —**the dogs** greyhound race meeting

doge (dōj) *n.* formerly, chief magistrate in Venice

dogey ('dōgi) *n.* young calf

doggerel ('dogərəl) *n.* slipshod, unpoetic or trivial verse

doggo ('dogō) *adv.* —**lie doggo** *inf.* keep quiet, still, hidden

dogie ('dōgi) *n.* motherless calf (*pl.* **-gies**)

dogma ('dogmə) *n.* **1.** article of belief, *esp.* one laid down authoritatively by church **2.** body of beliefs (*pl.* **-s, -ata** (-ətə)) —**dog'matic(al)** *a.* **1.** asserting opinions with arrogance **2.** relating to dogma —**dog'matically** *adv.* —**'dogmatism** *n.* arrogant assertion of opinion —**'dogmatist** *n.* —**'dogmatize** *v.*

doily *or* **doyley** ('doili) *n.* small cloth, paper, piece of lace to place under cake, dish *etc.*

Dolby ('dolbi, 'dōl-) *n.* trade name for system used in tape recorders which reduces noise level on recorded or broadcast sound

dolce ('dōlchā) *a. Mus.* sweet

doldrums ('dōldrəmz, 'dol-) *pl.n.* **1.** state of depression, dumps **2.** region of light winds and calms near the equator

dole (dōl) *n.* **1.** charitable gift **2.** (*usu. with* the) *inf.* payment under unemployment insurance —*vt.* **3.** (*usu. with* out) deal out sparingly

doleful ('dōlfəl) *a.* dreary, mournful —**'dolefully** *adv.*

doll (dol) *n.* **1.** child's toy image of human being **2.** *sl.* attractive girl or woman —**doll up** dress up in latest fashion or smartly

dollar ('dolər) *n.* monetary unit of U.S. and many other countries —**dollar-a-year** *a.* earning token salary, usu. for public service —**dollar day** day on which seller offers goods for one dollar per item —**dollar diplomacy** the use of financial resources to enhance political transactions

dollop ('doləp) *n. inf.* semisolid lump

dolly ('doli) *n.* **1.** child's word for doll **2.** wheeled support for motion-picture or TV camera **3.** any of various metal devices used as aids in hammering, riveting

dolman sleeve ('dōlmən, 'dol-) sleeve that is wide at armhole and tapers to tight wrist

dolmen ('dōlmən, 'dol-) *n.* **1.** *see* CROMLECH (sense 1) **2.** stone table

dolomite ('dōləmīt, 'dol-) *n.* type of limestone

dolor ('dōlər, 'dol-) *n.* grief, sadness, distress —**'dolorous** *a.* —**'dolorously** *adv.*

dolphin ('dolfin) *n.* sea mammal, smaller than whale, with beaklike snout —**dolphi'narium** *n.* pool or aquarium for dolphins

dolt (dōlt) *n.* stupid fellow —**'doltish** *a.*

-dom (*comb. form*) **1.** state, condition, as in *freedom* **2.** rank, office or domain of, as in *earldom* **3.** collection of persons, as in *officialdom*

domain (də'mān) *n.* **1.** lands held or ruled over **2.** sphere, field of influence **3.** province

dome (dōm) *n.* **1.** rounded vault forming a roof **2.** something of this shape

Domesday Book ('dōōmzdā, 'dōmz-) record of survey of England in 1086

domestic (də'mestik) *a.* **1.** of, in the home **2.** home-loving **3.** (of animals) tamed, kept by man **4.** of, in one's own country, not foreign —*n.* **5.** house servant —**do'mesticate** *vt.* **1.** tame (animals) **2.** accustom to home life **3.** adapt to an environment —**domesti'cation** *n.* —**domes'ticity** *n.*

domicile ('domisīl) *n.* person's regular place of abode —**'domiciled** *a.* living —**domiciliary** (domi'silieri) *a.* of a dwelling place

dominate ('domināt) *vt.* **1.** rule, control, sway **2.** (of heights) overlook —*vi.* **3.** control, be the most powerful or influential member or part of something —**'dominant** *a./n.*

—**domi'nation** *n.* —**domi'neer** *vi.* act imperiously, tyrannize

Dominica (domi'nēkə) *n.* country in Caribbean Sea in the Windward group of the West Indies located between Martinique and Guadeloupe

Dominican (də'minikən) *n.* **1.** friar or nun of the order of St. Dominic —*a.* **2.** pert. to this order

Dominican Republic country in the West Indies occupying the eastern portion of the island of Hispaniola (the western portion forming the Republic of Haiti)

dominion (də'minyən) *n.* **1.** sovereignty, rule **2.** territory of government

Dominion Day *see* **Canada Day** *at* CANADA

dominoes ('dominōz) *pl.n.* **1.** (*with sing. v.*) any of several games in which matching halves of dominoes are laid together —*sing.* **2.** small rectangular block used in dominoes, divided on one side into 2 equal areas, each either blank or marked with one to six dots **3.** cloak with eye mask for masquerading —**domino theory** theory that event in one place, *esp.* political takeover, will influence occurrence of similar events elsewhere

don[1] (don) *vt.* put on (clothes) (**-nn-**)

don[2] (don) *n.* **1.** fellow or tutor of college **2.** Sp. title, Sir —**'donnish** *a.* of or resembling university don, *esp.* denoting pedantry or fussiness

Doña ('donyə) *n.* Sp. title of address equivalent to *Mrs.* or *Madam*

donate (dō'nāt) *v.* give —**do'nation** *n.* gift to fund —**'donor** *n.*

done (dun) *pp. of* DO[1]

Donegal tweed ('donigōl) tweed with colored flecks woven into the fabric

dong (dong) *n.* **1.** imitation of sound of bell —*vi.* **2.** make such sound

Don Juan ('don 'hwän, 'wän, 'jōōən) **1.** legendary Sp. nobleman and philanderer **2.** successful seducer of women

donkey ('dongki) *n.* ass (*pl.* **-s**) —**donkey engine** auxiliary engine —**donkey jacket** short, thick jacket, oft. worn by workmen —**donkey's years** *inf.* a long time —**donkeywork** *n.* drudgery

Donna ('donə) *n.* It. title of address equivalent to *Madam*

Don Quixote ('don kē'hōtē, 'kwiksət) impractical idealist

doodad ('dōōdad) *n.* **1.** small item whose common name is unknown or forgotten **2.** trivial ornament

doodle ('dōōdəl) *v.* **1.** scribble absentmindedly —*n.* **2.** picture *etc.* drawn aimlessly —**'doodlebug** *n.* **1.** *see* V-1 **2.** diviner's rod

doom (dōōm) *n.* **1.** fate, destiny **2.** ruin **3.** judicial sentence, condemnation **4.** the Last Judgment —*vt.* **5.** sentence, condemn **6.** destine to destruction or suffering —**'doomsday** *n.* the day of the Last Judgment

door (dör) *n.* hinged or sliding barrier to close any entrance —**'doorjamb** *n.* one of two vertical members forming sides of door frame (*also* **'doorpost**) —**'doorman** *n.* man employed to attend doors of certain buildings —**'doormat** *n.* **1.** mat at entrance for wiping shoes on **2.** *sl.* person who offers little resistance to ill-treatment —**'doorstop** *n.* any device which prevents open door from moving —**'doorway** *n.* entrance with or without door —**'dooryard** *n.* yard next to house door —**door to door 1.** (of selling *etc.*) from one house to next **2.** (of journeys *etc.*) direct

dopa ('dōpə) *n.* amino acid found in the broad bean: used for the treatment of Parkinson's disease

dope (dōp) *n.* 1. kind of varnish 2. drug, *esp.* illegal, narcotic drug 3. *inf.* information 4. *inf.* stupid person —*vt.* 5. drug (*esp.* racehorse) —'**dopey** *or* '**dopy** *a. inf.* 1. foolish 2. drugged 3. half asleep —**dope out** figure out

Doppelgänger ('dopəlgengər) *n. Legend* ghostly duplicate of living person

Doppler effect ('doplər) change in apparent frequency of sound or light wave *etc.* as result of relative motion between observer and source (*also* **Doppler shift**)

Doric ('dorik) *a.* 1. of the inhabitants of Doris, in ancient Greece, or their dialect —*n.* 2. dialect of Dorians 3. style of Gr. architecture 4. rustic dialect —**Dorian** ('dōriən) *a./n.* (member) of early Gr. race

dormant ('dörmənt) *a.* 1. not active, in state of suspension 2. sleeping —'**dormancy** *n.*

dormer ('dörmər) *n.* upright window set in sloping roof

dormitory ('dörmitöri) *n.* sleeping room with many beds —**dormitory town** town whose inhabitants travel elsewhere to work

dormouse ('dörmows) *n.* small hibernating mouselike rodent

dorp (dörp) *n.* SA small town

dorsal ('dörsəl) *a. Anat., zool.* of, on back

Dorset vinny ('dörsit 'vini), **Blue Dorset**, *or* **Blue vinny** hard, blue-veined cheese made from skimmed cow's milk orig. from England

dory ('döri) *n.* deep-bodied type of fish, *esp.* John Dory

dose (dōs) *n.* 1. amount (of drug *etc.*) administered at one time 2. *inf.* instance or period of something unpleasant, *esp.* disease —*vt.* 3. give doses to —'**dosage** *n.* —**do'simeter** *n.* device for measuring radiation

doss (dos) *inf. n.* 1. temporary bed —*vi.* 2. sleep in dosshouse 3. sleep —'**dosshouse** *n.* cheap lodging house

dossier ('dosyā) *n.* set of papers on some particular subject or event

dot[1] (dot) *n.* 1. small spot, mark —*vt.* 2. mark with dots 3. sprinkle 4. *sl.* hit (**-tt-**) —'**dotty** *a.* 1. *sl.* crazy 2. *sl.* (*with* about) extremely fond (of) 3. marked with dots —**dotted swiss** sheer crisp cotton fabric with woven dots

dot[2] (dot) *n.* dowry

dote (dōt) *vi.* 1. (*with* on *or* upon) be passionately fond (of) 2. be silly or weak-minded —'**dotage** *n.* senility —'**dotard** *n.* —'**doting** *a.* blindly affectionate

dotterel ('dotərəl) *n.* kind of plover

dottle ('dotəl) *n.* plug of tobacco left in pipe after smoking

Douay Version (dōō'ā) English translation of the Bible used by Roman Catholics

double ('dubəl) *a.* 1. of two parts, layers *etc.*, folded 2. twice as much or as many 3. of two kinds 4. designed for two users 5. ambiguous 6. deceitful —*adv.* 7. twice 8. to twice the amount or extent 9. in a pair —*n.* 10. person or thing exactly like, or mistakable for, another 11. quantity twice as much as another 12. sharp turn 13. running pace —*pl.* 14. game between 2 pairs of players —*v.* 15. make, become double 16. increase twofold 17. fold in two 18. get round, sail round (headland *etc.*) —*vi.* 19. turn sharply —'**doubly** *adv.* —**double agent** spy employed simultaneously by two opposing sides —**double-barreled** *a.* 1. (of gun) having two barrels 2. serving two purposes; ambiguous —**double bass** largest and lowest-toned instrument of violin family —**double boiler** saucepan in two detachable parts in which food in upper part is cooked slowly by water boiling in lower part —**double-breasted** *a.*

(of garment) having overlapping fronts —**double-check** *v.* check again; verify —**double check** 1. second examination or verification 2. *Chess* simultaneous check from two pieces —**double chin** fold of fat under chin —**double-cross** *vt.* cheat; betray —**double-crosser** *n.* —**double dagger** character (‡) used in printing to indicate cross-reference —**double-dealing** *n.* artifice, duplicity —**double-decker** *n.* thing or structure having two decks, layers or levels —**double-edged** *a.* 1. acting in two ways 2. (of remark *etc.*) having two possible interpretations 3. (of knife *etc.*) having cutting edge on either side of blade —**double entry** book-keeping system in which transaction is entered as debit in one account and as credit in another —**double exposure** accidental or deliberate repeat exposure of film, creating double image —**double helix** pair of parallel helices with common axis, *esp.* in structure of DNA molecule —**double indemnity** provision for payment of twice value of life-insurance policy in the event of accidental death —**double jeopardy** subjecting person to being tried twice for the same offense —**double-jointed** *a.* having unusually flexible joints permitting abnormal degree of motion —**double play** baseball play resulting in two players' being put out —**double pneumonia** pneumonia affecting both lungs —**double-quick** *a./adv.* very fast —**double standard** set of principles that allows greater freedom to one person or group than another —**double take** delayed reaction to a remark, situation *etc.* —**double talk** 1. rapid speech with mixture of nonsense syllables and real words; gibberish 2. empty, deceptive or ambiguous talk —'**doublethink** *n.* accepting as true two different versions of a factual matter at the same time by disciplining the mind to ignore the inconsistency between them —**double time** 1. doubled wage rate for working on public holidays *etc.* 2. *Mus.* two beats per bar 3. *U.S. Army* fast march; slow running pace, keeping in step —**double or nothing** a gamble on paying twice the amount risked or nothing at all

double entendre (än'tändrə) word or phrase with two meanings, one usu. indelicate

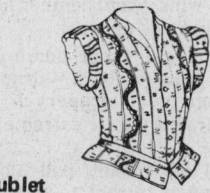

doublet

doublet ('dublit) *n.* 1. close-fitting body garment formerly worn by men 2. one of two words from same root but differing in form and usu. in meaning, as *warden* and *guardian* 3. false gem of thin layer of gemstone fused on to base of glass *etc.*

doubloon (du'blōōn) *n.* ancient Sp. gold coin

doubt (dowt) *vt.* 1. hesitate to believe 2. call into question 3. suspect —*vi.* 4. be wavering or uncertain in belief or opinion —*n.* 5. uncertainty, wavering in belief 6. state of affairs giving cause for uncertainty —'**doubter** *n.* —'**doubtful** *a.* —'**doubtfully** *adv.* —'**doubtless** *adv./a.*

douche (dōōsh) *n.* 1. jet or spray of water applied to (part of) body —*vt.* 2. give douche to

dough (dō) *n.* 1. flour or meal kneaded with water 2. *sl.* money —'**doughy** *a.* —'**doughnut**

n. sweetened and fried ball or ring-shaped piece of dough

doughty ('dowti) *a.* valiant —'**doughtily** *adv.* —'**doughtiness** *n.* boldness

dour (dōōr) *a.* grim, stubborn, severe

douse *or* **dowse** (dows, dowz) *vt.* 1. thrust into water 2. extinguish (light)

dovecote

dove (duv) *n.* bird of pigeon family —**dovecot** ('duvkot) *or* **dovecote** ('duvkōt, -kot) *n.* house for doves —'**dovetail** *n.* 1. joint made with fan-shaped tenon —*v.* 2. fit closely, neatly, firmly together

dowager ('dowəjər) *n.* widow with title or property derived from deceased husband

dowdy ('dowdi) *a.* 1. unattractively or shabbily dressed —*n.* 2. woman so dressed

dowel ('dowəl) *n.* wooden, metal peg, *esp.* joining two adjacent parts

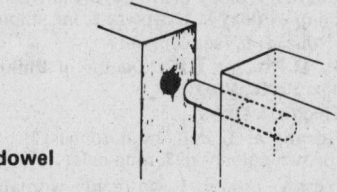

dowel

dower ('dowər) *n.* 1. widow's share for life of husband's estate —*vt.* 2. endow —'**dowry** *n.* 1. property wife brings to husband at marriage 2. any endowment

Dow-Jones average (dow'jōnz) *Fin.* index compiled from relative daily movement of prices of selected common stocks

down[1] (down) *adv.* 1. to, in, or toward, lower position 2. below the horizon 3. (of payment) on the spot, immediate —*prep.* 4. from higher to lower part of 5. at lower part of 6. along —*a.* 7. depressed, miserable —*vt.* 8. knock, pull, push down 9. *inf.* drink, *esp.* quickly —'**downward** *a./adv.* —'**downwards** *adv.* —'**downcast** *a.* 1. dejected 2. looking down —'**downer** *n.* depressant, *esp.* barbiturate —'**downfall** *n.* 1. sudden loss of health, reputation *etc.* 2. fall of rain, snow *etc.*, *esp.* sudden heavy one —'**downgrade** *vt.* 1. reduce in importance or value, *esp.* to demote (person) to poorer job 2. speak of disparagingly —*n.* 3. *chiefly* US downward slope —**down'hearted** *a.* discouraged; dejected —'**down'hill** *a.* 1. going or sloping down —*adv.* 2. toward bottom of hill; downward —*n.* 3. downward slope of hill; descent 4. skiing race downhill —**down payment** deposit paid on item purchased on hire-purchase *etc.* —'**downpour** *n.* heavy fall of rain —'**downright** *a.* 1. plain, straightforward —*adv.* 2. quite, thoroughly —'**down'stage** *a./adv.* at, to front of stage —'**down'stairs** *adv.* 1. down the stairs; to or on lower floor —*n.* 2. lower or ground floor 3. UK *inf.* servants of household collectively —'**down'stream** *adv./a.* in or toward lower part of stream; with current —**down-to-earth** a. sensible; practical; realistic —**'downtrodden** a. 1. subjugated; oppressed 2. trodden down —**'down'wind** adv./a. in same direction toward which wind is blowing; with wind from behind —**down and out** finished, defeated —**down under** inf. Australia and New Zealand —**go downhill** inf. decline; deteriorate —**have a down on** inf. have grudge against —**on the downgrade** waning in importance etc.

down² (down) n. 1. soft underfeathers, hair or fiber 2. fluff —**'downy** a.

down³ (down) n. obs. hill, esp. sand dune (also **downs**) —**'downland** n. open high land (also **downs**)

Downing Street ('downing) 1. street in London: official residences of prime minister of Great Britain and chancellor of the exchequer 2. inf. prime minister; British Government

Down's syndrome (downz) Pathol. chromosomal abnormality resulting in flat face and nose, short stubby fingers, vertical fold of skin at inner edge of eye and mental retardation (also **mongolism**)

dowry ('dowri) n. see DOWER

dowse (dowz) vi. use divining rod —**'dowser** n. water diviner —**dowsing rod** divining rod

doxology (dok'soləji) n. short hymn of praise to God

doyen ('doiən) n. senior member of a body or profession (**doyenne** (doi'en) fem.)

doyley ('doili) n. see DOILY

doz. dozen

doze (dōz) vi. 1. sleep drowsily, be half-asleep —n. 2. nap —**'dozy** a. 1. drowsy 2. inf. stupid

dozen ('duzən) n. (set of) twelve

D.Phil., D.Ph., or **DPh** Doctor of Philosophy (also **Ph.D., PhD**)

Dr. 1. Doctor 2. Drive

drab¹ (drab) a. 1. dull, monotonous 2. of a dingy brown color —n. 3. mud color

drab² (drab) obs. n. 1. slatternly woman 2. whore —vi. 3. consort with prostitutes (**-bb-**)

drachma ('drakmə) n. monetary unit of Greece (pl. **-s, -mae** (-mē))

Draconian (drā'kōniən) a. (oft. **d-**) 1. like the laws of Draco 2. very harsh, cruel

draft (draft, dräft) n. 1. current of air between apertures in room etc. 2. act or action of drawing 3. dose of medicine 4. act of drinking 5. quantity drunk at once 6. inhaling 7. depth of ship in water 8. the drawing in of, or fish taken in, net 9. preliminary plan or layout for work to be executed 10. design, sketch 11. rough copy of document 12. order for money 13. detachment of men, esp. troops, reinforcements —vt. 14. make sketch, plan or rough design of 15. make rough copy of (writing etc.) 16. select for compulsory military service —v. 17. detach (military personnel) from one unit to another —a. 18. for drawing 19. drawn —**'drafty** a. full of air currents —**draft horse** horse for vehicles carrying heavy loads —**'draftsman** n. one who makes drawings, plans etc. —**'draftsmanship** n.

drag (drag) vt. 1. pull along with difficulty or friction 2. trail on ground 3. sweep with net or grapnels 4. protract —vi. 5. lag, trail 6. (oft. with on or out) be tediously protracted (**-gg-**) —n. 7. check on progress 8. checked motion 9. iron shoe to check wheel 10. type of carriage 11. lure for hounds to hunt 12. kind of harrow 13. sledge, net, grapnel, rake 14. inf. tedious person or thing 15. sl. women's clothes worn by man (esp. **in in drag**) —**'dragnet** n. 1. fishing net to be dragged along sea floor 2. comprehensive

search, esp. by police for criminal etc. —**'dragster** n. automobile designed, modified for drag racing —**drag race** race where automobiles are timed over measured distance —**drag racing**

draggle ('dragəl) v. 1. make or become wet or dirty by trailing on ground —vi. 2. lag; dawdle

dragoman ('dragəmən) n. in some Middle Eastern countries, esp. formerly, professional interpreter or guide (pl. **-s, -men**)

dragon ('dragən) n. 1. mythical fire-breathing monster, like winged crocodile 2. type of large lizard —**'dragonfly** n. long-bodied insect with gauzy wings

dragoon (drə'gōōn) n. 1. cavalryman of certain regiments —vt. 2. oppress 3. coerce

drain (drān) vt. 1. draw off (liquid) by pipes, ditches etc. 2. dry 3. drink to dregs 4. empty, exhaust —vi. 5. flow off or away 6. become rid of liquid —n. 7. channel for removing liquid 8. sewer 9. depletion, strain —**'drainage** n. —**'drainboard** n. sloping grooved surface at side of sink for draining washed dishes etc. (also **'drainer**) —**'drainpipe** n. pipe for carrying off rainwater etc. —**drainpipe trousers** or **'drainpipes** pl.n. trousers with narrow legs

drake (drāk) n. male duck

Dralon ('drālon) n. trade name for acrylic fiber, esp. as velvet for draperies and upholstery

dram (dram) n. 1. small draft of strong drink 2. see **fluid dram** at FLUID

drama ('drämə) n. 1. stage play 2. art or literature of plays 3. playlike series of events —**dra'matic** a. 1. pert. to drama 2. suitable for stage representation 3. with force and vividness of drama 4. striking 5. tense 6. exciting —**'dramatist** n. writer of plays —**dramati'zation** n. —**'dramatize** vt. adapt (novel) for acting

Dramamine ('draməmēn) n. trade name for dimenhydrinate, an antihistamine used to treat and prevent motion sickness

dramatis personae ('drämətis pər'sōnē) characters in play

dramaturgy ('dramətərji) n. technique of writing and producing plays —**drama'turgic(al)** a. —**'dramaturge** n. playwright

Drambuie (dram'bōōi) n. Scottish liqueur made from whisky and heather honey

drank (drangk) pt. of DRINK

drape (drāp) vt. 1. cover, adorn with cloth 2. arrange in graceful folds —**'draper** n. dealer in cloth, linen etc. —**'drapery** n.

drastic ('drastik) a. 1. extreme, forceful 2. severe

draw (drö) vt. 1. pull, pull along, haul 2. inhale 3. entice, attract 4. delineate, portray with pencil etc. 5. frame, compose, draft, write 6. bring (upon, out etc.) 7. get by lot 8. (of ship) require (depth of water) 9. take from (well, barrel etc.) 10. receive (money) 11. bend (bow) —vi. 12. pull, shrink 13. make, admit current of air 14. make pictures with pencil etc. 15. finish game with equal points, goals etc., tie 16. write orders for money 17. come, approach (near) (**drew** pt., **drawn** pp.) —n. 18. act of drawing 19. casting of lots 20. game or contest ending in a tie —**'drawable** a. —**drawer** ('dröər) n. 1. one who or that which draws 2. (drör) sliding box in table or chest —pl. (drörz) 2-legged undergarment —**'drawing** n. 1. art of depicting in line 2. sketch so done 3. art of making drawings —**'drawback** n. anything that takes away from satisfaction; snag —**'drawbridge** n. hinged bridge that can be raised or lowered —**drawing account** money available in

advance of actual earnings esp. for traveling expenses —**drawing room** 1. formal reception room in house 2. private room in railroad car —**'drawstring** n. cord etc. run through hem around opening, so that when it is pulled tighter, the opening closes —**draw near** approach —**draw out** lengthen —**draw up** 1. arrange 2. stop

drawl (dröl) v. 1. speak or utter (words) slowly —n. 2. such speech —**'drawlingly** adv.

drawn (drön) v. 1. pp. of DRAW —a. 2. haggard, tired or tense in appearance

dray (drā) n. low cart without sides for heavy loads

dread (dred) vt. 1. fear greatly —n. 2. awe, terror —a. 3. feared, awful —**'dreadful** a. disagreeable, shocking, bad —**'dreadnought** n. large battleship mounting heavy guns

dream (drēm) n. 1. vision during sleep 2. fancy 3. reverie 4. aspiration 5. very pleasant idea, person, thing —vi. 6. have dreams —vt. 7. see, imagine in dreams 8. think of as possible (**dreamt** (dremt) or **dreamed** pt./pp.) —**'dreamer** n. —**'dreamless** a. —**'dreamy** a. 1. given to daydreams, unpractical, vague 2. inf. wonderful

dreary ('drēəri) a. dismal, dull —**drear** a. Lit. dreary —**'drearily** adv. —**'dreariness** n. gloom

dreck (drek) n. inf. cheap, worthless trash

dredge¹ (drej) v. 1. bring up (mud etc.) from sea bottom 2. deepen (channel) by dredge —vt. 3. search for, produce (obscure, remote, unlikely material) —n. 4. form of scoop or grab —**'dredger** n. ship for dredging

dredge² (drej) vt. sprinkle with flour etc. —**'dredger** n.

dregs (dregz) pl.n. 1. sediment, grounds 2. worthless part

drench (drench) vt. 1. wet thoroughly, soak 2. make (animal) take dose of medicine —n. 3. soaking 4. dose for animal

Dresden ('drezdən) n. 1. city in East Germany 2. delicate and decorative porcelain ware made near Dresden (also **Dresden china**) —a. 3. of Dresden china

dress (dres) vt. 1. clothe 2. array for show 3. trim, smooth, prepare surface of 4. prepare (food) for table 5. put dressing on (wound) 6. align (troops) —vi. 7. put on one's clothes 8. form in proper line —n. 9. one-piece garment for woman 10. clothing 11. clothing for ceremonial evening wear —**'dresser** n. 1. one who dresses, esp. actors or actresses 2. surgeon's assistant 3. kitchen sideboard —**'dressing** n. 1. something applied to something else, as sauce to food, ointment to wound, manure to land etc. 2. inf. scolding, as in dressing down —**'dressy** a. 1. stylish 2. fond of dress —**dress coat** cutaway coat worn by men as evening dress —**dressing room** room, esp. one in theater for changing costumes and make-up —**dressing station** Mil. first-aid post close to combat area —**dressing table** —**'dressmaker** n. —**dress rehearsal** 1. last rehearsal of play etc. using costumes etc. as for first night 2. any full-scale practice —**dress suit** man's evening suit, esp. tails

dressage (drə'säzh) n. method of training horse in special maneuvers to show obedience

drew (drōō) pt. of DRAW

dribble ('dribəl) v. 1. (allow to) flow in drops, trickle 2. work (basketball) forward with continuous bounces —vi. 3. run at the mouth —n. 4. trickle, drop —**'driblet** n. small portion or installment

dried (drīd) pt./pp. of DRY

drier ('drīər) *comp. of* DRY

driest ('drīist) *sup. of* DRY

drift (drift) *vi.* **1.** be carried as by current of air, water **2.** move aimlessly or passively —*n.* **3.** process of being driven by current **4.** slow current or course **5.** deviation from course **6.** tendency **7.** meaning **8.** wind-heaped mass of snow, sand *etc.* **9.** material driven or carried by water —'**drifter** *n.* **1.** one who, that which drifts **2.** *inf.* aimless person with no fixed job *etc.* —'**driftwood** *n.* wood washed ashore by sea

drill¹ (dril) *n.* **1.** boring tool or machine **2.** exercise of soldiers or others in handling of arms and maneuvers **3.** routine teaching —*v.* **4.** bore, pierce (hole) in (material) (as if) with drill **5.** exercise in military and other routine —*vi.* **6.** practice routine

drill² (dril) *n.* **1.** machine for sowing seed **2.** small furrow for seed **3.** row of plants —*v.* **4.** sow (seed) in drills or furrows

drill³ (dril) *n.* coarsely woven twilled fabric

drill⁴ (dril) *n.* W Afr. monkey

drink (dringk) *v.* **1.** swallow (liquid) **2.** take (intoxicating liquor), *esp.* to excess —*vt.* **3.** absorb (**drank** *pt.*, **drunk** *pp.*) —*n.* **4.** liquid for drinking **5.** portion of this **6.** act of drinking **7.** intoxicating liquor or excessive consumption of it —'**drinkable** *a.* —'**drinker** *n.* —**drink to** *or* **drink the health of** express good wishes *etc.* by drinking a toast to

drip (drip) *v.* **1.** fall or let fall in drops (-**pp**-) —*n.* **2.** act of dripping **3.** drop **4.** *Med.* intravenous administration of solution **5.** *inf.* dull, insipid person —'**dripping** *n.* **1.** melted fat that drips from roasting meat —*a.* **2.** very wet —**drip-dry** *a.* (of fabric) drying free of creases if hung up while wet —'**dripstone** *n.* projection over window or door to stop dripping of water

drive (drīv) *vt.* **1.** urge in some direction **2.** make move and steer (vehicle, animal *etc.*) **3.** urge, impel **4.** fix by blows, as nail **5.** chase **6.** convey in vehicle **7.** hit (ball) with force as in golf, tennis —*vi.* **8.** keep machine, animal going, steer it **9.** be conveyed in vehicle **10.** rush, dash, drift fast (**drove, driven** ('drivən), '**driving**) —*n.* **11.** act, action of driving **12.** journey in vehicle **13.** private road leading to house **14.** capacity for getting things done **15.** united effort, campaign **16.** means by which automobile is propelled **17.** forceful stroke or sustained effort —'**driver** *n.* **1.** one that drives **2.** *Golf* club used for tee shots —**drive-in** *a.* **1.** denoting public facility or service designed for use by patrons in cars —*n.* **2.** establishment designed to be used in such a manner —**driver's license** official document authorizing person to drive motor vehicle —'**driveway** *n.* path for vehicles, oft. connecting house with public road —**driving belt** belt that communicates motion to machinery

drivel ('drivəl) *vi.* **1.** run at mouth or nose **2.** talk nonsense —*n.* **3.** silly or senseless talk —'**driveler** *n.*

drizzle ('drizəl) *vi.* **1.** rain in fine drops —*n.* **2.** fine, light rain

drogue (drōg) *n.* **1.** any funnel-like device, *esp.* of canvas, used as sea anchor **2.** small parachute **3.** wind indicator **4.** windsock towed behind target aircraft **5.** funnel-shaped device on end of refueling hose of tanker aircraft to receive probe of aircraft being refueled

droll (drōl) *a.* funny, odd, comical —'**drollery** *n.* —'**drolly** *adv.*

dromedary ('droməderi, 'drum-) *n.* one-humped camel bred *esp.* for racing

drone (drōn) *n.* **1.** male of honey bee **2.** lazy idler **3.** deep humming **4.** bass pipe of bagpipe **5.** its note —*vi.* **6.** hum **7.** talk in monotonous tone

drongo ('dronggō) *n.* black tropical bird

drool (drōōl) *vi.* slaver, drivel

droop (drōōp) *vi.* **1.** hang down **2.** wilt, flag —*vt.* **3.** let hang down —*n.* **4.** drooping condition —'**droopy** *a.*

drop (drop) *n.* **1.** globule of liquid **2.** very small quantity **3.** fall, descent **4.** distance through which thing falls **5.** thing that falls, as gallows platform —*vt.* **6.** let fall **7.** let fall in drops **8.** utter casually **9.** set down, unload **10.** discontinue —*vi.* **11.** fall **12.** fall in drops **13.** lapse **14.** come or go casually (-**pp**-) —'**droplet** *n.* —'**dropper** *n.* **1.** small tube having bulb at one end for dispensing drops of liquid **2.** person or thing that drops —'**droppings** *pl.n.* dung of rabbits, sheep, birds *etc.* —'**dropout** *n.* person who fails to complete course of study or one who rejects conventional society

dropsy ('dropsi) *n. see* EDEMA —'**dropsical** *a.*

droshky ('droshki) *or* **drosky** ('droski) *n.* open four-wheeled carriage, formerly used in Russia

dross (dros) *n.* **1.** scum of molten metal **2.** impurity, refuse **3.** anything of little or no value

drought (drowt) *n.* long spell of dry weather

drove¹ (drōv) *pt. of* DRIVE

drove² (drōv) *n.* **1.** herd, flock, crowd, *esp.* in motion —*v.* **2.** drive (cattle *etc.*) *esp.* a long distance —'**drover** *n.* driver of cattle

drown (drown) *v.* **1.** die from suffocation caused by water in the lungs —*vt.* **2.** get rid of as by submerging in liquid **3.** (*sometimes with* out) make (sound) inaudible by louder sound

drowsy ('drowzi) *a.* **1.** half asleep **2.** lulling **3.** dull —**drowse** *v.* —'**drowsily** *adv.* —'**drowsiness** *n.*

drub (drub) *vt.* thrash, beat (-**bb**-) —'**drubbing** *n.* beating

drudge (druj) *vi.* **1.** work at menial or distasteful tasks, slave —*n.* **2.** one who drudges, hack —'**drudgery** *n.*

drug (drug) *n.* **1.** substance used in the treatment of disease **2.** narcotic **3.** commodity which is unsalable because of overproduction —*vt.* **4.** mix drugs with **5.** administer drug to, *esp.* one inducing unconsciousness (-**gg**-) —**drug abuse** compulsive use of substances capable of causing harm, *esp.* narcotics, stimulants, chemical solvents —**drug addict** person abnormally dependent on drugs —'**drugstore** *n.* pharmacy where wide variety of goods is available

drugget ('drugit) *n.* coarse woolen fabric, *esp.* used for carpeting

druid ('drōōid) *n.* (*sometimes* D-) **1.** member of ancient order of Celtic priests **2.** Eisteddfod official —**dru'idic(al)** *a.* —'**druidism** *n.*

drum (drum) *n.* **1.** percussion instrument of skin stretched over round hollow frame, played by beating with sticks **2.** any of various things shaped like drum **3.** eardrum —*vi.* **4.** play drum —*v.* **5.** tap, thump continuously (-**mm**-) —'**drummer** *n.* one who plays drum —'**drumfire** *n.* heavy continuous rapid artillery fire —**drum major** leader of marching band —**drum majorette** (mājə'ret) **1.** girl or woman who leads a marching band **2.** baton twirler accompanying a marching band —'**drumstick** *n.* **1.** stick for beating drum **2.** lower joint of cooked fowl's leg —**drum out** expel (from club *etc.*) —**drum up** obtain (support *etc.*) by solicitation or canvassing

drunk (drungk) *a.* **1.** overcome by strong drink **2.** *fig.* overwhelmed by strong emotion —*v.* **3.** *pp. of* DRINK —'**drunkard** *n.* one given to excessive drinking —'**drunken** *a.* **1.** intoxicated **2.** habitually drunk **3.** caused by, showing intoxication —'**drunkenness** *n.*

drupe (drōōp) *n.* fruit that has fleshy or fibrous part around stone that encloses seed, as peach *etc.*

dry (drī) *a.* **1.** without moisture **2.** rainless **3.** not yielding milk or other liquid **4.** cold, unfriendly **5.** caustically witty **6.** having prohibition of alcoholic drink **7.** uninteresting **8.** needing effort to study **9.** lacking sweetness (as wines) **10.** (of fruit) without fleshy walls, *eg* peas, beans, nuts —*vt.* **11.** remove water, moisture from —*vi.* **12.** become dry **13.** evaporate (**dried, 'drying**) —'**dryer** *or* '**drier** *n.* **1.** person or thing that dries **2.** apparatus for removing moisture —'**dryly** *or* '**drily** *adv.* —'**dryness** *n.* —**dry battery** electric battery without liquid —**dry cell** primary cell in which electrolyte is in form of paste or is treated in some way to prevent spilling —**dry-clean** *vt.* clean (clothes) with solvent other than water —**dry-cleaner** *n.* —**dry dock** dock that can be pumped dry for work on ship's bottom —**dry farming** methods of producing crops in areas of low rainfall —**dry fly** *Angling* artificial fly designed to be floated on surface of water —**dry ice** solid carbon dioxide —**dry measure** unit or system of units for measuring dry goods, such as grains *etc.* —**dry point 1.** needle for engraving without acid **2.** engraving so made —**dry rot** fungoid decay in wood —**dry run** practice, rehearsal in simulated conditions —**drystone** *a.* (of wall) made without mortar —**dry out 1.** make or become dry **2.** *inf.* (cause to) undergo treatment for alcoholism or drug addiction

dryad ('drīəd, -ad) *n.* wood nymph

dryly ('drīli) *adv. see* DRY

D.Sc. Doctor of Science

D.S.C. Distinguished Service Cross

D.S.M. *Mil.* Distinguished Service Medal

D.S.O. Distinguished Service Order

D.T.'s *inf.* delirium tremens

dual ('dyōōəl, 'dōō-) *a.* **1.** twofold **2.** of two, double, forming pair —'**dualism** *n.* recognition of two independent powers or principles, *eg* good and evil, mind and matter —**du'ality** *n.*

dub (dub) *vt.* **1.** confer knighthood on **2.** give title to **3.** provide (motion picture) with soundtrack not in original language **4.** smear with grease, dubbin (-**bb**-) —'**dubbin** *or* '**dubbing** *n.* grease for making leather supple

dubious ('dyōōbiəs, 'dōō-) *a.* **1.** causing doubt, not clear or decided **2.** of suspect character —**du'biety** *n.* uncertainty, doubt

ducal ('dyōōkəl, 'dōō-) *a.* of duke or duchy

ducat ('dukət) *n.* former gold coin of Italy *etc.*

duchess ('duchis) *n.* duke's wife, ex-wife or widow

duchy ('duchi) *n.* territory of duke, dukedom

duck¹ (duk) *n.* **1.** common swimming bird (**drake** *masc.*) —*v.* **2.** plunge (someone) under water **3.** bob down —'**duckling** *n.* —**duck-billed platypus** aquatic burrowing egg-laying mammal of Aust. and Tasmania with dense fur, bony ducklike beak and flattened tail —'**duckweed** *n.* plant that floats on ponds *etc.*

duck² (duk) *n.* **1.** strong linen or cotton fabric —*pl.* **2.** trousers made of this fabric

duck[3] (duk) *n.* amphibious vehicle used in World War II

duct (dukt) *n.* channel, tube —**ductile** ('duktil) *a.* **1.** capable of being drawn into wire **2.** flexible and tough **3.** docile —**duc'tility** *n.* —**'ductless** *a.* (of glands) secreting directly certain substances essential to health

dud (dud) *n.* **1.** futile, worthless person or thing **2.** shell that fails to explode —*a.* **3.** worthless

dude (dyōōd, dōōd) *n.* tourist, *esp.* in ranch district —**dude ranch** ranch serving as guesthouse and showplace

dudgeon ('dujən) *n.* anger, indignation, resentment

duds (dudz) *pl.n. inf.* clothes

due (dyōō, dōō) *a.* **1.** owing **2.** proper to be given, inflicted *etc.* **3.** adequate, fitting **4.** under engagement to arrive, be present **5.** timed (for) —*adv.* **6.** (with points of compass) exactly —*n.* **7.** person's right **8.** (*usu. pl.*) charge, fee *etc.* —**'duly** *adv.* **1.** properly **2.** fitly **3.** rightly **4.** punctually —**due to 1.** attributable to **2.** caused by

duel ('dyōōəl, 'dōōəl) *n.* **1.** arranged fight with deadly weapons, between two persons **2.** keen two-sided contest —*vi.* **3.** fight in duel —**'duelist** *or* **'duellist** *n.*

duenna (dyōō'enə, dōō-) *n.* older woman acting as companion and chaperone, *esp.* to younger woman in Spanish or Portuguese household

duet (dyōō'et, dōō-) *n.* piece of music for two performers —**du'ettist** *n.*

duff[1] (duf) *n.* kind of boiled pudding

duff[2] (duf) *vt.* **1.** manipulate, alter (article) so as to make it look like new **2.** mishit, *esp.* at golf —*a.* **3.** *sl.* bad, useless

duffel *or* **duffle** ('dufəl) *n.* **1.** coarse woolen cloth **2.** coat made of this —**duffel bag** large cylindrical cloth bag for clothing *etc.*

duffer ('dufər) *n.* stupid inefficient person

dug[1] (dug) *pt./pp. of* DIG

dug[2] (dug) *n.* udder, teat of animal

dugong ('dōōgong) *n.* whalelike mammal of tropical seas

dugout ('dugowt) *n.* **1.** covered excavation to provide shelter for troops *etc.* **2.** canoe of hollowed-out tree **3.** *Sport* covered enclosure where players wait when not on the field

duiker *or* **duyker** ('dīkər) *n.* small Afr. antelope (*also* **'duikerbok**)

duke (dyōōk, dōōk) *n.* **1.** nobleman of high rank **2.** sovereign of small state called duchy ('duchess *fem.*) —**'dukedom** *n.*

dukes (dyōōks, dōōks) *pl.n. sl.* fists

dulcet ('dulsit) *a.* (of sounds) sweet, melodious

dulcimer ('dulsimər) *n.* percussion instrument consisting of set of strings stretched over sounding board, played with two hammers

dull (dul) *a.* **1.** stupid **2.** insensible **3.** sluggish **4.** tedious **5.** lacking liveliness or variety **6.** gloomy, overcast —*v.* **7.** make or become dull —**'dullard** *n.* —**'dully** *adv.*

duly ('dyōōli, 'dōō-) *adv. see* DUE

dumb (dum) *a.* **1.** incapable of speech **2.** silent **3.** *inf.* stupid —**'dumbly** *adv.* —**'dumbness** *n.* —**'dumbbell** *n.* weight for exercises —**dumb'found** *vt.* confound into silence —**dumb show** acting without words —**'dumbwaiter** *n.* **1.** stand placed near dining table to hold food; revolving circular tray placed on table to hold food **2.** small elevator, usu. hand-operated, for conveying food and dishes between floors

dumdum ('dumdum) *n.* soft-nosed expanding bullet

dummy ('dumi) *n.* **1.** tailor's or dressmaker's model **2.** imitation object **3.** bridge hand exposed on table and played by partner **4.** one secretly acting for another **5.** figure used by football players for tackling practice **6.** prototype of book, indicating appearance of finished product; designer's layout of page —*a.* **7.** sham, bogus —**dummy run** experimental run; practice; rehearsal

dump (dump) *vt.* **1.** throw down in mass **2.** deposit **3.** unload **4.** send (low-priced goods) for sale abroad —*n.* **5.** refuse heap **6.** *inf.* dirty, unpleasant place **7.** temporary depot of stores or munitions —*pl.* **8.** low spirits, dejection

dumpling ('dumpling) *n.* small round pudding of dough, oft. fruity —**'dumpy** *a.* short, stout —**dumpy level** surveyor's leveling instrument

dun[1] (dun) *vt.* **1.** persistently press (debtor) for payment of debts (**-nn-**) —*n.* **2.** one who duns

dun[2] (dun) *a.* **1.** of dull grayish brown —*n.* **2.** this color **3.** horse of this color

dunce (duns) *n.* slow learner, stupid pupil

dunderhead ('dundərhed) *n.* blockhead —**'dunderheaded** *a.*

dune (dyōōn, dōōn) *n.* sand hill on coast or in desert

dung (dung) *n.* **1.** excrement of animals; manure —*vt.* **2.** manure (ground) —**'dunghill** *n.* **1.** heap of dung **2.** foul place, condition or person

dungaree (dunggə'rē) *n.* **1.** coarse cotton fabric —*pl.* **2.** overalls made of this material

dungeon ('dunjən) *n.* **1.** underground cell or vault for prisoners, donjon **2.** formerly, tower or keep of castle

dunk (dungk) *vt.* **1.** dip (bread *etc.*) in liquid before eating it **2.** submerge

dunlin ('dunlin) *n.* small sandpiper

dunnage ('dunij) *n.* material for packing cargo

dunnock ('dunək) *n.* hedge sparrow

duo ('dyōōō, 'dōōō) *n.* pair of performers (*pl.* **-s, dui** ('dyōōē, 'dōōē))

duodecimo (dyōōō'desimō, dōōō-) *n.* **1.** size of book in which each sheet is folded into 12 leaves **2.** book of this size (*pl.* **-s**) —*a.* **3.** of this size —**duo'decimal** *a.* —**duodecimal system** numeration system whose base is 12, the numbers 10 and 11 being denoted by special symbols and regarded as digits

duodenum (dyōōō'dēnəm, dōōō-) *n.* upper part of small intestine —**duo'denal** *a.*

duologue ('dyōōōlog, 'dōō-) *n.* **1.** part or all of play in which speaking roles are limited to two actors **2.** *rare* dialogue

dupe (dyōōp, dōōp) *n.* **1.** victim of delusion or sharp practice —*vt.* **2.** deceive for advantage, impose upon

duple ('dyōōpəl, 'dōō-) *a.* **1.** *rare* double **2.** *Mus.* (of time or music) having two beats in bar

duplex ('dyōōpleks, 'dōō-) *a.* **1.** twofold —*n.* **2.** apartment on two floors

duplicate ('dyōōplikāt, 'dōō-) *vt.* **1.** make exact copy of **2.** double —*a.* ('dyōōplikit, 'dōō-) **3.** double **4.** exactly the same as something else —*n.* ('dyōōplikit, 'dōō-) **5.** exact copy —**dupli'cation** *n.* —**'duplicator** *n.* machine for making copies —**du'plicity** *n.* deceitfulness, double-dealing, bad faith

durable ('dyōōrəbəl, 'dōō-) *a.* lasting, resisting wear —**dura'bility** *n.* —**'durably** *adv.* —**durable goods** goods that require infrequent replacement (*also* **'durables**)

dura mater ('dyōōrə 'mātər, 'dōōrə) outermost and toughest of three membranes covering brain and spinal cord (*also* **'dura**)

durance ('dyōōrəns, 'dōō-) *n. obs.* imprisonment

duration (dyōō'rāshən, dōō-) *n.* length of time something lasts

durbar ('dərbär, dər'bär) *n.* formerly, court of native ruler or governor in India or levée at such court

duress (dyōō'res, dōō-) *n.* compulsion by use of force or threats

during ('dyōōəring, 'dōō-) *prep.* throughout, in the time of, in the course of

durst (dərst) *obs. pt. of* DARE

dusk (dusk) *n.* **1.** darker stage of twilight **2.** partial darkness —**'duskily** *adv.* —**'dusky** *a.* **1.** dark **2.** dark-colored

dust (dust) *n.* **1.** fine particles, powder of earth or other matter, lying on surface or blown along by wind **2.** ashes of the dead —*vt.* **3.** sprinkle with powder **4.** rid of dust —**'duster** *n.* **1.** cloth for removing dust **2.** woman's lightweight coat —**'dusty** *a.* covered with dust —**'dustbowl** *n.* region stripped of vegetation by drought and erosion —**dust cover 1.** large cloth used to protect furniture from dust (*also* **'dustsheet**) **2.** removable paper cover to protect bound book (*also* **dust jacket**) —**'dustpan** *n.* short-handled hooded shovel for sweepings —**dust-up** *n. inf.* fight; argument —**dust up** attack

Dutch (duch) *a.* pert. to the Netherlands, its inhabitants or its language —**Dutch auction** auction method in which item is offered at high price and gradually reduced until buyer is found —**Dutch courage** drunken bravado —**Dutch elm disease** fungal disease of elm trees characterized by withering of foliage and stems —**Dutch oven 1.** iron or earthenware container with cover, used for stews *etc.* **2.** metal box, open in front, for cooking in front of open fire —**Dutch treat** meal *etc.* where each person pays his own share —**Dutch uncle** *inf.* person who criticizes or reproves frankly and severely —**in Dutch** in trouble

duty ('dyōōti, 'dōō-) *n.* **1.** moral or legal obligation **2.** that which is due **3.** tax on goods **4.** military service **5.** one's proper employment —**'duteous** *a.* —**'dutiable** *a.* liable to customs duty —**'dutiful** *a.* —**duty-bound** *a.* morally obliged —**duty-free** *a./adv.* with exemption from customs or excise duties

D.V. *Deo volente*

dwarf (dwôrf) *n.* **1.** very undersized person **2.** mythological, small, manlike creature (*pl.* **-s, dwarves**) —*a.* **3.** unusually small, stunted —*vt.* **4.** make seem small by contrast **5.** make stunted —**'dwarfish** *a.* —**'dwarfism** *n.* abnormally small stature, commonly caused by disease of bones or glands

dwell (dwel) *vi.* **1.** live, make one's abode (in) **2.** fix one's attention, write or speak at length (on) (**dwelt** *pt./pp.*) —**'dweller** *n.* —**'dwelling** *n.* house

dwindle ('dwindəl) *vi.* grow less, waste away, decline

Dy *Chem.* dysprosium

Dyak ('dīak) *n. see* DAYAK

dye (dī) *vt.* **1.** impregnate (cloth *etc.*) with coloring matter **2.** color thus (**dyed, 'dyeing**) —*n.* **3.** coloring matter in solution or which may be dissolved for dyeing **4.** tinge, color —**'dyeing** *n.* process or industry of coloring yarns *etc.* —**'dyer** *n.* —**dyed-in-the-wool** *a.* **1.** extreme or unchanging in opinion *etc.* **2.** (of fabric) made of dyed yarn

dying ('dīing) *v.* **1.** *pr.p. of* DIE[1] —*a.* **2.** relating to or occurring at moment of death

dyke[1] (dīk) *n. see* DIKE

dyke[2] (dīk) *n. offens.* lesbian

dynamics (dɪ'namiks) *pl.n.* **1.** (*with sing. v.*) branch of physics dealing with force as producing or affecting motion **2.** physical forces —**dy'namic** *a.* **1.** of, relating to motive force, force in operation **2.** energetic and forceful —**dy'namical** *a.* —**dy'namically** *adv.* —**'dynamism** *n.* **1.** *Philos.* theory that attempts to explain phenomena in terms of immanent force or energy **2.** forcefulness of energetic personality

dynamite ('dīnəmīt) *n.* **1.** high-explosive mixture —*vt.* **2.** blow up with this —**'dyna-miter** *n.*

dynamo ('dīnəmō) *n.* **1.** machine to convert mechanical into electrical energy, generator of electricity **2.** *inf.* energetic, hard-working person (*pl.* **-s**) —**dyna'mometer** *n.* instrument to measure energy expended

dynasty ('dīnəsti) *n.* line, family, succession of hereditary rulers —**'dynast** *n.* —**dy'nastic** *a.* of dynasty

dyne (dīn) *n.* cgs unit of force

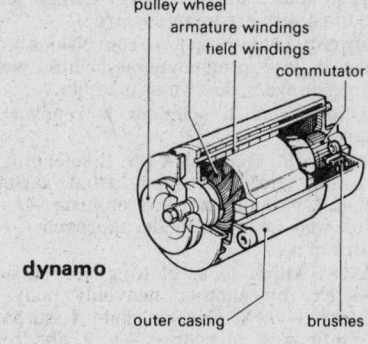

pulley wheel
armature windings
field windings
commutator

dynamo

outer casing   brushes

Dynel ('dīnəl) *n.* trade name for acrylic fiber

dys- (*comb. form*) **1.** diseased; abnormal **2.** difficult; painful **3.** bad

dysentery ('disənteri) *n.* painful inflammation of large intestine usu. with severe diarrhea

dysfunction (dis'fungkshən) *n.* abnormal, impaired functioning, *esp.* of bodily organ

dyslexia (dis'leksiə) *n.* impaired ability to read —**dys'lexic** *a.*

dysmenorrhea (dismenə'rēə) *n.* abnormally painful menstruation

dyspepsia (dis'pepsiə) *n.* indigestion —**dys-'peptic** *a./n.*

dysprosium (dis'prōziəm) *n. Chem.* metallic element *Symbol* Dy, at. wt. 162.5, at. no. 66

dystrophy ('distrəfi) *n.* wasting of body tissues, *esp.* muscles

dz. dozen

Dzhudesmo (joo'dezmō) *n. see* LADINO (sense 1)

Ee

e *or* **E** (ē) *n.* **1.** fifth letter of English alphabet **2.** any of several speech sounds represented by this letter, as in *he, bet* (*pl.* **e's, E's** *or* **Es**)

e 1. *Math.* transcendental number used as base of natural logarithms **2.** electron

E 1. *Mus.* third note of scale of C major; major or minor key having this note as its tonic **2.** *Phys.* energy; electromotive force **3.** East **4.** Eastern **5.** English **6.** Egypt(ian)

e. engineer(ing)

ea. each

each (ēch) *a./pron.* every (one) taken separately

eager ('ēgər) *a.* **1.** having a strong wish (for something) **2.** keen, anxious or impatient —**'eagerly** *adv.* —**'eagerness** *n.* —**eager beaver** *inf.* person who displays conspicuous diligence

eagle ('ēgəl) *n.* **1.** large bird with keen sight which preys on small birds and animals **2.** *Golf* score of two strokes under par for a hole —**'eaglet** *n.* young eagle —**eagle-eyed** *a.* having keen eyesight

ear¹ (ēər) *n.* **1.** organ of hearing and balance **2.** external part of it **3.** sense of hearing **4.** sensitiveness to sounds **5.** attention —**'ear-ache** *n.* acute pain in ear —**'eardrum** *n. see* **tympanic membrane** *at* TYMPANUM —**ear duster** baseball pitched close to or at the batter's head —**'earmark** *vt.* **1.** assign, reserve for definite purpose **2.** make identification mark on ear of (sheep *etc.*) —*n.* **3.** any distinguishing mark —**'earmuffs** *pl.n.* ear coverings for protection against cold or noise —**'earphone** *n.* receiver for radio *etc.* held to or put in ear —**'earring** *n.* ornament for lobe of ear —**'earshot** *n.* hearing distance —**'earsplitting** *a.* piercingly loud —**ear trumpet** trumpet-shaped instrument formerly used as hearing aid

—**'earwig** *n.* small insect with pincerlike tail —**be all ears** listen closely —**be up to the ears (in something)** *inf.* be deeply involved (in something) —**have one's ear to the ground** be alert to trends

ear² (ēər) *n.* spike, head of corn

earl (ərl) *n. Brit.* nobleman ranking next below marquis —**'earldom** *n.* his domain, title

early ('ərli) *a./adv.* **1.** before expected or usual time **2.** in first part, near or nearer beginning of some portion of time —**early bird** *inf.* one who arrives or rises early

earn (ərn) *vt.* **1.** obtain by work or merit **2.** gain —**'earnings** *pl.n.*

earnest¹ ('ərnist) *a.* **1.** serious, ardent **2.** sincere —**'earnestly** *adv.* —**in earnest** serious, determined

earnest² ('ərnist) *n.* **1.** money paid over in token to bind bargain, pledge **2.** pledge

earth (ərth) *n.* **1.** planet or world we live on **2.** ground, dry land **3.** mold, soil, mineral **4.** fox's hole **5.** wire connecting electrical apparatus to earth —*vt.* **6.** cover with earth **7.** connect electrically with earth —**'earthen** *a.* made of clay or earth —**'earthly** *a.* possible, feasible —**'earthy** *a.* **1.** of earth **2.** uninhibited **3.** vulgar —**earth closet** toilet in which earth is used to cover excreta —**'earthenware** *n.* porous white ceramic ware to which a shiny glaze is fused —**'earthquake** *n.* convulsion of earth's surface —**earth science** any of various sciences, such as geology, concerned with structure *etc.* of the earth —**'earthwork** *n.* bank of earth in fortification —**'earth-worm** *n.* terrestrial annelid that burrows in soil —**come back** *or* **down to earth** return to reality from fantasy

ease (ēz) *n.* **1.** comfort **2.** freedom from

constraint, annoyance, awkwardness, pain or trouble **3.** idleness —*v.* **4.** make or become less burdensome **5.** give bodily or mental ease to **6.** (cause to) move carefully or gradually —*vt.* **7.** slacken **8.** relieve of pain —**'easement** *n. Law* right of way *etc.* over another's land —**'easily** *adv.* —**'easiness** *n.* **1.** quality or condition of being easy to accomplish *etc.* **2.** ease or relaxation of manner —**'easy** *a.* **1.** not difficult **2.** free from pain, care, constraint or anxiety **3.** compliant **4.** characterized by low demand **5.** fitting loosely **6.** *inf.* having no preference for any particular course of action —**easy chair** comfortable upholstered armchair —**easy-going** *a.* **1.** not fussy **2.** indolent

easel ('ēzəl) *n.* frame to support artist's canvas *etc.*

east (ēst) *n.* **1.** part of horizon where sun rises **2.** eastern lands, orient —*a.* **3.** on, in or near east **4.** coming from east —*adv.* **5.** from or to east —**'easterly** *a./adv.* from or to east —**'eastern** *a.* of, dwelling in, east —**'eastern-er** *n.* —**'easting** *n.* distance eastwards of a point from a given meridian —**'eastward** *a./n.* —**'eastwards** *or* **'eastward** *adv.* —**Eastern Church 1.** any of Christian Churches of former Byzantine Empire **2.** any Church owing allegiance to Orthodox Church —**eastern hemisphere** (*oft.* **E- H-**) **1.** that half of the globe containing Europe, Asia, Afr. and Aust. **2.** lands in this, *esp.* Asia —**Eastern Seaboard** states on the Atlantic shore: Maine, New Hampshire, Massachusetts, Rhode Island, Connecticut, New York, Pennsylvania, Delaware, Maryland, Virginia, North and South Carolina, and Georgia —**Eastern Standard Time** time as reckoned from 75th to 90th meridians west of Greenwich —**East Germany** *see* GERMAN DEMOCRATIC REPUBLIC

Easter ('ēstər) *n.* movable festival of the Resurrection of Christ —**Easter egg** chocolate egg or hen's egg with its shell painted, given as gift at Easter —**'Eastertide** *n.* Easter season

easy ('ēzi) *a. see* EASE

eat (ēt) *v.* 1. chew and swallow 2. gnaw —*vt.* 3. consume, destroy 4. wear away (ate *pt.,* 'eaten *pp.*) —**'eatable** *a.* —**'eating** *n.* 1. food, *esp.* in relation to quality or taste —*a.* 2. suitable for eating —**eats** *pl.n. sl.* articles of food —**eat one's words** take back something said

eau de Cologne (ō də kə'lōn) *Fr.* light perfume

eau de vie (ō də 'vē) brandy

eaves (ēvz) *pl.n.* overhanging edges of roof —**'eavesdrop** *vi.* listen secretly —**'eavesdropper** *n.* —**'eavesdropping** *n.*

ebb (eb) *vi.* 1. flow back 2. decay —*n.* 3. flowing back of tide 4. decline, decay —**ebb tide**

ebony ('ebəni) *n.* 1. hard black wood —*a.* 2. made of, black as ebony —**'ebonite** *n.* vulcanite —**'ebonize** *vt.* make color of ebony

ebullient (i'bŏolyənt, i'bul-) *a.* 1. exuberant 2. boiling —**e'bullience** *n.* —**ebullition** (ebə'lishən) *n.* 1. boiling 2. effervescence 3. outburst

eccentric (ik'sentrik) *a.* 1. odd, unconventional 2. irregular 3. not placed, or not having axis placed, centrally 4. not circular (in orbit) —*n.* 5. odd, unconventional person 6. mechanical contrivance to change circular into to-and-fro movement —**ec'centrically** *adv.* —**eccen'tricity** *n.*

Eccles. *Bible* Ecclesiastes

Ecclesiastes (iklēzi'astēz) *n. Bible* 21st book of the O.T., authorship traditionally ascribed to Solomon, the theme of which is the excellence of wisdom

ecclesiastic (iklēzi'astik) *n.* 1. clergyman —*a.* 2. of, relating to the Christian Church —**ecclesi'astical** *a.* —**ecclesi'ology** *n.* science of church building and decoration

eccrinology (ekri'noləji) *n.* branch of physiology that relates to bodily secretions

E.C.G. 1. electrocardiogram 2. electrocardiograph

echelon ('eshəlon) *n.* 1. level, grade, of responsibility or command 2. formation of troops, planes *etc.* in parallel divisions, each slightly to left or right of the one in front

echidna (i'kidnə) *n.* spine-covered mammal of Aust. and New Guinea (*pl.* -s, -nae (-nē)) (*also* **spiny anteater**)

echinoderm (i'kīnōdərm) *n.* any member of a phylum of invertebrate animals with spiny skins and globular star-shaped bodies such as starfish, sea urchin and sea cucumber

echo ('ekō) *n.* 1. repetition of sounds by reflection 2. close imitation (*pl.* -es) —*vt.* 3. repeat as echo, send back the sound of 4. imitate closely —*vi.* 5. resound 6. be repeated ('echoed, 'echoing) —**echoic** (e'kōik) *a.* 1. characteristic of or resembling echo 2. onomatopoeic —**echo chamber** room with walls that reflect sound, used to make acoustic measurements and in recording (*also* **reverberation chamber**) —**echolo'cation** *n.* determination of position of object by measuring reflected sound —**echo sounder** —**echo sounding** system of ascertaining depth of water by measuring time required to receive echo from sea bottom or submerged object —**echo viruses** group of viruses infecting the gastrointestinal tract *esp.* of children

Echo ('ekō) *n.* word used in communications for the letter *e*

éclair (ā'klāər, i'klāər) *n.* finger-shaped, iced cake filled with cream or custard

eclampsia (i'klampsiə) *n.* convulsions and comas in late pregnancy associated with group of disorders known as toxemia

éclat (ā'klä) *n.* 1. splendor 2. renown 3. acclamation

eclectic (e'klektik, i'klek-) *a.* 1. selecting 2. borrowing one's philosophy from various sources 3. catholic in views or taste —*n.* 4. person who favors eclectic approach —**ec'lecticism** *n.*

eclipse (i'klips) *n.* 1. blotting out of sun, moon *etc.* by another heavenly body 2. obscurity —*vt.* 3. obscure, hide 4. surpass —**e'cliptic** *a.* 1. of eclipse —*n.* 2. apparent path of sun

eclogue ('eklog) *n.* short poem, *esp.* pastoral dialogue

eco- (*comb. form*) ecology; ecological, as in *ecosphere*

ecology (i'koləji) *n.* science of plants and animals in relation to their environment —**eco'logical** *a.* —**e'cologist** *n.* specialist in or advocate of ecological studies

econ. 1. economical 2. economics 3. economy

economy (i'konəmi) *n.* 1. careful management of resources to avoid unnecessary expenditure or waste 2. sparing, restrained or efficient use 3. system of interrelationship of money, industry and employment in a country —**eco'nomic** *a.* 1. of economics 2. profitable 3. economical —**eco'nomical** *a.* 1. not wasteful of money, time, effort *etc.* 2. frugal —**eco'nomically** *adv.* —**eco'nomics** *pl.n.* 1. (*with sing. v.*) study of economies of nations 2. (*with pl. v.*) financial aspects —**e'conomist** *n.* specialist in economics —**e'conomize** *v.* limit or reduce (expense, waste *etc.*)

ecosystem ('ēkōsistəm, 'ekō-) *n. Ecol.* system involving interactions between community and its nonliving environment

ecru ('ekrōō, 'akrōō) *n./a.* (of) color of unbleached linen, beige

ecstasy ('ekstəsi) *n.* 1. exalted state of feeling, mystic trance 2. frenzy —**ec'static** *a.* —**ec'statically** *adv.*

E.C.T. electroconvulsive therapy

ecto- (*comb. form*) outer, outside, as in *ectoplasm*

-ectomy (*comb. form*) surgical excision of part, as in *appendectomy*

ectoplasm ('ektōplazəm) *n.* in spiritualism, supposedly a semiluminous plastic substance which exudes from medium's body

Ecuador ('ekwədōr) *n.* country in S Amer. bounded on the north by Colombia, on the east and south by Peru and on the west by the Pacific Ocean —**Ecua'doran** or **Ecua'dorian** *a./n.*

ecumenical (ekyōō'menikəl) *a.* of the Christian Church throughout the world, *esp.* with regard to its unity —**ecu'menicalism, ecu'menicism** or **ecu'menism** *n.*

eczema (ig'zēmə, 'eksimə) *n.* any of group of transient or chronic skin disorders characterized by redness, swelling, blisters and scaling

ed. 1. edited 2. edition (*pl.* eds.) 3. editor (*pl.* eds.) 4. education

-ed¹ (*comb. form*) forming past tense of most English verbs

-ed² (*comb. form*) forming past participle of most English verbs

-ed³ (*comb. form*) possessing or having characteristics of, as in *salaried, red-blooded*

Edam ('ēdəm) *n.* firm cheese of mild flavor made from cow's milk, molded into a ball

and covered with red wax, orig. from Holland

E.D.C. European Defence Community

Edda ('edə) *n.* collection of old Icelandic myths

eddy ('edi) *n.* 1. small whirl in water, smoke *etc.* —*vi.* 2. move in whirls ('eddied, 'eddying)

edelweiss ('ādəlwīs, -vīs) *n.* white-flowered alpine plant with woolly leaves

edema (i'dēmə) *n.* swelling in body tissues, due to accumulation of fluid (*pl.* -mata (-mətə))

Eden ('ēdən) *n.* 1. garden in which Adam and Eve were placed at the Creation 2. any delightful, happy place or state

edentate (ē'dentāt) *n.* 1. any mammal of the order *Edentata*, which have few or no teeth, such as anteater —*a.* 2. of the order *Edentata*

edge (ej) *n.* 1. border, boundary 2. cutting side of blade 3. sharpness 4. advantage 5. acrimony, bitterness —*vt.* 6. give edge or border to 7. move gradually —*vi.* 8. advance sideways or gradually —**'edgeways** or **'edgewise** *adv.* —**'edging** *n.* —**'edgy** *a.* irritable, sharp or keen in temper —**on edge** 1. nervy, irritable 2. excited

edelweiss

edible ('edibəl) *a.* eatable, fit for eating —**edi'bility** *n.*

edict ('ēdikt) *n.* order proclaimed by authority, decree

edifice ('edifis) *n.* building, *esp.* big one

edify ('edifī) *vt.* improve morally, instruct (-fied, -fying) —**edifi'cation** *n.* improvement of mind or morals

edit ('edit) *vt.* prepare (book, motion picture, tape *etc.*) for publication or broadcast —**e'dition** *n.* 1. form in which something is published 2. number of copies of new publication printed at one time —**'editor** *n.* —**edi'torial** *a.* 1. of editor —*n.* 2. article stating opinion of newspaper *etc.*

edit. 1. edited 2. edition 3. editor

EDP emotionally disturbed person

E.D.P. electronic data processing

educate ('ejəkāt) *vt.* 1. provide schooling for 2. teach 3. train mentally and morally 4. train 5. improve, develop —**educa'bility** or **educata'bility** *n.* —**'educable** or **'educatable** *a.* capable of being trained or educated —**'educated** *a.* 1. having education, *esp.* a good one 2. cultivated —**edu'cation** *n.* —**edu'cational** *a.* —**edu'cationally** *adv.* —**'educative** *a.* —**'educator** *n.* —**educated guess** guess based on experience or information

educe (i'dyōōs, -'dōōs) *vt.* 1. bring out, elicit, develop 2. infer, deduce —**e'ducible** *a.* —**eduction** (i'dukshən) *n.*

Edwardian (ed'wōrdiən) *a.* of reign (1901-10) of Edward VII, king of Great

Britain and Ireland —**Ed'wardianism** n.

-ee (comb. form) **1.** recipient of action, as in assignee **2.** person in specified state or condition, as in absentee

EEC European Economic Community

EEG electroencephalogram

eel (ēl) n. snakelike fish

e'en (ēn) adv./n. Poet., obs. even, evening

-eer or **-ier** (comb. form) **1.** person who is concerned with something specified, as in auctioneer, engineer, profiteer **2.** be concerned with something specified, as in electioneer

e'er (ār) adv. Poet., obs. ever

eerie ('ēəri) a. **1.** weird, uncanny **2.** causing superstitious fear

efface (i'fās) vt. wipe or rub out —**ef'faceable** a. —**ef'facement** n.

effect (i'fekt) n. **1.** result, consequence **2.** efficacy **3.** impression **4.** condition of being operative —pl. **5.** property **6.** lighting, sounds etc. to accompany film, broadcast etc. —vt. **7.** bring about, accomplish —**ef'fective** a. **1.** having power to produce effects **2.** in effect, operative **3.** serviceable **4.** powerful **5.** striking —**ef'fectively** adv. —**ef'fectual** a. **1.** successful in producing desired effect **2.** satisfactory **3.** efficacious —**ef'fectually** adv. —**ef'fectuate** vt.

effeminate (i'feminit) a. (of man or boy) womanish, unmanly —**ef'feminacy** n.

efferent ('efərənt) a. conveying outward or away

effervesce (efər'ves) vi. **1.** give off bubbles **2.** be in high spirits —**effer'vescence** n. —**effer'vescent** a.

effete (e'fēt, i'fēt) a. worn-out, feeble

efficacious (efi'kāshəs) a. **1.** producing or sure to produce desired effect **2.** effective **3.** powerful **4.** adequate —**'efficacy** n. **1.** potency **2.** force **3.** efficiency

efficient (i'fishənt) a. capable, competent, producing effect —**ef'ficiency** n. —**ef'ficiently** adv.

effigy ('efiji) n. image, likeness

effloresce (eflö'res) vi. burst into flower —**efflo'rescence** n. —**efflo'rescent** a.

effluent ('eflōōənt) n. **1.** liquid discharged as waste **2.** stream flowing from larger stream, lake etc. —a. **3.** flowing out —**'effluence** or **efflux** ('efluks) n. —**ef'fluvium** n. something flowing out invisibly, esp. affecting lungs or sense of smell (pl. **-ia** (-iə))

effort ('efərt) n. **1.** exertion **2.** endeavor, attempt **3.** something achieved —**'effortless** a.

effrontery (i'fruntəri) n. brazen impudence

effulgent (i'fuljənt) a. radiant, shining brightly —**ef'fulgence** n.

effusion (i'fyōōzhən) n. (unrestrained) outpouring —**ef'fuse** v. pour out, shed —**ef'fusive** a. gushing, demonstrative —**ef'fusively** adv. —**ef'fusiveness** n.

eft (eft) n. dial., obs. newt

EFT electronic funds transfer

EFTA ('eftə) European Free Trade Association

e.g. exempli gratia (Lat., for example)

egalitarian (igali'teriən) a. **1.** believing that all people should be equal **2.** promoting this ideal —n. **3.** adherent of egalitarian principles —**egali'tarianism** n.

egg[1] (eg) n. **1.** oval or round object produced by female of bird or reptile from which young emerge, esp. egg of domestic fowl, used as food **2.** ovum —**'eggbeater** n. **1.** hand-operated utensil for stirring or mixing eggs **2.** helicopter —**egg cup 1.** small cup for holding boiled egg to be eaten out of the shell **2.** cup composed of two small bowls joined at bottoms, one for holding upright a soft-boiled egg, the other larger bowl for holding a soft-boiled egg emptied into it —**egg foo young** (fōō yung) Chinese-American type of omelet filled with a chicken, shellfish or meat and vegetable mixture —**'egghead** n. inf. intellectual —**'eggnog** n. drink made of eggs, milk, sugar, spice, and brandy, rum etc. —**'eggplant** n. perennial plant yielding a large smooth dark purple egg-shaped fruit eaten as a vegetable —**egg roll** Chinese dish made of dough wrapped around chopped vegetables and meat or shellfish and deep-fried —**'eggshell** n. **1.** outer layer of bird's egg —a. **2.** (of paint) having mat finish —**good egg** friendly, helpful person

egg[2] (eg) vt. —**egg on 1.** encourage, urge **2.** incite

eglantine ('egləntīn) n. sweet brier

ego ('ēgō, 'egō) n. **1.** the self **2.** the conscious thinking subject **3.** one's image of oneself **4.** morale —**'egoism** n. **1.** systematic selfishness **2.** theory that bases morality on self-interest —**'egoist** n. —**ego'istic(al)** a. —**'egotism** n. **1.** selfishness **2.** self-conceit —**'egotist** n. —**ego'tistic(al)** a. —**ego'centric** a. **1.** self-centred **2.** egoistic **3.** centered in the ego —**ego trip** inf. something undertaken to boost person's own image or appraisal of himself

egregious (i'grējəs) a. **1.** outstandingly bad, blatant **2.** (esp. of mistake etc.) absurdly obvious

egress ('ēgres) n. **1.** way out **2.** departure

egret ('ēgrit) n. **1.** lesser white heron **2.** down of dandelion

Egypt ('ējipt) n. country in Africa bounded east by Israel, the Gulf of Aqaba and the Red Sea, south by Sudan, west by Libya and north by the Mediterranean —**Egyptian** (i'jipshən) a./n. —**Egyp'tologist** n. —**Egyp'tology** n. study of archaeology and language of ancient Egypt

eh (ā) interj. exclamation expressing surprise or inquiry, or to seek confirmation of statement or question

EHF extremely high frequency

eider or **eider duck** ('īdər) n. Arctic duck —**'eiderdown** n. **1.** its breast feathers **2.** quilt (stuffed with feathers)

eight (āt) n. **1.** cardinal number one above seven **2.** eight-oared boat **3.** its crew —a. **4.** amounting to eight —**eigh'teen** a./n. eight more than ten —**eigh'teenth** a./n. —**eigh'teenthly** adv. —**'eightfold** a./adv. —**eighth** a./n. ordinal number of eight —**'eighthly** adv. —**'eightieth** a./n. —**'eighty** a./n. ten times eight —**eightfold path** tenets of Buddhism —**eightsome reel** Scottish dance for eight people —**figure of eight 1.** a skating figure **2.** any figure shaped as 8

einsteinium (īn'stīniəm) n. Chem. transuranic element Symbol E, at. wt. 254, at. no. 99

Eire ('erə) n. the Republic of Ireland

Eisenhower ('īzənhowər) n. **Dwight** (dwīt) **David.** the 34th President of the U.S. (1953-61)

eisteddfod (ī'stedhvod) n. **1.** annual congress of Welsh bards **2.** local gathering for competition in music and other performing arts

either ('ēdhər, 'īdhər) a./pron. **1.** one or the other **2.** one of two **3.** each —adv./conj. **4.** bringing in first of alternatives or strengthening an added negation

ejaculate (i'jakyəlāt) v. **1.** eject (semen) **2.** exclaim, utter suddenly —**ejacu'lation** n. —**e'jaculatory** a.

eject (i'jekt) vt. **1.** throw out **2.** expel, drive out —**e'jection** n. —**e'jectment** n. —**e'jector** n. —**ejection seat** seat, esp. in military aircraft, that ejects occupant in emergency

eke out (ēk) **1.** make (supply) last, esp. by frugal use **2.** supply deficiencies of **3.** make with difficulty (a living etc.)

elaborate (i'labərit) a. **1.** carefully worked out, detailed **2.** complicated —vi. (i'labərāt) **3.** expand —vt. (i'labərāt) **4.** work out in detail **5.** take pains with —**elabo'ration** n.

élan (ā'län) n. **1.** dash **2.** ardor **3.** impetuosity

eland ('ēlənd) n. largest S Afr. antelope, resembling elk

elapse (i'laps) vi. (of time) pass

elastic (i'lastik) a. **1.** resuming normal shape after distortion, springy **2.** flexible —n. **3.** tape, fabric, containing interwoven strands of flexible rubber —**e'lasticated** a. —**elas'ticity** n.

elation (i'lāshən) n. **1.** high spirits **2.** pride —**e'late** vt. (usu. passive) **1.** raise the spirits of **2.** make happy **3.** exhilarate

elbow ('elbō) n. **1.** joint between fore and upper parts of arm (esp. outer part of it) **2.** part of sleeve covering this —vt. **3.** shove, strike with elbow —**elbow grease** hard work —**'elbowroom** n. sufficient room

elder[1] ('eldər) a. comp. of OLD **1.** older, senior —n. **2.** person of greater age **3.** old person **4.** official of certain churches —**'elderly** a. growing old —**'eldest** a. sup. of OLD oldest

elder[2] ('eldər) n. white-flowered tree —**'elderberry** n. **1.** fruit of elder **2.** elder (tree)

El Dorado (el də'rädō) fictitious country rich in gold

eldritch ('eldrich) a. **1.** hideous **2.** weird **3.** uncanny **4.** haggish

elect (i'lekt) vt. **1.** choose by vote **2.** choose —a. **3.** appointed but not yet in office **4.** chosen, select, choice —**e'lection** n. choosing, esp. by voting —**election'eer** vi. busy oneself in political elections —**e'lective** a. appointed, filled or chosen by election —**e'lector** n. one who elects —**e'lectoral** a. —**e'lectorate** n. body of electors —**e'lectorship** n.

elect. or **elec. 1.** electric(al) **2.** electricity

electricity (ilek'trisiti) n. **1.** form of energy associated with stationary or moving electrons or other charged particles **2.** electric current or charge **3.** science dealing with electricity —**e'lectric** a. **1.** derived from, produced by, producing, transmitting or powered by electricity **2.** excited, emotionally charged —**e'lectrical** a. —**elec'trician** n. one trained in installation etc. of electrical devices —**electrifi'cation** n. —**e'lectrify** vt. —**electric blanket** blanket containing electric heating element —**electric chair** chair in which criminals sentenced to death are electrocuted —**electric eel** eel-like freshwater fish of N South Amer., having electric organs in body —**electric eye** see PHOTOCELL —**electric fire** appliance that supplies heat by means of electrically operated metal coil —**electric guitar** see GUITAR —**electric organ** Mus. organ in which sound is produced by electric devices instead of wind —**electric shock** effect of an electric current passing through body

electro- or sometimes before vowel **electr-** (comb. form) by, caused by electricity, as in electrotherapy. Such words are not given here where the meaning may easily be inferred from the simple word

electrocardiograph (ilektrō'kärdiōgraf) n. instrument for recording electrical activity of heart —**electro'cardiogram** n. tracing produced by this

electroconvulsive therapy (ilektrōkən-'vulsiv) *see* **shock therapy** *at* SHOCK¹

electrocute (i'lektrəkyōōt) *vt.* execute, kill by electricity —**electro'cution** *n.*

electrode (i'lektrōd) *n.* conductor by which electric current enters or leaves battery, vacuum tube *etc.*

electrodynamics (ilektrōdī'namiks) *pl.n.* (*with sing. v.*) dynamics of electricity

electroencephalograph (ilektrōin'sefələ-graf) *n.* instrument for recording electrical activity of brain —**electroen'cephalogram** *n.* tracing produced by this

electrolyte (i'lektrōlīt) *n.* substance capable of furnishing ions when dissolved in water

electrolyze (i'lektrōlīz) *vt.* decompose by electricity —**elec'trolysis** *n.*

electromagnet (ilektrō'magnit) *n.* magnet containing coil of wire through which electric current is passed —**electromag'netic** *a.* —**electro'magnetism** *n.* 1. magnetism produced by electric current 2. branch of

electromagnet

physics concerned with interaction of electric and magnetic fields

electromotive (ilektrō'mōtiv) *a.* of, concerned with or producing electric current —**electromotive force** *Phys.* 1. source of energy that can cause current to flow in electrical circuit 2. rate at which energy is drawn from this source

electron (i'lektron) *n.* tiny bit of exceedingly small mass and negative electric charge —**elec'tronic** *a.* 1. of electrons or electronics 2. using devices, such as semiconductors, transistors or valves, dependent on action of electrons —**elec'tronics** *pl.n.* 1. (*with sing. v.*) technology concerned with development of electronic devices and circuits 2. science of behavior and control of electrons —**electronic brain** *inf.* electronic computer —**electronic data processing** data processing largely performed by electronic equipment —**electronic music** music consisting of sounds produced by electric currents prerecorded on magnetic tape —**electronic organ** *Mus.* keyboard instrument in which sounds are produced by electronic or electrical means —**electron microscope** microscope that uses electrons and electron lenses to produce magnified image —**electron tube** electrical device, such as valve, in which flow of electrons between electrodes takes place —**electron volt** unit of energy used in nuclear physics

electroplate (i'lektrōplāt) *vt.* 1. coat with silver *etc.* by electrolysis —*n.* 2. articles electroplated

electroscope (i'lektrōskōp) *n.* instrument to show presence or kind of electricity

electroshock therapy (i'lektrōshok) *see* **shock therapy** *at* SHOCK¹

electrostatics (ilektrō'statiks) *n.* branch of physics concerned with static electricity —**electro'static** *a.*

electrotype (i'lektrōtīp) *n.* 1. art of producing copies of type *etc.* by electric deposition of copper upon mould 2. copy so produced

electrum (i'lektrəm) *n.* alloy of gold and silver used in jewelry *etc.*

eleemosynary (eli'mosineri) *a.* 1. charitable 2. dependent on charity

elegant ('eligənt) *a.* 1. graceful, tasteful 2. refined —**'elegance** *n.*

elegy ('eliji) *n.* lament for the dead in poem or song —**elegiac** (eli'jīək) *a.* 1. suited to elegies 2. plaintive —**elegiacs** (eli'jīəks) *pl.n.* elegiac verses

element ('elimənt) *n.* 1. substance which cannot be separated into other substances by chemical techniques 2. component part 3. small amount, trace 4. heating wire in electric kettle, stove *etc.* 5. proper abode or sphere 6. situation in which person is happiest or most effective (*esp. in* **in** *or* **out of one's element**) —*pl.* 7. powers of atmosphere 8. rudiments, first principles —**ele'mental** *a.* 1. fundamental 2. of powers of nature —**ele'mentary** *a.* rudimentary, simple —**elementary particle** any of several entities, such as electrons *etc.*, that are less complex than atoms —**elementary school** school comprising the first six or eight grades

elephant ('elifənt) *n.* huge four-footed, thick-skinned animal with ivory tusks and long trunk —**elephan'tiasis** *n.* disease with hardening of skin and enlargement of legs *etc.* —**ele'phantine** *a.* unwieldy, clumsy, heavily big

elevate ('elivāt) *vt.* raise, lift up, exalt —**ele'vation** *n.* 1. raising 2. height, *esp.* above sea level 3. angle above horizon, as of gun 4. drawing of one side of building *etc.* —**'elevator** *n.* platform, compartment *etc.* raised or lowered in vertical shaft to transport persons or goods in a building

eleven (i'levən) *n.* 1. number next above 10 2. team of 11 persons —*a.* 3. amounting to eleven —**e'levenfold** *a./adv.* —**e'levenses** *pl.n. inf.* light mid-morning snack —**e'leventh** *a.* ordinal number of eleven —**eleven-plus** *n.* UK *esp.* formerly, examination taken by children aged 11 or 12, that selects suitable candidates for grammar schools —**eleventh hour** latest possible time

elf (elf) *n.* 1. fairy 2. woodland sprite (*pl.* **elves**) —**'elfin, 'elfish, 'elvish** *or* **'elflike** *a.* roguish, mischievous

elicit (i'lisit) *vt.* 1. draw out, evoke 2. bring to light

elide (i'līd) *v.* omit (a vowel or syllable) at beginning or end of word—**e'lision** *n.*

eligible ('elijəbəl) *a.* 1. fit or qualified to be chosen 2. suitable, desirable —**eligi'bility** *n.*

eliminate (i'limināt) *vt.* remove, get rid of, set aside —**elimi'nation** *n.* —**e'liminator** *n.* one who, that which, eliminates

elision (i'lizhən) *n. see* ELIDE

elite (ā'lēt, i-) *n.* 1. choice or select body 2. the pick or best part of society 3. typewriter typesize (12 letters to inch) —*a.* 4. of or suitable for an elite —**e'litism** *n.* 1. belief that society should be governed by an elite 2. pride in being one of an elite group

elixir (i'liksər) *n.* 1. preparation sought by alchemists to change base metals into gold, or to prolong life 2. sovereign remedy

Elizabethan (ilizə'bēthən) *a.* 1. of reigns of Elizabeth I (queen of England, 1558-1603) or Elizabeth II (queen of Great Britain and N Ireland since 1952) 2. of style of architecture used in England during reign of Elizabeth I —*n.* 3. person who lived in England during reign of Elizabeth I

elk (elk) *n.* 1. N Amer. deer similar to European red deer (*also* **wapiti**) 2. deer of Europe and Asia resembling moose 3. (E-)

member of a society called the Benevolent and Protective Order of Elks

ell (el) *n.* obsolete unit of length, approximately 45 inches

Ellice Islands ('elis) *former name for* TUVALU

ellipse (i'lips) *n.* oval —**el'lipsoid** *n.* 1. geometric surface whose plane sections are ellipses or circles 2. solid having this shape —**ellip'soidal** *a.* —**el'liptical** *a.* 1. relating to or having the shape of an ellipse 2. relating to or resulting from ellipsis 3. (of speech *etc.*) very concise, obscure; circumlocutory (*also* **el'liptic**) —**el'liptically** *adv.*

ellipsis (i'lipsis) *n. Gram.* omission of parts of word or sentence (*pl.* **ellipses** (i'lipsēz))

elm (elm) *n.* 1. tree with serrated leaves 2. its wood

elocution (elə'kyōōshən) *n.* art of public speaking, voice management —**elo'cutionist** *n.* 1. teacher of this 2. specialist in verse speaking

elongate ('ēlonggāt) *vt.* lengthen, extend, prolong —**elon'gation** *n.*

elope (i'lōp) *vi.* run away from home with lover —**e'lopement** *n.*

eloquence ('eləkwəns) *n.* fluent, powerful use of language —**'eloquent** *a.* —**'eloquently** *adv.*

El Salvador (el 'salvədör) country in Central America bounded south by the Pacific, west by Guatemala and north by Honduras —**Salva'doran, Salva'dorean,** *or* **Salva'dorian** *a./n.*

else (els) *adv.* 1. besides, instead 2. otherwise —**'elsewhere** *adv.* in or to some other place

elucidate (i'lōōsidāt) *vt.* throw light upon, explain —**eluci'dation** *n.* —**e'lucidatory** *a.*

elude (i'lōōd) *vt.* 1. escape, slip away from, dodge 2. baffle —**e'lusion** *n.* 1. act of eluding 2. evasion —**e'lusive** *a.* difficult to catch hold of, deceptive —**e'lusively** *adv.* —**e'lusory** *a.*

elver ('elvər) *n.* young eel

elves (elvz) *n., pl. of* ELF

Elysium (i'liziəm) *n.* 1. *Gr. myth.* dwelling place of blessed after death (*also* **Elysian fields**) 2. state or place of perfect bliss

em (em) *n. Print.* the square of any size of type

em- (*comb. form*) *see* EN-

'em (əm) *pron. inf.* them

emaciate (i'māsiāt) *v.* make or become abnormally thin —**emaci'ation** *n.*

emanate ('emənāt) *vi.* issue, proceed, originate —**ema'nation** *n.* —**emanative** ('emənātiv) *a.*

emancipate (i'mansipāt) *vt.* set free —**emanci'pation** *n.* 1. act of setting free, *esp.* from social, legal restraint 2. state of being set free —**emanci'pationist** *n.* advocate of emancipation, *esp.* of slaves or women —**e'mancipator** *n.* —**emancipatory** (i'mansi-pətöri) *a.*

emasculate (i'maskyəlāt) *vt.* 1. castrate 2. enfeeble, weaken —**emascu'lation** *n.* —**e'masculative** *a.*

embalm (im'bäm, -'bälm) *vt.* preserve (corpse) from decay by use of chemicals, herbs *etc.* —**em'balmment** *n.*

embankment (im'bangkmənt) *n.* artificial mound carrying road, railroad, or serving to dam water

embargo (em'bärgō) *n.* 1. order stopping movement of ships 2. suspension of commerce 3. ban (*pl.* **-es**) —*vt.* 4. put under embargo 5. requisition

embark (em'bärk) *v.* 1. put, go, on board ship, aircraft *etc.* 2. (*with* **on** *or* **upon**) commence (new project, venture *etc.*) —**embar'kation** *n.*

embarrass (im'barəs) vt. 1. perplex, disconcert 2. abash 3. confuse 4. encumber 5. involve in financial difficulties —em'barrassment n.

embassy ('embəsi) n. 1. office, work or official residence of ambassador 2. deputation

embattle (im'batəl) vt. 1. deploy (troops) for battle 2. fortify (position etc.)

embed or **imbed** (im'bed) vt. fix fast in something solid

embellish (im'belish) vt. adorn, enrich —em'bellishment n.

ember ('embər) n. 1. glowing cinder —pl. 2. red-hot ashes

Ember days days appointed by Church for fasting in each quarter

embezzle (im'bezəl) vt. divert fraudulently, misappropriate (money in trust etc.) —em'bezzlement n. —em'bezzler n.

embitter (im'bitər) vt. make bitter —em'bitterment n.

emblazon (im'blāzən) vt. adorn richly, esp. heraldically

emblem ('embləm) n. 1. symbol 2. badge, device —emblem'atic a. —emblem'atically adv.

embody (im'bodi) vt. 1. give body, concrete expression to 2. represent, include, be expression of (em'bodied, em'bodying) —em'bodiment n.

embolden (im'bōldən) vt. make bold

embolism ('embəlizəm) n. clot or other obstruction carried in the bloodstream until it becomes lodged in a vessel too narrow to permit passage

embolus ('embələs) n. material, such as blood clot, that impedes circulation (pl. -li (-lī))

emboss (im'bos) vt. mold, stamp or carve in relief

embrace (im'brās) vt. 1. clasp in arms, hug 2. seize, avail oneself of, accept 3. comprise —n. 4. act of embracing

embrasure (im'brāzhər) n. 1. opening in wall for cannon 2. beveling of wall at sides of window

embrocation (embrō'kāshən) n. lotion for rubbing limbs etc. to relieve pain —'embrocate vt.

embroider (im'broidər) vt. 1. ornament with needlework 2. embellish, exaggerate (story) —em'broidery n.

embroil (im'broil) vt. 1. bring into confusion 2. involve in hostility —em'broilment n.

embryo ('embriō) n. 1. unborn or undeveloped offspring, germ 2. undeveloped thing (pl. -s) —embry'ologist n. —embry'ology n. study of development of the individual from the egg —embry'onic a.

embus (im'bus) v. (esp. of troops) put into, mount bus (-ss-)

emend (i'mend) vt. remove errors from, correct —emen'dation n. —'emendator n. —e'mendatory a.

emerald ('emərəld, 'emrəld) n. 1. bright green precious stone —a. 2. of the color of emerald —**Emerald Isle** Poet. Ireland

emerge (i'mərj) vi. 1. come up, out 2. rise to notice 3. come into view 4. come out on inquiry —e'mergence n. —e'mergent a. —e'mersion n. 1. act or instance of emerging 2. Astron. reappearance of celestial body after eclipse or occultation

emergency (i'mərjənsi) n. 1. sudden unforeseen thing or event needing prompt action 2. difficult situation 3. exigency, crisis

emeritus (i'meritəs) a. retired, honorably

discharged but retaining one's title (eg professor) on honorary basis

emery ('eməri) n. hard mineral used for polishing —**emery board** nail file of cardboard coated with crushed emery —**emery cloth** stiff paper coated with finely powdered emery

emetic (i'metik) n./a. (denoting) drug which causes vomiting

emf electromotive force

-emia or **-hemia** (comb. form) blood, esp. specified condition of blood in diseases, as in leukemia

emigrate ('emigrāt) vi. go and settle in another country —'emigrant n. —emi'gration n. —'emigratory a.

émigré ('emigrā) n. emigrant, esp. one forced to leave his country for political reasons

éminence grise (āmēnās 'grēz) Fr. person who wields power and influence unofficially (pl. éminences grises (āmēnās 'grēz))

eminent ('eminənt) a. distinguished, notable —'eminence n. 1. distinction 2. height 3. rank 4. fame 5. rising ground 6. (E-) title of cardinal —'eminently adv.

emir (i'mēər) n. (in Islamic world) 1. independent ruler or chieftain 2. military commander or governor 3. male descendant of Mohammed —e'mirate n.

emissary ('emiseri) n. agent, representative (esp. of government) sent on mission

emit (i'mit) vt. give out, put forth (-tt-) —e'mission n. —e'mitter n.

Emmenthal ('eməntäl) or **Emmenthaler** ('eməntälər) n. hard cheese, pale yellow in color with large, shiny holes and a nutty, sweet flavor, orig. from Switzerland (also **Swiss cheese**)

emollient (i'molyənt) a. 1. softening, soothing —n. 2. ointment or other softening application

emolument (i'molyəmənt) n. salary, pay, profit from work

emotion (i'mōshən) n. mental agitation, excited state of feeling, as joy, fear etc. —e'mote vi. inf. display exaggerated emotion, as in acting —e'moter n. —e'motional a. 1. given to emotion 2. appealing to the emotions —e'motive a. tending to arouse emotion

Emp. 1. Emperor 2. Empire 3. Empress

empanel or **impanel** (im'panəl) vt. Law 1. enter on list (names of persons to be summoned for jury service) 2. select (jury) from such list —em'panelment or im'panelment n.

empathy ('empəthi) n. power of understanding, imaginatively entering into, another's feelings —em'pathic or empa'thetic a.

emperor ('empərər) n. ruler of an empire ('empress fem.) —**emperor penguin** Antarctic penguin, the largest known, reaching a height of 1.3 m (4 ft.)

emphasis ('emfəsis) n. 1. importance attached 2. stress on words 3. vigor of speech, expression (pl. -ses (-sēz)) —'emphasize vt. —em'phatic a. 1. forceful, decided 2. stressed —em'phatically adv.

emphysema (emfi'zēmə) n. distension of the terminal air sacs of the lungs

empire ('empīər) n. large territory, esp. aggregate of states under supreme ruler, supreme control —**empire-builder** n. inf. person who seeks extra power, esp. by increasing his staff —**empire-building** n./a. —**empire style** style of decorative arts of French First Empire (1804-14) characterized by clarity, balance and restraint, and motifs from classical antiquity

empirical (em'pirikəl) a. relying on experiment or experience, not on theory —em'piric a. 1. empirical —n. 2. one who relies solely on experience and observation —em'pirically adv. —empiricism (em'pirisizəm) n.

emplacement (im'plāsmənt) n. 1. putting in position 2. gun platform

emplane (im'plān) v. board or put on board airplane

employ (im'ploi) vt. 1. provide work for (a person) in return for money, hire 2. keep busy 3. use (em'ployed, em'ploying) —em'ploy'ee n. —em'ployer n. —em'ployment n. 1. an employing, being employed 2. work, trade 3. occupation

emporium (em'pōriəm) n. 1. large general shop 2. centre of commerce (pl. -s, -ria (-riə))

empower (im'powər) vt. 1. enable 2. authorize

empress ('empris) n. see EMPEROR

empty ('empti) a. 1. containing nothing 2. unoccupied 3. senseless 4. vain, foolish —v. 5. make, become devoid of content 6. discharge (contents) (into) ('emptied, 'emptying) —'empties pl.n. empty boxes, bottles etc. —'emptiness n. —**empty-handed** a. 1. carrying nothing in hands 2. having gained nothing —**empty-headed** a. lacking sense

empyrean (empī'rēən) n. 1. obs. in ancient cosmology, highest part of the heavens 2. Poet. heavens; sky —a., also empy'real 3. of sky 4. heavenly, sublime

emu ('emyōo) n. large Aust. flightless bird like ostrich

emulate ('emyəlāt) vt. 1. strive to equal or excel 2. imitate —emu'lation n. 1. rivalry 2. competition —'emulative a. —'emulator n. —'emulous a. eager to equal or surpass another or his deeds

emulsion (i'mulshən) n. 1. light-sensitive coating of film 2. milky liquid with oily or resinous particles in suspension 3. paint etc. in this form —e'mulsifier n. substance used to disperse particles of an oily, fatty or other substance in a liquid —e'mulsify v. (e'mulsified, e'mulsifying) —e'mulsive a.

en (en) n. Print. unit of measurement, half an em

en- or **em-** (comb. form) put in, into, on, as in enrage. Such words are not given here where the meaning may easily be inferred from the simple word

-en¹ (comb. form) cause to be; become; cause to have, as in blacken, heighten

-en² (comb. form) of; made of; resembling, as in ashen, wooden

enable (in'ābəl) vt. make able, authorize, empower, supply with means (to do something) —**enabling act** legislative act conferring certain powers on person or organization

enact (in'akt) vt. 1. make law 2. represent or perform as in a play —en'actment n.

enamel (i'naməl) n. 1. glasslike coating applied to metal etc. to preserve surface 2. coating of teeth 3. any hard outer coating —vt. 4. decorate with enamel 5. ornament with glossy variegated colors, as if with enamel 6. portray in enamel

enamor (in'amər) vt. 1. inspire with love 2. charm 3. bewitch

en bloc (ä 'blok) Fr. 1. in a lump or block 2. all together

enc. 1. enclosed 2. enclosure

encamp (in'kamp) v. set up (in) camp —en'campment n. camp

encapsulate (in'kapsəlāt) vt. 1. enclose in capsule 2. put in concise or abridged form

encase (in'kās) *vt.* place or enclose as in case —**en'casement** *n.*

encaustic (in'kôstik) *a.* 1. with colors burnt in —*n.* 2. art of ornament by burnt-in colors

-ence *or* **-ency** (*comb. form*) action, state, condition, quality, as in *benevolence, residence, patience, fluency, permanency*

enceinte (on'sant) *a.* pregnant

encephalitis (insefə'lītis) *n.* inflammation of brain —**encephalitic** (insefə'litik) *a.*

encephalo- *or before vowel* **encephal-** (*comb. form*) brain, as in *encephalogram, encephalitis*

encephalogram (in'sefələgram) *n.* x-ray photograph of brain

enchain (in'chān) *vt.* 1. bind with chains 2. hold fast or captivate (attention *etc.*) —**en'chainment** *n.*

enchant (in'chänt) *vt.* 1. bewitch 2. delight —**en'chanter** *n.* (**-tress** *fem.*) —**en'chantment** *n.*

enchilada (enchi'lädə) *n.* Mexican dish of tortilla filled with meat, served with chili sauce

encircle (in'sərkəl) *vt.* 1. surround 2. enfold 3. go round so as to encompass —**en'circlement** *n.*

enclave ('enklāv) *n.* portion of territory entirely surrounded by foreign land

enclitic (en'klitik) *a.* 1. pronounced as part of another word —*n.* 2. enclitic word or form

enclose *or* **inclose** (in'klōz) *vt.* 1. shut in 2. surround 3. envelop 4. place in with something else (in letter *etc.*) —**en'closure** *or* **in'closure** *n.* —**enclosed order** Christian religious order whose members do not go into the outside world

encomium (en'kōmiəm) *n.* 1. formal praise 2. eulogy —**en'comiast** *n.* one who composes encomiums —**encomi'astic** *a.* —**encomi'astically** *adv.*

encompass (in'kumpəs) *vt.* 1. surround, encircle 2. contain

encore ('ongkôr) *interj.* 1. again, once more —*n.* 2. call for repetition of song *etc.* 3. the repetition —*vt.* 4. ask to repeat

encounter (in'kowntər) *vt.* 1. meet unexpectedly 2. meet in conflict 3. be faced with (difficulty) —*n.* 4. casual or unexpected meeting 5. hostile meeting; contest —**encounter group** group of people who meet to develop self-awareness and mutual understanding by openly expressing feelings *etc.*

encourage (in'kurij) *vt.* 1. hearten, animate, inspire with hope 2. embolden —**en'couragement** *n.*

encroach (in'krōch) *vi.* 1. intrude (on) as usurper 2. trespass —**en'croachment** *n.*

encrust *or* **incrust** (in'krust) *v.* cover with or form a crust or hard covering

encumber *or* **incumber** (in'kumbər) *vt.* 1. hamper 2. burden —**en'cumbrance** *or* **in'cumbrance** *n.* impediment, burden

-ency (*comb. form*) *see* -ENCE

encyclical (en'siklikəl) *a.* 1. sent to many persons or places —*n.* 2. circular letter, *esp.* from Pope

encyclopedia *or* **encyclopaedia** (ensīklō'pēdiə) *n.* book, set of books of information on all subjects, or on every branch of subject, usu. arranged alphabetically —**encyclo'pedic** *or* **encyclo'paedic** *a.* —**encyclo'pedist** *or* **encyclo'paedist** *n.*

end (end) *n.* 1. limit 2. extremity 3. conclusion, finishing 4. fragment 5. latter part 6. death 7. event, issue 8. purpose, aim 9. *Sport* either of the defended areas of a playing field *etc.* —*vt.* 10. put an end to —*vi.* 11. come to an end, finish —**'ending** *n.*

—**'endless** *a.* —**'endmost** *a.* nearest end; most distant —**'endways** *adv.* —**'endpapers** *pl.n.* blank pages at beginning and end of book —**end product** final result of process *etc., esp.* in manufacturing —**end run** play in football in which the ball carrier tries to run wide of the opponents to reach the goal line —**end of steel C** (town at) point to which railroad tracks have been laid —**end it all** *inf.* commit suicide

endanger (in'dānjər) *vt.* put in danger or peril —**en'dangerment** *n.*

endear (in'dēər) *vt.* make dear or beloved —**en'dearing** *a.* —**en'dearingly** *adv.* —**en'dearment** *n.* 1. loving word 2. tender affection

endeavor (in'devər) *vi.* 1. try, strive —*n.* 2. attempt, effort

endemic (en'demik) *a.* 1. regularly occurring in a country or district —*n.* 2. endemic disease

endive ('endīv) *n.* curly-leaved chicory used as salad

endo- *or before vowel* **end-** (*comb. form*) within, as in *endocardium, endocrine.* Such words are not given here where the meaning may easily be inferred from the simple word

endocardium (endō'kärdiəm) *n.* lining membrane of the heart

endocrine ('endōkrin, -krīn) *a.* of those glands (thyroid, pituitary *etc.*) which secrete hormones directly into bloodstream

endogenous (en'dojinəs) *a. Biol.* developing or originating within an organism —**en'dogeny** *n.*

endorphin (en'dôrfin) *n.* chemical occurring in brain, which has similar effect to morphine

endorse *or* **indorse** (in'dôrs) *vt.* 1. sanction 2. confirm 3. write (*esp.* sign name) on back of 4. record (conviction) on (driver's license) —**endor'sation** *n.* **C** approval, support —**en'dorsement** *or* **in'dorsement** *n.*

endow (in'dow) *vt.* 1. provide permanent income for 2. furnish (with) —**en'dowment** *n.* —**endowment policy** life insurance that provides for payment of specified sum to policyholder at designated date or to his beneficiary should he die before this date

endue *or* **indue** (in'dyoo, -'doo) *vt.* invest, furnish (with quality *etc.*)

endure (in'dyooər, -'dooər) *vt.* 1. undergo 2. tolerate, bear —*vi.* 3. last —**en'durable** *a.* —**en'durance** *n.* act or power of enduring —**en'during** *a.* 1. permanent 2. having forbearance —**en'duringness** *n.*

enema ('enimə) *n.* medicine, liquid injected into rectum

enemy ('enəmi) *n.* 1. hostile person 2. opponent 3. armed foe 4. hostile force

energy ('enərji) *n.* 1. capacity to do work *esp.* the capacity of a force to set a body of matter in motion 2. source(s) of power, as oil, coal *etc.* 3. capacity of machine, battery *etc.* for work or output of power —**ener'getic** *a.* —**ener'getically** *adv.* —**'energize** *vt.* give vigor to

enervate ('enərvāt) *vt.* weaken, deprive of vigor —**ener'vation** *n.* lassitude, weakness

enfant terrible (ãfã te'rēbl) *Fr.* person given to unconventional conduct or indiscreet remarks (*pl.* **enfants terribles** (ãfã te'rēbl))

enfeeble (in'fēbəl) *vt.* weaken, debilitate —**en'feeblement** *n.*

enfilade ('enfilād) *n.* fire from artillery, sweeping line from end to end

enfold *or* **infold** (in'fōld) *vt.* 1. cover by enclosing 2. embrace —**en'folder** *or* **in'folder** *n.*

enforce (in'fôrs) *vt.* 1. compel obedience to 2. impose (action) upon 3. drive home —**en'forceable** *a.* —**en'forcement** *n.*

enfranchise (in'franchīz) *vt.* 1. give right of voting to 2. give parliamentary representation to 3. set free —**en'franchisement** *n.*

Eng. 1. England 2. English

eng. 1. engine 2. engineer 3. engineering

engage (in'gāj) *vt.* 1. employ 2. reserve, hire 3. bind by contract or promise 4. order 5. pledge oneself 6. betroth 7. undertake 8. attract 9. occupy 10. bring into conflict 11. interlock —*vi.* 12. employ oneself (in) 13. promise 14. begin to fight —**en'gaged** *a.* 1. betrothed 2. in use 3. occupied, busy —**en'gagement** *n.* —**en'gaging** *a.* charming

engender (in'jendər) *vt.* 1. give rise to 2. beget 3. rouse

engine ('enjin) *n.* 1. any machine to convert energy into mechanical work, as steam engine 2. railroad locomotive 3. fire engine —**engi'neer** *n.* 1. one who is in charge of engines, machinery *etc.* or construction work (*eg* roads, bridges) or installation of plant 2. one who originates, organizes something 3. driver of railroad locomotive —*vt.* 4. construct as engineer 5. contrive —**engi'neering** *n.*

England ('ingglənd) *n.* country in W Europe in S Great Britain bordered north by Scotland, east by the North Sea, south by the English Channel and west by Wales and the Irish Sea: part of United Kingdom —**'English** *n.* 1. the language of Britain, the U.S.A., most parts of the Commonwealth and certain other countries 2. (*with pl.v.*) the people of England —*a.* 3. relating to England —**English horn** an alto oboe

engorge (in'gôrj) *vt.* 1. *Pathol.* congest with blood 2. eat (food) greedily 3. gorge (oneself) —**en'gorgement** *n.*

engr. 1. engineer 2. engraved 3. engraver 4. engraving

engraft (in'graft) *vt.* 1. graft on 2. plant deeply 3. incorporate

engrain (in'grān) *vt. see* INGRAIN

engrave (in'grāv) *vt.* 1. cut in lines on metal for printing 2. carve, incise 3. impress deeply —**en'graver** *n.* —**en'graving** *n.* copy of picture printed from engraved plate

engross (in'grōs) *vt.* 1. absorb (attention) 2. occupy wholly 3. write out in large letters or in legal form 4. corner —**en'grossment** *n.*

engulf (in'gulf) *vt.* swallow up

enhance (in'hans) *vt.* heighten, intensify, increase value or attractiveness of —**en'hancement** *n.*

enigma (i'nigmə) *n.* 1. puzzling thing or person 2. riddle —**enig'matic(al)** *a.* —**enig'matically** *adv.*

enjambment *or* **enjambement** (in'jammənt) *n.* in verse, continuation of sentence beyond end of line

enjoin (in'join) *vt.* 1. command 2. forbid, prohibit

enjoy (in'joi) *vt.* 1. delight in 2. take pleasure in 3. have use or benefit of —*v. refl.* 4. be happy —**en'joyable** *a.* —**en'joyment** *n.*

enkindle (in'kindəl) *vt.* 1. set on fire; kindle 2. excite to activity or ardor; arouse

enlarge (in'lärj) *vt.* 1. make bigger 2. reproduce on larger scale, as photograph —*vi.* 3. grow bigger 4. talk, write in greater detail 5. be capable of reproduction on larger scale —**en'largeable** *a.* —**en'largement** *n.* —**en'larger** *n.* optical instrument for enlarging photographs

enlighten (in'lītən) *vt.* 1. give information to 2. instruct, inform 3. *Poet.* shed light on —**en'lightenment** *n.*

enlist (in'list) v. (persuade to) enter armed forces —**en'listment** n.

enliven (in'līvən) vt. brighten, make more lively, animate

en masse (Fr. ã 'mas) 1. in a group, body 2. all together

enmesh (in'mesh) or **immesh** vt. entangle

enmity ('enmiti) n. ill will, hostility

ennoble (i'nōbəl) vt. make noble, elevate —**en'noblement** n.

ennui ('on'wē) n. boredom

enormous (i'nôrməs) a. very big, vast —**e'normity** n. 1. a gross offense 2. great wickedness 3. inf. great size

enough (i'nuf) a. 1. as much or as many as need be 2. sufficient —n. 3. sufficient quantity —adv. 4. (just) sufficiently

enounce (i'nowns) vt. 1. state 2. enunciate, proclaim —**e'nouncement** n.

en passant (on pa'sän) Fr. in passing, by the way

enplane (in'plān) vi. board aircraft

enquire (in'kwīər) v. see INQUIRE

enrapture (in'rapchər) vt. 1. delight excessively 2. charm —**en'rapt** or **en'raptured** a. entranced

enrich (in'rich) vt. 1. make rich 2. add to —**en'richment** n.

enroll or **enrol** (in'rōl) vt. 1. write name of on roll or list 2. engage, enlist, take in as member 3. enter, record —vi. 4. become member —**en'rollment** n.

en route (on 'rōōt) Fr. on the way

ensconce (in'skons) vt. 1. place snugly 2. establish in safety

ensemble (on'sombəl) n. 1. whole 2. all parts taken together 3. woman's complete outfit 4. company of actors, dancers etc. 5. Mus. group of soloists performing together 6. Mus. concerted passage 7. general effect —adv. 8. all together or at once

enshrine (in'shrīn) vt. 1. set in shrine 2. preserve with great care and sacred affection

enshroud (in'shrowd) vt. cover or hide as with shroud

ensign ('ensīn) n. 1. (also 'ensən) naval or military flag 2. badge 3. (in U.S. Navy and coastguard) commissioned officer ranking above chief warrant officer and below lieutenant junior grade

ensilage ('ensilij) n. the process of making silage

enslave (in'slāv) vt. make into slave —**en'slavement** n. bondage —**en'slaver** n.

ensnare or **insnare** (in'snāər) vt. 1. capture in snare or trap 2. trick into false position 3. entangle

ensue (in'sōō) vi. follow, happen after

en suite (ã 'suēt) forming a set or single unit

ensure (en'shōōr) vt. 1. make safe or sure 2. make certain to happen 3. secure

E.N.T. Med. ear, nose and throat

-ent (comb. form) causing or performing action or existing in certain condition; agent that performs action, as in astringent, dependent

entablature (en'tabləchōōr) n. Archit. part of classical temple above columns, having architrave, frieze and cornice

entail (in'tāl) vt. 1. involve as result, necessitate 2. Law restrict (ownership of property) to designated line of heirs

entangle (in'tanggəl) vt. 1. ensnare 2. perplex —**en'tanglement** n.

entente (Fr. ã'tãt) n. friendly understanding between nations —**entente cordiale** (kor'dyal) 1. friendly understanding between

political powers 2. (oft. E- C-) understanding reached by France and Britain in April 1904 over colonial disputes

enter ('entər) vt. 1. go, come into 2. penetrate 3. join 4. write in, register —vi. 5. go, come in 6. join a party etc. 7. begin —'entrance n. 1. going, coming in 2. door, passage to enter 3. right to enter 4. fee paid for this —'entrant n. one who enters, esp. contest —'entry n. 1. entrance 2. entering 3. item entered, eg in account, list

enteric (en'terik) or **enteral** ('entərəl) a. of intestines —ente'ritis n. bowel inflammation

enterprise ('entərprīz) n. 1. bold or difficult undertaking 2. bold spirit 3. force of character in launching out 4. business, company —'enterprising a.

entertain (entər'tān) vt. 1. amuse, divert 2. receive as guest 3. maintain 4. consider favorable 5. take into consideration —enter'tainer n. —enter'taining a. serving to entertain; amusing —enter'tainment n.

enthrall or **enthral** (in'thrôl) vt. captivate, thrill, hold spellbound —en'thrallment n.

enthrone (en'thrōn) vt. 1. place on throne 2. honor; exalt 3. assign authority to —en'thronement n.

enthusiasm (in'thyōōziazəm, -'thōō-) n. ardent eagerness, zeal —en'thuse v. (cause to) show enthusiasm —en'thusiast n. ardent supporter —enthusi'astic a. —enthusi'astically adv.

entice (in'tīs) vt. allure, attract, inveigle, tempt —en'ticement n. —en'ticing a. alluring

entire (in'tīər, 'entīər) a. 1. whole, complete 2. unbroken —en'tirely adv. —entirety (in'tīriti, -'tīərti) n.

entitle (in'tītəl) vt. 1. give claim to 2. qualify 3. give title to 4. style

entity ('entiti) n. 1. thing's being or existence 2. reality 3. thing having real existence

entomb (in'tōōm) vt. 1. place in or as if in tomb; bury 2. serve as tomb for —en'tombment n.

entomology (entə'moləji) n. study of insects —entomo'logical a. —ento'mologist n. —ento'mologize vi.

entourage (ontōō'räzh) n. 1. associates, retinue 2. surroundings

entozoon (entō'zōon) n. internal parasite (pl. -zoa (-'zōə)) —entozoic (entō'zōik) a.

entr'acte ('ontrakt) n. 1. interval between acts of play etc. 2. esp. formerly, entertainment during such interval

entrails ('entrālz) pl.n. 1. bowels, intestines 2. inner parts

entrain (in'trān) v. board or put aboard train —en'trainment n.

entrance¹ ('entrəns) n. see ENTER

entrance² (in'trans) vt. 1. delight 2. throw into a trance

entrap (in'trap) vt. 1. catch or snare as in trap 2. trick into difficulty etc. (-pp-) —en'trapment n.

entreat (in'trēt) vt. 1. ask earnestly 2. beg, implore —en'treaty n. earnest request

entrée ('ontrā) n. 1. (dish served before) main course of meal 2. right of access, admission

entrench or **intrench** (in'trench) vt. 1. establish in fortified position with trenches 2. establish firmly —en'trenchment or in'trenchment n.

entrepreneur (ontrəprə'nər) n. person who attempts to profit by risk and initiative

entropy ('entrəpi) n. 1. unavailability of the

heat energy of a system for mechanical work 2. measurement of this

entrust or **intrust** (in'trust) vt. 1. commit, charge (with) 2. (oft. with to) put into care or protection of

entwine (in'twīn) vt. 1. plait, interweave 2. wreathe 3. embrace

enumerate (i'nyōōmərāt, -'nōō-) vt. 1. mention one by one 2. count —enumer'ation n. —e'numerative a. —e'numerator n.

enunciate (i'nunsiāt) vt. 1. state clearly 2. proclaim 3. pronounce —enunci'ation n. —e'nunciative a. —e'nunciator n.

enure (in'yōōr, in'ōōr) vt. see INURE

enuresis (enyōō'rēsis) n. involuntary discharge of urine, esp. during sleep —enuretic (enyōō'retik) a.

envelop (in'veləp) vt. 1. wrap up, enclose 2. surround 3. encircle —en'velopment n.

envelope ('envəlōp, 'on-) n. 1. folded, gummed cover of letter 2. covering, wrapper

envenom (in'venəm) vt. 1. put poison, venom in 2. embitter

environ (in'vīrən) vt. surround —en'vironment n. 1. surroundings 2. conditions of life or growth —environ'mental a. —environ'mentalist n. ecologist —en'virons pl.n. districts round town etc., outskirts

envisage (in'vizij) vt. 1. conceive of as possibility 2. visualize

envoi or **envoy** ('envoi) n. concluding stanza in ballade

envoy ('envoi) n. 1. messenger 2. diplomatic representative of rank below ambassador

envy ('envi) vt. 1. grudge (another's good fortune, success or qualities) 2. feel jealous of ('envied, 'envying) —n. 3. bitter contemplation of another's good fortune 4. jealousy 5. object of this feeling —'enviable a. arousing envy —'envious a. full of envy

enzyme ('enzīm) n. substance which catalyzes a reaction in a living system

Eocene ('ēəsēn) a. 1. of second epoch of Tertiary period, during which hooved mammals appeared —n. 2. Eocene epoch or rock series

eolith ('ēəlith) n. early flint implement —Eo'lithic a. of the period before Stone Age

eon ('ēən, 'ēon) n. 1. age, very long period of time 2. eternity

-eous (comb. form) relating to or having nature of, as in gaseous

EP 1. extended-play 2. electroplate

epaulet or **epaulette** (epə'let, 'epəlet) n. shoulder ornament formerly on uniform

épée ('epā) n. sword similar to foil but with heavier blade —'épéeist n.

epergne (i'pərn) n. ornamental centerpiece for table, holding flowers etc.

Eph. Bible Ephesians

ephedrine (i'fedrin) n. drug used to treat asthma, hay fever and other allergic disorders

ephemeral (i'femərəl) a. short-lived, transient —e'phemeron n. ephemeral thing (pl. -s, -ra (-rə)) (also e'phemera (pl. -s, -rae (-rē))) —e'phemerous a.

Ephesians (i'fēzhənz) pl.n. (with sing. v.) Bible 10th book of the N.T., epistle written by St. Paul to Christians of Ephesus from his captivity at Rome about 60 A.D.

epi-, eph-, or before vowel **ep-** (comb. form) 1. upon; above, as in epidermis 2. in addition to, as in epiphenomenon 3. after, as in epilogue 4. near, as in epicalyx

epic ('epik) n. 1. long poem or story telling of achievements of hero or heroes 2. film etc.

about heroic deeds —*a.* **3.** of, like, an epic **4.** impressive, grand

epicene ('episēn) *a.* common to both sexes

epicenter ('episentər) *n.* focus of earthquake —**epi'central** *a.*

epicure ('epikyŏŏər) *n.* one delighting in eating and drinking —**epicu'rean** *a.* **1.** of Epicurus, who taught that pleasure, in the shape of practice of virtue, was highest good **2.** given to refined sensuous enjoyment —*n.* **3.** such person or philosopher —**epicu'reanism** *n.* —**'epicurism** *n.*

epicycle ('episīkəl) *n.* circle whose center moves on circumference of greater circle

epidemic (epi'demik) *a.* **1.** (*esp.* of disease) prevalent and spreading rapidly **2.** widespread —*n.* **3.** widespread occurrence of a disease **4.** rapid development, spread or growth of something —**epi'demical** *a.* —**epidemiological** (epidēmiə'lojikəl) *a.* —**epidemiologist** (epidēmi'oləjist) *n.* —**epidemiology** (epidēmi'oləji) *n.* branch of medical science concerned with epidemic diseases —**epidemic parotitis** (parō'tītis) mumps

epidermis (epi'dərmis) *n.* outer skin

epidiascope (epi'dīəskōp) *n.* optical device for projecting magnified image on to screen

epidural (epi'dyŏŏrəl, -'dŏŏrəl) *n./a.* (of) spinal anesthetic used for relief of pain during childbirth

epiglottis (epi'glotis) *n.* cartilage that covers opening of larynx in swallowing —**epi'glottic** *a.*

epigram ('epigram) *n.* concise, witty poem or saying —**epigram'matic(al)** *a.* —**epigram'matically** *adv.* —**epi'grammatist** *n.*

epigraph ('epigraf) *n.* inscription

epilepsy ('epilepsi) *n.* disorder of nervous system causing fits and convulsions —**epi'leptic** *n.* **1.** sufferer from this —*a.* **2.** of, subject to, this

epilogue ('epilog) *n.* short speech or poem at end, *esp.* of play

epinephrine *or* **epinephrin** (epi'nefrin) *n.* hormone secreted by medulla of the adrenal gland which mobilizes the body for strenuous or emergency activity, used medicinally as stimulant *etc.* (*also* **adrenaline**)

Epiphany (i'pifəni) *n.* festival of the announcement of Christ to the Magi, celebrated Jan. 6th

epiphysis (i'pifisis) *n.* pineal body

epiphyte ('epifīt) *n.* plant which grows on another without being parasitic

Epis. 1. Episcopal; Episcopalian (*also* **Episc.**) **2.** Epistle

episcopal (i'piskəpəl) *a.* **1.** of bishop **2.** ruled by bishops —**e'piscopacy** *n.* government by body of bishops —**Episco'palian** *a.* **1.** of branch of Anglican Church in the U.S. —*n.* **2.** member or adherent of Protestant Christian denomination whose doctrine is based on the Apostles' Creed and in which practice ranges from rationalist to acceptance of most Roman Catholic dogma and is part of the Anglican Communion —**e'piscopate** *n.* **1.** bishop's office, see, or duration of office **2.** body of bishops

episode ('episōd) *n.* **1.** incident **2.** section of (serialized) book, television program *etc.* —**episodic(al)** (epi'sodik(əl)) *a.*

epistemology (ipisti'moləji) *n.* study of source, nature and limitations of knowledge —**epistemo'logical** *a.* —**episte'mologist** *n.*

epistle (i'pisəl) *n.* **1.** letter, *esp.* of apostle **2.** poem in letter form —**epistolary** (i'pistəleri) *a.* —**epistoler** (i'pistələr) *n.*

epitaph ('epitaf) *n.* memorial inscription on tomb

epithelium (epi'thēliəm) *n.* tissue covering external and internal surfaces of body (*pl.* **-s, -lia** (-liə)) —**epi'thelial** *or* **epi'thelioid** *a.*

epithet ('epithet) *n.* additional, descriptive word or name —**epi'thetic(al)** *a.*

epitome (i'pitəmi) *n.* **1.** typical example **2.** summary —**e'pitomist** *n.* —**e'pitomize** *vt.* typify

epoch ('epək, 'epok) *n.* **1.** beginning of period **2.** period, era, *esp.* one of notable events —**'epochal** *a.*

epode ('epōd) *n.* third, or last, part of lyric ode

eponym ('epənim) *n.* **1.** name, *esp.* place name, derived from name of real or mythical person **2.** name of person from which such name is derived —**e'ponymous** *a.* —**e'ponymously** *adv.* —**e'ponymy** *n.*

epoxy ('epoksi, e'poksi) *a. Chem.* of, consisting of, or containing oxygen atom joined to two different groups that are themselves joined to other groups —**epoxy resin** any of various thermosetting synthetic resins containing epoxy groups: used in surface coatings, adhesives *etc.*

epsilon ('epsilon) *n.* fifth letter of Gr. alphabet (E, ϵ)

Epsom salts ('epsəm) medicinal preparation of hydrated magnesium sulfate, used as purgative *etc.*

equable ('ekwəbəl) *a.* **1.** even-tempered, placid **2.** uniform —**equa'bility** *n.* —**'equably** *adv.*

equal ('ēkwəl) *a.* **1.** the same in number, size, merit *etc.* **2.** identical **3.** fit or qualified **4.** evenly balanced —*n.* **5.** one equal to another —*vt.* **6.** be equal to —**equality** (i'kwoliti) *n.* **1.** state of being equal **2.** uniformity —**equali'zation** *n.* —**'equalize** *v.* make, become, equal —**'equally** *adv.*

equanimity (ēkwə'nimiti, ekwə-) *n.* calmness, composure, steadiness

equate (i'kwāt) *vt.* **1.** make equal **2.** bring to a common standard —**equation** (i'kwāzhən, -shən) *n.* in chemistry and mathematics, statement asserting the equality of two expressions or two numbers

equator (i'kwātər) *n.* imaginary circle round earth equidistant from the poles —**equa'torial** *a.*

Equatorial Guinea country in Africa bounded west by the Atlantic, north by Cameroon and east and south by Gabon

equerry ('ekwəri, i'kweri) *n.* **1.** officer in attendance on sovereign **2.** officer in royal household in charge of horses

equestrian (i'kwestriən) *a.* **1.** of, skilled in, horse-riding **2.** mounted on horse —*n.* **3.** rider

equi- (*comb. form*) equal, at equal, as in *equidistant*. Such words are not given here where the meaning can easily be inferred from the simple word

equiangular (ēkwi'anggyŏŏlər) *a.* having equal angles

equilateral (ēkwi'latərəl) *a.* having equal sides

equilibrium (ēkwi'libriəm) *n.* state of steadiness, equipoise or stability (*pl.* **-s, -ria** (-riə))

equine ('ekwīn) *a.* of, like a horse

equinox ('ēkwinoks) *n.* **1.** time when sun crosses equator and day and night are equal —*pl.* **2.** points at which sun crosses equator —**equinoctial** (ēkwi'nokshəl) *a.*

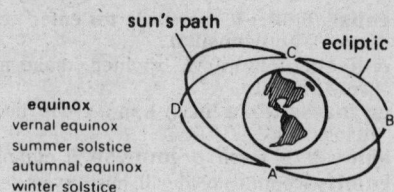

sun's path

ecliptic

equinox

A vernal equinox
B summer solstice
C autumnal equinox
D winter solstice

equip (i'kwip) *vt.* supply, fit out, array (**-pp-**) —**equipage** ('ekwipij) *n.* **1.** carriage, horses and attendants **2.** *obs.* outfit, requisites —**e'quipment** *n.*

equipoise ('ekwipoiz) *n.* **1.** perfect balance **2.** counterpoise **3.** equanimity —*vt.* **4.** counterbalance

equisetum (ekwi'sētəm) *n.* genus of primitive plant comprising the horsetail and scouring rush

equitation (ekwi'tāshən) *n.* study and practice of riding and horsemanship

equity ('ekwiti) *n.* **1.** fairness **2.** ownership right in property **3.** (E-) actors' union —**'equitable** *a.* fair, reasonable, just —**'equitably** *adv.* —**equity capital** corporate earnings or individual savings available for investment in new enterprise (*also* **venture capital**)

equiv. equivalent

equivalent (i'kwivələnt) *a.* **1.** equal in value **2.** having the same meaning or result **3.** tantamount **4.** corresponding —**e'quivalence** *or* **e'quivalency** *n.*

equivocal (i'kwivəkəl) *a.* **1.** of double or doubtful meaning **2.** questionable **3.** liable to suspicion —**equivo'cality** *n.* —**e'quivocate** *vi.* use equivocal words to mislead —**equivo'cation** *n.* —**e'quivocator** *n.*

er (ə, ər) *interj.* sound made when hesitating in speech

Er *Chem.* erbium

E.R. Elizabeth Regina (*Lat.*, Queen Elizabeth)

-er¹ (*comb. form*) **1.** person or thing that performs specified action, as in *reader* **2.** person engaged in profession *etc.*, as in *writer* **3.** native or inhabitant of, as in *Londoner* **4.** person or thing having certain characteristic, as in *newcomer*

-er² (*comb. form*) forming comparative degree of adjective or adverb, as in *deeper, faster*

era ('ēərə) *n.* **1.** system of time in which years are numbered from particular event **2.** time of the event **3.** memorable date, period

ERA 1. equal rights amendment **2.** *Baseball* earned run average

eradicate (i'radikāt) *vt.* **1.** wipe out, exterminate **2.** root out —**e'radicable** *a.* —**eradi'cation** *n.* —**e'radicative** *a./n.* —**e'radicator** *n.*

erase (i'rās) *vt.* **1.** rub out **2.** remove, *eg* recording from magnetic tape —**e'raser** *n.* —**e'rasure** *n.*

erbium ('ərbiəm) *n. Chem.* metallic element Symbol Er, at. wt. 167.3, at. no. 68

ere (āər) *prep./conj.* **1.** *Poet.* before **2.** sooner than —**ere'long** *adv. obs., poet.* before long; soon

erect (i'rekt) *a.* **1.** upright —*vt.* **2.** set up **3.** build —**e'rectile** *a.* —**e'rection** *n. esp.* an erect penis —**e'rector** *n.*

eremite ('erimīt) *n.* Christian hermit or recluse —**eremitic(al)** (eri'mitik(əl)) *a.* —**'eremitism** *n.*

erg (ərg) *n.* cgs unit of work or energy

ergo ('ərgō) *adv.* therefore

ergonomics (ərgə'nomiks) *pl.n.* (*with sing. v.*) study of relationship between workers and their environment

ergot ('ərgət, -got) *n.* 1. disease of grain *esp.* rye 2. diseased seed used as drug —'**ergotism** *n.* disease caused by eating ergot-infested bread

erica ('erikə) *n.* genus of plants including heathers

Erin ('erin) *n. obs., poet.* Ireland

ermine ('ərmin) *n.* 1. stoat in northern regions, *esp.* in winter 2. its white winter fur

erne *or* **ern** (ərn) *n.* fish-eating sea eagle

erode (i'rōd) *v.* 1. wear away —*vt.* 2. eat into —e'**rosion** *n.* —e'**rosive** *a.*

erogenous (i'rojinəs) *a.* sensitive to sexual stimulation

erotic (i'rotik) *a.* relating to, or treating of, sexual pleasure —e'**rotica** *n.* sexual literature or art —e'**roticism** *n.*

err (er, ər) *vi.* 1. make mistakes 2. be wrong 3. sin —er'**ratic** *a.* irregular in movement, conduct *etc.* —er'**ratically** *adv.* —**erratum** (e'rätəm) *n.* printing mistake noted for correction (*pl.* -**ta** (-tə)) —er'**roneous** *a.* mistaken, wrong —'**error** *n.* 1. mistake 2. wrong opinion 3. sin

errand ('erənd) *n.* 1. short journey for simple business 2. purpose of such journey 3. the business, mission of messenger —**errand boy**

errant ('erənt) *a.* 1. wandering in search of adventure 2. erring —'**errancy** *n.* erring state or conduct —'**errantry** *n.* state or conduct of knight errant

ersatz ('äərzats, 'erzats) *a.* substitute, imitation

Erse (ərs) *n.* 1. *see* **Gaelic** at GAEL —*a.* 2. of or relating to Gaelic language

erst (ərst) *adv.* of old, formerly

eruct (i'rukt) *v.* 1. belch 2. (of volcano) pour out (fumes or volcanic matter) —**eruc'tation** *n.*

erudite ('eryədīt, 'erə-) *a.* learned —**erudition** (eryə'dishən, erə-) *n.* learning

erupt (i'rupt) *vi.* burst out —e'**ruption** *n.* 1. bursting out, *esp.* volcanic outbreak 2. rash on the skin —e'**ruptive** *a.*

-ery *or* **-ry** (*comb. form*) 1. place of business or activity, as in *bakery, refinery* 2. class or collection of things, as in *cutlery* 3. qualities, actions, as in *snobbery, trickery* 4. practice, occupation, as in *husbandry* 5. state, condition, as in *slavery*

erysipelas (eri'sipiləs) *n.* acute skin infection caused by streptococcus

erythema (eri'thēmə) *n.* patchy inflammation of skin —**erythematic** (erithi'matik) *or* ery'**thematous** *a.*

erythrocyte (i'rithrəsīt) *n.* red blood cell of vertebrates that transports oxygen and carbon dioxide —**erythrocytic** (irithrə'sitik) *a.*

Es *Chem.* einsteinium

escalate ('eskəlāt) *v.* increase, be increased, in extent, intensity *etc.*

escalator ('eskəlātər) *n.* moving staircase —**escalator clause** clause in contract stipulating adjustment in wages *etc.* in event of large rise in cost of living *etc.*

escallop (i'skolop, i'skal-) *see* SCALLOP

escape (i'skāp) *vi.* 1. get free 2. get off safely 3. go unpunished 4. find way out —*vt.* 5. elude 6. be forgotten by —*n.* 7. escaping —**escapade** ('eskəpād) *n.* wild (mischievous) adventure —**es'capement** *n.* 1. mechanism consisting of toothed wheel and anchor, used in timepieces to provide periodic impulses to pendulum or balance 2. any similar mechanism that regulates movement —**es'capism**

n. taking refuge in fantasy to avoid facing disagreeable facts —**escapologist** (iskä-'poləjist) *n.* entertainer specializing in freeing himself from confinement —**escape clause** clause releasing signatory to contract under certain conditions —**escape hatch** means of emergency exit from shop *etc.* —**escape velocity** minimum velocity necessary for a body to escape from the gravitational field of the earth *etc.*

escarp (i'skärp) *n.* steep bank under rampart —**es'carpment** *n.* 1. steep hillside 2. escarp

-escent (*a. comb. form*) beginning to be, do, show *etc.*, as in *convalescent, luminescent* —-**escence** (*n. comb. form*)

eschatology (eskə'toləji) *n.* study of death, judgment and last things —**eschato'logical** *a.*

escheat (is'chēt) *Law n.* 1. reversion of property to state in absence of legal heirs 2. property so reverting —*v.* 3. take (land) by escheat or (of land) revert by escheat —**es'cheatable** *a.* —**es'cheatage** *n.*

eschew (is'chōō) *vt.* avoid, abstain from, shun

eschscholtzia (is'kolshə) *n.* garden plant with bright flowers, California poppy

escort ('eskört) *n.* 1. armed guard for traveler *etc.* 2. person or persons accompanying another —*vt.* (is'kört) 3. accompany or attend as escort

escritoire ('eskritwär) *n.* type of writing desk

esculent ('eskyələnt) *a.* edible

escutcheon (i'skuchən) *n.* 1. shield with coat of arms 2. ornamental plate round keyhole *etc.* —**blot on one's escutcheon** stain on one's honor

Esdras ('ezdrəs) *n. Bible* Ezra and Nehemiah in the Douay Version of the O.T.

-ese (*comb. form*) place of origin, language, style, as in *Cantonese, Japanese, journalese*

Eskimo ('eskimō) *n.* 1. one of aboriginal race inhabiting N Amer., Greenland *etc.* (*pl.* -**s**) 2. their language 3. *sl.* a Jew

esophagus

esophagus (i'sofəgəs) *n.* gullet, canal from mouth to stomach (*pl.* -**gi** (-gī, -jī)) —**esophageal** (isofə'jēəl) *a.*

esoteric (esə'terik) *a.* 1. abstruse, obscure 2. secret 3. restricted to initiates

E.S.P. extrasensory perception

esp. especially

espadrille ('espədril) *n.* canvas shoe, *esp.* with braided cord sole

espalier (i'spalyər) *n.* 1. shrub, (fruit) tree trained to grow flat, as against wall *etc.* 2. trellis for this

esparto (i'spärtō) *n.* kind of grass yielding fiber used for making rope *etc.*

especial (i'speshəl) *a.* 1. pre-eminent, more than ordinary 2. particular —**es'pecially** *adv.*

Esperanto (espə'rantō) *n.* artificial language designed for universal use —**Espe-'rantist** *n.* one who uses Esperanto

espionage ('espiənäzh) *n.* 1. spying 2. use of secret agents

esplanade ('esplənäd, -näd) *n.* level space, *esp.* one used as public promenade

espouse (i'spowz) *vt.* 1. support, embrace (cause *etc.*) 2. *obs.* marry —**es'pousal** *n.*

espresso (e'spresō) *n.* strong coffee made by forcing steam through ground coffee beans

esprit (i'sprē) *n.* 1. spirit 2. animation —**esprit de corps** (də 'kör) attachment, loyalty to the society *etc.* one belongs to

espy (i'spī) *vt.* catch sight of (**es'pied, es'pying**) —**es'pial** *n.* observation

Esq. Esquire

-esque (*comb. form*) specified character, manner, style or resemblance, as in *picturesque, Romanesque, statuesque*

esquire ('eskwīər, is'kwīər) *n.* 1. gentleman's courtesy title used on letters 2. formerly, squire

-ess (*comb. form*) female, as in *actress*

essay ('esā; *def. 3 also* e'sā) *n.* 1. prose composition 2. short treatise 3. attempt —*vt.* (e'sā) 4. try, attempt 5. test (**es'sayed, es'saying**) —'**essayist** *n.*

essence ('esəns) *n.* 1. all that makes thing what it is 2. existence, being 3. entity, reality 4. extract got by distillation —**es'sential** *a.* 1. necessary, indispensable 2. inherent 3. of, constituting essence of thing —*n.* 4. indispensable element 5. chief point —**essenti'ality** *n.* —**essential oil** any of various volatile oils in plants, having odor *etc.* of plant from which they are extracted

E.S.T. Eastern Standard Time

est. 1. established 2. estimate(d)

-est (*comb. form*) forming superlative degree of adjective or adverb, as in *fastest*

establish (i'stablish) *vt.* 1. make secure 2. set up 3. settle 4. prove —**es'tablishment** *n.* 1. permanent organized body, full number of regiment *etc.* 2. household 3. business 4. public institution —**the Establishment** group, class of people holding authority within a society

estate (i'stāt) *n.* 1. landed property 2. person's property 3. area of property development, *esp.* of houses or factories 4. class as part of nation 5. rank, state, condition of life —**estate tax** tax levied on property of deceased before it is transferred to the heirs

esteem (i'stēm) *vt.* 1. think highly of 2. consider —*n.* 3. favorable opinion, regard, respect

ester ('estər) *n. Chem.* organic compound produced by reaction between acid and alcohol

Esther ('estər) *n. Bible* 17th book of the O.T., telling the story of Esther who became queen to Xerxes and saved the Jews from massacre which is commemorated annually in the feast of Purim

estimate ('estimāt) *vt.* 1. form approximate idea of (amounts, measurements *etc.*) 2. form opinion of 3. quote probable price for —*n.* ('estimit) 4. approximate judgment of amounts *etc.* 5. amount *etc.* arrived at 6. opinion 7. price quoted by contractor —'**estimable** *a.* worthy of regard —**esti'mation** *n.* 1. opinion, judgment 2. esteem

estivate ('estivāt) *vi.* spend the summer, *esp.* in dormant condition —'**estival** *a.* rare of summer —**esti'vation** *n.*

estrange (i'strānj) *vt.* 1. lose affection of 2. alienate —**es'trangement** *n.*

estrogen ('estrəjən) *n.* hormone in females *esp.* controlling changes, cycles in reproductive organs

estrus ('estrəs) *or* **estrum** ('estrəm) *n. see* HEAT (sense 5)

estuary ('eschŏŏəri) n. tidal mouth of river, inlet —'**estuarine** a.

-et (comb. form) small, lesser, as in islet, baronet

eta ('ātə, 'ētə) n. seventh letter in Gr. alphabet (H, η)

E.T.A. estimated time of arrival

et al. 1. et alibi (Lat., and elsewhere) 2. et alii (Lat., and others)

etc. et cetera

et cetera (et 'setərə, 'setrə) Lat. and the rest, and other things —**et'ceteras** pl.n. miscellaneous extras

etch (ech) v. 1. make (engraving) by eating away surface of metal plate with acids etc. —vt. 2. imprint vividly —'**etcher** n. —'**etching** n.

eternal (i'tərnəl) a. 1. without beginning or end 2. everlasting 3. changeless —e'**ternally** adv. —e'**ternity** n. —**eternal triangle** emotional relationship in which there are conflicts involving a man and two women or a woman and two men —**eternity ring** ring, esp. one set all around with stones to symbolize continuity —**the Eternal City** Rome

ethane ('ethān) n. odorless flammable gaseous alkane obtained from natural gas and petroleum

ether ('ēthər) n. 1. colorless volatile liquid used as anesthetic 2. intangible fluid formerly supposed to fill all space 3. the clear sky, region above clouds —**ethereal** (i'thēəriəl) a. 1. light, airy 2. heavenly, spiritlike —**ethereality** (ithēəri'aliti) n. —**ethereali'zation** n. —**etherealize** (i'thēəriəlīz) vt. 1. make or regard as being ethereal 2. add ether to or make into ether

ethical ('ethikəl) a. relating to morals —'**ethically** adv. —'**ethics** pl.n. 1. (with sing. v.) science of morals 2. moral principles, rules of conduct —**ethical drug** drug which can only be bought on physician's prescription

Ethiopia (ēthi'ōpiə) n. country in Africa bounded northeast by the Red Sea, east by Djibouti and Somalia, south by Kenya and west by Sudan —**Ethi'opian** a. 1. of Ethiopia —n. 2. native of Ethiopia 3. Amharic —n./a. 4. obs. Negro

ethnic ('ethnik) a. of race or relating to classification of humans into social, cultural etc. groups —'**ethnics** pl.n. minority groups distinguished by culture —**ethno'graphic** a. —**eth'nography** n. description of races of men —**ethno'logical** a. —**eth'nology** n. the study of human races

ethology (e'tholəji) n. scientific study of animal behavior in its natural state

ethos ('ēthos) n. distinctive character, spirit etc. of people, culture etc.

ethyl ('ethil) n. (C₂H₅) radical of ordinary alcohol and ether —'**ethylene** n. poisonous gas used as anesthetic and fuel —**ethyl alcohol** see ALCOHOL (sense 1)

etiolate ('ētiəlāt) v. 1. Bot. whiten (green plant) through lack of sunlight 2. (cause to) become pale and weak —**etio'lation** n.

etiology (ēti'oləji) n. study of causes, esp. inquiry into origin of disease —**etio'logical** a.

etiquette ('etikit, -ket) n. conventional code of conduct or behavior

Eton collar ('ētən) broad stiff white collar worn outside Eton jacket

Eton crop short mannish hair style worn by women in 1920s

Eton jacket waist-length jacket, open in front, formerly worn by pupils of Eton College, public school for boys in S England

Etruscan (i'truskən) or **Etrurian** (i'trŏŏriən) n. 1. member of ancient people of Etruria in central Italy 2. language of ancient Etruscans —a. 3. of Etruria, Etruscans, their culture or their language —**Etruscan art** tomb painting and artifacts produced between 7th and 3rd centuries B.C. by Etruscans

et seq. 1. et sequens (Lat., and the following) 2. (also et seqq.) et sequentia (Lat., and those that follow)

-ette (comb. form) 1. small, as in cigarette 2. female, as in majorette 3. imitation, as in Leatherette

étude ('ātyōōd, -tōōd) n. short musical composition, study, intended often as technical exercise

ety., etym., or **etymol.** 1. etymological 2. etymology

etymology (eti'moləji) n. 1. tracing, account of, formation of word's origin, development 2. science of this —**etymo'logical** a. —**etymo'logically** adv. —**ety'mologist** n.

Eu Chem. europium

eu- (comb. form) well, as in eugenic, euphony

eucalyptus (yōōkə'liptəs) or **eucalypt** ('yōōkəlipt) n. mostly Aust. genus of tree, the gum tree, yielding timber and oil, used medicinally from leaves

Eucharist ('yōōkərist) n. 1. Christian sacrament of the Lord's Supper 2. the consecrated elements —**Eucha'ristic** a.

euchre ('yōōkər) n. family of card games for four players (two partnerships) played usu. with 32 cards from a standard deck by omitting all cards below seven in which the object is to win tricks with a card of the highest rank in a plain suit or the trump suit

Euclidean (yōō'klidiən) a. denoting system of geometry based on axioms of Gr. mathematician Euclid —**Euclidean geometry** the study of three classes of objects, ie points, lines and planes (which are not defined) and their relations to each other

eugenic (yōō'jenik) a. relating to, or tending towards, production of fine offspring —**eu'genicist** n. —**eu'genics** pl.n. (with sing. v.) this science

Euler circles ('oilər) concentric or enclosing circles used to show relations between sets and subsets

eulogy ('yōōləji) n. 1. speech or writing in praise of person 2. praise —'**eulogist** n. —**eulo'gistic** a. —**eulo'gistically** adv. —'**eulogize** v.

eunuch ('yōōnək) n. castrated man, esp. formerly one employed in harem —'**eunuchoidism** n. glandular disturbance marked by development of female physical traits in men

euphemism ('yōōfimizəm) n. 1. substitution of mild term for offensive or hurtful one 2. instance of this —'**euphemist** n. —**euphe'mistic** a. —**euphe'mistically** adv. —'**euphemize** v.

euphonium (yōō'fōniəm) n. brass musical instrument larger than the cornet with the oval bell pointing backwards, used in brass bands

euphony ('yōōfəni) n. pleasantness of sound —**euphonic** (yōō'fonik) or **euphonious** (yōō'fōniəs) a. pleasing to ear

euphoria (yōō'fōriə) n. sense of wellbeing or elation —**euphoric** (yōō'forik) a.

euphuism ('yōōfyōōizəm) n. affected highflown manner of writing, esp. in imitation of Lyly's Euphues (1580) —**euphu'istic** a.

Eur. Europe(an)

Eurasian (yōō'rāzhən, -shən) a. 1. of mixed European and Asiatic descent 2. of Europe and Asia —n. 3. one of this descent

Euratom (yōō'ratəm) n. European Atomic Energy Commission

eureka (yōō'rēkə) interj. exclamation of triumph at finding something

eurhythmics or **eurythmics** (yōō'ridhmiks) pl.n. (with sing. v.) system of training through physical movement to music —**eu'rhythmy** or **eu'rythmy** n.

Euro- ('yōōrō-) or before vowel **Eur-** (comb. form) Europe; European

Eurodollar ('yōōrōdolər) n. U.S. dollar as part of European holding

European (yōōrə'pēən) n./a. (native) of Europe —**European Atomic Energy Commission** authority established by Common Market to develop peaceful uses of nuclear energy —**European Economic Community** association of a number of European nations for trade

europium (yōō'rōpiəm) n. Chem. metallic element Symbol Eu, at. wt. 152.0, at. no. 63

eurythmics (yōō'ridhmiks) n. see EURHYTHMICS

Eustachian tube (yōō'stāshən) passage leading from pharynx to middle ear

euthanasia (yōōthə'nāzhə) n. 1. gentle, painless death 2. putting to death in this way, esp. to relieve suffering

euthenics (yōō'theniks) pl.n. (with sing. v.) science of the relation of environment to human beings

eV electronvolt

evacuate (i'vakyōōāt) vt. 1. empty 2. cause to withdraw 3. discharge —**evacu'ation** n. —**evacu'ee** n. person moved from danger area, esp. in time of war

evade (i'vād) vt. 1. avoid, escape from 2. elude —e'**vasion** n. 1. subterfuge 2. excuse 3. equivocation —e'**vasive** a. elusive, not straightforward —e'**vasively** adv.

evaluate (i'valyōōāt) vt. find or judge value of —**evalu'ation** n.

evanesce (evə'nes) vi. fade away —**eva'nescence** n. —**eva'nescent** a. fleeting, transient

evangelical (ēvan'jelikəl) a. 1. of, or according to, gospel teaching 2. of Protestant sect which maintains salvation by faith —n. 3. member of evangelical sect —**evan'gelicalism** n. —e'**vangelism** n. —e'**vangelist** n. 1. writer of one of the four gospels 2. ardent, zealous preacher of the gospel 3. revivalist —**evangeli'zation** n. —e'**vangelize** vt. 1. preach gospel to 2. convert

evaporate (i'vapərāt) vi. 1. turn into, pass off in, vapor —vt. 2. turn into vapor —**evapo'ration** n. conversion of liquid into gaseous state at surface —e'**vaporative** a. —e'**vaporator** n. —**evaporated milk** milk from which some of the water has been evaporated

evasion (i'vāzhən) n. see EVADE

eve (ēv) n. 1. evening before (festival etc.) 2. time just before (event etc.) 3. obs. evening

Eve (ēv) n. the first woman, and wife of Adam

even¹ ('ēvən) a. 1. flat, smooth 2. uniform in quality, equal in amount, balanced 3. divisible by two 4. impartial —vt. 5. make even 6. smooth 7. equalize —adv. 8. equally 9. simply 10. notwithstanding —'**evens** a./adv. 1. (of bet) winning identical sum if successful 2. (of runner) offered at such odds —**even-handed** a. fair; impartial —**even-handedly** adv. —**even-handedness** n.

even² ('ēvən) n. obs. eve; evening —'**evensong** n. evening prayer

evening ('ēvning) n. 1. the close of day or early part of night 2. decline, end —**evening**

dress attire for formal occasion during evening —**evening paper** daily newspaper published at or after noon —**evening star** planet, usu. Venus, seen in west just after sunset

event (i'vent) n. 1. happening 2. notable occurrence 3. issue, result 4. any one contest in series in sporting program —e'**ventful** a. full of exciting events —e'**ventual** a. 1. resulting in the end 2. ultimate 3. final —**eventu'ality** n. possible event —e'**ventually** adv. —e'**ventuate** vi. 1. turn out 2. happen 3. end —**in the event that** if it should happen that

ever ('evər) adv. 1. always 2. constantly 3. at any time —**ever'more** adv. —'**evergreen** n./a. (tree or shrub) bearing foliage throughout year —**ever'lasting** a. 1. eternal 2. lasting for an indefinitely long period —**ever'lastingly** adv.

every ('evri) a. 1. each of all 2. all possible —'**everybody** pron. —'**every'day** a. usual, ordinary —'**Everyman** n. (oft. e-) ordinary person; common man —'**everyone** pron. —'**everything** pron. —'**everywhere** adv. to or in all places

evict (i'vikt) vt. expel by legal process, turn out —e'**viction** n. —e'**victor** n.

evident ('evidənt) a. plain, obvious —'**evidence** n. 1. ground of belief 2. sign, indication 3. testimony —vt. 4. indicate, prove —evi'**dential** a. —'**evidently** adv. —**in evidence** conspicuous

evil ('ēvəl) a. 1. bad, harmful —n. 2. what is bad or harmful 3. sin —'**evilly** adv. —**evil'doer** n. sinner —**evil-eyed** a. —**the evil eye** 1. look superstitiously supposed to have power of inflicting harm etc. 2. power to inflict harm etc. by such a look

evince (i'vins) vt. show, indicate

eviscerate (i'visərāt) vt. 1. remove internal organs 2. deprive of meaning or significance —**eviscer'ation** n. —e'**viscerator** n.

evoke (i'vōk) vt. 1. draw forth 2. call to mind —**evocation** (evə'kāshən) n. —**evocative** (i'vokətiv) a.

evolve (i'volv) v. 1. develop or cause to develop gradually —vi. 2. undergo slow changes in process of growth —**evolution** (evə'lōōshən, ēvə-) n. 1. evolving 2. development of species from earlier forms —**evolutional** (evə'lōōshənəl, ēvə-) a. —**evolutionary** (evə'lōōshəneri, ēvə-) a. —**evolutionist** (evə'lōōshənist, ēvə-) n.

ewe (yōō) n. female sheep

ewer ('yōōər) n. pitcher, water jug with wide spout

ex¹ (eks) prep. 1. Fin. excluding; without 2. Comm. without charge to buyer until removed from —**ex cathedra** (kə'thēdrə) 1. with authority 2. (of papal pronouncements) defined as infallibly true —**ex gratia** ('grāshə) given as favor, esp. where no legal obligation exists —**ex hypothesi** (hī'pothəsi) in accordance with hypothesis stated —**ex libris** ('lēbris) from the library of —**ex officio** (ə'fishiō) by right of position or office —**ex post facto** ('faktō) having retrospective effect

ex² (eks) n. inf. ex-wife, ex-husband etc.

ex-, e-, or **ef-** (comb. form) out from, from, out of, formerly, as in exclaim, evade, effusive, exodus. Such words are not given here where the meaning may easily be inferred from the simple word

ex. 1. example 2. except(ed) 3. extra

exacerbate (ig'zasərbāt) vt. 1. aggravate, make worse 2. embitter —**exacer'bation** n.

exact (ig'zakt) a. 1. precise, accurate, strictly correct —vt. 2. demand, extort 3. insist upon 4. enforce —ex'**acting** a. making rigorous or excessive demands —ex'**action** n. 1. act of exacting 2. that which is exacted, as excessive work etc. 3. oppressive demand —ex'**actitude** n. —ex'**actly** adv. —ex'**actness** n. 1. accuracy 2. precision —ex'**actor** n.

exaggerate (ig'zajərāt) vt. 1. magnify beyond truth, overstate 2. enlarge 3. overestimate —**exagger'ation** n. —ex'**aggerative** a. —ex'**aggerator** n.

exalt (ig'zölt) vt. 1. raise up 2. praise 3. make noble, dignify —**exal'tation** n. 1. an exalting 2. elevation in rank, dignity or position 3. rapture

exam (ig'zam) examination

examine (ig'zamin) vt. 1. investigate 2. look at closely 3. ask questions of 4. test knowledge or proficiency of 5. inquire into —**exami'nation** n. —**exami'nee** n. —**ex'aminer** n.

example (ig'zampəl) n. 1. thing illustrating general rule 2. specimen 3. model 4. warning 5. precedent 6. instance

exasperate (ig'zaspərāt) vt. 1. irritate, enrage 2. intensify, make worse —**exasper'ation** n.

Excalibur (ek'skalibər) n. the sword of King Arthur

excavate ('ekskəvāt) vt. 1. hollow out 2. unearth 3. make (hole) by digging —**exca'vation** n. —'**excavator** n.

exceed (ik'sēd) vt. 1. be greater than 2. go beyond 3. surpass —ex'**ceeding** a. 1. very great; exceptional; excessive —adv. 2. obs. to a great or unusual degree —ex'**ceedingly** adv. 1. very 2. greatly

excel (ik'sel) vt. 1. surpass, be better than —vi. 2. be very good, pre-eminent (-ll-) —'**excellence** n. —'**Excellency** n. title borne by ambassadors and R.C. bishops and archbishops —'**excellent** a. very good

except (ik'sept) prep. 1. not including 2. but —conj. 3. obs. unless —vt. 4. leave or take out 5. exclude —ex'**cepting** prep. not including —ex'**ception** n. 1. thing excepted, not included in a rule 2. objection —ex'**ceptionable** a. open to objection —ex'**ceptional** a. not ordinary, esp. much above average —ex'**ceptionally** adv.

excerpt ('eksərpt, 'egzərpt) n. 1. quoted or extracted passage from book etc. —vt. (ek'sərpt, eg'zərpt) 2. extract, quote (passage from book etc.) —ex'**cerption** n.

excess (ik'ses, 'ekses) n. 1. an exceeding 2. amount by which thing exceeds 3. too great amount 4. intemperance, immoderate conduct —ex'**cessive** a. —ex'**cessively** adv.

exchange (iks'chānj) vt. 1. give (something) in return for something else 2. barter —n. 3. giving one thing and receiving another 4. thing given for another 5. building where merchants meet for business 6. central telephone office where connections are made etc. —**exchangea'bility** n. —ex'**changeable** a. —**exchange rate** rate at which currency unit of one country may be exchanged for that of another

exchequer (iks'chekər) n. UK government department in charge of revenue

excise¹ ('eksīz, -sis) n. duty charged on goods during manufacture or before sale

excise² (ik'sīz) vt. cut out, cut away —**excision** (ik'sizhən) n.

excite (ik'sīt) vt. 1. arouse to strong emotion, stimulate 2. rouse up, set in motion 3. Elec. magnetize poles of —**excita'bility** n. —ex'**citable** a. —ex'**citably** adv. —**exci'tation** n. —ex'**cited** a. emotionally or sexually aroused —ex'**citedness** n. —ex'**citement** n. —ex'**citing** a. 1. thrilling 2. rousing to action

exclaim (ik'sklām) vi. 1. speak suddenly —v. 2. cry out —**exclamation** (eksklə'māshən) n. —**exclamatory** (iks'klamətöri) a. —**exclamation point** punctuation mark ! used after exclamations and vehement commands

exclude (ik'sklōōd) vt. 1. shut out 2. debar 3. reject, not consider —ex'**clusion** n. —ex'**clusive** a. 1. excluding 2. inclined to keep out (from society etc.) 3. sole, only 4. select —n. 5. something exclusive, esp. story appearing only in one newspaper —ex'**clusively** adv.

excommunicate (ekskə'myōōnikāt) vt. cut off from the sacraments of the Church —**excommuni'cation** n.

excoriate (ik'sköriāt) vt. 1. strip (skin) from (person or animal) 2. denounce vehemently —**excori'ation** n.

excrement ('ekskrimənt) n. 1. waste matter from body, esp. from bowels 2. dung —**excreta** (ik'skrētə) pl.n. excrement —**excrete** (ik'skrēt) vt. discharge from the system —**excretion** (ik'skrēshən) n. —**excretory** ('ekskrətöri) a. —**excretory system** structures collectively removing waste from the animal body

excrescent (ik'skresənt) a. 1. growing out of something 2. redundant —ex'**crescence** n. unnatural outgrowth

excruciate (ik'skrōōshiāt) vt. torment acutely, torture in body or mind —ex'**cruciating** a. —**excruci'ation** n.

exculpate ('ekskulpāt, ek'skulpāt) vt. free from blame, acquit —**excul'pation** n. —ex'**culpatory** a.

excursion (ik'skərzhən) n. 1. journey, ramble, trip for pleasure 2. digression —ex'**cursive** a. 1. tending to digress 2. involving detours —ex'**cursiveness** n. —ex'**cursus** n. digression (pl. **-es, -sus** (rare))

excuse (ik'skyōōz) vt. 1. forgive, overlook 2. try to clear from blame 3. seek exemption for 4. set free, remit —n. (ik'skyōōs) 5. that which serves to excuse 6. apology —ex'**cusable** a.

exec. 1. executive 2. executor

execrate ('eksikrāt) vt. 1. loathe, detest 2. denounce, deplore 3. curse —'**execrable** a. abominable, hatefully bad —exe'**cration** n. —'**execrative** or '**execratory** a.

execute ('eksikyōōt) vt. 1. inflict capital punishment on, kill 2. carry out, perform 3. make, produce 4. sign (document) —ex'**ecutant** n. performer, esp. of music —exe'**cution** n. —exe'**cutioner** n. one employed to execute criminals —ex'**ecutive** n. 1. person in administrative position 2. executive body 3. committee carrying on business of society etc. —a. 4. carrying into effect, esp. of branch of government enforcing laws —ex'**ecutor** n. person appointed to carry out provisions of a will (**ex'ecutrix** fem.)

exegesis (eksi'jēsis) n. explanation, esp. of Scripture (pl. **-geses** (-'jēsēz)) —**exegetic(al)** (eksi'jetik(əl)) a.

exemplar (ig'zemplär, -plər) n. model type —**exem'plarily** adv. —ex'**emplary** a. 1. fit to be imitated, serving as example 2. commendable 3. typical —**exemplifi'cation** n. —ex'**emplify** vt. 1. serve as example of 2. illustrate 3. exhibit 4. make attested copy of (**-fied, -fying**)

exempt (ig'zempt) vt. 1. free 2. excuse —a. 3. freed (from), not liable (for) 4. not affected (by) —ex'**emption** n.

exequies ('eksikwiz) pl.n. funeral rites or procession

exercise ('eksərsīz) vt. 1. use, employ 2. give exercise to 3. carry out, discharge 4. trouble, harass —*vi.* **5.** take exercise —*n.* **6.** use of limbs for health **7.** practice for training **8.** task for training **9.** lesson **10.** employment **11.** use (of limbs, faculty *etc.*)

exert (ig'zɔrt) *vt.* **1.** apply (oneself) diligently, make effort **2.** bring to bear —**ex'ertion** *n.* effort, physical activity

exeunt ('eksiunt) *Lat. Theat.* they leave the stage: stage direction —**exeunt omnes** ('omnäz) they all go out

exfoliate (eks'fōliāt) *v.* peel in scales, layers

exhale (eks'hāl) *v.* **1.** breathe out **2.** give, pass off as vapor

exhaust (ig'zöst) *vt.* **1.** tire out **2.** use up **3.** empty **4.** draw off **5.** treat, discuss thoroughly —*n.* **6.** used steam or fluid from engine **7.** waste gases from internal-combustion engine **8.** passage for, or coming out of this —**exhausti'bility** *n.* —**ex'haustible** *a.* —**ex'haustion** *n.* **1.** state of extreme fatigue **2.** limit of endurance —**ex'haustive** *a.* comprehensive

exhibit (ig'zibit) *vt.* **1.** show, display **2.** manifest **3.** show publicly (oft. in competition) —*n.* **4.** thing shown, *esp.* in competition or as evidence in court —**exhi'bition** *n.* **1.** display, act of displaying **2.** public show (of works of art *etc.*) —**exhi'bitionism** *n.* —**exhi'bitionist** *n.* one with compulsive desire to draw attention to himself or to expose genitals publicly —**exhibition'istic** *a.* —**ex'hibitor** *n.* one who exhibits, *esp.* in show —**ex'hibitory** *a.*

exhilarate (ig'zilərāt) *vt.* enliven, gladden —**exhila'ration** *n.* high spirits, enlivenment

exhort (ig'zört) *vt.* urge, admonish earnestly —**exhor'tation** *n.* —**ex'horter** *n.*

exhume (ig'zyōōm, -'zōōm; iks'hyōōm, -'yōōm) *vt.* unearth (what has been buried), disinter —**exhu'mation** *n.*

exigent ('eksijənt) *a.* **1.** exacting **2.** urgent, pressing —'**exigence** *or* '**exigency** *n.* **1.** pressing need **2.** emergency —'**exigible** *a.* liable to be exacted or demanded

exiguous (ig'zigyōōəs) *a.* scanty, meager

exile ('egzīl, 'eksīl) *n.* **1.** banishment, expulsion from one's own country **2.** long absence abroad **3.** one banished or permanently living away from his home or country —*vt.* **4.** banish, expel

exist (ig'zist) *vi.* be, have being, live —**ex'istence** *n.* —**ex'istent** *a.*

existential (egzi'stenchəl, eksi-) *a.* **1.** of existence **2.** *Philos.* based on personal experience **3.** of existentialism —**exis'tentialism** *n.* theory which holds that man is free and responsible for his own acts

exit ('egzit, 'eksit) *n.* **1.** way out **2.** going out **3.** death **4.** actor's departure from stage —*vi.* **5.** go out

exo- (*comb. form*) external, outside, or beyond, as in *exothermal*

exocrine ('eksəkrin) *a.* of gland (*eg* salivary, sweat) secreting its products through ducts

Exod. *Bible* Exodus

exodus ('eksədəs) *n.* **1.** the departure of many people **2.** (E-) the departure of the Israelites from Egypt led by Moses **3.** (E-) *Bible* 2nd book of the O.T., account of the founding of the nation of Israel and the building of the tabernacle

exonerate (ig'zonərāt) *vt.* **1.** free, declare free, from blame **2.** exculpate **3.** acquit —**exoner'ation** *n.* —**ex'onerative** *a.*

exophthalmos (eksof'thalməs) *n.* protrusion of the eyeball

exorbitant (ig'zörbitənt) *a.* very excessive, inordinate, immoderate —**ex'orbitance** *n.* —**ex'orbitantly** *adv.*

exorcise *or* **-ize** ('eksörsīz) *vt.* **1.** cast out

(evil spirits) by invocation **2.** free (person) of evil spirits —**exorcism** ('eksörsizəm) *n.* —**exorcist** ('eksörsist) *n.*

exordium (eg'zördiəm) *n.* introductory part of a speech or treatise (*pl.* **-s, -ia** (-iə)) —**ex'ordial** *a.*

exoteric (eksə'terik) *a.* **1.** understandable by the many **2.** ordinary, popular

exotic (ig'zotik) *a.* **1.** brought in from abroad, foreign **2.** rare, unusual, having strange or bizarre allure —*n.* **3.** exotic plant *etc.* —**ex'otica** *pl.n.* (collection of) exotic objects —**ex'oticism** *n.* —**exotic dancer** striptease or belly dancer

expand (ik'spand) *v.* **1.** increase **2.** spread out **3.** dilate **4.** develop —**ex'pandable** *or* **ex'pandible** *a.* —**ex'panse** *n.* **1.** wide space **2.** open stretch of land —**expansi'bility** *n.* —**ex'pansible** *a.* —**ex'pansion** *n.* —**ex'pansionism** *n.* practice of expanding economy or territory of country —**ex'pansionist** *n./a.* —**expansion'istic** *a.* —**ex'pansive** *a.* **1.** wide **2.** extensive **3.** friendly, talkative

expatiate (ek'spāshiāt) *vi.* **1.** speak or write at great length **2.** enlarge —**expati'ation** *n.*

expatriate (eks'patriāt) *vt.* **1.** banish, exile **2.** withdraw (oneself) from one's native land —*a./n.* (eks'patriāt, -it) **3.** (person) exiled or banished from his native country —**expatri'ation** *n.*

expect (ik'spekt) *vt.* **1.** regard as probable **2.** look forward to **3.** await **4.** hope for —**ex'pectancy** *n.* **1.** state or act of expecting **2.** that which is expected **3.** hope —**ex'pectant** *a.* looking or waiting for, *esp.* for birth of child —**ex'pectantly** *adv.* —**expec'tation** *n.* **1.** act or state of expecting **2.** prospect of future good **3.** what is expected **4.** promise **5.** value of something expected —*pl.* **6.** prospect of fortune or profit by will

expectorate (ik'spektərāt) *v.* spit out (phlegm *etc.*) —**ex'pectorant** *Med. a.* **1.** promoting secretion, liquefaction or expulsion of sputum from respiratory passages —*n.* **2.** expectorant drug or agent —**expecto'ration** *n.*

expedient (ik'spēdiənt) *a.* **1.** fitting, advisable, politic, suitable, convenient —*n.* **2.** something suitable, useful, *esp.* in emergency —**ex'pediency** *n.* —**ex'pediently** *adv.*

expedite ('ekspidīt) *vt.* **1.** help on, hasten **2.** dispatch —**expedition** (ekspi'dishən) *n.* **1.** journey for definite (oft. scientific or military) purpose **2.** people, equipment comprising expedition **3.** excursion **4.** promptness —**expeditionary** (ekspi'dishəneri) *a.* —**expeditious** (ekspi'dishəs) *a.* prompt, speedy

expel (ik'spel) *vt.* **1.** drive, cast out **2.** exclude **3.** discharge (-ll-) —**expulsion** (ik'spulshən) *n.* —**expulsive** (ik'spulsiv) *a.*

expend (ik'spend) *vt.* **1.** spend, pay out **2.** use up —**ex'pendable** *a.* likely, or meant, to be used up or destroyed —**ex'penditure** *n.* —**ex'pense** *n.* **1.** cost **2.** (cause of) spending —*pl.* **3.** charges, outlay incurred —**ex'pensive** *a.* high-priced, costly, dear —**expense account 1.** arrangement by which expenses are refunded to employee by employer **2.** record of such expenses

experience (ik'spēəriəns) *n.* **1.** observation of facts as source of knowledge **2.** being affected consciously by event **3.** the event **4.** knowledge, skill, gained from life, by contact with facts and events —*vt.* **5.** undergo, suffer, meet with —**ex'perienced** *a.* skilled, expert, capable —**experi'ential** *a.*

experiment (ik'sperimənt) *n.* **1.** test, trial, something done in the hope that it may succeed, or to test theory —*vi.* (ik'speriment) **2.** make experiment —**ex-**

peri'mental *a.* —**experi'mentalist** *n.* —**experi'mentally** *adv.*

expert ('ekspərt) *n.* **1.** one skillful, knowledgeable, in something **2.** authority —*a.* **3.** practiced, skillful —**expertise** (ekspər'tēz) *n.*

expiate ('ekspiāt) *vt.* **1.** pay penalty for **2.** make amends for —**expi'ation** *n.* —'**expiator** *n.* —'**expiatory** *a.*

expire (ik'spīər) *vi.* **1.** come to an end **2.** give out breath **3.** die —*vt.* **4.** breathe out —**expiration** (ekspi'rāshən) *n.* —**ex'piratory** *a.* —**ex'piry** *n.* end

explain (ik'splān) *vt.* **1.** make clear, intelligible **2.** interpret **3.** elucidate **4.** give details of **5.** account for —**explanation** (eksplə'nāshən) *n.* —**explanatory** (iks'planətöri) *or* **explanative** (iks'planativ) *a.*

expletive ('eskplətiv) *n.* **1.** exclamation **2.** oath —*a.* **3.** serving only to fill out sentence *etc.*

explicable (ek'splikəbəl, 'eksplik-) *a.* explainable —'**explicate** *vt.* develop, explain —**ex'plicative** *or* **ex'plicatory** *a.*

explicit (ik'splisit) *a.* **1.** stated in detail **2.** stated, not merely implied **3.** outspoken **4.** clear, plain **5.** unequivocal

explode (ik'splōd) *vi.* **1.** go off with bang **2.** burst violently **3.** (of population) increase rapidly —*vt.* **4.** make explode **5.** discredit, expose (a theory *etc.*) —**ex'plosion** *n.* —**ex'plosive** *a./n.*

exploit ('eksploit) *n.* **1.** brilliant feat, deed —*vt.* (ik'sploit) **2.** turn to advantage **3.** make use of for one's own ends —**exploi'tation** *n.* —**ex'ploiter** *n.*

explore (ik'splör) *vt.* **1.** investigate **2.** examine **3.** scrutinize **4.** examine (country *etc.*) by going through it —**explo'ration** *n.* —**exploratory** (ik'splörətöri) *a.* —**ex'plorer** *n.*

explosion (ik'splōzhən) *n. see* EXPLODE

expo ('ekspō) *n. inf.* exposition, large international exhibition

exponent (ik'spönənt) *n. see* EXPOUND

export (ek'spört, 'ekspört) *vt.* **1.** send (goods) out of the country —*n./a.* ('ekspört) **2.** (of) goods or services sold to foreign country or countries —**expor'tation** *n.* —**ex'porter** *n.*

expose (ik'spōz) *vt.* **1.** exhibit **2.** disclose, reveal **3.** lay open **4.** leave unprotected **5.** subject (photographic plate or film) to light —**ex'posed** *a.* **1.** not concealed **2.** without shelter from the elements **3.** vulnerable —**ex'posure** *n.* **1.** act of exposing or condition of being exposed **2.** position or outlook of building **3.** lack of shelter from weather, *esp.* cold **4.** exposed surface **5.** *Photog.* act of exposing film or plate to light *etc.*; area on film or plate that has been exposed **6.** *Photog.* intensity of light falling on film or plate multiplied by time of exposure; combination of lens aperture and shutter speed used in taking photograph **7.** appearance before public, as on TV

exposé (ekspō'zā) *n.* newspaper article *etc.* disclosing scandal, crime *etc.*

exposition (ekspə'zishən) *n. see* EXPOUND

expostulate (ik'sposchəlāt) *vi.* **1.** remonstrate **2.** reason (in a kindly manner) —**expostu'lation** *n.* —**ex'postulatory** *a.*

expound (ik'spownd) *vt.* explain, interpret —**exponent** (ik'spönənt) *n.* **1.** one who sets out facts or interprets something **2.** one favoring a particular policy **3.** *Math.* small, raised number showing the power of a factor —**expo'nential** *a.* —**expo'sition** *n.* **1.** explanation, description **2.** exhibition of goods *etc.* —**expositor** (ik'spozitər) *n.* one who explains, interpreter —**expository** (ik'spozitöri) *a.* explanatory

express (ik'spres) *vt.* 1. put into words 2. make known or understood by words, behavior *etc.* 3. squeeze out —*a.* 4. definitely stated 5. specially designed 6. clear 7. positive 8. speedy 9. (of messenger) specially sent off 10. (of train) fast and making few stops —*adv.* 11. specially 12. on purpose 13. with speed —*n.* 14. express train or messenger 15. rapid parcel delivery service —**ex'pressible** *a.* —**ex'pression** *n.* 1. expressing 2. word, phrase 3. look, aspect 4. feeling 5. utterance —**ex'pressionism** *n.* theory that art depends on expression of artist's creative self, not on mere reproduction —**ex'pressive** *a.* —**ex'pressly** *adv.* —**ex'pressway** *n.* urban highway usu. divided with controlled access and departure lanes

expresso (ik'spresō) *n. see* ESPRESSO

expropriate (eks'prōpriāt) *vt.* 1. dispossess 2. take out of owner's hands —**expropri'ation** *n.* —**ex'propriator** *n.*

expulsion (ik'spulshən) *n. see* EXPEL

expunge (ik'spunj) *vt.* strike out, erase —**ex'punction** *n.*

expurgate ('ekspərgāt) *vt.* remove objectionable parts from (book *etc.*), purge —**expur'gation** *n.* —'**expurgator** *n.* —**ex'purgatory** *a.*

exquisite (ek'skwizit, 'ekskwizit) *a.* 1. of extreme beauty or delicacy 2. keen, acute 3. keenly sensitive —**ex'quisitely** *adv.*

ex-serviceman *n.* man who has served in the armed forces

extant ('ekstənt, ek'stant) *a.* still existing

extempore (ik'stempəri) *a./adv.* without previous thought or preparation —**extempo'raneous** *a.* —**ex'temporary** *a.* —**extempori'zation** *n.* —**ex'temporize** *vi.* 1. speak without preparation —*vt.* 2. devise for the occasion

extend (ik'stend) *vt.* 1. stretch out, lengthen 2. prolong in duration 3. widen in area, scope 4. accord, grant —*vi.* 5. reach 6. cover a certain area 7. have a certain range or scope 8. become larger or wider —**ex'tendable**, **ex'tendible**, *or* **ex'tensible** *a.* that can be extended —**ex'tension** *n.* 1. stretching out, prolongation, enlargement 2. expansion 3. continuation, additional part, as of telephone *etc.* —**ex'tensive** *a.* wide, large, comprehensive —**ex'tensor** *n.* straightening muscle —**ex'tent** *n.* 1. space or degree to which thing is extended 2. size 3. compass 4. volume —**extended family** nuclear family together with blood relatives, oft. spanning three or more generations —**extended-play** *a.* denoting phonograph record played at 45 r.p.m.

extenuate (ik'stenyōōāt) *vt.* make less blameworthy, mitigate —**extenu'ation** *n.* —**ex'tenuatory** *a.*

exterior (ik'stēəriər) *n.* 1. the outside 2. outward appearance —*a.* 3. outer, outward, external —**exteriori'zation** *n. Surg.* temporary exposure of structure outside the body —**ex'teriorize** *vt.* —**exterior angle** 1. angle of polygon contained between one side extended and adjacent side 2. any of four angles made by transversal that are outside region between two intersected lines

exterminate (ik'stərmināt) *vt.* destroy utterly, annihilate, root out, eliminate —**extermi'nation** *n.* —**ex'terminator** *n.* destroyer

external (ik'stərnəl) *a.* outside, outward —**externali'zation** *n.* —**ex'ternalize** *vt.* 1. make external 2. *Psychol.* attribute (one's feelings) to one's surroundings —**ex'ternally** *adv.*

extinct (ik'stingkt) *a.* 1. having died out or come to an end 2. no longer existing 3. quenched, no longer burning —**ex'tinction** *n.*

extinguish (ik'stinggwish) *vt.* 1. put out, quench 2. wipe out —**ex'tinguishable** *a.* —**ex'tinguisher** *n.* device, *esp.* spraying liquid or foam, used to put out fires

extirpate ('ekstərpāt) *vt.* 1. root out 2. destroy utterly —**extir'pation** *n.* —'**extirpator** *n.*

extol *or* **extoll** (ik'stōl) *vt.* praise highly (-ll-)

extort (ik'stört) *vt.* 1. get by force or threats 2. wring out 3. exact —**ex'tortion** *n.* —**ex'tortionate** *a.* (of prices *etc.*) excessive, exorbitant —**ex'tortioner** *n.*

extra ('ekstrə) *a.* 1. additional 2. larger, better, than usual —*adv.* 3. additionally 4. more than usually —*n.* 5. extra thing 6. something charged as additional 7. *Cine.* person hired for crowd scenes

extra- (*comb. form*) beyond, as in *extradition, extramural, extraterritorial.* Such words are not given here where the meaning may easily be inferred from the simple word

extract (ik'strakt) *vt.* 1. take out, *esp.* by force 2. obtain against person's will 3. get by pressure, distillation *etc.* 4. deduce 5. derive 6. copy out, quote —*n.* ('ekstrakt) 7. passage from book, motion picture *etc.* 8. matter got by distillation 9. concentrated solution —**ex'traction** *n.* 1. extracting, *esp.* of tooth 2. ancestry —**ex'tractor** *n.*

extracurricular (ekstrəkə'rikyələr) *a.* 1. taking place outside normal school timetable 2. beyond regular duties *etc.*

extradition (ekstrə'dishən) *n.* delivery, under treaty, of foreign fugitive from justice to authorities concerned —**extraditable** ('ekstrədītəbəl) *a.* —**extradite** ('ekstrədīt) *vt.* 1. surrender (alleged offender) for trial to foreign state 2. procure extradition of

extramural (ekstrə'myōōrəl) *a.* situated outside walls or boundaries of a place, *eg* sports, medical care

extraneous (ik'strāniəs) *a.* 1. not essential 2. irrelevant 3. added from without, not belonging

extraordinary (ik'strördəneri) *a.* 1. out of the usual course 2. additional 3. unusual, surprising, exceptional —**extraordi'narily** *adv.*

extrapolate (ik'strapəlāt) *v.* 1. infer (something not known) from known facts 2. *Math.* estimate (a value) beyond known values

extrasensory (ekstrə'sensəri) *a.* of perception apparently gained without use of known senses

extraterrestrial (ekstrəti'restriəl) *a.* of, or from outside the earth's atmosphere

extravagant (ik'stravigənt) *a.* 1. wasteful 2. exorbitant 3. wild, absurd —**ex'travagance** *n.* —**ex'travagantly** *adv.* —**extrava'ganza** *n.* elaborate, lavish, entertainment, display *etc.*

extravert ('ekstrəvərt) *n. see* EXTROVERT

extreme (ik'strēm) *a.* 1. of high or highest degree 2. severe 3. going beyond moderation 4. at the end 5. outermost —*n.* 6. utmost degree 7. thing at one end or the other, first and last of series —**ex'tremely** *adv.* —**ex'tremism** *n.* —**ex'tremist** *n.* 1. advocate of extreme measures —*a.* 2. of immoderate or excessive actions, opinions *etc.* —**extremity** (ik'stremiti) *n.* 1. end —*pl.* 2. hands and feet 3. utmost distress 4. extreme measures —**extreme unction** sacrament in which dying person is anointed by priest

extricate ('ekstrikāt) *vt.* disentangle, unravel, set free —'**extricable** *a.* —**extri'cation** *n.*

extrinsic (ek'strinzik, -sik) *a.* accessory, not belonging, not intrinsic —**ex'trinsically** *adv.*

extrovert *or* **extravert** ('ekstrəvərt) *n.* one who is interested in other people and things rather than his own feelings —**extro'version** *or* **extra'version** *n.*

extrude (ik'strōōd) *vt.* 1. squeeze, force out 2. (*esp.* of molten metal or plastic *etc.*) shape by squeezing through suitable nozzle or die

exuberant (ig'zōōbərənt) *a.* 1. high-spirited, vivacious 2. prolific, abundant, luxurious —**ex'uberance** *n.* —**ex'uberantly** *adv.*

exude (ig'zōōd) *vi.* 1. ooze out —*vt.* 2. give off (moisture) —**exudation** (eksyōō'dāshən, eksōō-) *n.* —**ex'udative** *a.*

exult (ig'zult) *vi.* 1. rejoice 2. triumph —**ex'ultancy** *n.* —**ex'ultant** *a.* triumphant —**exul'tation** *n.*

-ey (*comb. form*) *see* -Y¹, -Y²

eye
(A, conjunctiva; B, cornea; C, aqueous humour; D, pupil; E, crystalline lens; F, iris; G, ciliary body; H, sclera; I, choroid; J, retina; K, vitreous body; L, forea centralis; M, optic nerve)

eye (ī) *n.* 1. organ of sight 2. look, glance 3. attention 4. aperture 5. view 6. judgment 7. watch, vigilance 8. thing, mark resembling eye 9. slit in needle for thread —*vt.* 10. look at 11. observe —'**eyeless** *a.* —'**eyelet** *n.* 1. small hole through which rope or cord is passed 2. ring reinforcing this —'**eyeball** *n.* ball of eye —**eye bank** place for storage of corneas removed from the recently dead for transplanting to the eyes of those with corneal defects —'**eyebrow** *n.* ridge or fringe of hair above eye —**eye-catcher** *n.* —**eye-catching** *a.* striking —'**eyeful** *n. inf.* 1. view, glance *etc.* 2. beautiful sight, *esp.* a woman —'**eyeglasses** *pl.n.* lenses to assist sight —'**eyehole** *n.* 1. hole through which rope *etc.* is passed 2. *inf.* cavity containing eyeball 3. peephole —'**eyelash** *n.* hair fringing eyelid —**eyelet embroidery** eyelets decorated with needlework to form a fabric —'**eyelid** *n.* either of two muscular folds of skin that can be moved to cover exposed portion of eyeball —'**eyeliner** *n.* cosmetic used to outline eyes —**eye-opener** *n. inf.* 1. surprising news 2. revealing statement —'**eyepiece** *n.* lens or lenses in optical instrument nearest eye of observer —**eye shadow** colored cosmetic put on around the eyes —'**eyeshot** *n.* range of vision —'**eyesight** *n.* ability to see —'**eyesore** *n.* thing that annoys one to see —'**eyestrain** *n.* fatigue of eyes —'**eyetooth** *n.* canine tooth —'**eyewash** *n. inf.* deceptive talk *etc.*, nonsense —'**eyewitness** *n.* one who saw something for himself —**an eye for an eye** retributive justice; retaliation —**eyeball to eyeball** confronting another closely —**up to the eyeballs (in something)** deeply occupied (with something)

eyrie ('ēəri, 'āəri) *n. see* AERIE

Ezech. *Bible* Ezechiel

Ezechiel (i'zēkyəl) *n. Bible* Ezekiel in the Douay Version of the O.T.

Ezekiel (i'zēkyəl) *n. Bible* 26th book of the O.T., written by the prophet Ezekiel concerning the fate of the nation of Israel after the Babylonian captivity

Ezra ('ezrə) *n. Bible* 15th book of the O.T., a postexilic book relating the experiences of the Jews as they reunited

Ff

f *or* **F** (ef) *n.* **1.** sixth letter of English alphabet **2.** speech sound represented by this letter, as in *fat* (*pl.* **f's, F's** *or* **Fs**)

f, f/, *or* **f:** f-number

f. *Mus.* forte

f. *or* **F. 1.** female **2.** *Gram.* feminine **3.** folio (*pl.* **ff.** *or* **FF.**) **4.** following (page) (*pl.* **ff.**) **5.** franc **6.** furlong

F 1. *Mus.* fourth note of scale of C major; major or minor key having this note as its tonic **2.** Fahrenheit **3.** *Chem.* fluorine **4.** *Phys.* force **5.** farad **6.** *Genetics* generation of filial offspring, F_1 being first generation **7.** Fellow

fa (fä) *n. Mus.* **1.** in fixed system of solmization, the note F **2.** in movable do system, the fourth note of a major scale

FAA Federal Aviation Agency

fable ('fābəl) *n.* **1.** short story with moral, *esp.* one with animals as characters **2.** tale **3.** legend **4.** fiction; lie —*v.* **5.** tell (fables) —*vi.* **6.** tell lies —*vt.* **7.** talk of in manner of fable —**fabulist** ('fabyəlist) *n.* writer of fables —**fabulous** ('fabyələs) *a.* **1.** amazing **2.** *inf.* extremely good **3.** told of in fables

fabric ('fabrik) *n.* **1.** cloth **2.** texture **3.** frame, structure —**'fabricate** *vt.* **1.** build **2.** frame **3.** construct **4.** invent (lie *etc.*) **5.** forge (document) —**fabri'cation** *n.* —**'fabricator** *n.*

facade *or* **façade** (fə'säd) *n.* **1.** front of building **2.** *fig.* outward appearance

face (fās) *n.* **1.** front of head **2.** distorted expression **3.** outward appearance **4.** front, upper surface or chief side of anything **5.** dial of a clock *etc.* **6.** dignity **7.** *inf.* make-up (*esp.* in **put one's face on**) **8.** *Print.* printing surface of type character; style or design of character on type (*also* **'typeface**) —*vt.* **9.** look or front toward **10.** meet (boldly) **11.** give a covering surface to —*vi.* **12.** turn —**'faceless** *a.* without a face **2.** anonymous —**'facer** *n.* person or thing that faces —**facet** ('fasit) *n.* **1.** one side of many-sided body, *esp.* cut gem **2.** one aspect —**facial** ('fāshəl) *a.* **1.** pert. to face —*n.* **2.** cosmetic treatment for face —**'facing** *n.* **1.** piece of material used *esp.* to conceal seam and prevent fraying **2.** (*usu. pl.*) collar, cuffs *etc.* of military uniform jacket **3.** outer layer or coat of material applied to surface of wall —**face card** king, queen or jack at cards —**face-lift** *n.* **1.** operation to tighten skin of face to remove wrinkles **2.** improvement, renovation —**face-saving** *a.* maintaining dignity —**face value 1.** value on face of commercial paper or coin **2.** apparent value —**face the music** face unpleasant consequences bravely —**face up to** accept (unpleasant fact *etc.*) —**on the face of it** to all appearances

facetious (fə'sēshəs) *a.* **1.** (sarcastically) witty **2.** humorous, given to jesting, *esp.* at inappropriate time

-facient (*comb. form*) state; quality, as in *absorbefacient*

facile ('fasil) *a.* **1.** easy **2.** working easily **3.** easy-going **4.** superficial, silly —**fa'cilitate** *vt.* make easy, help progress of —**facili'tation** *n.* —**fa'cility** *n.* **1.** easiness **2.** dexterity

—*pl.* **3.** opportunities, good conditions **4.** means, equipment for doing something

facsimile (fak'simili) *n.* **1.** exact copy **2.** telegraphic system in which document is scanned photoelectrically and resulting signals are transmitted and reproduced photographically after reception **3.** image produced by this means

fact (fakt) *n.* **1.** thing known to be true **2.** deed **3.** reality —**'factual** *a.* —**as a matter of fact, in (point of) fact** in reality or actuality —**fact of life** (*esp.* unpleasant) inescapable truth

faction¹ ('fakshən) *n.* **1.** (dissenting) minority group within larger body **2.** dissension —**'factious** *a.* of or producing factions

faction² ('fakshən) *n.* dramatization of factual event

factitious (fak'tishəs) *a.* **1.** artificial **2.** specially made up **3.** unreal

factor ('faktər) *n.* **1.** something contributing to a result **2.** one of numbers which multiplied together give a given number **3.** agent, dealer —**fac'torial** *Math. n.* **1.** product of all positive integers from one up to and including given integer —*a.* **2.** of factorials or factors —**fac'totum** *n.* man-of-all-work

factory ('faktəri) *n.* building where things are manufactured —**factory ship** fishing vessel that processes its catch before returning to port

faculty ('fakəlti) *n.* **1.** inherent power **2.** power of the mind **3.** ability, aptitude **4.** teaching staff and administrators with academic qualifications at an institution for learning **5.** members of profession **6.** authorization —**'facultative** *a.* **1.** optional **2.** contingent

fad (fad) *n.* **1.** short-lived fashion **2.** whim —**'faddish** *or* **'faddy** *a.*

fade (fād) *vi.* **1.** lose color, strength **2.** wither **3.** grow dim **4.** disappear gradually —*vt.* **5.** cause to fade —**'fadeless** *a.* —**fade-in, fade-out** *n.* **1.** *Rad.* variation in strength of signals **2.** *T.V.*, *cine.* gradual appearance and disappearance of picture

faeces ('fēsēz) *pl.n.* see FECES

faerie *or* **faery** ('fāəri) *obs., poet. n.* **1.** fairyland —*a./n.* **2.** see FAIRY

Faeroe *or* **Faroe Islands** ('fārō, 'fer-) self-governing region of kingdom of Denmark —**Faero'ese** *or* **Faro'ese** *a./n.*

fag (fag) *n.* **1.** *inf.* boring task **2.** *sl.* cigarette **3.** *sl.* male homosexual **4.** UK *esp.* formerly, young public school boy who performs menial chores for older boy or prefect —*v.* **5.** *inf.* (*esp. with* out) tire —*vi.* **6.** do menial tasks for a senior boy in school (-gg-) —**fag end** last part, inferior remnant

faggot ('fagət) *n. sl.* male homosexual

fagot *or* **faggot** ('fagət) *n.* bundle of sticks tied together —**'fagoting** *or* **'faggoting** *n.* fabric decoration in which threads are tied in bundles after crosswise threads have been withdrawn

Fah. *or* **Fahr.** Fahrenheit

Fahrenheit ('farənhīt) *a.* measured by thermometric scale with freezing point of water 32°, boiling point 212°

faïence (fā'äns, fī-) *n.* glazed earthenware or china

fail (fāl) *vi.* **1.** be unsuccessful **2.** stop operating or working **3.** be below the required standard **4.** be insufficient **5.** run short **6.** be wanting when in need **7.** lose power **8.** die away **9.** become bankrupt —*vt.* **10.** disappoint, give no help to **11.** neglect **12.** judge (candidate) to be below required standard —**'failing** *n.* **1.** deficiency **2.** fault —*prep.* **3.** in default of —**'failure** *n.* —**fail-safe** *a.* (of device) ensuring safety or remedy of malfunction in machine, weapon *etc.* —**without fail** certainly

faille (fīl, 'fīəl) *n.* ribbed silk or rayon fabric

fain (fān) *obs. a.* **1.** glad, willing; constrained —*adv.* **2.** gladly

faint (fānt) *a.* **1.** feeble, dim, pale **2.** weak **3.** dizzy, about to lose consciousness —*vi.* **4.** lose consciousness temporarily —*n.* **5.** an instance of this (*also* syncope) —**faint-hearted** *a.* timid

fair¹ (fāər) *a.* **1.** just, impartial **2.** according to rules, legitimate **3.** blond(e) **4.** beautiful **5.** ample **6.** of moderate quality or amount **7.** unblemished **8.** plausible **9.** middling **10.** (of weather) favorable —*adv.* **11.** honestly **12.** absolutely; quite —**'fairing** *n.* *Aviation* streamlined casing, or any part so shaped that it provides streamline form —**'fairly** *adv.* **1.** moderately **2.** as deserved; justly **3.** positively —**'fairness** *n.* —**fair copy** neat copy of corrected document —**fair-haired boy** boy or man favored by person or group —**Fair Isle** intricate multicolored pattern knitted with Shetland wool —**fair play** (abidance by) established standard of decency —**'fairway** *n.* **1.** navigable channel **2.** *Golf* trimmed turf between rough —**fair-weather** *a.* **1.** suitable for use in fair weather only **2.** unreliable in difficult situations —**the fair sex** women collectively

fair² (fāər) *n.* **1.** traveling entertainment with sideshows, amusements *etc.* **2.** large exhibition of commercial or industrial products **3.** periodical market often with amusements —**'fairground** *n.*

fairy ('fāəri) *n.* **1.** imaginary small creature with powers of magic **2.** *sl.* male homosexual —*a.* **3.** of fairies **4.** like fairy, beautiful and delicate —**fairy godmother** benefactress, *esp.* unknown —**'fairyland** *n.* —**fairy ring** circle of darker color in grass —**fairy tale 1.** story of imaginary beings and happenings, *esp.* as told to children **2.** highly improbable account

fait accompli (fe takō'plē) *Fr.* something already done that cannot be altered

faith (fāth) *n.* **1.** trust **2.** belief (without proof) **3.** religion **4.** promise **5.** loyalty, constancy —**'faithful** *a.* constant, true —**'faithfully** *adv.* —**'faithless** *a.* —**faith healing** method of treating illness by religious faith and prayer

fake (fāk) *vt.* **1.** conceal defects of by artifice **2.** touch up **3.** counterfeit **4.** sham —*n.* **5.** fraudulent object, person, act —*a.* **6.** not genuine —**'faker** *n.* **1.** one who deals in fakes **2.** swindler

fakir (fə'kēər) *n.* 1. member of Islamic religious order 2. Hindu ascetic

Falange ('falanj) *n.* Fascist movement in Spain —**Fa'langist** *n./a.*

falchion ('fölchən) *n.* broad curved medieval sword

falcon ('falkən, 'föl-) *n.* small bird of prey, *esp.* trained in hawking for sport —**'falconer** *n.* one who keeps, trains or hunts with falcons —**'falconry** *n.* hawking

falderal ('foldərol) *n. see* FOLDEROL

Falkland Islands ('fölklənd) crown colony of United Kingdom situated in S Atlantic Ocean about 480 miles northeast of Cape Horn

fall (föl) *vi.* 1. drop, come down freely 2. become lower 3. decrease 4. hang down 5. come to the ground, cease to stand 6. perish 7. collapse 8. be captured 9. revert 10. lapse 11. be uttered 12. become 13. happen (**fell** *pt.*, **'fallen** *pp.*) —*n.* 14. falling 15. amount that falls 16. amount of descent 17. decrease 18. collapse, ruin 19. drop 20. (*oft. pl.*) cascade 21. cadence 22. yielding to temptation 23. autumn 24. rope of hoisting tackle —**fall guy** *inf.* victim of confidence trick —**falling sickness** *or* **evil** *former name for* epilepsy —**falling star** *inf.* meteor —**'fallout** *n.* radioactive particles spread as result of nuclear explosion —**fall for** *inf.* 1. fall in love with 2. be taken in by —**fall out** 1. disagree 2. leave place in rank

fallacy ('faləsi) *n.* 1. incorrect, misleading opinion or argument 2. flaw in logic 3. illusion —**fallacious** (fə'lāshəs) *a.* —**falli'bil-ity** *n.* —**'fallible** *a.* liable to error —**'fallibly** *adv.*

fallen ('fölən) *v.* 1. *pp. of* FALL —*a.* 2. having sunk in reputation or honor 3. killed in battle with glory —**fallen arch** collapse of arch formed by instep of foot, resulting in flat feet

Fallopian tube (fə'lōpiən) either of pair of tubes through which egg cells pass from ovary to womb (*also* **oviduct**)

fallow[1] ('falō) *a.* 1. plowed and harrowed but left without crop 2. uncultivated 3. neglected

fallow[2] ('falō) *a.* brown or reddish-yellow —**fallow deer** deer of this color

false (föls) *a.* 1. wrong, erroneous 2. deceptive 3. faithless 4. sham, artificial —**'falsehood** *n.* lie —**'falsely** *adv.* —**'false-ness** *n.* faithlessness —**falsifi'cation** *n.* —**'falsify** *vt.* 1. alter fraudulently 2. misrepresent 3. disappoint (hopes *etc.*) (**'falsified, 'falsifying**) —**'falsity** *n.* —**false pretenses** misrepresentation of facts to gain advantage (*esp. in* **under false pretenses**)

falsetto (föl'setō) *n.* high-pitched voice above natural range (*pl.* -**s**)

Falstaffian (föl'stafiən) *a.* like Shakespeare's Falstaff, fat, convivial and boasting

falter ('föltər) *vi.* 1. hesitate 2. waver 3. stumble —**'falteringly** *adv.*

fame (fām) *n.* 1. reputation 2. renown —**famed** *a.* —**'famous** *a.* 1. widely known 2. *inf.* excellent

familiar (fə'milyər) *a.* 1. well-known 2. frequent, customary 3. intimate 4. closely acquainted 5. unceremonious 6. impertinent, too friendly —*n.* 7. familiar friend 8. familiar demon —**famili'arity** *n.* —**familiari'zation** *n.* —**fa'miliarize** *vt.* —**fa'miliarly** *adv.*

family ('famili, 'famli) *n.* 1. group of parents and children, or near relatives 2. person's children 3. all descendants of common ancestor 4. household 5. group of allied objects 6. *Biol.* taxonomic division of plants and animals ranking above a genus and below an order —**fa'milial** *a.* —**family man** married man who has children, *esp.* one who is devoted to his family —**family name** surname, *esp.* representing family honor —**family planning** control of number of children in family, *esp.* by contraception —**family tree** chart showing relationships and lines of descent of family (*also* **genealogical tree**)

famine ('famin) *n.* 1. extreme scarcity of food 2. starvation 3. acute shortage of anything —**'famished** *a.* very hungry

famous ('fāməs) *a. see* FAME

fan[1] (fan) *n.* 1. instrument for producing current of air, *esp.* for ventilating or cooling 2. folding object of paper *etc.* used, *esp.* formerly, for cooling the face 3. outspread feathers of a bird's tail —*vt.* 4. blow or cool with fan —*v.* 5. spread out like fan (-**nn**-) —**fan belt** belt that drives cooling fan in internal-combustion engine —**'fanjet** *n. see* TURBOFAN —**'fanlight** *n.* (fan-shaped) window over door —**'fantail** *n.* kind of bird (*esp.* pigeon) with fan-shaped tail —**fan vaulting** *Archit.* vaulting having ribs that radiate, like those of fan, from top of capital (*also* **palm vaulting**)

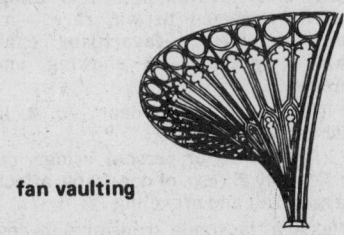

fan vaulting

fan[2] (fan) *n. inf.* 1. devoted admirer 2. enthusiast, particularly for sport *etc.*

fanatic (fə'natik) *a.* 1. filled with abnormal enthusiasm, *esp.* in religion —*n.* 2. fanatic person —**fa'natical** *a.* —**fa'natically** *adv.* —**fa'naticism** *n.*

fancy ('fansi) *a.* 1. ornamental, not plain 2. of whimsical or arbitrary kind —*n.* 3. whim, caprice 4. liking, inclination 5. imagination 6. mental image —*vt.* 7. imagine 8. be inclined to believe 9. *inf.* have a liking for (**'fancied, 'fancying**) —*interj.* 10. exclamation of surprise (*also* **fancy that**) —**'fancier** *n.* one with liking and expert knowledge (respecting some specific thing) —**'fanciful** *a.* —**'fancifully** *adv.* —**fancy dress** costume worn at masquerades *etc.* representing historical figure *etc.* —**fancy-free** *a.* having no commitments —**fancy goods** small decorative gifts —**fancy man** *sl.* 1. woman's lover 2. pimp —**fancy woman** *sl.* 1. mistress 2. prostitute

fandango (fan'danggō) *n.* 1. lively Sp. dance with castanets 2. music for this dance (*pl.* -**s**)

fanfare ('fanfaor) *n.* 1. a flourish of trumpets or bugles 2. ostentatious display

fang (fang) *n.* 1. snake's poison tooth 2. long, pointed tooth

fantasy ('fantəsi, -zi) *n.* 1. power of imagination, *esp.* extravagant 2. mental image 3. fanciful invention or design —**fantasia** (fan'tāzhə) *n.* fanciful musical composition —**'fantasize** *v.* —**fan'tastic** *a.* 1. quaint 2. grotesque 3. extremely fanciful, wild 4. *inf.* very good 5. *inf.* very large —**fan'tastically** *adv.*

FAO Food and Agriculture Organization (of the United Nations)

far (fär) *adv.* 1. at or to a great distance or advanced point 2. at or to a remote time 3. by very much —*a.* 4. distant 5. more distant (**'farther, 'further** *comp.*, **'farthest, 'fur-thest** *sup.*) —**'faraway** *a.* 1. distant 2. absent-minded —**Far East** countries of E Asia, including China, Japan *etc.* —**Far Eastern** *a.* —**far-fetched** *a.* incredible —**far-flung** *a.* 1. widely distributed 2. far distant; remote —**Far North** Arctic and sub-Arctic regions —**far-off** *a.* remote; distant —**far-out** *a. sl.* 1. bizarre, avant-garde 2. wonderful —**far'sighted** *a.* possessing prudence and foresight —**far'sightedness** *n.* hypermetropia —**far and away** by a very great margin —**far out** *sl.* expression of amazement or delight

farad ('farad, -rəd) *n.* unit of electrical capacity —**faradaic** (farə'dāik) *a.*

farce[1] (färs) *n. see* FORCEMEAT

farce[2] (färs) *n.* 1. comedy of boisterous humor 2. absurd and futile proceeding —**'farcical** *a.* ludicrous —**'farcically** *adv.*

fare (faor) *n.* 1. charge for passenger's transport 2. passenger 3. food —*vi.* 4. get on 5. happen 6. travel, progress —**fare'well** *interj.* 1. goodbye —*n.* 2. leave-taking

farina (fə'rēnə) *n.* 1. flour or meal made from cereal grain 2. any powdery or mealy substance —**farinaceous** (fari'nāshəs) *a.* 1. mealy 2. starchy

farm (färm) *n.* 1. tract of land for cultivation or rearing livestock 2. unit of land, water, for growing or rearing a particular crop, animal *etc.* —*v.* 3. cultivate (land) 4. rear (livestock) on farm —**'farmer** *n.* —**farm hand** person hired to work on farm —**'farmhouse** *n.* —**'farmstead** *n.* farm or part of farm consisting of main buildings together with adjacent grounds —**'farmyard** *n.* —**farm out** 1. send (work) to be done by others 2. put into care of others

faro ('faorō) *n.* card game

farrago (fə'rägō) *n.* medley, hodgepodge (*pl.* -**s**)

farrier ('fariər) *n.* one who shoes, cares for horses —**'farriery** *n.* his art

farrow ('farō) *n.* 1. litter of pigs —*v.* 2. give birth to (litter)

fart (färt) *vulgar n.* 1. (audible) emission of gas from anus —*vi.* 2. break wind

farther ('färdhər) *adv./a. comp. of* FAR further —**'farthermost** *a.* most distant —**'farthest** *adv./a. sup. of* FAR furthest

farthing ('färdhing) *n.* UK formerly, coin worth quarter of penny

farthingale ('färdhin-gāl, 'färdhinggāl) *n. Hist.* hoop worn under skirts

farthingale

fasces ('fasēz) *pl.n.* 1. bundle of rods bound together round ax, forming Roman badge of authority 2. emblem of It. fascists

fascia ('fāshiə) *n.* 1. flat surface above shop window 2. *Archit.* long flat surface between moldings under eaves 3. face of wood or stone in a building 4. dashboard (*pl.* -**ciae** (-shiē))

fascinate ('fasināt) *vt.* 1. attract and delight by rousing interest and curiosity 2. render motionless, as with a fixed stare —**fasci'na-tion** *n.*

Fascism ('fashizəm) *n.* **1.** authoritarian political system opposed to democracy and liberalism **2.** (*oft.* **f-**) behavior (*esp.* by those in authority) supposedly typical of this system —**'Fascist** *a./n.*

fashion ('fashən) *n.* **1.** (latest) style, *esp.* of dress *etc.* **2.** manner, mode **3.** form, type —*vt.* **4.** shape, make —**'fashionable** *a.* —**'fashionably** *adv.*

fast[1] (fast) *a.* **1.** (capable of) moving quickly **2.** permitting, providing, rapid progress **3.** ahead of true time **4.** *obs.* dissipated **5.** firm, steady **6.** permanent —*adv.* **7.** rapidly **8.** tightly —**'fastness** *n.* **1.** fast state **2.** fortress, stronghold —**'fastback** *n.* automobile with back forming continuous slope from roof to rear —**fast-breeder reactor** nuclear reactor that uses little or no moderator and produces more fissionable material than it consumes —**fast food** food, *esp.* hamburgers *etc.*, prepared and served very quickly

fast[2] (fast) *vi.* **1.** go without food, or some kinds of food —*n.* **2.** act or period of fasting —**'fasting** *n.*

fasten ('fasən) *vt.* **1.** attach, fix, secure —*vi.* **2.** become joined **3.** (*usu. with* on) seize (upon) —**'fastening** *n.* something that fastens, such as clasp

fastidious (fa'stidiəs) *a.* **1.** hard to please **2.** discriminating, particular

fat (fat) *n.* **1.** oily edible substance **2.** fat part —*a.* **3.** having too much fat **4.** containing fat, greasy **5.** profitable **6.** fertile (**'fatter** *comp.*, **'fattest** *sup.*) —*vt.* **7.** feed (animals) for slaughter (**-tt-**) —**'fatness** *n.* —**'fatten** *v.* —**'fatty** *a./n.* —**'fathead** *n. inf.* dolt, idiot —**fat stock** livestock fattened and ready for market —**fatty acid** any of class of aliphatic carboxylic acids, such as palmitic acid

fate (fāt) *n.* **1.** power supposed to predetermine events **2.** goddess of destiny **3.** destiny **4.** person's appointed lot or condition **5.** death; destruction —*vt.* **6.** preordain —**'fatal** *a.* **1.** deadly, ending in death **2.** destructive **3.** disastrous **4.** inevitable —**'fatalism** *n.* **1.** belief that everything is predetermined **2.** submission to fate —**'fatalist** *n.* —**fatal'istic** *a.* —**fatal'istically** *adv.* —**fatality** (fə'taliti, fə-) *n.* **1.** accident resulting in death **2.** person killed in war, accident —**'fatally** *adv.* —**'fateful** *a.* **1.** fraught with destiny **2.** prophetic

father ('fädhər) *n.* **1.** male parent **2.** forefather, ancestor **3.** (**F-**) God **4.** originator, early leader **5.** priest, confessor **6.** oldest member of a society —*vt.* **7.** beget **8.** originate **9.** pass as father or author of **10.** act as father to —**'fatherhood** *n.* —**'fatherless** *a.* —**'fatherly** *a.* —**father-in-law** *n.* husband's or wife's father —**'fatherland** *n.* **1.** person's native country **2.** country of person's ancestors —**Father's Day** day for honoring fathers *usu.* the 3rd Sunday in June

fathom ('fadhəm) *n.* **1.** measure of six feet of water —*vt.* **2.** sound (water) **3.** get to bottom of, understand —**'fathomable** *a.* —**'fathomless** *a.* too deep to fathom

fatigue (fə'tēg) *n.* **1.** weariness **2.** toil **3.** weakness of metals *etc.* subjected to stress **4.** soldier's nonmilitary duty —*pl.* **5.** special clothing worn by military personnel to carry out such duties —*vt.* **6.** weary

fatuous ('fachōōəs) *a.* very silly, idiotic —**'fatuity** (fə'tyōōiti, -'tōō-) *n.*

faucet ('fôsit) *n.* device for allowing water to emerge from a pipe in a controlled flow

fault (fôlt) *n.* **1.** defect **2.** flaw **3.** misdeed **4.** blame, culpability **5.** blunder, mistake **6.** *Tennis* ball wrongly served **7.** *Geol.* break in strata —*vt.* **8.** find fault in —*v.* **9.** (cause to) undergo fault —*vi.* **10.** commit a fault

—**'faultily** *adv.* —**'faultless** *a.* —**'faultlessly** *adv.* —**'faulty** *a.* —**to a fault** excessively

faun (fôn) *n.* mythological woodland being with tail and horns

fauna ('fônə) *n.* animals of region or period collectively (*pl.* **-s, -ae** (-ē))

Fauves (fōv) *pl.n.* —**les Fauves** (lā). *orig.* a contemptuous name for a group of French postimpressionist painters who showed their work at the Salon d'Automne in 1905 so-called because of their use of strident color, violent distortions and broad, bold brush strokes

faux pas ('fō 'pä) social blunder or indiscretion (*pl.* **faux pas** ('fō 'päz))

favor ('favər) *n.* **1.** goodwill **2.** approval **3.** especial kindness **4.** partiality **5.** small gift or toy given to guest at party *etc.* **6** *Hist.* badge or knot of ribbons —*vt.* **7.** regard or treat with favor **8.** oblige **9.** treat with partiality **10.** aid **11.** support **12.** resemble —**'favorable** *a.* **1.** advantageous, encouraging, promising **2.** giving consent —**'favorably** *adv.* —**'favored** *a.* **1.** treated with favor **2.** having appearance (as specified), as in *ill-favored* —**favorite** ('favərit) *n.* **1.** favored person or thing **2.** horse *etc.* expected to win race —*a.* **3.** chosen, preferred —**favoritism** ('favər-itizəm) *n.* practice of showing undue preference

fawn[1] (fôn) *n.* **1.** young deer —*a.* **2.** light grayish-brown

fawn[2] (fôn) *vi.* **1.** (of person) cringe, court favor servilely **2.** (*esp.* of dog) show affection by wagging tail and groveling

Fax (faks) *n.* facsimile transmission device which transmits printed material by telephone

fay (fā) *n.* fairy, sprite

F.B.I. Federal Bureau of Investigation

FCA Farm Credit Administration

FCC Federal Communications Commission

FDA Food and Drug Administration

FDIC Federal Deposit Insurance Corporation

Fe *Chem.* iron

fealty ('fēəlti) *n.* **1.** fidelity of vassal to his lord **2.** loyalty

fear (fēər) *n.* **1.** dread, alarm, anxiety, unpleasant emotion caused by coming evil or danger —*vi.* **2.** have this feeling, be afraid —*vt.* **3.** regard with fear **4.** shrink from **5.** revere —**'fearful** *a.* **1.** afraid **2.** causing fear **3.** *inf.* very unpleasant —**'fearfully** *adv.* —**'fearless** *a.* intrepid —**'fearlessly** *adv.* —**'fearsome** *a.*

feasible ('fēzəbəl) *a.* **1.** able to be done **2.** likely —**feasi'bility** *n.* —**'feasibly** *adv.*

feast (fēst) *n.* **1.** banquet, lavish meal **2.** religious anniversary **3.** something very pleasant, sumptuous —*vi.* **4.** partake of banquet; fare sumptuously —*vt.* **5.** regale with feast **6.** provide delight for —**'feaster** *n.*

feat (fēt) *n.* **1.** notable deed **2.** surprising or striking trick

feather ('fedhər) *n.* **1.** one of the barbed shafts which form covering of birds **2.** anything resembling this —*vt.* **3.** provide, line with feathers —*vi.* **4.** grow feathers —*v.* **5.** turn (oar) edgeways —**'feathery** *a.* —**feather bed** mattress filled with feathers —**feather'bed** *vi.* require employer to hire more persons than needed to perform task —**'featherbrain** *or* **'featherhead** *n.* frivolous or forgetful person —**'featherbrained** *or* **'featherheaded** *a.* —**'featherstitch** *n.* embroidery stitch producing pattern of branches along a stem —**'featherweight** *n.* very light person or thing, *esp.* boxer (between bantamweight and lightweight)

weighing not more than 126 lbs. —**feather one's nest** enrich oneself —**the white feather** cowardice

feature ('fēchər) *n.* **1.** (*usu. pl.*) part of face **2.** characteristic or notable part of anything **3.** main or special item —*vt.* **4.** portray **5.** *Cine.* present in leading role in a motion picture **6.** give prominence to —*vi.* **7.** be prominent —**'featureless** *a.* without striking features

Feb. February

febrile ('febril, 'fē-) *a.* of fever

February ('febyōōəri, -brōō-) *n.* second month of year (normally containing 28 days; in leap year, 29)

feces *or* **faeces** ('fēsēz) *pl.n.* excrement, bodily waste —**fecal** *or* **faecal** ('fēkəl) *a.*

feckless ('feklis) *a.* spiritless; weak; irresponsible

feculent ('fekyələnt) *a.* full of sediment, turbid —**'feculence** *n.*

fecund ('fekənd, 'fēk-) *a.* fertile, fruitful, fertilizing —**'fecundate** *vt.* fertilize, impregnate —**fecun'dation** *n.* —**fecundity** (fi'kunditi) *n.*

fed (fed) *pt./pp.* of FEED —**fed up** bored, dissatisfied

Fed. *or* **fed.** **1.** Federal **2.** Federation **3.** Federated

federal ('fedərəl) *a.* of or like the government of states which are united but retain internal independence —**'federalism** *n.* —**'federalist** *n./a.* —**'federate** *v.* form into, become, a federation —**fede'ration** *n.* **1.** league **2.** federal union —**federal style** American architectural style of about 1780–1820 characterized by symmetrical facades, smooth surfaces, and restrained classical ornament

fee (fē) *n.* payment for professional and other services

feeble ('fēbəl) *a.* **1.** weak **2.** lacking strength or effectiveness, insipid —**'feebly** *adv.* —**'feeble-minded** *a.* **1.** lacking in intelligence **2.** mentally defective

feed (fēd) *vt.* **1.** give food to **2.** supply, support —*vi.* **3.** take food (**fed** *pt./pp.*) —*n.* **4.** feeding **5.** fodder, pasturage **6.** allowance of fodder **7.** material supplied to machine **8.** part of machine taking in material —**'feeder** *n.* **1.** one who or that which feeds **2.** child's bib **3.** tributary channel —**'feedback** *n.* **1.** return of part of output of electrical circuit or loudspeakers. In **negative feedback** rise in output energy reduces input energy; in **positive feedback** increase in output energy reinforces input energy **2.** information received in response to inquiry *etc.* —**'feedlot** *n.* area, building where cattle are fattened for market

feel (fēl) *vt.* **1.** perceive, examine by touch **2.** experience **3.** find (one's way) cautiously **4.** be sensitive to **5.** believe, consider —*vi.* **6.** have physical or emotional sensation of (something) (**felt** *pt./pp.*) —*n.* **7.** act or instance of feeling **8.** quality or impression of something perceived by feeling **9.** sense of touch —**'feeler** *n.* **1.** special organ of touch in some animals **2.** proposal put forward to test others' opinion **3.** that which feels —**'feeling** *n.* **1.** sense of touch **2.** ability to feel **3.** physical sensation **4.** emotion **5.** sympathy, tenderness **6.** conviction or opinion not solely based on reason —*pl.* **7.** susceptibilities —*a.* **8.** sensitive, sympathetic, heartfelt —**feel for** show sympathy or compassion toward —**feel like** have an inclination for

feet (fēt) *n., pl.* of FOOT

feign (fān) *v.* pretend, sham

feint[1] (fānt) *n.* **1.** sham attack or blow meant to deceive opponent **2.** semblance, pretense —*vi.* **3.** make feint

feint[2] (fānt) *n. Print.* narrowest rule used in production of ruled paper

feldspar ('feldspär, 'felspär) *or* **felspar** *n.* crystalline mineral found in granite *etc.* —**feldspathic** (feld'spathik, fel'spath-) *or* **fel'spathic** *a.*

felicity (fi'lisiti) *n.* 1. great happiness, bliss 2. appropriate expression or style —**fe'licitate** *vt.* congratulate —**felici'tation** *n.* (*usu. in pl.*) —**fe'licitous** *a.* 1. apt, well-chosen 2. happy

feline ('fēlīn) *a./n.* (of, relating to) a member of the cat family —**felinity** (fi'liniti) *n.*

fell[1] (fel) *pt. of* FALL

fell[2] (fel) *vt.* 1. knock down 2. cut down (tree) —**'feller** *n.*

fell[3] (fel) *a. obs.* fierce, terrible —**one fell swoop** a single hasty action or occurrence

fell[4] (fel) *n.* skin or hide with hair

fell[5] (fel) *n.* mountain, stretch of moorland, *esp.* in N of England

fellatio (fi'lāshiō) *n.* sexual activity in which penis is stimulated by partner's mouth

felloe ('felō) *or* **felly** *n.* outer part (or section) of wheel

fellow ('felō) *n.* 1. man, boy 2. person 3. comrade, associate 4. counterpart, like thing 5. member (of society, college *etc.*) —*a.* 6. of the same class, associated —**'fellowship** *n.* 1. fraternity 2. friendship 3. in university *etc.*, research post; special scholarship —**fellow traveler** 1. companion on journey 2. non-Communist who sympathizes with Communism

felon ('felən) *n.* one guilty of felony —**fe'lonious** *a.* —**'felony** *n.* serious crime

felspar ('felspär) *n. see* FELDSPAR

felt[1] (felt) *pt./pp. of* FEEL

felt[2] (felt) *n.* 1. soft, matted fabric made by bonding fibers chemically and by pressure 2. thing made of this —*vt.* 3. make into, or cover with, felt —*vi.* 4. become matted like felt —**felt-tip pen** pen whose writing point is made from pressed fibers (*also* **fiber-tip pen**)

fem. feminine

female ('fēmāl) *a.* 1. of sex which bears offspring 2. relating to this sex —*n.* 3. one of this sex

feminine ('feminin) *a.* 1. of women 2. womanly 3. denoting class or type of grammatical inflection in some languages —**femi'ninity** *n.* —**'feminism** *n.* advocacy of equal rights for women —**'feminist** *n./a.*

femur ('fēmər) *n.* thighbone —**'femoral** *a.* of the thigh

fen[1] (fen) *n.* tract of marshy land, swamp —**'fenny** *a.*

fen[2] (fen) *n.* monetary unit of the People's Republic of China, worth one hundredth of a yuan

fence (fens) *n.* 1. structure of wire, wood *etc.* enclosing an area 2. *Machinery* guard, guide 3. *sl.* dealer in stolen property —*vt.* 4. erect fence on or around 5. (*with* in) enclose —*vi.* 6. fight (as sport) with swords 7. avoid question *etc.* 8. *sl.* deal in stolen property —**'fencing** *n.* close-combat sport involving personal offense and defense between two persons using swords

fend (fend) *vt.* 1. (*usu. with* off) ward off, repel —*vi.* 2. provide (for oneself *etc.*) —**'fender** *n.* 1. low metal frame in front of fireplace 2. name for various protective devices 3. frame 4. edge 5. buffer 6. guard over wheel of automobile

fenestration (feni'strāshən) *n.* arrangement of windows in a building

Fenian ('fēniən) *n.* 1. formerly, member of Irish revolutionary organization founded in

U.S.A. in 19th century to fight for independent Ireland —*a.* 2. of Fenians

fennel ('fenəl) *n.* yellow-flowered fragrant herb

fenugreek ('fenyəgrēk) *n.* heavily scented leguminous plant

-fer (*n. comb. form*) person or thing that bears something specified, as in *crucifer*, *conifer* —**-ferous** (*a. comb. form*) bearing, producing, as in *coniferous*

feral[1] ('fēərəl) *a.* wild, uncultivated

feral[2] ('fēərəl) *a. obs.* funereal, gloomy

fermata (fer'mätə) *n. Mus.* pause (*pl.* **-s, -te** (-ti))

ferment ('fərment) *n.* 1. leaven, substance causing thing to ferment 2. excitement, tumult —*v.* (fər'ment) 3. (cause to) undergo chemical change with effervescence, liberation of heat and alteration of properties, *eg* process of wine-making and bread-making 4. (cause to) become excited—**fermen'tation** *n.*

fermium ('fərmiəm) *n. Chem.* transuranic element *Symbol* Fm, at. wt. 253, at. no. 100

fern (fərn) *n.* class of pteridophytes of various sizes, distinguished by large leaves and complicated structure —**'fernery** *n.* place for growing ferns —**'ferny** *a.* full of ferns

ferocious (fə'rōshəs) *a.* fierce, savage, cruel —**ferocity** (fə'rositi) *n.*

ferret ('ferit) *n.* 1. tamed animal like weasel, used to catch rabbits, rats *etc.* —*vt.* (*usu. with* out) 2. drive out with ferrets 3. search out —*vi.* 4. search about, rummage

ferric ('ferik) *a.* pert. to, containing, iron —**fer'riferous** *a.* yielding iron —**'ferrous** *a.* of or containing iron in divalent state —**ferruginous** (fə'rōōjinəs, fe-) *a.* 1. containing iron 2. reddish-brown —**ferro'concrete** *n.* concrete strengthened by framework of metal

Ferris wheel ('feris) in fairground, large, vertical wheel with seats for riding

ferro- (*comb. form*) 1. property or presence of iron, as in *ferromagnetism* 2. presence of iron in divalent state, as in *ferrocyanide*

ferrocene ('ferōsēn) *n.* 1. crystalline stable organometallic coordination compound 2. analogous compound with heavy metal

ferrule ('ferəl) *n.* metal cap to strengthen end of stick *etc.*

ferry ('feri) *n.* 1. boat *etc.* for transporting people, vehicles, across body of water, *esp.* as repeated or regular service 2. place for ferrying —*v.* 3. carry, travel, by ferry —*vt.* 4. convey (passengers *etc.*) (**'ferried, 'ferrying**) —**'ferryman** *n.*

fertile ('fərtil) *a.* 1. (capable of) producing offspring, bearing crops *etc.* 2. fruitful, producing abundantly 3. inventive —**fer'tility** *n.* —**fertili'zation** *n.* —**'fertilize** *vt.* make fertile —**'fertilizer** *n.*

ferule ('ferəl) *n.* 1. flat piece of wood, such as ruler, formerly used in some schools to cane children on hand —*vt.* 2. punish with ferule

fervent ('fərvənt) *a.* ardent, vehement, intense —**'fervency** *n.* —**'fervently** *adv.* —**'fervor** *n.*

fervid ('fərvid) *a.* 1. very hot, burning 2. fervent —**'fervidly** *adv.*

fescue ('feskyōō) *n.* grass used as pasture, with stiff narrow leaves

fess *or* **fesse** (fes) *n. Her.* horizontal band across shield

festal ('festəl) *a.* 1. of feast or holiday 2. merry, gay —**'festally** *adv.*

fester ('festər) *v.* 1. (cause to) form pus —*vi.* 2. rankle 3. become embittered

festival ('festivəl) *n.* 1. day, period set aside for celebration, *esp.* of religious feast 2.

organized series of events, performances *etc.*, usu. in one place —**'festive** *a.* 1. joyous, merry 2. of feast —**fes'tivity** *n.* 1. gaiety, mirth 2. rejoicing —*pl.* 3. festive proceedings

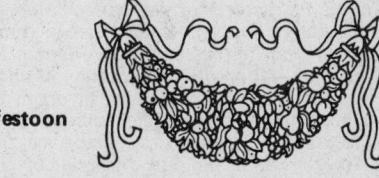

festoon

festoon (fe'stōōn) *n.* 1. chain of flowers, ribbons *etc.* hung in curve between two points —*vt.* 2. form into, adorn with festoons

fetch[1] (fech) *vt.* 1. go and bring 2. draw forth 3. be sold for —*n.* 4. trick —**'fetching** *a.* attractive —**fetch up** 1. *inf.* arrive 2. *sl.* vomit (food *etc.*)

fetch[2] (fech) *n.* ghost or apparition of living person

fete *or* **fête** (fāt, fet) *n.* 1. gala, bazaar *etc.*, *esp.* one held out of doors 2. festival, holiday, celebration —*vt.* 3. feast 4. honor with festive entertainment

fetid *or* **foetid** ('fetid) *a.* stinking

fetish *or* **fetich** ('fetish, 'fētish) *n.* 1. (inanimate) object believed to have magical powers 2. excessive attention to something 3. object, activity, to which excessive devotion is paid

fetlock ('fetlok) *n.* projection behind and above horse's hoof, or tuft of hair on this

fetter ('fetər) *n.* 1. chain or shackle for feet 2. check, restraint —*pl.* 3. captivity —*vt.* 4. chain up 5. restrain, hamper

fettle ('fetəl) *n.* condition, state of health

fetus *or* **foetus** ('fētəs) *n.* unborn or unhatched young of vertebrate, *esp.* human embryo three months after conception —**'fetal** *or* **'foetal** *a.*

feud (fyōōd) *n.* 1. bitter, lasting, mutual hostility, *esp.* between two families or tribes 2. vendetta —*vi.* 3. carry on feud

feudal ('fyōōdəl) *a.* 1. of, like, medieval social and economic system based on holding land from superior in return for service 2. *inf.* very old-fashioned —**'feudalism** *n.*

fever ('fēvər) *n.* 1. elevation of body temperature above 98.6°F 2. intense nervous excitement —**'fevered** *a.* —**'feverish** *a.* 1. having fever 2. accompanied by, caused by, fever 3. in a state of restless excitement —**'feverishly** *adv.* —**fever blisters** *see* cold sore *at* COLD —**'feverfew** *n.* bushy plant with white flower heads —**fever pitch** 1. very fast pace 2. intense excitement —**fever therapy** treatment of disease by elevating body temperature

few (fyōō) *a.* 1. not many —*n.* 2. small number —**a good few, quite a few** several

fey (fā) *a.* 1. clairvoyant, visionary 2. *esp. Scot.* fated to die

fez (fez) *n.* red, brimless, orig. Turkish tasseled cap (*pl.* **'fezzes**)

ff *Mus.* fortissimo

ff. 1. folios 2. and the following (pages *etc.*)

FFV First Family of Virginia

FHA Federal Housing Administration

fiancé (fēon'sā) *n.* person engaged to be married (**fian'cée** *fem.*)

Fianna Fáil ('fēənə 'fäl) the Irish Republican Party

fiasco (fē'äskō) *n.* breakdown, total failure (*pl.* **-s, -es**)

fiat ('fēət, -at, -ät; 'fīət, -at) *n.* 1. decree 2. official permission

fib (fib) *n.* 1. trivial lie, falsehood —*vi.* 2. tell fib (-bb-) —'**fibber** *n.*

fiber ('fibər) *n.* 1. elongated, thick-walled cell which strengthens tissue in plants and animals 2. substance that can be spun (*eg* wool, cotton) —'**fibril** *n.* 1. small fiber or part of fiber 2. *Biol.* root hair —'**fibroid** *a.* 1. *Anat.* (of structures or tissues) containing or resembling fibers —*n.* 2. benign tumor derived from fibrous connective tissue (*also* fi'**broma**) —fi'**brosis** *n.* formation of abnormal amount of fibrous tissue in organ *etc.* —fibro'**sitis** *n.* rheumatic condition of the soft tissues —'**fibrous** *a.* made of fiber —'**fiberboard** *n.* building material of compressed plant fibers —'**fiberglass** *n.* material made of fine glass fibers —**fiber optics** use of bundles of long transparent glass fibers in transmitting light

Fibonacci series (fēbə'nächi) the series of numbers in which each term is the sum of the two preceding terms, *ie* 0, 1, 1, 2, 3, 5, 8, 13, 21

fibrin ('fibrin) *n.* insoluble protein in blood, causing coagulation —fi'**brinogen** *n.* globulin produced in the liver, present in blood plasma and converted into fibrin during clotting of blood

fibroma (fi'brōmə) *n. see* fibroid *at* FIBER

fibula ('fibyələ) *n.* slender outer bone of lower leg (*pl.* **-lae** (-lē), **-s**) —'**fibular** *a.*

fickle ('fikəl) *a.* changeable, inconstant —'**fickleness** *n.*

fiction ('fikshən) *n.* 1. prose, literary works of the imagination 2. invented statement or story —'**fictional** *a.* —'**fictionalize** *vt.* make into fiction —fic'**titious** *a.* 1. not genuine, false 2. imaginary 3. assumed

fiddle ('fidəl) *n.* 1. *inf.* violin 2. triviality 3. *inf.* illegal, fraudulent arrangement —*vi.* 4. play fiddle 5. make idle movements, fidget, trifle —*v.* 6. *sl.* cheat, contrive —'**fiddling** *a.* trivial —'**fiddly** *a.* small, awkward to handle —**fiddler crab** burrowing crab of Amer. coastal regions, male of which has one pincerlike claw enlarged —'**fiddlesticks** *interj.* nonsense

Fidei Defensor ('fidiĭ di'fensör) *Lat.* Defender of the Faith

fidelity (fi'deliti) *n.* 1. faithfulness 2. quality of sound reproduction

fidget ('fijit) *vi.* 1. move restlessly 2. be uneasy —*n.* 3. (*oft. pl.*) nervous restlessness, restless mood 4. one who fidgets —'**fidgety** *a.*

fiduciary (fi'dyōōshieri, -'dōō-) *a.* 1. held, given in trust 2. relating to trustee —*n.* 3. trustee

fie (fi) *interj. obs., jocular* exclamation of distaste or mock dismay

field (fēld) *n.* 1. area of (farming) land 2. enclosed piece of land 3. tract of land rich in specified product (*eg goldfield*) 4. players in a game or sport collectively 5. all competitors but the favorite 6. battlefield 7. area over which electric, gravitational, magnetic force can be exerted 8. surface of shield, coin *etc.* 9. sphere of knowledge 10. range, area of operation 11. *Sport* stop or return (ball) 12. send (player, team) on to sportsfield —*vi.* 13. *Sport* (of player or team) act or take turn as fielder(s) —'**fielder** *n.* —**field day** 1. day of maneuvers, outdoor activities 2. important occasion —**field event** any track-and-field activity except a race —'**fieldfare** *n.* Eurasian thrush with pale gray head and rump —**field glasses** binoculars —**field hockey** game played on turf by two teams of 11 players using curved sticks to propel a small hard ball into opponents' goal —**field house** building

enclosing area suitable for athletic events and usu. with facilities for dressing —**fielding average** measure of fielding ability of a baseball player, *eg* a player with 10 errors in 600 chances has a fielding average of .984 —**field judge** football official whose duties include timing intermission periods and time-outs —**field officer** officer holding rank of major, lieutenant colonel or colonel —**field trip** visit made by teacher and students to a place away from school for educational purposes —**field work** 1. work done in field by students to gain first-hand experience of subject 2. gathering of anthropological and sociological data —**field of view** area visible through optical instrument

fiend (fēnd) *n.* 1. demon, devil 2. wicked person 3. person very fond of or addicted to something, *eg fresh-air fiend, drug fiend* —'**fiendish** *a.* 1. wicked 2. *inf.* difficult; unpleasant

fierce (fēərs) *a.* 1. savage, wild, violent 2. rough 3. severe 4. intense —'**fiercely** *adv.* —'**fierceness** *n.*

fiery ('fiəri) *a.* 1. consisting of fire 2. blazing, glowing, flashing 3. irritable 4. spirited ('**fierier** *comp.,* '**fieriest** *sup.*) —'**fierily** *adv.*

fiesta (fi'estə) *n.* (*esp.* in Spain and Latin America) 1. (religious) celebration 2. carnival

FIFA ('fēfə) Fédération Internationale de Football Association

fife (fif) *n.* small transverse flute with finger holes used in marching bands —'**fifer** *n.*

fifteen (fif'tēn) *see* FIVE

fig (fig) *n.* 1. soft, pear-shaped fruit 2. tree bearing it 3. something of negligible value

fig. 1. figurative(ly) 2. figure

fight (fit) *v.* 1. contend (with) in battle or in single combat 2. maintain (cause *etc.*) against opponent —*vt.* 3. resolve by combat (**fought** *pt./pp.*) —*n.* 4. battle, struggle or physical combat 5. quarrel, dispute, contest 6. resistance 7. boxing match —'**fighter** *n.* 1. one who fights 2. *Mil.* aircraft designed for destroying other aircraft —**fighting chance** chance of success dependent on struggle

figment ('figmənt) *n.* invention, purely imaginary thing

figure ('figyər) *n.* 1. numerical symbol 2. amount, number 3. form, shape 4. bodily shape 5. appearance, *esp.* conspicuous appearance 6. character, personage 7. space enclosed by lines or surfaces 8. diagram, illustration 9. likeness, image 10. pattern, movement in dancing, skating, *etc.* 11. abnormal form of expression for effect in speech, *eg* metaphor —*vt.* 12. calculate, estimate 13. *inf.* consider 14. represent by picture or diagram 15. ornament —*vi.* 16. (*oft. with* in) show, appear, be conspicuous, be included —figu'**ration** *n.* 1. *Mus.* florid ornamentation of musical passage 2. instance of representing figuratively, as by allegory 3. figurative representation 4. decorating with design —'**figurative** *a.* 1. metaphorical 2. full of figures of speech —'**figuratively** *adv.* —**figurine** (figyə'rēn, figə-) *n.* statuette —'**figurehead** *n.* 1. nominal leader 2. ornamental figure under bowsprit of ship —**figure of speech** expression of language by which literal meaning of word is not employed

figwort ('figwərt) *n.* plant related to foxglove, having small greenish flowers

Fiji ('fējē) *n.* country in S Pacific Ocean comprising about 332 islands and islets lying between 15° and 22° S latitude and 174° and 177° longitude

filament ('filəmənt) *n.* 1. fine wire in electric light bulb and radio valve which is heated by electric current 2. threadlike body

filariasis (filə'riəsis) *n.* infection by any of a species of threadlike roundworms

filbert ('filbərt) *n.* 1. N temperate shrub with edible nuts 2. this nut (*also* '**hazelnut,** '**cobnut**)

filch (filch) *vt.* steal, pilfer

file[1] (fil) *n.* 1. box, folder, clip *etc.* holding papers for reference 2. papers so kept 3. information about specific person, subject 4. orderly line, as of soldiers, one behind the other —*vt.* 5. arrange (papers *etc.*) and put them away for reference 6. send (copy) to a newspaper 7. bring (suit) in lawcourt —*vi.* 8. register as candidate in primary election —'**filing** *n.* —**single** (*or* **Indian**) **file** single line of people one behind the other

file[2] (fil) *n.* 1. roughened tool for smoothing or shaping —*vt.* 2. apply file to, smooth, polish —'**filing** *n.* 1. action of using file 2. scrap of metal removed by file

filial ('filiəl, 'filyəl) *a.* of, befitting, son or daughter —'**filially** *adv.*

filibuster ('filibustər) *n.* 1. process of obstructing legislation by using delaying tactics —*v.* 2. obstruct (legislation) with delaying tactics —*vi.* 3. engage in unlawful military action

filigree ('filigrē) *or* **filagree** ('filəgrē) *n.* fine tracery or openwork of metal, usu. gold or silver wire

Filipino (fili'pēnō) *n.* 1. native of the Philippines (*pl.* **-s**) —*a.* 2. of the Philippines

fill (fil) *vt.* 1. make full 2. occupy completely 3. hold, discharge duties of 4. stop up 5. satisfy, fulfill —*vi.* 6. become full —*n.* 7. full supply 8. as much as desired 9. soil *etc.* to bring area of ground up to required level —'**filler** *n.* 1. person or thing that fills 2. object or substance used to add weight *etc.* or to fill in gap 3. paste used for filling in cracks *etc.* before painting 4. inner portion of cigar 5. *Journalism* space-filling item in newspaper *etc.* —'**filling** *n.* 1. act or instance of filling 2. something used to fill cavity or container 3. food mixture to fill cake, pastry or sandwich 4. yarn for shuttle or interlacing warp —**filling station** garage selling gasoline *etc.* —**fill in** 1. complete contents of (outlined drawing or writing) 2. complete (form of application) 3. *inf.* inform fully 4. (*with* for) *inf.* substitute —**fill the bill** *inf.* supply all that is wanted

fillet ('filit) *n.* 1. boneless slice of meat, fish 2. narrow strip —*vt.* 3. cut into fillets, bone —'**filleted** *a.*

fillip ('filip) *n.* 1. stimulus 2. sudden release of finger bent against thumb 3. snap so produced —*vt.* 4. stimulate 5. give fillip to

Fillmore ('filmör) *n.* **Millard.** the 13th President of the U.S. (1850-53)

filly ('fili) *n.* female horse under four years old

film (film) *n.* 1. thin coating or covering layer 2. (single roll of) light-sensitive strip or sheet used for taking photographs or making a motion picture 3. a motion picture —*a.* 4. connected with the motion-picture industry —*vt.* 5. make motion picture of (a subject) 6. photograph with motion-picture camera —*v.* 7. cover or become covered with film —'**filmy** *a.* 1. membranous 2. gauzy —**film star** movie star —**film strip** strip of film composed of images projected separately as slides

filter ('filtər) *n.* 1. cloth or other material, or a device, permitting fluid to pass but retaining solid particles 2. anything performing similar function —*v.* **3.** (*oft. with* out) remove or separate (suspended particles *etc.*) from (liquid, gas *etc.*) by action of filter —*vi.* **4.** pass slowly (as if) through filter —'**filtrate** *n.* filtered gas or liquid —**filter paper** porous paper for filtering liquids —**filter tip 1.** attachment to mouth end of cigarette for trapping impurities **2.** cigarette having such attachment —**filter-tipped** *a.*

filth (filth) *n.* **1.** disgusting dirt **2.** pollution **3.** obscenity —'**filthily** *adv.* —'**filthiness** *n.* —'**filthy** *a.* **1.** unclean **2.** foul

fin (fin) *n.* **1.** propelling or steering organ of fish **2.** anything like this, *eg* stabilizing plane of airplane

fin. 1. finance **2.** financial

finagle (fi'nāgəl) *inf. vt.* **1.** get or achieve by craftiness —*v.* **2.** use trickery on (person) —**fi'nagler** *n.*

final ('fīnəl) *a.* **1.** at the end **2.** conclusive —*n.* **3.** game, heat, examination *etc.* coming at end of series —**finale** (fi'näli, -'näli) *n.* **1.** closing part of musical composition, opera *etc.* **2.** termination —'**finalist** *n.* contestant who has reached last stage of competition —**fi'nality** *n.* —'**finalize** *v.* —'**finally** *adv.*

finance (fi'nans, 'fīnans) *n.* **1.** management of money **2.** (*also pl.*) money resources —*vt.* **3.** find capital for —**fi'nancial** *a.* of finance —**fi'nancially** *adv.* —**fi'nancier** *n.*

finch (finch) *n.* one of family of small singing birds

find (fīnd) *vt.* **1.** come across, light upon **2.** obtain **3.** realize **4.** experience, discover **5.** discover by searching **6.** supply (as funds) **7.** *Law* give a verdict (upon) (**found** *pt./pp.*) —*n.* **8.** finding **9.** (valuable) thing found —'**finder** *n.* —'**finding** *n.* judicial verdict —**find out 1.** gain knowledge of (something); learn **2.** detect crime, deception *etc.* of (someone)

fine¹ (fīn) *a.* **1.** choice, of high quality, excellent **2.** delicate **3.** subtle **4.** pure **5.** in small particles **6.** slender **7.** handsome **8.** showy **9.** *inf.* healthy, at ease, comfortable **10.** free from rain —*vt.* **11.** make clear or pure **12.** refine **13.** thin —'**finely** *adv.* —'**fineness** *n.* —'**finery** *n.* showy dress —**finesse** (fi'nes) *n.* elegant, skillful management —**fine art** art produced for its aesthetic value —**fine-drawn** *a.* **1.** (of distinctions *etc.*) precise; subtle **2.** (of wire *etc.*) drawn out until very fine —'**fine'spun** *a.* **1.** spun out to fine thread **2.** excessively subtle or refined —**fine-tooth comb** comb with fine, closely set teeth —**go over** *or* **through with a fine-tooth comb** examine very thoroughly

fine² (fīn) *n.* **1.** sum fixed as penalty —*vt.* **2.** punish by fine —**in fine 1.** in conclusion **2.** in brief

fines herbes (*Fr.* fēn 'zerb) mixture of finely chopped herbs, used to flavor omelets *etc.*

finger ('finggər) *n.* **1.** one of the jointed branches of the hand **2.** any of various things like this —*vt.* **3.** touch or handle with fingers —'**fingering** *n.* **1.** *Mus.* technique of using one's fingers **2.** *Mus.* numerals in musical part indicating this **3.** fine wool yarn for manufacture of stockings *etc.* —'**fingerboard** *n.* part of musical instrument on which fingers are placed —**finger bowl** small bowl filled with water for rinsing fingers at table after meal —**finger plate** ornamental plate above door handle to prevent finger marks —'**fingerprint** *n.* impression of tip of finger, *esp.* as used for identifying criminals

finial ('fīniəl) *n. Archit.* ornament at apex of pinnacles, gables, spires *etc.*

finicky ('finiki) *or* **finicking** *a.* **1.** fastidious, fussy **2.** too fine

finis ('finis) *Lat.* end, *esp.* of book

finish ('finish) *v.* **1.** bring, come to an end, conclude —*vt.* **2.** complete **3.** perfect **4.** kill —*n.* **5.** end **6.** way in which thing is finished, as an *oak finish* of furniture **7.** final appearance —'**finisher** *n.* —**finishing school** private school for girls that teaches social graces

finite ('fīnīt) *a.* bounded, limited —**finite set** set containing a limited number of elements

Finland ('finlənd) *n.* country in N Europe bounded east by the U.S.S.R., south by the Baltic Sea, west by the Gulf of Bothnia and Sweden and north by Norway —**Finn** *n.* native of Finland —'**Finnish** *a.* **1.** of Finland —*n.* **2.** official language of Finland

finnan haddock ('finən) *or* **haddie** ('hadi) smoked haddock

fiord (fē'ôrd) *n. see* FJORD

fipple ('fipəl) *n.* wooden plug forming flue in end of pipe —**fipple flute** generic name for musical instruments of the flageolet or recorder type

fir (fər) *n.* **1.** kind of coniferous resinous tree **2.** its wood

fire ('fīər) *n.* **1.** state of burning, combustion, flame, glow **2.** mass of burning fuel **3.** destructive burning, conflagration **4.** device for heating a room *etc.* **5.** ardor, keenness, spirit **6.** shooting of firearms —*vt.* **7.** discharge (firearm) **8.** propel from firearm **9.** *inf.* dismiss from employment **10.** bake **11.** make burn **12.** supply with fuel **13.** inspire **14.** explode —*vi.* **15.** discharge firearm **16.** begin to burn —'**firing** *n.* **1.** process of baking ceramics *etc.* in kiln **2.** act of stoking fire or furnace **3.** discharge of firearm **4.** something used as fuel —**fire alarm** device to give warning of fire —'**firearm** *n.* gun, rifle, pistol *etc.* —'**fireball** *n.* **1.** ball-shaped discharge of lightning **2.** region of hot ionized gas at center of nuclear explosion **3.** *Astron.* large bright meteor **4.** *sl.* energetic person —'**firebomb** *n. see* INCENDIARY (sense 6) —'**firebrand** *n.* **1.** burning piece of wood **2.** energetic (troublesome) person —'**firebreak** *n.* strip of cleared land to arrest progress of bush or grass fire —'**firebrick** *n.* refractory brick made of fire clay, for lining furnaces *etc.* —'**firebug** *n. inf.* person who intentionally sets fire to buildings *etc.* —**fire clay** heat-resistant clay used in making of firebricks *etc.* —'**firecracker** *n.* small cardboard container filled with explosive powder —'**firecrest** *n.* small European warbler —'**firedamp** *n.* explosive hydrocarbon gas forming in mines —**fire department** organized, usu. municipal, body responsible for preventing and putting out fires —'**firedog** *n.* either of pair of metal stands used to support logs in open fire —**fire drill** rehearsal of procedures for escape from fire —**fire-eater** *n.* **1.** performer who simulates swallowing of fire **2.** belligerent person —**fire engine** vehicle with apparatus for extinguishing fires —**fire escape** means, *esp.* outside metal stairs, for escaping from burning buildings —'**firefly** *n.* insect giving off intermittent glow —'**fireguard** *n.* **1.** fire screen **2.** one who watches for and extinguishes fires —**fire hall** fire station —**fire irons** tongs, poker and shovel —'**fireman** *n.* **1.** member of fire department **2.** stoker **3.** assistant to locomotive driver —'**fireplace** *n.* recess in room for fire —'**fireplug** *n.* hydrant placed on sidewalk —**fire ship** burning vessel sent drifting against enemy ships —**fire station** building housing fire apparatus —'**firetrap** *n.* building unsafe in case of fire —'**firework** *n.*

1. (*oft. pl.*) device to give spectacular effects by explosions and colored sparks —*pl.* **2.** outburst of temper, anger —**firing line 1.** *Mil.* positions from which fire is delivered **2.** leading position in an activity —**firing squad** detachment sent to fire volleys at military funeral, or to shoot criminal —**under fire 1.** under attack **2.** under criticism

firkin ('fərkin) *n.* **1.** small cask **2.** UK measure of 9 gallons

firm¹ (fərm) *a.* **1.** solid **2.** fixed, stable **3.** steadfast **4.** resolute **5.** settled —*v.* **6.** make, become firm

firm² (fərm) *n.* **1.** commercial enterprise **2.** partnership

firmament ('fərməmənt) *n.* expanse of sky, heavens

first (fərst) *a.* **1.** earliest in time or order **2.** foremost in rank or position **3.** most excellent **4.** highest, chief —*n.* **5.** beginning **6.** first occurrence of something **7.** highest place in competition —*adv.* **8.** before others in time, order *etc.* —'**firstly** *adv.* —**first aid** help given to injured person before arrival of doctor —**first base 1.** base that must be touched first in order to score a run at baseball **2.** player defending this base **3.** first step in a course of action —**first class** *n.* **1.** class of highest value, quality *etc.* —*a.* **2.** of highest class **3.** excellent **4.** of most comfortable class of accommodation in hotel, train *etc.* —**first-class** *adv.* by first-class means of transportation *etc.* —**first cousin** son or daughter of one's aunt or uncle —**first-day cover** *Philately* envelope postmarked on first day of issue of its stamps —**first finger** finger next to thumb —**first fruits 1.** first results or profits of undertaking **2.** earliest fruits gathered and offered to Deity in gratitude for fruitfulness —**first-hand** *a.* obtained directly from the first source —**first lady** (*oft.* F- L-) wife or official hostess of state governor or U.S. president —**first mate** *or* **officer** officer of merchant vessel immediately below captain —**first name** personal or Christian name —**first night** first public performance of a play or opera —**first offender** person convicted of criminal offense for first time —**first person** grammatical category of pronouns and verbs used by speaker to refer to himself —**first-rate** *a.* of highest class or quality —**first string** the best players of an athletic team —**first water 1.** finest quality of precious stone **2.** best quality

firth (fərth) *or* **frith** *n. esp.* in Scotland, arm of the sea, river estuary

fiscal ('fiskəl) *a.* of finances —**fiscal year** annual period at end of which firm's accounts are made up

fish (fish) *n.* **1.** cold-blooded egg-laying aquatic vertebrate with scaly skin, gills and paired fins **2.** its flesh as food (*pl.* **fish, -es**) —*vi.* **3.** (attempt to) catch fish **4.** search (for something) **5.** (*with* for) try to get information indirectly —'**fisher** *n.* —'**fishery** *n.* **1.** business of fishing **2.** fishing ground —'**fishy** *a.* **1.** of, like, or full of fish **2.** dubious, open to suspicion —**fish-and-chips** *pl.n. esp.* UK fried fish and French fries —**fish cake** fried flattened ball of flaked fish mixed with mashed potatoes —'**fisherman** *n.* one who catches fish for a living or for pleasure —**fish-eye lens** *Photog.* lens of small focal length, that covers almost 180° —**fish-kettle** *n.* oval pot for cooking fish —**fish meal** ground dried fish used as fertilizer *etc.* —'**fishmonger** *n.* seller of fish —'**fishskin** *n.* disease in which skin is coarse, dry and scaly (*also* **ichthy'osis**) —**fish slice 1.** fish carver **2.** flat-bladed utensil for turning or lifting food in frying —**fish story** unbelievable tale —**'fishwife** *n.* coarse, scolding woman —**have other fish to fry** have more important matters to attend to

fishplate ('fishplāt) *n.* piece of metal holding rails together

fission ('fishən, 'fizh-) *n.* splitting of an atomic nucleus into two approximately equal parts accompanied by the release of great amounts of energy —**'fissionable** *a.* capable of undergoing nuclear fission —**fissiparous** (fi'sipərəs) *a.* reproducing by fission

fissure ('fishər) *n.* cleft, split, cleavage —**fissile** ('fisil) *a.* 1. capable of splitting 2. tending to split

fist (fist) *n.* clenched hand —**'fisticuffs** *pl.n.* fighting

fistula ('fischələ) *n.* pipelike ulcer (*pl.* -**s**, -**lae** (-lē))

fit¹ (fit) *vt.* 1. be suited to 2. be properly adjusted to 3. arrange, adjust, apply, insert 4. supply, furnish —*vi.* 5. be correctly adjusted or adapted 6. be of right size (-**tt**-) —*a.* 7. well-suited, worthy 8. qualified 9. proper, becoming 10. ready 11. in good condition or health ('**fitter** *comp.*, '**fittest** *sup.*) —*n.* 12. way anything fits, its style 13. adjustment —**'fitly** *adv.* —**'fitment** *n.* piece of furniture —**'fitness** *n.* —**'fitted** *a.* 1. designed for excellent fit 2. (of carpet) cut to cover floor completely 3. (of furniture) built to fit particular space —**'fitter** *n.* 1. one who, that which, makes fit 2. one who supervises making and fitting of garments 3. mechanic skilled in fitting up metalwork —**'fitting** *a.* 1. appropriate, suitable, proper —*n.* 2. fixture 3. apparatus 4. action of fitting —**fit in** 1. give place or time to 2. belong or conform, *esp.* after adjustment

fit² (fit) *n.* 1. seizure with convulsions, spasms, loss of consciousness *etc.*, of epilepsy, hysteria *etc.* 2. sudden passing attack of illness 3. passing state, mood —**'fitful** *a.* spasmodic, capricious —**'fitfully** *adv.* —**have or throw a fit** *inf.* become very angry

five (fīv) *a./n.* cardinal number after four —**fif'teen** *a./n.* ten plus five —**fif'teenth** *a./n.* —**fifth** (fifth) *a./n.* ordinal number of five —**fifthly** ('fifthli) *adv.* —**fiftieth** ('fiftiith) *a./n.* —**fifty** ('fifti) *a./n.* five tens —**'fiver** *n. inf.* 5-dollar bill —**fifth column** organization spying for enemy within country at war —**fifty-fifty** *a./adv. inf.* in equal parts —**five-o'clock shadow** beard growth visible late in day on man's shaven face —**'fivepins** *pl.n.* bowling game played *esp.* in Canada —**five-star** *a.* of the highest class —**five-star general** a general of the army —**Five-Year Plan** in socialist economies, government plan for economic development over five-year period

fix (fiks) *vt.* 1. fasten, make firm or stable 2. set, establish 3. appoint, assign, determine 4. make fast 5. repair 6. *inf.* influence the outcome of unfairly or by deception 7. *inf.* bribe 8. *inf.* give (someone) his just deserts —*vi.* 9. become firm or solidified 10. determine —*n.* 11. difficult situation 12. position of ship, aircraft ascertained by radar, observation *etc.* 13. *sl.* dose of narcotic drug —**fix'ation** *n.* 1. act of fixing 2. preoccupation, obsession 3. situation of being set in some way of acting or thinking —**'fixative** *a.* 1. capable of, or tending to fix —*n.* 2. fluid sprayed over drawings to prevent smudging *etc.* 3. substance added to liquid to make it less volatile —**fixed** *a.* 1. attached so as to be immovable 2. stable 3. steadily directed 4. established as to relative position 5. always at same time 6. (of ideas *etc.*) firmly maintained 7. (of element) held in chemical combination 8. (of substance)

nonvolatile 9. arranged 10. *inf.* equipped; provided for 11. *inf.* illegally arranged —**fixedly** ('fiksidli) *adv.* intently —**'fixity** *n.* —**'fixture** *n.* 1. thing fixed in position 2. thing attached to house 3. date for sporting event 4. the event —**fixed star** star whose position appears to be stationary over long period of time —**fix (someone) up** attend to (someone's) needs —**fix up** arrange

fizz (fiz) *vi.* 1. hiss, splutter —*n.* 2. hissing noise 3. effervescent liquid, such as soda water, champagne —**'fizzle** *vi.* 1. splutter weakly —*n.* 2. fizzling noise 3. fiasco —**'fizzy** *a.* effervescent —**fizzle out** *inf.* come to nothing, fail

fjord *or* **fiord** (fē'ôrd) *n. esp.* in Norway, long, narrow inlet of sea

FL Florida

fl. 1. floor 2. *floruit* (*Lat.*, (he or she) flourished) 3. fluid

Fla. Florida

flabbergast ('flabərgast) *vt.* overwhelm with astonishment

flabby ('flabi) *a.* 1. hanging loose, limp 2. out of condition, too fat 3. feeble 4. yielding

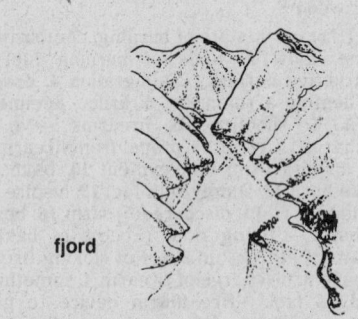

fjord

—**flab** *n. inf.* unsightly fat on the body —**'flabbiness** *n.*

flaccid ('flaksid, 'flasid) *a.* flabby, lacking firmness —**flac'cidity** *n.*

flag¹ (flag) *n.* 1. banner, piece of bunting attached to staff or halyard as standard or signal 2. small paper emblem sold on flag days —*vt.* 3. decorate or mark with flag(s) 4. send or communicate (messages *etc.*) by flag signals (-**gg**-) —**flag day** day on which small flags or emblems are sold in streets for charity —**'flagpole** *or* **'flagstaff** *n.* pole on which flag is hoisted and displayed (*pl.* -**poles** *or* -**staffs**, -**staves** (-stāvz)) —**'flagship** *n.* 1. admiral's ship 2. most important ship of fleet —**flag down** warn or signal (vehicle) to stop —**flag of convenience** national flag flown by ship registered in that country to gain financial or legal advantage —**flag of truce** white flag indicating invitation to enemy to negotiate

flag² (flag) *n.* any plant with sword-shaped leaves, *esp.* the iris —**'flaggy** *a.*

flag³ (flag) *n.* 1. flat slab of stone —*pl.* 2. pavement of flags —*vt.* 3. furnish (floor *etc.*) with flagstones (-**gg**-) —**'flagstone** *n.*

flag⁴ (flag) *vi.* 1. droop, fade 2. lose vigor (-**gg**-)

flagellate¹ ('flajəlit) *n.* any microorganism having whiplike appendages

flagellate² ('flajilāt) *vt.* scourge, flog —**'flagellant** *n.* one who scourges himself, *esp.* in religious penance —**flagel'lation** *n.* —**'flagellator** *n.*

flagellum (flə'jeləm) *n.* 1. *Biol.* whiplike outgrowth from cell that acts as organ of locomotion 2. *Bot.* long thin shoot (*pl.* -**la** (-lə), -**s**)

flageolet (flajə'let) *n.* small musical instrument similar to the recorder with four finger holes in front and two thumb holes in back

flagon ('flagən) *n.* large bottle of wine *etc.*

flagrant ('flāgrənt) *a.* glaring, scandalous, blatant —**'flagrancy** *n.* —**'flagrantly** *adv.*

flail (flāl) *n.* 1. instrument for threshing corn by hand —*v.* 2. beat with, move as, flail

flair (flāər) *n.* 1. natural ability 2. elegance

flak *or* **flack** (flak) *n.* 1. anti-aircraft fire 2. *inf.* adverse criticism

flake (flāk) *n.* 1. small, thin piece, *esp.* particle of snow 2. piece chipped off —*v.* 3. (cause to) peel off in flakes —**'flaky** *a.* —**flake out** *inf.* collapse, sleep from exhaustion

flambé (fläm'bā) *a.* (of food) served in flaming brandy *etc.*

flamboyant (flam'boiənt) *a.* 1. florid, gorgeous, showy 2. exuberant, ostentatious

flame (flām) *n.* 1. burning gas, *esp.* above fire 2. visible burning 3. passion, *esp.* love 4. *inf.* sweetheart —*vi.* 5. give out flames, blaze 6. shine 7. burst out —**'flaming** *a.* 1. burning with flames 2. glowing brightly 3. ardent 4. *inf.* a common intensifier —**flame-thrower** *n.* weapon that ejects stream of burning fluid

flamenco (flə'mengkō) *n.* Sp. dance to guitar (*pl.* -**s**)

flamingo (flə'minggō) *n.* large pink bird with long neck and legs (*pl.* -**s**, -**es**)

flammable ('flaməbəl) *a.* liable to catch fire

flange (flanj) *n.* 1. projecting flat rim, collar or rib —*v.* 2. provide with or take form of flange

flank (flangk) *n.* 1. part of side between hips and ribs 2. side of anything, *eg* body of troops —*vt.* 3. guard or strengthen on flank 4. attack flank of 5. be at, move along either side of

flannel ('flanəl) *n.* 1. soft woolen fabric for clothing, *esp.* trousers —*pl.* 2. trousers *etc.* made of flannel —**flanne'lette** *n.* cotton fabric imitating flannel —**'flannelly** *a.* —**flannel-mouthed** *a.* speaking insincerely

flap (flap) *v.* 1. move (wings, arms *etc.*) as bird flying 2. (cause to) sway —*vt.* 3. strike with flat object —*vi.* 4. *inf.* be agitated, flustered (-**pp**-) —*n.* 5. act of flapping 6. broad piece of anything hanging from hinge or loosely from one side 7. movable part of aircraft wing 8. *inf.* state of excitement or panic —**'flapper** *n.* in 1920s, young woman, *esp.* one flaunting unconventional behavior —**'flapjack** *n.* pancake

flare (flāər) *vi.* 1. blaze with unsteady flame 2. *inf.* (*with* up) suddenly burst into anger 3. spread outward, as bottom of skirt —*n.* 4. instance of flaring 5. signal light —**flare-path** *n.* area lit up to facilitate landing or takeoff of aircraft —**flare-up** *n.* 1. sudden burst of fire 2. *inf.* sudden burst of emotion —**flare up** 1. burst suddenly into fire 2. *inf.* burst into anger

flash (flash) *n.* 1. sudden burst of light or flame 2. sudden short blaze 3. very short time 4. brief news item 5. ribbon; badge 6. display —*vi.* 7. break into sudden flame 8. gleam 9. burst into view 10. move very fast 11. appear suddenly 12. *sl.* expose oneself indecently —*vt.* 13. cause to gleam 14. emit (light *etc.*) suddenly —*a.* 15. showy (*also* '**flashy**) 16. sham —**'flasher** *n.* 1. something which flashes 2. *sl.* someone who indecently exposes himself —**'flashing** *n.* weatherproof material used to cover valleys between slopes of roof *etc.* —**'flashback** *n.* break in continuity of book, play or motion picture, to introduce what has taken place previously —**'flashbulb** *n. Photog.* small light bulb triggered, *usu.* electrically, to produce bright flash of light —**'flashcube** n. boxlike camera attachment, holding four flashbulbs, that turns so that each flashbulb can be used —**'flashlight** n. 1. small battery-powered light 2. Photog. brief bright light emitted by electronic flash (also flash) —**flash point** temperature at which a vapor ignites —**flash in the pan** person etc. that enjoys only short-lived success

flask (flask) n. narrow-necked bottle often fitted with top to be carried in a pocket

flat¹ (flat) a. 1. level 2. spread out 3. at full length 4. smooth 5. downright 6. dull, lifeless 7. Mus. below pitch 8. (of tire) deflated, punctured 9. (of battery) fully discharged, dead (**'flatter** comp., **'flattest** sup.) —adv. 10. completely, utterly; absolutely —n. 11. flat object, surface or part 12. Mus. tone or note produced below pitch 13. punctured tire 14. shallow box for raising seedlings —**'flatly** adv. —**'flatness** n. —**'flatten** v. —**'flatfish** n. type of fish which swims along sea floor on one side of body with both eyes on uppermost side —**'flatfoot** n. 1. condition in which instep arch of foot is flattened 2. sl. policeman (pl. -s, -feet) —**'flatiron** n. iron for pressing clothes —**flat race** race over level ground with no jumps —**flat spin** 1. aircraft spin in which longitudinal axis is more nearly horizontal than vertical 2. inf. state of confusion —**'flatware** n. 1. table utensils such as knives, forks and spoons 2. serving dishes, esp. silver, that are more or less flat —**'flatworm** n. any member of a phylum of invertebrate animals with flattened bodies including tapeworms and liver flukes —**flat out** at, with maximum speed or effort

flat² (flat) n. apartment on one floor of building

flatter ('flatər) vt. 1. fawn on 2. praise insincerely 3. gratify vanity of 4. represent too favorably —**'flatterer** n. —**'flattery** n.

flatulent ('flachələnt) a. 1. suffering from, generating (excess) gases in intestines 2. pretentious —**'flatulence** n. 1. flatulent condition 2. verbosity, emptiness

flaunt (flönt) v. 1. show off 2. wave proudly

flautist ('flötist) n. UK flute player

flavescent (flə'vesənt) a. yellowish; turning yellow

flavor ('flāvər) n. 1. mixed sensation of smell and taste 2. distinctive taste, savor 3. undefinable characteristic, quality of anything —vt. 4. give flavor to 5. season —**'flavoring** n.

flaw¹ (flö) n. 1. crack 2. defect, blemish —vt. 3. make flaw in —**'flawless** a. perfect

flaw² (flö) n. sudden gust of wind; squall

flax (flaks) n. 1. plant grown for its textile fiber and seeds 2. its fibers, spun into linen thread —**'flaxen** a. 1. of flax 2. light yellow, straw-colored

flay (flā) vt. 1. strip skin off 2. criticize severely

flea (flē) n. small, wingless, jumping, blood-sucking insect —**'fleabag** n. unkempt person, horse etc. —**'fleabite** n. 1. insect's bite 2. trifling injury 3. trifle —**flea-bitten** a. 1. bitten by flea 2. mean, worthless 3. scruffy —**flea market** market for cheap goods

fleck (flek) n. 1. small mark, streak or particle —vt. 2. mark with flecks

fled (fled) pt./pp. of FLEE

fledged (flejd) a. 1. (of birds) able to fly 2. experienced, trained —**'fledgling** n. 1. young bird 2. inexperienced person

flee (flē) v. run away (from) (**fled, 'fleeing**)

fleece (flēs) n. 1. whole sheep's wool —vt. 2. rob —**'fleecy** a. —**fleece-lined** a. (of knitted fabric) napped on one side

fleet¹ (flēt) n. 1. number of warships organized as unit 2. number of ships, trucks etc. operating together

fleet² (flēt) a. swift, nimble —**'fleeting** a. passing, transient —**'fleetingly** adv.

Fleet Street (flēt) 1. street in London where many newspaper offices are situated 2. Brit. journalism or journalists collectively

Flemish ('flemish) n. 1. language spoken by Flemings, almost identical to Dutch —a. 2. of Flanders —**'Fleming** n. native of Flanders, medieval principality in the Low Countries, or of Flemish-speaking Belgium —**the Flemish** the Flemish people

flense (flens), **flench** (flench), or **flinch** (flinch) vt. strip (esp. whale) of flesh

flesh (flesh) n. 1. soft part, muscular substance, between skin and bone 2. in plants, pulp 3. fat 4. sensual appetites —**'fleshily** adv. —**'fleshly** a. 1. carnal 2. material —**'fleshy** a. plump 2. pulpy —**'fleshpots** pl.n. (places catering for) self-indulgent living —**flesh wound** wound affecting superficial tissues —**in the flesh** in person; actually present

fleur-de-lis or **fleur-de-lys** (flərdə'lē) n. 1. heraldic lily with three petals 2. iris (pl. **fleurs-de-lis** or **fleurs-de-lys** (flərdə'lēz))

flew (flōō) pt. of FLY¹

flews (flōōz) pl.n. fleshy hanging lip of bloodhound or similar dog

flex (fleks) n. 1. instance or act of flexing —v. 2. bend, be bent —**flexi'bility** n. —**'flexible** a. 1. easily bent 2. manageable 3. adaptable —**'flexibly** adv. —**'flexion** n. 1. bending 2. bent state —**'flextime** n. system permitting variation in starting and finishing times of work, providing an agreed number of hours is worked over a specified period

flibbertigibbet ('flibərtijibit) n. flighty, gossiping person

flick (flik) vt. 1. strike lightly, jerk —n. 2. light blow 3. jerk 4. sl. motion picture —**flick knife** knife with retractable blade that springs out when button is pressed

flicker ('flikər) vi. 1. burn, shine, unsteadily 2. waver, quiver —n. 3. unsteady light or movement

flight (flīt) n. 1. act or manner of flying through air 2. number flying together, as birds 3. journey in aircraft 4. smallest air force unit 5. power of flying 6. swift movement or passage 7. sally 8. distance flown 9. feather etc. fitted to arrow or dart to give it stability in flight 10. stairs between two landings 11. running away —**flight attendant** person attending passengers on an airplane —**flight deck** 1. crew compartment in airliner 2. upper deck of aircraft carrier where aircraft take off —**flight path** the planned course of something, esp. aircraft, in flight —**flight pay** extra allowance paid to military personnel on flight duty —**flight plan** statement of details of intended journey filed by a pilot with an authority —**flight recorder** electronic device in aircraft storing information about its flight

flighty ('flīti) a. 1. frivolous 2. erratic

flimsy ('flimzi) a. 1. frail, weak 2. thin 3. easily destroyed —**'flimsily** adv.

flinch (flinch) vi. shrink, draw back, wince

fling (fling) v. 1. throw, send, move, with force (**flung** pt./pp.) —n. 2. throw 3. hasty attempt 4. spell of indulgence 5. vigorous dance

flint (flint) n. 1. hard steel-gray stone 2. piece of this 3. hard substance used (as flint) for striking fire —**'flintily** adv. —**'flinty** a. 1. like or consisting of flint 2. hard, cruel —**'flintlock** n. 1. gunlock in which charge is ignited by spark produced by flint in hammer 2. firearm having such lock

flintlock

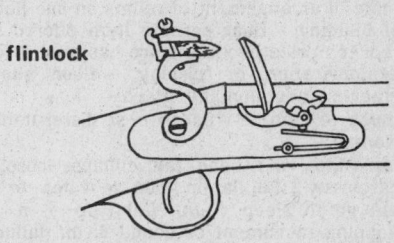

flip (flip) vt. 1. throw or flick lightly 2. turn over —vi. 3. sl. fly into rage or emotional outburst (also **flip one's lid** or **top**) (**-pp-**) —n. 4. instance, act, of flipping 5. drink with beaten egg —a. 6. inf. flippant; pert —**'flippancy** n. —**'flippant** a. treating serious things lightly —**'flippantly** adv. —**'flipper** n. 1. limb, fin for swimming —pl. 2. fin-shaped rubber devices worn on feet to help in swimming —**flip side** less important side of pop record

flirt (flərt) vi. 1. toy, play with another's affections 2. trifle, toy (with) —n. 3. person who flirts —**flir'tation** n. —**flir'tatious** a.

flit (flit) vi. 1. pass lightly and rapidly 2. dart 3. inf. go away hastily, secretly (**-tt-**)

flitch (flich) n. side of bacon

float (flōt) vi. 1. rest, drift on surface of liquid 2. be suspended freely 3. move aimlessly —vt. 4. (of liquid) support, bear alone 5. in commerce, get (company) started 6. Fin. allow (currency) to fluctuate against other currencies in accordance with market forces —n. 7. anything small that floats (esp. to support something else, eg fishing net) 8. motor vehicle carrying tableau etc. in parade 9. sum of money used to provide change —**'floating** a. 1. having little or no attachment 2. (of organ etc.) displaced and abnormally movable 3. uncommitted, un-fixed 4. Fin. (of capital) available for current use; (of debt) short-term and unfunded; (of currency) free to fluctuate against other currencies in accordance with market forces —**flo'tation** or **floa'tation** n. act of floating, esp. floating of company —**floating rib** any rib of lower two pairs of ribs, which are not attached to breastbone —**floating voter** voter of no fixed political allegiance

flocculent ('flokyələnt) a. like tufts of wool

flock¹ (flok) n. 1. number of animals of one kind together 2. body of people 3. religious congregation —vi. 4. gather in a crowd

flock² (flok) n. 1. lock, tuft of wool etc. 2. wool refuse for stuffing cushions etc. —**'flocking** n. method of applying raised patterns to fabric, leather, paper etc. by adhesive —**'flocky** a.

floe (flō) n. sheet of floating ice

flog (flog) vt. beat with whip, stick etc. (**-gg-**)

flood (flud) n. 1. inundation, overflow of water 2. rising of tide 3. outpouring 4. flowing water —vt. 5. inundate 6. cover, fill with water —vi. 7. arrive, move etc. in great numbers —**'floodgate** n. gate, sluice for letting water in or out —**'floodlight** n. broad, intense beam of artificial light —**'floodlit** a. —**flood tide** 1. the rising tide 2. fig. peak of prosperity

floor (flör) n. 1. lower surface of room 2. set of rooms on one level, story 3. flat space 4. (right to speak in) legislative hall or formal meeting —vt. 5. supply with floor 6. knock down 7. confound —**'flooring** n. material for floors —**floor leader** legislator chosen by political party to direct activities on legislative floor —**floor manager** person at political convention who coordinates support for his candidate —**floor plan** drawing to scale of arrangement of rooms on one floor of building —**floor sample** item offered at reduced price because store has used it for demonstration or display —**floor show** entertainment in nightclub *etc.*

floozy *or* **floozie** ('flōōzi) *n. sl.* disreputable woman

flop (flop) *vi.* 1. bend, fall, collapse loosely, carelessly 2. fall flat on floor, on water *etc.* 3. *inf.* go to sleep 4. *inf.* fail (-pp-) —*n.* 5. flopping movement or sound 6. *inf.* failure —'**floppily** *adv.* —'**floppiness** *n.* —'**floppy** *a.* limp, unsteady —**floppy disk** flexible magnetic disk that stores information and can be used to store data in memory of digital computer

flora ('flōrə) *n.* 1. plants of a region 2. list of them (*pl.* -**s**, -**rae** (-rē)) —'**floral** *a.* of flowers —**flo'rescence** *n.* state or time of flowering —'**floret** *n.* small flower forming part of composite flower —**flori'bunda** *n.* type of rose whose flowers grow in large clusters —**flori'cultural** *a.* —'**floriculture** *n.* cultivation of flowers —**flori'culturist** *n.* —**florist** ('flōrist) *n.* dealer in flowers

Florentine ('flörəntēn) *a.* 1. of Florence in Italy 2. of dishes cooked with spinach —*n.* 3. native of Florence —**Florence flask** ('flörəns) glass laboratory vessel

florid ('florid) *a.* 1. with red, flushed complexion 2. ornate

Florida ('flöridə) *n.* South Atlantic state of the U.S.: ratified the Constitution in 1845. Abbrev.: **Fla., FL** (with ZIP code)

florin ('florin) *n.* formerly, Brit. silver two-shilling piece

floss (flos) *n.* 1. mass of fine, silky fibers, *eg* of cotton, silk 2. fluff —'**flossy** *a.* light and downy

flotation *or* **floatation** (flō'tāshən) *n. see* FLOAT

flotilla (flō'tilə) *n.* 1. fleet of small vessels 2. group of destroyers

flotsam ('flotsəm) *n.* 1. floating wreckage 2. discarded waste objects

flounce[1] (flowns) *vi.* 1. go, move abruptly and impatiently —*n.* 2. fling, jerk of body or limb

flounce[2] (flowns) *n.* ornamental gathered strip on woman's garment

flounder[1] ('flowndər) *vi.* 1. plunge and struggle, *esp.* in water or mud 2. proceed in bungling, hesitating manner —*n.* 3. act of floundering

flounder[2] ('flowndər) *n.* flatfish

flour ('flowər) *n.* 1. powder prepared by sifting and grinding wheat *etc.* 2. fine soft powder —*vt.* 3. sprinkle with flour —'**flouriness** *n.* —'**floury** *a.*

flourish ('flurish) *vi.* 1. thrive 2. be in the prime —*vt.* 3. brandish, wave about 4. display —*n.* 5. ornamental curve 6. showy gesture in speech *etc.* 7. waving of hand, weapon *etc.* 8. fanfare (of trumpets)

flout (flowt) *vt.* 1. show contempt for, mock 2. defy

flow (flō) *vi.* 1. glide along as stream 2. circulate, as the blood 3. move easily 4. move in waves 5. hang loose 6. be present in abundance —*n.* 7. act, instance of flowing 8. quantity that flows 9. rise of tide 10. ample supply —**flow chart** diagram showing sequence of operations in industrial *etc.* process

flower ('flowər) *n.* 1. part of plant from which fruit is developed 2. bloom, blossom 3. ornamentation 4. choicest part, pick —*pl.* 5.

chemical sublimate —*vi.* 6. produce flowers 7. bloom 8. come to prime condition —*vt.* 9. ornament with flowers —'**flowered** *a.* 1. having flowers 2. decorated with floral design —'**floweret** *n.* floret —'**flowery** *a.* 1. abounding in flowers 2. full of fine words, ornamented with figures of speech —**flower girl** small girl attendant at wedding

flown (flōn) *pp. of* FLY[1]

fl. oz. fluid ounce(s)

flu (flōō) *n.* influenza

fluctuate ('flukchōōāt) *v.* 1. vary —*vi.* 2. rise and fall, undulate —**fluctu'ation** *n.*

flue (flōō) *n.* passage or pipe for smoke or hot air, chimney

fluent ('flōōənt) *a.* 1. speaking, writing a given language easily and well 2. easy, graceful

fluff (fluf) *n.* 1. soft, feathery stuff 2. down 3. *inf.* mistake —*v.* 4. make or become soft, light 5. *inf.* make mistake (in) —'**fluffy** *a.*

Fluflon ('fluflon) *n.* trade name for a stretch nylon yarn

flügelhorn ('flōōgəlhörn) *n.* musical instrument resembling the cornet, but with a wider bore, played in brass bands

fluid ('flōōid) *a.* 1. flowing easily 2. not solid —*n.* 3. gas or liquid —**flu'idity** *n.* —**fluid dram** ⅛ of fluid ounce —**fluid drive** automobile transmission using oil to transmit power —**fluid mechanics** branch of physics concerned with the properties of liquids and gases —**fluid ounce** unit of capacity ¹⁄₁₆ of pint

fluke[1] (flōōk) *n.* 1. flat triangular point of anchor —*pl.* 2. whale's tail

fluke[2] (flōōk) *n.* 1. stroke of luck, accident —*vt.* 2. gain, make, hit by accident or by luck —'**fluky** *a.* 1. uncertain 2. got by luck

fluke[3] (flōōk) *n.* 1. flatfish 2. parasitic worm

flume (flōōm) *n.* narrow (artificial) channel for water

flummery ('fluməri) *n.* 1. nonsense, idle talk, humbug 2. dish of milk, flour, eggs *etc.*

flummox ('fluməks) *vt.* bewilder, perplex

flung (flung) *pt./pp. of* FLING

flunk (flungk) *inf. v.* 1. (cause to) fail to reach required standard (in) —*vi.* 2. (*with* out) be dismissed from school

flunky *or* **flunkey** ('flungki) *n.* 1. servant, *esp.* liveried manservant 2. servile person

fluorescence (flōōə'resəns) *n.* emission of light or other radiation from substance when bombarded by particles (electrons *etc.*) or other radiation, as in fluorescent lamp —**fluo'resce** *vi.* —**fluo'rescent** *a.* —**fluorescent lamp** lamp in which ultraviolet radiation from electrical gas discharge causes layer of phosphor on tube's inside surface to fluoresce —**fluoroscope** *n.* device consisting of fluorescent screen and x-ray source that enables x-ray image of person *etc.* to be observed directly —**fluo'roscopy** *n.* examination of person *etc.* by means of fluoroscope

fluorite ('flōōərīt, 'flōōr-) *or* **fluorspar** ('flōōərspär, 'flōōr-) *n.* mineral containing fluorine —'**fluoridate** *vt.* —**fluori'dation** *n.* —'**fluoride** *n.* salt containing fluorine, *esp.* as added to domestic water supply as protection against tooth decay —'**fluorinate** *vt.* treat or cause to combine with fluorine —'**fluorine** *n. Chem.* nonmetallic element Symbol F, at. wt. 190, at. no. 9

fluorocarbon (flōōərō'kärbən, flōōrō-) *n.* substance containing both fluorine and carbon atoms used in refrigeration and air-conditioning units

flurry ('fluri) *n.* 1. squall, gust 2. bustle, commotion 3. death struggle of whale 4.

fluttering (as of snowflakes) —*vt.* 5. agitate, bewilder, fluster ('**flurried, 'flurrying**)

flush[1] (flush) *vi.* 1. blush 2. (of skin) redden 3. flow suddenly or violently —*vt.* 4. cleanse (*eg* toilet) by rush of water 5. excite —*n.* 6. reddening, blush 7. rush of water 8. excitement 9. elation 10. glow of color 11. freshness, vigor —*a.* 12. full 13. *inf.* having plenty of money 14. *inf.* well supplied 15. level with surrounding surface

flush[2] (flush) *vt.* cause to leave cover and take flight

flush[3] (flush) *n. Poker* hand of cards all of one suit —**royal flush** an ace-high straight flush —**straight flush** hand of five cards in sequence in the same suit

fluster ('flustər) *v.* 1. make or become nervous, agitated —*n.* 2. state of confusion or agitation

flute (flōōt) *n.* 1. orchestral woodwind instrument in the form of a straight pipe, held horizontally and played through a hole located near one end. Toward the other end are a number of finger holes covered with keys 2. groove, channel —*vi.* 3. play on flute —*vt.* 4. make grooves in —'**fluted** *a.* —'**fluting** *n.* —'**flutist** *or* '**flautist** *n.* flute player

flutter ('flutər) *v.* 1. flap (as wings) rapidly without flight or in short flights 2. be or make excited, agitated —*vi.* 3. quiver —*n.* 4. flapping movement 5. nervous agitation 6. *inf.* modest wager

fluvial ('flōōviəl) *a.* of rivers

flux (fluks) *n.* 1. discharge 2. constant succession of changes 3. substance mixed with metal to clean, aid adhesion in soldering *etc.* 4. measure of strength in magnetic field

fly[1] (flī) *vi.* 1. move through air on wings or in aircraft 2. pass quickly 3. rush 4. flee, run away —*vt.* 5. operate (aircraft) 6. cause to fly 7. set flying —*v.* 8. float loosely (**flew** *pt.,* **flown** *pp.*) —*n.* 9. (zipper or buttons fastening) opening in trousers 10. flap in garment or tent 11. flying —'**flier** *or* '**flyer** *n.* 1. person or thing that flies 2. aviator, pilot 3. *inf.* long, flying leap 4. rectangular step in straight flight of stairs 5. *Athletics inf.* flying start —'**flying** *a.* hurried, brief —'**flyaway** *a.* 1. (of hair *etc.*) loose and fluttering 2. frivolous, flighty; giddy —**fly ball** baseball batted up into the air (*also* fly) —**fly-by-night** *inf. a.* 1. untrustworthy, *esp.* in finance —*n.* 2. untrustworthy person —**fly-fish** *vi.* fish with artificial fly as lure —**fly front** flap of material at garment opening concealing fastening —**flying boat** airplane fitted with floats instead of landing wheels —**flying buttress** *Archit.* arched or slanting structure attached at only one point to a mass of masonry —**flying colors** conspicuous success —**flying doctor** (*esp.* Aust.) doctor visiting patients in outback areas by aircraft —**flying fish** fish with winglike fins used for gliding above the sea —**flying fox** large fruit-eating bat —**flying saucer** unidentified (disk-shaped) flying object, supposedly from outer space —**flying squad** special detachment of police, soldiers *etc.*, ready to act quickly —**flying start** start to race in which competitor is already traveling at speed as he passes starting line —**flying tackle** football tackle in which player hurls himself at ball carrier —'**flyleaf** *n.* blank leaf at beginning or end of book —'**flyover** *n.* low-altitude flight as demonstration by one or more airplanes —'**flypaper** *n.* paper with sticky and poisonous coating to trap flies —**fly sheet** sheet of instructions —**fly spray** liquid sprayed from aerosol to destroy flies

—'**flytrap** n. 1. insectivorous plant 2. device for catching flies —'**flyweight** n. 1. professional boxer weighing not more than 112 lbs. (51 kg); amateur boxer weighing 106-112 lbs. (48-51 kg) 2. in Olympic wrestling, wrestler weighing not more than 115 lbs. (52 kg) —'**flywheel** n. heavy wheel regulating speed of machine —**fly in the face of** act in defiance of —**fly the coop** sl. leave secretly —**go fly a kite!** sl. go away!

flying fish

fly² (flī) n. two-winged insect, esp. common housefly —'**flyblown** a. infested with larvae of blowfly —'**flycatcher** n. small insect-eating songbird

Fm Chem. fermium

FM frequency modulation

fm. 1. fathom (also **fm**) 2. from

FMB Federal Maritime Board

FMCS Federal Mediation and Conciliation Service

f-number or **f number** n. Photog. numerical value of relative aperture

fo. folio

foal (fōl) n. 1. young of horse, ass etc. —v. 2. bear (foal)

foam (fōm) n. 1. collection of small bubbles on liquid 2. froth of saliva or sweat 3. light cellular solid used for insulation, packing etc. —v. 4. (cause to) produce foam —vi. 5. be very angry (esp. in **foam at the mouth**) —'**foamy** a. —**foam rubber** rubber treated to form firm, spongy foam

fob (fob) n. 1. short watch chain 2. small pocket in waistband of trousers or vest

f.o.b. or **F.O.B.** Comm. free on board

fob off 1. ignore, dismiss (someone or something) in offhand (insulting) manner 2. dispose of (-**bb**-)

fo'c'sle ('fōksəl) n. see FORECASTLE

focus ('fōkəs) n. 1. point at which rays meet after being reflected or refracted (also **focal point**) 2. state of optical image when it is clearly defined 3. state of instrument producing such image 4. point of convergence 5. point on which interest, activity is centered (pl. -**es**, **foci** ('fōsī)) —vt. 6. bring to focus, adjust 7. concentrate —vi. 8. come to focus 9. converge —'**focal** a. of, at focus —**focal length** or **distance** distance from focal point of lens to reflecting surface

fodder ('fodər) n. bulk food for livestock

foe (fō) n. enemy

foetid ('fetid) a. see FETID

foetus ('fetəs) n. see FETUS

fog (fog) n. 1. thick mist 2. dense watery vapor in lower atmosphere 3. cloud of anything reducing visibility —vt. 4. cover in fog 5. puzzle (-**gg**-) —'**foggy** a. —'**fogbound** a. prevented from operation by fog —'**fog-horn** n. instrument to warn ships in fog

Foggy Bottom the U.S. Department of State

fogy or **fogey** ('fōgi) n. old-fashioned person

foible ('foibəl) n. minor weakness; idiosyncrasy

foil¹ (foil) vt. baffle, defeat, frustrate —'**foilable** a.

foil² (foil) n. 1. metal in thin sheet 2. anything which sets off another thing to advantage 3. Archit. small arc between cusps

foil³ (foil) n. light, slender, flexible sword tipped by button

foist (foist) vt. (usu. with off or on) sell, pass off (inferior or unwanted thing) as valuable

fold¹ (fōld) vt. 1. double up, bend part of 2. interlace (arms) 3. wrap up 4. clasp (in arms) 5. Cooking mix gently —vi. 6. become folded 7. admit of being folded 8. inf. fail —n. 9. folding 10. coil 11. winding 12. line made by folding 13. crease 14. foldlike geological formation —'**folder** n. binder, file for loose papers —'**foldaway** a. (of bed etc.) able to be folded away when not in use —**folding door** door in form of hinged leaves that can be folded one against another

fold² (fōld) n. 1. enclosure for sheep 2. body of believers, church

-**fold** (comb. form) having so many parts; being so many times as much or as many, as in hundredfold

folderol or **falderal** ('foldərol) n. 1. showy but worthless trifle 2. nonsense

foliage ('fōliij) n. leaves collectively, leafage —**foli'aceous** a. of or like leaf —'**foliate** a. leaflike, having leaves —**foli'ation** n. 1. Bot. process of producing leaves; state of being in leaf; arrangement of leaves in leaf bud 2. Archit. ornamentation consisting of cusps and foils 3. consecutive numbering of leaves of book 4. Geol. arrangement of constituents of rock in leaflike layers

folio ('fōliō) n. 1. sheet of paper 19 × 25 inches folded in half to make two leaves of book 2. book more than 12 inches in height 3. page in an account book 4. page number (pl. -**s**)

folk (fōk) n. 1. race of people —pl. 2. people in general 3. family, relatives —'**folksy** a. 1. of or like ordinary people 2. friendly; affable 3. affectedly simple —**folk art** art of past and present peasant societies characterized by naive subject matter and lively style —**folk dance** —**folk etymology** gradual change in form of word through influence of more familiar word with which it becomes associated —'**folklore** n. tradition, customs, beliefs popularly held —**folk music** 1. music passed on from generation to generation 2. any music composed in this idiom —**folk song** 1. song handed down among common people 2. modern song in folk idiom

Folle blanche (fol blänsh) dry white table wine

follicle ('folikəl) n. 1. small sac 2. seed vessel —**fol'licular** a.

follow ('fōlō) v. 1. go or come after —vt. 2. accompany, attend on 3. keep to (path etc.) 4. take as guide, conform to 5. engage in 6. have a keen interest in 7. be consequent on 8. grasp meaning of —vi. 9. come next 10. result —'**follower** n. 1. disciple 2. supporter —'**following** a. 1. about to be mentioned —n. 2. body of supporters —**follow-through** n. in ball games, continuation of stroke after impact with ball —**follow-up** n. something done to reinforce initial action

folly ('foli) n. 1. foolishness 2. foolish action, idea etc. 3. useless, extravagant structure

foment (fō'ment) vt. 1. foster, stir up 2. bathe with hot lotions —**fomen'tation** n.

fond (fond) a. 1. tender, loving 2. obs. credulous 3. obs. foolish —'**fondly** adv. —'**fondness** n. —**fond of** having liking for

fondant ('fondənt) n. 1. soft sugar mixture for candies 2. candy made of this

fondle ('fondəl) vt. caress

fondue or **fondu** (fon'dyōō, -'dōō; 'fondyōō, -dōō) n. 1. preparation of Swiss cheese flavored with wine used as hot dip for bread cubes 2. cubes of meat or fruit cooked in a hot liquid —**fondue fork** long fork with identifying color used for dipping fondue —**fondue pan** receptacle usu. heated by alcohol lamp for preparing fondue

font (font) n. 1. bowl for baptismal water, usu. on pedestal 2. assortment of printing type of one size

fontanel or **fontanelle** (fontə'nel) n. soft, membranous gap between bones of baby's skull

food (fōōd) n. 1. any substance except water incorporated by a living organism for its maintenance 2. what one eats 3. mental or spiritual nourishment —**food chain** series of organisms each feeding on a lower member —**food poisoning** acute illness caused by food that is naturally poisonous or contaminated by bacteria —**food processor** kitchen appliance for preparing foods by grinding, shredding, liquidizing etc. —**food stamps** stamps distributed by federal government for purchasing food —'**foodstuff** n. food —**food value** nutritional power of food

fool (fōōl) n. 1. silly, empty-headed person 2. dupe 3. simpleton 4. Hist. jester, clown 5. dessert of puréed fruit mixed with cream etc. —vt. 6. delude, dupe —vi. 7. act as fool —'**foolery** n. 1. habitual folly 2. act of playing the fool 3. absurdity —'**foolish** a. 1. ill-considered, silly 2. stupid —'**foolishly** adv. —'**foolhardiness** n. —'**foolhardy** a. foolishly adventurous —'**foolproof** a. proof against failure —**fool's cap** 1. jester's or dunce's cap 2. this as watermark —'**foolscap** n. size of paper about 13 inches by eight inches which formerly had this mark —**fool's errand** fruitless undertaking —**fool's gold** any of various yellow minerals mistaken for gold —**fool's paradise** illusory happiness

foot (fōōt) n. 1. lowest part of leg, from ankle down 2. lowest part of anything, base, stand 3. end of bed etc. 4. infantry 5. measure of twelve inches 6. division of verse (pl. **feet**) —v. 7. dance (also **foot it**) —vt. 8. walk over (esp. in **foot it**) 9. pay cost of (esp. in **foot the bill**) —'**footage** n. 1. length in feet 2. length, extent, of film used —'**footing** n. 1. basis, foundation 2. firm standing, relations, conditions —pl. 3. (concrete) foundations for walls of buildings —**foot-and-mouth disease** infectious viral disease in sheep, cattle etc. —'**football** n. 1. outdoor game played by two teams of usu. 11 players each, each team attempting to carry or kick a large inflated ball over the other team's goal line (see **Australian Rules** at AUSTRALIA, RUGBY, SOCCER) 2. the ball —'**footballer** n. —'**footboard** n. 1. treadle or foot-operated lever on machine 2. vertical board at foot of bed —**foot brake** brake operated by pressure on foot pedal —'**footbridge** n. narrow bridge for pedestrians —'**footfall** n. sound of footstep —**foot fault** Tennis fault of overstepping baseline while serving —'**foothill** n. (oft. pl.) low hill at foot of mountain —'**foothold** n. 1. place affording secure grip for the foot 2. secure position from which progress may be made —'**footlights** pl.n. lights across front of stage —'**footloose** a. free from any ties —'**footman** n. liveried servant —'**footnote** n. note of reference or explanation printed at foot of page —'**footpad** n. obs. robber, highwayman —'**footpath** n. narrow path for pedestrians —**foot-pound** n. amount of energy required to raise weight of one pound to height of one foot —'**footprint** n. mark left by foot —'**footrest** n. something that provides support for feet —'**footsore** a. having sore feet, esp. from walking —'**footwear** n. anything worn to cover feet —'**footwork** n. skillful use of feet, as in sports etc.

fop (fop) *n.* man excessively concerned with fashion —**'foppery** *n.* —**'foppish** *a.* —**'foppishly** *adv.*

for (för; *unstressed* fər) *prep.* 1. intended to reach 2. directed or belonging to 3. because of 4. instead of 5. toward 6. on account of 7. in favor of 8. respecting 9. during 10. in search of 11. in payment of 12. in the character of 13. in spite of —*conj.* 14. because —**for it** *inf.* liable for punishment or blame

for- (*comb. form*) from, away, against, as in *forswear, forbid.* Such words are not given here where the meaning may easily be inferred from the simple word

forage ('forij) *n.* 1. food for cattle and horses —*vi.* 2. collect forage 3. make roving search

foramen (fə'rāmən) *n.* natural hole, *esp.* in bone (*pl.* -**ramina** (-'ramınə), **-s**)

forasmuch as ('förəzmuch) *conj.* seeing that

foray ('forā) *n.* 1. raid, inroad —*vi.* 2. make one —**'forayer** *n.*

forbear[1] ('förbāər) *n. see* FOREBEAR

forbear[2] (för'bāər) *v.* 1. (*esp. with* from) cease; refrain (from) —*vi.* 2. be patient (**for'bore** *pt.,* **for'borne** *pp.*) —**for'bearance** *n.* self-control; patience —**for'bearing** *a.*

forbid (fər'bid) *vt.* prohibit, refuse to allow (**forbade** (fər'bād), **for'bidden** *pp.,* **for'bidding** *pr.p.*) —**for'bidding** *a.* 1. uninviting 2. threatening

force (förs) *n.* 1. strength, power 2. compulsion 3. that which is exerted on a motionless body of matter to put it in motion or to change the velocity of a body if it is already in motion 4. mental or moral strength 5. body of troops, police *etc.* 6. group of people organized for particular task or duty 7. effectiveness, operative state 8. violence —*vt.* 9. constrain, compel 10. produce by effort, strength 11. break open 12. urge, strain 13. drive 14. hasten maturity of —**forced** *a.* 1. accomplished by great effort 2. compulsory 3. unnatural 4. strained —**'forceful** *a.* 1. powerful 2. persuasive —**'forcible** *a.* 1. done by force 2. efficacious, compelling, impressive 3. strong —**'forcibly** *adv.* —**force-feed** *vt.* force (person or animal) to eat or swallow (food)

forcemeat ('försmēt) *n.* mixture of chopped ingredients used for stuffing (*also* **farce**)

forceps ('försips) *pl.n.* surgical pincers

ford (förd) *n.* 1. shallow place where river may be crossed —*vt.* 2. cross (river *etc.*) over shallow area —**'fordable** *a.*

Ford (förd) *n.* **Gerald Rudolph.** the 38th President of the U.S. (1974-77)

fore[1] (för) *a.* 1. in front (**former, 'further** *comp.,* **'foremost, first, 'furthest** *sup.*) —*n.* 2. front part

fore[2] (för) *interj.* golfer's warning

fore- (*comb. form*) previous, before, front

fore-and-aft *a.* placed in line from bow to rear of ship

forearm ('förärm) *n.* 1. arm between wrist and elbow —*vt.* (för'ärm) 2. arm by stockpiling weapons

forebear *or* **forbear** ('förbāər) *n.* ancestor

forebode (för'bōd) *vt.* indicate in advance —**fore'boding** *n.* anticipation of evil

forecast ('förkast) *vt.* 1. estimate beforehand (*esp.* weather); prophesy —*n.* 2. prediction

forecastle *or* **fo'c's'le** ('fōksəl) *n.* 1. forward raised part of ship 2. sailors' quarters

foreclose (för'klōz) *vt.* 1. take away power of redeeming (mortgage) 2. prevent 3. shut out, bar —**fore'closure** *n.*

forecourt ('förkört) *n.* courtyard, open space, in front of building

forefather ('förfädhər) *n.* ancestor

forefinger ('förfinggər) *n.* finger next to thumb

forefoot ('förfŏŏt) *n.* either of front feet of quadruped

forefront ('förfrunt) *n.* 1. extreme front 2. position of most prominence or action

foregather (för'gadhər) *vi. see* FORGATHER

forego[1] (för'gō) *vt.* precede in time, place (-'**went** *pt.,* -'**gone** *pp.,* -'**going** *pr.p.*) —**fore'going** *a.* going before, preceding —**fore'gone** *a.* 1. determined beforehand 2. preceding —**foregone conclusion** result that might have been foreseen

forego[2] (för'gō) *vt. see* FORGO

foreground ('förgrownd) *n.* part of view, *esp.* in picture, nearest observer

forehand ('förhand) *a.* (of stroke in racket games) made with inner side of wrist leading

forehead ('förid) *n.* part of face above eyebrows and between temples

foreign ('forin) *a.* 1. not of, or in, one's own country 2. relating to, or connected with other countries 3. irrelevant 4. coming from outside 5. unfamiliar, strange —**'foreigner** *n.* —**foreign aid** economic assistance to another country —**foreign correspondent** person reporting news from another country —**foreign exchange** 1. process of settling debts between countries 2. the currency of other countries —**Foreign Legion** body of foreign volunteers in an army, *esp.* the French army —**foreign service** field personnel of U.S. Department of State

foreknow (för'nō) *vt.* know in advance —**foreknowledge** (för'nolij) *n.*

foreland ('förlənd) *n.* 1. headland, promontory 2. land lying in front of something, such as water

foreleg ('förleg) *n.* either of front legs of horse or other quadruped

forelimb ('förlim) *n.* either of front limbs of vertebrate

forelock ('förlok) *n.* lock of hair above forehead

foreman ('förmən) *n.* 1. one in charge of work 2. leader of jury

foremast ('förmast; *Naut.* 'förməst) *n.* mast nearest bow

foremost ('förmōst) *a./adv.* first in time, place, importance *etc.*

forenoon ('förnōōn) *n.* morning

forensic (fə'rensik, -zik) *a.* of courts of law —**forensic medicine** application of medical knowledge in legal matters

foreordain (förör'dān) *vt.* determine (events *etc.*) in future —**foreordination** (förördi'nāshən) *n.*

forepaw ('förpö) *n.* either of front feet of most land mammals that do not have hooves

foreplay ('förplā) *n.* sexual stimulation before intercourse

forerunner ('förrunər) *n.* one who goes before, precursor

foresail ('försāl; *Naut.* 'försəl) *n. Naut.* 1. aftermost headsail of fore-and-aft rigged vessel 2. lowest sail set on foremast of square-rigged vessel

foresee (för'sē) *vt.* see beforehand (-'**saw** *pt.,* -'**seen** *pp.*)

foreshadow (för'shadō) *vt.* show, suggest beforehand

foreshore ('förshör) *n.* part of shore between high and low tide marks

foreshortening (för'shörtəning) *n.* the application of the rules of perspective to an individual form to create the illusion of depth and dimensionality

foresight ('försīt) *n.* 1. foreseeing 2. care for future

foreskin ('förskin) *n.* skin that covers tip of penis

forest ('forist) *n.* 1. area with heavy growth of trees and plants 2. these trees 3. *fig.* something resembling forest —*vt.* 4. plant, create forest in (an area) —**fores'tation** *n.* planting of trees over wide area —**'forester** *n.* one skilled in forestry —**'forestry** *n.* study, management of forest planting and maintenance

forestall (för'stöl) *vt.* 1. anticipate 2. prevent, guard against in advance

foretaste ('förtāst) *n.* 1. anticipation 2. taste beforehand

foretell (för'tel) *vt.* prophesy (**fore'told** *pt./pp.*)

forethought ('förthöt) *n.* thoughtful consideration of future events

foretoken ('förtōkən) *n.* 1. sign of future event —*vt.* (för'tōkən) 2. foreshadow

foretop ('förtop; *Naut.* 'förtəp) *n.* platform at top of foremast

for ever *or* **forever** (fə'revər, fö-) *adv.* 1. always 2. eternally —*n.* 3. a long time

forewarn (för'wörn) *vt.* warn, caution in advance

forewent (för'went) *pt. of* FOREGO[1], FOREGO[2]

foreword ('förwərd) *n.* preface

forfeit ('förfit) *n.* 1. thing lost by crime or fault 2. penalty, fine —*a.* 3. lost by crime or fault —*vt.* 4. lose by penalty —**'forfeiture** *n.*

forgather *or* **foregather** (för'gadhər) *vi.* 1. meet together, assemble 2. associate

forgave (fər'gāv) *pt. of* FORGIVE

forge[1] (förj) *n.* 1. place where metal is worked, smithy 2. furnace, workshop for melting or refining metal —*vt.* 3. shape (metal) by heating in fire and hammering 4. make, shape 5. invent 6. make a fraudulent imitation of, counterfeit —**'forger** *n.* —**'forgery** *n.* 1. forged document, bank note *etc.* 2. the making of it

forge[2] (förj) *vi.* advance steadily

forget (fər'get) *vt.* 1. lose memory of 2. neglect, overlook (**for'got** *pt.,* **for'gotten** *or* **for'got** *pp.,* **for'getting** *pr.p.*) —**for'getful** *a.* liable to forget —**for'getfully** *adv.* —**forget-me-not** *n.* plant with small blue flower

forgive (fər'giv) *v.* 1. cease to blame or hold resentment (against) —*vt.* 2. pardon —**for'giveness** *n.* —**for'giving** *a.* willing to forgive

forgo *or* **forego** (för'gō) *vt.* go without, give up (-'**went** *pt.,* -'**gone** *pp.,* -'**going** *pr.p.*)

forgot (fər'got) *pt./pp. of* FORGET —**for'gotten** *pp. of* FORGET

fork (förk) *n.* 1. pronged instrument for eating food 2. pronged tool for digging or lifting 3. division into branches 4. point of this division 5. one of the branches —*vi.* 6. branch —*vt.* 7. dig, lift, throw with fork 8. make fork-shaped —**forked** *a.* 1. having fork or forklike parts 2. zigzag —**'forklift** *n.* vehicle having two power-operated horizontal prongs that can be raised and lowered —**fork out, over** *or* **up** *inf.* pay out (money)

forlorn (fər'lörn) *a.* 1. forsaken 2. desperate —**forlorn hope** anything undertaken with little hope of success

form (förm) *n.* 1. shape 2. visible appearance 3. visible person or animal 4. structure 5. nature 6. species, kind 7. regularly drawn up document, *esp.* printed one with blanks for particulars 8. condition, *esp.* good condition 9. model for fitting clothes 10. customary way of doing things 11. set order of words 12. long seat without back, bench 13. hare's nest 14. *Print.* frame for type —*vt.* 15. shape, mold

16. arrange, organize 17. train 18. shape in the mind, conceive 19. go to make up, make part of —*vi.* 20. come into existence or shape —**for'mation** *n.* 1. forming 2. thing formed 3. structure, shape, arrangement 4. military order —**'formative** *a.* 1. of, relating to, development 2. serving or tending to form 3. used in forming —**'formless** *a.* —**form letter** standard letter for dealing with routine matters

-form (*comb. form*) having shape or form of; resembling, as in *cruciform, vermiform*

formal (**'fôrmǝl**) *a.* 1. ceremonial 2. according to rule 3. of outward form or routine 4. of, for, formal occasions 5. according to rule that does not matter 6. precise; stiff —**'formalism** *n.* 1. quality of being formal 2. exclusive concern for form, structure, technique in an activity, *eg* art —**'formalist** *n.* —**for'mality** *n.* 1. observance required by custom or etiquette 2. condition or quality of being formal 3. conformity to custom, conventionality, mere form 4. in art, precision, stiffness, as opposed to originality —**formali'zation** *n.* —**'formalize** *vt.* 1. make formal 2. make official or valid 3. give definite form to —**'formally** *adv.*

formaldehyde (**fôr'maldihῑd**) *n.* colorless, poisonous, pungent gas, used in making antiseptics and in chemistry —**'formalin** *n.* solution of formaldehyde in water, used as disinfectant, preservative *etc.*

format (**'fôrmat**) *n.* 1. size and shape of book 2. organization of television show *etc.*

former (**'fôrmǝr**) *a.* 1. earlier in time 2. of past times 3. first named —*n.* 4. first named thing, person or fact —**'formerly** *adv.* previously

Formica (**fôr'mῑkǝ**) *n.* trade name for type of laminated sheet used to make heat-resistant surfaces

formic acid (**'fôrmik**) acid found in insects (*esp.* ants) and some plants used in textile manufacture

formidable (**'fôrmidǝbǝl, fôr'mid-**) *a.* 1. to be feared 2. overwhelming, terrible, redoubtable 3. likely to be difficult, serious —**'formidably** *adv.*

Formosa (**fôr'mōsǝ**) *n. former name for* TAIWAN

formula (**'fôrmyǝlǝ**) *n.* 1. set form of words setting forth principle, method or rule for doing, producing something 2. human milk substitute for feeding infant 3. specific category of car in motor racing 4. recipe 5. *Science, math.* rule, fact expressed in symbols and figures (*pl.* **-ulae** (-yǝlē), **-s**) —**'formulary** *n.* collection of formulas —**'formulate** *vt.* 1. reduce to, express in formula, or in definite form 2. devise —**formu'lation** *n.* —**'formulator** *n.*

fornication (**fôrni'kāshǝn**) *n.* sexual intercourse outside marriage —**'fornicate** *vi.*

forsake (**fǝ'rsāk**) *vt.* 1. abandon, desert 2. give up (**for'sook, for'saken, for'saking**)

forsooth (**fǝr'sōōth**) *adv. obs.* in truth

forswear (**fôr'swāǝr**) *vt.* 1. renounce 2. deny —*v. refl.* 3. perjure (**-'swore** *pt.*, **-'sworn** *pp.*)

forsythia (**fǝr'sithiǝ**) *n.* widely cultivated shrub with yellow flowers

fort (**fôrt**) *n.* fortified place, stronghold —**hold the fort** *inf.* guard something temporarily

forte¹ (**fôrt, 'fôrtᾱ**) *n.* one's strong point, that in which one excels

forte² (**'fôrti**) *adv. Mus.* loudly (**for'tissimo** *sup.*)

forth (**fôrth**) *adv.* 1. onward 2. into view —**'forth'coming** *a.* 1. about to come 2. ready

when wanted 3. willing to talk, communicative —**forth'with** *adv.* at once, immediately

forthright (**'fôrthrῑt**) *a.* direct, outspoken

fortieth (**'fôrtiith**) *see* FOUR

fortify (**'fôrtifῑ**) *vt.* 1. strengthen 2. provide with defensive works (**fortified, 'fortifying**) —**fortifi'cation** *n.*

fortitude (**'fôrtityōōd, -tōōd**) *n.* courage in adversity or pain, endurance

fortnight (**'fôrtnῑt**) *n.* two weeks —**'fortnightly** *a./adv.*

FORTRAN (**'fôrtran**) *Comp. formula translator*, high-level language for writing scientific programs

fortress (**'fôrtris**) *n.* fortified place, *eg* castle, stronghold

fortuitous (**fôr'tyōōitǝs, -'tōō-**) *a.* accidental, by chance —**for'tuitously** *adv.* —**for'tuity** *n.*

fortune (**'fôrchǝn**) *n.* 1. good luck 2. prosperity, wealth 3. chance, luck —**'fortunate** *a.* —**'fortunately** *adv.* —**fortune-hunter** *n.* person seeking fortune, *esp.* by marriage —**fortune-teller** *n.* one who predicts a person's future

forty (**'fôrti**) *see* FOUR —**forty winks** short sleep, nap

forum (**'fôrǝm**) *n.* (place or medium for) meeting, assembly for open discussion or debate

forward (**'fôrwǝrd**) *a.* 1. lying in front of something 2. onward 3. presumptuous, impudent 4. advanced, progressive 5. relating to the future —*n.* 6. player placed in forward position in various team games, *eg* football —*adv.* 7. toward the future 8. toward the front, to the front 9. into view 10. (**'fôrwǝrd**; *Naut.* **'fôrǝrd**) at, in fore part of ship 11. onward, so as to make progress —*vt.* 12. help forward 13. send, dispatch —**'forwardly** *adv.* pertly —**'forwardness** *n.* —**'forwards** *adv.*

forwent (**fôr'went**) *pt. of* FORGO

fosse *or* **foss** (**fos**) *n.* ditch; moat

fossil (**'fosǝl**) *n.* 1. remnant or impression of animal or plant, *esp.* prehistoric one, preserved in earth 2. *inf.* person, idea *etc.* that is outdated and incapable of change —*a.* 3. of, like or forming fossil 4. dug from earth 5. *inf.* antiquated —**'fossilize** *v.* 1. turn into fossil —*vt.* 2. petrify —**fossil fuel** fuel derived from materials formed over a long period of time from the remains of living organisms, *eg* petroleum, natural gas and coal

foster (**'fostǝr**) *vt.* 1. promote growth or development of 2. bring up (child) *esp.* not one's own —**foster brother, sister, father, mother, parent, child** one related by upbringing, not blood

fought (**fôt**) *pt./pp. of* FIGHT

foul (**fowl**) *a.* 1. loathsome, offensive 2. stinking 3. dirty 4. unfair 5. (of weather) wet, rough 6. obscene, disgustingly abusive 7. charged with harmful matter, clogged, choked —*n.* 8. act of unfair play 9. the breaking of a rule —*adv.* 10. unfairly —*v.* 11. make, become foul 12. jam —*vt.* 13. collide with —**'foully** *adv.* —**foul ball** baseball hit outside the foul lines —**foul line** 1. in baseball, one of two lines extending from home plate marking the boundary 2. in basketball, one of two lines on the court at which player stands to take foul shot —**foul play** 1. violent crime, *esp.* murder 2. violation of rules in game —**foul shot** in basketball, a throw at the basket without interference by opponents, awarded as a penalty against them —**fall foul of** 1. get into trouble with 2. (of ships) collide with

foulard (**fōō'lärd**) *n.* soft light fabric of silk or rayon

found¹ (**fownd**) *pt./pp. of* FIND —**found object** something found, not looked for, incorporated into works of art by the Dadaists and surrealists (*also* **objet trouvé**)

found² (**fownd**) *vt.* 1. establish, institute 2. lay base of 3. base, ground —**foun'dation** *n.* 1. basis 2. base, lowest part of building 3. founding 4. endowed institution *etc.* 5. cosmetic used as base for make-up —**'founder** *n.* —**foundation garment** woman's under-garment worn to shape and support figure (*also* **foun'dation**) —**foundation stone** one of stones forming foundation of building, *esp.* stone laid with public ceremony

found³ (**fownd**) *vt.* 1. melt and run into mold 2. cast —**'founder** *n.* —**'foundry** *n.* 1. place for casting 2. art of this

founder (**'fowndǝr**) *vi.* 1. collapse 2. sink 3. become stuck as in mud *etc.*

foundling (**'fowndling**) *n.* deserted infant

fount (**fownt**) *n.* fountain

fountain (**'fowntin**) *n.* 1. jet of water, *esp.* ornamental one 2. spring 3. source —**'fountainhead** *n.* source —**fountain pen** pen with ink reservoir

four (**fôr**) *n./a.* cardinal number next after three —**'fortieth** *a./n.* —**'forty** *n./a.* four tens —**four'teen** *n./a.* four plus ten —**four'teenth** *a.* —**fourth** *a.* ordinal number of four —**'fourthly** *adv.* —**Four Freedoms** freedom of expression, of worship, from want, from fear —**Four-H** *or* **4-H club** club for *head, heart, hands,* and *health,* organization sponsored by Deptartment of Agriculture for rural youth —**Four Hundred** formerly, the most exclusive social set in New York City —**four-in-hand** *n.* 1. road vehicle drawn by four horses and driven by one driver 2. four-horse team 3. long narrow necktie tied in flat slipknot with ends dangling —**four-leaf clover** clover with four leaves rather than three, supposed to bring good luck —**four-letter word** any of several short English words referring to sex or excrement: regarded generally as offensive —**four-poster** *n.* bed with four posts for curtains *etc.* —**'four'score** *a./n. obs.* eighty —**'foursome** *n.* 1. group of four people 2. game or dance for four people —**four'square** *a.* firm, steady —**four-stroke** *n.* internal-combustion engine firing once every four strokes of piston —**fourth-class mail** class of mail sent at cheapest rate —**fourth estate** (*sometimes* F-E-) journalists; journalism —**on all fours** on hands and knees —**the Fourth** July 4th, Independence Day

fowl (**fowl**) *n.* 1. domestic cock or hen 2. bird, its flesh —*vi.* 3. hunt wild birds —**'fowler** *n.* —**fowling piece** light gun

fox (**foks**) *n.* 1. wild animal of the dog family related to wolf with pointed snout, reddish or gray fur and a bushy tail 2. its pelt, *esp.* silver fox 3. cunning person 4. (F-) member of Amerindian people formerly living in Wisconsin —*vt.* 5. perplex 6. repair (shoe) by renewing top 7. mislead —*vi.* 8. act craftily —**'foxy** *a.* 1. of or resembling fox, *esp.* in craftiness 2. of reddish-brown color 3. (of grapes) having sharp flavor 4. (of woman) physically attractive —**'foxglove** *n.* genus of erect biennial or perennial plants grown for ornament and as a source of digitalis —**'foxhole** *n. sl.* in war, small trench giving protection —**'foxhound** *n.* dog bred for hunting foxes —**fox-hunting** *n.* —**fox terrier** small dog now mainly kept as pet —**'foxtrot** *n.* 1. (music for) ballroom dance 2. (F-) word used in communications for the letter *f* —*vi.* 3. perform foxtrot

foyer (**'foiǝr, 'foiᾱ**) *n.* entrance hall in theaters, hotels *etc.*

F.P. *or* **f.p. 1.** freezing point (*also* **fp**) **2.** fully paid

FPC Federal Power Commission

f.p.s. 1. feet per second **2.** foot-pound-second

Fr *Chem.* francium

fr. 1. fragment **2.** franc **3.** from

Fr. 1. Father **2.** Frater (*Lat.* brother) **3.** French **4.** Friday

fracas ('frākəs, 'fra-) *n.* noisy quarrel; uproar; brawl

fraction ('frakshən) *n.* **1.** any indicated quotient of two quantities, *esp.* any algebraic expression with a numerator and a denominator **2.** fragment, piece —**'fractional** *a.* **1.** constituting a fraction **2.** forming but a small part **3.** insignificant

fractious ('frakshəs) *a.* **1.** unruly **2.** irritable

fracture ('frakchər) *n.* **1.** breakage, part broken **2.** breaking of bone **3.** breach, rupture —*v.* **4.** break

fragile ('frajil) *a.* **1.** breakable **2.** frail, delicate —**fra'gility** *n.*

fragment ('fragmənt) *n.* **1.** piece broken off **2.** small portion **3.** incomplete part —*v.* ('fragment) **4.** (cause to) break into fragments —**'fragmentary** *a.*

fragrant ('frāgrənt) *a.* sweet-smelling —**'fragrance** *n.* scent —**'fragrantly** *adv.*

frail (frāl) *a.* **1.** fragile, delicate **2.** infirm, in weak health **3.** morally weak —**'frailly** *adv.* —**'frailty** *n.*

frambesia (fram'bēzhiə) *n.* yaws

frame (frām) *n.* **1.** that in which thing is set, as square of wood round picture *etc.* **2.** structure **3.** build of body **4.** constitution **5.** mood **6.** individual exposure on strip of film **7.** *Pool etc.* wooden triangle used to set up balls, balls when set up or single game finished when all balls have been potted —*vt.* **8.** put together, make **9.** adapt **10.** put into words **11.** put into frame **12.** *sl.* conspire to incriminate on false charge —**frame-up** *n. sl.* **1.** plot **2.** manufactured evidence —**'framework** *n.* **1.** structure into which completing parts can be fitted **2.** supporting work

franc (frangk; *Fr.* frä) *n.* monetary unit of France, Switzerland and other countries

France (frans) *n.* country in Europe bounded north by the English Channel, northeast by Belgium and Luxembourg, east by the Federal Republic of Germany, Switzerland and Italy, south by the Mediterranean (with Monaco as a coastal enclave), southwest by Spain and Andorra and west by the Atlantic Ocean

franchise ('franchīz) *n.* **1.** right of voting **2.** citizenship **3.** privilege or right, *esp.* right to sell certain goods

Franciscan (fran'siskən) *n.* monk or nun of the order founded by St. Francis of Assisi in 1209

francium ('fransiəm) *n. Chem.* radioactive element of alkali-metal group *Symbol* Fr, at. wt. 223, at. no. 87

Franco- ('frangkō-) (*comb. form*) France; French, as in *Franco-Prussian*

francolin ('frangkəlin) *n.* Afr. or Asian partridge

frangipani (franji'pani, -'päni) *n.* tropical Amer. shrub (*pl.* **-s, -'pani**)

frank (frangk) *a.* **1.** candid, outspoken **2.** sincere —*n.* **3.** official mark on letter either canceling stamp or ensuring delivery without stamp —*vt.* **4.** mark letter thus —**'frankly** *adv.* candidly —**'frankness** *n.* —**franking machine** machine that prints marks on letters *etc.* indicating that postage has been paid

Frank (frangk) *n.* member of group of W

Germanic peoples who gradually conquered most of Gaul and Germany in late 4th century A.D. —**'Frankish** *n.* **1.** ancient W Germanic language of Franks —*a.* **2.** of Franks or their language

Frankenstein's monster ('frangkinstīnz) creation or monster that brings disaster and is beyond the control of its creator

frankfurter *or* **frankforter** ('frangkfərtər) *n.* cured cooked sausage of beef or beef and pork (*also* **hot dog**)

frankincense ('frangkinsens) *n.* aromatic gum resin burned as incense

frantic ('frantik) *a.* **1.** distracted with rage, grief, joy *etc.* **2.** frenzied —**'frantically** *adv.*

frappé (fra'pā) *n.* **1.** drink consisting of liqueur *etc.* poured over crushed ice **2.** thick milk shake —*a.* **3.** (*esp.* of drinks) chilled

fraternal (frə'tərnəl) *a.* of brother; brotherly —**fra'ternally** *adv.* —**fra'ternity** *n.* **1.** brotherliness **2.** brotherhood **3.** men's student organization for usu. social purposes —**frater'ni'zation** *n.* —**'fraternize** *vi.* associate, make friends —**fratri'cidal** *a.* —**'fratricide** *n.* killing, killer of brother or sister

Frau (frow) *n.* married German woman: usu. used as title equivalent to *Mrs.* (*pl.* **Frauen** ('frowən), **-s**)

fraud (fröd) *n.* **1.** criminal deception **2.** swindle, imposture **3.** *inf.* person who acts in false or deceitful way —**'fraudulence** *n.* —**'fraudulent** *a.*

fraught (fröt) *a.* —**fraught with** filled with, involving

fray[1] (frā) *n.* **1.** fight **2.** noisy quarrel

fray[2] (frā) *v.* **1.** wear through by rubbing **2.** make, become ragged at edge

frazil ('frāzil) *n.* **C** broken spikes of ice formed in turbulent water

frazzle ('frazəl) *inf. v.* **1.** make or become exhausted **2.** make or become irritated —*n.* **3.** exhausted state

freak (frēk) *n.* **1.** abnormal person, animal, thing —*a.* **2.** oddly different from what is normal —**'freakish** *or* (*inf.*) **'freaky** *a.* —**freak out** *inf.* (cause to) hallucinate, be wildly excited *etc.*

freckle ('frekəl) *n.* **1.** light brown spot on skin, *esp.* caused by sun **2.** any small spot —*v.* **3.** mark or become marked in freckles —**'freckled** *a.*

free (frē) *a.* **1.** able to act at will, not under compulsion or restraint **2.** (*with* from) not restricted or affected by **3.** not subject to cost or tax **4.** independent **5.** not exact or literal **6.** generous **7.** not in use **8.** (of person) not occupied, having no engagement **9.** loose, not fixed —*vt.* **10.** set at liberty **11.** (*with* of *or* from) remove (obstacles, pain *etc.*), rid (of) (**freed, 'freeing**) —**'freebie, 'freebee,** *or* **'freeby** *n. sl.* anything that is free of charge —**'freedom** *n.* —**'freely** *adv.* —**'freeboard** *n.* space between deck of vessel and waterline —**free enterprise** economic system in which commercial organizations compete for profit with little state control —**free flight** flight of rocket *etc.* when engine has ceased to produce thrust —**free-for-all** *n.* brawl —**'freehand** *a.* drawn without guiding instruments —**free kick** in football, place kick awarded for foul or infringement —**'freelance** *a./n.* **1.** (of) self-employed, unattached person —*vi.* **2.** work as freelance —*adv.* **3.** as freelance —**free-living** *a.* **1.** given to indulgence of appetites **2.** (of animals *etc.*) not parasitic —**free'load** *vi.* eat, drink *etc.* at another's expense —**free love** practice of sexual relationships without fidelity to single partner —**'freemartin** *n.* calf incapable of reproducing —**'Freemason** *n.* member of secret fraternity for mutual help —**free ride**

---

something obtained without cost —**free speech** right to express opinions publicly —**free'standing** *a.* not attached to or supported by another object —**'freestyle** *n.* race, as in swimming, in which each participant may use style of his or her choice —**free'thinker** *n.* skeptic who forms his own opinions, *esp.* in religion —**free trade** international trade free of protective tariffs —**free verse** unrhymed verse without metrical pattern —**'freeway** *n.* **1.** expressway with controlled access **2.** toll-free highway —**free'wheel** *vi.* coast —**free will 1.** apparent human ability to make choices not externally determined **2.** doctrine that human beings have such freedom of choice **3.** ability to make choice without coercion —**free-will** *a.* voluntary; spontaneous —**free on board** (of shipment of goods) delivered on board ship *etc.* without charge to buyer —**the Free World** non-Communist countries collectively

freesia ('frēzhə) *n.* plant with fragrant, tubular flowers

freeze (frēz) *v.* **1.** change (by reduction of temperature) from liquid to solid, as water to ice —*vt.* **2.** preserve (food *etc.*) by extreme cold, as in freezer **3.** fix (prices *etc.*) —*vi.* **4.** feel very cold **5.** become rigid as with fear **6.** stop (**froze, 'frozen, 'freezing**) —**'freezer** *n.* insulated cabinet for long-term storage of perishable foodstuffs —**frozen** ('frōzən) *a.* (of credits *etc.*) unrealizable —**freeze-dry** *vt.* preserve (substance) by rapid freezing and subsequently drying in vacuum —**freezing point** temperature at which liquid becomes solid, 32°F or 0°C for water

freight (frāt) *n.* **1.** commercial transport (*esp.* by railroad, ship) **2.** cost of this **3.** goods so carried —*vt.* **4.** send as or by freight —**'freightage** *n.* money paid for freight —**'freighter** *n.*

French (french) *n.* **1.** Romance language spoken by people of France and some Canadians, Belgians and Swiss —*a.* **2.** of France —**French Canadian** Canadian citizen whose native language is French —**French-Canadian** *a.* of French Canadians —**French chalk** variety of talc used to mark cloth or remove grease stains —**French dressing** salad dressing of oil and vinegar —**French fries** potatoes cut into thin strips and fried in deep fat —**French horn** orchestral brass instrument with a narrow conical tube wound twice in a circle, funnel-shaped mouthpiece, and a flaring bell —**French leave** unauthorized leave —**French toast** sliced bread dipped in egg-and-milk batter and sautéed —**French window** pair of exterior windows reaching to the floor, opening in the middle and used as a door

frenetic (fri'netik) *a.* frenzied

frenzy ('frenzi) *n.* **1.** violent mental derangement **2.** wild excitement —**'frenzied** *a.*

frequent ('frēkwənt) *a.* **1.** happening often **2.** common **3.** numerous —*vt.* (fre'kwent) **4.** go often to —**'frequency** *n.* **1.** rate of occurrence **2.** in radio *etc.*, cycles per second of alternating current —**fre'quentative** *a.* expressing repetition —**'frequently** *adv.* —**frequency modulation** *Rad.* method of transmitting information in which frequency of carrier wave is varied

fresco ('freskō) *n.* **1.** method of painting in watercolor on plaster of wall before it dries **2.** painting done thus (*pl.* **-es, -s**)

fresh (fresh) *a.* **1.** not stale **2.** new **3.** additional **4.** different **5.** recent **6.** inexperienced 7. pure 8. not pickled, frozen *etc.* 9. not faded or dimmed 10. not tired 11. (of wind) strong 12. *inf.* impudent 13. *inf.* arrogant —'**freshen** *v.* —'**freshet** *n.* 1. rush of water at river mouth 2. flood of river water —'**freshly** *adv.* —'**freshman** *n.* first-year student —'**freshness** *n.* —'**freshwater** *a.* 1. of or living in fresh water 2. (*esp.* of sailor who has not sailed on sea) inexperienced 3. little known

fret[1] (fret) *v.* 1. irritate or be irritated 2 worry (**-tt-**) —*n.* 3. irritation —'**fretful** *a.* irritable, (easily) upset

fret[2] (fret) *n.* 1. repetitive geometrical pattern 2. small bar on fingerboard of guitar *etc.* —*vt.* 3. ornament with carved pattern (**-tt-**) —**fret saw** saw with narrow blade and fine teeth, used for fretwork —'**fretwork** *n.* carved or open woodwork in ornamental patterns and devices

Freudian ('froidiən) *a.* pert. to Austrian psychologist Sigmund Freud, or his theories —**Freudian slip** any action, such as slip of tongue, that may reveal unconscious thought

Fri. Friday

friable ('friəbəl) *a.* easily crumbled —**fria'bility** *or* '**friableness** *n.*

friar ('friər) *n.* member of mendicant religious order —'**friary** *n.* house of friars

fricassee ('frikəsē, frikə'sē) *n.* 1. dish of pieces of chicken or meat, fried or stewed and served with rich sauce —*vt.* 2. cook thus

fricative ('frikətiv) *n.* 1. consonant produced by partial occlusion of air stream, such as (f) or (z) —*a.* 2. relating to fricative

friction ('frikshən) *n.* 1. rubbing 2. resistance met with by body moving over another 3. clash of wills *etc.*, disagreement —'**friction-al** *a.*

Friday ('friidi) *n.* sixth day of week —**Good Friday** the Friday before Easter

fried (friid) *pt./pp.* of FRY[1]

Friedman's disease ('frēdmənz) *see* NARCO-LEPSY

friend (frend) *n.* 1. one well known to another and regarded with affection and loyalty 2. intimate associate 3. supporter 4. (F-) Quaker —'**friendless** *a.* —'**friendliness** *n.* —'**friendly** *a.* 1. having disposition of a friend, kind 2. favorable —'**friendship** *n.* —**Friends of the Earth** organization of environmentalists and conservationists

frier ('friər) *n. see* **fryer** *at* FRY[1]

frieze[1] (frēz) *n.* ornamental band, strip (on wall)

frieze[2] (frēz) *n.* kind of coarse woolen cloth

frigate ('frigit) *n.* 1. old (sailing) warship corresponding to modern cruiser 2. fast destroyerlike warship equipped for escort and antisubmarine duties —**frigate bird** bird of tropical and subtropical seas, with wide wingspan

fright (friit) *n.* 1. sudden fear 2. shock 3. alarm 4. grotesque or ludicrous person or thing —*vt.* 5. *obs.* frighten —'**frighten** *vt.* cause fear, fright in —'**frightful** *a.* 1. terrible, calamitous 2. shocking 3. *inf.* very great, very large —'**frightfully** *adv. inf.* 1. terribly 2. very —'**frightfulness** *n.*

frigid ('frijid) *a.* 1. formal, dull 2. (sexually) unfeeling 3. cold —**fri'gidity** *n.* —'**frigidly** *adv.* —**frigid zone** cold region inside Arctic or Antarctic Circle

Frigidaire (friji'dāər) *n.* trade name, but used to refer to any domestic refrigerator

frill (fril) *n.* 1. fluted strip of fabric gathered at one edge 2. ruff of hair, feathers around neck of dog, bird *etc.* 3. fringe 4. (*oft. pl.*) unnecessary words, politeness; superfluous

thing; adornment —*vt.* 5. make into, decorate with frill

fringe (frinj) *n.* 1. ornamental edge of hanging threads, tassels *etc.* 2. anything like this 3. edge, limit —*vt.* 4. adorn with fringe 5. be fringe for —*a.* 6. (of theater *etc.*) unofficial, unconventional, extra —**fringe benefit** benefit provided by employer to supplement employee's regular pay

frippery ('fripəri) *n.* 1. finery 2. trivia

Frisbee ('frizbē) *n.* trade name for plastic disk thrown with spinning motion for recreation

Frisian ('frizhən, 'frēzhən) *n.* 1. language spoken in NW Netherlands and adjacent islands 2. speaker of this language —*a.* 3. of this language or its speakers

frisk (frisk) *vi.* 1. move, leap playfully —*vt.* 2. wave briskly 3. *inf.* search (person) for concealed weapons *etc.* —*n.* 4. playful antic or movement 5. *inf.* instance of frisking a person —'**friskily** *adv.* —'**frisky** *a.*

fritillary ('fritileri) *n.* 1. bulbous plant with purple or white bell-shaped flowers 2. butterfly with black spots on orange wings

fritter[1] ('fritər) *vt.* (*usu. with* away) waste

fritter[2] ('fritər) *n.* piece of food fried in batter

frivolous ('frivələs) *a.* 1. not serious, flippant 2. unimportant —**fri'volity** *n.*

frizz (friz) *vt.* 1. crisp, curl into small curls —*n.* 2. frizzed hair —'**frizzy** *a.* crimped

frizzle ('frizəl) *v.* fry, toast or grill with sizzling sound

fro (frō) *adv.* away, from (*only in* **to and fro**)

frock (frok) *n.* 1. long cloak worn by monks and friars 2. woman's or girl's dress —*vt.* 3. invest with office of priest —**frock coat** man's double-breasted skirted coat not cut away in front

frog[1] (frog) *n.* tailless amphibious animal developed from tadpole —'**frogman** *n.* swimmer equipped for swimming, working underwater —'**frogmarch** *n.* any method of moving person against his will

frog[2] (frog) *n.* 1. fastening of knot or button and loop 2. attachment to belt to carry sword

frolic ('frolik) *n.* 1. merrymaking —*vi.* 2. behave playfully ('**frolicked,** '**frolicking**) —'**frolicsome** *a.*

from (from; *unstressed* frəm) *prep.* expressing point of departure, source, distance, cause, change of state *etc.*

frond (frond) *n.* large leaf, finely divided *esp.* of fern and palm

front (frunt) *n.* 1. fore part 2. position directly before or ahead 3. seaside promenade 4. battle line or area 5. *Met.* dividing line between two air masses of different characteristics 6. outward aspect, bearing 7. *inf.* something serving as a respectable cover for another, *usu.* criminal activity 8. field of activity 9. group with common goal —*v.* 10. look, face (on to) —*vt.* 11. *inf.* be a cover for —*a.* 12. of, at the front —'**frontage** *n.* 1. facade of building 2. extent of front —'**frontal** *a.* —**fron'tier** *n.* part of country which borders on another —'**frontispiece** *n.* illustration facing title page of book —'**front-runner** *n. inf.* leader in race *etc.*

frost (frost) *n.* 1. frozen dew or mist 2. act or state of freezing 3. weather in which temperature falls below point at which water turns to ice —*v.* 4. cover, be covered with frost or something similar in appearance —*vt.* 5. give slightly roughened surface to —'**frostily** *adv.* —'**frosting** *n.* 1. icing 2. rough or matt finish on glass *etc.* —'**frosty** *a.* 1. accompanied by frost 2. chilly, cold 3.

unfriendly —'**frostbite** *n.* destruction of tissue, *esp.* of fingers, ears *etc.*, by cold

froth (froth) *n.* 1. collection of small bubbles, foam 2. scum 3. idle talk —*v.* 4. (cause to) foam —'**frothily** *adv.* —'**frothy** *a.*

froward ('frōərd) *a.* obstinate; contrary

frown (frown) *vi.* 1. wrinkle brows —*n.* 2. act of frowning 3. show of dislike or displeasure

frowsty ('frowsti) *a.* stale, musty

frowsy *or* **frowzy** ('frowzi) *a.* 1. dirty 2. unkempt

froze (frōz) *pt.* of FREEZE —'**frozen** *pp.* of FREEZE

FRS Federal Reserve System

fructify ('fruktifi) *v.* (cause to) bear fruit ('**fructified,** '**fructifying**) —**fructifi'cation** *n.*

fructose ('fruktōs) *n.* crystalline sugar occurring in many fruits (*also* **levulose**)

frugal ('frōōgəl) *a.* 1. sparing, thrifty, economical 2. meager —**fru'gality** *n.* —'**frugally** *adv.*

fruit (frōōt) *n.* 1. seed and its envelope, *esp.* edible one 2. vegetable products 3. (*usu. in pl.*) result, benefit —*vi.* 4. bear fruit —'**fruitful** *a.* 1. bearing fruit in abundance 2. productive, prolific 3. producing results or profits —**fruition** (frōō'ishən) *n.* 1. enjoyment 2. realization of hopes —'**fruitless** *a.* 1. unproductive 2. without fruit —'**fruity** *a.* 1. of or resembling fruit 2. (of voice) mellow, rich

frump (frump) *n.* dowdy woman —'**frumpish** *or* '**frumpy** *a.*

frustrate ('frustrāt) *vt.* 1. thwart, balk 2. disappoint —**frus'tration** *n.*

frustum ('frustəm) *n. Geom.* part of the solid between two parallel lines cutting the solid (*pl.* **-s, -ta** (-tə))

fry[1] (frī) *vt.* 1. cook with fat —*vi.* 2. be cooked thus (**fried,** '**frying**) —*n.* 3. fried meat 4. dish of anything fried —'**fryer** *or* '**frier** *n.* 1. one that fries 2. utensil for deep-frying foods —**frying pan** shallow pan for frying —**out of the frying pan into the fire** from bad situation to worse one

fry[2] (frī) *n.* young fishes —**small fry** young or insignificant beings

f-stop *n.* any of settings for f-number of camera

ft. 1. feet 2. foot 3. fort

FTC Federal Trade Commission

fth. *or* **fthm.** fathom

fuchsia ('fyōōshə) *n.* ornamental shrub with purple-red flowers

fuddle ('fudəl) *v.* 1. (cause to) be intoxicated, confused —*n.* 2. this state

fuddy-duddy ('fudidudi) *n. inf.* (elderly) dull person

fudge[1] (fuj) *n.* soft, creamy candy made of milk, butter and sugar —**hot fudge** warm chocolate sauce served on ice cream

fudge[2] (fuj) *vt.* 1. make, do carelessly or dishonestly 2. fake

fuel (fyōōəl) *n.* 1. material for burning as source of heat or power 2. something which nourishes —*vt.* 3. provide with fuel —**fuel cell** cell in which chemical energy is converted directly into electrical energy —**fuel injection** system for introducing fuel directly into the combustion chambers of internal-combustion engine without use of carburetor

fugitive ('fyōōjitiv) *n.* 1. one who flees, *esp.* from arrest or pursuit —*a.* 2. fleeing, elusive

fugue (fyōōg) *n.* musical composition in which themes are repeated in different parts

führer *or* **fuehrer** ('fūrər) *n.* leader, title of Ger. dictator, *esp.* Hitler

-ful (*comb. form*) 1. full of; characterized by, as in *painful, restful* 2. able or tending to, as in *useful* 3. as much as will fill thing specified, as in *mouthful*

fulcrum ('fŏŏlkrəm, 'ful-) *n.* point on which lever is placed for support (*pl.* **-cra** (-krə))

fulfill *or* **fulfil** (fŏŏl'fil) *vt.* 1. satisfy 2. carry out 3. obey —**ful'fillment** *n.*

full¹ (fŏŏl) *a.* 1. containing as much as possible 2. abundant 3. complete 4. ample 5. plump 6. (of garment) of ample cut —*adv.* 7. very 8. quite 9. exactly —**'fullness** *n.* —**'fully** *adv.* —**'fulsome** *a.* excessive —**'fullback** *n. Football etc.* defensive player or position held by this player —**full-blooded** *a.* 1. (*esp.* of horses) of unmixed ancestry 2. having great vigor —**full-blown** *a.* 1. characterized by fullest or best development 2. in full bloom —**full-bodied** *a.* having full rich flavor or quality —**full-fledged** *a.* 1. (of bird) having acquired adult feathers and being able to fly 2. completely developed 3. of full rank or status —**full house** 1. *Poker* hand with three cards of same value and another pair 2. *theater etc.* filled to capacity 3. in bingo *etc.*, set of numbers needed to win —**full-scale** *a.* 1. (of plan *etc.*) of actual size 2. using all resources —**full stop** *see* PERIOD (sense 6) —**full-time** *a.* for entire time appropriate to activity —**full time** *adv.* 1. on full-time basis —*n.* 2. end of match —**fully fashioned** (of stockings *etc.*) shaped so as to fit closely

full² (fŏŏl) *v.* become or make (cloth *etc.*) more compact during manufacture through shrinking and pressing —**fuller's earth** absorbent clay

fulmar ('fŏŏlmər) *n.* Arctic sea bird

fulminate ('fŏŏlmināt, 'ful-) *vi.* 1. (*esp. with* against) criticize harshly —*n.* 2. chemical compound exploding readily —**fulmi'nation** *n.*

fulsome ('fŏŏlsəm) *a. see* FULL¹

fumble ('fumbəl) *vi.* 1. grope about —*vt.* 2. handle awkwardly —*n.* 3. awkward attempt

fume (fyŏŏm) *vi.* 1. be angry 2. emit smoke or vapor —*n.* 3. smoke 4. vapor —**'fumigate** *vt.* apply fumes or smoke to, *esp.* for disinfection —**fumi'gation** *n.* —**'fumigator** *n.*

fumitory ('fyŏŏmitōri) *n.* plant with spurred flowers

fun (fun) *n.* anything enjoyable, amusing *etc.* —**'funnily** *adv.* —**'funny** *a.* 1. comical 2. odd, difficult to explain

function ('fungkshən) *n.* 1. work a thing is designed to do 2. (large) social event 3. duty 4. profession 5. *Math.* quantity whose value depends on varying value of another —*vi.* 6. operate, work —**'functional** *a.* 1. having a special purpose 2. practical, necessary 3. capable of operating —**'functionary** *n.* official

fund (fund) *n.* 1. stock or sum of money 2. supply, store —*pl.* 3. money resources —*vt.* 4. in financial, business dealings, furnish money to in form of fund

fundamental (fundə'mentəl) *a.* 1. of, affecting, or serving as the base 2. essential, primary —*n.* 3. basic rule or fact —**funda-** ment *n.* 1. buttocks 2. foundation —**funda-'mentalism** *n.* —**funda'mentalist** *n.* one laying stress on belief in literal and verbal inspiration of Bible and other traditional creeds —**fundamental particle** *see* **elementary particle** *at* ELEMENT

funeral ('fyŏŏnərəl) *n.* (ceremony associated with) burial or cremation of dead —**funereal** (fyŏŏ'nēəriəl) *a.* 1. like a funeral 2. dark 3. gloomy —**funeral director** undertaker —**funeral home** place where dead are prepared for burial or cremation and placed on view

fungus ('funggəs) *n.* any of a large group of lower plants lacking chlorophyll and reproducing by spores, *eg* molds, yeasts, mushrooms (*pl.* **fungi** ('funjī, 'funggī), **-es**) —**'fungal** *or* **'fungous** *a.* —**'fungicide** ('funjisīd) *n.* fungus destroyer —**'fungoid** *a.* resembling fungus

funicular (fyŏŏ'nikyələr) *n.* cable railway on mountainside with two counterbalanced cars

funk (fungk) *n.* panic (*esp. in* blue funk)

funky ('fungki) *a. inf.* (of jazz, pop *etc.*) passionate and soulful, reminiscent of early blues

funnel ('funəl) *n.* 1. cone-shaped vessel or tube 2. chimney of locomotive or ship 3. ventilating shaft —*v.* 4. (cause to) move as through funnel —*vt.* 5. concentrate, focus

funny ('funi) *a. see* FUN —**funny bone** area near elbow where sharp tingling sensation is experienced when struck

fur (fər) *n.* 1. soft hair of animal 2. garment *etc.* of dressed skins with such hair 3. furlike coating —*vt.* 4. cover with fur (**-rr-**) —**'furrier** *n.* dealer in furs —**'furry** *a.* of, like fur

fur. furlong

furbelow ('fərbilō) *n.* 1. flounce, ruffle 2. (*oft. pl.*) showy ornamentation —*vt.* 3. put furbelow on (garment *etc.*)

furbish ('fərbish) *vt.* clean up

furcate ('fərkāt) *a.* forked, branching

furious ('fyŏŏriəs) *a.* 1. extremely angry 2. violent —**'furiously** *adv.* —**'furiousness** *n.*

furl (fərl) *vt.* roll up and bind (sail, umbrella *etc.*)

furlong ('fərlong) *n.* unit of distance equal to 220 yards

furlough ('fərlō) *n.* leave of absence

furnace ('fərnis) *n.* 1. apparatus for applying great heat to metals 2. closed structure for producing heat 3. hot place

furnish ('fərnish) *vt.* 1. fit up (house) with furniture 2. equip 3. supply, yield —**furnishings** *pl.n.* furniture, carpets *etc.* with which room is furnished —**'furniture** *n.* movable contents of a house or room

furor ('fyŏŏrôr) *n.* 1. public outburst, *esp.* of protest 2. sudden enthusiasm

furrow ('furō) *n.* 1. trench as made by plow 2. groove —*vt.* 3. make furrows in

further ('fərdhər) *adv. comp. of* FAR *and* FORE¹ 1. more 2. in addition 3. at or to a greater distance or extent —*a. comp. of* FAR *and* FORE¹ 4. more distant 5. additional —*vt.* 6. help forward, promote —**'furtherance** *n.* —**'furtherer** *n.* —**'furthermore** *adv.* besides —**'furthermost** *a.* —**'furthest** *a./adv. sup. of* FAR, FORE¹

furtive ('fərtiv) *a.* stealthy, sly, secretive —**'furtively** *adv.*

fury ('fyŏŏri) *n.* 1. wild rage, violent anger 2. violence of storm *etc.* 3. (*usu. pl.*) snake-haired avenging deity

furze (fərz) *n.* prickly shrub, gorse

fuscous ('fuskəs) *a.* dark-colored

fuse (fyŏŏz) *v.* 1. blend by melting 2. melt with heat 3. amalgamate 4. (cause to) fail as a result of blown fuse —*n.* 5. soft wire, with low melting point, used as safety device in electrical systems 6. device (*orig.* combustible cord) for igniting bomb *etc.* —**fusi'bility** *n.* —**'fusible** *a.* —**'fusion** *n.* 1. melting 2. state of being melted 3. union of things, as atomic nuclei, as if melted together

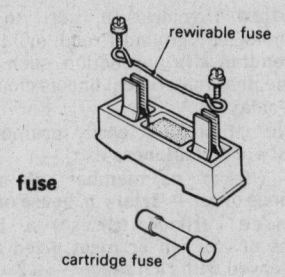

rewirable fuse

fuse

cartridge fuse

fuselage ('fyŏŏsiläzh, -zi-) *n.* body of aircraft

fusil ('fyŏŏzil) *n.* light flintlock musket —**fusi'lier** *n.* soldier of certain regiments —**fusil'lade** *n.* continuous discharge of firearms

fuss (fus) *n.* 1. needless bustle or concern 2. complaint, objection —*vi.* 3. make fuss —**'fussily** *adv.* —**'fussiness** *n.* —**'fussy** *a.* 1. particular 2. faddy 3. overmeticulous 4. overelaborate

fustian ('fuschən) *n.* 1. thick cotton cloth 2. inflated language

fusty ('fusti) *a.* 1. moldy 2. smelling of damp 3. old-fashioned —**'fustily** *adv.* —**'fustiness** *n.*

futile ('fyŏŏtil) *a.* 1. useless, ineffectual 2. trifling —**fu'tility** *n.*

future ('fyŏŏchər) *n.* 1. time to come 2. what will happen 3. tense of verb indicating this 4. likelihood of development —*a.* 5. that will be 6. of, relating to, time to come —**'futurism** *n.* movement in art marked by revolt against tradition —**'futurist** *n./a.* —**futur'istic** *a.* ultramodern —**fu'turity** *n.* —**future perfect** *Gram. a.* 1. denoting tense of verbs describing action that will have been performed by certain time —*n.* 2. future perfect tense; verb in this tense

fuze (fyŏŏz) *vt.* equip with a fuse

fuzz (fuz) *n.* 1. fluff 2. fluffy or frizzed hair 3. blur 4. *sl.* police(man) —**'fuzzy** *a.* 1. fluffy 2. frizzy 3. blurred, indistinct

fwd. forward

-fy (*comb. form*) make; become, as in *beautify*

Gg

g *or* **G** (jē) *n.* **1.** seventh letter of English alphabet **2.** speech sound represented by this letter, usu. as in *grass,* or as in *page* (*pl.* **g's, G's** *or* **Gs**)

g 1. gram(s) **2.** (acceleration due to) gravity

G 1. *Mus.* fifth note of scale of C major; major or minor key having this note as its tonic **2.** gravitational constant **3.** *Phys.* conductance **4.** German **5.** giga **6.** good **7.** *sl.* grand (thousand dollars)

Ga *Chem.* gallium

GA Georgia

gabardine ('gabərdēn) *n.* **1.** fine twill cloth like serge used *esp.* for raincoats **2.** *Hist.* loose upper garment worn by Jews (*also* **gaberdine**)

gabble ('gabəl) *v.* **1.** talk, utter inarticulately or too fast ('**gabbled, 'gabbling**) —*n.* **2.** such talk —**gab** *vi.* **1.** talk excessively; chatter (**-bb-**) —*n.* **2.** idle or trivial talk —'**gabby** *a.* *inf.* talkative —**gift of the gab** eloquence, loquacity

gable ('gābəl) *n.* triangular upper part of wall at end of ridged roof (*also* **gable end**)

Gabon (ga'bōn) *n.* country in Africa bounded west by the Atlantic Ocean, north by Equatorial Guinea and Cameroon and east and south by Congo

gad (gad) *vi.* (*esp. with* about) go around in search of pleasure (**-dd-**) —'**gadabout** *n.* pleasure-seeker

gadfly ('gadflī) *n.* **1.** cattle-biting fly **2.** worrying person

gadget ('gajit) *n.* **1.** small mechanical device **2.** object valued for its novelty or ingenuity —'**gadgetry** *n.*

gadoid ('gādoid) *a.* **1.** of order of marine fishes typically having pectoral and pelvic fins close together and small cycloid scales —*n.* **2.** gadoid fish

gadolinium (gadə'liniəm) *n. Chem.* metallic element *Symbol* Gd, at. wt. 157.3, at. no. 64

gadroon (gə'drōōn) *n.* **1.** *Archit.* carved or indented convex molding **2.** decorative border formed by convex series of curves, *esp.* in furniture and silver ware

gadwall ('gadwöl) *n.* duck related to mallard

Gael (gāl) *n.* one who speaks Gaelic —**Gaelic** ('gālik, 'ga-) *n.* **1.** language of Ireland and Scottish Highlands —*a.* **2.** of Gaels, their language or customs

gaff (gaf) *n.* **1.** stick with iron hook for landing fish **2.** spar for top of fore-and-aft sail —*vt.* **3.** seize (fish) with gaff

gaffe (gaf) *n.* social blunder, *esp.* tactless remark

gaffer ('gafər) *n.* **1.** old man **2.** technician in charge of lighting in motion picture or television production

gag[1] (gag) *vt.* **1.** stop up (person's mouth) with cloth *etc.* —*vi.* **2.** *sl.* retch, choke (**-gg-**) —*n.* **3.** cloth *etc.* put into, tied across mouth

gag[2] (gag) *n.* joke, funny story, gimmick

gaga ('gägä) *a. sl.* **1.** senile **2.** crazy

gage[1] (gāj) *n.* **1.** pledge, thing given as security **2.** challenge, or something symbolizing one

gage[2] (gāj) *see* GAUGE

gaggle ('gagəl) *n.* **1.** flock of geese **2.** *inf.* disorderly crowd

gaiety ('gāəti) *n. see* GAY

gain (gān) *vt.* **1.** obtain, secure **2.** obtain as profit **3.** win **4.** earn **5.** reach —*v.* **6.** increase, improve —*vi.* **7.** (*usu. with* on *or* upon) get nearer **8.** (of watch, machine *etc.*) operate too fast —*n.* **9.** profit **10.** increase, improvement —'**gainful** *a.* profitable; lucrative —'**gainfully** *adv.*

gainsay (gān'sā) *vt.* deny; contradict (**gain-'said, gain'saying**)

gait (gāt) *n.* **1.** manner of walking **2.** pace

gaiter ('gātər) *n.* covering of leather, cloth *etc.* for lower leg

gal *or* **gal.** gallon

Gal. *Bible* Galatians

gala ('gālə, 'galə, 'gälə) *n.* **1.** festive occasion **2.** show **3.** competitive sporting event

galah (gə'lä) *n. Aust.* gray cockatoo with reddish breast

galantine ('galəntēn) *n.* cold dish of meat or poultry, boned, cooked, then pressed and glazed

Galatians (gə'lāshənz) *pl.n.* (*with sing. v.*) *Bible* 9th book of the N.T., epistle written by St. Paul to Christians of central Asia Minor in Galatia

galaxy ('galəksi) *n.* **1.** system of stars bound by gravitational forces **2.** splendid gathering, *esp.* of famous people —**ga'lactic** *a.*

gale (gāl) *n.* **1.** strong wind **2.** *inf.* loud outburst, *esp.* of laughter

galena (gə'lēnə) *n.* bluish-gray or black mineral consisting of lead sulfide: principal ore of lead

gall[1] (göl) *n.* **1.** *inf.* impudence **2.** bitterness —**gall bladder** sac attached to liver, reservoir for bile —'**gallstone** *n.* hard secretion in gall bladder or ducts leading from it (*also* **biliary calculus**)

gall[2] (göl) *n.* **1.** painful swelling, *esp.* on horse **2.** sore caused by chafing —*vt.* **3.** make sore by rubbing **4.** vex, irritate —'**galling** *a.* irritating, exasperating, humiliating

gall[3] (göl) *n.* abnormal outgrowth on trees *etc.*

gallant ('galənt) *a.* **1.** fine, stately, brave **2.** (gə'lant, gə'länt) (of man) very attentive to women; chivalrous —*n.* (gə'lant, gə'länt, 'galənt) **3.** lover, suitor **4.** fashionable young man —'**gallantly** *adv.* —'**gallantry** *n.*

galleon ('galiən) *n.* large, high-built sailing ship of war

gallery ('galəri) *n.* **1.** covered walk with side openings, colonnade **2.** platform or projecting upper floor in church, theater *etc.* **3.** group of spectators **4.** long, narrow platform on outside of building **5.** room or rooms for special purposes, *eg* showing works of art **6.** passage in wall, open to interior of building **7.** horizontal passage, as in mine *etc.*

galley ('gali) *n.* **1.** one-decked vessel with sails and oars, usu. rowed by slaves or criminals **2.** kitchen of ship or aircraft **3.** large rowing boat **4.** *Print.* tray for holding composed type —**galley proof** printer's proof in long slip form —**galley slave 1.** one condemned to row in galley **2.** drudge

galliard ('galyərd) *n.* **1.** dance in triple time for two persons **2.** music for this dance

Gallic ('galik) *a.* **1.** of ancient Gaul **2.** French —'**Gallicism** *n.* French word or idiom

gallinaceous (gali'nāshəs) *a.* of order of birds, including domestic fowl, pheasants *etc.,* having heavy rounded body and strong legs

gallium ('galiəm) *n. Chem.* metallic element *Symbol* Ga, at. wt. 69.7, at. no. 31

gallivant ('galivant) *vi.* gad about

Gallo- ('galō-) (*comb. form*) Gaul; France, as in *Gallo-Roman*

gallon ('galən) *n.* unit of liquid measure comprising four quarts or 231 cubic inches

gallop ('galəp) *v.* **1.** go, ride at gallop —*vi.* **2.** move fast —*n.* **3.** horse's fastest pace with all four feet off the ground at once in each stride **4.** ride at this pace —'**galloper** *n.* —'**galloping** *a.* **1.** at a gallop **2.** speedy, swift

gallows ('galōz) *n.* structure, usu. of two upright beams and crossbar, *esp.* for hanging criminals

Gallup Poll ('galəp) method of finding out public opinion by questioning a cross section of the population

galoot (gə'lōōt) *n. inf.* silly, clumsy person

galore (gə'lör) *adv.* in plenty

galoshes (gə'loshiz) *pl.n.* waterproof overshoes

galumph (gə'lumpf, -'lumf) *vi. inf.* leap or move about clumsily or joyfully

galvanic (gal'vanik) *a.* **1.** of, producing, concerning electric current, *esp.* when produced chemically **2.** *inf.* resembling effect of electric shock; startling —'**galvanize** *vt.* **1.** stimulate to action; excite; startle **2.** cover (iron *etc.*) with protective zinc coating —**galva'nometer** *n.* instrument for detecting or measuring small electric currents

Gamay (ga'mā) *n.* **1.** red, light-bodied table wine **2.** grape used to make this wine

Gambia ('gambia) *n.* —**The Gambia** country in Africa bounded west by the Atlantic Ocean and on all other sides by Senegal

gambit ('gambit) *n.* **1.** *Chess* opening involving offer of a pawn **2.** any opening maneuver, comment *etc.* intended to secure an advantage

gamble ('gambəl) *vi.* **1.** play games of chance to win money **2.** act on expectation of something —*n.* **3.** risky undertaking **4.** bet, wager —'**gambler** *n.*

gamboge (gam'bōj, -'bōōzh) *n.* gum resin used as yellow pigment

gambol ('gambəl) *vi.* **1.** skip, jump playfully —*n.* **2.** playful antic

game[1] (gām) *n.* **1.** diversion, pastime **2.** jest **3.** contest for amusement **4.** scheme, strategy **5.** animals or birds hunted **6.** their flesh —*a.* **7.** brave **8.** willing —*vi.* **9.** gamble —'**gamester** *n.* gambler —'**gaming** *n.* gambling —'**gamy** *or* '**gamey** *a.* **1.** having smell or flavor of game **2.** *inf.* spirited; plucky; brave —'**gamecock** *n.* fowl bred for fighting —'**game-**

keeper n. man employed to breed and take care of game —**game laws** laws governing hunting and preservation of game —**game plan** design for course of action —**game point** state in a game when one side needs only one point to win —**'gamesmanship** n. inf. art of winning games or defeating opponents by cunning practices without actually cheating

game² (gām) a. lame, crippled

gamete (gə'mēt, 'gamēt) n. Biol. sexual cell that unites with another for reproduction

gamin ('gamin) n. street urchin

gamine (ga'mēn) n. slim, boyish girl; elfish tomboy

gamma ('gamə) n. third letter of Gr. alphabet (Γ, γ) —**gamma globulin** group of proteins in blood plasma that includes most of the antibodies used by the body to combat disease —**gamma ray** invisible, highly penetrative, light ray emitted during radioactive disintegration

gammon ('gamən) n. 1. double victory in backgammon in which player throws off all his pieces before his opponent throws any —vt. 2. score such a victory over

gamut ('gamət) n. whole range or scale

gander ('gandər) n. 1. male goose 2. inf. a quick look (esp. in take (or have) a gander)

gang (gang) n. 1. (criminal) group 2. organized group of workmen —vi. 3. (esp. with together) form gang —**gang up on** inf. combine against

gangling ('ganggling) or **gangly** a. lanky, awkward in movement

ganglion ('gangglion) n. 1. mass of nerve tissue outside brain and spinal cord 2. cyst on tendon 3. center of activity (pl. -**glia** (-gliə), -**s**)

gangplank ('gangplangk) n. portable bridge for boarding or leaving vessel

gangrene ('ganggrēn) n. death of body tissue as result of inadequate blood supply —**gangrenous** ('ganggrinəs) a.

gangster ('gangstər) n. 1. member of criminal gang 2. notorious or hardened criminal

gangue (gang) n. valueless and undesirable material in ore

gangway ('gangwā) n. 1. gangplank 2. passage between row of seats —interj. 3. clear a path

gannet ('ganit) n. predatory sea bird

ganoid ('ganoid) a./n. (fish) with smooth, hard, enameled, bony scales, eg sturgeon

gantry ('gantri) n. 1. structure to support crane, railroad signals etc. 2. framework beside rocket on launching pad (also **gantry scaffold**)

GAO General Accounting Office

gap (gap) n. 1. breach, opening, interval 2. cleft 3. empty space

gape (gāp) vi. 1. stare in wonder 2. open mouth wide, as in yawning 3. be, become wide open —n. 4. act of gaping

garage (gə'räzh, -'räj) n. 1. (part of) building to house motor vehicles 2. refueling and repair center for motor vehicles —vt. 3. leave (vehicle) in garage —**garage sale** sale of used objects held in or near family garage

garb (gärb) n. 1. dress 2. fashion of dress —vt. 3. dress, clothe

garbage ('gärbij) n. 1. food waste 2. useless material —**garbage in, garbage out** Comp. faulty input results in faulty output

garbanzo (gär'banzō) n. chickpea (pl. -**s**)

garble ('gärbəl) vt. jumble or distort (story, account etc.)

garçon (Fr. gar'sō) n. waiter, esp. French

garden ('gärdən) n. 1. ground for growing flowers, fruit, or vegetables —vi. 2. cultivate garden —**'gardener** n. —**'gardening** n. —**garden-variety** a. ordinary, everyday

gardenia (gär'dēnyə) n. (sub)tropical shrub with fragrant white or yellow flowers

Garfield ('gärfēld) n. **James Abram.** the 20th President of the U.S. (Mar.–Sept. 1881)

garfish ('gärfish) n. elongated bony fish

garganey ('gärgəni) n. small Eurasian duck related to mallard

gargantuan (gär'ganchōoən) a. (sometimes G-) immense, enormous, huge

gargle ('gärgəl) vi. 1. wash throat with liquid kept moving by the breath —vt. 2. wash (throat) thus —n. 3. gargling 4. preparation for this purpose

gargoyle ('gärgoil) n. carved (grotesque) face on waterspout, esp. on Gothic church

garish ('gāərish) a. 1. showy 2. gaudy

garland ('gärlənd) n. 1. wreath of flowers worn or hung as decoration —vt. 2. decorate with garlands

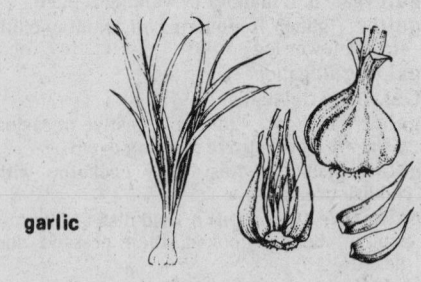

garlic

garlic ('gärlik) n. (bulb of) plant with strong smell and taste, used in cooking and seasoning

garment ('gärmənt) n. article of clothing —**Garment District** area in New York City where clothing is made and sold wholesale

garner ('gärnər) vt. store up, collect, as if in granary

garnet ('gärnit) n. red semiprecious stone

garnish ('gärnish) vt. 1. adorn, decorate (esp. food) —n. 2. material for this

garret ('garit) n. room on top floor, attic

garrison ('garisən) n. 1. troops stationed in town, fort etc. 2. fortified place —vt. 3. station (troops) in (fort etc.) —**garrison cap** folding, wedge-shaped cap worn as part of soldier's uniform (also **overseas cap**)

garrotte or **garotte** (gə'rot) n. 1. Spanish capital punishment by strangling 2. apparatus for this —vt. 3. execute, kill thus —**gar'rotter** or **ga'rotter** n.

garrulous ('garələs, 'garyə-) a. (frivolously) talkative —**garrulity** (gə'rōoliti, ga-) n. loquacity

garter ('gärtər) n. band worn round leg to hold up sock or stocking —**garter stitch** knitting with all rows in knit stitch

gas (gas) n. 1. airlike substance with the capacity to expand indefinitely and not liquefy or solidify at ordinary temperatures 2. fossil fuel in form of gas, used for heating or lighting 3. gaseous anesthetic 4. poisonous or irritant substance dispersed through atmosphere in warfare etc. 5. inf. gasoline 6. inf. accelerator pedal in motor vehicle (pl. -**es**, **'gasses**) —vt. 7. project gas over 8. poison with gas —vi. 9. inf. talk idly, boastfully (-**ss-**) —**'gaseous** a. of, like gas —**'gassy** a. —**'gasbag** n. sl. person who talks idly —**gas chamber** airtight room into which poison gas is introduced to kill people —**gas**

mask mask with chemical filter to guard against poisoning by gas —**gas meter** apparatus for measuring amount of gas passed through it —**ga'someter** n. laboratory apparatus for measuring gases —**gas plant** dittany —**gas range** cooking stove that uses gas as fuel —**gas station** place that sells gasoline, oil, tires etc. and provides other services for motor vehicles (also **filling station, service station**) —**gas tank 1.** tank for storing gas or gasoline **2.** tank containing gasoline supply in a gasoline-engine vehicle —**'gasworks** pl.n. (with sing. v.) plant where gas, esp. coal gas, is made

gash (gash) n. 1. gaping wound, slash —vt. 2. cut deeply

gasket ('gaskit) n. rubber, asbestos etc. used as seal between metal faces, esp. in engines

gasohol (gasə'höl) n. mixture of small proportion of alcohol to gasoline used as fuel for internal-combustion engine

gasoline or **gasolene** ('gasəlēn, gasə'lēn) n. by-product of crude oil used mainly as fuel for internal-combustion engine

gasp (gasp) vi. 1. catch breath with open mouth, as in exhaustion or surprise —n. 2. convulsive catching of breath

gastric ('gastrik) a. of stomach —**gas'trectomy** n. partial or complete removal of the stomach —**gastroente'ritis** n. inflammation of stomach and intestines —**'gastronome** or **gas'tronomist** n. gourmet —**gastro'nomical** a. —**ga'stronomy** n. art of good eating —**gastric juice** digestive fluid secreted by stomach, containing hydrochloric acid etc. —**gastric ulcer** ulcer of stomach lining

gastro- or oft. before vowel **gastr-** (comb. form) stomach, as in gastroenteritis, gastritis

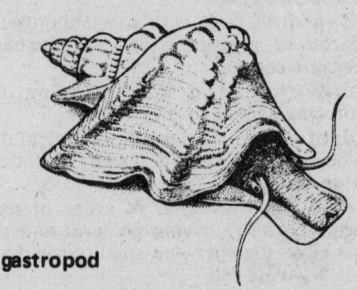

gastropod

gastropod ('gastrəpod) n. any mollusk with a single, sometimes vestigial, shell

gate (gāt) n. 1. opening in wall, fence etc. 2. barrier for closing it 3. sluice 4. any entrance or way out 5. (entrance money paid by) those attending sporting event —**gate-crash** v. enter (meeting, social function etc.) uninvited —**'gatehouse** n. house built at or over gateway —**gate-leg table** table with leaves supported by hinged leg swung out from frame —**'gateway** n. means of entrance and exit

gather ('gadhər) v. 1. (cause to) assemble 2. increase gradually 3. draw together —vt. 4. collect 5. learn, understand 6. draw (material) into small tucks or folds —**'gathering** n. assembly

GATT (gat) General Agreement on Tariffs and Trade

gauche (gōsh) a. tactless, blundering —**gaucherie** (gōshə'rē) n. awkwardness, clumsiness

gaucho ('gowchō) n. S Amer. cowboy (pl. -**s**) —**gaucho pants** mid-calf-length wide-bottomed culottes

gaudy ('gôdi) a. showy in a tasteless way —**'gaudily** adv. —**'gaudiness** n.

gauge *or* **gage** (gāj) *n.* **1.** standard measure, as of diameter of wire, thickness of sheet metal *etc.* **2.** distance between rails of railroad **3.** capacity, extent **4.** instrument for measuring such things as wire, rainfall, height of water in boiler *etc.* —*vt.* **5.** measure **6.** estimate

Gaul (gôl) *n.* **1.** native of Gaul, region in Roman times stretching from N Italy to S Netherlands **2.** Frenchman

gaunt (gônt) *a.* lean, haggard

gauntlet ('gôntlit) *n.* **1.** armored glove **2.** glove covering part of arm —**run the gauntlet 1.** formerly, run as punishment between two lines of men striking at runner with sticks *etc.* **2.** be exposed to criticism or unpleasant treatment **3.** undergo ordeal —**throw down the gauntlet** offer challenge

gauss (gows) *n.* unit of density of magnetic field (*pl.* **gauss**)

gauze (gôz) *n.* **1.** thin transparent fabric of silk, wire *etc.* **2.** cotton surgical dressing —'**gauzy** *a.*

gave (gāv) *pt. of* GIVE

gavel ('gavəl) *n.* mallet of presiding officer or auctioneer

gavotte (gə'vot) *n.* **1.** lively dance **2.** music for it

gawk (gôk) *vi.* stare stupidly —'**gawky** *a.* clumsy, awkward

gawp (gôp) *vi. sl.* **1.** stare stupidly **2.** gape

gay (gā) *a.* **1.** merry **2.** lively **3.** cheerful **4.** bright **5.** light-hearted **6.** showy **7.** given to pleasure **8.** *inf.* homosexual —'**gaiety** *n.* **1.** state or condition of being gay **2.** festivity; merrymaking —'**gaily** *adv.*

gaze (gāz) *vi.* **1.** look fixedly —*n.* **2.** fixed look

gazebo (gə'zābō, -'zēbō) *n.* summerhouse, turret on roof, with extensive view (*pl.* **-s**, **-es**)

gazelle (gə'zel) *n.* small graceful antelope

gazetteer (gazi'tēər) *n.* geographical dictionary

G.B. Great Britain

GCA ground-controlled approach

G clef *see* treble clef *at* TREBLE

Gd *Chem.* gadolinium

GDR German Democratic Republic

Ge *Chem.* germanium

gear (gēər) *n.* **1.** set of wheels working together, *esp.* by engaging cogs **2.** connection by which engine, motor *etc.* is brought into work **3.** arrangement by which driving wheel of cycle or motor vehicle performs more or fewer revolutions relative to pedals, pistons *etc.* **4.** equipment **5.** clothing **6.** goods, utensils **7.** apparatus, tackle, tools **8.** rigging **9.** harness —*vt.* **10.** adapt (one thing) so as to conform with another **11.** provide with gear **12.** put in gear —'**gearing** *n.* **1.** assembly of gears for transmitting motion **2.** act or technique of providing gears to transmit motion —'**gearbox** *n.* case protecting gearing of bicycle or motor vehicle —**gear lever** *or* '**gearshift** *n.* lever used to move gearwheels relative to each other in motor vehicle *etc.* —'**gearwheel** *n.* toothed wheel in system of gears (*also* **gear**) —**in gear** connected up and ready for work —**out of gear 1.** disconnected, out of working order **2.** upset

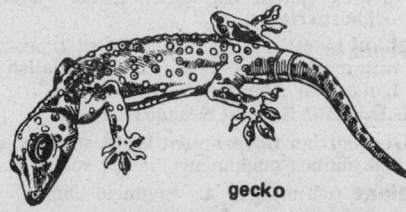

gecko

gecko ('gekō) *n.* insectivorous lizard of warm regions (*pl.* **-s**, **-es**)

gee (jē) *interj.* **1.** exclamation to horse *etc.* to encourage it to turn to right, go on or go faster (*also* **gee up**) —*vt.* **2.** (*usu. with* up) move (horse *etc.*) ahead; urge on

geese (gēs) *n., pl. of* GOOSE

geezer ('gēzər) *n. inf.* old (eccentric) man

Geiger counter ('gīgər) *or* **Geiger-Müller counter** (-'myōōlər, -'milər, -'mulər) instrument for detecting radioactivity, cosmic radiation and charged atomic particles

geisha ('gāshə, 'gē-) *n.* in Japan, professional female companion for men

gel (jel) *n.* **1.** jellylike substance —*vi.* **2.** form a gel (**-ll-**)

gelatin *or* **gelatine** ('jelətin) *n.* **1.** substance prepared from animal bones *etc.*, producing edible jelly **2.** anything resembling this —**ge'latinous** *a.* like gelatin or jelly

geld (geld) *vt.* castrate —'**gelding** *n.* castrated horse

gelid ('jelid) *a.* very cold

gelignite ('jelignīt) *n.* powerful explosive consisting of dynamite in gelatin form

gelt (gelt) *n. sl.* money

gem (jem) *n.* **1.** precious stone, *esp.* when cut and polished **2.** treasure —*vt.* **3.** adorn with gems (**-mm-**)

geminate ('jemināt) *v.* double, pair, repeat —**gemi'nation** *n.*

Gemini ('jeminē, -nī) *n.* (twins) 3rd sign of zodiac, operative May 21st–June 20th

gemma ('jemə) *n.* asexual reproductive structure in mosses *etc.* that becomes detached from parent and develops into new individual (*pl.* **-mae** (-mē))

gemsbok ('gemzbok) *n.* S Afr. oryx

gen. **1.** gender **2.** general **3.** genitive **4.** genus

Gen. **1.** General **2.** *Bible* Genesis

-gen (*comb. form*) **1.** producing; that which produces, as in *hydrogen* **2.** something produced, as in *antigen*

gendarme ('zhondärm) *n.* policeman in France

gender ('jendər) *n.* **1.** sex, male or female **2.** grammatical classification of nouns

gene (jēn) *n.* basic unit of heredity, segment of DNA molecule —**genetic** (ji'netik) *a.* —**ge'netics** *pl.n.* (*with sing. v.*) scientific study of heredity and variation in organisms —**genetic code** relationship between base-unit sequence in RNA, or DNA parents, and sequence of amino-acid residues in proteins —**genetic engineering** alteration of structure of chromosomes in living organisms

genealogy (jēni'aləji) *n.* **1.** account of descent from ancestors **2.** pedigree **3.** study of pedigrees —**genea'logical** *a.* —**gene'alogist** *n.*

genera ('jenərə) *n., pl. of* GENUS

general ('jenərəl, 'jenrəl) *a.* **1.** common, widespread **2.** not particular or specific **3.** applicable to all or most **4.** not restricted to one department **5.** usual, prevalent **6.** miscellaneous **7.** dealing with main element only **8.** vague, indefinite —*n.* **9.** army officer of rank above colonel —**gene'rality** *n.* **1.** general principle **2.** vague statement **3.** indefiniteness —**generali'zation** *n.* **1.** general conclusion from particular instance **2.** inference —'**generalize** *vt.* **1.** reduce to general laws —*vi.* **2.** draw general conclusions —'**generally** *adv.* —**General Assembly 1.** main deliberative body of the United Nations **2.** (**g- a-**) supreme governing body of many Protestant denominations, *esp.* the Presbyterian Church (U.S.) —**general election** any election for city, state or federal officials held at specified intervals —**general practitioner** nonspecialist physician —**general-purpose** *a.* having a variety of uses —**general strike** strike by all or most of workers of country *etc.*

generalissimo (jenərə'lisimō, jenrə-) *n.* supreme commander of combined military, naval and air forces in some countries (*pl.* **-s**)

generate ('jenərāt) *vt.* **1.** bring into being **2.** produce —**gene'ration** *n.* **1.** bringing into being **2.** all persons born about same time **3.** average time between two such generations (about 30 years) —'**generative** *a.* —'**generator** *n.* **1.** apparatus for producing steam, electricity *etc.* **2.** begetter —**generation gap** years separating one generation from next, *esp.* regarded as representing difference in outlook and lack of understanding between them

generic (ji'nerik) *a.* belonging to, characteristic of class or genus —**ge'nerically** *adv.*

generous ('jenərəs, 'jenrəs) *a.* **1.** liberal, free in giving **2.** abundant —**gene'rosity** *n.* —'**generously** *adv.*

genesis ('jenisis) *n.* **1.** origin **2.** mode of formation (*pl.* **-eses** (-isēz))

Genesis ('jenisis) *n. Bible* 1st book of the O.T., account of the creation of the world, the fall of man and the promise of redemption

-genesis (*comb. form*) genesis, development, generation, as in *biogenesis, parthenogenesis*

genet ('jenit) *n.* catlike mammal of Afr. and S Europe

Geneva Convention (ji'nēvə) **1.** international agreement, formulated in 1864, establishing code for wartime treatment of sick or wounded: revised to cover maritime warfare and prisoners of war **2.** *see* **Universal Copyright Convention** *at* UNIVERSAL

genial ('jēnyəl) *a.* **1.** cheerful, warm in behavior **2.** mild, conducive to growth —**geni'ality** *n.* —'**genially** *adv.*

genie ('jēni) *n.* in fairy tales, servant appearing by, and working, magic

genital ('jenitəl) *a.* relating to sexual organs or reproduction —'**genitals** *or* **genitalia** (jeni'tālyə) *pl.n.* the sexual organs

genitive ('jenitiv) *a./n.* possessive (case) —**genitival** (jeni'tīvəl) *a.*

genius ('jēnyəs, -niəs) *n.* **1.** (person with) exceptional power or ability, *esp.* of mind **2.** distinctive spirit or nature (of nation *etc.*)

genocide ('jenəsīd) *n.* murder of a nationality or ethnic group

-genous (*comb. form*) **1.** yielding; generating, as in *erogenous* **2.** generated by; issuing from, as in *endogenous*

genre ('zhänrə) *n.* **1.** kind **2.** sort **3.** style **4.** painting of homely scene

gent (jent) *inf. n.* **1.** gentleman —*pl.* **2.** men's public toilet

genteel (jen'tēl) *a.* **1.** well-bred **2.** stylish **3.** affectedly proper —**gen'teelly** *adv.*

gentian ('jenchən) *n.* plant, *usu.* with blue flowers —**gentian violet** violet dye used as antiseptic *etc.*

Gentile ('jentīl) *a.* **1.** of race other than Jewish **2.** heathen —*n.* **3.** person, *esp.* Christian, who is not a Jew **4.** (among Mormons) person who is not a Mormon

gentle ('jentəl) *a.* **1.** mild, quiet, not rough or severe **2.** soft and soothing **3.** courteous **4.** moderate **5.** gradual **6.** noble **7.** well-born —**gen'tility** *n.* **1.** noble birth **2.** respectability, politeness —'**gentleness** *n.* **1.** quality of being gentle **2.** tenderness —'**gently** *adv.* —'**gentlefolk** *or* '**gentlefolks** *pl.n.* persons regarded as being of good breeding —'**gen-**

tleman *n.* 1. chivalrous well-bred man 2. man of good social position 3. man (used as a mark of politeness) —**'gentlemanly** *or* **'gentlemanlike** *a.* —**gentlemen's agreement** agreement binding by honor but not valid in law —**'gentlewoman** *n.*

gentry ('jentri) *pl.n.* aristocracy —**gentri-fi'cation** *n.* rise in amenity of decaying urban neighborhoods through the movement of middle-class families into the area

genuflect ('jenyəflekt) *vi.* bend knee, *esp.* in worship —**genu'flection** *n.*

genuine ('jenyŏoin) *a.* 1. real, true, not fake; authentic 2. sincere 3. pure

genus ('jēnəs) *n.* 1. *Biol.* taxonomic division of plants and animals below family and above species 2. the first word of a scientific name in binomial nomenclature class, order, group (*pl.* **-es, 'genera**)

geo- (*comb. form*) earth, as in *geomorphology*

geocentric (jēō'sentrik) *a. Astron.* 1. measured, seen from the earth 2. having the earth as center —**geo'centrically** *adv.*

geode ('jēŏd) *n.* 1. cavity lined with crystals 2. stone containing this

geodesic (jēə'desik, -'dē-) *n.* the shortest distance between 2 points on a curved surface —**geodesic dome** light but strong hemispherical construction formed from set of polygons

geodesy (ji'odisi) *n.* science of measuring the earth's surface

geog. 1. geographer 2. geographic(al) 3. geography

geography (ji'ogrəfi) *n.* science of earth's form, physical features, climate, population *etc.* —**ge'ographer** *n.* —**geo'graphic(al)** *a.* —**geo'graphically** *adv.* —**geographical mile** *see* MILE

geoid ('jēoid) *n.* 1. hypothetical surface that corresponds to mean sea level, extending under continents 2. shape of the earth

geol. 1. geologic(al) 2. geologist 3. geology

geology (ji'olǝji) *n.* science of earth's crust, rocks, strata *etc.* —**geo'logical** *a.* —**geo'logically** *adv.* —**ge'ologist** *n.*

geometry (ji'omitri) *n.* science of properties and relations of lines, surfaces, solids and angles —**geo'metric(al)** *a.* —**geo'metrically** *adv.* —**geome'trician** *n.* —**geometric mean** middle term of a geometric progression —**geometric progression** sequence of numbers, each of which differs from succeeding one by constant ratio, as 1, 2, 4, 8 —**geometric series** such numbers written as sum

geophysics (jēə'fiziks) *pl.n.* (*with sing. v.*) science dealing with the physics of the earth —**geo'physical** *a.* —**geo'physicist** *n.*

George Cross (jörj) British award for bravery

georgette (jör'jet) *n.* fine fabric with dull crepelike surface

Georgia ('jörjǝ) *n.* South Atlantic state of the U.S.: ratified the Constitution in 1788. Abbrev.: **GA** (with ZIP code)

Georgian ('jörjǝn) *a.* of the times of the four Georges (1714-1830) or of George V (1910-36)

georgic ('jörjik) *n.* poem on rural life, *esp.* one by Virgil

geostationary (jēō'stāshǝneri) *a.* (of satellite) in orbit around earth so it remains over same point on surface

geotropism (ji'otrǝpizǝm) *n.* response of plant part to stimulus of gravity

Ger. 1. German 2. Germany

geranium (ji'rāniəm) *n.* 1. common cultivated plant with red, pink or white flowers, pelargonium 2. strong pink color

gerbil

gerbil *or* **gerbille** ('jǝrbil) *n.* burrowing desert rodent of Asia and Afr. with long hind legs adapted for leaping

gerent ('jēǝrǝnt) *n.* ruler, governor, director

gerfalcon ('jǝrfalkǝn, -föl-) *n. see* GYRFALCON

geriatrics (jeri'atriks) *pl.n.* (*with sing. v.*) branch of medicine dealing with old age and its diseases —**geri'atric** *a./n.* old (person) —**geria'trician** *n.*

germ (jǝrm) *n.* 1. microbe, *esp.* causing disease 2. elementary thing 3. rudiment of new organism, of animal or plant —**germi-'cidal** *a.* —**'germicide** *n.* substance for destroying disease germs —**germ cell** sexual reproductive cell —**germ theory** theory that certain diseases are caused by specific microbes —**germ warfare** use of bacteria against enemy

german ('jǝrmǝn) *a.* 1. of the same parents 2. closely akin (*only in* **brother-, sister-, cousin-german**)

German ('jǝrmǝn) *n./a.* (language or native) of Germany —**Ger'manic** *n.* 1. branch of Indo-European family of languages including Dutch, German *etc.* 2. unrecorded language from which these languages developed (*also* **Proto-Germanic**) —*a.* 3. of this group of languages 4. of Germany, German language or any people that speaks Germanic language —**German measles** *see* RUBELLA —**German shepherd** large wolflike breed of dog

German Democratic Republic country in Europe bounded north by the Baltic Sea, east by Poland, south by Czechoslovakia and south and west by the Federal Republic of Germany (*also* **East Germany**)

germander (jǝr'mandǝr) *n.* European plant having two-lipped flowers with very small upper lip

germane (jǝr'mān) *a.* relevant, pertinent

germanium (jǝr'māniǝm) *n. Chem.* metallic element *Symbol* Ge, at. wt. 72.6, at. no. 32

Germany ('jǝrmǝni) *n.* —**Federal Republic of Germany** country in Europe bounded north by the North Sea, Denmark and the Baltic Sea, east by the German Democratic Republic, Czechoslovakia and Austria, south by Austria and Switzerland and west by France, Luxembourg, Belgium and the Netherlands (*also* **West Germany**)

germinate ('jǝrmināt) *v.* (cause to) sprout or begin to grow —**germi'nation** *n.* —**'germinative** *a.*

gerontology (jerǝn'tolǝji) *n.* scientific study of ageing and problems of elderly people —**geron'tologist** *n.*

gerrymander (jeri'mandǝr, 'jerimandǝr) *vt.* 1. divide constituencies of (voting area) so as to give one party unfair advantage 2. manipulate or adapt to one's advantage —*n.* 3. act or result of gerrymandering

gerund ('jerǝnd) *n.* noun formed from verb, *eg* living

gerundive (ji'rundiv) *n.* 1. in Latin grammar, adjective formed from verb, expressing desirability *etc.* of activity denoted by verb —*a.* 2. of gerund or gerundive

gesso ('jesō) *n.* 1. white ground of plaster and size, used to prepare panels *etc.* for painting *etc.* 2. any white substance, *esp.* plaster of Paris, that forms ground when mixed with water

Gestapo (ge'stäpō) *n.* secret state police in Nazi Germany

gestate (je'stāt) *v.* carry (developing young) in uterus during pregnancy —**ges'tation** *n.* period of pregnancy in mammals

gesticulate (je'stikyǝlāt) *vi.* use expressive movements of hands and arms when speaking —**gesticu'lation** *n.*

gesture ('jeschǝr) *n.* 1. movement to convey meaning 2. indication of state of mind —*vi.* 3. make such a movement

get (get) *vt.* 1. obtain, procure 2. contract 3. catch 4. earn 5. cause to go or come 6. bring into position or state 7. induce 8. engender 9. *inf.* understand —*vi.* 10. succeed in coming or going 11. (*oft. with* to) reach, attain 12. become (**got** *pt.,* **got** *or* **gotten** *pp.,* **'getting** *pr.p.*) —**'getaway** *n.* escape —**get-together** *n. inf.* small informal social gathering —**get-up** *n. inf.* 1. costume, outfit 2. arrangement of book *etc.* —**get-up-and-go** *n. inf.* energy, drive —**get across** (cause to) be understood —**get at** 1. gain access to 2. mean, intend 3. annoy 4. criticize 5. influence —**get by** *inf.* manage, *esp.* in spite of difficulties —**get on** 1. grow late 2. (of person) grow old 3. make progress, manage, fare 4. (*oft. with* with) establish friendly relationship 5. (*with* with) continue to do —**get (one's) goat** *sl.* make (one) angry, annoyed —**get one's own back** *inf.* obtain one's revenge —**have got** possess —**have got to** must, have to

geum ('jēǝm) *n.* garden plant with orange, yellow or white flowers

geyser ('gīzǝr) *n.* hot spring throwing up spout of water from time to time

Ghana ('gänǝ, 'gan-) *n.* country in Africa bounded south by Atlantic, west by Ivory Coast and Burkina-Faso, north by Burkina-Faso and east by Togo

ghastly ('gastli) *a.* 1. *inf.* unpleasant 2. deathlike, pallid 3. *inf.* unwell 4. horrible —*adv.* 5. sickly

ghat (göt) *n.* (in India) 1. stairs leading down to river 2. mountain pass

ghee (gē) *n.* clarified butter or vegetable fat used in cuisine of India, Pakistan and Bangladesh

gherkin ('gǝrkin) *n.* small cucumber used in pickling

ghetto ('getō) *n.* densely populated (*esp.* by one racial group) slum area (*pl.* **-s, -es**)

ghost (gōst) *n.* 1. spirit, dead person appearing again 2. specter 3. semblance 4. faint trace 5. one who writes work to appear under another's name —*v.* 6. ghostwrite —*vt.* 7. haunt —**'ghostly** *a.* —**ghost town** deserted town, *esp.* one in western U.S.A. that was formerly a boom town —**'ghostwrite** *v.* write (article *etc.*) on behalf of person who is then credited as author (*also* **ghost**) —**'ghostwriter** *n.*

ghoul (gōol) *n.* 1. malevolent spirit 2. person with morbid interests 3. fiend —**'ghoulish** *a.* 1. of or like ghoul 2. horrible

G.H.Q. *Mil.* General Headquarters

GI (*short for* **Government Issue**, stamped on U.S. military equipment) *inf.* U.S. soldier

giant ('jīǝnt) *n.* 1. mythical being of superhuman size 2. very tall person, plant *etc.* —*a.* **3.** huge —**gi'gantic** *a.* enormous, huge —**gi'gantism** *n.* abnormal growth of the skeleton caused by disorder of the endocrine glands

giaour ('jowər) *n. derogatory* non-Muslim, *esp.* Christian

gib (gib) *n.* **1.** metal wedge, pad or thrust bearing let into steam engine crosshead —*vt.* **2.** fasten or supply with gib (-**bb**-)

Gib (jib) *n. inf.* Gibraltar

gibber ('jibər) *vi.* **1.** make meaningless sounds with mouth **2.** jabber, chatter —**'gibberish** *n.* meaningless speech or words

gibbet ('jibit) *n.* **1.** gallows **2.** post with arm on which executed criminals were formerly hung **3.** death by hanging —*vt.* **4.** hang on gibbet **5.** hold up to scorn

gibbon ('gibən) *n.* small tailless arboreal ape of E Indies and southern Asia

gibbous ('jibəs, 'gib-) *a.* **1.** (of moon *etc.*) more than half illuminated **2.** hunchbacked **3.** bulging —**'gibbousness** or **gibbosity** (ji'bositi, gi-) *n.*

gibe or **jibe** (jīb) *v.* **1.** utter taunts (at) **2.** mock **3.** jeer —*n.* **4.** provoking remark

giblets ('jiblits) *pl.n.* internal edible parts of fowl, as liver, gizzard *etc.*

Gibraltar (ji'brôltər) *n.* crown colony of United Kingdom with area of 2 ¹/₂ sq. mi. at the extreme south of Spain and the western entrance to the Mediterranean

Gibson ('gibsən) *n.* drink made of gin and vermouth and garnished with a cocktail onion

giddy ('gidi) *a.* **1.** dizzy, feeling as if about to fall **2.** liable to cause this feeling **3.** flighty, frivolous —**'giddily** *adv.* —**'giddiness** *n.*

gift (gift) *n.* **1.** thing given, present **2.** faculty, power —*vt.* **3.** present, endow, bestow —**'gifted** *a.* talented —**gift certificate** voucher given as present which recipient can exchange for gift

gig (gig) *n.* **1.** light, two-wheeled carriage **2.** *inf.* single booking of musicians to play at concert *etc.* **3.** cluster of fish hooks

giga- ('jigə-, 'gigə-) (*comb. form*) 10⁹, as in *gigavolt*

gigantic (jī'gantik) *a. see* GIANT

giggle ('gigəl) *vi.* **1.** laugh nervously, foolishly —*n.* **2.** such a laugh **3.** joke

GIGO ('gigō) *Comp.* garbage in, garbage out

gigolo ('jigəlō, 'zhig-) *n.* **1.** man kept by (older) woman **2.** man paid to escort women

gigot ('jigət) *n.* **1.** leg of lamb or mutton **2.** leg-of-mutton sleeve

Gilchrist's disease ('gilkrists) *see* BLASTOMYCOSIS

gild¹ (gild) *vt.* **1.** put thin layer of gold on **2.** make falsely attractive (**'gilded** *pt.*, **gilt** or **'gilded** *pp.*) —**gilt** *a.* **1.** gilded —*n.* **2.** thin layer of gold applied in gilding **3.** superficial appearance —**gilt-edged** *a.* **1.** (of securities) dated over short, medium, or long term, and characterized by minimum risk and usu. issued by Government **2.** (of books *etc.*) having gilded edges

gild² (gild) *n. see* GUILD

gill¹ (gil) *n.* (*usu. pl.*) breathing organ in fish

gill² (jil) *n.* liquid measure comprising 4 fluid ounces, equal to 7.219 cubic inches or 118.291 milliliters

gillie, ghillie, or **gilly** ('gili) *n.* in Scotland, attendant for hunting or fishing

gill-over-the-ground (jil-) *n. see* **ground ivy** *at* GROUND¹

gillyflower or **gilliflower** ('jiliflowər) *n.* fragrant flower

gilt (gilt) *n.* young female pig

gimbals ('jimbəlz, 'gim-) *pl.n.* pivoted rings, for keeping things, *eg* compass, horizontal at sea

gimcrack ('jimkrak) *a.* **1.** cheap; shoddy —*n.* **2.** cheap showy trifle

gimlet ('gimlit) *n.* boring tool, usu. with screw point —**'gimlet-eyed** *a.* having a piercing glance

gimmick ('gimik) *n.* clever device, stratagem *etc.*, *esp.* designed to attract attention or publicity

gimp or **guimpe** (gimp) *n.* narrow fabric or braid used as edging or trimming

gin¹ (jin) *n.* spirit flavored with juniper berries —**gin rummy** form of rummy for two players in which 'gin' is called by player melding all ten cards

gin² (jin) *n.* **1.** primitive engine in which vertical shaft is turned to drive horizontal beam in a circle **2.** machine for separating cotton from seeds **3.** snare, trap

ginger ('jinjər) *n.* **1.** plant with hot-tasting spicy root used in cooking *etc.* **2.** the root **3.** *inf.* spirit, mettle **4.** light reddish-yellow color —**'gingery** *a.* **1.** of, like ginger **2.** hot **3.** high-spirited **4.** reddish —**ginger ale** ginger-flavored carbonated drink —**ginger beer** drink resembling ginger ale but with stronger ginger flavor —**'gingerbread** *n.* cake flavored with ginger —**ginger snap** crisp cookie flavored with ginger

gingerly ('jinjərli) *adv.* **1.** cautiously, warily, reluctantly —*a.* **2.** cautious, reluctant or timid

gingham ('gingəm) *n.* cotton cloth, usu. checked, woven from dyed yarn

gingivitis (jinji'vītis) *n.* inflammation of gums

ginkgo or **gingko** ('gingkō, 'gingkgō) *n.* ornamental Chinese tree (*pl.* -**es**)

ginseng ('jinsang, -seng) *n.* **1.** plant of China or of N Amer., whose roots are used medicinally **2.** root of this plant or substance obtained from root

gip (jip) *see* GYP

Gipsy ('jipsi) *n. see* GYPSY

giraffe (ji'raf) *n.* Afr. ruminant animal, with spotted coat and very long neck and legs

gird¹ (gərd) *vt.* **1.** put belt round **2.** fasten (clothing) thus **3.** equip with sword **4.** prepare (oneself) **5.** encircle (**girt, 'girded** *pt./pp.*) —**'girder** *n.* large beam, *esp.* of steel

gird² (gərd) *dial. v.* **1.** jeer (at); mock —*n.* **2.** taunt; gibe

girdle ('gərdəl) *n.* **1.** corset **2.** waistband **3.** anything that surrounds, encircles —*vt.* **4.** surround, encircle

girl (gərl) *n.* **1.** female child **2.** young (unmarried) woman —**'girlhood** *n.* —**'girlie** *a. inf.* (of magazine) featuring nude or scantily dressed women —**'girlish** *a.* —**girl Friday** female employee with wide range of secretarial and clerical duties —**'girlfriend** *n.* **1.** female friend with whom male is romantically or sexually involved **2.** any female friend —**Girl Scout** member of U.S. organization for girls founded in 1912 to foster citizenship, character, health and skills

girt¹ (gərt) *pt./pp. of* GIRD¹

girt² (gərt) *vt.* **1.** bind; encircle; gird **2.** measure girth of

girth (gərth) *n.* **1.** measurement around something **2.** leather or cloth band put around horse's belly to hold saddle *etc.* —*vt.* **3.** surround, secure with girth

gist (jist) *n.* substance, main point (of remarks *etc.*)

give (giv) *vt.* **1.** bestow, confer ownership of, make present of **2.** deliver **3.** impart **4.** assign **5.** yield, supply **6.** utter, emit **7.** be host of (party *etc.*) **8.** make over **9.** cause to have —*vi.* **10.** yield, give way, move (**gave, 'given, 'giving**) —*n.* **11.** yielding, elasticity —**give-**

and-take *n.* **1.** mutual concessions, shared benefits and cooperation **2.** smoothly flowing exchange of ideas and talk —**'giveaway** *n.* **1.** betrayal or disclosure, *esp.* when unintentional —*a.* **2.** very cheap (*esp. in* giveaway prices) —**give and take** make mutual concessions —**give away 1.** donate or bestow as gift *etc.* **2.** sell very cheaply **3.** reveal, betray **4.** fail to use (opportunity) through neglect **5.** present (bride) formally to her husband in marriage ceremony —**give or take** plus or minus —**give up 1.** acknowledge defeat **2.** abandon

gizzard ('gizərd) *n.* part of bird's stomach

Gjetost ('yetöst) *n. see* MYSOST

glabrous ('glābrəs) *a. Biol.* without hairs or any unevenness; smooth

glacé (gla'sā) *a.* **1.** crystallized, candied, iced **2.** glossy

glacier ('glāshər, -zhər) *n.* river of ice, slow-moving mass of ice formed by accumulated snow in mountain valleys —**glacial** ('glāshəl) *a.* **1.** of ice, or of glaciers **2.** very cold —**glaciated** ('glāshiātid) *a.* —**glaciation** (glāshi'āshən, -si-) *n.* —**glacial period** time when large part of earth's surface was covered by ice

glad (glad) *a.* **1.** pleased **2.** happy, joyous **3.** giving joy —**'gladden** *vt.* make glad —**'gladly** *adv.* —**'gladness** *n.* —**glad eye** *inf.* inviting or seductive glance (*esp. in* give (someone) the glad eye) —**'gladrags** *pl.n. sl.* clothes for special occasions

glade (glād) *n.* clear, grassy space in wood or forest

gladiator ('gladiātər) *n.* trained fighter in Roman arena

gladiolus (gladi'ōləs) *n.* kind of iris, with sword-shaped leaves (*pl.* -**lus, -li** (-lī))

glair (glâər) *n.* **1.** white of egg **2.** sticky substance —*vt.* **3.** smear with white of egg —**'glairy** *a.*

glamour or **glamor** ('glamər) *n.* alluring charm, fascination —**'glamorize** or **'glamourize** *vt.* make appear glamorous —**'glamorous** or **'glamourous** *a.*

glance (glans) *vi.* **1.** look rapidly or briefly **2.** allude briefly to or touch on subject **3.** (*usu. with* off) glide off (something struck) —*n.* **4.** brief look **5.** flash **6.** gleam **7.** sudden (deflected) blow

gland (gland) *n.* one of various small organs controlling different bodily functions by chemical means —**'glanders** *n.* contagious horse disease —**'glandular** *a.* —**glandular fever** acute disease characterized by fever, swollen lymph nodes *etc.* (*also* **infectious mononucleosis**)

glare (glâər) *vi.* **1.** look fiercely **2.** shine brightly, intensely **3.** be conspicuous —*n.* **4.** angry stare **5.** dazzling light —**'glaring** *a.*

glass (glas) *n.* **1.** hard transparent substance made by fusing sand, soda, potash *etc.* **2.** things made of it **3.** tumbler **4.** its contents **5.** lens **6.** mirror **7.** telescope **8.** barometer **9.** microscope —*pl.* **10.** eyeglasses —**'glassily** *adv.* —**'glassiness** *n.* —**'glassy** *a.* **1.** like glass **2.** expressionless —**glass-blower** *n.* —**glass-blowing** *n.* process of shaping molten glass by blowing air into it through tube —**glass harmonica** musical instrument consisting of series of graded glass disks which produces sound by rubbing the fingers against the wetted rims —**'glasshouse** *n.* **1.** greenhouse **2.** *inf.* army prison —**glass wool** spun glass in fluffy mass used for thermal insulation and filtering air

Glaswegian (glas'wējən) *a.* **1.** of Glasgow, city in Scotland —*n.* **2.** native or inhabitant of Glasgow

glaucoma (glow'kōmə, glŏ-) *n.* eye disorder in which there is an increase in the fluid pressure within the eye leading to progressive loss of vision and eventual blindness —**glau'comatous** *a.*

glaucous ('glôkəs) *a.* 1. *Bot.* covered with waxy or powdery bloom 2. bluish-green

glaze (glāz) *vt.* 1. furnish with glass 2. cover with glassy substance —*vi.* 3. become glassy —*n.* 4. transparent coating 5. substance used for this 6. glossy surface —**glazier** ('glāzhər) *n.* person who glazes windows

gleam (glēm) *n.* 1. slight or passing beam of light 2. faint or momentary show —*vi.* 3. give out gleams

glean (glēn) *v.* 1. pick up (facts *etc.*) 2. gather (useful remnants of crop) in cornfields after harvesting —**'gleaner** *n.* —**'gleanings** *pl.n.*

glebe (glēb) *n.* land belonging to parish church or benefice

glee (glē) *n.* 1. mirth, merriment 2. musical composition for three or more voices —**'gleeful** *a.* —**'gleefully** *adv.* —**glee club** choral society

glen (glen) *n.* narrow valley, usu. wooded and with a stream, *esp.* in Scotland

glengarry (glen'gari) *n.* Scottish woolen boat-shaped cap with ribbons hanging down back

glib (glib) *a.* 1. fluent but insincere or superficial 2. plausible —**'glibly** *adv.* —**'glibness** *n.*

glide (glīd) *vi.* 1. pass smoothly and continuously 2. (of airplane) move without use of engines —*n.* 3. smooth, silent movement 4. *Mus.* sounds made in passing from tone to tone —**'glider** *n.* aircraft without engine which moves in air currents —**'gliding** *n.* sport of flying gliders

glimmer ('glimər) *vi.* 1. shine faintly, flicker —*n.* 2. glow or twinkle of light —**'glimmering** *n.* 1. faint gleam of light 2. faint idea, notion

glimpse (glimps) *n.* 1. brief or incomplete view —*vt.* 2. catch glimpse of

glint (glint) *v.* 1. flash 2. glance, glitter 3. reflect —*n.* 4. bright gleam; flash

glissade (gli'säd, -'sād) *n.* 1. gliding dance step 2. slide, usu. on feet down slope of ice —*vi.* 3. perform glissade

glisten ('glisən) *vi.* gleam by reflecting light

glister ('glistər) *vi./n. obs.* glitter

glitter ('glitər) *vi.* 1. shine with bright quivering light, sparkle 2. be showy —*n.* 3. luster 4. sparkle —**glitter ice** C ice formed from freezing rain

gloaming ('glōming) *n. Scot., poet.* evening twilight

gloat (glōt) *vi.* regard, dwell (on) with smugness or malicious satisfaction

glob (glob) *n. inf.* soft lump or mass

globe (glōb) *n.* 1. sphere with map of earth or stars 2. heavenly sphere, *esp.* the earth 3. ball, sphere —**'global** *a.* —**'globular** ('globyələr) *a.* globe-shaped —**globule** ('globyōōl) *n.* 1. small round particle 2. drop —**'globetrotter** *n.* (habitual) worldwide traveler —**the globe** the world; the earth

globulin ('globyəlin) *n.* class of proteins found in all living organisms

glockenspiel ('glokənspēl, -shpēl) *n.* percussion instrument of metal bars which are struck with hammers

glomerate ('glomərit) *a.* 1. gathered into rounded mass 2. *Anat.* (*esp.* of glands) conglomerate in structure

glomerulonephritis (gləmeryəlōni'frītis, -merə-) *n.* kidney infection affecting children and young adults

gloom (glōōm) *n.* 1. darkness 2. melancholy, depression —**'gloomily** *adv.* —**'gloomy** *a.*

glory ('glōri) *n.* 1. renown, honorable fame 2. splendor 3. exalted or prosperous state 4. heavenly bliss —*vi.* 5. take pride ('gloried, 'glorying) —**glorifi'cation** *n.* —**'glorify** *vt.* 1. make glorious 2. invest with glory (-ified, -ifying) —**'glorious** *a.* 1. illustrious 2. splendid 3. excellent 4. delightful —**'gloriously** *adv.* —**glory hole** *inf.* untidy cupboard, room or receptacle for storage

gloss¹ (glos) *n.* 1. surface shine, luster —*vt.* 2. put gloss on 3. (*esp. with* over) (try to) cover up, pass over (fault, error) —**'glossiness** *n.* —**'glossy** *a.* 1. smooth, shiny —*n.* 2. photograph printed on shiny paper

gloss² (glos) *n.* 1. marginal interpretation of word 2. comment, explanation —*vt.* 3. interpret 4. comment 5. (*oft. with* over) explain away —**'glossary** *n.* list of items peculiar to a field of knowledge with explanations

glossitis (glo'sītis) *n.* inflammation of the tongue

glottis ('glotis) *n.* human vocal apparatus, larynx (*pl.* **-es, -tides** (-tidēz)) —**'glottal** or **'glottic** *a.*

glove (gluv) *n.* 1. (*oft. pl.*) covering for the hand —*vt.* 2. cover with, or as with glove —**glove compartment** small storage area in dashboard of automobile —**the gloves** 1. boxing gloves 2. boxing

glow (glō) *vi.* 1. give out light and heat without flames 2. shine 3. experience feeling of wellbeing or satisfaction 4. be or look hot 5. burn with emotion —*n.* 6. shining heat 7. warmth of color 8. feeling of wellbeing 9. ardor —**glow-worm** *n.* female insect giving out green light

glower ('glowər) *vi.* 1. scowl —*n.* 2. sullen or angry stare

gloxinia (glok'siniə) *n.* tropical plant with large bell-shaped flowers

glucose ('glōōkōs, -kōz) *n.* 1. type of sugar found in fruit *etc.* 2. syrup made from cornstarch

glue (glōō) *n.* 1. any natural or synthetic adhesive 2. any sticky substance —*vt.* 3. fasten with glue —**'gluey** *a.*

glum (glum) *a.* sullen, moody, gloomy

glut (glut) *n.* 1. surfeit, excessive amount —*vt.* 2. feed, gratify to the full or to excess 3. overstock (market *etc.*) with commodity (-tt-)

gluten ('glōōtən) *n.* protein present in strong wheat flour —**'glutinous** *a.* sticky, gluey

glutton¹ ('glutən) *n.* 1. greedy person 2. one with great liking or capacity for something —**'gluttonous** *a.* like glutton, greedy —**'gluttony** *n.*

glutton² ('glutən) *n.* wolverine

glycerin, glycerine ('glisərin), *or* **glycerol** ('glisərŏl) *n.* colorless sweet liquid with wide application in chemistry and industry

glycogen ('glīkəjən) *n.* polysaccharide consisting of glucose units: form in which carbohydrate is stored in animals —**glyco'genesis** *n.* —**glyco'genic** *a.*

glyptic ('gliptik) *a.* pert. to carving, *esp.* on precious stones

gm. gram

G-man *n.* 1. FBI agent 2. *Irish* political detective

GMT Greenwich Mean Time

gnarled (närld) *or* **gnarly** *a.* 1. knobby, rugged 2. (*esp.* of hands) twisted

gnash (nash) *vt.* grind (teeth) together as in anger or pain

gnat (nat) *n.* small, biting, two-winged fly

gnaw (nô) *v.* 1. bite or chew steadily 2. (*esp. with* at) cause distress (to)

gneiss (nīs) *n.* coarse-grained metamorphic rock

gnome (nōm) *n.* legendary creature like small old man —**Gnomes of Zürich** important Swiss financial institutions

gnomic ('nōmik) *a.* of or like an aphorism

gnomon ('nōmon) *n.* 1. stationary arm that projects shadow on sundial 2. geometric figure remaining after parallelogram has been removed from corner of larger parallelogram 3. term of a certain kind of arithmetical progression

gnostic ('nostik) *a.* 1. of, relating to knowledge, *esp.* spiritual knowledge —*n.* 2. (G-) adherent of Gnosticism —**'Gnosticism** *n.* religious movement characterized by belief in intuitive spiritual knowledge: regarded as heresy by Christian Church

GNP Gross National Product

gnu (nyōō, nōō) *n.* S Afr. antelope somewhat like ox (*pl.* **-s, gnu**)

go¹ (gō) *vi.* 1. move along, make way 2. be moving 3. depart 4. function 5. make specified sound 6. fail, give way, break down 7. elapse 8. be kept, put 9. be able to be put 10. result 11. (*with* toward) contribute to (result) 12. (*with* toward) tend to 13. be accepted, have force 14. become (**went** *pt.*, **gone** *pp.*) —*n.* 15. going 16. energy, vigor 17. attempt 18. turn —**'goer** *n.* 1. person who attends something regularly, as in *moviegoer* 2. person or thing that goes, *esp.* very fast —**'going** *n.* 1. departure; farewell 2. condition of road surface with regard to walking *etc.* 3. *inf.* speed, progress *etc.* —*a.* 4. thriving (*esp. in* **a going concern**) 5. current; accepted 6. available —**goner** ('gonər) *n.* person beyond help or recovery, *esp.* person about to die —**go-ahead** *n.* 1. *inf.* permission to proceed —*a.* 2. enterprising, ambitious —**go-between** *n.* person who acts as intermediary for two people or groups —**go-cart** *n.* 1. baby stroller 2. baby walker 3. handcart, pushcart 4. vehicle used in soapbox derby —**go-getter** *n. inf.* ambitious person —**go-go dancer** dancer, usu. scantily dressed, who performs rhythmic and oft. erotic modern dance routines in nightclubs *etc.* —**going-over** *n. inf.* 1. check; examination; investigation 2. castigation; thrashing (*pl.* **goings-over**) —**goings-on** *pl.n. inf.* 1. actions or conduct, *esp.* regarded with disapproval 2. happenings or events, *esp.* mysterious or suspicious —**go down** 1. move to lower place or level; sink, decline, decrease *etc.* 2. be received or accepted 3. be remembered or recorded (*esp. in* **go down in history**) —**go down on** perform fellatio or cunnilingus on

go² (gō) *n.* board game for two players played with 181 stones each on a board with 19 equidistant lines parallel to one edge and 19 lines at right angles to them, the object of the game being to occupy the territory of the board —**go moku** ('mōkōō) *or* **bang** game played on go board whose object is to place five stones in a row

goad (gōd) *n.* 1. spiked stick for driving cattle 2. anything that urges to action 3. incentive —*vt.* 4. urge on 5. torment

goal (gōl) *n.* 1. end of race 2. object of effort 3. posts through which ball is to be driven in football *etc.* 4. the score so made —**'goalkeeper** *n. Sport* player in goal whose duty is to prevent ball from entering it

goat (gōt) *n.* four-footed animal with long hair, horns and beard —**goa'tee** *n.* pointed tuftlike beard growing on chin —**goat-herd** *n.* —**'goatsucker** *n.* nightjar —**get (someone's) goat** *sl.* annoy (someone)

gob (gob) *n.* 1. lump 2. (*usu. pl*) large amount *sl.* —**'gobbet** *n.* lump (of food) —**'gobble** *v.* eat hastily, noisily or greedily

gobble ('gobəl) n. 1. throaty, gurgling cry of the turkey-cock —vi. 2. make this sound —'**gobbler** n. male turkey

gobbledygook or **gobbledegook** (gobəldi-'gōōk, -'gōōk) n. pretentious language, esp. as used by officials

goblet ('goblit) n. drinking cup

goblin ('goblin) n. Folklore small, usu. malevolent being

goby ('gōbi) n. small spiny-finned fish having ventral fins modified as sucker

god (god) n. 1. superhuman being worshiped as having supernatural power 2. object of worship, idol 3. (G-) in monotheistic religions, the Supreme Being, creator and ruler of the universe ('**goddess** fem.) —'**godlike** a. —'**godliness** n. —'**godly** a. devout, pious —'**godchild** n. person sponsored by adults at baptism ('**godson** or '**goddaughter**) —**god-fearing** a. religious, good —'**godforsaken** a. hopeless, dismal —'**godhead** n. divine nature or deity —'**godparent** n. sponsor at baptism ('**godfather** or '**godmother**) —'**godsend** n. something unexpected but welcome —**God'speed** interj./n. expression of good wishes for person's success and safety

godetia (gə'dēshə) n. annual garden plant

godwit ('godwit) n. large shore bird of N regions

gofer ('gōfər) n. person in office who runs errands

goffer ('gōfər) vt. 1. press pleats into (frill) 2. decorate (edges of book) —n. 3. ornamental frill made by pressing pleats 4. decoration formed by goffering books

goggle ('gogəl) vi. 1. (of eyes) bulge 2. stare —pl.n. 3. protective eyeglasses —**goggle-eyed** a. having bulging eyes

Goidelic (goi'delik) n. 1. N group of Celtic languages, consisting of Irish Gaelic, Scottish Gaelic and Manx —a. 2. of or characteristic of this group of languages

goiter ('goitər) n. enlargement of thyroid gland.

gold (gōld) n. 1. Chem. yellow noble metal used for coins, jewelry and as a medium of exchange Symbol Au, at. wt. 197.0, at. no. 79 2. coins made of this 3. wealth 4. beautiful or precious thing 5. color of gold —a. 6. of, like gold —'**golden** a. —'**goldcrest** n. Eurasian songbird with yellow crown —**gold-digger** n. woman skillful in extracting money from men —**golden age 1.** Class. myth. first and best age of mankind, when existence was happy, prosperous and innocent 2. most flourishing period, esp. in history of art or nation —**golden boy** or **girl** a popular or successful person —**golden eagle** large eagle of mountainous regions of N hemisphere —**Golden Fleece** Gr. myth. fleece of winged ram stolen by Jason and Argonauts —**golden hamster** tawny species of hamster, popular as pet and used as laboratory animal —**golden handshake** inf. money given to employee on retirement or for loss of employment —**golden mean** middle course between extremes —'**goldenrod** n. tall plant with golden flower spikes —**golden rule** important principle of action —**golden wedding** fiftieth wedding anniversary —'**goldfield** n. place where gold deposits are known to exist —'**goldfish** n. any of various ornamental pond or aquarium fish —**gold mine 1.** place where gold is mined 2. a source of great wealth —**gold plate 1.** thin coating of gold, usu. produced by electroplating 2. vessels or utensils made of gold —**gold-plate** vt. —**gold reserve** gold held by central bank to guarantee value of a country's currency —**gold rush** large-scale migration of people to territory where gold

has been found —'**goldsmith** n. 1. dealer in articles made of gold 2. artisan who makes such articles —**gold standard** financial arrangement whereby currencies of countries accepting it are expressed in fixed terms of gold

Gold Coast former name of GHANA (also **Togoland**)

golf (golf) n. 1. outdoor game in which player attempts to propel a small resilient ball with clubs around a turfed course with widely spaced holes in regular progression with the smallest number of strokes —vi. 2. play this game —'**golfer** n. —**golf club 1.** long-shafted club with wood or metal head used to strike golf ball 2. (premises of) association of golf players, usu. having its own course and facilities —**golf course** area of open land on which golf is played —**golf links** golf course located by the sea

Golf (golf) n. word used in communications for the letter g

Goliath (gə'līəth) n. Bible Philistine giant killed by David with stone from sling

golly ('goli) interj. exclamation of mild surprise

-gon (comb. form) figure having specified number of angles, as in pentagon

gonad ('gōnad) n. gland producing gametes —**gonado'tropin** n. hormone which stimulates the gonads

gondola ('gondələ) n. Venetian canal boat —**gondo'lier** n. person who propels gondola

gone (gon) pp. of GO¹

gonfalon ('gonfələn, -lən) n. 1. banner hanging from crossbar, used esp. by certain medieval Italian republics 2. battle flag suspended crosswise on staff, usu. having serrated edge

gong (gong) n. 1. orchestral percussion instrument consisting of large circular bronze disk with turned edge and struck with a heavy bass-drum beater 2. anything used thus

gonorrhea (gonə'rēə) n. a venereal disease

good (gōōd) a. 1. commendable 2. right 3. proper 4. excellent 5. beneficial 6. well-behaved 7. virtuous 8. kind 9. financially safe or secure 10. adequate 11. sound 12. valid ('**better** comp., **best** sup.) —n. 13. benefit 14. wellbeing 15. profit —pl. 16. property 17. wares —'**goodly** a. large, considerable —'**goodness** n. —**Good Book** the Bible —**Good Conduct Medal** U.S. Army medal awarded to enlisted men for meritorious service —**Good Friday** see FRIDAY —**good-hearted** a. kind and generous —**Good Samaritan 1.** N.T. figure in one of Christ's parables who is example of compassion toward those in distress 2. kindly person who helps another in difficulty —**good sort** inf. agreeable person —**good turn** helpful, friendly act; good deed; favor —**good will 1.** kindly feeling, heartiness 2. value of a business in reputation etc. over and above its tangible assets —**goody-goody** n. 1. inf. smugly virtuous or sanctimonious person —a. 2. smug and sanctimonious

goodbye (gōōd'bī) interj./n. form of address on parting

gooey ('gōōi) a. inf. sticky, soft —**goo** n. inf. 1. sticky substance 2. coy or sentimental language or ideas

goof (gōōf) inf. n. 1. mistake 2. stupid person —vi. 3. make mistake —'**goofy** a. silly, sloppy

goon (gōōn) n. inf. stupid fellow

goosander (gōō'sandər) n. type of duck

goose (gōōs) n. 1. web-footed bird 2. its flesh 3. simpleton (pl. **geese**) —**goose flesh**

bristling of skin due to cold, fright —**goose step** formal parade step

gooseberry ('gōōsberi, 'gōōz-; -bri) n. 1. thorny shrub 2. its hairy fruit 3. inf. unwelcome third party (oft. in play gooseberry)

gopher ('gōfər) n. various species of Amer. burrowing rodents

Gordian knot ('gördiən) 1. in Greek legend, complicated knot, tied by King Gordius, that Alexander the Great cut with sword 2. intricate problem (esp. in cut the Gordian knot)

gore¹ (gör) n. (dried) blood from wound —'**gorily** adv. —'**gory** a. 1. horrific; bloodthirsty 2. involving bloodshed and killing 3. covered in gore

gore² (gör) vt. pierce with horns

gore³ (gör) n. 1. triangular piece inserted to shape garment —vt. 2. shape thus

Gore-tex ('görteks) n. trade name for laminated fabric used for protection from rain

gorge (görj) n. 1. ravine 2. disgust, resentment —vi. 3. eat greedily —'**gorget** n. armor, ornamentation or clothing for throat —**gorge oneself** stuff oneself with food

gorgeous ('görjəs) a. 1. splendid, showy, dazzling 2. inf. extremely pleasing

Gorgon ('görgən) n. terrifying or repulsive woman

Gorgonzola (görgən'zōlə) n. a semihard, blue-veined cheese made from cow's milk, with a rich, piquant flavor, orig. from Italy

gorilla (gə'rilə) n. largest anthropoid ape, found in Afr.

gormandize ('görməndīz) v. eat (food) hurriedly or like a glutton

gorse (görs) n. prickly shrub

gory ('göri) a. see GORE¹

gosh (gosh) interj. exclamation of mild surprise or wonder

goshawk ('gos-hök) n. large hawk

gosling ('gozling) n. young goose

gospel ('gospəl) n. 1. unquestionable truth 2. (G-) any of first four books of New Testament

gossamer ('gosəmər) n. 1. filmy substance like spider's web 2. thin gauze or silk fabric

gossip ('gosip) n. 1. idle (malicious) talk about other persons, esp. regardless of facts 2. one who talks thus (also '**gossipmonger**) —vi. 3. engage in gossip 4. chatter —**gossip column** part of newspaper devoted to gossip about well-known people

got (got) pt./pp. of GET

Goth (goth) n. 1. member of East Germanic people who invaded Roman Empire from 3rd to 5th cent. 2. rude or barbaric person —'**Gothic** a. 1. Archit. of the pointed arch style common in Europe from 12th-16th centuries 2. of Goths 3. (sometimes g-) barbarous 4. (sometimes g-) of literary style characterized by gloom, the grotesque, and the supernatural —n. 5. (of type) German black letter 6. bold type style without serifs

gotten ('gotən) pp. of GET

gouache (gwäsh) n. 1. painting technique using opaque watercolor in which pigments are bound with glue (also **body color**) 2. paint used in this technique 3. painting done by this method

Gouda ('gōōdə) n. a firm cheese of mild flavor made from cow's milk, shaped like disk and covered with red wax, orig. from Holland

gouge (gowj) vt. (usu. with out) 1. scoop out 2. force out —n. 3. chisel with curved cutting edge

goulash ('gŏōlăsh, -lash) *n.* stew of meat and vegetables seasoned with paprika (*also* **Hungarian goulash**)

gourds

gourd (gŏrd, gŏōərd) *n.* **1.** trailing or climbing plant **2.** its large fleshy fruit **3.** its rind as vessel

gourmand ('gŏōərmănd, -mənd) *n.* glutton —'**gourmandize** *v.*

gourmet ('gŏōərmă, gŏōr'mă) *n.* **1.** connoisseur of wine, food **2.** epicure

gout (gowt) *n.* disease characterized by inflammation, *esp.* of joints —'**gouty** *a.*

Gov. *or* **gov. 1.** government **2.** governor

govern ('gŭvərn) *vt.* **1.** rule, direct, guide, control **2.** decide, determine **3.** be followed by (grammatical case *etc.*) —'**governable** *a.* —'**governance** *n.* act of governing —'**governess** *n.* woman teacher, *esp.* in private household —'**government** *n.* **1.** exercise of political authority in directing a people, state *etc.* **2.** system by which community is ruled **3.** body of people in charge of government of state **4.** ministry in a parliamentary system **5.** executive power **6.** control **7.** direction **8.** exercise of authority —**govern'mental** *a.* —**governor** ('gŭvnər, 'guvənər, 'guvərnər) *n.* **1.** one who governs, *esp.* one invested with supreme authority in state *etc.* **2.** chief administrator of an institution **3.** member of committee responsible for an organization or institution **4.** regulator for speed of engine

Govt. *or* **govt.** government

gown (gown) *n.* **1.** loose flowing outer garment **2.** woman's (long) dress **3.** official robe, as in university *etc.*

goy (goi) *n.* (among Jews) a non-Jew (*pl.* **goyim** ('goiim), **-s**)

G.P. General Practitioner

GPO 1. General Post Office **2.** Government Printing Office

Gr. 1. Grecian **2.** Greece **3.** Greek

gr. 1. grade **2.** grain **3.** gram **4.** gravity **5.** gross

grab (grab) *vt.* **1.** grasp suddenly **2.** snatch (**-bb-**) —*n.* **3.** sudden clutch **4.** quick attempt to seize **5.** device or implement for clutching —**grab bag** box or bag containing small prizes for which children search

grace (grās) *n.* **1.** charm, elegance **2.** accomplishment **3.** good will, favor **4.** sense of propriety **5.** postponement granted **6.** short thanksgiving before or after meal **7.** title of duke or archbishop —*pl.* **8.** affectation of manner (*esp. in* **airs and graces**) —*vt.* **9.** add grace to, honor —'**graceful** *a.* —'**gracefully** *adv.* —'**graceless** *a.* shameless, depraved —'**gracious** *a.* **1.** favorable **2.** kind **3.** pleasing **4.** indulgent, beneficent, condescending —'**graciously** *adv.* —**grace note** *Mus.* melodic ornament

Graces ('grāsiz) *pl.n. Gr. myth.* three sister goddesses, givers of charm and beauty

grade (grād) *n.* **1.** step, stage **2.** degree of rank *etc.* **3.** class **4.** mark, rating **5.** slope —*vt.* **6.** arrange in classes **7.** assign grade to **8.** level (ground), move (earth) with grader —**gradation** (grā'dāshən, grə-) *n.* **1.** series of degrees or steps **2.** each of them **3.** arrangement in steps **4.** in painting, gradual

passing from one shade *etc.* to another —'**grader** *n.* **1.** person or thing that grades **2.** machine with wide blade used in road making —**make the grade** succeed

gradient ('grādiənt) *n.* (degree of) slope

gradual ('grajŏōəl) *a.* **1.** taking place by degrees **2.** slow and steady **3.** not steep —'**gradually** *adv.*

graduate ('grajŏōāt) *vi.* **1.** complete successful course of study, *esp.* university —*vt.* **2.** divide into degrees **3.** mark, arrange according to scale —*n.* ('grajŏōit) **4.** holder of diploma, certificate or degree —**gradu'ation** *n.*

graffiti (grə'fētē) *pl.n.* (*oft.* obscene) writing, drawing on walls (*sing.* **graf'fito**)

graft (graft) *n.* **1.** shoot of plant set in stalk of another **2.** the process **3.** surgical transplant of skin to an area of body in need of tissue —*vt.* **4.** insert (shoot) in another stalk **5.** transplant (living tissue in surgery)

graham ('grāəm) *a. see* **whole-grain** *at* WHOLE

Grail (grāl) *n. see* **Holy Grail** *at* HOLY

grain (grān) *n.* **1.** seed, fruit of cereal plant **2.** wheat and allied plants **3.** small hard particle **4.** unit of weight, 0.002083 ounce (0.0648 gram) in avoirdupois, troy or apothecaries' system **5.** texture **6.** arrangement of fibers **7.** any very small amount **8.** natural temperament or disposition —'**grainy** *a.*

gram *or* **gramme** (gram) *n.* unit of weight in metric system, one thousandth of a kilogram, about the weight of one cubic centimeter of water at 4° Celsius

-gram (*comb. form*) drawing; something written or recorded, as in *hexagram, telegram*

gramineous (grə'miniəs) *a.* **1.** of or belonging to grass family **2.** resembling grass; grasslike (*also* **graminaceous** (grami'nāshəs))

graminivorous (grami'nivərəs) *a.* (of animals) feeding on grass

grammar ('gramər) *n.* **1.** science of structure and usages of language **2.** book on this **3.** correct use of words —**grammarian** (grə'meriən, -'mar-) *n.* —**gram'matical** *a.* according to grammar —**gram'matically** *adv.* —**grammar school** elementary school

grampus ('grampəs) *n.* **1.** cetacean related to killer whale common in northern seas **2.** giant whip scorpion of southern U.S.

granary ('granəri) *n.* **1.** storehouse for grain **2.** rich grain growing region

grand (grand) *a.* **1.** imposing **2.** magnificent **3.** majestic **4.** noble **5.** splendid **6.** eminent **7.** lofty **8.** chief, of chief importance **9.** final (total) —**grandeur** ('granjər) *n.* **1.** nobility **2.** magnificence **3.** dignity —**gran'diloquence** *n.* —**gran'diloquent** *a.* pompous in speech —**gran'diloquently** *adv.* —'**grandiose** *a.* **1.** imposing **2.** affectedly grand **3.** striking —**grandchild** ('granchīld, 'grand-) *n.* child of one's child (**grandson** ('gransun, 'grand-) *or* **granddaughter** ('grandôtər, 'granddôtər)) —**grand duke 1.** prince or nobleman who rules territory, state or principality **2.** son or male descendant in male line of Russian czar —**grandfather clock** long-pendulum clock in tall standing wooden case —**grand jury** jury, comprising 12 to 33 persons, designated to inquire into accusations of crime and ascertain whether evidence is adequate to found indictment —**Grand National** annual steeplechase race at Aintree racecourse at Liverpool, England —**grand opera** opera with serious plot and fully composed text —**grandparent** ('granpərənt, 'grand-; -per-) *n.* parent of

parent (**grandfather** ('granfädhər, 'grand-) *or* **grandmother** ('granmudhər, 'grand-)) —**grand piano** large harp-shaped piano with horizontal strings —**grand slam** *Bridge* bidding for and winning all thirteen tricks —**Grand Slam 1.** *Tennis* winning of Australian, French, U.S. and Wimbledon championships within a calendar year **2.** *Golf* winning of a group of championships **3.** *Baseball* a home run with runners on all bases —**grandstand** ('granstand, 'grand-) *n.* structure with tiered seats for spectators

grande dame (grăd 'dam) *Fr.* woman regarded as most experienced or prominent member of her profession *etc.*

grandee (gran'dē) *n.* Spanish nobleman of highest rank

grand mal ('gränd 'mäl) form of epilepsy characterized by convulsions and loss of consciousness

Grand Prix (*Fr.* grä 'prē) any of series of international formula motor races

grange (grānj) *n.* **1.** country house with farm buildings **2.** (**G-**) lodge or local branch of the "Patrons of Husbandry", an association founded in 1867 to promote the interests of agriculture

granite ('granit) *n.* hard crystalline igneous rock —**gra'nitic** *a.*

granivorous (grə'nivərəs, grā-) *a.* feeding on grain or seeds

granny ('grani) *n. inf.* grandmother —**granny glasses** eyeglasses with round lenses and thin wire frames —**granny knot** square knot with loops crossed wrongly and thus insecure

grant (grant) *vt.* **1.** consent to fulfill (request) **2.** permit **3.** bestow **4.** admit —*n.* **5.** something bestowed, *esp.* land or money for a special purpose —**gran'tee** *n.* —'**granter** *or* (*Law*) '**grantor** *n.* —**grant-in-aid** *n.* money granted by central to local government for program *etc.* (*pl.* **grants-in-aid**)

Grant (grant) *n.* **Ulysses Simpson.** the 18th President of the U.S. (1869-73)

granule ('granyŏol) *n.* small grain —'**granular** *a.* of or like grains —'**granulate** *vt.* **1.** form into grains —*vi.* **2.** take form of grains —**granu'lation** *n.*

granuloma (granyə'lōmə) *n.* tumorlike nodule which develops in response to infection or irritation

grape (grāp) *n.* fruit of vine —**grape hyacinth** plant with clusters of small, rounded blue flowers —'**grapeshot** *n.* bullets scattering when fired —'**grapevine** *n.* **1.** grape-bearing vine **2.** *inf.* unofficial means of conveying information

grapefruit ('grāpfrŏot) *n.* subtropical citrus fruit

graph (graf) *n.* drawing depicting relation of different numbers, quantities *etc.* (*also* **chart**)

-graph (*n. comb. form*) **1.** instrument that writes or records, as in *telegraph* **2.** writing, record; drawing, as in *autograph, lithograph* —**-grapher** (*n. comb. form*) **1.** person skilled in subject, as in *geographer, photographer* **2.** person who writes or draws in specified way, as in *stenographer, lithographer* —**-graphic(al)** (*a. comb. form*) —**-graphy** (*n. comb. form*) **1.** form of writing, representing *etc.*, as in *calligraphy, photography* **2.** art; descriptive science, as in *choreography, oceanography*

graphic ('grafik) *or* **graphical** *a.* **1.** vividly descriptive **2.** of, in, relating to, writing, drawing, painting *etc.* —'**graphics** *pl.n.* **1.** (*with sing. v.*) art of drawing in accordance with mathematical principles 2. (*with sing. v.*) study of writing systems 3. (*with pl. v.*) drawings *etc.* in layout of magazine or book —'**graphite** *n.* form of carbon (used in pencils) —**gra'phol-ogy** *n.* study of handwriting —**graphic arts** fine or applied visual arts based on drawing or use of line, *esp.* illustration and print-making —**graph paper** paper with intersect-ing lines for drawing graphs *etc.*

grapnel ('grapnǝl) *n.* 1. hooked iron instru-ment for seizing anything 2. small anchor with several flukes

grapple ('grapǝl) *v.* 1. come to grips, wrestle 2. cope, contend —*n.* 3. grappling 4. grapnel —**grappling iron** grapnel, *esp.* for securing ships

GRAS list (gras) the official Food and Drug Administration list of food additives which are *generally recognized as safe*

grasp (grasp) *v.* 1. (try, struggle to) seize hold (of) —*vt.* 2. understand —*n.* 3. act of grasping 4. grip 5. comprehension —'**grasp-ing** *a.* greedy, avaricious

grass (gras) *n.* 1. common type of plant with jointed stems and long narrow leaves (including cereals, bamboo *etc.*) 2. such plants grown as lawn 3. pasture 4. *sl.* marijuana —*vt.* 5. cover with grass —**grass hockey** C hockey played on field —'**grass-hopper** *n.* jumping, chirping insect —**grass roots** fundamentals —'**grassroots** *a.* coming from ordinary people, the rank and file —**grass widow** wife whose husband is absent

grate[1] (grāt) *vt.* 1. rub into small bits on rough surface —*vi.* 2. rub with harsh noise 3. have irritating effect —'**grater** *n.* utensil with rough surface for reducing substance to small particles

grate[2] (grāt) *n.* framework of metal bars for holding fuel in fireplace —'**grating** *n.* framework of parallel or latticed bars covering opening

grateful ('grātfǝl) *a.* 1. thankful 2. apprecia-tive 3. pleasing —'**gratefully** *adv.* —'**grate-fulness** *n.* —**gratitude** ('gratityōōd, -tōōd) *n.* sense of being thankful for favor

gratify ('gratifī) *vt.* 1. satisfy 2. please 3. indulge —**gratifi'cation** *n.*

gratin (*Fr.* gra'tē) 1. method of cooking to form light crust 2. dish so cooked

gratis ('gratis, 'grātis) *adv./a.* free, for nothing

gratuitous (grǝ'tyōōitǝs, -'tōō-) *a.* 1. given free 2. uncalled-for —**gra'tuitously** *adv.* —**gra'tuity** *n.* 1. gift of money for services rendered 2. donation

gravamen (grǝ'vāmǝn) *n.* 1. *Law* part of accusation weighing most heavily against accused 2. *Law* substance of complaint 3. *rare* grievance (*pl.* -**vamina** (-'vaminǝ))

grave[1] (grāv) *n.* 1. hole dug to bury corpse 2. *Poet.* death —'**gravestone** *n.* monument on grave —'**graveyard** *n.*

grave[2] (grāv) *a.* 1. serious, weighty 2. dignified, solemn 3. plain, dark in color 4. deep in note —'**gravely** *adv.*

grave[3] (grāv) *vt.* clean (ship's bottom) by scraping —**graving dock** dry dock

grave[4] (gräv) *n. Phonet.* accent (`) used to indicate quality of vowel, full pronunciation of syllable *etc.*

gravel ('gravǝl) *n.* 1. small stones 2. coarse sand —*vt.* 3. cover with gravel —'**gravelly** *a.*

graven ('grāvǝn) *a.* carved, engraved

Graves (gräv) *n.* 1. (*sometimes* g-) white or red wine from district around Bordeaux, France 2. dry or medium sweet white wine from any country

gravid ('gravid) *a.* pregnant

gravimetric (gravi'metrik) *a.* 1. of measure-ment by weight 2. *Chem.* of analysis of quantities by weight

gravitate ('gravitāt) *vi.* 1. move by gravity 2. tend (toward center of attraction) 3. sink, settle down —**gravi'tation** *n.*

gravity ('graviti) *n.* 1. force of attraction of one body for another, *esp.* of objects to the earth 2. heaviness 3. importance 4. serious-ness 5. staidness

gravy ('grāvi) *n.* 1. juices from meat in cooking 2. sauce for food made from these —**gravy boat** small boat-shaped vessel for serving gravy

gray *or* **grey** (grā) *a.* 1. of color between black and white, as ashes or lead 2. clouded 3. dismal 4. turning white 5. aged 6. intermediate, indeterminate —*n.* 7. gray color 8. gray or whitish horse —'**grayling** *n.* fish of salmon family —**Gray Friar** Francis-can friar —'**grayhen** *n.* female of black grouse —'**grayhound** *n.* swift slender dog used in coursing and racing —'**graylag** *or* **graylag goose** *n.* large gray Eurasian goose —**gray matter** 1. grayish tissue of brain and spinal cord, containing nerve cell bodies and fibers 2. *inf.* brains; intellect

graze[1] (grāz) *v.* feed on (grass, pasture) —**grazier** ('grāzhǝr) *n.* one who raises cattle for market —'**grazing** *n.* 1. vegetation on ranges or pastures that is available for livestock to feed upon 2. land on which this is growing

graze[2] (grāz) *vt.* 1. touch lightly in passing, scratch, scrape —*n.* 2. grazing 3. abrasion

grease (grēs) *n.* 1. soft melted fat of animals 2. thick oil as lubricant —*vt.* (grēs, grēz) 3. apply grease to —'**greaser** *n.* 1. *offens.* native or inhabitant of Latin America, esp. Mexican 2. swaggering aggressive white male of working-class background —'**greasi-ly** *adv.* —'**greasiness** *n.* —'**greasy** *a.* —**grease gun** appliance for injecting oil or grease into machinery —**grease monkey** *inf.* mechanic —'**greasepaint** *n.* theatrical make-up —**grease pencil** crayon-like pencil used to mark glossy surfaces —**grease the palm** (*or* **hand**) **of** bribe

great (grāt) *a.* 1. large, big 2. important 3. pre-eminent, distinguished 4. *inf.* excellent —'**greatly** *adv.* —'**greatness** *n.* —**great circle** circular section of sphere with radius equal to that of sphere —'**greatcoat** *n.* overcoat, *esp.* military —**Great Dane** breed of very large dog —**Great Russian** *n.* 1. *Linguis.* Russian 2. member of chief East Slavonic people of Russia —*a.* 3. of this people or their language —**great seal** (*oft.* G- S-) principal seal of nation *etc.* used to authenticate documents of highest impor-tance

great- (*comb. form*) indicates a degree further removed in relationship, as in *great-grandfather*

Great Lakes chain of five large lakes along U.S.-Canadian border

Great Plains region in central North America

Great Salt Lake strongly saline lake in Utah

Great White Father American Indian name for U.S. president

Great White Way theater section of New York City on Broadway

greave (grēv) *n.* (*oft. pl.*) armor for leg below knee

grebe (grēb) *n.* aquatic diving bird

Grecian ('grēshǝn) *a.* of (ancient) Greece —**Grecian profile** profile in which nose and forehead form almost straight line

Greco- *or* **Graeco-** (*comb. form*) Greek, as in *Greco-Roman*

Greece (grēs) *n.* country in S Europe bounded north by Albania, Yugoslavia and Bulgaria, east by Turkey and the Aegean Sea, south by the Mediterranean and west by the Ionian Sea

greed (grēd) *n.* excessive consumption of, desire for, food, wealth —'**greedily** *adv.* —'**greediness** *n.* voracity of appetite —'**greedy** *a.* 1. gluttonous 2. eagerly desirous 3. voracious 4. covetous

Greek (grēk) *n.* 1. native language of Greece —*a.* 2. of Greece, the Greeks or the Greek language —**Greek cross** cross with four arms of same length —**Greek gift** gift given with harmful intent —**Greek Orthodox Church** 1. established Church of Greece, in which Metropolitan of Athens has primacy of honor (*also* **Greek Church**) 2. *see* **Orthodox Church** *at* ORTHODOX

green (grēn) *a.* 1. of color between blue and yellow in the spectrum 2. grass-colored 3. emerald 4. unripe 5. inexperienced 6. gullible 7. envious —*n.* 8. color 9. area of grass —*pl.* 10. green vegetables —'**greenery** *n.* vegeta-tion —**green bean** string bean —**green-eyed** *a.* jealous, envious —**green-eyed monster** jealousy, envy —'**greenfinch** *n.* European finch with dull green plumage in male —'**greenfly** *n.* aphid —'**greengage** *n.* kind of plum —'**greenhorn** *n.* inexperienced person, newcomer —'**greenhouse** *n.* building mainly of glass, with heat and humidity regulated for raising plants —**greenhouse effect** the insulating action of an atmospheric sub-stance, *esp.* carbon dioxide, which permits the heat of the sun to pass through to the earth and prevents the heat from leaving —**green light** 1. signal to go, *esp.* green traffic light 2. permission to proceed with project *etc.* —**green manure** crop plowed into soil to fertilize it —**green pepper** green unripe fruit of sweet pepper —'**greenroom** *n.* room for actors when offstage —'**green-shank** *n.* large European sandpiper —**greens keeper** person responsible for golf course —**greenstick fracture** fracture in children in which bone is partly bent and splinters only on convex side of bend —'**greenstone** *n.* New Zealand jade —'**greensward** *n.* turf —**green thumb** unusual ability to raise plants

Greenland ('grēnlǝnd) *n.* division of Den-mark occupying an island in the N Atlantic separated from Canada by Baffin Bay, Davis Strait and the Labrador Sea

Greenwich Mean Time *or* **Greenwich Time** ('grinij) local time of 0° meridian passing through Greenwich, England: stand-ard time for Britain and basis for calculating times throughout world

greet (grēt) *vt.* 1. meet with expressions of welcome 2. accost, salute 3. receive —'**greeting** *n.*

gregarious (gri'gariǝs, -'ger-) *a.* 1. fond of company, sociable 2. living in flocks —**gre'gariousness** *n.*

Gregorian calendar (gri'görien) calendar introduced by Pope Gregory XIII in 1582 and still in use

Gregorian chant *see* PLAINSONG

gremlin ('gremlin) *n. sl.* imaginary being blamed for mechanical and other troubles

Grenada (grǝ'nādǝ) *n.* country in the Caribbean Sea occupying the most southerly of the Windward Islands

grenade (gri'nād) *n.* explosive shell or bomb, thrown by hand or shot from rifle —**grenadier** (grenǝ'dēǝr) *n.* formerly, gre-nade thrower

grenadine (grenə'dēn, 'grenədēn) n. syrup made from pomegranate juice, for sweetening and coloring drinks

grew (grōō) pt. of GROW

grey (grā) see GRAY

grid (grid) n. 1. network of horizontal and vertical lines, bars etc. 2. any interconnecting system of links 3. national network of electricity supply

griddle ('gridəl) n. flat iron plate for cooking

gridiron ('gridīərn) n. 1. frame of metal bars for cooking on 2. football field

grief (grēf) n. deep sorrow —**grievance** n. real or imaginary grounds for complaint —**grieve** vi. 1. feel grief —vt. 2. cause grief to —'**grievous** a. 1. painful, oppressive 2. very serious —**grief-stricken** a. stricken with grief; sorrowful

griffin ('grifin), **griffon,** or **gryphon** n. fabulous monster with eagle's head and wings and lion's body

grill (gril) n. 1. device on cooker to radiate heat downwards, broiler 2. food cooked under it 3. gridiron —v. 4. cook (food) under broiler —vt. 5. subject to severe questioning —'**grilling** a. 1. very hot —n. 2. severe cross-examination —'**grillroom** n. informal dining room in hotel

grille or **grill** (gril) n. grating, crosswork of bars over opening

grilse (grils) n. salmon at stage when it returns for first time from sea (pl. **-s, grilse**)

grim (grim) a. 1. stern 2. of stern or forbidding aspect, relentless 3. joyless —'**grimly** adv.

grimace ('grimis, gri'mās) n. 1. wry face —vi. 2. pull wry face

grimalkin (gri'môlkin, -'mal-) n. 1. old cat, esp. female cat 2. crotchety or shrewish old woman

grime (grīm) n. 1. ingrained dirt, soot —vt. 2. soil, dirty, blacken —'**grimy** a.

grin (grin) vi. 1. show teeth, as in laughter (**-nn-**) —n. 2. grinning smile

grind (grīnd) vt. 1. crush to powder 2. oppress 3. make sharp, smooth 4. grate —vi. 5. perform action of grinding 6. inf. work, esp. study hard 7. grate (**ground** pt./pp.) —n. 8. inf. hard work 9. act of grinding —'**grinder** n. —'**grindstone** n. stone used for grinding

gringo ('gringgō) n. offens. (among Spanish Americans) a foreigner, esp. North American (pl. **-s**)

grip (grip) n. 1. firm hold, grasp 2. grasping power 3. mastery 4. handle 5. suitcase or traveling bag (also '**handgrip**) —vt. 6. grasp or hold tightly 7. hold interest or attention of (**-pp-**)

gripe (grīp) vi. 1. inf. complain (persistently) —n. 2. intestinal pain (esp. in infants) 3. inf. complaint

grippe (grip) n. influenza

grisly ('grizli) a. grim, causing terror, ghastly

grist (grist) n. corn to be ground —**grist to (**or **for) the (**or **one's) mill** something which can be turned to advantage

gristle ('grisəl) n. cartilage, tough flexible tissue

grit (grit) n. 1. rough particles of sand 2. coarse sandstone 3. courage —n./a. 4. (**G-**) C inf. Liberal —pl. 5. wheat etc. coarsely ground —vt. 6. clench, grind (teeth) (**-tt-**) —'**grittiness** n. —'**gritty** a.

grizzle ('grizəl) v. make, become gray —'**grizzled** a. —'**grizzly** a. —'**grizzly bear** large North Amer. bear

groan (grōn) vi. 1. make low, deep sound of grief or pain 2. be in pain or overburdened —n. 3. groaning sound

groat (grōt) n. formerly, silver coin worth four pennies

groats (grōts) pl.n. hulled and crushed grain of oats, wheat or certain other cereals

grocer ('grōsər) n. dealer in foodstuffs —'**groceries** pl.n. commodities sold by grocer —'**grocery** n. trade, premises of grocer

grog (grog) n. spirit (esp. rum) and water —'**groggy** a. inf. unsteady, shaky, weak

groin (groin) n. 1. fold where legs meet abdomen 2. wall or jetty built out from river bank or shore to control erosion 3. Archit. edge made by intersection of two vaults —vt. 4. build with groins

groom (grōōm, grŏŏm) n. 1. person caring for horses 2. see **bridegroom** at BRIDE —vt. 3. tend or look after 4. brush or clean (esp. horse) 5. train (someone for something) —'**groomsman** n. friend attending bridegroom —**well-groomed** a. neat, smart

groove (grōōv) n. 1. narrow channel, hollow, esp. cut by tool 2. rut, routine —vt. 3. cut groove in —'**groovy** a. sl. fashionable, exciting

grope (grōp) vi. feel about, search blindly

grosbeak ('grōsbēk) n. finch with large powerful bill

grosgrain ('grōgrān) n. heavy ribbed silk or rayon fabric —**grosgrain ribbon** ribbon used for trimming and reinforcing clothes etc.

gros point (grō) 1. needlepoint stitch covering two horizontal and two vertical threads 2. work done in this stitch

gross (grōs) a. 1. very fat 2. total, not net 3. coarse 4. indecent 5. flagrant 6. thick, rank —n. 7. twelve dozen —'**grossly** adv. —**gross national product** total value of final goods and services produced annually by nation

grotesque (grō'tesk) a. 1. (horribly) distorted 2. absurd —n. 3. 16th-cent. decorative style using distorted human, animal and plant forms 4. grotesque person, thing —gro'**tesquely** adv.

grotto ('grotō) n. cave

grotty ('groti) a. inf. dirty, untidy, unpleasant

grouch (growch) inf. n. 1. persistent grumbler 2. discontented mood —vi. 3. grumble, be peevish

ground[1] (grownd) n. 1. surface of earth 2. soil, earth 3. (oft. pl.) reason, motive 4. coating to work on with paint 5. background, main surface worked on in painting, embroidery etc. 6. special area 7. bottom of sea —pl. 8. dregs, esp. from coffee 9. enclosed land round house —vt. 10. establish 11. instruct (in elements) 12. place on ground —vi. 13. run ashore —'**grounded** a. (of aircraft) unable or not permitted to fly —'**grounding** n. basic general knowledge of a subject —'**groundless** a. without reason —**ground ball** a batted baseball that rolls or bounces along the ground —**ground cloth** waterproof sheet for spreading on the ground (also '**groundsheet**) —**ground cover** low-growing perennial plants used as grass substitutes or to control erosion —**ground crew** group of people in charge of maintenance and repair of aircraft —**ground-effect machine** vehicle supported above surface of ground or water by cushion of air, used for mowing grass or traveling short distances (also **air-cushion vehicle**) —**ground floor** floor of building level or almost level with ground —'**groundhog** n. see **woodchuck** at WOOD —**ground ivy** trailing herb of the mint family with blue flowers (also **creeping Charlie, gill-over-the-ground**) —'**groundspeed** n. aircraft's

speed in relation to ground —**ground swell 1.** considerable swell of sea, oft. caused by distant storm **2.** rapidly developing general opinion —'**groundwork** n. **1.** preliminary work as foundation or basis **2.** ground or background of painting etc. —**get in on the ground floor** inf. be in project etc. from its inception

ground[2] (grownd) pt./pp. of GRIND

groundsel ('grownsəl) n. Eurasian yellow-flowered weed

group (grōōp) n. **1.** number of persons or things considered as collective unit **2.** number of persons bound together by common interests etc. **3.** small musical band of players or singers **4.** class **5.** two or more figures forming one artistic design —v. **6.** place, fall into group —**group therapy** simultaneous treatment of number of individuals brought together to share their problems in group discussion

grouper ('grōōpər) n. large bottom-feeding food fish of tropical seas (pl. **-s, grouper**)

grouse[1] (grows) n. **1.** game bird **2.** its flesh (pl. **grouse**)

grouse[2] (grows) vi. **1.** grumble, complain —n. **2.** complaint —'**grouser** n. grumbler

grout (growt) n. **1.** thin fluid mortar —vt. **2.** fill up with grout

grove (grōv) n. **1.** small group of trees **2.** road lined with trees

grovel ('grovəl, 'gruv-) vi. **1.** abase oneself **2.** lie face down

grow (grō) vi. **1.** develop naturally **2.** increase in size, height etc. **3.** be produced **4.** become by degrees —vt. **5.** produce by cultivation (**grew** pt., **grown** pp.) —**growth** n. **1.** growing **2.** increase **3.** what has grown or is growing —**growing pains 1.** pains in joints sometimes experienced by growing children **2.** difficulties besetting new enterprise in early stages —**grown-up** a./n. adult

growl (growl) vi. **1.** make low guttural sound of anger **2.** rumble **3.** murmur, complain —n. **4.** act or sound of growling

grub (grub) vt. **1.** (oft. with **up** or **out**) dig superficially **2.** root up —vi. **3.** dig, rummage **4.** plod (**-bb-**) —n. **5.** larva of insect **6.** sl. food —'**grubby** a. dirty

grudge (gruj) vt. **1.** be unwilling to give, allow —n. **2.** ill will

gruel ('grōōəl) n. food of oatmeal etc., boiled in milk or water —'**grueling** or '**gruelling** a./n. exhausting, severe (experience)

gruesome ('grōōsəm) a. fearful, horrible, grisly —'**gruesomeness** n.

gruff (gruf) a. rough in manner or voice, surly —'**gruffly** adv.

grumble ('grumbəl) vi. **1.** complain **2.** rumble, murmur **3.** make growling sounds —n. **4.** complaint **5.** low growl —'**grumbler** n.

grumpy ('grumpi) a. ill-tempered, surly —'**grumpily** adv.

grunt (grunt) vi. **1.** make sound characteristic of pig —n. **2.** deep, hoarse sound of pig **3.** gruff noise

Gruyère (grōō'yâr) n. a cooked, hard cheese, pale yellow in color, honeycombed with holes, made from whole cow's milk, orig. from Switzerland

gryphon ('grifən) n. see GRIFFIN

G.S. 1. General Staff **2.** ground speed

GSA General Services Administration

G-string n. **1.** very small covering for genitals **2.** Mus. string tuned to G

G-suit n. close-fitting garment worn by crew of high-speed aircraft, pressurized to prevent blackout during maneuvers

Guam (gwäm) n. island in the western Pacific Ocean, a territory of the U.S.

guanaco (gwə'näkŏ) *n.* cud-chewing S Amer. mammal closely related to domesticated llama (*pl.* **-s**)

guano ('gwänŏ) *n.* sea bird manure (*pl.* **-s**)

Guarani (gwärə'nē) *n.* Amerindian language spoken in Paraguay

guarantee (garən'tē) *n.* **1.** formal assurance, *esp.* in writing, that product *etc.* will meet certain standards, last for given time *etc.* —*vt.* **2.** give guarantee of, for something **3.** secure (against risk *etc.*) (**guaran'teed, guaran'teeing**) —**guaran'tor** *n.* one who undertakes fulfillment of another's promises —**'guaranty** *n.* **1.** pledge of responsibility for fulfilling another person's obligations in case of default **2.** thing given or taken as security for guaranty **3.** act of providing security **4.** guarantor —*v.* **5.** guarantee

guard (gärd) *vt.* **1.** protect, defend —*vi.* **2.** be careful, take precautions —*n.* **3.** person, group that protects, supervises, keeps watch **4.** sentry **5.** soldiers protecting anything **6.** protection **7.** screen for enclosing anything dangerous **8.** protector **9.** posture of defense —*pl.* **10.** (**G-**) any of certain British regiments —**'guarded** *a.* **1.** kept under surveillance **2.** prudent, restrained or non-committal —**'guardedly** *adv.* —**'guardian** *n.* **1.** keeper, protector **2.** person having custody of infant *etc.* —**'guardianship** *n.* care —**'guardhouse** *or* **'guardroom** *n.* place for stationing those on guard or for prisoners —**'guardsman** *n.* soldier in Guards

Guarnerius (gwär'nēərias, -'ner-) *n.* violin made by member of the Guarnerius family, called 'dark Strad'

Guatemala (gwäti'mälə) *n.* country in Central America bounded on the north and west by Mexico, south by the Pacific Ocean and east by El Salvador, Honduras and Belize

guava ('gwävə) *n.* tropical tree with fruit used to make jelly

gubernatorial (gōōbərnə'tôriəl, gyōō-) *a.* of or relating to governor

gudgeon[1] ('gujən) *n.* small freshwater fish

gudgeon[2] ('gujən) *n.* **1.** pivot bearing **2.** socket for rudder **3.** kind of connecting pin

guelder-rose (geldər'rōz) *n.* shrub with clusters of white flowers

guerdon ('gərdən) *n.* reward

Guernsey ('gərnzi) *n.* **1.** breed of cattle **2.** close-fitting knitted sweater

guerrilla *or* **guerilla** (gə'rilə) *n.* member of irregular armed force, *esp.* fighting established force, government *etc.*

guess (ges) *vt.* **1.** estimate without calculation **2.** conjecture, suppose **3.** consider, think —*vi.* **4.** form conjectures —*n.* **5.** estimate —**'guesstimate** *n.* estimate based on guesswork and experience —**'guesswork** *n.* **1.** set of conclusions *etc.* arrived at by guessing **2.** process of making guesses

guest (gest) *n.* **1.** one entertained at another's house **2.** one living in hotel —**guest of honor** person honored by a social occasion —**guest room** room in house reserved for guest

guff (guf) *n. sl.* silly talk

guffaw (gu'fō) *n.* **1.** burst of boisterous laughter —*vi.* **2.** laugh in this way

guide (gīd) *n.* **1.** one who shows the way **2.** adviser **3.** book of instruction or information **4.** contrivance for directing motion —*vt.* **5.** lead, act as guide to **6.** arrange —**'guidance** *n.* —**guided missile** missile whose flight path is controlled by radio or preprogrammed homing mechanism —**guide dog** dog trained to lead blind person —**'guideline** *n.* principle put forward to determine course of action —**guide word** word at head of page of alphabetical reference book giving the first or last word on the page

guidon ('gīdon, -dən) *n.* **1.** pennant, used as marker, *esp.* by cavalry regiments **2.** man or vehicle that carries this

guild *or* **gild** (gild) *n.* **1.** organization, club **2.** society for mutual help, or with common object **3.** *Hist.* society of merchants or tradesmen —**'guildhall** *n.* meeting place of guild or corporation

guilder ('gildər) *or* **gulden** ('gōōldən, 'gōōl-) *n.* **1.** standard monetary unit of Netherlands (*also* **'gilder**) **2.** former gold or silver coin of Germany, Austria or Netherlands (*pl.* **-s, -der** *or* **-s, -den**)

guile (gīl) *n.* cunning, deceit —**'guileful** *a.* —**'guilefully** *adv.* —**'guileless** *a.*

guillemot ('gilimot) *n.* species of sea bird

guillotine ('gilətēn) *n.* **1.** device for beheading **2.** machine for cutting paper **3.** in legislature, method of restricting length of debate by fixing time for taking vote —*vt.* **4.** behead **5.** use guillotine on **6.** limit (debate) by guillotine

guilt (gilt) *n.* **1.** fact, state of having done wrong **2.** responsibility for criminal or moral offense —**'guiltily** *adv.* —**'guiltiness** *n.* —**'guiltless** *a.* innocent —**'guilty** *a.* having committed an offense

guinea pig

guinea ('gini) *n.* formerly, Brit. gold coin worth 21 shillings —**guinea fowl** bird allied to pheasant —**guinea pig 1.** rodent originating in S Amer. **2.** *inf.* person or animal used in experiments —**guinea worm** tropical roundworm parasite in humans

Guinea ('gini) *n.* country in W Africa bounded northwest by Guinea-Bissau and Senegal, northeast by Mali, southeast by the Ivory Coast, south by Liberia and Sierra Leone and west by the Atlantic Ocean

Guinea-Bissau (ginibi'sow) *n.* country in Africa bounded north by Senegal, west by the Atlantic Ocean and east and south by Guinea

guipure (gi'pyōōr, -'pōōr) *n.* **1.** any of many types of lace that have their pattern connected by threads, rather than supported on net mesh (*also* **guipure lace**) **2.** heavy corded trimming; gimp

guise (gīz) *n.* external appearance, *esp.* one assumed

guitar (gi'tär) *n.* plucked, stringed musical instrument with a flat, waisted body, long fretted neck and six strings —**gui'tarist** *n.* —**bass guitar** guitar with 12 strings and lower register —**electric** *or* **steel guitar** guitar with solid body which merely supports the strings as sound is produced by an electric amplifying system —**Hawaiian guitar** ukulele

Gulag ('gōōlag) *n.* central administrative department of Soviet security service, responsible for prisons, labor camps *etc.*

gulch (gulch) *n.* **1.** ravine **2.** gully

gulf (gulf) *n.* **1.** large inlet of the sea **2.** chasm **3.** large gap —**Gulf Stream** warm ocean current flowing from Gulf of Mexico toward NW Europe (*also* **North Atlantic Drift**) —**'gulfweed** *n.* seaweed forming dense floating masses in tropical Atlantic waters, *esp.* Gulf Stream (*also* **sar'gasso, sargasso weed**)

gull[1] (gul) *n.* long-winged web-footed sea bird

gull[2] (gul) *n.* **1.** dupe, fool —*vt.* **2.** dupe, cheat —**gulli'bility** *n.* —**'gullible** *a.* easily imposed on, credulous

gullet ('gulit) *n.* food passage from mouth to stomach

gully ('guli) *n.* channel or ravine worn by water

gulp (gulp) *vt.* **1.** swallow eagerly —*vi.* **2.** gasp, choke —*n.* **3.** act of gulping

gum[1] (gum) *n.* firm flesh in which teeth are set —**'gummy** *a.* toothless —**'gumboil** *n.* abscess on gum

gum[2] (gum) *n.* **1.** sticky substance issuing from certain trees **2.** an adhesive **3.** chewing gum —*vt.* **4.** stick with gum (**-mm-**) —**'gummy** *a.* —**gum arabic** water-soluble gum obtained from some acacias used in manufacture of adhesives, confectionery and drugs —**gum resin** mixture of resin and gum obtained from various plants and trees —**'gumtree** *n.* any species of eucalyptus —**gum up the works** *inf.* impede progress —**up a gumtree** *sl.* in a difficult position

gumption ('gumpshən) *n.* **1.** resourcefulness **2.** shrewdness, sense

gun (gun) *n.* **1.** weapon with metal tube from which missiles are discharged by explosion **2.** cannon, pistol *etc.* —*vt.* **3.** (*oft. with* down) shoot **4.** race (engine of motor vehicle) —*vi.* **5.** hunt with gun (**-nn-**) —**'gunner** *n.* —**'gunnery** *n.* use or science of large guns —**'gunboat** *n.* small warship —**gunboat diplomacy** diplomacy conducted by threats of military intervention —**'guncotton** *n.* cellulose nitrate containing large amount of nitrogen: used as explosive —**gun dog** (breed of) dog used to find or retrieve game —**'gunman** *n.* armed criminal —**'gunmetal** *n.* **1.** alloy of copper and tin or zinc, formerly used for guns **2.** color of gunmetal: pewter gray —*a.* **3.** of this color —**'gunpoint** *n.* muzzle of gun —**'gunpowder** *n.* explosive mixture of saltpeter, sulfur and charcoal —**'gunrunner** *n.* —**'gunrunning** *n.* smuggling of guns and ammunition into country —**'gunshot** *n.* **1.** shot or range of gun —*a.* **2.** caused by missile from gun —**'gunstock** *n.* wooden handle or support to which is attached barrel of rifle —**gunwale** *or* **gunnel** ('gunəl) *n.* upper edge of ship's side —**at gunpoint** under threat of being shot

gunny ('guni) *n.* strong, coarse sacking made from jute

guppy ('gupi) *n.* small aquarium fish

gurgle ('gərgəl) *n.* **1.** bubbling noise —*vi.* **2.** utter, flow with gurgle

Gurkha ('gərkə) *n.* **1.** any of a warlike people in Nepal **2.** member of this people serving as soldier in British army

gurnard ('gərnərd) *n.* spiny armor-headed sea fish; sea robin

guru (gə'rōō, 'gōōrōō) *n.* **1.** Hindu spiritual teacher **2.** influential or revered teacher

gush (gush) *vi.* **1.** flow out suddenly and copiously, spurt —*n.* **2.** sudden and copious flow **3.** effusiveness —**'gusher** *n.* **1.** gushing person **2.** something, such as spurting oil well, that gushes

gusset ('gusit) *n.* triangle or diamond-shaped piece of material let into garment —**'gusseted** *a.*

gust (gust) *n.* **1.** sudden blast of wind **2.** burst of rain, anger, passion *etc.* —**'gusty** *a.*

gustation (gu'stāshən) *n.* act of tasting or faculty of taste —**'gustatory** *a.*

gusto ('gustō) *n.* enjoyment, zest

gut (gut) *n.* **1.** (*oft. pl.*) entrails, intestines **2.** material made from guts of animals, *eg* for violin strings *etc.* —*pl.* **3.** *inf.* essential, fundamental part **4.** courage —*vt.* **5.** remove guts from (fish *etc.*) **6.** remove, destroy contents of (house) (**-tt-**) —**'gutless** *a. inf.* lacking courage —**'gutsy** *a. inf.* **1.** greedy **2.** courageous

gutta-percha (gutə'pərchə) *n.* (tropical tree producing) whitish rubber substance

gutter ('gutər) *n.* **1.** shallow trough for carrying off water from roof or side of street —*vt.* **2.** make channels in —*vi.* **3.** flow in streams **4.** (of candle) melt away by wax forming channels and running down —**gutter press** journalism that relies on sensationalism —**'guttersnipe** *n.* **1.** neglected slum child **2.** mean vindictive person

guttural ('gutərəl) *a.* **1.** of, relating to, or produced in, the throat —*n.* **2.** guttural sound or letter

guy[1] (gī) *n. inf.* a man

guy[2] (gī) *n.* **1.** rope, chain to steady, secure something (*eg* tent) —*vt.* **2.** keep in position by guy —**'guyrope** *n.*

Guyana (gī'anə) *n.* country in South America bounded northeast by the Atlantic Ocean, east by Suriname, south and west by Brazil and west by Venezuela

guzzle ('guzəl) *v.* eat or drink greedily

gybe (jīb) *vi. see* JIBE[1]

gym (jim) *n.* **1.** gymnasium **2.** gymnastics —**gym shoes** rubber-soled shoes worn in gymnasium —**gym suit** clothing worn for gym class

gymnasium (jim'nāziəm) *n.* place equipped for muscular exercises, athletic training (*pl.* **-s, -nasia** (-'nāziə)) —**'gymnast** *n.* expert in gymnastics —**gym'nastics** *pl.n.* sport in which both prescribed and optional physical exercises must be performed in an artistic yet formally correct manner

gymnosperm ('jimnəspərm) *n.* seed-bearing plant in which ovules are borne naked on open scales: all conifers, sago palm, ginkgo, Mormon tea bush

gynecology (gīni'koləji) *n.* branch of medicine dealing with diseases and disorders of females, *esp.* the reproductive organs —**gyneco'logical** *or* **gyneco'logic** *a.* —**gyne'cologist** *n.*

gyp (jip) *sl. vt.* **1.** swindle, cheat, defraud (**-pp-**) —*n.* **2.** act of cheating **3.** person who gyps

gypsophila (jip'sofilə) *n.* garden plant with small white or pink flowers

gypsum ('jipsəm) *n.* crystalline sulfate of lime: source of plaster

Gypsy *or* **Gipsy** ('jipsi) *n.* one of wandering race originally from NW India, Romany

gyrate ('jīrāt) *vi.* move in circle, spirally, revolve —**gy'ration** *n.* —**gy'rational** *a.* —**gyratory** ('jīrətōri) *a.* revolving, spinning

gyrfalcon *or* **gerfalcon** ('jərfalkən, -föl-) *n.* large, rare falcon

gyro ('jīrō) *n.* **1.** *see* GYROCOMPASS **2.** *see* GYROSCOPE (*pl.* **-s**)

gyro- *or before vowel* **gyr-** (*comb. form*) **1.** rotating or gyrating motion, as in *gyroscope* **2.** gyroscope, as in *gyrocompass*

gyrocompass ('jīrōkumpəs) *n.* compass using gyroscope to indicate true north

gyroscope ('jīrəskōp) *n.* disk or wheel so mounted as to be able to rotate about any axis, *esp.* to keep disk (with compass *etc.*) level despite movement of ship *etc.* —**gyroscopic** (jīrə'skopik) *a.*

gyrostabilizer (jīrō'stābilīzər) *n.* gyroscopic device to prevent rolling of ship or airplane

gyve (jīv, gīv) *obs. vt.* **1.** shackle, fetter —*n.* **2.** (*usu. pl.*) fetter

Hh

h *or* **H 1.** eighth letter of English alphabet **2.** speech sound represented by this letter **3.** something shaped like an H

H 1. *Chem.* hydrogen **2.** (of pencils) hard

ha hectare

Habacuc ('habəkuk) *n. Bible* Habakkuk in the Douay Version of the O.T.

Habakkuk ('habəkuk) *n. Bible* 35th book of the O.T., written by the prophet Habakkuk, a group of psalms on the triumph of justice and divine mercy over evil

habeas corpus ('hābiəs 'körpəs) writ issued to produce prisoner in court

haberdasher ('habərdashər) *n.* dealer in articles of dress, ribbons, pins, needles *etc.* —**'haberdashery** *n.*

habiliments (hə'bilimənts) *pl.n.* dress

habit ('habit) *n.* **1.** settled tendency or practice **2.** constitution **3.** customary apparel, *esp.* of nun or monk **4.** woman's riding dress —**ha'bitual** *a.* **1.** formed or acquired by habit **2.** usual, customary —**ha'bitually** *adv.* —**ha'bituate** *vt.* accustom —**habitu'ation** *n.* —**habitué** (hə'bichōōā) *n.* constant visitor

habitable ('habitəbəl) *a.* fit to live in —**'habitant** *n.* **C** (descendant of) original French settler —**'habitat** *n.* natural home (of animal *etc.*) —**habi'tation** *n.* dwelling place

hachure (ha'shōōər) *n.* shading of short lines drawn on relief map to indicate gradients

hacienda (hasi'endə, asi'endə) *n.* ranch or large estate in Spanish Amer.

hack[1] (hak) *vt.* **1.** cut, chop (at) violently **2.** *Sport* foul by kicking the shins —*vi.* **3.** *inf.*

utter harsh, dry cough —*n.* **4.** cut or gash **5.** any tool used for shallow digging

hack[2] (hak) *n.* **1.** horse hired out for ordinary riding **2.** drudge, *esp.* writer of inferior literary works —**hack work** dull, repetitive work

hackle

hackle ('hakəl) *n.* **1.** neck feathers of turkey *etc.* —*pl.* **2.** hairs on back of neck of dog and other animals, which are raised in anger

hackney ('hakni) *n.* carriage or coach kept for hire

hackneyed ('haknid) *a.* (of words *etc.*) stale, trite because of overuse

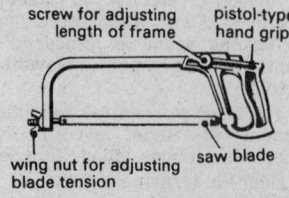

screw for adjusting length of frame   pistol-type hand grip

wing nut for adjusting blade tension   saw blade

hacksaw

hacksaw ('haksö) *n.* handsaw for cutting metal

had (had) *pt./pp. of* HAVE

haddock ('hadək) *n.* large, edible seafish

Hades ('hādēz) *n.* **1.** abode of the dead **2.** underworld **3.** hell

hadj (haj) *n. see* HAJJ

haemoglobin ('hēməglōbin) *n. see* HEMOGLOBIN

hafnium ('hafniəm) *n. Chem.* metallic element *Symbol* Hf, at. wt. 178.5, at. no. 72

haft (haft) *n.* **1.** handle (of knife *etc.*) —*vt.* **2.** provide with haft

hag (hag) *n.* **1.** ugly old woman **2.** witch —**hag-ridden** *a.* troubled, careworn

Haggadah (hə'gädə) *n. Judaism* reading at Passover Seder recounting Israel's bondage and flight from Egypt

Haggai ('hagī, 'hagī) *n. Bible* 37th book of the O.T., written by the prophet Haggai about 520 B.C. urging the renewal of work on restoring the temple after the Babylonian captivity

haggard ('hagərd) *a.* **1.** wild-looking **2.** anxious, careworn —*n.* **3.** *Falconry* untamed hawk

haggis ('hagis) *n.* Scottish dish made from sheep's heart, lungs, liver, chopped with oatmeal, suet, onion *etc.* and boiled in stomach-bag

haggle ('hagəl) *vi.* (*oft. with* over) bargain, wrangle (over price, terms *etc.*)

hagiology (hagi'oləji) *n.* literature of the lives and legends of saints —**hagi'ographer** *n.* —**hagi'ography** *n.* writing of this

ha-ha[1] ('hä'hä) *interj.* **1.** representation of the sound of laughter **2.** exclamation expressing derision, mockery *etc.*

ha-ha[2] ('hähä) *n.* sunken fence bordering garden *etc.,* that allows uninterrupted views from within

haiku ('hīkoo) *n.* epigrammatic Japanese verse form in 17 syllables (*pl.* **-ku**)

hail[1] (hāl) *n.* **1.** (shower of) pellets of ice **2.** intense shower, barrage —*v.* **3.** pour down as shower of hail —'**hailstone** *n.*

hail[2] (hāl) *vt.* **1.** greet, *esp.* enthusiastically **2.** acclaim, acknowledge **3.** call —**hail from** come from —**Hail Mary** ('mâəri) *R.C.* prayer to the Virgin Mary consisting of salutation and plea for her intercession (*also* **Ave Maria**)

hair (hâər) *n.* **1.** filament growing from skin of mammals **2.** such filaments collectively —'**hairiness** *n.* —'**hairy** *a.* —'**hairdo** *n.* way of dressing hair —'**hairdresser** *n.* one who attends to and cuts hair, *esp.* women's hair —'**hairline** *a./n.* very fine (line) —'**hairpiece** *n.* **1.** wig or toupee **2.** false hair attached to one's real hair to give it greater bulk or length —'**hairpin** *n.* pin for keeping hair in place —**hairpin bend** U-shaped turn of road —**hair-raising** *a.* terrifying —**hair's-breadth** *n.* very short margin or distance —**hair shirt** rough shirt worn as penance by religious ascetics —'**hairsplitting** *n.* making of overfine distinctions —'**hairspring** *n.* very fine, delicate spring in timepiece —'**hairstyle** *n.* —**hair trigger** trigger operated by light touch

Haiti ('hāti) *n.* country in the Caribbean occupying the western portion of the island of Hispaniola —**Haitian** ('hāshən, 'hātiən) *a./n.*

hajj *or* **hadj** (haj) *n.* pilgrimage to Mecca that every Muslim is required to make —'**hajji** *or* '**hadji** *n.* Muslim who has made pilgrimage to Mecca (*pl.* **-s**)

hake (hāk) *n.* edible fish of the cod family

Halakah (hä'läkə) *n.* codification of laws of the Talmud

halberd ('halbərd) *or* **halbert** *n.* combined spear and battleax

halcyon ('halsiən) *n.* bird fabled to calm the sea and to breed on floating nest, kingfisher —**halcyon days** time of peace and happiness

hale[1] (hāl) *a.* robust, healthy (*esp. in* **hale and hearty**)

hale[2] (hāl) *vt.* pull; drag —'**haler** *n.*

half (haf, häf) *n.* **1.** either of two equal parts of something (*pl.* **halves**) —*a.* **2.** forming half —*adv.* **3.** to the extent of half —**half-and-half** *n.* mixture of half one thing and half another thing, *esp.* half milk and half cream —'**halfback** *n.* **1.** in football, one of two backs who line up on each side of the fullback **2.** in field hockey, rugby and soccer, player behind forwards —**half-baked** *a.* **1.** underdone **2.** *inf.* immature, silly —**half-blood** *n.* **1.** relationship between individuals having only one parent in common; individual having such relationship **2.** half-breed —**half-breed** *or* **half-caste** *n.* person with parents of different races —**half-brother, -sister** *n.* brother (sister) by one parent only —**half-cock** *n.* halfway position of firearm's hammer when trigger is locked —**half-cocked** *a.* ill-prepared —**half-dollar** *n.* (coin representing) 50 cents —**half-hardy** *a.* (of plant) being able to withstand low but not freezing temperature —**half-hearted** *a.* unenthusiastic —**half-hitch** *n.* knot made by passing end of piece of rope around itself and through loop thus made —**half hour** thirty minutes —**half-life** *n.* time taken for half the atoms in radioactive material to decay —**half-mast** *n.* (of flag) halfway position to which flag is lowered on mast to mourn dead —**half measures** inadequate measures or actions —**half-moon** *n.* the moon when its disk is half illuminated —**half-nelson** *n.* hold in wrestling —**half shell** half of mollusk shell for serving shellfish on —**half-size** *n.* clothing size for the full-figured woman —**half sole** sole of boot or shoe from shank to toe —**half-timbered** *or* **half-timber** *a.* (of building) having exposed timber framework filled with brick —**half-time** *n. Sport* rest period between two halves of game —**half-title** *n.* title of book as printed on right-hand page preceding title page —'**halftone** *n.* illustration printed from relief plate, showing light and shadow by means of minute dots —**half-track** *n.* vehicle with caterpillar tracks on wheels that supply motive power only —**half-true** *a.* —**half-truth** *n.* partially true statement intended to mislead —**half volley** striking of ball the moment it bounces —'**half'way** *adv./a.* at or to half distance —**halfway house 1.** place to rest midway on journey **2.** halfway point in any progression **3.** center or hostel to facilitate readjustment to private life of released prisoners *etc.* —'**halfwit** *n.* **1.** mentally retarded person **2.** stupid person —**by halves** imperfectly —**go halves** share expenses *etc.* equally —**half seas over** *inf.* drunk —**meet halfway** compromise with

halibut ('halibət) *n.* large edible flatfish

halitosis (hali'tōsis) *n.* bad-smelling breath

hall (hōl) *n.* **1.** (entrance) passage **2.** large room or building belonging to particular group or used for particular purpose, *esp.* public assembly —'**hallway** *n.* hall or corridor —**Hall of Fame 1.** national shrine commemorating outstanding Americans at New York University in New York City **2.** place set aside to honor outstanding persons in any profession or location **3.** persons acclaimed as outstanding

hallelujah (hali'loōyə) *or* **alleluia** *n./interj.* exclamation of praise to God

hallmark ('hōlmärk) *n.* **1.** mark used to indicate standard of tested gold and silver **2.** mark of excellence **3.** distinguishing feature

hallo (hə'lō) *or* **halloo** (hə'loō) *n.* **1.** call to spur on hunting dogs —*vi.* **2.** shout loudly

hallow ('halō) *vt.* make or honor as holy —**Hallowe'en** *or* **Halloween** (halō'ēn) *n.* the evening of Oct. 31st, the day before Allhallows or All Saints' Day

hallucinate (hə'loōsināt) *vi.* suffer illusions —**halluci'nation** *n.* illusion —**hal'lucinatory** *a.* —**hal'lucinogen** *n.* usu. illicit substance taken to produce vivid mental imagery

hallux vulgus ('haləks 'vulgəs) bunion

halo ('hālō) *n.* **1.** circle of light round moon, sun *etc.* **2.** disk of light round saint's head in picture **3.** aura surrounding admired person, thing *etc.* (*pl.* **-es, -s**) —*vt.* **4.** surround with halo

halogen ('haləjən) *n.* group of elements comprising fluorine, chlorine, bromine, iodine, astatine (in ascending atomic no. order) —**ha'logenous** *a.*

halophyte ('haləfīt) *n.* plant which grows in soil or water containing a high proportion of salt

halothane ('haləthān) *n.* nonexplosive inhaled anesthetic

halt[1] (hōlt) *n.* **1.** interruption or end to progress *etc., esp.* as command to stop marching **2.** minor railroad station without station buildings —*v.* **3.** (cause to) stop

halt[2] (hōlt) *vi.* falter, fail —'**halting** *a.* hesitant, lame

halter ('hōltər) *n.* **1.** rope or strap with headgear to fasten horses or cattle **2.** low-cut dress style with strap passing behind neck **3.** noose for hanging a person —*vt.* **4.** put halter on

halvah *or* **halva** ('hälvä, 'hälvə) *n.* a sweet, sticky confection from the Middle East and India made of honey and sesame seeds or semolina and fruit

halve (hav, häv) *vt.* **1.** cut in half **2.** reduce to half **3.** share

halyard ('halyərd) *n.* rope for raising sail, signal flags *etc.*

ham (ham) *n.* **1.** meat, *esp.* salted or smoked, from thigh of pig **2.** actor adopting exaggerated, unconvincing style **3.** amateur radio enthusiast —*v.* **4.** overact (**-mm-**) —'**hammy** *a. inf.* **1.** (of actor) tending to overact **2.** (of play, performance *etc.*) overacted —**ham-fisted** *or* **ham-handed** *a.* clumsy —'**hamstring** *n.* **1.** tendon at back of knee —*vt.* **2.** cripple by cutting this —'**hamstrung** *a.* **1.** crippled **2.** thwarted —**hamstring muscle** any of three muscles at back of thigh that flex and rotate the leg

hamadryad (hamə'drīəd) *n. Class. myth.* nymph which inhabits tree and dies with it

hamburger ('hambərgər) *n.* broiled or fried patty of ground beef, *esp.* served in bread roll

Hamitic (ha'mitik, hə-) *n.* **1.** group of N Afr. languages related to Semitic —*a.* **2.** denoting this group of languages **3.** denoting Hamites, group of peoples of N Afr., including ancient Egyptians, supposedly descended from Noah's son Ham

hamlet ('hamlit) *n.* small village

hammer ('hamər) *n.* **1.** tool usu. with heavy head at end of handle, for beating, driving nails *etc.* **2.** machine with similar function **3.** contrivance for exploding charge of gun **4.** auctioneer's mallet **5.** metal ball on wire thrown in sports —*v.* **6.** strike (blows) with, or as with, hammer —'**hammerhead** *n.* shark with wide, flattened head —'**hammertoe** *n.* deformed toe —**hammer and sickle** emblem on flag of Soviet Union, representing industrial workers and peasants respectively —**hammer out** solve problem by full investigation of difficulties

hammock ('hamək) *n.* bed of canvas *etc.,* hung on cords

Hammond organ ('hamənd) trade name of musical instrument shaped like small piano with two keyboards which generates tone electronically

hamper[1] ('hampər) *n.* **1.** large covered basket **2.** large parcel, box *etc.* of food, wines *etc., esp.* one sent as Christmas gift

hamper[2] ('hampər) *vt.* impede, obstruct movements of

hamster ('hamstər) *n.* rodent with cheek pouches for carrying grain, sometimes kept as pet

hand (hand) *n.* **1.** extremity of arm beyond wrist **2.** side, quarter, direction **3.** style of writing **4.** cards dealt to player **5.** measure of four inches **6.** manual worker **7.** sailor **8.** help, aid **9.** pointer on dial **10.** applause —*vt.* **11.** pass **12.** deliver **13.** hold out —'**handful** *n.* **1.** small quantity or number **2.** *inf.* person or thing causing problems (*pl.* **-s**) —'**handily** *adv.* —'**handiness** *n.* **1.** dexterity **2.** state of being near, available —'**handy** *a.* **1.** convenient **2.** clever with the hands —'**handbag** *n.* **1.** woman's bag for personal articles **2.** bag for carrying in hand —'**handball** *n.* indoor or outdoor court game for two or four players in which object is to hit a small hard ball with a gloved hand against a wall so that opponent cannot return the ball before it bounces twice —**'handbill** n. small printed notice —**'handbook** n. small reference or instruction book —**'handcart** n. cart drawn or pushed by hand —**'handcuff** n. **1.** fetter for wrist, usu. joined in pair —vt. **2.** secure thus —**'handicraft** n. manual occupation or skill —**'handiwork** n. thing done by particular person —**handkerchief** ('hangkǝrchif, -chēf) n. **1.** small square of fabric carried in pocket for wiping nose etc. **2.** neckerchief —**handkerchief linen** see **Irish linen** at IRELAND —**hand-me-down** n. inf. **1.** something, esp. outgrown garment, passed down from one person to another **2.** anything already used by another —**hand-out** n. **1.** money, food etc. given free **2.** pamphlet giving news, information etc. —**hand-pick** vt. select with great care —**hand-picked** a. —**'handset** n. telephone mouthpiece and earpiece mounted as single unit —**hands-on** a. involving active participation and operating experience —**'handspring** n. gymnastic feat in which person leaps forward or backward into handstand and then on to his feet —**'handstand** n. act of supporting body in upside-down position by hands alone —**hand-to-hand** a./adv. at close quarters —**hand-to-mouth** a./adv. with barely enough money or food to satisfy immediate needs —**'handwriting** n. way person writes —**'handyman** n. **1.** man employed to do various tasks **2.** man skilled in odd jobs —**hand in glove with** very intimate with

handicap ('handikap) n. **1.** something that hampers or hinders **2.** race, contest in which chances are equalized by starts, weights carried etc. **3.** condition so imposed **4.** any physical disability —vt. **5.** hamper **6.** impose handicaps on (-pp-) —**'handicapped** a. physically or mentally disabled

handle ('handǝl) n. **1.** part of utensil etc. which is to be held —vt. **2.** touch, feel with hands **3.** manage **4.** deal with **5.** trade —**'handler** n. **1.** person who trains and controls animals **2.** trainer or second of boxer —**'handlebars** pl.n. curved metal bar used to steer bicycle, motorcycle etc.

handsome ('hansǝm) a. **1.** of fine appearance **2.** generous **3.** ample —**'handsomely** adv.

hang (hang) vt. **1.** suspend **2.** kill by suspension by neck (**hanged** pt./pp.) **3.** attach, set up (wallpaper, doors etc.) —vi. **4.** be suspended (**hung** pt./pp.) —**'hanger** n. frame on which garment etc. can be hung —**'hangdog** a. sullen, dejected —**hanger-on** n. sycophantic follower or dependant (pl. **hangers-on**) —**hang-glider** n. glider like large kite, with pilot hanging in frame below —**hang-gliding** n. —**'hangman** n. executioner —**'hangnail** n. piece of skin hanging loose at base or side of fingernail —**'hangover** n. aftereffects of too much drinking —**hang-up** n. inf. persistent emotional problem —**hang out** inf. reside, frequent

hangar ('hangǝr) n. building for aircraft

hank (hangk) n. coil, skein, length, esp. as measure of yarn

hanker ('hangkǝr) vi. (with for or after) have a yearning

hanky or **hankie** ('hangki) n. inf. handkerchief

hanky-panky (hangki'pangki) n. inf. **1.** trickery **2.** illicit sexual relations

Hansard ('hansǝrd, 'hansärd) n. official printed record of speeches, debates etc. in Brit., Aust. and other parliaments

Hanseatic League (hansi'atik) commercial organization of towns in N Germany formed to protect and control trade

Hansen's disease ('hansǝnz) leprosy

hansom ('hansǝm) n. (sometimes H-) two-wheeled horse-drawn cab for two to ride inside with driver mounted up behind

haphazard (hap'hazǝrd) a. **1.** random **2.** careless

hapless ('haplis) a. unlucky

haploid ('haploid) n. cell having half the basic number of chromosomes

happen ('hapǝn) vi. **1.** come about, occur **2.** chance (to do) —**'happening** n. occurrence, event

happy ('hapi) a. **1.** glad **2.** content **3.** lucky, fortunate **4.** apt —**'happily** adv. —**'happiness** n. —**happy-go-lucky** a. casual, light-hearted

hara-kiri (hari'kiri) n. in Japan, ritual suicide by disemboweling

harangue (hǝ'rang) n. **1.** vehement speech **2.** tirade —v. **3.** address (person or crowd) in angry, forceful or persuasive way

harass (hǝ'ras, 'harǝs) vt. worry, trouble, torment —**ha'rassment** n.

harbinger ('härbinjǝr) n. **1.** one who announces another's approach **2.** forerunner, herald

harbor ('härbǝr) n. **1.** shelter for ships **2.** shelter —vt. **3.** give shelter or protection to **4.** maintain (secretly) (esp. grudge etc.)

hard (härd) a. **1.** firm, resisting pressure **2.** solid **3.** difficult to understand **4.** harsh, unfeeling **5.** difficult to bear **6.** practical, shrewd **7.** heavy **8.** strenuous **9.** (of water) not making lather well with soap **10.** (of drugs) highly addictive —adv. **11.** vigorously **12.** with difficulty **13.** close —**'harden** v. —**'hardly** adv. **1.** unkindly, harshly **2.** scarcely, not quite **3.** only just —**'hardness** n. —**'hardship** n. **1.** ill luck **2.** severe toil, suffering **3.** instance of this —**'hardback** n. **1.** book bound in stiff covers —a. **2.** of or denoting hardback or publication of hardbacks (also **'casebound, 'hardbound, 'hardcover**) —**hard-bitten** a. inf. tough and realistic —**'hardboard** n. thin stiff sheet made of compressed sawdust and woodchips with one smooth face —**hard-boiled** a. **1.** (of egg) cooked sufficiently long to solidify white and yolk **2.** inf. (of person) experienced, unemotional, unsympathetic —**hard copy** Comp. output that can be read by eye —**hard core 1.** members of group who form intransigent nucleus resisting change **2.** material, such as broken stones, used to form foundation for road etc. —**hard-core** a. **1.** (of pornography) depicting sexual acts in explicit detail **2.** completely established in belief etc. —**hard court** tennis court with hard surface —**hard-headed** a. shrewd —**hard'hearted** a. unkind or intolerant —**hard'heartedness** n. —**hard labor** formerly, penalty of compulsory labor in addition to imprisonment —**hard line** uncompromising course or policy —**'hard'liner** n. —**hard palate** anterior bony portion of roof of mouth —**hard paste** basis of vitreous porcelain —**hard-pressed** a. **1.** in difficulties **2.** closely pursued —**hard sell** aggressive technique of selling or advertising —**'hardware** n. **1.** tools, implements **2.** necessary (parts of) machinery **3.** Comp. mechanical and electronic parts —**hard water** water with large concentration of ions esp. calcium, magnesium and iron —**hard wheat** wheat high in gluten for making bread —**'hardwood** n. heavy wood from certain deciduous trees, eg oak, teak —**hard of**

hearing rather deaf —**hard up** very short of money

Harding ('härding) n. **Warren Gamaliel.** the 29th President of the U.S. (1921-23)

hardy ('härdi) a. **1.** robust, vigorous **2.** bold **3.** (of plants) able to grow in the open all year round —**'hardihood** n. extreme boldness, audacity —**'hardily** adv. —**'hardiness** n.

hare (hāǝr) n. animal like large rabbit, with longer legs and ears, noted for speed —**'harebell** n. plant with slender stems and leaves and bell-shaped blue flowers —**hare-'brained** a. rash, wild —**hare'lip** n. fissure of upper lip (also **cleft lip**) —**hare and hounds** paper chase

Hare Krishna ('häri 'krishnǝ) member of religious movement founded by Swami Prabhupada in the U.S. in 1965, based on the founder's transcription of the Bhagavad Gita

harem ('harǝm, 'her-) n. **1.** women's part of Muslim dwelling **2.** one man's wives collectively —**harem pants** full trousers for women gathered at ankles —**harem skirt** full straight-cut skirt gathered or pleated onto a band at knees or ankles

haricot ('harikō) n. type of French bean that can be dried and stored

hark (härk) vi. listen —**hark back** return (to previous subject of discussion)

harken ('härkǝn) vi. see HEARKEN

harlequin ('härlikwin) n. **1.** stock comic character, esp. masked clown in diamond-patterned costume —a. **2.** multicolored

Harley Street ('härli) street in central London famous for its large number of medical specialists' consulting rooms

harlot ('härlǝt) n. whore, prostitute —**'harlotry** n.

harm (härm) n. **1.** damage, injury —vt. **2.** cause harm to —**'harmful** a. —**'harmfully** adv. —**'harmless** a. unable or unlikely to hurt —**'harmlessly** adv.

harmony ('härmǝni) n. **1.** agreement **2.** concord **3.** peace **4.** Mus. combination of notes to make chords **5.** melodious sound —**harmonic** (här'monik) a. **1.** of harmony —n. **2.** tone or note whose frequency is a multiple of its pitch —**harmonica** (här'monikǝ) n. small wind instrument played with mouth —**harmonics** (här'moniks) pl.n. **1.** (with sing. v.) science of musical sounds **2.** harmonious sounds —**har'monious** a. —**har'moniously** adv. —**'harmonist** n. —**har'monium** n. keyboard musical instrument whose tones are produced by thin metal tongues or reeds set in motion by foot-operated bellows —**harmoni'zation** n. —**'harmonize** vt. **1.** bring into harmony **2.** cause to agree **3.** reconcile —vi. **4.** be in harmony **5.** sing in harmony, as with other singers

harness ('härnis) n. **1.** equipment for attaching horse to cart, plow etc. **2.** any such equipment —vt. **3.** put on, in harness **4.** utilize energy or power of (waterfall etc.) —**in harness** in or at one's routine work

harp (härp) n. **1.** musical instrument of strings played by hand —vi. **2.** play on harp **3.** (with on or upon) dwell (on) continuously —**'harper** or **'harpist** n. —**'harpsichord** n. stringed keyboard instrument resembling grand piano but differing from it as sound is produced by plucking, not striking, the strings

harpoon (här'pōon) n. **1.** barbed spear with rope attached for catching whales —vt. **2.** catch, kill with or as if with a harpoon —**har'pooner** n. —**harpoon gun** gun for firing harpoon in whaling

harpy ('härpi) n. 1. monster with body of woman and wings and claws of bird 2. cruel, grasping person

harquebus ('härkwibəs) n. heavy portable gun of 15th cent. usu. fired from support (also **arquebus**)

harridan ('haridən) n. shrewish old woman, hag

harrier ('hariər) n. 1. hound used in hunting hares 2. falcon 3. cross-country runner

Harrison[1] ('harisən) n. **Benjamin.** the 23rd President of the U.S. (1889-93)

Harrison[2] ('harisən) n. **William Henry.** the 9th President of the U.S. (Mar.-Apr. 1841)

Harrison Narcotic Act federal law of 1914 controlling the sale of certain drugs

Harris tweed ('haris) trade name for tweed spun, dyed and woven on the island of Lewis with Harris

harrow ('harō) n. 1. implement for smoothing, leveling, or stirring up soil —vt. 2. draw harrow over 3. distress greatly —**harrowing** a. 1. heart-rending 2. distressful

harry ('hari) vt. 1. harass 2. ravage (-ried, -rying)

harsh (härsh) a. 1. rough, discordant 2. severe 3. unfeeling —**harshly** adv.

hart (härt) n. male deer —**hartshorn** ('härtshörn) n. material made from harts' horns, formerly chief source of ammonia

hartebeest ('härtibēst) n. Afr. antelope

harum-scarum (harəm'skarəm, herəm'skerəm) a. 1. reckless, wild 2. giddy

harvest ('härvist) n. 1. (season for) gathering in grain 2. gathering 3. crop 4. product of action —v. 5. reap and gather in (crop) —**harvester** n. —**harvest mite** chigger (also **red bug**)

has (haz) third person sing. pres. indicative of HAVE —**has-been** n. inf. person or thing that is no longer popular, successful etc.

hash (hash) n. 1. dish of preserved or cooked meat mixed with potatoes and browned 2. inf. hashish —vt. 3. cut up into small pieces 4. muddle, confuse —**hash browns** or **hash brown potatoes** diced boiled potatoes and onions formed into cake and fried —**hash-house** n. sl. cheap restaurant —**hash mark** 1. broken line on football field showing where ball may be returned to play 2. service stripe on uniform of enlisted personnel —**make a hash of** mess up, bungle —**settle a person's hash** get rid of or subdue a person

hashish ('hashēsh, -ish) n. resinous extract of Indian hemp, esp. used as hallucinogen

Hasid ('hasid) n. sect of Jews holding fundamental, mystical, reactionary views identified by dress and customs (pl. **'Hasidim**)

hasp (hasp) n. 1. clasp passing over staple for fastening door etc. —vt. 2. fasten, secure with hasp

hassle ('hasəl) inf. n. 1. quarrel 2. great deal of bother or trouble —vi. 3. quarrel, fight —vt. 4. harass (persistently)

hassock ('hasək) n. 1. kneeling-cushion 2. footstool for resting one's legs

hast (hast) obs. second person sing. pres. indicative of HAVE

haste (hāst) n. 1. speed, quickness, hurry —vi. 2. Poet. hasten —**hasten** ('hāsən) v. (cause to) hurry, increase speed —**hastily** adv. —**hasty** a.

hat (hat) n. head covering, usu. with brim —**hatter** n. dealer in, maker of hats —**hat trick** any three successive achievements, esp. in sport

hatch[1] (hach) v. 1. (of young, esp. of birds) (cause to) emerge from egg —vt. 2. contrive, devise —**hatchery** n.

hatch[2] (hach) n. 1. hatchway 2. trapdoor over it 3. opening in wall or door, as service hatch, to facilitate service of meals etc. between two rooms 4. lower half of divided door —**hatchback** n. automobile with single lifting door in rear —**hatchway** n. opening in deck of ship etc.

hatch[3] (hach) vt. 1. engrave or draw lines on for shading 2. shade with parallel lines

hatchet ('hachit) n. small ax —**hatchet job** inf. malicious verbal or written attack —**hatchet man** inf. person carrying out unpleasant assignments for another —**bury the hatchet** make peace

hate (hāt) vt. 1. dislike strongly, bear malice toward —n. 2. intense dislike 3. that which is hated —**hateful** a. detestable —**hatefully** adv. —**hatred** ('hātrid) n. extreme dislike, active ill will

hauberk ('höbərk) n. long coat of mail

haughty ('höti) a. proud, arrogant —**haughtily** adv. —**haughtiness** n.

haul (höl) vt. 1. pull, drag with effort —vi. 2. (of wind) shift —n. 3. hauling 4. something that is hauled 5. catch of fish 6. acquisition 7. distance (to be) covered —**haulage** n. 1. carrying of loads 2. charge for this —**haulier** n. firm, person that transports goods by road

haulm (höm) n. 1. stalks of beans, potatoes, grasses etc. collectively 2. single stem of such plant

haunch (hönch) n. 1. human hip or fleshy hindquarter of animal 2. leg and loin of venison

haunt (hönt) vt. 1. visit regularly 2. visit in form of ghost 3. recur to —n. 4. place frequently visited —**haunted** a. 1. frequented by ghosts 2. worried —**haunting** a. 1. (of memories) poignant or persistent 2. poignantly sentimental —**hauntingly** adv.

hautbois or **hautboy** ('ōboi) n. oboe

haute couture (ōt kōō'tür) Fr. high fashion

hauteur (hō'tər, ō'tər, hō'tər) n. haughty spirit

Havana cigar (hə'vanə) fine quality of cigar (also **Ha'vana**)

have (hav) vt. 1. hold, possess 2. be possessed, affected with 3. cheat, outwit 4. engage in 5. obtain 6. contain 7. allow 8. cause to be (done) 9. give birth to 10. as auxiliary, forms perfect and other tenses (pres. tense: I have, thou hast, he has, we, you, they have) (had, 'having) —**have to** be obliged to

haven ('hāvən) n. place of safety

Haverhill fever ('hāvəril) acute bacterial disease usu. transmitted by rat bites (also **streptobacillary fever**)

haversack ('havərsak) n. canvas bag for provisions etc., slung from shoulder when hiking

havoc ('havək) n. 1. devastation, ruin 2. inf. confusion, chaos

haw (hö) n. 1. fruit of hawthorn 2. hawthorn

Hawaii (hə'wäyē) n. Pacific state of the U.S., admitted to the Union in 1960. Abbrev.: **HI** (with ZIP code)

hawfinch ('höfinch) n. Eurasian finch

hawk[1] (hök) n. 1. small-to-medium bird of prey with very short wings and long tail 2. supporter, advocate of warlike policies —vi. 3. hunt with hawks 4. soar and swoop like hawk —**hawk-eyed** a. 1. having extremely keen sight 2. vigilant or observant

hawk[2] (hök) vt. offer (goods) for sale, as in street —**hawker** n.

hawk[3] (hök) vi. clear throat noisily

hawse (höz) n. part of ship's bows with holes for cables

hawser ('hözər) n. large rope or cable

hawthorn ('höthörn) n. thorny shrub or tree having pink or white flowers and reddish fruits (also **May, May tree**)

Hawthorne effect ('höthörn) the change in output or results in a situation purely as an effect of applying different stimuli

hay (hā) n. grass mown and dried —**haybox** n. box filled with hay in which heated food is left to finish cooking —**hay fever** allergic reaction to pollen, dust etc. —**haymaker** n. 1. person who cuts or turns hay 2. either of two machines, one designed to crush stems of hay, the other to break and bend them, in order to cause more rapid and even drying 3. Boxing sl. wild swinging punch —**haymaking** a./n. —**haystack** n. large pile of hay —**haywire** a. 1. crazy 2. disorganized

Hayes (hāz) n. **Rutherford Birchard.** the 19th President of the U.S. (1877-81)

hazard ('hazərd) n. 1. chance 2. risk, danger —vt. 3. expose to risk 4. run risk of —**hazardous** a. risky

haze (hāz) n. 1. mist, oft. due to heat 2. obscurity —**hazy** a. 1. misty 2. obscured 3. vague

hazel ('hāzəl) n. 1. bush bearing nuts 2. yellowish-brown color of the nuts —a. 3. light yellowish brown

Hb hemoglobin

H.B.C. Hudson's Bay Company

H-bomb hydrogen bomb

H.C.F. highest common factor

he (hē; unstressed ē) pron. 1. (third person masculine pronoun) person, animal already referred to 2. (comb. form) male, as in he-goat —**he-man** n. inf. strongly built muscular man

He Chem. helium

HE or **H.E.** 1. high explosive 2. His Eminence 3. His (or Her) Excellency

head (hed) n. 1. upper part of person's or animal's body, containing mouth, sense organs and brain 2. upper part of anything 3. chief of organization, school etc. 4. chief part 5. aptitude, capacity 6. culmination or crisis 7. leader 8. section of chapter 9. title 10. headland 11. person, animal considered as unit 12. white froth on beer etc. 13. inf. headache —a. 14. chief, principal 15. (of wind) contrary —vt. 16. be at the top, head of 17. lead, direct 18. provide with head 19. hit (ball) with head —vi. 20. (with for) make (for) 21. form a head —**header** n. 1. inf. headlong fall or dive 2. brick laid with end in face of wall 3. action of striking ball with head —**heading** n. 1. direction 2. title —**heads** adv. inf. with obverse side (of coin) uppermost —**heady** a. apt to intoxicate or excite —**headache** n. 1. continuous pain in head 2. inf. worrying circumstance —**headboard** n. vertical board at head of bed —**headdress** n. any head covering, esp. ornate one —**headgear** n. 1. hat, headdress etc. 2. any part of horse's harness worn on head —**head-hunter** n. —**head-hunting** n. 1. practice among certain peoples of removing heads of slain enemies and preserving them as trophies 2. (of company or corporation) recruitment of, or drive to recruit, new high-level personnel —**headland** n. promontory —**headlight** n. powerful lamp carried on front of locomotive, motor vehicle etc. —**headline** n. news summary, usu. in large type in newspaper —**head'long** adv. 1. with head foremost 2. with great haste —**head louse** louse that lives on the scalp of man —**head-on** adv./a. 1. (of collision etc.) front foremost 2. with directness —**headphones** pl.n. two earphones held in position by strap over head (*also* (*inf.*) **cans**) —**head pin** foremost pin in arrangement of bowling pins —'**headquarters** *pl.n.* 1. operational center of commander-in-chief 2. center of administration —'**headroom** *or* '**headway** *n.* clear space between decks —'**headshrinker** *n.* 1. *sl.* psychiatrist (*also* **shrink**) 2. head-hunter who shrinks heads of his victims —'**headstall** *n.* part of bridle that fits round horse's head —**head start** initial advantage in competitive situation —'**headstone** *n.* gravestone —'**headstrong** *a.* self-willed —'**headwaters** *pl.n.* tributary streams of river —'**headway** *n.* advance, progress —'**headwind** *n.* wind blowing directly against course of aircraft or ship —'**headword** *n.* key word placed at beginning of line *etc.* as in dictionary entry —**come to a head** reach a crisis —**head and shoulders** (**above**) clearly superior (to) —**put heads together** pool ideas

heal (hēl) *v.* make or become well —**health** (helth) *n.* 1. soundness of body 2. condition of body 3. toast drunk in person's honor —**healthily** ('helthili) *adv.* —**healthiness** ('helthinis) *n.* —**healthy** ('helthi) *a.* 1. of strong constitution 2. of or producing good health, wellbeing *etc.* 3. vigorous

heap (hēp) *n.* 1. pile of things lying one on another 2. great quantity —*vt.* 3. pile 4. load (with)

hear (hēər) *vt.* 1. perceive by ear 2. listen to 3. *Law* try (case) 4. heed —*vi.* 5. perceive sound 6. (*with* of *or* about) learn (**heard** (hərd) *pt./pp.*) —'**hearer** *n.* —'**hearing** *n.* 1. ability to hear 2. earshot 3. judicial examination —**hearing aid** 1. miniaturized amplifier designed to aid those with difficulty in hearing 2. any device serving the same purpose, *eg* ear trumpet —'**hearsay** *n.* 1. rumor —*a.* 2. based on hearsay —**hear! hear!** exclamation of approval, agreement

hearken *or* **harken** ('härkən) *vi.* listen

hearse (hərs) *n.* funeral carriage for carrying coffin to grave

heart (härt) *n.* 1. organ which makes blood circulate 2. seat of emotions and affections 3. mind, soul, courage 4. central part 5. playing card marked with symbol of heart 6. one of these marks —*pl.* 7. (*with sing. v.*) any of family of card games for two to six players each playing for himself, played with standard 52-card deck in which the object is to avoid taking certain cards or tricks —'**hearten** *v.* make, become cheerful —'**heartily** *adv.* —'**heartless** *a.* unfeeling —'**hearty** *a.* 1. friendly 2. vigorous 3. in good health 4. satisfying the appetite —'**heartache** *n.* intense anguish or mental suffering —**heart attack** sudden severe malfunction of heart —'**heartbreak** *n.* intense and overwhelming grief or disappointment —'**heartbreaking** *a.* —'**heartburn** *n.* burning sensation originating in the upper abdomen and moving behind the breastbone —**heart failure** 1. inability of heart to pump adequate amount of blood to tissues 2. sudden cessation of heartbeat, resulting in death —'**heartfelt** *a.* sincerely and strongly felt —'**heartfree** *a.* with the affections free or disengaged —**heart-lung machine** device which duplicates functions of heart and lungs —**heart-rending** *a.* 1. overwhelming with grief 2. agonizing —**heart-searching** *n.* examination of one's feelings or conscience —'**heartsease** *n.* wild pansy —**heart-throb** *n.* *sl.* object of infatuation —**heart-to-heart** *a.* 1. (*esp.* of conversation) concerned with personal problems —*n.* 2. intimate conversation —**heart-warming** *a.* 1. pleasing; gratifying 2. emotionally moving —'**heartwood** *n.*

central core of dark hard wood in tree trunks —**by heart** memorized —**take to heart** be deeply troubled by —**wear one's heart on one's sleeve** let one's feelings show

hearth (härth) *n.* 1. part of room where fire is made 2. home

heat (hēt) *n.* 1. hotness 2. sensation of this 3. hot weather or climate 4. warmth of feeling, anger *etc.* 5. sexual excitement caused by readiness to mate in female animals (*also* **estrus, estrum**) 6. one of many races *etc.* to decide persons to compete in finals —*v.* 7. make, become hot —'**heated** *a.* angry —'**heatedly** *adv.* —'**heater** *n.* any device for supplying heat, such as a convector —**heat cramp** painful contractions following heavy loss of body salts through perspiration —**heat exhaustion** inability of the circulatory system to adapt to additional demand of cooling the skin in a hot climate —**heat pump** device for extracting heat from substance that is at slightly higher temperature than its surroundings and delivering it to factory *etc.* at much higher temperature —**heat stroke** the breakdown of the heat-regulating mechanisms of the body, always fatal when untreated —**heat wave** continuous spell of abnormally hot weather

heath (hēth) *n.* 1. tract of wasteland 2. low-growing evergreen shrub

heathen ('hēdhən) *a.* 1. not adhering to a religious system 2. pagan 3. barbarous 4. unenlightened —*n.* 5. heathen person (*pl.* **-s,** '**heathen**) —'**heathendom** *n.* —'**heathenish** *a.* 1. of or like heathen 2. rough 3. barbarous —'**heathenism** *n.*

heather ('hedhər) *n.* shrub growing on heaths and mountains —'**heathery** *a.*

heave (hēv) *vt.* 1. lift with effort 2. throw (something heavy) 3. utter (sigh) —*vi.* 4. swell, rise 5. feel nausea —*n.* 6. act or effort of heaving

heaven ('hevən) *n.* 1. abode of God 2. place of bliss 3. (*also pl.*) sky —'**heavenly** *a.* 1. lovely, delightful, divine 2. beautiful 3. of or like heaven

heavy ('hevi) *a.* 1. weighty, striking, falling with force 2. dense 3. sluggish 4. difficult, severe 5. sorrowful 6. serious 7. dull —'**heavily** *adv.* —'**heaviness** *n.* —**heavy-duty** *a.* made to withstand hard wear, bad weather *etc.* —**heavy-handed** *a.* 1. clumsy 2. harsh and oppressive —**heavy-hearted** *a.* sad; melancholy —**heavy industry** basic, large-scale industry producing metal, machinery *etc.* —**heavy-metal** *a.* of type of rock music characterized by strong beat and amplified instrumental effects —**heavy water** deuterium oxide, water in which normal hydrogen content has been replaced by deuterium

Heb. 1. Hebrew 2. *Bible* Hebrews

hebdomadal (heb'domədəl) *a.* weekly

Hebrew ('hēbrōō) *n.* 1. member of an ancient Semitic people 2. their language 3. its modern form, used in Israel —**He'braic(al)** *a.* of or characteristic of Hebrews, their language or culture

Hebrews ('hēbrōōz) *pl.n.* (*with sing. v.*) *Bible* 19th book of the N.T., epistle of disputed authorship espousing the perfection of Christ

heckle ('hekəl) *v.* interrupt or try to annoy (speaker) by questions, taunts *etc.*

hectare ('hektåər, -tär) *n.* metric unit of area: one hundred ares or 10 000 square meters, equal to 2.47 acres

hectic ('hektik) *a.* rushed, busy

hecto- *or before vowel* **hect-** (*comb. form*) one hundred, *esp.* in metric system, as in *hectoliter, hectometer*

hector ('hektər) *vt.* 1. bully —*vi.* 2. bluster —*n.* 3. blusterer

heddle ('hedəl) *n. Weaving* one of set of frames of vertical wires

hedge (hej) *n.* 1. fence of bushes —*vt.* 2. surround with hedge 3. obstruct 4. hem in 5. guard against risk of loss in (bet *etc.*), *esp.* by laying bets with other bookmakers —*vi.* 6. make or trim hedges 7. be evasive 8. secure against loss —'**hedgehog** *n.* small Old World mammal covered with spines —'**hedgerow** *n.* bushes forming hedge —**hedge sparrow** small brownish songbird

hedonism ('hēdənizəm) *n.* 1. doctrine that pleasure is the chief good 2. indulgence in sensual pleasure —**he'donics** *pl.n.* (*with sing. v.*) 1. branch of psychology concerned with the study of pleasant and unpleasant sensations 2. in philosophy, study of pleasures —'**hedonist** *n.* —**hedo'nistic** *a.*

heed (hēd) *vt.* take notice of —'**heedful** *a.* —'**heedless** *a.* careless

heehaw ('hēhô, 'hē'hô) *interj.* imitation or representation of braying sound of donkey

heel[1] (hēl) *n.* 1. hinder part of foot 2. part of shoe supporting this 3. *sl.* undesirable person —*vt.* 4. supply with heel 5. touch (ground, ball) with heel —'**heelball** *n.* mixture of beeswax and lampblack used by shoemakers and in taking rubbings, *esp.* brass rubbings —**heel spur** bony growth on the heel bone

heel[2] (hēl) *v.* 1. (of ship) (cause to) lean to one side —*n.* 2. heeling, list

hefty ('hefti) *a.* 1. bulky 2. weighty 3. strong

hegemony (hi'jeməni, -'gem-) *n.* leadership, political domination —**hegemonic** (hejə'monik, hegə-) *a.*

hegira *or* **hejira** (hi'jīrə, 'hejirə) *n.* 1. flight of Mohammed from Mecca to Medina in 622 A.D. 2. escape or flight

heifer ('hefər) *n.* young cow

height (hīt) *n.* 1. measure from base to top 2. quality of being high 3. elevation 4. highest degree 5. (*oft. pl.*) hilltop —'**heighten** *vt.* 1. make higher 2. intensify

Heimlich maneuver ('hīmlik) applying manual pressure to the lower chest to dislodge a foreign object from the windpipe

heinous ('hānəs) *a.* atrocious, extremely wicked, detestable

heir (āər) *n.* person entitled to inherit property or rank ('**heiress** *fem.*) —'**heirloom** *n.* thing that has been in family for generations

Helanca (hə'langkə) *n.* trade name for nylon stretch yarn

held (held) *pt./pp.* of HOLD[1]

helical ('helikəl) *a.* spiral

helicopter ('helikoptər) *n.* aircraft made to rise vertically by pull of airscrew revolving horizontally —'**heliport** *n.* airport for helicopters

helio- *or before vowel* **heli-** (*comb. form*) sun, as in *heliocentric*

heliocentric (hēliō'sentrik) *a.* 1. having sun at its center 2. measured in relation to sun —**helio'centrically** *adv.*

heliograph ('hēliəgraf) *n.* signaling apparatus employing mirror to reflect sun's rays

heliostat ('hēliəstat) *n.* astronomical instrument used to reflect light of sun in constant direction

heliotherapy (hēliō'therəpi) *n.* therapeutic use of sunlight

heliotrope ('hēliətrōp, 'helyə-) *n.* 1. plant with purple flowers 2. bluish-violet to purple color —**heliotropic** (hēlia'trōpik, -'tropik) a. growing, turning toward source of light

helium ('hēliəm) n. Chem. noble gas present in the sun's atmosphere Symbol He, at. wt. 4.003, at. no. 2

helix ('hēliks) n. **1.** spiral **2.** incurving fold that forms margin of external ear **3.** see VOLUTE (sense 1) (pl. **helices** ('helisēz), -es)

hell (hel) n. **1.** abode of the damned **2.** abode of the dead generally **3.** place or state of wickedness, misery or torture —'**hellish** a./adv. —'**hellbent** a. (with on) inf. strongly or rashly intent —'**hellfire** n. **1.** torment of hell, envisaged as eternal fire —a. **2.** characterizing sermons that emphasize this —**Hell's Angel** member of motorcycle gang who typically dress in leather clothing, noted for their lawless behavior

hellebore ('helibōr) n. plant with white flowers that bloom in winter, Christmas rose

Hellenic (he'lenik, hə-) a. pert. to inhabitants of Greece —'**Hellenist** n.

hello (hə'lō, he-) interj. expression of greeting or surprise

helm (helm) n. tiller, wheel for turning ship's rudder

helmet ('helmit) n. defensive or protective covering for head (also **helm**)

helminth ('helminth) n. parasitic worm, esp. nematode or fluke —**hel'minthic** a.

Helot ('helət) n. **1.** in ancient Sparta, member of class of serfs owned by state **2.** (usu. **h**-) serf or slave —'**Helotism** n. —'**Helotry** n.

help (help) vt. **1.** aid, assist **2.** support **3.** succor **4.** remedy, prevent —n. **5.** act of helping or being helped **6.** person or thing that helps —'**helper** n. —'**helpful** a. —'**helping** n. single portion of food taken at meal —'**helpless** a. **1.** useless, incompetent **2.** unaided **3.** unable to help —'**helplessly** adv. —'**helpmate** or '**helpmeet** n. **1.** helpful companion **2.** husband or wife

helter-skelter (heltər'skeltər) adv./a./n. **1.** (in) hurry and confusion —n. **2.** high spiral slide at fairground

helve (helv) n. handle of hand tool such as ax or pick

hem[1] (hem) n. **1.** border of cloth, esp. one made by turning over edge and sewing it down —vt. **2.** sew thus **3.** (usu. with in) confine, shut in (-mm-) —'**hemstitch** n. **1.** ornamental stitch —v. **2.** decorate (hem etc.) with hemstitches

hem[2] (hem) n./interj. **1.** representation of sound of clearing throat, used to gain attention etc. —vi. **2.** utter this sound (-mm-) —**hem** (or **hum**) **and haw** hesitate in speaking

hematite ('hēmətīt) n. ore of iron

hematology (hēmə'tolaji) n. branch of medicine concerned with diseases of blood

hematoma (hēmə'tōmə) n. tumorlike swelling resulting from the escape of blood from a ruptured vessel into the tissues

hemi- (comb. form) half, as in hemisphere

hemiplegia (hemi'plējiə) n. paralysis of one side of the body

hemisphere ('hemisfēər) n. **1.** half sphere **2.** half of celestial sphere **3.** half of the earth —**hemispheric(al)** (hemi'sfēərik(əl), -'sferik-(əl)) a.

hemistich ('hemistik) n. half line of verse

hemlock ('hemlok) n. **1.** either of two native N Amer. trees of the pine family: one in the northwest, the other in the east **2.** poisonous European perennial herb naturalized sporadically in wet places throughout N Amer. **3.** native poisonous herb of wet habitats (also **water hemlock**) —**ground hemlock** low spreading yew of eastern N Amer.

hemo- (comb. form) blood

hemoglobin ('hēməglōbin) n. coloring and oxygen-bearing matter of red blood corpuscles

hemolytic streptococci (hēmə'litik) bacteria which cause several illnesses in humans

hemophilia (hēmə'filiə) n. hereditary tendency to intensive bleeding as blood fails to clot —**hemo'philiac** a./n.

hemorrhage ('hemərij) n. profuse bleeding

hemorrhoids ('heməroidz) pl.n. swollen veins in rectum (also **piles**)

hemp (hemp) n. **1.** Indian plant **2.** its fiber used for rope etc. **3.** any of several narcotic drugs made from varieties of hemp —'**hempen** a. made of hemp or rope

hen (hen) n. female of domestic fowl and others —'**henpeck** vt. (of woman) harass (a man, esp. husband) by nagging

hence (hens) adv. **1.** from this point **2.** for this reason —**hence'forward** or '**henceforth** adv. from now onward

henchman ('henchmən) n. trusty follower

henge (henj) n. circular monument, oft. containing circle of stones

henna ('henə) n. **1.** flowering shrub **2.** reddish dye made from it

henotheism ('henəthēizəm) n. belief in one god (of several) as special god of one's family, tribe etc.

henry ('henri) n. unit of electrical inductance

heparin ('hepərin) n. compound produced by liver that inhibits clotting of the blood

hepatic (hi'patik) a. pert. to the liver —**hepa'titis** n. inflammation of the liver

hepta- or before vowel **hept-** (comb. form) seven, as in heptameter

heptagon ('heptəgon) n. figure with seven angles —**hep'tagonal** a.

heptarchy ('heptärki) n. rule by seven

her (hər; unstressed ər) a. objective and possessive case of SHE —**hers** pron. of her —**her'self** pron.

herald ('herəld) n. **1.** messenger, envoy **2.** officer who makes royal proclamations, arranges ceremonies, regulates armorial bearings etc. —vt. **3.** announce **4.** proclaim approach of —**he'raldic** a. —'**heraldry** n. study of (right to have) heraldic bearings

herb (ərb) n. **1.** plant with soft stem which dies down after flowering **2.** plant used in cooking or medicine —**her'baceous** a. **1.** of, like herbs **2.** flowering perennially —'**herbage** n. **1.** herbs **2.** grass **3.** pasture —'**herbal** a. **1.** of herbs —n. **2.** book on herbs —'**herbalist** n. **1.** writer on herbs **2.** dealer in medicinal herbs —**her'barium** n. collection of dried plants (pl. -s, -ia (-iə)) —'**herbicide** n. chemical which destroys plants —**her'bivorous** a. feeding on plants

Hercules ('hərkyəlēz) n. mythical hero noted for strength —**herculean** (hərkyə'lēən) a. requiring great strength, courage etc.

herd (hərd) n. **1.** company of animals, usu. of same species, feeding or traveling together **2.** herdsman —v. **3.** collect or be collected together —vt. **4.** tend (livestock) —**herd instinct** Psychol. inborn tendency to associate with others and follow group's behavior —'**herdsman** n.

here (hēər) adv. **1.** in this place **2.** at or to this point —**here'after** adv. **1.** in time to come —n. **2.** future existence —**here'by** adv. by means of or as result of this —'**heretofore** adv. before —**here'with** adv. together with this

heredity (hi'rediti) n. the transmission of physical traits from parent organisms to their offspring through genes —**here'dita-**

-ment n. property that can be inherited —**heredi'tarily** adv. —**he'reditary** a. **1.** descending by inheritance **2.** holding office by inheritance **3.** that can be transmitted from one generation to another

heresy ('herəsi) n. opinion contrary to orthodox opinion or belief —'**heretic** n. one holding opinions contrary to orthodox faith —**he'retical** a. —**he'retically** adv.

heritage ('heritij) n. **1.** what may be or is inherited **2.** anything from past, esp. owned or handed down by tradition —'**heritable** a. that can be inherited

hermaphrodite (hər'mafrədīt) n. **1.** animal or flower that has both male and female reproductive organs **2.** person having both male and female characteristics

hermetic (hər'metik) or **hermetical** a. sealed so as to be airtight —**her'metically** adv.

hermit ('hərmit) n. one living in solitude, esp. from religious motives —'**hermitage** n. his abode —**hermit crab** soft-bodied crustacean living in and carrying about empty shells of mollusks

hernia ('hərniə) n. projection of (part of) organ through lining encasing it (pl. -s, -iae (-iē)) —'**hernial** a.

hero ('hēərō) n. **1.** one greatly regarded for achievements or qualities **2.** principal character in play etc. **3.** illustrious warrior **4.** demigod (pl. -es) (**heroine** ('herōin) fem.) —**heroic** (hi'rōik) a. **1.** of, like hero **2.** courageous, daring —**heroically** (hi'rōikəli) adv. —**heroics** (hi'rōiks) pl.n. extravagant behavior —**heroism** ('herōizəm) n. **1.** qualities of hero **2.** courage, boldness —**heroic verse** type of verse suitable for epic or heroic subjects —**hero worship 1.** admiration of heroes or of great men **2.** excessive admiration of others —**hero-worship** vt. feel admiration or adulation for

heroin ('herōin) n. white crystalline derivative of morphine, a highly addictive narcotic

heron ('herən) n. long-legged wading bird —'**heronry** n. place where herons breed

herpes ('hərpēz) n. any of several virus diseases characterized by blister formation on the skin or mucous membranes

Herr (German her) n. German man: used before name as title equivalent to Mr (pl. **Herren** ('herən))

herring ('hering) n. important food fish of northern hemisphere —'**herringbone** n. stitch or pattern of zigzag lines —**herring gull** common gull that has white plumage with black-tipped wings

hertz (hərts) n. unit of frequency (pl. **hertz**)

hesitate ('hezitāt) vi. **1.** hold back **2.** feel or show indecision **3.** be reluctant —'**hesitancy** or **hesi'tation** n. **1.** wavering **2.** doubt **3.** stammering —'**hesitant** a. undecided, pausing —'**hesitantly** adv.

hessian ('hesiən) n. burlap

hest (hest) n. behest, command

hetaera (hi'tēərə) or **hetaira** (hi'tīrə) n. esp. in ancient Greece, prostitute, esp. educated courtesan (pl. -taerae (-'tēərē) or -tairai (-'tīrī))

hetero- (comb. form) other; different, as in heterosexual

heterodox ('hetərədoks) a. not orthodox —'**heterodoxy** n.

heterodyne ('hetərədīn) v. **1.** Electron. mix (two alternating signals) to produce two signals having frequencies corresponding to sum and difference of original frequencies —a. **2.** produced by, operating by, or involved in heterodyning two signals

heterogeneous (hetərə'jēniəs) a. composed of diverse elements —**heteroge'neity** n.

heteromorphic (hetərə'mörfik) a. Biol. 1. differing from normal form 2. (esp. of insects) having different forms at different stages of life cycle —**hetero'morphism** n.

heterosexual (hetərō'seksh̆ōōəl) n. person sexually attracted to members of the opposite sex —**heterosexu'ality** n.

heuchera ('hoikərə) n. genus of N Amer. plants of the saxifrage family; alumroot

heuristic (hyŏō'ristik) a. 1. (of methods of teaching) encouraging students to find out things for themselves 2. (in solving problems by computer) proceeding by trial and error

hew (hyōō) v. chop, cut with ax (**hewn, hewed** pp.) —**'hewer** n.

HEW Health, Education and Welfare: U.S. government agency

hexa- or before vowel **hex-** (comb. form) six, as in hexachord

hexagon ('heksəgon) n. figure with six angles —**hex'agonal** a.

hexagram ('heksəgram) n. star-shaped figure formed by extending sides of regular hexagon to meet at six points

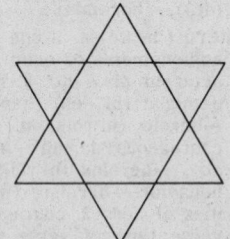

hexagram

hexameter (hek'samitər) n. line of verse of six feet

hexapod ('heksəpod) n. insect

hey (hā) interj. expression indicating surprise, dismay, discovery etc.—**'heyday** n. bloom, prime —**hey presto** exclamation used by conjurers to herald climax of trick

Hf Chem. hafnium

HF, H.F., hf, or **h.f.** high frequency

hf. half

Hg Chem. mercury

H.H. 1. His (or Her) Highness 2. His Holiness (title of Pope)

HI Hawaii

hiatus (hī'ātəs) n. break or gap where something is missing —**hiatus hernia** part of intestinal tract that slips in and out of gap in diaphragm (pl. **-es, hi'atus**)

hibernate ('hībərnāt) vi. pass the winter, esp. in a torpid state —**hiber'nation** n. —**'hibernator** n.

Hibernian (hī'bərniən) a./n. Irish (person)

hibiscus (hī'biskəs, hi-) n. 1. flowering (sub)tropical shrub 2. Rose of Sharon

hiccup ('hikup) n. 1. spasm of the breathing organs with an abrupt coughlike sound —vi. 2. make a hiccup or hiccups (also **'hiccough**)

hick (hik) inf. a. 1. rustic 2. unsophisticated —n. 3. person like this

hickory ('hikəri) n. 1. N Amer. nut-bearing tree 2. its tough wood

hide[1] (hīd) vt. 1. put, keep out of sight 2. conceal, keep secret —vi. 3. conceal oneself (**hid** (hid) pt., **hidden** ('hidən) or **hid** pp., **'hiding** pr.p.) —n. 4. place of concealment, eg for birdwatcher —**'hideaway** n. hiding place or secluded spot —**hide-out** n. hiding place

hide[2] (hīd) n. skin of animal —**'hiding** n. sl. thrashing —**'hidebound** a. 1. restricted, esp.

by petty rules etc. 2. narrow-minded 3. (of tree) having bark so close that it impedes growth

hideous ('hidiəs) a. repulsive, revolting —**'hideously** adv.

hie (hī) v. obs. hasten (**hied** pt./pp., **'hying** or **'hieing** pr.p.)

hierarchy ('hīərärki) n. system of persons or things arranged in graded order —**hier'archic(al)** a.

hieratic (hīə'ratik) a. 1. of priests 2. of cursive form of hieroglyphics used by priests in ancient Egypt —n. 3. hieratic script of ancient Egypt —**hier'atically** adv.

hieroglyphic (hīərə'glifik) a. 1. of a system of picture writing, esp. as used in ancient Egypt —n. 2. symbol representing object, concept, or sound 3. symbol, picture, difficult to decipher —**'hieroglyph** n.

hi-fi ('hī'fī) inf. a. 1. see high-fidelity at HIGH —n. 2. high-fidelity equipment

higgledy-piggledy (higəldi'pigəldi) adv./a. inf. in confusion

high (hī) a. 1. tall, lofty 2. far up 3. (of roads) main 4. (of meat) tainted 5. (of season) well advanced 6. (of sound) acute in pitch 7. expensive 8. of great importance, quality, or rank 9. inf. in state of euphoria, esp. induced by drugs 10. inf. bad-smelling —adv. 11. far up 12. strongly, to a great extent 13. at, to a high pitch 14. at a high rate —**'highly** adv. —**'highness** n. 1. quality of being high 2. (H-) title of prince or princess —**'highball** n. long iced drink consisting of liquor base with soda water etc. —**high beam** headlight with a long range —**'highbrow** sl. n. 1. intellectual, esp. intellectual snob —a. 2. intellectual 3. difficult 4. serious —**'highchair** n. long-legged chair for child, esp. one with table-like tray —**High Church** party within Church of England emphasizing authority of bishops and importance of sacraments, rituals and ceremonies —**higher education** education and training at colleges, universities etc. —**high explosive** extremely powerful chemical explosive —**highfa'lutin** or **highfa'luting** a. inf. pompous or pretentious —**high-fidelity** a. of high-quality sound-reproducing equipment —**high-flier** or **high-flyer** n. 1. person extreme in aims, ambition etc. 2. person of great ability, esp. in career —**high-flown** a. extravagant, bombastic —**high frequency** radio frequency lying between 30 and 3 megahertz —**High German** standard German language, historically developed from the form of W Germanic spoken in S Germany —**high-handed** a. domineering, dogmatic —**high jump** athletic event in which competitor has to jump over high bar —**Highland** ('hīlənd) a. of, from the Highlands of Scotland —**highland(s)** ('hīlənd(z)) (pl.)n. relatively high ground —**high-level language** Comp. language suitable for problem solving where a single instruction can correspond to several instructions —**'highlight** n. 1. lightest or brightest area in painting, photograph etc. 2. outstanding feature —vt. 3. bring into prominence —**highly strung** excitable, nervous —**High Mass** solemn and elaborate sung Mass —**high-minded** a. having or characterized by high moral principles —**high-mindedness** n. —**high-powered** a. 1. (of optical instrument or lens) having high magnification 2. dynamic and energetic —**high-pressure** a. 1. having, using, or designed to withstand pressure above normal 2. inf. (of selling) persuasive in aggressive and persistent manner —**high priest** 1. Judaism priest of highest rank 2. head of cult —**high school** secondary school —**high seas** open seas,

outside jurisdiction of any one nation —**high-sounding** a. pompous, imposing —**high-spirited** a. vivacious, bold or lively —**high-tension** a. carrying or operating at relatively high voltage —**high tide** 1. tide at its highest level 2. culminating point —**high time** latest possible time —**high treason** act of treason directly affecting sovereign or state —**high water** 1. high tide 2. state of any stretch of water at its highest level —**'highway** n. 1. main road 2. ordinary route —**'highwayman** n. formerly, robber on road, esp. mounted

hijack or **highjack** ('hījak) vt. 1. divert or wrongfully take command of (vehicle or its contents) while in transit 2. rob —**'hijacker** or **'highjacker** n.

hike (hīk) vi. 1. walk a long way (for pleasure) in country —vt. 2. pull (up), hitch —n. 3. long walk —**'hiker** n.

hilarity (hi'lariti) n. cheerfulness, gaiety —**hilarious** (hi'lariəs, -'ler-) a.

hill (hil) n. 1. natural elevation, small mountain 2. mound —**'hillock** n. little hill —**'hilly** a. —**'hillbilly** n. unsophisticated (country) person

hilt (hilt) n. handle of sword etc. —**to the hilt** to the full

hilum ('hīləm) n. Bot. scar on seed marking its point of attachment to seed stalk (pl. **-la** (-lə))

him (him; unstressed im) pron. objective case of HE —**him'self** pron. emphatic form of HE

hind[1] (hīnd) or **hinder** ('hīndər) a. at the back, posterior —**'hindquarter** n. 1. one of two back quarters of carcass of beef etc. —pl. 2. rear, esp. of four-legged animal —**'hindsight** n. 1. ability to understand, after something has happened, what should have been done 2. firearm's rear sight

hind[2] (hīnd) n. female of deer

hinder ('hindər) vt. obstruct, impede, delay —**'hindrance** n.

Hindi ('hindi) n. language of N central India —**'Hindu** or **'Hindoo** n. person who adheres to **Hinduism,** the dominant religion of India —**Hindustani** or **Hindostani** (hindōō'stani, -'stäni) n. 1. dialect of Hindi spoken in Delhi 2. all spoken forms of Hindi and Urdu considered together —a. 3. of or relating to these languages or Hindustan

hinge (hinj) n. 1. movable joint, as that on which door hangs —vt. 2. attach with, or as with, hinge —vi. 3. turn, depend (on)

hinny ('hini) n. sterile hybrid offspring of male horse and female donkey

hint (hint) n. 1. slight indication or suggestion —v. 2. (sometimes with at) suggest indirectly

hinterland ('hintərland) n. district lying behind coast, or near city, port etc.

hip[1] (hip) n. 1. (oft. pl.) either side of body below waist and above thigh 2. angle formed where sloping sides of roof meet 3. fruit of rose, esp. wild —**'hipbone** n. large flaring bone forming half of pelvis in mammals composed of ilium, ischium and pubis which become consolidated in the adult (also **innominate bone**)

hip[2] (hip) a. sl. 1. aware of or following latest trends 2. informed

hippeastrum (hipi'astrəm) n. genus of tropical and subtropical bulbs of lily family related to and often sold as amaryllis, with strap-shaped leaves and stout flower stems carrying funnel-shaped flowers, widely grown as house plant

hippie or **hippy** ('hipi) n. (young) person whose behavior, dress etc. implies rejection of conventional values

hippo ('hipō) n. inf. hippopotamus (pl. **-s**)

Hippocratic oath (hipə'kratik) oath taken by doctor to observe code of medical ethics

hippodrome ('hipədrōm) n. arena for equestrian display

hippogriff ('hipəgrif) n. legendary griffinlike creature with horse's body

hippopotamus (hipə'potəməs) n. large Afr. animal living in rivers (pl. **-es, -mi** (-mī))

hire ('hīər) vt. 1. obtain temporary use of by payment 2. engage for wage —n. 3. hiring or being hired 4. payment for use of something —'**hireling** n. one who serves for wages

hirsute ('hərsōōt) a. hairy —**hirsutism** ('hərsitizəm) n. unusual growth of hair on females

his (hiz; unstressed iz) pron./a. belonging to him

Hispanic (hi'spanik) a. of or derived from Spain or the Spanish —**Hi'spanicism** n.

hispid ('hispid) a. 1. rough with bristles or minute spines 2. bristly, shaggy —**his'pidity** n.

hiss (his) vi. 1. make sharp sound of letter s, esp. in disapproval —vt. 2. express disapproval of, deride thus —n. 3. sound like that of prolonged s —'**hissing** n.

hist. 1. historian 2. historical 3. history

histamine ('histəmēn) n. substance released by body tissues, sometimes creating allergic reactions

histogeny (hi'stojəni) n. formation and development of organic tissues

histogram ('histəgram) n. graph using vertical columns to illustrate frequency distribution

histology (hi'stoləji) n. branch of biology concerned with the structure of tissues —**his'tologist** n.

histoplasmosis (histoplaz'mōsis) n. disease caused by infection with a soil fungus

history ('histəri) n. 1. record of past events 2. study of these 3. past events 4. train of events, public or private 5. course of life or existence 6. systematic account of phenomena —**his'torian** n. writer of history —**historic** (hi'storik) a. noted in history —**historical** (hi'storikəl) a. 1. of, based on, history 2. belonging to the past —**historically** (hi'storikəli) adv. —**histo'ricity** n. historical authenticity —**histori'ographer** n. 1. official historian 2. one who studies historical method

histrionic (histri'onik) a. excessively theatrical, insincere, artificial in manner —**histri'onics** pl.n. behavior like this

hit (hit) vt. 1. strike with blow or missile 2. affect injuriously 3. reach —vi. 4. strike a blow 5. (with upon) light (upon) (**hit, 'hitting**) —n. 6. blow 7. inf. success —'**hitter** n. —**hit-and-run** a. 1. denoting motor-vehicle accident in which driver leaves scene without stopping 2. (of attack etc.) relying on surprise allied to rapid departure from scene of operations —**hit-and-run play** baseball play in which base runner moves off as soon as the pitcher begins to pitch and the batter swings —**hit man** hired assassin —**hit parade** list of currently most popular songs, ranked in order of sales per record —**hit it off** get along (with person) —**hit or miss** casual; haphazard —**hit the hay** sl. go to bed —**hit the nail on the head** express the truth exactly —**hit the trail** or **road** inf. 1. proceed on journey 2. leave

hitch (hich) vt. 1. fasten with loop etc. 2. raise, move with jerk —vi. 3. be caught or fastened —n. 4. difficulty 5. knot, fastening 6. jerk —'**hitchhike** or **hitch** vi. travel by begging free rides

hither ('hidhər) adv. 1. to or toward this place (esp. in **come hither**) —a. 2. obs. situated on this side —'**hitherto** adv. up to now or to this time

hive (hīv) n. 1. structure in which bees live or are housed 2. fig. place swarming with busy occupants —v. 3. gather, place bees, in hive —**hive away** store, keep —**hive off** 1. transfer 2. dispose of

hives (hīvz) pl.n. urticaria

H.M. His (or Her) Majesty

H.M.C.S. His (or Her) Majesty's Canadian Ship

H.M.S. His (or Her) Majesty's Service or Ship

H.M.S.O. UK His (or Her) Majesty's Stationery Office

ho (hō) interj. 1. imitation or representation of sound of deep laugh (also **ho-ho**) 2. exclamation used to attract attention etc.

Ho Chem. holmium

hoard (hörd) n. 1. stock, store, esp. hidden away —vt. 2. amass and hide away 3. store

hoarding ('hörding) n. 1. large board for displaying advertisements 2. temporary wooden fence round building or piece of ground

hoarse (hörs) a. rough, harsh-sounding, husky —'**hoarsely** adv. —'**hoarseness** n.

hoary ('höri) a. 1. gray with age 2. grayish-white 3. of great antiquity 4. venerable —'**hoarfrost** n. frozen dew

hoax (hōks) n. 1. practical joke 2. deceptive trick —vt. 3. play trick upon 4. deceive —'**hoaxer** n.

hob (hob) n. 1. flat-topped casing of fireplace 2. top area of cooking stove —'**hobnail** n. large-headed nail for boot soles

hobble ('hobəl) vi. 1. walk lamely —vt. 2. tie legs of (horse etc.) together —n. 3. straps or ropes put on an animal's legs to prevent it straying 4. limping gait

hobbledehoy ('hobəldihoi) n. obs. rough, ill-mannered clumsy youth

hobby ('hobi) n. 1. favorite occupation as pastime 2. small falcon —'**hobbyhorse** n. 1. toy horse 2. favorite topic, preoccupation

hobgoblin ('hobgoblin) n. mischievous fairy

hobnob ('hobnob) vi. (oft. with **with**) 1. be familiar 2. obs. drink (**-bb-**)

hobo ('hōbō) n. shiftless, wandering person (pl. **-s, -es**)

Hobson's choice ('hobsənz) choice of taking what is offered or nothing at all

hock¹ (hok) n. 1. backward-pointing joint on leg of horse etc., corresponding to human ankle —vt. 2. disable by cutting tendons of hock

hock² (hok) n. dry white wine

hock³ (hok) inf. vt. 1. pawn, pledge —n. 2. state of being in pawn —'**hocker** n. —**in hock** 1. in prison 2. in debt 3. in pawn

hockey ('hoki) n. 1. see **field hockey** at FIELD 2. see **ice hockey** at ICE

hocus-pocus (hōkəs'pōkəs) n. 1. trickery 2. mystifying jargon

hod (hod) n. 1. small trough on a staff for carrying mortar, bricks etc. 2. tall, narrow coal scuttle

hodgepodge ('hojpoj) n. medley

Hodgkin's disease ('hojkinz) disease of unknown origin marked by enlargement of the lymph glands, considered by some to be a form of cancer

hoe (hō) n. 1. tool for weeding, breaking ground etc. —v. 2. dig, weed or till (surface soil) with hoe (**hoed, 'hoeing**)

hog (hog) n. 1. pig, esp. castrated male for fattening 2. greedy, dirty person —vt. 3. inf. eat, use selfishly (**-gg-**) —'**hogback** n. 1. narrow ridge with steep sides (also **hog's back**) 2. Archaeol. tomb with sloping sides —'**hogshead** n. 1. large cask 2. liquid measure, having several values, used esp. for alcoholic beverages —'**hogwash** n. 1. nonsense 2. pig food

hogan ('hōgən) n. dwelling of logs and mud used by Navaho Indians

Hogmanay (hogmə'nā) n. in Scotland, last day of year

Hohokum (hō'hōkəm) n. Amerindian culture of Arizona of 800 A.D.

hoick (hoik) vt. raise abruptly and sharply

hoi polloi ('hoi pə'loi) 1. the common mass of people 2. the masses

hoist (hoist) vt. raise aloft, raise with tackle etc.

hoity-toity (hoiti'toiti) a. inf. arrogant, haughty

hokum ('hōkəm) n. sl. 1. claptrap; bunk 2. obvious or hackneyed material of a sentimental nature in motion picture etc.

hold¹ (hōld) vt. 1. keep fast, grasp 2. support in or with hands etc. 3. maintain in position 4. have capacity for 5. own, occupy 6. carry on 7. detain 8. celebrate 9. keep back 10. believe —vi. 11. cling 12. remain fast or unbroken 13. (with **to**) abide (by) 14. keep 15. remain relevant, valid or true (**held** pt./pp.) —n. 16. grasp 17. influence —'**holder** n. —'**holding** n. (oft. pl.) property, such as land or stocks and shares —'**holdall** n. valise or case for carrying clothes etc. —'**holdfast** n. clamp —**holding company** company formed to hold stock of other companies, which it then controls —**holding pattern** circular route for aircraft awaiting landing —'**holdup** n. 1. armed robbery 2. delay

hold² (hōld) n. space in ship or aircraft for cargo

hole (hōl) n. 1. hollow place, cavity 2. perforation 3. opening 4. inf. unattractive place 5. inf. difficult situation —vt. 6. make holes in 7. drive into a hole —vi. 8. go into a hole —'**holey** a. —**hole-and-corner** a. inf. furtive or secretive

holiday ('holidā) n. day or other period of rest from work etc., esp. spent away from home

Holland ('holənd) n. 1. popular name for the Netherlands 2. (h-) linen fabric —'**Hollands** n. spirit, gin

holler ('holər) inf. v. 1. shout or yell (something) —n. 2. shout; call

hollow ('holō) a. 1. having a cavity, not solid 2. empty 3. false 4. insincere 5. not full-toned —n. 6. cavity, hole, valley —vt. 7. make hollow, make hole in 8. excavate —**hollow back** see LORDOSIS —'**hollowware** or '**holloware** n. dishes, esp. silver serving dishes, having depth and volume

holly ('holi) n. evergreen shrub with prickly leaves and red berries

hollyhock ('holihok) n. tall plant bearing many large flowers

holmium ('hōlmiəm) n. Chem. metallic element Symbol Ho, at. wt. 164.9, at. no. 67

holm oak (hōm, hōlm) evergreen Mediterranean oak tree

holocaust ('holəköst, 'holə-) n. 1. great destruction of life, esp. by fire 2. (oft. **H-**) murder of Jews by the Nazis during World War II

holograph ('hōləgraf, 'holə-) n. document wholly written by the signer

holography (hŏ'logrəfi) *n.* science of using lasers to produce photographic record (**hologram**) which can reproduce a three-dimensional image

Holstein ('hŏlstīn) *n.* one of breed of large black-and-white dairy cattle

holster ('hŏlstər) *n.* leather case for pistol, hung from belt *etc.*

holt (hŏlt) *n. Poet.* wood, wooded hill

holy ('hŏli) *a.* 1. belonging, devoted to God 2. free from sin 3. divine 4. consecrated —'**holily** *adv.* —'**holiness** *n.* 1. sanctity 2. (H-) Pope's title —**holier-than-thou** *a.* offensively sanctimonious or self-righteous —**Holy Communion** service of the Eucharist —**holy day** day of religious festival —**Holy Ghost** *or* **Spirit** third person of Trinity —**Holy Grail** cup or dish used by Christ at the Last Supper —**holy orders** 1. sacrament whereby person is admitted to Christian ministry 2. grades of Christian ministry 3. status of ordained Christian minister —**Holy See** *R.C.Ch.* 1. the see of the pope as bishop of Rome 2. Roman curia —**Holy Week** week before Easter —**the Holy Land** Palestine

homage ('homij) *n.* 1. tribute, respect, reverence 2. formal acknowledgment of allegiance

homburg ('hombərg) *n.* man's hat of felt with dented crown and stiff upturned brim

home (hŏm) *n.* 1. dwelling place 2. residence 3. native place 4. institution for the elderly, infirm *etc.* —*a.* 5. of one's home, country *etc.* —*adv.* 6. to, at one's home 7. to the point —*v.* 8. direct or be directed on to a point or target —'**homeless** *a.* —'**homely** *a.* plain —'**homeward** *a./adv.* —'**homewards** *adv.* —'**homing** *a. Zool.* of ability to return home after traveling great distances —**home-brew** *n.* alcoholic drink made at home —**home economics** study of diet, budgeting and other subjects concerned with running a home —**home plate** baseball base at which batter stands: last of four a base runner must touch to score a run —**home rule** 1. self-government 2. partial autonomy sometimes granted to national minority or colony —**home run** baseball hit that allows batter to make complete circuit of bases and score a run —'**homesick** *a.* depressed by absence from home —'**homesickness** *n.* —'**homespun** *a.* 1. domestic 2. simple —*n.* 3. cloth made of homespun yarn —'**homestead** *n.* 1. house with outbuildings, *esp.* on farm 2. house and land occupied by owner and exempt from seizure and forced sale for debt —'**homesteader** *n.* —'**homework** *n.* school work to be done at home —**homing pigeon** domestic pigeon developed for its homing instinct, used for racing (*also* '**homer**) —**bring home to** impress deeply upon —**home and dry** safe or successful

homeo- *or* **homoio-** (*comb. form*) like, similar, as in *homeomorphism*

homeopathy (hŏmi'opəthi) *n.* treatment of disease by small doses of drug that produces, in healthy person, symptoms similar to those of disease being treated —'**homeopath** *n.* one who believes in or practices homeopathy —**homeo'pathic** *a.* —**homeo'pathically** *adv.*

homeostasis (hŏmiŏ'stăsis) *n.* the tendency of all living organisms to maintain a steady state for continued functioning

homicide ('homisīd) *n.* 1. killing of human being 2. killer —**homi'cidal** *a.*

homily ('homili) *n.* 1. sermon 2. religious discourse —**homi'letic** *a.* —**homi'letics** *pl.n.* (*with sing. v.*) art of preaching

hominid ('hominid) *n./a.* (of or relating to) man and his ancestors

hominoid ('hominoid) *a.* 1. manlike 2. of or belonging to primate family, which includes anthropoid apes and man —*n.* 3. hominoid animal

Homo ('hŏmŏ) *n.* genus to which modern man belongs —**Homo sapiens** ('sapiənz, 'săpiənz, -enz) specific name of modern man

homo- (*comb. form*) same, as in *homosexual.* Such words are not given here where the meaning may easily be inferred from the simple word

homogeneous (hŏmə'jēniəs, -nyəs) *a.* 1. formed of uniform parts 2. similar, uniform 3. of the same nature —**homoge'neity** *n.* —**homogenize** (hŏ'mojinīz, hə-) *vt.* break up fat globules (in milk and cream) to distribute them evenly

homograph ('homəgraf) *n.* one of group of words spelt in the same way but having different meanings —**homo'graphic** *a.*

homologous (hŏ'moləgəs, hə-) *a.* having the same relation, relative position *etc.* —'**homologue** *or* '**homolog** *n.* homologous thing

homonym ('homənim) *n.* word of same form as another, but having different meaning —**homo'nymic** *or* **ho'monymous** *a.*

homophone ('hŏməfŏn) *n.* a word of the same sound as another, but having different spelling

homosexual (hŏmə'sekshŏŏəl) *n.* 1. person sexually attracted to members of the same sex —*a.* 2. of or relating to homosexuals or homosexuality —**homosexu'ality** *n.*

Hon *or* **Hon.** 1. Honorable 2. (*also* **h-**) honorary

Honduras (hon'dyŏŏrəs, -'dŏŏ-) *n.* country in Central America bounded north by the Caribbean, east and southeast by Nicaragua, west by Guatemala, southwest by El Salvador and south by the Pacific Ocean —**Hon'duran** *n./a.* (native or inhabitant) of Honduras

hone (hŏn) *n.* 1. whetstone —*vt.* 2. sharpen with hone

honest ('onist) *a.* 1. not cheating, lying, stealing *etc.* 2. genuine 3. without pretension —'**honestly** *adv.* —'**honesty** *n.* 1. quality of being honest 2. plant with silvery seed pods

honey ('huni) *n.* sweet fluid made by bees —'**honeyed** *or* '**honied** *a. Poet.* 1. flattering or soothing 2. made sweet or agreeable 3. full of honey —'**honeybee** *n.* any of various social bees widely domesticated as source of honey and beeswax —'**honeycomb** *n.* 1. wax structure in hexagonal cells in which bees place honey, eggs *etc.* 2. raised effect on cloth resembling honeycomb —*vt.* 3. fill with cells or perforations —'**honeydew** *n.* 1. sweet sticky substance found on plants 2. type of sweet melon —'**honeymoon** *n.* journey taken by newly-wedded pair —'**honeysuckle** *n.* climbing plant

Hong Kong (hong kong) crown colony of the United Kingdom 20 miles east of the mouth of the Pearl River and 80 miles south of Canton

honk (hongk) *n.* 1. call of wild goose 2. any sound like this, *esp.* sound of automobile horn —*vi.* 3. make this sound

honky ('hongki) *n.* (among Blacks) White person

honky-tonk ('hongkitongk) *n.* 1. *sl.* cheap disreputable nightclub *etc.* 2. style of ragtime piano-playing

honor ('onər) *n.* 1. personal integrity 2. renown 3. reputation 4. sense of what is right or due 5. chastity 6. high rank or position 7. source, cause of honor 8. pleasure, privilege —*pl.* 9. mark of respect 10. distinction in examination —*vt.* 11. respect highly 12.

confer honor on 13. accept or pay (bill *etc.*) when due —'**honorable** *a.* —'**honorably** *adv.* —**hono'rarium** *n.* a fee (*pl.* **-s, -ia** (-iə) —'**honorary** *a.* 1. conferred for the sake of honor only 2. holding position without pay or usual requirements 3. giving services without pay —**hono'rific** *a.* conferring honor —**honor roll** 1. list of names of persons deserving honor, *esp.* students 2. public display of names of local citizens who have served in the armed forces —**honor society** society for recognition of academic achievement, *esp.* of undergraduates —**honor system** system whereby members of institution are trusted to abide by the rules without supervision

hooch *or* **hootch** (hŏŏch) *n. sl.* alcoholic drink, *esp.* when illicitly distilled

hood (hŏŏd) *n.* 1. covering for head and neck, oft. part of cloak or gown 2. hoodlike thing as (adjustable) top of automobile, baby carriage *etc.* 3. metal cover of automobile engine —'**hooded** *a.* covered with or shaped like hood —**hooded crow** crow that has gray body and black head, wings, and tail —'**hoodwink** *vt.* deceive

hoodlum ('hŏŏdləm, 'hŏŏd-) *n.* gangster, bully —**hood** *n. sl.* hoodlum

hoodoo ('hŏŏdŏŏ) *n.* 1. voodoo 2. cause of bad luck

hooey ('hŏŏi) *n./interj. sl.* nonsense

hoof (hŏŏf) *n.* horny casing of foot of horse *etc.* (*pl.* **-s, hooves**) —**on the hoof** (of livestock) alive

hoo-ha ('hŏŏhä) *n.* needless fuss, bother *etc.*

hook (hŏŏk) *n.* 1. bent piece of metal used to suspend, hold, or pull something 2. something resembling hook in shape or function 3. curved cutting tool 4. *Boxing* blow delivered with bent elbow —*vt.* 5. grasp, catch, hold, as with hook 6. fasten with hook 7. *Golf* drive (ball) widely to the left —**hooked** *a.* 1. shaped like hook 2. caught 3. *sl.* addicted —'**hooker** *n. sl.* prostitute —**hook-up** *n.* linking of radio, television stations —'**hookworm** *n.* infestation with intestinal roundworm

hookah ('hŏŏkə) *n.* oriental pipe in which smoke is drawn through water and long tube

hooligan ('hŏŏligən) *n.* violent, irresponsible (young) person —'**hooliganism** *n.*

hoop (hŏŏp) *n.* 1. rigid circular band of metal, wood *etc.* 2. such a band used for binding barrel *etc.*, for use as toy, or for jumping through as in circus acts —*vt.* 3. bind with hoops 4. encircle —**go through the hoop(s)** *inf.* go through an ordeal or test

hoopla ('hŏŏplä) *n.* 1. commotion 2. communication intended to confuse

hoopoe ('hŏŏpŏŏ) *n.* bird with large crest

hooray (hŏŏ'rā) *interj. see* HURRAH

Hoosier ('hŏŏzhər) *n.* native or resident of Indiana

hoot (hŏŏt) *n.* 1. owl's cry or similar sound 2. cry of disapproval or derision 3. *inf.* funny person or thing —*vi.* 4. utter hoot, *esp.* in derision

Hoover ('hŏŏvər) *n.* **Herbert Clark.** the 31st President of the U.S. (1929-33)

hooves (hŏŏvz) *n., pl. of* HOOF

hop[1] (hop) *vi.* 1. spring on one foot 2. *inf.* move quickly (**-pp-**) —*n.* 3. leap, skip 4. one stage of journey 5. *inf.* dance —'**hopscotch** *n.* children's game of hopping in pattern drawn on ground

hop[2]

hop² (hop) n. 1. climbing plant with bitter cones used to flavor beer etc. —pl. 2. the cones

hope (hōp) n. 1. expectation of something desired 2. thing that gives, or object of, this feeling —v. 3. feel hope —'**hopeful** a. —'**hopefully** adv. inf. it is hoped —'**hopeless** a. —**young hopeful** promising boy or girl

Hopi ('hōpi) n. 1. (member of) Amerindian people of northeastern Arizona (pl. **Hopi, -s**) 2. the Uto-Aztecan language of the Hopi

hopper ('hopər) n. 1. one who hops 2. device for feeding material into mill or machine, or grain into railroad truck etc. 3. mechanical hop-picker

horal ('hôrəl) a. 1. pert. to an hour 2. hourly

horde (hôrd) n. large crowd, esp. moving together

horehound ('hôrhownd) n. plant with bitter juice used to flavor candy

horizon (hə'rīzən) n. 1. boundary of part of the earth seen from any given point 2. line where earth and sky seem to meet 3. boundary of mental outlook —**horizontal** (hori'zontəl) a. parallel with horizon, level —**horizontally** (hori'zontəli) adv.

hormone ('hôrmōn) n. 1. substance secreted by certain glands which stimulates organs of the body 2. synthetic substance with same effect

horn (hôrn) n. 1. hard projection on heads of certain animals, eg cows 2. substance of horns 3. various things made of, or resembling it 4. wind instrument orig. made of horn 5. device, esp. in motor vehicle, emitting sound as warning etc. —**horned** a. having horns —'**horny** a. 1. of, like or hard as horn 2. having horn(s) 3. sl. sexually aroused —'**hornbeam** n. tree with smooth gray bark —'**hornbill** n. type of bird with horny growth on large bill —'**hornbook** n. page bearing religious text or alphabet, held in frame with thin window of horn over it —**horn of plenty** see CORNUCOPIA —'**hornpipe** n. lively dance, esp. associated with sailors

hornblende ('hôrnblend) n. mineral consisting of silica, with magnesia, lime or iron

hornet ('hôrnit) n. any large social wasp

horologe ('horəlôj) n. rare any timepiece —**ho'rology** n. art or science of clockmaking and measuring time

horoscope ('horəskōp) n. 1. observation of, or scheme showing disposition of planets etc., at given moment, esp. birth, by which character and abilities of individual are predicted 2. telling of person's fortune by this method

horror ('horər) n. 1. terror 2. loathing, fear 3. its cause —**hor'rendous** a. horrific —'**horrible** a. exciting horror, hideous, shocking —'**horribly** adv. —'**horrid** a. 1. unpleasant, repulsive 2. inf. unkind —**hor'rific** a. particularly horrible —'**horrify** vt. move to horror (**-ified, -ifying**)

hors d'oeuvre (ör 'dərv) small dish served before main meal

horse (hôrs) n. 1. four-legged herbivorous mammal with flowing mane and tail, ranging in size from 24 inches to 68 inches at the shoulders. Domesticated species are used to carry loads, to pull vehicles and for riding 2. cavalry 3. vaulting-block 4. frame for support etc. —vt. 5. provide with horse or horses —'**horsy** or '**horsey** a. 1. having to do with horses 2. devoted to horses or horse racing —**horse brass** decorative brass ornament, orig. attached to horse's harness —**horse chestnut** tree with conical clusters of white or pink flowers and large nuts —'**horseflesh** n. 1. horses collectively 2. flesh of horse, esp. edible horse meat —'**horsefly**

n. large, bloodsucking fly —**horse laugh** harsh boisterous laugh —'**horseman** n. rider on horse ('**horsewoman** fem.) —'**horseplay** n. rough or rowdy play —'**horsepower** n. unit of power of engine etc. 550 foot-pounds per second —'**horseradish** n. plant with pungent root —**horse sense** see **common sense** at COMMON —'**horseshoe** n. 1. protective U-shaped piece of iron nailed to horse's hoof 2. thing so shaped —**horseshoe pitching** game played by two or four players in which horseshoes are thrown toward an iron stake at each end of a court —'**horsetail** n. primitive plant with erect jointed stems with whorls of small leaves around the joints: a garden weed —**horse about** or **around** inf. play roughly, boisterously

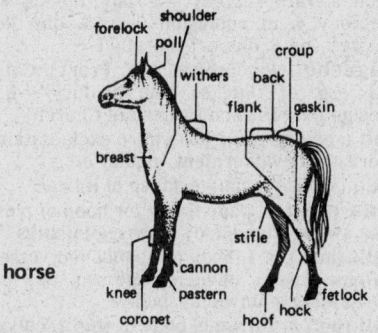

horse

hortatory ('hôrtətôri) or **hortative** ('hôrtətiv) a. tending to exhort; encouraging —**hor'tation** n.

horticulture ('hôrtikulchər) n. art or science of gardening —**horti'cultural** a. —**horti'culturist** n.

Hos. Bible Hosea

hosanna or **hosannah** (hō'zanə) n./interj. cry of praise, adoration

hose (hōz) n. 1. flexible tube for conveying liquid or gas 2. stockings —vt. 3. water with hose —**hosier** ('hōzhər) n. dealer in stockings etc. —**hosiery** ('hōzhəri) n. stockings etc.

Hosea (hō'zāə, -'zēə) n. Bible 28th book of the O.T., written by the prophet Hosea in which he uses his domestic life as an analogy for the relationship between God and man

hospice ('hospis) n. obs. 1. traveler's house of rest kept by religious order 2. place for care of the dying

hospital ('hospitəl) n. institution for care of sick —**hospitali'zation** n. —'**hospitalize** vt. place for care in hospital

hospitality (hospi'taliti) n. friendly and liberal reception of strangers or guests —**hos'pitable** a. welcoming, kindly —**hos'pitably** adv.

host¹ (hōst) n. 1. one who entertains another ('**hostess** fem.) 2. innkeeper 3. compere of show 4. animal, plant on which parasite lives —v. 5. be host of (party, program etc.)

host² (hōst) n. large number

Host (hōst) n. consecrated bread of the Eucharist

hosta ('hostə, 'hōstə) n. plantain lily

hostage ('hostij) n. person taken or given as pledge or security

hostel ('hostəl) n. supervised lodging esp. for youth traveling by bicycle or on foot —'**hostelry** n. obs. inn

hostile ('hostil) a. 1. opposed, antagonistic 2. warlike 3. of or relating to an enemy 4. unfriendly —**hos'tility** n. 1. enmity —pl. 2. acts of warfare

hot (hot) a. 1. of high temperature, very warm, giving or feeling heat 2. angry 3.

severe 4. recent, new 5. much favored 6. spicy 7. sl. good, quick, smart 8. sl. stolen ('**hotter** comp., '**hottest** sup.) —'**hotly** adv. —'**hotness** n. —**hots** n. sl. lust —**hot air** inf. boastful, empty talk —'**hotbed** n. 1. bed of enclosed soil heated by fermenting manure 2. any place encouraging growth —**hot-blooded** a. passionate, excitable —'**hotcap** n. small translucent cover for forcing or protecting outdoor plants —**hot dog** frankfurter in long split roll —'**hotfoot** vi./adv. (go) quickly —'**hothead** n. hasty, intemperate person —**hot-headed** a. impetuous, rash or hot-tempered —**hot-headedness** n. —'**hothouse** n. 1. heated greenhouse 2. any place encouraging growth —**hot line** direct communication link between heads of government etc. —**hot money** capital that is transferred from one commercial center to another seeking best opportunity for short-term gain —'**hotplate** n. 1. solid disk on electric stove 2. portable device for cooking or keeping food warm —**hot potato** situation likely to cause trouble to person dealing with it —**hot rod** automobile with engine that has been modified to produce increased power —**hot seat** 1. inf. difficult or dangerous position 2. sl. electric chair —**hot-foot it** go quickly —**in hot water** inf. in trouble —**make it hot for** cause trouble for —**sell like hot cakes** sell readily

hotchpotch ('hochpoch) n. 1. dish of many ingredients 2. hodgepodge

hotel (hō'tel, 'hōtel) n. 1. commercial establishment providing lodging and meals 2. (H-) word used in communications for the letter h —**hotel keeper** or **ho'telier** n.

Hottentot ('hotəntot) n. 1. member of a people of southwest Africa related to the Bushmen (pl. **-tot, -s**) 2. the 'click' language of the Khoisan family spoken by the Hottentot

hough (hok) see HOCK¹

hound (hownd) n. 1. any of class of purebred dogs defined by the American Kennel Club, typically with large drooping ears, which hunt by scent and are used in the chase —vt. 2. chase, pursue 3. urge on —**houndstooth check** or **hound's tooth check** ('howndz-'tŏŏth, 'hownz-) medium-sized broken-check fabric pattern

hour ('owər) n. 1. twenty-fourth part of day 2. sixty minutes 3. time of day 4. appointed time —pl. 5. fixed periods for work, prayers etc. 6. book of prayers —'**hourly** adv. 1. every hour 2. frequently —a. 3. frequent 4. happening every hour —'**hourglass** n. 1. device consisting of two transparent chambers linked by narrow channel, containing quantity of sand that takes specified time to trickle from one chamber to the other —a. 2. well-proportioned with small waist

houri ('hŏŏri) n. beautiful nymph of the Muslim paradise (pl. **-s**)

house (hows) n. 1. building for human habitation 2. building for other specified purpose 3. legislative or other assembly 4. (H-) family, esp. royal 5. business firm 6. theater audience —v. (howz) 7. give or receive shelter, lodging or storage —vt. (howz) 8. cover; contain —**housing** ('howzing) n. 1. (providing of) houses 2. part or structure designed to cover, protect, contain —**house arrest** confinement to one's own home rather than in prison —'**houseboat** n. boat for living in on river etc. —'**housebound** a. unable to leave one's house —'**housebreak** vt. teach acceptable behavior to (esp. pets) —'**housebreaker** n. burglar —'**housecoat** n. woman's long loose garment for casual wear at home —'**housefly** n. pestiferous two-winged insect found throughout the world —**'household** *n.* persons living in house collectively —**'householder** *n.* **1.** occupier of house as his dwelling **2.** head of household —**household name** *or* **word** person or thing that is very well known —**'househusband** *n.* married man who runs household while wife earns income —**'housekeeper** *n.* person managing affairs of household —**'housekeeping** *n.* running household —**housemaid's knee** inflammation and swelling of bursa in front of kneecap —**'houseman** *n.* man who performs general domestic duties —**House of Commons** UK, C lower chamber of Parliament —**House of Lords** UK upper chamber of Parliament, composed of the peers of the realm —**House of Representatives** the lower legislative branch of the U.S. Congress, of many states and of some other countries —**house organ** periodical published by business for its employees —**house plant** plant for growing indoors —**house-proud** *a.* preoccupied with appearance of one's house —**'housetop** *n.* roof of house —**'housewarming** *n.* party to celebrate entry into new house or premises —**'housewife** *n.* **1.** married woman who runs a household **2.** ('huzif) small sewing kit for traveling —**'housework** *n.* work of running home, such as cleaning *etc.* —**on the house** at owner's expense —**put one's house in order** make the necessary reforms

hove (hōv) *chiefly Naut. pt./pp. of* HEAVE

hovel ('huvəl, 'hov-) *n.* small, wretched usu. dirty house

hover ('huvər, 'hov-) *vi.* **1.** (of bird *etc.*) hang in the air **2.** loiter **3.** be in state of indecision —**'Hovercraft** *n.* trade name for ground-effect machine used to cross short stretches of water

how (how) *adv.* **1.** in what way **2.** by what means **3.** in what condition **4.** to what degree —**howbeit** (how'bēit) *adv. obs.* nevertheless —**how'ever** *adv.* **1.** nevertheless **2.** in whatever way, degree **3.** all the same

howdah ('howdə) *n.* (canopied) seat on elephant's back

howitzer ('howitsər) *n.* short gun firing shells at high elevation

howl (howl) *vi.* **1.** utter long loud cry —*n.* **2.** such cry —**'howler** *n.* **1.** one that howls **2.** *inf.* stupid mistake —**'howling** *a. inf.* great

hoyden ('hoidən) *n.* wild, boisterous girl, tomboy —**'hoydenish** *a.*

hoyle (hoil) *n.* compendium of rules of indoor (*esp.* card) games —**according to hoyle** following the rules, correctly

H.P. 1. half pay **2.** high pressure **3.** horsepower (*also* **hp**)

H.Q. *or* **h.q.** headquarters

hr. *or* **hr** hour

H.R.H. His (*or* Her) Royal Highness

HT *Phys.* high tension

huarache (wə'rächi, hə-) *n.* low-heeled sandal with upper made of interwoven leather thongs

hub (hub) *n.* **1.** middle part of wheel, from which spokes radiate **2.** central point of activity

hubble-bubble ('hubəlbubəl) *n.* **1.** *see* HOOKAH **2.** turmoil **3.** gargling sound

hubbub ('hubub) *n.* **1.** confused noise of many voices **2.** uproar

hubris ('hyōōbris) *or* **hybris** *n.* pride or arrogance —**hu'bristic** *or* **hy'bristic** *a.*

huckaback ('hukəbak) *n.* coarse absorbent linen or cotton fabric used for towels *etc.* (*also* **huck**)

huckster ('hukstər) *n.* **1.** person using aggressive or questionable methods of selling —*vt.* **2.** sell (goods) thus

huddle ('hudəl) *n.* **1.** crowded mass **2.** *inf.* impromptu conference —*v.* **3.** heap, crowd together **4.** hunch (oneself)

hue (hyōō) *n.* **1.** color or gradation of color **2.** aspect of color which permits classification

hue and cry 1. public uproar, outcry **2.** formerly, loud outcry usu. in pursuit of wrongdoer

huff (huf) *n.* **1.** passing mood of anger —*v.* **2.** make or become angry, resentful —*vi.* **3.** blow, puff heavily —**'huffily** *adv.* —**'huffy** *a.*

hug (hug) *vt.* **1.** clasp tightly in the arms **2.** cling to **3.** keep close to (**-gg-**) —*n.* **4.** fond embrace

huge (hyōōj, yōōj) *a.* very big —**'hugely** *adv.* very much

hugger-mugger ('hugərmugər) *n.* **1.** confusion **2.** *rare* secrecy —*a./adv. obs.* **3.** with secrecy **4.** in confusion —*vt.* **5.** *obs.* keep secret —*vi.* **6.** *obs.* act secretly

Huguenot ('hyōōgənot) *n.* **1.** French Calvinist, *esp.* of 16th or 17th century —*a.* **2.** designating French Protestant Church

huh (*spelling pron.* hu) *interj.* exclamation of derision, bewilderment, inquiry *etc.*

hula ('hōōlə) *n.* native dance of Hawaii

Hula-Hoop *n.* trade name for hoop of plastic *etc.* swung round body by wriggling hips

hulk (hulk) *n.* **1.** body of abandoned vessel **2.** *offens.* large, unwieldy person or thing —**'hulking** *a.* unwieldy, bulky

hull (hul) *n.* **1.** frame, body of ship **2.** calyx of strawberry, raspberry or similar fruit **3.** shell, husk —*vt.* **4.** remove shell, hull from **5.** pierce hull of (vessel *etc.*)

hullabaloo ('huləbəlōō) *n.* uproar, clamor, row

hum (hum) *vi.* **1.** make low continuous sound as bee **2.** *sl.* be very active —*vt.* **3.** sing with closed lips (**-mm-**) —*n.* **4.** humming sound **5.** *sl.* great activity **6.** in radio, disturbance affecting reception —**'hummingbird** *n.* member of family of very small colorful New World birds found from Arctic N Amer. to tip of S Amer. which are notable for ability to hover while feeding on nectar

human ('hyōōmən, 'yōō-) *a.* of, relating to, or characteristic of mankind —**humane** (hyōō'mān, yōō-) *a.* **1.** benevolent, kind **2.** merciful —**'humanism** *n.* **1.** belief in human effort rather than religion **2.** interest in human welfare and affairs **3.** classical literary culture —**'humanist** *n.* —**humani'tarian** *n.* **1.** philanthropist —*a.* **2.** having the welfare of mankind at heart —**hu'manity** *n.* **1.** human nature **2.** human race **3.** kindliness —*pl.* **4.** study of literature, philosophy, the arts —**'humanize** *vt.* **1.** make human **2.** civilize —**'humanly** *adv.* —**'humanoid** *a.* **1.** like human being in appearance —*n.* **2.** being with human rather than anthropoid characteristics **3.** in science fiction, robot or creature resembling human being —**'humankind** *n.* whole race of man

humble ('humbəl) *a.* **1.** lowly, modest —*vt.* **2.** bring low, abase, humiliate —**'humbly** *adv.* —**humble pie** apology or retraction made under duress —**eat humble pie** be forced to submit to humiliation

humbug ('humbug) *n.* **1.** impostor **2.** sham, nonsense, deception —*vt.* **3.** deceive; defraud (**-gg-**)

humdinger ('hum'dingər) *n. sl.* excellent person or thing

humdrum ('humdrum) *a.* commonplace, dull, monotonous

humeral ('hyōōmərəl) *a.* of shoulder —**'humerus** *n.* long bone between elbow and shoulder (*pl.* **-meri** (-mərī))

humid ('hyōōmid, 'yōō-) *a.* moist, damp

—**hu'midifier** *n.* device for increasing amount of water vapor in air in room *etc.* —**hu'midify** *vt.* —**hu'midity** *n.*

humiliate (hyōō'miliāt, yōō-) *vt.* lower dignity of, abase, mortify —**humili'ation** *n.*

humility (hyōō'militi, yōō-) *n.* **1.** state of being humble **2.** meekness

hummock ('humək) *n.* **1.** low knoll, hillock **2.** ridge of ice

humor ('hyōōmər, 'yōōmər) *n.* **1.** faculty of saying or perceiving what excites amusement **2.** state of mind, mood **3.** temperament **4.** *obs.* any of various fluids of body —*vt.* **5.** gratify, indulge —**'humorist** *n.* person who acts, speaks, writes humorously —**'humorous** *a.* funny, amusing —**'humorously** *adv.*

hump (hump) *n.* **1.** normal or deforming lump, *esp.* on back **2.** hillock **3.** *inf.* dejection —*vt.* **4.** make hump-shaped **5.** *sl.* carry, heave —**'humpback** *n.* person with hump —**'hump-backed** *a.* having a hump

humph (*spelling pron.* humf) *interj.* exclamation of annoyance, indecision *etc.*

humus ('hyōōməs, 'yōō-) *n.* decayed vegetable and animal matter

Hun (hun) *n.* **1.** member of Asiatic nomadic peoples who invaded Europe in 4th and 5th centuries A.D. **2.** *inf. derog.* German **3.** *inf.* vandal —**Hunlike** *a.* —**Hunnish** *a.*

hunch (hunch) *n.* **1.** intuition or premonition **2.** hump —*vt.* **3.** thrust, bend into hump —**'hunchback** *n.* **1.** curvature of the spine in which back is rounded (*also* **kyphosis**) **2.** person with this condition

hundred ('hundrəd) *n./a.* cardinal number, ten times ten —**'hundredfold** *a./adv.* —**'hundredth** *a./n.* ordinal number of a hundred —**'hundredweight** *n.* weight of 100 lbs. (45.4 kg.)

hung (hung) *v.* **1.** *pt./pp. of* HANG —*a.* **2.** (of jury *etc.*) unable to decide **3.** not having majority —**hung-over** *a. inf.* suffering from aftereffects of excessive drinking —**hung up** *inf.* **1.** delayed **2.** emotionally disturbed

Hungary ('hunggəri) *n.* country in Europe bounded north by Czechoslovakia, northeast by the U.S.S.R., east by Romania, south by Yugoslavia and west by Austria —**Hun'garian** *n./a.* **1.** (native or inhabitant) of Hungary —*n.* **2.** language of Hungary which is the major member of the Ugric branch of Finno-Ugrian

hunger ('hunggər) *n.* **1.** discomfort, exhaustion from lack of food **2.** strong desire —*vi.* **3.** (usu. *with* for *or* after) have great desire (for) —**'hungrily** *adv.* —**'hungry** *a.* having keen appetite —**hunger strike** refusal of all food, as protest

hunk (hungk) *n.* thick piece

hunker ('hungkər) *vi.* squat (down)

hunkers ('hungkərz) *pl.n. dial.* haunches

hunt (hunt) *v.* **1.** (seek out to) kill or capture for sport or food **2.** search (for) —*n.* **3.** chase, search **4.** (party organized for) hunting —**'hunter** *n.* **1.** one who hunts ('**huntress** *fem.*) **2.** horse, dog bred for hunting —**'huntsman** *n.* man in charge of pack of hounds

hurdle ('hərdəl) *n.* **1.** portable frame of bars for temporary fences or for jumping over **2.** obstacle —*pl.* **3.** race over hurdles —*vi.* **4.** race over hurdles —**'hurdler** *n.* one who races over hurdles

hurdy-gurdy ('hərdi'gərdi) *n.* mechanical (musical) instrument (eg barrel organ)

hurl (hərl) *vt.* throw violently —**hurly-burly** *n.* loud confusion

hurling ('hərling) *n.* traditional Irish game resembling field hockey but differing in that the ball may be struck with the hand and kicked when off the ground and may be balanced in the stick and hurled

Huron ('hyŏŏrən, 'hŏŏ-) *n.* **1.** confederacy of Amerindian peoples of St. Lawrence valley **2.** member of any of these peoples (*pl.* **-ron, -s**)

hurrah (hŏŏ'rŏ, -'rä) *or* **hooray** *interj.* exclamation of joy or applause

hurricane ('hurikăn, 'hurikən) *n.* very strong, potentially destructive wind or storm —**hurricane lamp** lamp with glass covering round flame

hurry ('huri) *v.* **1.** (cause to) move or act in great haste ('**hurried, 'hurrying**) —*n.* **2.** undue haste **3.** eagerness —'**hurriedly** *adv.*

hurst (hərst) *n. obs.* **1.** wood **2.** sandbank

hurt (hərt) *vt.* **1.** injure, damage, give pain to **2.** wound feelings of, distress —*vi.* **3.** *inf.* feel pain (**hurt** *pt./pp.*) —*n.* **4.** wound, injury, harm —'**hurtful** *a.*

hurtle ('hərtəl) *vi.* **1.** move rapidly **2.** rush violently **3.** whirl

husband ('huzbənd) *n.* **1.** married man —*v.* **2.** economize, manage or use to best advantage —'**husbandry** *n.* **1.** farming **2.** economy

hush (hush) *v.* **1.** make or be silent —*n.* **2.** stillness **3.** quietness —**hush-hush** *a. inf.* secret —**hush up** suppress (rumors, information), make secret

husk (husk) *n.* **1.** dry covering of certain seeds and fruits **2.** worthless outside part —*vt.* **3.** remove husk from —'**husky** *a.* **1.** rough in tone, hoarse **2.** dry as husk, dry in the throat **3.** of, full of, husks **4.** *inf.* big and strong

husky ('huski) *n.* **1.** Arctic sled dog **2. C** *sl.* Inuit

hussar (hə'zär, -'sär) *n.* lightly armed cavalry soldier

hussy ('husi, -zi) *n.* brazen girl or young woman

hustings ('hustingz) *pl.n.* **1.** platform from which political speeches are made **2.** political campaigning

hustle ('husəl) *v.* **1.** push about, jostle, hurry —*vi.* **2.** *sl.* solicit —*n.* **3.** instance of hustling —'**hustler** *n.*

hut (hut) *n.* any small house or shelter, usu. of wood or metal

hutch (huch) *n.* boxlike pen for rabbits *etc.*

hyacinth ('hīəsinth) *n.* **1.** bulbous plant with bell-shaped flowers, *esp.* purple-blue **2.** this blue **3.** orange gem jacinth

hyaena (hī'ēnə) *n. see* HYENA

hyaline ('hīəlin) *a.* clear, translucent

hyaluronidase (hīlyŏŏ'ronidās) *n.* enzyme which breaks down tissue thus enabling therapeutic liquids to be absorbed efficiently

hybrid ('hībrid) *n.* **1.** offspring of two plants or animals of different species **2.** mongrel —*a.* **3.** crossbred —'**hybridism** *n.* —'**hybridize** *v.* (cause to) produce hybrids; crossbreed

hybris ('hībris, 'he-) *n. see* HUBRIS

hydatid ('hīdətid) *a./n.* (of) watery cyst, resulting from development of tapeworm larva causing serious disease (in man)

hydra ('hīdrə) *n.* **1.** fabulous many-headed water serpent **2.** any persistent problem **3.** freshwater polyp (*pl.* **-s, -drae** (-drē)) —**hydra-headed** *a.* hard to root out

hydrangea (hī'drănjə) *n.* ornamental shrub with pink, blue, or white flowers

hydrant ('hīdrənt) *n.* pipe with valve and spout at which water may be drawn from a main pipe

hydrate ('hīdrāt) *n.* **1.** chemical compound containing water that is chemically combined with substance —*v.* **2.** (cause to) undergo treatment or impregnation with water —**hy'dration** *n.* —'**hydrator** *n.*

hydraulic (hī'drŏlik) *a.* concerned with, operated by, pressure transmitted through liquid in pipe —**hy'draulics** *pl.n.* (*with sing. v.*) science of mechanical properties of liquid in motion

Hydro ('hīdrō) *n.* **C** hydroelectric power company

hydro- *or before vowel* **hydr-** (*comb. form*) **1.** water, as in *hydroelectric* **2.** presence of hydrogen, as in *hydrocarbon*

hydrocarbon (hīdrə'kärbən) *n.* compound of hydrogen and carbon

hydrocephalus (hīdrō'sefələs) *or* **hydrocephaly** (hīdrō'sefəli) *n.* accumulation of cerebrospinal fluid within ventricles of brain —**hydrocephalic** (hīdrōsə'falik) *or* **hydro-'cephalous** *a.*

hydrochloric acid (hīdrə'klorik) strong colorless acid used in many industrial and laboratory processes

hydrocyanic acid (hīdrōsī'anik) *see* **hydrogen cyanide** *at* HYDROGEN

hydrodynamics (hīdrōdī'namiks) *pl.n.* (*with sing. v.*) science of the motions of system wholly or partly fluid

hydroelectric (hīdrōi'lektrik) *a.* pert. to generation of electricity by use of water

hydrofoil ('hīdrəfoil) *n.* fast, light vessel with hull raised out of water at speed by vanes in water

hydrogen ('hīdrijən) *n. Chem.* gaseous element *Symbol* H, at. wt. 1.0, at. no. 1 —**hy'drogenate** *v.* (cause to) undergo reaction with hydrogen —**hydrogen'ation** *n.* —**hydrogen bomb** atom bomb of enormous power —**hydrogen cyanide** colorless poisonous liquid with faint odor of bitter almonds, used for making plastics and as war gas —**hydrogen peroxide** colorless liquid used as antiseptic and bleach

hydrography (hī'drogrəfi) *n.* description of waters of the earth —**hy'drographer** *n.* —**hydro'graphic** *a.*

hydrology (hī'droləji) *n.* study of distribution, use *etc.* of the water of the earth and its atmosphere —**hydrologic** (hīdrə'lojik) *a.* —**hy'drologist** *n.*

hydrolysis (hī'drolisis) *n.* decomposition of chemical compound reacting with water

hydrometer (hī'dromitər) *n.* device for measuring relative density of liquid

hydronephrosis (hīdrōni'frōsis) *n.* dilation of parts of kidney by dammed-up urine

hydrophilic (hīdrə'filik) *a. Chem.* tending to dissolve in, mix with, or be wetted by water —'**hydrophile** *n.*

hydrophobia (hīdrə'fōbiə) *n.* rabies

hydrophone ('hīdrəfōn) *n.* instrument for detecting sound through water

hydroplane ('hīdrəplān) *n.* **1.** speedboat with hull raised partly out of water **2.** seaplane **3.** vane controlling motion of submarine *etc.*

hydroponics (hīdrə'poniks) *pl.n.* (*with sing. v.*) science of cultivating plants in water without using soil

hydrosphere ('hīdrəsfēər) *n.* watery part of earth's surface, including oceans, lakes, water vapor in atmosphere *etc.*

hydrostatics (hīdrə'statiks) *pl.n.* (*with sing. v.*) branch of science concerned with mechanical properties and behavior of fluids that are not in motion —**hydro'static** *a.*

hydrotherapy (hīdrə'therəpi) *n. Med.* treatment of disease by external application of water

hydrotropism (hī'drotrəpizəm) *n.* directional growth of plants in response to water

hydrous ('hīdrəs) *a.* containing water

hydroxide (hī'droksīd) *n. Chem.* any compound containing OH group, *eg* NaOH (sodium hydroxide)

hydrozoan (hīdrə'zōən) *n.* **1.** any coelenterate of the class *Hydrozoa*, which includes hydra and Portuguese man-of-war —*a.* **2.** of *Hydrozoa*

hyena

hyena *or* **hyaena** (hī'ēnə) *n.* nocturnal carnivorous mammal of Asia and Africa having howl like wild laughter

hygiene ('hījēn) *n.* **1.** principles and practice of health and cleanliness **2.** study of these principles —**hygienic** (hīji'enik) *a.* —**hygienically** (hīji'enikəli) *adv.* —**hy'gienist** *n.*

hygrometer (hī'gromitər) *n.* instrument for measuring humidity of air

hygroscopic (hīgrə'skopik) *a.* readily absorbing moisture from the atmosphere

hymen ('hīmən) *n.* **1.** membrane partly covering vagina of virgin **2.** (**H-**) Greek god of marriage

hymenopterous (hīmi'noptərəs) *a.* of large order of insects having two pairs of membranous wings —**hyme'nopteran** *n.* any hymenopterous insect (*pl.* **-tera** (-tərə))

hymn (him) *n.* **1.** song of praise, *esp.* to God —*vt.* **2.** praise in song —**hymnal** ('himnəl) *a.* **1.** of hymns —*n.* **2.** book of hymns (*also* **hymn book**) —**hymnodist** ('himnədist) *n.* —**hymnody** ('himnədi) *n.* singing or composition of hymns

hyoscyamine (hīə'sīəmēn) *n.* poisonous alkaloid occurring in belladonna and related plants and used like atropine

hype¹ (hīp) *sl. n.* **1.** hypodermic syringe **2.** drug addict —*vi.* **3.** (*with* up) inject oneself with drug

hype² (hīp) *sl. n.* **1.** deception; racket **2.** intensive or exaggerated publicity or sales promotion —*vt.* **3.** market or promote, using exaggerated or intensive publicity

hyper- (*comb. form*) over, above, excessively, as in *hyperactive*. Such words are not given here where the meaning may easily be inferred from the simple word

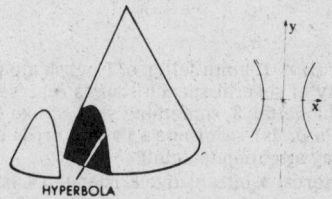

HYPERBOLA

hyperbola (hī'pərbələ) *n.* curve (in two parts) produced when double right circular cone is cut by plane making larger angle with the base than the side makes (*pl.* **-s, -le** (-lē))

hyperbole (hī'pərbəli) *n.* rhetorical exaggeration —**hyperbolic(al)** (hīpər'bolik(əl)) *a.*

Hyperborean (hīpər'bōriən) *a./n.* (inhabitant) of extreme north

hypercritical (hīpər'kritikəl) *a.* too critical —**hyper'criticism** *n.*

hyperglycemia (hīpərglī'sēmiə) *n.* abnormally large amount of sugar in blood —**hypergly'cemic** *a.*

hyperhidrosis (hīpərhi'drōsis, -hī-) *n.* excessive sweating

hyperinsulinism (hīpər'insəlinizəm) *n.* overproduction of insulin

hypermetropia (hīpərmi'trōpiə) *n.* condition in which images come to a focus behind the retina of the eye resulting in better vision for distant objects (*also* **hyperopia, farsightedness**) —**hypermetropic** (hīpərmi-'tropik) *a.*

hyperon ('hīpəron) *n. Phys.* any baryon that is not a nucleon

hyperopia (hīpə'rōpiə) *n. see* HYPERMETROPIA —**hyperopic** (hīpə'rōpik, -'ropik) *a.*

hypersensitive (hīpər'sensitiv) *a.* unduly vulnerable emotionally or physically

hypersonic (hīpər'sonik) *a.* concerned with or having velocity of at least five times that of sound in same medium under the same conditions —**hyper'sonics** *n.*

hypertension ('hīpərtenchən) *n.* abnormally high blood pressure

hypertrophy (hī'pərtrəfi) *n.* 1. enlargement of organ or part resulting from increase in size of cells —*v.* 2. (cause to) undergo this condition

hyperventilation (hīpərventi'lāshən) *n.* increase in rate of breathing, sometimes resulting in cramp and dizziness

hyphen ('hīfən) *n.* short line (-) indicating that two words or syllables are to be connected or separated —**'hyphenate** *vt.* —**'hyphenated** *a.* joined by hyphen

hypno- *or before vowel* **hypn-** (*comb. form*) 1. sleep, as in *hypnophobia* 2. hypnosis, as in *hypnotherapy*

hypnosis (hip'nōsis) *n.* induced state like deep sleep in which subject acts on external suggestion (*pl.* **-ses** (-sēz)) —**hypnotic**

(hip'notik) *a./n.* (of, relating to) drug which induces sleep —**'hypnotism** *n.* —**'hypnotist** *n.* —**'hypnotize** *vt.* affect with hypnosis —**hypno'therapy** *n.* use of hypnosis in treatment of physical or mental disorders

hypo ('hīpō) *n.* sodium thiosulfate, used as fixer in developing photographs

hypo- *or before vowel* **hyp-** (*comb. form*) under, below, less, as in *hypocrite, hyphen.* Such words are not given here where meaning may easily be inferred from simple word

hypocaust ('hīpōköst) *n.* ancient Roman underfloor heating system

hypochondria (hīpə'kondriə) *or* **hypochondriasis** (hīpəkən'drīəsis) *n.* morbid preoccupation about one's own health —**hypo'chondriac** *a./n.* —**hypochon'driacal** *a.*

hypocrisy (hi'pokrəsi) *n.* 1. assuming of false appearance of virtue 2. insincerity —**'hypocrite** *n.* —**hypo'critical** *a.* —**hypo'critically** *adv.*

hypodermic (hīpə'dərmik) *a.* 1. introduced, injected beneath the skin —*n.* 2. hypodermic syringe or needle

hypogastric (hīpə'gastrik) *a.* relating to, situated in, lower part of abdomen

hypoglycemia (hīpōglī'sēmiə) *n.* abnormally low concentration of sugar in the blood

hypogonadism (hīpō'gonədizəm) *n.* partial or complete lack of functioning of the sex glands

hypostasis (hī'postəsis) *n.* 1. *Metaphys.* essential nature of anything 2. *Christianity* any of the three persons of the Godhead 3. accumulation of blood in organ or part as result of poor circulation (*pl.* **-ses** (-sēz)) —**hypostatic** (hīpə'statik) *or* **hypo'statical** *a.*

hypotension ('hīpōtenchən) *n.* abnormally low blood pressure —**hypo'tensive** *a.*

hypotenuse (hī'potinyōōs, -nōōs, -nyōōz, -nōōz) *n.* side of a right-angled triangle opposite the right angle

hypothecate (hī'pothikāt) *vt.* 1. *see* **hypothesize** *at* HYPOTHESIS 2. *Law* pledge (personal property) as security for debt without transferring possession —**hypothe'cation** *n.* —**hy'pothecator** *n.*

hypothermia (hīpō'thərmiə) *n.* condition of having body temperature reduced to dangerously low level

hypothesis (hī'pothisis) *n.* 1. suggested explanation of something 2. assumption as basis of reasoning (*pl.* **-eses** (-isēz)) —**hy'pothesize** *v.* —**hypo'thetical** *a.* —**hypo'thetically** *adv.*

hypso- *or before vowel* **hyps-** (*comb. form*) height, as in *hypsometry*

hypsography (hip'sogrəfi) *n.* branch of geography dealing with altitudes

hypsometer (hip'somitər) *n.* instrument for measuring altitudes —**hyp'sometry** *n.* science of measuring altitudes

hyrax ('hīraks) *n.* genus of hoofed but rodent-like animals (*pl.* **-es, hyraces** ('hīrəsēz))

hyssop ('hisəp) *n.* small aromatic herb

hysterectomy (histə'rektəmi) *n.* surgical operation for removing the uterus

hysteresis (histə'rēsis) *n. Phys.* lag or delay in changes in variable property of a system

hysteria (hi'steriə, -'stēəriə) *n.* 1. mental disorder with emotional outbursts 2. any frenzied emotional state 3. fit of crying or laughing —**hys'terical** *a.* —**hys'terically** *adv.* —**hys'terics** *pl.n.* fits of hysteria

Hz hertz

Ii

i *or* **I** (ī) *n.* 1. ninth letter of English alphabet 2. any of several speech sounds represented by this letter 3. something shaped like I (*pl.* **i's, I's** *or* **Is**) —**dot one's i's and cross one's t's** pay attention to detail

i 1. interest 2. intransitive 3. island(s) 4. isle(s)

I (ī) *pron.* the pronoun of the first person singular

I 1. *Chem.* iodine 2. *Phys.* current 3. *Phys.* isospin 4. Roman numeral, one

IA Iowa

-ia (*comb. form*) 1. in place names, as in *Columbia* 2. in names of diseases, as in *pneumonia* 3. in words denoting condition or quality, as in *utopia* 4. in names of botanical genera and zoological classes, as in *Reptilia* 5. in collective nouns borrowed from Latin, as in *regalia*

IAEA International Atomic Energy Agency

-ial (*comb. form*) of or relating to, as in *managerial*

iamb ('īam, 'īamb) *or* **iambus** (ī'ambəs) *n.* metrical foot of short and long syllable (*pl.* **'iambs** *or* **-buses, -bi** (-bī)) —**i'ambic** *a.*

IATA (ī'ätə, ē'ätə) International Air Transport Association

-iatrics *or* **-iatry** (*n. comb. form*) medical care or treatment, as in *pediatrics, psychiatry* —**-iatric(al)** (*a. comb. form*)

iatrogenic (īatrə'jenik) *a.* (of a disease) induced inadvertently by a physician

Iberian (ī'bēəriən) *a.* of Iberia, *ie* Spain and Portugal

ibex ('ībeks) *n.* wild goat with large horns (*pl.* **-es, 'ibex**)

ibid. *or* **ib.** ibidem (*Lat.,* in the same place)

ibis ('ībis) *n.* storklike bird

-ible (*a. comb. form*) *see* -ABLE —**-ibly** (*adv. comb. form*) —**-ibility** (*n. comb. form*)

i/c 1. in charge (of) 2. internal combustion

-ic (*comb. form*) 1. of, relating to or

resembling, as in *periodic* (*also* **-ical**) 2. *Chem.* indicating that element is chemically combined in higher of two possible valence states, as in *ferric*

ICA International Cooperation Administration

-ical (*a. comb. form*) *see* -IC (sense 1) —**-ically** (*adv. comb. form*)

ICBM intercontinental ballistic missile

ICC 1. Interstate Commerce Commission 2. Indian Claims Commission

ice (īs) *n.* 1. frozen water 2. frozen confection, ice cream —*v.* 3. (*oft. with* up, over *etc.*) cover, become covered with ice —*vt.* 4. cool with ice 5. cover with icing —**'icicle** *n.* tapering spike of ice hanging where water has dripped —**'icily** *adv.* —**'iciness** *n.* —**'icing** *n.* semisolid flavored sweet mixture used to coat cakes and cookies (*also* **frosting**) —**'icy** *a.* 1. covered with ice 2. cold 3. chilling —**ice age** *see* **glacial period** *at*

GLACIER —**'iceberg** *n.* large floating mass of ice —**'icebox** *n.* **1.** refrigerator **2.** insulated cabinet packed with ice for storing food —**'icebreaker** *n.* **1.** vessel for breaking up ice in bodies of water (*also* **'iceboat**) **2.** device for breaking ice into smaller pieces —**'icecap** *n.* mass of glacial ice that permanently covers polar regions *etc.* —**ice cream** sweetened frozen dessert made from cream, eggs *etc.* —**ice floe** sheet of floating ice —**ice hockey** indoor or outdoor game played by two teams of six players wearing ice skates whose object is to score points by propelling a disk called a puck into the opponents' goal —**ice pack 1.** bag *etc.* containing ice, applied to part of body to reduce swelling *etc.* **2.** *see* **pack ice** at PACK —**ice skate** boot having steel blade fitted to sole to enable wearer to glide over ice —**ice-skate** *vi.* glide over ice on ice skates —**ice-skater** *n.* —**on thin ice** unsafe; vulnerable

Iceland ('Island, -land) *n.* country occupying a large island in the N Atlantic Ocean close to the Arctic Circle —**'Icelander** *n.* native or inhabitant of Iceland —**Ice'landic** *a.* **1.** of, or relating to Iceland —*n.* **2.** language of Iceland, which is a Scandinavian language

ichneumon (ik'nyōōmən, -'nōō-) *n.* grayish-brown mongoose

ichor ('īkōr) *n.* **1.** *Gr. myth.* fluid said to flow in veins of gods **2.** *Pathol.* foul-smelling watery discharge from wound or ulcer —**'ichorous** *a.*

ichthyology (ikthi'olǝji) *n.* scientific study of fish —**ichthyosaurus** (ikthiǝ'sörǝs) *n.* prehistoric marine animal (*pl.* **-i** (-ī))

icicle ('īsikǝl) *n.* *see* ICE

icon *or* **ikon** ('īkon) *n.* image, representation, *esp.* of religious figure —**i'conoclasm** *n.* —**i'conoclast** *n.* **1.** one who attacks established principles *etc.* **2.** breaker of icons —**icono'clastic** *a.* —**ico'nography** *n.* **1.** icons collectively **2.** study of icons —**ico'nostasis** *n.* icon-covered screen in Greek or Russian Orthodox Church that separates sanctuary from public areas

icono- *or before vowel* **icon-** (*comb. form*) image; likeness, as in *iconology*

ichthyosis (ikthi'ōsis) *n.* skin disease characterized by dry and scaly skin (*also* **fish skin**)

icterus ('iktǝrǝs) *n.* condition in which bile pigments accumulate in body fluids tinting skin and whites of eyeballs a greenish yellow (*also* **jaundice**)

ictus ('iktǝs) *n.* **1.** *Prosody* metrical or rhythmical stress in verse feet, as contrasted with stress accent on words **2.** *Med.* sudden attack or stroke (*pl.* **-es, -tus**) —**'ictal** *a.*

id (id) *n.* *Psychoanal.* the mind's instinctive energies

ID 1. Idaho **2.** identification

-id (*comb. form*) member of zoological family, as in *cyprinid*

Idaho ('īdǝhō) *n.* Mountain state of the U.S., admitted to the Union in 1890. Abbrev.: **ID** (with ZIP code)

idea (ī'dēǝ) *n.* **1.** notion in the mind **2.** conception **3.** vague belief **4.** plan, aim —**i'deal** *n.* **1.** conception of something that is perfect **2.** perfect person or thing —*a.* **3.** perfect **4.** visionary **5.** existing only in idea —**i'dealism** *n.* **1.** tendency to seek perfection in everything **2.** philosophy that mind is the only reality —**i'dealist** *n.* **1.** one who holds doctrine of idealism **2.** one who strives after the ideal **3.** impractical person —**ideal'istic** *a.* —**ideali'zation** *n.* —**i'dealize** *vt.* portray as ideal —**i'deally** *adv.*

idée fixe (ēdā 'fēks) *Fr.* fixed idea; obsession (*pl.* **idées fixes** (ēdā 'fēks))

idem ('īdem, 'idem) *Lat.*, the same

identity (ī'dentiti) *n.* **1.** individuality **2.** being the same, exactly alike —**i'dentical** *a.* very same —**i'dentically** *adv.* —**i'dentifiable** *a.* —**identifi'cation** *n.* —**i'dentify** *vt.* **1.** establish identity of **2.** treat as identical —*v.* **3.** associate (oneself) (**i'dentified, i'dentifying**) —**identification parade** group of persons assembled for purpose of discovering whether witness can identify suspect

ideo- (*comb. form*) idea; ideas, as in *ideology*

ideogram ('idiǝgram) *or* **ideograph** ('idiǝgraf) *n.* picture, symbol, figure *etc.* suggesting an object without naming it —**ide'ography** *n.* representation of things by ideograms

ideology (īdi'olǝji) *n.* body of ideas, beliefs of group, nation *etc.* —**ideo'logical** *a.*

ides (īdz) *n.* the 15th of March, May, July and Oct. and the 13th of other months of the Ancient Roman calendar

id est (id est) *Lat.*, that is

idiocy ('idiǝsi) *n. see* IDIOT

idiom ('idiǝm) *n.* **1.** way of expression natural or peculiar to a language or group **2.** characteristic style of expression —**idio-'matic** *a.* **1.** using idioms **2.** colloquial

idiosyncrasy (idiǝ'singkrǝsi) *n.* peculiarity of mind, temper or disposition in a person

idiot ('idiǝt) *n.* **1.** mentally deficient person **2.** foolish, senseless person —**'idiocy** *n.* **1.** state of being an idiot **2.** foolish act or remark —**idi'otic** *a.* utterly senseless or stupid —**idi'otically** *adv.* —**idiot box** television —**idiot card** *sl.* card for prompting television performer

idle ('īdǝl) *a.* **1.** unemployed **2.** lazy **3.** useless; vain **4.** groundless —*vi.* **5.** be idle **6.** (of engine) run slowly with gears disengaged —*vt.* **7.** (*esp. with* away) waste —**'idleness** *n.* —**'idler** *n.* —**'idly** *adv.*

idol ('īdǝl) *n.* **1.** image of deity as object of worship **2.** object of excessive devotion —**i'dolater** *n.* worshiper of idols (**i'dolatress** *fem.*) —**i'dolatrous** *a.* —**i'dolatry** *n.* —**'idolize** *vt.* **1.** love or venerate to excess **2.** make an idol of

idyll *or* **idyl** ('īdil) *n.* **1.** short descriptive poem of picturesque or charming scene or episode, *esp.* of rustic life **2.** charming or picturesque scene or event —**i'dyllic** *a.* **1.** of, like, idyll **2.** delightful —**i'dyllically** *adv.*

i.e. id est

if (if) *conj.* **1.** on condition or supposition that **2.** whether **3.** although —*n.* **4.** uncertainty, doubt (*esp. in* **ifs and buts**)

-iferous (*comb. form*) containing, yielding, as in *carboniferous*

igloo

igloo ('iglu:) *n.* Eskimo house built of soil, wood or stone or of snow and ice

igneous ('igniǝs) *a.* (*esp. of rocks*) formed as molten rock cools and hardens

ignis fatuus ('ignis 'fachōōǝs) will-o'-the-wisp (*pl.* **ignes fatui** ('ignēz 'fachōōī))

ignite (ig'nīt) *v.* (cause to) burn —**ignition** (ig'nishǝn) *n.* **1.** act of kindling or setting on fire **2.** in internal-combustion engine, means of firing explosive mixture, usu. electric spark

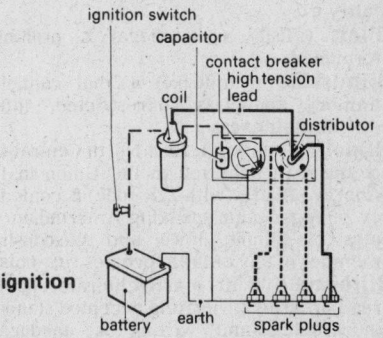

ignition

ignoble (ig'nōbǝl) *a.* **1.** mean, base **2.** of low birth —**ig'nobly** *adv.*

ignominy ('ignǝmini) *n.* **1.** dishonor, disgrace **2.** shameful act —**igno'minious** *a.*

ignore (ig'nör) *vt.* disregard; leave out of account —**ignoramus** (ignǝ'rāmǝs) *n.* ignorant person (*pl.* **-es**) —**ignorance** *n.* lack of knowledge —**ignorant** *a.* **1.** lacking knowledge **2.** uneducated **3.** unaware —**'ignorantly** *adv.*

iguana (i'gwänǝ) *n.* large tropical American tree-climbing lizard

ikebana (ikǝ'bänǝ) *n.* Japanese decorative art of flower arrangement

ikon ('īkon) *n. see* ICON

IL Illinois

il- (*comb. form*) *see* IN-¹, IN-²

ileum ('iliǝm) *n.* lower part of small intestine (*pl.* **-ea** (-iǝ)) —**'ileac** *a.* —**'ileus** *n.* interference with normal flow of intestinal contents caused by mechanical obstruction or by disturbance of blood or nerve supply

ilex ('īleks) *n.* any of genus of trees or shrubs such as holly and inkberry

ilium ('iliǝm) *n.* uppermost and widest of three sections of hipbone (*pl.* **-ia** (-iǝ)) —**'iliac** *a.*

ilk (ilk) *a.* same —**of that ilk 1.** of the same type or class **2.** *Scot.* of the place of the same name

ill (il) *a.* **1.** not in good health **2.** bad, evil **3.** faulty **4.** unfavorable —*n.* **5.** evil, harm **6.** mild disease —*adv.* **7.** badly **8.** hardly, with difficulty —**'illness** *n.* —**ill-advised** *a.* imprudent, injudicious —**ill-bred** *a.* badly brought up; lacking good manners —**ill-considered** *a.* done without due consideration; not thought out —**ill-disposed** *a.* (*oft. with* toward) not kindly disposed —**ill fame** bad reputation —**ill-fated** *a.* unfortunate —**ill-favored** *a.* ugly, deformed —**ill-founded** *a.* not founded on true or reliable premises; unsubstantiated —**ill-gotten** *a.* obtained dishonestly —**ill-mannered** *a.* boorish, uncivil —**ill-natured** *a.* naturally unpleasant and mean —**ill-omened** *a.* unlucky, inauspicious —**ill-starred** *a.* unlucky, ill-fated —**ill-timed** *a.* inopportune —**ill-treat** *vt.* treat cruelly —**ill-use** ('il'yōōz) *vt.* **1.** use badly or cruelly; abuse —*n.* ('il'yōōs), *also* **ill-usage 2.** harsh or cruel treatment; abuse —**ill will** unkind feeling, hostility —**house of ill fame** brothel

Ill. Illinois

illegal (i'lēgǝl) *a.* **1.** forbidden by law; unlawful; illicit **2.** unauthorized or prohibited by code of official or accepted rules —**ille'gality** *n.* —**il'legally** *adv.*

illegible (i'lejibǝl) *a.* unable to be read or deciphered —**illegi'bility** *n.*

illegitimate (ili'jitimit) a. 1. born out of wedlock 2. unlawful 3. not regular —**ille'gitimacy** n.

illiberal (i'libərəl) a. 1. narrow-minded; prejudiced; intolerant 2. not generous; mean 3. lacking in culture or refinement —**illiber'ality** n.

illicit (i'lisit) a. 1. illegal 2. prohibited, forbidden

illimitable (i'limitəbəl) a. that cannot be limited, boundless, unrestricted, infinite —**il'limitableness** n.

Illinois (ili'noi) n. 1. East North Central state of the U.S., admitted to the Union in 1818. Abbrev.: **Ill., IL** (with ZIP code) 2. confederacy of Algonquian-speaking Amerindian peoples of Illinois, Iowa and Wisconsin 3. member of any of these peoples (pl. **-nois**)

illiterate (i'litərit) a. 1. not literate, unable to read or write 2. violating accepted standards in reading and writing 3. uneducated, ignorant, uncultured —n. 4. illiterate person —**il'literacy** n.

illogical (i'lojikəl) a. 1. characterized by lack of logic, senseless; unreasonable 2. disregarding logical principles —**illogi'cality** or **il'logicalness** n. —**il'logically** adv.

illuminate (i'lōōmināt) vt. 1. light up 2. clarify 3. decorate with lights 4. decorate with gold and colors —**il'luminant** n. agent of lighting —**illumi'nation** n. —**il'luminative** a.

illus. or **illust.** 1. illustrated 2. illustration

illusion (i'lōōzhən) n. deceptive appearance or belief —**il'lusionist** n. conjurer —**il'lusory** or **il'lusive** a. false

illustrate (i'ləstrāt) vt. 1. provide with pictures or examples 2. exemplify —**illus'tration** n. 1. picture, diagram 2. example 3. act of illustrating —**illustrative** a. providing explanation —**illustrator** n.

illustrious (i'lustriəs) a. famous, distinguished, exalted

im- (comb. form) see IN-¹, IN-²

image ('imij) n. 1. representation or likeness of person or thing 2. optical counterpart, as in mirror 3. double, copy 4. general impression 5. mental picture created by words, esp. in literature 6. personality presented to the public by a person —vt. rare 7. make image of 8. reflect —**'imagery** n. images collectively, esp. in literature

imagine (i'majin) vt. 1. picture to oneself 2. think 3. conjecture —**i'maginable** a. —**i'maginary** a. existing only in fancy —**imagi'nation** n. 1. faculty of making mental images of things not present 2. fancy —**im'aginative** a. —**im'aginatively** adv.

imago (i'māgō) n. 1. last, perfected state of insect life 2. image (pl. **-s, imagines** (i'māgənēz))

imam (i'mäm) n. 1. leader of prayers in mosque 2. (**I-**) title of any of various Muslim leaders

imbalance (im'baləns) n. lack of balance, proportion

imbecile ('imbisil) n. 1. idiot —a. 2. idiotic —**imbe'cility** n.

imbed (im'bed) vt. see EMBED

imbibe (im'bīb) vt. 1. drink in 2. absorb —vi. 3. drink

imbricate ('imbrikit) a. lying over each other in regular order, like tiles or shingles on roof (also **'imbricated**) —**imbri'cation** n.

imbroglio (im'brōlyō) n. complicated situation, plot (pl. **-s**)

imbue (im'byōō) vt. inspire

IMF International Monetary Fund

imitate ('imitāt) vt. 1. take as model 2. mimic, copy —**'imitable** a. —**imi'tation** n. 1.

act of imitating 2. copy of original 3. likeness 4. counterfeit —**'imitative** a. —**'imitator** n.

immaculate (i'makyōōlit) a. 1. spotless 2. pure 3. unsullied

immanent ('imənənt) a. existing within, inherent —**'immanence** n.

immaterial (imə'tēəriəl) a. 1. unimportant, trifling 2. not consisting of matter 3. spiritual

immeasurable (i'mezhərəbəl) a. incapable of being measured, esp. by virtue of great size; limitless —**immeasura'bility** or **im'measurableness** n. —**im'measurably** adv.

immediate (i'mēdiət) a. 1. occurring at once 2. direct, not separated by others —**im'mediacy** n. —**im'mediately** adv.

immemorial (imi'mōriəl) a. beyond memory

immense (i'mens) a. huge, vast —**im'mensely** adv. —**im'mensity** n. vastness

immerse (i'mərs) vt. 1. dip, plunge into liquid 2. involve, engross —**im'mersion** n. immersing —**immersion foot** circulatory disturbance arising from prolonged exposure to below-freezing cold and dampness (also **trench foot**)

immesh (i'mesh) vt. see ENMESH

immigrate ('imigrāt) vi. come into country as settler —**'immigrant** n./a. —**immi'gration** n.

imminent ('iminənt) a. 1. liable to happen soon 2. close at hand —**'imminence** n. —**'imminently** adv.

immobilize (i'mōbilīz) vt. 1. make immobile 2. Fin. convert (circulating capital) into fixed capital —**immobili'zation** n. —**im'mobilizer** n.

immolate ('iməlāt) vt. kill, sacrifice —**immo'lation** n.

immoral (i'morəl) a. 1. corrupt 2. promiscuous 3. indecent 4. unethical —**immo'rality** n.

immortal (i'mörtəl) a. 1. deathless 2. famed for all time —n. 3. immortal being 4. god 5. one whose fame will last —**immor'tality** n. —**im'mortalize** vt.

immune (i'myōōn) a. 1. able to resist (disease etc.) 2. secure 3. exempt —**im'munity** n. 1. state of being immune 2. freedom from prosecution, tax etc. —**immuni'zation** n. process of making immune to disease —**'immunize** vt. make immune —**immu'nology** n. branch of biology concerned with study of immunity

immure (i'myōōər) vt. imprison, wall up

immutable (i'myōōtəbəl) a. unchangeable

imp (imp) n. 1. little devil 2. mischievous child —**'impish** a. of or like an imp; mischievous

imp. 1. imperative 2. imperfect

impact ('impakt) n. 1. collision 2. profound effect —vt. (im'pakt) 3. drive, press —**im'pacted** a. 1. (of tooth) wedged against another tooth below gum 2. (of fracture) having jagged broken ends wedged into each other

impair (im'pāər) vt. weaken, damage —**im'pairment** n.

impala

impala (im'palə) n. antelope of southern Afr.

impale (im'pāl) vt. 1. pierce with sharp instrument 2. combine (two coats of arms) by placing them side by side with line between —**im'palement** n.

impanel (im'panəl) vt. Law 1. enter on list (names of persons to be summoned for jury service) 2. select (jury) from such list —**im'panelment** n.

impart (im'pärt) vt. 1. communicate (information etc.) 2. give

impartial (im'pärshəl) a. 1. not biased or prejudiced 2. fair —**imparti'ality** n.

impassable (im'pasəbəl) a. 1. not capable of being passed 2. blocked, as mountain pass

impasse ('impas, im'pas) n. 1. deadlock 2. place, situation, from which there is no outlet

impassible (im'pasəbəl) a. rare 1. not susceptible to pain or injury 2. impassive; unmoved —**impassi'bility** or **im'passibleness** n.

impassioned (im'pashənd) a. deeply moved, ardent

impassive (im'pasiv) a. 1. showing no emotion 2. calm —**impas'sivity** n.

impasto (im'pastō) n. 1. paint applied thickly, so that brush marks are evident 2. technique of painting in this way

impeach (im'pēch) vt. 1. charge with crime 2. call to account 3. denounce —**im'peachable** a. —**im'peachment** n.

impeccable (im'pekəbəl) a. without flaw or error —**impecca'bility** n.

impecunious (impi'kyōōnyəs, -niəs) a. poor —**impecuni'osity** n.

impede (im'pēd) vt. hinder —**im'pedance** n. Elec. measure of opposition offered to flow of alternating current —**impediment** (im'pedimənt) n. 1. obstruction 2. defect —**impedimenta** (impedi'mentə) pl.n. 1. any objects that impede progress, esp. baggage and equipment carried by army 2. Law obstructions to making of contract, esp. of marriage

impel (im'pel) vt. 1. induce, incite 2. drive, force (**-ll-**) —**im'peller** n.

impend (im'pend) vi. 1. threaten, be imminent 2. (with over) rare hang —**im'pending** a.

impenitent (im'penitənt) a. not sorry or penitent; unrepentant —**im'penitence** n.

imperative (im'perətiv) a. 1. necessary 2. peremptory 3. expressing command —n. 4. imperative mood —**im'peratively** adv.

imperceptible (impər'septibəl) a. too slight, subtle, gradual etc. to be perceived —**impercepti'bility** n. —**imper'ceptibly** adv.

imperfect (im'pərfikt) a. 1. exhibiting or characterized by faults, mistakes etc.; defective 2. not complete or finished; deficient 3. Gram. denoting tense of verbs usu. used to describe continuous or repeated past actions or events 4. Law legally unenforceable 5. Mus. proceeding to dominant from tonic, subdominant or any chord other than dominant 6. Mus. of or relating to all intervals other than fourth, fifth and octave —n. 7. Gram. (verb in) imperfect tense —**imper'fection** n. 1. condition or quality of being imperfect 2. fault, defect

imperial (im'pēəriəl) a. 1. of empire or emperor 2. majestic 3. denoting weights and measures established by law, the customary system in U.S. —**im'perialism** n. 1. extension of empire 2. belief in colonial empire —**im'perialist** a./n. —**imperial'istic** a.

imperil (im'peril) vt. bring into peril, endanger

imperious (im'pēəriəs) *a.* domineering; haughty; dictatorial

impermeable (im'pərmiəbəl) *a.* (of substance) not allowing passage of fluid through interstices —**impermea'bility** *n.*

impersonal (im'pərsənəl) *a.* 1. objective, having no personal significance 2. devoid of human warmth, personality *etc.* 3. (of verb) without personal subject —**imperson'ality** *n.*

impersonate (im'pərsənāt) *vt.* 1. pretend to be (another person) 2. imitate 3. play the part of —**imperson'ation** *n.* —**im'persona-tor** *n.*

impertinent (im'pərtinənt) *a.* insolent, rude —im'pertinence *n.* —**im'pertinently** *adv.*

imperturbable (impər'tərbəbəl) *a.* calm, not excitable —**imper'turbably** *adv.*

impervious (im'pərviəs) *a.* 1. not affording passage 2. (*oft. with* to) not receptive (to feeling, argument *etc.*) —**im'perviously** *adv.* —**im'perviousness** *n.*

impetigo (impi'tēgō, -'tīgō) *n.* contagious skin disease

impetuous (im'pechŏŏəs) *a.* likely to act without consideration, rash —**impetu'osity** *n.* —**im'petuously** *adv.*

impetus ('impitəs) *n.* 1. force with which body moves 2. impulse

impinge (im'pinj) *vi.* 1. (*usu. with* on *or* upon) encroach 2. (*usu. with* on, against *or* upon) collide (with) —**im'pingement** *n.*

impious ('impiəs) *a.* irreverent, profane, wicked —**impiety** (im'pīiti) *n.* 1. lack of reverence or proper respect for a god 2. any lack of proper respect 3. impious act

implacable (im'plakəbəl) *a.* 1. not to be appeased 2. unyielding —**implaca'bility** *n.*

implant (im'plant) *vt.* 1. insert, fix —*n.* ('implant) 2. anything implanted, *esp.* surgically, such as tissue graft

implement ('implimənt) *n.* 1. tool, instrument, utensil —*vt.* ('impliment) 2. carry out (instructions *etc.*); put into effect

implicate ('implikāt) *vt.* 1. involve, include 2. imply 3. *rare* entangle —**impli'cation** *n.* something implied —**im'plicit** *a.* 1. implied but not expressed 2. absolute and unreserved

implode (im'plōd) *v.* collapse inward

implore (im'plör) *vt.* entreat earnestly

imply (im'plī) *vt.* 1. indicate by hint, suggest 2. mean (**im'plied, im'plying**)

impolitic (im'politik) *a.* not politic or expedient —**im'politicly** *adv.*

imponderable (im'pondərəbəl, -drəbəl) *a.* 1. unable to be weighed or assessed —*n.* 2. something difficult or impossible to assess —**impondera'bility** *n.* —**im'ponderably** *adv.*

import (im'pört, 'impört) *vt.* 1. bring in, introduce (*esp.* goods from foreign country) 2. imply —*n.* ('impört) 3. thing imported 4. meaning 5. importance 6. C *sl.* sportsman not native to area where he plays —**im'portable** *a.* —**impor'tation** *n.* —**im'porter** *n.*

important (im'pörtənt) *a.* 1. of great consequence 2. momentous 3. pompous —**im'portance** *n.* —**im'portantly** *adv.*

importune (impər'tyŏŏn, -'tŏŏn, im'pör-chən) *vt.* request, demand of (someone) persistently —**im'portunate** *a.* persistent —**im'portunately** *adv.* —**impor'tunity** *n.*

impose (im'pōz) *vt.* 1. levy (tax, duty *etc.*) —*vi.* 2. (*usu. with* on *or* upon) take advantage (of), practice deceit (on) —**im'posing** *a.* impressive —**impo'sition** *n.* 1. that which is imposed 2. tax 3. burden 4. deception —'impost *n.* duty, tax on imports

impossible (im'posəbəl) *a.* 1. incapable of being done or experienced 2. absurd 3. unreasonable —**impossi'bility** *n.* —**im'possibly** *adv.*

impost ('impōst) *n. Archit.* member at top of column that supports arch

impostor *or* **imposter** (im'postər) *n.* deceiver, one who assumes false identity —**im'posture** *n.*

impotent ('impətənt) *a.* 1. powerless 2. (of males) incapable of sexual intercourse —'impotence *n.* —'impotently *adv.*

impound (im'pownd) *vt.* 1. take legal possession of and, oft., place in a pound (automobiles, animals *etc.*) 2. confiscate

impoverish (im'povərish) *vt.* make poor or weak —**im'poverishment** *n.*

impracticable (im'praktikəbəl) *a.* 1. incapable of being put into practice or accomplished 2. unsuitable for desired use —**impractica'bility** *n.* —**im'practicably** *adv.*

impractical (im'praktikəl) *a.* 1. not practical or workable 2. not gifted with practical skills —**impracti'cality** *n.* —**im'practically** *adv.*

imprecation (impri'kāshən) *n.* 1. invoking of evil 2. curse —'imprecate *v.*

impregnable (im'pregnəbəl) *a.* 1. proof against attack 2. unassailable 3. unable to be broken into —**impregna'bility** *n.* —**im'pregnably** *adv.*

impregnate (im'pregnāt) *vt.* 1. saturate, infuse 2. make pregnant —**impreg'nation** *n.*

impresario (imprə'säriō) *n.* organizer of public entertainment; manager of opera, ballet *etc.* (*pl.* **-s**)

impress[1] (im'pres) *vt.* 1. affect deeply, usu. favorably 2. imprint, stamp 3. fix —*n.* ('impres) 4. act of impressing 5. mark impressed —**impressi'bility** *n.* —**im'press-ible** *a.* —**im'pression** *n.* 1. effect produced, *esp.* on mind 2. notion, belief 3. imprint 4. a printing 5. total of copies printed at once 6. printed copy —**impressiona'bility** *n.* —**im'pressionable** *a.* susceptible to external influences —**im'pressionism** *n.* art style that renders general effect without detail —**im'pressionist** *n.* —**impression'istic** *a.* —**im'pressive** *a.* making deep impression

impress[2] (im'pres) *vt.* press into service

imprest (im'prest) *vt.* 1. advance on loan by government —*n.* 2. money advanced by government

imprimatur (impri'mätŏŏr, im'primə-tyŏŏr, -tŏŏr) *n.* license to print book *etc.*

imprint ('imprint) *n.* 1. mark made by pressure 2. characteristic mark 3. publisher's or printer's name and address in book *etc.* —*vt.* (im'print) 4. produce (mark) on (surface) by pressure, printing or stamping 5. fix in mind

imprison (im'prizən) *vt.* put in prison —**im'prisonment** *n.*

improbity (im'prōbiti) *n.* dishonesty, wickedness, unscrupulousness

impromptu (im'promptyŏŏ, -tŏŏ) *adv./a.* 1. extempore; unrehearsed —*n.* 2. improvisation

improper (im'propər) *a.* 1. lacking propriety; not seemly or fitting 2. unsuitable for certain use or occasion; inappropriate 3. irregular; abnormal —**impropriety** (imprə-'prīiti) *n.* 1. lack of propriety; indecency 2. improper act or use 3. state of being improper —**improper fraction** fraction in which numerator is greater than denominator, as ⁷⁄₆

improve (im'prŏŏv) *v.* make or become better in quality, standard, value *etc.* —**im'provable** *a.* —**im'provement** *n.* —**im'prover** *n.*

improvident (im'providənt) *a.* 1. thriftless; imprudent 2. negligent —**im'providence** *n.*

improvise ('imprəvīz) *v.* 1. perform or make quickly from materials at hand 2. perform (poem, piece of music *etc.*), composing as one goes along —**improvi'sation** *n.* —'im-proviser *or* 'improvisor *n.*

impudent ('impyədənt) *a.* disrespectful, impertinent —'impudence *n.* —'impudently *adv.*

impugn (im'pyŏŏn) *vt.* call in question, challenge

impulse ('impuls) *n.* 1. sudden inclination to act 2. sudden application of force 3. motion caused by it 4. stimulation of nerve moving muscle —**im'pulsion** *n.* impulse —**im'pulsive** *a.* given to acting without reflection, rash

impunity (im'pyŏŏniti) *n.* freedom, exemption from injurious consequences or punishment

impurity (im'pyŏŏriti) *n.* 1. quality of being impure 2. impure thing or element 3. *Electron.* small quantity of element added to pure semiconductor crystal to control its electrical conductivity

impute (im'pyŏŏt) *vt.* ascribe, attribute —**imputa'bility** *n.* —**impu'tation** *n.* 1. that which is imputed as a charge or fault 2. reproach, censure

in (in) *prep.* 1. expresses inclusion within limits of space, time, circumstance, sphere *etc.* —*adv.* 2. in or into some state, place *etc.* 3. *inf.* in vogue *etc.* —*a.* 4. *inf.* fashionable —**in for** about to be affected by —**ins and outs** intricacies, complications; details

In *Chem.* indium

IN Indiana

in. 1. inch(es) 2. inlet

in-[1], **il-, im-,** *or* **ir-** (*comb. form*) 1. not; non-, as in *incredible, illegal, imperfect, irregular* 2. lack of, as in *inexperience.* See the list below

in-[2], **il-, im-,** *or* **ir-** (*comb. form*) 1. in; into; toward; within; on, as in *infiltrate, immigrate* 2. having intensive or causative function, as in *inflame, imperil*

in absentia (in ab'senchə) *Lat.* in absence of (someone indicated)

imma'ture	im'patient	im'prudent	in'applicable	incom'patible	incon'spicuous
im'miscible	im'penetrable	im'pure	inap'propriate	incom'plete	in'constant
im'mobile	im'permanent	ina'bility	inar'ticulate	incompre'hensible	incon'testable
im'moderate	imper'missible	inac'cessible	inar'tistic	incon'clusive	in'continent
im'modest	im'plausible	in'accurate	inat'tentive	incon'siderable	incon'venience
im'mov(e)able	impo'lite	in'adequate	in'audible	incon'siderate	incon'venient
im'palpable	impre'cise	inad'missible	in'capable	incon'sistent	incor'rect
im'patience	im'probable	inad'visable	in'comparable	incon'solable	incor'ruptible

inadvertent (inəd'vərtənt) a. 1. not attentive 2. negligent 3. unintentional —**inad'vertence** or **inad'vertency** n. —**inad'vertently** adv.

inalienable (in'ālyənəbəl) a. not able to be transferred to another —**inaliena'bility** n.

inamorata (inamə'rätə) n. woman with whom one is in love; lover (pl. **-s**)

inane (i'nān) a. foolish, silly, vacant —**inanition** (inə'nishən) n. 1. exhaustion 2. silliness —**inanity** (i'naniti) n.

inanimate (in'animit) a. 1. lacking qualities of living beings 2. appearing dead 3. lacking vitality

inapposite (in'apəzit) a. not appropriate or pertinent

inapt (in'apt) a. 1. not apt or fitting 2. lacking skill; inept —**in'aptitude** or **in'aptness** n.

inasmuch as (inəz'much) seeing that

inaugurate (in'ögyərāt, -gərāt) vt. 1. begin, initiate the use of, esp. with ceremony 2. admit to office —**in'augural** a. —**in'augural-ly** adv. —**inaugu'ration** n. 1. act of inaugurating 2. ceremony to celebrate the initiation or admission of

inauspicious (inö'spishəs) a. not auspicious; unlucky; unfavorable —**inaus'piciously** adv.

inboard ('inbörd) a. inside hull or bulwarks

inborn ('in'börn) a. existing from birth; inherent

inbreed ('in'brēd) v. breed from union of closely related individuals ('**in'bred** pt./pp.) —'**in'bred** a. 1. produced as result of inbreeding 2. inborn, ingrained —'**inbreeding** n.

inc. 1. inclusive 2. incorporated 3. increase

incalculable (in'kalkyələbəl) a. beyond calculation; very great

in camera in secret or private session

incandescent (inkan'desənt) a. 1. glowing with heat, shining 2. (of artificial light) produced by glowing filament —**incan'desce** vi. glow —**incan'descence** n.

incantation (inkan'tāshən) n. magic spell or formula, charm

incapacitate (inkə'pasitāt) vt. 1. disable; make unfit 2. disqualify —**inca'pacity** n.

incarcerate (in'kärsərāt) vt. imprison —**incarce'ration** n. —**in'carcerator** n.

incarnate (in'kärnāt) vt. 1. embody in flesh, esp. in human form —a. (in'kärnit, -nāt) 2. embodied in flesh, in human form 3. typified —**incar'nation** n.

incendiary (in'sendieri) a. 1. of malicious setting on fire of property 2. creating strife, violence etc. 3. designed to cause fires —n. 4. fire raiser 5. agitator 6. bomb filled with flammable substance —**in'cendiarism** n.

incense¹ ('insens) n. 1. gum, spice giving perfume when burned 2. its smoke —vt. 3. burn incense to 4. perfume with it

incense² (in'sens) vt. enrage

incentive (in'sentiv) n. 1. something that arouses to effort or action 2. stimulus

inception (in'sepshən) n. beginning

incessant (in'sesənt) a. unceasing

incest ('insest) n. sexual intercourse between two people too closely related to marry —**in'cestuous** a.

inch¹ (inch) n. 1. one twelfth of foot, or 0.0254 meter —v. 2. move very slowly

inch² (inch) n. Scot., Irish small island

inchoate (in'köāt, 'inköāt) a. 1. just begun 2. undeveloped

incident ('insidənt) n. 1. event, occurrence —a. (usu. with to) 2. naturally attaching (to) 3. striking, falling (upon) —'**incidence** n. 1. degree, extent or frequency of occurrence 2. a falling on, or affecting —**inci'dental** a. occurring as a minor part or an inevitable accompaniment or by chance —**inci'dental-ly** adv. 1. by chance 2. by the way —**inci'dentals** pl.n. accompanying items —**incidental music** background music for motion picture etc.

incinerate (in'sinərāt) vt. burn up complete-ly; reduce to ashes —**inciner'ation** n. —**in'cinerator** n. furnace or apparatus for incinerating something, esp. refuse

incipient (in'sipiənt) a. beginning

incise (in'sīz) vt. produce (lines etc.) by cutting into surface of (something) with sharp tool —**incision** (in'sizhən) n. 1. act of incising 2. cut, gash, notch 3. cut made with knife during surgical operation —**incisive** (in'sīsiv) a. 1. (of remark etc.) keen, biting 2. sharp —**in'cisor** n. cutting tooth

incite (in'sīt) vt. stir up or provoke to action —**inci'tation** or **in'citement** n.

incl. 1. including 2. inclusive

inclement (in'klemənt) a. (of weather) stormy, severe, cold —**in'clemency** n.

incline (in'klīn) v. 1. lean, slope 2. (cause to) be disposed —vt. 3. bend or lower (head etc.) —n. ('inklīn) 4. slope —**inclination** (inkli-'nāshən) n. 1. liking, tendency, preference 2. sloping surface 3. degree of deviation —**inclined plane** plane whose angle to horizontal is oblique

inclose (in'klöz) vt. see ENCLOSE

include (in'klood) vt. 1. have as (part of) contents 2. comprise 3. add in 4. take in —**in'clusion** n. —**in'clusive** a. including (everything) —**in'clusively** adv.

incognito (inkog'nētö) or (fem.) **incognita** adv./a. 1. under assumed identity —n. 2. assumed identity (pl. **-s**)

incognizant (in'kognizənt) a. unaware —**in'cognizance** n.

incoherent (inkö'hēərənt) a. 1. lacking clarity, disorganized 2. inarticulate —**inco'herence** n. —**inco'herently** adv.

income ('inkum) n. 1. amount of money, esp. annual, from salary, investments etc. 2. receipts —**income tax** personal tax levied on annual income

incoming ('inkuming) a. 1. coming in 2. about to come into office; next 3. (of interest etc.) being received; accruing

incommensurable (inkə'mensərəbəl, -'mench-) a. 1. incapable of being measured comparatively 2. incommensurate 3. Math.

having no common factor other than 1 —n. 4. something incommensurable —**incom-mensura'bility** n.

incommensurate (inkə'mensərit, -'mench-) a. 1. disproportionate 2. incommensurable

incommode (inkə'möd) vt. trouble, inconvenience, disturb —**incom'modious** a. 1. cramped 2. inconvenient

incommunicado (inkəmyöoni'kädö) a./adv. deprived (by force or by choice) of communication with others

incomparable (in'kompərəbəl, -prəbəl) a. 1. beyond or above comparison; matchless; unequaled 2. lacking basis for comparison; not having qualities or features that can be compared —**incompara'bility** or **in'compa-rableness** n. —**in'comparably** adv.

incompetent (in'kompitənt) a. 1. not possessing necessary ability, skill etc. to do or carry out task; incapable 2. marked by lack of ability, skill etc. 3. Law not legally qualified —n. 4. incompetent person —**in'competence** or **in'competency** n.

incongruous (in'konggrööəs) or **incongru-ent** a. 1. not appropriate 2. inconsistent, absurd —**incon'gruity** n. —**in'congruously** adv.

inconsequential (inkonsi'kwenchəl) or **in-consequent** (in'konsikwənt) a. 1. illogical 2. irrelevant; trivial

incontrovertible (inkontrə'vərtəbəl) a. undeniable; indisputable

incorporate (in'körpərāt) v. 1. include 2. unite into one body 3. form into corporation —**incorpo'ration** n.

incorporeal (inkör'pöriəl) a. 1. without material form, body or substance 2. spiritual, metaphysical 3. Law having no material existence —**incorpo'reity** or **incorpore'ality** n.

incorrigible (in'korijəbəl) a. 1. beyond correction or reform 2. firmly rooted —**incorrigi'bility** n.

increase (in'krēs) v. 1. make or become greater in size, number etc. —n. ('inkrēs) 2. growth, enlargement —**in'creasingly** adv. more and more

incredible (in'kredəbəl) a. 1. unbelievable 2. inf. marvelous; amazing

incredulous (in'krejöoləs) a. unbelieving —**incre'dulity** n.

increment ('inkrimənt) n. increase, esp. one of a series

incriminate (in'krimināt) vt. 1. imply guilt of 2. charge with crime —**in'criminatory** a.

incrust (in'krust) v. see ENCRUST

incubate ('ingkyəbāt, 'inkyə-) vt. 1. provide (eggs, embryos, bacteria etc.) with heat or other favorable condition for development —vi. 2. develop in this way —**incu'bation** n. —'**incubator** n. apparatus for artificially hatching eggs, for rearing premature babies

incubus ('ingkyəbəs, 'inkyə-) n. 1. nightmare; obsession 2. (orig.) demon believed to afflict sleeping person (pl. **-bi** (-bī), **-es**)

inculcate (in'kulkāt, 'inkulkāt) vt. impress on the mind —**incul'cation** n. —**in'culcator** n.

in'curable	indis'putable	ines'sential	inex'tinguishable	inof'fensive	insta'bility
inde'cipherable	indis'tinct	inex'act	in'fertile	in'sanitary	insub'stantial
inde'cision	indis'tinguishable	inex'cusable	infer'tility	in'sensitive	insuf'ficient
inde'cisive	inef'ficient	inex'pedient	in'formal	in'separable	insur'mountable
inde'finable	ine'lastic	inex'pensive	in'frequent	insig'nificant	in'tangible
in'definite	in'elegant	inex'perience	in'gratitude	insin'cere	in'tolerable
inde'structible	in'equable	inex'perienced	inhos'pitable	in'soluble	in'tolerant
indis'cernible	in'equitable	in'expert	inju'dicious	in'solvent	in'variable

inculpate (in'kulpāt, 'inkulpāt) vt. incriminate; cause blame to be imputed to —**incul'pation** n. —**in'culpatory** a.

incumbent (in'kumbənt) a. 1. lying, resting —n. 2. holder of office, esp. church benefice —**in'cumbency** n. 1. obligation 2. office or tenure of incumbent —**it is incumbent on** it is the duty of

incumber (in'kumbər) vt. see ENCUMBER

incur (in'kər) vt. 1. fall into 2. bring upon oneself (**-rr-**) —**in'cursion** n. 1. invasion 2. penetration

incus ('ingkəs) n. the middle bone in a chain of three bones in the ear of a mammal (pl. **incudes** (ing'kyōōdēz))

incuse (in'kyōōz, -'kyōōs) vt. 1. impress by striking or stamping —a. 2. hammered —n. 3. impression made by stamping

ind. 1. independent 2. index 3. indicative

Ind. 1. Independent 2. India 3. Indian 4. Indiana 5. Indies

indebted (in'detid) a. 1. owing gratitude (for help, favors etc.) 2. owing money —**in'debtedness** n.

indecent (in'dēsənt) a. 1. offensive to standards of decency, esp. in sexual matters 2. unseemly, improper (esp. **in indecent haste**) —**in'decency** n. 1. state or quality of being indecent 2. indecent act etc. —**indecent exposure** offense of indecently exposing one's body, esp. genitals, in public

indeed (in'dēd) adv. 1. in truth, really, in fact, certainly —interj. 2. denoting surprise, doubt etc.

indefatigable (indi'fatigəbəl) a. untiring —**inde'fatigably** adv.

indefeasible (indi'fēzəbəl) a. that cannot be lost or annulled —**indefeasi'bility** n.

indefensible (indi'fensəbəl) a. not justifiable or defensible —**inde'fensibly** adv.

indelible (in'delibəl) a. 1. that cannot be blotted out, effaced or erased 2. producing such a mark —**indeli'bility** n. —**in'delibly** adv.

indelicate (in'delikit) a. 1. coarse 2. embarrassing, tasteless

indemnity (in'demniti) n. 1. compensation for loss 2. security against loss —**indemnifi'cation** n. —**in'demnify** vt. 1. give indemnity to 2. compensate (**in'demnified, in'demnifying**)

indent (in'dent) v. 1. set (written matter etc.) in from margin etc. 2. notch (edge, border etc.); make (something) jagged 3. cut (document in duplicate) so that irregular lines may be matched 4. make an order upon (someone) or for (something) —n. ('indent) 5. notch 6. order, requisition —**inden'tation** n. 1. hollowed, notched or cut place, as an edge or coastline 2. series of hollows, notches or cuts 3. act of indenting; condition of being indented 4. leaving of space or amount of space left between margin and start of indented line (also **in'dention, 'indent**) —**in'dention** n. indentation (on page) —**in'denture** n. 1. indented document 2. contract, esp. one binding apprentice to master —vt. 3. bind thus

independent (indi'pendənt) a. 1. not subject to others 2. self-reliant 3. free 4. valid in itself 5. politically of no party —**inde'pendence** or **inde'pendency** n. 1. being independent 2. self-reliance 3. self-support —**inde'pendently** adv. —**Independence Day** July 4th, U.S. national holiday in commemoration of the adoption of the Declaration of Independence —**independent clause** Gram. main or coordinate clause

in-depth a. carefully worked out, detailed, thorough

indescribable (indi'skrībəbəl) a. 1. beyond description 2. too intense etc. for words —**inde'scribably** adv.

indeterminate (indi'tərminit) a. 1. uncertain 2. inconclusive 3. incalculable 4. Math. (of an equation) having more than one variable

index ('indeks) n. 1. alphabetical list of references, usu. at end of book 2. pointer, indicator 3. Math. exponent (pl. **-es, 'indices**) —vt. 4. provide (book) with index 5. insert in index —**index finger** finger next to thumb (also **'forefinger**) —**index number** number used to compare some quantity, such as cost of living, at different times

India ('indiə) n. 1. country in Asia bounded northwest by Pakistan, north by China, Tibet, Nepal and Bhutan, east by Burma, southeast, south and southwest by the Indian Ocean 2. word used in communications for the letter i —'**Indian** n./a. 1. (of, or relating to) Amerindian 2. (native or inhabitant) of India —'**Indic** a. 1. denoting, belonging to or relating to branch of Indo-European languages —n. 2. this group of languages —'**Indiaman** n. formerly, merchant ship engaged in trade with India —**Indian club** bottle-shaped club, usu. used by gymnasts etc. —**Indian corn** maize —**Indian file** single file —**Indian giver** person who gives something and then takes it back —**Indian hemp** cannabis —**Indian ink** very dark black (drawing) ink —**Indian list** C inf. list of people to whom liquor may not be sold —**Indian Ocean** ocean south of Asia, east of Africa and west of Australia —**Indian pipe** white leafless saprophytic plant of U.S. and Asia —**Indian pudding** baked dessert made of cornmeal, milk and molasses —**Indian red** moderate-to-strong brownish red —**Indian summer** period of unusually warm weather in fall —**Indian wrestling** contest in which seated opponents clasp hands with elbows on the table and attempt to force each other's hand down —**India paper** extremely thin, opaque printing paper used esp. for Bibles and dictionaries —**India rubber** rubber, eraser

Indiana (indi'anə) n. East North central state of the U.S., admitted to the Union in 1816. Abbrev: **Ind., IN** (with ZIP code)

indicate ('indikāt) vt. 1. point out 2. state briefly 3. signify —**indi'cation** n. 1. sign 2. token 3. explanation —**in'dicative** a. 1. (with of) pointing (to) 2. Gram. stating fact —n. 3. Gram. (verb in) indicative mood —'**indicator** n. 1. one who, that which, indicates 2. on vehicle, flashing light showing driver's intention to turn

indices ('indisēz) n., pl. of INDEX

indict (in'dīt) vt. accuse, esp. by legal process —**in'dictable** a. —**in'dictment** n.

indifferent (in'difrənt, -fərənt) a. 1. uninterested 2. unimportant 3. neither good nor bad 4. inferior 5. neutral —**in'difference** n.

indigenous (in'dijinəs) a. born in or natural to a country —**indigene** ('indijēn) n. 1. aborigine 2. native

indigent ('indijənt) a. poor; needy —'**indigence** n. poverty

indigestion (indī'jeschən, -di-) n. (discomfort, pain caused by) difficulty in digesting food —**indi'gestible** a.

indignant (in'dignənt) a. 1. moved by anger and scorn 2. angered by sense of injury or injustice —**in'dignantly** adv. —**indig'nation** n. —**in'dignity** n. humiliation; insult, slight

indigo ('indigō) n. 1. blue dye obtained from plant 2. the plant (pl. **-s, -es**) —a. 3. deep blue

indirect (indi'rekt, -dī-) a. 1. deviating from direct course or line 2. not coming as direct effect or consequence 3. not straightforward, open or fair —**indi'rectly** adv. —**indi'rectness** n. —**indirect discourse** reporting of something said by conveying what was meant rather than repeating exact words —**indirect object** Gram. noun, pronoun or noun phrase indicating recipient or beneficiary of action of verb and its direct object —**indirect tax** tax levied on goods or services rather than on individuals or companies

indiscreet (indi'skrēt) a. not discreet; imprudent; tactless —**indiscretion** (indi-'skreshən) n. 1. characteristic or state of being indiscreet 2. indiscreet act, remark etc.

indiscrete (indi'skrēt, in'diskrēt) a. not divisible or divided into parts

indiscriminate (indi'skriminit) a. 1. lacking discrimination 2. jumbled

indispensable (indi'spensəbəl) a. necessary; essential

indisposition (indispə'zishən) n. 1. sickness 2. disinclination —**indis'pose** vt. —**indis'posed** a. 1. unwell, not fit 2. disinclined

indissoluble (indi'solyəbəl) a. permanent

indium ('indiəm) n. Chem. metallic element Symbol In, at. wt. 114.8, at. no. 49

individual (indi'vijōōəl) a. 1. single 2. characteristic of single person or thing 3. distinctive —n. 4. single person or thing, esp. when regarded as distinct from others —**indi'vidualism** n. principle of asserting one's independence —**indi'vidualist** n. —**individual'istic** a. —**individu'ality** n. 1. distinctive character 2. personality —**indi'vidualize** vt. make (or treat as) individual —**indi'vidually** adv. singly

Indo- ('indō-) (comb. form) India; Indian, as in Indo-European

indoctrinate (in'doktrināt) vt. implant beliefs in the mind of

Indo-European a./n. (denoting) the most geographically widespread and numerically important family of languages which includes English; a member of the Germanic branch

indolent ('indələnt) a. lazy —'**indolence** n.

indomitable (in'domitəbəl) a. unyielding

Indonesia (indō'nēzhə, -shə) n. 1. country in southern Pacific consisting of the islands of Sumatra, Java and Madura, Celebes, Borneo, Lesser Sundas, Moluccas, the western half of New Guinea and some 3000 smaller islands and islets 2. Malay archipelago —**Indo'nesian** n./a. 1. (native or inhabitant) of Indonesia —n. 2. language of Indonesia which is a member of the Malayo-Polynesian family, differing from Malay in its transcription

indoor ('indōr) a. 1. within doors 2. under cover —**in'doors** adv. inside or into house or other building

indorse (in'dōrs) vt. see ENDORSE

indubitable (in'dyōōbitəbəl, -'dōō-) a. beyond doubt; certain —**in'dubitably** adv.

induce (in'dyōōs, -'dōōs) vt. 1. persuade 2. bring on 3. cause 4. produce by induction —**in'ducement** n. incentive, attraction

induct (in'dukt) vt. install in office —**in'ductance** n. —**in'duction** n. 1. an inducting 2. general inference from particular instances 3. production of electric or magnetic state in body by its being near (not touching) electrified or magnetized body 4. in internal-combustion engine, part of the piston's action which draws gas from carburetor —**in'ductive** a. —**in'ductively** adv. —**in'ductor** n. —**induction coil** transformer for producing high voltage from low voltage

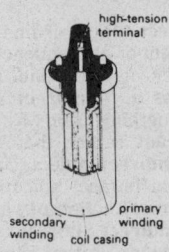

induction coil high-tension terminal / secondary winding / primary winding / coil casing

indue (in'dyōō, -'dōō) vt. see ENDUE

indulge (in'dulj) vt. 1. gratify 2. give free course to 3. pamper, spoil —**in'dulgence** n. 1. an indulging 2. extravagance 3. something granted as a favor or privilege 4. R.C.Ch. remission of temporal punishment due after absolution —**in'dulgent** a. —**in'dulgently** adv.

indurate ('indyərāt, -də-) v. 1. make or become hard or callous 2. make or become hardy —a. ('indyərit, -də-) 3. hardened, callous, or unfeeling —**'indurative** a.

industry ('indəstri) n. 1. manufacture, processing etc. of goods 2. branch of this 3. diligence, habitual hard work —**in'dustrial** a. of industries, trades —**in'dustrialist** n. person engaged in control of industrial enterprise —**in'dustrialize** v. —**in'dustrious** a. diligent —**industrial design** application of aesthetic principles to the design of machine-made articles, with standards independent of those for hand-made objects —**industrial medicine** branch of medicine dealing with medical care of workers (also **occupational medicine**) —**Industrial Revolution** transformation in 18th and 19th centuries of Brit. and other countries into industrial nations

-ine (comb. form) 1. of, relating to or belonging to, as in saturnine 2. consisting of; resembling, as in crystalline 3. indicating any of various classes of chemical compounds, as in chlorine, nicotine, glycerine (also **-in**) 4. indicating feminine form, as in heroine

inebriate (in'ēbriāt) vt. 1. make drunk; intoxicate —a. (in'ēbriit) 2. drunken —n. (in'ēbriit) 3. habitual drunkard —**inebri'a-tion** or **inebriety** (ini'brīīti) n. drunkenness

inedible (in'edibəl) a. 1. not eatable 2. unfit for food —**inedi'bility** n.

ineducable (in'ejəkəbəl) a. incapable of being educated, esp. through mental retardation

ineffable (in'efəbəl) a. 1. too great or sacred for words 2. unutterable —**ineffa'bility** n. —**in'effably** adv.

ineligible (in'elijəbəl) a. not fit or qualified (for something) —**ineligi'bility** n.

ineluctable (ini'luktəbəl) a. (esp. of fate) incapable of being avoided; inescapable

inept (in'ept) a. 1. absurd 2. out of place 3. clumsy —**in'eptitude** n.

inequality (ini'kwoliti) n. 1. state or quality of being unequal 2. lack of smoothness or regularity 3. Math. statement indicating that value of one quantity or expression is not equal to another

inert (in'ərt) a. 1. without power of action or resistance 2. slow, sluggish 3. chemically unreactive —**inertia** (in'ərshə, -shiə) n. 1. inactivity 2. property by which matter continues in its existing state of rest or motion in straight line, unless that state is changed by external force —**in'ertly** adv. —**in'ertness** n. —**inertial guidance** guidance of aircraft or spacecraft by use of automatic instruments carried by craft

inescapable (ini'skāpəbəl) a. incapable of being escaped or avoided

inestimable (in'estiməbəl) a. too good, too great to be estimated

inevitable (in'evitəbəl) a. 1. unavoidable 2. sure to happen —**inevita'bility** n. —**in'evitably** adv.

inexorable (in'eksərəbəl) a. relentless —**in'exorably** adv.

inexpiable (in'ekspiəbəl) a. 1. incapable of being expiated 2. obs. implacable

inexplicable (inik'splikəbəl, in'eksplikəbəl) a. impossible to explain

in extenso (in ik'stensō) Lat. at full length

in extremis (in ik'strāmis, ik'strēmis) Lat. at the point of death

inextricable (iniks'trikəbəl, in'ekstrikəbəl) a. 1. not able to be escaped from 2. not able to be disentangled etc. 3. extremely involved or intricate —**inextrica'bility** or **inex'tricableness** n. —**inex'tricably** adv.

inf. 1. infinitive 2. informal 3. information

infallible (in'faləbəl) a. 1. unerring 2. not liable to fail 3. certain, sure —**infalli'bility** n. —**in'fallibly** adv.

infamous ('infəməs) a. 1. notorious 2. shocking —**'infamously** adv. —**'infamy** n.

infant ('infənt) n. very young child —**'infancy** n. —**in'fanticide** n. 1. murder of newborn child 2. person guilty of this —**'infantile** a. childish —**infantile paralysis** poliomyelitis

infante (in'fanti) n. formerly, son of king of Spain or Portugal, esp. one not heir to throne —**infanta** (in'fantə) n. 1. formerly, daughter of king of Spain or Portugal 2. wife of infante

infantry ('infəntri) n. foot soldiers

infatuate (in'fachōōāt) vt. inspire with folly or foolish passion —**in'fatuated** a. foolishly enamored —**infatu'ation** n.

infect (in'fekt) vt. 1. affect (with disease) 2. contaminate —**in'fection** n. —**in'fectious** a. catching, spreading, pestilential —**infectious hepatitis** acute infectious viral disease, usu. benign, transmitted by food or water contaminated by fecal matter —**infectious mononucleosis** acute infectious disease characterized by fever, sore throat, swollen lymph nodes etc. (also **glandular fever**)

infelicitous (infi'lisitəs) a. unfortunate; unsuitable —**infe'licity** n. 1. being infelicitous 2. unsuitable or inapt remark etc.

infer (in'fər) vt. deduce, conclude (**-rr-**) —**'inference** n. —**infer'ential** a. deduced

inferior (in'fēəriər) a. 1. of poor quality 2. lower —n. 3. one lower (in rank etc.) —**inferi'ority** n. —**inferiority complex** Psychoanal. sense of inferiority, lack of confidence

infernal (in'fərnəl) a. 1. devilish 2. hellish 3. inf. irritating, confounded —**in'fernally** adv.

inferno (in'fərnō) n. 1. region of hell 2. conflagration (pl. **-s**)

infest (in'fest) vt. inhabit or overrun in dangerously or unpleasantly large numbers —**infes'tation** n.

infidelity (infi'deliti) n. 1. unfaithfulness 2. religious disbelief 3. disloyalty 4. treachery —**'infidel** n. 1. unbeliever —a. 2. rejecting a specific religion, esp. Christianity or Islam 3. of unbelievers or unbelief

infield ('infēld) n. 1. area of baseball field enclosed by base lines 2. area inside running track or racetrack —**'infielder** n.

infighting ('infīting) n. 1. Boxing combat at close quarters 2. intense conflict, as between members of same organization —**'infighter** n.

infiltrate (in'filtrāt, 'infiltrāt) v. 1. trickle through —vt. 2. (cause to) gain access

surreptitiously 3. cause to pass through pores —**infil'tration** n.

infin. infinitive

infinite ('infinit) a. boundless —**'infinitely** adv. exceedingly —**infini'tesimal** a. extremely, infinitely small —**in'finitude** n. state or quality of being infinite —**in'finity** n. unlimited and endless extent

infinitive (in'finitiv) a./n. (denoting) verb form with characteristics of noun and verb and in English used with to

infirm (in'fərm) a. 1. physically weak 2. mentally weak 3. irresolute —**in'firmary** n. hospital; sick quarters —**in'firmity** n.

infix ('infiks, in'fiks) vt. 1. fix firmly in 2. instill, inculcate 3. Gram. insert (affix) into middle of word —n. ('infiks) 4. Gram. affix inserted into middle of word

in flagrante delicto (in flə'granti di'liktō) while committing the offense

inflame (in'flām) vt. 1. rouse to anger, excitement 2. cause inflammation in —vi 3. become inflamed —**inflammability** (inflamə'biliti) n. —**inflammable** (in'flaməbəl) a. 1. flammable 2. excitable —**inflammation** (inflə'māshən) n. reaction of body to irritant by pain, heat, swelling and redness —**inflammatory** (in'flamətöri) a.

inflate (in'flāt) v. 1. blow up with air, gas 2. swell —vt. 3. cause economic inflation of (prices etc.) —vi. 4. undergo economic inflation —**in'flatable** a. —**in'flation** n. increase in prices and fall in value of money —**in'flationary** a.

inflect (in'flekt) vt. 1. modify (words) to show grammatical relationships 2. bend inward —**in'flection** n. 1. modification of word 2. modulation of voice

inflexible (in'fleksəbəl) a. 1. incapable of being bent 2. stern —**inflexi'bility** n.

inflict (in'flikt) vt. 1. impose 2. deliver forcibly —**in'fliction** n. 1. inflicting 2. punishment

in-flight a. provided during flight in aircraft

inflorescence (inflə'resəns) n. 1. flowering part of a plant 2. Bot. arrangement of flowers on stem

inflow ('inflō) n. 1. something, such as liquid or gas, that flows in 2. act of flowing in; influx

influence ('inflōōəns) n. 1. effect of one person or thing on another 2. power of person or thing having an effect 3. thing, person exercising this —vt. 4. sway 5. induce 6. affect —**influ'ential** a.

influenza (inflōō'enzə) n. contagious feverish virus disease marked by muscular pain and inflammation of the respiratory system

influx ('influks) n. 1. a flowing in 2. inflow

info ('infō) inf. information

infold (in'fōld) vt. see ENFOLD

inform (in'förm) vt. 1. tell 2. animate —vi. 3. (oft. with on or against) give information (about) —**in'formant** n. one who tells —**infor'mation** n. 1. facts acquired through experience or study 2. knowledge of specific and timely events or situations; news 3. act of informing; condition of being informed 4. office, agency etc. providing information 5. charge or complaint made by prosecuting officer 6. Comp. results derived from processing of data according to programmed instructions 7. Comp. information operated on by computer program (also **'data**) —**infor'mational** a. —**in'formative** a. —**in'formed** a. having much knowledge of something —**in'former** n. 1. person who informs against someone, esp. criminal 2. person who provides information —**information retrieval** techniques of storing and recovering facts, esp. by the use of computerized systems —**information technology** technology concerned with collecting and storing information, *esp.* by computer or electronically —**information theory** theory that deals statistically with coding, transmitting, storing, retrieving and decoding information

infra ('infrə) *adv.* 1. below 2. under 3. after —**infra dig** *inf.* beneath one's dignity —**infra'red** *a.* denoting rays below red end of visible spectrum —**infra'sonic** *a.* having frequency below that of sound

infraction (in'frakshən) *n.* infringement

infrangible (in'franjibəl) *a.* 1. incapable of being broken 2. not capable of being violated or infringed —**infrangi'bility** *or* in'**frangibleness** *n.*

infrastructure ('infrəstrukchər) *n.* basic structure or fixed-capital items of an organization or economic system

infringe (in'frinj) *vt.* transgress, break —in'**fraction** *n.* breach, violation —in'**fringement** *n.*

infuriate (in'fyŏŏriāt) *vt.* enrage

infuse (in'fyŏŏz) *v.* 1. soak to extract flavor *etc.* —*vt.* 2. instill, charge —in'**fusible** *a.* capable of being infused —in'**fusion** *n.* 1. an infusing 2. liquid extract obtained

infusible (in'fyŏŏzəbəl) *a.* not fusible; not easily melted; having high melting point —**infusi'bility** *or* in'**fusibleness** *n.*

-ing[1] (*comb. form*) 1. action of, process of, result of or something connected with verb, as in *meeting, wedding, winnings* 2. something used in, consisting of, involving *etc.*, as in *tubing, soldiering*

-ing[2] (*comb. form*) 1. forming present participle of verbs, as in *walking, believing* 2. forming participial adjectives, as in *growing boy, sinking ship* 3. forming adjectives not derived from verbs, as in *swashbuckling*

ingenious (in'jēnyəs) *a.* 1. clever at contriving 2. cleverly contrived —in'**geniously** *adv.* —inge'**nuity** *n.*

ingénue ('anjənŏŏ, 'än-) *n.* 1. artless girl or young woman 2. actress playing such a part

ingenuous (in'jenyŏŏəs) *a.* 1. frank 2. naive, innocent —in'**genuously** *adv.*

ingest (in'jest) *vt.* take (food or liquid) into the body —in'**gestible** *a.* —in'**gestion** *n.*

inglenook ('inggəlnŏŏk) *n.* corner by a fireplace

inglorious (in'glöriəs) *a.* dishonorable, shameful, disgraceful

ingot ('inggət) *n.* brick of cast metal, *esp.* gold

ingrain *or* **engrain** (in'grān) *vt.* 1. implant deeply 2. *obs.* dye, infuse deeply —in'**grained** *or* en'**grained** *a.* 1. deep-rooted 2. inveterate 3. (*esp.* of dirt) worked into or through fiber, grain, pores *etc.*

ingratiate (in'grāshiāt) *v. refl.* get (oneself) into favor —in'**gratiatingly** *adv.*

ingredient (in'grēdiənt) *n.* component part of a mixture

ingress ('in-gres) *n.* 1. entry 2. means or right of entrance

ingrown ('in-grōn) *a.* 1. (*esp.* of toenail) grown abnormally into flesh 2. grown within; native; innate

inhabit (in'habit) *vt.* dwell in —in'**habitable** *a.* —in'**habitant** *n.* —inhabi'**tation** *n.*

inhale (in'hāl) *v.* breathe in (air *etc.*) —in'**halant** *a.* 1. (*esp.* of medicinal preparation) inhaled for its therapeutic effect 2. inhaling —*n.* 3. inhalant medicinal preparation —inha'**lation** *n.* —in'**haler** *n.* device producing and assisting inhalation of therapeutic vapors

inhere (in'hēər) *vi.* 1. (of qualities) exist 2. (of rights) be vested —in'**herence** *n.* —in'**herent** *a.* existing as an inseparable part

inherit (in'herit) *vt.* 1. receive as heir 2. derive from parents —*vi.* 3. succeed as heir —**inherita'bility** *or* in'**heritableness** *n.* —in'**heritable** *a.* 1. capable of being transmitted by heredity 2. capable of being inherited —in'**heritance** *n.* —in'**heritor** *n.* (in'**heritress** *or* in'**heritrix** *fem.)*

inhesion (in'hēzhən) *n.* inherence

inhibit (in'hibit) *vt.* 1. restrain (impulse, desire *etc.*) 2. hinder (action) 3. forbid —**inhibition** (ini'bishən, inhi-) *n.* 1. repression of emotion, instinct 2. a stopping or retarding —in'**hibitory** *a.*

inhuman (in'hyŏŏmən, -'yŏŏ-) *a.* 1. cruel, brutal 2. not human —inhu'**manity** *n.*

inhume (in'hyŏŏm) *vt.* bury, inter —inhu'**mation** *n.*

inimical (i'nimikəl) *a.* 1. unfavorable 2. unfriendly; hostile

inimitable (i'nimitəbəl) *a.* defying imitation

iniquity (i'nikwiti) *n.* 1. gross injustice 2. wickedness, sin —in'**iquitous** *a.* 1. unfair, unjust 2. sinful 3. *inf.* outrageous

initial (i'nishəl) *a.* 1. of, occurring at the beginning —*n.* 2. initial letter, *esp.* of person's name —*vt.* 3. mark, sign with one's initials —in'**itialize** *vt. Comp.* set (program) to starting position or value —in'**itially** *adv.* —**initial teaching alphabet** alphabet of 44 characters for teaching beginners to read English

initiate (i'nishiāt) *vt.* 1. originate, begin 2. admit into closed society 3. instruct in elements of something —*n.* (i'nishiit, -āt) 4. initiated person —initi'**ation** *n.* —in'**itiative** *n.* 1. first step, lead 2. ability to act independently —*a.* 3. originating —in'**itiatory** *a.*

inject (in'jekt) *vt.* introduce (*esp.* fluid, medicine *etc.* with syringe) —in'**jection** *n.*

injunction (in'jungkshən) *n.* 1. judicial order to restrain 2. authoritative order

injury ('injəri) *n.* 1. physical damage or harm 2. wrong —'**injurable** *a.* —'**injure** *vt.* 1. do harm or damage to 2. offend, *esp.* by injustice —'**injured** *a.* —in'**jurious** *a.* —in'**juriously** *adv.* —**injury time** *Soccer* extra time added on to compensate for time spent attending to injured players during match

injustice (in'justis) *n.* 1. want of justice 2. wrong 3. injury 4. unjust act

ink (ingk) *n.* 1. fluid used for writing or printing —*vt.* 2. mark with ink 3. cover, smear with ink —'**inker** *n.* —'**inky** *a.* 1. resembling ink, *esp.* in color; dark; black 2. of, containing or stained with ink —'**inkstand** *n.* —'**inkwell** *n.* vessel for holding ink

inkling ('ingkling) *n.* hint, slight knowledge or suspicion

inlaid ('in'lād) *a.* decorated with inset pattern

inland ('inland, -lənd) *n.* 1. interior of country —*a.* 2. in interior of country 3. away from the sea 4. within a country —*adv.* 5. in or toward the inland

in-law *n.* relative by marriage

inlay (in'lā) *vt.* 1. embed 2. decorate with inset pattern (in'**laid** *pt./pp.*) —*n.* ('inlā) 3. inlaid piece or pattern

inlet ('inlet, -lət) *n.* 1. entrance 2. mouth of creek 3. piece inserted

in loco parentis (in 'lōkō pə'rentis) *Lat.* in place of a parent

inmate ('inmāt) *n.* occupant, *esp.* of prison, hospital *etc.*

inmost ('inmōst) *a. sup. of* IN most inward, deepest

inn (in) *n.* 1. tavern 2. country hotel —'**innkeeper** *n.* —**Inns of Court** 1. four societies admitting to English Bar 2. their buildings

innards ('inərdz) *pl.n. inf.* internal organs or working parts (*orig.* '**inwards**)

innate (i'nāt, 'ināt) *a.* 1. inborn 2. inherent

inner ('inər) *a.* 1. lying within —*n.* 2. ring next to bull's-eye on target —'**innermost** *a.* —**inner city** sections of a large city in or near its center —**inner man** 1. mind; soul 2. *jocular* stomach; appetite (**inner woman** *fem.*) —**inner tube** rubber air tube of pneumatic tire

inning ('ining) *n.* 1. division of baseball game in which a team is at bat until it has three outs —*pl.* 2. similar division of cricket game

innocent ('inəsənt) *a.* 1. pure 2. guiltless 3. harmless —*n.* 4. innocent person, *esp.* young child —'**innocence** *n.* —'**innocently** *adv.*

innocuous (i'nokyŏŏəs) *a.* harmless

innominate bone (i'nominit) *see* **hipbone** *at* HIP[1]

innovate ('inəvāt) *vt.* introduce (changes, new things) —inno'**vation** *n.* —'**innovator** *n.*

innuendo (inyŏŏ'endō) *n.* 1. allusive remark, hint 2. indirect accusation (*pl.* **-es**)

innumerable (i'nyŏŏmərəbəl, i'nyŏŏmrəbəl; -'nŏŏ-) *or* **innumerous** *a.* countless; very numerous

inoculate (i'nokyŏŏlāt) *vt.* immunize by injecting vaccine —inocu'**lation** *n.*

inoperable (in'opərəbəl, -'oprə-) *a.* 1. unworkable 2. *Med.* that cannot be operated on —in'**operative** *a.* 1. not operative 2. ineffective

inopportune (inopər'tyŏŏn, -'tŏŏn) *a.* badly timed

inordinate (in'ördinit) *a.* excessive

inorganic (inör'ganik) *a.* 1. not having structure or characteristics of living organisms 2. of substances without carbon the study of which is a branch of chemistry

inpatient ('inpāshənt) *n.* patient that stays in hospital

in perpetuum (in pər'petyŏŏəm) *Lat.* for ever

input ('inpŏŏt) *n.* 1. act of putting in 2. that which is put in, as resource needed for industrial production *etc.* 3. data *etc.* fed into a computer

inquest ('inkwest) *n.* 1. legal or judicial inquiry presided over by a coroner 2. detailed inquiry or discussion

inquietude (in'kwītyŏŏd, -tŏŏd) *n.* restlessness, uneasiness, anxiety —in'**quiet** *a.*

inquire (in'kwīər) *vi.* seek information —in'**quirer** *n.* —in'**quiry** *n.* 1. question 2. investigation

inquisition (inkwi'zishən) *n.* 1. searching investigation, official inquiry 2. (I-) *Hist.* tribunal for suppression of heresy —in'**quisitor** *n.* —inquisi'**torial** *a.*

inquisitive (in'kwizitiv) *a.* 1. curious 2. prying

in re (in 'rā, 'rē) in the matter of: used *esp.* in bankruptcy proceedings

inroad ('inrōd) *n.* incursion

inrush ('inrush) *n.* sudden, usu. overwhelming, inward flow or rush; influx

ins. 1. inches 2. insurance

insane (in'sān) *a.* 1. mentally deranged; crazy 2. senseless —in'**sanely** *adv.* 1. like a lunatic, madly 2. excessively —**insanity** (in'saniti)

insatiable (in'sāshəbəl) *or* **insatiate** (in'sāshiit) *a.* incapable of being satisfied

inscribe (in'skrīb) vt. 1. write, engrave (in or on something) 2. mark 3. dedicate 4. trace (figure) within another —**inscription** (in-'skripshən) n. 1. inscribing 2. words inscribed on monument etc.

inscrutable (in'skrōōtəbəl) a. 1. mysterious, impenetrable 2. affording no explanation —**inscruta'bility** n. —**in'scrutably** adv.

insect ('insekt) n. any of a class of small arthropods with three pairs of legs, head, thorax and abdomen and two or four wings —**in'secticide** n. substance for killing insects —**insec'tivorous** a. insect-eating

insecure (insi'kyōōər) a. 1. not safe or firm 2. anxious, not confident

inseminate (in'semināt) vt. implant semen into —**artificial insemination** impregnation of the female by artificial means

insensate (in'sensāt, -sit) a. 1. without sensation, unconscious 2. unfeeling

insensible (in'sensəbəl) a. 1. unconscious 2. without feeling 3. not aware 4. not perceptible —**insensi'bility** n. —**in'sensibly** adv. imperceptibly

insert (in'sərt) vt. 1. introduce 2. place or put in, into or between —n. ('insərt) 3. something inserted —**in'sertion** n.

in-service a. denoting training that is given to employees during the course of employment

inset ('inset) n. 1. something extra inserted, esp. as decoration —vt. ('inset, in'set) 2. set or place in or within; insert

inshore ('in'shôr) adv./a. near shore

inside ('in'sīd) n. 1. inner side, surface or part —a. ('insīd) 2. of, in, or on inside —adv. (in'sīd) 3. in or into the inside 4. sl. in prison —prep. (in'sīd) 5. within, on inner side of

insidious (in'sidiəs) a. 1. stealthy, treacherous 2. unseen but deadly —**in'sidiously** adv.

insight ('insīt) n. mental penetration, discernment

insignia (in'signiə) pl.n. badges, emblems of honor or office (sing. **in'signia**)

insinuate (in'sinyōōāt) vt. 1. hint 2. work (oneself) into favor 3. introduce gradually or subtly —**insinu'ation** n.

insipid (in'sipid) a. 1. dull, spiritless 2. tasteless —**insi'pidity** n.

insist (in'sist) vi. (oft. with on or upon) 1. demand persistently 2. maintain 3. emphasize —**in'sistence** n. —**in'sistent** a.

in situ (in 'sitōō) Lat. in its original position

insofar (insō'fär) adv. (usu. with as) to the degree or extent (that)

insole ('insōl) n. 1. inner sole of shoe or boot 2. loose additional inner sole to give extra warmth or make shoe fit

insolent ('insələnt) a. arrogantly impudent —'insolence n. —'insolently adv.

insomnia (in'somniə) n. sleeplessness —**in'somniac** a./n.

insomuch (insə'much) adv. to such an extent

insouciant (in'sōōsiənt) a. indifferent, careless, unconcerned —**in'souciance** n.

inspect (in'spekt) vt. examine closely or officially —**in'spection** n. —**in'spector** n. —**in'spectorate** n. body of inspectors

inspire (in'spīər) vt. 1. animate, invigorate 2. arouse, create feeling, thought in 3. give rise to —vi. 4. breathe in, inhale —**inspiration** (inspi'rāshən) n. 1. good idea 2. creative influence or stimulus

inspirit (in'spirit) vt. animate, put spirit into, encourage

inst. (instant) of the current month

install or **instal** (in'stôl) vt. 1. have (apparatus) put in 2. establish 3. place

(person in office etc.) with ceremony —**installation** (instə'lāshən) n. 1. act of installing 2. that which is installed

installment (in'stôlmənt) n. 1. payment of part of debt 2. any of parts of a whole delivered in succession —**installment plan** arrangement for paying in installments

instance ('instəns) n. 1. example, particular case 2. request 3. stage in proceedings —vt. 4. cite —**for instance** for or as an example

instant ('instənt) n. 1. moment, point of time —a. 2. immediate 3. urgent 4. (of foods) requiring little preparation —**instan'taneous** a. happening in an instant —**instan'taneously** adv. —**in'stanter** adv. at once —'instantly adv. at once

instead (in'sted) adv. 1. in place 2. as a substitute

instep ('instep) n. arched part of foot between toes and ankle

instigate ('instigāt) vt. 1. incite, urge 2. bring about —**insti'gation** n. —**in'stigator** n.

instill (in'stil) vt. implant; inculcate —**instil'lation** n. —**in'stillment** n.

instinct (in'stingkt) n. 1. inborn impulse or propensity 2. unconscious skill 3. intuition —**in'stinctive** a. —**in'stinctively** adv.

institute ('instityōōt, -tōōt) vt. 1. establish, found 2. appoint 3. set going —n. 4. society for promoting some public object, esp. scientific 5. its building —'instituter or 'institutor n. —**insti'tution** n. 1. an instituting 2. establishment for care or education, hospital, college etc. 3. an established custom or law or (inf.) person —**insti'tutional** a. 1. of institutions 2. routine —**insti'tutionalize** vt. 1. subject to (adverse) effects of confinement in institution 2. place in an institution —v. 3. make or become an institution

instruct (in'strukt) vt. 1. teach 2. inform 3. order —**in'struction** n. 1. teaching 2. order —pl. 3. directions —**in'structive** a. 1. informative 2. useful —**in'structively** adv. —**in'structor** n. (**in'structress** fem.)

instrument ('instrəmənt) n. 1. tool, implement, means, person, thing used to make, do, measure etc. 2. mechanism for producing musical sound 3. legal document —**instru'mental** a. 1. acting as instrument or means 2. helpful 3. belonging to, produced by musical instruments —**instru'mentalist** n. player of musical instrument —**instrumen'tality** n. agency, means —**instru'mentally** adv. —**instrumen'tation** n. arrangement of music for instruments

insubordinate (insə'bôrdinit) a. 1. not submissive 2. mutinous, rebellious —**insubordi'nation** n.

insufferable (in'sufərəbəl) a. intolerable; unendurable —**in'sufferably** adv.

insular ('insyələr, 'insələr) a. 1. of an island 2. remote, detached 3. narrow-minded; prejudiced —**insu'larity** n.

insulate ('insəlāt) vt. 1. prevent or reduce transfer of electricity, heat, sound etc. to or from (body or device) by surrounding with nonconducting material 2. isolate, detach —**insu'lation** n. —'**insulator** n.

insulin ('insəlin) n. pancreatic hormone essential for using sugar —**insulin shock** state of collapse resulting from administration of too much insulin thus causing decrease in blood sugar

insult (in'sult) vt. 1. behave rudely to 2. offend —n. ('insult) 3. offensive remark 4. affront —**in'sulting** a. —**in'sultingly** adv.

insuperable (in'sōōpərəbəl, -prəbəl) a. 1. that cannot be got over or surmounted 2. unconquerable —**in'superably** adv.

insupportable (insə'pôrtəbəl) a. 1. incapable of being endured; intolerable; insufferable 2. incapable of being supported or justified; indefensible

insure (in'shōōər) vi. 1. contract for payment in event of loss, death etc. by payment of premiums —vt. 2. obtain insurance for 3. (with against) make safe (against) —**in'surable** a. —**in'surance** n. —**in'surer** n. —**insurance policy** contract of insurance

insurgent (in'sərjənt) a. 1. in revolt —n. 2. rebel —**in'surgence** or **insur'rection** n. revolt

int. 1. interest 2. interior 3. internal 4. international

intact (in'takt) a. 1. untouched 2. uninjured

intaglio (in'talyō) n. 1. engraved design 2. gem so cut (pl. -**s**, -**gli** (-lyē))

intake ('intāk) n. 1. what is taken in 2. quantity taken in 3. opening for taking in 4. in motor vehicle, air passage into carburetor

integer ('intijər) n. 1. whole number 2. whole of anything

integral ('intigrəl) a. constituting an essential part of a whole —**'integrate** v. 1. combine into one whole 2. unify diverse elements (of community etc.) —**inte'gration** n. —**integral calculus** branch of mathematics concerned with finding the limit of a sum of terms —**integrated circuit** tiny electronic circuit, usu. on silicon chip

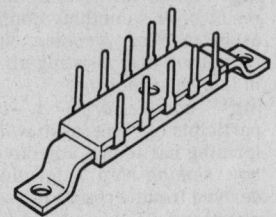

integrated circuit

integrity (in'tegriti) n. 1. honesty 2. original perfect state

integument (in'tegyəmənt) n. natural covering, skin, rind, husk

intellect ('intilekt) n. power of thinking and reasoning —**intel'lectual** a. 1. of, appealing to intellect 2. having good intellect —n. 3. one endowed with intellect and attracted to intellectual things —**intellectu'ality** n.

intelligent (in'telijənt) a. 1. having, showing good intellect 2. quick at understanding 3. informed —**in'telligence** n. 1. quickness of understanding 2. mental power or ability 3. intellect 4. information, news, esp. military information —**in'telligently** adv. —**intelli'gentsia** n. intellectual or cultured classes —**intelligi'bility** n. —**in'telligible** a. understandable —**in'telligibly** adv. —**intelligence quotient** range of numbers used to define relative mental ability as measured by standard tests of intelligence

intemperate (in'tempərit, -prit) a. 1. drinking alcohol to excess 2. immoderate 3. unrestrained —**in'temperance** n.

intend (in'tend) v. propose, mean (to do, say etc.) —**in'tended** a. 1. planned, future —n. 2. inf. proposed spouse

intense (in'tens) a. 1. very strong or acute 2. emotional —**intensifi'cation** n. —**in'tensify** v. 1. make or become stronger 2. increase (**in'tensified, in'tensifying**) —**in'tensity** n. 1. intense quality 2. strength —**in'tensive** a. characterized by intensity or emphasis on specified factor —**in'tensively** adv.

intent (in'tent) n. 1. purpose —a. 2. concentrating 3. resolved, bent 4. preoccupied, absorbed —**in'tention** *n*. purpose, aim —**in'tentional** *a*. —**in'tently** *adv*. —**in'tentness** *n*.

inter (in'tər) *vt*. bury (**-rr-**) —**in'terment** *n*.

inter- (*comb. form*) between, among, mutually as in *interglacial, interrelation*. Such words are not given here where the meaning may easily be inferred from the simple word

intercol'legiate	interga'lactic
intercom'municate	intergovern'mental
inter'company	inter'knit
intercon'nect	inter'mesh
intercon'nection	inter'mingle
interdenomi'national	inter'mix
interdepart'mental	inter'racial
interde'pend	interuni'versity
interde'pendence	inter'war
inter'flow	inter'weave

interact (intər'akt) *vi*. act on each other —**inter'action** *n*.

inter alia ('intər 'ālia) *Lat*. among other things

interbreed (intər'brēd) *v*. breed within a related group

intercede (intər'sēd) *vi*. plead (in favor of), mediate —**intercession** (intər'seshən) *n*. —**intercessor** (intər'sesər) *n*.

intercept (intər'sept) *vt*. 1. cut off 2. seize, stop in transit —**inter'ception** *n*. —**inter'ceptor** *or* **inter'cepter** *n*. 1. one who, that which intercepts 2. fast fighter plane, missile *etc*.

interchange (intər'chānj) *v*. 1. (cause to) exchange places —*n*. ('intərchānj) 2. highway junction —**inter'changeable** *a*. able to be exchanged in position or use

intercom ('intərkom) *n*. internal telephonic system

intercommunion (intərkə'myōōnyən) *n*. association between Churches, involving *esp*. mutual reception of Holy Communion

intercontinental (intərkonti'nentəl) *a*. 1. connecting continents 2. (of missile) able to reach one continent from another

intercourse ('intərkörs) *n*. 1. mutual dealings; communication 2. copulation

interdict ('intərdikt) *n*. 1. decree of Pope restraining clergy from performing divine service 2. formal prohibition —*vt*. (intər'dikt) 3. prohibit, forbid 4. restrain —**inter'diction** *n*.

interdisciplinary (intər'disiplineri) *a*. involving two or more academic disciplines

interest ('intrist, -tərist) *n*. 1. concern, curiosity 2. thing exciting this 3. sum paid for use of borrowed money 4. (*oft. pl.*) benefit, advantage 5. (*oft. pl.*) right, share —*vt*. 6. excite curiosity or concern of 7. cause to become involved in something; concern —'**interested** *a*. 1. showing or having interest 2. personally involved or implicated —'**interesting** *a*. —'**interestingly** *adv*.

interface ('intərfās) *n*. area, surface, boundary linking two systems

interfere (intər'fēər) *vi*. 1. meddle, intervene 2. clash 3. (*with* with) *euphemistic* assault sexually —**inter'ference** *n*. 1. act of interfering 2. *Rad*. interruption of reception by atmospherics or by unwanted signals

interferon (intər'fēəron) *n*. a protein produced by the body that stops the development of an invading virus

interim ('intərim) *n*. 1. meantime —*a*. 2. temporary, intervening

interior (in'tēəriər) *a*. 1. inner 2. inland 3. indoors —*n*. 4. inside 5. inland region —**interior angle** angle of polygon contained between two adjacent sides —**interior design** colors, furniture *etc*. of interior of house *etc*.

interject (intər'jekt) *vt*. interpose (remark *etc*.) —**inter'jection** *n*. 1. exclamation 2. interjected remark

interlace (intər'lās) *vt*. unite, as by lacing together —**inter'lacement** *n*.

interlard (intər'lärd) *vt*. intersperse

interleave (intər'lēv) *vt*. insert, as blank leaves in book, between other leaves —'**interleaf** *n*. extra leaf

interlining ('intərlīning) *n*. material used between lining and outer fabric of *esp*. outdoor garment

interlock (intər'lok) *v*. 1. lock together firmly —*n*. ('intərlok) 2. fabric constructed by interlocking two ribbed fabrics

interlocutor (intər'lokyətər) *n*. one who takes part in conversation —**interlo'cution** *n*. dialogue —**inter'locutory** *a*.

interloper ('intərlōpər) *n*. one intruding in another's affairs

interlude ('intərlōōd) *n*. 1. interval (in play *etc*.) 2. something filling an interval

intermarry (intər'mari) *vi*. 1. (of families, races, religions) become linked by marriage 2. marry within one's family —**inter'marriage** *n*.

intermediate (intər'mēdiit) *a*. coming between; interposed —**inter'mediary** *n*./*a*.

intermezzo (intər'metsō) *n*. short performance between acts of play or opera (*pl*. **-s, -mezzi** (-'metsē))

interminable (in'tərminəbəl) *a*. endless

intermit (intər'mit) *v*. stop for a time (**-tt-**) —**inter'mission** *n*. 1. short period between events or activities; pause 2. act of intermitting; state of being intermitted —**inter'mittent** *a*. occurring at intervals

intern (in'tərn) *vt*. 1. confine to special area or camp —*n*. ('intərn) 2. internee 3. advanced student or recent graduate undergoing supervised practical training, *esp*. in medicine (*also* '**interne**) —**inter'nee** *n*. person who is interned, *esp*. enemy citizen in wartime or terrorism suspect —**in'ternment** *n*.

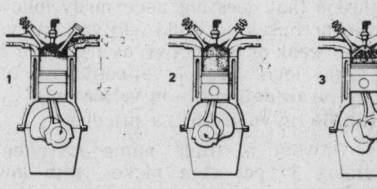

internal-combustion engine
(1. induction stroke; 2. compression stroke; 3. power stroke; 4. exhaust stroke)

internal (in'tərnəl) *a*. 1. inward 2. interior 3. of a nation's domestic as opposed to foreign affairs —**in'ternally** *adv*. —'**internist** *n*. physician specializing in internal medicine —**internal-combustion engine** heat engine in which combustion occurs within engine rather than in an external furnace —**internal medicine** branch of medicine concerned with treatment of diseases, *esp*. of adults, not requiring surgical intervention —**internal revenue** revenue of a government from any domestic source —**Internal Revenue Ser-**vice division of the U.S. Department of the Treasury that collects income and excise taxes and enforces revenue laws

international (intər'nashənəl) *a*. 1. of relations between nations —*n*. 2. game or match between teams of different countries —**inter'nationalism** *n*. ideal or practice of cooperation and understanding between nations —**inter'nationalist** *n*. —**inter'nationally** *adv*. —**international nautical mile** unit of distance in sea and air navigation equal to 6067.1033 feet or 1.852 kilometers (*also* **international air mile**) —**International Phonetic Alphabet** series of signs and letters for representation of human speech sounds —**international pitch** *Mus*. tuning standard of 440 vibrations per second for A above middle C

internecine (intər'nesēn, -'nēsīn) *a*. 1. mutually destructive 2. deadly

interplanetary (intər'planiteri) *a*. of, linking planets

interplay ('intərplā) *n*. 1. action and reaction of two things, sides *etc*. upon each other 2. interaction 3. reciprocation

Interpol ('intərpol) International Criminal Police Organization

interpolate (in'tərpəlāt) *vt*. 1. insert (new, *esp*. misleading matter) in (book *etc*.) 2. interject (remark) 3. *Math*. estimate (a value) between known values —**interpo'lation** *n*.

interpose (intər'pōz) *vt*. 1. insert 2. say as interruption 3. put in the way —*vi*. 4. intervene —**interpo'sition** *n*.

interpret (in'tərprit) *vt*. 1. explain 2. *Art* render, represent —*vi*. 3. translate, *esp*. orally —**interpre'tation** *n*. —**in'terpreter** *n*.

interregnum (intə'regnəm) *n*. 1. interval between reigns 2. gap in continuity (*pl*. **-na** (-nə), **-s**)

interrelate (intərri'lāt) *v*. place in or come into mutual or reciprocal relationship —**interre'lation** *n*.

interrogate (in'terəgāt) *vt*. question, *esp*. closely or officially —**interro'gation** *n*. —**inter'rogative** *a*. 1. questioning —*n*. 2. word used in asking question —**in'terrogator** *n*. —**inter'rogatory** *a*. 1. of inquiry —*n*. 2. question, set of questions —**interrogation point** *see* **question mark** *at* QUESTION

interrupt (intə'rupt) *v*. 1. break in (upon) —*vt*. 2. stop the course of 3. block —**inter'ruption** *n*.

interscholastic (intərskə'lastik) *a*. 1. (of sports events, competitions *etc*.) occurring between two or more schools 2. representative of various schools

intersect (intər'sekt) *vt*. 1. divide by passing across or through —*vi*. 2. meet and cross —**inter'section** *n*. point where lines, roads cross

interspace (intər'spās) *vt*. 1. make or occupy space between —*n*. ('intərspās) 2. space between or among things —**interspatial** (intər'spāshəl) *a*.

intersperse (intər'spərs) *vt*. sprinkle (something) with or (something) among or in —**inter'spersion** *n*.

interstate (intər'stāt) *a*. 1. between, involving two or more states —*n*. 2. interstate highway —**interstate highway system** road system that links all states of the U.S.

interstellar (intər'stelər) *a*. (of the space) between stars

interstice (in'tərstis) *n*. chink, gap, crevice —**inter'stitial** *a*.

intertrigo (intər'trīgō) *n*. inflammation caused by repeated friction between two opposing skin surfaces

intertwine (intər'twIn) v. twist together, entwine

interurban (intər'ərbən) a. between or connecting cities

interval ('intərvəl) n. 1. intervening time or space 2. pause, break 3. Mus. difference in pitch between two tones

intervene (intər'vēn) vi. 1. come into a situation in order to change it 2. (with on or between) be, come (between or among) 3. occur in meantime 4. interpose —**intervention** (intər'venchən) n.

interview ('intərvyōō) n. 1. meeting, esp. formally arranged and involving questioning of a person —vt. 2. have interview with —**interview'ee** n. —'**interviewer** n.

intestate (in'testāt, -tit) a. 1. not having made a will 2. (of property) not disposed of by will —**in'testacy** n.

intestine (in'testin) n. (usu. pl.) lower part of alimentary canal between stomach and anus —**in'testinal** a. —**intestinal obstruction** see **ileus** at ILEUM

intimate[1] ('intimit) a. 1. closely acquainted, familiar 2. private 3. extensive 4. having sexual relations —n. 5. intimate friend —'**intimacy** n.

intimate[2] ('intimāt) vt. 1. announce 2. imply —**inti'mation** n. notice

intimidate (in'timidāt) vt. 1. frighten into submission 2. deter by threats —**intimi'dation** n. —**in'timidator** n.

into ('intōō; unstressed 'intə) prep. 1. expresses motion to a point within 2. indicates change of state 3. indicates coming up against, encountering 4. indicates arithmetical division

intone (in'tōn) or **intonate** vt. 1. chant 2. recite in monotone —**into'nation** n. 1. modulation of voice 2. quality of a musical sound, esp. regarding pitch 3. intoning 4. accent

in toto (in 'tōtō) Lat. totally, entirely, completely

intoxicate (in'toksikāt) vt. 1. make drunk 2. excite to excess —**in'toxicant** a./n. (anything) causing intoxication —**intoxi'cation** n.

intr. intransitive

intra- (comb. form) within, as in intrastate

intractable (in'traktəbəl) a. 1. difficult to influence 2. hard to control

intramural (intrə'myōōrəl) a. operating within or involving those within boundaries, esp. of school or college

intransigent (in'transijənt) a. uncompromising, obstinate

intransitive (in'transitiv) a. denoting a verb that does not require direct object —**intransi'tivity** or **in'transitiveness** n.

intrauterine (intrə'yōōtərin) a. within the womb (see also IUD)

intravenous (intrə'vēnəs) a. into a vein

in-tray n. tray for incoming papers etc. requiring attention

intrench (in'trench) vt. see ENTRENCH

intrepid (in'trepid) a. fearless, undaunted —**intre'pidity** n.

intricate ('intrikit) a. involved, puzzlingly entangled —'**intricacy** n. —'**intricately** adv.

intrigue ('intrēg, in'trēg) n. 1. underhand plot 2. secret love affair —vi. (in'trēg) 3. carry on intrigue —vt. (in'trēg) 4. interest, puzzle

intrinsic (in'trinzik, -sik) a. inherent; essential —**in'trinsically** adv.

intro. or **introd.** 1. introduction 2. introductory

intro- (comb. form) into, within, as in introduce, introvert

introduce (intrə'dyōōs, -'dōōs) vt. 1. make acquainted 2. present 3. bring in 4. bring forward 5. bring into practice 6. insert —**intro'duction** n. 1. an introducing 2. presentation of one person to another 3. preliminary section or treatment 4. Mus. opening passage in movement or composition, that precedes main material —**intro'ductory** a. preliminary

introit ('introit, -troit) n. Eccles. anthem sung as priest approaches altar

introspection (intrə'spekshən) n. examination of one's own thoughts —**intro'spective** a.

introvert ('introvərt) n. Psychoanal. one who looks inward rather than at the external world —**intro'versible** a. —**intro'version** n. —**intro'versive** a. —'**introverted** a.

intrude (in'trōōd) v. thrust (oneself) in uninvited —**in'truder** n. —**in'trusion** n. —**in'trusive** a.

intrust (in'trust) vt. see ENTRUST

intuition (intyōō'ishən, intōō-) n. 1. immediate mental apprehension without reasoning 2. immediate insight —**in'tuit** vt. —**in'tuitive** a.

intussusception (intəsə'sepshən) n. condition in which one segment of intestine is telescoped into another

Inuit ('inyōōit) n. Eskimo of N Amer. or Greenland

inundate ('inundāt) vt. 1. flood 2. overwhelm —**inun'dation** n.

inure or **enure** (i'nyōōər, i'nōōər) vt. accustom, esp. to hardship, danger etc.

in vacuo (in 'vakyōō) Lat. in vacuum

invade (in'vād) v. 1. enter (a country etc.) by force with hostile intent —vt. 2. overrun 3. pervade —**in'vader** n. —**in'vasion** n. 1. act of invading with armed forces 2. any encroachment or intrusion 3. onset of something harmful, esp. disease

invalid[1] ('invəlid) n. 1. one suffering from chronic ill health —a. 2. ill, suffering from sickness or injury —vt. 3. cause to become an invalid

invalid[2] (in'valid) a. 1. not valid; having no cogency or legal force 2. Logic having conclusion that does not necessarily follow from its premises; not valid —**in'validate** vt. 1. render weak or ineffective, as argument 2. take away legal force or effectiveness of; annul —**invali'dation** n. —**in'validator** n.

invaluable (in'valyōōəbəl) a. priceless

Invar (in'vär) n. trade name for steel containing 30 per cent nickel, with low coefficient of expansion

invasion (in'vāzhən) n. see INVADE

inveigh (in'vā) vi. speak violently —**invective** (in'vektiv) n. abusive speech or writing, vituperation

inveigle (in'vāgəl, -'vē-) vt. entice, seduce, wheedle —**in'veiglement** n.

invent (in'vent) vt. 1. devise, originate 2. fabricate (falsehoods etc.) —**in'vention** n. 1. that which is invented 2. ability to invent 3. contrivance 4. deceit; lie —**in'ventive** a. resourceful; creative —**in'ventively** adv. —**in'ventor** n.

inventory ('invəntōri) n. 1. detailed list of goods etc. —vt. 2. make list of

invert (in'vərt) vt. 1. turn upside down 2. reverse position, relations of —**inverse** (in'vərs, 'invərs) a. 1. inverted 2. opposite —**in'versely** adv. —**in'version** n.

invertebrate (in'vərtibrit, -brāt) n. animal without a backbone —**invertebrate biology** study of such animals

invest (in'vest) vt. 1. lay out (money, time, effort etc.) for profit or advantage 2. install 3. endow 4. obs. clothe 5. Poet. cover, as with garment —**in'vestiture** n. formal installation of person in office or rank —**in'vestment** n. 1. investing 2. money invested 3. stocks and bonds bought —**in'vestor** n. —**investment company** company that invests its funds in other companies and issues its own securities against these investments

investigate (in'vestigāt) vt. inquire into; examine —**investi'gation** n. —**in'vestigator** n.

inveterate (in'vetərit) a. 1. deep-rooted; long-established 2. confirmed —**in'veteracy** n.

invidious (in'vidiəs) a. likely to cause ill will or envy —**in'vidiously** adv.

invigilate (in'vijilāt) vi. supervise examination candidates —**in'vigilator** n.

invigorate (in'vigərāt) vt. give vigor to, strengthen

invincible (in'vinsəbəl) a. unconquerable —**invinci'bility** n.

inviolable (in'vīələbəl) a. 1. not to be profaned; sacred 2. unalterable —**in'violate** a. 1. unhurt 2. unprofaned 3. unbroken

invisible (in'vizəbəl) a. 1. not visible; not able to be perceived by eye 2. concealed from sight; hidden 3. not easily seen or noticed 4. kept hidden from public view; secret; clandestine 5. Econ. of services, such as insurance and freight, rather than goods —n. 6. Econ. invisible item of trade; service —**invisi'bility** or **in'visibleness** n. —**in'visibly** adv.

invite (in'vīt) vt. 1. request the company of 2. ask courteously 3. ask for 4. attract, call forth —n. ('invīt) 5. inf. invitation —**invitation** (invi'tāshən) n. —**in'viting** a. tempting; alluring; attractive

invoice ('invois) n. 1. a list of goods or services sold, with prices —vt. 2. present with an invoice 3. make an invoice of

invoke (in'vōk) vt. 1. call on 2. appeal to 3. ask earnestly for 4. summon —**invo'cation** n.

involuntary (in'volənteri) a. 1. not done voluntarily 2. unintentional 3. instinctive

involute ('involōōt) a. 1. complex 2. coiled spirally 3. rolled inward (also **invo'luted**) —n. 4. Math. curve with inward spiral —**invo'lution** n.

involve (in'volv) vt. 1. include 2. entail 3. implicate (person) 4. concern 5. entangle —**in'volved** a. 1. complicated 2. concerned —**in'volvement** n.

inward ('inwərd) a. 1. internal 2. situated within 3. spiritual, mental —adv. 4. toward the inside 5. into the mind (also '**inwards**) —pl.n. 6. see INNARDS —'**inwardly** adv. 1. in the mind 2. internally

iodine ('īədīn, 'īədin, 'īədēn) n. Chem. nonmetallic element Symbol I, at. wt. 126.9, at. no. 53 —**iodide** ('īədīd) n. 1. salt of hydriodic acid, containing the iodide ion 2. compound containing an iodine atom —'**iodize** vt. treat with iodine or iodide —**iodoform** (ī'ōdəfōrm, ī'od-) n. antiseptic

I.O.M. Isle of Man

ion ('īən, -on) n. charged particle formed from an atom or group of atoms through the gain or loss of one or more electrons —**i'onic** a. —**ioni'zation** n. the loss of one or more outer electrons of an atom causing it to become electrically positively charged, or the gain of one or more extra electrons, causing the atom to become negatively charged —'**ionize** v. change or become changed into ions —**i'onosphere** n. region of atmosphere 60 to 100 km above earth's surface

-ion (*comb. form*) action, process, state, as in *creation, objection*

Ionic (I'onik) *a. Archit.* distinguished by scroll-like decoration on columns

iota (I'ōtə) *n.* **1.** ninth letter in Gr. alphabet (I, ι) **2.** (*usu. with* not one *or* an) very small amount

IOU *n.* signed paper acknowledging debt

-ious (*comb. form*) characterized by; full of, as in *ambitious, suspicious*

I.O.W. Isle of Wight

Iowa ('Iōə) *n.* West North Central state of the U.S., admitted to the Union in 1846. Abbrev.: **IA** (with ZIP code)

IPA International Phonetic Alphabet

ipecac ('ipikak) *or* **ipecacuanha** (ĕpikakyōō'anyə) *n.* S Amer. plant yielding an emetic

ipso facto ('ipsō 'faktō) *Lat.* by that very fact

I.Q. intelligence quotient

Ir *Chem.* iridium

Ir. **1.** Ireland **2.** Irish

IR **1.** information retrieval **2.** internal revenue

ir- (*comb. form*) see IN-[1], IN-[2]

I.R.A. Irish Republican Army

Iran (i'rän, -'ran, I'ran) *n.* country in western Asia bounded north by the U.S.S.R. and the Caspian Sea, east by Afghanistan and Pakistan, south by the Gulf of Oman and the Persian Gulf, and west by Iraq and Turkey —**Iranian** (i'rāniən) *a./n.* **1.** (native or inhabitant) of Iran —*n.* **2.** branch of Indo-European languages to which Persian, the official language of Iran, belongs

Iraq (i'räk, -rak) *n.* country in Middle East bounded north by Turkey, east by Iran, southeast by the Persian Gulf, south by Kuwait and Saudi Arabia and west by Jordan and Syria —**I'raqi** *n.* **1.** native or inhabitant of Iraq (*pl.* **-s**) —*a.* **2.** of Iraq

irascible (i'rasibəl) *a.* hot-tempered —**irasci'bility** *n.* —**i'rascibly** *adv.*

IRBM intermediate-range ballistic missile

ire ('Iər) *n.* anger, wrath —**i'rate** *a.* angry

Republic of Ireland

Ireland ('Iərlənd) *n.* **1. Republic of Ireland.** country lying in the N Atlantic in the smaller of the British Isles, separated from Great Britain by the Irish Sea to the east and bounded northeast by Northern Ireland **2.** island made up of Republic of Ireland and Northern Ireland —**Irish** *a.* **1.** of Ireland, its people or their language —*n.* **2.** Irish Gaelic —**Irish coffee** coffee mixed with whiskey and topped with cream —**Irish Gaelic** Goidelic language of the Celts of Ireland; official language of Republic of Ireland since 1921 —**Irish linen** very fine lightweight fabric woven from Irish flax (*also* **handker-**

chief linen) —**Irish moss** carrageen —**Irish stew** stew made of mutton, potatoes, onions *etc.* —**Irish tweed** tweed with white warp and colored weft threads

iridaceous (iri'dāshəs, I-) *a.* belonging to iris family

iridescent (iri'desənt) *a.* exhibiting changing colors like those of the rainbow —**iri'descence** *n.*

iridium (i'ridiəm) *n. Chem.* noble metallic element *Symbol* Ir, at. wt. 192.2, at. no. 77

iris

iris ('Iris) *n.* **1.** circular membrane of eye containing pupil **2.** (*also* **flag**) plant with sword-shaped leaves and showy flowers (*pl.* **-es, irides** ('Iridēz, 'iri-))

irk (ərk) *vt.* irritate, vex —**'irksome** *a.* tiresome

iron ('Iərn) *n.* **1.** *Chem.* metallic element *Symbol* Fe, at. wt. 55.9, at. no. 26 **2.** tool *etc.* of this metal **3.** appliance used, when heated, to smooth cloth **4.** metal-headed golf club **5.** splintlike support for malformed leg **6.** great hardness, strength or resolve —*pl.* **7.** fetters —*a.* **8.** of, like iron **9.** inflexible, unyielding **10.** robust —*v.* **11.** smooth, cover, fetter *etc.* with iron or an iron —**'irony** *a.* of, resembling, or containing iron —**Iron Age** era of iron implements beginning in central Europe from about the 7th cent. B.C. until the Christian era —**iron'clad** *a.* protected with or as with iron —**Iron Curtain 1.** guarded border between countries of Soviet bloc and the rest of Europe **2.** (**i- c-**) any barrier that separates communities or ideologies —**iron hand** harsh or rigorous control —**ironing board** board, usu. on legs, with suitable covering on which to iron clothes —**iron lung** apparatus for administering artificial respiration for a prolonged period —**iron maiden** medieval instrument of torture, consisting of enclosed space lined with iron spikes —**iron pyrites 1.** fool's gold **2.** marcasite —**iron rations** emergency food supplies —**'ironstone** *n.* **1.** any rock consisting mainly of iron-bearing ore **2.** tough durable earthenware —**'ironwood** *n.* **1.** the hop hornbeam, deciduous tree of the birch family of eastern N Amer. **2.** tough wood of this tree —**'ironwork** *n.* work done in iron, *esp.* decorative work —**'ironworks** *pl.n.* (*sometimes with sing. v.*) building in which iron is smelted, cast or wrought —**irons in the fire** projects, undertakings —**strike while the iron is hot** act when opportunity knocks

irony ('Irəni) *n.* **1.** (*usu.* humorous or mildly sarcastic) use of words to mean the opposite of what is said **2.** event, situation opposite of that expected —**i'ronic(al)** *a.* of, using irony

Iroquoian (irə'kwoiən) *n.* Amerindian language family spoken in upper New York state, Oklahoma and North Carolina

Iroquois ('irəkwoi, -kwä) *n.* **1.** Amerindian

confederacy of New York comprising Cayuga, Mohawk, Oneida, Onondaga, Seneca and later Tuscaroro tribes **2.** any member of these peoples (*pl.* **-ois**)

irradiate (i'rādiāt) *vt.* **1.** treat by irradiation **2.** shine upon, throw light upon, light up —**irradi'ation** *n.* impregnation by x-rays, light rays

irrational (i'rashənəl) *a.* **1.** inconsistent with reason or logic **2.** incapable of reasoning **3.** *Math.* of real number which cannot be expressed as a ratio of two integers —**irration'ality** *n.*

irreconcilable (irekən'sIləbəl, i'rekənsI-) *a.* **1.** not able to be reconciled; incompatible —*n.* **2.** person or thing that is implacably hostile **3.** (*usu. pl.*) one of various principles *etc.* that are incapable of being brought into agreement —**irreconcila'bility** *n.* —**irrecon'cilably** *adv.*

irrecoverable (iri'kuvərəbəl, -'kuvrə-) *a.* **1.** not able to be recovered or regained **2.** not able to be remedied or rectified

irredeemable (iri'dēməbəl) *a.* **1.** (of bonds *etc.*) without date of redemption of capital; incapable of being bought back directly or paid off **2.** (of paper money) not convertible into specie **3.** (of loss) not able to be recovered; irretrievable **4.** not able to be improved or rectified; irreparable —**irre'deemably** *adv.*

irredentist (iri'dentist) *n.* **1.** (*sometimes* I-) person, *esp.* member of 19th-century It. association, who favored acquisition of territory that had once been part of his country —*a.* **2.** of irredentism —**irre'dentism** *n.*

irreducible (iri'dyōōsibəl, -'dōōs-) *a.* **1.** not able to be reduced or lessened **2.** not able to be brought to simpler or reduced form **3.** *Math.* (of polynomial) unable to be factorized into polynomials of lower degree —**irreduci'bility** *n.*

irrefrangible (iri'franjəbəl) *a.* **1.** inviolable **2.** in optics, not susceptible to refraction

irrefutable (iri'fyōōtəbəl, i'refyətəbəl) *a.* that cannot be refuted, disproved

irreg. irregular(ly)

irregular (i'regyələr) *a.* **1.** lacking uniformity or symmetry; uneven in shape, arrangement *etc.* **2.** not occurring at expected or equal intervals **3.** differing from normal or accepted practice or routine **4.** (of formation, inflections or derivations of word) not following usual pattern of formation in language **5.** (of troops) not belonging to regular forces —*n.* **6.** soldier not in regular army —**irregu'larity** *n.*

irrelevant (i'reləvənt) *a.* not relating or pertinent to matter at hand; not important —**ir'relevance** *or* **ir'relevancy** *n.*

irremissible (iri'misəbəl) *a.* **1.** unpardonable; inexcusable **2.** that must be done, as through duty or obligation —**irremissi'bility** *n.*

irreparable (i'repərəbəl, i'reprəbəl) *a.* not able to be repaired or remedied

irreplaceable (iri'plāsəbəl) *a.* not able to be replaced

irrepressible (iri'presəbəl) *a.* not capable of being repressed, controlled or restrained —**irrepressi'bility** *n.* —**irre'pressibly** *adv.*

irreproachable (iri'prōchəbəl) *a.* not deserving reproach; blameless

irresistible (iri'zistəbəl) *a.* **1.** not able to be resisted or refused; overpowering **2.** very fascinating or alluring —**irre'sistibly** *adv.*

irresolute (i'rezəlōōt) *a.* lacking resolution; wavering; hesitating —**ir'resolutely** *adv.* —**ir'resoluteness** *or* **irreso'lution** *n.*

irrespective (iri'spektiv) a. —**irrespective of** without taking account of

irresponsible (iri'sponsəbəl) a. 1. not showing or done with due care for consequences of one's actions or attitudes; reckless 2. not capable of bearing responsibility —**irresponsi'bility** or **irre'sponsibleness** n. —**irre'sponsibly** adv.

irretrievable (iri'trēvəbəl) a. not able to be retrieved, recovered or repaired —**irretriev-a'bility** n. —**irre'trievably** adv.

irreverence (i'revərəns) n. 1. lack of due respect or veneration 2. disrespectful remark or act —**ir'reverent** a.

irreversible (iri'vərsəbəl) a. 1. not able to be reversed 2. not able to be revoked or repealed 3. Chem., phys. capable of changing or producing change in one direction only —**irreversi'bility** n. —**irre'versibly** adv.

irrevocable (i'revəkəbəl) a. not able to be changed, undone, altered

irrigate ('irigāt) vt. water by artificial channels, pipes etc. —**irri'gation** n. —'**irrigator** n.

irritate ('iritāt) vt. 1. annoy 2. inflame 3. stimulate —'**irritable** a. easily annoyed —'**irritably** adv. —'**irritant** a./n. (person or thing) causing irritation —**irri'tation** n.

irrupt (i'rupt) vi. 1. enter forcibly 2. increase suddenly —**ir'ruption** n.

IRS Internal Revenue Service

is (iz) third person singular, present indicative of BE

is. 1. island 2. isle

Isa. Bible Isaiah

Isaiah (I'zāə) n. Bible 23rd book of the O.T., first of the prophetic books, written by Isaiah; oft. called the Old Testament Gospel as it is about the judgment of God and the deliverance of man

Isaias (I'zāəs) n. Bible Isaiah in the Douay Version of the O.T.

I.S.B.N. or **ISBN** International Standard Book Number

ischium ('iskiəm) n. curved bone forming base of each half of pelvis

-ish (comb. form) 1. of a nationality, as in Scottish 2. oft. derogatory having manner or qualities of; resembling, as in slavish, boyish 3. somewhat; approximately, as in yellowish, sevenish 4. concerned or preoccupied with, as in bookish

isinglass ('Izin-glas, 'Izingglas) n. kind of gelatin obtained from some freshwater fishes

Islam (is'läm) n. Muslim faith or world —**Is'lamic** a. —**Islamic art** Muslim art, typically nonfigurative, highly ornamental, using texts from the Koran for decoration

island ('Ilənd) n. 1. piece of land surrounded by water 2. anything like this, as raised piece for pedestrians in middle of road —'**islander** n. inhabitant of island

isle (Il) n. island —'**islet** n. little island

ism ('izəm) n. inf., oft. derogatory unspecified doctrine, system or practice

-ism (comb. form) 1. action, process, result, as in criticism 2. state; condition, as in paganism 3. doctrine, system, body of principles and practices, as in Leninism, spiritualism 4. behavior; characteristic quality, as in heroism 5. characteristic usage, esp. of language, as in Scotticism

isobar ('Isəbär) n. line on map connecting places of equal mean barometric pressure —**iso'baric** a.

isochronal (I'sokrənəl) or **isochronous** a. 1. having same duration; equal in time 2. occurring at equal time intervals; having uniform period of vibration —**i'sochronism** n.

isolate ('Isəlāt) vt. place apart or alone —**iso'lation** n. —**iso'lationism** n. policy of not participating in international affairs —**iso'lationist** n./a.

isomer ('Isəmər) n. substance with same molecules as another but different atomic arrangement —**iso'meric** a. —**i'somerism** n.

isometric (Isə'metrik) a. 1. having equal dimensions 2. relating to muscular contraction without external movement —**iso'metrics** pl.n. (with sing. v.) system of isometric exercises

isomorphism (Isə'mörfizəm) n. 1. Biol. similarity of form 2. Chem. existence of two or more substances of different composition in similar crystalline form 3. Math. one-to-one correspondence between elements of two or more sets —**iso'morphic** or **iso'morphous** a.

isoniazid (Isō'nIəzid) n. drug for oral treatment of tuberculosis

isosceles (I'sosilēz) a. (of triangle) having two sides equal

isotherm ('Isəthərm) n. line on map connecting points of equal mean temperature

isotope ('Isətōp) n. atom of element having a different nuclear mass and atomic weight from other atoms in same element —**isotopic** (Isə'topik, -'tōpik) a.

isotropic (Isə'trōpik, -'tropik) or **isotropous** (I'sotrəpəs) a. 1. having uniform physical properties in all directions 2. Biol. not having predetermined axes —**i'sotropy** n.

Israel ('izriəl) n. 1. country in Middle East bounded west by Egypt and the Mediterranean, north by Lebanon, east by Syria and Jordan 2. ancient kingdom of Jews in this region —**Israeli** (iz'rāli) n./a. —'**Israelite** n. Bible member of ethnic group claiming descent from Jacob; Hebrew —**Children of Israel** the Jewish people or nation

issue ('ishyoo) n. 1. sending or giving out officially or publicly 2. number or amount so given out 3. discharge 4. offspring, children 5. topic of discussion 6. question, dispute 7. outcome, result —vi. 8. go out 9. result (in) 10. arise (from) —vt. 11. emit, give out, send out 12. distribute 13. publish —**take issue** disagree

-ist (comb. form) 1. person who performs certain action or is concerned with something specified, as in soloist 2. person who practices in specific field, as in physicist 3. person who advocates particular doctrine, system etc.; of doctrine advocated, as in socialist 4. person characterized by specified trait, tendency etc.; of such a trait, as in purist —**-istic** (a. comb. form)

isthmus ('isməs) n. neck of land between two seas

it (it) pron. neuter pronoun of the third person —**its** a. belonging to it —**it'self** pron. emphatic form of IT

It. 1. Italian 2. Italy

i.t.a. or **I.T.A.** initial teaching alphabet

ital. Print. italic

italic (i'talik) a. (of type) sloping —**i'talicize** vt. put in italics —**i'talics** pl.n. italic type, now used for emphasis etc.

Italy ('itəli) n. country in southern Europe occupying a long peninsula extending into the Mediterranean, bounded east by Yugoslavia, north by Austria and Switzerland and west by France —**Italian** (i'talyən) n./a. 1. (native or inhabitant) of Italy —n. 2. language of Italy, which is a Romance language —**I'talianate** or **Italia'nesque** a. Italian in style or character

itch (ich) n. 1. irritation in the skin 2. restless desire —vi. 3. feel or produce irritating or tickling sensation 4. have a restless desire (to do something) —'**itchy** a.

-ite (comb. form) 1. native or inhabitant of, as in Israelite 2. follower or advocate of; supporter of group, as in Luddite, laborite 3. Biol. division of body or organ, as in neurite 4. mineral; rock, as in nephrite, peridotite 5. commercial product, as in vulcanite

item ('Itəm) n. 1. single thing in list, collection etc. 2. piece of information 3. entry in account etc. —adv. ('Item, 'Itəm) 4. also —'**itemize** vt.

iterate ('itərāt) vt. repeat —**iter'ation** n. —**iterative** ('itərātiv, 'itərətiv) a.

itinerant (I'tinərənt, i-) a. 1. traveling from place to place 2. working for a short time in various places 3. traveling on circuit —**i'tineracy** n. —**i'tinerary** n. 1. record, line of travel 2. route 3. guidebook

-itis (comb. form) inflammation of specified part, as in tonsillitis

-ity (comb. form) state; condition, as in technicality

IUD intrauterine device (for contraception)

-ive (comb. form) tendency, inclination, character, quality, as in divisive, festive, massive

ivory ('Ivəri, -vri) n. 1. hard white substance of the tusks of elephants etc. 2. yellowish-white color; cream —a. 3. yellowish-white; cream —'**ivories** pl.n. sl. 1. piano keys 2. teeth 3. dice —**ivory tower** seclusion, remoteness

Ivory Coast country in Africa bounded west by Liberia and Guinea, north by Mali and Burkina-Faso, east by Ghana and south by the Gulf of Guinea —**Ivory Coaster**

ivy ('Ivi) n. climbing evergreen plant —'**ivied** a. covered with ivy

-ize (comb. form) 1. cause to become, resemble or agree with, as in legalize 2. become; change into, as in crystallize 3. affect in specified way; subject to, as in hypnotize 4. act according to some principle, policy etc., as in economize

j *or* **J** (jā) *n.* **1.** tenth letter of English alphabet **2.** speech sound represented by this letter (*pl.* **j's, J's** *or* **Js**)

J 1. joule(s) **2.** *Cards* jack **3.** journal

JA joint account

J.A. judge advocate

jab (jab) *vt.* **1.** poke roughly **2.** thrust, stab abruptly (**-bb-**) —*n.* **3.** poke **4.** *inf.* injection

jabber ('jabər) *vi.* **1.** chatter **2.** talk rapidly, incoherently —**'jabberwocky** *n.* nonsense, *esp.* in verse

jabot (zha'bō, 'zhabō) *n.* frill, ruffle at throat or breast of garment

jacaranda (jakə'randə) *n.* S Amer. tree with fernlike leaves and pale purple flowers

jacinth ('jāsinth, 'jas-) *n.* reddish-orange semi-precious stone

jack (jak) *n.* **1.** fellow, man **2.** *inf.* sailor **3.** male of some animals **4.** device for lifting heavy weight, *esp.* automobile **5.** various mechanical appliances **6.** lowest court card, with picture of page boy **7.** *Bowls* ball aimed at **8.** socket and plug connection in electronic equipment **9.** small flag, *esp.* national, at sea —*vt.* **10.** (*usu. with* up) lift (an object) with a jack —**Jack Frost** personification of frost —**jack-in-the-box** *n.* toy consisting of figure on tight spring in box, which springs out when lid is opened (*pl.* **jack-in-the-boxes, jacks-in-the-box**) —**jack of all trades** person who undertakes many kinds of work (*pl.* **jacks of all trades**) —**jack-o'-lantern** *n.* **1.** lantern made from hollowed pumpkin, cut to represent human face **2.** will-o'-the-wisp —**Jack Tar** *chiefly lit.* sailor

jackal ('jakəl, -ȯl) *n.* wild, gregarious animal of Asia and Afr. closely allied to dog

jackanapes ('jakənāps) *n.* **1.** conceited impertinent person **2.** mischievous child **3.** *obs.* monkey

jackass ('jakas) *n.* **1.** the male of the ass **2.** blockhead —**laughing jackass** the Aust. kookaburra

jackboot ('jakbōōt) *n.* large riding boot coming above knee

jackdaw ('jakdō) *n.* European bird of crow family

jacket ('jakit) *n.* **1.** outer garment, short coat **2.** outer casing, cover —**'jacketed** *a.*

jackhammer ('jak-hamər) *n.* pneumatic hammer

jackknife ('jaknīf) *n.* **1.** pocketknife **2.** dive with sharp bend at waist in midair —*vi.* **3.** (of trailer truck) go out of control in such a way that trailer forms right angle to tractor

jackpot ('jakpot) *n.* large prize, accumulated stake, as pool in poker —**hit the jackpot** win a jackpot; achieve great success, *esp.* through luck

jack rabbit hare

jacks (jaks) *pl.n.* game in which bone or metal pieces (**jackstones**) are thrown and picked up between bounces of small ball

Jackson ('jaksən) *n.* **Andrew.** the 7th President of the U.S. (1829-37)

Jacobean (jakə'bēən) *a.* of the reign of James I (1603-25)

Jacobite ('jakəbīt) *n.* adherent of Stuarts after overthrow of James II

Jacquard ('jakärd) *n.* **1.** fabric in which design is incorporated into the weave **2.** loom for weaving such fabrics

Jacuzzi (jə'kōōzi) *n.* **1.** trade name for device which swirls water in bath **2.** bath containing such a device

jade¹ (jād) *n.* **1.** ornamental semiprecious stone, usu. dark green **2.** this color

jade² (jād) *n.* **1.** old worn-out horse **2.** *obs., offens.* woman considered to be disreputable —**'jaded** *a.* **1.** tired **2.** off color

jag¹ (jag) *n.* sharp or ragged projection —**jagged** ('jagid) *a.*

jag² (jag) *n. sl.* **1.** intoxication from drugs or liquor **2.** bout of drinking, drug-taking *etc.*

J.A.G. judge advocate general

jaguar ('jagyōōär) *n.* medium-sized, black-marked feline of the New World (*also* **American leopard**)

jai alai ('hīlī, hī ə'lī) court game in which the ball is caught in a wicker racket and hurled against the walls of the enclosed arena

jail (jāl) *n.* **1.** building for confinement of criminals or suspects —*vt.* **2.** send to, confine in prison —**'jailer** *or* **'jailor** *n.* —**'jailbird** *n.* hardened criminal

jalopy (jə'lopi) *n. inf.* decrepit old automobile

jalousie ('jaləsē) *n.* **1.** adjustable blind or shutter constructed from angled slats to allow ventilation and to prevent the ingress of rain **2.** window made of angled slats of glass

jam (jam) *vt.* **1.** pack together **2.** (*oft. with* on) apply fiercely **3.** squeeze **4.** *Rad.* block (another station) with impulses of equal wavelength —*v.* **5.** (cause to) stick together and become unworkable —*vi.* **6.** *sl.* play in jam session (**-mm-**) —*n.* **7.** fruit preserved by boiling with sugar **8.** crush **9.** hold-up of traffic **10.** awkward situation —**jam-packed** *a.* filled to capacity —**jam session** (improvised) jazz or pop music session

Jamaica (jə'mākə) *n.* country in Caribbean comprising an island in the Greater Antilles 90 miles south of the east end of Cuba —**Ja'maican** *n./a.*

jamb (jam) *n.* side and head lining of door, window *etc.*

jamboree (jambə'rē) *n.* **1.** celebration, spree **2.** national or international rally of Boy Scouts

James (jāmz) *n. Bible* 20th book of the N.T., epistle addressed to converted Jews living around the Mediterranean, written by a half-brother of Jesus

Jan. January

jangle ('janggəl) *v.* **1.** (cause to) sound harshly, as bell —*vt.* **2.** produce jarring effect on —*n.* **3.** harsh sound

janitor ('janitər) *n.* **1.** caretaker **2.** doorkeeper (**'janitress** *fem.*)

January ('janyōōeri) *n.* first month

japan (jə'pan) *n.* **1.** very hard, *usu.* black varnish —*vt.* **2.** cover with this (**-nn-**)

Japan (jə'pan) *n.* country lying in Pacific off the east coast of Asia comprising four main islands and many smaller islands, separated from Korea by the Korea Strait and from the U.S.S.R. by La Pérouse Strait —**Japa'nese** *a.* **1.** of Japan —*n.* **2.** native or inhabitant of Japan (*pl.* **-ese**) **3.** the language of Japan, which is the only member of its family

jape (jāp) *n./vi.* joke

japonica (jə'ponikə) *n.* shrub with red flowers (*also* **Japanese quince**)

jar¹ (jär) *n. usu.* round vessel of glass, earthenware *etc.*

jar² (jär) *v.* **1.** (cause to) vibrate suddenly, violently —*vt.* **2.** have disturbing, painful effect on (**-rr-**) —*n.* **3.** jarring sound **4.** shock *etc.*

jardinière (järdi'nēər, zhärdi'nyâər) *n.* ornamental pot for growing plants

jargon ('järgən) *n.* **1.** specialized language concerned with particular subject **2.** pretentious or nonsensical language

Jas. James

jasmine ('jazmin) *n.* any of a genus of tender and hardy, deciduous and evergreen shrubs and climbers of the olive family grown for their white or yellow flowers, many of which are strongly fragrant

jasper ('jaspər) *n.* red, yellow, dark green or brown quartz used as gemstone

jaundice ('jöndis) *n.* **1.** symptom marked by yellowness of skin (*also* **'icterus**) **2.** bitterness, ill humor **3.** prejudice —*vt.* **4.** make prejudiced, bitter *etc.*

jaunt (jönt) *n.* **1.** short pleasurable excursion —*vi.* **2.** go on such an excursion —**jaunting car** formerly, light, two-wheeled, one-horse vehicle used in Ireland

jaunty ('jönti) *a.* **1.** sprightly **2.** brisk **3.** smart, trim —**'jauntily** *adv.*

Java ('javə) *n.* **1.** island of Indonesia **2.** (**j-**) *sl.* brewed coffee —**Java'nese** *a.* **1.** of Java —*n.* **2.** native or inhabitant of Java (*pl.* **-ese**) **3.** Malayan language of Java

javelin ('javlin) *n.* spear, *esp.* for throwing in sporting events

jaw (jö) *n.* **1.** one of bones in which teeth are set —*pl.* **2.** mouth **3.** gripping part of vise *etc.* **4.** *fig.* narrow opening of gorge or valley —*vi.* **5.** *sl.* talk lengthily

jay

jay (jā) *n.* woodland bird of Europe, N Afr. and N Asia with raucous voice —**'jaywalk** *vi.* walk in or across street carelessly or illegally —**'jaywalker** *n.*

jazz (jaz) *n.* syncopated music and dance —**'jazzy** *a.* flashy, showy —**jazz up 1.** play as jazz **2.** make more lively, appealing

JC junior college

JCS joint chiefs of staff

jct junction

JD 1. junior dean **2.** doctor of jurisprudence; doctor of law(s) **3.** justice department **4.** juvenile delinquent

JDL Jewish Defense League

jealous ('jeləs) *a.* **1.** distrustful of the faithfulness (of) **2.** envious **3.** suspiciously watchful —**'jealously** *adv.* —**'jealousy** *n.*

jeans (jēnz) *pl.n.* casual trousers with yoke at back, *esp.* made of denim

Jeep (jēp) *n.* trade name for light four-wheel-drive utility vehicle

jeer (jēər) *v.* **1.** scoff —*n.* **2.** scoff, taunt, gibe

Jefferson ('jefərsən) *n.* **Thomas.** the 3rd President of the U.S. (1801-09)

Jehovah (ji'hōvə) *n. O.T.* God —**Jehovah's Witness** member of Christian sect which believes end of world is near

jejune (ji'jōōn) *a.* **1.** simple, naive **2.** meager

Jekyll and Hyde ('jekəl; hīd) person with two distinct personalities, one good, the other evil

jell (jel) *v.* **1.** congeal —*vi.* **2.** *inf.* assume definite form

Jello ('jelō) *n.* trade name for gelatin dessert usu. flavored and colored like fruit

jelly ('jeli) *n.* **1.** semitransparent food made with gelatin, becoming softly stiff as it cools **2.** anything of the consistency of this —**'jellybean** *n.* bean-shaped candy with chewy filling and hard sugar coating —**'jellyfish** *n.* jellylike small sea animal

jenny ('jeni) *n.* **1.** female ass **2.** female wren

jeopardy ('jepərdi) *n.* (*usu.* with in) danger —**'jeopardize** *vt.* endanger

Jer. *Bible* Jeremiah

jerboa (jər'bōə) *n.* **1.** small Afr. burrowing rodent resembling a mouse **2.** desert rat

jeremiad (jeri'mīəd) *n.* lamentation; complaint

Jeremiah (jerə'mīə) *n. Bible* 24th book of the O.T., written by a major prophet who lived at the time of the fall of Jerusalem

Jeremias (jerə'mīəs) *n. Bible* Jeremiah in the Douay Version of the O.T.

jerk[1] (jərk) *n.* **1.** sharp, abruptly stopped movement **2.** twitch **3.** sharp pull **4.** *sl.* stupid person —*v.* **5.** move or throw with a jerk —**'jerkily** *adv.* —**'jerkiness** *n.* —**'jerky** *a.* uneven, spasmodic

jerk[2] (jərk) *vt.* **1.** preserve (beef *etc.*) by cutting into strips and drying in sun —*n.* **2.** jerked meat (*also* **'jerky**)

jerkin ('jərkin) *n.* sleeveless jacket, *esp.* of leather

jerry-built ('jeri-) *a.* of flimsy construction with cheap materials —**jerry-builder** *n.*

jerry can flat-sided can for storing or transporting motor fuel *etc.*

jersey ('jərzi) *n.* **1.** plain machine-knitted fabric of natural or man-made fibers **2.** circular-knitted sweater **3.** (J-) breed of cattle

jessamine ('jesəmin) *n.* jasmine

jest (jest) *n./vi.* joke —**'jester** *n.* joker, *esp.* employed by medieval ruler

Jesuit ('jezhōōit) *n.* member of Society of Jesus, order founded by Ignatius Loyola in 1534 —**Jesu'itical** *a.* of Jesuits

Jesus ('jēzəs) *n.* **1.** ?4 B.C.-?29 A.D., founder of Christianity, believed by Christians to be the Son of God (*also* **Jesus Christ, Jesus of Nazareth**) —*interj.* **2.** used to express intense surprise, dismay *etc.* (*also* **Jesus wept**)

jet[1] (jet) *n.* **1.** stream of liquid, gas *etc.*, shot from small hole **2.** the small hole **3.** spout, nozzle **4.** aircraft driven by jet propulsion —*vt.* **5.** throw out —*vi.* **6.** shoot forth —*v.* **7.** transport or be transported by jet (**-tt-**) —**jet lag** fatigue caused by crossing time zones in jet aircraft —**jet-propelled** *a.* driven by jet propulsion —**jet propulsion** propulsion by thrust provided by jet of gas or liquid —**jet set** rich, fashionable social set,

members of which travel widely for pleasure —**'jetsetter** *n.*

jet[2] (jet) *n.* hard black coal capable of brilliant polish —**jet-black** *a.* glossy black

jetsam ('jetsəm) *n.* cargo thrown overboard to lighten ship and later washed ashore —**'jettison** *vt.* **1.** abandon **2.** throw overboard

jetty ('jeti) *n.* small pier, wharf

Jew (jōō) *n.* **1.** person of Hebrew religion or ancestry **2.** *inf., offens.* miser (**'Jewess** *fem.*) —**'Jewish** *a.* —**'Jewry** *n.* the Jewish people —**jew's-harp** *n.* small musical instrument held between teeth and played by finger

jewel ('jōōəl) *n.* **1.** precious stone **2.** ornament containing one **3.** precious thing —**'jeweler** *n.* dealer in jewels —**'jewelry** *n.* items of bodily adornment other than clothing

jewfish ('jōōfish) *n.* large fish of tropical and temperate waters

Jezebel ('jezəbəl) *n.* **1.** *O.T.* wife of Ahab, king of Israel **2.** (*sometimes* **j-**) shameless or scheming woman

j.g. junior grade

jib (jib) *n.* **1.** triangular sail set forward of mast **2.** projecting arm of crane or derrick —*vi.* **3.** object to proceeding **4.** (of horse, person) stop and refuse to go on (**-bb-**) —**'jibber** *n.* —**jib boom** spar from end of bowsprit

jibe[1] (jīb) *or* **jib** (jib) *vi.* **1.** (of boom of fore-and-aft sail) swing over to other side with following wind **2.** alter course thus

jibe[2] (jīb) *vi. inf.* agree; accord; harmonize

jiffy ('jifi) *n. inf.* very short period of time

Jiffy bag ('jifi) trade name for padded envelope

jig[1] (jig) *n.* **1.** lively dance **2.** music for it **3.** small mechanical device **4.** mechanical device used as guide for cutting *etc.* **5.** *Angling* any of various lures —*vi.* **6.** dance jig **7.** make jerky up-and-down movements (**-gg-**) —**'jigger** *n.* —**'jigsaw** *n.* machine fretsaw —**jigsaw (puzzle)** picture stuck on board and cut into interlocking pieces with jigsaw —**in jig time** right away —**the jig is up** *sl.* success is hopeless

jig[2] (jig) *n. offens.* a Negro

jigger ('jigər) *n.* 1½ oz. glass for spirits

jiggery-pokery ('jigəri'pōkəri) *n. inf.* trickery, nonsense

jiggle ('jigəl) *v.* move (up and down *etc.*) with short jerky movements

jilt (jilt) *vt.* cast off (lover)

jim crow ('jim 'krō) (*oft.* J- C-) **1.** policy or practice of segregating Negroes **2.** *offens.* Negro

jimjams ('jimjamz) *pl.n.* **1.** *sl.* delirium tremens **2.** state of nervous tension or anxiety

jimmy ('jimi) *n.* short steel crowbar, pinchbar

jingle ('jinggəl) *n.* **1.** mixed metallic noise, as of shaken chain **2.** catchy, rhythmic verse, song *etc.* —*v.* **3.** (cause to) make jingling sound

jingo ('jinggō) *n.* **1.** loud, bellicose patriot **2.** jingoism (*pl.* **-es**) —**'jingoism** *n.* chauvinism —**jingo'istic** *a.* —**by jingo** exclamation of surprise

jinks (jinks) *pl.n.* boisterous merrymaking (*esp.* in **high jinks**)

jinni (ji'nē, 'jini) *or* **jinn** (jin) *n.* spirit in Muslim mythology who could assume human or animal form (*pl.* **jinn, jinns**) (*also* **djinni, djinn, djin**)

jinx (jinks) *n.* **1.** force, person, thing bringing bad luck —*vt.* **2.** be or put a jinx on

jitney ('jitni) *n.* small passenger bus following a regular route at varying hours —**jitney cab** automobile run as jitney

jitters ('jitərz) *pl.n.* worried nervousness, anxiety —**'jittery** *a.* nervous —**'jitterbug** *n.* **1.** fast jerky Amer. dance popular in 1940s **2.** person who dances jitterbug —*vi.* **3.** perform such dance

jiujitsu *or* **jiujutsu** (jōō'jitsōō) *n. see* JUJITSU

Jivaro ('hēvərō) *n.* Amerindian language spoken in Peru and Ecuador

jive (jīv) *n.* **1.** fast jazz music **2.** dancing to jazz music **3.** jargon of jazz musicians and jazz fans **4.** glib, deceptive talk

Jn *or* **Jno** John

JND just noticeable difference

job (job) *n.* **1.** piece of work, task **2.** post, office **3.** *inf.* difficult task **4.** *inf.* crime, *esp.* robbery —**'jobber** *n.* stockjobber —**'jobbing** *a.* doing single, particular jobs for payment —**'jobless** *a./pl.n.* unemployed (people) —**job lot 1.** assortment sold together **2.** miscellaneous collection

Job (jōb) *n. Bible* 18th book of the O.T., a poetical book of the Bible written by the man whose name has become synonymous with patience —**Job's comforter** person who adds to distress while purporting to give sympathy

jockey ('joki) *n.* **1.** professional rider in horse races (*pl.* **-s**) —*v.* **2.** (*esp.* with for) maneuver ('jockeyed, 'jockeying)

jockstrap ('jokstrap) *n.* piece of elasticated material worn by men, *esp.* athletes, to support genitals (*also* **athletic supporter**)

jocose (jə'kōs) *a.* waggish, humorous —**jo'cosely** *adv.* —**jocosity** (jə'kositi) *n.* —**jocular** ('jokyələr) *a.* **1.** joking **2.** given to joking —**jocularity** (jokyə'lariti) *n.*

jocund ('jokənd) *a.* merry, cheerful —**jo'cundity** *n.*

jodhpurs ('jodpərz) *pl.n.* tight-legged riding breeches —**jodhpur boot** ankle-high shoe fastened with buckle at side

Joel ('jōəl) *n. Bible* 29th book of the O.T., a prophetic book built around the plague of locusts present at the time of its writing

jog (jog) *vi.* **1.** run slowly or move at a trot, *esp.* for physical exercise —*vt.* **2.** jar, nudge **3.** remind, stimulate (**-gg-**) —*n.* **4.** jogging —**'jogger** *n.* —**'jogging** *n.* —**jog trot** slow regular trot

joggle ('jogəl) *v.* **1.** move to and fro in jerks **2.** shake —*n.* **3.** act of joggling

john (jon) *n. sl.* toilet

John (jon) *n. Bible* **1.** the 4th book of the N.T., the Gospel of John **2.** the 23rd, 24th and 25th books of the N.T., epistles written by John **3.** the apostle, writer of the Gospel, the epistles and Revelation

John Bull personification of the English nation

Johnson[1] ('jonsən) *n.* **Andrew.** the 17th President of the U.S. (1865-69)

Johnson[2] ('jonsən) *n.* **Lyndon Baines.** the 36th President of the U.S. (1963-69)

Johnston and Sand Islands ('jonsən, -stən) a territory of the U.S. in the south Pacific Ocean

joie de vivre (zhwad 'vēvr) *Fr.* enjoyment of life, ebullience

join (join) *vt.* **1.** put together, fasten, unite **2.** become member of —*vi.* **3.** become united, connected **4.** (with up) enlist **5.** (*usu.* with in) take part —*n.* **6.** joining **7.** place of joining —**'joiner** *n.* **1.** maker of finished woodwork **2.** one who joins —**'joinery** *n.* joiner's work

joint (joint) *n.* **1.** arrangement by which two things fit together, rigidly or loosely **2.** place of this **3.** meat for roasting, oft. with bone **4.** *inf.* house, place *etc.* **5.** *sl.* disreputable bar or nightclub **6.** *sl.* marijuana cigarette —*a.* **7.** common **8.** shared by two or more —*vt.* **9.**

connect by joints **10.** divide at the joints —'**jointly** adv. —**joint-stock company** business enterprise whose owners are issued shares of transferable stock —**out of joint 1.** dislocated **2.** disorganized

jointure ('joinchər) n. Law property settled on wife for her use after husband's death

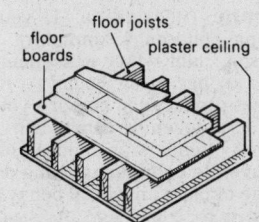

floor joists
floor boards
plaster ceiling

joist

joist (joist) n. one of the parallel beams stretched from wall to wall on which to fix floor or ceiling —'**joisted** a.

joke (jōk) n. **1.** thing said or done to cause laughter **2.** something said or done merely in fun **3.** ridiculous or humorous circumstance —vi. **4.** make jokes —'**joker** n. **1.** one who jokes **2.** sl. fellow **3.** extra card in pack, counting as highest or wild card in some games

jolly ('joli) a. **1.** jovial **2.** festive, merry —vt. **3.** (esp. with along) (try to) make (person, occasion etc.) happier ('**jollied, 'jollying**) —**jollifi'cation** n. merrymaking —'**jollity** n.

Jolly Roger pirates' flag with white skull and crossbones on black field

jolt (jōlt) n. **1.** sudden jerk **2.** bump **3.** shock —v. **4.** move, shake with jolts —'**jolty** a.

Jon. Bible Jonah

Jonah ('jōnə) n. **1.** Bible 32nd book of the O.T., written by the prophet who was swallowed by a great fish **2.** person believed to bring bad luck to those around him

Jonas ('jōnəs) n. Bible Jonah in the Douay Version of the O.T.

jonquil ('jonkwil, 'jong-) n. **1.** fragrant yellow or white narcissus —a. **2.** pale yellow

Jordan ('jôrdən) n. country in Middle East bounded south by Saudi Arabia, west by Israel, north by Syria and east by Iraq —**Jordanian** (jôr'dāniən) n./a.

Josh. Bible Joshua

Joshua ('joshəwə, -shwə) n. Bible 6th book of the O.T., in which the successor to Moses describes the return to Palestine

joss (jos) n. Chinese idol —**joss house** Chinese temple —**joss stick** stick of Chinese incense

jostle ('josəl) v. knock or push against (someone)

Josue ('joshəwi, -shwi) n. Bible Joshua in the Douay Version of the O.T.

jot (jot) n. **1.** small amount, whit —vt. **2.** write briefly; make note of (**-tt-**) —'**jotter** n. notebook

joule (jōōl) n. unit of energy equal to work done when a force of one newton acts over a distance of one meter

journal ('jэrnəl) n. **1.** daily newspaper or other periodical **2.** daily record **3.** logbook **4.** part of axle or shaft resting on the bearings —**journa'lese** n. journalists' jargon **2.** high-flown style, full of clichés —**journalism** n. editing, writing in periodicals —**journalist** n. —**journa'listic** a.

journey ('jэrni) n. **1.** traveling from one place to another; excursion **2.** distance traveled —vi. **3.** travel

journeyman ('jэrnimən) n. craftsman or artisan employed by another

---

joust (jowst) Hist. n. **1.** encounter with lances between two mounted knights —vi. **2.** engage in joust

Jove (jōv) n. see JUPITER (sense 1) —'**Jovian** a. —**by Jove** exclamation of surprise

jovial ('jōviəl) a. convivial, merry, gay

jowl (jowl) n. **1.** cheek, jaw **2.** outside of throat when prominent

joy (joi) n. **1.** gladness, pleasure, delight **2.** cause of this —'**joyful** a. —'**joyless** a. —'**joyous** a. **1.** having happy nature or mood **2.** joyful —'**joyously** adv. —**joy ride** trip, esp. in stolen automobile —'**joystick** n. inf. control column of aircraft

J.P. Justice of the Peace

Jr. Junior

Jth. Bible Judith

jubilate ('jōōbilāt) vi. rejoice —'**jubilant** a. exultant —'**jubilantly** adv. —**jubi'lation** n.

jubilee ('jōōbilē) n. time of rejoicing, esp. 25th or 50th anniversary

Jud. Bible Judges

Judaic (jōō'dāik) a. of the Jews or Judaism —'**Judaism** n. **1.** religion of the Jews **2.** religious and cultural traditions of the Jews **3.** the Jews collectively —'**Judaize** vt. **1.** make Jewish —v. **2.** conform or bring into conformity with Judaism

Judas ('jōōdəs) n. **1.** N.T. apostle who betrayed Jesus to his enemies for 30 pieces of silver **2.** person who betrays a friend; traitor

judder ('judər) inf. vi. **1.** shake, vibrate —n. **2.** a vibrating motion

Jude (jōōd) n. Bible 26th book of the N.T., an epistle exhorting believers to guard against apostasy

Judesmo (jōō'dezmō) n. see LADINO (sense 1)

judge (juj) n. **1.** officer appointed to try cases in court of law **2.** one who decides in dispute, contest etc. **3.** one able to form reliable opinion, arbiter **4.** umpire **5.** in Jewish history, ruler —vi. **6.** act as judge —vt. **7.** act as judge of **8.** try, estimate **9.** decide —'**judgment** or '**judgement** n. **1.** faculty of judging **2.** sentence of court **3.** opinion **4.** misfortune regarded as sign of divine displeasure —**Judgment Day** occasion of Last Judgment by God at end of world

Judges ('jujiz) pl.n. (with sing. v.) Bible 7th book of the O.T., describing a period of 400 years during which the people of Israel suffered repeated judgments by God for their sins

judicature ('jōōdikəchōōər) n. **1.** administration of justice **2.** body of judges —**ju'dicial** a. **1.** of, or by, a court or judge **2.** having qualities proper to a judge **3.** discriminating —**ju'dicially** adv. —**ju'diciary** n. system of courts and judges —**ju'dicious** a. well-judged, sensible, prudent

Judith ('jōōdith) n. Bible 18th book in the Douay Version of the O.T.

judo ('jōōdō) n. modern sport derived from jujitsu eliminating dangerous techniques

jug (jug) n. **1.** vessel for liquids, with handle and small spout **2.** its contents **3.** sl. prison —vt. **4.** stew (esp. hare) in jug (**-gg-**)

juggernaut ('jugərnöt) n. any irresistible, destructive force

juggle ('jugəl) v. **1.** throw and catch (several objects) so most are in the air simultaneously **2.** manage, manipulate (accounts etc.) to deceive —n. **3.** act of juggling —'**juggler** n.

jugular vein ('jugyələr) one of three large veins of the neck returning blood from the head

---

juice (jōōs) n. **1.** liquid part of vegetable, fruit or meat **2.** inf. electric current **3.** inf. gasoline **4.** vigor, vitality —'**juicy** a. succulent

jujitsu, jujutsu, or **jiujutsu** (jōō'jitsōō) n. system of weaponless combat and self-defense

juju ('jōōjōō) n. **1.** object superstitiously revered by certain W Afr. peoples and used as charm or fetish **2.** power associated with juju

jujube ('jōōjōōb) n. **1.** any of several spiny trees that have yellowish flowers and dark red edible fruits **2.** fruit of any of these trees **3.** lozenge of gelatin, sugar etc.

jukebox ('jōōkboks) n. automatic, coin-operated phonograph

Jul. July

julep ('jōōlip) n. **1.** tall drink of liquor, sugar, crushed ice and flavoring, esp. mint **2.** sweet drink of syrup, flavoring and water

Julian ('jōōlyən) a. of Julius Caesar —**Julian calendar** calendar as adjusted by Julius Caesar in 46 B.C., in which the year was made to consist of 365 days, 6 hours, instead of 365 days

julienne (jōōli'en) a. **1.** (of vegetables or meats) cut into thin strips —n. **2.** clear meat soup containing julienne vegetables

Juliett (jōōli'et) n. word used in communications for the letter j

July (jōō'lī) n. seventh month

jumble ('jumbəl) v. **1.** mingle, mix in confusion **2.** remember in confused form —n. **3.** confused heap, muddle **4.** sale

jumbo ('jumbō) n. inf. **1.** elephant **2.** anything very large (pl. **-s**) —**jumbo jet** inf. large jet-propelled airliner

jump (jump) v. **1.** (cause to) spring, leap (over) **2.** pass or skip (over) —vi. **3.** move hastily **4.** rise steeply **5.** parachute from aircraft **6.** start, jerk (with astonishment etc.) **7.** (of faulty film etc.) make abrupt movements —vt. **8.** come off (tracks, rails etc.) **9.** inf. attack without warning —n. **10.** act of jumping **11.** obstacle to be jumped **12.** distance, height jumped **13.** sudden nervous jerk or start **14.** sudden rise in prices —'**jumper** n. **1.** one who, that which jumps **2.** dress without sleeves or collar, usu. worn over blouse or sweater **3.** wire for making or breaking electrical circuit —'**jumpy** a. nervous —**jumper cables** cables for carrying current from one battery to another —**jump jet** inf. fixed-wing jet aircraft that can land and take off vertically —**jump rope** rope used in children's game in which player jumps over twirling rope —**jump suit** one-piece garment of trousers and top —**jump the gun** start before permitted time —**one jump ahead** one step ahead of one's rival

Jun. 1. June **2.** junior (also **jun.**)

junction ('jungkshən) n. **1.** railroad station etc. where lines, routes join **2.** place of joining **3.** joining

juncture ('jungkchər) n. state of affairs

June (jōōn) n. sixth month

jungle ('junggəl) n. **1.** tangled vegetation of equatorial forest **2.** land covered with it **3.** tangled mass **4.** condition of intense competition, struggle for survival —'**jungly** a.

junior ('jōōnyər) a. **1.** younger **2.** of lower standing —n. **3.** junior person —**junior college** college offering two-year curriculum —**junior high school** school including usu. grades 7, 8 and 9 —**Junior League** organization of women under the age of 40 for voluntary civic and social service —**junior varsity** athletic team for those not eligible for the varsity

juniper ('jōōnipər) *n.* evergreen shrub with berries yielding oil of juniper, used for medicine and gin making

junk[1] (jungk) *n.* **1.** discarded, useless objects **2.** *inf.* nonsense **3.** *sl.* narcotic drug —**'junkie** *or* **'junky** *n. sl.* drug addict —**junk food** food eaten in addition to or instead of regular meals, oft. with low nutritional value

junk[2] (jungk) *n.* Chinese sailing vessel

junket ('jungkit) *n.* **1.** curdled milk flavored and sweetened —*vi.* **2.** feast, picnic

junta ('hŏōntə, 'jun-, 'hun-) *n.* group of military officers holding power in a country

Jupiter ('jōōpitər) *n.* **1.** Roman chief of gods **2.** largest of the planets

Jurassic (jŏō'rasik) *a.* **1.** of second period of Mesozoic era —*n.* **2.** Jurassic period or rock system

juridical (jŏō'ridikəl) *a.* of law or administration of justice; legal

jurisdiction (jŏōəris'dikshən) *n.* **1.** administration of justice **2.** authority **3.** territory covered by it —**juris'prudence** *n.* science of, skill in, law —**'jurist** *n.* one skilled in law —**ju'ristic(al)** *a.*

jury ('jŏōəri) *n.* **1.** body of persons sworn to render verdict in court of law **2.** body of judges of competition —**'juror** *or* **'juryman** *n.* one of jury —**jury box** enclosure in court where jury sit

jury- (*comb. form*) *chiefly naut.* makeshift, as in *jury-rigged*

just (just) *a.* **1.** fair **2.** upright, honest **3.** proper, right, equitable —*adv.* **4.** exactly **5.** barely **6.** at this instant **7.** merely, only **8.** really —**'justice** *n.* **1.** quality of being just **2.** fairness **3.** judicial proceedings **4.** judge, magistrate —**jus'ticiary** *a.* **1.** of administration of justice —*n.* **2.** officer or administrator of justice; judge —**'justifiable** *a.* —**'justifiably** *adv.* —**justifi'cation** *n.* —**'justify** *vt.* **1.** prove right, true or innocent **2.** vindicate **3.** excuse (**-ified, -ifying**) —**'justly** *adv.* —**justice of the peace** lay magistrate whose function is to preserve peace in his area, try summarily minor cases, administer oaths and perform marriages

jut (jut) *vi.* **1.** (*oft. with* out) project, stick out (**-tt-**) —*n.* **2.** projection

jute (jōōt) *n.* fiber of certain plants, used for rope, canvas *etc.*

juvenile ('jōōvinil) *a.* **1.** young **2.** of, for young children **3.** immature —*n.* **4.** young person, child —**juve'nescence** *n.* —**juve'nescent** *a.* becoming young —**'juve'nilia** *pl.n.* works produced in author's youth —**juve'nility** *n.* —**juvenile court** court dealing with young offenders or children in need of care —**juvenile delinquent** young person guilty of some offense, antisocial behavior *etc.*

juxtapose ('jukstəpōz) *vt.* put side by side —**juxtapo'sition** *n.* contiguity, being side by side

JV junior varsity

Kk

k *or* **K** (kā) *n.* **1.** 11th letter of English alphabet **2.** speech sound represented by this letter, as in *kitten* (*pl.* **k's, K's** *or* **Ks**)

k 1. kilo **2.** *Math.* unit vector along *z*-axis **3.** knit

K 1. kelvin **2.** *Chess* king **3.** *Chem.* potassium **4.** *Phys.* kaon **5.** one thousand **6.** *Comp.* unit of 1024 words, bytes or bits

kabob ('kābob, kə'bob) *or* **kebab** *n.* cubes of marinated meat or vegetables placed on a skewer and cooked with radiant heat

Kabuki (kə'bōōki, 'käbōōki) *n.* traditional Japanese popular drama performed in highly conventional manner

kachina (kə'chēnə) *n.* in Pueblo culture, doll symbolizing powers and manifestations of nature and ancestors

Kaddish ('kädish) *n. Judaism* **1.** prayer closing synagogue service **2.** prayer of mourners for the dead **3.** *inf.* son

Kaffir *or* **Kafir** ('kafər) *n.* **SA** *offens.* any Black African

Kaiser ('kīzər) *n.* (*sometimes* k-) *Hist.* **1.** any of three German emperors **2.** any Austro-Hungarian emperor

kalanchoe (kalən'kōi) *n.* succulent plant with red, pink or yellow flowers

kale (kāl) *n.* type of cabbage

kaleidoscope (kə'līdəskōp) *n.* **1.** optical toy for producing changing symmetrical patterns by multiple reflections of colored glass chips *etc.*, in inclined mirrors enclosed in tube **2.** any complex, frequently changing pattern —**kaleidoscopic** (kəlīdə'skopik) *a.* swiftly changing

Kamasutra (kämə'sōōtrə) *n.* ancient Hindu text on erotic pleasure

kamikaze (kämi'käzi) *n.* (*oft.* K-) suicidal attack, *esp.* as in World War II, by Japanese pilots

Kampuchea (kampōō'chēə) *n.* country in southeast Asia bounded north by Laos and Thailand, west by Thailand, east by Vietnam and south by the Gulf of Thailand

Kan. *or* **Kans.** Kansas

kangaroo (kanggə'rōō) *n.* **1.** Aust. marsupial with very strongly developed hind legs for jumping —*vi.* **2.** *inf.* (of motor vehicle) move forward with sudden jerks —**kangaroo court** irregular, illegal court

Kansas ('kanzəs) *n.* Central state of the U.S., admitted to the Union in 1861. Abbrev.: **Kan., Kans., KS** (with ZIP code)

kaolin ('kāəlin) *n.* fine white clay used for porcelain and medicinally

kaon ('kāon) *n.* meson that has rest mass of about 996 or 964 electron masses (*also* **K-meson**)

kapok

kapok ('kāpok) *n.* **1.** tropical tree **2.** fiber from its seed pods used to stuff cushions *etc.*

kappa ('kapə) *n.* tenth letter in Gr. alphabet (Κ, κ)

kaput (kä'pŏŏt) *a. inf.* ruined, broken, no good

karakul ('karəkəl) *n.* **1.** tightly curled, lustrous coat of young lambs from Russia, SW Africa or China used for clothing (*also* **astrakhan, Persian lamb**) **2.** sheep of this breed —**karakul cloth** heavy woolen fabric resembling this

karat *or* **carat** ('karət) *n.* measure of fineness for gold equal to $\frac{1}{24}$ part of pure gold in any alloy

karate (kə'räti) *n.* system of self-defense using hands, arms, feet and legs as sole weapons

kart (kärt) *n.* light low-framed vehicle with small wheels and engine for recreational racing (**karting**) (*also* **go-cart, go-kart**)

kasbah ('kazbä) *n. see* CASBAH

katydid ('kātidid) *n.* green long-horned grasshopper living in trees in N Amer.

kauri ('kowri) *n.* large N.Z. pine giving valuable timber (*pl.* **-s**)

kava ('kävə) *n.* **1.** Polynesian shrub **2.** beverage prepared from the aromatic roots of this shrub

kayak ('kīak) *n.* **1.** Eskimo canoe made of sealskins stretched over frame **2.** any canoe of this design

kazoo (kə'zōō) *n.* cigar-shaped toy musical instrument producing nasal sound

kc kilocycle

K.C. King's Counsel

kcal kilocalorie

kea ('kēə) *n.* large New Zealand parrot with brownish-green plumage

kebab ('kābäb, kə'bäb) *n. see* KABOB

kedge (kej) *n.* **1.** small anchor —*vt.* **2.** move (ship) by cable attached to kedge

kedgeree (kejə'rē) *n.* dish of fish cooked with rice, eggs *etc.*

keel (kēl) *n.* lowest longitudinal support on which ship is built —**'keelhaul** *vt.* **1.** formerly, punish by hauling under keel of ship **2.** rebuke severely —**keelson** ('kelsən, 'kēl-) *n.* line of timbers or plates bolted to keel —**keel over 1.** turn upside down **2.** *inf.* collapse suddenly —**on an even keel** well-balanced; steady

keen[1] *a.* **1.** sharp **2.** acute **3.** eager **4.** shrewd **5.** strong —**'keenly** *adv.* —**'keenness** *n.*

keen[2] (kēn) *n.* **1.** funeral lament —*vi.* **2.** wail over the dead

keep (kēp) *vt.* **1.** retain possession of, not lose **2.** store **3.** cause to continue **4.** take charge of **5.** maintain **6.** detain **7.** provide upkeep of **8.** reserve —*vi.* **9.** remain good **10.** remain **11.** continue (**kept** *pt./pp.*) —*n.* **12.** living or support **13.** charge or care **14.** central tower of castle, stronghold —**'keeper** *n.* —**'keeping** *n.* **1.** harmony, agreement **2.** care, charge, possession —**'keepsake** *n.* gift that evokes memories of person or event

keg (keg) *n.* **1.** small barrel **2.** metal container for beer

kelp (kelp) *n.* **1.** large seaweed **2.** its ashes, yielding iodine

kelt (kelt) *n.* salmon that has recently spawned

Keltic ('keltik) *n. see* CELTIC

kelvin ('kelvin) *n.* unit of temperature —**Kelvin temperature** temperature on a scale where absolute zero (-273.15° Celsius) is taken as zero degrees

ken (ken) *n.* **1.** range of knowledge —*v.* **2.** in Scotland, know (**kenned** or **kent** *pt./pp.*)

kendo ('kendō) *n.* Japanese form of fencing using wooden staves

Kennedy ('kenədi) *n.* **John Fitzgerald.** the 35th President of the U.S. (1961-63)

kennel ('kenəl) *n.* **1.** house, shelter for dog —*pl.* **2.** place for breeding, boarding dogs —*vt.* **3.** put into kennel

kentledge ('kentlij) *n. Naut.* scrap metal used as ballast

Kentucky (kən'tuki) *n.* East South Central state of the U.S., admitted to the Union in 1792. Abbrev.: **KY** (with ZIP code) —**Kentucky Derby** *see* DERBY (sense 1)

Kenya ('kenyə, 'kēn-) *n.* country in Africa bounded north by Ethiopia, west by Uganda, south by Tanzania and east by Somalia and the Indian Ocean —**'Kenyan** *n./a.*

kepi ('kāpē) *n.* military cap with circular top and visor (*pl.* **-s**)

kept (kept) *pt./pp. of* KEEP

keratitis (kerə'tītis) *n.* inflammation of the cornea

kerchief ('kərchif) *n.* **1.** head-cloth **2.** scarf

kermes ('kərmis) *n.* insect used for red dyestuff

kernel ('kərnəl) *n.* **1.** inner seed of nut or fruit stone **2.** central, essential part

kerosine or **kerosene** ('kerəsēn) *n.* fuel oil distilled from petrolatum, also used as solvent

kestrel ('kestrəl) *n.* small falcon

ketch (kech) *n.* two-masted sailing vessel

ketchup ('kechəp, 'kach-, 'kats-) *n. see* CATSUP

ketone ('kētōn) *n.* one of class of chemical compounds with the general formula $R'COR$, where R and R' are organic groups, the simplest ketone being acetone —**ketonic** (kē'tonik) *a.* —**ke'tosis** *n.* disturbance of body chemistry produced by the use of fat as a source of energy

kettle ('ketəl) *n.* metal vessel with spout and handle, *esp.* for boiling water —**'kettledrum** *n.* musical instrument made of membrane stretched over copper hemisphere (*also* **timpani**) —**a fine kettle of fish** awkward situation, mess

key[1] (kē) *n.* **1.** instrument for operating lock, winding clock *etc.* **2.** something providing control, explanation, means of achieving an end *etc.* **3.** main note or tonal center of musical composition **4.** operating lever of typewriter, piano, flute *etc.* **5.** system of identifying characteristics **6.** means of solving encoded material —*vt.* **7.** provide symbols on (map *etc.*) to assist identification of positions on it **8.** scratch (plaster surface) to provide bond for plaster or paint **9.** insert (copy, information) by keystroke —*a.* **10.** vital **11.** most important —**'keyboard** *n.* set of keys on piano *etc.* —**'keyhole** *n.* aperture in lock case into which key is inserted —**'keynote** *n.* **1.** dominant idea **2.** basic note of musical key —**key punch** device having keyboard operated manually to transfer data onto punched cards *etc.* (*also* **card punch**) —**key-punch** *vt.* transfer (data) by key punch —**key signature** *Mus.* sharps or flats at beginning of each stave line to indicate key —**'keystone** *n.* **1.** central stone of arch **2.** something necessary to connect other related things —**'keystroke** *n.* depression of single key on keyboard of typewriter, computer *etc.* —**key word** significant word used to facilitate indexing of documents

key[2] (kē) *n. see* CAY

Keynesianism ('kānziənizəm) *n.* group of theories and programs of J.M. Keynes (1883-1946) and his followers, *esp.* advocacy of government intervention to maintain high employment —**'Keynesian** *n./a.* (denoting) one who supports the economic ideas propounded by Keynes

kg or **kg.** kilogram

K.G.B. Soviet secret police

khaki ('kaki, 'kä-) *a.* **1.** dull yellowish-brown —*n.* **2.** dull yellowish-brown color **3.** hard-wearing fabric of this color, used *esp.* for military uniforms (*pl.* **-s**)

khan (kän) *n.* **1.** formerly, (title borne by) medieval Chinese emperors and Mongol and Turkic rulers **2.** title of respect borne by important personages in Afghanistan and central Asia

Khmer (kmâər) *n.* member of a people of Kampuchea

kHz kilohertz

kibble ('kibəl) *vt.* grind into small pieces

kibbutz (ki'bŏŏts) *n.* Jewish communal agricultural settlement in Israel (*pl.* **kibbutzim** (kibŏŏt'sēm)) —**kib'butznik** *n.* **1.** member of kibbutz **2.** enthusiast about kibbutzim

kibitzer ('kibitsər, ki'bit-) *n.* **1.** *inf.* one who watches a game of cards without comment **2.** person giving unsolicited advice

kibosh ('kībosh) *n. sl.* —**put the kibosh on 1.** silence **2.** get rid of **3.** defeat

kick (kik) *vi.* **1.** strike out with foot **2.** (*sometimes with* against) be recalcitrant **3.** recoil —*vt.* **4.** strike or hit with foot **5.** score (goal) with a kick **6.** *inf.* free oneself of (habit *etc.*) —*n.* **7.** foot blow **8.** recoil **9.** excitement, thrill —**'kickback** *n.* **1.** strong reaction **2.** money paid illegally for favors done *etc.* —**'kickoff** *n.* **1.** place kick from center of field in football **2.** time at which first such kick is due to take place —**kick pleat** inverted pleat at back of narrow skirt —**'kickstand** *n.* short metal bar which when kicked into vertical position holds stationary cycle upright —**kick turn** skiing turn in

stationary position used to change direction —**kick off 1.** start game of football **2.** *inf.* begin (discussion *etc.*) —**kick the bucket** *sl.* die —**kick the habit** give up a habit —**kick (someone) upstairs** promote (someone) to an apparently better position

kid (kid) *n.* **1.** young goat **2.** leather of its skin **3.** *inf.* child —*vt.* **4.** tease; deceive —*vi.* **5.** behave, speak in fun (**-dd-**) —**kid glove** glove made of kidskin —**'kid'glove** *a.* **1.** overdelicate **2.** diplomatic; tactful —**handle with kid gloves** treat with great tact or caution

kidnap ('kidnap) *vt.* seize and hold to ransom (**-pp-**) —**'kidnapper** *n.*

kidney ('kidni) *n.* **1.** either of the pair of organs which secrete urine **2.** animal kidney used as food **3.** nature, kind (*esp.* **in of the same** or **a different kidney**) (*pl.* **-s**) —**kidney bean** any large bean seed of the cultivated plant, *esp.* a large dark red one —**kidney machine** machine carrying out functions of kidney (*also* **artificial kidney, dialysis machine**) —**kidney stones** calculi

kilim (kē'lēm) *n.* type of pileless rug woven in Near East with identical pattern on both sides

kill (kil) *vt.* **1.** deprive of life **2.** destroy **3.** neutralize **4.** pass (time) **5.** weaken; dilute **6.** *inf.* exhaust **7.** *inf.* cause to suffer pain **8.** *inf.* quash, defeat, veto —*n.* **9.** act or time of killing **10.** animals *etc.* killed in hunt —**'killer** *n.* one who, that which, kills —**'killing** *inf. a.* **1.** very tiring **2.** very funny —*n.* **3.** sudden success, *esp.* on stock market —**killer whale** ferocious toothed whale most common in cold seas —**kill-joy** *n.* person who spoils other people's pleasure

kiln (kiln, kil) *n.* furnace, oven

kilo ('kēlō) *n.* kilogram (*pl.* **-s**)

Kilo ('kēlō) *n.* word used in communications for the letter *k*

kilo- (*comb. form*) one thousand, as in *kiloliter, kilometer*

kilocycle ('kiləsīkəl) *n. short for* kilocycle per second: former unit of frequency equal to 1 kilohertz

kilogram ('kēləgram, 'kilə-) *n.* basic unit of mass in metric system equal to 1000 grams or 2.205 pounds

kilohertz ('kiləhərts, 'kēlə-) *n.* one thousand cycles per second

kiloton ('kēlōtun, 'kilō-) *n.* **1.** one thousand tons **2.** explosive power, *esp.* of nuclear weapon, equal to power of 1000 tons of TNT

kilowatt ('kiləwot) *n. Elec.* one thousand watts —**kilowatt-hour** *n.* unit of energy equal to work done by power of 1000 watts in one hour

kilt (kilt) *n.* usu. tartan knee-length skirt, deeply pleated, worn orig. by Scottish Highlanders

kimono

kimono (ki'mōnə, -nō) *n.* **1.** loose, wide-sleeved Japanese robe, fastened with sash **2.** European garment like this (*pl.* **-s**)

kin (kin) *n.* **1.** family, relatives —*a.* **2.** related by blood —**kindred** ('kindrid) *n.* **1.** relationship by blood **2.** relatives collectively —*a.* **3.** similar **4.** related —'**kinsfolk** *pl.n.* —'**kinship** *n.*

-kin (*comb. form*) small, as in *lambkin*

kind (kīnd) *n.* **1.** genus, sort, class —*a.* **2.** sympathetic, considerate **3.** good, benevolent **4.** gentle —'**kindliness** *n.* —'**kindly** *a.* **1.** kind, genial —*adv.* **2.** in a considerate or humane way —'**kindness** *n.* —**kind-hearted** *a.* kindly, readily sympathetic —**in kind 1.** (of payment) in goods rather than money **2.** with something similar

kindergarten ('kindərgärtən) *n.* class, school for children of about four to six years old

kindle ('kindəl) *vt.* **1.** set on fire **2.** inspire, excite —*vi.* **3.** catch fire —'**kindling** *n.* wood, straw *etc.* to kindle fire

kinematic (kini'matik) *a.* of motion without reference to mass or force —**kine'matics** *pl.n.* (*with sing. v.*) science of this —**kine'matograph** *n. see* **cinematograph** *at* CINEMA

kinetic (ki'netik) *a.* of motion in relation to force —**ki'netics** *pl.n.* (*with sing. v.*) science of this —**kinetic art**, *esp.* sculpture, that moves or has moving parts —**kinetic energy** energy created by movement

king (king) *n.* **1.** male sovereign ruler of independent state, monarch **2.** piece in game of chess whose capture loses the game **3.** highest face card, with picture of a king **4.** *Checkers* two pieces on top of one another, allowed freedom of movement —'**kingdom** *n.* **1.** state ruled by king **2.** realm **3.** sphere —'**kingly** *a.* **1.** royal **2.** appropriate to a king —**Kings** *pl.n.* (*with sing. v.*) *Bible* 11th and 12th books of the O.T., which record the reign of Solomon and division of the kingdom and the captivity of the northern tribes by Assyria —'**kingship** *n.* —**King Charles spaniel** toy breed of spaniel with very long ears —'**kingcup** *n.* any of several yellow-flowered plants, *esp.* buttercup —'**kingfisher** *n.* small bird of Europe or tropical regions with bright plumage which dives for fish —**King James Version** the Authorized Version of the Bible used by Protestants, published in 1611 in the reign of King James I —'**kingpin** *n.* **1.** swivel pin **2.** central or front pin in bowling **3.** *inf.* chief person or thing —**king post** beam in roof framework rising from tie beam to the ridge —**king-size** or **king-sized** *a.* **1.** large **2.** larger than standard size

kink (kingk) *n.* **1.** tight twist in rope, wire, hair *etc.* **2.** crick, as of neck **3.** *inf.* eccentricity —*v.* **4.** make, become kinked —'**kinky** *a.* **1.** full of kinks **2.** *inf.* eccentric, *esp.* given to deviant (sexual) practices

kiosk ('kēosk) *n.* **1.** small, sometimes movable booth selling drinks, cigarettes, newspapers *etc.* **2.** public telephone booth

Kiowa ('kīōwö, -wä) *n.* **1.** member of Amerindian people of Colorado, Kansas, New Mexico, Oklahoma and Texas (*pl.* **-wa, -s**) **2.** the Uto-Aztecan language of this people

kipper ('kipər) *vt.* **1.** cure (fish) by splitting open, rubbing with salt and drying or smoking —*n.* **2.** kippered fish

Kiribati (kiri'bas) *n.* country occupying a large expanse of the central Pacific comprising Banaba Island, the 16 Gilbert Islands, the 8 Phoenix Islands and 8 of the 11 Line Islands

kirk (kərk) *n.* in Scotland, church

Kirsch (kēərsh) *n.* brandy made from cherries

kismet ('kizmet, -mit) *n.* fate, destiny

kiss (kis) *n.* **1.** touch or caress with lips **2.** light touch —*vt.* **3.** touch with the lips as an expression of love, greeting *etc.* —*vi.* **4.** join lips with another person in act of love or desire —'**kisser** *n.* **1.** one who kisses **2.** *sl.* mouth; face —**kiss of life** mouth-to-mouth resuscitation

kist (kist) *n.* large wooden chest

kit (kit) *n.* **1.** outfit, equipment **2.** personal effects, *esp.* of traveler **3.** set of pieces of equipment sold ready to be assembled —'**kitbag** *n.* bag for holding soldier's or traveler's kit

kitchen ('kichin) *n.* room used for preparing and cooking food —**kitch'enette** *n.* small room (or part of larger room) used for cooking —**kitchen garden** garden for raising vegetables, herbs *etc.*

kite (kīt) *n.* **1.** light papered frame flown in wind **2.** *sl.* airplane **3.** large hawk

kith (kith) *n.* acquaintance, kindred (*only in* **kith and kin**)

kithara ('kithərə) *n.* foremost stringed instrument of the ancient Greeks and legendary instrument of their god Apollo, with a U-shaped frame, a crossbar between the arms and at least five strings

kitsch (kich) *n.* vulgarized, pretentious art, literature *etc.*, usu. with popular, sentimental appeal

kitten ('kitən) *n.* young cat —'**kittenish** *a.* **1.** like kitten; lively **2.** (of woman) flirtatious, *esp.* coyly

kittiwake ('kitiwāk) *n.* type of seagull

kitty ('kiti) *n.* **1.** kitten or cat **2.** in some gambling games, pool **3.** communal fund

kiva ('kēvə) *n.* Pueblo Indian ceremonial structure, usu. round and partly underground

kiwi ('kēwē) *n.* **1.** N.Z. flightless bird having long beak, stout legs and weakly barbed feathers **2.** brown, hairy, oval fruit **3.** *inf.* New Zealander (*pl.* **-s**)

kl. kiloliter

klaxon ('klaksən) *n.* formerly, powerful electric motor horn

Klein bottle (klīn) bottle-shaped figure which is enclosed, but has no inside or outside, no edges and one surface, formed by inserting the end of a tapering tube through one side of the tube making the ends contiguous

kleptomania (kleptə'māniə) *n.* compulsive tendency to steal *esp.* when there is no obvious motivation —**klepto'maniac** *n.*

klipspringer ('klipspringər) *n.* small agile Afr. antelope

km *or* **km.** kilometer

knack (nak) *n.* **1.** acquired facility or dexterity **2.** trick **3.** habit

knacker ('nakər) *n.* buyer of worn-out horses *etc.*, for killing —'**knackered** *a. sl.* exhausted

knapsack ('napsak) *n.* soldier's or traveler's bag to strap to the back, rucksack

knapweed ('napwēd) *n.* plant having purplish thistle-like flowers

knave (nāv) *n.* **1.** jack at cards **2.** *obs.* rogue —'**knavery** *n.* villainy —'**knavish** *a.*

knead (nēd) *vt.* **1.** work (flour) into dough **2.** work, massage —'**kneader** *n.*

knee (nē) *n.* **1.** joint between thigh and lower leg **2.** part of garment covering knee **3.** lap —*vt.* **4.** strike, push with knee —'**kneecap** *n.* bone in front of knee (*also* **patella**)

kneel (nēl) *vi.* fall, rest on knees (**knelt** *pt./pp.*)

knell (nel) *n.* **1.** sound of a bell, *esp.* at funeral or death **2.** portent of doom

knelt (nelt) *pt./pp. of* KNEEL

knew (nyoo, noo) *pt. of* KNOW

knickerbocker ('nikərbokər) *n.* **1.** (**K-**) native or resident of New York City or New York state —*pl.* **2.** knickers

knickers ('nikərz) *pl.n.* loose-fitting breeches gathered at knees

knick-knack ('niknak) *n.* trifle, trinket

knife (nīf) *n.* **1.** cutting blade, *esp.* one in handle, used as implement or weapon (*pl.* **knives**) —*vt.* **2.** cut or stab with knife —**knife edge** critical, possibly dangerous situation

knight (nīt) *n.* **1.** man of rank below baronet, having right to prefix *Sir* to his name **2.** member of medieval order of chivalry **3.** champion **4.** piece in chess —*vt.* **5.** confer knighthood on —'**knighthood** *n.* —'**knightly** *a.*

knit (nit) *v.* **1.** form (garment *etc.*) by putting together series of loops with knitting needles **2.** draw together **3.** unite ('**knitted, knit** *pt./pp.*, '**knitting** *pr.p.*) —'**knitter** *n.* —'**knitting** *n.* **1.** knitted work **2.** act of knitting —'**knitwear** *n.* knitted clothing, *esp.* sweaters

knives (nīvz) *n., pl. of* KNIFE

knob (nob) *n.* rounded lump, *esp.* at end or on surface of anything —'**knobby** *or* '**knobbly** *a.*

knock (nok) *vt.* **1.** strike, hit **2.** *inf.* disparage —*vi.* **3.** rap audibly **4.** (of engine) make metallic noise, pink —*n.* **5.** blow, rap —'**knocker** *n.* **1.** metal appliance for knocking on door **2.** person or thing that knocks —**knock-kneed** *a.* having incurved legs —'**knockout** *n.* **1.** blow *etc.* that renders unconscious, *esp.* in boxing **2.** *inf.* person or thing overwhelmingly attractive —**knock down 1.** strike to ground with blow, as in boxing **2.** in auctions, declare (article) sold **3.** demolish **4.** dismantle for ease of transport **5.** *inf.* reduce (price *etc.*) —**knocked up** *inf.* pregnant —**knock off** *inf.* **1.** cease work **2.** make hurriedly **3.** kill **4.** steal —**knock out 1.** render unconscious, *esp.* in boxing **2.** *inf.* overwhelm, amaze

knockwurst ('nokwərst) *n.* short thick smoked sausage

knoll (nōl) *n.* small rounded hill, mound

knot[1] (not) *n.* **1.** fastening of strands by looping and pulling tight **2.** cockade, cluster **3.** small closely knit group **4.** tie, bond **5.** hard lump, *esp.* of wood where branch joins or has joined **6.** unit of speed of one International Nautical Mile (6076.1155 feet or 1852 meters) per hour **7.** difficulty —*vt.* **8.** tie with knot, in knots (**-tt-**) —'**knotty** *a.* **1.** full of knots **2.** puzzling, difficult —'**knothole** *n.* hole in wood where knot has been

knot[2] (not) *n.* small northern sandpiper with gray plumage

know (nō) *vt.* **1.** be aware of **2.** have information about **3.** be acquainted with **4.** recognize **5.** have experience of, understand —*vi.* **6.** have information or understanding (**knew** *pt.*, **known** *pp.*) —'**knowable** *a.* —'**knowing** *a.* cunning, shrewd —'**knowingly** *adv.* **1.** shrewdly **2.** deliberately —'**knowledge** ('nolij) *n.* **1.** knowing **2.** what one knows **3.** learning —**knowledgeable** ('nolijəbəl) *a.* well-informed —**known** *a.* identified —**know-how** *n. inf.* practical knowledge, experience, aptitude —**know-it-all** *n. inf.* person who pretends or appears to know a great deal —**in the know** *inf.* informed

knuckle ('nukəl) *n.* **1.** bone at finger joint **2.** knee joint of calf or pig —*vt.* **3.** strike with knuckles —**knuckle-duster** *n.* metal appliance worn on knuckles to add force to blow —**knuckle down** *inf.* get down (to work) —**knuckle under** yield, submit —**near the knuckle** *inf.* approaching indecency

knur (nər) *n.* **1.** knot in wood **2.** hard lump

knurl (nərl) *vt.* **1.** impress with series of fine ridges or serrations —*n.* **2.** small ridge, *esp.* one of series —**knurled** *a.* **1.** serrated **2.** gnarled

koala (kō'älə, kə'wäl-) *n.* tailless arboreal Aust. marsupial mammal feeding almost exclusively on eucalyptus leaves (*also* **koala bear**)

kohl (kōl) *n.* black powder used *esp.* in Eastern countries for darkening the eyelids

kohlrabi (kōl'rabi, -'räbi) *n.* type of cabbage with edible stem

koine (koi'nā, kē'nē) *n.* **1.** (K-) the Greek language consisting of an amalgamation of dialects spoken during the time of the Roman Empire (c. 31 B.C.-476 A.D.) **2.** a lingua franca

kokanee (kō'kani) *n.* salmon of N Amer. lakes

kola ('kōlə) *n. see* COLA

kolinsky (kə'linski) *n.* **1.** any of various Asian minks **2.** rich tawny fur of this animal

Kol Nidre (kōl 'nidrā, kōl; -rə) *Judaism* the prayer chanted just before sunset on Yom Kippur eve

komatik (kō'matik) *n.* C Eskimo sledge with wooden runners

koodoo ('kōōdōō) *n. see* KUDU

kook (kōōk) *n. inf.* eccentric or foolish person —'**kooky** *or* '**kookie** *a.*

kookaburra ('kōōkəburə) *n.* large Aust. kingfisher with cackling cry (*also* **laughing jackass**)

kopeck *or* **kopek** ('kōpek) *n.* Soviet monetary unit, one hundredth of rouble

Koran (kə'ran, -'rän) *n.* sacred book of Muslims (*also* **Alkoran, Alcoran**)

Korea (kə'rēə) *n.* country in Asia bounded north by the demilitarized zone separating it from North Korea, east by the Sea of Japan, south by the Korea Strait separating it from Japan and west by the Yellow Sea —**Ko'rean** *n./a.* **1.** (native or inhabitant) of Korea —*n.* **2.** language of Korea, which is the only member of its branch

Korsakoff's psychosis ('körsəkofs) severe mental disturbance seen mainly in chronic alcoholics marked by loss of memory and degeneration of nervous tissue (*also* **amnestic confabulatory syndrome**)

kosher ('kōshər) *a.* **1.** permitted, clean, good, as of food *etc.*, conforming to the Jewish dietary law **2.** *inf.* legitimate, authentic —*n.* **3.** kosher food

kowtow (kow'tow) *n.* **1.** former Chinese custom of touching ground with head in respect **2.** submission —*vi.* (*esp. with* to) **3.** prostrate oneself **4.** be obsequious, fawn (on)

Kr *Chem.* krypton

kraal (krōl, kräl) *n.* SA **1.** hut village, *esp.* one surrounded by fence **2.** corral

kraken ('kräkən) *n.* mythical Norwegian sea monster

Kraut (krowt) *a./n. sl., offens.* German

Krebs cycle (krebz) series of chemical reactions occurring in the tissues of mammals by which food is made available for energy (*also* **citric acid cycle, tricarboxylic acid cycle**)

Kremlin ('kremlin) *n.* **1.** fortress within Russian town, *esp.* Moscow **2.** central government of Soviet Union

krill (kril) *n.* small shrimplike marine animal

kris (krēs) *n.* Malayan and Indonesian knife with scalloped edge

krona ('krōnə) *n.* standard monetary unit of Sweden and Iceland (*pl.* **-nor** (-nör, -nər))

krone ('krōnə) *n.* standard monetary unit of Norway and Denmark (*pl.* **-ner** (-nər))

krypton ('kripton) *n. Chem.* noble gaseous element *Symbol* Kr, at. wt. 83.80, at. no. 36

KS Kansas

Kt *Chess* knight (*also* **N**)

kudos ('kyōōdos, 'kōōdos) *n.* **1.** fame **2.** credit

kudu *or* **koodoo** ('kōōdōō) *n.* Afr. antelope with spiral horns

Ku Klux Klan (kōō kluks 'klan, kyōō) **1.** secret organization of White Southerners formed after U.S. Civil War to fight Black emancipation **2.** secret organization of White Protestant Americans, mainly in South, who use violence against Blacks, Jews *etc.*

kukri ('kōōkri) *n.* heavy, curved Gurkha knife

kulak (kōō'lak, kyōō-; 'kōōlak, 'kyōō-) *n.* independent well-to-do Russian peasant

kümmel ('kiməl) *n.* cumin-flavored German liqueur

kumquat ('kumkwot) *n.* **1.** small Chinese tree **2.** its round orange fruit

kung fu ('kōōng 'fōō) Chinese martial art combining techniques of judo and karate

Kuwait (kə'wāt) *n.* country in Middle East situated on the northwestern coast of the Arabian Gulf —**Ku'waiti** *n./a.*

kvass (kə'väs, kfäs) *n.* Russian beer made from barley, malt and rye

kW *or* **kw** kilowatt

kwashiorkor (kwäshi'örkər) *n.* severe malnutrition of young children, resulting from dietary deficiency of protein

kWh, kwh, *or* **kw-h** kilowatt-hour

KWIC (kwik) *Comp.* key word in context (*esp. in* **KWIC index**)

KWOC (kwok) *Comp.* key word out of context

KY Kentucky

kymograph ('kīməgraf) *n.* instrument for recording on graph pressure, oscillations, sound waves

Kymric ('kimrik) *a. see* CYMRIC

kyphosis (kī'fōsis) *n. see* **hunchback** (sense 1) *at* HUNCH

Ll

l *or* **L** (el) *n.* **1.** 12th letter of English alphabet **2.** speech sound represented by this letter **3.** something shaped like L (*pl.* **l's, L's** *or* **Ls**)

L 1. lambert **2.** large **3.** Latin **4.** *Phys.* length **5.** pound (*usually written:* £) **6.** longitude **7.** *Electron.* inductor (in circuit diagrams) **8.** *Phys.* latent heat **9.** *Phys.* self-inductance **10.** Roman numeral, 50

L. *or* **l. 1.** lake **2.** left **3.** line (*pl.* **LL.** *or* **ll.**) **4.** liter

la (lä) *n. Mus.* **1.** in fixed system of solmization, the note A **2.** in movable do system, the sixth note of a major scale

La *Chem.* lanthanum

LA 1. Los Angeles **2.** Louisiana

laager ('lägər) *n.* SA encampment surrounded by wagons

lab (lab) *inf.* laboratory

Lab. Labrador

label ('lābəl) *n.* **1.** slip of paper, metal *etc.*, fixed to object to give information about it **2.** brief, descriptive phrase or term —*vt.* **3.** fasten label to **4.** mark with label **5** describe or classify in a word or phrase

labiate ('lābiit, -āt) *n.* **1.** plant of family *Labiatae*, having square stems, aromatic leaves and two-lipped corolla —*a.* **2.** of family *Labiatae*

labium ('lābiəm) *n.* **1.** lip; liplike structure **2.** any of four lip-shaped folds of vulva, comprising outer pair (**labia majora**) and inner pair (**labia minora**) (*pl.* **-bia** (-biə)) —'**labial** *a.* **1.** of the lips **2.** pronounced with the lips —*n.* **3.** speech sound pronounced thus

labor ('lābər) *n.* **1.** exertion of body or mind **2.** task **3.** workers collectively **4.** effort, pain of childbirth or time taken for this —*vi.* **5.** work hard **6.** strive **7.** maintain normal motion with difficulty **8.** (*esp.* of ship) be tossed heavily —*vt.* **9.** stress to excess —'**labored** *a.* uttered, done, with difficulty —'**laborer** *n.* one who labors, *esp.* man doing manual work for wages —**la'borious** *a.* tedious —**la'boriously** *adv.* —**labor-saving** *a.* eliminating or lessening physical labor —**Labour Party 1.** Brit. political party, generally supporting interests of organized labor **2.** similar party in various other countries

laboratory ('labrətöri) *n.* place for scientific investigations or for manufacture of chemicals

Labrador ('labrədör) *n.* breed of large, smooth-coated retriever dog (*also* **Labrador retriever**)

laburnum (lə'bərnəm) *n.* tree with yellow hanging flowers

labyrinth ('labərinth) *n.* **1.** network of tortuous passages, maze **2.** inexplicable difficulty **3.** perplexity **4.** inner ear —**laby-'rinthine** a. —**labyrin'thitis** n. inflammation of the inner ear characterized by loss of balance and nausea

lac¹ (lak) n. resinous substance secreted by some insects

lac² (lăk) n. one hundred thousand (of rupees)

lace (lās) n. **1.** fine patterned openwork fabric **2.** cord, usu. one of pair, to draw edges together, eg to tighten shoes etc. **3.** ornamental braid —vt. **4.** fasten with laces **5.** flavor with spirit —'**lacy** a. fine, like lace

lacerate ('lasərāt) vt. **1.** tear, mangle **2.** distress —'**lacerable** a. —**lacer'ation** n.

lachrymal or **lacrimal** ('lakriməl) a. of tears —'**lachrymatory** or '**lacrimatory** a. causing tears or inflammation of eyes —'**lachrymose** a. tearful —'**lachrymosely** adv.

lack (lak) n. **1.** deficiency, need —vt. **2.** need, be short of —'**lackluster** a. lacking brilliance or vitality

lackadaisical (lakə'dāzikəl) a. **1.** languid, listless **2.** lazy, careless

lackey ('laki) n. **1.** servile follower **2.** footman (pl. **-s**) —vi. **3.** be or play, the lackey **4.** (with for) wait (upon)

laconic (lə'konik) a. **1.** using, expressed in few words **2.** brief, terse **3.** offhand, not caring —**la'conically** adv. —**la'conicism** n.

lacquer ('lakər) n. **1.** hard varnish —vt. **2.** coat with this

lacrimal ('lakriməl) a. see LACHRYMAL

lacrosse (lə'kros) n. goal game played with crosse

lactic ('laktik) a. of milk —'**lactate** vi. secrete milk —**lac'tation** n. —**lac'tometer** n. instrument for measuring purity and density of milk —'**lactose** n. white crystalline substance occurring in milk —**lactic acid** colorless syrupy acid found in sour milk etc.

lacuna (lə'kyōōnə, -'kōōnə) n. gap, missing part, esp. in document or series (pl. **-nae** (-nē), **-s**)

lad (lad) n. boy, young fellow

ladder ('ladər) n. frame of two poles connected by rungs, used for climbing —**ladder back** type of chair in which back is constructed of horizontal slats between two uprights

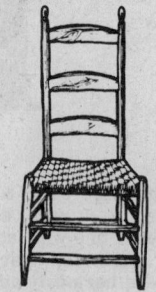

ladder back

lade (lād) vt. **1.** load **2.** ship **3.** burden, weigh down ('**laden** pp.) —'**lading** n. cargo, freight

la-di-da or **la-de-da** (lädē'dä) a. inf. affecting exaggeratedly genteel manners or speech

Ladino (lə'dēnō) n. **1.** (also **Judesmo, Dzhudesmo**) a dialect of Spanish and Portuguese, the vernacular of Sephardic Jews **2.** (l-) Spanish-speaking Latin American person (pl. **-s**)

ladle ('lādəl) n. **1.** spoon with long handle and large bowl —vt. **2.** (oft. with out) serve out (as) with ladle

lady ('lādi) n. **1.** female counterpart of gentleman **2.** polite term for a woman **3.** title of some women of rank —'**ladies** or **ladies' room** n. inf. women's public toilet —'**ladyship** n. title of a lady —'**ladybug** n. small beetle, usu. red with black spots —**Lady Day** Feast of the Annunciation, March 25th —'**ladyfinger** n. small finger-shaped sponge cake —**lady-in-waiting** n. lady who attends queen or princess (pl. **ladies-in-waiting**) —**lady-killer** n. inf. man who believes he is irresistible to women —'**ladylike** a. **1.** gracious **2.** well-mannered —**lady's-slipper** n. orchid with reddish or purple flowers —**Our Lady** the Virgin Mary

lag¹ (lag) vi. **1.** (oft. with behind) go too slowly, fall behind (**-gg-**) —n. **2.** lagging, interval of time between events —'**laggard** n. one who lags —'**lagging** a. loitering, slow

lag² (lag) vt. wrap (boiler, pipes etc.) with insulating material (**-gg-**) —'**lagging** n. this material

lag³ (lag) n. sl. convict (esp. in old lag)

lager ('lägər) n. light-bodied type of beer

lagoon (lə'gōōn) n. saltwater lake, enclosed by atoll, or separated by sandbank from sea

laic ('lāik) a. secular, lay —**laici'zation** n. —'**laicize** vt. render secular or lay

laid (lād) pt./pp. of LAY² —**laid-back** a. relaxed in style or character; easy-going and unhurried —**laid paper** paper with regular mesh impressed upon it

lain (lān) pp. of LIE¹

lair (laər) n. resting place, den of animal

laird (laərd) n. Scottish landowner —'**laird-ship** n. estate

laissez faire or **laisser faire** (lesā 'faər) Fr. **1.** principle of nonintervention, esp. by government in commercial affairs **2.** indifference

laity ('lāiti) n. laymen, the people as opposed to clergy

lake¹ (lāk) n. expanse of inland water —'**lakelet** n.

lake² (lāk) n. red pigment

lam¹ (lam) vt. sl. beat, hit (**-mm-**) —'**lamming** n. beating, thrashing

lam² (lam) n. sl. —**on the lam** making an escape

Lam. Bible Lamentations

lama ('lämə) n. Buddhist priest in Tibet or Mongolia —'**Lamaism** n. form of Buddhism of Tibet and Mongolia —'**Lamaist** n./a. —'**lamasery** n. monastery of lamas

lamb (lam) n. **1.** young of the sheep **2.** its meat **3.** innocent or helpless creature —vi. **4.** (of sheep) give birth —'**lambkin** n. **1.** small lamb **2.** term of affection for child —'**lamblike** a. meek, gentle —**lamb's ears** hardy perennial garden plant with woolly leaves and small purple flowers in dense whorls —'**lambskin** n. **1.** skin of lamb, esp. with wool still on **2.** material or garment prepared from this —**lamb's wool** soft, virgin wool from seven-month-old lamb having superior spinning qualities —**Lamb of God** (among Christians) Jesus

lambaste or **lambast** (lam'bāst) vt. **1.** beat **2.** reprimand

lambda ('lamdə) n. 11th letter in Gr. alphabet (Λ, λ)

lambent ('lambənt) a. **1.** (of flame) flickering softly **2.** glowing

lambert ('lambərt) n. cgs unit of illumination

lame (lām) a. **1.** crippled in a limb, esp. leg **2.** limping **3.** (of excuse etc.) unconvincing —vt. **4.** cripple —**lame duck 1.** disabled, weak person or thing **2.** elected official or body of officials remaining in office between election and inauguration of successor(s)

lamé (lä'mā) n./a. (fabric) interwoven with gold or silver thread

lamella (lə'melə) n. thin plate or scale esp. of mushroom gill or mollusk gill (pl. **-lae** (-lē), **-s**) —**la'mellar** or **lamellate** (lə'melit, 'lamilāt) a.

lament (lə'ment) v. **1.** feel, express sorrow (for) —n. **2.** passionate expression of grief **3.** song of grief —'**lamentable** a. deplorable —**lamen'tation** n.

Lamentations (lamən'tāshənz) pl.n. (with sing. v.) Bible 25th book of the O.T., written by Jeremiah, describing the capture and destruction of Jerusalem by the Babylonians

lamina ('laminə) n. thin plate, scale, flake (pl. **-nae** (-nē), **-s**) —**laminate** ('lamināt) vt. **1.** make (sheet of material) by bonding together two or more thin sheets **2.** split, beat, form into thin sheets **3.** cover with thin sheet of material —n. ('laminit, -nāt) **4.** laminated sheet —**lami'nation** n.

Lammas ('laməs) n. Aug. 1st, formerly a harvest festival

lammergeier or **lammergeyer** ('lamər-gīər) n. type of rare vulture

lamp (lamp) n. **1.** any of various appliances (esp. electrical) that produce light, heat, radiation etc. **2.** formerly, vessel holding oil burned by wick for lighting —'**lampblack** n. pigment made from soot —'**lamplight** n. —'**lamppost** n. post supporting lamp in street —'**lampshade** n.

lampoon (lam'pōōn) n. **1.** satire ridiculing person, literary work etc. —vt. **2.** satirize, ridicule —**lam'pooner** or **lam'poonist** n.

lamprey ('lampri) n. fish like an eel with a sucker mouth

lanceolate

lance (lans) n. **1.** horseman's spear —vt. **2.** pierce with lance or lancet —**lanceolate** ('lansiəlāt) a. lance-shaped, tapering —'**lancer** n. formerly, cavalry soldier armed with lance —'**lancers** pl.n. (with sing. v.) **1.** quadrille for eight or sixteen couples **2.** music for this dance —'**lancet** n. pointed two-edged surgical knife

land (land) n. **1.** solid part of earth's surface **2.** ground, soil **3.** country **4.** property consisting of land —pl. **5.** estates —vi. **6.** come to land, disembark **7.** bring an aircraft or (of aircraft) come from air to land or water **8.** alight, step down **9.** arrive on ground **10.** C be legally admitted as immigrant —vt. **11.** bring to land **12.** bring to some point or condition **13.** inf. obtain **14.** catch **15.** inf. strike —'**landed** a. possessing, consisting of lands —'**landing** n. **1.** act of landing **2.** platform between flights of stairs **3.** a landing stage —'**landless** a. '**landward** a./adv. —'**landfall** n. ship's approach to land at end of voyage —**land grant** tract of land given by government, usu. for colleges —**land-grant college** college or university in the U.S. entitled to federal government support under certain laws —**landing gear** undercarriage —**landing stage** floating wharf —'**landlocked** a. enclosed by land —'**landlord** or '**landlady** n. person who lets land, houses etc. —'**landlubber** n. person ignorant of the sea and ships —'**landmark** n. **1.** boundary mark, conspicuous object, as guide for direction etc. **2.** event, decision etc. considered as important stage in development of something —'**landmass** n. large continuous area of land —**land mine** Mil. explosive charge placed in ground, usu. detonated by stepping or driving on it —**land-poor** a. needing money while owning land —**land reform** program, esp. by national government, to redistribute large holdings of land to the landless —'**landscape** n. 1. piece of inland scenery 2. picture of it 3. prospect —v. 4. create, arrange (garden, park etc.) —**landscape gardener** —**landscape painter** —'**landslide** n. 1. falling of soil, rock etc. down mountainside 2. overwhelming electoral victory —'**landsman** n. fellow countryman —**land of milk and honey** land of natural fertility promised to Israelites by God —**land on one's feet** emerge safely from a risky situation —**see how the land lies** ascertain the facts before acting

landau ('landow, -dō) n. four-wheeled carriage with folding top

lane (lān) n. 1. narrow road or street 2. specified route followed by shipping or aircraft 3. area of road for one stream of traffic

lang. language

language ('langgwij) n. 1. system of sounds, symbols etc. for communicating thought 2. specialized vocabulary used by a particular group 3. style of speech or expression —**language laboratory** room equipped with tape recorders etc. for learning foreign languages

languish ('langgwish) vi. 1. be or become weak or faint 2. be in depressing or painful conditions 3. droop, pine —'**languid** a. 1. lacking energy, interest 2. spiritless, dull —'**languidly** adv. —'**languor** ('langgər) n. 1. want of energy or interest 2. faintness 3. tender mood 4. softness of atmosphere —'**languorous** ('langgərəs) a.

lank (langk) a. 1. lean and tall 2. greasy and limp —'**lanky** a. tall, thin and ungainly

lanolin ('lanəlin) n. grease from wool used in ointments etc.

lantern ('lantərn) n. 1. transparent case for lamp or candle 2. erection on dome or roof to admit light —**lantern jaw** long hollow jaw that gives face drawn appearance —**lantern-jawed** a. —**lanthorn** ('lantərn) n. obs. lantern

lanthanum ('lanthənəm) n. Chem. metallic element Symbol La, at. wt. 138.9, at. no. 57 —**lanthanide series** class of 15 chemically related elements (**lanthanides**) with atomic numbers from 57 (lanthanum) to 71 (lutetium)

lanyard ('lanyərd) n. 1. short cord for securing knife or whistle 2. short nautical rope 3. cord for firing cannon

Laos ('laōs, 'lāos, 'lāos) n. country in Asia bounded in the north by China, east by Vietnam, south by Kampuchea and west by Thailand and Burma —**Laotian** (lā'ōshən) a./n.

lap[1] (lap) n. 1. the part between waist and knees of a person when sitting 2. fig. place where anything lies securely 3. single circuit of racecourse, track 4. stage or part of journey 5. single turn of wound thread etc. —vt. 6. enfold, wrap round 7. overtake (opponent) to be one or more circuits ahead (-pp-) —'**lappet** n. flap, fold —'**lapdog** n. small pet dog —**lap joint** joint made by placing one member over another and fastening together (also **lapped joint**) —**lap of honor** ceremonial circuit of racing track etc. by winner of race

lap[2] (lap) v. 1. (oft. with up) drink by scooping up with tongue 2. (of waves etc.) beat softly (-pp-)

lapel (lə'pel) n. part of front of coat etc. folded back toward shoulders

lapidary ('lapideri) a. 1. of stones 2. engraved on stone —n. 3. cutter, engraver of stones

lapis lazuli ('lapis 'lazyəlē) bright blue stone or pigment

lapse (laps) n. 1. fall (in standard, condition, virtue etc.) 2. slip 3. mistake 4. passing (of time etc.) —vi. 5. fall away 6. end, esp. through disuse

lapwing ('lapwing) n. type of plover

larboard ('lärbərd) n./a. obs. port (side of ship)

larceny ('lärsini) n. theft

larch (lärch) n. deciduous coniferous tree

lard (lärd) n. 1. prepared pig's fat —vt. 2. insert strips of bacon in (meat) 3. intersperse, decorate (speech) (with strange words etc.) —'**lardy** a.

larder ('lärdər) n. storeroom or cupboard for food

large (lärj) a. 1. broad in range or area 2. great in size, number etc. 3. liberal 4. generous —adv. 5. in a big way —'**largely** adv. —**lar'gess** or **lar'gesse** n. 1. bounty 2. gift 3. donation —**large-scale** a. 1. wide-ranging, extensive 2. (of maps and models) constructed or drawn to big scale —**at large** 1. free, not confined 2. in general 3. fully

largo ('lärgō) a./adv. Mus. to be performed moderately slowly

lariat ('lariət) n. lasso

lark[1] (lärk) n. any of a family of ground-nesting songbirds of which the meadowlark and prairie horned lark are found in N Amer. —'**larkspur** n. plant with spikes of blue, pink or white flowers

lark[2] (lärk) n. 1. frolic, spree —vi. 2. indulge in lark —'**larky** a.

larrigan ('larigən) n. knee-high moccasin boot worn by trappers etc.

larva ('lärvə) n. insect in immature but active stage (pl. -ae (-ē)) —'**larval** a. —'**larviform** a.

larynx ('laringks) n. part of throat containing vocal cords (pl. **larynges** (lə'rinjēz), **-es**) —**laryn'geal** a. 1. of larynx 2. Phonet. articulated at larynx; glottal —**laryn'gitis** n. inflammation of larynx

lasagna or **lasagne** (lə'zänyə) n. pasta formed in wide, flat sheets

lascar ('laskər) n. E Indian seaman

lascivious (lə'siviəs) a. lustful

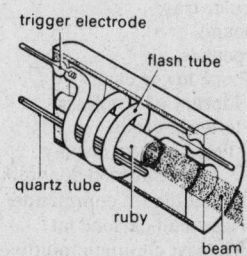

laser

trigger electrode

flash tube

quartz tube

ruby

beam

laser ('lāzər) n. light amplification by stimulated emission of radiation: device that amplifies focused coherent light waves and concentrates them in narrow intense beam

lash[1] (lash) n. 1. stroke with whip 2. flexible part of whip 3. eyelash —vt. 4. strike with whip, thong etc. 5. dash against (as waves) 6. attack verbally, ridicule 7. flick, wave sharply to and fro —'**lashing** n. 1. whipping, flogging 2. scolding —**lash out** 1. burst into or resort to verbal or physical attack 2. inf. be extravagant, as in spending

lash[2] (lash) vt. fasten or bind tightly with cord etc. —'**lashing** n. rope etc. used for binding or securing —**lash-up** n. temporary connection of equipment for experimental or emergency use

lass (las) n. girl —'**lassie** n. inf. little lass; girl

Lassa fever ('lasə) serious viral disease of Central W Afr., characterized by high fever etc.

lassitude ('lasityōōd, -tōōd) n. weariness

lasso ('lasō, la'sōō) n. 1. rope with noose for catching cattle etc. (pl. **-s**, **-es**) —vt. 2. catch (as) with lasso ('**lassoed**, '**lassoing**)

last[1] (last) a./adv. 1. after all others, coming at the end 2. most recent(ly) —a. 3. sup. of LATE 4. only remaining —n. 5. last person or thing —'**lastly** adv. finally —**last-ditch** a. made or done as last desperate effort in face of opposition —**last name** family name —**last rites** see extreme unction at EXTREME —**on its last legs** at the end of its usefulness —**the Last Judgment** in Christian belief, the day God will judge all men, living and dead —**the last straw** final irritation or problem that stretches one's endurance or patience beyond limit —**the Last Supper** the meal eaten by Jesus and his disciples the night of his betrayal —**the last word** 1. the final statement in a dispute 2. a definitive statement 3. the latest fashion

last[2] (last) vi. continue, hold out, remain alive or unexhausted, endure —'**lasting** a. permanent; enduring —'**lastingly** adv.

last[3] (last) n. model of foot on which shoes are made, repaired

Lastex ('lasteks) n. trade name for yarn made from combination of rubber with silk, cotton or rayon

lat. latitude

latch (lach) n. 1. fastening for door, consisting of bar, catch for it, and lever to lift it 2. small lock with spring action —vt. 3. fasten with latch —**latchkey child** child who has to let himself in at home after school as his parents are out at work

late (lāt) a. 1. coming after the appointed time 2. delayed 3. that was recently but now is not 4. recently dead 5. recent in date 6. of late stage of development (**later** comp., '**latest**, **last** sup.) —adv. 7. after proper time 8. recently 9. at, till late hour —'**lately** adv. not long since —'**latish** a. rather late —**Late Greek** Greek language from about 3rd to 8th century A.D. —**Late Latin** form of written Latin used from 3rd to 7th century A.D.

lateen sail (lə'tēn) triangular sail on long yard hoisted to head of mast

latent ('lātənt) a. 1. existing but not developed 2. hidden

lateral ('latərəl) a. of, at, from the side —'**laterally** adv.

laterite ('latərīt) n. dark red rock or clay formed by weathering of rock in tropical regions

latex ('lāteks) n. sap or fluid of plants, esp. of rubber tree (pl. **-es**, **latices** ('lātisēz, 'lat-)) —**laticiferous** (lati'sifərəs) a. bearing or containing latex or sap

lath (lath) n. thin strip of wood —'**lathing** n. —'**lathy** a. 1. like a lath 2. tall and thin

lathe (lādh) n. machine for turning object while it is being shaped

lather ('ladhər) n. 1. froth of soap and water 2. frothy sweat —vi. 3. form lather —vt. 4. inf. beat

Latin ('latin) n. 1. language of ancient Romans —a. 2. of ancient Romans 3. of, in their language 4. speaking a Romance language —'**Latinism** n. word, idiom imitating Latin —**La'tinity** n. 1. manner of writing

Latin 2. Latin style —**Latin alphabet** alphabet used for writing Latin and adapted for writing many modern languages including English —**Latin America** those areas of Amer. whose official languages are Spanish and Portuguese: S Amer., Central Amer., Mexico and certain islands in the Caribbean —**Latin American**

latitude ('latityōōd, -tōōd) n. **1.** angular distance on meridian reckoned N or S from equator **2.** deviation from a standard **3.** freedom from restriction **4.** scope —pl. **5.** regions —lati'tudinal a. —latitudi'narian a. claiming, showing latitude of thought, esp. in religion —latitudi'narianism n.

latrine (lə'trēn) n. in army etc., toilet

latter ('latər) a. **1.** second of two **2.** later **3.** more recent —n. **4.** second or last-mentioned person or thing —'latterly adv. —**Latter-Day Saint** Mormon

lattice ('latis) n. **1.** structure of strips of wood, metal etc. crossing with spaces between **2.** window so made —'latticed a.

laud (lôd) Lit. n. **1.** praise, song of praise —vt. **2.** praise, glorify —lauda'bility n. —'laudable a. praiseworthy —'laudably adv. —lau'dation n. **1.** praise **2.** honor paid —'laudatory a. expressing, containing praise

laudanum ('lôdənəm) n. tincture of opium

laugh (laf, läf) vi. **1.** make sounds instinctively expressing amusement, merriment or scorn —n. **2.** such sound —'laughable a. ludicrous —'laughably adv. —'laughter n. —**laughing gas** nitrous oxide as anesthetic —**laughing hyena** spotted hyena, so called from its cry —**laughing jackass** see KOOKABURRA —**laughing stock** object of general derision

launch¹ (lônch) vt. **1.** set afloat **2.** set in motion **3.** begin **4.** propel (missile, spacecraft) into space **5.** hurl, send —vi. **6.** enter on course —'launcher n. installation, vehicle, device for launching rockets, missiles etc. —**launch pad** platform from which spacecraft etc. is launched

launch² (lônch) n. large power-driven boat

Laundromat ('lôndrəmat) n. trade name for launderette

laundry ('lôndri) n. **1.** place for washing clothes, esp. as a business **2.** clothes etc. for washing —'launder vt. **1.** wash and iron **2.** legitimize (money obtained from criminal activity) —launder'ette n. place equipped with laundry equipment that customers may use for a fee

laureate ('lôriit) a. crowned with laurels —'laureateship n. post of poet laureate —**poet laureate** UK poet with appointment to Royal Household, nominally to compose verses on important royal occasions

laurel ('lôrəl) n. **1.** glossy-leaved shrub, bay tree —pl. **2.** its leaves, emblem of victory or merit

lava ('lävə) n. molten matter thrown out by volcanoes, solidifying as it cools

lavatory ('lavətöri) n. **1.** fixed washbowl with running water and drainpipe **2.** bathroom

lave (lāv) vt. obs. wash, bathe

lavender ('lavəndər) n. **1.** shrub with fragrant flowers **2.** color of the flowers, pale lilac —**lavender water** perfume or toilet water made from flowers of lavender plant

lavish ('lavish) a. **1.** giving or spending profusely **2.** very, too abundant —vt. **3.** spend, bestow profusely

law (lô) n. **1.** rule binding on community **2.** system of such rules **3.** legal science **4.** knowledge, administration of it **5.** inf. (member of) police force **6.** general principle deduced from facts **7.** invariable

sequence of events in nature —'lawful a. allowed by law —'lawfully adv. —'lawless a. **1.** ignoring laws **2.** violent —'lawlessly adv. —'lawyer n. professional expert in law —**law-abiding** a. **1.** obedient to laws **2.** well-behaved —'lawgiver n. one who makes laws —'lawsuit n. prosecution of claim in court

lawn¹ (lôn) n. stretch of carefully tended grass, esp. around house —**lawn mower** hand- or power-operated machine for cutting grass —**lawn tennis** tennis played on grass court

lawn² (lôn) n. fine soft cotton fabric

lawrencium (lô'rensiəm) n. Chem. transuranic element Symbol Lr, at. wt. 257, at. no. 103

lawyer ('lôyər, 'loiər) n. see LAW

lax (laks) a. **1.** not strict **2.** lacking precision **3.** loose, slack —'laxative a. **1.** having loosening effect on bowels —n. **2.** agent stimulating evacuation of feces —'laxity or 'laxness n. **1.** slackness **2.** looseness of (moral) standards —'laxly adv.

lay¹ (lā) pt. of LIE¹ —'layabout n. lazy person, loafer

lay² (lā) vt. **1.** deposit, set, cause to lie **2.** sl. have sexual intercourse with (laid, 'laying) —n. sl. **3.** female sexual partner —'layer n. **1.** single thickness of some substance, as stratum or coating on surface **2.** laying hen **3.** shoot of plant pegged down or partly covered with earth to encourage root growth —vt. **4.** propagate (plants) by making layers —lay-off n. —'layout n. arrangement, esp. of matter for printing —**lay by** store for future use —**lay it on the line** sl. speak out without reserve —**lay off** dismiss (staff) during slack period —**lay on 1.** provide, supply **2.** apply **3.** strike —**lay out 1.** display **2.** expend **3.** prepare for burial **4.** sl. knock out —**lay waste** devastate

lay³ (lā) n. minstrel's song

lay⁴ (lā) a. **1.** not clerical or professional **2.** of or done by persons not clergymen —'layman n. ordinary person —**lay reader 1.** Ch. of England person licensed by bishop to conduct religious services other than Eucharist **2.** R.C.Ch. layman chosen to read epistle at Mass

layette (lā'et) n. clothing, accessories etc. for newborn child

lay figure 1. jointed figure of the body used by artists **2.** nonentity

lazy ('lāzi) a. averse to work, indolent —**laze** vi. indulge in laziness —'lazily adv. —'laziness n. —**lazy Susan** ('sōōzən) revolving circular tray

lb. pound

lbs. pounds

l.c. Print. lower case

L.C. Library of Congress

L/C letter of credit

LCD liquid crystal display

L.C.D. least common denominator

LCDR lieutenant commander

LCL less-than-carload lot

L.C.M. least common multiple

LD lethal dose

L-dopa ('el'dōpə) n. drug used to treat Parkinson's disease

L.D.S. 1. Latter-Day Saint **2.** laus Deo semper (Lat., praise be to God for ever)

lea (lē, lā) n. Poet. piece of meadow or open ground

leach (lēch) v. **1.** remove or be removed from substance by percolating liquid **2.** (cause to) lose soluble substances by action of percolating liquid —n. **3.** act or process of leaching **4.** substance that is leached or constituents removed by leaching **5.** porous vessel for leaching

lead¹ (lēd) vt. **1.** guide, conduct **2.** persuade **3.** direct **4.** control —vi. **5.** be, go, play first **6.** (with to) result (in) **7.** give access (led (led), 'leading) —n. **8.** leading **9.** that which leads or is used to lead **10.** example **11.** front or principal place, role etc. **12.** cable bringing current to electric instrument —'leader n. —'leadership n. —**leading light** inf. important or outstanding person, esp. in organization —**leading question** question worded to prompt answer desired —**leading tone** Mus. **1.** seventh degree of major or minor scale (also sub'tonic) **2.** esp. in cadences, note that tends most naturally to resolve to note lying one semitone above —**lead time** time between design of product and its production

lead² (led) n. **1.** Chem. metallic element Symbol Pb, at. wt. 207.2, at. no. 82 **2.** plummet, used for sounding depths of water **3.** graphite —pl. **4.** lead-covered piece of roof **5.** strips of lead used to widen spaces in printing etc. —vt. **6.** cover, weight or space with lead ('leaded, 'leading) —'leaden a. **1.** of, like lead **2.** heavy **3.** dull —'leadsman n. sailor who heaves the lead —**lead poisoning 1.** acute or chronic poisoning by lead, characterized by abdominal pain etc. **2.** sl. death or injury resulting from being shot with bullets

leaf (lēf) n. **1.** organ of photosynthesis in plants, consisting of a flat, usu. green blade on stem **2.** two pages of book etc. **3.** thin sheet **4.** flap, movable part of table etc. (pl. **leaves** (lēvz)) —v. **5.** (oft. with through) turn through (pages etc.) cursorily —'leafless a. —'leaflet n. **1.** small leaf **2.** single sheet, often folded, of printed matter for distribution, handbill —'leafy a.

league¹ (lēg) n. **1.** agreement for mutual help **2.** parties to it **3.** federation of clubs etc. **4.** inf. class, level —vi. **5.** form an alliance; combine in an association —'leaguer n. member of league —**not in the same league (as)** inferior (to)

league² (lēg) n. obs. measure of distance varying from 2½ to 4½ miles

leak (lēk) n. **1.** hole, defect, that allows escape or entrance of liquid, gas, radiation etc. **2.** disclosure **3.** sl. act of urinating —vi. **4.** let fluid etc. in or out **5.** (of fluid etc.) find its way through leak —vt. **6.** let escape —v. **7.** (oft. with out) (allow to) become known little by little —'leakage n. **1.** leaking **2.** gradual escape or loss —'leaky a.

lean¹ (lēn) a. **1.** lacking fat **2.** thin **3.** meager **4.** (of mixture of fuel and air) with too little fuel —n. **5.** lean part of meat, mainly muscular tissue

lean² (lēn) v. **1.** rest (against) **2.** bend, incline —vi. **3.** (with to or toward) tend (toward) **4.** (with on or upon) depend, rely (on) —'leaning n. tendency —**lean-to** n. room, shed built against existing wall

leap (lēp) vi. **1.** spring, jump —vt. **2.** spring over (leapt or leaped pt./pp.) —n. **3.** jump —'leapfrog n. **1.** game in which player vaults over another bending down —v. **2.** (cause to) advance by jumps or stages (-gg-) —**leap year** year with Feb. 29th as extra day, occurring every fourth year

learn (lərn) vt. **1.** gain knowledge of or acquire skill in (something) by study, practice or teaching —vi. **2.** gain knowledge **3.** be taught **4.** (oft. with of or about) find out —learned ('lərnid) a. **1.** erudite, deeply read **2.** showing much learning —'learnedly ('lərnidli) adv. —'learner n. —'learning n. knowledge got by study

lease (lēs) n. **1.** contract by which land or property is rented for stated time by owner to tenant —vt. **2.** let, rent by, take on lease —'leasehold n. property held on lease

leash (lēsh) *n.* **1.** thong for holding a dog **2.** set of three animals held in leash —*vt.* **3.** hold in, secure by leash

least (lēst) *sup. of* LITTLE *a.* **1.** smallest —*n.* **2.** smallest one —*adv.* **3.** in smallest degree

leather (ledhər) *n.* prepared skin of animal —'**leathery** *a.* like leather, tough —'**leather-back** *n.* largest existing sea turtle —'**leather-jacket** *n.* crane-fly grub —'**leatherwood** *n.* N Amer. shrub with tough, leathery bark formerly used as emergency fiber for thongs

leave[1] (lēv) *vt.* **1.** go away from **2.** deposit **3.** allow to remain **4.** entrust **5.** bequeath —*vi.* **6.** go away, set out (**left, 'leaving**)

leave[2] (lēv) *n.* **1.** permission **2.** permission to be absent from work, duty **3.** period of such absence **4.** formal parting —**leave of absence 1.** leave from work or duty, *esp.* for a long time **2.** this period of time —**leave-taking** *n.* act of departing; farewell —**by** *or* **with your leave** with your permission

leave[3] (lēv) *vi.* produce or grow leaves (**leaved, 'leaving**)

leaven ('levən) *n.* **1.** yeast **2.** *fig.* transforming influence —*vt.* **3.** raise with leaven **4.** taint; modify

Lebanon ('lebənon) *n.* country in Middle East bounded on the north and east by Syria, west by the Mediterranean and south by Israel —**Leba'nese** *n./a.*

lecher ('lechər) *n.* man given to lewdness —**lech** *vi. inf.* (*usu. with* after) behave lecherously (toward) —'**lecherous** *a.* **1.** lewd **2.** provoking lust **3.** lascivious —'**lecherously** *adv.* —'**lecherousness** *n.* —'**lechery** *n.*

lecithin ('lesithin) *n.* one of a class of phosphorus-containing fats found in animal tissues, egg yolk and soybeans used in the manufacture of pharmaceuticals, cosmetics, margarine and chocolate (*also* **phosphatidyl choline**)

lectern ('lektərn) *n.* reading desk, *esp.* in church

lection ('lekshən) *n.* **1.** difference in copies of manuscript or book **2.** reading —'**lectionary** *n.* book, list of scripture lessons for particular days —'**lector** *n.* reader

lecture ('lekchər) *n.* **1.** instructive discourse **2.** speech of reproof —*vi.* **3.** deliver discourse —*vt.* **4.** reprove —'**lecturer** *n.* —'**lectureship** *n.* appointment as lecturer

LED light-emitting diode

ledge (lej) *n.* **1.** narrow shelf sticking out from wall, cliff *etc.* **2.** ridge, rock below surface of sea

ledger ('lejər) *n.* **1.** book of debit and credit accounts, chief account book of firm **2.** flat stone —**ledger line** *Mus.* short line, above or below stave

lee (lē) *n.* **1.** shelter **2.** side of anything, *esp.* ship, away from wind —'**leeward** *a./n.* **1.** (on) lee side —*adv.* **2.** toward this side —**lee shore** shore toward which wind is blowing —'**leeway** *n.* **1.** leeward drift of ship **2.** room for free movement within limits **3.** loss of progress

leech[1] (lēch) *n.* **1.** species of bloodsucking worm **2.** *Hist.* physician —'**leechcraft** *n.*

leech[2] (lēch) *n.* edge of a sail

leek (lēk) *n.* **1.** plant like onion with long bulb and thick stem **2.** this as Welsh emblem

leer (lēər) *vi.* **1.** glance with malign, sly or lascivious expression —*n.* **2.** such glance —'**leery** *a.* **1.** *chiefly dial.* knowing, sly **2.** *sl.* (*with* of) suspicious, wary

lees (lēz) *pl.n.* **1.** sediment of wine *etc.* **2.** dregs of liquor

left[1] (left) *a.* **1.** denoting the side that faces west when the front faces north **2.** opposite to the right —*n.* **3.** the left hand or part **4.**

Pol. reforming or radical party (*also* **left wing**) —*adv.* **5.** on or toward the left —'**leftist** *n./a.* (person) of the political left —**left-handed** *a.* **1.** using left hand with greater ease than right **2.** performed with left hand **3.** designed for use by left hand **4.** awkward, clumsy **5.** ironically ambiguous **6.** turning from right to left; anticlockwise —*adv.* **7.** with left hand —**left-hander** *n.*

left[2] (left) *pt./pp. of* LEAVE[1]

leg (leg) *n.* **1.** one of limbs on which person or animal walks, runs, stands **2.** part of garment covering leg **3.** anything which supports, as leg of table **4.** stage of journey —'**leggings** *pl.n.* covering of leather or other material for legs —'**leggy** *a.* **1.** long-legged **2.** (of plants) straggling —'**legroom** *n.* room to move legs comfortably, as in aircraft —**give someone a leg up** help someone to get over an obstacle or difficulty —**has not a leg to stand on** has no facts to support argument

legacy ('legəsi) *n.* **1.** anything left by will, bequest **2.** thing handed down to successor —**lega'tee** *n.* recipient of legacy

legal ('lēgəl) *a.* of, appointed or permitted by, or based on, law —**legal'ese** *n.* conventional language in which legal documents are written —'**legalism** *n.* strict adherence to law, *esp.* letter of law rather than its spirit —**legal'istic** *a.* —**le'gality** *n.* —**legali'zation** *n.* —'**legalize** *vt.* make legal —'**legally** *adv.* —**legal tender** currency that creditor must by law accept in redemption of debt

legate ('legit) *n.* ambassador, *esp.* papal —'**legateship** *n.* —**le'gation** *n.* **1.** diplomatic minister and his staff **2.** his residence

legato (li'gätō) *adv. Mus.* smoothly

legend ('lejənd) *n.* **1.** traditional story or myth **2.** traditional literature **3.** famous, renowned, person or event **4.** inscription —'**legendary** *a.*

legerdemain (lejərdə'mān) *n.* **1.** juggling, conjuring, sleight of hand **2.** trickery

leghorn ('leghörn, 'legörn, 'legərn) *n.* **1.** kind of straw **2.** hat made of it **3.** (L-) breed of fowls

legible ('lejəbəl) *a.* easily read —**legi'bility** *n.* —'**legibly** *adv.*

legion ('lējən) *n.* **1.** body of infantry in Roman army **2.** various modern military bodies **3.** association of veterans **4.** large number —*a.* **5.** very numerous —'**legionary** *a./n.* —**legion'naire** *n.* (*oft.* L-) member of military force or association —**Legion-naire's disease** bacterial infection of the lungs

legislator ('lejislātər) *n.* maker of laws —'**legislate** *vi.* make laws —**legis'lation** *n.* **1.** act of legislating **2.** laws which are made —'**legislative** *a.* —'**legislature** *n.* body that makes laws of a state —**legislative assembly** (*oft.* L- A-) single-chamber legislature in most Canad. provinces

legitimate (li'jitimit) *a.* **1.** born in wedlock **2.** lawful, regular **3.** fairly deduced —*vt.* (li'jitimāt) **4.** make legitimate —**le'gitimacy** *n.* —**le'gitimateness** *n.* —**legiti'mation** *n.* —**le'gitimism** *n.* —**le'gitimist** *n.* supporter of hereditary title to monarchy —**le'gitimize** *vt.* legitimate

leguan ('legōän) *n.* large S Afr. lizard

legume ('legyōōm, li'gyōōm) *n.* **1.** any plant bearing capsules or pods with opposing sutures which can open to discharge its seeds **2.** the fruit, including table vegetables such as peas and beans, from such a plant —**le'guminous** *a.* (of plants) pod-bearing

lei (lā, 'lāē) *n.* garland of flowers

leishmaniasis (lēshmə'nīəsis) *n.* any of

number of conditions caused by infection with parasites transmitted by blood-sucking sandflies which have bitten infected mammals

leisure ('lēzhər) *n.* **1.** freedom from occupation **2.** spare time —'**leisured** *a.* with plenty of spare time —'**leisurely** *a.* **1.** deliberate, unhurried —*adv.* **2.** slowly

leitmotiv *or* **leitmotif** ('lītmōtēf) *n. Mus.* recurring theme associated with some person, situation, thought

L.E.M. (lem) lunar excursion module

lemming ('leming) *n.* rodent of arctic regions

lemon ('lemən) *n.* **1.** pale yellow acid fruit **2.** tree bearing it **3.** its color **4.** *sl.* useless or defective person or thing —**lemon'ade** *n.* drink made from lemon juice —**lemon sole** European flatfish highly valued as food

lemur ('lēmər) *n.* nocturnal animal like monkey

lend (lend) *vt.* **1.** give temporary use of **2.** let out for hire or interest **3.** give, bestow (**lent, 'lending**) —'**lender** *n.* —**lends itself to** is suitable for

length (lengkth, length) *n.* **1.** quality of being long **2.** measurement from end to end **3.** duration **4.** extent **5.** piece of a certain length —'**lengthen** *v.* **1.** make, become longer **2.** draw out —'**lengthily** *adv.* —'**lengthwise** *adv./a.* in direction of length —'**lengthy** *a.* (over)long —**at length 1.** in full detail **2.** at last

lenient ('lēniənt) *a.* mild, tolerant, not strict —'**lenience** *or* '**leniency** *n.* —'**leniently** *adv.*

lenity ('leniti) *n.* **1.** mercy **2.** clemency

lens (lenz) *n.* piece of glass or similar material with one or both sides curved, used to converge or diverge light rays in cameras, eyeglasses, telescopes *etc.* (*pl.* -es)

lent (lent) *pt./pp. of* LEND

Lent (lent) *n.* period of fasting from Ash Wednesday to Easter Eve —'**Lenten** *a.* of, in or suitable to Lent

lentil ('lentil) *n.* edible seed of leguminous plant —**len'ticular** *a.* like lentil

lento ('lentō) *adv. Mus.* slowly

Leo ('lēō) *n.* (lion) 5th sign of zodiac, operative *c.* Jul. 22nd–Aug. 21st

leonine ('lēənīn) *a.* like a lion

leopard ('lepərd) *n.* large, tawny black-spotted feline of southern Asia and Africa ('**leopardess** *fem.*)

leotard ('lēətärd) *n.* tight-fitting garment covering most of body, worn by acrobats, dancers *etc.*

leper ('lepər) *n.* **1.** one suffering from leprosy **2.** person ignored or despised —'**leprosy** *n.* chronic infectious disease characterized by formation of painful inflamed nodules beneath skin and disfigurement and wasting of infected parts (*also* **Hansen's disease**) —'**leprous** *a.*

Lepidoptera (lepi'doptərə) *pl.n.* order of insects with four wings covered with fine gossamer scales, as moths, butterflies —**lepi'dopterist** *n.* person who studies or collects moths and butterflies —**lepi'dopter-ous** *a.*

leprechaun ('leprəkon, -kön) *n.* mischievous elf of Irish folklore

lepton ('lepton) *n. Phys.* any of group of elementary particles and their antiparticles, that participate in weak interactions

leptospiroses (leptōspī'rōsēz) *pl.n.* group of diseases caused by strains of corkscrew-shaped microorganisms, found in bodies of wild rodents or domestic animals, which contaminate water and soil with urine

lesbian ('lezbiən) *n.* homosexual woman —**'lesbianism** *n.*

lese-majesty ('lēz'majisti) *n.* 1. treason 2. taking of liberties

lesion ('lēzhən) *n.* 1. injury 2. injurious change in texture or action of an organ of the body

Lesotho (lə'sōtō) *n.* country in Africa bounded west by the Orange Free State, north by the Orange Free State and Natal, east by Natal and East Griqualand and south by the Cape Province

less (les) *comp. of* LITTLE *a.* 1. not so much —*n.* 2. smaller part, quantity 3. a lesser amount —*adv.* 4. to a smaller extent or degree —*prep.* 5. after deducting, minus —**'lessen** *v.* diminish, reduce —**'lesser** *a.* 1. less 2. smaller 3. minor

-less (*comb. form*) 1. without; lacking, as in *speechless* 2. not able to (do something) or not able to be (done, performed *etc.*), as in *countless*

lessee (le'sē) *n.* one to whom lease is granted

lesson ('lesən) *n.* 1. installment of course of instruction 2. content of this 3. experience that teaches 4. portion of Scripture read in church

lessor ('lesör, le'sör) *n.* grantor of a lease

lest (lest) *conj.* 1. in order that not 2. for fear that

let[1] (let) *vt.* 1. allow, enable, cause to 2. allow to escape 3. grant use of for rent, lease —*vi.* 4. be leased —*v. aux.* 5. used to express a proposal, command, threat, assumption (**let, 'letting**) —**'letdown** *n.* disappointment —**let-up** *n. inf.* lessening, abatement —**let down** 1. lower 2. disappoint 3. undo, shorten and resew (hem) 4. untie (long hair that is bound up) and allow to fall loose 5. deflate —**let off** 1. allow to disembark or leave 2. explode or fire (bomb *etc.*) 3. excuse from (work *etc*) 4. *inf.* allow to get away without expected punishment *etc.* —**let's** let us: used to express suggestion *etc.* by speaker to himself and hearers

let[2] (let) *n.* 1. hindrance 2. in some games, minor infringement or obstruction of ball requiring replaying of point

lethal ('lēthəl) *a.* deadly

lethargy ('lethərji) *n.* 1. apathy, want of energy or interest 2. unnatural drowsiness —**le'thargic** *a.* —**le'thargically** *adv.*

letter ('letər) *n.* 1. alphabetical symbol 2. written message 3. strict meaning, interpretation —*pl.* 4. literature 5. knowledge of books —*vt.* 6. mark with, in, letters —**'lettered** *a.* learned —**letter bomb** explosive device in envelope, detonated when envelope is opened —**'letterhead** *n.* sheet of writing paper printed with one's address, name *etc.* —**letter-perfect** *a.* 1. correct in every detail 2. (of speaker *etc.*) knowing one's text perfectly —**'letterpress** *n.* matter printed from a raised surface —**letter of credit** letter issued by bank entitling bearer to draw funds from that bank or its agencies —**letter of the law** exact requirements of law, in contrast to spirit or purpose of legislation

lettuce ('letis) *n.* plant grown for use in salad

leucocyte ('lōōkəsīt) *n. see* LEUKOCYTE —**leucocy'tosis** *n.* abnormal increase of white blood cells in the blood

leucoma (lōō'kōmə) *n. see* LEUKOMA

leucotomy (lōō'kotəmi) *n. see* **lobotomy** *at* LOBE

leukemia (lōō'kēmiə) *n.* a progressive blood

disease marked by the uncontrollable increase of leukocytes

leukocyte *or* **leucocyte** ('lōōkəsīt) *n.* any white blood corpuscle

leukoma *or* **leucoma** (lōō'kōmə) *n.* dense, white opacity of the cornea

leukopenia (lōōkə'pēniə) *n.* the abnormal decrease of white blood cells in the blood

leukoplakia (lōōkō'plākiə) *n.* whitish, thickened plaques of mucous membranes developed in response to irritation

leukorrhea (lōōkə'rēə) *n.* whitish discharge from female genital tract

Lev. *Bible* Leviticus

Levant (li'vant) *n. old name for* area of E Mediterranean now occupied by Lebanon, Syria and Israel —**le'vanter** *n.* (*sometimes* L-) 1. easterly wind in W Mediterranean area 2. inhabitant of the Levant —**Levantine** ('levəntīn) *a./n.*

levee[1] ('levi, lə've, lə'vā) *n.* 1. Brit. sovereign's reception for men only 2. *Hist.* reception held by sovereign on rising

levee[2] ('levi) *n.* 1. natural or artificial river embankment 2. landing place

level ('levəl) *a.* 1. horizontal 2. even in surface 3. consistent in style, quality *etc.* —*n.* 4. horizontal line or surface 5. instrument for showing, testing horizontal plane 6. position on scale 7. standard, grade 8. horizontal passage in mine —*vt.* 9. make level 10. bring to same level 11. knock down 12. aim (gun or accusation *etc.*) —*vi.* 13. *inf.* (*esp. with* with) be honest, frank —**'leveler** *or* **'leveller** *n.* advocate of social equality —**level-headed** *a.* not apt to be carried away by emotion

lever ('levər) *n.* 1. rigid bar pivoted about a fulcrum to transfer a force with mechanical advantage 2. handle pressed, pulled *etc.* to operate something —*vt.* 3. pry, move with lever —**'leverage** *n.* 1. action, power of lever 2. influence 3. power to accomplish something 4. advantage

leveret ('levərit, -vrit) *n.* young hare

leviathan (li'vīəthən) *n.* 1. sea monster 2. anything huge or formidable

levitation (levi'tāshən) *n.* the power of raising a solid body into the air supernaturally —**'levitate** *v.* (cause to) do this

Leviticus (li'vitikəs) *n. Bible* 3rd book of the O.T., setting out the feasts and codifying the rules of behavior for Jews

levity ('leviti) *n.* 1. inclination to make a joke of serious matters, frivolity 2. facetiousness

levulose ('levyəlōs) *n.* fructose

levy ('levi) *vt.* 1. impose (tax) 2. raise (troops) (**'levied, 'levying**) —*n.* 3. imposition or collection of taxes 4. enrolling of troops 5. amount, number levied

lewd (lōōd) *a.* 1. lustful 2. indecent —**'lewdly** *adv.* —**'lewdness** *n.*

lexicon ('leksikon, -kən) *n.* dictionary —**'lexical** *a.* —**lexi'cographer** *n.* writer of dictionaries —**lexi'cography** *n.*

ley (lē, lā) *n.* 1. arable land temporarily under grass 2. line joining two prominent points in landscape, thought to be line of prehistoric track (*also* **ley line**)

Leyden jar ('līdən) *Phys.* early type of capacitor consisting of glass jar with lower part of inside and outside coated with tinfoil

L.F. *Rad.* low frequency

LG *or* **L.G.** Low German

Lhasa apso ('läsə) small dog of Tibetan breed with long straight coat

Li *Chem.* lithium

liable ('līəbəl) *a.* 1. answerable 2. exposed 3. subject 4. likely —**lia'bility** *n.* 1. state of being liable, obligation 2. hindrance, disadvantage —*pl.* 3. debts

liaison ('lēəzon, li'āzon) *n.* 1. union 2. connection 3. intimacy, *esp.* secret —**li'aise** *vi.* communicate and maintain contact —**liaison officer** officer who keeps units of troops in touch

liana (li'änə) *n.* climbing plant of tropical forests

liar ('līər) *n. see* LIE[2]

lib (lib) *inf.* liberation

lib. 1. liber (*Lat.*, book) 2. librarian 3. library

Lib. Liberal

libation (lī'bāshən) *n.* drink poured as offering to the gods

libel ('lībəl) *n.* 1. published statement falsely damaging person's reputation —*vt.* 2. defame falsely —**'libelous** *or* **'libellous** *a.* defamatory

liberal ('libərəl, 'librəl) *a.* 1. (*also* L-) of political party favoring democratic reforms or favoring individual freedom 2. generous 3. tolerant 4. abundant 5. (of education) designed to develop general cultural interests —*n.* 6. one who has liberal ideas or opinions —**'liberalism** *n.* —**libe'rality** *n.* munificence —**'liberalize** *v.* —**'liberally** *adv.*

liberate ('libərāt) *vt.* set free —**libe'ration** *n.* —**'liberator** *n.*

Liberia (lī'bēriə) *n.* country in Africa bounded south by the Atlantic, west by Sierra Leone, north by Guinea and east by the Ivory Coast —**Li'berian** *n./a.*

libertarian (libər'teriən) *n.* 1. believer in freedom of thought *etc.*, or in free will —*a.* 2. of, like a libertarian —**liber'tarianism** *n.*

libertine ('libərtēn) *n.* 1. morally dissolute person —*a.* 2. dissolute —**'libertinism** *n.*

liberty ('libərti) *n.* 1. freedom —*pl.* 2. rights, privileges —**at liberty** 1. free 2. having the right —**take liberties** be presumptuous

libido (li'bēdō) *n.* 1. life force 2. emotional craving, *esp.* of sexual origin (*pl.* **-s**) —**libidinous** (li'bidinəs) *a.* lustful

Libra ('lībrə, 'lēbrə) *n.* 1. (balance) 7th sign of zodiac, operative c. Sept. 22nd-Oct. 22nd 2. (l-) *Hist.* a pound weight (*pl.* **librae** ('lībrē, 'lēbrī))

library ('lībreri) *n.* 1. room, building where books are kept 2. collection of books, phonograph records *etc.* 3. reading, writing room in house —**li'brarian** *n.* keeper of library —**li'brarianship** *n.*

libretto (li'bretō) *n.* words of an opera (*pl.* **-s, -ti** (-tē)) —**li'brettist** *n.*

Libya ('libiə) *n.* country in Africa bounded north by the Mediterranean, west by Tunisia and Algeria, south by Niger and Chad and east by Sudan and Egypt —**'Libyan** *n./a.*

lice (līs) *n., pl. of* LOUSE

license ('līsəns) *n.* 1. (document, certificate giving) leave, permission 2. excessive liberty 3. dissoluteness 4. writer's, artist's transgression of rules of his art (*oft.* **poetic license**) —*vt.* 5. grant license to —**licen'see** *n.* holder of license —**li'centiate** *n.* one licensed to practice art, profession

licentious (lī'senchəs) *a.* 1. dissolute 2. sexually immoral —**li'centiously** *adv.*

lichee ('līchē) *n. see* LITCHI

lichen ('līkən) *n.* plant organism formed by symbiotic association of an alga and a fungus —**'lichened** *a.* —**liche'nology** *n.* —**lichen planus** ('plānəs) skin disorder marked by flat-topped, violet-colored, pinhead-sized raised spots

lich-gate (lich-) *n. see* LYCH-GATE

licit ('lisit) *a. rare* lawful

lick (lik) *vt.* 1. pass the tongue over 2. touch lightly 3. *sl.* defeat 4. *sl.* flog, beat —*n.* 5. act of licking 6. small amount (*esp.* of paint *etc.*) 7. block or natural deposit of salt or other chemical licked by cattle *etc.* **8.** *inf.* speed —'**licking** *n. sl.* beating

licorice ('likərish, 'likrish; -ris) *n.* **1.** leguminous plant of Europe and Asia **2.** sweet-tasting dried root of this plant used in confectionery, medicine *etc.* —**licorice stick** *sl.* clarinet

lid (lid) *n.* **1.** movable cover **2.** cover of the eye **3.** *sl.* hat

lido ('lēdō) *n.* pleasure center with swimming and boating (*pl.* **-s**)

lie¹ (lī) *vi.* **1.** be horizontal, at rest **2.** be situated **3.** remain, be in certain state or position **4.** exist, be found **5.** recline (**lay, lain,** '**lying**) —*n.* **6.** state (of affairs *etc.*) **7.** direction

lie² (lī) *vi.* **1.** make false statement (**lied,** '**lying**) —*n.* **2.** deliberate falsehood —'**liar** *n.* person who tells lies —**give the lie to** disprove —**white lie** untruth said without evil intent

Liechtenstein ('liktənshtīn, -stīn) *n.* country in Europe bounded east by Austria and west by Switzerland —'**Liechtensteiner** *n.*

Liederkranz ('lēdərkrants) *n.* trade name for creamy cheese with edible russet crust which develops a robust odor as it changes from white to cream

lief (lēv, lēf) *adv.* **1.** *rare* gladly, willingly —*a.* *obs.* **2.** ready; glad **3.** dear, beloved

liege (lēj) *a.* **1.** bound to render or receive feudal service **2.** faithful —*n.* **3.** lord **4.** vassal, subject

lien (lēn, 'lēən) *n.* right to hold another's property until claim is met

lieu (lōō) *n.* place —**in lieu (of)** instead (of)

lieutenant (lōō'tenənt) *n.* **1.** deputy **2.** fire- or police-department officer below captain **3.** commissioned officer in armed forces ranking below one specified, as in *lieutenant colonel, lieutenant commander, lieutenant general* **4.** navy or coastguard officer below lieutenant commander and above lieutenant junior grade —**first lieutenant** officer in army, air force or marine corps ranking below captain and above second lieutenant —**second lieutenant** commissioned officer of the lowest rank in army, air force or marine corps —**lieutenant governor 1.** elected U.S. state official substituting for governor when necessary **2. C** representative of Crown in province appointed by federal government —**lieutenant junior grade** navy or coastguard officer above ensign

life (līf) *n.* **1.** active principle of existence of animals and plants, animate existence **2.** time of its lasting **3.** history of such existence **4.** way of living **5.** vigor, vivacity (*pl.* **lives**) —'**lifeless** *a.* **1.** dead **2.** inert **3.** dull —**life belt** buoyant device to keep afloat person in danger of drowning —'**lifeblood** *n.* **1.** blood, considered as vital to life **2.** essential or animating force —'**lifeboat** *n.* boat for rescuing people at sea, escaping from sinking ship *etc.* —**life buoy** buoyant device for keeping person afloat in emergency —'**lifeguard** *n.* person at beach or pool to protect bathers —**life insurance** insurance providing for payment of specified sum to named beneficiary on death of policyholder —**life jacket** sleeveless jacket worn to keep person afloat —'**lifelike** *a.* closely resembling life —'**lifeline** *n.* **1.** line thrown or fired aboard vessel for hauling in hawser for breeches buoy **2.** line by which deep-sea diver is raised or lowered **3.** vital line of access or communication —'**lifelong** *a.* lasting a lifetime —**life preserver** life belt; life jacket —**life-size** *or* **life-sized** *a.* representing actual size —**life style** particu-

lar attitudes, habits *etc.* of person or group —'**lifetime** *n.* length of time person, animal or object lives or functions

lift (lift) *vt.* **1.** raise in position, status, mood, volume *etc.* **2.** take up and remove **3.** exalt spiritually **4.** *inf.* steal —*vi.* **5.** rise —*n.* **6.** raising apparatus **7.** act of lifting **8.** ride in automobile *etc.* as passenger **9.** air force acting at right angles on aircraft wing, so lifting it **10.** *inf.* feeling of cheerfulness, uplift —'**liftoff** *n.* **1.** initial movement of rocket from launching pad **2.** instant at which this occurs —**lift off** (of rocket) leave launching pad

ligament ('ligəmənt) *n.* band of tissue joining bones —'**ligature** *n.* **1.** anything which binds **2.** thread for tying up artery **3.** *Print.* character of two or more joined letters

light¹ (līt) *a.* **1.** of, or bearing little weight **2.** not severe **3.** gentle **4.** easy, requiring little effort **5.** trivial **6.** (of industry) producing small, usu. consumer goods, using light machinery —*adv.* **7.** in light manner —*vi.* **8.** alight (from vehicle *etc.*) **9.** (*with* on *or* upon) come by chance (upon) ('**lighted, lit** *pt./pp.*) —'**lighten** *vt.* reduce, remove (load *etc.*) —'**lightly** *adv.* —'**lightness** *n.* —**lights** *pl.n.* lungs of butchered animals —**light-fingered** *a.* having nimble fingers, *esp.* for thieving or picking pockets —**light flyweight** amateur boxer weighing not more than 48 kg (106 lbs.) —**light-headed** *a.* **1.** dizzy, inclined to faint **2.** delirious —**light-hearted** *a.* carefree —**light heavyweight 1.** professional boxer weighing 72.5-79.5 kg (160-175 lbs.) **2.** amateur boxer weighing 75-81 kg (165-179 lbs.) **3.** wrestler weighing usu. 87-97 kg (192-214 lbs.) —**light middleweight** amateur boxer weighing 67-71 kg (148-157 lbs.) —**light-minded** *a.* frivolous —**light muscat** dry or semisweet white table wine —'**lightweight** *n./a.* (person) of little weight or importance —**light welterweight** amateur boxer weighing 60-63.5 kg (132-140 lbs.)

light² (līt) *n.* **1.** electromagnetic radiation by which things are visible **2.** source of this, lamp **3.** window **4.** mental vision **5.** light part of anything **6.** means or act of setting fire to something **7.** understanding —*pl.* **8.** traffic lights —*a.* **9.** bright **10.** pale, not dark —*vt.* **11.** set burning **12.** give light to —*vi.* **13.** take fire **14.** brighten ('**lighted, lit** *pt./pp.*) —'**lighten** *vt.* give light to —'**lighting** *n.* apparatus for supplying artificial light —'**lightning** *n.* visible discharge of electricity in atmosphere —'**lighthouse** *n.* tower with a light to guide ships —**light year** *Astron.* distance light travels in one year, about six million million miles

lighter ('lītər) *n.* **1.** device for lighting cigarettes *etc.* **2.** flat-bottomed boat for unloading ships

ligneous ('ligniəs) *a.* of, or of the nature of, wood —'**lignite** *n.* woody or brown coal

lignin ('lignin) *n.* organic substance which forms characteristic part of all woody fibers

lignum vitae ('lignəm 'vītī) *Lat.* **1.** tropical tree **2.** its extremely hard wood

like¹ (līk) *a.* **1.** resembling **2.** similar to **3.** characteristic of —*adv.* **4.** in the manner of —*pron.* **5.** similar thing —'**likelihood** *n.* probability —'**likely** *a.* **1.** probable **2.** hopeful, promising —*adv.* **3.** probably —'**liken** *vt.* compare —'**likeness** *n.* **1.** resemblance **2.** portrait —'**likewise** *adv.* **1.** in addition; moreover; also **2.** in like manner

like² (līk) *vt.* find agreeable, enjoy, love —'**likable** *or* '**likeable** *a.* —'**liking** *n.* **1.** fondness **2.** inclination, taste

-like (*comb. form*) **1.** resembling, similar to,

as in *lifelike* **2.** having characteristics of, as in *childlike*

lilac ('līlək) *n.* **1.** shrub of the olive family cultivated for its panicles of highly scented flowers in white, pink or pale purple **2.** a variable color ranging near pale purple —*a.* **3.** of this color

Lilliputian (lili'pyōōshən) *a.* **1.** diminutive —*n.* **2.** midget, pygmy

lilt (lilt) *vi.* **1.** (of melody) have a lilt **2.** move lightly —*n.* **3.** rhythmical effect in music, swing —'**lilting** *a.*

lily ('lili) *n.* any of a genus of the lily family, erect bulbous perennials with showy flowers in late summer that are native to the northern hemisphere and cultivated widely in a variety of sizes —**lily-livered** *a.* cowardly; timid —**lily pad** floating leaf of water lily —**lily-white** *a.* **1.** of a pure white **2.** *inf.* pure; irreproachable —**lily of the valley** low perennial plant with fragrant, white bell-like flowers

Lima ('lēmə) *n.* word used in communications for the letter *l*

limb¹ (lim) *n.* **1.** arm or leg **2.** wing **3.** branch of tree —**limbed** *a.* **1.** having limbs **2.** having specified number or kind of limbs

limb² (lim) *n.* **1.** edge of sun or moon **2.** edge of sextant

limber¹ ('limbər) *n.* detachable front of gun carriage

limber² ('limbər) *a.* pliant, lithe —**limber up** loosen stiff muscles by exercises

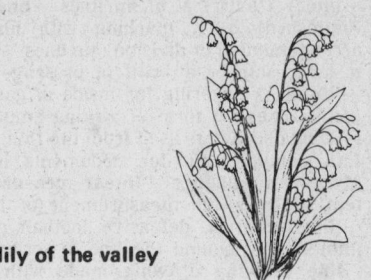

lily of the valley

limbo¹ ('limbō) *n.* **1.** (*oft.* **L**-) *R.C.Ch.* region intermediate between Heaven and Hell for the unbaptized **2.** intermediate, indeterminate place or state (*pl.* **-s**)

limbo² ('limbō) *n.* W Indian dance in which dancers pass under a bar (*pl.* **-s**)

Limburger ('limbərgər) *n.* a semihard, fermented, cow's-milk cheese with a full flavor orig. from Belgium

lime¹ (līm) *n.* **1.** any of certain calcium compounds used in making fertilizer, cement —*vt.* **2.** treat (land) with lime —'**limy** *a.* of, like or smeared with birdlime —'**limekiln** *n.* kiln in which calcium carbonate is calcined to produce quicklime —'**limelight** *n.* **1.** formerly, intense white light obtained by heating lime **2.** glare of publicity —'**limestone** *n.* sedimentary rock used in building

lime² (līm) *n.* small, greenish-yellow citrus fruit —'**limey** *n. sl.* Englishman —'**limy** *a.* —**lime juice** juice of lime prepared as drink

lime³ (līm) *n.* tree, the linden

limerick ('limərik) *n.* self-contained, nonsensical, humorous verse of five lines

limit ('limit) *n.* **1.** utmost extent or duration **2.** boundary —*vt.* **3.** restrict, restrain, bound —'**limitable** *a.* —**limi'tation** *n.* —'**limited** *a.* **1.** restricted; confined **2.** without scope; narrow **3.** (of governing powers *etc.*) restricted or checked, by or as if by constitution, laws or assembly —'**limitless** *a.* —**limited liability** liability limited by law

limn (lim) *vt.* paint; depict; draw —**limner** ('limnər, 'limər) *n.*

limo ('limō) *n. inf.* limousine (*pl.* -**s**)

limousine ('liməzēn, limə'zēn) *n.* large, luxurious automobile

limp[1] (limp) *a.* without firmness or stiffness —**'limply** *adv.*

limp[2] (limp) *vi.* 1. walk lamely —*n.* 2. limping gait

limpet ('limpit) *n.* shellfish which sticks tightly to rocks

limpid ('limpid) *a.* 1. clear 2. translucent —**lim'pidity** *n.* —**'limpidly** *adv.*

linchpin ('linchpin) *n.* 1. pin to hold wheel on its axle 2. essential person or thing

Lincoln ('lingkən) *n.* **Abraham.** the 16th President of the U.S. (1861-65)

linden ('lindən) *n.* deciduous tree with fragrant flowers, the lime

line (līn) *n.* 1. long narrow mark 2. stroke made with pen *etc.* 3. continuous length without breadth 4. row 5. series, course 6. telephone connection 7. progeny 8. province of activity 9. shipping company 10. railroad track 11. any class of goods 12. cord 13. string 14. wire 15. advice, guidance —*vt.* 16. cover inside of 17. mark with lines 18. bring into line 19. be, form border, edge of —**'linage** *n.* number of lines in piece of written or printed matter —**lineage** ('liniij) *n.* descent from, descendants of an ancestor —**lineal** ('liniəl) *a.* of lines 2. in direct line of descent —**lineament** ('liniəmənt) *n.* feature —**linear** ('liniər) *a.* of, in lines —**lineation** (lini'āshən) *n.* 1. marking with lines 2. arrangement of or division into lines —**'liner** *n.* large ship or aircraft of passenger line —**'lining** *n.* covering for inside of garment *etc.* —**Linear B** form of writing employing syllabic characters used from the 15th to the 12th centuries B.C. for documents in the Mycenean language —**linear measure** system of units for measurement of length —**'linebacker** *n.* defensive football player immediately behind the line of scrimmage —**line drawing** drawing made with lines only —**'lineman** *n.* football player in the forward line —**line printer** electro-mechanical device that prints a line of characters at a time —**line score** score of baseball game showing hits, runs and errors of each team —**'linesman** *n.* in some sports, official who helps referee, umpire —**line-up** *n.* 1. row or arrangement of people or things assembled for particular purpose 2. members of team taking part in a game —**get a line on** obtain all relevant information about —**line of credit** maximum credit allowed to borrower or holder of charge card —**line of fire** flight path of missile discharged from firearm —**line up 1.** form, put into or organize line-up **2.** produce, organize and assemble **3.** align —**out of line** inappropriate

linen ('linin) *a.* 1. made of flax —*n.* 2. cloth made of flax 3. linen articles collectively 4. sheets, tablecloths *etc.;* shirts (orig. made of linen)

ling[1] (ling) *n.* slender food fish

ling[2] (ling) *n.* heather

-ling (*comb. form*) 1. person or thing associated with group, activity or quality specified, as in *nestling, underling* 2. diminutive, as in *duckling*

linger ('linggər) *vi.* delay, loiter, remain long

lingerie (länzhə'rä) *n.* women's underwear or nightwear

lingo ('linggō) *n. inf.* language, speech, *esp.* applied to dialects (*pl.* -**es**)

lingua franca ('linggwə 'frangkə) language used for communication between people of different mother tongues (*pl.* **lingua francas, linguae francae** ('linggwē 'frangkē))

lingual ('linggwəl) *a.* 1. of the tongue or language —*n.* 2. sound made by the tongue, as *d, l, t* —**'linguist** *n.* one skilled in languages or language study —**lin'guistic** *a.* of languages or their study —**lin'guistics** *pl.n.* (*with sing. v.*) study, science of language

liniment ('linimənt) *n.* embrocation

link (lingk) *n.* 1. ring of a chain 2. connection 3. unit of measure, 7.92 in. —*vt.* 4. join with, as with, link 5. intertwine —*vi.* 6. be so joined —**'linkage** *n.* —**'linkman** *n.* presenter of television or radio program consisting of number of outside broadcasts from different locations

links (lingks) *pl.n.* golf course

linnet ('linit) *n.* songbird of finch family

linoleum (li'nōliəm) *n.* floor covering of burlap with smooth, hard, decorative coating of powdered cork, linseed oil *etc.* —**linoleum block 1.** design carved in relief on mounted linoleum **2.** a print from this

linseed ('linsēd) *n.* seed of flax plant —**linseed oil** yellow oil extracted from it

linsey-woolsey (linzi'wŏŏlzi) *n.* rough fabric of linen warp and coarse wool or cotton filling

lint (lint) *n.* 1. shreds or bits of thread 2. staple cotton fiber

lintel ('lintəl) *n.* top piece of door or window

lion ('līən) *n.* large social feline of Africa and S Asia with a shaggy mane in the adult male ('**lioness** *fem.*) —**'lionize** *vt.* treat as celebrity —**lion-hearted** *a.* brave —**the lion's share** largest portion

lip (lip) *n.* 1. either edge of the mouth 2. edge or margin 3. *sl.* impudence —**lip-reading** *n.* method of understanding spoken words by interpreting movements of speaker's lips —**lip service** insincere tribute or respect —**'lipstick** *n.* cosmetic preparation in stick form, for coloring lips —**lip sync** (singk) synchronizing lip movements with recorded sound

lipoma (li'pōmə) *n.* slow-growing tumor of fat tissue

lipotropic factors (lipō'trōpik) substances preventing or reversing abnormal accumulation of fat in the liver

liqueur (li'kyŏŏər -'kŏŏər; *Fr.* lē'kœr) *n.* alcoholic liquor flavored and sweetened

liquid ('likwid) *a.* 1. fluid, not solid or gaseous 2. flowing smoothly 3. (of assets) in form of money or easily converted into money —*n.* 4. matter in fluid phase in which surface is free, volume is definite, and shape determined by the container —**lique'faction** *n.* —**'liquefy** *v.* make or become liquid —**li'quescence** *n.* —**li'quescent** *a.* tending to become liquid —**'liquidize** *v.* —**'liquidizer** *n.* kitchen appliance with blades for puréeing vegetables, blending liquids *etc.* (*also* **'blender**) —**liquid air** air reduced to liquid state on application of increased pressure at low temperature —**liquid crystal display** display of numbers, *esp.* in electronic calculator, using cells containing a liquid with crystal-line properties, that change their reflectivity when an electric field is applied to them —**liquid gold** suspension of finely-divided gold particles in oil, used chiefly in gilding —**liquid measure** system of units for measuring volumes of liquids or their containers

liquidate ('likwidāt) *vt.* 1. pay (debt) 2. arrange affairs of and dissolve (company) 3. wipe out, kill —**liqui'dation** *n.* 1. process of clearing up financial affairs 2. state of being bankrupt —**'liquidator** *n.* official appointed to liquidate business —**li'quidity** *n.* state of being able to meet financial obligations

liquor ('likər) *n.* 1. alcoholic drink 2. juice produced by boiling food

liquorice ('likərish, 'likrish; -ris) *n. see* LICORICE

lira ('lēərə; *It.* 'lēra) *n.* monetary unit of Italy and Turkey (*pl.* **lire** ('lēəri; *It.* 'lērā), -**s**)

lisle (līl) *n.* fine hand-twisted cotton thread

lisp (lisp) *vi.* 1. speak with faulty pronunciation of 's' and 'z' 2. speak falteringly —*n.* 3. such pronunciation or speech

lissome *or* **lissom** ('lisəm) *a.* 1. supple 2. agile

list[1] (list) *n.* 1. inventory, register 2. catalog 3. edge of cloth —*pl.* 4. field for combat —*vt.* 5. place on list —**list price** selling price of merchandise as quoted in catalog or advertisement

list[2] (list) *vi.* 1. (of ship) lean to one side —*n.* 2. inclination of ship

listen ('lisən) *vi.* try to hear, attend (to) —**'listener** *n.*

listless ('listlis) *a.* indifferent, languid —**'listlessly** *adv.*

lit (lit) *pt./pp. of* LIGHT[1], LIGHT[2]

litany ('litəni) *n.* prayer with responses from congregation

litchi

litchi, lichee, *or* **lychee** ('līchē) *n.* 1. Chinese tree with red edible fruits 2. fruit of this tree, which has whitish juicy pulp (*also* **litchi nut**)

liter ('lētər) *n.* unit of volume in metric system, exactly 1000 cm³, 1m³ or 10 deciliters or approximately 0.908 dry quart and 1.057 liquid quarts

literal ('litərəl) *a.* 1. according to sense of actual words, not figurative 2. exact in wording 3. of letters —**'literalism** *n.* 1. disposition to take words and statements in literal sense 2. literal or realistic portrayal in art or literature —**'literally** *adv.*

literate ('litərit) *a.* 1. able to read and write 2. educated —*n.* 3. literate person —**'literacy** *n.* —**literati** (litə'rātē) *pl.n.* scholarly, literary people

literature ('litərichŏŏər, 'litri-; -chər) *n.* 1. books and writings, *esp.* of particular country, period or subject 2. *inf.* printed material —**lite'rarily** *adv.* —**'literary** *a.* of or learned in literature

lithe (līdh, līth) *a.* supple, pliant —**'lithesome** *a.* lissome, supple

lithium ('lithiəm) *n. Chem.* metallic element *Symbol* Li, at. wt. 6.9, at. no. 3

litho ('līthō) *n.* 1. lithography 2. lithograph (*pl.* -**s**) —*a.* 3. lithographic —*adv.* 4. lithographically

litho- *or before vowel* **lith-** (*comb. form*) stone, as in *lithograph*

lithography (li'thogrəfi) *n.* method of printing from metal or stone block using the antipathy of grease and water —**'lithograph** *n.* 1. print so produced —*vt.* 2. print thus —**li'thographer** *n.* —**litho'graphic** *a.*

lithotomy (lith'otəmi) *n.* operation to remove stones from urinary bladder

litigate ('litigāt) vt. 1. contest in law —vi. 2. carry on a lawsuit —**litigant** n./a. (person) conducting a lawsuit —**liti'gation** n. lawsuit —**litigious** (li'tijəs) a. 1. given to engaging in lawsuits 2. disputatious

litmus ('litməs) n. blue dye turned red by acids and restored to blue by alkali —**litmus paper**

litotes ('lītətēz) n. ironical understatement for rhetorical effect (pl. **-tes**)

Litt.D. or **Lit.D.** 1. Doctor of Letters 2. Doctor of Literature

litter ('litər) n. 1. untidy refuse 2. odds and ends 3. young of animal produced at one birth 4. straw etc. as bedding for animals 5. portable couch 6. kind of stretcher for wounded —v. 7. strew (with) litter 8. give birth to (young) —**litterbug** n. sl. person who drops refuse in public places

little ('litəl) a. 1. small, not much (**less, least**) —n. 2. small quantity —adv. 3. to a small extent 4. not much or often 5. not at all (**less, least**) —**Little Bear, Little Dipper** Ursa Minor —**little people** Folklore small supernatural beings, such as leprechauns —**little slam** Bridge bidding for and winning twelve tricks (also **small slam**)

littoral ('litərəl) a. 1. pert. to the seashore —n. 2. coastal district

liturgy ('litərji) n. prescribed form of public worship —**li'turgical** a.

live[1] (liv) v. 1. have life 2. pass one's life 3. continue in life 4. continue, last 5. dwell 6. feed —**livable** or **liveable** a. 1. suitable for living in 2. tolerable —**liver** n. person who lives in specified way —**living** n. 1. action of being in life 2. people now alive 3. way of life 4. means of living 5. church benefice —**living room** room in house used for relaxation and entertainment —**living wage** wage adequate to maintain person and his family in reasonable comfort —**live down** overcome (past misdeeds)

live[2] (līv) a. 1. living, alive 2. active, vital 3. flaming 4. (of rail etc.) carrying electric current 5. (of broadcast) transmitted during the actual performance —**liveliness** n. —**lively** a. brisk, active, vivid —**liven** vt. (esp. with up) make (more) lively —**live oak** evergreen oak of southeastern U.S. —**livestock** n. domestic animals —**live wire** 1. wire carrying electric current 2. able, very energetic person

livelihood ('līvlihŏŏd) n. 1. means of living 2. subsistence, support

livelong ('liv'long) a. lasting throughout the whole day

liver ('livər) n. 1. organ secreting bile 2. animal liver as food —**liverish** a. 1. unwell, as from liver upset 2. cross, touchy, irritable —**liver fluke** parasitic flatworm inhabiting bile ducts of sheep, cattle etc. —**liver sausage** sausage made of pork liver and seasonings —**liver spots** light brown spots on skin of usu. middle-aged or older persons —**liverwurst** ('livərwərst) n. liver sausage

liverwort ('livərwərt) n. simple land plant resembling moss but lacking radial symmetry

livery ('livəri) n. 1. distinctive dress of person or group, esp. servant(s) 2. allowance of food for horses 3. a livery stable —**liveried** a. (esp. of servants etc.) wearing livery —**liveryman** n. member of a London guild —**livery stable** stable where horses are kept at a charge or hired out

lives (līvz) n., pl. of LIFE

livid ('livid) a. 1. of a bluish pale color 2. discolored, as by bruising 3. inf. angry, furious

lizard ('lizərd) n. four-footed reptile

L.L. 1. Late Latin 2. Low Latin

llama ('lämə) n. woolly animal used as beast of burden in S Amer.

LL.B. Bachelor of Laws

LL.D. Doctor of Laws

Lloyd's (loidz) n. association of London underwriters originally concerned with marine insurance and shipping information and now subscribing a variety of insurance policies and publishing daily list (**Lloyd's List**) of shipping data and news

loach (lōch) n. carplike freshwater fish

load (lōd) n. 1. burden 2. amount usu. carried at once 3. actual load carried by vehicle 4. resistance against which engine has to work 5. amount of electrical energy drawn from a source —vt. 6. put load on or into 7. charge (gun) 8. weigh down —**loaded** a. 1. carrying a load 2. (of dice) dishonestly weighted 3. biased 4. (of question) containing hidden trap or implication 5. sl. wealthy 6. sl. drunk

loadstar ('lōdstär) n. see lodestar at LODE

loadstone ('lōdstōn) n. see lodestone at LODE

loaf[1] (lōf) n. 1. mass of bread as baked 2. shaped mass of food (pl. **loaves**)

loaf[2] (lōf) vi. idle, loiter —**loafer** n. idler

Loafer ('lōfər) n. trade name for shoe resembling a moccasin

loam (lōm) n. fertile soil

loan (lōn) n. 1. act of lending 2. thing lent 3. money borrowed at interest 4. permission to use —vt. 5. lend, grant loan of

loath or **loth** (lōth, lōdh) a. unwilling, reluctant —**loathe** (lōdh) vt. hate, abhor —**loathing** ('lōdhing) n. 1. disgust 2. repulsion —**loathsome** ('lōthsəm, 'lōdhsəm) a. disgusting

loaves (lōvz) n., pl. of LOAF[1]

lob (lob) n. 1. in tennis etc., shot pitched high in air —v. 2. throw, pitch (shot) thus (**-bb-**)

lobby ('lobi) n. 1. corridor into which rooms open 2. passage or room in legislative building, esp. houses of parliament of Britain and Aust., to which the public has access or one of two rooms where members indicate their vote 3. group which tries to influence members of lawmaking assembly —**lobbying** n. frequenting lobby to collect news or influence members —**lobbyist** n. person employed by particular interest to lobby

lobe (lōb) n. 1. any rounded projection 2. subdivision of body organ 3. soft, hanging part of ear —**lobar** a. of lobe —**lobate** a. 1. having or resembling lobes 2. (of birds) having separate toes each fringed with weblike lobe —**lobed** a. —**lo'bectomy** n. surgical removal of a lobe of an organ —**lo'botomy** n. any of various surgical methods of treating certain mental disorders (also **prefrontal lobotomy, leucotomy**)

lobelia (lō'bēlyə, -liə) n. garden plant with blue, red or white flowers

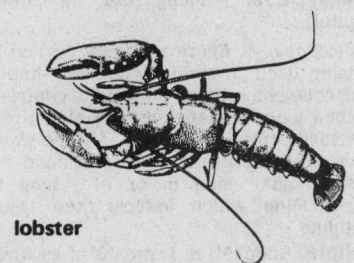

lobster

lobster ('lobstər) n. shellfish with long tail and claws, turning red when boiled

lobworm ('lobwərm) n. lugworm

local ('lōkəl) a. 1. of, existing in particular place 2. confined to a definite spot, district or part of the body 3. of place —n. 4. person belonging to a district 5. inf. (nearby) pub —**locale** (lō'kal) n. scene of event —**lo'cality** n. 1. place, situation 2. district —**'localize** vt. assign, restrict to definite place —**'locally** adv. —**local anesthetic** anesthetic which produces insensibility in one part of body —**local color** behavior etc. characteristic of a certain region or time, introduced into novel etc. to supply realism

locate ('lōkāt, lō'kāt) vt. 1. attribute to a place 2. find the place of 3. situate —**lo'cation** n. 1. placing 2. situation 3. site of motion-picture production away from studio 4. SA Black Afr. or Colored township —**locative** ('lokətiv) a./n. (of) grammatical case denoting 'place where'

loch (lok, lokh) n. Scottish lake or long narrow bay

loci ('lōsī) n., pl. of LOCUS

lock[1] (lok) n. 1. appliance for fastening door, lid etc. 2. mechanism for firing gun 3. enclosure in river or canal for moving boats from one level to another 4. extent to which vehicle's front wheels will turn 5. appliance to check the revolution of a wheel 6. interlocking 7. block, jam —vt. 8. fasten, make secure with lock 9. join firmly 10. cause to become immovable 11. embrace closely —vi. 12. become fixed or united 13. become immovable —**locker** n. small cupboard with lock —**lockkeeper** n. person tending lock on river or canal —**locknut** n. second nut used on top of first on bolt to prevent it shaking loose —**lockout** n. exclusion of workmen by employers as means of coercion —**locksmith** n. one who makes and mends locks —**lockup** n. sl. prison —**lock, stock and barrel** completely

lock[2] (lok) n. tress of hair

locket ('lokit) n. small hinged pendant for portrait etc.

lockjaw ('lokjō) n. tetanus

loco ('lōkō) inf. locomotive

locoism ('lōkōizəm) n. disease of domestic livestock marked by erratic behavior caused by eating locoweed (also **loco, loco disease**) —**'loco** a. crazy —**'locoweed** n. any of various leguminous plants of southwestern U.S. causing locoism

locomotive (lōkə'mōtiv) n. 1. engine for pulling carriages on railroad tracks —a. 2. having power of moving from place to place —**loco'motion** n. action, power of moving

locomotor ataxia (lōkə'mōtər ə'taksiə) tabes dorsalis

locum tenens ('lōkəm 'tēnenz) Lat. substitute, esp. for doctor or clergyman during absence (pl. **locum tenentes** (tə'nentēz)) (also **'locum**) —**locum tenency**

locus ('lōkəs) n. 1. exact place or locality 2. Math. any set of points that satisfy certain conditions and no points that do not 3. position of gene in a chromosome (pl. **loci**)

locust ('lōkəst) n. destructive winged insect —**locust bean** bean-shaped fruit of locust tree —**locust tree** 1. N. Amer. leguminous tree having prickly branches, white flowers and reddish-brown seed pods 2. the carob

locution (lō'kyōōshən) n. 1. a phrase 2. speech 3. mode or style of speaking

lode (lōd) n. a vein of ore —**'lodestar** or **'loadstar** n. Pole Star —**'lodestone** or **'loadstone** n. magnetic iron ore

loden ('lōdən) n. 1. thick soft woolen cloth used for outer clothing 2. dull grayish green

lodge (loj) *n*. 1. house, cabin used seasonally or occasionally, *eg* for hunting, skiing 2. gatekeeper's house 3. meeting place of branch of Freemasons *etc*. 4. the branch 5. beaver's or otter's dwelling —*vt*. 6. house 7. deposit 8. bring (a charge *etc*.) against someone —*vi*. 9. live in another's house at fixed charge 10. come to rest —'**lodger** *n*. —'**lodging** *n*. rented room(s) in another person's house —'**lodgment** *or* '**lodgement** *n*. lodging, being lodged

loft (loft) *n*. 1. space between top story and roof 2. gallery in church *etc*. —*vt*. 3. send (golf ball *etc*.) high —'**loftily** *adv*. haughtily —'**loftiness** *n*. —'**lofty** *a*. 1. of great height, elevated 2. haughty

log[1] (log) *n*. 1. portion of felled tree stripped of branches 2. detailed record of voyages, time traveled *etc*. of ship, aircraft *etc*. 3. apparatus used formerly for measuring ship's speed —*vt*. 4. keep a record of 5. travel (specified distance, time) (**-gg-**) —'**logger** *n*. lumberjack —'**logging** *n*. cutting and transporting logs to river —'**logbook** *n*.

log[2] (log) *n*. logarithm

logan ('lōgən) *n*. C *see* BOGAN

loganberry ('lōgənberi) *n*. 1. trailing prickly plant, cross between raspberry and blackberry 2. its purplish-red fruit

logarithm ('logəridhəm) *n*. the exponent of the power to which a fixed number is to be raised to produce a given number —**loga-'rithmic** *a*.

loggerhead ('logərhed) *n*. —**at loggerheads** quarreling, disputing

loggia ('lōjiə, 'löjä) *n*. covered, arcaded gallery (*pl*. **-s**, **loggie** ('löjä))

logic ('lojik) *n*. 1. art or philosophy of reasoning 2. reasoned thought or argument 3. coherence of various facts, events *etc*. —'**logical** *a*. 1. of logic 2. according to reason 3. reasonable 4. apt to reason correctly —'**logically** *adv*. —lo'**gician** *n*.

logistics (lō'jistiks, lə-) *pl.n*. (*with sing. or pl. v.*) 1. the transport, housing and feeding of troops 2. organization of any project, operation —lo'**gistical** *a*.

logo ('logō) *n*. company emblem or motto (*pl*. **-s**)

Logos ('lōgos, -gōs) *n*. the Divine Word incarnate, Christ

-logue *or* **-log** (*comb. form*) 1. speech or discourse of particular kind, as in *monologue* 2. field of specialist study, as in *pedagogue*, *sinologue*

-logy (*n. comb. form*) 1. science or study of, as in *musicology* 2. writing, discourse or body of writings, as in *trilogy, phraseology, martyrology* —'**logical** *or* **-logic** (*a. comb. form*) —'**logist** (*n. comb. form*)

loin (loin) *n*. 1. part of body between ribs and hip 2. cut of meat from this —*pl*. 3. hips and lower abdomen —'**loincloth** *n*. garment covering loins only

loiter ('loitər) *vi*. 1. dawdle, hang about 2. idle —'**loiterer** *n*.

loll (lol) *vi*. 1. sit, lie lazily 2. (*esp*. of the tongue) hang out —*vt*. 3. hang out (tongue)

lollipop *or* **lollypop** ('lolipop) *n*. hard candy on small wooden stick

London ('lundən) *n*. the capital of England and of the United Kingdom —**London broil** broiled flank steak cut across the grain in thin slices

lone (lōn) *a*. solitary —'**loneliness** *n*. —'**lonely** *a*. 1. sad because alone 2. unfrequented 3. solitary, alone —'**loner** *n*. *inf*. one who prefers to be alone —'**lonesome** *a*. lonely

long[1] (long) *a*. 1. having length, *esp*. great length, in space or time 2. extensive 3. protracted —*adv*. 4. for a long time —'**longbow** *n*. *esp*. in medieval England, large powerful hand-drawn bow —**long division** process of dividing one number by another and putting steps down in full —**long-drawn-out** *a*. overprolonged, extended —'**longhair** *a*. *inf*. of intellectuals or their tastes, *esp*. preferring classical music to jazz *etc*. (*also* **long-haired**) —'**longhand** *n*. writing of words, letters *etc*. in full —**long-headed** *a*. astute; shrewd; sagacious —**long johns** *inf*. underpants with long legs —**long jump** athletic contest in which competitors try to cover farthest distance possible with running jump from fixed board or mark —**long-playing** *a*. (of record) to be played at 33 1/3 revolutions per minute, a microgroove record —**long-range** *a*. 1. of the future 2. able to travel long distances without refueling 3. (of weapons) designed to hit distant target —**long shot** competitor, undertaking, bet *etc*. with small chance of success —**long-standing** *a*. existing for a long time —**long-term** *a*. 1. lasting or extending over a long time 2. *Fin*. maturing after a long period —**long ton** the imperial ton (2240 lbs.) —**long wave** radio wave with wavelength greater than 1000 meters —**long-winded** *a*. tediously loquacious —**the long and the short of it** all that needs to be said

long[2] (long) *vi*. have keen desire, yearn —'**longing** *n*. yearning

long. longitude

longeron ('lonjəron) *n*. long spar running fore and aft in body of aircraft

longevity (lon'jeviti) *n*. long existence or life

longitude ('lonjityōōd, -'tōōd) *n*. distance east or west from Greenwich meridian —**longi'tudinal** *a*. 1. of length or longitude 2. lengthwise

longshoreman ('longshörmən) *n*. person who loads and unloads ships at a seaport

loofah ('lōōfə) *n*. 1. pod of plant used as sponge 2. the plant

look (lōōk) *vi*. 1. direct, use eyes 2. face 3. seem 4. (*with* for) search 5. (*with* for) hope 6. (*with* after) take care (of) —*n*. 7. looking 8. view 9. search 10. (*oft. pl.*) appearance —**looker-on** *n*. spectator —**looking glass** mirror —'**lookout** *n*. 1. guard 2. place for watching 3. prospect 4. watchman 5. *inf*. worry, concern —**good looks** beauty —**look after** tend —**look down on** despise

loom[1] (lōōm) *n*. 1. machine for weaving 2. middle part of oar

loom[2] (lōōm) *vi*. 1. appear dimly 2. seem ominously close 3. assume great importance

loon[1] (lōōn) *n*. any of several large fish-eating diving birds of N Amer. best known for its haunting cry

loon[2] (lōōn) *n*. *inf*. stupid, foolish person —'**loony** *a./n*. —**loony bin** *inf*. mental hospital

loop (lōōp) *n*. 1. figure made by curved line crossing itself 2. similar rounded shape in cord, rope *etc*. crossed on itself 3. contraceptive coil 4. aerial maneuver in which aircraft describes complete circle 5. *Figure skating* curve crossing itself made on single edge —*vt*. 6. make loop in or of —**loop line** railroad line which leaves, then rejoins, main line

loophole ('lōōphōl) *n*. 1. means of escape, of evading rule without infringing it 2. vertical slit in wall, *esp*. for defense

loose (lōōs) *a*. 1. not tight, fastened, fixed or tense 2. slack 3. vague 4. dissolute —*vt*. 5. free 6. unfasten 7. slacken —*vi*. 8. (*with* off) shoot, let fly (bullet *etc*.) —'**loosely** *adv*. —'**loosen** *v*. make or become loose —'**looseness** *n*. —'**loose-jointed** *a*. 1. supple and easy in movement 2. loosely built; with ill-fitting joints —'**loose-leaf** *a*. (of binder *etc*.) capable of being opened to allow removal and addition of pages —**on the loose** 1. free 2. *inf*. on a spree

loot (lōōt) *n./v*. plunder

lop[1] (lop) *vt*. (*usu. with* off) 1. cut away (twigs and branches) from tree 2. chop (off) (**-pp-**)

lop[2] (lop) *vi*. hang limply (**-pp-**) —**lop-eared** *a*. having drooping ears —'**lop'sided** *a*. with one side lower than the other, badly balanced

lope (lōp) *vi*. run with long, easy strides

loquacious (lō'kwāshəs) *a*. talkative —lo'**quacity** (lō'kwasiti) *n*.

loquat ('lōkwot) *n*. 1. Asian evergreen tree of rose family 2. its yellow edible fruit

lor (lör) *interj*. *nonstandard* exclamation of surprise or dismay

loran ('lörən) *n*. radio navigation system operating over long distances

lord (lörd) *n*. 1. British nobleman, peer of the realm 2. feudal superior 3. one ruling others 4. owner 5. God —*v*. 6. be domineering (*esp. in* **lord it over someone**) —'**lordliness** *n*. —'**lordly** *a*. 1. imperious, proud 2. fit for a lord —'**lordship** *n*. 1. rule, ownership 2. domain 3. title of some noblemen —**Lord Mayor** mayor in City of London and certain other boroughs —**Lord Spiritual** archbishop or bishop in the House of Lords (*pl*. **Lords Spiritual**) —**Lord Temporal** peer who is not archbishop or bishop in the House of Lords (*pl*. **Lords Temporal**) —**the Lord's Day** Christian Sabbath; Sunday —**the Lord's Prayer** prayer taught by Jesus Christ to his disciples (*also* **Our Father, Pater'noster**) —**the Lord's Supper** *see* **Holy Communion** *at* HOLY

lordosis (lör'dōsis) *n*. exaggeration of normal forward curve of lower spine (*also* **hollow back**)

lore (lör) *n*. 1. learning 2. body of facts and traditions

lorgnette (lör'nyet) *n*. pair of eyeglasses mounted on long handle

lorikeet ('löriket) *n*. small parrot

loris ('löris) *n*. tree-dwelling, nocturnal Asian animal (*pl*. **-ris**)

lorn (lörn) *a*. *poet*. 1. abandoned 2. desolate

lory ('löri) *n*., **lowry**, *or* **lowrie** *n*. small, brightly colored parrot of Aust. and Indonesia

lose (lōōz) *vt*. 1. be deprived of, fail to retain or use 2. let slip 3. fail to get 4. (of clock *etc*.) run slow by (specified amount) 5. be defeated in —*vi*. 6. suffer loss (**lost** *pt./pp*., '**losing** *pr.p*.) —'**loser** *n*. 1. person or thing that loses 2. *inf*. person or thing that seems destined to fail *etc*. —**loss** (los) *n*. 1. a losing 2. what is lost 3. harm or damage resulting from losing —**lost** (lost) *a*. 1. unable to be found 2. unable to find one's way 3. bewildered 4. not won 5. not utilized

lot (lot) *pron*. 1. great number —*n*. 2. collection 3. large quantity 4. share 5. fate 6. destiny 7. item at auction 8. one of a set of objects used to decide something by chance (*esp. in* **to cast lots**) 9. area of land —*pl*. 10. *inf*. great numbers or quantity —*adv*. 11. *inf*. a great deal

loth (lōth, lōdh) *a*. *see* LOATH

lotion ('lōshən) *n*. liquid for washing wounds, improving skin *etc*.

lotos ('lōtəs) *n*. *see* LOTUS

lottery ('lotəri) *n*. 1. method of raising funds by selling tickets and prizes by chance 2. gamble

lotto ('lotō) *n.* game of chance like bingo

lotus *or* **lotos** ('lōtəs) *n.* **1.** legendary plant whose fruits induce forgetfulness when eaten **2.** Egyptian water lily —**lotus-eater** *n. Gk myth.* one of people encountered by Odysseus in N Afr. who lived in indolent forgetfulness, drugged by fruit of legendary lotus —**lotus position** seated cross-legged position in yoga

loud (lowd) *a.* **1.** strongly audible **2.** noisy **3.** obtrusive —'**loudly** *adv.* —'**loud'mouth** *n. inf.* person who brags or talks too loudly —'**loud'mouthed** *a.* —'**loud'speaker** *n.* instrument for converting electrical signals into sound audible at a distance

lough (lok, lokh) *n.* in Ireland, lake

Louisiana (looēzi'anə) *n.* West South Central state of the U.S., admitted to the Union in 1812. *Abbrev.:* **LA** (with ZIP code)

lounge (lownj) *vi.* **1.** sit, lie, walk or stand in a relaxed manner —*n.* **2.** living room of house **3.** general waiting, relaxing area in airport, hotel *etc.* —'**lounger** *n.* loafer

loup cervier (loō sər'vyā) *see* **Canada lynx** *at* CANADA

lour ('lowər) *see* LOWER

lourie ('lowri) *n.* S Afr. bird with bright plumage

louse (lows) *n.* parasitic insect (*pl.* **lice**) —**lousy** ('lowzi) *a.* **1.** *sl.* nasty, unpleasant **2.** (*with* with) *sl.* (too) generously provided, thickly populated (with) **3.** *sl.* bad, poor **4.** having lice

lout (lowt) *n.* crude, oafish person —'**loutish** *a.*

louver ('loōvər) *n./a.* **1.** (of) one of a set of boards or panes set parallel and slanted to admit air but not rain —*n.* **2.** ventilating structure of these

lovage ('luvij) *n.* European umbelliferous plant used for flavoring food

love (luv) *n.* **1.** warm affection **2.** benevolence **3.** charity **4.** sexual passion **5.** sweetheart **6.** *Tennis etc.* score of nothing —*vt.* **7.** admire passionately **8.** delight in —*vi.* **9.** be in love —'**lovable** *or* '**loveable** *a.* —'**loveless** *a.* —'**loveliness** *n.* —'**lovely** *a.* beautiful, delightful —'**lover** *n.* —'**loving** *a.* **1.** affectionate **2.** tender —'**lovingly** *adv.* —'**lovebird** *n.* **1.** small parrot **2.** *inf.* lover (*usu. pl.*) —**love child** *euphemistic* illegitimate child, bastard —**love-in-a-mist** *n.* garden plant with pale blue flowers —**love letter** —'**lovelorn** *a.* forsaken by, pining for a lover —**love seat** armchair or sofa for two persons —'**lovesick** *a.* pining or languishing because of love —'**lovesickness** *n.* —**loving cup** bowl formerly passed round at banquet —**make love (to)** have sexual intercourse (with)

low¹ (lō) *a.* **1.** not tall, high or elevated **2.** humble **3.** coarse, vulgar **4.** dejected **5.** ill **6.** not loud **7.** moderate **8.** cheap —'**lower** *vt.* **1.** cause, allow to descend **2.** move down **3.** degrade —*vi.* **4.** diminish —*a.* **5.** below in position or rank **6.** at an early stage, period of development —'**lowliness** *n.* —'**lowly** *a.* modest, humble —**low beam** short range of automobile headlight —'**low'born** *a. rare* of ignoble or common parentage —**low'bred** *a.* vulgar —'**lowbrow** *n./a.* (one) having no intellectual or cultural interests —'**lowdown** *n. inf.* inside information —**low-down** *a. inf.* base, shabby, dishonorable —**lower-case** *a.* **1.** of small letters —*vt.* **2.** print with lower-case letters —**lower class** social stratum having lowest position in social hierarchy —'**lower-class** *a.* **1.** of lower class **2.** inferior; vulgar —**lower house** one of houses of bicameral legislature, usu. the larger and more representative (*also* **lower chamber**) —**lower plant** nonflowering plant —**low**

frequency radio waveband with frequency between 30 and 300 kilohertz —**Low German** language of N Germany, spoken *esp.* in rural areas (*also* '**Plattdeutsch**) —**low-grade** *a.* of inferior quality —**low-key** *a.* subdued, restrained, not intense —**lowland** ('lōlənd) *n.* low-lying country —**lowlander** ('lōləndər) *n.* —**Low Mass** Mass that has simplified ceremonial form and is spoken rather than sung —**low-minded** *a.* having vulgar or crude mind and character —**low profile** position or attitude characterized by deliberate avoidance of prominence or publicity —**low season** period of low activity, *esp.* of resorts —**low-tension** *a.* carrying, operating at low voltage —**low tide 1.** tide at lowest level or time at which it reaches this **2.** lowest point —**low water 1.** low tide **2.** state of any stretch of water at its lowest level

low² (lō) *n.* **1.** cry of cattle, bellow —*vi.* **2.** (of cattle) utter their cry, bellow

lower *or* **lour** ('lowər) *vi.* **1.** look gloomy or threatening, as sky **2.** scowl —*n.* **3.** scowl, frown

lowrie ('lowri) *n. see* LORY

lox¹ (loks) *n.* smoked salmon

lox² (loks) *n. short for* liquid oxygen, *esp.* when used as oxidizer for rocket fuels

loyal ('loiəl) *a.* faithful, true to allegiance —'**loyalist** *n.* —'**Loyalist** *n.* C.United Empire Loyalist —'**loyally** *adv.* —'**loyalty** *n.* —**loyal toast** toast drunk in pledging allegiance to sovereign, usu. after meal

lozenge ('lozinj) *n.* **1.** rhombus, diamond figure **2.** small medicated candy shaped like this

LP long-playing (record)

LPG *or* **LP gas** liquid petroleum gas

Lr *Chem.* lawrencium

LSD 1. lysergic acid diethylamide (hallucinogenic drug) **2.** librae, solidi, denarii (*Lat.,* pounds, shillings, pence)

Lt. Lieutenant

ltd. Limited

Lu *Chem.* lutetium

lubber ('lubər) *n.* **1.** clumsy fellow **2.** unskilled seaman

lubricate ('loōbrikāt) *vt.* **1.** oil, grease **2.** make slippery —'**lubricant** *n.* substance used for this —**lubri'cation** *n.* —'**lubricator** *n.* —**lu'bricity** *n.* **1.** slipperiness, smoothness **2.** lewdness

lucent ('loōsənt) *a.* bright, shining

lucerne (loō'sərn) *n.* alfalfa

lucid ('loōsid) *a.* **1.** clear **2.** easily understood **3.** sane —**lu'cidity** *or* '**lucidness** *n.* —'**lucidly** *adv.*

Lucite ('loōsīt) *n.* trade name for acrylic resin that is used as a glass substitute in sheet form

luck (luk) *n.* **1.** fortune, good or bad **2.** good fortune **3.** chance —'**luckily** *adv.* fortunately —'**luckless** *a.* having bad luck —'**lucky** *a.* having good luck

lucre ('loōkər) *n. usu. facetious* money, wealth —'**lucrative** *a.* very profitable —**filthy lucre** *inf.* money

Luddite ('ludīt) *n.* **1.** orig. member of band of workmen organized to destroy machinery believing that its use led to unemployment **2.** person opposed to technological advance

ludicrous ('loōdikrəs) *a.* absurd, laughable, ridiculous

luff (luf) *n.* **1.** the part of fore-and-aft sail nearest mast —*v.* **2.** sail (ship) into wind so that sails flap —*vi.* **3.** (of sails) flap

lug¹ (lug) *v.* drag (something heavy) with effort (**-gg-**)

lug² (lug) *n.* **1.** projection, tag serving as handle or support **2.** *inf.* ear

luggage ('lugij) *n.* traveler's trunks and other baggage

lugger ('lugər) *n.* working boat (*eg* fishing, prawning lugger) orig. fitted with lugsail

lugsail ('lugsāl, -səl) *n.* oblong sail fixed on yard which hangs slanting on mast

lugubrious (loō'goōbriəs) *a.* mournful, doleful, gloomy —**lu'gubriously** *adv.*

lugworm ('lugwərm) *n.* large worm used as bait

Luke (loōk) *n. Bible* 3rd book of the N.T.: synoptic gospel presenting Christ as a man among men in this account written by the author of Acts

lukewarm ('loōk'wôrm) *a.* **1.** moderately warm, tepid **2.** unenthusiastic

lull (lul) *vt.* **1.** soothe, sing (to sleep) **2.** make quiet —*vi.* **3.** become quiet, subside —*n.* **4.** brief time of quiet in storm *etc.* —'**lullaby** ('lulⱥbī) *n.* lulling song, *esp.* for children

lumbar ('lumbər) *a.* relating to body between lower ribs and hips —**lumbago** (lum'bāgō) *n.* rheumatism in the lower part of the back

lumber ('lumbər) *n.* **1.** disused articles, useless rubbish **2.** sawn timber —*vi.* **3.** move heavily —*vt.* **4.** *inf.* burden with something unpleasant —'**lumberjack** *n.* man who fells trees and prepares logs for transport to mill —'**lumberyard** *n.* place where lumber and other building materials are sold

lumen ('loōmin) *n.* SI unit of luminous flux (*pl.* **-s, -mina** (-minə))

luminous ('loōminəs) *a.* **1.** bright **2.** shedding light **3.** glowing **4.** lucid —'**luminary** *n.* **1.** learned person **2.** heavenly body giving light —**lumi'nescence** *n.* emission of light at low temperatures by process (*eg* chemical) not involving burning —**lumi'nosity** *n.*

lump (lump) *n.* **1.** shapeless piece or mass **2.** swelling **3.** large sum —*vt.* **4.** (*oft. with* together) throw (together) in one mass or sum —*vi.* **5.** move heavily —'**lumpish** *a.* **1.** clumsy **2.** stupid —'**lumpy** *a.* **1.** full of lumps **2.** uneven —**lump sum** relatively large sum of money, paid at one time —**lump it** *inf.* put up with something

lunar ('loōnər) *a.* relating to the moon —**lunar module** module used to carry astronauts from spacecraft to surface of moon and back

lunatic ('loōnətik) *a.* **1.** insane —*n.* **2.** insane person —'**lunacy** *n.* —**lunatic asylum** *old name for* institution for mentally ill —**lunatic fringe** extreme, radical section of group *etc.*

lunch (lunch) *n.* **1.** meal taken in the middle of the day —*v.* **2.** eat, entertain to lunch —**luncheon** ('lunchən) *n.* a lunch

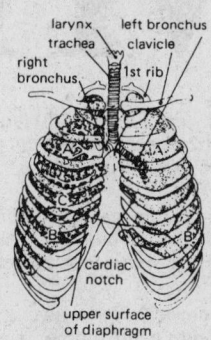

lungs
A upper lobes
B lower lobes
C middle lobe of right lung

larynx
trachea
left bronchus
clavicle
right bronchus
1st rib
cardiac notch
upper surface of diaphragm

lung (lung) *n.* one of the two organs of respiration in vertebrates —'**lungfish** *n.* type of fish with air-breathing lung —'**lungworm** *n.* parasitic worm infesting lungs of some animals —'**lungwort** *n.* flowering plant

lunge (lunj) *vi.* 1. thrust with sword *etc.* —*n.* 2. such thrust 3. sudden movement of body, plunge

lupine[1] *or* **lupin** ('lōōpin) *n.* leguminous plant with tall spikes of flowers

lupine[2] ('lōōpīn) *a.* like a wolf

lupus ('lōōpəs) *n.* skin disease characterized by skin lesions —**lupus erythematosus** (erithēmə'tōsəs) inflammatory disease of the connective or supporting tissues of the body —**lupus vulgaris** (vul'gāris) tuberculosis of the skin

lurch (lərch) *n.* 1. sudden roll to one side —*vi.* 2. stagger —**leave in the lurch** leave in difficulties

lurcher ('lərchər) *n.* crossbred dog trained to hunt silently

lure (lōōr) *n.* 1. something which entices 2. bait 3. power to attract —*vt.* 4. entice 5. attract

Lurex ('lōōəreks, 'lōōr-) *n.* trade name for metallic thread made from plastic-coated aluminum

lurid ('lōōrid) *a.* 1. vivid in shocking detail, sensational 2. pale, wan 3. lit with unnatural glare —'**luridly** *adv.*

lurk (lərk) *vi.* lie hidden —'**lurking** *a.* (of suspicion) not definite

luscious ('lushəs) *a.* 1. sweet, juicy 2. extremely pleasurable or attractive

lush[1] (lush) *a.* (of grass *etc.*) luxuriant and juicy, fresh

lush[2] (lush) *n. sl.* 1. heavy drinker 2. alcoholic —'**lushy** *a.*

lust (lust) *n.* 1. strong desire for sexual gratification 2. any strong desire —*vi.* 3. have passionate desire —'**lustful** *a.* —'**lustily** *adv.* —'**lusty** *a.* vigorous, healthy

luster *or* **lustre** ('lustər) *n.* 1. gloss, sheen 2. splendor 3. renown 4. glory 5. glossy material 6. metallic pottery glaze —'**lustrous** *a.* shining, luminous

lustration (lus'trāshən) *n.* purification by sacrifice —'**lustral** *a.* used in lustration —'**lustrate** *vt.*

lute[1] (lōōt) *n.* plucked stringed musical instrument with body in the shape of a halved pear from which extends a fretted angled neck —'**lutenist** *or* '**lutist** *n.*

lute[2] (lōōt) *n.* 1. composition to make joints airtight —*vt.* 2. close with lute

lutetium (lōō'tēshiəm) *n. Chem.* metallic element *Symbol* Lu, at. wt. 175.0, at. no. 71

Lutheran ('lōōthərən) *n.* 1. member of Protestant Christian denomination believing that salvation is by faith alone through grace —*a.* 2. of Lutheran Church —'**Lutheranism** *n.*

lutz (lōōts) *n. Ice-skating* jump from one skate with complete turn in air and return to other skate

lux (luks) *n.* SI unit of illumination (*pl.* **lux**)

luxe (lōōks, luks; *Fr.* lüks) *n. see* DE LUXE

Luxembourg *or* **Luxemburg** ('luksəmbərg) *n.* country in Europe bounded west by Belgium, south by France and east by West Germany —'**Luxembourger** *or* '**Luxemburger** *n.* —**Luxem'bourgian** *or* **Luxem'burgian** *a.*

luxury ('lukshəri, 'lugzhəri) *n.* 1. possession and use of costly, choice things for enjoyment 2. enjoyable but not necessary thing 3. comfortable surroundings —**luxuriance** (lug'zhōōriəns, luk'shōōr-) *n.* abundance, proliferation —**luxuriant** (lug'zhōōriənt, luk'shōōr-) *a.* 1. growing thickly 2. abundant —**luxuriantly** (lug'zhōōriəntli, luk'shōōr-) *adv.* —**luxuriate** (lug'zhōōriāt, luk'shōōr-) *vi.* 1. indulge in luxury 2. flourish profusely 3. take delight —**luxurious** (lug'zhōōriəs, luk'shōōr-) *a.* 1. fond of luxury 2. self-indulgent 3. sumptuous —**luxuriously** (lug'zhōōriəsli, luk'shōōr-) *adv.*

lyceum (lī'sēəm) *n.* public building for concerts *etc.*

lychee ('līchē) *n. see* LITCHI

lych-gate ('lichgāt) *n.* roofed gate of churchyard (*also* **lich-gate**)

Lycra ('līkrə) *n.* trade name for synthetic elastic polyurethane fiber

lyddite ('lidīt) *n.* powerful explosive used in shells

lye (lī) *n.* water made alkaline with wood ashes *etc.* for use as cleaning agent

lying ('līing) *pr.p. of* LIE[1], LIE[2] —**lying-in** *n.* confinement in childbirth (*pl.* **lyings-in**)

lymph (limf) *n.* colorless bodily fluid, mainly of white blood cells —**lym'phatic** *a.* 1. of lymph 2. flabby, sluggish —*n.* 3. vessel in the body conveying lymph —**lymph node** any of numerous bean-shaped masses of tissue, situated along course of lymphatic vessels

lymphogranuloma venereum ('limfōgranyə'lōma və'nēəriəm) infectious venereal disease caused by virus-like organism

lynch (linch) *vt.* put to death without trial —**lynch law** procedure of self-appointed court trying and executing accused

lynx

lynx (lingks) *n.* animal of cat family —**lynxeyed** *a.* having keen sight

lyre ('līər) *n* instrument like harp —**lyric** ('lirik) *n.* 1. lyric poem —*pl.* 2. words of popular song —**lyric(al)** ('lirik(əl)) *a.* 1. of short personal poems expressing emotion 2. of lyre 3. meant to be sung —**lyricist** ('lirisist) *n.* —**lyrist** ('lirist) *n.* 1. lyric poet 2. ('līərist) player on lyre —'**lyrebird** *n.* Aust. bird, the male of which displays tail shaped like a lyre —**wax lyrical** express great enthusiasm

lysogeny (lī'sojəni) *n.* the coexistence between a virus and a bacterium

-lyte (*n. comb. form*) substance that can be decomposed or broken down, as in *electrolyte* —**-lytic** (*a. comb. form*) loosening, dissolving, as in *paralytic*

Mm

m *or* **M** (em) *n.* 1. 13th letter of English alphabet 2. speech sound represented by this letter (*pl.* **m's, M's** *or* **Ms**)

m meter(s)

M 1. Mach 2. mega- 3. *Currency* mark(s) 4. million 5. Roman numeral, 1000

m. 1. male 2. married 3. masculine 4. mile 5. minute

M. 1. Medieval 2. Monsieur

ma (mä, mö) *n. inf.* mother

MA 1. Massachusetts 2. Maritime Administration

M.A. Master of Arts

ma'am (mäm) *n.* madam

Mac *or* **Macc** Maccabees

Mac-, Mc- *or* **M'-** (*comb. form*) in surnames of Gaelic origin, son of, as in *MacDonald*

macabre (mə'käbər, -brə) *a.* gruesome, ghastly

macadam (mə'kadəm) *n.* road surface made of pressed layers of small broken stones —**ma'cadamize** *vt.* pave (road) with this

macaroni (makə'rōni) *n.* pasta in long, thin tubes (*pl.* **-s, -es**)

macaroon (makə'rōōn) *n.* cookie made of egg white, sugar and almonds or coconut

macaw (mə'kö) *n.* kind of parrot

Maccabees ('makəbēz) *pl.n.* (*with sing. v.*)

Bible 45th and 46th books in the Douay Version of the O.T.

mace[1] (mās) *n.* 1. staff with metal head 2. staff of office

mace[2] (mās) *n.* spice made of the husk of the nutmeg

macerate ('masərāt) *v.* 1. soften by soaking 2. (cause to) waste away —**mace'ration** *n.*

Mach. *Bible* Machabees

Machabees ('makəbēz) *pl.n. see* MACCABEES

machete (mə'sheti, -'chēti, -'shet) *n.* broad, heavy knife used for cutting or as a weapon

Machiavellian (makiə'veliən) *a.* politically unprincipled, crafty, perfidious, subtle, deeplaid

machination (maki'nāshən) n. (usu. pl.) plotting, intrigue —'**machinate** v. lay or devise (plots)

machine (mə'shēn) n. **1.** apparatus combining action of several parts to apply mechanical force **2.** controlling organization **3.** mechanical appliance **4.** vehicle —vt. **5.** sew, print, shape etc. with machine —**ma-'chinery** n. **1.** parts of machine collectively **2.** machines —**ma'chinist** n. one who makes or works machines —**machine gun** gun firing repeatedly and continuously with an automatic loading and firing mechanism —**machine-readable** a. (of data) in a form that can be directly fed into a computer —**machine shop** workshop in which machine tools are operated —**machine tool** power-driven machine, such as lathe, for cutting or shaping metals etc.

machismo (mä'chēzmō, -'chiz-) n. strong or exaggerated masculine pride or masculinity (oft. **macho** ('mächō))

Mach (number) (mäk) n. the ratio of the air speed of an aircraft to the velocity of sound under given conditions

mackerel ('makrəl) n. edible sea fish with blue and silver stripes —**mackerel shark** see PORBEAGLE

mackinaw ('makinō) n. **1.** heavy blanket cloth, usu. plaid with nap on both sides **2.** short coat made from this or similar fabric **3.** blanket formerly distributed to Indians by U.S. government **4.** flat-bottomed boat

macramé (makrə'mā) n. ornamental work of knotted cord

macro- or before vowel **macr-** (comb. form) **1.** large, long, or great in size or duration, as in macroscopic **2.** Pathol. abnormal enlargement, as in macrocephaly

macrobiotic (makrōbī'otik) a. of dietary system advocating whole grain and vegetables in belief that it will prolong life

macrocosm ('makrəkozəm) n. **1.** the universe **2.** any large, complete system

macron ('mākron, 'makron, -krən) n. diacritical mark (−) placed over letter to represent long vowel

macroscopic (makrə'skopik) a. **1.** visible to the naked eye **2.** concerned with large units —**macro'scopically** adv.

mad (mad) a. **1.** suffering from mental disease, insane **2.** wildly foolish **3.** very enthusiastic **4.** excited **5.** inf. furious, angry —'**madden** vt. make mad —'**madly** adv. —'**madness** n. **1.** insanity **2.** folly —'**madhouse** n. inf. **1.** mental hospital or asylum **2.** state of uproar or confusion —'**madman** n.

Madagascar (madə'gaskər) n. country lying off the southeast of Africa from which it is separated by the Mozambique channel by the least distance of 250 miles —**Mada'gascan** n./a.

madam ('madəm) n. polite form of address to a woman used without name, esp. in correspondence (pl. **mesdames**)

madame (mə'dam, ma'dam, 'madəm) n. married Frenchwoman (pl. **mesdames**)

madcap ('madkap) n. **1.** reckless person —a. **2.** reckless

madder ('madər) n. **1.** climbing plant **2.** its root **3.** red dye made from this

made (mād) pt./pp. of MAKE —**made-up** a. **1.** invented **2.** wearing make-up **3.** put together

Madeira (mə'dēərə, -'dera) n. rich sherry wine

madeleine ('madələn) n. small rich cake shaped like a shell

mademoiselle (madmwə'zel, mam'zel) n. **1.** young unmarried French girl or woman **2.** French teacher or governess

Madison ('madisən) n. **James.** the 4th President of the U.S. (1809-17)

Madonna (mə'donə) n. **1.** the Virgin Mary **2.** picture or statue of her

madras (mə'dräs) n. woven cotton fabric available in varying weights and patterns, usu. stripes and plaids

madrepore ('madripör) n. kind of coral

madrigal ('madrigəl) n. **1.** unaccompanied part song **2.** short love poem or song

maelstrom ('mālstrəm, -strom) n. **1.** great whirlpool **2.** turmoil

maenad ('mēnad) n. Class. lit. frenzied female worshiper of Dionysus

maestoso (mī'stōsō) adv. Mus. grandly, in majestic manner

maestro ('mīstrō) n. **1.** outstanding musician, conductor **2.** man regarded as master of any art (pl. -**tri** (-trē), -**s**)

Mafia ('mäfiə, 'maf-) n. **1.** international secret criminal organization, orig. Italian **2.** (**m-**) clique, faction —**Mafi'oso** n. member of the Mafia

magazine ('magəzēn, magə'zēn) n. **1.** periodical publication with stories and articles by different writers **2.** appliance for supplying cartridges automatically to gun **3.** storehouse for explosives or arms

magenta (mə'jentə) a./n. (of) deep purplish-red color

maggot ('magət) n. grub, larva —'**maggoty** a. infested with maggots

magi ('mājī) pl.n. **1.** priests of ancient Persia **2.** the wise men from the East at the Nativity (sing. -**gus** (-gəs))

magic ('majik) n. **1.** art of supposedly invoking supernatural powers to influence events etc. **2.** any mysterious agency or power **3.** witchcraft, conjuring —a. **4.** magical, enchanting —'**magical** a. —'**magically** adv. —**ma'gician** n. one skilled in magic, wizard, conjurer, enchanter —**magic lantern** early form of projector using slides —**magic square** array of numbers in the form of a square characterized by the fact that every row and column and each diagonal has the same sum

magistrate ('majistrāt, -strit) n. **1.** civil officer administering law **2.** justice of the peace —**magis'terial** a. **1.** of, referring to magistrate **2.** dictatorial —'**magistracy** n. **1.** office of magistrate **2.** magistrates collectively

magma ('magmə) n. **1.** paste or suspension consisting of finely divided solid dispersed in liquid **2.** molten rock inside earth's crust

Magna Charta ('magnə 'kärtə) charter obtained from King John in 1215 establishing the English people's right to personal and political liberty

magna cum laude ('mägnə koom 'lowdə) Lat. (esp. of college or university degree) with great distinction

magnanimous (mag'naniməs) a. noble, generous, not petty —**magna'nimity** n.

magnate ('magnāt, -nit) n. influential or wealthy person

magnesium (mag'nēziəm) n. Chem. metallic element Symbol Mg, at. wt. 24.3, at. no. 12 —**mag'nesia** n. white powder compound of this, used in medicine

magnet ('magnit) n. **1.** piece of iron, steel having properties of attracting iron, steel and pointing north and south when suspended **2.** lodestone —**mag'netic** a. **1.** with properties of magnet **2.** exerting powerful attraction —**mag'netically** adv. —'**magnetism** n. **1.** magnetic phenomena **2.** science of magnetic phenomena **3.** personal charm or power of attracting others —'**magnetite** n.

black magnetizable mineral that is important source of iron —**magneti'zation** n. —'**magnetize** vt. **1.** make into a magnet **2.** attract as if by magnet **3.** fascinate —**magneto** (mag'nētō) n. apparatus for ignition in internal-combustion engine (pl. -**s**) —**magne'tometer** n. instrument used to measure magnetic force —'**magnetron** n. two-electrode electronic valve used with applied magnetic field to generate high-power microwave oscillations —**magnetic field** field of force surrounding permanent magnet or moving charged particle —**magnetic mine** mine designed to activate when magnetic field is detected —**magnetic needle** magnetized rod used in certain instruments for indicating direction of magnetic field —**magnetic north** direction in which compass needle points, usu. at angle from direction of true north —**magnetic pole 1.** either of two places on the earth's surface in the polar regions toward which a compass will point **2.** either pole of a magnet —**magnetic storm** sudden severe disturbance of earth's magnetic field —**magnetic tape** long coated plastic strip for recording sound or video signals

Magnificat (mag'nifikat) n. hymn of Virgin Mary in Luke 1. 46-55

magnificent (mag'nifisənt) a. **1.** splendid **2.** stately, imposing **3.** excellent —**mag'nificence** n. —**mag'nificently** adv.

magnify ('magnifī) vt. **1.** increase apparent size of, as with lens **2.** exaggerate **3.** make greater (-**fied, -fying**) —**magnifi'cation** n.

magniloquent (mag'niləkwənt) a. **1.** speaking pompously **2.** grandiose —**mag'niloquence** n.

magnitude ('magnityōod, -tōod) n. **1.** importance **2.** greatness, size

magnolia (mag'nōlyə) n. shrub or tree with large white, sweet-scented flowers

magnum ('magnəm) n. large wine bottle (approx. 1½ quarts)

magnum opus great work of art or literature

magpie ('magpī) n. black-and-white bird

Magyar ('magyär) n. **1.** member of prevailing people in Hungary **2.** native speech of Hungary —a. **3.** pert. to Magyars

maharaja or **maharajah** (mähə'räjə) n. former title of some Hindu princes ranking above a raja

maharani or **maharanee** (mähə'ränē) n. **1.** wife of maharaja **2.** woman holding rank of maharaja

maharishi (mə'härishi) n. Hindu religious teacher or mystic

mahatma (mə'hätmə) n. **1.** Hinduism man of saintly life with supernatural powers **2.** one endowed with great wisdom and power

mah-jongg (mä'zhong, -'jong) n. game for four players played with 144 tiles comprising 108 suit tiles, 28 honors and 8 flowers or seasons, the object of which is to obtain sets of tiles

mahlstick ('mölstik) n. see MAULSTICK

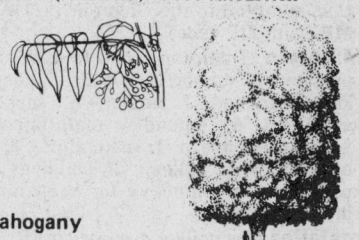

mahogany

mahogany (mə'hogəni) n. tree yielding reddish-brown wood

mahout (mə'howt) *n.* in India and E Indies, elephant driver or keeper

maiden ('mādən) *n.* **1.** *Lit.* young unmarried woman —*a.* **2.** unmarried **3.** of, suited to maiden **4.** first **5.** having blank record —**maid** *n.* **1.** *Lit.* young unmarried woman **2.** woman servant —**'maidenhood** *n.* —**'maidenly** *a.* modest —**'maidenhair** *n.* fern with delicate stalks and fronds —**'maidenhead** *n.* **1.** hymen **2.** virginity —**maiden name** woman's surname before marriage —**maid of honor 1.** principal unmarried attendant of bride **2.** unmarried lady attending queen or princess

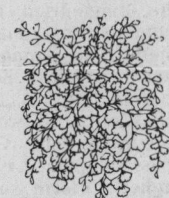

maidenhair

mail¹ (māl) *n.* **1.** letters *etc.* transported and delivered by the post office **2.** letters *etc.* conveyed at one time **3.** the postal system **4.** train, ship *etc.* carrying mail —*vt.* **5.** send by mail —**mail box 1.** public box for holding postal matter to be transmitted **2.** private box for holding letters *etc.* delivered by mailman —**'mailman** *n.* man who delivers, and sometimes collects, mail (*also* **'postman**) —**mail order 1.** order for merchandise sent by mail **2.** system of buying and selling merchandise through mail

mail² (māl) *n.* armor of interlaced rings or overlapping plates —**mailed** *a.* covered with mail

maillot (mī'ō, mä'yō) *n.* woman's one-piece bathing suit

maim (mām) *vt.* cripple, mutilate

main (mān) *a.* **1.** chief, principal, leading —*n.* **2.** principal pipe, line carrying water, electricity *etc.* **3.** chief part **4.** strength, power **5.** *obs.* open sea —**'mainly** *adv.* for the most part, chiefly —**main chance** one's own interests (*usu. in* **have an eye to the main chance**) —**main clause** *Gram.* clause that can stand alone as sentence —**main force** physical strength —**mainland** ('mānland, -lənd) *n.* stretch of land which forms main part of a country —**main line 1.** principal railroad line or highway **2.** *sl.* main vein into which narcotic drug can be injected —**'mainline** *vi. sl.* inject drug thus —**'mainmast** *n.* principal mast in ship —**mainsail** ('mānsāl; *Naut.* 'mānsəl) *n.* lowest sail of mainmast —**'mainspring** *n.* **1.** chief spring of watch or clock **2.** chief cause or motive —**'mainstay** *n.* **1.** rope from mainmast **2.** chief support —**'mainstream** *n.* **1.** main current (of river, cultural trend *etc.*) —*a.* **2.** of style of jazz that lies between traditional and modern

Maine (mān) *n.* New England state of the U.S., admitted to the Union in 1820. Abbrev.: **ME** (with ZIP code)

maintain (mān'tān) *vt.* **1.** carry on **2.** preserve **3.** support **4.** sustain **5.** keep up **6.** keep supplied **7.** affirm **8.** support by argument **9.** defend —**main'tainable** *a.* —**'maintenance** *n.* **1.** maintaining **2.** means of support **3.** upkeep of buildings *etc.* **4.** provision of money for separated or divorced spouse

maiolica (mə'yolikə) *n. see* MAJOLICA

maisonette (māzə'net) *n.* **1.** small house **2.** apartment occupying two floors

maître d'hôtel (mātrə dō'tel, metrə) *Fr.* head waiter or waitress

maize (māz) *n.* Indian corn

Maj. Major

majesty ('majisti) *n.* **1.** stateliness **2.** sovereignty **3.** grandeur —**ma'jestic** *a.* **1.** splendid **2.** regal —**ma'jestically** *adv.*

majolica (mə'jolikə) *or* **maiolica** *n.* type of ornamented Italian pottery

major ('mājər) *n.* **1.** army officer ranking next above captain **2.** major scale in music **3.** principal field of study at university *etc.* **4.** person of legal majority —*a.* **5.** greater in number, quality, extent **6.** significant, serious —*vi.* **7.** (*usu. with* in) do one's principal study (in particular subject) —**ma'jority** *n.* **1.** greater number **2.** larger party voting together **3.** excess of the vote on one side **4.** coming of age **5.** rank of major —**major-domo** (-'dōmō) *n.* house steward (*pl.* **-s**) —**major general** *Mil.* officer immediately junior to lieutenant general —**major scale** *Mus.* scale with semitones instead of whole tones after third and seventh notes

make (māk) *vt.* **1.** construct **2.** produce **3.** create **4.** establish **5.** appoint **6.** amount to **7.** cause to (do something) **8.** accomplish **9.** reach **10.** earn —*vi.* **11.** tend (**made**, **'making**) —*n.* **12.** brand, type, style —**'Maker** *n.* title given to God (as Creator) —**'making** *n.* **1.** creation —*pl.* **2.** necessary requirements or qualities —**make-believe** *n.* fantasy or pretense —**make-shift** *n.* temporary expedient —**make-up** *n.* **1.** cosmetics **2.** characteristics **3.** layout —**'makeweight** *n.* trifle added to make something stronger or better —(**go to**) **meet one's Maker** die —**make believe** pretend; enact fantasy —**make up 1.** compose **2.** compile **3.** complete **4.** compensate **5.** apply cosmetics **6.** invent —**on the make** *sl.* **1.** intent on gain **2.** in search of sexual partner

mako ('mākō) *n.* type of shark (*pl.* **-s**)

Mal *Bible* Malachi

mal- (*comb. form*) ill, badly, as in *malformation, malfunction*

malabsorption syndrome (maləb'sörp-shən) disease in which digestive tract is unable to absorb certain nutrients

malacca (mə'lakə) *a.* of brown cane used for walking stick or umbrella handle

Malachi ('maləkī) *n. Bible* 39th book of the O.T., last book in the English Canon, written by the prophet Malachi, stating the final message from God to a rebellious people

Malachias (malə'kīəs) *n. Bible* Malachi in the Douay Version of the O.T.

malachite ('maləkīt) *n.* green mineral used as gemstone and to make ornaments

maladjusted (malə'justid) *a.* **1.** *Psychol.* unable to meet the demands of society **2.** badly adjusted —**malad'justment** *n.*

maladministration (malədminis'trāshən) *n.* inefficient or dishonest administration

maladroit (malə'droit) *a.* clumsy, awkward

malady ('malədi) *n.* disease

Malagasy Republic (malə'gasi) *former name for* MADAGASCAR

malaise (mə'lāz, ma'lāz) *n.* vague, unlocated feeling of discomfort

malapropism ('maləpropizəm) *n.* ludicrous misuse of word

malapropos (malaprə'pō) *a./adv.* inappropriate(ly)

malaria (mə'leriə) *n.* infectious disease caused by parasites transmitted by mosquitoes —**ma'larial** *a.*

Malathion (malə'thīon, -on) *n.* trade name for insecticide consisting of organic phosphate

Malawi (mə'läwi) *n.* country in Africa bounded north by Tanzania, south by Mozambique, west by Zambia and south and west by Lake Malawi —**Ma'lawian** *n./a.*

Malaysia (mə'lāzhə) *n.* country in the Indian Ocean occupying a peninsula in the Indian Ocean bounded north by Thailand and the northern part of the island of Borneo —**Malay** (mə'lā) *n./a.* **1.** (native or inhabitant) of Malaysia, eastern Sumatra and parts of Borneo —*n.* **2.** the language of the Malays which is a branch of the Malayo-Polynesian family —**Ma'layan** *n./a.* —**Ma'laysian** *n./a.*

malcontent (malkən'tent) *a.* **1.** actively discontented —*n.* **2.** malcontent person

Maldives ('möldēvz, 'mal-; -dīvz, -divz) *pl.n.* —**Republic of Maldives** country lying in the Indian Ocean consisting of about 2000 low-lying coral islands 400 miles southwest of Sri Lanka —**Maldivian** (möl'diviən, mal-) *n./a.*

male (māl) *a.* **1.** of sex producing gametes which fertilize female gametes **2.** of men or male animals —*n.* **3.** male person or animal

malediction (mali'dikshən) *n.* curse

malefactor ('malifaktər) *n.* criminal

maleficent (mə'lefisənt) *a.* harmful, hurtful —**ma'leficence** *n.*

malevolent (mə'levələnt) *a.* full of ill will —**ma'levolence** *n.*

Mali ('mäli, 'mali) *n.* country in Africa bounded west by Senegal, northwest by Mauritania, northeast by Algeria, east by Niger and south by Burkina-Faso, the Ivory Coast and Guinea —**Malian** *n./a.*

malice ('malis) *n.* **1.** ill will **2.** spite —**ma'licious** *a.* **1.** intending evil or unkindness **2.** spiteful **3.** moved by hatred —**ma'liciously** *adv.*

malign (mə'līn) *a.* **1.** evil in influence or effect —*vt.* **2.** slander, misrepresent —**malignancy** (mə'lignənsi) *n.* —**malignant** (mə'lignant) *a.* **1.** feeling extreme ill will **2.** (of disease) resistant to therapy —**malignantly** (mə'lignəntli) *adv.* —**malignity** (mə'ligniti) *n.* malignant disposition

malinger (mə'linggər) *vi.* feign illness to escape duty —**ma'lingerer** *n.*

mall (möl) *n.* **1.** level, shaded walk **2.** street, shopping area closed to vehicles

mallard ('malərd) *n.* wild duck

malleable ('maliəbəl) *a.* **1.** capable of being hammered into shape **2.** adaptable —**malle-a'bility** *n.*

mallet ('malit) *n.* **1.** (wooden) hammer **2.** croquet or polo stick

mallow ('malō) *n.* wild plant with purple flowers

malmsey ('mämzi, 'mälm-) *n.* strong sweet wine

malnutrition (malnyōō'trishən, -nōō-) *n.* inadequate nutrition

malodorous (mal'ōdərəs) *a.* evil-smelling

malpractice (mal'praktis) *n.* negligent treatment by a professional, *esp.* doctor or dentist, resulting in injury

malt (mölt) *n.* **1.** grain used for brewing —*v.* **2.** make into or become malt —**'maltster** *n.* maker of malt

Malta ('möltə) *n.* country in the Mediterranean comprising the islands of Malta, Gozo and Comina and some islets about 60 miles south of Sicily —**Mal'tese** *n./a.* **1.** (native or inhabitant) of Malta —*n.* **2.** the Semitic language of the Maltese **3.** breed of toy dogs with long white silky coat (*pl.* **-tese**) —**Maltese cross** cross with triangular arms that taper toward center

maltreat (mal'trēt) *vt.* treat badly, handle roughly —**mal'treatment** *n.*

mama *or* **mamma** ('mämə) *n.* **1.** mother **2.** *sl.* wife, woman

mamba ('mämbə, 'mam-) *n.* deadly S Afr. snake

mambo ('mambō) *n.* Latin Amer. dance like rumba (*pl.* **-s**)

mamma ('mamə) *n.* milk-secreting organ of female mammals: breast in women, udder in cows *etc.* (*pl.* **-mae** (-mē)) —'**mammary** *a.*

mammal ('maməl) *n.* member of class of warm-blooded vertebrates which suckle their young with milk —**mammalian** (mə'māliən, ma-) *a.*

mammilla (ma'milə) *n.* **1.** nipple **2.** any nipple-shaped prominence (*pl.* **-lae** (-lē)) —'**mammillary** *a.*

mammon ('mamən) *n.* **1.** wealth regarded as source of evil **2.** (**M-**) false god of covetousness —'**mammonism** *n.* —'**mammonist** *n.*

mammoth ('maməth) *n.* **1.** extinct animal like an elephant —*a.* **2.** colossal

man (man) *n.* **1.** human being **2.** person **3.** human race **4.** adult male **5. SA** *sl.* any person **6.** manservant **7.** piece used in chess *etc.* (*pl.* **men**) —*vt.* **8.** supply (ship *etc.*) with necessary men **9.** fortify (**-nn-**) —'**manful** *a.* brave, vigorous —'**manfully** *adv.* —'**manhood** *n.* —'**manlike** *a.* —'**manliness** *n.* —'**manly** *a.* —'**mannish** *a.* like a man —**man Friday 1.** loyal male servant or assistant **2.** any factotum, *esp.* (*also* **girl Friday, person Friday**) —'**manhandle** *vt.* treat roughly —'**manhole** *n.* opening through which man may pass to a drain, sewer *etc.* —'**man-hour** *n.* unit of work in industry, equal to work done by one man in one hour —'**manhunt** *n.* organized search for fugitive —'**mankind** *n.* human beings in general —**man-of-war** *or* **man o' war** *n.* **1.** warship **2.** *see* **Portuguese man-of-war** *at* PORTUGAL —'**manpower** *n.* **1.** power of human effort **2.** available number of workers —'**manslaughter** *n.* culpable homicide without malice aforethought —**man in the street** typical person —**man of letters 1.** writer **2.** scholar —**man of the world** man of wide experience

mana ('mänə) *n.* **1.** generalized supernatural force or power in objects or persons **2.** moral authority

manacle ('manəkəl) *n.* **1.** fetter, handcuff —*vt.* **2.** shackle

manage ('manij) *v.* **1.** be in charge (of), administer **2.** succeed in (doing) —*vt.* **3.** control **4.** handle, cope with **5.** conduct, carry on —'**manageable** *a.* —'**management** *n.* **1.** those who manage, as board of directors *etc.* **2.** administration **3.** skillful use of means **4.** conduct —'**manager** *n.* **1.** one in charge of business, institution, actor *etc.* ('**manageress** *fem.*) **2.** one who manages efficiently —**mana'gerial** *a.* —'**managing** *a.* having administrative control

mañana (mə'nyänə) *Sp.* **1.** tomorrow **2.** some other and later time

manatee

manatee ('manətē) *n.* large, plant-eating aquatic mammal

Manchu ('manchōō, man'chōō) *n.* **1.** member of Mongoloid people of Manchuria (*pl.* **-s, -chu**) **2.** language of this people

Mancunian (man'kyōōniən) *n.* **1.** native or inhabitant of Manchester, England —*a.* **2.** of Manchester, England

mandala ('mundələ) *n.* any of various designs, usu. circular, symbolizing the universe

mandamus (man'dāməs) *n.* writ from superior to lower court, officer, corporation *etc.* commanding that a specific thing be done

mandarin ('mandərin) *n.* **1.** *Hist.* Chinese high-ranking bureaucrat **2.** *fig.* any high government official **3.** Chinese variety of orange **4.** (**M-**) Beijing, formerly Peking, dialect which is the official pronunciation of the Chinese language —**mandarin duck** Asian duck, the male of which has brightly colored patterned plumage and crest

mandate ('mandāt) *n.* **1.** command of, or commission to act for, another **2.** commission from United Nations to govern a territory **3.** instruction from electorate to representative or government —'**mandated** *a.* committed to a mandate —**mandatory** ('mandətöri) *n.* **1.** holder of a mandate —*a.*, *also* '**mandatary 2.** compulsory

mandible ('mandibəl) *n.* **1.** lower jawbone **2.** either part of bird's beak —**man'dibular** *a.* of, like mandible

mandolin (mandə'lin) *n.* plucked musical instrument descended from the lute but with a smaller almost straight neck

mandrake ('mandrāk) *or* **mandragora** (man'dragərə) *n.* narcotic plant

mandrel *or* **mandril** ('mandrəl) *n.* **1.** axis on which material is supported in a lathe **2.** rod round which metal is cast or forged

mandrill ('mandril) *n.* large blue-faced baboon

mane (mān) *n.* long hair on neck of horse, lion *etc.* —**maned** *a.*

maneuver (mə'nōōvər, -'nyōōvər) *n.* **1.** contrived, complicated, perhaps deceptive plan or action **2.** skillful management —*vt.* **3.** contrive or accomplish with skill or cunning —*vi.* **4.** manipulate situations *etc.* in order to gain some end —*v.* **5.** (cause to) perform maneuvers

manganese ('manggənēz, -nēs) *n.* *Chem.* metallic element *Symbol* Mn, at. wt. 54.9, at. no. 25

mange (mānj) *n.* any of various contagious skin diseases caused by mites affecting humans and domestic animals —'**mangy** *or* '**mangey** *a.* scruffy, shabby

mangel ('manggəl) *n.* coarse beet grown for cattle (*also* **mangel-wurzel** (-wərzəl))

manger ('mānjər) *n.* eating trough in stable

mangle ('manggəl) *vt.* mutilate, spoil, hack

mango ('manggō) *n.* **1.** tropical fruit **2.** tree bearing it (*pl.* **-s, -es**)

mangrove

mangrove ('man-grōv, 'mang-) *n.* tropical tree which grows on muddy banks of estuaries

Manhattan (man'hatən) *n.* **1.** borough of New York City **2.** (*sometimes* **m-**) cocktail made of whiskey, sweet vermouth and sometimes bitters

mania ('māniə) *n.* **1.** madness **2.** prevailing craze —'**maniac, maniacal** (mə'nīəkəl) *or*

manic ('manik) *a.* affected by mania —'**maniac** *n. inf.* **1.** mad person **2.** crazy enthusiast —**manic-depressive** *a. Psych.* **1.** pert. to mental disorder characterized by alternation between extreme confidence and deep depression —*n.* **2.** person afflicted with this disorder

manicure ('manikyōōr) *n.* **1.** treatment and care of fingernails and hands —*vt.* **2.** apply such treatment to —'**manicurist** *n.* one doing this professionally

manifest ('manifest) *a.* **1.** clearly revealed, visible, undoubted —*vt.* **2.** make manifest —*n.* **3.** list of cargo for customs —**manifes·'tation** *n.* —'**manifestly** *adv.* clearly —**mani·'festo** *n.* declaration of policy by political party, government, or movement (*pl.* **-s, -es**)

manifold ('manifōld) *a.* **1.** numerous and varied —*n.* **2.** in internal-combustion engine, pipe with several outlets —*vt.* **3.** make copies of (document)

Manila (mə'nilə) *n.* **1.** fiber used for ropes **2.** tough paper

manipulate (mə'nipyəlāt) *vt.* **1.** handle **2.** deal with skillfully **3.** manage **4.** falsify —**manipu'lation** *n.* **1.** act of manipulating, working by hand **2.** skilled use of hands —**ma'nipulative** *a.* —**ma'nipulator** *n.*

manitou *or* **manitu** ('manitōō) *n.* Algonquian concept denoting the supernatural force of the natural world

manna ('manə) *n.* **1.** food of Israelites in the wilderness **2.** any spiritual or divine nourishment

mannequin ('manikin) *n.* **1.** woman who wears clothing displayed at fashion show; model **2.** life-size dummy of human body used to fit or display clothes **3.** *Arts see* LAY FIGURE (sense 1)

manner ('manər) *n.* **1.** way thing happens or is done **2.** sort, kind **3.** custom **4.** style —*pl.* **5.** social behavior —'**mannered** *a.* having idiosyncrasies or mannerisms; affected —'**mannerism** *n.* person's distinctive habit, trait —'**mannerly** *a.* polite

manor ('manər) *n.* **1.** *Hist.* land belonging to a lord **2.** feudal unit of land —**ma'norial** *a.* —**manor house** residence of lord of manor

manqué (mong'kā) *Fr.* unfulfilled; would-be

mansard ('mansärd) *n.* roof with break in its slope, lower part being steeper than upper —'**mansarded** *a.*

manse (mans) *n.* **1.** house of minister in some religious denominations **2.** mansion

mansion ('manchən) *n.* large house

mantel ('mantəl) *n.* structure around fireplace —**mantel shelf** *or* '**mantelpiece** *n.* shelf at top of mantel

mantilla (man'tēya, man'tilə) *n.* in Spain, (lace) scarf worn as headdress

mantis ('mantis) *n.* genus of insects including the stick insects and leaf insects (*pl.* **mantes** ('mantēz))

mantissa (man'tisə) *n.* decimal part of common logarithm

mantle ('mantəl) *n.* **1.** loose cloak **2.** covering **3.** incandescent gauze around gas jet —*vt.* **4.** cover **5.** conceal

mantra ('mantrə) *n.* *Hinduism* word or formula to be recited or sung as aid to meditation

manual ('manyōōəl) *a.* **1.** of, or done with, the hands **2.** by human labor, not automatic —*n.* **3.** handbook **4.** textbook **5.** organ keyboard

manufacture (manyə'fakchər) *vt.* **1.** process, make (materials) into finished articles **2.** produce (articles) **3.** invent, concoct —*n.* **4.** making of articles, materials, *esp.* in large quantities **5.** anything produced from raw materials —**manu'facturer** *n.* owner of factory

manumit (manyə'mit) *vt.* free from slavery (-tt-) —**manu'mission** *n.*

manure (mə'nyŏŏər, mə'nŏŏər) *vt.* 1. enrich (land) —*n.* 2. dung or chemical fertilizer used to enrich land

manuscript ('manyəskript) *n.* 1. book, document, written by hand 2. copy for printing —*a.* 3. handwritten

Manx (mangks) *a.* 1. of Isle of Man —*n.* 2. Manx language —**Manx cat** tailless breed of cat —'**Manxman** *n.*

many ('meni) *a.* 1. numerous (**more** *comp.*, **most** *sup.*) —*n.* 2. large number

Maoism ('mowizəm) *n.* form of Marxism advanced by Mao Tse-tung (in Pinyin, Mao Ze Dong) in China —'**Maoist** *n./a.*

Maori ('mowri) *n.* 1. member of New Zealand native race (*pl.* **-s, -ri**) 2. their language

map (map) *n.* 1. flat representation of the earth or some part of it, or of the heavens —*vt.* 2. make a map of 3. (*with* **out**) plan (-pp-)

maple ('māpəl) *n.* 1. any of family and genus of deciduous trees or shrubs of N temperate zone with green, purple or golden lobed leaves and winged seeds borne in pairs 2. hard light-colored wood of a maple used for flooring and furniture —**maple leaf** national emblem of Canada —**maple sugar** sugar made by boiling maple syrup —**maple syrup** syrup made by boiling sap of maple, *esp.* sugar maple

maquis (ma'kē, mä-) *n.* 1. scrubby undergrowth of Mediterranean countries 2. (*oft.* **M-**) name adopted by French underground resistance movement in World War II

mar (mär) *vt.* spoil, impair (-rr-)

Mar. March

marabou ('marəbōō) *n.* 1. kind of stork 2. its soft white lower tail feathers, used to trim hats *etc.* 3. kind of silk

maraca (mə'räkə, -'rakə) *n.* percussion instrument of gourd containing dried seeds *etc.*

maraschino (marə'skēnō) *n.* 1. liqueur made from bitter wild cherries 2. large red cherry preserved in syrup (*pl.* **-s**)

marathon ('marəthon) *n.* 1. long-distance race 2. endurance contest

maraud (mə'röd) *vi.* 1. make raid for plunder —*v.* 2. pillage —**ma'rauder** *n.*

marble ('märbəl) *n.* 1. kind of limestone capable of taking polish 2. slab of, sculpture in this 3. small ball used in children's game —'**marbled** *a.* having mottled appearance, like marble —'**marbly** *a.*

marc (märk) *n.* 1. remains of grapes *etc.* that have been pressed for wine-making 2. brandy distilled from these

marcasite ('märkəsīt) *n.* 1. pale yellow crystallized iron pyrites 2. polished form of steel or white metal used for making jewelry

march[1] (märch) *vi.* 1. walk with military step 2. go, progress —*vt.* 3. cause to march —*n.* 4. action of marching 5. distance marched in day 6. tune to accompany marching —**marching orders** 1. *Mil.* instructions about march, its destination *etc.* 2. *inf.* any notice of dismissal, *esp.* from employment —**march-past** *n.* review of troops as they march past a saluting point

march[2] (märch) *n.* 1. border or frontier —*vi.* 2. (*oft. with* **upon** *or* **with**) share a common border (with)

March (märch) *n.* third month —**March hare** hare during its breeding season, noted for its excitable behavior

marchioness ('märshənis) *n.* wife, ex-wife or widow of marquis

Mardi Gras ('märdi grä) 1. festival of Shrove Tuesday 2. revelry celebrating this

mare[1] (mār) *n.* female horse —**mare's nest** supposed discovery which proves worthless

mare[2] ('märā) *n.* (**M-** *when part of name*) huge dry plain on surface of moon (*pl.* **maria** ('märiə))

margarine ('märjərin, -rēn) *n.* butter substitute made from vegetable fats

margin ('märjin) *n.* 1. border, edge 2. space round printed page 3. amount allowed beyond what is necessary —'**marginal** *a.*

marguerite (märgə'rēt) *n.* large daisy

marigold ('marigōld) *n.* plant with yellow flowers

marijuana *or* **marihuana** (mari'wänə, -'hwänə) *n.* dried flowers and leaves of hemp plant, used as narcotic

marimba (mə'rimbə) *n.* a percussion instrument similar to but larger than the xylophone, used by bands

marina (mə'rēnə) *n.* mooring facility for yachts and pleasure boats

marinade (mari'nād) *n.* seasoned, flavored liquid used to soak fish, meat *etc.* before cooking —'**marinate** *v.*

marine (mə'rēn) *a.* 1. of the sea or shipping 2. used at, found in sea —*n.* 3. shipping, fleet 4. soldier trained for land or sea combat —**mariner** ('marinər) *n.* sailor

marionette (mariə'net) *n.* puppet worked with strings

marital ('maritəl) *a.* relating to a husband or to marriage

maritime ('maritīm) *a.* 1. connected with seafaring, naval 2. bordering on the sea 3. (of climate) having small temperature differences between summer and winter —**Maritime Provinces** certain of the Canadian provinces with coasts facing the Gulf of St. Lawrence or Atlantic (*also* '**Maritimes**)

marjoram ('märjərəm) *n.* aromatic herb

mark[1] (märk) *n.* 1. line, dot, scar *etc.* 2. sign, token 3. inscription 4. letter, number showing evaluation of schoolwork *etc.* 5. indication 6. target —*vt.* 7. make a mark on 8. be distinguishing mark of 9. indicate 10. notice 11. watch 12. assess, *eg* examination paper 13. stay close to (sporting opponent) to hamper his play —**marked** *a.* 1. obvious, evident, or noticeable 2. singled out, *esp.* as target of attack 3. *Linguis.* distinguished by specific feature, as in phonology —**markedly** ('märkidli) *adv.* —'**marker** *n.* 1. one who, that which keeps score at games 2. counter used at card playing *etc.* —'**marksman** *n.* skilled shot

mark[2] (märk) *n.* German coin

Mark (märk) *n.* *Bible* 2nd book of the N.T., synoptic gospel presenting Jesus in the role of servant in the chronology of His life written by a disciple

market ('märkit) *n.* 1. assembly, place for buying and selling 2. demand for goods 3. center for trade —*vt.* 4. offer or produce for sale —'**marketable** *a.* —'**marketing** *n.* business of selling goods, including advertising, packaging *etc.* —**market research** analysis of data relating to demand for product

marl (märl) *n.* 1. soil rich in calcium carbonate used as fertilizer —*vt.* 2. fertilize with it

marline *or* **marlin** ('märlin) *n.* two-strand cord —'**marlinspike** *or* '**marlinespike** *n.* pointed tool, *esp.* for unraveling rope to be spliced

marmalade ('märməlād) *n.* sweet jelly usu.

made of oranges, lemons *etc.* incorporating shreds of rind

marmoreal (mär'möriəl) *or* **marmorean** *a.* of or like marble

marmoset ('märməset, -zet) *n.* small bushy-tailed monkey

marmot ('märmət) *n.* any of various N Amer. burrowing rodents living in colonies (*also* **rockchuck**)

maroon[1] (mə'rōōn) *n.* 1. brownish crimson —*a.* 2. of this color

maroon[2] (mə'rōōn) *vt.* 1. leave (person) on deserted island or coast 2. isolate, cut off by any means

marquee (mär'kē) *n.* large tent

marquetry *or* **marqueterie** ('märkitri) *n.* inlaid work, wood mosaic

marquis ('märkwis, mär'kē) *n.* nobleman of rank below duke —**marquisate** ('märkwizit) *n.*

marquise (mär'kēz) *n.* 1. in various countries, marchioness 2. gemstone cut in pointed oval shape

Marrano (mə'ränō) *n.* Spanish or Portuguese Jew forcibly converted to Christianity in the 15th cent. (*pl.* **-s**)

marrow ('marō) *n.* 1. fatty substance inside bones 2. vital part —'**marrowy** *a.* —'**marrowfat** *n.* large pea

marry ('mari) *v.* 1. take (someone as husband or wife) in marriage 2. unite closely —*vt.* 3. join as husband and wife ('**married**, '**marrying**) —**marriage** ('marij) *n.* 1. state of being married 2. wedding —**marriageable** ('marijəbəl) *a.* —**marriage bureau** business concern set up to introduce people wishing to get married —**marriage guidance** advice given to couples who have problems in their married life

Mars (märz) *n.* 1. Roman god of war 2. planet nearest but one to earth —**Martian** ('märshən) *n.* 1. supposed inhabitant of Mars —*a.* 2. of Mars

marsala (mär'sälə) *n.* fortified dessert wine

Marseillaise (märsə'lāz) *n.* the French national anthem

marsh (märsh) *n.* low-lying wet land —'**marshy** *a.* —**marsh gas** gas composed of methane produced when vegetation decomposes under water —**marshmallow** ('märshmelō) *n.* confection orig. made from root of **marsh mallow,** shrubby plant growing near marshes

marshal *or* **marshall** ('märshəl) *n.* 1. high officer of state 2. law enforcement officer —*vt.* 3. arrange in due order 4. conduct with ceremony —**marshaling yard** railroad depot for freight trains

marsupial (mär'sōōpiəl) *n.* 1. animal that carries its young in pouch, *eg* kangaroo —*a.* 2. of marsupials —**mar'supium** *n.* external pouch in most female marsupials (*pl.* **-pia** (-piə))

mart (märt) *n.* 1. place of trade 2. market

Martello tower (mär'telō) round fort, for coast defense

marten ('märtin) *n.* 1. weasel-like animal 2. its fur

martial ('märshəl) *a.* 1. relating to war 2. warlike, brave —**court martial** *see* COURT —**martial law** law enforced by military authorities in times of danger or emergency

martin ('märtin) *n.* species of swallow

martinet (märti'net) *n.* strict disciplinarian

martingale ('märtin-gāl, 'märtinggāl) *n.* strap to prevent horse from throwing up its head

martini (mär'tēni) *n.* 1. cocktail containing gin and vermouth decorated with maraschino cherry 2. (**M-**) trade name for Italian vermouth (*pl.* **-s**)

Martinique (märti'nēk) *n.* an overseas department of France situated in the Lesser Antilles between Dominica and St. Lucia —**Marti'nican** *n./a.*

Martinmas ('märtinmǝs) *n.* feast of St. Martin, Nov. 11th

martlet ('märtlit) *n. Her.* bird without feet

martyr ('märtǝr) *n.* 1. one put to death for his beliefs 2. one who suffers in some cause 3. one in constant suffering —*vt.* 4. make martyr of —**'martyrdom** *n.* —**martyr'ology** *n.* list, history of Christian martyrs

marvel ('märvǝl) *vi.* 1. wonder —*n.* 2. wonderful thing —**'marvelous** *or* **'marvellous** *a.* 1. amazing 2. wonderful

Marxism ('märksizǝm) *n.* state socialism as conceived by Karl Marx —**'Marxian** *a.* —**'Marxist** *n./a.*

Maryland ('merilǝnd) *n.* South Atlantic state of the U.S.: ratified the Constitution in 1788. Abbrev.: **MD** (with ZIP code)

marzipan ('märtsipän, -pan, 'märzipan) *n.* paste of almonds, sugar *etc.* used in candy, cakes *etc.*

Masai (mä'sĪ, 'mäsĪ) *n.* 1. member of Negroid pastoral people living chiefly in Kenya and Tanzania (*pl.* **-s**, **-'sai**) 2. language of this people

masc. masculine

mascara (ma'skarǝ) *n.* cosmetic for darkening eyelashes

mascot ('maskot, -kǝt) *n.* thing supposed to bring luck

masculine ('maskyǝlin) *a.* 1. relating to males 2. manly 3. of the grammatical gender of words referring to males or things conventionally regarded as male

maser ('māzǝr) *n.* device for amplifying microwaves

mash (mash) *n.* 1. meal mixed with warm water 2. warm food for horses *etc.* 3. soft pulpy mass or consistency —*vt.* 4. make into a mash 5. crush into soft mass or pulp

mashie *or* **mashy** ('mashi) *n. Golf* iron club with deep sloping blade for lob shots

mask (mask) *n.* 1. covering for face 2. *Surg.* covering for nose and mouth 3. disguise, pretense —*vt.* 4. cover with mask 5. hide, disguise —**masking tape** adhesive tape used to protect surfaces surrounding an area to be painted

maskanonge ('maskǝnonj), **maskelonge** ('maskǝlonj), *or* **maskinonge** ('maskinonj) *n. see* MUSKELLUNGE

masochism ('masǝkizǝm) *n.* abnormal condition where pleasure (*esp.* sexual) is derived from pain, humiliation *etc.* —**'masochist** *n.* —**maso'chistic** *a.*

mason ('māsǝn) *n.* 1. worker in stone 2. (**M-**) Freemason —**Masonic** (mǝ'sonik) *a.* of Freemasonry —**'masonry** *n.* 1. stonework 2. (**M-**) Freemasonry

masque *or* **mask** (mask) *n. Hist.* form of theatrical performance —**masquerade** (maskǝ'rād) *n.* 1. masked ball —*vi.* 2. appear in disguise

mass (mas) *n.* 1. quantity of matter 2. dense collection of this 3. large quantity or number —*v.* 4. form into a mass —**'massive** *a.* large and heavy —**'massy** *a.* solid, weighty —**mass market** market for mass-produced goods —**mass-market** *a.* of mass market —**mass media** means of communication to large numbers of people, such as television, newspapers *etc.* —**mass-produce** *vt.* produce (standardized articles) in large quantities —**mass production** —**mass spectrometer** instrument in which ions are separated by

electric or magnetic fields according to their ratios of charge to mass (*also* **'spectroscope**) —**the masses** the populace

Mass (mas) *n.* service of the Eucharist, *esp.* in R.C. Church

Massachusetts (masǝ'chōōsits) *n.* New England state of the U.S.: ratified the Constitution in 1788. Abbrev.: **Mass., MA** (with ZIP code)

massacre ('masǝkǝr) *n.* 1. indiscriminate, large-scale killing, *esp.* of unresisting people —*vt.* 2. kill indiscriminately

massage (mǝ'säzh, -'säj) *n.* 1. rubbing and kneading of muscles *etc.* as curative treatment —*vt.* 2. apply this treatment to 3. manipulate (figures *etc.*) in order to deceive —**masseur** (ma'sǝr) *n.* one who practices massage (**masseuse** (ma'sǝz, -'sǝrz, -'sōōz) *fem.*)

massé ('masi) *n. Billiards* stroke with cue upright

massif (ma'sēf) *n.* compact group of mountains

mast[1] (mast) *n.* 1. pole for supporting ship's sails 2. tall upright support for antenna *etc.* —**'masthead** *n.* 1. *Naut.* head of mast 2. name of newspaper, its proprietors, staff *etc.*, printed at top of front page —*vt.* 3. raise (sail) to masthead

mast[2] (mast) *n.* fruit of beech, oak *etc.* used as pig fodder

mastectomy (ma'stektǝmi) *n.* surgical removal of a breast

master ('mastǝr) *n.* 1. one in control 2. employer 3. head of household 4. owner 5. document *etc.* from which copies are made 6. captain of merchant ship 7. expert 8. great artist 9. teacher —*vt.* 10. overcome 11. acquire knowledge of or skill in —**'masterful** *a.* imperious, domineering —**'masterly** *a.* showing great competence —**'mastery** *n.* 1. full understanding 2. expertise 3. authority 4. victory —**master key** key that opens many different locks —**'mastermind** *vt.* 1. plan, direct —*n.* 2. very intelligent person, *esp.* one who directs an undertaking —**'masterpiece** *n.* outstanding work, *orig.* the test piece by which a craftsman was admitted to his guild —**'masterstroke** *n.* outstanding piece of strategy *etc.* —**Master of Arts** (*or* **Science** *etc.*) 1. degree given by university *usu.* to postgraduate 2. person who has this degree —**master of ceremonies** person who presides over public ceremony *etc.*, introducing events *etc.*

mastic ('mastik) *n.* 1. gum obtained from certain trees 2. puttylike substance

masticate ('mastikāt) *v.* chew —**masti'cation** *n.* —**'masticatory** *a.*

mastiff

mastiff ('mastif) *n.* large dog

mastitis (ma'stĪtis) *n.* inflammation of breast or udder

mastodon ('mastǝdon) *n.* 1. extinct elephant-like mammal 2. anything unusually large

mastoid ('mastoid) *a.* 1. nipple-shaped —*n.* 2. prominence on bone behind human ear —**mastoid'ectomy** *n.* surgical removal of

infected mastoid —**mastoi'ditis** *n.* inflammation of mastoid

masturbate ('mastǝrbāt) *v.* stimulate (one's own or one's partner's) genital organs —**mastur'bation** *n.*

mat[1] (mat) *n.* 1. small rug 2. piece of fabric to protect another surface or to wipe feet on *etc.* 3. thick tangled mass —*v.* 4. form into such mass (**-tt-**) —**on the mat** *inf.* called up for reprimand

mat[2] *or* **matt** (mat) *a.* dull, lusterless, not shiny

matador ('matǝdör) *n.* man who slays bull in bullfights

match[1] (mach) *n.* 1. contest, game 2. equal 3. person, thing exactly corresponding to another 4. marriage 5. person regarded as eligible for marriage —*vt.* 6. get something corresponding to (color, pattern *etc.*) 7. oppose, put in competition with 8. join (in marriage) —*vi.* 9. correspond —**'matchless** *a.* unequaled —**'matchboard** *n.* long, flimsy board tongued and grooved for lining work —**'matchmaker** *n.* one who tries to bring about a marriage —**match play** *Golf* scoring according to number of holes won and lost

match[2] (mach) *n.* 1. small stick with head which ignites when rubbed 2. fuse —**'matchbox** *n.* —**'matchlock** *n.* early musket fired by fuse —**'matchwood** *n.* small splinters

mate[1] (māt) *n.* 1. comrade 2. husband, wife 3. one of pair 4. officer in merchant ship 5. *inf.* common Brit. and Aust. term of address, *esp.* between males —*v.* 6. marry or join in marriage 7. pair —**'matey** *a. inf.* friendly, sociable

mate[2] (māt) *n./vt. Chess* checkmate

maté *or* **mate** ('mätā) *n.* 1. tealike beverage drunk in South America 2. shrub or tree from which this drink is made 3. leaves and shoots of this tree

mater ('mātǝr) *n.* UK *sl.* mother

material (mǝ'tēǝriǝl) *n.* 1. substance from which thing is made 2. cloth, fabric —*a.* 3. of matter or body 4. affecting physical wellbeing 5. unspiritual 6. important, essential —**ma'terialism** *n.* 1. excessive interest in, desire for money and possessions 2. doctrine that nothing but matter exists, denying independent existence of spirit —**ma'terialist** *a./n.* —**material'istic** *a.* —**ma'terialize** *vi.* 1. come into existence or view —*vt.* 2. make material —**ma'terially** *adv.* appreciably

matériel *or* **materiel** (mǝtēǝri'el) *n.* equipment of organization, *esp.* of military force

maternal (mǝ'tǝrnǝl) *a.* of, related through mother —**ma'ternity** *n.* motherhood

math (math) *n. inf.* mathematics

mathematics (mathǝ'matiks) *pl.n.* (*with sing. v.*) science of number, quantity, shape and space —**mathe'matical** *a.* —**mathe'matically** *adv.* —**mathema'tician** *n.*

matinée (mati'nā) *n.* afternoon performance in theater —**matinée coat** short coat for baby

matins ('matinz) *pl.n.* morning prayers

matriarch ('mātriärk) *n.* mother as head and ruler of family —**matri'archal** *a.* —**'matriarchy** *n.* society with matriarchal government and descent reckoned in female line

matricide ('matrisĪd, 'mā-) *n.* 1. the crime of killing one's mother 2. one who does this

matriculate (mǝ'trikyǝlāt) *v.* enroll, be enrolled in a college or university —**matricu'lation** *n.*

matrimony ('matrimōni) *n.* marriage —**matri'monial** *a.*

matrix ('mātriks) *n.* **1.** substance, situation in which something originates, takes form, or is enclosed **2.** intercellular substance of bone, cartilage *etc.* **3.** mold for casting **4.** *Math.* rectangular array of elements set out in rows and columns (*pl.* **matrices** ('mātrisēz, 'ma-))

matron ('mātrən) *n.* **1.** married woman **2.** woman who superintends domestic arrangements of public institution, boarding school *etc.* —'**matronly** *a.* sedate —**matron of honor** married woman serving as chief attendant to bride

matt (mat) *a. see* MAT²

Matt. *Bible* Matthew

matter ('matər) *n.* **1.** anything that has weight and occupies space **2.** physical or bodily substance **3.** affair, business **4.** cause of trouble **5.** substance of book *etc.* **6.** pus —*vi.* **7.** be of importance, signify —**matter-of-fact** *a.* unimaginative or emotionless —**matter of fact** fact that is undeniably true —**as a matter of fact** actually; in fact

Matthew ('mathyōō) *n. Bible* 1st book of the N.T., synoptic gospel presenting Jesus as fulfillment of the O.T. promises of Redeemer and King of Israel, written by a disciple

mattock ('matək) *n.* tool like pick with ends of blades flattened for cutting, hoeing

mattress ('matris) *n.* **1.** stuffed flat case, often with springs, or foam-rubber pad, used as part of bed **2.** underlay

mature (mə'tyōōr, -'tōōr, -'chōōr) *a.* **1.** ripe, completely developed **2.** grown-up —*v.* **3.** bring, come to maturity —*vi.* **4.** (of bill) fall due —**matu'ration** *n.* process of maturing —**ma'turity** *n.* full development

matutinal (machōō'tīnəl) *a.* of, occurring in, or during morning

matzo ('mätsō) *n.* flat, unleavened bread resembling a soda cracker

maudlin ('mödlin) *a.* weakly or tearfully sentimental

maul (möl) *vt.* **1.** handle roughly **2.** beat; bruise —*n.* **3.** heavy wooden hammer

maulstick *or* **mahlstick** ('mölstik) *n.* light stick with ball at one end, held in left hand to support right hand while painting

maunder ('möndər) *vi.* talk, act aimlessly, dreamily

maundy ('möndi) *n.* **1.** foot-washing ceremony on Thursday before Easter **2.** royal alms given on that day

Mauritania (möri'tāniə, mor-; -nyə) *n.* country in Africa bounded west by the Atlantic Ocean, north by Western Sahara, northeast by Algeria, east and southeast by Mali, and south by Senegal —**Mauri'tanian** *n./a.*

Mauritius (mö'rishəs) *n.* country in the Indian Ocean about 500 miles east of Madagascar comprising two islands —**Mau'ritian** *n./a.*

mausoleum (mösə'lēəm) *n.* stately building as a tomb (*pl.* **-s, -lea** (-'lēə))

mauve (mōv) *a./n.* (of) pale purple color

maven ('māvən) *or* **mavin** *n. inf.* expert; connoisseur

maverick ('mavərik) *n.* **1.** unbranded steer, stray cow **2.** independent, unorthodox person

mavin ('māvin) *n. see* MAVEN

maw (mö) *n.* stomach, crop

mawkish ('mökish) *a.* **1.** weakly sentimental, maudlin **2.** sickly

max. maximum

maxi ('maksi) *n.* **1.** long skirt, dress, or coat —*a.* **2.** large, considerable

maxilla (mak'silə) *n.* jawbone (*pl.* **-lae** (-lē)) —'**maxillary** *a.* of the jaw

maxim ('maksim) *n.* **1.** general truth, proverb **2.** rule of conduct, principle

maximum ('maksiməm) *n.* **1.** greatest size or number **2.** highest point (*pl.* **-s, -ma** (-mə)) —*a.* **3.** greatest —'**maximize** *vt.*

maxwell ('makswel, 'makswəl) *n.* cgs unit of magnetic flux

may (mā) *v. aux.* expresses possibility, permission, opportunity *etc.* (**might** *pt.*) —**maybe** ('mābē) *adv.* perhaps; possibly

May (mā) *n.* **1.** fifth month **2.** hawthorn or its flowers —'**mayfly** *n.* short-lived flying insect, found near water —'**maypole** *n.* pole set up for dancing round on **May Day**, first day of May —**May queen** girl chosen to preside over May-Day celebrations

Maya ('mīə) *n.* **1.** member of Amerindian people of Yucatán, Belize and N Guatemala (*pl.* **-ya, -s**) **2.** language of this people

Mayday (mā'dā, 'mādā) *n.* international radiotelephone distress signal

mayhap ('māhap) *adv. obs.* perhaps

mayhem ('māhem) *n.* **1.** depriving person by violence of limb, member or organ, or causing mutilation of body **2.** any violent destruction **3.** confusion

mayonnaise (māənāz, māə'nāz) *n.* creamy sauce of egg yolks, oil *etc., esp.* for salads

mayor (māər) *n.* head of municipality —'**mayoral** *a.* —'**mayoralty** *n.* (time of) office of mayor —'**mayoress** *n.* **1.** mayor's wife **2.** lady mayor

maze (māz) *n.* **1.** labyrinth **2.** network of paths, lines **3.** state of confusion

mazel ('mäzəl) *n. inf.* luck —**mazel tov** (töf) expression of felicitation or congratulations

mazurka *or* **mazourka** (mə'zərkə) *n.* **1.** lively Polish dance like polka **2.** music for it

MB Manitoba

M.B. Bachelor of Medicine

M.C. **1.** Master of Ceremonies **2.** Military Cross

M.C.C. Marylebone Cricket Club

McKinley (mə'kinli) *n.* **William.** the 25th President of the U.S. (1897-1901)

Md *Chem.* mendelevium

MD Maryland

M.D. Doctor of Medicine

me¹ (mē; *unstressed* mi) *pron.* objective case of pronoun I

me² (mē) *n. Mus. see* MI

ME Maine

ME *or* **M.E.** Middle English

M.E. **1.** Marine Engineer **2.** Mechanical Engineer **3.** Methodist Episcopal **4.** Mining Engineer **5.** in titles, Most Excellent

mea culpa ('māä 'kŏŏlpä) *Lat.* my fault

mead¹ (mēd) *n.* alcoholic drink made from honey

mead² (mēd) *n. obs., poet.* meadow

meadow ('medō) *n.* piece of grassland —'**meadowsweet** *n.* plant with dense heads of small fragrant flowers

meager ('mēgər) *a.* **1.** lean, thin **2.** scanty, insufficient

meal¹ (mēl) *n.* **1.** occasion when food is served and eaten **2.** the food —**meal ticket** person, situation *etc.* providing source of livelihood or income

meal² (mēl) *n.* grain ground to powder —'**mealy** *a.* —**mealy-mouthed** *a.* euphemistic, insincere in what one says

mealie ('mēli) *n. SA* maize

mean¹ (mēn) *vt.* **1.** intend **2.** signify —*vi.* **3.** have the intention of behaving (**meant** *pt./pp.,* '**meaning** *pr.p.*) —'**meaning** *n.* **1.** sense, significance —*a.* **2.** expressive —'**meaningful** *a.* of great meaning or significance —'**meaningless** *a.*

mean² (mēn) *a.* **1.** ungenerous, petty **2.** miserly, niggardly **3.** unpleasant **4.** callous **5.** shabby **6.** ashamed —'**meanly** *adv.* —'**meanness** *n.*

mean³ (mēn) *n.* **1.** thing which is intermediate **2.** middle point —*pl.* **3.** that by which thing is done **4.** money **5.** resources —*a.* **6.** intermediate in time, quality *etc.* **7.** average —**means test** inquiry into person's means to decide eligibility for pension, grant *etc.* —'**meantime** *or* '**meanwhile** *adv./n.* (during) time between one happening and another —**by all means** certainly —**by no means** not at all

meander (mi'andər) *vi.* **1.** flow windingly **2.** wander aimlessly

meant (ment) *pt./pp. of* MEAN¹

measles ('mēzəlz) *n.* highly contagious virus disease marked by eruptions of skin (*also* **rubeola**) —'**measly** *a.* **1.** *inf.* poor, wretched, stingy **2.** of measles

measure ('mezhər) *n.* **1.** size, quantity **2.** vessel, rod, line *etc.* for ascertaining size or quantity **3.** unit of size or quantity **4.** course, plan of action **5.** law **6.** poetical rhythm **7.** musical time **8.** *Poet.* tune **9.** *obs.* dance —*vt.* **10.** ascertain size, quantity of **11.** indicate measurement of **12.** estimate **13.** bring into competition against —*vi.* **14.** make measurement(s) **15.** be (so much) in size or quantity —'**measurable** *a.* —'**measured** *a.* **1.** determined by measure **2.** steady **3.** rhythmical **4.** carefully considered —'**measurement** *n.* **1.** measuring **2.** size —*pl.* **3.** dimensions

meat (mēt) *n.* **1.** animal flesh as food **2.** food —'**meaty** *a.* **1.** (tasting) of, like meat **2.** brawny **3.** full of import or interest

Mecca ('mekə) *n.* **1.** holy city of Islam **2.** place that attracts visitors

mechanic (mi'kanik) *n.* **1.** one employed in working with machinery **2.** skilled workman —*pl.* **3.** scientific theory of motion —**me'chanical** *a.* **1.** concerned with machines or operation of them **2.** worked, produced (as though) by machine **3.** acting without thought —**me'chanically** *adv.* —**mecha'nician** *n.* —**mechanical drawing** drawing done with T squares, scales *etc.*

mechanism ('mekənizəm) *n.* **1.** structure of machine **2.** piece of machinery —**mechani'zation** *n.* —'**mechanize** *vt.* **1.** equip with machinery **2.** make mechanical, automatic **3.** *Mil.* equip with armored vehicles —'**mechanized** *a.*

mechlorethamine (məklörə'thämin) *n. see* **nitrogen mustard** *at* NITROGEN

Med (med) *n. inf.* Mediterranean region

med. **1.** medical **2.** medicine **3.** medieval **4.** medium

M.Ed. Master of Education

medal ('medəl) *n.* piece of metal with inscription *etc.* used as reward or memento —'**medalist** *or* '**medallist** *n.* **1.** winner of a medal **2.** maker of medals —**me'dallion** *n.* **1.** large medal **2.** any of various things like this in decorative work

meddle ('medəl) *vi.* interfere, busy oneself unnecessarily —'**meddlesome** *a.*

media ('mēdiə) *n., pl. of* MEDIUM, used *esp.* of the mass media, radio, television *etc.* —**media event** event staged for or exploited by the mass media

mediaeval (mēdi'ēvəl, medi-) *a. see* MEDIEVAL

medial ('mēdiəl) *a.* **1.** in the middle **2.** pert. to a mean or average —'**median** *a./n.* middle (point or line) —**median strip** space, oft. landscaped, dividing opposing traffic on a highway

mediate ('mēdiăt) vi. 1. intervene to reconcile —vt. 2. bring about by mediation —a. ('mēdiit) 3. depending on mediation —medi'ation n. 1. intervention in behalf of another 2. act of going between —'mediator n.

medicine ('medisin) n. 1. drug or remedy for treating disease 2. science of preventing, diagnosing, alleviating, or curing disease —'medic n. inf. 1. doctor 2. medical orderly 3. medical student —'medical a. —'medically adv. —me'dicament n. remedy —'medicate vt. impregnate with medicinal substances —medi'cation n. —'medicative a. healing —me'dicinal a. curative —'medico n. inf. 1. doctor 2. medical student (pl. -s) —medical electronics use of technology in diagnosis and treatment of human disease —medicine ball heavy ball for physical training —medicine man witch doctor

medieval or **mediaeval** (mēdi'ēvəl, medi-) a. of Middle Ages —medi'evalism or medi'aevalism n. 1. spirit of Middle Ages 2. cult of medieval ideals —medi'evalist or medi'aevalist n. student of Middle Ages —Medieval Greek Greek language from 7th cent. A.D.-1204 —Medieval Latin Latin language as used throughout Europe in Middle Ages

mediocre (mēdi'ōkər) a. 1. neither bad nor good, ordinary, middling 2. second-rate —mediocrity (mēdi'okriti) n.

meditate ('meditāt) vi. 1. be occupied in thought 2. reflect deeply on spiritual matters —medi'tation n. 1. thought 2. absorption in thought 3. religious contemplation —'meditative a. 1. thoughtful 2. reflective —'meditatively adv.

Mediterranean (meditə'rāniən) n. 1. short for **Mediterranean Sea**, sea between S Europe, N Afr., and SW Asia 2. native or inhabitant of Mediterranean country —a. 3. of Mediterranean Sea

medium ('mēdiəm) a. 1. between two qualities, degrees etc., average —n. 2. middle quality, degree 3. intermediate substance conveying force 4. means, agency of communicating news etc. to public, as radio, newspapers etc. 5. person through whom communication can supposedly be held with spirit world 6. surroundings, environment (pl. -s, 'media) —medium waves Rad. waves between 100 and 1000 meters

medlar ('medlər) n. 1. tree with fruit like small apple 2. the fruit, eaten when decayed

medley ('medli) n. miscellaneous mixture (pl. -s)

medulla (mi'dulə) n. 1. marrow 2. pith 3. inner tissue —medullary ('medələri) a.

Medusa (mi'dyōōsə, -'dōōsə; -zə) n. 1. Myth. Gorgon whose head turned beholders into stone 2. (m-) jellyfish (pl. -sae (-sē, -zē))

meek (mēk) a. submissive, humble —'meekly adv. —'meekness n.

meerkat ('mēərkat) n. S Afr. mongoose

meerschaum ('mēərshəm) n. 1. white substance like clay 2. tobacco pipe bowl made of this

meet[1] (mēt) vt. 1. come face to face with, encounter 2. satisfy 3. pay —vi. 4. come face to face 5. converge at specified point 6. assemble 7. come into contact (met pt./pp.) —n. 8. meeting, esp. for sports —'meeting n. 1. assembly 2. encounter

meet[2] (mēt) a. obs. fit, suitable

mega- (comb. form) 1. denoting 10⁶, as in megawatt 2. in computer technology, denoting 2²⁰ (1 048 576), as in megabyte 3. large, great, as in megalith

megadeath ('megədeth) n. death of a million people, esp. in nuclear war

megahertz ('megəhərts) n. one million hertz (pl. 'megahertz)

megalith ('megəlith) n. great stone —mega'lithic a.

megalomania (megəlō'māniə) n. desire for, delusions of grandeur, power etc. —megalo'maniac a./n.

megalopolis (megə'lopəlis) n. urban complex, usu. comprising several towns —megalopolitan (megəlō'politən) a./n.

megamouth ('megəmowth) n. plankton-feeding shark found in Pacific

megaphone ('megəfōn) n. cone-shaped instrument to amplify voice

megaton ('megətun) n. 1. one million tons 2. explosive power of 1 000 000 tons of TNT

megohm ('megōm) n. Elec. one million ohms

meiosis (mī'ōsis) n. cell division in which the chromosomes of sperm and egg are reduced from the number characteristic of the species to one half so that the resulting zygote will have the correct number of chromosomes (pl. -ses (-sēz)) —meiotic (mī'otik) a.

melamine ('meləmēn) n. colorless crystalline compound used in making synthetic resins —melamine resin resilient kind of plastic

melancholy ('melənkoli) n. 1. sadness, dejection, gloom —a. 2. gloomy, dejected —melancholia (melən'kōliə) n. mental disease accompanied by depression —'melancholic n./a.

Melanesian (melə'nēzhən) a. 1. of Melanesia, its people, or their languages —n. 2. native or inhabitant of Melanesia 3. group or branch of languages spoken in Melanesia

mélange (mā'lāzh) Fr. mixture

melanin ('melənin) n. dark pigment found in hair, skin etc. of humans and other animals —mela'noma n. tumor containing melanin which may be benign or cancerous —mela'nosis n. excessive deposits of melanin in the tissues

Melba toast ('melbə) very thin crisp toast

meld (meld) v. 1. (in card games) declare (cards, which then score points) —n. 2. act of melding 3. set of cards for melding

melee or **mêlée** ('mālā, mā'lā) n. confused, noisy fight or crowd

melioidosis (mēlioi'dōsis) n. disease of humans and animals caused by bacteria found in soil and water

meliorate ('mēlyərāt, -liə-) v. improve —melio'ration n. —'meliorism n. doctrine that the world may be improved by human effort —'meliorist n.

mellifluous (me'liflōōəs, mə-) or **mellifluent** a. (of sound) smooth, sweet —mel'lifluence n.

mellophone ('meləfōn) n. musical instrument played in a brass band resembling the French horn

mellow ('melō) a. 1. ripe 2. softened by age, experience 3. soft, not harsh 4. genial, gay —v. 5. make, become mellow

melodeon (mi'lōdiən) n. Mus. 1. small accordion 2. keyboard instrument similar to harmonium

melodrama ('melədrämə) n. 1. play full of sensational and startling situations, often highly emotional 2. overdramatic behavior, emotion —melodra'matic a.

melody ('melədi) n. 1. series of musical notes which make tune 2. sweet sound —melodic (mi'lodik) a. 1. of or relating to melody 2. of or relating to part in piece of music —me'lodious a. 1. pleasing to the ear 2. tuneful —'melodist n. 1. singer 2. composer

melon ('melən) n. large, fleshy, juicy fruit

melt (melt) v. 1. (cause to) become liquid by heat 2. dissolve 3. soften 4. (cause to) waste away 5. blend —vi. 6. disappear ('melted pt./pp., 'molten pp.) —'melting a. 1. softening 2. languishing 3. tender —melting point temperature at which solid turns into liquid —'meltwater n. melted snow or ice

melton ('meltən) n. heavy smooth woolen fabric with short nap

mem. 1. member 2. memoir 3. memorandum 4. memorial

member ('membər) n. 1. any of individuals making up body or society 2. limb 3. any part of complex whole —'membership n. —Member of Parliament UK member of House of Commons or similar legislative body

membrane ('membrān) n. thin flexible tissue in plant or animal body —'membranous a.

memento (mi'mentō) n. thing serving to remind, souvenir (pl. -s, -es) —memento mori ('mōrē) object intended to remind people of death

memo ('memō) n. memorandum (pl. -s)

memoir ('memwär) n. 1. autobiography, personal history or biography 2. record of events

memory ('meməri) n. 1. faculty of recollecting, recalling to mind 2. recollection 3. thing remembered 4. length of time one can remember 5. commemoration 6. part or faculty of computer which stores information —memorabilia (memərə'biliə) pl.n. memorable events or things (sing. -rabile (-'rabili)) —'memorable a. worthy of remembrance, noteworthy —'memorably adv. —memo'randum n. 1. note to help the memory etc. 2. informal letter 3. note of contract (pl. -s, -da (-də)) —me'morial a. 1. of, preserving memory —n. 2. thing, esp. a monument, which serves to keep in memory —me'morialist n. —me'morialize vt. commemorate —'memorize vt. commit to memory

men (men) n., pl. of MAN

menace ('menis) n. 1. threat —v. 2. threaten

ménage (mā'näzh) n. persons of a household —ménage à trois (mānazh a 'trwa) Fr. sexual arrangement involving married couple and lover of one of them (pl. ménages à trois (mānazh a 'trwa))

menagerie (mi'najəri) n. exhibition, collection of wild animals

mend (mend) vt. 1. repair, patch 2. reform, correct, put right —vi. 3. improve, esp. in health —n. 4. repaired breakage, hole —on the mend regaining health

mendacious (men'dāshəs) a. untruthful —mendacity (men'dasiti) n. (tendency to) untruthfulness

mendelevium (mendi'lēviəm) n. Chem. transuranic element Symbol Mv, at. wt. 256, at. no. 101

mendicant ('mendikənt) a. 1. begging —n. 2. beggar —'mendicancy or men'dicity n. begging

menhir ('menhēər) n. single, upright monumental stone, monolith

menial ('mēniəl) a. 1. of work requiring little skill 2. of household duties or servants 3. servile —n. 4. servant 5. servile person

Ménière's disease (mən'yerz, 'menyərz) progressive disorder of the inner ear characterized by severe vertigo, tinnitus and deafness

meninges (mi'ninjēz) pl.n. three membranes that envelop brain and spinal cord (sing. meninx ('mēningks)) —meningeal (menin'jēəl) *a.* —**meningi'oma** *n.* tumor of the meninges —**meningitis** (menin'jītis) *n.* inflammation of the membranes of the brain

meniscus (mi'niskəs) *n.* 1. curved surface of liquid 2. curved lens

menopause ('menəpöz) *n.* period of gradual decline in activity of female reproductive organs

menorah (mi'nörə) *n.* branched candelabrum used in Jewish celebrations

menses ('mensēz) *n.* 1. menstruation 2. matter discharged during menstruation (*pl.* 'menses)

menstruation (menstrŏŏ'āshən) *n.* approximately monthly discharge of blood and cellular debris from womb of nonpregnant woman —'**menstrual** *a.* —'**menstruate** *vi.*

mensuration (mensə'rāshən, menchə-) *n.* measuring, *esp.* of areas

-ment (*comb. form*) 1. state; condition; quality, as in *enjoyment* 2. result or product of action, as in *embankment* 3. process; action, as in *management*

mental ('mentəl) *a.* 1. of, done by the mind 2. *inf.* feeble-minded, mad —**men'tality** *n.* state or quality of mind —'**mentally** *adv.*

menthol ('menthöl) *n.* organic compound found in peppermint, used medicinally

mention ('menchən) *vt.* 1. refer to briefly, speak of —*n.* 2. acknowledgment 3. reference to or remark about person or thing —'**mentionable** *a.* fit or suitable to be mentioned

mentor ('mentör) *n.* wise, trusted adviser, guide

menu ('menyŏŏ) *n.* list of dishes to be served, or from which to order

meow, miaow (mi'ow), *or* **miaul** (mi'owl) *vi.* 1. (of cat) make characteristic crying sound —*interj.* 2. imitation of this sound

meperidine (mə'peridēn) *n.* synthetic pain-relieving drug with sedative and antispasmodic properties: a morphine substitute (*also* **Demerol**)

mercantile ('mərkəntēl, -tīl) *a.* of, engaged in trade, commerce

mercenary ('mərsineri) *a.* 1. influenced by greed 2. working merely for reward —*n.* 3. hired soldier

mercer ('mərsər) *n. esp.* formerly, dealer in fabrics —'**mercery** *n.* his trade, goods

mercerize ('mərsərīz) *vt.* give luster to (cotton fabrics) by treating with chemicals —'**mercerized** *a.*

merchant ('mərchənt) *n.* 1. one engaged in trade 2. wholesale trader —**merchandise** ('mərchəndīz, -dīs) *n.* his wares —'**merchantman** *n.* trading ship —**merchant navy** ships engaged in a nation's commerce

Mercurochrome (mər'kyŏŏrəkröm) *n.* trade name for red organic compound used to disinfect skin and mucous membranes

mercury ('mərkyəri) *n.* 1. *Chem.* metallic element *Symbol* Hg, at. wt. 200.8, at. no. 80 (*also* **quicksilver**) 2. (**M-**) *Roman myth.* messenger of the gods 3. (**M-**) planet nearest to sun —**mer'curial** *a.* 1. relating to, containing mercury 2. lively, changeable

mercy ('mərsi) *n.* refraining from infliction of suffering by one who has right, power to inflict it, compassion —'**merciful** *a.* —'**merciless** *a.* —**mercy killing** *see* EUTHANASIA

mere[1] (mēər) *a.* 1. only 2. not more than 3. nothing but —'**merely** *adv.*

mere[2] (mēər) *n. obs.* lake

meretricious (meri'trishəs) *a.* 1. superficially or garishly attractive 2. insincere

merganser (mər'gansər) *n.* large, crested diving duck

merge (mərj) *v.* (cause to) lose identity or be

absorbed —'**merger** *n.* 1. combination of business firms into one 2. absorption into something greater

meridian (mə'ridiən) *n.* 1. circle of the earth passing through poles 2. imaginary circle in sky passing through celestial poles 3. highest point reached by star *etc.* 4. period of greatest splendor —*a.* 5. of meridian 6. at peak of something

meringue (mə'rang) *n.* 1. baked mixture of white of eggs and sugar 2. cake of this

merino (mə'rēnö) *n.* 1. breed of sheep originating in Spain (*pl.* **-s**) 2. long, fine wool of this sheep 3. yarn or cloth made from this wool

merit ('merit) *n.* 1. excellence, worth 2. quality of deserving reward —*pl.* 3. excellence —*vt.* 4. deserve —**meri'tocracy** *n.* 1. rule by persons chosen for their superior talents or intellect 2. persons constituting such group —**meri'torious** *a.* deserving praise

merlin ('mərlin) *n.* small falcon

merlot (mər'lö) *n.* dry red wine from grape grown in Bordeaux and California

mermaid ('mərmād) *n.* imaginary sea creature with upper part of woman and lower part of fish

merry ('meri) *a.* joyous, cheerful —'**merrily** *adv.* —'**merriment** *n.* —**merry-go-round** *n.* roundabout

mésalliance (māzal'yäns) *n.* marriage with person of lower social status

mescal (me'skal) *n.* small, bluish-green cactus native to southwest U.S. and Mexico (*also* **peyote**) —**mescaline** ('meskəlin, -lēn) *n.* psychedelic drug obtained from this plant —**mescal buttons** rounded parts of stem yielding mescaline

mesdames (mā'däm, -'dam) *n., pl. of* MADAM, MADAME

mesdemoiselles (mādmwə'zel) *n., pl. of* MADEMOISELLE

mesembryanthemum (mizembri'anthiməm) *n.* low-growing plant with daisylike flowers of various colors

mesh (mesh) *n.* 1. (one of the open spaces of, or wires *etc.* forming) network, net —*v.* 2. entangle, become entangled 3. (of gears) engage —*vi.* 4. coordinate

meshugge (mə'shŏŏgə) *a. inf.* crazy, obsessed, phobic, bizarre —**meshugene** (mə'shŏŏgənə) *n.* meshugge male —**meshugener** (mə'shŏŏgənər) *n.* meshugge female

mesmerism ('mezmərizəm) *n. former term for* HYPNOTISM —**mes'meric** *a.* —'**mesmerist** *n.* —'**mesmerize** *vt.* 1. hypnotize 2. fascinate, hold spellbound

meso- *or before vowel* **mes-** (*comb. form*) middle or intermediate, as in *mesomorph*

Mesolithic (mezə'lithik, mēz-, mēs-, mes-) *n.* 1. period between Paleolithic and Neolithic —*a.* 2. of or relating to Mesolithic

meson ('mezon, 'mēz-, 'mēs-, 'mes-) *n.* elementary atomic particle of small mass and very short life

Mesozoic (mezə'zöik, mēz-, mēs-, mes-) *a.* of, denoting, or relating to era of geological time that began 225 000 000 years ago and lasted about 155 000 000 years

mess (mes) *n.* 1. untidy confusion 2. trouble, difficulty 3. group in armed services who regularly eat together 4. place where they eat —*vi.* 5. make mess 6. *Mil.* eat in a mess —*vt.* 7. muddle —'**messy** *a.* —**mess about** *or* **around** potter about

message ('mesij) *n.* 1. communication sent 2. meaning, moral 3. errand —'**messenger** *n.* bearer of message

Messiah (mi'sīə) *n.* 1. Jews' promised deliverer 2. Christ —**Messianic** (mesi'anik) *a.*

messieurs (mə'syə, mā'syə; mə'səərz) *n., pl. of* MONSIEUR

Messrs. ('mesərz) *n., pl. of* MR.

mestizo (me'stēzö) *n.* person of mixed European and Amerindian ancestry (*pl.* **-s**)

met (met) *pt./pp. of* MEET[1]

met. 1. meteorological 2. meteorology 3. metropolitan

meta- *or sometimes before vowel* **met-** (*comb. form*) change, as in *metamorphose, metathesis*

metabolism (mi'tabəlizəm) *n.* chemical process of living organism *esp.* energy production, tissue synthesis, formation and excretion of waste products —**meta'bolic** *a.* —**me'tabolize** *v.*

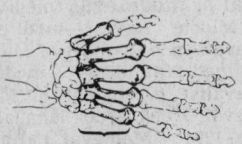

metacarpus

metacarpus (metə'kärpəs) *n.* 1. skeleton of hand between wrist and fingers 2. corresponding bones in other vertebrates (*pl.* **-pi** (-pī)) —**meta'carpal** *a./n.*

metal ('metəl) *n.* 1. mineral substance, opaque, fusible and malleable, capable of conducting heat and electricity 2. *Chem.* such a substance in a pure state, as distinguished from alloys —**me'tallic** *a.* —'**metalloid** *n.* 1. nonmetallic element that has some of properties of metal —*a.* (*also* **metal'loidal**) 2. of or being metalloid 3. resembling metal —**metal'lurgic** *or* **metal'lurgical** *a.* —**metallurgist** *n.* —'**metallurgy** *n.* scientific study of extracting, refining metals, and their structure and properties

metamorphosis (metə'mörfəsis) *n.* change of shape, character *etc.* (*pl.* **-phoses** (-fəsēz)) —**meta'morphic** *a.* (*esp.* of rocks) changed in texture, structure by heat, pressure *etc.* —**meta'morphose** *v.* transform

metaphor ('metəför, -fər) *n.* 1. figure of speech in which term is transferred to something it does not literally apply to 2. instance of this —**meta'phorical** *a.* figurative —**meta'phorically** *adv.*

metaphysics (metə'fiziks) *pl.n.* (*with sing. v.*) branch of philosophy concerned with being and knowing —**meta'physical** *a.* —**metaphy'sician** *n.*

metastasis (mi'tastəsis) *n. Pathol.* spreading of disease, *esp.* cancer cells, from one part of body to another (*pl.* **-ses** (-sēz)) —**metastatic** (metə'statik) *a.*

metatarsus

metatarsus (metə'tärsəs) *n.* 1. skeleton of foot between toes and ankle 2. corresponding bones in other vertebrates (*pl.* **-si** (-sī)) —**meta'tarsal** *a./n.*

metate (mə'täti) *n.* stone for grinding maize

metathesis (mi'tathəsis) *n.* transposition, *esp.* of letters in word, *eg* Old English *bridd* gives modern *bird* (*pl.* **-eses** (-əsēz))

metazoan (metə'zōən) n. 1. any animal having a body composed of many cells —a. (*also* **meta'zoic**) 2. of or relating to metazoans

mete (mēt) vt. measure —**mete out** 1. distribute 2. allot as punishment

metempsychosis (mitemsi'kōsis, mitemp-si-; metəmsi'kōsis) n. migration of soul from one body to another (*pl.* **-ses** (-sēz)) —**metempsy'chosist** n.

meteor ('mētiər) n. small, fast-moving celestial body, visible as streak of incandescence if it enters earth's atmosphere —**mete'oric** a. 1. of, like meteor 2. brilliant but short-lived —**'meteorite** n. fallen meteor —**'meteoroid** n. any of small celestial bodies that are thought to orbit sun —**meteor'oidal** a.

meteorology (mētiə'roləji) n. study of earth's atmosphere, *esp.* for weather forecasting —**meteoro'logical** a. —**meteor'ologist** n.

meter ('mētər) n. 1. basic unit of length in metric system defined by path of speed of light during specific interval 2. instrument for recording consumption of gas, electricity *etc.* 3. *Mus.* basic scheme of beats within a measure —**'metric** a. of system of weights and measures in which meter is a unit —**metrical** ('metrikəl) a. of measurement of poetic meter —**metricate** ('metrikāt) v. convert (measuring system *etc.*) from nonmetric to metric units —**metrication** (metri'kāshən) n. —**metric ton** *see* TONNE

Meth. Methodist

methane ('methān) n. flammable gas, compound of carbon and hydrogen

methanol ('methənōl) n. colorless, poisonous liquid used as solvent and fuel (*also* **methyl alcohol**)

methinks (mi'thingks) v. impers. obs. it seems to me (**me'thought** pt.)

method ('methəd) n. 1. way, manner 2. technique 3. orderliness, system —**me'thodical** a. orderly —**'methodize** vt. reduce to order —**metho'dology** n. particular method or procedure

Methodist ('methədist) n./a. (member) of Protestant Christian denomination derived from system of faith and practice initiated by John Wesley and his followers in 1738 —**'Methodism** n.

methyl ('methil) n. (compound containing) a saturated hydrocarbon group of atoms —**'methylate** vt. 1. combine with methyl 2. mix with methanol —**methyl alcohol** *see* METHANOL —**methylated spirits** ethyl alcohol contaminated with methyl alcohol to make it undrinkable

meticulous (mi'tikyələs) a. (over)particular about details

métier ('metyā) n. 1. profession, vocation 2. forte

métis (mā'tēs) n. person of mixed blood

metonymy (mi'tonimi) n. figure of speech in which thing is replaced by another associated with it, *eg the Crown* for *the king* —**meto'nymical** a.

metric ('metrik) a. *see* METER

Metro ('metrō) n. **C** metropolitan city administration

metronome ('metrənōm) n. instrument which marks musical time by means of ticking pendulum

metropolis (mi'tropəlis) n. chief city of a country, region —**metro'politan** a. 1. of metropolis —n. 2. bishop with authority over other bishops of a province

-metry (*n. comb. form*) process or science of

measuring, as in *geometry* —**-metric** (a. comb. form)

mettle ('metəl) n. courage, spirit —**'mettlesome** a. high-spirited

mew[1] (myōō) n. 1. cry of cat, gull —vi. 2. utter this cry

mew[2] (myōō) n. any sea gull, *esp.* common gull

Mex. 1. Mexican 2. Mexico

Mexico ('meksikō) n. country in Central America bounded north by the U.S.A., west and southwest by the Pacific, south by Guatemala and Belize and east by the Gulf of Mexico —**'Mexican** n./a.

mezuza (mə'zōōzə) n. small oblong container holding printed verses from Deuteronomy fixed to door jamb, sometimes worn as ornament

mezzanine ('mezənēn) n. intermediate story, balcony between two main stories, *esp.* between first and second floors

mezzo ('metsō) adv. *Mus.* moderately; quite —**mezzo-soprano** n. voice, singer between soprano and contralto (*pl.* **-s**)

mezzotint ('metsōtint) n. 1. method of engraving by scraping roughened surface 2. print so made

mf *Mus.* mezzo forte

MF 1. *Rad.* medium frequency. 2. Middle French

mfr. 1. manufacture 2. manufacturer

mg *or* **mg.** milligram(s)

Mg *Chem.* magnesium

Mgr. 1. manager 2. Monseigneur 3. Monsignor

MHG Middle High German

MHS Mohs' scale

MHz megahertz

mi (mē) n. *Mus.* 1. in fixed system of solmization, the note E 2. in movable do system, the third note of a major scale

MI Michigan

Miami (mī'ami) n. member of Algonquian-speaking Amerindian people orig. of Wisconsin and Indiana (*pl.* **Miami, -s**)

miaow (mi'ow) *see* MEOW

miasma (mī'azmə, mi-) n. unwholesome or foreboding atmosphere (*pl.* **-mata** (-mətə), **-s**) —**miasmatic** (mīəz'matik) a.

mica ('mīkə) n. mineral found as glittering scales, plates

Micah ('mīkə) n. *Bible* 33rd book of the O.T., written by the prophet Micah, displaying the character and acts of Jehovah in relation to the nation of Israel

mice (mīs) n., *pl. of* MOUSE

Mich. Michigan

Michaelmas ('mikəlməs) n. feast of Archangel St. Michael, 29th September —**Michaelmas daisy** common garden flower of aster family

Micheas ('mīkiəs) n. *Bible* Micah in the Douay Version of the O.T.

Michigan ('mishigən) n. East North Central state of the U.S., admitted to the Union in 1837. Abbrev.: **Mich., MI** (with ZIP code)

mick (mik) n. offens. Irishman

Mickey Finn (fin) sl. drink containing drug to make drinker unconscious

micro ('mīkrō) n. inf. 1. microcomputer 2. microprocessor (*pl.* **-s**)

micro- *or before vowel* **micr-** (*comb. form*) 1. small or minute, as in *microdot* 2. magnification or amplification, as in *microscope, microphone* 3. involving use of microscope, as in *microscopy* 4. one millionth, as in *microfarad* (millionth of a farad)

microbe ('mīkrōb) n. 1. minute organism 2. disease germ —**mi'crobial** a.

microbiology (mīkrōbi'oləji) n. branch of biology involving study of microorganisms —**microbio'logic(al)** a.

Microcard ('mīkrōkärd) n. trade name for card having microcopies of printed data

microcephaly (mīkrō'sefəli) n. condition in which the brain is small and undeveloped

microchip ('mīkrōchip) n. small wafer of silicon *etc.* containing electronic circuits (*also* **chip**)

microcircuit ('mīkrōsərkit) n. miniature electronic circuit, *esp.* integrated circuit —**'microcircuitry** n.

microcomputer (mīkrōkəm'pyōōtər) n. computer in which central processing unit is contained in one or more silicon chips

microcopy ('mīkrōkopi) n. minute photographic replica useful for storage because of its small size

microcosm ('mīkrəkozəm) *or* **microcosmos** (mīkrə'kozməs) n. 1. miniature representation, model *etc.* of some larger system 2. the microscopic or even smaller world —**micro'cosmic** a.

microdot ('mīkrōdot) n. extremely small microcopy

microelectronics ('mīkrōilek'troniks) pl.n. (with sing. v.) branch of electronics concerned with microcircuits

microfauna ('mīkrōfōnə) n. minute animals living in sand and gravel below the sea's surface

microfiche ('mīkrōfēsh) n. microfilm in sheet form

microfilm ('mīkrəfilm) n. miniaturized recording of manuscript, book on roll of film

microgroove ('mīkrōgrōōv) n. 1. narrow groove of long-playing phonograph record —a. 2. (of a record) having such grooves

micrometer (mī'kromitər) n. instrument for measuring very small distances or angles

microminiaturization (mīkrōminiəchōōri'zāshən) n. production of small components and circuits and equipment in which they are used

micron ('mīkron) n. unit of length, one millionth of a meter

microorganism (mīkrō'örgənizəm) n. smallest and simplest form of life, *eg* bacteria, yeasts, protozoa *etc.*

microphone ('mīkrəfōn) n. instrument for amplifying, transmitting sounds

microprint ('mīkrəprint) n. greatly reduced photographic copy of print, read by magnifying device

microprocessor (mīkrō'prōsesər) n. integrated circuit acting as central processing unit in small computer

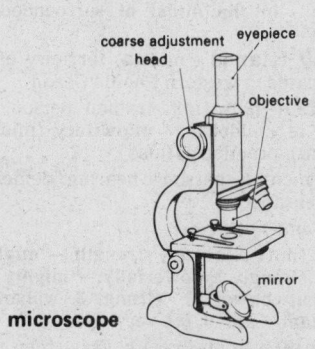

coarse adjustment eyepiece
head
objective
mirror

microscope

microscope ('mīkrəskōp) n. instrument by which very small body is magnified and made visible —**microscopic** (mīkrə'skopik) a. 1. of microscope 2. very small —**microscopy** (mī'kroskəpi) n. use of microscope

microstructure ('mīkrōstrukchər) n. structure on microscopic scale, *esp.* of alloy as observed by etching, polishing *etc.* under microscope

microsurgery (mīkrō'sərjəri) n. minute surgical dissection or manipulation of individual cells under a microscope

microwave ('mīkrəwāv) n. electromagnetic wave with wavelength of a few centimeters, used in radar, cooking *etc.*

micturate ('mikchərat) vi. urinate —**micturition** (mikchə'rishən) n.

mid (mid) a. intermediate, in the middle of —'**midday** n. noon —**midland** ('midlənd) n. 1. interior of a country —*pl.* 2. central England —'**midnight** n. twelve o'clock at night —**midnight sun** sun visible at midnight during summer inside Arctic and Antarctic circles —'**midshipman** n. naval officer of lowest commissioned rank —'**mid**'**summer** n. 1. summer solstice 2. middle of summer —'**midway** a./adv. halfway —'**mid**'**winter** n.

midden ('midən) n. 1. dunghill 2. rubbish heap

middle ('midəl) a. 1. equidistant from two extremes 2. medium, intermediate —n. 3. middle point or part —'**middling** a. 1. mediocre 2. moderate —adv. 3. inf. moderately —**middle age** period of life between youth and old age, usu. considered to be between ages of 40 and 60 —**middle-aged** a. —**Middle Ages** period from end of Roman Empire to Renaissance, roughly A.D. 500–1500 —**middle C** Mus. note written on first ledger line below treble staff or first ledger line above bass staff —**middle class** social class of businessmen, professional people *etc.* —**middle-class** a. —**middle ear** sound-conducting part of ear —**Middle East** (loosely) area around E Mediterranean, *esp.* Israel and Arab countries from Turkey to N Afr. and eastward to Iran —**Middle Eastern** —**Middle English** English language from about 1100 to about 1450 —**Middle High German** High German from about 1200 to about 1500 —**Middle Low German** Low German from about 1200 to about 1500 —'**middleman** n. trader between producer and consumer —**middle-of-the-road** a. not extreme; moderate —'**middleweight** n. 1. professional boxer weighing 154–160 lbs. (70–72.5 kg); amateur boxer weighing 157–165 lbs. (71–75 kg) 2. wrestler weighing usu. 172–192 lbs. (78–87 kg)

midget ('mijit) n. very small person or thing

midi ('midi) a. (of skirt *etc.*) reaching to below knee or midcalf

midriff ('midrif) n. middle part of body

midst (midst) prep. 1. in the middle of —n. 2. middle —**in the midst of** surrounded by, among

Midway Islands ('midwā) territory of the U.S. located in western Pacific Ocean

midwife ('midwīf) n. trained person who assists at childbirth —**midwifery** (mid'wifəri) n. art, practice of this

mien (mēn) n. person's bearing, demeanor or appearance

might[1] (mīt) pt. of MAY

might[2] (mīt) n. power, strength —'**mightily** adv. 1. strongly 2. powerfully —'**mighty** a. 1. of great power 2. strong 3. valiant 4. important —adv. 5. inf. very

mignonette (minyə'net) n. gray-green plant with sweet-smelling flowers

migraine ('mīgrān) n. severe recurring headache marked by nausea and visual disturbances and usu. on one side of head

migrate ('mīgrāt, mī'grāt) vi. move from one place to another —'**migrant** n./a. —**mi**'**gration** n. 1. act of passing from one place, condition to another 2. number migrating together —'**migratory** a. 1. of, capable of migration 2. (of animals) changing from one place to another according to season

mikado (mi'kädō) n. (oft. **M**-) Japanese emperor

mike (mīk) n. inf. microphone

Mike (mīk) n. word used in communications for the letter m

milady (mi'lādi) n. formerly, continental title used for English gentlewoman

milch (milk, milch) a. giving, kept for milk

mild (mīld) a. 1. not strongly flavored 2. gentle, merciful 3. calm or temperate —'**mildly** adv. —'**mildness** n. —**mild steel** any strong tough steel that contains low quantity of carbon

mildew ('mildyōō, -dōō) n. 1. destructive fungus on plants or things exposed to damp —v. 2. become tainted, affect with mildew

mile (mīl) n. measure of length, 1760 yards, 1.609 km —'**mileage** n. 1. distance in miles 2. traveling expenses per mile 3. miles traveled (per gallon of gasoline) 4. inf. advantage, profit, use —'**milestone** n. 1. stone marker showing distance 2. significant event, achievement —**nautical mile** see NAUTICAL

milfoil ('milfoil) n. yarrow

milieu (mēl'yə, -'yōō) n. environment, condition in life

military ('militeri) a. 1. of, for, soldiers, armies or war 2. of style of dress marked by severe cut, brass buttons, epaulettes *etc.* —n. 3. armed services —'**militancy** n. —'**militant** a. 1. aggressive, vigorous in support of cause 2. prepared, willing to fight —'**militarism** n. enthusiasm for military force and methods —'**militarist** n. —'**militarize** vt. convert to military use —**militia** (mi'lishə) n. military force of citizens for home service

militate ('militāt) vi. (esp. with against) have strong influence, effect (on)

milium ('miliəm) n. whitish lump in the skin due to a blocked duct in an oil gland (pl. -**ia** (-iə))

Milium ('miliəm) n. trade name for metal-insulated fabric used for lining outer clothing and curtains

milk (milk) n. 1. white fluid with which mammals feed their young 2. fluid in some plants —vt. 3. draw milk from —'**milky** a. 1. containing, like milk 2. (of liquids) opaque, clouded —**milk-and-water** a. weak, feeble, or insipid —'**milkmaid** n. esp. formerly, woman working with cows or in dairy —**milk run** Aeron. inf. routine and uneventful flight —**milk shake** frothy drink made of milk, flavoring and ice cream —'**milksop** n. effeminate fellow —**milk teeth** first set of teeth in young mammals —**Milky Way** luminous band of stars *etc.* stretching across sky, the galaxy —**milk of magnesia** suspension of magnesium hydroxide in water, used as laxative (also **magnesia magma**)

mill (mil) n. 1. factory 2. machine for grinding, pulverizing corn, paper *etc.* —vt. 3. put through mill 4. cut fine grooves across edges of (eg coins) —vi. 5. move in confused manner, as cattle or crowds of people —'**miller** n. —'**millpond** n. pool formed by damming stream to provide water to turn mill wheel —'**millrace** n. current of water driving mill wheel —'**millstone** n. flat circular stone for grinding

millennium (mi'leniəm) n. 1. period of a thousand years during which some claim Christ is to reign on earth 2. period of a thousand years 3. period of peace, happiness (pl. -**s**, -**ia** (-iə))

millet ('milit) n. a cereal grass

milli- (comb. form) thousandth, as in *milliliter*

milliard ('milyärd, 'miliärd) n. in England, France, and Germany, the name for one billion, the number one followed by nine zeros: 1 000 000 000

millibar ('milibär) n. unit of atmospheric pressure

milligram ('miligram) n. thousandth part of a gram

millimeter ('milimētər) n. thousandth part of a meter

milliner ('milinər) n. maker of, dealer in women's hats, ribbons *etc.* —'**millinery** n. his goods or work

million ('milyən) n. 1000 thousand —**million**'**aire** n. 1. owner of a million dollars, pounds *etc.* 2. very rich man —'**millionth** a./n.

millipede ('miliped) n. any of various terrestrial arthropods having a cylindrical body composed of 20 to 100 segments each with two pairs of legs

milt (milt) n. reproductive secretion of male fish

mime (mīm) n. 1. acting without the use of words —v. 2. act in mime

mimic ('mimik) vt. 1. imitate (person, manner *etc.*), esp. for satirical effect ('**mimicked**, '**mimicking**) —n. 2. one who, or animal which does this, or is adept at it —a. 3. imitative, simulated —**mi**'**metic** a. 1. of, resembling, or relating to imitation 2. Biol. of or exhibiting protective resemblance to another species —'**mimicry** n. mimicking

mimosa (mi'mōsə, mī-; -zə) n. genus of plants with fluffy, yellow flowers and sensitive leaves

min. 1. minim 2. minimum 3. minute

mina ('mīnə) n. see MYNAH

minaret (minə'ret, 'minəret) n. tall slender tower of mosque

minatory ('minətöri) or **minatorial** a. threatening or menacing

mince (mins) vt. 1. cut, chop small 2. soften or moderate (words *etc.*) —vi. 3. walk, speak in affected manner —'**mincing** a. affected in manner —'**mincemeat** n. mixture of currants, spices, suet *etc.* —**mince pie** pie containing mincemeat

mind (mīnd) n. 1. thinking faculties as distinguished from the body, intellectual faculties 2. memory, attention 3. intention 4. opinion 5. sanity —vt. 6. take offense at 7. care for 8. attend to 9. be cautious, careful about 10. be concerned, troubled about —vi. 11. be careful —'**mindful** a. 1. heedful 2. keeping in memory —'**mindless** a. stupid, careless —**mind-reader** n. person seemingly able to discern thoughts of another —**mind's eye** visual memory or imagination

mine[1] (mīn) pron. belonging to me

mine[2] (mīn) n. 1. deep hole for digging out coal, metals *etc.* 2. in war, hidden deposit of explosive to blow up ship *etc.* 3. profitable source —vt. 4. dig from mine 5. make mine in or under 6. place explosive mines in, on —vi. 7. make, work in mine —'**miner** n. one who works in a mine —'**minefield** n. area of land or sea containing mines —'**minelayer** n. ship for laying mines —'**minesweeper** n. ship for clearing away mines

mineral ('minərəl, 'minrəl) n. 1. chemical element or compound occurring naturally as a product of inorganic processes 2. atom of substance other than carbon, hydrogen, oxygen and nitrogen in living system 3. any of various homogeneous substances, *esp.* coal, salt, water or gas, obtained from the ground **4.** anything neither animal nor vegetable —**'mineralist** *n.* —**minera'logical** *a.* —**mine'ralogy** *n.* science of minerals —**mineral oil** oil of mineral origin, *esp.* refined petrolatum jelly, used as a laxative —**mineral water** water impregnated with minerals or gases

minestrone (mini'strōni) *n.* thick vegetable soup usu. containing beans and pasta

mingle ('minggəl) *v.* mix, blend, unite, merge

mingy ('minji) *a. inf.* miserly, stingy, or niggardly

mini ('mini) *n.* something small or miniature —**'miniskirt** *n.* very short skirt, one at least four inches above knee

mini- (*comb. form*) smaller or shorter than standard size

miniature ('miniəchōōər) *n.* **1.** small painted portrait **2.** anything on small scale —*a.* **3.** small-scale, minute —**'miniaturist** *n.* —**'miniaturize** *vt.* make or construct on a very small scale

minim ('minim) *n.* **1.** unit of fluid measure, one sixtieth of a fluid dram **2.** *Mus.* half note

minimize ('minimīz) *vt.* bring to, estimate at smallest possible amount —**'minimal** *a.* —**'minimum** *n.* **1.** lowest size or quantity (*pl.* **-s, -ma** (-mə)) —*a.* **2.** least possible —**minimum wage** lowest wage that employer is permitted to pay by law or union contract

minion ('minyən) *n.* **1.** favorite **2.** servile dependent

minister ('ministər) *n.* **1.** diplomatic representative **2.** clergyman —*vi.* **3.** (*oft. with* to) attend to needs (of), take care (of) —**'ministrant** *a./n.* —**minis'tration** *n.* rendering help, *esp.* to sick —**'ministry** *n.* **1.** office of clergyman **2.** period of service of minister **3.** act of ministering

miniver ('minivər) *n.* a white fur used in ceremonial costumes

mink (mingk) *n.* **1.** variety of weasel **2.** its (brown) fur

Minnesota (mini'sōtə) *n.* West North Central state of the U.S., admitted to the Union in 1858. Abbrev.: **Minn., MN** (with ZIP code)

minnow ('minō) *n.* small freshwater fish

Minoan (mi'nōən) *a.* **1.** of Bronze Age culture of Crete from about 3000 B.C. to about 1100 B.C. —*n.* **2.** Cretan belonging to Minoan culture

minor ('mīnər) *a.* **1.** lesser **2.** under age —*n.* **3.** person below age of legal majority **4.** minor scale in music —**minority** (mi'nöriti) *n.* **1.** lesser number **2.** smaller party voting together **3.** ethical or religious group in a minority in any state **4.** state of being a minor —**minor arts** generally all art forms not painting, sculpture or architecture —**minor scale** *Mus.* scale with semitones instead of whole tones after second and seventh notes

Minotaur ('minətör) *n.* fabled monster, half bull, half man

minster ('minstər) *n.* **1.** *Hist.* monastery church **2.** cathedral, large church

minstrel ('minstrəl) *n.* **1.** medieval singer, musician, poet —*pl.* **2.** performers of Negro songs —**'minstrelsy** *n.* **1.** art, body of minstrels **2.** collection of songs

mint¹ (mint) *n.* **1.** place where money is coined —*vt.* **2.** coin, invent

mint² (mint) *n.* aromatic plant —**mint julep** tall drink of bourbon, ice, sugar and mint

minuet (minyōō'et) *n.* **1.** stately dance in moderate triple time **2.** music for it

minus ('mīnəs) *prep.* **1.** less, with the deduction of, deprived of —*a.* **2.** lacking **3.** negative —*n.* **4.** the sign of subtraction (-)

minuscule ('minəskyōōl) *n.* **1.** lower-case letter **2.** writing using such letters —*a.* **3.** relating to, printed in, or written in small letters **4.** very small —**minuscular** (mi'nuskyələr) *a.*

minute¹ (mī'nyōōt, -'nōōt) *a.* **1.** very small **2.** precise —**mi'nutely** *adv.* —**minutiae** (mi'nyōōshiē, -'nōō-) *pl.n.* trifles, precise details

minute² ('minit) *n.* **1.** 60th part of hour or degree **2.** moment **3.** memorandum —*pl.* **4.** record of proceedings of meeting *etc.* —*vt.* **5.** make minute of **6.** record in minutes —**minute steak** small steak that can be cooked quickly

minx (mingks) *n.* bold, flirtatious woman

minyan ('minyən) *n. Judaism* the ten male Jews required for a religious service (*pl.* **minyanim** (minyə'nēm))

Miocene ('mīəsēn) *a.* **1.** of or denoting fourth epoch of Tertiary period —*n.* **2.** this epoch or rock system

miracle ('mirəkəl) *n.* **1.** supernatural event **2.** marvel —**mi'raculous** *a.* —**mi'raculously** *adv.* —**miracle drug** newly discovered drug that has startling therapeutic effect (*also* **wonder drug**) —**miracle play** drama (*esp.* medieval) based on sacred subject

mirage (mi'räzh) *n.* deceptive image in atmosphere, *eg* of lake in desert

mire ('mīər) *n.* **1.** swampy ground, mud —*vt.* **2.** stick in, dirty with mud

mirror ('mirər) *n.* **1.** glass or polished surface reflecting images —*vt.* **2.** reflect —**mirror image 1.** image as observed in mirror **2.** object that corresponds to another in reverse as does image in mirror

mirth (mərth) *n.* merriment, gaiety —**'mirthful** *a.* —**'mirthless** *a.*

mis- (*comb. form*) wrong(ly), bad(ly). See the list below

misadventure (misəd'venchər) *n.* unlucky chance

misalliance (misə'līəns) *n.* unsuitable alliance or marriage —**misal'ly** *v.*

misanthrope ('misənthrōp) *n.* hater of mankind —**misanthropic** (misən'thropik) *a.* —**mi'santhropy** *n.*

misappropriate (misə'prōpriāt) *vt.* **1.** put to dishonest use **2.** embezzle —**misappropri'ation** *n.*

misbegotten (misbi'gotən) *a.* **1.** unlawfully obtained **2.** badly conceived or designed **3.** *Lit., dial.* illegitimate; bastard

miscarry (mis'kari) *vi.* **1.** bring forth young prematurely **2.** go wrong, fail —**mis'carriage** *n.*

miscast (mis'kast) *v.* **1.** distribute (acting parts) wrongly —*vt.* **2.** assign to unsuitable role

miscegenation (miseji'nāshən, misiji'nā-) *n.* interbreeding of races

miscellaneous (misə'lāniəs) *a.* mixed, assorted —**mis'cellany** *n.* **1.** collection of assorted writings in one book **2.** medley

mischance (mis'chans) *n.* unlucky event

mischief ('mischif) *n.* **1.** annoying behavior **2.** inclination to tease, disturb **3.** harm **4.** source of harm or annoyance —**'mischievous** *a.* **1.** (of a child) full of pranks **2.** disposed to mischief **3.** having harmful effect

miscible ('misibəl) *a.* capable of mixing

misconception (miskən'sepshən) *n.* wrong idea, belief

miscreant ('miskriənt) *n.* wicked person, evildoer, villain

misdemeanor (misdi'mēnər) *n.* **1.** formerly, offense less grave than a felony **2.** minor offense

misdoubt (mis'dowt) *v. obs.* doubt or suspect

mise en scène (mēz ă 'sen) *Fr.* **1.** arrangement of scenery *etc.* in play; stage setting **2.** environment of event

miser ('mīzər) *n.* **1.** hoarder of money **2.** stingy person —**'miserliness** *n.* —**'miserly** *a.* **1.** avaricious **2.** niggardly

miserable ('mizərəbəl) *a.* **1.** very unhappy, wretched **2.** causing misery **3.** worthless **4.** squalid —**'miserableness** *n.* —**'misery** *n.* **1.** great unhappiness **2.** distress **3.** poverty

misericord *or* **misericorde** (mi'zerikörd) *n.* ledge projecting from underside of hinged seat of choir stall in church, on which occupant can support himself while standing

misfire (mis'fīər) *vi.* fail to fire, start, function successfully

misfit ('misfit) *n. esp.* person not suited to his environment or work

misgiving (mis'giving) *n.* (*oft. pl.*) feeling of fear, doubt *etc.*

misguided (mis'gīdid) *a.* foolish, unreasonable

mishap ('mis-hap) *n.* minor accident

mishmash ('mishmash) *n.* confused collection or mixture

mislay (mis'lā) *vt.* put in place which cannot later be remembered

mislead (mis'lēd) *vt.* **1.** give false information to **2.** lead astray (**mis'led** *pt./pp.*) —**mis'leading** *a.* deceptive

misnomer (mis'nōmər) *n.* **1.** wrong name or term **2.** use of this

misogamy (mi'sogəmi) *n.* hatred of marriage —**mi'sogamist** *n.*

misogyny (mi'sojini) *n.* hatred of women —**mi'sogynist** *n.*

misrepresent (misrepri'zent) *vt.* portray in wrong or misleading light

misrule (mis'rōōl) *vt.* **1.** govern inefficiently or without justice —*n.* **2.** inefficient or unjust government **3.** disorder

miss (mis) *vt.* **1.** fail to hit, reach, find, catch, or notice **2.** not be in time for **3.** omit **4.** notice or regret absence of **5.** avoid —*vi.* **6.** (of engine) misfire —*n.* **7.** fact, instance of missing —**'missing** *a.* **1.** lost **2.** absent —**missing link 1.** hypothetical extinct animal intermediate between anthropoid apes and man **2.** any missing section or part in series

Miss (mis) *n.* **1.** title of unmarried woman **2.** (m-) girl

Miss. Mississippi

missal ('misəl) *n.* book containing prayers *etc.* of the Mass

---

missile ('misil) *n.* that which may be thrown, shot, homed to damage, destroy —**guided missile** *see* GUIDE

mission ('mishən) *n.* 1. specific task or duty 2. calling in life 3. delegation 4. sending or being sent on some service 5. those sent —**'missionary** *n.* 1. one sent to a place, society to spread religion —*a.* 2. of, like missionary or religious mission

missis ('misiz, -is) *n. see* MISSUS

Mississippi (misi'sipi) *n.* East South Central state of the U.S., admitted to the Union in 1817. Abbrev.: **Miss., MS** (with ZIP code)

missive ('misiv) *n.* letter

Missouri (mi'zōōri, -'zōōrə) *n.* West North Central state of the U.S., admitted to the Union in 1821. Abbrev.: **Mo., MO** (with ZIP code)

misspend (mis'spend) *v.* spend thoughtlessly or wastefully (-**'spending**, -**'spent**)

missus *or* **missis** ('misiz, -is) *n.* (*usu. with* the) one's wife or wife of person addressed or referred to

mist (mist) *n.* water vapor in fine drops —**'mistily** *adv.* —**'misty** *a.* 1. full of mist 2. dim 3. obscure

mistake (mi'stāk) *n.* 1. error, blunder —*vt.* 2. fail to understand 3. form wrong opinion about 4. take (person or thing) for another —**mis'taken** *a.* 1. wrong in opinion *etc.* 2. arising from error in judgment *etc.*

mister ('mistər) *n.* title of courtesy to a man

mistle thrush ('misəl) European thrush with brown back and spotted breast

mistletoe

mistletoe ('misəltō) *n.* evergreen parasitic plant with white berries, which grows on trees

mistook (mi'stŏŏk) *pt. of* MISTAKE

mistral ('mistrəl, mi'sträl) *n.* strong, dry, N wind in France

mistress ('mistris) *n.* 1. object of man's illicit love 2. woman with mastery or control 3. woman owner 4. woman teacher 5. *obs.* title given to married woman

mistrial (mis'trīəl) *n. Law* trial made void because of some error

mistrust (mis'trust) *vt.* 1. have doubts or suspicions about —*n.* 2. distrust —**mis'trustful** *a.*

misunderstanding (misundər'standing) *n.* 1. failure to understand properly 2. disagreement —**misunder'stood** *a.* not properly or sympathetically understood

mite (mīt) *n.* 1. very small arachnid 2. anything very small 3. small but well-meant contribution

miter ('mītər) *n.* 1. bishop's headdress 2. joint between two pieces of wood *etc.* meeting at right angles —*vt.* 3. join with, shape for a miter joint 4. put miter on

mitigate ('mitigāt) *vt.* make less severe —**miti'gation** *n.* —**mitigating circumstances** circumstances which lessen the culpability of an offender

mitosis (mī'tōsis) *n.* cell division by which growth takes place in all living organisms in which nuclear genetic material is equally divided between two daughter cells —**mitotic** (mī'totik) *a.*

mitt (mit) *n.* 1. glove leaving fingers bare 2. baseball catcher's glove 3. *sl.* hand

mitten ('mitən) *n.* glove with two compartments, one for thumb and one for fingers

mix (miks) *vt.* 1. put together, combine, blend, mingle —*vi.* 2. be mixed 3. associate —**mixed** *a.* composed of different elements, races, sexes *etc.* —**'mixer** *n.* one who, that which mixes —**'mixture** *n.* —**mixed bag** *inf.* something composed of diverse elements, people *etc.* —**mixed blessing** situation *etc.* having advantages and disadvantages —**mixed doubles** *Tennis* game with man and woman as partners on each side —**mixed grill** dish of broiled chops, sausages, bacon *etc.* —**mixed marriage** marriage between persons of different races or religions —**mixed media** 1. the use of several different materials in a work of art 2. performances combining song, dance, sound, light, speech *etc.* —**mixed-up** *a. inf.* confused —**mix-up** *n.* confused situation

mizzen *or* **mizen** ('mizən) *n.* lowest fore-and-aft sail on aftermost mast of ship —**mizzenmast** ('mizənmast; *Naut.* 'mizənməst) *n.* aftermost mast on full-rigged ship

mks units metric system of units based on the meter, kilogram and second

ml milliliter(s)

M.L. Medieval Latin

M.L.A. C Member of the Legislative Assembly

M.Litt. Master of Letters

Mlle *or* **Mlle.** Mademoiselle (*pl.* **Mlles, Mlles.**)

mm millimeter(s)

Mme *or* **Mme.** Madame (*pl.* **Mmes, Mmes.**)

Mn *Chem.* manganese

MN Minnesota

MNA *or* **M.N.A. C** Member of the National Assembly

mnemonic (ni'monik) *a.* 1. helping the memory —*n.* 2. something intended to help the memory

mo (mō) *n. inf.* moment

Mo *Chem.* molybdenum

MO *or* **Mo.** Missouri

M.O. Medical Officer

-mo (*comb. form*) in bookbinding, indicating book size by specifying number of leaves formed by folding one sheet of paper, as in *sixteenmo*

moa ('mōə) *n.* any of various extinct flightless birds of New Zealand

moan (mōn) *n.* 1. low murmur, usually of pain —*v.* 2. utter (words *etc.*) with moan —*vi.* 3. lament

moat (mōt) *n.* 1. deep wide ditch, *esp.* round castle —*vt.* 2. surround with moat

mob (mob) *n.* 1. disorderly crowd of people 2. mixed assembly —*vt.* 3. attack in mob, hustle or ill-treat (-**bb-**) —**'mobster** *n. sl.* gangster

mobcap ('mobkap) *n.* formerly, woman's large cotton cap with pouched crown

mobile ('mōbil) *a.* 1. capable of movement 2. easily moved or changed —*n.* 3. hanging structure of card, plastic *etc.*, designed to move in air currents —**mo'bility** *n.*

mobilize ('mōbilīz) *vi.* 1. (of armed services) prepare for military service —*vt.* 2. organize for a purpose —**mobilization** (mōbili'zāshən) *n.* in war time, calling up of men and women for active service

Möbius strip ('mōbiəs) a surface with only one side and one edge made by putting a single twist in a long, rectangular strip of paper and pasting the ends together

moccasin ('mokəsin) *n.* 1. flat shoe based on Amerindian footwear where leather is placed under foot, brought around side and pleated on to a U-shaped vamp 2. *see* **water moccasin** *at* WATER 3. snake resembling water moccasin —**moccasin flower** any of several lady's-slippers, *esp.* orchid found in N Amer. woodlands

mocha ('mōkə) *n.* 1. type of strong, dark coffee 2. this flavor

mock (mok) *vt.* 1. make fun of, ridicule 2. mimic —*vi.* 3. scoff —*n.* 4. act of mocking 5. laughing stock —*a.* 6. sham, imitation —**'mocker** *n.* —**'mockery** *n.* 1. derision 2. travesty —**mocking bird** N Amer. bird which imitates songs of others —**mock orange** shrub with white fragrant flowers —**mock turtle soup** imitation turtle soup made from calf's head —**mock-up** *n.* scale model —**put the mockers on** *inf.* ruin chances of success of

mod¹ (mod) *a.* of any fashion in dress regarded as stylish

mod² (mod) *n.* annual Highland Gaelic meeting with musical and literary competitions

mod. 1. moderate 2. modern

mod cons (konz) *inf.* modern conveniences

mode (mōd) *n.* 1. method, manner 2. prevailing fashion 3. *Mus.* any of various scales of notes within one octave —**'modal** *a.* 1. of or relating to mode or manner 2. *Gram.* expressing distinction of mood 3. *Metaphys.* of or relating to form of thing as opposed to its substance *etc.* 4. *Mus.* of or relating to mode —**mo'dality** *n.* —**'modish** *a.* in the fashion —**modiste** (mō'dēst) *n.* fashionable dressmaker or milliner

model ('modəl) *n.* 1. miniature representation 2. pattern 3. person or thing worthy of imitation 4. person employed by artist to pose, or by dress designer to display clothing —*vt.* 5. make model of 6. mold —*v.* 7. display (clothing) for dress designer

modem ('mōdem) *n. Comp.* coupler used with telephone or on direct line for transmitting information from one computer to another

moderate ('modərit) *a.* 1. not going to extremes, temperate, medium —*n.* 2. person of moderate views —*v.* ('modərāt) 3. make, become less violent or excessive 4. preside (over) —**mode'ration** *n.* —**'moderator** *n.* 1. mediator 2. president of Presbyterian body 3. arbitrator

moderato (modə'rätō) *adv. Mus.* 1. at moderate tempo 2. direction indicating that tempo specified be used with restraint

modern ('modərn) *a.* 1. of present or recent times 2. in, of current fashion —*n.* 3. person living in modern times —**'modernism** *n.* (support of) modern tendencies, thoughts *etc.* —**'modernist** *n.* —**mo'dernity** *n.* —**moderni'zation** *n.* —**'modernize** *vt.* bring up to date —**modern art** term for realist painting beginning in mid-19th century —**Modern English** English language since about 1450 —**modern languages** current European languages as subject of study

modest ('modist) *a.* 1. not overrating one's qualities or achievements 2. shy 3. moderate, not excessive 4. decorous, decent —**'modestly** *adv.* —**'modesty** *n.*

modicum ('modikəm) *n.* small quantity

modify ('modifī) *vt.* 1. change slightly 2. tone down (-**fied**, -**fying**) —**modifi'cation** *n.* —**'modifier** *n. esp.* word qualifying another

modulate ('mojəlāt) *vt.* 1. regulate 2. vary in tone —*vi.* 3. change key of music —**modu'lation** *n.* 1. modulating 2. *Electron.* superimposing signals on to high-frequency carrier **3.** *Mus.* the change of key within a composition —**'modulator** *n.*

module ('mojōōl) *n.* (detachable) unit, section, component with specific function —**'modular** *a.* designed or constructed to a standardized scale or to standard parts

modulus ('mojələs) *n.* **1.** *Phys.* coefficient expressing specified property of specified substance **2.** *Math.* number by which logarithm to one base is multiplied to give the corresponding logarithm to another base **3.** *Math.* integer that can be divided exactly into the difference between two other integers (*pl.* **-li** (-lī))

modus operandi ('mōdəs opə'randē) *Lat.* method of operating, tackling task (*pl. modi operandi* ('mōdē))

modus vivendi (vi'vendē) *Lat.* working arrangement between conflicting interests (*pl. modi vivendi* ('mōdē))

Mogen David ('mōgən 'dövid) double triangle forming the six-pointed star of David: a symbol of Jewry and of the state of Israel

mogul ('mōgul, mō'gul) *n.* important or powerful person

mohair ('mōhåər) *n.* **1.** fine cloth of goat's hair **2.** hair of Angora goat

Mohammed (mō'hamid) *n. see* MUHAMMAD

Mohawk ('mōhök) *n.* **1.** Amerindian people of Mohawk River valley, New York **2.** member of this people (*pl.* **-hawk, -s**) **3.** Iroquoian language of this people

Mohican (mō'hēkən) *n.* member of Amerindian people of upper Hudson River valley, New York (*pl.* **-can, -s**)

Mohs' scale (mōz) a scale measuring the resistance of substances to being scratched ranging from 1 (talc) to 10 (diamond)

moiety ('moiiti) *n.* a half

moire ('moiər, mör, mwär) *n.* fabric, usu. silk, having watered effect —**moiré** (mö'rā, mwä'rā) *a.* **1.** having watered or wavelike pattern —*n.* **2.** such pattern, impressed on fabrics by means of engraved rollers **3.** any fabric having such pattern, moire

moist (moist) *a.* damp, slightly wet —**moisten** ('moisən) *v.* —**'moisture** *n.* liquid, *esp.* diffused or in drops —**'moisturize** *vt.* add, restore moisture to (skin *etc.*)

mol *Chem.* mole

molar ('mōlər) *a.* **1.** (of teeth) for grinding —*n.* **2.** molar tooth

molasses (mə'lasiz) *n.* syrup, by-product of process of sugar refining

mold¹ (mōld) *n.* **1.** hollow object in which metal *etc.* is cast **2.** pattern for shaping **3.** character **4.** shape, form —*vt.* **5.** shape or pattern —**'molding** *n.* **1.** molded object **2.** ornamental edging **3.** decoration —**'moldboard** *n.* curved blade of plow

mold² (mōld) *n.* fungoid growth caused by dampness —**'moldy** *a.* stale, musty

mold³ (mōld) *n.* loose or surface earth —**'molder** *vi.* decay into dust

mole¹ (mōl) *n.* small dark protuberant spot on the skin

mole² (mōl) *n.* **1.** small burrowing animal **2.** spy, informer —**'molehill** *n.* small mound of earth thrown up by burrowing mole —**make a mountain out of a molehill** exaggerate an unimportant matter out of all proportion

mole³ (mōl) *n.* **1.** pier or breakwater **2.** causeway **3.** harbor within this

mole⁴ (mōl) *n.* SI unit of amount of substance

molecule ('molikyōōl) *n.* **1.** smallest particle of a substance, either element or compound, in ordinary existence **2.** very small particle

—**mo'lecular** *a.* of, inherent in molecules —**molecular biology** science concerned with biological structure at the level of the molecule —**molecular weight** sum of all atomic weights of atoms in a molecule

molest (mə'lest) *vt.* pester, interfere with so as to annoy or injure —**molestation** (mōle'stāshən) *n.*

moll (mol) *n. sl.* **1.** gangster's female accomplice **2.** prostitute

mollify ('molifī) *vt.* calm down, placate, soften (**-fied, -fying**) —**mollifi'cation** *n.*

mollusk *or* **mollusc** ('moləsk) *n.* any member of a phylum (*Mollusca*) of invertebrate animals with a soft body and usu. external shell including oysters, snails, clams, squids and octopuses

mollycoddle ('molikodəl) *vt.* pamper

Molotov cocktail ('molətöf) primitive bomb made of bottle filled with usu. gasoline with a wick that is ignited at time of hurling

molt (mōlt) *v.* **1.** cast or shed (fur, feathers *etc.*) —*n.* **2.** molting

molten ('mōltən) *a.* **1.** liquefied; melted **2.** made by having been melted —*v.* **3.** *pp. of* MELT

molto ('mōltō) *adv. Mus.* very

molybdenum (mə'libdinəm) *n. Chem.* metallic element *Symbol* Mo, at. wt. 95.9, at. no. 42

moment ('mōmənt) *n.* **1.** very short space of time **2.** (present) point in time —**momentarily** *adv.* —**'momentary** *a.* lasting only a moment —**moment of force** effective tendency of a force to rotate a body to which it is applied —**moment of truth** moment when person or thing is put to test

momentous (mō'mentəs) *a.* of great importance

momentum (mō'mentəm) *n.* **1.** force of a moving body **2.** impetus gained from motion (*pl.* **-ta** (-tə), **-s**)

Mon. Monday

Monaco ('monəkō) *n.* country in Europe, an enclave in France, on the Mediterranean —**Monegasque** (moni'gask) *n./a.*

monad ('mōnad) *n.* **1.** *Philos.* any fundamental singular metaphysical entity **2.** single-celled organism **3.** atom, ion, or radical with valency of one —**monadic** (mō'nadik) *a.*

monandrous (mə'nandrəs, mo-) *a.* **1.** having only one male sexual partner over a period of time **2.** (of plants) having flowers with only one stamen —**mo'nandry** *n.*

monarch ('monərk) *n.* sovereign ruler of a state —**mon'archic** *a.* —**'monarchist** *n.* supporter of monarchy —**'monarchy** *n.* **1.** state ruled by sovereign **2.** his rule

monastery ('monəsteri) *n.* house occupied by a religious order —**mo'nastic** *a.* **1.** relating to monks, nuns, or monasteries —*n.* **2.** monk, recluse —**mo'nasticism** *n.*

monaural (mo'nörəl) *a.* relating to, having, or hearing with only one ear

Monday ('mundi) *n.* second day of the week, or first of working week

money ('muni) *n.* bank notes, coin *etc.*, used as medium of exchange (*pl.* **-s, -ies**) —**monetarism** ('monitərizəm) *n.* theory that inflation is caused by increase in money supply —**monetarist** ('monitərist) *n./a.* —**monetary** ('moniteri) *a.* —**monetization** (moniti'zāshən) *n.* —**monetize** ('monitīz) *vt.* make into, recognize as money —**'moneyed** *or* **'monied** *a.* rich —**'moneybags** *n. sl.* very rich person —**money-grubbing** *a. inf.* seeking greedily to obtain money —**'moneylender** *n.* person who lends money at interest as a living —**money-spinner** *n. inf.* enterprise, idea *etc.* that is source of wealth

monger ('munggər) *n.* trader or dealer: usu. in compounds, as in *ironmonger*

Mongolia (mon'gōlyə, mong-; -'gōliə) *n.* country in Asia bounded north by the U.S.S.R., east, south and west by China —**Mon'golian** *n./a.* **1.** (native or inhabitant) of Mongolia —*n.* **2.** the Altaic language of the Mongolians

mongolism ('monggəlizəm) *or* **Mongolianism** (mong'gōliənizəm) *n.* Down's syndrome —**'mongol** *n./a.* (one) afflicted with this —**'mongoloid** *a.* relating to or characterized by mongolism

Mongoloid ('monggəloid) *a.* of major racial group of mankind, including most of peoples of Asia, Eskimos, and N Amer. Indians

mongoose ('mon-gōōs, 'monggōōs) *n.* small animal of Asia and Afr. noted for killing snakes (*pl.* **-s**)

mongrel ('munggrəl, 'monggrəl) *n.* **1.** animal, *esp.* dog, of mixed breed, hybrid —*a.* **2.** of mixed breed

monitor ('monitər) *n.* **1.** person or device which checks, controls, warns or keeps record of something **2.** pupil assisting teacher with odd jobs in school **3.** television set used in a studio for checking program being transmitted **4.** type of large lizard —*vt.* **5.** watch, check on —**mo'nition** *n.* warning —**'monitory** *a.*

monk (mungk) *n.* one of a religious community of men bound by vows of poverty *etc.* —**'monkish** *a.* —**'monkshood** *n.* poisonous plant with hooded flowers

monkey ('mungki) *n.* **1.** long-tailed primate **2.** mischievous child —*vi.* **3.** meddle, fool —**monkey business** *inf.* mischievous or dishonest behavior or acts —**monkey puzzle** coniferous tree with sharp stiff leaves —**monkey wrench** spanner with movable jaws

mono ('monō) *a.* **1.** monophonic —*n.* **2.** monophonic sound

mono- *or before vowel* **mon-** (*comb. form*) single, as in *monosyllabic*

monochrome ('monəkrōm) *n.* **1.** representation in one color —*a.* **2.** of one color —**monochro'matic** *a.*

monocle ('monəkəl) *n.* single eyeglass

monocotyledon (monəkoti'lēdən) *n.* any of various flowering plants having single embryonic seed leaf and leaves with parallel veins —**monocoty'ledonous** *a.*

monocular (mo'nokyələr) *a.* one-eyed

monocyte ('monəsīt) *n.* large phagocytic leukocyte formed in bone marrow or spleen

monoecious (mə'nēshəs) *a.* (of plants) having male and female reproductive organs carried separately on the same plant

monogamy (mə'nogəmi) *n.* custom of being married to one person at a time

monogram ('monəgram) *n.* design of letters interwoven

monograph ('monəgraf) *n.* short book on single subject

monogyny (mə'nojini) *n.* having only one female sexual partner over a period of time —**mo'nogynous** *a.*

monolith ('monəlith) *n.* monument consisting of single standing stone

monologue ('monəlog) *n.* **1.** dramatic composition with only one speaker **2.** long speech by one person

monomania (monə'māniə) *n.* excessive preoccupation with one thing

monomial (mo'nōmiəl) *n.* **1.** *Math.* expression consisting of single term —*a.* **2.** consisting of single algebraic term

mononucleosis (monōnyōōkli'ōsis, -nōō-) n. 1. *Pathol.* presence of large number of monocytes in blood 2. *see* **infectious mononucleosis** *at* INFECT

monophonic (monə'fonik) a. 1. (of reproduction of sound) using only one channel between source and loudspeaker (*also* **mo'naural**) 2. *Mus.* of style of musical composition consisting of single melodic line

monoplane ('monəplān) n. airplane with one pair of wings

monopoly (mə'nopəli) n. 1. exclusive possession of trade, privilege *etc.* 2. (M-) trade name for board game for two to six players —**mo'nopolist** n. —**mo'nopolize** vt. claim, take exclusive possession of

monorail ('monərāl) n. railroad with cars running on or suspended from single rail

monosodium glutamate (monə'sōdiəm 'glōōtəmāt) white crystalline substance used as food flavoring

monosyllable ('monəsiləbəl) n. word of one syllable

monotheism ('monəthēizəm) n. belief in only one God —**'monotheist** n.

monotone ('monətōn) n. continuing on one note —**mo'notonous** a. lacking in variety, dull, wearisome —**mo'notony** n.

monovalent (monə'vālənt) a. *Chem.* 1. having valency of one 2. having only one valency (*also* **uni'valent**) —**mono'valence** *or* **mono'valency** n.

monoxide (mə'noksīd) n. oxide that contains one oxygen atom per molecule

Monroe (mən'rō) n. **James.** the 5th President of the U.S. (1821-25)

Monseigneur (mōse'nyœr) *Fr.* title given to French bishops, prelates, and princes (*pl.* **Messeigneurs** (māse'nyœr))

monsieur (məs'yə) n. French title of address equivalent to *sir* when used alone or *Mr.* before name

Monsignor (mon'sēnyər) n. *R.C.Ch.* ecclesiastical title attached to certain offices and prefixed to surname

monsoon (mon'sōōn) n. 1. seasonal wind of SE Asia 2. very heavy rainfall season

monster ('monstər) n. 1. fantastic imaginary beast 2. misshapen animal or plant 3. very wicked person 4. huge person, animal or thing —a. 5. huge —**mon'strosity** n. 1. monstrous being 2. deformity 3. distortion —**'monstrous** a. 1. of, like monster 2. unnatural 3. enormous 4. horrible —**'monstrously** adv.

monstrance ('monstrəns) n. *R.C.Ch.* vessel in which consecrated Host is exposed for adoration

Mont. Montana

montage (mon'tāzh) n. 1. elements of two or more pictures imposed upon a single background to give a unified effect 2. method of editing a motion picture

Montana (mon'tanə) n. Mountain state of the U.S., admitted to the Union in 1889. Abbrev.: **Mont., MT** (with ZIP code)

montbretia (mon'brēshə) n. plant with orange flowers on long stems

Montezuma's revenge (monti'zōōməz) diarrhea, *esp.* contracted in Mexico by tourist

month (munth) n. 1. one of twelve periods into which the year is divided 2. period of moon's revolution —**'monthly** a. 1. happening or payable once a month —adv. 2. once a month —n. 3. magazine published every month

Montserrat (montsə'rat) n. crown colony of the United Kingdom lying in the Caribbean Sea 25 miles southwest of Antigua

monument ('monyəmənt) n. anything that commemorates, *esp.* a building or statue —**monu'mental** a. 1. vast, lasting 2. of or serving as monument —**monumental mason** maker and engraver of tombstones

moo (mōō) n. 1. cry of cow —vi. 2. make this noise, low

mooch (mōōch) vi. *sl.* loaf, slouch

mood[1] (mōōd) n. state of mind and feelings —**'moody** a. 1. gloomy, pensive 2. changeable in mood

mood[2] (mōōd) n. *Gram.* form indicating function of verb

Moog synthesizer (mōōg, mōg) trade name for electrophonic instrument operated by keyboard and pedals

moon (mōōn) n. 1. satellite which takes lunar month to revolve around earth 2. any secondary planet —vi. 3. (*oft. with* around) go about dreamily —**'moony** a. 1. *inf.* dreamy or listless 2. of or like moon —**'mooncalf** n. 1. born fool; dolt 2. person who idles time away (*pl.* **-calves**) —**'moonlight** n. 1. light of moon —vi. 2. hold two paid occupations —**moonlight flit** hurried departure by night to escape from one's creditors —**'moonscape** n. general surface of moon or representation of it —**'moonshine** n. 1. whiskey illicitly distilled 2. nonsense —**'moonshot** n. launching of spacecraft *etc.* to moon —**'moonstone** n. transparent semiprecious stone —**'moonstruck** a. deranged

moor[1] (mōōər) n. tract of open uncultivated land, often hilly and heather-clad —**'moorhen** n. water bird

moor[2] (mōōər) v. secure (ship) with chains or ropes —**'moorage** n. place, charge for mooring —**'moorings** pl.n. 1. ropes *etc.* for mooring 2. something providing stability, security

Moor (mōōər) n. member of race in Morocco and adjoining parts of N Afr.

moose (mōōs) n. N Amer. deer, like elk

moot (mōōt) a. 1. that is open to argument, debatable —vt. 2. bring for discussion —n. 3. meeting

mop (mop) n. 1. bundle of yarn, cloth *etc.* on end of stick, used for cleaning 2. tangle (of hair *etc.*) —vt. 3. clean, wipe with mop or other absorbent stuff (**-pp-**)

mope (mōp) vi. be gloomy, apathetic

moped ('mōped) n. light motorized bicycle

moquette (mō'ket) n. thick fabric used for upholstery *etc.*

moraine (mə'rān) n. accumulated mass of debris, earth, stones *etc.*, deposited by glacier

moral ('mörəl, 'morəl) a. 1. pert. to right and wrong conduct 2. of good conduct —n. 3. practical lesson, *eg* of fable —pl. 4. habits with respect to right and wrong, *esp.* in matters of sex —**'moralist** n. teacher of morality —**mo'rality** n. 1. good moral conduct 2. moral goodness or badness 3. kind of medieval drama, containing moral lesson —**'moralize** vi. 1. write, talk about moral aspect of things 2. interpret morally —**'morally** adv. —**moral philosophy** branch of philosophy dealing with ethics —**moral victory** triumph that is psychological rather than practical

morale (mə'ral) n. degree of confidence, hope of person or group

morass (mə'ras) n. 1. marsh 2. mess

moratorium (morə'töriəm) n. 1. act authorizing postponement of payments *etc.* 2. delay (*pl.* **-ria** (-riə))

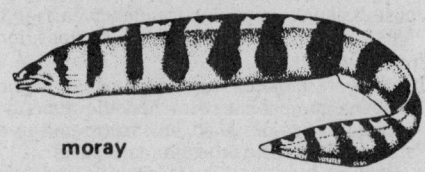

moray

moray (mə'rā, 'mörā) n. large, voracious eel

morbid ('mörbid) a. 1. unduly interested in death 2. gruesome 3. diseased

mordant ('mördənt) a. 1. biting 2. corrosive 3. scathing —n. 4. substance that fixes dyes

more (mör) comp. of MANY *and* MUCH a. 1. greater in quantity or number —adv. 2. to a greater extent 3. in addition —pron. 4. greater or additional amount or number —**more'over** adv. besides, further

morel (mə'rel, mö'rel) n. edible fungus in which mushroom has pitted cap

morello (mə'relō) n. variety of small dark sour cherry (*pl.* **-s**)

mores ('möräz) pl.n. customs and conventions embodying fundamental values of society *etc.*

morganatic marriage (mörgə'natik) marriage of king or prince in which wife does not share husband's rank or possessions and children do not inherit from father

morgue (mörg) n. mortuary

moribund ('moribund) a. 1. dying 2. stagnant

Mormon ('mörmən) n. member of Church of Latter-Day Saints whose authority is the Bible, Book of Mormon, revelations to Joseph Smith by the Angel Moroni in 1827 and certain pronouncements of the 1st Presidency (*also* **Latter-Day Saint**) —**'Mormonism** n.

mornay (mör'nā) a. denoting cheese sauce used in various dishes

morning ('mörning) n. early part of day until noon —**morn** n. *Poet.* morning —**morning dress** formal day dress for men, comprising cutaway frock coat, usu. with gray trousers and top hat —**morning-glory** n. plant with trumpet-shaped flowers which close in late afternoon —**morning sickness** inf. nausea occurring shortly after rising during early months of pregnancy —**morning star** planet, usu. Venus, seen just before sunrise —**the morning after** inf. aftereffects of excess, *esp.* hangover

Morocco (mə'rokō) n. 1. country in Africa bounded east and southeast by Algeria, southwest by Western Sahara, northwest by the Atlantic Ocean and north by the Mediterranean Sea 2. (m-) fine goatskin leather —**Mo'roccan** n./a.

moron ('möron) n. 1. mentally deficient person 2. inf. fool —**mo'ronic** a.

morose (mə'rōs) a. sullen, moody

morphine ('mörfēn) *or* **morphia** ('mörfiə) n. narcotic extract of opium, drug used to induce sleep and relieve pain

morphology (mör'foləji) n. 1. science of structure of organisms 2. form and structure of words of a language —**morpho'logical** a.

morris dance ('moris) English folk dance

morrow ('morō) n. *Poet.* next day

Morse (mörs) n. system of telegraphic signaling in which letters of alphabet are represented by combinations of dots and dashes, or short and long flashes

morsel ('mörsəl) n. fragment, small piece

mortal ('mörtəl) a. 1. subject to death 2. causing death —n. 3. mortal creature —**mor'tality** n. 1. state of being mortal 2. great loss of life 3. death rate —**'mortally**

adv. **1.** fatally **2.** deeply, intensely —**mortal sin** *R.C.Ch.* sin meriting damnation

mortar ('mörtər) *n.* **1.** mixture of lime, sand and water for holding bricks and stones together **2.** small cannon firing over short range **3.** vessel in which substances are pounded —**'mortarboard** *n.* **1.** board for holding mortar **2.** square academic cap

mortgage ('mörgij) *n.* **1.** conveyance of property as security for debt with provision that property be reconveyed on payment within agreed time —*vt.* **2.** convey by mortgage **3.** pledge as security —**mortga-'gee** *n.* —**mortgagor** (mörgi'jör) *or* **'mortgager** *n.*

mortify ('mörtifī) *vt.* **1.** humiliate **2.** subdue by self-denial —*vi.* **3.** (of flesh) be affected with gangrene (**-fied, -fying**) —**mortifi'ca-tion** *n.*

mortise *or* **mortice** ('mörtis) *n.* **1.** hole in piece of wood *etc.* to receive the tongue (tenon) and end of another piece —*vt.* **2.** make mortise in **3.** fasten by mortise and tenon —**mortise lock** lock embedded in door

mortuary ('mörchŏŏəri) *n.* **1.** building where corpses are kept before burial —*a.* **2.** of, for burial

mosaic (mō'zāik) *n.* **1.** picture or pattern of small bits of colored stone, glass *etc.* **2.** this process of decoration

Mosaic (mō'zāik) *a.* of Moses

Moselle (mō'zel) *n.* light white wine

Moslem ('mozləm) *see* MUSLIM

mosque (mosk) *n.* Muslim temple

mosquito (mə'skētō) *n.* any of various kinds of flying, biting insects of which the adult female sucks the blood of birds and mammals (*pl.* **-es**)

moss (mos) *n.* **1.** simple land plant without roots, reproducing by spores **2.** peat bog, swamp —**'mossy** *a.* covered with moss —**moss agate** agate with mosslike markings —**moss stitch** knitting stitch made up of alternate knit and purl stitches

most (mōst) *sup. of* MUCH *and* MANY *a.* **1.** greatest in size, number, or degree —*n.* **2.** greatest number, amount, or degree —*adv.* **3.** in the greatest degree **4.** almost —**'mostly** *adv.* for the most part, generally, on the whole —**Most Reverend** courtesy title applied to archbishops

M.O.T. Member of Our Tribe: used by Jews

mote (mōt) *n.* tiny speck

motel (mō'tel) *n.* roadside hotel with accommodation for motorists and vehicles

motet (mō'tet) *n.* short sacred vocal composition

moth (moth) *n.* **1.** usu. nocturnal insect like butterfly **2.** its grub —**'mothy** *a.* infested with moths —**'mothball** *n.* **1.** small ball of camphor or naphthalene to repel moths from stored clothing *etc.* —*vt.* **2.** put in mothballs **3.** store, postpone *etc.* —**'motheaten** *a.* **1.** eaten, damaged by grub of moth **2.** decayed, scruffy

mother ('mudhər) *n.* **1.** female parent **2.** head of religious community of women —*a.* **3.** natural, native, inborn —*vt.* **4.** act as mother to —**'motherhood** *n.* —**'motherly** *a.* —**Mother Carey's chicken** ('kariz, 'keriz) *see* **storm petrel** (sense 1) *at* STORM —**mother country 1.** original country of colonists or settlers **2.** person's native country —**mother earth 1.** earth as a mother, particularly in its fertility **2.** soil; ground —**mother-in-law** *n.* mother of one's husband or wife —**mother of pearl** iridescent lining of certain shells —**Mother's Day** day for honoring mothers, usu. the 2nd Sunday in May —**mother tongue 1.** language

first learned by child **2.** language from which another has evolved

motif (mō'tēf) *n.* **1.** dominating theme **2.** recurring design

motion ('mōshən) *n.* **1.** process or action or way of moving **2.** proposal in meeting **3.** application to judge —*v.* **4.** signal or direct by sign —**'motionless** *a.* still, immobile —**motion sickness** disorder marked by headache, dizziness, sweating, nausea, pallor or cold sweats caused by reaction to movement (*also* **airsickness, carsickness, seasickness**)

motive ('mōtiv) *n.* **1.** that which makes person act in particular way **2.** inner impulse —*a.* **3.** causing motion —**'motivate** *vt.* **1.** instigate **2.** incite —**moti'vation** *n.* —**motive power 1.** any source of energy used to produce motion **2.** means of supplying power to engine *etc.*

mot juste (mō 'zhŭst) *Fr.* appropriate word or expression (*pl.* *mots justes* (mō 'zhŭst))

motley ('motli) *a.* **1.** miscellaneous, varied **2.** multicolored —*n.* **3.** motley color or mixture **4.** jester's particolored dress

motocross ('mōtōkros) *n.* motorcycle race over rough course

motor ('mōtər) *n.* **1.** that which imparts movement **2.** machine to supply motive power **3.** automobile —*vi.* **4.** travel by automobile —**'motoring** *n.* —**'motorist** *n.* user of automobile —**'motorize** *vt.* **1.** equip with motor **2.** provide with motor transport —**'motorboat, 'motorcar, 'motorcycle, motor scooter** *n.* vehicles driven by motor —**motorcade** ('mōtərkād) *n.* parade of motor vehicles —**motor nerve** nerve which controls muscular movement

mottle ('motəl) *vt.* **1.** mark with blotches, variegate —*n.* **2.** arrangement of blotches **3.** blotch on surface

motto ('motō) *n.* **1.** saying adopted as rule of conduct **2.** short inscribed sentence **3.** word or sentence on heraldic crest (*pl.* **-s, -es**)

moue (mōō) *Fr.* pouting look

moufflon (mōō'flon) *n.* wild mountain sheep

mound (mownd) *n.* **1.** heap of earth or stones **2.** small hill

mount (mownt) *vi.* **1.** rise **2.** increase **3.** get on horseback —*vt.* **4.** get up on **5.** frame (picture) **6.** fix, set up **7.** provide with horse —*n.* **8.** that on which thing is supported or fitted **9.** horse **10.** hill

mountain ('mowntin) *n.* **1.** hill of great size **2.** surplus —**mountain'eer** *n.* one who lives among or climbs mountains —**mountain-'eering** *n.* technique of climbing high places of the earth —**'mountainous** *a.* very high, rugged —**mountain lion** cougar —**Mountain Standard Time** time as reckoned from the 105th to 120th meridians west of Greenwich

mountebank ('mowntibangk) *n.* charlatan, fake

Mountie ('mownti) *n. inf.* member of Royal Canadian Mounted Police

mourn (mörn) *v.* feel, show sorrow (for) —**'mourner** *n.* —**'mournful** *a.* sad, dismal —**'mournfully** *adv.* —**'mourning** *n.* **1.** grieving **2.** conventional signs of grief for death **3.** clothes of mourner —**mourning band** piece of black material, *esp.* armband, worn to indicate mourning

mouse (mows) *n.* **1.** small rodent (*pl.* **mice**) —*vi.* (mowz) **2.** catch, hunt mice **3.** prowl —**'mouser** *n.* cat used for catching mice —**'mousy** *or* **'mousey** *a.* **1.** like mouse, *esp.* in color **2.** meek, shy —**'mousetrap** *n.* **1.** any trap for catching mice **2.** *inf.* cheese of indifferent quality

mousse (mōōs) *n.* sweet dish of flavored cream whipped and chilled

mousseline (mōōsə'lēn) *n.* sheer fabric resembling muslin —**mousseline de laine** (də 'len) lightweight plain-weave woolen cloth, oft. printed —**mousseline de soie** (də 'swä) silk or rayon muslin, crisper and firmer than chiffon

moustache ('mustash, məs'tash) *n. see* MUSTACHE

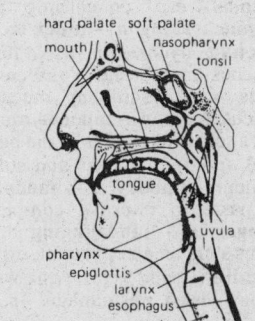

mouth

mouth (mowth) *n.* **1.** opening in head for eating, speaking *etc.* **2.** opening into anything hollow **3.** outfall of river **4.** entrance to harbor *etc.* —*vt.* (mowdh) **5.** declaim, *esp.* in public **6.** form (words) with lips without speaking **7.** take, move in mouth —**'mouthful** *n.* **1.** as much as is held in mouth at one time **2.** small quantity, as of food **3.** word *etc.* difficult to say —**mouth organ** harmonica —**'mouthpiece** *n.* **1.** end of anything placed between lips, *eg* pipe **2.** spokesman —**'mouthwash** *n.* solution for cleansing mouth

move (mōōv) *vt.* **1.** change position of **2.** stir emotions of **3.** incite **4.** propose for consideration —*vi.* **5.** change places **6.** change one's dwelling **7.** take action —*n.* **8.** a moving **9.** motion toward some goal —**'movable** *or* **'moveable** *a./n.* —**'movement** *n.* **1.** process, action of moving **2.** moving parts of machine **3.** division of piece of music

movie ('mōōvi) *n.* **1.** motion picture —*pl.* **2.** place where motion picture is shown **3.** the motion-picture industry and medium —**movie star** popular motion-picture actor or actress

mow (mō) *v.* cut (grass *etc.*) (**mown** *pp.*) —**'mower** *n.* man or machine that mows

Mozambique (mōzəm'bēk) *n.* country in Africa bounded east by the Indian Ocean, south by South Africa, southwest by Swaziland, west by South Africa and Zimbabwe and north by Zambia, Malawi and Tanzania —**Mozam'bican** *n./a.*

Mozzarella (motsə'relə) *n.* a semisoft cheese from cow's milk, notable for its elasticity when melted, orig. from Italy

mp *or* **m.p.** *Mus.* mezzo piano

M.P. 1. Member of Parliament **2.** Military Police **3.** Mounted Police

m.p.g. miles per gallon

m.p.h. miles per hour

M.Phil. *or* **M.Ph.** Master of Philosophy

Mr. ('mistər) mister

Mrs. ('misiz, -is) title of married woman

MS Mississippi

Ms. (miz) title used instead of Miss or Mrs.

MS. *or* **ms.** manuscript (*pl.* **MSS.** *or* **mss.**)

M.Sc. Master of Science

M.S.T. Mountain Standard Time

MT Montana

Mt. *or* **mt.** Mount

mu (myōō, mōō) *n.* 12th letter in Gr. alphabet (M, μ)

much (much) *a.* **1.** existing in quantity —*n.* **2.** large amount **3.** a great deal **4.** important matter —*adv.* **5.** in a great degree **6.** nearly (**more** *comp.*, **most** *sup.*)

mucilage ('myōōsilij) *n.* glue

muck (muk) *n.* **1.** cattle dung **2.** unclean refuse —'**mucky** *a.* **1.** dirty **2.** messy **3.** unpleasant —'**muckamuck** *n.* arrogant person —'**muckrake** *vi.* seek out and expose scandal, *esp.* concerning public figures —'**muckraking** *n.* —**muck up** ruin, spoil

mucus ('myōōkəs) *n.* viscid fluid secreted by mucous membrane —**mu'cosity** *n.* —'**mucous** *a.* **1.** resembling mucus **2.** secreting mucus **3.** slimy —**mucous membrane** lining of canals and cavities of the body

mud (mud) *n.* **1.** wet and soft earth **2.** *inf.* slander —'**muddy** *a.* —'**mudpack** *n.* cosmetic paste to improve complexion —'**mudslinger** *n.* —'**mudslinging** *n.* casting malicious slurs on an opponent, *esp.* in politics

muddle ('mudəl) *vt.* **1.** (*esp. with* up) confuse **2.** bewilder **3.** mismanage —*n.* **4.** confusion **5.** tangle

Muenster ('munstər, 'mōōn-) *n.* a semihard, whole-milk cheese, cylindrical in shape with a brick-red rind, orig. from Alsace

muesli ('myōōzli) *n.* mixture of rolled oats, dried fruit *etc.* eaten with milk

muezzin (mōō'ezin) *n.* crier who summons Muslims to prayer

muff[1] (muf) *n.* tube-shaped covering to keep the hands warm

muff[2] (muf) *vt.* miss, bungle, fail in

muffin ('mufin) *n.* small cup-shaped sweet bread roll, usually eaten hot with butter

muffle ('mufəl) *vt.* wrap up, *esp.* to deaden sound —'**muffler** *n.* **1.** scarf **2.** device to reduce noise of engine exhaust *etc.*

mufti ('mufti) *n.* plain clothes as distinguished from uniform, *eg* of soldier

mug[1] (mug) *n.* drinking cup

mug[2] (mug) *n. sl.* **1.** face **2.** fool, simpleton, one easily imposed upon —*vt.* **3.** *inf.* rob violently (**-gg-**) —'**mugger** *n.*

muggy ('mugi) *a.* damp and stifling

mugwump ('mugwump) *n.* person who sits on the fence concerning party politics

Muhammad (mō'hamid) *n.* prophet, and founder of Islam —**Mu'hammadan** *a./n.* Muslim —**Mu'hammadanism** *n.* another word (not in Muslim use) for ISLAM

mukluk ('mukluk) *n.* **1.** Eskimo's soft (sealskin) boot **2.** knitted boot with soft leather soles for indoor wear

mulatto (myōō'lato, mōō-) *n.* child of one White and one Black parent (*pl.* **-s, -es**)

mulberry ('mulberi, -bəri) *n.* **1.** tree whose leaves are used to feed silkworms **2.** its purplish fruit

mulch (mulch) *n.* **1.** straw, leaves *etc.*, spread as protection for roots of plants —*vt.* **2.** protect thus

mulct (mulkt) *vt.* **1.** defraud **2.** fine

mule[1] (myōōl) *n.* **1.** animal which is cross between horse and ass **2.** hybrid **3.** spinning machine —**muleteer** (myōōli'tēər) *n.* mule driver —'**mulish** *a.* obstinate

mule[2] (myōōl) *n.* backless shoe or slipper

mull[1] (mul) *vt.* heat (wine) with sugar and spices —**mull over** think over, ponder

mull[2] (mul) *n.* light muslin fabric of soft texture

mullah ('mulə, 'mōōlə) *n.* Muslim theologian

mullein ('mulin) *n.* plant with tall spikes of yellow flowers

mullet ('mulit) *n.* edible sea fish

mulligatawny (muligə'tōni) *n.* vegetable or meat soup flavored with curry powder

mullion ('mulyən) *n.* upright dividing bar in window —'**mullioned** *a.*

multangular (mul'tanggyōōlər) *or* **multiangular** *a.* having many angles

multi- (*comb. form*) many, as in *multiracial, multistory.* Such words are omitted where the meaning may easily be found from the simple word

multifarious (multi'fariəs, -'fer-) *a.* of various kinds or parts —**multi'fariously** *adv.*

multilateral (multi'latərəl, multī-; -'latrəl) *a.* **1.** of or involving more than two nations or parties **2.** having many sides

multinational (multi'nashənəl, multī-) *a.* (of large business company) operating in several countries

multiple ('multipəl) *a.* **1.** having many parts —*n.* **2.** quantity which contains another an exact number of times —**multipli'cand** *n. Math.* number to be multiplied —**multipli'cation** *n.* —**multi'plicity** *n.* variety, greatness in number —'**multiplier** *n.* **1.** person or thing that multiplies **2.** number by which multiplicand is multiplied **3.** *Phys.* any instrument, as photomultiplier, for increasing effect —'**multiply** *vt.* **1.** increase in number **2.** add (a number) to itself a given number of times —*vi.* **3.** increase in number or amount (**-plied, -plying**) —**multiple-choice** *a.* having a number of possible given answers out of which the correct one must be chosen —**multiple personality** condition in which individual leads two or more distinct and separate existences —**multiple sclerosis** disease of the human nervous system affecting persons between ages of 10 and 50 —**multiplication table** one of group of tables giving results of multiplying two numbers together

multiplex ('multipleks) *a.* **1.** having many elements or parts **2.** capable of transmitting numerous messages over same wire or channel

multitude ('multityōōd, -tōōd) *n.* **1.** great number **2.** great crowd **3.** populace —**multi'tudinous** *a.* very numerous

mum (mum) *n. inf.* **1.** mother **2.** large shaggy chrysanthemum flower

mumble ('mumbəl) *vi.* **1.** speak indistinctly —*v.* **2.** mutter

mumbo jumbo ('mumbō) **1.** foolish religious reverence or incantation **2.** meaningless or unnecessarily complicated language

mummer ('mumər) *n.* actor in dumb show —**mum** *a.* **1.** silent —*v.* **2.** act in mime (**-mm-**) —'**mummery** *n.* dumb-show acting

mummy ('mumi) *n.* embalmed body, *esp.* as prepared for burial in ancient Egypt —'**mummify** *v.* (**-fied, -fying**)

mumps (mumps) *pl.n.* infectious virus disease occurring chiefly in children usu. attacking salivary glands (*also* **epidemic parotitis**)

mun. municipal

munch (munch) *v.* **1.** chew noisily and vigorously **2.** crunch

mundane (mun'dān, 'mundān) *a.* **1.** ordinary, everyday **2.** belonging to this world, earthly

mung bean (mung) **1.** E Asian bean plant grown for forage: source of bean sprouts **2.** seed of this plant

municipal (myōō'nisipəl) *a.* belonging to affairs of city or town —**munici'pality** *n.* **1.** city or town with local self-government **2.** its governing body

munificent (myōō'nifisənt) *a.* very generous —**mu'nificence** *n.* bounty

muniments ('myōōnimənts) *pl.n.* title deeds, documents verifying ownership

munition (myōō'nishən) *n.* (*usu. pl.*) military stores

muon ('myōōon) *n.* positive or negative elementary particle with mass 207 times that of electron

mural ('myōōrəl) *n.* **1.** painting on a wall —*a.* **2.** of or on a wall

murder ('mərdər) *n.* **1.** unlawful premeditated killing of human being —*vt.* **2.** kill thus —'**murderer** *n.* ('**murderess** *fem.*) —'**murderous** *a.*

murk *or* **mirk** (mərk) *n.* thick darkness —'**murky** *or* '**mirky** *a.* gloomy

murmur ('mərmər) *n.* **1.** low, indistinct sound —*vi.* **2.** make such a sound **3.** complain —*vt.* **4.** utter in a low voice

Murphy's law ('mərfiz) notion that if anything is liable to go wrong, it will

murrain ('murin) *n.* cattle plague

mus. **1.** museum **2.** music(al)

Mus.B. *or* **Mus.Bac.** Bachelor of Music

muscat ('muskat, -kət) *n.* **1.** musk-flavored grape **2.** raisin —**musca'tel** *n.* **1.** muscat **2.** strong wine made from it

muscle ('musəl) *n.* **1.** specialized tissue in humans and other animals concerned with movement **2.** system of muscles —**muscular** ('muskyələr) *a.* **1.** with well-developed muscles **2.** strong **3.** of, like muscle —**musculature** ('muskyələchōōər) *n.* **1.** arrangement of muscles in organ or part **2.** total muscular system of organism —**muscle-bound** *a.* with muscles stiff through overdevelopment —'**muscleman** *n.* **1.** man with highly developed muscles **2.** henchman employed by gangster *etc.* to intimidate or use violence upon victims —**muscular dystrophy** inherited disease of several types involving progressive degeneration of skeletal muscle —**muscle in** *inf.* force one's way in

Muscovy (mus'kōvi) *or* **musk duck** large crested widely domesticated S Amer. duck

Mus.D. *or* **Mus.Doc.** Doctor of Music

muse (myōōz) *vi.* **1.** ponder **2.** consider meditatively **3.** be lost in thought —*n.* **4.** state of musing or abstraction **5.** reverie

Muse (myōōz) *n.* one of the nine goddesses inspiring learning and the arts

museum (myōō'zēəm) *n.* (place housing) collection of natural, artistic, historical or scientific objects —**museum piece 1.** object fit to be kept in museum **2.** *inf.* person or thing regarded as antiquated

mush (mush) *n.* **1.** soft pulpy mass **2.** *inf.* cloying sentimentality —'**mushy** *a.*

mushroom ('mushrōōm, -rōōm) *n.* **1.** any edible fungus with fruiting body consisting of stalked cap with gills —*vi.* **2.** shoot up rapidly **3.** expand —**mushroom cloud** mushroom-shaped cloud produced by nuclear explosion

music ('myōōzik) *n.* **1.** art form using melodious and harmonious combination of notes **2.** laws of this **3.** composition in this art —'**musical** *a.* **1.** of, like music **2.** interested in, or with instinct for, music **3.** pleasant to ear —*n.* **4.** show, motion picture in which music plays essential part —'**musically** *adv.* —**mu'sician** *n.* —**musi'cologist** *n.* —**musi'cology** *n.* scientific study of music —**musical chairs** party game in which players walk around chairs to music, there being one fewer chairs than players: when music stops, player without a chair is eliminated —**musical comedy** light dramatic entertainment with songs, dances *etc.* —**music** *or* **musical box** mechanical instrument that plays tunes by means of pins on revolving cylinder striking tuned teeth of comblike metal plate —**music hall** vaudeville theater

musk (musk) *n.* 1. scent obtained from gland of **musk deer** 2. any of various plants with similar scent —'**musky** *a.* —'**muskmelon** *n.* any of several varieties of melon, such as cantaloupe, having ribbed or warty rind and musky aroma —**musk ox** ox of Arctic Amer. —'**muskrat** *n.* 1. N Amer. rodent found near water 2. its fur —**musk rose** rose cultivated for its white musk-scented flowers

muskeg ('muskeg) *n.* C boggy hollow

muskellunge ('muskəlunj) *or* **muskallonge** ('muskəlonj) *n.* large game and food fish of pike family found in lakes and rivers of eastern and midwestern N Amer. (*also* **maskanonge, maskelonge, maskinonge**)

musket ('muskit) *n. Hist.* infantryman's gun —**muske'teer** *n.* —'**musketry** *n.* (use of) small firearms

Muskogean (mus'kōgiən) *n.* Amerindian language family spoken orig. in southeastern U.S., now in Oklahoma

Muslim ('muzlim, 'mŏŏs-, 'mŏŏz-) *or* **Moslem** *n.* 1. follower of religion of Islam —*a.* 2. of religion, culture *etc.* of Islam

muslin ('muzlin) *n.* fine cotton fabric —'**muslined** *a.*

mussel ('musəl) *n.* 1. marine bivalve mollusk 2. freshwater bivalve mollusk

must[1] (must; *unstressed* məst, məs) *v. aux.* 1. be obliged to, or certain to —*n.* 2. something one must do

must[2] (must) *n.* 1. newly-pressed grape juice 2. unfermented wine

mustache *or* **moustache** ('mustash, məs'tash) *n.* hair on the upper lip —**mustache cup** cup with partial cover to protect drinker's mustache

mustang ('mustang) *n.* wild horse

mustard ('mustərd) *n.* 1. powder made from the seeds of a plant, used in paste as a condiment 2. the plant —**mustard gas** poisonous gas causing blistering —**mustard plaster** irritant preparation used to stimulate blood flow

mustargen ('mustərjən) *n. see* **nitrogen mustard** *at* NITROGEN

muster ('mustər) *v.* 1. assemble —*n.* 2. assembly, *esp.* for exercise, inspection

musty ('musti) *a.* moldy, stale —**must** *or* '**mustiness** *n.*

mutate ('myōōtāt, myōō'tāt) *v.* (cause to) undergo mutation —'**mutable** *a.* liable to change —'**mutant** *n.* mutated animal, plant *etc.* —**mu'tation** *n.* change in the genetic material of a living organism which can be inherited

mute (myōōt) *a.* 1. dumb 2. silent —*n.* 3. dumb person 4. *Mus.* contrivance to soften tone of instruments —'**muted** *a.* 1. (of sound) muffled 2. (of light) subdued —'**mutely** *adv.*

mutilate ('myōōtilāt) *vt.* 1. deprive of a limb or other part 2. damage, deface —**muti'lation** *n.* —'**mutilator** *n.*

mutiny ('myōōtini) *n.* 1. rebellion against authority, esp. against officers of disciplined body —*vi.* 2. commit mutiny ('**mutinied**, '**mutinying**) —**muti'neer** *n.* —'**mutinous** *a.* rebellious

mutt (mut) *n. inf.* 1. stupid person 2. dog

mutter ('mutər) *vi.* 1. speak with mouth nearly closed, indistinctly 2. grumble —*vt.* 3. utter in such tones —*n.* 4. act, sound of muttering

mutton ('mutən) *n.* flesh of sheep used as food —**mutton bird** migratory seabird —'**muttonchops** *pl.n.* side whiskers trimmed in shape of chops —'**muttonhead** *n. sl.* fool

mutual ('myōōchōōəl) *a.* 1. done, possessed *etc.* by each of two with respect to the other 2. reciprocal 3. *inf.* common to both or all —'**mutually** *adv.*

muumuu ('mōōmōō) *n.* loose dress in bright colors and patterns adapted from dresses orig. given to Hawaiian women by missionaries

Muzak ('myōōzak) *n.* trade name for recorded light music played in shops *etc.*

muzzle ('muzəl) *n.* 1. mouth and nose of animal 2. cover for these to prevent biting 3. open end of gun —*vt.* 4. put muzzle on 5. silence, gag

muzzy ('muzi) *a.* indistinct, confused, muddled

MV 1. mean variation 2. motor vessel

MVA Missouri Valley Authority

MW megawatt(s)

MWe megawatts electric

Mx *Phys.* maxwell

my (mī) *a.* belonging to me —**my'self** *pron.* emphatic or reflexive form of I

myalgia (mī'aljiə) *n.* pain in a muscle

myasthenia gravis (mīəs'thēniə 'grävis) rare disease marked by muscle weakness and fatigue

mycelium (mī'sēliəm) *n.* vegetative body of fungi (*pl.* **-lia** (-liə)) —**my'celial** *a.*

Mycenaean (mīsi'nēən) *a.* 1. of ancient Mycenae or its inhabitants 2. of Aegean civilization of Mycenae (1400 to 1100 B.C.)

mycology (mī'koləji) *n.* science of fungi

mycorrhiza (mīkə'rīzə) *n.* symbiosis between roots of a higher plant and a fungus

mynah *or* **myna** ('mīnə) *n.* Indian bird related to starling

myopia (mī'ōpiə) *n.* near-sightedness —**myopic** (mī'opik) *a.*

myositis (mīə'sītis) *n.* muscular pain or discomfort of unknown origin

myosotis (mīə'sōtis) *n.* any of genus of plants of the borage family, *eg* forget-me-not

Myr million years

myriad ('miriəd) *a.* 1. innumerable —*n.* 2. large indefinite number

myriapod ('miriəpod) *n.* 1. any of group of terrestrial arthropods having long segmented body, such as the centipede —*a.* 2. of or belonging to this group

myrmidon ('mərmidon, -dən) *n.* follower or henchman

myrrh (mər) *n.* aromatic gum, formerly used as incense

myrtle ('mərtəl) *n.* 1. flowering evergreen shrub 2. periwinkle

myself (mī'self) *pron. see* MY

Mysost ('mīsost) *n.* a hard cheese, oft. brown in color, from goat's milk, orig. produced in all Scandinavian countries (*also* **Gjetost, Primost**)

mystery ('mistəri, -tri) *n.* 1. obscure or secret thing 2. anything strange or inexplicable 3. religious rite —**mys'terious** *a.* —**mys'teriously** *adv.* —**mystery play** medieval drama based on biblical incidents

mystic ('mistik) *n.* 1. one who seeks divine, spiritual knowledge, *esp.* by prayer, contemplation *etc.* —*a.* 2. of hidden meaning, *esp.* in religious sense —'**mystical** *a.* —'**mysticism** *n.*

mystify ('mistifī) *vt.* bewilder, puzzle (**-fied, -fying**) —**mystifi'cation** *n.*

mystique (mi'stēk) *n.* aura of mystery, power *etc.*

myth (mith) *n.* 1. tale with supernatural characters or events 2. invented story 3. imaginary person or object —'**mythical** *a.* —**mytho'logical** *a.* —**my'thologist** *n.* —**my'thology** *n.* 1. myths collectively 2. study of them

myxedema (miksi'dēmə) *n.* illness caused by severe thyroxine deficiency

myxomatosis (miksōmə'tōsis) *n.* contagious, fatal disease of rabbits caused by a virus sometimes introduced as biological control

Nn

n *or* **N** (en) *n.* **1.** 14th letter of English alphabet **2.** speech sound represented by this letter (*pl.* **n's, N's** *or* **Ns**)

n (en) *a.* indefinite number (of) —**nth** (enth) *a.* **1.** *Math.* of unspecified ordinal number, usu. greatest in series **2.** *inf.* being last or most extreme of long series —**to the nth degree** *inf.* to the utmost extreme

N 1. *Chess* knight **2.** *Chem.* nitrogen **3.** *Phys.* newton **4.** north(ern)

n. 1. neuter **2.** noun **3.** number

Na *Chem.* sodium

nab (nab) *vt. inf.* **1.** arrest (criminal) **2.** catch suddenly (**-bb-**)

nacre ('nākər) *n.* **1.** mother-of-pearl **2.** shellfish

nadir ('nādēər, 'nādər) *n.* **1.** point opposite the zenith **2.** lowest point

nae (nā) *a. Scots word for* NO (sense 1)

nag[1] (nag) *v.* **1.** scold or annoy constantly **2.** cause pain to constantly (**-gg-**) —*n.* **3.** nagging **4.** one who nags

nag[2] (nag) *n.* **1.** *inf.* horse **2.** small horse for riding

Nahum ('nāhəm) *n. Bible* 34th book of the O.T., written by the prophet Nahum, dealing with the judgment upon the city of Nineveh

naiad ('nāəd, 'nīəd, -ad) *n.* water nymph (*pl.* **-s, -ades** (-ədēz))

naïf *or* **naif** (nä'ēf) *a. see* NAIVE

nail (nāl) *n.* **1.** horny shield at ends of fingers, toes **2.** claw **3.** small metal spike for fixing wood *etc.* —*vt.* **4.** fix, stud with nails **5.** *inf.* catch —**'nailfile** *n.* small file used to trim nails —**nail set** punch for driving head of nail below or flush with surrounding surface

nainsook ('nānsŏŏk) *n.* soft fine cotton, oft. mercerized

naive, naïve (nä'ēv), **naïf,** *or* **naif** *a.* simple, unaffected, ingenuous —**naiveté, naïveté** (näēvə'tā), *or* **naivety** (nä'ēvəti) *n.*

naked ('nākid) *a.* **1.** without clothes **2.** exposed, bare **3.** undisguised —**'nakedly** *adv.* —**'nakedness** *n.* —**naked eye** the eye unassisted by any optical instrument

namby-pamby (nambi'pambi) *a.* **1.** weakly **2.** sentimental **3.** insipid —*n.* **4.** namby-pamby person

name (nām) *n.* **1.** word by which person, thing *etc.* is denoted **2.** reputation **3.** title **4.** credit **5.** family **6.** famous person —*vt.* **7.** give name to **8.** call by name **9.** entitle **10.** appoint **11.** mention **12.** specify —**'nameless** *a.* **1.** without a name **2.** indescribable **3.** too dreadful to be mentioned **4.** obscure —**'namely** *adv.* that is to say —**name-calling** *n.* speaking abusively to or about a person —**name day** *R.C.Ch.* feast day of saint whose name one bears —**name-dropper** *n.* —**name-dropping** *n. inf.* referring frequently to famous people, *esp.* as though they were intimate friends, in order to impress others —**'nameplate** *n.* small panel on door bearing occupant's name —**'namesake** *n.* person with same name as another —**name of the game** object of the activity

Namibia (nə'mibiə) *n.* country in Africa bounded north by Angola and Zambia, east by Botswana, Southeast by South Africa, and west by the Atlantic

nance ('nans) *n. offens.* effeminate or homosexual boy or man

nankeen (nan'kēn) *or* **nankin** ('nan'kin) *n.* **1.** buff-colored cotton fabric —*pl.* **2.** trousers made of this

nanny ('nani) *n.* UK child's nurse —**nanny goat** she-goat

nano- (*comb. form*) one billionth (10^{-9}), as in *nanosecond*

nap[1] (nap) *vi.* **1.** take short sleep, *esp.* in daytime (**-pp-**) —*n.* **2.** short sleep

nap[2] (nap) *n.* downy surface on cloth made by projecting fibers

nap[3] (nap) *n.* card game of the whist family

napalm ('nāpäm, 'nāpälm) *n.* jellied gasoline, highly inflammable, used in bombs *etc.*

nape (nāp) *n.* back of neck

naphtha ('nafthə, 'nap-) *n.* liquid distilled from crude petroleum used as solvent for cleaning and as raw material for gasoline —**'naphthalene** *n.* white crystalline product distilled from coal tar or petroleum, used in disinfectants, mothballs *etc.*

napkin ('napkin) *n.* cloth, paper for wiping fingers or lips at table

narcissus

narcissus (när'sisəs) *n.* genus of bulbous plants including daffodil, jonquil, *esp.* one with white flowers (*pl.* **-cissi** (-'sisī)) —**'narcissism** *n.* abnormal love and admiration of oneself —**'narcissist** *n.*

narcolepsy ('närkəlepsi) *n.* illness marked by sudden short spells of overpowering sleepiness (*also* **Friedman's disease**)

narcotic (när'kotik) *n.* **1.** any of a group of drugs, including morphine and opium, producing numbness and stupor, used medicinally but addictive —*a.* **2.** of narcotics or narcosis —**narcosis** (när'kōsis) *n.* effect of narcotic

nard (närd) *n.* **1.** *see* spikenard at SPIKE **2.** plant whose aromatic roots were formerly used in medicine

Narraganset (narə'gansit) *n.* member of Algonquian-speaking Amerindian people of Rhode Island (*pl.* **-set, -s**)

narrate ('närāt, na'rāt) *vt.* relate, recount, tell (story) —**nar'ration** *n.* —**'narrative** *n.* **1.** account, story —*a.* **2.** relating —**'narrator** *n.*

narrow ('närō) *a.* **1.** of little breadth, *esp.* in comparison to length **2.** limited **3.** barely adequate or successful —*v.* **4.** make, become narrow —**'narrowly** *adv.* —**'narrowness** *n.*

—**'narrows** *pl.n.* narrow part of straits —**'narrowback** *n. inf.* (among Irish) recent immigrant to the U.S.A. from Ireland —**narrow-minded** *a.* **1.** illiberal **2.** bigoted —**narrow-mindedness** *n.* prejudice, bigotry

narwhal ('närwäl, -wəl) *or* **narwhale** ('närwäl) *n.* arctic whale with tusk developed from teeth

NASA ('nasə) National Aeronautics and Space Administration

nasal ('nāzəl) *a.* **1.** of nose —*n.* **2.** sound partly produced in nose —**'nasalize** *vt.* make nasal in sound —**'nasally** *adv.*

nascent ('nasənt, 'nā-) *a.* **1.** just coming into existence **2.** springing up

nasturtium

nasturtium (nə'stərshəm) *n.* **1.** genus of plants which includes the watercress **2.** trailing garden plant with red or orange flowers

nasty ('nasti) *a.* foul, disagreeable, unpleasant —**'nastily** *adv.* —**'nastiness** *n.*

nat. 1. national **2.** native **3.** natural

natal ('nātəl) *a.* of birth

natatory ('nātətöri) *or* **natatorial** (nātə'töriəl, nat-) *a.* of swimming —**na'tation** *n.*

nation ('nāshən) *n.* people or race organized as a state —**national** ('nashənəl) *a.* **1.** belonging or pert. to a nation **2.** public, general —*n.* **3.** member of a nation —**nationalism** ('nashənəlizəm) *n.* **1.** loyalty, devotion to one's country **2.** movement for independence of state, people, ruled by another —**nationalist** ('nashənəlist) *n./a.* —**nationality** (nashə'naliti) *n.* **1.** national quality or feeling **2.** fact of belonging to particular nation —**nationalization** (nashənəli'zāshən) *n.* acquisition and management of industries by the State —**nationalize** ('nashənəlīz) *vt.* convert (private industry, resources *etc.*) to state control —**nationally** ('nashənəli) *adv.* —**national debt** total financial obligations incurred by nation's central government —**National Foundation** foundation established in 1938 to conduct research for prevention of poliomyelitis and care for sufferers. The program is now expanded to include prevention of birth defects and virus diseases —**National Guard** U.S. military reserve force maintained by the states but available for federal use —**national park** area of land controlled by the state to preserve its natural beauty *etc.* —**National Safety Council** nonprofit cooperative organization chartered by Congress which furnishes leadership to the national safety movement

native ('nātiv) a. **1.** inborn **2.** born in particular place **3.** found in pure state **4.** that was place of one's birth —n. **5.** one born in a place **6.** member of indigenous race of a country **7.** species of plant, animal *etc.* originating in a place —**Native American** American Indian, Amerindian

nativity (nə'tiviti) n. **1.** birth **2.** time, circumstances of birth **3.** (N-) birth of Christ

NATO ('nātō) North Atlantic Treaty Organization

natterjack ('natərjak) n. small European toad

natty ('nati) a. neat and smart; spruce —'**nattily** adv.

nature ('nāchər) n. **1.** innate or essential qualities of person or thing **2.** class, sort **3.** life force **4.** (oft. N-) power underlying all phenomena in material world **5.** material world as a whole **6.** natural unspoilt scenery or countryside, and plants and animals in it **7.** disposition, temperament —**natural** ('nachrəl) a. **1.** of, according to, occurring in, provided by, nature **2.** inborn **3.** normal **4.** unaffected **5.** illegitimate —n. **6.** something, somebody well suited for something **7.** Mus. character (♮) used to remove effect of a sharp or flat preceding it —**naturalism** ('nachrəlizəm) n. **1.** movement, esp. in art and literature, advocating realism **2.** belief that all religious truth is based on study of natural causes and processes —**naturalist** ('nachrəlist) n. student of natural history —**naturalistic** (nachrə'listik) a. of or imitating nature in effect or characteristics —**naturalization** (nachrəli'zāshən) n. —**naturalize** ('nachrəlīz) vt. **1.** admit to citizenship **2.** accustom to new climate —**naturally** ('nachrəli) adv. **1.** of or according to nature **2.** by nature **3.** of course —**natural childbirth** system of childbirth involving minimum use of drugs for which mother has undergone training —**natural gas** gaseous mixture, consisting mainly of methane, trapped below ground; used extensively as fuel —**natural history** study of animals and plants —**natural law** principle of law or action considered as derived from nature or right reason and binding in human society —**natural number** any of positive integers 1, 2, 3, 4,... —**natural resources** naturally occurring materials such as coal *etc.* —**natural science** any of sciences that are involved in study of physical world, including biology, physics *etc.* —**natural selection** process resulting in survival of those individuals from population of animals *etc.* that are best adapted to prevailing environmental conditions —**nature trail** path through countryside of particular interest to naturalists

Naugahyde ('nōgəhīd) n. trade name for a vinyl material imitating leather, oft. used for upholstery

naught (nöt) n. **1.** obs. nothing **2.** cipher 0 —**set at naught** defy, disregard

naughty ('nöti) a. **1.** disobedient, not behaving well **2.** inf. mildly indecent —'**naughtily** adv.

Nauru (nä'ōōrōō) n. country lying in the south Pacific Ocean comprising an island lying at 0° 32′ S latitude and 166° 56′ E longitude

nausea ('nōziə, -shə, -siə, -zhə) n. feeling that precedes vomiting —'**nauseate** vt. sicken —'**nauseous** ('nōshəs, 'nōziəs) a. **1.** disgusting **2.** causing nausea

nautical ('nötikəl) a. **1.** of seamen or ships **2.** marine —**nautical mile** measure of length used in navigation, 1.852 km, 2022 yards

nautilus ('nötiləs) n. univalvular mollusk of warm seas (pl. -es, -tili (-tilī))

Navaho or **Navajo** ('navəhō) n. **1.** member of Amerindian people of northern New Mexico and Arizona (pl. -ho or -jo, -s) **2.** the Athapascan language of this people

naval ('nāvəl) a. see NAVY

nave[1] (nāv) n. main part of church

nave[2] (nāv) n. hub of wheel

navel ('nāvəl) n. small scar, depression in middle of abdomen where umbilical cord was attached (also **umbilicus**)

navigate ('navigāt) v. **1.** plan, direct, plot path or position of (ship etc.) **2.** travel —'**navigable** a. —**navi'gation** n. **1.** science of directing course of seagoing vessel, or of aircraft in flight **2.** shipping —'**navigator** n. one who navigates

navy ('nāvi) n. **1.** fleet **2.** warships of country with their crews and organization —a. **3.** navy-blue —'**naval** a. of the navy —**navy-blue** a. very dark blue

Nazi ('nätsi) n. **1.** member of the National Socialist political party in Germany, 1919–45 **2.** one who thinks, acts like a Nazi (pl. -s) —a. **3.** of Nazis —'**Nazism** or '**Naziism** n. Nazi doctrine

Nb Chem. niobium

NB 1. Nebraska **2.** New Brunswick

NB, N.B., or **n.b.** nota bene

NBS National Bureau of Standards

NC North Carolina

N.C.O. noncommissioned officer

Nd Chem. neodymium

ND North Dakota

N.D.P. C New Democratic Party

Ne Chem. neon

NE 1. northeast(ern) **2.** Nebraska

Neanderthal (ni'andərtöl, -thöl) a. of Middle Paleolithic man

neap (nēp) a. low —**neap tide** the low tide at the first and third quarters of the moon

Neapolitan (nēə'politən) n. **1.** native or inhabitant of Naples —a. **2.** of Naples —**Neapolitan ice cream** brick of ice cream with different flavors in layers

near (nēər) prep. **1.** close to —adv. **2.** at or to a short distance —a. **3.** close at hand **4.** closely related **5.** narrow, so as barely to escape **6.** stingy **7.** closer (of two); left (of pair) —v. **8.** approach —'**nearly** adv. **1.** closely **2.** almost —'**nearness** n. —**near'by** a. adjacent —**Near East** see **Middle East** at MIDDLE **2.** formerly, Balkan States and area of Ottoman Empire —**near'sightedness** n. condition in which images come to a focus in front of the retina (also **myopia**)

neat (nēt) a. **1.** tidy, orderly **2.** efficient **3.** precise, deft **4.** cleverly worded **5.** undiluted **6.** simple and elegant **7.** sl. pleasing; admirable; excellent —'**neaten** vt. make neat; tidy —'**neatly** adv. —'**neatness** n.

neath (nēth) prep. obs. beneath

N.E.B. New English Bible

Nebraska (ni'braskə) n. West North Central state of the U.S., admitted to the U.S. in 1867. Abbrev.: **Nebr., NB** (with ZIP code)

nebula ('nebyələ) n. Astron. diffuse cloud of particles, gases (pl. -s, -ulae (-yəlē)) —'**nebulous** a. **1.** cloudy **2.** vague, indistinct

necessary ('nesiseri) a. **1.** needful, requisite, that must be done **2.** unavoidable, inevitable —**neces'sarily** adv. —**ne'cessitate** vt. make necessary —**ne'cessitous** a. poor, needy, destitute —**ne'cessity** n. **1.** something needed, requisite **2.** constraining power or state of affairs **3.** compulsion **4.** poverty

neck (nek) n. **1.** part of body joining head to shoulders **2.** narrower part of a bottle etc. **3.** narrow piece of anything between wider parts —vi. **4.** sl. embrace, cuddle —'**neckerchief** n. kerchief for the neck —'**necklet** n.

neck ornament, piece of fur etc. —**necklace** ('neklis) n. ornament round the neck —'**necktie** n. long narrow piece of material worn knotted around collar of shirt

necro- or before vowel **necr-** (comb. form) death, dead body, dead tissue, as in necrosis

necromancy ('nekrəmansi) n. magic, esp. by communication with dead —'**necromancer** n. wizard

necrophilia (nekrə'filiə) n. sexual attraction for or intercourse with dead bodies (also **necro'mania, ne'crophilism**)

necropolis (nə'kropəlis, ne-) n. cemetery (pl. -es, -oleis (-əlās))

nectar ('nektər) n. **1.** honey of flowers **2.** drink of the gods —'**nectary** n. honey gland of flower

nectarine

nectarine (nektə'rēn) n. smooth-skinned peach

née or **nee** (nā) a. indicating maiden name of married woman

need (nēd) vt. **1.** want, require —n. **2.** (state, instance of) want **3.** requirement **4.** necessity **5.** poverty —'**needful** a. necessary, requisite —'**needless** a. unnecessary —**needs** adv. of necessity (esp. in **needs must** or **must needs**) —'**needy** a. poor, in want

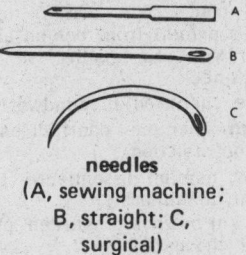

needles
(A, sewing machine;
B, straight; C,
surgical)

needle ('nēdəl) n. **1.** pointed pin with an eye and no head, for sewing **2.** long, pointed pin for knitting **3.** pointer of gauge, dial **4.** magnetized bar of compass **5.** stylus for phonograph **6.** leaf of fir or pine **7.** obelisk **8.** inf. hypodermic syringe —vt. **9.** inf. goad, provoke —'**needlecord** n. corduroy fabric with narrow ribs —'**needlepoint** n. **1.** embroidery done on canvas with various stitches so as to resemble tapestry **2.** point lace —'**needlework** n. embroidery, sewing

ne'er (nāər) adv. Lit. never —**ne'er-do-well** n. worthless person

nefarious (ni'fariəs, -'fer-) a. wicked

neg. negative(ly)

negate (ni'gāt) vt. deny, nullify —**ne'gation** n. contradiction, denial

negative ('negətiv) a. **1.** expressing denial or refusal **2.** lacking enthusiasm, energy, interest **3.** not positive **4.** (of electrical charge) having the same polarity as the charge of an electron —n. **5.** negative word or statement **6.** Photog. picture made by action of light on chemicals in which lights and shades are reversed —vt. **7.** disprove, reject —**negative feedback** see **feedback** at FEED

neglect (ni'glekt) vt. 1. disregard, take no care of 2. omit through carelessness —vi. 3. fail (to do) —n. 4. fact of neglecting or being neglected —**ne'glectful** a.

negligee or **negligé** (negli'zhā) n. 1. woman's light, gauzy dressing gown 2. easy, informal attire

negligence ('neglijəns) n. 1. neglect 2. carelessness —**'negligent** a. —**'negligible** a. 1. able to be disregarded 2. very small or unimportant

negotiate (ni'gōshiāt) vi. 1. discuss with view to mutual settlement —vt. 2. arrange by conference 3. transfer (bill, check etc.) 4. get over, past, around (obstacle) —**ne'gotiable** a. —**negoti'ation** n. 1. treating with another on business 2. discussion 3. transference (of bill, check etc.) —**ne'gotiator** n.

Negro ('nēgrō) n. member of Black orig. Afr. race (pl. **-es**) ('**Negress** fem.) —**negritude** ('negritōōd, 'nē-; -tyōōd) n. 1. fact of being a Negro 2. awareness and cultivation of Negro culture etc. —'**Negroid** a. of or like a Negro

negus ('nēgəs) n. hot drink of port and lemon juice

Nehemiah (nēhə'mīə, nēə'mīə) n. Bible 16th book of the O.T., completing the story of the return to Palestine after the exile

neigh (nā) n. 1. cry of horse —vi. 2. utter this cry

neighbor ('nābər) n. one who lives near another —'**neighborhood** n. 1. district 2. people of a district 3. region round about —'**neighboring** a. situated nearby —'**neighborly** a. 1. as or befitting a good or friendly neighbor 2. friendly 3. sociable 4. helpful

neither ('nēdhər, 'nīdhər) a./pron. 1. not the one or the other —adv. 2. not on the one hand 3. not either —conj. 4. not

nelson ('nelsən) n. wrestling hold in which wrestler places his arm(s) under his opponent's arm(s) from behind and exerts pressure with his palms on back of opponent's neck

nematode ('nematōd) n. roundworm

nem. con. nemine contradicente (Lat., without contradiction)

nem. diss. nemine dissentiente (Lat., without dissent, unanimously)

nemesia (ni'mēzhə) n. garden plant with flowers of various colors

Nemesis ('nemisis) n. 1. retribution 2. the goddess of vengeance (pl. **-ses** (-sēz))

neo- or sometimes before vowel **ne-** (comb. form) new, later, revived in modified form, based upon

neodymium (nēō'dimiəm) n. Chem. metallic element Symbol Nd, at. wt. 144.2, at. no. 60

Neolithic (nēə'lithik) a. of the later Stone Age

neologism (ni'oləjizəm) or **neology** n. new-coined word or phrase —**ne'ologize** vi.

neon ('nēon) n. Chem. element, noble gas Symbol Ne, at. wt. 83.80, at. no. 36 —**neon lamp** or **sign** illumination device containing neon and other gases

neophyte ('nēəfīt) n. 1. new convert 2. beginner, novice

Nepal (nə'pöl, -'pol) n. country in Asia bounded north by Tibet, east by India and West Bengal, south and west by India —**Nepalese** (nepə'lēz, -'lēs) n./a. (native or inhabitant) of Nepal

nephew ('nefyōō) n. brother's or sister's son

nephritis (ni'frītis) n. inflammation of a kidney

nephrosis (ni'frōsis) n. kidney condition marked by protein in the urine and edema

nepotism ('nepətizəm) n. undue favoritism toward one's relations

Neptune ('neptyōōn, -tōōn) n. 1. god of the sea 2. planet second farthest from sun

neptunium (nep'tyōōniəm, -'tōōniəm) n. Chem. metallic element Symbol Np, at. wt. 237, at. no. 93

nerve (nərv) n. 1. sinew, tendon 2. fiber or bundle of fibers conveying feeling, impulses to motion etc. to and from brain and other parts of body 3. assurance 4. coolness in danger 5. audacity —pl. 6. irritability, unusual sensitiveness to fear, annoyance etc. —vt. 7. give courage or strength to —'**nerveless** a. 1. without nerves 2. useless 3. weak 4. paralyzed —'**nervous** a. 1. excitable, timid 2. apprehensive, worried 3. of the nerves —'**nervously** adv. —'**nervousness** n. —'**nervy** a. 1. nervous 2. jumpy 3. irritable 4. on edge —**nerve cell** see NEURON —**nerve center** 1. group of nerve cells associated with specific function 2. principal source of control over any complex activity —**nerve gas** poisonous gas that has paralyzing effect on central nervous system that can be fatal —**nerve-racking** or **nerve-wracking** a. very distressing, exhausting or harrowing —**nervous breakdown** condition of mental, emotional disturbance, disability —**nervous system** system of specialized tissue controlling internal activities of organism and regulating interaction with environment

ness (nes) n. headland, cape

-ness (comb. form) state, condition, quality, as in greatness, selfishness

nest (nest) n. 1. place in which bird lays and hatches its eggs 2. animal's breeding place 3. snug retreat —vi. 4. make, have a nest —**nest egg** (fund of) money in reserve

nestle ('nesəl) vi. settle comfortably, usu. pressing in or close to something

nestling ('nestling) n. bird too young to leave nest

net[1] (net) n. 1. openwork fabric of meshes of cord etc. 2. piece of it used to catch fish etc. —vt. 3. cover with, or catch in, net (**-tt-**) —'**netting** n. string or wire net

net[2] (net) a. 1. left after all deductions 2. free from deduction —vt. 3. gain, yield as clear profit (**-tt-**) —**net profit** gross profit minus all operating costs not included in calculation of gross profit

nether ('nedhər) a. lower —'**nethermost** a. farthest down; lowest —**nether world** 1. underworld 2. hell (also **nether regions**)

Netherlands ('nedhərləndz) pl.n. (with sing. v.) —**the Netherlands** country in Europe bounded north and west by the North Sea, south by Belgium and east by West Germany —'**Netherland**, '**Netherlandic**, or '**Netherlandish** a. —'**Netherlander** n.

Netherlands Antilles (an'tilēz) pl.n. (with sing. v.) —**the Netherlands Antilles** division of the Kingdom of the Netherlands comprising two groups of islands in the Caribbean

netsuke ('netsəki) n. carved wooden or ivory toggle or button worn in Japan

nettle ('netəl) n. 1. plant with stinging hairs on the leaves —vt. 2. irritate, provoke —**nettle rash** urticaria

network ('netwərk) n. 1. system of intersecting lines, roads etc. 2. interconnecting group of people or things 3. in broadcasting, group of stations connected to transmit same programs simultaneously

Neufchatel (nyōōshə'tel, nōō-) n. soft cow's-milk cheese with a mild flavor orig. from France

neural ('nyōōrəl, 'nōōrəl) a. of the nerves

neuralgia (nyōō'raljə, nōō-) n. pain in, along nerves, esp. of face and head —**neu'ralgic** a.

neuritis (nyōō'rītis, nōō-) n. disorder of nerves excluding those of brain and spinal cord caused by disease, mechanical pressure, vitamin deficiency etc.

neuro- or before vowel **neur-** (comb. form) nerve; nervous system, as in neurology

neurology (nyōō'roləji, nōō-) n. science, study of nerves —**neu'rologist** n.

neuron ('nyōōron, 'nōō-, 'nyōōə-, 'nōōə-) or **neurone** ('nyōōrōn, 'nōō-, 'njōōə-, 'nōōə-) n. cell specialized to conduct nerve impulses (also **nerve cell**) —**neu'ronic** a.

neurosis (nyōō'rōsis, nōō-) n. relatively mild mental disorder (pl. **-ses** (-sēz)) —**neurotic** (nyōō'rotik, nōō-) a. 1. suffering from nervous disorder 2. abnormally sensitive —n. 3. neurotic person

neurosurgery (nyōōrō'sərjəri, nōōrō-) n. branch of surgery concerned with nervous system —**neuro'surgical** a.

neuter ('nyōōtər, 'nōōtər) a. 1. neither masculine nor feminine —n. 2. neuter word 3. neuter gender —vt. 4. castrate, spay (domestic animal)

neutral ('nyōōtrəl, 'nōōtrəl) a. 1. taking neither side in war, dispute etc. 2. without marked qualities 3. belonging to neither of two classes —n. 4. neutral nation or a subject of one 5. neutral gear —**neu'trality** n. —'**neutralize** vt. 1. make ineffective 2. counterbalance —**neutral gear** in vehicle, position of gears that leaves transmission disengaged

neutrino (nyōō'trēnō, nōō-) n. Phys. stable elementary particle with zero rest mass (pl. **-s**)

neutron ('nyōōtron, 'nōō-) n. electrically neutral particle of the nucleus of an atom

Nevada (nə'vadə) n. Mountain state of the U.S., admitted to the Union in 1864. Abbrev.: Nev., NV (with ZIP code)

never ('nevər) adv. at no time —**never'more** adv. Lit. never again —**neverthe'less** adv. for all that, notwithstanding

nevus ('nēvəs) n. birthmark (pl. **nevi** ('nēvī))

new (nyōō, nōō) a. 1. not existing before, fresh 2. that has lately come into some state or existence 3. unfamiliar, strange —adv. 4. recently, fresh (usu. '**newly**) —'**newly** adv. —'**newness** n. —'**newcomer** n. recent arrival —**New Deal** policies for social reform and economic recovery in U.S. initiated by Franklin D. Roosevelt —**New English Bible** translation of Bible by British interdenominational committee first published in 1970 —'**new'fangled** a. of new fashion —**new math** approach to mathematics in which basic principles of set theory are introduced in elementary school —**new moon** moon when it appears as narrow waxing crescent —'**newspeak** n. language of bureaucrats and politicians, regarded as deliberately ambiguous and misleading —**New Testament** second part of the Bible concerned with the life and teaching of Jesus and the early Christian church —**New Year** first day or days of year —**New Year's Day** January 1st, U.S. national holiday —**the New World** the Americas; western hemisphere

newel ('nyōōəl, 'nōōəl) n. 1. central pillar of winding staircase 2. post at top or bottom of staircase rail

New Hampshire ('hampshər) New England state of the U.S.: ratified the Constitution in 1788. Abbrev.: NH (with ZIP code)

New Jersey ('jərzi) Middle Atlantic state of the U.S.: ratified the Constitution in 1787. Abbrev.: NJ (with ZIP code)

New Mexico ('meksikō) Mountain state of the U.S., admitted to the Union in 1912. Abbrev.: N. Mex., NM (with ZIP code)

news (nyōōz, nōōz) n. 1. report of recent

happenings, tidings **2.** interesting fact not previously known —**'newsy** *a.* full of news —**news agency** organization that provides news reports for subscribing newspapers *etc.* —**'newsboy** *n.* boy who delivers or sells newspapers —**'newscast** *n.* news broadcast —**'newscaster** *n.* —**news flash** brief item of important news, oft. interrupting radio or television program —**'newsletter** *n.* **1.** printed periodical bulletin circulated to members of group (*also* **news-sheet**) **2.** *Hist.* written or printed account of news —**'newspaper** *n.* periodical, usu. daily or weekly, publication containing news —**'newsprint** *n.* paper of the kind used for newspapers *etc.* —**'newsreel** *n.* short movie giving news —**'newsstand** *n.* stand from which newspapers are sold —**'newsworthy** *a.* sufficiently interesting or important to be reported as news

newt (nyo͞ot, no͞ot) *n.* small, tailed amphibious creature

newton ('nyo͞otən, 'no͞otən) *n.* SI unit of force

New York (york) Middle Atlantic state of the U.S.: ratified the Constitution in 1788. Abbrev.: **NY** (with ZIP code)

New Zealand ('zēlənd) country lying in the South Pacific southeast of Australia comprising North and South Islands, Stewart Island, Chatham Islands and other islands as well as territories overseas —**New Zealander** ('zēləndər)

next (nekst) *a./adv.* **1.** nearest **2.** immediately following —**next door** at or to adjacent house, apartment *etc.* —**next-of-kin** *n.* nearest relative

nexus ('neksəs) *n.* tie, connection, link (*pl.* **'nexus**)

Nez Percé (nez pərs, nes pãrs; *Fr.* nā per'sā) **1.** member of Amerindian people of Idaho, Washington and Oregon **2.** Penutian language of this people

NF Newfoundland

NH New Hampshire

Ni *Chem.* nickel

nib (nib) *n.* **1.** (split) pen point **2.** bird's beak —*pl.* **3.** crushed cocoa beans

nibble ('nibəl) *v.* **1.** take little bites (of) —*n.* **2.** little bite

nibs (nibz) *n.* mock title of respect, as in *his nibs*

Nicaragua (nikə'rägwə) *n.* country in Central America bounded east by the Atlantic, south by Costa Rica, west by the Pacific and north by El Salvador and Honduras —**Nica'raguan** *n./a.*

nice (nīs) *a.* **1.** pleasant **2.** friendly, kind **3.** attractive **4.** subtle, fine **5.** careful, exact **6.** difficult to decide —**'nicely** *adv.* —**nicety** ('nīsiti) *n.* **1.** minute distinction or detail **2.** subtlety **3.** precision

niche (nich) *n.* **1.** recess in wall **2.** suitable place in life, public estimation *etc.*

nick (nik) *vt.* **1.** make notch in, indent **2.** *sl.* steal —*n.* **3.** notch **4.** exact point of time —**in good nick** *inf.* in good condition

nickel ('nikəl) *n.* **1.** *Chem.* metallic element *Symbol* Ni, at. wt. 58.7, at. no. 28 **2.** five-cent piece —**nickel silver** white alloy containing copper, zinc and nickel (*also* **German silver**)

nicker ('nikər) *vi.* **1.** (of horse) neigh softly **2.** snigger

nicknack ('nik,nak) *n. see* KNICK-KNACK

nickname ('niknām) *n.* familiar name added to or replacing an ordinary name

nicotine ('nikətēn) *n.* liquid alkaloid obtained from leaves of tobacco plant —**'nicotinism** *n.* tobacco poisoning

nictitate ('niktitāt) *or* **nictate** ('niktāt) *v.* blink —**nicti'tation** *or* **nic'tation** *n.*

niece (nēs) *n.* brother's or sister's daughter

niello (nē'elō) *n.* black alloy of lead, silver, copper and sulfur used to decorate metal objects

nifty ('nifti) *a. inf.* **1.** neat, smart **2.** quick

Niger ('nījər) *n.* country in Africa bounded north by Algeria and Libya, east by Chad, south by Nigeria, southwest by Benin and Burkina-Faso and west by Mali —**Nigerois** (nēzhər'wä, -zher-) *n.*

Nigeria (nī'jēəriə) *n.* country in Africa bounded north by Niger, northeast by Lake Chad, east by Cameroon, south by the Atlantic and west by Benin and Niger —**Ni'gerian** *n./a.*

niggard ('nigərd) *n.* mean, stingy person —**'niggardly** *a./adv.*

nigger ('nigər) *n. offens.* Negro

niggle ('nigəl) *vi.* **1.** find fault continually —*vt.* **2.** annoy —**'niggling** *a.* **1.** petty **2.** irritating and persistent

nigh (nī) *a./adv./prep. obs., poet.* near

night (nīt) *n.* **1.** time of darkness between sunset and sunrise **2.** end of daylight **3.** dark —**'nightie** *n.* nightdress —**'nightly** *a.* **1.** happening, done every night **2.** of the night —*adv.* **3.** every night **4.** by night —**nights** *adv. inf.* at night, *esp.* regularly —**night blindness** *Pathol.* inability to see normally in dim light (*also* **nyctalopia**) —**'nightcap** *n.* **1.** cap worn in bed **2.** late-night (alcoholic) drink —**'nightclub** *n.* establishment for dancing, music *etc.* opening late at night —**'nightdress** *n.* woman's loose robe worn in bed —**'nightfall** *n.* approach of darkness; dusk —**'nightingale** *n.* any of various old world thrushes noted for sweet singing, *esp.* at night —**'nightmare** *n.* **1.** very bad dream **2.** terrifying experience —**night school** educational institution that holds classes in evening —**'nightshade** *n.* any of various plants of potato family, some of them with very poisonous berries —**'nightspot** *n. inf.* nightclub —**'nightstick** *n.* short club carried by uniformed member of police —**'nighttime** *n.* —**night watch 1.** guard kept at night, *esp.* for security **2.** period of time watch is kept

NIH National Institutes of Health

nihilism ('nīilizəm, 'nīhilizəm) *n.* **1.** rejection of all religious and moral principles **2.** opposition to all constituted authority or government —**'nihilist** *n.* —**nihil'istic** *a.*

-nik (*comb. form*) *inf., oft. offens.* person associated with specified state or quality: *beatnik, jognik, richnik*

nil (nil) *n.* nothing, zero

nimble ('nimbəl) *a.* agile, active, quick, dexterous —**'nimbly** *adv.*

nimbus ('nimbəs) *n.* **1.** rain or storm cloud **2.** cloud of glory, halo (*pl.* **-bi** (-bī), **-es**)

nincompoop ('ninkəmpo͞op, 'ning-) *n.* fool, simpleton

nine (nīn) *a./n.* cardinal number next above eight —**nine'teen** *a./n.* nine more than ten —**nine'teenth** *a.* —**'ninetieth** *a.* —**'ninety** *a./n.* nine tens —**ninth** (nīnth) *a.* —**'ninthly** ('nīnthli) *adv.* —**nine-days wonder** something that arouses great interest but only for short period —**'ninepins** *pl.n.* (*with sing. v.*) game where wooden pins are set up to be knocked down by rolling ball, skittles —**nineteenth hole** *Golf sl.* bar in golf clubhouse

niobium (nī'ōbiəm) *n. Chem.* metallic element *Symbol* Nb, at. wt. 92.9, at. no. 41 (*formerly* **columbium**)

nip (nip) *vt.* **1.** pinch sharply **2.** detach by pinching, bite **3.** check growth of (plants) thus **4.** *sl.* steal —*vi.* **5.** *inf.* hurry (-pp-) —*n.* **6.** pinch **7.** check to growth **8.** sharp coldness of

weather **9.** short drink —**'nipper** *n.* **1.** thing (*eg* crab's claw) that nips **2.** *inf.* small child —*pl.* **3.** pincers —**'nippy** *a. inf.* **1.** cold **2.** quick

nipple ('nipəl) *n.* **1.** point of a breast, teat **2.** anything like this

Nippon ('nipon) *n.* Japan —**Nippo'nese** *a./n.*

nisei (nē'sā, 'nēsā) *n.* person whose parents immigrated to the U.S.A. from Japan (*pl.* **nisei, -s**)

nit (nit) *n.* **1.** egg of louse or other parasite **2.** *inf.* nitwit —**nitty-gritty** *n. inf.* basic facts, details —**'nitwit** *n. inf.* fool

niter ('nītər) *n.* **1.** potassium nitrate **2.** sodium nitrate

nitrogen ('nītrəjən) *n. Chem.* gaseous element *Symbol* N, at. wt. 14.0, at. no. 7 —**'nitrate** *n.* compound of nitric acid and an alkali —**'nitric** *or* **'nitrous** *a.* —**'nitrify** *vt.* **1.** treat or cause to react with nitrogen **2.** treat (soil) with nitrates **3.** (of nitrobacteria) convert (ammonium compounds) into nitrates by oxidation —**ni'trogenous** *a.* of, containing nitrogen —**nitric acid** corrosive liquid —**nitrobac'teria** *pl.n.* soil bacteria involved in nitrification —**nitrogen cycle** natural circulation of nitrogen by living organisms —**nitrogen mustard** anticancer drug related to sulfur mustard gas used in warfare (*also* **mustargen, mechlorethamine**) —**nitroglycerin** *or* **nitroglycerine** (nītrə'glisərin) *n.* explosive liquid —**nitrous oxide** gas with sweet smell, used as anesthetic in dentistry (*also* **laughing gas**)

nix (niks) *sl. n.* **1.** nothing —*vt.* **2.** reject (proposal, plan)

Nixon ('niksən) *n.* **Richard Milhous.** the 37th President of the U.S. (1969-74)

NJ New Jersey

NLRB National Labor Relations Board

NM *or* **N. Mex.** New Mexico

NNE north-northeast

NNW north-northwest

no (nō) *a.* **1.** not any, not a **2.** not at all —*adv.* **3.** expresses negative reply to question or request —*n.* **4.** refusal **5.** denial **6.** negative vote or voter (*pl.* **-es**) —**no-go** *a. sl.* **1.** not functioning properly **2.** hopeless —**no-man's-land** *n.* **1.** waste or unclaimed land **2.** contested land between two opposing forces —**no-one** *or* **no one** *pron.* nobody —**no-trump Cards** *n.* **1.** bid or contract to play without trumps (*also* **no-trumps**) —*a.* **2.** (of hand) of balanced distribution suitable for playing without trumps (*also* **no-trumper**) —**'noway** *adv. sl.* not at all

No¹ *or* **Noh** (nō) *n.* traditional Japanese drama evolved from Shinto rites

No² *Chem.* nobelium

No. number (*pl.* **Nos.**)

nob (nob) *n. sl.* **1.** member of upper classes **2.** head

nobelium (nō'bēliəm) *n. Chem.* transuranic element *Symbol* No, at. wt. 254, at. no. 102

noble ('nōbəl) *a.* **1.** of the nobility **2.** showing, having high moral qualities **3.** impressive, excellent —*n.* **4.** member of the nobility —**no'bility** *n.* **1.** class holding special rank, usu. hereditary, in state **2.** quality of being noble —**'nobly** *adv.* —**noble gas** gaseous element that almost never combines with other elements (*also* **rare gas**) —**'nobleman** *n.* —**noble metal** metallic element not corroding or tarnishing in air or water and highly resistant to chemical action

noblesse oblige (nō'bles ə'blēzh) *oft. ironic* supposed obligation of nobility to be honorable and generous

nobody ('nōbədi) *pron.* **1.** no person —*n.* **2.** person of no importance

nock (nok) *n.* 1. notch on arrow that fits on bowstring 2. groove at either end of bow that holds bowstring —*vt.* 3. fit (arrow) on bowstring

nocturnal (nok'tərnəl) *a.* 1. of, in, by, night 2. active by night

nocturne ('noktərn) *n.* 1. dreamy piece of music 2. night scene

nod (nod) *v.* 1. bow (head) slightly and quickly in assent, command *etc.* —*vi.* 2. let head droop with sleep (**-dd-**) —*n.* 3. act of nodding —**nodding acquaintance** slight knowledge of person or subject —**nod off** *inf.* fall asleep

node (nōd) *n.* 1. knot or knob 2. point at which curve crosses itself —'**nodal** *a.* —'**nodical** *a.*

nodule ('nojōōl) *n.* 1. little knot 2. rounded irregular mineral mass

Noel (nō'el) *n.* 1. Christmas 2. (**n-**) Christmas carol

nog[1] (nog) *n.* beverage made with beaten eggs, usu. with alcoholic liquor, such as *eggnog*

nog[2] (nog) *n.* 1. peg or block 2. stump —'**nogging** *n.* horizontal timber member in framed construction

noggin ('nogin) *n.* 1. small amount of liquor 2. small mug 3. *inf.* head

Noh (nō) *n. see* No[1]

noise (noiz) *n.* 1. any sound, *esp.* disturbing one 2. clamor, din 3. loud outcry 4. talk; interest —*vt.* 5. (*usu. with* abroad *or* about) spread (gossip *etc.*) —'**noiseless** *a.* without noise, quiet, silent —'**noisily** *adv.* —'**noisy** *a.* 1. making much noise 2. clamorous

noisome ('noisəm) *a.* 1. (*esp.* of smells) offensive 2. harmful, noxious

nom. nominative

nomad ('nōmad) *n.* 1. member of tribe with no fixed dwelling place 2. wanderer —**no-**'**madic** *a.*

nom de plume (nom də 'plōōm) *Fr.* writer's assumed name, pen name, pseudonym (*pl.* **noms de plume**)

nomenclature ('nōmənkləchər) *n.* terminology of particular science *etc.*

nominal ('nominəl) *a.* 1. in name only 2. (of fee *etc.*) small, insignificant 3. of a name or names —'**nominalism** *n.* philosophical theory that general word, such as *dog*, is merely name and does not denote real object, the general idea 'dog' —'**nominalist** *n.* —'**nominally** *adv.* 1. in name only 2. not really

nominate ('nomināt) *vt.* 1. propose as candidate 2. appoint to office —**nomi**'**nation** *n.* —'**nominative** *a./n.* (of) case of nouns, pronouns when subject of verb —'**nominator** *n.* —**nomi**'**nee** *n.* candidate

non- (*comb. form*) negatives the idea of the simple word. See the list below

nonage ('nonij, 'nōnij) *n.* 1. *Law* state of being under any of various ages at which person may legally enter into certain transactions 2. any period of immaturity

nonagenarian (nōnəji'neriən) *a.* 1. aged between ninety and ninety-nine —*n.* 2. person of such age

nonaligned (nonə'līnd) *a.* (of states *etc.*) not part of a major alliance or power bloc

nonce (nons) *n.* —**nonce word** word coined for single occasion —**for the nonce** 1. for the occasion only 2. for the present

nonchalant (nonshə'länt, 'nonshələnt, -lənt) *a.* casually unconcerned, indifferent, cool —**noncha**'**lance** *n.*

noncombatant (nonkəm'batənt, non'kombətənt) *n.* 1. civilian during war 2. member of army who does not fight, *eg* doctor, chaplain

noncommissioned officer (nonkə'mishənd) *Mil.* subordinate officer, risen from the ranks

noncommittal (nonkə'mitəl) *a.* avoiding definite preference or pledge

non compos mentis ('non 'kompəs 'mentis) *Lat.* of unsound mind

nondescript (nondi'skript) *a.* lacking distinctive characteristics, indeterminate

none (nun) *pron.* 1. no-one, not any —*a.* 2. no —*adv.* 3. in no way —**nonesuch** *or* **nonsuch** ('nunsuch) *n. obs.* matchless person or thing; nonpareil —**nonethe**'**less** *adv.* despite that, however

nonentity (non'entiti) *n.* 1. insignificant person, thing 2. nonexistent thing

nonevent ('nonivent, noni'vent) *n.* disappointing or insignificant occurrence, *esp.* one predicted to be important

nonferrous (non'ferəs) *a.* 1. denoting metal other than iron 2. not containing iron

nonflammable (non'flaməbəl) *a.* 1. incapable of burning 2. not easily set on fire

nonintervention (nonintər'venchən) *n.* refusal to intervene, *esp.* abstention by state from intervening in affairs of other states

noniron (non'īərn) *a.* not requiring ironing

nonnuclear (non'nyōōkliər, -'nōō-) *a.* not operated by or using nuclear energy

nonpareil (nonpə'rel) *a.* 1. unequaled, matchless —*n.* 2. person or thing unequaled or unrivaled 3. *Print.* 6-point type or 6-point space 4. small chocolate disk covered with tiny beads of colored sugar 5. one of the beads of sugar used to decorate cakes and cookies

nonpartisan (non'pärtizən) *a.* not supporting any single political party

nonplus ('non'plus) *vt.* disconcert, confound or bewilder completely (**-ss-**)

nonproliferation (nonprəlifər'āshən) *n.* limitation of production *esp.* of nuclear weapons

nonrepresentational (nonreprizen'tāshənəl) *a.* *Art* abstract

nonsectarian (nonsek'teriən) *a.* not sectarian; not confined to any specific religion

nonsense ('nonsens, -səns) *n.* 1. lack of sense 2. absurd language 3. absurdity 4. silly conduct —**non**'**sensical** *a.* 1. ridiculous 2. meaningless 3. without sense

non sequitur ('non 'sekwitər) *Lat.* statement with little or no relation to what preceded it

nonstarter (non'stärtər) *n.* 1. horse that fails to run in race for which it has been entered 2. person or thing that has little chance of success

nonsuch ('nunsuch) *n. see* **nonesuch** *at* NONE

non-U *a.* (*esp.* of language) not characteristic of upper class

nonunion (non'yōōnyən) *a.* 1. not belonging to trade union 2. not favoring or employing union labor 3. not produced by union labor

noodle[1] ('nōōdəl) *n.* strip of pasta served in soup *etc.*

noodle[2] ('nōōdəl) *n.* simpleton, fool

nook (nōōk) *n.* sheltered corner, retreat

noon (nōōn) *n.* midday, twelve o'clock —'**noonday** *n.* noon —'**noontide** *n.* the time about noon

noose (nōōs) *n.* 1. running loop 2. snare —*vt.* 3. catch, ensnare in noose, lasso

nor (nör; *unstressed* nər) *conj.* and not

nor' *or* **nor** (nör) north (*esp.* in compounds)

Nor. 1. Norman 2. north 3. Norway 4. Norwegian

Nordic ('nördik) *a.* pert. to peoples of Germanic stock

norm (nörm) *n.* 1. average level of achievement 2. rule or authoritative standard 3. model 4. standard type or pattern —'**normal** *a.* 1. ordinary 2. usual 3. conforming to type —*n.* 4. *Geom.* perpendicular —**nor**'**mality** *n.* —**normali**'**zation** *n.* —'**normalize** *vt.* 1. bring or make into normal state 2. bring into conformity with standard 3. heat (steel) above critical temperature and allow it to cool in air to relieve internal stresses; anneal —'**normally** *adv.* —'**normative** *a.* creating or prescribing norm or standard

Norman ('nörmən) *n.* 1. in Middle Ages, member of people of Normandy in N France, descended from 10th-century Scandinavian conquerors of the country and native French 2. native of Normandy 3. medieval Norman and English dialect of Old French (*also* **Norman French**) —*a.* 4. of Normans or their dialect of French 5. of Normandy 6. denoting Romanesque architecture used in Britain from Norman Conquest until 12th century, characterized by massive masonry walls *etc.*

Norse (nörs) *a.* 1. of ancient and medieval Scandinavia 2. of Norway —*n.* 3. N group of Germanic languages, spoken in Scandinavia 4. any of these languages, *esp.* in ancient or medieval forms —'**Norseman** *n. see* VIKING —**the Norse** 1. Norwegians 2. Vikings

north (nörth) *n.* 1. direction to the right of person facing the sunset 2. part of the world, of country *etc.* toward this point 3. person occupying this position in game —*adv.* 4. toward or in the north —*a.* 5. to, from or in the north —**northerly** ('nördhərli) *a.* 1. of or situated in north —*n.* 2. wind from the north

nonac'ceptance	noncom'pliance	nonex'istent	nonoper'ational	non'resident	non'taxable
nonag'gression	noncon'secutive	non'fiction	non'party	nonre'sistant	non'technical
nonalco'holic	noncon'tagious	nonin'fectious	non'payment	nonre'turnable	non'toxic
nonap'pearance	noncon'tributory	nonin'flammable	non-playing	nonse'lective	nontrans'ferable
nonbe'liever	noncontro'versial	nonmag'netic	non'poisonous	non'shrink(able)	non'tropical
nonbel'ligerent	noncooper'ation	nonma'lignant	non'porous	non'slip	non'venomous
non'breakable	nonde'livery	non'member	non'profit-making	non'smoker	non'verbal
non-Catholic	nondenomi'national	non'metal	non'racial	non'standard	non'violent
noncom'bustible	non'drinker	non'militant	non'reader	non'stick	non'voter
non'communist	non'driver	non-negotiable	non'registered	non'stop	
noncom'petitive	nones'sential	nonob'servance	nonrepre'sentative	non'swimmer	

—**northern** ('nördhərn) a. —**northerner** ('nördhərnər) n. person from the north —**northward** ('nördhwərd; Naut. 'nördhərd) a./n./adv. —**northwards** ('nördhwərdz) adv. —**northeast** (north'ēst; Naut. nör'ēst) n. **1.** direction midway between north and east **2.** (oft. N-) area lying in or toward this direction —a. **3.** (sometimes N-) of northeastern part of specified country etc. **4.** in, toward or facing northeast **5.** (esp. of wind) from northeast (also north'eastern) —adv. **6.** in, to, toward or (esp. of wind) from northeast —**North'east** n. areas or regions lying to northeast of implied point of orientation —**northeaster** (north'ēstər; Naut. nör'ēstər) n. strong wind or storm from northeast —**northern hemisphere** (oft. N-H-) half of globe lying north of equator —**northern lights** aurora borealis —**north-northeast** n. **1.** direction midway between north and northeast —a./adv. **2.** in, from or toward this direction —**north-northwest** n. **1.** direction midway between northwest and north —a./adv. **2.** in, from or toward this direction —**North Pole 1.** northernmost point on earth's axis **2.** Astron. point of intersection of earth's extended axis and northern half of celestial sphere (also north celestial pole) —**northwest** (north'west; Naut. nör'west) n. **1.** direction midway between north and west **2.** (oft. N-) area lying in or toward this direction —a. **3.** (sometimes N-) of northwestern part of specified country etc. (also north'western) —a./adv. **4.** in, to, toward or (esp. of wind) from northwest —**northwester** (north'westər; Naut. nör'westər) n. strong wind or storm from northwest —**the North Star** see **Pole Star** at POLE²

North Carolina (karə'līnə) South Atlantic state of the U.S.: ratified the Constitution in 1789. Abbrev.: **NC** (with ZIP code)

North Dakota (də'kōtə) West North Central state of the U.S., admitted to the Union in 1889. Abbrev.: **ND** (with ZIP code)

Northern Rhodesia former name of ZAMBIA

North Korea country in Asia bounded north by China, east by the Sea of Japan, west by the Yellow Sea and south by Korea from which it is separated by a demilitarized zone

Norw. 1. Norway **2.** Norwegian

Norway ('nörwā) n. country in Europe bounded north by the Arctic Ocean, east by the U.S.S.R., Finland and Sweden, south by the Skagerrak Straits and west by the North Sea —**Norwegian** (nör'wējən) n./a. **1.** (native or inhabitant) of Norway —n. **2.** language of Norway which is a Scandinavian language

Nos. numbers

nose (nōz) n. **1.** organ of smell, used also in breathing, as opening to balance pressure on eardrum, and sounding board to form speech sounds **2.** any projection resembling a nose, as prow of ship, aircraft etc. —v. **3.** (cause to) move forward slowly and carefully —vt. **4.** touch with nose **5.** smell, sniff —vi. **6.** smell **7.** (with into, around, about etc.) pry —'**nosy** or '**nosey** a. inf. inquisitive —'**nosebag** n. bag fastened around head of horse in which feed is placed —'**noseband** n. detachable part of horse's bridle that goes around nose —**nose dive** downward sweep of aircraft —'**nosegay** n. bunch of flowers

nosh (nosh) n. **1.** a snack **2.** anything eaten between meals —'**nosher** n. **1.** one who eats between meals **2.** one with a sweet tooth —**nosh-up** n. UK large and satisfying meal

nostalgia (no'staljə) n. **1.** longing for return of past events **2.** homesickness —**nos'talgic** a.

nostril ('nostril) n. one of the two external openings of the nose

nostrum ('nostrəm) n. **1.** quack medicine **2.** secret remedy

not (not) adv. expressing negation, refusal, denial —**not proven** ('prōvən) a third verdict available to Scottish courts, returned when there is insufficient evidence to convict

nota bene ('nōtə 'bēni) Lat. note well

notable ('nōtəbəl) a. **1.** worthy of note, remarkable —n. **2.** person of distinction —**nota'bility** n. an eminent person —'**notably** adv.

notary ('nōtəri) n. person authorized to draw up deeds, contracts

notation (nō'tāshən) n. **1.** representation of numbers, quantities, by symbols **2.** set of such symbols **3.** C footnote, memorandum

notch (noch) n. **1.** V-shaped cut or indentation **2.** inf. step, grade —vt. **3.** make notches in

note (nōt) n. **1.** brief comment or record **2.** short letter **3.** symbol for musical sound **4.** single tone **5.** sign **6.** indication, hint **7.** fame **8.** notice **9.** regard —pl. **10.** brief jottings written down for future reference —vt. **11.** observe, record **12.** heed —'**noted** a. well-known —'**notelet** n. folded card with printed design on front, for writing short letter —'**notebook** n. small book with blank pages for writing —'**notepaper** n. paper for writing notes —'**noteworthy** a. **1.** worth noting **2.** remarkable

nothing ('nuthing) pron. **1.** no thing **2.** not anything, nought —adv. **3.** not at all, in no way —'**nothingness** n.

notice ('nōtis) n. **1.** observation **2.** attention, consideration **3.** warning, intimation, announcement **4.** advance notification of intention to end a contract etc., as of employment **5.** review —vt. **6.** observe, mention **7.** give attention to —'**noticeable** a. **1.** conspicuous **2.** attracting attention **3.** appreciable

notify ('nōtifī) vt. **1.** report **2.** give notice of or to (-**fied**, -**fying**) —'**notifiable** a. —**notifi-'cation** n.

notion ('nōshən) n. **1.** concept **2.** opinion **3.** whim —'**notional** a. speculative, imaginary, abstract

notorious (nō'tōriəs) a. **1.** known for something bad **2.** well-known —**notoriety** (nōtə'rīiti) n. discreditable publicity

notwithstanding (notwith'standing) prep. **1.** in spite of —adv. **2.** all the same —conj. **3.** although

nougat ('nōōgət) n. chewy candy containing nuts, fruit etc.

nought (nöt) n. **1.** nothing **2.** cipher 0

noun (nown) n. word used as name of person, idea, or thing, substantive

nourish ('nurish) vt. **1.** feed **2.** nurture **3.** tend **4.** encourage —'**nourishment** n.

nouveau riche (nōōvo 'rēsh) Fr. person who has acquired wealth recently and is regarded as vulgarly ostentatious (pl. **nouveaux riches** (nōōvo 'rēsh))

Nov. November

nova ('nōvə) n. star that suddenly becomes brighter then loses brightness through months or years (pl. **-vae** (-vē), **-s**)

novel¹ ('novəl) n. fictitious tale in book form —**nove'lette** n. **1.** short novel **2.** trite, oversentimental novel —'**novelist** n. writer of novels

novel² ('novəl) a. **1.** new, recent **2.** strange —'**novelty** n. **1.** newness **2.** something new or unusual **3.** small ornament, trinket

novella (nō'velə) n. **1.** short narrative tale, esp. one having satirical point **2.** short novel (pl. **-s**, **-le** (-li))

November (nō'vembər) n. **1.** eleventh month **2.** word used in communications for the letter n

novena (nō'vēnə) n. R.C.Ch. prayers, services, lasting nine consecutive days (pl. **-nae** (-nē))

novice ('novis) n. **1.** one new to anything **2.** beginner **3.** candidate for admission to religious order —**novitiate** (nō'vishit) n. **1.** probationary period **2.** part of religious house for novices **3.** novice

Novocain ('nōvəkān) n. trade name for procaine hydrochloride

now (now) adv. **1.** at the present time **2.** immediately **3.** recently (oft. with just) —conj. **4.** seeing that, since —'**nowadays** adv. in these times, at present

Nowel or **Nowell** (nō'el) n. see NOEL

nowhere ('nōwāər) adv. not in any place or state

nowise ('nōwīz) adv. not in any manner or degree

noxious ('nokshəs) a. poisonous, harmful

nozzle ('nozəl) n. pointed spout, esp. at end of hose

Np Chem. neptunium

NRA National Rifle Association

NS Nova Scotia

NSA National Shipping Authority

NSC National Security Council

NSF National Science Foundation

N.S.P.C.A. National Society for the Prevention of Cruelty to Animals

N.S.P.C.C. National Society for the Prevention of Cruelty to Children

N.S.T. Newfoundland Standard Time

N.T. 1. New Testament **2.** no-trump

nt. wt. or **nt wt** net weight

nu (nyōō, nōō) n. 13th letter in Gr. alphabet (N, ν)

nuance ('nyōōäns, nōō'äns) n. delicate shade of difference, in color, tone of voice etc.

nub (nub) n. **1.** small lump **2.** main point (of story etc.)

nubile ('nyōōbil, 'nōō-) a. marriageable

nucleon ('nyōōklion, 'nōō-) n. proton or neutron

nucleus ('nyōōkliəs, 'nōō-) n. **1.** center, kernel **2.** beginning meant to receive additions **3.** core of the atom (pl. **-lei** (-līī)) —'**nuclear** a. of, pert. to atomic nucleus —**nucle'onics** pl.n. (with sing. v.) branch of physics dealing with applications of nuclear energy —**nuclear bomb** bomb whose force is due to uncontrolled nuclear fusion or nuclear fission —**nuclear disarmament** elimination of nuclear weapons from country's armament —**nuclear energy** energy released by nuclear fission —**nuclear family** Sociol., anthropol. primary social unit consisting of parents and their offspring —**nuclear fission** disintegration of the atom —**nuclear fusion** reaction in which two nuclei combine to form nucleus with release of energy (also '**fusion**) —**nuclear physics** branch of physics concerned with structure of nucleus and particles of which it consists —**nuclear reaction** change in structure and energy content of atomic nucleus by interaction with another nucleus, particle —**nuclear reactor** see REACT —**nucleic acid** (nyōō'klēik, nōō-; -'klā-) substance whose molecules contain information which guides the synthesis of proteins —**nucleo'protein** n. large complex combination of proteins and nucleic acids found in all living cells

nude (nyōōd, nōōd) *n.* **1.** state of being naked **2.** (picture, statue *etc.* of) naked person —*a.* **3.** naked —**'nudism** *n.* practice of nudity —**'nudist** *n.* —**'nudity** *n.*

nudge (nuj) *vt.* **1.** touch slightly with elbow —*n.* **2.** such touch

nugatory ('nyōōgətöri, 'nōō-) *a.* trifling, futile

nugget ('nugit) *n.* rough lump of native gold

nuisance ('nyōōsəns, 'nōō-) *n.* something or someone harmful, offensive, annoying or disagreeable

null (nul) *a.* of no effect, void —**'nullify** *vt.* **1.** cancel **2.** make useless or ineffective (**-fied, -fying**) —**'nullity** *n.* state of being null and void —**null set** *Math.* set having no members (*also* **empty set**)

num. 1. number **2.** numeral

Num. Numbers

numb (num) *a.* **1.** deprived of feeling, *esp.* by cold —*vt.* **2.** make numb **3.** deaden —**'numbskull** *n. see* NUMSKULL

number ('numbər) *n.* **1.** sum, aggregate **2.** word or symbol saying how many **3.** single issue of a paper *etc.* issued in regular series **4.** classification as to singular or plural **5.** song, piece of music **6.** performance **7.** company, collection **8.** identifying number, as of particular house, telephone *etc.* **9.** *sl.* measure, correct estimation —*vt.* **10.** count **11.** class, reckon **12.** give a number to **13.** amount to —**'numberless** *a.* countless —**number crunching** the performing of complicated calculations involving large numbers, *esp.* at high speed by computer —**number one** *n.* **1.** *inf.* oneself —*a.* **2.** first in importance, urgency *etc.* —**Number Ten** 10 Downing Street, British prime minister's official London residence

Numbers ('numbərz) *pl.n.* (*with sing. v.*) *Bible* 4th book of the O.T., continuing the story of the deliverance, describing the 40 years wandering in the desert

numeral ('nyōōmərəl, 'nōō-) *n.* sign or word denoting a number —**'numerable** *a.* able to be numbered or counted —**'numeracy** *n.* —**numerate** ('nyōōmərit, 'nōō-) *a.* **1.** able to use numbers, *esp.* in calculations —*vt.* ('nyōōmərāt, 'nōō-) **2.** count —**nume'ration** *n.* —**'numerator** *n.* top part of fraction, figure showing how many of the fractional units are taken —**nu'merical** *a.* of, in respect

of, number or numbers —**nume'rology** *n.* study of numbers, and of their supposed influence on human affairs —**'numerous** *a.* many

numismatic (nyōōmiz'matik, nōō-) *a.* of coins —**numis'matics** *pl.n.* (*with sing. v.*) the study of coins —**nu'mismatist** *n.*

numskull *or* **numbskull** ('numskul) *n.* dolt, dunce

nun (nun) *n.* woman living (in convent) under religious vows —**'nunnery** *n.* convent of nuns —**nun's veiling** very lightweight worsted dress fabric

nuncio ('nunsiō, 'nōōn-) *n.* ambassador of the Pope (*pl.* **-s**)

nunny bag ('nuni) C small sealskin haversack

nuptial ('nupshəl, -chəl) *a.* of, relating to marriage —**'nuptials** *pl.n.* (*sometimes with sing. v.*) **1.** marriage **2.** wedding ceremony

nurse (nərs) *n.* **1.** person trained for care of sick or injured **2.** woman tending another's child —*vt.* **3.** act as nurse to **4.** suckle **5.** pay special attention to **6.** harbor (grudge *etc.*) —**'nursery** *n.* **1.** room for children **2.** rearing place for plants —**'nursemaid** *n.* woman employed to look after children (*also* **nurse**) —**'nurseryman** *n.* one who raises plants for sale —**nursery rhyme** short traditional verse or song for children —**nursery school** school for young children —**nursery slope** gentle slope for beginners in skiing —**nursing home** private hospital or residence for aged or infirm persons

nurture ('nərchər) *n.* **1.** bringing up **2.** education **3.** rearing **4.** nourishment —*vt.* **5.** bring up **6.** educate

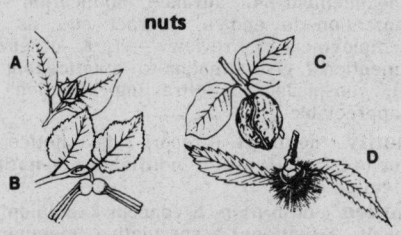

nuts

(A, beech; B, hazel; C, walnut; D, sweet chestnut)

nut (nut) *n.* **1.** seed consisting of hard shell and kernel **2.** hollow metal collar into which a screw fits **3.** *inf.* head **4.** *inf.* eccentric or crazy person —*vi.* **5.** gather nuts (**-tt-**) —**'nutty** *a.* **1.** of, like nut **2.** pleasant to taste and bite **3.** *sl.* insane, crazy (*also* **nuts**) —**'nutcase** *n. sl.* insane or foolish person —**'nutcracker** *n.* **1.** (*oft. pl.*) device for cracking shells of nuts **2.** Old World or North American bird having speckled plumage and feeding on nuts *etc.* —**'nuthatch** *n.* small songbird —**'nutmeg** *n.* aromatic seed of Indian tree —**'nutshell** *n.* shell around kernel of nut —**in a nutshell** in essence; briefly —**nuts and bolts** *inf.* essential or practical details

nutria ('nyōōtriə, 'nōō-) *n.* fur of coypu

nutrient ('nyōōtriənt, 'nōō-) *a.* **1.** nourishing —*n.* **2.** something nutritious

nutriment ('nyōōtrimənt, 'nōō-) *n.* nourishing food —**nu'trition** *n.* **1.** branch of biology concerned with relation of food substances to body function and health **2.** nutriment —**nu'tritionist** *n.* —**nu'tritious** *or* **'nutritive** *a.* **1.** nourishing **2.** promoting growth

nux vomica ('nuks 'vomikə) seed of tree which yields strychnine

nuzzle ('nuzəl) *v.* **1.** burrow, press with nose —*vi.* **2.** nestle

NV Nevada

NW northwest(ern)

N.W.T. Northwest Territories (of Canada)

NY New York

Nyasaland (nI'asəland) *n. former name of* MALAWI

nyctalopia (niktə'lōpiə) *n. see* **night blindness** *at* NIGHT

nylon ('nIlon) *n.* **1.** synthetic material used for fabrics, bristles, ropes *etc.* —*pl.* **2.** stockings made of this

nymph (nimf) *n.* legendary semidivine maiden of sea, woods, mountains *etc.*

nymphomania (nimfə'mániə) *n.* abnormally intense sexual desire in women —**nympho'maniac** *n.*

N.Z. *or* **N. Zeal.** New Zealand

Oo

o *or* **O** (ō) *n.* **1.** 15th letter of English alphabet **2.** any of several speech sounds represented by this letter, as in *code, pot, cow* or *form* **3.** something shaped like O; zero (*pl.* **o's, O's** *or* **Os**)

O¹ 1. *Chem.* oxygen **2.** human blood type of ABO group **3.** Old

O² (ō) *interj.* **1.** *see* OH **2.** exclamation introducing invocation, entreaty, wish *etc.* —**O Canada** the Canadian national anthem

o' (ə) *prep. inf.* of

O'- (*comb. form*) in surnames of Irish Gaelic origin, descendant of, as in *O'Corrigan*

oaf (ōf) *n.* **1.** lout **2.** dolt

oak (ōk) *n.* **1.** common, deciduous forest tree —*pl.* **2.** (**O-**) horse race for fillies held annually at Epsom —**'oaken** *a.* of oak —**oak apple** round gall on oak trees —**oak wilt** fungal disease of oak trees

oakum ('ōkəm) *n.* loose fiber got by unraveling old rope

oar (ör) *n.* **1.** wooden lever with broad blade worked by the hands to propel boat **2.** oarsman —*v.* **3.** row —**'oarsman** *n.* —**'oarsmanship** *n.* skill in rowing

OAS Organization of American States

oasis (ō'āsis) *n.* fertile spot in desert (*pl.* **oases** (ō'āsēz))

oast (ōst) *n.* kiln for drying hops

oat (ōt) *n.* **1.** (*usu. pl.*) grain of cereal plant **2.** the plant —**'oaten** *a.* —**'oatmeal** *n.*

oath (ōth) *n.* **1.** confirmation of truth of statement by naming something sacred **2.** curse (*pl.* **oaths** (ōdhz, oths))

OAU Organization of African Unity

ob. 1. (on tombstones *etc.*) obiit (*Lat.*, he or she died) **2.** obiter (*Lat.*, incidentally, in passing) **3.** oboe

ob- (*comb. form*) inverse; inversely, as in *obovate*

Obadiah (ōbə'dīə) *n. Bible* 31st book of the O.T., written by the prophet Obadiah to show judgment on the nation of Edom

obbligato (obli'gätō) *Mus. a.* **1.** not to be omitted —*n.* **2.** essential part in score (*pl.* **-s, -ti** (-tē))

obdurate ('obdyŏŏrit, 'obdərit) *a.* stubborn, unyielding —**'obduracy** *or* **'obdurateness** *n.*

obedience (ō'bēdiəns, ə-) *n.* submission to authority —**o'bedient** *a.* **1.** willing to obey **2.** compliant **3.** dutiful —**o'bediently** *adv.*

obeisance (ō'bēsəns, ə-; -'bā-) *n.* bow; curtsy

obelisk ('obilisk) *n.* tapering rectangular stone column with pyramidal apex

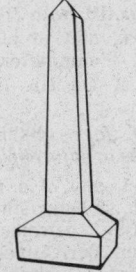

obelisk

obese (ō'bēs) *a.* very fat, corpulent —**o'besity** *n.* result of imbalance between food consumption and energy needs

obey (ō'bā, ə-) *vt.* **1.** do the bidding of **2.** act in accordance with —*vi.* **3.** do as ordered **4.** submit to authority

obfuscate ('obfuskāt) *vt.* **1.** perplex **2.** darken

obituary (ə'bichŏŏəri) *n.* **1.** notice, record of death **2.** biographical sketch of deceased person, *esp.* in newspaper (*also* (*inf.*) **o'bit**)

obj. 1. object **2.** objective

object¹ ('objikt) *n.* **1.** material thing **2.** that to which feeling or action is directed **3.** end, aim **4.** *Gram.* word dependent on verb or preposition —**object lesson** lesson with practical and concrete illustration —**no object** not an obstacle or hindrance

object² (əb'jekt) *vt.* **1.** state in opposition —*vi.* **2.** feel dislike or reluctance (to something) —**ob'jection** *n.* —**ob'jectionable** *a.* **1.** disagreeable **2.** justly liable to objection —**ob'jector** *n.*

objective (əb'jektiv) *a.* **1.** external to the mind **2.** impartial —*n.* **3.** thing or place aimed at —**objec'tivity** *n.*

objet d'art (obzhe 'dar) *Fr.* small object considered to be of artistic worth (*pl.* **objets d'art** (obzhe 'dar))

objet trouvé (obzhe trōō'vā) *Fr.* found object

oblate¹ (ob'lāt, 'oblāt) *a.* (of sphere) flattened at the poles

oblate² ('oblāt) *n.* person dedicated to religious work

oblation (ə'blāshən) *n.* offering —**ob'lational** *a.*

oblige (ə'blīj) *vt.* **1.** bind morally or legally to do service to **2.** compel —**obligate** ('obligāt) *vt.* **1.** bind, *esp.* by legal contract **2.** put under obligation —**obligation** (obli'gāshən) *n.* **1.** binding duty, promise **2.** debt of gratitude —**obligatory** (ə'bligətöri, o-) *a.* **1.** required **2.** binding —**o'bliging** *a.* ready to serve others, civil, helpful, courteous

oblique (ō'blēk, ə-) *a.* **1.** slanting **2.** indirect —**o'bliquely** *adv.* —**obliquity** (ō'blikwiti, ə-) *n.* **1.** slant **2.** dishonesty —**oblique angle** angle not a right angle

obliterate (ə'blitərāt) *vt.* blot out, efface, destroy completely —**oblite'ration** *n.*

oblivion (ə'bliviən) *n.* forgetting or being forgotten —**ob'livious** *a.* **1.** forgetful **2.** unaware

oblong ('oblong) *a.* **1.** rectangular, with adjacent sides unequal —*n.* **2.** oblong figure

obloquy ('obləkwi) *n.* **1.** reproach, abuse **2.** disgrace **3.** detraction

obnoxious (ob'nokshəs, əb-) *a.* offensive, disliked, odious

oboe ('ōbō) *n.* orchestral woodwind instrument formed like a conical pipe with holes closed by keys and a double-reeded mouthpiece —**'oboist** *n.* —**oboe d'amore** (dä'mörā) larger type of oboe used in 18th century

obs. 1. observation **2.** obsolete

obscene (ob'sēn, əb-) *a.* **1.** indecent, lewd **2.** repulsive —**obscenity** (ob'seniti, əb-) *n.*

obscure (ob'skyŏŏər, əb-) *a.* **1.** unclear, indistinct **2.** unexplained **3.** dark, dim **4.** humble —*vt.* **5.** make unintelligible **6.** dim **7.** conceal —**ob'scurant** *n.* one who opposes enlightenment or reform —**ob'scurantism** *n.* —**ob'scurity** *n.* **1.** indistinctness **2.** lack of intelligibility **3.** darkness **4.** obscure, *esp.* unrecognized, place or position **5.** retirement

obsequies ('obsikwiz) *pl.n.* funeral rites

obsequious (əb'sēkwiəs) *a.* servile, fawning

observe (əb'zərv) *vt.* **1.** notice, remark **2.** watch **3.** note systematically **4.** keep, follow —*vi.* **5.** make a remark —**ob'servable** *a.* —**ob'servably** *adv.* —**ob'servance** *n.* **1.** paying attention **2.** keeping —**ob'servant** *a.* quick to notice —**obser'vation** *n.* **1.** action, habit of observing **2.** noticing **3.** remark —**ob'servatory** *n.* place for watching stars *etc.* —**ob'server** *n.*

obsess (əb'ses) *vt.* haunt, fill the mind of —**ob'session** *n.* **1.** fixed idea **2.** domination of the mind by one idea —**ob'sessive** *a.*

obsidian (əb'sidiən) *n.* fused volcanic rock, forming hard, dark, natural glass

obsolete (obsə'lēt, 'obsəlēt) *a.* disused, out of date —**obso'lescent** *a.* going out of use

obstacle ('obstəkəl) *n.* **1.** hindrance **2.** impediment, barrier, obstruction

obstetrics (əb'stetriks, ob-) *pl.n.* (*with sing. v.*) branch of medicine concerned with childbirth and care of women before and after childbirth —**ob'stetric(al)** *a.* —**obste'trician** *n.*

obstinate ('obstinit) *a.* **1.** stubborn **2.** self-willed **3.** unyielding **4.** hard to overcome or cure —'**obstinacy** *n.* —**'obstinately** *adv.*

obstreperous (əb'strepərəs) *a.* unruly, noisy, boisterous

obstruct (əb'strukt) *vt.* **1.** block up **2.** hinder, impede —**ob'struction** *n.* —**ob'structionist** *n.* one who deliberately opposes transaction of business —**ob'structive** *a.*

obtain (əb'tān) *vt.* **1.** get **2.** acquire **3.** procure by effort —*vi.* **4.** be customary —**ob'tainable** *a.* procurable

obtrude (əb'trōōd) *v.* thrust forward unduly —**ob'trusion** *n.* —**ob'trusive** *a.* forward, pushing —**ob'trusively** *adv.*

obtuse (ob'tyŏŏs, əb-; -'tŏŏs) *a.* **1.** dull of perception **2.** stupid **3.** (of angle) greater than right angle **4.** not pointed —**ob'tusely** *adv.*

obverse ('obvərs, ob'vərs) *n.* **1.** fact, idea *etc.* which is the complement of another **2.** side of coin, medal *etc.* that has the principal design —*a.* **3.** facing the observer **4.** complementary, opposite

obviate ('obviāt) *vt.* remove, make unnecessary

obvious ('obviəs) *a.* **1.** clear, evident **2.** wanting in subtlety

ocarina (okə'rēnə) *n.* popular musical instrument in the shape of an egg, a bird, or a sweet potato with a protruding mouthpiece and a number of fingerholes

occasion (ə'kāzhən) *n.* **1.** time when thing happens **2.** reason, need **3.** opportunity **4.** special event —*vt.* **5.** cause —**oc'casional** *a.*

1. happening, found now and then **2.** produced for some special event, as *occasional music* —**oc'casionally** *adv.* sometimes, now and then

Occident ('oksidənt) *n.* the West —**Occi'dental** *a.*

occlude (ə'klōōd) *vt.* shut in or out —**oc'clusion** *n.* —**oc'clusive** *a.* serving to occlude —**occluded front** *Met.* line occurring where cold front of depression has overtaken warm front, raising warm sector from ground level (*also* **oc'clusion**)

occult (ə'kult, o'kult, 'okult) *a.* **1.** secret, mysterious **2.** supernatural —*n.* **3.** esoteric knowledge —*vt.* (ə'kult, o'kult) **4.** hide from view —**occul'tation** *n.* eclipse —**oc'cultism** *n.* study of supernatural —**oc'cultness** *n.* mystery

occupy ('okyəpī) *vt.* **1.** inhabit, fill **2.** employ **3.** take possession of (**-pied, -pying**) —**occupancy** *n.* **1.** fact of occupying **2.** residing —**'occupant** *n.* —**occu'pation** *n.* **1.** employment **2.** pursuit **3.** fact of occupying **4.** seizure —**occu'pational** *a.* **1.** pert. to occupation, *esp.* of diseases arising from a particular occupation **2.** pert. to use of occupations, *eg* craft, hobbies *etc.* as means of rehabilitation —**'occupier** *n.* tenant —**occupational medicine** *see* **industrial medicine** *at* INDUSTRY —**occupational therapy** *Med.* therapeutic use of crafts, hobbies *etc.*, *esp.* in rehabilitation of emotionally disturbed patients

occur (ə'kər) *vi.* **1.** happen **2.** come to find (**-rr-**) —**oc'currence** *n.* happening

OCDM Office of Civil and Defense Mobilization

ocean ('ōshən) *n.* **1.** great body of water **2.** large division of this **3.** the sea —**oceanic** (ōshi'anik) *a.* —**ocean'ographer** *n.* —**ocean'ography** *n.* study of physical and biological features of the sea —**ocean'ology** *n.* study of the sea, *esp.* of its economic geography —**ocean-going** *a.* (of ship, boat *etc.*) suited for travel on ocean

ocelot ('osilot, 'ō-) *n.* medium-sized feline with fawn, black-bordered spots on a yellow body of the southwest U.S. and western South America

oche ('oki) *n. Darts* mark on floor behind which player must stand to throw

ocher ('ōkər) *n.* various earths used as yellow or brown pigments —**ochreous** ('ōkərəs, 'ōkriəs), **'ocherous,** *or* **'ochery** *a.*

o'clock (ə'klok) *adv.* by the clock

OCR optical character reader *or* recognition

Oct. October

oct- (*comb. form*) eight

octagon ('oktəgon) *n.* plane figure with eight angles —**oc'tagonal** *a.*

octahedron (oktə'hēdrən) *n.* solid figure with eight sides (*pl.* **-s, -dra** (-drə))

octane ('oktān) *n.* ingredient of motor fuel —**octane number** a number usually between 0 and 100 which indicates the relative performance of a fuel in an internal-combustion engine

octave ('oktiv) *n.* **1.** *Mus.* eighth note above or below given note **2.** this space **3.** eight lines of verse

octavo (ok'tāvō) *n.* book in which each sheet is folded three times forming eight leaves (*pl.* **-s**)

octennial (ok'teniəl) *a.* lasting, happening every eight years

octet (ok'tet) *n.* **1.** group of eight **2.** music for eight instruments or singers

October (ok'tōbər) *n.* tenth month

octogenarian (oktəji'neriən) *or* **octogenary** (ok'tojineri) *n.* **1.** person aged between eighty and ninety —*a.* **2.** of an octogenarian

octopus

octopus ('oktəpəs) *n.* mollusk with eight arms covered with suckers —**'octopod** *n./a.* (mollusk) with eight arms

octoroon (oktə'rōōn) *n.* person of one-eighth Negro ancestry

octosyllable ('oktəsiləbəl) *n.* word, line of verse of eight syllables

ocular ('okyələr) *a.* of eye or sight —**'ocularly** *adv.*

oculist ('okyəlist) *n. Med. obs.* ophthalmologist

O.D. *Med.* overdose

odd (od) *a.* **1.** strange, queer **2.** incidental, random **3.** that is one in addition when the rest have been divided into equal groups **4.** not even **5.** not part of a set —**'oddity** *n.* **1.** odd person or thing **2.** quality of being odd —**'oddment** *n.* (*oft. pl.*) **1.** remnant **2.** trifle —**odds** *pl.n.* (*with on or against*) **1.** advantage conceded in betting **2.** likelihood —**oddjobman** *or* **odd-jobber** *n.* person who does casual work, *esp.* domestic repairs —**odds-on** *a.* **1.** (of chance, horse *etc.*) rated at even money or less to win **2.** regarded as more or most likely to win, happen *etc.* —**odds and ends** odd fragments or scraps

ode (ōd) *n.* lyric poem on particular subject

odium ('ōdiəm) *n.* hatred, widespread dislike —**'odious** *a.* hateful, repulsive, obnoxious

odometer (ō'domitər) *n.* device for measuring distance traveled *esp.* in automobile

odor ('ōdər) *n.* smell —**odo'riferous** *a.* spreading an odor —**'odorless** *a.* —**'odorous** *a.* **1.** fragrant **2.** scented

Odyssey ('odisi) *n.* **1.** Homer's epic describing Odysseus' return from Troy **2.** any long adventurous journey

OE, O.E., *or* **OE.** Old English (language)

O.E.C.D. Organization for Economic Co-operation and Development

Oedipus complex ('edipəs, 'ēdipəs) *Psychoanal.* usu. unconscious desire of child to possess sexually parent of opposite sex —**'oedipal** *or* **oedi'pean** *a.*

o'er (ōər, ör) *prep./adv. Poet.* over

oeuvre ('œvrə) *Fr.* total output of artist, musician or writer —**oeuvre catalog** definitive list of artist's, musician's or writer's output

of (ov; *unstressed* əv) *prep.* removal, separation, ownership, attribute, material, quality

off (of) *adv.* **1.** away —*prep.* **2.** away from —*a.* **3.** not operative **4.** canceled or postponed **5.** bad, sour *etc.* **6.** more distant (of two); right (of pair) —**'offing** *n.* part of sea visible to observer on ship or shore —**'offbeat** *n.* **1.** *Mus.* any of normally unaccented beats in bar —*a.* **2.** unusual, unconventional or eccentric —**off chance** slight possibility —**off color** slightly ill —**off cut** piece of paper, wood *etc.* remaining after main pieces have been cut; remnant —**'offhand** *a.* **1.** without previous thought **2.** curt (*also* **'offhanded**) —**off key 1.** *Mus.* not in correct key; out of tune **2.** out of keeping; discordant —**off line 1.** of or concerned with part of computer system not connected to central processing unit but controlled by computer

storage device **2.** disconnected from computer —**off-peak** *a.* of or relating to services as used outside periods of intensive use —**offset** ('ofset) *n.* **1.** that which counterbalances, compensates **2.** method of printing **3.** narrow horizontal or sloping surface formed where wall is reduced in thickness toward top —*vt.* ('ofset, of'set) **4.** counterbalance, compensate for **5.** print (text *etc.*) using offset process **6.** construct offset in (wall) —**'offshoot** *n.* **1.** shoot or branch growing from main stem of plant **2.** something that develops from principal source —**'offside** *a./adv. Sport* illegally forward —**'offspring** *n.* children, issue —**off-the-peg** *a.* (of clothing) ready to wear; not produced especially for person buying —**in the offing** likely to happen soon —**on the off chance** with the hope

off. **1.** office **2.** officer **3.** official

offal ('ofəl) *n.* **1.** edible entrails of animal **2.** refuse

offend (ə'fend) *vt.* **1.** hurt feelings of, displease —*vi.* **2.** do wrong —**of'fender** *n.* —**of'fense** *n.* **1.** wrong **2.** crime **3.** insult —**of'fensive** *a.* **1.** causing displeasure **2.** aggressive —*n.* **3.** position or movement of attack

offer ('ofər) *vt.* **1.** present for acceptance or refusal **2.** tender **3.** propose **4.** attempt —*vi.* **5.** present itself —*n.* **6.** offering, bid —**'offerer** *or* **'offeror** *n.* —**'offering** *n.* **1.** something that is offered **2.** contribution **3.** sacrifice, as of animal, to deity —**'offertory** *n.* **1.** offering of the bread and wine at the Eucharist **2.** collection in church service

office ('ofis) *n.* **1.** room(s), building, in which business, clerical work *etc.* is done **2.** commercial or professional organization **3.** official position **4.** service **5.** duty **6.** form of worship —*pl.* **7.** task **8.** service —**'officer** *n.* **1.** one in command in army, navy, ship *etc.* **2.** official

official (ə'fishəl) *a.* **1.** with, by, authority —*n.* **2.** one holding office, *esp.* in public body —**of'ficialdom** *n.* officials collectively, or their attitudes, work, usu. in contemptuous sense —**officia'lese** *n.* language characteristic of official documents, *esp.* when verbose

officiate (ə'fishiāt) *vi.* **1.** perform duties of office **2.** perform ceremony

officious (ə'fishəs) *a.* **1.** importunate in offering service **2.** interfering

oft (oft) *adv.* often (*obs., poet.* except in combinations such as *oft-repeated* and *oft-recurring*)

often ('ofən) *adv.* many times, frequently

ogee arch ('ōjē) pointed arch with S-shaped curve on both sides

ogle ('ōgəl) *v.* **1.** stare, look (at) amorously —*n.* **2.** this look —**'ogler** *n.*

ogre ('ōgər) *n.* **1.** *Folklore* man-eating giant **2.** monster —**'ogress** *fem.*)

oh (ō) *interj.* exclamation of surprise, pain *etc.*

Ohio (ō'hīō) *n.* East North Central state of the U.S., admitted to the Union in 1803. Abbrev.: **Oh., OH** (with ZIP code)

ohm (ōm) *n.* unit of electrical resistance —**'ohmic** *a.* —**'ohmmeter** *n.*

O.H.M.S. UK On His (*or* Her) Majesty's Service

-oid (*comb. form*) likeness, resemblance, similarity, as in *anthropoid*

oil (oil) *n.* **1.** any of a number of viscous liquids with smooth, sticky feel and wide variety of uses **2.** petroleum **3.** any of variety of petroleum derivatives, *esp.* as fuel or lubricant —*vt.* **4.** lubricate with oil **5.** apply oil to —**'oily** a. **1.** soaked in or smeared with oil or grease **2.** consisting of, containing or resembling oil **3.** flatteringly servile or obsequious —**oil cake** stock feed consisting of compressed linseed —**'oilcloth** n. waterproof material made by treating cotton fabric with drying oil or synthetic resin —**'oilfield** n. area containing reserves of petroleum —**'oilfired** a. (of central heating etc.) using oil as fuel —**oil painting 1.** picture painted with oil paints **2.** art of painting with oil paints —**oil rig** see RIG (sense 6) —**'oilskin** n. cloth treated to make it waterproof —**oil slick** mass of floating oil covering area of water —**oil well** boring into earth or sea bed for extraction of petroleum —**well oiled** sl. drunk

ointment ('ointmənt) n. greasy preparation for healing or beautifying the skin

Ojibwa (ō'jibwä) n. **1.** member of Amerindian people of Michigan (pl. **-wa, -s**) **2.** Algonquian language of this people (also **Chippewa**)

OK Oklahoma

O.K. irf. a./adv. **1.** all right —n. **2.** approval —vt. **3.** approve (**O.K.ing** (ō'kāing), **O.K.ed** (ō'kād))

okapi (ō'käpi) n. Afr. animal like short-necked giraffe (pl. **-s, -pi**)

Oklahoma (ōklə'hōmə) n. West South Central state of the U.S., admitted to the Union in 1907. Abbrev.: **Okla., OK** (with ZIP code)

okra ('ōkrə) n. **1.** annual plant with yellow-and-red flowers and edible pods **2.** pod of this plant, eaten in soups, stews etc.

old (ōld) a. **1.** aged, having lived or existed long **2.** belonging to earlier period (**'older, 'elder** comp., **'oldest, 'eldest** sup.) —**'olden** a. old —**'oldie** n. inf. old song, movie, person etc. —**'oldish** a. —**old age** period during which life cycle is drawing toward conclusion —**Old Bailey** Central Criminal Court of England —**old country** country of origin of immigrant or immigrant's ancestors —**Old English** English language from time of earliest Saxon settlements in fifth century A.D. to about 1100 (also **Anglo-Saxon**) —**old-fashioned** a. **1.** in style of earlier period, out of date **2.** fond of old ways —n. **3.** cocktail containing spirit, bitters, fruit etc. —**Old Glory** the U.S. flag —**old guard 1.** group that works for long-established principles etc. **2.** conservative element in political party or other groups —**old hat** old-fashioned; trite —**old maid** elderly spinster —**old man 1.** inf. father; husband **2.** (sometimes **O- M-**) inf. man in command, such as employer, foreman etc. **3.** jocular affectionate term used in addressing man —**old master 1.** one of great European painters before 19th cent. **2.** painting by one of these —**Old Nick** inf., jocular Satan —**old school** group of people favoring traditional ideas etc. —**Old Testament** collection of books comprising sacred Scriptures of Hebrews; first part of Christian Bible —**old wives' tale** belief passed on as piece of traditional wisdom —**Old World** eastern hemisphere —**old-world** a. of former times, esp. quaint or traditional

oleaginous (ōli'ajinəs) a. **1.** oily, producing oil **2.** unctuous, fawning —**ole'aginousness** n.

oleander ('ōliandər, ōli'andər) n. poisonous evergreen flowering shrub

oleo- (comb. form) oil, as in oleomargarine

olfactory (ol'faktəri, ōl-) a. of smelling

oligarchy ('oligärki) n. government by a few —**'oligarch** n. —**oli'garchic(al)** a.

Oligocene ('oligōsēn, 'ōli-; ə'lig-) a. **1.** of third epoch of Tertiary period —n. **2.** Oligocene epoch or rock series

olive ('oliv) n. **1.** evergreen tree **2.** its oil-yielding fruit **3.** its wood —a. **4.** grayish-green —**olive branch** any offering of peace or conciliation —**olive oil** pale yellow oil extracted from olives, used in medicines etc.

Olympian (ə'limpiən) a. **1.** of Mount Olympus or classical Greek gods **2.** majestic in manner or bearing **3.** of ancient Olympia or its inhabitants —n. **4.** god of Mount Olympus **5.** inhabitant of ancient Olympia

Olympic (ə'limpik) a. **1.** of Olympic Games **2.** of ancient Olympia —**Olympic Games 1.** Panhellenic festival, held every fourth year in honor of Zeus at ancient Olympia **2.** series of competitive sports events held every four years for amateur athletes

Omaha ('ōməhô, -hä) n. member of Siouan-speaking Amerindian people of northeastern Nebraska (pl. **-ha, -s**)

Oman (ō'män, ō'man) n. country in the Middle East bounded south and east by the Arabian Sea, west by the People's Republic of Yemen and north by Saudi Arabia

omega (ō'megə) n. **1.** last letter in Gr. alphabet (Ω, ω) **2.** end

omelet or **omelette** ('omlit) n. dish of eggs beaten up and fried with seasoning

omen ('ōmən) n. prophetic object or happening —**ominous** ('ominəs) a. boding evil, threatening

omicron ('omikron, 'ōmikron) n. 15th letter in Gr. alphabet (O, o)

omit (ō'mit) vt. **1.** leave out, neglect **2.** leave undone (**-tt-**) —**o'mission** n. —**o'missive** a.

omni- (comb. form) all

omnibus ('omnibus, -bəs) n. **1.** large road vehicle traveling on set route and taking passengers at any stage (also **bus**) **2.** book containing several works —a. **3.** serving, containing several objects

omnidirectional (omnidi'rekshənəl, omnī-; -dī-) a. in radio, denotes transmission, reception in all directions

omnipotent (om'nipətənt) a. all-powerful —**om'nipotence** n.

omnipresent (omni'prezənt) a. present everywhere —**omni'presence** n.

omniscient (om'nishənt) a. knowing everything —**om'niscience** n.

omnivorous (om'nivərəs) a. **1.** devouring all foods **2.** not fastidious

on (on) prep. **1.** above and touching, at, near, toward etc. **2.** attached to **3.** concerning **4.** performed upon **5.** during **6.** taking regularly —a. **7.** operating **8.** taking place —adv. **9.** so as to be on **10.** forward **11.** continuously **12.** in progress —**'oncoming** a. **1.** coming nearer in space or time; approaching —n. **2.** approach; onset —**'ongoing** a. **1.** actually in progress **2.** continually moving forward —**on line** of or concerned with peripheral device that is directly connected to and controlled by central processing unit of computer —**'onrush** n. forceful forward rush or flow —**'onset** n. **1.** violent attack **2.** assault **3.** beginning —**'onslaught** n. attack —**on stream** (of manufacturing process, equipment etc.) in or about to go into operation or production —**'onward** a. **1.** advanced or advancing —adv. **2.** in advance, ahead, forward —**'onwards** adv.

ON Ontario

on- (comb. form) on, as in onlooker

onager ('onəjər) n. wild ass

Onandaga (ōnən'dägə) n. member of Iroquoian-speaking Amerindian people of upper New York state (pl. **-ga, -s**)

onanism ('ōnənizəm) n. masturbation

once (wuns) adv. **1.** one time **2.** formerly **3.** ever —**once-over** n. inf. quick examination —**at once** immediately; simultaneously

onchocerciasis (ongkōsər'kīəsis) n. infection with a worm transmitted by black flies which bite humans, eventually resulting in blindness

one (wun) a. **1.** lowest cardinal number **2.** single **3.** united **4.** only, without others **5.** identical —n. **6.** number or figure 1 **7.** unity **8.** single specimen —pron. **9.** particular but not stated person **10.** any person —**'oneness** n. **1.** unity **2.** uniformity **3.** singleness —**one'self** pron. —**one-armed bandit** inf. slot machine operated by pulling down lever at one side —**one-horse** a. inf. small; obscure —**one-night stand 1.** performance given only once at any one place **2.** inf. sexual encounter lasting only one night —**one-sided** a. **1.** partial **2.** uneven —**one-track** a. **1.** inf. obsessed with one idea, subject etc. **2.** having or consisting of single track —**one-way** a. denoting system of traffic circulation in one direction only

onerous ('onərəs, 'ō-) a. burdensome

onion ('unyən) n. edible bulb of pungent flavor

only ('ōnli) a. **1.** being the one specimen —adv. **2.** solely, merely, exclusively —conj. **3.** but then, excepting that

onomatopoeia (onəmatə'pēə) n. formation of a word by using sounds that resemble or suggest the object or action to be named —**onomato'poeic** or **onomatopoetic** (onəmatəpō'etik) a.

onto or **on to** ('ontoo; unstressed 'ontə) prep. **1.** on top of **2.** aware of

ontology (on'toləji) n. science of being or reality —**onto'logical** a. —**on'tologist** n.

onus ('ōnəs) n. responsibility, burden

onyx ('oniks) n. variety of chalcedony with parallel regular color bands used as gemstone

oodles ('ōōdəlz) pl.n. inf. abundance

oolite ('ōəlīt) n. any sedimentary rock, esp. limestone, consisting of tiny spherical grains within fine matrix —**oolitic** (ōə'litik) a.

ooze (ōōz) vi. **1.** pass slowly out —v. **2.** exude (moisture etc.) —n. **3.** sluggish flow **4.** wet mud, slime —**'oozy** a.

op. 1. opera **2.** operation **3.** opus

o.p. or **O.P.** out of print

opal ('ōpəl) n. gemstone displaying variegated colors —**opa'lescent** a.

opaque (ō'pāk) a. not allowing the passage of light, not transparent —**opacity** (ō'pasiti) n.

op. cit. opere citato (Lat., in the work cited)

OPEC ('ōpek) Organization of Petroleum Exporting Countries

open ('ōpən) a. **1.** not shut or blocked up **2.** without lid or door **3.** bare **4.** undisguised **5.** not enclosed, covered or exclusive **6.** spread out, accessible **7.** frank, sincere —vt. **8.** set open, uncover, give access to **9.** disclose, lay bare **10.** begin **11.** make a hole in —vi. **12.** become open **13.** begin —n. **14.** clear space, unenclosed country **15.** Sport competition in which all may enter —**'opening** n. **1.** hole, gap **2.** beginning **3.** opportunity —a. **4.** first **5.** initial —**'openly** adv. without concealment —**open-and-shut** a. easily decided or solved —**open-ended** a. without definite limits, as of duration or amount —**open-handed** a. generous —**open-hearted** a. frank, magnanimous —**open-heart surgery** surgical repair of heart during which blood circulation is oft. maintained mechanically —**open-minded** a. unprejudiced —**open-plan** a. having no or few dividing walls between areas —**open prison** prison without restraints to prevent absconding —**open secret** something that is supposed to be secret but is widely known —**open verdict** coroner's verdict not stating cause (of death) —**'openwork** n. pattern with interstices

opera ('opərə, 'oprə) n. musical drama —**oper'atic** a. of opera —**ope'retta** n. light, comic opera —**opera glasses** small binoculars used by audiences in theaters etc.

operation (opə'rāshən) n. 1. working, way things work 2. scope 3. act of surgery 4. military action —**opera'bility** n. —**'operable** a. 1. capable of being treated by surgical operation 2. capable of being put into practice —**'operate** vt. 1. cause to function 2. control functioning of —vi. 3. work 4. produce an effect 5. perform act of surgery 6. exert power —**ope'rational** a. 1. of operation(s) 2. working —**'operative** a. 1. working —n. 2. worker, esp. with a special skill —**'operator** n. —**operating room** room in which surgical operations are performed —**operations research** analysis of problems in business involving quantitative techniques

operculum (ō'pərkyələm) n. lid; cover (pl. **-s, -la** (-lə))

ophidian (ō'fidiən) a. 1. snakelike 2. of suborder of reptiles which comprises snakes —n. 3. any reptile of this suborder

ophthalmic (of'thalmik) a. of eyes —**oph'thalmia** n. inflammation of eye —**ophthal'mologist** n. medical practitioner specializing in diagnosis and treatment of eye diseases —**ophthal'mology** n. study of eye and its diseases —**oph'thalmoscope** n. instrument for examining interior of eye

opiate ('ōpiit) see OPIUM

opinion (ə'pinyən) n. 1. what one thinks about something 2. belief, judgment —**opine** (ō'pīn) vt. 1. think —vi. 2. utter opinion —**o'pinionated** a. stubborn in one's opinions, dogmatic

opium ('ōpiəm) n. addictive narcotic drug made from poppy —**'opiate** n. 1. drug containing opium 2. narcotic —a. 3. inducing sleep 4. soothing

opossum (ə'posəm) or **possum** n. small Amer. and Aust. marsupial

opp. 1. opposed **2.** opposite

opponent (ə'pōnənt) n. adversary, antagonist

opportune (opər'tyōōn, -'tōōn) a. seasonable, well-timed —**oppor'tunism** n. policy of doing what is expedient at the time regardless of principle —**oppor'tunist** n./a. —**oppor'tunity** n. 1. favorable time or condition 2. good chance

oppose (ə'pōz) vt. 1. resist, withstand 2. contrast 3. set against —**op'poser** n. —**'opposite** a. 1. contrary 2. facing 3. diametrically different 4. adverse 5. Bot. (of leaves) growing in pairs on either side of a

opposite (sense 5)

stem —n. 6. the contrary —prep./adv. 7. facing 8. on the other side —**oppo'sition** n. 1. antithesis 2. resistance 3. obstruction 4. hostility 5. group opposing another 6. party opposing that in power —**opposite number** person holding corresponding position on another side or situation

oppress (ə'pres) vt. 1. govern with tyranny 2. weigh down —**op'pression** n. 1. act of oppressing 2. severity 3. misery —**op'pres-**

sive a. 1. tyrannical 2. hard to bear 3. heavy 4. (of weather) hot and tiring —**op'pressively** adv. —**op'pressor** n.

opprobrium (ə'prōbriəm) n. disgrace —**op'probrious** a. 1. reproachful 2. shameful 3. abusive

oppugn (ə'pyōōn) vt. call into question, dispute

opt (opt) vi. make a choice —**'optative** a. 1. expressing wish or desire —n. 2. mood of verb expressing wish

opt. 1. optical **2.** optional

optic ('optik) a. 1. of eye or sight —n. 2. eye —pl. 3. (with sing. v.) science of sight and light —**'optical** a. —**op'tician** n. maker of, dealer in spectacles, optical instruments —**optical character reader** computer device enabling characters, usu. printed on paper, to be optically scanned and input to storage device —**optic nerve** bundle of nerve fibers which conduct visual impulses from eye to brain

optimism ('optimizəm) n. 1. disposition to look on the bright side 2. doctrine that good must prevail in the end 3. belief that the world is the best possible world —**'optimist** n. —**opti'mistic** a. —**opti'mistically** adv.

optimum ('optiməm) a./n. the best, the most favorable (pl. **-s, -ma** (-mə))

option ('opshən) n. 1. choice 2. preference 3. thing chosen 4. in business, purchased privilege of either buying or selling things at specified price within specified time —**'optional** a. leaving to choice

optometrist (op'tomitrist) n. person usu. not medically qualified, testing eyesight, prescribing corrective lenses etc. —**op'tometry** n. measurement of the visual power of the eye

opulent ('opyələnt) a. 1. rich 2. copious —**'opulence** n. riches, wealth

opus ('ōpəs) n. 1. work 2. musical composition (pl. **opera** ('ōpərə, 'op-), **-es**)

or (ör; unstressed ər) conj. 1. introducing alternatives 2. if not

OR Oregon

O.R. 1. operating room **2.** operational research **3.** owner's risk

-or¹ (comb. form) person or thing that does what is expressed by verb, as in actor, sailor

-or² (comb. form) state, condition, activity, as in terror, error, behavior, labor

oracle ('orəkəl) n. 1. divine utterance, prophecy, oft. ambiguous, given at shrine of god 2. the shrine 3. wise or mysterious adviser —**o'racular** a. 1. of oracle 2. prophetic 3. authoritative 4. ambiguous

oral ('ōrəl, 'orəl) a. 1. spoken 2. by mouth —n. 3. spoken examination —**'orally** adv.

orange ('orinj) n. 1. bright reddish-yellow round fruit 2. tree bearing it 3. fruit's color —**orange'ade** n. effervescent orange-flavored drink —**'orangery** n. building, such as greenhouse, in which orange trees are grown —**orange pekoe** ('pēkō) black tea from smallest top leaves, grown in India and Sri Lanka

Orangeman ('orinjmən) n. member of society founded as secret order in Ireland to uphold Protestantism

orangutan (ə'rangətan) n. large Indonesian ape

orator ('orətər) n. 1. maker of speech 2. skillful speaker —**o'ration** n. formal speech —**ora'torical** a. of orator or oration —**'oratory** n. 1. speeches 2. eloquence 3. small private chapel

oratorio (orə'töriō) n. semidramatic composition of sacred music (pl. **-s**)

orb (örb) n. globe, sphere —**or'bicular** a.

orbit ('örbit) n. 1. track of planet, satellite, comet etc., around another heavenly body 2. field of influence, sphere 3. eye socket —v. 4. move in, or put into, an orbit

Orcadian (ör'kādiən) n. 1. native or inhabitant of the Orkneys —a. 2. of or relating to the Orkneys

orchard ('örchərd) n. 1. area for cultivation of fruit trees 2. the trees

orchestra ('örkistrə) n. 1. band of musicians 2. place for such a band in theater etc. (also **orchestra pit**) 3. all seating for spectators on the main floor —**or'chestral** a. —**'orchestrate** vt. 1. compose or arrange (music) for orchestra 2. organize, arrange

orchid ('örkid) n. genus of various flowering plants

orchitis (ör'kītis) n. inflammation of the testis

ordain (ör'dān) vt. 1. admit to Christian ministry 2. confer holy orders upon 3. decree, enact 4. destine —**ordi'nation** n.

ordeal (ör'dēl) n. 1. severe, trying experience 2. Hist. form of trial by which accused underwent severe physical test

order ('ördər) n. 1. regular or proper arrangement or condition 2. sequence 3. peaceful condition of society 4. rank, class 5. group 6. command 7. request for something to be supplied 8. mode of procedure 9. instruction 10. monastic society 11. Biol. taxonomic division of plants and animals ranking above a family and below a class —vt. 12. command 13. request (something) to be supplied or made 14. arrange —**'orderliness** n. —**'orderly** a. 1. tidy 2. methodical 3. well-behaved —n. 4. hospital attendant 5. soldier following officer to carry orders —**'ordinal** a. 1. showing position in a series —n. 2. ordinal number —**ordinal number** number denoting order, quality or degree in group, such as first, second, third

ordinance ('ördnəns) n. 1. decree, rule 2. rite, ceremony

ordinary ('ördəneri) a. 1. usual, normal 2. common 3. plain 4. commonplace —n. 5. bishop in his province —**ordi'narily** adv.

ordinate ('ördinit) n. vertical or y-coordinate of point in two-dimensional system of Cartesian coordinates

ordnance ('ördnəns) n. 1. big guns, artillery 2. military stores —**Ordnance Survey** official geographical survey of Britain

Ordovician (ördə'vishən) a. 1. of, denoting or formed in second period of Paleozoic era —n. 2. Ordovician period or rock system

ordure ('örjər) n. 1. dung 2. filth

ore (ör) n. naturally occurring mineral which yields metal

Oreg. Oregon

oregano (ə'regənō) n. herb, variety of marjoram

Oregon ('örigən, 'or-) n. Pacific state of the U.S., admitted to the Union in 1859. Abbrev.: **Oreg., OR** (with ZIP code)

organ ('örgən) n. 1. large complex musical keyboard instrument in which sound is produced by means of a number of pipes arranged in sets or stops, supplied with air from a bellows 2. structure of animal or plant carrying out particular function. 3. means of action 4. medium of information, esp. newspaper —**or'ganic** a. 1. of, derived from, living organisms 2. of bodily organs 3. affecting bodily organs 4. having vital organs 5. Chem. of compounds formed from carbon 6. grown with fertilizers derived from animal or vegetable matter 7. organized, systematic —**or'ganically** adv. —**'organist** n. organ player —**organ loft** gallery in church etc. for an organ —**organ transplantation** transplantation of body's organs and tissues to replace or restore functions lost by injury, disease or old age

organdy or **organdie** ('örgəndi) n. light, transparent muslin with a crisp finish

organize ('örgənīz) vt. 1. give definite structure to 2. get up, arrange 3. put into working order 4. unite in a society —**'organism** n. 1. organized body or system 2. plant, animal —**organi'zation** n. 1. act of organizing 2. body of people, society —**'organizer** n.

organza (ör'ganzə) n. thin, stiff transparent fabric of silk or synthetic fiber

orgasm ('örgazəm) n. sexual climax

orgy ('örji) n. 1. drunken or licentious revel, debauch 2. act of immoderation, overindulgence

oriel ('öriəl) n. 1. projecting part of an upper room with a window 2. the window

orient ('öriənt) n. 1. (O-) the East 2. luster of best pearls —a. 3. rising 4. (O-) Eastern —vt. ('örient) 5. place so as to face East 6. adjust or align (oneself etc.) according to surroundings or circumstances 7. position or set (map etc.) with reference to compass etc. —ori'ental a./n. —ori'entalist n. expert in Eastern languages and history —'orientate vt. orient —orien'tation n. —orien'teering n. competitive sport involving compass and map-reading skills

orifice ('orifis) n. opening, mouth of a cavity, eg pipe

orig. 1. origin 2. original(ly)

origami (öri'gämi) n. Japanese art of paper folding

origin ('orijin) n. 1. beginning 2. source 3. parentage

original (ə'rijinəl) a. 1. primitive, earliest 2. new, not copied or derived 3. thinking or acting for oneself 4. eccentric —n. 5. pattern, thing from which another is copied 6. unconventional or strange person —origi'nality n. power of producing something individual to oneself —o'riginally adv. at first, in the beginning —**original sin** Theol. state of sin held to be innate in mankind as descendants of Adam

originate (ə'rijināt) v. come or bring into existence, begin —origi'nation n. —o'riginator n.

oriole ('öriōl) n. any of various New World birds of which the males are black and orange or yellow

orison ('örisən, 'or-; -zən) n. prayer

Orlon ('örlon) n. trade name for acrylic fabric used for clothing etc.

ormolu ('örməlōō) n. 1. gilded bronze 2. gold-colored alloy 3. articles of these

ornament ('örnəmənt) n. 1. any object used to adorn or decorate 2. decoration —vt. ('örnəment) 3. adorn —orna'mental a.

ornate (ör'nāt) a. highly decorated or elaborate

ornery ('örnəri) a. dial., inf. 1. stubborn; vile-tempered 2. low; treacherous 3. ordinary

ornithology (örni'tholəji) n. science of birds —ornitho'logical a. —orni'thologist n.

orotund ('orətund) a. 1. full, clear and musical 2. pompous

orphan ('örfən) n. child bereaved of one or both parents —'orphanage n. institution for care of orphans —'orphanhood n.

orrery ('orəri) n. mechanical model of solar system to show revolutions, planets etc.

orris ('oris) n. any of various kinds of iris

ortho- or before vowel **orth-** (comb. form) right, correct

orthodontics (örthə'dontiks) or **orthodontia** (örthə'donchiə) n. branch of dentistry concerned with correcting irregularities of teeth —ortho'dontic a. —ortho'dontist n.

orthodox ('örthədoks) a. 1. holding accepted views 2. conventional —'orthodoxy n. —**Orthodox Church** 1. collective body of Eastern Churches that were separated from western Church in 11th cent. and are in communion with either Patriarch of Moscow or Patriarch of Constantinople 2. the Orthodox Church in America, which has been autonomous since 1970

orthography (ör'thogrəfi) n. correct spelling

orthopedics (örthə'pēdiks) pl.n. (with sing. v.) branch of surgery concerned with disorders of spine and joints and repair of deformities of these parts —ortho'pedic a.

orthopterous (ör'thoptərəs) a. of large order of insects, including crickets, locusts and grasshoppers, having leathery forewings and membranous hind wings

ortolan ('örtələn) n. a small bird, esp. as table delicacy

-ory[1] (comb. form) 1. place for, as in observatory 2. something having specified use, as in directory

-ory[2] (comb. form) of, relating to; characterized by; having effect of, as in contributory

oryx ('oriks) n. large Afr. antelope (pl. -es, -yx)

Os Chem. osmium

O.S. 1. Old Style 2. Ordinary Seaman 3. outsize 4. (also **OS**) Old Saxon (language)

Osage (ō'sāj) n. 1. member of Amerindian people of Missouri (pl. -s, Osage) 2. Siouan language of this people

Oscar ('oskər) n. 1. any of several small gold statuettes awarded annually in U.S.A. for outstanding achievements in the motion-picture industry 2. word used in communications for the letter o

oscillate ('osilāt) vi. 1. swing to and fro 2. waver 3. fluctuate (regularly) —oscil'lation n. —'oscillator n. —'oscillatory a. —os'cilloscope n. electronic instrument producing visible representation of rapidly changing quantity

osculate ('oskyəlāt) v. jocular kiss —'oscular a. —oscu'lation n. —'osculatory a.

Osee ('ōzē, ō'zāə) n. Bible Hosea in the Douay Version of the O.T.

osier ('ōzhər) n. species of willow used for basketwork

-osis (comb. form) 1. process; state, as in metamorphosis 2. diseased condition, as in tuberculosis 3. formation or development of something, as in fibrosis

osmium ('ozmiəm) n. Chem. noble metal Symbol Os, at. wt. 192.2, at. no. 76

osmosis (oz'mōsis, os-) n. the passage of water through a permeable membrane from a low-to-high concentrate of solutions —os'motic (oz'motik, os-) a.

osprey ('ospri, -prā) n. 1. fishing hawk 2. plume

osseous ('osiəs) a. 1. of, like bone 2. bony —ossifi'cation n. —'ossify v. 1. turn into bone —vi. 2. grow rigid (-fied, -fying)

osteitis deformans (osti'ītis di'förmənz) see PAGET'S DISEASE

ostensible (o'stensibəl) a. 1. apparent 2. professed —os'tensibly adv.

ostentation (ostən'tāshən) n. show, pretentious display —osten'tatious a. 1. given to display 2. showing off —osten'tatiously adv.

osteo- or before vowel **oste-** (comb. form) bone(s)

osteoarthritis (ostiōär'thrītis) n. arthritis produced by degeneration of the cartilage found at the junction of bones and the overgrowth of bone at the margin

osteochondritis (ostiōkon'drītis) n. condition in which there is limited destruction of bone, usu. following injury

osteomalacia (ostiōmə'lāshiə) n. abnormal condition of bone marked by abundance of fibrous matrix and cartilage and mineral deficiency

osteomyelitis (ostiōmī'lītis) n. infection of bone by microorganisms

osteopathy (osti'opəthi) n. art of treating disease by removing structural derangement by manipulation, esp. of spine —'osteopath n. one skilled in this art

osteoporosis (ostiōpə'rōsis) n. disorder of bone caused by decreased matrix and mineral portions

ostler ('oslər) or **hostler** n. Hist. stableman at an inn

ostracize ('ostrəsīz) vt. exclude, banish from society, exile —'ostracism n. social boycotting

ostrich ('ostrich) n. large swift-running flightless Afr. bird

O.T. 1. occupational therapy 2. Old Testament 3. overtime

other ('ŭdhər) a. 1. not this 2. not the same 3. alternative, different —pron. 4. other person or thing —'otherwise adv. 1. differently 2. in another way —conj. 3. or else, if not —'otherworldly a. 1. of or relating to spiritual or imaginative world 2. impractical, unworldly

otiose ('ōshiōs, 'ōtiōs) a. 1. superfluous 2. useless

otitis (ō'tītis) n. inflammation of ear

Oto-Manguean (ōtə'mänggēən) n. Amerindian language family spoken in southern Mexico

otosclerosis (ōtōsklī'rōsis) n. disease of unknown cause marked by deposits of bone in the ear resulting in progressive deafness

Ottawa ('otəwə) n. member of Siouan-speaking Amerindian people orig. of Michigan and southern Ontario and now of Oklahoma (pl. -s, -wa)

otter ('otər) n. furry aquatic fish-eating mammal

Ottoman ('otəmən) a. 1. Turkish —n. 2. Turk (pl. -s) 3. (o-) cushioned, backless seat, storage box (pl. -s) 4. (o-) heavy corded silk or synthetic fabric with flat crosswise ribs

oubliette (ōōbli'et) n. dungeon entered by trapdoor

ouch (owch) interj. exclamation of sudden pain

ought (öt) v. aux. 1. expressing duty, obligation or advisability 2. be bound

Ouija

Ouija ('wējə) n. trade name for board with letters and symbols used to obtain messages at seances

ounce (owns) n. a weight, sixteenth of avoirdupois pound (28.4 grams), twelfth of apothecaries' or troy pound (31.1 grams)

our ('owər) a. belonging to us —'ours pron. —**Our Father** see the Lord's Prayer at LORD —our'self pron. myself, used in regal or formal style —**our'selves** *pl. pron.* emphatic or reflexive form of WE

-ous (*comb. form*) 1. having; full of, as in *dangerous, spacious* 2. *Chem.* indicating that element is chemically combined in lower of two possible valency states, as in *ferrous*

ousel ('ōōzəl) *n. see* OUZEL

oust (owst) *vt.* put out, expel

out (owt) *adv.* 1. from within, away 2. wrong 3. on strike —*a.* 4. not worth considering 5. not allowed 6. unfashionable 7. unconscious 8. not in use, operation *etc.* 9. at an end 10. not burning 11. *Sport* dismissed —'**outer** *a.* away from the inside —'**outermost** *or* '**outmost** *a.* on extreme outside —'**outing** *n.* pleasure excursion —'**outward** *a./adv.* —'**outwardly** *adv.* —'**outwards** *adv.* —**out-and-out** *a.* thoroughgoing; complete —**outer space** any region of space beyond atmosphere of earth —**out-of-the-way** *a.* 1. distant from more populous areas 2. uncommon or unusual —**out of date** no longer valid, current, or fashionable —**out of pocket** 1. having lost money, as in a commercial enterprise 2. without money to spend 3. (of expenses) unbudgeted and paid for in cash

out- (*comb. form*) 1. beyond, in excess, as in *outclass, outdistance, outsize* 2. so as to surpass or defeat, as in *outfox, outmaneuver* 3. outside, away from, as in *outpatient, outgrowth.* See the list below

outback ('owt'bak) *n.* A remote, sparsely populated country

outbalance (owt'baləns) *vt.* 1. outweigh 2. exceed in weight

outboard ('owtbörd) *a.* (of boat's engine) mounted outside stern

outbreak ('owtbrāk) *n.* sudden occurrence, *esp.* of disease or strife

outbuilding ('owtbilding) *n.* structure for storage *etc.* away from main premises of house or factory

outburst ('owtbərst) *n.* bursting out, *esp.* of violent emotion

outcast ('owtkast) *n.* 1. someone rejected —*a.* 2. rejected, cast out

outclass (owt'klas) *vt.* excel, surpass

outcome ('owtkum) *n.* result

outcrop ('owtkrop, owt'krop) *Geol. n.* 1. rock coming out of stratum to the surface —*vi.* (owt'krop) 2. come out to the surface (-**pp**-)

outcry ('owtkrī) *n.* 1. widespread or vehement protest —*vt.* (owt'krī) 2. cry louder or make more noise than

outdo (owt'dōō) *vt.* surpass or exceed in performance (-'**doing,** -'**did,** -'**done**)

outdoors (owt'dörz) *adv.* in the open air —'**out'door** *a.*

outfall ('owtföl) *n.* mouth of river

outfit ('owtfit) *n.* 1. equipment 2. clothes and accessories 3. *inf.* group or association regarded as a unit —'**outfitter** *n.* one who deals in outfits

outflank (owt'flangk) *vt.* 1. get beyond the flank of (enemy army) 2. circumvent

outgoing ('owtgōing) *a.* 1. departing 2. friendly, sociable

outgrow (owt'grō) *vt.* 1. become too large or too old for 2. surpass in growth (-'**grew,** -'**grown,** -'**growing**)

outhouse ('owt-hows) *n.* 1. outbuilding 2. outdoor privy

outlandish (owt'landish) *a.* queer, extravagantly strange

outlaw ('owtlö) *n.* 1. one beyond protection of the law 2. exile, bandit —*vt.* 3. make (someone) an outlaw 4. ban —'**outlawry** *n.*

outlay ('owtlā) *n.* expenditure

outlet ('owtlet, -lit) *n.* 1. opening, vent 2. means of release or escape 3. market for product or service

outline ('owtlīn) *n.* 1. rough sketch 2. general plan 3. lines enclosing visible figure —*vt.* 4. sketch 5. summarize

outlook ('owtlōōk) *n.* 1. point of view 2. probable outcome 3. view

outlying ('owtlīing) *a.* distant, remote

outmoded (owt'mōdid) *a.* no longer fashionable or accepted

output ('owtpōōt) *n.* 1. quantity produced 2. *Comp.* information produced

outrage ('owtrāj) *n.* 1. violation of others' rights 2. gross or violent offense or indignity 3. anger arising from this —*vt.* 4. offend grossly 5. insult 6. injure, violate —**out'rageous** *a.*

outré (ōō'trā) *a.* 1. extravagantly odd 2. bizarre

outrigger ('owtrigər) *n.* 1. frame, *esp.* with float attached, outside boat's gunwale 2. frame on rowing boat's side with rowlock 3. boat equipped with such a framework

outright ('owtrīt) *a.* 1. undisputed 2. downright 3. positive —*adv.* (owt'rīt) 4. completely 5. instantly 6. openly

outset ('owtset) *n.* beginning

outside ('owt'sīd) *n.* 1. exterior 2. C settled parts of Canada —*adv.* (owt'sīd) 3. not inside 4. in the open air —*a.* ('owt'sīd) 5. on exterior 6. remote, unlikely 7. greatest possible, probable —**out'sider** *n.* 1. person outside specific group 2. contestant thought unlikely to win —**outside broadcast** *T.V., rad.* broadcast not made from studio

outskirts ('owtskərts) *pl.n.* outer areas, districts, *esp.* of city

outspan ('owtspan) *n.* **SA** 1. unyoking of oxen 2. area for rest

outspoken (owt'spōkən) *a.* frank, candid

outstanding (owt'standing) *a.* 1. excellent 2. remarkable 3. unsettled, unpaid

outstrip (owt'strip) *vt.* outrun, surpass

outwit (owt'wit) *vt.* get the better of by cunning

outwork ('owtwərk) *n.* part of fortress outside main wall

ouzel *or* **ousel** ('ōōzəl) *n.* 1. type of thrush 2. kind of diving bird

ouzo ('ōōzō) *n.* strong aniseed-flavored spirit from Greece

ova ('ōvə) *n., pl. of* OVUM

oval ('ōvəl) *a.* 1. egg-shaped, elliptical —*n.* 2. something of this shape

ovary ('ōvəri) *n.* female egg-producing organ —**o'varian** *a.*

ovation (ō'vāshən) *n.* enthusiastic burst of applause

oven ('uvən) *n.* heated chamber for baking in

over ('ōvər) *adv.* 1. above, above and beyond, going beyond, in excess, too much, past, finished, in repetition, across, downwards *etc.* —*prep.* 2. above 3. on, upon 4. more than, in excess of, along *etc.* —*a.* 5. upper, outer

over- (*comb. form*) too, too much, in excess, above, to a prostrate position. See the list below

overall ('ōvəröl) *n.* 1. (*also pl.*) loose garment worn as protection against dirt *etc.* —*a.* (ōvər'öl, 'ōvəröl) 2. total

overbalance (ōvər'baləns) *v.* 1. lose or cause to lose balance —*n.* ('ōvərbaləns) 2. excess of weight, value *etc.*

overbearing (ōvər'bāəring) *a.* domineering

overblown (ōvər'blōn) *a.* excessive, bombastic

overboard ('ōvərbörd) *adv.* from a vessel into the water

overcast ('ōvərkast) *a.* covered over, *esp.* by clouds

overcheck ('ōvərchek) *n.* (in textiles) checked pattern laid over another checked pattern

overcoat ('ōvərkōt) *n.* warm coat worn over outer clothing

overcome (ōvər'kum) *vt.* 1. conquer 2. surmount 3. make incapable or powerless —*vi.* 4. be victorious

overdrive ('ōvərdrīv) *n.* 1. very high gear in motor vehicle used at high speeds to reduce wear —*vt.* (ōvər'drīv) 2. drive too hard or too far; overwork (-'**driving,** -'**drove,** -'**driven**)

overhaul (ōvər'höl) *vt.* 1. examine and set in

out'bid	'outpost
out'box	out'rank
out'distance	out'reach
out'face	'outrider
'outfield	out'rival
out'fight	out'run
'outflow	out'shine
out'fox	'outsize
'outgrowth	out'smart
out'last	'out'spread
out'live	out'stare
outma'neuver	'outstation
out'match	out'stretch
out'number	out'value
out'pace	out'vote
out'play	out'weigh

overa'bundance	over'eat
over'act	over'emphasize
overam'bitious	over'estimate
over'anxious	overex'cite
over'awe	overex'ert
over'book	overex'pand
over'burden	overex'penditure
overca'pacity	over'fill
over'cautious	over'flow v.
over'charge	'overflow n.
'overcoat	'overgarment
over'compensate	over'grow
over'confident	over'hang
overcon'sumption	over'hasty
over'cook	overin'dulge
over'crowd	overin'dulgence
over'curious	overin'sistent
overde'pendent	over'joy
overde'velop	over'lay
over'do	over'lie
'overdose	over'load v.
over'due	'overload n.
over'eager	'overlord

over'many	over'size
over'modest	over'sleep
over'much	over'specialize
over'night	over'spend
'overpass	over'spill v.
over'pay	'overspill n.
over'play	over'stay
overpopu'lation	over'steer v.
over'praise	'oversteer n.
over'price	over'step
overpro'duce	over'stock v.
overpro'duction	'overstock n.
over'rate	over'stretch
over'reach	over'tire
overre'act	over'top
over'ripe	over'trump
over'run	over'turn
over'sensitive	over'use
over'shadow	over'value
'overshoe	over'weight
over'shoot	over'work v.
oversimplifi'cation	'overwork n.
over'simplify	over'zealous

order, repair **2.** overtake —*n.* ('ōvərhōl) **3.** thorough examination, *esp.* for repairs

overhead ('ōvərhed) *a.* **1.** over one's head, above —*adv.* (ōvər'hed) **2.** aloft, above —'**overheads** *pl.n.* expenses of running a business, over and above cost of manufacturing and of raw materials

overhear (ōvər'hēər) *vt.* hear (person, remark *etc.*) without knowledge of speaker (-'**hearing,** -'**heard**)

overkill ('ōvərkil) *n.* capacity, advantage greater than required

overland ('ōvərland) *a./adv.* by land

overlap (ōvər'lap) *v.* **1.** (of two things) extend or lie partly over (each other) **2.** cover and extend beyond (something) —*vi.* **3.** coincide partly in time, subject *etc.* (-**pp-**) —*n.* ('ōvərlap) **4.** part that overlaps or is overlapped **5.** amount, length *etc.* overlapping

overleaf ('ōvərlēf) *adv.* on other side of page

overlook (ōvər'lōok) *vt.* **1.** fail to notice **2.** disregard **3.** look over

overpower (ōvər'pouər) *vt.* **1.** conquer by superior force **2.** have such strong effect on as to make ineffective **3.** supply with more power than necessary —**over**'**powering** *a.*

override (ōvər'rīd) *vt.* **1.** set aside, disregard **2.** cancel **3.** trample down

overrule (ōvər'rōōl) *vt.* **1.** disallow arguments of (person) by use of authority **2.** rule or decide against (decision *etc.*) **3.** prevail over; influence **4.** exercise rule over

overseas (ōvər'sēz) *a.* **1.** foreign **2.** from or to a place over the sea (*also* **over**'**sea**) —*adv.* **3.** beyond the sea; abroad —**overseas cap** *see* **garrison cap** *at* GARRISON

overseer ('ōvərsēər) *n.* supervisor —**over**-'**see** *vt.* supervise

oversight ('ōvərsīt) *n.* **1.** failure to notice **2.** mistake

overt (ō'vərt, 'ōvərt) *a.* open, unconcealed

overtake (ōvər'tāk) *vt.* **1.** come up with in pursuit **2.** catch up

overthrow (ōvər'thrō) *vt.* **1.** upset, overturn **2.** defeat (-'**threw,** -'**thrown,** -'**throwing**) —*n.* ('ōvərthrō) **3.** ruin **4.** defeat **5.** fall

overtime ('ōvərtīm) *n.* **1.** time at work, outside normal working hours **2.** payment for this time

overtone ('ōvərtōn) *n.* **1.** additional meaning, nuance **2.** *Mus., Acoustics* any tone in harmonic series produced by fundamental tone

overture ('ōvərchōōər) *n.* **1.** *Mus.* orchestral introduction **2.** opening of negotiations **3.** formal offer

overweening (ōvər'wēning) *a.* thinking too much of oneself

overwhelm (ōvər'welm) *vt.* **1.** crush **2.** submerge, engulf —**over**'**whelming** *a.* **1.** decisive **2.** irresistible —**over**'**whelmingly** *adv.*

overwrought (ōvər'röt) *a.* **1.** overexcited **2.** too elaborate

ovi- *or* **ovo-** (*comb. form*) egg; ovum, as in *oviform*

oviduct ('ōvidukt) *n.* tube through which ova are conveyed from ovary (*also* (in mammals) **Fallopian tube**) —**oviducal** (ōvi-'dyōōkəl, -'dōōkəl) *or* **ovi**'**ductal** *a.*

oviform ('ōviförm) *a.* egg-shaped

ovine ('ōvīn) *a.* of, like, sheep

oviparous (ō'vipərəs) *a.* laying eggs

ovoid ('ōvoid) *a.* egg-shaped

ovoviviparous ('ōvōvī'vipərəs) *a.* (of certain reptiles, fishes *etc.*) producing eggs that hatch within body of mother —**ovovivi**-'**parity** *n.*

ovule ('ovyōōl) *n.* unfertilized seed —'**ovulate** *vi.* produce, discharge egg from ovary —**ovu**'**lation** *n.*

ovum ('ōvəm) *n.* female egg cell, in which development of fetus takes place (*pl.* **ova**)

owe (ō) *vt.* be bound to repay, be indebted for —'**owing** *a.* owed, due —**owing to** caused by, as a result of

owl (owl) *n.* night bird of prey —'**owlet** *n.* young owl —'**owlish** *a.* solemn and dull

own (ōn) *a.* **1.** denoting possession —*vt.* **2.** possess **3.** acknowledge —*vi.* **4.** confess —'**owner** *n.* —'**ownership** *n.* possession

ox (oks) *n.* **1.** large cloven-footed and usu. horned farm animal **2.** bull or cow (*pl.* **oxen**) —'**oxbow** *n.* **1.** U-shaped harness collar of ox **2.** lake formed from deep bend of river —'**oxeye** *n.* daisylike plant —'**oxtail** *n.* skinned tail of ox, used *esp.* in soups and stews —'**oxtongue** *n.* **1.** any of various plants having bristly tongue-shaped leaves **2.** tongue of ox, braised or boiled as food

oxalis (ok'salis) *n.* genus of plants —**ox**'**alic** *a.* —**oxalic acid** poisonous acid derived from oxalis

Oxbridge ('oksbrij) *n.* Brit. universities of Oxford and Cambridge, *esp.* considered as prestigious academic institutions

oxen ('oksən) *n., pl. of* ox

Oxfam ('oksfam) Oxford Committee for Famine Relief

Oxford cloth ('oksfərd) heavy cotton cloth used for shirts

oxide ('oksīd) *n.* compound of oxygen and one other element —**oxidate** ('oksidāt) *v.* —**oxidation** (oksi'dāshən) *n.* act or process of oxidizing —**oxidization** (oksidi'zāshən) *n.* —**oxidize** ('oksidīz) *v.* (cause to) combine with oxide, rust

oxygen ('oksijən) *n. Chem.* gaseous element *Symbol* O, at. wt. 16.0, at. no. 8 —'**oxygenate** *or* '**oxygenize** *vt.* combine- or treat with oxygen —**oxya**'**cetylene** *a.* denoting flame used for welding produced by mixture of oxygen and acetylene —**oxygen tent** *Med.* transparent enclosure covering patient, into which oxygen is released to help maintain respiration

oxymoron (oksi'mörən) *n.* figure of speech in which two ideas of opposite meaning are combined to form an expressive phrase or epithet, as in *cruel kindness* (*pl.* -**mora** (-'mörə))

oxytocin (oksi'tōsin) *n.* hormone secreted by pituitary gland which enables lactation

oyez (ō'yā, ō'yes) *n.* call, uttered three times by public crier or court official

oyster

oyster ('oistər) *n.* edible bivalve mollusk —'**oystercatcher** *n.* shore bird —**oyster plant** salsify

oyster catcher

oz *or* **oz.** ounce

ozone ('ōzōn) *n.* form of oxygen with pungent odor —'**ozonize** *vt.* —**ozone layer** layer of ozone in the upper atmosphere which absorbs harmful radiation from the sun

Pp

p or **P** (pē) n. 1. 16th letter of English alphabet 2. speech sound represented by this letter (pl. **p's, P's** or **Ps**) —**mind one's p's and q's** be careful to use polite language

p 1. page 2. UK pence 3. UK penny 4. Mus. piano (softly)

P 1. Chess pawn 2. Chem. phosphorus 3. pressure

Pa Chem. protactinium

PA Pennsylvania

P.A. 1. personal assistant 2. power of attorney 3. press agent 4. private account 5. public-address system 6. publicity agent 7. Publishers Association 8. purchasing agent

p.a. per annum

pace (pās) n. 1. step 2. its length 3. rate of movement 4. walk, gait —vi. 5. step —vt. 6. set speed for 7. cross, measure with steps —'**pacer** n. one who sets the pace for another —'**pacemaker** n. esp. electronic device surgically implanted in those with heart disease

pachyderm ('pakidərm) n. thick-skinned animal, eg elephant —**pachy'dermatous** a. thick-skinned, stolid

Pacific (pə'sifik) n. (short for **Pacific Ocean**) world's largest ocean, bordered by America, Asia and Australia, divided by equator into North Pacific and South Pacific —**Pacific Standard Time** time as reckoned from the 120th meridian west of Greenwich

pacify ('pasifī) vt. 1. calm 2. restore to peace (-**ified, -ifying**) —**pa'cific** a. 1. peaceable 2. calm, tranquil —**pacifi'cation** n. —**pa'cificatory** a. tending to make peace —'**pacifier** n. 1. person or thing that pacifies 2. baby's dummy or teething ring —'**pacifism** n. —'**pacifist** n. 1. advocate of abolition of war 2. one who refuses to participate in war

pack (pak) n. 1. bundle 2. band of animals 3. large set of people or things 4. set of, container for, retail commodities 5. set of playing cards 6. mass of floating ice —v. 7. put (articles) together in suitcase etc. 8. press tightly together, cram —vt. 9. make into a bundle 10. fill with things 11. fill (meeting etc.) with one's own supporters 12. (oft. with off or away) order off —'**package** n. 1. parcel 2. set of items offered together —vt. 3. wrap in or put into package —'**packet** n. 1. small parcel 2. small container (and contents) 3. sl. large sum of money —**package store** store selling alcoholic beverages for consumption outside its premises —**packet** (**boat**) n. mail-boat —'**packhorse** n. horse for carrying goods —**pack ice** loose floating ice which has been compacted together —**pack saddle** saddle for carrying goods

pact (pakt) n. covenant, agreement, compact

pad¹ (pad) n. 1. piece of soft stuff used as a cushion, protection etc. 2. block of sheets of paper 3. foot or sole of various animals 4. place for launching rockets 5. sl. residence —vt. 6. make soft, fill in, protect etc. with pad or padding (-**dd**-) —'**padding** n. 1. material used for stuffing 2. literary matter put in simply to increase quantity —**padded cell** room, esp. in mental hospital, with padded surfaces, in which violent inmates are placed

pad² (pad) vi. 1. walk with soft step 2. travel slowly (-**dd**-) —n. 3. sound of soft footstep

paddle¹ ('padəl) n. 1. short oar with broad blade at one or each end —v. 2. move by, as with, paddles 3. row gently —**paddle tennis** indoor or outdoor court game played by two or four persons using wooden or plastic paddles instead of standard tennis rackets —**paddle wheel** wheel with crosswise blades striking water successively to propel ship

paddle² ('padəl) vi. 1. walk with bare feet in shallow water —n. 2. act of paddling

paddock ('padək) n. small grass field or enclosure

paddy ('padi) n. rice growing or in the husk —**paddy field** field where rice is grown

padlock ('padlok) n. 1. detachable lock with hinged hoop to go through staple or ring —vt. 2. fasten thus

padre ('pādrā, -ri) n. 1. priest, clergyman 2. chaplain with the armed forces

paean ('pēən) n. song of triumph or thanksgiving

paella (pä'elə, -'alyə) n. Spanish dish of rice, shellfish and chicken cooked and served in a large shallow pan

pagan ('pāgən) a./n. heathen —'**paganism** n.

page¹ (pāj) n. one side of leaf of book etc.

page² (pāj) n. 1. boy servant or attendant —vt. 2. summon by loudspeaker announcement —'**pager** n. device carried on person so that he or she can be summoned —'**pageboy** n. medium-length hair style with ends of hair curled under

pageant ('pajənt) n. 1. show of persons in costume in procession, dramatic scenes etc., usu. illustrating history 2. brilliant show —'**pageantry** n.

Paget's disease ('pajits) chronic bone disease of unknown origin marked by thickening, enlargement and painful deformation (also **osteitis deformans**)

paginate ('pajināt) vt. number pages of —**pagi'nation** n.

pagoda (pə'gōdə) n. pyramidal temple or tower of Chinese or Indian type

paid (pād) pt./pp. of PAY —**put paid to** inf. end, destroy

pail (pāl) n. bucket —'**pailful** n.

pain (pān) n. 1. bodily or mental suffering 2. penalty or punishment —pl. 3. trouble, exertion —vt. 4. inflict pain upon —'**pained** a. having or expressing pain or distress, esp. mental or emotional —'**painful** a. —'**painfully** adv. —'**painless** a. —'**painlessly** adv. —'**painkiller** n. drug, as aspirin, that reduces pain —'**painstaking** a. diligent, careful

paint (pānt) n. 1. coloring matter spread on a surface with brushes, roller, spray gun etc. —vt. 2. portray, color, coat, or make picture of, with paint 3. apply make-up to 4. describe —'**painter** n. —'**painting** n. picture in paint

painter¹ ('pāntər) n. cougar

painter² ('pāntər) n. line at bow of boat for tying it up

pair (pāər) n. 1. set of two, esp. existing or generally used together —v. 2. (oft. with off) group or be grouped in twos

paisley ('pāzli) n. pattern of small curving shapes

Paiute ('pīyōōt, 'pīōōt) n. 1. member of Amerindian people of northeastern Arizona, southern Utah and southeastern Nevada 2. Shoshonean language of this people

pajamas (pə'jäməz) pl.n. sleeping or lounging suit

Pakistan (paki'stan, päki'stän) n. country in Asia bounded northwest by Afghanistan, north by the U.S.S.R. and China, east by India and south by the Arabian Sea —**Paki'stani** n./a.

pal (pal) n. inf. friend —'**pally** a. inf. on friendly terms

palace ('palis) n. 1. residence of king, bishop etc. 2. stately mansion —**pa'latial** a. 1. like a palace 2. magnificent —'**palatine** a. with royal privileges

paladin ('palədin) n. Hist. knight errant

palanquin (palən'kēn) n. covered litter, formerly used in Orient, carried on shoulders of four men

palate ('palit) n. 1. roof of mouth 2. sense of taste —'**palatable** a. agreeable to eat —'**palatal** or '**palatine** a. 1. of the palate 2. made by placing tongue against palate —n. 3. palatal sound

palatial (pə'lāshəl) a. see PALACE

palaver (pə'lavər, -'lävər) n. 1. fuss 2. conference, discussion

pale¹ (pāl) a. 1. wan, dim, whitish —vi. 2. whiten 3. lose superiority or importance —'**paleface** n. derogatory term for White person, said to have been used by N Amer. Indians

pale² (pāl) n. stake, boundary —'**paling** n. upright plank making up fence

paleo- or before vowel **pale-** (comb. form) old, ancient, prehistoric, as in paleography

Paleocene ('paliōsēn) a. 1. of first epoch of Tertiary period —n. 2. Paleocene epoch or rock series

Paleolithic (paliō'lithik) a. of the old Stone Age

paleontology (palion'toləji) n. study of past geological periods and fossils —**paleonto'logical** a.

Paleozoic (paliō'zōik) a. 1. of geological time that began with Cambrian period and lasted until end of Permian period —n. 2. Paleozoic era

Palestinian (pali'stiniən) a. 1. of Palestine, former country in Middle East —n. 2. native or inhabitant of this area 3. descendant of inhabitant of this area, displaced when Israel became state

palette ('palit) n. 1. surface on which artist sets out and mixes pigments 2. range of colors used by an artist —**palette knife** spatula with thin flexible blade, used in painting etc.

palindrome ('palindrōm) n. word, verse or sentence that is the same when read backward or forward

palisade (pali'sād) *n.* **1.** fence of stakes —*vt.* **2.** enclose or protect with one

pall[1] (pöl) *n.* **1.** cloth spread over a coffin **2.** depressing, oppressive atmosphere —**'pall-bearer** *n.* one carrying, attending coffin at funeral

pall[2] (pöl) *vi.* **1.** become tasteless or tiresome **2.** cloy

palladium (pə'lādiəm) *n. Chem.* white noble metal *Symbol* Pd, at. wt. 106.4, at. no. 46

pallet[1] ('palit) *n.* **1.** straw mattress **2.** small bed

pallet[2] ('palit) *n.* portable platform for storing and moving goods

palliate ('paliāt) *vt.* **1.** relieve without curing **2.** excuse —**palli'ation** *n.* —**palliative** ('paliātiv, 'palyə-) *a.* **1.** giving temporary or partial relief —*n.* **2.** that which excuses, mitigates or alleviates

pallid ('palid) *a.* pale, wan, colorless —**'pallor** *n.* paleness

palmate

palm (päm, pälm) *n.* **1.** inner surface of hand **2.** tropical tree **3.** leaf of the tree as symbol of victory —*vt.* **4.** conceal in palm of hand **5.** pass off by trickery —**palmate** ('palmāt, 'pälmāt, 'pämāt) *or* **'palmated** *a.* **1.** shaped like open hand **2.** *Bot.* having five lobes that spread out from common point **3.** (of water birds) having three toes connected by web —**'palmist** *n.* —**'palmistry** *n.* fortune-telling from lines on palm of hand —**'palmy** *a.* flourishing, successful —**palm oil** oil obtained from fruit of certain palms —**Palm Sunday** Sunday before Easter —**palm off** (*oft. with* on) **1.** offer, sell or spend fraudulently **2.** divert in order to be rid of

palomino (palə'mēnō) *n.* golden horse with white mane and tail (*pl.* **-s**)

palpable ('palpəbəl) *a.* **1.** obvious **2.** certain **3.** that may be touched or felt —**'palpably** *adv.*

palpate ('palpāt) *vt. Med.* examine by touch

palpitate ('palpitāt) *vi.* **1.** throb **2.** pulsate violently —**palpi'tation** *n.* **1.** throbbing **2.** violent, irregular beating of heart

palsy ('pölzi) *n.* paralysis

paltry ('pöltri) *a.* worthless, contemptible, trifling

pampas ('pampəz, -pəs) *n.* (*oft. with pl. v.*) vast grassy treeless plains in S Amer.

pamper ('pampər) *vt.* overindulge, spoil by coddling

pamphlet ('pamflit) *n.* thin unbound book usu. on some topical subject

pan[1] (pan) *n.* **1.** broad, shallow vessel **2.** depression in ground, *esp.* where salt forms —*vt.* **3.** wash (gold ore) in pan **4.** *inf.* criticize harshly (**-nn-**) —**'pantile** *n.* curved roofing tile —**pan out** result

pan[2] (pan) *v.* move (motion-picture camera) slowly while filming to cover scene, follow moving object *etc.* (**-nn-**)

pan- (*comb. form*) all, as in *panacea, pantomime.* Such words are not given here where the meaning may easily be inferred from simple word

panacea (panə'sēə) *n.* universal remedy, cure for all ills

panache (pə'nash, -'näsh) *n.* dashing style

panama ('panəmä) *n.* **1.** fine straw from a palmlike plant from Ecuador **2.** cotton and wool cloth for summer suits

Panama ('panəmä) *n.* country in Central America bounded north by the Caribbean, east by Colombia, south by the Pacific and west by Costa Rica —**Panamanian** (panə'mäniən) *n./a.* (native or inhabitant) of Panama

Pan-American *a.* of North, South and Central America collectively —**Pan-American games** series of sports events for amateur athletes of the western hemisphere held every four years

pancake ('pankāk) *n.* **1.** thin cake of batter fried in pan **2.** flat cake or stick of compressed make-up —*vi.* **3.** *Aviation* make flat landing by dropping in a level position

panchromatic (pankrō'matik) *a. Photog.* sensitive to light of all colors

pancreas ('pangkriəs) *n.* gland behind stomach and liver which secretes enzymes to aid digestion and hormones into the blood stream —**pancre'atic** *a.* —**pancrea'titis** *n.* inflammation of this gland

panda ('pandə) *n.* **1.** reddish-brown carnivore of the Himalayas resembling and related to raccoon, with long fur and bushy tail marked with pale rings (*also* **lesser panda**) **2.** large black-and-white herbivore of Tibet and western China resembling bear, but related to raccoon, and symbol of the World Wildlife Fund (*also* **giant panda**)

pandemic (pan'demik) *a.* (of disease) occurring over wide area

pandemonium (pandi'mōniəm) *n.* scene of din and uproar

pander ('pandər) *v.* **1.** (*esp. with* to) give gratification (to weakness or desires) —*n.* **2.** pimp

pandit ('pundit; *spelling pron.* 'pandit) *n. see* PUNDIT (sense 2)

P. & L. profit and loss

pane (pān) *n.* single piece of glass in window or door

panegyric (pani'jirik) *n.* speech of praise —**pane'gyrical** *a.* laudatory —**pane'gyrist** *n.*

panel ('panəl) *n.* **1.** compartment of surface, usu. raised or sunk, *eg* in door **2.** any distinct section of something, *eg* of body of automobile **3.** strip of material inserted in garment **4.** group of persons as team in quiz game *etc.* **5.** list of jurors, doctors *etc.* **6.** thin board with picture on it —*vt.* **7.** adorn with panels —**'paneling** *n.* paneled work —**'panelist** *n.* member of panel —**panel game** quiz *etc.* played by group of people, *esp.* on TV

pang (pang) *n.* **1.** sudden pain, sharp twinge **2.** compunction

pangolin ('panggəlin, pan'gōlin, pang'gōlin) *n.* mammal with scaly body and long snout for feeding on ants *etc.* (*also* **scaly anteater**)

panic ('panik) *n.* **1.** sudden and infectious fear **2.** extreme fright **3.** unreasoning terror —*a.* **4.** of fear *etc.* —*v.* **5.** feel or cause to feel panic (**-icked, -icking**) —**'panicky** *a.* **1.** inclined to panic **2.** nervous —**'panicmonger** *n.* one who starts panic —**panic-stricken** *or* **panic-struck** *a.*

panicle ('panikəl) *n.* compound raceme, as in oat

panjandrum (pan'jandrəm) *n.* pompous self-important man

pannier ('panyər, 'paniər) *n.* basket carried by beast of burden, bicycle, or on person's shoulders

panoply ('panəpli) *n.* complete, magnificent array —**'panoplied** *a.*

panorama (panə'ramə, -'rämə) *n.* **1.** unobstructed or complete view of a region **2.** continuous painting, usu. a landscape, around the walls of a room or rolled on a cylinder —**pano'ramic** *a.* —**panoramic sight** form of periscopic sight used by marksmen

panpipes ('panpīps) *pl.n.* primitive wind instrument comprising a number of graded pipes, made from bamboo canes or clay, bound together in the form of a raft

pansy ('panzi) *n.* **1.** flower, species of violet **2.** *inf.* effeminate man

pant (pant) *vi.* **1.** gasp for breath **2.** yearn, long **3.** throb —*n.* **4.** gasp

pantaloon (pantə'lōōn) *n.* **1.** in pantomime, foolish old man who is the butt of clown —*pl.* **2.** *inf.* baggy trousers

pantechnicon (pan'teknikən) *n.* large van, *esp.* for carrying furniture

pantheism ('panthiizəm) *n.* identification of God with the universe —**'pantheist** *n.* —**panthe'istic** *a.* —**'pantheon** *n.* temple of all gods

panther ('panthər) *n.* variety of leopard

panties ('pantiz) *pl.n.* woman's or child's undergarment with closed crotch covering lower trunk —**panty hose** ('panti) garment for woman combining hosiery and panties

pantograph ('pantəgraf) *n.* instrument for copying maps *etc.* to any scale

pantomime ('pantəmīm) *n.* **1.** UK theatrical show, usu. produced at Christmastime, oft. founded on fairy tale **2.** dramatic entertainment in dumb show

pantry ('pantri) *n.* room for storing food or utensils

pants (pants) *pl.n.* **1.** undergarment for lower trunk **2.** trousers

panzer ('panzər; *Ger.* 'pantsər) *a.* **1.** of fast mechanized armored units employed by German army in World War II —*n.* **2.** vehicle belonging to panzer unit, *esp.* tank —*pl.* **3.** armored troops

pap[1] (pap) *n.* **1.** soft food for infants, invalids *etc.* **2.** pulp, mash **3.** SA maize porridge

pap[2] (pap) *n.* **1.** breast **2.** nipple

papa ('päpə) *n. inf.* father

Papa ('päpə) *n.* word used in communications for the letter *p*

papacy ('pāpəsi) *n.* **1.** office of Pope **2.** papal system —**'papal** *a.* of, relating to, the Pope

Papago ('päpəgō) *n.* **1.** member of Amerindian people of southern Arizona (*pl.* **-go, -s**) **2.** Uto-Aztecan language of the Papago

Papanicolaou's stain (päpə'nēkəlowz) *see* PAP SMEAR

papaw *or* **pawpaw** ('päpö, 'pöpö) *n.* **1.** tree bearing melon-shaped fruit **2.** its fruit

paper ('pāpər) *n.* **1.** material made by pressing pulp of rags, straw, wood *etc.* into thin, flat sheets **2.** printed sheet of paper **3.** newspaper **4.** article, essay **5.** set of examination questions —*pl.* **6.** documents *etc.* —*vt.* **7.** cover, decorate with paper —**'paperback** *n.* book with flexible covers —**'paperboy** *n.* boy employed to deliver newspapers ('papergirl *fem.*) —**paper chase** cross-country run in which runner lays trail of paper for others to follow —**'paperclip** *n.* clip for holding sheets of paper together, *esp.* one of bent wire —**'paperhanger** *n.* person who hangs wallpaper as occupation —**'paperknife** *n.* knife with comparatively blunt blade for opening sealed envelopes *etc.* —**paper money** paper currency issued by government or central bank as legal tender —**'paperweight** *n.* small heavy object to prevent loose papers from scattering —**'paperwork** *n.* clerical work, such as writing of reports or letters

papier-mâché (păpərmə'shā, papyāmə'shā) *n.* pulp from rags or paper mixed with size, shaped by molding and dried hard

papilla (pə'pilə) *n.* **1.** small projection of tissue at base of hair *etc.* **2.** any similar protuberance (*pl.* **-lae** (-lē)) —**'papillary, 'papillate** *or* **'papillose** *a.*

papoose (pa'pōōs, pə-) *n.* N Amer. Indian child

paprika (pə'prēkə, pa-) *n.* (powdered seasoning prepared from) type of red pepper

Pap smear (pap) test for cancer of the womb by examining cells from its neck (*also* **Papanicolaou's stain**)

Papua New Guinea ('papyōōə, 'păpōōə) country lying in the South Pacific occupying the eastern part of the island of New Guinea, bordering the Netherlands Antilles

papyrus

papyrus (pə'pīrəs) *n.* **1.** species of reed **2.** (manuscript written on) kind of paper made from this plant (*pl.* **-ri** (-rī), **-es**)

par (pär) *n.* **1.** equality of value or standing **2.** face value (of stocks) **3.** *Golf* estimated standard score —**'parity** *n.* **1.** equality **2.** analogy —**par value** value imprinted on face of stock certificate or bond and used to assess dividend *etc.*

par. 1. paragraph **2.** parallel **3.** parenthesis

para- *or before vowel* **par-** (*comb. form*) beside, beyond, as in *paradigm, parallel, parody*

parable ('parəbəl) *n.* allegory, story with a moral lesson —**para'bolic(al)** *a.* of parable

parabola (pə'rabələ) *n.* section of cone cut by

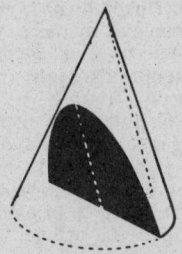

parabola

plane parallel to the cone's side —**para'bolic** *a.* of parabola

parachute ('parəshōōt) *n.* **1.** apparatus extending like umbrella used to retard the descent of a falling body —*v.* **2.** land or cause to land by parachute —**'parachutist** *n.*

parade (pə'rād) *n.* **1.** display **2.** muster of troops **3.** parade ground **4.** public walk —*vi.* **5.** march —*vt.* **6.** display

paradigm ('parədīm) *n.* example, model —**paradigmatic** (parədig'matik) *a.*

paradise ('parədīs) *n.* **1.** Heaven **2.** state of bliss **3.** Garden of Eden

paradox ('parədoks) *n.* **1.** antinomy **2.** self-contradictory or false statement —**para'doxical** *a.*

paraffin ('parəfin) *n.* waxlike or liquid hydrocarbon mixture used as fuel, solvent, in candles *etc.*

paragon ('parəgon, -gən) *n.* pattern or model of excellence

paragraph ('parəgraf) *n.* **1.** section of chapter or book **2.** short notice, as in newspaper —*vt.* **3.** arrange in paragraphs

Paraguay ('parəgwī, -gwā) *n.* country in South America bounded east by Brazil, east, south and west by Argentina and north by Bolivia —**Para'guayan** *n./a.* (native or inhabitant) of Paraguay

parakeet *or* **parrakeet** ('parəkēt) *n.* small long-tailed parrot

Paralipomenon (parəli'pomənon) *n. Bible* Chronicles in the Douay Version of the O.T.

parallax ('parəlaks) *n.* apparent difference in object's position or direction as viewed from different points

parallel ('parəlel) *a.* **1.** continuously at equal distances **2.** precisely corresponding —*n.* **3.** line equidistant from another at all points **4.** thing exactly like another **5.** comparison **6.** line of latitude —*vt.* **7.** represent as similar, compare —**'parallelism** *n.* —**paral'lelogram** *n.* four-sided plane figure with opposite sides parallel —**parallel bars** *Gymnastics* pair of wooden bars on uprights used for exercises

paralysis (pə'ralisis) *n.* incapacity to move or feel, due to damage to nervous system (*pl.* **-yses** (-isēz)) —**para'lytic** *a./n.* (person) afflicted with paralysis —**'paralyze** *vt.* **1.** afflict with paralysis **2.** cripple **3.** make useless or ineffectual —**infantile paralysis** poliomyelitis

paramedical (parə'medikəl) *a.* **1.** of persons working in various capacities in support of medical profession **2.** of professionals in allied fields, *eg* technicians, chiropodists, physiotherapists *etc.*

parameter (pə'ramitər) *n.* any constant limiting factor

paramilitary (parə'militeri) *a.* of civilian group organized on military lines or in support of the military

paramount ('parəmownt) *a.* supreme, eminent, pre-eminent, chief

paramour ('parəmōōər) *n. esp.* formerly, illicit lover, mistress

parang ('pärang) *n.* heavy Malay knife

paranoia (parə'noiə) *n.* mental disease with delusions of fame, grandeur, persecution —**paranoiac** (parə'noiak, -ik) *a./n.* —**'paranoid** *a.* **1.** of paranoia **2.** *inf.* exhibiting fear of persecution *etc.* —*n.* **3.** person afflicted with paranoia

parapet ('parəpit, -pet) *n.* low wall, railing along edge of balcony, bridge *etc.*

paraphernalia (parəfər'nālyə) *pl.n.* (*sometimes with sing. v.*) **1.** personal belongings **2.** odds and ends of equipment

paraphrase ('parəfrāz) *n.* **1.** expression of meaning of passage in other words **2.** free translation —*vt.* **3.** put into other words

paraplegia (parə'plējə) *n.* paralysis of lower half of body —**para'plegic** *n./a.*

parapsychology (parəsī'koləji) *n.* study of subjects pert. to extrasensory perception, *eg* telepathy

paraquat ('parəkwot) *n.* fast-acting herbicide which becomes inactive when in contact with soil

parasite ('parəsīt) *n.* **1.** animal or plant living in or on another **2.** self-interested hanger-on —**parasitic** (parə'sitik) *a.* of the nature of, living as, parasite —**'parasitism** *n.*

parasol ('parəsöl, -sol) *n.* sunshade

parataxis (parə'taksis) *n.* arrangement of sentences which omits connecting words

parathion (parə'thīən, -on) *n.* toxic oil used as insecticide

parathyroid gland (parə'thīroid) one of two bean-shaped structures in front of neck essential to life as they secrete hormones controlling bone development and maintain calcium and phosphate metabolism

paratroops ('parətrōōps) *pl.n.* troops trained to descend by parachute

paratyphoid fever (parə'tīfoid) infectious disease contracted by eating contaminated food with symptoms resembling typhoid fever

parboil ('pärboil) *vt.* boil until partly cooked

parcel ('pärsəl) *n.* **1.** packet of goods, *esp.* one enclosed in paper **2.** quantity dealt with at one time **3.** piece of land —*vt.* **4.** wrap up **5.** divide into parts

parch (pärch) *v.* **1.** dry by heating **2.** make, become hot and dry **3.** scorch **4.** roast slightly

parchment ('pärchmənt) *n.* **1.** sheep, goat, calf skin prepared for writing **2.** manuscript of this

pardon ('pärdən) *vt.* **1.** forgive, excuse —*n.* **2.** forgiveness **3.** release from punishment —**'pardonable** *a.* —**'pardonably** *adv.*

pare (pāər) *vt.* **1.** trim, cut edge or surface of **2.** decrease bit by bit —**'paring** *n.* piece pared off, rind

paregoric (parə'görik) *n.* narcotic preparation containing small amount of opium used to treat colic, earache, teething pain and diarrhea (*also* **camphorated opium tincture**)

parent ('parənt, 'per-) *n.* father or mother —**'parentage** *n.* descent, extraction —**pa'rental** *a.* —**'parenthood** *n.* —**parent teacher association** group of parents of children at school and their teachers formed in order to foster better understanding between them *etc.*

parenthesis (pə'renthisis) *n.* word or sentence inserted in passage independently of grammatical sequence and usu. marked off by brackets, dashes, or commas —**pa'rentheses** *pl.n.* round brackets, ( ), used for this —**pa'renthesize** *vt.* **1.** place in parentheses **2.** insert as parenthesis **3.** intersperse with parentheses —**paren'thetical** *a.*

par excellence (par ekse'läs) *Fr.* to degree of excellence; beyond comparison

pariah (pə'rīə, 'pariə) *n.* social outcast

parietal (pə'rīitəl) *a.* of the walls of bodily cavities, *eg* skull

pari-mutuel (pari'myōōchōōəl) *n.* system of betting in which those who have bet on winners of race share in total amount wagered less percentage for management (*pl.* **pari-mutuels, paris-mutuels** (pari'myōōchōōəlz))

parish ('parish) *n.* **1.** district under one clergyman **2.** (in Louisiana) a county —**pa'rishioner** *n.* inhabitant of parish

parity ('pariti) *n. see* PAR

park (pärk) *n.* **1.** large area of land in natural state preserved for recreational use **2.** large enclosed piece of ground, usu. with grass or woodland, attached to country house or for public use **3.** space in camp for military supplies —*vt.* **4.** leave for a short time **5.** maneuver (vehicle) into a suitable space **6.** arrange or leave in a park —**parking lot** area where vehicles may be left for a time —**parking meter** timing device, usu. coin-operated, that indicates how long vehicle may be left parked —**parking ticket** summons served for parking offense —**'parkland** *n.* grassland with scattered trees

parka ('pärkə) *n.* warm waterproof coat, oft. with hood

Parkinson's disease ('pärkinsənz) progressive chronic disorder of central nervous system characterized by impaired muscular coordination and tremor (*also* **'parkinsonism**)

Parkinson's law notion, expressed facetiously as law of economics, that work expands to fill time available

parlance ('pärləns) *n.* 1. way of speaking, conversation 2. idiom

parley ('pärli) *n.* 1. meeting between leaders or representatives of opposing forces to discuss terms —*vi.* 2. hold discussion about terms

parliament ('pärləmənt) *n.* 1. the legislature of the United Kingdom 2. any similar legislative assembly —**parliamen'tarian** *n.* member of parliament —**parlia'mentary** *a.*

parlor ('pärlər) *n.* 1. sitting room, room for receiving company in small house 2. place for milking cows 3. room or shop as business premises, *esp.* hairdresser *etc.*

Parmesan ('pärmizän, -zan, -zən) *n.* the hardest cheese, made of cow's milk, with mild flavor, best grated, orig. from Italy (*also* **Parmigiano** (pärmi'jänō), **Reggiano Lodigiano**)

parochial (pə'rōkiəl) *a.* 1. narrow, provincial 2. of a parish —**pa'rochialism** *n.*

parody ('parədi) *n.* 1. composition in which author's style is made fun of by imitation 2. travesty —*vt.* 3. write parody of (**-odied, -odying**) —**'parodist** *n.*

parole (pə'rōl) *n.* 1. early freeing of prisoner on condition he is of good behavior 2. word of honor —*vt.* 3. place on parole

parotid (pə'rotid) *a.* 1. relating to or situated near parotid gland —*n.* 2. parotid gland —**parotid gland** large salivary gland in front of and below each ear

-parous (*comb. form*) giving birth to, as in *oviparous*

paroxysm ('parəksizəm) *n.* sudden violent attack of pain, rage, laughter

parquet ('pärkā) *n.* 1. flooring of wooden blocks arranged in pattern 2. method of preventing warping of wood by reinforcement —**parquetry** ('pärkitri) *n.*

parr (pär) *n.* salmon up to two years of age (*pl.* **-s, parr**)

parrakeet ('parəkēt) *n. see* PARAKEET

parricide ('parisīd) *n.* murder or murderer of a parent

parrot ('parət) *n.* 1. any of several related birds with short hooked beak, some varieties of which can imitate speaking 2. unintelligent imitator —**parrot fever** *or* **disease** *see* **psittacosis** *at* PSITTACINE

parry ('pari) *vt.* 1. ward off, turn aside (**'parried, 'parrying**) —*n.* 2. act of parrying, *esp.* in fencing

parse (pärs, pärz) *vt.* 1. describe (word) 2. analyze (sentence) in terms of grammar

parsec ('pärsek) *n.* unit of length used in expressing distance of stars

parsimony ('pärsimōni) *n.* 1. stinginess 2. undue economy —**parsi'monious** *a.* sparing

parsley ('pärsli) *n.* herb used for seasoning, garnish *etc.*

parsnip ('pärsnip) *n.* edible yellow root vegetable

parson ('pärsən) *n.* 1. clergyman of parish or church 2. clergyman —**'parsonage** *n.* parson's house —**parson's nose** fatty extreme end portion of tail of fowl when cooked

part (pärt) *n.* 1. portion, section, share 2. division 3. actor's role 4. duty 5. (*oft. pl.*) region 6. interest 7. division between sections of hair on head —*v.* 8. divide 9. separate —**'parting** *n.* 1. separation 2. leave-taking —**'partly** *adv.* in part —**part of speech** class of words sharing important syntactic or semantic features; group of words in language that may occur in similar positions or fulfill similar functions in sentence —**part song** song for several voices singing in harmony (*also* **canon, round**) —**part-time** *a.* 1. for less than entire time appropriate to activity —*adv.* 2. on part-time basis —**part-timer** *n.*

part. 1. participle 2. particular

partake (pär'tāk) *vi.* 1. (*with* of) take or have share (in) 2. take food or drink (**-'took, -'taken, -'taking**)

parterre (pär'tâər) *n.* 1. ornamental arrangement of beds in a flower garden 2. the pit of a theater

parthenogenesis (pärthinō'jenisis) *n.* the reproduction of an individual plant or animal from an unfertilized ovule or ovum —**parthenoge'netic** *a.*

Parthian shot ('pärthiən) hostile remark or gesture delivered while departing

partial ('pärshəl) *a.* 1. not general or complete 2. prejudiced 3. (*with* to) fond (of) —**parti'ality** *n.* 1. favoritism 2. fondness —**'partially** *adv.* partly

participate (pər'tisipāt, pär-) *v.* (*with* in) 1. share (in) 2. take part (in) —**par'ticipant** *n.* —**partici'pation** *n.* —**par'ticipator** *n.*

participle ('pärtisipəl) *n.* adjective made by inflection from verb and keeping verb's relation to dependent words —**parti'cipial** *a.*

particle ('pärtikəl) *n.* 1. minute portion of matter 2. least possible amount 3. minor part of speech in grammar, prefix, suffix —**particle accelerator** device to impart high velocity to an elementary particle, increasing its energy

parti-colored (pärti'kulərd) *a.* differently colored in different parts, variegated

particular (pər'tikyələr) *a.* 1. relating to one, not general 2. distinct 3. minute 4. very exact 5. fastidious —*n.* 6. detail, item —*pl.* 7. detailed account 8. items of information —**particu'larity** *n.* —**par'ticularize** *vt.* mention in detail —**par'ticularly** *adv.*

partisan ('pärtizən, -sən) *n.* 1. adherent of a party 2. guerrilla, member of resistance movement —*a.* 3. adhering to faction 4. prejudiced

partition (pər'tishən, pär-) *n.* 1. division 2. interior dividing wall —*vt.* 3. divide, cut into sections

partitive ('pärtitiv) *a.* 1. *Gram.* indicating that noun involved in construction refers only to part of what it otherwise refers to 2. serving to separate or divide into parts —*n.* 3. *Gram.* partitive linguistic element or feature

partner ('pärtnər) *n.* 1. ally or companion 2. a member of a partnership 3. one that dances with another 4. a husband or wife 5. *Golf, Tennis etc.* one who plays with another against opponents —*vt.* 6. (cause to) be a partner (of) —**'partnership** *n.* association of persons for business *etc.*

partridge ('pärtrij) *n.* any of various game birds of the grouse family

parturition (pärtə'rishən, pärchə-, pärtyŏŏ-) *n.* 1. act of bringing forth young 2. childbirth —**par'turient** *a.* 1. of childbirth 2. giving birth 3. producing new idea *etc.*

party ('pärti) *n.* 1. social assembly 2. group of persons traveling or working together 3. group of persons united in opinion 4. side 5. person —*a.* 6. of, belonging to, a party or faction —**party line** 1. telephone line serving two or more subscribers 2. policies of political party —**party wall** common wall separating adjoining premises

parulis (pə'rōōlis) *n.* gumboil

parvenu *or* (*fem.*) **parvenue** ('pärvənyŏŏ, -nōō) *n.* 1. one newly risen into position of notice, power, wealth 2. upstart

pas (pä) *n.* dance step or movement, *esp.* in ballet (*pl.* **pas**)

pascal ('paskəl) *n.* SI unit of pressure

Paschal ('paskəl) *a.* of the Passover or Easter

pasha ('päshə, 'pashə) *n.* formerly, high official of Ottoman Empire or modern Egyptian kingdom: placed after name when used as title

Pashto ('pushtō) *n.* the Iranian language of the Pathan people which is the chief vernacular of eastern Afghanistan and adjacent parts of Pakistan

pasqueflower ('paskflowər) *n.* 1. small purple-flowered plant of N and Central Europe and W Asia 2. any of several related N Amer. plants

pass (pas) *vt.* 1. go by, beyond, through *etc.* 2. exceed 3. be accepted by 4. undergo successfully 5. spend 6. transfer 7. exchange 8. disregard 9. undergo (examination) successfully 10. bring into force, sanction (a parliamentary bill *etc.*) —*vi.* 11. go 12. be transferred from one state or person to another 13. elapse —*n.* 14. way, *esp.* a narrow and difficult way 15. permit, license, authorization 16. successful result from test 17. condition 18. *Sport* transfer of ball —**'passable** *a.* (just) acceptable —**'passing** *a.* 1. transitory 2. cursory, casual —**'passbook** *n.* bankbook —**passer-by** *n.* person that is passing by, *esp.* on foot (*pl.* **passers-by**) —**'passkey** *n.* 1. any of various keys, *esp.* latchkey 2. master key 3. skeleton key —**pass up** ignore, neglect; reject

passage ('pasij) *n.* 1. channel, opening 2. way through, corridor 3. part of book *etc.* 4. journey, voyage, fare 5. enactment of law by parliament *etc.* 6. *rare* conversation; dispute —**'passageway** *n.* way, *esp.* one in or between buildings; passage

Passamaquoddy (pasəmə'kwodi) *n.* (member of) Algonquian-speaking Amerindian people of Maine, which is a member of Abnaki confederacy (*pl.* **-dy, -s**)

passé (pa'sā) *a.* 1. out of date 2. past the prime

passenger ('pasinjər) *n.* 1. traveler, *esp.* by public conveyance 2. one of a team who does not pull his weight

passerine ('pasərīn) *a./n.* (member) of the order of perching bird

passim ('pasim) *Lat.* everywhere, throughout

passion ('pashən) *n.* 1. ardent desire, *esp.* sexual 2. any strongly felt emotion 3. suffering (*esp.* that of Christ) —**'passionate** *a.* (easily) moved by strong emotions —**'passionflower** *n.* tropical Amer. plant —**passion fruit** edible fruit of passionflower —**Passion play** play depicting Passion of Christ

passive ('pasiv) *a.* 1. unresisting 2. submissive 3. inactive 4. denoting grammatical mood of verb in which the action is suffered by the subject —**pas'sivity** *n.* —**passive resistance** resistance to government *etc.* without violence, as by fasting, demonstrating or refusing to cooperate

Passover ('pasōvər) *n.* Jewish spring holiday commemorating the liberation of the Jews from slavery in Egypt (*also* **Pesach**)

passport ('paspört) *n.* official document granting permission to pass, travel abroad *etc.*

password ('paswərd) *n.* 1. word, phrase, to distinguish friend from enemy 2. countersign

past (past) *a.* 1. ended 2. gone by 3. elapsed —*n.* 4. bygone times —*adv.* 5. by 6. along —*prep.* 7. beyond 8. after —**past master** 1. person with talent for, or experience in a particular activity 2. person who has held office of master in guild *etc.* —**past participle** participial form of verbs used to modify noun that is logically object of verb, also used in certain compound tenses and passive forms of verb —**past perfect** *Gram. a.* 1. denoting tense of verbs used in relating past events where action had already occurred at time of action of main verb that is itself in past tense —*n.* 2. past perfect tense 3. verb in this tense

pasta ('pästə) *n.* any of several variously shaped edible preparations of dough, *eg* spaghetti

paste (pāst) *n.* 1. soft composition, as toothpaste 2. soft plastic mixture or adhesive 3. fine glass to imitate gems —*vt.* 4. fasten with paste —**'pasty** *a.* 1. like paste 2. white 3. sickly —**'pasteboard** *n.* stiff thick paper

pastel (pa'stel) *n.* 1. colored crayon 2. art of drawing with crayons 3. pale, delicate color —*a.* 4. delicately tinted

pastern ('pastərn) *n.* part of horse's foot between fetlock and hoof

pasteurize ('paschəriz, 'pastə-) *vt.* sterilize by heat —**pasteuri'zation** *n.*

pastiche (pa'stēsh) *or* **pasticcio** (pa-'stēchō) *n.* 1. literary, musical, artistic work composed of parts borrowed from other works and loosely connected together 2. work imitating another's style

pastille (pa'stēl) *or* **pastil** ('pastəl) *n.* 1. lozenge 2. aromatic substance burnt as fumigator

pastime ('pastim) *n.* 1. that which makes time pass agreeably 2. recreation

pastor ('pastər) *n.* clergyman in charge of a congregation —**'pastoral** *a.* 1. of, or like, shepherd's or rural life 2. of office of pastor —*n.* 3. poem describing rural life —**pasto-rale** (pastə'räl) *n. Mus.* 1. composition evocative of rural life 2. musical play based on rustic story (*pl.* **-s, -rali** (*It.* -'räle)) —**'pastorate** *n.* office, jurisdiction of pastor

pastry ('pāstri) *n.* article of food made chiefly of flour, fat and water

pasture ('paschər) *n.* 1. grass for food of cattle 2. ground on which cattle graze —*v.* 3. (cause to) graze —**'pasturage** *n.* (right to) pasture

pasty ('pasti) *n.* small pie of meat and crust, baked without a dish

pat[1] (pat) *vt.* 1. tap (**-tt-**) —*n.* 2. light, quick blow 3. small mass, as of butter, beaten into shape

pat[2] (pat) *adv.* 1. exactly 2. fluently 3. opportunely —*a.* 4. glib 5. exactly right

pat. patent(ed)

patch (pach) *n.* 1. piece of cloth sewn on garment 2. spot 3. plot of ground 4. protecting pad for the eye 5. small contrasting area 6. short period —*vt.* 7. mend 8. repair clumsily —**'patchy** *a.* 1. of uneven quality 2. full of patches —**patch test** test to detect skin sensitivity to contact with irritants or allergic agents —**'patchwork** *n.* 1. work composed of pieces sewn together 2. jumble

patchouli *or* **patchouly** ('pachəli, pə'chōō-li) *n.* 1. Indian herb 2. perfume made from it

pate (pāt) *n.* 1. head 2. top of head

pâté (pä'tā, pa'tā) *n.* spread of finely minced liver *etc.* —**pâté de foie gras** (*Fr.* pätā də fwa 'grä) smooth rich paste made from liver of specially fattened goose (*pl.* **pâtés de foie gras** (*Fr.* pätā))

patella (pə'telə) *n.* kneecap (*pl.* **patellae** (pə'telē)) —**pa'tellar** *a.*

paten ('patən) *n.* plate for bread in the Eucharist

patent ('patənt) *n.* 1. deed securing to person exclusive right to invention —*a.* 2. open 3. (*also* 'pātənt) evident; manifest 4. open to public perusal, as in *letters patent* —*vt.* 5. secure a patent for —**paten'tee** *n.* one that has a patent —**patently** ('patəntli, 'pātəntli) *adv.* obviously —**patent leather** (imitation) leather processed to give hard, glossy surface —**patent medicine** medicine with patent, available without prescription —**Patent Office** government department that issues patents

pater ('pātər) *n.* **UK** *sl.* father

paterfamilias (pātərfə'miliəs) *n.* father of a family (*pl.* **patresfamilias** (pätrēzfə'miliəs, pätrās-))

paternal (pə'tərnəl) *a.* 1. fatherly 2. of a father —**pa'ternalism** *n.* authority exercised in a way that limits individual responsibility —**paternal'istic** *a.* —**pa'ternity** *n.* 1. relation of a father to his offspring 2. fatherhood —**paternity test** blood or tissue test used to determine whether a man is the father of a particular child

paternoster ('patərnostər, pätər'nostər) *n.* 1. (P-) Lord's Prayer 2. beads of rosary 3. type of elevator with platforms rising and falling in an endless moving chain

path (path, päth) *n.* 1. way or track 2. course of action —**'pathway** *n.* 1. path 2. *Biochem.* chain of reactions associated with particular metabolic process

-path (*comb. form*) 1. person suffering from specified disease or disorder, as in *neuropath* 2. practitioner of particular method of treatment, as in *osteopath*

pathetic (pə'thetik) *a.* 1. affecting or moving tender emotions 2. distressingly inadequate —**pa'thetically** *adv.* —**pathetic fallacy** *Lit.* presentation of nature *etc.* as possessing human feelings

pathogenic (pathə'jenik) *a.* producing disease —**pa'thogeny** *n.* mode of development of disease

pathology (pə'tholəji) *n.* science of diseases —**patho'logical** *a.* 1. of the science of disease 2. due to disease 3. *inf.* compulsively motivated

pathos ('pāthos) *n.* power of exciting tender emotions

-pathy (*n. comb. form*) 1. feeling, perception, as in *telepathy* 2. disease, as in *psychopathy* 3. method of treating disease, as in *osteopathy* —**-pathic** (*a. comb. form*)

patient ('pāshənt) *a.* 1. bearing trials calmly —*n.* 2. person under medical treatment —**'patience** *n.* quality of enduring

patina ('patinə) *n.* 1. fine layer on a surface 2. sheen of age on woodwork

patio ('patiō) *n.* paved area adjoining house (*pl.* **-s**)

patois ('patwä; *Fr.* pa'twa) *n.* regional dialect (*pl.* **patois** ('patwäz; *Fr.* pa'twa))

pat. pend. patent pending

patriarch ('pātriärk) *n.* father and ruler of family, *esp.* Biblical —**patri'archal** *a.* venerable —**'patriarchy** *n.* 1. form of social organization in which male is head of family and descent, kinship and title are traced through male line 2. society governed by such system

patrician (pə'trishən) *n.* 1. noble of ancient Rome 2. one of noble birth —*a.* 3. of noble birth

patricide ('patrisid) *n.* murder or murderer of father

patriot ('pātriət, -ot) *n.* one that loves his country and maintains its interests —**patri'otic** *a.* inspired by love of one's country —**'patriotism** *n.*

patrol (pə'trōl) *n.* 1. regular circuit by guard 2. person, small group patrolling 3. unit of Scouts —*v.* 4. go round on guard or reconnoitering (**-ll-**)

patron ('pātrən) *n.* 1. one who sponsors or aids artists, charities *etc.* 2. protector 3. regular customer 4. guardian saint 5. one that has disposition of church living *etc.* —**patronage** ('patrənij) *n.* support given by, or position of, a patron —**'patronize** *vt.* 1. assume air of superiority toward 2. frequent as customer 3. encourage —**'patronizing** *a.* condescending

patronymic (patrə'nimik) *n.* name derived from that of father or ancestor

patter ('patər) *vi.* 1. make noise, as sound of quick, short steps 2. tap in quick succession 3. pray, talk rapidly —*n.* 4. quick succession of taps 5. *inf.* glib, rapid speech

pattern ('patərn) *n.* 1. arrangement of repeated parts 2. design 3. shape to direct cutting of cloth *etc.* 4. model 5. specimen —*vt.* 6. (*with* on, after) model 7. decorate with pattern

paucity ('pösiti) *n.* 1. scarcity 2. smallness of quantity 3. fewness

paunch (pönch) *n.* belly

pauper ('pöpər) *n.* poor person, *esp.*, formerly, one supported by the public —**'pauperism** *n.* 1. destitution 2. extreme poverty

pause (pöz) *vi.* 1. cease for a time —*n.* 2. stop or rest

pavane *or* **pavan** (pə'vän, -'van) *n.* 1. slow, stately dance of 16th and 17th centuries 2. music for this dance

pave (pāv) *vt.* 1. form surface on with stone or brick 2. prepare, make easier (*esp. in* **pave the way**) —**'pavement** *n.* 1. paved floor, footpath 2. material for paving

pavilion (pə'vilyən) *n.* 1. clubhouse on playing field *etc.* 2. building for housing exhibition *etc.* 3. large ornate tent

pavlova (pav'lōvə) *n.* meringue cake with whipped cream and fruit

paw (pö) *n.* 1. foot of animal —*v.* 2. scrape with forefoot —*vt.* 3. handle roughly 4. stroke with the hands

pawl (pöl) *n.* pivoted lever shaped to engage with ratchet wheel to prevent motion in particular direction

pawn[1] (pön) *vt.* 1. deposit (article) as security for money borrowed —*n.* 2. article deposited —**'pawnbroker** *n.* lender of money on goods pledged

pawn[2] (pön) *n.* 1. piece in chess 2. *fig.* person used as mere tool

Pawnee (pö'nē) *n.* member of Siouan-speaking Amerindian people orig. of Kansas and Nebraska, now of Oklahoma (*pl.* **-nee, -s**)

pawpaw ('popö, 'pö-) *n. see* PAPAW

pax (paks) *n. chiefly R.C.Ch.* 1. kiss of peace 2. small plate formerly used to convey kiss of peace from celebrant at Mass to those attending it

pay (pā) *vt.* 1. give (money *etc.*) for goods or services rendered 2. compensate 3. give, bestow 4. be profitable to 5. (*with* out) release bit by bit, as rope 6. (*with* out) spend —*vi.* 7. be remunerative or profitable (**paid, 'paying**) —*n.* 8. wages 9. paid employment

—**'payable** a. **1.** justly due **2.** profitable —**pay'ee** n. person to whom money is paid or due —**'payment** n. discharge of debt —**pay'ola** n. inf. **1.** bribe given to secure special treatment, esp. to disc jockey to promote commercial product **2.** practice of paying or receiving such bribes —**paying guest** boarder, lodger, esp. in private house —**'payload** n. **1.** part of cargo earning revenue **2.** explosive power of missile etc. —**'paymaster** n. official of government etc., responsible for payment of wages and salaries —**'payoff** n. **1.** final settlement, esp. in retribution **2.** inf. climax, consequence or outcome of events etc. **3.** final payment of debt etc. **4.** time of such payment **5.** inf. bribe —**pay packet 1.** envelope containing employee's wages **2.** the wages —**'payroll** n. **1.** list of employees, specifying salary or wage of each **2.** total of these amounts or actual money equivalent —**pay off 1.** pay all that is due in wages etc. and discharge from employment **2.** pay complete amount of (debt etc.) **3.** turn out to be profitable **4.** take revenge on (person) or for (wrong done) **5.** inf. give bribe to

Pb Chem. lead

p.c. 1. per cent **2.** postcard

Pd Chem. palladium

pd. paid

PE Prince Edward Island

P.E. physical education

pea (pē) n. **1.** fruit, growing in pods, of climbing plant **2.** the plant —**pea-green** a. of shade of green like color of green peas —**pea jacket** or **'peacoat** n. sailor's short heavy woolen overcoat —**pea'souper** n. inf. thick fog

peace (pēs) n. **1.** freedom from war **2.** harmony **3.** quietness of mind **4.** calm **5.** repose —**'peaceable** a. disposed to peace —**'peaceably** adv. —**'peaceful** a. **1.** free from war, tumult **2.** mild **3.** undisturbed —**'peacefully** adv. —**'peacemaker** n. person who establishes peace, esp. between others —**peace offering 1.** something given to adversary in hope of procuring or maintaining peace **2.** Judaism sacrificial meal shared between offerer and Jehovah —**peace pipe** pipe smoked by N Amer. Indians, esp. as token of peace (also **'calumet**)

peach[1] (pēch) n. **1.** stone fruit of delicate flavor **2.** inf. anything very pleasant **3.** pinkish-yellow color —**'peachy** a. **1.** like peach **2.** inf. fine, excellent

peach[2] (pēch) vi. sl. become informer

peacock ('pēkok) n. **1.** male of bird ('**peafowl**) with fanlike tail, brilliantly colored ('**peahen** fem.) —vi. **2.** strut about or pose, like a peacock

peak (pēk) n. **1.** pointed end of anything, esp. hill's sharp top **2.** point of greatest development etc. **3.** sharp increase **4.** projecting piece on front of cap —v. **5.** (cause to) form, reach peaks —**peaked** or **'peaky** a. **1.** like, having a peak **2.** sickly, wan, drawn —**peak hour** time at which maximum occurs, either in amount of traffic or demand for gas etc. —**peak load** maximum load on electrical power-supply system

peal (pēl) n. **1.** loud sound or succession of loud sounds **2.** changes rung on set of bells **3.** chime —v. **4.** sound loudly

peanut ('pēnut) n. **1.** pea-shaped nut that ripens underground —pl. **2.** inf. trifling amount of money

pear (pâər) n. **1.** tree yielding sweet, juicy fruit **2.** the fruit —**pear-shaped** a. shaped like a pear, heavier at the bottom than the top

pearl (pərl) n. hard, lustrous structure found in several mollusks, esp. pearl oyster and used as jewel —**'pearly** a. like pearls —**pearl barley** barley with skin ground off —**pearl diver** or **fisher** person who dives for pearl-bearing mollusks

peasant ('pezənt) n. member of low social class, esp. in rural district —**'peasantry** n. peasants collectively

pease (pēz) n. obs., dial. pea (pl. **pease**)

peat (pēt) n. **1.** decomposed vegetable substance found in bogs **2.** turf of it used for fuel —**peat moss** any of various mosses, esp. sphagnum, that grow in wet places and decay to form peat (see also SPHAGNUM)

pebble ('pebəl) n. **1.** small roundish stone **2.** pale, transparent rock crystal **3.** grainy, irregular surface —vt. **4.** pave, cover with pebbles

pecan (pi'kän, -'kan; 'pēkan) n. **1.** N Amer. tree, species of hickory, allied to walnut **2.** its edible nut

peccadillo (pekə'dilō) n. **1.** slight offense **2.** petty crime (pl. **-es, -s**)

peccary

peccary ('pekəri) n. vicious Amer. animal allied to pig

peck[1] (pek) n. **1.** fourth part of bushel, 2 gallons **2.** great deal

peck[2] (pek) v. **1.** pick, strike with or as with beak **2.** nibble —vt. **3.** inf. kiss quickly —n. **4.** act, instance of pecking —**'peckish** a. inf. hungry

pectin ('pektin) n. gelatinizing substance obtained from ripe fruits —**'pectic** a. **1.** congealing **2.** denoting pectin

pectoral ('pektərəl) a. **1.** of the breast —n. **2.** chest medicine **3.** breastplate —**pectoral fin** either of pair of fins, situated just behind head in fishes —**pectoral girdle** bony arch supporting forelimbs of a vertebrate (also **shoulder girdle**)

peculate ('pekyəlāt) v. **1.** embezzle **2.** steal —**pecu'lation** n. —**'peculator** n.

peculiar (pi'kyōōlyər) a. **1.** strange **2.** particular **3.** (with to) belonging (to) —**peculi'arity** n. **1.** oddity **2.** characteristic **3.** distinguishing feature

pecuniary (pi'kyōōnieri) a. relating to, or consisting of, money

-ped or **-pede** (comb. form) foot or feet, as in quadruped, centipede

pedagogue or **pedagog** ('pedəgog) n. **1.** schoolmaster **2.** pedant —**pedagogic** (pedə'gojik, -'gōj-) a. —**pedagogy** ('pedəgōji, -goji) n. principles, practice or profession of teaching

pedal ('pedəl) n. **1.** something to transmit motion from foot **2.** foot lever to modify tone or swell of musical instrument **3.** Mus. note, usu. bass, held through successive harmonies —a. ('pēdəl) **4.** of a foot —v. **5.** propel (bicycle) by using pedals —vi. **6.** use pedals

pedalo ('pedəlō) n. small watercraft with paddle wheel propelled by foot pedals (pl. **-s, -es**)

pedant ('pedənt) n. one who overvalues, or insists on, petty details of book-learning, grammatical rules etc. —**pe'dantic** a.

peddle ('pedəl) v. go round selling (goods)

—**'peddler** n. one who sells, esp. narcotic drugs

pederast ('pedərast) n. man who has homosexual relations with boy —**'pederasty** n.

pedestal

pedestal ('pedistəl) n. base of column, pillar

pedestrian (pi'destriən) n. **1.** one who walks on foot —a. **2.** going on foot **3.** commonplace; dull, uninspiring —**pe'destrianism** n. the practice of walking —**pe'destrianize** vt. convert into area for use of pedestrians only —**pedestrian crossing** UK crosswalk —**pedestrian precinct** area for pedestrians only to shop etc.

pedi- (comb. form) foot, as in pedicure

pediatrics (pēdi'atriks) n. branch of medicine dealing with diseases and disorders of children —**pedia'trician** n.

pediculosis (pədikyə'lōsis) n. infestation by lice

pedicure ('pedikyōōər) n. medical or cosmetic treatment of feet

pedigree ('pedigrē) n. **1.** register of ancestors **2.** genealogy

pediment ('pedimənt) n. triangular part over Greek portico etc. —**pedi'mental** a.

pedo- or before vowel **ped-** (comb. form) child, children, as in pedophilia

pedophilia (pēdə'filiə) n. condition of being sexually attracted to children —**pedophile** ('pēdəfil) or **pedo'philiac** n./a.

peduncle ('pēdungkəl, pi'dungkəl) n. **1.** flower stalk **2.** stalklike structure

peek (pēk) vi./n. peep, glance

peel (pēl) vt. **1.** strip off skin, rind or any form of covering from —vi. **2.** come off, as skin, rind —n. **3.** rind, skin —**peeled** a. inf. (of eyes) watchful

peen (pēn) n. **1.** end of hammer head opposite striking face, oft. rounded or wedge-shaped —vt. **2.** strike with peen of hammer or stream of metal shot

peep[1] (pēp) vi. **1.** look slyly or quickly —n. **2.** such a look —**'peeper** n. **1.** person who peeps **2.** (oft. pl.) sl. eye —**Peeping Tom** man who furtively observes women undressing; voyeur —**'peepshow** n. box with peephole through which series of pictures can be seen

peep[2] (pēp) vi. **1.** cry, as chick, chirp —n. **2.** such a cry

peer[1] (pēr) n. **1.** nobleman **2.** one of the same rank ('**peeress** fem.) —**'peerage** n. **1.** body of peers **2.** rank of peer —**'peerless** a. without match or equal —**peer group** social group composed of individuals of approximately same age

peer[2] (pēr) vi. look closely and intently

peevish ('pēvish) a. **1.** fretful **2.** irritable —**peeved** a. inf. sulky, irritated —**'peevishly** adv. —**'peevishness** n. annoyance

peewit or **pewit** ('pēwit) n. see LAPWING

peg (peg) n. **1.** nail or pin for joining, fastening, marking etc. **2.** (mark of) level, standard etc. —vt. **3.** fasten with pegs **4.** stabilize (prices) **5.** inf. throw —vi. **6.** (with away) persevere (-gg-) —**'pegboard** n. **1.** board having pattern of holes into which small pegs can be fitted, used for playing certain games or keeping score **2.** see solitaire (sense 3) *at* SOLITARY **3.** hardboard perforated by pattern of holes in which articles may be hung, as for display —**peg leg** *inf.* **1.** artificial leg, *esp.* one made of wood **2.** person with artificial leg —**peg out** *sl.* die

peignoir (pān'wär) *n.* lady's dressing gown, jacket, wrapper

pejorative (pi'jörətiv, -'jor-; 'pējər-) *a.* (of words *etc.*) with unpleasant, disparaging connotation

Pekingese *or* **Pekinese** (pēkə'nēz, pēking'ēz) *n.* small Chinese dog (*also* **peke**) —**Peking man** ('pē'king) extinct man of Pleistocene period

pelargonium (pelär'gōniəm) *n.* any of a genus of tender perennials commonly referred to as geraniums when grown as houseplants, with red, white or pink flowers

pelf (pelf) *n. contemptuous* money; wealth

pelican ('pelikən) *n.* large, fish-eating water-fowl with large pouch beneath its bill

pelisse (pə'lēs, pe-) *n.* **1.** fur-trimmed cloak **2.** loose coat, usu. fur-trimmed, worn *esp.* by women in early 19th cent.

pellagra (pə'lagrə, -'lā-) *n.* disease caused by dietary deficiency of niacin, characterized by scaling of skin *etc.*

pellet ('pelit) *n.* little ball, pill

pellicle ('pelikəl) *n.* thin skin, film

pell-mell ('pel'mel) *adv.* in utter confusion, headlong

pellucid (pə'loōsid) *a.* **1.** translucent **2.** clear —**pellu'cidity** *n.*

pelmet

pelmet ('pelmit) *n.* ornamental drapery or board, concealing curtain rail

pelt¹ (pelt) *vt.* **1.** strike with missiles —*vi.* **2.** throw missiles **3.** rush **4.** fall persistently, as rain

pelt² (pelt) *n.* raw hide or skin

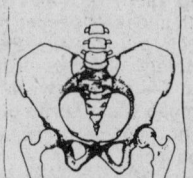

pelvis

pelvis ('pelvis) *n.* basin-shaped structure holding some abdominal organs in skeleton of vertebrate (*pl.* **-es, -ves** (-vēz)) —**'pelvic** *a.* pert. to pelvis —**pelvic girdle** bony arch supporting hind or lower limbs of vertebrate

pemmican *or* **pemican** ('pemikən) *n.* **1.** concentrated food used by Amerindians made of pounded lean dried meat mixed with smelted fat **2.** similar preparation used for emergency rations

pemphigus vulgaris ('pemfigəs vul'gäris) serious skin disorder of adult life of unknown origin

pen¹ (pen) *n.* **1.** instrument for writing —*vt.* **2.** compose **3.** write (**-nn-**) —**'penknife** *n.* small knife with one or more blades that fold into

handle —**'penmanship** *n.* style or technique of writing by hand —**pen name** author's pseudonym —**pen pal** person with whom one exchanges letters, oft. person in another country whom one has not met —**'pen-pusher** *n.* clerk involved with boring paperwork

pen² (pen) *n.* **1.** small enclosure, as for sheep —*vt.* **2.** put, keep in enclosure (**-nn-**)

pen³ (pen) *n.* female swan

Pen. Peninsula

penal ('pēnəl) *a.* of, incurring, inflicting, punishment —**'penalize** *vt.* **1.** impose penalty on **2.** handicap —**penalty** ('penəlti) *n.* **1.** punishment for crime or offense **2.** forfeit **3.** *Sport* handicap or disadvantage imposed for infringement of rule *etc.* —**penal code** codified body of laws that relate to crime and punishment

penance ('penəns) *n.* **1.** suffering submitted to as expression of penitence **2.** repentance

penchant ('penchənt; *Fr.* pä'shä) *n.* inclination, decided taste

pencil ('pensəl) *n.* **1.** instrument as of graphite, for writing *etc.* **2.** *Optics* narrow beam of light —*vt.* **3.** paint or draw **4.** mark with pencil

pendant ('pendənt) *n.* hanging ornament —**'pendent** *a.* **1.** suspended, hanging **2.** projecting

pending ('pending) *prep.* **1.** during, until —*a.* **2.** awaiting settlement **3.** undecided **4.** imminent

pendulous ('penjələs, 'pendyələs, 'pendələs) *a.* hanging, swinging —**'pendulum** *n.* suspended weight swinging to and fro, *esp.* as regulator for clock

penetrate ('penitrāt) *vt.* **1.** enter into **2.** pierce **3.** arrive at the meaning of —**pene-tra'bility** *n.* quality of being penetrable —**'penetrable** *a.* capable of being entered or pierced —**'penetrating** *a.* **1.** sharp **2.** easily heard **3.** subtle **4.** quick to understand —**pene'tration** *n.* insight, acuteness —**'penetrative** *a.* **1.** piercing **2.** discerning —**'penetrator** *n.*

penguin ('penggwin) *n.* flightless, short-legged swimming bird

penicillin (peni'silin) *n.* antibiotic drug effective against a wide range of diseases, infections

peninsula (pi'ninsələ, -'ninchələ) *n.* portion of land nearly surrounded by water —**pe-'ninsular** *a.*

penis ('pēnis) *n.* male organ of copulation (and of urination) in man and mammals (*pl.* **-es, penes** ('pēnēz))

penitent ('penitənt) *a.* **1.** affected by sense of guilt —*n.* **2.** one that repents of sin —**'penitence** *n.* **1.** sorrow for sin **2.** repentance —**peni'tential** *a.* of, or expressing, penitence —**peni'tentiary** *a.* **1.** relating to penance, or to the rules of penance —*n.* **2.** prison

Pennacook ('penəkoŏk) *n.* (member of) Algonquian-speaking Amerindian people of New Hampshire (*pl.* **-cook, -s**)

pennant ('penənt) *n.* long narrow flag

pennon ('penən) *n.* small pointed or swallow-tailed flag

Pennsylvania (pensil'vānyə, -niə) *n.* Middle Atlantic state of the U.S.: ratified the Constitution in 1787. Abbrev.: **PA** (with ZIP code)

penny ('peni) *n.* bronze coin, 100th part of dollar (*pl.* **'pennies**) —**'penniless** *a.* **1.** having no money **2.** poor —**Penny Black** first postage stamp, issued in Brit. in 1840 —**penny-pincher** *n. inf.* person who is excessively careful with money —**penny-**

pinching *n./a.* —**penny-wise** *a.* greatly concerned with saving small sums of money —**bad penny** someone or something unwanted —**penny-wise and pound-foolish** careful about trifles but wasteful in large ventures —**pretty penny** considerable sum of money

Penobscot (pə'nobskot) *n.* member of Algonquian-speaking Amerindian people of Maine, member of Abnaki confederacy (*pl.* **-scot, -s**)

penology (pi'noləji) *n.* study of punishment and prevention of crime

pension¹ ('penchən) *n.* **1.** regular payment to old people, retired public officials, soldiers *etc.* —*vt.* **2.** grant pension to —**'pensioner** *n.*

pension² (pä'syö) *Fr.* **1.** continental boarding house **2.** (full) board

pensive ('pensiv) *a.* **1.** thoughtful with sadness **2.** wistful

penstemon (pen'stēmən) *n. see* PENTSTEMON

pent (pent) *a.* shut up, kept in —**pent-up** *a.* not released, repressed

penta- (*comb. form*) five, as in *pentagon, pentameter*

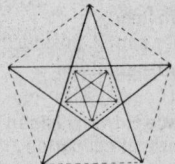

pentacle

pentacle ('pentəkəl) *n.* **1.** star-shaped figure with five points **2.** such figure used by Pythagoreans, black magicians *etc.* (*also* **'pentagram, 'pentangle**)

pentagon ('pentəgon) *n.* **1.** plane figure having five angles **2.** (**P-**) building in Virginia containing the U.S. Department of Defense **3.** (**P-**) the U.S. military establishment —**pen-'tagonal** *a.*

pentameter (pen'tamitər) *n.* verse of five metrical feet

Pentateuch ('pentətyoŏk, -toŏk) *n.* the first five books of the O.T. comprising Genesis, Exodus, Leviticus, Numbers and Deuteronomy

pentathlon (pen'tathlən, -lon) *n.* athletic contest of five events

pentatonic scale (pentə'tonik) *Mus.* scale consisting of five notes

Pentecost ('pentikost) *n.* **1.** Whitsuntide **2.** Jewish harvest festival on 50th day after Passover —**Pente'costal** *a.* **1.** denoting a mainly Protestant Christian movement, now with various organized forms, emphasizing the immediate presence of God in the Holy Spirit **2.** of Pentecost or influence of Holy Ghost —*n.* **3.** member of a Pentecostal Church —**Pente'costalist** *n./a.*

penthouse ('pent-hows) *n.* apartment or other structure on top, or top floor, of building

pentode ('pentōd) *n. Electron.* five-electrode thermionic valve, having anode, cathode and three grids

pentothal sodium ('pentəthöl) barbiturate used for anesthesia and to produce relaxed state in psychotherapy (*also* **sodium pentothal**)

pentstemon (pent'stēmən) *or* **penstemon** *n.* bright-flowered garden plant

penult ('pēnult, pi'nult) *n.* last syllable but one of word —**pe'nultimate** *a.* next before the last

penumbra (pi'numbrə) *n.* **1.** imperfect shadow **2.** in an eclipse, the partially shadowed region which surrounds the full shadow

penury ('penyəri) n. 1. extreme poverty 2. extreme scarcity —**pe'nurious** a. 1. niggardly, stingy 2. poor, scanty

peony ('pēəni) n. any of genus of N Amer. plants with showy red, pink or white flowers

people ('pēpəl) pl.n. 1. persons generally 2. community, nation 3. family —n. 4. race —vt. 5. stock with inhabitants, populate

pep (pep) n. 1. vigor 2. energy 3. enthusiasm —vt. (usu. with up) 4. impart energy to 5. speed up (-**pp**-) —**pep pill** inf. tablet containing stimulant —**pep talk** inf. enthusiastic talk designed to increase confidence, production etc.

pepper ('pepər) n. 1. fruit of climbing plant, which yields pungent aromatic spice 2. various slightly pungent vegetables, eg capsicum —vt. 3. season with pepper 4. sprinkle, dot 5. pelt with missiles —**'peppery** a. 1. having the qualities of pepper 2. irritable —**pepper-and-salt** a. 1. (of cloth etc.) marked with fine mixture of black and white 2. (of hair) streaked with gray —**'peppercorn** n. 1. dried pepper berry 2. something trifling —**pepper mill** hand mill used to grind peppercorns —**'peppermint** n. 1. plant noted for aromatic pungent liquor distilled from it 2. a sweet flavored with this

pepperidge ('pepərij) n. see **black gum** at BLACK

pepsin ('pepsin) n. enzyme produced in stomach, which, when activated by acid, breaks down proteins

peptic ('peptik) a. relating to digestion or digestive juices

peptide ('peptīd) n. 1. chain of two or more amino acids 2. antibiotic substance isolated from microorganisms

peptone ('peptōn) n. one of a group of compounds obtained by partial decomposition of proteins used commercially as food supplements

Pequot ('pēkwot) n. member of Algonquian-speaking Amerindian people of Connecticut

per (pər) prep. 1. for each 2. by 3. in manner of

per- (comb. form) through, thoroughly, as in perfect, perspicacious

peradventure ('pərədvenchər) obs. adv. 1. by chance; perhaps —n. 2. chance; doubt

perambulate (pə'rambyəlāt) vt. 1. walk through or over 2. traverse —vi. 3. walk about —**per'ambulator** n. baby carriage

per annum ('anəm) Lat. by the year

percale (pər'kāl) n. closely woven cotton fabric with smooth finish used for bedclothes

per capita ('kapitə) of or for each person

perceive (pər'sēv) vt. 1. obtain knowledge of through senses 2. observe 3. understand —**per'ceivable** a. —**percepti'bility** n. —**per'ceptible** a. discernible, recognizable —**per'ception** n. 1. faculty of perceiving 2. intuitive judgment —**per'ceptive** a.

percentage (pər'sentij) n. proportion or rate per hundred —**per cent** in each hundred —**per'centile** n. one of 99 actual or notional values of a variable dividing its distribution into 100 groups with equal frequencies (also **'centile**)

perception (pər'sepshən) n. see PERCEIVE

perch¹ (pərch) n. any of a family of freshwater fishes

perch² (pərch) n. 1. resting place, as for bird 2. formerly, measure of 5½ yards —vt. 3. place, as on perch —vi. 4. alight, settle on fixed body 5. roost 6. balance

perchance (pər'chans) adv. Poet. perhaps

percipient (pər'sipiənt) a. 1. having faculty of perception 2. perceiving —n. 3. one who perceives

percolate ('pərkəlāt) v. 1. pass through fine mesh as liquor 2. permeate 3. filter —**perco'lation** n. —**'percolator** n. coffeepot with filter

percussion (pər'kushən) n. 1. collision 2. impact 3. vibratory shock —**per'cussionist** n. Mus. person who plays percussion instrument —**percussion cap** detonator consisting of paper or thin metal cap containing material that explodes when struck —**percussion instrument** one played by being struck, eg drum, cymbals, piano

perdition (pər'dishən) n. spiritual ruin

peregrinate ('perigrināt) vi. travel about, roam —**peregri'nation** n.

peregrine ('perigrin) n. type of falcon

peremptory (pə'remptəri) a. 1. authoritative, imperious 2. forbidding debate 3. decisive

perennial (pə'reniəl) a. 1. lasting through the years 2. perpetual, unfailing —n. 3. plant living at least 3 years —**pe'rennially** adv.

perfect ('pərfikt) a. 1. complete 2. finished 3. whole 4. unspoilt 5. faultless 6. correct, precise 7. excellent 8. of highest quality —n. 9. tense denoting a complete act —vt. (pər'fekt) 10. improve 11. finish 12. make skillful —**per'fectable** a. capable of becoming perfect —**per'fection** n. 1. state of being perfect 2. faultlessness —**per'fectionism** n. 1. Philos. doctrine that man can attain perfection in this life 2. demand for highest standard of excellence —**per'fectionist** n. —**'perfectly** adv. —**perfect number** number that is the sum of all its divisors, eg 6 and 28 —**perfect participle** past participle

perfidy ('pərfidi) n. treachery, disloyalty —**per'fidious** a.

perforate ('pərfərāt) vt. make holes in, penetrate —**perfo'ration** n.

perforce (pər'förs) adv. of necessity

perform (pər'förm) vt. 1. bring to completion 2. accomplish; fulfill 3. represent on stage —vi. 4. function 5. act part 6. play, as on musical instrument —**per'formance** n. —**per'former** n.

perfume ('pərfyoom) n. 1. agreeable scent 2. fragrance —vt. (pər'fyoom) 3. imbue with an agreeable odor, scent —**per'fumer** n. —**per'fumery** n. perfumes in general

perfunctory (pər'fungktəri) a. 1. superficial 2. hasty 3. done indifferently

pergola ('pərgələ) n. 1. area covered by plants growing on trellis 2. the trellis

perhaps (pər'haps; inf. praps) adv. possibly

peri- (comb. form) round, as in perimeter, period, periphrasis

perianth ('perianth) n. outer part of flower, consisting of calyx and corolla

pericardium (peri'kärdiəm) n. membrane enclosing the heart (pl. -**dia** (-diə)) —**pericardiac** or **pericardial** a. —**pericar'ditis** n. inflammation of pericardium

peridot ('peridō) n. yellowish-green semiprecious stone, a variety of chrysolite

perigee ('perijē) n. point in its orbit around earth when moon or satellite is nearest earth

perihelion (peri'hēlyən) n. point in orbit of planet or comet when nearest to sun (pl. -**lia** (-lyə))

peril ('peril) n. 1. danger 2. exposure to injury —**'perilous** a. full of peril, hazardous

perimeter (pə'rimitər) n. 1. the total outer boundary of a space or structure 2. boundary

of a figure —**perimeter fence** enclosure for the space bound

perineum (peri'nēəm) n. 1. region of body between anus and genital organs 2. surface of human trunk between thighs (pl. -**nea** (-'nēə))

period ('pēəriəd) n. 1. particular portion of time 2. a series of years 3. single occurrence of menstruation 4. cycle 5. conclusion 6. full stop (.) at end of sentence 7. complete sentence —a. 8. (of furniture, dress, play etc.) belonging to particular time in history —**peri'odic** a. recurring at regular intervals —**peri'odical** a./n. 1. (of) publication issued at regular intervals —a. 2. of a period 3. periodic —**perio'dicity** n. —**periodic law** principle that chemical properties of elements are periodic functions of their atomic numbers —**periodic table** tabular organization of the properties of elements in horizontal rows (periods) and vertical columns (groups)

peripatetic (peripə'tetik) a. itinerant, walking, traveling about

periphery (pə'rifəri) n. 1. circumference 2. surface, outside —**pe'ripheral** a. 1. minor, unimportant 2. of periphery

periphrasis (pə'rifrəsis) n. 1. roundabout speech or phrase 2. circumlocution (pl. -**rases** (-rəsēz)) —**peri'phrastic** a.

periscope ('periskōp) n. instrument, used esp. in submarines, for giving view of objects on different level —**periscopic** (peri'skopik) a.

perish ('perish) vi. 1. die, waste away 2. decay, rot —**perisha'bility** n. —**'perishable** a. 1. that will not last long —pl.n. 2. perishable food —**'perishing** a. 1. inf. (of weather etc.) extremely cold 2. sl. confounded

peristalsis (peri'stölsis, -'stolsis, -'stalsis) n. succession of waves of involuntary muscular contraction of various bodily tubes, esp. of alimentary tract (pl. -**ses** (-sēz))

peristyle ('peristīl) n. 1. range of pillars surrounding building, square etc. 2. court within this

peritoneum (peritə'nēəm) n. membrane lining internal surface of abdomen (pl. -**s**, -**nea** (-'nēə)) —**perito'nitis** n. inflammation of peritoneum

periwig ('periwig) n. Hist. wig

periwinkle ('periwingkəl) n. 1. myrtle 2. small edible shellfish (also **'winkle**)

perjure ('pərjər) vt. render (oneself) guilty of perjury —**'perjury** n. 1. crime of false testimony on oath 2. false swearing

perk¹ (pərk) n. inf. perquisite

perk² (pərk) vi. inf. (of coffee) percolate

perky ('pərki) a. lively, cheerful, jaunty, gay —**perk up** make, become cheerful

perm (pərm) n. inf. see PERMANENT (sense 3)

permafrost ('pərməfrost) n. permanently frozen ground

permanent ('pərmənənt) a. 1. continuing in same state 2. lasting —n. 3. (treatment of hair producing) long-lasting style (also **permanent wave**) —**'permanence** or **'permanency** n. fixedness

permanganate (pər'manggənāt) n. salt of an acid of manganese

permeate ('pərmiāt) vt. 1. pervade, saturate 2. pass through pores of —**'permeable** a. admitting of passage of fluids

Permian ('pərmiən) a. 1. of last period of Paleozoic era, between Carboniferous and Triassic periods —n. 2. Permian period or rock system

permit (pər'mit) vt. 1. allow 2. give leave to (-**tt**-) —n. ('pərmit) 3. warrant or license to

do something **4.** written permission —**per-
'missible** a. allowable —**per'mission** n.
authorization, leave, liberty —**per'missive** a.
(too) tolerant, lenient, esp. sexually

permute (pər'myōōt) vt. change sequence of
—**permu'tation** n. **1.** mutual transference **2.**
Math. arrangement of a number of quan-
tities in every possible order

pernicious (pər'nishəs) a. **1.** wicked or
mischievous **2.** extremely hurtful **3.** having
quality of destroying or injuring —**pernicious anemia** form of anemia characterized
by lesions of spinal cord, weakness, diarrhea
etc.

pernickety (pər'nikiti) a. inf. fussy, fastidious about trifles

pernio (pər'niō) n. chilblain (pl. **perniones**
(pərni'ōnēz))

peroration (perər'āshən) n. concluding part
of oration —**'perorate** vi.

peroxide (pə'roksīd) n. **1.** oxide of a given
base containing greatest quantity of oxygen
2. see **hydrogen peroxide** at HYDROGEN

perpendicular

perpendicular (pərpən'dikyələr) a. **1.** at
right angles to the plane of the horizon **2.** at
right angles to given line or surface **3.** of
style of English Gothic architecture characterized by vertical lines **4.** exactly upright
—n. **5.** line falling at right angles on another
line or plane

perpetrate ('pərpitrāt) vt. perform or be
responsible for (deception, crime etc.)
—**perpe'tration** n. —**'perpetrator** n.

perpetual (pər'pechōōəl) a. **1.** continuous **2.**
lasting for ever —**per'petually** adv. —**per-
'petuate** vt. **1.** make perpetual **2.** not allow to
be forgotten —**perpetu'ation** n. —**perpetuity**
(pərpə'tyōōiti, -'tōō-) n. —**perpetual motion**
motion of hypothetical mechanism that
continues indefinitely without any external
source of energy

perplex (pər'pleks) vt. **1.** puzzle, bewilder **2.**
make difficult to understand —**per'plexity** n.
puzzled or tangled state

perquisite ('pərkwizit) n. **1.** any incidental
benefit from a certain type of employment **2.**
casual payment in addition to salary

Perrier water ('periā) trade name for
mineral water, orig. from France

perry ('peri) n. fermented drink made from
pears

per se (sā) Lat. by or in itself

persecute ('pərsikyōōt) vt. **1.** oppress because of race, religion etc. **2.** subject to
persistent ill-treatment —**perse'cution** n.
—**'persecutor** n.

persevere (pərsi'vēər) vi. (oft. with in)
persist, maintain effort —**perse'verance** n.
persistence

Persia ('pərzhə) n. former name of IRAN
—**'Persian** a. **1.** of ancient Persia or modern
Iran —n. **2.** native or inhabitant of modern
Iran; Iranian **3.** language of Iran or Persia in
any of ancient or modern forms —**Persian
cat** long-haired domestic cat —**Persian lamb**
see KARAKUL

persimmon (pər'simən) n. **1.** any of several
tropical trees typically having hard wood **2.**
its fruit

persist (pər'sist) vi. (oft. with in) continue in
spite of obstacles or objections —**per'sistence** or **per'sistency** n. —**per'sistent** a. **1.**
persisting **2.** steady **3.** persevering **4.** lasting

person ('pərsən) n. **1.** individual (human)
being **2.** body of human being **3.** Gram.
classification, or one of the classes, of
pronouns and verb forms according to the
person speaking, spoken to, or spoken of
—**per'sona** n. assumed character (pl. **-nae**
(-nē) —**'personable** a. good-looking —**'personage** n. notable person —**'personal** a. **1.**
individual, private, or one's own **2.** of,
relating to grammatical person —**perso'nality** n. **1.** distinctive character **2.** a celebrity
—**'personalize** vt. **1.** endow with personal or
individual qualities **2.** mark with person's
initials, name etc. **3.** take personally **4.**
personify —**'personally** adv. in person
—**'personalty** n. personal property —**'personate** vt. pass oneself off as —**perso'nation**
n. —**personal property** Law all property
except land and interests in land that pass to
heir —**in person** actually present

persona non grata (pər'sōnə non 'gratə,
'grätə) Lat. **1.** unacceptable or unwelcome
person **2.** diplomat who is not acceptable to
government to whom he is accredited (pl.
personae non gratae (pər'sōnē non 'gratē,
'grätē))

personify (pər'sonifī) vt. **1.** represent as
person **2.** typify (-**ified**, -**ifying**) —**personifi-
'cation** n.

personnel (pərsə'nel) n. **1.** staff employed in
a service or institution **2.** department that
interviews or keeps records of employees

perspective (pər'spektiv) n. **1.** mental view
2. art of drawing on flat surface to give effect
of solidity and relative distances and sizes **3.**
drawing in perspective

perspicacious (pərspi'kāshəs) a. having
quick mental insight —**perspicacity** (pərspi'kasiti) n.

perspicuous (pər'spikyōōəs) a. **1.** clearly
expressed **2.** lucid **3.** plain **4.** obvious
—**perspi'cuity** n.

perspire (pər'spīər) vi. sweat —**perspiration**
(pərspə'rāshən) n. sweating

persuade (pər'swād) vt. **1.** bring (one to do
something) by argument, charm etc. **2.**
convince —**per'suasion** n. **1.** art, act of
persuading **2.** way of thinking or belief
—**per'suasive** a.

pert (pərt) a. forward, saucy

pertain (pər'tān) vi. (oft. with to) **1.** belong,
relate, have reference (to) **2.** concern

pertinacious (pərti'nāshəs) a. obstinate,
persistent —**pertinacity** (pərti'nasiti) or
perti'naciousness n. doggedness, resolution

pertinent ('pərtinənt) a. relating to the
matter at hand —**'pertinence** or **'pertinency**
n. relevance

perturb (pər'tərb) vt. **1.** disturb greatly **2.**
alarm —**per'turbable** a. —**pertur'bation** n.
agitation of mind

pertussis (pər'tusis) n. whooping cough

Peru (pə'rōō) n. country in South America
bounded east by Brazil and Bolivia, south by
Chile, west by the Atlantic Ocean and
Ecuador and north by Colombia —**Pe'ruvian**
n./a. (native or inhabitant) of Peru

peruke (pə'rōōk) n. Hist. wig

peruse (pə'rōōz) vt. read, esp. in slow and
careful, or leisurely, manner —**pe'rusal** n.

pervade (pər'vād) vt. **1.** spread through **2.** be
rife among —**per'vasion** n. —**per'vasive** a.

pervert (pər'vərt) vt. **1.** turn to wrong use **2.**
lead astray —n. ('pərvərt) **3.** one who shows
unhealthy abnormality, esp. in sexual mat-

ters —**per'verse** a. **1.** obstinately or unrea-
sonably wrong **2.** self-willed **3.** headstrong **4.**
wayward —**per'versely** adv. —**per'version**
n.

pervious ('pərviəs) a. **1.** permeable **2.**
penetrable, giving passage

Pesach ('päsäk) n. see PASSOVER

peseta (pə'sātə; pä'sätä) n. monetary unit of
Spain

peso ('pāsō) n. monetary unit of Mexico etc.
(pl. **pesos** ('pāsōz; Sp. 'päsos))

pessary ('pesəri) n. **1.** instrument used to
support mouth and neck of uterus **2.**
appliance to prevent conception **3.** vaginal
suppository

pessimism ('pesimizəm) n. **1.** tendency to
see the worst side of things **2.** theory that
everything turns to evil —**'pessimist** n.
—**pessi'mistic** a.

pest (pest) n. **1.** troublesome or harmful
thing, person or insect **2.** rare plague
—**'pesticide** n. chemical for killing pests,
esp. insects —**pes'tiferous** a. **1.** troublesome
2. bringing plague

pester ('pestər) vt. trouble or vex persistently, harass

pestilence ('pestiləns) n. epidemic disease,
esp. bubonic plague —**'pestilent** a. **1.**
troublesome **2.** deadly —**pesti'lential** a.

pestle ('pesəl) n. **1.** instrument with which
things are pounded in a mortar —v. **2.** pound
with pestle

pet[1] (pet) n. **1.** animal kept for companionship etc. **2.** person regarded with affection
—vt. **3.** make pet of —v. **4.** inf. hug, embrace,
fondle (**-tt-**)

pet[2] (pet) n. fit of sulkiness, esp. at what is felt
to be a slight; pique —**'pettish** a. peevish,
petulant

Pet. Bible Peter

petal ('petəl) n. white or colored leaflike part
of flower —**'petaled** a.

petard (pi'tärd) n. formerly, an explosive
device

peter ('pētər) vi. —**peter out** inf. disappear,
lose power gradually

Peter ('pētər) n. Bible 21st and 22nd books of
the N.T., epistles written by St. Peter to the
Jews between 60 and 70 A.D.

Peter Pan youthful or immature man

Peter principle notion that in every
hierarchy each employee tends to rise to his
level of incompetence, thus every post tends
to be filled by a person incompetent to
execute its duties

pethidine ('pethidēn) n. water-soluble drug
used as analgesic (also **me'peridine**)

petiole ('petiōl) n. **1.** stalk by which leaf is
attached to plant **2.** Zool. slender stalk or
stem, as between thorax and abdomen of
ants —**'petiolate** a.

petit ('peti) a. Law small, petty —**petit
bourgeois** n. **1.** section of middle class with
lowest social status, as shopkeepers etc. **2.**
member of this stratum (pl. **petits bourgeois**
('peti 'bōōərzhwäz)) (also **petite bourgeoisie, petty bourgeoisie**) —a. **3.** of petit
bourgeois, esp. indicating sense of self-
righteousness etc. —**petit four** any of various
small fancy cakes and biscuits (pl. **petits
fours** ('peti 'förz)) —**petit jury** jury of 12
persons impaneled to determine facts of
case and decide issue pursuant to direction
of court on points of law (also **petty jury**)
—**petit mal** (mal) mild form of epilepsy
characterized by periods of impairment or
loss of consciousness for up to 30 seconds
—**petit point 1.** small diagonal needlepoint
stitch used for fine detail **2.** work done with
such stitches

petite (pə'tēt) *a.* (of women) small, dainty

petition (pi'tishən) *n.* 1. entreaty, request, *esp.* one presented to sovereign or parliament —*vt.* 2. present petition to —**pe'titionary** *a.*

petrel ('petrəl) *n.* any of a family of sea birds

petrify ('petrifī) *vt.* 1. turn to stone 2. *fig.* make motionless with fear 3. make dumb with amazement (**-ified, -ifying**) —**petri'faction** *or* **petrifi'cation** *n.*

petrochemical (petrō'kemikəl) *n.* 1. any substance, such as acetone or ethanol, obtained from petroleum —*a.* 2. of petrochemicals; related to petrochemistry —**pet-ro'chemistry** *n.*

petrocurrency ('petrōkurənsi) *n.* currency oil-producing countries acquire as profit from oil sales to other countries

petrodollar ('petrōdolər) *n.* money earned by country by exporting of petroleum

petrolatum (petrə'lātəm) *n.* translucent gelatinous substance obtained from petroleum

petroleum (pə'trōliəm) *n.* mineral oil used as a lubricant, rust preventive in machinery, in manufacturing cosmetics and in medicine as a protective dressing —**petroleum jelly** *see* PETROLATUM

petrology (pe'troləji) *n.* study of rocks and their structure

petticoat ('petikōt) *n.* women's undergarment worn under skirts, dresses *etc.*

pettifogger ('petifogər) *n.* 1. low-class lawyer 2. one given to mean dealing in small matters

petty ('peti) *a.* 1. unimportant, trivial 2. small-minded, mean 3. on a small scale —**petty cash** cash kept by firm to pay minor incidental expenses —**petty jury** *see* **petit jury** *at* PETIT —**petty officer** noncommissioned officer in Navy

petulant ('pechələnt) *a.* given to small fits of temper, peevish —**'petulance** *or* **'petulancy** *n.*

petunia (pi'tyōōnyə, -'tōōnyə) *n.* any plant of tropical Amer. genus with funnel-shaped purple or white flowers

pew (pyōō) *n.* 1. fixed seat in church 2. *inf.* chair, seat

pewit *or* **peewit** ('pēwit) *n. see* LAPWING

pewter ('pyōōtər) *n.* 1. alloy of tin and lead 2. ware made of this

peyote (pā'ōti) *or* **peyotl** (pā'ōtəl) *n. see* MESCAL

pH potential of hydrogen; measure of acidity or alkalinity of solution

PHA Public Housing Administration

phagocyte ('fagəsīt) *n.* blood cell that ingests and destroys foreign particles, bacteria and other cells —**phagocytic** (fagə'sitik) *a.*

phagocytosis (fagəsi'tōsis) *n.* ingestion of small particles by certain cells, *eg* leukocytes

phalanx ('fālangks) *n.* body of men formed in close array (*pl.* **-es, phalanges** (fa'lanjēz))

phalarope ('falərōp) *n.* any of a family of small wading birds

phallus ('faləs) *n.* 1. penis 2. symbol of it used in primitive rites (*pl.* **-es, -li** (-lī)) —**'phallic** *a.* —**'phallicism** *n.*

phantasm ('fantazəm) *n.* 1. vision of absent person 2. illusion —**phantasma'goria** *or* **phan'tasmagory** *n.* 1. crowd of dim or unreal figures 2. exhibition of illusions —**phan'tasmal** *a.* —**'phantasy** *n. see* FANTASY

phantom ('fantəm) *n.* 1. apparition, specter, ghost 2. fancied vision

Pharaoh ('fãərō) *n.* title of ancient Egyptian kings

Pharisee ('farisē) *n.* 1. sanctimonious person 2. hypocrite —**phari'saic(al)** *a.*

pharmaceutical (färmə'sōōtikəl) *or* **pharmaceutic** *a.* of pharmacy —**pharma'ceutics** *pl.n.* (*with sing. v.*) science of pharmacy —**'pharmacist** *n.* person qualified to dispense drugs —**pharma'cology** *n.* science concerned with the development of drugs, their use and the mechanism of their action —**pharmacopeia** (färməkə'pēə) *n.* official book with list and directions for use of drugs —**'pharmacy** *n.* 1. preparation and dispensing of drugs 2. dispensary

pharos ('fãəros) *n.* marine lighthouse or beacon

pharynx ('faringks) *n.* cavity forming back part of mouth and terminating in gullet (*pl.* **pharynges** (fə'rinjēz)) —**pharyn'geal** *or* **pha'ryngal** *a.* —**pharyn'gitis** *n.* inflammation of pharynx

phase (fāz) *n.* 1. any distinct or characteristic period or stage in a development or chain of events —*vt.* 2. arrange, execute in stages or to coincide with something else

Ph.D. Doctor of Philosophy (*also* **D.Phil.**)

pheasant ('fezənt) *n.* any of various game birds with bright plumage

pheno- *or before vowel* **phen-** (*comb. form*) 1. showing, manifesting, as in *phenotype* 2. indicating that molecule contains benzene rings, as in *phenobarbital*

phenobarbital (fēnō'bärbitōl) *n.* drug inducing sleep

phenol ('fēnōl) *n.* carbolic acid

phenomenon (fi'nominon) *n.* 1. anything appearing or observed 2. remarkable person or thing (*pl.* **phenomena** (fi'nominə)) —**phe-'nomenal** *a.* 1. relating to phenomena 2. remarkable 3. recognizable or evidenced by senses —**phe'nomenalism** *n.* 1. theory that only phenomena are real and can be known 2. tendency to think about things as phenomena only —**phe'nomenalist** *n./a.*

pheromone ('ferəmōn) *n.* substance secreted by one insect which affects the behavior of another insect of the same species

phew (fyōō, fōō) *interj.* exclamation of relief, surprise *etc.*

phi (fī) *n.* 21st letter in Gr. alphabet (Φ, φ) (*pl.* **-s**)

phial ('fīəl) *n.* small bottle for medicine *etc.*

Phil. 1. *Bible* Philippians 2. Philippines 3. Philadelphia

philander (fi'landər) *vi.* (of man) flirt with women

philanthropy (fi'lanthrəpi) *n.* 1. practice of doing good to one's fellow men 2. love of mankind —**philan'thropic** *a.* loving mankind, benevolent —**phi'lanthropist** *or* **'philanthrope** *n.*

philately (fi'latəli) *n.* stamp collecting —**phila'telic** *a.* —**phi'latelist** *n.*

-phile *or* **-phil** (*comb. form*) person or thing having fondness for something specified, as in *bibliophile*

Philemon (fi'lēmon, fī-) *n. Bible* 18th book of the N.T., epistle written by St. Paul during his imprisonment addressed to Philemon

philharmonic (filər'monik, filhär-, filär-) *a.* 1. fond of music 2. (**P-** *when part of name*) denoting orchestra, choir *etc.* devoted to music

philhellene (fil'helēn) *n.* 1. lover of Greece and Greek culture 2. *European hist.* supporter of cause of Greek national independence —**philhel'lenic** *a.*

Philippians (fi'lipiənz) *pl.n.* (*with sing. v.*) *Bible* 11th book of the N.T., epistle written by St. Paul to Christians of Philippi (Macedonia)

philippic (fi'lipik) *n.* bitter or impassioned speech of denunciation; invective

Philippines (fili'pēnz) *n.* country lying in the Pacific comprising 7100 islands and islets situated between 21° 25′ and 4° 23′ north latitude and between 116° and 127° east longitude —**Fili'pino** *a.* 1. of the Philippines —*n.* 2. native or inhabitant of the Philippines (*pl.* **-s**)

Philistine ('filistēn) *n.* 1. ignorant, smug person 2. member of non-Semitic people who inhabited ancient Philistia —*a.* 3. (*sometimes* **p-**) boorishly uncultured 4. of the ancient Philistines —**'philistinism** *n.*

Phillips ('filips) *n.* trade name for screw that has two slots crossing at center of head which can only be manipulated with a special screwdriver

philo- *or before vowel* **phil-** (*comb. form*) love of, as in *philology, philanthropic*

philology (fi'loləji) *n.* science of structure and development of languages —**philo'logical** *a.* —**phi'lologist** *or* **phi'lologer** *n.*

philos. 1. philosopher 2. philosophical

philosophy (fi'losəfi) *n.* 1. pursuit of wisdom 2. study of realities and general principles 3. system of theories on nature of things or on conduct 4. calmness of mind —**phi'losopher** *n.* one who studies, possesses or originates philosophy —**philo'sophic(al)** *a.* 1. of, like philosophy 2. wise, learned 3. calm, stoical —**phi'losophize** *vi.* 1. reason like philosopher 2. theorize 3. moralize

philter *or* **philtre** ('filtər) *n.* love potion

phlebitis (fli'bītis) *n.* inflammation of a vein

phlebotomy (fli'botəmi) *n.* the technique of withdrawing blood to treat disease (*also* **bloodletting**)

phlegm (flem) *n.* 1. viscid substance formed by mucous membrane and ejected by coughing *etc.* 2. calmness, sluggishness —**phlegmatic(al)** (fleg'matik(əl)) *a.* 1. not easily agitated 2. composed

phloem ('flōem) *n.* tissue in higher plants that conducts food substances to all parts of plant

phlogiston (flō'jistən) *n.* hypothetical substance formerly thought to be present in all combustible materials

phlox (floks) *n.* any of chiefly N Amer. genus of flowering plants (*pl.* **phlox, -es**)

phobia ('fōbiə) *n.* 1. fear, aversion 2. unreasoning dislike

-phobia (*n. comb. form*) extreme abnormal fear of or aversion to, as in *acrophobia, claustrophobia* —**-phobe** (*n. comb. form*) one that fears or hates, as in *xenophobe* —**-phobic** (*a. comb. form*)

Phoenician (fə'nishən, -'nēshən) *n.* 1. member of ancient Semitic people of NW Syria 2. extinct language of this people —*a.* 3. of Phoenicia, Phoenicians or their language

phoenix ('fēniks) *n.* 1. legendary bird 2. unique thing

phone (fōn) *n./v. inf.* telephone —**phone-in** *n. Rad., T.V.* program in which listeners' or viewers' questions, comments *etc.* are telephoned to studio and broadcast live as part of discussion

-phone (*n. comb. form*) 1. device giving off sound, as in *telephone* —(*a. comb. form*) 2. speaking a particular language, as in *Francophone* —**-phonic** (*a. comb. form*)

phoneme ('fōnēm) *n. Linguis.* one of set of speech sounds in a language, that serve to distinguish one word from another —**pho-'nemic** *a.* —**pho'nemics** *pl.n.* (*with sing. v.*) aspect of linguistics concerned with classification and analysis of phonemes of a language

phonetic (fə'netik) *a.* of vocal sounds —**phone'tician** *or* **'phonetist** *n.* —**pho'netics** *pl.n.* (*with sing. v.*) science of vocal sounds

phoney ('fōni) *a.* see PHONY

phono- *or before vowel* **phon-** (*comb. form*) sounds, as in *phonology*

phonograph ('fōnəgraf) *n.* instrument recording and reproducing sounds —**phono-'graphic** *a.*

phonology (fə'noləji) *n.* 1. study of speech sounds and their development 2. system of sounds in a language —**phono'logic(al)** *a.* —**pho'nologist** *n.*

phony *or* **phoney** ('fōni) *a. inf.* 1. counterfeit, sham, fraudulent 2. suspect

phosphatidyl choline (fosfə'tīdil 'kōlēn) *see* LECITHIN

phosphorus ('fosfərəs) *n.* 1. *Chem.* metalloid element *Symbol* P, at. wt. 31.0, at. no. 15 2. phosphorescent substance or body that shines in the dark —**'phosphate, 'phosphide, 'phosphite** *n.* compounds of phosphorus —**'phosphor** *n.* substance capable of emitting light when irradiated with particles of electromagnetic radiation —**phospho'resce** *vi.* exhibit phosphorescence —**phospho'rescence** *n.* faint glow in the dark —**phos'phoric** *a.* of or containing phosphorus with valence of five —**'phosphorous** *a.* of or containing phosphorus in trivalent state

photo ('fōtō) *n. inf.* photograph (*pl.* **-s**) —**photo finish** photo taken at end of race to show placing of contestants

photo- (*comb. form*) light, as in *photometer, photosynthesis*

photocell ('fōtəsel) *n.* device in which photoelectric or photovoltaic effect or photoconductivity is used to produce current or voltage when exposed to light or other electromagnetic radiation (*also* **photoelectric cell, electric eye**)

photochemistry (fōtō'kemistri) *n.* study of chemical action of light

photoconductivity (fōtōkonduk'tiviti) *n.* change in electrical conductivity of certain substances as a result of absorption of electromagnetic radiation

photocopy ('fōtəkopi) *n.* 1. photographic reproduction —*vt.* 2. make photocopy of —**'photocopier** *n.* instrument using lightsensitive photographic materials to reproduce written, printed or graphic work

photoelectricity (fōtōilek'trisiti) *n.* electricity produced or affected by action of light —**photoe'lectric** *a.* of electric or electronic effects caused by light or other electromagnetic radiation —**photoe'lectrically** *adv.* —**photoelectric cell** *see* PHOTOCELL

photoelectron (fōtōi'lektron) *n.* electron liberated from metallic surface by action of beam of light

photoflood ('fōtōflud) *n.* highly incandescent tungsten lamp used for indoor photography, television *etc.*

photogelatin (fōtō'jelətin) *n. see* COLLOTYPE

photogenic (fōtə'jenik) *a.* (*esp.* of person) capable of being photographed attractively

photograph ('fōtəgraf) *n.* 1. picture made by chemical action of light on sensitive film —*vt.* 2. take photograph of —**pho'tographer** *n.* —**photo'graphic** *a.* —**pho'tography** *n.*

photogravure (fōtəgrə'vyŏŏr, -'vŏŏr) *n.* 1. process of etching, product of photography 2. picture so reproduced

photolithography (fōtōli'thogrəfi) *n.* art of printing from photographs transferred to stone or metal plate —**photolitho'graphic** *a.*

photometer (fō'tomitər) *n.* instrument for measuring intensity of light —**pho'tometry** *n.*

photomontage (fōtōmon'tazh) *n.* 1. technique of producing composite picture by combining several photographs 2. composite picture so produced

photon ('fōton) *n.* pulse of light energy

photosensitive (fōtō'sensitiv) *a.* sensitive to electromagnetic radiation, *esp.* light —**photosensi'tivity** *n.* —**photo'sensitize** *vt.*

Photostat ('fōtəstat) *n.* 1. trade name for apparatus for obtaining direct, facsimile, photographic reproductions of documents, manuscripts, drawings *etc.*, without printing from negatives —*vt.* 2. take Photostat copy of

photosynthesis (fōtō'sinthisis) *n.* process by which green plant manufactures sugar from carbon dioxide and water in the presence of light

phototropism (fō'totrəpizəm) *n.* growth response of plant parts to stimulus of light

photovoltaic effect (fōtōvol'tāik) effect when electromagnetic radiation falls on thin film of one solid deposited on surface of dissimilar solid producing a difference in potential between the two materials

phrase (frāz) *n.* 1. group of words 2. pithy expression 3. mode of expression —*vt.* 4. express in words —**phraseology** (frāzi'oləji) *n.* manner of expression, choice of words —**phrasal verb** phrase consisting of verb and preposition, oft. with meaning different to the parts (*eg* take in)

phrenology (fri'noləji) *n.* 1. formerly, study of skull's shape 2. theory that character and mental powers are indicated by shape of skull —**phreno'logical** *a.* —**phre'nologist** *n.*

PHS Public Health Service

phthisis ('thīsis, 'thisis) *n. see* **tuberculosis** *at* TUBERCLE

phylactery (fi'laktəri) *n.* leather case containing religious texts worn by Jewish men

phylloxera (filok'sēərə, fi'loksərə) *n.* any of several plant lice which attack leaves and roots of grapevines

phylum ('fīləm) *n.* 1. major taxonomic division of animals and plants that contain one or more classes 2. group of related language families or linguistic stocks (*pl.* **-la** (-lə))

phys. 1. physical 2. physician 3. physics 4. physiological 5. physiology

physic ('fizik) *n.* 1. *rare* medicine, *esp.* cathartic —*pl.* 2. (*with sing. v.*) science of properties of matter and energy —**'physical** *a.* 1. bodily, as opposed to mental or moral 2. material 3. of physics of body —**'physically** *adv.* —**phy'sician** *n.* qualified medical practitioner —**'physicist** *n.* one skilled in, or student of physics —**physical change** alteration that does not affect the molecular composition of a substance —**physical chemistry** chemistry concerned with way in which physical properties of substances depend on their chemical structure, properties and reactions —**physical education** training and practice in sports, gymnastics *etc.* —**physical geography** branch of geography that deals with natural features of earth's surface —**physical science** any science concerned with nonliving matter, such as physics, chemistry *etc.* —**physical training** method of keeping fit by following course of bodily exercises

physiognomy (fizi'onəmi, fizi'ognəmi) *n.* 1. judging character by face 2. face 3. outward appearance of something

physiography (fizi'ogrəfi) *n.* science of the earth's surface —**physi'ographer** *n.*

physiology (fizi'oləji) *n.* science of normal function of living things —**physi'ologist** *n.*

physiotherapy (fiziō'therəpi) *n.* therapeutic use of physical means, as massage *etc.* —**physio'therapist** *n.*

physique (fi'zēk) *n.* bodily structure, constitution and development

pi[1] (pī) *n.* 1. 16th letter in Gr. alphabet (Π, π) 2. *Math.* ratio of circumference of circle to its diameter (*pl.* **-s**)

pi[2] *or* **pie** (pī) *n.* 1. jumbled pile of printer's type 2. jumbled mixture (*pl.* **pies**) —*vt.* 3. spill and mix (set type) indiscriminately 4. mix up (**pied** *pt./pp.*, **'piing, 'pieing** *pr.p.*)

pia mater ('pīə 'mātər) innermost of three membranes that cover brain and spinal cord

pian (pi'an, pi'än, pyän) *n. see* YAWS

piano (pi'anō) *n.* 1. (*orig.* **pianoforte** (pi'anəfört)) musical instrument with strings which are struck by hammers worked by keys (*pl.* **-s**) —*a./adv.* (pi'anō) 2. *Mus.* to be performed softly —**pia'nissimo** *a./adv. Mus.* to be performed very quietly —**'pianist** *n.* performer on piano

piazza (pi'azə; *It.* 'pyattsa) *n.* square, marketplace

pibroch ('pēbrok, -brokh) *n.* form of bagpipe music

pica ('pīkə) *n.* 1. printing type of 6 lines to the inch (*also* **em, pica em**) 2. formerly, size of type equal to 12 point 3. typewriter type size (10 letters to inch)

picador ('pikədör) *n.* mounted bullfighter with lance

picaresque (pikə'resk) *a.* (of fiction) episodic and dealing with adventures of rogues

piccalilli (pikə'lili) *n.* pickle of mixed vegetables in mustard sauce

piccaninny (pikə'nini) *n. see* PICKANINNY

piccolo ('pikəlō) *n.* woodwind instrument of flute family pitched an octave higher than flute (*pl.* **-s**)

pick[1] (pik) *vt.* 1. choose, select carefully 2. pluck, gather 3. peck at 4. pierce with something pointed 5. find occasion for —*n.* 6. act of picking 7. choicest part —**picked** *a.* selected with care —**'pickings** *pl.n.* 1. gleanings 2. odds and ends of profit —**'picky** *a. inf.* fussy; finicky —**'picklock** *n.* instrument for opening locks —**pick-me-up** *n. inf.* 1. tonic 2. stimulating drink —**'pickpocket** *n.* one who steals from another's pocket —**pick-up** *n.* 1. device for conversion of mechanical energy into electric signals, as in phonograph *etc.* 2. small truck —**pick on** find fault with —**pick up** 1. raise, lift 2. collect 3. improve, get better 4. accelerate

pick[2] (pik) *n.* tool with curved iron crossbar and wooden shaft, used for breaking up hard ground or masonry —**'pickax** *n.* pick

pickaback ('pikəbak) *n. see* PIGGYBACK

pickaninny *or* **piccaninny** (pikə'nini) *n. offens.* small Negro child

picket ('pikit) *n.* 1. prong, pointed stake 2. party of labor unionists posted to deter would-be workers during strike —*vt.* 3. post as picket 4. beset with pickets 5. tether to peg —**picket fence** fence of pickets —**picket line** line of people acting as pickets

pickle ('pikəl) *n.* 1. food preserved in brine, vinegar *etc.* 2. liquid used for preserving 3. awkward situation —*pl.* 4. pickled vegetables —*vt.* 5. preserve in pickle —**'pickled** *a. inf.* drunk

picnic ('piknik) *n.* 1. pleasure excursion during which food is consumed outdoors —*vi.* 2. take part in picnic (**'picnicked, 'picnicking**)

picot ('pēkō) *n.* any of pattern of small loops, as on lace

picric acid ('pikrik) powerful acid used in dyeing, medicine and as ingredient in certain explosives

Pict (pikt) *n.* member of ancient race of NE Scotland —**'Pictish** *a.*

pictograph ('piktəgraf) *n.* **1.** picture or symbol standing for word or group of words **2.** chart on which symbols are used to represent values (*also* **'pictogram**)

picture ('pikchər) *n.* **1.** drawing or painting **2.** mental image **3.** beautiful or picturesque object —*vt.* **4.** represent in, or as in, a picture —**pic'torial** *a.* **1.** of, in, with, painting or pictures **2.** graphic —*n.* **3.** newspaper with pictures —**pic'torially** *adv.* —**picturesque** (pikchə'resk) *a.* **1.** such as would be effective in picture **2.** striking, vivid —**picture card** *see* face card *at* FACE —**picture molding 1.** edge around framed picture **2.** molding or rail near top of wall from which pictures are hung (*also* **picture rail**) —**picture postcard** postcard with picture on one side —**picture window** large window having single pane of glass, usu. facing view

piddling ('pidling) *a. inf.* petty; trifling

pidgin ('pijin) *n.* lingua franca based on reduced English, French, Spanish or Portuguese vocabulary and smattering of native words —**Pidgin English 1.** language used by traders in Orient **2.** official language of Papua New Guinea

pie (pī) *n.* **1.** baked dish of meat or fruit *etc.*, usu. with pastry crust **2.** *obs.* magpie —**pie chart** circular graph divided into sectors proportional to magnitudes of quantities represented —**pie in the sky** *inf.* illusory hope of some future good

piebald ('pībōld) *a.* **1.** irregularly marked with black and white **2.** motley —*n.* **3.** piebald horse or other animal —**pied** *a.* **1.** piebald **2.** variegated

piece (pēs) *n.* **1.** bit, part, fragment **2.** single object **3.** literary or musical composition *etc.* **4.** *sl.* young woman **5.** small object used in checkers, chess *etc.* —*vt.* **6.** (*with* together) mend, put together —**piece goods** goods, *esp.* fabrics, made in standard widths and lengths —**'piecemeal** *adv.* by, in, or into pieces, a bit at a time —**'piecework** *n.* work paid for according to quantity produced

pièce de résistance (pyes də rāzēs'täs) *Fr.* principal item

pied-à-terre (pyätä'ter) *Fr.* apartment or other lodging for occasional use (*pl.* ***pieds-à-terre*** (pyätä'ter))

pier (pēər) *n.* **1.** structure running into sea as landing stage **2.** piece of solid upright masonry, *esp.* supporting bridge —**pier glass** tall narrow mirror designed to hang on wall between windows

pierce (pēərs) *vt.* **1.** make hole in **2.** make a way through —**'piercing** *a.* keen, penetrating

Pierce (pēərs) *n.* **Franklin.** the 14th President of the U.S. (1853-57)

Pierrot ('pēərō; *Fr.* pye'rō) *n.* pantomime character, clown

piety ('pīəti) *n.* **1.** godliness **2.** devoutness, goodness **3.** dutifulness —**'pietism** *n.* exaggerated or affected piety

piezoelectricity (pēəzōilek'trisiti) *n. Phys.* **1.** production of electricity or electric polarity by applying mechanical stress to certain crystals **2.** converse effect in which stress is produced in crystal as result of applied potential difference

piffle ('pifəl) *n. inf.* rubbish, twaddle, nonsense

pig (pig) *n.* **1.** wild or domesticated mammal killed for pork, ham, bacon **2.** *inf.* greedy, dirty person **3.** *sl.* policeman **4.** oblong mass of smelted metal —*vi.* **5.** (of sow) produce litter (**-gg-**) —**'piggery** *n.* **1.** place for keeping, breeding pigs **2.** greediness —**'piggish** *a.* **1.** dirty **2.** greedy **3.** stubborn —**'piggy** *n.* child's word for a pig —**'piglet** *n.* young pig —**piggy bank** child's bank shaped like pig with slot for coins —**pig-headed** *a.* obstinate —**pig iron** crude iron produced in blast furnace and poured into molds —**'pigskin** *n.* **1.** skin of domestic pig **2.** leather made of this skin **3.** *inf.* football —*a.* **4.** made of pigskin —**'pigsty** *or* **'pigpen** *n.* **1.** pen for pigs; sty **2.** untidy place —**'pigswill** *n.* waste food *etc.* fed to pigs (*also* **pig's wash**) —**'pigtail** *n.* braid of hair hanging from back or either side of head

pigeon ('pijin) *n.* **1.** bird of many wild and domesticated varieties, oft. trained to carry messages **2.** *inf.* concern, responsibility (*oft. in* **it's his, her** *etc.* **pigeon**) —**'pigeonhole** *n.* **1.** compartment for papers in desk *etc.* —*vt.* **2.** defer **3.** classify —**pigeon-toed** *a.* with feet, toes turned inward

piggyback ('pigibak) *or* **pickaback** *n.* ride on back of man or animal, given to child

pigment ('pigmənt) *n.* coloring matter, paint or dye —**pigmen'tation** *n.* **1.** coloration in plants, animals or man caused by presence of pigments **2.** deposition of pigment in animals, plants or man

pigmy ('pigmi) *see* PYGMY

pike[1] (pīk) *n.* any of various types of large, predatory freshwater fishes

pike[2] (pīk) *n.* spear formerly used by infantry

pilaf *or* **pilaff** (pi'läf) *n.* any Turkish dish based on sautéed rice simmered in broth and seasonings

pilaster ('pīlastər, pi'lastər) *n.* square column, usu. set in wall

pilau *or* **pilaw** (pi'lō) *n. see* PILAF

pilchard ('pilchərd) *n.* small sea fish like the herring

pile[1] (pīl) *n.* **1.** heap **2.** great mass of building —*vt.* **3.** heap (up), stack (load) —*vi.* **4.** (*with* in, out, off *etc.*) move in a group —**pile-up** *n. inf.* multiple collision of vehicles —**atomic pile** nuclear reactor —**pile up 1.** gather or be gathered in pile **2.** *inf.* (cause to) crash

pile[2] (pīl) *n.* beam driven into the ground, *esp.* as foundation for building in water or wet ground —**'piledriver** *n.* machine for driving down piles

pile[3] (pīl) *n.* **1.** nap of cloth, *esp.* of velvet, carpet *etc.* **2.** down

piles (pīlz) *pl.n.* varicosed veins of rectum, hemorrhoids

pilfer ('pilfər) *v.* steal in small quantities

pilgrim ('pilgrim) *n.* **1.** one who journeys to sacred place **2.** wanderer, wayfarer —**'pilgrimage** *n.* —**the Pilgrim Fathers** *or* **Pilgrims** English Puritans who founded Plymouth Colony in Massachusetts

pill (pil) *n.* **1.** small ball of medicine swallowed whole **2.** anything disagreeable which has to be endured —**'pilling** *n.* the gathering of fibers into small balls on the surface of a fabric —**'pillbox** *n.* **1.** small box for pills **2.** small round hat —**the pill** oral contraceptive

pillage ('pilij) *v.* **1.** plunder, ravage, sack —*n.* **2.** seizure of goods, *esp.* in war **3.** plunder

pillar ('pilər) *n.* **1.** slender, upright structure, column **2.** prominent supporter

pillion ('pilyən) *n.* seat, cushion, for passenger behind rider of motorcycle or horse

pillory ('piləri) *n.* **1.** frame with holes for head and hands in which offender was formerly confined and exposed to public abuse and ridicule —*vt.* **2.** expose to ridicule and abuse **3.** set in pillory (**'pilloried, 'pillorying**)

pillow ('pilō) *n.* **1.** cushion for the head, *esp.* in bed —*vt.* **2.** lay on, or as on, pillow —**'pillowcase** *or* **'pillowslip** *n.* removable washable cover for pillow

pilot ('pīlət) *n.* **1.** person qualified to fly an aircraft or spacecraft **2.** one qualified to take charge of ship entering or leaving harbor **3.** steersman **4.** guide —*a.* **5.** experimental and preliminary —*vt.* **6.** act as pilot to **7.** steer —**'pilotage** *n.* **1.** act of piloting ship or aircraft **2.** pilot's fee —**pilot fish** small fish of tropical and subtropical seas which oft. accompanies sharks —**pilot house** *Naut.* enclosed structure on bridge of vessel from which it can be navigated; wheelhouse —**pilot lamp** small light in electric circuit that lights when current is on —**pilot light 1.** small auxiliary flame lighting main burner in gas appliance *etc.* **2.** small electric light as indicator

pilpul ('pilpəl) *n. Judaism* **1.** intensive argument used in discussion of passages in the Talmud **2.** hairsplitting

pilule ('pilyōōl) *n.* small pill

Pima ('pēmə) *n.* **1.** (member of) Amerindian people of southern Arizona (*pl.* **-ma, -s**) **2.** the Uto-Aztecan language of the Pima —**Pima cotton** variety of cotton grown in southwestern U.S. used *esp.* for clothing

pimento (pi'mentō) *n.* **1.** allspice **2.** sweet red pepper (*pl.* **-s**) (*also* **pimiento** (pi'mentō, -'myen-))

pi-meson ('pī'mezon) *n. see* PION

pimp (pimp) *n.* **1.** one who solicits for prostitute —*vi.* **2.** act as pimp

pimpernel ('pimpərnel, -nəl) *n.* any of several plants with small scarlet, blue or white flowers closing in dull weather

pimple ('pimpəl) *n.* small pus-filled spot on skin

pin (pin) *n.* **1.** short thin piece of stiff wire with point and head, for fastening **2.** wooden or metal peg or rivet —*vt.* **3.** fasten with pin **4.** seize and hold fast (**-nn-**) —**'pinball machine** electrically operated table game, where small ball is shot through various obstacles —**'pincushion** *n.* small cushion in which pins are stuck ready for use —**'pinhead** *n.* **1.** head of pin **2.** something very small **3.** *sl.* stupid person —**pin money** trivial sum —**'pinpoint** *vt.* mark exactly —**'pinprick** *n.* **1.** slight puncture made (as if) by pin **2.** small irritation —*vt.* **3.** puncture (as if) with pin —**'pinstripe** *n.* in textiles, very narrow stripe in fabric or fabric itself —**pin tuck** narrow, ornamental fold, *esp.* on shirt fronts *etc.* —**'pinwheel** *n.* child's toy of paper or plastic mounted on stick designed to revolve when blown by wind —**on pins and needles** in a state of anxious suspense —**pins and needles** *inf.* tingling sensation in fingers *etc.* caused by return of normal blood circulation after its temporary impairment

pinafore ('pinəfōr) *n.* sleeveless garment fastened at back and worn as apron or dress

pince-nez (pans'nā; *Fr.* pēs'nā) *n.* eyeglasses kept on nose by spring (*pl.* **pince-nez**)

pincers

pincers ('pinsərz) *pl.n.* **1.** tool for gripping, composed of two limbs crossed and pivoted **2.** claws of lobster *etc.*

pinch (pinch) *vt.* **1.** nip, squeeze **2.** stint **3.** *inf.* steal **4.** *inf.* arrest —*n.* **5.** nip **6.** as much as can be taken up between finger and thumb **7.** stress **8.** emergency —**'pinchbar** *n.* crowbar that serves as fulcrum

pinchbeck ('pinchbek) *n.* **1.** zinc and copper alloy —*a.* **2.** counterfeit, flashy

pine[1] (pīn) *n.* 1. any of a family of evergreen coniferous trees 2. its wood —**pine cone** seed-producing structure of pine tree

pine[2] (pīn) *vi.* 1. yearn 2. waste away with grief

pineal ('pīniəl) *a.* shaped like pine cone —**pineal body** glandlike structure located in center of brain, function still unknown (*also* **epiphysis**)

pineapple ('pīnapəl) *n.* 1. tropical plant with spiny leaves bearing large edible fruit 2. the fruit

ping (ping) *n.* 1. short high-pitched resonant sound, as of bullet striking metal or sonar echo —*vi.* 2. make such noise

Ping-Pong ('pingpong) *n.* trade name for table tennis

pinion[1] ('pinyən) *n.* 1. bird's wing —*vt.* 2. disable or confine by binding wings, arms *etc.*

pinion[2] ('pinyən) *n.* small cogwheel

pink (pingk) *n.* 1. pale reddish color 2. garden plant 3. best condition, fitness —*a.* 4. of color pink —*vt.* 5. pierce 6. ornament with perforations or scalloped, indented edge —*vi.* 7. (of engine) knock

pinkie *or* **pinky** ('pingki) *n.* little finger

pinnace ('pinis) *n.* ship's tender

pinnacle ('pinəkəl) *n.* 1. highest pitch or point 2. mountain peak 3. pointed turret on buttress or roof

pinnate ('pināt) *a.* 1. like feather 2. (of compound leaves) having leaflets growing opposite each other in pairs on either side of stem

pinochle ('pēnukəl) *n.* card game usu. for four players in two partnerships played with deck of 48 cards comprising two each of ace, king, queen, jack, ten and nine in the four familiar suits the object of which is to score points by melding and taking tricks

piñon *or* **pinyon** ('pinyōn, -yon, -yən; pin'yon) *n.* any of various low-growing pines of western N Amer. with edible seeds (*pl.* **-s, piñones** (pin'yōnĕz)) —**piñon nuts** the edible seeds of the piñon

Pinot noir (pē'nō nwär) 1. red table wine 2. grape used to make this wine

pint (pīnt) *n.* liquid measure, half a quart, ⅛ gallon (.473 liter) —**pint-size** *or* **pint-sized** *a.* *inf.* very small

pintle ('pintəl) *n.* pivot pin

pinto ('pintō) *a.* 1. marked with patches of white; piebald —*n.* 2. pinto horse (*pl.* **-s**)

pin-up *n.* *inf.* picture of sexually attractive person, *esp.* (partly) naked

Pinyin ('pin'yin) *n.* official system of romanizing Chinese

pion ('pīon) *or* **pi-meson** *n.* *Phys.* meson having positive or negative charge and rest mass 273 times that of electron, or no charge and rest mass 264 times that of electron

pioneer (pīə'nēər) *n.* 1. explorer 2. early settler 3. originator 4. one of advance party preparing road for troops —*vi.* 5. act as pioneer or leader

pious ('pīəs) *a.* 1. devout 2. righteous

pip[1] (pip) *n.* seed in fruit

pip[2] (pip) *n.* 1. high-pitched sound used as time signal on radio 2. spot on playing cards, dice or dominoes 3. *inf.* star on junior officer's shoulder showing rank

pip[3] (pip) *n.* disease of fowl

pipe (pīp) *n.* 1. tube of metal or other material 2. tube with small bowl at end for smoking tobacco 3. musical instrument, whistle 4. wine cask —*pl.* 5. bagpipe —*v.* 6. play on pipe 7. utter (something) shrilly —*vt.* 8. convey by pipe 9. ornament with a piping

or fancy edging —'**piper** *n.* player of pipe or bagpipe —'**piping** *n.* 1. system of pipes 2. decoration of icing on cake 3. fancy edging or trimming on clothing 4. act or art of playing pipe, *esp.* bagpipe —'**pipeclay** *n.* 1. white clay used in manufacture of tobacco pipes *etc.* and for whitening leather *etc.* —*vt.* 2. whiten with pipeclay —**pipe cleaner** short length of thin wires twisted so as to hold tiny tufts of yarn: used to clean stem of tobacco pipe —**pipe dream** fanciful, impossible plan *etc.* —'**pipeline** *n.* 1. long pipe for transporting oil, water *etc.* 2. means of communication —**in the pipeline** 1. yet to come 2. in process of completion *etc.* —**pipe down** *sl.* stop talking, making noise *etc.* —**pipe up** 1. commence singing or playing musical instrument 2. speak up, *esp.* in shrill voice

pipette (pī'pet) *n.* slender glass tube to transfer fluids from one vessel to another

pipit ('pipit) *n.* any of various songbirds, *esp.* meadow pipit

pippin ('pipin) *n.* any of several kinds of apple

pipsqueak ('pipskwēk) *n.* *inf.* insignificant or contemptible person or thing

piquant ('pēkənt, -känt) *a.* 1. pungent 2. stimulating —'**piquancy** *or* '**piquantness** *n.*

pique (pēk) *n.* 1. feeling of injury, baffled curiosity or resentment —*vt.* 2. hurt pride of 3. irritate 4. stimulate

piqué (pi'kā, 'pēkā) *n.* firm cotton fabric with lengthwise corded effect

piranha (pi'ranyə, -'ränyə, -'ränə) *n.* any of various small voracious freshwater fishes of tropical Amer.

pirate ('pīrit) *n.* 1. sea robber 2. publisher *etc.* who infringes copyright —*n./a.* 3. (person) broadcasting illegally —*vt.* 4. use or reproduce (artistic work *etc.*) illicitly —'**piracy** *n.* —**piratic(al)** (pi'ratik(əl), pī-) *a.* —**piratically** (pi'ratikəli, pī-) *adv.*

piroshki *or* **pirozhki** (pirəsh'kē) *pl.n.* finger-sized, crescent-shaped pastries filled with savory mixture usu. served with Russian soups

pirouette (pirŏō'et) *n.* 1. spinning round on the toe —*vi.* 2. perform pirouette

Pisces ('pīsĕz, 'pī-) *pl.n.* (fishes) 12th sign of zodiac, operative *c.* Feb. 19th-Mar. 20th —**piscatorial** (piskə'töriəl) *or* **piscatory** ('piskətöri) *a.* of fishing or fishes —**piscine** ('pīsēn) *a.* of fish

pistachio (pi'stashiō, -'stäshiō) *n.* 1. small hard-shelled, greenish, sweet-tasting nut 2. tree producing it 3. pale green color (*pl.* **-s**)

pistil ('pistil) *n.* seed-bearing organ of flower —'**pistillate** *a.* (of plants) 1. having pistils but no anthers 2. producing pistils

pistol ('pistəl) *n.* 1. small firearm for one hand —*vt.* 2. shoot with pistol

piston ('pistən) *n.* in internal-combustion engine, steam engine *etc.*, cylindrical part propelled to and fro in hollow cylinder by pressure of gas *etc.* to convert reciprocating motion to rotation

pit[1] (pit) *n.* 1. deep hole in ground 2. mine or its shaft 3. depression 4. part of theater occupied by orchestra (*also* **orchestra pit**) 5. enclosure where animals were set to fight 6. servicing, refueling area at auto racecourse —*vt.* 7. set to fight, match 8. mark with small dents or scars (**-tt-**) —'**pitfall** *n.* 1. any hidden danger 2. covered pit for catching animals or men —'**pithead** *n.* top of mine shaft and buildings *etc.* around it

pit[2] (pit) *n.* 1. stone of cherry *etc.* —*vt.* 2. extract stone from (fruit) (**-tt-**)

pit-a-pat (pitiʹpat) *adv.* 1. with quick light

taps —*vi.* 2. make quick light taps (**-tt-**) —*n.* 3. such taps

Pitcairn Island ('pitkaərn) administrative district of New Zealand lying in the South Pacific equidistant from New Zealand and Panama

pitch[1] (pich) *vt.* 1. cast or throw 2. set up 3. set the key of (a tune) —*vi.* 4. fall headlong 5. (of ship) plunge lengthwise —*n.* 6. act of pitching 7. degree, height, intensity 8. slope 9. distance airscrew advances during one revolution 10. distance between threads of screw, teeth of saw *etc.* 11. acuteness of tone 12. *Sport* field of play 13. station of street vendor *etc.* 14. *inf.* persuasive sales talk —'**pitcher** *n.* *Baseball* player who delivers ball to batter —**pitched battle** 1. battle ensuing from deliberate choice of time and place 2. any fierce encounter, *esp.* one with large numbers —'**pitchfork** *n.* 1. fork for lifting hay *etc.* —*vt.* 2. throw with, as with, pitchfork —**pitch pipe** small pipe that sounds note or notes of standard frequency —**pitch in** 1. cooperate; contribute 2. begin energetically —**pitch into** 1. assail physically or verbally 2. get on with doing (something)

pitch[2] (pich) *n.* 1. dark sticky substance obtained from tar or turpentine —*vt.* 2. coat with this —'**pitchy** *a.* 1. covered with pitch 2. black as pitch —**pitch-black** *or* **pitch-dark** *a.* very dark —**pitch pine** any of various kinds of resinous pine

pitchblende ('pichblend) *n.* dark massive mineral yielding uranium and radium

pitcher ('pichər) *n.* large jug —**pitcher plant** insectivorous plant with leaves modified to form pitcher-like organs that attract and trap insects

pith (pith) *n.* 1. soft innermost tissue in a plant 2. essential substance, most important part —'**pithily** *adv.* —'**pithless** *a.* —'**pithy** *a.* 1. terse, cogent, concise 2. consisting of pith —**pith helmet** lightweight hat made of pith that protects wearer from sun (*also* to'pi)

piton ('pēton) *n.* *Mountaineering* metal spike that may be driven into crevice and used to secure rope *etc.*

pitressin (pi'tresin) *n.* *see* VASOPRESSIN

pittance ('pitəns) *n.* 1. small allowance 2. inadequate wages

pitter-patter ('pitərpatər) *n.* 1. sound of light rapid taps or pats, as of raindrops —*vi.* 2. make such sound —*adv.* 3. with such sound

pituitary (pi'tyŏōiteri, -'tŏō-) *a.* of, pert. to, endocrine gland at base of brain

pity ('piti) *n.* 1. sympathy, sorrow for others' suffering 2. regrettable fact —*vt.* 3. feel pity for ('**pitied**, '**pitying**) —'**piteous** *a.* 1. deserving pity 2. sad, wretched —'**pitiable** *a.* —'**pitiably** *adv.* —'**pitiful** *a.* 1. woeful 2. contemptible —'**pitiless** *a.* feeling no pity, hard, merciless

pityriasis rosea (piti'rīəsis rō'zēə) common skin disease of unknown origin marked by red scaly areas resembling ringworm

più (pyŏō) *adv.* *Mus.* more (quickly *etc.*)

pivot ('pivət) *n.* 1. shaft or pin on which thing turns —*vt.* 2. furnish with pivot —*vi.* 3. hinge on pivot —'**pivotal** *a.* 1. of, acting as, pivot 2. of crucial importance

pixie *or* **pixy** ('piksi) *n.* fairy

pizza ('pētsə) *n.* dish, *orig.* It., of baked disk of dough covered with wide variety of savory toppings —**pizzeria** (pētsə'rēə) *n.* place selling pizzas

pizzicato (pitsi'kätō) *a./n.* *Mus.* (note, passage) played by plucking string of violin *etc.* with finger

pl. 1. place 2. plate 3. plural

placard ('plakärd) *n.* 1. paper or card with

notice on one side for posting up or carrying; poster —*vt.* **2.** post placards on **3.** advertise, display on placards

placate ('plăkāt) *vt.* conciliate, pacify, appease —'**placatory** *a.*

place (plās) *n.* **1.** locality, spot **2.** position **3.** stead **4.** duty **5.** town, village, residence, buildings **6.** office, employment **7.** seat, space —*vt.* **8.** put in particular place **9.** set **10.** identify **11.** make (order, bet *etc.*) —'**placement** *n.* **1.** act of placing or state of being placed **2.** arrangement, position **3.** process of finding employment —**place kick** *Football* kick in which ball is placed in position before it is kicked —**place-kick** *v.* kick (ball) in this way —**place mat** small mat serving as individual table cover for person at meal —**place setting** flatware, tableware and glassware laid for one person at dining table

placebo (plə'sēbō) *n.* inactive substance given to unsuspecting patient as active drug (*pl.* **-s, -es**)

placenta (plə'sentə) *n.* organ formed in uterus during pregnancy, providing nutrients for fetus; afterbirth (*pl.* **-s, -tae** (-tē)) —pla'**cental** *a.*

placer ('plasər) *n.* surface sediment containing particles of gold or some other valuable mineral

placid ('plasid) *a.* **1.** calm **2.** equable —pla'**cidity** *n.* mildness, quiet

placket ('plakit) *n.* opening at top of skirt *etc.* fastened with buttons, zipper *etc.*

plagiarism ('plājərizəm) *n.* act of taking ideas, passages *etc.* from an author and presenting them as one's own —'**plagiarize** *v.*

plague (plāg) *n.* **1.** highly contagious disease, *esp.* bubonic plague **2.** *inf.* nuisance **3.** affliction —*vt.* **4.** trouble, annoy

plaice (plās) *n.* European flatfish

plaid (plad) *n.* **1.** long Highland cloak or shawl **2.** checked or tartan pattern

plain (plān) *a.* **1.** flat, level **2.** unobstructed, not intricate **3.** clear, obvious **4.** easily understood **5.** simple **6.** ordinary **7.** without decoration **8.** not beautiful —*n.* **9.** tract of level country —*adv.* **10.** clearly —'**plainly** *adv.* —'**plainness** *n.* —**plain chocolate** chocolate with slightly bitter flavor and dark color —**plain clothes** civilian dress, as opposed to uniform —**plain sailing** unobstructed course of action —**plain speaking** frankness, candor

plainsong ('plānsong) *n.* style of unison unaccompanied vocal music used in medieval Church

plaint (plānt) *n.* **1.** *Law* statement of complaint **2.** *obs.* lament —'**plaintiff** *n. Law* one who sues in court —'**plaintive** *a.* sad, mournful

plait (plăt, plāt) *n.* **1.** braid of hair, straw *etc.* —*vt.* **2.** form or weave into plaits

plan (plan) *n.* **1.** scheme **2.** way of proceeding **3.** project, design **4.** drawing of horizontal section **5.** diagram, map —*vt.* **6.** make plan of **7.** arrange beforehand (**-nn-**)

planchette (plan'shet) *n.* small board used in spiritualism

plane

plane[1] (plān) *n.* **1.** smooth surface **2.** a level **3.** carpenter's tool for smoothing wood —*vt.* **4.** make smooth with plane —*a.* **5.** perfectly flat or level —'**planar** *a.* **1.** of plane **2.** lying in one plane; flat —'**planer** *n.* planing machine

plane[2] (plān) *vi.* **1.** (of airplane) glide **2.** (of boat) rise and partly skim over water —*n.* **3.** wing of airplane **4.** airplane

plane[3] (plān) *n.* sycamore

planet ('planit) *n.* heavenly body revolving round the sun —'**planetary** *a.* of planets

planetarium (plani'teriəm) *n.* **1.** an apparatus that shows the movement of sun, moon, stars and planets by projecting lights on the inside of a dome **2.** building in which the apparatus is housed (*pl.* **-s, -ia** (-iə))

plangent ('planjənt) *a.* resounding

plank (plangk) *n.* **1.** long flat piece of sawn timber —*vt.* **2.** cover with planks

plankton ('plangktən) *n.* minute animal and vegetable organisms floating in ocean

planography (plā'nogrəfi) *n.* process of printing from a flat surface

plant (plant) *n.* **1.** any living organism feeding on inorganic substances and without power of locomotion **2.** such an organism that is smaller than tree or shrub **3.** equipment or machinery needed for manufacture **4.** building and equipment for manufacturing purposes **5.** heavy vehicles used for road building *etc.* —*vt.* **6.** set in ground to grow **7.** support, establish **8.** stock with plants **9.** *sl.* hide, *esp.* to deceive or observe —'**planter** *n.* **1.** one who plants **2.** ornamental pot or stand for house plants —**plant kingdom** the plant species of the world collectively

plantain[1]

plantain[1] ('plantin) *n.* cosmopolitan weed with broad leaves and yellow flowers

plantain[2] ('plantin) *n.* **1.** tropical plant like banana **2.** its fruit

plantation (plan'tāshən) *n.* **1.** estate for cultivation of tea, tobacco *etc.* **2.** wood of planted trees **3.** *formerly,* colony

plantigrade ('plantigrād) *a.* walking on soles of feet

plaque (plak) *n.* **1.** ornamental plate, tablet **2.** plate of clasp or brooch **3.** filmy deposit on surfaces of teeth, conducive to decay

-plasm (*n. comb. form*) *Biol.* material forming cells, as in *protoplasm* —-**plasmic** (*a. comb. form*)

plasma ('plazmə) *or* **plasm** ('plazəm) *n.* clear yellowish fluid portion of blood —'**plasmic** *a.* —**plasma expander** substance used as temporary substitute for whole blood to prevent loss of fluids

plaster ('plastər) *n.* **1.** mixture of lime, sand *etc.* for coating walls *etc.* **2.** piece of fabric spread with medicinal or adhesive substance —*vt.* **3.** apply plaster to **4.** apply like plaster —'**plastered** *a. sl.* intoxicated; drunk —'**plasterer** *n.* —'**plasterboard** *n.* thin board in form of layer of plaster compressed between two layers of fiberboard, used to form or

cover walls *etc.* —**plaster of Paris** ('paris) **1.** white powder that sets to hard solid when mixed with water, used for sculptures and casts *etc.* **2.** hard plaster produced when this powder is mixed with water

plastic ('plastik) *n.* **1.** any of a group of synthetic products derived from casein, cellulose *etc.,* which can be readily molded into any form and are extremely durable —*a.* **2.** made of plastic **3.** easily molded, pliant **4.** capable of being molded **5.** produced by molding **6.** *sl.* superficially attractive yet unoriginal or artificial —**plasticity** (pla-'stisiti) *n.* ability to be molded —**plasticizer** ('plastisīzər) *n.* any of number of substances added to materials to soften and improve flexibility *etc.* —**plastic surgery** repair or reconstruction of missing or malformed parts of the body for medical or cosmetic reasons

plate (plāt) *n.* **1.** shallow round dish **2.** flat thin sheet of metal, glass *etc.* **3.** utensils of gold or silver **4.** device for printing **5.** illustration in book **6.** device used by dentists to straighten children's teeth **7.** *inf.* set of false teeth —*vt.* **8.** cover with thin coating of gold, silver or other metal —'**plateful** *n.* —'**plater** *n.* —**plate glass** kind of thick glass used for mirrors, windows *etc.*

plateau (pla'tō, 'platō) *n.* **1.** tract of level high land, tableland **2.** period of stability (*pl.* **-s, -eaux** (-ōz))

platelet ('plātlit) *n.* minute particle occurring in blood of vertebrates and involved in clotting of blood

platen ('platən) *n.* **1.** *Print.* plate by which paper is pressed against type **2.** roller in typewriter

platform ('platförm) *n.* **1.** raised level surface or floor, stage **2.** raised area in station from which passengers board trains **3.** political program

platinum ('platinəm) *n. Chem.* grayish-white noble metal *Symbol* Pt., at. wt. 195.1, at. no. 78 —**platinum-blond** *or* **platinum-blonde** *a.* **1.** (of hair) of pale silver-blond color **2.** having hair of this color

platitude ('platityōōd, -tōōd) *n.* commonplace remark —**plati'tudinous** *a.*

Platonic (plə'tonik) *a.* **1.** of Plato or his philosophy **2.** (*oft.* **p-**) (of love) purely spiritual, friendly —**Platonism** ('platənizəm) *n.* **1.** teachings of Plato, Gr. philosopher, and his followers **2.** philosophical theory that meanings of general words are real entities (forms) and describe particular objects *etc.* by virtue of some relationship of these to form —**Platonist** ('platənist) *n.*

platoon (plə'tōōn) *n.* body of soldiers employed as unit

platter ('platər) *n.* flat dish

platypus ('platipəs) *n. see* **duck-billed platypus** *at* DUCK[1]

plaudit ('plödit) *n.* act of applause, handclapping

plausible ('plözəbəl) *a.* **1.** apparently fair or reasonable **2.** fair-spoken —**plausi'bility** *n.*

play (plā) *vi.* **1.** amuse oneself **2.** take part in game **3.** behave carelessly; trifle **4.** act a part on the stage **5.** perform on musical instrument **6.** move with light or irregular motion, flicker *etc.* —*vt.* **7.** contend with in game **8.** take part in (game) **9.** act the part of **10.** perform (music) **11.** perform on (instrument) **12.** use, work (instrument) —*n.* **13.** dramatic piece or performance **14.** sport **15.** amusement **16.** manner of action or conduct **17.** activity **18.** brisk or free movement **19.** gambling —'**player** *n.* —'**playful** *a.* lively —'**playback** *n.* **1.** act or process of reproducing recording, *esp.* on magnetic tape 2. part of tape recorder serving to or used for reproducing recorded material —'**playbill** *n.* 1. poster or bill advertising play 2. program of play —'**playboy** *n.* man, *esp.* of private means, who devotes himself to the pleasures of nightclubs, female company *etc.* —'**playground** *n.* 1. outdoor area for children's play, *esp.* one having swings *etc.* or adjoining school 2. place popular as resort —'**playgroup** *n.* group of young children playing regularly under adult supervision —'**playhouse** *n.* theater —**playing card** one of set of 52 cards used in card games —'**playmate** *or* '**playfellow** *n.* friend or partner in play or recreation —**play-off** *n.* 1. *Sport* extra contest to decide winner when competitors are tied 2. contest or series of games to determine championship —'**playpen** *n.* small enclosure, usu. portable, in which young child can be left to play in safety —'**plaything** *n.* toy —'**playwright** *n.* author of plays —**play back** reproduce (recorded material) on (magnetic tape) by means of tape recorder —**play off** 1. (*usu.* *with* against) manipulate as if playing game 2. take part in play-off —**play on words** pun

plaza ('plazə, 'plāzə) *n.* 1. open space or square 2. complex of shops *etc.*

plea (plē) *n.* 1. entreaty 2. statement of prisoner or defendant 3. excuse —**plead** *vi.* 1. make earnest appeal 2. address court of law —*vt.* 3. bring forward as excuse or plea ('**pleaded** *or* **pled** (pled), '**pleading**)

please (plēz) *vt.* 1. be agreeable to 2. gratify 3. delight —*vi.* 4. like, be willing —*adv.* 5. word of request —**pleasance** ('plezəns) *n.* secluded part of garden —**pleasant** ('plezənt) *a.* pleasing, agreeable —**pleasantly** ('plezəntli) *adv.* —**pleasantry** ('plezəntri) *n.* joke, humor —**pleasurable** ('plezhərəbəl) *a.* giving pleasure —**pleasure** ('plezhər) *n.* 1. enjoyment, satisfaction 2. will, choice

pleat (plēt) *n.* 1. any of various types of fold made by doubling material back on itself —*vt.* 2. make, gather into pleats

plebeian (plə'bēən) *a.* 1. belonging to the common people 2. low or rough —*n.* 3. one of the common people (*also* (*offens. sl.*) **pleb** (pleb))

plebiscite ('plebisīt, -sit) *n.* decision by direct voting of the electorate

plectrum ('plektrəm) *or* **plectron** ('plektrən) *n.* small implement for plucking strings of guitar *etc.* (*pl.* **-tra** (-trə), **-s**)

pledge (plej) *n.* 1. promise 2. thing given over as security 3. toast —*vt.* 4. promise formally 5. bind or secure by pledge 6. give over as security

Pleiocene ('plīəsēn) *n. see* PLIOCENE

Pleistocene ('plīstəsēn) *a.* 1. of glacial period of formation —*n.* 2. Pleistocene epoch or rock series

plenary ('plēnəri, 'plen-) *a.* 1. complete, without limitations, absolute 2. (of meeting *etc.*) with all members present

plenipotentiary (plenipə'tenchəri) *a./n.* (envoy) having full powers

plenitude ('plenityōōd, -tōōd) *n.* 1. completeness, entirety 2. abundance

plenty ('plenti) *n.* 1. abundance 2. quite enough —'**plenteous** *a.* 1. ample 2. rich 3. copious —'**plentiful** *a.* abundant

plenum ('plenəm, 'plēnəm) *n.* 1. space as considered to be full of matter (opposed to vacuum) 2. condition of fullness (*pl.* **-s, -na** (-nə))

plethora ('plethərə) *n.* oversupply

pleura ('plōōrə) *n.* membrane lining the chest and covering the lungs (*pl.* **pleurae** ('plōōrē)) —'**pleurisy** *n.* inflammation of the pleura

pliable ('plīəbəl) *a.* easily bent or influenced —**plia'bility** *n.* —'**pliancy** *n.* —'**pliant** *a.* pliable

pliers ('plīərz) *pl.n.* tool with hinged arms and jaws for gripping

plight[1] (plīt) *n.* 1. distressing state 2. predicament

plight[2] (plīt) *vt.* promise —**plight one's troth** make a promise, *esp.* of marriage

plinth (plinth) *n.* 1. square slab at base of column 2. narrow rectangular platform to form toe space on furniture and appliances

Pliocene *or* **Pleiocene** ('plīəsēn) *a.* 1. of the most recent tertiary deposits —*n.* 2. Pliocene epoch or rock series

plissé (pli'sā) *n.* 1. fabric with wrinkled finish, achieved by treatment involving caustic soda 2. such finish on fabric

P.L.O. Palestine Liberation Organization

plod (plod) *vi.* walk or work doggedly (**-dd-**)

plop (plop) *n.* 1. sound of object falling into water without splash —*v.* 2. (cause to) fall with such sound (**-pp-**)

plosion ('plōzhən) *n. Phonet.* sound of abrupt break or closure, *esp.* audible release of stop (*also* **ex'plosion**) —'**plosive** *Phonet.* *a.* 1. accompanied by plosion —*n.* 2. plosive consonant; stop

plot[1] (plot) *n.* 1. secret plan, conspiracy 2. essence of story, play *etc.* —*vt.* 3. devise secretly 4. mark position of 5. make map of —*vi.* 6. conspire (**-tt-**)

plot[2] (plot) *n.* small piece of land

plover ('pluvər) *n.* any of various shore birds, typically with round head, straight bill and long pointed wings

plow (plow) *n.* 1. implement for turning up soil 2. similar implement for clearing snow *etc.* —*vt.* 3. turn up with plow, furrow —*vi.* 4. (*with* through) work (at) slowly —'**plowman** *n.* —'**plowshare** *n.* blade of plow

ploy (ploi) *n.* 1. stratagem 2. occupation 3. prank

pluck (pluk) *vt.* 1. pull, pick off 2. strip 3. sound strings of (guitar *etc.*) with fingers, plectrum —*n.* 4. courage 5. sudden pull or tug —'**pluckily** *adv.* —'**plucky** *a.* courageous

plug (plug) *n.* 1. thing fitting into and filling a hole 2. *Elec.* device connecting appliance to electricity supply 3. tobacco pressed hard 4. *inf.* recommendation, advertisement —*vt.* 5. stop with plug 6. *inf.* advertise (product, show *etc.*) by constant repetition, as on television 7. *sl.* punch 8. *sl.* shoot —*vi.* 9. *inf.* (*with* away) work hard (**-gg-**) —**plug in** connect (electrical appliance) with power source by means of plug

plum (plum) *n.* 1. stone fruit 2. tree bearing it 3. choicest part, piece, position *etc.* —*a.* 4. choice 5. of dark reddish-purple color —'**plummy** *a.* of plums

plumage ('plōōmij) *n. see* PLUME

plumb (plum) *n.* 1. ball of lead (**plumb bob**) attached to string used for sounding, finding the perpendicular *etc.* —*a.* 2. perpendicular —*adv.* 3. perpendicularly 4. exactly 5. downright 6. honestly 7. exactly —*vt.* 8. set exactly upright 9. find depth of 10. reach, undergo 11. equip with, connect to plumbing system —'**plumber** *n.* worker who attends to water and sewage systems —'**plumbing** *n.* 1. trade of plumber 2. system of water and sewage pipes —'**plumbline** *n.* cord with plumb attached

plume (plōōm) *n.* 1. feather 2. ornament of feathers or horsehair —*vt.* 3. furnish with plumes 4. pride (oneself) —'**plumage** *n.* bird's feathers collectively

plummet ('plumit) *vi.* 1. plunge headlong —*n.* 2. plumbline

plump[1] (plump) *a.* 1. of rounded form, moderately fat, chubby —*v.* 2. (*oft.* *with* up *or* out) make, become plump

plump[2] (plump) *vi.* 1. sit, fall abruptly —*vt.* 2. drop, throw abruptly —*adv.* 3. suddenly 4. heavily 5. directly —**plump for** choose, vote only for

plunder ('plundər) *vt.* 1. take by force 2. rob systematically —*vi.* 3. rob —*n.* 4. pillage 5. booty, spoils

plunge (plunj) *vt.* 1. put forcibly —*vi.* 2. throw oneself 3. enter, rush with violence 4. descend very suddenly —*n.* 5. dive —'**plunger** *n.* 1. rubber suction cap to unblock drains 2. pump piston —**take the plunge** *inf.* 1. embark on risky enterprise 2. get married

plunk (plungk) *v.* 1. pluck (string of banjo *etc.*) 2. drop suddenly

pluperfect (plōō'pərfikt) *a./n.* (tense) expressing action completed before past point of time

plural ('plōōrəl) *a.* 1. of, denoting more than one person or thing —*n.* 2. word in its plural form —'**pluralism** *n.* 1. holding of more than one appointment, vote *etc.* 2. coexistence of different social groups *etc.* in one society —'**pluralist** *n./a.* —**plu'rality** *n.* majority of votes *etc.*

plus (plus) *prep.* 1. with addition of (*usu.* indicated by the sign +) —*a.* 2. to be added 3. positive —**plus fours** men's baggy knickerbockers reaching below knee

plush (plush) *n.* 1. fabric with long nap, long-piled velvet —*a.* 2. luxurious

Pluto[1] ('plōōtō) *n. Gr. myth.* god of underworld; Hades —**Plu'tonian** *a.* pert. to Pluto or the infernal regions, dark —**plutonic** (plōō'tonik) *a.* (of igneous rocks) derived from magma that has cooled and solidified below surface of earth

Pluto[2] ('plōōtō) *n.* second smallest planet and farthest known from sun

plutocracy (plōō'tokrəsi) *n.* 1. government by the rich 2. state ruled thus 3. wealthy class —'**plutocrat** *n.* wealthy man —**pluto'cratic** *a.*

plutonium (plōō'tōniəm) *n. Chem.* transuranic element *Symbol* Pu, at. wt. 242, at. no. 94

pluvial ('plōōviəl) *a.* of, caused by the action of rain

ply[1] (plī) *vt.* 1. wield 2. work at 3. supply pressingly 4. urge 5. keep busy —*vi.* 6. go to and fro, run regularly (**plied, 'plying**)

ply[2] (plī) *n.* 1. fold or thickness 2. strand of yarn —'**plywood** *n.* board of thin layers of wood glued together with grains at right angles

Pm *Chem.* promethium

p.m. *or* **P.M.** 1. post meridiem (*Lat.*, after noon) 2. postmortem

PMS premenstrual syndrome

PMT premenstrual tension

pneumatic (nyōō'matik, nōō-) *a.* of, worked by, inflated with wind or air —**pneu'matics** *pl.n.* (*with sing. v.*) branch of physics concerned with mechanical properties of gases, *esp.* air

pneumoconiosis ('nyōōmōkōni'ōsis, 'nōō-) *n.* any lung disorder caused by inhaling dust particles

pneumonia (nyōō'mōnyə, nōō-) *n.* inflammation of the lungs

pneumothorax (nyōōmə'thōraks, nōōmə-) *n.* the presence of air between the lung and chest wall, formerly induced as treatment for tuberculosis

Po *Chem.* polonium

P.O. 1. Petty Officer 2. Post Office

poach[1] (pōch) *vt.* 1. catch (game) illegally 2.

trample, make swampy or soft —*vi.* 3. trespass for purpose of poaching 4. encroach

poach[2] (pōch) *vt.* simmer (eggs, fish *etc.*) gently in water *etc.* —'**poacher** *n.*

pock (pok) *n.* pustule, as in smallpox *etc.*

pocket ('pokit) *n.* 1. small bag inserted in garment 2. cavity filled with ore *etc.* 3. socket, cavity, pouch or hollow 4. mass of water or air differing from that surrounding it 5. isolated group or area —*vt.* 6. put into one's pocket 7. appropriate, steal —*a.* 8. small —'**pocketbook** *n.* 1. small bag or case for money, papers *etc.* 2. handbag —'**pocket-knife** *n.* small knife with one or more blades that fold into handle —**pocket money** money for small, occasional expenses

poco ('pōkō; *It.* 'pōkō) *or* **un poco** *a./adv. Mus.* little; to a small degree

pod (pod) *n.* 1. long seed vessel, as of peas, beans *etc.* —*vi.* 2. form pods —*vt.* 3. shell (-dd-)

-pod *or* **-pode** (*comb. form*) indicating certain type or number of feet, as in *arthropod, tripod*

podiatry (pə'dīətri) *n.* paramedical specialty dealing with diagnosis and treatment of disorders of the feet (*also* **chiropody**)

podium ('pōdiəm) *n.* small raised platform (*pl.* **-s, -dia** (-diə))

poem ('pōim) *n.* imaginative composition in rhythmic lines —**poesy** ('pōizi) *n.* poetry —'**poet** *n.* writer of poems —**poetaster** ('pōitastər) *n.* would-be or inferior poet —**po'etic(al)** *a.* —**po'etically** *adv.* —'**poetry** *n.* art or work of poet, verse —**poetic justice** fitting retribution —**poetic license** justifiable departure from conventional rules of form, fact *etc.*, as in poetry

pogey *or* **pogy** ('pōgi) *n.* C *sl.* 1. unemployment insurance 2. dole

pogo stick ('pōgō) stout pole with handle at top, steps for feet and spring at bottom, so that user can spring up, down and along on it

pogrom ('pōgrəm) *n.* organized persecution and massacre, *esp.* of Jews in Russia

poignant ('poinyənt, -nənt) *a.* 1. moving 2. biting, stinging 3. vivid 4. pungent —'**poignancy** *or* '**poignance** *n.*

poinciana (poinsi'anə) *n.* tropical tree with scarlet flowers

poinsettia (poin'setə, -'setiə) *n. orig.* Amer. shrub, widely cultivated for its clusters of scarlet bracts, resembling petals

point (point) *n.* 1. dot, mark 2. punctuation mark 3. item, detail 4. unit of value 5. position, degree, stage 6. moment 7. gist of an argument 8. purpose 9. striking or effective part or quality 10. essential object or thing 11. sharp end 12. single unit in scoring 13. headland 14. one of direction marks of compass 15. movable rail changing train to other rails 16. fine kind of lace 17. act of pointing 18. unit of academic credit 19. printing unit, one twelfth of a pica —*pl.* 20. electrical contacts in distributor of engine —*vi.* 21. show direction or position by extending finger 22. direct attention 23. (of dog) indicate position of game by standing facing it —*vt.* 24. aim, direct 25. sharpen 26. fill up joints of (brickwork *etc.*) with mortar 27. give value to (words *etc.*) —'**pointed** *a.* 1. sharp 2. direct, telling —'**pointedly** *adv.* —'**pointer** *n.* 1. index 2. indicating rod *etc.* used for pointing 3. indication 4. dog trained to point —'**pointless** *a.* 1. blunt 2. futile, irrelevant —**point-blank** *a.* 1. aimed horizontally 2. plain, blunt —*adv.* 3. with level aim (there being no necessity to elevate for distance) 4. at short range —**point of no return** 1. point at which irreversible commitment must be made to action *etc.* 2.

point in journey at which, if one continues, supplies will be insufficient for return to starting place —**point of order** question raised in meeting as to whether rules governing procedures are being breached (*pl.* **points of order**) —**point of view** 1. position from which someone or something is observed 2. mental viewpoint or attitude (*pl.* **points of view**)

pointillism ('pwantēizəm, 'pointilizəm) *n.* technique of painting elaborated from impressionism, in which dots of unmixed color are juxtaposed on white ground so that from distance they fuse in viewer's eye into appropriate intermediate tones —**pointillist** (pwantē'ēst, 'pointəlist) *n./a.*

poise (poiz) *n.* 1. composure 2. self-possession 3. balance, equilibrium, carriage (of body *etc.*) —*v.* 4. (cause to) be balanced or suspended —*vt.* 5. hold in readiness

poison ('poizən) *n.* 1. substance which kills or injures when introduced into living organism —*vt.* 2. give poison to 3. infect 4. pervert, spoil —'**poisoner** *n.* —'**poisonous** *a.* —**poison control center** center, usu. in hospital, coordinating data on all aspects of poisoning and making such information available to physicians —**poison ivy** N Amer. shrub or climbing plant that causes itching rash on contact —**poison oak** either of two plants, vine found on west coast of U.S. and shrub in central and eastern U.S. with same effect as poison ivy —**poison-pen letter** malicious anonymous letter —**poison sumac** shrub found in swamps from Maine to Florida with same effect as poison ivy

poke[1] (pōk) *vt.* 1. push, thrust with finger, stick *etc.* 2. thrust —*vi.* 3. make thrusts 4. pry —*n.* 5. act of poking —'**poker** *n.* metal rod for poking fire —'**poky** *or* '**pokey** *a.* small, confined, cramped

poke[2] (pōk) *n.* —**pig in a poke** something bought *etc.* without previous inspection

poker ('pōkər) *n.* any of various card games in which player with highest card or hand wins the pool or kitty —**poker face** *inf.* face without expression, as of poker player concealing value of his cards —**poker-faced** *a.*

pol. 1. political 2. politics

Pol. 1. Poland 2. Polish

Poland ('pōlənd) *n.* country in Europe bounded north by the Baltic Sea, east by the U.S.S.R., south by Czechoslovakia and west by the German Democratic Republic —**Pole** *n.* native or inhabitant of Poland —'**Polish** *n./a.* 1. (of) Polish language which is a branch of Balto-Slavic —*a.* 2. of Poles and Poland

Poland

polar ('pōlər) *a.* see POLE[2]

Polaris (pə'laris, -'läris) *n.* 1. brightest star

in constellation Ursa Minor, situated slightly less than 1° from north celestial pole (*also* **Pole Star, North Star**) 2. type of Amer. ballistic missile, usu. fired by submarine

Polaroid ('pōləroid) *n.* trade name for: 1. type of material which polarizes light 2. camera that develops print very quickly inside itself

polder ('pōldər, 'pol-) *n.* land reclaimed from the sea

pole[1] (pōl) *n.* 1. long rounded piece of wood *etc.* —*vt.* 2. propel with pole —**pole-vault** *vi.* perform or compete in the pole vault —**pole-vaulter** *n.* —**the pole vault** field event in which competitors attempt to clear high bar with aid of long flexible pole

pole[2] (pōl) *n.* 1. either of the ends of axis of earth or celestial sphere 2. either of opposite ends of magnet, electric cell *etc.* —'**polar** *a.* 1. pert. to the N and S pole, or to magnetic poles 2. directly opposite in tendency, character *etc.* —**po'larity** *n.* —**polari'zation** *n.* —'**polarize** *vt.* give polarity to —**polar bear** white Arctic bear —**polar circle** either Arctic Circle or Antarctic Circle —**the Pole Star** star closest to N celestial pole at any particular time, at present Polaris

poleax ('pōlaks) *n.* 1. battle-ax —*vt.* 2. hit, fell as with poleax

polecat ('pōlkat) *n.* small animal of weasel family

polemic (pə'lemik) *a.* 1. controversial (*also* **po'lemical**) —*n.* 2. war of words, argument —**po'lemics** *pl.n.* (*with sing. v.*) art or practice of dispute or argument

police (pə'lēs) *n.* 1. the civil force which maintains public order —*vt.* 2. keep in order —**police dog** dog trained to help police —**po'liceman** *n.* member of police force (**po'licewoman** *fem.*) —**police state** state or country in which repressive government maintains control through police —**police station** office or headquarters of police force of district

policy[1] ('polisi) *n.* 1. course of action adopted, *esp.* in state affairs 2. prudence

policy[2] ('polisi) *n.* insurance contract

poliomyelitis (pōliōmīə'lītis) *n.* disease of spinal cord characterized by fever and sometimes paralysis (*also* **infantile paralysis**)

polish ('polish) *vt.* 1. make smooth and glossy 2. refine —*n.* 3. shine 4. polishing 5. substance for polishing 6. refinement

Politburo ('politbyŏŏrō) *n.* 1. executive committee of a Communist Party 2. supreme policy-making authority in most Communist countries

polite (pə'līt) *a.* 1. showing regard for others in manners, speech *etc.* 2. refined, cultured —**po'litely** *adv.* —**po'liteness** *n.* courtesy

politic ('politik) *a.* 1. wise 2. shrewd 3. expedient 4. cunning —**po'litical** *a.* of the state or its affairs —**poli'tician** *n.* one engaged in politics —'**politics** *pl.n.* 1. (*with sing. v.*) art of government 2. political affairs or life —'**polity** *n.* 1. form of government 2. organized state 3. civil government —**political asylum** refuge given to someone for political reasons —**political economy** former name for economics —**political prisoner** someone imprisoned for holding or expressing particular political beliefs —**political science** study of state, government and politics —**political scientist**

Polk (pōk) *n.* **James Knox.** the 11th President of the U.S. (1845-49)

polka ('pōlkə) *n.* 1. lively dance in 2/4 time 2. music for it —**polka dot** one of pattern of bold spots on fabric *etc.*

poll (pōl) *n*. 1. voting 2. counting of votes 3. number of votes recorded 4. canvassing of sample of population to determine general opinion 5. (top of) head —*vt*. 6. receive (votes) 7. take votes of 8. lop, shear 9. cut horns from (animals) —*vi*. 10. vote —**'pollster** *n*. one who conducts polls

pollard ('polərd) *n*. 1. hornless animal of normally horned variety 2. tree on which a close head of young branches has been made by polling —*vt*. 3. make a pollard of

pollen ('polən) *n*. fertilizing dust of flower —**'pollinate** *vt*. —**pollen count** measure of pollen present in air over 24-hour period

pollute (pə'lōōt) *vt*. 1. make foul 2. corrupt 3. desecrate —**pol'lutant** *n*. —**pol'lution** *n*.

polo ('pōlō) *n*. game in which two teams of players on horseback attempt to drive a ball through goals set up at each end of a turf field —**polo neck** 1. collar on garment, worn rolled over to fit closely round neck 2. sweater with such collar

polonaise (polə'nāz) *n*. 1. Polish dance 2. music for it

polonium (pə'lōniəm) *n. Chem*. transuranic element *Symbol* Po, at. wt. 210.0, at. no. 84

poltergeist ('pōltərgīst) *n*. noisy mischievous spirit

poltroon (pol'trōōn) *n*. abject coward

poly- (*comb. form*) many, as in *polysyllabic*

polyandry ('poliandri) *n*. polygamy in which woman has more than one husband

polyanthus (poli'anthəs) *n*. cultivated primrose

polychrome ('polikrōm) *a*. 1. having various colors —*n*. 2. work of art in many colors —**polychro'matic** *a*.

polycythemia (polisī'thēmiə) *n*. the increase in number of red cells in the blood

polyester ('poliestər) *n*. any of large class of synthetic materials used as plastics, textile fibers *etc*.

polygamy (pə'ligəmi) *n*. custom of being married to several persons at same time —**po'lygamist** *n*.

polyglot ('poliglot) *a*. speaking, writing in several languages

polygon ('poligon) *n*. figure with many angles or sides —**po'lygonal** *a*.

polygraph ('poligraf) *n*. 1. instrument for recording pulse rate and perspiration, used *esp*. as lie detector 2. device for producing copies of written matter

polygyny (pə'lijəni) *n*. polygamy in which man has more than one wife

polyhedron (poli'hēdrən) *n*. solid figure contained by many faces (*pl*. -**s, -dra** (-drə))

polymath ('polimath) *n*. person of great and varied learning

polymer ('polimər) *n*. substance whose molecules are made up of many structural units held together by interatomic bonds —**poly'meric** *a*. of polymer —**polymeri'zation** *n*. —**'polymerize** *v*.

polymorphous (poli'mörfəs) *or* **polymorphic** *a*. 1. having, taking or passing through many different forms or stages 2. exhibiting or undergoing polymorphism

Polynesian (poli'nēzhən, -shən) *a*. 1. of Polynesia, group of Pacific islands, its people or any of their languages —*n*. 2. member of people of Polynesia, generally of Caucasoid features with light skin and wavy hair 3. branch of Malayo-Polynesian family of languages, including Maori and Hawaiian

polynomial (poli'nōmiəl) *a*. 1. of two or more names or terms —*n*. 2. mathematical expression consisting of sum of terms each of which is product of constant and one or more variables raised to positive or zero integral power 3. mathematical expression consisting of sum of a number of terms (*also* **multi'nomial**)

polyp ('polip) *n*. 1. sea anemone or allied animal 2. tumor with branched roots (*also* **'polypus**)

polyphase ('polifāz) *a*. (of alternating current of electricity) possessing number of regular sets of alternations

polyphony (pə'lifəni) *n*. polyphonic style of composition or piece of music utilizing it —**poly'phonic** *a*. 1. *Mus*. composed of relatively independent parts; contrapuntal 2. many-voiced

polysaccharide (poli'sakərīd) *n*. organic compound composed of monosaccharides found widely distributed in nature, *eg* cellulose, starch and glycogen

polystyrene (poli'stīrēn) *n*. synthetic material used *esp*. as white rigid foam for packing *etc*.

polytechnic (poli'teknik) *n*. 1. college dealing mainly with various arts and crafts —*a*. 2. of or relating to technical instruction

polytheism ('polithēizəm) *n*. belief in many gods —**'polytheist** *n*.

polyunsaturated ('poliun'sachərātid) *a*. of group of fats that do not form cholesterol in blood

polyurethane (poli'yōōrəthān) *n*. class of synthetic materials, oft. in foam or flexible form

polyvalent (poli'vālənt) *a*. having more than one valency

pomace ('pumis) *n*. 1. pulpy residue of apples or similar fruit after crushing and pressing, as in cider-making 2. any pulpy substance left after crushing *etc*.

pomade (pō'mād, -'mäd) *n*. 1. perfumed oil or ointment applied to hair, to make it smooth and shiny —*vt*. 2. put pomade on

pomander ('pōmandər, pō'mandər) *n*. (container for) mixture of sweet-smelling herbs *etc*.

pomegranate ('pomigranit, 'pomgranit) *n*. 1. tree cultivated for its edible fruit 2. its fruit with thick rind containing many seeds in red pulp

pomelo ('poməlō) *n. see* GRAPEFRUIT (*pl*. -**s**)

Pomeranian (pomə'rāniən) *n*. breed of toy dog

pommel ('puməl, 'pom-) *n*. 1. front of saddle 2. knob of sword hilt —*vt*. 3. *see* PUMMEL

pommy ('pomi) *n*. (*sometimes* P-) **A, NZ** *sl*. British person (*also* **pom**)

pomp (pomp) *n*. splendid display or ceremony

pompon ('pompon) *or* **pompom** ('pompom) *n*. tuft of ribbon, wool, feathers *etc*. decorating hat, shoe *etc*.

pompous ('pompəs) *a*. 1. self-important 2. ostentatious 3. (of language) inflated, stilted —**pom'posity** *n*.

poncho ('ponchō) *n*. 1. square or oblong blanket-like fabric with opening in middle for head 2. waterproof garment resembling poncho (*pl*. -**s**)

pond (pond) *n*. small body, pool or lake of still water

ponder ('pondər) *v*. 1. muse, meditate, think over 2. consider, deliberate (on)

ponderous ('pondərəs) *a*. 1. heavy, unwieldy 2. boring

pongee (pon'jē) *n*. soft unbleached washable silk woven from filaments of wild silkworms

pontiff ('pontif) *n*. 1. Pope 2. high priest 3. bishop —**pon'tifical** *a*. —**pontificate** (pon-'tifikit) *n*. 1. dignity or office of pontiff —*vi*. (pon'tifikāt) 2. speak bombastically (*also* **'pontify**) 3. act as pontiff

pontoon (pon'tōōn) *n*. flat-bottomed boat or metal drum for use in supporting temporary bridge

pony ('pōni) *n*. 1. horse of small breed 2. very small glass, *esp*. for liqueurs —**'ponytail** *n*. long hair tied in one bunch at back of head

poodle ('pōōdəl) *n*. pet dog with long curly hair oft. clipped fancifully —**poodle cloth** fabric made of wool and mohair with loops on surface

Pooh-Bah ('pōōbä) *n*. pompous official

pooh-pooh ('pōōpōō) *vt*. express disdain or scorn for; dismiss, belittle

pool¹ (pōōl) *n*. 1. small body of still water 2. deep place in river or stream 3. puddle 4. swimming pool

pool² (pōōl) *n*. 1. common fund or resources 2. group of people, *eg* typists, any of whom can work for any of several employers 3. aggregate of money or chips at stake in game of cards consisting usu. of contributions from each player (*also* **kitty, pot**) 4. cartel 5. variety of billiards —*vt*. 6. put in common fund

poop (pōōp) *n*. ship's stern

poor (pōōr, pör) *a*. 1. having little money 2. unproductive 3. inadequate, insignificant 4. needy 5. miserable, pitiable 6. feeble 7. not fertile —**'poorly** *adv*. 1. badly —*a*. 2. *inf*. not in good health —**'poorness** *n*. —**poor box** box, *esp*. in church, used for collection of alms or money for poor —**'poorhouse** *n*. formerly, publicly maintained institution offering accommodation to the poor

pop¹ (pop) *vi*. 1. make small explosive sound 2. *inf*. go or come unexpectedly or suddenly —*vt*. 3. cause to make small explosive sound 4. put or place suddenly (-**pp**-) —*n*. 5. small explosive sound 6. *inf*. nonalcoholic fizzy drink —**'popper** *n*. 1. person or thing that pops 2. container for cooking popcorn in —**'popcorn** *n*. 1. any kind of maize that puffs up when roasted 2. the roasted product —**'popgun** *n*. toy gun that fires pellet or cork by means of compressed air

pop² (pop) *n. inf*. 1. father 2. old man

pop³ (pop) *n*. 1. music of general appeal, *esp*. to young people —*a*. 2. *inf*. popular —**pop art** American art movement of 1960s which used commercial illustration techniques to portray imagery from popular culture and commercial art

pop. 1. popular 2. population

pope (pōp) *n*. (*oft*. P-) bishop of Rome and head of R.C. Church —**'popery** *n. offens*. papal system, doctrines —**'popish** *a. derogatory* belonging to or characteristic of Roman Catholicism

popeyed ('pop'īd) *a*. 1. having bulging, prominent eyes 2. staring in astonishment

popinjay ('popinjā) *n*. 1. conceited or talkative person 2. *obs*. parrot

poplar ('poplər) *n*. 1. any of a genus of slender fast-growing trees of the willow family 2. the wood from these trees 3. the tulip tree or its wood

poplin ('poplin) *n*. corded fabric *usu*. of cotton

poppadom *or* **poppadum** ('popədəm) *n*. thin, round, crisp Indian bread

poppet ('popit) *n*. 1. mushroom-shaped valve lifted from seating by applying axial force to stem (*also* **poppet valve**) 2. *Naut*. temporary supporting brace for vessel hauled on land

poppy ('popi) *n*. bright-flowered plant yielding opium

poppycock ('popikok) *n. inf*. nonsense

Popsicle ('popsikəl) n. trade name for flavored colored water frozen onto two flat sticks

populace ('popyələs) n. (sometimes with pl. v.) the common people, the masses

popular ('popyələr) a. 1. finding general favor 2. of, by the people —**popu'larity** n. state or quality of being generally liked —**populari'zation** n. —'**popularize** vt. make popular —'**popularly** adv. —**popular front** (oft. **P- F-**) left-wing group or party that opposes spread of fascism

populate ('popyəlāt) vt. fill with inhabitants —**popu'lation** n. 1. inhabitants 2. the number of such inhabitants —'**populous** a. thickly populated or inhabited

porbeagle ('pörbēgəl) n. any of several sharks of northern seas (also **mackerel shark**)

porcelain ('pörslin) n. fine ceramic ware, china —**porcelain enamel** vitreous enamel

porch (pörch) n. covered approach to entrance of building

porcine ('pörsīn) a. of, like pigs

porcupine ('pörkyəpīn) n. any of various rodents covered with long, pointed quills

pore[1] (pör) vi. 1. fix eye or mind 2. (with over) study closely

pore[2] (pör) n. minute opening, esp. in skin —**po'rosity** n. —'**porous** a. 1. allowing liquid to soak through 2. full of pores

pork (pörk) n. pig's flesh used as food —'**porker** n. pig raised for food —'**porky** a. fleshy, fat —**porkpie hat** hat with round flat crown and brim that can be turned up or down

porn (pörn) or **porno** n. inf. pornography

pornography (pör'nogrəfi) n. indecent literature, pictures etc. —**por'nographer** n. —**porno'graphic** a. —**porno'graphically** adv.

porphyria (pör'firiə) n. any of group of rare inborn diseases which block hemoglobin formation

porphyry ('pörfiri) n. reddish stone with embedded crystals

porpoise ('pörpəs) n. blunt-nosed sea mammal like dolphin (pl. -poise, -s)

porridge ('porij) n. 1. soft food of oatmeal etc. boiled in water 2. sl. imprisonment

porringer ('porinjər) n. small dish, oft. with handle, for soup, porridge etc.

port[1] (pört) n. 1. harbor, haven 2. town with harbor

port[2] (pört) n. 1. left side of ship or aircraft (also (formerly) '**larboard**) —v. 2. turn to left side of ship

port[3] (pört) n. strong red wine

port[4] (pört) n. opening in side of ship —'**porthole** n. small opening or window in side of ship

port[5] (pört) Mil. vt. 1. carry (rifle etc.) diagonally across body —n. 2. this position

Port. 1. Portugal 2. Portuguese

portable ('pörtəbəl) n./a. (something) easily carried

portage ('pörtij) n. (cost of) transport

portal ('pörtəl) n. large doorway or imposing gate

portcullis (pört'kulis) n. defense grating to raise or lower in front of castle gateway

Port-du-Salut (pördəsəl'yōō, -sə'lōō) or **Port-Salut** n. a semihard, fermented and flat, round whole-milk cheese orig. from France

portend (pör'tend) vt. foretell, be an omen of —'**portent** n. 1. omen, warning 2. marvel —**por'tentous** a. 1. ominous, threatening 2. pompous

porter[1] ('pörtər) n. 1. person employed to carry burden, eg on railroad 2. doorkeeper —'**porterage** n. (charge for) carrying of supplies

porter[2] ('pörtər) n. dark sweet ale brewed from black malt —'**porterhouse** n. thick choice steak of beef cut from middle ribs or sirloin (also **porterhouse steak**)

portfolio (pört'fōliō) n. 1. flat portable case for loose papers 2. office of minister of state (pl. -s)

portico ('pörtikō) n. 1. colonnade 2. covered walk (pl. -es, -s)

portière (Fr. por'tyer) n. curtain hung in doorway

portion ('pörshən) n. 1. part 2. share 3. helping 4. destiny, lot —vt. 5. divide into shares —'**portionless** a.

portly ('pörtli) a. bulky, stout

portmanteau (pört'mantō) n. leather suitcase, esp. one opening into two compartments (pl. -s, -teaux (-tōz)) —**portmanteau word** word formed by joining together beginning and end of two other words (also **blend**)

portray (pör'trā) vt. make pictures of, describe —**portrait** ('pörtrit, -trāt) n. likeness of (face of) individual —**portraiture** ('pörtrichōōər, -chər) n. —**por'trayal** n. act of portraying

Portugal ('pörchigəl) n. country in Europe bounded north and east by Spain and south and west by the Atlantic —**Portu'guese** n./a. 1. (native or inhabitant) of Portugal —n. 2. language of Portugal, which is a Romance language —**Portuguese man-of-war** sea animal with stinging tentacles

pose (pōz) vt. 1. place in attitude 2. put forward —vi. 3. assume attitude, affect or pretend to be a certain character —n. 4. attitude, esp. one assumed for effect —'**poser** n. one who poses —**poseur** (pō'zər) n. one who assumes affected attitude to create impression

poser ('pōzər) n. puzzling question

posh (posh) a. inf. 1. smart, elegant, stylish 2. upper-class or genteel

posit ('pozit) vt. lay down as principle

position (pə'zishən) n. 1. place 2. situation 3. location, attitude 4. status 5. state of affairs 6. employment 7. strategic point 8. Mus. vertical spacing or layout of written notes in chord —vt. 9. place in position

positive ('pozitiv) a. 1. certain, sure 2. definite, absolute, unquestionable 3. utter, downright 4. confident 5. not negative 6. greater than zero 7. Elec. having deficiency of electrons —n. 8. something positive 9. Photog. print in which lights and shadows are not reversed —'**positively** adv. —'**positivism** n. philosophy recognizing only matters of fact and experience —'**positivist** a./n. (one) believing in this —**positive discrimination** provision of special opportunities for disadvantaged group —**positive feedback** see **feedback** (sense 1) at FEED

positron ('pozitron) n. positive electron

poss. 1. possession 2. possessive 3. possible 4. possibly

posse ('posi) n. 1. body of men, esp. for maintaining law and order 2. C group of trained horsemen who perform at rodeos

possess (pə'zes) vt. 1. own 2. (of evil spirit etc.) have mastery of —**pos'session** n. 1. act of possessing 2. thing possessed 3. ownership —**pos'sessive** a. 1. of, indicating possession 2. with excessive desire to possess, control —n. 3. possessive case in grammar

possible ('posibəl) a. 1. that can, or may, be, exist, happen or be done 2. worthy of

consideration —n. 3. possible candidate —**possi'bility** n. —'**possibly** adv. perhaps

possum ('posəm) n. see OPOSSUM —**play possum** pretend to be dead, asleep etc. to deceive opponent

post[1] (pōst) n. 1. upright pole of timber or metal fixed firmly, usu. to support or mark something —vt. 2. display 3. put up (notice etc.) on wall etc. —'**poster** n. 1. large advertising bill 2. one who posts bills —**poster paints** or **colors** lusterless paints used for writing posters etc.

post[2] (pōst) n. 1. official carrying of letters or parcels 2. collection or delivery of these 3. office 4. situation 5. point, station, place of duty 6. place where soldier is stationed 7. place held by body of troops 8. fort —vt. 9. put into official box for carriage by post 10. supply with latest information 11. station (soldiers etc.) in particular spot 12. transfer (entries) to ledger —adv. 13. in haste —'**postage** n. charge for mailing an item —'**postal** a. —**postage stamp** printed paper label with gummed back for attaching to mail as official indication that required postage has been paid —**postal card** preprinted card purchased at post office —**Postal Service** U.S. government corporation responsible for transportation and delivery of mail —'**postcard** n. 1. message on illustrated card without envelope —vt. 2. send postcard to —'**postman** n. mailman —**postman's knock** parlor game involving exchange of kisses —'**postmark** n. official mark with name of office etc. stamped on letters —'**postmaster** or '**postmistress** n. official in charge of local post office —**postmaster general** executive head of postal service in certain countries (pl. **postmasters general**) —**post office** place where postal business is conducted —'**post-paid** adv./a. with postage prepaid

post- (comb. form) after, behind, later than, as in postwar. Such compounds are not given here where the meaning can easily be found from the simple word

postdate (pōst'dāt) vt. assign date to (event etc.) that is later than actual date

posterior (po'stēəriər, po-) a. 1. later 2. hinder —n. 3. the buttocks

posterity (po'steriti) n. 1. later generations 2. descendants

postern ('pōstərn, 'postərn) n. 1. private entrance 2. small door, gate

postexilic (pōstig'zilik) a. O.T. existing or occurring after Babylonian exile of Jews (587-539 B.C.)

postgraduate (pōst'grajōōit) a. 1. carried on after graduation —n. 2. student taking course of study after graduation

posthaste ('pōst'hāst) adv. 1. with great haste —n. 2. obs. great haste

posthumous ('poschəməs, 'postyəməs, 'postəməs) a. 1. occurring after death 2. born after father's death 3. (of book etc.) published after author's death —'**posthumously** adv.

posthypnotic suggestion (pōst-hip'notik) suggestion made to subject while in hypnotic trance, to be acted upon some time after emerging from trance

postilion or **postillion** (pō'stilyən) n. Hist. man riding one of pair of horses drawing a carriage

postimpressionism (pōstim'preshənizəm) n. movement in painting at end of 19th cent. which rejected naturalism and momentary effects of impressionism but adapted its use of pure color to paint subjects with greater subjective emotion —**postim'pressionist** a.

of Paul Cézanne, Vincent Van Gogh, Paul Gauguin and neoimpressionists

post meridiem (mə'ridiəm) *see* P.M. (sense 1)

postmortem (pōst'mörtəm) *n.* 1. analysis of recent event —*a.* 2. taking place after death —**postmortem examination** medical examination of dead body

postnasal drip (pōst'nāzəl) the discharge of fluid secretions into the back part of the nose and throat from nasal and sinus tissues

postnatal (pōst'nātəl) *a.* after birth

post-obit (pōst'ōbit) *a.* taking effect after death

postoperative (pōst'opərətiv) *a.* of period following surgical operation

postpartum depression (pōst'pärtəm) condition sometimes occurring after childbirth, marked by weeping, sensitivity and depression

postpone (pōst'pōn, pōs'pōn) *vt.* put off to later time, defer —**post'ponement** *n.*

postprandial (pōst'prandiəl) *a.* after-dinner

postscript ('pōsskript) *n.* 1. note added at end of letter, after signature 2. supplement added to book, document *etc.*

postulant ('poschələnt) *n.* candidate for admission to religious order

postulate ('poschəlāt) *vt.* 1. take for granted 2. lay down as self-evident 3. stipulate —*n.* ('poschəlit) 4. proposition assumed without proof 5. prerequisite —**postu'lation** *n.*

posture ('poschər) *n.* 1. attitude, position of body —*vi.* 2. pose

posy ('pōzi) *n.* bunch of flowers

pot (pot) *n.* 1. round vessel 2. cooking vessel 3. trap, *esp.* for crabs, lobsters 4. *sl.* cannabis 5. *see* POOL² (sense 3) —*pl.* 6. *inf.* a lot —*vt.* 7. put into, preserve in pot (**-tt-**) —**'potted** *a.* 1. preserved in a pot 2. *inf.* abridged —**'pot'bellied** *a.* —**'potbelly** *n.* 1. enlarged protruding abdomen (*also* **beer belly**) 2. one having such an abdomen —**'potboiler** *n. inf.* artistic work of little merit produced quickly to make money —**pot-bound** *a.* (of pot plant) having grown to fill all available root space and lacking room for continued growth —**'potherb** *n.* any plant having leaves, stems *etc.* that are used in cooking —**'pothole** *n.* 1. pitlike cavity in rocks, usu. limestone, produced by faulting and water action 2. hole worn in road —**'pothook** *n.* 1. S-shaped hook for suspending pot over fire 2. long hook for lifting hot pots *etc.* 3. S-shaped mark, oft. made by children when learning to write —**'pothunter** *n.* 1. person who hunts for profit without regard to rules of sport 2. *inf.* person who enters competitions for sole purpose of winning prizes —**'pot'luck** *n.* 1. whatever food is available without special preparation 2. choice dictated by lack of alternative (*esp. in* **take potluck**) —**pot plant** plant grown in flowerpot —**pot roast** meat cooked slowly in covered pot with little water —**'potsherd** *n.* broken fragment of pottery —**pot shot** easy or random shot

potable ('pōtəbəl) *a.* drinkable

potage (po'tazh; *English* pō'täzh) *Fr.* thick soup

potash ('potash) *n.* 1. alkali used in soap *etc.* 2. crude potassium carbonate

potassium (pə'tasiəm) *n. Chem.* metallic element *Symbol* k, at. wt. 39.1, at. no. 19 —**potassium nitrate** crystalline compound used in gunpowders, fertilizers and as preservative (*also* **'salt'peter, 'niter**)

potato (pə'tātō) *n.* plant with tubers grown for food (*pl.* **-es**) —**potato chip** very thin fried slice of potato, eaten cold —**sweet potato** 1. trailing plant 2. its edible sweetish tubers

potent ('pōtənt) *a.* 1. powerful, influential 2. (of male) capable of sexual intercourse —**'potency** *n.* 1. physical or moral power 2. efficacy

potentate ('pōtəntāt) *n.* ruler

potential (pə'tenchəl) *a.* 1. latent, that may or might but does not now exist or act —*n.* 2. possibility 3. amount of potential energy 4. *Elec.* level of electric pressure —**potenti'ality** *n.* —**potential difference** difference in electric potential between two points in electric field

pother ('podhər) *n.* 1. commotion, fuss 2. choking cloud of smoke *etc.*

potion ('pōshən) *n.* dose of medicine or poison

potpourri (pōpoŏ'rē) *n.* 1. mixture of rose petals, spices *etc.* 2. musical, literary medley (*pl.* **-s**)

pottage ('potij) *n.* thick soup containing vegetables and meat

potter ('potər) *n.* maker of ceramic ware —**'pottery** *n.* 1. earthenware and stoneware 2. place where it is made 3. art of making it —**potter's wheel** device with horizontal rotating disk, on which clay is molded by hand —**the Potteries** region of W central England in which china industries are concentrated

pouch (powch) *n.* 1. small bag 2. *Anat.* any sac, pocket or pouchlike cavity —*vt.* 3. put into pouch

poult-de-soie (pōōdə'swä) *n.* fine corded silk or rayon

poultice ('pōltis) *n.* soft composition of mustard, kaolin *etc.*, applied hot to sore or inflamed parts of body

poultry ('pōltri) *n.* domestic fowls collectively —**'poulterer** *n.* dealer in poultry

pounce (powns) *vi.* 1. spring suddenly, swoop —*n.* 2. swoop or sudden descent

pound¹ (pownd) *vt.* 1. beat, thump 2. crush to pieces or powder —*vi.* 3. walk, run heavily

pound² (pownd) *n.* 1. unit of troy and apothecaries' weight equal to 0.373 kg 2. unit of avoirdupois weight equal to 0.454 kg 3. monetary unit in U.K. —**'poundage** *n.* charge of so much per pound of weight

pound³ (pownd) *n.* 1. enclosure for stray animals or officially removed vehicles 2. confined space —**'poundage** *n.* 1. confinement within an enclosure or boundary 2. fee required to free animal from pound

poundal ('powndəl) *n.* unit of force in the foot-pound-second system

pour (pör) *vi.* 1. come out in a stream, crowd *etc.* 2. flow freely 3. rain heavily —*vt.* 4. give out in a stream, crowd *etc.* 5. cause to run out

pourboire (pōōr'bwar) *Fr.* tip; gratuity

pout¹ (powt) *v.* 1. thrust out (lips) —*vi.* 2. look sulky —*n.* 3. act of pouting —**'pouter** *n.* pigeon with power of inflating its crop

pout² (powt) *n.* type of food fish (*pl.* **pout, -s**)

poverty ('povərti) *n.* 1. state of being poor 2. poorness 3. lack of means 4. scarcity —**poverty line** level of income below which one is classified as poor by federal government standards —**poverty-stricken** *a.* suffering from extreme poverty

P.O.W. prisoner of war

powder ('powdər) *n.* 1. solid matter in fine dry particles 2. medicine in this form 3. gunpowder 4. face powder *etc.* —*vt.* 5. apply powder to 6. reduce to powder; pulverize —**'powdery** *a.* —**powder keg** 1. small barrel to hold gunpowder 2. potential source of violence *etc.* —**powder puff** soft pad for applying cosmetic powder —**powder room** ladies' toilet

power ('powər) *n.* 1. ability to do or act 2. strength 3. authority 4. control 5. person or thing having authority 6. mechanical energy 7. electricity supply 8. rate of doing work 9. product from continuous multiplication of number by itself —**'powered** *a.* having or operated by mechanical or electrical power —**'powerful** *a.* —**'powerless** *a.* —**'powerhouse** *or* **power station** *n.* installation for generating and distributing electric power —**power of attorney** 1. legal authority to act for another person in certain specified matters 2. document conferring such authority

powwow ('powwow) *n.* 1. Amerindian ceremony of celebration (cure of disease, success in hunting or war *etc.*) 2. council or conference of or with Amerindians 3. *inf.* any meeting —*vi.* 4. hold a powwow

pox (poks) *n.* 1. one of several diseases marked by pustular eruptions of skin 2. *inf.* syphilis

pp *or* **pp.** pianissimo

pp. pages

p.p. 1. parcel post 2. past participle 3. prepaid 4. postpaid 5. by delegation to 6. on prescriptions, after meal

ppd. 1. postpaid 2. prepaid

P.P.S. *or* **p.p.s.** post postscriptum

PQ Quebec

Pr *Chem.* praseodymium

pr. 1. pair (*pl.* **prs.**) 2. present 3. price 4. pronoun

P.R. public relations

practical ('praktikəl) *a.* 1. given to action rather than theory 2. relating to action or real existence 3. useful 4. in effect though not in name 5. virtual —**practica'bility** *n.* —**'practicable** *a.* that can be done, used *etc.* —**'practically** *adv.* —**prac'titioner** *n.* one engaged in a profession —**practical joke** trick usu. intended to make victim appear foolish

practice *or* **practise** ('praktis) *n.* 1. habit 2. mastery, skill 3. exercise of art or profession 4. action, not theory —*vt.* 5. do repeatedly, work at to gain skill 6. do habitually 7. put into action —*vi.* 8. exercise oneself 9. exercise profession

praetor ('prētər) *n.* in ancient Rome, senior magistrate ranking just below consul

pragmatic (prag'matik) *a.* 1. concerned with practical consequence 2. of the affairs of state —**prag'matical** *a.* —**'pragmatism** *n.*

prairie dog

prairie ('prāəri) *n.* large treeless tract of grassland of Central U.S.A. and Canad. —**prairie dog** small N Amer. rodent inhabiting burrows in grasslands —**prairie schooner** canvas-covered wagon used by early Americans to cross the continent

praise (prāz) *n.* 1. commendation 2. fact, state of being praised —*vt.* 3. express approval, admiration of 4. speak well of 5. glorify —**'praiseworthy** *a.*

praline ('prälēn) *n.* sweet composed of nuts and sugar

prance (prans) *vi.* 1. swagger 2. caper 3. walk with bounds —*n.* 4. prancing

prank (prangk) *n.* mischievous trick or escapade, frolic

prase (prāz) *n.* light green translucent chalcedony

praseodymium (prāziō'dimiəm) *n. Chem.* metallic element *Symbol* Pr, at. wt. 140.9, at. no. 59

prate (prāt) *vi.* **1.** talk idly, chatter —*n.* **2.** idle or trivial talk

prattle ('pratəl) *vi.* **1.** talk like child —*n.* **2.** trifling, childish talk —**'prattler** *n.* babbler

prawn

prawn (prön) *n.* edible sea crustacean like shrimp but larger

praxis ('praksis) *n.* practice, *esp.* as opposed to theory (*pl.* **-es, praxes** ('praksēz))

pray (prā) *vt.* **1.** ask earnestly, entreat —*vi.* **2.** offer prayers, *esp.* to God —**prayer** (prāər) *n.* **1.** action, practice of praying to God **2.** earnest entreaty —**prayer rug** small carpet on which Muslim kneels while saying prayers (*also* **prayer mat**) —**prayer wheel** Buddhism *esp.* in Tibet, wheel or cylinder inscribed with prayers, each revolution of which is counted as uttered prayer —**praying mantis** *or* **mantid** *see* MANTIS

pre- (*comb. form*) before, beforehand, as in *prenatal, prerecord, preshrunk.* Such compounds are not given here where the meaning can easily be found from the simple word

preach (prēch) *vi.* **1.** deliver sermon **2.** give moral, religious advice —*vt.* **3.** set forth in religious discourse **4.** advocate —**'preacher** *n.*

preamble ('prēambəl, prē'ambəl) *n.* introductory part of story *etc.*

prebend ('prebənd) *n.* stipend of canon or member of cathedral chapter —**pre'bendal** *a.* —**'prebendary** *n.* holder of this

Precambrian (prē'kambriən) *a.* **1.** of earliest geological era, which lasted for about 4 000 000 000 years before Cambrian period —*n.* **2.** Precambrian era

precarious (pri'kariəs, -'ker-) *a.* insecure, unstable, perilous

precaution (pri'köshən) *n.* **1.** previous care to prevent evil or secure good **2.** preventive measure —**pre'cautionary** *a.*

precede (pri'sēd) *vt.* go, come before in rank, order, time *etc.* —**precedence** ('presidəns) *n.* priority in position, rank, time *etc.* —**precedent** ('presidənt) *n.* previous example or occurrence taken as rule

precentor (pri'sentər) *n.* leader of singing choir or congregation

precept ('presept) *n.* rule for conduct, maxim —**pre'ceptor** *n.* instructor —**precep-'torial** *a.*

precinct ('presingkt) *n.* **1.** enclosed, limited area **2.** area in town, oft. closed to traffic, reserved for particular activity **3.** administrative area of city —*pl.* **4.** environs

precious ('preshəs) *a.* **1.** beloved, cherished **2.** of great value, highly valued **3.** rare —**preci'osity** *n.* overrefinement in art or literature —**'preciously** *adv.* —**'preciousness** *n.* —**precious metal** gold, silver or platinum —**precious stone** (in jewelry trade) diamond, emerald, ruby, sapphire, pearl and sometimes black opal

precipice ('presipis) *n.* very steep cliff or rockface —**precipitous** (pri'sipitəs) *a.* sheer

precipitant (pri'sipitənt) *a.* **1.** hasty, rash **2.** abrupt —**pre'cipitance** *or* **pre'cipitancy** *n.*

precipitate (pri'sipitāt) *vt.* **1.** hasten happening of **2.** throw headlong **3.** *Chem.* cause to be deposited in solid form from solution —*a.* (pri'sipitit) **4.** too sudden **5.** rash, impetuous —*n.* (pri'sipitit) **6.** substance chemically precipitated —**pre'cipitately** *adv.* —**precipi'tation** *n.* rain, snow, sleet *etc.*

précis (prā'sē, 'prāse) *n.* abstract, summary (*pl.* **précis** (prā'sēz, 'prāsēz))

precise (pri'sīs) *a.* **1.** definite **2.** particular **3.** exact, strictly worded **4.** careful in observance **5.** punctilious, formal —**pre'cisely** *adv.* —**precision** (pri'sizhən) *n.* accuracy

preclude (pri'klōōd) *vt.* **1.** prevent from happening **2.** shut out

precocious (pri'kōshəs) *a.* developed, matured early or too soon —**precocity** (pri'kositi) *or* **pre'cociousness** *n.*

precognition (prēkog'nishən) *n. Psychol.* alleged ability to foresee future events —**pre'cognitive** *a.*

pre-Columbian art (prēkə'lumbiən) the indigenous art of North, Central and South America before 1492

preconceive (prēkən'sēv) *vt.* form an idea of beforehand —**precon'ception** *n.*

precondition (prēkən'dishən) *n.* necessary or required condition

precursor (pri'kərsər) *n.* one who or that which precedes —**pre'cursive** *or* **pre'cursory** *a.*

pred. predicate

predate (prē'dāt) *vt.* **1.** affix date to (document *etc.*) that is earlier than actual date **2.** assign date to (event *etc.*) that is earlier than actual or previously assigned date of occurrence **3.** be or occur at earlier date than; precede in time

predatory ('predətōri) *a.* **1.** hunting, killing other animals *etc.* for food **2.** plundering —**'predator** *n.* predatory animal

predecease (prēdi'sēs) *vt.* die before (some other person)

predecessor ('prēdisesər) *n.* **1.** one who precedes another in an office or position **2.** ancestor

predestine (prē'destin) *vt.* decree beforehand, foreordain —**predesti'nation** *n.*

predetermine (prēdi'tərmin) *vt.* **1.** determine beforehand **2.** influence, bias —**predetermi'nation** *n.*

predicament (pri'dikəmənt) *n.* perplexing, embarrassing or difficult situation

predicant ('predikənt) *a.* **1.** of preaching —*n.* **2.** member of religious order founded for preaching, *esp.* Dominican

predicate ('predikāt) *vt.* **1.** affirm, assert **2.** (*with* on *or* upon) base (argument *etc.*) —*n.* ('predikit) **3.** that which is predicated **4.** *Gram.* statement made about a subject —**'predicable** *a.* **1.** capable of being predicated —*n.* **2.** quality that can be predicated **3.** *Logic* any of five general forms of attribution, namely genus, species, differentia, property and accident —**predi'cation** *n.* —**'predicative** *a.*

predict (pri'dikt) *vt.* foretell, prophesy —**pre'dictable** *a.* —**pre'diction** *n.*

predilection (predi'lekshən, prē-) *n.* preference, liking, partiality

predispose (prēdi'spöz) *vt.* **1.** incline, influence **2.** make susceptible

predominate (pri'domināt) *vi.* be main or controlling element —**pre'dominance** *n.* —**pre'dominant** *a.* chief

pre-eminent (pri'eminənt) *a.* excelling all others, outstanding —**pre-eminence** *n.* —**pre-eminently** *adv.*

pre-empt (pri'empt) *vt.* acquire in advance of or to exclusion of others —**pre-emption** *n.* —**pre-emptive** *a.*

preen (prēn) *vt.* **1.** (of birds) trim (feathers) with beak, plume **2.** smarten (oneself)

pref. **1.** preface **2.** preference **3.** prefix

prefabricate (prē'fabrikāt) *vt.* manufacture (buildings *etc.*) in shaped sections, for rapid assembly on site —**pre'fab** *n.* prefabricated building, *esp.* house

preface ('prefis) *n.* **1.** introduction to book *etc.* —*vt.* **2.** introduce —**'prefatory** *a.*

prefect ('prēfekt) *n.* person put in authority —**'prefecture** *n.* office, residence, district of a prefect

prefer (pri'fər) *vt.* **1.** like better **2.** promote (**-rr-**) —**preferable** ('prefərəbəl) *a.* more desirable —**preferably** ('prefərəbli) *adv.* —**preference** ('prefərəns, 'prefrəns) *n.* —**preferential** (prefə'renchəl) *a.* giving, receiving preference —**pre'ferment** *n.* promotion, advancement

prefigure (prē'figyər) *vt.* exhibit, suggest by previous types, foreshadow —**pre'figurative** *a.*

prefix ('prēfiks) *n.* **1.** preposition or particle put at beginning of word or title —*vt.* (prē'fiks, 'prēfiks) **2.** put as introduction **3.** put before word to make compound

prefrontal lobotomy (prē'fruntəl) *see* **lobotomy** *at* LOBE

pregnant ('pregnant) *a.* **1.** carrying fetus in womb **2.** full of meaning, significance **3.** inventive —**'pregnancy** *n.*

prehensile (prē'hensil, -sīl) *a.* capable of grasping —**prehen'sility** *n.*

prehistoric (prēhi'storik) *or* **prehistorical** *a.* before period in which written history begins —**pre'history** *n.*

prejudge (prē'juj) *vt.* judge beforehand, *esp.* without sufficient evidence

prejudice ('prejədis) *n.* **1.** preconceived opinion **2.** bias, partiality **3.** injury likely to happen to person or his rights as result of others' action or judgment —*vt.* **4.** influence **5.** bias **6.** injure —**preju'dicial** *a.* **1.** injurious **2.** disadvantageous

prelate ('prelit) *n.* bishop or other church dignitary of equal or higher rank —**'prelacy** *n.* his office —**prelatical** (pri'latikəl) *a.*

preliminary (pri'limineri) *a.* **1.** preparatory, introductory —*n.* **2.** introductory, preparatory statement, action **3.** eliminating contest held before main competition

prelims ('prēlimz, prə'limz) *pl.n.* pages of book, such as title page *etc.* before main text (*also* **front matter**)

prelude ('prelyōōd) *n.* **1.** *Mus.* introductory movement **2.** performance, event *etc.* serving as introduction —*v.* **3.** serve as prelude to (something) —*vt.* **4.** introduce

premarital (prē'maritəl) *a.* occurring before marriage

premature (premə'tyōōər, -'tōōər, -'chōōər) *a.* **1.** happening, done before proper time **2.** impulsive, hasty **3.** (of infant) born before end of full period of gestation

premeditate (pri'meditāt) *vt.* consider, plan beforehand —**premedi'tation** *n.*

premenstrual (prē'menstrōōəl) *a.* of period in menstrual cycle just before menstruation

premier (pri'mēər, 'premiər) *n.* **1.** prime minister **2.** head of government of Aust. state —*a.* **3.** chief, foremost **4.** first —**pre'miership** *n.*

premiere (pri'myāər, -'mēər; primi'āər) *n.* first public performance of a play, motion picture *etc.*

premise ('premis) *n.* **1.** *Logic* proposition from which inference is drawn (*also* **'premiss**) —*pl.* **2.** house, building with its belongings 3. *Law* beginning of deed —*vt.* ('premis, pri'mīz) 4. state by way of introduction

premium ('prēmiəm) *n.* 1. bonus 2. sum paid for insurance 3. excess over nominal value 4. great value or regard

premonition (premə'nishən) *n.* presentiment, foreboding

prenatal (prē'nātəl) *a.* occurring, existing or taking place before birth

preoccupy (prē'okyəpI) *vt.* occupy to the exclusion of other things (**-pying, -pied**) —**preoccu'pation** *n.* mental concentration or absorption

preordain (prēōr'dān) *vt.* ordain or decree beforehand

prep. 1. preparation 2. preparatory 3. preposition

prepare (pri'pāər) *vt.* 1. make ready 2. make —*vi.* 3. get ready —**preparation** (prepə'rāshən) *n.* 1. making ready beforehand 2. something that is prepared, as a medicine 3. at school, (time spent) preparing work for lesson —**preparatory** (pri'parətöri) *a.* 1. serving to prepare 2. introductory —**preparedness** (pri'paridnis, -'per-) *n.* state of being prepared —'**preppie** *or* '**preppy** *n./a.* (denoting) one who apparently has a preparatory-school background —**preparatory school** private secondary school preparing students for college (*also* **prep school**)

prepay (prē'pā) *vt.* pay in advance

prepense (pri'pens) *a.* usu. in legal contexts, premeditated (*esp. in* **malice prepense**)

preponderate (pri'pondərāt) *vi.* be of greater weight or power —**pre'ponderance** *n.* superiority of power, numbers *etc.*

preposition (prepə'zishən) *n.* word marking relation between noun or pronoun and other words —**prepo'sitional** *a.*

prepossess (prēpə'zes) *vt.* 1. preoccupy or engross mentally 2. impress, *esp.* favorably, beforehand —**prepos'sessing** *a.* inviting favorable opinion, attractive, winning —**prepos'session** *n.*

preposterous (pri'postərəs) *a.* utterly absurd, foolish

prepuce ('prēpyoōs) *n.* 1. retractable fold of skin covering tip of penis; foreskin 2. similar fold of skin covering tip of clitoris

Pre-Raphaelite (prē'rafiəlIt) *n.* 1. member of **Pre-Raphaelite Brotherhood,** association of painters and writers founded in 1848 to revive qualities of It. painting before Raphael —*a.* 2. of Pre-Raphaelite painting and painters

prerequisite (prē'rekwizit) *n./a.* (something) required as prior condition

prerogative (pri'rogətiv) *n.* 1. peculiar power or right, *esp.* as vested in sovereign —*a.* 2. privileged

pres. 1. present (time) 2. presidential

Pres. President

presage ('presij) *n.* 1. omen, indication of something to come —*vt.* ('presij, pri'sāj) 2. foretell

presbyopia (prezbi'ōpiə) *n.* progressively diminishing ability of the eye to focus, *esp.* on near objects; long-sightedness

presbyter ('prezbitər) *n.* 1. elder in early Christian church 2. priest 3. member of a presbytery —**Presby'terian** *a./n.* (member) of Protestant Christian church emphasizing sovereignty and justice of God in highly structured representational system of ministers and lay persons —**Presby'terianism** *n.* —'**presbytery** *n.* 1. church court composed of all ministers within a certain district and one ruling elder from each church 2. *R.C.Ch.* priest's house

prescience ('preshiəns, 'preshəns, 'presiəns) *n.* foreknowledge —'**prescient** *a.*

prescribe (pri'skrib) *v.* 1. set out rules (for) 2. order 3. ordain 4. order use of (medicine) —**prescription** (pri'skripshən) *n.* 1. prescribing 2. thing prescribed 3. written statement of it —**prescriptive** (pri'skriptiv) *a.*

present[1] ('prezənt) *a.* 1. that is here 2. now existing or happening —*n.* 3. present time or tense —'**presence** *n.* 1. being present 2. appearance, bearing —'**presently** *adv.* 1. soon —**presence of mind** ability to remain calm and act constructively during crises —**present-day** *a.* of modern day; current —**present participle** participial form of verbs used adjectivally when action it describes is contemporaneous with that of main verb of sentence and also used in formation of certain compound tenses —**present perfect** *Gram. see* PERFECT (sense 9)

present[2] (pri'zent) *vt.* 1. introduce formally 2. show 3. give 4. offer 5. point, aim —*n.* ('prezənt) 6. gift —**pre'sentable** *a.* fit to be seen —**presentation** (prēzen'tāshən, prezən-) *n.*

presentiment (pri'zentimənt) *n.* sense of something (*esp.* evil) about to happen

preserve (pri'zərv) *vt.* 1. keep from harm, injury or decay 2. maintain 3. pickle —*n.* 4. special area 5. that which is preserved, as fruit *etc.* 6. place where game is kept for private fishing, shooting —**preservation** (prezər'vāshən) *n.* —**pre'servative** *n.* 1. chemical added to perishable foods, drinks *etc.* to prevent them from rotting —*a.* 2. tending to preserve 3. having quality of preserving

preside (pri'zId) *vi.* 1. be chairman 2. (*with* over) superintend —**presidency** ('prezidənsi) *n.* —**president** ('prezidənt) *n.* head of society, company, republic *etc.* —**presidential** (prezi'denchəl) *a.*

presidium (pri'sidiəm) *n.* 1. (*oft.* **P-**) in Communist countries, permanent committee of larger body, such as legislature, that acts for it when it is in recess 2. collective presidency

press[1] (pres) *vt.* 1. subject to push or squeeze 2. smooth by pressure or heat 3. urge steadily, earnestly —*vi.* 4. bring weight to bear 5. throng 6. hasten —*n.* 7. a pressing 8. machine for pressing, *esp.* printing machine 9. printing house 10. art or process of printing 11. newspapers collectively 12. crowd 13. stress 14. large cupboard —'**pressing** *a.* 1. urgent 2. persistent —**press agent** person employed to secure publicity —**press conference** interview for press reporters given by politician *etc.* —**press gallery** area for newspaper reporters, *esp.* in legislative assembly —'**pressman** *n.* 1. printer who attends to the press 2. journalist —**press-up** *n.* exercise in which body is alternately raised and lowered by arms only, trunk being kept straight (*also* **push-up**)

press[2] (pres) *vt.* force to serve in navy or army —**press gang** formerly, body of men employed to press men into naval service

pressure ('preshər) *n.* 1. act of pressing 2. influence 3. authority 4. difficulties 5. *Phys.* thrust per unit area —**pressuri'zation** *n.* in aircraft, maintenance of normal atmospheric pressure at high altitudes —'**pressurize** *vt.* —**pressure cooker** vessel like saucepan which cooks food rapidly by steam under pressure —**pressure group** organized group which exerts influence on policies, public opinion *etc.*

prestidigitation (prestidiji'tāshən) *n. see* **sleight of hand** *at* SLEIGHT —**presti'digitator** *n.*

prestige (pre'stēzh) *n.* 1. reputation based on high achievement, character, wealth *etc.* 2. power to impress or influence —**prestigious** (pre'stijəs) *a.*

presto ('prestō) *adv.* 1. *Mus.* quickly 2. immediately (*esp. in* **hey presto**)

prestressed (prē'strest) *a.* (of concrete) containing stretched steel cables for strengthening

presume (pri'zoōm) *vt.* 1. take for granted —*vi.* 2. take liberties —**pre'sumably** *adv.* 1. probably 2. doubtlessly —**presumption** (pri'zumpshən) *n.* 1. forward, arrogant opinion or conduct 2. strong probability —**presumptive** (pri'zumptiv) *a.* that may be assumed as true or valid until contrary is proved —**presumptuous** (pri'zumpchoōəs) *a.* forward, impudent, taking liberties —**presumptuously** (pri'zumpchoōəsli) *adv.* —**heir presumptive** heir whose right may be defeated by birth of nearer relative

presuppose (prēsə'pōz) *vt.* assume or take for granted beforehand —**presuppo'sition** *n.*

pretend (pri'tend) *vt.* 1. claim or allege (something untrue) 2. make believe, as in play —*vi.* 3. lay claim (to) —**pre'tender** *n.* claimant (to throne) —'**pretense** *or* '**pretence** *n.* 1. simulation 2. pretext —**pre'tension** *n.* —**pre'tentious** *a.* 1. making claim to special merit or importance 2. given to outward show

preter- (*comb. form*) beyond, more than

preterit *or* **preterite** ('pretərit) *a.* 1. past 2. expressing past state or action —*n.* 3. past tense

preternatural (prētər'nachrəl) *a.* 1. out of ordinary way of nature 2. abnormal, supernatural

pretext ('prētekst) *n.* excuse

pretty ('priti) *a.* 1. having beauty that is attractive rather than imposing 2. charming —*adv.* 3. fairly, moderately —'**prettify** *vt.* make pretty, *esp.* in trivial way; embellish —'**prettily** *adv.* —'**prettiness** *n.*

pretzel ('pretsəl) *n.* brittle biscuit usu. in form of knot or stick

prevail (pri'vāl) *vi.* 1. gain mastery 2. triumph 3. be in fashion, generally established —**pre'vailing** *a.* 1. widespread 2. predominant —**prevalence** ('prevələns) *n.* —**prevalent** ('prevələnt) *a.* extensively existing, rife

prevaricate (pri'varikāt) *vi.* 1. make evasive or misleading statements 2. tell lie(s) —**prevari'cation** *n.* —**pre'varicator** *n.*

prevent (pri'vent) *vt.* stop, hinder —**pre'ventable** *a.* —**pre'vention** *n.* —**pre'ventive** *a.* preventing, or serving to prevent, *esp.* disease (*also* **pre'ventative**) —**preventive medicine** medical specialty dealing with prevention of disease

preview ('prēvyoō) *n.* 1. advance showing 2. showing of scenes from forthcoming motion picture

previous ('prēviəs) *a.* 1. earlier 2. preceding 3. *inf.* hasty —'**previously** *adv.* before

prey (prā) *n.* 1. animal hunted and killed by another carnivorous animal 2. victim —*vi.* (*oft. with* **upon**) 3. seize for food 4. treat as prey 5. afflict, obsess

price (prIs) *n.* 1. that for which thing is bought or sold 2. cost 3. value 4. reward 5. odds in betting —*vt.* 6. fix, ask price for —'**priceless** *a.* 1. invaluable 2. *inf.* very funny —'**pricey** *or* '**pricy** *a. inf.* expensive —**price control** establishment of maximum price levels for basic goods and services by government —**at any price** whatever the price or cost

prick (prik) vt. 1. pierce slightly with sharp point 2. cause to feel mental pain 3. mark by prick —v. 4. (usu. with up) erect (ears) —n. 5. slight hole made by pricking 6. pricking or being pricked 7. sting 8. remorse 9. that which pricks 10. sharp point —'**prickle** n. 1. thorn, spike —vi. 2. feel tingling or pricking sensation —'**prickly** a. —**prickly heat** inflammation of skin with stinging pains —**prickly pear** 1. tropical cactus having flattened or cylindrical spiny joints and oval fruit 2. fruit of prickly pear

pride (prīd) n. 1. too high an opinion of oneself, inordinate self-esteem 2. worthy self-esteem 3. feeling of elation or great satisfaction 4. something causing this 5. group (of lions) —v.refl. 6. take pride

prie-dieu (prē'dyə) n. piece of furniture consisting of low surface for kneeling upon and narrow front surmounted by rest, for use when praying

priest (prēst) or (fem.) **priestess** n. official minister of religion, clergyman —'**priest-hood** n. —'**priestly** a.

prig (prig) n. self-righteous person who professes superior culture, morality etc. —'**priggery** n. —'**priggish** a.

prim (prim) a. very restrained, formally prudish

prima ('prēmə) a. first —**prima ballerina** leading female ballet dancer —**prima donna** ('primə 'donə, 'prēmə) 1. principal female singer in opera 2. inf. temperamental person (pl. -s)

primacy ('prīməsi) n. 1. state of being first in rank, grade etc. 2. office of archbishop

prima facie ('primə 'fāshə, -'fāshi) Lat. at first sight

primal ('praiməl) a. 1. of earliest age 2. first, original —pri'**marily** adv. —'**primary** a. 1. chief 2. of the first stage, decision etc. 3. elementary —**primary accent** or **stress** Linguis. strongest accent in word or breath group —**primary colors** red, yellow and blue, which can produce all other colors, but cannot themselves be made from any combination of other colors —**primary election** 1. election in which voters directly nominate the candidate of their own party for office 2. election where voters of the same political party select delegates to a nominating convention

primate ('prīmāt) n. 1. one of order of mammals comprising man, apes, monkeys, marmosets and lemurs 2. archbishop or the highest ranking bishop of a province

prime[1] (prīm) a. 1. fundamental 2. original 3. chief 4. best —n. 5. first, best part of anything 6. youth 7. full health and vigor —vt. 8. prepare (gun, engine, pump etc.) for use 9. fill up, eg with information, liquor —'**priming** n. powder mixture used for priming gun —**prime meridian** the 0° meridian from which other meridians are calculated, usu. taken to pass through Greenwich —**Prime Minister** 1. the chief executive of a parliamentary government 2. chief minister of ruler or state —**prime number** integer that cannot be divided into other integers but is only divisible by itself or 1

prime[2] (prīm) vt. prepare for paint with preliminary coating of oil, size etc. —'**primer** or '**priming** n. paint etc. for priming

primer ('primər) n. elementary school book or manual

primeval (prī'mēvəl) a. of the earliest age of the world

primitive ('primitiv) a. 1. of an early undeveloped kind, ancient 2. crude, rough

primogeniture (prīmō'jenichŏŏr, -chər) n.

the exclusive right of inheritance by the first-born, usu. son —**primo'genital** a. —**pri-mo'genitor** n. 1. forefather; ancestor 2. earliest parent or ancestor, as of race

primordial (prī'mördiəl) a. existing at or from the beginning

Primost ('prēmōst) n. see MYSOST

primp (primp) v. dress (oneself), esp. in fine clothes; prink

primrose ('primrōz) n. 1. any of various pale yellow spring flowers of the genus Primula 2. this color —a. 3. of this color —**primrose path** pleasurable way of life

primula ('primyələ) n. genus of plants of cosmopolitan distribution of over 500 species and countless hybrids, all with 5-petaled flowers

prince (prins) n. 1. male member of royal or noble family 2. ruler, chief 3. person of high standing or privilege, as in prince of the church ('**princess** fem.) —'**princely** a. 1. generous, lavish 2. stately 3. magnificent —'**princess** a. (of dress) cut to follow curves of body with no seam at waistline —**Prince of Darkness** the devil —**Prince of Peace** Jesus Christ —**Prince of Wales** title usu. conferred on heir to British throne —**Prince-of-Wales check** woven fabric with large, open-check pattern with colored overcheck

principal ('prinsipəl) a. 1. chief in importance —n. 2. person for whom another is agent 3. head of institution, esp. school or college 4. sum of money lent and yielding interest 5. chief actor —**princi'pality** n. country ruled by a prince —**principal parts** Gram. main inflected forms of verb, from which all other inflections may be deduced

principle ('prinsipəl) n. 1. moral rule 2. settled reason of action 3. uprightness 4. fundamental truth or element

prink (pringk) v. 1. dress (oneself etc.) finely; deck out —vi. 2. preen oneself

print (print) vt. 1. reproduce (words, pictures etc.) by pressing inked types on blocks to paper etc. 2. produce thus 3. write in imitation of this 4. impress 5. Photog. produce (pictures) from negatives 6. stamp (fabric) with colored design —n. 7. printed matter 8. printed lettering 9. written imitation of printed type 10. photograph 11. impression, mark left on surface by thing that has pressed against it 12. printed cotton fabric —'**printer** n. one engaged in printing —'**printing** n. 1. business or art of producing printed matter 2. printed text 3. copies of book etc. printed at one time (also im'**pression**) 4. form of writing in which letters resemble printed letters —**printed circuit** electronic circuit with wiring printed on an insulating base —**printed matter** printed material eligible for special postage rates —**printer's devil** apprentice or errand boy in printing establishment —**printing press** machine for printing —**print-out** n. printed information from computer, tele-printer etc. —**out of print** no longer available from publisher

prior ('prīər) a. 1. earlier —n. 2. chief of religious house or order (-ess fem.) —pri'**ority** n. 1. precedence 2. something given special attention —'**priory** n. monastery, nunnery under prior, prioress

prise (prīz) vt. see PRIZE[1] (senses 6, 7)

prism ('prizəm) n. 1. transparent body bounded in part by two plane faces which are not parallel 2. something which refracts light 3. in geometry, polyhedron two of whose faces are polygons that lie on parallel planes and whose other faces are parallelo-

grams intersecting on parallel lines —**pris-'matic** a. 1. of prism shape 2. (of color) such as is produced by refraction through prism, rainbow-like, brilliant

prison ('prizən) n. jail —'**prisoner** n. 1. one kept in prison 2. captive —**prisoner of war** person, esp. serviceman, captured by enemy in time of war —**prisoner's base** children's game where members of opposing sides are captured and can only be freed in specified ways

prissy ('prisi) a. inf. fussy, prim

pristine ('pristēn, pris'tēn) a. 1. original 2. primitive 3. unspoiled, good

private ('prīvit) a. 1. secret, not public 2. reserved for, belonging to, or concerning, an individual only 3. personal 4. secluded 5. denoting soldier of lowest rank —n. 6. soldier or marine one grade above a recruit —'**privacy** n. —'**privately** adv. —privati'**zation** n. —'**privatize** vt. take into or return to private ownership (a company or concern previously owned by the State) —**private eye** inf. private detective —**private first class** enlisted man in the army or marines above the rank of private and below the rank of corporal —**private parts** or '**privates** pl.n. genitals —**private school** school under financial and managerial control of private body or charitable trust

privateer (prīvə'tēər) n. Hist. 1. privately owned armed vessel authorized by government to take part in war 2. captain of such ship

privation (prī'vāshən) n. 1. loss or lack of comforts or necessities 2. hardship 3. act of depriving —'**privative** ('privətiv) a.

privet ('privit) n. any of various ornamental shrubs with half-evergreen leaves and white flowers

privilege ('privilij) n. 1. advantage or favor that only a few obtain 2. right, advantage belonging to person or class —'**privileged** a. enjoying special right or immunity

privy ('privi) a. 1. admitted to knowledge of secret —n. 2. toilet, esp. outhouse 3. Law person having interest in an action —'**privily** adv. —**privy council** council of state of monarch or governor

prize[1] (prīz) n. 1. reward given for success in competition 2. thing striven for 3. thing won, eg in lottery etc. —a. 4. winning or likely to win a prize —vt. 5. value highly 6. force open by levering 7. obtain with difficulty —'**prize-fight** n. boxing match for money —'**prize-fighter** n.

prize[2] (prīz) n. ship, property captured in (naval) warfare

pro[1] (prō) adv./prep. in favor (of)

pro[2] (prō) n. 1. professional 2. prostitute (pl. -s) —a. 3. professional

pro- (comb. form) for, instead of, before, in front, as in proconsul, pronoun, project. Such compounds are not given here where the meaning may easily be found from the simple word

probable ('probəbəl) a. likely —proba'**bility** n. 1. ratio of number of ways in which an event can occur in a specified form to the total ways in which the event can occur 2. anything that has appearance of truth 3. branch of mathematics —'**probably** adv.

probate ('prōbāt) n. 1. proving of authenticity of will 2. certificate of this —**probate court** court for the probate of wills, administration of estates, and related matters

probation (prō'bāshən) n. 1. system of dealing with lawbreakers, esp. juvenile ones, by placing them under supervision of probation officer for stated period 2. testing of candidate before admission to full membership —**pro'bationer** *n.* person on probation —**probation officer** officer of court who supervises offenders placed on probation

probe (prōb) *vt.* 1. search into, examine, question closely —*n.* 2. that which probes, or is used to probe 3. thorough inquiry

probity ('prōbiti) *n.* honesty, uprightness, integrity

problem ('probləm) *n.* 1. matter *etc.* difficult to deal with or solve 2. question set for solution 3. puzzle —**proble'matic(al)** *a.* 1. questionable; uncertain 2. disputable

proboscis (prə'bosis) *n.* trunk or long snout, *eg* of elephant (*pl.* **-es, proboscides** (prə-'bosidēz))

procaine hydrochloride ('prōkān) local or general anesthetic administered by injection or intravenously in conjunction with adrenaline

proceed (prə'sēd) *vi.* 1. go forward, continue 2. be carried on 3. go to law —**pro'cedural** *a.* —**pro'cedure** *n.* 1. act, manner of proceeding 2. conduct —**pro'ceeding** *n.* 1. act or course of action 2. transaction —*pl.* 3. minutes of meeting 4. methods of prosecuting charge, claim *etc.* —**'proceeds** *pl.n.* price or profit

process ('prōses) *n.* 1. series of actions or changes 2. method of operation 3. state of going on 4. action of law 5. outgrowth —*vt.* 6. handle, treat, prepare by special method of manufacture *etc.* —**pro'cession** *n.* 1. regular, orderly progress 2. train of persons in formal order

proclaim (prə'klām) *vt.* announce publicly, declare —**proclamation** (proklə'māshən) *n.*

proclivity (prō'kliviti) *n.* inclination, tendency

proconsul (prō'konsəl) *n. Hist.* governor of province

procrastinate (prə'krastināt, prō-) *vi.* put off (an action) until later, delay —**procrasti-'nation** *n.* —**pro'crastinator** *n.*

procreate ('prōkriāt) *v.* produce (offspring) —**procre'ation** *n.*

Procrustean (prə'krustiən, prō-) *a.* compelling uniformity by violence

proctology (prok'toləji) *n.* branch of medicine concerned with anus and rectum

proctor ('proktər) *n.* 1. steward, proxy 2. university official with disciplinary powers

procure (prə'kyōōər) *vt.* 1. obtain, acquire 2. provide 3. bring about —*vi.* 4. act as pimp —**pro'curable** *a.* —**procuration** (prokyə-'rāshən) *n.* —**procurator** ('prokyōōrātər) *n.* one who manages another's affairs —**pro-'curement** *n.* —**pro'curer** *n.* 1. one who procures 2. pimp

prod (prod) *vt.* 1. poke with something pointed (**-dd-**) —*n.* 2. prodding 3. goad 4. pointed instrument

prodigal ('prodigəl) *a.* 1. wasteful 2. extravagant —*n.* 3. spendthrift —**prodi'gality** *n.* reckless extravagance

prodigy ('prodiji) *n.* 1. person with some marvelous gift 2. thing causing wonder —**pro'digious** *a.* 1. very great, immense 2. extraordinary —**pro'digiously** *adv.*

produce (prə'dyōōs, -'dōōs) *vt.* 1. bring into existence 2. yield 3. make 4. bring forward 5. manufacture 6. exhibit 7. present on stage, screen, television 8. *Geom.* extend in length —*n.* ('prodōōs, 'prō-; -dyōōs) 9. that which is yielded or made —**pro'ducer** *n.* person who produces, *esp.* play, motion picture *etc.* —**product** ('produkt) *n.* 1. result of process of manufacture 2. number resulting from multiplication —**pro'duction** *n.* 1. producing

2. things produced —**pro'ductive** *a.* 1. fertile 2. creative 3. efficient —**productivity** (produk'tiviti) *n.*

proem ('prōem) *n.* introduction or preface, such as to work of literature

Prof. Professor

profane (prō'fān, prə-) *a.* 1. irreverent, blasphemous 2. not sacred —*vt.* 3. pollute, desecrate —**profanation** (profə'nāshən) *n.* —**profanity** (prō'faniti, prə-) *n.* profane talk or behavior, blasphemy

profess (prə'fes) *vt.* 1. affirm, acknowledge 2. confess publicly 3. assert 4. claim, pretend —**professedly** (prə'fesidli) *adv.* avowedly —**pro'fession** *n.* 1. calling or occupation, *esp.* learned, scientific or artistic 2. a professing 3. vow of religious faith on entering religious order —**pro'fessional** *a.* 1. engaged in a profession 2. engaged in a game or sport for money —*n.* 3. paid player —**pro'fessor** *n.* 1. teacher of highest rank in university 2. *inf.* one who teaches or professes special knowledge in any art, sport or occupation requiring skill —**professorial** (prōfi'sōriəl, profi-) *a.* —**professoriate** (prōfi'sōriit, profi-) *n.* body of university professors —**pro'fessorship** *n.*

proffer ('profər) *vt./n.* offer

proficient (prə'fishənt) *a.* skilled; expert —**pro'ficiency** *n.*

profile ('prōfīl) *n.* 1. outline, *esp.* of face, as seen from side 2. brief biographical sketch 3. verbal, numerical or graphical summary or analysis

profit ('profit) *n.* 1. (*oft. pl.*) money gained 2. benefit obtained —*v.* 3. benefit —**'profitable** *a.* yielding profit —**profi'teer** *n.* 1. one who makes excessive profits at the expense of the public —*vi.* 2. make excessive profits —**'profitless** *a.* —**profit-sharing** *n.* system in which portion of net profit of business is distributed to employees, usu. in proportion to wages or length of service

profligate ('profligit) *a.* 1. dissolute 2. reckless, wasteful —*n.* 3. dissolute person —**'profligacy** *n.*

pro forma ('prō 'förmə) *Lat.* for the sake of, as a matter of form —**pro forma invoice** invoice presented at time of payment

profound (prə'fownd) *a.* 1. very learned 2. deep —**profundity** (prə'funditi) *n.*

profuse (prə'fyōōs) *a.* abundant, prodigal —**pro'fusion** *n.*

progeny ('projini) *n.* children —**progenitor** (prō'jenitər) *n.* ancestor

progesterone (prō'jestərōn) *n.* hormone which prepares uterus for pregnancy and prevents further ovulation

prognathous ('prognəthəs, prog'nāthəs) *or* **prognathic** (prog'nathik) *a.* with projecting lower jaw

prognosis (prog'nōsis) *n.* 1. art of foretelling course of disease by symptoms 2. forecast (*pl.* **-noses** (-'nōsēz)) —**prognostic** (prog'nostik) *a.* 1. of, serving as prognosis —*n.* 2. *Med.* any symptom used in making prognosis 3. sign of some future occurrence —**prognosticate** (prog'nostikāt) *vt.* foretell —**prognostication** (prognosti'kāshən) *n.*

program ('prōgram) *n.* 1. plan, detailed notes of intended proceedings 2. broadcast on radio or television 3. syllabus or curriculum 4. detailed instructions for computer —*vt.* 5. feed program into (computer) 6. arrange detailed instructions for (computer) (**-mm-**) —**'programmer** *n.*

progress ('progris, -gres) *n.* 1. onward movement 2. development —*vi.* (prə'gres) 3. go forward 4. improve —**pro'gression** *n.* 1. moving forward 2. advance, improvement 3.

increase or decrease of numbers or magnitudes according to fixed law 4. *Mus.* regular succession of chords —**pro'gressive** *a.* 1. progressing by degrees 2. favoring political or social reform 3. *Gram.* designating form of verb expressing action or state

prohibit (prō'hibit, prə-) *vt.* forbid —**prohibition** (prōi'bishən) *n.* 1. act of forbidding 2. interdict 3. interdiction of supply and consumption of alcoholic drinks —**pro'hibitive** *a.* 1. tending to forbid or exclude 2. (of prices) very high —**pro'hibitory** *a.*

project ('projekt) *n.* 1. plan, scheme 2. design —*vt.* (prə'jekt) 3. plan 4. throw 5. cause to appear on distant background —*vi.* (prə'jekt) 6. stick out, protrude —**projectile** (prə'jektil) *n.* 1. heavy missile, *esp.* shell or ball —*a.* 2. designed for throwing —**projection** (prə'jekshən) *n.* —**projectionist** (prə-'jekshənist) *n.* operator of motion-picture projector —**projector** (prə'jektər) *n.* 1. apparatus for projecting photographic images, motion pictures, slides on screen 2. one that forms scheme or design

prolapse (prō'laps, 'prōlaps) *n.* falling, slipping down of internal part of body from normal position (*also* **pro'lapsus**)

prolate ('prōlāt) *a.* having polar diameter greater than the equatorial diameter

prolegomena (prōle'gominə) *pl.n.* introductory remarks prefixed to book; preface

proletariat (prōli'teriit, -'tar-; -iat) *n.* 1. all wage earners collectively 2. lowest class of community, working class —**prole'tarian** *a./n.*

proliferate (prə'lifərāt) *v.* grow or reproduce rapidly —**prolifer'ation** *n.*

prolific (prə'lifik) *a.* 1. producing fruit, offspring *etc.* in abundance 2. producing constant or successful results 3. fruitful

prolix (prō'liks, 'prōliks) *a.* (of speech *etc.*) wordy, long-winded —**pro'lixity** *n.*

prologue ('prōlog) *n.* introductory act or event

prolong (prə'long) *vt.* lengthen, protract —**prolongation** (prōlong'gāshən) *n.*

prom (prom) *n. inf.* dance at school or college

promenade (promə'nād, -'näd) *n.* 1. leisurely walk 2. place made or used for this —*vi.* 3. take leisurely walk 4. go up and down

promethium (prə'mēthiəm) *n. Chem.* metallic element Symbol Pm, at. wt. 147, at. no. 61

prominent ('prominənt) *a.* 1. sticking out 2. conspicuous 3. distinguished —**'prominence** *n.*

promiscuous (prə'miskyōōs) *a.* 1. indiscriminate, *esp.* in sexual relations 2. mixed without distinction —**promiscuity** (promi-'skyōōiti) *n.*

promise ('promis) *v.* 1. give undertaking or assurance (of) —*vi.* 2. be likely —*n.* 3. undertaking to do or not to do something 4. potential —**'promising** *a.* showing good signs, hopeful —**'promissory** *a.* containing promise —**Promised Land** 1. *O.T.* land of Canaan, promised by God to Abraham and his descendants as their heritage 2. *Christianity* heaven 3. place where one expects to find greater happiness —**promissory note** written promise to pay sum to person named

promontory ('proməntöri) *n.* point of high land jutting out into the sea, headland

promote (prə'mōt) *vt.* 1. help forward 2. move up to higher rank or position 3. work for 4. encourage sale of —**pro'moter** *n.* —**pro'motion** *n.* 1. advancement 2. preferment

prompt (prompt) *a.* 1. done at once 2. acting with alacrity 3. punctual 4. ready —*vt.* 5.

urge, suggest —v. 6. help out (actor or speaker) by reading or suggesting next words —'**prompter** n. —'**promptitude** or '**promptness** n. —'**promptly** adv.

promulgate ('promʌlgāt) vt. proclaim, publish —**promul'gation** n. —'**promulgator** n.

pron. 1. pronoun 2. pronunciation

prone (prōn) a. 1. lying face or front downward 2. inclined —'**proneness** n.

prong (prong) n. single spike of fork or similar instrument

pronghorn ('pronghörn) n. deerlike antelope found in treeless country in W North America from southern Canada to northern Mexico

pronoun ('prōnown) n. word used to replace noun —**pro'nominal** a. pert. to, like pronoun

pronounce (prə'nowns) vt. 1. utter formally 2. form with organs of speech 3. say distinctly 4. declare —vi. 5. give opinion or decision —**pro'nounceable** a. —**pro'nounced** a. strongly marked, decided —**pro'nouncement** n. declaration —**pronunci'ation** n. 1. manner in which word etc. is pronounced 2. articulation 3. phonetic transcription of a word

pronto ('prontō) adv. inf. at once, immediately, quickly

proof (prŏof) n. 1. evidence 2. thing which proves 3. test, demonstration 4. trial impression from type or engraved plate 5. Photog. print from a negative 6. standard of strength of alcoholic drink —a. 7. giving impenetrable defense 8. of proved strength —'**proofread** v. read and correct (proofs) —'**proofreader** n. —'**proofreading** n.

-**proof** (comb. form) impervious to; resisting effects of, as in waterproof

prop[1] (prop) vt. 1. support, sustain, hold up (-**pp**-) —n. 2. pole, beam etc. used as support

prop[2] (prop) n. propeller —'**prop'jet** n. see TURBOPROP

prop[3] (prop) n. (theatrical) property

prop. 1. proper(ly) 2. property 3. proposition 4. proprietor

propaganda (propə'gandə) n. organized dissemination of information to spread particular doctrines, principles, information etc. —**propa'gandist** a./n.

propagate ('propəgāt) vt. 1. reproduce, breed, spread by sowing, breeding etc. 2. transmit —vi. 3. breed, multiply —**propa'gation** n. —'**propagative** a.

propane ('prōpān) n. colorless, flammable gas occurring naturally in crude petroleum

propel (prə'pel) vt. cause to move forward (-**ll**-) —**pro'pellant** or **pro'pellent** n. something causing propulsion, eg rocket fuel —**pro'peller** n. revolving shaft with blades for driving ship or aircraft —**pro'pulsion** n. act of driving forward —**pro'pulsive** or **pro'pulsory** a. tending, having power to propel 2. urging on

propensity (prə'pensiti) n. 1. inclination or bent 2. tendency 3. disposition

proper ('propər) a. 1. appropriate 2. correct 3. conforming to etiquette, decorous 4. strict 5. (of noun) denoting individual person or place —'**properly** adv. —**proper fraction** fraction in which numerator is greater than denominator

property ('propərti) n. 1. that which is owned 2. estate whether in lands, goods or money 3. quality, attribute of something 4. article used on stage in play etc.

prophet ('profit) n. 1. inspired teacher or revealer of Divine Will 2. foreteller of future (-**ess** fem.) —**prophecy** ('profisi) n. prediction, prophetic utterance —**prophesy** ('profisī) v. foretell —**prophetic** (prə'fetik) a.

prophylactic (prōfi'laktik, profi-) n./a. 1. (something) done or used to ward off disease —n. 2. condom —**prophy'laxis** n.

propinquity (prə'pingkwiti) n. nearness, proximity, close kinship

propitiate (prō'pishiāt) vt. appease, gain favor of —**propiti'ation** n. —**pro'pitiatory** a. —**pro'pitious** a. favorable, auspicious

proponent (prə'pōnənt) n. one who advocates something

proportion (prə'pörshən) n. 1. part of whole 2. the equality of 2 ratios, eg 1 is to 2 as 4 is to 8 3. correct relation in size and/or amount of degree between one thing and another —pl. 4. dimensions —vt. 5. arrange proportions of —**pro'portional** a. —**pro'portional** or **pro'portionate** a. 1. having a due proportion 2. corresponding in size, number etc. —**pro'portionally** adv. —**proportional representation** representation of parties in elective body in proportion to votes they win

propose (prə'pōz) vt. 1. put forward for consideration 2. nominate 3. intend —vi. 4. offer marriage —**pro'posal** n. —**pro'poser** n. —**proposition** (propə'zishən) n. 1. offer 2. statement, assertion 3. theorem 4. suggestion of terms 5. inf. thing to be dealt with

propound (prə'pownd) vt. put forward for consideration or solution

proprietor (prə'prīətər) n. owner (-**tress**, -**trix** fem.) —**pro'prietary** a. 1. belonging to owner 2. made by firm with exclusive rights of manufacture

propriety (prə'prīəti) n. properness, correct conduct, fitness

propulsion (prə'pulshən) n. see PROPEL

pro rata ('rātə, 'rätə) Lat. in proportion

prorate (prō'rāt) vt. divide proportionately

prorogue (prə'rōg) vt. dismiss (parliament) at end of session without dissolution

prosaic (prō'zāik) a. commonplace, unromantic

pros and cons various arguments in favor of and against motion, course of action etc.

proscenium (prō'sēniəm) n. arch or opening framing stage (pl. -**nia** (-niə))

proscribe (prō'skrīb) vt. outlaw, condemn —**proscription** (prō'skripshən) n.

prose (prōz) n. speech or writing without rhyme or meter —'**prosily** adv. —'**prosiness** n. —'**prosy** a. tedious, dull

prosecute ('prosikyŏot) vt. carry on, bring legal proceedings against —**prose'cution** n. —'**prosecutor** n. (-**trix** fem.)

proselyte ('prosilīt) n. convert —**proselytism** ('prosilītizəm, -lit-) n. —**proselytize** ('prosilitīz) v.

prosody ('prosədi) n. system, study of versification —'**prosodist** n.

prospect ('prospekt) n. 1. (sometimes pl.) expectation, chance for success 2. view, outlook 3. likely customer or subscriber 4. mental view —v. 5. explore, esp. for gold —**pro'spective** a. 1. anticipated 2. future —**pro'spectively** adv. —'**prospector** n. —**pro'spectus** n. circular describing company, school etc.

prosper ('prospər) v. (cause to) do well —**pros'perity** n. good fortune, wellbeing —'**prosperous** a. 1. doing well, successful 2. flourishing, rich, well-off —'**prosperously** adv.

prostaglandin (prostə'glandin) n. any of group of biological compounds which act on smooth muscle of the vascular and reproductive systems

prostate ('prostāt) n. gland accessory to male generative organs

prosthesis (pros'thēsis, 'prosthisis) n. (re-

placement of part of body with) artificial substitute (pl. -**ses** (-sēz))

prostitute ('prostityŏot, -tŏot) n. 1. one who offers sexual intercourse in return for payment —vt. 2. make a prostitute of 3. put to unworthy use —**prosti'tution** n.

prostrate ('prostrāt) a. 1. lying flat 2. crushed, submissive, overcome —vt. 3. throw flat on ground 4. reduce to exhaustion —**pros'tration** n.

Prot. Protestant

protactinium (prōtak'tiniəm) n. Chem. metallic element Symbol Pa, at. wt. 231.0, at. no. 91

protagonist (prō'tagənist) n. 1. leading character 2. principal actor 3. champion of a cause

protasis ('protəsis) n. introductory clause of conditional sentence (pl. -**ses** (-sēz))

protean ('prōtiən, prō'tēən) a. 1. variable 2. versatile

protect (prə'tekt) vt. defend, guard, keep from harm —**pro'tection** n. —**pro'tectionist** n. one who advocates protecting industries by taxing competing imports —**pro'tective** a. —**pro'tector** n. 1. one who protects 2. regent —**pro'tectorate** n. 1. relation of state to territory it protects and controls 2. such territory 3. office, period of protector of a state

protégé or (fem.) **protégée** ('prōtizhā) n. one under another's care, protection or patronage

protein ('prōtēn) n. any of various kinds of organic compound which form most essential part of food of living creatures —**proteinuria** (prōtən'yŏoriə, -'ŏoriə) n. protein in the urine, usu. indicating kidney disease

pro tempore ('prō 'tempəri) Lat. for the time being (also **pro tem**)

protest ('prōtest) n. 1. declaration or demonstration of objection —vi. (prə'test) 2. object —v. (prə'test) 3. make declaration (against) 4. assert formally —**protes'tation** n. strong declaration

Protestant ('protistənt) a. 1. belonging to any branch of the Western Church outside the Roman Catholic Church —n. 2. member of such a church —'**Protestantism** n.

prothrombin (prō'thrombin) n. substance important in blood clotting

proto- or sometimes before vowel **prot-** (comb. form) first, as in prototype

protocol ('prōtəkol) n. 1. diplomatic etiquette 2. draft of terms signed by parties as basis of formal treaty 3. plan for medical or scientific experiment

proton ('prōton) n. positively charged particle in nucleus of atom

protoplasm ('prōtəplazəm) n. substance that is living matter of all animal and plant cells —**proto'plasmic** a.

prototype ('prōtətīp) n. 1. original or model after which thing is copied 2. pattern

protozoan (prōtə'zōən) n. minute animal of lowest and simplest class (pl. -**zoa** (-'zōə))

protract (prə'trakt) vt. 1. lengthen 2. prolong 3. delay 4. draw to scale —**pro'tracted** a. 1. long-drawn-out 2. tedious —**pro'traction** n. —**pro'tractor** n. instrument for measuring angles on paper

protrude (prō'trŏod) v. stick out, (cause to) project —**pro'trusile** a. Zool. capable of being thrust forward —**pro'trusion** n. —**pro'trusive** a. thrusting forward —**pro'trusively** adv.

protuberant (prō'tyŏobərənt, -'tŏo-) a. bulging out —**pro'tuberance** or **pro'tuberancy** n. bulge, swelling

proud (prowd) *a.* **1.** feeling or displaying pride **2.** arrogant **3.** gratified **4.** noble **5.** self-respecting **6.** stately —**'proudly** *adv.* —**proud flesh** flesh growing around healing wound

Prov. 1. Provençal **2.** *Bible* Proverbs **3.** Province **4.** Provost

prove (prōōv) *vt.* **1.** establish validity of **2.** demonstrate, test —*vi.* **3.** turn out (to be *etc.*) **4.** (of dough) rise in warm place before baking (**proved, 'proven** *pp.*) —**proving ground** place for testing new equipment *etc.*

provenance ('provinəns) *n.* place of origin, source

Provençal (provən'säl; *Fr.* provä'sal) *a.* **1.** of Provence, former province of SE France, its dialect of French or its Romance language —*n.* **2.** language of Provence, closely related to French and Italian, belonging to Romance group of Indo-European family **3.** native or inhabitant of Provence

provender ('provindər) *n.* fodder

proverb ('provərb) *n.* short, pithy, traditional saying in common use —**pro'verbial** *a.*

Proverbs ('provərbz) *pl.n.* (*with sing. v.*) *Bible* 20th book of the O.T., written by Solomon, a guide for moral practice outside of the place of worship

provide (prə'vīd) *vi.* **1.** make preparation —*vt.* **2.** supply, equip, prepare, furnish, give —**pro'vider** *n.* —**pro'viding** *or* **pro'vided** *conj.* (*sometimes with* that) on condition or understanding (that)

provident ('providənt) *a.* **1.** thrifty **2.** showing foresight —**'providence** *n.* **1.** kindly care of God or nature **2.** foresight **3.** economy —**provi'dential** *a.* strikingly fortunate, lucky —**provi'dentially** *adv.*

province ('provins) *n.* **1.** division of a country, district **2.** sphere of action —*pl.* **3.** any part of country outside capital —**pro'vincial** *a.* **1.** of a province **2.** unsophisticated **3.** narrow in outlook —*n.* **4.** unsophisticated person **5.** inhabitant of province —**pro'vincialism** *n.* **1.** narrowness of outlook **2.** lack of refinement **3.** idiom peculiar to province

provision (prə'vizhən) *n.* **1.** a providing, *esp.* for the future **2.** thing provided —*pl.* **3.** food **4.** *Law* articles of instrument or statute —*vt.* **5.** supply with food —**pro'visional** *a.* **1.** temporary **2.** conditional

proviso (prə'vīzō) *n.* condition (*pl.* -s, -es)

provoke (prə'vōk) *vt.* **1.** irritate **2.** incense **3.** arouse **4.** excite **5.** cause —**provocation** (provə'kāshən) *n.* —**pro'vocative** (prə'vokətiv) *a.*

Provolone (prōvə'lōni) *n.* a hard, mellow cheese, usu. smoked after drying, orig. from Italy

provost ('provōst, 'provəst) *n.* **1.** one who superintends or presides **2.** head of certain colleges

prow (prow) *n.* bow of vessel

prowess ('prowis) *n.* **1.** bravery, fighting capacity **2.** skill

prowl (prowl) *vi.* **1.** roam stealthily, *esp.* in search of prey or booty —*n.* **2.** act of prowling —**'prowler** *n.* —**on the prowl 1.** moving about stealthily **2.** pursuing members of opposite sex

prox. proximo

proximate ('proksimit) *a.* nearest, next, immediate —**prox'imity** *n.* —**'proximo** *adv.* in the next month

proxy ('proksi) *n.* **1.** authorized agent or substitute **2.** writing authorizing one to act as this

prude (prōōd) *n.* one who affects excessive modesty or propriety —**'prudery** *n.* —**'prudish** *a.*

prudent ('prōōdənt) *a.* **1.** careful, discreet **2.** sensible —**'prudence** *n.* **1.** habit of acting with careful deliberation **2.** wisdom applied to practice —**pru'dential** *a.*

prune[1] (prōōn) *n.* dried plum

prune[2] (prōōn) *vt.* **1.** cut out (dead parts, excessive branches *etc.*) from **2.** shorten, reduce —**pruning hook** tool with curved blade terminating in hook, used for pruning

prurient ('prōōriənt) *a.* **1.** given to, springing from lewd thoughts **2.** having unhealthy curiosity or desire —**'prurience** *or* **'pruriency** *n.*

pruritus (prōō'rītəs) *n.* intense itching —**pruritic** (prōō'ritik) *a.*

prussic acid ('prusik) extremely poisonous aqueous solution of hydrogen cyanide

pry (prī) *vi.* **1.** make furtive or impertinent inquiries **2.** look curiously —*vt.* **3.** force open (**pried, 'prying**)

P.S. postscript (*also* **p.s.**)

Ps. *or* **Psa.** *Bible* Psalm(s)

psalm (säm, sälm) *n.* **1.** sacred song **2.** (P-) any of the sacred songs making up the Book of Psalms in the Bible —**'psalmist** *n.* writer of psalms —**'psalmody** *n.* art, act of singing sacred music —**Psalter** ('sôltər) *n.* **1.** book of psalms **2.** copy of the Psalms as separate book —**psaltery** ('sôltəri) *n.* obsolete stringed instrument like lyre

Psalms (sämz, sälmz) *pl.n.* (*with sing. v.*) *Bible* 19th book of the O.T., collection of 150 psalms, many of which were written by David for worship

psephology (se'foləji) *n.* statistical and sociological study of elections

pseud (sōōd) *inf. n.* **1.** false or pretentious person —*a.* **2.** sham, fake (*also* **'pseudo**)

pseudo- *or sometimes before vowel* **pseud-** (*comb. form*) sham, as in *pseudo-Gothic, pseudomodern.* Such compounds are not given here where the meaning may easily be inferred from the simple word

pseudonym ('sōōdənim) *n.* false, fictitious name —**pseudonymous** (sōō'doniməs) *a.*

psi (sī, psī) *n.* 23rd letter in Gr. alphabet (Ψ, ψ), transliterated as *ps*

psittacine ('sitəsīn) *a.* pert. to, like parrots —**psitta'cosis** *n.* dangerous infectious disease, virus of which is carried by parrots

psoriasis (sə'rīəsis) *n.* skin disease characterized by formation of reddish spots and patches covered with silvery scales

psst (pst) *interj.* exclamation of beckoning, *esp.* made surreptitiously

P.S.T. Pacific Standard Time

psyche ('sīki) *n.* human mind or soul

psychedelic (sīki'delik) *a.* **1.** of or causing hallucinations **2.** like intense colors *etc.* experienced during hallucinations

psychic ('sīkik) *a.* **1.** sensitive to phenomena lying outside range of normal experience **2.** of soul or mind **3.** that appears to be outside region of physical law (*also* **'psychical**) —**psychiatry** (si'kīətri, sī-) *n.* medical treatment of mental diseases —**psychoa'nalysis** *n.* method of studying and treating mental disorders —**psycho'analyst** *n.* —**psycho'analyze** *vt.* treat by psychoanalysis —**psychogenic** (sīkə'jenik) *a. Psychol.* (*esp.* of disorders or symptoms) of mental, rather than organic origin —**psychoki'nesis** *n.* (in parapsychology) alteration of state of object supposedly by mental influence alone —**psycho'logical** *a.* of psychology **2.** of the mind —**psy'chologist** *n.* —**psy'chology** *n.* **1.** study of mind **2.** *inf.* person's mental make-up —**psy'chometry** *n.* **1.** measurement, testing of psychological processes **2.** supposed ability to divine unknown person's qualities

by handling object used or worn by him —**'psychopath** *n.* person afflicted with severe mental disorder causing him to commit antisocial, oft. violent acts —**psycho'pathic** *a.* —**'psychopharma'cology** *n.* study of effect of drugs on the mind —**psy'chosis** *n.* severe mental disorder in which person's contact with reality becomes distorted (*pl.* -**choses** (-'kōsēz)) —**psychoso'matic** *a.* of physical disorders thought to have psychological causes —**psycho'therapy** *n.* treatment of disease by psychological, rather than by physical, means —**psychological moment** most appropriate time for producing desired effect —**psychological warfare** military application of psychology, *esp.* to manipulation of morale in time of war —**psychosomatic medicine** branch of psychiatry dealing with physical illnesses that result from emotional conflicts

psycho ('sīkō) *sl. n.* **1.** psychopath (*pl.* -**s**) —*a.* **2.** psychopathic

psycho- *or sometimes before vowel* **psych-** (*comb. form*) mind, psychological or mental processes, as in *psychology, psychosomatic*

Pt *Chem.* platinum

pt. 1. part **2.** pint **3.** point

Pt. 1. Point **2.** Port

P.T. 1. physical therapy **2.** physical training

P.T.A. parent teacher association

ptarmigan ('tärmigən) *n.* bird of grouse family which turns white in winter (*pl.* -**s, -gan**)

Pte. Private (soldier)

pteridophyte (tə'ridəfīt) *n.* any of phylum of plants comprising ferns, club mosses, horsetails and quillworts

ptero- (*comb. form*) wing, as in *pterodactyl*

pterodactyl (terə'daktil) *n.* extinct flying reptile with batlike wings

P.T.O. *or* **p.t.o.** please turn over

ptomaine ('tōmān) *n.* any of group of poisonous alkaloids found in decaying matter

ptyalin ('tīəlin) *n.* enzyme found in saliva which breaks down starch

Pu *Chem.* plutonium

pub (pub) *n.* UK public house, building with bar(s) and license to sell alcoholic drinks —**pub-crawl** *sl. n.* **1.** drinking tour of number of pubs or bars —*vi.* **2.** make such tour

pub. 1. public **2.** publication **3.** published **4.** publisher **5.** publishing

puberty ('pyōōbərti) *n.* sexual maturity —**'pubertal** *a.*

pubes ('pyōōbēz) *n.* **1.** region above external genital organs, covered with hair from time of puberty **2.** pubic hair (*pl.* **'pubes**) **3.** *pl. of* PUBIS

pubescent (pyōō'besənt) *a.* **1.** arriving or arrived at puberty **2.** (of certain plants and animals or their parts) covered with fine short hairs or down —**pu'bescence** *n.*

pubic ('pyōōbik) *a.* of the pubes or pubis

pubis ('pyōōbis) *n.* bone forming front of each half of pelvis (*pl.* -**bes** (-bēz))

public ('publik) *a.* **1.** of or concerning the public as a whole **2.** not private **3.** open to general observation or knowledge **4.** accessible to all **5.** serving the people —*n.* **6.** the community or its members —**'publican** *n.* keeper of public house —**'publicly** *adv.* —**public-address system** system of microphones, amplifiers and loudspeakers for increasing sound level, used in auditoriums *etc.* (*also* **P.A. system**) —**public enemy** notorious person, such as criminal, regarded as menace to public —**public health** organized efforts of community to protect its members against disease —**Public Health**

Service chief health agency of U.S. government, which works closely with states, sets standards for sanitation, maintains quarantine services *etc.* —**public house** UK pub —**public relations** promotion of good relations of an organization or authority with the general public —**public school 1.** in England and Wales, private independent fee-paying school **2.** in some Canad. provinces, a local elementary school —**public servant** elected or appointed holder of public office —**public spirit** interest in and devotion to welfare of community —**public-spirited** *a.* having or showing active interest in good of community —**public transport** trains, buses *etc.* that have fixed routes and are available to general public

publicist ('publisist) *n.* **1.** writer on public concerns **2.** journalist —**pub'licity** *n.* **1.** process of attracting public attention **2.** attention thus gained —*a.* **3.** pert. to advertisement —'**publicize** *vt.* advertise

publish ('publish) *vt.* **1.** prepare and issue for sale (books, music *etc.*) **2.** make generally known **3.** proclaim —**publi'cation** *n.* —'**publisher** *n.*

puce (py$\overline{oo}$s) *a./n.* purplish-brown (color)

puck[1] (puk) *n.* rubber disk used instead of ball in ice hockey

puck[2] (puk) *n.* mischievous sprite —'**puckish** *a.*

pucka ('puk∂) *a. see* PUKKA

pucker ('puk∂r) *v.* **1.** gather into wrinkles —*n.* **2.** crease, fold

pudding ('p$\overline{oo}$ding) *n.* **1.** sweet, usu. cooked dessert, oft. made from flour or other cereal **2.** soft savory dish with pastry or batter **3.** kind of sausage

puddle ('pud∂l) *n.* **1.** small muddy pool **2.** rough cement for lining ponds *etc.* —*vt.* **3.** line with puddle **4.** make muddy

pudendum (py$\overline{oo}$'dend∂m) *n.* (*oft. pl.*) human external genital organs, *esp.* of female (*pl.* -**da** (-d∂)) —**pu'dendal** *or* '**pudic** *a.*

pudgy ('puji) *a.* plump and short

pueblo (p$\overline{oo}$'eblō, 'pweblō) *n.* **1.** communal dwelling consisting of continuous flat-roofed houses in groups occupied by Amerindians of southwestern U.S. **2.** Amerindian village of southwestern U.S. **3.** (**P-**) (member of) group of Amerindian peoples of southwestern U.S. (*pl.* -**s**)

puerile ('py$\overline{oo}$$\partial$ril) *a.* **1.** childish **2.** foolish **3.** trivial

puerperium (py$\overline{oo}$$\partial$r'pē$\partial$ri$\partial$m) *n.* period of about six weeks after childbirth —**puerperal** (py$\overline{oo}$'∂rp∂r∂l) *a.* —**puerperal fever** blood poisoning caused by infection during childbirth

Puerto Rico ('pört∂ 'rēkō, 'pwertō) island in the West Indies, Commonwealth of the U.S. —**Puerto Rican** (native or inhabitant) of Puerto Rico

puff (puf) *n.* **1.** short blast of breath, wind *etc.* **2.** its sound **3.** type of pastry **4.** laudatory notice or advertisement —*vi.* **5.** blow abruptly **6.** breathe hard —*vt.* **7.** send out in a puff **8.** blow out, inflate **9.** advertise **10.** smoke hard —**puffed** *a.* **1.** breathless; winded **2.** puffy —'**puffy** *a.* **1.** short-winded **2.** swollen —**puff adder 1.** large venomous Afr. viper that inflates its body when alarmed **2.** N Amer. nonvenomous snake that inflates its body when alarmed (*also* **hognose snake**) —'**puffball** *n.* ball-shaped fungus —**puff paste** dough for making a rich flaky pastry

puffin ('pufin) *n.* any of various sea birds with large brightly colored beaks

pug (pug) *n.* **1.** small snub-nosed dog **2.** *sl.* boxer —**pug nose** snub nose

pugilism ('py$\overline{oo}$jiliz∂m) *n.* art, practice or profession of fighting with fists; boxing —'**pugilist** *n.* —**pugi'listic** *a.*

pugnacious (pug'nāsh∂s) *a.* given to fighting —**pugnacity** (pug'nasiti) *n.*

puissant ('pwis∂nt, 'py$\overline{oo}$is∂nt) *a. Poet.* powerful, mighty —'**puissance** *n.* show-jumping competition over very high fences

puke (py$\overline{oo}$k) *sl. vi.* **1.** vomit —*n.* **2.** act of vomiting

pukka *or* **pucka** ('puk∂) *a. Anglo-Indian* properly or perfectly done, constructed *etc.*; good; genuine

pulchritude ('pulkrity$\overline{oo}$d, -t$\overline{oo}$d) *n. Lit.* beauty

pule (py$\overline{oo}$l) *vi.* whine; whimper

Pulitzer Prize ('p$\overline{oo}$lits∂r) any of annual prizes awarded for achievements in American journalism, letters and music

pull (p$\overline{oo}$l) *vt.* **1.** exert force on (object) to move it toward source of force **2.** strain, stretch **3.** tear **4.** propel by rowing —*n.* **5.** act of pulling **6.** force exerted by it **7.** draft of liquor **8.** *inf.* power, influence —**pull in 1.** (of train) arrive **2.** (of automobile *etc.*) draw in to side of road, stop **3.** attract **4.** *sl.* arrest —**pull off** *inf.* carry through to successful issue —**pull out 1.** withdraw **2.** extract **3.** (of train) depart **4.** (of automobile *etc.*) move away from side of road; move out to overtake —**pull (someone's) leg** *inf.* make fun of (someone) —**pull up 1.** tear up **2.** recover lost ground **3.** improve **4.** come to a stop **5.** halt **6.** reprimand

pullet ('p$\overline{oo}$lit) *n.* young hen

pulley ('p$\overline{oo}$li) *n.* wheel with groove in rim for cord, used to raise weights by downward pull

Pullman ('p$\overline{oo}$lm∂n) *n.* railroad saloon car (*pl.* -**s**) (*also* **Pullman car**)

pullover ('p$\overline{oo}$lōv∂r) *n.* sweater without fastening, to be pulled over head

pulmonary ('p$\overline{oo}$lm∂neri, 'pul-) *a.* **1.** of lungs **2.** having lungs or lunglike organs —**pulmonary embolism** obstruction of artery in lung by embolus or foreign substance

pulp (pulp) *n.* **1.** soft, moist, vegetable or animal matter **2.** flesh of fruit **3.** any soft soggy mass —*vt.* **4.** reduce to pulp

pulpit ('p$\overline{oo}$lpit) *n.* raised (enclosed) platform for preacher

pulsar ('pulsär) *n.* small dense star emitting radio waves

pulse[1] (puls) *n.* **1.** movement of blood in arteries corresponding to heartbeat, discernible to touch, *eg* in wrist **2.** any regular beat or vibration —'**pulsate** *vi.* throb, quiver —**pul'sation** *n.*

pulse[2] (puls) *n.* edible seeds of pod-bearing plants, *eg* beans

pulverize ('pulv∂rīz) *vt.* **1.** reduce to powder **2.** smash, demolish —**pulveri'zation** *n.*

puma ('py$\overline{oo}$m∂, 'p$\overline{oo}$m∂) *n.* cougar

pumice ('pumis) *n.* light porous variety of volcanic rock used to scour, smooth and polish (*also* **pumice stone**)

pummel ('pum∂l) *vt.* strike repeatedly

pump[1] (pump) *n.* **1.** appliance in which piston and handle are used for raising water, or putting in or taking out air, liquid *etc.* —*vt.* **2.** raise, put in, take out *etc.* with pump **3.** empty by means of pump **4.** extract information from —*vi.* **5.** work pump **6.** work like pump

pump[2] (pump) *n.* low-cut shoe without laces or straps

pumpernickel ('pump∂rnik∂l) *n.* sour black bread made of coarse rye flour

pumpkin ('pumpkin) *n.* any of several varieties of gourd, eaten *esp.* as vegetable

pun (pun) *n.* **1.** humorous use of words that have the same sound, but have different meanings —*vi.* **2.** make pun (-**nn**-) —'**punster** *n.*

punch[1] (punch) *n.* **1.** tool for perforating or stamping **2.** blow with fist **3.** *inf.* vigor —*vt.* **4.** stamp, perforate with punch **5.** strike with fist —'**punchball** *n.* stuffed or inflated ball or bag, either suspended or supported by flexible rod, that is punched for exercise, *esp.* boxing training —**punch card** *or* **punched card** card on which data can be coded in form of punched holes —**punch-drunk** *or* (*inf.*) '**punchy** *a.* dazed, as by repeated blows —**punch line** culminating part of joke *etc.*, that gives it its point —**punch tape** strip of paper used in computers *etc.* for recording information in form of punched holes

punch[2] (punch) *n.* drink of spirits or wine with fruit juice, spice *etc.* —**punch bowl** bowl in which punch is mixed and served

punctilious (pungk'tili∂s) *a.* **1.** making much of details of etiquette **2.** very exact, particular

punctual ('pungkch$\overline{oo}$$\partial$l) *a.* in good time, not late, prompt —**punctu'ality** *n.* —'**punctually** *adv.*

punctuate ('pungkch$\overline{oo}$āt) *vt.* **1.** insert punctuation marks into **2.** interrupt at intervals —**punctu'ation** *n.* marks, *eg* commas, colons *etc.*, put in writing to assist in making sense clear

puncture ('pungkch∂r) *n.* **1.** small hole made by sharp object, *esp.* in tire **2.** act of puncturing —*vt.* **3.** prick hole in, perforate

pundit *or* **pandit** ('pundit) *n.* **1.** self-appointed expert **2.** Brahman learned in Sanskrit and, *esp.* in Hindu religion, philosophy or law

pungent ('punj∂nt) *a.* **1.** biting **2.** irritant **3.** piercing **4.** tart **5.** caustic —'**pungency** *n.*

punish ('punish) *vt.* **1.** cause (someone) to suffer for offense **2.** inflict penalty on **3.** use or treat roughly —'**punishable** *a.* —'**punishment** *n.* —**punitive** ('py$\overline{oo}$nitiv) *a.* inflicting or intending to inflict punishment

punk[1] (pungk) *a./n.* **1.** inferior, rotten, worthless (person or thing) **2.** petty (hoodlum) **3.** (of) style of rock music

punk[2] (pungk) *n.* **1.** sticklike or coiled substance that smolders when lit **2.** dried decayed wood or other substance that smolders when ignited: used as tinder

punkah *or* **punka** ('pungk∂) *n.* **1.** fan made of palm leaf or leaves **2.** large fan made of palm leaves *etc.* worked mechanically to cool room

punt[1] (punt) *n.* **1.** flat-bottomed, square-ended boat, propelled by pushing with pole —*vt.* **2.** propel thus

punt[2] (punt) *Sport vt.* **1.** kick (ball) before it touches ground, when let fall from hands —*n.* **2.** such a kick

punt[3] (punt) *vi.* gamble, bet —'**punter** *n.* **1.** one who punts **2.** professional gambler **3.** *inf.* customer or client, *esp.* prostitute's client

puny ('py$\overline{oo}$ni) *a.* small and feeble

pup (pup) *n.* young of certain animals, *eg* dog

pupa ('py$\overline{oo}$p∂) *n.* stage between larva and adult in metamorphosis of insect, chrysalis (*pl.* **pupae** ('py$\overline{oo}$pē)) —'**pupal** *a.*

pupil[1] ('py$\overline{oo}$p∂l) *n.* **1.** person being taught **2.** opening in iris of eye

puppet ('pupit) *n.* small doll or figure of person *etc.* controlled by operator's hand —**puppe'teer** *n.* —'**puppetry** *n.* —**puppet show** show with puppets worked by hidden showman —**puppet state** state that appears independent but is controlled by another

puppy ('pupi) n. young dog —**puppy fat** fatty tissue in child or adolescent, usu. disappearing with age

purblind ('pɜrblīnd) a. 1. partly or nearly blind 2. lacking in insight or understanding

purchase ('pɜrchis) vt. 1. buy —n. 2. act of buying 3. what is bought 4. leverage, grip

purdah ('pɜrdə) n. 1. Muslim, Hindu custom of keeping women in seclusion 2. screen, veil to achieve this

pure (pyŏŏr) a. 1. unmixed, untainted 2. simple 3. spotless 4. faultless 5. innocent 6. concerned with theory only —**'purely** adv. —**purifi'cation** n. —**pu'rificatory** a. —**'purify** v. make, become pure, clear or clean (-**ified**, -**ifying**) —**'purism** n. excessive insistence on correctness of language —**'purist** n. —**'purity** n. state of being pure —**purebred** ('pyŏŏr'bred) a. 1. denoting pure strain obtained through many generations of controlled breeding —n. ('pyŏŏr-bred) 2. purebred animal

purée (pyŏŏ'rā) n. 1. pulp of cooked fruit or vegetables —vt. 2. make (cooked foods) into purée

purgatory ('pɜrgətöri) n. place or state of torment, pain or distress, esp. temporary —**purga'torial** a.

purge (pɜrj) vt. 1. make clean, purify 2. remove, get rid of 3. clear out —n. 4. act, process of purging 5. removal of undesirable members from political party, army etc. —**purgation** (pɜr'gāshən) n. —**purgative** ('pɜrgətiv) a./n.

Purim ('pŏŏrim) n. Judaism Feast of Lots commemorating the rescue of the Persian Jews from Haman's plot to exterminate them

purine ('pyŏŏərēn) n. ring-structured compound, building block of DNA and RNA

Puritan ('pyŏŏritən) n. 1. Hist. member of extreme Protestant party 2. (p-) person of extreme strictness in morals or religion —**puri'tanic(al)** a. 1. strict in the observance of religious and moral duties 2. overscrupulous —**'puritanism** n.

purl¹ ('pɜrl) n. 1. stitch that forms ridge in knitting —v. 2. knit in purl

purl² (pɜrl) vi. flow with burbling sound, swirl, babble

purlieus ('pɜrlyŏŏz, -lŏŏz) pl.n. outlying parts, outskirts

purlin ('pɜrlin) n. horizontal beam that provides support for rafters of roof

purloin (pɜr'loin) vt. 1. steal 2. pilfer

purple ('pɜrpəl) n./a. (of) color between blue and red —**Purple Heart** 1. decoration awarded to members of U.S. Armed Forces for wound received in action 2. sl. amphetamine pill

purport (pɜr'pört) vt. 1. claim to be (true etc.) 2. signify, imply —n. ('pɜrpört) 3. meaning 4. apparent meaning 5. significance

purpose ('pɜrpəs) n. 1. reason, object 2. design 3. aim, intention —vt. 4. intend —**'purposely** adv. —**purpose-built** a. made to serve specific purpose —**on purpose** intentionally

purr (pɜr) n. 1. (esp. of cats) make low vibrant sound, usu. considered as expressing pleasure etc. —vi. 2. utter this sound

purse (pɜrs) n. 1. pocketbook, small bag for money 2. resources 3. money as prize —vt. 4. pucker (mouth, lips etc.) in wrinkles —vi. 5. become wrinkled and drawn in —**'purser** n. ship's officer who keeps accounts —**purse strings** control of expenditure (esp. in **hold** or **control the purse strings**)

purslane ('pɜrslin) n. plant used (esp. formerly) in salads and as potherb

pursue (pɜr'sŏŏ) vt. 1. run after 2. chase 3. aim at 4. engage in 5. continue 6. follow —vi. 7. go in pursuit 8. continue —**pur'suance** n. carrying out —**pur'suant** adj. chiefly law in agreement or conformity —**pur'suer** n. —**pur'suit** n. 1. running after, attempt to catch 2. occupation

purulent ('pyŏŏryələnt, 'pyŏŏrələnt) a. see at PUS

purvey (pɜr'vā) vt. supply (provisions) —**pur'veyance** n. —**pur'veyor** n.

purview ('pɜrvyŏŏ) n. scope, range

pus (pus) n. yellowish discharge produced by suppuration —**purulence** ('pyŏŏryələns, 'pyŏŏrələns) n. —**'purulent** a. 1. forming, discharging pus 2. septic

push (pŏŏsh) vt. 1. move, try to move away by pressure 2. drive, impel 3. inf. sell (esp. narcotic drugs) illegally —vi. 4. make thrust 5. advance with steady effort —n. 6. thrust 7. persevering self-assertion 8. big military advance 9. sl. dismissal —**'pusher** n. —**'pushing** or (inf.) **'pushy** a. given to pushing oneself —**push button** electrical switch operated by pressing button, which closes or opens circuit —**push-button** a. 1. operated by push button 2. initiated as simply as by pressing button —**'pushchair** n. esp. UK (collapsible) chair-shaped carriage for baby —**'pushover** n. sl. 1. something easily achieved 2. person etc. easily taken advantage of or defeated —**push-start** vt. 1. start (motor vehicle) by pushing while in gear, thus turning engine —n. 2. this process

pusillanimous (pyŏŏsi'laniməs) a. cowardly —**pusilla'nimity** n.

puss (pŏŏs) n. cat (also **'pussy**) —**pussy willow** willow tree with silvery silky catkins

pussyfoot ('pŏŏsifŏŏt) vi. inf. 1. move stealthily 2. act indecisively, procrastinate

pustule ('puschŏŏl, -tyŏŏl, -tŏŏl) n. pimple containing pus —**'pustular** a. —**pustulate** ('puschəlāt, 'pustyə-, 'pustə-) v. 1. (cause to) form into pustules —a. ('puschəlit, 'pustyə-, 'pustə-) 2. covered with pustules

put (pŏŏt) vt. 1. place 2. set 3. express 4. throw (esp. shot) (**put**, **'putting**) —n. 5. throw —**put-down** n. cruelly critical remark —**put-up** a. dishonestly or craftily prearranged (esp. in **put-up job**) —**put across** express successfully —**put down** 1. make written record of 2. repress 3. consider 4. attribute 5. put (animal) to death because of old age or illness 6. table on agenda 7. sl. reject, humiliate —**put off** 1. postpone 2. disconcert 3. repel —**put up** 1. erect 2. accommodate 3. nominate

putative ('pyŏŏtətiv) a. reputed, supposed —**'putatively** adv.

putrid ('pyŏŏtrid) a. 1. decomposed 2. rotten —**'putrefy** v. make or become rotten (-**efied**, -**efying**) —**putre'faction** n. —**pu'trescence** n. —**pu'trescent** a. becoming rotten —**pu'tridity** n.

Putsch (pŏŏch) n. surprise attempt to overthrow the existing power, political revolt

putt (put) vt. strike (golf ball) along ground in direction of hole —**'putter** n. golf club for putting —**putting green** 1. on golf course, area of closely mown grass at end of fairway where hole is 2. area of smooth grass with several holes for putting games

puttee ('puti) n. strip of cloth wound round leg like bandage, serving as gaiter

putto ('pŏŏtō) n. figure of naked baby boy, sometimes with wings, common in Renaissance art (pl. **putti** ('pŏŏtē))

putty ('puti) n. 1. paste of whiting and oil as used by glaziers 2. jeweler's polishing powder —vt. 3. fix, fill with putty (-**ied**, -**ying**)

puzzle ('puzəl) v. 1. perplex or be perplexed —n. 2. bewildering, perplexing question, problem or toy —**'puzzlement** n.

PVC polyvinyl chloride (synthetic thermoplastic material used in insulation, shoes etc.)

pye-dog ('pīdog) n. ownerless half-wild Asian dog

pyelonephritis (pīəlōni'frītis) n. infection of the kidney

pyemia (pī'ēmiə) n. form of blood poisoning —**py'emic** a.

pygmy or **pigmy** ('pigmi) n. 1. abnormally undersized person 2. (P-) member of one of dwarf peoples of Equatorial Afr. —a. 3. undersized

pylon ('pīlon, -lən) n. towerlike erection, esp. to carry electric cables

pyo- or before vowel **py-** (comb. form) pus, as in pyosis

pyorrhea (pīə'rēə) n. inflammation of the gums with discharge of pus and loosening of teeth

pyramid ('pirəmid) n. 1. massive structure with square base and four triangular faces meeting at apex 2. solid geometrical figure having a polygon as base whose sides are triangles sharing a common apex —vt. 3. build up in the form of a pyramid 4. increase rapidly on a broadening base —**py'ramidal** a.

pyre ('pīər) n. pile of wood for burning a dead body

pyrethrum (pī'rēthrəm) n. 1. any of several types of cultivated chrysanthemums 2. insecticide made from it

pyretic (pī'retik) a. of fever

Pyrex ('pīreks) n. trade name for glassware resistant to heat and chemicals

pyridoxine (piri'doksēn) n. vitamin B_6

pyrite ('pīrīt) n. yellow mineral consisting of iron sulfide in cubic crystalline form

pyrites (pi'rītēz, pī-) n. 1. see PYRITE 2. any of a number of other disulfides of metals, esp. of copper and tin (pl. **py'rites**)

pyro- or before vowel **pyr-** (comb. form) 1. fire or heat, as in pyromania, pyrometer 2. Chem. new substance obtained by heating another, as in pyroboric acid 3. Min. having property that changes upon application of heat; having flame-colored appearance, as in pyroxylin

pyrogenic (pīrō'jenik) or **pyrogenous** (pī'rojinəs) a. 1. produced by or producing heat 2. causing or resulting from fever

pyrography (pī'rogrəfi) n. 1. art of burning designs on wood or leather with heated tools 2. design made by this process

pyromania (pīrō'māniə) n. uncontrollable impulse and practice of setting things on fire —**pyro'maniac** n.

pyrometer (pī'romitər) n. instrument for measuring very high temperature —**py'rometry** n.

pyrotechnics (pīrə'tekniks) pl.n. 1. (with sing. v.) manufacture of fireworks 2. (with sing. or pl. v.) firework display —**pyro'technist** n.

Pyrrhic victory ('pirik) victory won at excessive cost

Pythagorean theorem (pithagə'rēən, pī-) proposition that in right-angled triangle square of length of hypotenuse equals sum of squares of other two sides

python ('pīthon, -thən) n. large snake that crushes its prey

pyx (piks) n. 1. vessel in which consecrated Host is preserved 2. (also **pyx chest**) box in Brit. Royal Mint holding specimen coins kept to be tested for weight

Qq

q *or* **Q** (kyōō) *n.* **1.** 17th letter of English alphabet **2.** speech sound represented by this letter (*pl.* **q's, Q's** *or* **Qs**)

Q 1. *Chess* Queen **2.** Question **3.** Quebec

q. 1. quart **2.** quarter **3.** quarto (*pl.* **qq., Qq.**) (*also* **Q.**) **4.** question

Qatar ('kätər, 'gät-) *n.* country in Middle East occupying a peninsula in the Persian Gulf, bounded by Saudi Arabia to the south

Q.E.D. quod erat demonstrandum (*Lat.,* which was to be proved)

Qld. Queensland

Q.M. Quartermaster

qr. 1. quarter **2.** quire (*pl.* **qrs.**)

qt. 1. quart (*pl.* **qt., qts.**) **2.** quantity

q.t. *inf.* quiet —**on the q.t.** secretly

qto quarto

qua (kwä, kwā) *prep.* in the capacity of

quack (kwak) *n.* **1.** harsh cry of duck **2.** pretender to medical or other skill —*vi.* **3.** (of duck) utter cry

quack grass perennial grass, a garden weed which spreads very rapidly by means of trailing underground stems which root at every node (*also* **quick grass, twitch grass, witch grass**)

quad (kwod) *n.* **1.** quadrant **2.** *inf.* quadruplet **3.** quadrangle **4.** quadraphonic

quadrangle ('kwodranggəl) *n.* **1.** four-sided figure **2.** four-sided courtyard in a building —**quad'rangular** *a.*

quadrant ('kwodrənt) *n.* **1.** quarter of circle **2.** instrument for taking angular measurements —**quadrate** *vt.* make square —**quadratic** (kwo'dratik) *a.* (of equation) involving square of unknown quantity

quadraphonic (kwodrə'fonik) *a.* (of a sound system) using four independent speakers

quadrennial (kwo'dreniəl) *a.* **1.** lasting four years **2.** occurring every four years —*n.* **3.** period of four years

quadri- *or before vowel* **quadr-** (*comb. form*) four

quadrilateral (kwodri'latərəl) *a.* **1.** four-sided —*n.* **2.** four-sided figure

quadrille (kwo'dril, kwə-) *n.* **1.** square dance **2.** music played for it

quadrillion (kwo'drilyən) *n.* **1.** in Amer. and France, number represented as one followed by 15 zeros (10^{15}) **2.** in Brit. and Germany, number represented as one followed by 24 zeros (10^{24})

quadriplegia (kwodri'plējiə) *n.* paralysis of all four limbs (*also* **tetra'plegia**) —**quadri-'plegic** *a.*

quadrivalent (kwodri'vālənt) *a. Chem.* having four valencies (*also* **tetra'valent**) —**quadri'valency** *or* **quadri'valence** *n.*

quadroon (kwo'drōōn) *n.* person of one quarter Negro ancestry

quadruped ('kwodrəped) *n.* four-footed animal —**quad'rupedal** *a.*

quadruple (kwo'drōōpəl, 'kwodrəpəl) *a.* **1.** fourfold **2.** consisting of four parts —*v.* **3.** make, become four times as much —*n.* **4.** quantity or number four times as great as another —**quad'ruplicate** *a.* fourfold

quadruplet (kwo'drōōplit, -'drup-; 'kwodrōō-plit) *n.* one of four offspring born at one birth

quaff (kwof) *v.* drink heartily or in one draft

quag (kwag) *n.* bog, swamp

quagga ('kwagə) *n.* recently extinct member of horse family

quail[1] (kwāl) *vi.* flinch; cower

quail²

quail[2] (kwāl) *n.* small game bird resembling domestic fowl (**bobwhite quail** sometimes considered a songbird, **California quail** sometimes pet, **Gambrel's quail** protected by law)

quaint (kwānt) *a.* **1.** interestingly old-fashioned or odd **2.** curious **3.** whimsical —**'quaintly** *adv.* —**'quaintness** *n.*

quake (kwāk) *vi.* shake, tremble

Quaker ('kwākər) *n.* member of Christian sect, the **Society of Friends** ('**Quakeress** *fem.*)

qualify ('kwolifī) *vi.* **1.** make oneself competent —*vt.* **2.** moderate **3.** limit **4.** make competent **5.** ascribe quality to **6.** describe (**-fied, -fying**) —**qualifi'cation** *n.* **1.** thing that qualifies, attribute **2.** restriction **3.** qualifying

quality ('kwoliti) *n.* **1.** attribute, characteristic, property **2.** degree of excellence **3.** rank —**'qualitative** *a.* depending on quality —**qualitative analysis** *Chem.* decomposition of substance to determine kinds of constituents present; result obtained by such determination —**quality control** control of relative quality of manufactured product, usu. by statistical sampling techniques

qualm (kwäm, kwälm) *n.* **1.** misgiving **2.** sudden feeling of sickness —**'qualmish** *a.*

quandary ('kwondri) *n.* state of perplexity; puzzling situation; dilemma

quantity ('kwontiti) *n.* **1.** size, number, amount **2.** specified or considerable amount —**'quantify** *vt.* discover, express quantity of —**'quantitative** *a.* **1.** involving considerations of amount or size **2.** capable of being measured **3.** *Prosody* of metrical system based on length of syllables —**'quantum** *n.* desired or required amount (*pl.* **-ta**) —**quantitative analysis** *Chem.* decomposition of substance to determine amount of each constituent; result obtained by such determination —**quantum theory** theory that, in radiation, energy of electrons is discharged not continuously but in discrete units or quanta

quarantine ('kworəntēn) *n.* **1.** isolation to prevent spreading of infection —*vt.* **2.** put, keep in quarantine

quark (kwörk, kwärk) *n. Phys.* any of several hypothetical particles thought to be fundamental units of matter

quarrel[1] ('kworəl) *n.* **1.** angry dispute **2.** argument —*vi.* **3.** argue **4.** find fault —**'quarrelsome** *a.*

quarrel[2] ('kworəl) *n.* **1.** crossbow arrow **2.** diamond-shaped pane

quarry[1] ('kwori) *n.* **1.** object of hunt or pursuit **2.** prey

quarry[2] ('kwori) *n.* **1.** excavation where stone *etc.* is got from ground for building *etc.* —*v.* **2.** get (stone *etc.*) from quarry ('**quarried, 'quarrying**)

quart (kwört) *n.* **1.** measure of liquid capacity equal to two pints or one quarter of a gallon, measuring 57.75 cubic inches, and equivalent to .946 liter **2.** measure of dry capacity equal to two pints or one eighth of a peck, measuring 67.201 cubic inches and equivalent to 1.101 liters

quarter ('kwörtər) *n.* **1.** fourth part **2.** 25 cents **3.** region, district **4.** mercy —*pl.* **5.** lodgings —*vt.* **6.** divide into quarters —*v.* **7.** billet or be billeted in lodgings —**'quarterly** *a.* **1.** happening, due *etc.* each quarter of year —*n.* **2.** quarterly periodical —**quar'tet** *n.* **1.** group of four musicians **2.** music for four performers —**'quarto** *n.* **1.** size of book in which sheets are folded into four leaves (*pl.* **-s**) —*a.* **2.** of this size —**'quarterback** *n.* member of football team who calls the signals —**'quarterdeck** *n.* after part of upper deck used *esp.* for official, ceremonial purposes —**quarter'final** *n.* round before semifinal in competition —**quarter horse** small, powerful breed of horse —**'quarter-master** *n.* officer responsible for stores —**quarter note** *Mus.* one fourth of time value of whole note —**quarter rest** pause in music lasting as long as quarter note —**'quarter-staff** *n.* long staff for fighting (*pl.* **-staves**)

quartz (kwörts) *n.* stone of pure crystalline silica —**'quartzite** *n.* quartz rock

quasar ('kwāzär, -sär) *n.* extremely distant starlike object emitting powerful radio waves

quash (kwosh) *vt.* **1.** annul **2.** reject **3.** subdue forcibly

quasi- ('kwāzī-) (*comb. form*) seemingly, resembling but not actually being, as in *quasi-scientific*

quassia ('kwoshə) *n.* tropical Amer. tree

quaternary ('kwotərneri, kwə'tərnəri) *a.* **1.** of the number four **2.** having four parts **3.** (Q-) *Geol.* of most recent period, after Tertiary —*n.* **4.** (Q-) Quaternary period or rock system

quatrain ('kwotrān) *n.* four-line stanza, *esp.* rhymed alternately

quatrefoil ('katərfoil) *n.* **1.** leaf composed of four leaflets **2.** *Archit.* carved ornament having four arcs arranged about common center

quattrocento (kwätrō'chentō) *n.* the 15th century., *esp.* when referring to Italian art and literature

quaver ('kwāvər) *vt.* **1.** say or sing in tremulous tones —*vi.* **2.** tremble, shake, vibrate

quay (kē) *n.* **1.** solid, fixed landing stage **2.** wharf

queasy ('kwēzi) *a.* inclined to, or causing, sickness

Quebec (kwi'bek) *n.* word used in communications for the letter *q*

Quechua ('kechōōə, kə'chōōə) *n.* Amerindian language spoken in Peru, Bolivia and Ecuador

queen (kwēn) *n.* 1. king's wife 2. female sovereign 3. piece in chess 4. fertile female bee, wasp *etc.* 5. face card with picture of a queen, ranking between king and jack 6. *inf.* male homosexual 7. female domestic cat —'**queenly** *a./adv.* —**Queen Anne** (an) 1. of architecture, furniture and silver ware in the reign of Queen Anne of England (1702-14) 2. of American architectural style of late 19th cent. combining many materials and styles —**Queen Anne's lace** wild carrot —**queen consort** wife of reigning king —**queen dowager** widow of king —**queen mother** widow of former king who is also mother of reigning sovereign —**Queen's Counsel** in Canad., honorary title which may be bestowed by government on lawyers with long experience —**queen's highway** in Canad., main road maintained by provincial government —**queen-size** *a.* smaller than king-size

Queens (kwēnz) *n.* borough of New York City

Queen Anne (sense 1)

Queensberry rules ('kwēnzberi) 1. code of rules followed in modern boxing 2. *inf.* gentlemanly conduct, *esp.* in dispute

queer (kwēər) *a.* 1. odd, strange 2. *inf.* homosexual —*n.* 3. *inf.* homosexual —*vt. inf.* 4. spoil 5. interfere with

quell (kwel) *vt.* 1. crush, put down 2. allay 3. pacify

quench (kwench) *vt.* 1. slake 2. extinguish, put out 3. suppress

quern (kwərn) *n.* stone hand mill

querulous ('kweryələs, 'kwerələs) *a.* 1. fretful 2. peevish, whining

query ('kwēəri) *n.* 1. question 2. mark of interrogation —*vt.* 3. question ('**queried**, '**querying**)

quest (kwest) *n./vi.* search

question ('kweschən) *n.* 1. sentence seeking for answer 2. that which is asked 3. interrogation 4. inquiry 5. problem 6. point for debate 7. debate, strife —*vt.* 8. ask questions of, interrogate 9. dispute 10. doubt —'**questionable** *a.* doubtful, *esp.* not clearly true or honest —**questionnaire** (kweschə'nāər) *n.* list of questions drawn up for formal answer —**question mark** 1. punctuation mark ?, used at end of questions *etc.* where doubt or ignorance is implied 2. this mark used for any other purpose, as to draw attention to possible mistake (*also* **interrogation point**)

queue (kyōō) *n.* 1. line of waiting persons, vehicles 2. pigtail worn by Chinese males under order of Manchus —*vi.* 3. (*with* up) wait in queue

quibble ('kwibəl) *n.* 1. trivial objection —*vi.* 2. make this

quiche (kēsh) *n.* open unsweetened pastry shell filled with rich custard flavored with cheese, onion, bacon *etc.*

quick (kwik) *a.* 1. rapid, swift 2. keen 3. brisk 4. hasty —*n.* 5. sensitive flesh 6. innermost feelings (*esp. in* **cut to the quick**) —*adv.* 7. *inf.* rapidly —'**quicken** *v.* make, become faster or more lively —'**quickie** *n. inf.* anything made, done *etc.* rapidly or in haste —'**quickly** *adv.* —**quick bread** any biscuit, bread, cake, doughnut, pancake or waffle leavened with baking powder —**quick-freeze** *vt.* freeze (food) rapidly enough so that ice crystals formed are too small to rupture cells —**quick grass** *see* QUACK GRASS —'**quicklime** *n.* calcium oxide —'**quicksand** *n.* loose wet sand easily yielding to pressure and engulfing persons, animals *etc.* —'**quicksilver** *n.* mercury —'**quickstep** *n.* 1. ballroom dance —*vi.* 2. perform this dance —**quick-tempered** *a.* irascible —**quick time** rate of marching in which 120 steps are taken in one minute —**quick-witted** *a.* having keenly alert mind —**quick-wittedness** *n.* —**the quick** *obs.* living people

quid (kwid) *n.* piece of tobacco suitable for chewing

quiddity ('kwiditi) *n.* 1. essential nature 2. petty or trifling distinction; quibble

quid pro quo (kwid prō 'kwō) *Lat.* something given in exchange

quiescent (kwI'esənt, kwi-) *a.* 1. at rest, inactive, inert 2. silent —**qui'escence** *or* **qui'escency** *n.*

quiet ('kwIət) *a.* 1. with little or no motion or noise 2. undisturbed 3. not showy or obtrusive —*n.* 4. state of peacefulness, absence of noise or disturbance —*v.* 5. make, become quiet —'**quieten** *v.* make, become quiet —'**quietly** *adv.* —'**quietness** *or* '**quietude** *n.*

quietism ('kwIətizəm) *n.* passive attitude to life, *esp.* as form of religion —'**quietist** *n.*

quietus (kwI'ētəs) *n.* 1. anything that serves to quash, eliminate or kill 2. release from life; death 3. discharge or settlement of debts, duties *etc.*

quill (kwil) *n.* 1. large feather 2. hollow stem of this 3. pen, plectrum made from feather 4. spine of porcupine —'**quillwort** *n.* lower plant resembling a tuft of grass found in eastern U.S.

quilt (kwilt) *n.* 1. padded coverlet —*vt.* 2. stitch (two pieces of cloth) with pad between

quince (kwins) *n.* 1. acid pear-shaped fruit 2. tree bearing it

quincunx ('kwinkungks) *n.* group of five objects arranged in shape of rectangle with one at each corner and fifth in center

quindecillion (kwindi'silyən) *n.* 1. in Amer. and France, number represented as one followed by 48 zeros 2. in Brit. and Germany, number represented as one followed by 90 zeros

quinine ('kwinīn) *n.* bitter drug made from bark of tree, used to treat fever, and as tonic

Quinquagesima (kwingkə'jesimə) *n.* Sunday 50 days before Easter

quinquennial (kwin'kweniəl) *a.* 1. lasting five years 2. occurring every five years —*n.* 3. period of five years

quinquereme ('kwingkwirēm) *n.* ancient Roman galley with five banks of oars

quinsy ('kwinzi) *n.* inflammation of throat or tonsils

quint (kwint) *n. inf.* quintuplet

quintessence (kwin'tesəns) *n.* 1. purest form, essential feature 2. embodiment —**quintes'sential** *a.*

quintet (kwin'tet) *n.* 1. set of five singers or players 2. composition for five voices or instruments

quintillion (kwin'tilyən) *n.* 1. in Amer. and France, number represented as one followed by 18 zeros (10¹⁸) 2. in Brit. and Germany, number represented as one followed by 30 zeros (10³⁰)

quintuple (kwin'tyōōpəl, -'tōō-; 'kwintəpəl) *v.* 1. multiply by five —*a.* 2. five times as much or as many; fivefold 3. consisting of five parts —*n.* 4. quantity or number five times as great as another —**quin'tuplicate** *a.*

quintuplet (kwin'tuplit, -'tyōō-, -'tōō-; 'kwintəplit) *n.* one of five offspring born at one birth

quip (kwip) *n.* 1. witty saying —*vi.* 2. make quip (-pp-)

quipu ('kēpōō) *n.* device consisting of cord with attached strings of various colors used by ancient Peruvians for recording events and for calculating

quire ('kwIər) *n.* 24 sheets of paper of the same size and quality

quirk (kwərk) *n.* 1. individual peculiarity of character 2. unexpected twist or turn

quisling ('kwizling) *n.* traitor who aids occupying enemy force

quit (kwit) *vi.* 1. stop doing a thing 2. depart —*vt.* 3. leave, go away from 4. cease from (**quit** *or* '**quitted** *pt./pp.*) —*a.* 5. free, rid —**quits** *a.* on equal or even terms by repayment *etc.* —'**quittance** *n.* 1. discharge 2. receipt —'**quitter** *n.* one lacking perseverance

quite (kwIt) *adv.* 1. wholly, completely 2. very considerably 3. somewhat, rather —*interj.* 4. exactly, just so

quiver¹ ('kwivər) *vi.* 1. shake, tremble —*n.* 2. quivering 3. vibration

quiver² ('kwivər) *n.* carrying case for arrows

quixotic (kwik'sotik) *a.* unrealistically and impractically optimistic, idealistic, chivalrous

quiz (kwiz) *n.* 1. short written or oral test 2. entertainment in which general or specific knowledge of players is tested by questions —*vt.* 3. question, interrogate (-zz-) —'**quizzical** *a.* 1. questioning 2. mocking

quod (kwod) *n. sl.* prison

quoin (koin, kwoin) *n.* 1. external corner of building 2. small wedge for locking printing type into form

quoit (kwāt, koit, kwoit) *n.* 1. ring for throwing at peg as a game —*pl.* 2. (*with sing. v.*) the game

quondam ('kwondəm, -dam) *a.* of an earlier time; former

quorum ('kwörəm) *n.* number that must be present in meeting to make its transactions valid

quota ('kwōtə) *n.* 1. share to be contributed or received 2. specified number, quantity, which may be imported or admitted

quote (kwōt) *vt.* 1. copy or repeat passages from 2. refer to, *esp.* to confirm view 3. state price for (commodity, stock or bond) —'**quotable** *a.* —**quo'tation** *n.* —**quotation mark** either of punctuation marks used to begin or end quotation, respectively " and " or ' and '

quoth (kwōth) *v. obs.* said

quotidian (kwō'tidiən) *a.* 1. daily 2. everyday, commonplace

quotient ('kwōshənt) *n.* number resulting from dividing one number by another

q.v. quod vide (*Lat.*, which see)

qwerty *or* **QWERTY** ('kwərti) *n. inf.* standard typewriter keyboard

Rr

r¹ *or* **R** (är) *n.* **1.** 18th letter of English alphabet **2.** speech sound represented by this letter (*pl.* **r's, R's** *or* **Rs**) —**the three Rs** three skills regarded as fundamentals of education: reading, writing and arithmetic

r² *or* **R 1.** rabbi **2.** radius **3.** rare **4.** Republican **5.** *Phys., electron.* resistance **6.** right **7.** river **8.** roentgen *or* röntgen **9.** *Chess* rook **10.** run

R 1. *Chem.* radical **2.** rand **3.** rupee **4.** Réaumur (scale) **5.** Royal **6.** *Chem.* gas constant

R. 1. Regina (*Lat.,* Queen) **2.** Rex (*Lat.,* King) **3.** *Chem.* any organic group

Ra *Chem.* radium

R.A. 1. Royal Academy **2.** Royal Artillery

rabbet ('rabit) *see* REBATE²

rabbi ('rabī) *n.* Jewish learned man, spiritual leader (*pl.* **-s**) —**rabbinical** (rə'binikəl) *or* **rab'binic** *a.*

rabbit ('rabit) *n.* **1.** small burrowing rodent like hare —*vi.* **2.** hunt rabbits —**rabbit fever** *see* TULAREMIA —**rabbit punch** sharp blow to back of neck

rabble ('rabəl) *n.* **1.** crowd of vulgar, noisy people **2.** mob —**rabble-rouser** *n.* person who manipulates passions of mob; demagogue

Rabelaisian (rabə'lāzhən, -ziən) *a.* **1.** of or resembling work of François Rabelais, Fr. writer, characterized by broad, oft. bawdy humor and sharp satire —*n.* **2.** student or admirer of Rabelais

rabid ('rabid, 'rā-) *a.* **1.** relating to or having rabies **2.** furious **3.** mad **4.** fanatical —**'rabidly** *adv.* —**'rabidness** *n.*

rabies ('rābēz) *n.* fatal virus disease of central nervous system transmitted by the bite of an infected warm-blooded animal

raccoon (ra'kōōn, rə-) *n.* nocturnal tree-dwelling N Amer. omnivorous mammal with grayish-brown fur, sharp snout and bushy ringed tail

race¹ (rās) *n.* **1.** contest of speed, as in running, swimming *etc.* **2.** contest, rivalry **3.** strong current of water, *esp.* leading to waterwheel —*pl.* **4.** meeting for horse racing —*vt.* **5.** cause to run rapidly —*vi.* **6.** run swiftly **7.** (of engine, pedal *etc.*) move rapidly and erratically, *esp.* on removal of resistance —**'racer** *n.* **1.** person, vehicle, animal that races **2.** any of various Amer. snakes —**'racetrack** *n.* long broad track, over which horses are raced

race² (rās) *n.* **1.** group of people of common ancestry with distinguishing physical features, skin color *etc.* **2.** species **3.** type —**'racial** *a.* —**'racialism** *or* **'racism** *n.* **1.** belief in innate superiority of particular race **2.** antagonism toward members of different race based on this belief —**'racialist** *or* **'racist** *a./n.* —**race riot** riot caused by racial animosity

raceme (rā'sēm, rə-) *n.* cluster of flowers along a central stem, as in foxglove

rack¹ (rak) *n.* **1.** framework for displaying or holding baggage, books, hats, bottles *etc.* **2.** *Mech.* straight bar with teeth on its edge, to work with pinion **3.** instrument of torture by stretching —*vt.* **4.** stretch on rack or wheel **5.**

torture **6.** stretch, strain —**'racking** *a.* agonizing —**rack-and-pinion** *n.* **1.** device for converting rotary into linear motion and vice versa, in which gearwheel (pinion) engages with flat toothed bar (rack) —*a.* **2.** (of type of steering gear in motor vehicles) having track rod with rack along part of its length that engages with pinion attached to steering column —**rack railway** mountain railway having middle rail fitted with rack that engages pinion on locomotive (*also* **cog railway**)

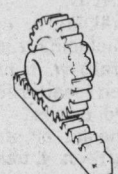

rack-and-pinion

rack² (rak) *n.* destruction (*esp. in* **rack and ruin**)

racket¹ ('rakit) *n.* **1.** loud noise, uproar **2.** occupation by which money is made illegally —**racket'eer** *n.* one making illegal profits —**racket'eering** *n.* —**'rackety** *a.* noisy

racket² *or* **racquet** ('rakit) *n.* **1.** bat used in tennis *etc.* —*pl.n.* **2.** (*with sing. v.*) racket game played by two players in which points are scored by server (*also* **hard rackets**) —**racket games** indoor racket-and-ball games played in walled enclosures having surfaces of cement or boards including court tennis, rackets and squash rackets

raconteur (rakon'tər) *n.* skilled storyteller

racy ('rāsi) *a.* **1.** spirited **2.** lively **3.** having strong flavor **4.** spicy **5.** piquant —**'racily** *adv.* —**'raciness** *n.*

radar ('rādär) *n.* radio detecting and ranging, system for detecting the presence, position or movement of objects by sending out radio waves that they reflect

raddled ('radəld) *a.* (*esp.* of person) unkempt or run-down in appearance

radial ('rādiəl) *a. see* RADIUS

radiate ('rādiāt) *v.* **1.** emit, be emitted in rays —*vi.* **2.** spread out from center —**'radiance** *n.* **1.** brightness **2.** splendor —**'radiant** *a.* **1.** beaming **2.** shining **3.** emitting rays —*n.* **4.** point or object that emits radiation, *esp.* part of heater that gives out heat **5.** *Astron.* the point in space from which a meteor shower appears to emanate —**radi'ation** *n.* **1.** transmission of heat, light *etc.* from one body to another **2.** particles, rays, emitted in nuclear decay **3.** act of radiating —**'radiator** *n.* **1.** that which radiates, *esp.* heating apparatus for rooms **2.** cooling apparatus of automobile engine —**radiant energy** energy emitted or propagated in form of particles or electromagnetic radiation —**radiation sickness** illness caused by overexposure of body to ionizing radiations from radioactive material *etc.* —**radiation therapy** use of x-ray apparatus and other sources of high-energy radiation in treatment of human and animal diseases

radical ('radikəl) *a.* **1.** fundamental, thorough **2.** extreme **3.** *Math.* of roots of numbers or quantities —*n.* **4.** person of extreme (political) views **5.** radicle **6.** *Math.* number expressed as root of another **7.** group of atoms of several elements which remain unchanged in a series of chemical compounds —**'radicalism** *n.* —**radical sign** symbol √ placed before number or quantity to indicate extraction of root, *esp.* square root

radicle ('radikəl) *n. Bot.* root

radio ('rādiō) *n.* **1.** use of electromagnetic waves for broadcasting, communication *etc.* **2.** device for receiving, amplifying radio signals **3.** broadcasting, content of radio program —*vt.* **4.** transmit (message *etc.*) by radio —**radio'active** *a.* emitting invisible rays that penetrate matter —**radioac'tivity** *n.* disintegration of the nuclei of the atoms of certain elements during which rays and elementary particles are emitted —**radio astronomy** astronomy in which radio telescope is used to detect and analyze radio signals received on earth from radio sources in space —**radiocarbon dating** technique for determining age of organic materials based on their content of radioisotope ¹⁴C acquired from atmosphere when they formed part of living plant (*see also* **carbon dating** *at* CARBON) —**radio'chemical** *a.* —**radio'chemist** *n.* —**radio'chemistry** *n.* chemistry of radioactive elements and their compounds —**radio frequency 1.** any frequency that lies in range 10 kilohertz to 300 000 megahertz and can be used for broadcasting **2.** frequency transmitted by particular radio station —**'radiograph** *n.* image produced on sensitized film or plate by radiation —**radi'ographer** *n.* —**radi'ography** *n.* production of image on film or plate by radiation —**radio'isotope** *n.* radioactive isotope —**radi'ologist** *n.* —**radi'ology** *n.* science of use of rays in medicine —**radioscopic** (rādiō'skopik) *a.* —**radi'oscopy** *n. see* fluoroscopy *at* FLUORESCENCE —**radiosonde** ('rādiōsond) *n.* airborne instrument to send meteorological information back to earth by radio —**radio'telegraph** *v./n.* —**radiote'legraphy** *n.* telegraphy in which messages (usu. in Morse code) are transmitted by radio waves —**radio'telephone** *n.* **1.** device for communications by means of radio waves —*v.* **2.** telephone (person) by radiotelephone —**radiote'lephony** *n.* —**radio telescope** instrument used in radio astronomy to pick up and analyze radio waves from space and to transmit radio waves —**radio'therapy** *n.* diagnosis and treatment of disease by x-rays

radio- (*comb. form*) **1.** denoting radio, broadcasting or radio frequency, as in *radiotelegraphy* **2.** indicating radioactivity or radiation, as in *radiochemistry*

radish ('radish) *n.* pungent root vegetable

radium ('rādiəm) *n. Chem.* metallic element *Symbol* Ra, at. wt. 226.1, at. no. 88

radius ('rādiəs) *n.* **1.** straight line from center to circumference of circle **2.** bone on the thumb side of a human forearm (*pl.* **radii**

('rādiĭ), -es) —'**radial** a. 1. arranged like radii of circle 2. of ray or rays 3. of radius —'**radian** n. SI unit of plane angle; angle between two radii of circle that cut off on circumference arc equal in length to radius —**radial-ply** a. (of pneumatic tire) having fabric cords in outer casing running radially, enabling sidewalls to be flexible

radon ('rādon) n. Chem. gaseous element Symbol Rn, at. wt. 222.0 at. no. 86

RAF (nonstandard raf) or **R.A.F.** Royal Air Force

raffia or **raphia** ('rafiə) n. prepared palm fiber for making mats etc.

raffish ('rafish) a. disreputable

raffle ('rafəl) n. 1. lottery in which an article is assigned by lot to one of those buying tickets —vt. 2. dispose of by raffle

raft (raft) n. floating structure of logs, planks etc.

rafter ('raftər) n. one of main beams of roof

rag[1] (rag) n. 1. fragment of cloth 2. torn piece 3. inf. newspaper etc., esp. one considered worthless 4. piece of ragtime music —pl. 5. tattered clothing —**ragged** ('ragid) a. 1. shaggy 2. torn 3. clothed in torn clothes 4. lacking smoothness —**ragbag** n. confused assortment —**ragtag** n. derogatory common people; rabble (esp. in **ragtag and bobtail**) —**ragtime** n. style of jazz piano music —**rag trade** inf. clothing industry, trade —**ragwort** n. European plant with yellow daisylike flowers (see also GROUNDSEL)

rag[2] (rag) vt. 1. tease 2. torment 3. play practical jokes on (-gg-) —n. 4. period of carnival with procession etc. organized by students to raise money for charities

rag[3] (rag) Jazz n. 1. piece of ragtime music —vt. 2. compose or perform in ragtime (-gg-)

ragamuffin ('ragəmufin) n. ragged, dirty person

rage (rāj) n. 1. violent anger or passion 2. fury —vi. 3. speak, act with fury 4. proceed violently and without check (as storm, battle etc.) 5. be widely and violently prevalent —**all the rage** very popular

raglan ('raglən) a. (of sleeve) cut in two sections, with point at neckline and seam down the center of the arm, used mainly in suits and overcoats

ragout (ra'gōō) n. highly seasoned stew of meat and vegetables

raid (rād) n. 1. rush, attack 2. foray —vt. 3. make raid on —**raider** n.

rail[1] (rāl) n. horizontal bar, esp. as part of fence, track etc. —'**railing** n. fence, barrier made of rails supported by posts —**railhead** n. farthest point to which railroad line extends —'**railroad** n. 1. track of iron rails on which trains run 2. company operating railroad —**off the rails** inf. 1. astray 2. on wrong track 3. in error 4. leading reckless, dissipated life

rail[2] (rāl) vi. (with at or against) 1. utter abuse 2. scoff 3. scold 4. reproach —'**raillery** n. banter

rail[3] (rāl) n. any of various kinds of marsh bird

raiment ('rāmənt) n. obs. clothing

rain (rān) n. 1. moisture falling in drops from clouds 2. fall of such drops —vi. 3. fall as rain —vt. 4. pour down like rain —'**rainy** a. —'**rainbow** n. arch of prismatic colors in sky —'**raincoat** n. light water-resistant overcoat —'**rainfall** n. 1. precipitation in form of raindrops 2. Met. amount of precipitation in specified place and time —'**rainforest** n. dense forest found in tropical areas of heavy

rainfall —**rain gauge** instrument for measuring rainfall —**rainy day** future time of need, esp. financial

raise (rāz) vt. 1. lift up 2. set up 3. build 4. increase 5. elevate 6. promote 7. heighten, as pitch of voice 8. breed into existence 9. levy, collect 10. end (siege)

raisin ('rāzən) n. dried grape

raison d'être (rezō 'detr) Fr. reason or justification for existence (pl. **raisons d'être** (rezō 'detr))

raj (räj) n. rule, sway, esp. in India —'**raja** or '**rajah** n. Indian prince or ruler

rake[1] (rāk) n. 1. tool with long handle and crosspiece with teeth for gathering hay, leaves etc. —vt. 2. gather, smooth with rake 3. sweep, search over 4. sweep with shot —**rake-off** n. inf. monetary commission, esp. illegal

rake[2] (rāk) n. dissolute or dissipated man —'**rakish** a. dissolute; profligate

rake[3] (rāk) n. 1. slope, esp. backward, of ship's funnel etc. —v. 2. incline from perpendicular —'**rakish** a. appearing dashing or speedy

raku ('räkōō) n. coarse-grained Japanese pottery notable for its refined rusticity

rally[1] ('rali) vt. 1. bring together, esp. what has been scattered, as routed army or dispersed troops —vi. 2. come together 3. regain health or strength, revive ('**rallied**, '**rallying**) —n. 4. act of rallying 5. assembly, esp. outdoor, of any organization 6. Tennis lively exchange of strokes

rally[2] ('rali) v. mock or ridicule (someone) in good-natured way; chaff; tease

ram (ram) n. 1. male sheep 2. hydraulic machine 3. battering engine —vt. 4. force, drive 5. strike against with force 6. stuff 7. strike with ram (-mm-) —'**ramrod** n. 1. rod for cleaning barrel of rifle etc. 2. rod for ramming in charge of muzzle-loading firearm

RAM (ram) Comp. random access memory

ramada (rə'mädə) n. shelter with open sides

Ramadan ('ramədän) n. 1. 9th Islamic month 2. strict fasting observed during this time

ramble ('rambəl) vi. 1. walk without definite route 2. wander 3. talk incoherently 4. spread in random fashion —n. 5. rambling walk —'**rambler** n. 1. climbing rose 2. one who rambles

rambutan (ram'bōōtən) n. 1. SE Asian tree 2. its bright red edible fruit

ramekin or **ramequin** ('ramikin) n. 1. small fireproof dish 2. savory food baked in it

ramify ('ramifī) v. 1. spread in branches, subdivide —vi. 2. become complex (-**ified**, -**ifying**) —**ramifi'cation** n. 1. branch, subdivision 2. process of branching out 3. consequence

ramp (ramp) n. gradual slope joining two level surfaces

rampage ('rampāj, ram'pāj) vi. 1. dash about violently —n. (ram'pāj) 2. angry or destructive behavior —**ram'pageous** a. —**on the rampage** behaving violently or destructively

rampant ('rampənt) a. 1. violent 2. rife 3. rearing

rampart ('rampärt) n. 1. mound, wall for defense —vt. 2. defend with rampart

rampike ('rampīk) n. C tall tree, burnt or bare of branches

ramshackle ('ramshakəl) a. tumbledown, rickety, makeshift

ran (ran) pt. of RUN

ranch (ranch) n. 1. Amer. cattle farm —vi. 2. live or work on a ranch —'**rancher** n.

rancherie ('ranchəri) n. C Indian reservation

rancid ('ransid) a. (of food) having unpleasant smell or taste —**ran'cidity** n.

rancor ('rangkər) n. bitter, inveterate hate —'**rancorous** a. 1. malignant 2. virulent

rand (rand, rond, ront) n. monetary unit of S Afr.

R & B rhythm-and-blues

R & D research and development

random ('randəm) a. made or done by chance, without plan —**at random** haphazard(ly)

randy ('randi) a. sl. sexually aroused

rang (rang) pt. of RING[2]

range (rānj) n. 1. limits 2. row 3. scope, sphere 4. distance missile can travel 5. distance of mark shot at 6. place for shooting practice or rocket testing 7. rank 8. kitchen stove —vt. 9. set in row 10. classify 11. roam —vi. 12. extend 13. roam 14. pass from one point to another 15. fluctuate (as prices) —'**ranger** n. official in charge of or patrolling park etc. —'**rangy** a. 1. with long, slender limbs 2. spacious —'**rangefinder** n. instrument for finding distance away of given object

rani or **ranee** (rä'nē, 'räni) n. queen or princess; wife of raja

rank[1] (rangk) n. 1. line 2. place where taxis wait 3. order 4. social class 5. status 6. relative place or position —pl. 7. common soldiers 8. great mass or majority of people (also **rank and file**) —vt. 9. draw up in rank, classify —vi. 10. have rank, place 11. have certain distinctions

rank[2] (rangk) a. 1. growing too thickly, coarse 2. offensively strong 3. rancid 4. vile 5. flagrant —'**rankly** adv.

rankle ('rangkəl) vi. fester, continue to cause anger, resentment or bitterness

ransack ('ransak) vt. 1. search thoroughly 2. pillage, plunder

ransom ('ransəm) n. 1. release from captivity by payment 2. amount paid —vt. 3. pay ransom for —'**ransomer** n.

rant (rant) vi. 1. rave in violent, high-sounding language —n. 2. noisy, boisterous speech 3. wild gaiety —'**ranter** n.

ranunculus (rə'nungkyələs) n. any of a genus of plants that includes buttercup, crowfoot and spearwort

rap[1] (rap) n. 1. smart slight blow —vt. 2. give rap to (-pp-) —**take the rap** sl. suffer punishment, whether guilty or not

rap[2] (rap) n. the least amount (esp. in **not care a rap**)

rapacious (rə'pāshəs) a. 1. greedy 2. grasping —**rapacity** (rə'pasiti) n.

rape[1] (rāp) vt. 1. force (woman) to submit unwillingly to sexual intercourse —n. 2. act of raping 3. any violation or abuse

rape[2] (rāp) n. plant with oil-yielding seeds, also used as fodder (also '**colza, cole**)

rapid ('rapid) a. 1. quick, swift —pl.n. 2. part of river with fast, turbulent current —**ra'pidity** or '**rapidness** n. —'**rapidly** adv. —**rapid eye movement** movement of eyeballs during sleep, while sleeper is dreaming

rapier ('rāpiər) n. fine-bladed sword used as thrusting weapon

rapine ('rapin, -pīn) n. plunder

rapport (ra'pōr) n. harmony, agreement

rapprochement (raprosh'mä) Fr. reestablishment of friendly relations between nations

rapscallion (rap'skalyən) n. rascal, rogue

rapt (rapt) a. engrossed, spellbound —'**rapture** n. ecstasy —'**rapturous** a.

raptorial (rap'töriǝl) *a.* **1.** predatory **2.** of the order of birds of prey

rare[1] (rāǝr) *a.* **1.** uncommon **2.** infrequent **3.** of uncommon quality **4.** (of atmosphere) having low density, thin —**'rarely** *adv.* seldom —**'rareness** *n.* —**rarity** ('rariti, 'rer-) *n.* **1.** anything rare **2.** rareness —**rare earth 1.** any oxide of lanthanide **2.** any element of lanthanide series (*also* **rare-earth element**) —**rare gas** *see* **noble gas** *at* NOBLE

rare[2] (rāǝr) *a.* (of meat) lightly cooked

rarebit ('rāǝrbit) *n. see* **Welsh rabbit** *at* WALES

rarefy ('rāǝrifī) *v.* **1.** make, become thin, rare or less dense —*vt.* **2.** refine (**-fied, -fying**) —**rare'faction** *or* **rarefi'cation** *n.*

raring ('rāǝring) *a.* enthusiastically willing, ready

rascal ('raskǝl) *n.* **1.** rogue **2.** naughty (young) person —**ras'cality** *n.* roguery, baseness —**'rascally** *a./adv.*

raschel (rä'shel) *n.* **1.** type of knitting machine producing ribbed jersey **2.** the fabric produced

rase (rāz) *vt. see* RAZE

rash[1] (rash) *a.* hasty, reckless, incautious —**'rashly** *adv.*

rash[2] (rash) *n.* **1.** skin eruption **2.** outbreak, series of (unpleasant) occurrences

rasp (rasp) *n.* **1.** harsh, grating noise **2.** coarse file —*vt.* **3.** scrape with rasp —*vi.* **4.** grate upon **5.** irritate **6.** make scraping noise **7.** speak in grating voice

raspberry ('razberi, -bǝri) *n.* **1.** red, juicy, edible berry **2.** plant which bears it **3.** *inf.* spluttering noise with tongue and lips to show contempt

Rastafarian (rastǝ'fariǝn) *n.* **1.** member of Jamaican cult that regards Ras Tafari, former emperor of Ethiopia, Haile Selassie, as God —*a.* **2.** of Rastafarians —**'Rasta** *a./n.*

rat (rat) *n.* **1.** small rodent **2.** *inf.* contemptible person, *esp.* deserter, informer *etc.* —*vi.* **3.** inform **4.** (*with* on) betray **5.** (*with* on) desert, abandon **6.** hunt rats (**-tt-**) —**'ratter** *n.* **1.** dog or cat that catches and kills rats **2.** *inf.* worker who works during strike; blackleg; scab (*also* **rat**) —**'ratty** *a. sl.* **1.** mean, ill-tempered, irritable **2.** (of hair) straggly, unkempt, greasy —**rat-bite fever 1.** *see* HAVERHILL FEVER **2.** acute infectious febrile disease caused by bite of rat infected with *Spirillum minus* bacterium —**ratcatcher** *n.* one whose job is to drive away or destroy vermin, *esp.* rats —**rat race** continual hectic competitive activity —**'ratsbane** *n.* rat poison, *esp.* arsenic oxide —**smell a rat** have suspicions of some treacherous practice

ratchet wheel

ratchet ('rachit) *n.* set of teeth on bar or wheel allowing motion in one direction only

rate[1] (rāt) *n.* **1.** proportion between two things **2.** charge **3.** degree of speed *etc.* —*pl.* **4. UK** local tax on property —*vt.* **5.** value **6.** estimate value of **7. UK** assess for local taxation —**'ratable** *or* **'rateable** *a.* **1.** that can be rated **2. UK** liable to pay rates —**'ratepayer** *n.*

rate[2] (rāt) *vt.* scold, chide

rather ('radhǝr, 'rä-) *adv.* **1.** to some extent **2.** preferably **3.** more willingly

ratify ('ratifī) *vt.* confirm (**-ified, -ifying**) —**ratifi'cation** *n.*

rating ('rāting) *n.* **1.** valuing or assessing **2.** fixing a rate **3.** classification, *esp.* of ship **4.** angry rebuke

ratio ('rāshō, -shiō) *n.* **1.** proportion **2.** quantitative relation

ratiocinate (rati'osināt) *vi.* reason —**ratioci'nation** *n.*

ration ('rashǝn) *n.* **1.** fixed allowance of food *etc.* —*vt.* **2.** supply with, limit to certain amount

rational ('rashnǝl, -shǝnǝl) *a.* **1.** reasonable, sensible **2.** capable of thinking, reasoning —**rationale** (rashǝ'nal) *n.* reasons given for actions *etc.* —**'rationalism** *n.* philosophy which regards reason as only guide or authority —**'rationalist** *n.* —**ratio'nality** *n.* —**rationali'zation** *n.* —**'rationalize** *vt.* **1.** justify by plausible reasoning **2.** reorganize to improve efficiency *etc.* —**'rationally** *adv.*

ratline ('ratlin) *n. Naut.* any of light lines tied across shrouds of sailing vessel for climbing aloft

rattan (ra'tan) *n.* **1.** climbing palm with jointed stems **2.** cane made of this

rattle ('ratǝl) *vi.* **1.** give out succession of short sharp sounds **2.** clatter —*vt.* **3.** shake briskly causing a sharp clatter of sounds *inf.* confuse, fluster —*n.* **5.** succession of short sharp sounds **6.** baby's toy filled with small pellets for making this sound **7.** set of horny rings in rattlesnake's tail —**'rattling** *adv. inf.* very —**'rattlesnake** *n.* poisonous snake —**'rattletrap** *n. inf.* broken-down old vehicle, *esp.* automobile

raucous ('rökǝs) *a.* **1.** hoarse **2.** harsh

raunchy ('rönchi) *a.* **1.** lecherous, smutty **2.** slovenly; dirty

ravage ('ravij) *vt.* **1.** lay waste, plunder —*n.* **2.** destruction

rave (rāv) *vi.* **1.** talk wildly, as in delirium **2.** write or speak (about) enthusiastically —*n.* **3.** enthusiastic or extravagant praise —**'raving** *a.* **1.** delirious; frenzied **2.** *inf.* exciting admiration —*adv.* **3.** so as to cause raving —**rave-up** *n. sl.* party

ravel ('ravǝl) *vt.* **1.** entangle **2.** fray out **3.** disentangle

raven[1] ('rāvǝn) *n.* black bird like crow —*a.* **2.** jet-black

raven[2] ('ravǝn) *v.* seek (prey, plunder) —**'ravening** *a.* (of animals) voracious; predatory —**'ravenous** *a.* very hungry

ravine (rǝ'vēn) *n.* narrow steep-sided valley worn by stream, gorge

ravioli (ravi'ōli) *n.* small cases of pasta filled with highly seasoned chopped meat or vegetables

ravish ('ravish) *vt.* **1.** enrapture **2.** commit rape upon —**'ravishing** *a.* lovely, entrancing

raw (rö) *a.* **1.** uncooked **2.** not manufactured or refined **3.** skinned **4.** inexperienced, unpracticed, as recruits **5.** sensitive **6.** chilly —**'raw'boned** *a.* having lean bony physique —**raw deal** unfair or dishonest treatment —**'rawhide** *n.* **1.** untanned hide **2.** whip made of this —**in the raw 1.** *inf.* without clothing; naked **2.** in natural or unmodified state

ray[1] (rā) *n.* **1.** single line or narrow beam of light, heat *etc.* **2.** any of set of radiating lines —*vi.* **3.** come out in rays **4.** radiate

ray[2] (rā) *n.* marine fish, oft. very large, with winglike pectoral fins and whiplike tail

rayon ('rāon) *n.* (fabric made of) synthetic fiber

raze *or* **rase** (rāz) *vt.* **1.** destroy completely **2.** wipe out, delete **3.** level

razor ('rāzǝr) *n.* sharp instrument for shaving or for cutting hair —**'razorbill** *n.* N Atlantic auk

razzle-dazzle (razǝl'dazǝl) *or* **razzmatazz** (razmǝ'taz) *n. sl.* **1.** noisy or showy fuss or activity **2.** spree; frolic

Rb *Chem.* rubidium

R.C. 1. Red Cross **2.** Roman Catholic

R.C.A.F. Royal Canadian Air Force

R.C.M.P. Royal Canadian Mounted Police

R.C.N. Royal Canadian Navy

Rd. Road

re[1] (rā) *n. Mus.* **1.** in fixed system of solmization, the note D **2.** in movable do system, the second note of a major scale

re[2] (rā, rē) *prep.* with reference to, concerning

Re *Chem.* rhenium

re- (*comb. form*) again. See the list below

REA Rural Electrification Administration

reach (rēch) *vt.* **1.** arrive at **2.** extend as far as **3.** succeed in touching **4.** attain to —*vi.* **5.** stretch out hand **6.** extend —*n.* **7.** act of reaching **8.** power of touching **9.** grasp, scope **10.** range **11.** stretch of river between two bends —**'reachable** *a.* —**reach-me-down** *n.* **1.** *see* **hand-me-down** *at* HAND **2.** ready-made garment

react (ri'akt) *vi.* act in return, opposition or toward former state —**re'actance** *n. Elec.* resistance in coil, apart from ohmic resistance, due to current reacting on itself —**re'action** *n.* **1.** any action resisting another **2.** counter or backward tendency **3.** mental depression following overexertion **4.** *inf.* response **5.** chemical or nuclear change —**re'actionary** *n./a.* (person) opposed to change, *esp.* in politics *etc.* —**re'active** *a.* chemically active —**nuclear reactor** apparatus in which nuclear reaction is maintained and controlled to produce nuclear energy

read (rēd) *vt.* **1.** look at and understand (written or printed matter) **2.** learn by reading **3.** interpret mentally **4.** read and utter **5.** interpret **6.** study **7.** understand (any indicating instrument) **8.** (of instrument) register —*vi.* **9.** be occupied in reading **10.** find mentioned in reading (**read** (red) *pt./pp.*) —**reada'bility** *n.* —**'readable** *a.* that can be read, or read with pleasure —**'reader** *n.* **1.** one who reads **2.** school textbook **3.** one who reads manuscripts submitted to publisher **4.** one who reads printer's proofs —**'readership** *n.* all readers of particular publication or author —**'reading** *n.* —**read-out** *n.* **1.** retrieving of information from computer memory or storage device **2.** information retrieved —**read between the lines** *inf.* deduce a meaning that is implied —**read out 1.** read aloud **2.** expel from political party *etc.* **3.** retrieve information from computer memory or storage device

ready ('redi) *a.* **1.** prepared for use or action **2.** willing, prompt —**'readily** *adv.* **1.** promptly **2.** willingly —**'readiness** *n.* —**ready-made** *a.* **1.** made for purchase and immediate use by customer **2.** extremely convenient; ideally suited **3.** unoriginal, conventional —*n.* **4.** ready-made article, *esp.* garment —**ready reckoner** table of numbers used to facilitate simple calculations, *esp.* for working out interest *etc.*

Reagan ('rāgǝn) *n.* **Ronald Wilson.** the 40th President of the U.S. from 1981

reagent (rē'ājǝnt) *n.* chemical substance that reacts with another and is used to detect presence of the other —**re'agency** *n.*

real (rēǝl) *a.* **1.** existing in fact **2.** happening **3.** actual **4.** genuine **5.** (of property) consisting of land and houses —**'realism** *n.* **1.** regarding things as they are **2.** artistic treatment with this outlook —**'realist** n. —**rea'listic** a. —**reality** (rē'aliti) n. real existence —**'really** adv. —**'realty** n. real estate —**real estate** landed property —**real tennis** see **court tennis** at COURT

realize ('rēəlīz) vt. **1.** apprehend, grasp significance of **2.** make real **3.** convert into money —**reali'zation** n.

realm (relm) n. **1.** kingdom, domain **2.** province, sphere

ream[1] (rēm) n. **1.** twenty quires of paper: 480, 500 or 516 sheets —pl. **2.** inf. large quantity of written matter

ream[2] (rēm) vt. enlarge, bevel out, as hole in metal —**'reamer** n. tool for this

reap (rēp) v. **1.** cut and gather (harvest) —vt. **2.** receive as fruit of previous activity —**'reaper** n.

rear[1] (rēər) n. **1.** back part **2.** part of army, procession etc. behind others —**'rearmost** a. —**rear admiral** lowest flag rank in certain navies —**'rearguard** n. troops protecting rear of army —**rear-view mirror** mirror on motor vehicle enabling driver to see traffic behind —**'rearward** a. **1.** toward or in rear —adv. **2.** toward or in rear (also **'rearwards**) —n. **3.** position in rear, esp. rear division of military formation

rear[2] (rēər) vt. **1.** care for and educate (children) **2.** breed **3.** erect —vi. **4.** rise, esp. on hind feet

reason ('rēzən) n. **1.** ground, motive **2.** faculty of thinking **3.** sanity **4.** sensible or logical thought or view —vi. **5.** think logically in forming conclusions **6.** (usu. with with) persuade by logical argument into doing etc. —**'reasonable** a. **1.** sensible, not excessive **2.** suitable **3.** logical —**'reasoning** n. **1.** drawing of conclusions from facts etc. **2.** arguments, proofs etc. so adduced

reassure (rēə'shōōər) vt. restore confidence to

rebate[1] ('rēbāt) n. **1.** discount, refund —vt. ('rēbāt, ri'bāt) **2.** deduct

rebate[2] ('rabit, 'rēbāt) or **rabbet** n. **1.** recess, groove cut into piece of timber to join with matching piece —vt. **2.** cut rebate in

rebel (ri'bel) vi. **1.** revolt, resist lawful authority, take arms against ruling power (-ll-) —n. ('rebəl) **2.** one who rebels **3.** insurgent —a. ('rebəl) **4.** in rebellion —**re'bellion** n. organized open resistance to authority —**re'bellious** a. —**re'belliously** adv.

rebirth (rē'bərth) n. **1.** revival, renaissance **2.** second or new birth

rebore ('rēbōr) n. boring of cylinder to regain true shape

rebound ('rē'bownd, ri'bownd) vi. **1.** spring back **2.** misfire, esp. so as to hurt perpetrator

(of plan, deed etc.) —n. ('rēbownd, ri'bownd) **3.** act of springing back or recoiling **4.** return

rebuff (ri'buf) n. **1.** blunt refusal **2.** check —vt. **3.** snub

rebuke (ri'byōōk) vt. **1.** reprove, reprimand, find fault with —n. **2.** reprimand, scolding

rebus ('rēbəs) n. riddle in which names of things etc. are represented by pictures standing for syllables etc. (pl. **-es**)

rebut (ri'but) vt. refute, disprove (-tt-) —**re'buttal** n.

rec. 1. receipt **2.** recipe **3.** record

recalcitrant (ri'kalsitrənt) a./n. willfully disobedient (person) —**re'calcitrance** n.

recall (ri'köl) vt. **1.** recollect, remember **2.** call, summon, order back **3.** annul, cancel **4.** revive, restore —n. **5.** summons to return **6.** ability to remember

recant (ri'kant) v. withdraw (statement, opinion etc.) —**recan'tation** n.

recap ('rēkap, ri'kap) v. **1.** recapitulate (-pp-) —n. ('rēkap) **2.** recapitulation

recapitulate (rēkə'pichəlāt) vt. **1.** state again briefly **2.** repeat —**recapitu'lation** n.

recce ('reki) sl. n. **1.** reconnaissance —v. **2.** reconnoiter

recd. or **rec'd.** received

recede (ri'sēd) vi. **1.** go back **2.** become distant **3.** slope backward **4.** start balding

receipt (ri'sēt) n. **1.** written acknowledgment of money received **2.** receiving or being received —vt. **3.** acknowledge payment of in writing

receive (ri'sēv) vt. **1.** take, accept, get **2.** experience **3.** greet (guests) —**re'ceivable** a. —**re'ceiver** n. **1.** officer appointed to take public money **2.** one who takes stolen goods knowing them to have been stolen **3.** equipment in telephone, radio or television that converts electrical signals into sound and light

recent ('rēsənt) a. **1.** that has lately happened **2.** new **3.** (R-) of second and most recent epoch of Quaternary period, which began 10 000 years ago (also **'Holocene**) —n. **4.** (R-) Recent epoch or rock series (also **'Holocene**) —**'recently** adv.

receptacle (ri'septəkəl) n. vessel, place or space to contain anything

reception (ri'sepshən) n. **1.** receiving **2.** manner of receiving **3.** welcome **4.** formal party **5.** area for receiving guests, clients etc. **6.** in broadcasting, quality of signals received —**re'ceptionist** n. person who receives guests, clients etc. —**reception room 1.** room in house suitable for entertaining guests **2.** room in hotel suitable for receptions etc.

receptive (ri'septiv) a. able, quick, willing to receive new ideas, suggestions etc. —**receptivity** (rēsep'tiviti) or **re'ceptiveness** n.

recess ('rēses, ri'ses) n. **1.** niche, alcove **2.** hollow **3.** secret, hidden place **4.** remission or suspension of business **5.** vacation

recession (ri'seshən) n. **1.** period of reduction in trade **2.** act of receding —**re'cessive** a. receding

recessional (ri'seshənəl) n. hymn sung while clergy retire

recherché (rəsher'shā, rə'shāərshā) a. **1.** of studied elegance **2.** exquisite **3.** choice

recidivism (ri'sidivizəm) n. habitual relapse into crime —**re'cidivist** n./a.

recipe ('resipē) n. **1.** directions for cooking a dish **2.** prescription **3.** expedient

recipient (ri'sipiənt) a. **1.** that can or does receive —n. **2.** one who, that which receives —**re'cipience** or **re'cipiency** n.

reciprocal (ri'siprəkəl) a. **1.** complementary **2.** mutual **3.** moving backward and forward **4.** alternating —**re'ciprocally** adv. —**re'ciprocate** vt. **1.** give and receive mutually **2.** return —vi. **3.** move backward and forward —**recipro'cation** n. —**reciprocity** (resi'prositi) n.

recite (ri'sīt) vt. repeat aloud, esp. to audience —**re'cital** n. **1.** musical performance, usu. by one person **2.** act of reciting **3.** narration of facts etc. **4.** story **5.** public entertainment of recitations etc. —**recitation** (resi'tāshən) n. **1.** recital, usu. from memory, of poetry or prose **2.** recountal —**recitative** (resitə'tēv) n. musical declamation —**re'citer** n.

reckless ('reklis) a. heedless, incautious —**'recklessness** n.

reckon ('rekən) v. **1.** count —vt. **2.** include **3.** consider **4.** think, deem —vi. **5.** make calculations —**'reckoner** n. —**'reckoning** n. **1.** counting, calculating **2.** settlement of account etc. **3.** bill, account **4.** retribution for one's actions (esp. **in day of reckoning**) **5.** Navigation see **dead reckoning** at DEAD

reclaim (ri'klām) vt. **1.** make fit for cultivation **2.** bring back **3.** reform **4.** demand the return of —**re'claimable** a.

recline (ri'klīn) vi. sit, lie back or on one's side

recluse ('reklōōs, ri'klōōs) n. **1.** hermit —a. **2.** living in complete retirement —**re'clusion** n. —**re'clusive** a.

recognize ('rekəgnīz) vt. **1.** know again **2.** treat as valid **3.** notice, show appreciation of —**recognition** (rekəg'nishən) n. —**'recognizable** a. —**recognizance** (ri'kognizəns) n. **1.** avowal **2.** bond by which person undertakes before court to observe some condition **3.** obs. recognition

recoil (ri'koil) vi. **1.** draw back in horror etc. **2.** go wrong so as to hurt the perpetrator **3.** (esp. of gun when fired) rebound —n. ('rēkoil, ri'koil) **4.** backward spring **5.** retreat **6.** recoiling

---

re'activate	reas'semble	recon'nection	redistri'bution	re-enter	reim'pose
read'dress	reas'sert	recon'sider	re'do	re-equip	rein'terpret
read'just	reas'sertion	recon'struct	re'draft	re-examine	reinterpre'tation
read'mission	reas'sess	recon'struction	re'draw	re'fill v.	reintro'duce
read'mit	reas'sessment	recon'vene	re-echo	'refill n.	reintro'duction
reaf'firm	rea'waken	re-cover	re-educate	re'float	re'kindle
reaffir'mation	re'bid v.	re-create	re-elect	re'forest	re'lay v.
rea'lign	'rebid n.	re'decorate	re-election	re'form	'relay n.
rea'lignment	re'born	rede'ploy	re-emerge	re'fuel	re'light
re'allocate	re'build	rede'sign	re-emergence	re'furnish	re'load
reap'pear	re'calculate	rede'velop	re-emphasize	re'gain	relo'cate
reap'pearance	re'capture	rede'velopment	re-employ	re'gather	relo'cation
reap'praisal	re'cast	redi'rect	re-enact	re'grow	re'marriage
reap'praise	re'charge	redi'rection	re-enactment	re'harden	re'marry
rear'range	recom'mence	redis'cover	re-enforce	re'heat	re'match v.
rear'rangement	recon'nect	redis'tribute	re-enforcement	re'house	'rematch n.

recollect (rekə'lekt) *vt.* call back to mind, remember —**recol'lection** *n.*

recommend (rekə'mend) *vt.* 1. advise, counsel 2. praise, commend 3. make acceptable —**recommen'dation** *n.*

recompense ('rekəmpens) *vt.* 1. reward 2. compensate, make up for —*n.* 3. compensation 4. reward 5. requital

reconcile ('rekənsīl) *vt.* 1. bring back into friendship 2. adjust, settle, harmonize —**'reconcilable** *a.* —**'reconcilement** *n.* —**reconciliation** (rekənsili'āshən) *n.*

recondite ('rekəndīt, ri'kondīt) *a.* obscure, abstruse, little known

recondition (rekən'dishən) *vt.* restore to good condition or working order

reconnoiter *or* **reconnoitre** (rekə'noitər) *vt.* 1. make preliminary survey of 2. survey position of (enemy) —*vi.* 3. make reconnaissance —**reconnaissance** (ri'konizəns, -səns) *n.* 1. examination or survey for military or engineering purposes 2. scouting

reconstitute (rē'konstityōot, -tōot) *vt.* restore (food) to former state, *esp.* by addition of water to a concentrate

record ('rekərd, -kôrd) *n.* 1. being recorded 2. document or other thing that records 3. disk with indentations which phonograph transforms into sound 4. best recorded achievement 5. known facts about person's past —*vt.* (ri'kôrd) 6. put in writing 7. register —*v.* (ri'kôrd) 8. preserve (sound, TV programs *etc.*) on plastic disk, magnetic tape *etc.* for reproduction on playback device —**re'corder** *n.* 1. one who, that which records 2. type of flute which is held vertically and blown through mouthpiece containing fipple which leaves only a narrow slit for passage of breath, usu. made in soprano (descant), treble (alto), tenor and bass sizes 3. judge in certain courts —**re'cording** *n.* 1. process of making records from sound 2. something recorded, *eg* radio or TV program —**record-player** *n.* machine for playing phonograph records —**for the record** for the sake of strict factual accuracy —**off the record** confidential or confidentially

recorder (sense 2)

recount[1] (ri'kownt) *vt.* tell in detail

recount[2] (rē'kownt) *v.* 1. count (votes *etc.*) again —*n.* ('rēkownt) 2. second or further count, *esp.* of votes

recoup (ri'kōop) *vt.* 1. recompense, compensate 2. recover (what has been expended or lost)

re'model	re'settle
re'number	re'shuffle
re'occupy	re'spray *v.*
re'open	'respray *n.*
re'order	re'start
reorgani'zation	re'stock
re'organize	re'surface
re'pack	re'think *v.*
re'paint	'rethink *n.*
re'paper	re'trial
re'phrase	re'try
re'plant	re'type
re'print *v.*	reu'nite
'reprint *n.*	re'use
re'route	re'visit
re'set	re'wind

recourse ('rēkôrs, ri'kôrs) *n.* 1. (resorting to) source of help 2. *Law* right of action or appeal

recover (ri'kuvər) *vt.* 1. regain, get back —*vi.* 2. get back health —**re'coverable** *a.* —**re'covery** *n.*

recreant ('rekriənt) *a.* 1. cowardly, disloyal —*n.* 2. recreant person 3. renegade —**'recreance** *or* **'recreancy** *n.*

recreation (rekri'āshən) *n.* agreeable or refreshing occupation, relaxation, amusement —**'recreative** *a.*

recriminate (ri'krimināt) *vi.* make countercharge or mutual accusation —**recrimi'nation** *n.* mutual abuse and blame —**re'criminative** *or* **re'criminatory** *a.*

recrudesce (rēkrōo'des) *vi.* break out again —**recru'descence** *n.* —**recru'descent** *a.*

recruit (ri'krōot) *n.* 1. newly enlisted soldier 2. one newly joining society *etc.* —*vt.* 3. enlist (fresh soldiers *etc.*) —**re'cruitment** *n.*

rectangle ('rektanggəl) *n.* oblong four-sided figure with four right angles —**rec'tangular** *a.* shaped thus

rectify ('rektifī) *vt.* 1. put right, correct, remedy 2. purify (**-fied, -fying**) —**rectifi'cation** *n.* 1. act of setting right 2. refining by repeated distillation 3. *Elec.* conversion of alternating current into direct current —**'rectifier** *n.* thing that rectifies

rectilinear (rekti'liniər) *or* **rectilineal** *a.* 1. in straight line 2. characterized by straight lines

rectitude ('rektityōod) *n.* 1. moral uprightness 2. honesty of purpose

recto ('rektō) *n.* right-hand page of book, front of leaf (*pl.* **-s**)

rector ('rektər) *n.* 1. clergyman with care of parish 2. head of certain institutions, chiefly academic —**'rectorship** *n.* —**'rectory** *n.* rector's house

rectum ('rektəm) *n.* final section of large intestine (*pl.* **-s, -ta** (-tə)) —**'rectal** *a.*

recumbent (ri'kumbənt) *a.* lying down —**re'cumbence** *or* **re'cumbency** *n.*

recuperate (ri'kyōopərāt, -'kōo-) *vi.* 1. recover from illness, convalesce —*v.* 2. restore, be restored from losses *etc.* —**recuper'ation** *n.*

recur (ri'kər) *vi.* 1. happen again 2. return again and again 3. go or come back in mind (**-rr-**) —**re'currence** *n.* repetition —**re'current** *a.*

recusant ('rekyəzənt) *n.* 1. one who refused to conform to rites of Established Anglican Church —*a.* 2. obstinate in refusal

recycle (rē'sīkəl) *vt.* 1. reprocess (manufactured substance) for use again 2. reuse

red (red) *a.* 1. of color varying from crimson to orange and seen in blood, rubies, glowing fire *etc.* —*n.* 2. the color 3. *inf.* communist —**'redden** *vt.* 1. make red —*vi.* 2. become red 3. flush —**'reddish** *a.* —**red blood cell** *see* ERYTHROCYTE —**red-blooded** *a.* 1. vigorous 2. virile —**'redbreast** *n.* robin —**red bug** chigger —**red carpet** 1. strip of red carpeting laid for important dignitaries to walk on 2. deferential treatment accorded to person of importance —**'redcoat** *n.* 1. *obs.* soldier 2. **C** *inf.* Mountie —**Red Crescent** emblem of Red Cross Society in Muslim country —**Red Cross** international humanitarian organization providing medical care for war casualties, famine relief *etc.* —**red deer** large deer formerly widely distributed in woodlands of Europe and Asia —**Red Ensign** national flag of Canad. until 1965 —**'redfish** *n.* any of various types of fish —**red flag** 1. emblem of communist party 2. (R- F-) their song 3. danger signal —**red-**

handed *a.* *inf.* (caught) in the act —**red hat** broad-brimmed crimson hat given to cardinals as symbol of rank —**'redhead** *n.* person with red hair —**'redheaded** *a.* —**red herring** topic introduced to divert attention from main issue —**red-hot** *a.* 1. (*esp.* of metal) heated to temperature at which it glows red 2. extremely hot 3. keen, excited, eager 4. furious; violent 5. very recent or topical —**red-hot poker** garden plant with tall spikes of red or orange flowers —**red lead** (led) red poisonous insoluble oxide of lead —**redletter day** memorably important or happy occasion —**red light** 1. signal to stop, *esp.* traffic signal 2. danger signal 3. red lamp hanging outside house indicating it is a brothel —**red-light district** district containing many brothels —**red pepper** 1. pepper plant cultivated for its hot pungent red podlike fruits 2. this fruit 3. ripe red fruit of sweet pepper 4. *see* CAYENNE PEPPER —**red rag** provocation; something that infuriates —**'redshank** *n.* large European sandpiper —**red shift** shift in spectral lines of stellar spectrum toward red end of visible region relative to wavelength of these lines in terrestrial spectrum —**'redskin** *n.* *inf.* Amer. Indian —**'redstart** *n.* 1. European songbird of thrush family 2. N Amer. warbler —**red tape** excessive adherence to official rules —**'redwing** *n.* small European thrush having speckled breast and reddish flanks —**'redwood** *n.* giant coniferous tree of California —**in the red** *inf.* in debt —**see red** *inf.* be angry

redeem (ri'dēm) *vt.* 1. buy back 2. set free 3. free from sin 4. make up for —**re'deemable** *a.* —**redemption** (ri'dempshən) *n.* —**The Redeemer** Jesus Christ

redeploy (rēdi'ploi) *v.* assign new positions or tasks to (labor *etc.*) —**rede'ployment** *n.*

redolent ('redələnt) *a.* 1. smelling strongly, fragrant 2. reminiscent —**'redolence** *n.*

redouble (rē'dubəl) *v.* 1. increase, multiply, intensify 2. *Bridge* double a second time

redoubt (ri'dowt) *n.* detached outwork in fortifications

redoubtable (ri'dowtəbəl) *a.* dreaded, formidable

redound (ri'downd) *vi.* 1. contribute 2. recoil

redress (ri'dres) *vt.* 1. set right 2. make amends for —*n.* 3. compensation, amends

reduce (ri'dyōos, -'dōos) *vt.* 1. bring down, lower 2. lessen, weaken 3. bring by force or necessity to some state or action 4. slim 5. simplify 6. dilute —*vi.* 7. *Chem.* separate substance from others with which it is combined —**re'ducible** *a.* —**reduction** (ri'dukshən) *n.* —**reducing agent** substance used to deoxidize or lessen density of another substance

redundant (ri'dundənt) *a.* 1. superfluous 2. (of worker) deprived of job because it is no longer needed —**re'dundancy** *n.*

reduplicate (ri'dyōoplikāt, -'dōo-) *v.* 1. make or become double; repeat 2. repeat (sound or syllable) in word or (of sound or syllable) be repeated —*a.* (ri'dyōoplikit, -'dōo-) 3. doubled; repeated 4. (of petals or sepals) having margins curving outward —**redupli'cation** *n.*

reed (rēd) *n.* 1. any of various marsh or water plants 2. tall straight stem of one 3. *Mus.* vibrating cane or metal strip of certain wind instruments —**'reedy** *a.* 1. full of reeds 2. like reed instrument 3. harsh and thin in tone —**'reedbuck** *n.* S Afr. antelope with buff coat —**reed bunting** common European bunting that has brown streaked plumage —**reed organ** *see* **harmonium** *at* HARMONY

reef (rēf) n. 1. ridge of rock or coral near surface of sea 2. vein of ore 3. part of sail which can be rolled up to reduce area —vt. 4. take in a reef of —**reefer** n. 1. sailor's jacket 2. sl. hand-rolled cigarette, esp. containing cannabis —**reef knot** knot consisting of two overhand knots turned opposite ways (also **square knot**)

reef knot

reek (rēk) n. 1. strong (unpleasant) smell —vi. 2. emit fumes 3. smell

reel (rēl, rēəl) n. 1. spool on which film is wound 2. Cine. portion of motion picture 3. winding apparatus 4. bobbin 5. thread wound on this 6. lively dance 7. music for it 8. act of staggering —vt. 9. wind on to reel 10. draw (in) by means of reel —vi. 11. stagger, sway, rock —**reel off** recite, write fluently, quickly

re-entry (rē'entri) n. 1. retaking possession of land etc. 2. return of spacecraft into earth's atmosphere

reeve¹ (rēv) n. 1. Hist. manorial steward or official 2. **C** president of local (rural) council

reeve² (rēv) vt. pass (rope) through hole, in block etc.

reeve³ (rēv) n. female of ruff (bird)

ref. 1. referee 2. reference 3. reformed

refectory (ri'fektəri, -tri) n. room for meals in college etc. —**re'fection** n. meal —**refectory table** long narrow dining table supported by two trestles

refer (ri'fər) vi. 1. relate, allude —vt. 2. send for information 3. trace, ascribe 4. submit for decision (-rr-) —**referable** ('refərəbəl) or **re'ferrable** a. —**referee** (refə'rē) n. 1. arbitrator 2. person willing to testify to someone's character etc. 3. umpire —v. 4. act as referee (in) —**reference** ('refərəns, 'refrəns) n. 1. act of referring 2. citation or direction in book 3. appeal to judgment of another 4. testimonial 5. one to whom inquiries as to character etc. may be made —**referendum** (refə'rendəm) n. submitting of question to electorate (pl. **-s, -da** (-də)) —**referent** ('refərənt) n. object or idea to which word or phrase refers —**re'ferral** n. act, instance of referring —**reference library** library where books may be consulted but not taken away by readers

refine (ri'fīn) vt. purify —**re'fined** a. 1. not coarse or vulgar; genteel, elegant, polite 2. freed from impurities; purified —**re'finement** n. 1. subtlety 2. improvement, elaboration 3. fineness of feeling, taste or manners —**re'finer** n. —**re'finery** n. place where sugar, oil etc. is refined

refit (rē'fit) v. 1. make or be made ready for use again by repairing etc. (-tt-) —n. ('rēfit) 2. repair or re-equipping, as of ship, for further use

reflation (rē'flāshən) n. (steps taken to) produce) increase in economic activity of country etc.

reflect (ri'flekt) vt. 1. throw back, esp. rays of light 2. cast (discredit etc.) upon —vi. 3. meditate —**re'flection** n. 1. act of reflecting 2. return of rays of heat, light or waves of sound from surface 3. image of object given back by mirror etc. 4. conscious thought 5. meditation 6. expression of thought —**re'flective** a. 1. meditative, quiet, contemplative 2. throwing back images —**re'flector** n. polished surface for reflecting light etc.

reflex ('rēfleks) n. 1. reflex action 2.

reflected image 3. reflected light, color etc. —a. 4. (of muscular action) involuntary 5. reflected 6. bent back —**re'flexive** a. Gram. denoting agent's action on himself —**reflex action** involuntary response to (nerve) stimulation

reflux ('rēfluks) n. flowing back, ebb —**refluence** ('reflōōəns) n. —**refluent** ('reflōōənt) a. returning, ebbing

reform (ri'förm) vt. 1. improve 2. reconstruct —vi. 3. abandon evil practices —n. 4. improvement —**reformation** (refər'māshən) n. —**re'formatory** n. 1. institution for reforming juvenile offenders —a. 2. reforming —**re'former** n.

refract (ri'frakt) vt. change course of (light etc.) passing from one medium to another —**re'fraction** n. —**re'fractive** a.

refractory (ri'fraktəri) a. 1. unmanageable 2. difficult to treat or work 3. Med. resistant to treatment 4. resistant to heat

refrain¹ (ri'frān) vi. abstain

refrain² (ri'frān) n. chorus

refresh (ri'fresh) vt. 1. give freshness to 2. revive 3. renew 4. brighten 5. provide with refreshment —**re'fresher** n. that which refreshes —**re'freshment** n. 1. that which refreshes, esp. food, drink 2. restorative

refrigerate (ri'frijərāt) vt. 1. freeze 2. cool —**re'frigerant** n. 1. refrigerating substance —a. 2. causing cooling or freezing —**refriger'ation** n. —**re'frigerator** n. apparatus in which foods, drinks are kept cool

refuge ('refyōōj) n. shelter, protection, sanctuary —**refu'gee** n. one who seeks refuge, esp. in foreign country

refulgent (ri'fōōljənt, -'ful-) a. shining, radiant —**re'fulgence** n. —**re'fulgency** n. splendor

refund (ri'fund) vt. 1. pay back —n. ('rēfund) 2. return of money to purchaser or amount so returned

refurbish (ri'fərbish) vt. furbish, furnish or polish anew

refuse¹ (ri'fyōōz) v. decline, deny, reject —**re'fusal** n. 1. denial of anything demanded or offered 2. option

refuse² ('refyōōs) n. rubbish, useless matter

refute (ri'fyōōt) vt. disprove —**re'futable** a. —**refutation** (refyōō'tāshən) n.

regal ('rēgəl) a. of, like a king —**regalia** (ri'gālyə) pl.n. (sometimes with sing. v.) 1. insignia of royalty, as used at coronation etc. 2. emblems of high office, an order etc. —**re'gality** n. —**'regally** adv.

regale (ri'gāl) vt. 1. give pleasure to 2. feast —**re'galement** n.

regard (ri'gärd) vt. 1. look at 2. consider 3. relate to 4. heed —n. 5. look 6. attention 7. particular respect 8. esteem —pl. 9. expression of good will —**re'gardful** a. heedful, careful —**re'garding** prep. in respect of; on the subject of —**re'gardless** a. 1. heedless —adv. 2. in spite of everything

regatta (ri'gātə, -'gatə) n. meeting for yacht or boat races

regenerate (ri'jenərāt) v. 1. (cause to) undergo spiritual rebirth 2. reform morally 3. reproduce, re-create 4. reorganize —a. (ri'jenərit) 5. born anew —**regener'ation** n. —**re'generative** a. —**re'generator** n.

regent ('rējənt) n. 1. ruler of kingdom during absence, minority etc. of its monarch —a. 2. ruling —**'regency** n. status of, (period of) office of regent —**regency style** eclectic architectural and decorative style named for Prince Regent (later George IV) seen from late 18th cent. to about 1830

reggae ('regā) n. style of popular West Indian music with strong beat

Reggiano Lodigiano (re'jänō lōdē'jänō) see PARMESAN

regicide ('rejisīd) n. 1. one who kills a king 2. this crime

regime or **régime** (rā'zhēm) n. 1. system of government, administration 2. see REGIMEN (sense 1)

regimen ('rejimən) n. 1. prescribed system of diet etc. (also **re'gime**) 2. rule

regiment ('rejimənt) n. 1. organized body of troops as unit of army —vt. ('rejiment) 2. discipline, organize rigidly or too strictly —**regi'mental** a. of regiment —**regi'mentals** pl.n. uniform

region ('rējən) n. 1. area, district 2. stretch of country 3. part of the body 4. sphere, realm 5. (oft. **R-**) administrative division of a country —**'regional** a. —**regional enteritis** see CROHN'S DISEASE

register ('rejistər) n. 1. list 2. catalog 3. roll 4. device for registering 5. written record 6. range of voice or instrument —v. 7. show, be shown on meter, face etc. —vt. 8. enter in register 9. record 10. show 11. set down in writing 12. Print., photog. cause to correspond precisely —**'registrar** n. keeper of a register —**regis'tration** n. —**'registry** n. 1. registering 2. place where registers are kept, esp. of births, marriages, deaths —**registered mail** 1. Postal Service facility by which compensation is paid for loss of or damage to mail for which registration fee has been paid 2. mail sent by this service

regorge (ri'görj) vt. vomit up

regress (ri'gres) vi. 1. return, revert to former place, condition etc. —n. ('regres) 2. movement in backward direction —**re'gression** n. 1. act of returning 2. retrogression —**re'gressive** a. falling back —**re'gressively** adv.

regret (ri'gret) vt. 1. feel sorry, distressed for loss of or on account of (-tt-) —n. 2. sorrow, distress for thing done or left undone or lost —**re'gretful** a. —**re'grettable** a.

regular ('regyələr) a. 1. normal 2. habitual 3. done, occurring, according to rule 4. periodical 5. straight, level 6. living under rule 7. belonging to standing army —n. 8. regular soldier 9. inf. regular customer —**regu'larity** n. —**'regularize** v.

regulate ('regyəlāt) vt. 1. adjust 2. arrange 3. direct 4. govern 5. put under rule —**regu'lation** n. —**'regulator** n. contrivance to produce uniformity of motion, as flywheel, governor valve etc.

regurgitate (rē'gərjitāt) v. 1. vomit 2. bring back (swallowed food) into mouth —**regurgi'tation** n.

rehabilitate (rēə'bilitāt) vt. 1. help (person) to readjust to society after period of illness, imprisonment etc. 2. restore to reputation or former position 3. make fit again 4. reinstate —**rehabili'tation** n.

rehash (rē'hash) vt. 1. rework, reuse —n. 2. old materials presented in new form

rehearse (ri'hərs) vt. 1. practice (play etc.) 2. repeat aloud 3. say over again 4. train, drill —**re'hearsal** n.

Reich (rīk) n. 1. Holy Roman Empire (962-1806) (**First Reich**) 2. Hohenzollern empire in Germany from 1871 to 1918 (**Second Reich**) 3. Nazi dictatorship in Germany from 1933-45 (**Third Reich**)

reign (rān) n. 1. period of sovereign's rule —vi. 2. be sovereign 3. be supreme

reimburse (rēim'bərs) vt. 1. refund 2. pay back —**reim'bursement** n.

rein (rān) n. 1. (oft. pl.) narrow strap

attached to bit to guide horse **2.** instrument for governing —*vt.* **3.** check, manage with reins **4.** control —**give (a) free rein** remove restraints

reincarnation (rēinkär'nāshən) *n.* **1.** rebirth of soul in successive bodies **2.** one of series of such transmigrations —**rein'carnate** *vt.*

reindeer

reindeer ('rāndēər) *n.* large deer of northern regions of America, Asia and Europe, oft. domesticated and used as food source (*pl.* **-deer, -s**)

reinforce (rēin'förs) *vt.* **1.** strengthen with new support, material, force **2.** strengthen with additional troops, ships *etc.* —**rein'forcement** *n.* —**reinforced concrete 1.** concrete strengthened internally by steel bars **2.** ferroconcrete

reinstate (rēin'stāt) *vt.* replace, restore, re-establish —**rein'statement** *n.*

reiterate (rē'itərāt) *vt.* repeat again and again —**reiter'ation** *n.* repetition

reject (ri'jekt) *vt.* **1.** refuse to accept **2.** put aside **3.** discard **4.** renounce —*n.* ('rējekt) **5.** person or thing rejected as not up to standard —**re'jection** *n.* refusal

rejig (rē'jig) *vt.* **1.** re-equip (factory, plant) **2.** *inf.* rearrange (**-gg-**)

rejoice (ri'jois) *v.* **1.** make or be joyful, merry —*vt.* **2.** exult **3.** gladden

rejoin (ri'join) *vt.* **1.** reply **2.** (rē'join) join again —**re'joinder** *n.* answer, retort

rejuvenate (ri'jōōvināt) *vt.* restore to youth —**rejuve'nation** *n.* —**rejuve'nescence** *n.* process of growing young again

relapse (ri'laps) *vi.* **1.** fall back (into evil, illness *etc.*) —*n.* **2.** act or instance of relapsing

relate (ri'lāt) *vt.* **1.** narrate, recount **2.** establish relation between —*vi.* (with to) **3.** have reference or relation **4.** form sympathetic relationship —**re'lated** *a.* **1.** connected; associated **2.** connected by kinship or marriage

relation (ri'lāshən) *n.* **1.** relative quality or condition **2.** connection by blood or marriage **3.** connection (between things) **4.** act of relating **5.** narrative —**re'lationship** *n.* —**relative** ('relətiv) *a.* **1.** dependent on relation to something else, not absolute **2.** having reference or relation —*n.* **3.** one connected by blood or marriage **4.** relative word or thing —**relatively** ('relətivli) *adv.* —**relativity** (relə'tiviti) *n.* **1.** state of being relative **2.** subject of two theories of Albert Einstein, dealing with relationships of space, time and motion and acceleration and gravity

relax (ri'laks) *vt.* **1.** make loose or slack —*vi.* **2.** become loosened or slack **3.** ease up from effort or attention **4.** become more friendly, less strict —**relax'ation** *n.* **1.** relaxing recreation **2.** alleviation **3.** abatement

relay ('rēlā) *n.* **1.** fresh set of people or animals relieving others **2.** *Elec.* device for making or breaking local circuit **3.** *Rad., T.V.*

broadcasting station receiving programs from another station —*vt.* ('rēlā, ri'lā) **4.** pass on, as message ('relayed, 'relaying) —**relay race** race between teams of which each runner races part of distance

release (ri'lēs) *vt.* **1.** give up, surrender, set free **2.** permit public showing of (motion picture *etc.*) —*n.* **3.** setting free **4.** releasing **5.** written discharge **6.** permission to show publicly **7.** motion picture, record *etc.* newly issued

relegate ('religāt) *vt.* **1.** banish, consign **2.** demote —**rele'gation** *n.*

relent (ri'lent) *vi.* give up harsh intention, become less severe —**re'lentless** *a.* **1.** pitiless **2.** merciless

relevant ('relivənt) *a.* having to do with the matter in hand, to the point —'**relevance** *n.*

reliable (ri'līəbəl) *a. see* RELY

relic ('relik) *n.* **1.** thing remaining, *esp.* as memorial of saint **2.** memento —*pl.* **3.** remains, traces **4.** *obs.* dead body —'**relict** *n. obs.* widow

relief (ri'lēf) *n.* **1.** alleviation, end of pain, distress *etc.* **2.** money, food given to victims of disaster, poverty *etc.* **3.** release from duty **4.** one who relieves another from work or duty **5.** bus, plane *etc.* that carries passengers when a scheduled service is full **6.** freeing of besieged city *etc.* **7.** projection of carved design from surface **8.** distinctness, prominence —**re'lieve** *vt.* bring or give relief to —**relief map** map showing elevations and depressions of country in relief

religion (ri'lijən) *n.* system of belief in, worship of a supernatural power or god —**religiose** (ri'lijiōs) *a.* affectedly or extremely pious; sanctimoniously religious —**religiosity** (riliji'ositi) *n.* —**re'ligious** *a.* **1.** pert. to religion **2.** pious **3.** conscientious —**re'ligiously** *adv.* **1.** in religious manner **2.** scrupulously **3.** conscientiously

relinquish (ri'lingkwish) *vt.* **1.** give up, abandon **2.** surrender or renounce (claim, right *etc.*) —**re'linquishment** *n.*

reliquary ('relikweri) *n.* case or shrine for holy relics

relish ('relish) *vt.* **1.** enjoy, like —*n.* **2.** liking, gusto **3.** savory taste **4.** taste, flavor

relive (rē'liv) *vt.* experience (sensation *etc.*) again, *esp.* in imagination —**re'livable** *a.*

reluctant (ri'luktənt) *a.* unwilling, disinclined —**re'luctance** *n.*

rely (ri'lī) *vi.* **1.** depend **2.** (with on) trust (**re'lied, re'lying**) —**relia'bility** *n.* —**re'liable** *a.* trustworthy, dependable —**re'liance** *n.* **1.** trust **2.** confidence **3.** dependence —**re'liant** *a.* confident

REM rapid eye movement

remain (ri'mān) *vi.* **1.** stay, be left behind **2.** continue **3.** abide **4.** last —**re'mainder** *n.* **1.** what is left after subtraction —*vt.* **2.** offer (end of consignment of goods, material *etc.*) at reduced prices —**re'mains** *pl.n.* **1.** relics, *esp.* of ancient buildings **2.** dead body

remand (ri'mand) *vt.* send back, *esp.* into custody —**remand home** *or* **center** place of detention for young delinquents

remark (ri'märk) *vi.* **1.** make casual comment —*vt.* **2.** comment, observe **3.** say **4.** take notice of —*n.* **5.** observation, comment —**re'markable** *a.* noteworthy, unusual —**re'markably** *adv.* **1.** exceedingly **2.** unusually

remedy ('remidi) *n.* **1.** means of curing, counteracting or relieving disease, trouble *etc.* —*vt.* **2.** put right (**-edied, -edying**) —**remediable** (ri'mēdiəbəl) *a.* —**remedial** (ri'mēdiəl) *a.* designed, intended to correct specific disability, handicap *etc.*

remember (ri'membər) *vt.* **1.** retain in, recall to memory **2.** have in mind —**re'membrance** *n.* **1.** memory **2.** token **3.** souvenir **4.** reminiscence —**Remembrance Day** C statutory holiday observed on Nov. 11th in memory of the dead of both World Wars

remind (ri'mīnd) *vt.* **1.** cause to remember **2.** put in mind —**re'minder** *n.*

reminisce (remi'nis) *vi.* talk, write of past times, experiences *etc.* —**remi'niscence** *n.* **1.** remembering **2.** thing recollected —*pl.* **3.** memoirs —**remi'niscent** *a.* reminding, suggestive

remiss (ri'mis) *a.* negligent, careless —**re'missly** *adv.*

remit (ri'mit) *v.* **1.** send (money) for goods, services *etc., esp.* by mail **2.** refrain from exacting (penalty) —*vt.* **3.** give up **4.** restore, return **5.** slacken **6.** *obs.* forgive (**-tt-**) —*n.* (ri'mit, 'rēmit) **7.** area of competence, authority —**re'missible** *a.* —**re'mission** *n.* **1.** abatement **2.** reduction in length of prison term **3.** pardon, forgiveness —**re'mittance** *n.* **1.** sending of money **2.** money sent —**re'mittence** *n.* —**re'mittent** *a.* (of symptoms of disease) characterized by periods of diminished severity —**re'mittently** *adv.*

remnant ('remnənt) *n.* **1.** (*oft. pl.*) fragment or small piece remaining **2.** oddment

remonstrate (ri'monstrāt, 'remənstrāt) *vi.* protest, reason, argue —**re'monstrance** *n.*

remorse (ri'mörs) *n.* regret and repentance —**re'morseful** *a.* —**re'morsefully** *adv.* —**re'morseless** *a.* pitiless

remote (ri'mōt) *a.* **1.** far away, distant **2.** aloof **3.** slight —**re'motely** *adv.* —**remote control** control of apparatus from a distance by electrical device

remove (ri'mōōv) *vt.* **1.** take away or off **2.** transfer **3.** withdraw —*vi.* **4.** go away, change residence —*n.* **5.** degree of difference —**re'movable** *a.* —**re'moval** *n.*

remunerate (ri'myōōnərāt) *vt.* reward, pay —**remuner'ation** *n.* —**re'munerative** *a.*

renaissance (renə'sons, -'zons) *or* **renascence** (ri'nasəns, -'nā-) *n.* revival, rebirth, *esp.* (**R-**) revival of learning in 14th-16th centuries

renal ('rēnəl) *a.* of the kidneys

renascent (ri'nasənt, -'nā-) *a.* springing up again into being

rend (rend) *v.* **1.** tear, wrench apart **2.** burst, break, split (**rent, 'rending**)

render ('rendər) *vt.* **1.** submit, present **2.** give in return, deliver up **3.** cause to become **4.** portray, represent **5.** melt down **6.** cover with plaster

rendezvous ('rondivōō) *n.* **1.** meeting place **2.** appointment **3.** haunt **4.** assignation (*pl.* **-vous** (-vōōz)) —*vi.* **5.** meet, come together

rendition (ren'dishən) *n.* **1.** performance **2.** translation

renegade ('renigād) *n.* **1.** deserter **2.** outlaw **3.** rebel

renege (ri'nēg) *vi.* go back (on promise *etc.*)

renew (ri'nyōō, -'nōō) *vt.* **1.** begin again **2.** reaffirm **3.** make valid again **4.** make new **5.** revive **6.** restore to former state **7.** replenish —*vi.* **8.** be made new **9.** grow again —**renewa'bility** *n.* —**re'newable** *a.* —**re'newal** *n.* **1.** revival, restoration **2.** regeneration

rennet ('renit) *n.* preparation for curdling milk

renounce (ri'nowns) *vt.* **1.** give up, cast off, disown **2.** abjure **3.** resign, as title or claim —**renunci'ation** *n.* **1.** act or instance of renouncing **2.** formal declaration renouncing something

renovate ('renəvāt) vt. restore, repair, renew, do up —**reno'vation** n.

renown (ri'nown) n. fame —**re'nowned** a.

rent[1] (rent) n. 1. payment for use of land, buildings, machines etc. —vt. 2. hold by lease 3. hire 4. let —**'rental** n. sum payable as rent

rent[2] (rent) n. 1. tear 2. fissure —v. 3. pt./pp. of REND

renunciation (rinunsi'āshən) n. see RENOUNCE

rep[1] (rep) a./n. repertory (company, theater, group)

rep[2] (rep) n. representative

repaid (rē'pād) pt./pp. of REPAY

repair[1] (ri'pāər) vt. 1. make whole, sound again 2. mend 3. patch 4. restore —n. 5. act or process of repairing —**re'pairable** a. —**reparation** (repə'rāshən) n. 1. repairing 2. amends, compensation

repair[2] (ri'pāər) vi. (usu. with to) resort, go

repartee (repər'tē, -pär-) n. 1. witty retort 2. interchange of witty retorts

repast (ri'past) n. meal

repatriate (rē'pātriāt, -'pat-) vt. send (someone) back to his own country —**repatri'ation** n.

repay (rē'pā) vt. 1. pay back, refund 2. make return for (**re'paid, re'paying**) —**re'payable** a. —**re'payment** n.

repeal (ri'pēl) vt. 1. revoke, annul, cancel —n. 2. act of repealing

repeat (ri'pēt) vt. 1. say, do again 2. reproduce —vi. 3. recur —n. 4. act, instance of repeating, esp. TV show broadcast again —**re'peatedly** adv. 1. again and again 2. frequently —**re'peater** n. 1. firearm that may be discharged many times without reloading 2. timepiece that strikes hours —**repe'tition** n. 1. act of repeating 2. thing repeated 3. piece learnt by heart and repeated —**repetitious** (repi'tishəs) a. repeated unnecessarily —**repetitive** (ri'petitiv) a. repeated

repel (ri'pel) vt. 1. drive back, ward off, refuse 2. be repulsive to (**-ll-**) —**re'pellent** a. 1. distasteful 2. resisting (water etc.) —n. 3. that which repels, esp. chemical to repel insects

repent (ri'pent) vi. 1. wish one had not done something 2. feel regret for deed or omission —vt. 3. feel regret for —**re'pentance** n. contrition —**re'pentant** a.

repercussion (rēpər'kushən) n. 1. (oft. pl.) indirect effect, oft. unpleasant 2. recoil 3. echo

repertory ('repərtöri) n. 1. repertoire, collection 2. store —**repertoire** ('repərtwär) n. stock of plays, songs etc. that player or company can give —**repertory company** or **theater** (theater with) permanent company producing succession of plays

repetition (repi'tishən) n. see REPEAT

repine (ri'pīn) vi. fret, complain

replace (ri'plās) vt. 1. substitute for 2. put back —**re'placement** n.

replay ('rēplā) n. 1. immediate reshowing on TV of incident in sport, esp. in slow motion (also **action replay**) 2. replaying of a match —vt. (rē'plā) 3. play again

replenish (ri'plenish) vt. fill up again —**re'plenishment** n.

replete (ri'plēt) a. filled, gorged —**re'pletion** n. complete fullness

replica ('replikə) n. 1. exact copy 2. facsimile, duplicate —**'replicate** vt. make, be a copy of

reply (ri'plī) v. 1. answer (**re'plied, re'plying**) —n. 2. an answer; response

report (ri'pört) n. 1. account, statement 2. written statement of child's progress at school 3. rumor 4. repute 5. bang —vt. 6. announce, relate 7. make, give account of 8. take down in writing 9. complain about —vi. 10. make report 11. act as reporter 12. present oneself (to) —**re'porter** n. one who reports, esp. for newspaper

repose (ri'pōz) n. 1. peace 2. composure 3. sleep —vi. 4. rest —vt. 5. lay at rest 6. place 7. rely, lean (on) —**repository** (ri'pozitöri) n. 1. place where valuables are deposited for safety 2. store

repossess (rēpə'zes) vt. take back possession of (property), esp. for nonpayment of money due on installment plan —**repos'session** n.

repoussé (rəpōō'sā, rə'pōōsā) a. 1. embossed 2. hammered into relief from reverse side —n. 3. metal work so produced

reprehend (repri'hend) vt. find fault with —**repre'hensible** a. deserving censure 2. unworthy —**repre'hension** n. censure

represent (repri'zent) vt. 1. stand for 2. deputize for 3. act, play 4. symbolize 5. make out to be 6. call up by description or portrait —**represen'tation** n. —**repre'sentative** n. 1. one chosen to stand for group 2. traveling salesman —a. 3. typical

repress (ri'pres) vt. keep down or under, quell, check —**re'pression** n. restraint —**re'pressive** a.

reprieve (ri'prēv) vt. 1. suspend execution of (condemned person) 2. give temporary relief to —n. 3. postponement or cancellation of punishment 4. respite 5. last-minute intervention

reprimand ('reprimand) n. 1. formal admonition —vt. 2. admonish formally

reprisal (ri'prīzəl) n. retaliation

reproach (ri'prōch) vt. 1. blame, rebuke —n. 2. scolding, upbraiding 3. expression of this 4. thing bringing discredit —**re'proachful** a.

reprobate ('reprəbāt) a. 1. depraved 2. cast off by God —n. 3. depraved or disreputable person —vt. 4. disapprove of, reject —**repro'bation** n.

reproduce (rēprə'dyōōs, -'dōōs) vt. 1. produce copy of 2. bring (new individuals) into existence 3. re-create, produce anew —vi. 4. propagate 5. generate —**repro'ducible** a. —**repro'duction** n. 1. process of reproducing 2. that which is reproduced 3. facsimile, as of painting etc. —**repro'ductive** a.

reprove (ri'prōōv) vt. censure —**re'proof** n.

reptile ('reptil, -tīl) n. cold-blooded, air-breathing vertebrate with horny scales or plates, as snake, tortoise etc. —**reptilian** (rep'tiliən) a.

republic (ri'publik) n. state without monarch in which supremacy of people or their elected representatives is formally acknowledged —**re'publican** a./n. —**re'publicanism** n.

repudiate (ri'pyōōdiāt) vt. 1. reject authority or validity of 2. cast off, disown

repugnant (ri'pugnənt) a. 1. offensive 2. distasteful 3. contrary —**re'pugnance** n. 1. dislike, aversion 2. incompatibility

repulse (ri'puls) vt. 1. drive back 2. rebuff 3. repel —n. 4. driving back, rejection, rebuff —**re'pulsion** n. 1. distaste, aversion 2. Phys. force separating two objects —**re'pulsive** a. loathsome, disgusting

repute (ri'pyōōt) vt. reckon, consider —n. 2. reputation, credit —**reputable** ('repyətəbəl) a. 1. of good repute 2. respectable —**reputation** (repyə'tāshən) n. 1. estimation in which person is held 2. character 3. good name —**re'puted** a. generally reckoned or considered; supposed —**re'putedly** adv.

request (ri'kwest) n. 1. asking 2. thing asked for —vt. 3. ask

Requiem ('rekwiəm) n. 1. Mass for the dead 2. music for this

requiescat in pace (rekwi'eskat in 'päke) Lat. may he (or she) rest in peace

require (ri'kwīər) vt. 1. want, need 2. demand —**re'quirement** n. 1. essential condition 2. specific need 3. want

requisite ('rekwizit) a. 1. necessary 2. essential —n. 3. something indispensable; necessity

requisition (rekwi'zishən) n. 1. formal demand, eg for materials or supplies —vt. 2. demand (supplies) 3. press into service

requite (ri'kwīt) vt. repay —**re'quital** n.

reredos ('rerədos, 'rēərədos, 'rēərdos) n. ornamental screen behind altar

rerun (rē'run) vt. 1. broadcast or put on (motion picture etc.) again 2. run (race etc.) again —n. ('rērun) 3. motion picture etc. that is broadcast again; repeat 4. race that is run again

rescind (ri'sind) vt. cancel, annul —**re'scindment** or **rescission** (ri'sizhən) n.

rescue ('reskyōō) vt. bring out of danger etc., deliver, extricate (**-cuing, -cued**) —n. 2. act or instance of rescuing —**'rescuer** n. —**'rescuing** n.

research (ri'sərch) n. 1. investigation, esp. scientific study to discover facts —v. 2. carry out investigations (on, into) —**re'searcher** n.

resemble (ri'zembəl) vt. 1. be like 2. look like —**re'semblance** n.

resent (ri'zent) vt. 1. show, feel indignation at 2. retain bitterness about —**re'sentful** a. —**re'sentment** n.

reserve (ri'zərv) vt. 1. hold back, set aside, keep for future use —n. 2. (also pl.) something, esp. money, troops etc., kept for emergencies 3. area of land reserved for particular purpose or for use by particular group of people etc. (also **reser'vation**) 4. reticence, concealment of feelings or friendliness —**reservation** (rezər'vāshən) n. 1. reserving 2. thing reserved 3. doubt 4. exception; limitation —**re'served** a. not showing feelings, lacking cordiality —**re'servist** n. one serving in reserve —**reserve price** minimum price acceptable to owner of property being auctioned

reservoir ('rezərvwär) n. 1. enclosed area for storage of water, esp. for community supplies 2. receptacle for liquid, gas etc. 3. place where anything is kept in store

reside (ri'zīd) vi. dwell permanently —**residence** ('rezidəns) n. 1. home 2. house —**resident** ('rezidənt) a./n. —**residential** (rezi'denchəl) a. 1. (of part of town) consisting mainly of residences 2. of, connected with residence 3. providing living accommodation

residue ('rezidyōō, -dōō) n. what is left, remainder —**residual** (ri'zijōōəl) a. —**residuary** (ri'zijōōeri) a. —**residuum** (ri'zijōōəm) n. formal residue (pl. **-ua** (-ōōə))

resign (ri'zīn) vt. 1. give up 2. reconcile (oneself) —vi. 3. give up office, employment etc. —**resignation** (rezig'nāshən) n. 1. resigning 2. being resigned, submission —**re'signed** a. content to endure

resilient (ri'zilyənt) a. 1. (of an object) capable of returning to normal after stretching etc.; elastic 2. (of a person) recovering quickly from shock etc. —**re'silience** or **re'siliency** n.

resin ('rezin) n. sticky substance formed in and oozing from plants, esp. firs and pines (also **'rosin**) —**'resinous** a. of, like resin

resist (ri'zist) v. 1. withstand 2. oppose —**re'sistance** n. 1. act of resisting 2. opposition 3. hindrance 4. Elec. opposition offered by circuit to passage of current through it —**re'sistant** a. —**re'sistible** a. —**resis'tivity** n. measure of electrical resistance —**re'sistor** n. component of electrical circuit producing resistance

resit (rē'sit) vt. 1. sit (examination) again —n. ('rēsit) 2. examination one must sit again

resolute ('rezəlōōt) a. determined —'**resolutely** adv. —**reso'lution** n. 1. resolving 2. firmness 3. purpose or thing resolved upon 4. decision of court or vote of assembly

resolve (ri'zolv) vi. 1. make up one's mind 2. decide with effort of will —vt. 3. form by resolution of vote 4. separate component parts of 5. make clear —n. 6. resolution 7. fixed purpose —**resoluble** (ri'zolyəbəl) or **re'solvable** a. able to be resolved or analyzed —**re'solved** a. fixed in purpose or intention; determined —**resolvedly** (ri'zol-vidli) adv. —**re'solvent** a./n. —**re'solver** n.

resonance ('rezənəns) n. 1. echoing, esp. in deep tone 2. sound produced by body vibrating in sympathy with neighboring source of sound —'**resonant** a. —'**resonate** v. —'**resonator** n.

resort (ri'zört) vi. 1. have recourse 2. (with to) frequent —n. 3. place of recreation, eg beach 4. recourse 5. frequented place, haunt

resound (ri'zownd) vi. echo, go on sounding —**re'sounding** a. 1. echoing 2. thorough

resource (ri'sörs, -'zörs) n. 1. capability, ingenuity 2. that to which one resorts for support 3. expedient —pl. 4. source of economic wealth 5. stock that can be drawn on 6. means of support, funds —**re'sourceful** a. —**re'sourcefully** adv. —**re'sourcefulness** n.

respect (ri'spekt) n. 1. deference, esteem 2. point, aspect 3. reference, relation —vt. 4. treat with esteem 5. show consideration for —**respecta'bility** n. —**re'spectable** a. 1. worthy of respect, decent 2. fairly good —**re'specter** n. —**re'spectful** a. —**re'specting** prep. concerning —**re'spective** a. 1. relating separately to each of those in question 2. several, separate —**re'spectively** adv.

respire (ri'spīər) v. breathe —**respirable** ('respirəbəl) a. —**respiration** (respə'rāshən) n. —**respirator** ('respərātər) n. apparatus worn over mouth and breathed through as protection against dust, poison gas etc. or to provide artificial respiration —**respiratory** ('respərətöri) a.

respite ('respit, ri'spīt) n. 1. pause 2. interval 3. suspension of labor 4. delay 5. reprieve

resplendent (ri'splendənt) a. 1. brilliant, splendid 2. shining —**re'splendence** or **re'splendency** n.

respond (ri'spond) vi. 1. answer 2. act in answer to any stimulus 3. react —**re'spondent** a. 1. replying —n. 2. one who answers 3. defendant —**re'sponse** n. answer —**re'sponsive** a. readily reacting to some influence —**re'sponsiveness** n.

responsible (ri'sponsəbəl) a. 1. liable to answer (for) 2. accountable 3. dependable 4. involving responsibility 5. of good credit or position —**responsi'bility** n. 1. state of being answerable 2. duty 3. charge 4. obligation

rest[1] (rest) n. 1. repose 2. freedom from exertion etc. 3. that on which anything rests or leans 4. pause, esp. in music 5. support —vi. 6. take rest 7. be supported —vt. 8. give rest to 9. place on support —'**restful** a. —'**restless** a.

rest[2] (rest) n. 1. remainder 2. others —vi. 3. remain 4. continue to be

restaurant ('restərənt, 'restəront, -tront) n. commercial establishment serving food

—**restaurateur** (restərə'tər) n. keeper of restaurant

restitution (resti'tyōōshən, -'tōō-) n. 1. giving back or making up 2. reparation, compensation

restive ('restiv) a. 1. restless 2. resisting control, impatient

restore (ri'stör) vt. 1. build up again, renew 2. re-establish 3. give back —**restoration** (restə'rāshən) n. —**re'storative** a. restoring —n. 2. medicine to strengthen etc. —**re'storer** n.

restrain (ri'strān) vt. 1. check, hold back 2. prevent 3. confine —**re'straint** n. restraining, control, esp. self-control

restrict (ri'strikt) vt. limit, bound —**re'striction** n. 1. limitation 2. restraint 3. rule —**re'strictive** a. —**restrictive clause** Gram. relative clause that restricts the number of possible referents of its antecedent —**restrictive practices** agreements to limit competition or output in industry

result (ri'zult) vi. 1. follow as consequence 2. happen 3. end —n. 4. effect, outcome —**re'sultant** a. arising as result

resume (ri'zōōm) v. begin again —**résumé** ('rezəmā) n. 1. curriculum vitae 2. summary, abstract —**resumption** (ri'zumpshən) n. 1. resuming 2. fresh start —**resumptive** (ri'zumptiv) a.

resurgence (ri'sərjəns) n. rising again —**re'surgent** a.

resurrect (rezə'rekt) vt. 1. restore to life, resuscitate 2. use once more (something discarded etc.) —**resur'rection** n. 1. rising again (esp. from dead) 2. revival

resuscitate (ri'susitāt) vt. revive to life, consciousness —**resusci'tation** n.

retail ('rētāl) n. 1. sale of goods in small quantities —adv. 2. by retail —v. 3. sell, be sold, retail 4. (ri'tāl) recount —'**retailer** n.

retain (ri'tān) vt. 1. keep 2. engage services of —**re'tainer** n. 1. fee to retain professional adviser, esp. barrister 2. Hist. follower of nobleman etc. —**retention** (ri'tenchən) n. —**retentive** (ri'tentiv) a. capable of retaining, remembering —**retaining wall** wall constructed to hold back earth etc. (also **re'vetment**)

retake (rē'tāk) vt. 1. take back, capture again 2. Cine. shoot (scene) again 3. tape (recording) again —n. ('rētāk) 4. Cine. rephotographed scene 5. retaped recording

retaliate (ri'tāliāt) vi. 1. repay someone in kind 2. revenge oneself —**retali'ation** n. —**re'taliative** or **re'taliatory** a.

retard (ri'tärd) vt. 1. make slow or late 2. keep back 3. impede development of —**retar'dation** n. —**re'tarded** a. underdeveloped, esp. mentally

retch (rech) vi. try to vomit

reticent ('retisənt) a. 1. reserved in speech 2. uncommunicative —'**reticence** n.

reticulate (ri'tikyəlit) a. 1. made or arranged like a net (also **re'ticular**) —v. (ri'tikyəlāt) 2. make, be like net —**reticu'lation** n. —**reticuloendothelial system** (ri-'tikyəlōendə'thēliəl) vast widely distributed network of cells which form a major link in body defense against infection

retina ('retinə) n. light-sensitive membrane at back of eye (pl. -s, -nae (-nē)) —**retinal** detachment partial or complete separation of the retina from its attachment

retinue ('retinyōō, -nōō) n. band of followers or attendants

retire (ri'tīər) vi. 1. give up office or work 2. go away 3. withdraw 4. go to bed —vt. 5. cause to retire —**re'tired** a. that has retired from office etc. —**re'tirement** n. —**re'tiring** a. unobtrusive, shy

retort

retort (ri'tört) vt. 1. reply 2. repay in kind, retaliate 3. hurl back (charge etc.) —vi. 4. reply with countercharge —n. 5. vigorous reply or repartee 6. vessel with bent neck used for distilling

retouch (rē'tuch) vt. touch up, improve by new touches, esp. of paint etc.

retrace (rē'trās) vt. go back over (a route etc.) again

retract (ri'trakt) v. draw back, recant —**re'tractable** or **re'tractible** a. —**re'tractile** a. capable of being drawn in —**re'traction** n. drawing or taking back, esp. of statement etc. —**re'tractor** n. 1. muscle 2. surgical instrument

retread (rē'tred) vt. 1. renovate (worn rubber tire) (-'treaded, -'treading) —n. ('rētred) 2. renovated tire

retreat (ri'trēt) vi. 1. move back from any position 2. retire —n. 3. act of, or military signal for, retiring, withdrawal 4. place to which anyone retires, esp. for religious contemplation 5. period of seclusion, esp. for religious contemplation 6. refuge 7. sunset call on bugle

retrench (ri'trench) v. 1. reduce (expenditure), esp. by dismissing staff —vt. 2. cut down —**re'trenchment** n.

retribution (retri'byōōshən) n. 1. recompense, esp. for evil deeds 2. vengeance —**retributive** (ri'tribyətiv) a.

retrieve (ri'trēv) vt. 1. fetch back again 2. restore 3. rescue from ruin 4. recover (esp. information) from computer 5. regain —**re'trievable** a. —**re'trieval** n. —**re'triever** n. dog trained to retrieve game

retro- (comb. form) 1. back; backward, as in retroactive 2. located behind, as in retro-choir

retroact ('retrōakt) vi. 1. react 2. act in opposite direction —**retro'active** a. applying or referring to the past —**retro'actively** adv.

retrochoir ('retrōkwīər) n. space in large church or cathedral behind high altar

retrograde ('retrəgrād) a. 1. going backward, reverting 2. reactionary —**retro'gress** vi. 1. go back to earlier, esp. worse, condition; degenerate, deteriorate 2. move backward; recede —**retro'gression** n. —**retro'gressive** a.

retrolental fibroplasia (retrō'lentəl fībrə'plāzhə) eye disease formerly causing blindness in infants subjected to excess oxygen supply

retrorocket ('retrōrokit) n. rocket engine to slow or reverse spacecraft etc.

retrospect ('retrəspekt) n. looking back, survey of past —**retro'spection** n. —**retro'spective** a.

retroussé (rətrōō'sā, rə'trōōsā) a. (of nose) turned upward, pug

retsina (ret'sēnə) n. Greek wine

return (ri'tərn) vi. 1. go, come back —vt. 2. give, send back 3. report officially 4. elect —n. 5. returning, being returned 6. profit 7. official report 8. return ticket —**return ticket** ticket allowing passenger to travel to and from a place

reunion (rē'yōōnyən) n. gathering of people who have been apart

rev (rev) inf. n. 1. revolution (of engine) —v. 2. (oft. with up) increase speed of revolution (of) (-vv-)

Rev. 1. *Bible* Revelation 2. Reverend

revaluate (rē'valyōōāt) *v.* adjust exchange value of (currency) upward —**revalu'ation** *n.*

revamp (rē'vamp) *vt.* renovate, restore

reveal (ri'vēl) *vt.* 1. make known 2. show —**revelation** (revə'lāshən) *n.*

reveille ('revəli) *n.* morning bugle call *etc.* to waken soldiers

revel ('revəl) *vi.* 1. take pleasure (in) 2. make merry —*n.* 3. (*usu. pl.*) merrymaking —'**reveler** *n.* —'**revelry** *n.* festivity

Revelation (revə'lāshən) *n. Bible* 27th book of the N.T., the last book of the Bible, written by St. John the Divine, considered a book on prophecy about the world to come

revenge (ri'venj) *n.* 1. retaliation for wrong done 2. act that satisfies this 3. desire for this —*vt.* 4. avenge 5. make retaliation for —*v.refl.* 6. avenge oneself —**re'vengeful** *a.* 1. vindictive 2. resentful

revenue ('revinyōō, -nōō) *n.* income, *esp.* of state, as taxes *etc.* —**Internal Revenue Service** *see at* INTERNAL

reverberate (ri'vərbərāt) *v.* echo, resound, throw back (sound *etc.*) —**reverber'ation** *n.*

revere (ri'vēər) *vt.* hold in great regard or religious respect —**reverence** ('revərəns) *n.* 1. revering 2. awe mingled with respect and esteem 3. veneration —**reverend** ('revərənd) *a.* (*esp.* as prefix to clergyman's name) worthy of reverence —**reverent** ('revərənt, 'revrənt) *a.* showing reverence —**reverential** (revə'renchəl) *a.* marked by reverence

reverie ('revəri) *n.* daydream, absent-minded state

revers (ri'vēər) *n.* part of garment which is turned back, *eg* lapel (*pl.* -**vers** (-'vēərz))

reverse (ri'vərs) *v.* 1. (of vehicle) (cause to) move backward —*vt.* 2. turn upside down or other way round 3. change completely —*n.* 4. opposite, contrary 5. side opposite, obverse 6. defeat 7. reverse gear —*a.* 8. opposite, contrary —**re'versal** *n.* —**re'versible** *a.* —**reverse gear** mechanism enabling vehicle to move backward —**reversing light** light on rear of motor vehicle to provide illumination when reversing

revert (ri'vərt) *vi.* 1. return to former state 2. come back to subject 3. refer (to) a second time 4. turn backward —**re'version** *n.* (of property) rightful passing to owner or designated heir *etc.* —**re'verted** *a.* —**re'vertible** *a.*

review (ri'vyōō) *vt.* 1. examine 2. look back on 3. reconsider 4. hold, make, write review of —*n.* 5. general survey 6. critical notice of book *etc.* 7. periodical with critical articles 8. inspection of troops 9. *see* REVUE —**re'viewer** *n.* writer of reviews

revile (ri'vīl) *vt.* be viciously scornful of, abuse —**re'viler** *n.*

revise (ri'vīz) *vt.* 1. look over and correct 2. restudy (work done previously) in preparation for examination 3. change, alter —**re'viser** *n.* —**revision** (ri'vizhən) *n.* 1. re-examination for purpose of correcting 2. revising of notes, subject for examination 3. revised copy —**revisionism** (ri'vizhənizəm) *n.* 1. (*sometimes* R-) moderate, nonrevolutionary version of Marxism developed in Germany around 1900 2. (*sometimes* R-) in Marxist-Leninist ideology, dangerous departure from true interpretation of Marx's teachings 3. advocacy of revision of some political theory *etc.* —**revisionist** (ri'vizhənist) *n./a.* —**re'visory** *a.* of revision

revive (ri'vīv) *v.* bring, come back to life, vigor, use *etc.* —**re'vival** *n.* reviving, *esp.* of religious fervor —**re'vivalist** *n./a.*

revoke (ri'vōk) *vt.* 1. take back, withdraw 2. cancel —**revocable** ('revəkəbəl) *a.* —**revocation** (revə'kāshən) *n.* repeal

revolt (ri'vōlt) *n.* 1. rebellion —*vi.* 2. rise in rebellion 3. feel disgust —*vt.* 4. affect with disgust —**re'volting** *a.* disgusting, horrible

revolve (ri'volv) *vi.* 1. turn round, rotate 2. be centered (on) —*vt.* 3. rotate —**revolution** (revə'lōōshən) *n.* 1. violent overthrow of government 2. great change 3. complete rotation, turning or spinning round —**revolutionary** (revə'lōōshəneri) *a./n.* —**revolutionize** (revə'lōōshənīz) *vt.* 1. change considerably 2. bring about revolution in —**revolving door** door that rotates about vertical axis, *esp.* with four leaves at right angles to each other

revolver (ri'volvər) *n.* repeating pistol with revolving magazine

revue *or* **review** (ri'vyōō) *n.* theatrical entertainment with topical sketches and songs

revulsion (ri'vulshən) *n.* 1. sudden violent change of feeling 2. marked repugnance or abhorrence

reward (ri'wörd) *vt.* 1. pay, make return to (someone) for service, conduct *etc.* —*n.* 2. something given in return for a deed or service rendered —**re'warding** *a.* giving personal satisfaction, worthwhile

rewire (rē'wīər) *vt.* provide (house *etc.*) with new wiring

RF radio frequency

Rh 1. *Chem.* rhodium 2. rhesus (*esp. in* **Rh factor** (*see also* **rhesus factor** *at* RHESUS))

rhapsody ('rapsədi) *n.* enthusiastic or high-flown (musical) composition or utterance —**rhapsodic** (rap'sodik) *a.* —'**rhapsodist** *n.* —**rhapsodize** ('rapsədīz) *v.*

rhea ('rēə) *n.* S Amer. three-toed ostrich

rhebok ('rēbok) *n.* brownish-gray S Afr. antelope

rhenium ('rēniəm) *n. Chem.* metallic element *Symbol* Re, at. wt. 186.2, at. no. 75

rheostat ('rēəstat) *n.* instrument for regulating the value of the resistance in an electric circuit

rhesus ('rēsəs) *n.* small, long-tailed monkey of S Asia —**rhesus factor** feature distinguishing different types of human blood (*also* **Rh factor**)

rhetoric ('retərik) *n.* 1. art of effective speaking or writing 2. artificial or exaggerated language —**rhe'torical** *a.* (of question) not requiring an answer —**rheto'rician** *n.*

rheum (rōōm) *n.* 1. watery discharge, mucus 2. catarrh —'**rheumy** *a.*

rheumatism ('rōōmətizəm) *n.* painful inflammation of joints or muscles —**rheu'matic** *a./n.* —'**rheumatoid** *a.* of, like rheumatism —**rheumatic fever** disease characterized by inflammation and pain in joints —**rheumatoid arthritis** chronic disease characterized by inflammation and swelling of joints

Rh factor *see* **rhesus factor** *at* RHESUS

rhinestone ('rīnstōn) *n.* imitation gem made of paste

Rhine wine (rīn) dry wine, usu. white, from the vineyards bordering the River Rhine in Germany

rhinitis (rī'nītis) *n.* inflammation of the mucous membranes lining the nasal passages

rhino ('rīnō) *n.* rhinoceros (*pl.* -**s**, '**rhino**)

rhino- *or before vowel* **rhin-** (*comb. form*) nose, as in *rhinology*

rhinoceros (rī'nosərəs, ri-) *n.* large thick-skinned animal with one or two horns on nose (*pl.* -**es**, -**ros**)

rhizome ('rīzōm) *n.* thick horizontal underground stem whose buds develop into new plants (*also* '**rootstock**, '**rootstalk**)

rhizome

rho (rō) *n.* 17th letter in Gr. alphabet (P, ρ) (*pl.* -**s**)

Rhode Island (rōd) New England state of the U.S.: ratified the Constitution in 1790. Abbrev.: **RI** (with ZIP code)

Rhodes scholar (rōdz) person holding a Rhodes scholarship, endowed by Cecil J. Rhodes, to study at Oxford University, England

rhodium ('rōdiəm) *n. Chem.* grayish-white noble metal *Symbol* Rh, at. wt. 102.9, at. no. 45 —'**rhodic** *a.*

rhododendron (rōdə'dendrən) *n.* any of various evergreen flowering shrubs

rhombus ('rombəs) *n.* equilateral but not right-angled parallelogram, diamond-shaped figure (*pl.* -**es**, -**bi** (-bī)) —**rhombohedron** (rombō'hēdrən) *n.* six-sided prism whose sides are parallelograms —'**rhomboid** *n./a.* —**rhom'boidal** *a.*

rhubarb ('rōōbärb) *n.* 1. garden plant of which the fleshy stalks are cooked and used as fruit 2. laxative from root of allied Chinese plant

rhumb line (rum) 1. imaginary line on surface of sphere that intersects all meridians at same angle 2. course navigated by vessel or aircraft that maintains uniform compass heading (*also* **rhumb**)

rhyme (rīm) *n.* 1. identity of sounds at ends of lines of verse, or in words 2. word or syllable identical in sound to another 3. verse marked by rhyme —*vt.* 4. use (word) to make rhymes —**rhymester** ('rīmstər) *or* '**rhymer** *n.* poet, *esp.* one considered mediocre; poetaster, versifier —**rhyme scheme** pattern of rhymes used in piece of verse, usu. indicated by letters —**rhyming slang** slang in which word is replaced by word or phrase that rhymes with it

rhythm ('ridhəm) *n.* measured beat or flow, *esp.* of words, music *etc.* —'**rhythmic(al)** *a.* —'**rhythmically** *adv.* —**rhythm-and-blues** *n.* kind of popular music derived from or influenced by blues —**rhythm method** method of contraception by restricting sexual intercourse to days in woman's menstrual cycle when conception is considered least likely to occur

RI Rhode Island

R.I. 1. Regina et Imperatrix (*Lat.,* Queen and Empress) 2. Rex et Imperator (*Lat.,* King and Emperor) 3 Royal Institution

ria ('rēə) *n.* long narrow inlet of sea coast, being former valley submerged by sea

rib[1] (rib) *n.* 1. one of paired curved bony rods stiffening the body of most vertebrates protecting heart, lungs *etc.* 2. cut of meat including rib(s) 3. curved timber of framework of boat 4. raised series of rows in knitting *etc.* —*vt.* 5. furnish, mark with ribs 6. knit to form rib pattern (-**bb**-) —'**ribbing** *n.* —'**ribcage** *n.* wall of chest consisting of ribs and connective tissue

rib[2] (rib) *vt. inf.* tease, ridicule (-**bb**-)

ribald ('ribəld) *a.* 1. irreverent, scurrilous 2. indecent —*n.* 3. ribald person —'**ribaldry** *n.* vulgar, indecent talk

ribbon ('ribən) *n.* **1.** narrow band of fabric used for trimming, tying *etc.* **2.** long strip or line of anything

riboflavin (rĪbə'flāvin) *n.* form of vitamin B

ribonucleic acid (rĪbōnyŏŏ'klēik, -nŏŏ-; -'klā-) *see* RNA

rice (rĪs) *n.* **1.** cereal plant **2.** its seeds as food —**rice paper** fine, edible paper

rich (rich) *a.* **1.** wealthy **2.** fertile **3.** abounding **4.** valuable **5.** (of food) containing much fat or sugar **6.** mellow **7.** amusing —*n.* **8.** the wealthy classes —**'riches** *pl.n.* wealth —**'richly** *adv.*

Richmond ('richmənd) *n.* borough of New York City

Richter scale ('riktər) logarithmic scale ranging from one to ten for expressing intensity of earthquake

rick[1] (rik) *n.* stack of hay *etc.*

rick[2] (rik) *vt./n.* sprain, wrench

rickets ('rikits) *n.* disease of children marked by softening of bones, bandy legs *etc.*, caused by vitamin D deficiency —**'rickety** *a.* **1.** shaky, insecure, unstable **2.** suffering from rickets

rickettsia (ri'ketsiə) *n.* any of group of microorganisms between bacteria and viruses in size activated only in presence of living cells —**rickettsial diseases** diseases transmitted by lice, fleas *etc.*, including typhus and spotted fever —**rickettsial pox** infectious disease resembling chickenpox transmitted by mites

ricksha *or* **rickshaw** ('rikshō) *n.* light two-wheeled man-drawn Asian vehicle

ricochet ('rikəshā) *vi.* **1.** (of bullet) rebound or be deflected by solid surface or water —*n.* **2.** bullet or shot to which this happens

Ricotta (ri'kotə) *n.* creamy, soft cheese with mild flavor orig. from Italy

rid (rid) *vt.* **1.** clear, relieve **2.** free **3.** deliver (**rid, 'ridding**) —**'riddance** *n.* **1.** clearance **2.** act of ridding **3.** deliverance **4.** relief

ridden ('ridən) *pp. of* RIDE

-ridden (*comb. form*) afflicted by, affected by, as in *disease-ridden*

riddle[1] ('ridəl) *n.* **1.** question made puzzling to test one's ingenuity **2.** enigma **3.** puzzling thing, person —*vi.* **4.** speak in, make riddles

riddle[2] ('ridəl) *vt.* **1.** pierce with many holes —*n.* **2.** coarse sieve for gravel *etc.* —**'riddled with** full of, *esp.* holes

ride (rĪd) *v.* **1.** sit on and control or propel (horse, bicycle *etc.*) —*vi.* **2.** go on horseback or in vehicle **3.** lie at anchor **4.** be carried on or across —*vt.* **5.** travel over (**rode, 'ridden, 'riding**) —*n.* **6.** journey on horse *etc.*, or in any vehicle **7.** riding track —**'rider** *n.* **1.** one who rides **2.** supplementary clause **3.** addition to a document **4.** mathematical problem on given proposition —**'riderless** *a.* —**riding crop** short whip with handle at one end for opening gates —**riding lamp** *or* **light** light on vessel showing it is at anchor

ridge (rij) *n.* **1.** long, narrow hill **2.** long, narrow elevation on surface **3.** line of meeting of two sloping surfaces —*v.* **4.** form into ridges —**'ridgepole** *n.* **1.** timber along ridge of roof, to which rafters are attached **2.** horizontal pole at apex of tent

ridiculous (ri'dikyələs) *a.* deserving to be laughed at; absurd, foolish —**'ridicule** *n.* **1.** language or behavior intended to humiliate or mock —*vt.* **2.** laugh at, deride

riding ('rĪding) *n.* **1.** (**R-** *when part of name*) former administrative district of Yorkshire **2. C** parliamentary constituency

riesling ('rēzling) *n.* **1.** dry white wine **2.** type of grape used to make this wine

rife (rĪf) *a.* prevalent, common

riffle ('rifəl) *v.* flick through (pages *etc.*) quickly

riffraff ('rifraf) *n.* disreputable people, *esp.* collectively; rabble

rifle ('rĪfəl) *vt.* **1.** search and rob **2.** ransack **3.** make spiral grooves in (gun barrel *etc.*) —*n.* **4.** firearm with long barrel —**'rifling** *n.* **1.** arrangement of grooves in gun barrel **2.** pillaging

rift (rift) *n.* crack, split, cleft —**rift valley** long narrow valley resulting from subsidence of land between two faults

rig (rig) *vt.* **1.** provide (ship) with spars, ropes *etc.* **2.** equip **3.** set up, *esp.* as makeshift **4.** arrange in dishonest way (**-gg-**) —*n.* **5.** way ship's masts and sails are arranged **6.** apparatus for drilling for oil and gas **7.** horse-drawn vehicle —**'rigger** *n.* —**'rigging** *n.* ship's spars and ropes —**'rigout** *n. inf.* person's clothing or costume, *esp.* bizarre outfit —**rig out 1.** (*oft. with* with) equip or fit out (with) **2.** dress or be dressed

rigamarole ('rigəmərōl) *n. see* RIGMAROLE

right (rĪt) *a.* **1.** just **2.** in accordance with truth and duty **3.** true **4.** correct **5.** proper **6.** of side that faces east when front is turned to north **7.** *Pol.* conservative or reactionary (*also* **right-wing**) **8.** straight **9.** upright **10.** of outer or more finished side of fabric —*vt.* **11.** bring back to vertical position **12.** do justice to —*vi.* **13.** come back to vertical position —*n.* **14.** claim, title *etc.* allowed or due **15.** what is right, just or due **16.** conservative political party **17.** *Boxing* punch, blow with right hand —*adv.* **18.** straight **19.** properly **20.** very **21.** on or to right side —**'rightful** *a.* —**'rightly** *adv.* —**right angle** angle of 90° —**right-hand** *a.* **1.** of, located on or moving toward the right **2.** for use by right hand —**right-handed** *a.* **1.** using right hand with greater skill than left **2.** performed with right hand **3.** for use by right hand **4.** turning from left to right —**right-minded** *a.* holding opinions or principles that accord with what is right or with opinions of speaker —**Right Reverend** title of high ecclesiastical official —**right triangle** triangle one angle of which is right angle —**right whale** large gray or black whalebone whale with large head and no dorsal fin —**right-hand man** most valuable assistant —**right of way** *Law* **1.** right to pass over someone's land **2.** path used (*pl.* **rights of way**)

righteous ('rĪchəs) *a.* **1.** just, upright **2.** godly **3.** virtuous **4.** good **5.** honest —**'righteousness** *n.*

rigid ('rijid) *a.* **1.** inflexible **2.** harsh, stiff —**ri'gidity** *n.*

rigmarole ('rigmərōl) *or* **rigamarole** *n.* **1.** meaningless string of words **2.** long, complicated procedure

Rigmel shrunk ('rigməl) trade name for shrinking process which limits subsequent shrinking to 1 per cent in any dimension

rigor[1] ('rigər) *n.* sudden coldness attended by shivering —**rigor mortis** ('mörtis) stiffening of body after death

rigor[2] ('rigər) *n.* **1.** harshness, severity, strictness **2.** hardship —**'rigorous** *a.* stern, harsh, severe

rile (rĪl) *vt. inf.* anger, annoy

rill (ril) *n.* small stream

rim (rim) *n.* **1.** edge, border, margin **2.** outer ring of wheel —**rimmed** *a.* bordered, edged

rime (rĪm) *n.* hoarfrost —**'rimy** *a.*

rind (rĪnd) *n.* outer coating of fruits *etc.*

rinderpest ('rindərpest) *n.* malignant infectious disease of cattle

ring[1] (ring) *n.* **1.** circle of gold *etc.*, *esp.* for finger **2.** any circular band, coil, rim *etc.* **3.**

people or things arranged so as to form circle **4.** group of people working together to advance their own interests **5.** enclosed area, *esp.* roped-in square for boxing —*vt.* **6.** put ring round **7.** mark (bird *etc.*) with ring —**'ringer** *n.* **1.** one who rings bells **2.** *sl.* person, thing apparently identical to another (*esp. in* **dead ringer**) —**'ringlet** *n.* curly lock of hair —**'ringbark** *v.* kill (tree) by cutting bark round trunk —**ring finger** third finger, *esp.* of left hand, on which wedding ring is worn —**'ringleader** *n.* instigator of mutiny, riot *etc.* —**'ringmaster** *n.* master of ceremonies in circus —**ring road** main road that bypasses a town (center) —**'ringside** *n.* **1.** row of seats nearest boxing or wrestling ring **2.** any place affording close uninterrupted view —**'ringworm** *n.* fungal skin disease in circular patches

ring[2] (ring) *vi.* **1.** give out clear resonant sound, as bell **2.** resound —*vt.* **3.** cause (bell) to sound **4.** call (person) by telephone (**rang** *pt.,* **rung** *pp.*) —*n.* **5.** a ringing **6.** telephone call

rink (ringk) *n.* **1.** sheet of ice for skating or curling **2.** floor for roller skating

rinkhals ('ringk-hows) *n.* S Afr. ring-necked cobra

rinse (rins) *vt.* **1.** remove detergent from (washed clothing, hair *etc.*) by applying clean water **2.** wash lightly —*n.* **3.** a rinsing **4.** liquid to tint hair

riot ('rĪət) *n.* **1.** tumult, disorder **2.** loud revelry **3.** disorderly, unrestrained disturbance **4.** profusion —*vi.* **5.** make, engage in riot —**'riotous** *a.* unruly, rebellious, wanton

rip[1] (rip) *vt.* **1.** cut, tear away, slash, rend (**-pp-**) —*n.* **2.** rent, tear —**'ripcord** *n.* cord pulled to open parachute —**rip-roaring** *a. inf.* characterized by excitement, intensity or boisterous behavior —**'ripsaw** *n.* saw with coarse teeth (used for cutting wood along grain) —**rip-off** *n. sl.* act of stealing, overcharging *etc.* —**rip off** *sl.* **1.** steal **2.** overcharge

rip[2] (rip) *n.* strong current, *esp.* one moving away from the shore

R.I.P. *requiescat in pace*

riparian (ri'periən, rĪ-) *a.* of, on banks of river

ripe (rĪp) *a.* **1.** ready to be reaped, eaten *etc.* **2.** matured **3.** (of judgment *etc.*) sound —**'ripen** *v.* **1.** make or grow ripe —*vi.* **2.** mature

riposte (ri'pōst) *n.* **1.** verbal retort **2.** counterstroke **3.** *Fencing* quick lunge after parry

ripple ('ripəl) *n.* **1.** slight wave, ruffling of surface **2.** sound like ripples of water —*vi.* **3.** flow, form into little waves **4.** (of sounds) rise and fall gently —*vt.* **5.** form ripples on

rise (rĪz) *vi.* **1.** get up **2.** move upward **3.** appear above horizon **4.** reach higher level **5.** increase in value or price **6.** rebel **7.** adjourn **8.** originate; begin (**rose, risen** ('rizən), **'rising**) —*n.* **9.** rising **10.** slope upward **11.** increase, *esp.* of wages —**'riser** *n.* **1.** one who rises, *esp.* from bed **2.** vertical part of step —**'rising** *n.* **1.** revolt —*a.* **2.** increasing in rank, maturity

risible ('rizibəl) *a.* **1.** inclined to laugh **2.** laughable —**risi'bility** *n.*

risk (risk) *n.* **1.** chance of disaster or loss —*vt.* **2.** venture **3.** put in jeopardy **4.** take chance of —**'riskily** *adv.* —**'risky** *a.* **1.** dangerous **2.** hazardous —**take** *or* **run a risk** proceed in an action regardless of danger involved

risotto (ri'sotō, -'zotō) *n.* dish of rice cooked in stock and served with various other ingredients

risqué (ri'skǎ) a. suggestive of indecency

rite (rīt) n. formal practice or custom, esp. religious —**ritual** ('richōōəl) n. 1. prescribed order or book of rites 2. regular, stereotyped action or behavior —a. 3. concerning rites —**ritualism** ('richōōəlizəm) n. practice of ritual —**ritualist** ('richōōəlist) n.

ritzy ('ritsi) a. sl. luxurious; elegant

rival ('rīvəl) n. 1. one that competes with another for favor, success etc. —vt. 2. vie with —a. 3. in position of rival —**'rivalry** n. keen competition

rive (rīv) v. (usu. as pp./a. **riven**) 1. split asunder 2. tear apart (**rived** pt., **rived**, **'riven** pp., **'riving** pr.p.) —**riven** ('rivən) a. split

river ('rivər) n. 1. large natural stream of water 2. copious flow —**river basin** area drained by river and its tributaries —**'riverbed** n. channel in which river flows or has flowed

rivet ('rivit) n. 1. bolt for fastening metal plates, the end being put through holes and then beaten flat —vt. 2. fasten with rivets 3. cause to be fixed or held firmly, esp. (fig.) in surprise, horror etc. —**'riveter** n.

Riviera (rivi'erə) n. 1. resort area along northern Mediterranean coast in France and Italy 2. any opulent seaside resort area

rivulet ('rivyəlit, 'rivəlit) n. small stream

R.M. C Rural Municipality

rms or **r.m.s.** root mean square

Rn Chem. radon

RNA Biochem. ribonucleic acid; any of group of nucleic acids, present in all living cells, that play essential role in synthesis of proteins

roach (rōch) n. European freshwater fish (pl. **roach, -es**)

road (rōd) n. 1. track, way prepared for passengers, vehicles etc. 2. direction, way 3. street —**'roadster** n. 1. obs. touring car 2. kind of bicycle —**'roadblock** n. barricade across road to stop traffic for inspection etc. —**road hog** selfish, aggressive driver —**'roadholding** n. extent to which motor vehicle is stable and does not skid, esp. on sharp bends etc. —**'roadhouse** n. public house, restaurant on country route —**road metal** broken stones used in macadamizing roads —**road sense** sound judgment in driving road vehicles —**road show** 1. Rad. live program, usu. with audience participation, transmitted from radio van taking particular show on the road 2. group of entertainers on tour —**'roadside** n./a. —**'roadstead** n. Naut. partly sheltered anchorage (also **roads**) —**road test** test to ensure that vehicle is roadworthy, esp. after repair etc., by driving it on roads —**road-test** vt. test (vehicle) in this way —**'roadway** n. 1. surface of road 2. part of road used by vehicles —**'roadworks** pl.n. repairs to road, esp. blocking part of road —**'roadworthy** a. (of vehicle) mechanically sound —**hit the road** sl. start or resume traveling —**one for the road** a last alcoholic drink before leaving

roam (rōm) v. wander about —**'roamer** n.

roan (rōn) a. 1. (of horses) having coat in which main color is thickly interspersed with another, esp. bay, sorrel or chestnut mixed with white or gray —n. 2. horse having such a coat

roar (rōr) vi. 1. make or utter loud, deep, hoarse sound, as of lion —v. 2. (of people) utter (something) with loud deep cry, as in anger or triumph —n. 3. such a sound —**'roaring** a. 1. inf. brisk and profitable —adv. 2. noisily

roast (rōst) v. 1. bake, cook in closed oven 2. cook by exposure to open fire 3. make, be

very hot —n. 4. roasted joint —a. 5. roasted —**'roaster** n. 1. oven etc. for roasting meat 2. chicken etc. suitable for roasting —**'roasting** n. esp. inf. severe criticism, scolding

rob (rob) vt. 1. plunder, steal from 2. pillage, defraud (**-bb-**) —**'robber** n. —**'robbery** n.

robe (rōb) n. 1. any long outer garment, oft. denoting rank or office —vt. 2. dress —vi. 3. put on robes, vestments

robin ('robin) n. small brown bird with red breast (also (**robin**) **redbreast**)

robot ('rōbot) n. 1. automated machine, esp. performing functions in human manner 2. person of machine-like efficiency —**ro'botic** a. of or like robot —**ro'botics** pl.n. (with sing. v.) study of use of robots —**'robotize** vt. 1. equip (factory) with robots 2. turn (human) into robot

Rob Roy (rob roi) a Manhattan made with Scotch whisky

robust (rō'bust, 'rōbust) a. sturdy, strong —**ro'bustious** a. obs. 1. rough; boisterous 2. strong, robust, stout —**ro'bustness** n.

roc (rok) n. monstrous bird of Arabian mythology

rock¹ (rok) n. 1. stone 2. large rugged mass of stone 3. hard candy in sticks —**'rockery** n. mound or grotto of stones or rocks for plants in garden —**'rocky** a. 1. having many rocks 2. rugged —**rock bottom** lowest possible level —**rock-bound** a. hemmed in or encircled by rocks (also (poet.) **rock-girt**) —**'rockchuck** n. see MARMOT —**rock crystal** transparent colorless quartz —**rock garden** garden featuring rocks or rockeries —**rock plant** plant that grows on rocks or in rocky ground —**rock rabbit** SA hyrax —**rock salmon** various food fishes, esp. dogfish —**rock salt** mineral consisting of sodium chloride in crystalline form, occurring in sedimentary beds etc.: important source of table salt (also **'halite**)

rock² (rok) v. 1. (cause to) sway to and fro 2. reel or sway or cause (someone) to reel or sway, as with shock or emotion —vi. 3. dance in rock-and-roll style —n. 4. rocking motion 5. rock-and-roll —**'rocker** n. curved piece of wood etc. on which thing may rock —**'rocky** a. 1. weak, unstable 2. inf. (of person) dizzy; nauseated —**rock-and-roll** or **rock-'n'-roll** n. 1. type of pop music of 1950s as blend of rhythm-and-blues and country-and-western 2. dancing performed to such music —**rocking horse** toy horse mounted on rockers, on which child can rock to and fro in seesaw movement —**off one's rocker** inf. insane

rocket¹ ('rokit) n. 1. self-propelling device powered by burning of explosive contents, used as firework, for display, signaling, line carrying, weapon etc. 2. vehicle propelled by rocket engine, as weapon or carrying spacecraft —vi. 3. move fast, esp. upward, as rocket —**'rocketry** n.

rocket² ('rokit) n. any of several kinds of flowering plant

Rocky Mountain spotted fever ('roki) severe rickettsial disease transmitted by ticks

rococo (rə'kōkō) a. (oft. **R-**) 1. of furniture, architecture etc. having much conventional decoration in style of early 18th-cent. work in Europe 2. tastelessly florid

rod (rod) n. 1. slender cylinder of metal, wood etc. 2. cane 3. unit of length equal to 5½ yards

rode (rōd) pt. of RIDE

rodent ('rōdənt) n. any gnawing animal, eg rat

rodeo ('rōdiō, rə'dāō) n. public performance of competitive games and skills of the cowboy (pl. **-s**)

rodomontade (rodəmon'tād, rōdə-; -'täd) Lit. n. 1. boastful words or behavior —vi. 2. boast; rant

roe¹ (rō) n. small species of deer

roe² (rō) n. mass of eggs in fish

roentgen or **röntgen** ('rentgən, 'rənt-; -jən) n. measuring unit of radiation dose

rogation (rō'gāshən) n. (usu. pl.) Christianity solemn supplication, esp. in form of ceremony prescribed by Church —**Rogation Days** three days preceding Ascension Day

roger ('rojər) interj. 1. Telecomm. etc. message received and understood 2. expression of agreement

rogue (rōg) n. 1. scoundrel 2. mischief-loving person, oft. child 3. wild beast of savage temper, living apart from herd —**'roguery** n. —**'roguish** a. —**rogues' gallery** collection of portraits of known criminals kept by police for identification purposes

roister ('roistər) vi. 1. be noisy or boisterous 2. brag, bluster or swagger —**'roisterer** n. reveler

role or **rôle** (rōl) n. 1. actor's part 2. specific task or function

roll (rōl) v. 1. move by turning over and over —vt. 2. wind round 3. smooth out with roller —vi. 4. move, sweep along 5. undulate 6. (of ship) swing from side to side 7. (of aircraft) turn about a line from nose to tail in flight —n. 8. act of lying down and turning over and over or from side to side 9. piece of paper etc. rolled up 10. any object thus shaped, as in meat roll 11. official list or register, esp. of names 12. bread baked into small oval or round 13. continuous sound, as of drums, thunder etc. —**'roller** n. 1. cylinder of wood, stone, metal etc. used for pressing, crushing, smoothing, supporting thing to be moved, winding thing on etc. 2. long wave of sea 3. any of various Old World birds that have blue, green and brown plumage and erratic flight —**'rolling** a. 1. having gentle rising and falling slopes 2. reverberating 3. that may be turned up or down 4. sl. extremely rich —adv. 5. sl. swaying, staggering (esp. in **rolling drunk**) —**roll call** act, time of calling over list of names, as in schools or army —**rolled gold** metal coated with thin layer of gold —**roller bearings** bearings of hardened steel rollers —**roller coaster** (in amusement parks) narrow railway with open carriages that run swiftly over route of sharp curves and steep inclines —**roller skate** skate with wheels instead of runner —**roller skating** —**roller towel** loop of towel on roller —**rolling mill** 1. mill or factory where ingots of heated metal are passed between rollers to produce sheets or bars of a required cross section and form 2. machine used for this purpose —**rolling pin** cylindrical roller for dough —**rolling stock** locomotives, carriages etc. of railroad —**rolling stone** restless or wandering person —**roll-on** a. 1. (of deodorant etc.) dispensed by means of revolving ball fitted into neck of container —n. 2. woman's foundation garment —**roll-top** a. (of desk) with flexible lid sliding in grooves —**roll up** inf. appear, turn up

rollick ('rolik) vi. 1. behave in carefree or boisterous manner —n. 2. boisterous or carefree escapade —**'rollicking** a.

roly-poly ('rōli'pōli) a. round, plump

ROM (rom) Comp. read only memory

rom. Print. roman (type)

Rom. Bible Romans

romaine (rō'mān) n. lettuce with long slender leaves (also **cos lettuce**)

Roman ('rōmən) a. of Rome or Church of Rome —**Roman alphabet** alphabet evolved by ancient Romans for writing of Latin and still used for writing most of languages of Western Europe —**Roman candle** firework that produces continuous shower of sparks punctuated by colored balls of fire —**Roman Catholic** member of Christian Church traditionally founded by Jesus who named St. Peter the first Vicar and whose authority is the Pope and tradition as recorded in scripture and expressed in Church councils —**Roman nose** nose having high prominent bridge —**Roman numerals** letters I, V, X, L, C, D, M used to represent numbers in manner of Romans —**roman type** plain upright letters, ordinary style of printing

romance (rō'mans, rə-; 'rōmans) n. 1. love affair, esp. intense and happy one 2. mysterious or exciting quality 3. tale of chivalry 4. tale with scenes remote from ordinary life 5. literature like this 6. picturesque falsehood —vi. 7. exaggerate, fantasize —**ro'mancer** n. —**ro'mantic** a. 1. characterized by romance 2. of or dealing with love 3. (of literature etc.) preferring passion and imagination to proportion and finish —n. 4. romantic person 5. person whose tastes in art, literature etc. lie mainly in romanticism —**ro'manticism** n. —**ro'manticist** n. —**ro'manticize** v.

Romance (rō'mans, rə-; 'rōmans) a. 1. of vernacular language of certain countries, developed from Latin, as French, Spanish etc. —n. 2. this group of languages

Romanesque (rōmə'nesk) a./n. (in) style of round-arched vaulted architecture of period between Classical and Gothic

Romania (rō'māniə) n. country in eastern Europe bounded north by the U.S.S.R., east by the U.S.S.R. and the Black Sea, south by Bulgaria and west by Yugoslavia and Hungary —**Ro'manian** n./a. 1. (native or inhabitant) of Romania —n. 2. language of Romania, which is a Romance language

Romans ('rōmənz) pl.n. (with sing. v.) Bible 6th book of the N.T., epistle written by St. Paul to Christians of Rome and considered the foundation of Christian theology

Romany ('roməni, 'rō-) n. 1. Gypsy 2. Gypsy language —a. 3. of the Gypsies or their language

Romeo ('rōmiō) n. word used in communications for the letter r

romp (romp) vi. 1. run, play wildly, joyfully —n. 2. spell of romping —**'rompers** pl.n. child's one-piece garment consisting of trousers and bib with straps —**romp home** win easily

rondavel (ron'dävəl) n. SA circular building, oft. thatched

rondo ('rondō) n. piece of music with leading theme to which return is continually made (pl. -s)

röntgen ('rentgən, 'rənt-; -jən) n. see ROENTGEN

rood (rōod) n. 1. the Cross 2. crucifix 3. quarter of acre —**rood screen** screen separating nave from choir

roof (rōof) n. 1. outside upper covering of building 2. top, covering part of anything —vt. 3. put roof on, over —**'roofing** n. 1. material used to construct roof 2. act of constructing roof —**roof rack** rack attached to roof of motor vehicle for carrying luggage etc. —**'rooftree** n. see ridgepole at RIDGE —**hit** (or **raise** or **go through**) **the roof** inf. become extremely angry

rook¹ (rōok) n. 1. bird of crow family —vt. 2. sl. swindle, cheat —**'rookery** n. colony of rooks

rook² (rōok) n. chessman (also 'castle)

rookie ('rōoki) n. inf. recruit, esp. in army

room (rōom, rōom) n. 1. space 2. space enough 3. division of house 4. scope, opportunity —pl. 5. lodging —**'roomy** a. spacious —**'roommate** n. person with whom one shares room or lodging —**room service** service in hotel providing meals etc. in guests' rooms

Roosevelt¹ ('rōzəvəlt) n. Franklin Delano. the 32nd President of the U.S. (1933-45)

Roosevelt² ('rōzəvəlt) n. Theodore. the 26th President of the U.S. (1901-09)

roost (rōost) n. 1. perch for fowls —vi. 2. perch —**'rooster** n. domestic cock —**come home to roost** have unfavorable repercussions

root (rōot) n. 1. part of plant that grows down into earth and conveys nourishment to plant 2. plant with edible root, eg carrot 3. vital part 4. source, origin, original cause of anything 5. Anat. embedded portion of tooth, nail, hair etc. 6. primitive word from which other words are derived 7. Math. factor of a quantity which, when multiplied by itself the number of times indicated, gives the quantity —v. 8. (cause to) take root —vt. 9. pull by roots —vi. 10. dig, burrow —**'rootless** a. having no roots or ties —**root mean square** square root of average of squares of set of numbers —**'rootstock** n. 1. see RHIZOME 2. see STOCK (sense 6) 3. Biol. basic structure from which offshoots have developed —**root out** remove or eliminate completely

root for inf. cheer, applaud, encourage —**'rooter** n.

rope (rōp) n. 1. thick cord —vt. 2. secure, mark off with rope —**'ropiness** n. —**'ropy** a. 1. inf. inferior, inadequate 2. inf. not well 3. (of liquid) sticky and stringy —**'ropewalk** n. long narrow shed where ropes are made —**know the ropes** know details or procedures, as of job

Roquefort ('rōkfərt) n. semisoft sheep's-milk cheese with blue-green mold veining imported from France

rorqual ('rörkwəl) n. whalebone whale with dorsal fin and series of grooves along throat and chest (also 'finback)

rosacea (rō'zāshə) n. skin disease of adults marked by redness, pus pimples and swollen blood vessels of the face

rosaceous (rō'zāshəs) a. 1. of Rosaceae, family of plants typically having five-petaled flowers, including rose, strawberry etc. 2. like rose, esp. rose-colored

rosary ('rōzəri) n. 1. R.C.Ch. series of prayers 2. string of beads for counting these prayers as they are recited 3. rose garden

rose¹ (rōz) n. 1. shrub, climbing plant usu. with prickly stems and fragrant flowers 2. the flower, national floral emblem of U.S. 3. perforated flat nozzle for hose etc. 4. pink color —a. 5. of this color —**roseate** ('rōziit, -āt) a. rose-colored, rosy —**ro'sette** n. 1. rose-shaped bunch of ribbon 2. rose-shaped architectural ornament —**'rosy** a. 1. flushed 2. hopeful, promising —**rose-colored** a. 1.

rosette

having color of rose 2. unwarrantably optimistic —**rose-water** n. 1. scented water made by distillation of rose petals or by

impregnation with oil of roses —a. 2. elegant or delicate, esp. excessively so —**rose window** circular window with series of mullions branching from center —**'rosewood** n. fragrant wood —**rose of Sharon** ('sharən, 'sher-) 1. creeping shrub native to SE Europe but widely cultivated, with large yellow flowers 2. hardy hibiscus

rose² (rōz) pt. of RISE

rosé (rō'zā) n. pink wine

rosemary ('rōzmeri) n. evergreen fragrant flowering shrub

Rosh Hashanah (rōsh hə'shōnə, rosh hə'shänə; Hebrew 'rosh hasha'na) Jewish New Year

Rosicrucian (rōzi'krōoshən) n. 1. member of secret order devoted to occult beliefs —a. 2. of the Rosicrucians or Rosicrucianism —**Rosi'crucianism** n.

rosin ('rozin) n. resin

roster ('rostər) n. 1. list or plan showing turns of duty —vt. 2. place on roster

rostrum ('rostrəm) n. 1. platform, stage, pulpit 2. beak or bill of bird (pl. -s, -tra (-trə))

rot (rot) v. 1. (cause to) decompose naturally —vt. 2. corrupt (-tt-) —n. 3. decay, putrefaction 4. any disease producing decomposition of tissue 5. inf. nonsense —**'rotten** a. 1. decomposed, putrid 2. corrupt

rota ('rōtə) n. roster, list

rotary ('rōtəri) a. 1. (of movement) circular 2. operated by rotary movement —**Ro'tarian** n. member of Rotary Club —**'rotate** v. (cause to) move round center or on pivot —**ro'tation** n. 1. rotating 2. regular succession —**'rotatory** a. —**'rototill** vt. —**'Rototiller** n. trade name for a mechanical cultivator with rotary blades —**Rotary Club** one of international association of businessmen's clubs

ROTC Reserve Officer Training Corps

rote (rōt) n. —**rote learning** method of learning by repetition —**by rote** from memory

rotisserie (rō'tisəri) n. (electrically driven) rotating spit for cooking meat

rotor ('rōtər) n. revolving portion of a dynamo motor or turbine

rotten ('rotən) a. see ROT

rotund (rō'tund) a. 1. round 2. plump 3. sonorous —**ro'tundity** n.

rotunda (rō'tundə) n. circular building or room, esp. with dome

rouble ('rōobəl) n. see RUBLE

roué (rōo'ā) n. debauched or lecherous man; rake

rouge (rōozh) n. 1. red powder, cream used to color cheeks —vt. 2. color with rouge

rough (ruf) a. 1. not smooth, of irregular surface 2. violent, stormy, boisterous 3. rude 4. uncivil 5. lacking refinement 6. approximate 7. in preliminary form —vt. 8. make rough 9. plan out approximately 10. (with it) live without usual comforts etc. —n. 11. rough state or area 12. sketch —**'roughage** n. unassimilated portion of food promoting proper intestinal action —**'roughen** v. —**'roughly** adv. —**rough-and-ready** a. 1. crude, unpolished or hastily prepared, but sufficient for purpose 2. (of person) without formality or refinement —**rough-and-tumble** n. 1. fight or scuffle without rules —a. 2. characterized by disorderliness and disregard for rules —**rough diamond** trustworthy but unsophisticated person —**rough-dry** a. 1. (of clothing or linen) dried ready for pressing —vt. 2. dry (clothing etc.) without ironing —**rough-hew** vt. shape roughly —**'roughhouse** n. sl. fight, row —**'roughneck** n. inf. 1. tough, coarse male 2. skilled worker other than driller in oilfield —**rough'shod** a. (of horse) shod with rough-bottomed shoes to prevent sliding —**ride roughshod over** treat harshly and without consideration

roulette (rōō'let) n. game of chance played with revolving wheel and ball

round (rownd) a. 1. spherical 2. cylindrical 3. circular 4. curved 5. full, complete 6. roughly correct 7. large, considerable 8. plump 9. positive —adv. 10. with circular or circuitous course —n. 11. thing round in shape 12. recurrent duties 13. stage in competition 14. customary course, as of mailman 15. game (of golf) 16. one of several periods in boxing match etc. 17. cartridge for firearm 18. rung 19. movement in circle —prep. 20. about 21. on all sides of —v. 22. make, become round —vt. 23. move round —**'roundly** adv. 1. plainly 2. thoroughly —**'roundabout** a. indirect; devious —**round dance** 1. dance in which dancers form circle 2. ballroom dance in which couples revolve —**round figure** or **number** whole number, usu. multiple of ten —**'Roundhead** n. English hist. supporter of Parliament against Charles I during Civil War —**round lot** unit of trading on the stock exchange —**round robin** tournament in which each competitor plays against every other participant —**round-shouldered** a. denoting faulty posture characterized by drooping shoulders and slight forward bending of back —**round table** meeting of parties or people on equal terms for discussion —**round-the-clock** a. throughout day and night —**round trip** trip to place and back again —**'roundup** n. 1. act of gathering together cattle etc. for branding, counting or selling 2. inf. any similar act of bringing together —**'roundworm** n. any member of a phylum of invertebrate animals with cylindrical, elongated bodies parasitic in plants or animals or free-living in soil or water, such as hookworm and filiaria (also **nematode**) —**round up** 1. drive (cattle) together 2. collect and arrest (criminals)

roundel ('rowndəl) n. 1. poem consisting of three stanzas each of three lines with refrain after first and third 2. small disk —**'roundelay** n. simple song with refrain

rouse (rowz) vt. 1. wake up, stir up, excite to action 2. cause to rise —vi. 3. waken

rout¹ (rowt) n. 1. overwhelming defeat, disorderly retreat 2. noisy rabble —vt. 3. scatter and put to flight

rout² (rowt) v. 1. dig over or turn up (something), esp. (of animal) with snout; root —vt. 2. (usu. with out or up) find by searching 3. (usu. with out) drive out 4. (oft. with out) hollow or gouge out —vi. 5. search, poke, rummage

route (rōōt, rowt) n. road, chosen way

routine (rōō'tēn) n. 1. regularity of procedure, unvarying round 2. regular course —a. 3. ordinary, regular

rove (rōv) v. wander, roam —**'rover** n. 1. one who roves 2. pirate

row¹ (rō) n. 1. number of things in a straight line 2. rank 3. file 4. line

row² (rō) v. 1. propel (boat) by oars —n. 2. spell of rowing —**'rowboat** n.

row³ (row) inf. n. 1. dispute 2. disturbance —vi. 3. quarrel noisily

rowan ('rowən, 'rōən) n. small deciduous tree, native to Europe, producing bright red berries (also (**European**) **mountain ash**)

rowdy ('rowdi) a. 1. disorderly, noisy and rough —n. 2. person like this

rowel ('rowəl) n. small wheel with points on spur

rowlock ('roḷək) n. appliance on gunwale of boat serving as point of leverage for oar

royal ('roiəl) a. 1. of, worthy of, befitting, patronized by, king or queen 2. splendid —**'royalist** n. supporter of monarchy —**'royalty** n. 1. royal dignity or power 2. royal persons 3. payment to owner of land for right to work minerals, or to inventor for use of his invention 4. payment to author depending on sales —**Royal Air Force** air force of Great Britain —**royal blue** (of) deep blue color —**royal jelly** substance secreted by pharyngeal glands of worker bees and fed to all larvae when very young and to larvae destined to become queens throughout their development —**Royal Marines** UK corps of soldiers trained in amphibious warfare —**Royal Navy** navy of Great Britain —**royal palm** palm tree of tropical Amer. having tall trunk with tuft of feathery pinnate leaves

r.p.m. revolutions per minute

R.R. 1. Right Reverend 2. C Rural Route

R.S. UK Royal Society

R.S.A. Republic of South Africa

RSFSR Russian Soviet Federated Socialist Republic

R.S.V. Revised Standard Version (of the Bible)

R.S.V.P. répondez s'il vous plaît (Fr., please reply)

Ru Chem. ruthenium

rub (rub) vt. 1. apply pressure to with circular or backward and forward movement 2. clean, polish, dry, thus 3. pass hand over 4. abrade, chafe 5. remove by friction —vi. 6. come into contact accompanied by friction 7. become frayed or worn by friction (-bb-) —n. 8. rubbing 9. impediment —**'rubbing** n. impression taken of incised or raised surface by laying paper over it and rubbing with wax etc.

rubato (rōō'bätō) Mus. n. 1. flexibility of tempo in performance (pl. -s) —a./adv. 2. to be played with flexible tempo

rubber¹ ('rubər) n. 1. coagulated sap of rough, elastic consistency, of certain tropical trees (also **India rubber, gum elastic,** '**caoutchouc**) 2. piece of rubber etc. used for erasing 3. thing for rubbing 4. person who rubs 5. condom —a. 6. made of rubber —**'rubberize** vt. coat, impregnate, treat with rubber —**'rubbery** a. —**rubber band** continuous loop of thin rubber, used to hold papers etc. together —**'rubberneck** sl. n. 1. person who gapes inquisitively 2. sightseer, tourist —vi. 3. stare in naive or foolish manner —**rubber plant** 1. plant with glossy leathery leaves, cultivated as house plant in Europe and N Amer. 2. any of several tropical trees, sap of which yields crude rubber —**rubbersheet geometry** see TOPOLOGY (sense 1) —**rubber stamp** 1. device for imprinting dates etc. 2. automatic authorization

rubber² ('rubər) n. 1. series of odd number of games or contests at various games 2. two out of three games won

rubbish ('rubish) n. 1. waste material 2. anything worthless 3. trash, nonsense —**'rubbishy** a. valueless

rubble ('rubəl) n. 1. fragments of stone etc. 2. builders' rubbish

rubella (rōō'belə) n. mild contagious virus disease which may cause severe damage to an unborn child (also **German measles**)

rubeola (rōōbi'ōlə) n. see MEASLES

rubicund ('rōōbikənd) a. of reddish color; ruddy

rubidium (rōō'bidiəm) n. Chem. metallic element Symbol Rb, at. wt. 85.5, at. no. 37

ruble or **rouble** ('rōōbəl) n. monetary unit of Soviet Union

rubric ('rōōbrik) n. 1. title, heading 2. direction in liturgy 3. instruction

ruby ('rōōbi) n. 1. precious red gem 2. its color —a. 3. of this color —**ruby wedding** fortieth wedding anniversary

ruche (rōōsh) n. strip of pleated or frilled lace etc. used to decorate blouses etc.

ruck¹ (ruk) n. 1. crowd 2. common herd 3. rank and file

ruck² (ruk) n. 1. crease —v. 2. make, become wrinkled

rucksack ('ruksak) n. pack carried on back (also **back pack**)

ruction ('rukshən) n. inf. noisy disturbance

rudder ('rudər) n. flat piece hinged to boat's stern or rear of aircraft used to steer

ruddy ('rudi) a. 1. of fresh or healthy red color 2. rosy 3. florid

rude (rōōd) a. 1. impolite 2. coarse 3. vulgar 4. primitive 5. roughly made 6. uneducated 7. sudden, violent —**'rudely** adv.

rudiments ('rōōdimənts) pl.n. elements, first principles —**rudi'mentary** a.

rue¹ (rōō) v. 1. grieve (for) —vt. 2. regret 3. deplore —vi. 4. repent —n. 5. obs. repentance —**'rueful** a. 1. sorry 2. regretful 3. dejected 4. deplorable —**'ruefully** adv.

rue² (rōō) n. plant with evergreen bitter leaves

ruff¹ (ruf) n. 1. starched and frilled collar 2. natural collar of feathers, fur etc. on some birds and animals 3. type of shore bird —**'ruffle** vt. 1. rumple, disorder 2. annoy, put out 3. frill, pleat —n. 4. frilled trimming

ruff² (ruf) n./v. Cards trump

ruffian ('rufiən) n. violent, lawless person —**'ruffianism** n. —**'ruffianly** a.

rufous ('rōōfəs) a. reddish-brown

rug (rug) n. 1. small, oft. shaggy or thick-piled floor mat 2. thick woolen wrap, coverlet

rugby ('rugbi) n. game of the football family played by two teams of 15 players in which the object is to score points by carrying the oval, leather-covered ball over the opponent's goal line or kicking it over the crossbar and between uprights on the goal line

rugged ('rugid) a. 1. rough 2. broken 3. unpolished 4. harsh, austere

ruin ('rōōin) n. 1. decay, destruction 2. downfall 3. fallen or broken state 4. loss of wealth, position etc. —pl. 5. ruined buildings etc. —vt. 6. reduce to ruins 7. bring to decay or destruction 8. spoil 9. impoverish —**rui'nation** n. —**'ruinous** a. causing or characterized by ruin or destruction —**'ruinously** adv.

rule (rōōl) n. 1. principle 2. precept 3. authority 4. government 5. what is usual 6. control 7. measuring stick —vt. 8. govern 9. decide 10. mark with straight lines 11. draw (line) —**'ruler** n. 1. one who governs 2. stick for measuring or ruling lines —**'ruling** n. 1. decision of someone in authority, such as judge 2. one or more parallel ruled lines —a. 3. controlling or exercising authority 4. predominant —**rule of thumb** rough and practical approach, based on experience, rather than theory

rum (rum) n. spirit distilled from sugar cane

rumba ('rumbə, 'rōōm-) n. 1. rhythmic dance, orig. Cuban 2. music for it

rumble ('rumbəl) vi. 1. make noise as of distant thunder, heavy vehicle etc. —n. 2. such noise

rumbustious (rum'buschəs) a. boisterous, unruly

ruminate ('rōōmināt) vi. 1. chew cud 2. ponder, meditate —**'ruminant** a./n. cud-chewing (animal) —**rumi'nation** *n.* quiet meditation and reflection —**'ruminative** *a.*

rummage ('rumij) *v.* **1.** search thoroughly —*n.* **2.** act of rummaging

rummy ('rumi) *n.* any of family of card games played with one or two standard decks of 52 cards in which the object is to form matched sets or sequences, the deduction of which will bring the value of the unmatched cards to a lower total than that of the opponent(s)

rumor ('rōōmər) *n.* **1.** hearsay, common talk, unproved statement —*vt.* **2.** put round as, by way of, rumor

rump (rump) *n.* **1.** hindquarters of mammal, not including legs **2.** person's buttocks

rumple ('rumpəl) *v./n.* crease, wrinkle

rumpus ('rumpəs) *n.* **1.** disturbance **2.** noise and confusion

run (run) *vi.* **1.** move with more rapid gait than walking **2.** go quickly **3.** flow **4.** flee **5.** compete in race, contest, election **6.** revolve **7.** continue **8.** function **9.** travel according to schedule **10.** fuse **11.** melt **12.** spread **13.** have certain meaning —*vt.* **14.** cross by running **15.** expose oneself to (risk *etc.*) **16.** cause to run **17.** (of newspaper) print, publish **18.** land and dispose of (smuggled goods) **19.** manage **20.** operate (**ran** *pt.,* **run** *pp.,* **'running** *pr.p.*) —*n.* **21.** act, spell of running **22.** rush **23.** tendency, course **24.** period **25.** sequence **26.** heavy demand **27.** enclosure for domestic fowls, animals **28.** ride in automobile **29.** series of unraveled stitches **30.** score of one at baseball **31.** steep snow-covered course for skiing *etc.* —**'runner** *n.* **1.** racer **2.** messenger **3.** curved piece of wood on which sledge slides **4.** blade of ice skate **5.** slender stem of plant running along ground forming new roots at intervals **6.** strip of lace *etc.* placed on table for decoration **7.** strip of carpet —**'running** *a.* **1.** continuous **2.** consecutive **3.** flowing **4.** discharging **5.** effortless **6.** entered for race **7.** used for running —*n.* **8.** act of moving or flowing quickly **9.** management —**'runny** *a.* tending to flow or exude moisture —**'runabout** *n.* small light vehicle or aircraft —**'runaway** *n.* **1.** person or animal that runs away **2.** act or instance of running away —*a.* **3.** rising rapidly, as prices **4.** (of race *etc.*) easily won —**'rundown** *n.* summary —**run-down** *a.* exhausted —**runner-up** *n.* contestant finishing race or competition in second place (*pl.* **runners-up**) —**running board** ledge beneath doors of some automobiles and other conveyances —**running head** *Print.* heading printed at top of every page of book —**running knot** knot that moves or slips easily —**running repairs** repairs that do not (greatly) interrupt operations —**run-of-the-mill** *a.* ordinary —**run-up** *n.* **1.** approach run by athlete for long jump, pole vault *etc.* **2.** preliminary or preparatory period —**'runway** *n.* level stretch where aircraft take off and land —**run about** move busily from place to place —**run away** **1.** take flight; escape **2.** go away; depart **3.** (of horse) gallop away uncontrollably —**run away with** **1.** abscond or elope with **2.** make off with; steal **3.** escape from control of **4.** win easily or be assured of victory in (competition) —**run down** **1.** stop working **2.** reduce **3.** exhaust **4.** denigrate —**run up** **1.** amass; incur **2.** make by sewing together quickly **3.** hoist —**in the running** having a fair chance in a competition

rune (rōōn) *n.* **1.** character of earliest Germanic alphabet **2.** magic sign —**'runic** *a.*

rung[1] (rung) *n.* crossbar or spoke, *esp.* in ladder

rung[2] (rung) *pp. of* RING[2]

runnel ('runəl) *n.* **1.** gutter **2.** small brook or rivulet

running ('runing) *see* RUN

Runnymede ('runimēd) *n.* place where Magna Charta was granted

runt (runt) *n.* **1.** smallest young animal in litter **2.** *offens.* undersized person

rupee (rōō'pē) *n.* monetary unit of India, Pakistan, Sri Lanka *etc.*

rupture ('rupchər) *n.* **1.** breaking, breach **2.** hernia —*v.* **3.** break **4.** burst, sever

rural ('rōōrəl) *a.* of the country —**'ruralize** *v.* —**rural route** mail service in rural area

ruse (rōōs, rōōz) *n.* stratagem, trick

rush[1] (rush) *vt.* **1.** impel, carry along violently and rapidly **2.** take by sudden assault —*vi.* **3.** cause to hurry **4.** move violently or rapidly —*n.* **5.** rushing, charge **6.** hurry **7.** eager demand **8.** heavy current (of air, water *etc.*) —*a.* **9.** done with speed **10.** characterized by speed —**rush hour** period at beginning and end of day when many people are traveling to and from work

rush[2] (rush) *n.* **1.** marsh plant with slender pithy stem **2.** the stems used as material for baskets —**'rushy** *a.* full of rushes

rusk (rusk) *n.* slice of sweet, dried bread cooked again in oven, zwieback

Russ. Russia(n)

russet ('rusit) *a.* **1.** reddish-brown —*n.* **2.** the color

Russian ('rushən) *n.* **1.** official language of Soviet Union: Indo-European language belonging to East Slavonic branch **2.** native or inhabitant of Russia or Soviet Union —*a.* **3.** of Russia or Soviet Union —**Russian Revolution** uprising in Russia in March 1917 in which the czar's government collapsed —**Russian roulette** **1.** act of bravado in which person spins cylinder of revolver loaded with only one cartridge and presses trigger with barrel against his own head **2.** any foolish or potentially suicidal undertaking —**Russian wolfhound** *see* BORZOI

rust (rust) *n.* **1.** reddish-brown coating formed on iron by oxidation **2.** disease of plants —*v.* **3.** contract, affect with rust —**'rusty** *a.* **1.** coated with, affected by, or consisting of rust **2.** of rust color **3.** out of practice —**'rustproof** *a.*

rustic ('rustik) *a.* **1.** of or as of country people **2.** rural **3.** of rude manufacture **4.** made of untrimmed branches —*n.* **5.** countryman, peasant —**'rusticate** *vi.* live a country life —**rusti'cation** *n.* —**rus'ticity** *n.*

rustle ('rusəl) *vi.* **1.** make sound as of blown dead leaves *etc.* —*vt.* **2.** steal (cattle) —*n.* **3.** soft fluttering or crackling sound —**'rustler** *n.* cattle thief

rut[1] (rut) *n.* **1.** furrow made by wheel **2.** settled habit or way of living **3.** groove —**'rutty** *a.*

rut[2] (rut) *n.* **1.** periodic sexual excitement among animals —*vi.* **2.** be under influence of this (**-tt-**)

Ruth (rōōth) *n. Bible* 8th book of the O.T., story of Moabite woman who remained loyal to her mother-in-law, Naomi, after death of her husband

ruthenium (rōō'thēniəm) *n. Chem.* rare white noble metal *Symbol* Ru, at. wt. 101.1, at. no. 44

ruthless ('rōōthlis) *a.* pitiless, merciless —**'ruthlessly** *adv.*

R.V. Revised Version (of the Bible)

Rwanda (rōō'ändə) *n.* country in Africa bounded south by Burundi, west by Zaïre, north by Uganda and east by Tanzania —**Rw'andan** *n./a.*

-ry (*comb. form*) *see* -ERY

rye (rī) *n.* **1.** grain used for fodder and bread **2.** plant bearing it **3.** whiskey made from rye —**rye bread** bread made entirely or partly from rye flour

rye-grass *n.* any of various kinds of grasses cultivated for fodder

Ss

s *or* **S** (es) *n*. **1.** 19th letter of English alphabet **2.** speech sound represented by this letter, either voiceless, as in *sit*, or voiced, as in *dogs* **3.** something shaped like S (*pl.* **s's, S's** *or* **Ss**)

S 1. Society **2.** South(ern) **3.** *Chem.* sulfur **4.** *Phys.* entropy **5.** *Phys.* siemens **6.** *Phys.* strangeness

s. 1. second (of time) **2.** shilling **3.** singular **4.** son **5.** succeeded

-'s (*comb. form*) **1.** forming possessive singular of nouns and some pronouns, as in *man's* **2.** forming possessive plural of nouns whose plurals do not end in *-s*, as in *children's* **3.** forming plural of numbers, letters, or symbols, as in *20's*

-s' (*comb. form*) forming possessive of plural nouns and some singular nouns ending in sounded s, as in *girls'; for goodness' sake*

S.A. 1. Salvation Army **2.** South Africa **3.** South Australia **4.** *Sturmabteilung*: Nazi terrorist militia

Sabbath ('sabəth) *n*. **1.** Jewish and Christian day of worship and rest **2.** Sunday —**sab'bati-cal** *a./n*. (denoting) leave granted to university staff *etc*. for study

saber *or* **sabre** ('sābər) *n*. curved cavalry sword —**saber rattling** display of armed force —**saber-toothed tiger** extinct cat with curved swordlike upper canine teeth

sable ('sābəl) *n*. **1.** small weasel-like Arctic animal **2.** its fur **3.** black (*pl.* **-s, 'sable**) —*a*. **4.** black, in heraldry

sabot (sa'bō, 'sabō) *n*. shoe made of wood, or with wooden sole

sabotage ('sabətäzh) *n*. **1.** intentional damage done to roads, machines *etc*., *esp*. secretly in war —*vt*. **2.** carry out sabotage on **3.** destroy, disrupt —**saboteur** (sabə'tər) *n*.

sac (sak) *n*. pouchlike structure in an animal or vegetable body

saccharin ('sakərin) *n*. artificial sweetener —**saccharine** ('sakərin, -rēn, -rīn) *a. lit., fig.* excessively sweet

sacerdotal (sasər'dōtəl) *a*. of priests

sachet (sa'shā) *n*. small envelope or bag, *esp*. one holding liquid, as shampoo

sack¹ (sak) *n*. **1.** large bag, *orig*. of coarse material **2.** pillaging **3.** *inf.* dismissal **4.** *sl.* bed **5.** loose straight dress tapering to below knees —*vt*. **6.** pillage (captured town) **7.** *inf.* dismiss —**'sacking** *n*. material for sacks —**'sackcloth** *n*. coarse fabric used for sacks —**sackcloth and ashes** public display of extreme grief

sack² (sak) *n. obs.* dry white wine from SW Europe

sacrament ('sakrəmənt) *n*. one of certain ceremonies of Christian Church, *esp*. Eucharist —**sacra'mental** *a*.

sacred ('sākrid) *a*. **1.** dedicated, regarded as holy **2.** set apart, reserved **3.** inviolable **4.** connected with, intended for religious use —**'sacredly** *adv*. —**'sacredness** *n*. —**sacred cow** *inf.* person *etc*. held to be beyond criticism

sacrifice ('sakrifīs) *n*. **1.** giving something up for sake of something else **2.** act of giving up **3.** thing so given up **4.** making of offering

to a god **5.** thing offered —*vt*. **6.** offer as sacrifice **7.** give up **8.** sell at very cheap price —**sacrificial** (sakri'fishəl) *a*.

sacrilege ('sakrilij) *n*. misuse, desecration of something sacred —**sacrilegious** (sakri'lijəs) *a*. **1.** profane **2.** desecrating

sacristan ('sakristən) *or* **sacrist** ('sakrist, 'sā-) *n*. official in charge of vestments and sacred vessels of church —**'sacristy** *n*. room where sacred vessels *etc*. are kept

sacrosanct ('sakrōsangkt) *a*. **1.** preserved by religious fear against desecration or violence **2.** inviolable —**sacro'sanctity** *n*.

sacrum

sacrum ('sakrəm, 'sākrəm) *n*. five vertebrae forming compound bone at base of spinal column (*pl.* **-cra** (-krə)) —**sacro'iliac** *a./n*. (of) joint of lower back above largest bone of pelvis

sad (sad) *a*. **1.** sorrowful **2.** unsatisfactory, deplorable —**'sadden** *vt*. make sad

saddle ('sadəl) *n*. **1.** rider's seat to fasten on horse, bicycle *etc*. **2.** anything resembling a saddle, *esp*. marking on backs of various animals **3.** cut of meat including the two loins **4.** ridge of hill —*vt*. **5.** put saddle on **6.** lay burden, responsibility on —**'saddler** *n*. maker of saddles *etc*. —**'saddlery** *n*. —**'saddlebag** *n*. small bag attached to saddle of bicycle *etc*. —**saddle shoe** lace-up shoe with contrasting band of leather across instep —**saddle soap** soft soap for preserving and cleaning leather —**saddle stitch** decorative running stitch made with thick thread —**'saddletree** *n*. frame of saddle

Sadducee ('sajəsē, 'sadyəsē) *n. Judaism* member of ancient Jewish sect, denying resurrection of dead and validity of oral tradition

sadism ('sādizəm) *n*. form of (sexual) perversion marked by love of inflicting pain —**'sadist** *n*. —**sadistic** (sə'distik) *a*. —**sado-'masochism** *n*. sadistic and masochistic elements in one person —**sadomaso'chistic** *a*.

s.a.e. stamped addressed envelope

safari (sə'färi) *n*. **1.** (party making) overland (hunting) journey, *esp*. in Afr. (*pl.* **-s**) —*a*. **2.** denoting style of dress marked by belted vented jackets and pleated pockets with buttoned flaps

safe (sāf) *a*. **1.** protected **2.** uninjured, out of danger **3.** not involving risk **4.** trustworthy **5.** sure, reliable **6.** cautious —*n*. **7.** strong lockable container **8.** ventilated cupboard for meat *etc*. —**'safely** *adv*. —**'safety** *n*. —**safe-conduct** *n*. passport, permit to pass somewhere —**safe-cracker** *n*. person who breaks open and robs safes —**safe-deposit** *or* **safety-deposit box** box in bank vault for safe storage of money *etc*. —**'safeguard** *n*. **1.**

protection —*vt*. **2.** protect —**safety belt** belt worn by person and attached to object, worn to prevent injury —**safety glass** glass made unsplinterable by lamination with plastic —**safety lamp** miner's oil lamp in which flame is surrounded by metal gauze to prevent it igniting combustible gas —**safety match** match that will light only when struck against prepared surface —**safety pin** spring clasp with covering catch, designed to shield point when closed —**safety razor** razor with guard over blade —**safety valve 1.** valve in pressure vessel that allows fluid to escape at excess pressure **2.** harmless outlet for emotion *etc*.

safflower ('saflowər) *n*. thistle-like plant with flowers used for dye, oil

saffron ('safrən) *n*. **1.** crocus **2.** orange-colored flavoring obtained from it **3.** the color —*a*. **4.** orange

sag (sag) *vi*. **1.** sink in middle **2.** hang sideways **3.** curve downward under pressure **4.** give way **5.** tire **6.** (of clothing) hang loosely (**-gg-**) —*n*. **7.** droop

saga ('sägə) *n*. **1.** legend of Norse heroes **2.** any long (heroic) story

sagacious (sə'gāshəs) *a*. wise —**sa'gaciously** *adv*. —**sagacity** (sə'gasiti) *n*.

sage¹ (sāj) *n*. **1.** very wise man —*a*. **2.** wise —**'sagely** *adv*.

sage² (sāj) *n*. **1.** any of various shrubs of the mint family **2.** their aromatic grayish-green leaves used in cooking

sagebrush ('sājbrush) *n*. aromatic plant of West N Amer.

Sagittarius (saji'teriəs) *n*. (archer) 9th sign of zodiac, operative *c*. Nov. 22nd-Dec. 20th

sago ('sāgō) *n*. starchy cereal from powdered pith of palm (**sago palm**), used for puddings and as thickening agent

said (sed) *pt./pp.* of SAY

sail (sāl) *n*. **1.** piece of fabric stretched to catch wind for propelling ship *etc*. **2.** act of sailing **3.** journey upon the water **4.** ships collectively **5.** arm of windmill —*vi*. **6.** travel by water **7.** move smoothly **8.** begin voyage —*vt*. **9.** navigate —**'sailor** *n*. **1.** member of ship's crew, *esp*. of rank below officer **2.** one who sails —**'sailcloth** *n*. **1.** fabric from which sails are made **2.** canvas-like cloth used for clothing *etc*.

saint (sānt) *n*. **1.** (title of) person formally recognized (*esp*. by R.C. Church) after death as having gained by holy deeds a special place in heaven **2.** exceptionally good person —**'sainted** *a*. **1.** canonized **2.** sacred —**'saint-liness** *n*. holiness —**'saintly** *a*. —**Saint Andrew's Cross** ('androoz) X-shaped cross —**Saint Bernard** (bər'närd) breed of large working dog orig. from Swiss Alps —**Saint Patrick's Day** ('patriks) March 17th, in honor of the patron saint of Ireland —**Saint Valentine's Day** Feb. 14th; observed as day for sending valentines —**Saint Vitus's dance** ('vītəsiz) *see* CHOREA

Saint Christopher Nevis ('kristəfər 'nēvis) *n*. country lying in Caribbean forming part of the Lesser Antilles (*also* **St. Kitts-Nevis**)

Saint Helena (əl'ēnə, hə'lēnə) crown colony of United Kingdom lying in the south Atlantic 1200 miles from the west coast of Africa at about 5° W longitude and 15° S latitude

Saint Lucia ('lōōshə) country lying in east Caribbean comprising a small island in the Lesser Antilles

Saint Vincent and the Grenadines ('vinsənt; grenə'dēnz) country lying in the eastern Caribbean comprising the island of St. Vincent and the Northern Grenadines

saithe (sāth) *n.* coalfish

sake[1] (sāk) *n.* **1.** cause, account **2.** end, purpose —**for the sake of 1.** in behalf of **2.** to please or benefit

sake[2], **saké**, *or* **saki** ('säki) *n.* Japanese alcoholic drink made of fermented rice

salaam (sə'läm) *n.* **1.** bow of salutation, mark of respect in East —*vt.* **2.** salute

salacious (sə'lāshəs) *a.* excessively concerned with sex, lewd —**salacity** (sə'lasiti) *n.*

salad ('saləd) *n.* mixed vegetables, or fruit, used as food usu. without cooking —**salad days** period of youth and inexperience —**salad dressing** oil, vinegar, herbs *etc.* mixed together as sauce for salad

salamander ('saləmandər) *n.* **1.** variety of lizard **2.** mythical lizard-like fire spirit

salami (sə'lämi) *n.* highly-spiced sausage of pork or beef

salary ('saləri) *n.* fixed regular payment to persons employed usu. in nonmanual work —**'salaried** *a.*

salchow ('sölkō) *n. Figure skating* jump from inner backward edge of one foot with full turn in air, returning to outer backward edge of opposite foot

sale (sāl) *n.* **1.** selling **2.** selling of goods at unusually low prices **3.** auction —**'salable** *or* **'saleable** *a.* capable of being sold —**'salesman** *n.* man employed to sell goods or services in a store or in a defined territory —**'salesmanship** *n.* art of selling or presenting goods in most effective way —**sales talk** persuasion used in selling —**sales tax** tax paid by buyer and collected by seller for city or state

salicin ('salisin) *n.* substance obtained from poplars and used in medicine —**sali'cylic** *a.* —**salicylic acid** white crystalline substance used in manufacture of aspirin, and as fungicide

salient ('sālyənt, -liənt) *a.* **1.** prominent, noticeable **2.** jutting out —*n.* **3.** salient angle, *esp.* in fortification —**'salience** *or* **'saliency** *n.*

saline ('sālēn, -līn) *a.* **1.** containing, consisting of a chemical salt, *esp.* common salt **2.** salty —**salinity** (sā'liniti, sə-) *n.*

Salish ('salish) *n.* Amerindian language family spoken in Pacific Northwest, Montana and Wyoming

saliva (sə'līvə) *n.* liquid which forms in mouth —**salivary** ('saliveri) *a.* —**salivate** ('salivāt) *v.* —**salivary glands** in humans, three pairs of glands in lower jaw: parotid, submaxillary, and sublingual —**saliva test** test for use of drugs in athletes, race horses *etc.*

Salk vaccine (sölk, sök) vaccine against poliomyelitis made from killed viruses

sallow[1] ('salō) *a.* of unhealthy pale or yellowish color

sallow[2] ('salō) *n.* tree or low shrub allied to the willow

sally ('sali) *n.* **1.** rushing out, *esp.* by troops **2.** outburst **3.** witty remark —*vi.* **4.** rush **5.** set out ('**sallied**, '**sallying**)

salmagundi (salmə'gundi) *n.* **1.** mixed salad dish of cooked meats, eggs, beetroot *etc.* **2.** miscellany

salmon ('samən) *n.* **1.** large silvery fish with orange-pink flesh valued as food **2.** color of its flesh, a yellowish pink —*a.* **3.** of this color —'**salmonberry** *n.* salmon-colored raspberry of Pacific coast

salmonella (salmə'nelə) *n.* any of genus of bacteria causing disease, *esp.* food poisoning (*pl.* -**lae** (-lē))

salon (sə'lon, 'salon) *n.* **1.** (reception room for) guests in fashionable household **2.** commercial premises of hairdressers, beauticians *etc.*

saloon (sə'lōōn) *n.* **1.** principal cabin or public room in passenger ship **2.** public room for buying and consuming alcoholic beverages

salpiglossis (salpi'glosis) *n.* any of small genus of plants of the nightshade family with bright funnel-shaped flowers

salsify ('salsifi) *n.* purple-flowered plant with edible root (*also* **oyster plant, vegetable oyster**)

salt (sölt) *n.* **1.** white powdery or granular crystalline substance consisting mainly of sodium chloride, used to season or preserve food **2.** chemical compound of acid and metal **3.** wit —*vt.* **4.** season, sprinkle with, preserve with salt —'**saltless** *a.* —'**saltness** *n.* —'**salty** *a.* of, like salt —'**saltbush** *n.* shrub that grows in alkaline desert regions —'**saltcellar** *n.* small vessel for salt at table —**salt lick** deposit, block of salt licked by game, cattle *etc.* —'**saltpan** *n.* depression encrusted with salt after draining away of water —'**salt'peter** *n.* **1.** sodium nitrate used as meat preservative **2.** potassium nitrate used in gunpowder —'**salt'water** *a.* —**old salt** sailor —**salt away** *or* **down** hoard or save (money, valuables *etc.*) —**with a pinch, grain, of salt** allowing for exaggeration —**worth one's salt** efficient

SALT (sölt) Strategic Arms Limitation Talks

saltant ('saltənt) *a.* **1.** leaping **2.** dancing —**sal'tation** *n.* —'**saltatory** *a.*

salubrious (sə'lōōbriəs) *a.* favorable to health, beneficial —**sa'lubrity** *n.*

Saluki (sə'lōōki) *n.* tall hound with silky coat

salutary ('salyəteri) *a.* wholesome, resulting in good —**salu'tarily** *adv.*

salute (sə'lōōt) *vt.* **1.** greet with words or sign **2.** acknowledge with praise —*vi.* **3.** perform military salute —*n.* **4.** word, sign by which one person greets another **5.** motion of arm as mark of respect to superior *etc.* in military usage **6.** firing of guns as military greeting of honor —**salutation** (salyə'tāshən) *n.*

Salvadoran (salvə'dörən), **Salvadorean**, *or* **Salvadorian** (salvə'döriən) *see* EL SALVADOR

salvage ('salvij) *n.* **1.** act of saving ship or other property from danger of loss **2.** property so saved —*vt.* **3.** rescue, save from wreck or ruin

salvation (sal'vāshən) *n.* (*esp.* of soul) fact or state of being saved —**Salvation Army** Christian body organized for evangelism and social work among poor

salve (sav, säv, salv) *n.* **1.** healing ointment —*vt.* **2.** anoint with salve **3.** soothe

salver ('salvər) *n.* (silver) tray for presentation of food, letters *etc.*

salvia ('salviə) *n.* any of a large, widely distributed plant of the mint family grown for ornament

salvo ('salvō) *n.* simultaneous discharge of guns *etc.* (*pl.* -**s, -es**)

sal volatile (sal və'latili) preparation of ammonia used to revive persons who faint *etc.*

SAM (sam) surface-to-air missile

Sam. *Bible* Samuel

Samaritan (sə'maritən) *n.* **1.** native of ancient Samaria **2.** benevolent person

samarium (sə'meriəm, -'mar-) *n. Chem.* metallic element *Symbol* Sm, at. wt. 150.4, at. no. 62

samba ('sambə) *n.* **1.** dance of S Amer. origin **2.** music for it

Sam Browne belt (sam brown) leather belt having supporting belt over right shoulder, formerly used to support sword, now part of dress uniform of many military or civil forces

same (sām) *a.* (*usu. with* the) **1.** identical, not different, unchanged **2.** uniform **3.** just mentioned previously —'**sameness** *n.* **1.** similarity **2.** monotony

samite ('samīt) *n.* rich silk cloth

Samoa (sə'mōə) *n.* group of islands in south Pacific Ocean of which the eastern part is a territory of the U.S. —**Sa'moan** *n./a.*

samovar ('saməvär) *n.* Russian tea urn

Samoyed ('saməyed, 'samoied) *n.* dog with thick white coat and tightly curled tail

sampan ('sampan) *n.* small oriental boat

samphire ('samflər) *n.* herb found on rocks by sea shore

sample ('sampəl) *n.* **1.** specimen —*vt.* **2.** take, give sample of **3.** try **4.** test **5.** select —'**sampler** *n.* beginner's exercise in embroidery —'**sampling** *n.* **1.** the taking of samples **2.** sample

Samson ('samsən) *n.* **1.** *O.T.* judge of Israel, who performed herculean feats of strength until he was betrayed by his mistress Delilah **2.** any man of outstanding physical strength

Samuel ('samyōōəl) *n. Bible* 9th and 10th books of the O.T.: accounts of the reunification of the people of Israel and Samuel's yielding to their demand for a king. As a result Saul was established on the throne and David anointed as a future king

samurai ('samərī, 'samyərī) *n.* member of ancient Japanese warrior caste (*pl.* -**rai**)

sanatorium (sanə'töriəm) *n. see* **sanitarium** *at* SANITARY

sanctify ('sangktifī) *vt.* **1.** set apart as holy **2.** free from sin (-**fied, -fying**) —**sanctifi'cation** *n.* —'**sanctity** *n.* **1.** saintliness **2.** sacredness **3.** inviolability —'**sanctuary** *n.* **1.** holy place **2.** part of church nearest altar **3.** formerly, place where fugitive was safe from arrest or violence **4.** place protected by law where animals *etc.* can live without interference —'**sanctum** *n.* **1.** sacred place or shrine **2.** person's private room (*pl.* -**s, -ta**)

sanctimonious (sangkti'mōniəs) *a.* making a show of piety, holiness —'**sanctimony** *or* **sancti'moniousness** *n.*

sanction ('sangkshən) *n.* **1.** permission, authorization **2.** penalty for breaking law —*pl.* **3.** boycott or other coercive measure, *esp.* by one state against another regarded as having violated a law, right *etc.* —*vt.* **4.** allow, authorize, permit

sand (sand) *n.* **1.** substance consisting of small grains of rock or mineral, *esp.* on beach or in desert —*pl.* **2.** stretches or banks of this, usu. forming sea shore —*vt.* **3.** polish, smooth with sandpaper **4.** cover, mix with sand —'**sander** *n.* **1.** vehicle equipped to sand roads **2.** power tool for smoothing surfaces —'**sandy** *a.* **1.** like sand **2.** sand-colored **3.** consisting of, covered with sand —'**sandbag** *n.* bag filled with sand or earth, used as protection against gunfire *etc.* and as weapon —**sand bar** ridge of sand in lake, river or sea, built up by action of water —'**sandblast** *n.* **1.** jet of sand blown from a nozzle under pressure for cleaning, grinding *etc.* —*vt.* **2.** clean or decorate (surface) with sandblast —**sand box** receptacle containing sand for children to play in —'**sandman** *n.* in folklore, magical person supposed to put children to sleep by sprinkling sand in their eyes —**sand martin** small brown European songbird with white underparts —'**sandpaper** *n.* paper with sand stuck on it for scraping or polishing wood *etc.* —'**sandpiper** *n.* shore bird resembling plover —'**sandstone** *n.* sedimentary rock composed of sand consolidated with such materials as quartz, hematite and clay minerals —'**sandstorm** *n.* strong wind that whips up clouds of sand —**sand yacht** wheeled boat with sails, built to be propelled over sand

sandal ('sandəl) *n.* shoe consisting of sole attached by straps

sandalwood ('sandəlwŏŏd) *n.* sweet-scented wood of S Asia

sanderling ('sandərling) *n.* small sandpiper that frequents sandy shores

sandwich ('sanwich, 'sandwich) *n.* **1.** two slices of bread with meat or other substance between —*vt.* **2.** insert between two other things —**sandwich board** one of two connected boards hung over shoulders in front of and behind person to display advertisements —**sandwich man** man who carries sandwich board

sane (sān) *a.* **1.** of sound mind **2.** sensible, rational —**sanity** ('saniti) *n.*

Sanforizing ('sanfərīzing) *n.* trade name for method of preshrinking fabric using a patented process

sang (sang) *pt. of* SING

sang-froid (*Fr.* sā'frwa) *n.* composure; self-possession

Sangreal ('san'grāəl, 'sang-) *n. see* **Holy Grail** *at* HOLY

sangria (sang'grēə) *n.* Sp. drink of red wine and fruit juice, sometimes laced with brandy

sanguine ('sanggwin) *a.* **1.** cheerful, confident **2.** ruddy in complexion —'**sanguinary** *a.* **1.** accompanied by bloodshed **2.** bloodthirsty

Sanhedrin (san'hedrin, sän-; san'hēdrin; 'sanidrin) *n. Judaism* supreme judicial, ecclesiastical, and administrative council of Jews in New Testament times

sanitary ('saniteri) *a.* helping protection of health against dirt *etc.* —'**sanatory** *or* '**sanative** *a.* curative —**sani'tarium** *or* **sana'torium** *n.* health resort (*pl.* **-s, -ria** (-riə)) —**sani'tation** *n.* measures, apparatus for preservation of public health —**sanitary napkin** absorbent pad worn externally by women during menstruation

sank (sangk) *pt. of* SINK

San Marino (san mə'rēnō) country of Europe landlocked in central Italy, 12 miles from the Adriatic Sea —**San Marinese** (san mari'nēz)

sans (sanz) *prep.* without —**sans-culotte** (sanskyŏŏ'lot, -kŏŏ-) *n.* **1.** revolutionary of poorer class during French Revolution **2.** any revolutionary extremist

sansei (sän'sā) *n.* person whose grandparents immigrated to the U.S.A. from Japan (*pl.* **sansei, -s**)

Sanskrit ('sanskrit) *n.* ancient language of inhabitants of N India, Pakistan and part of Ceylon

Santa Claus ('santi klŏz, 'santə) legendary patron saint of children, who brings presents at Christmas

São Tomé e Principe (sown tə'mā ā 'prinsipə) country lying in Atlantic Ocean about 120 miles off the west coast of Gabon

sap[1] (sap) *n.* **1.** moisture which circulates in plants **2.** energy —*vt.* **3.** drain of sap (**-pp-**) —'**sapless** *a.* —'**sapling** *n.* young tree

sap[2] (sap) *vt.* **1.** undermine **2.** destroy insidiously **3.** weaken (**-pp-**) —*n.* **4.** trench dug in order to approach or undermine enemy position

sap[3] (sap) *n. inf.* gullible person —'**sappy** *a.*

sapid ('sapid) *a.* **1.** having pleasant taste **2.** agreeable or engaging —**sa'pidity** *n.*

sapient ('sāpiənt) *a.* (*usu. ironical*) wise, discerning, shrewd, knowing —'**sapience** *n.*

saponify (sə'ponifī) *Chem. v.* **1.** convert (fat) into soap by treatment with alkali —*vi.* **2.** undergo reaction in which ester is hydrolyzed to acid and alcohol as result of treatment with alkali —**saponifi'cation** *n.*

Sapphic ('safik) *a.* **1.** of Sappho, 6th-cent. B.C. Grecian poetess **2.** of meter associated with Sappho —*n.* **3.** Sapphic verse —'**sapphism** *n.* lesbianism

sapphire ('safīər) *n.* **1.** blue precious stone **2.** deep blue —*a.* **3.** of sapphire (blue) **4.** denoting 45th anniversary

saprophyte ('saprəfīt) *n.* plant that lives on dead organic matter —**saprophytic** (saprō'fitik) *a.*

saraband *or* **sarabande** ('sarəband) *n.* **1.** slow, stately Sp. dance **2.** music for it

Saracen ('sarəsən) *n.* **1.** Arabian **2.** adherent of Islam in Syria and Palestine **3.** infidel —**Saracenic** (sarə'senik) *a.*

sarcasm ('särkazəm) *n.* **1.** bitter or wounding ironic remark **2.** such remarks **3.** taunt; sneer **4.** irony **5.** use of such expressions —**sar'castic** *a.* —**sar'castically** *adv.*

sarcoidosis (särkoi'dōsis) *n.* disease of adults marked by formation of nodules and scar tissue in lungs and many other parts of the body

sarcoma (sär'kōmə) *n.* malignant tumor arising from connective tissue (*pl.* **-s, -mata** (-mətə)) —**sar'comatous** *a.*

sarcophagus (sär'kofəgəs) *n.* stone coffin (*pl.* **-gi** (-gī), **-es**)

sard (särd) *or* **sardius** ('särdiəs) *n.* precious stone, variety of chalcedony

sardine (sär'dēn) *n.* small fish of herring family, usu. preserved in oil

sardonic (sär'donik) *a.* characterized by irony, mockery or derision

sardonyx (sär'doniks, 'särdəniks) *n.* variety of onyx with deep orange-red layers used as gemstone

Sargasso Sea (sär'gasō) calm area of water in N Atlantic, northeast of the West Indies —**sargasso** *or* **sargasso weed** *n. see* **gulfweed** *at* GULF

sargassum (sär'gasəm) *n.* gulfweed, type of floating seaweed

saris

sari ('säri) *n.* length of fabric wound around the body worn by Southern Asian women (*pl.* **-s**)

sarong (sə'rong) *n.* skirtlike garment worn in Asian and Pacific countries

sarsaparilla (sasəpə'rilə, saspə-; särs-) *n.* (flavor of) drink, *orig.* made from aromatic root of tropical Amer. prickly climbing plant

sartorial (sär'tôriəl) *a.* of tailor, tailoring or men's clothing

sash[1] (sash) *n.* decorative belt or ribbon, wound around the body

sash[2] (sash) *n.* wooden window frame opened by moving up and down in grooves

saskatoon (saskə'tōōn) *n.* Canad. shrub with purplish berries

sassafras ('sasəfras) *n.* laurel-like tree with aromatic bark used medicinally

Sassenach ('sasənak, -nakh) *n. Scot.* English person

sat (sat) *pt./pp. of* SIT

SAT Standard Achievement Test

Sat. 1. Saturday **2.** Saturn

Satan ('sātən) *n.* the devil —**satanic(al)** (sə'tanik(əl)) *a.* devilish, fiendish —**satanically** (sə'tanikəli) *adv.* —'**Satanism** *n.* **1.** worship of Satan **2.** satanic disposition —'**Satanist** *n./a.*

satchel ('sachəl) *n.* small bag, *esp.* for school books

sate (sāt) *vt.* satisfy (a desire or appetite) fully or excessively

sateen (sa'tēn) *n.* glossy linen or cotton fabric that resembles satin

satellite ('satəlīt) *n.* **1.** celestial body or man-made projectile orbiting planet **2.** person, country *etc.* dependent on another

satiate ('sāshiāt) *vt.* **1.** satisfy to the full **2.** surfeit —'**satiable** *a.* —**sati'ation** *n.* —**satiety** (sə'tīiti) *n.* feeling of having had too much

satin ('satin) *n.* fabric (of silk, rayon *etc.*) with glossy surface on one side —'**satiny** *a.* of, like satin —'**satinwood** *n.* any of various tropical trees that yield hard satiny wood

satire ('satīər) *n.* **1.** composition in which vice, folly or foolish person is held up to ridicule **2.** use of ridicule or sarcasm to expose vice and folly —**satiric(al)** (sə'tirik(əl)) *a.* **1.** of nature of satire **2.** sarcastic **3.** bitter —**satirist** ('satərist) *n.* —**satirize** ('satīrīz) *vt.* **1.** make object of satire **2.** censure thus

satisfy ('satisfī) *vt.* **1.** content, meet wishes of **2.** pay **3.** fulfill, supply adequately **4.** convince (**-fied, -fying**) —**satis'faction** *n.* —**satis'factory** *a.*

saturate ('sachərāt) *vt.* **1.** soak thoroughly **2.** cause to absorb maximum amount **3.** *Chem.* cause (substance) to combine to its full capacity with another **4.** shell or bomb heavily —**satu'ration** *n.* act, result of saturating

Saturday ('satərdi) *n.* seventh day of week

Saturn ('satərn) *n.* **1.** Roman god **2.** one of planets —**Saturnalia** (satər'nālyə, -liə) *n.* **1.** ancient festival of Saturn **2.** (*also* s-) noisy revelry, orgy —'**saturnine** *a.* **1.** gloomy **2.** sluggish in temperament, dull, morose

satyr ('sātər, 'satər) *n.* **1.** woodland deity, part man, part goat **2.** lustful man —**satyric** (sā'tirik, sa-) *a.*

sauce (sôs) *n.* **1.** liquid added to food to enhance flavor **2.** *inf.* impudence —*vt.* **3.** add sauce to **4.** *inf.* be cheeky, impudent to —'**saucily** *adv.* —'**saucy** *a.* impudent —'**saucepan** *n.* cooking pot with long handle

saucer ('sôsər) *n.* **1.** curved plate put under cup **2.** shallow depression

Saudi Arabia ('sowdi) country in Middle East bounded west by the Red Sea, south by Yemen and the People's Republic of Yemen, east by the People's Republic of Yemen and Oman, and north by the United Arab Emirates, the Persian Gulf, Kuwait, Iraq and Jordan —'**Saudi** *n./a.* —**Saudi Arabian**

sauerkraut ('sowərkrowt) *n.* Ger. dish of finely shredded and pickled cabbage

sauna ('sownə, 'sönə) *n.* kind of steam bath, *orig.* Finnish

saunter ('söntər) *vi.* 1. walk in leisurely manner, stroll —*n.* 2. leisurely walk or stroll

-saur *or* **-saurus** (*comb. form*) lizard, as in *dinosaur*

saurian ('söriən) *n.* one of the order of reptiles including the alligator, lizard *etc.*

sausage ('sösij) *n.* ground and seasoned meat enclosed in thin tube of animal intestine or synthetic material

sauté (sö'tā, sō-) *a.* fried quickly with little fat

Sauternes (sō'tərn) *n.* sweet white Fr. wine

savage ('savij) *a.* 1. wild 2. ferocious 3. brutal 4. uncivilized, primitive —*n.* 5. member of savage tribe, barbarian —*vt.* 6. attack ferociously —'**savagely** *adv.* —'**savagery** *n.*

savanna *or* **savannah** (sə'vanə) *n.* extensive open grassy plain

savant (sa'vänt, sə-; sə'vant, 'savənt) *n.* man of learning

save (sāv) *vt.* 1. rescue, preserve 2. protect 3. secure 4. keep for future, lay by 5. prevent need of 6. spare 7. except —*vi.* 8. lay by money —*prep.* 9. except —*conj.* 10. *obs.* but —'**saving** *a.* 1. frugal 2. thrifty 3. delivering from sin 4. excepting 5. compensating —*prep.* 6. excepting —*n.* 7. economy —*pl.* 8. money, earnings put by for future use —**savings bank** bank that accepts savings of depositors and pays interest on the deposits —**savings bond** a nontransferable registered bond issued by the U.S. government

savior ('sāvyər) *n.* 1. person who rescues another 2. (S-) Christ

savoir-faire (savwär'fâər; *Fr.* savwar'fer) ability to do, say, the right thing in any situation

savor ('sāvər) *n.* 1. characteristic taste 2. flavor 3. odor 4. distinctive quality —*vi.* 5. have particular smell or taste 6. (*with* of) have suggestion (of) —*vt.* 7. give flavor to 8. have flavor of 9. enjoy, appreciate —'**savory** *a.* 1. attractive to taste or smell 2. not sweet

savory ('sāvəri) *n.* aromatic herb used in cooking

savoy cabbage (sə'voi) variety of cabbage with wrinkled leaves

savvy ('savi) *sl. v.* 1. understand —*n.* 2. wits, intelligence

saw[1] (sö) *n.* 1. tool for cutting wood *etc.* by tearing it with toothed edge —*vt.* 2. cut with saw —*vi.* 3. make movements of sawing (**sawed, sawn, 'sawing**) —'**sawyer** *n.* 1. one who saws timber 2. felled tree projecting from stream bed —'**sawbones** *n. sl.* surgeon or doctor —'**sawdust** *n.* fine wood fragments made in sawing —'**sawfish** *n.* fish of tropical waters armed with toothed snout —'**sawhorse** *n.* stand for supporting timber during sawing —'**sawmill** *n.* apparatus for sawing logs

saw[2] (sö) *pt. of* SEE[1]

saw[3] (sö) *n.* wise saying, proverb

sawn (sön) *pp. of* SAW[1]

sax (saks) *inf.* saxophone

saxhorn ('saks-hörn) *n.* any of family of brass instruments, developed by Adolphe Sax, upright with three pistons standing on top of the tube —**sax tuba** bass saxhorn

saxifrage ('saksifrij, -frāj) *n.* any of genus of low, spreading perennials with basal leaves grown in Alpine or rock gardens

Saxon ('saksən) *n.* 1. member of West Germanic people who settled widely in Europe in the early Middle Ages —*a.* 2. of this people or their language

saxophone ('saksəfōn) *n.* metal woodwind instrument with a conical bore, using a single reed, available in six sizes, played in bands

say (sā) *vt.* 1. speak 2. pronounce 3. state 4. express 5. take as example or as near enough 6. make a case for (said *pt./pp.*, 'saying *prp.*, **says** (sez) *3rd pers. sing. pres. ind.*) —*n.* 7. what one has to say 8. chance of saying it 9. share in decision —'**saying** *n.* maxim, proverb

Sb *Chem.* antimony

SBA Small Business Administration

Sc *Chem.* scandium

SC South Carolina

sc. 1. scale 2. scene 3. science 4. screw 5. scruple (unit of weight)

s.c. *Print.* small capital letters

S.C. 1. Signal Corps 2. C Social Credit

scab (skab) *n.* 1. crust formed over wound 2. skin disease 3. disease of plants 4. *offens.* one who works during strike —'**scabby** *a.*

scabbard ('skabərd) *n.* sheath for sword or dagger

scabies ('skābēz) *n.* contagious skin disease —'**scabious** *a.* having scabies, scabby

scabrous ('skabrəs, 'skā-) *a.* 1. having rough surface 2. thorny 3. indecent 4. risky

scaffold ('skafəld) *n.* 1. temporary platform for workmen 2. gallows —'**scaffolding** *n.* (material for building) scaffold

scalar ('skālər) *n./a.* (variable quantity, *eg* time) having magnitude but no direction

scalawag ('skaliwag) *n. inf.* scamp, rascal

scald (sköld) *vt.* 1. burn with hot liquid or steam 2. clean, sterilize with boiling water 3. heat (liquid) almost to boiling point —*n.* 4. injury by scalding

scale[1] (skāl) *n.* 1. one of the thin, overlapping plates covering fishes and reptiles 2. thin flake 3. incrustation which forms in boilers *etc.* —*vt.* 4. remove scales from —*vi.* 5. come off in scales —'**scaly** *a.* resembling or covered in scales

scale[2] (skāl) *n.* 1. (*chiefly in pl.*) weighing instrument —*vt.* 2. weigh in scales 3. have weight of

scale[3] (skāl) *n.* 1. graduated table or sequence of marks at regular intervals used as reference or for fixing standards, as in making measurements, in music *etc.* 2. ratio of size between a thing and a model or map of it 3. (relative) degree, extent —*vt.* 4. climb —*a.* 5. proportionate —**scale up** *or* **down** increase or decrease proportionately in size

scalene ('skālēn) *a.* (of triangle) with three unequal sides

scallion ('skalyən) *n.* young onion before enlargement of the bulb

scallop ('skoləp, 'skal-) *or* **scollop** ('skoləp) *n.* 1. any of various marine mollusks 2. the edible muscle of the scallop 3. edging in small curves like edge of scallop shell —*vt.* 4. shape like scallop shell 5. cook in scallop shell or dish like one

scalp (skalp) *n.* 1. skin and hair of top of head —*vt.* 2. cut off scalp of

scalpel ('skalpəl) *n.* small surgical knife

scam (skam) *n.* confidence game, swindle

scamp (skamp) *n.* 1. mischievous person or child —*vt.* 2. skimp

scamper ('skampər) *vi.* 1. run about 2. run hastily from place to place —*n.* 3. act of scampering

scan (skan) *vt.* 1. look at carefully, scrutinize 2. measure or read (verse) by metrical feet 3. examine, search by systematically varying the direction of a radar or sonar beam 4. glance over quickly —*vi.* 5. (of verse) conform to metrical rules (-nn-) —*n.* 6. scanning —'**scanner** *n.* device, *esp.* electronic, which scans —'**scansion** *n.* analysis of metrical structure of verse

Scand. Scandinavia(n)

scandal ('skandəl) *n.* 1. action, event generally considered disgraceful 2. malicious gossip —'**scandalize** *vt.* shock —'**scandalous** *a.* outrageous, disgraceful —'**scandalmonger** *n.* person who spreads gossip *etc.*

Scandinavian (skandi'nāviən) *a.* 1. of Scandinavia, its inhabitants or their languages which are mutually intelligible Germanic languages —*n.* 2. native or inhabitant of Denmark, Iceland, Norway or Sweden

scandium ('skandiəm) *n. Chem.* metallic element *Symbol* Sc, at. wt. 45.0, at. no. 21

scant (skant) *a.* barely sufficient or not sufficient —'**scantily** *adv.* —'**scanty** *a.*

scapegoat ('skāpgōt) *n.* person bearing blame due to others

scapegrace ('skāpgrās) *n.* mischievous person

scapula ('skapyələ) *n.* shoulder blade (*pl.* -**lae** (-lē), -**s**) —'**scapular** *a.* 1. of scapula —*n.* 2. part of habit of certain religious orders in R.C. Church

scar[1] (skär) *n.* 1. mark left by healed wound, burn or sore 2. change resulting from emotional distress —*v.* 3. mark, heal with scar (-rr-)

scar[2] (skär) *n.* bare craggy rock formation

scarab ('skarəb) *n.* 1. sacred beetle of ancient Egypt 2. gem cut in shape of this

scarce (skâərs) *a.* 1. hard to find 2. existing or available in insufficient quantity 3. uncommon —'**scarcely** *adv.* 1. only just 2. not quite 3. definitely or probably not —'**scarceness** *or* '**scarcity** *n.*

scare (skâər) *vt.* 1. frighten —*n.* 2. fright, sudden panic —'**scary** *a.* —'**scarecrow** *n.* 1. thing set up to frighten birds from crops 2. badly dressed or miserable-looking person —'**scaremonger** *n.* one who spreads alarming rumors

scarf[1] (skärf) *n.* long narrow strip, large piece of material to put round neck, head *etc.* (*pl.* -**s, scarves**)

scarf[2] (skärf) *n.* 1. part cut away from each of two pieces of timber to be jointed longitudinally 2. joint so made (*pl.* -**s**) —*vt.* 3. cut or join in this way —'**scarfing** *n.*

scarify ('skarifī, 'skeri-) *vt.* 1. scratch, cut slightly all over 2. lacerate 3. stir surface soil of 4. criticize mercilessly (-**fied, -fying**) —scarifi'cation *n.*

scarlatina (skärlə'tēnə) *n.* scarlet fever

scarlet ('skärlit) *n.* 1. brilliant red color 2. cloth or clothing of this color, *esp.* military uniform —*a.* 3. of this color 4. immoral, *esp.* unchaste —**scarlet fever** infectious bacterial disease, formerly major cause of death in children, now controlled by antibiotics (*also* **scarlatina**)

scarp (skärp) *n.* 1. steep slope 2. inside slope of ditch in fortifications

scarves (skärvz) *n., pl. of* SCARF[1]

scat[1] (skat) *vi. inf.* (*usu. imp.*) go away (-**tt**-)

scat[2] (skat) *n. Jazz* singing characterized by improvised vocal sounds instead of words

scathe (skādh) (*usu. now as pp./a.* **scathed** & **un'scathed**) *n.* 1. injury, harm, damage —*vt.* 2. injure, damage —'**scathing** *a.* 1. harshly critical 2. cutting 3. damaging

Scaticook ('skatikŏok) *n.* Algonquian-speaking Amerindian people of Connecticut

scatology (ska'toləji) *n.* 1. scientific study of excrement, *esp.* in medicine and pale-ontology 2. preoccupation with obscenity, *esp.* in form of references to excrement —**scato'logical** *a.*

scatter ('skatər) *vt.* 1. throw in various directions 2. put here and there —*vi.* 3. separate and move in various directions —*n.* 4. sprinkling —'**scatty** *a. inf.* silly, useless —'**scatterbrain** *n.* silly, careless person

scavenge ('skavinj) *v.* search for (anything usable), *usu.* among discarded material —'**scavenger** *n.* 1. person who scavenges 2. animal, bird which feeds on refuse

scene (sēn) *n.* 1. place of action of novel, play *etc.* 2. place of any action 3. subdivision of play 4. view 5. episode 6. display of strong emotion —**scenario** (si'narió, -'ner-) *n.* summary of plot (of play *etc.*) or plan (*pl.* -**s**) —'**scenery** *n.* 1. natural features of district 2. constructions of wood, canvas *etc.* used on stage to represent a place where action is happening —'**scenic** *a.* 1. picturesque 2. of or on the stage

scent (sent) *n.* 1. distinctive smell, *esp.* pleasant one 2. trail, clue 3. perfume —*vt.* 4. detect or track by or as if by smell 5. suspect, sense 6. fill with fragrance

scepter ('septər) *n.* 1. ornamental staff as symbol of royal power 2. royal dignity

schedule ('skejŏōl, -jŏōl) *n.* 1. plan of procedure for a project 2. list 3. timetable —*vt.* 4. enter in schedule 5. plan to occur at certain time —**on schedule** on time

schema ('skēmə) *n.* overall plan or diagram (*pl.* -**mata** (-mətə)) —**sche'matic** *a.* present-ed as plan or diagram —'**schematize** *vt.*

scheme (skēm) *n.* 1. plan, design 2. project 3. outline —*v.* 4. devise, plan, *esp.* in underhand manner —'**schemer** *n.*

scherzo ('skāərtsō) *n. Mus.* light playful composition (*pl.* -**s**, -**zi** (-tsē))

Schick test (shik) test for susceptibility to diphtheria

schism ('sizəm, 'skiz-) *n.* (group resulting from) division in political party, church *etc.* —**schis'matic** *n./a.*

schist (shist) *n.* crystalline rock which splits into layers —'**schistose** *a.*

schistosomiasis (shistəsŏ'mīəsis) *n.* severe infectious disease caused by flatworm infestation transmitted to humans by snails (*also* **bilharzia, snail fever**)

schizo ('skitsō) *inf. a.* 1. schizophrenic —*n.* 2. schizophrenic person (*pl.* -**s**)

schizo- *or before vowel* **schiz-** (*comb. form*) indicating cleavage, split, or division, as in *schizophrenia*

schizophrenia (skitsə'frēniə) *n.* mental disorder involving deterioration of, confusion about personality —'**schizoid** *a.* of schizo-phrenia —**schizophrenic** (skitsə'frenik) *a./n.*

schmaltz *or* **schmalz** (shmŏlts, shmolts) *see* SHMALZ

schnapps (shnaps) *n.* 1. spirit distilled from potatoes 2. *inf.* any strong spirit

schnitzel ('shnitsəl) *n.* thin slice of meat, *esp.* veal

scholar ('skolər) *n. see* SCHOOL¹

scholium ('skōliəm) *n.* 1. marginal annota-tion 2. note 3. comment (*pl.* -**lia** (-liə)) —'**scholiast** *n.* 1. commentator 2. annotator

school¹ (skŏōl) *n.* 1. institution for teaching children or for giving instruction in any

subject 2. buildings of such institution 3. group of thinkers, writers, artists *etc.* with principles or methods in common —*vt.* 4. educate 5. bring under control, train —'**scholar** *n.* 1. learned person 2. one taught in school 3. one quick to learn —**scholarly** ('skolərli) *a.* learned, erudite —**scholarship** ('skolərship) *n.* 1. learning 2. prize, grant to student for payment of school or college fees —**scholastic** (skə'lastik) *a.* 1. of schools or scholars, or education 2. pedantic —'**school-ing** *n.* 1. education 2. training of animal, *esp.* of horse for dressage —'**schoolhouse** *n.* 1. building used as school 2. house attached to school —'**schoolman** *n.* medieval philoso-pher —'**schoolmarm** *n. inf.* 1. woman schoolteacher 2. woman considered old-fashioned or prim —'**schoolmaster** *n.* 1. man who teaches school 2. edible snapper of Gulf of Mexico and tropical Atlantic —'**school-mistress** *n.* woman who teaches school —'**schoolteacher** *n.* person who teaches school

school² (skŏōl) *n.* shoal (of fish, whales *etc.*)

schooner ('skŏōnər) *n.* 1. fore-and-aft rigged vessel with two or more masts 2. tall glass

schottische ('shotish, sho'tēsh) *n.* 1. 19th-century German dance 2. music for this

schwa (shwä) *n.* 1. central vowel represent-ed in International Phonetic Alphabet by (ə), *eg* 'a' in *around* 2. symbol (ə) used to represent this sound

sciatica (sI'atikə) *n.* 1. neuralgia of hip and thigh 2. pain in sciatic nerve —**sci'atic** *a.* 1. of the hip 2. of sciatica

science ('sIəns) *n.* 1. systematic study and knowledge of natural or physical phenom-ena 2. any branch of study concerned with observed material facts —**scien'tific** *a.* 1. of the principles of science 2. systematic —**scien'tifically** *adv.* —'**scientist** *n.* person versed in natural sciences —**science fiction** stories set in a fantasy world making imaginative use of scientific knowledge

Scientology (sIən'toləji) *n.* religious cult based on belief that self-awareness is paramount

sci-fi ('sI'fī) *n. inf.* science fiction

scimitar

scimitar ('simitər) *n.* oriental curved sword

scintilla (sin'tilə) *n. rare* minute amount

scintillate ('sintilāt) *vi.* 1. give off sparks 2. be animated, witty, clever —**scintil'lation** *n.* —**scintillation counter** instrument for de-tecting and measuring intensity of high-energy radiation

scion ('sIən) *n.* 1. descendant, heir 2. slip for grafting

scission ('sizhən) *n.* act of cutting, dividing, splitting —'**scissile** *a.*

scissors ('sizərz) *pl.n.* 1. cutting instrument of two blades pivoted together (*also* **pair of scissors**) —*n./a.* 2. (with) scissor-like action of limbs in swimming, athletics *etc.* —**scis-sor-like** *a.*

scleroderma (sklerə'dərmə) *n.* progressive disease of the connective tissues of the body

sclerosis (skli'rōsis) *n.* a hardening of bodily organs, tissues *etc.* (*pl.* -**ses** (-sēz)) —**sclera** ('sklerə) *n.* firm white fibrous membrane that forms outer covering of eyeball —**sclerotic** (skli'rotik) *a.* 1. of sclera 2. of or having sclerosis —*n.* 3. sclera

scoff¹ (skof) *vi.* 1. (*oft. with* at) express derision (for) —*n.* 2. derision 3. mocking words —'**scoffer** *n.*

scoff² (skof) *v. sl.* eat rapidly

scold (skōld) *v.* 1. find fault (with) —*vt.* 2. reprimand, be angry with —*n.* 3. one who does this

scoliosis (skŏli'ōsis) *n.* lateral curvature of the spine

scollop ('skoləp) *see* SCALLOP

sconce¹ (skons) *n.* bracket candlestick on wall

sconce² (skons) *n.* small protective fortifica-tion

scone (skōn, skon) *n.* small plain cake baked on griddle or in oven

scoop (skŏōp) *n.* 1. small shovel-like tool for ladling, hollowing out *etc.* 2. *sl.* profitable deal 3. *Journalism* exclusive news item —*vt.* 4. ladle out 5. hollow out, rake in with scoop 6. make sudden profit 7. beat (rival newspaper *etc.*)

scoot (skŏōt) *vi. sl.* move off quickly —'**scooter** *n.* 1. child's vehicle propelled by pushing on ground with one foot 2. light motorcycle (*also* **motor scooter**)

scope (skōp) *n.* 1. range of activity or application 2. opportunity

-scope (*n. comb. form*) indicating instrument for observing or detecting, as in *microscope* —**-scopic** (*a. comb. form*)

scopolamine (skō'poləmēn) *n.* drug ob-tained from plants of nightshade family used as preanesthetic and as 'truth drug'

scorbutic (skōr'byŏōtik) *a.* of or having scurvy —**scor'butically** *adv.*

scorch (skōrch) *v.* 1. burn, be burnt, on surface 2. parch 3. shrivel 4. wither —*n.* 5. slight burn —'**scorcher** *n. inf.* very hot day

score (skōr) *n.* 1. points gained in game, competition 2. group of 20 3. (*esp. pl.*) a lot 4. copy of musical composition 5. mark or notch, *esp.* to keep tally 6. reason, account 7. grievance —*v.* 8. gain (points) in game —*vt.* 9. mark 10. (*with* out) cross out 11. arrange music for —*vi.* 12. keep tally of points 13. succeed —'**scorecard** *n.* 1. card on which scores are recorded 2. card identifying players in sports match

scoria ('skōriə) *n.* 1. solidified lava contain-ing many cavities 2. refuse obtained from smelted ore (*pl.* -**riae** (-riē))

scorn (skōrn) *n.* 1. contempt, derision —*vt.* 2. despise —'**scorner** *n.* —'**scornful** *a.* derisive —'**scornfully** *adv.*

Scorpio ('skōrpió) *n.* (scorpion) 8th sign of zodiac, operative *c.* Oct. 23rd-Nov. 21st

scorpion ('skōrpiən) *n.* small lobster-shaped animal with sting at end of jointed tail

Scot. 1. Scotland 2. Scottish

scotch (skoch) *vt.* 1. put an end to 2. *obs.* wound

scoter ('skōtər) *n.* sea duck of northern regions

scot-free *a.* without harm or loss

Scotland ('skotlənd) *n.* division of the United Kingdom in N Great Britain —**Scot** *n.* native of Scotland —**Scotch** (skoch) *n.* whisky made in Scotland —'**Scottie** *or* '**Scotty** *n.* 1. Scottish terrier 2. *inf.* Scotsman —'**Scottish** *or* **Scots** *a.* —**Scotland Yard** headquarters of police force of metropolitan London —'**Scotsman** *n.* —**Scots** *or* **Scotch pine** 1. coniferous tree of Europe and W and N Asia 2. its wood —**Scottish terrier** small long-haired breed of terrier

scoundrel ('skowndrəl) *n.* villain, black-guard —'**scoundrelly** *a.*

scour¹ ('skowər) *vt.* 1. clean, polish by rubbing 2. clear or flush out —**scouring rush** primitive plant resembling horsetail but taller, used for cleaning as stems contain embedded silica

scour² ('skow∂r) v. move rapidly along or over (territory) in search of something

scourge (sk∂rj) n. 1. whip, lash 2. severe affliction 3. pest 4. calamity —vt. 5. flog 6. punish severely

scout (skowt) n. 1. one sent out to reconnoiter 2. Boy Scout; Girl Scout —vi. 3. go out, act as scout 4. reconnoiter

scow (skow) n. unpowered barge

scowl (skowl) vi. 1. frown gloomily or sullenly —n. 2. angry or gloomy expression

scrabble ('skrab∂l) vi. 1. scrape with hands, claws in disorderly manner —n. 2. (S-) trade name for word game where object is to form interlocking words by using letters with designated values

scrag (skrag) n. 1. lean person or animal 2. lean end of a neck of mutton —'scraggy a. thin, bony

scraggly ('skragli) a. untidy

scram (skram) vi. inf. (oft. imp.) go away hastily, get out (-mm-)

scramble ('skramb∂l) vi. 1. move along or up by crawling, climbing etc. 2. struggle with others 3. run with football after protection has been broken down —vt. 4. mix up 5. cook (eggs) beaten up with milk 6. render (speech) unintelligible by electronic device —n. 7. scrambling 8. rough climb 9. disorderly proceeding —'scrambler n. electronic device that renders speech unintelligible during transmission

scrap (skrap) n. 1. small piece or fragment 2. waste material 3. inf. fight —vt. 4. break up, discard as useless —vi. 5. inf. fight (-pp-) —'scrappy a. 1. unequal in quality 2. badly finished —'scrapbook n. book in which newspaper cuttings etc. are kept —scrap heap pile of waste material

scrape (skrāp) vt. 1. rub with something sharp 2. clean, smooth thus 3. grate 4. scratch 5. rub with harsh noise —n. 6. act, sound of scraping 7. inf. awkward situation, esp. as result of escapade —'scraper n. 1. instrument for scraping 2. contrivance on which mud is scraped from shoes etc.

scratch (skrach) vt. 1. score, make narrow surface wound on with claws, nails, or anything pointed 2. make marks on with pointed instruments 3. scrape (skin) with nails to relieve itching 4. remove, withdraw from list, race etc. —vi. 5. use claws or nails, esp. to relieve itching —n. 6. wound, mark or sound made by scratching 7. line or starting point —a. 8. got together at short notice 9. impromptu —'scratchy a.

scrawl (skröl) vt. 1. write, draw untidily —n. 2. thing scrawled 3. careless writing

scrawny ('skröni) a. thin, bony

scream (skrēm) vi. 1. utter piercing cry, esp. of fear, pain etc. 2. be very obvious —vt. 3. utter in a scream —n. 4. shrill, piercing cry 5. inf. very funny person or thing

scree (skrē) n. 1. loose shifting stones 2. slope covered with these

screech (skrēch) vi./n. scream —screech owl 1. small N Amer. owl having reddish-brown or gray plumage 2. UK any owl that utters screeching cry

screed (skrēd) n. 1. long (tedious) letter, passage or speech 2. thin layer of cement

screen (skrēn) n. 1. device to shelter from heat, light, draft, observation etc. 2. anything used for such purpose 3. mesh over doors, windows to keep out insects 4. white or silvered surface on which photographic images are projected 5. maneuver in some sports to impede opponent legally 6. wooden or stone partition in church —vt. 7. shelter, hide 8. protect from detection 9. show

(motion picture) 10. scrutinize 11. examine (group of people) for presence of disease, weapons etc. 12. examine for political motives 13. Elec. protect from stray electric or magnetic fields —'screenplay n. script for motion picture, including instructions for sets and camera work —screen process see silk-screen at SILK —the screen the motion-picture industry

screw (skrōō) n. 1. (nail-like device or cylinder with) spiral thread cut to engage similar thread or to bore into material (wood etc.) to pin or fasten 2. anything resembling a screw in shape, esp. in spiral form 3. propeller 4. twist —vt. 5. fasten with screw 6. twist around 7. inf. extort —'screwy a. inf. crazy, eccentric —'screwball sl. n. 1. eccentric person —a. 2. odd; eccentric —'screwdriver n. tool for turning screws —put the screws on compel by applying pressure on (debtor) —screw up 1. distort 2. inf. bungle

scribble ('skrib∂l) v. 1. write, draw careless-ly —vi. 2. make meaningless marks with pen or pencil —n. 3. something scribbled —'scribbly a.

scribe (∂krīb) n. 1. writer 2. copyist —v. 3. scratch a line on (a surface) with pointed instrument

scrimmage ('skrimij) n. scuffle

scrimp (skrimp) vt. 1. make too small or short 2. treat meanly —'scrimpy a.

script (skript) n. 1. (system or style of) handwriting 2. written characters 3. written text of motion picture, play or radio or television program 4. answer paper in examination

scripture ('skripch∂r) n. 1. sacred writings 2. the Bible —'scriptural a.

scrofula ('skrofy∂l∂) n. tuberculosis of lymphatic glands of neck —'scrofulous a.

scroll (skrōl) n. 1. roll of parchment or paper 2. list 3. ornament shaped thus

Scrooge (skrōōj) n. miserly person

scrotum ('skrōt∂m) n. pouch containing testicles (pl. -ta (-t∂)) —'scrotal a.

scrounge (skrownj) v. inf. get (something) without cost, by begging —'scrounger n.

scrub¹ (skrub) vt. 1. clean with hard brush and water 2. scour 3. inf. cancel, get rid of (-bb-) —n. 4. scrubbing —'scrubber n. 1. person or thing that scrubs 2. apparatus for purifying gas

scrub² (skrub) n. 1. stunted trees 2. brushwood —'scrubby a. 1. covered with scrub 2. stunted 3. inf. messy

scrub typhus infectious disease caused by rickettsia transmitted to humans by mites

scruff (skruf) n. nape (of neck)

scruffy ('skrufi) a. unkempt or shabby

scrumptious ('skrumpsh∂s) a. inf. very pleasing; delicious —'scrumptiously adv.

scrumpy ('skrumpi) n. rough dry cider

scrunch (skrunch) v. 1. crumple or crunch or be crumpled or crunched —n. 2. act or sound of scrunching

scruple ('skrōōp∂l) n. 1. doubt or hesitation about what is morally right 2. apothecaries' weight of 20 grains —vi. 3. hesitate —'scrupulous a. 1. extremely conscientious 2. thorough, attentive to small points

scrutiny ('skrōōtini) n. 1. close examination 2. critical investigation 3. official examination of votes etc. 4. searching look —scruti-'neer n. person who examines —'scrutinize vt. examine closely

scuba ('skyōōb∂, 'skōōb∂) n./a. (relating to) self-contained underwater breathing apparatus

scud (skud) vi. 1. run fast 2. run before the wind (-dd-)

scuff (skuf) vi. 1. drag, scrape with feet in walking —vt. 2. scrape with feet 3. graze —n. 4. act, sound of scuffing —pl. 5. thong sandals —scuffed a. (of shoes) scraped or slightly grazed

scuffle ('skuf∂l) vi. 1. fight in disorderly manner 2. shuffle —n. 3. disorderly struggle

scull (skul) n. 1. oar used in stern of boat 2. short oar used in pairs —v. 3. propel, move by means of scull(s)

scullery ('skul∂ri) n. place for washing dishes etc. —'scullion n. helper in kitchen

sculpture ('skulpch∂r) n. 1. art of forming figures in relief or solid 2. product of this art —vt. 3. represent by sculpture —sculpt v. —'sculptor n. —'sculptural a. with qualities proper to sculpture

scum (skum) n. 1. froth or other floating matter on liquid 2. waste part of anything 3. vile person(s) or thing(s) —'scummy a.

scupper ('skup∂r) n. 1. hole in ship's side level with deck to carry off water —vt. 2. inf. ruin, destroy, kill

scurf (sk∂rf) n. flaky matter on scalp, dandruff

scurrilous ('skuril∂s) a. coarse, indecently abusive —scur'rility n.

scurry ('skuri) vi. 1. run hastily ('scurried, 'scurrying) —n. 2. bustling haste 3. flurry

scurvy ('sk∂rvi) n. 1. disease caused by lack of vitamin C —a. 2. mean, contemptible

scut (skut) n. short tail of hare or other animal

scuttle¹ ('skut∂l) n. fireside container for coal

scuttle² ('skut∂l) vi. 1. rush away —n. 2. hurried pace, run

scuttle³ ('skut∂l) vt. cause (ship) to sink by making holes in bottom

scythe (sīdh) n. 1. manual implement with long curved blade for cutting grass —vt. 2. cut with scythe

SD South Dakota

Se Chem. selenium

SE southeast(ern)

sea anemone

sea (sē) n. 1. mass of salt water covering greater part of earth 2. broad tract of this 3. waves 4. swell 5. large quantity 6. vast expanse —sea anchor Naut. device dragged in water to slow vessel —sea anemone sea animal with suckers like petals —'seaboard n. territory bordering sea coast —sea cow 1. dugong or manatee 2. obs. walrus —sea cucumber echinoderm with elongated body covered with leathery skin and cluster of tentacles at oral end —sea dog experienced or old sailor —'seafaring a. occupied in sea voyages —'seafood n. edible saltwater fish or shellfish —sea-girt a. Lit. surrounded by sea —sea gull gull —sea horse fish with bony plated body and horselike head —sea kale European coastal plant with edible asparagus-like shoots —sea legs inf. 1. ability to maintain one's balance on board ship 2. ability to resist seasickness —sea level level of surface of sea, taken to be mean level between high and low tide —**sea lion** any of large-eared seals of Pacific —**'seaman** n. sailor —**'seamanship** n. skill in navigating, maintaining and operating vessel —**sea mile** see **nautical mile** at NAUTICAL —**'seaplane** n. aircraft that lands on and takes off from water —**Sea Scout** member of Scouting program teaching seamanship —**'seashell** n. empty shell of marine mollusk —**'seasick** a. —**'seasickness** n. see **motion sickness** at MOTION —**'seaside** n. place, esp. resort, on coast —**sea urchin** marine animal with globular body enclosed in rigid, spiny test —**'seaweed** n. 1. mass of marine or freshwater plants 2. marine alga, esp. kelp —**'seaworthy** a. in fit condition to put to sea

sea horse

seal[1] (sēl) n. 1. device impressed on piece of wax etc., fixed to letter etc. as mark of authentication 2. impression thus made 3. device, material preventing passage of water, air, oil etc. (also **'sealer**) —vt. 4. affix seal to 5. ratify, authorize 6. mark with stamp as evidence of some quality 7. keep close or secret 8. settle 9. make watertight, airtight etc. —**sealing wax** hard material made of shellac and turpentine that softens when heated

seal[2] (sēl) n. 1. amphibious furred carnivorous mammal with flippers as limbs —vi. 2. hunt seals —**'sealer** n. person or ship engaged in sealing —**'sealskin** n. skin, fur of seals

seam (sēm) n. 1. line of junction of two edges, eg of two pieces of cloth, or two planks 2. thin layer, stratum —vt. 3. mark with furrows or wrinkles —**'seamless** a. —**'seamstress** ('sēmstris, 'sem-) or **sempstress** ('sempstris, 'semstris) n. woman who sews and makes clothing, esp. professionally —**'seamy** a. 1. sordid 2. marked with seams

seance ('sāons) n. meeting of spiritualists

sear (sēər) vt. 1. scorch, brand with hot iron 2. deaden

search (sərch) v. 1. look over or through (a place etc.) to find something —vt. 2. probe into, examine —n. 3. act of searching 4. quest —**'searcher** n. —**'searching** a. 1. keen 2. thorough 3. severe —**'searchlight** n. powerful electric light with concentrated beam —**search warrant** legal document authorizing search of premises for stolen goods etc.

season ('sēzən) n. 1. one of four divisions of year (spring, summer, fall and winter), which have characteristic weather conditions 2. period during which thing takes place, grows, is active etc. 3. proper time —vt. 4. flavor with salt, herbs etc. 5. make reliable or ready for use 6. make experienced —**'seasonable** a. 1. appropriate for the season 2. opportune 3. fit —**'seasonal** a. depending on, varying with seasons —**'seasoning** n. flavoring —**season ticket** ticket for series of journeys, events etc. within a certain time

seat (sēt) n. 1. thing for sitting on 2. buttocks 3. base 4. right to sit (eg in council etc.) 5. place where something is located, centered 6. locality of disease, trouble etc. 7. country house —vt. 8. bring to or place on seat 9.

provide sitting accommodation for 10. install firmly —**seat belt** belt worn in automobile, aircraft etc. to secure seated passenger

SEATO ('sētō) South East Asia Treaty Organization

sebaceous (si'bāshəs) a. 1. of, pert. to fat 2. secreting fat, oil —**sebaceous cyst** round or oval swelling caused by blocking of oil glands of skin (also **wen**)

sec[1] (sek) a. 1. (of wines) dry 2. (of champagne) of medium sweetness

sec[2] (sek) inf. second (of time)

sec[3] (sek) secant

sec. 1. second (of time) 2. secondary 3. secretary 4. section 5. sector

S.E.C. Securities and Exchange Commission

secant ('sēkant, -kənt) n. Math. 1. (of angle) the reciprocal of its cosine 2. line that intersects a curve

secede (si'sēd) vi. withdraw formally from federation, Church etc. —**secession** (si'seshən) n. —**secessionist** (si'seshənist) n.

seclude (si'klōōd) vt. guard from, remove from sight, view, contact with others —**se'cluded** a. 1. remote 2. private —**se'clusion** n.

second[1] ('sekənd) a. 1. next after first 2. alternate 3. additional 4. of lower quality —n. 5. person or thing coming second 6. attendant 7. sixtieth part of minute 8. unit of time 9. moment 10. (esp. pl.) inferior goods —vt. 11. support 12. support (motion in meeting) so that discussion may be in order —**'seconder** n. —**'secondly** adv. —**second-best** a. next to best —**second chamber** upper house of bicameral legislative assembly —**second class** class next in value etc. to first —**second-class** a. 1. of grade next to best in quality etc. 2. shoddy or inferior 3. (of accommodations in hotel, on aircraft etc.) next in quality to first-class 4. of mail that consists mainly of newspapers etc. —adv. 5. by second-class mail etc. —**Second Coming** or **Advent** Christian theol. prophesied return of Christ to earth at Last Judgment —**second cousin** child of first cousin of either of one's parents —**second fiddle** inf. 1. second violin in string quartet 2. person who has secondary status —**second hand** pointer on face of timepiece that indicates seconds —**second-hand** a. 1. bought after use by another 2. not original 3. dealing in goods that are not new —adv. 4. not directly —**second lieutenant** commissioned officer of lowest rank in army, air force and marine corps, below first lieutenant —**second nature** habit etc. long practiced so as to seem innate —**second person** grammatical category of pronouns and verbs used when referring to individual(s) being addressed —**second-rate** a. 1. mediocre 2. second in importance etc. —**second sight** faculty of seeing events before they occur —**second thought** revised opinion on matter already considered —**second wind** (wind) 1. return of breath at normal rate, esp. following exertion 2. renewed ability to continue in effort —**come off second-best** inf. be defeated in competition

second[2] ('sekənd) vt. transfer (employee, officer) temporarily

secondary ('sekənderi) a. 1. of less importance 2. developed from, or dependent on, something else —**secon'darily** adv. —**secondary color** color formed by mixing two primary colors in equal parts: orange, green or violet —**secondary road** 1. road not of primary importance 2. feeder road

secret ('sēkrit) a. 1. kept, meant to be kept from knowledge of others 2. hidden 3.

private —n. 4. thing kept secret —**'secrecy** n. keeping or being kept secret —**'secretive** a. given to having secrets; uncommunicative, reticent —**'secretiveness** n. —**'secretly** adv. —**secret agent** person employed in espionage —**secret police** police force that operates secretly to check subversion —**secret service** government department that conducts intelligence or counterintelligence operations

secretary ('sekrəteri) n. 1. person employed by individual or organization to deal with papers and correspondence, keep records, prepare business etc. 2. head of a U.S. government department —**secre'tarial** a. —**secre'tariat** n. 1. body of secretaries 2. building occupied by secretarial staff —**'secretaryship** n. —**secretary bird** large Afr. bird of prey

secretary bird

secrete (si'krēt) vt. 1. hide, conceal 2. (of gland etc.) collect and supply (particular substance in body) —**se'cretion** n. —**se'cretory** a.

sect (sekt) n. 1. group of people (within religious body etc.) with common interest 2. faction —**sec'tarian** a. 1. of a sect 2. narrow-minded

section ('sekshən) n. 1. part cut off 2. division 3. portion 4. distinct part of city, country, people etc. 5. cutting 6. drawing of anything as if cut through —**'sectional** a.

sector ('sektər) n. 1. part, subdivision 2. part of circle enclosed by two radii and the arc which they cut off

secular ('sekyələr) a. 1. worldly 2. lay, not religious 3. not monastic 4. lasting for, or occurring once in, an age 5. centuries old —**'secularism** n. —**'secularist** n. one who believes that religion should have no place in civil affairs —**seculari'zation** n. —**'secularize** vt. transfer from religious to lay possession or use

secure (si'kyōōr) a. 1. safe 2. free from fear, anxiety 3. firmly fixed 4. certain 5. sure, confident —vt. 6. gain possession of 7. make safe 8. free (creditor) from risk of loss 9. make firm —**se'curely** adv. —**se'curity** n. 1. state of safety 2. protection 3. that which secures 4. assurance 5. anything given as bond, caution or pledge 6. one that becomes surety for another —**security risk** person deemed to be threat to state security

sedan (si'dan) n. enclosed automobile for four or more persons including the driver —**sedan chair** Hist. closed chair for one person, carried on poles by bearers

sedate[1] (si'dāt) a. 1. calm, collected 2. serious

sedate[2] (si'dāt) vt. make calm by sedative —**se'dation** n. —**sedative** ('sedətiv) a. 1. having soothing or calming effect —n. 2. sedative drug

sedentary ('sedənteri) a. 1. done sitting down 2. sitting much 3. (of birds) not migratory

sedge (sej) n. plant like coarse grass growing

in swampy ground —**sedge warbler** European songbird having streaked brownish plumage with white eye stripes

sedilia (sə'dēlyə) *pl.n.* (*with sing. v.*) stone seats on south side of altar for priests

sediment ('sedimənt) *n.* **1.** matter which settles to the bottom of liquid **2.** matter deposited from water, ice or wind —**sedi-'mentary** *a.*

sedition (si'dishən) *n.* speech or action threatening authority of a state —**se'ditious** *a.*

seduce (si'dyōōs, -'dōōs) *vt.* **1.** persuade to commit some (wrong) deed, *esp.* sexual intercourse **2.** tempt **3.** attract —**se'ducer** *n.* (**seductress** (si'duktris) *fem.*) —**seduction** (si'dukshən) *n.* —**seductive** (si'duktiv) *a.* **1.** alluring **2.** winning

sedulous ('sejələs) *a.* **1.** diligent **2.** industrious **3.** persevering, persistent —**se'dulity** *n.*

sedum ('sēdəm) *n.* rock plant

see[1] (sē) *vt.* **1.** perceive with eyes or mentally **2.** observe **3.** watch **4.** find out **5.** consider **6.** have experience of **7.** interview **8.** make sure **9.** accompany —*vi.* **10.** have power of sight **11.** consider **12.** understand (**saw, seen, 'seeing**) —**'seeing** *conj.* since, in view of the fact that

see[2] (sē) *n.* diocese, office or jurisdiction of bishop

seed (sēd) *n.* **1.** reproductive germs of plants **2.** one grain of this **3.** such grains saved or used for sowing **4.** origin **5.** sperm **6.** *obs.* offspring —*vt.* **7.** sow with seed **8.** arrange (draw for lawn tennis or other tournament) so that best players do not meet in early rounds —*vi.* **9.** produce seed —**'seedling** *n.* young plant raised from seed —**'seedy** *a.* **1.** shabby **2.** (of plant) at seed-producing stage **3.** *inf.* unwell, ill —**seed pearl** tiny pearl weighing less than a quarter of a grain

seek (sēk) *vt.* **1.** make search or inquiry for —*vi.* **2.** search (**sought, 'seeking**)

seem (sēm) *vi.* **1.** appear (to be or to do) **2.** look **3.** appear to one's judgment —**'seeming** *a.* apparent but not real —**'seemingly** *adv.*

seemly ('sēmli) *a.* becoming and proper —**'seemliness** *n.*

seen (sēn) *pp. of* SEE[1]

seep (sēp) *vi.* trickle through slowly, as water, ooze

seer (sēər) *n.* prophet

seersucker ('sēərsukər) *n.* light cotton fabric with slightly crinkled surface

seesaw ('sēsö) *n.* **1.** game in which children sit at opposite ends of plank supported in middle and swing up and down **2.** plank used for this —*vi.* **3.** move up and down

seethe (sēdh) *vi.* **1.** boil, foam **2.** be very agitated **3.** be in constant movement (as large crowd *etc.*) (**seethed, 'seething**)

segment ('segmənt) *n.* **1.** piece cut off **2.** section —*v.* ('segment) **3.** divide into segments —**seg'mental** *a.* —**segmen'tation** *n.*

segregate ('segrigāt) *vt.* set apart from the rest —**segre'gation** *n.*

seigneur (sā'nyər; *Fr.* se'nyœr) *n.* **1.** member of landed gentry in Canada **2.** feudal lord of the manor —**sei'gneurial** *a.*

seine (sān) *n.* type of large fishing net

seismic ('sīzmik) *a.* pert. to earthquakes —**'seismograph** *n.* instrument that records earthquakes (*also* seis'mometer) —**seismo-'logic(al)** *a.* pert. to seismology —**seis'mologist** *n.* person versed in seismology —**seis-'mology** *n.* science of earthquakes

seismo- *or before vowel* **seism-** (*comb. form*) earthquake, as in *seismology*

seize (sēz) *vt.* **1.** grasp **2.** lay hold of **3.** capture —*vi.* **4.** (of mechanical parts) stick tightly through overheating —**'seizable** *a.* —**'seizure** *n.* **1.** act of taking, *esp.* by warrant, as goods **2.** sudden onset of disease

seldom ('seldəm) *adv.* not often, rarely

select (si'lekt) *vt.* **1.** pick out, choose —*a.* **2.** choice, picked **3.** exclusive —**se'lection** *n.* —**se'lective** *a.* —**selec'tivity** *n.* —**se'lector** *n.*

selenium (si'lēniəm) *n. Chem.* metalloid element *Symbol* Se, at. wt. 79.0, at. no. 34 —**se'lenic** *a.*

self (self) *pron.* **1.** used reflexively or to express emphasis (*pl.* **selves**) —*a.* **2.** (of color) same throughout, uniform —*n.* **3.** one's own person or individuality (*pl.* **selves**) —**'selfish** *a.* **1.** concerned unduly over personal profit or pleasure **2.** lacking consideration for others **3.** greedy —**'selfishly** *adv.* —**'selfless** *a.* **1.** having no regard to self **2.** unselfish

self- (*comb. form*) of oneself or itself. See the list above

self-abnegation *n.* denial of one's own interests

self-abuse *n.* **1.** misuse of one's own abilities *etc.* **2.** euphemism for **masturbation** (*see at* MASTURBATE)

self-aggrandizement *n.* act of increasing one's own power *etc.* —**self-aggrandizing** *a.*

self-assertion *n.* act of putting forward one's own opinions *etc.*, *esp.* in aggressive manner —**self-asserting** *a.* —**self-assertive** *a.*

self-assurance *n.* confidence in validity *etc.* of one's own opinions *etc.* —**self-assured** *a.*

self-conscious *a.* **1.** unduly aware of oneself **2.** conscious of one's acts or states

self-determination *n.* the right of person or nation to decide for himself or itself

self-discipline *n.* disciplining of one's own feelings, desires *etc.* —**self-disciplined** *a.*

self-educated *a.* educated through one's own efforts without formal instruction

self-effacement *n.* act of making oneself, one's actions *etc.* inconspicuous —**self-effacing** *a.*

self-employed *a.* earning one's living in one's own business —**self-employment** *n.*

self-expression *n.* expression of one's own personality *etc.* as in painting *etc.* —**self-expressive** *a.*

self-government *n.* government of country *etc.* by its own people —**self-governed** *a.* —**self-governing** *a.*

selfheal ('selfhēl) *n.* any of several European herbaceous plants reputedly having healing powers

self-important *a.* having unduly high opinion of one's own importance *etc.* —**self-importance** *n.*

self-improvement *n.* improvement of one's status, education *etc.* by one's own efforts

self-induced *a.* induced by oneself or itself

self-interest *n.* **1.** one's personal interest or advantage **2.** act of pursuing one's own interest

self-made *a.* having achieved wealth, status *etc.* by one's own efforts

self-opinionated *a.* **1.** having unduly high regard for oneself or one's own opinions **2.** clinging stubbornly to one's own opinions

self-possessed *a.* calm, composed —**self-possession** *n.*

self-propelled *a.* (of vehicle) provided with its own source of tractive power

self-respect *n.* proper sense of one's own dignity and integrity

self-righteous *a.* smugly sure of one's own virtue

self-rising *a.* (of flour) having leavening agent and salt already added

self-sacrifice *n.* sacrifice of one's own desires *etc.* for sake of wellbeing of others —**self-sacrificing** *a.*

selfsame ('selfsām) *a.* very same

self-satisfied *a.* having or showing complacent satisfaction with oneself, one's own actions *etc.* —**self-satisfaction** *n.*

self-sealing *a.* **1.** (*esp.* of envelope) designed to become sealed by pressure only **2.** (of tire) capable of sealing itself after being pierced

self-seeking *n.* **1.** act of seeking one's own profit or interest —*a.* **2.** having exclusive preoccupation with one's own profit or interest —**self-seeker** *n.*

self-service *a./n.* (of) restaurant *etc.* where customers serve themselves

self-starter *n.* **1.** electric motor used to start internal-combustion engine **2.** switch that operates this motor

self-styled *a.* claiming to be of specified nature, profession *etc.*

self-sufficient *or* **self-sufficing** *a.* **1.** sufficient in itself **2.** relying on one's own powers

self-will *n.* **1.** obstinacy **2.** willfulness —**self-willed** *a.* headstrong

self-winding *a.* (of wrist watch) winding automatically

sell (sel) *vt.* **1.** hand over for a price **2.** stock, have for sale **3.** make (someone) accept **4.** *inf.* betray, cheat —*vi.* **5.** find purchasers (**sold, 'selling**) —*n.* **6.** *inf.* hoax —**'seller** *n.* —**'sellout** *n.* **1.** disposing of completely by selling **2.** betrayal

seltzer ('seltsər) *n.* aerated mineral water

selvage *or* **selvedge** ('selvij) *n.* finished, nonfraying edge of cloth

selves (selvz) *n., pl. of* SELF

semantic (si'mantik) *a.* relating to meaning of words or symbols —**se'mantics** *pl.n.* (*with sing. v.*) study of linguistic meaning

semaphore ('semaför) *n.* **1.** post with movable arms for signaling **2.** system of signaling by human or mechanical arms

semblance ('semblans) *n.* **1.** (false) appearance **2.** image, likeness

self-abasement	self-confidence	self-evident	self-raised
self-absorbed	self-confident	self-explanatory	self-realization
self-absorption	self-contained	self-help	self-regard
self-addressed	self-control	self-indulgence	self-reliance
self-adhesive	self-deception	self-indulgent	self-reliant
self-appointed	self-defeating	self-inflicted	self-reproach
self-appraisal	self-defense	self-instructed	self-restraint
self-approbation	self-delusion	self-justification	self-righting
self-catering	self-denial	self-knowledge	self-selection
self-centered	self-doubt	self-pity	self-set
self-complacent	self-engrossed	self-portrait	self-supporting
self-confessed	self-esteem	self-preservation	self-taught

semen ('sēmən) *n.* fluid carrying sperm of male animals

semester (si'mestər) *n.* **1.** period of six months **2.** either of two usu. 18-week periods of academic instruction **—semester hour** unit of academic credit

semi- (*comb. form*) half, partly, not completely, as in *semicircle*

semiannual (semi'anyŏŏəl, semī-) *a.* **1.** occurring every half-year **2.** lasting for half a year **—semi'annually** *adv.*

semicircle ('semisərkəl) *n.* half of circle **—semi'circular** *a.* **—semicircular canal** *Anat.* any of three looped fluid-filled membranous tubes that comprise labyrinth of ear

semicolon ('semikōlən) *n.* punctuation mark (;)

semiconductor (semikən'duktər, semī-) *n.* **1.** substance, as silicon, having electrical conductivity that increases with temperature **2.** device, as transistor, dependent on properties of such substance

semidetached (semidi'tacht, semī-) *a./n.* (of) house joined to another on one side only

semifinal (semi'fīnəl) *n.* match, round *etc.* before final

Semillon (sāmi'yon) *n.* **1.** semisweet white wine **2.** grape used to make this wine

seminal ('seminəl) *a.* **1.** capable of developing **2.** influential, important **3.** rudimentary **4.** of semen or seed

seminar ('seminär) *n.* meeting of group (of students) for discussion

seminary ('semineri) *n.* **1.** college for priests **2.** finishing school for young women

Seminole ('seminōl) *n.* member of Amerindian people of Florida (*pl.* **-s, -nole**)

semiprecious (semi'preshəs, semī-) *a.* (of gemstones) having less value than precious stones

semiprofessional (semiprə'feshnəl, -shənəl; semī-) *a.* **1.** (of person) engaged in activity or sport part time but for pay **2.** (of activity or sport) engaged in by semiprofessionals **3.** of person whose activities are professional in some respects *—n.* **4.** semiprofessional person

semiskilled (semi'skild, semī-) *a.* partly skilled, trained but not for specialized work

Semite ('semīt) *n.* member of group of people now inhabiting the Middle East including Arabs and Jews **—Semitic** (si'mitik) *a.* **1.** of languages including Amharic, Arabic and Hebrew and speakers of these languages **2.** Jewish

semitone ('semitōn, 'semī-) *n. Mus.* difference in pitch between any two immediately adjacent keys on piano

semitrailer ('semitrālər, 'semī-) *n.* type of trailer that has wheels only at rear, front end being supported by towing vehicle

semivowel ('semivowəl) *n. Phonet.* vowel-like sound that acts like consonant, as (w) in *well* and (j), represented as *y*, in *yell* (*also* **glide**)

semolina (semə'lēnə) *n.* milled product of hard wheat used *esp.* for pasta

sempervivum (sempər'vīvəm) *n.* plant with ornamental rosettes of leaves

sempre ('semprā) *adv. Mus.* always; consistently

Sen. *or* **sen. 1.** senate **2.** senator **3.** senior

senate ('senit) *n.* **1.** upper council of state, university *etc.* **2.** (S-) upper house of U.S. Congress **—'senator** *n.* **—sena'torial** *a.*

send (send) *vt.* **1.** cause to go or be conveyed **2.** dispatch **3.** transmit (by radio) (**sent, 'sending**) **—'sendoff** *n. inf.* demonstration of good wishes to person about to set off on

journey *etc.* **—send-up** *n.* parody or imitation **—send off 1.** cause to depart **2.** *Soccer, rugby etc.* (of referee) dismiss (player) from field of play for some offense **—send up** *sl.* **1.** send to prison **2.** make fun of, *esp.* by doing parody of

Seneca ('senikə) *n.* (member of) Iroquoian-speaking Amerindian people of upper New York state (*pl.* **Seneca, -s**)

Senegal (seni'gôl) *n.* country in Africa bounded north and northeast by Mauritania, east by Mali, south by Guinea and Guinea-Bissau and west by the Atlantic Ocean with The Gambia forming an enclave on that shore **—Senegalese** (senigə'lēz) *n./a.*

senescent (si'nesənt) *a.* **1.** growing old **2.** characteristic of old age **—se'nescence** *n.*

senile ('sēnīl) *a.* showing weakness of old age **—senility** (si'niliti) *n.*

senior ('sēnyər) *a.* **1.** superior in rank or standing **2.** older *—n.* **3.** superior **4.** elder person **—seni'ority** *n.*

senna ('senə) *n.* **1.** tropical plant **2.** its dried leaves or pods, used as laxative

señor (sā'nyör; *Sp.* sā'nyor) *n.* Sp. title of respect, like Mr. (*pl.* **-s, -ñores** (*Sp.* -'nyorās)) **—se'ñora** *n.* Mrs. **—seño'rita** *n.* Miss

sensation (sen'sāshən) *n.* **1.** operation of sense, feeling, awareness **2.** excited feeling, state of excitement **3.** exciting event **4.** strong impression **5.** commotion **—sen'sational** *a.* **1.** producing great excitement **2.** melodramatic **3.** of perception by senses **—sen'sationalism** *n.* **1.** use of sensational language *etc.* to arouse intense emotional excitement **2.** doctrine that sensations are basis of all knowledge

sense (sens) *n.* **1.** any of bodily faculties of perception or feeling **2.** sensitiveness of any or all of these faculties **3.** ability to perceive, mental alertness **4.** consciousness **5.** meaning **6.** coherence, intelligible meaning **7.** sound practical judgment *—vt.* **8.** perceive **9.** understand **—'senseless** *a.* **—'senselessly** *adv.* **—sense organ** structure in animals that is specialized for receiving external stimuli and transmitting them to brain

sensible ('sensibəl) *a.* **1.** reasonable **2.** perceptible by senses **3.** aware, mindful **4.** considerable, appreciable **—sensi'bility** *n.* ability to feel, *esp.* emotional or moral feelings **—'sensibly** *adv.*

sensitive ('sensitiv) *a.* **1.** open to, acutely affected by, external impressions **2.** easily affected or altered **3.** easily upset by criticism **4.** responsive to slight changes **—'sensitively** *adv.* **—sensi'tivity** *or* 'sensitiveness** *n.* **—'sensitize** *vt.* make sensitive, *esp.* make (photographic film *etc.*) sensitive to light

sensor ('sensör, 'sensər) *n.* device that responds to stimulus

sensory ('sensəri) *or* **sensorial** (sen'söriəl) *a.* relating to organs, operation, of senses **—sensory deprivation** extended isolation accompanied by exclusion of sensory input such as light, sound and tactile impulses

sensual ('senchŏŏəl) *a.* **1.** of senses only and not of mind **2.** given to pursuit of pleasures of sense **3.** self-indulgent **4.** licentious **—'sensualism** *n.* **—'sensualist** *n.* **—sensu'ality** *n.*

sensuous ('senchŏŏəs) *a.* stimulating, or apprehended by senses, *esp.* in aesthetic manner

sent (sent) *pt./pp. of* SEND

sentence ('sentəns) *n.* **1.** combination of words, which is complete as expressing a thought **2.** judgment passed on criminal by court or judge *—vt.* **3.** pass sentence on, condemn **—sen'tential** *a.* of sentence **—sen-**

'tentious *a.* **1.** full of axioms and maxims **2.** pithy **3.** pompously moralizing **—sen'tentiously** *adv.* **—sen'tentiousness** *n.*

sentient ('senchiənt, -chənt; 'sentiənt) *a.* **1.** capable of feeling **2.** feeling **3.** thinking **—'sentience** *or* 'sentiency** *n.*

sentiment ('sentimənt) *n.* **1.** tendency to be moved by feeling rather than reason **2.** verbal expression of feeling **3.** mental feeling, emotion **4.** opinion **—senti'mental** *a.* **1.** given to indulgence in sentiment and in its expression **2.** weak **3.** of sentiment **—senti'mentalist** *n.* **—sentimen'tality** *n.* **—senti'mentalize** *v.*

sentinel ('sentinəl) *n.* sentry

sentry ('sentri) *n.* soldier on watch **—sentry box** small shelter in which sentry may stand to be sheltered from weather

sepal ('sēpəl, 'sepəl) *n.* leaf or division of the calyx of a flower

separate ('sepərāt) *vt.* **1.** part **2.** divide **3.** sever **4.** put apart **5.** occupy place between *—vi.* **6.** withdraw, become parted *—a.* ('seprit, 'sepərit) **7.** disconnected, apart **8.** distinct, individual *—'* **separable** *a.* **—separately** ('sepritli, 'sepəritli) *adv.* **—sepa'ration** *n.* **1.** disconnection **2.** *Law* living apart of married people without divorce **—'separatism** *n.* **—'separatist** *n.* person who advocates secession from organization, union *etc.* **—'separator** *n.* **1.** that which separates **2.** apparatus for separating cream from milk **—separate school C** school for a large religious minority

Sephardi (sə'färdi) *n.* **1.** Spanish or Portuguese Jew or descendant of Sephardim **2.** member of Ashkenazic Hasidim who use part of the Sephardic liturgy (*pl.* **Se'phardim**)

sepia ('sēpiə) *n.* **1.** reddish-brown pigment made from a fluid secreted by the cuttlefish *—a.* **2.** of this color

sepoy ('sēpoi) *n.* formerly, Indian soldier in service of Brit.

sepsis ('sepsis) *n.* presence of pus-forming bacteria in body

Sept. September

September (sep'tembər) *n.* 9th month

septennial (sep'teniəl) *a.* lasting, occurring every seven years

septet (sep'tet) *n.* **1.** music for seven instruments or voices **2.** group of seven performers

septic ('septik) *a.* **1.** of, caused by, sepsis **2.** (of wound) infected **—septicemia** (septi'sēmiə) *n.* blood poisoning **—septic tank** tank for containing sewage to be decomposed by anaerobic bacteria

septuagenarian (septyŏŏəji'neriən, septŏŏə-) *a.* **1.** aged between seventy and seventy-nine *—n.* **2.** person of this age

Septuagesima (septŏŏə'jesimə) *n.* third Sunday before Lent

septum ('septəm) *n. Biol., anat.* dividing partition between two tissues or cavities (*pl.* **-ta** (-tə))

septuple (sep'tyŏŏpəl, -'tŏŏ-; 'septəpəl) *a.* **1.** seven times as much or many **2.** consisting of seven parts or members *—vt.* **3.** multiply by seven **—sep'tuplicate** *n./a.*

sepulcher ('sepəlkər) *n.* tomb, burial vault **—se'pulchral** *a.* **1.** of burial, or the grave **2.** mournful **3.** gloomy **—'sepulture** *n.* burial

sequel ('sēkwəl) *n.* **1.** consequence **2.** continuation, *eg* of story

sequence ('sēkwəns) *n.* **1.** arrangement of things in successive order **2.** section, episode of film story **—'sequent** *or* se'quential** *a.*

sequester (si'kwestər) vt. 1. separate 2. seclude 3. put aside —**sequestrate** ('sēkwəstrāt, 'sek-; si'kwes-) vt. 1. confiscate 2. divert or appropriate income of (property) to satisfy claims against its owner —**seques-'tration** n.

sequin ('sēkwin) n. 1. small ornamental shiny disk on dresses etc. 2. formerly, Venetian gold coin

sequoia (si'kwoiə) n. giant Californian coniferous tree

seraglio (se'ralyō, -'räl-) or **serail** (sə'rī) n. harem, palace, of Turkish sultan (pl. **-s**)

seraph ('serəf) n. member of highest order of angels (pl. **-s, -aphim** (-əfim)) —**se'raphic** a.

Serbian ('sərbiən) a. 1. of Serbia, its people or their dialect of Serbo-Croatian —n. 2. dialect of Serbo-Croatian spoken in Serbia 3. native or inhabitant of Serbia (also **Serb**) —**Serbo-Croatian** or **Serbo-Croat** (-'krōat) n. 1. chief official language of Yugoslavia —a. 2. of this language which is written in the Cyrillic alphabet

serenade (seri'nād) n. 1. sentimental piece of music or song of type addressed to woman by lover, esp. at evening —v. 2. sing serenade (to)

serendipity (serən'dipiti) n. faculty of making fortunate discoveries by accident

serene (si'rēn) a. 1. calm, tranquil 2. unclouded 3. quiet, placid —**se'renely** adv. —**serenity** (si'reniti) n.

serf (sərf) n. one of class of medieval laborers bound to, and transferred with, land —**'serfdom** or **'serfhood** n.

serge (sərj) n. strong hard-wearing twilled worsted fabric

sergeant ('särjənt) n. 1. noncommissioned officer in army, air force or marine corps 2. police officer below captain —**sergeant major** title of three highest noncommissioned officers in army, air force and marine corps: sergeant major of the army etc. command sergeant major and sergeant major

series ('sēərēz) n. 1. sequence 2. set (eg of radio, TV programs with same characters, setting, but different stories) (pl. **-ries**) —**'serial** n. 1. story or play produced in successive episodes or installments 2. periodical publication —a. 3. of, in or forming a series —**'serialize** vt. publish, present as serial —**seriatim** (sēəri'ātim, -'atim) adv. one after another

serif ('serif) n. Print. small line finishing off stroke of letter

seriocomic (sēəriō'komik) a. mixing serious and comic elements —**serio'comically** adv.

serious ('sēəriəs) a. 1. thoughtful 2. earnest, sincere 3. of importance 4. giving cause for concern —**'seriously** adv.

sermon ('sərmən) n. 1. discourse of religious instruction or exhortation spoken or read from pulpit 2. any similar discourse —**'sermonize** vi. 1. talk like preacher 2. compose sermons

serotonin (sēərə'tōnin) n. compound found in many venoms and many tissues of the human body

serpent ('sərpənt) n. Lit. snake —**'serpentine** a. 1. like, shaped like, serpent —n. 2. any of several kinds of green-to-black rock

serrate ('serāt, sə'rāt) a. having notched, sawlike edge —**ser'rated** a. —**ser'ration** n.

serried ('serid) a. in close order, shoulder to shoulder

serum ('sēərəm) n. watery animal fluid, esp. thin part of blood as used for inoculation or vaccination (pl. **-s, -ra** (-rə)) —**se'rosity** n. —**'serous** a. of or producing serum —**serum sickness** allergic reaction to injected animal serums used for treatment or immunization

serval ('sərvəl) n. feline Afr. mammal

serve (sərv) vt. 1. work for, under 2. attend to (customers) in store etc. 3. provide 4. provide (guests) with (food etc.) 5. present (food etc.) in particular way 6. provide with regular supply of 7. pay homage to 8. go through (period of service etc.) 9. suit 10. Tennis etc. put (ball) into play —vi. 11. be member of military unit —n. 12. Tennis etc. act of serving ball —**'servant** n. personal or domestic attendant —**'service** n. 1. the act of serving, helping, assisting 2. system organized to provide for needs of public 3. maintenance of vehicle 4. use 5. readiness, availability for use 6. set of dishes etc. 7. form, session, of public worship —pl. 8. armed forces —vt. 9. overhaul —**'serviceable** a. 1. in working order, usable 2. durable —**'serving** n. portion of food or drink —**service charge** or **fee** percentage of bill added to total to pay for service —**'serviceman** n. 1. member of the armed forces 2. service-station attendant —**'serviceperson** n. —**service station** place supplying fuel, oil, maintenance for motor vehicles (also **filling station, gas station**) —**service tree** Eurasian rosaceous tree with white flowers and brown edible apple-like fruits

servile ('sərvil, -vīl) a. 1. without independence 2. cringing, fawning 3. menial —**ser'vility** n.

servitude ('sərvityōōd, -tōōd) n. bondage, slavery

servomechanism ('sərvōmekənizəm) n. device for converting small mechanical force into larger force, esp. in steering mechanisms

servomotor ('sərvōmōtər) n. motor that supplies power to servomechanism

sesame ('sesəmi) n. E Indian annual plant with seeds used as flavoring and for making oil

sesqui- (comb. form) one and a half, as in sesquicentennial

sessile ('sesīl) a. 1. (of flowers or leaves) having no stalk 2. (of animals such as barnacle) permanently attached —**sessility** (se'siliti) n.

session ('seshən) n. 1. meeting of court etc. 2. assembly 3. continuous series of such meetings 4. any period devoted to an activity

sestet (se'stet) n. 1. Prosody last six lines of sonnet 2. see SEXTET (sense 1)

set (set) vt. 1. put or place in specified position or condition 2. cause to sit 3. fix 4. point 5. put up 6. make ready 7. establish 8. prescribe, allot 9. put to music 10. (of hair) arrange while wet, so that it dries in position —vi. 11. become firm or fixed 12. (of sun) go down 13. have direction (**set, 'setting**) —a. 14. fixed, established 15. deliberate 16. formal 17. arranged beforehand 18. unvarying —n. 19. act or state of being set 20. bearing, posture 21. Rad., T.V. complete apparatus for reception or transmission 22. Theat., cine. organized settings and equipment to form ensemble of scene 23. number of things, persons associated as being similar, complementary or used together 24. Math. group of numbers, objects etc. with at least one common property —**'setback** n. anything that hinders or impedes —**set piece** 1. work of literature etc. intended to create impressive effect 2. display of fireworks —**'setscrew** n. screw that fits into coupling, cam etc. and prevents motion of part

relative to shaft on which it is mounted —**set-to** n. inf. brief disagreement or fight —**'setup** n. 1. position 2. organization —**set to** 1. begin working 2. start fighting —**set up** establish

sett or **set** (set) n. badger's burrow

settee (se'tē) n. 1. long seat with back support 2. sofa

setter ('setər) n. any of various breeds of sporting dog

setting ('seting) n. 1. background 2. surroundings 3. scenery and other stage accessories 4. act of fixing 5. decorative metalwork holding precious stone etc. in position 6. tableware and flatware for (single place at) table 7. descending below horizon of sun 8. music for song

settle¹ ('setəl) vt. 1. arrange, put in order 2. establish, make firm or secure 3. make quiet or calm 4. decide upon 5. end (dispute etc.) 6. pay 7. bestow (property) by legal deed —vi. 8. come to rest 9. subside and become firm or compact 10. become clear 11. take up residence 12. sink to bottom 13. come to agreement —**'settlement** n. 1. act of settling 2. place newly inhabited 3. money bestowed legally 4. subsidence (of building) —**'settler** n. colonist

settle² ('setəl) n. seat, usu. made of wood with high back and arms

seven ('sevən) a./n. cardinal number, next after six —**seven'teen** a./n. ten and seven —**'seventh** a. ordinal number of seven —**'seventy** a./n. ten times seven —**seven seas** all the oceans of the world —**seventh heaven** 1. final state of eternal bliss 2. state of supreme happiness

sever ('sevər) v. 1. divide —vt. 2. cut off —**'severance** n. —**severance pay** compensation paid by a firm to employee for loss of employment

several ('sevrəl) a. 1. some, a few 2. separate; individual 3. various 4. different —pron. 5. indefinite small number —**'severally** adv. apart from others

severe (si'vēər) a. 1. strict; rigorous 2. hard to do 3. harsh 4. austere 5. extreme —**se'verely** adv. —**severity** (si'veriti) n.

seviche (sə'vēchä) n. cubes of fish marinated in lime or lemon juice served as accompaniment or appetizer to main course or snack

sew (sō) v. 1. join (pieces of fabric etc.) with needle and thread —vt. 2. make by sewing (**sewed** pt., **sewed, sewn** pp., **'sewing** pr.p.) —**'sewing** n.

sewage ('sōōij) n. refuse, waste matter, excrement conveyed in sewer —**'sewer** n. underground drain to remove waste water and refuse —**'sewerage** n. 1. arrangement of sewers 2. sewage —**sewage farm** place where sewage is treated, esp. for use as manure

sex (seks) n. 1. state of being male or female 2. males or females collectively 3. sexual intercourse —a. 4. concerning sex —vt. 5. ascertain sex of —**'sexism** n. discrimination on basis of sex —**'sexist** n./a. —**'sexless** a. 1. having no sexual differentiation 2. having no sexual appeal or desires —**'sexual** a. —**'sexually** adv. —**'sexy** a. inf. provoking or intended to provoke sexual interest —**sex appeal** quality of attracting opposite sex —**sex change** change of sex, esp. involving medical or surgical treatment to alter sexual characteristics to those of opposite sex —**sex chromosome** chromosome determining sex of animals —**sexual intercourse** act in which male's penis is inserted into female's vagina

sex- (*comb. form*) six, as in *sextet*

sexagenarian (seksəji'neriən) *a.* **1.** aged between sixty and sixty-nine —*n.* **2.** person of this age

Sexagesima (seksə'jesimə) *n.* second Sunday before Lent

sextant ('sekstənt) *n.* navigator's instrument for measuring elevations of heavenly body *etc.*

sextet (seks'tet) *n.* **1.** music for six instruments or voices **2.** group of six performers

sexton ('sekstən) *n.* official in charge of a church, oft. acting as grave digger

sextuple (seks'työöpəl, -'töö-; 'sekstəpəl) *n.* **1.** quantity or number six times as great as another —*a.* **2.** six times as much or as many **3.** consisting of six parts or members —**sex'tuplet** *n.* **1.** one of six offspring born at one birth **2.** *Mus.* group of six notes played in time value of four

Seychelles (sā'shelz, sā'shel) *pl.n.* country lying in the Indian Ocean north of Madagascar comprising 112 islands and islets

SF *or* **sf** science fiction

sforzando (sför'tsändö) *Mus. a./adv.* **1.** to be played with emphasis —*n.* **2.** symbol, mark *etc.* indicating this

Sgt. Sergeant

sh (sh) *interj.* exclamation to request silence or quiet

shabby ('shabi) *a.* **1.** faded, worn, ragged **2.** poorly dressed **3.** mean, dishonorable **4.** dirty —'**shabbily** *adv.* —'**shabbiness** *n.*

shack (shak) *n.* rough hut —**shack up** (*usu.* **with** with) *sl.* live (*esp.* with lover)

shackle ('shakəl) *n.* (*oft. pl.*) **1.** metal ring or fastening for prisoner's wrist or ankle **2.** anything that confines —*vt.* **3.** fasten with shackles **4.** hamper

shad (shad) *n.* any of several important food fishes of N Amer. and Europe resembling herring

shade (shād) *n.* **1.** partial darkness **2.** shelter, place sheltered from light, heat *etc.* **3.** darker part of anything **4.** depth of color **5.** tinge **6.** ghost **7.** screen **8.** anything used to screen **9.** window blind —*pl.* **10.** *sl.* sunglasses —*vt.* **11.** screen from light, darken **12.** represent (shades) in (drawing) —'**shady** *a.* **1.** shielded from sun **2.** dim **3.** dubious **4.** dishonest **5.** dishonorable

shadow ('shadō) *n.* **1.** dark figure projected by anything that intercepts rays of light **2.** patch of shade **3.** slight trace **4.** indistinct image **5.** gloom **6.** inseparable companion —*vt.* **7.** cast shadow over **8.** follow and watch closely —'**shadowy** *a.*

shaft (shaft) *n.* **1.** straight rod, stem **2.** handle **3.** arrow **4.** ray, beam (of light) **5.** revolving rod for transmitting power **6.** one of the bars between which horse is harnessed **7.** entrance boring of mine

shag[1] (shag) *n.* **1.** matted wool or hair **2.** long-napped cloth **3.** coarse shredded tobacco —'**shaggy** *a.* **1.** covered with rough hair or wool **2.** tousled, unkempt

shag[2] (shag) *n.* any of various varieties of cormorant

shagreen (sha'grēn) *n.* **1.** rough skin of certain sharks and rays **2.** rough grainy leather made from certain animal hides

shah (shä) *n.* formerly, ruler of Iran

Shahaptian (shə'haptiən) *n.* Amerindian linguistic family of Oregon, Washington and Idaho

shake (shāk) *v.* **1.** (cause to) move with quick vibrations **2.** grasp the hand (of another) in greeting —*vi.* **3.** sway; totter —*vt.* **4.** upset **5.** wave, brandish (**shook**, '**shaken**) —*n.* **6.** act

of shaking **7.** vibration **8.** jolt **9.** *inf.* short period of time, jiffy —'**shaker** *n.* **1.** person or thing that shakes **2.** container from which condiment is shaken **3.** container in which ingredients of alcoholic drinks are shaken together —'**shakily** *adv.* —'**shaky** *a.* unsteady, insecure

shale (shāl) *n.* flaky, sedimentary rock

shall (shal; *unstressed* shəl) *v. aux.* makes compound tenses or moods to express obligation, command, condition or intention (**should** *pt.*)

shallot (shə'lot) *n.* kind of small onion

shallow ('shalō) *a.* **1.** not deep **2.** having little depth of water **3.** superficial **4.** not sincere —*n.* **5.** shallow place —'**shallowness** *n.*

shalom aleichem (shöləm ə'lākəm) *Hebrew* peace be to you: used by Jews as greeting or farewell (*oft. also* **shalom** (shä'löm))

sham (sham) *a./n.* **1.** imitation, counterfeit —*vi.* **2.** pretend —*v.* **3.** feign (-mm-)

shaman ('shämən) *n.* **1.** priest of shamanism **2.** medicine man of similar religion (*pl.* **-s**) —'**shamanism** *n.* religion of certain peoples of northern Asia, based on belief in good and evil spirits who can be controlled only by shamans

shamble ('shambəl) *vi.* walk in shuffling, awkward way

shambles ('shambəlz) *pl.n.* (*with sing. v.*) messy, disorderly thing or place

shame (shām) *n.* **1.** emotion caused by consciousness of guilt or dishonor in one's conduct or state **2.** cause of disgrace **3.** ignominy **4.** pity, hard luck —*vt.* **5.** cause to feel shame **6.** disgrace **7.** force by shame —'**shameful** *a.* disgraceful —'**shamefully** *adv.* —'**shameless** *a.* **1.** with no sense of shame **2.** indecent —'**shame'faced** *a.* ashamed

shammy ('shami) *n. see* CHAMOIS (sense 2)

shampoo (sham'pöö) *n.* **1.** any of various preparations of liquid detergent for washing hair, carpets *etc.* **2.** this process —*vt.* **3.** use shampoo to wash

shamrock ('shamrok) *n.* any three-leaved plant used as an Irish emblem

shamus ('shäməs, 'shāməs) *n. inf.* **1.** private detective **2.** caretaker of a synagogue

shandygaff ('shandigaf) *n.* mixed drink, *esp.* beer diluted with soft drink

shanghai (shang'hī) *vt.* force, trick (someone) into doing something

Shangri La ('shranggri 'lä) a place where life approaches perfection

shank (shangk) *n.* **1.** lower leg **2.** tibia **3.** stem of thing

shantung (shan'tung) *n.* soft, natural Chinese silk

shanty[1] ('shanti) *n.* **1.** temporary wooden building **2.** crude dwelling

shanty[2] ('shanti) *n.* sailor's song with chorus

shape (shāp) *n.* **1.** external form or appearance **2.** mold, pattern **3.** *inf.* condition, *esp.* of physical fitness —*vt.* **4.** form, mold, fashion, make —*vi.* **5.** develop (**shaped, 'shaping**) —'**shapeless** *a.* —'**shapely** *a.* well-proportioned

SHAPE (shāp) Supreme Headquarters Allied Powers Europe

shard (shärd) *or* **sherd** *n.* broken fragment, *esp.* of earthenware

share[1] (shāər) *n.* **1.** portion, quota, lot **2.** unit of ownership in public company —*v.* **3.** give, take a share (of) **4.** join with others in doing, using (something)

share[2] (shāər) *n.* blade of plow

shark (shärk) *n.* **1.** large usu. predatory sea fish **2.** person who cheats others

sharkskin ('shärkskin) *n.* stiff rayon fabric

sharp (shärp) *a.* **1.** having keen cutting edge or fine point **2.** keen **3.** not gradual or gentle **4.** brisk **5.** clever **6.** harsh **7.** dealing cleverly but unfairly **8.** shrill **9.** strongly marked, *esp.* in outline —*adv.* **10.** promptly —*n.* **11.** *Mus.* note half a tone above natural pitch **12.** *sl.* cheat, swindler —'**sharpen** *vt.* make sharp —'**sharper** *n.* person who cheats or swindles —'**sharply** *adv.* —'**sharpness** *n.* —**sharp practice** dishonest dealings —**sharp-set** *a.* **1.** set to give acute cutting angle **2.** keenly hungry —'**sharpshooter** *n.* marksman —**sharp-witted** *a.* having or showing keen intelligence

shatter ('shatər) *v.* **1.** break in pieces —*vt.* **2.** ruin (plans *etc.*) **3.** disturb (person) greatly

shave (shāv) *v.* **1.** cut close (*esp.* hair of face or head) —*vt.* **2.** pare away **3.** graze **4.** reduce (**shaved, 'shaven, 'shaving**) —*n.* **5.** shaving —'**shaver** *n.* **1.** person or thing that shaves **2.** electrical implement for shaving —'**shavings** *pl.n.* parings —**close** *or* **near shave** narrow escape

Shavian ('shāviən) *a.* **1.** of or like George Bernard Shaw, his works, ideas *etc.* —*n.* **2.** admirer of Shaw or his works

shawl (shöl) *n.* piece of fabric to cover woman's shoulders or wrap baby

Shawnee (shö'nē) *n.* **1.** member of Amerindian people orig. of the central Ohio valley (*pl.* **-ee, -s**) **2.** language of this people

she (shē) *pron.* 3rd person singular feminine pronoun

sheaf (shēf) *n.* **1.** bundle, *esp.* corn **2.** loose leaves of paper (*pl.* **sheaves**)

shear (shēər) *vt.* **1.** clip hair, wool from **2.** cut (through) **3.** fracture (**sheared** *pt.*, **shorn, sheared** *pp.*, '**shearing** *pr.p.*) —'**shearer** *n.* —**shears** *pl.n.* **1.** large pair of scissors **2.** any of various analogous cutting instruments

shearwater ('shēərwötər) *n.* any of various sea birds having long wings and a hooked bill

sheath (shēth) *n.* **1.** close-fitting cover, *esp.* for knife or sword **2.** enclosing structure of body or plant part **3.** close-fitting dress (*pl.* **sheaths** (shēdhz)) —**sheathe** *vt.* put into sheath

sheave (shēv) *n.* wheel with grooved rim, *esp.* one used as pulley

sheaves (shēvz) *n., pl. of* SHEAF

shebang (shi'bang) *n. sl.* situation, matter (*esp. in* **the whole shebang**)

shebeen *or* **shebean** (shə'bēn) *n.* **1.** *Irish, Scot.,* **SA** place where alcohol is sold illegally **2.** in S Afr., place where Black Afr. men engage in social drinking

shed[1] (shed) *n.* roofed shelter used as store or workshop

shed[2] (shed) *v.* **1.** (cause to) pour forth (*eg* tears, blood) —*vt.* **2.** cast off (**shed, 'shedding**)

sheen (shēn) *n.* gloss —'**sheeny** *a.*

sheep (shēp) *n.* ruminant animal bred for wool and meat (*pl.* **sheep**) —'**sheepish** *a.* embarrassed, shy —**sheep-dip** *n.* (deep trough containing) solution in which sheep are immersed to kill vermin and germs in fleece —'**sheepdog** *n.* any of various breeds of dog, *orig.* for herding sheep —'**sheepfold** *n.* pen or enclosure for sheep —'**sheepshank** *n.* knot *etc.* made in rope to shorten it temporarily

sheer[1] (shēər) *a.* **1.** perpendicular **2.** (of material) very fine, transparent **3.** absolute, unmitigated

sheer[2] (shēər) *vi.* deviate from course, swerve, turn aside

sheet[1] (shēt) *n.* 1. broad length of fabric to cover bed 2. broad piece of any thin material 3. large expanse —*vt.* 4. cover with sheet —**sheet music** printed copy of short composition or piece

sheet[2] (shēt) *n.* rope fastened in corner of sail —**sheet anchor** large anchor for emergency

Sheffield plate ('shefēld) objects made by fusing a thin sheet of silver to a thin sheet of copper

shegetz ('shāgits) *n.* a male goy

sheikh *or* **sheik** (shēk, shāk) *n.* Arab chief

shekel ('shekəl) *n.* 1. Hebrew weight and silver coin 2. (*oft. pl.*) *inf.* money, cash

shelf (shelf) *n.* 1. board fixed horizontally (on wall *etc.*) for holding things 2. ledge (*pl.* **shelves**) —**shelf life** length of time packaged food *etc.* will last without deteriorating

shell (shel) *n.* 1. hard outer case (*esp.* of egg, nut *etc.*) 2. husk 3. explosive projectile 4. outer part of structure left when interior is removed —*vt.* 5. take shell from 6. take out of shell 7. fire at with shells —**shellfish** *n.* any edible water animal with a shell —**shell shock** *see* **combat fatigue** at COMBAT —**shell out** *inf.* pay up

shellac (shə'lak) *n.* 1. resin usu. produced in thin plates for use as varnish —*vt.* 2. coat with shellac (-'lacked, -'lacking)

shelter ('sheltər) *n.* 1. place, structure giving protection 2. protection 3. refuge; haven —*vt.* 4. give protection to 5. act as shelter for —*vi.* 6. take shelter

shelve (shelv) *vt.* 1. put on a shelf 2. put off, defer indefinitely 3. cease to employ —*vi.* 4. slope gradually —**'shelving** *n.* 1. material for making shelves 2. set of shelves

shelves (shelvz) *n., pl. of* SHELF

shenanigan (shi'nanigən) *n. sl.* 1. frolicking 2. act of playing tricks *etc.*

shepherd ('shepərd) *n.* 1. man who tends sheep (**'shepherdess** *fem.*) —*vt.* 2. guide, watch over —**shepherd's-purse** *n.* plant with white flowers

sherbet ('shərbət) *n.* fruit-flavored frozen dessert

sherd (shərd) *n. see* SHARD

sheriff ('sherif) *n.* 1. law enforcement officer 2. **C** municipal officer who enforces court orders *etc.* —**'sheriffdom** *n.*

Sherpa ('shərpə) *n.* member of a Tibetan people (*pl.* **-s**, **'Sherpa**)

sherry ('sheri) *n.* fortified wine

Shetland pony ('shetlənd) very small sturdy breed of pony

shewbread *or* **showbread** ('shōbred) *n.* consecrated unleavened bread formerly placed in Tabernacle on Sabbath

shield (shēld) *n.* 1. piece of armor carried on arm 2. any protection used to stop blows, missiles *etc.* 3. any protective device 4. sports trophy —*vt.* 5. cover, protect

shift (shift) *v.* 1. (cause to) move, change position —*n.* 2. relay of workers 3. time of their working 4. evasion 5. expedient 6. removal 7. woman's underskirt or dress —**'shiftiness** *n.* —**'shiftless** *a.* lacking in resource or character —**'shifty** *a.* 1. evasive 2. of dubious character

shikse ('shiksə) *n.* a female goy

shillelagh *or* **shillala** (shə'lāli) *n.* in Ireland, cudgel

shilling ('shiling) *n.* 1. former Brit. coin, now 5p 2. monetary unit in various countries

shilly-shally ('shilishali) *vi.* 1. waver —*n.* 2. wavering, indecision

shim (shim) *n.* 1. thin washer used to adjust clearance for gears *etc.* —*vt.* 2. modify

clearance on (gear *etc.*) by use of shims (**-mm-**)

shimmer ('shimər) *vi.* 1. shine with quivering light —*n.* 2. such light 3. glimmer

shimmy ('shimi) *n.* 1. Amer. ragtime dance with much shaking of hips and shoulders 2. abnormal wobbling motion in motor vehicle

shin (shin) *n.* 1. front of lower leg —*v.* 2. climb with arms and legs —*vt.* 3. kick on shin (**-nn-**) —**'shin'bone** *n.* tibia

shindig ('shindig) *or* **shindy** ('shindi) *n. inf.* row; noisy disturbance

shine (shīn) *vi.* 1. give out, reflect light 2. perform very well, excel —*vt.* 3. cause to shine by polishing (**shone**, **'shining**) —*n.* 4. brightness, luster 5. polishing —**'shiner** *n.* 1. something that shines, such as polishing device 2. small N Amer. freshwater cyprinid fish 3. *inf.* black eye —**'shiny** *a.*

shingle[1] ('shinggəl) *n.* 1. wooden roof tile —*vt.* 2. cover with shingles

shingle[2] ('shinggəl) *n.* mass of pebbles

shingles ('shinggəlz) *n.* disease causing inflammation along a nerve

Shinto ('shintō) *n.* native Japanese religion characterized by the veneration of nature and of ancestors —**'Shintoism** *n.*

ship (ship) *n.* 1. large sea-going vessel —*vt.* 2. put on or send by ship —*vi.* 3. embark 4. take service in ship (**-pp-**) —**'shipment** *n.* 1. act of shipping 2. goods shipped —**'shipper** *n.* company *etc.* in business of shipping freight —**'shipping** *n.* 1. freight transport business 2. ships collectively —**'shipboard** *a.* taking place, used, or intended for use aboard ship —**'shipmate** *n.* sailor who serves on same ship as another —**'ship'shape** *a.* orderly, trim —**'shipwreck** *n.* 1. destruction of ship through storm, collision *etc.* —*vt.* 2. cause to undergo shipwreck —**'shipwright** *n.* artisan skilled in tasks required to build vessels —**'shipyard** *n.* place for building and repair of ships

-ship (*comb. form*) 1. state, condition, as in *fellowship* 2. rank, office, position, as in *lordship* 3. craft, skill, as in *scholarship*

shire horse ('shīər) large heavy breed of carthorse

shirk (shərk) *vt.* evade, try to avoid (duty *etc.*)

shirr (shər) *vt.* 1. gather (fabric) into parallel rows —*n.* 2. series of gathered rows decorating dress *etc.*

shirt (shərt) *n.* garment for upper part of body —**'shirty** *a. sl.* annoyed —**shirt-tail** *n.* part of shirt that extends below waist —**'shirtwaist** *n.* woman's garment with bodice resembling shirt

shish kebab (shish) *see* KABOB

shiver[1] ('shivər) *vi.* 1. tremble, usu. with cold or fear; shudder; vibrate —*n.* 2. act, state of shivering

shiver[2] ('shivər) *v.* 1. break in pieces —*n.* 2. splinter

shlemiel (shlə'mēl) *n. inf.* clumsy or unlucky person

shlep (shlep) *vt.* drag, carry (**-pp-**) —*n.* 2. unkempt person 3. petty thief 4. hobo, bum

shlock (shlok) *n. inf.* poor-quality article, junk, trash

shmalz (shmölts, shmolts) *inf. n.* 1. excessive sentimentality 2. rendered chicken fat —*vi.* 3. convey inappropriate emotion —*a.* 4. corny, mawkish, trite

shmeer (shmēər) *inf. n.* 1. bribe 2. the entire deal —*vt.* 3. spread, smear 4. bribe

shmoos (shmо̄о̄s) *inf. n.* 1. aimless, friendly chat —*vi.* 2. engage in a heart-to-heart talk

shnook (shno͝ok) *n. inf.* 1. *see* SHLEMIEL 2. timid, unassertive person

shnorer ('shnörər) *n. inf.* 1. cadger 2. chiseler, compulsive haggler —**shnor** *vi.* beg

shoal[1] (shōl) *n.* 1. stretch of shallow water 2. sandbank, sandbar —*v.* 3. make, become shallow

shoal[2] (shōl) *n.* 1. large number of fish swimming together —*vi.* 2. form shoal

shock[1] (shok) *vt.* 1. horrify —*n.* 2. violent or damaging blow 3. emotional disturbance 4. state of weakness, illness, caused by physical or mental shock 5. paralytical stroke 6. collision 7. effect on sensory nerves of electric discharge —**'shocker** *n.* person or thing that shocks or distresses —**'shocking** *a.* 1. causing shock, disgust *etc.* 2. *inf.* very bad or terrible —**shock absorber** device, *esp.* in automobiles, to absorb shocks —**shock therapy** *or* **treatment** treatment of certain psychotic conditions by injecting drugs or by passing electric current through brain

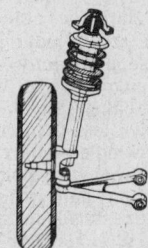

shock absorber

shock[2] (shok) *n.* group of corn sheaves placed together

shock[3] (shok) *n.* 1. mass of hair —*a.* 2. shaggy —**'shockheaded** *a.*

shod (shod) *pt./pp. of* SHOE

shoddy ('shodi) *a.* 1. worthless, trashy 2. second-rate 3. made of poor material

shoe (sho͞o) *n.* 1. covering for foot, not enclosing ankle 2. metal rim or curved bar put on horse's hoof 3. any of various protective plates or undercoverings —*vt.* 4. protect, furnish with shoe or shoes (**shod** *pt./pp.,* **'shoeing** *pr.p.*) —**'shoehorn** *n.* curved plastic or metal implement, inserted at back of shoe, used to ease in heel —**'shoestring** *a./n.* very small (amount of money *etc.*) —**'shoetree** *n.* wooden or metal block inserted into shoe to preserve shape

shofar ('shōfär, -fər) *n. Judaism* trumpet made from ram's horn, used by Jews throughout history to mark important occasions

shogun ('shōgən) *n.* Japanese hereditary military dictator and virtual ruler before 1868

shone (shōn) *pt./pp. of* SHINE

shoo (sho͞o) *interj.* 1. go away —*vt.* 2. drive away

shook (sho͝ok) *pt. of* SHAKE

shoot (sho͞ot) *vt.* 1. hit, wound, kill with missile fired from weapon 2. send, slide, push rapidly —*v.* 3. discharge (weapon) 4. photograph, film —*vi.* 5. hunt 6. sprout (**shot**, **'shooting**) —*n.* 7. young branch 8. shooting competition 9. hunting expedition —**'shooter** *n.* 1. person that shoots 2. revolver —**'shooting** *n.* sport in which small arms are fired for accuracy at stationary targets —**shooting star** *inf.* meteor —**shooting stick** device resembling walking stick, having spike at one end and folding seat at other

shop (shop) *n.* 1. place for retail sale of goods and services 2. workshop, works building —*vi.* 3. visit stores to buy (**-pp-**) —**'shopkeeper** *n.* person who owns or manages shop

—**'shoplifter** *n.* one who steals from shop —**shopping center 1.** area of town where most of shops are situated **2.** complex of stores, restaurants *etc.* with adjoining parking lot —**'shopsoiled** *a.* faded *etc.* from being displayed in shop —**shop steward** labor union representative of workers in factory *etc.* —**'shoptalk** *n.* conversation concerning one's work, *esp.* outside business hours —**'shopwalker** *n.* overseer who directs customers *etc.* —**talk shop** talk of one's business *etc.* at unsuitable moments

shore¹ (shōr) *n.* edge of sea or lake

shore² (shōr) *vt.* (*oft. with* up) prop (up)

shorn (shōrn) *pp. of* SHEAR

short (shört) *a.* **1.** not long **2.** not tall **3.** brief, hasty **4.** not reaching quantity or standard required **5.** wanting, lacking **6.** abrupt, rude **7.** friable —*adv.* **8.** suddenly, abruptly **9.** without reaching end —*n.* **10.** short circuit **11.** shortstop —*pl.* **12.** short trousers —**'shortage** *n.* deficiency —**'shorten** *v.* —**'shortening** *n.* butter, lard or other fat, used in cake mixture *etc.* to make pastry light —**'shortly** *adv.* **1.** soon **2.** briefly —**'shortbread** *n.* sweet, brittle cake made of butter, flour and sugar —**'shortcake** *n.* quick bread —**short-change** *vt.* **1.** give less than correct change to **2.** *sl.* cheat, swindle —**short circuit** faulty connection between two points in electric circuit, establishing path of low resistance through which excessive current can flow —**short-circuit** *v.* **1.** develop or cause to develop short circuit —*vt.* **2.** bypass (procedure *etc.*) —**'shortcoming** *n.* failing, defect —**short cut 1.** shorter route than usual one **2.** means of saving time or effort —**short-cut** *vi.* use short cut —**'shortfall** *n.* failure to meet requirement —**'shorthair** *n.* domestic cat with short dense coat —**'shorthand** *n.* method of rapid writing by signs or contractions —**short-handed** *a.* lacking the usual or necessary number of workers, helpers —**'shorthorn** *n.* short-horned breed of cattle with several regional varieties —**short-lived** *a.* living or lasting only for a short time —**short-range** *a.* of limited extent in time or distance —**short shrift** summary treatment —**short-sighted** *a.* **1.** relating to or suffering from myopia **2.** lacking foresight —**'shortstop** *n.* baseball player defending infield —**short-tempered** *a.* easily moved to anger —**short-term** *a.* **1.** extending over limited period **2.** *Fin.* extending over or maturing within short period of time —**short ton** ton (2000 lbs.) —**short wave** radio wave between 10 and 100 meters —**short-winded** *a.* **1.** tending to run out of breath, *esp.* after exertion **2.** (of speech or writing) abrupt —**have by the short hairs** *sl.* have at one's mercy

Shoshone (shə'shōni, shə'shōn, 'shōshōn) *or* **Shoshoni** (shə'shōni) *n.* **1.** group of Amerindian peoples *orig.* ranging through California, Colorado, Utah, Nebraska and Kansas **2.** member of any of these peoples (*pl.* **-s, -ne** *or* **-ni**) —**Sho'shonean** *n.* language family of Uto-Aztecan phylum

shot (shot) *n.* **1.** act of shooting **2.** missile **3.** lead in small pellets **4.** marksman, shooter **5.** try, attempt **6.** photograph **7.** short film sequence **8.** dose **9.** *inf.* injection —*a.* **10.** woven so that color is different, according to angle of light —*v.* **11.** *pt./pp. of* SHOOT —**'shotgun** *n.* **1.** firearm with unrifled bore used mainly for hunting small game —*a.* **2.** involving coercion or duress —**shot put** athletic event in which contestants hurl heavy metal ball as far as possible

should (shŏŏd) *pt. of* SHALL

shoulder ('shōldər) *n.* **1.** part of body to which arm or foreleg is attached **2.** anything resembling shoulder **3.** side of road —*vt.* **4.** undertake **5.** bear (burden) **6.** accept (responsibility) **7.** put on one's shoulder —*vi.* **8.** make way by pushing —**shoulder blade** either of pair of large triangular bones lying at upper back of body (*also* **scapula**) —**shoulder girdle** pectoral girdle

shout (showt) *n.* **1.** loud cry —*v.* **2.** utter (cry *etc.*) with loud voice

shove (shuv) *vt.* **1.** push **2.** *inf.* put —*n.* **3.** push —**shove off** *inf.* go away

shovel ('shuvəl) *n.* **1.** instrument for scooping, lifting earth *etc.* —*vt.* **2.** lift, move (as) with shovel —**'shoveler** *n.* duck with spoon-shaped bill

show (shō) *vt.* **1.** expose to view **2.** point out **3.** display, exhibit **4.** explain; prove **5.** guide **6.** accord (favor *etc.*) —*vi.* **7.** appear **8.** be noticeable (**showed, shown, 'showing**) —*n.* **9.** display, exhibition **10.** public spectacle **11.** theatrical or other entertainment **12.** indication **13.** competitive event **14.** ostentation **15.** semblance **16.** pretense —**'showily** *adv.* —**'showy** *a.* **1.** gaudy **2.** ostentatious —**show business** entertainment industry (*also* (*inf.*) **show biz**) —**'showcase** *n.* **1.** glass case used for displaying and protecting objects in museum *etc.* **2.** setting in which anything may be displayed to best advantage —**'showdown** *n.* **1.** confrontation **2.** final test —**'showman** *n.* **1.** one employed in, or owning, show at fair *etc.* **2.** one skilled at presenting anything in effective way —**show-off** *n.* —**'showpiece** *n.* **1.** anything exhibited **2.** anything prized as fine example of its type —**show off 1.** exhibit to invite admiration **2.** behave in such a way as to make an impression —**show up 1.** reveal **2.** expose **3.** *inf.* embarrass **4.** *inf.* arrive

shower ('showər) *n.* **1.** short fall of rain **2.** anything coming down like rain **3.** kind of bath in which person stands while being sprayed with water **4.** party to present gifts to a person —*vt.* **5.** bestow liberally —*vi.* **6.** take bath in shower —**'showery** *a.*

shrank (shrangk) *pt. of* SHRINK

shrapnel ('shrapnəl) *n.* **1.** shell filled with pellets which scatter on bursting **2.** shell splinters

shred (shred) *n.* **1.** fragment, torn strip **2.** small amount —*vt.* **3.** cut, tear to shreds (**shred** *or* **'shredded, 'shredding**)

shrew

shrew (shrōō) *n.* **1.** any of various small, insectivorous rodents having long, pointed nose and sometimes poor eyesight **2.** bad-tempered woman **3.** scold —**'shrewish** *a.* nagging

shrewd (shrōōd) *a.* **1.** astute, intelligent **2.** crafty

shriek (shrēk) *n.* **1.** shrill cry **2.** piercing scream —*v.* **3.** screech

shrift (shrift) *n.* **1.** confession **2.** absolution

shrike (shrīk) *n.* bird of prey

shrill (shril) *a.* **1.** piercing, sharp in tone —*v.* **2.** utter (words *etc.*) in such tone —**'shrilly** *adv.*

shrimp (shrimp) *n.* **1.** small edible crustacean **2.** *inf.* undersized person —*vi.* **3.** fish for shrimps

shrine (shrīn) *n.* place (building, tomb, alcove) of worship, usu. associated with saint

shrink (shringk) *vi.* **1.** become smaller **2.** retire, flinch, recoil —*vt.* **3.** make smaller (**shrank** *pt.,* **'shrunken, shrunk** *pp.,* **'shrinking** *pr.p.*) —*n.* **4.** *sl.* psychiatrist —**'shrinkage** *n.* —**shrink-wrap** *vt.* package (product) in flexible plastic wrapping designed to shrink about its contours

shrivel ('shrivəl) *vi.* shrink and wither

shroud (shrowd) *n.* **1.** sheet, wrapping, for corpse **2.** anything which covers, envelops like shroud —*pl.* **3.** set of ropes to masthead —*vt.* **4.** put shroud on **5.** screen, veil **6.** wrap up

Shrovetide ('shrōvtīd) *n.* the three days preceding Lent —**Shrove Tuesday** day before Ash Wednesday

shrub (shrub) *n.* bushy plant —**'shrubbery** *n.* plantation, part of garden, filled with shrubs

shrug (shrug) *vi.* **1.** raise shoulders, as sign of indifference, ignorance *etc.* —*vt.* **2.** move (shoulders) thus **3.** (*with* off) dismiss as unimportant (**-gg-**) —*n.* **4.** shrugging

shrunk (shrungk) *pp. of* SHRINK

shtetl ('shtetl) *n.* any of the former Jewish village communities of Eastern Europe, *esp.* in czarist Russia (*pl.* **shtetlach** ('shtetläk))

shuck (shuk) *n.* shell, husk, pod

shudder ('shudər) *vi.* **1.** shake, tremble violently, *esp.* with horror —*n.* **2.** shuddering, tremor

shuffle ('shufəl) *vi.* **1.** move feet without lifting them **2.** act evasively —*vt.* **3.** mix (cards) **4.** (*with* off) evade, pass to another —*n.* **5.** shuffling **6.** rearrangement —**'shuffler** *n.*

shul (shōōl) *n. inf.* synagogue

shun (shun) *vt.* **1.** avoid **2.** keep away from (**-nn-**)

shunt (shunt) *vt.* **1.** push aside **2.** divert **3.** move (train) from one line to another

shush (shush, shŏŏsh) *interj.* **1.** be quiet, hush —*vt.* **2.** silence or calm by saying "shush"

shut (shut) *v.* **1.** close —*vt.* **2.** bar **3.** forbid entrance to (**shut, 'shutting**) —**'shutter** *n.* **1.** movable window screen, usu. hinged to frame **2.** device in camera admitting light as required to film or plate —**'shuteye** *n. sl.* sleep —**shut down** close or stop (factory, machine *etc.*)

shuttle ('shutəl) *n.* **1.** instrument which threads weft between threads of warp in weaving **2.** similar appliance in sewing machine **3.** plane, bus *etc.* traveling to and fro over short distance —**'shuttlecock** *n.* small, light cone with cork stub and fan of feathers used in badminton

shy¹ (shī) *a.* **1.** awkward in company **2.** timid, bashful **3.** reluctant **4.** scarce, lacking (*esp.* in card games, not having enough money for bet *etc.*) —*vi.* **5.** start back in fear **6.** show sudden reluctance (**shied, 'shying**) —*n.* **7.** start of fear by horse —**'shyly** *adv.* —**'shyness** *n.*

shy² (shī) *vt./n.* throw (**shied, 'shying**)

Shylock ('shīlok) *n.* heartless or demanding creditor

shyster ('shīstər) *n. sl.* dishonest, deceitful person *esp.* lawyer

si (sē) *or* **ti** *n. Mus.* **1.** in fixed system of solmization, the note B **2.** in movable do system, the seventh note of a major scale

Si *Chem.* silicon

SI *Fr.* Système International (d'Unités): the 1960 revision of the International Metric System where the basic units of length, volume and mass are the meter, cubic meter and kilogram

Siam (sī'am) *n. former name of* THAILAND —**Sia'mese** *n./a.* —**Siamese cat** breed of cat with blue eyes —**Siamese twins** twins born joined to each other by some part of body

sibilant ('sibilənt) *a.* 1. hissing —*n.* 2. speech sound with hissing effect

sibling ('sibling) *n.* person's brother or sister

sibyl ('sibil) *n.* woman endowed with spirit of prophecy —**sibylline** ('sibilīn) *a.* occult

sic (sik) *Lat.* thus: used to indicate that something has been quoted exactly

sick (sik) *a.* 1. inclined to vomit 2. not well or healthy, physically or mentally 3. *inf.* macabre, sadistic, morbid 4. *inf.* bored, tired 5. *inf.* disgusted —**'sicken** *v.* 1. make, become sick —*vt.* 2. disgust; nauseate —**'sickening** *a.* 1. causing sickness or revulsion 2. *inf.* extremely annoying —**'sickly** *a.* 1. unhealthy 2. inducing nausea —**'sickness** *n.* —**'sickbay** *n.* place set aside for treating sick people, *esp.* in ships

sickle ('sikəl) *n.* reaping hook —**sickle cell anemia** inherited form of anemia in which large number of red blood cells become sickle-shaped

side (sīd) *n.* 1. one of the surfaces of object, *esp.* upright inner or outer surface 2. either surface of thing having only two 3. part of body that is to right or left 4. region nearer or farther than, or right or left of, dividing line *etc.* 5. region 6. aspect or part 7. one of two parties or sets of opponents 8. sect, faction 9. line of descent traced through one parent 10. *sl.* insolence, arrogance, pretentiousness —*a.* 11. at, in the side 12. subordinate, incidental —*vi.* 13. (*usu. with* with) take up cause (of) —**'siding** *n.* short line of rails on which trains or wagons are shunted from main line —**side arms** weapons carried on person, by belt or holster, such as sword, pistol *etc.* —**'sideboard** *n.* piece of furniture for holding dishes *etc.* in dining room —**'sideburns** *pl.n.* man's whiskers grown down either side of face in front of ears —**'sidecar** *n.* small car attached to side of motorcycle —**'sidekick** *n. sl.* close friend or follower —**'sidelight** *n.* light displayed by ships under weigh at night —**'sideline** *n.* 1. *Sport* boundary of playing area 2. subsidiary interest or activity —**'side'long** *a.* 1. lateral, not directly forward —*adv.* 2. obliquely —**'side-saddle** *n.* riding saddle orig. designed for women riders in skirts, who sit with both legs on same side of horse —**'sideshow** *n.* 1. small show offered in conjunction with larger attraction, as at circus 2. subordinate event —**'sideslip** *n.* skid —**'sidesman** *n. Anglican Ch.* man elected to help parish churchwarden —**'side'splitting** *a.* 1. producing great mirth 2. (of laughter) very hearty —**'sidestep** *v.* 1. step aside from or out of way of (something) —*vt.* 2. dodge —**side step** movement to one side, as in boxing *etc.* —**'sidetrack** *v.* 1. distract or be distracted from main topic —*n.* 2. digression —**'sidewalk** *n.* paved walk alongside street —**'sideways** *adv.* 1. to or from the side 2. laterally (*also* **'sidewise**)

sidereal (sī'dēəriəl) *a.* relating to, fixed by, stars

sidle ('sīdəl) *vi.* 1. move in furtive or stealthy manner 2. move sideways

SIDS sudden infant death syndrome

siege (sēj) *n.* besieging of town or fortified place

siemens ('sēmənz) *n.* derived SI unit of electrical conductance

sienna (si'enə) *n.* (pigment of) brownish-yellow color

sierra (si'erə) *n.* range of mountains with jagged peaks

Sierra (si'erə) *n.* word used in communications for the letter *s*

Sierra Leone (lē'ōn) country in Africa bounded northwest, north and northeast by Guinea, southeast by Liberia and southwest by the Atlantic Ocean —**Sierra Leonean** (lē'ōniən)

siesta (si'estə) *n.* rest, sleep in afternoon

sieve (siv) *n.* 1. device with network or perforated bottom for sifting —*vt.* 2. sift 3. strain

sift (sift) *vt.* 1. separate (*eg* with sieve) coarser portion from finer 2. examine closely

sigh (sī) *vi./n.* (utter) long audible breath —**sigh for** yearn for, grieve for

sight (sīt) *n.* 1. faculty of seeing 2. seeing 3. thing seen 4. view 5. glimpse 6. device for guiding eye 7. spectacle 8. *inf.* pitiful or ridiculous object 9. *inf.* large number, great deal —*vt.* 10. catch sight of 11. adjust sights of (gun *etc.*) —**'sightless** *a.* —**sight-read** *v.* play, sing (music) at first sight —**'sightsee** *v.* visit (place) to look at interesting sights —**'sightseeing** *n.*

sigma ('sigmə) *n.* 1. 18th letter in Gr. alphabet (Σ, σ or, when final, ς), consonant, transliterated as *S* 2. *Math.* symbol Σ, indicating summation

sign (sīn) *n.* 1. mark, gesture *etc.* to convey some meaning 2. (board, placard bearing) notice, warning *etc.* 3. symbol 4. omen 5. evidence —*vt.* 6. put one's signature to 7. ratify —*vi.* 8. make sign or gesture 9. affix signature —**sign language** any system of communication by signs, *esp.* used by deaf —**'signpost** *n.* 1. post bearing sign that shows way, as at roadside 2. something that serves as indication —*vt.* 3. mark with signposts

signal ('signəl) *n.* 1. sign to convey order or information, *esp.* on railroad 2. that which in first place impels any action 3. *Rad. etc.* sequence of electrical impulses transmitted or received —*a.* 4. remarkable, striking —*vt.* 5. make signals to —*vi.* 6. give orders *etc.* by signals —**'signalize** *vt.* make notable —**'signally** *adv.* —**signal box** 1. building containing signal levers for railroad lines 2. control point for large area of railroad system —**'signalman** *n.* railroad employee in charge of signals

signatory ('signətöri) *n.* one of those who sign agreements, treaties

signature ('signichōōər, -chər) *n.* 1. person's name written by himself 2. act of writing it —**signature tune** tune associated with particular program, person *etc.*

signet ('signit) *n.* small seal —**signet ring** finger ring bearing signet

significant (sig'nifikənt) *a.* 1. revealing 2. designed to make something known 3. important —**sig'nificance** *n.* 1. import, weight 2. meaning —**sig'nificantly** *adv.* —**signifi'cation** *n.* meaning —**significant figures** 1. figures of number that express magnitude to specified degree of accuracy 2. number of such figures

signify ('signifī) *vt.* 1. mean 2. indicate 3. denote 4. imply —*vi.* 5. be of importance ('signified, 'signifying)

signor *or* **signior** (sēn'yör; *It.* sēny'nyōr) *n. It.* title of respect, like Mr. (*pl.* -s, -gnori (*It.* -'nyōrē)) —**signora** (sēn'yörə; *It.* sēny'nyōra) *n.* Mrs. (*pl.* -s, -re (*It.* -rā))

—**signorina** (sēnyə'rēnə; *It.* sēnynyo'rēna) *n.* Miss (*pl.* -s, -ne (*It.* -nā))

Sikh (sēk) *n.* member of Indian religious sect

silage ('sīlij) *n.* fodder crop harvested while green and stored in state of partial fermentation

silence ('sīləns) *n.* 1. absence of noise 2. refraining from speech —*vt.* 3. make silent 4. put a stop to —**'silencer** *n.* device to reduce noise of firearm —**'silent** *a.*

silhouette (siloō'et) *n.* 1. outline of object seen against light 2. profile portrait in black

silica ('silikə) *n.* naturally occurring dioxide of silicon —**siliceous** *or* **silicious** (si'lishəs) *a.* —**sili'cosis** *n.* lung disease caused by inhaling silica dust over a long period —**silica gel** form of silica with property of great absorbency used to dry atmosphere and articles

silicon ('silikən) *n. Chem.* metalloid element *Symbol* Si, at. wt. 28.1, at. no. 14 —**'silicone** *n.* large class of synthetic substances, related to silicon and used in chemistry, industry and medicine —**silicon chip** *see* CHIP (sense 4)

silk (silk) *n.* 1. fiber made by larvae (**silkworm**) of certain moth 2. thread, fabric made from this —**'silken** *a.* 1. made of, like silk 2. soft 3. smooth 4. dressed in silk —**'silkily** *adv.* —**'silkiness** *n.* —**'silky** *a.* —**silk hat** man's top hat covered with silk —**silk-screen** *n.* stencil process of printing a design through screen of fine mesh cloth

sill (sil) *n.* 1. ledge beneath window 2. bottom part of door or window frame

sillabub ('siləbub) *n. see* SYLLABUB

silly ('sili) *a.* 1. foolish 2. trivial 3. feeble-minded —**'silliness** *n.*

silo ('sīlō) *n.* 1. pit, tower for storing fodder or grain 2. underground missile launching site (*pl.* -s)

silt (silt) *n.* 1. mud deposited by water —*v.* 2. fill, be choked with silt —**sil'tation** *n.* —**'silty** *a.*

Silurian (sī'lōōriən) *a.* 1. of or formed in third period of Paleozoic era, during which fishes first appeared —*n.* 2. Silurian period or rock system

silvan ('silvən) *a. see* SYLVAN

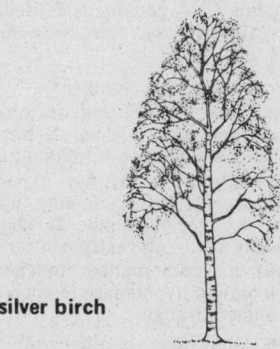

silver birch

silver ('silvər) *n.* 1. *Chem.* metallic element *Symbol* Ag, at. wt. 107.9, at. no. 47 2. things made of it 3. silver coins 4. flatware —*a.* 5. made of silver 6. resembling silver or its color 7. having pale luster, as moon 8. soft, melodious, as sound 9. bright —*vt.* 10. coat with silver —**'silvery** *a.* —**silver birch** tree having silvery-white peeling bark —**silver jubilee** 25th anniversary —**silver lining** hopeful aspect of otherwise desperate situation —**silver plate** 1. thin layer of silver deposited on base metal 2. articles, *esp.*

tableware, made of silver plate —**silver-plate** vt. coat (metal etc.) with silver —**silver point** method of drawing in which great delicacy is achieved by using a silver-tipped drawing implement —**silver screen** inf. **1.** motion-picture industry **2.** screen on to which movies are projected —**'silversmith** n. craftsman who makes articles of silver —**silver wedding** 25th wedding anniversary

silviculture ('silvikulchər) n. branch of forestry concerned with cultivation of trees

simian ('simiən) a. of, like apes

similar ('similər) a. resembling, like —**simi'larity** n. likeness, close resemblance

simile ('simili) n. comparison of one thing with another, using as or like, esp. in poetry

similitude (si'milityōōd, -tōōd) n. **1.** outward appearance, likeness **2.** guise

simmer ('simər) v. **1.** keep or be just bubbling or just below boiling point —vi. **2.** be in state of suppressed anger or laughter

simper ('simpər) v. **1.** smile, utter in silly or affected way —n. **2.** simpering smile

simple ('simpəl) a. **1.** not complicated **2.** plain **3.** not combined or complex **4.** ordinary, mere **5.** guileless **6.** stupid —**'simpleness** n. —**'simpleton** n. foolish person —**sim'plicity** n. **1.** simpleness **2.** clearness **3.** artlessness —**simplifi'cation** n. —**'simplify** vt. make simple, plain or easy (**-plified**, **-plifying**) —**sim'plistic** a. very simple, naive —**'simply** adv. —**simple fracture** fracture in which broken bone does not pierce skin —**simple interest** interest paid on principal alone —**simple-minded** a. **1.** stupid; feeble-minded **2.** mentally defective **3.** unsophisticated —**simple-mindedness** n. —**simple sentence** sentence consisting of single main clause

simulate ('simyəlāt) vt. **1.** make pretense of **2.** reproduce, copy (esp. conditions of particular situation) —**simu'lation** n. —**'simulator** n.

simultaneous (sīməl'tāniəs) a. occurring at the same time —**simultaneity** (sīməltə'nēiti) or **simul'taneousness** n. —**simul'taneously** adv.

sin¹ (sin) n. **1.** transgression of divine or moral law, esp. committed consciously **2.** offense against principle or standard —vi. **3.** commit sin (**-nn-**) —**'sinful** a. **1.** of nature of sin **2.** guilty of sin —**'sinfully** adv. —**'sinner** n. —**sin bin** C sl. penalty box used in ice hockey —**Sin City** Las Vegas, Nevada

sin² Math. sine

SIN C Social Insurance Number

since (sins) prep. **1.** during or throughout period of time after —conj. **2.** from time when **3.** because —adv. **4.** from that time

sincere (sin'sēər) a. **1.** not hypocritical, actually moved by or feeling apparent emotions **2.** true, genuine **3.** unaffected —**sin'cerely** adv. —**sincerity** (sin'seriti) n.

sine (sīn) n. mathematical function, esp. ratio of length of hypotenuse to opposite side in right-angled triangle

sinecure ('sīnikyōōər) n. office with pay but minimal duties

sine die ('sīni 'dīi) Lat. with no date, indefinitely postponed

sine qua non ('sini kwä 'non, 'sīni kwä 'non) Lat. essential condition or requirement

sinew ('sinyōō) n. **1.** tough, fibrous cord joining muscle to bone —pl. **2.** muscles, strength —**'sinewy** a. **1.** stringy **2.** muscular

sing (sing) vi. **1.** utter musical sounds **2.** hum, whistle, ring —vt. **3.** utter (words) with musical modulation **4.** celebrate in song or poetry (**sang, sung, 'singing**) —**'singer** n.

—**'singsong** n. **1.** informal singing session —a. **2.** monotonously regular in tone, rhythm

Singapore ('singgəpōr) n. country in Indian Ocean consisting of Singapore Island and 54 islets lying at southern tip of Malaysia —**Singaporean** (singgə'pōriən) n./a.

singe (sinj) vt. **1.** burn surface of (**singed, 'singeing**) —n. **2.** act or effect of singeing

Singh (sing) n. title assumed by Sikh on becoming full member of community

single ('singgəl) a. **1.** one only **2.** alone, separate **3.** unmarried **4.** for one **5.** formed of only one part, fold etc. **6.** denoting ticket for train etc. valid for outward journey only **7.** wholehearted, straightforward —n. **8.** single thing **9.** phonograph record with one short item on each side **10.** single ticket —vt. **11.** (with out) pick (out) —**'singleton** n. **1.** Bridge etc. original holding of one card only in suit **2.** single object as distinguished from pair or group **3.** Math. set containing only one member —**'singly** adv. —**single-breasted** a. (of garment) overlapping only slightly and with one row of fastenings —**single entry** Book-keeping entered in one account only —**single file** persons, things arranged in one line —**single-handed** a./adv. without assistance —**single-minded** a. having but one aim or purpose —**single-mindedness** n.

singular ('singgyələr) a. **1.** remarkable **2.** unusual **3.** unique **4.** denoting one person or thing —**singu'larity** n. something unusual —**'singularly** adv. **1.** particularly **2.** peculiarly

Sinhalese (singgə'lēz, sinhə-, sinə-) n. **1.** member of people living chiefly in Sri Lanka **2.** language of this people which is descended from Sanskrit —a. **3.** of this people or their language

sinister ('sinistər) a. **1.** threatening **2.** evil-looking **3.** wicked **4.** unlucky **5.** Her. on left-hand side

sink (singk) vi. **1.** become submerged (in water) **2.** drop, give way **3.** decline in value, health etc. **4.** penetrate —vt. **5.** cause to sink **6.** make by digging out **7.** invest (**sank** pt., **sunk, 'sunken** pp., **'sinking** pr.p.) —n. **8.** receptacle with pipe for carrying away waste water **9.** cesspool **10.** place of corruption, vice —**'sinker** n. weight for fishing line —**sinking fund** money set aside at intervals for payment of particular liability at fixed date

Sinn Fein ('shin 'fān) the movement for Irish independence —**Sinn Feiner** ('fānər) —**Sinn Feinism** ('fānizəm)

Sino- (comb. form) Chinese, of China, as in Sino-Tibetan

Sinology (sī'noləji) n. study of Chinese history, language, culture etc. —**Sinological** (sīnə'lojikəl) a. —**Si'nologist** n.

sinuous ('sinyōōəs) a. **1.** curving **2.** devious **3.** lithe —**'sinuate** a. —**sinu'osity** n.

sinus ('sīnəs) n. cavity, esp. any of air passages in bones of skull —**sinu'sitis** n. infection of air cavities of bones of skull connecting with nasal passages

Sion ('sīən) n. see ZION

Siouan ('sōōən) n. Amerindian language family spoken in northern Midwest, Montana and Oklahoma

Sioux (sōō) n. see DAKOTA

sip (sip) v. **1.** drink in very small portions (**-pp-**) —n. **2.** small drink

siphon ('sīfən) n. **1.** device, esp. bent tube, which uses atmospheric or gaseous pressure to draw liquid from container —vt. **2.** draw off thus **3.** draw off in small amounts

sir (sər) n. **1.** polite term of address for a man **2.** (S-) title of knight or baronet

sire ('sīər) n. **1.** male parent, esp. of horse or domestic animal **2.** term of address to king —vt. **3.** beget

siren ('sīərən) n. **1.** device making loud wailing noise, esp. giving warning of danger **2.** legendary sea nymph who lured sailors to destruction **3.** alluring woman

Sirius ('siriəs) n. brightest star in sky, lying in constellation Canis Major (also **Dog Star**)

sirloin ('sərloin) n. prime cut of loin of beef

sirocco (si'rokō) n. hot oppressive wind beginning in N Afr. and reaching S Europe (pl. -s)

sisal ('sīsəl) n. (fiber of) plant used in making ropes

siskin ('siskin) n. small olive-green bird of finch family

sissy ('sisi) a./n. weak, cowardly (person)

sister ('sistər) n. **1.** daughter of same parents **2.** woman fellow-member, esp. of religious body —a. **3.** closely related, similar —**'sisterhood** n. **1.** relation of sister **2.** order, band of women —**'sisterly** a. —**sister-in-law** n. **1.** sister of husband or wife **2.** brother's wife

sit (sit) vi. **1.** adopt posture or rest on buttocks, thighs **2.** perch **3.** (of bird) cover eggs to hatch them **4.** pose for portrait **5.** occupy official position **6.** hold session **7.** remain **8.** keep watch over baby etc. —vt. **9.** take (examination) (**sat, 'sitting**) —**'sitter** n. **1.** person or animal that sits **2.** person who is posing for portrait **3.** see baby-sitter at BABY —**'sitting** n. **1.** continuous period of being seated **2.** in canteen etc., such period during which one of two or more meals is served **3.** meeting, esp. of official body **4.** incubation period of bird's eggs during which mother sits on them —**sit-down** a. (of meal etc.) eaten while sitting down at table —**sit-down strike** strike in which employees refuse to leave their place of employment —**sit-in** n. protest involving refusal to move from place —**sitting duck** inf. person or thing in defenseless position —**sit down 1.** adopt sitting posture **2.** (with under) suffer (insults etc.) without protest —**sit in** protest by sit-in

sitar (si'tär) n. stringed musical instrument, esp. of India

site (sīt) n. **1.** place, location **2.** space for, with, a building —vt. **3.** locate in specific place

situate ('sichōōāt) vt. place, locate —**situ'ation** n. **1.** place, position **2.** state of affairs **3.** employment, post —**situation comedy** comedy based on humorous situations that could arise in day-to-day life

six (siks) a./n. cardinal number one more than five —**six'teen** n./a. six and ten —**sixth** a. **1.** ordinal number of six —n. **2.** sixth part —**'sixty** n./a. six times ten —**Six Counties** Northern Ireland —**six-shooter** n. inf. revolver with six chambers —**sixth sense** any supposed means of perception, such as intuition

size¹ (sīz) n. **1.** bigness, dimensions **2.** one of series of standard measurements of clothing etc. **3.** inf. state of affairs —vt. **4.** arrange according to size —**'sizable** or **'sizeable** a. quite large —**size up** inf. assess (person, situation etc.)

size² (sīz) n. **1.** gluelike sealer, filler —vt. **2.** coat, treat with size

sizzle ('sizəl) vi./n. (make) hissing, spluttering sound, as of frying —**'sizzler** n. inf. hot day

SK Saskatchewan

skat (skät, skat) n. card game of the euchre family for three, four or five players but with only three actually playing

skate¹ (skāt) n. **1.** steel blade attached to

boot, for gliding over ice —vi. 2. glide as on skates —'**skateboard** n. small board mounted on roller-skate wheels

skate²

skate² (skāt) n. large marine ray
skedaddle (ski'dadəl) vi. inf. scamper off
skein (skān) n. 1. quantity of yarn, wool etc. in loose knot 2. flight of wildfowl
skeleton ('skelitən) n. 1. bones of animal 2. bones separated from flesh and preserved in their natural position 3. very thin person 4. outline, draft, framework 5. nucleus —a. 6. reduced to a minimum 7. drawn in outline 8. not in detail —'**skeletal** a. —**skeleton key** key filed down so as to open many different locks
skeptic ('skeptik) n. 1. one who maintains doubt or disbelief 2. agnostic 3. unbeliever —'**skeptical** a. —'**skepticism** n.
skerry ('skeri) n. rocky island or reef
sketch (skech) n. 1. rough drawing 2. brief account 3. essay 4. short humorous play —v. 5. make sketch (of) —'**sketchy** a. 1. omitting detail 2. incomplete 3. inadequate
skew (skyōō) vi. 1. move obliquely —a. 2. slanting 3. crooked —'**skew'whiff** a. inf. 1. aslant 2. crooked
skewbald ('skyōōbôld) a. (esp. of horse) white and any other color (except black) in patches
skewer ('skyōōər, skyōōər) n. 1. pin to fasten meat together —vt. 2. pierce or fasten with skewer
ski (skē) n. 1. long runner fastened to foot for sliding over snow or water (pl. -s, ski) —vi. 2. slide on skis (**skied**, '**skiing**) —**ski jump** ramp overhanging slope from which skiers compete to make longest jump —**ski-jump** vi.
skid (skid) v. 1. (cause (esp. vehicle) to) slide (sideways) out of control with wheels not revolving (-dd-) —n. 2. instance of this 3. device to facilitate sliding, eg in moving heavy objects —**skid row** sl. dilapidated section of city inhabited by vagrants etc.
skiddoo or **skidoo** (ski'dōō) vi. go away. leave
skidoo (ski'dōō) n. C snowmobile
skiff (skif) n. small boat
skill (skil) n. practical ability, cleverness, dexterity —**skilled** a. having, requiring knowledge, united with readiness and dexterity —'**skillful** a. expert, masterly, adroit —'**skillfully** adv.
skillet ('skilit) n. small frying pan
skim (skim) vt. 1. remove floating matter from surface of (liquid) 2. glide over lightly and rapidly 3. read thus —vi. 4. move thus (-mm-) —**skim** or **skimmed milk** milk from which cream has been removed
skimp (skimp) v. 1. give short measure (on) 2. do (thing) imperfectly —'**skimpy** a. 1. meager 2. scanty
skin (skin) n. 1. outer covering of vertebrate body, lower animal or fruit 2. animal skin used as material or container 3. film on surface of cooling liquid etc. 4. complexion

—vt. 5. remove skin of (-nn-) —'**skinless** a. —**skinned** a. 1. stripped of skin 2. having skin of specified kind —'**skinner** n. 1. dealer in hides 2. furrier —'**skinny** a. thin —**skin-deep** a. 1. superficial 2. slight —**skin diving** underwater swimming using breathing apparatus —**skin flick** motion picture containing much nudity and explicit sex scenes —'**skinflint** n. miser, niggard —**skin graft** transplant of piece of healthy skin to wound to form new skin —'**skin'tight** a. fitting close to skin —**keep one's eyes skinned** watch carefully
skip¹ (skip) vi. 1. leap lightly 2. jump a rope as it is swung under one —vt. 3. pass over, omit (-pp-) —n. 4. act of skipping
skip² (skip) n. 1. large open container for builders' rubbish etc. 2. large bucket, container for transporting men, materials in mines etc.
skipper ('skipər) n. 1. captain of ship, plane or team —vt. 2. captain
skirl (skərl) n. sound of bagpipes
skirmish ('skərmish) n. 1. fight between small parties, small battle —vi. 2. fight briefly or irregularly
skirt (skərt) n. 1. woman's garment hanging from waist 2. lower part of woman's dress, coat etc. 3. outlying part 4. sl. woman —vt. 5. border 6. go round —'**skirting** n. material for women's skirts
skit (skit) n. satire, esp. theatrical burlesque
skittish ('skitish) a. frisky, frivolous
skittles ('skitəlz) pl.n. ninepins
skivvy ('skivi) n. female servant who does menial work
skua ('skyōōə) n. large predatory gull
skulk (skulk) vi. 1. sneak out of the way 2. lurk

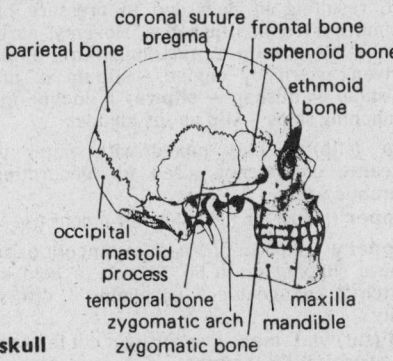

parietal bone — coronal suture — bregma — frontal bone — sphenoid bone — ethmoid bone — occipital — mastoid process — temporal bone — zygomatic arch — maxilla — mandible — zygomatic bone
skull

skull (skul) n. skeleton of head of vertebrate forming bony case protecting brain and chief sense organs and supporting jaw —**skull and crossbones** picture of human skull above two crossed thighbones, used as warning of danger or death —'**skullcap** n. close-fitting cap
skullduggery (skul'dugəri) n. inf. trickery

skunk

skunk (skungk) n. 1. small N Amer. animal which emits evil-smelling fluid 2. sl. contemptible person

sky (skī) n. 1. apparently dome-shaped expanse extending upward from the horizon 2. outer space 3. heavenly regions (pl. **skies**) —vt. 4. hit (cricket ball) high —'**skydiving** n. parachute jumping with delayed opening of parachute —**sky-high** a./adv. 1. at or to unprecedented level —adv. 2. high into air —'**skyjack** vt. hijack (an aircraft) —'**skylark** n. 1. lark, noted for singing while hovering at great height —vi. 2. inf. romp or play jokes —'**skylight** n. window in roof or ceiling —'**skyline** n. 1. line at which earth and sky appear to meet 2. outline of trees etc. seen against sky —'**skyscraper** n. very tall building —**blow sky-high** destroy
Skye terrier (skī) short-legged breed of terrier with long wiry hair
slab (slab) n. thick, broad piece
slack (slak) a. 1. loose 2. sluggish 3. careless, negligent 4. not busy —n. 5. loose part, as of rope —vi. 6. be idle or lazy —'**slacken** v. 1. make or become looser 2. make or become slower —'**slacker** n. person who evades work —'**slackly** adv. —**slack water** period of still water around turn of tide
slacks (slaks) pl.n. informal trousers worn by men or women
slag (slag) n. 1. refuse of smelted metal 2. sl. coarse woman —**slag heap** hillock of waste matter from coal-mining etc.
slain (slān) pp. of SLAY
slake (slāk) vt. 1. satisfy (thirst, desire etc.) 2. combine (lime) with water to produce calcium hydroxide
slalom ('släləm) n. race over winding course in skiing etc.
slam (slam) v. 1. shut noisily 2. bang —vt. 3. hit 4. dash down 5. inf. criticize harshly (-mm-) —n. 6. (noise of) this action 7. sl. jail (also '**slammer**) 8. Bridge winning of all tricks by one side
slander ('slandər) n. 1. false or malicious statement about person —v. 2. utter such statement (about) —'**slanderer** n. —'**slanderous** a.
slang (slang) n. 1. colloquial language —vt. 2. sl. scold, abuse violently
slant (slant) v. 1. slope —vt. 2. put at angle 3. write, present (news etc.) with bias —n. 4. slope 5. point of view 6. idea —a. 7. sloping, oblique —'**slantwise** or '**slantways** adv.
slap (slap) n. 1. blow with open hand or flat instrument —vt. 2. strike thus 3. inf. put (on, down) carelessly or messily (-pp-) —'**slap'dash** a. careless and abrupt —'**slaphappy** a. inf. 1. cheerfully irresponsible 2. dazed as if from repeated blows —'**slapstick** n. boisterous knockabout comedy
slash (slash) vt. 1. gash 2. lash 3. cut, slit 4. criticize unmercifully —n. 5. gash 6. cutting stroke
slat (slat) n. narrow strip of wood or metal as in blinds etc.
slate (slāt) n. 1. kind of stone which splits easily in flat sheets 2. piece of this for covering roof or, formerly, for writing on —vt. 3. cover with slates 4. abuse —'**slating** n. severe reprimand
slater ('slātər) n. woodlouse
slattern ('slatərn) n. slut —'**slatternly** a. slovenly, untidy
slaughter ('slôtər) n. 1. killing —vt. 2. kill —'**slaughterous** a. —'**slaughterhouse** n. place for killing animals for food
Slav (släv) n. member of any of peoples of E Europe or Soviet Asia who speak Slavonic language —**Sla'vonic** or '**Slavic** n. 1. branch of Indo-European family of languages, including Bulgarian, Russian, Polish, Czech etc. —a. 2. of this group of languages

slave (slāv) n. 1. captive, person without freedom or personal rights 2. one dominated by another or by a habit etc. —vi. 3. work like slave —'**slaver** n. person, ship engaged in slave traffic —'**slavery** n. —'**slavish** a. servile —**slave-driver** n. 1. esp. formerly, person forcing slaves to work 2. employer demanding excessively hard work from employees

slaver ('slavər) vi. 1. dribble saliva from mouth 2. fawn —n. 3. saliva running from mouth

slaw (slö) n. coleslaw

slay (slā) vt. 1. kill 2. inf. impress, esp. by being very funny (**slew, slain, 'slaying**)

sleazy ('slēzi) a. sordid

sled (sled) n. 1. vehicle on runners for sliding on snow 2. toboggan —v. 3. convey, travel by sled (**-dd-**)

sledge (slej) n. heavy hammer with long handle (also '**sledgehammer**)

sleek (slēk) a. glossy, smooth, shiny

sleep (slēp) n. 1. unconscious state regularly occurring in man and animals 2. period spend sleeping —vi. 3. take rest in sleep (**slept, 'sleeping**) —'**sleeper** n. 1. one who sleeps 2. railroad sleeping car —'**sleepily** adv. —'**sleepiness** n. —'**sleepless** a. —'**sleepy** a. —**sleeping bag** large well-padded bag for sleeping in, esp. outdoors —**sleeping car** railroad car fitted with compartments containing bunks for sleeping in —**sleeping partner** partner in business who does not play active role (also **silent partner**) —**sleeping pill** drug used to induce sleep —**sleeping sickness** Afr. disease spread by tsetse fly —'**sleepwalk** vi. walk while asleep

sleet (slēt) n. rain and snow or hail falling together

sleeve (slēv) n. 1. part of garment which covers arm 2. case surrounding shaft 3. phonograph record cover —vt. 4. furnish with sleeves —**sleeved** a. —'**sleeveless** a. —**have (something) up one's sleeve** have (something) prepared secretly for emergency

sleight (slīt) n. 1. dexterity 2. trickery 3. deviousness —**sleight of hand** 1. (manual dexterity in) conjuring, juggling 2. legerdemain

slender ('slendər) a. 1. of small width relative to length or height 2. feeble

slept (slept) pt./pp. of SLEEP

sleuth (slooth) n. 1. detective 2. tracking dog (also '**sleuthhound**) —vt. 3. track

slew (sloo) pt. of SLAY

slice (slīs) n. 1. thin flat piece cut off 2. share 3. flat culinary tool —vt. 4. cut into slices 5. cut cleanly 6. hit (ball) with bat etc. at angle

slick (slik) a. 1. smooth 2. smooth-tongued 3. flattering 4. superficially attractive 5. sly —vt. 6. make glossy, smooth —n. 7. slippery area 8. patch of oil on water

slide (slīd) vi. 1. slip smoothly along 2. glide, as over ice 3. deteriorate morally —v. 4. pass imperceptibly (**slid** (slid) pt., **slid, slidden** ('slidən) pp., '**sliding** pr.p.) —n. 5. sliding 6. surface, track for sliding 7. sliding part of mechanism 8. piece of glass holding object to be viewed under microscope 9. photographic transparency 10. ornamental clip to hold hair in place, hair slide —**slide rule** instrument of two parts, one of which slides upon the other, for rapid calculations —**sliding scale** schedule for automatically varying one thing (eg wages) according to fluctuations of another (eg cost of living)

slight (slīt) a. 1. small, trifling 2. not substantial, fragile 3. slender —vt. 4. disregard 5. neglect —n. 6. indifference 7. act of discourtesy —'**slightly** adv.

slim (slim) a. 1. small in width relative to height or length 2. small in amount or quality —v. 3. make or become slim by diet and exercise (**-mm-**)

slime (slīm) n. greasy, thick, liquid mud or similar substance —'**slimy** a. 1. like slime 2. fawning

sling (sling) n. 1. strap, loop with string attached at each end for hurling stone 2. bandage for supporting wounded limb 3. rope, belt etc. for hoisting, carrying weights —vt. 4. throw 5. hoist, swing by rope (**slung, 'slinging**) —'**slingback** n. shoe with strap instead of full covering for heel

slink (slingk) vi. move stealthily (**slunk, 'slinking**) —'**slinky** a. 1. sinuously graceful 2. (of clothing etc.) figure-hugging

slip¹ (slip) v. 1. (cause to) move smoothly, easily, quietly 2. pass out of (mind etc.) 3. (of motor vehicle clutch) engage partially, fail —vi. 4. lose balance by sliding 5. fall from person's grasp 6. (usu. with up) make mistake 7. decline in health, morals —vt. 8. put on or take off easily, quickly 9. let go (anchor etc.) 10. dislocate (bone) (**-pp-**) —n. 11. act or occasion of slipping 12. mistake 13. petticoat 14. small piece of paper 15. plant cutting 16. launching slope on which ships are built 17. covering for pillow —'**slippy** a. see SLIPPERY (sense 1) —'**slipknot** n. knot tied so that it will slip along rope round which it is made (also **running knot**) —**slip-on** a. 1. (of garment or shoe) easily put on or removed —n. 2. slip-on garment or shoe —**slipped disk** herniated intervertebral disk, oft. resulting in pain due to pressure on spinal nerves —'**slipshod** a. slovenly, careless —'**slipstream** n. Aviation stream of air driven astern by engine —**slip-up** n. inf. mistake or mishap —'**slipway** n. incline for launching ships —**slip up** inf. blunder

slip² (slip) n. clay mixed with water to creamy consistency, used for decorating ceramic ware

slipper ('slipər) n. light shoe for indoor use

slippery ('slipəri, -pri) a. 1. so smooth as to cause slipping or to be difficult to hold or catch 2. changeable 3. unreliable 4. crafty, wily

slit (slit) vt. 1. make long straight cut in 2. cut in strips (**slit, 'slitting**) —n. 3. long narrow cut or opening

slither ('slidhər) vi. slide unsteadily (down slope etc.)

sliver ('slivər) n. 1. thin small piece torn off something 2. splinter

slivovitz ('slivəvits, 'slē-) n. plum brandy

slob (slob) n. inf. stupid, coarse person

slobber ('slobər) or **slabber** ('slabər) vi. 1. slaver 2. be weakly and excessively demonstrative —n. 3. running saliva 4. maudlin speech —'**slobbery** or '**slabbery** a.

slob ice C sludgy masses of floating ice

sloe (slō) n. blue-black, sour fruit of blackthorn —**sloe-eyed** a. having dark slanted or almond-shaped eyes

slog (slog) vt. 1. hit vigorously, esp. at cricket —vi. 2. work or study with dogged determination 3. move, work with difficulty (**-gg-**) —n. 4. tiring walk 5. long exhausting work 6. heavy blow

slogan ('slōgən) n. distinctive phrase (in advertising etc.)

sloop (sloop) n. 1. small one-masted vessel 2. Hist. small warship

slop (slop) vi. 1. spill —vt. 2. spill, splash (**-pp-**) —n. 3. liquid spilt 4. liquid food 5. dirty liquid —pl. 6. liquid refuse —'**sloppy** a. 1. careless, untidy 2. sentimental 3. wet, muddy

slope (slōp) vt. 1. place slanting —vi. 2. lie in, follow an inclined course 3. go furtively —n. 4. inclined portion of ground 5. upward, downward inclination

slosh (slosh) n. 1. watery mud, snow etc. 2. sl. heavy blow —v. 3. splash —vt. 4. hit —**sloshed** a. sl. drunk

slot (slot) n. 1. narrow hole or depression 2. slit for coins —vt. 3. put in slot 4. sort 5. inf. place in series, organization (**-tt-**) —**slot machine** automatic machine worked by insertion of coin

sloth (slōth, slôth) n. 1. sluggish S Amer. animal 2. sluggishness —'**slothful** a. lazy, idle

slouch (slowch) vi. 1. walk, sit etc. in lazy or ungainly, drooping manner —n. 2. drooping bearing 3. incompetent or slovenly person —a. 4. (of hat) with wide, flexible brim

slough¹ (sloo) n. 1. bog 2. (sloo, slow) C hole where water collects

slough² (sluf) n. skin shed by snake —v. 2. shed (skin) —**slough off** cast off (cares etc.)

sloven ('sluvən) n. dirty, untidy person —'**slovenly** a. 1. untidy 2. careless 3. disorderly —adv. 4. in slovenly manner

slow (slō) a. 1. lasting a long time 2. moving at low speed 3. behind the true time 4. dull —v. 5. (cause to) decrease in speed —'**slowly** adv. —'**slowness** n. —'**slowcoach** n. person slow in moving, acting, deciding etc. —**slow-motion** a. (of motion-picture or television image) showing movement greatly slowed down

slowworm ('slōwərm) n. small legless lizard, blindworm

sludge (sluj) n. 1. slush, ooze 2. sewage

slue (sloo) n. see SLOUGH¹ (sense 2)

slug¹ (slug) n. 1. land snail with no shell 2. bullet —'**sluggard** n. lazy, idle person —'**sluggish** a. 1. slow 2. lazy, inert 3. not functioning well —'**sluggishness** n.

slug² (slug) vt. 1. hit, slog (**-gg-**) —n. 2. heavy blow 3. portion of spirits —'**slugger** n. hard-hitting boxer, slogger

sluice (sloos) n. 1. gate, door to control flow of water —vt. 2. pour water over, through

slum (slum) n. 1. squalid street or neighborhood —vi. 2. visit slums (**-mm-**)

slumber ('slumbər) vi./n. sleep —'**slumberer** n.

slump (slump) vi. 1. fall heavily 2. relax ungracefully 3. decline suddenly in value, volume or esteem —n. 4. sudden decline 5. (of prices etc.) sharp fall 6. depression

slung (slung) pt./pp. of SLING

slunk (slungk) pt./pp. of SLINK

slur (slər) vt. 1. pass over lightly 2. run together (words, musical notes) 3. disparage (**-rr-**) —n. 4. slight, stigma 5. Mus. curved line above or below notes to be slurred

slurp (slərp) v. inf. eat, drink noisily

slurry ('sluri) n. muddy liquid mixture, such as cement, mud etc.

slush (slush) n. 1. watery, muddy substance 2. excess sentimentality —**slush fund** fund for financing bribery, corruption

slut (slut) n. dirty (immoral) woman —'**sluttish** a. —'**sluttishness** n.

sly (slī) a. 1. wily, knowing 2. secret, deceitful —'**slyly** or '**slily** adv. —'**slyness** n.

Sm Chem. samarium

smack¹ (smak) n. 1. taste, flavor 2. sl. heroin —vi. (with of) 3. have taste (of) 4. be suggestive (of)

smack² (smak) *vt.* **1.** slap **2.** open and close (lips) with loud sound —*n.* **3.** smacking slap **4.** crack **5.** such sound **6.** loud kiss —*adv.* **7.** *inf.* squarely; directly —**'smacker** *n. sl.* **1.** loud kiss **2.** pound note or dollar bill

smack³ (smak) *n.* small sailing vessel, usu. for fishing

small (smöl) *a.* **1.** little **2.** unimportant; petty **3.** short **4.** weak **5.** mean —*n.* **6.** small slender part, *esp.* of the back —*pl.* **7.** *inf.* personal laundry, underwear —**'smallness** *n.* —**small change 1.** coins, *esp.* those of low value **2.** *rare* person or thing of little importance —**small hours** hours just after midnight —**small-minded** *a.* having narrow views; petty —**'smallpox** *n.* contagious disease —**small-scale** *a.* **1.** of limited size **2.** (of map *etc.*) giving small representation of something —**small slam** *Bridge* bidding for and winning twelve tricks (*also* **little slam**) —**small talk** light, polite conversation —**small-time** *a. inf.* insignificant; petty —**small-timer** *n.*

smarm (smärm) *vi. inf.* fawn —**'smarmy** *a. inf.* unpleasantly suave; fawning

smart (smärt) *a.* **1.** astute **2.** brisk **3.** clever, witty **4.** impertinent **5.** well dressed **6.** fashionable **7.** causing stinging pain —*v.* **8.** feel, cause pain —*n.* **9.** sharp pain —**'smarten** *v.* —**'smartly** *adv.* —**'smartness** *n.* —**smart aleck** (ʹalik) *or* **ass** *inf.* conceited person, know-it-all

smash (smash) *vt.* **1.** break violently **2.** strike hard **3.** ruin **4.** destroy —*vi.* **5.** break **6.** dash violently —*n.* **7.** heavy blow **8.** collision (of vehicles *etc.*) **9.** total financial failure **10.** *inf.* popular success —**smashed** *a. sl.* very drunk or affected by drugs —**'smasher** *n. inf.* attractive person, thing —**'smashing** *a.* excellent

smattering (ʹsmatəring) *n.* slight superficial knowledge

smear (smeər) *vt.* **1.** rub with grease *etc.* **2.** smudge, spread with dirt, grease *etc.* —*n.* **3.** mark made thus **4.** sample of secretion for medical examination **5.** slander

smell (smel) *vt.* **1.** perceive by nose **2.** *fig.* suspect —*vi.* **3.** give out odor **4.** use nose (**smelt** *or* **smelled, 'smelling**) —*n.* **5.** faculty of perceiving odors by nose **6.** anything detected by sense of smell —**'smelly** *a.* with strong (unpleasant) smell —**smelling salts** preparation of ammonium carbonate that has stimulant action when sniffed in cases of faintness *etc.*

smelt¹ (smelt) *vt.* extract (metal) from (ore) —**'smeltery** *n.*

smelt² (smelt) *n.* fish of salmon family

smew (smyōō) *n.* type of duck

smilax (ʹsmīlaks) *n.* **1.** climbing shrub having slightly lobed leaves and berry-like fruits **2.** much branched vine of S Afr. with glossy green foliage

smile (smīl) *n.* **1.** curving or parting of lips in pleased or amused expression —*vi.* **2.** wear, assume a smile **3.** (*with* on) approve, favor

smirch (smərch) *vt.* **1.** dirty, sully **2.** disgrace, discredit —*n.* **3.** stain **4.** disgrace

smirk (smərk) *n.* **1.** smile expressing scorn, smugness —*vi.* **2.** give such smile

smite (smīt) *vt.* **1.** strike **2.** attack **3.** afflict **4.** affect, *esp.* with love or fear (**smote, 'smitten, 'smiting**)

smith (smith) *n.* worker in iron, gold *etc.* —**smithy** (ʹsmithi, ʹsmidhi) *n.* blacksmith's workshop

smithereens (smidhəʹrēnz) *pl.n.* small bits

smitten (ʹsmitən) *pp. of* SMITE

smock (smok) *n.* **1.** loose outer garment —*vt.* **2.** gather by sewing in honeycomb pattern

smog (smog) *n.* mixture of smoke and fog

smoke (smōk) *n.* **1.** cloudy mass of suspended particles that rises from fire or anything burning **2.** spell of tobacco smoking —*vi.* **3.** give off smoke **4.** inhale and expel tobacco smoke —*vt.* **5.** use (tobacco) by smoking **6.** expose to smoke (*esp.* in curing fish *etc.*) —**'smoker** *n.* —**'smokily** *adv.* —**'smoky** *a.* —**smoke screen 1.** *Mil.* cloud of smoke produced to obscure movements **2.** something said or done to conceal truth —**'smokestack** *n.* chimney that conveys smoke into air

smolder (ʹsmōldər) *vi.* **1.** burn slowly without flame **2.** (of feelings) exist in suppressed state

smolt (smōlt) *n.* young salmon at stage when it migrates from fresh water to sea

smooch (smōōch) *vi./n. inf.* kiss, cuddle

smooth (smōōdh) *a.* **1.** not rough, even of surface or texture **2.** sinuous **3.** flowing **4.** calm, soft, soothing **5.** suave, plausible **6.** free from jolts —*vt.* **7.** make smooth **8.** quieten —**'smoothly** *adv.* —**smooth-spoken** *a.* speaking in gently persuasive manner —**smooth-tongued** *a.* suave or persuasive in speech

smorgasbord (ʹsmörgəsbörd) *n.* buffet meal of assorted dishes

smote (smōt) *pt. of* SMITE

smother (ʹsmudhər) *vt.* **1.** suffocate by cutting off from air **2.** envelop **3.** suppress —*vi.* **4.** be suffocated by being cut off from air

smudge (smuj) *vt.* **1.** make smear, stain, dirty mark on —*n.* **2.** smear or dirty mark

smug (smug) *a.* self-satisfied, complacent

smuggle (ʹsmugəl) *vt.* **1.** import, export without paying customs duties **2.** conceal, take secretly

smut (smut) *n.* **1.** piece of soot, particle of dirt **2.** lewd or obscene talk *etc.* **3.** disease of grain —*vt.* **4.** blacken, smudge (-tt-) —**'smutty** *a.* **1.** soiled with smut, soot **2.** obscene, lewd

Sn *Chem.* tin

snack (snak) *n.* light, hasty meal —**snack bar** bar at which snacks are served

snaffle (ʹsnafəl) *n.* **1.** jointed bit for bridle —*vt.* **2.** put snaffle on

snag (snag) *n.* **1.** difficulty **2.** sharp protuberance **3.** hole, loop in fabric caused by sharp object **4.** obstacle (*eg* tree branch *etc.* in river bed) —*vt.* **5.** catch, damage on snag (-gg-)

snail (snāl) *n.* **1.** slow-moving mollusk with shell **2.** slow, sluggish person —**snail-like** *a.* —**snail fever** *see* SCHISTOSOMIASIS —**snail's pace** very slow rate

snake (snāk) *n.* **1.** long scaly limbless reptile —*vi.* **2.** move like snake —**'snaky** *a.* of, like snakes —**snake charmer** entertainer who appears to charm snakes by playing music —**snakes and ladders** obstacle game governed by throw of dice and instructions printed on the board on which it is played

snap (snap) *v.* **1.** break suddenly **2.** (cause to) make cracking sound **3.** bite (at) suddenly **4.** speak (words) suddenly, angrily (-pp-) —*n.* **5.** act of snapping **6.** fastener **7.** *inf.* snapshot **8.** *inf.* easy task **9.** brief period, *esp.* of cold weather —*a.* **10.** sudden, unplanned, arranged quickly —**'snapper** *n.* **1.** perchlike fish **2.** decorated paper tube filled with party favors which pops when pulled apart —**'snappy** *a.* **1.** irritable **2.** *sl.* quick **3.** *sl.* well-dressed, fashionable —**'snapdragon** *n.* plant with flowers that can be opened like a mouth —**snap fastener** fastening device with projecting knob on one part that snaps into hole on other part —**'snapshot** *n.* photograph

snare¹ (snaər) *n.* **1.** (noose used as) trap —*vt.* **2.** catch with one

snare² (snaər) *n. Mus.* set of gut strings wound with wire fitted across bottom of drum to increase vibration —**snare drum** cylindrical double-headed drum with snares

snarl (snärl) *n.* **1.** growl of angry dog **2.** tangle, knot —*vi.* **3.** utter snarl **4.** grumble —**snarl-up** *n. inf.* confusion, obstruction, *esp.* traffic jam

snatch (snach) *vt.* **1.** make quick grab or bite at **2.** seize, catch —*n.* **3.** grab **4.** fragment **5.** short spell

snazzy (ʹsnazi) *a. inf.* stylish, flashy

sneak (snēk) *vi.* **1.** slink **2.** move about furtively **3.** act in mean, underhand manner —*n.* **4.** mean, treacherous person **5.** petty informer —**'sneaking** *a.* secret but persistent —**sneak thief** person who steals articles from premises which he enters through open windows *etc.*

sneakers (ʹsnēkərz) *pl.n.* canvas shoes with flexible soles

sneer (snēər) *n.* **1.** scornful, contemptuous expression or remark —*vi.* **2.** assume scornful expression —*v.* **3.** speak or utter contemptuously

sneeze (snēz) *vi.* **1.** emit breath through nose with sudden involuntary spasm and noise —*n.* **2.** sound or act of sneezing

snicker (ʹsnikər) *see* SNIGGER

snide (snīd) *a.* malicious, supercilious

sniff (snif) *vi.* **1.** inhale through nose with sharp hiss **2.** (*with* at) express disapproval *etc.* by sniffing —*vt.* **3.** take up through nose **4.** smell —*n.* **5.** act or sound of sniffing —**'sniffle** *vi.* sniff noisily through nose, *esp.* when suffering from a cold in the head, snuffle

snifter (ʹsniftər) *n.* **1.** pear-shaped glass with bowl that narrows toward the top so that aroma of brandy *etc.* is retained **2.** *inf.* small alcoholic drink

snigger (ʹsnigər) *n.* **1.** sly, disrespectful laugh, *esp.* partly stifled —*vi.* **2.** utter such laugh

snip (snip) *v.* **1.** cut (bits off) (-pp-) —*n.* **2.** act, sound of snipping **3.** bit cut off **4.** *inf.* bargain **5.** *inf.* certainty —**'snippet** *n.* shred, fragment, clipping —**snips** *pl.n.* tool for cutting

snipe (snīp) *n.* **1.** wading bird —*v.* **2.** shoot at (enemy) from cover **3.** (*with* at) criticize, attack (person) slyly —**'sniper** *n.*

snitch (snich) *inf. vt.* **1.** steal —*vi.* **2.** inform on someone —*n.* **3.** telltale

snivel (ʹsnivəl) *vi.* **1.** sniffle to show distress **2.** whine

snob (snob) *n.* one who offensively judges others by social rank *etc.* —**'snobbery** *n.* —**'snobbish** *a.* of, like snob —**'snobbishly** *adv.*

snood (snōōd) *n.* pouchlike hat, worn at back of head to hold woman's hair

snook (snōōk) *n.* rude gesture, made by putting one thumb to nose with fingers outstretched (*esp. in* **cock a snook at**)

snooker (ʹsnōōkər) *n.* **1.** variety of pool played with 15 red balls and 6 balls of other colors —*vt.* **2.** hoodwink

snoop (snōōp) *vi.* **1.** pry, meddle **2.** peer —*n.* **3.** one who acts thus **4.** act or instance of snooping

snooty (ʹsnōōti) *a. sl.* haughty

snooze (snōōz) *vi.* **1.** take short sleep, be half asleep —*n.* **2.** nap

snore (snör) *vi.* **1.** breathe noisily when asleep —*n.* **2.** noise of snoring

snorkel (ʹsnörkəl) *n.* **1.** tube for breathing underwater —*vi.* **2.** swim, fish using this

snort (snört) *vi.* 1. make (contemptuous) noise by driving breath through nostrils —*n.* 2. such noise

snot (snot) *n. vulg.* mucus from nose —'**snotty** *a.* spitefully unpleasant

snout (snowt) *n.* animal's nose

snow (snō) *n.* 1. frozen vapor which falls in flakes 2. *sl.* cocaine —*v.* 3. fall, sprinkle as snow —*vt.* 4. let fall, throw down like snow 5. cover with snow 6. *inf.* mislead, charm insincerely, persuade —'**snowy** *a.* 1. of, like snow 2. covered with snow 3. very white —'**snowball** *n.* 1. snow pressed into hard ball for throwing —*vi.* 2. increase rapidly in importance *etc.* 3. play, fight with snowballs —'**snowberry** *n.* shrub with small pink flowers and white berries —**snow blindness** temporary blindness due to brightness of snow —'**snowdrift** *n.* bank of deep snow —'**snowdrop** *n.* small, white, bell-shaped spring flower —'**snowfall** *n.* 1. fall of snow 2. *Met.* amount of snow received in specified place and time —**snow fence** fence erected in winter to protect from drifting snow —'**snowflake** *n.* 1. one of mass of ice crystals that fall as snow 2. any of various European plants that have white bell-shape of flowers —**snow goose** white N Amer. goose —**snow-in-summer** *n.* rock plant with white flowers —**snow line** elevation above which snow does not melt —'**snowman** *n.* figure shaped out of snow —'**snowmobile** *n.* any automotive vehicle for traveling on snow —'**snowplow** *n.* 1. implement or vehicle for clearing away snow 2. stemming with both skis to slow or stop —'**snowshoe** *n.* light wooden frame with strips of leather stretched across it for walking or running on deep snow —**snow under** 1. cover and block with snow 2. *fig.* overwhelm

snub (snub) *vt.* 1. insult (*esp.* by ignoring) intentionally (-**bb**-) —*n.* 2. snubbing, rebuff —*a.* 3. short and blunt

snuff[1] (snuf) *n.* powdered tobacco for inhaling through nose

snuff[2] (snuf) *vt.* extinguish (*esp.* light from candle) —'**snuffer** *n.* 1. cone-shaped implement for extinguishing candles —*pl.* 2. instrument resembling scissors for trimming wick of candle —**snuff it** *sl.* die

snuffle ('snufəl) *vi.* breathe noisily or with difficulty

snug (snug) *a.* warm, comfortable —'**snuggle** *v.* lie close to, for warmth or affection —'**snugly** *adv.*

snye (snī) *n.* C side channel of river

so[1] (sō) *adv.* 1. to such an extent 2. in such a manner 3. very 4. the case being such 5. accordingly —*conj.* 6. therefore 7. in order that 8. with the result that —*interj.* 9. well —**so-and-so** *n. inf.* 1. person whose name is forgotten or ignored 2. *euphemistic* person or thing regarded as unpleasant —**so-called** *a.* called by but doubtfully deserving the name —**so long** *inf.* farewell; goodbye

so[2] (sō) *n. Mus. see* SOL

So. south(ern)

soak (sōk) *v.* 1. make, become or be thoroughly wet, *esp.* by immersion in liquid —*vt.* 2. absorb 3. drench —*vi.* 4. lie in liquid —*n.* 5. soaking 6. *sl.* habitual drunkard

soap (sōp) *n.* 1. compound of alkali and oil used in washing —*vt.* 2. apply soap to —'**soapy** *a.* —'**soapbox** *n.* crate used as platform for speech-making —**soapbox derby** race for children down ramped course on hand-made motorless vehicles made by drivers —**soap opera** radio or television serial of domestic life —'**soapstone** *n.* massive compact variety of talc, used for making hearths *etc.* (*also* **steatite**)

soar (sōr) *vi.* 1. fly high 2. increase, rise (in price *etc.*)

sob (sob) *vi.* 1. catch breath, *esp.* in weeping (-**bb**-) —*n.* 2. sobbing —**sob story** tale of personal distress told to arouse sympathy

sober ('sōbər) *a.* 1. not drunk 2. temperate 3. subdued 4. dull, plain 5. solemn —*v.* 6. make, become sober —'**soberly** *adv.* —**so'briety** *n.* state of being sober

sobriquet ('sōbrikā) *n.* 1. nickname 2. assumed name

Soc. *or* **soc.** Society

soccer ('sokər) *n.* football game played by two teams of 11 players each of which attempts to score points by propelling a round ball into the other's goal (*also* **association football**)

sociable ('sōshəbəl) *a.* 1. friendly 2. convivial —**socia'bility** *n.* —'**sociably** *adv.*

social ('sōshəl) *a.* 1. living in communities 2. relating to society 3. sociable —*n.* 4. informal gathering —'**socialite** *n.* member of fashionable society —**sociali'zation** *n.* —'**socialize** *v.* —'**socially** *adv.* —**social contract** *or* **compact** agreement entered into by. individuals, that results in formation of state and entails surrender of some personal liberties —**Social Register** trade name for directory of eminent persons in a community —**social science** study of society and of relationship of individual members within society, including economics, history, psychology *etc.* —**social security** state provision for the unemployed, aged *etc.* —**social services** welfare activities organized by state —**social studies** (*with sing. v.*) study of how people live and organize themselves in society, embracing geography, economics *etc.* —**social work** work to improve welfare of others

socialism ('sōshəlizəm) *n.* political system which advocates public ownership of means of production, distribution and exchange —'**socialist** *n./a.* —**socia'listic** *a.*

society (sə'sīəti) *n.* 1. living associated with others 2. those so living 3. companionship 4. company 5. association 6. club 7. fashionable people collectively

socio- (*comb. form*) denoting social or society, as in *socioeconomic*

socioeconomic (sōsiōekə'nomik, -ēkə-) *a.* of or involving both economic and social factors

sociology (sōsi'oləji) *n.* study of societies

sociopolitical (sōsiōpə'litikəl) *a.* of or involving both political and social factors

sock[1] (sok) *n.* cloth covering for foot

sock[2] (sok) *sl. vt.* 1. hit —*n.* 2. blow

socket ('sokit) *n.* hole or recess for something to fit into

Socratic (sə'kratik) *a.* of, like Gr. philosopher Socrates

sod (sod) *n.* 1. lump of earth with grass 2. *sl.* person considered obnoxious 3. *sl.* person, as specified

soda ('sōdə) *n.* 1. compound of sodium 2. soda water —**soda fountain** 1. counter that serves drinks, snacks *etc.* 2. apparatus dispensing soda water —**soda water** water charged with carbon dioxide

sodden ('sodən) *a.* 1. soaked 2. drunk 3. heavy and doughy

sodium ('sōdiəm) *n. Chem.* metallic element *Symbol* Na, at. wt. 23.0, at. no. 11 —**sodium bicarbonate** *or* **sodium hydrogen carbonate** chemical compound used in baking powder *etc.* (*also* **bicarbonate of soda**) —**sodium carbonate** soluble crystalline compound used in manufacture of glass, ceramics, soap and paper, and as cleansing agent —**sodium chloride** common table salt —**sodium**

hydroxide white strongly alkaline solid used in manufacture of rayon, paper, aluminum, soap and sodium compounds —**sodium pentothal** *see* PENTOTHAL SODIUM

Sodom ('sodəm) *n.* 1. *O.T.* city that, with Gomorrah, traditionally typifies depravity 2. this city as representing homosexuality 3. any place notorious for depravity

sodomy ('sodəmi) *n.* anal intercourse —'**sodomite** *n.*

sofa ('sōfə) *n.* upholstered seat with back and arms, for two or more people

soft (soft) *a.* 1. yielding easily to pressure 2. mild 3. easy 4. subdued 5. quiet, gentle 6. (too) lenient 7. oversentimental 8. feebleminded 9. (of water) containing few mineral salts 10. (of drugs) not liable to cause addiction —**soften** ('sofən) *v.* 1. make, become soft or softer —*vt.* 2. mollify 3. lighten 4. mitigate 5. make less loud —'**softly** *adv.* gently, quietly —'**softy** *or* '**softie** *n. inf.* person who is sentimental, weakly foolish or lacking in physical endurance —'**softball** *n.* bat-and-ball game resembling baseball, but played on a smaller field, with a smaller bat and a larger ball, and consisting of seven innings. Pitching must be underhand —**soft-boiled** *a.* (of egg) boiled for a short time so that yolk remains soft —**soft drink** drink that is nonalcoholic —**soft'hearted** *a.* easily moved to pity —**soft palate** posterior fleshy portion of roof of mouth —**soft-pedal** *vt.* 1. mute tone of (piano) 2. *inf.* make (something) less obvious by deliberately failing to emphasize it —**soft pedal** foot-operated lever on piano that causes fewer of strings to sound —**soft sell** method of selling based on indirect suggestion or inducement —**soft-shoe** *a.* (of tap-dancing) done without metal pieces on shoes —**soft soap** flattery —**soft spot** sentimental fondness —'**software** *n.* computer programs, tapes *etc.* for a particular computer system —'**softwood** *n.* wood of coniferous tree

soggy ('sogi) *a.* 1. soaked with liquid 2. damp and heavy

soigné *or* (*fem.*) **soignée** (swä'nyā) *a.* well-groomed

soil[1] (soil) *n.* 1. earth, ground 2. country, territory

soil[2] (soil) *v.* 1. make, become dirty —*vt.* 2. tarnish, defile —*n.* 3. dirt 4. sewage 5. stain

soiree (swä'rā) *n.* private evening party, *esp.* with music

sojourn ('sōjərn, sō'jərn) *vi.* 1. stay for a time —*n.* 2. short stay —'**sojourner** *n.*

sol (sol) *n. Mus.* 1. in fixed system of solmization, the note G 2. in movable do system, the fifth note of a major scale

solace ('solis) *n./vt.* comfort in distress

solar ('sōlər) *a.* of the sun —**solari'zation** *n.* —'**solarize** *vt.* affect by sunlight —**solar cell** cell that produces electricity from sun's rays —**solar plexus** ('pleksəs) network of nerves at pit of stomach —**solar system** system containing sun and heavenly bodies held in its gravitational field

solarium (sō'lariəm, sə-; -'ler-) *n.* 1. room built mainly of glass to give exposure to sun 2. (place with) bed for acquiring suntan by artificial means

sold (sōld) *pt./pp. of* SELL

solder ('sodər) *n.* 1. easily melted alloy used for joining metal —*vt.* 2. join with solder —**soldering iron**

soldier ('sōljər) *n.* 1. one serving in army —*vi.* 2. serve in army 3. (*with* on) persist doggedly —'**soldierly** *a.* —'**soldiery** *n.* troops —**soldier of fortune** man who seeks money or adventure as soldier

sole[1] (sōl) a. 1. one and only, unique 2. solitary —**'solely** adv. 1. alone 2. only 3. entirely

sole[2] (sōl) n. 1. underside of foot 2. underpart of boot etc. —vt. 3. fit with sole

sole[3] (sōl) n. small edible flatfish

solecism ('solisizəm) n. breach of grammar or etiquette

solemn ('soləm) a. 1. serious 2. formal 3. impressive —**solemnity** (sə'lemniti) n. —**solemnization** ('soləmni'zāshən) n. —**solemnize** ('soləmnīz) vt. 1. celebrate, perform 2. make solemn —**'solemnly** adv.

solenoid ('sōlinoid) n. coil of wire as part of electrical apparatus used to control doors

sol-fa ('sol'fä) n. Mus. system of syllables sol, fa etc. sung in scale

solicit (sə'lisit) vt. 1. request 2. accost 3. urge 4. entice —**solici'tation** n. —**so'licitor** n. —**so'licitous** a. 1. anxious 2. eager 3. earnest —**so'licitude** n.

solid ('solid) a. 1. not hollow 2. compact 3. composed of one substance 4. firm 5. massive 6. reliable —n. 7. body of three dimensions 8. substance not liquid or gas —**soli'darity** n. 1. unity of interests 2. united state —**solidifi'cation** n. —**so'lidify** v. 1. make, become solid or firm 2. harden (-**ified**, -**ifying**) —**so'lidity** n. —**'solidly** adv. —**solid geometry** branch of geometry concerned with solid geometric figures —**solid-state** a. (of electronic device) consisting chiefly of semiconductor materials and controlled by means of their electrical properties

solidus ('solidəs) n. short stroke (/) used in text to separate items (pl. -**di** (-dī)) (also **diagonal, virgule**)

soliloquy (sə'liləkwi) n. esp. in drama, thoughts spoken by person while alone —**so'liloquize** v.

solipsism ('sōlipsizəm, 'sol-) n. doctrine that self is the only thing known to exist —**'solipsist** n.

solitary ('soliteri) a. 1. alone, single —n. 2. hermit —**'solitaire** n. 1. precious stone, esp. diamond, set alone in a ring 2. card game for one person in which cards have to be played in a prescribed manner 3. board game for one person in which pegs have to be brought to a particular arrangement —**'solitude** n. 1. state of being alone 2. loneliness —**solitary confinement** isolation imposed on prisoner —**double solitaire** solitaire game adapted for two persons

solo ('sōlō) n. 1. music for one performer (pl. -**s**, -**li** (-lē)) 2. card game like whist (pl. -**s**) —a. 3. not concerted 4. unaccompanied, alone 5. piloting airplane alone —**'soloist** n.

Solomon Islands ('soləmən) country lying in south Pacific comprising an archipelago east of New Guinea within the area 5° to 12°30' S latitude and 155°30' to 169°45' E longitude

solstice ('solstis) n. either shortest (winter) or longest (summer) day of year —**solstitial** (sol'stishəl) a.

solve (solv) vt. 1. work out answer to 2. find answer to —**solubility** (solyə'biliti) n. —**soluble** ('solyəbəl) a. 1. capable of being dissolved in liquid 2. able to be solved or explained —**solute** ('solyōōt) n. 1. substance dissolved in solution —a. 2. Bot. unattached —**solution** (sə'lōōshən) n. 1. answer to problem 2. dissolving 3. liquid with something dissolved in it —**'solvable** a. —**'solvency** n. —**'solvent** a. 1. able to meet financial obligations —n. 2. liquid with power of dissolving

Somalia (sō'mälia) n. country in Africa bounded north by the Gulf of Aden, east and south by the Indian Ocean and west by Kenya —**So'malian** n./a.

somatic (sō'matik) a. 1. of the body, as distinct from the mind 2. of animal body or body wall as distinct from viscera, limbs and head

somber ('sombər) a. dark, gloomy

sombrero (səm'brāərō, som-) n. wide-brimmed hat (pl. -**s**)

some (sum; unstressed səm) a. 1. denoting an indefinite number, amount or extent 2. one or other 3. amount of 4. certain 5. approximately —pron. 6. portion, quantity —**'somebody** pron. 1. some person —n. 2. important person —**'somehow** adv. by some means unknown —**'someone** pron. some person —**'something** pron. 1. thing not clearly defined 2. indefinite amount, quantity or degree —**'sometime** adv. 1. formerly 2. at some (past or future) time —a. 3. former —**'sometimes** adv. 1. occasionally 2. now and then —**'somewhat** adv. to some extent, rather —**'somewhere** adv.

somersault ('sumərsolt) n. tumbling head over heels

somnambulist (som'nambyəlist) n. sleepwalker —**som'nambulism** n. —**somnambu-'listic** a.

somnolent ('somnələnt) a. 1. drowsy 2. causing sleep —**somnolence or 'somnolen-cy** n.

son (sun) n. male child —**'sonny** n. familiar term of address to boy or man —**son-in-law** n. daughter's husband

sonar ('sōnär) n. sound navigating ranging device that detects submerged objects by reflected vibrations

sonata (sə'nätə) n. piece of music in several movements —**sonatina** (sonə'tēnə) n. short sonata

son et lumière (sōn ā lōō'myäər) Fr. entertainment staged at night at famous place, building, giving dramatic history of it with lighting and sound effects

song (song) n. 1. singing 2. poem etc. for singing —**'songster** n. 1. singer 2. songbird ('songstress fem.) —**'songbird** n. 1. passerine bird with highly developed vocal organs and usu. musical call 2. any bird with musical call —**Song of Solomon** Bible 22nd book of the O.T., written by Solomon, delineating the perfect picture of true love

sonic ('sonik) a. pert. to sound waves —**sonic barrier** see **sound barrier** at SOUND[1] —**sonic boom** explosive sound caused by aircraft traveling at supersonic speed

sonnet ('sonit) n. fourteen-line poem with definite rhyme scheme —**sonne'teer** n. writer of this

sonorous (sə'nōrəs, 'sonərəs) a. giving out (deep) sound, resonant —**sonority** (sə'nōriti) n. —**so'norously** adv.

soon (sōōn) adv. 1. in a short time 2. before long 3. early, quickly

soot (sōōt) n. black powdery substance formed by burning of coal etc. —**'sooty** a. of, like soot

sooth (sōōth) n. truth —**'soothsayer** n. one who foretells future, diviner

soothe (sōōdh) vt. 1. make calm, tranquil 2. relieve (pain etc.)

sop (sop) n. 1. piece of bread etc. soaked in liquid 2. concession, bribe —vt. 3. steep in water etc. 4. soak (up) (-**pp**-) —**'sopping** a. completely soaked —**'soppy** a. inf. oversentimental

sophist ('sofist) n. fallacious reasoner, quibbler —**'sophism** n. specious argument —**so'phistical** a. —**'sophistry** n.

sophisticate (sə'fistikāt) vt. 1. make artificial, spoil, falsify, corrupt —n. (sə'fistikit, -kāt) 2. sophisticated person —**so'phisticated** a. 1. having refined or cultured tastes, habits 2. worldly 3. superficially clever 4. complex —**sophisti'cation** n.

sophomore ('sofmōr) n. student in second year at college or high school

Sophonias (sofə'nīəs) n. Bible Zephaniah in the Douay Version of the O.T.

-sophy (n. comb. form) indicating knowledge or intellectual system, as in philosophy —**-sophic** or **-sophical** (a. comb. form)

soporific (sopə'rifik) a. 1. causing sleep (esp. by drugs) —n. 2. drug or other agent that induces sleep

soprano (sə'pranō, -'pränō) n. 1. highest voice in women and boys 2. singer with this voice 3. musical part for it (pl. -**s**)

sorbet ('sorbit) n. (fruit-flavored) water ice

sorcerer ('sorsərər) or (fem.) **sorceress** ('sorsəris) n. magician —**'sorcery** n. witchcraft, magic

sordid ('sordid) a. 1. mean, squalid 2. ignoble, base —**'sordidly** adv. —**'sordidness** n.

sore (sōr) a. 1. painful 2. causing annoyance 3. severe 4. distressed 5. annoyed —adv. 6. obs. grievously, intensely —n. 7. sore place, ulcer, boil etc. —**'sorely** adv. 1. grievously 2. greatly

sorghum ('sorgəm) n. kind of grass cultivated for fodder, smother crop and production of syrup

sorority (sə'rōriti) n. social club or society for women

sorrel ('sorəl) n. 1. plant 2. reddish-brown color 3. horse of this color —a. 4. of this color

sorrow ('sorō) n. 1. pain of mind, grief, sadness —vi. 2. grieve —**'sorrowful** a.

sorry ('sori) a. 1. feeling pity or regret 2. distressed 3. miserable, wretched 4. mean, poor —**'sorrily** adv. —**'sorriness** n.

sort (sort) n. 1. kind or class —vt. 2. classify

sortie ('sorti) n. sally by besieged forces

SOS 1. international code signal of distress 2. call for help

so-so a. inf. mediocre

sostenuto (sostə'nōōtō, sōs-) a./adv. Mus. in smooth sustained manner

sot (sot) n. habitual drunkard

sotto voce ('sotō 'vōchi) It. in an undertone

sou (sōō) n. 1. former French coin 2. small amount of money

soubrette (sōō'bret) n. 1. minor female role in comedy 2. any flirtatious girl

soufflé (sōō'flā, 'sōōflā) n. dish of eggs beaten to froth, flavored and baked

sough (sow) n. low murmuring sound as of wind in trees

sought (sot) pt./pp. of SEEK

souk (sōōk) n. open-air market place, esp. in N Afr. and Middle East

soul (sōl) n. 1. spiritual and immortal part of human being 2. example, pattern 3. person —**'soulful** a. full of emotion or sentiment —**'soulless** a. 1. mechanical 2. lacking sensitivity or nobility 3. heartless, cruel —**soul-destroying** a. (of occupation etc.) monotonous —**soul food** inf. food, as yams etc., traditionally eaten by Blacks —**soul mate** person for whom one has deep affinity —**soul music** type of Black music resulting from addition of jazz and gospel to urban blues style —**soul-searching** n. deep or critical examination of one's motives, actions etc.

sound¹ (sownd) *n.* **1.** what is heard **2.** noise —*vi.* **3.** make sound **4.** seem **5.** resonate with a certain quality —*vt.* **6.** cause to sound **7.** utter —**sound barrier** large increase in resistance encountered by aircraft approaching speed of sound —**sound effect** sound artificially produced to create theatrical effect, as in plays, motion pictures *etc.* —**sounding board 1.** thin wooden board in violin *etc.* designed to reflect sound **2.** person *etc.* used to test new idea *etc.* —**sound track** recorded sound accompaniment of motion picture *etc.* —**sound wave** wave that propagates sound

sound² (sownd) *a.* **1.** in good condition **2.** solid **3.** of good judgment **4.** legal **5.** solvent **6.** thorough **7.** effective **8.** watertight **9.** deep —'**soundly** *adv.* thoroughly

sound³ (sownd) *vt.* **1.** measure depth of (well, sea *etc.*) **2.** probe —'**soundings** *pl.n.* measurements taken by sounding —**sound out** ascertain views of

sound⁴ (sownd) *n.* channel, strait

soup (soōp) *n.* liquid food made by boiling meat, vegetables *etc.* —'**soupy** *a.* **1.** like soup **2.** murky **3.** sentimental —**soup kitchen** place where food, *esp.* soup, is served to destitute people —**soup up** *inf.* **1.** enliven **2.** increase power of (an engine)

soupçon (soōp'sō) *Fr.* small amount

sour ('sowər) *a.* **1.** acid **2.** gone bad **3.** rancid **4.** peevish **5.** disagreeable —*v.* **6.** make, become sour —'**sourly** *adv.* —'**sourness** *n.* —**sour ball** hard round candy with tart flavor —**sour cream** commercially fermented cream —'**sourdough** *n.* **1.** dough leavened by culture of mild yeast **2.** pioneer, *esp.* old-timer in Alaska —**sour grapes** attitude of despising something because one cannot have it oneself —**sour gum** *see* **black gum** at BLACK —'**sourpuss** *n.* sullen, sour-faced person —**sour salt** citric acid crystals used for flavoring

source (sörs) *n.* **1.** origin, starting point **2.** spring

sousaphone ('soōzəfōn) *n.* brass musical instrument, largest of those resembling the cornet, carried over the shoulder, with a wide, conspicuous bell, used in a brass band

souse (sows) *v.* **1.** plunge, drench or be drenched **2.** pickle —*n.* **3.** sousing **4.** brine for pickling

soutane (soō'tän, -'tan) *n.* cassock

south (sowth) *n.* **1.** cardinal point opposite north **2.** region, part of country *etc.* lying to that side —*a./adv.* **3.** (that is) toward south —**southerly** ('sudhərli) *a.* **1.** toward south —*n.* **2.** wind from the south —**southern** ('sudhərn) *a.* in south —**Southerner** ('sudhərnər) *n.* (*sometimes* s-) native or inhabitant of south of any specified region —'**southward** *adv.* —'**Southdown** *n.* breed of sheep —**south'east** *n.* **1.** point of compass midway between south and east —*a.* **2.** (*sometimes* S-) denoting southeastern part of specified country *etc.* **3.** in, toward or facing southeast —*adv.* **4.** in, to, toward or (*esp.* of wind) from southeast —**Southern Cross** small constellation in S hemisphere whose four brightest stars form cross —**southern hemisphere** (*oft.* S- H-) that half of earth lying south of equator —**southern lights** aurora australis —'**southpaw** *inf.* **1.** any left-handed person —*a.* **2.** of or relating to southpaw —**South Pole** southernmost point on earth's axis —**South Seas** seas south of equator —**south-southeast** *n.* **1.** point on compass midway between southeast and south —*a./adv.* **2.** in, from or toward this direction —**south-southwest** *n.* **1.** point on compass midway between south and southwest —*a./adv.* **2.** in, from or toward this

direction —**south'west** *n.* **1.** point on compass midway between west and south —*a.* **2.** (*sometimes* S-) of or denoting southwestern part of specified country *etc.* **3.** in or toward southwest —*adv.* **4.** in, to, toward or (*esp.* of wind) from southwest —**South'west** *n.* (*usu. with* the) southwestern part of the U.S.

South Africa —**Republic of South Africa** country in Africa bounded north by Botswana and Zimbabwe, northeast by Mozambique and Swaziland, east by the Indian Ocean, south and west by the Atlantic and northwest by Namibia

South Carolina (karə'līnə) South Atlantic state of the U.S.: ratified the Constitution in 1788. Abbrev.: **SC** (with ZIP code)

South Dakota (də'kōtə) West North Central state of the U.S., admitted to the Union in 1889. Abbrev.: **SD** (with ZIP code)

South West Africa *see* NAMIBIA

souvenir ('soōvənēər, soōvə'nēər) *n.* keepsake, memento

sou'wester (sow'westər) *n.* waterproof hat

sovereign ('sovrin) *n.* **1.** king, queen **2.** former Brit. gold coin worth 20 shillings —*a.* **3.** supreme **4.** efficacious —'**sovereignty** *n.* **1.** supreme power and right to exercise it **2.** dominion **3.** independent state

soviet ('sōviət, 'sov-) *n.* **1.** elected council at various levels of government in U.S.S.R. **2.** (S-) citizen of U.S.S.R. —*a.* **3.** (S-) of U.S.S.R., its people or its government —'**sovietism** *n.*

Soviet Union Russia; U.S.S.R.

sow¹ (sō) *vi.* **1.** scatter, plant seed —*vt.* **2.** scatter, deposit (seed) **3.** spread abroad (**sowed** *pt.,* **sown** or **sowed** *pp.,* '**sowing** *pr.p.*)

soybean ('soi'bēn) *n.* edible bean used as meat substitute, in making soy sauce *etc.* —**soy sauce** (soi) salty, dark brown sauce made from fermented soybeans, used *esp.* in Oriental cookery (*also* **soya sauce** ('soiə))

sp. 1. special **2.** species (*pl.* **spp.**) **3.** specific **4.** specimen **5.** spelling

spa (spä) *n.* **1.** medicinal spring **2.** place or resort with such a spring

space (spās) *n.* **1.** extent **2.** room **3.** period **4.** empty place **5.** area **6.** expanse **7.** region beyond earth's atmosphere —*vt.* **8.** place at intervals —**spacious** ('spāshəs) *a.* roomy, extensive —**space age** period in which exploration of space has become possible —**space-age** *a.* ultramodern —'**spacecraft** or '**spaceship** *n.* vehicle for travel beyond earth's atmosphere —'**spaceman** *n.* —**space shuttle** vehicle designed to carry men and materials to space stations *etc.* —**space station** any manned artificial satellite designed to orbit earth and provide base for scientific research in space —'**spacesuit** *n.* sealed, pressurized suit worn by astronaut —**space-time** *n. Phys.* continuum having three spatial coordinates and one time coordinate that together specify location of particle or event (*also* **space-time continuum**)

spade¹ (spād) *n.* tool for digging —'**spadework** *n.* arduous preparatory work

spade² (spād) *n.* leaf-shaped black symbol on playing card

spadix ('spādiks) *n.* spike of small flowers on fleshy stem, whole being enclosed in spathe (*pl.* **spadices** ('spādisēz))

spaghetti (spə'geti) *n.* pasta in form of long strings

Spain (spān) *n.* country in Europe bounded north by the Bay of Biscay and the Pyrenees, east and south by the Mediterranean and the Straits of Gibraltar, southwest by the

Atlantic and west by Portugal and the Atlantic —**Spaniard** ('spanyərd) *n.* native or inhabitant of Spain —**Spanish** ('spanish) *a.* **1.** of Spain —*n.* **2.** language of Spain and most of Central and South America: the Romance language with the largest number of speakers —**Spanish America** parts of America colonized by Spaniards and now chiefly Spanish-speaking —**Spanish fly 1.** European blister beetle, the dried bodies of which yield cantharides **2.** cantharides —**Spanish Main 1.** mainland of Spanish America **2.** Caribbean Sea

span (span) *n.* **1.** space from thumb to little finger as measure **2.** extent, space **3.** stretch of arch *etc.* **4.** distance from wingtip to wingtip (*also* '**wingspan**) —*vt.* **5.** stretch over **6.** measure with hand (**-nn-**)

spandex ('spandeks) *n.* synthetic elastomeric fiber

spangle ('spanggəl) *n.* **1.** small shiny metallic ornament —*vt.* **2.** decorate with spangles

spaniel ('spanyəl) *n.* any of several breeds of dog with long ears and silky hair

spank (spangk) *vt.* **1.** slap with flat of hand, *esp.* on buttocks —*n.* **2.** one or series of these slaps —'**spanking** *n.* **1.** series of spanks —*a.* **2.** quick, lively **3.** large, fine

spar¹ (spär) *n.* pole, beam, *esp.* as part of ship's rigging

spar² (spär) *vi.* **1.** box **2.** dispute, *esp.* in fun (**-rr-**) —*n.* **3.** sparring —**sparring partner** person who practices with boxer during training

spar³ (spär) *n.* any of various kinds of crystalline mineral

spare (spāər) *vt.* **1.** leave unhurt **2.** show mercy **3.** abstain from using **4.** do without **5.** give away —*a.* **6.** additional **7.** in reserve **8.** thin, lean **9.** scanty —*n.* **10.** spare part (for machine) —'**sparing** *a.* economical, careful —'**sparerib** *n.* cut of pork ribs with most of meat trimmed off

spark (spärk) *n.* **1.** small glowing or burning particle **2.** flash of light produced by electrical discharge **3.** vivacity, humor **4.** trace **5.** in internal-combustion engines, electric spark (in spark plug) which ignites explosive mixture in cylinder —*vi.* **6.** emit sparks —*vt.* **7.** (*oft. with* off) kindle, excite —**spark plug** device screwed into cylinder head of internal-combustion engine to ignite explosive mixture by means of electric spark

sparkle ('spärkəl) *vi.* **1.** glitter **2.** effervesce **3.** scintillate —*n.* **4.** small spark **5.** glitter **6.** flash **7.** luster —'**sparkler** *n. inf.* sparkling gem

sparrow ('sparō) *n.* small brownish bird —**sparrow grass** *inf.* asparagus —**sparrow hawk** hawk that hunts small birds

sparse (spärs) *a.* thinly scattered

Spartan ('spärtən) *a.* **1.** of ancient Gk. city of Sparta, its inhabitants or their culture **2.** (*sometimes* s-) very strict or austere **3.** (*sometimes* s-) possessing courage and resolve

spasm ('spazəm) *n.* **1.** sudden convulsive (muscular) contraction **2.** sudden burst of activity *etc.* —**spas'modic** *a.* occurring in spasms

spastic ('spastik) *a.* **1.** affected by spasms, suffering cerebral palsy —*n.* **2.** person who has cerebral palsy

spat¹ (spat) *pt./pp.* of SPIT¹

spat² (spat) *n.* short gaiter

spat³ (spat) *n.* petty quarrel

spate (spāt) *n.* **1.** rush, outpouring **2.** flood

spathe (spādh) *n.* large sheathlike leaf enclosing flower cluster

spatial ('spāshəl) a. of, in space

spatter ('spatər) vt. 1. splash, cast drops over —vi. 2. be scattered in drops —n. 3. slight splash 4. sprinkling

spatula ('spachələ) n. utensil with broad, flat blade used for various purposes

spawn (spŏn) n. 1. eggs of fish or frog 2. fragments of mycelia used to propagate mushrooms —vi. 3. (of fish or frog) cast eggs —vt. 4. produce, engender

spay (spā) vt. remove ovaries from (animal)

speak (spēk) vi. 1. utter words 2. converse 3. deliver discourse —vt. 4. utter 5. pronounce 6. express 7. communicate in (**spoke, 'spoken, 'speaking**) —'**speakable** a. —'**speaker** n. 1. one who speaks 2. one who specializes in speech-making 3. (oft. S-) official chairman of many legislative bodies 4. loudspeaker —'**speakeasy** n. place where alcoholic drink was sold illicitly during Prohibition

spear (spēər) n. 1. long pointed weapon 2. slender shoot, as of asparagus —vt. 3. transfix, pierce, wound with spear —'**spearhead** n. 1. leading force in attack, campaign —vt. 2. lead, initiate (attack, campaign etc.)

spearmint ('spēərmint) n. type of mint

spec. 1. special 2. specification 3. speculation

special ('speshəl) a. 1. beyond the usual 2. particular, individual 3. distinct 4. limited —'**specialism** n. —'**specialist** n. one who devotes himself to special subject or branch of subject —speciali'**zation** n. —'**specialize** vi. 1. be specialist —vt. 2. make special —'**specially** adv. —'**specialty** n. special product, skill, characteristic etc. —**special delivery** delivery of mail outside time of scheduled delivery

specie ('spēshē) n. coined, as distinct from paper, money

species ('spēshēz; Lat. 'spēshiēz) n. 1. sort, kind, esp. of animals etc. 2. class 3. subdivision 4. Biol. group of plants or animals able to reproduce among themselves (pl. -**cies**)

specific (spi'sifik) a. 1. definite 2. exact in detail 3. characteristic of a thing or kind —spe'**cifically** adv. —specifi'**cation** n. detailed description of something to be made, done —'**specify** vt. state definitely or in detail (-**ified, -ifying**) —**specific gravity** ratio of density of substance to that of water

specimen ('spesimin) n. 1. part typifying whole 2. individual example 3. Med. sample of tissue, urine etc. taken for diagnostic examination

specious ('spēshəs) a. deceptively plausible, but false —'**speciously** adv. —'**speciousness** n.

speck (spek) n. 1. small spot, particle —vt. 2. spot —'**speckle** n./vt. speck

spectacle ('spektəkəl) n. 1. public display or performance 2. thing exhibited 3. ridiculous sight —pl. 4. pair of lenses for correcting defective sight —spec'**tacular** a. 1. impressive 2. showy 3. grand 4. magnificent —n. 5. lavishly produced performance —spec'**tator** n. one who looks on

specter ('spektər) n. 1. ghost 2. image of something unpleasant —'**spectral** a. ghostly

spectrum ('spektrəm) n. 1. image formed by light or sound in which the parts are arranged according to wavelength or frequency 2. continuous sequence or range (pl. -**tra**) —'**spectroscope** n. instrument for producing, examining spectra —spec'**troscopist** n. —spec'**troscopy** n. study of spectra by use of spectroscopes etc.

speculate ('spekyəlāt) vi. 1. guess, conjecture 2. engage in (risky) commercial transactions —specu'**lation** n. —'**speculative** a. given to, characterized by speculation —'**speculator** n.

speculum ('spekyələm) n. 1. mirror 2. reflector of polished metal, esp. in reflecting telescopes 3. instrument for dilating body passages (pl. -**la** (-lə), -**s**) —'**specular** a.

sped (sped) pt./pp. of SPEED

speech (spēch) n. 1. act, faculty of speaking 2. words, language 3. conversation 4. discourse 5. (formal) talk given before audience —'**speechify** vi. make speech, esp. long and tedious one (-**ified, -ifying**) —'**speechless** a. 1. dumb 2. at a loss for words

speed (spēd) n. 1. swiftness 2. rate of progress 3. degree of sensitivity of photographic film 4. sl. amphetamine —vi. 5. move quickly 6. drive vehicle at high speed 7. obs. succeed —vt. 8. further 9. expedite (**sped** or '**speeded** pt./pp.) —'**speedily** adv. —'**speeding** n. driving (vehicle) at high speed, esp. over legal limit —'**speedo** n. inf. speedometer (pl. -**s**) —'**speedy** a. 1. quick 2. rapid 3. nimble 4. prompt —'**speedball** n. game combining features of soccer and basketball with elements of Amer. football played on standard field by two teams of 11 players whose object is to move the round ball in the direction of the opponents' goal —'**speedboat** n. light, fast motorboat —**speed limit** maximum permitted speed at which vehicle may travel on certain roads —**speed'ometer** n. instrument to show speed of vehicle —'**speedway** n. track for motorcycle racing —'**speedwell** n. any plant of the genus Veronica with small, usu. blue flowers

speleology (spēli'oləji) n. study, exploring of caves —speleo'**logical** a.

spell¹ (spel) vt. 1. give letters of in order 2. read letter by letter 3. indicate, result in (**spelled** or **spelt** pt./pp., '**spelling** pr.p.) —'**spelling** n. —**spell out** make explicit

spell² (spel) n. 1. magic formula 2. enchantment —'**spellbound** a. enchanted, entranced

spell³ (spel) n. (short) period of time, work

spelt (spelt) pt./pp. of SPELL¹

spend (spend) vt. 1. pay out 2. pass (time) on activity etc. 3. use up completely (**spent** pt./pp., '**spending** pr.p.) —'**spender** n. —**spent** a. used up, exhausted —'**spendthrift** n. wasteful person

sperm (spərm) n. 1. male reproductive cell 2. semen —**spermaceti** (spərmə'sēti, -'seti) n. white, waxy substance obtained from oil from head of sperm whale —**sper'matic** a. of sperm —**spermatozoon** (spərmatə'zōon) n. any of male reproductive cells released in semen during ejaculation (pl. -**zoa** (-'zōə)) (also **sperm, 'zoosperm**) —'**spermicide** n. drug etc. that kills sperm —**sperm whale** large, toothed whale hunted for sperm oil, spermaceti and ambergris (also '**cachalot**)

spew (spyōō) v. vomit

sphagnum ('sfagnəm) n. moss that grows in bogs

sphere (sfēər) n. 1. ball, globe 2. range 3. field of action 4. status 5. position 6. province —**spherical** ('sfeərikəl, 'sfer-) a. —'**spheroid** n. 1. geometric surface produced by rotating ellipse about one of its two axes —a. 2. shaped like but not exactly a sphere

sphincter ('sfingktər) n. ring of muscle surrounding opening of hollow bodily organ

sphinx (sfingks) n. 1. statue in Egypt with lion's body and human head 2. (S-) monster with woman's head and lion's body 3. enigmatic person (pl. -**es, sphinges** ('sfinjēz))

sphygmomanometer (sfigmōmə'nomitər) n. instrument for measuring blood pressure

spice (spīs) n. 1. aromatic or pungent vegetable substance 2. spices collectively 3. anything that adds flavor, relish, piquancy, interest etc. —vt. 4. season with spices, flavor —'**spicily** adv. —'**spicy** a. 1. flavored with spices 2. inf. slightly indecent, risqué

spick-and-span or **spic-and-span** (spikən'span) a. 1. neat, smart 2. new-looking

spider ('spīdər) n. small eight-legged creature which spins web to catch prey —'**spidery** a. —**spider plant** hardy house plant with long thin leaves

spiel (spēl) inf. n. 1. glib (sales) talk —vi. 2. deliver spiel, recite —'**spieler** n.

spigot ('spigət) n. peg, plug

spike (spīk) n. 1. sharp point 2. sharp pointed object 3. long flower cluster with flowers attached directly to the stalk —vt. 4. pierce, fasten with spike 5. render ineffective 6. add alcohol to (drink) —'**spiky** a. —'**spikenard** n. 1. aromatic Indian plant with rose-purple flowers 2. aromatic ointment obtained from this plant

spill¹ (spil) v. 1. (cause to) pour, flow over, fall out, esp. unintentionally 2. upset —vi. 3. be lost or wasted (**spilt** (spilt) or **spilled** pt./pp.) —n. 4. fall 5. amount spilt —'**spillage** n.

spill² (spil) n. thin strip of wood, twisted paper etc. for lighting fires etc.

spin (spin) v. 1. (cause to) revolve rapidly 2. whirl —vt. 3. twist into thread 4. (with out) prolong 5. inf. tell (a story) —vi. 6. fish with lure (**spun**, obs. **span** (span) pt., **spun** pp., '**spinning** pr.p.) —n. 7. spinning 8. (of aircraft) descent in dive with continued rotation 9. rapid run or ride 10. in skating, rapid turning on the spot 11. angular momentum of elementary particle —'**spinner** n. 1. person or thing that spins 2. fishing lure with fin or wing that revolves —**spinne'ret** n. any of several organs in spiders etc. through which silk threads are exuded —'**spinning** n. act, process of drawing out and twisting into threads, as wool, cotton, flax etc. —**spinning jenny** early type of spinning frame with several spindles —**spinning wheel** household machine with large wheel turned by treadle for spinning wool etc. into thread —**spin-off** n. any product or development derived incidentally from application of existing knowledge or enterprise

spina bifida ('spīnə 'bīfidə) congenital condition in which meninges of spinal cord protrude through gap in backbone

spinach ('spinich) n. 1. annual plant with edible leaves 2. the leaves, eaten boiled as vegetable

spindle ('spindəl) n. rod, axis for spinning —'**spindly** a. 1. long and slender 2. attenuated —'**spindlelegs** or '**spindleshanks** pl.n. 1. long thin legs 2. person who has such legs

spindrift ('spindrift) n. spray blown along surface of sea

spine (spīn) n. 1. backbone 2. thin spike, esp. on fish etc. 3. ridge 4. back of book —'**spinal** a. —'**spineless** a. 1. lacking spine 2. cowardly —'**spiny** a. 1. (of animals) having or covered with quills or spines 2. (of plants) covered with spines 3. troublesome —**spinal column** structure in vertebrates consisting of vertebrae protecting the spinal cord and uniting skull, rib cage, shoulder and pelvic girdles into skeleton (also **backbone**) —**spinal cord** cord of nerve tissue within spinal canal, which together with brain forms central nervous system —**spine-chiller** n. motion picture etc. that arouses terror

spinel or **spinelle** (spi'nel) n. hard crystalline mineral of various colors used as gemstone

spinet ('spinit, spi'net) n. 1. small modern piano 2. oblong pianoforte of 19th cent. 3. harpsicord with one manual

spinnaker ('spinəkər; Naut. 'spangkər) n. large yacht sail

spinney ('spini) n. small wood

spinster ('spinstər) n. unmarried woman

spiracle ('spirəkəl, 'spīrə-) n. Zool. opening for breathing

spiral ('spīrəl) n. 1. continuous curve drawn at ever-increasing distance from fixed point 2. anything resembling this —a. 3. having shape of spiral —'**spirally** adv.

spirant ('spīrənt) a. 1. Phonet. see FRICATIVE —n. 2. fricative consonant

spire ('spīər) n. 1. pointed part of steeple 2. pointed stem

spirea or **spiraea** (spī'rēə) n. any of various plants with small white or pink flower sprays

spirit ('spirit) n. 1. life principle animating body 2. disposition 3. liveliness 4. courage 5. frame of mind 6. essential character or meaning 7. soul 8. ghost 9. liquid got by distillation, alcohol —pl. 10. emotional state 11. strong alcoholic drink, eg whiskey —vt. 12. (usu. with away or off) carry away mysteriously —'**spirited** a. lively —'**spiritless** a. listless, apathetic —'**spiritual** a. 1. given to, interested in things of the spirit —n. 2. Negro sacred song, hymn —'**spiritualism** n. belief that spirits of the dead communicate with the living —'**spiritualist** n. —spiritu'ality n. —'**spiritually** adv. —'**spirituous** a. alcoholic —**spirit gum** glue made from gum dissolved in ether —**spirit lamp** lamp that burns methylated or other spirits —**spirit level** glass tube containing bubble in liquid, used to check horizontal, vertical surfaces —**spirits of salts** hydrochloric acid

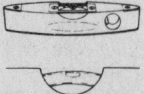

spirit level

spirochete ('spirəkēt) n. spiral bacterium with flexible cell wall found in mud and water and as parasite in animals producing diseases, eg syphilis, yaws, leptospirosis

spirt (spərt) see SPURT

spit¹ (spit) vi. 1. eject saliva —vt. 2. eject from mouth (**spat, spit** pt./pp., '**spitting** pr.p.) —n. 3. spitting, saliva —'**spittle** n. saliva —**spit'toon** n. vessel to spit into —'**spitfire** n. person with fiery temper —**spitting image** inf. person who bears physical resemblance to another —**spit and polish** inf. punctilious attention to neatness, discipline etc., esp. in armed forces

spit² (spit) n. 1. sharp rod to put through meat for roasting 2. sandy point projecting into the sea —vt. 3. thrust through (**-tt-**)

spite (spīt) n. 1. malice —vt. 2. thwart spitefully —'**spiteful** a. —'**spitefully** adv. —**in spite of** regardless of; notwithstanding

splake (splāk) n. type of hybrid Canad. trout

splash (splash) v. 1. scatter (liquid) about, on or over (something) —vt. 2. print, display prominently —n. 3. sound of water being scattered 4. patch, esp. of color 5. (effect of) extravagant display 6. small amount —'**splashdown** n. 1. controlled landing of spacecraft on water 2. time scheduled for this event —**splash down**

splat (splat) n. wet, slapping sound

splatter ('splatər) v./n. spatter

splay (splā) a. 1. spread out 2. slanting 3. turned outward —v. 4. spread out 5. twist outward —n. 6. slant surface 7. spread —**splay'footed** a. flat and broad (of foot)

spleen (splēn) n. 1. organ in abdomen 2. anger 3. irritable or morose temper —**splenetic** (spli'netik) a. —'**spleenwort** n. any of various ferns

splendid ('splendid) a. 1. magnificent 2. brilliant 3. excellent —'**splendidly** adv. —'**splendor** n.

splice (splīs) vt. 1. join by interweaving strands 2. join (wood) by overlapping 3. sl. join in marriage —n. 4. spliced joint

spline (splīn) n. narrow groove, ridge, strip, esp. joining wood etc.

splint (splint) n. rigid support for broken limb etc.

splinter ('splintər) n. 1. thin fragment of glass, wood etc. —v. 2. break into fragments, shiver —**splinter group** group that separates from main party, organization, oft. after disagreement

split (split) v. 1. break asunder 2. separate 3. divide —vi. 4. sl. depart; leave (**split, 'splitting**) —n. 5. crack, fissure 6. dessert of fruit and ice cream —'**splitting** a. 1. (of headache) acute 2. (of head) assailed by overpowering unbearable pain —**split infinitive** in English grammar, infinitive used with another word between to and verb —**split-level** a. (of house etc.) having floor level of one part about half story above floor level of adjoining part —**split personality** 1. tendency to change rapidly in mood or temperament 2. schizophrenia —**split second** infinitely small period of time —**split-second** a. made or arrived at in infinitely short time

splotch (sploch) n./vt. splash, daub —'**splotchy** a.

splurge (splərj) v. 1. spend (money) extravagantly —n. 2. ostentatious display, esp. of wealth 3. bout of unrestrained extravagance

splutter ('splutər) vi. 1. make hissing, spitting sounds —vt. 2. utter incoherently with spitting sounds —n. 3. process or noise of spluttering 4. spluttering incoherent speech

spode (spōd) n. (sometimes S-) china or porcelain manufactured by Josiah Spode, English potter, or his company

spoil (spoil) vt. 1. damage, injure 2. damage manners or behavior of (esp. child) by indulgence 3. pillage —vi. 4. go bad (**spoiled** or **spoilt** pt./pp., '**spoiling** pr.p.) —n. 5. booty 6. waste material, esp. in mining (also '**spoilage**) —'**spoiler** n. slowing device on aircraft wing etc. —'**spoilsport** n. inf. one who spoils pleasure of other people —**spoiling for** eager for

spoke¹ (spōk) pt. of SPEAK —'**spoken** pp. of SPEAK —'**spokesman** n. one deputed to speak for others

spoke² (spōk) n. radial bar of wheel

spoliation (spōli'āshən) n. 1. act of spoiling 2. robbery 3. destruction

spondee ('spondē) n. metrical foot consisting of two long syllables (ˉ ˉ)

sponge (spunj) n. 1. freshwater or marine invertebrate 2. its skeleton, or a synthetic substance like it, used to absorb liquids 3. raised yeast dough 4. pad used in surgery to absorb fluid —vt. 5. wipe with sponge —vi. 6. live at expense of others —v. 7. cadge —'**sponger** n. sl. one who cadges or lives at expense of others —'**spongy** a. 1. spongelike 2. wet and soft —**sponge cake** type of light cake

sponsor ('sponsər) n. 1. one promoting, advertising something 2. one who agrees to give money to a charity on completion of specified activity by another 3. one taking responsibility (esp. for welfare of child at baptism, ie godparent) 4. guarantor —vt. 5. act as sponsor for —'**sponsorship** n.

spontaneous (spon'tāniəs) a. 1. voluntary 2. natural 3. not forced 4. produced without external force —**spontaneity** (spontə'nēiti, -'nā-) n. —spon'**taneously** adv. —spon'**taneousness** n. —**spontaneous combustion** ignition of substance as result of internal oxidation processes

spoof (spōof) n. 1. mild satirical mockery 2. trick, hoax

spook (spōok) n. ghost —'**spooky** a.

spool (spōol) n. reel, bobbin

spoon (spōon) n. 1. implement with shallow bowl at end of handle for eating or serving food etc. —vt. 2. lift with spoon —'**spoonful** n. —'**spoonbill** n. any of several wading birds having long horizontally flattened bill —**spoon-feed** vt. 1. feed with spoon 2. spoil 3. provide (person) with ready-made opinions etc.

spoonerism ('spōonərizəm) n. amusing transposition of initial consonants, eg 'half-warmed fish' for 'half-formed wish'

spoor (spōor, spōr) n. 1. trail of animal, esp. wild animals —v. 2. follow spoor (of)

sporadic (spə'radik) or **sporadical** a. 1. intermittent 2. scattered —spo'**radically** adv.

spore (spōr) n. minute reproductive body of flowerless plant or protozoan

sporran ('sporən) n. pouch worn in front of kilt

sport (spōrt) n. 1. game, activity for pleasure, competition, exercise 2. enjoyment 3. mockery 4. cheerful person, good loser —vt. 5. wear, esp. ostentatiously —vi. 6. frolic 7. play (sport) —'**sporting** a. 1. of sport 2. behaving with fairness, generosity —'**sportive** a. playful —'**sporty** a. 1. stylish, loud or gay 2. relating to or appropriate to sportsman —**sporting chance** sufficient prospect of success to justify the attempt —**sports car** fast (open) car —**sports jacket** man's casual jacket —'**sportsman** n. 1. one who engages in sport 2. good loser

spot (spot) n. 1. small mark 2. blemish 3. pimple 4. place 5. (difficult) situation 6. inf. small quantity —vt. 7. mark with spots 8. detect 9. observe (**-tt-**) —'**spotless** a. 1. unblemished 2. pure —'**spotlessly** adv. —'**spotty** a. 1. with spots 2. uneven —**spot check** random examination —'**spotlight** n. 1. powerful light illuminating small area 2. center of attention —**spot-weld** vt. 1. join (two pieces of metal) by electrically generated heat —n. 2. weld so formed

spouse (spows, spowz) n. husband or wife —**spousal** ('spowzəl) n. marriage

spout (spowt) v. 1. pour out —vi. 2. sl. speechify —n. 3. projecting tube or lip for pouring liquids 4. copious discharge

sprain (sprān) n./vt. wrench or twist (of muscle etc.)

sprang (sprang) pt. of SPRING

sprat (sprat) n. small sea fish

sprawl (sprōl) vi. 1. lie or sit about awkwardly —v. 2. spread in rambling, unplanned way —n. 3. sprawling

spray¹ (sprā) n. 1. (device for producing) fine drops of liquid —vt. 2. sprinkle with shower of fine drops —**spray gun** device that sprays fluid in finely divided form by atomizing it in air jet

spray² (sprā) *n.* **1.** branch, twig with buds, flowers *etc.* **2.** floral ornament, brooch *etc.* like this

spread (spred) *v.* **1.** extend **2.** stretch out **3.** open out **4.** scatter **5.** distribute or be distributed **6.** unfold —*vt.* **7.** cover (**spread, 'spreading**) —*n.* **8.** extent **9.** increase **10.** ample meal **11.** food which can be spread on bread *etc.* —**spread-eagle** *a.* with arms and legs outstretched (*also* **spread-eagled**)

spree (sprē) *n.* **1.** session of overindulgence **2.** romp

sprig (sprig) *n.* **1.** small twig **2.** ornamental design like this **3.** small nail

sprightly ('sprītli) *a.* lively, brisk —**'sprightliness** *n.*

spring (spring) *vi.* **1.** leap **2.** shoot up or forth **3.** come into being **4.** appear **5.** grow **6.** become bent or split —*vt.* **7.** produce unexpectedly **8.** set off (trap) (**sprang, sprung, 'springing**) —*n.* **9.** leap **10.** recoil **11.** piece of coiled or bent metal with much resilience **12.** flow of water from earth **13.** first season of year —**'springy** *a.* elastic —**'springboard** *n.* flexible board for diving —**spring-clean** *v.* clean (house) thoroughly —**spring-cleaning** *n.* —**springer spaniel** breed of spaniel with silky coat, used for flushing or springing game —**spring tide** high tide at new or full moon

springbok

springbok ('springbok) *n.* **1.** S Afr. antelope **2.** (**S-**) South African national sportsman

sprinkle ('springkəl) *vt.* scatter small drops on, strew —**'sprinkler** *n.* —**'sprinkling** *n.* small quantity or number

sprint (sprint) *vi.* **1.** run short distance at great speed —*n.* **2.** such run, race

sprit (sprit) *n.* small spar set diagonally across fore-and-aft sail in order to extend it —**spritsail** ('spritsāl; *Naut.* 'spritsəl) *n.* sail extended by sprit

sprite (sprīt) *n.* fairy, elf

sprocket ('sprokit) *n.* **1.** projection on wheel or capstan for engaging chain **2.** wheel with sprockets (*also* **sprocket wheel**)

sprout (sprowt) *v.* **1.** put forth (shoots) —*vi.* **2.** spring up —*n.* **3.** shoot

spruce¹ (sprōōs) *n.* variety of fir

spruce² (sprōōs) *a.* neat in dress

sprue (sprōō) *n.* disease of the small intestine marked by impaired absorption of nutrients

sprung (sprung) *pp. of* SPRING

spry (sprī) *a.* nimble, vigorous

spud (spud) *n. inf.* potato

spume (spyōōm) *n./vi.* foam, froth

spun (spun) *pt./pp. of* SPIN

spunk (spungk) *n.* courage, spirit

spur (spər) *n.* **1.** pricking instrument attached to horseman's heel **2.** incitement **3.** stimulus **4.** projection on cock's leg **5.** projecting mountain range **6.** railroad branch line or siding —*vt.* **7.** ride hard (**-rr-**)

spurious ('spyŏŏriəs) *a.* not genuine

spurn (spərn) *vt.* reject with scorn, thrust aside

spurt *or* **spirt** (spərt) *v.* **1.** send, come out in jet —*vi.* **2.** rush suddenly —*n.* **3.** jet **4.** short sudden effort, *esp.* in race

sputnik ('spŏŏtnik, 'sput-) *n.* any of series of Russian satellites

sputter ('sputər) *v.* splutter

sputum ('spyŏŏtəm, 'spŏŏtəm) *n.* spittle (*pl.* **-ta** (-tə))

spy (spī) *n.* **1.** one who watches (*esp.* in rival countries, companies *etc.*) and reports secretly —*vi.* **2.** act as spy —*vt.* **3.** catch sight of (**spied, 'spying**) —**'spyglass** *n.* small telescope

Sq. 1. Square **2.** Squadron

squab (skwob) *n.* **1.** young unfledged bird, *esp.* pigeon **2.** short fat person **3.** well-stuffed cushion —*a.* **4.** (of birds) unfledged **5.** short and fat

squabble ('skwobəl) *vi.* **1.** engage in petty, noisy quarrel, bicker —*n.* **2.** petty quarrel

squad (skwod) *n.* small party, *esp.* of soldiers —**'squadron** *n.* basic unit of air force fighting group

squalid ('skwolid) *a.* mean and dirty —**'squalor** *n.*

squall (skwôl) *n.* **1.** harsh cry **2.** sudden gust of wind **3.** short storm —*vi.* **4.** yell

squander ('skwondər) *vt.* spend wastefully, dissipate

square (skwâər) *n.* **1.** equilateral rectangle **2.** area of this shape **3.** in town, open space (of this shape) **4.** product of a number multiplied by itself **5.** instrument for drawing right angles —*a.* **6.** square in form **7.** honest **8.** straight, even **9.** level, equal **10.** denoting a measure of area **11.** *inf.* old-fashioned, conservative —*vt.* **12.** make square **13.** find square of **14.** pay **15.** bribe —*vi.* **16.** fit, suit —**'squarely** *adv.* —**square dance** any of various formation dances in which couples form squares —**square-dance** *vi.* perform such dance —**square deal** any transaction *etc.* that is honest and fair —**square measure** unit or system of units for measuring areas —**square meter** *etc.* area equal to that of square with sides one meter *etc.* long —**square root** number that, multiplied by itself, gives number of which it is factor

squash (skwosh) *vt.* **1.** crush flat **2.** pulp **3.** suppress **4.** humiliate —*n.* **5.** juice of crushed fruit **6.** crowd **7.** any of various edible gourds —**squash rackets** (*with sing. v.*) indoor racket-and-ball game for (usually) two players in which ball is struck off wall(s) of court and in which only the server can score points

squat (skwot) *vi.* **1.** sit on heels **2.** act as squatter (**-tt-**) —*a.* **3.** short and thick —**'squatter** *n.* one who settles on land or occupies house without permission

squaw (skwô) *n.* N Amer. Indian woman

squawk (skwôk) *n.* **1.** short harsh cry, *esp.* of bird —*vi.* **2.** utter this cry

squeak (skwēk) *vi./n.* (make) short shrill sound

squeal (skwēl) *n.* **1.** long piercing squeak —*vi.* **2.** make one **3.** *sl.* confess information (about another)

squeamish ('skwēmish) *a.* **1.** easily made sick **2.** easily shocked **3.** overscrupulous

squeegee ('skwējē) *or* **squilgee** ('skwējē, 'skwiljē) *n.* **1.** tool with rubber blade for clearing water (from glass *etc.*), spreading wet paper *etc.* —*vt.* **2.** press, smooth with squeegee

squeeze (skwēz) *vt.* **1.** press **2.** wring **3.** force

4. hug **5.** subject to extortion —*n.* **6.** act of squeezing **7.** period of hardship, difficulty caused by financial weakness

squelch (skwelch) *vi.* **1.** make, walk with wet sucking sound, as in walking through mud —*n.* **2.** squelching sound

squib (skwib) *n.* **1.** small firework that hisses before exploding **2.** insignificant person

squid (skwid) *n.* type of cuttlefish

squiggle ('skwigəl) *n.* **1.** wavy, wriggling mark —*vi.* **2.** wriggle **3.** draw squiggle

squill (skwil) *n.* **1.** Mediterranean plant of lily family **2.** its bulb, used medicinally as expectorant

squint (skwint) *vi.* **1.** have the eyes turned in different directions **2.** glance sideways —*n.* **3.** this eye disorder **4.** glance —*a.* **5.** having a squint

squire ('skwīər) *n.* country gentleman

squirm (skwərm) *vi.* **1.** wriggle **2.** be embarrassed —*n.* **3.** squirming movement

squirrel ('skwirəl) *n.* **1.** any of various arboreal rodents with gray or reddish-brown fur and bushy tail. **2.** its bushy pelt

squirt (skwərt) *v.* **1.** force (liquid) or (of liquid) be forced through narrow opening —*n.* **2.** jet **3.** *inf.* short or insignificant person

Sr *Chem.* strontium

Sr. *or* **Sr 1.** Senior **2.** Sister

Sri Lanka (srē 'längkə) country lying off the southeast coast of India in the Indian Ocean —**Sri Lankan** ('längkən)

SS 1. Saints **2.** paramilitary organization within Nazi party that provided Hitler's bodyguard, security forces, concentration camp guards *etc.* **3.** (*also* **S.S.**) steamship

SSA Social Security Administration

SSE south-southeast

SSR Soviet Socialist Republic

SSS Selective Service System

SSW south-southwest

St. *or* **St 1.** Saint **2.** Strait **3.** Street

stab (stab) *v.* **1.** pierce, strike (at) with pointed weapon (**-bb-**) —*n.* **2.** blow, wound so inflicted **3.** sudden sensation, *eg* of fear **4.** attempt

stabilize ('stābilīz) *vt.* make steady, restore to equilibrium, *esp.* of money values, prices and wages —**stabili'zation** *n.* —**'stabilizer** *n.* device to maintain equilibrium of ship, aircraft *etc.*

stable¹ ('stābəl) *n.* **1.** building for horses **2.** race horses of particular owner, establishment **3.** such establishment —*vt.* **4.** put into stable

stable² ('stābəl) *a.* **1.** firmly fixed **2.** steadfast, resolute —**stability** (stə'biliti) *n.* **1.** steadiness **2.** ability to resist change of any kind —**'stably** *adv.*

staccato (stə'kätō) *a.* **1.** *Mus.* with notes sharply separated **2.** abrupt

stack (stak) *n.* **1.** ordered pile, heap **2.** chimney —*vt.* **3.** pile in stack **4.** control (aircraft waiting to land) so that they fly at different altitudes

stadium ('stādiəm) *n.* open-air arena for athletics *etc.* (*pl.* **-s, -dia** (-diə))

staff (staf) *n.* **1.** body of officers or workers employed by a company *etc.*; personnel (*pl.* **-s**) **2.** pole (*pl.* **-s, staves**) **3.** set of five lines on which music is written (*pl.* **-s, staves**) —*vt.* **4.** supply with personnel —**staff sergeant** noncommissioned officer who ranks: in Army, above sergeant and below sergeant first class; in Air Force, above airman first class and below technical sergeant; in Marine Corps, above sergeant and below gunnery sergeant

stag (stag) *n.* **1.** male deer —*a.* **2.** for men only

stage (stāj) *n.* 1. period, division of development 2. raised floor or platform 3. (platform of) theater 4. scene of action 5. stopping place on road, distance between two of them 6. separate unit of space rocket that can be jettisoned —*vt.* 7. put (play) on stage 8. arrange, bring about —**'staging** *n.* any temporary structure used in building, *esp.* platforms supported by scaffolding —**'stagy** *a.* theatrical —**'stagecoach** *n.* formerly, four-wheeled horse-drawn vehicle used to carry passengers *etc.* on regular route —**stage fright** panic that may beset person about to appear in front of audience —**'stagehand** *n.* person who sets stage, moves props *etc.* in theatrical production —**stage-manage** *v.* 1. work as stage manager for (play *etc.*) —*vt.* 2. arrange or supervise from behind the scenes —**stage manager** person who supervises stage arrangements of theatrical production —**stage-struck** *a.* infatuated with glamor of theatrical life —**stage whisper** loud whisper intended to be heard by audience

stagger ('stagər) *vi.* 1. walk unsteadily —*vt.* 2. astound 3. arrange in overlapping or alternating positions, times 4. distribute over a period —*n.* 5. act of staggering —*pl.* 6. form of vertigo 7. disease of horses —**'staggering** *a.* astounding

stagnate ('stagnāt) *vi.* cease to flow or develop —**'stagnant** *a.* 1. sluggish 2. not flowing 3. foul, impure —**stag'nation** *n.*

staid (stād) *a.* of sober and quiet character, sedate —**'staidly** *adv.* —**'staidness** *n.*

stain (stān) *vt.* 1. spot, mark 2. apply liquid coloring to (wood *etc.*) 3. bring disgrace upon —*n.* 4. spot, mark, discoloration 5. moral taint —**'stainless** *a.* —**stained glass** glass colored with metallic oxides and joined with lead strips to form design —**stainless steel** rustless steel alloy

stairs (stāərz) *pl.n.* set of steps, *esp.* as part of house —**'staircase** *n.* structure enclosing stairs —**'stairway** *n.* stairs —**'stairwell** *n.* vertical shaft that contains stairs

stake (stāk) *n.* 1. sharpened stick or post 2. money wagered or contended for —*vt.* 3. secure, mark out with stakes 4. wager, risk —**stake out** *sl.* keep under surveillance

stalactite (stə'laktīt, 'stalǝktīt) *n.* lime deposit like icicle on roof of cave

stalagmite (stə'lagmīt, 'stalǝgmīt) *n.* lime deposit like pillar on floor of cave

stale (stāl) *a.* 1. old, lacking freshness 2. hackneyed 3. lacking energy, interest through monotony —**'stalemate** *n.* 1. *Chess* position in chess when neither player can win as the player to move can only move his king into check 2. deadlock, impasse

stalk¹ (stök) *n.* 1. plant's stem 2. anything like this

stalk² (stök) *v.* 1. follow, approach (game *etc.*) stealthily —*vi.* 2. walk in stiff and stately manner —*n.* 3. stalking —**'stalking-horse** *n.* pretext

stall (stöl) *n.* 1. compartment in stable *etc.* 2. erection for display and sale of goods 3. seat in chancel of church 4. finger sheath —*vt.* 5. put in stall 6. hinder 7. stick fast —*v.* 8. delay 9. stop unintentionally (motor engine) 10. lose flying speed (of aircraft) —*vi.* 11. prevaricate

stallion ('stalyǝn) *n.* male horse, *esp.* one used for breeding

stalwart ('stölwǝrt) *a.* 1. strong 2. brave 3. staunch —*n.* 4. stalwart person

stamen ('stāmǝn) *n.* male organ of flowering plant (*pl.* **-s, stamina** ('stāminǝ, 'staminǝ))

stamina ('staminǝ) *n.* power of endurance, vitality

stammer ('stamǝr) *v.* 1. speak, say with repetition of syllables —*n.* 2. habit of so speaking —**'stammerer** *n.*

stamp (stamp) *vi.* 1. put down foot with force —*vt.* 2. impress mark on 3. affix postage stamp to 4. fix (in memory) 5. reveal, characterize —*n.* 6. stamping with foot 7. imprinted mark 8. appliance for marking 9. piece of gummed paper printed with device as evidence of postage *etc.* 10. character —**stamping ground** habitual meeting or gathering place

stampede (stam'pēd) *n.* 1. sudden frightened rush, *esp.* of herd of cattle 2. headlong rush of a crowd 3. **C** rodeo —*vi.* 4. cause, take part in stampede

stance (stans) *n.* 1. manner, position of standing 2. attitude 3. point of view

stanch (stönch, stänch) *vt.* *see* STAUNCH (sense 1)

stanchion ('stanchǝn) *n.* 1. upright bar, support —*vt.* 2. support

stand (stand) *v.* 1. have, take, set in upright position —*vi.* 2. remain 3. be situated 4. remain firm or stationary 5. cease to move 6. adhere to principles 7. offer oneself as a candidate 8. (*with* for) be symbol *etc.* (of) —*vt.* 9. endure 10. *inf.* provide free, treat to (**stood, 'standing**) —*n.* 11. holding firm 12. position 13. halt 14. something on which thing may be placed 15. structure from which spectators watch sport *etc.* 16. stop made by pop group *etc.* —**'standing** *n.* 1. reputation, status 2. duration —*a.* 3. erect 4. permanent, lasting 5. stagnant 6. performed from stationary position, as in *standing jump* —**stand-by** *n.* person or thing that is ready for use or can be relied on in emergency —**stand-in** *n.* person, thing that acts as substitute —**stand'offish** *a.* reserved or aloof —**'standstill** *n.* complete cessation of movement —**stand by** 1. be available and ready to act if needed 2. be present as onlooker 3. be faithful to —**stand in** deputize —**stand over** 1. watch closely 2. postpone

standard ('standǝrd) *n.* 1. accepted example of something against which others are judged 2. degree, quality 3. flag 4. weight or measure to which others must conform 5. post —*a.* 6. usual, regular 7. average 8. of recognized authority, competence 9. accepted as correct —**standardi'zation** *n.* —**'standardize** *vt.* regulate by a standard —**standard-bearer** *n.* 1. man who carries a standard 2. leader of party *etc.* —**standard gauge** railroad track with distance of 56½ inches between lines —**standard time** official local time of region or country determined by distance from Greenwich of line of longitude passing through area —**standard of living** level of subsistence or material welfare of community, person *etc.*

standpoint ('standpoint) *n.* 1. point of view, opinion 2. mental attitude

stank (stangk) *pt. of* STINK

stannary ('stanǝri) *n.* place or region where tin is mined or worked

stannous ('stanǝs) *a.* of, containing tin

stanza ('stanzǝ) *n.* group of lines of verse

staphylococcus (stafilō'kokǝs) *n.* spherical bacterium usu. growing in grapelike clusters, a major cause of common infections (*pl.* **-cocci** (-'koksī))

staple ('stāpǝl) *n.* 1. U-shaped piece of wire used to fasten papers, cloth *etc.* 2. short length of stiff wire formed into U-shape with pointed ends, used for holding hasp to post, securing electrical cables *etc.* 3. main product 4. fiber 5. pile of wool *etc.* —*a.* 6. principal 7. regularly produced or made for market —*vt.* 8. fasten with staple 9. sort, classify (wool *etc.*) according to length of fiber —**'stapler** *n.* small device for fastening papers together

star (stär) *n.* 1. celestial body, seen as twinkling point of light 2. asterisk (*) 3. celebrated player, actor *etc.* 4. medal, jewel *etc.* of apparent shape of star —*vt.* 5. adorn with stars 6. mark (with asterisk) 7. feature as star performer —*vi.* 8. play leading role (in motion picture *etc.*) (**-rr-**) —*a.* 9. leading, most important, famous —**'stardom** *n.* —**'starlet** *n.* young actress who is projected as potential star —**'starry** *a.* covered with stars —**star-crossed** *a.* dogged by ill luck —**'starfish** *n.* small star-shaped sea creature —**'stargaze** *vi.* 1. observe stars 2. daydream —**'stargazing** *n./a.* —**starry-eyed** *a.* given to naive wishes, judgments *etc.* —**Star-Spangled Banner** 1. national anthem of the United States 2. Stars and Stripes —**star-studded** *a.* featuring large proportion of well-known performers —**Star of David** Mogen David —**Stars and Stripes** the U.S. flag

starboard ('stärbǝrd) *n.* 1. right-hand side of ship, looking forward —*a.* 2. of, on this side

starch (stärch) *n.* 1. substance forming the main food element in bread, potatoes *etc.*, and used mixed with water, for stiffening certain fabrics —*vt.* 2. stiffen thus —**'starchy** *a.* 1. containing starch 2. stiff 3. formal 4. prim

stare (stāǝr) *vi.* 1. look fixedly 2. gaze with wide-open eyes —*n.* 3. staring, fixed gaze —**stare one in the face** be obvious or visible to one —**stare out** abash by staring at

stark (stärk) *a.* 1. blunt, bare 2. desolate 3. absolute —*adv.* 4. completely

starling ('stärling) *n.* glossy black speckled songbird

start (stärt) *vt.* 1. begin 2. set going —*vi.* 3. begin, *esp.* journey 4. make sudden movement —*n.* 5. beginning 6. abrupt movement 7. advantage of a lead in a race —**'starter** *n.* 1. electric motor starting automobile engine 2. competitor in, supervisor of, start of race

startle ('stärtǝl) *vt.* surprise, frighten or alarm suddenly

starve (stärv) *v.* (cause to) suffer or die from hunger —**star'vation** *n.*

stash (stash) *vt. inf.* put away, hide

-stat (*comb. form*) device that causes something to remain stationary or constant, as in *thermostat*

state (stāt) *n.* 1. condition 2. place, situation 3. politically organized people 4. government 5. rank 6. pomp —*vt.* 7. express in words —**'stated** *a.* 1. fixed 2. regular 3. settled —**'stateless** *a.* 1. without nationality 2. without state or states —**'stately** *a.* dignified, lofty —**'statement** *n.* 1. expression in words 2. account —**state attorney** *or* **state's attorney** legal officer representing a state in court proceedings —**state-of-the-art** *a.* (of hi-fi equipment *etc.*) up-to-the-minute —**'stateroom** *n.* 1. private cabin on ship 2. large room in palace, mansion, used for ceremonial occasions —**'stateside** *a.* denoting continental U.S. —**'statesman** *n.* respected political leader —**states' rights** all rights not vested in the federal government by the Constitution of the U.S. —**state tree** tree selected as emblem for a state

static ('statik) *a.* 1. motionless, inactive 2. pert. to bodies at rest or in equilibrium 3. *Comp.* (of a memory) not needing its contents refreshed periodically —*n.* 4. electrical interference in radio reception —*pl.* 5. (*with sing. v.*) branch of physics —**'statically** *adv.*

station ('stāshən) *n.* **1.** place where thing stops or is placed **2.** stopping place for railroad trains **3.** local office for police force, fire brigade *etc.* **4.** place equipped for radio or television transmission **5.** bus garage **6.** post, employment **7.** status **8.** position in life —*vt.* **9.** put in position —'**stationary** *a.* **1.** not moving, fixed **2.** not changing —**Stations of the Cross** series of 14 images representing the events of Christ's Passion —**station wagon** automobile longer than sedan with open trunk area

stationer ('stāshənər) *n.* dealer in writing materials *etc.* —'**stationery** *n.*

statistics (stə'tistiks) *pl.n.* **1.** numerical facts collected systematically and arranged **2.** (*with sing. v.*) the study of them —**sta'tistical** *a.* —**sta'tistically** *adv.* —**statis'tician** *n.* one who compiles and studies statistics

statue ('stachōō) *n.* solid carved or cast image of person, animal *etc.* —'**statuary** *n.* statues collectively —**statuesque** (stachōō'esk) *a.* **1.** like statue **2.** dignified —**statu'ette** *n.* small statue

stature ('stachər) *n.* **1.** bodily height **2.** greatness

status ('stātəs) *n.* **1.** position, rank **2.** prestige **3.** relation to others —**status quo** (kwō) existing state of affairs —**status symbol** possession regarded as proof of owner's wealth *etc.*

statute ('stachōōt) *n.* written law —'**statutory** *a.* enacted, defined or authorized by statute

staunch (stönch) *vt.* **1.** stop flow of (blood) (*also* **stanch**) —*a.* **2.** trustworthy, loyal

Staunton ('stöntən) *a.* denoting pattern of chessmen used in tournament and club play

stave (stāv) *n.* **1.** one of the pieces forming barrel **2.** verse, stanza **3.** *Mus.* staff —*vt.* **4.** (*usu. with* in) burst or force (hole in something) **5.** (*with* off) ward (off) (**stove, staved** *pt./pp.,* '**staving** *pr.p.*)

staves (stāvz) *n., pl. of* STAFF, STAVE

stay' (stā) *vi.* **1.** remain **2.** sojourn **3.** pause **4.** wait **5.** endure —*vt.* **6.** stop **7.** hinder **8.** postpone (**stayed,** '**staying**) —*n.* **9.** remaining, sojourning **10.** check **11.** restraint **12.** deterrent **13.** postponement —**stay-at-home** *a./n.* (person) enjoying quiet and unadventurous use of leisure —**staying power** endurance

stay² (stā) *n.* **1.** support, prop **2.** rope supporting mast *etc.* —*pl.* **3.** formerly, laced corsets

stead (sted) *n. rare* place —**stand (someone) in good stead** be useful or of good service to (someone)

steady ('stedi) *a.* **1.** firm **2.** regular **3.** temperate **4.** industrious **5.** reliable —*vt.* **6.** make steady —'**steadily** *adv.* —'**steadiness** *n.* —'**steadfast** *a.* firm, fixed, unyielding —'**steadfastly** *adv.* —**steady state** *Phys.* condition of system when some or all of quantities describing it are independent of time —**steady (on)** be careful

steak (stāk) *n.* **1.** thick slice of meat **2.** slice of fish

steal (stēl) *v.* **1.** take (something) without right or leave —*vi.* **2.** move silently (**stole,** '**stolen,** '**stealing**)

stealth (stelth) *n.* secret or underhand procedure, behavior —'**stealthily** *adv.* —'**stealthy** *a.*

steam (stēm) *n.* **1.** vapor of boiling water **2.** *inf.* power, energy —*vi.* **3.** give off steam **4.** rise in vapor **5.** move by steam power —*vt.* **6.** cook or treat with steam —'**steamer** *n.* **1.** steam-propelled ship **2.** vessel for cooking or treating with steam —'**steamy** *a.* **1.** of, full of,

or covered with steam **2.** *inf.* lustful —**steam bath** room or enclosure that can be filled with steam in which people bathe to induce sweating and refresh or cleanse themselves —**steam-engine** *n.* engine worked or propelled by steam —**steam iron** electric iron that emits steam to facilitate pressing and ironing —'**steam'roller** *n.* **1.** large roller, *orig.* moved by steam, for leveling road surfaces *etc.* **2.** any great power used to crush opposition —*vt.* **3.** crush —'**steamship** *n.*

stearin ('stēərin) *n.* **1.** colorless crystalline ester, present in fats and used in soap and candles (*also* **tri'stearin**) **2.** fat in its solid form

steatite ('stēətīt) *n.* soapstone

steatopygia (stēətə'pījiə) *n.* hereditary condition of overdevelopment of the buttocks

steatorrhea (stēətə'rēə) *n.* excessive secretion of fat in the stool

steed (stēd) *n. Poet.* horse

steel (stēl) *n.* **1.** hard and malleable metal made by mixing carbon in iron **2.** tool, weapon of steel **3.** C railroad track, line —*vt.* **4.** harden —'**steely** *a.* —**steel band** type of band consisting mainly of percussion instruments made from oildrums —**steel guitar** *see* GUITAR —**steel wool** woven mass of fine steel fibers, used for cleaning or polishing

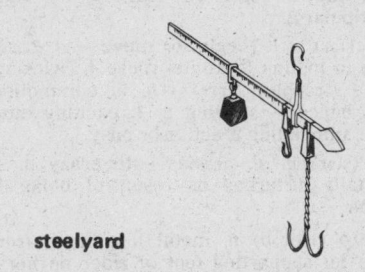

steelyard

steelyard ('stēlyärd) *n.* kind of balance with unequal arms

steep' (stēp) *a.* **1.** rising, sloping abruptly **2.** precipitous **3.** *inf.* difficult **4.** (of prices) very high or exorbitant **5.** *inf.* unreasonable —'**steepen** *v.* —'**steeply** *adv.*

steep² (stēp) *vt.* **1.** soak, saturate —*vi.* **2.** be soaked —*n.* **3.** act or process of steeping **4.** the liquid used for this purpose

steeple ('stēpəl) *n.* church tower with spire —'**steeplechase** *n.* **1.** horse race with ditches and fences to jump **2.** foot race with hurdles *etc.* to jump —'**steeplejack** *n.* one who builds, repairs chimneys, steeples *etc.*

steer' (stēər) *vt.* **1.** guide, direct course of (vessel, motor vehicle *etc.*) —*vi.* **2.** direct one's course —'**steerage** *n.* **1.** effect of a helm **2.** formerly, cheapest accommodation on ship —**steering committee** committee set up to prepare topics to be discussed, order of business *etc.* for legislative assembly *etc.* —**steering gear, wheel** *etc.* mechanism for steering —'**steersman** *n.* helmsman of vessel

steer² (stēər) *n.* castrated male ox

stein (stīn) *n.* earthenware beer mug

stele (stēl, 'stēli) *n.* ancient carved stone pillar or slab (*pl.* **stelae** ('stēlē), **steles** ('stēliz, stēlz))

stellar ('stelər) *a.* of stars

stem' (stem) *n.* **1.** stalk, trunk **2.** long slender part, as in tobacco pipe **3.** part of word to

which inflections are added **4.** foremost part of ship

stem² (stem) *vt.* check, stop, dam up (**-mm-**)

stench (stench) *n.* offensive smell

stencil ('stensəl) *n.* **1.** thin sheet of plastic or metal pierced with pattern, which is brushed over with paint or ink, leaving pattern on surface under it **2.** pattern produced by this process —*vt.* **3.** mark (surface) with stencil

Sten gun (sten) light sub-machine-gun

stenography (stə'nogrəfi) *n.* shorthand writing —**ste'nographer** *n.* —**steno'graphic** *a.*

stentorian (sten'töriən) *a.* (of voice) very loud

step (step) *vi.* **1.** move and set down foot **2.** proceed (in this way) —*vt.* **3.** measure in paces (**-pp-**) —*n.* **4.** act of stepping **5.** sound made by stepping **6.** mark made by foot **7.** manner of walking **8.** series of foot movements forming part of dance **9.** gait **10.** pace **11.** measure, act, stage in proceeding **12.** board, rung *etc.* to put foot on **13.** degree in scale **14.** mast socket **15.** promotion —*pl.* **16.** stepladder —'**stepladder** *n.* four-legged ladder having broad flat steps —**stepping stone 1.** one of series of stones acting as footrests for crossing streams *etc.* **2.** circumstance that assists progress toward some goal

stepchild ('stepchīld) *n.* child of husband or wife by former marriage —'**stepbrother** *n.* —'**stepfather** *n.* —'**stepmother** *n.* —'**stepsister** *n.*

stephanotis (stefə'nōtis) *n.* climbing shrub with fragrant waxy flowers

steppe (step) *n.* (*oft. pl.*) extensive treeless plain in European and Asiatic Russia

-ster (*comb. form*) **1.** indicating person who is engaged in certain activity, as in *prankster* **2.** indicating person associated with or being something specified, as in *mobster, youngster*

stere (stēər) *n.* cubic meter

stereo- *or sometimes before vowel* **stere-** (*comb. form*) three-dimensional quality or solidity, as in *stereoscope*

stereophonic (steriə'fonik, stēər-) *a.* (of sound reproduction) using two or more separate microphones to feed two or more loudspeakers through separate channels in order to give spatial effect to sound —'**stereo** *a./n.* (of, for) stereophonic phonograph *etc.*

stereoscope ('steriəskōp, 'stēər-) *n.* optical instrument for viewing two-dimensional pictures, giving illusion of depth and relief —**stereoscopic** (steriə'skopik, stēər-) *a.*

stereotype ('steriətīp, 'stēər-) *n.* **1.** metal plate for printing cast from set-up type **2.** something (monotonously) familiar, conventional, predictable —*vt.* **3.** make stereotype of —'**stereotyped** *a.* **1.** lacking originality or individuality **2.** reproduced from or on stereotype printing plate

sterile ('steril) *a.* **1.** unable to produce fruit, crops, young *etc.* **2.** free from (harmful) germs —**ste'rility** *n.* —**sterili'zation** *n.* process or act of making sterile —'**sterilize** *vt.* render sterile

sterling ('stərling) *a.* **1.** genuine, true **2.** of solid worth, dependable **3.** in British money —*n.* **4.** British money —**sterling silver** alloy of 925 parts silver to 75 parts base metal

stern' (stərn) *a.* severe, strict

stern² (stərn) *n.* rear part of ship

sternum ('stərnəm) *n.* breastbone (*pl.* **-na** (-nə), **-s**)

steroid ('stēəroid) *n.* any of group of naturally occurring substances, *eg* sex hormones, cholesterol, digitalis, cortisone, with basic structure of 17 carbon atoms in four fused ring systems, producing variety of physiological effects on human body

stertorous ('stərtərəs) *a.* **1.** with sound of heavy snoring **2.** breathing in this way

stet (stet) *Lat.*, let it stand (proofreader's direction to cancel alteration previously made)

stethoscope ('stethəskōp) *n.* instrument for listening to action of heart, lungs *etc.*

stetson ('stetsən) *n.* type of broad-brimmed felt hat

stevedore ('stēvidör) *n.* one who loads or unloads ships

stew (styōō, stōō) *n.* **1.** food cooked slowly in closed vessel **2.** state of excitement, agitation or worry —*v.* **3.** cook by stewing —**stewed** *a.* **1.** (of fish *etc.*) cooked by stewing **2.** *sl.* drunk

steward ('styōōərd, 'stōōərd) *n.* **1.** one who manages another's property **2.** official managing race meeting, assembly *etc.* **3.** attendant on ship's or aircraft's passengers ('**stewardess** *fem.*)

stick (stik) *n.* **1.** long, thin piece of wood **2.** anything shaped like a stick **3.** *inf.* person, as in *good stick* —*vt.* **4.** pierce, stab **5.** place, fasten, as by pins, glue **6.** *inf.* tolerate, abide —*vi.* **7.** adhere **8.** come to stop, jam **9.** remain **10.** be fastened (**stuck** *pt./pp.*) —'**sticker** *n.* adhesive label, poster —'**sticky** *a.* **1.** covered with, like adhesive substance **2.** (of weather) warm, humid **3.** *inf.* difficult, unpleasant —**stick insect** insect that resembles a twig —**stick-in-the-mud** *n. inf.* person who lacks initiative or imagination —**stick-up** *n. sl.* robbery at gunpoint —**stick out** protrude —**stick up** *sl.* rob, *esp.* at gunpoint —**stick up for** *inf.* support or defend

stickleback ('stikəlbak) *n.* small fish with sharp spines on back

stickler ('stiklər) *n.* (*usu. with* for) person who insists on something

stiff (stif) *a.* **1.** not easily bent or moved **2.** rigid **3.** awkward **4.** difficult **5.** thick, not fluid **6.** formal **7.** stubborn **8.** unnatural **9.** strong or fresh, as breeze **10.** *inf.* excessive —*n.* **11.** *sl.* corpse —'**stiffen** *v.* —'**stiffly** *adv.* —'**stiffness** *n.* —**stiff-necked** *a.* obstinate, stubborn

stifle ('stīfəl) *vt.* smother, suppress

stigma ('stigmə) *n.* distinguishing mark, *esp.* of disgrace (*pl.* **-s, stigmata** (stig'mätə, 'stigmətə)) —'**stigmatism** *n.* —'**stigmatize** *vt.* mark with stigma

stile (stīl) *n.* arrangement of steps for climbing a fence

stiletto (sti'letō) *n.* **1.** small dagger **2.** small boring tool **3.** very high heel on woman's shoe, tapering to very narrow tip (*pl.* **-s**) —*a.* **4.** thin, pointed like stiletto

still[1] (stil) *a.* **1.** motionless **2.** noiseless **3.** at rest —*vt.* **4.** quiet —*adv.* **5.** to this time **6.** yet **7.** even —*n.* **8.** photograph, *esp.* of motion-picture scene —'**stillness** *n.* —**still'born** *a.* born dead —**still life** painting of inanimate objects

still[2] (stil) *n.* apparatus for distilling —**still room** pantry, store room in large house

stilt (stilt) *n.* **1.** pole with footrests for walking raised from ground **2.** long post supporting building *etc.* **3.** shore bird similar to avocet but having straight bill —'**stilted** *a.* stiff in manner, pompous —'**stiltedly** *adv.*

Stilton ('stiltən) *n.* semihard, double cream, inoculated blue-mold cheese, *orig.* from England

stimulus ('stimyələs) *n.* **1.** something that rouses to activity **2.** incentive (*pl.* **-uli** (-yəlī, -yəlē)) —'**stimulant** *n.* drug *etc.* acting as a stimulus —'**stimulate** *vt.* rouse up, spur

—'**stimulating** *a.* acting as stimulus —**stimu'lation** *n.* —'**stimulative** *a./n.*

sting (sting) *vt.* **1.** thrust sting into **2.** cause sharp pain to **3.** *sl.* impose upon by asking for money **4.** overcharge —*vi.* **5.** feel sharp pain (**stung, 'stinging**) —*n.* **6.** (wound, pain, caused by) sharp pointed organ, oft. poisonous, of certain insects and animals —'**stingray** *n.* ray having whiplike tail bearing serrated venomous spine capable of inflicting painful weals

stingy ('stinji) *a.* **1.** niggardly **2.** avaricious —'**stingily** *adv.* —'**stinginess** *n.*

stink (stingk) *vi.* **1.** give out strongly offensive smell **2.** *sl.* be abhorrent (**stank, stunk, 'stinking**) —*n.* **3.** such smell, stench **4.** *inf.* fuss, bother —'**stinker** *n. sl.* **1.** difficult or unpleasant person or thing **2.** something of very poor quality —**stink bomb** small bomb containing liquid with offensive smell

stint (stint) *v.* **1.** be frugal, miserly to (someone) with (something) —*n.* **2.** allotted amount of work or time **3.** limitation, restriction

stipend ('stīpend) *n.* salary, *esp.* of clergyman —sti'**pendiary** *a.* receiving stipend

stipple ('stipəl) *vt.* **1.** engrave, paint in dots —*n.* **2.** this process

stipulate ('stipyəlāt) *vt.* specify in making a bargain —**stipu'lation** *n.* proviso, condition —'**stipulator** *n.*

stipule ('stipyōōl) *n.* small paired outgrowth occurring at base of leaf or its stalk —'**stipular** *a.*

stir[1] (stər) *v.* **1.** (begin to) move —*vt.* **2.** set, keep in motion **3.** excite; rouse **4.** (*with* up) cause (trouble) (**-rr-**) —*n.* **5.** commotion, disturbance —'**stirring** *a.* **1.** exciting emotions; stimulating **2.** active or busy

stir[2] (stər) *n. sl.* prison —**stir-crazy** *a. sl.* mentally disturbed as result of being in prison

stirrup ('stirəp) *n.* metal loop hung from strap for supporting foot of rider on horse (*also* **stirrup iron**) —**stirrup pump** hand-operated pump, base of cylinder of which is placed in bucket of water: used in fighting fires

stitch (stich) *n.* **1.** movement of needle in sewing *etc.* **2.** its result in the work **3.** sharp pain in side **4.** least fragment (of clothing) —*vt.* **5.** sew, fasten *etc.* with stitches

stoat (stōt) *n.* the ermine in its brown summer coat

stock (stok) *n.* **1.** goods, material stored, *esp.* for sale or later use **2.** reserve, fund **3.** financial shares in, or capital of, company *etc.* **4.** standing, reputation **5.** farm animals, livestock **6.** plant, stem from which cuttings are taken **7.** handle of gun, tool *etc.* **8.** liquid broth produced by boiling meat *etc.* **9.** flowering plant **10.** lineage —*pl.* **11.** *Hist.* frame to secure feet, hands (of offender) **12.** frame to support ship during construction —*a.* **13.** kept in stock **14.** standard, hackneyed —*vt.* **15.** keep (goods) for sale **16.** supply with livestock, fish *etc.* —'**stocky** *a.* thickset —'**stockbreeder** *n.* person who breeds livestock as occupation —'**stockbroker** *n.* agent for buying, selling shares in companies —**stock car** ordinary car strengthened and modified for a form of racing in which cars often collide —**stock certificate** certificate signifying ownership of one or more shares in a corporation —**stock exchange** institution for buying and selling shares —'**stockman** *n.* man experienced in driving, handling cattle, sheep —**stock market** stock exchange —'**stockpile** *v.* acquire and store large

quantity of (something) —**stock-still** *a.* motionless —'**stocktaking** *n.* examination, counting and valuing of goods in shop *etc.* —'**stockyard** *n.* yard with pens or covered buildings where farm animals are assembled, sold *etc.* —**stock in trade 1.** goods necessary for carrying on business **2.** anything constantly used by someone as part of his occupation, trade *etc.*

stockade (sto'kād) *n.* enclosure of stakes, barrier

stockinet (stoki'net) *n.* machine-knitted elastic fabric

stocking ('stoking) *n.* one of pair of close-fitting coverings for legs and feet —'**stockinged** *a.*

stodgy ('stoji) *a.* (*esp.* of food) heavy, dull —**stodge** *n.* heavy, solid food

stoic ('stōik) *a.* **1.** capable of much self-control, great endurance without complaint —*n.* **2.** stoical person —'**stoical** *a.* —'**stoicism** ('stōisizəm) *n.*

stoke (stōk) *v.* feed, tend (fire or furnace) —'**stoker** *n.* —'**stokehold** *n. Naut.* **1.** coal bunker for ship's furnace **2.** hold for ship's boilers; fire room —'**stokehole** *n.* **1.** stokehold **2.** hole in furnace through which it is stoked

stole[1] (stōl) *pt. of* STEAL —'**stolen** *pp. of* STEAL

stole[2] (stōl) *n.* long scarf or shawl

stolid ('stolid) *a.* **1.** hard to excite **2.** heavy, slow, apathetic —**sto'lidity** *n.* —'**stolidly** *adv.*

stoma ('stōmə) *n.* **1.** *Bot.* epidermal pore in plant leaves, that controls passage of gases through plant **2.** *Zool., anat.* mouth or mouthlike part (*pl.* '**stomata**)

stomach ('stumək) *n.* **1.** sac forming chief digestive organ in any animal **2.** appetite **3.** desire, inclination —*vt.* **4.** put up with —**stomach pump** suction device for removing stomach contents —**stomach ache** pain in stomach or abdomen

stomp (stomp) *vi. inf.* stamp

stone (stōn) *n.* **1.** (piece of) rock **2.** gem **3.** hard seed of fruit **4.** hard deposit formed in kidneys, bladder **5.** grindstone, millstone —*vt.* **6.** throw stones at **7.** free (fruit) from stones —**stoned** *a. sl.* stupefied by alcohol or drugs —'**stonily** *adv.* —'**stony** *or* '**stoney** *a.* **1.** of, like stone **2.** hard **3.** cold —**Stone Age** period in human culture identified by use of stone implements —**stone-blind** *a.* completely blind —'**stonechat** *n.* common European songbird —**stone-cold** *a.* completely cold —**stone-cold sober** completely sober —'**stonecrop** *n.* any of the sedums *esp.* useful as rock and wall plants —**stone deaf** completely deaf —'**stonemason** *n.* person skilled in preparing stone for building —**stone's throw** short distance —'**stoneware** *n.* hard, opaque vitrified ceramic ware —**stony-broke** *a. sl.* with no money left

stood (stōōd) *pt./pp. of* STAND

stooge (stōōj) *n.* **1.** *Theat. etc.* performer who is always the butt of another's jokes **2.** *sl.* one taken advantage of by another

stook (stōōk) *n.* group of sheaves set upright in field to dry

stool (stōōl) *n.* **1.** backless chair **2.** excrement —**stool pigeon 1.** living or dummy pigeon used as decoy **2.** police informer

stoop (stōōp) *vi.* **1.** lean forward or down, bend **2.** swoop **3.** abase, degrade oneself —*n.* **4.** stooping carriage of the body

stop (stop) *vt.* **1.** check, bring to halt **2.** prevent **3.** interrupt **4.** suspend **5.** desist from **6.** fill up (an opening) —*vi.* **7.** cease, come to a halt **8.** stay (**-pp-**) —*n.* **9.** stopping or becoming stopped **10.** punctuation mark, *esp.*

full stop 11. any device for altering or regulating pitch 12. set of pipes in organ having tones of a distinct quality —'**stoppage** n. —'**stopper** n. plug for closing bottle etc. —'**stopgap** n. temporary substitute —'**stoplight** n. taillight of a vehicle that lights up as the driver steps on the brake pedal to slow down or stop —'**stopoff** or '**stopover** n. short break in journey —'**stopwatch** n. watch which can be stopped for exact timing of race

store (stōr) vt. 1. stock, furnish, keep —n. 2. shop 3. abundance 4. stock 5. department store 6. place for keeping goods 7. warehouse —pl. 8. stocks of goods, provisions —'**storage** n. —**storage battery** accumulator —'**storehouse** n.

stork (störk) n. large wading bird

storm (störm) n. 1. violent weather with wind, rain, hail, sand, snow etc. 2. assault on fortress 3. violent outbreak, discharge —vt. 4. assault 5. take by storm —vi. 6. rage —'**stormy** a. 1. like storm 2. (emotionally) violent —**storm center** 1. center of cyclonic storm etc. where pressure is lowest 2. center of disturbance or trouble —**storm door** additional door outside ordinary door, providing extra insulation against wind etc. —**storm petrel** or **stormy petrel** 1. any of various small sea birds typically having dark plumage and paler underparts 2. person who brings trouble —**storm-trooper** n. 1. member of Nazi S.A. 2. member of force of shock troops

story ('stōri) n. 1. (book, piece of prose etc.) telling about events, happenings 2. inf. lie 3. horizontal division of a building (also 'storey) —'**storybook** n. book containing stories, esp. for children —'**storyteller** n.

stoup (stōōp) n. small basin near church door for holy water

stout (stowt) a. 1. fat 2. sturdy 3. resolute —n. 4. kind of beer —'**stoutly** adv. —'**stoutness** n. —'**stout'hearted** a. brave

stove¹ (stōv) n. apparatus for cooking, heating etc. —'**stovepipe** n. 1. pipe that serves as flue to stove 2. man's tall silk hat

stove² (stōv) pt./pp. of STAVE

stow (stō) vt. pack away —'**stowage** n. —'**stowaway** n. one who hides in ship to obtain free passage

strabismus (strə'bizməs) n. abnormal parallel alignment of one or both eyes, characterized by turning inward or outward from nose (also **squint**)

straddle ('stradəl) vt. 1. bestride —vi. 2. spread legs wide —n. 3. act or position of straddling

Stradivarius (stradi'variəs, -'ver-) n. 1. violin or cello made by member of the Stradivarius family (also **Strad**) 2. **Antonius**. 1644-1737, violin-maker of Cremona, pupil of Nicolò Amati

strafe (strāf) vt. attack (esp. with bullets, rockets) from air

straggle ('stragəl) vi. stray, get dispersed, linger —'**straggler** n.

straight (strāt) a. 1. without bend 2. honest 3. level 4. in order 5. (of spirits) undiluted, neat 6. expressionless 7. (of drama, actor etc.) serious 8. sl. heterosexual —n. 9. straight state or part —adv. 10. direct —'**straighten** v. —**straighta'way** adv. immediately (also **straight away**) —**straight face** serious facial expression, esp. one that conceals impulse to laugh —**straight-faced** a. —**straight-'forward** a. 1. open, frank 2. simple 3. honest —**straight'forwardly** adv. —**straight man** subsidiary actor who acts as stooge to comedian

strain¹ (strān) vt. 1. stretch tightly 2. stretch to full or to excess 3. filter —vi. 4. make great effort —n. 5. stretching force 6. violent effort 7. injury from being strained 8. burst of music or poetry 9. great demand 10. (condition caused by) overwork, worry etc. 11. tone of speaking or writing —**strained** a. —'**strainer** n. 1. filter, sieve 2. stretcher, tightener

strain² (strān) n. 1. breed or race 2. esp. Biol. type 3. trace, streak

strait (strāt) n. 1. channel of water connecting two larger areas of water —pl. 2. position of difficulty or distress —a. 3. narrow 4. strict —'**straiten** vt. 1. make strait, narrow 2. press with poverty —'**straitjacket** n. jacket to confine arms of violent person —**strait-laced** a. 1. austere, strict 2. puritanical

strand¹ (strand) v. 1. run aground 2. leave, be left helpless or in difficulties —n. 3. Poet. shore

strand² (strand) n. one of individual fibers or threads of string, wire etc.

strange (strānj) a. 1. odd, queer 2. unaccustomed 3. foreign 4. uncommon 5. wonderful 6. singular —'**strangely** adv. —'**strangeness** n. —'**stranger** n. 1. unknown person 2. foreigner 3. (with to) one unaccustomed (to)

strangle ('stranggəl) vt. 1. kill by squeezing windpipe 2. suppress —**strangu'lation** n. strangling —'**stranglehold** n. 1. wrestling hold in which wrestler's arms are pressed against opponent's windpipe 2. complete control over person or situation

strap (strap) n. 1. strip, esp. of leather —vt. 2. fasten, beat with strap (-**pp**-) —'**strapping** a. tall and well-made —'**straphanger** n. in bus, train, one who has to stand, steadying himself with strap provided for this

strata ('strātə, 'stratə) n., pl. of STRATUM

stratagem ('stratijəm) n. plan, trick —**strategic(al)** (strə'tējik(əl)) a. —'**strategist** n. —'**strategy** n. 1. art of war 2. overall plan

strathspey (strath'spā) n. type of Scottish dance with gliding steps

stratosphere ('stratəsfēər) n. upper part of the atmosphere, approx. 15 miles above earth's surface

stratum ('strātəm, 'stratəm) n. 1. layer, esp. of rock 2. class in society (pl. -**s**, -**ta**) —**stratification** (stratifi'kāshən) n. —'**stratify** ('stratifī) v. form, deposit in layers (-**ified**, -**ifying**)

stratus ('strātəs, 'stratəs) n. gray layer cloud (pl. -**ti** (-tī))

straw (strö) n. 1. stalks of grain 2. single stalk 3. long, narrow tube used to suck up liquid —**strawberry** ('ströberi, -bəri) n. 1. any of various temperature zone plants bearing a soft juicy fruit with seeds on the surface 2. the usu. red conical fruit —**strawberry blonde** (of hair) reddish blonde —**strawberry mark** soft vascular red birthmark

stray (strā) vi. 1. wander 2. digress 3. get lost —a. 4. strayed 5. occasional, scattered —n. 6. stray animal

streak (strēk) n. 1. long line or band 2. element, trace —vt. 3. mark with streaks —vi. 4. move fast —'**streaky** a. 1. having streaks 2. striped

stream (strēm) n. 1. flowing body of water or other liquid 2. steady flow 3. current or flow of air —vi. 4. flow 5. run with liquid 6. float, wave in the air —'**streamer** n. 1. (paper) ribbon 2. narrow flag —**stream of consciousness** 1. Psychol. continuous flow of ideas, feelings etc. forming content of individual's consciousness 2. literary technique that reveals flow of thoughts and feelings of

characters through long passages of soliloquy

streamlined ('strēmlīnd) a. (of automobile, plane etc.) built so as to offer least resistance to air

street (strēt) n. public thoroughfare in town or village, usu. lined with houses —'**streetwalker** n. prostitute

strength (strength) n. 1. quality of being strong 2. power 3. capacity for exertion or endurance 4. vehemence 5. force 6. full or necessary number of people —'**strengthen** v. make or become stronger —**on the strength of** 1. relying on 2. because of

strenuous ('strenyōōəs) a. 1. energetic 2. earnest —'**strenuously** adv.

streptobacillary fever (streptōbə'siləri) see HAVERHILL FEVER

streptococcus (streptō'kokəs) n. any of genus of bacteria that produces lactic acid from the fermentation of sugars, producing cheese and butter and causing disease, eg pneumonia, erysipelas (pl. -**cocci** (-'koksī))

streptomycin (streptə'mīsin) n. antibiotic drug produced by soil microorganism

stress (stres) n. 1. emphasis 2. strain 3. impelling force 4. effort 5. tension —vt. 6. emphasize 7. accent 8. put mechanical stress on

stretch (strech) vt. 1. extend 2. exert to utmost 3. tighten, pull out 4. reach out —vi. 5. reach 6. have elasticity —n. 7. stretching, being stretched, expanse 8. spell —'**stretcher** n. 1. person, thing that stretches 2. appliance on which ill, wounded or dead person is carried 3. wooden frame on which canvas for a painting is stretched

strew (strōō) vt. scatter over surface, spread (**strewed** pt., **strewed** or **strewn** pp., '**strewing** pr.p.)

strewth (strōōth) interj. expression of surprise or dismay

stria ('strīə) n. small channel or threadlike line in surface of shell or other object (pl. **striae** ('strīē)) —**striate** ('strīit) a. 1. streaked, furrowed, grooved (also '**striated**) —vt. ('strīāt) 2. mark with streaks 3. score —**stri'ation** n.

stricken ('strikən) a. 1. seriously affected by disease, grief, famine 2. afflicted —v. 3. pp. of STRIKE

strict (strikt) a. 1. not lax or indulgent 2. defined 3. without exception —'**strictly** adv.

stricture ('strikchər) n. 1. critical remark 2. constriction

stride (strīd) vi. 1. walk with long steps (**strode, stridden** ('stridən), '**striding**) —n. 2. single step 3. its length 4. regular pace

strident ('strīdənt) a. 1. harsh in tone 2. loud 3. urgent

strife (strīf) n. 1. conflict 2. quarreling

strike (strīk) v. 1. hit (against) 2. ignite 3. (of snake) bite 4. (of plants) (cause to) take root 5. attack 6. hook (fish) 7. sound (time) as bell in clock etc. —vt. 8. affect 9. arrive at, come upon 10. enter mind of 11. discover (gold, oil etc.) 12. dismantle, remove 13. make (coin) —vi. 14. cease work as protest or to make demands (**struck** pt., '**stricken, struck** pp., '**striking** pr.p.) —n. 15. act of striking —'**striker** n. —'**striking** a. noteworthy, impressive —'**strikebreaker** n. person who tries to make strike ineffectual by working —'**strikebreaking** n./a. —**strike pay** or **benefit** allowance paid by labor union to members on strike —**strike off** remove

Strine (strīn) n. humorous transliteration of Australian pronunciation

string (string) n. 1. (length of) thin cord or other material 2. strand, row 3. series 4. fiber in plants —pl. 5. conditions —vt. 6. provide with, thread on string 7. form in line, series (**strung, 'stringing**) —**stringed** a. (of musical instruments) furnished with strings —**'stringer** n. 1. Archit. horizontal timber beam used for structural purposes 2. Naut. longitudinal structural brace for strengthening hull of vessel 3. part-time journalist retained by newspaper to cover particular area —**'stringy** a. 1. like string 2. fibrous —**string course** Archit. ornamental projecting band or continuous molding along wall (also **'cordon**)

stringent ('strinjənt) a. strict, rigid, binding —**'stringency** n. severity —**'stringently** adv.

strip (strip) vt. 1. lay bare, take covering off 2. dismantle 3. deprive —vi. 4. undress (**-pp-**) —n. 5. long, narrow piece 6. act of undressing or performing striptease —**'stripper** n. —**strip poker** game of poker in which loser of a hand removes an article of clothing —**'striptease** n. cabaret or theater act in which person undresses

stripe (strīp) n. 1. narrow mark, band 2. chevron as symbol of military rank —**'stripy** a.

stripling ('stripling) n. youth

strive (strīv) vi. try hard, struggle, contend (**strove, striven** ('strivən), **'striving**)

strobe (strōb) n. apparatus which produces high-intensity flashing light

stroboscope ('strōbəskōp) n. 1. instrument producing intense flashing light 2. similar device synchronized with shutter of camera so that series of still photographs can be taken of moving object —**stroboscopic(al)** (strōbə'skopik(əl)) a.

strode (strōd) pt. of STRIDE

stroke (strōk) n. 1. blow 2. sudden action, occurrence 3. apoplexy 4. mark of pen, pencil, brush etc. 5. chime of clock 6. completed movement in series 7. act, manner of striking (ball etc.) 8. style, method of swimming 9. rower sitting nearest stern setting the rate of rowing 10. act of stroking —vt. 11. set stroke for (rowing crew) 12. pass hand lightly over

stroll (strōl) vi. 1. walk in leisurely or idle manner —n. 2. leisurely walk

strong (strong) a. 1. powerful 2. robust 3. healthy 4. difficult to break 5. noticeable 6. intense 7. emphatic 8. not diluted 9. having a certain number —**'strongly** adv. —**strong-arm** inf. a. 1. of or involving physical force or violence —vt. 2. show violence toward —**'strongbox** n. box or safe in which valuables are locked for safety —**'stronghold** n. fortress —**strong language** swearing

strontium ('stronchiəm, -chəm; 'strontiəm) n. Chem. metallic element Symbol Sr, at. wt. 87.6, at. no. 38 —**strontium 90** radioactive isotope of strontium present in fallout of nuclear explosions

strop (strop) n. 1. leather for sharpening razors —vt. 2. sharpen on strop (**-pp-**) —**'stroppy** a. sl. angry, awkward

strophe ('strōfi) n. division of ode —**strophic** ('strōfik, 'strof-) a.

strove (strōv) pt. of STRIVE

struck (struk) pt./pp. of STRIKE

structure ('strukchər) n. 1. (arrangement of parts in) construction, building etc. 2. form 3. organization —vt. 4. give structure to —**'structural** a.

strudel ('stroodəl) n. thin sheet of dough usu. filled with apple and baked

struggle ('strugəl) vi. 1. contend 2. fight 3. proceed, work, move with difficulty and effort —n. 4. act of struggling

strum (strum) v. stroke strings of (guitar etc.) (**-mm-**)

strumpet ('strumpit) n. obs. promiscuous woman

strung (strung) pt./pp. of STRING

strut (strut) vi. 1. walk affectedly or pompously (**-tt-**) —n. 2. brace 3. rigid support, usu. set obliquely 4. strutting gait

strychnine ('striknīn, -nin, -nēn) n. poison obtained from nux vomica seeds —**'strychnic** a.

stub (stub) n. 1. remnant of anything, eg pencil, cigarette etc. 2. counterfoil of check etc. —vt. 3. strike (toes) against fixed object 4. extinguish by pressing against surface (**-bb-**) —**'stubby** a. short, broad

stubble ('stubəl) n. 1. stumps of cut grain after reaping 2. short growth of beard

stubborn ('stubərn) a. unyielding, obstinate

stucco ('stukō) n. plaster (pl. **-s, -es**) —**'stuccoed** a.

stuck (stuk) pt./pp. of STICK —**stuck-up** a. inf. conceited; snobbish

stud¹ (stud) n. 1. nail with large head 2. removable double-headed button 3. vertical wall support —vt. 4. set with studs (**-dd-**)

stud² (stud) n. set of animals, esp. horses, kept for breeding —**'studbook** n. book giving pedigree of horses —**stud farm**

studio ('styoodiō, 'stoodiō) n. 1. workroom of artist, photographer etc. 2. building, room where motion pictures, television or radio shows are made, broadcast (pl. **-s**) —**studio couch** upholstered couch that can be converted into double bed

study ('studi) vi. 1. be engaged in learning —vt. 2. make study of 3. try constantly to do 4. consider 5. scrutinize (**'studied, 'studying**) —n. 6. effort to acquire knowledge 7. subject of this 8. room to study in 9. book, report etc. produced as result of study 10. carefully worked-out detail in drawing, painting or clay model for proposed work of art —**student** ('styoodənt, 'stoo-) n. one who studies —**'studied** a. carefully designed, premeditated —**'studious** ('styoodiəs, 'stoo-) a. 1. fond of study 2. thoughtful 3. painstaking 4. deliberate

stuff (stuf) vi. 1. eat (large amount) —vt. 2. pack, cram, fill (completely) 3. fill with seasoned mixture 4. fill (animal's skin) with material to preserve lifelike form —n. 5. material, fabric 6. any substance —**'stuffing** n. material for stuffing, esp. seasoned mixture for inserting in poultry etc. before cooking —**'stuffy** a. 1. lacking fresh air 2. inf. dull, conventional —**do your stuff** inf. do what is required or expected of you

stultify ('stultifī) vt. make ineffectual (**-ified, -ifying**) —**stultifi'cation** n.

stumble ('stumbəl) vi. 1. trip and nearly fall 2. falter —n. 3. act of stumbling —**stumbling block** obstacle

stump (stump) n. 1. remnant of tree, tooth etc. when main part has been cut away 2. one of uprights of wicket in cricket —vt. 3. confuse, puzzle —vi. 4. walk heavily, noisily —**'stumpy** a. short and thickset

stun (stun) vt. 1. knock senseless 2. amaze (**-nn-**) —**'stunner** n. inf. person or thing of great beauty, quality etc. —**'stunning** a.

stung (stung) pt./pp. of STING

stunk (stungk) pp. of STINK

stunt¹ (stunt) vt. check growth of, dwarf —**'stunted** a. 1. underdeveloped 2. undersized

stunt² (stunt) n. 1. feat of dexterity or daring 2. anything spectacular, unusual, done to gain publicity —**stunt man** professional acrobat substituted for actor when dangerous scenes are filmed

stupefy ('styoopifī, 'stoo-) vt. 1. make insensive, lethargic 2. astound (**-efied, -efying**) —**stupe'faction** n.

stupendous (styoo'pendəs, stoo-) a. 1. astonishing, amazing 2. huge

stupid ('styoopid, 'stoo-) a. 1. slow-witted 2. silly 3. dazed or stupefied

stupor ('styoopər, 'stoo-) n. 1. dazed state 2. insensibility

sturdy ('stərdi) a. 1. robust 2. strongly built 3. vigorous —**'sturdily** adv. —**'sturdiness** n.

sturgeon

sturgeon ('stərjən) n. fish yielding caviar and isinglass

stutter ('stutər) v. 1. speak (word etc.) with difficulty 2. stammer —n. 3. act or habit of stuttering

sty¹ (stī) n. 1. place in which pigs are kept 2. hovel, dirty place

sty² or **stye** (stī) n. inflammation on edge of eyelid

Stygian ('stijiən) a. 1. of river Styx in Hades 2. gloomy 3. infernal

style (stīl) n. 1. manner of writing, doing etc. 2. designation 3. sort 4. elegance, refinement 5. superior manner, quality 6. design —vt. 7. shape, design 8. adapt 9. designate —**'stylish** a. fashionable —**'stylishly** adv. —**'stylist** n. 1. one cultivating style in literary or other execution 2. designer 3. hairdresser —**sty'listic** a. —**'stylize** vt. give conventional stylistic form to

stylus ('stīləs) n. 1. writing instrument 2. in phonograph, tiny point running in groove of record (pl. **-li** (-lī), **-es**)

stymie ('stīmi) vt. hinder, thwart

styptic ('stiptik) a./n. (designating) a substance that stops bleeding

styrene ('stīrēn) n. colorless liquid used in making synthetic rubber, plastics

suave (swäv) a. smoothly polite, affable, bland —**'suavity** n.

sub (sub) n. 1. subeditor 2. submarine 3. subscription 4. substitute 5. inf. advance payment of wages, salary —vi. 6. inf. serve as substitute —v. 7. inf. grant or receive (advance payment) —vt. 8. subedit (**-bb-**)

sub- (comb. form) under, less than, in lower position, subordinate, forming subdivision, as in subaqua, subeditor, subheading, subnormal, subsoil. Such words are not given here where the meaning may be easily inferred from the simple word

subcommittee ('subkəmiti, subkə'miti) n. section of committee functioning separately from main body

subconscious (sub'konchəs) a. 1. acting, existing without one's awareness —n. 2. Psychol. that part of human mind unknown, or only partly known, to possessor

subcontinent ('sub'kontinənt) n. large land mass that is distinct part of continent —**subconti'nental** a.

subcontract ('sub'kontrakt) n. 1. subordinate contract under which supply of materials or labor is let out to someone other than party to main contract —vi. (sub'kontrakt, subkən'trakt) 2. (oft. with for) enter into subcontract —vt. (sub'kontrakt, subkən'trakt) 3. let out (work) on subcontract —sub'contractor n.

subculture ('subkulchər) n. subdivision of national culture with distinct integrated network of behavior, beliefs and attitudes

subcutaneous (subkyōō'tāniəs) a. under the skin

subdivide (subdi'vīd, 'subdivīd) vt. divide again —subdivision (subdi'vizhən, 'subdivizhən) n.

subdominant (sub'dominənt) Mus. n. 1. fourth degree of major or minor scale 2. key or chord based on this —a. 3. of the subdominant

subdue (səb'dyōō, -'dōō) vt. 1. win control over; conquer 2. overcome 3. render less intense or less conspicuous (-'dued, -'duing)

subedit (sub'edit) v. edit and correct (written or printed material) —sub'editor n. person who checks and edits copy, esp. on newspaper

subfusc (sub'fusk, 'subfusk) a. devoid of brightness; drab, dull or dark

subject ('subjikt) n. 1. theme, topic 2. that about which something is predicated 3. conscious self 4. one under power of another —a. 5. owing allegiance 6. subordinate 7. dependent 8. liable —vt. (səb'jekt) 9. cause to undergo 10. make liable 11. subdue —sub'jection n. act of bringing, or state of being, under control —sub'jective a. 1. based on personal feelings, not impartial 2. of the self 3. existing in the mind 4. displaying artist's individuality —subjec'tivity n.

subjoin (sub'join) vt. add to end of something written etc.

sub judice (sŏŏb 'yōōdikā, sub 'jōōdisi) Lat. under judicial consideration

subjugate ('subjigāt) vt. 1. force to submit 2. conquer —subju'gation n. —'subjugator n.

subjunctive (səb'jungktiv) Gram. n. 1. mood used mainly in subordinate clauses expressing wish, possibility —a. 2. in, of that mood

sublease ('sub'lēs, 'sublēs) n. 1. lease of property made by lessee of that property —v. 2. grant sublease of (property); sublet

sublet ('sub'let) vt. (of tenant) let whole or part of what he has rented to another

sublimate ('sublimāt) vt. 1. Psychol. direct energy (esp. sexual) into activities considered more socially acceptable 2. refine —n. 3. Chem. material obtained when substance is sublimed —subli'mation n.

sublime (sə'blīm) a. 1. elevated 2. eminent 3. majestic 4. inspiring awe 5. exalted —v. 6. Chem. (cause to) change from solid to vapor —sub'limely adv. —sublimity (sə'blimiti) or su'blimeness n.

subliminal (sub'liminəl) a. resulting from processes of which the individual is not aware

sub-machine-gun n. portable automatic gun with short barrel

submarine ('submərēn, submə'rēn) n. 1. (war)ship which can travel (and attack from) below surface of sea and remain submerged for long periods —a. 2. below surface of sea

submerge (səb'mərj) or **submerse** (səb'mərs) v. place, go under water —sub'mergence or sub'mersion n. —sub'mersible or sub'mergible a. 1. able to be submerged 2. capable of operating under water etc. —n. 3. warship designed to operate under water

submit (səb'mit) vt. 1. surrender 2. put forward for consideration —vi. 3. surrender 4. defer (-tt-) —sub'mission n. —sub'missive a. meek, obedient

subordinate (sə'bördinit) a. 1. of lower rank or less importance —n. 2. inferior 3. one under order of another —vt. (sə'bördināt) 4. make, treat as subordinate —sub'ordinately adv. —subordi'nation n. —subordinate clause Gram. clause with adjectival, adverbial or nominal function, rather than one that functions as separate sentence in its own right

suborn (sə'börn) vt. bribe to do evil —subornation (subör'nāshən) n. —sub'orner n.

subplot ('subplot) n. subordinate plot in novel, motion picture etc.

subpoena (sə'pēnə) n. 1. writ requiring attendance at court of law —vt. 2. summon by such order (-naed, -naing)

sub rosa ('rōzə) in secret

subscribe (səb'skrīb) vt. 1. pay, promise to pay (contribution) —v. 2. write (one's name) at end of document —sub'scriber n. —subscription (səb'skripshən) n. 1. subscribing 2. money paid

subscript ('subskript) a. 1. Print. (of character) printed below base line —n. 2. subscript character (also sub'index)

subsection ('subseksh ən) n. division of a section

subsequent ('subsikwənt) a. later, following or coming after in time —'subsequence n.

subservient (səb'sərviənt) a. submissive, servile —sub'servience n.

subset ('subset) n. mathematical set contained within larger set

subside (səb'sīd) vi. 1. abate, come to an end 2. sink 3. settle 4. collapse —subsidence (səb'sīdəns, 'subsidəns) n.

subsidiary (səb'sidieri) a. 1. supplementing 2. secondary 3. auxiliary —n. 4. subsidiary person or thing

subsidize ('subsidīz) vt. 1. help financially 2. pay grant to —'subsidy n. money granted

subsist (səb'sist) vi. exist, sustain life —sub'sistence n. 1. the means by which one supports life 2. livelihood

subsonic (sub'sonik) a. concerning speeds less than that of sound

substance ('substəns) n. 1. matter with uniform properties 2. particular kind of matter 3. chief part, essence 4. wealth —sub'stantial a. 1. considerable 2. of real value 3. solid, big 4. important 5. really existing —substanti'ality n. —sub'stantially adv. —sub'stantiate vt. bring evidence for, confirm, prove —substanti'ation n. —'substantive a. 1. having independent existence 2. real, fixed —n. 3. noun

substitute ('substityōōt, -tōōt) v. 1. put, serve in exchange (for) —n. 2. thing, person put in place of another 3. deputy —substi'tution n.

substratum ('substrātəm, -stratəm) n. 1. that which is laid or spread under 2. layer of earth lying under another 3. basis (pl. -ta (-tə), -s)

subsume (səb'sōōm) vt. incorporate (idea, case etc.) under comprehensive heading, classification

subtenant (sub'tenənt) n. person who rents property from tenant —sub'tenancy n.

subtend (səb'tend) vt. Geom. be opposite to and delimit

subterfuge ('subtərfyōōj) n. trick, lying excuse used to evade something

subterranean (subtə'rāniən) a. underground (also subter'restrial)

subtitle ('subtītəl) n. 1. secondary title of book 2. (oft. pl.) Cine. text or fragment of translation appearing at the bottom of the screen

subtle ('sutəl) a. 1. not immediately obvious 2. ingenious, acute 3. crafty 4. intricate 5. delicate 6. making fine distinctions —'subtlety n. —'subtly adv.

subtonic (sub'tonik) n. Mus. seventh degree of major or minor scale

subtract (səb'trakt) vt. take away, deduct —sub'traction n.

subtrahend ('subtrəhend) n. number to be subtracted from another number (minuend)

subtropical (sub'tropikəl) a. of regions bordering on the tropics

suburb ('subərb) n. residential area on outskirts of city —su'burban a./n. —su'burbia n. 1. suburbs or people living in them considered as an identifiable community or class in society 2. life, customs etc. of suburban people

subvention (səb'venchən) n. subsidy

subvert (səb'vərt) vt. 1. overthrow 2. corrupt —sub'version n. —sub'versive a.

subway ('subwā) n. 1. underground passage 2. underground railway

succeed (sək'sēd) vi. 1. accomplish purpose 2. turn out satisfactorily 3. follow —vt. 4. follow, take place of —success (sək'ses) n. 1. favorable accomplishment, attainment, issue or outcome 2. successful person or thing —successful (sək'sesfəl) a. —successfully (sək'sesfəli) adv. —succession (sək'seshən) n. 1. following 2. series 3. succeeding —successive (sək'sesiv) a. following in order, consecutive —successively (sək'sesivli) adv. —successor (sək'sesər) n.

succinct (sək'singkt) a. terse, concise

succor ('sukər) vt./n. help in distress

succubus ('sukyəbəs) n. female demon fabled to have sexual intercourse with sleeping men (pl. -bi (-bī))

succulent ('sukyələnt) a. 1. juicy, full of juice 2. (of plant) having thick, fleshy leaves —n. 3. such plant —'succulence or 'succulency n.

succumb (sə'kum) vi. 1. yield, give way 2. die

such (such) a. 1. of the kind or degree mentioned 2. so great, so much 3. so made etc. 4. of the same kind —such and such particular thing that is unspecified —'suchlike inf. a. 1. such —pron. 2. other such things

suck (suk) vt. 1. draw into mouth 2. hold, dissolve in mouth 3. draw in —n. 4. sucking —'sucker n. 1. person, thing that sucks 2. organ, appliance which adheres by suction 3. shoot coming from root or base of stem of plant 4. inf. person easily deceived or taken in

suckle ('sukəl) v. feed from the breast —'suckling n. unweaned infant

sucrose ('sōōkrōs, -krōz) n. sugar

suction ('sukshən) n. 1. drawing or sucking of air or fluid 2. force produced by difference in pressure

Sudan (sōō'dan) n. —Democratic Republic of Sudan country in Africa bounded north by Egypt, northeast by the Red Sea, east by Eritrea and Ethiopia, south by Kenya, Uganda and Zaïre, west by the Central African Republic and Chad and northwest by Libya —Suda'nese n./a.

sudden ('sudən) a. 1. done, occurring unexpectedly 2. abrupt, hurried —'suddenly adv. —'suddenness n. —sudden infant death syndrome unexplained death of infant during sleep (also crib death)

sudorific (sōodə'rifik) *a.* 1. causing perspiration —*n.* 2. medicine that produces sweat

suds (sudz) *pl.n.* froth of soap and water, lather

sue (sōo) *vt.* 1. prosecute 2. seek justice from 3. beseech —*vi.* 4. make application or entreaty (**sued, 'suing**)

suede (swād) *n.* leather with soft, velvety finish

suet ('sōoit) *n.* hard animal fat from around the kidney

suffer ('sufər) *v.* 1. undergo, endure, experience (pain *etc.*) —*vt.* 2. *obs.* allow —'**sufferable** *a.* —'**sufferance** *n.* toleration —'**sufferer** *n.*

suffice (sə'fīs) *v.* be adequate, satisfactory (for) —**sufficiency** (sə'fishənsi) *n.* adequate amount —**sufficient** (sə'fishənt) *a.* enough, adequate

suffix ('sufiks) *n.* 1. letter or word added to end of word —*vt.* ('sufiks, sə'fiks) 2. add, annex to the end

suffocate ('sufəkāt) *v.* 1. kill, be killed by deprivation of oxygen 2. smother —**suffo'cation** *n.*

suffrage ('sufrij) *n.* vote or right of voting —'**suffragist** *n.* one claiming a right of voting (**suffra'gette** *fem.*)

suffuse (sə'fyōoz) *vt.* well up and spread over —**suf'fusion** *n.*

sugar ('shŏogər) *n.* 1. sweet crystalline vegetable substance —*vt.* 2. sweeten, make pleasant (with sugar) —'**sugary** *a.* —**sugar candy** confection made by boiling pure sugar until it hardens —**sugar cane** plant from whose juice sugar is obtained —**sugar daddy** *sl.* wealthy (elderly) man who pays for (*esp.* sexual) favors of younger person —**sugar loaf** conical mass of hard refined sugar

suggest (sə'jest) *vt.* 1. propose 2. call up the idea of —**suggesti'bility** *n.* —**sug'gestible** *a.* easily influenced —**sug'gestion** *n.* 1. hint 2. proposal 3. insinuation of impression, belief *etc.* into mind —**sug'gestive** *a.* containing, open to suggestion, *esp.* of something indecent

suicide ('sōoisīd) *n.* 1. act or instance of killing oneself intentionally 2. person who does this —**sui'cidal** *a.*

suit (sōot) *n.* 1. set of clothing 2. garment worn for particular event, purpose 3. one of four sets in block of cards 4. action at law —*v.* 5. make, be fit or appropriate (for) 6. be acceptable (to) —**suita'bility** *n.* —'**suitable** *a.* 1. fitting, proper 2. convenient 3. becoming —'**suitably** *adv.* —'**suitcase** *n.* flat rectangular traveling case

suite (swēt) *n.* 1. matched set, *esp.* of furniture 2. set of rooms 3. retinue

suitor ('sōotər) *n.* 1. man who courts woman 2. one who sues 3. petitioner

sukiyaki (ski'yäki, sōoki'yäki) *n.* dish of thin slices of meat and vegetables cooked in soy sauce, sake and sugar in a chafing dish

sulfa drug ('sulfə) sulfonamide used to treat bacterial infections

sulfate ('sulfāt) *n.* salt formed by sulfuric acid in combination with any base

sulfonamide (sul'fonəmīd) *n.* any of group of drugs used as internal germicides in treatment of many bacterial diseases

sulfone ('sulfōn) *n.* any of group of drugs used to treat leprosy

sulfur ('sulfər) *n. Chem.* nonmetallic element *Symbol* S, at. wt. 32.1, at. no. 16 —'**sulfide** *n.* compound of sulfur with more electropositive element —'**sulfite** *n.* salt or ester of acid —**sulfitic** (sul'fitik) *a.*

—**sulfuric** (sul'fyōŏərik) *a.* —**sulfurous** ('sulfyərəs, -fərəs) *a.* —**sulfur dioxide** colorless soluble pungent gas used in manufacture of sulfuric acid, preservation of foodstuffs, bleaching and disinfecting —**sulfuric acid** colorless oily corrosive liquid used in manufacture of fertilizers, dyes and explosives

sulk (sulk) *vi.* 1. be silent, resentful, *esp.* to draw attention to oneself —*n.* 2. sulky mood —'**sulkily** *adv.* —'**sulky** *a.*

sullen ('sulən) *a.* 1. unwilling to talk or be sociable; morose 2. dismal, dull —'**sullenly** *adv.*

sully ('suli) *vt.* stain, tarnish, disgrace ('**sullied, 'sullying**)

sultan ('sultən) *n.* ruler of Muslim country —**sul'tana** *n.* 1. sultan's wife 2. kind of raisin —'**sultanate** *n.* 1. territory or country ruled by sultan 2. office, rank or jurisdiction of sultan

sultry ('sultri) *a.* 1. (of weather) hot, humid 2. (of person) looking sensual

sum (sum) *n.* 1. amount 2. problem in arithmetic —*v.* 3. add up 4. (*with* up) make summary of (**-mm-**) —**summing-up** *n.* summary of main points of speech *etc.* —**sum total** 1. total obtained by adding up sum or sums 2. everything included

sumac ('sōomak, 'shōo-) *n.* shrub with clusters of green flowers and red hairy fruits

summa cum laude ('sōomə kōom 'lowdə) *Lat.* with the greatest distinction, *esp.* of college or university degree

summary ('suməri) *n.* 1. abridgment or statement of chief points of longer document, speech *etc.* 2. abstract —*a.* 3. done quickly —**sum'marily** *adv.* 1. speedily 2. abruptly —'**summarize** *vt.* 1. make summary of 2. present briefly and concisely —**sum'mation** *n.* adding up

summer ('sumər) *n.* 1. second, warmest season —*vi.* 2. pass the summer —'**summery** *a.* —**summer camp** camp providing recreational or educational activities for children in residence —'**summerhouse** *n.* small building in garden or park, used for shade in summer —**summer school** academic course *etc.* held during summer —**summer solstice** 1. time at which sun is at its northernmost point in sky; June 21st 2. *Astron.* point on celestial sphere at which ecliptic is furthest north from celestial equator —'**summertime** *n.* the season of summer or period resembling it

summit ('sumit) *n.* 1. highest point or part 2. peak —**summit conference** meeting of heads of governments

summon ('sumən) *vt.* 1. demand attendance of 2. call on 3. bid (witness) appear in court 4. gather up (energies *etc.*) —'**summons** *n.* 1. call 2. authoritative demand

sumptuous ('sumpchōoəs) *a.* 1. lavish, magnificent 2. costly —'**sumptuary** *a.* pert. to or regulating expenditure —'**sumptuously** *adv.* —'**sumptuousness** *n.*

sun (sun) *n.* 1. luminous body round which earth and other planets revolve 2. its rays —*vt.* 3. expose to sun's rays (**-nn-**) —'**sunless** *a.* —'**sunny** *a.* 1. like the sun 2. warm 3. cheerful —'**sunbathing** *n.* exposure of whole or part of body to sun's rays —'**sunbeam** *n.* ray of sun —'**sunburn** *n.* inflammation of skin due to excessive exposure to sun —'**sundial** *n.* device indicating time during hours of sunlight by means of pointer that casts shadow on to surface marked in hours —'**sundown** *n.* sunset —'**sunfish** *n.* sea fish with large rounded body —'**sunflower** *n.* plant with large golden flowers —'**sun-**

sunflower

glasses *pl.n.* glasses with darkened or polarizing lenses that protect eyes from sun's glare —**sun-god** *n.* sun considered as personal deity —**sun lamp** lamp that generates infrared-to-ultraviolet rays —'**sunrise** *n.* 1. daily appearance of sun above horizon 2. atmospheric phenomena accompanying this appearance 3. time at which sun rises at particular locality —'**sunset** *n.* 1. daily disappearance of sun below horizon 2. atmospheric phenomena accompanying this disappearance 3. time at which sun sets at particular locality —'**sunshade** *n.* device, *esp.* parasol or awning, serving to shade from sun —'**sunshine** *n.* 1. light or warmth received directly from sun 2. light-hearted term of affection —'**sunshiny** *a.* —'**sunspot** *n.* dark patch appearing temporarily on sun's surface —'**sunstroke** *n.* frequently fatal condition caused by prolonged exposure to intensely hot sun —'**suntan** *n.* browning of skin by exposure to sun

Sun. Sunday

sundae ('sundi) *n.* ice cream topped with syrup and chopped nuts

Sunday ('sundi) *n.* 1. first day of week 2. Christian Sabbath —**Sunday best** one's best clothes —**Sunday school** school for religious instruction of children

sunder ('sundər) *vt.* separate, sever

sundry ('sundri) *a.* several, various —'**sundries** *pl.n.* odd items not mentioned in detail

sung (sung) *pp. of* SING

sunk (sungk) *pp. of* SINK

sup (sup) *vt.* 1. take by sips —*vi.* 2. take supper (**-pp-**) —*n.* 3. mouthful of liquid

sup. 1. above 2. superior 3. *Gram.* superlative 4. supplement 5. supplementary 6. supply

super ('sōopər) *a. inf.* very good

super- (*comb. form*) above, greater, exceeding(ly), as in *superhuman, superman, superstore, supertanker.* Such compounds are not given here where the meaning may be inferred from the simple word

superable ('sōopərəbəl) *a.* 1. capable of being overcome 2. surmountable

superannuate (sōopər'anyōoāt) *vt.* 1. pension off 2. discharge or dismiss as too old —**super'annuated** *a.* —**superannu'ation** *n.* 1. pension given on retirement 2. contribution by employee to pension

superb (sōo'pərb) *a.* 1. splendid 2. grand 3. impressive —**su'perbly** *adv.*

supercargo (sōopər'kärgō, 'sōopərkärgō) *n.* officer on merchant ship in charge of cargo

supercharge ('sōopərchärj) *vt.* charge, fill to excess —'**supercharged** *a.* —'**supercharger** *n.* in internal-combustion engine, device to ensure complete filling of cylinder with explosive mixture when running at high speed

supercilious (sōopər'siliəs) *a.* displaying arrogant pride, scorn, indifference

superconductivity (sōopərkonduk'tiviti) *n. Phys.* property of certain substances that have almost no electrical resistance at temperatures close to absolute zero —**supercon'ductive** *or* **supercon'ducting** *a.* —**supercon'ductor** *n.*

supercool (sōōpərˈkōōl) v. Chem. cool without freezing or crystallization to temperature below that at which freezing or crystallization should occur

superego (sōōpərˈēgō, -ˈegō) n. Psychoanal. that part of the unconscious mind that acts as conscience for the ego

supererogation (sōōpərerəˈgāshən) n. 1. performance of work in excess of that required 2. R.C.Ch. prayers, devotions etc. beyond those prescribed as obligatory

superficial (sōōpərˈfishəl) a. 1. of or on surface 2. not careful or thorough 3. without depth —**superfici'ality** n.

superfluous (sōōˈpərflōōəs) a. 1. extra, unnecessary 2. excessive 3. left over —**super'fluity** n. 1. superabundance 2. unnecessary amount —**su'perfluously** adv.

superheat (sōōpərˈhēt) vt. 1. heat (vapor, esp. steam) to temperature above its saturation point for given pressure 2. heat (liquid) to temperature above its boiling point without boiling occurring 3. overheat —**super'heater** n.

superheterodyne receiver (sōōpərˈhetərə-dīn) radio receiver that combines two radio-frequency signals by heterodyne action to produce signal above audible frequency limit

superimpose (sōōpərimˈpōz) vt. 1. set or place on or over something else 2. (usu. with on or upon) add (to) —**superimpo'sition** n.

superintend (sōōpərinˈtend) vt. 1. have charge of 2. overlook 3. manage —**superin'tendence** n. —**superin'tendent** n.

superior (sōōˈpēəriər) a. 1. greater in quality or quantity 2. upper, higher in position, rank or quality 3. showing consciousness of being so —**superi'ority** n. quality of being higher, greater or more excellent

superlative (sōōˈpərlətiv) a. 1. of, in highest degree or quality 2. surpassing 3. Gram. denoting form of adjective, adverb meaning 'most' —n. 4. Gram. superlative degree of adjective or adverb

supermarket (ˈsōōpərmärkit) n. large self-service store selling chiefly food and household goods

supernatural (sōōpərˈnachərəl) a. 1. being beyond the powers or laws of nature 2. miraculous —**super'naturally** adv.

supernova (sōōpərˈnōvə) n. star that explodes and is for a few days up to one hundred million times brighter than sun (pl. -vae (-vē), -s)

supernumerary (sōōpərˈnyōōməreri, -ˈnōō-) a. 1. in excess of normal number, extra —n. 2. extra person or thing 3. person hired for walk-on part in drama or opera

superphosphate (sōōpərˈfosfāt) n. chemical fertilizer

superpose (sōōpərˈpōz) vt. Geom. place (one figure) upon another so that their perimeters coincide

superpower (ˈsōōpərpowər) n. an extremely powerful state

superscribe (ˈsōōpərskrīb, sōōpərˈskrīb) vt. write (inscription etc.) above, on top of or outside —**superscription** (sōōpərˈskripshən) n.

superscript (ˈsōōpərskript) n./a. (character) printed, written above the line

supersede (sōōpərˈsēd) vt. 1. take the place of 2. set aside, discard, supplant —**supersession** (sōōpərˈseshən) n.

supersonic (sōōpərˈsonik) a. denoting speed greater than that of sound

superstition (sōōpərˈstishən) n. religion, opinion or practice based on belief in luck or magic —**super'stitious** a. —**super'stitiously** adv.

superstructure (ˈsōōpərstrukchər) n. 1. structure above foundations 2. part of ship above deck

supervene (sōōpərˈvēn) vi. happen, as an interruption or change —**supervention** (sōōpərˈvenchən) n.

supervise (ˈsōōpərvīz) vt. 1. oversee 2. direct 3. inspect and control 4. superintend —**supervision** (sōōpərˈvizhən) n. —**'supervisor** n. —**super'visory** a.

supine (sōōˈpīn) a. 1. lying on back with face upward 2. indolent —n. (ˈsōōpīn) 3. Latin verbal noun

supper (ˈsupər) n. 1. (light) evening meal, esp. when main meal is at midday 2. social event featuring supper

supplant (səˈplänt) vt. 1. take the place of, esp. unfairly 2. oust —**sup'planter** n.

supple (ˈsupəl) a. 1. pliable 2. flexible 3. compliant —**'supply** or **'supplely** adv.

supplement (ˈsuplimənt) n. 1. thing added to fill up, supply deficiency, esp. extra part added to book etc. 2. additional number of periodical, usu. on special subject 3. separate, oft. illustrated section published periodically with newspaper —vt. (ˈsupliment) 4. add to 5. remedy deficiency of —**supple'mentary** a. additional —**supplementary angle** either of two angles whose sum is 180°

suppliant (ˈsupliənt) a. 1. petitioning —n. 2. petitioner

supplicate (ˈsuplikāt) v. 1. beg humbly —vt. 2. entreat —**suppli'cation** n. —**'supplicatory** a.

supply (səˈplī) vt. 1. furnish 2. make available 3. provide (sup'plied, sup'plying) —n. 4. supplying, substitute 5. stock, store

support (səˈpört) vt. 1. hold up 2. sustain 3. assist —n. 4. supporting, being supported 5. means of support —**sup'portable** a. —**sup'porter** n. adherent —**sup'porting** a. (of motion-picture etc. role) less important —**sup'portive** a.

suppose (səˈpōz) vt. 1. assume as theory 2. take for granted 3. accept as likely 4. (in passive) be expected, obliged 5. (in passive) ought —**supposed** (səˈpōzid, -ˈpōzd) a. —**supposedly** (səˈpōzidli) adv. —**suppo'sition** n. 1. assumption 2. belief without proof 3. conjecture —**suppo'sitious** or **supposititious** (səpoziˈtishəs) a. sham, spurious, counterfeit

suppository (səˈpozitöri) n. medication (in capsule) for insertion in orifice of body

suppress (səˈpres) vt. 1. put down, restrain 2. crush 3. keep or withdraw from publication —**sup'pression** n.

suppurate (ˈsupyərāt) vi. fester, form pus —**suppu'ration** n.

supra- (comb. form) above, over, as in supranational. Such words are not given here where the meaning may easily be inferred from the simple word

supreme (səˈprēm, sōō-) a. 1. highest in authority or rank 2. utmost —**supremacy** (səˈpreməsi, sōō-) n. position of being supreme —**su'premely** adv. —**Supreme Being** God —**Supreme Commander** military commander of all allied forces —**Supreme Court** the highest court in the U.S. and of most states

Supt. or **supt.** superintendent

sur-¹ (comb. form) over, above; beyond, as in surcharge

sur-² (comb. form) see SUB-

surcease (ˈsərsēs, sərˈsēs) v. 1. (cause to) cease —n. 2. cessation

surcharge (ˈsərchärj) n. 1. additional charge —vt. 2. subject to additional charge

surd (sərd) n. 1. Math. sum containing one or more irrational roots of numbers 2. Phonet. voiceless consonant —a. 3. of or relating to surd

sure (shōōər, shör) a. 1. certain 2. trustworthy 3. without doubt —adv. 4. inf. certainly —**'surely** adv. —**surety** (ˈshōōəriti, ˈshōōərti) n. one who makes himself responsible for another's obligations —**sure-fire** a. inf. certain to succeed or meet expectations —**sure-footed** a. 1. unlikely to fall, slip or stumble 2. not likely to err or fall

surf (sərf) n. 1. waves breaking on shore —vi. 2. swim in, ride surf —**'surfer** n. —**'surfboard** n. board used in sport of riding over surf —**'surfboarding** n. sport of riding a board on the fast-moving incline of a wave (also 'surfing)

surface (ˈsərfis) n. 1. outside face of body 2. exterior 3. plane 4. top, visible side 5. superficial appearance, outward impression —a. 6. involving the surface only 7. going no deeper than surface —v. 8. (cause to) come to surface —vt. 9. put a surface on —**surface tension** property of liquids caused by intermolecular forces near surface leading to apparent presence of surface film

surfeit (ˈsərfit) n. 1. excess 2. disgust caused by excess —vt. 3. feed to excess

surge (sərj) n. 1. wave 2. sudden increase 3. Elec. sudden rush of current in circuit —vi. 4. move in large waves 5. swell, billow

surgeon (ˈsərjən) n. medical practitioner who specializes in surgery —**'surgery** n. branch of medicine concerned with the treatment of disease or disorder by physical intervention —**'surgical** a. —**'surgically** adv. —**surgeon general** 1. chief medical officer of any of the armed forces (pl. **surgeons general**) 2. (S- G-) head of U.S. Bureau of Public Health or a state health agency

Suriname (sōōriˈnämə) n. country in South America bounded north by the Atlantic, east by French Guiana, west by Guyana and south by Brazil

surly (ˈsərli) a. 1. gloomily morose 2. ill-natured 3. cross and rude —**'surlily** adv. —**'surliness** n.

surmise (sərˈmīz) v./n. guess, conjecture

surmount (sərˈmownt) vt. get over, overcome —**sur'mountable** a.

surname (ˈsərnām) n. family name

surpass (sərˈpas) vt. 1. go beyond 2. excel 3. outstrip —**sur'passable** a. —**sur'passing** a. 1. excellent 2. exceeding others

surplice (ˈsərplis) n. loose white vestment worn by clergy and choristers

surplus (ˈsərpləs) n. what remains over in excess

surprise (sərˈprīz) vt. 1. cause surprise to 2. astonish 3. take, come upon unexpectedly 4. startle (someone) into action thus —n. 5. what takes unawares 6. something unexpected 7. emotion aroused by being taken unawares

surrealism (səˈrēəlizəm) n. movement in art and literature emphasizing expression of the unconscious —**sur'real** a. —**sur'realist** n./a.

surrender (səˈrendər) vt. 1. hand over, give up —vi. 2. allow oneself to yield 3. cease resistance 4. capitulate —n. 5. act of surrendering

surreptitious (surəpˈtishəs) a. 1. done secretly or stealthily 2. furtive —**surrep'titiously** adv.

surrogate (ˈsurəgāt, -git) n. 1. deputy, esp. of bishop 2. substitute

surround (sə'rownd) *vt.* **1.** be, come all round, encompass **2.** encircle **3.** hem in —*n.* **4.** border, edging —**sur'roundings** *pl.n.* conditions, scenery *etc.* around a person, place, environment

surtax ('sörtaks) *n.* additional tax

surveillance (sər'vāləns) *n.* close watch, supervision —**sur'veillant** *a./n.*

survey (sər'vā, 'sörvā) *vt.* **1.** scrutinize **2.** inspect, examine **3.** measure, map (land) —*n.* ('sörvā, sər'vā) **4.** a surveying **5.** inspection **6.** report incorporating results of survey —**sur'veyor** *n.*

survive (sər'vīv) *vt.* **1.** outlive **2.** come through alive —*vi.* **3.** continue to live or exist —**sur'vival** *n.* continuation of existence of persons, things *etc.* —**sur'vivor** *n.* one left alive when others have died —**survival of the fittest** natural selection

susceptible (sə'septəbl) *a.* **1.** yielding readily **2.** capable **3.** impressionable —**suscepti'bility** *n.*

suspect (sə'spekt) *vt.* **1.** doubt innocence of **2.** have impression of existence or presence of **3.** be inclined to believe **4.** mistrust —*a.* ('suspekt) **5.** of suspected character —*n.* ('suspekt) **6.** suspected person

suspend (sə'spend) *vt.* **1.** hang up **2.** cause to cease for a time **3.** debar from an office or privilege **4.** keep inoperative **5.** sustain in fluid —**sus'penders** *pl.n.* straps worn over shoulders to hold up trousers —**suspended animation** temporary cessation of vital functions —**suspended sentence** prison sentence that is not served by offender unless he commits further offense during its currency

suspense (sə'spens) *n.* **1.** state of uncertainty, *esp.* while awaiting news, an event *etc.* **2.** anxiety, worry —**sus'pension** *n.* **1.** state of being suspended **2.** springs on axle of body of vehicle **3.** dispersion of liquid or solid in liquid in which the dispersed substance does not dissolve —**sus'pensory** *a.* —**suspension bridge** bridge suspended from cables that hang between two towers and are anchored at both ends

suspicion (sə'spishən) *n.* **1.** suspecting, being suspected **2.** slight trace —**sus'picious** *a.*

sustain (sə'stān) *vt.* **1.** keep, hold up **2.** endure **3.** keep alive **4.** confirm —**sus'tainable** *a.* —**sustenance** ('sustənəns) *n.* food

suture ('sōōchər) *n.* **1.** act of sewing **2.** sewing up of a wound **3.** material used for this **4.** a joining of the bones of the skull —**'sutural** *a.*

suzerain ('sōōzərən, -rān) *n.* **1.** sovereign with rights over autonomous state **2.** feudal lord —**suzerainty** ('sōōzərənti, -rānti) *n.*

svelte (sfelt) *a.* **1.** lightly built, slender **2.** sophisticated

SW *or* **S.W.** southwest(ern)

Sw. 1. Sweden **2.** Swedish

swab (swob) *n.* **1.** mop **2.** pad of surgical wool *etc.* for cleaning, taking specimen *etc.* **3.** *sl.* low or unmannerly fellow —*vt.* **4.** clean with swab (-bb-) —**'swabber** *n.*

swaddle ('swodəl) *vt.* swathe —**swaddling clothes** long strips of cloth for wrapping newborn baby

swag (swag) *n.* **1.** garland or drapery suspended between two points and hanging in an arc **2.** *sl.* stolen property **3.** A *inf.* bag carried by swagman —**'swagman** *n.* **A** itinerant vagrant worker

swagger ('swagər) *vi.* **1.** strut **2.** boast —*n.* **3.** strutting gait **4.** boastful, overconfident manner —**swagger stick** short cane or stick carried on occasion by army officers

Swahili (swä'hēli) *n.* **1.** Bantu language widely used as lingua franca throughout E and central Afr. **2.** member of people speaking this language (*pl.* **-s, -li**) —**Swa'hilian** *a.*

swain (swān) *n.* rustic lover

swallow[1] ('swolō) *vt.* **1.** cause, allow to pass down gullet **2.** engulf **3.** suppress, keep back **4.** *inf.* believe gullibly —*n.* **5.** act of swallowing

swallow[2] ('swolō) *n.* migratory bird with forked tail and skimming manner of flight —**'swallowtail** *n.* **1.** butterfly having tail-like extension of each hind wing **2.** forked tail of swallow or similar bird

swam (swam) *pt. of* SWIM

swami ('swämi) *n.* in India, title of respect for Hindu saint or religious teacher (*pl.* **-es, -s**)

swamp (swomp) *n.* **1.** bog —*vt.* **2.** entangle in swamp **3.** overwhelm **4.** flood —**'swampy** *a.*

swan (swon) *n.* **1.** large, web-footed water bird with graceful curved neck —*vi.* **2.** *inf.* stroll idly (-nn-) —**'swannery** *n.* —**swan dive** dive in which diver arches back and stretches arms sideways —**swan's-down** *n.* **1.** fine soft down feathers of swan, used to trim clothing *etc.* **2.** thick soft fabric of wool with silk, cotton or rayon **3.** cotton fabric with heavy nap —**swan song 1.** fabled song of a swan before death **2.** last act *etc.* before death

swank (swangk) *vi. sl.* **1.** swagger **2.** show off —**'swanky** *a. sl.* **1.** smart **2.** showy

swap (swop) *n./v. inf.* **1.** exchange **2.** barter (-pp-)

sward (sword) *or* **swarth** (swörth) *n.* green turf

swarm[1] (swörm) *n.* **1.** large cluster of insects **2.** vast crowd —*vi.* **3.** (of bees) be on the move in swarm **4.** gather in large numbers

swarm[2] (swörm) *v.* climb (rope *etc.*) by grasping with hands and knees

swarthy ('swördhi) *a.* dark-complexioned

swashbuckler ('swoshbuklər) *n.* swaggering daredevil person —**'swashbuckling** *a.*

swastika ('swostikə) *n.* form of cross with arms bent at right angles: form with counterclockwise arms used as emblem by Amerindians and in Orient; form with clockwise arms official symbol of Nazi Party and the Third Reich

swat (swot) *vt.* **1.** hit smartly **2.** kill, *esp.* insects (-tt-)

swatch (swoch) *n.* sample of cloth or other material

swathe (swādh) *vt.* cover with wraps or bandages

sway (swā) *v.* **1.** swing unsteadily **2.** (cause to) vacillate in opinion *etc.* —*vt.* **3.** influence opinion *etc.* of —*n.* **4.** control **5.** power **6.** swaying motion

Swaziland ('swäziland) *n.* country in Africa bounded north, west and south by South Africa and east by Mozambique

swear (swâr) *vt.* **1.** promise on oath **2.** cause to take an oath —*vi.* **3.** declare **4.** curse (**swore, sworn, 'swearing**) —**'swearword** *n.* socially taboo word of a profane, obscene or insulting character

sweat (swet) *n.* **1.** moisture oozing from, forming on skin, *esp.* in humans —*v.* **2.** (cause to) exude sweat —*vi.* **3.** toil **4.** *inf.* worry —*vt.* **5.** employ at wrongfully low wages (**sweat** *or* **'sweated** *pt./pp.,* **'sweating** *pr.p.*) —**'sweaty** *a.* —**'sweatband** *n.* **1.** band of material set in hat to protect it from sweat **2.** piece of cloth tied around forehead to keep sweat out of eyes or around wrist to keep hands dry, as in sports —**sweat shirt** long-sleeved knitted cotton sweater —**'sweatshop** *n.* workshop where employees work long hours for low wages

sweater ('swetər) *n.* knitted or crocheted jacket or pullover

Sweden ('swēdən) *n.* country in Europe bounded east by the Gulf of Bothnia, south by the Baltic Sea, west and northwest by Norway and northeast by Finland —**Swede** *n.* —**'Swedish** *a.* **1.** of Sweden —*n.* **2.** language of Sweden which is a Scandinavian language

sweep (swēp) *vi.* **1.** effect cleaning with broom **2.** pass quickly or magnificently **3.** extend in continuous curve —*vt.* **4.** clean with broom **5.** carry impetuously (**swept, 'sweeping**) —*n.* **6.** act of cleaning with broom **7.** sweeping motion **8.** wide curve **9.** range **10.** long oar **11.** one who cleans chimneys —**'sweeping** *a.* **1.** wide-ranging **2.** without limitations, reservations —**sweep** *or* **'sweepstake** *n.* gamble in which winner takes stakes contributed by all

sweet (swēt) *a.* **1.** tasting like sugar **2.** agreeable **3.** kind, charming **4.** fresh, fragrant **5.** in good condition **6.** tuneful **7.** gentle, dear, beloved —*n.* **8.** small piece of sweet food —**'sweeten** *v.* —**'sweetener** *n.* **1.** sweetening agent, *esp.* one that is sugar-free **2.** *sl.* bribe —**'sweetish** *a.* —**'sweetly** *adv.* —**'sweetbread** *n.* animal's pancreas used as food —**'sweetbrier** *n.* wild rose —**sweet corn** variety of maize —**'sweetheart** *n.* lover —**'sweetmeat** *n.* sweetened delicacy, *eg* small cake, candy —**sweet pea** plant of pea family with bright flowers —**sweet potato 1.** trailing plant **2.** its edible, sweetish, starchy tubers —**sweet-talk** *vt. inf.* coax, flatter —**sweet tooth** strong liking for sweet foods —**sweet william** ('wilyəm) garden plant with flat flower clusters

swell (swel) *v.* **1.** expand —*vi.* **2.** be greatly filled with pride, emotion (**swelled, 'swollen, 'swelling**) —*n.* **3.** act of swelling or being swollen **4.** wave of sea **5.** mechanism in organ to vary volume of sound **6.** *sl.* person of high social standing —*a.* **7.** *sl.* smart, fine —**swell'headed** *a. inf.* having inflated view of one's own worth

swelter ('sweltər) *vi.* be oppressed with heat

swept (swept) *pt./pp. of* SWEEP

swerve (swörv) *vi.* **1.** swing round, change direction during motion **2.** turn aside (from duty *etc.*) —*n.* **3.** swerving

swift (swift) *a.* **1.** rapid, quick, ready —*n.* **2.** bird like a swallow —**'swiftly** *adv.*

swig (swig) *n.* **1.** large swallow of drink —*v.* **2.** drink thus (-gg-)

swill (swil) *v.* **1.** drink greedily —*vt.* **2.** pour water over or through —*n.* **3.** liquid pig food **4.** greedy drinking **5.** rinsing

swim (swim) *vi.* **1.** support and move oneself in water **2.** float **3.** be flooded **4.** have feeling of dizziness —*vt.* **5.** cross by swimming **6.** compete in by swimming (**swam, swum, 'swimming**) —*n.* **7.** spell of swimming —**'swimmer** *n.* —**'swimming** *n.* act of propelling the body through water with arm and leg motion without artificial aid —**'swimmingly** *adv.* successfully, effortlessly —**swimming pool** artificial pool for swimming —**'swimsuit** *n.* swimming garment

swindle ('swindəl) *n./v.* cheat —**'swindler** *n.*

swine (swīn) *n.* **1.** pig **2.** contemptible person (*pl.* **swine**) —**'swinish** *a.* —**swine fever** infectious viral disease of pigs —**'swineherd** *n.*

swing (swing) *v.* **1.** (cause to) move to and fro **2.** (cause to) pivot, turn **3.** hang **4.** arrange, play (music) with (jazz) rhythm —*vi.* **5.** be hanged **6.** hit out (at) (**swung** *pt./pp.*) —*n.* **7.** act, instance of swinging **8.** seat hung to swing on **9.** fluctuation (*esp.* in voting pattern) **10.** C train of freight sleds, canoes —**'swinger** n. inf. **1.** person regarded as modern, lively **2.** one who indulges freely in sex

swingeing ('swinjing) a. esp. UK **1.** severe **2.** huge

swingletree ('swinggəltrē) n. crossbar in horse's harness to which ends of traces are attached (also **'whiffletree**)

swipe (swīp) v. **1.** (sometimes with at) strike with wide, sweeping or glancing blow —vt. **2.** sl. steal

swirl (swərl) v. **1.** (cause to) move with eddying motion —n. **2.** such motion

swish (swish) v. **1.** (cause to) move with audible hissing sound —n. **2.** the sound —a. **3.** inf. fashionable, smart

Swiss (swis) see SWITZERLAND

switch (swich) n. **1.** mechanism to complete or interrupt electric circuit etc. **2.** abrupt change **3.** flexible stick or twig **4.** tufted end of animal's tail **5.** tress of false hair —vi. **6.** shift, change **7.** swing —vt. **8.** affect (current etc.) with switch **9.** change abruptly **10.** strike with switch —**'switchback** n. road, railroad with steep rises and descents —**'switchboard** n. installation for establishing or varying connections in telephone and electric circuits

Switzerland ('switsərlənd) n. country in Europe bounded south by Italy, east by France, north by West Germany and west by Austria —**Swiss** n./a. (native or inhabitant) of Switzerland —**Swiss chard** see CHARD —**Swiss cheese** hard, yellow cheese with many holes made from half-skimmed cow's milk

swivel ('swivəl) n. **1.** mechanism of two parts which can revolve the one on the other —v. **2.** turn (on swivel)

swizzle ('swizəl) n. an alcoholic drink containing gin or rum —**swizzle stick** small rod used to agitate effervescent drink to facilitate escape of carbon dioxide

swollen ('swōlən) pp. of SWELL

swoon (swōōn) vi./n. faint

swoop (swōōp) vi. **1.** dive, as hawk —n. **2.** act of swooping **3.** sudden attack

swoosh (swōōsh) vi. **1.** make rustling, swirling sound, esp. when moving, pouring out —n. **2.** swirling, rustling sound or movement

sword (sörd) n. weapon with long blade for cutting or thrusting —**sword dance** dance in which performers dance nimbly over swords on ground or brandish them in the air —**'swordfish** n. fish with elongated sharp upper jaw, like sword —**'swordplay** n. **1.** action or art of fighting with sword **2.** verbal sparring —**sword swallower** person who swallows or appears to swallow swords, in a circus etc.

swore (swör) pt. of SWEAR —**sworn** pp. of SWEAR

swum (swum) pp. of SWIM

swung (swung) pt./pp. of SWING

sybarite ('sibərīt) n. person who loves luxury —**sybaritic** (sibə'ritik) a.

sycamore ('sikəmör) n. family of plane trees native to eastern U.S., California and southern Arizona grown widely throughout U.S. as street trees

sycophant ('sikəfənt) n. one using flattery to gain favors —**'sycophancy** n. —**syco'phantic** a.

Sydenham's chorea ('sidənəmz) see CHOREA

syllable ('siləbəl) n. division of word as unit for pronunciation —**syl'labic** a. —**syl'labify** vt.

syllabub or **sillabub** ('siləbub) n. **1.** sweet frothy dish of cream, sugar and wine **2.** something insubstantial

syllabus ('siləbəs) n. **1.** outline of a course of study **2.** program, list of subjects studied on course (pl. **-es, -bi** (-bī))

syllogism ('siləjizəm) n. form of logical reasoning consisting of two premises and conclusion —**syllo'gistic** a.

sylph (silf) n. **1.** slender, graceful woman **2.** sprite —**'sylphlike** a.

sylvan or **silvan** ('silvən) a. of forests, trees

Sylvaner (sil'vanər) n. **1.** semisweet white table wine **2.** grape used to make this wine

sym- see SYN-

symbiosis (simbī'ōsis, -bi-) n. living together of two organisms of different kinds, esp. to their mutual benefit —**symbiotic** (simbī'otik, -bi-) a.

symbol ('simbəl) n. **1.** thing representing or typifying something **2.** letter, figure or sign used in mathematics etc. to represent a quantity etc. —**sym'bolic** a. —**sym'bolically** adv. —**'symbolism** n. **1.** use of, representation by symbols **2.** movement in art holding that work of art should express idea in symbolic form —**'symbolist** n./a. —**'symbolize** v.

symmetry ('simitri) n. **1.** proportion between parts **2.** balance of arrangement between two sides **3.** order —**sym'metrical** a. **1.** having due proportion in parts **2.** harmonious **3.** regular

sympathy ('simpəthi) n. **1.** feeling for another in pain etc. **2.** compassion, pity **3.** sharing of emotion, interest, desire etc. **4.** fellow feeling —**sympa'thectomy** n. operation to sever fibers of sympathetic nervous system —**sympa'thetic** a. —**sympa'thetically** adv. —**'sympathize** vi. —**sympathetic magic** type of magic in which it is sought to produce large-scale effect by performing some small-scale ceremony resembling it, as pouring of water on altar to induce rainfall —**sympathetic nervous system** part of nervous system controlling secretion, contraction of smooth muscle and blood vessels etc.

symphony ('simfəni) n. **1.** composition for full orchestra **2.** harmony of sounds —**symphonic** (sim'fonik) a. —**symphonious** (sim'fōniəs) a. harmonious —**symphonic poem** extended orchestral composition, based on nonmusical material, such as work of literature or folk tale —**symphony orchestra** large orchestra comprising strings, brass, woodwind, harp and percussion

symposium (sim'pōziəm) n. **1.** conference, meeting **2.** discussion, writings on a given topic (pl. **-s, -sia** (-ziə))

symptom ('simptəm) n. **1.** change in body indicating its state of health or disease **2.** sign, token —**sympto'matic** a.

syn- or **sym-** (comb. form) with, together, alike

synagogue ('sinəgog) n. (place of worship of) Jewish congregation

synchromesh ('singkrōmesh) a. (of gearbox) having device that synchronizes speeds of gears before they engage

synchronize ('singkrənīz) vt. **1.** make agree in time —vi. **2.** happen at same time —**'synchronism** n. —**synchroni'zation** n. —**'synchronous** a. simultaneous

synchrotron ('singkrətron) n. device for acceleration of stream of electrons

syncopate ('singkəpāt) vt. accentuate (weak beat in bar of music) —**synco'pation** n.

syncope ('singkəpi) n. **1.** fainting **2.** elision of letter(s) from middle of word

syncretize ('singkritīz) v. attempt to combine characteristic teachings, beliefs, or practices of (differing systems of religion or philosophy) —**syncreti'zation** n.

syndicate ('sindikit) n. **1.** body of people, delegates associated for some enterprise —vt. ('sindikāt) **2.** form into syndicate **3.** publish in many newspapers at the same time —**'syndicalism** n. economic movement aiming at combination of workers in all trades to enforce demands of labor

syndrome ('sindrōm) n. **1.** combination of several symptoms in disease **2.** symptom, set of symptoms or characteristics

synecdoche (sin'ekdəki) n. figure of speech by which whole of thing is put for part or part for whole, eg sail for ship

synod ('sinəd, 'sinod) n. **1.** church council **2.** convention

synonym ('sinənim) n. word with same meaning as another —**syno'nymity** n. —**synonymous** (si'noniməs) a.

synopsis (si'nopsis) n. summary, outline (pl. **-ses** (-sēz)) —**syn'optic** a. **1.** of, like synopsis **2.** having same viewpoint

syntax ('sintaks) n. part of grammar treating of arrangement of words in sentence —**syn'tactic** a. —**syn'tactically** adv.

synthesis ('sinthisis) n. putting together, combination (pl. **-theses** (-thisēz)) —**'synthesize** v. (cause to) combine into a whole —**'synthesizer** n. **1.** see MOOG SYNTHESIZER **2.** person or thing that synthesizes —**synthetic** (sin'thetik) a. **1.** artificial **2.** of synthesis —**synthetic detergent** synthetic substance other than soap cabable of soaplike cleaning action

syphilis ('sifilis) n. contagious venereal disease —**syphi'litic** a.

syphon ('sīfən) n. bottle for holding carbonated water

Syria ('siriə) n. country in Middle East bounded west by the Mediterranean and Lebanon, south by Israel and Jordan, east by Iraq and north by Turkey —**'Syrian** n./a.

syringe (si'rinj, 'sirinj) n. **1.** instrument for drawing in liquid by piston and forcing it out in fine stream or spray **2.** squirt —vt. **3.** spray, cleanse with syringe

syrup ('sirəp) n. **1.** thick solution obtained in process of refining sugar **2.** any liquid like this, esp. in consistency —**'syrupy** a.

system ('sistəm) n. **1.** complex whole, organization **2.** method **3.** classification —**syste'matic** a. methodical —**syste'matically** adv. —**'systematize** vt. **1.** reduce to system **2.** arrange methodically —**systemic** (si'stemik) a. affecting entire body or organism —**systems analysis** analysis of methods involved in scientific and industrial operations, usu. with computer, so that improved system can be designed

systole ('sistəli) n. contraction of heart and arteries for expelling blood and carrying on circulation —**systolic** (si'stolik) a. **1.** contracting **2.** of systole

Tt

t or **T** (tē) *n.* **1.** 20th letter of English alphabet **2.** speech sound represented by this letter **3.** something shaped like T (*pl.* **t's, T's** or **Ts**) —**to a T** in every detail; perfectly

t 1. tense **2.** ton

T 1. absolute temperature **2.** *Chem.* tritium **3.** surface tension **4.** tablespoon

ta (tä) *interj.* **UK** *inf.* thank you

Ta *Chem.* tantalum

Taal (täl) *n.* **SA** language, *esp.* Afrikaans

tab¹ (tab) *n.* tag, label, short strap —**keep tabs on** *inf.* keep watchful eye on

tab² (tab) **1.** tabulator **2.** tablet

tabard ('tabərd) *n.* (herald's) short tunic open at sides

tabby ('tabi) *n./a.* (cat) with markings of stripes *etc.* on lighter background

tabernacle ('tabərnakəl) *n.* **1.** portable shrine of Israelites **2.** *R.C.Ch.* receptacle containing consecrated Host **3.** place of worship not called a church

tabes dorsalis ('tābēz dör'salis) late manifestation of syphilis involving spinal cord resulting in progressive failure of lower limbs

table ('tābəl) *n.* **1.** piece of furniture consisting of flat board supported by legs **2.** food **3.** set of facts, figures arranged in lines or columns —*vt.* **4.** lay on table **5.** suspend discussion of (bill *etc.*) indefinitely **6. UK** submit (motion *etc.*) for consideration by meeting —**'tablecloth** *n.* cloth for covering table —**'tableland** *n.* plateau, high flat area —**'tablespoon** *n.* spoon used for serving food *etc.* —**table tennis** ball game played on table with small bats and light hollow ball

tableau ('tablō) *n.* **1.** group of persons, silent and motionless, arranged to represent some scene **2.** dramatic scene (*pl.* **-leaux** (-lōz))

table d'hôte ('täbəl 'dōt) *Fr.* (meal) with limited choice of dishes, at a fixed price

tablet ('tablit) *n.* **1.** pill of compressed powdered medicinal substance **2.** flattish cake of soap *etc.* **3.** slab of stone, wood *etc.*, *esp.* used formerly for writing on

tabloid ('tabloid) *n.* illustrated popular small-sized newspaper with terse, sensational headlines

taboo or **tabu** (tə'boo) *a.* **1.** forbidden; disapproved of —*n.* **2.** prohibition resulting from social conventions *etc.* **3.** thing prohibited —*vt.* **4.** place under taboo

tabor or **tabour** ('tābər) *n.* small drum, used *esp.* in Middle Ages, struck with one hand while other held pipe

tabular ('tabyələr) *a.* shaped, arranged like a table —**'tabulate** *vt.* arrange (figures, facts *etc.*) in tables —**tabu'lation** *n.* —**'tabulator** *n.* **1.** device for setting stops that locate column margins on typewriter **2.** *Comp.* machine that reads data from punched cards *etc.*, producing lists, tabulations or totals

tachism ('tashizəm) *n.* action painting

tacho- (*comb. form*) speed, as in *tachometer*

tachometer (ta'komitər) *n.* device for measuring speed, *esp.* of revolving shaft (in automobile) and hence revolutions per minute

tacit ('tasit) *a.* **1.** implied but not spoken **2.** silent —**'tacitly** *adv.* —**'taciturn** *a.* **1.** talking little **2.** habitually silent —**taci'turnity** *n.*

tack¹ (tak) *n.* **1.** small nail **2.** long, loose, temporary stitch **3.** *Naut.* course of ship obliquely to windward **4.** course, direction **5.** *inf.* food —*vt.* **6.** nail with tacks **7.** stitch (garment) with long, loose temporary stitches, baste **8.** append, attach —*v.* **9.** sail to windward

tack² (tak) *n.* riding harness for horses

tackle ('takəl) *n.* **1.** equipment, apparatus, *esp.* lifting appliances with ropes **2.** *Sport* physical challenge of opponent —*vt.* **3.** take in hand **4.** grapple with **5.** challenge

tacky¹ ('taki) *a.* sticky, not quite dry —**'tackiness** *n.*

tacky² ('taki) *a. inf.* **1.** shabby, shoddy **2.** ostentatious and vulgar

tact (takt) *n.* **1.** skill in dealing with people or situations **2.** delicate perception of the feelings of others —**'tactful** *a.* —**'tactfully** *adv.* —**'tactless** *a.* —**'tactlessly** *adv.*

tactics ('taktiks) *pl.n.* **1.** (*with sing. v.*) art of handling troops, ships in battle **2.** adroit management of a situation **3.** plans for this —**'tactical** *a.* —**tac'tician** *n.*

tactile ('taktil) *a.* of the sense of touch

tadpole ('tadpōl) *n.* immature frog, in its first state before gills and tail are absorbed

taffeta ('tafitə) *n.* smooth, stiff fabric of silk, rayon *etc.*

taffrail ('tafrāl) *n.* **1.** rail at stern of ship **2.** flat ornamental part of stern

Taffy ('tafi) *n. sl.* Welshman

Taft (taft) *n.* **William Howard.** the 27th President of the U.S. (1909-13)

tag¹ (tag) *n.* **1.** label identifying or showing price of something **2.** ragged, hanging end **3.** pointed end of shoelace *etc.* **4.** trite quotation **5.** any appendage —*vt.* **6.** append, add (on) —*vi.* **7.** (*usu. with* on or along) trail behind (-gg-)

tag² (tag) *n.* **1.** children's game where one being chased becomes chaser upon being touched by chaser —*vt.* **2.** touch (-gg-) —**tag wrestling** wrestling match for teams of two, where one partner may replace the other upon being touched on hand

tageles (ta'jētēz) *n.* plant with yellow or orange flowers

t'ai chi ch'uan or **tai chi chuan** (tī jē chōo'än, tī chē) Chinese system of disciplined movements practiced as aid to meditation or for exercise (*also* **t'ai chi**)

tail (tāl) *n.* **1.** flexible prolongation of animal's spine **2.** lower or inferior part of anything **3.** appendage **4.** rear part of aircraft **5.** *inf.* person employed to follow and spy on another —*pl.* **6.** reverse side of coin **7.** *inf.* tail coat —*vt.* **8.** remove tail of **9.** *inf.* follow closely, trail —**tailed** *a.* —**'tailings** *pl.n.* waste left over from some (*eg* industrial) process —**'tailless** *a.* —**'tailboard** *n.* removable or hinged rear board on vehicle —**tail coat** man's evening dress jacket —**tail end** last part —**'tailgate** *n.* **1.** gate used to control flow of water at lower end of lock **2.** tailboard —*v.* **3.** drive very close behind (vehicle) —**'taillight** *n.* light, *usu.* red, at rear of vehicle —**'tailpiece** *n.* **1.** extension or appendage that lengthens or completes something **2.** decorative design at foot of page *etc.* **3.** piece of wood to which strings of violin *etc.* are attached at lower end **4.** short beam or rafter with one end embedded in wall —**'tailpipe** *n.* pipe from which exhaust gases are discharged, *esp.* at rear of motor vehicle —**'tailplane** *n.* stabilizing surface at rear of aircraft —**'tailspin** *n.* spinning dive of aircraft —**'tailwind** *n.* wind blowing in same direction as course of aircraft or ship —**tail off** diminish gradually, dwindle —**turn tail** run away

tailor ('tālər) *n.* maker of outer clothing, *esp.* for men —**'tailored** *a.* **1.** having simple lines, as some women's garments **2.** specially fitted —**'tailorbird** *n.* tropical Asian warbler that builds nest by sewing together large leaves using plant fibers —**tailor-made** *a.* **1.** made by tailor **2.** well-fitting **3.** appropriate —*n.* **4.** *inf.* factory-made cigarette

taint (tānt) *v.* **1.** affect or be affected by pollution *etc.* —*n.* **2.** defect, flaw **3.** infection, contamination

Taiwan ('tī'wän) *n.* country in Asia situated on an island between the East and South China Seas (*also* **Republic of China**) —**Taiwa'nese** *n./a.*

take (tāk) *vt.* **1.** grasp, get hold of **2.** get, receive **3.** assume **4.** adopt **5.** accept **6.** understand **7.** consider **8.** carry, conduct **9.** use **10.** capture **11.** consume **12.** require —*vi.* **13.** be effective **14.** please (**took, 'taken, 'taking**) —*n.* **15.** *esp. Cine.* (recording of) scene, sequence photographed without interruption —**'taking** *a.* charming —**'takings** *pl.n.* earnings, receipts —**'takeaway UK, A, NZ** *a.* **1.** sold for consumption away from premises **2.** selling food for consumption away from premises —*n.* **3.** shop or restaurant that sells such food —**take-off** *n.* **1.** instant at which aircraft becomes airborne **2.** commencement of flight **3.** *inf.* act of mimicry —**'takeover** *n.* act of assuming power, control *etc.* —**take after** resemble in appearance or character —**take down 1.** write down **2.** dismantle **3.** humiliate —**take in 1.** understand **2.** make (garment *etc.*) smaller **3.** deceive —**take in vain 1.** blaspheme **2.** mention (person's name) —**take off 1.** (of aircraft) leave ground **2.** *inf.* go away **3.** *inf.* mimic —**take over 1.** assume control or management (of) **2.** *Print.* move (copy) to next line —**take to** become fond of

talc (talk) *n.* **1.** soft mineral of magnesium silicate **2.** talcum powder —**talcum powder** powder, *usu.* scented, to absorb body moisture, deodorize *etc.*

tale (tāl) *n.* **1.** story, narrative, report **2.** fictitious story —**tell tales 1.** tell fanciful lies **2.** report malicious stories *etc.*, *esp.* to someone in authority

talent ('talənt) *n.* **1.** natural ability or power **2.** ancient weight or money **3.** *inf.* (*esp.* attractive) members of opposite sex —**'tal-**

ented *a.* gifted —**talent scout** person whose occupation is searching for talented sportsmen, performers *etc.* for engagement as professionals

talis ('tălis) *n. Judaism* prayer shawl used by Jewish males at certain religious services (*pl.* **taleysem** (tă'lăsəm))

talisman ('talismən, 'talizmən) *n.* **1.** object supposed to have magic power **2.** amulet (*pl.* **-s**) —**talis'manic** *a.*

talk (tôk) *vi.* **1.** express, exchange ideas *etc.* in words **2.** spread rumors or gossip —*vt.* **3.** express in speech **4.** discuss **5.** speech, lecture **6.** conversation **7.** rumor —**'talkative** *a.* fond of talking —**'talker** *n.* —**talking book** recording of book, designed to be used by the blind —**talking-to** *n. inf.* reproof —**talk back** answer boldly or impudently —**talk into** persuade to by talking —**talk out of** dissuade from by talking

tall (tôl) *a.* **1.** high, of great stature **2.** incredible, untrue (*esp. in* **tall story**) —**'tallboy** *n.* high chest of drawers —**tall order** demand which is difficult to accomplish

tallow ('talō) *n.* **1.** melted and clarified animal fat —*vt.* **2.** smear with this

tally ('tali) *vi.* **1.** correspond one with the other **2.** keep score (**-lied, -lying**) —*n.* **3.** record, account, total number —**'tallier** *n.*

tally-ho (tali'hō) *interj.* huntsman's cry to urge on hounds

Talmud ('tălmŏŏd) *n.* body of Jewish law —**Tal'mudic** *a.*

talon ('talən) *n.* claw

tamarind ('tamərind) *n.* **1.** tropical tree **2.** its pods containing sour brownish pulp

tamarisk ('tamərisk) *n.* ornamental, evergreen tree or shrub with slender branches, very small leaves and spiky flowers

tambour ('tambŏŏr) *n.* **1.** *Real tennis* sloping buttress on one side of receiver's end of court **2.** embroidery frame consisting of two hoops over which fabric is stretched while being worked **3.** embroidered work done on such frame **4.** sliding door on desks *etc.*, made of thin strips of wood glued on to canvas backing **5.** *Archit.* wall that is circular in plan, *esp.* supporting dome or surrounded by colonnade **6.** drum —*v.* **7.** embroider on tambour

tambourine (tambə'rēn) *n.* flat half-drum with jingling disks of metal attached

tame (tăm) *a.* **1.** not wild, domesticated **2.** subdued **3.** uninteresting —*vt.* **4.** make tame —**'tamely** *adv.* **1.** in a tame manner **2.** without resisting —**'tamer** *n.*

Tamil ('tamil) *n.* **1.** member of a people of S India and Sri Lanka **2.** language of this people (*pl.* **-s, 'Tamil**) —*a.* **3.** of this people

tam-o'-shanter ('taməshantər) *n.* Scottish brimless wool cap with bobble in center

tamp (tamp) *vt.* pack, force down by repeated blows

tamper ('tampər) *vi.* (*usu. with* **with**) interfere improperly, meddle

tampon ('tampon) *n.* **1.** plug of lint, cotton *etc.* inserted in wound, body cavity, to stop flow of blood, absorb secretions *etc.* **2.** two-headed drumstick

tan¹ (tan) *a./n.* **1.** (of) brown color of skin after long exposure to rays of sun *etc.* —*v.* **2.** (cause to) go brown —*vt.* **3.** (of animal hide) convert to leather by chemical treatment **4.** *inf.* beat, flog (**-nn-**) —**'tanner** *n.* —**'tannery** *n.* place where hides are tanned —**'tannic** *a.* of tan, tannin or tannic acid —**'tannin** *n.* vegetable substance used as tanning agent —**'tanbark** *n.* bark of certain trees, yielding

tannin —**tannic acid** astringent derived from oak bark *etc.*, used in tanning *etc.*

tan² (tan) *Trig.* tangent

tanager ('tanəjər) *n.* any of family of Amer. songbirds having short thick bill and, in male, brilliantly colored plumage

tandem ('tandəm) *n.* bicycle for two riders, one behind the other

tandoor (tăn'dŏŏr) *n.* clay oven in which food is cooked, usu. over charcoal (*pl.* **tan'doori**) —**tan'doori** *a.* cooked in a tandoor

tang (tang) *n.* **1.** strong pungent taste or smell **2.** trace, hint **3.** spike, barb —**'tangy** *a.*

Tanganyika and Zanzibar (tanggə'nyĕkə, 'zanzibăr) *former name of* TANZANIA —**Tanga'nyikan** *n./a.*

tangent ('tanjənt) *n.* **1.** line that touches a curve without cutting **2.** divergent course **3.** *Trig.* ratio of side opposite given acute angle in right-angled triangle to adjacent side —*a.* **4.** touching, meeting without cutting —**tan'gential** *a.* —**tan'gentially** *adv.*

tangerine ('tanjərēn, tanjə'rēn) *n.* **1.** Asian citrus tree **2.** its fruit, a variety of orange **3.** reddish-orange color

tangible ('tanjəbəl) *a.* **1.** that can be touched **2.** definite **3.** palpable; concrete —**tangi'bility** *n.*

tangle ('tanggəl) *n.* **1.** confused mass or situation —*vt.* **2.** twist together in muddle —*vi.* **3.** contend

tango ('tanggō) *n.* dance of S Amer. origin (*pl.* **-s**)

Tango ('tanggō) *n.* word used in communications for the letter *t*

tangram ('tanggrəm, 'tan-grəm) *n.* Chinese puzzle comprising square cut in five triangles, a square and a rhomboid capable of being recombined to represent many figures

tank (tangk) *n.* **1.** storage vessel for liquids or gas **2.** armored motor vehicle moving on tracks **3.** cistern **4.** reservoir —**'tanker** *n.* ship, plane or truck for carrying liquid in bulk —**tank farming** *see* HYDROPONICS —**tank up** *sl.* imbibe large quantity of alcoholic drink

tankard ('tangkərd) *n.* large drinking cup of metal or glass, usu. with hinged lid

tanner ('tanər) *n.* UK *inf.* sixpence

tannin ('tanin) *n. see* TAN¹

tansy ('tanzi) *n.* yellow-flowered aromatic herb

tantalize ('tantəlīz) *vt.* torment by appearing to offer something desired —**'tantalus** *n.* UK case in which bottles may be locked with their contents visible

tantalum ('tantələm) *n. Chem.* metallic element *Symbol* Ta, at. wt. 181.0, at. no. 73

tantamount ('tantəmownt) *a.* **1.** equivalent in value or signification **2.** equal, amounting

tantrum ('tantrəm) *n.* childish outburst of temper

Tanzania (tanzə'nēə) *n.* country in Africa bounded northeast by Kenya, north by Lake Victoria and Uganda, northwest by Rwanda and Burundi, west by Lake Tanganyika, southwest by Zambia and Malawi and south by Mozambique —**Tanza'nian** *n./a.*

Taoism ('dowizəm, 'tow-) *n.* system of religion and philosophy based on teachings of Lao-tse, Chinese philosopher, and advocating simple, honest life and noninterference with course of natural events —**'Taoist** *n./a.* —**Tao'istic** *a.*

tap¹ (tap) *v.* **1.** strike lightly but with some noise (**-pp-**) —*n.* **2.** slight blow, rap —**tap dance** step dance in which performer wears shoes equipped with metal pieces that make

rhythmic sound on stage as he dances —**tap-dance** *vi.* perform tap dance —**tap-dancer** *n.* —**tap-dancing** *n.*

tap² (tap) *n.* **1.** valve with handle to regulate or stop flow of fluid in pipe *etc.* **2.** stopper, plug permitting liquid to be drawn from cask *etc.* **3.** steel tool for forming internal screw threads —*vt.* **4.** put tap in **5.** draw off (as) with tap **6.** make secret connection to (telephone wire) to overhear conversation on it **7.** make connection to (pipe, drain *etc.*) **8.** form internal threads in **9.** ask (someone) for money; obtain (money) from someone (**-pp-**) —**'taproom** *n.* bar or bar room

tape (tăp) *n.* **1.** narrow long strip of fabric, paper *etc.* **2.** magnetic recording of music *etc.* —*vt.* **3.** record (speech, music *etc.*) —**tape deck** platform supporting spools *etc.* of tape recorder, incorporating motor and playback, recording and erasing heads —**tape machine** telegraphic device that records current stock quotations electronically or on ticker tape —**tape measure** tape of fabric or metal, marked off in centimeters, inches *etc.* —**tape recorder** apparatus for recording sound on magnetized tape and playing it back —**tape recording 1.** act of recording on magnetic tape **2.** magnetized tape used for this **3.** music *etc.* so recorded —**'tapeworm** *n.* long flat worm parasitic in animals and man —**have (someone) taped** *inf.* have (someone) sized up, have measure of (someone)

taper ('tăpər) *vi.* **1.** become gradually thinner toward one end —*n.* **2.** thin candle **3.** long wick covered with wax; spill **4.** a narrowing

tapestry ('tapistri) *n.* fabric decorated with designs in colors woven by needles, not in shuttles —**'tapestried** *a.*

tapioca (tapi'ōkə) *n.* beadlike starch made from cassava root, used *esp.* in puddings and as a thickening agent

tapir ('tăpər) *n.* Amer. animal with elongated snout, allied to pig

tappet ('tapit) *n.* in internal-combustion engine, short steel rod conveying movement imparted by the lift of a cam to the valve stem

taproot ('taprŏŏt) *n.* large single root growing straight down

tar¹ (tär) *n.* **1.** thick black liquid distilled from coal *etc.* —*vt.* **2.** coat, treat with tar (**-rr-**)

tar² (tär) *n. inf.* sailor

tarantella (tarən'telə) *n.* **1.** lively It. dance **2.** music for it

tarantula (tə'ranchələ) *n.* any of various large (poisonous) hairy spiders (*pl.* **-s, -lae** (-lē))

tarboosh (tär'bŏŏsh) *n.* felt brimless cap, usu. red and oft. with silk tassel, worn by Muslim men

tardy ('tärdi) *a.* **1.** slow **2.** late —**'tardily** *adv.*

tare¹ (tăr) *n.* **1.** weight of wrapping or container for goods **2.** unladen weight of vehicle

tare² (tăr) *n.* **1.** vetch **2.** weed

target ('tärgit) *n.* **1.** mark to aim at in shooting *etc.* **2.** thing aimed at **3.** object of criticism **4.** butt —**target language** language into which text *etc.* is translated

Tarheel ('tärhēl) *n.* nickname for native or resident of North Carolina

tariff ('tarif) *n.* **1.** tax levied on imports *etc.* **2.** list of charges **3.** method of charging for supply of services, *eg* electricity

Tarmac ('tärmak) *n.* trade name for mixture of tar, bitumen and crushed stones rolled to give hard, smooth surface

tarn (tärn) *n.* small mountain lake

tarnish ('tärnish) *v.* 1. (cause to) become stained, lose shine or become dimmed or sullied —*n.* 2. discoloration, blemish

taro ('tärō) *n.* 1. widely cultivated tropical plant with broad leaves and edible rootstock 2. its edible rootstock

tarot ('tarō) *n.* one of special set of cards now used mainly by fortune-tellers

tarpaulin (tär'pölin) *n.* (sheet of) heavy hard-wearing waterproof fabric

tarragon ('taragon) *n.* aromatic herb

tarry ('tari) *vi.* 1. linger, delay 2. stay behind (**-ried, -rying**)

tarsier ('tärsiä, -siər) *n.* nocturnal tree-dwelling mammal of Indonesia *etc.*

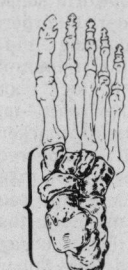

tarsus

tarsus ('tärsəs) *n.* 1. bones of ankle and heel collectively 2. corresponding part in other mammals *etc.* 3. connective tissue supporting free edge of each eyelid (*pl.* **-si** (-sī)) —'**tarsal** *a.* 1. of tarsus or tarsi —*n.* 2. tarsal bone

tart[1] (tärt) *n.* 1. pie or flan filled with fruit, jam *etc.* 2. *inf., offens.* promiscuous woman, *esp.* prostitute

tart[2] (tärt) *a.* 1. sour, bitter 2. sharp

tartan ('tärtən) *n.* 1. woolen cloth woven in pattern of colored checks, *esp.* in colors, patterns associated with Scottish clans 2. such pattern

tartar[1] ('tärtər) *n.* 1. crust deposited on teeth 2. deposit formed during fermentation of wine —**tar'taric** *a.* —**tartaric acid** colorless crystalline acid found in many fruits

tartar[2] ('tärtər) *n.* vicious-tempered person, difficult to deal with

Tartar ('tärtər) *see* TATAR

tartar sauce mayonnaise sauce mixed with chopped herbs, capers *etc.*

Tas. Tasmania

task (task) *n.* 1. piece of work (*esp.* unpleasant or difficult) set or undertaken —*vt.* 2. assign task to 3. exact —**task force** naval or military unit dispatched to carry out specific undertaking —'**taskmaster** *n.* overseer —**take to task** reprove

Taslan ('taslən) *n.* trade name for bulking process which makes loops in yarn

Tasmanian devil (taz'mäniən) small, ferocious, carnivorous marsupial of Tasmania

Tass (tas) *n.* principal news agency of Soviet Union

tassel ('tasəl) *n.* 1. ornament of fringed knot of threads *etc.* 2. tuft

taste (tāst) *n.* 1. sense by which flavor, quality of substance is detected by the tongue 2. this act or sensation 3. (brief) experience of something 4. small amount 5. preference, liking 6. power of discerning, judging 7. discretion, delicacy —*v.* 8. observe or distinguish the taste of (a substance) 9. take small amount of (food *etc.*) into mouth —*vt.* 10. experience —*vi.* 11. have specific flavor —'**tasteful** *a.* 1. in good style 2. with, showing good taste —'**tastefully** *adv.*

—'**tasteless** *a.* —'**taster** *n.* 1. person who samples food or drink for quality 2. device used in tasting or sampling 3. *esp.* formerly, person employed to taste food and drink prepared for king *etc.* to test for poison —'**tasty** *a.* pleasantly or highly flavored —**taste bud** small organ of taste on tongue

tat[1] (tat) *v.* make (something) by tatting (-**tt**-) —'**tatter** *n.* —'**tatting** *n.* type of handmade lace

tat[2] (tat) *n.* 1. ragged, shoddy article 2. tattiness

Tatar ('tätər) *or* **Tartar** *n.* 1. member of Mongoloid people who established powerful state in central Asia in 13th century 2. descendant of this people, now scattered throughout Soviet Union 3. Turkic language or dialect spoken by this people —*a.* 4. of Tatars

tatter ('tatər) *v.* 1. make or become ragged, worn to shreds —*n.* 2. ragged piece

tattle ('tatəl) *vi./n.* gossip, chatter —'**tattle-tale** *n.* 1. scandalmonger, gossip —*a.* 2. telltale

tattoo[1] (ta'tōō) *n.* 1. formerly, beat of drum and bugle call 2. military spectacle or pageant

tattoo[2] (ta'tōō) *vt.* 1. mark (skin) in patterns *etc.* by pricking and filling punctures with indelible colored inks (-'**tooed,** -'**tooing**) —*n.* 2. mark so made

tatty ('tati) *a.* shabby, worn-out —'**tattiness** *n.*

tau (tow, tö) *n.* 19th letter in Gr. alphabet (T, τ)

taught (töt) *pt./pp. of* TEACH

taunt (tönt) *vt.* 1. provoke, deride with insulting words *etc.* 2. tease; tantalize —*n.* 3. instance of this

taupe (tōp) *n.* brownish-gray color

Taurus ('törəs) *n.* (bull) 2nd sign of zodiac, operative *c.* Apr. 21st-May 20th

taut (töt) *a.* 1. drawn tight 2. under strain —'**tauten** *vt.* make tight or tense

tauto- *or before vowel* **taut-** (*comb. form*) identical, same, as in *tautology*

tautology (tö'toləji) *n.* repetition of same thing in other words in same sentence —**tauto'logical** *a.*

tavern ('tavərn) *n.* 1. premises licensed to sell alcoholic beverages 2. inn

tawdry ('tödri) *a.* showy, but cheap and without taste, flashy —'**tawdrily** *adv.* —'**tawdriness** *n.*

tawny ('töni) *a./n.* (of) light (yellowish) brown —**tawny owl** European owl having reddish-brown plumage and round head

tax (taks) *n.* 1. compulsory payments by wage earners, companies *etc.* imposed by government to raise revenue 2. heavy demand (on something) —*vt.* 3. impose tax on 4. strain 5. accuse, blame —'**taxable** *a.* —**tax'ation** *n.* levying of taxes —**tax-deductible** *a.* legally deductible from income before tax assessment —**tax-free** *a.* exempt from taxation —'**taxpayer** *n.* —**tax return** statement of personal income for tax purposes

taxi ('taksi) *n.* 1. taxicab (*pl.* **-s**) —*vi.* 2. (of aircraft) run along ground under its own power 3. go in taxicab (**taxied** *pt./pp.,* '**taxying,** '**taxiing** *pr.p.*) —'**taxicab** *n.* motor vehicle for hire with driver —'**taximeter** *n.* meter fitted to taxicab to register fare, based on length of journey —**taxi stand** place where taxicabs wait to be hired

taxidermy ('taksidərmi) *n.* art of stuffing, mounting animal skins to give them lifelike appearance —**taxi'dermal** *or* **taxi'dermic** *a.* —'**taxidermist** *n.*

taxonomy (tak'sonəmi) *n.* science, practice of classifying by structure, *esp.* living organisms —**taxo'nomic** *a.*

taxoplasmosis (taksōplaz'mōsis) *n.* infectious disease affecting humans, dogs, cats, chickens and other animals whose method of transmission is unknown and which may be congenital

Taylor ('tālər) *n.* **Zachary.** the 12th President of the U.S. (1849-50)

Tb *Chem.* terbium

T.B. *or* **t.b.** tuberculosis

T-bone steak steak cut from sirloin of beef, containing T-shaped bone

tbs. *or* **tbsp.** tablespoon(ful)

Tc *Chem.* technetium

tch *interj./n.* 1. clicking sound made with tongue, to express disapproval *etc.* —*vi.* 2. utter tch's

Te *Chem.* tellurium

tea (tē) *n.* 1. dried leaves of plant cultivated *esp.* in (sub)tropical Asia 2. infusion of it as beverage 3. any of various herbal infusions 4. tea, cakes *etc.* as light afternoon meal 5. main evening meal —**tea bag** small porous bag of paper containing tea leaves —**tea ball** perforated metal ball filled with tea leaves and used to make tea —'**teacup** *n.* 1. cup out of which tea may be drunk 2. amount teacup will hold, usu. six fluid ounces (*also* '**teacupful**) —'**teahouse** *n.* restaurant where tea and light refreshments are served —**tea leaf** 1. dried leaf of tea shrub, used to make tea 2. (*usu. pl.*) shredded parts of these leaves, *esp.* after infusion —**tea party** social gathering at which tea is served —'**teapot** *n.* container with lid, spout and handle, in which tea is made —'**teaspoon** *n.* 1. small spoon for stirring tea *etc.* 2. cooking measure equal to five milliliters or ⅓ of a tablespoon —**tea tree** Aust., N.Z. tree —**tea wagon** small table on wheels for serving tea or holding dishes

teach (tēch) *vt.* 1. instruct 2. educate 3. train 4. impart knowledge of —*vi.* 5. act as teacher (**taught,** '**teaching**) —'**teacher** *n.* —'**teaching** *n.* —**teaching machine** machine that presents information and questions to user, registers answers, and indicates whether these are correct or acceptable

teak (tēk) *n.* 1. tall evergreen tree of SE Asia 2. very hard wood obtained from it

teal (tēl) *n.* 1. type of small duck 2. greenish-blue color

team (tēm) *n.* 1. set of animals, players of game *etc.* associated in activity —*v.* 2. (*usu. with* up) (cause to) make a team —'**teamster** *n.* driver of team of draft animals —**team-mate** *n.* fellow member of team —**team spirit** subordination of individual desire for good of team —'**teamwork** *n.* cooperative work by team acting as unit

tear[1] (tēər) *n.* drop of fluid appearing in and falling from eye —'**tearful** *a.* 1. inclined to weep 2. involving tears —'**tearless** *a.* —'**teardrop** *n.* —**tear gas** irritant gas causing abnormal watering of eyes and temporary blindness —**tear-jerker** *n. inf.* excessively sentimental motion picture *etc.*

tear[2] (tāər) *vt.* 1. pull apart, rend —*vi.* 2. become torn 3. rush (**tore, torn,** '**tearing**) —*n.* 4. hole, cut; split —**tear away** persuade (oneself or someone else) to leave

tease (tēz) *vt.* 1. tantalize, irritate, bait 2. pull apart fibers of —*n.* 3. one who teases —'**teaser** *n.* annoying or puzzling problem —'**teasing** *a.*

teasel ('tēzəl) *n.* plant with prickly leaves and head

teat (tēt) *n.* mammary gland; nipple

tech (tek) *a./n. inf.* technical (school, college or institute)

tech. 1. technical **2.** technology

technetium (tek'nēshiəm) *n. Chem.* metallic element *Symbol* Tc, at. wt. 99, at. no. 43

technical ('teknikəl) *a.* **1.** of, specializing in industrial, practical or mechanical arts and applied sciences **2.** skilled in practical and mechanical arts **3.** belonging to particular art or science **4.** according to letter of the law —**techni'cality** *n.* **1.** point of procedure **2.** state of being technical —**'technically** *adv.* —**tech'nician** *n.* one skilled in technique of an art —**technique** (tek'nēk) *n.* **1.** method of performance in an art **2.** skill required for mastery of subject —**technical knockout** *Boxing* judgment of knockout given when boxer is in referee's opinion too badly beaten to continue

Technicolor ('teknikulər) *n.* trade name for color process in motion pictures

techno- (*comb. form*) **1.** craft; art, as in *technology, technography* **2.** technological; technical, as in *technocracy*

technocracy (tek'nokrəsi) *n.* **1.** government by technical experts **2.** group of these experts

technology (tek'noləji) *n.* **1.** application of practical, mechanical sciences to industry, commerce **2.** technical methods, skills, knowledge —**techno'logical** *a.* —**tech'nologist** *n.*

tectonic (tek'tonik) *a.* of construction or building —**tec'tonics** *pl.n.* (*with sing. v.*) art, science of building

teddy bear ('tedi) child's soft toy bear (*also* **'teddy**)

Te Deum (tā 'dāəm, tē 'dēəm) **1.** ancient Latin hymn in rhythmic prose **2.** musical setting of this hymn **3.** service of thanksgiving in which recital of this hymn forms central part

tedious ('tēdiəs) *a.* causing fatigue or boredom, monotonous —**'tedium** *n.* monotony

tee (tē) *n.* **1.** *Golf* slightly raised ground from which first stroke of hole is made **2.** small peg supporting ball for this stroke **3.** target in some games (*eg* quoits) —**tee off** make first stroke of hole in golf

teem (tēm) *vi.* **1.** abound, swarm, be prolific **2.** pour, rain heavily

teens (tēnz) *pl.n.* years of life from 13 to 19 —**'teenage** *a.* —**'teenager** *n.* young person between 13 and 19 —**'teenybopper** *n. sl.* young teenager, usu. girl, who avidly follows fashions

teeny ('tēni) *a.* extremely small; tiny (*also* **teeny-weeny** (tēni'wēni), **teensy-weensy** (tēnsi'wēnsi))

tee shirt *see* T-SHIRT

teeter ('tētər) *vi.* **1.** seesaw or make similar movements **2.** vacillate

teeth (tēth) *n., pl. of* TOOTH —**teethe** (tēdh) *vi.* (of baby) grow first teeth —**teething** ('tēdhing) *n.* eruption of the "milk" or deciduous teeth in infancy —**teething ring** hard ring on which babies may bite while teething —**teething troubles** problems, difficulties at first stage of something

teetotal ('tē'tōtəl) *a.* pledged to abstain from alcohol —**tee'totaler** *n.* —**tee'totalism** *n.*

Teflon ('teflon) *n.* trade name for polymer used to make nonstick coatings on cooking utensils

tel. 1. telegram **2.** telegraph(ic) **3.** telephone

tele- *or before vowel* **tel-** (*comb. form*) at a distance, from far off, as in *telescope*

telecast ('telikast) *vi./n.* (broadcast) television program

telecommunications (telikəmyōōni'kā-shənz) *pl.n.* (*with sing. v.*) science and technology of communications by telephony, radio, television *etc.*

telegram ('teligram) *n.* message sent by telegraph

telegraph ('teligraf) *n.* **1.** electrical apparatus for transmitting messages to a distance **2.** any signaling device for transmitting messages —*v.* **3.** communicate by telegraph —*vt.* **4.** C cast (votes) illegally by impersonating registered voters —**tele'graphic** *a.* —**tele'graphically** *adv.* —**te'legraphist** *n.* one who works telegraph —**te'legraphy** *n.* **1.** science of telegraph **2.** use of telegraph

telekinesis (teliki'nēsis, -kī-) *n.* **1.** movement of a body caused by thought or willpower **2.** ability to cause such movement —**telekinetic** (teliki'netik, -kī-) *a.*

teleology (teli'oləji, tēli-) *n.* **1.** doctrine of final causes **2.** belief that things happen because of the purpose or design that will be fulfilled by them —**teleo'logic(al)** *a.*

telepathy (ti'lepəthi) *n.* action of one mind on another at a distance —**tele'pathic** *a.* —**tele'pathically** *adv.*

telephone ('telifōn) *n.* **1.** apparatus for communicating sound to hearer at a distance —*v.* **2.** communicate, speak by telephone —**telephonic** (teli'fonik) *a.* —**te'lephony** *n.* —**telephone booth** soundproof enclosure having public telephone —**telephone directory** book listing names, addresses and telephone numbers of subscribers in particular area

telephoto (teli'fōtō) *a.* (of lens) producing magnified image of distant object —**telepho'tography** *n.* process or technique of photographing distant objects using telephoto lens

teleprinter ('teliprintər) *n. see* TELETYPEWRITER

TelePrompTer ('telipromptər) *n. T.V.* trade name for device to enable speaker to refer to his script out of sight of the cameras

telescope ('teliskōp) *n.* **1.** optical instrument for magnifying distant objects —*v.* **2.** slide or drive together, *esp.* parts designed to fit one inside the other **3.** make smaller, shorter —**telescopic** (teli'skopik) *a.*

teletypewriter (teli'tīpwrītər) *n.* apparatus capable of being used over telephone networks to send and receive signals and to produce hard copy

television ('telivizhən) *n.* **1.** system of producing on screen images of distant objects, events *etc.* by electromagnetic radiation **2.** device for receiving this transmission and converting it to optical images **3.** program *etc.* viewed on television set —**'televise** *vt.* **1.** transmit by television **2.** make, produce as television program

telex ('teleks) *n.* **1.** international communication service by means of teletypewriters connected through automatic exchanges —*vt.* **2.** transmit (message) by telex

tell (tel) *vt.* **1.** let know **2.** order, direct **3.** narrate, make known **4.** discern **5.** distinguish **6.** count —*vi.* **7.** give account **8.** be of weight, importance **9.** *inf.* reveal secrets (**told, 'telling**) —**'teller** *n.* **1.** narrator **2.** bank cashier —**'telling** *a.* effective, striking —**'telltale** *n.* **1.** sneak **2.** automatic indicator —*a.* **3.** revealing

tellurian (tə'lōōriən, te-) *a.* of the earth —**tel'luric** *a.* —**tel'lurium** *n. Chem.* metalloid element *Symbol* Te, at. wt. 127.6, at. no. 52 —**tellurous** ('telyərəs; tə'lōōrəs, te-) *a.*

temerity (ti'meriti) *n.* boldness, audacity

temp (temp) *inf.* *n.* **1.** one employed on temporary basis —*vi.* **2.** work as temp

temp. 1. temperature **2.** temporary

temper ('tempər) *n.* **1.** frame of mind **2.** anger, oft. noisy **3.** mental constitution **4.** degree of hardness of steel *etc.* —*vt.* **5.** restrain, qualify, moderate **6.** harden **7.** bring to proper condition —**'tempered** *a.* having temper or temperament as specified, as in *ill-tempered*

tempera ('tempərə) *n.* painting medium in which pigment is dissolved with egg white and combined with egg yolk

temperament ('tempərəmənt) *n.* **1.** natural disposition **2.** excitability; moodiness; anger —**tempera'mental** *a.* **1.** given to extremes of temperament, moody **2.** of, occasioned by temperament **3.** *inf.* working erratically and inconsistently; unreliable —**tempera'mentally** *adv.*

temperate ('tempərit) *a.* **1.** not extreme **2.** showing, practicing moderation —**'temperance** *n.* **1.** moderation **2.** abstinence, *esp.* from alcohol —**'temperately** *adv.* —**Temperate Zone** parts of earth's surface lying between Arctic Circle and tropic of Cancer and between Antarctic Circle and tropic of Capricorn

temperature ('tempərchōōər, 'tempri-; -chər) *n.* **1.** degree of heat or coldness **2.** *inf.* (abnormally) high body temperature

tempest ('tempist) *n.* violent storm —**tem'pestuous** *a.* **1.** turbulent **2.** violent, stormy —**tem'pestuously** *adv.*

template *or* **templet** ('templit) *n.* mold, pattern to help shape something accurately

temple[1] ('tempəl) *n.* **1.** building for worship **2.** shrine

temple[2] ('tempəl) *n.* flat part on either side of forehead

tempo ('tempō) *n.* rate, rhythm, *esp.* in music (*pl.* **-s, -pi** (-pē))

temporal[1] ('tempərəl) *a.* **1.** of time **2.** of this life or world, secular **3.** *Gram.* of tense or linguistic expression of time —**tempo'rality** *n.*

temporal[2] ('tempərəl) *a. Anat.* of temple or temples —**temporal bone** either of two compound bones forming sides of skull

temporary ('tempəreri) *a.* lasting, used only for a time —**tempo'rarily** *adv.*

temporize ('tempərīz) *vi.* **1.** use evasive action; hedge; gain time by negotiation *etc.* **2.** conform to circumstances —**'temporizer** *n.*

tempt (tempt) *vt.* **1.** try to persuade, entice, *esp.* to something wrong or unwise **2.** dispose, cause to be inclined —**temp'tation** *n.* **1.** act of tempting **2.** thing that tempts —**'tempter** *n.* (**'temptress** *fem.*) —**'tempting** *a.* attractive, inviting

tempus fugit ('tempəs 'fyōōjit) *Lat.* time flies

ten (ten) *n./a.* cardinal number next after nine —**tenth** *a./n.* ordinal number —**tengallon hat** cowboy's broad-brimmed felt hat with high crown —**tenpins** ('tenpinz) *pl.n.* (*with sing. v.*) bowling game in which bowls are rolled down lane to knock over ten target pins —**the Ten Commandments** *O.T.* commandments summarizing basic obligations of man toward God and his fellow men

ten. *Mus.* **1.** tenor **2.** tenuto

tenable ('tenəbəl) *a.* able to be held, defended, maintained

tenacious (ti'nāshəs) *a.* **1.** holding fast **2.** retentive **3.** stubborn —**tenacity** (ti'nasiti) *n.*

tenant ('tenənt) *n.* one who holds lands, house *etc.* on rent or lease —**'tenancy** *n.* —**'tenantry** *n.* body of tenants —**tenant farmer** person who farms land rented from another, rent usu. taking form of crops *etc.*

tench (tench) *n.* freshwater game fish

tend[1] (tend) vi. 1. be inclined 2. be conducive 3. go or move (in particular direction) —**'tendency** n. inclination, bent —**ten'dentious** or **ten'dencious** a. having, showing tendency or bias, controversial

tend[2] (tend) vt. take care of, watch over —**'tender** n. 1. small boat carried by yacht or ship 2. carriage for fuel and water attached to steam locomotive 3. one who tends, eg bar tender

tender[1] ('tendər) a. 1. not tough or hard 2. easily injured 3. gentle, loving, affectionate 4. delicate, soft —**'tenderize** vt. soften (meat) by pounding or by treating with substance made for this purpose —**'tenderly** adv. —**'tenderness** n. —**'tenderfoot** n. newcomer, esp. to ranch etc. —**'tenderloin** n. tenderest muscle of loin of pork etc.

tender[2] ('tendər) vt. 1. offer —vi. 2. make offer or estimate —n. 3. offer 4. offer or estimate for contract to undertake specific work 5. what may legally be offered in payment

tendon ('tendən) n. sinew attaching muscle to bone etc.

tendril ('tendril) n. 1. slender curling stem by which climbing plant clings to anything 2. curl, as of hair

tenement ('tenəmənt) n. building divided into separate apartments (also **tenement building**)

tenet ('tenit, 'tēnit) n. doctrine, belief

Tennessee (tenə'sē) n. East South Central state of the U.S., admitted to the Union in 1796. Abbrev.: **Tenn., TN** (with ZIP code)

tennis ('tenis) n. game in which ball is struck with racket by players on opposite sides of net, lawn tennis —**tennis elbow** strained muscle as a result of playing tennis —**tennis shoe** sneaker

tenon ('tenən) n. tongue put on end of piece of wood etc. to fit into a mortise —**tenon saw**

tenor ('tenər) n. 1. male voice between alto and bass 2. music for, singer with this 3. saxophone etc. intermediate between alto and baritone or bass 4. general course, meaning

tenosynovitis ('tenōsinə'vītis) n. inflammation of sheath enveloping certain tendons

tense[1] (tens) n. modification of verb to show time of action

tense[2] (tens) a. 1. stretched tight, strained; taut 2. emotionally strained —v. 3. make, become tense —**'tensile** a. 1. of tension 2. capable of being stretched —**'tension** n. 1. stretching 2. strain when stretched 3. emotional strain or excitement 4. hostility 5. suspense 6. Elec. voltage —**tensile strength** measure of ability of material to withstand longitudinal stress

tent (tent) n. portable shelter of canvas —**tent dress** dress widening from shoulders in shape of tent —**tent stitch** see **petit point** at PETIT

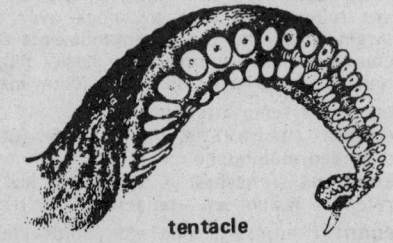

tentacle

tentacle ('tentəkəl) n. elongated, flexible organ of some animals (eg octopus) used for grasping, feeding etc.

tentative ('tentətiv) a. 1. done as a trial 2. experimental, cautious —**'tentatively** adv.

tenterhooks ('tentərhŏŏks) pl.n. —**on tenterhooks** in anxious suspense

tenuous ('tenyŏŏəs) a. 1. flimsy, uncertain 2. thin, fine, slender —**te'nuity** n.

tenure ('tenyər, 'tenyŏŏər) n. (length of time of) possession, holding of office, position etc.

tenuto (tə'nŏŏtō) a./adv. Mus. (of note) to be held for or beyond its full time value

tepee ('tēpē) n. Amerindian cone-shaped tent of animal skins

tepid ('tepid) a. 1. moderately warm, lukewarm 2. half-hearted

tequila (ti'kēlə) n. Mexican alcoholic spirit

ter. 1. terrace 2. territory

terbium ('tərbiəm) n. Chem. metallic element Symbol Tb, at. wt. 158.9, at no. 65

tercel ('tərsəl) or **tiercel** n. male falcon or hawk, esp. as used in falconry

tercentenary (tərsen'tenəri) or **tercentennial** a./n. (of) three hundredth anniversary

tergiversate (tər'jivərsāt) vi. 1. change sides or loyalties 2. be evasive or ambiguous —tergiver'sation n.

term (tərm) n. 1. expression 2. limited period of time 3. period during which courts sit, schools are open etc. 4. limit, end —pl. 5. conditions 6. mutual relationship —vt. 7. name, designate —**terms of reference** specific limits of responsibility that determine activities of investigating body etc.

termagant ('tərməgənt) n. shrewish woman; scold

terminal ('tərminəl) a. 1. at, forming an end 2. pert. to, forming a terminus 3. (of disease) ending in death —n. 4. terminal part or structure 5. extremity 6. point where current enters, leaves electrical device (eg battery) 7. device permitting operation of computer at some distance from it —**terminal velocity** 1. constant maximum velocity reached by body falling under gravity through fluid, esp. atmosphere 2. velocity of missile or projectile when it reaches target 3. maximum velocity attained by rocket etc. flying in parabolic flight path 4. maximum velocity that aircraft can attain

terminate ('tərmināt) v. bring, come to an end —**'terminable** a. —**termi'nation** n.

terminology (tərmi'noləji) n. 1. set of technical terms or vocabulary 2. study of terms —**termino'logical** a.

terminus ('tərminəs) n. 1. finishing point 2. farthest limit 3. railroad station, bus station etc. at end of long-distance line (pl. **-ni** (-nī), **-es**)

termite ('tərmīt) n. insect, many species of which feed on and damage living trees and wooden structures (also **white ant**)

tern (tərn) n. sea bird like gull

ternary ('tərnəri) a. 1. consisting of three 2. proceeding in threes

Terpsichore (tərp'sikəri) n. Muse of dance and choral song —**Terpsichorean** (tərpsikə'rēən, -'kŏriən) oft. jocular a. 1. of dancing (also **Terpsicho'real**) —n. 2. dancer

Terr. 1. Terrace 2. Territory

terrace ('terəs) n. 1. raised level place 2. level cut out of hill 3. row, street of houses built on raised or sloping ground or as one block 4. (oft. pl.) unroofed tier for spectators at football stadium —vt. 5. form into, furnish with terrace

terra cotta ('terə 'kotə) 1. hard unglazed pottery 2. its color, brownish red

terra firma ('fərmə) Lat. firm ground; dry land

terrain (tə'rān) n. area of ground, esp. with reference to its physical character

terra incognita (inkog'nētə, in'kognitə) Lat. unexplored or unknown area

terrapin

terrapin ('terəpin) n. type of aquatic turtle

terrazzo (te'razō, -'rätsō) n. floor, wall finish of chips of stone set in mortar and polished

terrene (te'rēn) a. 1. of earth; worldly; mundane 2. rare of earth; earthy —n. 3. land 4. rare earth

terrestrial (tə'restriəl) a. 1. of the earth 2. of, living on land

terrible ('terəbəl) a. 1. serious 2. dreadful, frightful 3. excessive 4. causing fear —**'terribly** adv.

terrier ('teriər) n. small dog of various breeds, orig. for following quarry into burrow

terrific (tə'rifik) a. 1. very great 2. inf. good, excellent 3. terrible, awe-inspiring

terrify ('terifī) vt. fill with fear, dread

terrine (tə'rēn, te-) n. 1. oval earthenware cooking dish 2. food cooked or served in such dish, esp. pâté

territory ('teritôri) n. 1. region 2. geographical area under control of a political unit, esp. a sovereign state 3. area of knowledge —**terri'torial** a. of territory —**territorial waters** waters over which nation exercises jurisdiction

terror ('terər) n. 1. great fear 2. inf. troublesome person or thing —**'terrorism** n. 1. use of violence, intimidation to achieve ends 2. state of terror —**'terrorist** n./a. —**'terrorize** vt. force, oppress by fear, violence

terry ('teri) n./a. (pile fabric) with the loops uncut (used to make towels, curtains and clothing)

terse (tərs) a. 1. expressed in few words, concise 2. abrupt

tertiary ('tərshieri, -shəri) a. 1. third in degree, order etc. 2. (T-) of Tertiary period or rock system —n. 3. (T-) geological period before Quaternary —**tertiary colors** colors produced by mixing secondary colors

tessellate ('tesilāt) vt. 1. make, pave, inlay with mosaic of small tiles 2. (of identical shapes) fit together exactly —**'tessellated** a. —**tessel'lation** n. —**tessera** ('tesərə) n. small cube of glass, marble or stone used in mosaic (pl. **-ae** (-ē))

test (test) vt. 1. put to the proof 2. carry out test(s) on —n. 3. critical examination 4. means of trial —**'testing** a. difficult —**test case** lawsuit viewed as means of establishing precedent —**test match** one of series of international sports contests, esp. cricket —**test paper** 1. Chem. paper impregnated with indicator for chemical tests 2. question sheet of test 3. paper completed by test candidate —**test pilot** pilot who flies aircraft of new design to test performance in air —**test tube** narrow cylindrical glass vessel used in scientific experiments —**test-tube baby** baby conceived outside womb and subsequently implanted in womb

testament ('testəmənt) n. 1. Law will 2. declaration 3. (T-) one of the two main divisions of the Bible —**testa'mentary** a.

thermos

testate ('testāt, 'testit) a. having left a valid will —'**testacy** n. state of being testate —'**testator** n. maker of will ('**testatrix** fem.)

testicle ('testikəl) n. either of two male reproductive glands

testify ('testifĭ) v. 1. declare 2. bear witness (to) (-**fied, -fying**)

testimony ('testimōni) n. 1. affirmation 2. evidence —**testi'monial** n. 1. certificate of character, ability etc. 2. tribute given by person expressing regard for recipient —a. 3. of testimony or testimonial

testis ('testis) n. testicle (pl. **testes** ('testēz)) —**tes'tosterone** n. male sex hormone

testy ('testi) a. irritable, short-tempered —'**testily** adv.

tetanus ('tetənəs) n. serious bacterial disease producing muscular spasms, contractions (also '**lockjaw**)

tetchy ('techi) a. cross, irritable, touchy —'**tetchiness** n.

tête-à-tête ('tātə'tāt) n. 1. private conversation between two people 2. small sofa for two people, esp. S-shaped (pl. -**s**, -**tête**) —adv. ('tātə'tāt) 3. intimately; in private

tether ('tedhər) n. 1. rope or chain for fastening (grazing) animal —vt. 2. tie up with rope —**be at the end of one's tether** have reached limit of one's endurance

tetra- or before vowel **tetr-** (comb. form) four, as in tetrameter

tetracycline (tetrə'sīklēn) n. any of group of antibiotic drugs used to treat wide range of diseases

tetrad ('tetrad) n. group or series of four

tetraethyl lead (tetrə'ethil led) colorless oily insoluble liquid used in gasoline to prevent knocking

tetragon ('tetrəgon) n. figure with four angles and four sides —**te'tragonal** a. —**tetra'hedron** n. solid contained by four plane faces

tetralogy (te'traləji) n. series of four related works, as in drama or opera

tetrameter (te'tramitər) n. Prosody 1. line of verse consisting of four metrical feet 2. verse composed of such lines

Teuton ('tyōōtən, 'tōōtən) n. 1. member of ancient Germanic people from Jutland who migrated to S Gaul in 2nd century B.C. 2. member of any Germanic-speaking people, esp. German —a. 3. Teutonic —**Teu'tonic** a. 1. German 2. of ancient Teutons

Texas ('teksəs) n. West South Central state of the U.S., admitted to the Union in 1845. Abbrev.: **Tex., TX** (with ZIP code)

text (tekst) n. 1. (actual words of) book, passage etc. 2. passage of Scriptures etc., esp. as subject of discourse —'**textual** a. of, in a text —'**textbook** n. book of instruction on particular subject —**textual criticism** 1. scholarly study of manuscripts, esp. of Bible, to establish original text 2. literary criticism emphasizing close analysis of text

textile ('tekstīl) n. 1. any fabric or cloth, esp. woven —a. 2. of (the making of) fabrics

Textralizing ('tekstrəlīzing) n. trade name for texturing process applied to yarns

texture ('tekschər) n. 1. surface of material, esp. as perceived by sense of touch 2. character, structure 3. consistency —vt. 4. give distinctive texture to

Th Chem. thorium

-th[1] (comb. form) 1. action or its consequence, as in growth 2. quality, as in width

-th[2] or **-eth** (comb. form) forming ordinal numbers, as in fourth, thousandth

Thailand ('tīland) n. country in Asia bounded west by Burma and the Indian Ocean, east by the Gulf of Thailand and Kampuchea and east and north by Laos —**Thai** n./a. 1. (native or inhabitant) of Thailand (pl. **Thai**) —n. 2. language of Thailand which is probably a Sino-Tibetan language

thalidomide (thə'lidəmīd) n. drug formerly used as sedative, but found to cause abnormalities in developing fetus

thallium ('thaliəm) n. Chem. metallic element Symbol Tl, at. wt. 204.4, at. no. 81 —'**thallic** a.

thallophyte ('thaləfīt) n. any of phylum of plants comprising algae and fungi

than (dhan; unstressed dhən) conj. introduces second part of comparison

thane or **thegn** (thān) n. Hist. nobleman holding lands in return for certain services

thank (thangk) vt. 1. express gratitude to 2. say thanks to 3. hold responsible —'**thankful** a. grateful, appreciative —'**thankless** a. 1. having, bringing no thanks 2. unprofitable —**thanks** pl.n. words of gratitude —**Thanksgiving Day** national public holiday in Canad. and U.S.: fourth Thursday in November in U.S., second Monday in October in Canad.

that (dhat; unstressed dhət) a. 1. demonstrates or particularizes (pl. **those**) —demonstrative pron. 2. particular thing meant (pl. **those**) —adv. 3. as —relative pron. 4. which, who —conj. 5. introduces noun or adverbial clauses

thatch (thach) n. 1. reeds, straw etc. used as roofing material —vt. 2. roof (a house) with reeds, straw etc. —'**thatcher** n.

thaw (thö) v. 1. melt 2. (cause to) unfreeze 3. defrost —vi. 4. become warmer or more genial —n. 5. a melting (of frost etc.)

the (stressed or emphatic dhē; unstressed before consonant dhə; unstressed before vowel dhi) the definite article

theater ('thēətər) n. 1. place where plays etc. are performed 2. drama, dramatic works generally 3. large room with (tiered) seats, used for lectures etc. —**theatrical** (thi'atrikəl) a. 1. of, for the theater 2. exaggerated, affected —**theatrically** (thi'atrikəli) adv. —**theatricals** (thi'atrikəlz) pl.n. amateur dramatic performances

thee (dhē) pron. obs. objective and dative of THOU[1]

theft (theft) n. stealing

their (dhāər) a. belonging to them —**theirs** pron. something or someone belonging to them

theism ('thēizəm) n. belief in creation of universe by one god —'**theist** n. —**the'istic(al)** a.

them (dhem; unstressed dhəm) pron. 1. objective case of THEY 2. those persons or things —**them'selves** pron. emphatic and reflexive form of THEY

theme (thēm) n. 1. main idea or topic of conversation, book etc. 2. subject of composition 3. recurring melody in music —**the'matic** a.

then (dhen) adv. 1. at that time 2. next 3. that being so

thence (dhens) adv. from that place, point of reasoning etc.

theo- or before vowel **the-** (comb. form) God; gods, as in theology

theocracy (thi'okrəsi) n. government by a deity or a priesthood —**theo'cratic** a.

theodolite (thi'odəlīt) n. surveying instrument for measuring angles

theology (thi'oləji) n. systematic study of religion(s) and religious belief(s) —**theologian** (thēə'lōjən) n. —**theo'logical** a. —**theo'logically** adv.

theorem ('thēərəm) n. proposition which can be demonstrated by argument —**theore'matic** or **theo'remic** a.

theory ('thēəri) n. 1. supposition to account for something 2. system of rules and principles 3. rules and reasoning etc. as distinguished from practice —**theo'retic(al)** a. 1. based on theory 2. speculative, as opposed to practical —**theo'retically** adv. —**theore'tician** n. student or user of theory rather than practical aspects of subject —'**theorist** n. —'**theorize** vi. form theories, speculate

theosophy (thi'osəfi) n. any of various religious, philosophical systems claiming possibility of intuitive insight into divine nature

therapy ('therəpi) n. healing treatment (usu. in comb. forms as radiotherapy) —**therapeutic** (therə'pyōōtik) a. 1. of healing 2. serving to improve or maintain health —**therapeutics** (therə'pyōōtiks) pl.n. (with sing. v.) art of healing —'**therapist** n.

there (dhāər) adv. 1. in that place 2. to that point —**therea'bouts** or **therea'bout** adv. near that place, time etc. —**there'after** adv. from that time on; after that time —**there'by** adv. by that means —'**therefore** adv. in consequence, that being so —**there'in** adv. Formal, law in or into that place etc. —**there'of** adv. Formal, law 1. of or concerning that or it 2. from or because of that —**there'to** adv. 1. Formal, law to that or it 2. obs. in addition to that —**there'under** adv. Formal, law 1. in documents etc., below that or it; subsequently in that; thereafter 2. under terms or authority of that —'**thereupon** adv. at that point, immediately afterward —**there'with** or '**therewithal** adv. 1. Formal, law with or in addition to that 2. rare thereupon 3. obs. by means of or on account of that

therm (thərm) n. unit of measurement of heat —'**thermal** a. 1. of, pert. to heat 2. hot, warm (esp. of spring etc.) 3. (of garments) specially made so as to have exceptional heat-retaining qualities —'**thermic** a.

thermion ('thərmiən) n. Phys. ion emitted by incandescent body —**thermi'onic** a. pert. to thermion —**thermionic valve** electronic valve in which electrons are emitted from a heated rather than a cold cathode

thermo- or before vowel **therm-** (comb. form) related to, caused by or producing heat, as in thermometer

thermocouple ('thərmōkupəl) n. 1. device for measuring temperature consisting of pair of wires of different metals joined at both ends 2. similar device with only one junction between two dissimilar metals

thermodynamics (thərmōdī'namiks) pl.n. (with sing. v.) the science that deals with the interrelationship and interconversion of different forms of energy

thermoelectricity (thərmōilek'trisiti) n. electricity developed by the action of heat —**thermoe'lectric(al)** a. 1. of conversion of heat energy to electrical energy 2. of conversion of electrical energy

thermometer (thər'momitər) n. instrument to measure temperature —**thermo'metric** a.

thermonuclear (thərmō'nyōōkliər, -'nōōkliər) a. involving nuclear fusion

thermoplastic (thərmō'plastik) n. 1. plastic that retains its properties after being melted and solidified —a. 2. (of plastic etc.) becoming soft when heated and rehardening on cooling without appreciable change of properties

thermos ('thərmos) n. vacuum bottle

thermosetting ('thɔrmōseting) *a.* (of material, *esp.* synthetic plastic) hardening permanently after one application of heat and pressure

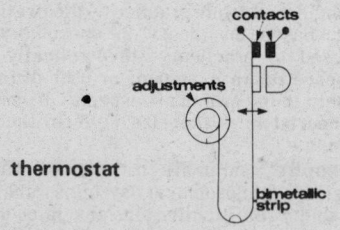

thermostat

thermostat ('thɔrmɔstat) *n.* apparatus for automatically regulating temperature —**thermo'static** *a.*

thesaurus (thi'sörɔs) *n.* **1.** book containing lists of synonyms and sometimes antonyms **2.** dictionary of selected words, topics (*pl.* **-es, -ri** (-rī))

these (dhēz) *pron., pl. of* THIS

thesis ('thēsis) *n.* **1.** written work submitted for degree, diploma **2.** theory maintained in argument (*pl.* **theses** ('thēsēz))

Thespian ('thespiɔn) *a.* **1.** theatrical —*n.* **2.** actor, actress

Thess. *Bible* Thessalonians

Thessalonians (thesɔ'lōnyɔnz) *pl.n.* (*with sing. v.*) *Bible* 13th and 14th books of the N.T., epistles written by St. Paul to the church at Thessalonica

theta ('thâtɔ, 'thētɔ) *n.* eighth letter in Gr. alphabet (θ, θ)

they (dhā) *pron.* the third person plural pronoun

thick (thik) *a.* **1.** having great thickness, not thin **2.** dense, crowded **3.** having dense consistency **4.** (of voice) throaty **5.** *inf.* stupid, insensitive **6.** *inf.* friendly (*esp.* in **thick as thieves**) —*n.* **7.** busiest, most intense part —**'thicken** *v.* **1.** make, become thick —*vi.* **2.** become more involved, complicated —**'thickening** *n.* **1.** something added to liquid to thicken it **2.** thickened part or piece —**'thicket** *n.* thick growth of small trees —**'thickly** *adv.* —**'thickness** *n.* **1.** dimensions of anything measured through it, at right angles to length and breadth **2.** state of being thick **3.** layer —**'thickhead** *n.* **1.** stupid or ignorant person; fool **2.** Aust. or SE Asian songbird —**thick'headed** *a.* —**thick'headedness** *n.* —**thick'set** *a.* **1.** sturdy and solid of body **2.** set closely together —**thick-skinned** *a.* insensitive to criticism or hints; not easily upset or affected

thief (thēf) *n.* one who steals (*pl.* **thieves** (thēvz)) —**thieve** *v.* steal —**'thievish** *a.*

thigh (thī) *n.* upper part of leg —**'thigh'bone** *n.* bone of hind or lower limb (*also* **femur**)

thimble ('thimbɔl) *n.* cap protecting end of finger when sewing

thin (thin) *a.* **1.** of little thickness **2.** slim, lean **3.** of little density **4.** sparse; fine **5.** loose, not close-packed **6.** *inf.* unlikely —*v.* **7.** make, become thin (**-nn-**) —**'thinner** *n.* —**'thinness** *n.* —**thin-skinned** *a.* sensitive to criticism or hints; easily upset or affected

thine (dhīn) *pron./a.* (thing) belonging to thee

thing (thing) *n.* **1.** material object **2.** any possible object of thought **3.** preoccupation, obsession (*esp.* in **have a thing about**) —**thingumabob** ('thingɔmɔbob), **thingamajig** *or* **thingumajig** ('thingɔmɔjig) *n. inf.* person or thing the name of which is unknown,

temporarily forgotten or deliberately overlooked

think (thingk) *vi.* **1.** have one's mind at work **2.** reflect, meditate **3.** reason **4.** deliberate **5.** imagine **6.** hold opinion —*vt.* **7.** conceive, consider in the mind **8.** believe **9.** esteem (**thought, 'thinking**) —**'thinkable** *a.* able to be conceived, considered, possible, feasible —**'thinker** *n.* —**'thinking** *a.* reflecting —**think-tank** *n.* group of experts studying specific problems

thio- *or before vowel* **thi-** (*comb. form*) sulfur, *esp.* denoting replacement of oxygen atom with sulfur atom, as in *thiol, thiosulfate*

thiopentone sodium (thiō'pentōn) *or* **thiopental sodium** (thiō'pental) barbiturate drug used as intravenous general anesthetic (*also* **sodium pentothal**)

third (thɔrd) *a.* **1.** ordinal number corresponding to *three* —*n.* **2.** third part —**third degree** *see* DEGREE —**third dimension** dimension of depth by which solid object may be distinguished from two-dimensional drawing or picture of it —**third party** *Law, insurance etc.* person involved by chance or only incidentally in legal proceedings *etc.* —**third person** grammatical category of pronouns and verbs used when referring to objects or individuals other than speaker or his addressee(s) —**third-rate** *a.* mediocre, inferior —**Third World** developing countries of Afr., Asia, Latin Amer.

thirst (thɔrst) *n.* **1.** desire to drink **2.** feeling caused by lack of drink **3.** craving, yearning —*vi.* **4.** feel lack of drink —**'thirstily** *adv.* —**'thirsty** *a.*

thirteen (thɔr'tēn) *n./a.* three plus ten —**Thirteen Colonies** the colonies of British North America that joined in the American Revolution and became the United States

thirty ('thɔrti) *n./a.* three times ten

this (dhis) *demonstrative a./pron.* denotes thing, person near, or just mentioned (*pl.* **these**)

thistle ('thisɔl) *n.* prickly plant with dense flower heads —**'thistledown** *n.* mass of feathery plumed seeds produced by thistle

thither ('thidhɔr, 'dhidhɔr) *or* **thitherward** *adv. obs.* to or toward that place

thixotropic (thiksɔ'tropik, -'tropik) *a.* (of certain liquids, as paints) having property of thickening if left undisturbed but becoming less viscous when stirred

tho *or* **tho'** (dhō) *poet. see* THOUGH

thole¹ (thōl) *or* **tholepin** ('thōlpin) *n.* wooden pin set upright in gunwale of rowing boat to serve as fulcrum in rowing

thole² (thōl) *vt. dial.* put up with; bear **2.** suffer

thong (thong) *n.* **1.** narrow strip of leather, strap **2.** rubber-soled sandal attached to foot by thong between big toe and next toe

thorax ('thöraks) *n.* part of body between neck and belly —**thoracic** (thɔ'rasik) *a.*

Thorazine ('thörɔzēn) *n.* trade name for chlorpromazine

thorium ('thöriɔm) *n. Chem.* metallic element *Symbol* Th, at. wt. 232.0, at. no. 90

thorn (thörn) *n.* **1.** prickle on plant **2.** spine **3.** bush noted for its thorns **4.** *fig.* anything which causes trouble or annoyance (*esp.* in **thorn in one's side** *or* **flesh**) —**'thorny** *a.*

thorough ('thɔrō) *a.* **1.** careful, methodical **2.** complete, entire —**'thoroughly** *adv.* —**'thoroughbred** *a.* **1.** of pure breed —*n.* **2.** purebred animal, *esp.* horse —**'thoroughfare** *n.* **1.** road or passage open at both ends **2.** right of way —**'thorough'going** *a.* **1.** extremely thorough **2.** absolute; complete

those (dhōz) *pron., pl. of* THAT

thou¹ (dhow) *pron. obs.* the second person singular pronoun (*pl.* **ye, you**)

thou² (thow) *n.* **1.** thousandth of inch **2.** *inf.* thousand (*pl.* **-s, thou**)

though (dhō) *conj.* **1.** in spite of the fact that, even if —*adv.* **2.** nevertheless

thought (thöt) *n.* **1.** process of thinking **2.** what one thinks **3.** product of thinking **4.** meditation —*v.* **5.** *pt./pp. of* THINK —**'thoughtful** *a.* **1.** considerate **2.** showing careful thought **3.** engaged in meditation **4.** attentive —**'thoughtless** *a.* inconsiderate, careless, heedless —**thought transference** *Psychol. see* TELEPATHY

thousand ('thowzɔnd) *n./a.* cardinal number, ten hundred

thrall (thröl) *n.* **1.** slavery **2.** slave, bondsman —*vt.* **3.** enslave —**'thralldom** *or* **'thraldom** *n.* bondage

thrash (thrash) *vt.* **1.** beat, whip soundly **2.** defeat soundly —*v.* **3.** *see* THRESH (sense 1) —*vi.* **4.** move, plunge, *esp.* arms, legs in wild manner —**thrash out 1.** argue about from every angle **2.** solve by exhaustive discussion

thread (thred) *n.* **1.** fine cord **2.** fine strand, filament or fiber of some material **3.** ridge cut spirally on screw **4.** theme, meaning —*vt.* **5.** put thread into **6.** fit film, magnetic tape *etc.* into (machine) **7.** put on thread **8.** pick (one's way *etc.*) —**'threadbare** *a.* **1.** worn, with nap rubbed off **2.** meager **3.** shabby

threat (thret) *n.* **1.** declaration of intention to harm, injure *etc.* **2.** person or thing regarded as dangerous —**'threaten** *vt.* **1.** utter threats against **2.** menace

three (thrē) *n./a.* cardinal number, one more than two —**'threesome** *n.* group of three —**three-D** *or* **3-D** *n.* three-dimensional effect —**three-dimensional** *a.* **1.** having three dimensions **2.** simulating the effect of depth —**three-legged race** race in which pairs of competitors run with adjacent legs tied together —**threepenny bit** *or* **threepenny bit** ('threpni, -ɔni; 'thrip-, 'thrup-) former twelve-sided Brit. coin valued at three old pence —**three-ply** *a.* having three layers (as wood) or strands (as wool) —**three-quarter** *a.* **1.** being three quarters of something **2.** being of three quarters the normal length —**'three'score** *n./a. obs.* sixty

threnody ('threnɔdi) *or* **threnode** ('thrēnōd, 'thren-) *n.* ode, song or speech of lamentation, *esp.* for dead —**'threnodist** *n.*

thresh (thrash, thresh) *v.* **1.** beat, rub (wheat, *etc.*) to separate grain from husks and straw —*vi.* **2.** toss and turn; thrash

threshold ('threshōld, 'threshhōld) *n.* **1.** bar of stone or wood forming bottom of doorway **2.** entrance **3.** starting point **4.** point at which a stimulus is perceived, or produces a response

threw (thrōō) *pt. of* THROW

thrice (thrīs) *adv.* three times

thrift (thrift) *n.* **1.** saving, economy **2.** genus of plant, sea pink —**'thrifty** *a.* economical, frugal, sparing

thrill (thril) *n.* **1.** sudden sensation of excitement and pleasure —*v.* **2.** (cause to) feel a thrill —*vi.* **3.** vibrate, tremble —**'thriller** *n.* book, motion picture *etc.* with story of mystery, suspense —**'thrilling** *a.* exciting

thrips (thrips) *n.* small slender-bodied insect that feeds on plant sap (*pl.* **thrips**)

thrive (thrīv) *vi.* **1.** grow well **2.** flourish, prosper (**throve, thrived** *pt.,* **thriven** ('thrivɔn), **thrived** *pp.,* **'thriving** *pr.p.*)

thro' *or* **thro** (thrōō) *Poet. see* THROUGH

throat (thrōt) *n.* **1.** front of neck **2.** either or both of passages through it —**'throaty** *a.* (of voice) hoarse

throb (throb) *vi.* **1.** beat, quiver strongly, pulsate (**-bb-**) —*n.* **2.** pulsation, beat; vibration

throes (thrōz) *pl.n.* condition of violent pangs, pain *etc.* —**in the throes of** *inf.* in the process of

thrombin ('thrombin) *n.* substance important in blood clotting

thromboangiitis obliterans (thrombōanji'Itis ō'blitǝranz) *see* BUERGER'S DISEASE

thrombophlebitis (thrombōfli'bItis) *n.* formation of blood clot in wall of inflamed vein

thrombosis (throm'bōsis) *n.* formation of clot of coagulated blood in blood vessel or heart

throne (thrōn) *n.* **1.** ceremonial seat, powers and duties of king or queen —*vt.* **2.** place on throne, declare king *etc.*

throng (throng) *n./v.* crowd

throstle ('throsǝl) *n. see* THRUSH¹

throttle ('throtǝl) *n.* **1.** device controlling amount of fuel entering engine and thereby its speed —*vt.* **2.** strangle **3.** suppress **4.** restrict (flow of liquid *etc.*)

through (thrōō) *prep.* **1.** from end to end, from side to side of **2.** between the sides of **3.** in consequence of **4.** by means or fault of —*adv.* **5.** from end to end **6.** to the end —*a.* **7.** completed **8.** *inf.* finished **9.** continuous **10.** (of transport, traffic) not stopping —**through'out** *adv./prep.* in every part (of) —**'throughput** *n.* quantity of material processed, *esp.* by computer —**through ticket** ticket for whole of journey —**through train, bus** *etc.* train, bus *etc.* which travels whole (unbroken) length of long journey —**carry through** accomplish

throve (thrōv) *pt. of* THRIVE

throw (thrō) *vt.* **1.** fling, cast **2.** move, put abruptly, carelessly **3.** give, hold (party *etc.*) **4.** cause to fall **5.** shape on potter's wheel **6.** move (switch, lever *etc.*) **7.** *inf.* baffle, disconcert (**threw, thrown, 'throwing**) —*n.* **8.** act or distance of throwing —**'throwaway** *a.* **1.** said incidentally, *esp.* for rhetorical effect; casual —*n.* **2.** anything that can be thrown away or discarded **3.** handbill —**throw away 1.** get rid of; discard **2.** fail to make good use of; waste —**'throwback** *n.* **1.** one who, that which reverts to character of an ancestor **2.** this process

thrum (thrum) *v.* **1.** strum rhythmically but without expression on (musical instrument) —*vi.* **2.** drum incessantly (**-mm-**) —*n.* **3.** repetitive strumming

thrush¹ (thrush) *n.* songbird

thrush² (thrush) *n.* **1.** fungal disease of mouth, *esp.* in infants **2.** vaginal infection caused by same fungus **3.** foot disease of horses

thrust (thrust) *vt.* push, drive —*v.* **2.** (make a) stab —*vi.* **3.** push one's way (**thrust, 'thrusting**) —*n.* **4.** lunge, stab with pointed weapon *etc.* **5.** cutting remark **6.** propulsive force or power

thud (thud) *n.* **1.** dull heavy sound —*vi.* **2.** make thud (**-dd-**)

thug (thug) *n.* brutal, violent person —**'thuggery** *n.* —**'thuggish** *a.*

thuja ('thyōōjǝ, 'thōōjǝ) *n.* any of various coniferous trees of N Amer. and E Asia

thulium ('thyōōliǝm, 'thōō-) *n. Chem.* metallic element *Symbol* Tm, at. wt. 168.9, at. no. 69

thumb (thum) *n.* **1.** first, shortest, thickest finger of hand —*vt.* **2.** handle, dirty with thumb **3.** signal for (ride in vehicle) **4.** flick through (pages of book *etc.*) —**thumb index** series of indentations cut into fore-edge of book to facilitate quick reference —**thumb-index** *vt.* furnish with thumb index

—**'thumbnail** *n.* **1.** nail of thumb —*a.* **2.** concise and brief —**'thumbscrew** *n.* **1.** instrument of torture that pinches or crushes thumbs **2.** screw with projections on head enabling it to be turned by thumb and forefinger

thump (thump) *n.* **1.** dull heavy blow **2.** sound of one —*vt.* **3.** strike heavily —*vi.* **4.** throb, beat or pound violently —**'thumping** *a. sl.* huge; excessive

thunder ('thundǝr) *n.* **1.** loud noise accompanying lightning —*vi.* **2.** rumble with thunder **3.** make noise like thunder —*vt.* **4.** utter loudly —**'thundering** *a. sl.* very great; excessive —**'thunderous** *a.* —**'thundery** *a.* sultry —**'thunderbolt** *or* **'thunderclap** *n.* **1.** lightning flash followed by peal of thunder **2.** anything totally unexpected and unpleasant —**'thundercloud** *n.* electrically charged cumulonimbus cloud associated with thunderstorms —**'thunderstorm** *n.* storm with thunder and lightning and usu. heavy rain or hail —**'thunderstruck** *a.* amazed

thurible ('thyōōribǝl, 'thōōr-) *n. see* CENSER

Thurs. Thursday

Thursday ('thǝrzdi) *n.* fifth day of week

thus (dhus) *adv.* **1.** in this way **2.** therefore

thwack (thwak) *vt./n.* whack

thwart (thwört) *vt.* **1.** foil, frustrate —*adv.* **2.** *obs.* across —*n.* **3.** seat across a boat

thy (dhI) *a.* belonging to thee —**thy'self** *pron.* emphatic form of THOU¹

thyme (tIm) *n.* aromatic herb

thymol ('thImöl) *n.* white crystalline substance obtained from thyme and used as antiseptic *etc.*

thymus ('thImǝs) *n.* small ductless gland in upper part of chest (*pl.* **-es, -mi** (-mI))

thyroid ('thIroid) *a.* **1.** of thyroid gland **2.** of largest cartilage of larynx —*n.* **3.** thyroid gland **4.** preparation of thyroid gland of certain animals, used to treat hypothyroidism —**thyroid-blocking drug** any of group of compounds inhibiting manufacture or release of hormones from thyroid gland (*also* **antithyroid drug**) —**thyroid gland** endocrine gland controlling body growth, situated in humans at base of throat

thyroxine (thI'roksēn) *n.* iodine containing hormone of the thyroid gland

ti (tē) *n. see* SI

Ti *Chem.* titanium

tiara (ti'arǝ) *n.* jeweled head ornament, coronet

tibia ('tibiǝ) *n.* inner and thicker of two bones of the leg below the knee (*also* **shinbone**) (*pl.* **-biae** (-biē), **-s**) —**'tibial** *a.*

tic (tik) *n.* spasmodic twitch in muscles, *esp.* of face —**tic douloureux** (dōōlǝ'rōō) *see* TRIGEMINAL NEURALGIA

tick¹ (tik) *n.* **1.** slight tapping sound, as of watch movement **2.** small mark (✓) —*vt.* **3.** mark with tick —*vi.* **4.** make ticking sound —**'ticker** *n.* **1.** *sl.* heart **2.** *sl.* watch **3.** person or thing that ticks **4.** tape machine —**ticker tape** continuous paper ribbon —**'ticktock** *n.* **1.** ticking sound as made by clock —*vi.* **2.** make ticking sound

tick² (tik) *n.* arachnid related to and larger than mite, parasitic at all stages of development

tick³ (tik) *n.* mattress case —**'ticking** *n.* strong material for mattress covers

tick⁴ (tik) *n. inf.* credit, account

ticket ('tikit) *n.* **1.** card, paper entitling holder to admission, travel *etc.* **2.** label **3.** summons served for parking or traffic offense **4.** list of candidates of one party for election —*vt.* **5.** attach label to **6.** issue tickets to

tickle ('tikǝl) *vt.* **1.** touch, stroke, poke (person, part of body *etc.*) to produce laughter *etc.* **2.** please, amuse (*oft. in* **tickle one's fancy**) —*vi.* **3.** be irritated, itch —*n.* **4.** act, instance of this **5. C** narrow strait —**'ticklish** *a.* **1.** sensitive to tickling **2.** requiring care or tact

tidbit ('tidbit) *n.* **1.** tasty morsel of food **2.** pleasing scrap (of scandal *etc.*)

tiddlywinks ('tidliwingks) *pl.n.* game of trying to flip small plastic disks into cup

tide (tId) *n.* **1.** rise and fall of sea happening twice each lunar day **2.** stream **3.** season, time —**'tidal** *a.* of, like tide —**tidal wave** great wave, *esp.* produced by earthquake —**'tidemark** *n.* mark left by highest or lowest point of tide —**tide someone over** help someone for a while, *esp.* by loan *etc.*

tidings ('tIdingz) *pl.n.* news

tidy ('tIdi) *a.* **1.** orderly, neat **2.** *inf.* of fair size —*vt.* **3.** put in order

tie (tI) *vi.* **1.** make an equal score —*vt.* **2.** fasten, bind, secure **3.** restrict (**tied, 'tying**) —*n.* **4.** that with which anything is bound **5.** restriction, restraint **6.** bond, link **7.** drawn game, contest **8.** match, game in eliminating competition —**tie-dyeing** *n.* way of dyeing cloth in patterns by tying sections tightly so they will not absorb dye —**'tiepin** *n.* ornamental pin used to pin ends of tie to shirt —**tie-up** *n.* **1.** link, connection **2.** standstill **3.** *inf.* traffic jam —**tie up 1.** bind securely (as if) with string *etc.* **2.** moor (vessel) **3.** engage attentions of **4.** conclude (organization of something) **5.** come or bring to complete standstill **6.** commit (funds *etc.*) and so make unavailable for other uses **7.** subject (property) to conditions that prevent sale *etc.*

tier (tēǝr) *n.* row, rank, layer

tiercel ('tēǝrsǝl) *n. see* TERCEL

tiff (tif) *n.* petty quarrel

tiffin ('tifin) *n.* in India, light meal, *esp.* at midday

tiger ('tIgǝr) *n.* large, tawny, black-striped feline of Asia —**'tigress** *n.* **1.** female tiger **2.** fierce, cruel or wildly passionate woman —**tiger lily** lily plant cultivated for its flowers, which have black-spotted orange petals —**tiger moth** moth with wings conspicuously marked with stripes and spots —**tiger's-eye** *or* **'tigereye** *n.* semiprecious golden-brown stone

tight (tIt) *a.* **1.** taut, tense **2.** closely fitting **3.** secure, firm **4.** not allowing passage of water *etc.* **5.** cramped **6.** *inf.* miserly **7.** *inf.* drunk —**'tighten** *v.* —**'tightly** *adv.* —**tights** *pl.n.* one-piece clinging garment covering body from waist to feet —**tight'fisted** *a.* miserly —**tight'knit** *a.* **1.** closely integrated **2.** organized carefully —**tight-lipped** *a.* **1.** secretive; taciturn **2.** with lips pressed tightly together, as through anger —**'tightrope** *n.* rope stretched taut above the ground, on which acrobats perform

tigon ('tIgǝn) *or* **tiglon** ('tiglǝn) *n.* offspring of tiger and lioness

tike (tIk) *n. see* TYKE

tiki ('tēkē) *n.* amulet, figurine of Maori cultures

tilde ('tildǝ) *n.* diacritical mark (˜) placed over letter to indicate nasal sound, as in Sp. *señor*

tile (tIl) *n.* **1.** flat piece of ceramic, plastic *etc.* material used for roofs, walls, floors, fireplaces *etc.* —*vt.* **2.** cover with tiles —**tiled** *a.* —**'tiling** *n.* —**on the tiles** *inf.* on a spree, *esp.* of drinking or debauchery

till¹ (til) *prep.* **1.** up to the time of —*conj.* **2.** to the time that

till² (til) *vt.* cultivate —**'tillage** *n.* —**'tiller** *n.*

till[3] (til) *n.* **1.** drawer for money in shop counter **2.** cash register

tiller ('tilər) *n.* lever to move rudder of boat

tilt (tilt) *v.* **1.** incline, slope, slant **2.** tip up —*vi.* **3.** take part in medieval combat with lances **4.** thrust, aim —*n.* **5.** slope, incline **6.** *Hist.* combat for mounted men with lances, joust

tilth (tilth) *n.* **1.** tilled land **2.** condition of soil

Tim. *Bible* Timothy

timber ('timbər) *n.* **1.** wood for building *etc.* **2.** trees suitable for the sawmill —'**timbered** *a.* **1.** made of wood **2.** covered with trees —**timber limit 1.** C area to which rights of cutting trees are limited **2.** timber line —**timber line** geographical limit beyond which trees will not grow

timbre *or* **timber** ('tambər, 'timbər) *n.* **1.** *Mus.* quality of sound **2.** *Phonet.* tone differentiating one vowel *etc.* from another

time (tīm) *n.* **1.** existence as a succession of states **2.** hour **3.** duration **4.** period **5.** point in duration **6.** opportunity **7.** occasion **8.** leisure **9.** tempo —*vt.* **10.** choose time for **11.** note time taken by —'**timeless** *a.* **1.** unaffected or unchanged by time; ageless **2.** eternal —'**timely** *a.* at opportune or appropriate time —'**timer** *n.* person, device for recording or indicating time —'**timing** *n.* regulation of actions or remarks in relation to others to produce best effect, as in theater *etc.* —**time and motion study** analysis of industrial or work procedures to determine most efficient methods of operation (*also* **time and motion, time study, motion study**) —**time bomb** bomb designed to explode at prearranged time —**time clock** clock which records, by punching or stamping **timecards** inserted into it, time of arrival or departure of employees —**time exposure 1.** exposure of photographic film for a relatively long period, usu. a few seconds **2.** photograph produced by such exposure —**time-honored** *a.* respectable because old —**time-lag** *n.* period of time between cause and effect —**time off** period when one is absent from work for vacation, through sickness *etc.* —**time-out** *n.* **1.** *Sport* interruption in play during which players rest, discuss tactics *etc.* **2.** period of rest; break —'**timepiece** *n.* device, such as watch or clock, which measures and indicates time —'**timeserver** *n.* person who compromises and changes his opinions *etc.* to suit current fashions —**time sharing 1.** system by which users at different terminals of computer can apparently communicate with it at same time **2.** system of part-ownership of vacation home, whereby each participant owns property for particular period every year —**time signature** *Mus.* sign, usu. consisting of two figures, one above other, after key signature, indicating tempo —'**timetable** *n.* plan showing hours of work, times of arrival and departure *etc.* —'**timeworn** *a.* **1.** showing adverse effects of overlong use or of old age **2.** hackneyed; trite —**time zone** region throughout which same standard time is used —**on time 1.** at the expected or scheduled time **2.** payable in installments —**time and a half** rate of pay equaling one and a half times normal rate, oft. for overtime

timid ('timid) *a.* **1.** easily frightened **2.** lacking self-confidence —ti'**midity** *or* '**timidness** *n.* —'**timidly** *adv.* —'**timorous** *a.* **1.** timid **2.** indicating fear

Timothy ('timəthi) *n.* *Bible* 15th and 16th books of the N.T., epistles written by St. Paul to the minister in charge of the churches at Ephesus

timpani ('timpəni) *pl.n.* set of kettledrums —'**timpanist** *n.*

tin (tin) *n.* **1.** *Chem.* metallic element *Symbol* Sn, at. no. 50 **2.** container made of tin or tinned iron —*vt.* **3.** put in tin, *esp.* for preserving (food); can **4.** coat with tin (-**nn**-) —'**tinny** *a.* **1.** (of sound) thin, metallic **2.** cheap, shoddy —'**tinfoil** *n.* **1.** thin foil made of tin or alloy of tin and lead **2.** thin foil made of aluminum; used for wrapping foodstuffs —**tin god 1.** self-important person **2.** person erroneously regarded as holy or venerable —**tin lizzie** ('lizi) *inf.* old or decrepit automobile —**tin plate** thin steel sheet coated with layer of tin that protects steel from corrosion —**tin-plate** *vt.* coat with layer of tin —'**tinpot** *a.* *inf.* inferior, worthless —'**tinsmith** *n.* person who works with tin or tin plate

tincture ('tingkchər) *n.* **1.** solution of medicinal substance in alcohol **2.** color, stain —*vt.* **3.** color, tint

tinder ('tindər) *n.* dry, easily burning material used to start fire —'**tinderbox** *n.* **1.** formerly, box for holding tinder, *esp.* one fitted with flint and steel **2.** touchy or explosive person or thing

tine (tīn) *n.* tooth, spike of fork, antler, harrow *etc.*

tinea ('tiniə) *n.* ringworm —**tinea pedis** ('pedis) athlete's foot —**tinea capitis** ('kapitis) ringworm of the scalp —**tinea corporis** ('körpəris) ringworm of the body —**tinea cruris** ('krōōris) ringworm of the body creases, *esp.* groin

ting (ting) *n.* **1.** sharp sound, as of bell **2.** tinkling —*vi.* **3.** tinkle —**ting-a-ling** *n.* sound of small bell

tinge (tinj) *n.* **1.** slight trace, flavor —*vt.* **2.** color, flavor slightly

tingle ('tinggəl) *vi.* **1.** feel thrill or pricking sensation —*n.* **2.** sensation of tingling

tinker ('tingkər) *n.* **1.** formerly, traveling mender of pots and pans —*vi.* **2.** fiddle, meddle (*eg* with machinery), oft. inexpertly —**tinker's damn** *or* **cuss** *sl.* slightest heed (*esp. in* **not give a tinker's damn** *or* **cuss**)

tinkle ('tingkəl) *v.* **1.** (cause to) give out series of light sounds like small bell —*n.* **2.** this sound or action

tinnitus ('tinitəs) *n.* noises in the ear

tinsel ('tinsəl) *n.* **1.** glittering, metallic substance for decoration **2.** anything sham and showy

tint (tint) *n.* **1.** color **2.** shade of color **3.** tinge —*vt.* **4.** dye, give tint to

tintinnabulation (tintinabyə'lāshən) *n.* act or instance of ringing or pealing of bells

tiny ('tīni) *a.* very small, minute

-tion (*comb. form*) state, condition, action, process, result, as in *election, prohibition*

tip[1] (tip) *n.* **1.** slender or pointed end of anything **2.** piece of metal, leather *etc.* protecting an extremity —*vt.* **3.** put a tip on (-**pp**-)

tip[2] (tip) *n.* **1.** small present of money given for service rendered **2.** helpful piece of information **3.** warning, hint —*vt.* **4.** give tip to (-**pp**-) —'**tipster** *n.* one who sells tips about races —**tip-off** *n.* warning or hint, *esp.* given confidentially and based on inside information —**tip off**

tip[3] (tip) *vt.* **1.** tilt, upset **2.** touch lightly —*vi.* **3.** topple over (-**pp**-) —*n.* **4.** UK place where rubbish is dumped

tippet ('tipit) *n.* covering for the neck and shoulders

tipple ('tipəl) *v.* **1.** drink (alcohol) habitually, *esp.* in small quantities —*n.* **2.** alcoholic drink —'**tippler** *n.*

tipsy ('tipsi) *a.* (slightly) drunk

tiptoe ('tiptō) *vi.* **1.** walk on ball of foot and toes **2.** walk softly

tiptop ('tip'top) *a.* of the best quality or highest degree

tirade (tī'rād) *n.* long speech, generally vigorous and hostile, denunciation

tire[1] ('tīər) *vt.* **1.** reduce energy of, *esp.* by exertion **2.** bore **3.** irritate —*vi.* **4.** become tired, wearied, bored —**tired** *a.* **1.** fatigued **2.** no longer fresh; hackneyed —'**tireless** *a.* unable to be tired —'**tirelessly** *adv.* —'**tiresome** *a.* wearisome, irritating, tedious —'**tiring** *a.*

tire[2] ('tīər) *n.* **1.** (inflated) rubber ring over rim of wheel of road vehicle **2.** metal band on rim of cartwheel

tissue ('tishōō) *n.* **1.** substance of animal body, plant *etc.* **2.** fine, soft paper, *esp.* used as handkerchief *etc.* **3.** fine woven fabric

tit[1] (tit) *n.* any of numerous small, active Old World songbirds *esp.* bluetit *etc.*

tit[2] (tit) *n.* **1.** *vulgar sl.* female breast **2.** *sl.* despicable, stupid person

Tit. *Bible* Titus

titan ('tītən) *n.* person of great strength or size —ti'**tanic** *a.* huge, epic

titanium (tī'tāniəm) *n.* *Chem.* metallic element *Symbol* Ti, at. wt. 47.9, at. no. 22

tit for tat blow for blow, retaliation

tithe (tīdh) *n.* **1.** *esp. Hist.* tenth part of agricultural produce paid for the upkeep of the clergy or as tax —*vt.* **2.** exact tithes from —**tithe barn** formerly, large barn where agricultural tithe of parish was stored

Titian ('tishən) *a.* of reddish-gold color, auburn

titillate ('titilāt) *vt.* tickle, stimulate agreeably —**titil'lation** *n.* —'**titillator** *n.*

titivate *or* **tittivate** ('titivāt) *v.* dress or smarten up —**titi'vation** *or* **titti'vation** *n.*

title ('tītəl) *n.* **1.** name of book **2.** heading **3.** name **4.** appellation denoting rank **5.** legal right or document proving it **6.** *Sport* championship —'**titled** *a.* of the aristocracy —**title deed** legal document as proof of ownership —'**titleholder** *n.* person who holds title, *esp.* sporting championship —**title page** page in book that gives title, author, publisher *etc.* —**title role** role of character after whom play *etc.* is named

titration (tī'trāshən) *n.* operation in which measured amount of one solution is added to known quantity of another solution until reaction between the two is complete —'**titrate** *vt.* measure volume or concentration of (solution) by titration

titter ('titər) *vi.* **1.** laugh in suppressed way —*n.* **2.** such laugh

tittle ('titəl) *n.* whit, detail

tittle-tattle *n./vi.* gossip

titular ('tichələr) *a.* **1.** pert. to title **2.** nominal **3.** held by virtue of a title

Titus ('tītəs) *n.* *Bible* 17th book of the N.T., epistle written by St. Paul to Titus while Titus was ministering on the isle of Crete

tizzy ('tizi) *n.* *inf.* state of confusion, anxiety

Tl *Chem.* thallium

Tm *Chem.* thulium

TN Tennessee

tn. ton(s)

TNT trinitrotoluene

to (tōō; *unstressed* tŏŏ, tə) *prep.* **1.** toward, in the direction of **2.** as far as **3.** used to introduce a comparison, ratio, indirect object, infinitive mood *etc.* —*adv.* **4.** to the required or normal state or position —**to and fro 1.** back and forth **2.** here and there —**toing and froing**

toad (tōd) *n.* animal like large frog

toadflax ('tōdflaks) *n.* perennial plant having yellow-orange flowers (*also* **butter-and-eggs**)

toadstool ('tōdstōōl) *n.* poisonous fungus resembling mushroom

toady ('tōdi) *n.* **1.** one who flatters, ingratiates himself —*vi.* **2.** do this ('**toadied,** '**toadying**)

toast (tōst) *n.* **1.** slice of bread crisped and browned on both sides by heat **2.** tribute, proposal of health, success *etc.* made by company of people and marked by drinking together **3.** person toasted —*vt.* **4.** crisp and brown (as bread) **5.** drink toast to **6.** dry or warm at fire —'**toaster** *n.* electrical device for toasting bread —'**toastmaster** *n.* person who introduces speakers, proposes toasts *etc.* at public dinners ('**toastmistress** *fem.*)

Tob. *Bible* Tobias

tobacco (tə'bakō) *n.* **1.** plant with leaves used for smoking or chewing or in snuff **2.** the prepared leaves (*pl.* **-s, -es**) —to'**bacconist** *n.* one who sells tobacco products

Tobias (tə'bīəs) *n. Bible* 17th book in the Douay Version of the O.T.

toboggan (tə'bogən) *n.* **1.** sled of thin boards curving up at front end with handrails at side **2.** sharp decline —*vi.* **3.** slide on toboggan **4.** decline suddenly and sharply (in value)

toby jug ('tōbi) mug in form of stout, seated man

toccata (tə'kätə) *n.* rapid piece of music for keyboard instrument

tocsin ('toksin) *n.* alarm signal, bell

today (tə'dā) *n.* **1.** this day —*adv.* **2.** on this day **3.** nowadays

toddle ('todəl) *vi.* **1.** walk with unsteady, short steps **2.** *inf.* stroll —*n.* **3.** toddling —'**toddler** *n.* child beginning to walk

toddy ('todi) *n.* sweetened mixture of liquor, hot water *etc.*

to-do *n. inf.* fuss, commotion (*pl.* **-s**)

toe (tō) *n.* **1.** digit of foot **2.** anything resembling toe in shape or position —*vt.* **3.** reach, touch or kick with toe —'**toecap** *n.* reinforced covering for toe of shoe —'**toehold** *n.* **1.** small foothold to facilitate climbing **2.** any means of gaining access, support *etc.* **3.** wrestling hold in which opponent's toe is held and leg twisted —**toe the line** conform

toffee ('tofi) *n.* chewy candy made of boiled sugar *etc.* —**toffee-apple** *n.* apple fixed on stick and coated with toffee

tofu ('tōfōō) *n.* soybean curd

toga ('tōgə) *n.* loose outer garment worn by ancient Romans

together (tə'gedhər) *adv.* **1.** in company **2.** simultaneously —*a./adv.* **3.** *inf.* (well) organized —to'**getherness** *n.* feeling of closeness or affection from being united with other people

toggle ('togəl) *n.* **1.** small wooden, metal peg fixed crosswise on cord, wire *etc.* and used for fastening as button **2.** any similar device —**toggle joint** device consisting of two arms pivoted at common joint and at outer ends, and used to apply pressure by straightening angle between two arms —**toggle switch** electric switch having projecting lever that is manipulated in particular way to open or close circuit

Togo ('tōgō) *n.* country in Africa bounded west by Ghana, north by Burkina-Faso, east by Benin and south by the Bight of Benin —'**Togolander** *n.* —**Togo**'**lese** *n./a.*

Togoland ('tōgōland) *n. former name of* GHANA (*also* **Gold Coast**)

togs (togz) *pl.n. inf.* clothing

toil (toil) *n.* **1.** heavy work or task —*vi.* **2.** labor —'**toilsome** *or* '**toilful** *a.* laborious —'**toilworn** *a.* **1.** weary with toil **2.** hard and lined

toilet ('toilit) *n.* **1.** fixture usu. consisting of water-flushed bowl used for defecation and urination **2.** process of washing, dressing **3.** articles used for this —'**toiletry** *n.* object or cosmetic used in making up *etc.* —**toilet paper** thin absorbent paper, oft. wound in roll round cardboard cylinder (**toilet roll**), used for cleaning oneself after defecation or urination —**toilet training** training of young child to use toilet when he needs to discharge bodily waste —**toilet water** form of liquid perfume lighter than cologne

Tokay (tō'kā) *n.* dessert wine made by blending angelica, port and sherry

token ('tōkən) *n.* **1.** sign or object used as evidence **2.** symbol **3.** piece used as money —*a.* **4.** nominal, slight —'**tokenism** *n.* practice of making only token effort or doing no more than minimum, *esp.* to comply with law

told (tōld) *pt./pp. of* TELL

tolerate ('tolərāt) *vt.* **1.** put up with **2.** permit —'**tolerable** *a.* **1.** bearable **2.** fair, moderate —'**tolerably** *adv.* —'**tolerance** *n.* (degree of) ability to endure stress, pain, radiation *etc.* —'**tolerant** *a.* **1.** disinclined to interfere with others' ways or opinions **2.** forbearing **3.** broad-minded —'**tolerantly** *adv.* —**tole**'**ration** *n.*

toll[1] (tōl) *vt.* **1.** make (bell) ring slowly at regular intervals **2.** announce (death) thus —*vi.* **3.** ring thus —*n.* **4.** tolling sound

toll[2] (tōl) *n.* **1.** tax, *esp.* for the use of bridge or road **2.** loss, damage incurred through accident, disaster *etc.* —'**tollgate** *n.* gate across toll road or bridge at which travelers must stop and pay

toluene ('tolyōōēn) *n.* volatile flammable liquid obtained from petroleum and coal tar

tolulosis (tolə'lōsis) *n. see* CRYPTOCOCCOSIS

tom (tom) *n.* male of some animals, *esp.* cat

tomahawk ('tomihôk) *n.* **1.** fighting axe of N Amer. Indians —*vt.* **2.** strike, kill with tomahawk

tomato (tə'mātō) *n.* **1.** plant with red or yellow fruit **2.** the fruit, used in salads *etc.* (*pl.* **-es**)

tomb (tōōm) *n.* **1.** grave **2.** monument over grave —'**tombstone** *n.* gravestone

tomboy ('tomboi) *n.* girl who acts, dresses in boyish way

Tom, Dick, and (or) Harry ordinary, undistinguished or common person (*esp. in* **every Tom, Dick, and Harry; any Tom, Dick, or Harry**)

tome (tōm) *n.* large book or volume

tomfoolery (tom'fōōləri) *n.* nonsense, silly behavior

tommy ('tomi) *n. sl.* private soldier in Brit. army —**Tommy gun** type of sub-machine-gun —'**tommyrot** *n.* utter nonsense

tomorrow (tə'morō) *adv./n.* (on) the day after today

tom-tom *n.* any long and narrow small-headed drum beaten with the hands

ton (tun) *n.* **1.** measure of weight, 1016 kg (2240 lbs.) (*also* **long ton**) **2.** measure of weight, 907 kg (2000 lbs.) (*also* **short ton**) **3.** metric ton **4.** *inf.* any large quantity —'**tonnage** *n.* **1.** carrying capacity **2.** charge per ton **3.** ships collectively

tondo ('tondō) *n.* circular painting or sculptured medallion (*pl.* **tondi** ('tondē))

tone (tōn) *n.* **1.** quality of musical sound **2.** quality of hue **3.** general character, style **4.**

healthy condition —*vt.* **5.** give tone to —*v.* **6.** blend, harmonize —'**tonal** *a.* —to'**nality** *n.* —**tone-deaf** *a.* unable to distinguish differences in musical pitch —**tone deafness** —**tone poem** orchestral work based on story, legend *etc.*

tong (tong) *n.* formerly, secret society of Chinese Americans

Tonga ('tonggə) *n.* protectorate of the United Kingdom lying in the South Pacific and comprising about 169 islands lying between 15° and 23°30' S latitude and 173° and 177° W longitude —'**Tongan** *a./n.*

tongs (tongz) *pl.n.* large pincers, *esp.* for handling coal, sugar

tongue-and-groove joint

tongue (tung) *n.* **1.** muscular organ inside mouth, used for speech, taste *etc.* **2.** various things shaped like this **3.** language; speech; voice —**tongue-and-groove joint** joint made by means of tongue along edge of one board that fits into groove along edge of another board —**tongue-lash** *vt.* reprimand severely; scold —**tongue-lashing** *n./a.* —**tongue-tie** *n.* congenital condition in which tongue has restricted mobility as result of abnormally short fold of skin under tongue —**tongue-tied** *a.* **1.** speechless, *esp.* with embarrassment or shyness **2.** having condition of tongue-tie —**tongue twister** sentence or phrase difficult to articulate clearly and quickly

tonic ('tonik) *n.* **1.** medicine to improve bodily tone or condition **2.** *Mus.* first keynote of scale —*a.* **3.** invigorating, restorative **4.** of tone —**tonic sol-fa** method of teaching music, by which syllables are used as names for notes of major scale in any key —**tonic water** *or* **tonic** mineral water oft. containing quinine

tonight (tə'nīt) *n.* **1.** this night **2.** the coming night —*adv.* **3.** on this night

tonne (tun) *n.* metric ton, 1000 kg

tonsil ('tonsəl) *n.* gland in throat —'**tonsillar** *a.* —**tonsil**'**lectomy** *n.* surgical removal of tonsils —**tonsil**'**litis** *n.* inflammation of tonsils

tonsorial (ton'sôriəl) *a. oft. jocular* of barbering or hairdressing

tonsure ('tonchər) *n.* **1.** shaving of part of head as religious or monastic practice **2.** part shaved —*vt.* **3.** shave thus

too (tōō) *adv.* **1.** also, in addition **2.** in excess, overmuch

took (tōōk) *pt. of* TAKE

tool (tōōl) *n.* **1.** implement or appliance for mechanical operations **2.** servile helper **3.** means to an end —*vt.* **4.** work on with tool **5.** indent design on (leather book cover *etc.*) —'**tooling** *n.* **1.** decorative work **2.** setting up *etc.* of tools, *esp.* for machine operation

toot (tōōt) *v.* **1.** (cause to) give short blast, hoot or whistle —*n.* **2.** short sound of horn, trumpet *etc.*

tooth (tōōth) *n.* **1.** bonelike projection in gums of upper and lower jaws of vertebrates **2.** any of various pointed things like this **3.** prong, cog (*pl.* **teeth**) —'**toothsome** *a.* of delicious or appetizing appearance, flavor or smell —'**toothy** *a.* having or showing numerous, large or projecting teeth —'**toothache** *n.* pain in or about tooth

—'**toothbrush** n. small brush, usu. with long handle, for cleaning teeth —**tooth-comb** n. small comb with teeth close together —'**toothpaste** n. paste for cleaning teeth, applied with toothbrush —'**toothpick** n. small sharp sliver of wood etc. for extracting pieces of food from between teeth

tootle ('to͞otəl) inf. v. 1. toot —n. 2. soft hoot or series of hoots

top[1] (top) n. 1. highest part, summit 2. highest rank 3. first in merit 4. garment for upper part of body 5. lid, stopper of bottle etc. 6. platform on ship's mast —vt. 7. cut off, pass, reach, surpass top of 8. provide top for (-pp-) —'**topless** a. (of costume or woman) with no covering for breasts —'**topmost** a. 1. supreme 2. highest —'**topping** n. 1. something that tops something else, esp. sauce or garnish for food —a. 2. high or superior in rank, degree etc. —**top brass** inf. 1. high-ranking army officers 2. important officials —'**topcoat** n. outdoor coat worn over suit etc. —**top dog** inf. leader or chief of group —**top-drawer** a. of highest standing, esp. socially —**top-dress** vt. spread soil, fertilizer etc. on surface of (land) —**top dressing** —**top-flight** a. of superior or excellent quality —**topgallant** (top'galənt; Naut. tə'galənt) n. 1. mast on square-rigger above topmast or extension of topmast 2. sail set on yard of topgallant mast —a. 3. of topgallant —**top gear** 1. highest forward ratio of gearbox in motor vehicle 2. highest speed, greatest energy etc. (also **top**) —**top hat** man's hat with tall cylindrical crown —**top-heavy** a. 1. unbalanced 2. with top too heavy for base —'**topknot** n. 1. crest, tuft, chignon etc. on top of head 2. European flatfish —**top-level** a. of those on highest level of influence or authority —**topmast** ('topmast; Naut. 'topməst) n. mast next above lower mast on sailing vessel —**top'notch** a. excellent, first-class —**topsail** ('topsāl; Naut. 'topsəl) n. square sail carried on yard set on topmast —**top-secret** a. needing highest level of secrecy, security —'**top'side** n. 1. uppermost side 2. (oft. pl.) part of ship's sides above water line 3. (oft. pl.) part of ship above decks —**Top Sider** trade name for shoe worn for sailing —'**topsoil** n. surface layer of soil

top[2] (top) n. toy which spins on tapering point

topaz ('tōpaz) n. 1. gemstone of any of various colors, esp. yellow —a. 2. of color of yellow topaz

tope[1] (tōp) v. consume (liquor) as regular habit, usu. in large quantities —'**toper** n.

tope[2] (tōp) n. small gray shark of European coastal waters

topi (tō'pē, 'tōpē; -pi) n. lightweight hat made of pith (pl. -s)

topiary ('tōpieri) a. 1. (of shrubs) shaped by cutting or pruning, made ornamental by trimming or training —n. 2. topiary work 3. topiary garden —'**topiarist** n.

topic ('topik) n. subject of discourse, conversation etc. —'**topical** a. 1. up-to-date, having news value 2. of topic

topography (tə'pogrəfi) n. (description of) surface features of a place —to'**pographer** n. —topo'**graphic** a. —topo'**graphically** adv.

topology (tə'poləji) n. 1. branch of mathematics concerned with the properties of geometric figures that remain unchanged even when distorted (also **rubber-sheet geometry**) 2. study of topography of given place 3. anatomy of any specific bodily area, structure or part —topo'**logic(al)** a. —to'**pologist** n.

topple ('topəl) v. (cause to) fall over, collapse

topsy-turvy (topsi'tərvi) a. 1. upside down 2. in confusion

toque (tōk) n. 1. small round hat 2. C knitted cap

tor (tör) n. high, rocky hill

Torah ('tōrə) n. 1. the Pentateuch 2. scroll on which this is written 3. whole body of Jewish sacred writings and tradition, including oral expositions of the Law

torch (törch) n. 1. burning brand etc. 2. any apparatus burning with hot flame (eg for welding) —'**torchbearer** n. —**torch singer** —**torch song** sentimental song, usu. sung by woman —**carry a torch for** be in love with, esp. unrequitedly

tore (tör) pt. of TEAR[2] —**torn** pp. of TEAR[2]

toreador ('toriədör) n. bullfighter

torment (tör'ment) vt. 1. torture in body or mind 2. afflict 3. tease —n. ('törment) 4. suffering, torture, agony of body or mind —tor'**mentor** n.

tornado (tör'nādō) n. 1. whirlwind 2. violent storm (pl. -es, -s)

torpedo (tör'pēdō) n. 1. cylindrical, self-propelled underwater missile with explosive warhead, fired esp. from submarine (pl. -es) —vt. 2. strike, sink with, as with, torpedo

torpid ('törpid) a. sluggish, apathetic —tor'**pidity** or '**torpidness** n. —'**torpor** n. torpid state

torque (törk) n. 1. collar, similar ornament of twisted gold or other metal 2. Mech. any rotating or twisting force

torr (tör) n. unit of pressure equal to one millimeter of mercury (133.322 newtons per square meter)

torrent ('torənt) n. 1. rushing stream 2. downpour —tor'**rential** a. 1. resembling a torrent 2. overwhelming

torrid ('torid) a. 1. parched, dried with heat 2. highly emotional —tor'**ridity** or '**torridness** n. —**Torrid Zone** land between tropics

torsion ('törshən) n. twist, twisting

torso ('törsō) n. 1. (statue of) body without head or limbs 2. trunk (pl. -s, -si (-si))

tort (tört) n. Law private or civil wrong

torticollis (törti'kolis) n. condition in which neck is twisted and head tilted

tortilla (tör'tēə) n. thin Mexican pancake

tortoise ('törtəs) n. four-footed reptile covered with shell of horny plates —**tortoiseshell** ('törtəshel) n. 1. mottled brown shell of hawksbill turtle used commercially —a. 2. of yellowish-brown mottled color 3. made of tortoiseshell

tortuous ('törcho͞oəs) a. 1. winding, twisting 2. involved, not straightforward —tortu'**osity** n.

torture ('törchər) n. 1. infliction of severe pain —vt. 2. subject to torture —'**torturer** n. —**torture chamber**

Tory ('töri) n. 1. member of Brit., Canad. conservative party 2. politically reactionary person

toss (tos) vt. 1. throw up, about —vi. 2. be thrown, fling oneself about —n. 3. act of tossing —**toss-up** n. 1. instance of tossing up coin 2. inf. even chance or risk —**toss up** spin (coin) in air to decide between alternatives by guessing which side will fall uppermost

tot[1] (tot) n. 1. very small child 2. small quantity, esp. of drink

tot[2] (tot) v. (with up) total; add (-tt-)

total ('tōtəl) n. 1. whole amount 2. sum, aggregate —a. 3. complete, entire, full, absolute —v. 4. (sometimes with to) amount —vt. 5. add up —to'**tality** n. —'**totalizator** or '**totalizer** n. machine to operate system of betting on racecourse in which money is paid out to winners in proportion to their stakes

totalitarian (tōtali'teriən) a. of dictatorial, one-party government

tote[1] (tōt) totalizator

tote[2] (tōt) vt. haul, carry —**tote bag** large handbag or shopping bag

totem ('tōtəm) n. tribal badge or emblem —to'**temic** a. —**totem pole** post carved, painted with totems, esp. by Amer. Indians

totter ('totər) vi. 1. walk unsteadily 2. begin to fall

toucan ('to͞okan) n. tropical Amer. bird with large bill

touch (tuch) n. 1. sense by which qualities of object etc. are perceived by touching 2. characteristic manner or ability 3. touching 4. slight blow, stroke, contact, amount etc. —vt. 5. come into contact with 6. put hand on 7. reach 8. affect emotions of 9. deal with, handle 10. eat, drink 11. inf. (try to) borrow from —vi. 12. be in contact 13. (with on) refer (to) —**touched** a. 1. moved to sympathy or emotion 2. showing slight insanity —'**touching** a. 1. emotionally moving —prep. 2. concerning —'**touchy** a. easily offended, sensitive —'**touchdown** n. 1. moment at which landing aircraft or spacecraft comes into contact with landing surface 2. American football scoring play for six points achieved by being in possession of ball in opponents' end zone —'**touchline** n. side line of pitch in some games —'**touchstone** n. criterion —**touch-type** vi. type without looking at keyboard —**touch-typist** n. —'**touchwood** n. tinder —**touch and go** precarious (situation) —**touch down** 1. (of aircraft etc.) land 2. Rugby place ball behind goal line, as when scoring try

touché (to͞o'shā) interj. orig. in fencing, acknowledgment that blow, witty remark etc. has been successful

tough (tuf) a. 1. strong, resilient, not brittle 2. sturdy 3. able to bear hardship, strain 4. difficult 5. needing effort to chew 6. sl. rough, uncivilized, violent 7. inf. unlucky, unfair —n. 8. inf. rough, violent person —'**toughen** v. —'**toughness** n.

toupee (to͞o'pā) n. wig or piece of false hair that covers bald patch

tour (to͞or) n. 1. traveling round 2. journey to one place after another 3. excursion —v. 4. make tour (of) —'**tourism** n. 1. tourist travel 2. this as an industry —'**tourist** n. one who travels for pleasure —'**touristy** a. inf., oft. derogatory abounding in or designed for tourists —**touring car** large open automobile, usu. seating driver and four passengers

tour de force (to͞or də 'förs) Fr. brilliant stroke, achievement

tourmaline ('to͞orməlin, -lēn) n. gemstone of variable color

tournament ('to͞ornəmənt) n. 1. competition, contest usu. with several stages to decide overall winner 2. Hist. contest between knights on horseback —'**tourney** n. Hist. knightly tournament

tourniquet ('to͞ornikət) n. bandage, surgical instrument to constrict artery and stop bleeding

tousle ('towzəl) vt. 1. tangle, ruffle 2. treat roughly —n. 3. disorderly, tangled or rumpled state 4. disheveled or disordered mass, esp. of hair

tout (towt) vi. 1. solicit custom (usu. in undesirable fashion) 2. obtain and sell information about race horses —n. 3. one who touts

tow[1] (tō) vt. 1. drag along behind, esp. at end

of rope —*n.* **2.** towing or being towed **3.** vessel, vehicle in tow —**'towage** *n.* —**'tow-bar** *n.* metal bar attached to automobile for towing trailer *etc.* —**'towpath** *n.* path beside canal, river, *orig.* for towing —**'towrope** *n.* rope or cable used for towing vehicle or vessel (*also* **'towline**)

tow² (tō) *n.* fiber of hemp, flax —**tow-headed** *a.* with pale-colored or rumpled hair

toward (tōrd, tə'wōrd) *prep.* **1.** in direction of **2.** with regard to **3.** as contribution to (*also* **towards**)

towel ('towəl) *n.* **1.** cloth or paper for wiping off moisture after washing —*vt.* **2.** dry or wipe with towel —**'toweling** *n.* material used for making towels —**throw in the towel** give up completely

tower ('towər) *n.* **1.** tall strong structure *oft.* forming part of church or other large building **2.** fortress —*vi.* **3.** stand very high **4.** loom —**'towering** *a.* **1.** very tall; lofty **2.** outstanding, as in importance or stature **3.** (of rage) intense

town (town) *n.* collection of dwellings *etc.*, larger than village and smaller than city —**'township** *n.* **1.** small town **2.** C land-survey area —**town clerk** chief administrative officer of town —**town crier** formerly, person employed to make public announcements in streets —**town hall** chief building in which municipal business is transacted, *oft.* with hall for public meetings —**town planning** comprehensive planning of physical and social development of town —**'townspeople** *pl.n.*

toxic ('toksik) *a.* **1.** poisonous **2.** due to poison —**tox'emia** *n.* blood poisoning —**tox'icity** *n.* strength of a poison —**toxi'cology** *n.* study of poisons —**'toxin** *n.* poison of bacterial origin —**'toxoid** *n.* bacterial poison that has been made harmless without removing its ability to stimulate the production of antibodies

toxophily (tok'sofili) *n.* archery —**tox'ophilite** *n.*

toy (toi) *n.* **1.** something designed to be played with **2.** (miniature) replica —*a.* **3.** very small —*vi.* **4.** act idly —**toy dog** purebred dog characterized by diminutiveness

trace¹ (trās) *n.* **1.** track left by anything **2.** indication **3.** minute quantity —*vt.* **4.** follow course, track of **5.** find out **6.** make plan of **7.** draw or copy exactly, *esp.* using tracing paper —**'tracer** *n.* **1.** person or thing that traces **2.** ammunition that can be observed when in flight by burning of chemical substances in base of projectile **3.** *Med.* radioactive isotope introduced into body to study metabolic processes *etc.* by following its progress with Geiger counter or other detector **4.** investigation to trace missing cargo *etc.* —**'tracery** *n.* interlaced ornament, *esp.* stonework of Gothic window —**'tracing** *n.* traced copy of drawing —**trace element** chemical element needed by all living organisms in minute quantities —**tracer bullet** bullet which leaves visible trail so that aim can be checked —**tracing paper** transparent paper placed over drawing, map *etc.* to enable exact copy to be taken

trace² (trās) *n.* **1.** chain, strap by which horse pulls vehicle **2.** *Angling* short piece of gut, nylon attaching hook or fly to line

trachea ('trākiə) *n.* windpipe (*pl.* **tracheae** ('trākiē)) —**'tracheal** *or* **'tracheate** *a.* —**trache'otomy** *n.* surgical incision into trachea

trachoma (trə'kōmə) *n.* highly contagious virus disease of the eyes

track (trak) *n.* **1.** mark, line of marks, left by passage of anything **2.** path, rough road **3.** course **4.** railroad line **5.** distance between two road wheels on one axle **6.** circular jointed metal band driven by wheels as on tank, bulldozer *etc.* **7.** course for running or racing **8.** separate section on phonograph record —*vt.* **9.** follow trail or path of **10.** (*with* down) find thus —**track-and-field** *a.* of series of competitive events comprising running for speed, jumping for height or distance and throwing for distance —**track events** athletic sports held on a track —**track record** past accomplishments of person, company *etc.* —**track shoe** light running shoe fitted with steel spikes for better grip —**'tracksuit** *n.* warm, two-piece garment worn *esp.* by athletes

Tracrium ('trākriəm) *n.* trade name for atracurium

tract¹ (trakt) *n.* **1.** wide expanse, area **2.** *Anat.* system of organs *etc.* with particular function

tract² (trakt) *n.* treatise or pamphlet, *esp.* religious one —**'tractate** *n.* short tract

tractable ('traktəbəl) *a.* easy to manage, docile, amenable

traction ('trakshən) *n.* **1.** action of drawing, pulling **2.** force applied to produce tension on part of body by various means in medical treatment —**traction engine** steam-powered locomotive used, *esp.* formerly, for drawing heavy loads along roads or over rough ground

tractor ('traktər) *n.* motor vehicle for hauling, pulling *etc.*

trade (trād) *n.* **1.** commerce, business **2.** buying and selling **3.** any profitable pursuit **4.** those engaged in trade —*vi.* **5.** engage in trade —*vt.* **6.** buy and sell **7.** barter **8.** exchange (one thing) for another —**'trader** *n.* —**trade-in** *n.* used article given in part payment for new —**'trademark** *or* **trade name** *n.* name, symbol or other mark registered and legally restricted to use by owner —**trade price** price of commodities as sold by wholesalers to retailers —**trade secret** secret formula, process *etc.* known and used to advantage by only one manufacturer —**'tradesman** *n.* **1.** shopkeeper **2.** skilled worker —**trade union** society of workers for protection of their interests —**trade wind** wind blowing constantly toward equator in certain parts of globe —**trading stamp** stamp given by some retail organizations to customers, redeemable for merchandise or cash

tradescantia (tradis'kanchiə) *n.* widely cultivated plant with striped variegated leaves

tradition (trə'dishən) *n.* **1.** unwritten body of beliefs, facts *etc.* handed down from generation to generation **2.** custom, practice of long standing **3.** process of handing down —**tra'ditional** *a.* —**tra'ditionally** *adv.*

traduce (trə'dyōōs, -'dōōs) *vt.* slander

traffic ('trafik) *n.* **1.** vehicles passing to and fro in street, town *etc.* **2.** (illicit) trade —*vi.* **3.** trade, *esp.* in illicit goods (*eg* drugs) (**'trafficked, 'trafficking**) —**'trafficker** *n.* trader —**traffic lights** set of colored lights at road junctions *etc.* to control flow of traffic

tragedy ('trajidi) *n.* **1.** sad or calamitous event **2.** dramatic, literary work dealing with serious, sad topic and with ending marked by (inevitable) disaster —**tra'gedian** *n.* actor in, writer of tragedies (**tragedi'enne** *fem.*) —**'tragic** *a.* **1.** of, in manner of tragedy **2.** disastrous **3.** appalling —**'tragically** *adv.* —**tragi'comedy** *n.* play with both tragic and comic elements

trail (trāl) *vt.* **1.** drag behind one **2.** follow or hunt (animal or person) by following marks or tracks —*vi.* **3.** be drawn behind **4.** hang, grow loosely —*n.* **5.** track, trace **6.** thing that trails **7.** rough, ill-defined track in wild country —**'trailer** *n.* **1.** vehicle towed by another vehicle **2.** large enclosed vehicle for living in, pulled by automobile **3.** *Cine.* advertisement of forthcoming motion picture **4.** trailing plant —**'trailblazer** *n.* **1.** pioneer in particular field **2.** person who blazes trail

train (trān) *vt.* **1.** educate, instruct, exercise **2.** cause to grow in particular way **3.** aim (gun *etc.*) —*vi.* **4.** follow course of training, *esp.* to achieve physical fitness for athletics —*n.* **5.** line of railroad vehicles joined to locomotive **6.** succession, *esp.* of thoughts, events *etc.* **7.** procession of animals, vehicles *etc.* traveling together **8.** trailing part of dress **9.** body of attendants —**trai'nee** *n.* one training to be skilled worker, *esp.* in industry —**'trainer** *n.* **1.** person who trains athletes **2.** piece of equipment employed in training, such as simulated aircraft cockpit **3.** person who schools race horses —**'training** *n.* —**'trainbearer** *n.* attendant who holds up train of dignitary's robe —**train spotter** person who collects numbers of railroad locomotives

traipse (trāps) *vi. inf.* walk wearily

trait (trāt) *n.* characteristic feature

traitor ('trātər) *n.* one who betrays or is guilty of treason —**'traitorous** *a.* **1.** disloyal **2.** guilty of treachery —**'traitorously** *adv.*

trajectory (trə'jektəri) *n.* line of flight, (curved) path of projectile

trammel ('traməl) *n.* **1.** anything that restrains or holds captive **2.** type of compasses —*vt.* **3.** restrain, hinder

tramp (tramp) *vi.* **1.** travel on foot, *esp.* as vagabond or for pleasure **2.** walk heavily —*n.* **3.** (homeless) person who travels about on foot **4.** walk **5.** tramping **6.** vessel that takes cargo wherever shippers desire **7.** *sl.* prostitute; promiscuous woman

trample ('trampəl) *v.* tread (on) and crush under foot

trampoline (trampə'lēn, 'trampəlēn) *n.* tough canvas sheet stretched horizontally with elastic cords *etc.* to frame, for gymnastic, acrobatic use

trance (trans) *n.* **1.** unconscious or dazed state **2.** state of ecstasy or total absorption

tranquil ('trangkwil) *a.* calm, quiet —**'tranquilize** *vt.* make calm —**'tranquilizer** *n.* drug which induces calm, tranquil state —**tran'quillity** *or* **tran'quility** *n.* —**'tranquilly** *adv.*

trans. **1.** transaction **2.** transferred **3.** transitive **4.** translated **5.** translator **6.** transport(ation) **7.** transverse

trans- (*comb. form*) across, through, beyond, on the other side, as in *transatlantic*

transact (trans'akt, tranz-) *vt.* **1.** carry through **2.** negotiate **3.** conduct (affair *etc.*) —**trans'action** *n.* **1.** performing of any business **2.** that which is performed **3.** single sale or purchase —*pl.* **4.** proceedings **5.** reports of a society

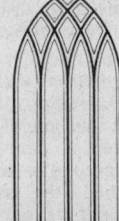

tracery

transatlantic (transət'lantik, tranz-) *a.* **1.** on or from the other side of the Atlantic **2.** crossing the Atlantic

transceiver (tran'sēvər) *n.* combined radio transmitter and receiver

transcend (tran'send) *vt.* **1.** rise above **2.** exceed, surpass —**tran'scendence** *n.* —**tran'scendent** *a.* —**transcen'dental** *a.* **1.** surpassing experience **2.** supernatural **3.** abstruse —**transcen'dentalism** *n.* —**transcendental meditation** technique, based on Hindu traditions, for relaxing and refreshing mind and body through silent repetition of mantra

transcribe (tran'skrīb) *vt.* **1.** copy out **2.** transliterate, translate **3.** record for later broadcast **4.** arrange (music) for different instrument —**'transcript** *n.* copy —**tran'scription** *n.* **1.** act or instance of transcribing or state of being transcribed **2.** something transcribed **3.** representation in writing of actual pronunciation of word *etc.* using phonetic symbols

transducer (trans'dyōōsər, tranz-; -'dōōsər) *n.* any device that converts one form of energy into another

transept ('transept) *n.* **1.** transverse part of cruciform church **2.** either of its arms

transfer (trans'fər) *v.* **1.** move, send from one person, place *etc.* to another (-**rr**-) —*n.* ('transfər) **2.** removal of person or thing from one place to another **3.** design which can be transferred from one surface to another by pressure, heat *etc.* —**trans'ferable** *or* **trans'ferrable** *a.* —**transference** (trans'fərəns, 'transfərəns) *n.* transfer

transfigure (trans'figyər) *vt.* alter appearance of —**transfiguration** (transfigyə'rāshən, -figə-) *n.*

transfix (trans'fiks) *vt.* **1.** astound, stun **2.** pierce

transform (trans'förm) *vt.* change shape, character of —**transfor'mation** *n.* —**trans'former** *n. Elec.* apparatus for changing voltage of alternating current

transfuse (trans'fyōōz) *vt.* convey from one vessel to another, *esp.* blood from healthy person to one injured or ill —**trans'fusion** *n.*

transgress (trans'gres, tranz-) *vt.* **1.** break (law) —*vi.* **2.** sin —**trans'gression** *n.* —**trans'gressor** *n.*

tranship (tran'ship) *v. see* TRANSSHIP

transient ('tranchənt, 'tranziənt) *a.* fleeting, not permanent —**'transience** *n.*

transistor (tran'zistər) *n.* **1.** *Electron.* small, semiconducting device used to amplify electric currents **2.** portable radio using transistors —**tran'sistorize** *v.* **1.** convert to use or manufacture of transistors and other solid-state components —*vt.* **2.** equip with transistors and other solid-state components

transit ('transit, 'tranz-) *n.* passage, crossing —**transition** (tran'sishən, tran'zishən) *n.* change from one state to another —**transitional** (tran'sishnəl, tran'zishnəl; -ənəl) *a.* —**'transitive** *a.* (of verb) requiring direct object —**'transitory** *a.* not lasting long, transient —**transit camp** camp in which refugees *etc.* live temporarily

translate (trans'lāt, tranz-) *vt.* **1.** turn from one language into another **2.** interpret **3.** transfer (a bishop) to another see —**trans'lation** *n.* —**trans'lator** *n.*

transliterate (trans'litərāt, tranz-) *vt.* write in the letters of another alphabet —**translit-er'ation** *n.*

translucent (trans'lōōsənt, tranz-) *a.* letting light pass through, semitransparent —**trans'lucence** *n.*

transmigrate (trans'mīgrāt, tranz-) *vi.* (of soul) pass into another body —**transmi'gration** *n.*

transmit (trans'mit, tranz-) *vt.* **1.** send, cause to pass to another place, person *etc.* **2.** communicate **3.** send out (signals) by means of radio waves **4.** broadcast (radio, television program) (-**tt**-) —**trans'mission** *n.* **1.** transference **2.** gear by which power is communicated from engine to road wheels —**trans'mitter** *n.* **1.** person or thing that transmits **2.** equipment used for generating and amplifying radio-frequency carrier, modulating carrier with information and feeding it to antenna for transmission **3.** microphone in telephone that converts sound waves into audio-frequency electrical signals **4.** device that converts mechanical movements into coded electrical signals transmitted along telegraph circuit

transmogrify (trans'mogrifī, tranz-) *vt. inf.* change completely *esp.* into bizarre form

transmute (trans'myōōt, tranz-) *vt.* change in form, properties or nature —**transmu'tation** *n.*

transom ('transəm) *n.* **1.** crosspiece **2.** lintel

transparent (trans'parənt, -'per-) *a.* **1.** letting light pass without distortion **2.** that can be seen through distinctly **3.** obvious —**trans'parence** *n.* —**trans'parency** *n.* **1.** quality of being transparent **2.** photographic slide **3.** picture made visible by light behind it —**trans'parently** *adv.*

transpire (tran'spīər) *vi.* **1.** become known **2.** *inf.* happen **3.** (of plants) give off water vapor through leaves —**transpiration** (transpə'rāshən) *n.*

transplant (trans'plant) *vt.* **1.** move and plant again in another place **2.** transfer (organ) surgically from one body to another —*n.* ('transplant) **3.** surgical transplanting of organ **4.** anything transplanted —**transplan'tation** *n.*

transponder (tran'spondər) *n.* radio or radar transmitter-receiver that transmits signals automatically when it receives predetermined signals

transport (trans'pört) *vt.* **1.** convey from one place to another **2.** *Hist.* banish, as criminal, to penal colony **3.** enrapture —*n.* ('transpört) **4.** means of conveyance **5.** ships, aircraft *etc.* used in transporting stores, troops *etc.* **6.** a ship *etc.* so used **7.** ecstasy, rapture or any powerful emotion —**transpor'tation** *n.* **1.** transporting **2.** *Hist.* deportation to penal colony

transpose (trans'pōz) *vt.* **1.** change order of, interchange **2.** put (music) into different key —**trans'posal** *n.* —**transpo'sition** *n.*

transsexual (trans'sekshōōəl) *n.* **1.** person who is completely identified with opposite sex **2.** person who has undergone medical procedures to alter sexual characteristics to those of opposite sex

transship (tran'ship, trans'ship) *or* **tranship** *v.* move from one ship, train *etc.* to another

transubstantiation (transəbstanchi'āshən) *n.* doctrine that substance of bread and wine changes into substance of Christ's body when consecrated in Eucharist

transuranic (transhə'ranik), **transuranian** (transhə'rāniən), *or* **transuranium** *a.* **1.** (of element) having atomic number greater than that of uranium **2.** of behavior of transuranic elements

transverse (trans'vərs, tranz-) *a.* **1.** lying across **2.** at right angles

transvestite (trans'vestīt, tranz-) *n.* person seeking sexual pleasure by wearing clothing normally worn by opposite sex

trap[1] (trap) *n.* **1.** snare, device for catching game *etc.* **2.** anything planned to deceive, betray *etc.* **3.** arrangement of pipes to prevent escape of gas **4.** movable opening, *esp.* through ceiling *etc.* **5.** *Hist.* two-wheeled carriage **6.** *sl.* mouth —*vt.* **7.** catch, ensnare (-**pp**-) —**'trapper** *n.* one who traps animals for their fur —**trap door** door in floor or roof

trap[2] (trap) *vt.* (*oft. with* out) dress, adorn (-**pp**-)

trapeze (tra'pēz, trə-) *n.* horizontal bar suspended from two ropes for use in gymnastics, acrobatic exhibitions *etc.* —**trapeze dress** tent-shaped dress with stiff full skirt molding body to high bust and falling free from shoulders at back

trapezoid ('trapəzoid) *n.* quadrilateral figure with only two sides parallel —**trapezium** (trə'pēziəm) *n.* quadrilateral with no parallel sides (*pl.* **-s, -zia** (-ziə))

trappings ('trapingz) *pl.n.* equipment, ornaments

Trappist ('trapist) *n.* member of Cistercian order of monks who observe strict silence

trash (trash) *n.* **1.** anything without value **2.** worthless person(s) —*vt.* **3.** destroy (a person's character) —**'trashy** *a.*

trauma ('trowmə, 'trömə) *n.* **1.** nervous shock **2.** injury (*pl.* **-ta** (-tə), **-s**) —**trau'matic** *a.* of, causing, caused by trauma

travail (trə'vāl, 'travāl) *vi./n.* labor, toil

travel ('travəl) *vi.* **1.** go, move from one place to another —*n.* **2.** act of traveling, *esp.* as tourist **3.** *Machinery* distance component is permitted to move —*pl.* **4.** (account of) traveling —**'traveler** *n.* —**'travelogue** *or* **'travelog** *n.* motion picture *etc.* about travels —**travel agency** agency that arranges and negotiates vacations *etc.* for travelers —**travel agent** —**traveler's check** check sold by bank *etc.* to bearer, who signs it on purchase and can cash it abroad by signing it again —**traveling fellowship** fellowship which requires recipient to pursue study or research away from his or her normal place of study or research —**traveling salesman** salesman who travels within assigned territory to sell merchandise or solicit orders for commercial enterprise he represents by direct personal contact with (potential) customers

traverse (trə'vərs, tra-; 'travərs) *vt.* **1.** cross, go through or over —*vi.* **2.** (of gun) move laterally —*n.* ('travərs) **3.** anything set across **4.** partition **5.** *Mountaineering* face, steep slope to be crossed from side to side —*a.* ('travərs; trə'vərs, tra-) **6.** being, lying across

travesty ('travisti) *n.* **1.** farcical, grotesque imitation **2.** mockery —*vt.* **3.** make, be a travesty of (-**estied, -estying**)

travois (trə'voi, 'travoi) *n.* vehicle used by Plains Indians comprising two trailing poles bearing a platform or net for the load

trawl (tröl) *n.* **1.** net dragged at deep levels behind special boat, to catch fish —*vi.* **2.** fish with one —**'trawler** *n.* trawling vessel

tray (trā) *n.* **1.** flat board, usu. with rim, for carrying things **2.** any similar utensil

treachery ('trechəri) *n.* deceit, betrayal —**'treacherous** *a.* **1.** disloyal **2.** unreliable, dangerous —**'treacherously** *adv.*

tread (tred) *vt.* **1.** set foot on **2.** trample —*vi.* **3.** walk **4.** (*sometimes with* on) repress (**trod** *pt.*, **'trodden** *or* **trod** *pp.*, **'treading** *pr.p.*) —*n.* **5.** treading **6.** fashion of walking **7.** upper surface of step **8.** part of rubber tire in contact with ground —**'treadmill** *n.* **1.** *Hist.* cylinder turned by treading on steps projecting from it **2.** dreary routine *etc.*

treadle ('tredǝl) *n.* lever worked by foot to turn wheel

treason ('trēzǝn) *n.* **1.** violation by subject of allegiance to sovereign or state **2.** treachery; disloyalty —**'treasonable** *or* **'treasonous** *a.* constituting treason —**'treasonably** *adv.*

treasure ('trezhǝr) *n.* **1.** riches **2.** stored wealth or valuables —*vt.* **3.** prize, cherish **4.** store up —**'treasurer** *n.* official in charge of funds —**'treasury** *n.* **1.** place for treasure **2.** (T-) government department in charge of finance —**treasure-trove** *n.* treasure found hidden with no evidence of ownership

treat (trēt) *n.* **1.** pleasure, entertainment given —*vt.* **2.** deal with, act toward **3.** give medical treatment to **4.** give (someone) gift, food *etc.* at one's own expense —*vi.* **5.** negotiate **6.** (*with* of) discourse (on) —**'treatment** *n.* **1.** method of counteracting a disease **2.** act or mode of treating **3.** manner of handling an artistic medium

treatise ('trētis, -iz) *n.* book discussing a subject, formal essay

treaty ('trēti) *n.* signed contract between states *etc.*

treble ('trebǝl) *a.* **1.** threefold, triple **2.** *Mus.* high-pitched —*n.* **3.** soprano voice **4.** part of music for it **5.** singer with such voice —*v.* **6.** increase threefold —**'trebly** *adv.* —**treble clef** *Mus.* clef that establishes G fifth above middle C as being on second line of staff

tree (trē) *n.* **1.** large perennial plant with woody trunk **2.** beam **3.** anything (*eg* genealogical chart) resembling tree or tree's structure —*vt.* **4.** force, drive up tree —**tree creeper** small songbird

trefoil (sense 2)

trefoil ('trēfoil, 'tref-) *n.* **1.** plant with three-lobed leaf, clover **2.** carved ornament like this

trek (trek) *n.* **1.** long difficult journey, *esp.* on foot **2.** migration by ox wagon —*vi.* **3.** make a trek (-kk-) —**'trekker** *n.*

trellis ('trelis) *n.* **1.** lattice or grating of light bars fixed crosswise —*vt.* **2.** screen, supply with one

tremble ('trembǝl) *vi.* **1.** quiver, shake **2.** feel fear, anxiety —*n.* **3.** involuntary shaking, quiver, tremor —**'trembler** *n.* trembling spring that makes electrical contact when shaken

tremendous (tri'mendǝs) *a.* **1.** vast, immense **2.** *inf.* exciting, unusual **3.** *inf.* excellent

tremolo ('tremǝlō) *n.* quivering or vibrating effect in singing or playing (*pl.* -s)

tremor ('tremǝr) *n.* **1.** quiver **2.** shaking **3.** minor earthquake

tremulous ('tremyǝlǝs) *a.* **1.** quivering slightly **2.** timorous, agitated

trench (trench) *n.* **1.** long narrow ditch, *esp.* as shelter in war —*vt.* **2.** cut grooves or ditches in —**trench coat** double-breasted waterproof coat —**trench foot** *see* **immersion foot** *at* IMMERSE

trenchant ('trenchǝnt) *a.* cutting, incisive, biting

trencher ('trenchǝr) *n. Hist.* wooden plate on which food was served —**'trencherman** *n.* person who enjoys food; hearty eater

trend (trend) *n.* **1.** direction, tendency, inclination, drift **2.** fashion; mode —**'trendiness** *n.* —**'trendy** *a./n. inf.* consciously

fashionable (person) —**'trendsetter** *n.* person or thing that creates or may create new fashion —**'trendsetting** *a.*

trephine ('trefīn) *n.* **1.** instrument for cutting circular pieces, *esp.* from skull —*vt.* **2.** remove circular section of bone, *esp.* from skull, of (someone)

trepidation (trepi'dāshǝn) *n.* fear, anxiety

trespass ('trespǝs, -pas) *vi.* **1.** intrude (on property *etc.* of another) **2.** transgress, sin —*n.* **3.** wrongful entering on another's land **4.** wrongdoing —**'trespasser** *n.*

tress (tres) *n.* long lock of hair

trestle ('tresǝl) *n.* board fixed on pairs of spreading legs and used as support

Trevira (trǝ'vēǝrǝ) *n.* trade name for polyester fiber

tri- (*comb. form*) three, as in *trisect*

triad ('trīad) *n.* **1.** group of three **2.** *Chem.* element, radical with valency of three

trial ('trīǝl, trīl) *n.* **1.** act of trying, testing **2.** experimental examination **3.** *Law* investigation of case before judge **4.** thing, person that strains endurance or patience —**trial and error** method of discovery *etc.* based on practical experiment and experience rather than theory —**trial balance** *Book-keeping* statement of all debit and credit balances in ledger of double-entry system

triangle ('trīanggǝl) *n.* **1.** figure with three angles **2.** percussion musical instrument —**tri'angular** *a.* —**triangulate** (trī'anggyǝlāt) *vt.* **1.** survey by method of triangulation **2.** calculate trigonometrically **3.** divide into triangles **4.** make triangular —*a.* (trī'anggyǝlit) **5.** marked with or composed of triangles —**triangu'lation** *n.* method of surveying in which area is divided into triangles, one side and all angles of which are measured and lengths of other lines calculated trigonometrically

Triassic (trī'asik) *a.* **1.** of first period of Mesozoic era —*n.* **2.** Triassic period or rock system (*also* **'Trias**)

triathlon (trī'athlǝn, -lon) *n.* athletic event comprising swimming, cycling and running

tribe (trīb) *n.* **1.** race **2.** subdivision of race of people —**'tribal** *a.*

tribulation (tribyǝ'lāshǝn) *n.* **1.** misery, trouble, affliction, distress **2.** cause of this

tribune ('tribyōōn) *n.* person or institution upholding public rights —**tribunal** (trī'byōōnǝl, tri-) *n.* **1.** lawcourt **2.** body appointed to inquire into and decide specific matter **3.** seat of judge

tributary ('tribyǝteri) *n.* **1.** stream flowing into another —*a.* **2.** auxiliary **3.** contributory **4.** paying tribute

tribute ('tribyōōt) *n.* **1.** sign of honor or recognition **2.** tax paid by one state to another

trice (trīs) *n.* moment —**in a trice** instantly

triceps ('trīseps) *n.* muscle having three heads, *esp.* one that extends forearm (*pl.* -es, -ceps)

trichina (tri'kīnǝ) *n.* minute parasitic worm (*pl.* -nae (-nē)) —**trichinosis** (triki'nōsis) *n.* infestation by trichinae transmitted by eating contaminated pork

trichomonas (trikǝ'mōnǝs) *n.* single-celled organism causing disease in reproductive organs of cattle and humans

trichromatic (trīkrō'matik) *or* **trichromic** (trī'krōmik) *a.* **1.** involving combination of three primary colors **2.** of normal color vision **3.** having three colors —**tri'chromatism** *n.*

trick (trik) *n.* **1.** deception **2.** prank **3.** mannerism **4.** illusion **5.** feat of skill or

cunning **6.** knack **7.** cards played in one round **8.** spell of duty —*vt.* **9.** cheat, hoax, deceive —**'trickery** *n.* —**'trickster** *n.* —**'tricky** *a.* **1.** difficult, needing careful handling **2.** crafty

trickle ('trikǝl) *v.* (cause to) run, flow, move in thin stream or drops

tricolor ('trīkulǝr) *a.* **1.** three-colored —*n.* **2.** tricolor flag (*eg* of France)

tricot ('trēkō) *n.* thin rayon or nylon fabric knitted or resembling knitting

tricycle ('trīsikǝl) *n.* three-wheeled vehicle operated by pedals

trident ('trīdǝnt) *n.* three-pronged fork or spear

triennial (trī'eniǝl) *a.* happening every, or lasting, three years

trifle ('trīfǝl) *n.* **1.** insignificant thing or matter **2.** small amount **3.** dessert of sponge cake, whipped cream *etc.* —*vi.* **4.** toy **5.** act, speak idly —**'trifler** *n.* —**'trifling** *a.* **1.** insignificant, petty **2.** frivolous; idle

trig. **1.** trigonometry **2.** trigonometrical —**trig station** *or* **point** landmark which surveyor uses

trigeminal neuralgia (trī'jeminǝl) nerve disorder marked by attacks of severe stabbing pains of the face (*also* **tic douloureux**)

trigger ('trigǝr) *n.* **1.** catch which releases spring, *esp.* to fire gun —*vt.* **2.** (*oft. with* off) start, set in action *etc.* —**trigger-happy** *a.* tending to irresponsible, ill-considered behavior, *esp.* in use of firearms

trigonometry (trigǝ'nomitri) *n.* branch of mathematics dealing with relations of sides and angles of triangles —**trigono'metrical** *a.*

trike (trīk) tricycle

trilateral (trī'latǝrǝl) *a.* having three sides —**tri'laterally** *adv.*

trilby ('trilbi) *n.* man's soft felt hat

trill (tril) *vi.* **1.** sing with quavering voice **2.** sing lightly —*n.* **3.** such singing or sound

trillion ('trilyǝn) *n.* in the U.S. and France, 10^{12}: the numeral 1 followed by 12 zeros; in Britain and Germany, 10^{18}: the numeral 1 followed by 18 zeros

trilobite ('trīlǝbīt) *n.* extinct marine arthropod abundant in Paleozoic times, having segmented exoskeleton divided into three parts —**trilobitic** (trīlǝ'bitik) *a.*

trilogy ('trilǝji) *n.* series of three related (literary) works

trim (trim) *a.* **1.** neat, smart **2.** slender **3.** in good order —*vt.* **4.** shorten slightly by cutting, prune **5.** decorate **6.** adjust **7.** put in good order **8.** adjust balance of (ship, aircraft) (-mm-) —*n.* **9.** decoration **10.** order, state of being trim **11.** haircut that neatens existing style **12.** upholstery, accessories in automobile **13.** edging material, as inside woodwork round doors, windows *etc.* —**'trimming** *n.* (*oft. pl.*) decoration, addition

trimaran ('trīmǝran) *n.* three-hulled vessel

Trinidad and Tobago ('trinidad; tǝ'bāgō) country lying in the Caribbean off the coast of Venezuela comprising the islands of Trinidad and Tobago —**Trinidadian** (trini'dādiǝn, -'dadiǝn) *n./a.*

trinitrotoluene (trīnītrō'tolyōōēn) *or* **trinitrotoluol** (trīnītrō'tolyōōol) *n.* a high explosive derived from toluene

trinity ('triniti) *n.* **1.** the state of being threefold **2.** (T-) the three persons of the Godhead —**trini'tarian** *n./a.* —**Trinity Sunday** Sunday after Whit Sunday

trinket ('tringkit) *n.* small ornament, trifle —**'trinketry** *n.*

trio ('trēō) *n.* **1.** group of three **2.** music for three parts (*pl.* -s)

triode ('trīŏd) *n. Electron.* three-electrode valve

trip (trip) *n.* 1. (short) journey for pleasure 2. stumble 3. switch 4. *inf.* hallucinatory experience caused by drug —*v.* 5. (*oft. with* up) (cause to) stumble 6. (cause to) make false step, mistake —*vi.* 7. run lightly; skip; dance 8. *inf.* take hallucinatory drugs —*vt.* 9. operate (switch) (**-pp-**) —**'tripper** *n.* tourist

tripartite (trī'pärtīt) *a.* having, divided into three parts

tripe (trīp) *n.* 1. stomach of cow *etc.* prepared for food 2. *inf.* nonsense

triphosphopyridine nucleotide (trīfosfō'pīridēn 'nyōōkliotīd, 'nōōkliotīd) coenzyme found in tissues of body where it participates in energy-producing reactions

triplane ('trīplān) *n.* airplane with three wings one above another

triple ('tripəl) *a.* 1. threefold —*v.* 2. treble —**'triplet** *n.* 1. three of a kind 2. one of three offspring born at one birth —**'triply** *adv.* —**triple jump** athletic event in which competitor has to perform hop, step and jump in continuous movement —**triple point** *Chem.* temperature and pressure at which three phases of substance are in equilibrium

triplicate ('triplikit) *a.* 1. threefold —*vt.* ('triplikāt) 2. make threefold —*n.* 3. state of being triplicate 4. one of set of three copies —**tripli'cation** *n.*

tripod ('trīpod) *n.* stool, stand *etc.* with three feet

tripos ('trīpos) *n.* degree examination at Cambridge University, England

triptych ('triptik) *n.* carving, set of pictures, *esp.* altarpiece, on three panels hinged side by side

trireme ('trīrēm) *n.* ancient Gr. galley with three banks of oars on each side

trisect ('trīsekt, trī'sekt) *vt.* divide into three (equal) parts —**tri'section** *n.*

trite (trīt) *a.* hackneyed, banal

tritium ('tritiəm) *n.* radioactive isotope of hydrogen

triumph ('trīəmf) *n.* 1. great success 2. victory 3. exultation —*vi.* 4. achieve great success or victory 5. exult —**tri'umphal** *a.* celebrating triumph —**tri'umphant** *a.* experiencing or displaying triumph

triumvirate (trī'umvirit) *n.* joint rule by three persons

trivalent (trī'vālənt) *a. Chem.* 1. having valency of three 2. having three valencies (*also* **ter'valent**) —**tri'valency** *n.*

trivet ('trivit) *n.* metal bracket or stand for pot or kettle

trivia ('triviə) *pl.n.* petty, unimportant things, details —**'trivial** *a.* 1. of little consequence 2. commonplace —**trivi'ality** *n.*

trochee ('trōkē) *n.* in verse, foot of two syllables, first long and second short —**tro'chaic** *a.*

trod (trod) *pt. of* TREAD —**'trodden** *or* **trod** *pp. of* TREAD

troglodyte ('troglədīt) *n.* cave dweller

troika ('troikə) *n.* 1. Russian vehicle drawn by three horses abreast 2. three horses harnessed abreast 3. triumvirate

Trojan ('trōjən) *n./a.* 1. (inhabitant) of ancient Troy 2. steadfast or persevering (person) —**Trojan Horse** 1. *Gr. myth.* hollow wooden figure of horse left outside Troy by Greeks and dragged inside by Trojans. Men concealed inside opened city to final Greek assault 2. trap intended to undermine enemy

troll[1] (trōl) *vt.* fish for by dragging baited hook or lure through water

troll[2] (trōl) *n.* supernatural being in Scandinavian mythology and folklore

trolley bus ('troli) bus deriving power from overhead electric wire but not running on rails

trollop ('troləp) *n.* promiscuous or slovenly woman

trombone (trom'bōn) *n.* deep-toned brass wind instrument with sliding tube —**trom'bonist** *n.*

trompe l'oeil (trômp'ləi) painting that creates the illusion of being that which is depicted

troop (trōōp) *n.* 1. group or crowd of persons or animals 2. unit of cavalry —*pl.* 3. soldiers —*vi.* 4. move in a troop, flock —**'trooper** *n.* 1. mounted policeman 2. state policeman

trope (trōp) *n.* figure of speech

trophy ('trōfi) *n.* 1. prize, award, as shield, cup 2. memorial of victory, hunt *etc.*

-trophy (*n. comb. form*) certain type of nourishment or growth, as in *dystrophy* —**-trophic** (*a. comb. form*)

tropic ('tropik) *n.* 1. either of two lines of latitude at 23½° N (**tropic of Cancer**) or 23½° S (**tropic of Capricorn**) —*pl.* 2. area of earth's surface between these lines —**'tropical** *a.* 1. pert. to, within tropics 2. (of climate) very hot —**tropical medicine** branch of medicine dealing with diseases of tropics and subtropics —**'tropicbird** *n.* tropical aquatic bird having long tail feathers and white plumage with black markings

tropism ('trōpizəm) *n.* response of organism, *esp.* plant, to external stimulus by growth in direction determined by stimulus

troposphere ('trōpəsfēər, 'trop-) *n.* lowest atmospheric layer, in which air temperature decreases normally with height at about 6.5°C per km

trot (trot) *vi.* 1. (of horse) move at medium pace, lifting feet in diagonal pairs 2. (of person) run easily with short strides (**-tt-**) —*n.* 3. trotting, jog —**'trotter** *n.* 1. horse trained to trot in race 2. foot of certain animals, *esp.* pig

troth (troth, trōth, trôth) *n. obs.* fidelity, truth

Trotskyism ('trotskiizəm) *n.* theory of communism of Leon Trotsky, Russian revolutionary and writer, in which he called for immediate worldwide revolution by proletariat —**'Trotskyite** *or* **'Trotskyist** *n./a.*

troubadour ('trōōbədôr, -dōōər) *n.* one of school of early poets and singers

trouble ('trubəl) *n.* 1. state or cause of mental distress, pain, inconvenience *etc.* 2. care, effort —*vt.* 3. be trouble to —*vi.* 4. be inconvenienced, concerned 5. be agitated 6. take pains; exert oneself —**'troublesome** *a.* —**'troubleshooter** *n.* person who locates cause of trouble and removes or treats it, as in running of machine —**'troubleshooting** *n./a.*

trough (trof) *n.* 1. long open vessel, *esp.* for animals' food or water 2. hollow between two waves 3. *Met.* area of low pressure

trounce (trowns) *vt.* beat thoroughly, thrash

troupe (trōōp) *n.* company of performers —**'trouper** *n.* 1. member of troupe 2. dependable worker or associate

trousers ('trowzərz) *pl.n.* two-legged outer garment with legs reaching to the ankles

trousseau ('trōōsō) *n.* bride's outfit of clothing (*pl.* **-seaux** (-sōz), **-s**)

trout (trowt) *n.* freshwater sport and food fish

trowel ('trowəl) *n.* small tool like spade for spreading mortar, lifting plants *etc.*

troy weight (troi) system of weights based on ounce of 20 pennyweights or 480 grains to the ounce and 12 ounces to the pound

truant ('trōōənt) *n.* 1. one absent without leave, *esp.* child so absenting himself or herself from school —*a.* 2. being or relating to truant —**'truancy** *n.*

Trubenizing ('trōōbənizing) *n.* (formerly, trade name for) process for making collars and cuffs on shirts permanently stiff

truce (trōōs) *n.* 1. temporary cessation of fighting 2. respite, lull

truck[1] (truk) *n.* wheeled (motor) vehicle for moving goods

truck[2] (truk) *n.* 1. barter 2. dealing (*esp. in* **have no truck with**) 3. payment of workmen in goods 4. *inf.* rubbish

truckle ('trukəl) *vi.* yield weakly

truckle bed low bed on wheels, stored under larger bed

truculent ('trukyələnt) *a.* aggressive, defiant

trudge (truj) *vi.* 1. walk laboriously —*n.* 2. laborious or wearisome walk

true (trōō) *a.* 1. in accordance with facts 2. faithful 3. exact, correct 4. genuine —**'truism** *n.* self-evident truth —**'truly** *adv.* 1. exactly 2. really 3. sincerely —**truth** *n.* 1. state of being true 2. something that is true —**'truthful** *a.* 1. accustomed to speak the truth 2. accurate, exact —**'truthfully** *adv.* —**true-blue** *a.* unwaveringly or staunchly loyal —**true blue** one who is true-blue

truffle ('trufəl) *n.* 1. edible fungus growing underground 2. soft candy made of a chocolate mixture

truism ('trōōizəm) *n. see* TRUE

Truman ('trōōmən) *n.* **Harry S** the 33rd President of the U.S. (1945-53)

trump[1] (trump) *n.* 1. card of suit temporarily ranking above others —*v.* 2. play trump card on (plain suit) —**trump up** invent, concoct —**turn up** *or* **out trumps** turn out (unexpectedly) well, successfully

trump[2] (trump) *n.* 1. trumpet 2. blast on trumpet —**the last trump** final trumpet call on Day of Judgment

trumpery ('trumpəri) *a.* 1. showy but worthless —*n.* 2. worthless finery 3. trash, rubbish

trumpet ('trumpit) *n.* 1. metal wind instrument like horn —*vi.* 2. blow trumpet 3. make sound like one, as elephant —*vt.* 4. proclaim, make widely known

truncate ('trungkāt, trung'kāt) *vt.* cut short —**'truncated** *a.* 1. (of cone *etc.*) having apex or end removed by plane intersection 2. shortened (as if) by cutting off (*also* **'truncate**)

truncheon ('trunchən) *n.* 1. short thick club or baton 2. staff of office or authority —*vt.* 3. cudgel

trundle ('trundəl) *vt.* roll, as a thing on little wheels

trunk (trungk) *n.* 1. main stem of tree 2. person's body without or excluding head and limbs 3. box for clothing *etc.* 4. elephant's proboscis —*pl.* 5. man's swimsuit —**trunk line** main line of railroad, canal, telephone *etc.*

truss (trus) *vt.* 1. (*oft. with* up) fasten, tie —*n.* 2. support 3. medical device of belt *etc.* to hold hernia in place 4. package, bundle (of hay *etc.*) 5. cluster of flowers at end of single stalk

trust (trust) *n.* 1. confidence 2. firm belief 3. reliance 4. combination of producers to reduce competition and keep up prices 5. care, responsibility 6. property held for another —*vt.* 7. rely on 8. believe in 9. consign for care —*v.* 10. expect, hope

—**trus'tee** *n.* one legally holding property on another's behalf —**trus'teeship** *n.* —**'trustful** *a.* 1. inclined to trust 2. credulous —**'trustworthy** *a.* 1. reliable, dependable, honest 2. safe —**'trusty** *a.* 1. faithful 2. reliable —**trust fund** money, securities *etc.* held in trust

Trust Territory of the Pacific islands and atolls including the Carolines, the Marshalls and Marianas in the Pacific Ocean, a UN trust territory administered by the U.S.

truth (trŌŌth) *n.* see TRUE

try (trī) *vi.* 1. attempt, endeavor —*vt.* 2. attempt 3. test 4. make demands upon 5. investigate (case) 6. examine (person) in court of law 7. purify; refine (as metals) (**tried, 'trying**) —*n.* 8. attempt, effort 9. *Rugby* score gained by touching ball down over opponent's goal line —**tried** *a.* 1. proved 2. afflicted —**'trying** *a.* 1. upsetting, annoying 2. difficult —**'tryout** *n.* —**trysail** ('trīsāl; *Naut.* 'trīsəl) *n.* small fore-and-aft sail set on sailing vessel in foul weather to help keep her head to wind —**try on** 1. put on (garment) to find out whether it fits *etc.* 2. *inf.* attempt to deceive or fool (*esp. in* **try it on**) —**try out** 1. test; put to experimental use 2. (*usu. with* for) (of actor *etc.*) undergo test; submit (actor *etc.*) to test to determine suitability for role *etc.*

trypanosome (tri'panəsōm) *n.* protozoon with spindle-shaped body and single flagellum, blood parasite of vertebrates causing disease, *eg* sleeping sickness —**African trypanosomiasis** (tripanəsə'mīəsis) sleeping sickness transmitted by tsetse fly

tryst (trist) *n.* 1. appointment to meet 2. place appointed

tsar (zär) *n.* see CZAR

tsetse fly ('tsetsi) *Afr.* bloodsucking fly whose bite transmits various diseases to man and animals

T-shirt *or* **tee shirt** *n.* informal (short-sleeved) sweater, *usu.* of cotton

tsimmes ('tsimis) *n.* 1. a fruit or vegetable stew 2. a state of confusion 3. a complicated or overelaborated procedure

tsores *or* **tsuris** ('tsorəs) *pl.n.* (*sometimes with sing. v.*) *inf.* troubles, worries, afflictions

tsp. teaspoon

T square T-shaped ruler for drawing parallel lines, right angles *etc.*

tub (tub) *n.* 1. open wooden vessel like bottom half of barrel 2. small round container 3. bath 4. *inf.* old, slow ship *etc.* —**'tubby** *a.* 1. plump 2. shaped like tub

tuba ('tyŌŌbə, 'tŌŌbə) *n.* valved brass wind instrument of low pitch

tube (tyŌŌb, tŌŌb) *n.* 1. long, narrow, hollow cylinder 2. flexible cylinder with cap to hold liquids, pastes 3. UK (*sometimes* T-) underground electric railway, *esp.* in London 4. *sl.* television set —**'tubing** *n.* 1. tubes collectively 2. length of tube 3. system of tubes 4. fabric in form of tube —**'tubular** *a.* like tube

tuber ('tyŌŌbər, 'tŌŌbər) *n.* swollen stem or root, usu. underground, of plant —**'tuberous** *a.*

tubercle ('tyŌŌbərkəl, 'tŌŌbərkəl) *n.* 1. any small rounded nodule on skin *etc.* 2. small lesion of tissue, *esp.* produced by tuberculosis —**tu'bercular** *a.* —**tu'berculin** *n.* extraction from bacillus used to test for and treat tuberculosis —**tubercu'losis** *n.* bacterial disease affecting lungs, skin, lymph glands, brain and blood stream (*also* **consumption, phthisis**)

tuck (tuk) *vt.* 1. push, fold into small space 2. gather, stitch in folds 3. draw, roll together —*n.* 4. stitched· fold 5. *inf.* food —**'tucker** *n.* strip of linen or lace formerly worn across bosom by women —**tuck in** 1. put to bed and make snug 2. thrust loose ends or sides of (something) into confining space 3. *inf.* eat, *esp.* heartily

Tudor ('tyŌŌdər, 'tŌŌdər) *a.* 1. of the English royal house ruling 1485-1603 2. in, resembling style of this period, *esp.* of architecture

Tues. Tuesday

Tuesday ('tyŌŌzdi, 'tŌŌzdi) *n.* third day of week

tufa ('tyŌŌfə, 'tŌŌfə) *n.* porous rock formed as deposit from springs *etc.*

tuff (tuf) *n.* hard volcanic rock consisting of consolidated fragments of lava

tuffet ('tufit) *n.* small mound or seat

tuft (tuft) *n.* bunch of feathers, threads *etc.*

tug (tug) *vt.* 1. pull hard or violently 2. haul 3. jerk forward (-**gg**-) —*n.* 4. violent pull 5. ship used to tow other vessels —**tug of war** contest in which two teams pull against one another on a rope

tuition (tyŌŌ'ishən, tŌŌ-) *n.* 1. teaching, instruction 2. private coaching —**tu'itional** *a.*

tularemia (tyŌŌlə'rēmiə, tŌŌlə-) *n.* bacterial disease transmitted to humans by contact, ingestion and insects from infected rabbits, rodents and other wild animals

tulip ('tyŌŌlip, 'tŌŌlip) *n.* any of several bulbous plants native to Asia with bright cup-shaped flowers —**tulip tree** N Amer. forest tree with tulip-shaped greenish-yellow flowers and long conelike fruits

tulle (tŌŌl) *n.* kind of fine thin silk or lace

tullibee ('tuləbē) *n.* Canad. whitefish

tumble ('tumbəl) *v.* 1. (cause to) fall, roll, twist *etc.*, *esp.* in play —*vt.* 2. rumple, disturb —*n.* 3. fall 4. somersault —**'tumbler** *n.* 1. stemless drinking glass 2. acrobat 3. spring catch in lock —**tumble-down** *a.* dilapidated —**tumble to** *inf.* realize, understand

tumbril *or* **tumbrel** ('tumbrəl) *n.* open cart for taking victims of French Revolution to guillotine

tumefy ('tyŌŌmifī, 'tŌŌ-) *v.* (cause to) swell —**tu'mescence** *n.* —**tu'mescent** *a.* (becoming) swollen

tummy ('tumi) *n.* *inf.* stomach

tumor ('tyŌŌmər, 'tŌŌmər) *n.* abnormal growth in or on body

tumult ('tyŌŌmult) *n.* violent uproar, commotion —**tu'multuous** *a.*

tumulus ('tyŌŌmyələs, 'tŌŌ-) *n.* burial mound, barrow (*pl.* -**li** (-lī))

tun (tun) *n.* 1. large cask 2. measure of liquid

tuna

tuna ('tyŌŌnə, 'tŌŌnə) *n.* any of various large marine food fishes

tundra ('tundrə) *n.* vast treeless zone between icecap and timber line of N Amer. and Eurasia

tune (tyŌŌn, tŌŌn) *n.* 1. melody 2. quality of being in pitch 3. adjustment of musical instrument 4. concord 5. frame of mind —*vt.* 6. put in tune 7. adjust (machine) to obtain most efficient running 8. adjust (radio circuit) —**'tuneful** *a.* —**'tunefully** *adv.* —**'tuner** *n.* —**tune-up** *n.* adjustments to

engine to improve performance —**tuning fork** two-pronged metal fork that when struck produces pure note of constant specified pitch —**tune in** adjust (radio, television) to receive (a station, program) —**tune up** 1. adjust (musical instrument) to particular pitch 2. tune (instruments) to common pitch 3. adjust (engine) in (motor vehicle) to improve performance

tungsten ('tungstən) *n.* *Chem.* metallic element *Symbol* W, at. wt. 183.9, at. no. 74

tunic ('tyŌŌnik, 'tŌŌnik) *n.* 1. close-fitting jacket forming part of uniform 2. loose hiplength or kneelength garment

Tunisia (tyŌŌ'nēzhiə, tŌŌ-) *n.* country in Africa bounded north and east by the Mediterranean Sea, west by Algeria and south by Libya —**Tu'nisian** *n./a.*

tunnel ('tunəl) *n.* 1. underground passage, *esp.* as track for railroad line 2. burrow of a mole *etc.* —*vt.* 3. make tunnel through —*vi.* 4. (*with* through, under *etc.*) make or force a way (through or under something) —**'tunneler** *n.*

tup (tup) *n.* male sheep, ram

tupik ('tŌŌpək) *n.* C tent used as summer shelter by Eskimos

turban ('tərbən) *n.* 1. in certain countries, man's headdress, made by coiling length of cloth round head or a cap 2. woman's hat like this

turbid ('tərbid) *a.* 1. muddy, not clear 2. disturbed —**tur'bidity** *or* **'turbidness** *n.*

turbine ('tərbin, -bīn) *n.* rotary engine driven by steam, gas, water or air playing on blades

turbo- (*comb. form*) of, relating to, or driven by a turbine, as in *turbofan*

turbofan ('tərbōfan) *n.* 1. bypass engine in which large fan driven by turbine forces air rearward around exhaust gases to increase propulsive thrust 2. aircraft driven by turbofans 3. fan in such engine

turbojet ('tərbōjet) *n.* 1. turbojet engine 2. aircraft powered by turbojet engines —**turbojet engine** gas turbine in which exhaust gases provide propulsive thrust to drive aircraft

turboprop ('tərbōprop) *n.* 1. gas turbine for driving aircraft propeller 2. aircraft powered by turboprops

turbot ('tərbət) *n.* large European flatfish

turbulent ('tərbyələnt) *a.* 1. in commotion 2. swirling 3. riotous —**'turbulence** *n.* *Met.* instability of atmosphere causing gusty air currents *etc.*

tureen (tə'rēn) *n.* serving dish for soup

turf (tərf) *n.* 1. short grass with earth bound to it by matted roots 2. grass, *esp.* as lawn (*pl.* -**s, turves**) 3. territory, *esp.* area claimed by juvenile gang —*vt.* 4. lay with turf —**turf accountant** bookmaker —**the turf** 1. horse racing 2. racecourse —**turf out** *inf.* dismiss, throw out

turgid ('tərjid) *a.* 1. swollen, inflated 2. bombastic —**tur'gescent** *a.* —**tur'gidity** *n.*

turkey ('tərki) *n.* 1. large bird reared for its flesh 2. *inf.* unsuccessful theatrical performance. 3. *sl.* stupid, incompetent or unappealing person

Turkey ('tərki) *n.* country in Europe and Asia bounded west by the Aegean Sea and Greece, north by Bulgaria and the Black Sea, east by the U.S.S.R. and Iran and south by Iraq, Syria and the Mediterranean —**Turk** *n.* —**'Turkic** *a.* of the branch of Altaic stretching from northern Siberia to Turkey —**'Turkish** *n./a.* 1. of Turkey —*n.* 2. language of Turkey which is a Turkic language —**Turkish bath** steam bath —**Turkish coffee**

very strong black coffee —**Turkish delight** gelatin flavored and coated with powdered sugar —**Turkish towel** towel made of terry cloth

Turkoman or **Turcoman** ('tɔrkəmən) n. member of group of peoples living in the Turkmen, Uzbek and Kazakh republics of the U.S.S.R. (pl. **-s**)

Turks and Caicos Islands ('kākəs) crown colony of the United Kingdom forming an archipelago southeast of the Bahamas

turmeric ('tɔrmərik) n. **1.** Asian plant **2.** powdered root of this used as dye, medicine and condiment

turmoil ('tɔrmoil) n. confusion and bustle, commotion

turn (tɔrn) v. **1.** move around, rotate **2.** change, reverse, alter position or direction (of) —vi. **3.** (oft. with into) change in nature, character etc. **4.** (of milk) become rancid or sour —vt. **5.** make, shape on lathe —n. **6.** act of turning **7.** inclination **8.** period, spell **9.** turning **10.** short walk **11.** (part of) rotation **12.** performance —'**turner** n. —'**turning** n. road, path leading off main route —'**turnabout** n. **1.** act of turning so as to face different direction **2.** reversal of opinion etc. —'**turncoat** n. one who forsakes his party or principles —**turning circle** smallest circle in which vehicle can turn —**turning point 1.** moment when course of events is changed **2.** point at which there is change in direction or motion —'**turnkey** n. obs. keeper of keys, esp. in prison; warder, jailer —**turn-off** n. **1.** road etc. branching off from main thoroughfare **2.** something or someone that turns one off —**turn-on** n. something or someone that turns one on —'**turnout** n. **1.** number of people appearing for some purpose, occasion **2.** way in which person is dressed, equipped —'**turnover** n. **1.** total sales made by business over certain period **2.** rate at which staff leave and are replaced **3.** small pasty —'**turnpike** n. highway with tollgates —'**turnstile** n. revolving gate for controlling admission of people —'**turnstone** n. shore bird that lifts up stones in search of food —'**turntable** n. revolving platform, esp. of phonograph —**turn-up** n. unexpected or chance occurrence —**turn down** refuse —**turn off 1.** leave (road etc.) **2.** (of road etc.) deviate from (another road etc.) **3.** cause (something) to cease operating by turning knob etc. **4.** inf. cause (person etc.) to feel dislike or distaste for (something) —**turn on 1.** cause (something) to operate by turning knob etc. **2.** depend or hinge on **3.** become hostile; retaliate **4.** inf. produce (charm etc.) suddenly or automatically **5.** sl. arouse emotionally or sexually **6.** sl. take or become intoxicated by drugs **7.** sl. introduce to drugs —**turn up 1.** appear **2.** be found **3.** increase (flow, volume)

turnip ('tɔrnip) n. plant with globular root used as food

turpentine ('tɔrpəntīn) n. **1.** resin got from certain trees **2.** oil, spirits made from this

turpitude ('tɔrpityōod, -tōod) n. depravity

turps (tɔrps) turpentine

turquoise or **turquois** ('tɔrkwoiz, -koiz) n. **1.** bluish-green or greenish-gray gemstone **2.** variable color averaging light greenish blue —**turquoise blue** color of the stone turquoise —**turquoise green** color averaging light bluish green

turret ('turit) n. **1.** small tower **2.** revolving armored tower for guns on warship, tank etc.

turtle ('tɔrtəl) n. sea tortoise —'**turtleneck** n. **1.** round high close-fitting neck on sweater **2.** sweater itself

turtledove ('tɔrtəlduv) n. **1.** Old World dove having brown plumage with speckled wings and long dark tail **2.** gentle or loving person

tusk (tusk) n. long pointed side tooth of certain animals (eg elephant, wild boar etc.) —'**tusker** n. animal with tusks fully developed

tussle ('tusəl) n./vi. fight, struggle

tussock ('tusək) n. **1.** clump of grass **2.** tuft —'**tussocky** a.

tutelage ('tyōotilij, 'tōo-) n. act, office of tutor or guardian —'**tutelary** or '**tutelar** a.

tutor ('tyōotər, 'tōotər) n. **1.** one teaching individuals or small groups —v. **2.** teach thus —**tu'torial** n. period of instruction with tutor

tutti ('tōoti, 'tōoti) a./adv. Mus. to be performed by whole orchestra, choir etc.

tutti-frutti (tōoti'frōoti) n. ice cream containing small pieces of candied fruits

tutu ('tōotōo) n. short, stiff skirt worn by ballerinas

Tuvalu (tōo'välōo) n. country lying in South Pacific comprising nine islands lying between 5°30' and 11° S latitude and 180° E longitude —**Tuva'luan** a./n.

tu-whit tu-whoo (tə'wit tə'wōo) imitation of sound made by owl

tuxedo (tuk'sēdō) n. semiformal evening suit for men (pl. **-s**)

TV 1. television **2.** sl. transvestite

TVA Tennessee Valley Authority

twaddle ('twodəl) n. silly talk

twain (twān) n. obs. two —**in twain** asunder

twang (twang) n. **1.** vibrating metallic sound **2.** nasal speech —v. **3.** (cause to) make such sounds

tweak (twēk) vt. **1.** pinch and twist or pull —n. **2.** a tweaking

twee (twē) a. inf. excessively sentimental, sweet, pretty

tweed (twēd) n. **1.** rough-surfaced cloth used for clothing —pl. **2.** suit of tweed —'**tweedy** a. **1.** of tweed **2.** showing fondness for hearty outdoor life, usu. associated with wearers of tweeds

tweet (twēt) n./vi. chirp —'**tweeter** n. loudspeaker reproducing high-frequency sounds

tweezers ('twēzərz) pl.n. small forceps or tongs

twelve (twelv) n./a. cardinal number two more than ten —**twelfth** a./n. ordinal number —**Twelfth Day** Jan. 6th, twelfth day after Christmas; feast of Epiphany —**twelve-tone** a. of type of serial music which uses as musical material tone row formed by 12 semitones of chromatic scale

twenty ('twenti) n./a. cardinal number, twice ten —'**twentieth** a./n. ordinal number —**twenty-four-hour time** measuring day beginning at midnight expressed as 0000 used widely in scientific work, in operations of the armed forces and in all travel timetables in Europe —**twenty questions** word-guessing parlor game in which guesser attempts to discover word selected by other players within 20 questions —**twenty-twenty** or **20/20 vision** normal standard of vision

twerp or **twirp** (twɔrp) n. inf. silly person

twice (twīs) adv. two times

twiddle ('twidəl) v. **1.** fiddle —vt. **2.** twist

twig¹ (twig) n. small branch, shoot

twig² (twig) v. inf. notice; understand (**-gg-**)

twilight ('twīlīt) n. soft light after sunset —'**twilit** a. —**twilight zone 1.** inner-city area where houses have become dilapidated **2.** any indefinite or transitional condition or area

twill (twil) n. fabric woven so as to have surface of parallel ridges

twin (twin) n. **1.** one of pair, esp. of two children born together —a. **2.** being a twin —v. **3.** pair, be paired

twine (twīn) v. **1.** twist, coil round —n. **2.** string, cord

twinge (twinj) n. **1.** momentary sharp, shooting pain **2.** qualm

twinkle ('twingkəl) vi. **1.** shine with dancing or quivering light, sparkle —n. **2.** twinkling **3.** flash **4.** gleam of amusement in eyes —'**twinkling** n. very brief time

twirl (twɔrl) v. **1.** turn or twist round quickly **2.** whirl —vt. **3.** twiddle —n. **4.** rotating; being rotated; whirl, twist **5.** something wound around or twisted; coil **6.** written flourish

twist (twist) v. **1.** make, become spiral, by turning with one end fast **2.** distort, change **3.** wind —n. **4.** thing twisted **5.** dance popular in 1960s, in which dancers vigorously twist the hips —'**twister** n. inf. swindler —'**twisty** a.

twit (twit) n. **1.** inf. foolish person —vt. **2.** taunt (**-tt-**)

twitch (twich) v. **1.** give momentary sharp pull or jerk (to) —n. **2.** such pull or jerk **3.** spasmodic jerk, spasm

twitch grass see QUACK GRASS

twitter ('twitər) vi. **1.** (of birds) utter succession of tremulous sounds —n. **2.** such succession of notes

two (tōo) n./a. cardinal number, one more than one —'**twofold** a./adv. —'**twosome** n. **1.** two together, esp. two people **2.** match between two people —**two-edged** a. **1.** having two cutting edges **2.** (esp. of remark) having two interpretations —**two-faced** a. **1.** double-dealing, deceitful **2.** with two faces —**two-ply** a. **1.** made of two layers, strands etc. —n. **2.** two-ply knitting yarn etc. —**two-step** n. **1.** ballroom dance in duple time **2.** music for such dance —**two-stroke** a. (of internal-combustion engine) making one explosion to every two strokes of piston —**two-time** v. inf. deceive (someone, esp. lover) by carrying on relationship with another —**two-timer** n.

TX Texas

-ty¹ (comb. form) multiple of ten, as in sixty, seventy

-ty² (comb. form) state, condition, quality, as in cruelty

tycoon (tī'kōon) n. powerful, influential businessman

tyke or **tike** (tīk) n. **1.** inf. small, cheeky child **2.** small (mongrel) dog

Tyler ('tīlər) n. **John.** the 10th President of the U.S. (1841-45)

tympani ('timpəni) pl.n. see TIMPANI

tympanum ('timpənəm) n. **1.** cavity of middle ear **2.** tympanic membrane **3.** any diaphragm resembling that in middle ear in function **4.** Archit. recessed space, esp. triangular, bounded by cornices of pediment **5.** recessed space bounded by arch and lintel of doorway or window below it **6.** Mus. drum **7.** scoop wheel for raising water (pl. **-s, -na** (-nə)) —**tym'panic** a. —**tympanic membrane** thin membrane separating external ear from middle ear

Tynwald ('tinwəld, 'tīn-) n. Parliament of Isle of Man

type (tīp) n. **1.** class, sort **2.** model; pattern **3.** characteristic build **4.** specimen **5.** block bearing letter used for printing **6.** such pieces collectively —vt. **7.** print with typewriter **8.** typify **9.** classify —'**typist** n. one who operates typewriter —'**typo** n. inf. error in typing —'**typecast** vt. cast (actor) in same kind of role continually —'**typeface** n. **1.** printing surface of any type character **2.** style or design of character on type (also **face**) —'**typescript** n. typewritten document or copy —**'typesetter** *n.* **1.** person who sets type; compositor **2.** typesetting machine —**'typewrite** *v.* —**'typewriter** *n.* keyed writing machine

-type (*comb. form*) **1.** type, form, as in *archetype* **2.** printing type; photographic process, as in *collotype*

typhoid ('tīfoid) *n.* **1.** acute infectious disease, affecting *esp.* intestines —*a., also* **ty'phoidal 2.** resembling typhus —**'typhus** *n.* rickettsial disease occurring in epidemic (louse-borne) and endemic (flea-borne from mice and rats) forms —**Typhoid Mary** ('mãəri) person who is an unknowing source of contamination

typhoon (tı'fōōn) *n.* violent tropical storm or cyclone —**typhonic** (tı'fonik) *a.*

typical ('tipikəl) *or* **typic** *a.* **1.** true to type **2.** characteristic —**'typically** *adv.*

typify ('tipifī) *vt.* serve as type or model of (**-ified, -ifying**)

typography (tı'pogrəfi) *n.* **1.** art of printing **2.** style of printing —**ty'pographer** *n.* —**typo'graphical** *a.*

tyrannosaur (ti'ranəsör) *or* **tyrannosaurus** (tiranə'sörəs) *n.* large carnivorous two-footed dinosaur common in N Amer. in Upper Jurassic and Cretaceous times

tyrant ('tīrənt) *n.* **1.** oppressive or cruel ruler

2. one who forces his will on others cruelly and arbitrarily —**tyrannical** (ti'ranikəl) *a.* **1.** despotic **2.** ruthless —**tyrannically** (ti'ranikəli) *adv.* —**tyrannicide** (ti'ranisīd) *n.* **1.** slayer of tyrant **2.** his deed —**tyrannize** ('tirənīz) *v.* exert ruthless or tyrannical authority (over) —**tyrannous** ('tirənəs) *a.* —**tyranny** ('tirəni) *n.* despotism

Tyrian ('tiriən) *n.* **1.** native of ancient Tyre, port in S Lebanon and center of ancient Phoenician culture —*a.* **2.** of ancient Tyre

tyro ('tīrō) *n.* novice, beginner (*pl.* **-s**)

tzar (zär) *n. see* CZAR

Uu

u *or* **U** (yōō) *n.* **1.** 21st letter of English alphabet **2.** any of several speech sounds represented by this letter, as in *mute, cut* or *minus* **3.** something shaped like U (*pl.* **u's, U's** *or* **Us**)

U 1. united **2.** unionist **3.** university **4.** UK universal (used to describe category of film certified as suitable for viewing by anyone) **5.** *Chem.* uranium

U.A.E. United Arab Emirates

ubiquitous (yōō'bikwitəs) *a.* **1.** everywhere at once **2.** omnipresent —**u'biquity** *n.*

U-boat *n.* German submarine

u.c. *Print.* upper case

udder ('udər) *n.* milk-secreting organ of cow *etc.*

UFO unidentified flying object

Uganda (yōō'gandə, ōō'gandə; -'gän-) *n.* country in Africa bounded north by Sudan, east by Kenya, south by Tanzania and west by Zaïre —**U'gandan** *n./a.*

ugh (ug, əkh, ə) *interj.* exclamation of disgust, annoyance *etc.*

ugly ('ugli) *a.* **1.** unpleasant or repulsive to the sight, hideous **2.** ill-omened **3.** threatening —**'uglify** *v.* —**'ugliness** *n.* —**ugly duckling** person or thing, initially ugly or unpromising, that changes into something beautiful or admirable

UHF ultrahigh frequency

U.K. United Kingdom

ukase (yōō'kās, -'kāz) *n.* in imperial Russia, edict of czar

Ukrainian (yōō'krāniən) *a.* **1.** of Ukraine —*n.* **2.** East Slavonic language of Ukrainians **3.** native or inhabitant of Ukraine

ukulele (yōōkə'lāli) *n.* small four-stringed guitar, *esp.* of Hawaii

ulcer ('ulsər) *n.* open sore on skin, mucous membrane that is slow to heal —**'ulcerate** *v.* make, form ulcer(s) —**'ulcerated** *a.* —**ulce'ration** *n.* —**'ulcerative** *a.* —**'ulcerous** *a.* —**ulcerative colitis** inflammation of colon resulting in formation of ulcers

ulna ('ulnə) *n.* bone of the human forearm on the little finger side (*pl.* **ulnae** ('ulnē), **-s**)

Ulster ('ulstər) *n.* **1.** Northern Ireland **2.** (**u-**) man's heavy double-breasted overcoat —**'Ulsterite** *n.* —**'Ulsterman** *n.*

ult. 1. ultimate **2.** ultimo

ulterior (ul'tēəriər) *a.* **1.** lying beneath, beyond what is revealed or evident (*eg* motives) **2.** situated beyond

ultimate ('ultimit) *a.* **1.** last **2.** highest **3.** most significant **4.** fundamental —**'ultimately** *adv.* —**ultimatum** (ulti'mātəm) *n.* **1.** final proposition **2.** final terms offered (*pl.* **-s, -ta** (-tə)) —**'ultimo** *adv.* in last month

ultra ('ultrə) *a.* **1.** extreme, *esp.* in beliefs or opinions —*n.* **2.** extremist

ultra- (*comb. form*) beyond, excessive(ly), extreme(ly) as in *ultramodern*

ultrahigh frequency (ultrə'hī) (band of) radio waves of very short wavelength

ultramarine (ultrəmə'rēn) *n.* blue pigment

ultrasonic (ultrə'sonik) *a.* of sound waves beyond the range of human ear —**ultra'sonics** *pl.n.* (*with sing. v.*) branch of physics concerned with ultrasonic waves (*also* **super'sonics**)

ultrasound ('ultrəsownd) *n.* ultrasonic waves, used in cleaning metallic parts, echo sounding, medical diagnosis *etc.*

ultraviolet (ultrə'vīəlit) *a.* of electromagnetic radiation, *eg* of sun *etc.*, beyond limit of visibility at violet end of spectrum

ululate ('ulyəlāt) *vi.* howl, wail —**'ululant** *a.* —**ulu'lation** *n.*

umbel ('umbəl) *n.* umbrella-like flower cluster with stalks springing from central point —**umbel'liferous** *a.*

umber ('umbər) *n.* dark brown pigment

umbilical (um'bilikəl) *a.* of (region of) navel —**umbilicus** (umbi'līkəs, um'bilikəs) *n.* **1.** *Biol.* hollow structure, such as cavity at base of gastropod shell **2.** *Anat.* navel (*pl.* **-bilici** (-bi'līkī, -sī; -'bilikī, -sī)) —**umbilical cord 1.** cordlike structure connecting fetus with placenta of mother **2.** cord joining astronaut to spacecraft *etc.*

umbra ('umbrə) *n.* **1.** region of complete shadow due to obstruction of light by opaque object, *esp.* shadow cast by moon onto earth during solar eclipse **2.** darker inner region of sunspot (*pl.* **-brae** (-brē), **-s**) —**'umbral** *a.*

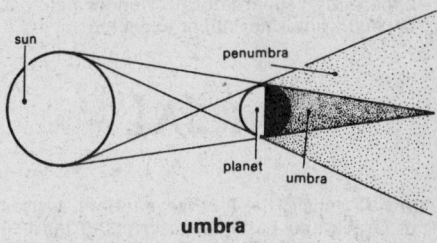

umbra

umbrage ('umbrij) *n.* offense, resentment (*esp. in* give *or* take umbrage)

umbrella (um'brelə) *n.* **1.** folding circular cover of nylon *etc.* on stick, carried in hand to protect against rain, heat of sun **2.** anything shaped or functioning like an umbrella

umiak ('ōōmiak) *n.* Eskimo boat made of skins, usu. propelled by paddles

umlaut ('ōōmlowt) *n.* **1.** mark (¨) placed over vowel in some languages, such as German **2.** *esp.* in Germanic languages, change of vowel within word caused by assimilating influence of vowel or semivowel in preceding or following syllable

umpire ('umpīər) *n.* **1.** person chosen to decide question, or to decide disputes and enforce rules in a game —*v.* **2.** act as umpire in or for (game *etc.*)

umpteen ('ump'tēn) *a. inf.* many —**ump'teenth** *n./a.*

UN United Nations

un- (*comb. form*) not, contrary to, opposite of, reversal of an action, removal from, release, deprivation. See the list below

unaccountable (unə'kowntəbəl) *a.* that cannot be explained

unaffected[1] (unə'fektid) *a.* unpretentious, natural —**unaf'fectedly** *adv.*

unaffected[2] (unə'fektid) *a.* not affected

unanimous (yŏŏ'nanimǝs) a. 1. in complete agreement 2. agreed by all —una'nimity n. —u'nanimously adv.

unassailable (unǝ'sāləbǝl) a. 1. able to withstand attack 2. irrefutable —unas'sailably adv.

unassuming (unǝ'sooming) a. not pretentious, modest

unattached (unǝ'tacht) a. 1. not connected with any specific thing, group etc. 2. not engaged or married

unavailing (unǝ'vāling) a. useless, futile

unaware (unǝ'wāǝr) a. not aware, uninformed —una'wares adv. 1. without previous warning 2. unexpectedly

unbend (un'bend) v. 1. release or be released from restraints of formality 2. inf. relax (mind) or (of mind) become relaxed 3. make or become straight from original bent shape (-'bent, -'bending) —un'bending a. 1. rigid, inflexible 2. characterized by sternness or severity

unbidden (un'bidǝn) a. 1. not commanded; voluntary, spontaneous 2. not invited

unbosom (un'boozǝm) vt. tell or reveal (one's secrets etc.)

unbounded (un'boundid) a. having no boundaries or limits —un'boundedly adv.

unbridled (un'brīdǝld) a. 1. with all restraints removed 2. (of horse etc.) wearing no bridle

unburden (un'bǝrdǝn) vt. 1. remove load or burden from 2. relieve, make free (one's mind, oneself etc.) of worry etc. by revelation or confession

uncalled-for a. unnecessary; unwarranted

uncanny (un'kani) a. 1. characterized by apparently supernatural wonder etc. 2. beyond what is normal or expected

UNCIAL

uncial ('unshǝl) a. 1. of large letters, as used in Greek and Latin manuscripts of third to ninth centuries, that resemble modern capitals but are more rounded —n. 2. uncial letter or manuscript —'uncially adv.

uncle ('ungkǝl) n. 1. brother of father or mother 2. husband of aunt —Uncle Sam personification of American nation

uncompromising (un'komprǝmīzing) a. not prepared to compromise —un'compromisingly adv.

unconscionable (un'konchǝnǝbǝl) a. 1. unscrupulous, unprincipled 2. excessive

unconscious (un'konchǝs) a. 1. insensible 2. not aware 3. not knowing 4. of thoughts, memories etc. of which one is not normally aware —n. 5. these thoughts —un'consciously adv. —un'consciousness n.

uncounted (un'kowntid) a. 1. innumerable 2. not counted

uncouth (un'kooth) a. 1. clumsy, boorish 2. without ease or polish

uncover (un'kuvǝr) vt. 1. remove cover, top etc. from 2. reveal, disclose —v. 3. take off (one's head covering), esp. as mark of respect

unction ('ungkshǝn) n. 1. anointing 2. excessive politeness 3. soothing words or thoughts —'unctuous a. 1. slippery, greasy 2. oily in manner, ingratiating

undeceive (undi'sēv) vt. reveal truth to (someone mistaken, misled)

under ('undǝr) prep. 1. below, beneath 2. bound by, included in 3. less than 4. subjected to 5. known by 6. in the time of —adv. 7. in lower place or condition —a. 8. lower —under way 1. in progress 2. Naut. in motion in direction headed

under- (comb. form) beneath, below, lower, too little, as in underground, underbid. See the list below

undera'chieve	'underpants
under'bid v.	'underpart
'underbid n.	under'priced
'underclothes	under'sea
under'do	under'sexed
under'done	under'shoot
underem'ployed	under'sized
under'foot	'underskirt
'undergarment	under'staffed
under'lie	under'state
under'manned	under'value
under'nourish	under'water
under'paid	under'weight

underage (undǝr'āj) a. below required age, esp. below legal age for voting or drinking

undercarriage ('undǝrkarij) n. landing gear of aircraft

undercoat ('undǝrkōt) n. coat of paint applied before top coat

undercover ('undǝrkuvǝr) a. done or acting in secret

undercurrent ('undǝrkurǝnt) n. 1. current that lies beneath another current 2. opinion, emotion etc. lying beneath apparent feeling or meaning

undercut (undǝr'kut) v. 1. charge less than (competitor) in order to obtain trade 2. cut

away under part of (something) 3. Sport hit (ball) in such a way as to impart backspin —n. ('undǝrkut) 4. act of cutting underneath 5. Sport stroke that imparts backspin to ball

underdeveloped (undǝrdi'velǝpt) a. 1. immature; undersized 2. relating to societies lacking economical and industrial development necessary to advance 3. Photog. (of film etc.) processed in developer for less than required time

underdog ('undǝrdog) n. 1. losing competitor in contest etc. 2. person in position of inferiority

underestimate (undǝr'estimāt) vt. 1. make too low an estimate of 2. think insufficiently highly of —n. (undǝr'estimit) 3. too low an estimate —underesti'mation n.

underexpose (undǝrik'spōz) vt. 1. Photog. expose (film etc.) for too short a period or with insufficient light 2. fail to subject to appropriate publicity —underex'posure n.

undergo (undǝr'gō) vt. experience, endure, sustain (-'went, -'gone, -'going)

undergraduate (undǝr'grajōōit) n. student member of university or college who has not taken degree

underground ('undǝrgrownd) a. 1. under the ground 2. secret —adv. (undǝr'grownd) 3. under earth's surface 4. secretly —n. 5. secret but organized resistance to government in power 6. railway system under the ground

undergrowth ('undǝrgrōth) n. small trees, bushes etc. growing beneath taller trees in wood or forest

underhand ('undǝrhand) a. 1. secret, sly 2. Sport of style of throwing, bowling or serving in which hand is swung below shoulder level

underlay (undǝr'lā) vt. 1. place (something) under or beneath 2. support by something laid beneath (-'laid, -'laying) —n. ('undǝrlā) 3. lining, support etc. laid underneath something else 4. felt, rubber etc. laid beneath carpet to increase insulation

underline ('undǝrlīn, undǝr'līn) vt. 1. put line under 2. emphasize

underling ('undǝrling) n. subordinate

underlying (undǝr'līing) a. 1. concealed but detectable 2. fundamental; basic 3. lying under

undermine (undǝr'mīn) vt. 1. wear away base, support of 2. weaken insidiously

underneath (undǝr'nēth) adv. 1. below —prep. 2. under —a. 3. lower —n. 4. lower part, surface etc.

underpass ('undǝrpas) n. section of road passing under another road, railroad line etc.

una'bated	unap'preciated	un'bind	un'christian	uncon'firmed	un'curl
una'bridged	unap'proachable	un'blemished	un'circumcised	uncon'nected	un'damaged
unac'ceptable	un'armed	un'blinking	un'civil	un'conquered	un'daunted
unac'companied	una'shamed	un'block	un'claimed	uncon'trollable	unde'cided
unac'customed	un'asked	un'bolt	un'clear	uncon'trolled	unde'feated
unac'knowledged	unat'tainable	un'born	un'clothe	uncontro'versial	unde'fended
unac'quainted	unat'tended	un'breakable	un'cluttered	uncon'ventional	unde'manding
una'dorned	unat'tractive	un'broken	un'coil	uncon'vincing	undemo'cratic
una'dulterated	un'authorized	un'buckle	un'combed	unco'operative	unde'monstrative
unad'venturous	una'vailable	uncared-for	un'comfortable	unco'ordinated	unde'niable
una'fraid	un'balanced	un'ceasing	uncom'mitted	un'cork	unde'served
un'aided	un'bearable	un'censored	un'common	uncor'roborated	unde'serving
unal'loyed	un'beaten	un'censured	uncom'municative	un'couple	unde'sirable
un'alterable	unbe'coming	un'certain	uncom'plaining	un'critical	unde'tected
unam'biguous	unbe'lievable	un'challenged	un'complicated	un'crowned	unde'terred
un'answerable	unbe'liever	uncharacte'ristic	uncompli'mentary	un'cultivated	unde'veloped
unap'pealing	unbe'lieving	un'charitable	uncon'cerned	un'cultured	undi'minished
un'appetizing	un'biased	un'checked	uncon'ditional	un'curbed	un'disciplined

underpin (undər'pin) *vt.* **1.** support from beneath, *esp.* by prop **2.** give corroboration or support to (-**nn**-)

underprivileged (undər'privilijd) *a.* lacking rights and advantages of other members of society

undershirt ('undərshərt) *n.* upper undergarment for males, usu. with short sleeves, worn between skin and shirt

underside ('undərsīd) *n.* bottom or lower surface

understand (undər'stand) *v.* **1.** know and comprehend **2.** realize —*vt.* **3.** infer **4.** take for granted (-'stood, -'standing) —**under'standable** *a.* —**under'standably** *adv.* —**under'standing** *n.* **1.** intelligence **2.** opinion **3.** agreement —*a.* **4.** sympathetic

understudy ('undərstudi) *n.* **1.** one prepared to take over theatrical part from performer if necessary —*vt.* **2.** act as understudy (to) or learn (part) thus

undertake (undər'tāk) *vt.* **1.** make oneself responsible for **2.** enter upon **3.** promise (-'took, -'taken, -'taking) —**under'taker** *n.* one who arranges funerals —**under'taking** *n.* **1.** that which is undertaken **2.** project **3.** guarantee

undertone ('undərtōn) *n.* **1.** quiet, dropped tone of voice **2.** underlying tone or suggestion

undertow ('undərtō) *n.* **1.** backwash of wave **2.** current beneath surface moving in different direction from surface current

underwear ('undərwāər) *n.* garments worn next to skin (*also* '**underclothes**)

underworld ('undərwərld) *n.* **1.** criminals and their associates **2.** *Myth.* abode of the dead

underwrite ('undərrīt, undər'rīt) *vt.* **1.** agree to pay **2.** accept liability in (insurance policy) (-'wrote, -'written, -'writing) —'**underwriter** *n.* **1.** one that underwrites **2.** agent for insurance company who assesses risks

undies ('undiz) *pl.n. inf.* women's underwear

undo (un'dōō) *vt.* **1.** untie, unfasten **2.** reverse **3.** cause downfall of (-'did, -'done, -'doing) —**un'doing** *n.* —**un'done** *a.* **1.** ruined **2.** not performed

undoubted (un'dowtid) *a.* certain; indisputable —**un'doubtedly** *adv.*

undue (un'dyōō, -'dōō) *a.* **1.** excessive **2.** improper; illegal —**un'duly** *adv.* immoderately

undulate ('unjəlāt) *v.* move up and down like waves —'**undulant** *a.* —**undu'lation** *n.* —'**undulatory** *a.* —**undulant fever** *see* BRUCELLOSIS

unearth (un'ərth) *vt.* **1.** dig up **2.** discover

unearthly (un'ərthli) *a.* **1.** ghostly; eerie **2.** heavenly; sublime **3.** ridiculous or unreasonable (*esp. in* **unearthly hour**) —**un'earthliness** *n.*

uneasy (un'ēzi) *a.* **1.** anxious **2.** uncomfortable

unemployed (unim'ploid) *a.* having no paid employment, out of work —**unem'ployment** *n.*

unerring (un'ering) *a.* **1.** not missing the mark **2.** consistently accurate

UNESCO (yōō'neskō) United Nations Educational, Scientific and Cultural Organization

unexceptionable (unik'sepshnəbəl, -shən-əbəl) *a.* beyond criticism or objection —**unex'ceptionably** *adv.*

unexceptional (unik'sepshnəl, -shənəl) *a.* **1.** ordinary or normal **2.** subject to or allowing no exceptions —**unex'ceptionally** *adv.*

unfortunate (un'fôrchənit) *a.* **1.** causing or attended by misfortune **2.** unlucky or unhappy **3.** regrettable; unsuitable —*n.* **4.** unlucky person —**un'fortunately** *adv.*

unfounded (un'fowndid) *a.* **1.** (of ideas, allegations *etc.*) baseless **2.** not yet established —**un'foundedly** *adv.*

unfrock (un'frok) *vt.* deprive (person in holy orders) of ecclesiastical status

ungainly (un'gānli) *a.* awkward, clumsy

unguarded (un'gärdid) *a.* **1.** unprotected; vulnerable **2.** open; frank **3.** incautious

unguent ('unggwənt) *n.* ointment

ungulate ('unggyəlit, 'un-gyəlit, -lāt) *n.* any of large group of mammals all of which have hooves

unhinge (un'hinj) *vt.* **1.** remove (door *etc.*) from its hinges **2.** unbalance (person, his mind *etc.*)

unholy (un'hōli) *a.* **1.** not holy or sacred **2.** immoral or depraved **3.** *inf.* outrageous; unnatural

uni- (*comb. form*) one, as in *unicorn*, *uniform*. Such words are not given here where the meanings may easily be inferred from the simple word

UNICEF ('yōōnisef) United Nations International Children's Emergency Fund

unicellular (yōōni'selyələr) *a.* (of organisms and certain algae) consisting of single cell —**unicellu'larity** *n.*

unicorn ('yōōnikörn) *n.* mythical horselike animal with single long horn

uniform ('yōōnifôrm) *n.* **1.** identifying clothing worn by members of same group, *eg* soldiers, nurses *etc.* —*a.* **2.** not changing, unvarying **3.** regular, consistent **4.** conforming to same standard or rule —**uni'formity** *n.* sameness —'**uniformly** *adv.*

Uniform ('yōōnifôrm) *n.* word used in communications for the letter *u*

unify ('yōōnifī) *v.* make or become one (-**ified, -ifying**) —**unifi'cation** *n.* —**Unification Church** religious sect founded by Rev. Sun Myung Moon, S Korean industrialist and religious leader

unilateral (yōōni'latərəl) *a.* **1.** one-sided **2.** (of contract) binding one party only —**uni'laterally** *adv.*

unimpeachable (unim'pēchəbəl) *a.* unquestionable as to honesty, truth *etc.*

union ('yōōnyən) *n.* **1.** joining into one **2.** state of being joined **3.** result of being joined **4.** federation, combination of societies *etc.* **5.** labor union **6.** in set theory, the set containing all the members of two given sets only —'**unionism** *n.* —'**unionist** *n.* supporter of union —'**unionize** *v.* organize (workers) into labor union —**Union Jack** national flag of United Kingdom

Union of Soviet Socialist Republics country in Europe and Asia bounded north by the Arctic Ocean, east by the Pacific Ocean, south by China, Mongolia, Afghanistan, Iran, Turkey, the Black Sea, Romania and Hungary and west by Czechoslovakia, Poland, the Baltic Sea, Finland and Norway

unique (yōō'nēk) *a.* **1.** being only one of its kind **2.** unparalleled

unisex ('yōōniseks) *a.* of clothing, hairstyle, hairdressers *etc.* that can be worn or used by either sex

unison ('yōōnisən) *n.* **1.** *Mus.* singing *etc.* of same note as others **2.** agreement, harmony, concord

unit ('yōōnit) *n.* **1.** single thing or person **2.** standard quantity **3.** group of people or things with one purpose —**Uni'tarian** *n.* member of Christian body that denies doctrine of the Trinity —**Uni'tarianism** *n.* —'**unitary** *a.*

unite (yōō'nīt) *vt.* **1.** join into one, connect **2.** associate **3.** cause to adhere —*vi.* **4.** become one **5.** combine —'**unity** *n.* **1.** state of being one **2.** harmony **3.** agreement, uniformity **4.** combination of separate parts into connected whole **5.** *Math.* the number one —**United Church of Christ** Protestant Christian denomination created by ecumenical union in 1957 of Congregationalist, Evangelical and Reformed Churches representing both Calvinist and Lutheran traditions —**United Empire Loyalist** American colonist who settled in Canada during American Revolution from loyalty to Britain —**United Nations Organization** organization formed in 1945 to promote peace and international cooperation

United Arab Emirates (i'mēərits, ä'mēərits) country in Middle East bounded

---

undis'covered	unex'plained	un'freeze	unhy'gienic	uninter'rupted	unlooked-for
undis'puted	un'failing	un'furl	uni'dentified	unin'vited	un'lucky
undis'turbed	un'fair	un'godly	uni'maginable	unin'viting	un'made
un'drinkable	un'faithful	un'governable	uni'maginative	un'justified	un'make
un'dying	unfa'miliar	un'gracious	unim'paired	un'kind	un'manageable
un'earned	un'fashionable	ungram'matical	unim'portant	un'known	un'manned
un'eatable	un'fasten	un'grateful	unim'pressed	un'labeled	un'mannerly
uneco'nomic	un'fathomable	un'hallowed	unin'formed	un'ladylike	un'marked
un'educated	un'favorable	un'happy	unin'habited	un'lawful	un'married
une'motional	un'feeling	un'harmed	unin'hibited	un'learned	un'mask
un'ending	un'feigned	un'healthy	un'injured	un'leash	un'mentionable
un'equal	un'finished	un'heard	unin'spired	un'lettered	un'merciful
un'equaled	un'fit	unheard-of	unin'sured	un'like	un'merited
une'quivocal	un'flinching	un'heated	unin'telligent	un'likely	unmis'takable
un'ethical	un'fold	un'heeded	unin'telligible	un'limited	un'moved
un'even	unfore'seen	un'helpful	unin'tended	un'lined	un'musical
une'ventful	unfor'gettable	un'hurried	unin'tentional	un'load	un'named
unex'pected	unfor'givable	un'hurt	un'interesting	un'lock	unneces'sarily

north by the Persian Gulf, east by Oman, south and west by Saudi Arabia and northwest by Qatar

United Kingdom of Great Britain and Northern Ireland country lying in N Atlantic comprising England, Scotland and Wales occupying the island of Great Britain and the northeast portion of the smaller of the British Isles in which is located Northern Ireland, bounded south and west by the Republic of Ireland

United States of America country in North America bounded north by Canada, east by the Atlantic, south by the Gulf of Mexico, the Rio Grande and Mexico and west by the Pacific

Univ. University

univalent (yōōni'vālənt) a. 1. (of chromosome during meiosis) not paired with its homologue 2. *Chem. see* MONOVALENT —**uni-'valency** n.

universe ('yōōnivərs) n. 1. all existing things considered as constituting systematic whole 2. human beings collectively —**uni'versal** a. 1. relating to all things or all people 2. applying to all members of a community —**univer'sality** n. —**uni'versally** adv. —**Universal Copyright Convention** agreement formulated in 1952 under auspices of UNESCO for reciprocal protection of copyright among contracting states. The symbol ⓒ is used to indicate that the work concerned is protected (*also* **Geneva Convention, UNESCO Convention**) —**universal joint** or **coupling** form of coupling between two rotating shafts allowing freedom of movement in all directions

university (yōōni'vərsiti) n. educational institution with teaching and research facilities comprising graduate and professional schools awarding master's degrees and doctorates and an undergraduate division awarding bachelor's degrees

unjust (un'just) a. not in accordance with accepted standards of justice; unfair —**un-'justly** adv.

unkempt (un'kempt) a. of rough or uncared-for appearance

unless (un'les) conj. except under the circumstances that

unloose (un'lōōs) or **unloosen** vt. 1. release 2. loosen (hold, grip etc.) 3. unfasten, untie

unman (un'man) vt. 1. cause to lose nerve etc. 2. make effeminate 3. remove men from (**-nn-**)

unmitigated (un'mitigātid) a. not diminished in intensity, severity etc.

unnatural (un'nachərəl) a. 1. abnormal 2. not in accordance with accepted standards

of behavior 3. uncanny; supernatural 4. affected, forced 5. inhuman, monstrous —**un'naturally** adv.

unnerve (un'nərv) vt. cause to lose courage, confidence etc.

unparalleled (un'parəleld) a. unequaled

unprincipled (un'prinsipəld) a. lacking moral precepts

unquote (un'kwōt) interj. expression used parenthetically to indicate that preceding quotation is finished

unravel (un'ravəl) vt. undo, untangle

unread (un'red) a. 1. (of book etc.) not yet read 2. (of person) having read little

unregenerate (unri'jenərit) a. 1. unrepentant 2. obstinately adhering to one's own views —**unre'generacy** n. —**unre'generately** adv.

unremitting (unri'miting) a. never slackening or stopping

unrest (un'rest) n. troubled or rebellious state of discontent

unroll (un'rōl) v. 1. open out (something rolled or folded) or (of something rolled etc.) become unwound —vi. 2. become visible or apparent, esp. gradually

unruly (un'rōōli) a. badly behaved, ungovernable, disorderly

unsaturated (un'sachərātid) a. 1. not saturated 2. (of chemical compound, esp. organic compound) containing one or more double or triple bonds and thus capable of undergoing addition reactions —**unsatu'ration** n.

unsavory (un'sāvəri) a. distasteful, disagreeable

unsightly (un'sītli) a. ugly

unspeakable (un'spēkəbəl) a. 1. incapable of expression in words 2. indescribably bad or evil 3. not to be uttered —**un'speakably** adv.

unstructured (un'strukchərd) a. without formal or systematic organization

unstrung (un'strung) a. 1. emotionally distressed 2. (of stringed instrument) with strings detached

unstudied (un'studid) a. 1. natural 2. (*with* in) without knowledge or training

unsung (un'sung) a. 1. not acclaimed or honored 2. not yet sung

untenable (un'tenəbəl) a. (of theories etc.) incapable of being maintained, defended

unthinkable (un'thingkəbəl) a. 1. out of the question 2. inconceivable 3. unreasonable

untie (un'tī) v. 1. unfasten or free (knot or something that is tied) or (of knot etc.) become unfastened —vt. 2. free from restriction (**-'tied, -'tying**)

until (un'til) conj. 1. to the time that 2. (with a negative) before —prep. 3. up to the time of

unto ('untə, 'untōō) prep. obs. to

untold (un'tōld) a. 1. incapable of description 2. incalculably great in number or quantity 3. not told

untouched (un'tucht) a. 1. not touched 2. not harmed —**un'touchable** a. 1. not able to be touched —n. 2. esp. formerly, noncaste Hindu, forbidden to be touched by one of caste

untoward (un'tōrd, 'untōrd, untə'wörd) a. awkward, inconvenient

unutterable (un'utərəbəl) a. incapable of being expressed in words —**un'utterably** adv.

unwell (un'wel) a. not well, ill

unwieldy (un'wēldi) a. 1. awkward, big, heavy to handle 2. clumsy

unwitting (un'witing) a. 1. not knowing 2. not intentional

up (up) prep. 1. from lower to higher position 2. along —adv. 3. in or to higher position, source, activity etc. 4. indicating completion ('**upper** comp., '**uppermost** sup.) —'**upward** a./adv. —'**upwards** or '**upward** adv. —**up-and-coming** a. promising continued or future success; enterprising —'**uphill** a. 1. inclining; sloping 2. requiring protracted effort —adv. 3. up incline or slope 4. against difficulties —n. 5. rising incline —**up-to-date** a. modern; fashionable —**up against** confronted with

up- (comb. form) up, upper, upward, as in uproot, upgrade. Such words are not given here where the meaning may easily be inferred from the simple word

upbeat (upbēt) n. 1. Mus. unaccented beat; upward gesture of conductor's baton indicating this —a. 2. inf. cheerful; optimistic

upbraid (up'brād) vt. scold, reproach

upbringing ('upbringing) n. rearing and education of children

update (up'dāt) vt. bring up to date

upgrade ('upgrād, up'grād) vt. 1. promote to higher position 2. improve — n. ('upgrād) 3. upward slope

upheaval (up'hēvəl) n. sudden or violent disturbance

uphold (up'hōld) vt. 1. maintain 2. support (**up'held, up'holding**)

upholster (up'hōlstər) vt. fit springs, padding and coverings on (chairs etc.) —**up'holsterer** n. —**up'holstery** n.

upkeep ('upkēp) n. act, process or cost of keeping something in good repair

upland ('uplənd) n. high land

---

un'necessary	un'pleasant	un'qualified	un'saddle	un'sheathe	unsub'stantiated
un'noticed	un'pleasing	un'questionable	un'safe	un'skilled	unsuc'cessful
unob'servant	un'plumbed	un'real	un'said	un'skillful	un'suitable
unob'served	un'popular	unrea'listic	un'salable	un'sociable	un'sure
unob'tainable	un'practiced	un'reasonable	unsatis'factory	un'social	unsur'passed
unob'trusive	un'precedented	un'registered	un'scathed	unso'licited	unsus'pected
un'occupied	unpre'dictable	unre'lenting	un'scheduled	un'solved	unsus'pecting
unof'ficial	unpre'pared	unre'liable	unscien'tific	unso'phisticated	un'sweetened
un'opened	unprepos'sessing	unre'pentant	un'scramble	un'sound	unsympa'thetic
unop'posed	unpre'tentious	unrepre'sentative	un'screw	un'sparing	unsyste'matic
un'organized	un'printable	unre'quited	un'scrupulous	un'specified	un'tainted
un'orthodox	unpro'ductive	unre'served	un'seasonable	un'spoken	un'tamed
un'pack	unpro'fessional	unre'solved	un'seat	un'sporting	un'tangle
un'paid	un'profitable	unre'strained	un'seemly	un'stable	un'tapped
un'pardonable	un'promising	un'righteous	unself'conscious	un'steady	un'taught
un'pick	unpro'pitious	un'ripe	un'selfish	un'stinted	un'taxed
un'pin	unpro'tected	un'rivaled	un'settle	un'string	un'thinking
un'playable	unpro'voked	un'ruffled	un'shakable	un'stuffy	un'throne

uplift (up'lift) *vt.* **1.** raise aloft —*n.* ('uplift) **2.** a lifting up **3.** mental, social or emotional improvement —*a.* ('uplift) **4.** designating brassiere for lifting and supporting breasts

upon (ə'pon) *prep.* on

upper ('upər) *a. comp. of* UP **1.** higher, situated above —*n.* **2.** upper part of boot or shoe —'**uppermost** *a. sup. of* UP —**upper-case** *a.* of or relating to capital letters used in setting or production of printed or typed matter —'**uppercut** *n.* short-arm upward blow —**the upper hand** position of control

uppish ('upish) *a. inf.* **1.** self-assertive **2.** arrogant **3.** affectedly superior

upright ('uprīt) *a.* **1.** erect **2.** honest, just —*adv.* **3.** vertically —*n.* **4.** thing standing upright, *eg* post in framework **5.** upright piano —**upright piano** piano with rectangular vertical case

uprising ('uprīzing) *n.* rebellion, revolt

uproar ('uprör) *n.* tumult, disturbance —up'**roarious** *a.* rowdy —up'**roariously** *adv.*

uproot (up'rōōt) *vt.* **1.** pull up by or as if by the roots **2.** displace (person or persons) from native or habitual surroundings

upset (up'set) *vt.* **1.** overturn **2.** distress **3.** disrupt **4.** make ill (up'set, up'setting) —*n.* ('upset) **5.** unexpected defeat **6.** confusion **7.** trouble **8.** overturning

upshot ('upshot) *n.* outcome, end

upside down ('upsīd) **1.** turned over completely; inverted **2.** in disorder or chaos

upsilon ('yōōpsilon, 'upsilon) *n.* 20th letter in Gr. alphabet (Υ, υ), vowel transliterated as *y* or *u*

upstage ('up'stāj) *a.* **1.** of back of stage —*vt.* (up'stāj) **2.** *inf.* draw attention away from (another) to oneself

upstanding (up'standing) *a.* **1.** of good character **2.** upright and vigorous in build

upstart ('upstärt) *n.* one suddenly raised to wealth, power *etc.*

uptake ('uptāk) *n.* **1.** shaft *etc.* used to convey smoke or gases, *esp.* one that connects furnace to chimney **2.** lifting up —**quick** (*or* **slow**) **on the uptake** *inf.* quick (or slow) to understand or learn

uptight ('up'tīt) *a. inf.* **1.** displaying tense nervousness, irritability **2.** repressed

upturn ('uptərn, up'tərn) *v.* **1.** turn or cause to turn over or upside down —*vt.* **2.** create disorder in **3.** direct upward —*n.* ('uptərn) **4.** upward trend or improvement

uranium (yōō'rāniəm) *n. Chem.* metallic element *Symbol* U, at. wt. 238.0, at. no. 92

urban ('ərbən) *a.* relating to town or city —'**urbanize** *vt.* change (countryside) to residential or industrial area

---

un'tidy	un'warranted
un'timely	un'wary
un'trained	un'washed
un'troubled	un'wavering
un'true	un'welcome
un'trustworthy	un'wept
un'truthful	un'wholesome
un'tutored	un'willing
un'twist	un'wind
un'typical	un'wise
un'usable	un'workable
un'used	un'worldly
un'usual	un'worn
un'utilized	un'worthy
un'veil	un'wrap
un'verified	un'written
un'voiced	un'yielding
un'wanted	un'zip

urbane (ər'bān) *a.* elegant, sophisticated —**urbanity** (ər'baniti) *n.*

urchin ('ərchin) *n.* mischievous, unkempt child

Urdu ('ōōərdōō, 'ər-) *n.* official language of Pakistan, belonging to Indic branch of Indo-European family of languages, closely related to Hindi

urea (yōō'rēə) *n.* product of animal (including human) metabolism excreted in urine

ureter ('yōō'ritər) *n.* tube that conveys urine from kidney to urinary bladder or cloaca —**ureteral** (yōō'rētərəl) *or* **ureteric** (yōōri'terik) *a.*

urethra (yōō'rēthrə) *n.* canal conveying urine from bladder out of body (*pl.* -**thrae** (-thrē), -**s**)

urge (ərj) *vt.* **1.** exhort earnestly **2.** entreat **3.** drive on —*n.* **4.** strong desire —'**urgency** *n.* —'**urgent** *a.* **1.** pressing **2.** needing attention at once —'**urgently** *adv.*

urine ('yōōrin) *n.* fluid excreted by kidneys to bladder and passed as waste from body —**u'remia** *n.* urine in the blood —'**uric** *a.* —'**urinal** *n.* (place with) sanitary fitting(s) used by men for urination —'**urinary** *a.* —'**urinate** *vi.* discharge urine —**uri'nation** *n.* —**uric acid** compound manufactured in tissues from proteins and purines and excreted by most vertebrates and some lower animals —**urinary bladder** muscular sac located in lower part of abdomen which collects and stores urine

urn (ərn) *n.* **1.** vessel like vase, *esp.* for ashes of the dead **2.** large container with tap for making and dispensing tea, coffee *etc.*

urogenital (yōōrō'jenitəl) *a.* of urinary and genital organs and their functions (*also* **genito'urinary**)

Ursa Major ('ərsə 'mājər) extensive conspicuous constellation in N hemisphere. The seven brightest stars form Great Bear or Big Dipper

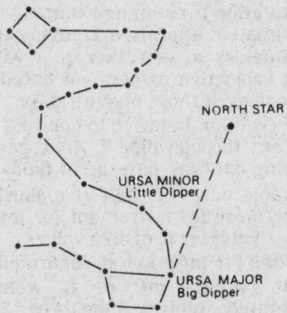

Ursa Minor ('ərsə 'mīnər) small faint constellation, brightest star of which is Pole Star (*also* **Little Bear, Little Dipper**)

ursine ('ərsīn) *a.* of, like a bear

Uruguay ('yōōrəgwī, -gwā; 'ōōrəgwī) *n.* country in South America bounded northeast by Brazil, southeast by the Atlantic, south by the Río de la Plata and west by Argentina —**Uru'guayan** *n./a.*

Urundi (ōō'rōōndi) *n. former name of* BURUNDI

us (us) *pron. pl.* the objective case of WE

U.S. United States

U.S.A. United States of America

U.S.C.G. United States Coast Guard

use (yōōz) *vt.* **1.** employ, avail oneself of **2.** exercise **3.** exploit **4.** consume —*n.* (yōōs) **5.** employment, application to a purpose **6.** need to employ **7.** serviceableness **8.** profit **9.** habit —'**usable** *or* '**useable** *a.* fit for use

—**usage** ('yōōsij, -zij) *n.* **1.** act of using **2.** custom **3.** customary way of using —**used** *a.* second-hand, not new —**useful** ('yōōsfəl) *a.* **1.** of use **2.** helpful **3.** serviceable —**usefully** ('yōōsfəli) *adv.* —**usefulness** ('yōōsfəlnis) *n.* —**useless** ('yōōslis) *a.* —**uselessly** ('yōōslisli) *adv.* —**uselessness** ('yōōslisnis) *n.* —**user-friendly** *a.* (of computers) easy to operate —**used to** (yōōst) *a.* **1.** accustomed to —*vt.* **2.** did so formerly

usher ('ushər) *n.* **1.** doorkeeper, one showing people to seats *etc.* (**ushe'rette** *fem.*) —*vt.* **2.** introduce, announce **3.** inaugurate

U.S.I.A. United States Information Agency

U.S.M.C. United States Marine Corps

U.S.S.R. Union of Soviet Socialist Republics

usual ('yōōzhōōəl) *a.* habitual, ordinary —'**usually** *adv.* **1.** as a rule **2.** generally, commonly

usurp (yōō'sərp, -'zərp) *vt.* seize wrongfully —**usur'pation** *n.* violent or unlawful seizing of power —**u'surper** *n.*

usury ('yōōzhəri) *n.* **1.** lending of money at excessive interest **2.** such interest —'**usurer** *n.* moneylender —**u'surious** *a.*

Utah ('yōōtö) *n.* Mountain state of the U.S., admitted to the Union in 1896. Abbrev.: **UT** (with ZIP code)

Ute (yōōt) *n.* **1.** member of Amerindian people *orig.* ranging through Utah, Colorado, Arizona and New Mexico (*pl.* **Ute, -s**) **2.** the language of this people (of Uto-Aztecan phylum)

utensil (yōō'tensəl) *n.* vessel, implement, *esp.* in domestic use

uterus ('yōōtərəs) *n.* womb (*pl.* **uteri** ('yōōtərī)) —**uterine** ('yōōtərīn) *a.* of the uterus

utilidor (yōō'tilədər; *Canad.* -dör) *n.* C above-ground insulated casing for pipes

utility (yōō'tiliti) *n.* **1.** usefulness **2.** benefit **3.** useful thing —*a.* **4.** made for practical purposes —**utili'tarian** *a.* **1.** useful rather than beautiful **2.** of utilitarianism —*n.* **3.** believer in utilitarianism —**utili'tarianism** *n.* doctrine that morality of actions is to be tested by their utility, *esp.* that the greatest good of the greatest number should be the sole end of public action —**utili'zation** *n.* —'**utilize** *vt.* make use of —**utility room** room used for storage, laundry *etc.*

utmost ('utmōst) *or* **uttermost** *a.* **1.** to the highest degree **2.** extreme, furthest —*n.* **3.** greatest possible amount

Uto-Aztecan (yōōtō'aztekən) *n.* Amerindian language family spoken throughout the Amer. southwest and Mexico

Utopia (yōō'tōpiə) *n.* (*sometimes* **u-**) imaginary state with perfect political and social conditions or constitution —U'**topian** *a.* (*sometimes* **u-**) ideally perfect but impracticable

utter[1] ('utər) *vt.* **1.** express, emit audibly, say **2.** put in circulation (forged bank notes, counterfeit coin) —'**utterance** *n.* **1.** act of speaking **2.** expression in words **3.** spoken words

utter[2] ('utər) *a.* complete, total, absolute —'**utterly** *adv.*

uttermost ('utərmōst) *see* UTMOST

U-turn *n.* **1.** U-shaped turn by vehicle in order to go in opposite direction **2.** reversal of political policy

U.V. ultraviolet

uvula ('yōōvyələ) *n.* pendent fleshy part of soft palate (*pl.* -**lae** (-lē), -**s**) —'**uvular** *a.*

uxorious (uk'söriəs) *a.* excessively fond of one's wife

V v

v or **V** (vē) n. **1.** 22nd letter of English alphabet **2.** speech sound represented by this letter, as in *vote* **3.** something shaped like V (*pl.* **v's, V's** or **Vs**)

v volt

V *Chem.* vanadium

v. 1. verb **2.** verse **3.** versus **4.** very **5.** vide

V-1 *n.* flying robot bomb invented by Germans in World War II (*also* **'doodlebug, 'buzzbomb**)

VA 1. Veterans Administration **2.** Virginia

vacant ('vākənt) *a.* **1.** without thought, empty **2.** unoccupied —**'vacancy** *n.* **1.** state of being unoccupied **2.** unfilled post, accommodation *etc.* —**'vacantly** *adv.*

vacate ('vākāt, vā'kāt) *vt.* quit, leave empty —**va'cation** *n.* **1.** time when universities and law courts are closed **2.** period in which break is taken from work or studies, for rest, travel or recreation **3.** act of vacating — *vi.* **4.** take or spend vacation

vaccinate ('vaksināt) *vt.* inoculate with vaccine as protection against a specific disease —**vacci'nation** *n.* —**'vaccinator** *n.* —**vaccine** (vak'sēn, 'vaksēn) *n.* treated microorganisms used for immunization

vacillate ('vasilāt) *vi.* **1.** fluctuate in opinion **2.** waver **3.** move to and fro —**vacil'lation** *n.* **1.** indecision **2.** wavering **3.** unsteadiness

vacuum ('vakyŏŏm) *n.* **1.** place, region containing no matter and from which all or most air, gas has been removed (*pl.* **-s, -ua** (-yŏŏə)) —*v.* **2.** clean with vacuum cleaner —**va'cuity** *n.* —**'vacuous** *a.* **1.** vacant **2.** expressionless **3.** unintelligent —**vacuum bottle** double-walled cylinder with vacuum between walls, for keeping contents of inner flask at temperature at which they were inserted —**vacuum cleaner** apparatus for removing dust by suction —**vacuum-packed** *a.* packed in airtight container to maintain freshness *etc.* —**vacuum pump** pump for producing low gas pressure —**vacuum tube** or **valve** part of radio or television which controls flow of current

vade mecum ('vādi 'mēkəm, 'vādi 'mākəm) handbook *etc.* carried on person for immediate use when needed

vagabond ('vagəbond) *n.* **1.** person with no fixed home **2.** wandering beggar or thief —*a.* **3.** like a vagabond

vagary ('vāgəri, və'gāəri) *n.* **1.** something unusual, erratic **2.** whim

vagina (və'jīnə) *n.* passage from womb to exterior —**vaginal** ('vajinəl) *a.*

vagrant ('vāgrənt) *n.* **1.** vagabond —*a.* **2.** wandering, *esp.* without purpose —**'vagrancy** *n.*

vague (vāg) *a.* **1.** indefinite, uncertain **2.** indistinct **3.** not clearly expressed **4.** absent-minded

vain (vān) *a.* **1.** conceited **2.** worthless, useless **3.** unavailing **4.** foolish —**'vainly** *adv.*

vainglory ('vān-glöri, vān'glöri) *n.* boastfulness, vanity —**vain'glorious** *a.*

valance ('valəns) *n.* **1.** short curtain round base of bed *etc.* **2.** short frame or piece of fabric used to conceal curtain fixtures

vale (vāl) *n.* *Poet.* valley

valediction (vali'dikshən) *n.* farewell —**valedic'torian** *n.* student, usu. one ranking highest in the graduating class, who delivers the valedictory at commencement exercises —**vale'dictory** *n.* **1.** farewell address —*a.* **2.** parting, farewell

valency ('vālənsi) or **valence** ('vāləns) *n.* *Chem.* combining power of element or atom

valentine ('valəntīn) *n.* (one receiving) card, gift, expressing affection on Saint Valentine's Day, Feb. 14th

valet ('valit, 'valā) *n.* gentleman's personal servant

valetudinarian (valityŏŏdi'neriən, -tŏŏ-) or **valetudinary** (vali'tyŏŏdineri, -'tŏŏ-) *a.* **1.** sickly **2.** infirm —*n.* **3.** person obliged or disposed to live the life of an invalid

valiant ('valyənt) *a.* brave, courageous

valid ('valid) *a.* **1.** sound **2.** capable of being justified **3.** of binding force in law —**va'lidity** *n.* **1.** soundness **2.** power to convince **3.** legal force —**'validate** *vt.* make valid

valise (və'lēs) *n.* traveling bag

valley ('vali) *n.* **1.** low area between hills **2.** river basin

valor ('valər) *n.* bravery —**'valorous** *a.*

value ('valyŏŏ) *n.* **1.** desirability of a thing, oft. in respect of usefulness, exchangeability *etc.* **2.** utility **3.** equivalent **4.** importance —*pl.* **5.** principles, standards —*vt.* **6.** estimate value of **7.** hold in respect **8.** prize —**'valuable** *a.* **1.** precious **2.** worthy **3.** capable of being valued —*n.* **4.** (*usu. pl.*) valuable thing —**valu'ation** *n.* estimated worth —**'valued** *a.* **1.** estimated; appraised **2.** highly thought of —**'valueless** *a.* —**'valuer** *n.* —**value judgment** subjective assessment based on one's own values or those of one's class

valve (valv) *n.* **1.** device to control passage of fluid *etc.* through pipe **2.** *Anat.* part of body allowing one-way passage of fluids **3.** any of separable parts of shell of mollusk **4.** *Mus.* device on brass instrument for lengthening tube —**'valvular** *a.* of, like valves

vamoose (və'mŏŏs) *vi. sl.* depart quickly

vamp¹ (vamp) *inf. n.* **1.** woman who deliberately allures men —*v.* **2.** exploit (man) as vamp

vamp² (vamp) *n.* **1.** something patched up **2.** front part of shoe upper —*vt.* **3.** patch up, rework

vampire ('vampīər) *n.* **1.** in folklore, corpse that rises from dead to drink blood of the living **2.** bat that sucks blood of animals

van¹ (van) *n.* **1.** covered vehicle, *esp.* for goods **2.** detachable, transportable structure; passenger cabin

van² (van) *n.* vanguard

vanadium (və'nādiəm) *n.* *Chem.* metallic element *Symbol* V, at. wt. 51.0, at. no. 23

Van Buren (van 'byŏŏrən) **Martin.** the 8th President of the U.S. (1837-41)

vandal ('vandəl) *n.* one who wantonly and deliberately damages or destroys —**'vandalism** *n.* —**'vandalize** *vt.*

Vandyke beard (van'dīk) short pointed beard (*also* **Van'dyke**)

vane (vān) *n.* **1.** flate plate or blade of metal mounted on vertical axis in exposed position to indicate wind direction **2.** blade of propeller **3.** fin on bomb *etc.* **4.** sight on quadrant

vanguard ('van-gärd) *n.* leading, foremost group, position *etc.*

vanilla (və'nilə) *n.* **1.** tropical climbing orchid **2.** its seed (pod) **3.** essence of this for flavoring

vanish ('vanish) *vi.* **1.** disappear **2.** fade away —**vanishing act 1.** unannounced or unauthorized disappearance **2.** illusion by magician —**vanishing cream** cosmetic cream that is colorless once applied, used as foundation or cleansing cream —**vanishing point 1.** point to which parallel lines appear to converge **2.** point at which something disappears

vanity ('vaniti) *n.* **1.** excessive pride or conceit **2.** ostentation —**vanity case** woman's small hand case for carrying cosmetics *etc.* —**vanity plate** *inf.* automobile license plate bearing owner's name or other distinctive word —**vanity press** publishing house that publishes books at the author's expense

vanquish ('vangkwish) *vt.* **1.** subdue in battle **2.** conquer, overcome —**vanquishable** *a.* —**'vanquisher** *n.*

vantage ('vantij) *n.* advantage

Vanuatu (vanŏŏ'ätŏŏ) *n.* country lying in S Pacific roughly 500 miles west of Fiji and 1100 miles east of Australia

vapid ('vapid) *a.* flat, dull, insipid —**va'pidity** *n.*

vapor ('vāpər) *n.* **1.** gaseous form of a substance more familiar as liquid or solid **2.** steam, mist **3.** invisible moisture in air —**'vaporize** *v.* convert into, pass off in, vapor —**'vaporizer** *n.* —**'vaporous** *a.*

variable ('veriəbəl, 'var-) *see* VARY

varicella (vari'selə) *n. see* **chickenpox** at CHICK

varicose ('varikōs) *a.* (of vein) denoting dilation caused by failure of valves in the vein

variegate ('veriəgāt, 'verigāt, 'var-) *vt.* diversify by patches of different colors —**'variegated** *a.* streaked, spotted, dappled —**varie'gation** *n.*

variety (və'rīiti) *n.* **1.** state of being varied or various **2.** diversity **3.** varied assortment **4.** sort, kind

variola (veri'ōlə, vari-; və'rīələ) *n.* smallpox or cowpox

various ('veriəs, 'var-) *a.* manifold, diverse, of several kinds

varlet ('värlit) *n.* formerly, menial servant, rascal

varmint ('värmint) *n. inf.* obnoxious person or animal

varnish ('värnish) *n.* **1.** resinous solution put on a surface to make it hard and shiny —*vt.* **2.** apply varnish to

varsity ('värsiti) *n.* main athletic team of school, college or university

vary ('veəri) *v.* (cause to) change, diversify, differ, deviate (**'varied, 'varying**) —**vari'ability** *n.* —**'variable** *a.* **1.** changeable **2.** unsteady; fickle —*n.* **3.** something subject to

variation —'**variance** *n.* state of discord, discrepancy —'**variant** *a.* 1. different —*n.* 2. difference in form 3. alternative form or reading —**vari'ation** *n.* 1. alteration 2. extent to which thing varies 3. modification —**vari'ational** *a.* —'**varied** *a.* 1. diverse 2. modified 3. variegated

vas (vas) *n. Anat.* vessel, tube carrying bodily fluid (*pl.* **vasa** ('vāzə)) —**vas deferens** ('defərənz, -renz) duct within each testis that conveys spermatozoa to ejaculatory duct (*pl.* **vasa deferentia** (defə'renchiə))

vascular ('vaskyələr) *a.* of, with vessels for conveying sap, blood *etc.*

vase (vās) *n.* vessel, jar as ornament or for holding flowers

vasectomy (və'sektəmi) *n.* surgical removal of part of vas bearing sperm from testicle

Vaseline ('vasilēn) *n.* trade name for jelly-like petroleum product

vasoconstrictor (vāzōkən'striktər) *n.* drug which constricts the blood vessels

vasodilator (vāzōdī'lātər, -di-) *n.* drug that expands blood vessels

vasopressin (vāzō'presin) *n.* hormone of pituitary gland which helps control volume of urine production (*also* **pitressin**)

vassal ('vasəl) *n.* 1. holder of land by feudal tenure 2. dependent —'**vassalage** *n.*

vast (vast) *a.* very large —'**vastly** *adv.* —'**vastness** *n.*

vat (vat) *n.* large tub, tank

Vatican City State ('vatikən) sovereign state forming an enclave in Rome under the absolute powers of the Pope —'**Vatican** *n.* 1. Pope's palace 2. papal authority

vaudeville ('vōdəvil, 'vōdvil; 'vod-, 'vōd-) *n.* theatrical entertainment with songs, juggling acts, dance *etc.*

vault

vault[1] (vōlt) *n.* 1. arched roof 2. arched apartment 3. cellar 4. burial chamber 5. place for storing valuables —*vt.* 6. build with arched roof —'**vaulting** *n.* one or more vaults in building or such structures collectively

vault[2] (vōlt) *v.* 1. spring, jump over (object) with the hands resting on something —*n.* 2. such jump —'**vaulting** *a.* 1. excessively confident 2. used to vault

vaunt (vônt) *v./n.* boast

vb. verb

VC Vietcong

VCR video cassette recorder

VD venereal disease

V Day day of victory

VDU visual display unit

veal (vēl) *n.* calf flesh as food

vector ('vektər) *n.* 1. quantity (*eg* force) having both magnitude and direction 2. disease-carrying organism, *esp.* insect 3. compass direction, course

veer (vēər) *vi.* 1. change direction 2. change one's mind

vegan ('vējən, -an; 'vēgən) *n.* strict vegetarian, who does not eat animal products

vegetable ('vejtəbəl) *n.* 1. plant, *esp.* edible one 2. *inf.* person who has lost use of his mental faculties, limbs *etc.* 3. *inf.* dull person —*a.* 4. of, from, concerned with plants —**vegetable oil** any of group of oils obtained from plants —**vegetable oyster** salsify

vegetarian (veji'teriən) *n.* 1. one who does not eat meat —*a.* 2. not eating meat; without meat —**vege'tarianism** *n.*

vegetate ('vejitāt) *vi.* 1. (of plants) grow, develop 2. (of person) live dull, unproductive life —**vege'tation** *n.* 1. plants collectively 2. plants growing in a place 3. process of plant growth —'**vegetative** *a.*

vehement ('vēimənt) *a.* 1. marked by intensity of feeling 2. vigorous 3. forcible —'**vehemence** *n.* —'**vehemently** *adv.*

vehicle ('vēikəl, 'vēhikəl) *n.* 1. means of conveying 2. means of expression 3. medium —**vehicular** (vē'hikyələr) *a.*

veil (vāl) *n.* 1. light material to cover face or head 2. mask, cover —*vt.* 3. cover with, as with, veil —**veiled** *a.* disguised —**take the veil** become a nun

vein (vān) *n.* 1. tube in body taking blood to heart 2. rib of leaf or insect's wing 3. fissure in rock filled with ore 4. streak 5. distinctive trait, strain *etc.* 6. mood —*vt.* 7. mark with streaks —'**veiny** *a.* —**venation** (ve'nāshən, vē-) *n.* 1. arrangement of veins in leaf *etc.* 2. such veins collectively —'**venous** *a.* of veins

Velcro ('velkrō) *n.* trade name for fastening consisting of two strips of nylon fabric, one having tiny hooked threads and the other a coarse surface, that form strong bond when pressed together

veld *or* **veldt** (velt, felt) *n.* elevated grassland in S Afr. —**veldskoen** ('veltskōōn, 'felt-) *n.* **SA** ankle-length boot *orig.* of raw hide

vellum ('veləm) *n.* 1. parchment of calfskin used for manuscripts or bindings 2. paper resembling this

velocipede (vi'losipēd) *n.* early form of bicycle

velocity (vi'lositi) *n.* 1. rate of motion in given direction 2. speed

velodrome ('vēlədrōm, 'vel-) *n.* area with banked track for cycle racing

velour *or* **velours** (və'lōōər) *n.* 1. fabric with velvety finish 2. fur felt with long nap, used *esp.* for hats

velum ('vēləm) *n.* 1. membranous covering or organ 2. soft palate (*pl.* **vela** ('vēlə))

velvet ('velvit) *n.* silk or cotton fabric with thick, short pile —**velve'teen** *n.* cotton fabric resembling velvet —'**velvety** *a.* 1. of, like velvet 2. soft and smooth

vena cava ('vēnə 'kāvə) either of two large veins that convey oxygen-depleted blood to heart (*pl.* **venae cavae** ('vēnē 'kāvē))

venal ('vēnəl) *a.* 1. guilty of taking, prepared to take, bribes 2. corrupt —**ve'nality** *n.*

vend (vend) *vt.* sell —'**vendible** *a.* 1. salable, marketable —*n.* 2. (*usu. pl.*) *rare* salable object —'**vendor** *n.* —**vending machine** machine that automatically dispenses goods when money is inserted

vendetta (ven'detə) *n.* bitter, prolonged feud

veneer (vi'nēər) *n.* 1. thin layer of fine wood 2. superficial appearance —*vt.* 3. cover with veneer

venerable ('venərəbəl) *a.* worthy of reverence —'**venerate** *vt.* look up to, respect, reverence —**vener'ation** *n.*

venereal (vi'nēəriəl) *a.* 1. (of disease) transmitted by sexual intercourse 2. infected with venereal disease 3. of genitals or sexual intercourse

venery[1] ('venəri) *n. obs.* pursuit of sexual gratification

venery[2] ('venəri) *n. Hist.* art, practice of hunting

Venetian (vi'nēshən) *a.* 1. of Venice, port in NE Italy —*n.* 2. native or inhabitant of Venice —**Venetian blind** window blind made of thin horizontal slats arranged to turn so as to admit or exclude light

Venezuela (veni'zwālə) *n.* country in South America bounded north by the Caribbean, east by Guyana, south by Brazil and south and southwest by Colombia —**Vene'zuelan** *n./a.*

vengeance ('venjəns) *n.* 1. revenge 2. retribution for wrong done —'**vengeful** *a.*

venial ('vēniəl) *a.* pardonable

venison ('venisən, -zən) *n.* flesh of deer as food

Venn diagrams (ven) diagrams using overlapping circles to show relationships between sets

venom ('venəm) *n.* 1. poison 2. spite —'**venomous** *a.* poisonous

venous ('vēnəs) *a. see* VEIN

vent[1] (vent) *n.* 1. small hole or outlet —*vt.* 2. give outlet to 3. utter 4. pour forth

vent[2] (vent) *n.* vertical slit in garment, *esp.* at back of jacket

ventilate ('ventilāt) *vt.* 1. supply with fresh air 2. bring into discussion —**venti'lation** *n.* —'**ventilator** *n.*

ventral ('ventrəl) *a.* abdominal

ventricle ('ventrikəl) *n.* cavity, hollow in body, *esp.* in heart or brain —**ven'tricular** *a.*

ventriloquist (ven'triləkwist) *n.* one who can so speak that the sounds seem to come from some other person or place —**ven'triloquism** *n.*

venture ('venchər) *vt.* 1. expose to hazard 2. risk —*vi.* 3. dare 4. have courage (to do something or go somewhere) —*n.* 5. risky undertaking 6. speculative commercial undertaking —'**venturesome** *or* '**venturous** *a.*

venue ('venyōō) *n.* 1. *Law* district in which case is tried 2. meeting place 3. location

Venus ('vēnəs) *n.* 1. Roman goddess of love 2. planet between earth and Mercury —**Venus's flytrap** insect-eating plant

veracious (və'rāshəs) *a.* 1. truthful 2. true —**veracity** (və'rasiti) *n.*

veranda *or* **verandah** (və'randə) *n.* open or partly enclosed porch on outside of house

verb (vərb) *n.* part of speech used to express action or being —'**verbal** *a.* 1. of, by, or relating to words spoken rather than written 2. of, like a verb —'**verbalism** *n.* 1. verbal expression; phrase; word 2. exaggerated emphasis on importance of words 3. statement lacking real content —'**verbalize** *vt.* 1. put into words —*vi.* 2. speak —'**verbally** *adv.* —**verbatim** (vər'bātim) *adv./a.* word for word, literal(ly) —**verbal noun** noun derived from verb

verbascum (vər'baskəm) *n.* perennial garden plant

verbena (vər'bēnə) *n.* 1. genus of fragrant, beautiful plants 2. their characteristic scent

verbiage ('vərbiij) *n.* excess of words —**verbose** (vər'bōs) *a.* long-winded —**verbosity** (vər'bositi) *n.*

verdant ('vərdənt) *a.* green and fresh —'**verdure** *n.* 1. greenery 2. freshness —'**verdurous** *a.*

verdict ('vərdikt) *n.* 1. decision of a jury 2. opinion reached after examination of facts

verdigris ('vərdigrēs, -gris) *n.* green film on copper

verdure ('vərjər) *n. see* VERDANT

verge (vərj) *n.* **1.** edge **2.** brink **3.** tiling projected over gable of building —*vi.* **4.** (*with* on) come close (to) **5.** (*sometimes with* on) be on the border (of)

verger ('vərjər) *n.* **1.** caretaker and attendant in church **2.** bearer of wand of office

verify ('verifī) *vt.* **1.** prove, confirm truth of **2.** test accuracy of (-**ified, -ifying**) —'**verifiable** *a.* —**verifi'cation** *n.*

verily ('verili) *adv. obs.* **1.** truly **2.** in truth

verisimilitude (verisi'milityōod, -tōod) *n.* **1.** appearance of truth **2.** likelihood —**veri'similar** *a.* probable; likely

veritable ('veritəbəl) *a.* actual, true, genuine —'**veritably** *adv.*

verity ('veriti) *n.* **1.** truth **2.** reality **3.** true assertion

vermi- (*comb. form*) worm, as in *vermicide, vermiform, vermifuge*

vermicelli (vərmi'cheli, -'seli) *n.* pasta in fine strands

vermicide ('vərmisīd) *n.* substance to destroy worms —**ver'micular** *a.* **1.** resembling form, motion or tracks of worms **2.** of worms —'**vermiform** *a.* shaped like a worm (*eg* **vermiform appendix**)

vermiculite (vər'mikyəlīt) *n.* granular substance formed by subjecting mica to heat, used in horticulture for its water-retaining property

vermilion (vər'milyən) *a./n.* (of) bright red color or pigment

vermin ('vərmin) *n.* (*with pl. v.*) injurious animals, parasites *etc.* —'**verminous** *a.*

Vermont (vər'mont) *n.* New England state of the U.S., admitted to the Union in 1791. Abbrev.: **Vt., VT** (with ZIP code)

vermouth (vər'mōoth) *n.* wine flavored with aromatic herbs *etc.*

vernacular (vər'nakyələr) *n.* **1.** commonly spoken language or dialect of particular country or place —*a.* **2.** of vernacular **3.** native

vernal ('vərnəl) *a.* of spring

vernier ('vərniər) *n.* sliding scale for obtaining fractional parts of subdivision of graduated scale

veronica (və'ronikə) *n.* genus of plants including speedwell

verruca (və'rōokə) *n.* wart

versatile ('vərsətil) *a.* **1.** capable of or adapted to many different uses, skills *etc.* **2.** liable to change —**versa'tility** *n.*

verse (vərs) *n.* **1.** stanza or short subdivision of poem or the Bible **2.** poetry **3.** line of poetry —**versifi'cation** *n.* —'**versifier** *n.* —'**versify** *v.* turn (something) into verse (**-ified, -ifying**) —**versed in** skilled in

version ('vərzhən, -shən) *n.* **1.** description from certain point of view **2.** translation **3.** adaptation

verso ('vərsō) *n.* back of sheet of printed paper, left-hand page (*pl.* -**s**)

versus ('vərsəs) *prep.* against

vertebra ('vərtibrə) *n.* single section of backbone (*pl.* -**brae** (-brē), -**s**) —'**vertebral** *a.* of the spine —'**vertebrate** *n./a.* (of) animal with backbone, such as fish, amphibians, reptiles, birds and mammals —'**vertebrate biology** the study of this phylum (*Chordata*)

vertex ('vərteks) *n.* summit (*pl.* -**es, vertices** ('vərtisēz))

vertical ('vərtikəl) *a.* **1.** at right angles to the horizon **2.** upright **3.** overhead —'**vertically** *adv.*

vertigo ('vərtigō) *n.* giddiness (*pl.* -**es, vertigines** (vər'tijinēz)) —**vertiginous** (vər'tijinəs) *a.* dizzy

vertu (vər'tōo) *n. see* VIRTU

verve (vərv) *n.* **1.** enthusiasm **2.** spirit **3.** energy, vigor

very ('veri) *a.* **1.** exact, ideal **2.** same **3.** complete **4.** actual —*adv.* **5.** extremely, to great extent —**very high frequency** radio frequency or band lying between 300 and 30 megahertz —**very low frequency** radio frequency band or radio frequency lying between 30 and 3 kilohertz

vesicle ('vesikəl) *n.* small blister, bubble or cavity —**ve'sicular** *a.*

vespers ('vespərz) *n.* **1.** evening church service **2.** evensong

vessel ('vesəl) *n.* **1.** any object used as container, *esp.* for liquids **2.** ship, large boat **3.** tubular structure conveying liquids (*eg* blood) in body

vest (vest) *n.* **1.** sleeveless garment worn under jacket or coat —*vt.* **2.** place **3.** bestow **4.** confer **5.** clothe —'**vestment** *n.* robe or official garment —**vested interest** strong personal interest in particular state of affairs

vestal ('vestəl) *a.* pure, chaste —**vestal virgin** in ancient Rome, one of virgin priestesses whose lives were dedicated to Vesta and to maintaining sacred fire in her temple

vestibule ('vestibyōol) *n.* entrance hall, lobby

vestige ('vestij) *n.* small trace, amount —**ves'tigial** *a.*

vestry ('vestri) *n.* room in church for keeping vestments, holding meetings *etc.*

vet (vet) *n.* **1.** veterinarian —*vt.* **2.** examine **3.** check (-**tt-**)

vet. 1. veteran **2.** veterinarian

vetch (vech) *n.* plant of bean family

veteran ('vetərən) *n.* **1.** one who has served a long time, *esp.* in fighting services —*a.* **2.** long-serving

veterinarian (vetəri'neriən) *n.* person qualified and licensed to treat disorders and diseases of animals, *esp.* livestock and pets (*also* **vet**) —'**veterinary** *a.* of, relating to the science of treating injured and diseased animals

veto ('vētō) *n.* **1.** power of rejecting piece of legislation or preventing it from coming into effect **2.** any prohibition (*pl.* -**es**) —*vt.* **3.** enforce veto against **4.** forbid with authority

vex (veks) *vt.* **1.** annoy **2.** distress —**vex'ation** *n.* **1.** cause of irritation **2.** state of distress —**vex'atious** *a.* —**vexed** *a.* **1.** cross, annoyed **2.** much discussed

VHF *or* **vhf** very high frequency

V.I. Vancouver Island

via ('vīə, 'vēə) *prep.* by way of

viable ('vīəbəl) *a.* **1.** practicable **2.** able to live and grow independently —**via'bility** *n.*

viaduct ('vīədukt) *n.* bridge over valley for a road or railroad

vial ('vīəl) *n. see* PHIAL

viands ('vīəndz) *pl.n.* food

viaticum (vī'atikəm) *n.* **1.** Holy Communion as administered to person dying or in danger of death **2.** *rare* provisions or travel allowance for journey (*pl.* -**ca** (-kə), -**s**)

vibes (vībz) *pl.n. inf.* **1.** vibrations **2.** vibraphone

vibraphone ('vībrəfōn) *n.* musical instrument like xylophone, but with electronic resonators, that produces a gentle vibrato

vibrate ('vībrāt) *v.* **1.** (cause to) move to and fro rapidly and continuously **2.** give off (light or sound) by vibration —*vi.* **3.** oscillate **4.** quiver —'**vibrant** *a.* **1.** throbbing **2.** vibrating **3.** appearing vigorous, lively —**vi'bration** *n.* **1.** a vibrating —*pl.* **2.** *inf.* instinctive feelings about a place, person *etc.* —**vibrato** (vi'brätō) *n.* vibrating effect in music (*pl.* -**s**) —'**vibrator** *n.* **1.** device for producing vibratory motion, as in massage **2.** such a device with vibrating part or tip, used as dildo —'**vibratory** *a.*

viburnum (vī'bərnəm) *n.* subtropical shrub with white flowers and berry-like fruits

vicar ('vikər) *n.* clergyman in charge of parish —'**vicarage** *n.* vicar's house —**vicarial** (vī'keriəl, vi-; -'kar-) *a.* of vicar —**vicar apostolic** *R.C. Ch.* titular bishop having jurisdiction in missionary countries (*pl.* **vicars apostolic**) —**vicar general** official appointed to assist bishop of diocese in administrative or judicial duties (*pl.* **vicars general**) —**Vicar of Christ** *R.C.Ch.* the Pope

vicarious (vī'keriəs, vi-; -'kar-) *a.* **1.** obtained, enjoyed or undergone at second hand through sympathetic participation in another's experiences **2.** suffered, done *etc.* as substitute for another —**vi'cariously** *adv.*

vice[1] (vīs) *n.* **1.** evil or immoral habit or practice **2.** criminal immorality, *esp.* prostitution **3.** fault, imperfection —**vice squad** police division which deals with enforcement of gaming and prostitution laws

vice[2] (vīs) *n. inf.* **1.** person who serves as deputy to another **2.** person succeeding another

vice- (*comb. form*) in place of, second to, as in *vice-chairman, viceroy*. Such compounds are not given here where meaning may be inferred from simple word

vice admiral commissioned officer in navy or coastguard ranking above a rear admiral and whose insignia is three stars

vicegerent (vīs'jēərənt) *n.* **1.** person appointed to exercise all or some of authority of another **2.** *R.C.Ch.* representative of God or Christ on earth, such as pope —*a.* **3.** invested with or characterized by delegated authority —**vice'gerency** *n.*

vice president officer ranking immediately below president and serving as his deputy —**vice-presidency** *n.*

viceroy ('vīsroi) *n.* ruler acting for king in province or dependency (**vicereine** ('vīsrān) *fem.*) —**vice'regal** *a.* of viceroy —'**viceroyalty** *n.*

vice versa (vīsi 'vərsə) *Lat.* conversely, the other way round

vichy water ('vishi) **1.** (*sometimes* V- w-) mineral water from Vichy in France, reputed to be beneficial to health **2.** any sparkling mineral water resembling this

vicinage ('visənij) *n. rare* **1.** residents of particular neighborhood **2.** vicinity

vicinity (vi'siniti) *n.* neighborhood

vicious ('vishəs) *a.* **1.** wicked, cruel **2.** ferocious, dangerous **3.** leading to vice —'**viciously** *adv.* —**vicious circle 1.** situation in which attempt to resolve one problem creates new problems that lead back to original situation **2.** *Logic* invalid form of reasoning in which conclusion is derived from premise orig. deduced from same conclusion **3.** *Logic* circular definition

vicissitude (vi'sisityōod, -tōod) *n.* **1.** change of fortune —*pl.* **2.** ups and downs of fortune —**vicissi'tudinous** *a.*

vibraphone

victim ('viktim) *n.* **1.** person or thing killed, injured *etc.* as result of another's deed, or accident, circumstances *etc.* **2.** person cheated **3.** sacrifice —**victimi'zation** *n.* —**'victimize** *vt.* **1.** punish unfairly **2.** make victim of

victor ('viktər) *n.* **1.** conqueror **2.** winner —**vic'torious** *a.* having defeated an adversary —**'victory** *n.* winning of battle *etc.*

Victor ('viktər) *n.* word used in communications for the letter *v*

victoria (vik'töriə) *n.* four-wheeled horse-drawn carriage with folding hood

Victorian (vik'töriən) *a.* **1.** of Victoria, queen of Great Brit. and Ireland, or period of her reign (1837-1901) **2.** exhibiting characteristics popularly attributed to Victorians, *esp.* prudery *etc.* **3.** of Victoria (state in Aust. or any of the cities) —*n.* **4.** person who lived during reign of Queen Victoria **5.** inhabitant of Victoria (state or any of the cities) —**Victoria Day** Monday preceding May 24th: national holiday in Canad. in commemoration of Queen Victoria's birthday

victual ('vitəl) *n.* **1.** (*usu. pl.*) food —*v.* **2.** supply with or obtain food —**'victualler** *or* **'victualer** *n.*

vicuña (vi'kōōnyə, vĪ-; -'kyōōnə, -'kōōnə) *n.* **1.** S Amer. animal like llama **2.** fine, light cloth made from its wool

vide ('vĪdi) *Lat.* see —**vide infra** see below —**vide supra** see above

videlicet (vi'deliset) *Lat.* namely

video ('vidiō) *a.* **1.** relating to or used in transmission or production of television image —*n.* **2.** apparatus for recording television programs *etc.* —**video cassette** cassette containing video tape —**video cassette recorder** tape recorder for vision and sound signals using magnetic tape in closed plastic cassettes, for recording and playing back television programs and motion pictures (*also* **video**) —**'videodisc** *or* **'videodisk** *n.* disk stored with information, which one plays like a phonograph record, the result being translated, in sound and vision, on to TV set —**'videophone** *n.* telephonic device in which there is both verbal and visual communication between parties —**video tape** magnetic tape on which to record television program —**video tape recorder**

vie (vĪ) *vi.* (*with* with *or* for) contend, compete (against or for someone, something) (**vied, 'vying**)

Vietnam (vē'et'näm, vyet-) *n.* country in Asia bounded north by China, east and south by the South China Sea and west by Kampuchea and Laos —**Vi'et'cong** *n.* in Vietnam War, (member of) Communist-led guerrilla force and revolutionary army of South Vietnam —**Vietna'mese** *n./a.* **1.** (native or inhabitant) of Vietnam —*n.* **2.** language of Vietnam whose linguistic affiliation is uncertain

view (vyōō) *n.* **1.** survey by eyes or mind **2.** range of vision **3.** picture **4.** scene **5.** opinion **6.** purpose —*vt.* **7.** look at **8.** survey **9.** consider —**'viewer** *n.* **1.** one who views **2.** one who watches television **3.** optical device to assist viewing of photographic slides —**'viewfinder** *n.* device on camera enabling user to see what will be included in photograph —**'viewpoint** *n.* **1.** way of regarding a subject **2.** position commanding view of landscape

vigil ('vijil) *n.* **1.** a keeping awake, watch **2.** eve of feast day —**'vigilance** *n.* —**'vigilant** *a.* watchful, alert —**vigilance committee** self-appointed body of citizens organized to maintain order *etc.*

vigilante (viji'lanti) *n.* one, *esp.* as member of group, who unofficially takes it upon himself to enforce law

vignette (vi'nyet) *n.* **1.** short literary essay, sketch **2.** photograph or portrait with the background shaded off

vigor ('vigər) *n.* **1.** force, strength **2.** energy, activity —**'vigorous** *a.* **1.** strong **2.** energetic **3.** flourishing —**'vigorously** *adv.*

Viking ('vĪking) *n.* medieval Scandinavian seafarer, raider, settler

vile (vĪl) *a.* **1.** very wicked, shameful **2.** disgusting **3.** despicable —**'vilely** *adv.* —**'vileness** *n.* —**vilification** (vilifi'kāshən) *n.* —**vilify** ('vilifĪ) *vt.* **1.** speak ill of **2.** slander (**-ified, -ifying**)

villa ('vilə) *n.* **1.** large, luxurious, country house **2.** detached or semidetached suburban house

village ('vilij) *n.* small group of houses in country area —**'villager** *n.*

villain ('vilən) *n.* **1.** wicked person **2.** *inf.* mischievous person —**'villainous** *a.* **1.** wicked **2.** vile —**'villainy** *n.*

villein ('vilən) *n.* in medieval Europe, peasant personally bound to his lord, to whom he paid dues and services in return for land —**'villeinage** *n.*

vim (vim) *n. inf.* force, energy

vinaigrette (vini'gret) *n.* **1.** small bottle of smelling salts **2.** type of salad dressing

Vincent's disease *or* **angina** ('vinsənts) ulcerative condition of mouth, throat and gums with thick membrane-like coating

vinculum ('vingkyələm) *n.* **1.** line drawn above group of mathematical terms, used as equivalent to parentheses or brackets around them **2.** *Anat.* bandlike structure, *esp.* uniting two or more parts (*pl.* **-la** (-lə))

vindicate ('vindikāt) *vt.* **1.** clear of charges **2.** justify **3.** establish the truth or merit of —**'vindicable** *a.* capable of being vindicated; justifiable —**vindi'cation** *n.* —**'vindicator** *n.* —**'vindicatory** *a.*

vindictive (vin'diktiv) *a.* **1.** revengeful **2.** inspired by resentment

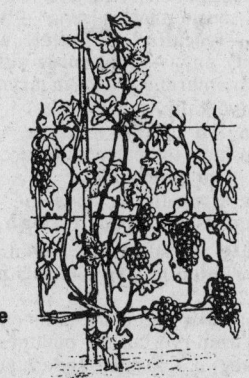
vine

vine (vĪn) *n.* climbing plant bearing grapes —**'vinery** *n.* **1.** hothouse for growing grapes **2.** vineyard **3.** vines collectively —**vi'nosity** *n.* distinctive and essential quality and flavor of wine —**vintage** ('vintij) *n.* **1.** gathering of the grapes **2.** the yield **3.** wine of particular year **4.** time of origin —*a.* **5.** best and most typical —**vintner** ('vintnər) *n.* dealer in wine —**vineyard** ('vinyərd) *n.* plantation of vines

vinegar ('vinigər) *n.* sour liquid usu. obtained from alcoholic liquors —**'vinegary** *a.* **1.** like vinegar **2.** sour **3.** bad-tempered

vini- *or before vowel* **vin-** (*comb. form*) wine, as in *viniculture*

viniculture ('vinikulchər) *n.* process or business of growing grapes and making wine

Vinland ('vinlənd) *n.* region in eastern N Amer. visited and described by Norsemen about 1000 A.D.

vinyl ('vĪnil) *n.* plastic material with variety of domestic and industrial uses

vinyon ('vinyon) *n.* any of various polyvinyl fibers

viol ('vĪəl) *n.* early stringed instrument preceding violin —**'violist** *n.* person who plays viola or viol

viola[1] (vi'ōlə) *n. see* VIOLIN

viola[2] (vĪ'ōlə, vi-; 'vĪələ) *n.* single-colored variety of pansy

violate ('vĪəlāt) *vt.* **1.** break (law, agreement *etc.*), infringe **2.** rape **3.** outrage, desecrate —**'violable** *a.* —**vio'lation** *n.* —**'violator** *n.*

violent ('vĪələnt) *a.* **1.** marked by, due to, extreme force, passion or fierceness **2.** of great force **3.** intense —**'violence** *n.* —**'violently** *adv.*

violet ('vĪəlit) *n.* **1.** plant with small bluish-purple or white flowers **2.** the flower **3.** bluish-purple color —*a.* **4.** of this color

violin (vĪə'lin) *n.* **1.** small four-stringed musical instrument —*a.* **2.** denoting family of string instruments constructed on same principles of producing sound —**vi'ola** *n.* large violin with lower range —**vio'linist** *n.* —**violoncello** (vĪələn'chelō) *n. see* CELLO —**viola da gamba** (vi'ōlə də 'gämbə, 'gambə) second largest and lowest member of viol family

V.I.P. very important person

viper ('vĪpər) *n.* **1.** common European venomous snake **2.** vicious, treacherous person

virago (vi'rägō) *n.* abusive woman (*pl.* **-es, -s**)

virgin ('vərjin) *n.* **1.** one who has not had sexual intercourse —*a.* **2.** without experience of sexual intercourse **3.** unsullied, fresh **4.** (of land) untilled —**'virginal** *a.* **1.** of, like virgin —*n.* **2.** (*oft. pl.*) type of spinet —**vir'ginity** *n.* —**Virgin Birth** doctrine that Jesus Christ was conceived solely by direct intervention of Holy Spirit so that Mary remained a virgin after his birth —**Virgin Mary** Mary, mother of Christ (*also* **the Virgin**)

Virginia (vər'jinyə) *n.* South Atlantic state of the U.S.: ratified the Constitution in 1788. Abbrev.: **VA** (with ZIP code) —**Virginia creeper** N Amer. deciduous climbing vine having palmate leaves and bluish-black berries (*also* **woodbine**)

Virgin Islands territory of the U.S. in the Caribbean

Virgo ('vərgō) *n.* (virgin) 6th sign of the zodiac operative c. Aug. 22nd-Sept. 21st

virgule ('vərgyōōl) *n.* solidus

virile ('viril) *a.* **1.** (of male) capable of copulation or procreation **2.** strong, forceful —**vi'rility** *n.*

virology (vĪ'roləji) *n. see* VIRUS

virtu *or* **vertu** (vər'tōō) *n.* **1.** taste or love for curios or works of fine art **2.** such objects collectively **3.** quality of being appealing to connoisseur (*esp. in* **articles of virtu, objects of virtu**)

virtual ('vərchōōəl) *a.* so in effect, though not in appearance or name —**'virtually** *adv.* practically, almost

virtue ('vərchōō) *n.* **1.** moral goodness **2.** good quality **3.** merit **4.** inherent power —**'virtuous** *a.* **1.** morally good **2.** chaste —**'virtuously** *adv.*

virtuoso (vərchōō'ōsō, -'ōzō) *n.* one with special skill, *esp.* in fine art (*pl.* **-s, -si** (-sē, -zē)) —**virtuosity** (vərchōō'ositi) *n.* great technical skill, *esp.* in a fine art, as music

virulent ('viryǝlǝnt, 'virǝlǝnt) a. 1. very infectious, poisonous etc. 2. malicious

virus ('vīrǝs) n. any single-celled disease-causing organic structure distinct from and oft. smaller than bacteria that can only reproduce in a living organism —'**viral** a. of virus —**vi'rology** n. study of viruses

visa ('vēzǝ) n. endorsement on passport permitting the bearer to travel into country of issuing government —'**visaed** a.

visage ('vizij) n. face

vis-à-vis ('vēzǝ'vē) Fr. 1. in relation to, regarding 2. opposite to

viscera ('visǝrǝ) pl.n. large internal organs of body, esp. of abdomen (sing. **viscus** ('viskǝs)) —'**visceral** a.

viscid ('visid) a. sticky, of a consistency like molasses —**vi'scidity** n.

viscose ('viskōs) n. (substance used to produce) synthetic fabric

viscount ('vīkownt) n. Brit. nobleman ranking below earl and above baron —'**viscountess** n. 1. wife, ex-wife or widow of viscount 2. noblewoman ranking below countess and above baroness

viscous ('viskǝs) a. thick and sticky —**vis-'cosity** n.

vise (vīs) n. fixed appliance with screw to apply controlled pressure to object held in jaws of vise

visible ('vizibǝl) a. that can be seen —**visi'bility** n. degree of clarity of atmosphere, esp. for navigation —'**visibly** adv.

vision ('vizhǝn) n. 1. sight 2. insight 3. dream 4. phantom 5. imagination —'**visionary** a. 1. marked by vision 2. impractical —n. 3. mystic 4. impractical person

visit ('vizit) v. 1. go, come and see, stay temporarily with (someone) —n. 2. stay 3. call at person's home etc. 4. official call —'**visitant** n. 1. ghost; apparition 2. visitor or guest, usu. from far away 3. migratory bird that is present in particular region only at certain times (also '**visitor**) —**visi'tation** n. 1. formal visit or inspection 2. affliction or plague —'**visitor** n.

visor or **vizor** ('vīzǝr) n. 1. front part of helmet made to move up and down before face 2. eyeshade, esp. on automobile 3. peak on cap

vista ('vistǝ) n. view, esp. distant view

visual ('vizhōōǝl) a. 1. of sight 2. visible —**visuali'zation** n. —'**visualize** vt. form mental image of —**visual aids** devices, such as motion pictures, slides etc., that display in visual form material to be understood or remembered

vital ('vītǝl) a. 1. necessary to, affecting life 2. lively, animated 3. essential 4. highly important —**vi'tality** n. life, vigor —'**vitalize** vt. 1. give life to 2. lend vigor to —'**vitally** adv. —'**vitals** pl.n. vital organs of body —**vital statistics** 1. data concerning human life or conditions affecting it, such as death rate 2. inf. measurements of woman's bust, waist and hips

vitamin ('vītǝmin) n. any of group of substances occurring in foodstuffs and essential to health

vitiate ('vishiāt) vt. 1. spoil 2. deprive of efficacy 3. invalidate —**viti'ation** n.

viticulture ('vitikulchǝr) n. 1. science, art or process of cultivating grapevines 2. study of (growing of) grapes —**viti'culturist** n.

vitreous ('vitriǝs) a. 1. of glass 2. glassy —**vitrifi'cation** n. —'**vitrify** v. convert or be converted into glass, or glassy substance (**-ified, -ifying**) —**vitreous humor** transparent gelatinous substance that fills eyeball between lens and retina

vitriol ('vitriǝl) n. 1. sulfuric acid 2. caustic speech —**vitri'olic** a.

vituperate (vī'tyōōpǝrāt, vi-; -'tōō-) vt. abuse in words, revile —**vituper'ation** n. —**vi'tuperative** a.

viva ('vēvǝ) interj. long live; up with (specified person or thing)

vivace (vē'vächā, -chi) a./adv. Mus. to be performed in brisk lively manner

vivacious (vi'vāshǝs) a. lively, gay, sprightly —**vivacity** (vi'vasiti) n.

vivarium (vī'variǝm, -'ver-) n. place where animals are kept under natural conditions for study etc. (pl. **-s, -ia** (-iǝ))

viva voce ('vīvǝ 'vōsi) Lat. adv. 1. by word of mouth —n. 2. oral examination (oft. '**viva**)

vivid ('vivid) a. 1. bright, intense 2. clear 3. lively, animated 4. graphic —'**vividly** adv.

vivify ('vivifī) vt. animate, inspire (**-ified, -ifying**)

viviparous (vī'vipǝrǝs, vi-) a. bringing forth young alive

vivisection (vivi'sekshǝn) n. dissection of, or operating on, living animals —'**vivisect** v. subject (animal) to vivisection —**vivi'sectionist** n. —'**vivisector** n.

vixen ('viksǝn) n. 1. female fox 2. spiteful woman —'**vixenish** a.

Viyella (vī'yelǝ) n. trade name for twill-weave cloth made of cotton and wool

viz. videlicet

vizier (vi'zēǝr) n. high official in some Muslim countries

vizor ('vīzǝr) n. see VISOR

V-J Day day marking Allied victory over Japan in World War II (Aug. 15th, 1945)

V.L. Vulgar Latin

VLF or **vlf** Rad. very low frequency

V neck neck on garment resembling shape of letter V —**V-neck** or **V-necked** a.

voc. or **vocat.** vocative

vocable ('vōkǝbǝl) n. word regarded as sequence of letters or spoken sounds

vocabulary (vō'kabyǝleri, vǝ-) n. 1. list of words, usu. in alphabetical order 2. stock of words used in particular language etc.

vocal ('vōkǝl) a. 1. of, with, or giving out voice 2. outspoken, articulate —n. 3. piece of popular music that is sung —'**vocalist** n. singer —'**vocalize** vt. utter with voice —'**vocally** adv. —**vocal cords** either of two pairs of membranous folds in larynx.

vocalic (vō'kalik) a. of vowel(s)

vocation (vō'kāshǝn) n. (urge, inclination, predisposition to) particular career, profession etc. —**vo'cational** a.

vocative ('vokǝtiv) n. in some languages, case of nouns used in addressing a person

vociferate (vō'sifǝrāt) v. exclaim, cry out —**vocifer'ation** n. —**vo'ciferous** a. shouting, noisy

vodka ('vodkǝ) n. colorless alcoholic liquor distilled from rye, corn or potatoes

vogue (vōg) n. 1. fashion, style 2. popularity

voice (vois) n. 1. sound given out by person in speaking, singing etc. 2. quality of the sound 3. expressed opinion 4. (right to) share in discussion 5. verbal form proper to relation of subject and action —vt. 6. give utterance to, express —'**voiceless** a. —**voice-over** n. voice of unseen commentator heard during television broadcast —'**voiceprint** n. graphic representation of person's voice recorded electronically

void (void) a. 1. empty 2. destitute 3. not legally binding —n. 4. empty space —vt. 5. make ineffectual or invalid 6. empty out

voile (voil) n. light semitransparent fabric

vol. volume

volatile ('volǝtil) a. 1. evaporating quickly 2. lively 3. fickle, changeable —**vola'tility** n. —**volatili'zation** n. —**vo'latilize** v. (cause to) evaporate

vol-au-vent (Fr. volō'vä) n. small, light pastry case with savory filling

volcano (vol'kānō) n. 1. hole in earth's crust through which lava, ashes, smoke etc. are discharged 2. mountain so formed (pl. **-es, -s**) —**volcanic** (vol'kanik) a. —**volcanology** (volkǝ'nolǝji) or **vulcanology** n. study of volcanoes and volcanic phenomena

vole (vōl) n. any of various small rodents resembling mice but with a short tail

volition (vō'lishǝn, vǝ-) n. 1. act, power of willing 2. exercise of the will —**vo'litional** a.

Volk (folk) n. SA Afrikaner people

volley ('voli) n. 1. simultaneous discharge of weapons or missiles 2. rush of oaths, questions etc. 3. Sport kick, stroke etc. at moving ball before it touches ground —v. 4. discharge or be discharged —vt. 5. utter 6. fly, strike etc. in volley —'**volleyball** n. game played indoors or outdoors by two teams of six players each who seek to score points by hitting a ball back and forth across a net

volt (vōlt) n. unit of electric potential —'**voltage** n. electric potential difference expressed in volts —'**voltmeter** n.

voltaic (vol'tāik) a. see GALVANIC (sense 1)

volte-face (volt'fäs) Fr. n. complete reversal of opinion or direction (pl. **volte-face**)

voluble ('volyǝbǝl) a. talking easily, readily and at length —**volu'bility** n. —'**volubly** adv.

volume ('volyǝm, -yōōm) n. 1. space occupied 2. bulk, mass 3. amount 4. power, fullness of voice or sound 5. control on radio etc. for adjusting this 6. book 7. part of book bound in one cover —**volu'metric** a. pert. to measurement by volume —**voluminous** (vǝ'lōōminǝs) a. bulky, copious

voluntary ('volǝnteri) a. 1. having, done by free will 2. done without payment 3. supported by freewill contributions 4. spontaneous —n. 5. organ solo in church service —**volun'tarily** adv. —**volun'teer** n. 1. one who offers service, joins force etc. of his own free will —v. 2. offer oneself or one's services

voluptuous (vǝ'lupchōōǝs) a. of, contributing to pleasures of the senses —**vo'luptuary** n. one given to luxury and sensual pleasures

volute (vǝ'lōōt) n. spiral or twisting turn, form or object

vomit ('vomit) v. 1. eject (contents of stomach) through mouth —n. 2. matter vomited

voodoo ('vōōdōō) n. 1. practice of black magic, esp. in W Indies, witchcraft —vt. 2. affect by voodoo

voracious (vō'rāshǝs) a. greedy, ravenous —**vo'raciously** adv. —**voracity** (vō'rasiti) n.

-vorous (a. comb. form) feeding on; devouring, as in carnivorous —**-vore** (n. comb. form)

vortex ('vörteks) n. 1. whirlpool 2. whirling motion (pl. **-es, vortices** ('vörtisēz))

votary ('vōtǝri) n. one vowed to service or pursuit ('**votaress** fem.) —'**votive** a. given, consecrated by vow

vote (vōt) n. 1. formal expression of choice 2. individual pronouncement 3. right to give it, in question or election 4. result of voting 5. that which is given or allowed by vote —v. 6. express, declare opinion, choice, preference etc. by vote 7. authorize, enact etc. by vote —'**voter** n.

vouch (vowch) vi. (usu. with for) guarantee, make oneself responsible (for) —'**voucher** n. 1. document proving correctness of item in accounts, or to establish facts **2.** ticket as substitute for cash —**vouch'safe** *vt.* condescend to grant or do

vow (vow) *n.* **1.** solemn promise, *esp.* religious one —*vt.* **2.** promise, threaten by vow

vowel ('vowəl) *n.* **1.** any speech sound pronounced without stoppage or friction of the breath **2.** letter standing for such sound, as *a, e, i, o, u*

vox (voks) *n.* voice; sound (*pl.* **voces** ('vōsēz)) —**vox populi** ('popyəlī) voice of the people; popular or public opinion

voyage ('voiij) *n.* **1.** journey, *esp.* long one, by sea or air —*vi.* **2.** make voyage —**'voyager** *n.* —**voyageur** (voiə'zhər, vwäyä'zhər; *Fr.* vwaya'zhœr) *n.* **C** guide, trapper in N regions

voyeur (vwä'yər) *n.* one obtaining sexual pleasure by watching sexual activities of others

vs. versus

V-sign *n.* gesture made by raising index and middle fingers with palm outward meaning victory or peace

V.S.O. very superior old (brandy)

V.S.O.P. very superior old pale (brandy)

VT *or* **Vt.** Vermont

VTOL ('vētol) vertical takeoff and landing

VTR video tape recorder

vulcanize ('vulkənīz) *vt.* treat (rubber) with sulfur at high temperature to increase its durability —**'vulcanite** *n.* rubber so hardened —**vulcani'zation** *n.* —**vulca'nology** *n.* *see* **volcanology** *at* VOLCANO

Vulg. Vulgate

vulgar ('vulgər) *a.* **1.** offending against good taste **2.** coarse **3.** common —**vulgarian** (vul'gariən, -'ger-) *n.* vulgar (rich) person —**'vulgarism** *n.* coarse, obscene word, phrase —**vulgarity** (vul'gariti) *n.* —**vulgari'zation** *n.* —**'vulgarize** *vt.* make vulgar or too common —**'vulgarly** *adv.* —**vulgar fraction** *see* **common fraction** *at* COMMON —**Vulgar Latin** any of dialects of Latin

spoken in Roman Empire other than classical Latin

Vulgate ('vulgāt, -git) *n.* fourth-century Latin version of the Bible

vulnerable ('vulnərəbəl) *a.* **1.** capable of being physically or emotionally wounded or hurt **2.** exposed, open to attack, persuasion *etc.* —**vulnera'bility** *n.*

vulpine ('vulpīn) *a.* **1.** of foxes **2.** foxy

vulture ('vulchər) *n.* large bird which feeds on carrion —**'vulturine** *or* **'vulturous** *a.* **1.** of vulture **2.** rapacious

vulva ('vulvə) *n.* external genitals of human female

vv. **1.** versus **2.** *Mus.* volumes

v.v. vice versa

vying ('vīing) *pr.p. of* VIE

Vyrene ('vīrēn, vī'rēn) *n.* trade name for stretch fiber

w *or* **W** ('dubəlyōō) *n.* **1.** 23rd letter of English alphabet **2.** speech sound represented by this letter, usu. semivowel, as in *web* (*pl.* **w's, W's** *or* **Ws**)

W **1.** *Chem.* tungsten **2.** energy

w. **1.** warden **2.** water **3.** watt **4.** week **5.** weight **6.** west(ern) **7.** white **8.** wide **9.** width **10.** wife

W. **1.** Wales **2.** Welsh

WA Washington

WAC Women's Army Corps

wacky ('waki) *a.* *sl.* eccentric or unpredictable

wad (wod) *n.* **1.** small pad of fibrous material **2.** thick roll of bank notes **3.** sum of money —*vt.* **4.** line, pad, stuff *etc.* with wad (**-dd-**) —**'wadding** *n.* stuffing

waddle ('wodəl) *vi.* **1.** walk like duck —*n.* **2.** this gait

wade (wād) *vi.* **1.** walk through something that hampers movement, *esp.* water **2.** proceed with difficulty —**'wader** *n.* **1.** person or bird that wades —*pl.* **2.** angler's high waterproof boots

Wade-Giles ('wād'jīlz) *n./a.* (of) system of transliterating the Chinese language into the Roman alphabet, superseded by Pinyin in some countries

Waf (waf) *n.* member of women's component of U.S. Air Force formed after World War II

wafer ('wāfər) *n.* **1.** thin, crisp biscuit **2.** thin slice of anything

waffle ('wofəl) *n.* kind of pancake with deep indentations on both sides —**waffle iron** utensil for cooking waffles, having two flat, studded plates hinged together

waft (woft, waft) *vt.* **1.** convey smoothly through air or water —*n.* **2.** breath of wind **3.** odor, whiff

wag (wag) *v.* **1.** (cause to) move rapidly from side to side (**-gg-**) —*n.* **2.** instance of wagging **3.** *inf.* humorous, witty person —**'waggish** *a.* —**'wagtail** *n.* small bird with wagging tail

wage (wāj) *n.* **1.** (*oft. pl.*) payment for work done —*vt.* **2.** engage in

wager ('wājər) *n./v.* bet

waggle ('wagəl) *v.* wag —**'waggly** *a.*

Wagnerian (väg'nēəriən) *a.* pert. to German composer Richard Wagner, his music or his theories

wagon ('wagən) *n.* **1.** four-wheeled vehicle for heavy loads **2.** railway freight truck —**'wagoner** *n.* —**wago'nette** *n.* four-wheeled horse-drawn vehicle with two lengthwise seats facing each other behind driver's seat

waif (wāf) *n.* homeless person, *esp.* child

wail (wāl) *v.* **1.** cry out —*vt.* **2.** lament —*n.* **3.** mournful cry

wainscot ('wānskət) *n.* **1.** wooden lining of walls of room —*vt.* **2.** line thus

waist (wāst) *n.* **1.** part of body between hips and ribs **2.** various narrow central parts —**'waistband** *n.* fabric or ribbon fitting around the waist of trousers or skirt —**'waistline** *n.* line, size of waist (of person, garment)

wait (wāt) *v.* **1.** stay in one place, remain inactive in expectation (of something) **2.** be prepared (for something) **3.** delay —*vi.* **4.** serve in restaurant *etc.* —*n.* **5.** act or period of waiting —*pl.* **6.** street musicians, carol singers —**'waiter** *n.* **1.** attendant on guests at hotel, restaurant *etc.* (**'waitress** *fem.*) **2.** one who waits —**waiting game** postponement of action in order to gain advantage —**waiting list** list of people waiting to obtain some object, treatment *etc.*

waive (wāv) *vt.* **1.** forgo **2.** not insist on —**'waiver** *n.* (written statement of) this act

wake¹ (wāk) *v.* **1.** rouse from sleep **2.** stir (up) (**woke, 'woken, 'waking**) —*n.* **3.** vigil **4.** watch beside corpse **5.** (*oft. pl.*) annual holiday in parts of N England —**'wakeful** *a.* —**'waken** *v.* wake

wake² (wāk) *n.* track or path left by anything that has passed, as track of turbulent water behind ship

Wake Island (wāk) territory of the U.S. in the western Pacific Ocean

Waldorf salad ('wöldörf) salad made usu. of diced apples, celery, nuts and mayonnaise

wale (wāl) *n.* **1.** raised mark left on skin after stroke of whip **2.** weave of fabric, such as ribs in corduroy **3.** *Naut.* ridge of planking along rail of ship —*v.* **4.** raise wales (on) by striking **5.** weave with wale

Wales (wālz) *n.* division of the United Kingdom in southwest Great Britain —**Welsh** *a./n.* —**'Welshman** *n.* —**Welsh rabbit** *or* **rarebit** savory dish of melted cheese on toast —**Welsh terrier** wire-haired breed of terrier with black-and-tan coat

walk (wök) *v.* **1.** (cause, assist to) move, travel on foot at ordinary pace —*vt.* **2.** cross, pass through by walking **3.** escort, conduct by walking —*n.* **4.** act, instance of walking **5.** path or other place or route for walking **6.** manner of walking **7.** occupation, career —**'walker** *n.* **1.** person who walks **2.** framework used as aid to walking, *esp.* for baby or crippled person **3.** escort, usu. male —**'walkabout** *n.* **1.** informal stroll by a public figure **2.** (of Aust. Aborigine) wandering —**walkie-talkie** *n.* portable radio set containing both transmission and receiver units —**walking stick** stick, cane carried to assist walking —**walk-on** *n.* small part in play

—'**walkout** *n.* **1.** strike **2.** act of leaving as a protest —'**walkover** *n.* unopposed or easy victory

wall (wöl) *n.* **1.** structure of brick, stone *etc.* serving as fence, side of building *etc.* **2.** surface of one **3.** anything resembling this —*vt.* **4.** enclose with wall **5.** block up with wall —'**wallboard** *n.* thin board made of materials, such as compressed wood fibers or gypsum plaster, used to cover walls *etc.* —'**wallflower** *n.* **1.** hardy perennial or subshrub of the cabbage family, oft. scented, grown as ornamental **2.** woman who remains seated at dance *etc.* for lack of partner —'**wallpaper** *n.* **1.** paper, usu. patterned, to cover interior walls —*v.* **2.** cover (surface) with wallpaper

wallaby

wallaby ('woləbi) *n.* any of various small species of kangaroo

wallet ('wolit) *n.* small folding case, *esp.* for paper money, documents *etc.*

walleyed ('wölīd) *a.* **1.** squinting **2.** having eyes with pale irises

Walloon (wo'lōōn) *n.* **1.** member of French-speaking people living chiefly in S and SE Belgium **2.** French dialect of Belgium —*a.* **3.** of Walloons or their dialect

wallop ('woləp) *inf. vt.* **1.** beat soundly **2.** strike hard —*n.* **3.** stroke or blow —'**walloper** *n. inf.* one who wallops —'**walloping** *inf. n.* **1.** thrashing —*adv.* **2.** very, greatly —*a.* **3.** great

wallow ('wolō) *vi.* **1.** roll (in liquid or mud) **2.** revel —*n.* **3.** act or instance of wallowing **4.** muddy place where animals wallow

Wall Street dominant financial interests of the U.S. economy

walnut ('wölnut) *n.* **1.** edible nut of north temperature zone tree **2.** the tree **3.** its wood **4.** the hickory nut **5.** any fruit or tree resembling the walnut

walrus ('wölrəs, 'wol-) *n.* either of two large marine mammals related to seals and found in Arctic seas (*pl.* **-es, -rus**)

waltz (wölts, wöls) *n.* **1.** ballroom dance **2.** music in triple time —*v.* **3.** dance or lead (someone) in or as in a waltz

wampum ('wompəm) *n.* **1.** beads made of shells, formerly used by N Amer. Indians as money and for ornament **2.** *sl.* money

wan (won) *a.* pale, sickly complexioned, pallid

wand (wond) *n.* stick, usu. straight and slender, *esp.* as carried by magician *etc.*

wander ('wondər) *v.* **1.** roam, ramble —*vi.* **2.** go astray, deviate —*n.* **3.** stroll —'**wanderer** *n.* —'**wanderlust** *n.* irrepressible urge to wander or travel

wane (wān) *vi./n.* **1.** decline **2.** (of moon) decrease in size

wangle ('wanggəl) *inf. vt.* **1.** manipulate, manage in skillful way —*n.* **2.** intrigue, trickery, something obtained by craft

Wankel engine ('vängkəl, 'wängkəl) type of rotary four-stroke internal-combustion engine without reciprocating parts

want (wont) *v.* **1.** desire —*vt.* **2.** lack —*n.* **3.** desire **4.** need **5.** deficiency —'**wanted** *a.* being sought, *esp.* by the police —'**wanting** *a.* **1.** lacking **2.** below standard

wanton ('wontən) *a.* **1.** dissolute **2.** without motive, thoughtless **3.** unrestrained —*n.* **4.** wanton person, *esp.* woman

wapiti ('wopiti) *n.* see ELK (sense 1) (*pl.* **wapiti, -s**)

war[1] (wör) *n.* **1.** fighting between nations **2.** state of hostility **3.** conflict, contest —*vi.* **4.** make war (**-rr-**) —'**warlike** *a.* **1.** of, for war **2.** fond of war —'**warrior** *n.* fighter —'**warbonnet** *n.* Amerindian ceremonial headdress with feathered extension down back —**war crime** crime committed in wartime in violation of accepted customs of war —**war cry 1.** cry used by attacking troops in war **2.** distinctive word, phrase used by political party *etc.* —'**warfare** *n.* hostilities —**war game 1.** notional tactical exercise for training military commanders, in which no military units are actually deployed **2.** game in which model soldiers are used to create battles in order to study tactics —'**warhead** *n.* part of missile *etc.* containing explosives —'**warhorse** *n.* **1.** horse used in battle **2.** *inf.* veteran soldier or politician —**war memorial** monument to those who die in war —'**warmonger** *n.* one fostering, encouraging war —**war paint 1.** painted decoration of face and body applied by certain N Amer. Indians before battle **2.** *inf.* cosmetics —'**warpath** *n.* route taken by N Amer. Indians on warlike expedition —'**warship** *n.* vessel armed, armored for naval warfare —'**wartime** *n./a.* —**on the warpath** *inf.* in a state of anger

war[2] warrant

warble ('wörbəl) *v.* sing with trills —'**warbler** *n.* **1.** person or bird that warbles **2.** kind of small songbird

ward (wörd) *n.* **1.** division of city **2.** minor under care of guardian **3.** guardianship **4.** bar in lock, groove in key that prevents incorrectly cut key opening lock —'**warder** *n.* jailer ('**wardress** *fem.*) —'**wardship** *n.* **1.** office of guardian **2.** state of being under guardian —'**wardroom** *n.* officers' mess on warship —**ward off** avert, repel

-ward *or* **-wards** (*comb. form*) indicating direction toward, as in *backward step*

warden ('wördən) *n.* person, officer in charge of building, institution, college *etc.*

wardrobe ('wördröb) *n.* **1.** piece of furniture for hanging clothes in **2.** person's supply of clothing **3.** costumes of theatrical company

ware (wâər) *n.* **1.** goods **2.** articles collectively —*pl.* **3.** goods for sale **4.** commodities **5.** merchandise —'**warehouse** *n.* storehouse for goods prior to distribution and sale

warlock ('wörlok) *n.* man who practices black magic

warm (wörm) *a.* **1.** moderately hot **2.** serving to maintain heat **3.** affectionate **4.** ardent **5.** earnest **6.** hearty **7.** (of color) having yellow or red base —*v.* **8.** make, become warm —'**warmly** *adv.* —**warmth** *n.* **1.** mild heat **2.** cordiality **3.** vehemence, anger —**warm-blooded** *a.* **1.** having constant body temperature independent of surroundings **2.** ardent —**warm-bloodedness** *n.* —**warm front** *Met.* advancing edge of warm air mass —**warming pan** metal container holding hot liquid or hot coals with a cover and long handle used to warm a bed

warming pan

warn (wörn) *vt.* **1.** put on guard **2.** caution, admonish **3.** give advance information to **4.** notify authoritatively —'**warning** *n.* **1.** hint of harm *etc.* **2.** admonition **3.** advance notice

warp (wörp) *v.* **1.** (cause to) twist (out of shape) **2.** pervert or be perverted —*n.* **3.** state, condition of being warped **4.** lengthwise threads on loom

warrant ('worənt) *n.* **1.** authority **2.** document giving authority —*vt.* **3.** guarantee **4.** authorize, justify —**warran'tee** *n.* person given warranty —**warran'tor** *n.* person, company giving warranty —'**warranty** *n.* **1.** guarantee of quality of goods **2.** security —**warrant officer 1.** officer in armed services who holds a rank between those of commissioned and noncommissioned officers **2.** commissioned officer ranking below ensign in the navy or coast guard and below a second lieutenant in the marine corps

warren ('worən) *n.* **1.** (burrows inhabited by) colony of rabbits **2.** crowded tenement or district **3.** maze of passageways or cubicles

wart (wört) *n.* small hard growth on skin caused by virus —**wart hog** kind of Afr. wild pig

wary ('wâəri) *a.* watchful, cautious, alert

was (woz; *unstressed* wəz) *pt.* first and third person sing. of BE

wash (wosh) *v.* **1.** clean (oneself, clothing *etc.*), *esp.* with water, soap *etc.* **2.** move, be moved by water —*vi.* **3.** be washable **4.** *inf.* be able to be proved true —*vt.* **5.** flow, sweep over, against —*n.* **6.** act of washing **7.** clothing washed at one time **8.** sweep of water, *esp.* set up by moving ship **9.** thin coat of color —'**washable** *a.* capable of being washed without damage *etc.* —'**washer** *n.* **1.** one who, that which, washes **2.** ring put under a nut —'**washing** *n.* clothing to be washed —'**washy** *a.* **1.** dilute **2.** watery **3.** insipid —**wash-and-wear** *a.* of or relating to fabric or clothing needing little or no ironing after washing —'**washboard** *n.* **1.** corrugated rectangular surface used for scrubbing clothes **2.** *Naut.* planklike shield fastened to gunwales of boat to prevent water from splashing over side —**wash drawing** pen-and-ink drawing that has been lightly brushed over with water —**washing soda** common name for sodium carbonate —'**washout** *n. inf.* complete failure —**washed out 1.** faded or colorless **2.** exhausted, pale

Washington[1] ('wöshingtən, 'wosh-) *n.* Pacific state of the U.S., admitted to the Union in 1889. Abbrev.: **Wash., WA** (with ZIP code)

Washington[2] ('wöshingtən, 'wosh-) *n.* **George.** the 1st President of the U.S. (1789-97)

wasp (wosp) *n.* striped stinging insect resembling bee —'**waspish** *a.* irritable, snappish —**wasp waist** very small waist

WASP *or* **Wasp** (wosp) *n.* White Anglo-Saxon Protestant: person descended from N European Protestant stock, *esp.* member of most privileged class of people in the U.S.

wassail ('wosəl, wo'sāl) *n.* **1.** formerly, toast made to person at festivities **2.** festivity when much drinking takes place **3.** alcoholic liquor drunk at such festivity, *esp.* spiced beer —*v.* **4.** drink health of (person) at wassail —*vi.* **5.** go from house to house singing carols at Christmas

Wassermann test ('wosərmən) diagnostic procedure used to detect syphilis

waste (wāst) vt. 1. expend uselessly, use extravagantly 2. fail to take advantage of 3. lay desolate 4. kill; injure severely —vi. 5. dwindle 6. pine away —n. 7. act of wasting 8. what is wasted 9. desert —a. 10. useless 11. desert 12. wasted —'**wastage** n. 1. loss by use or decay 2. reduction in numbers, esp. of work force —'**wasteful** a. extravagant —'**wastefully** adv. —'**wasting** a. reducing vitality, strength or robustness of body —'**wastrel** n. wasteful person, idler —'**wasteland** n. barren or desolate area of land

watch (woch) vt. 1. observe closely 2. guard —vi. 3. wait expectantly 4. be on watch —n. 5. portable timepiece for wrist, pocket etc. 6. state of being on the lookout 7. guard 8. spell of duty, esp. on shipboard where 24 hours is divided into six watches beginning at 12.30 a.m. —'**watchful** a. —'**watchfully** adv. —'**watchdog** n. 1. dog trained to guard property 2. person or group that acts as protector against inefficiency etc. —'**watch-maker** n. one skilled in making and repairing watches —'**watchman** n. man guarding building etc., esp. at night —**watch night** in Protestant churches, service held on night of Dec. 31st, to mark passing of old year —'**watchword** n. 1. password 2. rallying cry

water ('wôtər) n. 1. liquid form of compound of hydrogen and oxygen descending as rain, forming rivers, lakes and seas 2. body of water 3. river 4. lake 5. sea 6. tear 7. urine —vt. 8. put water on or into 9. irrigate, provide with water —vi. 10. salivate 11. (of eyes) fill with tears 12. take in or obtain water —'**watery** a. —**water bed** waterproof mattress filled with water —**water biscuit** cracker made mainly of flour and water —**water boy** person who keeps group supplied with water —'**waterbuck** n. Afr. antelope —**water buffalo** domesticated Asian buffalo —**water bug** any of various aquatic insects with grasping forelimbs and partially thickened wings —**water cannon** device for directing stream of water used to control crowds —**water chestnut** 1. tuber of a Chinese sedge 2. fruit of aquatic plant of primrose family —'**watercolor** n. 1. paint in which water is the solvent of the binding material 2. painting in this medium —**water cooler** device for supplying refrigerated drinking water —'**watercourse** n. natural or man-made channel through which water flows —'**waterfall** n. perpendicular descent of waters of a stream —'**waterfowl** n. 1. any aquatic freshwater bird, esp. duck, goose or swan 2. such birds collectively —'**waterfront** n. area of town abutting on a body of water —**water gauge** instrument that measures volume of water in tank —**water glass** 1. glass vessel for holding drinking water 2. device with glass bottom for examining objects in or under water 3. silicate of sodium used in commerce as cement, protective coating and fireproofing agent 4. water gauge —**water ice** frozen dessert of water, sugar and flavoring —**watering place** 1. place where animals, esp. livestock, come to drink 2. health or recreational resort featuring mineral springs 3. nightclub, bar or lounge where drink is available —**water jump** obstacle in race consisting of pool, stream or ditch —**water lily** any of genus of aquatic plants with showy flowers —'**waterline** n. any of several lines marked on outside of ship to correspond with surface of the water —'**waterlogged** a. saturated,

filled with water —**water main** pipe or conduit for conveying water —'**watermark** n. 1. mark indicating height to which water has risen 2. marking in paper produced by projecting design during manufacture 3. design or pattern of the marking —vt. 4. mark (paper) with watermark 5. impress in the manner of a watermark —'**watermelon** n. 1. large edible fruit with hard green rind and sweet watery reddish flesh 2. any vine of the gourd family bearing watermelons —**water moccasin** 1. venomous semiaquatic pit viper related to copperhead (also **cottonmouth, cottonmouth moccasin**) 2. Amer. snake living in or near water —**water ouzel** see DIPPER (sense 2) —**water pistol** toy pistol that squirts stream of water —**water polo** goal-type game played in water —**water power** 1. power latent in dynamic or static head of water as used to drive machinery 2. source of such power, such as dam —'**waterproof** a. 1. not letting water through —vt. 2. make waterproof —**water-repellent** a. (of fabric) having a finish that resists absorption of water —'**watershed** n. 1. drainage area 2. the point of change between two conditions, phases etc. —'**waterskiing** n. sport in which person on skis is towed by boat —'**waterspout** n. 1. pipe from which water is spouted 2. the water lifted from a body of water by a tornado —**water table** level below which ground is saturated with water —'**watertight** a. 1. so fitted as to prevent water entering or escaping 2. so worded that meaning cannot be misconstrued —**water vapor** invisible moisture in atmosphere —'**waterwheel** n. wheel driven by direct action of water —**water wings** air-filled device used to support body of swimmer —'**waterworks** pl.n. 1. (with sing. v.) system for storing, purifying and distributing water for community supply 2. (with pl. v.) crying, tears 3. (with pl. v.) urinary system

water wheel

Watergate ('wôtərgāt) n. political scandal, usu. involving abuse of power of office and concealment

Waterloo (wôtər'lōō) n. 1. town in Belgium, site of battle where Napoleon met his final defeat 2. total or crushing defeat (esp. in **meet one's Waterloo**)

watt (wot) n. unit of electric power —'**wattage** n. electric power expressed in watts —**watt-hour** n. unit of energy equal to one watt used for one hour —'**wattmeter** n. meter for measuring electric power in watts

wattle ('wotəl) n. 1. frame of woven branches etc. as fence 2. fleshy pendant lobe of neck of certain birds, eg turkey —**wattle and daub** form of wall construction consisting of interwoven twigs plastered with mixture of clay and water

waul or **wawl** (wôl) vi. cry or wail plaintively like cat

wave (wāv) v. 1. move to and fro, as hand in greeting or farewell 2. signal by waving 3. give, take shape of waves (as hair etc.) —n. 4. ridge and trough on water etc. 5. act,

gesture of waving 6. vibration, as in radio waves, of electric and magnetic forces alternating in direction 7. prolonged spell of something 8. upsurge 9. wavelike shape in the hair etc. —'**wavy** a. —'**waveband** n. range of wavelengths or frequencies used for particular type of radio transmission —'**wavelength** n. distance between same points of two successive sound waves

waver ('wāvər) vi. 1. hesitate, be irresolute 2. be, become unsteady —'**waverer** n.

WAVES (wāvz) Women Accepted for Volunteer Emergency Service (Women's Reserve, U.S. Naval Reserve)

wax[1] (waks) n. 1. yellow, soft, pliable material made by bees 2. this or similar substance used for sealing, making candles etc. 3. waxy secretion of ear —vt. 4. put wax on —'**waxen** a. 1. made of, treated with, or covered with wax 2. resembling wax in color or texture —'**waxy** a. like wax —**wax bean** yellowish string bean with waxy pod —'**waxbill** n. Afr. finchlike weaverbird —**waxed** or **wax paper** paper coated with wax to make it resist water and oil, used as wrapping —'**waxwing** n. small songbird —'**waxwork** n. lifelike figure, esp. of famous person, reproduced in wax

wax[2] (waks) vi. grow, increase

way (wā) n. 1. manner 2. method, means 3. track 4. direction 5. path 6. passage 7. course 8. route 9. progress 10. state or condition —'**waybill** n. document attached to goods in transit specifying their nature, point of origin, destination and rate to be charged —'**wayfarer** n. traveler, esp. on foot —'**waylay** vt. lie in wait for and accost, attack (-**laid**, -**laying**) —**way-out** a. inf. 1. extremely unconventional or experimental 2. excellent or amazing —'**wayside** n. 1. side or edge of a road —a. 2. situated by the wayside —'**wayward** a. capricious, perverse, willful —'**waywardly** adv. —'**waywardness** n. —**ways and means** 1. revenues and methods of raising revenues needed for functioning of state etc. 2. (W- a- M-) committee of legislature concerned with this purpose —**Way of the Cross** see **Stations of the Cross** at STATION

-ways (comb. form) indicating direction or manner, as in sideways

Wb Phys. weber

W.C. or **WC** without charge

WCTU Women's Christian Temperance Union

wd 1. wood 2. word 3. would

W.D. War Department

we (wē) pron. first person plural pronoun

weak (wēk) a. 1. lacking strength 2. feeble 3. fragile 4. defenseless 5. easily influenced 6. faint —'**weaken** v. —'**weakling** n. feeble creature —'**weakly** a. 1. weak 2. sickly —adv. 3. in a weak or feeble manner —'**weakness** n. —**weak-kneed** a. inf. yielding readily to force, intimidation etc.

weal[1] (wēl) n. streak left on flesh by blow of stick or whip

weal[2] (wēl) n. obs. prosperity or wellbeing (esp. in **the public weal, common weal**)

weald (wēld) n. obs. forested country

wealth (welth) n. 1. riches 2. abundance —'**wealthiness** n. —'**wealthy** a.

wean (wēn) vt. 1. accustom to food other than mother's milk 2. coax away

weapon ('wepən) n. 1. implement to fight with 2. anything used to get the better of an opponent

wear (wāər) vt. 1. have on the body 2. show 3. produce (hole etc.) by rubbing etc. 4. harass; weaken 5. inf. allow, tolerate —vi. 6. last 7.

become impaired by use **8.** (*with* on) (of time) pass slowly (**wore, worn, 'wearing**) —*n.* **9.** act of wearing **10.** things to wear **11.** damage caused by use **12.** ability to resist effects of constant use —**'wearer** *n.* —**wear and tear** depreciation or loss resulting from ordinary use

weary ('wēəri) *a.* **1.** tired, exhausted, jaded **2.** tiring **3.** tedious —*v.* **4.** make, become weary (**'wearied, 'wearying**) —**'wearily** *adv.* —**'weariness** *n.* —**'wearisome** *a.* causing weariness

weasel ('wēzəl) *n.* **1.** any of various small, fierce carnivores with long slender bodies **2.** cunning person **3.** tracked vehicle resembling tractor used in snow **4.** *sl.* informer —*vi.* **5.** evade an obligation, renege —**weasel words** ambiguous words intended to mislead

weather ('wedhər) *n.* **1.** day-to-day meteorological conditions, *esp.* temperature, cloudiness *etc.* of a place —*a.* **2.** toward the wind —*v.* **3.** affect or be affected by weather —*vt.* **4.** endure **5.** resist **6.** come safely through **7.** sail to windward of —**'weathering** *n.* mechanical and chemical breakdown of rocks by action of rain, cold *etc.* —**weather-beaten** *a.* showing signs of exposure to weather —**'weatherboard** *n.* timber boards used as external cladding of house; clapboard —**weather-bound** *a.* (of vessel, aircraft *etc.*) delayed by bad weather —**'weathercock** *n.* revolving vane to show which way wind blows —**weather eye 1.** vision of person trained to observe changes in weather **2.** *inf.* alert or observant gaze —**weather house** model house, usu. with two human figures, one that enters to foretell bad weather and one that enters to foretell good weather —**weather strip** thin strip of metal, felt *etc.* fitted between frame of door or window and opening part to exclude drafts and rain —**weather vane** vane designed to indicate direction in which wind is blowing

weave (wēv) *vt.* **1.** form into texture or fabric by interlacing, *esp.* on loom **2.** fashion, construct —*vi.* **3.** practice weaving **4.** make one's way, *esp.* with side-to-side motion (**wove** *or* **weaved, 'woven** *or* **weaved, 'weaving**) —**'weaver** *n.* **1.** person who weaves **2.** weaverbird —**'weaverbird** *n.* small Old World passerine songbird with short thick bill and dull plumage which builds covered nests

web (web) *n.* **1.** woven fabric **2.** net spun by spider **3.** membrane between toes of waterfowl, frogs *etc.* —**'webbing** *n.* strong fabric woven in strips

weber ('webər, 'vābər) *n.* SI unit of magnetic flux

wed (wed) *v.* **1.** marry —*vt.* **2.** unite closely (**'wedded, wed** *pt./pp.,* **'wedding**) —**'wedding** *n.* act of marrying, nuptial ceremony —**'wedlock** *n.* marriage

Wed. Wednesday

wedge (wej) *n.* **1.** piece of wood, metal *etc.,* thick at one end, tapering to a thin edge —*vt.* **2.** fasten, split with wedge **3.** stick by compression or crowding

Wedgwood ('wejwŏŏd) *n.* trade name for dinner ware and ornamental ceramic objects

Wednesday ('wenzdi) *n.* fourth day of week

wee (wē) *a.* small, little

weed (wēd) *n.* **1.** plant growing where undesired **2.** *inf.* tobacco **3.** *inf.* marijuana **4.** *inf.* thin, sickly person, animal —*vt.* **5.** clear of weeds —**'weedy** *a.* **1.** full of weeds **2.** *inf.* thin, weakly —**weed out** remove, eliminate what is unwanted

weeds (wēdz) *pl.n.* (widow's) mourning clothes

week (wēk) *n.* **1.** period of seven days, *esp.* one beginning on Sunday and ending on Saturday **2.** hours, days of work in seven-day period —**'weekly** *a./adv.* **1.** (happening, done, published *etc.*) once a week —*n.* **2.** newspaper or magazine issued every week —**'weekday** *n.* any day of week except Sunday and *usu.* Saturday —**'weekend** *n.* Saturday and Sunday, *esp.* considered as rest period

weep (wēp) *v.* **1.** shed (tears) —*vi.* **2.** grieve **3.** exude fluid (**wept, 'weeping**) —**'weepy** *a.* —**weeping willow** willow with drooping branches

weevil ('wēvil) *n.* any of numerous beetles with head prolonged to a snout, destructive to nuts, grain, fruit *etc.*

weft (weft) *n.* see WOOF[1]

weigh (wā) *vt.* **1.** find weight of **2.** consider **3.** raise (anchor) —*vi.* **4.** have weight **5.** be burdensome —**weight** *n.* **1.** force exerted on a quantity of matter by the gravity of the earth **2.** quality of heaviness **3.** heavy mass **4.** object of known mass for weighing **5.** unit of measurement of weight **6.** importance, influence —*vt.* **7.** add weight to —**'weightily** *adv.* —**'weighting** *n.* additional allowance payable in particular circumstances —**'weightlessness** *n.* having little or no weight, experienced *esp.* at great distances from earth because of reduced gravitational attraction (*also* **zero gravity**) —**'weighty** *a.* **1.** heavy **2.** onerous **3.** important **4.** momentous —**'weighbridge** *n.* machine for weighing vehicles *etc.* by means of metal plate set into road —**'weightlifting** *n.* sport of lifting barbells of specified weights in prescribed manner

weir (wēər) *n.* river dam

weird (wēərd) *a.* **1.** unearthly, uncanny **2.** strange, bizarre

welch (welch) *vi.* see WELSH

welcome ('welkəm) *a.* **1.** received gladly **2.** freely permitted —*n.* **3.** kindly greeting —*vt.* **4.** greet with pleasure **5.** receive gladly (**-comed, -coming**)

weld (weld) *vt.* **1.** unite (metal) by softening with heat **2.** unite closely —*n.* **3.** welded joint —**'welder** *n.* **1.** tradesman who welds **2.** machine used in welding

welfare ('welfâər) *n.* **1.** well-being **2.** government aid, *esp.* financial, for the needy —**welfare state** system in which the government takes responsibility for the social, economic *etc.* security of its citizens

well[1] (wel) *adv.* **1.** in good manner or degree **2.** suitably **3.** intimately **4.** fully **5.** favorably, kindly **6.** to a considerable degree —*a.* **7.** in good health **8.** suitable (**'better** *comp.,* **best** *sup.*) —*interj.* **9.** exclamation of surprise, interrogation *etc.* —**well-appointed** *a.* equipped or furnished well —**well-balanced** *a.* **1.** sane; sensible **2.** equally matched —**well-being** *n.* state of being well, happy or prosperous —**well-connected** *a.* having influential relatives —**well-disposed** *a.* having kindly or favorable feelings (toward) —**well-done** *a.* **1.** accomplished satisfactorily **2.** (of meat) cooked thoroughly —**well-earned** *a.* fully deserved —**well-grounded** *a.* **1.** thoroughly trained in rudiments of a subject **2.** based on good reasons —**well-heeled** *a.* *sl.* rich —**well-informed** *a.* knowledgeable —**well-intentioned** *a.* having benevolent intentions, usu. with unfortunate results —**well-kept** *a.* **1.** (of person) having a tidy, pleasing appearance **2.** (of room *etc.*) neat **3.** (of secret) not divulged —**well-nigh** *adv.* *poet.* almost —**well-off** *a.* **1.** in satisfactory state **2.** rich —**well-read** *a.* having read much —**well-rounded** *a.* **1.** varied and complete **2.** (of person) having developed many abilities **3.** symmetrical **4.** (of sentence) expressed well —**well-spoken** *a.* speaking fluently, graciously, aptly —**well-to-do** *a.* moderately wealthy —**well tried** proven to be satisfactory by long experience —**well-wisher** *n.* person who shows benevolence toward person, cause *etc.* —**well-wishing** *a./n.* —**well-worn** *a.* **1.** so much used as to be affected by wear **2.** hackneyed

well[2] (wel) *n.* **1.** hole sunk into the earth to reach water, gas, oil *etc.* **2.** spring **3.** any shaft like a well **4.** lowered floor forming seating area —*vi.* **5.** spring, gush —**'wellhead** *n.* **1.** source of well or stream **2.** source, fountainhead or origin —**'wellspring** *n.* **1.** source of spring or stream **2.** source of abundant supply

welsh (welsh) *or* **welch** *vi.* fail to pay debt or fulfill obligation —**'welsher** *or* **'welcher** *n.*

Welsh (welsh) *a./n.* see WALES

welt (welt) *n.* **1.** raised, strengthened seam **2.** weal —*vt.* **3.** provide with welt **4.** thrash

welter ('weltər) *vi.* **1.** roll or tumble —*n.* **2.** turmoil, disorder

welterweight ('weltərwāt) *n.* **1.** professional boxer weighing 140-147 lbs (63.5-66.5 kg); amateur boxer weighing 140-148 lbs (63.5-67 kg) **2.** wrestler weighing usu. 154-172 lbs (70-78 kg)

wen (wen) *n.* cyst, *esp.* on scalp

wench (wench) *n. now oft. facetious* young woman

wend (wend) *v.* go, travel

wendigo ('wendigo) *n.* **C** see SPLAKE

went (went) *pt. of* GO[1]

wept (wept) *pt./pp. of* WEEP

were (wər) imperfect indicative plural and subjunctive sing. and pl. of BE

werewolf ('wēərwŏŏlf, 'wâər-) *n.* in folklore, human being turned into wolf

weskit ('weskit) *n.* woman's sleeveless garment for the upper body

Wesleyan ('weslian, 'wez-) *a.* **1.** pert. to English preacher, John Wesley (1703-91), who founded Methodism **2.** of Methodism, *esp.* in its original form —*n.* **3.** follower of John Wesley **4.** member of Methodist Church —**'Wesleyanism** *n.*

west (west) *n.* **1.** part of sky where sun sets **2.** part of country *etc.* lying to this side **3.** occident —*a.* **4.** that is toward or in this region —*adv.* **5.** to the west —**'westerly** *a.* —**'western** *a.* **1.** of, in the west **2.** of dress based on clothes of working cowboys, *eg* jeans, high-heeled boots —*n.* **3.** motion picture, story *etc.* about cowboys or frontiersmen in western U.S. —**'westernize** *vt.* influence with customs, practices *etc.* of West —**'westward** *a./adv.* —**'westwards** *adv.* toward the west —**western hemisphere** (*oft.* **W- H-**) that half of the globe containing N and S Amer. —**go west** *inf.* **1.** disappear **2.** die **3.** be lost

West Germany see (Federal Republic of) GERMANY

Westminster ('westminstər) *n.* British Houses of Parliament

West Virginia East Central state of the U.S., admitted to the Union in 1863. Abbrev.: **W.Va., WV** (with ZIP code)

wet (wet) *a.* **1.** having water or other liquid on a surface or being soaked in it **2.** rainy **3.** (of paint, ink *etc.*) not yet dry **4.** permitting manufacture and sale of alcoholic liquors (**'wetter** *comp.,* **'wettest** *sup.*) —*vt.* **5.** make wet (**wet, 'wetted** *pt./pp.,* **'wetting** *pr.p.*) —*n.* **6.** moisture, rain —**'wetback** *n.* Mexican who enters U.S. illegally —**wet blanket** *inf.*

white

one depressing spirits of others —**wet dream** erotic dream accompanied by emission of semen —**wet nurse** woman suckling another's child —**wet suit** close-fitting rubber suit worn by divers *etc.*

wether ('wedhər) *n.* castrated ram

WFTU World Federation of Trade Unions

wh 1. which 2. white

WH watt-hour

whack (wak) *vt.* 1. strike with sharp resounding blow —*n.* 2. such blow 3. *inf.* share 4. *inf.* attempt —**whacked** *a.* exhausted —'**whacking** *a. inf.* big, enormous

whale (wāl) *n.* 1. any of order of large marine mammals with fishlike bodies and flattened heads 2. thing or idea with great magnitude 3. *Astron.* the constellation *Cetus* —'**whaler** *n.* man, ship employed in hunting whales —'**whaling** *n.* work or industry of hunting and processing whales for food, oil *etc.* —'**whalebone** *n.* 1. horny elastic substance from projections of upper jaw of certain whales 2. thin strip of this substance, or imitation in metal or plastic, used to stiffen bodices

wham (wam) *n.* 1. forceful blow or sound produced by it —*v.* 2. strike or cause to strike with great force (-**mm**-)

wharf (wôrf) *n.* platform at harbor, on river *etc.* for loading and unloading ships (*pl.* **wharves** (wôrvz), -**s**)

what (wot; *unstressed* wət) *pron.* 1. which thing 2. that which 3. request for statement to be repeated —*a.* 4. which 5. as much as 6. how great, surprising *etc.* —*interj.* 7. exclamation of surprise, anger *etc.* —**what-** '**ever** *pron.* 1. anything which 2. of what kind it may be —**whatso**'**ever** *a.* 1. at all: used as intensifier with indefinite pronouns and determiners such as *none, anybody* —*pron.* 2. *rare* whatever —'**whatnot** *n.* 1. *inf.* person, thing whose name is unknown, forgotten *etc.* 2. small stand with shelves

wheat (wēt) *n.* 1. grain of a cereal plant that yields flour for bread, cakes, pasta *etc.* 2. plant with dense spikes bearing the edible grain —'**wheaten** *a.* —**wheat bread** bread made from combined whole-grain and white flours —**wheat cake** pancake made of wheat flour —'**wheatear** *n.* any of various Old World thrushes —**wheat germ** embryo of wheat kernel

wheedle ('wēdəl) *v.* coax, cajole

wheel (wēl) *n.* 1. circular frame or disk (with spokes) revolving on axle 2. anything like a wheel in shape or function 3. act of turning 4. steering wheel —*v.* 5. (cause to) turn as if on axis 6. (cause to) move on or as if on wheels 7. (cause to) change course, *esp.* in opposite direction —'**wheelbarrow** *n.* barrow with one wheel —'**wheelbase** *n.* distance between front and rear hubs of vehicle —'**wheelchair** *n.* chair mounted on large wheels, used by people who cannot walk —**wheeler-dealer** *n.* manipulative person, *esp.* in business or politics —'**wheelhorse** *n.* 1. horse nearest the wheels (in a team) 2. reliable and effective person, *esp.* in politics —'**wheel-house** *n.* enclosed structure on vessel's bridge for steersman —'**wheelspin** *n.* revolution of wheels without full grip of road —'**wheelwright** *n.* person who makes or mends wheels as trade

wheeze (wēz) *vi.* 1. breathe with difficulty and whistling noise —*n.* 2. this sound 3. *inf.* trick, idea, plan —'**wheezy** *a.*

whelk (welk) *n.* any of several large spiral-shelled marine snails

whelp (welp) *n.* 1. young of certain animals, *esp.* of wolf or dog 2. *disparaging* youth 3. *jocular* child —*v.* 4. give birth to (whelps)

when (wen) *adv.* 1. at what time —*conj.* 2. at the time that 3. although 4. since —*pron.* 5. at which (time) —**when**'**ever** *adv./conj.* at whatever time —'**whensoever** *conj./adv. rare* whenever

whence (wens) *adv./conj. formal* 1. from what place or source 2. how

where (wāər) *adv./conj.* 1. at what place 2. at or to the place in which —'**whereabouts** *adv./conj.* 1. in what, which place —*n.* 2. present position —**where**'**as** *conj.* 1. considering that 2. while, on the contrary —**where**'**by** *conj.* by which —'**wherefore** *adv. obs.* 1. why 2. consequently —**where**'**of** *obs., formal adv.* 1. of what or which person or thing? —*pron.* 2. of which (person or thing) —'**whereupon** *conj.* at which point —**wher**'**ever** *adv./conj.* 1. where in the world 2. in what or which place 3. in any circumstances in which —'**wherewithal** *n.* necessary funds, resources *etc.*

whet (wet) *vt.* 1. sharpen 2. stimulate (-**tt**-) —'**whetstone** *n.* stone for sharpening tools

whether ('wedhər) *conj.* introduces the first of two alternatives, of which the second may be expressed or implied

whew (hwōō) *interj.* exclamation expressing relief, delight *etc.*

whey (wā) *n.* watery part of milk left after separation of curd, *esp.* in cheese making

which (wich) *a.* 1. used in requests for a selection from alternatives —*pron.* 2. which person or thing 3. the thing 'who' —**which**-'**ever** *pron.*

whiff (wif) *n.* 1. brief smell or suggestion of 2. puff of air —*vt.* 3. smell

Whig (wig) *n.* 1. member of the Amer. political party supporting the Revolution 2. **UK** member of 18th-cent. political party that sought to increase parliamentary power by limiting royal authority

while (wīl) *conj.* 1. in the time that 2. in spite of the fact that, although 3. whereas —*vt.* 4. pass (time, usu. idly) —*n.* 5. period of time —'**whilst** *conj.* while

whim (wim) *n.* sudden, passing fancy —'**whimsical** *a.* 1. fanciful 2. full of whims —**whimsi**'**cality** *n.* —'**whimsy** *or* '**whimsey** *n.* 1. whim 2. caprice —*a.* 3. quaint, comical or unusual, oft. in tasteless way

whimper ('wimpər) *vi.* 1. cry or whine softly 2. complain in this way —*n.* 3. such cry or complaint

whin (win) *n.* gorse

whine (wīn) *n.* 1. high-pitched plaintive cry 2. peevish complaint —*vi.* 3. utter this

whinny ('wini) *vi.* 1. neigh softly ('**whinnied,** '**whinnying**) —*n.* 2. gentle neigh

whip (wip) *vt.* 1. strike with whip 2. thrash 3. beat (cream, eggs) to a froth 4. lash 5. *inf.* pull, remove, insert *etc.* quickly 6. *inf.* steal —*vi.* 7. dart (-**pp**-) —*n.* 8. lash attached to handle for urging or punishing 9. member of legislature appointed by a political party to enforce party discipline, *esp.* to secure attendance at important sessions 10. elastic quality permitting bending in mast, fishing rod *etc.* 11. whipped dessert —'**whipping** *n.* 1. thrashing with whip or similar implement 2. cord used for binding or lashing 3. binding formed by wrapping rope *etc.* with cord or twine —'**whipcord** *n.* 1. strong worsted fabric with diagonally ribbed surface 2. hard twisted cord used for lashes of whips *etc.* —**whip hand** (*usu. with* the) 1. in driving horses *etc.*, hand holding whip 2. advantage or dominating position —'**whiplash** *n.* quick lash of whip or like that of whip —**whiplash injury** injury to neck as result of sudden jerking of unsupported head —'**whipper-snapper** *n.* insignificant but pretentious or

cheeky person, oft. young one. (*also* '**whipster**) —**whipping boy** scapegoat —**whip-round** *n. inf.* collection of money

whippet ('wipit) *n.* 1. small, swift purebred hound used for hunting rabbits and coursing 2. fast, light tank used in World War I

whir *or* **whirr** (wər) *v.* 1. (cause to) fly, spin *etc.* with buzzing or whizzing sound —*vi.* 2. bustle —*n.* 3. this sound 4. bustle

whirl (wərl) *v.* 1. swing rapidly round 2. drive or be driven at high speed —*vi.* 3. move rapidly in a circular course —*n.* 4. whirling movement 5. confusion, bustle, giddiness —'**whirligig** *n.* 1. spinning toy 2. merry-go-round —'**whirlpool** *n.* circular current, eddy —'**whirlwind** *n.* 1. wind whirling round while moving forward —*a.* 2. rapid or sudden —'**whirlybird** *n. inf.* helicopter

whisk (wisk) *vt.* 1. brush, sweep, beat lightly 2. beat to a froth —*v.* 3. move, remove, quickly —*n.* 4. light brush 5. egg-beating implement

whisker ('wiskər) *n.* 1. long stiff hair at side of mouth of cat or other animal 2. any of hairs on a man's face —**by a whisker** *inf.* only just

whiskey ('wiski) *n.* spirit distilled from fermented cereals (*Scot.,* **C** '**whisky**)

Whiskey ('wiski) *n.* word used in communications for the letter *w*

whisper ('wispər) *v.* 1. speak in soft, hushed tones, without vibration of vocal cords 2. rustle —*n.* 3. such speech 4. trace or suspicion 5. rustle

whist (wist) *n.* any of family of card games for four players in two partnerships played with standard 52-card deck in which the object is to win at least seven tricks out of 13 in play

whistle ('wisəl) *vi.* 1. produce shrill sound by forcing breath through rounded, nearly closed lips —*vt.* 2. utter, summon *etc.* by whistle —*n.* 3. such sound 4. any similar sound 5. instrument to make it —'**whistler** *n.* —**whistle stop** 1. minor railroad station where trains stop only on signal; small town having such a station 2. brief appearance in town, *esp.* by political candidate

whit (wit) *n.* jot, particle (*esp. in* **not a whit**)

white (wīt) *a.* 1. of the color of milk or table salt 2. pale 3. light in color 4. (**W**-) having a light-colored skin —*n.* 5. color of milk or table salt 6. white pigment 7. white part 8. clear fluid round yolk of egg 9. (**W**-) White person —'**whiten** *v.* —'**whiteness** *n.* —'**whiting** *n.* form of chalk used in polishing silver, whitewashing and making putty —'**whitish** *a.* —**white ant** termite —'**whitebait** *n.* young herring —**white blood cell** *see* LEUKOCYTE —'**whitecap** *n.* wave with white broken crest —**white-collar** *a.* denoting nonmanual salaried workers —**white dwarf** one of class of small faint stars of enormous density —**white elephant** useless, unwanted, gift or possession —**white feather** symbol or mark of cowardice —'**whitefish** *n.* any freshwater food fish related to salmon and trout —**white flag** white banner or cloth used as signal of surrender or truce —'**whitefly** *n.* very small, whitish fly with four wings, usu. found on the under surface of leaves —**white friar** Carmelite friar, so called because of white cloak that forms part of habit of this order —**white gold** pale alloy of gold resembling silver or platinum —**white goods** 1. household linen such as sheets, tablecloths *etc.* 2. large household appliances, such as refrigerators *etc.* —'**whitehead** *n. see* MILIUM —**white heat** 1. intense heat characterized by emission of white light 2. *inf.* state of intense excitement or activity —**white hope**

one expected to bring honor or glory to his group, team *etc.* —**white horse** whitecap —**white-hot** *a.* 1. at such high temperature that white light is emitted 2. *inf.* in state of intense emotion —**white lead** (led) any of various lead-containing pigments used chiefly as exterior paints —**white lie** minor, unimportant lie —**white matter** whitish tissue of brain and spinal cord, consisting mainly of nerve fibers —**white meat** any meat that is light in color, such as chicken or turkey breast —**white noise** sound or electrical noise that has relatively wide continuous range of frequencies of uniform intensity —**whiteout** *n.* condition of severely reduced visibility in snowy regions —**white pepper** condiment made from husked dried beans of pepper plant —**white sale** sale of white goods —**white sauce** thick sauce made from flour, butter, seasonings, and milk or stock —**white slave** woman, child forced or enticed away for purposes of prostitution —**white tie** 1. white bow tie worn as part of man's full evening dress 2. full evening dress for men —**whitewash** *n.* 1. substance for whitening walls *etc.* —*vt.* 2. apply this to 3. cover up, gloss over, suppress —**white whale** small white toothed whale of northern waters (*also* be'**luga**) —**whitewood** *n.* 1. tree with light-colored wood, such as the tulip tree 2. its wood —**show the white feather** act in cowardly manner —**the White House** 1. official Washington residence of president of U.S. 2. U.S. presidency —**White man's burden** supposed duty of White race to bring education and Western culture to non-White inhabitants of their colonies

Whitehall ('wIt-hōl) *n.* 1. street in London where main government offices are situated 2. British Government

whither ('widhər) *adv. Poet.* 1. to what place 2. to which

whiting ('wIting) *n.* 1. any of various marine food fishes found in seas around U.S. 2. hake 3. European food fish related to cod

whitlow ('witlō) *n.* abscess on finger, *esp.* round nail

Whitsun ('witsən) *n.* week following **Whit Sunday**, seventh Sunday after Easter (*also* **Pentecost**)

whittle ('witəl) *vt.* 1. cut, carve with knife 2. pare away —**whittle down** reduce gradually, wear (away)

whiz *or* **whizz** (wiz) *n.* 1. loud hissing sound 2. *inf.* person skillful at something —*vi.* 3. move with or make loud hissing sound 4. *inf.* move quickly —**whiz** *or* **whizz kid** *inf.* person who is outstandingly successful for his or her age

who (hōō) *pron.* relative and interrogative pronoun, always referring to persons —**who-dunit** (hōō'dunit) *n. inf.* detective story —**who'ever** *pron.* who, any one or every one that —**whoso'ever** *pron. formal* whoever

W.H.O. World Health Organization

whoa (wō) *interj.* command used, *esp.* to horses, to stop or slow down

whole (hōl) *a.* 1. complete 2. containing all elements or parts 3. entire 4. not defective or imperfect 5. healthy —*n.* 6. complete thing or system —'**wholly** *adv.* —'**wholesome** *a.* producing good effect, physically or morally —**whole-grain** *a.* of, pert. to flour which contains the whole of the grain (*also* **graham**) —'**whole'hearted** *a.* 1. sincere 2. enthusiastic —**whole number** 1. integer 2. natural number —'**wholesale** *n.* 1. sale of goods by large quantities to retailers —*a.* 2. dealing by wholesale 3. extensive —'**wholesaler** *n.* —**on the whole** 1. taking everything into consideration 2. in general

whom (hōōm) *pron.* objective case of WHO

whoop (hōōp) *n.* shout or cry expressing excitement *etc.*

whoopee ('wōōpē) *n. inf.* gay, riotous time —**make whoopee** 1. participate in wild noisy party 2. make love

whooping cough ('hōōping) infectious disease of mucous membrane lining air passages, marked by convulsive coughing with shrill crowing sound on breathing in (*also* **pertussis**)

whoops (wōōps) *interj.* exclamation of surprise or of apology

whopper ('wopər) *n. inf.* 1. anything unusually large 2. monstrous lie —'**whopping** *a.*

whore (hör) *n.* prostitute —'**whorehouse** *n.* brothel

whorl (wörl, wərl) *n.* 1. ring of leaves or petals 2. turn of spiral 3. anything forming part of circular pattern, *eg* lines of human fingerprint

whortleberry ('wərtəlberi) *n.* small Eurasian shrub of erica genus with edible sweet blackish berries

whose (hōōz) *pron.* possessive case of WHO and WHICH

whs *or* **whse** warehouse

whsle wholesale

why (wI) *adv.* for what cause or reason

WI Wisconsin

W.I. 1. West Indies 2. wrought iron 3. UK Women's Institute

WIA wounded in action

wick (wik) *n.* strip of thread feeding flame of lamp or candle with oil, grease *etc.*

wicked ('wikid) *a.* 1. evil, sinful 2. very bad 3. mischievous —'**wickedly** *adv.* —'**wickedness** *n.*

wicker(work) ('wikər(wərk)) *n.* woven cane *etc.*, basketwork

wicket ('wikit) *n.* 1. small gate 2. *Cricket* set of three stumps and bails 3. cricket pitch

wid widow *or* widower

wide (wId) *a.* 1. having a great extent from side to side, broad 2. having considerable distance between 3. spacious 4. liberal 5. vast 6. far from the mark 7. opened fully —*adv.* 8. to the full extent 9. far from the intended target —'**widely** *adv.* —'**widen** *v.* —**width** (width) *or* '**wideness** *n.* breadth —**wide-angle lens** lens system on camera that can cover angle of view of 60° or more —**wide-eyed** *a.* innocent or credulous —'**widespread** *a.* 1. extending over a wide area 2. common

widow ('widō) *n.* 1. woman whose husband is dead and who has not married again 2. *fig.* woman temporarily abandoned by husband, as in *golf widow* —*vt.* 3. make a widow of —'**widower** *n.* man whose wife is dead and who has not married again —'**widowhood** *n.*

wield (wēld) *vt.* 1. hold and use 2. brandish 3. manage

wife (wIf) *n.* a man's partner in marriage, married woman (*pl.* **wives**) —'**wifely** *a.*

wig (wig) *n.* artificial hair for the head

wigeon *or* **widgeon** ('wijən) *n.* Eurasian duck of marshes, swamps *etc.*

wiggle ('wigəl) *v.* 1. (cause to) move jerkily from side to side —*n.* 2. such movement —'**wiggly** *a.*

wigwam ('wigwam) *n.* N Amer. Indian's hut of Great Lakes region and eastward

wild (wIld) *a.* 1. not tamed or domesticated 2. not cultivated 3. savage 4. stormy 5. uncontrolled 6. random 7. excited 8. rash 9. frantic 10. *inf.* (of party *etc.*) rowdy, exciting 11. (of card, *esp.* joker or deuce, in some games) able to be given any value the holder pleases —'**wildly** *adv.* —'**wildness** *n.* —'**wildcat** *n.* 1. bobcat —*a.* 2. of sudden occurrence, *esp.* oil- or gas-well strike —**wild-goose chase** futile pursuit —'**wildlife** *n.* wild animals and plants collectively —**wild oats** *sl.* indiscretions of youth, *esp.* dissoluteness before settling down (*esp. in* **sow one's wild oats**) —**wild rice** tall aquatic N Amer. perennial grass or its edible grain —**Wild West** western U.S., *esp.* with reference to its frontier lawlessness

wildebeest ('wildibēst) *n.* gnu

wilderness ('wildərnis) *n.* 1. desert, waste place 2. state of desolation or confusion

wildfire ('wIldfIər) *n.* 1. raging, uncontrollable fire 2. anything spreading, moving fast

wile (wIl) *n.* trick —'**wily** *a.*

will (wil) *v. aux.* 1. forms moods and tenses indicating intention or conditional result (**would** *pt.*) —*vi.* 2. have a wish —*vt.* 3. wish 4. intend 5. leave as legacy —*n.* 6. faculty of deciding what one will do 7. purpose 8. volition 9. determination 10. wish 11. directions written for disposal of property after death —'**willful** *a.* 1. obstinate, self-willed 2. intentional —'**willfully** *adv.* —'**willfulness** *n.* —'**willing** *a.* 1. ready 2. given cheerfully —'**willingly** *adv.* —'**willingness** *n.* —'**willpower** *n.* ability to control oneself, one's actions, impulses

willies ('wiliz) *pl.n. sl.* nervousness, jitters, or fright (*esp. in* **give** (*or* **get**) **the willies**)

williwaw ('wiliwō) *n.* sudden violent gust of cold land air

will-o'-the-wisp (wiləðə'wisp) *n.* 1. brief pale flame or phosphorescence sometimes seen over marshes 2. elusive person or hope

willow ('wilō) *n.* 1. tree, such as the weeping willow with long thin flexible branches 2. its wood —'**willowy** *a.* lithe, slender, supple —'**willowherb** *n.* tall plant with mauve flowers

willy-nilly (wili'nili) *adv./a.* (occurring) whether desired or not

Wilson ('wilsən) *n.* **Woodrow**. the 28th President of the U.S. (1913-17)

wilt (wilt) *v.* (cause to) become limp, drooping or lose strength *etc.*

Wimbledon ('wimbəldən) *n.* residential area and shopping center in south London, location of All-England Lawn Tennis Championships

wimp (wimp) *n. inf.* feeble, ineffective person

wimple ('wimpəl) *n.* cloth wound around head to frame the face, now worn by some nuns

win (win) *vi.* 1. be successful, victorious —*vt.* 2. get by labor or effort 3. reach 4. allure 5. be successful in 6. gain the support, consent *etc.* of (**won**, '**winning**) —*n.* 7. victory, *esp.* in games —'**winner** *n.* —'**winning** *a.* charming —'**winnings** *pl.n.* sum won in game, betting *etc.*

wince (wins) *vi.* 1. flinch, draw back, as from pain *etc.* —*n.* 2. this act

winch (winch) *n.* 1. machine for hoisting or hauling using cable wound round drum —*vt.* 2. move (something) by using a winch

wind¹ (wind) *n.* 1. air in motion 2. breath 3. flatulence 4. idle talk 5. hint or suggestion 6. scent borne by air —*vt.* 7. render short of breath, *esp.* by blow *etc.* 8. get the scent of —'**windward** *n.* side against which wind is blowing —'**windy** *a.* 1. exposed to wind 2. flatulent 3. *inf.* talking too much —'**windbag** *n. sl.* voluble person who has little of interest to communicate —'**windbreak** *n.* fence, line of trees *etc.* serving as protection from wind —'**windfall** *n.* 1. unexpected good luck 2.

fallen fruit —**wind gauge** anemometer —**wind instrument** musical instrument played by blowing or air pressure —**'wind-jammer** n. large merchant sailing ship —**windmill** ('windmil, 'winmil) n. 1. wind-driven apparatus with fanlike sails for raising water, crushing grain etc. 2. imaginary opponent or evil —**'windpipe** n. passage from throat to lungs —**'windshield** n. protective sheet of glass etc. in front of driver or pilot —**'windsock** n. cone of material flown on mast at airfield to indicate wind direction (also **wind sleeve**) —**wind tunnel** chamber for testing aerodynamic properties of aircraft etc. in which current of air can be maintained at constant velocity

windjammer

wind² (wīnd) vi. 1. twine 2. meander —vt. 3. turn or coil around some object or point 4. wrap 5. make ready for working by tightening spring (**wound**, **'winding**) —n. 6. act of winding 7. single turn of something wound 8. a turn, curve —**winding sheet** sheet in which corpse is wrapped for burial; shroud —**wind-up** n. inf. 1. act of concluding 2. end —**wind down** 1. lower or move down by cranking 2. (of clock spring) become slack 3. diminish gradually in force or power —**wind up** 1. bring to or reach a conclusion 2. tighten spring of (clockwork mechanism) 3. inf. make nervous, tense etc. 4. inf. see LIQUIDATE (sense 2) 5. inf. end up (in specified state)

windlass ('windləs) n. winch, esp. simple one worked by a crank

window ('windō) n. 1. hole in wall (with glass) to admit light, air etc. 2. anything similar in appearance or function 3. area for display of goods behind glass of shop front —**window box** long narrow box, placed on windowsill, in which plants are grown —**window-dressing** n. 1. arrangement of goods in a shop window 2. deceptive display —**'windowpane** n. sheet of glass in window —**window-shop** vi. look at goods in shop windows without buying them (-pp-) —**'windowsill** n. sill below window

Windsor chair ('winzər) simple wooden chair, usu. having shaped seat, splayed legs, and back of many spindles

wine (wīn) n. fermented juice of grape etc. —**'wino** n. person who habitually drinks wine as means of getting drunk —**'wine-press** n. apparatus for extracting juice from grape —**'wineskin** n. skin of sheep or goat sewn up and used as holder for wine

wing (wing) n. 1. feathered limb a bird uses in flying 2. one of organs of flight of insect or some animals 3. main lifting surface of aircraft 4. lateral extension 5. side portion of building projecting from main central portion 6. one of sides of a stage 7. flank corps of army on either left or right side 8. inf. arm of human being 9. Sport (player on) either side of pitch 10. faction, esp. of political party —pl. 11. insignia worn by qualified aircraft pilot 12. sides of stage —vi. 13. fly 14. move, go very fast —vt. 15. disable,

wound slightly —**winged** a. having wings —**wing chair** chair having wings on each side of back —**'wingspan** n. see SPAN (sense 4)

wink (wingk) v. 1. close and open (an eye) rapidly, esp. to indicate friendliness or as signal —vi. 2. twinkle —n. 3. act of winking

winkle ('wingkəl) n. shellfish, periwinkle

winnow ('winō) vt. 1. blow free of chaff 2. sift, examine

winsome ('winsəm) a. charming, winning

winter ('wintər) n. 1. the coldest season —vi. 2. pass, spend the winter —**'wintry** or **'wintery** a. 1. of, like winter 2. cold —**'wintergreen** n. evergreen shrub, esp. subshrub of eastern N Amer., which has white, bell-shaped flowers and edible red berries —**winter solstice** time at which sun is at its southernmost point in sky appearing at noon at its lowest altitude above horizon. It occurs about Dec. 22nd —**winter sports** sports held in open air on snow or ice —**oil of wintergreen** aromatic compound, formerly made from the shrub but now synthesized: used medicinally and for flavoring

wipe (wīp) vt. 1. rub so as to clean —n. 2. wiping —**'wiper** n. 1. one that wipes 2. automatic wiping apparatus (esp. **windshield wiper**) —**wipe out** 1. erase 2. annihilate 3. sl. kill

wire ('wīər) n. 1. metal drawn into thin, flexible strand 2. something made of wire, eg fence 3. telegram —vt. 4. provide, fasten with wire 5. send by telegraph —**'wiring** n. system of wires —**'wiry** a. 1. like wire 2. lean and tough —**wire-gauge** n. 1. flat plate with slots in which standard wire sizes can be measured 2. standard system of sizes for measuring diameters of wires —**wire-haired** a. (of various breeds of dog) with short stiff hair —**'wiretap** v. tap (telephone wire etc.) to obtain information secretly

wireless ('wīərlis) n. 1. old-fashioned term for radio, radio set —a. 2. of or for radio

Wisconsin (wis'konsin) n. East North Central state of the U.S., admitted to the Union in 1848. Abbrev.: **Wis.**, **WI** (with ZIP code)

Wisd. Bible Wisdom of Solomon

wise¹ (wīz) a. 1. having intelligence and knowledge 2. sensible —**wisdom** ('wizdəm) n. 1. (accumulated) knowledge, learning 2. erudition —**'wisely** adv. —**'wiseacre** n. one who wishes to seem wise —**wisdom tooth** third molar usu. cut about 20th year

wise² (wīz) n. obs. manner

-wise (comb. form) 1. indicating direction or manner, as in clockwise, likewise 2. with reference to, as in businesswise

wisecrack ('wīzkrak) n. inf. flippant, (would-be) clever remark

wish (wish) vi. 1. have a desire —vt. 2. desire —n. 3. desire 4. thing desired —**'wishful** a. 1. desirous 2. too optimistic —**'wishbone** n. V-shaped bone above breastbone of fowl —**wishful thinking** erroneous belief that one's wishes are in accordance with reality

wishy-washy ('wishiwoshi) a. inf. 1. lacking in substance, force, color etc. 2. watery; thin

wisp (wisp) n. 1. light, delicate streak, as of smoke 2. twisted handful, usu. of straw etc. 3. stray lock of hair —**'wispy** a.

wisteria (wi'stēəriə) or **wistaria** (wis'tēəriə, -'ter-) n. climbing shrub with usu. mauve flowers

wistful ('wistfəl) a. 1. longing, yearning 2. sadly pensive —**'wistfully** adv.

wit¹ (wit) n. 1. ingenuity in connecting amusingly incongruous ideas 2. person gifted with this power 3. sense 4. intellect 5.

understanding 6. ingenuity 7. humor —**'witless** a. foolish —**'witticism** n. witty remark —**'wittily** adv. —**'wittingly** adv. 1. on purpose 2. knowingly —**'witty** a.

wit² (wit) v. obs. be or become aware of (something) —**to wit** that is to say; namely

witch (wich) n. 1. person, usu. female, believed to practice, practicing, or professing to practice (black) magic, sorcery 2. ugly, wicked woman 3. fascinating woman —**'witchery** n. —**'witchcraft** n. —**witch doctor** in certain societies, man appearing to cure or cause injury, disease by magic —**witch grass** see QUACK GRASS —**witch-hunt** n. rigorous campaign to expose dissenters on pretext of safeguarding public welfare —**witch-hunting** n./a.

witch- (comb. form) see WYCH-

witch hazel 1. any of genus of trees and shrubs of N Amer. having medicinal properties 2. astringent medicinal solution containing extract of bark and leaves of one of these shrubs, applied to treat bruises etc.

with (widh, with) prep. 1. in company or possession of 2. against 3. in relation to 4. through 5. by means of —**withal** (wi'dhôl) adv. also, likewise —**within** (wi'dhin) prep./adv. in, inside —**without** (wi'dhowt) prep. 1. lacking 2. obs. outside

withdraw (widh'drô) v. draw back or out (-**'drew**, -**'drawn**, -**'drawing**) —**with'drawal** n. —**with'drawn** a. reserved, unsociable

withe (with, widh, wīdh) n. 1. strong flexible twig, esp. of willow, suitable for binding things together —vt. 2. bind with withes

wither ('widhər) v. (cause to) wilt, dry up, decline —**'withering** a. (of glance etc.) scornful

withers ('widhərz) pl.n. ridge between a horse's shoulder blades

withhold (with'hōld, widh-) vt. 1. restrain 2. keep back 3. refrain from giving (-**'held**, -**'holding**) —**with'holder** n.

withstand (with'stand, widh-) vt. oppose, resist, esp. successfully (-**'stood**, -**'standing**)

withy ('widhi) n. 1. see WITHE (sense 1) 2. willow tree

witness ('witnis) n. 1. one who sees something 2. testimony 3. one who gives testimony —vi. 4. give testimony —vt. 5. see 6. attest to genuineness of 7. see and sign as having seen —**witness stand** place in court of law in which witnesses stand to give evidence

wives (wīvz) n., pl. of WIFE —**old wives' tale** superstitious tradition

wizard ('wizərd) n. 1. sorcerer, magician 2. expert —**'wizardry** n.

wizened ('wizənd) or **wizen** a. shriveled, wrinkled

wk. 1. week (pl. **wks.**) 2. work

wkly weekly

WL 1. waterline 2. wavelength

wm wattmeter

WNW west-northwest

W.O. warrant officer

w/o without

woad (wōd) n. 1. biennial plant of British Isles formerly grown for dye yielded by its leaves 2. blue dye from this plant

wobble ('wobəl) vi. 1. move unsteadily, sway —n. 2. an unsteady movement —**'wobbly** a.

WOC without compensation

woe (wō) n. grief —**'woebegone** a. looking sorrowful —**'woeful** a. 1. sorrowful 2. pitiful 3. wretched —**'woefully** adv.

wold (wōld) n. open downs, moorland

wolf (woolf) n. 1. wild predatory doglike animal of northern countries 2. inf. man who habitually tries to seduce women (pl. **wolves**

(wŏolvz)) —vt. 3. eat ravenously —'wolf-hound n. largest breed of dog, used formerly to hunt wolves —wolf whistle whistle by man expressing admiration for a woman —cry wolf raise false alarm

wolfram ('wŏolfrəm) n. tungsten

wolverine (wŏolvə'rēn) n. carnivorous mammal inhabiting Arctic regions

woman ('wŏomən) n. 1. adult human female 2. women collectively (pl. women ('wimin)) —'womanhood n. —'womanish a. effeminate —'womanize vi. inf. (of a man) indulge in many casual affairs with women —'womanizer n. —'womankind n. —'womanly a. of, proper to woman —Women's Liberation movement for removal of attitudes, practices that preserve social, economic etc. inequalities between women and men (also women's lib)

womb (wŏom) n. female organ of conception and gestation

wombat ('wombat) n. Aust. burrowing marsupial with heavy body, short legs and dense fur

won (wun) pt./pp. of WIN

wonder ('wundər) n. 1. emotion excited by amazing or unusual thing 2. marvel, miracle —vi. 3. be curious 4. feel amazement —'wonderful a. 1. remarkable 2. very fine —'wonderfully adv. —'wonderment n. surprise —'wondrous a. 1. inspiring wonder 2. strange —wonder drug see miracle drug at MIRACLE

wonky ('wongki) a. inf. 1. shaky, unsteady 2. groggy 3. askew 4. unreliable

wont (wŏnt, wŏnt) n. 1. custom —a. 2. accustomed —'wonted a. habitual, established

woo (wŏo) vt. court, seek to marry —'wooer n. suitor

wood (wŏod) n. 1. substance of trees, timber 2. firewood 3. tract of land with growing trees —'wooded a. having (many) trees —'wooden a. 1. made of wood 2. obstinate 3. without expression —'woody a. —'woodbine n. Virginia creeper —'woodcarver n. —'woodcarving n. 1. act of carving wood 2. work of art produced by carving wood —'woodchuck n. thickset marmot found east of Rockies from northern Canada to southern U.S. (also groundhog) —'woodcock n. game bird —'woodcut n. 1. engraving on wood 2. impression from this —woodland ('wŏodlənd) n. woods, forest —'woodlark n. Old World lark similar to skylark —'woodlouse n. small gray land crustacean with flattened elliptical body (pl. -lice) —'woodpecker n. climbing bird usu. with brightly colored plumage and strong chisel-like bill with which it bores into trees for insects —'woodpile n. heap of firewood —wood pulp finely pulped wood that has been digested by chemical, such as caustic soda, used in making paper and rayon —'woodruff n. plant, esp. sweet woodruff, which has small sweet-scented white flowers, used to flavor wine and in perfumery —wood screw screw with slotted head and gimlet point permitting it to be driven into wood with a screwdriver —wood sorrel Eurasian plant having compound leaves, underground creeping stem and white purple-veined flowers —woodwind ('wŏodwind) a./n. (of) wind instruments of orchestra whose tones are produced by opening and closing holes —'woodwork n. components made of wood, such as doors etc.

woof¹ (wŏof, wŏof) n. the threads that cross the warp in weaving

woof² (wŏof) interj. 1. imitation of bark of dog —vi. 2. (of dog) bark

woofer ('wŏofər) n. loudspeaker for reproducing low-frequency sounds

wool (wŏol) n. 1. soft hair of sheep, goat etc. 2. yarn spun from this —'woolen or 'woollen a. —'woolly or 'wooly a. 1. of wool 2. vague, muddled —n. 3. knitted woolen garment —'woolgathering a./n. daydreaming —'woolsack n. Lord Chancellor's seat in British House of Lords

woomera ('wŏomərə) n. 1. throwing stick used by Aust. Aborigines for propelling dart or spear 2. short club used as missile

woozy ('wŏozi) a. inf. 1. dazed or confused 2. experiencing dizziness, nausea etc. as result of drink —'woozily adv. —'wooziness n.

word (wərd) n. 1. unit of speech or writing regarded by users of a language as the smallest separate meaningful unit 2. term 3. message 4. brief remark 5. information 6. promise 7. command —vt. 8. express in words, esp. in particular way —'wordily adv. —'wording n. choice and arrangement of words —'wordy a. using more words than necessary, verbose —word blindness 1. alexia 2. dyslexia —word processing production of documents by electronic system including typing, text editing and storage —word processor installation for word processing, typically consisting of keyboard and VDU incorporating microprocessor, storage and processing capabilities

wore (wōr) pt. of WEAR

work (wərk) n. 1. labor 2. employment 3. occupation 4. task 5. toil 6. something made or accomplished 7. production of art or science 8. book 9. needlework —pl. 10. factory 11. total of person's deeds, writings etc. 12. inf. everything, full or extreme treatment 13. mechanism of clock etc. —vt. 14. cause to operate 15. make, shape —vi. 16. apply effort 17. labor 18. operate 19. be engaged in trade, profession etc. 20. turn out successfully 21. ferment —'workable a. —'worker n. —'working n. 1. operation or mode of operation of something 2. act or process of molding something pliable 3. (oft. pl.) part of mine or quarry that is being or has been worked —a. 4. of or concerned with person or thing that works 5. concerned with, used in, or suitable for work 6. capable of being operated or used —'workaday a. 1. ordinary 2. suitable for working days —worka'holic n. person obsessively addicted to work —work force 1. total number of workers employed by company on specific project etc. 2. total number of people who could be employed —'workhouse n. Hist. institution offering food, lodgings for unpaid menial work —working class social class consisting of wage earners, esp. manual —working-class a. —working party advisory committee studying specific problem, question —'workman n. manual worker —'workmanlike or 'workmanly a. appropriate to or befitting a good workman —'workmanship n. 1. skill of workman 2. way thing is finished 3. style —work-out n. session of physical exercise, esp. for training or practice —'workroom n. —'workshop n. place where things are made —'workshy a. not inclined to work —work station area in office etc. where one person works —work in 1. insert or become inserted 2. find space for —work of art 1. piece of fine art, as painting, sculpture 2. something that may be likened to piece of fine art, esp. in beauty etc. —work out 1. accomplish by effort 2. solve by reasoning or calculation 3. devise or formulate 4. prove satisfactory 5. happen as

specified 6. take part in physical exercise, as in training 7. remove all mineral in (mine etc.) that can be profitably exploited

world (wərld) n. 1. the universe 2. the planet earth 3. sphere of existence 4. mankind, people generally 5. society —'worldly a. 1. earthly 2. mundane 3. absorbed in the pursuit of material gain, advantage 4. carnal —World Bank popular name for International Bank for Reconstruction and Development, established in 1945 —world-beater n. person or thing that surpasses all others in his, her or its category; champion —World Court the Permanent Court of International Justice at the Hague, Netherlands —World Cup international association football championship competition held every four years between national teams —World Series annual series of baseball games between pennant winners of major leagues to decide U.S. professional championship —world-shaking a. of enormous significance; momentous —world war war involving many countries

worm (wərm) n. 1. small limbless creeping snakelike creature 2. anything resembling worm in shape or movement 3. inf. weak, despised person —pl. 4. (disorder caused by) infestation of worms, esp. in intestines —vi. 5. crawl —vt. 6. work (oneself) in insidiously 7. extract (secret) craftily 8. rid of worms —'wormy a. —'wormcast n. coil of earth excreted by earthworm —worm-eaten a. 1. full of holes gnawed by worms 2. old, antiquated —worm gear 1. device consisting of threaded shaft (worm) that mates with gear wheel (worm wheel) so that rotary motion can be transferred between two

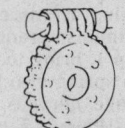

worm gear

shafts at right angles to each other 2. gear wheel driven by threaded shaft or worm (also worm wheel) —worm's-eye a. seen from below

wormwood ('wərmwŏod) n. 1. bitter herb 2. bitterness

worn (wōrn) pp. of WEAR —worn-out a. 1. worn or used until threadbare, valueless or useless 2. exhausted

worry ('wuri) vi. 1. be (unduly) concerned —vt. 2. trouble, pester, harass 3. (of dog) seize, shake with teeth ('worried, 'worrying) —n. 4. (cause of) anxiety, concern —'worrier n. —'worrisome a. 1. causing worry 2. tending to worry —worry beads string of beads that when played with supposedly relieves nervous tension

worse (wərs) a./adv. 1. comp. of BAD or BADLY —n. 2. inferior or less good person, thing or state —'worsen v. 1. make, grow worse —vt. 2. impair —vi. 3. deteriorate —worst a./adv. 1. sup. of BAD or BADLY —n. 2. least good or most inferior person, part or thing

worship ('wərship) vt. 1. show religious devotion to 2. adore 3. love and admire —n. 4. act of worshiping 5. title used to address mayor, magistrate etc. —'worshiper n. —'worshipful a.

worsted ('wŏostid) n. 1. smooth, twisted woolen yarn —a. 2. made of woolen yarn 3. spun from wool

wort (wərt) n. 1. obs. plant, herb 2. infusion of malt before fermentation

worth (wərth) a. 1. having or deserving to have value specified 2. meriting —n. 3. excellence 4. merit, value 5. virtue 6. usefulness 7. price 8. quantity to be had for a given sum —**worthily** ('wərdhili) adv. —**worthiness** ('wərdhinis) n. —**worthless** a. useless —**worthy** ('wərdhi) a. 1. virtuous 2. meriting —n. 3. one of eminent worth —**worth'while** a. worth the time, effort etc. involved

would (wŏŏd; unstressed wəd) v. aux. 1. expressing wish, intention, probability —v. 2. pt. of WILL —**would-be** a. wishing, pretending to be

wound[1] (wŏŏnd) n. 1. injury, hurt from cut, stab etc. —vt. 2. inflict wound on, injure 3. pain

wound[2] (wownd) pt./pp. of WIND[2]

wove (wōv) pt. of WEAVE

woven ('wōvən) pp. of WEAVE

wow (wow) interj. 1. exclamation of astonishment, admiration etc. —n. 2. inf. object of astonishment, admiration etc. 3. variation, distortion in pitch in phonograph etc.

WP 1. weather permitting 2. without prejudice 3. word processing 4. word processor

WPA Works Progress Administration

WPC watts per candle

w.p.m. or **WPM** words per minute

wpn weapon

W.R. warehouse receipt

wrack (rak) n. kelp

wrack

wraith (rāth) n. 1. apparition of a person seen shortly before or after death 2. specter

wrangle ('ranggəl) vi. 1. quarrel (noisily) 2. dispute 3. herd cattle —n. 4. noisy quarrel 5. dispute —**'wrangler** n. cowboy

wrap (rap) vt. 1. cover, esp. by putting something round 2. put round (-pp-) —**wrap** or **'wrapper** n. 1. loose garment 2. covering —**'wrapping** n. material used to wrap —**'wrapover, 'wraparound** or **'wrapround** a. (of garment, esp. skirt) not sewn up at one side, but worn wrapped round body and fastened so that open edges overlap

wrasse (ras) n. any of several edible marine fishes of warm seas

wrath (rath) n. anger —**'wrathful** a.

wreak (rēk) vt. 1. inflict (vengeance) 2. cause

wreath (rēth) n. something twisted into ring form, esp. band of flowers etc. as memorial or tribute on grave etc. —**wreathe** vt. 1. form into wreath 2. surround 3. wind round

wreck (rek) n. 1. destruction of ship 2. wrecked ship 3. ruin 4. something ruined —vt. 5. cause the wreck of —**'wreckage** n. —**'wrecker** n. 1. person or thing that destroys, ruins 2. person whose job is to demolish houses, dismantle old automobiles etc.

wren '(ren) n. any of numerous small N Amer. songbirds distributed throughout the U.S. of which one species has spread to Europe and Asia

wrench (rench) vt. 1. twist 2. distort 3. seize forcibly 4. sprain —n. 5. violent twist 6. tool for twisting, screwing or holding 7. sudden pain caused esp. by separation

wrest (rest) vt. 1. take by force 2. twist violently

wrestle ('resəl, 'rasəl) vi. 1. fight (esp. as sport) by grappling and trying to throw down 2. strive 3. struggle —n. 4. struggle, tussle —**'wrestler** n. —**'wrestling** n.

wretch (rech) n. 1. despicable person 2. miserable creature —**wretched** ('rechid) a. 1. miserable, unhappy 2. worthless —**wretchedly** ('rechidli) adv. —**wretchedness** ('rechidnis) n.

wriggle ('rigəl) vi. 1. move with twisting action, as worm 2. squirm —n. 3. this action

wright (rīt) n. obs. workman; maker; builder

wring (ring) vt. 1. twist 2. extort 3. pain 4. squeeze out (**wrung, 'wringing**) —**'wringer** n. machine consisting of two rollers between which wet clothes are run to squeeze out the water

wrinkle ('ringkəl) n. 1. slight ridge or furrow on surface 2. crease in the skin 3. fold 4. pucker 5. inf. (useful) trick, hint —v. 6. make, become wrinkled, pucker

wrist (rist) n. joint between hand and arm —**'wristlet** n. band worn on wrist — **wrist watch**

writ (rit) n. written command from law court or other authority.

write (rīt) vi. 1. mark paper etc. with the symbols which are used to represent words or sounds 2. compose 3. send a letter —vt. 4. set down in words 5. compose 6. communicate in writing 7. Comp. transcribe (data) on

an output medium 8. Comp. transfer (data) into a section of memory (**wrote, written** ('ritən), **'writing**) —**'writer** n. 1. one who writes 2. author —**write-off** n. 1. the deletion of an item from assets of a business 2. reduction in book value of an asset 3. inf. something damaged beyond repair —**write-up** n. written (published) account of something

writhe (rīdh) vi. 1. twist, squirm in or as in pain etc. 2. be acutely embarrassed (**writhed** pt., **writhed,** Poet. **writhen** ('ridhən) pp., **'writhing** pr.p.)

wrnt warrant

wrong (rong) a. 1. not right or good 2. not suitable 3. wicked 4. incorrect 5. mistaken 6. not functioning properly —n. 7. that which is wrong 8. harm 9. evil —vt. 10. do wrong to 11. think badly of without justification —**'wrongful** a. —**'wrongfully** adv. —**'wrongly** adv. —**'wrong'doer** n. one who acts immorally or illegally —**'wrong'doing** n. —**wrong font** error of using the wrong kind of type —**wrong-headed** a. 1. constantly wrong in judgment 2. foolishly stubborn

wrote (rōt) pt. of WRITE

wrought (rōt) v. 1. pt./pp. of WORK —a. 2. (of metals) shaped by hammering or beating —**wrought iron** form of iron that is tough, malleable and relatively soft

wrung (rung) pt./pp. of WRING

wry (rī) a. 1. turned to one side, contorted, askew 2. sardonic, dryly humorous —**'wryneck** n. migratory woodpecker

WSW west-southwest

WT 1. watertight 2. wireless telegraphy

wt. weight

wunderkind ('voondərkint) n. 1. child prodigy 2. person who succeeds in highly competitive field at an early age

WV or **W.Va.** West Virginia

WW 1. warehouse warrant 2. with warrants

w/w wall-to-wall

WY Wyoming

wych- or **witch-** (comb. form) (of tree) with pliant branches

wynd (wīnd) n. in Scotland, narrow lane, alley

Wyoming (wī'ōming) n. Mountain state of the U.S., admitted to the Union in 1890. Abbrev.: **Wyo., WY** (with ZIP code)

wyvern ('wīvərn) n. mythical creature usu. represented as two-legged winged dragon with a barbed tail

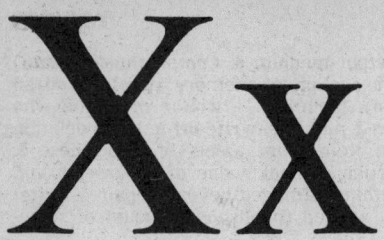

Xx

x *or* **X** (eks) *n.* **1.** 24th letter of English alphabet **2.** speech sound sequence represented by this letter, pronounced as *ks* or *gz* or, in initial position, *z*, as in *xylophone* (*pl.* **x's, X's** *or* **Xs**)

x¹ 1. first in order of class including *x, y, z* **2.** *Math.* unknown quantity

x² 1. cross **2.** ex **3.** experimental **4.** extra

X 1. Christ **2.** Christian **3.** Cross **4.** Roman numeral, 10 **5.** mark indicating error, a choice, a kiss, signature, position **6.** unknown, mysterious person, factor **7.** power of magnification **8.** multiplication symbol **9.** symbol indicating dimension

xanthine ('zanthēn) *n.* **1.** crystalline compound found in urine, blood and certain plants **2.** any of three derivatives of xanthine, which act as stimulants and diuretics

Xanthippe *or* **Xantippe** (zan'tipi) *n.* wife of the Greek philosopher Socrates, of proverbially shrewish nature

x-axis *n.* **1.** in a plane Cartesian coordinate system, the horizontal axis along which the abscissa is measured **2.** in a 3-dimensional Cartesian coordinate, the axis along which values of *x* are measured and at which both *y* and *z* equal zero

XC *Fin.* ex coupon

X chromosome chromosome for femaleness, usu. occurring paired in female cells and single in male cells of many animals

xcp *Fin.* ex coupon

XD *or* **x div** *Fin.* ex dividend

Xe *Chem.* xenon

xebec ('zēbek) *n.* Mediterranean sailing ship with long overhanging bow and stern

xeno- *or before vowel* **xen-** (*comb. form*) something strange or foreign, as in *xenogamy*

xenogamy (ze'nogəmi) *n.* **1.** pollination from another plant **2.** cross-fertilization

xenograft ('zenəgraft) *n.* tissue graft carried out between members of different species

xenon ('zēnon, 'zenon) *n.* *Chem.* noble gas present in the atmosphere (about one part in 170 million by volume) used for filling television and other luminescent tubes *Symbol* Xe, at. wt. 131.3, at. no. 54

xenophobia (zenə'fōbiə) *n.* dislike, hatred, fear, of strangers or aliens —**'xenophobe** *n.* person who is hostile to what is foreign

xerography (zi'rogrəfi) *n.* photocopying process —**xero'graphic** *a.* —**Xerox** ('zēəroks) *n.* trade name for xerographic copying process, machine

xerophyte ('zēərəfīt) *n.* plant able to grow in dry conditions —**'xeric** *a.*

x height height of lower-case letter x used to represent the main body of a lower-case letter

xi (zī, ksī) *n.* 14th letter in Gr. alphabet (Ξ, ξ) (*pl.* **-s**)

XI, x in, *or* **x int.** *Fin.* ex interest

XL 1. extra large **2.** extra long

Xmas ('krisməs, 'eksməs) Christmas

Xn Christian

Xnty Christianity

XR *Fin.* ex rights

x-ray *or* **X-ray** *n.* **1.** radiation of very short wavelengths, capable of penetrating solid bodies, and printing on photographic plate shadow picture of objects not permeable by rays —*vt.* **2.** photograph by x-rays —**x-ray astronomy** astronomy dealing with heavenly bodies by means of x-rays they emit —**x-ray crystallography** study and practice of determining the structure of a crystal by using x-rays —**x-ray diffraction** scattering of x-rays by atoms of a crystal that produces an interference effect so that the diffraction pattern gives information on the structure of the crystal —**x-ray star** luminous heavenly object emitting major part of its radiation in form of x-rays —**x-ray therapy** medical treatment using x-rays —**x-ray tube** vacuum tube in which concentrated stream of electrons strikes a metal target and produces x-rays

X ray word used in communications for the letter *x*

XS extra small

XW *Fin.* ex warrants

xylem ('zīləm, -lem) *n.* plant tissue that conducts water and mineral salts from roots to other parts

xylene ('zīlēn) *n.* aromatic hydrocarbon existing in three isomeric forms, all three being colorless flammable volatile liquids used as solvents *etc.*

xylograph ('zīləgraf) *n.* **1.** wood engraving **2.** impression from wood block

xyloid ('zīloid) *a.* **1.** pert. to wood **2.** woody

xylophone ('zīləfōn) *n.* orchestral percussion instrument consisting of graded hardwood bars tuned in chromatic scale mounted on a horizontal frame struck with hammers

xylose ('zīlōs, -lōz) *n.* white crystalline sugar found in wood and straw and used in dyeing, tanning, diabetic food *etc.*

Yy

y *or* **Y** (wī) *n.* **1.** 25th letter of English alphabet **2.** speech sound represented by this letter, usu. semivowel, as in *yawn*, or vowel, as in *symbol, shy* **3.** something shaped like Y (*pl.* **y's, Y's** *or* **Ys**)

y 1. yard(s) **2.** year(s) **3.** yen **4.** *Math.* y-axis or coordinate measured along y-axis in Cartesian coordinate system **5.** *Math.* algebraic variable

Y *Chem.* yttrium

-y¹ *or* **-ey** (*comb. form*) **1.** characterized by; consisting of; filled with; resembling, as in *sunny, sandy, smoky, classy* **2.** tending to; acting or existing as specified, as in *leaky, shiny*

-y², -ie, *or* **-ey** (*comb. form*) *inf.* **1.** denoting smallness and expressing affection and familiarity, as in *doggy, Jamie* **2.** person or thing concerned with or characterized by being, as in *groupie, goalie, fatty*

-y³ (*comb. form*) **1.** act of doing what is indicated by verbal element, as in *inquiry* **2.** state, condition, quality, as in *geography, jealousy*

YA young adult

yacht (yot) *n.* vessel propelled by sail or power, used for racing, pleasure *etc.* —**'yachtsman** *n.*

yahoo ('yähōō, 'yähōō) *n.* crude, coarse person

Yahweh ('yäwä, -vä) *n.* the God of the Hebrews

yak¹ (yak) *n.* shaggy-haired, long-horned ox of Central Asia

yak² (yak) *sl. n.* **1.** noisy, continuous, trivial talk —*vi.* **2.** chatter or talk in this way (**-kk-**)

Yakima ('yakimō) *n.* **1.** member of group of Shahaptian peoples, of lower Yakima valley in south central Washington (*pl.* **Yakima, -s**) 2. language of this people

yak

yam (yam) *n.* 1. moist-fleshed and usu. orange-fleshed sweet potato 2. edible starchy tuberous root of various plants used as staple food in tropical areas

Yang (yang) *n. see* YIN AND YANG

yank (yangk) *vt.* 1. jerk, tug; pull quickly —*n.* 2. quick tug

Yankee ('yangki) *n.* 1. native or inhabitant of New England 2. native or inhabitant of northern U.S. 3. native or inhabitant of U.S. 4. word used in communications for the letter *y*

yanqui ('yängki) *n.* citizen of U.S. who is not a Hispano-American

yap (yap) *vi.* 1. bark (as small dog) 2. talk idly; gossip (**-pp-**) —*n.* 3. sharp bark

Yaqui ('yäkē) *n.* (member of) Amerindian people of southern Arizona orig. from Sonora, Mexico (*pl.* **-qui, -s**)

yarborough ('yärbərə, -brə) *n. Bridge, whist* hand of 13 cards with no card higher than nine

yard[1] (yärd) *n.* 1. unit of length, 0.915 meter, three feet 2. (*usu. pl.*) great length or quantity 3. *sl.* one hundred dollars 4. spar slung across ship's mast to extend sails —**'yardage** *n.* 1. aggregate number of yards 2. length, extent or volume of goods measured in yards —**yard goods** fabrics sold by yard —**'yardstick** *n.* 1. graduated measuring stick 2. formula or standard of measurement or comparison

yard[2] (yärd) *n.* piece of enclosed ground, oft. attached to or adjoining building and used for some specific purpose, as garden, storage, holding livestock *etc.* —**'yardage** *n.* 1. use of yard 2. charge made for this —**'yardbird** *n.* 1. soldier assigned to menial task or restricted to limited area as punishment 2. untrained or inept enlisted man

yarmulke ('yäməkə, 'yärməlkə) *n. Judaism* man's skullcap worn at prayer, and by strongly religious Jews at all times

yarn (yärn) *n.* 1. continuous strand of twisted fibers or filaments 2. tale —*vi.* 3. tell a tale

yarrow ('yarō) *n.* large genus of hardy herbaceous perennials of the daisy family with many forms and colors

yashmak *or* **yasmac** ('yashmak) *n.* face veil worn by Muslim women

yaup (yöp) *see* YAWP

yaw (yö) *vi.* 1. (of aircraft *etc.*) turn about vertical axis 2. (of ship *etc.*) deviate temporarily from course

yawl (yöl) *n.* two-masted sailing vessel

yawn (yön) *vi.* 1. open mouth wide, *esp.* in sleepiness 2. gape —*n.* 3. a yawning

yawp *or* **yaup** (yöp) *n./vi.* (make) raucous noise

yaws (yöz) *pl.n.* contagious bacterial disease prevalent in tropics

y-axis *n.* reference axis of graph or two- or three-dimensional Cartesian coordinate system along which y-coordinate is measured

Yb *Chem.* ytterbium

YB yearbook

Y chromosome sex chromosome that occurs as one of pair with X chromosome in paired cells of males of many animals

yclept (i'klept) *a. obs.* called (by the name of)

yd yard (measure)

ye (yē) *pron. obs.* you

yea (yā) *interj. obs.* yes

yeah ('yeə, yaə) *interj.* yes

year (yēər) *n.* 1. time taken by one revolution of earth round sun, about 365 days 2. twelve months —**'yearling** *n.* animal one year old —**'yearly** *adv.* 1. every year, once a year —*a.* 2. happening *etc.* once a year —**'year-book** *n.* 1. school publication, usu. compiled by graduating class, that records the year's activities 2. reference book published annually and containing details of events of previous year —**Yearly Meeting** organization uniting several Quarterly Meetings of the Society of Friends

yearn (yərn) *vi.* 1. feel longing, desire 2. be filled with pity, tenderness —**'yearning** *n./a.*

yeast (yēst) *n.* 1. frothy yellowish substance consisting of cells of a fungus reproducing in a saccharin liquid to produce an alcoholic fermentation used in leavening dough and making alcoholic beverages 2. dried form of this 3. wild airborne cells of this fungus —**'yeasty** *a.* 1. frothy, foamy 2. exuberant

yegg (yeg) *n. inf.* 1. safe-cracker 2. robber

yell (yel) *v.* 1. cry out in loud shrill tone 2. *inf.* call —*n.* 3. loud shrill cry 4. *inf.* call

yellow ('yelō) *a.* 1. of the color of lemons, gold *etc.* 2. *inf.* cowardly —*n.* 3. portion of spectrum lying between green and orange —**yellow fever** acute infectious viral disease transmitted by mosquitoes (*also* **yellow jack**) —**'yellowhammer** *n.* small European bunting —**yellow jack** 1. flag raised by ship in quarantine 2. yellow fever —**yellow jacket** any of various small ground-nesting wasps —**yellow pages** classified telephone directory or section of directory that lists subscribers by business or service provided —**yellow peril** supposed danger from Oriental peoples —**yellow streak** cowardly trait —**'yellowwood** *n.* 1. any of various trees having yellowish wood or yielding a yellowish extract 2. the wood of such a tree

yelp (yelp) *vi./n.* (produce) quick, shrill cry

Yemen ('yemən) *n.* —**People's Democratic Republic of Yemen**. country in western Asia bounded north by Yemen Arab Republic and Saudi Arabia, east by Oman, south by the Gulf of Aden and west by the Yemen Arab Republic

Yemen Arab Republic country in western Asia bounded north by Saudi Arabia, south and east by the People's Democratic Republic of Yemen and west by the Red Sea

yen[1] (yen) *n.* Japanese monetary unit (*pl.* **yen**)

yen[2] (yen) *n. inf.* longing, craving

yenta ('yentə) *n.* vulgar, ill-tempered woman who gossips

yeoman ('yōmən) *n.* 1. *Hist.* farmer cultivating his own land 2. assistant, subordinate —**'yeomanry** *n.* 1. yeomen collectively 2. Brit. volunteer cavalry force, organized in 1761 for home defense —**yeoman of the guard** member of ceremonial bodyguard (**Yeomen of the Guard**) of British monarch

yerba maté ('yerbə 'mätā, 'yərbə) *see* MATÉ

yes (yes) *interj.* affirms or consents, gives an affirmative answer —**yes man** weak person willing to agree to anything

yeshiva (yə'shēvə) *n.* 1. rabbinical seminary 2. Hebrew secondary school (*pl.* **-s, yeshivoth** (yəshē'vōt))

yesterday ('yestərdi, -dā) *n.* 1. day before today 2. recent time —*adv.* 3. on the day before today

yet (yet) *adv.* 1. now 2. still 3. besides 4. hitherto 5. nevertheless —*conj.* 6. but, at the same time, nevertheless

yeti ('yeti) *n. see* **abominable snowman** *at* ABOMINATE

yew (yōō) *n.* 1. genus of evergreen trees with dark leaves 2. wood of any of these

Yggdrasil *or* **Ygdrasil** ('igdrəsil) *n.* in Norse legend, the great ash tree that supported the universe

Yiddish ('yidish) *a./n.* (of, in) dialect of mixed German and Hebrew, the vernacular of Ashkenazic Jews —**yid** *n. sl. offens.* Jew

yield (yēld) *vt.* 1. give or return as food 2. produce 3. provide 4. concede 5. give up, surrender —*vi.* 6. submit 7. (*with* to) comply (*with*) 8. surrender, give way —*n.* 9. amount produced, result 10. return, profit

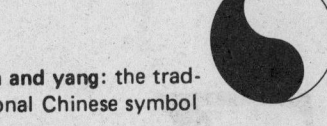

yin and yang: the traditional Chinese symbol

Yin and Yang (yin) two complementary principles of Chinese philosophy: Yin is negative, dark and feminine; Yang is positive, bright and masculine

Y.M.C.A. Young Men's Christian Association

Y.M.H.A. Young Men's Hebrew Association

YO year old

y.o. year(s) old

YOB year of birth

yodel ('yōdəl) *n.* 1. type of vocalization indigenous to mountain people of Switzerland and Tyrol marked by frequent and quick passing from low chest voice to high falsetto —*v.* 2. sing in a yodel

Yoga ('yōgə) *n.* 1. Hindu philosophical system aiming at spiritual, mental and physical well-being by means of certain physical and mental exercises 2. (y-) system of exercises for attaining bodily well-being (**Hatha yoga**) —**yogi** ('yōgi) *n.* one who practices yoga (*pl.* **-s, -gin** (-gin))

yogurt *or* **yoghurt** ('yōgərt) *n.* semisolid food, oft. flavored, made of whole or skimmed milk fermented by cultures of certain bacteria

yoicks (yoiks) *interj.* cry used in fox-hunting to urge on hounds

yoke (yōk) *n.* 1. wooden bar put across necks of two animals to hold them together and to which plow *etc.* may be attached 2. various objects like a yoke in shape or use 3. fitted part of garment, *esp.* round neck, shoulders 4. bond, tie 5. domination —*vt.* 6. put a yoke on 7. couple, unite

yokel ('yōkəl) *n.* naive or gullible inhabitant of small town or rural area

yolk (yōk) *n.* 1. yellow central part of egg 2. oily secretion of skin of sheep

Yom Kippur (yōm ki'pōōr; *Hebrew* yom ke'pōōr) Jewish holiday celebrated as day of fasting, when prayers of penitence are recited in synagogue (*also* **Day of Atonement**)

yon (yon) *a. obs., dial.* that or those over there —**'yonder** *a.* 1. yon —*adv.* 2. over there, in that direction

yoo-hoo ('yōōhōō) *interj.* call to attract attention

yore (yōr) *n. Poet.* the distant past

Yorkshire pudding ('yŏrkshēər) batter consisting of eggs, flour and milk baked in meat drippings

Yorkshire terrier purebred toy dog with long straight silky coat mostly bluish-gray but tan on head and chest

you (yōō; *unstressed* yŏō) *pron.* referring to person(s) addressed, or to unspecified person(s) —**you-all** *pron.* (*used chiefly in southern U.S.*) **1.** in addressing two or more persons **2.** addressing one person as representing another or others

young (yung) *a.* **1.** not far advanced in growth, life or existence **2.** not yet old **3.** immature **4.** junior **5.** recently formed **6.** vigorous —*n.* **7.** offspring —'**youngster** *n.* child

younker ('yungkər) *n.* **1.** young man **2.** youngster

your (yŏr, yŏŏər; *unstressed* yər) *a.* belonging to you —**yours** *pron.* —**your'self** *pron.* (*pl.* **your'selves**)

youth (yōōth) *n.* **1.** state or time of being young **2.** state before adult age **3.** young man **4.** young people —'**youthful** *a.* —**youth hostel** supervised lodging for young travelers

yowl (yowl) *vi./n.* (produce) mournful cry

yo-yo ('yŏyŏ) *n.* toy consisting of a spool attached to a string, by which it can be spun out and reeled in while attached to the finger (*pl.* **-s**)

yr 1. year **2.** younger **3.** your

yrs 1. years **2.** yours

Y.S.T. Yukon Standard Time

Y.T. C Yukon Territory

ytterbium (i'terbiəm) *n. Chem.* metallic element *Symbol* Yb, at. wt. 173.0, at. no. 70

yttrium ('itriəm) *n. Chem.* metallic element *Symbol* Y, at. wt. 88.9, at. no. 39

yuan (yōō'än) *n.* Chinese monetary unit (*pl.* **yuan**)

yucca ('yukə) *n.* genus of hardy and tender evergreen shrubs and small trees of the lily family with long leaves and flowers borne on an erect stem

Yugoslavia (yōōgō'släviə) *n.* country in Europe bounded north by Austria and Hungary, northeast by Romania, east by Bulgaria, south by Greece, and west by Albania, the Adriatic Sea, and Italy —**Yugo-'slavian** *n./a.*

yule (yōōl) *n.* (*sometimes* **Y-**) the Christmas festival or season

Yuma ('yōōmə) *n.* Amerindian language family of southwest U.S. and northern Mexico —'**Yuman** *a./n.*

Yuppie ('yupi) *n.* young urban (usu. upwardly mobile) professional

yurt (yōōrt) *n.* circular domed tent consisting of collapsible lattice framework covered with skins or felt used as dwelling by Mongol nomads in Siberia

Y.W.C.A. Young Women's Christian Association

Y.W.H.A. Young Women's Hebrew Association

Zz

z *or* **Z** (zē) *n.* **1.** 26th letter of English alphabet **2.** speech sound represented by this letter **3.** something shaped like Z (*pl.* **z's, Z's** *or* **Zs**)

z 1. zero **2.** zone **3.** *Math.* z-axis or coordinate measured along z-axis in Cartesian or cylindrical coordinate system **4.** *Math.* algebraic variable

Z *or* **ZD** zenith distance

Zach. *Bible* Zacharias

Zacharias (zakə'rīəs) *n. Bible* Zechariah in the Douay Version of the O.T.

Zaïre (zä'ēər) *n.* country in Africa bounded north by the Central African Republic, northeast by Sudan, east by Uganda, Rwanda, Burundi and Lake Tanganyika, south by Zambia, southwest by Angola, northwest by Congo —**Za'ïrian** *a./n.*

Zambia ('zambiə) *n.* country in Africa bounded north by Zaïre and Tanzania, east by Malawi, southeast by Mozambique, south by Zimbabwe and Namibia —'**Zambian** *a./n.*

zany ('zāni) *a.* comical, funny in unusual way

zarzuela (zär'zwālə) *n.* national type of Spanish opera, usu. light one-act comedy but occasionally dealing with serious dramatic subjects in two or three acts

ZD *see* Z

zeal (zēl) *n.* **1.** fervor **2.** keenness, enthusiasm —**zealot** ('zelət) *n.* **1.** fanatic **2.** enthusiast —**zealous** ('zeləs) *a.* **1.** ardent **2.** enthusiastic **3.** earnest —**zealously** ('zeləsli) *adv.*

zebra ('zēbrə) *n.* any of several fleet African mammals related to the horse but conspicuously striped

zebu ('zēbōō) *n.* humped Indian ox or cow

Zech. *Bible* Zechariah

Zechariah (zekə'rīə) *n. Bible* 38th book of the O.T., written by the prophet Zechariah in the 5th cent. B.C. about the coming of Christ

Zemstvo ('zemstvŏ) *n.* in czarist Russia, council composed of local elected officials

Zen (zen) *n.* form of Buddhism emphasizing meditation and physical work as means to enlightenment

zenana (zə'nänə) *n.* **1.** in India and Pakistan, women's part of high-caste dwelling **2.** lightweight quilted fabric used mainly for housecoats

zenith ('zēnith) *n.* **1.** point of the heavens directly above an observer **2.** point opposite nadir **3.** summit, peak **4.** climax —'**zenithal** *a.*

Zeph. *Bible* Zephaniah

Zephaniah (zefə'nīə) *n. Bible* 36th book of the O.T., written by the prophet Zephaniah about 5th cent. B.C. concerning the Day of the Lord

zephyr ('zefər) *n.* soft, gentle breeze

zeppelin ('zepəlin) *n.* large, cylindrical, rigid airship

zero ('zēərō) *n.* **1.** nothing **2.** figure 0 **3.** point on graduated instrument from which positive and negative quantities are reckoned **4.** the lowest point (*pl.* **-s, -es**) —**zero hour 1.** *Mil.* time set for start of attack *etc.* **2.** *inf.* critical time —**zero population growth** replacing of present population without increasing it

zest (zest) *n.* **1.** enjoyment **2.** excitement, interest, flavor **3.** peel of orange or lemon

zeta ('zātə, 'zētə) *n.* sixth letter in Gr. alphabet (Z, ζ)

Zeus (zōōs) *n.* supreme god of the ancient Greeks

ZI zone of interior

zibeline *or* **zibelline** ('zibəlēn) *n.* strongly colored cloth made from alpaca, mohair and camel's hair with lustrous long-napped finish

zigzag ('zigzag) *n.* **1.** line or course characterized by sharp turns in alternating directions —*vi.* **2.** move along in zigzag course (**-zagged** *pt./pp.*, **-zagging** *pr.p.*)

zilch (zilch) *inf. n.* **1.** nothing, zero —*a.* **2.** no

zillion ('zilyən) *n. inf.* extremely large, indeterminate number

Zimbabwe (zim'bäbwi) *n.* country in Africa located between northern border of Transvaal and the Zambesi River bordered on the east by Mozambique, on the west by Botswana —**Zim'babwean** *a./n.*

zinc (zingk) *n. Chem.* metallic element *Symbol* Zn, at. wt. 65.4, at. no. 30 —'**zincograph** *n.* —**zin'cographer** *n.* —**zin'cography** *n.* art or process of engraving zinc to form printing plate —**zinc ointment** medicinal ointment of zinc oxide, petrolatum and paraffin —**zinc oxide** white insoluble powder used as pigment in paints, cosmetics, glass *etc.* (*also* **flowers of zinc**)

Zinfandel ('zinfəndel) *n.* **1.** red, mediumbodied table wine **2.** grape used to make this wine

zing (zing) *inf. n.* **1.** short high-pitched buzzing sound **2.** vitality; zest —*vi.* **3.** make or move with high-pitched buzzing sound

zinjanthropus (zin'janthrəpəs) *n.* fossil hominid characterized by very low brow and large molars

zinnia ('ziniə) *n.* genus of annual and perennial plants and subshrubs of the daisy family grown for ornament

Zion ('zīən) *or* **Sion** *n.* **1.** hill on which Jerusalem stands **2.** Judaism **3.** Christian

Church **4.** heaven —**'Zionism** *n.* movement to found, support Jewish homeland in Palestine —**'Zionist** *n./a.*

zip (zip) *n.* **1.** energy and vigor **2.** sharp whizzing sound —*vi.* **3.** move with zip —*vt.* **4.** add speed and force to (**-pp-**)

zip code system combining 2-letter abbreviation for a State and 5-figure number identifying postal delivery areas in the U.S. —**zip-code** *vt.* furnish with a zip code

zipper ('zipər) *n.* device for fastening with two rows of flexible metal or nylon teeth, interlocked and opened by a sliding clip —**'zippered** *a.* equipped with zipper —**zip up** close with zipper (**-pp-**)

zircon ('zɔrkon) *n.* mineral used as gemstone and in industry —**zir'conium** *n. Chem.* metallic element *Symbol* Zr, at. wt. 91.2, at. no. 40

zither ('zidhər) *n.* stringed instrument of ancient origin consisting of flat wooden box over which are stretched 30 to 45 strings. Four or five melody strings can be stopped on a fretted fingerboard and are played with a plectrum while other strings are plucked for the accompaniment

zloty ('zloti) *n.* Polish monetary unit (*pl.* **-s**, **zloty**)

Zn 1. *Chem.* zinc **2.** azimuth

zodiac ('zōdiak) *n.* imaginary belt of the heavens along which the sun, moon, and chief planets appear to move, divided crosswise into twelve equal areas, called **signs of the zodiac,** each named after a constellation —**zodiacal** (zō'dɪəkəl) *a.*

zombie or **zombi** ('zombi) *n.* **1.** person appearing lifeless, apathetic *etc.* **2.** corpse supposedly brought to life by supernatural spirit

zone (zōn) *n.* **1.** region with particular characteristics or use **2.** any of the five belts into which tropics and arctic and antarctic circles divide the earth —**'zonal** *a.* —**zone defense** *Sport* system of defense in which each defensive player has an assigned zone

zonked (zongkt) *a. sl.* **1.** intoxicated by alcohol **2.** stupefied by drug

zoo (zōō) *n.* place where wild animals are kept, studied, bred and exhibited (*in full* **zoological gardens**)

zoo- or before vowel **zo-** (*comb. form*) animals, as in *zooplankton*

zoogeography (zōəji'ogrəfi) *n.* science of geographical distribution of animals

zoography (zō'ogrəfi) *n.* descriptive zoology —**zo'ographer** or **zo'ographist** *n.*

zooid ('zōoid) *n.* **1.** independent animal body, such as individual of coelenterate colony **2.** cell or body capable of spontaneous motion, produced by organism

zool. 1. zoological **2.** zoology

zoology (zō'oləji, zōō-) *n.* **1.** scientific study of animals **2.** characteristics of particular animals or of fauna of particular area —**zoo'logical** *a.* —**zo'ologist** *n.*

zoom (zōōm) *v.* **1.** (cause to) make loud buzzing, humming sound **2.** (cause to) go fast or rise, increase sharply —*vi.* **3.** (*with* in or out) use camera lens of adjustable focal length to make subject appear closer or further away —**zoom lens** lens used in this way

zoonosis (zō'onəsis) *n.* disease transmissible from lower animals to man in natural conditions (*pl.* **-ses** (-sēz))

zoophyte ('zōəfīt) *n.* plantlike animal, *eg* sponge —**zoophytic** (zōə'fitik) *a.*

zori ('zöri) *n.* flat sandal with thong between big and second toe, usu. made of rubber (*pl.* **zori**)

Zoroastrianism (zörō'astriənizəm) or **Zoro-astrism** *n.* dualistic religion founded by Persian prophet Zoroaster, based on concept of continuous struggle between Ahura Mazda, god of creation, light and goodness, and his archenemy, Angra Mainyu, spirit of evil and darkness

Zouave (zōō'äv) *n.* member of French infantry unit orig. composed of Algerians wearing brilliant uniform and conducting spirited drill

zoysia ('zoishə) *n.* any of a genus of creeping perennial grasses with fine wiry leaves including some used for lawns in warm regions

ZPG zero population growth

Zr *Chem.* zirconium

zucchetto (zōō'ketō) *n. R.C.Ch.* ecclesiastical skullcap, black for priest, purple for bishop, red for cardinal, white for the pope (*pl.* **-es**)

zucchini (zōō'kēni) *n.* **1.** cylindrical dark green summer squash **2.** the bushy plant bearing this fruit (*pl.* **zucchini, -s**)

Zulu ('zōōlōō) *n.* **1.** member of Bantu-speaking people of Natal **2.** Bantu language of the Zulus **3.** word used in communications for the letter *z*

Zuni ('zōōnē) or **Zuñi** ('zōōnyē) *n.* **1.** Amerindian people of western New Mexico **2.** member of this people (*pl.* **-i, -is**) **3.** language of this people —**'Zunian** or **'Zuñian** *a./n.*

zuppa inglese ('tsōōpə ing'glāzi) dessert made of sponge cake, rum-flavored custard, fruit and whipped cream

zwieback ('zwībak, 'zwē-) *n.* rich sweet bread that is sliced and baked again until it is dry and crisp

zygote ('zīgōt) *n.* fertilized egg cell

zymurgy ('zīmərji) *n.* chemistry of fermentation processes

APPENDIX OF
INDO-EUROPEAN ROOTS

Some of the etymologies in the main body of the Dictionary make cross-references in bold-face type to entries in this Appendix, which is drawn from the fully explained Appendix in the hard-bound edition of *The American Heritage Dictionary*.

The Appendix selectively represents the prehistoric ancestry of the English language. English, together with most of the languages of Europe and a number of others (see the chart on pages 362–3), is descended from a reconstructed language called *Indo-European*. This language probably belongs to the neolithic period, but the culture in which it was spoken has not been archaeologically identified. The linguistic reconstruction, however, based on 150 years of scholarly work, is firm and intricate.

The fundamental relationship of Indo-European to English is hereditary. Thus, the Indo-European word (or root) for "field" was

agro-; this, in the Germanic branch of the family (to which English belongs), changed to *akraz*, which in Old English changed to *æcer*, becoming ACRE in Modern English. This word is thus part of the *native* vocabulary, which has been in unbroken use, though with regularly changing phonetic forms, for at least 6,000 years. This Appendix lists a selection of such native words. The histories of the English words that have been borrowed from other Indo-European languages, chiefly from Germanic and Romance and from Latin and Greek, are not traced here.

Each boldface entry is an Indo-European root, followed by its meaning. If the meaning is enclosed in quotation marks, it is to be taken as an approximate abstraction rather than a precise meaning. Next, usually, comes a Germanic descendant of the root, then an Old English descendant of the Germanic form. Meanings are given to these only if they differ markedly from that of the root. Following the

Old English word is the Modern English form in SMALL CAPITALS. Each of these is a cross-reference to the etymology of the word in the main body of the Dictionary.

Homographic roots are given superscript numbers. When one of these numbers differs from the number given in the hard-bound edition of *The American Heritage Dictionary* (abbreviated AHD), the latter is given in brackets at the end of the entry.

An asterisk is placed before every unattested form (one that is not found in documents but has been reconstructed) except for the entry forms. Technical terms have been used as sparingly as possible in this Appendix. An o-grade form is one in which an *e* has changed to an *o*, and a zero-grade form is one in which an *e* has dropped out or an *ā* or an *ē* has been reduced to *ə* (schwa).

---

abel-. Apple. Gmc *aplu-*, *apal-*, in OE *æppel*: APPLE.

ad-. To, near, at. Gmc *at* in OE *æt*: AT.

agh-¹. To be depressed or afraid. Gmc *ag-* in OE *eglan*, to afflict: AIL.

agh-². A day. Gmc *dagaz* (initial *d-* obscure) in: **a.** OE *dæg*: DAY; **b.** OE *dagian*, to dawn: DAWN.

agro-. Field. Gmc *akraz* in OE *æcer*: ACRE.

agwesī. Ax. Gmc *akwesī* in OE *æx*: AX.

ais-. To wish. Gmc *aiskôn* in OE *āscian*, *ācsian*: ASK.

aiw-. Life, long life, eternity. Gmc *aiwi* in: **a.** OE *ā*, ever: NO¹; **b.** OE *æfre*, ever: EVER.

ak-. Sharp. **1.** Gmc *akjô* in OE *ecg*, sharp side: EDGE. **2.** Gmc *ahuz* in OE *ēar*, *æhher*, ear of grain: EAR².

akwā-. Water. Gmc *ahwjô*, *aujô*, "thing on the water," in OE *iegland (land*, LAND*)*: ISLAND.

al-¹. Beyond. Gmc *aljaz* in OE *elles*: ELSE.

al-². To grow. Gmc *alda-*, "grown," in OE *eald*, old: OLD. [AHD *al-³*.]

alu-. Intoxication. Gmc *aluth-* in OE *ealu*, ale: ALE.

ambhi. Around. Reduced form *bhi* in Gmc *bi* in OE *bī*, *bi*, *be*: BY.

an¹. On. Gmc *ana* in OE *an*, *on*: ON.

an². Demonstrative particle. Gmc *antharaz* in OE *ōther*: OTHER.

ank-. Also **ang-.** To bend. **1.** Gmc *ank-* in OE *anclēow* (and ON *ankula*): ANKLE. **2.** Gmc *ang-* in OE *angul*, fishhook: ANGLE¹.

anti. Against or in front of; also, an end. **1.** Gmc *andi-* in OE *and-*: UN-². **2.** Gmc *andjô* in OE *ende*, end: END.

apo-. Also **ap-.** Off, away. **1.** Gmc *af* in: **a.** OE *of*, off: OF, OFF; **b.** OE *ebba*, low tide: EBB. **2.** Gmc *aftar-* in OE *æfter*: AFTER. **3.** Variant *ēp-* in Gmc *eben-*, "the after or later time," in OE *æfen*, evening: EVENING.

apsā. Aspen. Gmc *aspôn* in OE *æspe*: ASPEN.

arkw-. Bow and arrow. Gmc *arhwô* in OE *arwe*, *earh*: ARROW.

as-. To burn. Gmc *askôn* in OE *æsce*: ASH¹.

aug-. To increase. **1.** Gmc *aukan* in OE *ēacan*, to increase: EKE. **2.** Variant forms *wogs-*, *wegs-*, in Gmc *wahsan* in: **a.** OE *weaxan*, to grow: WAX²; **b.** OE *wæst*, growth, size: WAIST. [AHD *aug-¹*.]

aukwh-. Also **aukw-.** Cooking pot. Gmc *uhwna-* in *ufna-* in OE *ofen*: OVEN.

awes-. Also **aus-.** To shine. **1.** Gmc *aust-* in OE *ēast*: EAST. **2.** Gmc *austrôn-*, dawn goddess worshiped at the vernal equinox, in OE *ēastre*: EASTER.

ayer-. Day, morning. **1.** Gmc *airiz* in OE *ēr*, before: EARLY, ERE. **2.** Gmc *airistaz* in OE *ērest*, earliest: ERST.

ayos-. A metal. Variant *ayes-* in Gmc *aiz* in OE *ār*, brass: ORE.

bend-. Protruding point. Gmc *pannja*, "structure of stakes," in OE *penn*: PEN².

beu-. Also **bheu-.** To swell. **1.** Gmc *puk-* in OE *pocc*, pustule: POCK. **2.** Form *bheu-* in: **a.** OE *bōsm*: BOSOM; **b.** OE *bŷle*: BOIL². [AHD *beu-¹*.]

bhā-¹. To shine. Gmc *baukna-*, beacon, signal, in: **a.** OE *bēacen*: BEACON; **b.** OE *bēcnan*: BECKON.

bhā-². To speak. Gmc *banwan* in OE *bannan*, to summon (and ON *banna*, to prohibit): BAN.

bha-bhā-. Broad bean. Variant *bha-un-* in Gmc *baunô* in OE *bēan*: BEAN.

bhad-. Good. Gmc comparative *batizô* in OE *betera*: BETTER.

bhāghu-. Elbow. Gmc *bôguz* in OE *bōg*: BOUGH.

bhāgo-. Beech tree. **1.** Gmc *bôkô*, "beech staff for carving runes on," in OE *bôc*: BOOK. **2.** Gmc *bôkjo* in OE *bēce*: BEECH.

bhar-. Projection, bristle. **1.** O-grade form *bhor-* in Gmc *barsaz*, "spiny fish," in OE *bærs*: BASS¹. **2.** Zero-grade form *bhṛ-* in Gmc *bursti-* in OE *byrst*: BRISTLE.

bhardhā. Beard. Gmc *bardaz* in OE *beard*: BEARD.

bhares-. Also **bhars-.** Barley. Gmc *barz-* in OE *bære*: BARLEY.

bhau-. To strike. Gmc *bautan* in OE *bēatan*: BEAT.

bhē-. To warm. Zero-grade form *bha-* in: **a.** Gmc *batham* in OE *bæth*: BATH; **b.** Gmc *bakan* in OE *bacan*: BAKE.

bhedh-¹. To dig. Gmc *badjam*, "garden plot, sleeping place," in OE *bedd*: BED.

bhedh-². To bend. **1.** Gmc *bidjan* in OE *biddan*, to pray: BID. **2.** Gmc *bidam* in OE *gebed*,

prayer: BEAD.

bhei-¹. Bee. Gmc *biôn* in OE *bēo*: BEE.

bhei-². To strike. Gmc *bhi-li-* in OE *bile*, bird's beak: BILL².

bheid-. To split. **1.** Gmc *bitiz* in OE *bite*, a bite: BIT². **2.** Gmc *bītô* in OE *bita*, piece bitten off: BIT¹. **3.** Gmc *bītan*, to bite, in: **a.** OE *bītan*: BITE; **b.** OE *biter*, "biting": BITTER. **4.** Gmc *bait-*, boat (< "split planking"), in OE *bāt* (and ON *bātr*): BOAT.

bheidh-. To persuade, compel. **1.** Gmc *bīdan*, "to trust, to await trustingly, to stay," in OE *bīdan*: BIDE. **2.** Gmc *baidjan* in OE *bædan*, to compel: BAD.

bhel-¹. To shine, flash; shining white; fire. **1.** Gmc *blaikjan* in OE *blǣcan*: BLEACH. **2.** Gmc *blas-* in OE *blǣse*, torch: BLAZE¹. **3.** Gmc *blend-*, "dazzle, blind," in OE *blind*: BLIND. **4.** Gmc *blisk-* in OE *blyscan*: BLUSH. **5.** Variant *bhleg-* in Gmc *blakaz*, "burned," in OE *blæc*: BLACK.

bhel-². To blow, swell; a round object. Zero-grade form *bhḷ-* in Gmc *bul-* in OE *bolla*: BOWL¹.

bhel-³. To thrive, bloom. Extended form *bhlē-*. **1.** O-grade form *bhlô-* in Gmc *blô-s-* in OE *blôstma*: BLOSSOM. **2.** Zero-grade form *bhla-* in Gmc *bladaz* in OE *blæd*, leaf: BLADE.

bhel-⁴. To yell. Gmc *bell-* in: **a.** OE *belle*: BELL; **b.** OE *belgan*: BELLOW.

bheld-. To strike. Zero-grade form *bhḷd-* in Gmc *bult-* in OE *bolt*, heavy arrow: BOLT¹.

bhelgh-. To swell. **1.** Gmc *balgiz* in OE *belig*, bellows: BELLY. **2.** Gmc *bolgstraz* in OE *bolster*: BOLSTER.

bhen-. To strike. Gmc *banôn* in OE *bana*: BANE.

bhendh-. To bind. **1.** Gmc *bindan* in OE *bindan*: BIND. **2.** O-grade form *bhondh-* in Gmc *band-* in OE *bendan*: BEND. **3.** Celtic *benna* in OE *binne*, basket: BIN.

bher-¹. To carry. **1.** Gmc *beran* in OE *beran*: BEAR¹. **2.** Gmc *bērô* in OE *bēr*: BIER. **3.** Gmc *barwôn* in OE *bearwe*, basket: BARROW. **4.** Gmc *bur-* in OE *byrthen*: BURDEN. **5.** Compound root *bhrenk-* in Gmc *brengan* in OE *bringan*: BRING.

bher-². To bore. Gmc *borôn* in OE *borian*:

bore¹.

bher-³. Brown. 1. Variant *bhrū-* in Gmc *brūnaz* in OE *brūn*: BROWN. 2. Redupl form *bhibhru-* in OE *beofor*: BEAVER. 3. Gmc *berō* in OE *bera*: BEAR².

bherdh-. To cut. Zero-grade form *bhr̥dh-* in Gmc *burd-* in OE *bord*: BOARD.

bherəg-. To shine; white. 1. Gmc *berhtaz* in OE *beorht*: BRIGHT. 2. Gmc *berkjōn*, "the white tree," in OE *birce*: BIRCH.

bherək-. To shine, glitter, hence to move jerkily. Variant *bhrek-.* 1. Gmc *bregdan* in OE *bregdan*: BRAID. 2. Gmc *brigdil-* in OE *brīdel*: BRIDLE.

bherg-. To growl. Gmc *berk-* in OE *beorcan*: BARK¹.

bhergh-¹. To hide, protect. 1. Zero-grade form *bhr̥gh-* in: a. Gmc *burgjan* in OE *byrgan*: BURY; b. Gmc *burgisli-* in OE *byrgels* (pl): BURIAL. 2. Gmc *borgēn* in OE *borgian*: BORROW.

bhergh-². High; hill. Zero-grade form *bhr̥gh-* in Gmc *burgs,* hill-fort, in OE *burg*: BOROUGH, BURG.

bheu-. To be, exist, dwell. 1. Extended form *bhwī-* in Gmc *biju* in OE *bēon*: BE. 2. Zero-grade form *bhu-* in Gmc *buthla,* dwelling, in OE *bold*: BUILD. 3. Lengthened form *bhū-* in Gmc *būram* in OE *būr,* a dwelling, and *gebūr,* dweller: BOWER; NEIGHBOR.

bheudh-. To be or make aware. 1. Gmc *bi-udan,* to proclaim, in OE *bēodan*: BID. 2. Gmc *budōn-* in OE *boda,* messenger: BODE¹. 3. Gmc *budilaz,* herald, in OE *bydel*: BEADLE.

bheug-. To swell; curved objects. 1. Gmc *bugōn-* in OE *boga*: BOW³. 2. Gmc *būgan* in OE *būgan,* to bend: BOW², BUXOM. [AHD *bheug-³.*]

bhlē-¹. To howl. Gmc *blē-t-* in OE *blǣtan*: BLEAT.

bhlē-². To blow, swell. Gmc *blē-.* 1. OE *blāwan*: BLOW¹. 2. OE *blǣdre*: BLADDER. 3. OE *blǣst*: BLAST.

bhoso-. Naked. Gmc *bazaz* in OE *bær*: BARE.

bhrāter-. Brother. Gmc *brōthar-* in OE *brōthor*: BROTHER.

bhreg-. To break. Gmc *brekan* in OE *brecan*: BREAK.

bhrem-. To project. Gmc *brema* in: a. OE *brōm*: BROOM; b. OE *brǣmbel*: BRAMBLE. [AHD *bhrem-².*]

bhres-. To burst. Gmc *brest-* in OE *berstan*: BURST.

bhreu-¹. To break up. 1. Gmc *briutan* in OE *brytel*: BRITTLE. 2. Gmc *briuthan* in OE *brēothan,* to deteriorate: BROTHEL.

bhreu-². To boil, burn; also to brew, cook. 1. Gmc *breuwan* in OE *brēowan*: BREW. 2. Gmc *braudam* in OE *brēad*: BREAD. 3. Gmc *brudam* in OE *broth*: BROTH. 4. Variant *bhrē-* in: a. Gmc *brōd-,* "a warming, hatching, rearing of young," in OE *brōd*: BROOD; b. Gmc *brōdjan,* "to rear," in OE *brēdan*: BREED; c. Gmc *brēthaz,* "warm air," in OE *brǣth*: BREATH. 5. Gmc *brenw-* in OE *beornan, byrnan,* and *bærnan*: BURN. 6. Gmc *brandaz* in OE *brand,* piece of burning wood: BRAND.

bhreus-¹. To swell. Gmc *briustam* in OE *brēost*: BREAST.

bhreus-². To break. Gmc *brūsjan* in OE *brȳsan*: BRUISE.

bhrū-. Eyebrow. Gmc *brūs* in OE *brū*: BROW.

bhudh-. Bottom. OE *botm*: BOTTOM.

bhugo-. Male animal. Gmc *bukkaz* in OE *buc, bucca*: BUCK¹.

dā-. To divide. Variant *dī-.* 1. Gmc *tīdiz,* "division of time," in: a. OE *tīd*: TIDE; b. OE *tīdan,* to happen: BETIDE. 2. Gmc *timo* in OE *tima*: TIME.

dail-. To divide. 1. Gmc *dailiz* in OE *dǣlan*:

---

deal¹. 2. Gmc *dailaz* in OE *dāl,* share: DOLE.

dakru-. A tear. Gmc *tahr-* in OE *tēar*: TEAR².

de-. Demonstrative stem. Gmc *tō* in OE *tō*: TO.

deigh-. Insect. Gmc *tīk-* in OE *ticia*: TICK².

deik-. To show. Variant *deig-.* 1. Gmc *taikjan* in OE *tǣcan*: TEACH. 2. Gmc *taiknam* in OE *tācen*: TOKEN.

dek-. "Fringe, tail." Gmc *taglaz* in OE *tægel*: TAIL. [AHD *dek-².*]

dekm̥. Ten. Gmc *tehun* in OE *tīen*: TEN.

del-¹. Long. Prob form *dlon-gho-* in Gmc *langaz* in: a. OE *long*: LONG¹; b. OE *langian,* "to grow longer, yearn": LONG².

del-². To recount. 1. Gmc *taljan* in OE *tellan*: TELL. 2. Gmc *talō* in OE *talu*: TALE. 3. OE *talian*: TALK.

demə-¹. To build. Gmc *timram,* building material, in OE *timber*: TIMBER.

demə-². To constrain, break in (horses), tame. O-grade form *dom-* in Gmc *tamaz* in OE *tam*: TAME.

denk-. To bite. 1. Gmc *tanhuz,* tenacious, in OE *tōh*: TOUGH. 2. Gmc *tanguz* in OE *tange*: TONGS.

dent-. Tooth. O-grade form *dont-* in Gmc *tanthuz* in OE *tōth*: TOOTH.

der-¹. To run, walk, step. 1. Gmc *tred-* in OE *tredan*: TREAD. 2. Gmc *trep-,* "something into which one steps, snare," in OE *træppe*: TRAP.

der-². To split. Gmc *teran* in OE *teran*: TEAR¹.

deru-. To be firm, solid; also "wood, tree." 1. Variant *drew-* in: a. Gmc *trewam* in OE *trēow*: TREE; b. Gmc *triuwō* in OE *trēow,* faith: TRUCE. 2. Variant *dreu-* in Gmc *triuwaz* in OE *trēowe*: TRUE. 3. Variant *drou-* in Gmc *traujam* in OE *trīg,* wooden board: TRAY. 4. Form *dru-ko-* in Gmc *trugaz* in OE *trog*: TROUGH. 5. Variant *derw-* in Gmc *terw-,* resin, pitch, in OE *teru*: TAR¹.

deuk-. To lead. 1. Gmc *tiuhan* in OE *tēon*: TUG. 2. Zero-grade form *duk-* in Gmc *tugōn* in OE *togian*: TOW¹, TAUT. 3. O-grade form *douk-* in: a. OE *tigan*: TIE; b. Gmc *tauhmjan̄,* to beget, in OE *tīeman*: TEEM; c. Gmc *tauhmaz,* descendant, family, in OE *tēam*: TEAM.

dhē-. To set, put. 1. O-grade form *dhō-* in: a. Gmc *dōn* in OE *dōn*: DO; b. Gmc *dōmaz* in OE *dōm*: DOOM; c. Gmc *domjan* in OE *dēman*: DEEM. 2. Gmc *dēdiz* in OE *dǣd*: DEED. [AHD *dhē-¹.*]

dheigh-. To knead. 1. Gmc *daigjōn* in OE *dǣge,* bread kneader: DAIRY. 2. Gmc *-dīg-* in OE *hlǣfdige,* "bread kneader, mistress of a household" (*hlǣf,* LOAF): LADY. 3. O-grade form *dhoigh-* in Gmc *daigaz* in OE *dāg*: DOUGH.

dhel-. A hollow. 1. Gmc *daljō* in OE *dell*: DELL. 2. Gmc *dalam* in OE *dæl*: DALE.

dhelbh-. To dig. Gmc *delban* in OE *delfan*: DELVE.

dher-¹. To make muddy; darkness. 1. Gmc *derk-* in OE *deorc*: DARK. 2. Zero-grade form *dhr̥-* in: a. Gmc *drah-sta-* in OE *drōs*: DROSS; b. Gmc *drab-* in OE *dreflian*: DRIVEL.

dher-². To drone, buzz. Gmc *drēn-,* male honeybee, in OE *drān*: DRONE¹. [AHD *dher-³.*]

dhers-. To be bold. Gmc *ders-* and *durs-* in OE *durran*: DARE.

dheu-¹. "To rise in a cloud as dust"; hence also dark colors, breath, confused perceptions, etc. 1. Extended form *dheus-* possibly in: a. Gmc *dus-* in OE *dysig*: DIZZY; b. Gmc *diuzam,* "breathing animal," in OE *dēor*: DEER. 2. Extended form *dhwens-* in OE *dust*: DUST. 3. Extended form *dhus-* in Gmc *duskaz* in OE *dox*: DUSK. 4. Extended form *dhoubh-* in: a. Gmc *daubaz* in OE *dēaf*: DEAF; b. Gmc *dūbōn,* "dark-colored bird," in OE *dūfe*: DOVE¹. 5.

Zero-grade form *dhu-* in Gmc *dumbaz* in OE *dumb*: DUMB. 6. Extended form *dhwel-* in Gmc *dwelan* in OE *dwellan,* to deceive: DWELL.

dheu-². To flow. Gmc *dauwaz* in OE *dēaw*: DEW.

dheu-³. To die. 1. O-grade form *dhou-* in Gmc *daudaz* in OE *dēad*: DEAD. 2. Extended zero-grade form *dhwi-* in Gmc *dwinan* in OE *dwīnan*: DWINDLE.

dheub-. Deep. 1. Gmc *diupaz* in OE *dēop*: DEEP. 2. Gmc *duppjan* in OE *dyppan*: DIP. 3. Gmc *dubjan* in OE *dȳfan* and *dufan*: DIVE.

dheubh-. Wedge. Gmc *dub-* in OE *dubbian*: DUB¹.

dhigw-. To fix. Gmc *dīk-* in OE *dīc*: DIKE, DITCH.

dhragh-. To drag. Gmc *dragan* in: a. OE *dragan* (and ON *draga*): DRAG, DRAW; b. OE *dræge*: DRAY.

dhreg-. To draw. Variant of dhragh-. 1. Gmc *drinkan* in OE *drincan*: DRINK. 2. Gmc *drankjan* in OE *drencan*: DRENCH.

dhrelbh-. To drive. Gmc *drīban* in OE *drīfan*: DRIVE.

dhreu-. To fall, drip. 1. Extended form *dhreus-* in Gmc *driusan* in OE *drēosan*: DRIZZLE. 2. O-grade form *dhrous-* in: a. Gmc *drauzaz* in OE *drēor*: DREARY; b. Gmc *drusjan* in OE *drūsian*: DROWSE. 3. Extended zero-grade form *dhrub-* in Gmc *drupan* in OE *dropa*: DROP.

dhreugh-. To deceive. Gmc *draugma-* in OE *drēam*: DREAM.

dhughəter-. Daughter. Gmc *dohtēr* in OE *dohtor*: DAUGHTER.

dhwen-. To make noise. Gmc *duniz* in OE *dyne*: DIN.

dhwer-. Door. Zero-grade form *dhur-* in Gmc *durunz* and *duram* in OE *dor*: DOOR.

dn̥ghū. Tongue. Gmc *tungōn* in OE *tunge*: TONGUE.

dwō. Two. 1. Gmc *twai,* two, in: a. OE *twā, tu*: TWO; b. OE *twēgen*: TWAIN; c. Gmc *twalif-,* "two left (over from ten)," in OE *twelf*: TWELVE. 2. Forms *dwis* and *dwi-* in: a. Gmc *twiyes* in OE *twige*: TWICE; b. Gmc *twēgentig,* "twice ten," in OE *twēntig*: TWENTY; c. Gmc *twihna,* "double thread," in OE *twīn*: TWINE; d. Gmc *twisnaz* in OE *getwinn*: TWIN; e. Gmc *twiga,* fork, in OE *twigge*: TWIG.

ed-. To eat. Gmc *itan* in OE *etan*: EAT.

eg. I. Gmc *eg* in OE *ic*: I.

ĕik-. To possess. 1. Gmc *aigan* in OE *āgan*: OUGHT¹, OWE. 2. Gmc *aiganaz* in OE *āgen*: OWN.

eis-. Ice. Gmc *īs-* in OE *īs*: ICE. [AHD *eis-².*]

el-¹. Elbow. O-grade form *ol-* in Gmc *alinobogōn-* in OE *elnboga*: ELBOW.

el-². Red, brown. 1. Gmc *elmo-* in OE *elm*: ELM. 2. Gmc *aliza* in OE *aler*: ALDER.

en. In. Gmc *in* in OE *in, inn*: IN, INN.

er-¹. To set in motion. 1. O-grade form *or-* in Gmc *arnja-* in OE *eornost*: EARNEST¹. 2. Variant root *rei-,* to flow, in zero-grade form *ri-* in Gmc *rinwan* in OE *rinnan*: RUN.

er-². Earth. Gmc *erthō* in OE *eorthe*: EARTH. [AHD *er-².*]

erə-. To row. Form *rē-* in: a. Gmc *rō-* in OE *rōwan*: ROW²; b. Gmc *rōthra* in OE *rōther*: RUDDER. [AHD *erə-¹.*]

es-. To be. 1. Gmc *izmi* in OE *eam*: AM. 2. Stem *si-* in Gmc *sijai-* in OE *sie*: YES. 3. Form *sont-* in: a. Gmc *santhaz* in OE *sōth*: SOOTH; b. Zero-grade *sn̥t-* in Gmc *sunjō,* sin (< a formula of repentance, "it is true, the sin is real") in OE *synn*: SIN¹.

esen-. Harvest. O-grade form *osn-* in Gmc *aznōn,* to do harvest work, serve as a laborer, in OE *earnian*: EARN.

eu-. Lacking. Extended form *wə-* in Gmc

*wanēn in OE *wanian*: WANE. [AHD *eu-²*.]

eudh-. Udder. Zero-grade form *ŭdh-* in Gmc *ŭthr-* in OE *ūder*: UDDER.

gal-¹. Bald. Gmc *kalwaz* in OE *calu*, bald: CALLOW.

gal-². To call, shout. Gmc *klat-* in OE *clatrian*: CLATTER.

gel-¹. To form into a ball. Gmc *klŭd-* in OE *clott*, lump: CLOT.

gel-². Bright. Extended form *glei-* in Gmc *klai-* in OE *clǣne*: CLEAN.

gel-³. Cold. 1. Gmc *kaliz* in OE *ciele*: CHILL. 2. Gmc *kaldaz* in OE *ceald*: COLD. 3. Gmc *kōl-* in OE *cōl*: COOL.

gembh-. Tooth. O-grade form *gombh-* in Gmc *kambaz* in OE *comb, camb*: COMB.

genə-. To give birth. Zero-grade form *gṇ-*. 1. Gmc *kunjam* in OE *cynn*: KIN. 2. Gmc *kuningaz*, "son of the royal kin," in OE *cyning*: KING. 3. Gmc *kundjaz* in OE *cynd, gecynd*, birth, nature: KIND². 4. Gmc *kundiz* in OE *gecynde*, natural: KIND¹.

genu-¹. Knee. Variant *gneu-* in: **a.** Gmc *kniwam* in OE *cnēo*: KNEE; **b.** Gmc *kniwljan* in OE *cnēowlian*: KNEEL.

genu-². Chin. Form *genw-* in Gmc *kinnuz* in OE *cinn*: CHIN.

geph-. Jaw. Gmc *kabal* in OE *ceafl*: JOWL¹.

ger-¹. To gather. Extended form *grem-* in Gmc *kram-* in OE *crammian*: CRAM.

ger-². To cry hoarsely. 1. Gmc *krē-* in: **a.** OE *crāwe*: CROW¹; **b.** OE *crāwan*: CROW²; **c.** OE *cracian*: CRACK. 2. Gmc *kranu-* in OE *cran*: CRANE. [AHD *ger-⁴*.]

gerebh-. To scratch. Variant *grebh-* in: **a.** Gmc *krabb-* in OE *crabba*: CRAB¹; **b.** Gmc *kerban* in OE *ceorfan*: CARVE.

geulo-. A glowing coal. Gmc *kolam* in OE *col*: COAL.

geus-. To choose. Gmc *kiusan* in OE *cēosan*: CHOOSE.

ghabh-. Also **ghebh-**. To give. Gmc *giban* in OE *giefan*: GIVE.

ghaido-. Goat. Gmc *gaitaz* in OE *gāt*: GOAT.

ghalgh-. Branch, rod. Gmc *galgōn* in OE *gealga*: GALLOWS.

ghans-. Goose. 1. Gmc *gans-* in OE *gōs*: GOOSE. 2. Gmc *ganr-* in OE *gandra*: GANDER. 3. Gmc *ganōtōn* in OE *ganot*: GANNET.

ghasto-. Rod. Gmc *gazdaz* in OE *gierd*: YARD¹.

ghē-. To let go. Gmc *gēn* in OE *gān*: GO.

ghedh-. To unite, join, fit. 1. Form *ghōdh-* in Gmc *gōdaz*, "fitting, suitable," in OE *gōd*: GOOD. 2. Gmc *gadurī* in OE *tōgædere*: TOGETHER. 3. Gmc *gadurōn* in OE *gaderian*: GATHER.

ghēi-. To yawn. Form *ghi-n-ā-* in Gmc *ginōn* in OE *geonian*: YAWN.

gheis-. Fear, amazement. O-grade form *ghois-* in Gmc *gaistaz* in OE *gāst*: GHOST.

ghel-¹. To call. Gmc *gel-* in: **a.** OE *giellan*: YELL; **b.** OE *gielpan*: YELP.

ghel-². To shine. 1. Gmc *gelwaz* in OE *geolu*: YELLOW. 2. Zero-grade form *ghḷ-* in Gmc *gultham* in OE *gold*: GOLD.

ghend-. Also **ghed-**. To seize. Gmc *getan* in: **a.** OE *begietan*: BEGET; **b.** OE *forgietan*: FORGET.

ghengh-. To go. Gmc *gang-* in OE *gang*: GANG.

gher-¹. Gut, entrail. Gmc *garnō*, string, in OE *gearn*: YARN.

gher-². To enclose. 1. Zero-grade form *ghṛ-* in Gmc *gurdjan* in: **a.** OE *gyrdan*: GIRD; **b.** OE *gyrdel*: GIRDLE. 2. O-grade form *ghor-* in Gmc *gardaz*, "enclosure," in OE *geard*: YARD².

gher-³. To call out. Form *ghred-* in Gmc *grōtjan* in OE *grētan*: GREET.

gher-⁴. Gray. Gmc *grēwaz* in OE *grǣg*: GRAY.

gher-⁵. To want. Gmc *gernjan* in OE *giernan*: YEARN. [AHD *gher-⁶*.]

ghēu-. To yawn. Gmc *gō-ma-* in OE *gōma*: GUM².

gheu(ə)-. To invoke (as a god). Zero-grade form *ghu-* in: **a.** Gmc *gudam* in OE *god*: GOD; **b.** Gmc *gud-igaz*, "possessed by a god," in OE *gydig*: GIDDY.

ghrē-. To grow, become green. 1. O-grade form *ghrō-* in: **a.** Gmc *grōwan* in OE *grōwan*: GROW; **b.** Gmc *grōnjaz* in OE *grēne*: GREEN. 2. Zero-grade form *ghrə-* in Gmc *grasam* in OE *græs*: GRASS.

ghrebh-. To dig, bury. 1. O-grade form *ghrobh-* in: **a.** Gmc *graban* in OE *grafan*: GRAVE³; **b.** Gmc *graba* in OE *græf*: GRAVE¹. 2. Gmc *grubjan* in OE *grybban*: GRUB. [AHD *ghrebh-²*.]

ghrelb-. To grip. 1. Gmc *grip-* in OE *gripe* and *gripa*: GRIP¹. 2. Gmc *grīpan* in OE *grīpan*: GRIPE. 3. O-grade form *ghroib-* in Gmc *graipjan* in OE *grāpian*: GROPE.

ghrem-. Angry. Gmc *grimmaz* in OE *grim*: GRIM.

ghren-. Also **gwhren-**. To grind. 1. Gmc *grindan* in OE *grindan*: GRIND. 2. Gmc *grinst-* in OE *grīst*: GRIST.

ghrēu-. To grind. 1. Gmc *griut-* in OE *grēot*: GRIT. 2. Gmc *grautaz*, "coarsely ground," in OE *grēat*: GREAT.

gleubh-. To split. 1. Gmc *kliuban* in OE *clēofan*: CLEAVE¹. 2. Gmc *klub-* in OE *clufu*: CLOVE².

gnō-. To know. 1. Extended form *gnōw-* in Gmc *knōw-* in OE *gecnāwan*: KNOW. 2. Zero-grade form *gnə-* in: **a.** Gmc *kunnan* in OE *cunnan*: CAN¹, CON², CUNNING; **b.** Gmc *kunth-* in OE *cūth*: UNCOUTH.

gras-. To devour. Gmc *krasjōn* in OE *cresse*: CRESS.

greut-. To compress. Gmc *krūdan* in OE *crūdan*: CROWD.

grə-no-. Grain. Gmc *kornam* in OE *corn*: CORN¹.

gwā-. To come. 1. Gmc *kuman* in OE *cuman*: COME. 2. Gmc *kuma-* in OE *wilcuma*: WELCOME.

gwel-. To live. Zero-grade form *gwi-* in Gmc *kwikwaz* in OE *cwic*, living: QUICK.

gwel-¹. To swallow. Gmc *kel-* in OE *ceolu*: JOWL². [AHD *gwel-⁵*.]

gwel-². To pierce. 1. O-grade form *gwol-* in Gmc *kwaljan* in OE *cwellan*: QUELL. 2. Zero-grade form *gwḷ-* in Gmc *kuljan* in OE *cyllan*: KILL.

gwen-. Woman. Lengthened form *gwēn-* in Gmc *kwēniz* in OE *cwēn*: QUEEN.

gwet-. To speak. Gmc *kwithan* in OE *cwethan*: BEQUEATH, QUOTH. [AHD *gwet-²*.]

gwou-. Cow. Form *gwōu-s* in Gmc *kōuz* in OE *cū*: COW¹.

gyeu-. To chew. Gmc *kewwan* in OE *cēowan*: CHEW.

gzhyes. Yesterday. Gmc *ges-ter-* in OE *geostran*: YESTER-.

kā-. To like, desire. Gmc *hōraz* in OE *hōre*: WHORE.

kād-. Hatred. Zero-grade form *kəd-* in Gmc *hatōn* in OE *hatian*: HATE.

kadh-. To cover. 1. Gmc *hattuz* in OE *hætt*: HAT. 2. Form *kōdh-* in: **a.** Gmc *hōda* in OE *hōd*: HOOD¹; **b.** Gmc *hōdjan* in OE *hēdan*: HEED.

kagh-. To catch; fence. Gmc *hagjō* in OE *hecg*: HEDGE.

kaghlo-. Hail. Gmc *haglaz* in OE *hagol*: HAIL¹.

kai-. Heat. 1. Gmc *haitaz* in OE *hāt*: HOT. 2. Gmc *haiti-* in OE *hǣtu*: HEAT.

kailo-. Whole, uninjured. 1. Gmc *hailaz* in OE *hāl*: HALE¹, WHOLE. 2. Gmc *hailithō* in OE

hǣlth: HEALTH. 3. Gmc *hailjan* in OE *hǣlan*: HEAL. 4. Gmc *hailagaz* in OE *hālig*: HOLY. 5. Gmc *hailagōn* in OE *hālgian*: HALLOW.

kaito-. Forest. 1. Gmc *haithiz* in OE *hǣth*: HEATH. 2. Gmc *haithinaz* in OE *hǣthen*: HEATHEN.

kan-. To sing. Gmc *hannī* in OE *hen*: HEN.

kap-. To grasp. 1. Gmc *habēn* in OE *habban*: HAVE. 2. Gmc *habukaz* in OE *heafoc*: HAWK¹. 3. Gmc *hafigaz*, "having weight," in OE *hefig*: HEAVY. 4. Gmc *hafjan* in OE *hebban*: HEAVE.

kapho-. Hoof. Form *kăp-o-* in Gmc *hōfaz* in OE *hōf*: HOOF.

kaput. Head. Gmc *haubidam* in OE *hēafod*: HEAD.

kar-. Hard. O-grade form *kor-* in Gmc *harduz* in OE *hard*: HARD. [AHD *kar-¹*.]

kas-. Gray. Gmc *hasōn* in OE *hara*: HARE.

kau-. To hew. 1. Gmc *hawwan* in OE *hēawan*: HEW. 2. Gmc *haujam* in OE *hīeg*: HAY. [AHD *kau-²*.]

keg-. Hook. Gmc *hōka-* in OE *hōc*: HOOK.

kē-. To sharpen. O-grade form *kō-* in Gmc *hainō* in OE *hān*, stone: HONE.

kei-¹. To lie; home. O-grade form *koi-* in Gmc *haima* in OE *hām*: HOME.

kei-². Color adjective. 1. O-grade form *koi-* in Gmc *hairaz* in OE *hār*: HOARFROST. 2. Zero-grade form *ki-* in Gmc *hiwan* in OE *hēo*: HUE¹.

kel-¹. Warm. Form *klē-* in Gmc *hlēwaz* in OE *hlēo*: LEE.

kel-². To strike. Extended o-grade form *kold-* in Gmc *haltōn* in OE *healtian*: HALT².

kel-³. To shout. Form *klā-* in Gmc *hlō-* in OE *hlōwan*: LOW².

kel-⁴. To cover. 1. Gmc *haljō*, "concealed place," in OE *hell*: HELL. 2. Gmc *hallō* in OE *heall*: HALL. 3. Zero-grade form *kḷ-* in Gmc *hul-* in: **a.** OE *hulu*: HULL; **b.** OE *hol*: HOLE; **c.** OE *holh*: HOLLOW.

kel-⁵. To prick. Gmc *hulin-* in OE *holen*: HOLLY. [AHD *kel-⁹*.]

kel-⁶. Hill. Zero-grade form *kḷ-* in Gmc *hulni-* in OE *hyll*: HILL. [AHD *kel-⁸*.]

kelb-. To help. Gmc *helpan* in OE *helpan*: HELP.

kelp-. To hold. O-grade form *kolp-* in: **a.** Gmc *halb-* in OE *helma*: HELM; **b.** Gmc *half-* in OE *hælftre*: HALTER.

kem-¹. Hornless. Gmc *hinthjō* in OE *hind*: HIND².

kem-². To compress. Gmc *hamjan* in OE *hemm*, a doubling over: HEM¹.

kenəko-. Yellow. Gmc *hunagam* in OE *hunig*: HONEY.

kenk-¹. Heel. 1. Gmc *hanha* in OE *hōh*: HOCK¹. 2. Gmc *hanhila* in OE *hēla*: HEEL¹. [AHD *kenk-³*.]

kenk-². To be hungry. Zero-grade form *kṇk-* in Gmc *hungruz* in OE *hungor*: HUNGER.

ker-¹. Horn, head. 1. Zero-grade form *kṛ-* in: **a.** Gmc *hurnaz* in OE *horn*: HORN; **b.** Gmc *hurznuta* in OE *hyrnet*: HORNET. 2. Extended form *keru-* in Gmc *herutaz* in OE *heorot*: HART.

ker-². "Loud noise, bird's cry." Zero-grade form *kṛ-*. 1. Gmc *hring-* in OE *hringan*: RING². 2. Gmc *hraik-* in OE *hrǣcan*: RETCH. 3. Gmc *hraban* in OE *hræfn*: RAVEN.

ker-³. Heat, fire. Gmc *herthō* in OE *heorth*: HEARTH. [AHD *ker-⁴*.]

kerd-. Heart. Gmc *hertōn-* in OE *heorte*: HEART. [AHD *kerd-¹*.]

kerdh-. Herd. Gmc *herdō* in OE *heord*: HERD.

kerp-. To harvest. Variant *karp-* in Gmc *harbistaz* in OE *hærfest*: HARVEST.

kert-. To entwine. Zero-grade form *kṛt-* in Gmc *hurdiz*, wicker frame, hurdle, in OE *hyrdel*: HURDLE.

keu-. To observe, see, hear. O-grade form

*kou-. 1. Extended form *kous- in Gmc *hausjan in: **a.** OE *hieran:* HEAR; **b.** OE *heorcian: HARK, HEARKEN. 2. Variant *skou-* in: **a.** Gmc *skauwon, to look at, in OE *scēawian:* SHOW; **b.** Gmc *skauniz, bright, in OE *sciene:* SHEEN. [AHD *keu-¹.*]

kĕwero-. North (wind). Gmc *skūra-, wind, storm, in OE *scūr:* SHOWER.

klĕg-. To sound, cry out. Variant *klak- in Gmc *hlahjan in OE *hliehhan:* LAUGH.

klei-. To lean. 1. Zero-grade form *kli- in: **a.** Gmc *hlid-, "that which bends over," in OE *hlid:* LID; **b.** Gmc *hlinēn in OE *hleonian:* LEAN¹. 2. O-grade form *kloi- in Gmc *hlaidr- in OE *hlǣdder:* LADDER.

kleng-. To bend. 1. Gmc *hlink- in OE *hlinc:* LINKS. 2. Gmc *hlank- in OE *hlanc:* LANK.

kleu-. To hear. Zero-grade form *klu-. 1. Gmc *hlusinōn in OE *hlysnan:* LISTEN. 2. Lengthened form *klū- in Gmc *hlūdaz in OE *hlūd:* LOUD. [AHD *kleu-¹.*]

ko-. "This." Variant *ki- in Gmc *hi- in: **a.** OE *he:* HE¹; **b.** OE *him:* HIM; **c.** OE *his:* HIS; **d.** OE *hire:* HER; **e.** OE *hit:* IT; **f.** OE *hēr:* HERE; **g.** OE *heonane:* HENCE; **h.** OE *hider:* HITHER.

konk-. To hang. Gmc *hanhan in OE *hangian* and *hon* (and ON *hanga*): HANG.

kormo-. Pain. Gmc *harmaz in OE *hearm:* HARM.

koselo-. Hazel. Gmc *haselaz in OE *hæsel:* HAZEL.

krapo-. Roof. Gmc *hrōfam in OE *hrōf:* ROOF.

krep-. Body. Gmc *hrifiz in OE *hrif:* MIDRIFF.

kreu-¹. Raw flesh. Form *krēw- in Gmc *hrēwaz in OE *hrēaw:* RAW.

kreu-². To strike. Gmc *hrewwan in OE *hrēowan:* RUE¹.

kreut-. Reed. Gmc *hriuda- in OE *hrēod:* REED.

kus-. A kiss. Gmc *kussjan in OE *cyssan:* KISS.

kwed-. To sharpen. Gmc *hwatjan in OE *hwettan:* WHET.

kwei-. To hiss. Gmc *hwĭ-n- and *hwis- in: **a.** OE *hwīnan in OE *hwīnan:* WHINE; **b.** OE *hwisprian:* WHISPER; **c.** OE *hwistlian:* WHISTLE. [AHD *kwei-⁴.*]

kweit-. White. 1. Gmc *hwītaz in OE *hwīt:* WHITE. 2. Gmc *hwaitjaz in OE *hwǣte:* WHEAT.

kwel-. To revolve. Redupl form *kwe-kwel-o- in OE *hwēol:* WHEEL. [AHD *kwel-¹.*]

kwerp-. To turn oneself. Gmc *hwarb- in OE *hwearf,* wharf (< "place where people move about"): WHARF.

kwetwer-. Four. O-grade form *kwetwor- prob in Gmc *petwor- in: **a.** OE *fēower:* FOUR; **b.** OE *fēowertig:* FORTY.

kweye-. Cozy, quiet. Variant *kwī- in Gmc *hwīlō in OE *hwīl:* WHILE.

kwo-. Stem of relative and interrogative pronouns. 1. Gmc *hwas, *hwasa, *hwam, in OE *hwā, hwæs, hwæm:* WHO, WHOSE, WHOM. 2. Gmc *hwat in OE *hwæt:* WHAT. 3. Gmc *hwī in OE *hwȳ:* WHY. 4. Gmc *hwa-līk- in OE *hwelc:* WHICH. 5. Gmc *hwō- in OE *hū:* HOW. 6. Gmc *hwan- in OE *hwenne* and *hwanon:* WHEN and WHENCE. 7. Gmc *hwithrē in OE *hwider:* WHITHER. 8. Gmc *hwar- in OE *hwǣr:* WHERE. 9. Gmc *hwatharaz in: **a.** OE *hwæther:* NEITHER, WHETHER; **b.** Gmc *aiwo gihwatharaz, "ever each of two," in OE *ǣghwǣther:* EITHER.

kwon-. Dog. Zero-grade form *kwn̥ in Gmc *hundaz in OE *hund:* HOUND.

lab-. To lick. Gmc *lapjan in OE *lapian:* LAP³.

las-. To be eager or wanton. 1. Gmc *lustuz in OE *lust:* LUST. 2. Gmc *lustjan in OE *lystan:* LISTLESS.

leb-. Lip. Gmc *lep- in OE *lippa:* LIP. [AHD *leb-².*]

legh-. To lie, lay. 1. Gmc *ligjan in OE *licgan:* LIE¹. 2. Gmc *lagjan in OE *lecgan:* LAY¹.

legwh-. Light. Gmc *līhtaz in OE *līht:* LIGHT².

lei-. Slimy. Gmc *lī- in: **a.** OE *slīm:* SLIME; **b.** OE *slipor:* SLIPPERY.

lēi-. To let go. 1. Form *lēd- in Gmc *lētan in OE *lǣtan:* LET¹. 2. Form *lǝd- in: **a.** Gmc *lataz in OE *læt, lætra, latost:* LATE, LATTER, LAST¹; **b.** Gmc *latjan in OE *lettan:* LET². [AHD *lēi-².*]

leigh-. To lick. Zero-grade form *lig- in Gmc *likkōn in OE *liccian:* LICK.

leikw-. To leave. O-grade form *loikw- in Gmc *laihwnjan in OE *lǣnan:* LEND.

leip-. To stick; adhere; fat. 1. Gmc *lībam, "continuance," in OE *līf:* LIFE. 2. Gmc *libēn, "to continue," in OE *libban:* LIVE¹. 3. Gmc *laibjan in OE *lǣfan:* LEAVE¹. 4. Gmc *librō in OE *lifer:* LIVER.

leis-. Track, furrow. O-grade form *lois-. 1. Gmc *laist-, "footprint," in OE *lāst:* LAST³. 2. Gmc *laistjan, "to follow a track," in OE *lǣstan:* LAST². 3. Gmc *laizō* in OE *lār:* LORE. 4. Gmc *liznōn in OE *leornian:* LEARN.

leit-. To detest. 1. Gmc *laithaz in OE *lāth:* LOATH. 2. Gmc *laithōn in OE *lāthian:* LOATHE.

leith-. To go forth. O-grade form *loit-. 1. Gmc *laidjan in OE *lǣdan:* LEAD¹. 2. Variant *loid- in Gmc *laidō in OE *lād,* course: LOAD, LODE, LIVELIHOOD.

lem-. Broken. Gmc *lamōn in OE *lama:* LAME. [AHD *lem-¹.*]

lendh-. Open land. Gmc *landam in OE *land:* LAND. [AHD *lendh-².*]

lento-. Flexible. Gmc *linthjaz in OE *līthe:* LITHE.

lep-. To be flat; palm. Form *lōp- in Gmc *galōfō in OE *glōf:* GLOVE. [AHD *lep-².*]

letro-. Leather. Gmc *lethram in OE *lether-:* LEATHER.

leu-. To cut apart. 1. Gmc *lausaz in OE *los:* LOSE, LOSS. 2. Gmc *ferliusan in OE *forlēosan:* FORLORN. [AHD *leu-¹.*]

leubh-. To care; love. 1. O-grade form *loubh- in Gmc *galaubjan in OE *gelēfan, belēfan:* BELIEVE. 2. Zero-grade form *lubh- in Gmc *lubō in OE *lufu:* LOVE.

leud-. Small. Gmc *lūt- in OE *lȳtel:* LITTLE.

leugh-. To lie. Gmc *liugan in OE *lēogan:* LIE².

leuk-. Light. Gmc *liuhtam in OE *līht:* LIGHT¹.

leup-. To break off. Gmc *laubaz in OE *lēaf:* LEAF.

lou-. To wash. 1. Gmc *laugō in OE *lēag:* LYE. 2. OE *lēathor:* LATHER.

lus-. Louse. Gmc *lus- in OE *lūs:* LOUSE.

mā-. Damp. Gmc *mōra- in OE *mōr:* MOOR². [AHD *mā-³.*]

mad-. Moist (as food). Gmc *mati- in OE *mete:* MEAT.

mag-. Also **mak-.** To knead, fit. 1. Gmc *makōn in OE *macian:* MAKE. 2. Gmc *ga-mak-ōn, "fitted together with (another), spouse," in OE *gemæcca:* MATCH¹. 3. Gmc *mangjan, to mix, in: **a.** OE *mengan:* MINGLE; **b.** OE *gemang:* AMONG, MONGREL.

magh-. To be able. 1. Gmc *mag- in OE *magan:* MAY¹. 2. Gmc *mah-ti- in OE *miht:* MIGHT¹. 3. Gmc *mag-ena in OE *mægen:* MAIN. [AHD *magh-¹.*]

maghu-. Young person. Form *magho- in Gmc *magadin- in OE *mægden:* MAIDEN.

mai-¹. To cut. 1. Gmc *ā-mait-jon, "the biter," in OE *ǣmette:* ANT. 2. Gmc *mīton- in OE *mīte:* MITE¹.

mai-². To soil. Gmc *mail-, a blemish, in OE *māl:* MOLE¹.

man-. Man. Extended form *manu- in Gmc *manna- in OE *mann:* MAN. [AHD *man-¹.*]

marko-. Horse. Gmc feminine *marhjōn in OE *mere:* MARE¹.

māter-. Mother. Gmc *mōthar- in OE *mōdor:* MOTHER.

me-. First person singular pronoun. 1. Gmc *mĕ- in OE *mē:* ME. 2. Possessive form *meino- in Gmc *mīn- in OE *mīn:* MINE², MY. [AHD *me-¹.*]

mĕ-¹. Mind, disposition. O-grade form *mō- in Gmc *mōthaz in OE *mōd:* MOOD¹.

mĕ-². To measure. 1. Gmc *mǣlaz, "appointed time," in OE *mǣl:* MEAL². 2. Extended form *mēn- in: **a.** Gmc *mǣnon in OE *mōna:* MOON; **b.** Gmc *mǣnōth- in OE *mōnath:* MONTH.

mĕ-³. Big. 1. Gmc comparative *maizōn- in OE *māra* and *māre:* MORE. 2. Gmc superlative *maista- in OE *mǣst:* MOST.

mĕ-⁴. To cut down grass. Gmc *mǣ- in OE *māwan:* MOW¹.

med-. To take appropriate measures. Gmc *metan in OE *metan:* METE.

medhu-. Honey; mead. Gmc *medu in OE *meodu:* MEAD¹.

medhyo-. Middle. Gmc *middila- in OE *middel:* MIDDLE.

meg-. Great. Gmc *mik- in OE *mycel:* MUCH.

mei-. To change, exchange. 1. O-grade form *moi- in Gmc *ga-maid-az, "changed for the worse, abnormal," in OE *gemād:* MAD. 2. Form *mit-to-, "changed, wrongly," in **a.** Gmc *missa- in OE *mis-:* MIS-; **b.** Gmc *missjan in OE *missan:* MISS¹. [AHD *mei-¹.*]

meigh-. To urinate. Gmc *mih-, urine, rain, in OE *mist:* MIST.

mei-no-. Opinion, intention. 1. Gmc *main-, complaint, in OE *mān: MOAN. 2. Gmc *mainjan, to intend, in OE *mǣnan:* MEAN¹.

mel-. Soft. 1. Extended form *meld- in: **a.** Gmc *meltan in OE *meltan:* MELT; **b.** Gmc *malta- in OE *mealt:* MALT. 2. Extended form *meldh- in Gmc *mildja- in OE *milde:* MILD. [AHD *mel-¹.*]

melǝ-. To crush, grind. Gmc *mel-wa-, flour, in OE *melu:* MEAL¹.

melg-. To milk. Gmc *meluk- in OE *milc:* MILK.

mēlo-. Also **smēlo-.** Small animal. Zero-grade form *smǝlo in Gmc *smal- in OE *smæl:* SMALL.

men-. To think. Zero-grade form *mn̥- in Gmc *ga-mundi- in OE *gemynd:* MIND. [AHD *men-¹.*]

menegh-. Copious. Gmc *managa- in OE *manig:* MANY.

menth-. To chew. Form *mn̥tho- in Gmc *muntha- in OE *mūth:* MOUTH.

mer-¹. To flicker. Gmc *murgana- in OE *morgen:* MORN.

mer-². To trouble. Gmc *marzjan in OE *merran:* MAR. [AHD *mer-⁴.*]

merg-. Boundary. Gmc *mark- in OE *mearc:* MARK¹.

meu-. Damp. Gmc *meus- in OE *mos:* MOSS.

mōd-. To meet. Gmc *mōtjan in OE *mētan:* MEET¹.

mon-. Neck. Gmc *manō in OE *manu:* MANE.

mori-. Body of water. Gmc *mariska- in OE *mersc:* MARSH.

mozgo-. Marrow. Gmc *mazgā- in OE *mærg:* MARROW.

mregh-mo-. Brain. Gmc *brag-na- in OE *brægen:* BRAIN.

mreghu-. Short. Zero-grade form *mr̥ghu- in: **a.** Gmc *murja-, short, pleasant, in OE *mirige:* MERRY; **b.** Gmc *murgithō in OE *myrgth:* MIRTH.

mū-. Mouse. Gmc *mūs- in OE *mūs:* MOUSE. [AHD *mū-¹.*]

nas-. Nose. Gmc *nasō in OE *nosu:* NOSE.

nāu-. To be exhausted. Zero-grade form *nǝu- in Gmc *naudi- in OE *nēod, nēd:* NEED. [AHD *nāu-¹.*]

n̥dher-. Under. Gmc *under- in OE *under:* UNDER.

ne. Not. 1. Gmc *ne- in OE *ne:* NO¹. 2. Zero-grade form *ŋ- in Gmc *un- in OE un-: UN-¹.

ned-. To bind, tie. O-grade form *nod- in: a. Gmc *nati- in OE net: NET¹; b. Gmc nat-ilō in OE netle: NETTLE.

nek-. To attain. O-grade form *nok- in Gmc *ga-nah- in OE genōg: ENOUGH. [AHD nek-².]

nekwt-. Night. O-grade form *nokwt- in Gmc *naht- in OE niht: NIGHT.

nem-. To take. Gmc *nem- in: a. OE niman: NUMB; b. OE nœmel and numol: NIMBLE. [AHD nem-².]

ner-. Under, on the left; north. Zero-grade form *nr̥ in Gmc north- in OE north: NORTH. [AHD ner-¹.]

nes-. Personal pronoun. Zero-grade form *ns- in: a. Gmc *uns in OE ūs: US; b. Gmc *un-sara- in OE ūre: OUR. [AHD nes-².]

nētr-. Snake. Gmc *nēthrō- in OE nædre: ADDER.

newŋ. Nine. Gmc *niwun in OE nigon: NINE.

newo-. New. Gmc *neuja- in OE nēowe: NEW.

nl. Down. 1. Gmc *nith- in OE nithan, neothan: BENEATH, UNDERNEATH. 2. Gmc *nitheraz in OE nither: NETHER.

nizdo-. Bird's nest. 1. Gmc *nist- in OE nest: NEST. 2. Gmc *nistilōn in OE nestlian: NESTLE.

nobh-. Navel. Gmc *nabalō in OE nafela: NAVEL.

nogh-. Nail. Gmc *nagla- in OE nægl: NAIL.

nogw-. Naked. Gmc *nakweda- in OE nacod: NAKED.

nomen-. Name. Gmc *namōn- in OE nama: NAME.

nu-. Now. Gmc *neuja- in OE nū: NOW.

ōg-. Fruit. Zero-grade form *əg- in Gmc *ak-ran- in OE æcern: ACORN.

oino-. One. 1. Gmc *ainaz in OE ān: A, AN, ONE. 2. Gmc *ain-lif-, "one left (beyond ten)," in OE endleofan: ELEVEN. 3. Gmc *ainigaz in OE ænig: ANY.

olto-. An oath. Gmc *aithaz in OE āth: OATH.

oktō. Eight. Gmc *ahtō in OE eahta: EIGHT.

okw-. To see. Gmc *augōn- in OE ēage: EYE.

ous-. Ear. Gmc *auzan- in OE ēare: EAR¹.

owi-. Sheep. Gmc awi- in OE ēowu: EWE.

pā-. To feed. 1. Gmc *fōdram in OE fōdor: FODDER. 2. Extended form *pāt- in: a. Gmc *fōd- in OE fōda: FOOD; b. Gmc *fōdjan in OE fēdan: FEED; c. Gmc *fōstra- in OE fōstor: FOSTER.

pag-. To fasten. Form *pa-n-g- in Gmc *fangiz in OE fang: FANG.

pan-. Fabric. Gmc *fanōn- in OE fana: VANE.

past-. Solid, firm. 1. Gmc *fastuz in OE fæst: FAST¹. 2. Gmc *fastinōn in OE fastnian: FASTEN. 3. Gmc *fasten, to hold fast, in OE fæstan: FAST².

ped-¹. Foot. 1. Lengthened o-grade form *pōd- in Gmc *fōt- in OE fōt: FOOT. 2. Gmc *feterō in OE feter: FETTER.

ped-². Container. O-grade form *pod- in Gmc *fatam in OE fæt: VAT.

peig-¹. Also peik-. To cut. Gmc *fīhala in OE fēol: FILE².

peig-². Also peik-. Evil-minded. 1. Zero-grade form *pig- in Gmc *fikala in OE ficol: FICKLE. 2. O-grade form *poik- in: a. Gmc *gafaihaz in OE gefāh: FOE; b. Gmc *faigjaz in OE fæge: FEY.

peisk-. Fish. Gmc *fiska- in OE fisc: FISH.

pel-¹. To thrust. Extended form *peld- in: a. Gmc *falt- in OE anfealt: ANVIL; b. Gmc *feltaz, "compressed wool," in OE felt: FELT¹. [AHD pel-⁶.]

pel-². Pale. Variant *pal- in Gmc *falwaz in OE fealo: FALLOW DEER.

pel-³. To fold. Extended form *pelt- in: a. Gmc *falthan in OE faldan: FOLD¹; b. Gmc *-falthaz in OE -feald: -FOLD.

pel-⁴. Skin. Gmc *fel-men- in OE filmen, membrane: FILM.

pel-⁵. Also pelə-. To fill. Zero-grade form *plə- in: a. Gmc *fullaz in OE full: FULL¹; b. Gmc *fulljan in OE fyllan: FILL. [AHD pel-⁸.]

pelə-. Flat; to spread. 1. Gmc *felthuz in OE feld: FIELD. 2. Variant *plā- in Gmc *flōruz in OE flōr: FLOOR. [AHD pelə-¹.]

penkwe. Five. 1. Gmc *fimfti in OE fīf: FIVE. 2. Gmc *fimftehun in OE fīftēne: FIFTEEN. 3. Gmc *fimfton in OE fīfta: FIFTH. 4. Gmc *fimftig in OE fīftig: FIFTY. 5. Gmc *fingwraz, "one of five," in OE finger: FINGER. 6. Form *pŋksti- in Gmc *fūstiz in OE fȳst: FIST.

pent-. To tread, go. Gmc *finthan in OE findan: FIND.

per¹. "Forward, through, before." 1. Gmc *ferra in OE feor: FAR. 2. Zero-grade form *pr- in: a. Gmc for in OE for: FOR; b. Gmc *furth- in OE forth: FORTH; c. Gmc *furthera- in OE furthor: FURTHER; d. Gmc *furma- in OE forma: FORMER; FOREMOST; e. Gmc *furista- in OE fyrst: FIRST. 3. Variant *para in Gmc *fora in: a. OE fore: FORE; b. OE beforan: BEFORE. 4. Variant *pro in: a. Gmc *fram in OE from: FROM; b. Gmc *framjan, "to come forward," in OE framian: FRAME.

per-². To lead, pass over. 1. O-grade form *por- in Gmc *faran in OE faran: FARE. 2. Zero-grade form *pr- in Gmc *furdu- in OE ford: FORD.

per-³. To risk. Gmc *fēraz, "danger," in OE fǣr: FEAR. [AHD per-⁵.]

perk-. To dig out. Zero-grade form *prk- in Gmc *furh- in OE furh: FURROW. [AHD perk-³.]

perkwu-. Oak. Zero-grade form *prkw- in Gmc *furhu- in OE fyrh: FIR.

pet-¹. To fly. Gmc *fethrō in OE fether: FEATHER.

pet-². To spread. O-grade form *pot- in Gmc *fathmaz in OE fæthm: FATHOM.

peyə-. To be fat. Form *poid- in Gmc *faitaz in OE fǣtt: FAT.

pəter. Father. Gmc *fadar in OE fæder: FATHER.

phol-. To fall. 1. Gmc *fallan in OE feallan: FALL. 2. Gmc *falljan, "to cause to fall," in OE fellan: FELL¹.

plat-. To spread. Variant *plad- in Gmc *flatjam in OE flett, floor: FLAT².

plek-. To plait. O-grade form *plok- in Gmc *flahsam in OE fleax: FLAX.

plēk-. Also pleik-. To tear. 1. Form *plak- in Gmc *flahan in OE flēan: FLAY. 2. Gmc *flaiskaz, "piece of torn flesh," in OE flæsc: FLESH.

pleu-. To flow. 1. Extended form *pleuk- in: a. Gmc *fliugan in OE flēogan: FLY¹; b. Gmc *fliugjō in OE flēoge: FLY²; c. Zero-grade form *pluk- in Gmc *flug-ti- in OE flyht and *flyht: FLIGHT¹, FLIGHT²; d. Gmc *fluglaz, fuglaz, in OE fugol: FOWL. 2. Extended form *pleud- in: a. Gmc *fliutan in OE flēotan: FLEET¹; b. Zero-grade form *plud- in Gmc *flut- in flotian and floterian: FLOAT, FLUTTER. 4. Forms *plōu-, *plō-, in: a. Gmc *flōwen in OE flōwan: FLOW; b. Gmc *flōdu in OE flōd: FLOOD.

pleus-. Fleece. Gmc *fliusaz in OE flēos: FLEECE.

plou-.˘ Flea. Extended form *plouk- in Gmc *flauhaz in OE flēah: FLEA.

pneu-. To breathe. Gmc *fniu- in OE fnēosan: SNEEZE.

pōl-. To feel. Gmc *fōljan in OE fēlan: FEEL.

pōu-. Few, little. 1. Variant *pau- in Gmc *fawaz in OE fēawe: FEW. 2. Variant *pu-lo-, "young of an animal," in Gmc *fulō in OE fola: FOAL.

preu-. To hop. Zero-grade form *pru- in Gmc *fru- in OE frogga: FROG.

preus-. To freeze. 1. Gmc *friusan in OE frēosan: FREEZE. 2. Zero-grade form *prus- in Gmc *frustaz in OE frost: FROST.

prī-. To love. Extended form *priy-. 1. Gmc *frijaz in OE frēo: FREE. 2. Gmc *frijand- in OE frēond: FRIEND. 3. Gmc *frije-dagaz in OE frigedæg: FRIDAY.

pu-. To rot. Form *pū-lo-. 1. Gmc *fūlaz in OE fūl: FOUL. 2. Gmc *fūlithō in OE fylth: FILTH. [AHD pu-².]

puk-. Bushy-haired. 1. Gmc *fuhsaz in OE fox: FOX. 2. Gmc *fuhson in OE fyxe: VIXEN. [AHD puk-².]

pūr-. Fire. Gmc *fūri- in OE fȳr: FIRE.

pūro-. Grain. OE fyrs: FURZE.

rebh-. To roof over. Gmc *reb-jōn, "covering of the chest cavity," in OE rib: RIB.

reg-¹. To move in a straight line. 1. Gmc *rehtaz in OE riht: RIGHT. 2. O-grade form *rog- in: a. Gmc *rakō in OE raca: RAKE¹; b. Gmc *rak-inaz in OE gerecenian: RECKON; c. Lengthened form *rōg- in Gmc *rōkja- in OE rēceleas: RECKLESS.

reg-². Moist. Variant *rek- in Gmc *regnaz in OE rēn: RAIN.

rei-¹. To scratch, cut. 1. Form *roig- in Gmc *raigwa in OE rāw: ROW. 2. Form *reipp- in Gmc *raipaz in OE rāp: ROPE. 3. Form *reib- in: a. Gmc *rīpja- in OE rīpe: RIPE; b. Gmc *rīpjan in OE rīpan: REAP.

rei-². Flecked. O-grade form *roi- in Gmc *raihaz in OE rā: ROE².

reidh-. To ride. 1. Gmc *rīdan in OE rīdan: RIDE. 2. O-grade form *roidh- in: a. Gmc *raid- in OE rād: RAID, ROAD; b. Gmc *raid-ja in OE rǣde: READY.

reig-. To reach. O-grade form *roidh- in Gmc *raikjan in OE rǣcan: REACH. [AHD reig-².]

rendh-. To tear up. 1. Gmc *randjan in OE rendan: REND. 2. Gmc *rind- in OE rinde: RIND.

rēp-. Stake, beam. Variant *rap- in Gmc *raftra- in OE ræfter: RAFTER. [AHD rēp-².]

rēt-. Post. O-grade form *rōt- in Gmc *rodd- in OE rodd: ROD.

reudh-. Red, ruddy. 1. O-grade form *roudh- in Gmc *raudaz in OE rēad: RED. 2. Zero-grade form *rudh- in: a. Gmc *rudō in OE rudu: RUDDY; b. Gmc *rūst- in OE rūst: RUST.

reug-. To belch, smoke. Gmc *riukan in OE rēocan: REEK.

rewə-. To open; space. Variant *rū- in Gmc *rūmaz in OE rūm: ROOM.

rezg-. To plait. Gmc *ruski- in OE rysc: RUSH².

ruk-. Rough. Form *rūk- in Gmc *rūhwaz in OE rūh: ROUGH. [AHD ruk-².]

sā-. To satisfy. Zero-grade form *sə-. 1. Gmc *sadaz in OE sæd, sated: SAD. 2. Gmc *sadōn in OE sadian: SATE¹.

sab-. Juice. Gmc *sapam in OE sæp: SAP¹.

sāg-. To seek out. 1. Gmc *sōkjan in OE sēcan: SEEK. 2. Gmc *sakō in OE sacu: SAKE¹. 3. Gmc *sakan in OE forsacan: FORSAKE.

sai-. Suffering. 1. Gmc *sairaz in OE sār: SORE. 2. Gmc *sairig- in OE sārig: SORRY.

sal-¹. Salt. Gmc *saltam in OE sealt: SALT.

sal-². Dirty. Gmc *salwaz in OE salo: SALLOW.

saus-. Dry. Gmc *sausaz in OE sēar: SEAR, SERE.

sāwel-. Sun. Variants *swen-, *sun-. 1. Gmc sunnōn in OE sunne: SUN. 2. Gmc *sunthaz in OE sūth: SOUTH.

sē-. To sow. 1. Gmc *sējan in OE sāwan: SOW¹. 2. Gmc *sēdiz in OE sǣd: SEED. [AHD sē-¹.]

sed-. To sit. 1. Gmc *sitan in OE sittan: SIT. 2. Gmc *setlaz in OE setl: SETTLE. 3. O-grade form *sod- in: a. Gmc *satjan in OE settan: SET¹; b. Gmc *sadulaz in OE sadol: SADDLE; c. Lengthened form *sōd- in Gmc *sōtam in OE sōt: SOOT. [AHD sed-¹.]

sek-. To cut. 1. Gmc *segithō in OE sīthe: SCYTHE. 2. O-grade form *sok- in Gmc *sagō in OE *sagu*: SAW[1].

sekw-[1]. To say. O-grade form **sokw-*. 1. Gmc **sawjan* in OE *secgan*: SAY. 2. Gmc **sagō* in OE *sagu*: SAW[2]. [AHD *sekw-*[3].]

sekw-[2]. To see. 1. Gmc **sehwan* in OE *sēon*: SEE[1]. 2. Gmc **sih-th* in OE *sihth*: SIGHT.

sel-[1]. To take. Gmc **saljan*, "to sell" (< "cause to take"), in OE *sellan*: SELL. [AHD *sel-*[3].]

sel-[2]. Of good mood. Gmc **sēl-* in OE *gesǣlig*: SILLY.

selp-. Fat. Gmc **salb-* in OE *salf*: SALVE.

sem-[1]. Form **smm-o-* in Gmc **sumaz* in OE *sum*: SOME.

sem-[2]. Summer. Form **smm-araz* in OE *sumor*: SUMMER. [AHD *sem-*[3].]

sen-. Separated. Zero-grade form **sn̥-*. 1. Gmc **sundrō* in OE *sunder*: ASUNDER. 2. Gmc **sundrōn* in OE *syndrian*: SUNDER. 3. Gmc **sundriga-* in OE *syndrig*: SUNDRY. [AHD *sen-*[2].]

sendhro-. Crystalline deposit. Gmc **sendra-* in OE *sinder*: CINDER.

sengw-. To sink. Gmc **sinkwan* in OE *sincan*: SINK.

sengwh-. To sing. 1. Gmc **singan* in OE *singan*: SING. 2. O-grade form **songwh-* in Gmc **sangwaz* in OE *sang*: SONG.

senk-. To burn. O-grade form **sonk-* in Gmc **sangjan* in OE *sengan*: SINGE.

sent-. To go. O-grade form **sont-* in Gmc **sandjan* in OE *sendan*: SEND.

septm̥. Seven. Gmc **sibum* in OE *seofon*: SEVEN.

seu-[1]. To seethe. Gmc **siuthan* in OE *sēothan*: SEETHE.

seu-[2]. Third person and reflexive pronoun. Form **sel-bho-* in Gmc **selbaz* in OE *self*: SELF.

seu-[3]. To give birth. Gmc **sunuz* in OE *sunu*: SON.

seu-[4]. To take liquid. Form **sūg-*. 1. Gmc **sūk-* in OE *sūcan*: SUCK. 2. Gmc **suk-* in OE *socian*: SOAK.

skei-. To cut. 1. Gmc **ski-nōn-* in OE *scinu*: SHIN. 2. Extended form **skeit-* in Gmc **skaith-* in OE *scēadan*: SHED[1].

skel-[1]. To cut. 1. Gmc **skaljō*, "piece cut off," in OE *scell*: SHELL. 2. Gmc **skelduz* in OE *scield*: SHIELD.

skel-[2]. To be under an obligation. O-grade form **skol-* in Gmc **skal-*, "I owe, I ought," in OE *sceal, sceolde*: SHALL, SHOULD.

skeng-. Crooked. Gmc **skankō* in OE *sceanca*: SHANK.

skep-. "To cut, scrape." 1. Gmc **skap-* in: a. OE *gesceap*: SHAPE; b. OE *-scipe*: -SHIP. 2. Gmc **skaftaz* in OE *sceaft*: SHAFT[1]. 3. Gmc **skabb-* in OE *sceabb*: SHABBY. 4. Gmc **skab-* in OE *sceafan*: SHAVE.

sker-[1]. To cut. 1. Gmc **skeran* in OE *sceran*: SHEAR. 2. Gmc **skar-* in: a. OE *scēar*: SHARE[2]; b. OE *scearu*: SHARE[1]. 3. Gmc **skĕr-* in OE *scĕara*: SHEARS. 4. Gmc **skardaz* in OE *sceard*: SHARD. 5. Extended form **skerd-* in Gmc **skurtaz* in: a. OE *scort*: SHORT; b. OE *scyrte*: SHIRT. 6. Extended form **skerbh-* in Gmc **skarpaz* in OE *scearp*: SHARP. 7. Gmc **skrub-* in OE *scrybb*: SHRUB.

sker-[2]. To turn, bend. 1. Form **skreng-* in Gmc **skrink-* in OE *scrincan*: SHRINK. 2. Form **skrengh-* in Gmc **hringaz* in OE *hring*: RING[1]. 3. Form **kreuk-* in Gmc **hrugjaz* in OE *hrycg*: RIDGE. [AHD *sker-*[3].]

skeru-. To cut. Variant **skreu-*. 1. Gmc **skraw-* in OE *scrēawa*: SHREW. 2. Gmc **skraud-* in OE *scrēade*: SHRED. 3. Gmc **skrūd-*, "piece of cloth," in OE *scrūd*: SHROUD.

skeu-. Also **keu-**. To cover. 1. Zero-grade form **ku-* in: a. Gmc **husōn-* in OE *hosa*: HOSE;

b. Gmc **huzdam* in OE *hord*: HOARD; c. Gmc **hūdiz* in OE *hȳd*: HIDE[2]. 2. Gmc **hūdjan* in OE *hȳdan*: HIDE[1].

skeubh-. To shove. 1. Gmc **skiuban* in OE *scūfan*: SHOVE. 2. Gmc **skub-ilōn-* in OE *scofl*: SHOVEL.

skeud-. To shoot, chase, throw. 1. Gmc **skiutan* in OE *scēotan*: SHOOT. 2. Gmc **skutaz* in OE *scot*: SHOT[1]. 3. Gmc **skuttjan* in OE *scytel*: SHUTTLE.

skeup-. Cluster. Gmc **skauf-* in OE *scēaf*: SHEAF.

skhed-. To split, scatter. Form **skod-* in Gmc **skat-* in OE *sceaterian*: SHATTER.

skī-. To gleam. 1. Gmc **skīnan* in OE *scīnan*: SHINE. 2. Gmc **skim-* in OE *scimerian*: SHIMMER.

skot-. Shade. Gmc **skadwaz* in OE *sceadu*: SHADE.

skwalo-. Big fish. Variant **kwal-* in Gmc **hwaliz* in OE *hwæl*: WHALE.

slagw-. Also **lagw-**. To seize. Gmc **lakkjan* in OE *læccan*: LATCH.

slak-. To strike. 1. Gmc **slahan* in OE *slēan*: SLAY. 2. Gmc **slagja-* in OE *slecg*: SLEDGE-HAMMER.

slēg-. To be slack. Zero-grade form **slǝg-* in Gmc **slak-* in OE *slæc*: SLACK.

sleidh-. Slippery. Gmc **slīdan* in OE *slīdan*: SLIDE.

slenk-. To wind. Variant **sleng-* in Gmc **slinkjan* in OE *slincan*: SLINK.

sleubh-. To slide. Gmc **sliub-* in OE *slēf*: SLEEVE.

smē-. To smear. Extended root **smeid-* in Gmc **smītan* in OE *smītan*: SMITE.

smeg-. To taste. Gmc **smak-* in OE *smæc*: SMACK[2].

smel-. To smile. Gmc **smer-* in OE *smearcian*: SMIRK.

smer-[1]. To remember. Zero-grade form **mr̥* in Gmc **murnōn* in OE *murnan*: MOURN.

smer-[2]. Grease. Gmc **smerwjan* in OE *smerian*: SMEAR. [AHD *smer-*[3].]

smerd-. Pain. Gmc **smertan* in OE *smeortan*: SMART.

smeug-. Smoke. Gmc **smuk-* in OE *smoca*: SMOKE.

smi-. To cut (as with a sharp instrument). Gmc **smithaz* in OE *smith*: SMITH.

snē-[1]. Also **ne-**. To spin, sew. Gmc **nēthlō* in OE *nǣdl*: NEEDLE.

snē-[2]. "Nose." Gmc **snuf-* in OE *snyflan*: SNIVEL.

sneg-. To creep; creeping thing. O-grade form **snog-*. 1. Gmc **snag-ila-* in OE *snægel*: SNAIL. 2. Gmc **snakan-* in OE *snaca*: SNAKE.

sneigwh-. Snow. O-grade form **snoigwh-* in Gmc **snaiwaz* in OE *snāw*: SNOW.

snēu-. Sinew. Variant **senw-* in Gmc **senawō* in OE *sinu*: SINEW.

so-. This. Form **syā* in Gmc **sō* in OE *sēo*: SHE.

spei-. Sharp point. 1. Gmc **spituz* in OE *spitu*: SPIT[2]. 2. Gmc **spī-ra-* in OE *spīr*: SPIRE[1]. 3. O-grade form **spoig-* in Gmc **spaikōn-* in OE *spāca*: SPOKE[1].

spēi-. To thrive. O-grade form **spōi-* in Gmc **spōdiz* in OE *spēd*: SPEED.

spel-[1]. To split, break off. Gmc **spilthjan* in OE *spillan*: SPILL.

spel-[2]. To recite. Gmc **spellam* in OE *spell*: SPELL[2]. [AHD *spel-*[3].]

spen-. To draw, stretch, spin. 1. Gmc **spinnan* in OE *spinnan*: SPIN. 2. Gmc **spin-ilōn-* in OE *spinel*: SPINDLE. 3. O-grade form **spon-* in Gmc **spanno-* in OE *span*: SPAN[1].

sper-[1]. Spear. Gmc **speru* in OE *spere*: SPEAR.

sper-[2]. To strew. Zero-grade form **spr̥-*. 1. Gmc **spr-* in OE *sprēawlian*: SPRAWL. 2. Form **spreut-* in Gmc **sprūt-* in: a. OE *sprūtan*:

SPROUT; b. OE *spryttan*: SPURT. 3. Form *spreit-* in Gmc **spraidjan* in OE *sprǣdan*: SPREAD. [AHD *sper-*[4].]

sper-[3]. Sparrow. O-grade form **spor-* in Gmc **sparwan-* in OE *spearwa*: SPARROW.

spergh-. To move, spring. Form **sprengh-* in Gmc **springan* in OE *springan*: SPRING.

sphē-. Long, flat piece of wood. 1. Gmc **spēnu-* in OE *spōn*: SPOON. 2. Form *spǝ-dh-* in Gmc **spadan* in OE *spadu*: SPADE[1].

spher-. Ankle. 1. Gmc **spurōn* in OE *spora*: SPUR. 2. Gmc **spurnōn* in OE *spurnan*, to kick: SPURN.

sping-. Also **ping-**. Gmc **finki-* in OE *finc*: FINCH.

splei-. To split. Gmc **flī-* in OE *flint*: FLINT.

spoimo-. Foam. Variant **poimo-* in Gmc **faimaz* in OE *fām*: FOAM.

spreg-. To speak. Gmc **sprek-, spek-*, in: a. OE *specan*: SPEAK; b. OE *sprǣc*: SPEECH.

spyeu-. To spit. 1. Gmc **spit-* in OE *spittan*: SPIT[1]. 2. Gmc **spiu-* in OE *spīwan*: SPEW. 3. Gmc **spāt-* in OE *spātl*: SPITTLE.

sreu-. To flow. O-grade form **srou-* in Gmc **straumaz* in OE *strēam*: STREAM.

stā-. To stand. Zero-grade form **stǝ-*. 1. Gmc **standan* in: a. OE *standan*: STAND; b. OE *understandan*: UNDERSTAND. 2. Gmc **stamniz* in OE *stemn*: STEM[1]. 3. Gmc **stadiz* in OE *stede*: STEAD. 4. Variant **steu-* in Gmc **stiurjan* in OE *stīeran*: STEER[1].

stāk-. To stand. Zero-grade form **stǝk-*. 1. Gmc **staga-* in OE *stæg*: STAY[3]. 2. Gmc **stahla-* in OE *stēli*: STEEL.

stebh-. Post; to place firmly on. 1. Gmc **stab-* in OE *stæf*: STAFF. 2. Form **steb-* in: a. Gmc **stap-* in OE *stæpe*: STEP; b. Gmc **stamp-* in OE *stampian*: STAMP.

steg-[1]. To cover. Variant o-grade form **tog-* in Gmc **thakjan* in OE *theccan*: THATCH.

steg-[2]. Stick. O-grade form **stog-* in Gmc **stak-* in OE *staca*: STAKE[1].

stegh-. To prick. 1. Form **stengh-* in Gmc **stengjan* in OE *stingan*: STING. 2. O-grade form **stogh-* in Gmc **stag-* in OE *stagga*: STAG.

stei-. Stone. O-grade form **stoi-* in Gmc **stainaz* in OE *stān*: STONE.

steig-. To stick. Zero-grade form **stig-*. 1. Gmc **stik-* in OE *sticca* and *stician*: STICK. 2. Gmc **stikiz* in OE *stice*: STITCH.

steigh-. To stride, step. 1. Gmc **stīgan* in OE *stīgan*: STY[2]. 2. O-grade form **stoigh-* in Gmc **staigrī* in OE *stǣger*: STAIR.

steip-. To compress. Gmc **stīfaz* in OE *stif*: STIFF.

stel-. To put, stand. Gmc **stilli-* in OE *stille*: STILL. [AHD *stel-*[1].]

stenǝ-. To thunder. Zero-grade form **stnǝ-* in Gmc **thunaraz* in OE *thunor*: THUNDER.

ster-[1]. Stiff. 1. O-grade form **stor-* in: a. Gmc **staren* in OE *starian*: STARE; b. Gmc **starkaz* in OE *stearc*: STARK; c. Gmc **starkjan* in OE *stercan*: STARCH. 2. Zero-grade form **str̥-* in: a. Gmc **sturkaz* in OE *storc*: STORK; b. Gmc **strūt-* in OE *strūtian*: STRUT. 3. Extended form **sterd-* in Gmc **stert-* in: a. OE *styrtan*: START; b. OE *steartlian*: STARTLE. 4. Gmc **sterban* in OE *steorfan*: STARVE. 5. Gmc **sternjaz* in OE *stierne*: STERN[1].

ster-[2]. To spread. 1. Form **streu-* in Gmc **striw-* in OE *strēon*: STRAIN[2]. 2. Form **strou-* in: a. Gmc **strawjan* in OE *strēowian*: STREW; b. Gmc **strāwam* in OE *strēaw*: STRAW.

ster-[3]. Star. Gmc **sterrōn* in OE *steorra*: STAR.

ster-[4]. To steal. 1. Gmc **stelan* in OE *stelan*: STEAL. 2. Gmc **stalkōjan* in OE *stealcian*: STALK[2].

stern-. A thorny plant. Form **tr̥-nu-* in Gmc **thurnu-* in OE *thorn*: THORN.

steu-. To push, stick, beat. 1. Extended forms

*steup-, *steub-, in: a. Gmc *staup- in OE stēap: STEEP¹; b. Gmc *staupilaz in OE stȳpel: STEEPLE; c. Gmc *stūp- in OE stūpian: STOOP¹; d. Gmc *stubb- in OE stybb: STUB. 2. Extended form *steud- in Gmc *stuntjan in OE styntan: STINT. 3. Extended form *steug- in Gmc *stuk-kaz in OE stocc: STOCK.

storos. Starling. Gmc *staraz in OE stær: STARLING.

streig-. To stroke, rub, press. 1. Gmc *strīkan in OE strīcan: STRIKE. 2. Gmc *strikōn- in OE strica: STREAK. 3. O-grade form *stroig- in Gmc *straik- in OE strāc: STROKE.

su-. Pig. 1. Gmc *swīnam in OE swīn: SWINE. 2. Celtic *sukko- in OE hogg: HOG. 3. Lengthened form *sū- in Gmc *sū- in OE sugu: SOW². [AHD su-¹.]

sūro-. Sour. Gmc *sūraz in OE sūr: SOUR.

swād-. Sweet. Gmc *swōtja- in OE swēte: SWEET.

swei-. To bend, turn. 1. Gmc *swip- in: a. OE swāpan: SWEEP, SWOOP; b. OE swift: SWIFT. 2. Gmc *swīf- in OE swifan: SWIVEL. 3. Gmc *swim- in OE swima: SQUEAMISH, SWIM². [AHD swei-².]

sweid-. To sweat. O-grade form *swoid- in Gmc *swaidjan in OE swǣtan: SWEAT. [AHD sweid-².]

sweks. Six. Gmc *seks in OE six: SIX.

swel-¹. To eat, drink. Gmc *swelgan in OE swelgan: SWALLOW¹.

swel-². To shine, burn. Gmc *swiltan in OE sweltan: SWELTER.

swel-³. Post. Gmc *suljō- in OE sylle: SILL.

swen-. To sound. O-grade form *swon- in Gmc *swanaz in OE swan: SWAN.

sweng-. To swing. Gmc *swingan in OE swingan: SWING.

swento-. Healthy. Form *sunto- in Gmc *sunth- in OE gesund: SOUND².

swer-¹. To talk. O-grade form *swor- in: a. Gmc *swarjan in OE swerian: SWEAR; b. Gmc *andswaru, "a swearing against," in OE andswaru: ANSWER.

swer-². To buzz. O-grade form *swor- in Gmc *swarmaz in OE swearm: SWARM.

swer-³. To pierce. Gmc *swerdam in OE sword: SWORD. [AHD swer-⁴.]

swerbh-. To turn, wipe off. Gmc *swerb- in OE sweorfan: SWERVE.

swergh-. To worry. Gmc *sorg- in OE sorh: SORROW.

swesor-. Sister. Form *swesr- in Gmc *swistr- in OE sweostor: SISTER.

swo-. So. 1. Gmc *swa- in OE swā: SO. 2. Gmc *swa-lik- in OE swylc: SUCH.

swordo-. Black, dirty. Gmc *swartaz in OE sweart: SWARTHY.

syū-. To bind, sew. 1. Gmc *siwjan in OE seowian: SEW. 2. Form *sū- in Gmc *saumaz in OE sēam: SEAM.

tā-. To melt. Gmc *thāwōn in OE thāwian: THAW.

tegu-. Thick. Gmc *thiku- in OE thicce: THICK.

ten-. To stretch. Zero-grade form *tn̥- in Gmc *thunniz in OE thynne: THIN.

ter-¹. To pass through. Zero-grade form *tr̥- in Gmc *thurh in OE thurh: THROUGH. [AHD ter-³.]

ter-². To rub, turn. 1. Gmc *thersk- in: a. OE therscan: THRESH; b. OE therscold: THRESHOLD. 2. Form *trē- in: a. Gmc *thrēw- in OE thrāwan: THROW; b. Gmc *thrēdu- in OE thrǣd: THREAD.

ters-. To dry. Zero-grade form *tr̥s- in Gmc *thurs- in OE thurst: THIRST.

teuə-. To swell. 1. Form *teuk- in Gmc *thiuham in OE thēoh: THIGH. 2. Form *teus- in Gmc *thus-hundi-, "swollen hundred," in OE thūsend: THOUSAND. 3. Form *tum- in OE thūma: THUMB.

to-. Demonstrative pronoun. 1. Gmc *thē- in OE thē: THE. 2. Gmc *thasi- in OE thes: THIS. 3. Gmc *thana- in OE thanne: THAN, THEN. 4. Gmc *thanana- in OE thanon: THENCE. 5. Gmc *thar in OE thēr: THERE. 6. Gmc *thathro in OE thider: THITHER. 7. Gmc *thai in OE thā (and ON their): THEY. 8. Gmc *thaim in OE thǣm (and ON theim): THEM. 9. Gmc *that in OE thæt: THAT. 10. Gmc *thus- in OE thus: THUS.

tong-. To think, feel. 1. Gmc *thankōn in: a. OE thancian: THANK; b. OE thencan: THINK. 2. Gmc *thauht- in OE thōht: THOUGHT.

trei-. Three. 1. Gmc *thrijiz in OE thrēo, thriga, thrītig, and thrēotine: THREE, THRICE, THIRTY, THIRTEEN. 2. Gmc *thrithjaz in OE thridda: THIRD.

treud-. To squeeze. Gmc *thriut- in OE thrēat: THREAT.

trozdos-. Thrush. Gmc *thruskjōn- in OE thrysce: THRUSH.

tu-. You, thou. 1. Form *tū in Gmc *thū in OE thū: THOU. 2. Form *twei-no- in Gmc *thūnaz in OE thīn: THINE, THY.

twei-. To agitate, toss. Extended form *tweid- in Gmc *thwīt- in OE thwītan: WHITTLE.

twengh-. To press in on. 1. Gmc *thwang- in OE thwang: THONG. 2. Gmc *twangjan in OE twengan: TWINGE.

twer-. To whirl. Variant *stur-. 1. Gmc *sturmaz in OE storm: STORM. 2. Gmc *sturjan in OE styrian: STIR. [AHD twer-¹.]

ud-. Up, out. 1. Gmc *ūt- in OE ūt: OUT. 2. Gmc *ūt-era- in OE ūtera: UTTER². 3. Gmc *bi-ūtana in OE būtan: BUT, ABOUT.

uper. Over. Gmc *uberi in OE ofer: OVER.

upo-. Under, up from under, over. 1. Gmc *upp- in OE up, uppe: UP. 2. Gmc *upanaz in OE open: OPEN. 3. Gmc *bi-ufana in OE abufan: ABOVE. 4. Gmc *ubilaz, "excessive," in OE yfel: EVIL. 5. Gmc *obaswa, "that which is above," in OE yfes: EAVES.

wā-. To wound. Zero-grade form *wn̥- in Gmc *wundaz in OE wund: WOUND¹. [AHD wā-².]

wāb-. To cry. Gmc *wōpjan in OE wēpan: WEEP.

wadh-. A pledge. Gmc *wadi- in OE weddian: WED.

wādh-. To go. Gmc *wathan in OE wadan: WADE.

wai. Alas. Gmc *wai in OE wā: WOE.

wal-. To be strong. Form *woldh- in Gmc *waldan in OE wieldan: WIELD.

we-. We. Gmc *wīz in OE wē: WE.

wē-. To blow. 1. Gmc *wedram in OE weder: WEATHER. 2. Gmc *windaz in OE wind: WIND¹.

webh-. To weave. 1. Gmc *weban in OE wefan: WEAVE. 2. O-grade form *wobh- in Gmc *wabjam in OE webb: WEB.

wed-. Water; wet. 1. O-grade form *wod- in: a. Gmc *watar- in OE wæter: WATER; b. Gmc *wat-skan in OE wæscan: WASH. 2. Form *wēd- in Gmc *wēd- in OE wǣt: WET. 3. Form *wend- in Gmc *wintruz in OE winter: WINTER. 4. Form *ud-ro- in Gmc *otraz in OE otor: OTTER. [AHD wed-¹.]

weg-. To be lively. O-grade form *wog-. 1. Gmc *waken in OE wacian and *wacan: WAKE¹. 2. Gmc *wakjan in OE wæccan: WATCH. [AHD weg-².]

wegh-. To go, transport. 1. Gmc *wigan in OE wegan: WEIGH¹. 2. Gmc *wihti- in OE wiht: WEIGHT. 3. Gmc *wegaz in OE weg: WAY.

wei-¹. To twist. Gmc *wī-ra- in OE wīr: WIRE.

wei-². To wither. Gmc *wis- in OE wisnian: WIZENED. [AHD wei-³.]

weid-. To see. 1. Gmc *wītan in OE witan: TWIT. 2. Gmc *wissaz in: a. OE wīs: WISE¹; b. OE wisdōm: WISDOM. 3. Gmc *wissōn- in OE wīse: WISE². 4. Zero-grade form *wid- in: a. Gmc *wit- in OE wit: WIT; b. Gmc *witan in OE witan: UNWITTING.

weidh-. To separate. Zero-grade form *widh- in Gmc *widewaz in OE widuwe: WIDOW.

weik-¹. To wind. Variant *weig-. Gmc *wikōn- "a series," in OE wice: WEEK. [AHD weik-⁴.]

weik-². "Divination, sorcery." Gmc *wikk- in OE wicce and wicca: WICKED, WITCH.

weip-. To vacillate. Variant *weib- in Gmc *wīpjan, "to move back and forth," in OE wīpian: WIPE.

weis-. To flow. Gmc *wisōn in OE wāse: OOZE². [AHD weis-¹.]

wekti-. Thing. Gmc *wihti- in OE wiht: NOT.

wel-¹. Wool. Gmc *wullō in OE wull: WOOL. [AHD wel-⁵.]

wel-². To wish, will. 1. Gmc *wel- in OE wel: WELL². 2. Gmc *wiljōn- in OE will: WILL¹. 3. Gmc *willjan in OE wyllan: WILL².

wel-³. To turn, roll. 1. O-grade form *wol- in Gmc *wall- in OE wælla: WELL¹. 2. Form *welw- in Gmc *walwōn in OE wealwian: WALLOW.

welt-. Wild. Gmc *wilthigaz in OE wilde: WILD.

wen-. To desire, strive for. 1. Gmc *winnan in OE winnan: WIN. 2. Zero-grade form *wn̥- in: a. Gmc *wunēn in OE wunian: WONT; b. Gmc *wunsk- in OE wȳscan: WISH. 3. Gmc *wanjan in OE wenian: WEAN.

wendh-. To turn, wind. 1. Gmc *windan in OE windan: WIND². 2. Gmc *wandjan in OE wendan: WEND. 3. Gmc *wandrōn in OE wandrian: WANDER.

weng-. To bend, curve. 1. Gmc *wink- in OE wincian: WINK. 2. Gmc *winkja in OE wince: WINCH. 3. Gmc *winkil- in OE -wincel: PERIWINKLE¹.

wer-¹. High, raised spot. Gmc *wartōn- in.OE wearte: WART.

wer-². To speak. Zero-grade form *wr̥- in Gmc *wurdam in OE word: WORD. [AHD wer-⁶.]

wer-³. To turn, bend. 1. Form *wert- in: a. Gmc *warth- in OE -weard: -WARD; b. Gmc *wurth-, "that which befalls one," in OE wyrd: WEIRD. 2. Form *wreit- in Gmc *writh- in: a. OE writha: WREATH; b. OE writhan: WRITHE; c. OE wrāth: WRATH. 3. Form *wergh-. a. Gmc *wurgjan in OE wyrgan: WORRY; b. Gmc *wreng- in OE wringan: WRING. 4. Root *wrei in Gmc *wrankjan in: a. OE wrencan: WRENCH; b. OE gewrinclian: WRINKLE. 5. Form *wreik-. a. Gmc *wrīg- in OE wrīgian: WRY; b. Gmc *wristiz in OE wrist: WRIST. 6. Form *wrizd- in Gmc *wraistjan in OE wrǣstan and wrǣstlian: WREST, WRESTLE. 7. Form *werb- in Gmc *werp- in OE weorpan: WARP. 8. Form *wermi- in Gmc *wurmiz in OE wyrm: WORM.

wer-⁴. To watch out for. O-grade form *wor-. 1. Gmc *waraz in: a. OE wær: WARY; b. OE gewær: AWARE. 2. Gmc *wardaz in OE weard: WARD.

wer-⁵. To cover. O-grade form *wor- in Gmc *war-n- in OE wearnian: WARN.

werg-. To do. Gmc *werkam in OE weorc: WORK. [AHD werg-¹.]

wers-. To confuse. Gmc *wersizōn- in OE wyrsa: WORSE.

wes-¹. To clothe. O-grade form *wos- in Gmc *wazjan in OE werian: WEAR. [AHD wes-⁴.]

wes-². Wet. Gmc *wōs- in OE wōs: OOZE¹.

wes-³. To delay; "to be." O-grade form *wos- in Gmc *wos- in OE wæs, wǣre, wǣron: WAS, WERE.

wespero-. Evening, night. Gmc *west- in OE west: WEST.

wi-. Apart, in half. 1. Gmc *wīdaz in OE wīd: WIDE. 2. Gmc *withrō in OE with: WITH.

widhu-. Tree. Gmc *widu- in OE wudu: WOOD.

wiros. Man. Gmc *weraldh-, "life or age of man," in OE weorold: WORLD.

wlkwo-. Wolf. Variant *wlpo- in Gmc *wulfaz

in OE *wulf:* WOLF.

wokso-. Wax. Gmc **wahsam* in OE *wæx:* WAX.

wopsă. Wasp. Variant **wospā* in Gmc **wosp-* in OE *wæsp:* WASP.

wreg-. To shove, drive. **1.** Gmc **wrekan* in OE *wrecan:* WREAK. **2.** O-grade form **wrog-* in Gmc **wrakjō,* "one pursued," in OE *wrecca:* WRETCH.

wrŏd-. To root, gnaw. Gmc **wrŏt-* in OE *wrŏtan:* ROOT². **wrughyo-.** Rye. Gmc **rugi-* in OE *ryge:* RYE.

yeg-. Ice. Gmc **jekilaz* in OE *gicel:* ICICLE.

yēro-. Year. Gmc **jēram* in OE *gēar:* YEAR.

yes-. To bubble. Gmc **jest-* in OE *gist,* yeast : YEAST.

yeu-. Young. **1.** Gmc **juwungaz* in OE *geong:* YOUNG. **2.** Gmc **jugunth-* in OE *geoguth:* YOUTH. [AHD *yeu-².*]

yeug-. To join. Zero-grade form **yug-* in Gmc **yukam* in OE *geoc:* YOKE.

yu-. You. Gmc **jūz* and **iww-* in OE *gē, ēow, ēower:* YE², YOU, YOUR. [AHD *yu-¹.*]

Word Division Dictionary

WORDBREAK RULES

1. Division of words should be minimized in leaded matter and avoided in double-leaded matter.

2. Except in narrow measures, wordbreaks should be avoided at the ends of more than two lines. Similarly, no more than two consecutive lines should end with the same word, symbol, group of numbers, etc.

3. In two-line centerheads, the first line should be centered and set as full as possible, but it is not set to fill the measure by unduly wide spacing. Wordbreaks should be avoided. Flush sideheads are set full measure and wordbreaks are permitted if unavoidable. They are not set ragged unless so indicated on copy.

4. The final word of a paragraph should not be divided.

5. Words should preferably be divided according to pronunciation; and to avoid mispronunciation, they should be divided so that the part of the word left at the end of the line will suggest the whole word: *capac-ity*, not *capa-city*; *extraor-dinary*, not *extra-ordinary*; *Wednes-day*, not *Wed-nesday*; *physi-cal*, not *phys-ical*; *service-man*, not *serv-iceman*.

6. Although WORD DIVISION lists beginning and ending one-letter syllables for pronunciation purposes, under no circumstances are words to be divided on a single letter (e.g., *usu-al-ly*, not *u-su-al-ly*; *imag-i-nary*, not *i-mag-i-nar-y*).

7. Division of short words (of five or fewer letters) should be avoided; two-letter divisions, including the carry-over of two-letter endings (*ed, el, en, er, es, et, fy, ic, in, le, ly, or,* and *ty*); should also be avoided. In narrow measure, however, a sounded suffix (e.g., *paint-ed*; not *rained*) or syllable of two letters may be carried over—only if unavoidable. (See rule 10.)

8. Words of two syllables are split at the end of the first syllable: *dispelled, con-quered*; words of three or more syllables, with a choice of division possible, divide preferably on the vowel: *particu-lar, sepa-rate.*

9. In words with short prefixes, divide on the prefix; e.g., *ac, co, de, dis, ex, in, non, on, pre, pro, re, un,* etc. (e.g. *non-essential*, not *nonessential; pre-selected*, not *prese-lected*).

If possible, prefixes and combining forms of more than one syllable are preserved intact: *anti, infra, macro, micro, multi, over, retro, semi,* etc. (e.g., *anti-monopoly*, not *antimo-nopoly; over-optimistic*, not *overop-timistic*). (For chemical prefixes, see rule 30.)

10. *Words ending in* -er.—Although two-letter carryovers are to be avoided (rule 7), many -er words which are derived from comparatives (*coarse, coarser; sharp, sharper*) have been listed to prevent a wrong wordbreak; e.g., *coars-er*, not *coar-ser.*

Nouns ending in -er (*adviser, bracer, keeper, perceiver, reader*) derived from action verbs are also listed to prevent a wrong division; e.g., *perceiv-er*, not *percei-ver.*

Except in narrow measure and if unavoidable, the above -er words are not divided unless division can be made on a prefix; e.g., *per-ceiver.*

11. *Words ending in* -or.—Generally, -or words with a consonant preceding are divided before the preceding consonant; e.g., *advi-sor* (legal), *fabricator, guaran-tor, interve-nor, simula-tor, tai-lor*; but *bail-or, bargain-or, con-sign-or, grant-or.*

12. The following suffixes are not divided: *ceous, cial, cient, cion, cious, scious, geous, gion, gious, sial, tial, tion, tious,* and *sion.*

13. The suffixes -able and -ible are usually carried over intact; but when the stem word loses its original form, these suffixes are divided according to pronunciation: *comfort-able, corrupt-ible, manage-able;* but *dura-ble, audi-ble.*

14. Words ending in -ing, with stress on the primary syllable, are preferably divided on the base word; e.g., *appoint-ing, combat-ing, danc-ing, engineer-ing, process-ing, program-ing, stencil-ing, trac-ing,* etc. However, present participles, such as *control-ling, forbid-ding, refer-ring,* with stress placed on the second syllable, divide between the doubled consonants (see also rule 16).

15. When the final consonant sound of a word belongs to a syllable ending with a silent vowel, the final consonant or consonants become part of the added suffix: *chuck-ling, han-dler, han-dling, crum-bling, twin-kled, twin-kling;* but *rollick-ing.*

16. When the addition of -ed, -er, -est, or of a similar ending, causes the doubling of a final consonant, the added consonant is carried over: *pit-ted, rob-ber, thin-nest, glad-den, controllable, transmit-table;* but *bless-ed* (adj.), *dwell-er, gross-est.*

17. Words with doubled consonants are usually divided between these consonants: *clas-sic, ruf-fian, neces-sary, rebel-lion;* but *call-ing, mass-ing.*

18. If formation of a plural adds a syllable ending in an *s* sound, the plural ending should not be carried over by itself: *hor-ses, voi-ces;* but *church-es, cross-es,* thus not breaking the base word (see also rule 7).

19. The digraphs *ai, ck, dg, gh, gn, ng, oa, ph, sh, tch,* and *th* are not split.

20. Do not divide contractions: *doesn't, haven't.*

21. Solid compounds are divided preferably between the members: *bar-keeper, hand-kerchief, proof-reader, humming-bird.*

22. Avoid a division which adds another hyphen to a hyphened compound: *court-martial*, not *court-martial; tax-supported*, not *tax-sup-ported.*

23. A word of one syllable is not split: *tanned, shipped, quenched, through, chasm, prism.*

24. Two consonants preceded and followed by a vowel are divided on the first consonant: *abun-dant, advan-tage, struc-ture;* but *attend-ant, accept-ance, depend-ence.*

25. When two adjoining vowels are sounded separately, divide between them: *cre-ation, gene-alogy.*

26. In breaking homonyms, distinction should be given to their relative functions: *pro-ject* (v.), *proj-ect* (n.); *pro-duce* (v.), *prod-uce* (n.); *stranger* (n.), *strang-er* (comparative adjective); *rec-ollect* (recall), *re-collect* (collect again); but *proc-ess* (n., v.); *pro-test* (n., v.).

27. *Words ending in* -meter.—In the large group of words ending in -meter, distinction should be made between metric system terms and terms indicating a measuring instrument. When it is necessary to divide metric terms, preserve the combining form -meter; e.g., *centi-meter, deca-meter, hecto-meter, kilo-meter.* Bu measuring instruments divide after the *m*: *al-tim-e-ter, ba-rom-e-ter, mi-crom-e-ter, mul-tim-e-ter,* etc. Derivatives of these -meter terms follow the same form; e.g., *mul-tim-e-ter, mul-tim-e-try.*

For orthographic reasons, however, several measuring instruments do not lend themselves to the general rule; e.g., *flow-meter, flux-meter, gauss-meter, taxi-meter, torque-meter, volt-meter, water-meter, watt-meter,* etc.

28. *Foreign languages.*—Rules for word division in foreign languages, by language, are printed in the 1967 GPO Style Manual (unabridged), pages 387–492.

29. *Chemical formulas.*—In chemical formulas, the hyphen has an important function. If a break is unavoidable in a formula, division is preferably made after an original hyphen to avoid the introduction of a misleading hyphen. If impractical to break on a hyphen, division may be made after an original comma, and no hyphen is added to indicate a runover. The following formula shows original hyphens and commas where division may be made. No letterspacing is used in a chemical formula, but to fill a line, a space is permitted on both sides of a hyphen.

1-(2,6,6-trimethylcyclohex-1- en -1- yl)-
3,7,12,16

30. *Chemical combining forms, prefixes, and suffixes.*—If possible, and subject to rules of good spacing, it is desirable to preserve as a unit such combining forms as follows:

aceto, anhydro, benzo, bromo, chloro, chromo, cincho, cyclo, dehydro, diazo, flavo, fluoro, glyco, hydroxy, iso, keto, methyl, naphtho, phospho, poly, silico, tetra, triazo.

The following suffixes are used in chemical printing. For patent and narrow measure composition, two-letter suffixes may be carried over.

al, an, ane, ase, ate, ene, ic, id, ide, in, ine, ite, ol, ole, on, one, ose, ous oyl, yl, yne.

31. *Mineral elements.*—When it is necessary to break mineral constituents, division should preferably be made before a center period and beginning parenthesis, and after inferior figures following a closing parenthesis; but elements within parentheses are not separated. In cases of unavoidable breaks, a hyphen is not added to indicate a runover.

$$Mg(UO_2)_2(SiO_3)_2(OH)_2 \cdot 6H_2O$$

32. The em dash is not used at the beginning of any line of type, unless it is required before a credit line or signature, or in lieu of opening quotation marks in foreign languages. (See rules 9.52, 9.53, p. 142, 1967 GPO Style Manual.)

33. Neither periods nor asterisks used as an ellipsis are overrun alone at the end of a paragraph. If necessary, run over enough preceding lines to provide a short word or part of a word to accompany the ellipsis. If a runback is possible, subject to rules of good spacing and word division, this method may be adopted.

34. Abbreviations and symbols should not be broken at the end of a line: *A.F. of L., A.T. & T., C. Cls. R., f.o.b., n.o.i.b.n., R. & D., r.p.m., WMAL.* Where unavoidable in narrow measures and AGO's, long symbols may be broken after letters denoting a complete word. Use no hyphens. COM SUB A C LANT (Commander Submarine Allied Command Atlantic).

35. Figures of less than six digits, decimals, and closely connected combinations of figures and abbreviations should not be broken at the end of a line: *$15,000, 34,575, 31.416, £8 4s. 7d., $10.25, 5,000 kw.-hr., A.D. 1952, 9 p.m., 18° F., NW¼.* If a break in six digits or over is unavoidable, divide on the comma or period,

retain it, and use a hyphen.

36. Closely related abbreviations and initials in proper names and accompanying titles should not be separated, nor should titles, such as *Rev., Mr., Esq., Jr., 2d,* be separated from surnames.

37. Avoid dividing proper names, but if inescapable, follow general rules for word division.

38. Divisional and subdivisional paragraph reference signs and figures, such as *§ 18, section (a)(1), page 363(b),* should not be divided, nor should such references be separated from the matter to which they pertain.

In case of an unavoidable break in a lengthy reference (e.g., *7(B)(1)(a)(i)*), division will be made after elements in parentheses, and no hyphen is used.

39. In dates, do not divide the month and day, but the year may be carried over.

40. In case of an unavoidable break in a land-description symbol group at the end of a line, use no hyphen and break after a fraction.

41. Avoid breaking longitude and latitude figures at the end of a line; space out the line instead. In case of an unavoidable break at end of line, use hyphen.

A

Aar-on
Aa-ron-ic
ab-a-ca
ab-a-cus
ab-a-lo-ne
a-ban-don
a-bat-a-ble
ab-a-tis
ab-at-toir
a-bet-ter
a-bet-tor (law)
ab-bre-vi-a-tor
ab-di-ca-tor
ab-do-men
ab-dom-i-nal
ab-dom-i-no-per-i-ne-al
ab-dom-i-nos-co-py
ab-duc-tor
a-be-ce-dar-i-an
A-bed-ne-go
ab-en-ter-ic
ab-er-om-e-ter
ab-er-ra-tion
a-bey-ance
ab-hor-rence
ab-hor-ri-ble
a-bid-ance
ab-i-et-ic
Ab-i-gail
Ab-i-lene
a-bil-i-ty
a-bi-ot-ic
a-bi-ot-ro-phy
ab-ju-ra-tion
ab-jur-a-to-ry
ab-la-tive
a-blep-si-a
ab-ne-ga-tor
ab-nor-mal-i-ty
ab-nor-mi-ty
a-bol-ish
ab-o-li-tion-ist
a-bom-i-na-ble
ab-o-rig-i-nes
a-bor-ti-cide
a-bort-in
a-bor-tive
ab-ra-ca-dab-ra
a-brad-ant
A-bra-ham

a-bran-chi-ate
ab-ra-si-om-e-ter
ab-ra-sion
ab-ra-sive
a-bridg-ment
ab-ro-ga-tive
ab-rupt
ab-scess
ab-scis-sa
ab-scis-sion
ab-scond
ab-sence
ab-sen-tee-ism
ab-sinthe
ab-sin-thin
ab-so-lu-tion
ab-so-lut-ism
ab-so-lu-tive
ab-so-lu-tize
ab-sol-u-to-ry
ab-sol-vent
ab-solv-er
ab-sorb-ate
ab-sorb-ent
ab-sorp-tance
ab-sorp-ti-om-e-ter
ab-ste-mi-ous
ab-sten-tious
ab-ster-gent
ab-sti-nence
ab-stract-er
ab-strac-tive
ab-struse
ab-surd-i-ty
a-bu-lo-ma-ni-a
a-bun-dance
a-bus-age
a-bu-sive
a-but-ting
a-bys-mal
a-byss-al
Ab-ys-sin-i-an
a-ca-cia
ac-a-dem-i-cal
a-cad-e-mi-cian
a-cad-e-my
a-camp-si-a
ac-a-na-ceous
ac-an-tha-ceous
a-can-thoid
ac-an-tho-ma
a-can-thus
a cap-pel-la

a-cap-su-lar
a-ca-pul-co
a-car-dite
ac-a-ri-a-sis
a-car-i-cid-al
ac-a-roid
a-cau-date
ac-ced-ence
ac-cel-er-ans
ac-cel-er-a-tive
ac-cel-er-a-tor
ac-cel-er-om-e-ter
ac-cend-i-ble
ac-cen-tu-a-tor
ac-cept-a-ble
ac-cept-ance
ac-cep-ta-tion
ac-cept-er
ac-cep-tor (law)
ac-ces-si-ble
ac-ces-so-ri-al
ac-ciac-ca-tu-ra
ac-ci-den-tal
ac-cla-ma-tion
ac-clam-a-to-ry
ac-cli-mate
ac-cli-ma-ti-za-tion
ac-cliv-i-ty
ac-cli-vous
ac-co-lade
ac-com-mo-dat-ing
ac-com-pa-ni-ment
ac-com-pa-nist
ac-com-plice
ac-com-plish
ac-cord-ance
ac-cor-di-on-ist
ac-couche-ment
ac-cou-cheur
ac-count-a-ble
ac-count-an-cy
ac-cou-ter
ac-cred-i-ta-tion
ac-cres-cence
ac-cre-tive
ac-cul-tur-ate
ac-cum-bent
ac-cu-mu-la-tive
ac-cu-mu-la-tor
ac-cu-ra-cy
ac-cursed (v.)
ac-curs-ed (adj.)
ac-cus-a-ble

ac-cu-sa-tive
ac-cu-sa-to-ry
ac-cus-er
ac-cus-tomed
ac-e-naph-thy-lene
a-ceph-a-lous (adj.)
a-ceph-a-lus (n.)
ac-er-bate
a-cer-bi-ty
ac-er-ose
ac-e-tab-u-lum
ac-et-al-de-hyde
a-cet-a-mide
ac-et-am-i-dine
ac-et-a-mi-do-cin-nam-ic
ac-et-an-i-lide
ac-et-ar-sone
ac-e-tate
ac-e-ta-to-so-da-lite
a-ce-tic
a-ce-ti-fy
ac-e-tin
ac-e-to-ac-et-an-i-lide
a-cet-o-in
ac-e-tol-y-sis
ac-e-tom-e-ter
ac-e-tom-e-try
ac-e-tone
ac-e-ton-yl-i-dene
ac-e-to-phe-net-i-dide
ac-e-to-phe-none
ac-e-to-pro-pi-o-nate
ac-e-to-pur-pu-rine
ac-e-tous
ac-e-tox-yl
a-ce-tum
ac-e-tyl-ac-e-tone
a-cet-y-late
a-cet-y-la-tor
ac-e-tyl-cho-line
a-cet-y-lene
a-cet-y-lide
ac-e-tyl-meth-yl-car-bi-nol
ac-e-tyl-phen-yl-hy-dra-zine
ac-e-tyl-sa-lic-y-late
ac-e-tyl-sal-i-cyl-ic
Ach-il-le-an
A-chil-les
a-chol-ic
ach-ro-mat-ic
ach-ro-ma-tic-i-ty

a-chro-ma-tin
a-chro-ma-tism
a-cic-u-lar
ac-i-dif-er-ous
ac-i-dim-e-ter
ac-i-dim-e-try
a-cid-i-ty
a-cid-o-phil
ac-i-doph-i-lus
ac-i-do-sis
a-cid-u-lous
ac-i-na-ceous
ac-knowl-edge-a-ble
ac-knowl-edg-ment
ac-o-lyte
a-con-ic
ac-o-nite
ac-o-nit-ic
a-con-i-tine
a-cou-me-ter
a-cou-me-try
a-con-ti-um
a-cous-tic
ac-ous-ti-cian
a-cous-ti-con
ac-quaint-ance
ac-quaint-ed
ac-qui-es-cence
ac-quire
ac-qui-si-tion
ac-quis-i-tive
ac-quit-tal
a-cre-age
ac-ri-bom-e-ter
ac-rid
ac-ri-dine
ac-ri-din-i-um
a-crid-i-ty
ac-ri-mo-ni-ous
ac-ro-bat-ic
ac-ro-gen
a-crog-e-nous
a-cro-le-in
ac-ro-lith
ac-ro-nym
a-crop-e-tal
ac-ro-pho-bi-a
a-croph-o-ny
a-crop-o-lis
a-cros-tic
a-crot-ic
ac-ryl-am-ide
ac-ry-late

a-cryl-ic
ac-ry-lo-ni-trile
a-cryl-o-yl
ac-ry-lyl
ac-tin-ic
ac-tin-ism
ac-tin-o-lite
ac-ti-no-bac-il-lo-sis
ac-ti-noid
ac-tin-o-lite
ac-ti-nom-e-ter
ac-ti-no-my-cin
ac-ti-no-my-co-sis
ac-ti-nos-co-py
ac-tion-om-e-ter
ac-ti-va-ble
ac-ti-va-tor
ac-tiv-ism
ac-tiv-ist
ac-tiv-i-ty
ac-to-my-o-sin
ac-tor
ac-tress
ac-tu-al-i-ty
ac-tu-ar-y
ac-tu-a-tor
a-cu-i-ty
a-cu-men
a-cu-mi-nate
a-cute-ness
a-cy-clic
ac-yl-ate
ad ab-sur-dum
ad-age
a-da-gio
ad-a-mant
ad-a-man-tine
A-dam-si-a
ad-ams-ite
Ad-am-son
a-dapt-a-ble
a-dapt-a-bil-i-ty
ad-ap-ta-tion
a-dapt-er
a-dapt-ive
ad-ap-tom-e-ter
a-dap-tor
ad-ax-i-al
add-a-ble
add-ed
ad-den-da
add-er (one who adds)
ad-der (snake)

ad-dict-ed	ad-ver-si-ty	al-ba-tross	al-lu-vi-um	a-mo-le	an-es-thet-ic
ad-dic-tion	ad-vert-ence	al-be-dom-e-ter	al-lyl-a-mine	am-o-rous	an-es-the-tist
ad-dit-a-ment	ad-ver-tise-ment	al-be-rene	al-lyl-ic	a-mor-phism	a-neu-ri-a
ad-di-tion	ad-ver-tis-er	al-be-scent	al-ma-nac	am-or-ti-za-tion	an-eu-rin
ad-di-tive	ad-vis-a-ble	al-bin-ic	al-might-y	A-moy-ese	an-eu-rysm
ad-di-to-ry	ad-vis-ic	al-bi-nism	al-mond	am-per-age	an-ga-ry
ad-dress-ee	ad-vis-er	al-bi-nos	al-mon-er	am-pere-me-ter	an-gel-ic
ad-dress-er	ad-vi-sor (law)	al-bo-lite	a-lo-di-um	am-per-o-met-ric	an-ger
Ad-dres-so-graph	ad-vi-so-ry	Al-bu-quer-que	a-lo-et-ic	am-per-om-e-try	an-gi-i-tis
ad-dres-sor (law)	ad-vo-ca-cy	al-bu-men (egg)	a-lo-gism	am-per-sand	an-gi-na pec-to-ris
ad-du-cent	ad-vo-ca-to-ry	al-bu-min (chemical)	a-lo-in	am-phet-a-mine	an-gi-o-car-di-og-ra-phy
ad-duc-i-ble	Ae-ge-an	al-bu-mi-nate	a-lo-pe-ci-a	am-phib-i-an	an-gi-o-cyst
ad-duc-tor	ae-o-li-an	al-bu-mi-nom-e-ter	Al-o-ys-i-us	am-phib-i-ol-o-gy	an-gi-om-e-ter
Ad-e-la	aer-ate	al-bu-mi-no-sis	al-pac-a	am-phib-i-ous	an-gi-op-a-thy
Ad-e-laide	aer-a-tor	al-bu-mi-nu-ri-a	al-pha-bet-i-cal	am-phi-bol-ic	an-gi-o-sis
Ad-el-bert	aer-i-al	al-bur-num	al-pha-bet-ize	am-phib-o-lite	an-gi-os-to-my
ad-e-nase	ae-rie	al-ca-mine	al-pha-mer-ic	am-phib-o-lous	an-gi-o-to-nin
a-de-ni-a	aer-if-er-ous	al-chem-ic	al-pha-tron	am-phi-dip-loi-dy	an-gler
a-den-i-form	aer-i-fi-ca-tion	al-che-mist	Al-pine	am-phi-ge-net-ic	An-gli-can
ad-e-nine	aer-o-bac-ter	al-che-my	Al-pin-ism	am-phig-e-nous	an-gli-cize
ad-e-ni-tis	aer-o-bic	al-co-hol-ism	al-read-y	am-phi-kar-y-on	An-go-lese
ad-e-no-car-ci-no-ma	aer-o-dy-nam-ic	al-co-hol-om-e-ter	al-sike	Am-phip-o-da	An-go-ra
ad-e-no-fi-bro-ma	aer-ol-o-gy	al-co-hol-om-e-try	al-tar	am-pho-ter-ic	an-gos-tu-ra
ad-e-noi-dal	aer-om-e-ter	al-co-hol-y-sis	al-ter	am-phot-er-ism	an-gry
ad-e-no-ma	aer-o-mo-tor	Al-deb-a-ran	al-ter-na-tive	am-pli-fi-er	ang-strom
ad-e-nom-a-tous	aer-o-nau-tics	al-de-hyd-ic	al-ter-na-tor	am-pli-tude	an-guish
ad-e-nop-a-thy	aer-on-o-my	al-de-hy-drol	al-tim-e-ter	am-poule	an-gu-lar-i-ty
a-den-o-sine	aer-o-scope	al-der-man	al-tim-e-try	am-pu-ta-tor	an-he-dral
ad-e-not-o-my	aer-os-co-py	Al-der-ney	al-ti-tu-di-nar-i-an	Am-ster-dam	an-hi-dro-sis
ad-e-nyl	ae-rose	Al-dine	al-to-geth-er	am-u-let	an-hi-drot-ic
ad-ept	aer-o-sol	al-do-fu-ran-o-side	al-trose	a-mu-si-a	an-hy-dride
a-dept-ness	aer-o-stat	al-dol-ase	a-lu-mi-na	a-mus-ing	an-hy-dro-bi-o-sis
ad-e-qua-cy	Aes-chy-le-an	al-don-ic	a-lu-min-i-um	a-myg-da-la-ce-ae	an-hy-drous
ad-her-min	af-fa-ble	a-le-a-to-ry	a-lu-mi-nize	a-myg-da-lin	an-i-lide
ad-her-ence	af-fec-ta-tion	a-lem-bi-cate	a-lu-mi-nous	a-myg-da-loi-dal	an-i-line
ad-her-ent	af-fect-er	a-lep-ric	a-lu-mi-num	am-y-la-ceous	a-nil-i-ty
ad-he-res-cent	af-fect-i-ble	a-lert-ness	a-lum-nus	am-y-lase	an-i-mad-ver-sion
ad-he-sion	af-fec-tion-ate	al-eu-drin	a-lun-dum	am-yl-ene	an-i-mal-cule
ad-he-sive	af-fer-ent	al-eu-rit-ic	al-u-nite	am-y-loi-dal	an-i-mal-ism
ad-i-a-bat-ic	af-fi-anced	al-eu-rom-e-ter	al-vo-o-lar	am-y-lol-do-sis	an-i-ma-tion
ad in-fi-ni-tum	af-fi-da-vit	al-eu-rone	Al-ve-o-li-tes	am-y-lol-y-sis	an-i-mism
ad-i-nole	af-fil-i-ate	A-leu-tian	a-lys-sum	am-y-lo-pec-tin	an-i-mos-i-ty
a-dip-a-mide	af-fin-i-ty	a-lex-i-a	a-mal-ga-mate	am-y-lose	an-i-on-ic
ad-i-pate	af-firm-ance	a-lex-in	a-mal-ga-ma-tor	a-nab-a-sine	an-i-on-ot-ro-py
a-dip-ic	af-fir-ma-tion	al-ge-bra-i-cal	a-man-u-en-sis	an-a-bi-o-sis	an-is-ate
ad-i-po-ni-trile	af-firm-a-tive	al-ge-fa-cient	am-a-ranth	an-a-bol-ic	an-ise
ad-i-po-sis	af-fla-tus	Al-ge-ri-an	am-a-ran-thine	a-nab-o-lism	an-i-seed
ad-i-pos-i-ty	af-flict-ive	al-ge-si-a	am-a-roid	a-nach-ro-nism	an-is-ette
ad-i-po-so-gen-i-tal	af-flu-ent	al-ge-sim-e-ter	am-a-ryl-lis	an-a-con-da	a-nis-ic
ad-i-po-yl	Af-ghan-i-stan	al-gi-nate	am-a-teur-ish	A-nac-re-on	a-nis-i-dine
ad-ja-cent	a-fi-ci-o-na-do	al-gin-ic	am-a-tol	a-nad-ro-mous	an-i-sot-ro-py
ad-jec-ti-val	a-for-ti-o-ri	al-gol-o-gy	am-a-to-ry	an-aer-o-bi-a	an-klet
ad-jec-tive	Af-ri-can-ize	al-gom-e-ter	a-maze-ment	an-aer-o-bic	an-ky-lo-sis
ad-ju-di-cate	af-ter	Al-go-rab	Am-a-zo-ni-an	a-nag-ly-phy	an-ky-los-to-ma
ad-junc-tive	a-gam-ic	al-go-rism	am-bas-sa-do-ri-al	an-a-glyp-tics	an-nal-ist
ad-ju-ra-tion	ag-a-ric	al-gra-phy	am-ber-gris	an-a-gog-ic	An-nam-ese
ad-jur-er	a-gar-i-cin-ic	a-li-as	am-ber-old	a-nal-cite	an-neal-er
ad-just-a-ble	ag-a-rin-ic	al-i-bi	am-bi-dex-trous	an-a-lep-tic	an-ni-hi-late
ad-just-er	Ag-as-siz	al-i-cy-clic	am-bi-ent	an-al-ge-si-a	an-ni-ver-sa-ry
ad-jus-tor (zoology)	ag-ate	al-i-dade	am-bi-gu-i-ty	an-al-ge-sic	an-no-ta-tor
ad-ju-tage	Ag-a-thin	al-ien-ate	am-big-u-ous	an-a-log-i-cal	an-nounc-er
ad-ju-tant	a-ga-ve	al-ien-ist	am-bip-a-rous	a-nal-o-gous	an-nu-al
ad-ju-vant	a-gen-cy	a-lif-er-ous	am-bi-tious	a-nal-o-gy	an-nu-i-tant
Ad-le-ri-an	a-gen-da	al-i-men-ta-ry	am-biv-a-lence	a-nal-y-sis	an-nu-lar
ad lib-i-tum	a-gen-ti-val	al-i-mo-ny	am-bling	an-a-lyst	an-nu-let
ad-min-is-tra-tor	a-geu-si-a	a-line-ment	am-blys-to-ma	an-a-lyt-i-cal	an-nun-ci-a-to-ry
ad-min-is-tra-trix	ag-er-a-tum	a-lin-er	am-bro-si-a	an-a-lyz-er	an-ode
ad-mi-ra-ble	ag-glom-er-ate	al-i-phat-ic	am-bu-lance	an-a-mor-pho-sis	an-od-ic
ad-mi-ral-ty	ag-glu-ti-nant	al-i-quot	am-bu-la-to-ry	An-a-ni-as	an-od-ize
ad-mi-ra-tion	ag-glu-ti-noid	al-i-vin-cu-lar	am-bus-cad-er	an-a-phy-lax-is	an-o-dyne
ad-mir-er	ag-gran-dize	a-liz-a-rin	a-me-ba	an-ar-chism	a-noint-ment
ad-mis-si-ble	ag-gra-vate	al-ka-li	a-me-bi-a-sis	an-ar-chis-tic	a-nom-a-lis-tic
ad-mit-tance	ag-gre-gate	al-ka-lim-e-ter	a-me-bic	an-ar-chy	a-nom-a-lous
ad-mon-ish	ag-gres-sive	al-ka-lin-i-ty	A-mel-ia	a-nas-to-mo-sis	a-nom-a-ly
ad-mo-ni-tion	ag-gres-sor	al-ka-loi-dal	a-me-lio-ra-tive	a-nas-to-mot-ic	an-o-nym-i-ty
ad-mon-i-to-ry	ag-griev-ance	al-ke-nyl	am-e-lo-blas-to-ma	an-a-tase	a-non-y-mous
ad nau-se-am	ag-ile	alk-ox-ide	a-me-na-ble	a-nath-e-ma	an-o-op-si-a
a-do-be	a-gil-i-ty	alk-ox-yl-ate	a-mend-a-to-ry	a-na-tom-i-cal	A-noph-e-les
ad-o-les-cent	ag-i-ta-tive	al-kyl-ate	a-men-i-ty	a-nat-o-mist	an-ox-i-a
Ad-olph	ag-i-ta-tor	al-kyl-ene	a-men-or-rhe-a	a-nat-o-my	an-ser-ine
A-do-nis	ag-it-prop	al-kyl-ic	am-ent (botany)	an-ces-tral	an-swer
a-dopt-er	a-glo-mer-u-lar	al-kyl-ize	am-en-ta-ceous	an-chor-age	ant-ac-id
a-dop-tive	ag-no-si-a	al-lan-to-in-ase	A-mer-i-can-a	an-cho-rite (hermit)	an-tag-o-nism
a-dor-a-ble	ag-nos-te-rol	al-le-ga-tion	A-mer-i-can-ism	an-chor-ite (rock)	Ant-arc-tic
ad-o-ra-tion	ag-nos-ti-cism	Al-le-ghe-ni-an	am-er-i-ci-um	an-cho-vy	An-tar-es
a-dor-er	ag-o-niz-ing	Al-le-ghe-ny	ames-ite	an-cient	an-te-ced-ent
a-dorn-ment	ag-o-ra-pho-bi-a	al-le-giance	am-e-thyst	an-cil-lar-y	an-te-di-lu-vi-an
ad-re-nal	a-grar-i-an	al-le-gor-i-cal	a-mi-a-ble	an-cy-lo-sto-mi-a-sis	an-te-lope
A-dren-a-lin	ag-ri-cul-tur-al	al-le-go-ry	am-i-ca-ble	An-da-lu-sian	an-te-pe-nul-ti-mate
a-dren-er-gen	ag-ri-mo-ny	al-le-gro	a-mi-cus cu-ri-ae	an-da-lu-site	an-te-ri-or
ad-re-ner-gic	ag-ro-nom-ic	al-ler-gen-ic	am-i-dase	An-da-man	ant-he-lion
a-dre-no-chrome	a-gron-o-mist	al-ler-gic	am-ide	an-de-site	ant-hel-min-tic
a-dre-no-cor-ti-co-troph-ic	a-gron-o-my	al-le-vi-ate	a-mid-ic	and-i-ron	an-them
A-dri-an	ag-ros-tol-o-gy	al-le-vi-a-tor	a-mi-do	An-dor-ran	an-ther-al
A-dri-at-ic	ag-ryp-not-ic	al-li-a-ceous	a-mi-do-gen	an-dor-ite	an-tho-cy-an-i-din
a-droit-ness	a-gu-ish	al-li-ga-tor	am-i-dol	An-do-ver	an-thog-e-nous
ad-sorb-ate	aide me-moire	al-lit-er-a-tive	am-i-dox-ime	an-dro-gen-ic-i-ty	an-tho-log-i-cal
ad-sorb-ent	ai-grette	al-lo-ca-ble	a-mi-go	an-drog-y-nous	an-thol-o-gy
ad-sorp-tive	ai-le-ron	al-lo-ca-tor	am-i-nate	An-drom-e-da	An-tho-ny
ad-u-la-tion	ai-lu-ro-phobe	al-log-a-my	a-mine	An-dro-mede	an-thra-cene
a-dul-ter-a-tor	air-i-ness	al-lom-er-ism	a-mi-no	an-dro-sin	an-thra-cif-er-ous
a-dult-i-cide	air-om-e-ter	al-lom-e-try	a-mi-no-ben-zo-ic	an-dro-stane	an-thra-cite
ad-um-brate	Ak-ti-en-ge-sell-schaft	al-lo-path	am-i-nol-y-sis	an-dros-te-rone	an-thra-co-sil-i-co-sis
ad va-lo-rem	Al-a-bam-i-an	al-lop-a-thy	am-i-nop-ter-in	an-ec-dot-al	an-thra-nil-ic
ad-vanc-er	al-a-bas-ter	al-loph-a-nate	a-mi-no-sal-i-cyl-ic	a-ne-mi-a	an-thran-o-yl
ad-van-ta-geous	a-lac-ri-ty	al-lo-se-mat-ic	am-me-ter	a-ne-mic	an-thra-pur-pu-rin
ad-vec-tive	al-a-me-da	al-lo-troph-ic	am-mo-ni-a	a-nem-o-gram	an-thra-qui-no-nyl
ad-ven-ience	al-a-mo	al-lot-ro-py	am-mo-ni-ate	an-e-mom-e-ter	an-thrax
Ad-vent-ist	a-la-mode	al-lot-ted	am-mo-nite	a-nem-o-ne	an-thro-poi-dal
ad-ven-ti-tious	a-la-nine	al-lot-tee	Am-mon-ites (Biblical)	a-nem-o-scope	an-thro-po-log-i-cal
ad-ven-tur-er	al-a-nyl	al-lot-ting	am-mo-ni-um	an-er-oid	an-thro-pol-o-gy
ad-verb-i-al	a-larm-ist	al-lur-ing	am-mu-ni-tion	an-es-the-sia	an-thro-pom-e-ter
ad-ver-sar-y	A-las-kan	al-lu-sive	am-ne-sia	an-es-the-si-om-e-ter	an-thro-po-met-ric
	Al-ba-ni-an	al-lu-vi-al	am-nes-ty	an-es-the-si-ol-o-gy	

an-thro-poph-a-gy
an-ti-bi-ot-ic
an-ti-cal
an-tic-i-pa-to-ry
an-ti-cli-nal
an-ti-gen-ic
an-ti-ge-nic-i-ty
An-tig-o-ne
An-ti-guan
an-ti-his-ta-min-ic
An-til-le-an
an-til-o-gism
an-ti-mo-ny
an-ti-pas-to
an-ti-pa-thet-ic
an-tip-a-thy
an-tiph-o-nal
an-tip-o-dal
an-ti-pode
an-tip-o-de-an
an-tip-o-des
an-ti-quar-i-an
an-ti-quate
an-tique
an-tiq-ui-ty
an-ti-sep-tic
an-tith-e-sis
an-ti-thet-i-cal
ant-ler
an-to-nym
Ant-werp
an-u-re-sis
anx-i-e-ty
anx-ious
a-or-tic
a-pache (Paris thug)
A-pach-e (Indian tribe)
a-pa-re-jo
a-part-heid
ap-as-tron
ap-a-thet-ic
ap-a-thy
ap-a-tite
Ap-en-nine
a-pe-ri-ent
a-pe-ri-od-ic
a-per-i-tif
ap-er-tom-e-ter
ap-er-tur-al
aph-a-nite
aph-a-nit-ic
a-pha-sia
a-phe-lion
aph-i-cide
aph-o-rism
a-phra-si-a
aph-ro-dis-i-ac
Aph-ro-di-te
a-pi-a-rist
a-pi-ar-y
ap-i-cal
a-pi-ose
ap-ish
a-piv-o-rous
ap-neu-sis
a-poc-a-lyp-tic
a-poc-o-pe
a-poc-ry-phal
Ap-o-des
ap-o-dic-tic
a-pog-a-my
ap-o-ge-an
ap-o-gee
a-pog-e-ny
A-pol-li-nar-is
A-pol-lo
a-pol-o-get-ic
ap-o-lo-gi-a
a-pol-o-gist
ap-o-pho-rom-e-ter
ap-o-phyl-lite
ap-o-plec-tic
a-po-plex-y
a-pos-ta-sy
a-pos-tate
a-pos-ta-tize
a pos-te-ri-o-ri
a-pos-tle
a-pos-to-late
ap-os-tol-ic
a-pos-tro-phe
ap-os-troph-ic
a-poth-e-car-y
a-poth-e-o-sis
Ap-pa-lach-ian
ap-pall-ing
ap-pa-nage
ap-pa-ra-tus
ap-par-eled
ap-par-ent
ap-pa-ri-tion
ap-pear-ance
ap-pel-lant
ap-pel-la-tion
ap-pend-age
ap-pend-ant
ap-pen-dec-to-my
ap-pen-di-cal
ap-pen-di-ci-tis
ap-pen-dix
ap-per-cep-tion
ap-pet-i-ble
ap-pe-tiz-er

ap-pe-tiz-ing
ap-pli-ca-ble
ap-pli-ca-tor
ap-pli-ca-to-ry
ap-pli-que
ap-pog-gia-tu-ra
ap-point-ee
ap-point-ive
ap-po-site
ap-pos-i-tive
ap-prais-al
ap-pre-ci-a-tive
ap-pre-hen-si-ble
ap-pre-hen-sive
ap-pren-tice
ap-proach-ing
ap-pro-ba-tion
ap-pro-pri-a-tive
ap-prov-al
ap-prox-i-mate
ap-pui
ap-pur-te-nance
a-pri-cot
A-pril
a pri-o-ri
ap-ro-pos
ap-sis
ap-te-ri-um
ap-ter-ous
ap-ti-tude
aq-ua-plane
aq-ua-relle
a-quar-i-um
A-quar-i-us
a-quat-ic
aq-ua-tint
aq-ua-vit
aq-ue-duct
a-que-ous
aq-ui-fer
aq-ui-line
a-ra-besque
A-ra-bic
a-rab-i-nose
Ar-ab-ize
ar-a-ble
A-rach-ni-da
a-rach-noi-dal
Ar-a-go-nese
a-rag-o-nite
ar-al-kox-y
ar-al-kyl-ate
Ar-a-ma-ic
A-rap-a-ho
A-rau-ca-ni-an
ar-bi-ter
ar-bi-tra-ble
ar-bi-trag-er
ar-bit-ra-ment
ar-bi-trar-y
ar-bi-tra-tor
ar-bo-re-al
ar-bo-res-cent
ar-bo-re-tum
ar-bo-ri-cul-tur-al
ar-bo-rize
ar-bor-vi-tae
ar-bu-tus
ar-cade
Ar-ca-di-an
ar-ca-num
ar-cha-ic
ar-che-o-log-i-cal
ar-che-ol-o-gy
arch-er-y
ar-che-typ-al
ar-che-us
Ar-chi-bald
ar-chi-e-pis-co-pa-cy
Ar-chi-me-de-an
ar-chi-pel-a-go
ar-chi-tec-tur-al
ar-chi-trave
ar-chives
ar-chi-vist
Arc-tic
Arc-tu-rus
ar-cu-ate
ar-dent
ar-dor
ar-du-ous
ar-e-al
a-re-na
ar-e-na-ceous
a-re-o-la
ar-gen-tal
ar-gen-te-ous
ar-gen-tif-er-ous
Ar-gen-ti-na
ar-gen-tite
ar-gen-tous
ar-gen-tum
ar-gil-la-ceous
ar-gil-lif-er-ous
ar-gil-lite
ar-gi-nine
ar-gol
ar-gon
Ar-go-naut
ar-go-sy
ar-gu-men-ta-tive
Ar-gy-rol
a-rid-i-ty

Ar-i-el
A-ri-es
A-ri-on
a-ris-tate
ar-is-toc-ra-cy
a-ris-to-crat-ic
Ar-is-to-te-li-an
Ar-is-tot-le
ar-ith-met-ic (adj.)
a-rith-me-tic (n.)
ar-ith-met-i-cal
ar-ith-mom-e-ter
Ar-i-zo-nan
Ar-kan-san
ark-ite (mineral)
ar-ma-da
ar-ma-dil-los
Ar-ma-ged-don
ar-ma-ment
ar-ma-men-tar-i-um
ar-ma-ture
Ar-me-ni-an
ar-mi-stice
ar-mor-er
ar-mo-ri-al
ar-mo-ry
ar-ni-ca
a-ro-ma
ar-o-mat-ic
ar-o-ma-ti-za-tion
a-rous-al
a-rous-ing
ar-raign
ar-range-ments
ar-rear-age
ar-rest-er
ar-res-tive
ar-rhyth-mi-a
ar-riv-al
ar-ro-gant
ar-ron-disse-ment
ar-roy-o
ar-se-nal
ar-se-nate
ar-se-nic (n.)
ar-sen-ic (adj.)
ar-sen-i-cal
ar-se-nide
ar-se-ni-ous
ar-se-ni-o-sid-er-ite
ar-se-no-ben-zene
ar-sine
ar-son-ist
ar-so-ni-um
ars-phen-a-mine
ar-te-ri-al
ar-te-ri-og-ra-phy
ar-te-ri-o-lar
ar-te-ri-o-scle-ro-sis
ar-te-ri-ot-o-my
ar-te-ri-tis
ar-ter-y
ar-te-sian
ar-thrit-ic
ar-thri-tis
ar-thro-dese
ar-throd-e-sis
ar-throg-e-nous
ar-throg-ra-phy
ar-throm-e-ter
ar-throp-a-thy
ar-thro-pod
Ar-throp-o-da
ar-ti-choke
ar-ti-cle
ar-tic-u-la-tor
ar-ti-fact
ar-ti-fice
ar-tif-i-cer
ar-ti-fi-cial
ar-til-ler-y
ar-ti-nite
ar-ti-san
art-ist
ar-tiste
ar-tis-ti-cal
art-ist-ry
A-run-del (Maryland)
Ar-y-an-ize
ar-yl-am-ine
ar-yl-ate
ar-yl-ene
as-a-fet-i-da
as-bes-to-sis
as-ca-ri-a-sis
as-car-i-dole
as-cend-an-cy
as-cend-ant
as-cend-er
as-cer-tain
as-cet-i-cism
as-cid-i-an
as-ci-tes
a-scor-bic
as-cribe
a-sep-sis
a-sep-tic
Ash-ke-na-zi
A-si-at-ic
as-i-nin-i-ty
a-skance
a-skew
as-pa-rag-i-nase
as-par-a-gine

as-par-a-gus
as-par-tic
as-pect
as-per-ate
as-perge
as-per-gil-lus
as-per-i-ty
as-per-sion
as-phal-tene
as-phal-tic
As-pi-dis-tra
as-pi-rant
as-pi-ra-tor
as-pi-ra-to-ry
as-pi-rin
As-ple-ni-um
as-sail-ant
As-sam-ese
as-sas-si-nate
as-sem-bla-ble
as-sem-bler
as-sem-bly
as-sen-tor
as-sert-i-ble
as-ser-tive
as-sess-ee
as-ses-sor
as-ses-so-ri-al
as-sev-er-ate
as-si-du-i-ty
as-sid-u-ous
as-si-ette
as-sign-a-ble
as-sig-nat
as-sig-na-tion
as-sign-ee
as-sign-or
as-sim-i-la-ble
as-sist-ant
as-so-ci-a-ble
as-so-ci-ate
as-so-nance
as-suage
as-sump-sit
as-sur-ance
As-syr-i-an
as-ta-tine
as-ter
as-te-ri-al
as-ter-isk
as-ter-oid
as-ter-oi-dal
as-the-ni-a
as-then-ic
asth-mat-ic
as-tig-mat-ic
a-stig-ma-tism
as-tig-mom-e-ter
as-ton-ish
as-tound-ing
as-tra-gal
as-trag-a-lus
as-tra-khan
as-tral
as-tric-tion
as-trin-gent
as-tri-on-ics
as-tro-ga-tor
as-trog-o-ny
as-troid
as-tro-labe
as-trol-o-ger
as-tro-log-i-cal
as-trol-o-gy
as-trom-e-try
as-tro-naut
as-tro-nau-tics
as-tron-o-mer
as-tro-nom-i-cal
as-tron-o-my
as-tro-sphere
As-tu-ri-an
as-tute
a-sun-der
a-sy-lum
a-sym-met-ri-cal
as-ymp-tote
as-ymp-tot-ic
a-syn-ap-sis
a-sys-to-le
At-a-brine
at-a-rac-tic
at-a-vism
at-a-vis-tic
a-tax-i-a
at-e-lier
a-the-is-ti-cal
ath-e-ne-um
A-the-ni-an
Ath-ens
ath-er-o-ma
ath-er-om-a-tous
ath-er-o-scle-ro-sis
ath-let-i-cal-ly
a-threp-si-a
ath-ro-cyte
ath-ro-gen-ic
At-lan-tic
At-lan-tite
at-mol-y-sis
at-mom-e-ter
at-mos-pher-i-cal

at-oll
a-tom-ic
a-tom-i-cal
at-o-mic-i-ty
at-om-ism
at-om-is-tic
at-om-iz-er
a-ton-al
a-tone-ment
at-o-ny
at-o-py
a-tre-si-a
a-tri-o-ven-tric-u-lar
a-tri-um
a-tro-cious
a-troc-i-ty
a-troph-ic
at-ro-phy
at-ro-pine
at-ro-pin-ize
at-ta-ché
at-tain-der
at-tem-per-a-tor
at-tend-ant
at-ten-tive
at-ten-u-a-tor
at-test-ant
at-tes-ta-tion
at-test-er
at-ti-tu-di-nize
at-tor-ney
at-tract-ant
at-trac-tive
at-trac-tor
at-trib-ut-a-ble
at-trib-ute (n.)
at-trib-ute (v.)
at-trib-u-tive
at-tri-tus
auc-tion-eer
auc-to-ri-al
au-da-cious
au-dac-i-ty
au-di-ble
au-di-ence
au-di-o-gen-ic
au-di-om-e-ter
au-di-om-e-try
au-di-to-ri-um
au-di-to-ry
Au-du-bon
au-gan-ite
au-ger
au-gite
au-gi-tite
aug-men-ta-tion
aug-ment-a-tive
aug-men-tor
au-gu-ry
au-gust
Au-gus-tin-i-an
au-ral
au-ra-mine
au-re-ate
au-re-li-an
au-re-o-e
Au-re-o-my-cin
au-ri-cle
au-ric-u-lar
au-ric-u-lo-pa-ri-e-tal
au-ro-ra bo-re-al-is
au-rum
aus-cul-tate
aus-pic-es
aus-pi-cious
aus-ten-it-ic
aus-ter-i-ty
Aus-tra-la-sian
Aus-tra-lian
Aus-tri-an
au-tar-chic
au-tar-chy
au-then-ti-cal-ly
au-then-ti-ca-tor
au-then-tic-i-ty
au-thor-i-tar-i-an
au-thor-i-ta-tive
au-thor-i-za-tion
au-thor-iz-er
au-tism
au-toc-ra-cy
au-to-ge-net-ic
au-to-gen-ic
au-tog-e-nous
au-to-gi-ro
au-to-graph
au-tog-ra-pher
au-tol-y-sate
au-to-mat-i-cal
au-to-mat-i-cal-ly
au-to-ma-tic-i-ty
au-to-ma-tion
au-tom-a-tism
au-tom-a-tist
au-tom-a-ti-za-tion
au-tom-a-ton
au-tom-a-tous
au-tom-ne-si-a
au-to-net-ics
au-to-nom-ic
au-ton-o-mous
au-toph-a-gous
au-toph-o-ny

au-top-sy
au-tos-co-py
au-tot-o-my
au-tox-i-diz-a-ble
au-tum-nal
aux-a-nom-e-ter
aux-il-ia-ry
aux-in
aux-o-chrom-ic
aux-om-e-ter
av-a-lanche
av-a-ri-cious
av-a-tar
av-e-nue
av-er-age
a-ver-sion
a-vert-i-ble
a-vi-an-ics
av-i-a-rist
a-vi-ar-y
a-vi-a-tor
a-vi-a-trix
av-i-din
a-vid-i-ty
A-vi-gnon-ese
a-vi-on-ics
av-o-ca-dos
a-vo-ca-tion
a-voc-a-to-ry
a-void-ance
av-oir-du-pois
a-vow-al
a-vun-cu-lar
a-wak-en
awk-ward
awn-ing (n., v.)
ax-i-al-ly
ax-il-lar-y
ax-i-o-mat-ic
Ax-min-ster
ax-o-lotl
ax-om-e-ter
a-za-lea
az-e-la-ic
a-ze-o-trop-ic
a-ze-ot-ro-py
Az-er-bai-ja-ni
az-ide
az-i-do-a-ce-tic
az-i-mi-no
az-i-muth-al
az-ine
az-o-im-ide
az-ole
az-o-meth-ane
a-zo-ni-um
A-zo-to-bac-ter
az-o-tom-e-ter
az-ox-y-ben-zene
Az-tec-an
az-u-lene
az-ure
az-u-rin
az-ur-ite
az-y-gous

B

ba-bas-su
bab-bitt
bab-bling
Ba-bel
bab-i-ru-sa
ba-boon
ba-bush-ka
Bab-y-lo-ni-an
bac-ca-lau-re-ate
bac-cha-na-lian
bac-chant
bac-cif-er-ous
bach-e-lor
bac-il-lar-y
ba-cil-li
ba-cil-lus
bac-i-tra-cin
ba-con
Ba-co-ni-an
bac-te-ri-a
bac-te-ri-cid-al
bac-te-ri-cid-in
bac-ter-id
bac-te-ri-o-log-i-cal
bac-te-ri-ol-o-gy
bac-te-ri-ol-y-sis
bac-te-ri-o-lyt-ic
bac-te-ri-os-co-py
bac-te-ri-um
bac-te-roi-dal
badg-er
bad-i-nage
Bae-de-ker
baf-fling
ba-gasse
bag-a-telle
ba-gel
ba-guette
Ba-ha-i
Ba-ha-ma
bail-ee
bail-er
Bai-ley
bail-iff
bail-i-wick
ba-ke-lite

bak-er-y
bak-sheesh
Ba-la-kla-va
bal-a-lai-ka
bal-anc-er
ba-la-ta
bal-brig-gan
bal-co-ny
bal-der-dash
bal-dric
Bal-e-ar-ic
ba-leen
Ba-li-nese
Bal-kan
balk-y
bal-lad-eer
bal-le-ri-na
bal-lis-tics
bal-lo-net
bal-loon-ist
bal-ma-caan
balm-i-ness
Bal-mor-al
bal-ne-al
ba-lo-ney
bal-sam
Bal-tic
Bal-ti-mor-e-an
bal-us-trade
bam-bi-no
bam-boo-zle
ba-nal (commonplace)
ban-al (governor)
ba-nal-i-ty
ba-nan-a
Ban-bury
ban-dag-er
ban-dan-na
ban-deau
band-er
ban-dit-ry
ban-do-leer
ban-dy-ing
ban-ga-lore
ban-gle
ban-ish
ban-is-ter
bank-er
bank-rupt-cy
ban-quet-er
ban-shee
ban-tam
ban-ter
bant-ling
ban-zai
bap-tis-mal
bap-tis-ter-y
bap-tiz-er
Bar-ab-bas
Bá-rá-ny
bar-a-the-a
Bar-ba-dos
bar-bar-i-an
bar-bar-ic
bar-ba-rism
bar-ba-rous
Bar-ba-ry
bar-be-cue
bar-ber
bar-bette
bar-bi-tal
bar-bi-tu-rate
bar-bi-tu-ric
bar-gain-er
bar-gain-or (law)
bar-ing
bar-ite
bar-i-tone
bar-i-to-sis
bar-i-um
bar-ken-tine
bark-er
Bark-hau-sen
Bar-kis
bark-om-e-ter
Bar-na-bas
bar-na-cle
bar-o-graph
ba-rom-e-ter
bar-o-met-ric
bar-o-met-ro-graph
bar-o-me-trog-ra-phy
ba-rom-e-try
bar-on-ess
bar-on-et
ba-ro-ni-al
ba-roque
bar-o-scope
ba-rouche
bar-ra-cu-da
bar-rage
bar-ra-try
bar-reled
bar-ren
bar-rette
bar-ri-cade
bar-ring
bar-ris-ter
bar-ter
Bart-lett
bar-y-lite
ba-ry-ta
ba-ryt-ic
bar-y-tron

ba-sal
ba-salt
ba-sal-tic
ba-sic
ba-si-cal-ly
ba-sic-i-ty
ba-sid-i-um
bas-il
ba-sil-i-ca
bas-i-lisk
ba-sin
ba-sis
Bas-ker-ville
bas-ket-ry
bas-si-net
bas-tar-dy
bas-tille
bas-ti-na-do
Ba-ta-vi-an
ba-teau
bath-o-lith-ic
ba-thom-e-ter
ba-thos
ba-thym-e-ter
bath-y-met-ric
ba-thym-e-try
bath-y-scaphe
ba-thys-mal
ba-tik
ba-tiste
ba-ton (n.)
bat-on (v.)
bau-ble
Bau-mé
baux-ite
baux-it-ic
Ba-var-i-an
bay-ard
bay-o-net
Ba-yonne
bay-ou
ba-zoo-ka
bdel-li-um
bea-con
bead-er
bea-dle
bea-gle
beak-er
bé-ar-naise
beat-er
be-a-tif-ic
be-at-i-fy
be-at-i-tude
Be-a-trice
beau-sé-ant
beau-te-ous
bea-ver
be-bee-rine
Bech-u-a-na-land
beck-on
Bec-que-rel
be-di-zen
Bed-ou-in
Be-el-ze-bub
Be-er-she-ba
Bee-tho-ven
bee-tle
beg-gar-y
be-gin-ning
beg-ohm
be-go-nia
be-hav-ior-al
be-he-moth
be-hold-en
bei-del-lite
be-lat-ed
be-lea-guered
bel-fry
Bel-gian
be-liev-er
bel-la-don-na
bel-li-cos-i-ty
bel-lig-er-ent
Be-na-res
ben-e-fac-tor
be-nef-i-cent
ben-e-fi-cial
ben-e-fi-ci-ar-y
ben-e-fi-ci-ate
ben-e-fit-ed
be-nev-o-lence
be-nign
be-nig-nant
be-ni-to-ite
Ben-ja-min
ben-ton-ite
benz-al-de-hyde
ben-zald-ox-ime
benz-am-ide
Ben-ze-drine
ben-zene-di-a-zo-ni-um
ben-ze-noid
ben-zil-ic
benz-im-id-a-zole
ben-zo-ate
ben-zo-fla-vine
ben-zo-ic
ben-zo-in
ben-zo-i-nat-ed
ben-zo-phe-none
ben-zo-sul-fi-mide
benz-ox-y-a-ce-tic

ben-zo-yl-ate
ben-zyl-ate
ben-zyl-ox-y
ber-ba-mine
ber-ber-ine
be-ret
ber-ga-mot
berg-schrund
ber-i-ber-i
Ber-ing
Berke-ley
berke-li-um
Ber-mu-da
Bern-ese
Ber-noul-li
Ber-tha
berth-ing
Ber-tram
be-ryl-li-um
ber-yl-loid
Bes-sa-ra-bi-an
Bes-se-mer
bes-tial
bes-ti-al-i-ty
be-stride
be-ta-cism
be-ta-ine
be-ta-tron
be-tel
Be-tel-geuse
Be-thes-da
be-troth-al
Beu-lah
bev-a-tron
bev-eled
bev-er-age
be-wil-der
bez-el
Bhu-ta-nese
Bi-a-fra
bi-ased
bi-be-lot
Bi-ble
Bib-li-cal
bib-li-o-graph-ic
bib-li-og-ra-phy
bib-li-o-phile
bib-u-lous
bi-car-bon-ate
bi-ceph-a-lous
bi-chlo-ride
bi-chro-mate
bick-er-ing
bi-cus-pid
bi-cy-clist
bi-cy-clo-al-kane
bi-fur-cat-ed
big-a-mous
big-ot-ry
bi-gua-nide
Bi-ki-ni
bil-i-ar-y
bil-i-cy-a-nin
bil-i-fi-ca-tion
bil-ious
bil-i-ru-bin
bil-i-ru-bi-ne-mi-a
bil-liards
bi-loc-u-lar
bi-met-al-lism
bi-na-ry
bin-au-ral
bind-er-y
bin-na-cle
bin-oc-u-lar
bi-no-mi-al
bi-og-e-ny
bi-o-graph-i-cal
bi-og-ra-phy
bi-o-log-i-cal
bi-ol-o-gist
bi-ol-y-sis
bi-om-e-ter
bi-o-met-ric
bi-om-e-try
bi-on-o-my
bi-op-sy
bi-os-co-py
bi-os-o-phy
bi-os-ter-ol
bi-ot-ic
bi-o-tin
bi-o-tite
bi-o-vu-lar
bip-a-rous
bi-par-ti-ble
bi-par-ti-ent
bi-par-tite
Bir-ming-ham
bis-cuit
bish-op-ric
bis-muth-ate
bis-muth-yl
bi-son
bit-er
bi-tu-men
bi-tu-mi-nous
bi-u-ret
bi-va-lent
biv-ouacked
bi-zarre
black-ened
blad-ed
blam-a-ble

Blan-chard
blanch-er
blan-dish
blan-ket
blar-ney
blas-phe-mous
blas-te-ma
blast-er
blas-tog-e-ny
Blas-to-my-ce-tes
blas-to-my-co-sis
blas-tu-la
bla-tant
blath-er-ing
blaz-er
bla-zon
blem-ish
blend-er
bleph-a-ral
bless-ed (adj.)
blessed (v.)
blind-er
blink-er
blis-ter
bloat-er
block-ade
blon-dine
bloom-er
bloop-er
blu-cher
bludg-eon
bluff-ing
blu-ing
blun-der-er
blus-ter
boat-swain
bob-bi-net
bo-cac-cio
bo-dhi-satt-va
bod-ice
bod-i-ly
bo-gey (golf term)
bo-gie (cart)
bo-gy (specter)
Bo-he-mi-an
boil-er
bois-ter-ous
bo-le-ro
bo-le-tus
Bo-liv-i-an
Bo-lo-gna
bo-lom-e-ter
Bol-she-vi-ki
Bol-she-vism
Bol-she-vist
bol-ster
bom-bard-ier
bom-bas-ti-cal
bom-ba-zine
bom-bi-nate
bo-na fi-de
bo-nan-za
Bo-na-parte
bond-age
Bond-er-ize
bo-ni-to
bo-nus
boo-by
boo-dler
Bool-e-an
boo-mer-ang
boor-ish
boost-er
boo-tee
boo-ty
booz-er
bo-rac-ic
bo-ra-cite
bo-rat-ed
bo-rax
Bor-deaux
bor-der
bo-re-al
Bor-ghe-se
bo-ric
bo-ride
Bor-ne-an
bor-ne-ol
born-ite
bor-nyl
bo-ron
bor-ough
Bor-zoi
bos-om
Bos-po-rus
boss-ism
Bos-to-ni-an
bo-tan-i-cal
bot-a-nist
bot-a-ny
both-er-a-tion
bo-tog-e-nin
bot-ry-oi-dal
Bot-swa-na
bot-u-lin-ic
bot-u-lism
bou-cle
bou-doir
Bou-gain-vil-le-a
bouil-la-baisse
boul-der
bou-le-vard
bound-a-ry

boun-te-ous
bou-quet
Bour-bon-ism
bour-geois
bour-geoi-sie
bou-ton-niere
bo-vine
bowd-ler-ize
bow-le
boy-sen-ber-ry
bra-ce-ro
brach-i-al
bra-chi-o-la
Brach-i-op-o-da
brach-y-ceph-a-lous
bra-chyp-ter-ous
brach-ysm
bra-chyt-ic
brac-ing
brack-et
brack-ish
brac-te-al
brag-ga-do-ci-o
Brah-man-ism
bram-ble
bran-chi-al
bran-chif-er-ous
Bran-chi-op-o-da
brand-er
bran-dish
bra-se-ro
bra-zier
braz-il (mining term)
bra-zil (wood, nut)
Bra-zil
Bra-zil-ian
breath-er
brec-ci-a
breez-i-ness
Bre-men
brems-strah-lung
brem-sung
brenn-schluss
breth-ren
Bret-on
bre-vet
bre-vi-ar-y
bre-vier
brev-i-ty
brew-er-y
Brew-ster
brib-er-y
brid-al
bri-dle
bri-dling
bri-er
bri-gade
brig-a-dier
brig-and-age
brig-an-tine
Brigh-ton
bril-liant
brin-dle
Bri-nell
bri-quet-ted
bri-sance
brisk-en
bris-ket
bris-tle
bris-tly
Brit-ain
Bri-tan-ni-a
Brit-ish
broad-cast-er
bro-cade
broc-co-li
bro-chure
broil-er
bro-ken
bro-ker-age
brom-ar-gy-rite
bro-mate
bro-me-lin
bro-mide
bro-mid-ic
bro-mi-dro-sis
bro-min-ate
bro-mi-na-tion
bro-mine
bro-mo-cre-sol
bro-mo-i-o-dide
bro-mo-met-ric
bro-mom-e-try
bron-chi-al
bron-chi-tis
bron-choph-o-ny
bron-chos-co-py
bron-co
bron-tom-e-ter
brood-er
broth-el
broth-er
brows-er
bru-cel-lo-sis
bru-cine

bruc-ite
bruis-er
bru-tal-ize
brut-ish
bu-bon-ic
buc-ca-neer
buc-ci-na-tor
Bu-chan-an
Bu-cha-rest
buck-et-ful
buck-ler
buck-ling
bu-col-ic
Bu-da-pest
Bud-dha
budg-er-i-gar
budg-et-ar-y
budg-et-eer
Bue-nos Ai-res
buf-fa-lo
buff-er
buf-fet
buff-ing
buf-foon-er-y
bu-gle
bul-ba-ceous
bul-bar
bul-bo-cap-nine
bul-bous
Bul-gar-i-an
bulg-er
bulk-er
bul-late
bull-doz-er
bul-le-tin
bul-lion
bull-ish
bul-lock
bul-ly-ing
bul-rush
bum-bling
bump-er
bump-i-ness
bump-om-e-ter
bump-tious
bun-combe
Bun-des-rat
bun-dler
bun-ga-low
bun-gee
bun-gler
bun-ion
bun-ker-age
bun-kum
bunt-ing (v.)
bun-ting (bird, flag)
buoy-ant
bur-bled
bur-den
bu-reau
bu-reauc-ra-cy
bu-reau-crat-ic
bu-ret
bur-gee
bur-geon
bur-gess
bur-gher
bur-glar-ize
bur-gla-ry
bur-go-mas-ter
Bur-gun-di-an
bur-i-al
bur-ied
bur-lesque
hur-ley
Bur-mese
burn-ers
bur-nish-er
bur-sar
bur-si-tis
Bu-run-di-an
bur-y-ing
bus-es
bush-el
bus-i-ly
busi-ness
bus-kin
bust-er
bus-tling
bu-ta-di-ene
bu-tal-de-hyde
bu-tane
bu-ta-no-ic
bu-ta-nol
butch-er
bu-te-nyl
bu-tox-yl
but-tress
bu-tyl-a-mine
bu-tyl-ene
bu-tyr-a-ceous
bu-tyr-ate
bu-tyr-ic
bu-tyr-in-ase
bu-tyr-o-lac-tone
bu-tyr-om-e-ter
bu-tyr-yl
bux-om
buzz-ard
buzz-er
Byel-o-rus-sia
By-ron-ic
bys-si-no-sis
Byz-an-tine

C

ca-bal
cab-a-la
cab-a-lis-ti-cal
ca-ban-a
ca-bane
cab-a-ret
cab-bage
ca-ber-net
cab-e-zon
cab-i-net
cab-bling
cab-o-chon
ca-boose
cab-o-tage
cab-ri-o-let
ca-bu-ya
ca-ca-o
cach-a-lot
ca-chec-tic
ca-chet
cach-in-na-tion
ca-chou
ca-cique
cack-ling
cac-o-dyl-ic
ca-cog-ra-phy
cac-o-mis-tle
ca-coph-o-ny
cad-a-lene
ca-das-tral
ca-dav-er-ous
ca-delle
ca-dence
ca-den-za
ca-det
cad-i-nene
Ca-diz
cad-mi-um
cad-re
ca-du-ca-ry
ca-du-ce-us
Cae-sar
cae-si-ous
caf-e-te-ri-a
caf-feine
Ca-ga-yan
cais-son
ca-jol-er-y
ca-la-di-um
cal-a-mine
ca-lam-i-tous
ca-lan-dri-a
ca-lash
cal-a-ver-ite
cal-car-e-ous
cal-cif-er-ol
cal-cif-er-ous
cal-ci-fi-ca-tion
cal-cim-e-ter
cal-ci-mine
cal-ci-na-tion
cal-cite
cal-ci-um
cal-cu-la-ble
cal-cu-la-tor
cal-cu-la-to-ry
cal-cu-lus
cal-dron
cal-e-fa-cient
cal-en-dar
cal-en-der
ca-len-du-lin
ca-les-cent
cal-i-ber
cal-i-brat-er
cal-i-bra-tor
ca-li-che
Cal-i-for-ni-an
cal-i-for-ni-um
ca-lig-i-nous
cal-i-per
ca-liph
cal-is-then-ics
calk-er
cal-li-graph-ic
cal-lig-ra-phy
cal-li-o-pe
cal-lous (adj.)
cal-lus (n.)
cal-lus-es
cal-o-mel
cal-o-res-cence
ca-lor-ic
cal-o-rie
ca-lor-i-fa-cient
cal-o-rif-ic
cal-o-rim-e-ter
cal-o-ri-met-ri-cal
cal-o-rize
ca-lum-ni-ate
cal-um-ny
Cal-va-ry
Cal-vin-ism
ca-ly-coid
ca-lyp-so
ca-lyp-tra
ca-lyx
ca-ma-ra-de-rie
cam-a-ril-la
ca-ma-ta
cam-ber
cam-bi-um

Cam-bo-di-an
cam-bric
cam-el-eer
ca-mel-o-pard
Cam-em-bert
cam-e-o
cam-er-a
Cam-e-roon
ca-mion
cam-i-sole
cam-o-mile
Ca-mor-ra
cam-ou-flage
cam-pa-ni-le
camp-er
cam-pha-nyl
cam-phoid
cam-pho-len-ic
cam-pho-ra-ceous
cam-phor-ene
cam-phor-ic
cam-pim-e-ter
cam-pus
Ca-naan
Can-a-da
Ca-na-di-an
ca-nai-gre
ca-naille
ca-nal-i-za-tion
ca-na-pe
ca-nard
ca-nar-y
ca-nas-ta
Ca-nav-er-al
can-celed
can-cel-ing
can-cel-la-tion
can-cer-ous
can-croid
can-de-la
can-de-la-brum
can-de-li-lla
can-did
can-di-date
can-died
can-dling
can-dor
ca-nes-cent
ca-nic-o-la
ca-nine
can-is-ter
can-ker
can-na-bi-nol
can-na-bis
can-ner-y
can-ni-bal-ize
can-non-ade
can-nu-lar
ca-noe-ist
can-on
ca-ñon (Spanish form for canyon)
can-on-ess
ca-non-i-cal
can-on-i-za-tion
Ca-no-pus
can-o-py
can-ta-bi-le
can-ta-loup
can-tan-ker-ous
can-ta-ta
can-ter (v.)
cant-er (n.)
can-thar-i-des
can-tha-ris
can-thus
can-ti-cle
can-ti-le-ver
can-ton-ment
Ca-nuck
can-vassed
can-vass-er
caou-tchouc
ca-pa-ble
ca-pa-cious
ca-pac-i-tance
ca-pac-i-tor
ca-par-i-son
cap-e-lin
ca-per
ca-pi-as
cap-il-la-ros-co-py
cap-il-lar-y
cap-i-tal-ist
cap-i-tal-i-za-tion
ca-pi-tan
ca-pit-u-la-tor
cap-no-di-um
ca-pon-ette
ca-pote
cap-ric
ca-pric-cio
ca-price
ca-pri-cious
Cap-ri-cor-nis
cap-ro-ate
ca-pro-ic
cap-ry-late
cap-ryl-ic
cap-ry-lyl
cap-sa-i-cin
cap-si-cum
cap-stan

cap-su-lar
cap-ti-va-tor
cap-u-chin
cap-y-bar-a
car-a-bi-neer
Ca-ra-cas
car-a-cul
ca-rafe
car-a-mel
car-a-pace
car-at
car-a-van-sa-ry
car-a-way
carb-ac-i-dom-e-ter
carb-alk-ox-yl
car-ba-mate
car-bam-ic
car-bam-ide
carb-am-i-do-hy-dan-to-in
car-ba-mine
carb-am-i-no
car-bam-o-yl
car-ba-nil-ic
car-ba-nil-ide
car-bar-sone
car-baz-ic
car-ba-zole
car-beth-ox-yl
car-bine
car-bi-nol
car-bo-cy-a-nine
car-bo-cy-clic
car-bo-di-i-mide
car-bol-ic
car-bo-lize
Car-bo-loy
car-bo-na-ceous
car-bon-ate
car-bon-ic
car-bon-if-er-ous
car-bo-ni-um
car-bon-ize
car-bon-yl
car-bon-y-late
Car-bo-run-dum
car-box-yl-ase
car-box-yl-ic
car-bun-cle
car-bu-rant
car-bu-ret-ed
car-bu-ret-or
car-bu-riz-er
car-byl-a-mine
car-cass
car-cin-o-gen
car-ci-no-gen-ic
car-ci-noid
car-ci-no-ma
car-ci-no-ma-to-sis
car-ci-no-ma-tous
car-ci-no-sis
car-da-mom
car-di-ac
Car-di-a-zol
car-di-nal
card-ing
car-di-o-gen-ic
car-di-og-ra-phy
Car-di-oid
car-di-ol-o-gy
car-di-om-e-ter
car-di-ot-o-my
car-di-tis
ca-reen
ca-reer
ca-ress-ive
car-et
Car-ib-be-an
car-i-bou
car-i-ca-tur-al
car-ies
car-il-lon-neur
ca-ri-na
car-i-nate
car-i-ous
Car-list
Car-mel-ite
car-min-a-tive
car-min-ic
car-nage
car-nal-i-ty
car-nau-ba
Car-ne-gie
car-ne-lian
car-ni-tine
car-ni-val
car-niv-o-rous
car-no-tite
car-oled
Car-o-lin-i-an
car-om
car-o-tene
ca-rot-e-noid
ca-rot-id
ca-rous-al
Car-pa-thi-an
car-pel
car-pen-try
carp-er
car-pho-lite
car-pho-sid-er-ite
car-po-go-ni-um
car-riage

car-ri-on
car-ron-ade
car-rou-sel
cart-age
car-tel-ize
car-ti-lag-i-nous
car-tog-ra-phy
car-ton
car-toon-ist
car-touche
car-tridge
car-un-cle
car-vene
carv-er
Car-ver
car-y-at-id
car-y-op-sis
ca-sa-ba
Ca-sa-blan-ca
cas-car-a
ca-sein-ate
ca-se-ous
cash-ew
cash-ier
cas-ing
ca-si-no
cas-ket
cas-se-role
cas-si-mere
Cas-si-o-pe-ian
cas-sit-er-ite
cas-ta-net
cas-tel-late
cast-er
cas-ti-ga-tor
cas-tile
Cas-til-ian
cas-tle
cas-tor-ite
cas-tra-tive
cas-u-al-ty
cas-u-ist-ry
ca-sus bel-li
cat-a-bol-ic
ca-tab-o-lism
cat-a-clys-mic
cat-a-di-op-tric
cat-a-falque
cat-a-lase
cat-a-lec-tic
cat-a-lep-tic
cat-a-loged
cat-a-log-ing
cat-a-ly-sis
cat-a-lyst
cat-a-lyt-i-cal-ly
cat-a-lyz-er
cat-a-ma-ran
cat-a-me-ni-al
cat-a-pult
cat-a-ract
ca-tarrh-al
ca-tas-tro-phe
cat-a-stroph-ic
Ca-taw-ba
cat-e-che-sis
cat-e-chet-i-cal
cat-e-chism
cat-e-chu-men-al
cat-e-chol
ca-te-na
cat-e-gor-i-cal
cat-e-go-rize
cat-e-nar-y
cat-e-noid
ca-ter-er
cat-er-pil-lar
cat-er-waul
ca-thar-sis
ca-thar-tic
Ca-thar-ti-dae
ca-thec-tic
ca-the-dral
ca-thep-sin
cath-e-ter-i-za-tion
cath-e-tom-e-ter
cath-ode
ca-thod-ic
cath-o-lic-i-ty
ca-thol-i-cism
cat-i-on-ic
Cau-ca-sian
cau-cus
cau-dal
cau-di-llo
cau-li-flow-er
caus-al
cau-sal-i-ty
cau-sa-tion
caus-a-tive
cause ce-le-bre
cau-se-rie
caus-tic-i-ty
cau-ter-i-za-tion
cav-al-cade
cav-a-lier
cav-al-ry
cav-a-ti-na
ca-ve-at
cav-ern-ous
cav-i-ar
cav-iled
cav-il-er
cav-i-ta-tion

Ca-vi-te
cav-i-ty
ca-vort
cay-enne
Ca-yu-ga
Cay-use
ce-cum
ce-dar
ce-drat
ce-drol
ce-du-la
ceil-om-e-ter
Cel-an-ese
Cel-e-bes
cel-e-brate
ce-leb-ri-ty
ce-ler-i-ty
cel-er-y
ce-les-tial
cel-es-tite
cc-li-ac
cel-i-ba-cy
ce-li-ot-o-my
ce-lite
cel-lif-er-ous
cel-lo-phane
cel-lu-lar
cel-lu-loid
cel-lu-lose
cel-lu-los-ic
Cel-si-us
Celt-ic
cel-ti-um
ce-men-ta-tion
ce-ment-er
ce-ment-ite
ce-men-ti-tious
cem-e-ter-y
ce-no-bi-an
cen-o-bite
Ce-no-zo-ic
cen-so-ri-ous
Cen-tau-rus
cen-ta-vo
cen-te-nar-i-an
cen-te-nar-y
cen-ten-ni-al
cen-tes-i-mal
cen-te-si-mo
cent-ge-ner
cen-ti-me-ter
cen-ti-pede
cen-tral-ize
cen-trif-u-gal
cen-tri-fuge
cen-tri-pe-tal
cen-troi-dal
cen-tu-ry
ce-phal-ic
ceph-a-lin
ceph-a-lo-di-um
ceph-a-lom-e-ter
ceph-a-lom-e-try
Ceph-e-id
ce-ram-ic
ce-ram-ist
ce-ram-i-um
ce-ra-ti-um
cer-a-to-sau-rus
Cer-ber-us
ce-re-al
cer-e-bel-lo-ru-bral
cer-e-bel-lum
cer-e-bral
cer-e-brate
cer-e-bro-side
cer-e-bro-spi-nal
cer-e-brum
cere-ment
cer-e-mo-ni-al
Ce-ren-kov
Ce-res
cer-e-sin
ce-rise
ce-ri-um
ce-ro-graph
ce-rog-ra-phy
ce-roid
ce-ro-lite
ce-rot-ic
cer-tain-ly
cer-tif-i-cate
cer-ti-fi-ca-tion
cer-ti-o-ra-ri
cer-ti-tude
ce-ru-le-an
ce-ru-men
ce-russ-ite
cer-van-tite
cer-vi-cal
ce-sar-e-an
ce-si-um
ces-sa-tion
Ce-ta-ce-a
ce-tane
ce-tene
ce-tyl
Cha-blis
Chad-i-an
chaf-er
chaff-er (one who chaffs or banters)
chaf-fer (trade term—

buying and selling)
Cha-gres
cha-grin
chair-maned
chaise longue
chal-ced-o-ny
chal-ce-don-yx
chal-co-py-rite
chal-dron
cha-let
chal-ice
chal-i-co-sis
cha-lyb-e-ate
cham-ber-lain
cham-bray
cha-me-le-on
cham-fer
cham-ois
cham-pi-gnon
cham-pi-on
chan-cel-ler-y
chan-cel-lor
chan-cer-y
chan-cre
chan-croi-dal
chan-de-lier
chan-delle
chan-dler
change-a-ble
chang-er
chan-neled
chan-teur
chan-ti-cleer
cha-ot-ic
chap-ar-ral
cha-peau
chap-el
chap-er-on
chap-lain
char-a-banc
char-ac-ter-is-tic
cha-rade
charge-a-ble
char-gé d'af-faires
charg-er
char-i-ly
char-i-ness
char-i-ot-eer
cha-ris-ma
char-is-mat-ic
char-i-ta-ble
cha-ri-va-ri
Char-ley
Char-lotte
charm-er
char-nel
char-ter
char-treuse
Cha-ryb-dis
chas-er
chas-sis
chas-ten
chas-tis-er
chas-ti-ty
cha-teau
cha-te-laine
Chat-ham
cha-toy-an-cy
Chau-ce-ri-an
chau-tau-qua
chau-vin-ism
check-ered
chedd-ite
Che-ha-lis
chei-li-tis
Che-ka
che-la-tion
chel-i-do-ni-um
che-li-form
che-lo-ne
Chel-ten-ham
chem-i-at-ric
chem-i-cal
che-mig-ra-phy
che-mise
chem-i-sette
chem-is-try
chem-o-sphere
chem-o-ther-a-py
chem-mot-ro-pism
che-mur-gic
chem-ur-gy
che-nille
Che-no-po-di-um
cher-ish
cher-no-zem
Cher-o-kee
che-root
cher-ub
che-ru-bic
cher-u-bim
Chesb-ire
Ches-ter
chev-a-lier
chev-i-ot
chev-ron
Chey-enne
chi-a-ro-scu-ro
chi-ca-ner-y
chick-en
chi-cle
chic-o-ry
chif-fon

chif-fo-nier
chi-gnon
chil-dren
Chil-e-an
chi-me-ra
chi-mer-i-cal
chim-pan-zee
Chi-nese
chi-noi-se-rie
Chi-nook
chin-qua-pin
Chi-ri-qui
chi-ro-graph
chi-rog-ra-pher
chi-ro-man-cy
chi-rop-o-dy
chi-ro-prac-tor
chi-rur-gi-cal
chis-eled
chis-el-ing
chi-tin-oid
chiv-al-rous
chlo-ral
chlor-al-um
chlor-a-lu-mi-nite
chlor-am-ide
chlor-am-ine
chlor-am-phen-i-col
chlo-rate
chlor-az-ide
chlor-co-sane
Chlo-rel-la
chlor-e-mi-a
chlor-en-chy-ma
Chlo-re-tone
chlo-ric
chlo-ride
chlo-ri-dize
chlor-im-ide
chlo-ri-nate (v.)
chlo-rin-ate (n.)
chlo-rine
chlo-rit-ic
chlo-ro-form
chlo-ro-gen-ic
chlo-rom-e-ter
chlo-rom-e-try
Chlo-ro-my-ce-tin
chlo-ro-phyll
chlo-ro-prene
chlo-ro-sis
chlo-ro-then
chlo-rous
choc-o-late
choic-est
chok-er
cho-lan-ic
chol-an-threne
cho-le-ate
cho-le-cal-cif-er-ol
cho-le-cys-tec-to-my
cho-le-cys-ti-tis
cho-le-cys-tog-ra-phy
cho-le-cys-to-ki-nin
cho-le-cys-tos-to-my
cho-le-ic
cho-le-mi-a
chol-er
chol-er-a
cho-le-ret-ic
chol-er-ic
cho-les-tane
cho-les-ta-nol
cho-les-ter-ic
cho-les-ter-ol
cho-lic
cho-lin-er-gic
cho-lin-es-ter-ase
chol-o-ge-net-ic
cho-los-co-py
chon-dri-o-som-al
chon-dri-o-some
chon-drit-ic
chon-dro-dite
chon-dro-dit-ic
chon-dro-ma
chon-drom-a-tous
chon-drot-o-my
chon-drule
cho-ral
cho-rale
chord-al
chor-date
chor-di-tis
chor-dot-o-my
cho-re-a
cho-re-og-ra-pher
cho-ri-o-men-in-gi-tis
cho-ri-sis
cho-ris-ter
cho-roi-dal
cho-roid-i-tis
cho-rol-o-gy
chor-tle
cho-rus
cho-sen
chow-der
chres-tom-a-thy
chris-ten
Chris-tian
Chris-ti-an-i-ty
chro-ma-mom-e-ter
chro-mate
chro-mat-ic

chro-ma-tic-i-ty
chro-ma-tin
chro-mat-o-gram
chro-ma-tog-ra-phy
chro-ma-tol-y-sis
chro-mat-o-lyt-ic
chro-mat-o-scope
chro-ma-to-sis
chro-mic
chro-mif-er-ous
chro-mi-nance
chro-mite
chro-mi-um
chro-mo-gen-ic
chro-mo-i-so-mer-ic
chro-mom-e-ter
chro-mos-co-py
chro-mo-som-al
chro-mo-trop-ic
chro-mous
chron-i-cler
chron-o-graph
chro-nog-ra-pher
chron-o-log-i-cal-ly
chro-nol-o-gy
chro-nom-e-ter
chron-o-met-ri-cal
chron-o-scope
chro-nos-co-py
chrys-a-lis
chrys-a-loid
chrys-an-the-mum
chrys-a-ro-bin
chry-sene
chrys-o-er-i-ol
chrys-o-graph
chry-sog-ra-phy
chry-so-i-dine
chrys-o-lite
chrys-o-phyll
chuck-ling
Church-ill
churl-ish
chut-ist
chy-la-ceous
chy-lo-sis
chy-mi-fy
chy-mo-tryp-sin
ci-ca-da
cic-a-tri-sive
cic-a-trix
cic-a-trize
cic-e-ro-ne (n.)
cic-e-rone (v.)
ci-der
ci-gar
cig-a-rette
cil-i-ar-y
cil-i-um
ci-mi-cid
cim-o-lite
cin-cho-loi-pon
cin-cho-me-ron-ic
cin-cho-na
cin-chon-a-mine
cin-cho-nine
cin-cho-phen
cinc-ture
Cin-der-el-la
cin-e-ma
cin-e-mat-o-graph
cin-e-ma-tog-ra-pher
cin-e-ole
cin-e-rar-i-a
ci-ne-re-ous
cin-na-bar
cin-nam-ic
cin-nam-o-yl
ci-pher
ci-pho-ny
cir-ci-nate
cir-clet
cir-cling
circ-o-var-i-an
cir-cuit-al
cir-cuit-ed
cir-cu-i-tous
cir-cuit-ry
cir-cu-lar-ize
cir-cu-la-to-ry
cir-cum-e-ter
cir-cum-fer-en-tial
cir-cum-lo-cu-tion
cir-cum-loc-u-to-ry
cir-cum-scrib-a-ble
cir-cum-stan-tial
cir-rho-sis
cis-tern
cit-a-ble
ci-ta-to-ry
cit-i-fy
cit-i-zen
cit-ral
cit-rate
cit-ric
cit-ri-nin
cit-ron
cit-ron-el-la
cit-rus
civ-et
civ-il

ci-vil-ian
civ-i-li-za-tion
claim-ant
clam-or-ous
clan-des-tine
clang-or
cla-queur
Clar-ence
clar-et
clar-i-fi-ca-tion
clar-i-net
clar-i-on
clas-si-cal
clas-si-fy
clas-tic
claus-tro-pho-bi-a
clav-a-cin
clav-i-cle
cla-vic-u-lar
cleans-er
cleans-ing
clear-ance
cleav-age
Clem-a-tis
clem-en-cy
Clem-en-tine
Cle-o-pa-tra
cler-gy-man
cler-i-cal
clev-er
clev-is
cli-an-thus
click-er
cli-ent-age
cli-en-tele
cli-mac-ter-ic
cli-mac-tic
cli-mat-ic
cli-ma-tize
cli-ma-to-log-i-cal
cli-ma-tol-o-gy
cli-ma-tom-e-ter
cli-max
climb-er
clin-i-cal
cli-ni-cian
clin-i-co-path-o-log-ic
clin-i-co-pa-thol-o-gy
clink-er
cli-no-he-dral
cli-nom-e-ter
cli-quish
clit-o-ris
cloi-son-ne
clois-ter
Clo-rox
Clos-trid-i-um
clo-sure
cloth-ier
clo-ture
clo-ven
clo-ver
clown-ish
clum-si-ness
clus-ter
cne-mi-al
co-ad-ju-tor
co-ag-u-la-tor
co-ag-u-lom-e-ter
co-a-les-cence
co-a-lite (v.)
Coal-ite (n.)
co-a-li-tion
co-arc-ta-tion
coast-al
coast-er
co-bal-a-min
co-bal-tic
co-balt-if-er-ous
co-bal-ti-ni-trite
co-bal-to-cal-cite
co-bal-tom-e-nite
co-bal-tous
cob-bler
co-bra
co-caine
coc-cid-i-oi-dal
coc-cid-i-oi-din
coc-cid-i-o-sis
coc-cin-ic
coc-ci-nite
coc-cyg-e-al
co-chin
coch-i-neal
coch-le-ar
cock-ade
cock-er-el
cock-le-bur
co-coa
co-co-nut
co-coon
co-deine
codg-er
cod-i-cil
cod-i-fy
co-di-mer
cod-ling
co-erc-i-ble
co-er-cive
co-e-val
co-gen-cy
cog-i-ta-tive
co-gnac
cog-na-tus

cog-ni-tive
cog-ni-za-ble
cog-no-men
co-gno-scen-ti
cog-nos-ci-ble
co-her-ence
co-he-si-ble
co-he-sive
co-in-ci-den-tal
col-an-der
col-chi-cine
Col-chi-cum
co-lec-ti-vo
col-ec-to-my
Co-le-op-te-ra
col-ick-y
col-i-se-um
co-li-tis
col-lab-o-ra-tor
col-la-gen-ase
col-lag-e-nous
col-laps-i-ble
col-lat-er-al
col-la-tor
col-league
col-lect-a-ble
col-lec-ta-ne-a
col-lec-tive
col-lec-tor
col-le-gi-ate
col-lier
col-li-ma-tor
col-li-sion
col-lo-di-on
col-loi-dal
col-lo-qui-al-ism
col-lo-quy
col-lu-sive
col-lu-vi-um
co-logne
Co-lom-bi-an
co-lo-met-ric
co-lom-e-try
co-lon
colo-nel
co-lo-ni-al
co-lon-ic
col-o-nize
col-on-nade
col-o-ny
col-o-phon
col-o-pho-ny
col-or
Col-o-rad-an
Col-o-ra-do
col-or-a-tu-ra
col-or-im-e-ter
col-or-i-met-ric
col-or-im-e-try
co-los-sal
Col-os-se-um
co-los-sus
co-los-to-my
co-los-trum
col-por-teur
Co-lum-bi-a
col-um-bif-er-ous
col-um-bine
co-lum-bite
co-lum-bi-um
col-umn
co-lum-nar
col-um-nist
co-lure
Co-man-che
co-ma-tose
co-mat-u-la
com-bat-ant
com-bat-ed
com-bat-ing
com-bat-ive-ness
com-ba-tiv-i-ty
comb-er
com-bin-a-ble
com-bi-na-tive
com-bu-rim-e-ter
com-bus-ti-ble
com-bus-tor
co-me-di-an
com-e-dy
co-mes-ti-ble
com-e-tar-y
co-met-ic
com-fort-a-ble
com-fort-er
com-i-cal
Com-in-form
com-ing
co-mique
com-i-ty
com-man-dant
com-man-deer
com-mand-er
com-man-do
com-mem-o-ra-tor
com-mend-a-ble
com-men-da-tion
com-mend-a-to-ry
com-men-su-ra-ble
com-men-tar-y
com-men-ta-tor
com-mer-cial
com-mi-na-to-ry
com-min-gle

com-mi-nute
com-mis-er-ate
com-mis-sar-i-at
com-mis-sar-y
com-mis-sion
com-mis-sur-al
com-mis-sur-ot-o-my
com-mit-ta-ble
com-mit-tee
com-mo-di-ous
com-mod-i-ty
com-mon-er
com-mon-sen-si-ble
com-mo-rant
com-mu-nal
com-mu-ni-ca-tive
com-mu-ni-ca-tor
com-mun-ion
com-mu-ni-que
com-mu-nism
Com-mu-nist
com-mu-nis-tic
com-mu-ni-ty
com-mut-a-ble
com-mu-ta-tion
com-mu-ta-tor
com-mut-er
com-pact-er
com-pact-i-ble
com-pac-tor
com-pan-ion
com-pa-ny
com-pa-ra-ble
com-par-a-tive
com-par-a-tor
com-par-i-son
com-par-o-scope
com-part-men-tal-ize
com-pat-i-ble
com-pel-ling
com-pen-di-um
com-pen-sa-ble
com-pen-sat-ing
com-pen-sa-to-ry
com-pe-tent
com-pe-ti-tion
com-pet-i-tor
com-pi-la-tion
com-pil-er
com-pla-cent
com-plain-ant
com-plai-sance
com-ple-men-tal
com-ple-men-ta-ry
com-ple-tive
com-plex-ion
com-pli-cate
com-plic-i-ty
com-pli-men-ta-ry
com-po-nent
com-pos-er
com-pos-ite
com-po-si-tion
com-pos-i-tor
com-po-sure
com-pound-er
com-pre-hend-i-ble
com-pre-hen-si-ble
com-press-i-ble
com-press-ing
com-pres-sive
com-pres-som-e-ter
com-pres-sor
com-pris-al
com-pro-mise
Comp-tom-e-ter
comp-trol-ler
com-pul-so-ry
com-put-er
com-put-ist
co-nal
co-na-tion
con-cat-e-na-tion
con-cav-er
con-ceiv-a-ble
con-cen-tra-tor
con-cen-tri-cal
con-cen-tric-i-ty
con-cep-tu-al
con-cer-ti-na
con-cert-ize
con-ces-sion-aire
con-chi-form
con-choi-dal
con-cho-log-i-cal
con-chol-o-gy
con-chyl-i-um
con-cil-i-a-to-ry
con-clu-sive
con-coct-er
con-com-i-tant
con-cord-ance
con-cord-ant
con-cres-cence
con-cret-er
con-cu-bi-nage
con-cu-pis-cence
con-cu-pis-ci-ble
con-dem-na-to-ry
con-den-sa-ble
con-den-sa-tion
con-dens-er
con-dens-ing
con-de-scen-sion

con-di-ment
con-do-lence
con-do-min-i-um
con-don-ance
con-du-ci-ble
con-duct-ance
con-duct-ed
con-duct-i-ble
con-duc-tiv-i-ty
con-duc-tom-e-ter
con-duc-tor
con-duit
con-du-ran-gin
con-dy-loid
con-el-rad
Con-es-to-ga
con-fec-tion-er-y
con-fed-er-a-tion
con-fes-sor
con-fi-dant (n.)
con-fi-dent (adj.)
con-fig-u-ra-tion
con-fin-er
con-firm-a-ble
con-fir-ma-tion
con-firm-a-to-ry
con-firm-er
con-fis-ca-to-ry
con-fla-gra-tion
con-flic-tive
con-flux-i-ble
con-form-a-ble
con-for-ma-tion
con-form-i-ty
Con-fu-cian-ism
con-fus-a-ble
con-fut-a-ble
con-fu-ta-tion
con-ge-la-tive
con-gel-i-fract
con-ge-ner
con-ge-nial
con-ge-ni-al-i-ty
con-gen-i-tal
con-ge-ries
con-gest-i-ble
con-glom-er-at-ic
Con-go-lese
con-grat-u-la-to-ry
con-gre-ga-tor
con-gres-sion-al
con-gru-i-ty
con-i-cal
co-nic-e-ine
co-nid-i-um
con-i-fer
con-nif-er-ous
Co-ni-oph-o-ra
co-ni-um
con-jec-tur-al
con-ju-gal
con-ju-gate
con-junc-ti-vi-tis
con-ju-ra-tion
con-jur-er
con-nect-a-ble
con-nect-er
Con-nect-i-cut-er
con-nec-tive
con-niv-ance
con-nois-seur
con-nu-bi-al
co-noi-dal
co-no-phor
con-quer-or
con-quin-a-mine
con-san-guin-e-ous
con-sci-en-tious
con-scion-a-ble
con-scious
con-se-cra-tor
con-sec-u-tive
con-se-nes-cence
con-sen-sus
con-se-quen-tial
con-ser-va-tion
con-serv-a-tive
con-ser-va-tor
con-serv-a-to-ry
con-sid-er-ate
con-sig-na-tion
con-sign-ee
con-sign-or
con-sist-ent
con-sis-to-ry
con-so-la-tion
con-sol-i-date
con-som-me
con-so-nant
con-sor-ti-um
con-spi-cu-i-ty
con-spic-u-ous
con-spir-a-cy
con-spi-ra-tion
con-sta-ble
con-stab-u-lar-y
con-stan-cy
con-stant-an
con-ster-na-tion
con-sti-pa-tion
con-stit-u-ent
con-sti-tu-tive
con-stric-tor

con-struc-tor
con-sul-ar
con-sul-ate
con-sult-ant
con-sul-ta-tion
con-sult-a-tive
con-sult-er
con-sum-er
con-sum-mate
con-sum-ma-to-ry
con-sump-ti-ble
con-tac-tor
con-ta-gious
con-tam-i-na-tor
con-tem-pla-tor
con-tem-po-ra-ne-ous
con-tempt-i-ble
con-temp-tu-ous
con-tend-er
con-ten-tious
con-test-ant
con-tes-ta-tion
con-tex-tur-al
con-ti-gu-i-ty
con-tig-u-ous
con-ti-nence
con-ti-nen-tal
con-tin-gen-cy
con-ti-nu-i-ty
con-tin-u-ous
con-tin-u-um
con-tor-tive
con-tra-band
con-tract-a-ble
con-tract-ile
con-trac-tor
con-tra-dict-er
con-tra-dic-tor
con-tra-dic-to-ry
con-trail
con-tra-ri-e-ty
con-trar-i-wise
con-tras-tive
con-trib-ut-ing
con-tri-bu-tion
con-trib-u-tor
con-triv-ance
con-triv-er
con-trol-la-ble
con-tro-ver-sy
con-tro-vert-i-ble
con-tu-ma-cious
con-tu-me-li-ous
con-tu-me-ly
con-tu-sion
co-nun-drum
co-nus
con-va-les-cence
con-vec-tor
con-ven-ience
con-ven-ien-cy
con-ver-gent
con-verg-ing
con-vers-a-ble
con-ver-sant
con-ver-sive
con-vert-er
con-vert-i-ble
con-vey-or
con-vic-tive
con-vin-ci-ble
con-vinc-ing
con-viv-i-al
con-vo-lute
con-vul-sive
con-y-rine
cool-ant
cool-er
Coo-lidge
coo-lie
coop-er-age
co-op-er-a-tive
co-or-di-na-tor
coot-ie
co-pai-ba
co-pal-ite
Co-pen-ha-gen
Co-per-ni-cus
cop-ies
co-pi-ous
co-pla-nar
co-pol-y-mer
co-po-lym-er-ize
co-pra
cop-ro-por-phy-rin
cop-ro-stane
co-pros-ta-nol
co-pros-ter-ol
cop-u-la-tive
co-quet-ry
co-quet-tish
co-qui-na
cor-al
Cor-a-mine
cord-age
cor-date
cor-dial
cor-dial-i-ty
cor-dil-le-ra
cord-ite
Cor-do-ba
cor-don
cor-do-van
cor-du-roy

cor-dyl-ite
co-re-op-sis
co-re-spond-ent
co-ri-a-ceous
co-ri-an-der
Cor-i-ci-din
Cor-inth
Co-rin-thi-an
cor-i-o-lis
cor-mo-rant
cor-mus
cor-ne-al
cor-nered
cor-net-ist
cor-nice
cor-nif-ic
Cor-nish
cor-nu-co-pi-a
co-rol-la
cor-ol-lar-y
co-ro-na
cor-o-nal
cor-o-nar-y
cor-o-na-tion
cor-o-nene
cor-o-ner
cor-o-net
co-ro-ni-um
cor-po-ral
cor-po-ra-tive
cor-po-re-al
cor-pu-lent
cor-pus-cle
cor-pus-cu-lar
cor-rect-a-ble
cor-rect-ant
cor-rec-tive
cor-rec-tor
cor-re-late
cor-rel-a-tive
cor-re-spond-ence
cor-ri-dor
cor-ri-gen-dum
cor-ri-gi-ble
cor-rob-o-ra-to-ry
cor-rod-i-ble
cor-ro-si-ble
cor-ro-sive
cor-ru-ga-tor
cor-rupt-i-ble
cor-rup-tive
cor-sage
corse-let
cor-tege
cor-ti-cate
cor-ti-cip-e-tal
cor-ti-ci-um
cor-ti-co-ad-re-nal-o-trop-ic
cor-ti-cos-ter-one
cor-ti-sone
co-run-dum
co-rus-cant
cor-us-ca-tion
cor-vus-ite
co-ryd-a-line
cor-ym-bose
cor-y-phee
co-ry-za
co-sa-lite
co-se-cant
co-sine
cos-me-col-o-gy
cos-met-i-cal
cos-me-ti-cian
cos-me-tol-o-gy
cos-mi-cal-i-ty
cos-mism
cos-mo-gon-ic
cos-mog-o-ny
cos-mog-ra-pher
cos-mo-graph-ic
Cos-mo-line
cos-mol-o-gy
cos-mo-naut
cos-mo-pol-i-tan
cos-mop-o-lite
cos-mo-ra-ma
cos-mo-ram-ic
cos-mos-o-phy
cos-mo-tron
Cos-ta Ri-can
cos-tive
cos-tum-er
co-tar-gine
co-te-rie
co-ter-mi-nous
co-til-lion
co-to-ne-as-ter
cot-tag-er
cot-y-le-don
couch-ant
cou-lomb
cou-lom-e-ter
cou-ma-rin
cou-ma-rone
coun-cil-or
coun-seled
coun-sel-or
coun-te-nance
count-er (who counts)
coun-ter (other mean-ings)

coun-ter-feit
count-ess
coun-try
coun-ty
cou-pler
cou-plet
cou-pling
cou-pon
cour-age
cou-ra-geous
cou-rant
cou-ri-er
cours-er
cour-te-ous
cour-te-san
cour-te-sy
cour-tier
cous-in
cou-tu-ri-er
cou-vert
cov-e-nant-er
cov-e-nan-tor (law)
Cov-en-try
cov-er-age
cov-ert-ly
cov-et-ous
cov-ey
cox-i-tis
Cox-sack-ie
cow-ard-ice
cowl-ing
coy-ote
coz-en
co-zi-ness
crack-ers
crack-ling
cra-dling
cra-nid-i-um
cra-ni-ec-to-my
cra-ni-o-graph
cra-ni-og-ra-pher
cra-ni-ol-o-gy
cra-ni-om-e-ter
cra-ni-os-co-py
cra-ni-um
cra-ter-i-form
cra-tic-u-lar
cra-vat
Cra-ven-ette
crawl-er
cray-on
cra-zy
cream-er-y
creas-er
cre-at-ic
cre-a-tine
cre-at-i-nine
cre-a-tiv-i-ty
crea-ture
cre-den-tial
cre-den-za
cred-i-ble
cred-it-a-ble
cred-i-tor
cre-do
cre-du-li-ty
cred-u-lous
creed-ite
creep-er
cre-ma-to-ry
Cre-mo-na
cre-nate
cren-a-ture
cren-eled
cren-el-lat-ed
cre-nit-ic
cren-u-lat-ed
cre-oph-a-gous
cre-o-sol
cre-o-sote
crep-i-tant
cre-pus-cu-lar
cres-cen-do
cres-cen-tic
cre-sol
cre-sor-ci-nol
cre-sot-ic
cres-o-tine
cres-yl-ate
cre-syl-ic
cre-ta-ceous
cre-tin-ism
cre-tonne
cre-vasse
crev-ice
cre-vic-u-lar
crib-el-late
cri-bel-lum
cri-ce-tus
crick-et-er
cri-coid
Cri-me-an
crim-i-nal-i-ty
crim-i-no-log-ic
crim-i-nol-o-gy
crim-i-not-ic
cring-er
crin-kle
cri-noi-dal
crin-o-line
cri-nos-i-ty
crip-pling
cris-pate

crisp-er
cris-tate
cri-te-ri-a
crit-i-cal
crit-i-cism
cri-tique
croak-er
cro-ce-tin
cro-cheted
cro-chet-ing
cro-cid-o-lite
croc-o-dile
croc-o-ite
cro-con-ic
cro-ny-ism
cro-qui-gnole
cro-ta-lar-i-o-sis
crotch-et-y
cro-ton-ate
cro-ton-o-yl
crou-pi-er
croup-ous
crou-ton
cru-cial
cru-ci-ble
cru-ci-fix
cru-ci-form
cru-di-ty
cruis-er
crul-ler
crum-bling
crum-ple
cru-ral
cru-sad-er
crus-ta-ceous
crust-al
crus-tose
cry-o-gen-ics
cry-om-e-ter
cry-o-phil-ic
cry-o-sco-py
crypt-a-nal-y-sis
cryp-ta-rithm
cryp-ti-cal
cryp-to-gram-mic
cryp-tog-ra-pher
cryp-to-graph-ic
cryp-tom-e-ter
crys-taled
crys-tal-lin-i-ty
crys-tal-lite
crys-tal-li-za-tion
crys-tal-liz-er
crys-tal-log-ra-phy
crys-tal-loi-dal
cten-o-phore
cte-tol-o-gy
cu-bi-cal
cu-bic-u-lum
cub-ism
cub-ist
cu-bi-tal
cu-bi-tus
cu-boi-dal
cuck-old
cuck-oo
cudg-eled
cui-rass
cui-sine
cul-i-nar-y
cull-ing
cul-mi-na-tion
cu-lotte
cul-pa-ble
cul-prit
cult-ism
cul-ti-va-tor
cul-tur-al
cu-mal-de-hyde
cum-ber-some
cum-brous
cu-mene
cu-me-nyl
cu-mic
cu-mi-dine
cum-in
cu-min-o-in
cu-mi-nol
cu-mi-nyl
cu-mo-yl
cu-mu-la-tive
cu-mu-lene
cu-mu-lo-nim-bus
cu-mu-lus
cu-ne-ate
cu-ne-i-form
cu-no-ni-a-ceous
cu-pid-i-ty
cu-po-la
cu-pram-mo-ni-um
cu-pre-ine
cu-pre-ous
cu-pric
cu-prif-er-ous
cu-prite
cu-pro-cy-a-nide
cu-proid
cu-pro-ri-va-ite
cu-prous
cur-a-ble
Cu-ra-çao
cu-ra-re
cu-rate

cu-ra-tive
cu-ra-tor
cur-cu-min
cur-dle
cu-rette
cur-few
cu-rie
cu-rine
cu-ri-os-i-ty
cu-ri-o-so
cu-ri-ous
cu-rite
cu-ri-um
curl-i-cue
curl-i-ness
cur-mudg eon
cur-ric-u-lums
cur-sive
cur-so-ry
cur-tain
cur-te-sy
cur-va-ceous
cur-va-ture
cur-vet-ted
cur-vi-lin-e-ar
cur-vom-e-ter
cush-ioned
cus-pa-rine
cus-pi-dal
cus-pi-dor
cuss-ed-ness
cus-tard
cus-to-di-an
cus-tom-ar-i-ly
cus-tom-ar-y
cus-tom-er
cu-ta-ne-ous
cu-ti-cle
cu-tic-u-lar
cy-an-a-mide
cy-a-nate
cy-an-e-ous
cy-an-ic
cy-a-ni-da-tion
cy-a-nide
cy-an-i-din
cy-a-nite
cy-an-o-gen
cy-a-no-ge-net-ic
cy-a-no-gua-ni-dine
cy-a-no-hy-drin
cy-a-nom-e-ter
cy-a-no-met-ric
cy-a-nope
cy-a-no-phy-cin
cy-a-no-sis
cy-a-nu-ric
cy-aph-e-nine
cy-ber-net-ics
cyc-la-mate
cy-cli-cal
cy-clic-i-ty
cy-cling
cy-clist
cy-cli-tis
cy-cli-za-tion
cy-clo-hex-i-mide
cy-clo-hex-yl-a-mine
cy-cloi-dal
cy-clol-y-sis
cy-clom-e-ter
cy-clon-ic
cy-clo-nite
Cy-clo-pe-an
cy-clo-ra-ma
cy-clo-ser-ine
cy-clot-o-my
cy-clo-tron
cyl-in-der
cyl-in-dra-ceous
cy-lin-dri-cal
cyl-in-dric-i-ty
cyl-in-drite
cy-mene
cy-mo-graph
cy-mose
cyn-i-cal
cyn-i-cism
cyn-o-don-tin
cy-no-sure
Cyn-thi-a
cy-press
Cyp-ri-an
Cyp-ri-ot (native of Cyprus)
Cy-prus
Cyr-e-na-ic
Cy-ril-lic
cys-tec-to-my
cys-te-ic
cys-teine
cys-tine
cys-ti-tis
cys-toid
cys-to-ma
cys-tom-e-ter
cys-to-scope
cys-tos-co-py
cy-tase
cyt-i-dine
cyt-i-dyl-ic
cyt-i-sine
cy-toc-i-dal

cy-to-ge-net-ics
cy-tog-e-nous
cy-tol-o-gy
cy-tol-y-sin
cy-tol-y-zate
cy-to-lyze
cy-tom-e-ter
cy-to-sine
czar-ism
Czech-o-slo-vak

D

dachs-hund
Da-cron
dac-tyl-ic
dac-tyl-o-graph
dac-ty-log-ra-phy
dac-ty-loid
dac-ty-lol-o-gy
dac-ty-los-co-py
dac-ty-lus
Dae-da-li-an
daf-fo-dil
da-guerre-o-type
dahl-ia
Da-ho-me-an
dain-ti-ness
Dai-qui-ri
dair-y
dai-sy
Da-kar
Da-kin
Dal-e-car-li-an
dal-li-ance
Dal-ma-tian
dam-a-scene
Da-mas-cus
dam-ask
dam-na-ble
damn-ing
Dam-o-cles
Da-mon
damp-en-er
damp-er
damp-ish
dam-son
danc-ing
dan-de-li-on
dan-druff
dan-ger-ous
dan-gling
Dan-ish
dan-seuse
dark-en
dar-ling
da-sheen
das-tard
da-sym-e-ter
da-tive
da-tum
da-tu-ric
daub-er
daugh-ter
dau-phin
Da-vi-son-ite
da-vit
daw-dler
daz-zling
dea-con-ess
deaf-en-ing
deal-er
de-ba-cle
de-bar-ka-tion
de-bat-a-ble
deb-au-chee
de-bauch-er-y
de-ben-ture
deb-ile
de-bil-i-tate
deb-it
deb-o-nair
de-bris
debt-or
de-but
deb-u-tante
dec-ade
dec-a-dence
dec-a-dent
dec-a-he-dral
dec-a-lage
de-cal-co-ma-ni-a
de-ca-les-cence
Dec-a-lin
dec-a-li-ter
dec-a-log
de-cam-e-ter (verse)
dec-am-e-ter (measure)
dec-a-me-tho-ni-um
de-ca-nal (adj.)
dec-a-nal (n.)
dec-ane
dec-a-no-ic
dec-a-no-yl
De-cap-o-da
de-cap-i-ta-tor
de-cant-er
dec-are
de-cath-lon
de-ce-dent
de-ceiv-er

de-cel-er-a-tor
de-cel-er-om-e-ter
de-cel-er-on
De-cem-ber
de-cen-cy
dec-ene
de-cen-na-ry
de-cen-ni-al
dec-e-nyl
de-cep-tive
dec-i-bel
de-cid-u-ous
dec-ile
dec-i-mal
dec-i-ma-tion
dec-i-me-ter
de-ci-pher
de-ci-sion
de-ci-sive
deck-led
dec-la-ma-tion
de-clam-a-to-ry
de-clar-ant
dec-la-ra-tion
de-clar-a-tive
de-clar-a-to-ry
de-clin-a-ble
dec-li-na-tion
de-clin-a-to-ry
dec-li-nom-e-ter
de-cli-vate
de-cliv-i-ty
de-cli-vous
de-coct-i-ble
de-coc-tive
de-cod-er
de-col-le-te
dec-o-ra-tive
dec-o-rous
de-co-rum
dec-re-ment
de-crem-e-ter
de-crep-i-tude
de-cre-tive
dec-re-to-ry
dec-yl-ene
de-cyl-ic
ded-i-ca-to-ry
de-duc-i-ble
de-duct-i-ble
de-fal-ca-tion
def-a-ma-tion
de-fam-a-to-ry
de-fat-i-ga-ble
de-fea-si-ble
def-e-ca-tor
de-fec-ti-bil-i-ty
de-fec-tive
de-fec-tor
de-fend-ant
de-fend-er
de-fen-si-ble
de-fen-sive
de-fer
def-er-ence
de-fer-ra-ble
de-fer-ves-cence
de-fi-bra-tor
de-fi-cient
def-i-cit
def-i-lade
de-file
de-fin-a-ble
def-i-ni-tion
de-fin-i-tive
def-la-gra-tion
de-fla-tion
de-flec-tive
de-flec-tom-e-ter
de-flec-tor
def-lo-ra-tion
def-lu-ent
de-fo-li-ate
de-form-a-ble
de-for-ma-tion
de-form-a-tive
de-for-me-ter
de-form-i-ty
de-frau-da-tion
de-frost-er
de-gen-er-a-tive
de-glu-ti-tion
deg-ra-da-tion
de-grade
de-guel-in
de-his-cent
de-hy-dra-tor
de-hy-dro-cho-late
de-hy-dro-cho-les-ter-ol
de-hy-dro-gen-ase
de-i-fi-ca-tion
de-is-tic
de-jeu-ner
Del-a-war-e-an
de-lec-ta-ble
del-e-gate
del-e-te-ri-ous
de-le-tion
de-lib-er-a-tive
del-i-ble
del-i-ca-cy
del-i-ca-tes-sen
de-li-cious

De-li-lah
de-lin-e-a-tor
de-lin-quen-cy
del-i-ques-cence
de-lir-i-ous
de-lir-i-um
de-lo-mor-phous
del-phi-nin
del-phin-i-um
Del-sar-ti-an
del-toi-dal
del-uge
de-lu-so-ry
dem-a-gog
dem-a-gog-ic
dem-a-gogu-er-y
de-mand-ant
de-mar-ca-tion
de-mean-or
de-men-tia
de-mer-it
de-mesne
dem-i-monde
de-mise
dem-i-tasse
de-mo-bi-li-za-tion
de-moc-ra-cy
dem-o-crat
de-moc-ra-tize
de-mog-ra-pher
de-mo-graph-ic
dem-oi-selle
de-mol-ish
dem-o-li-tion
de-mon-e-tize
de-mo-ni-a-cal
de-mon-ic
de-mon-stra-ble
dem-on-stra-tion
de-mon-stra-tive
dem-on-stra-tor
de-mor-al-ize
de-mul-cent
de-mur-rage
de-nar-i-us
de-na-ry
den-drit-ic
den-dro-lite
den-drol-o-gy
den-drom-e-ter
Den-eb
de-ner-vate
den-gue
de-ni-er (one who de-
 nies)
de-nier (coin; silk)
den-i-gra-to-ry
den-im
den-i-zen
de-nom-i-na-tive
de-nom-i-na-tor
de-noue-ment
den-sim-e-ter
den-si-tom-e-ter
den-si-ty
den-tal
den-ti-cle
den-tic-u-lar
den-ti-frice
den-tig-er-ous
den-tist-ry
de-nu-da-tion
de-nun-ci-a-tive
de-nun-ci-a-to-ry
de-o-dor-ant
de-o-dor-iz-er
de-ox-y-ri-bose
de-part-men-tal-ize
de-par-ture
de-pend-a-ble
de-pend-en-cy
de-pend-ent
de-perm-ing
de-phleg-ma-to-ry
dep-i-late
de-pil-a-to-ry
de-plor-a-ble
dep-lo-ra-tion
de-po-nent
de-por-ta-tion
de-port-ee
de-pos-al
de-pos-er
de-pos-i-tar-y
de-pos-it-ed
dep-o-si-tion
de-pos-i-to-ry
de-pot
dep-ra-va-tion
de-prav-i-ty
dep-re-ca-to-ry
de-pre-ci-ate
de-pre-da-tion
dep-re-da-to-ry
de-pres-sant
de-press-i-ble
de-pres-sor
de-priv-al
dep-ri-va-tion
depth-om-e-ter
dep-u-ra-tor
dep-u-tize
de-rac-i-nate
de-re-cho

der-e-lict
de-ri-gueur
de-ri-sive
der-i-va-tion
de-riv-a-tive
der-ma-ti-tis
der-mat-o-graph
der-ma-tol-o-gy
der-ma-to-sis
der-moi-dal
der-nier
der-o-gate
de-rog-a-to-ry
der-vish
des-cant
de-scend-ant
de-scend-er
de-scend-i-ble
de-scrib-a-ble
de-scrip-tive
des-cry
des-e-crat-er
des-e-de-ri-um
Des-er-et
de-sert (n., that which is
 deserved)
des-ert (n., adj., barren
 tract)
de-sert (v.)
de-sert-er
des-ic-cate
des-ic-ca-tor
de-sid-er-a-tum
des-ig-na-ble
des-ig-nat-a-ble
des-ig-na-tive
des-ig-na-tor
de-sign-ed-ly
des-ig-nee
de-sign-er
de-sip-i-ent
de-sir-a-ble
de-sist-ance
des-mo-di-um
des-mo-lase
des-mol-y-sis
des-mo-trop-ic
des-mot-ro-pism
des-o-la-tion
des-ox-y-cho-lic
des-ox-y-ri-bo-nu-cle-ase
de-spair
des-per-a-do
des-per-ate
des-pi-ca-ble
de-spis-a-ble
de-spis-er
de-spite
de-spoil
de-spo-li-a-tion
de-spond-ence
de-spond-ent
des-pot-i-cal
des-pot-ism
des-pu-ma-tion
des-qua-ma-tion
des-sert
des-ti-na-tion
des-ti-ny
des-ti-tute
de-stroy-er
de-struct-i-ble
de-struc-tive
de-struc-tor
des-ue-tude
des-ul-to-ry
des-yl
de-syn-ap-sis
de-tect-a-ble
de-tec-tive
de-tec-tor
de-ten-tive
de-ter-gent
de-te-ri-o-ra-tive
de-ter-mi-na-ble
de-ter-mi-nant
de-ter-min-er
de-ter-rence
de-test-a-ble
det-o-nant
det-o-na-tor
de-trac-tor
det-ri-men-tal
de-tri-tal
de-tri-tus
deu-ter-ide
deu-te-ri-um
deu-ter-on
Deu-ter-o-nom-ic
Deu-ter-on-o-my
deut-sche
dev-as-ta-tor
de-vel-op-men-tal
de-vi-a-tor
de-vice
dev-il-ish
dev-il-try
de-vi-ous
dev-i-see
de-vis-er
dev-i-sor (legal)
De-vo-ni-an
dev-o-tee

Dew-ar
dex-ter-i-ty
dex-tral-i-ty
dex-trin-ate
dex-trin-o-gen-ic
dex-tro-car-di-a
dex-tro-pi-mar-ic
dex-trorse
dex-trose
dex-trous
di-a-ban-tite
di-a-be-tes
di-a-bet-ic
di-a-bol-i-cal
di-ab-o-lism
di-ac-e-tyl
di-a-dem
di-ag-no-sis
di-ag-nos-ti-cian
di-ag-o-nal
di-a-gramed
di-a-gram-mat-i-cal
di-a-lec-tic
di-a-lec-tol-o-gy
di-a-log
di-a-lu-ric
di-al-y-sis
di-a-lyt-ic
di-a-lyz-er
di-am-e-ter
di-a-met-ri-cal
di-am-i-no-gen
di-a-mond
Di-an-a
di-a-nite
di-a-pa-son
di-a-per
di-aph-a-nom-e-ter
di-aph-a-nous
di-a-phon-ic
di-aph-o-re-sis
di-a-phragm
di-a-phrag-mat-ic
di-ar-rhe-a
di-a-ry
di-as-po-ra
di-a-spore
di-a-stase
di-as-ta-sis
di-a-stat-ic
di-a-stim-e-ter
di-as-to-le
di-a-stol-ic
di-as-to-mat-ic
di-as-tro-phe
di-a-stroph-ic
di-ath-e-sis
di-a-ther-my
di-a-thet-ic
di-a-tom
di-a-to-ma-ceous
di-at-o-mite
di-at-ro-pism
di-a-zine
di-a-zo-ic
di-az-o-im-ide
di-a-zole
di-az-o-meth-ane
di-a-zo-ni-um
di-az-o-tize
di-az-o-type
di-ba-sic
di-bro-mo-a-ce-tic
di-bu-caine
di-ce-tyl
di-chlone
di-chlo-ro-di-flu-o-ro-
 meth-ane
di-cho-tom-ic
di-chot-o-mous
di-chot-o-my
di-chro-mat-ic
di-con-dyl-ic
di-cot-y-le-don
di-cou-ma-rol
di-crot-ic
Dic-ta-phone
dic-ta-tor
dic-ta-to-ri-al
dic-tion-ar-y
Dic-to-graph
di-dac-tic
di-dym-i-um
di-er-e-sis
di-e-ret-ic
die-sel-ize
di-e-tar-y
di-e-tet-ic
di-e-ti-tian
dif-fer-en-tial
dif-fi-dence
dif-flu-ent
dif-frac-tion
dif-frac-tom-e-ter
dif-fran-gi-ble
dif-fus-er
dif-fus-i-ble
dif-fu-sive
di-gest-er
di-gest-i-ble
di-ges-tive
dig-i-tal
dig-i-tal-is

dig-i-tal-i-za-tion
dig-i-tal-ose
dig-i-ti-ner-vate
dig-it-iz-er
di-hy-dro-er-go-cor-nine
di-hy-dro-er-got-a-mine
di-hy-drox-y-a-ce-tic
di-he-dral
di-lap-i-dat-ed
di-lat-ant
dil-a-ta-tion
di-la-tion
dil-a-tom-e-ter
di-la-tor
dil-a-to-ry
di-lem-ma
dil-et-tan-te
dil-u-ent
di-lut-ant
di-lut-er
di-me-don
di-men-hy-dri-nate
di-men-si-ble
di-mer-cap-rol
di-mer-ic
di-meth-yl
di-mid-i-ate
di-min-ish
dim-i-nu-tion
di-min-u-tive
dim-i-ty
di-mor-phous
din-ghy
di-ni-tro-tol-u-ene
di-no-saur
di-oc-e-san
di-o-cese
Di-og-e-nes
di-op-side
di-op-ter
di-op-tom-e-ter
di-o-ra-ma
di-o-ram-ic
di-o-rite
di-par-tite
di-phen-yl
diph-the-ri-a
diph-the-rit-ic
diph-the-roid
diph-thong-al
di-pic-o-lin-ic
di-ple-gi-a
di-plex-er
dip-loi-dal
dip-loid-ize
di-plo-ma-cy
dip-lo-mat
di-plo-ma-tist
di-plo-sis
dip-o-dy
dip-so-ma-ni-a
dip-ter-al
di-rec-tiv-i-ty
di-rec-tor-ate
di-rec-to-ri-al
dir-i-gi-ble
dirn-dl
dirt-i-ness
dis-ap-peared
dis-ap-point-ed
dis-as-ter
dis-as-trous
dis-az-o
dis-burs-al
dis-burs-er
dis-cern-i-ble
dis-cerp-ti-ble
dis-ci-ple
dis-ci-pli-nar-i-an
dis-ci-pli-nar-y
dis-ci-plin-er
dis-clo-sure
dis-coi-dal
dis-com-fi-ture
dis-con-so-late
dis-cord-ant
dis-co-theque
dis-cour-sive
dis-crep-an-cy
dis-crete
dis-cre-tion-ar-y
dis-crim-i-na-ble
dis-crim-i-na-tor
dis-cur-sive
dis-cus
dis-cuss-ant
dis-cuss-i-ble
dis-cus-sion
dis-eas-es
di-seuse
dis-ha-bille
di-shev-eled
dis-in-fect-ant
dis-in-te-grate
dis-man-tle
dis-mis-sal
dis-par-ag-er
dis-par-ate
dis-par-i-ty
dis-patch-er
dis-pen-sa-ble

dis-pen-sa-ry
dis-pens-er
dis-per-sal
dis-pers-ant
dis-pers-er
dis-pers-i-ble
dis-per-sive
dis-per-sold
dis-pir-it
dis-pos-al
dis-put-a-ble
dis-pu-tant
dis-pu-ta-tious
dis-pu-ta-tive
dis-put-er
dis-qui-si-tion
dis-quis-i-tive
dis-rep-u-ta-ble
dis-re-pute
dis-rupt-er
dis-sat-is-fied
dis-sect-i-ble
dis-sec-tor
dis-sem-i-na-tive
dis-sen-sion
dis-sent-er
dis-sim-i-la-tive
dis-si-pat-er
dis-sol-u-ble
dis-so-lute
dis-solv-a-ble
dis-sol-vent
dis-so-nance
dis-suad-er
dis-sua-sive
dis-sym-me-try
dis-taff
dis-tant
dis-tem-per
dis-ten-si-ble
dis-ten-tion
dis-til-la-tion
dis-tilled
dis-till-er-y
dis-till-ing
dis-tinc-tive
dis-tin-guished
dis-to-ma-ta
dis-sto-ma-to-sis
dis-stom-a-tous
dis-tor-tive
dis-tract-er
dis-tract-i-ble
dis-trac-tive
dis-tress-ing
dis-trib-ut-a-ble
dis-trib-u-tar-y
dis-trib-ute
dis-trib-u-tee
dis-tri-bu-tion
dis-trib-u-tive
dis-trib-u-tor
dis-turb-ance
dis-turb-er
di-thi-o-nate
di-thi-o-nous
di-thi-zone
dith-y-ram-bic
di-tol-yl
di-u-re-sis
di-u-ret-ic
di-ur-nal
di-va-ga-tion
di-van
div-er
di-ver-gent
di-vers (several)
di-ver-si-ty
di-vert-er
di-vert-i-ble
di-ver-tic-u-lec-to-my
di-ver-tic-u-lo-sis
di-ver-tic-u-lum
di-ver-tise-ment
di-ver-tisse-ment
di-ver-tive
di-ver-tor (electricity)
di-vest-i-ble
di-ves-ti-ture
di-vid-ed
div-i-dend
di-vid-er
div-i-na-tion
di-vin-a-to-ry
di-vin-i-ty
di-vis-i-ble
di-vi-sion
di-vi-so-ry
di-vor-cee
di-vul-gence
do-blon
do-cent
doc-i-ble
doc-ile
do-cil-i-ty
dock-et
doc-o-sane
doc-tor-al
doc-tor-ate
doc-tri-naire
doc-tri-nal
doc-u-ment-a-ble
doc-u-men-ta-ry
do-de-cane

do-dec-a-no-ic
Do-dec-a-nese
do-dec-ant
do-de-cyl-ene
dodg-er
dog-ger-el
dog-mat-ic
dog-ma-tism
dog-ma-tize
dol-drum
dol-er-ite
dol-i-cho-ce-phal-ic
do-lo-mite
do-lo-rous
dol-phin
do-main
do-mes-ti-cate
do-mes-tic-i-ty
dom-i-cil-i-ar-y
dom-i-nant
dom-i-na-tor
dom-i-neer
Dom-i-ni-ca
do-min-i-cal
Do-min-i-can
dom-i-nie
do-min-ion
dom-i-no
do-na-ble
do-nee
don-keys
do-nor
doo-dle
Dopp-ler
Do-ri-an
Dor-ic
Dor-is
dor-mant
dor-mer
dor-mi-to-ry
Dor-o-the-a
dor-sal
dor-sa-lis
dos-age
do-sim-e-ter
do-sim-e-try
dos-sier
dot-age
dot-ard
dot-ing
dot-ish
dou-ble
dou-blet
dou-bling
dou-bloon
dou-bly
dough-ty
dou-rine
dow-a-ger
dow-eled
down-i-ness
dox-o-log-i-cal
dox-ol-o-gy
doy-en
doz-en
drag-on
dra-goon
drain-age
dra-ma
Dram-a-mine
dra-mat-ic
dra-ma-tis per-so-nae
dram-a-tize
drap-er-y
dream-i-ness
drear-i-ness
dredg-er
dredg-ing
dress-er
dri-er
drift-age
drift-er
drill-ing
drink-om-e-ter
driv-el-er
driv-en
driv-er
droll-er-y
drom-e-dar-y
drop-si-cal
drop-sonde
dro-som-e-ter
dro-ver
drows-i-ness
drudg-er-y
drunk-ard
drunk-en-ness
dru-pa-ceous
du-al-ism
du-ar-chy
du-bi-e-ty
du-bi-ous
du-bi-ta-ble
du-cal
duc-at
duch-ess
du-chesse
duc-ti-ble
duc-tile
dudg-eon
duf-fel-bag
duff-er
du-fre-nite
dul-ci-mer

dul-ci-tol
dul-lard
dull-er
dum-found
dump-er
dump-ling
dump-y
dun-ga-ree
Dun-ge-ness
dun-geon
du-nite
Dun-kard
Dun-stan
du-o-dec-i-mos
du-o-de-nal
du-o-de-ni-tis
du-o-de-num
du-op-o-ly
du-op-so-ny
du-plex-er
du-pli-ca-tive
du-pli-ca-tor
du-plic-i-ty
du-ra-bil-i-ty
du-ral-u-min
dur-ance
du-ra-tion
du-rene
du-ress
du-rom-e-ter
dur-yl
dusk-i-ness
dust-er
du-te-ous
du-ti-ful
du-ve-tyn
dwarf-ish
dwell-ing
dwin-dling
Dy-cril
dy-nam-e-ter
dy-nam-i-cal
dy-nam-ics
dy-na-mit-er
dy-na-mi-za-tion
dy-na-mom-e-ter
dy-na-mo-met-ric
dy-na-mom-e-try
dy-na-mos
dy-na-mo-tor
Dy-na-Soar
dy-nas-tic
dy-na-tron
Dy-nel
dy-node
dys-cra-site
dys-en-ter-y
dys-pep-si-a
dys-pho-ri-a
dysp-ne-a
dys-pro-si-um

E

ea-ger
ea-glet
ear-li-er
earn-er
ear-nest
earth-en-ware
ea-sel
eas-i-ly
Eas-ter
east-er (storm)
east-ern-er
eb-on-ite
eb-on-y
e-bul-lient
e-bul-li-om-e-ter
e-bul-li-o-scop-ic
e-bul-li-os-co-py
eb-ul-li-tion
ec-cen-tric-i-ty
ec-cle-si-as-ti-cal
ec-dys-i-al
ec-go-nine
ech-e-lon
e-chi-noid
e-chi-nus
ech-o-me-ter
ec-lamp-si-a
ec-lec-ti-cal
e-clip-tic
e-clo-sion
e-co-log-i-cal
e-col-o-gy
e-con-o-met-ric (adj.)
e-con-o-me-trics (n.)
eco-nom-i-cal
eco-nom-ics
e-con-o-mist
e-con-o-mize
ec-o-sphere
ec-sta-sy
ec-stat-ic
ec-to-der-moi-dal
ec-tog-e-nous
ec-to-pi-a
ec-top-ic
ec-to-plasm
ec-typ-al
Ec-ua-dor-an

ec-u-men-i-cal
ec-ze-ma
ec-zem-a-tous
e-del-weiss
e-de-ma
e-dem-a-tous
ed-i-ble
ed-i-fi-ca-tion
ed-i-fice
e-di-tion
ed-i-to-ri-al-ize
ed-u-ca-ble
ed-u-ca-tor
e-duc-i-ble
e-duc-tor
ce-ri-ly
ef-fac-ing
ef-fect-i-ble
ef-fec-tive
ef-fec-tu-al
ef-fem-i-nate
ef-fer-ves-cence
ef-fer-ves-ci-ble
ef-fi-ca-cious
ef-fi-ca-cy
ef-fi-cien-cy
ef-fi-cient
ef-fi-gy
ef-flo-res-cence
ef-flu-vi-um
ef-fron-ter-y
ef-ful-gence
ef-fu-si-om-e-ter
ef-fu-sive
e-gal-i-tar-i-an
e-go-cen-trism
e-go-ism
e-go-is-ti-cal
e-go-tism
e-go-tis-ti-cal
e-gre-gious
E-gyp-tol-o-gy
ei-co-sane
ei-der
ei-gen
eight-een
eight-i-eth
ei-ko-nom-e-ter
ein-stein-i-um
eis-e ge-sis
Ei-sen-how-er
ei-ther
e-jac-u-la-to-ry
e-jec-tive
e-jec-tor
e-lab-o-ra-tive
e-las-tic-i-ty
e-las-to-mer
e-las-tom-e-ter
e-las-to-sis
e-lat-er-in
ela-te-ri-um
el-der
el-e-cam-pane
e-lec-tion-eer
e-lec-tive
e-lec-tor-al
e-lec-tor-ate
e-lec-tri-cal
e-lec-tric-i-ty
e-lec-tri-fi-ca-tion
e-lec-tro-car-di-o-gram
e-lec-tro-cute
e-lec-trode
e-lec-tro-graph-ic
e-lec-trog-ra-phy
e-lec-trol-y-sis
e-lec-tro-lyte
e-lec-tro-lyt-i-cal
e-lec-trom-e-ter
e-lec-tron-i-cal-ly
e-lec-tron-ics
e-lec-troph-o-rus
e-lec-trot-o-nus
el-ee-mos-y-nar-y
el-e-gant
el-e-gi-ac
el-e-gy
el-e-men-tar-i-ly
el-e-men-ta-ry
el-e-phan-ti-a-sis
el-e-va-tor
el-ev-enth
el-e-von
elf-in
e-lic-it
el-i-gi-ble
e-lim-i-nant
e-lim-i-na-tor
e-lix-ir
E-liz-a-be-than
el-lip-soi-dal
el-lip-som-e-ter
el-lip-ti-cal
el-lip-tic-i-ty
e-lo-gi-um
e-lon-ga-tion
el-o-quent
e-lu-ci-date
e-lud-i-ble
e-lu-so-ry
e-lu-tri-ate
e-lu-vi-um
E-lyr-i-a

E-ly-sian
E-ly-si-um
e-ma-ci-ate
em-a-nate
e-man-ci-pate
em-a-nom-e-ter
e-mar-gi-nate
e-mas-cu-late
em-ba-cle
em-bar-go
em-bar-ka-tion
em-bar-ras (n.)
em-bar-rass (v.)
em-bed-ded
em-bla-zon
em-blem-at-i-cal
em-bold-en
em-bol-ic
em-bo-lism
em-bo-lus
em-boss-er
em-bou-chure
em-brac-er
em-bra-sure
em-broi-der-y
em-bry-ol-o-gy
em-bry-on-ic
e-mend-a-ble
e-men-da-tion
e-mend-a-to-ry
em-er-al-dine
e-mer-gen-cy
e-mer-i-tus
e-mer-sion
em-er-y
e-met-ic
em-e-tine
em-i-grant
em-i-gree
em-i-nence
em-is-sar-y
e-mis-siv-i-ty
e-mit-ter
em-o-din
e-mol-lient
e-mol-u-ment
e-mot-er
e-mo-tion-al-ize
em-path-ic
em-pa-thy
em-pen-nage
em-per-or
em-pha-sis
em-phat-ic
em-phy-se-ma
em-pir-i-cal
em-pi-ris-tic
em-ploy-ee
em-po-ri-um
em-press
emp-ti-ness
em-py-e-ma
em-py-re-an
em-py-reu-ma
em-u-la-tive
em-u-la-to-ry
em-u-lous
e-mul-si-fi-er
e-mul-sive
e-mul-soi-dal
en-a-bling
en-am-el-er
en-am-o-ra-to
en-am-ored
e-nan-thic
en-ar-gite
en-ar-thro-sis
en-cap-su-late
en-caus-tic
en-ceinte
en-ce-phal-ic
en-ceph-a-li-tis
en-ceph-a-lo-cele
en-ceph-a-lo-gram
en-ceph-a-lo-graph-ic
en-ceph-a-log-ra-phy
en-ceph-a-loid
en-chi-la-da
en-chym-a-tous
en-clos-er
en-clo-sure
en-col-gnure
en-co-mi-ast
en-co-mi-um
en-coun-ter
en-cour-age
en-cri-nal
en-crin-ic
en-cum-ber
en-cum-brance
en-cy-clo-pe-di-a
en-cys-ta-tion
end-ar-te-ri-tis
en-deav-ored
en-de-mi-al
en-dem-i-cal-ly
en-de-mic-i-ty
en-de-mi-ol-ogy
En-der-by
end-er-gon-ic
en-dive
en-do-car-di-tis

en-do-cri-nal
en-do-crine
en-do-crin-o-log-ic
en-do-cri-nol-o-gy
en-do-crin-o-path-ic
en-doc-ri-nous
en-doc-ri-nous
en-do-ge-net-ic
en-do-ge-nic-i-ty
en-dog-e-nous
en-do-me-tri-tis
en-do-plas-ma
en-dors-a-ble
en-dors-ee
en-dors-er
en-dos-co-py
en-drin
en-e-ma
en-er-get-i-cal-ly
en-er-giz-er
en-er-vate
en-fi-lade
en-force-a-ble
en-fran-chise
en-gen-der
en-gi-neer-ing
en-gine-ry
Eng-land
Eng-lish
en-grav-er
e-nig-mat-ic
e-nig-ma-tize
en-join-der
en-liv-en
en-mi-ty
en-nui
e-nor-mi-ty
e-nor-mous
en-rolled
en-roll-ee
en-sem-ble
en-sign
en-si-lage
en-ter-ic
en-ter-i-tis
en-ter-o-cri-nin
en-ter-os-to-my
en-thal-py
en-thu-si-asm
en-thu-si-as-tic
en-tire-ty
en-ti-ty
en-to-mo-log-i-cal
en-to-mol-o-gy
en-tou-rage
en-trails
en-trance
en-tree
en-tre-pre-neur-i-al
en-tro-py
e-nu-cle-ate
e-nu-mer-ate
e-nun-ci-a-tive
en-vel-op (v.)
en-ve-lope (n.)
en-vel-op-ment
en-vi-a-ble
en-vi-ous
en-vi-ron
en-vis-age
en-zy-mat-ic
en-zy-mol-o-gy
e-o-sin-o-phil
e-os-pho-rite
ep-a-go-ge
ep-au-let
ep-en-dy-ma
e-phed-rine
e-phem-er-al
e-phem-er-is
E-phra-im
Eph-ra-ta
ep-i-cal
ep-i-cu-re-an
ep-i-dem-i-cal
ep-i-de-mi-o-log-i-cal
ep-i-de-mi-ol-o-gy
ep-i-der-mis
ep-i-der-moi-dal
ep-i-dote
ep-i-du-ral
ep-i-ge-al
e-pig-e-nous
ep-i-glot-tis
e-pig-ra-pher
ep-i-la-tor
ep-i-lep-tic
ep-i-log
ep-i-mer-i-za-tion
ep-i-neph-rine
Ep-i-nine
E-piph-a-ny
e-piph-y-sis
ep-i-pter-ic
E-pi-rus
E-pis-co-pa-lian
ep-i-sco-tis-ter
ep-i-sod-ic
e-pis-ta-sis
ep-i-stat-ic
e-pis-te-mol-o-gy

e-pis-tle
e-pis-to-lar-y
ep-i-stome
e-pith-e-li-um
e-pith-e-sis
ep-i-thet
e-pit-o-me
ep-i-tom-i-cal
e-pit-ro-phv
ep-och-al
ep-ox-y
ep-si-lon
eq-ua-ble
e-qualed
e-qual-iz-er
e-qua-nim-i-ty
e-quat-ive
e-qua-to-ri-al
eq-uer-ry
e-ques-tri-an
e-qui-dis-tant
e-qui-lat-er-al
eq-ui-len-in
e-quil-i-bra-tion
e-qui-lib-rist
e-qui-lib-ri-stat
e-qui-lib-ri-um
e-qui-noc-tial
e-qui-nox
eq-ui-page
eq-ui-poise
e-quipped
eq-ui-ta-ble
eq-ui-ty
e-quiv-a-lent
e-quiv-o-cal
e-quiv-o-ca-tor
e-rad-i-ca-tor
e-ras-er
e-ra-sure
er-bi-um
Er-e-bus
e-rec-tile
e-rec-tor
er-e-ma-cau-sis
er-ga-tive
er-god-ic
er-go-gen-ic
er-gom-e-ter
er-go-no-vine
er-gos-ter-ol
er-got
er-got-a-mine
er-got-ic
er-go-tize
e-rin-e-um
er-in-ite
er-i-nose
er-i-o-dic-ty-ol
er-i-om-e-ter
Er-len-mey-er
er-mine
e-rod-i-ble
e-ro-sive
e-rot-i-cism
crr-a-bil-i-ty
er-ra-ta
er-rat-ic
er-ro-ne-ous
er-u-bes-cent
e-ru-cic
e-ruc-ta-tion
er-u-di-tion
e-rup-tiv-i-ty
er-y-sip-e-las
er-y-the-ma
er-y-them-a-tous
er-y-thrine
er-y-thrite
e-ryth-ri-tol
e-ryth-ro-cyte
er-y-thro-i-dine
er-y-thro-pi-a
e-ryth-ro-scope
er-y-throse
e-ryth-ro-sin
er-y-thro-sis
e-ryth-ru-lose
es-ca-drille
es-ca-la-tor
es-cal-loped
es-cap-a-ble
es-ca-pade
es-cap-ee
es-cap-ism
es-cap-ist
es-ca-role
es-carp-ment
es-cha-tol-o-gy
es-chy-nite
es-cri-toire
es-crow
es-cu-dos
es-cu-lent
es-cutch-eon
es-er-o-line
Es-ki-mos
e-soph-a-ge-al
e-soph-a-gi-tis
e-soph-a-go-scope
e-soph-a-gos-co-pist
e-soph-a-gus

es-o-ter-ic
es-pal-ier
es-pe-cial
Es-pe-ran-to
es-pi-o-nage
es-pla-nade
es-pous-al
es-pous-er
es-tab-lish
es-ter-ase
es-ter-ize
es-thet-ic
es-ti-ma-ble
es-ti-ma-tor
es-ti-va-tor
Es-to-nian
es-top-pel
es-to-vers
es-tra-di-ol
es-trange
es-tray
es-tro-gen-ic
es-tu-a-rine
es-tu-ar-y
e-ter-ni-ty
eth-ane
eth-a-nol-a-mine
eth-a-nol-y-sis
eth-e-nyl
e-the-re-al
e-the-re-ous
e-ther-ize
eth-i-cal
eth-i-on-ic
e-thi-o-nine
E-thi-o-pi-an
eth-moi-dal
eth-moid-i-tis
eth-ni-cal
eth-nog-e-ny
eth-no-graph-ic
eth-nog-ra-phy
eth-no-log-i-cal
eth-nol-o-gy
eth-ox-y-line
eth-yl-a-mine
eth-yl-ate
eth-yl-ene-di-a-mine
eth-yl-e-nic
eth-yl-e-phed-rine
eth-yl-i-dine
eth-y-nyl-a-tion
e-ti-o-late
e-ti-o-log-i-cal
e-ti-ol-o-gy
e-ti-o-phyl-lin
et-i-quette
et-y-mo-log-i-cal
et-y-mol-o-gy
eu-ca-lyp-tus
Eu-cha-rist
eu-chred
eu-chro-ite
eu-clase
Eu-clid-e-an
cu-da-lene
eu-di-om-e-ter
Eu-ge-nia
eu-gen-ic
eu-gen-ist
eu-ge-nol
eu-lo-gis-ti-cal
eu-lo-gize
eu-lo-gy
eu-nuch
eu-pa-to-rin
eu-pav-er-ine
eu-phe-mism
eu-pho-ni-um
eu-pho-ny
eu-pho-ri-a
Eur-a-sian
eu-re-ka
Eu-ro-pe-an
eu-ro-pi-um
eu-ryth-mics
Eu-sta-chi-an
eu-tha-na-si-a
eu-then-ics
eux-e-nite
e-vac-u-ate
e-vag-i-nate
ev-a-nes-cence
e-van-gel-i-cal
e-van-ge-list
e-van-ge-lize
e-vap-o-ra-tor
e-vap-o-rim-e-ter
e-va-si-ble
e-va-sive
e-ven-ing (making level)
eve-ning (close of day)
e-ven-tu-al-i-ty
e-ver-si-ble
ev-er-y
e-vic-tor
ev-i-denc-ing
ev-i-den-tial
e-vinc-i-ble
e-vis-cer-a-tor
ev-i-ta-ble
e-voc-a-to-ry
ev-o-lu-tion-ar-y
ev-o-lu-tion-ist

ex-ac-er-bat-ing
ex-ac-ti-tude
ex-ag-ger-ate
ex-al-ta-tion
ex-am-i-na-tion
ex-am-in-er
ex-as-per-ate
ex-ca-va-tor
ex-cel-len-cy
ex-cel-si-or
ex-cept-a-ble
ex-cerpt-er
ex-cerpt-i-ble
ex-ces-sive
ex-cheq-uer
ex-cip-i-ent
ex-cit-a-ble
ex-cit-ant
ex-cit-a-tive
ex-cit-er
ex-cla-ma-tion
ex-clam-a-to-ry
ex-clud-a-ble
ex-clu-so-ry
ex-co-ri-a-tion
ex-cre-ment
ex-cres-cence
ex-cre-to-ry
ex-cru-ci-ate
ex-cul-pa-to-ry
ex-cus-a-ble
ex-e-cra-to-ry
ex-ec-u-tant
ex-ec-u-ted
ex-ec-u-tive
ex-ec-u-to-ry
ex-e-ge-sis
ex-e-get-ic
ex-em-pla-ry
ex-empt-i-ble
ex-emp-tive
ex-e-qua-tur
ex-er-cis-er
ex-er-e-sis
ex-ert-ist
ex-hal-ant
ex-ha-la-tion
ex-haust-ed
ex-haust-i-ble
ex-haus-tive
ex-hib-it
ex-hi-bi-tion
ex-hib-i-tive
ex-hib-i-to-ry
ex-hil-a-ra-tive
ex-hor-ta-tion
ex-hort-a-to-ry
ex-hu-ma-tion
ex-i-gen-cy
ex-i-gi-ble
ex-i-gu-i-ty
ex-ig-u-ous
ex-ist-ence
ex-is-ten-tial-ism
ex li-bris
ex-o-don-ti-a
ex-o-dus
ex-og-e-nous
ex-on-er-ate
ex-o-pep-ti-dase
ex-or-bi-tant
ex-or-di-um
ex-o-ter-ic
ex-o-ther-mic-i-ty
ex-ot-ic
ex-pand-a-ble
ex-pand-er
ex-pan-si-ble
ex-pan-sive
ex-pa-ti-ate
ex-pa-tri-ate
ex-pect-an-cy
ex-pect-ant
ex-pec-ta-tion
ex-pec-ta-tive
ex-pec-to-ra-tor
ex-pe-di-en-cy
ex-pe-dit-er
ex-pe-di-tious
ex-pel-lee
ex-pel-ling
ex-pend-i-ture
ex-pen-sive
ex-pe-ri-ence
ex-per-i-men-tal
ex-per-i-ment-er
ex-per-tise (n.)
ex-pert-ize (v.)
ex-pi-a-to-ry
ex-pi-ra-tion
ex-pir-a-to-ry
ex-pla-na-tion
ex-plan-a-to-ry
ex-ple-tive
ex-pli-ca-ble
ex-pli-ca-tive
ex-pli-ca-tor
ex-plic-a-to-ry
ex-plic-it-ly
ex-plod-er
ex-ploi-ta-tion
ex-ploit-a-tive
ex-ploit-er
ex-plo-ra-tion

ex-plor-a-to-ry
ex-plo-si-ble
ex-plo-sim-e-ter
ex-plo-sive
ex-po-nen-tial
ex-port-a-ble
ex-por-ta-tion
ex-pose (v.)
ex-po-sé (n.)
ex-po-si-tion
ex-pos-i-to-ry
ex-pos-tu-late
ex-po-sure
ex-press-age
ex-press-er
ex-press-i-ble
ex-pres-sive
ex-pres-sor
ex-pug-na-to-ry
ex-pul-sive
ex-pur-ga-to-ry
ex-quis-ite
ex-sic-cate
ex-tem-po-ra-ne-i-ty
ex-tem-po-re
ex-tem-po-rize
ex-tend-a-ble
ex-tend-er
ex-ten-si-ble
ex-ten-som-e-ter
ex-ten-sor
ex-ten-u-a-tor
ex-te-ri-or-ize
ex-ter-mi-na-tor
ex-ter-nal-i-ty
ex-tinc-tive
ex-tin-guish-er
ex-tir-pa-tor
ex-tract-a-ble
ex-tract-ant
ex-trac-tive
ex-trac-tor
ex-tra-dit-a-ble
ex-tral-i-ty
ex-tra-ne-ous
ex-traor-di-nar-i-ly
ex-trap-o-lat-ed
ex-trap-o-la-to-ry
ex-tra-sen-so-ry
ex-trav-a-gance
ex-trav-a-sa-tion
ex-tre-mism
ex-trem-ist
ex-trem-i-ty
ex-tri-cate
ex-trin-sic
ex-tro-vert-ish
ex-tro-ver-tive
ex-trud-er
ex-tru-si-ble
ex-tu-ber-ance
ex-u-ber-ant
ex-u-da-tion
ex-ult-ant
ex-ul-ta-tion
ex-ur-bi-a
eye-le-teer
ey-ing

F

fa-ba-ceous
Fa-bi-an
fa-bled
fab-ri-ca-tor
Fab-ri-koid
fab-u-lous
fa-cade
face-a-ble
fac-er
fac-et-ed
fa-ce-tious
fa-cial
fa-cient
fa-ci-es
fac-ile
fa-cil-i-ty
fac-ing
fa-con-ne
fac-sim-i-le
fac-tic-i-ty
fac-tious
fac-ti-tious
fac-tor
fac-to-ri-al
fac-to-ry
fac-to-tum
fac-u-la
fac-ul-ty
fa-cun-di-ty
fade-om-e-ter
fad-er
fa-gine
fag-ot
Fahr-en-heit
fa-ience
fail-ure
fai-naigue
fair-y-like
fak-er (one who fakes)
fa-kir (dervish)
Fa-lan-gist
fal-cip-a-rum

fal-con-er
fal-la-cious
fal-la-cy
fall-en
fal-li-bil-i-ty
Fal-lo-pi-an
fal-set-tos
fal-si-fi-ca-tion
fal-si-ty
Fal-staff-i-an
fal-ter
fa-mil-iar
fa-mil-i-ar-i-ty
fa-mil-iar-ize
fam-i-ly
fam-ish
fa-mous
fam-u-lus
fa-nat-i-cal
fa-nat-i-cism
fan-ci-er
fan-ci-ful
Fan-euil
fan-gled
fan-ta-sia
fan-ta-size
fan-tas-tic
fan-ta-sy
far-ad
Far-a-day
fa-rad-ic
far-a-dism
far-ci-cal
fa-ri-na
far-i-na-ceous
far-i-nose
farm-er
far-ther
far-thing
far-thin-gale
fas-ces
fas-ci-cle
fas-cic-u-lar
fas-ci-na-tor
fas-ci-o-li-a-sis
fas-cism
Fas-cist
Fa-scis-ti
fash-ion-a-ble
fas-ten-er
fas-tid-i-ous
fas-tig-i-um
fa-tal-ism
fa-tal-i-ty
fa-ther
fath-om-a-ble
Fa-thom-e-ter
fat-i-ga-ble
fa-tigue
fa-tigu-ing-ly
Fat-i-ma
fa-tu-i-tous
fat-u-ous
fau-cal-ize
fau-cet
fau-nal
fau-vism
fa-ve-o-lus
fa-vism
fa-vor-ite
fa-vor-it-ism
fa-vrile
fa-yal-ite
fe-al-ty
fea-sance
fea-si-bil-i-ty
feath-er-ing
fea-tured
fe-bric-i-ty
fe-bric-u-la
fe-brif-ic
fe-brif-u-gal
feb-ri-fuge
fe-brif-u-gine
feb-rile
fe-bril-i-ty
Feb-ru-ar-y
fe-cal
fec-u-lent
fe-cund
fec-un-date
fe-cun-da-tive
fe-cun-di-ty
fed-er-a-cy
fed-er-al-ese
fed-er-a-tive
fee-ble
Feh-ling
feld-spath-ic
feld-spath-oi-dal
fe-li-cide
fe-lic-i-tate
fe-lic-i-tous
fe-line
fe-lin-i-ty
fel-on
fe-lo-ni-ous
fel-o-ny
felt-er
Felt-ham
fe-luc-ca
fem-i-ne-i-ty
fem-i-nin-i-ty
fem-i-nism

fem-o-ral
fe-mur
fen-chene
fen-chone
fen-chyl
fen-ci-ble
fend-er
fe-nes-tra
fen-es-tra-tion
Fe-ni-an
fe-ra-cious
Fer-di-nand
fer-ment-a-ble
fer-men-ta-tion
fer-ment-a-tive
fer-ment-er
fer-men-tive
fer-mi-um
fe-roc-i-ty
fer-rif-er-ous
fer-ri-na-trite
fer-rit-ic
fer-ri-tin
fer-ro-cene
fer-ro-cy-a-nide
fer-rom-e-ter
fer-ru-gi-nous
fer-rule
fer-til-i-ty
fer-til-iz-a-ble
fer-til-iz-er
fe-ru-lic
fer-va-nite
fer-ven-cy
fer-vor
fes-ter
fes-ti-val
fes-tiv-i-ty
fes-toon
fe-tal
fot-e-ri-ta
fe-ti-cide
fet-id
fe-tid-i-ty
fet-ish-ism
fe-tus
feu-dal-ism
feud-ist
feuil-le-ton
fe-ver-ous
fi-an-ce
Fi-ber-glas
fi-ber-ize
fi-bril-la-tion
fi-brin-o-gen-ic
fi-bri-nog-e-nous
fi-broid
fi-bro-in
fi-bro-sis
fi-bro-si-tis
fi-brous
fib-u-la
fick-le
fic-tile
fic-ti-tious
fid-dler
fi-del-i-ty
fidg-et-y
fi-du-ci-ar-y
field-er
fiend-ish
fi-er-y
fi-es-ta
fight-er
fig-ur-al
fig-u-ra-tion
fig-u-ra-tive
fig-u-rine
fil-a-men-tous
fi-lar-i-al
fil-a-ri-a-sis
fil-bert
fil-i-al
fil-i-bus-ter
fil-i-gree
Fil-i-pi-no
fill-er (filled)
fill-er (money unit)
fil-let
fil-o-selle
fil-ter-er
filth-i-ness
fil-tra-ble
fil-tra-tion
fi-na-ble
fi-na-gle
fi-nal-e
fi-nal-i-ty
fi-nan-cial
fin-an-cier
fi-nanc-ing
find-er
fin-er-y
fi-nesse
fin-ger
fin-i-cal
fin-ick-y
fi-nis
fin-ished
fi-nite
fin-i-tude
Finn-ish
fir-ing

fir-kin
fir-ma-ment
firm-er
fis-cal
fisch-er-ite
fish-er-y
fis-sion
fis-sip-a-rous
fis-sure
fist-i-cuff
fis-tu-la
fis-tu-lous
fix-a-tive
flac-cid-i-ty
flag-el-lant
flag-el-la-tor
flag-eo-let
fla-gi-tious
flag-on
fla-grant
flam-beau
flam-boy-ant
fla-min-go
flam-ma-ble
flang-er
flank-er
flap-er-on
flar-ing
flat-u-lence
flau-tist
flav-a-none
fla-van-throne
fla-ves-cence
fla-vi-an-ic
fla-vin
fla-vo-nol
fla-vo-pur-pu-rin
fla-vor
fledg-ling
fletch-er-ize
flex-i-bi-lize
flex-om-e-ter
flex-or
flex-ur-al
flick-er-y
flin-ders
flir-ta-tious
float-er
floc-cu-lant (n.)
floc-cu-la-tor
floc-cu-lent (adj.)
flood-om-e-ter
flo-ral
Flor-ence
flor-enc-ite
Flor-en-tine
flo-res-cence
flo-ret
flo-ri-cul-tur-al
Flor-i-da
Flo-rid-i-an
flor-id-ness
flo-rif-er-ous
flo-ri-gen
flor-in
flo-rist
flo-riv-o-rous
flor-u-lent
flo-tage
flo-ta-tion
flo-til-la
flot-sam
floun-der
flour-ish
fluc-tu-ate
flu-en-cy
fluff-i-ness
flu-id-i-ty
flu-mer-in
flu-o-bo-rate
flu-o-bo-rite
flu-o-ran-thene
flu-or-ap-a-tite
flu-o-rene
flu-o-re-nyl
flu-o-res-ce-in
flu-o-res-cence
flu-o-ri-date
flu-o-ride
flu-o-ri-dize
flu-o-ri-nate
flu-o-rine
flu-o-rite
flu-o-ro-a-ce-tic
flu-o-ro-graph-ic
flu-o-rog-ra-phy
flu-o-rom-e-ter
flu-o-ro-scope
flu-o-ros-co-py
flu-o-ro-sis
flu-o-sil-i-cate
flu-o-si-lic-ic
flus-ter
flut-ist
flu-vi-al
flu-vi-ol-o-gy
flux-i-ble
flux-ion-al
flux-me-ter
Foam-ite
fo-cal-ize
fo-com-e-ter
fo-cus-er
fo-cus-ing

foi-ble
fol-de-rol
fo-li-a-ceous
fo-li-age
fo-lic
fo-lin-ic
fo-li-o-late
fol-lic-u-lar
fol-lic-u-li-tis
fo-men-ta-tion
fon-dant
fond-ling
fool-er-y
fool-ish
foo-zle
for-age
fo-ra-men
fo-ram-i-na
Fo-ram-i-nif-er-a
fo-ram-i-nif-er-ous
fo-ram-i-nous
for-ay
for-bear-ance
for-ceps
forc-er
forc-i-ble
forc-ing
fore-clo-sure
for-eign-er
fo-ren-si-cal
fore-see-a-ble
for-est-a-tion
for-est-er
for-est-ry
for-feit-er
for-feit-ure
forg-er
for-ger-y
fo-rint
for-mal
form-al-de-hyde
For-ma-lin
for-mal-ist
for-mal-i-ty
for-mal-ize
form-am-ide
form-am-i-dine
form-ant
for-mate
for-ma-tion
form-a-tive
form-a-zan
form-er (one who forms)
for-mer (previous)
for-mic
For-mi-ca
for-mi-cide
for-mi-da-ble
for-mol-ize
For-mo-san
for-mu-la
for-mu-la-ri-za-ble
for-mu-lar-i-za-tion
for-mu-lar-y
for-mu-la-tor
for-myl-ate
for-ni-ca-tion
for-syth-i-a
for-ti-eth
for-ti-fi-ca-tion
for-ti-fy
for-tis-si-mo
for-ti-tude
for-tress
for-tu-i-tous
for-tu-i-ty
for-tu-nato
for-ty
fo-rum
fos-sil-if-er-ous
fos-sil-ize
fos-so-ri-al
fos-ter
fou-lard
foun-da-tion
found-er (n.)
foun-der (v.; also as n.,
　act of foundering)
found-ling
found-ry
foun-tain
Four-drin-i-er
Fou-ri-er
four-ra-gere
fo-ve-o-late
Fow-ler
fowl-er
fra-cas
frac-tion-ate
frac-tious
frac-tog-ra-phy
frac-tur-al
frag-ile
fra-gil-i-ty
frag-men-tal
frag-men-tar-y
frag-ment-ize
fra-grance
frail-ty
fram-er
fran-chise
fran-ci-um
fran-gi-ble
fran-gi-pan-i

frank-furt-er
fran-kin-cense
fran-ti-cal-ly
fra-ter-nal
fra-ter-ni-ty
frat-er-nize
frat-ri-ci-dal
fraud-u-lent
frau-lein
freck-led
free-dom
freez-er
freight-er
fre-net-ic
fren-zied
fre-quen-cy
fre-quen-ta-tion
fresh-et
Freud-i-an
fric-an-deau
fric-as-see
frig-ate
fright-ened
frig-id
Frig-i-daire
fri-gid-i-ty
frig-o-rim-e-ter
fris-ket
frisk-i-ly
fri-vol-i-ty
friv-o-lous
frizz-ing
frol-icked
fron-des-cence
front-age
fron-tal
fron-ta-lis
fron-tier
fron-tis-piece
fron-to-gen-e-sis
front-o-ly-sis
fron-to-pa-ri-e-tal
frost-i-ness
froth-i-ly
frow-zy
fro-zen
fruc-tif-er-ous
fruc-ti-fy
fruc-tose
fru-gal-i-ty
fruit-age
fru-i-tion
frump-ish
frus-trate
frus-tum
fru-tes-cence
fu-ca-ceous
fuch-sia
fuch-sin-o-phil
fu-coi-dal
fu-cos-ter-ol
fu-el-er
fu-ga-cious
fu-gac-i-ty
fu-gi-tive
ful-crum
ful-fill-ing
ful-gen-ic
ful-gide
ful-gu-rant
ful-gu-ra-tion
ful-gu-rite
fu-lig-i-nous
full-ness
ful-mi-nate
ful-mi-nic
ful-min-u-ric
fu-ma-rase
fu-mar-ic
fu-mar-o-yl
fum-bler
fu-mig-a-cin
fu-mi-ga-tor
fu-mu-lus
fu-nam-bu-list
fun-da-men-tal
fun-dus-co-py
fu-ner-al
fu-ne-re-al
fun-gi-ble
fun-gi-ci-dal
fun-giv-o-rous
fun-goid
fun-gous (adj.)
fun-gus (n.)
fu-ni-cle
fu-nic-u-lar
fun-neled
fu-ra-nose
fu-ran-o-side
fur-be-low
fur-bish
fur-fu-ra-ceous
fur-fu-ral
fur-fu-ryl-i-dene
fu-ri-ous
fur-long
fur-lough
fur-nace
fur-nish-er
fur-ni-ture
fu-ro-ic
fu-ror
fur-ring

fur-ther
fur-thest
fur-tive
fu-run-cle
fu-run-cu-lo-sis
fu-ryl
fu-sar-i-um
fu-see
fu-sel
fu-se-lage
fu-si-ble
fu-si-lier
fu-sil-lade
fu-sion
fu-so-spi-ro-chete
fus-tian
fu-tile
fu-til-i-ty
fu-tu-ram-ic
fu-tur-ist
fu-tu-ri-ty
fuzz-i-ness

G

gab-ar-dine (fabric)
ga-ba-rit
gab-er-dine (gown)
ga-bi-on
ga-bling
Ga-bon
Gab-o-nese
Ga-bri-el
gadg-et-eer
gadg-et-ry
gad-o-le-ic
gad-o-lin-i-um
Gael-ic
gaf-fer
gag-er
gai-ner (diving)
gain-er (one who gains)
Gains-bor-ough
gait-er (harness)
gai-ter (overshoe)
ga-lac-ta-gogue
ga-lac-tic
ga-lac-to-lip-id
gal-ac-tom-e-ter
gal-ac-ton-ic
ga-lac-to-poi-e-sis
ga-lac-tos-a-mine
ga-lac-to-sid-ase
gal-ac-to-sis
ga-lac-tu-ron-ic
Ga-la-pa-gos
gal-a-te-a
ga-lax-i-al
gal-ax-y
ga-le-gine
ga-le-na
ga-le-nic (mineral)
ga-len-ic (medicinal)
ga-le-no-bis-mu-tite
Ga-li-cian
Gal-i-le-an
gal-lant-ry
gal-le-in
gal-ler-y
gal-li-na-ceous
gal-li-nule
Gal-lip-o-li
gal-li-vant
gal-lo-cy-a-nine
gal-lop
gal-op
ga-lore
ga-losh
gal-van-ic
gal-va-nism
gal-va-ni-za-tion
gal-va-nom-e-ter
gal-va-no-met-ric
gal-van-o-scope
Gam-bi-an
gam-bling
gam-boled
game-ster
ga-mete
ga-met-ic
ga-me-to-cide
gam-e-toid
gam-in
gam-ing
gam-ut
gan-der
Gan-dha-ra
Gan-dhi
gan-gling
gan-gli-on-at-ed
gan-gli-on-ic
gan-gli-o-side
gan-gre-nous
gang-ster
gan-is-ter
ga-nom-a-lite
gant-let (track)
Gan-tri-sin
gan-try
gap-er
ga-rage
gar-an-cine
Ga-rand
gar-bage

gar-bling
gar-den-er
gar-de-nia
Gar-di-nol
gar-gan-tu-an
gar-gling
gar-goyle
gar-ish
gar-land
gar-lick-y
gar-ner
gar-ni-er-ite
gar-nish-ee
gar-ni-ture
gar-ru-li-ty
gas-con-ade
gas-e-ous
gas-i-fy
gas-ket
gas-o-line
gas-om-e-ter
gas-o-met-ric
gas-sing
gas-ter-o-sto-ma-ta
gas-tral-gi-a
gas-tra-li-um
gas-trec-to-my
gas-tric
gas-tri-tis
gas-tro-cne-mi-us
gas-tro-en-ter-os-to-my
gas-tro-in-tes-ti-nal
gas-trol-o-ger
gas-tro-nom-ic
gas-tron-o-my
gas-tro-pod
Gas-trop-o-da
gas-tros-co-py
gas-tros-to-my
gath-er-ing
Ga-tun
gau-che-rie
gau-chos
gaud-i-ness
gau-lei-ter
Gaull-ist
gaunt-let
ga-vage
gav-el-er
ga-votte
gawk-i-ness
ga-zelle
gaz-er
ga-zette
gaz-et-teer
Gei-ger
gei-sha
gel-a-tin-ase
gel-at-i-nate
ge-lat-i-ni-za-tion
ge-lat-i-niz-er
ge-lat-i-no-chlo-ride
ge-lat-i-nous
ge-la-tion
geld-ing
ge-lid-i-ty
gel-ig-nite
gel-ling
gel-ose
gel-se-mic
gem-i-na-tive
Gem-i-ni
gem-mif-er-ous
gen-dar-mer-y
gen-der
gen-e-al-o-gist
gen-e-al-o-gy
gen-er-a-lis-si-mo
gen-er-al-i-ty
gen-er-al-ize
gen-er-a-tor
ge-ner-i-cal
gen-er-os-i-ty
gen-e-sis
gen-et
ge-net-i-cal
Ge-ne-va
ge-nial
ge-ni-al-i-ty
gen-ic
ge-nic-u-late
ge-nie
gen-in
ge-ni-o-plas-ty
ge-nis-te-in
gen-i-tal
gen-i-tive
gen-i-to-u-ri-nar-y
ge-nius
Gen-o-a
gen-o-ci-dal
ge-nome
ge-no-mere
gen-o-type
genth-ite
gen-tian-in
gen-tian-ose
gen-til-i-ty
gen-ti-o-bi-ose
gen-tis-ic
gen-ti-sin
gent-ly
gen-try
gen-u-flec-to-ry

gen-u-ine
ge-nus
ge-o-ce-rite
ge-oc-ro-nite
ge-o-des-ic
ge-od-e-sy
ge-o-det-i-cal
ge-od-ic
ge-o-dim-e-ter
ge-og-e-nous
ge-og-nos-tic
ge-og-o-ny
ge-og-ra-pher
ge-o-graph-ic
ge-og-ra-phy
ge-oi-dal
ge-o-log-i-cal
ge-ol-o-gist
ge-ol-o-gy
ge-om-a-lism
ge-om-e-ter
ge-o-met-ri-cal
ge-om-e-triz-er
ge-om-e-try
ge-o-pon-ics
geor-gette
Geor-gian
ge-os-co-py
ge-ot-ri-cho-sis
ge-o-trop-ic
ge-ot-ro-pism
ge-ran-ic
ge-ra-ni-ol
ge-ra-ni-um
ge-ra-nyl
Ge-rard
ge-rat-ic
ger-a-tol-o-gy
ge-rent
ger-i-a-tri-cian
ger-i-at-rics
ger-mane
ger-ma-nite
ger-ma-ni-um
ger-mi-ci-dal
ger-mi-nal
ger-mi-na-tor
Ge-ron-i-mo
ger-on-toc-ra-cy
ge-ron-to-log-i-cal
ger-on-tol-o-gy
Ger-trude
ger-und
ger-un-di-val
ge-run-dive
ge-sell-schaft
Ge-stalt
Ge-sta-po
ges-ta-tion
ges-tic-u-late
ges-ture
Geth-sem-a-ne
gey-ser
Gha-na-ian
gher-kin
ghoul-ish
gibbs-ite
Gi-bral-tar
gi-gan-tic
gi-gan-tism
gild-er
gil-son-ite
gim-baled
gin-ger
ging-ham
gin-gi-val
gin-gi-vi-tis
gink-go
gin-seng
gi-raffe
Gi-rard
gird-er
gir-dling
girl-ish
gi-tal-in
gi-tox-i-gen-in
giv-en
gla-bres-cent
gla-brous
gla-cial
gla-ci-a-tion
gla-cier
gla-ci-ol-o-gy
gla-ci-om-e-ter
glad-i-a-tor
glad-i-o-lus
glam-or-ous
glam-our
glan-ders
glan-du-lar
glar-ing
glass-ine
glass-i-ness
glau-ber-ite
glau-co-cer-i-nite
glau-co-ma
glau-co-ma-tous
glau-co-nite
glau-cous
glaz-er
gla-zier
glis-ten
gloam-ing
glob-al-ism

glo-bal-i-ty
glo-boid
glob-u-lar
glob-ule
glob-u-lif-er-ous
glob-u-lin
glo-mer-u-lar
gloom-i-ly
glo-ri-fy
glo-ri-ous
glos-sa-ry
gloss-i-ness
gloss-me-ter
Glouces-ter
glov-er
glu-ca-mine
glu-car-ic
glu-cin-i-um
glu-ci-tol
glu-ci-tyl
glu-co-nate
glu-con-ic
glu-co-py-ran-o-side
glu-co-sa-mine
glu-cose
glu-co-si-dase
glu-co-side
glu-cu-ron-ic
glu-cu-ron-i-dase
glu-cu-ro-nide
glu-ey-ness
glu-ing
glut-a-con-ic
glu-ta-mate
glu-tam-ic
glu-ta-min-ase
glu-ta-mine
glu-ta-min-ic
glu-tam-o-yl
glu-ta-thi-one
glu-te-al
glu-ten
glu-te-nin
glu-ten-ous
glu-ti-nous
glyc-er-ate
gly-ce-mi-a
gly-ce-mic
glyc-er-al-de-hyde
gly-cer-ic
glyc-er-ide
glyc-er-in
glyc-er-ol
glyc-er-o-phos-phor-ic
glyc-er-yl
glyc-ide
gly-cid-ic
glyc-i-dol
gly-cine
gly-co-cy-a-mine
gly-co-gen
gly-co-gen-ol-y-sis
gly-co-gen-o-lyt-ic
gly-col-y-sis
gly-co-lyt-ic
gly-co-si-dase
glyc-u-re-sis
gly-cyl
gly-ox-yl-ic
glyp-tol-o-gy
gnath-ism
gneiss-oid
gnom-ish
gno-se-ol-o-gy
gno-sis
gnos-tic
goa-tee
gob-ble-dy-gook
gob-bler
Go-be-lin
gob-lin
Goe-thals
goi-ter
goi-tro-gen-ic
goi-tro-ge-nic-i-ty
goi-trous
gold-en
Go-li-ath
go-nad-ec-to-my
go-nad-o-tro-phin
gon-do-la
gon-fa-lon
go-nid-i-al
go-nid-i-um
go-ni-om-e-ter
go-ni-o-met-ric
gon-o-coc-ci
gon-or-rhe-al
goo-gol-plex
go-pher
gor-geous
go-ril-la
gor-lic
Go-shen
gos-pel-er
gos-sa-mer
gos-syp-i-trin
Goth-am-ite
Goth-ic
gour-man-diz-er
gov-ern-ess
gov-ern-men-tal
gov-er-nor
goy-a-zite

Graaf-i-an
grac-ile
gra-cious
gra-da-tion
grad-a-to-ry
grad-er
gra-di-ent
gra-di-om-e-ter
grad-u-al
grad-u-ate
graft-er
gra-ham
grai-ning (fish)
grain-ing (of grain)
gram-i-cid-in
gram-i-na-les
gram-ine
gra-min-e-ous
gram-mar-i-an
gram-mat-i-cal
gra-na-ry
gran-dam
gran-deur
gran-dil-o-quent
gran-di-ose
grang-er
gran-ite
gra-nit-ic
gran-o-blas-tic
gran-o-di-o-rite
grant-ee
grant-er
Grant-ham
grant-or
gran-u-lar-i-ty
gran-u-late
gran-ule
gran-u-lo-ma-to-sis
gran-u-lous
graph-eme
gra-phe-mic
graph-i-cal
graph-ite
gra-phit-ic
gra-phol-o-gy
graph-o-met-ric
grap-pling
grasp-er
grat-er
grat-i-cule
grat-i-fy
grat-in
gra-tis
grat-i-tude
gra-tu-i-tous
gra-va-men
grav-eled
grav-el-ly
grav-en
grav-id
gra-vid-i-ty
gra-vim-e-ter
grav-i-met-ri-cal-ly
gra-vim-e-try
grav-i-sphere
grav-i-tat-er
grav-i-tom-e-ter
grav-i-ty
gra-vure
graz-er
greas-er
greas-i-ness
Gre-cian
greed-i-ness
green-sward
gre-gar-i-ous
Gre-go-ri-an
grei-sen
gre-nade
gren-a-dier
gren-a-dine
Gresh-am
grid-i-ron
griev-ance
griev-ous
Gri-gnard
grill-age
grim-ace
gri-mal-kin
grind-er
grin-gos
griph-ite
gris-e-o-ful-vin
gris-tly
griz-zly
gro-cer-y
gro-per (fish)
grop-er
gro-schen
gros-grain
gro-tesque
gro-tes-que-rie
ground-ling
grou-per (fish)
group-er
grou-ser (timber; cleats)
grous-er
grout-er
grov-el-er
growl-er
grum-bler
gru-mose
grun-ion
Gru-yere

guai-ac
guai-a-col
Gua-ma-ni-an
gua-na-mine
gua-ni-dine
gua-nif-er-ous
gua-nine
gua-nyl-ic
gua-ra-ni
guar-an-tee (n., v.)
guar-an-ty (n.) (legal)
guard-i-an
Gua-te-ma-la
gua-va
gua-yu-le
gu-ber-na-to-ri-al
gudg-eon
guer-don
Guern-sey
guer-ril-la
guid-ance
gui-don
guil-lo-tine
guilt-i-ly
Guin-ea
gui-pure
gui-tar
gul-den
gul-li-ble
gu-lose
Gun-ite
gur-gi-ta-tion
gur-gling
gur-nard
gush-er
gus-set
gus-ta-to-ry
Gu-ten-berg
gut-tur-al
Guy-a-nese
gym-na-si-um
gym-nas-tic
gym-no-sto-ma-ta
gym-no-stom-a-tous
gyn-e-coc-ra-cy
gyn-e-col-o-gy
gyp-se-ous
gyp-sif-er-ous
gy-ra-to-ry
gy-roi-dal
gy-ro-scop-ic

H

ha-be-as
ha-ben-dum
hab-er-dash-er-y
ha-bil-i-ment
hab-it-a-ble
hab-i-ta-tion
ha-bit-u-al
ha-bit-u-e
ha-chure
ha-ci-en-da
hack-ler
Ha-des
haf-ni-um
Ha-ga-nah
hag-i-ol-o-gy
Hai-fa
hai-kwan
Hai-tian
ha-la-tion
hal-a-zone
hal-berd-ier
hal-cy-on
hal-i-but
ha-lide
hal-i-dom
hal-i-eu-tics
hal-i-ste-re-sis
ha-lite
hal-i-to-sis
hal-le-lu-jah
Hal-low-een
hal-lu-ci-na-tion
ha-lo
hal-o-gen-a-tion
ha-log-e-nous
hal-o-hy-drin
ha-lom-e-ter
ha-lot-ri-chite
halt-er (one who halts)
hal-ter (other meanings)
ham-burg-er
Ham-mar-skjold
ham-per
ham-ster
hand-i-cap
hand-i-craft
hand-i-ly
hand-i-work
han-dle-a-ble
han-dler
han-dling
hand-som-est
hang-ar
hang-er
han-ker
Han-o-ver
Ha-nuk-kah
hap-pi-ness

har-a-kir-i
ha-rangued
ha-rangu-er
har-assed
har-bin-ger
har-bor
hard-en-er
har-di-ness
Har-ding
har-dy
ha-rem
har-i-cot
hark-en
har-le-quin
har-ma-line
har-mo-ni-al
har-mon-i-ca
har-mo-ni-ous
har-mo-nize
har-ness
harp-ist
har-poon
harp-si-chord
har-te-beest
Hart-ley
har-um-scar-um
har-vest-er
hash-ish
has-sled
has-tate
has-ten
hast-i-ly
Hast-ings
hatch-er-y
hatch-et
ha-tred
haugh-ti-ness
hau-teur
Ha-va-na
ha-ven
hav-er-sack
hav-oc
Ha-wai-ian
haw-ser
haz-ard-ous
ha-zel
haz-ing
head-quar-ters
health-i-est
heart-i-ly
heat-er
hea-then
heath-er
heav-en
heav-i-ly
Heav-i-side
heb-dom-a-dal
He-bra-ic
He-brew
Heb-ri-des
Hec-a-te
hec-a-tomb
heck-ler
hec-o-gen-in
hec-tare
hec-to-li-ter
hec-to-me-ter
hed-er-in
he-don-ics
he-do-nism
he-do-nis-tic
he-do-nom-e-ter
he-dral
heg-e-mon-ic
he-gem-o-ny
he-gi-ra
heif-er
hei-li-gen-schein
hei-nous
Hel-e-na
hel-e-nin
he-li-a-cal
he-li-an-the-mum
he-li-an-thus
hel-i-cal
hel-i-ces
hel-i-coi-dal
Hel-i-con
hel-i-cop-ter
he-li-o-graph
he-li-og-ra-phy
he-li-om-e-ter
he-li-o-met-ric
he-li-om-e-try
he-li-o-pho-bic
he-li-o-trope
he-li-ot-ro-pism
hel-i-port
he-li-um
he-lix
he-lix-om-e-ter
Hel-len-ic
Hel-le-nism
Hel-les-pont
hel-min-thic
hel-min-tho-spo-rin
hel-ot-ism
hel-ter-skel-ter
hel-vite
hel-vol-ic
he-ma-cy-tom-e-ter
he-ma-fi-brite
he-mag-glu-ti-nin
he-mal-bu-men

he-man-gi-o-ma-to-sis
he-ma-poi-e-sis
he-mar-thro-sis
he-ma-tal
he-ma-te-in
he-mat-ic
hem-a-tin-om-e-ter
hem-a-tite
hem-a-tit-ic
hem-a-to-cele
hem-a-to-crit
hem-a-tog-e-nous
hem-a-to-lite
he-ma-tol-o-gy
hem-a-to-ma
hem-a-tom-e-ter
hem-a-to-por-phy-rin
hem-a-to-sis
hem-a-tox-y-lin
hem-i-ac-e-tal
hem-i-cy-clic
hem-i-he-dral
hem-i-kar-y-on
he-min
he-mip-ter-oid
hem-i-spher-ic
hem-i-stich-al
he-mo-chro-mo-gen
he-mo-chro-mom-e-ter
he-mo-co-ni-o-sis
he-mo-cy-a-nin
he-mo-cyte
he-mo-cy-tol-y-sis
he-mo-glo-bin
he-mo-glo-bi-nom-e-ter
he-mol-y-sin
he-mol-y-sis
he-mo-lyt-ic
he-mom-e-ter
hem-or-rhag-ic
hem-or-rhoi-dal
he-mo-sid-er-in
he-mo-sid-er-o-sis
he-mo-stat-ic
hemp-en
hen-e-quen
hep-a-rin
he-pat-i-ca
hep-a-ti-tis
hep-a-to-cu-pre-in
hep-a-to-fla-vin
hep-a-tos-co-py
hep-ta-dec-yl
hep-tag-o-nal
hep-tam-e-ter
hep-tar-chy
hep-tu-lose
hep-tyl-ene
her-ald
he-ral-dic
her-ba-ceous
herb-age
her-bar-i-um
her-bi-ci-dal
her-biv-o-rous
Her-cu-les
her-e-dit-a-ment
he-red-i-tar-y
Her-e-ford
her-e-sy
her-e-tic
he-ret-i-cal
her-it-age
her-maph-ro-dite
her-me-neu-tics
her-met-i-cal
her-mit-age
her-ne-ar-in
her-ni-a
her-ni-ot-o-my
he-ro-ic
her-o-ine
her-o-ism
her-on
her-pes
her-pe-tol-o-gy
Hertz-i-an
hes-i-tan-cy
hes-i-tat-er
hes-i-ta-tion
hes-per-i-din
Hes-per-is
Hes-sian
hess-ite
het-er-o-aux-in
het-er-o-cy-clic
het-er-o-dox-y
het-er-o-ge-ne-ous
het-er-og-e-nous
het-er-o-ki-ne-sis
het-er-ol-o-gy
het-er-ol-y-sis
het-er-o-ou-si-a
het-er-o-pol-y
het-er-os-co-py
hex-a-chlo-ro-eth-ane
hex-a-gon
hex-ag-o-nal
hex-am-e-ter
hex-a-no-yl
hex-es-trol
hex-os-a-mine
hex-u-lose

hex-u-ron-ic
hex-yl-ene
hi-a-tus
hi-ber-na-tor
hick-o-ry
hid-e-ous
hi-dro-sis
hi-drot-ic
hi-er-ar-chy
hi-er-o-glyph-ic
high-fa-lu-tin
hi-lar-i-ous
hill-ocked
hi-lus
Hi-ma-la-yan
hin-der (v.)
hind-er (adj.)
hin-drance
Hin-du-stan-i
hint-er
hin-ter-land
Hip-po-crat-ic
hip-po-pot-a-mus
hip-pu-ric
Hir-o-shi-ma
hir-su-tal
His-pa-ni-a
His-pan-ic
his-pa-ni-dad
his-tam-i-nase
his-ta-mine
his-ti-dine
his-to-log-i-cal
his-tol-o-gy
his-tol-y-sis
his-to-ri-an
his-tor-i-cal
his-to-ric-i-ty
his-to-ry
his-tri-on-ic
hith-er-to
hock-ey
hod-o-graph
Hoh-en-zol-lern
hoist-er
hold-er
hol-i-day
ho-li-ness
hol-lan-daise
Hol-land-er
hol-mi-um
hol-o-caust
hol-o-graph
hol-o-he-dral
hol-o-pho-tal
ho-loph-ra-sis
hol-ster
Hol-yoke
hom-age
ho-me-ol-o-gy
ho-me-o-path-ic
ho-me-op-a-thy
ho-me-o-sta-sis
hom-i-ci-dal
hom-i-ly
hom-ish
hom-o-cys-teine
ho-mog-a-my
ho-mo-ge-ne-i-ty
ho-mo-ge-ne-ous
ho-mog-e-ni-za-tion
ho-mog-e-niz-er
ho-mog-e-nous
hom-o-log
ho-mol-o-gous
ho-mol-y-sis
hom-o-nym-ic
ho-mo-thet-ic
Hon-du-ran
hon-ey
Hon-i-ton
Hon-o-lu-lu
hon-or-a-ble
hon-o-rar-i-um
hon-or-ar-y
hon-or-if-ic
Hoo-ver
ho-ra-ry
ho-ri-zon
hor-i-zon-tal
hor-mo-nal
hor-mon-ic
ho-rol-o-gy
hor-o-scope
ho-ros-co-py
hor-ren-dous
hor-rif-ic
hor-ta-to-ry
hor-ti-cul-tur-al
ho-san-na
ho-sier-y
hos-pi-ta-ble
hos-pi-tal-i-za-tion
hos-tage
host-al
hos-tel-ry
host-ess
hos-til-i-ty
hos-tler
Hou-dry
hous-ing

hov-el
hov-er
how-it-zer
howl-er
how-lite
hua-ra-che
huck-ster
Hue-ne-me
Hu-gue-not
hul-la-ba-loo
hu-man-i-tar-i-an
hu-man-ize
hum-bling
hu-mec-tant
hu-mer-us
hu-mid-i-ty
hu-mil-i-a-tion
hu-min
hum-ite
hu-mi-ture
hu-mor-ous
hu-mous (adj.)
hu-mu-lene
hu-mus (n.)
hun-dred
Hun-gar-i-an
hun-ger
hun-gry
hunt-er
hur-dler
hurl-er
Hu-ron
hur-ried-ly
hur-ter (bumper)
hurt-er
hur-tling
hus-band-ry
husk-i-ness
hust-ing
hus-tler
hy-a-cin-thine
Hy-a-des
hy-a-les-cence
hy-a-lin-i-za-tion
hy-a-li-no-sis
hy-al-o-gen
hy-al-o-phane
hy-a-lu-ro-nate
hy-a-lu-ron-i-dase
hy-brid-ize
hy-dan-to-in-ate
hy-da-tid-o-sis
hy-da-to-gen-ic
hy-drac-ry-late
hy-dra-cryl-ic
hy-dral-a-zine
hy-dra-mat-ic
hy-dra-mine
hy-dran-ge-a
hy-drar-gil-lite
hy-dras-ti-nine
hy-dra-tor
hy-drau-lic
hy-dra-zide
hy-draz-i-dine
hy-dra-zine
hy-dra-zin-i-um
hy-dra-zo-ate
hy-dra-zone
hy-dre-mi-a
hy-dri-od-ic
hy-dri-o-dide
hy-dro-ab-i-et-yl
hy-dro-cal-u-mite
hy-dro-cele
hy-dro-ce-phal-ic
hy-dro-ceph-a-lous (adj.)
hy-dro-ceph-a-lus (n.)
hy-dro-chlo-ric
hy-dro-flu-or-ide
hy-dro-form-ate
hy-dro-gen-a-tion
hy-dro-gen-a-tor
hy-drog-e-nous
hy-drog-no-sy
hy-drog-ra-pher
hy-dro-graph-ic
hy-dro-lase
hy-drol-o-gy
hy-drol-y-sate
hy-drol-y-sis
hy-dro-lyze
hy-drom-e-ter
hy-dro-met-ric
hy-dro-ni-um
hy-drop-a-thy
hy-dro-pho-bi-a
hy-dro-pon-ics
hy-drox-ide
hy-drox-im-i-no
hy-drox-y-am-i-no
hy-drox-y-bu-tyr-ic
hy-drox-yl-a-mine
hy-drox-yl-ate
hy-drox-y-zine
hy-e-tom-e-ter
hy-gi-en-ic
hy-gien-ist
hy-grom-e-ter
hy-gro-met-ric
hy-gro-scop-ic
hy-me-ne-al
hy-me-no-cal-lis

hy-per-bo-la
hy-per-bo-le
hy-per-bol-i-cal
hy-per-bo-loi-dal
hy-per-crit-i-cal
hy-per-e-mi-a
hy-per-go-lic-i-ty
hy-per-i-cin
hy-per-in
hy-per-o-pi-a
hy-per-sthenc
hy-per-ten-sive
hy-per-troph-ic
hy-per-tro-phy
hy-phen-ate
hyp-no-sis
hyp-not-ic
hyp-no-tism
hy-po-bro-mous
hy-po-chlo-rous
hy-po-chon-dri-a
hy-poc-ri-sy
hypo-crite
hy-po-der-mic
hy-poid
hy-po-i-o-dous
hy-po-mor-pho-sis
hy-pos-ta-sis
hy-pot-e-nuse
hy-poth-e-cate
hy-poth-e-sis
hy-po-thet-i-cal
hy-pox-e-mi-a
hy-pox-i-a
hyp-som-e-ter
hys-taz-a-rin
hys-ter-ec-to-my
hys-ter-e-sis
hys-te-ri-a
hys-ter-i-cal
hys-ter-or-rha-phy
hys-ter-os-co-py
hys-ter-ot-o-my
hy-ther-graph

I

i-at-ro-gen-ic
i-at-ro-ge-nic-i-ty
I-be-ri-an
Ice-land-er
Ice-lan-dic
ich-neu-mon
ich-nog-ra-phy
ich-thy-ol
ich-thy-o-sis
i-ci-cle
ic-ing
i-con-o-clast
i-co-nog-ra-phy
i-co-nol-a-try
i-co-nom-e-ter
i-con-o-scope
ic-ter-ic
I-da-ho-an
i-de-al-ism
i-de-al-ist
i-de-al-i-za-tion
i-den-ti-cal
i-den-ti-fi-a-ble
i-de-oc-ra-cy
i-de-og-ra-phy
i-de-o-log-i-cal
i-de-ol-o-gy
id-i-o-cy
i-di-o-gram-mat-ic
id-i-om
id-i-o-mat-ic
id-i-om-e-ter
id-i-o-path-ic
id-i-op-a-thy
id-i-o-syn-cra-sy
id-i-ot-i-cal
id-i-tol
i-dol-a-ter
i-dol-a-trous
i-dol-ize
i-dyl-lic
i-dyl-list
ig-loo
ig-ne-ous
ig-nit-a-ble
ig-nit-er
ig-ni-tron
ig-no-min-i-ous
ig-no-min-y
ig-no-ra-mus
ig-no-rance
Ig-o-rot
il-e-i-tis
il-e-os-to-my
il-e-um
il-leg-i-ble
il-lic-it
il-lim-it-a-ble
Il-li-nois-an
il-lu-mi-nant
il-lu-mi-na-tor
il-lu-min-er
il-lu-mi-nom-e-ter
il-lu-sive
il-lu-so-ry
il-lus-tra-tive

il-lu-vi-al
il-men-ite
I-lo-i-lo
im-age-ry
i-mag-i-na-ble
i-mag-i-nar-y
i-mag-i-na-tive
i-ma-go
im-be-cil-i-ty
im-bri-cate
im-bro-glio
im-id-az-ole
im-id-az-o-line
im-ide
im-i-do
im-in-az-ole
im-i-no
im-i-ta-tive
im-mac-u-late
im-ma-nence
im-mar-gin-ate
im-me-di-a-cy
im-mem-o-ra-ble
im-me-mo-ri-al
im-men-si-ty
im-men-su-ra-ble
im-mers-i-ble
im-mers-ing
im-mer-sion
im-mi-gra-tion
im-mi-nent
im-mis-ci-ble
im-mo-late
im-mu-ni-ty
im-mu-ni-za-tion
Im-mu-no-gen
im-mu-nol-o-gy
im-mu-ta-ble
im-pac-tive
im-pal-pa-ble
im-par-ta-tion
im-part-i-ble
im-pass-a-ble
im-pas-si-ble
im-pas-sive
im-pa-tience
im-pe-cu-ni-ous
im-ped-ance
im-ped-i-ble
im-ped-i-men-tal
im-pe-dom-e-ter
im-pe-dor
im-pel-ling
im-per-a-tive
im-pe-ra-tor
im-per-cep-ti-ble
im-per-fo-rate
im-pe-ri-al
im-per-iled
im-pe-ri-ous
im-per-scrip-ti-ble
im-per-son-a-tor
im-per-sua-si-ble
im-per-turb-a-ble
im-per-vi-ous
im-pe-ti-go
im-pet-u-os-i-ty
im-pe-tus
im-ping-er
im-ping-ing
im-pi-ous
imp-ish
im-plac-a-ble
im-plan-ta-tion
im-ple-men-tal
im-pli-cate
im-plic-it-ly
im-plo-sion
im-pol-i-tic
im-por-tance
im-por-tant
im-port-er
im-por-tu-nate
im-post-er
im-pos-tor (deceiver)
im-pos-ture
im-po-tence
im-pov-er-ish
im-prec-a-to-ry
im-preg-na-tor
im-pre-sar-i-o
im-pre-scrip-ti-ble
im-press-a-ble
im-press-i-ble
im-pres-sive
im-pri-ma-tur
im-promp-tu
im-prov-i-dent
im-prov-i-sa-tion
im-pro-vise
im-pu-dence
im-pul-sive
im-pu-ni-ty
im-pu-ri-ty
im-put-a-ble
im-pu-ta-tion
in-ad-vert-ent
in-am-o-ra-ta
in-an-i-mate
in-a-ni-tion
in-an-i-ty
in-au-gu-ra-tion
in-cal-cu-la-ble

in-ca-les-cent
in-can-des-cent
in-ca-pac-i-tate
in-car-cer-ate
in-car-nate
in-cen-di-ar-y
in-cen-tive
in-cep-tive
in-ces-tu-ous
in-cho-ate
in-ci-den-tal
in-cin-er-a-tor
in-cip-i-ent
in-ci-sive
in-ci-sor
in-cit-ant
in-ci-ta-tion
in-cit-er
in-clem-ent
in-clin-a-ble
in-cli-na-tion
in-cli-na-to-ry
in-cli-nom-e-ter
in-clud-a-ble
in-clu-sive
in-cog-ni-to
in-com-pa-ra-ble
in-com-pat-i-ble
in-con-cus-si-ble
in-con-gru-ous
in-cor-po-ra-tor
in-cor-ri-gi-ble
in-creas-er
in-cred-i-ble
in-cre-du-li-ty
in-cred-u-lous
in-cre-ment
in-crim-i-nate
in-crus-ta-tion
in-cu-ba-tor
in-cu-bous (adj.)
in-cu-bus (n.)
in-cum-bent
in-cu-nab-u-lum
in-cur-a-ble
in-cur-ra-ble
in-cur-sive
in-da-mine
in-da-zole
in-de-fat-i-ga-ble
in-dem-ni-fi-ca-tion
in-dene
in-den-ta-tion
in-dent-er
in-den-ture
in-de-pend-ent
in-de-struct-i-ble
In-di-an
In-di-an-a
In-di-an-ap-o-lis
In-di-an-i-an
in-di-can
in-di-ca-tion
in-dic-a-tive
in-di-ca-tor
in-di-ci-a
in-dic-o-lite
in-dict-a-ble
in-dict-er
In-dies
in-dig-e-nous
in-di-gent
in-di-gest-i-ble
in-di-go
in-dig-o-lite
In-di-go-sol
in-di-go-tin
in-di-ru-bin
in-dis-pen-sa-ble
in-dis-pu-ta-ble
in-dis-sol-u-ble
in-di-um
in-di-vid-u-al-ize
in-di-vis-i-ble
in-doc-tri-nate
in-dole-a-ce-tic
in-do-lent
in-do-line
in-do-lyl
in-dom-i-ta-ble
In-do-ne-sian
in-do-phe-nin
in-dox-yl
in-du-bi-ta-ble
in-duc-er
in-duc-i-ble
in-duct-ance
in-duct-ee
in-duc-tive
in-duc-tom-e-ter
in-duc-tor
in-duc-to-ri-um
in-dul-gence
in-du-line
in-du-ra-tive
in-dus-tri-al-i-za-tion
in-e-bri-ate
in-ef-fa-ble
in-ef-face-a-ble
in-e-luc-ta-ble
in-ep-ti-tude
in-ert-ance
in-er-tial

in-ev-i-ta-ble
in-ex-o-ra-ble
in-ex-press-i-ble
in-ex-pres-sive
in-ex-pung-i-ble
in-ex-tir-pa-ble
in-ex-tri-ca-ble
in-fa-mous
in-fan-ti-cide
in-fan-tile
in-fan-try
in-fat-u-ate
in-fect-ant
in-fect-i-ble
in-fec-tious
in-fec-tive
in-fe-lic-i-tous
in-fer-a-ble
in-fer-ence
in-fe-ri-or-i-ty
in-fer-nal
in-fest-ant
in-fes-ta-tion
in-fil-tra-tor
in-fil-trom-e-ter
in-fi-nite
in-fin-i-tes-i-mal
in-fin-i-ti-val
in-fin-i-ty
in-fir-ma-ry
in-fir-mi-ty
in-flat-a-ble
in-flect-i-ble
in-flict-er
in-flo-res-cence
in-flu-en-tial
in-for-mal-i-ty
in-for-ma-lize
in-form-ant
in-for-ma-tion
in-form-a-tive
in-form-er
in-fract-i-ble
in-fran-gi-ble
in-fring-er
in-fun-dib-u-lum
in-fu-ri-ate
in-fu-si-ble
in-fu-so-ri-al
in-ge-nious
in-ge-nue
in-ge-nu-i-ty
in-gen-u-ous
in-ges-tant
in-got
in-gra-ti-ate
in-grat-i-tude
in-gra-ves-cence
in-grav-i-date
in-gre-di-ent
in-gui-nal
in-gur-gi-tate
in-hab-it-a-bil-i-ty
in-hab-it-ant
in-hab-it-er
in-hal-ant
in-ha-la-tion
in-ha-la-tor
in-her-ent
in-her-it-a-ble
in-her-it-ance
in-hib-it-er
in-hi-bi-tion
in-hib-i-tor (chem.)
in-hib-i-to-ry
in-hos-pit-a-ble
in-im-i-cal
in-im-i-ta-ble
in-iq-ui-tous
i-ni-tial
i-ni-ti-a-tive
in-jec-tor
in-junc-tive
in-ju-ri-ous
in-kling
in me-mo-ri-am
in-nas-ci-ble
in-noc-u-ous
in-no-va-to-ry
in-nu-en-do
in-nu-mer-a-ble
in-oc-u-late
in-or-di-nate
i-no-si-tol
in per-so-nam
in-quir-er
in-quir-y
in-qui-si-tion
in-quis-i-tive
in-sa-tia-ble
in-scrib-a-ble
in-scrib-er
in-scru-ta-ble
in-sec-ti-ci-dal
in-sec-tiv-o-ra
in-sec-tiv-o-rous
in-sec-tol-o-gy
in-sem-i-na-tion
in-sen-sate
in-ser-tive
in-sid-i-ous
in-sig-ne
in-sig-ni-a

in-sig-nif-i-cant
in-sip-id
in-si-pid-i-ty
in-sist-ence
in-sist-er
in-so-lence
in-sol-u-ble
in-sol-vent
in-spec-tor
In-spec-to-scope
in-spir-a-ble
in-spi-ra-tion
in-spir-a-tive
in-stal-la-tion
in-stalled
in-stan-ta-ne-ous
in-sti-ga-tor
in-stinc-tive
in-sti-tu-tor
in-struct-i-ble
in-struc-tive
in-struc-tor
in-stru-men-tal-i-ty
in-su-lar
in-su-la-tor
in-su-lin
in-su-per-a-ble
in-sur-ance
in-sur-er
in-sur-gen-cy
in-tagl-io
in-tan-gi-ble
in-te-ger
in-te-gral
in-te-gra-tor
in-teg-ri-ty
in-teg-u-men-tal
in-tel-lec-tu-al
in-tel-li-gen-tsi-a
in-tend-ant
in-ten-si-fy
in-ten-si-tom-e-ter
in-ten-si-ty
in-ten-sive
in-ter-ca-lar-y
in-ter-cede
in-ter-cep-tor
in-ter-cos-tal
in-ter-est
in-ter-fer-ence
in-ter-fer-om-e-ter
in-ter-im
in-te-ri-or
in-ter-jec-tor
in-ter-jec-tur-al
in-ter-lin-gua
in-ter-loc-u-to-ry
in-ter-lop-er
in-ter-me-di-ate
in-ter-mi-na-ble
in-tern
in-ter-nal
in-ter-ne-cine
in-ter-nist
in-ter-po-lat-er
in-ter-pret-a-ble
in-ter-pre-ta-tive
in-ter-pret-er
in-ter-pre-tive
in-ter-ro-gate
in-ter-rog-a-to-ry
in-ter-rupt-ed
in-ter-rupt-er
in-ter-rupt-i-ble
in-ter-rupt-ing
in-ter-stic-es
in-ter-sti-tial
in-ter-ven-er
in-ter-ve-nor (law)
in-tes-tate
in-tes-ti-nal
in-ti-ma-cy
in-ti-mat-er
in-tim-i-da-tor
in-to-nate
In-tox-im-e-ter
in-trac-ta-ble
in-tran-si-gent (n., adj.)
in-trav-a-sa-tion
in-tra-ve-nous
in-trep-id
in-tre-pid-i-ty
in-tri-ca-cy
in-trigu-er
in-trigu-ing
in-trin-si-cal
in-tro-duc-to-ry
in-tro-spec-tive
in-tro-ver-si-ble
in-trud-er
in-tru-sive
in-tu-i-tive
in-tu-mes-cence
in-u-lase
in-un-da-tor
in-vad-er
in-va-lid (n., v., adj., not well)
in-val-i-date
in-val-id (adj., not valid)
in-va-lid-i-ty

in-var-i-a-ble
in-vec-tive
in-vei-gle
in-vent-a-ble
in-ven-tor
in-ven-to-ry
in-vert-ase
in-ver-te-brate
in-vert-er
in-vert-i-ble
in-ver-tor (muscle)
in-ves-ti-ga-tor
in-ves-ti-ture
in-ves-tor
in-vet-er-ate
in-vid-i-ous
in-vig-o-rate
in-vin-ci-ble
in-vi-o-la-ble
in-vis-i-ble
in-vi-ta-tion
in-vit-er
in-vo-ca-tion
in-voc-a-tive
in-vo-lu-cre
i-o-di-nate
i-o-dine
i-o-din-oph-i-lous
i-o-do-a-ce-tic
i-o-do-form
i-o-do-hy-drin
i-o-dom-e-try
i-o-do-ni-um
i-o-do-phthal-ein
i-o-do-pyr-a-cet
i-o-dox-y-ben-zene
i-od-y-rite
I-o-ni-an
I-on-ic
i-o-ni-um
i-on-i-za-tion
i-o-nom-e-ter
i-o-none
i-on-o-spher-ic
I-o-wan
ip-e-cac
I-ra-ni-an
i-ras-ci-ble
ir-i-dec-to-my
ir-i-des-cence
i-rid-ic
i-rid-i-um
i-ron-i-cal
i-ron-y (of iron)
i-ro-ny (sarcasm)
Ir-o-quois
ir-ra-di-ate
ir-rad-i-ca-ble
ir-rec-on-cil-a-ble
ir-re-duc-i-ble
ir-ref-ra-ga-ble
ir-ref-u-ta-ble
ir-re-me-di-a-ble
ir-rep-a-ra-ble
ir-re-press-i-ble
ir-re-sist-i-ble
ir-re-spon-si-ble
ir-re-vers-i-ble
ir-rev-o-ca-ble
ir-ri-ga-ble
ir-ri-tant
i-sa-go-ge
i-sa-gog-ics
I-sa-iah
i-sa-tin-ic
is-che-mi-a
i-sin-glass
Is-lam-ic
is-land-er
is-let
i-so-am-yl-ene
i-so-bar-ic
i-so-bath-y-therm
i-soch-ro-nal
i-so-chrone
i-soch-ro-nism
i-so-cla-site
i-so-cli-nal
i-so-drin
i-sog-a-mous
i-so-gly-co-sa-mine
i-sog-o-nal
i-so-gon-ic
i-so-lat-a-ble
i-so-leu-cine
i-so-mer-ic
i-so-mer-ize
i-so-met-ri-cal-ly
i-som-e-try
i-so-ni-a-zid
i-so-phthal-ic
i-so-pre-noid
i-so-pro-pe-nyl
i-so-pro-pyl
i-sos-ce-les
i-sos-ta-sy
i-so-ther-mal
i-so-top-ic
i-so-to-py
i-so-tron
Is-rae-li
Is-ra-el-ite
Is-tan-bul

isth-mus	Jun-ker	Kirch-hoff	lan-dau-let	leg-is-la-tor	lid-o-caine
it-a-con-ic	junk-er	Kirsch-ner	Lang-shan	leg-is-la-to-ri-al	Lie-der-kranz
I-tal-ian	jun-ket-eer	kitch-en-ette	lan-guage	le-git-i-ma-cy	lien-ee
i-tal-i-cize	Ju-pi-ter	Kjel-dahl	lan-guish	leg-ume	lien-or
i-tem-ize	Ju-ras-sic	Klam-ath (river, etc.)	lan-guor-ous	le-gu-mi-nous	lieu-ten-an-cy
it-er-ate	ju-rat	Klee-nex	lan-o-ce-ric	Leices-ter	lift-er
i-tin-er-ar-y	ju-rid-i-cal	klep-to-ma-ni-a	lan-o-lin	leish-ma-ni-a-sis	lig-a-men-tous
i-vo-ry	ju-ri-di-cial (obs.)	klys-tron	la-nos-ter-ol	lei-sure	li-ga-tion
	ju-ris-dic-tion	knav-ish	Lan-ston	lem-on-ade	lig-a-ture
J	ju-ris-pru-dence	knick-er-bock-er	lan-tern	lend-er	light-ened
	ju-ris-tic	knock-er	lan-tha-nide	length-en	light-en-ing (brighten-ing)
Ja-bot	ju-ror	knowl-edge-a-ble	lan-tha-num	le-ni-en-cy	
jack-al	jus-tice	knuck-led	lan-thi-o-nine	len-i-ty	light-er-age
jack-a-napes	jus-ti-ci-a-ble	kc-gas-in	lap-a-rot-o-my	Lent-en	light-ning (a flash)
jack-et	jus-ti-fi-ca-tion	Koh-i-noor	la-pel-er	len-ti-cel	lig-ne-ous
Ja-cob	jus-tif-i-ca-to-ry	kohl-ra-bi	lap-i-dar-y	len-tic-u-lar	lig-nes-cent
Jac-o-be-an	ju-ve-nes-cence	ko-jic	la-pis	len-ti-go	lig-nite
Ja-co-bi-an	ju-ve-nile	kok-sa-ghyz	lap-is la-zu-li	len-til	lig-num vi-tae
Jac-o-bin	ju-ve-nil-i-ty	ko-lin-sky	La-o-tian	Leom-in-ster	lig-ro-in
jac-o-net	jux-ta-po-si-tion	kol-khoz	Lar-a-mie	Leon-ard	lig-u-lar
Jac-quard		Kom-man-da-tu-ra	lar-ce-nous	Le-o-nar-desque	lik-a-ble
Jacque-mi-not	**K**	ko-nim-e-ter	lar-da-ceous	le-o-nine	lik-en
jag-uar		ko-ni-ol-o-gy	lar-der	leop-ard	li-la-ceous
jal-ap	Kad-iak	Koo-te-nay	larg-er	lep-er	lil-li-pu-tian
ja-lop-y	Kaf-fir	ko-peck	lar-gess	lep-i-do-cro-cite	lim-ber
jal-ou-sie	kai-nite	Ko-ran	larg-est	le-pid-o-lite	Lim-burg-er
Ja-mai-can	kai-nos-ite	Ko-re-an	lar-i-at	Lep-i-dop-ter-a	lime-ade
jam-bo-ree	kai-ser	ko-ru-na	lar-va	lep-i-do-sis	li-mic-o-lous
jan-gling	ka-lei-do-scop-ic	ko-sher	lar-vi-cid-al	lep-rol-o-gy	lim-i-ta-tion
jan-i-tor	kal-i-bo-rite	kreu-zer	lar-vic-o-lous	lep-ro-sar-i-um	lim-it-ed
Jan-u-ar-y	ka-lic-i-nite	kro-nen	lar-viv-o-rous	le-pro-sis	li-miv-o-rous
Ja-nus	ka-lig-e-nous	kro-ner	la-ryn-ge-al	lep-ro-sy	lim-ner
Ja-pan	Kal-i-spell	kryp-ton	lar-yn-gec-to-my	lep-rous	lim-nim-e-ter
Jap-a-nese	ka-mi-ka-ze	ku-lak	lar-yn-git-ic	lep-to-ceph-a-lus	lim-nol-o-gy
ja-panned	kan-ga-roo	Kuo-min-tang	lar-yn-gi-tis	lep-to-mat-ic	Li-moges
Ja-pon-i-ca	Kan-san	kur-to-sis	la-ryn-go-log-i-cal	lep-to-spi-ro-sis	lim-o-nene
jar-di-niere	ka-o-lin-ic	Ku-wait	lar-yn-gol-o-gy	le-sion	li-mo-nite
jar-gon-ize	ka-o-lin-ite	Ku-wai-ti	la-ryn-go-scope	Le-so-tho	lim-ou-sine
jar-ring	ka-pok	Kwaj-a-lein	lar-yn-gos-co-py	les-pe-de-za	lim-pid-i-ty
jas-mine	Ka-ră-chi	kwa-shi-or-kor	lar-yn-got-o-my	les-see	lin-a-ble
jas-per	kar-y-o-gam-ic	ky-mo-graph	lar-ynx	less-en	lin-age
jaun-dice	kar-y-og-a-my	ky-mog-ra-phy	las-civ-i-ous	less-er	lin-al-o-ol
jaunt-i-ly	kar-y-o-ki-ne-sis	kyn-u-ren-ine	las-si-tude	less-on	lin-a-mar-in
jav-a-nese	kar-y-ol-o-gy		Lat-a-ki-a	les-sor	Lin-coln
jav-e-lin	kar-y-ol-y-sis	**L**	la-teen	le-thal	lin-dane
jeal-ous-y	kar-y-o-mi-to-sis		la-ten-cy	leth-ane	lin-e-age
Jef-fer-so-ni-an	kar-y-o-some	lab-a-rum	lat-er	le-thar-gic	lin-e-al
Je-ho-vah	ka-tab-a-sis	lab-e-fac-tion	lat-er-al	leth-ar-gy	lin-e-a-ment
je-ju-nos-to-my	kat-a-bat-ic	la-beled	lat-er-ite	leu-cite	lin-e-ar-i-ty
je-ju-num	Ka-tan-gan	la-bel-er	la-tes-cent	leu-con-ic	lin-en
Je-kyll	Kath-a-rine	la-bi-al	lat-est	leu-cop-te-rin	lin-e-o-late
jeop-ard-ize	ka-ty-did	la-bile	la-tex	leu-co-sin	lin-er
jeop-ard-y	kay-ak	la-bi-lize	lath-er-ing	leu-co-sphe-nite	lin-ger
Je-ru-sa-lem	keep-er	la-bi-um	lat-i-cif-er-ous	leu-cot-o-my	lin-ge-rie
jes-sa-mine	ken-o-tron	lab-o-ra-to-ry	Lat-in-ize	leu-cov-o-rin	lin-gual
Jes-u-it	Ken-tuck-i-an	la-bor-er	la-tite	leu-ke-mi-a	lin-guis-tics
Je-sus	Ken-yan	la-bo-ri-ous	lat-i-tu-di-nous	leu-ke-mic	lin-guist-ry
jew-eled	ker-a-tin	lab-ra-dor-ite	la-trine	leu-ker-gy	link-age
Jez-e-bel	ke-rat-i-nous	la-bur-num	laud-a-ble	leu-ko-cyte	Lin-nae-us
jin-gling	ker-a-ti-tis	lab-y-rin-thine	lau-dan-i-dine	leu-ko-cyt-ic	li-no-le-ate
jin-rik-i-sha	Ker-a-tol	lac-er-ate	lau-da-nine	leu-ko-cy-to-sis	lin-o-le-ic
jock-ey	ker-a-tol-y-sis	lach-es	lau-dan-o-sine	leu-ko-poi-e-sis	li-no-le-in
jo-gos-i-ty	ker-a-to-sis	lach-ry-mose	lau-da-num	leu-ko-poi-et-ic	lin-o-le-nic
joc-u-lar	ker-chiefed	lack-a-dai-si-cal	laud-a-to-ry	leu-kor-rhe-a	li-no-le-um
joc-und	ker-mes-ite	la-con-ic	launch-er	leu-ko-sis	Li-no-type
jo-cun-di-ty	ker-neled	lac-o-nism	laun-der	lev-an	li-nox-yn
jodh-pur	ker-o-gen	lac-quer	Laun-der-om-e-ter	Le-vant	lin-tel
joh-nin	ker-o-sene	lac-ri-mal	laun-dress	Le-vant-er	lint-er
John-ston	ker-sey	la-crosse	Laun-dro-mat	Le-van-tine	li-on-ess
join-der	ke-ta-zine	lac-tal-bu-min	lau-rate	le-va-tor	li-on-ize
joint-er	Ketch-i-can	lac-tase	lau-re-ate	le-vee (reception)	lip-a-rid
join-ture	ke-tene	lac-te-al	lau-reled	lev-ee (dam)	li-pe-mi-a
jok-er	ke-ti-mine	lac-tes-cent	Lau-rence	lev-el-er	lip-ide
joke-ster	ke-to-gen-e-sis	lac-tif-er-ous	Lau-ren-tian	le-ver	lip-i-do-sis
Jo-nah	ke-to-glu-tar-ic	lac-to-fla-vin	lau-ric	le-ver-age	lip-o-chon-dri-on
jon-quil	ke-tol-y-sis	lac-tom-e-ter	lau-ro-len-ic	le-vi-a-than	lip-o-fus-cin
Jor-da-ni-an	ke-to-lyt-ic	lac-tose	lau-ryl	lev-i-ga-tor	li-pog-e-nous
jo-se-ite	ke-tone	la-cu-na	la-vage	lev-i-tat-ing	li-po-ic
Jo-seph	ke-to-side	la-cus-trine	lav-a-liere	lev-i-ty	lip-oi-do-sis
Jo-se-phine	ke-to-sis	lad-en-ing	lav-a-to-ry	le-vo-glu-co-san	li-pol-y-sis
Josh-u-a	Keynes-i-an	lad-ing	lav-en-der	lev-u-li-nate	lip-o-lyt-ic
jos-tled	kha-ki	la-di-no	lav-ish	lev-u-lin-ic	li-po-ma-to-sis
jos-tling	Khar-toum	la-dler	Law-rence	lev-u-lose	li-po-si-tol
jour-nal-ist	khe-dive	la-drone	law-renc-ite	lev-y-ing	lip-o-trop-ic
jour-ney	Khru-shchev	La-fay-ette	lay-ette	lew-is-ite	li-qua-tion
jo-vi-al-i-ty	kib-itz	la-ger	Laz-a-rus	lex-i-cog-ra-pher	liq-ue-fa-cient
ju-bi-lant	ki-bosh	la-gniappe	la-zi-ly	lex-i-co-graph-ic	liq-ue-fy
ju-bi-la-tion	kid-nap-er	la-goon-al	laz-u-rite	lex-i-cog-ra-phy	li-ques-cent
Ju-da-ism	kie-sel-guhr	la-gu-na	lead-er	lex-ig-ra-phy	li-queur
judg-ment	kill-er	lai-tance	lea-guer	li-ai-son	liq-uid
ju-di-ca-to-ry	kil-o-cy-cle	la-lop-a-thy	leak-age	li-bel-ant	liq-ui-da-tor
ju-di-ca-ture	kil-o-me-ter	la-ma-ser-y	learn-ed (adj.)	li-beled	li-quid-i-ty
ju-di-cial	kil-o-ton	lam-bent	leath-er-ine	li-bel-ous	liq-ui-dus
ju-di-ci-ar-y	kil-o-watt	lam-bre-quin	leav-en	lib-er-al-i-ty	liq-uor
ju-di-cious	ki-mo-no	la-mel-lar	Leb-a-nese	lib-er-a-tor	li-roc-o-nite
ju-gal	ki-nase	lam-el-late	le-bens-raum	lib-er-tar-i-an	lis-e-ran
jug-gler	kin-der-gar-ten	la-mel-lose	lech-er-ous	lib-er-tine	lisp-er
jug-gling	kin-der-gart-ner	la-ment	lec-i-thin-ase	lib-er-ty	lis-ten-er
jug-u-lar	kind-li-ness	lam-en-ta-ble	lec-tern	li-bid-i-nous	lis-ter-el-lo-sis
ju-jit-su	kin-dling	lam-en-ta-tion	lec-tur-er	li-bi-do	lis-ter-i-a
ju-jube	kin-dred	lam-i-na-graph	ledg-er	Li-bra	lis-ter-ize
Ju-lian	kin-e-mat-ics	lam-i-nal	le-dol	li-brar-i-an	lit-a-ny
Ju-li-enne	kin-e-scope	lam-i-nar-in	leg-a-cy	li-bra-to-ry	li-tchi
Ju-li-et	ki-ne-si-at-rics	lam-i-nate	le-gal-i-ty	li-bret-to	li-ter
Ju-lius	ki-ne-sics	lam-i-na-tor	le-gal-ize	Lib-y-an	lit-er-al-ly
jum-bled	kin-e-sim-e-ter	lam-i-ni-tis	leg-ate (n.)	li-can-ic	lit-er-a-ti
jump-er	ki-ne-si-o-log-ic	lam-poon	le-gate (v.)	li-cens-a-ble	lit-er-a-tim
junc-tur-al	ki-ne-si-ol-o-gy	lam-prey	leg-a-tee	li-censed	lit-er-a-ture
Ju-neau	kin-es-the-si-a	la-nat-o-side	le-ga-tion	li-cens-ee	lith-arge
jun-ior	ki-net-ic	Lan-ce-lot	leg-end-ar-y	li-cens-er	li-the-mi-a
ju-nior-i-ty	ki-ne-to-phone	lan-ce-o-lar	leg-er-de-main	li-cen-sor	lith-i-a
ju-ni-per	ki-ne-to-scope	lanc-er	le-ger-i-ty	li-cen-tious	li-thi-a-sis
Jun-ius	kin-e-to-sis	lan-cet	leg-i-ble	li-chen-in	li-thid-i-o-nite
	Kings-ton	lan-ci-nate	le-gion-naire	lic-o-rice	lith-i-um
			leg-is-la-tive		

lith-o-cho-lic
lith-o-graph
li-thog-ra-pher
lith-o-graph-ic
li-thog-ra-phy
lith-ol-a-pax-y
lith-o-log-ic
li-thol-o-gy
lith-o-pone
lith-o-sol
li-thot-o-my
li-thot-ri-ty
Lith-u-a-ni-an
li-thu-ri-a
lit-i-ga-ble
lit-i-ga-tor
li-ti-gious
lit-ter-a-teur
lit-to-ral
li-tur-gi-cal
lit-ur-gy
liv-a-ble
live-li-hood
liv-er-y
liv-id
Liv-ing-ston
Li-vo-ni-an
lix-iv-i-ate
liz-ard
lla-ma
load-er
load-om-e-ter
loaf-er
loath-er
lo-bar
lo-bate
lob-bied
lo-bec-to-my
lo-be-li-a
lo-be-line
lo-bot-o-my
lob-u-lar
lob-u-lose
lo-cale
lo-cal-i-ty
lo-cal-iz-er
lo-cant
lo-cat-er
loc-a-tive
lo-ca-tor
lock-age
lock-er
lo-co-mo-tive
loc-u-late
lo-cust
lodg-er
lo-ga-nin
log-a-rith-mic
log-i-cel
lo-gi-cian
lo-gis-ti-cian
lo-gis-tics
log-o-gram-mat-ic
lo-gom-a-chy
log-o-pe-dic
log-o-type
loi-ter
lol-li-pop
Lom-bar-dy
lone-li-ness
long-er
lon-ger (cask)
lon-ge-ron
long-est
lon-gev-i-ty
lon-gi-fo-lene
lon-gi-tu-di-nal
loos-en
loot-er
lo-phine
lop-sid-ed
lo-qua-cious
lo-quac-i-ty
lo-ran
lor-gnette
Los An-ge-les
los-er
los-ing
loss-er
Lo-thar-i-o
Lou-i-si-an-i-an
lous-i-ness
lou-ver
lov-a-ble
lox-o-drom-ic
loy-al-ist
loz-enge
lu-bri-ca-tor
lu-bric-i-ty
Lu-ci-fer
lu-cif-er-ase
lu-cite
lu-cra-tive
lu-cu-brate
lu-di-crous
lu-gu-bri-ous
lum-bar
lu-men
lu-miere
lu-mi-fla-vin
lu-mi-naire
lu-mi-nar-y
lu-mi-nes-cence

lu-mi-nif-er-ous
lu-mi-nom-e-ter
lu-mi-nos-i-ty
lu-mi-nous
lu-mis-ter-ol
lu-na-cy
lu-nar-i-an
lu-na-tic
lunch-eon
lu-nette
lu-nik
lu-nu-late
lu-pet-i-dine
lu-pin-ine
lu-pu-lone
lu-rid
lus-cious
Lu-si-ta-ni-a
lus-ter (shine)
lust-er (n.) (one that lusts)
lus-trous
lu-te-in-ize
lu-te-o-lin
lu-te-o-vi-res-cent
lu-te-ti-um
Lu-ther-an
lu-ti-din-ic
Lux-em-bourg-er
lux-u-ri-ant
lux-u-ri-ous
ly-ce-um
ly-co-pene
lydd-ite
lymph-ad-e-ni-tis
lymph-ad-e-nop-a-thy
lym-phan-gi-al
lym-phat-ic
lym-pho-cyte
lymph-oid
lym-pho-ma-to-sis
ly-o-phil-ic
ly-oph-i-lize
lyr-i-cal
ly-ser-gic
ly-sim-e-ter
ly-sine
ly-so-gen-ic

M

ma-ca-bre
mac-ad-am-ize
mac-a-ro-ni
mac-a-ron-ic
mac-a-roon
Ma-cas-sar
ma-caw
Mac-ca-be-an
Mac-e-do-ni-an
mac-er-a-tor
ma-che-te
Mach-i-a-vel-li-an
ma-chi-nal
mach-i-na-tion
ma-chin-er-y
ma-chin-ist
mack-er-el
mack-in-tosh
mac-ro-bi-o-sis
mac-ro-cosm
mac-ro-cy-clic
mac-ro-cy-to-sis
mac-ro-mol-e-cule
ma-cron
ma-crop-si-a
mac-ro-scop-ic
mac-u-la-ture
mad-am
ma-dame
Ma-dei-ra
ma-de-moi-selle
ma-don-na
Ma-dras
Ma-drid
mad-ri-gal
mael-strom
mae-stro
Ma-fi-a

maf-ic
mag-a-zine
Mag-da-len
Mag-de-burg
ma-gen-ta
mag-i-cal
ma-gi-cian
Ma-gi-not
ma-gis-ter
mag-is-te-ri-al
mag-is-tra-cy
mag-na-nim-i-ty
mag-nan-i-mous
mag-ne-sia
mag-ne-si-o-chro-mite
mag-ne-site
mag-ne-si-um
mag-ne-syn
mag-net-i-cal-ly
mag-net-ite
mag-net-ize
mag-ne-to-graph
mag-ne-tom-e-ter

mag-ne-to-met-ric
mag-ne-tom-e-try
mag-ne-tos
mag-ne-tron
mag-ni-fi-ca-tion
mag-nif-i-cence
mag-ni-fy
mag-nil-o-quent
mag-ni-tude
mag-no-lia
ma-guey
mah-jong
ma-hog-a-ny
Ma-hom-et
maid-en
mail-er
Main-er
main-te-nance
mai-so-nette
mai-tre d'ho-tel
ma-jes-tic
maj-es-ty
ma-jol-i-ca
ma-jor-i-ty
maj-us-cule
ma-jus-cu-lar
mak-er
mal-a-chite
mal-a-dy
Mal-a-ga
Mal-a-gas-y
mal-a-gue-na
mal-aise
ma-lar
ma-lar-i-al
ma-lar-i-om-e-try
mal-a-thi-on
Ma-la-wi
Ma-lay-an
Ma-lay-sian
ma-le-ate
mal-e-dic-tion
mal-e-fac-tor
ma-lef-i-cent
ma-le-ic
ma-lev-o-lent
mal-fea-sance
Ma-li-an
mal-ic
mal-ice
ma-li-cious
ma-lif-er-ous
ma-lign
ma-lig-nant
ma-lin-ger
mal-le-a-ble
mal-o-nate
ma-lo-nic
malt-ase
Mal-tese
mal-tha
Mal-thu-sian
malt-ose
mam-ma-li-an
mam-ma-lif-er-ous
mam-mal-o-gy
mam-ma-ry
mam-mif-er-ous
man-a-cle
man-age-a-ble
man-ag-er
man-a-ge-ri-al
Ma-na-gua
ma-ña-na
man-a-tee
Man-chu-ri-an
man-da-mus
man-da-rin-ate
man-da-to-ry
man-del-ate
man-di-ble
man-dib-u-lar
man-do-lin-ist
man-drake
man-drel
ma-nege
ma-neu-ver
man-ga-nate
man-ga-nese
man-gan-ic
man-ga-nif-er-ous
man-ga-nin
man-ga-nite
man-ga-no-site
man-ga-nous
man-ger
man-gler
man-gy
ma-ni-ac
ma-ni-a-cal
ma-ni-co-ba
man-i-cur-ist
man-i-fes-tant
man-i-fes-ta-tion
man-i-fold-er
man-i-kin
Ma-nil-a
ma-nil-la
man-i-oc
man-ip-u-la-tor
man-nu-ron-ic
ma-nom-e-ter
ma-nom-e-try

man-or
ma-no-ri-al
man-o-stat
man-sard
man-tel (arch)
man-tle (garment)
man-tling
man-u-al
man-u-duc-to-ry
man-u-fac-tur-er
ma-nure
ma-quette
ma-quis
mar-a-bou
ma-rac-a
mar-a-schi-no
ma-ras-mus
ma-raud-er
mar-bled
mar-ble-ize
mar-ca-site
mar-che-se
mar-chion-ess
mar-ga-rate
Mar-ga-ret
mar-gar-ic
mar-ga-rin
mar-ga-rite
mar-ga-ro-san-ite
mar-gin-al
mar-gi-na-li-a
mar-gin-ate
mar-gue-rite
Mar-i-an
Mar-i-co-pa
mar-i-gold
mar-i-hua-na
ma-rim-ba
ma-ri-na
ma-rine
mar-i-ner
Ma-ri-nist (of Marin)
ma-rin-ist (sea)
ma-ri-no-ra-ma
mar-i-o-nette
mar-i-tal
ma-rit-i-cide
mar-i-time
mar-jo-ram
Mar-jo-ry
mark-er
mar-ket-er
mar-la-ceous
marl-ite
mar-ma-lade
mar-mo-ra-ceous
mar-mo-re-al
mar-mo-set
ma-roon
mar-que-try
mar-quis
mar-qui-sette
mar-riage-a-ble
Mar-seil-laise
Mar-seilles
mar-shaled
mar-shal-er
mar-su-pi-al-ize
mar-tens-ite
mar-tial
mar-ti-net
mar-tin-gale
Mar-ti-ni
mar-tite
mar-tyr-ize
mar-vel-ous
Mar-y-land-er
Ma-sa-ryk
mas-cu-lin-i-ty
mask-er
mas-och-ism
mas-och-is-tic
Ma-son-ite
ma-son-ry
masque-rade
mas-quer-ade
Mas-sa-chu-setts-an
mas-sa-cred
mas-sag-er
mas-sive
mast-er (with masts)
mas-ter (owner, etc.)
mas-tic
mas-ti-cate
mas-tiff
mas-tit-ic
mas-ti-tis
mas-to-don
mas-toi-dal
mas-toid-i-tis
mas-toid-ot-o-my
ma-su-ri-um
mat-a-dor
mat-er
ma-te-ri-al-ize
ma-te-ri-a med-i-ca
ma-te-ri-el
ma-ter-ni-ty
math-e-mat-i-cal
math-e-ma-ti-cian
math-e-mat-ics
ma-thet-ic
mat-in-al
mat-i-nee

ma-tri-ar-chal
mat-ri-ces
ma-tri-ci-dal
na-tric-u-late
mat-ri-mo-ni-al
ma-trix
ma-tron
mat-ro-nym-ic
mat-u-ra-tion
mat-u-ra-tive
ma-tu-ri-ty
na-tu-ti-nal
mat-zoth
maud-lin
maul-er
maun-der
Mau-re-ta-ni-an
Mau-rice
Mau-ri-ti-us (island)
Mau-ser
mau-so-le-um
mau-vine
mav-er-ick
mawk-ish
max-i-miz-er
max-i-mum
may-on-naise
may-or-al-ty
maz-a-rine
ma-zur-ka
mea-con-ing
mead-ow
mea-ger
meal-y-mouthed
me-an-der
mea-sles
mea-sly
meas-ur-a-ble
meas-ured
me-a-tus
me-cap-rine
me-chan-i-cal
mech-a-ni-cian
mech-a-nism
mech-a-ni-za-tion
mech-a-no-mor-phic
me-com-e-ter
me-con-ic
mec-o-nin
me-co-ni-um
med-al-ist
me-dal-lion
med-dler
me-di-an
me-di-as-ti-ni-tis
me-di-as-ti-num
me-di-a-tor
me-di-ca-ble
med-ic-aid
med-i-cal
me-dic-a-ment
med-i-care
Med-i-ci
me-dic-i-nal
med-i-cine
me-di-e-val
Me-di-na
me-di-o-cre
me-di-oc-ri-ty
med-i-ta-tive
Med-i-ter-ra-ne-an
me-di-um
me-dul-la
med-ul-lar-y
meer-schaum
meg-a-lo-ma-ni-a
meg-a-lop-o-lis
meg-a-lo-pol-i-tan
meg-a-phone
meg-a-ton
meg-ohm-me-ter
me-grim
mei-o-nite
mei-ot-ic
mei-ster
me-lac-o-nite
mel-a-mine
mel-an-cho-li-a
mel-an-chol-y
me-lange
me-lan-ger
me-lan-ic
mel-a-nin
mel-a-no-ma-to-sis
mel-a-no-sis
mel-a-no-stib-i-an—
me-lan-ter-ite
me-lee
me-lez-i-tose
mel-i-bi-ose
mel-i-lite
me-lio-ra-tive
Me-lis-sa
mel-i-tose
mel-lif-lu-ous
mel-li-tate
mel-lit-ic
me-lod-ic
me-lo-di-on
me-lo-di-ous
mel-o-dra-ma
mel-o-dy
mel-o-ma-ni-a
mel-o-nite

mel-o-plas-ty
melt-er
mem-bra-nate
mem-bra-nous
me-men-tos
mem-oir
mem-o-ra-ble
mem-o-ran-dums
me-mo-ri-al-iz-ing
mem-o-riz-er
men-ace
men-a-di-one
me-nag-er-ie
me-naph-thone
men-da-cious
men-dac-i-ty
men-de-le-vi-um
Men-de-li-an
men-de-lye-ev-ite
mend-er
men-di-cant
men-dic-i-ty
men-ha-den
me-ni-al
Me-ni-ere
men-i-lite
me-nin-ge-al
me-nin-gi-o-ma
me-nin-git-ic
me-nin-gi-tis
me-nin-go-cele
me-nin-go-coc-cus
me-nin-go-my-e-li-tis
me-nis-cus
Men-non-ite
Me-nom-i-nee
men-o-pau-sal
me-no-rah
men-ses
men-stru-al
men-su-ra-ble
men-su-ral
men-su-ra-tion
men-tal-i-ty
men-tha-di-ene
men-thane
men-tha-nol
men-the-none
men-tho-lat-ed
men-thyl
men-ti-cide
me-per-i-dine
me-phen-e-sin
Meph-is-to-phe-li-an
me-phit-ic
me-phi-tis
me-pro-ba-mate
mer-al-lu-ride
mer-can-tile
mer-cap-to
mer-cap-tom-er-in
mer-cap-tu-ric
Mer-ca-tor
mer-ce-nar-y
mer-cer-ize
mer-chan-dise
mer-chant-a-ble
mer-cu-rate
mer-cu-ri-al
mer-cu-ric
mer-cu-rous
me-ren-gue
me-re-ol-o-gy
mer-e-tri-cious
mer-gan-ser
mer-gence
Mer-gen-tha-ler
merg-er
me-rid-i-an
me-rid-i-o-nal
me-ringue
mer-i-nos
mer-it-ed
mer-i-to-ri-ous
mer-o-crine
mer-o-gon-ic
me-rog-o-ny
mer-o-he-dral
Mer-o-pe
me-ro-pi-a
me-rot-o-mize
me-rox-ene
mer-sal-yl
Mer-thi-o-late
mes-al-liance
mes-ar-te-ri-tis
mes-en-ce-phal-ic
mes-en-ceph-a-lon
mes-en-chy-ma
mes-en-chym-a-tous
mes-en-chyme
mes-en-ter-ic
mes-en-ter-i-tis
me-sic
mes-i-dine
mes-i-tyl
me-sit-y-lene
mes-mer-ism
mes-o-blast
mes-o-car-di-a
mes-o-ce-phal-ic
mes-o-derm
mes-o-ite
mes-o-mer-ic

me-som-er-ism
mes-on
mes-o-phyll
mes-o-sphere
mes-ox-al-ic
mes-ox-a-lyl
Mes-o-zo-ic
mes-quite
mes-sage
mes-sen-ger
mes-si-an-ic
mes-ti-zos
mes-yl
me-tab-a-sis
met-a-bi-o-sis
met-a-bi-ot-ic
met-a-bol-ic
me-tab-o-lism
me-tab-o-liz-a-ble
met-a-bo-rate
met-a-car-pus
me-tag-ra-phy
met-al-de-hyde
met-al-lic
met-al-lif-er-ous
met-al-lize
met-al-log-ra-phy
met-al-lur-gi-cal
met-al-os-co-py
met-a-mer-ic
met-am-er-ism
met-a-mor-phism
met-a-mor-pho-sis
met-a-phor-i-cal
met-a-phys-ics
met-ar-te-ri-ole
met-a-so-ma-to-sis
met-a-sta-ble
me-tas-ta-sis
me-tath-e-sis
me-tem-psy-cho-sis
me-te-or-ic
me-te-or-ite
me-te-or-it-ics
me-te-or-o-graph
me-te-or-og-ra-phy
me-te-or-oid
me-te-or-o-log-i-cal
me-te-or-ol-o-gist
me-te-or-ol-o-gy
me-te-or-om-e-ter
me-te-or-o-scope
me-te-or-os-co-py
me-ter
meth-ac-ry-late
meth-a-cryl-ic
meth-a-done
meth-al-lyl
meth-ane
meth-a-nol
meth-a-no-lic
meth-a-nol-y-sis
meth-a-nom-e-ter
meth-an-the-line
me-the-na-mine
meth-ene
meth-ide
meth-i-on-ic
me-thi-o-nine
me-thi-um
meth-od
me-thod-i-cal
Meth-od-ist
meth-od-ize
meth-od-ol-o-gy
me-tho-ni-um
meth-ox-ide
me-thox-y-car-bon-yl
meth-ox-yl
Me-thu-se-lah
meth-yl-a-mine
meth-yl-ate
meth-yl-ene
meth-yl-en-i-mine
meth-yl-eth-yl-pyr-i-
   dine
me-thyl-i-dyne
meth-yl-naph-tha-lene
meth-yl-ol-u-re-a
me-tic-u-lous
me-tier
me-ton-y-my
me-top-ic
met-o-pon
met-o-pos-co-py
Met-ra-zol
met-ric
met-ri-cal
me-tri-tis
me-trol-o-gy
met-ro-nome
me-tro-nym-ic
met-ro-pole
me-trop-o-lis
met-ro-pol-i-tan
mev-a-lon-ic
mez-za-nine
mho-me-ter
mi-ar-gy-rite
mi-ca-ceous
mi-cel-lar
mi-celle
Mi-chael
Mich-ael-mas

Mich-i-gan-ite
mi-cri-nite
mi-cro-bi-al
mi-cro-cosm
mi-crog-ra-phy
mi-cro-lite
mi-cro-me-rit-ics
mi-crom-e-ter
mi-cro-met-ri-cal
mi-crom-e-try
mi-cro-mho
mi-cron-ize
mi-cro-phon-ic
mi-cro-pyle
mi-cro-scop-ic
mi-cros-co-py
mi-crot-o-my
mid-dling
midg-et
mi-gnon-ette
mi-graine
mi-grain-oid
mi-grant
mi-gra-tet-ics
mi-gra-to-ry
mi-ka-do
Mi-lan
Mil-a-nese
mil-i-a-ri-a
mil-i-ar-y
mi-lieu
mil-i-tant
mil-i-ta-rism
mil-i-tate
mi-li-tia
milk-er
mil-le-nar-y
mil-len-ni-um
mill-er
mil-les-i-mal
mil-let
mil-li-am-me-ter
mil-li-ner-y
mil-lion-aire
Mim-e-o-graph
mi-met-ic
mim-e-tite
mim-ick-er
mim-ic-ry
mi-mo-sa
mi-mo-sine
min-a-ble
min-a-ret
minc-ing
mi-nen-wer-fer
min-er
min-er-ag-ra-phy
min-er-al-iz-er
min-er-al-og-i-cal
min-er-al-o-gy
Mi-ner-va
min-e-stro-ne
mi-nette
min-gling
min-i-a-ceous
min-i-a-ture
Min-ic
min-i-mize
min-i-mum
min-ion
min-is-te-ri-al
min-is-try
min-i-track
Min-ne-so-tan
mi-nom-e-ter
mi-nor-i-ty
min-strel
mint-age
mint-er
min-u-et
mi-nus-cu-lar
min-us-cule
mi-nute (time)
mi-nute (small)
min-ute-ly (every min-
   ute)
mi-nute-ly (precisely)
mi-nu-ti-a
mi-o-sis
mi-ot-ic
mi-rab-i-lite
mir-a-cle
mi-rac-u-lous
mi-rage
mis-an-throp-ic
mis-an-thro-py
mis-ceg-e-na-tion
mis-cel-la-ne-ous
mis-cel-la-ny
mis-chie-vous
mis-ci-bil-i-ty
mis-cre-ant
mis-de-mean-or
mis-er-a-ble
Mis-e-re-re
mi-ser-ly
mis-er-y
mis-fea-sance
mis-no-mer
mi-sog-y-nist
mis-pri-sion
mis-sil-eer
mis-sile-ry
Mis-sis-sip-pi-an
mis-sive

Mis-sou-ri-an
mis-spelled
mis-tak-a-ble
mis-tak-en
mis-ter
mis-tle-toe
mis-tral
mis-tress
mi-ter
mit-i-ga-tor
mi-to-chon-dri-a
mi-to-sis
mi-tot-ic
mi-trail-leuse
mi-tral
mix-ture
mne-mon-ic
mo-bile
mo-bil-i-ty
mo-bi-li-za-tion
mo-bil-om-e-ter
mob-oc-ra-cy
moc-ca-sin
mo-cha
mock-er-y
mod-al-ism
mo-dal-i-ty
mod-eled
mod-er-a-tor
mod-ern-is-tic
mod-ern-ize
mod-es-ty
mod-i-cum
mod-i-fy
mod-ish
mo-diste
mod-u-la-bil-i-ty
mod-u-lar
mod-u-la-tor
mod-u-lus
mo-dus op-e-ran-di
Mo-ham-med-an
Mo-ha-ve
moi-e-ty
moi-re
moist-en-er
mois-ture
mo-lar-i-ty
mo-la-ry
mo-las-ses
mold-er
mo-lec-u-lar
mol-e-cule
mo-les-ta-tion
mol-ten
molt-er
mo-lyb-date
mo-lyb-de-num
mo-lyb-do-me-nite
mol-y-site
mo-men-tar-i-ly
mo-men-tar-y
mo-men-tous
mo-men-tum
mom-ism
Mon-a-can
mo-nad
mo-nad-ic
mo-nan-dry
mo-nar-chal
mo-nar-chi-cal
mon-ar-chist
mon-as-te-ri-al
mon-as-ter-y
mo-nas-tic
mon-a-tom-ic
mon-a-zite
mo-nel
mo-ne-sia
mon-e-tar-y
mon-e-tite
mon-e-tize
mon-eys
mon-ger
Mon-go-li-an
Mon-gol-oid
mon-grel
mon-i-ker
mo-nim-o-lite
mon-ism
mo-nis-tic
mon-i-to-ry
mon-keys
monk-ish
mon-o-ac-e-tin
mon-o-ac-id
mon-o-a-cid-ic
mon-o-am-ide
mon-o-a-mine
mon-o-chro-mous
mo-noch-ro-nous
mon-o-cle
mon-o-coque
mo-noc-ra-cy
mon-o-crot-ic
mo-noc-u-lar
mo-nog-a-my
mo-nog-o-ny
mon-o-gramed
mon-o-gram-mat-ic
mo-nog-ra-pher
mon-o-graph-ic
mo-nog-y-ny
mon-o-lith-ic

mon-o-log
mo-nol-o-gist
mo-nom-a-chy
mon-o-ma-ni-a
mon-o-mer
mon-o-me-ter
mo-no-mi-al
mon-o-nu-cle-o-sis
mon-o-plane
mo-nop-o-lize
mo-nop-so-ny
mon-o-rail
mon-o-the-ism
mon-o-tone
mo-not-o-nous
mo-not-ro-py
mon-ox-ide
mon-sei-gneur
mon-sieur
mon-si-gnor
mon-ster
mon-stros-i-ty
mon-strous
mon-tage
Mon-tan-an
Mon-te-ne-grin
Mon-tes-so-ri
mon-tic-u-lous
mont-mo-ril-lon-ite
Mon-tre-al
mon-troy-dite
mon-u-men-tal
mon-zo-nite
Moor-ish
mo-quette
mo-raine
mor-al
mo-rale
mor-al-ist
mo-ral-i-ty
mor-al-ize
mo-rass-ic
mor-a-to-ri-um
Mo-ra-vi-an
mo-ra-vite
mor-bid-i-ty
mor-bose
mor-da-cious
mor-dac-i-ty
mor-dant
mo-reen
mo-rel-lo
mo-ren-cite
mo-res
mor-ga-nat-ic
mor-i-bund
mo-rin-done
mo-rin-ite
Mor-mon-ite
morn-ing
Mo-roc-co
mo-ron-ic
mo-ros-i-ty
mor-pheme
mor-phe-mics
Mor-pheus
mor-phine
mor-phog-ra-phy
mor-pho-line
mor-pho-log-i-cal
mor-phol-o-gy
mor-phom-e-try
mor-pho-sis
mor-phot-o-my
mor-tal-i-ty
mort-ga-gee
mort-ga-gor
mor-ti-cian
mor-ti-fi-ca-tion
mor-tis-er
mor-tu-ar-y
mo-sa-i-cism
mo-ses-ite
mos-qui-toes
mo-tel
moth-er
mo-til-i-ty
mo-ti-vate
mo-tor
mo-to-ri-al
mou-lage
mou-lin
moun-tain-eer
moun-te-bank
mount-er
mourn-er
mous-er
mous-que-taire
mousse-line
mov-a-ble
mov-ant
mov-er
mov-ie
mu-ce-dine
mu-ced-i-nous
mu-cic
mu-cif-er-ous
mu-ci-lage
mu-ci-lag-i-nous
mu-cin-o-gen
mu-cin-oid
mu-ci-no-lyt-ic
mu-coi-dal

mu-co-i-tin
mu-co-lyt-ic
mu-con-ic
mu-co-sa
mu-cos-i-ty
mu-cous (adj.)
mu-cus (n.)
mud-dled
muf-fler
Muh-len-berg
mu-lat-toes
mulch-er
mu-le-teer
mul-ish
mul-li-ga-taw-ny
mull-ite
mul-ti-far-i-ous
mul-tif-er-ous
Mul-ti-graph
Mul-ti-lith
mul-til-o-quent
mul-tim-e-ter
mul-tim-e-try
mul-tip-a-rous
mul-ti-par-tite
mul-ti-ple
mul-ti-plic-a-ble
mul-ti-pli-ca-tion
mul-ti-plic-i-ty
mul-ti-tu-di-nous
mul-ti-va-lent
mum-bling
Mun-chau-sen
mun-dane
Mu-nich
mu-nic-i-pal
mu-nif-i-cent
mu-ni-tion
mu-ral
mu-rar-i-um
mur-der-ous
mu-rine
mur-mur-ous
mus-ca-dine
mus-ca-rine
mus-ca-tel
mus-cle
Mus-co-vite
mus-cu-lar
mus-cu-la-ture
mus-cu-lo-trop-ic
mu-se-ol-o-gy
mu-se-um
mu-si-cal
mu-si-col-o-gy
mus-ing
mus-ket-eer
mus-tache
mus-tard
mu-ta-bil-i-ty
mu-ta-gen-ic
mu-tant
mu-tase
mu-ta-tive
mu-ti-late
mu-ti-nous
mut-ism
mu-tu-al-ism
mu-zhik
muz-zling
my-al-gi-a
My-an-e-sin
my-as-the-ni-a
my-as-then-ic
my-ce-li-um
my-ce-to-ma
my-co-my-cin
my-co-sis
myc-ter-ic
my-dri-a-sine
my-dri-a-sis
myd-ri-at-ic
my-e-li-tis
my-e-lo-cyte
my-e-loid
my-e-lo-ma-to-sis
my-e-lom-a-tous
my-e-lop-a-thy
my-e-lo-sis
my-o-car-di-tis
my-op-a-thy
my-o-pi-a
my-op-ic
my-o-sin
my-o-si-tis
my-ot-o-my
myr-i-ad
myr-i-am-e-ter
my-ric-e-tin
my-ric-i-trin
myr-i-cyl
myr-in-gi-tis
myr-in-got-o-my
my-ris-tate
myr-mi-don
myrrh-ic
myr-tle
mys-te-ri-ous
mys-ter-y
mys-ti-cal
mys-ti-fi-ca-tion

mys-tique
myth-i-cal
myth-o-log-i-cal
my-thol-o-gy
myx-o-bac-te-ri-al
myx-o-ma-to-sis

N

na-bob
na-celle
na-cre-ous
na-crite
na-dir
nad-or-ite
Na-ga-sa-ki
nah-co-lite
nail-er
nain-sook
na-ive
na-ive-te
na-ked
nam-a-ble
na-no-gram
na-palm
na-per-y
na-phaz-o-line
naph-tha
naph-tha-lene
naph-tha-len-ic
naph-thal-ic
naph-thene
naph-the-nic
naph-thi-o-nate
naph-thi-on-ic
naph-thol-ate
naph-tho-res-or-cin-ol
naphth-ox-y-a-ce-tic
naph-tho-yl
naph-thyl-a-mine
naph-thy-lene
Na-ples
Na-po-le-on
na-prap-a-thy
nar-cis-sism
nar-co-lep-sy
nar-co-sis
nar-cot-ic
nar-co-tol-ine
na-res
nar-in-gen-in
na-rin-gin
Nar-ra-gan-sett
nar-rat-a-ble
nar-ra-tor
na-sa-lis
na-sal-i-ty
nas-cent
na-so-scope
nas-ti-ly
nas-tur-tium
na-tal
na-tant
na-ta-to-ri-al
na-ta-to-ri-um
Natch-ez
Na-than-iel
na-tion-al-ist
na-tiv-is-tic
na-tiv-i-ty
na-tri-um
na-tro-lite
na-troph-i-lite
nat-u-ral-ist
nat-u-ral-ize
na-ture
na-tur-o-path
na-tur-op-a-thy
naugh-ti-ness
nau-pli-us
nau-se-ate
nau-seous
nau-ti-cal
nau-ti-lus
nau-to-phone
Nav-a-ho
na-val
nav-ar
na-vel
na-vic-u-lar
nav-i-ga-ble
nav-i-ga-tor
na-vite
Naz-a-rene
na-zism
Ne-an-der-thal
Ne-a-pol-i-tan
near-est
ne-ar-thro-sis
Ne-bras-kan
neb-u-lar
ne-bu-li-um
neb-u-los-i-ty
neb-u-lous
nec-es-sar-i-ly
ne-ces-si-tate
ne-ces-si-tous
nec-ro-bi-o-sis
nec-ro-log-i-cal
ne-crol-o-gy
nec-ro-man-cy
ne-crop-o-lis
ne-crop-sy
ne-cros-co-py
nec-ro-sin

ne-cro-sis
ne-crot-ic
ne-crot-o-my
nec-tar-ine
nec-ta-ry
nee-dler
ne-far-i-ous
ne-ga-tion
neg-a-tive
neg-a-to-ry
neg-a-tron
ne-glect-er
neg-li-gee
neg-li-gence
neg-li-gi-ble
ne-go-ti-a-ble
ne-go-ti-a-tor
Ne-gress
Ne-grit-ic
Ne-gro
Ne-groid
Ne-gus
neigh-bor
nei-ther
ne-mat-ic
nem-a-to-ci-dal
nem-a-tode
nem-a-to-di-a-sis
nem-a-tol-o-gy
Nem-bu-tal
ne-mes-ic
nem-e-sis
ne-moph-i-ly
nem-o-ral
Ne-o-ant-er-gan
ne-o-ars-phen-a-mine
ne-o-dym-i-um
ne-og-a-my
ne-o-lith-ic
ne-o-log-i-cal
ne-ol-o-gy
ne-o-my-cin
ne-on-tol-o-gy
ne-o-phyte
ne-o-pla-si-a
ne-o-prene
ne-o-stig-mine
Ne-o-sy-neph-rine
ne-o-ter-ic
ne-ot-o-cite
Ne-pal
Nep-a-lese
ne-pen-the
neph-e-lin-ite
neph-e-lite
neph-e-lom-e-ter
neph-e-lo-scope
neph-ew
ne-phol-o-gy
neph-o-scope
ne-phrec-to-my
neph-ric
ne-phrid-i-al
neph-rite
ne-phrit-ic
ne-phri-tis
ne-phrol-o-gy
neph-rop-to-sis
ne-phro-sis
ne-phrot-ic
ne-phrot-o-my
nep-i-on-ic
ne-pot-ic
nep-o-tism
nep-tu-ni-um
ne-rit-ic
ne-rol-i-dol
nerv-ate
nerv-ine
ner-von-ic
nerv-ous
ner-vule
ne-science
nest-ling (n.)
nes-tling (v.)
Nes-tor
neth-er
Ne-trop-sin
net-tled
Neuf-châ-tel
neu-ral-gia
neur-as-the-ni-a
neur-as-then-ic
neu-rec-to-my
neu-rine
neu-rit-ic
neu-ri-tis
neu-ro-blas-to-ma
neu-ro-crine
neu-ro-gen-ic
neu-rog-ra-phy
neu-roid
neu-ro-log-i-cal
neu-rol-o-gy
neu-rol-y-sis
neu-ro-path-ic
neu-rop-a-thy
neu-ro-sis
neu-rot-ic
neu-rot-i-cism
neu-rot-o-my
neu-ro-trop-ic
neu-rot-ro-pism

neu-ter
neu-tral-i-ty
neu-tral-iz-er
neu-tri-no
neu-tro-dyne
neu-tron
Ne-vad-an
ne-vus
new-com-er
New-to-ni-an
New Zea-land-er
nex-us
ni-a-cin-a-mide
Ni-ag-a-ra
nib-b'ing
Nic-a-ra-guan
ni-ce-ty
nick-el-if-er-ous
nick-el-ine
nick-el-o-de-on
nic-o-tin-a-mide
nic-o-tin-ate
nic-o-tin-ic
nic-o-ti-no-yl
nic-o-tin-u-ric
ni-dic-o-lous
nid-i-fi-cate
ni-dol-o-gy
Nietz-sche-ism
Ni-ger
Ni-ge-ri-a
ni-ger-ite
night-in-gale
ni-gres-cence
ni-grine
ni-grom-e-ter
ni-gro-sine
ni-grous
ni-hi-list
ni-lom-e-ter
nim-bly
nim-bo-stra-tus
ni-mi-e-ty
Nin-hy-drin
Ni-o-be
ni-o-bic
ni-o-bi-um
nip-e-cot-ic
Nip-pon-ese
Nir-va-na
Ni-sei
ni-sin
ni-ter
ni-tra-mine
ni-trate
ni-tra-tor
ni-tric
ni-trid-ize
ni-tri-fi-ca-tion
ni-trite
ni-tro-an-i-line
ni-tro-fu-ra-zone
ni-tro-gen-ate
ni-tro-gen-ize
ni-trog-e-nous
ni-tro-lic
ni-trom-e-ter
ni-tro-ni-um
ni-tros-a-mine
ni-tro-sate
ni-tro-so
ni-tro-tol-u-ene
ni-tro-tol-u-ol
ni-trous
ni-trox-yl-ene
ni-tryl
No-bel
no-bel-i-um
no-bil-i-ty
no-blesse
no-bly
no-car-di-o-sis
no-cer-ite
no-ci-cep-tor
noc-tam-bu-list
noc-ti-lu-cine
noc-tiv-a-gant
noc-tur-nal
noc-turne
noc-u-ous
nod-al
no-dal-i-ty
nod-u-lar
nod-ule
no-e-ma-ta-chom-e-ter
nois-i-ly
noi-some
no-lo con-ten-de-re
no-mad-ic
no-men-cla-ture
no-mi-al
nom-i-nal-ize
nom-i-nat-ed
nom-i-na-tion
nom-i-na-tive
no-moc-ra-cy
nom-o-gram
nom-o-graph-ic
no-mog-ra-phy
non-a-co-sane
non-a-dec-ane
non-a-ge-nar-i-an
no-nane
non-a-no-ic

no-na-nol
non-cha-lance
non-de-script
non-ene
non-en-ti-ty
no-no-ic
non-pa-reil
non-plused
non pro-se-qui-tur
non se-qui-tur
non-yl-ene
no-nyl-ic
noo-dle
no-ol-o-gy
no-pi-nene
Nor-dic
nor-di-hy-dro-guai-a-ret-ic
nor-mal-i-ty
nor-mal-iz-er
nor-ma-tive
North-amp-ton
north-ern
North-um-ber-land
Nor-we-gian
no-se-lite
no-sog-ra-phy
no-sol-o-gist
nos-tal-gi-a
nos-tril
nos-trum
nos-y
no-ta-ble
no-tam
no-tar-i-al
no-ta-ry
notch-er
noth-ing
no-tice-a-ble
no-ti-fi-ca-tion
no-to-ri-e-ty
no-to-ri-ous
nou-gat
nour-ish
nou-veau
nov-el-ette
nov-el-ist
no-vel-la
nov-el-ty
No-vem-ber
no-ve-na
nov-ice
no-vi-ti-ate
no-vo-cain
nox-ious
Nu-bi-an
nu-cle-ar
nu-cle-ate
nu-cle-in-a-tion
nu-cle-og-o-ny
nu-cle-o-his-tone
nu-cle-o-lar
nu-cle-ol-y-sis
nu-cle-om-e-ter
nu-cle-on-ics
nu-cle-o-tid-ase
nu-cle-us
nu-clide
nu-clid-ic
nudg-er
nud-ism
nu-di-ty
nu-ga-to-ry
nui-sance
nul-li-ty
num-bered
nu-mer-al
nu-mer-a-tive
nu-mer-a-tor
nu-mer-i-cal
nu-mer-ol-o-gy
nu-mis-mat-ics
nu-mis-ma-tist
num-skull
nun-ci-a-ture
nup-tial
nup-ti-al-i-ty
Nur-em-berg
nurs-er
nurs-er-y
nur-tur-al
nu-tri-a
nu-tri-ent
nu-tri-lite
nu-tri-tious
nu-tri-tive
nyc-ta-lo-pi-a
ny-lon
nym-pha
nymph-al
nys-tag-mus
nys-ta-tin
ny-tril

O

oak-en
oa-kum
o-a-sis
ob-bli-ga-to
ob-du-ra-cy
ob-du-rate
o-be-di-ence
o-bei-sance

o-be-li-al
ob-e-lisk
o-be-si-ty
ob-fus-ca-to-ry
o-bit-u-ar-y
ob-jec-tee
ob-jec-tiv-ism
ob-jec-tiv-i-ty
ob-jec-tor
ob-ju-ra-tion
ob-jur-gate
ob-last
ob-la-to-ry
ob-li-ga-tor
o-blig-a-to-ry
ob-li-gee
o-blig-ing
ob-li-gor
o-blique
ob-liq-ui-ty
ob-lit-er-ate
ob-li-ves-cence
ob-liv-i-on
ob-liv-i-ous
ob-long-at-ed
ob-lo-quy
ob-mu-tes-cence
ob-nox-ious
ob-nu-bi-la-tion
ob-o-lus
ob-scen-i-ty
ob-scu-ran-tism
ob-scu-ri-ty
ob-se-qui-ous
ob-se-qui-ty
ob-se-quy
ob-serv-ance
ob-serv-ant
ob-ser-va-tion
ob-serv-a-to-ry
ob-serv-er
ob-ses-sion
ob-sid-i-an
ob-so-les-cence
ob-so-lete
ob-sta-cle
ob-ste-tri-cian
ob-stet-rics
ob-sti-na-cy
ob-strep-er-ous
ob-struc-tive
ob-struc-tor
ob-tru-sive
ob-tund-ent
ob-tu-ra-tor
ob-tu-si-ty
ob-ver-tend
oc-a-ri-na
oc-ca-sion
oc-ci-den-tal
oc-cip-i-ta-lis
oc-cip-i-to-pa-ri-e-tal
oc-ci-put
oc-clu-sal
oc-clu-sion
oc-cul-ta-tion
oc-cult-ism
oc-cu-pan-cy
oc-cu-pa-tive
oc-curred
oc-cur-rence
o-cea-nar-i-um
o-ce-an-ic
o-cean-o-graph-ic
o-cean-og-ra-phy
oc-el-late
o-ce-lot
o-cher-ous
och-loc-ra-cy
o-chro-no-sis
oc-ta-co-sane
oc-ta-dec-a-di-e-no-ic
oc-ta-dec-ane
oc-ta-dec-a-no-ic
oc-ta-dec-yl
oc-ta-gon
oc-tag-o-nal
oc-ta-he-dron
oc-ta-mer
oc-tam-er-ous
oc-tane
oc-tan-gu-lar
oc-ta-no-ate
oc-ta-nol
oc-ta-no-yl
oc-ta-vos
Oc-to-ber
oc-to-ge-nar-i-an
oc-tog-e-nar-y
oc-to-ic
Oc-top-o-da
oc-to-pus
oc-to-roon
oc-tose
oc-tu-ple
oc-tup-let
oc-tyl-ene
oc-u-lar
oc-u-list
oc-u-lo-gy-ric
o-da-lisque
odd-i-ty
o-dif-er-ous

o-di-om-e-ter
o-di-ous
od-ist
o-di-um
o-dom-e-ter
o-don-ti-tis
o-don-to-gen-ic
o-don-tol-o-gy
o-don-tom-e-ter
o-don-tot-o-my
o-dor-ant
o-dor-if-er-ous
o-dor-om-e-ter
o-dor-ous
Od-ys-sey
oed-i-pal
oe-nan-thic
oer-sted
of-fal
of-fend-er
of-fen-sive
of-fer-to-ry
of-fi-cer
of-fi-cial
of-fi-ci-ate
of-fic-i-nal
of-fi-cious
off-ing
of-ten
o-gi-val
o-gre-ish
O-hi-o-an
ohm-ic
ohm-me-ter
oil-er
oi-ti-ci-ca
o-ken-ite
O-ki-na-wan
O-kla-ho-man
ok-o-nite
o-kra
old-en
old-ster
o-le-ag-i-nous
o-le-an-der
o-le-an-drin
o-lec-ra-non
o-le-fin-ic
o-le-ic
o-le-in-ic
o-le-og-ra-phy
o-le-o-mar-ga-rine
o-le-om-e-ter
o-le-o-res-in
o-le-o-yl
ol-fac-tom-e-ter
ol-fac-to-ry
ol-i-gar-chi-cal
ol-i-gar-chy
ol-i-ge-mi-a
ol-i-go-chro-ne-mi-a
ol-i-go-clase
ol-i-go-dy-nam-ic
ol-i-go-nite
ol-i-gop-o-ly
ol-i-gop-so-ny
ol-i-va-ceous
ol-i-var-y
o-liv-en-ite
ol-i-ves-cence
ol-i-vine
O-lym-pi-an
O-ma-ha
om-bro-graph
om-brom-e-ter
om-buds-man
o-me-ga
om-e-let
o-men-ol-o-gy
om-i-cron
om-i-nous
o-mis-si-ble
o-mis-sion
o-mit-ted
om-ni-bus
om-nif-i-cence
om-nim-e-ter
om-nip-o-tence
om-ni-science
om-niv-o-rous
om-pha-li-tis
on-a-ger
on-co-gen-ic
on-cog-e-ny
on-col-o-gy
on-col-y-sis
on-com-e-ter
on-cot-o-my
on-dom-e-ter
on-du-le
O-nei-da
on-er-ous
on-ion
on-o-ma-si-ol-o-gy
on-o-mat-o-poe-ia
On-on-da-ga
On-tar-i-an
on-tog-e-ny
on-to-log-i-cal
on-tol-o-gy
on-y-chol-y-sis
on-y-cho-my-co-sis
on-y-choph-a-gy
on-y-cho-sis

o-ol-o-gy
o-pa-cim-e-ter
o-pac-i-ty
o-pal-es-cent
o-pal-ine
o-paqu-er
o-paqu-ing
o-pei-do-scope
op-er-a
op-er-a-ble
op-er-and
op-er-ate
op-er-at-ic
op-er-a-tive
op-er-a-tor
o-per-cu-lar
oph-i-cleide
o-phid-i-an
o-phi-ol-o-gy
o-phit-ic
oph-thal-mi-a
oph-thal-mic
oph-thal-mo-log-ic
oph-thal-mol-o-gy
oph-thal-mom-e-ter
oph-thal-mo-met-ric
oph-thal-mo-scope
oph-thal-mos-co-py
o-pi-an-ic
o-pi-ate
o-pin-ion-at-ed
o-pin-ion-a-tor
op-i-som-e-ter
o-pis-tho-gas-tric
o-pi-um
o-pos-sum
op-po-nent
op-por-tun-ism
op-por-tun-ist
op-por-tu-ni-ty
op-pos-al
op-po-site
op-press-i-ble
op-pres-sive
op-pres-sor
op-pro-bri-um
op-ti-cal
op-ti-cian
op-ti-mal-ize
op-ti-me
op-tim-e-ter
op-ti-mism
op-ti-mis-tic
op-ti-mum
op-tom-e-ter
op-to-met-ric
op-tom-e-try
op-u-lent
or-a-cle
o-rac-u-lar
o-ral-ly
or-ange
o-ran-ge-lo
or-ange-ry
o-rang-u-tan
o-ra-tion
o-ra-tor
or-a-tor-i-cal
or-a-to-ri-o
or-bic-u-lar
or-bit-al
or-bit-ed
or-bit-er
or-bit-ing
or-chard
or-ches-tra
or-chi-da-ceous
or-chid-ol-o-gy
or-cin-ol
or-deal
or-dered
or-di-nal
or-di-nance
or-di-nar-i-ly
or-di-nar-y
ord-nance
Or-do-vi-cian
Or-e-go-ni-an
or-gan-dy
or-gan-ic
or-ga-nism
or-gan-ist
or-ga-niz-a-ble
or-ga-ni-za-tion
or-ga-niz-er
or-gan-o-gel
or-ga-no-gen-ic
or-ga-nog-e-ny
or-ga-nog-ra-phy
or-ga-nos-co-py
or-gan-o-sol
or-gi-as-tic
o-ri-el
O-ri-ent
o-ri-en-tal
o-ri-en-ta-lia
o-ri-en-ta-tor
o-ri-en-tite
or-i-fi-cial
or-i-flamme
or-i-gin
o-rig-i-nal-i-ty
o-rig-i-nat-ing
o-rig-i-na-tive

o-ri-ole
O-ri-on
or-is-mol-o-gy
or-i-son
Or-lan-do
Or-le-ans
Or-lon
or-mo-lu
or-na-men-tal
or-ner-y
or-ni-thine
or-ni-tho-log-i-cal
or-ni-thol-o-gy
or-ni-thop-ter
or-ni-tho-rhyn-chus
or-ni-tho-sis
or-ni-thot-o-my
or-nith-u-ric
o-rog-e-ny
o-rog-ra-phy
o-ro-ide
o-rol-o-gy
o-rom-e-ter
or-o-met-ric
o-ro-tun-di-ty
or-phan-age
or-pi-ment
or-ris
or-sel-lin-ic
or-tha-nil-ic
or-thi-con
or-tho-ar-se-nate
or-tho-ben-zo-qui-none
or-tho-clase
or-tho-don-ti-a
or-tho-don-tist
or-tho-dox-y
or-tho-e-py
or-tho-for-mic
or-thog-o-nal
or-thog-ra-phy
or-thom-e-try
or-tho-pe-dic
or-tho-pe-dist
or-thop-ne-a
Or-thop-ter-a
or-thop-tics
or-tho-sis
or-tho-typ-ic
or-to-lan
o-ryc-tol-o-gy
o-ryc-tog-no-sy
o-sa-zone
Os-car
os-cil-la-tor
os-cil-la-to-ry
os-cil-lom-e-ter
os-cil-lo-scope
os-ci-tant
os-cu-la-to-ry
os-cu-lom-e-ter
O-si-ris
os-mi-dro-sis
os-mi-rid-i-um
os-mi-um
os-mom-e-ter
os-mo-met-ric
os-mom-e-try
os-mo-sis
os-mot-ic
os-phre-sis
os-prey
os-se-ous
os-si-cle
os-sic-u-lar
os-si-cu-lec-to-my
os-sif-i-ca-to-ry
os-si-fy
os-te-al
os-te-it-ic
os-te-i-tis
os-ten-si-ble
os-ten-ta-tious
os-te-o-chon-dro-sis
os-te-ol-o-gy
os-te-ol-y-sis
os-te-o-ma
os-te-o-ma-tous
os-te-om-e-try
os-te-o-my-e-li-tis
os-te-o-path
os-te-op-a-thy
os-te-ot-o-my
os-tra-cism
os-tra-cize
os-trich
o-tal-gi-a
o-the-o-scope
oth-er
o-ti-ose
o-ti-os-i-ty
o-ti-tis me-di-a
o-tog-e-nous
o-to-lar-yn-go-log-i-cal
o-to-lar-yn-gol-o-gy
o-tos-co-py
o-to-sis
oua-ba-in
ou-bli-ette
ou-ri-cu-ry
oust-er
out-er
out-land-ish
out-law-ry
out-ra-geous

out-rag-er
ou-trance
out-rid-er
out-sid-er
o-val-i-form
o-val-i-ty
o-var-i-an
o-var-i-ole
o-var-i-ot-o-my
o-va-ri-tis
o-va-ry
ov-en
o-ver-head
o-ver-land-er
o-ver-se-er
o-ver-ture
o-vi-ci-dal
o-vic-u-lar
O-vid-i-an
o-vi-na-tion
o-vip-a-ra
o-vi-par-i-ty
o-vip-a-rous
o-vi-pos-i-tor
o-vu-lar
o-vu-la-to-ry
ow-ing
own-er
ox-a-late
ox-al-ic
ox-al-u-ric
ox-a-lyl
ox-am-ide
ox-am-i-dine
ox-an-i-late
ox-a-nil-ic
ox-a-zine
ox-a-zol-i-dine
ox-i-dant
ox-i-dase
ox-i-da-tion
ox-ide
ox-i-dim-e-try
ox-i-diz-a-ble
ox-i-diz-er
ox-id-u-lat-ed
ox-im-e-ter
ox-i-met-ric
ox-in-dole
ox-o-ni-um
ox-o-phen-ar-sine
ox-y-a-can-thine
ox-y-a-cet-y-lene
ox-y-gen
ox-y-gen-ate
ox-y-gen-ize
ox-y-lu-cif-er-in
ox-y-tet-ra-cy-cline
ox-y-to-cin
oys-ter
Oz-al-id
O-zark-i-an
o-zo-ke-rite
o-zon-ate
o-zon-ide
o-zon-iz-er
o-zon-ol-y-sis
o-zo-no-sphere

P

pab-u-lum
pac-er
pa-chi-si
pach-no-lite
pach-y-der-ma-tous
pa-chym-e-ter
pac-i-fi-a-ble
pa-cif-ic
pac-i-fi-ca-tion
pa-cif-i-ca-to-ry
pac-i-fist
pac-i-fy
pack-ag-er
pack-et
pad-dling
pa-dre
pa-dro-ne
Pad-u-an
pae-an
pa-gan-ism
pag-eant-ry
pag-er
pag-i-nal
pag-i-nate
pag-ing
pa-go-da
pains-tak-ing
paint-er
Pais-ley
Pak-i-stan-i
pal-ace
pa-la-ceous
pal-a-din
pal-an-quin
pal-at-a-bil-i-ty
pal-at-a-ble
pal-a-tal-ize
pal-ate (roof of mouth)
pa-la-tial
pal-a-ti-nate
pal-a-tine
pal-a-ti-tis

pal-a-to-gram
pa-lav-er
pa-le-a-ceous
pa-le-og-ra-pher
pa-le-ol-o-gy
pa-le-on-tol-o-gy
Pa-le-o-zo-ic
Pal-es-tin-i-an
pal-ette (artist's board)
pal-frey
pa-lil-o-gy
pal-imp-sest
pal-in-drome
pal-i-sade
pal-la-di-um
pal-let (a bed)
pal-let-ize
pal-lette (armor)
pal-li-a-tive
pal-mate
palm-er
pal-met-to
palm-is-try
pal-mit-ic
pal-mit-o-le-ic
pal-o-mi-no
pal-pa-ble
pal-pi-tate
pal-sy
pal-try
pal-u-drine
pa-lus-trine
pal-y-nol-o-gy
pam-a-quine
Pam-e-la
pam-pas
pam-pe-an
pam-per
pam-phlet
pam-phlet-eer
pam-phlet-ize
pan-a-ce-a
pa-nache (headdress)
pa-na-che (food)
Pan-a-ma-ni-an
pan-a-ry
pan-a-tel-a
pan-car-di-tis
pan-chro-mat-ic
pan-cre-as
pan-cre-a-tec-to-my
pan-cre-a-tin
pan-cre-a-ti-tis
pan-cre-o-zy-min
pan-dem-ic
pan-de-mo-ni-um
pan-der
pan-e-gyr-ic
pan-e-gy-rize
pan-el-ist
pan-go-lin
pan-icked
pan-i-cle
pa-nic-u-late
pan-mne-si-a
pan-nic-u-li-tis
pan-nier
pa-no-cha
pan-o-ply
pan-o-ram-a
pan-o-ram-ic
pan-soph-ic
pan-tag-a-my
Pan-ta-gru-el
pan-ta-loon
pan-tarch-y
pan-te-the-ine
pan-the-ism
pan-the-on
pan-ther
pant-i-soc-ra-cy
pan-to-chro-mism
pan-to-graph
pan-tog-ra-pher
pan-to-ic
pan-tol-o-gy
pan-tom-e-ter
pan-to-mime
pan-to-then-ic
pan-to-yl
pan-try
pa-pa-cy
pa-pa-in-ase
Pa-pa-ni-co-laou
pa-par-chy
pa-pav-er-ine
pa-paw
pa-pay-a
pa-per
pa-pier ma-che
pa-pil-la
pap-il-lar-y
pap-il-lo-ma-to-sis
pap-il-lom-a-tous
pa-pism
pa-poose
pa-pri-ka
Pap-u-an
pap-u-lar
pap-y-ra-ceous
pap-y-rin
pa-py-rus
par-a-ban-ic
par-a-ba-sic

pa-rab-a-sis
par-a-bi-o-sis
par-a-ble
pa-rab-o-la
par-a-bol-i-cal
pa-rab-o-loi-dal
par-a-chor
par-a-chord-al
pa-rach-ro-nism
par-a-chut-ist
par-a-clete
pa-rad-er
par-a-digm
par-a-dise
par-a-di-si-a-cal
par-a-dox
par-af-fin-ic
par-a-gly-co-gen
par-a-go-ge
par-a-gog-ic
par-a-gon
pa-rag-o-nite
par-a-graph-er
Par-a-guay-an
par-a-keet
par-al-de-hyde
par-al-lac-tic
par-al-leled
par-al-lel-e-pi-ped
par-al-lel-e-pip-e-don
par-al-lel-ing
par-al-lel-om-e-ter
pa-ral-o-gize
pa-ral-y-sis
par-a-lyt-ic
par-a-lyzed
par-am-e-ter
par-a-mide
par-a-mi-no-ben-zo-ic
par-a-mor-phism
par-a-mour
par-a-noi-a
par-a-noi-ac
par-a-noi-dal
par-ant-he-lion
par-a-pet-ed
par-a-pha-si-a
par-a-pher-na-lia
par-a-phrase
pa-raph-ra-sis
pa-raph-y-sis
par-a-ple-gi-a
par-a-ple-gic
par-ap-sis
par-a-se-le-ne
par-a-sit-e-mi-a
par-a-sit-i-cal
par-a-sit-i-ci-dal
par-a-sit-ism
par-a-si-tize
par-a-si-to-sis
par-a-sol
pa-ras-tro-phy
par-celed
par-don-a-ble
par-e-gor-ic
pa-ren-chy-ma
par-en-chym-a-tous
par-ent-age
pa-ren-tal
par-en-ter-al
pa-ren-the-sis
par-en-thet-i-cal
par-er-gon
pa-re-sis
par-ret-ic
par-he-lion
pa-ri-ah
pa-ri-e-tal
pa-ri-e-to-fron-tal
par-i-mu-tu-el
par-i-nar-ic
par-ing
Par-is
par-ish
pa-rish-ion-er
Pa-ri-sian
Pa-ri-si-enne
par-i-son
par-i-ty
Park-er
park-er
par-lance
par-lia-men-tar-i-an
par-lia-men-ta-ry
par-lous
pa-ro-chi-al
par-o-dis-tic
par-o-dy
pa-rol
pa-role
pa-rol-ee
par-o-nych-i-a
par-o-nym
pa-ron-y-mous
pa-rot-id
pa-rot-i-dec-to-my
par-o-tit-ic
par-o-ti-tis
par-ox-ysm
par-ox-ys-mal
par-quet-ry
par-ri-ci-dal
par-si-mo-ni-ous

pars-ley
pars-nip
par-son-age
par-tage
par-tak-er
part-er
par-terre
Par-the-non
par-ti-al-i-ty
par-tial-ly
par-ti-bil-i-ty
par-tic-i-pant
par-tic-i-pa-tor
par-ti-cip-i-al
par-ti-ci-ple
par-ti-cle
par-tic-u-lar-i-ty
par-tic-u-late
par-ti-san
par-ti-tion-er
par-ti-tive
par-tridge
par-tu-ri-tion
pa-ru-lis
par-ve-nu
pas-chal
pas-i-graph-ic
pa-sig-ra-phy
pas-quin-ade
pass-a-ble
pas-sa-ca-glia
pas-sage
pas-sé
pas-sen-ger
pas-ser (bird)
pass-er
pas-si-ble
pas-sim-e-ter
pass-ing
pas-sion-ate
pas-si-va-tor
pas-siv-ist
pas-siv-i-ty
pas-som-e-ter
pass-o-ver
pas-tel
past-er
pas-tern
pas-teur-i-za-tion
pas-tiche
pas-tille
pas-time
pas-tor
pas-to-ral
pas-to-rale
pas-tor-ate
pas-tra-mi
pas-try
pas-tur-age
Pat-a-go-ni-an
Pa-taps-co
patch-er-y
patch-ou-li
pa-tel-la
pat-ent-ee
pat-en-tor
pa-ter-fa-mil-i-as
pa-ter-nal
pa-ter-ni-ty
pa-ter-nos-ter
pa-thet-ic
path-o-don-ti-a
path-o-gen-ic
path-o-ge-nic-i-ty
pa-thog-e-ny
pa-thog-no-my
path-o-log-i-cal
pa-thol-o-gist
pa-thol-o-gy
pa-thom-e-ter
pa-thos
pa-tho-sis
pa-tien-cy
pat-i-na
pat-i-o
pa-tois
pa-tri-ar-chal
pa-tri-arch-ate
pa-tri-arch-y
pa-tri-cian
pat-ri-cid-al
pat-ri-mo-ni-al
pat-ri-mo-ny
pa-tri-ot-ic
pa-tri-ot-ism
pa-tris-tic
pa-trolled
pa-trol-ling
pa-tron-age
pa-tron-ess
pat-ro-nite
pa-tron-ize
pat-ro-nym-ic
pa-tron-y-my
pa-troon
pat-terned
pau-ci-ty
Pau-li-na
Pau-line
Paul-ine (of Paul)
Paul-ist
pau-lo-post
pau-per-ize

paus-al
pav-er
pa-vil-ion
Pav-lov-i-an
pav-o-nite
pawn-ee (pledgee)
Paw-nee (Indian)
pay-ee
pay-o-la
peace-a-ble
peaked (topped)
peak-ed (pale)
pearl-es-cent
pearl-ite
peas-ant-ry
pe-can
pec-ca-ble
pec-ca-dil-lo
pec-cant
pec-ca-ry
pec-tin-ase
pec-ti-nate
pec-tin-ic
pec-to-lyt-ic
pec-to-ral
pec-to-ril-o-quy
pec-tous (chemistry)
pec-tus (zoology)
pe-cu-liar
pe-cu-li-ar-i-ty
pe-cu-ni-ar-y
ped-a-gog
ped-a-gog-i-cal
ped-a-gog-y
ped-aled
ped-al-ine
ped-ant
pe-dan-tic
ped-ant-ry
ped-dler
Pe-der-sen
ped-es-tal
pe-des-tri-an
pe-di-at-ric
pe-di-a-tri-cian
ped-i-cel
ped-i-cle
pe-dic-u-lar
Pe-dic-u-lar-is
pe-dic-u-lo-sis
pe-dic-u-lous (adj.)
Pe-dic-u-lus (n.)
ped-i-cure
ped-i-gree
ped-o-cal
pe-dol-o-gy
pe-dom-e-ter
ped-o-met-ri-cal
pe-dun-cu-lar
peel-er
peep-er
peer-age
pee-vish
Peg-a-sus
peg-ma-tite
peg-ma-tit-ic
peign-oir
pei-ram-e-ter
pej-o-ra-tive
Pe-king-ese
pe-koe
pe-lag-ic
pel-ar-go-nate
pel-ar-gon-ic
pel-ar-gon-i-din
pel-ar-go-nin
pel-er-ine
pel-i-can
pe-lisse
pel-la-gra
pel-let-er
pel-lu-cid-i-ty
pel-mat-o-gram
pe-lo-rus
pelt-er (n.)
pel-ter (v.)
pelt-ry
pel-vic
pel-vim-e-ter
pem-mi-can
pe-nal-ize
pen-al-ty
pen-ance
pe-na-tes
pench-ant
pen-ciled
pend-ant (n.)
pend-en-cy
pend-ent (adj.)
pen-du-los-i-ty
pen-du-lum
Pe-nel-o-pe
pen-e-tra-ble
pen-e-tram-e-ter
pen-e-tra-tive
pen-e-tra-tor
pen-e-trom-e-ter
pen-guin
pen-i-cil-lin
pen-i-cil-lin-ase
pen-i-cil-li-o-sis
pe-nin-su-lar
pen-i-tent
pen-i-ten-tia-ry

pen-ni-nite	per-i-met-ri-cal	pes-ti-ci-dal	phen-ox-ide	pho-tog-ra-pher	pierc-er
Penn-syl-va-nian	pe-rim-e-try	pes-tif-er-ous	phe-nox-y-a-ce-tic	pho-to-graph-ic	pi-e-ty
Pe-nob-scot	per-i-ne-al	pes-ti-lence	phen-tol-a-mine	pho-tog-ra-phy	pi-e-zom-e-ter
pe-no-log-i-cal	per-i-ne-or-rha-phy	pes-tle	phen-yl-ac-et-al-de-hyde	pho-to-gra-vure	pi-e-zom-e-try
pe-nol-o-gy	per-i-neph-ri-um	pes-tol-o-gy	phen-yl-ate	pho-tol-y-sis	pi-geon-eer
Pen-sa-co-la	per-i-ne-um	pet-al-if-er-ous	phen-yl-ene	pho-to-lyt-ic	pig-men-tar-y
pen-sive	pe-ri-od-ic (at intervals)	pet-al-ite	phen-yl-eph-rine	pho-tom-e-ter	pi-gnon
pent-ac-id	per-i-od-ic (chemistry)	pet-al-ous	phen-yl-eth-yl-ene	pho-to-met-ric	pik-er
pen-ta-cle	pe-ri-od-i-cal	pet-al-y	phe-nyl-ic	pho-tom-e-try	pi-las-ter
pen-tad	pe-ri-o-dic-i-ty	pe-tard	phen-yl-ke-to-nu-ric	pho-ton	pil-chard
pen-ta-dec-ane	per-i-os-te-um	pe-te-chi-al	phe-nyt-o-in	pho-to-nas-tic	pil-er
pen-ta-dec-yl	per-i-pa-tet-ic	Pe-ter	phe-o-chro-mo-cy-to-ma	pho-top-a-thy	pil-fer-age
pen-ta-e-ryth-ri-tol	pe-riph-er-al-ly	pet-i-o-lar	phe-o-phor-bide	phot-op-tom-e-ter	pil-grim-age
pen-ta-gon	pe-riph-er-y	pet-i-ole	phe-o-phy-tin	pho-to-stat-ed	pi-lif-er-ous
pen-tag-o-nal	per-i-phrase	pet-it	Phil-a-del-phi-an	pho-to-trop-ic	pil-lag-er
pen-ta-he-dral	pe-riph-ra-sis	pe-tite	phi-lan-der	pho-to-pho-re-sis	pil-lo-ry
pen-ta-hy-drite	pe-rip-ter-al	pe-ti-tion-er	phil-an-throp-ic	pho-tot-ro-pism	pi-lo-car-pi-dine
pen-ta-mer	pe-rip-ter-y	Pe-trar-chan	phi-lan-thro-pist	pho-tron-ic	pi-lose
pen-tam-er-al	pe-rique	Pe-trarch-ist	phi-lan-thro-py	phras-a-ble	pi-lo-sine
pen-tam-er-ous (adj.)	pe-ris-cil	pe-trel	phil-a-tel-ic	phra-se-o-gram	pi-los-i-ty
pen-tam-er-us (n.)	per-i-scop-ic	pe-tres-cence	phi-lat-e-list	phra-se-og-ra-phy	pi-lot-age
pen-tam-e-ter	per-ish	pe-tri	phi-lat-e-ly	phra-se-ol-o-gy	Pil-sner
pent-am-i-dine	per-i-som-al	pet-ri-fac-tion	**phil-har-mon-ic**	phras-er	pil-u-lar
pen-tane	pe-ris-sad	pe-tro-chem-i-cal	**phil-i-a-ter**	phras-ing	pim-an-threne
pen-ta-no-ic	per-i-stal-tic	pe-trog-e-ny	phil-lip-pic	phren-ic	pi-mar-ic
pen-ta-ploi-dic	per-i-sta-sis	pe-trog-ra-pher	Phil-ip-pine	phren-i-cot-o-my	pim-e-late
pen-tarch-y	per-i-sty-lar	pet-ro-graph-i-cal	Phil-is-tine	phre-ni-tis	pi-men-ta
pen-ta-rone	per-rit-o-my	pe-trog-ra-phy	phil-o-den-dron	phren-o-log-i-cal	pi-men-to
Pen-ta-teuch	per-i-to-ne-os-co-py	pet-rol	phil-o-graph	phre-nol-o-gy	pi-mien-to
pen-tath-lon	per-i-to-ne-um	pet-ro-lage	phi-log-y-ny	phren-o-sin	pim-ply
pen-ta-tom-ic	per-i-to-nit-ic	pet-ro-la-tum	phil-o-log-i-cal	Phryg-i-an	pin-a-coi-dal
pen-ta-va-lent	per-i-to-ni-tis	pet-ro-lene	phi-lol-o-gy	phtha-lam-ic	pin-a-col
Pen-te-cos-tal	per-i-win-kle	pe-tro-le-um	phil-o-pe-na	phthal-ate	pi-nac-o-late
pen-te-nyl	per-jur-er	pe-trol-ic	phi-los-o-pher	phthal-ein	pi-nac-o-lone
pen-ti-tol	per-ju-ri-ous	pet-ro-lif-er-ous	phil-o-soph-i-cal	phthal-ic	pin-a-cy-a-nol
pen-to-bar-bi-tal	per-ju-ry	pet-ro-lize	phi-los-o-phiz-er	phthal-im-ide	pi-nane
pen-tode	per-lite	pet-ro-log-ic	phi-los-o-phy	phthal-in	pin-cers
pen-tom-ic	per-ma-frost	pe-trol-o-gy	phil-ter	phthal-o-ni-trile	pinch-er
pen-to-san	Perm-al-loy	pe-tro-sal	phle-bit-ic	phthal-o-yl	pin-e-al
Pen-to-thal	per-ma-nent	pet-rous	phle-bi-tis	phthi-o-col	pi-nene
pent-ox-ide	per-man-ga-nate	pe-trox-o-lin	phleb-o-graph-ic	phthi-ri-a-sis	pin-er-y
pen-tryl	per-me-a-ble	pet-u-lant	phle-bog-ra-phy	phthis-ick-y	pi-nic
pen-tu-lose	per-me-am-e-ter	pe-tu-nia	phle-bot-o-my	phthis-i-ol-o-gy	pin-ion
pen-tyl-ene	Per-mi-an	pe-yo-te	phleg-mat-ic	phthi-sis	pi-nite
pen-tyl-i-dene	per-mis-si-ble	pha-com-e-ter	phlob-a-phene	phy-col-o-gy	pi-ni-tol
pe-nul-ti-mate	per-mit-tee	pha-e-ton	phlo-em	phy-lac-tery	pink-er
pe-num-bra	per-mut-a-ble	phag-o-cyte	phlo-gis-ton	phyl-lo-por-phy-rin	pin-na-cle
pe-nu-ri-ous	per-mu-ta-tor	phag-o-cyt-ic	phlog-o-pi-ti-za-tion	phy-lo-ge-net-ic	pi-no-cam-phe-ol
pe-nu-ry	per-ni-cious	phag-o-cy-to-sis	phlo-i-on-ic	phy-log-e-ny	pi-noch-le
pe-on-age	per-ni-o-sis	pha-lange	phlor-e-tin	phy-lum	pi-no-lin
pe-o-ny	per-o-ne-al	pha-lan-ge-al	phlor-i-zin-ize	phy-ma-to-sis	pi-ñon
peo-ple	Pe-ro-nist	pha-lanx	phlor-o-glu-cin-ol	phys-i-at-rics	pi-non-ic
Pe-o-ri-a	per-o-ra-tion	phal-loi-dine	phlo-rol	phys-ic	pi-no-syl-vin
pe-pi-no	pe-ro-sis	phan-er-ite	phlox-ine	phys-i-cal	pim-tle
pep-lum	per-ox-i-dase	phan-er-o-gam	pho-bi-a	phy-si-cian	pi-nyl
pep-si-gogue	per-ox-ide	phan-er-os-co-py	pho-bo-tax-is	phys-i-cist	pi-o-neered
pep-sin-if-er-ous	per-ox-y-a-ce-tic	phan-er-o-sis	phoe-be	phys-i-og-no-my	pi-os-i-ty
pep-sin-o-gen	per-ox-y-di-sul-fate	phan-o-tron	Phoe-ni-cian	phys-i-og-ra-phy	pi-ous
pep-ti-dase	per-pen-dic-u-lar	phan-tas-ma-go-ri-al	Phoe-nix	phys-i-o-log-i-cal	pip-age
pep-to-nate	per-pe-tra-tor	phan-tas-mal	phon-as-the-ni-a	phys-i-ol-o-gy	pi-pec-o-line
pep-to-nize	per-pet-u-al	phan-tom	phon-au-to-graph	phys-i-om-e-try	pip-er
pe-rac-e-tic	per-pe-tu-i-ty	phan-to-scope	pho-ne-mat-ic	phys-i-os-o-phy	pi-per-a-zine
per-am-bu-la-tor	per-qui-site	Phar-aoh	pho-ne-mic	phy-sique	pi-per-ic
per-bo-rate	per-se-cu-tion	phar-i-sa-i-cal	pho-ne-mic-i-ty	phy-so-car-pous	pi-per-i-dine
Per-bu-nan	per-se-cu-to-ry	Phar-i-see	pho-nen-do-scope	phy-so-stig-mine	pip-er-ine
per-ca-line	Per-se-id	phar-ma-ceu-ti-cal	pho-net-ic	phy-tase	pi-per-o-nyl-ic
per-ceiv-a-ble	per-se-i-tol	phar-ma-cist	pho-ne-ti-cian	Phy-tin	pip-er-ox-an
per-ceiv-er	per-se-ver-ance	phar-ma-cog-no-sy	Phone-vi-sion	phy-to-flu-ene	pi-per-y-lene
per-cent-age	per-sev-er-a-tive	phar-mac-o-lite	pho-ni-at-ric	phy-tog-a-my	pi-pet
per-cent-ile	Per-shing	phar-ma-col-o-gy	phon-ic	phy-to-gen-ic	pi-quan-cy
per-cep-ti-ble	Per-sian	phar-ma-co-peia	pho-no-gen-ic	phy-tol-o-gy	pi-qué (fabric)
per-cep-tive	per-si-flage	pha-ryn-ge-al	**pho-no-graph-i-cal**	phy-tom-e-ter	pi-quet
per-cep-tu-al	per-sist-ence	phar-yn-gi-tis	**pho-nog-ra-phy**	phy-to-met-ric	pi-ra-cy
perch-er	per-sist-er	pha-ryn-go-log-i-cal	pho-no-lite	phy-toph-a-gous	pi-ra-nha
Per-che-ron	per-snick-e-ty	phar-yn-gol-o-gy	pho-nol-o-gy	phy-to-sis	pi-rat-i-cal
per-chlo-rate	per-son-a-ble	pha-ryn-go-scope	pho-nom-e-ter	phy-tos-te-rol	pi-rogue
per-chlo-ryl	per-son-al-i-ty	phar-ynx	pho-nom-e-try	phy-tyl	pir-ou-ette
per-cip-i-ent	per-son-al-ty	phas-e-me-ter	pho-no-phore	pi-a-nis-si-mo	pis-ca-to-ri-al
per-co-la-tor	per-son-nel	pha-se-o-lin	pho-noph-o-rous	pi-an-ist	Pis-ces
per cu-ri-am	per-spec-tive	phas-er (one who phases)	pho-ny	pi-a-niste	pis-cine
per-cus-sive	per-spec-tom-e-ter	pha-sic	phor-bin	pi-a-nis-tic	pi-si-form
per-e-gri-nate	per-spi-ca-cious	pha-si-tron	pho-re-sis	pi-an-o-for-te	pis-tach-i-o
pe-rei-ra	per-spi-cac-i-ty	pha-sor (electrical)	pho-ret-ic	pi-as-sa-va	pis-til-late
pe-remp-tive	per-spi-cu-i-ty	pheas-ant	pho-rom-e-ter	pi-as-ter	pitch-er
pe-remp-to-ry	per-spic-u-ous	phel-lan-drene	pho-rom-e-try	pic-a-resque	pit-e-ous
pe-ren-ni-al	per-spir-a-ble	phen-ace-tin	pho-rone	pic-a-yune	pith-e-can-thro-poid
per-fect-er	per-spi-ra-tion	phen-a-cite	pho-rop-tor	Pic-ca-dil-ly	pith-e-col-o-gy
per-fect-i-ble	per-spir-a-tive	phen-a-cyl	phos-gen-ite	pic-ca-lil-li	pith-i-ness
per-fec-tor	per-spir-a-to-ry	phen-an-threne	phos-pham-ic	pic-e-in	pit-i-a-ble
per-fer-vid	per-suad-er	phen-an-thri-dine	phos-pha-tase	pi-cene	pi-tom-e-ter
per-fid-i-ous	per-sua-si-ble	phe-nan-thri-din-i-um	phos-pha-te-mi-a	pick-et-er	pi-ton
per-fi-dy	per-sua-sive	phe-nan-thro-line	phos-phat-ic	pick-led	pi-tu-i-tar-y
per-fo-ra-tor	perth-ite	phe-nan-thryl	phos-phi-nate	pick-ling	Pi-tu-i-trin
per-form-ance	per-ti-na-cious	phen-ar-sa-zine	phos-phin-ic	pic-nick-er	pi-val-ic
per-form-er	per-ti-nac-i-ty	phen-a-zine	phos-pho-a-mi-no-lip-ide	pic-o-line	piv-ot-al
per-fum-er-y	per-ti-nent	phe-net-i-dine	phos-pho-di-es-ter-ase	pic-o-lin-ic	piv-ot-er
per-func-to-ry	per-turb-a-ble	phen-e-tole	phos-pho-nate	pic-ram-ic	pix-i-lat-ed
per-i-anth	per-tur-ba-tion	phe-nic	phos-phon-ic	pic-ram-ide	piz-ze-ri-a
per-i-ar-thri-tis	per-turb-er	phen-mi-az-ine	phos-pho-rate	pic-rate	plac-a-ble
per-i-as-tron	pe-rus-al	phe-no-bar-bi-tal	phos-pho-re-al	pic-ric	plac-ard (n.)
per-i-car-di-tis	Pe-ru-vi-an	phe-no-cop-ic	phos-pho-res-cence	pic-ro-cro-cin	pla-card (v.)
per-i-car-di-um	per-va-sive	phe-no-crys-tic	phos-phor-ic	pic-ro-lon-ic	pla-cat-er
per-i-cla-site	per-ver-sion	phe-nol	phos-phor-o-gen	pic-rom-er-ite	pla-ca-to-ry
Per-i-cle-an	per-ver-si-ty	phe-no-lase	phos-pho-ro-gen-ic	pic-ryl	place-a-ble
pe-ric-o-pe	per-vert-i-ble	phe-no-late	phos-pho-rol-y-sis	pic-to-graph-ic	pla-ce-bo
per-i-cop-ic	per-vi-ca-cious	phe-no-lic	phos-pho-rous (adj.)	pic-tog-ra-phy	pla-cen-ta
pe-rid-i-um	per-vi-cac-i-ty	phe-no-log-i-cal	phos-pho-rus (n.)	pic-to-ri-al	plac-en-tar-y
pe-rid-o-tite	per-vi-ous	phe-nol-o-gy	phos-pho-ryl-ase	pic-tur-a-ble	plac-en-ti-tis
per-i-gee	per-y-lene	phe-nol-phthal-ein	phos-vi-tin	pic-tur-esque	plac-er
pe-rig-y-nous	pe-se-ta	phe-nom-e-nal	pho-tics	pic-ul	plac-id
per-i-he-lion	Pe-sha-war	phe-nom-e-no-log-i-cal	pho-to-chro-my	pid-dler	pla-cid-i-ty
per-iled	pes-sa-ry	phe-nom-e-nol-o-gy	pho-to-gen-ic	pi-ece de re-sis-tance	plack-et
per-il-ous	pes-si-mis-tic	phe-no-plast	pho-to-gram-me-try	piec-er	pla-coi-dal
pe-rim-e-ter	pes-tered	phe-no-type			

pla-gia-rism
pla-gia-rize
pla-gi-o-clase
pla-gi-o-nite
plagu-ed
pla-gui-ly
pla-guy
plain-tiff
plain-tive
plait-er
pla-nar-i-ty
pla-na-tion
plan-chet
plan-chette
pla-ner (tree)
plan-er
plan-et
plan-e-tar-i-um
plan-e-tar-y
plan-e-tes-i-mal
plan-et-oi-dal
plan-et-o-log-ic
plan-e-tol-o-gy
plan-gen-cy
pla-nig-ra-phy
pla-nim-e-ter
pla-ni-met-ric
plank-tiv-o-rous
pla-no-con-cave
plan-o-graph
pla-nog-ra-phy
pla-nom-e-ter
plan-o-sol
plan-tain
plan-tar
plan-ta-tion
plant-er
pla-num
pla-quette
plas-ma-pher-e-sis
plas-min-o-gen
plas-mo-di-a-sis
plas-mo-di-um
plas-mol-y-sis
plas-mo-lyt-ic
plas-ter
plas-ti-ca-tor
plas-ti-cim-e-ter
plas-tic-i-ty
plas-ti-ciz-er
plas-ti-line
plas-ti-noid
plas-ti-sol
plas-to-mer
plas-tom-e-ter
plas-tron
pla-teau
plat-ed
plat-en
plat-er
pla-ti-na
pla-tin-ic
plat-i-no-type
plat-i-num
plat-i-tu-di-nar-i-an
pla-ton-ic
Pla-to-nist
pla-toon
plat-y-nite
plat-y-pus
plau-dit
plau-si-ble
plead-er
pleas-ant-ry
pleas-ur-a-ble
pleat-er
ple-be-ian
pleb-i-scite
pledg-ee
pledge-or (law)
pledg-er
pledg-et
Ple-ia-des
plei-o-bar
plei-ot-ro-py
Pleis-to-cene
ple-na-ry
plen-i-po-ten-tia-ry
plen-i-tude
plen-te-ous
plen-ti-ful
ple-num
ple-o-nasm
ple-rot-ic
pleth-o-ra
ple-thor-ic
pleu-ral
pleu-ri-sy
pleu-rit-ic
pleu-ro-dont
plex-im-e-ter
plex-us
Pli-o-cene
plom-bage
plov-er
plu-ma-ceous
plum-age
plu-mate
plum-ba-gin
plum-ba-go
plum-bate
plumb-er
plum-bif-er-ous

plum-bite
plum-bous
plu-mose
plump-er
plun-der
plunge-er
plu-ral-i-ty
plu-ri-va-lent
plu-tar-chy
plu-toc-ra-cy
plu-to-crat
plu-to-nism
plu-to-ni-um
plu-vi-og-ra-phy
plu-vi-om-e-ter
plu-vi-o-met-ric
plu-vi-ous
Plym-outh
pneu-drau-lic
pneu-mat-ic
pneu-ma-tic-i-ty
pneu-ma-tol-y-sis
pneu-ma-tom-e-ter
pneu-ma-to-sis
pneu-mec-to-my
pneu-mo-coc-cus
pneu-mol-y-sis
pneu-mo-nia
pneu-mon-ic
pneu-mo-ni-tis
poach-er
po-choir
pock-et
po-dal-ic
po-di-a-trist
po-di-a-try
po-di-um
po-do-lite
pod-zol-ize
po-et-as-ter
po-et-i-cal
po-et-ry
po-go-not-ro-phy
po-grom
poign-an-cy
poign-ant
poi-ki-lit-ic
poi-kil-o-cy-to-sis
poin-ci-an-a
poin-set-ti-a
point-er
Poi-ret
pois-er
poi-son-ous
pok-er
po-lar
po-lar-im-e-ter
po-lar-i-met-ric
Po-la-ris
po-lar-i-scope
po-lar-i-stro-bom-e-ter
po-lar-i-ty
po-lar-iz-er
po-lar-o-graph-ic
po-lar-og-ra-phy
Po-lar-oid
po-lar-on
po-lem-ic
pol-e-mize
pol-er
po-li-a-nite
po-lic-ing
pol-i-cy
po-li-o-my-e-li-tis
po-li-o-sis
Pol-ish
pol-ish-er
Po-lit-bu-ro
po-lit-i-cal
pol-i-ti-cian
pol-i-tics
po-litz-er
pol-len-iz-er
poll-er
pol-li-na-tion
pol-li-nif-er-ous
pol-lin-i-um
pol-li-no-sis
pol-lu-cite
pol-lut-ant
pol-lut-er
pol-lu-tion
pol-o-naise
po-lo-ni-um
pol-troon
pol-y-a-cryl-ic
pol-y-am-ide
pol-y-an-dry
pol-y-ar-gy-rite
pol-y-ba-site
pol-y-chro-mat-ic
pol-y-chro-my
pol-y-clin-ic
pol-y-crase
pol-y-cy-the-mi-a
po-lyd-y-mite
pol-y-ene
pol-y-es-ter
pol-y-eth-yl-ene
pol-y-gam-ic
po-lyg-a-my
po-lyg-e-ny
pol-y-glot

pol-y-gon
po-lyg-o-nal
pol-y-graph-ic
po-lyg-ra-phy
pol-y-he-dral
pol-y-hi-dro-sis
pol-y-i-so-bu-tyl-ene
pol-y-i-so-top-ic
pol-y-kar-y-on
pol-y-mer-ic
po-lym-er-i-za-tion
po-lym-er-iz-er
po-lym-er-ous
pol-y-me-ter
pol-ym-nite
pol-y-mor-phous
Pol-y-ne-sian
pol-y-no-mi-al
pol-y-nu-cle-o-sis
pol-yp-ec-to-my
pol-yph-a-gous
po-lyph-o-ny
pol-y-ploi-dic
pol-yp-ous
pol-yp-tych
pol-y-pus
pol-y-so-ma-ty
pol-y-sty-rene
pol-y-tech-ni-cal
pol-y-trop-ic
pol-y-u-ro-nide
pol-y-va-lent
pol-y-vi-nyl
pom-ace
po-made
po-ma-tum
pome-gran-ate
Pom-er-a-ni-an
pom-meled
po-mo-log-i-cal
po-mol-o-gy
pom-pa-dour
pom-pa-no
Pom-pe-ian
pom-pos-i-ty
pomp-ous
Pon-a-pe-an
pon-cho
pond-age
pon-der-o-sa
pon-der-os-i-ty
pon-der-ous
pon-iard
pon-tage
pon-tif-i-cal
pon-tif-i-ca-tor
poo-dle
pop-e-line
pop-lit-e-al
pop-ping
pop-u-lace
pop-u-lar-i-ty
pop-u-lar-ize
pop-u-lous
por-ce-lain
por-ce-la-ne-ous
por-cine
por-cu-pine
po-ri-ci-dal
po-rif-er-ous
po-ri-tes
por-nog-ra-pher
por-no-graph-ic
po-rom-e-ter
po-ro-scope
po-ros-co-py
po-rose
po-ro-sim-e-ter
po-ros-i-ty
po-rot-ic
po-rous
por-phin
por-phy-rin
por-phy-rit-ic
por-phyr-ox-ine
por-phy-ry
por-poise
port-a-ble
por-tage
por-tal
por-ten-tous
por-ter
port-fo-li-o
por-ti-co
por-tiere
port-man-teau
por-trai-ture
Por-tu-guese
por-tu-lac-a
pos-er
po-seur
po-si-tion-er
pos-i-ti-val
pos-i-tiv-ism
pos-i-tro-ni-um
po-sol-o-gy
pos-sessed
pos-sess-es
pos-ses-sive
pos-ses-sor
pos-si-bil-i-ty
post-age

post-al
post-er
pos-te-ri-or
pos-ter-i-ty
pos-ter-o-dor-sal
post-hu-mous
pos-tu-lant
pos-tur-al
po-ta-ble
po-tage
po-tam-ic
pot-a-mog-ra-phy
pot-a-mom-e-ter
pot-ash
pot-as-sam-ide
po-tas-sic
po-tas-si-um
po-ta-to-ry
po-ten-cy
po-ten-tate
po-ten-ti-al-i-ty
po-ten-ti-om-e-ter
po-tom-e-ter
pot-pour-ri
pot-sherd
poul-tice
poul-try
pounc-er
pound-age
pound-er
pour-par-ler
pousse ca-fe
pout-er
pov-er-ty
pow-dered
pow-ered
poz-zo-la-nic
prac-ti-ca-ble
prac-ti-cal-i-ty
prac-tic-er
prac-ti-tion-er
prae-co-pe
prag-mat-ic
prag-ma-tism
prai-rie
prais-er
pra-line
pranc-er
pran-di-al
prank-ster
pra-se-o-dym-i-um
pras-oid
pra-tique
prat-tler
prax-e-ol-o-gy
pray-er
preach-er
pre-am-ble
pre-car-i-ous
prec-a-to-ry
pre-ced-a-ble
prec-e-dence
pre-ce-dent (adj.)
prec-e-dent (n., v.)
pre-ced-ing
pre-cep-tor
pre-ci-os-i-ty
pre-cious
prec-i-pice
pre-cip-i-tant
pre-cip-i-ta-tor
pre-cip-i-tin-o-gen
pre-cip-i-tous
Pre-cip-i-tron
pre-ci-sion
pre-ci-sive
pre-clu-sive
pre-co-cious
pre-coc-i-ty
pre-cor-di-um
pre-cur-sor
pre-da-ceous
pre-dac-i-ty
pred-a-to-ry
pred-e-ces-sor
pre-den-ta-ry
pre-des-ti-nate
pred-i-ca-ble
pre-dic-a-ment
pred-i-cate
pred-i-ca-to-ry
pre-dict-able
pre-dic-tion
pre-dic-tor
pred-i-lec-tion
pred-nis-o-lone
pred-ni-sone
pre-dom-i-nance
pre-emp-to-ry
pre-fab-ri-ca-tor
pref-ace
pref-a-to-ry
pre-fec-ture
pre-fer
pref-er-a-ble
pref-er-ence
pref-er-en-tial
pre-fer-ment
pre-for-ma-tion
preg-nan-cy
preg-nen-in-o-lone
preg-nen-o-lone
pre-hen-si-ble

pre-hen-sile
prehn-ite
prehn-i-tene
prehn-it-ic
prej-u-di-cial
prel-ate
pre-lim-i-nar-y
prel-ude
pre-lu-di-al
pre-ma-ture
pre-med-i-ta-tive
pre-mier
pre-miere
prem-ise (n.)
pre-mise (v.)
pre-mi-um
pre-mo-ni-tion
pre-mon-i-to-ry
prep-a-ra-tion
pre-par-a-to-ry
pre-par-er
pre-pon-der-ant
pre-po-si-tion (before)
prep-o-si-tion
pre-pos-ter-ous
pre-puce
pre-req-ui-site
pre-rog-a-tive
pres-age (n.)
pre-sage (v.)
pres-by-o-phre-ni-a
pres-by-o-pi-a
Pres-by-te-ri-an
pres-by-ter-y
pre-science
pre-scient
pre-scis-sion
pre-scrib-er
pre-scrip-ti-ble
pre-scrip-tive
pres-ent (adj. and n.)
present (v.; also as n., military term)
pre-sent-a-ble
pres-en-ta-tion
pres-en-ta-tive
pre-sent-er
pre-sen-ti-ment
pre-sen-tive
pres-er-va-tion
pre-serv-a-tive
pre-serv-er
pres-i-den-cy
pres-i-den-tial
pre-sid-i-o
pre-sid-i-um
press-er
pres-sor
pres-sur-ize
pres-ti-dig-i-ta-tor
pres-tig-i-ous
Pres-tone
pre-sum-a-ble
pre-sump-tion
pre-sump-tive
pre-sump-tu-ous
pre-tend-er
pre-tense
pre-ten-tious
pret-er-it
pret-er-i-tal
pre-ter-mit
pre-to-ri-al
pret-ti-ness
pret-zel
pre-vail
prev-a-lence
pre-var-i-ca-tor
pre-vent-a-tive
pre-vent-er
pre-ven-tive
pre-vi-ous
pric-er
prick-ling
pri-ma-cy
pri-ma fa-ci-e
pri-ma-quine
pri-mar-i-ly
pri-mar-y
pri-mate
Pri-ma-tes
pri-ma-tol-o-gy
pri-ma-ve-ral
prim-er
pri-me-val
prim-i-tiv-ism
pri-mo-gen-i-ture
pri-mor-di-al
prim-u-la-ver-in
prim-u-line
pri-mus
prin-cess
prin-ci-pal
prin-ci-ple
print-er-y
pri-or-i-ty
pri-o-ry
pris-mat-ic
pris-ma-toi-dal
pris-moi-dal
pri-som-e-ter
pris-on-er
pris-tine
pri-va-cy

pri-va-teer
pri-va-tion
priv-a-tive
pri-vat-ize
priv-et
priv-i-leged
priv-i-ty
priz-a-ble
prob-a-bil-i-ty
prob-a-ble
pro-ba-tion-er
pro-ba-tive
pro-bi-ty
prob-lem-at-i-cal
prob-o-la
pro-bos-cis
pro-caine
pro-ce-du-ral
pro-ce-dure
proc-ess (n., v.)
proc-ess-ing
pro-ces-sion
proc-es-sor
pro-claim
proc-la-ma-tion
pro-clam-a-to-ry
pro-clit-ic
pro-cliv-i-ty
pro-cli-vous
proc-ne-mi-al
pro-cras-ti-na-tor
pro-cre-a-tor
pro-crus-te-an
proc-ti-tis
proc-to-log-i-cal
proc-tol-o-gy
proc-to-ri-al
proc-to-scop-ic
proc-tos-co-py
pro-cur-a-ble
proc-u-ra-cy
proc-u-ra-to-ry
pro-cur-er
pro-cur-ess
prod-i-gal-i-ty
pro-dig-i-o-sin
pro-di-gious
prod-i-gy
pro-drome
pro-duce (v.)
prod-uce (n.)
pro-duc-er
pro-duc-i-ble
prod-uct (n.)
pro-duct-i-ble
pro-duc-tion
pro-duc-tiv-i-ty
prof-a-na-tion
pro-fan-i-ty
pro-fess-ant
pro-fessed
pro-fes-sion
pro-fes-sor
pro-fes-so-ri-al
prof-fered
pro-fi-cient
pro-fil-er
pro-fi-lo-graph
pro-fi-lom-e-ter
prof-it-a-ble
prof-it-eer
prof-it-er
prof-li-ga-cy
prof-li-gate
prof-lu-ence
pro-fun-di-ty
pro-fu-sion
pro-gen-i-tor
prog-e-ny
pro-ges-ter-one
prog-na-thous
prog-no-sis
prog-nos-ti-ca-tor
pro-gramed
pro-gram-er
pro-gram-ing
pro-gram-ist
pro-gram-mat-ic
prog-ress (n.)
pro-gress (v.)
pro-gres-sion
pro-gres-sive
pro-hib-it-er
pro-hi-bi-tion
pro-hib-i-tive
pro-hib-i-to-ry
proj-ect (n.)
pro-ject (v.)
pro-jec-tile
pro-jec-tive
pro-jec-tor
pro-ji-cient
pro-lam-in
pro-la-tive
pro-le-gom-e-non
pro-lep-sis
pro-le-tar-i-an
pro-lif-er-a-tive
pro-lif-ic
pro-li-fic-i-ty
pro-line
pro-lix
pro-log
pro-lon-ga-tion

pro-lu-so-ry
prom-e-nad-er
Pro-me-the-us
pro-me-thi-um
prom-i-nence
prom-is-cu-i-ty
pro-mis-cu-ous
prom-is-ee
prom-i-sor
prom-is-so-ry
Prom-i-zole
prom-on-to-ry
pro-mot-er
prompt-er
promp-ti-tude
pro-mul-ga-tion
pro-mul-ga-tor
pro-na-tor
pro-nom-i-nal
pro-no-tum
pro-nounce-a-ble
pro-nun-ci-a-tion
proof-er
pro-pa-di-ene
prop-a-ga-ble
prop-a-gan-dist
prop-a-ga-tor
pro-pam-i-dine
pro-pa-no-ic
pro-pa-nol
pro-par-gyl
pro-par-ox-y-tone
pro-pel-lant (n.)
pro-pel-lent (adj.)
pro-pel-ler
pro-pe-no-ic
pro-pen-si-ty
pro-pe-nyl
pro-per-din
prop-er-ly
prop-er-ty
proph-e-cy (n.)
proph-e-sy (v.)
proph-et
pro-phet-ic
pro-phy-lac-tic
pro-phy-lax-is
pro-pin-qui-ty
pro-pi-o-late
pro-pi-o-lic
pro-pi-o-nate
pro-pi-on-ic
pro-pi-o-ni-trile
pro-pi-o-nyl
pro-pi-on-y-late
pro-pi-ti-ate
pro-pi-tious
pro-po-de-um
pro-po-nent
pro-por-tion-ate
pro-pos-al
pro-pos-er
prop-o-si-tion
pro-pri-e-tar-y
pro-pri-e-tor
pro-pri-e-ty
pro-pox-y-ac-et-an-i-lide
pro-pul-sive
pro-pul-so-ry
pro-pyl-a-mine
pro-pyl-ene
pro-pyl-ic
prop-y-lite
pro ra-ta
pro-rat-a-ble
pro-rat-er
pro-ro-ga-tion
pro-rogue
pro-sa-i-cal-ly
pro-sce-ni-um
pro-scribe
pro-scrip-tive
pros-e-cu-to-ry
pros-e-cu-trix
pros-e-lyte
pros-e-lyt-iz-er
pro-sod-i-cal
pros-o-dy
pros-o-pite
pros-o-pla-si-a
pros-pect
pro-spec-tive
pros-pec-tor
pro-spec-tus
pros-per-i-ty
pros-per-ous
pro-spi-cience
pros-ta-tec-to-my
pros-tat-ic
pros-ta-ti-tis
pro-sthen-ic
pros-the-sis
pros-thet-ic
pros-the-tist
Pro-stig-min
pros-ti-tute
pros-tra-tor
prot-ac-tin-i-um
pro-ta-gon
pro-tag-o-nist
prot-a-mine
pro-ta-no-pi-a
pro-te-an
pro-te-ase

pro-tect-ant
pro-tec-tive
pro-tec-tor-ate
pro-te-ge
pro-te-ide
pro-tein
pro-tein-a-ceous
pro-tein-ase
pro tem-po-re
pro-te-ol-y-sin
Prot-er-o-zo-ic
pro-test
pro-tes-tant (law)
Prot-es-tant (religion)
prot-es-ta-tion
pro-test-er
pro-thon-o-tar-y
pro-throm-bin
pro-tide
pro-ti-um
pro-to-blast
pro-to-cat-e-chu-al-de-hyde
pro-to-clas-tic
pro-toc-neme
pro-to-col
pro-to-gen
pro-tog-y-ny
pro-ton-ate
pro-to-pine
pro-to-plas-mal
pro-to-trop-ic
pro-tot-ro-py
pro-to-type
pro-to-ver-a-trine
prot-ox-ide
pro-to-zo-a
pro-to-zo-i-a-sis
pro-tract-i-ble
pro-trac-tile
pro-trac-tor
pro-tru-si-ble
pro-tru-sive
pro-tu-ber-ance
proust-ite
prov-a-ble
prov-e-nance
prov-en-der
pro-ve-nience
prov-er
prov-erb
pro-ver-bi-al
pro-vide
prov-i-dence
prov-i-den-tial
pro-vid-er
prov-ince
pro-vin-cial
pro-vi-sion
pro-vi-so-ry
prov-o-ca-tion
pro-voc-a-tive
pro-voc-a-to-ry
pro-vost (military)
prov-ost-al
prow-ess
prowl-er
prox-i-mate
prox-im-i-ty
pru-dence
pru-den-tial
prud-er-y
prud-ish
pru-i-nes-cence
pru-na-sin
pru-nel-la
prun-er
pru-ne-tin
pru-ni-trin
pru-ri-ent
pru-rit-ic
pru-ri-tus
prus-si-ate
psalm-ist
psal-mod-ic
psal-ter-y
pseud-an-dry
pseud-ar-thro-sis
pseu-do-cu-mi-dine
pseu-do-i-o-none
pseu-do-nym
pseu-don-y-mous
pseu-dos-co-py
pseu-dos-to-ma
psil-an-thro-py
psi-lo-mel-ane
psi-lo-sis
psi-lot-ic
psit-ta-co-sis
psit-ta-cot-ic
pso-phom-e-ter
pso-ri-a-sis
pso-ro-sis
Psy-che
psy-che-om-e-try
psy-chi-at-ric
psy-chi-a-trist
psy-chi-a-try
psy-chi-cal
psy-cho-an-a-lyst
psy-cho-an-a-lyt-ic
psy-cho-an-a-lyze
psy-cho-gen-ic

psy-cho-ge-nic-i-ty
psy-cho-graph-ic
psy-chog-ra-phy
psy-cho-log-i-cal
psy-chol-o-gist
psy-chom-e-ter
psy-cho-met-ric
psy-cho-me-tri-cian
psy-chom-e-try
psy-cho-nom-ics
psy-cho-path-ic
psy-chop-a-thy
psy-cho-sis
psy-cho-so-mat-ic
psy-chot-ic
psy-chro-tine
psy-chrom-e-ter
psy-chrom-e-try
psyl-li-um
psyl-lyl
ptar-mi-gan
pter-i-dine
pter-o-dac-tyl
pte-ro-ic
pter-o-pod
Pte-rop-o-da
pter-o-yl
pte-ryg-i-um
pter-y-goid
Ptol-e-ma-ic
pto-maine
pto-sis
pu-ber-ty
pu-ber-u-lent
pu-ber-u-lon-ic
pu-bes-cent
pu-bic
pu-bi-ot-o-my
pub-li-ca-tion
pub-li-cist
pub-lic-i-ty
puck-ered
pu-den-dal
pueb-lo
pu-er-ile
pu-er-per-al
pu-er-pe-ri-um
puff-er
pu-gi-lism
pu-gi-list
pu-gi-lis-tic
pug-na-cious
pug-nac-i-ty
pu-is-sant
pul-chri-tu-di-nous
pu-le-gone
pu-li-cide
pul-ing
pull-er
pul-let
pul-lo-rum
pul-mom-e-ter
pul-mo-nar-y
pul-mon-ic
Pul-mo-tor
pulp-er
pul-pit-eer
pulp-ot-o-my
pulp-ous
pul-que
pul-sa-tance
pul-sa-to-ry
puls-er
pul-sim-e-ter
pul-som-e-ter
pul-ver-iz-er
pul-ver-u-lent
pul-vin-ic
pu-mi-cate
pum-ice
pu-mi-ceous
pump-age
pump-er
pum-per-nick-el
pun-cheon
punch-er
pun-chi-nel-lo
punc-tate
punc-ti-form
punc-til-i-o
punc-til-i-ous
punc-tu-al-i-ty
punc-tu-ate
punc-tur-a-ble
punc-tured
pun-dit
pun-gen-cy
Pu-nic
pu-nic-ic
pun-ish-er
pu-ni-tive
pun-ster
punt-er
Punx-su-taw-ney
pu-pa-tion
pu-pif-er-ous
pu-pil
pu-pil-late
pu-pil-lom-e-ter
pup-pet-eer
pup-pet-ry
pur-chas-er
pu-ree
pur-ga-tive

pur-ga-to-ry
purg-er
pu-ri-fi-ca-tion
pu-rine
pur-ist
pu-ris-tic
pu-ri-tan
pu-ri-ty
Pur-kin-je
pur-lieu
pur-lin
pur-loin
pu-ro-my-cin
pur-ples-cent
pur-plish
pur-pos-ive
pur-pu-ra
pur-pu-rin
pur-pu-rite
pur-pu-ro-gal-lin
pur-pu-rog-e-nous
purs-er
pur-su-ant
pur-suit-me-ter
pur-sui-vant
pur-te-nance
pu-ru-lence
pur-vey-or
pu-sil-la-nim-i-ty
pu-sil-lan-i-mous
pus-tu-lous
pu-ta-tive
pu-tre-fa-cient
pu-tre-fac-tion
pu-tres-cent
pu-tres-ci-ble
pu-tres-cine
pu-trid
put-ter (n., v.)
putt-er (golf club)
Puy-al-lup
puz-zler
pyc-nom-e-ter
pyc-no-sis
pyc-not-ic
py-e-lit-ic
py-e-li-tis
py-e-lo-graph-ic
Pyg-ma-li-on
pyg-my
pyk-rete
py-lor-ic
py-lo-ro-plas-ty
py-lo-rus
py-o-cy-a-nase
py-o-cy-a-nin
py-o-gen-ic
py-or-rhe-a
pyr-a-cene
Pyr-a-lin
pyr-a-mid
py-ram-i-dal
pyr-a-mid-er
pyr-a-mid-i-cal
py-ran
pyr-a-nom-e-ter
py-ran-o-side
pyr-ar-gy-rite
pyr-a-zin-a-mide
pyr-az-ine
pyr-az-olo
py-raz-o-lone
py-raz-o-lyl
py-rene
Pyr-e-ne-an
py-ren-em-a-tous
py-re-thrin
py-re-thrum
Py-rex
py-rex-in
pyr-ge-om-e-ter
pyr-he-li-om-e-ter
pyr-i-bole
py-rid-a-zine
py-rid-ic
pyr-i-dine
pyr-i-din-i-um
pyr-i-done
pyr-i-dyl
py-rim-i-dine
py-rite
py-ri-tes
py-rit-ic
py-rit-if-er-ous
py ri-to-he-dral
py-ro-cat-e-chu-ic
py-ro-gal-lol
py-ro-ge-na-tion
py-rog-ra-phy
py-ro-lu-site
py-rol-y-sis
py-ro-lyze
py-ro-ma-ni-a
py-rom-e-ter
py-rone
py-ro-sis
py-ro-sphere
py-ro-tech-nic
py-rox-ene
pyr-ox-i-dine
py-rox-y-lin
pyr-rhic
pyr-rol-i-dine

pyr-ro-line
pyr-ro-lo-pyr-i-dine
pyr-ro-lyl
pyr-uv-al-de-hyde
pyr-u-vic
py-ryl-i-um
Py-thag-o-re-an
Pyth-i-an
py-thon-ic

Q

quack-er-y
quad-ded
quad-ra-ges-i-mal
quad-ran-gle
quad-ran-gu-lar
quad-rant
quad-rat-ic
quad-ra-ture
quad-ra-tus
quad-ren-ni-al
quad-ric
quad-rille
quad-ril-lion
quad-ri-ple-gic
quad-ri-va-lent
quad-roon
quad-ru-ped
quad-ru-ple
quad-ru-plet
quad-ru-plex
quad-ru-pli-cate
quak-er
qual-i-fi-ca-tion
qua-lim-e-ter
qual-i-ta-tive
qualm-ish
quan-da-ry
quan-tile
quan-tim-e-ter
quan-ti-ta-tive
quan-ti-ty
quan-ti-za-tion
quan-tize
quan-tum
quar-an-tin-er
quar-reled
quar-tan
quar-tered
quar-tern
quar-tet
quar-tile
quartz-ite
quartz-it-ic
quartz-ose
qua-si
quas-si-a
qua-ter-nar-y
qua-ter-ni-on
qua-ter-ni-ty
qua-ter-ni-za-tion
qua-ter-phen-yl
qua-torze
quat-rain
qua-vered
que-brach-i-tol
que-bra-cho
quell-er
quench-er
quen-stedt-ite
quer-ce-tin
quer-ci-mer-i-trin
que-rist
quer-u-lous
que-ry
ques-tion-naire
quet-zal
queue-r
queu-ing
quib-bler
quick-en-ing
qui-es-cent
qui-e-tude
qui-e-tus
quin-a-chrine
quin-al-din-i-um
quin-a-mine
qui-naph-thol
qui-na-ry
quin-az-o-line
quin-i-dine
qui-nine
qui-nin-ic
qui-niz-a-rin
qui-noi-dine
qui-no-line
quin-o-line
quin-o-lin-yl
qui-nol-o-gy
quin-o-lyl
qui-none
qui-non-ize
qui-no-nyl
qui-no-va-tan-nic
qui-no-vose
quin-sy
quin-tal
quin-tant
quin-ter-ni-on
quint-es-sence
quin-tet
quin-tile
quin-tu-ple

quin-tu-plet
qui-nu-cli-dine
quip-ster
quiv-ered
quix-ot-ic
quix-o-tism
quiz-zi-cal
quon-dam
quo-rum
quot-a-ble
quo-ta-tion
quot-er
quo-tient

R

rab-bet-ed
rab-bin-ate
rab-id
ra-bid-i-ty
ra-bies
rac-coon
race-mate
ra-ceme
ra-ce-mic
rac-e-mi-za-tion
rac-e-mose
ra-chi-om-e-ter
ra-chis
ra-chit-ic
ra-chi-tis
ra-cial-ism
rac-ing
rac-ist
rack-et-eer
rack-et-y
ra-con
rac-on-teur
ra-dar
ra-di-ac
ra-di-al
ra-di-ant
ra-di-a-tor
rad-i-cal
rad-i-cand
rad-i-cle
ra-di-o
ra-di-o-graph-ic
ra-di-og-ra-phy
ra-di-o-i-so-tope
ra-di-o-log-i-cal
ra-di-ol-o-gy
ra-di-ol-y-sis
ra-di-om-e-ter
ra-di-o-met-ric
ra-di-on-ic
ra-di-o-nu-clide
ra-di-os-co-py
ra-di-o-sonde
rad-ish
ra-di-um
ra-di-us
ra-dome
ra-don
raf-fi-a
raf-fi-nase
raf-fi-nate
raf-fi-nose
raf-fled
raf-ter (roof)
raft-er (worker on rafts)
ra-gout
raid-er
rail-ler-y
rai-ment
rais-er
rai-sin
rais-ing
ra-jah
rak-er
rak-ish
Ra-leigh
ral-ston-ite
ram-bler
ram-bunc-tious
ram-e-kin
ram-ie
ram-i-fi-ca-tion
ra-mose
ram-pa-geous
ram-pag-er
ramp-ant
ram-part
ra-na-les
ranch-er
ran-che-ro
ran-cho
ran-cid-i-ty
ran-cor-ous
ran-dom-ize
rang-er
rang-ette
ra-nine
rank-er
ran-kled
ran-som-er
rant-er
ra-pa-cious
ra-pac-i-ty
ra-pa-ki-vi
rap-er
Raph-a-el

rap-id
ra-pid-i-ty
ra-pi-er
rap-ine
rap-proche-ment
rap-tur-ous
rar-e-fy
rar-i-ty
ras-cal-i-ty
rash-er
rasp-er
ras-ter
rat-a-ble
rat-a-fi-a
ratch-et
rat-er
rath-er
rat-i-fy
ra-tio
ra-ti-oc-i-na-tion
ra-ti-om-e-ter
ra-tion-ale
ra-tion-al-ize
rat-tler
rau-cous
rau-vite
Rau-wol-fi-a
rav-ag-er
rav-eled
rave-lin
rav-el-ing
ra-ven (bird)
rav-en (other meanings)
rav-en-ing
rav-en-ous
ra-vine
rav-ing
rav-ish-er
ra-win-sonde
ra-zon
ra-zor
re-act-ance
re-ac-tion-ar-y
re-ac-tive
re-ac-tor
read-er
read-i-ness
re-a-gent
re-a-gin
re-al-gar
re-al-ism
re-al-is-tic
re-al-ize
re-al-tor
ream-er
reap-er
rea-son-a-ble
Re-au-mur
re-bat-er
re-bel (v.)
reb-el (adj., n.)
re-bel-lious
re-but-ta-ble
re-cal-ci-trant
re-ca-les-cence
re-can-ta-tion
re-ca-pit-u-late
re-ced-ence
re-ced-er
re-ceipt-or
re-ceiv-a-ble
re-ceiv-er
re-cen-sion
re-cep-ta-cle
re-cep-ti-ble
re-cep-tiv-i-ty
re-cep-tor
re-cess-er
re-ces-sion-al
re-ces-sive
re-cher-che
re-cid-i-vist
Re-ci-fe
rec-i-pe
re-cip-i-ent
re-cip-ro-ca-ble
re-cip-ro-cal
rec-i-proc-i-ty
re-ci-sion
re-cit-al
rec-i-ta-tive
reck-on-ing
re-claim
rec-la-ma
rec-la-ma-tion
re-clin-a-ble
rec-li-na-tion
re-clin-er
rec-luse
re-clu-sive
rec-og-ni-tion
re-cog-ni-zance
rec-og-nize
rec-og-ni-zee
rec-og-niz-er
rec-og-ni-zor
re-col-lect (collect again)
rec-ol-lect (remember)
rec-om-men-da-tion
rec-om-mend-a-to-ry
rec-om-pens-er
re-con-cen-tra-do
rec-on-cil-a-ble

rec-on-cil-er
rec-on-cil-i-a-tion
rec-on-dite
re-con-nais-sance
rec-on-noi-ter
rec-ord (adj., n.)
re-cord (v.)
re-cord-a-ble
re-cor-da-tion
re-cord-er
re-coup
re-cov-er-y
rec-re-ant
re-cre-ate (refresh)
re-cre-ate (create again)
rec-re-ate
rec-re-a-tion
re-crim-i-na-to-ry
re-cru-des-cence
re-cruit-er
rec-tan-gle
rec-tan-gu-lar
rec-tan-gu-lom-e-ter
rec-ti-fi-er
rec-ti-lin-e-ar
rec-ti-tude
rec-tor-ate
rec-to-ry
rec-tum
re-cum-bent
re-cu-per-a-tive
re-cur-rence
re-cur-sive
rec-u-sant
re-dac-tor
re-demp-ti-ble
re-demp-tive
re-demp-tor
red-in-gote
red-o-lent
re-doubt-a-ble
re-dox
re-dress-a-ble
re-dress-er
re-duc-er
re-duc-i-ble
re-duc-tase
re-duc-tone
re-duc-tor
re-dun-dan-cy
reef-er
reel-er
re-fec-to-ry
ref-er-a-ble
ref-er-ee
ref-er-ence
ref-er-en-dum
ref-er-en-tial
re-fer-ring
re-fin-er-y
re-flec-tance
re-flect-i-ble
re-flec-tive
re-flec-tom-e-ter
re-flec-tom-e-try
re-flec-tor-ize
re-flex-iv-i-ty
ref-lu-ent
re-for-est-a-tion
re-form-a-ble
ref-or-ma-tion
re-form-a-to-ry
re-form-er
re-frac-tive
re-frac-tom-e-ter
re-frac-to-met-ric
re-frac-tom-e-try
re-frac-to-ry
re-fran-gi-ble
ref-re-na-tion
re-frig-er-ant
re-frig-er-at-ing
re-frig-er-a-tion
re-frig-er-a-tor
ref-uge
ref-u-gee
re-ful-gent
re-fus-al
ref-use (adj., n.)
re-fuse (v.)
re-fut-a-ble
ref-u-ta-tion
re-fut-er
re-ga-lia
re-gal-i-ty
re-ge-late
re-gen-cy
re-gen-er-a-tive
re-gen-er-a-tor
reg-i-cide
re-gime
reg-i-men
reg-i-men-tal
reg-i-men-ta-ry
Re-gi-na
re-gion-al
reg-is-tered
reg-is-tra-ble
reg-is-trar
reg-is-trate
reg-let
Re-gnault
reg-o-sol

re-gres-sive
re-gret-ta-ble
reg-u-lar-i-ty
reg-u-la-tive
reg-u-la-to-ry
reg-u-lus
re-gur-gi-tate
re-ha-bil-i-ta-tive
re-hears-al
re-hears-er
Re-ho-both
Reichs-tag
re-im-burs-a-ble
Rei-nec-ke
re-in-forced
re-it-er-ate
re-ject-a-ble
re-ject-er (one that rejects)
re-jec-tor (circuit)
re-joic-ing
re-join-der
re-ju-ve-na-tor
re-ju-ve-nes-cence
re-laps-er
re-lat-er
rel-a-tiv-ism
rel-a-tiv-i-ty
re-la-tor (law)
re-lax-om-e-ter
re-leas-er
rel-e-ga-ble
rel-e-vant
rel-ict (n.)
re-lict (adj.)
re-lief-er
re-liev-er
re-li-gion
re-li-gi-os-i-ty
re-li-gious
re-lin-quish
rel-i-quar-y
rel-ish
re-lu-cence
re-luc-tance
rel-uc-tiv-i-ty
re-lu-mine
re-main-der
rem-a-nence
re-mark-a-ble
re-me-di-a-ble
re-me-di-al
rem-e-di-less
rem-e-dy
re-mem-brance
re-mind-er
rem-i-nis-cence
rem-i-nis-cer
re-miss-i-ble
re-mis-sive
re-mit-tee
re-mod-eled
re-mon-strance
re-mon-stra-tive
re-mon-stra-tor
re-mov-al
re-mu-ner-a-ble
re-mu-ner-a-tive
ren-ais-sance
Re-nais-sant
re-nal
re-nas-cence
ren-der (v.)
rend-er (n.)
ren-dez-vous
rend-i-ble
ren-di-tion
ren-dzi-na
ren-e-gade
re-nege
ren-gue
re-nin
ren-o-va-tor
re-nowned
rent-al
rent-er (n.)
ren-ter (v.)
re-nun-ci-a-to-ry
re-pair-a-ble
rep-a-ra-ble
rep-a-ra-tion
rep-ar-tee
re-pa-tri-ate
re-peal-er
re-peat-er
re-pel-lant (n.)
re-pel-lent (adj.)
re-pent-ance
re-per-cus-sion
rep-er-to-ry
rep-e-tend
rep-e-ti-tion
re-pet-i-tive
re-place-a-ble
re-plen-ish-er
re-ple-tive
re-plev-in
re-plev-i-sor
rep-li-ca
rep-li-cate
re-port-er
re-por-to-ri-al
rep-o-si-tion (n.)
re-po-si-tion (v.)

re-pos-i-to-ry
rep-re-hen-si-ble
rep-re-hen-so-ry
rep-re-sen-ta-tion
rep-re-sent-a-tive
rep-re-sent-er
re-press-er
re-press-i-ble
re-pres-sive
re-priev-al
rep-ri-mand
re-pris-al
rep-ro-ba-cy
rep-ro-bate
re-pro-duc-er
re-pro-duc-i-ble
rep-til-i-an
re-pub-li-can
re-pu-di-a-tor
re-pug-nant
re-pul-sive
rep-u-ta-ble
rep-u-ta-tion
re-pute
re-quest-er
req-ui-em
re-qui-es-cat
re-quir-er
req-ui-site
req-ui-si-tion
re-quit-al
res-az-ur-in
re-scind
re-scis-sion
re-scrip-tive
res-cu-a-ble
re-sect-a-ble
re-sem-blance
re-sem-bler
res-ene
re-ser-pic
Re-ser-pine
res-er-va-tion
re-served
re-serv-ist
res-er-voir
re-side
res-i-dence
res-i-den-tial
re-sid-u-al
re-sid-u-ar-y
res-i-due
re-sid-u-um
re-sign
res-ig-na-tion
re-sil-ien-cy
re-sil-i-om-e-ter
res-in-a-ceous
res-in-ate
res-in-ic
res-in-if-er-ous
re-sin-i-fi-ca-tion
res-in-og-ra-phy
res-in-oid
res-in-ol
res-in-ous
res-i-pis-cence
re-sist-ance
re-sist-er (one that re-sists)
re-sist-i-ble
re-sis-tiv-i-ty
re-sis-tor (device)
res-ite (resin)
res-i-tol
res ju-di-ca-ta
res-ol
re-sol-u-ble
res-o-lute
re-sol-u-tive
re-solv-ent
re-solv-er
res-o-nance
res-o-na-tor
res-or-cin-ol
res-or-cyl-ic
re-sorp-tive
re-so-ru-fin
re-spect-a-ble
re-spect-er
re-spec-tive
res-pi-ra-ble
res-pi-ra-tion
res-pi-ra-tor
res-pi-ra-to-ry
res-pi-rom-e-ter
res-pite
re-splend-ent
re-spond-ent
re-spond-er
re-spons-er
re-spon-si-ble
re-spon-sive
re-spon-sor
re-spon-so-ry
res-tau-rant
res-tau-ra-teur
res-ti-tu-tion
res-tive
res-to-ra-tion
re-stor-a-tive
re-stric-tive
re-sult-ant

re-sume (v.)
ré-su-mé (n.)
re-sump-tive
re-sur-gent
res-ur-rec-tor
re-sus-ci-ta-ble
re-sus-ci-ta-tor
re-tal-i-a-to-ry
re-tard-ant
re-tar-da-tion
re-tard-ed
re-tene
re-ten-tive
re-ten-tor
ret-ger-site
re-ti-ar-y
ret-i-cence
ret-i-cle
re-tic-u-late
ret-i-cule
re-tic-u-lin
re-tic-u-li-tis
re-tic-u-lo-cy-to-sis
re-tic-u-lose
ret-i-form
ret-i-na
re-tin-a-lite
ret-i-nene
ret-i-ni-tis
ret-i-no-cho-roid-i-tis
ret-i-nop-a-thy
ret-i-nos-co-py
ret-i-nue
re-tir-al
re-tir-ee
ret-o-na-tion
re-tort-er
re-tract-a-ble
re-trac-tile
re-trac-tion
re-trac-tive
re-trac-tor
ret-ri-bu-tion
re-trib-u-tive
re-trib-u-to-ry
re-triev-a-ble
re-triev-al
re-triev-er
ret-ro-ac-tive
ret-ro-cede (v.i.)
re-tro-cede (v.t.)
ret-ro-ced-ence
ret-ro-ces-sion
ret-ro-gra-da-to-ry
ret-ro-gres-sive
re-tro-ne-cine
re-tror-sine
ret-ro-spec-tive
ret-ro-stal-sis
ret-rous-sé
ret-ro-vert-ed
re-turn-ee
re-un-ion
re-vanche
rev-eil-le
rev-e-la-tion
re-vel-a-to-ry
re-vel-ed
rev-el-ry
re-veng-er
rev-e-nue
re-ver-a-ble
re-ver-ber-a-to-ry
re-vere
rev-er-ence
rev-er-ie
re-ver-sal
re-vers-er
re-vers-i-ble
re-ver-sion
re-vert-er
re-vert-i-ble
re-vet-ment
re-vil-er
rev-i-res-cent
re-vised
re-vis-er
re-vi-sion
re-vi-so-ry
re-viv-al
re-viv-i-fy
rev-i-vis-cent
re-vi-vor
rev-o-ca-ble
rev-o-ca-tion
rev-o-ca-to-ry
re-vok-a-ble
re-vok-er
re-volt-er
rev-o-lu-ble
rev-o-lu-tion
re-volv-er
re-vul-sive
Rey-kja-vik
rey-nard
Reyn-olds
rhab-do-man-cer
rham-na-zin
rham-ni-nose
rham-no-side
rha-pon-ti-gen-in
rhap-sod-i-cal
rhap-so-dy

rhe-a-dine
rhe-ni-um
rhe-ol-o-gy
rhe-om-e-ter
rhe-o-stat
rhe-sus
rhet-o-ric
rhe-tor-i-cal
rhet-o-ri-cian
rheu-mat-ic
rheu-ma-tism
rheum-ic
rhig-o-lene
rhi-ni-tis
rhi-noc-er-os
rhi-nol-o-gy
rhi-nos-co-py
rhi-zoi-dal
rhi-zom-a-tous
rhi-zome
rhi-zop-ter-in
rhi-zot-o-my
rho-da-mine
rho-da-nate
Rho-de-sian
rho-di-nol
rho-dite
rho-di-um
rho-di-zon-ic
rho-do-chro-site
rho-do-den-dron
rhom-bo-clase
rhom-bo-he-dral
rhom-boi-dal
rhum-ba-tron
rhyme-ster
rhy-o-lite
rhyth-mi-cal
rib-al-dry
ri-bi-tyl
ri-bo-fla-vin
ri-bo-nu-cle-ase
ri-bo-side
ri-bu-lose
ric-er
ri-chell-ite
ric-in-o-le-ic
rick-ett-si-al
ric-o-cheted
rid-dled
rid-er
rid-i-cule
ri-dic-u-lous
rid-ing
ri-ding (political divi-sion)
rif-fling
ri-fling
right-cous
right-er
ri-gid-i-ty
rig-id-ly
rig-ma-role
rig-or-ous
ri-mose
rin-der-pest
ring-er
rins-a-ble
rins-er
ri-ot-ous
ri-par-i-an
rip-en
ri-pid-o-lite
rip-pled
ris-er
ris-i-bil-i-ty
ris-ing
ris-que
rit-u-al
ri-valed
ri-val-ry
riv-et-er
Riv-i-er-a
riv-u-let
Ri-yadh
road-ster
Ro-a-noke
roam-er
roast-er
Rob-ert
rob-in (bird)
ro-bin (chemistry)
ro-bi-nose
ro-bust
Ro-chelle
Roch-es-ter
rock-et-eer
rock-et-er
rock-et-ry
rock-oon
ro-co-co
ro-den-ti-ci-dal
Rod-er-ick
roe-bling-ite
roent-gen-o-graph
roent-gen-og-ra-phy
roent-gen-ol-o-gy
roent-gen-om-e-ter
roent-gen-om-e-try
roent-gen-o-scope
roent-gen-os-co-py
rog-a-to-ry
Rog-er
ro-gnon

rogu-er-y
rogu-ish
roist-er-er
Ro-land
roll-er
rol-lick-ing
ro-maine
ro-manc-er
Ro-man-esque
Ro-man-ism
ro-ma-ni-um
ro-man-ti-cism
ro-man-ti-cist
Rom-a-ny
ro-me-ite
Ro-me-o
Rom-ish
romp-er
ron-deau
ro-ne-o-graph
ron-geur
roof-er
rook-er-y
Roo-se-velt
roost-er
rop-er
Roque-fort
ro-rif-er-ous
Ror-schach
ro-sa-ceous
Ros-a-lind
Ros-a-mond
ro-sa-ry
rosch-er-ite
ro-se-ate
ro-se-o-la
ro-sette
Rosh Ha-sha-na
Ros-i-cru-cian
ros-in-ate
ros-i-ness
ro-sol-ic
ros-ter
ros-trum
ros-y
ro-tal
ro-tam-e-ter
Ro-tar-i-an
ro-ta-ry
ro-tat-a-ble
ro-ta-tive
ro-ta-tor
ro-ta-to-ry
ro-te-noid
ro-te-none
Ro-tif-er-a
ro-tis-ser-ie
ro-to-graph
ro-to-gra-vure
ro-tor
ro-tun-da
ro-tun-di-ty
rough-en
rough-er
rough-om-e-ter
rou-lade
rou-leau
rou-lette
roun-del
round-er
rout-er
rou-tine
ro-ver (robber)
rov-er
row-dy-ism
row-eled
roy-al-ist
ru-ba-to
ru-be-an-ic
ru-be-fa-cient
ru-be-o-la
rub-e-ryth-ric
ru-bes-cent
ru-bi-cun-di-ty
ru-bid-i-um
ru-big-i-nous
ru-ble
ru-brene
ru-bric
ru-bri-ca-tor
ru-di-men-ta-ry
ru-fes-cence
ruf-fi-an
ruf-fier
ruf-fling
ru-fos-i-ty
ru-fous
ru-gos-i-ty
ru-gu-lose
ru-ined
ru-in-ing
ru-in-ous
rul-a-ble
rul-er
Ru-ma-ni-an
rum-bler
ru-mi-nant
rum-mag-er
ru-mor
rump-er
rum-pled
rum-pus
run-ci-ble
ru-nic

ru-pee
ru-pic-o-lous
rup-tured
ru-ral
ru-rig-e-nous
Rus-sian
rus-ti-ca-tor
rus-tic-i-ty
rust-i-ness
rus-tler
rus-tling
ru-ta-ba-ga
ru-ta-ceous
ru-te-car-pine
Ru-the-ni-an
ru-then-ic
ru-the-ni-um
ruth-er-ford-ine
ru-tile
ru-tin-ose
ru-ty-lene
Rwan-dan
ry-an-o-dine
Ry-u-kyu-an

S

sab-a-dine
Sab-ba-tar-i-an
sab-bat-i-cal
sa-ber
Sa-bine
sab-ine (pine)
sab-i-nene
sa-bi-no
sab-o-tage
sa-bra
sab-u-lous
sa-bu-tan
sac-cha-rate
sac-char-ic
sac-cha-ride
sac-cha-rif-er-ous
sac-cha-rim-e-ter
sac-cha-rin-ate
sac-cha-rin-ic
sac-cha-rom-e-ter
sac-cha-rose
sac-er-do-tal
sa-chem
sa-chet
sac-ral
sac-ra-men-tal
sac-ra-men-ta-ry
sa-cred
sac-ri-fi-cial
sac-ri-fic-ing
sac-ri-le-gious
sac-ris-tan
sac-ris-ty
sac-ro-il-i-ac
sac-ro-sanct
sac-rum
sad-dler-y
sa-dism
sa-dis-tic
Saeng-er-fest
sa-fa-ri
safe-ty
saf-flor-ite
saf-fron
saf-ra-nine
sa-ga-cious
sa-gac-i-ty
sag-a-more
sag-a-pe-num
sag-e-nite
Sag-it-tar-i-us
Sa-ha-ra
sail-or
sa-laam
sal-a-ble
sa-la-cious
sal-ad
sal-a-man-der
sa-la-mi
sal-a-ried
sal-e-ra-tus
sal-i-cin
sal-i-cyl-am-ide
sa-lic-y-late
sal-i-cyl-ic
sa-lic-y-lide
sal-i-cyl-ize
sal-i-cyl-o-yl
sal-i-cyl-u-ric
sa-lient
sal-i-gen-in
sa-lim-e-ter
sal-i-na-tion
sa-line
sa-lin-i-ty
sa-lin-o-gen-ic
sal-i-nom-e-ter
Salis-bur-y
sa-li-va
sal-i-var-y
sal-i-va-tion
sa-li-vous
salm-on
Sal-mo-nel-la
sal-mo-nel-lo-sis
salm-ons-ite

Sal-ol
Sa-lo-me
sa-lon
sal-pin-gec-to-my
sal-pin-gi-tis
sal-si-fy
sal-ta-to-ri-al
salt-er-y
salt-pe-ter
sa-lu-bri-ous
sa-lu-bri-ty
sal-u-tar-y
sal-u-ta-tion
sa-lu-ta-to-ry
sa-lute
sal-va-ble
Sal-va-dor-an
sal-vage-a-ble
sal-vag-er
Sal-var-san
sal-ver
sal-vi-a-nin
sal vo-la-ti-le
sal-vor
sam-a-ra
Sa-mar-i-tan
sa-mar-i-um
sam-bu-ni-grin
Sa-mo-an
sam-o-var
Sam-o-yed
sam-pler
sa-mu-rai
san-a-to-ri-um
sanc-ti-fi-ca-tion
sanc-ti-mo-ni-ous
sanc-tion-er
sanc-ti-ty
sanc-tu-ar-y
sanc-tum
san-daled
sand-er
sand-i-ness
san-dust
San-for-ize
san-guin-a-rine
san-gui-nar-y
san-guin-e-ous
san-guin-o-lent
San-he-drin
san-i-dine
san-i-tar-i-um
san-i-tar-y
san-i-tiz-er
san-i-ty
San-skrit
san-ta-lene
san-ta-lol
san-te-none
san-to-nin
sa-phe-nous
sap-id
sa-pid-i-ty
sa-pi-ence
sap-o-gen-in
sap-o-na-ceous
sa-pon-i-fi-ca-tion
sap-o-nin
sap-o-rif-ic
sap-phir-ine
sap-ro-gen-ic
sap-ro-ge-nic-i-ty
sa-prog-e-nous
sap-ro-pel-ic
Sar-ah
Sa-ran
sar-casm
sar-cas-tic
sar-coid-o-sis
sar-col-y-sis
sar-co-ma
sar-co-ma-to-sis
sar-com-a-tous
sar-coph-a-gus
sar-cop-side
sar-co-sine
sar-dine
sar-don-ic
sar-don-yx
sar-ki-nite
sar-men-to-gen-in
sa-rong
sar-sa-pa-ril-la
sar-to-ri-al
sar-to-ri-us
Sar-tri-an
sas-sa-fras
sas-so-lite
sa-tan-i-cal
satch-el
sa-teen
sat-el-lit-ed
sat-el-lit-oid
sat-el-lit-o-sis
sat-el-loid
sa-tia-ble
sa-ti-ate
sa-ti-e-ty
sat-in-et
sat-in-ize
sat-ire
sa-tir-i-cal
sat-i-rize
sat-is-fac-to-ri-ly

sat-is-fy
sa-trap
sat-u-ra-ble
sat-u-ra-tor
Sat-ur-day
Sat-urn
sat-ur-na-lian
Sa-tur-ni-an
sat-ur-nine
sat-yr
sa-tyr-ic
sau-cer
sau-ci-ness
Sau-di A-ra-bi-a
sau-er-bra-ten
sau-er-kraut
saun-ter
sau-rel
sau-ri-an
sau-sage
saus-su-rite
sau-ted
sau-terne
sav-a-ble
sav-age-ry
sa-van-na
sa-vant
sav-ing
sav-ior
Sav-iour
sa-voir faire
sa-vor-y
Sa-voy-ard
sax-i-frage
sax-o-phone
scab-bler
sca-bies
sca-bres-cent
scab-rous
sca-lar
scald-er
sca-le-no-he-dral
scal-er
scal-loped
scal-pel
scalp-er
scam-per
scan-dal-ize
scan-dal-ous
Scan-di-na-vi-an
scan-di-um
scan-ner
scant-ling
scap-o-lite
scap-u-la
scar-ab
scar-ci-ty
scarf-er
scar-i-fy
scar-i-ous
scar-la-ti-na
scar-let
scat-o-log-i-cal
sca-tol-o-gy
scat-tered
scav-eng-er
sce-nar-i-o
sce-nar-ist
sce-ner-y
sce-ni-cal
sce-no-graph
sce-nog-ra-phy
scent-er
scep-ter
sched-ule
schee-lite
sche-ma
sche-mat-ic
sche-ma-tist
sche-mat-o-graph
Sche-ring
schiff-li
schis-mat-ic
schist-oid
schist-ose
schis-to-some
schis-to-so-mi-a-sis
schiz-oid-ism
schiz-o-phre-ni-a
schiz-o-phren-ic
schle-miel
schlie-ren
Schnei-der
scho-la can-to-rum
schol-ar
scho-las-tic
schoo-ner
schor-la-ceous
schot-tische
schra-dan
schrei-ner-ize
Schro-ding-er
schroec-king-er-ite
Schweit-zer
schwei-zer
sci-at-i-ca
sci-en-tif-ic
sci-en-tist
scil-i-cet
scil-li-ro-side
scim-i-tar
scin-tig-ra-phy
scin-til-la-tor
scin-til-lom-e-ter

sci-oph-i-lous
sci-re fa-ci-as
scis-sors
sclar-e-ol
scle-rec-to-my
scle-ren-chy-ma
scle-ri-tis
scle-ro-ma
scle-rom-e-ter
scle-ro-sis
scle-ro-tal
scle-rot-ic
scle-rot-o-my
scob-i-nate
scoff-er
scold-er
scol-e-cite
sco-li-o-sis
sconc-i-ble
scoop-er
scoot-er
sco-pa-rin
scoph-o-ny
sco-pine
sco-pol-a-mine
sco-po-le-tin
scop-u-lite
scor-bu-tic
sco-ri-a-ceous
sco-ri-fi-ca-tion
scorn-er
scor-o-dite
scor-per
Scor-pi-o
scor-pi-on
scor-za-lite
sco-to-ma
sco-tom-a-tous
scoun-drel
scourg-er
scrab-bler
scram-bling
scrap-er
scratch-er
scrawl-er
scream-er
screen-er
scrib-bler
scrib-er
scrip-tur-al
scriv-en-er
scrof-u-la
scrof-u-lo-sis
scro-tum
scru-ple
scru-pu-lous
scru-ti-nize
scru-ti-ny
scuf-fling
scul-ler-y
sculp-tor
sculp-tur-al
scum-bled
scur-ril-i-ty
scur-ri-lous
scur-vi-ly
scut-tle-butt
scu-tum
seal-ant
seal-er
seal-ine
seam-stress
se-ance
sea-son-a-ble
seat-er
seb-a-cate
se-ba-ceous
se-bac-ic
seb-or-rhe-a
sec-a-lose
se-cant
se-ced-er
se-clu-sive
Sec-o-nal
sec-ond-ar-i-ly
sec-ond-ar-y
sec-ond-er
se-cre-cy
se-cret
se-cre-ta-gogue
sec-re-tar-i-al
se-cre-tin
se-cre-tive
se-cre-to-ry
sec-tar-i-an
sec-til-i-ty
sec-tion-al-ize
sec-tor-al
sec-to-ri-al
sec-u-lar-ize
se-cund
se-cun-date
se-cu-ri-ty
se-dan
se-date
sed-a-tive
sed-en-tar-y
sed-i-men-ta-ry
se-di-tious
se-duc-er
se-duc-i-ble
se-duc-tive
se-du-li-ty
sed-u-lous

seed-ling
seek-er
seep-age
seg-men-tal
seg-re-ga-ble
Seid-litz
sei-gnior-age
sei-sin
seis-mic-i-ty
seis-mo-graph
seis-mog-ra-phy
seis-mo-log-i-cal
seis-mol-o-gy
seis-mom-e-ter
seis-mo-met-ric
seiz-er
sei-zin
seiz-ing
sei-zor (law)
sei-zure
sel-dom
se-lect-ance
se-lect-ee
se-lec-tiv-i-ty
se-lec-tor
sel-e-nate
se-len-ic
sel-e-nide
se-le-ni-ous
sel-e-nite
se-le-ni-um
se-le-no-bis-muth-ite
sel-e-no-graph-ic
sel-e-nog-ra-phy
se-le-no-lite
se-le-no-log-i-cal
sel-e-nol-o-gy
sel-e-no-ni-um
sel-e-no-sis
self-ish
sell-er
sel-syn
Selt-zer
sel-vage
se-man-ti-cist
sem-a-phor-ist
se-ma-si-ol-o-gy
sem-blance
se-mei-ol-o-gy
se-mes-ter
sem-i-dine
sem-i-nal
sem-i-nar-y
sem-i-nif-er-ous
Sem-i-nole
Sem-ite
Se-mit-ic
Sem-i-tism
sem-o-li-na
sen-a-ry
sen-a-to-ri-al
send-er
se-ne-cic
se-ne-ci-o-nine
se-ne-ci-o-sis
Sen-e-gal-ese
se-nes-cence
sen-e-schal
se-nhor (Portuguese)
se-nile
se-nil-i-ty
sen-ior
se-nior-i-ty
se-nor
se-no-ri-ta
sen-sa-tion
sen-si-bil-i-ty
sen-sile
sen-si-tiv-i-ty
sen-si-tiz-er
sen-si-tom-e-ter
sen-so-ri-um
sen-so-ry
sen-su-al-i-ty
sen-su-ous
sen-tence
sen-ten-tious
sen-tience
sen-ti-men-tal
sen-ti-neled
sen-try
se-paled
sep-al-oid
sep-a-ra-ble
sep-a-ra-tee
sep-a-rat-ist
sep-a-ra-tor
se-phar-dic
se-pi-a
Sep-tem-ber
sep-ten-a-ry
sep-ti-ce-mi-a
sep-ti-mal
sep-tu-a-ge-nar-i-an
sep-tu-a-ges-i-ma
sep-tu-ple
sep-tu-plet
sep-tu-pli-cate
sep-ul-cher
se-pul-chral
sep-ul-ture
se-quac-i-ty
se-que-la
se-quen-tial

se-ques-tered	Sho-sho-ne	si-pid-i-ty	so-lan-der	sou-ve-nir	spi-nes-cence
se-ques-tra-tor	shoul-dered	si-ren	so-lan-i-dine	sov-er-eign	spin-et
se-ra-glio	shov-eled	si-ri-a-sis	so-la-nine	so-vi-et-ism	spin-or
ser-al	shov-er	Sir-i-us	so-la-no	sov-khoz	spi-nose
ser-aph	show-er-y	si-roc-cos	so-lar	Soxh-let	spi-nos-i-ty
se-raph-ic	shriev-al-ty	sir-up	so-lar-ism	so-zol-ic	spi-nous
ser-a-phim	Shrin-er	si-sal	so-lar-i-um	spa-cious	spin-ster
Ser-bi-an	shrink-age	sis-y-phe-an	so-lar-i-za-tion	spa-cis-tor	spin-thar-i-scope
ser-e-nad-er	shrink-er	si-tol-o-gy	so-las-o-nine	spa-ghet-ti	spi-nu-les-cent
ser-en-dip-i-ty	shriv-eled	si-to-ste-rol	sol-dered	spall-er	spir-a-cle
se-rene	shriv-ing	sit-u-at-ed	sol-dier	span-drel	spi-rac-u-lar
se-ren-i-ty	Shrop-shire	si-tus	sol-e-cism	span-gled	spi-raled
ser-geant	shuf-fled	siz-a-ble	sol-emn	Span-iard	spi-re-a
se-ri-al	shy-ster	siz-zled	so-lem-ni-ty	span-iel	spi-reme
se-ri-a-tim	si-a-log-ra-phy	skat-ole	sol-em-nize	spank-er	Spi-ri-fer
se-ri-ceous	si-al-o-li-thi-a-sis	skeet-er	so-le-noi-dal	sparg-er	spi-rif-er-ous
ser-i-cin	Si-a-mese	skel-e-ton-ize	sol-fe-ri-no	spark-let	spir-it-ed
ser-i-cite	Si-be-ri-an	skep-ti-cal	so-lic-i-ta-tion	spar-kling	spir-it-u-al
se-ries	sib-i-lant	skep-ti-cism	so-lic-i-tor	spar-si-ty	spir-i-tu-el
ser-i-graph	sib-i-la-to-ry	skew-er	so-lic-it-ous	Spar-tan	spir-it-u-ous
se-rig-ra-pher	sib-ling	ski-am-e-try	so-lic-i-tude	spar-te-ine	spi-ro-chete
se-rig-ra-phy	sib-yl-line	ski-as-co-py	sol-id	spas-mod-ic	spi-ro-chet-o-sis
ser-ine	Si-cil-ian	skill-ful-ness	sol-i-dar-ic	spas-mol-y-sis	spi-ro-graph
se-rin-ga	sick-en-ing	skimp-i-ly	sol-i-da-ris-tic	spas-mo-lyt-ic	spi-rom-e-ter
ser-in-gal	sick-led	skir-mish	sol-i-dar-i-ty	spas-tic-i-ty	spi-ro-met-ric
se-ri-ous	si-de-re-al	skirt-er	so-lid-i-fy	spa-tial	spi-ro-pen-tane
ser-mon-ize	sid-er-ite	skit-tish	so-lid-i-ty	spa-ti-og-ra-phy	splanch-ni-cec-to-my
se-ro-log-ic	sid-er-og-ra-pher	skiv-er	sol-i-dus	spat-u-la	splen-dent
se-rol-o-gy	sid-er-o-graph-ic	skul-dug-ger-y	so-lig-e-nous	spav-in	splen-did
se-ro-si-tis	sid-er-o-na-trite	skulk-er	so-lil-o-quy	spawn-er	splen-dif-er-ous
se-ro-ton-in	sid-er-o-sis	slack-ened	so-li-lu-nar	speak-er	splen-dor-ous
se-rous	sid-ing	slak-er	sol-ip-sism	spe-cial-ist	sple-net-ic
ser-pen-tin-ite	si-dled	slan-der-ous	sol-i-taire	spe-ci-al-i-ty	sple-nic
ser-pig-i-nous	si-er-o-zem	slat-tern	sol-i-tar-y	spe-cial-i-za-tion	sple-ni-tis
se-rum	Si-er-ra Le-one	slaugh-ter	sol-i-tude	spe-cial-ty	sple-ni-um
serv-ant	siev-er	slav-er-y	so-lod-ize	spe-ci-e (in sort)	splic-er
serv-er	sift-er	slav-ish	so-lo-ist	spe-cie (coin)	splin-tered
serv-ice-a-ble	sight-er	Sla-von-ic	Sol-o-mon	spe-cif-i-cal-ly	spo-di-um
ser-vi-ent	sig-ma-tism	sleep-er	sol-o-netz	spec-i-fi-ca-tion	spod-u-mene
ser-vile	sig-moid-ec-to-my	slen-der	so-lo-ni-an	spec-i-fic-i-ty	spoil-age
ser-vil-i-ty	sig-moid-os-to-my	slic-er	sol-stice	spec-i-fi-er	spoil-er
ser-vi-tor	sig-naled	slick-en-side	sol-sti-tial	spec-i-men	spo-ken
ser-vi-tude	sig-nal-ize	slick-er	sol-u-bil-i-ty	spe-ci-os-i-ty	spo-li-a-tion
ser-vo-mo-tor	sig-na-to-ry	slid-a-ble	sol-u-bi-liz-er	spe-cious	spon-dy-li-tis
ses-a-me	sig-nif-i-cant	slid-om-e-ter	so-lum	speck-led	spong-er
ses-a-min	sig-ni-fi-ca-tion	sling-er	sol-ute	spec-ta-cle	spon-gi-ness
ses-a-moid-i-tis	si-gnor	slith-er-y	so-lu-tion	spec-tac-u-lar	spon-gi-ol-o-gy
ses-a-mo-lin	si-gno-ra	sliv-er	sol-u-tiz-er	spec-ta-tor	spon-si-ble
ses-qui-pe-da-lian	si-lage	slo-gan	solv-a-ble	spec-ter	spon-sor
ses-sile	sil-ane	slop-ing	sol-ven-cy	spec-trog-ra-phy	spon-ta-ne-i-ty
ses-sion	si-lenc-er	Slo-vak-i-an	sol-vent	spec-trom-e-ter	spon-ta-ne-ous
se-ta-ceous	si-le-si-a	slov-en	sol-vol-y-sis	spec-trom-e-try	spoon-er-ism
se-ti-ger	si-lex	Slo-ve-ni-an	So-ma-li	spec-tro-scope	spo-rad-ic
se-tig-er-ous	sil-hou-ette	sludg-er	so-mat-ic	spec-tros-co-py	spo-ri-ci-dal
set-tler	sil-i-cate	slum-ber-ous	so-ma-ti-za-tion	spec-trum	spo-rif-er-ous
sev-en-ti-eth	sil-i-ca-ti-za-tion	smart-en	so-ma-to-gen-ic	spec-u-la-tive	spo-ro-gen-ic
sev-er-al	sil-i-ca-tor	smell-er	som-bre-ro	spec-u-la-tor	spo-ro-phyll
sev-ered	sil-i-ceous	smelt-er	som-er-sault	spec-u-lum	spo-ro-zo-an
se-ver-i-ty	si-lic-ic	smi-la-gen-in	som-nam-bu-list	speed-er	spor-tive
sew-age	sil-i-cide	smi-lax	som-nil-o-quy	speed-om-e-ter	spor-u-la-tion
sew-er-age	si-lic-i-dize	smith-er-eens	som-niv-o-len-cy	speed-ster	spor-ule
sex-a-ge-nar-i-an	sil-i-cif-er-ous	Smith-so-ni-an	som-no-lent	spe-le-ol-o-gy	spout-er
sex-ag-e-nar-y	si-lic-i-fy	smok-er	so-na-ble	spel-ter	spring-er
sex-tant	sil-i-co-mag-ne-sio-flu-o-rite	smol-dered	so-nar	spe-lunk-er	sprin-kler
sex-tu-ple	sil-i-con	smor-gas-bord	so-na-ta	Spen-ce-ri-an	sprin-kling
sex-tu-plet	sil-i-cone	smoth-ered	song-ster	spend-er	sprint-er
sex-tu-pli-cate	sil-i-co-sis	smudg-er	son-ic	Spen-gle-ri-an	sprock-et
sfer-ics	sil-i-cot-ic	smug-gler	so-nif-er-ous	sper-ma-ce-ti	spu-mes-cence
sfor-zan-do	silk-en	snarl-ish	son-net-eer	sper-mat-ic	spu-mous
shack-led	sil-li-man-ite	snatch-er	son-o-buoy	sper-ma-tif-er-ous	spu-ri-ous
shad-er	si-lox-ane	sneak-i-ness	so-nom-e-ter	sper-ma-tin	spur-tive
shad-ow	sil-ta-tion	sneez-er	So-no-ra	sper-ma-ti-za-tion	spu-tum
Sha-drach	Si-lu-ri-an	snick-er-ing	so-no-rant	sper-ma-to-cele	squad-ron
sha-green	sil-ver	sniff-er	son-o-res-cent	sper-ma-to-ci-dal	squa-lene
shak-er	sil-vi-cul-tur-al	snif-ter	son-o-rif-er-ous	sper-ma-to-cyte	squal-id-i-ty
Shake-spear-e-an	sim-i-lar-i-ty	snip-er	so-nor-i-ty	sper-ma-to-rhe-a	squal-or
sham-bles	sim-i-le (like)	sniv-el-er	so-no-rous	sper-ma-to-zo-id	squa-mous
shank-er	si-mi-le (music)	snob-ber-y	soon-est	sperm-ine	squan-dered
shap-er	si-mil-i-tude	Sno-ho-mish	Soph-ist	sperm-ism	squawk-er
shap-om-e-ter	si-mon-ize	snoop-er-y	so-phis-ti-cat-ed	sphal-er-ite	squeal-er
shar-a-ble	si-mo-ny	snor-kel	soph-ist-ry	sphe-nog-ra-phy	squeam-ish
sharp-en-ing	si-moom	snort-er	soph-o-mor-ic	sphe-noi-dal	squee-gee
sharp-er	sim-pat-i-co	snuf-fled	sop-o-rif-er-ous	spher-al	squeez-er
shat-tered	sim-per	snug-gled	sop-o-rif-ic	spher-i-cal	squint-er
shav-er	sim-pler	soak-age	so-pra-no	spho-ric-i-ty	squirt-er
sheath-er	sim-plex	soap-er	sor-be-fa-cient	sphe-roi-dal	sta-bi-la-tor
sheep-ish	sim-plic-i-ty	so-ber	sor-bent	sphe-roid-ic-i-ty	sta-bile
sheet-age	sim-pli-fy	so-bri-e-ty	sorb-ic	sphe-rom-e-ter	stab-i-lim-e-ter
shek-el	sim-u-la-crum	so-bri-quet	sor-bi-tan	spher-u-lite	sta-bil-i-ty
shel-lack-ing	sim-u-la-tor	so-cia-ble	sor-bite	sphinc-ter-ot-o-my	sta-bi-li-za-tion
shel-tered	si-mul-cast	so-cial-is-tic	sor-bi-tol	sphin-gom-e-ter	sta-bi-liz-er
shelv-ing	si-mul-ta-ne-ous	so-ci-a-try	sor-bose	sphin-go-sine	sta-bled
she-nan-i-gan	Si-na-it-ic	so-ci-e-ty	sor-bo-side	sphyg-mo-ma-nom-e-ter	stac-ca-to
shep-herd	si-nap-ic	so-ci-oc-ra-cy	sor-cer-er	sphyg-mom-e-ter	stach-y-drine
Sher-a-ton	sin-a-pine	so-ci-o-log-ic	sor-cer-y	spic-i-ness	sta-dim-e-ter
sher-bet	sin-ar-quism	so-ci-ol-o-gist	sor-did	spic-u-lar	sta-di-um
sher-iff	sin-cer-i-ty	so-ci-om-e-try	sor-ghum	spi-der	staff-er
shib-bo-leth	si-ne-cure	so-ci-op-a-thy	so-ri-tes	spie-gel-ei-sen	stag-mom-e-ter
shield-er	sin-ew	sock-dol-a-ger	so-rit-i-cal	spiel-er	stain-er
shift-er	sing-er	sock-et	So-rop-ti-mist	spig-ot	Sta-kha-nov-ite
shi-kim-ic	sin-gly	Soc-ra-tes	so-ror-i-cide	spike-nard	sta-lac-tite
shil-le-lagh	sin-gu-lar-i-ty	So-crat-ic	so-ror-i-ty	spik-i-ness	stal-ac-tit-ic
shil-ling	Sin-ha-lese	so-da-lite	so-ro-sis	spi-lite	sta-lag-mite
shin-er	sin-is-tral	so-dal-i-ty	sort-er	spill-er	stal-ag-mit-ic
shin-gled	sink-age	so-dam-ide	sor-tie	spil-ler (fish)	stal-ag-mom-e-ter
shirk-er	sink-er	so-dar	sor-ti-lege	spi-lo-ma	Sta-lin-grad
shirr-ing	si-nom-e-nine	so-di-um	so-ste-nu-to	spi-lo-site	sta-men
shiv-ered	sin-ter	sod-om-y	sou-brette	spi-na-ceous	stam-i-na
shock-er	sin-u-ous	so-far	souf-fle	spin-ach	stam-pede
sho-far	si-nus-i-tis	soft-en-er	soun-der (herd of swine)	spi-nal	stamp-er
shoot-er	si-nus-oi-dal	soi-gne	sound-er	spi-na-ste-rol	stan-chion
sho-ran	si-phon-age	soi-ree	sou-tache	spi-nate	stand-ard-i-za-tion
short-en		so-journ-er	south-er-ly	spin-dler	stand-ing
short-om-e-ter		sol-ace	south-ern-er	spi-nel	sta-nine

stan-nite
sta-pes
Staph-y-lo-coc-cus
staph-y-lot-o-my
sta-pler
starch-er
sta-re de-ci-sis
star-ling
star-lite
start-er
star-tling
star-va-tion
sta-sis
stat-ed
stat-i-cal-ly
sta-tion-ar-y
sta-tion-er-y
sta-tis-ti-cal
stat-is-ti-cian
stat-i-tron
sta-tom-e-ter
sta-tor
stat-o-scope
stat-u-ar-y
stat-u-esque
stat-ure
sta-tus
stat-ute
stat-u-to-ry
stau-ro-lite
stau-ro-scop-ic
stead-i-ness
stealth-i-ness
steam-er
ste-a-rate
ste-ar-ic
ste-a-rin
ste-a-rit-ic
ste-ar-o-yl
ste-a-ryl
ste-a-tite
ste-a-tol-y-sis
ste-a-to-sis
steep-er
stee-ple
steer-age
Ste-fan
Stel-lite
sten-ciled
ste-nog-ra-pher
sten-o-graph-ic
ste-nog-ra-phy
ste-n-o-ha-line
ste-nom-e-ter
ste-no-sis
sten-o-typ-ist
sten-to-ri-an
Ste-phen
ste-ra-di-an
ster-co-bi-lin-o-gen
ster-co-rite
ster-cu-lic
ster-e-og-no-sis
ster-e-og-ra-pher
ster-e-o-graph-ic
ster-e-om-e-ter
ster-e-om-e-try
ster-e-o-phon-ic
ster-e-oph-o-ny
ster-e-op-ti-con
ster-e-o-scope
ster-e-os-co-py
ster-e-ot-o-my
ster-e-o-typ-er
ster-ic
ster-ile
ste-ril-i-ty
ster-i-li-za-tion
ster-let
ster-ling
ster-num
ster-nu-ta-to-ry
ste-roi-dal
ste-rol
ster-to-rous
ste-thom-e-ter
steth-o-scope
ste-thos-co-py
Steu-ben
ste-ve-dore
Ste-ven-son
ste-vi-o-side
stew-ard
sthen-ic
stib-a-mine
stib-ine
sti-bin-ic
stib-i-o-pal-la-di-nite
sti-bon-ic
sti-bo-ni-um
stib-o-phen
sti-chom-e-try
stick-ler
stiff-en-er
sti-fling
stig-mas-ter-ol
stig-mat-ic
stig-ma-tism
stig-ma-tize
stil-bene
stil-bes-trol
sti-let-to
stilp-no-mel-ane

stim-u-lant
stim-u-la-tive
stim-u-la-tor
stim-u-lus
sting-er
sting-y (stinging)
stin-gy (close)
stink-er
sti-pend
sti-pen-di-ar-y
sti-pes
stip-i-tat-ic
stip-pled
stip-u-la-tion
stip-ule
stitch-er
stock-ade
sto-gy
sto-i-cal
stoi-chi-o-met-ric
stoi-chi-om-e-try
stok-er
stol-id
sto-lid-i-ty
stom-ach
sto-mach-ic
sto-ma-ti-tis
sto-ma-tol-o-gy
ston-i-ness
stop-pled
stor-age
stor-ied
sto-ri-ette
storm-i-ness
sto-ver
stow-age
stra-bis-mom-e-ter
stra-bis-mus
strad-dler
strag-gler
straight-en-er
strain-er
strait-ened
stra-mo-ni-um
strand-er
stran-ger (n.)
strang-er (adj.)
stran-gler
stran-gu-late
strat-a-gem
stra-te-gi-cal
strat-e-gist
strat-e-gy
strat-i-fi-ca-tion
strat-i-graph-ic
stra-tig-ra-phy
stra-to-cu-mu-lus
strat-o-sphere
strat-o-spher-ic
stra-tum
stra-tus
streak-i-ness
stream-er
strength-en-ing
stren-u-ous
strep-o-gen-in
strep-ta-mine
strep-to-coc-cic
strep-to-coc-co-sis
strep-to-my-cin
strep-to-thri-cin
stretch-er
stri-at-ed
stric-ture
stri-dent
strid-u-lous
stri-gose
strik-er
strin-gent
string-er
strip-er
strob-i-la-ceous
strob-o-scop-ic
strob-o-tron
stro-ga-noff
strok-er
stro-mat-ic
stro-ma-tin
stron-gy-lo-sis
stron-ti-an-if-er-ous
stron-ti-an-ite
stron-ti-um
stro-phan-thi-din
stro-phe
stroph-ic
struc-tur-al
strug-gled
strum-pet
strych-nine
stub-born-ness
stu-dent
stud-ied
stu-di-ous
stul-ti-fy
stum-bling
stump-age
stu-pe-fa-cient
stu-pe-fy
stu-pen-dous
stu-pid-i-ty
stu-por
stur-di-ly
stur-geon
stut-tered

Styg-i-an
sty-let
styl-ish
sty-lis-tic
styl-ize
sty-lo-graph-ic
sty-lom-e-try
sty-lus
sty-mie
styp-tic
sty-rac-i-tol
styr-e-nate
sty-rene
sty-ryl
sua-si-ble
suav-i-ty
su-ber-ate
su-ber-ic
su-ber-in
su-ber-ose
su-ber-yl-ar-gi-nine
sub-jec-tiv-ism
sub-ju-gate
sub-junc-tive
sub-lim-a-ble
sub-li-mate
sub-lime
sub-lim-i-nal
sub-lim-i-ty
sub-li-mize
sub-merged
sub-mer-gence
sub-mer-gi-ble
sub-mer-sal
sub-mersed
sub-mers-i-ble
sub-or-di-nate
sub-or-na-tion
sub-pe-naed
sub-ro-gate
sub-scrib-er
sub-ser-vi-ent
sub-sid-ence
sub-sid-i-ar-y
sub-si-dize
sub-sist-ence
sub-son-ic
sub-stan-tial
sub-stan-tive
sub-stit-u-ent
sub-sti-tut-a-ble
sub-sti-tu-tive
sub-sump-tive
sub-ti-lin
sub-tle-ty
sub-tract-er
sub-trac-tive
sub-ur-ban
sub-ver-sive
sub-vert-er
sub-vert-i-ble
suc-ce-da-ne-ous
suc-ce-dent
suc-ces-sive
suc-ces-sor
suc-cin-a-mate
suc-ci-nam-ic
suc-cin-a-mide
suc-ci-nate
suc-cin-ic
suc-ci-nyl
suc-cu-lence
suck-ler
su-cre
su-crose
suc-to-ri-al
su-da-men
Su-da-nese
su-da-to-ry
su-do-rif-er-ous
suf-fic-er
suf-fi-cien-cy
suf-fo-ca-tive
suf-fra-gist
suf-fus-a-ble
suf-fu-sive
sug-ar
sug-gest-i-ble
sug-ges-tive
su-i-ci-dal
sui ge-ner-is
suit-a-ble
suit-or
su-ki-ya-ki
sul-fa-cet-a-mide
sul-fa-di-az-ine
sul-fa-gua-ni-dine
sul-fa-mer-a-zine
sul-fa-meth-yl-thi-az-ole
sul-fam-ic
sulf-am-ide
sul-fam-o-yl
sul-fa-nil-a-mide
sul-fa-nil-ic
sul-fan-i-lyl
sul-fa-pyr-i-dine
sulf-ars-phen-a-mine
sul-fat-ase
sul-fa-thi-az-ole
sul-fen-ic
sulf-hy-dryl
sul-fide
sul-fi-nyl

Sul-fo-nal
sul-fon-a-mide
sul-fo-nat-ed
sul-fo-na-tor
sul-fon-eth-yl-meth-ane
sul-fon-ic
sul-fo-ni-um
sulf-ox-ide
sul-fu-re-ous
sul-fur-et-ed
sul-fu-ric
sul-fu-rize
sul-fu-rous
sul-fur-yl
sulk-i-ness
sul-tan-ate
sul-try
su-mac
Su-ma-tran
sum-mar-i-ly
sum-ma-rize
sum-ma-ry
sum-mit-ry
sump-tu-ar-y
sun-der
sun-dry
sunk-en
su-per-a-ble
su-perb
su-per-cil-i-ous
su-per-er-o-gate
su-per-e-rog-a-to-ry
su-per-fi-cial
su-per-flu-ous
su-per-in-tend-ent
su-pe-ri-or-i-ty
su-per-la-tive
su-per-nal
su-per-na-tant
su-per-nat-u-ral
su-per-nu-mer-ar-y
su-per-se-de-as
su-per-se-dure
su-per-sen-si-ble
su-per-son-ic
su-per-sti-tious
su-per-ve-nience
su-per-vis-ee
su-per-vi-so-ry
su-pi-na-tor
sup-ple-men-tal
sup-ple-men-ta-ry
sup-ple-tive
sup-pli-ca-to-ry
sup-port-ive
sup-pos-al
sup-po-si-tion
sup-pos-i-ti-tious
sup-pos-i-to-ry
sup-press-i-ble
sup-pres-sor
sup-pu-ra-tive
su-pra
su-prem-a-cy
sur-a-min
sur-cin-gle
sur-e-ty
sur-fac-er
sur-fac-ing
sur-fac-tant
sur-feit
sur-geon
sur-ger-y
sur-gi-cal
Su-ri-nam-ese
sur-li-ness
sur-mis-a-ble
sur-plice
sur-plus-age
sur-pris-a-ble
sur-re-al-ist
sur-ren-der
sur-rep-ti-tious
sur-ro-gate
sur-veil-lance
sur-viv-al
sur-vi-vor
sus-cep-ti-bil-i-ty
sus-pend-er
sus-pen-si-ble
sus-pen-so-ry
sus-pi-cious
sus-pi-ra-tion
sus-te-nance
su-sur-rus
su-tur-al
su-ze-rain
swad-dled
swamp-er
swank-i-ness
swarth-i-ness
swas-ti-ka
sweat-er
Swe-den
Swed-ish
sweep-er
sweet-ened
swel-ter
swift-er
swin-dler
swin-dling
swin-ish
switch-er

Swit-zer-land
swiv-eled
Syb-a-rite
Syb-a-rit-ic
syc-a-more
sych-no-car-pous
syc-o-phan-cy
sy-co-sis
sy-e-nite
syl-la-bar-y
syl-lab-ic
syl-lab-i-fi-ca-tion
syl-la-bize
syl-la-ble
syl-lo-gism
syl-lo-gis-ti-cal
Syl-phon
syl-van-ite
Syl-ves-ter
syl-ves-trene
syl-vite
sym-bi-o-sis
sym-bi-ot-ic
sym-bol-i-cal
sym-bol-ism
sym-bol-ize
sym-bol-o-gy
sym-met-ri-cal
sym-me-trize
sym-me-try
sym-pa-thec-to-my
sym-pa-thet-ic
sym-path-i-co-trop-ic
sym-pa-thin
sym-pa-thiz-er
sym-pa-tho-lyt-ic
sym-pa-thy
sym-phon-ic
sym-pho-ni-ous
sym-pho-nize
sym-pho-ny
sym-phy-sis
sym-phyt-ic
sym-po-si-um
symp-to-mat-ic
symp-tom-a-tize
symp-tom-a-tol-o-gy
syn-a-gogue
syn-apse
syn-ar-thro-sis
syn-chon-drot-o-my
syn-chro-nism
syn-chro-ni-za-tion
syn-chro-niz-er
syn-chro-no-graph
syn-chro-nous
syn-chro-ny
syn-chrop-ter
syn-chro-scope
syn-chro-tron
syn-cli-nal
syn-co-pa-tion
syn-co-pe
syn-des-mo-sis
syn-di-cal-ism
syn-di-cate
syn-drome
syn-ec-do-che
syn-e-col-o-gy
syn-er-e-sis
syn-er-gis-ti-cal
syn-es-the-si-a
syn-ge-nite
syn-od-al
syn-od-i-cal
syn-o-nym
syn-on-y-mous
syn-on-y-my
syn-op-sis
syn-op-tic
syn-o-vi-tis
syn-tec-tic
syn-the-sis
syn-the-siz-er
syn-the-tase
syn-thet-i-cal
syn-thol
syn-to-ni-za-tion
syph-i-lit-ic
syph-i-lol-o-gy
Syr-a-cuse
Syr-i-an
sy-rin-ga
sy-ringe
sy-rin-ge-al
sy-rin-gic
sy-rin-gin
syr-in-gi-tis
syr-in-got-omy
syr-inx
sys-tem-at-i-cal
sys-tem-a-tize
sys-tem-ic
sys-to-le
sys-tol-ic
sy-zyg-i-al
syz-y-gy

T

tab-ard
Ta-bas-co
tab-er-na-cle
tab-er-nan-thine

ta-bes dor-sa-lis
ta-bet-ic
tab-i-net
tab-leaux
ta-ble d'hote
tab-let
ta-bling
tab-loid
ta-boo
tab-o-ret
tab-u-lar
tab-u-la-tor
ta-chis-to-scope
tach-o-graph
ta-chom-e-ter
tach-o-met-ric
ta-chom-e-try
tach-y-car-di-a
tach-y-gen-ic
tach-y-graph-om-e-ter
ta-chyg-ra-phy
ta-chym-e-ter
tach-y-met-ric
ta-chys-ter-ol
tac-it
tac-i-tur-ni-ty
tack-ling
tac-o-nite
tac-ti-cal
tac-ti-cian
tac-tic-i-ty
tac-til-i-ty
tac-tom-e-ter
tac-to-sol
taf-fe-ta
Ta-ga-log
tag-a-tose
tag-e-tone
Ta-hi-tian
tail-er
tai-lored
Tai-wan-ese
tak-ing
talc-ose
tal-ent
ta-les (law)
tal-i-pes
tal-is-man
tal-i-tol
talk-a-tive
talk-er
tal-lage
tall-ate
tal-lith
Tal-mud-ic
tal-on
ta-lon-ic
tal-ose
ta-lus
ta-ma-le
tam-a-rack
tam-a-rind
tam-bour
tam-bou-rine
tamp-er (n.)
tam-per (v.)
Tam-pi-co
tam-pon-ade
tan-a-ce-tin
tan-a-ger
Ta-nan-a-rive
tan-dem
Tan-gan-yi-kan
tan-ge-los
tan-gen-tial
tan-ger-e-tin
tan-ger-ine
tan-gi-ble
tan-gled
tank-age
tan-kard
tank-er
tan-nom-e-ter
tan-ta-lite
tan-ta-liz-er
tan-ta-lum
tan-ta-mount
tan-trum
Tan-za-ni-a
ta-per
tap-er (device; one who tapes)
tap-es-try
ta-pe-tum
tap-i-o-ca
ta-pir
tap-ster
tar-an-tel-la
ta-ran-tu-la
ta-rax-e-in
tar-di-ness
tar-get-eer
tar-iff
tar-nish
tar-pau-lin
tar-pon
tar-sal
tars-ec-to-my
tar-sor-rha-phy
tar-sus
tar-tan
tar-tar-e-ous
tar-tar-ic
tar-tar-ous

tar-tram-ic
tar-tra-mide
tar-trat-ed
ta-sim-e-ter
Tas-ma-ni-an
tas-ma-nite
tas-seled
tast-er
tat-ter-de-ma-lion
tat-too-er
tau-rine
tau-ro-cho-late
tau-rom-a-chy
Tau-rus
tau-ryl
tau-to-log-i-cal
tau-tol-o-gy
tau-to-mer-ic
tau-tom-er-ism
tau-to-met-ric
tau-toph-o-ny
tav-ern
taw-dry
tax-i-der-mist
tax-ied
tax-i-fo-lin
tax-i-ing
tax-i-me-ter
tax-o-nom-ic
tax-on-o-my
Tche-by-cheff
team-ster
tea-seled
teas-er
tech-ne-ti-um
tech-ni-cal
tech-ni-cian
tech-nique
tech-noc-ra-cy
tech-no-log-i-cal
tech-nol-o-gy
tec-ton-ics
tec-ton-ite
te-di-ous
te-di-um
tee-ter
tee-to-tal-er
Tef-lon
teg-men-tal
Te-he-ran
Te-huan-te-pec-er
Tel-Au-to-graph
te-leg-ra-pher
tel-e-graph-ic
tel-e-ki-ne-sis
tel-em-e-ter
tel-e-met-ric
tel-e-me-try
tel-e-mo-tor
tel-e-o-log-i-cal
tel-e-ol-o-gy
tel-e-path-ic
te-lep-a-thy
tel-e-phon-ic
te-leph-o-ny
tel-e-ran
tel-e-scope
tel-e-scop-ic
te-les-co-py
tel-es-the-si-a
tel-e-vi-sion
tel-e-vi-sor
tell-er
tel-lu-ri-an
tel-lu-ride
tel-lu-ri-um
tel-lu-rom-e-ter
tel-lu-ro-ni-um
te-lome
tel-o-mer-i-za-tion
tel-pher-age
tem-blor
te-mer-i-ty
tem-per-a-men-tal
tem-per-ate
tem-per-a-ture
tem-pered
tem-pes-tu-ous
tem-plar
tem-plet
tem-po-ral
tem-po-rar-i-ly
tem-po-rar-y
tem-po-riz-er
tempt-a-ble
tempt-er
tempt-ress
ten-a-ble
te-na-cious
te-nac-i-ty
ten-an-cy
ten-ant-ry
tend-en-cy
tend-er (one who at-tends; ship)
ten-der (soft; offer)
ten-der-iz-er
ten-der-om-e-ter
ten-di-ni-tis
ten-don
ten-dril
ten-e-bres-cence
ten-e-brous
ten-e-ment

Ten-er-iffe
ten-et
te-nien-te
Ten-ite
Ten-nes-se-an
ten-o-de-sis
ten-on
ten-or
te-not-o-my
ten-si-ble
ten-sil-i-ty
ten-sim-e-ter
ten-si-om-e-ter
ten-so-ri-al
ten-ta-cle
ten-ta-tive
tent-age
ten-ter (drying frame)
tent-er
ten-ter-hook
te-nu-i-ty
ten-u-lin
ten-u-ous
ten-ure
te-pa-che
te-pee
teph-ro-sin
tep-id
te-pid-i-ty
te-qui-la
ter-a-con-ic
ter-a-cryl-ic
ter-a-to-log-i-cal
ter-a-tol-o-gy
ter-a-to-ma
ter-bi-um
ter-cen-te-nar-y
ter-e-ben-thene
te-reb-ic
ter-e-bin-thi-nate
ter-e-bin-thine
ter-eph-thal-ic
ter-gite
ter-gi-ver-sa-tor
ter-ma-gant
term-er
ter-mi-na-ble
ter-mi-nal
ter-mi-na-tor
ter-mi-nol-o-gy
ter-mi-nus
ter-mite
ter-mit-ic
ter-na-ry
ter-op-ter-in
ter-pene
ter-pe-nyl-ic
ter-pi-nene
ter-pin-e-ol
ter-pin-o-lene
ter-pi-nyl
terp-sich-o-re
terp-si-cho-re-an
ter-ra-pin
ter-rar-i-um
terre-plein
ter-res-tri-al
ter-ri-bly
ter-rif-ic
ter-rig-e-nous
ter-ri-to-ri-al
ter-ror-ism
ter-tian
ter-ti-ar-y
ter-tile
tes-sel-lat-ed
test-a-ble
tes-ta-ceous
tes-ta-men-ta-ry
tes-ta-tor
test-er
tes-ter (canopy)
tes-tic-u-lar
tes-ti-fy
tes-ti-mo-ni-al
tes-ti-ness
tes-tos-ter-one
te-tan-ic
tet-a-no-gen-ic
tet-a-nus
tet-a-ny
te-tar-toi-dal
teth-ered
tet-ra-bro-mo
tet-ra-cene
tet-ra-chlo-ro
te-trac-id
tet-ra-co-sa-no-ic
tet-ra-cy-cline
tet-rad
te-trad-ic
tet-ra-eth-yl
tet-ra-gon
tet-rag-o-nal
tet-ra-he-dral
tet-ra-hy-dro-fu-ran
tet-ra-kis-a-zo
te-tral-o-gy
tet-ra-mine
tet-ra-ni-tro-meth-ane
tet-ra-ple-gi-a
tet-ra-ploi-dy
te-trar-chic

te-trar-chy
tet-ra-som-a-ty
tet-ra-thi-o-nate
tet-ra-va-lent
tet-ra-zine
tet-ra-zo-li-um
te-traz-o-lyl
tet-ra-zone
tet-ri-tol
te-tron-ic
tet-rose
te-trox-ide
tet-ryl
Teu-ton-ic
Tex-an
tex-tile
tex-tu-al
tex-tur-al
Thai-land
thal-a-mot-o-my
thal-as-som-e-ter
thal-lif-er-ous
thal-line
thal-li-um
than-a-to-sis
thau-ma-site
thau-ma-tur-gy
the-a-ter
the-at-ri-cal
the-mat-i-cal-ly
then-o-yl
the-oc-ra-cy
the-o-crat-ic
the-od-o-lite
The-o-do-si-a
the-o-lo-gian
the-ol-o-gy
the-oph-a-gy
the-o-rem
the-o-re-mat-ic
the-o-ret-i-cal
the-o-re-ti-cian
the-o-rize
the-os-o-phy
ther-a-peu-ti-cal-ly
ther-a-pist
the-ri-at-rics
ther-mal
therm-i-on-ic
therm-is-tor
Ther-mit
ther-mo-chro-mism
ther-mo-du-ric
ther-mog-ra-pher
ther-mo-graph-ic
ther-mol-y-sis
ther-mo-lyt-ic
ther-mom-e-ter
ther-mo-met-ri-cal-ly
ther-mom-e-try
ther-moph-i-ly
ther-mo-scop-ic
ther-mo-stat
ther-mo-ther-a-py
the-sau-rus
the-sis
thes-pi-an
the-tin
the-ve-tin
thi-am-ide
thi-am-i-nase
thi-a-mine
thi-a-naph-thene
thi-an-threne
thi-a-zole
thi-az-o-line
thi-a-zol-sul-fone
thick-en-ing
thiev-ish
thi-mer-o-sal
think-er
thi-o-fla-vine
thi-o-naph-thene
thi-on-ic
Thi-o-nine
thi-o-ni-um
thi-oph-e-nine
thi-o-u-ra-cil
thi-o-u-re-a
thirst-i-ness
thir-ti-eth
this-tle
thith-er
thi-u-ro-ni-um
thix-ot-ro-py
Thom-as
Tho-mism
thon-zyl-a-mine
tho-rac-ic
tho-rac-i-co-lum-bar
tho-ra-co-scope
tho-ra-cos-to-my
tho-ri-ate
tho-rif-er-ous
tho-rite
tho-ri-um
tho-ron
thor-ough
thou-sand
thrash-er
thread-er
threat-en-ing
thre-i-tol
thre-node

thren-o-dy
thre-o-nine
thresh-er
thresh-old
thrift-i-ness
thrill-er
throat-i-ness
throm-bin
throm-bo-an-gi-i-tis
throm-bo-cy-to-sis
throm-bo-plas-tin
throm-bo-sis
throm-bot-ic
throm-bus
throt-tled
thrust-er (one that thrusts)
thrus-tor (machine)
thu-co-lite
thu-ja-pli-cin
thu-jyl
thu-li-um
thump-er
thun-der-ous
thu-ri-ble
thu-rif-er-ous
thy-mi-dine
thy-mi-dyl-ic
thy-mine
thy-mol-phthal-ein
thy-mo-nu-cle-ic
thy-mus
Thy-ra-tron
thy-rite
thy-roi-dal
thy-roid-ec-to-my
thy-roid-i-tis
thy-ro-nine
thy-rot-ro-phin
ti-ar-a
Ti-bet-an
tib-i-al
tick-et-er
tick-i-ci-dal
tick-lish
tid-al
ti-di-ness
ti-ding (news)
tid-ing (tide)
Ti-flis
ti-ger-ish
tight-en-er
tig-lal-de-hyde
ti-gnon
ti-go-nin
ti-gress
ti-grine
ti-grol-y-sis
till-a-ble
till-age
till-er
tilt-er
tim-bered
tim-brel
tim-er
tim-id
ti-mid-i-ty
tim-o-rous
tim-o-thy
tim-pa-nist
tin-cal-co-nite
tinc-to-ri-al
tinc-ture
tin-der
tin-gled
tin-ker
tin-kling
tin-seled
tint-er
tin-tin-nab-u-lous
tint-om-e-ter
tip-ster
ti-queur
ti-rade
ti-rail-leur
Tish-chen-ko
ti-ta-nate
ti-tan-ic
ti-ta-nif-er-ous
ti-ta-ni-um
ti-ter
tith-er
Ti-tian
tit-il-late
ti-tled
ti-trat-a-ble
ti-tra-tion
ti-trim-e-ter
ti-tri-met-ri-cal-ly
tit-u-lar-i-ty
toast-er
to-bac-co-nist
to-bog-gan-er
to-col-o-gy
to-coph-er-ol
toc-sin
tod-dler
to-geth-er
tog-gler
To-go-lese
toil-er
toi-let-ry
to-ken
To-ky-o

tol-bu-ta-mide
tol-er-a-ble
tol-er-a-tion
tol-i-dine
tol-u-ene
to-lu-i-dine
tol-u-ol
to-lu-ric
tol-u-yl-ene
tol-yl-ene
to-mat-i-dine
tom-a-tine
to-men-tose
to-mog-ra-phy
ton-al
to-nal-i-ty
to-neme
ton-er
to-net-ics
tongu-er
tongu-ing
ton-ic
to-nic-i-ty
to-nite (explosive)
ton-neau
ton-o-log-i-cal
to-nom-e-ter
ton-o-met-ric
to-nom-e-try
ton-sil-lec-to-my
ton-sil-li-tis
ton-sil-lot-o-my
ton-so-ri-al
ton-tine
to-nus
tool-er
to-paz-ine
to-pec-to-my
to-per
to-pi-ar-y
top-i-cal
to-pog-ra-pher
top-o-graph-i-cal
to-pog-ra-phy
top-o-log-i-cal
to-pol-o-gy
to-pon-y-my
top-sy-tur-vy
tor-chon
to-re-a-dor
to-ric
to-rin-gin
tor-men-tor
tor-na-do
to-roi-dal
tor-pe-do
tor-pid-i-ty
tor-por-if-ic
torqu-er
torqu-ing
torque-me-ter
tor-ren-tial
tor-si-bil-i-ty
tor-si-om-e-ter
tor-sion-al
tor-ti-lla
tor-som-e-ter
tor-toise
tor-tu-os-i-ty
tor-tu-ous
tor-tur-ous
tos-yl-ate
tot-a-ble
to-tal-i-tar-i-an-ism
to-tal-i-ty
to-tal-iz-er
to-ta-quine
to-tem-ism
tou-ché
tough-en
tou-pee
tour-ist
tour-ma-line
tour-na-ment
tour-ni-quet
tou-sled
tout-er
tow-age
to-ward
tow-eled
tow-ered
tox-e-mi-a
tox-e-mic
tox-ic-i-ty
tox-i-co-log-i-cal
tox-i-col-o-gist
tox-i-co-sis
tox-if-er-ous
tox-i-l-ge-nic-i-ty
tox-in
trac-er-y
tra-che-al
tra-che-i-tis
tra-che-ot-o-my
tra-cho-ma
tra-chyt-ic
trac-ing
track-age
trac-ta-ble
trac-tile
trac-tor
trad-er
tra-dev-man
tra-di-tion-al

tra-duc-er
tra-duc-i-ble
traf-fic-a-ble
traf-fick-er
trag-a-can-thin
tra-ge-di-an
tra-ge-di-enne
trag-e-dy
trag-i-cal
trail-er
train-ee
trai-tor-ous
trai-tress
traj-ect (n.)
tra-ject (v.)
tra-jec-tile
tra-jec-to-ry
tram-meled
tramp-er
tram-po-line
tran-quil-iz-er
tran-quil-li-ty
trans-ac-tion
trans-am-i-nase
trans-at-lan-tic
trans-ceiv-er
tran-scend-ent
tran-scen-den-tal
tran-scrib-er
tran-script
trans-duc-er
trans-duc-tor
tran-sect
trans-fer-a-ble
trans-fer-ase
trans-fer-ee
trans-fer-ence
trans-ferred
trans-for-ma-tion
trans-form-er
trans-fus-a-ble
trans-gres-sor
tran-sient
tran-sil-ience
tran-sis-tor
tran-sit-er
tran-si-tion
tran-si-tive
tran-si-to-ry
tran-si-tron
trans-la-tive
trans-la-tor
trans-lit-er-a-tor
trans-lu-cen-cy
trans-mis-si-ble
trans-mis-som-e-ter
trans-mit-ta-ble
trans-mog-ri-fy
trans-mut-a-ble
tran-som
tran-son-ic
tran-spar-ent
tran-spir-a-ble
tran-spi-ra-tion
tran-spire
tran-spi-rom-e-ter
trans-plan-ta-tion
trans-pon-der
trans-por-ta-tion
trans-pose
trans-ship
trans-u-da-tion
trans-ver-sal
trans-vers-er
trans-vert-er
trans-vert-i-ble
tra-pe-zi-um
trap-e-zoi-dal
trau-mat-ic
trau-ma-tism
trav-ail
trav-eled
trav-el-er
trav-el-og
tra-vers-a-ble
tra-vers-al
trav-erse (n.)
tra-verse (v.)
trav-er-tine
trav-es-ty
trawl-er
treach-er-ous
treach-er-y
trea-cle
trea-son-a-ble
treas-ur-a-ble
treas-ur-er
treas-ur-y
treat-er
trea-tise
tre-bled
tre-foil
tre-ha-lose
trel-lised
Trem-a-to-da
trem-bling
tre-men-dous
trem-e-tol
trem-o-lo
trem-or
trem-u-lous
trench-ant
tren-cher (board; cap)

trench-er (digger)
tre-pan
tre-phine
treph-o-cyte
treph-one
trep-i-da-tion
tre-pid-i-ty
trep-o-ne-ma-to-sis
trep-o-ne-mi-ci-dal
tres-pass-er
tres-tle
tri-an-gu-lar
tri-ar-yl-meth-ane
tri-a-zine
tri-az-i-nyl
tri-a-zole
tri-az-o-lyl
trib-al
tri-bom-e-ter
tri-bro-mo-eth-yl
trib-u-la-tion
tri-bu-nal
trib-une
trib-u-tar-y
trib-ute
tri-chi-a-sis
tri-chi-na
trich-i-no-sis
tri-chit-ic
tri-chlo-ride
tri-chlo-ro-meth-ane
trich-o-mo-ni-a-sis
tri-cho-sis
tri-chot-o my
trick-er-y
trick-ster
tri-cli-no-he-dric
tri-cy-cle
tri-dec-yl-ene
tri-dent
tri-eth-a-nol-a-mine
tri-far-i-ous
tri-fling
trig-o-nal
tri-go-ni-tis
trig-o-nom-e-ter
trig-o-no-met-ric
trig-o-nom-e-try
tri-ha-lide
tri-he-dral
tri-hy-dric
tri-ke-tone
tri-lo-bite
tri-log-ic
tril-o-gy
tri-mer-ide
tri-mes-ic
tri-meth-yl-ene-tri-ni-tra-mine
tri-met-ro-gon
tri-na-ry
Trin-i-dad
tri-ni-tro-tol-u-ene
trin-i-ty
trin-ket
tri-no-mi-al
Tri-o-nal
tri-part-i-ble
tri-par-tite
tri-phen-yl-ene
tri-phib-i-ous
triph-thong
tri-ple-gi-a
tri-plet
trip-li-cate
trip-loi-dy
tri-pod
trip-o-dal
tri-pod-ic
trip-tych
tri-so-mic
tri-syl-lab-ic
tri-thi-o-nate
trit-i-um
trit-u-ra-tor
tri-tyl
tri-um-phant
tri-um-vi-rate
tri-va-lent
triv-et
triv-i-al
tro-car
tro-chan-ter
tro-che
troch-e-am-e-ter
troch-le-ar
tro-choi-dal
tro-chom-e-ter
trog-lo-dyte
Tro-jan
trom-bi-di-a-sis
tro-mom-e-ter
tro-nom-e-ter
troop-er
tro-pane
tro-pe-ine
troph-ic
tro-phy
trop-i-cal
tro-pism
trop-o-lone
tro-pom-e-ter
tro-po-sphere
trop-tom-e-ter
tro-pyl
trou-ba-dour
trou-bled
trou-blous
trou-sers
trous-seau
tro-ver
trow-eled
tru-an-cy
Truck-ee
truck-ling
truc-u-lent
trump-er-y
trum-pet-er
trun-cat-ed
trun-cheon
trun-dle
truss-ing
trust-ee
tru-xi-llic
tryp-a-no-ci-dal
tryp-a-no-so-ma
tryp-ar-sa-mide
tryp-o-graph
tryp-sin-o-gen
tryp-to-phan
tset-se
tsu-nam-i
tsu-tsu-ga-mu-shi
tu-bec-to-my
tu-ber-cle
tu-ber-cu-lar
tu-ber-cu-lo-sis
tu-ber-cu-lous
tu-ber-os-i-ty
tu-bi-fa-cient
tub-ing
tu-bo-cu-ra-rine
tu-bu-lar
Tuc-son
tu-fa-ceous
tuff-a-ceous
tuft-er
Tui-ler-ies
tu-la-re-mi-a
tu-lip
tum-bler
tum-bling
tum-brel
tu-me-fa-cient
tu-mes-cent
tu-mid
tu-mor
tu-mul-tu-ous
tun-a-ble
tung-sten
tung-stite
tu-nicked
Tu-ni-si-an
tun-neled
tun-nel-er
tu-pe-lo
tu-ran-ose
tur-ban
tur-bi-dim-e-ter
tur-bi-di-met-ric
tur-bid-i-ty
tur-bi-nate
tur-bine
tur-bi-nec-to-my
tur-bo-charg-er
tur-bu-la-tor
tur-bu-lence
tu-reen
tur-ges-cence
tur-gid-i-ty
tur-key
Turk-ish
tur-mer-ic
tur-nip
tur-pen-tine
tur-pi-tude
tur-quoise
tur-tle
tu-te-lage
tu-tored
tu-to-ri-al
Tu-tu-i-lan
tu-yere
tweet-er
tweez-ers
twen-ti-eth
twin-kling
twist-er
Twitch-ell
ty-ing
tym-pan-ic
tym-pa-nist
tym-pa-num
tyn-dall-om-e-ter
typ-a-ble
typh-li-tis
ty-phoi-dal
ty-phoon
ty-phus
typ-i-cal
typ-i-fy
ty-pog-ra-pher
ty-po-graph-ic
ty-pog-ra-phy
ty-po-nym
ty-poth-e-tae
ty-ra-mine
ty-ran-ni-cal
tyr-an-nize
tyr-an-ny
ty-rant
ty-ro-ci-dine
Ty-rode
Ty-ro-le-an
Tyr-o-lese
ty-ro-sin-ase
ty-ro-sine
ty-ro-sin-o-sis

U

u-biq-ui-tous
u-biq-ui-ty
u-dom-e-ter
U-gan-dan
U-krain-i-an
u-ku-le-le
ul-cer-a-tive
ul-nar
ul-na-re
u-lot-o-my
ul-ster
ul-te-ri-or
ul-ti-ma-cy
ul-ti-ma-tum
ul-tra-ma-rine
ul-tra-son-ic
ul-u-late
U-lys-ses
um-bel-lif-er-one
um-ber
um-bil-i-cal
um-bil-i-cus
um-bra-geous
um-brel-la
u-mo-ho-ite
um-pire
u-na-nim-i-ty
u-nan-i-mous
u-na-ry
un-cial
un-ci-na-ri-a-sis
un-ci-nate
un-cle
unc-tu-ous
un-dec-yl-ene
un-dec-y-len-ic
un-der-tak-er
un-du-la-to-ry
un-guen-tous
un-gui-nous
u-ni-bi-va-lent
u-nic-i-ty
u-ni-corn
u-ni-fi-ca-tion
u-ni-form-i-ty
un-ion-ism
u-nip-a-rous
u-nip-o-tent
u-nique-ly
u-ni-son
u-nit-a-ble
u-ni-tar-i-an
u-ni-tar-y
u-nit-ed
u-nit-ize
u-ni-va-lent
u-ni-ver-sal-i-ty
u-ni-ver-si-ty
u-niv-o-cal
un-prec-e-dent-ed
un-re-quit-a-ble
up-heav-al
up-hol-ster-er
Up-per Vol-tan
up-roar-i-ous
u-ra-chus
u-ra-cil
u-ra-nate
U-ra-ni-an
u-ran-ic
u-ra-nif-er-ous
u-ra-nin-ite
u-ra-nite
u-ra-ni-um
u-ra-nog-ra-phy
u-ra-nol-o-gy
u-ra-nom-e-try
u-ra-nos-co-py
u-ra-nous
U-ra-nus
u-ra-nyl
u-ra-zine
ur-ban-i-ty
ur-bi-cul-ture
ur-chin
u-re-am-e-ter
u-re-mi-a
u-re-om e-ter
u-re-ter-i-tis
u-re-thane
u-re-thra
u-re-thri-tis
u-ret-ic
u-re-yl-ene
ur-gen-cy
u-ri-col-y-sis
u-ri-co-lyt-ic
u-ri-nal-y-sis
u-ri-nar-y
u-ri-nate
u-ri-no-cry-os-co-py
u-ri-nol-o-gy
u-ri-nom-e-ter
u-ro-bi-lin-o-gen
u-ro-fla-vin
u-ro-gen-i-tal
u-rog-ra-phy
u-ro-leu-cic
u-ro-li-thi-a-sis
u-ro-li-thol-o-gy
u-ro-log-ic
u-rol-o-gist
u-ro-poi-e-sis
u-ro-poi-et-ic
u-ro-por-phy-rin
u-ros-co-py
u-rot-ro-pine
ur-si-gram
ur-ti-car-i-a
us-a-ble
us-que-baugh
us-ti-la-gin-e-ous
u-su-al-ly
u-su-fruct
u-su-rer
u-su-ri-ous
u-sur-pa-tion
u-surp-er
u-su-ry
U-tah-an
u-ten-sil
u-ter-ine
u-ter-og-ra-phy
u-ter-us
u-til-i-tar-i-an
u-til-i-ty
u-ti-li-za-tion
u-ti-liz-er
u-to-pi-an
u-tri-cle
u-tric-u-lar
u-ve-i-tis
u-vi-ton-ic
u-vu-la
ux-or-i-cide
ux-o-ri-ous
u-zar-i-gen-in
u-za-rin

V

va-can-cy
vac-ci-na-tor
vac-il-la-tion
vac-u-ist
va-cu-i-ty
vac-u-om-e-ter
vac-u-um
va-de me-cum
vag-a-bond-age
va-gar-i-ous
va-gar-y
va-gi-na
vag-i-nal
vag-i-nec-to-my
vag-i-ni-tis
va-got-o-my
va-gran-cy
va-guish
val-ance
val-e-dic-to-ri-an
va-lence
va-len-ci-a
Va-len-ci-ennes
va-lent
val-en-tine
val-er-ate
va-le-ri-an
va-ler-ic
va-le-ryl
val-et
val-e-tu-di-nar-i-an
val-iant
val-i-da-tion
va-lid-i-ty
va-line
va-lise
val-or-i-za-tion
val-or-ous
val-u-a-ble
val-vate
val-vu-lar
val-vu-li-tis
val-vu-lot-o-my
va-nad-ic
van-a-dif-er-ous
va-na-di-um
Van-cou-ver
van-dal-ism
va-nil-la
van-ish
van-i-ty
van-quish-er
van-tage
vap-id
va-pid-i-ty
va-pog-ra-phy
va-por-im-e-ter
va-por-i-za-tion
va-por-iz-er
va-por-ous
var-i-a-bil-i-ty
Var-i-ac
var-i-ant
var-i-at-ed
var-i-a-tion
var-i-co-cele
var-i-cose
var-ied
var-i-e-gat-ed
va-ri-e-tal
va-ri-e-ty
var-i-o-lite
var-i-o-loid
var-i-om-e-ter
var-i-ous
var-is-tor
Var-i-typ-er
var-nish-er
vas-cu-lar
vas-ec-to-my
vas-e-line
vas-o-dil-a-tin
vas-o-di-la-tor
vas-o-mo-tor
vas-sal-age
vas-ti-tude
Vat-i-can
va-tic-i-nal
vaude-ville
vec-to-ri-al
veg-e-ta-ble
veg-e-tar-i-an
veg-e-ta-tive
ve-he-mence
ve-hi-cle
ve-hic-u-lar
vel-lum
vel-o-cim-e-ter
ve-loc-i-pede
ve-loc-i-ty
ve-lom-e-ter
ve-lours
ve-lum
vel-vet-een
ve-nal-i-ty
ve-na-tion
vend-ee
vend-er
ven-det-ta
vend-i-ble
ven-dor
ve-neer-er
ven-e-nif-er-ous
ven-er-a-ble
ve-ne-re-al
ve-ne-re-ol-o-gy
ven-er-y
Ve-ne-tian
venge-ance
ve-ni-al
ve-ni-re fa-ci-as
ven-i-son
ven-om-ous
ve-nous
ven-ter (abdomen)
vent-er (utters)
ven-ti-la-tor
ven-tom-e-ter
ven-tral
ven-tri-cle
ven-tric-u-lar
ven-tri-lo-qui-al
ven-tril-o-quism
ven-tril-o-quist
ven-tur-er
ven-tu-ri
ven-tur-ous
ven-ue
ven-ule
ven-u-lose
Ve-nu-si-an
ve-ra-cious
ve-rac-i-ty
ve-ran-da
ver-a-scope
ver-a-tral-de-hyde
ver-a-tram-ine
ve-rat-ric
ve-rat-ro-yl
Ve-ra-trum
ver-a-tryl-i-dene
ver-bal (adj.)
verb-al (n.) (part of speech)
ver-bal-i-ty
ver-bal-iz-er
ver-ba-tim
ver-be-na
ver-be-na-lin
ver-bi-age
ver-bile
ver-bos-i-ty
ver-bo-ten
ver-dant
ver-di-gris
ver-dur-ous
verg-er
ver-i-fi-a-ble
ver-i-fi-ca-tion
ver-i-si-mil-i-tude
ver-i-ta-ble
Ver-i-tas
ve-ri-tas
ver-i-ty
ver-mi-cel-li
ver-mi-ci-dal
ver-mic-u-lar
ver-mic-u-lite
ver-mi-form
ver-mif-u-gal
ver-mi-fuge
ver-mil-ion
ver-mi-no-sis
ver-min-ous
Ver-mont-er
ver-mouth
ver-nac-u-lar
ver-nal
ver-ni-er
ve-ron-i-ca
ver-ru-co-sis
ver-sa-til-i-ty
ver-sic-u-lar
ver-si-fi-ca-tion
ver-si-fi-er
ver-sus
ver-te-bra
ver-ti-cal
ver-tic-i-ty
ver-tig-i-nous
ver-ti-go
ves-i-cant
ves-i-ca-to-ry
ves-i-cle
ve-sic-u-lar
ves-per-al
ves-tal
vest-ed
ves-tib-u-lar
ves-ti-bule
ves-ti-bu-li-tis
ves-tig-i-al
ves-ti-ture
ves-try
ves-tur-al
Ve-su-vi-us
vet-er-an
vet-er-i-nar-i-an
vex-a-tious
vi-a-bil-i-ty
vi-a do-lo-ro-so
vi-a-duct
vi-bran-cy
vi-bra-to-ry
vib-ri-o-sis
vi-brom-e-ter
vi-bur-num
vic-ar-age
vi-car-i-ous
vice-ge-rent
vice-roy
vi-ce ver-sa
Vi-chy-ite
vi-chys-soise
vi-ci-a-nin
vi-ci-a-nose
vic-i-nage
vic-i-nal
vi-cin-i-ty
vi-cious
vi-cis-si-tude
vic-tim-ize
vic-to-ri-an
vic-to-ri-ous
vict-ualed
vict-ual-er
vi-cu-na
vi-de-li-cet
vid-e-o
Vi-et-nam-ese
vig-i-lance
vig-i-lan-te
vig-i-lan-tism
vi-gnette
vi-gnet-ter
vig-or-ous
vi-king
vi-la-yet
vil-i-fi-er
vil-lag-er
vil-lain-ous
vi-na-ceous
vin-ai-grette
vin-ci-ble
vin-cu-lum
vin-di-ca-ble
vin-di-ca-to-ry
vin-dic-tive
vin-e-gar
vin-er-y
vin-i-cul-tur-al
vi-nif-er-a
vin-ol-o-gy
vin-om-e-ter
vi-nous
vin-tag-er
vint-ner
vi-nyl-a-tion
vi-nyl-ene
vi-nyl-i-dene
Vi-nyl-ite
vi-nyl-o-gous
vi-o-la-ble
vi-o-la-ceous
vi-o-lan-throne
vi-o-la-tor
vi-o-lence
vi-o-les-cent
vi-o-lin-ist
vi-o-lon-cel-lo

vi-o-lu-ric	vo-cif-er-ous	war-bler	whor-tle-ber-ry	xan-thate	yt-tro-tan-ta-lite
vi-os-ter-ol	voic-ing	war-den	wick-ed-ly	xan-the-nyl	Yu-go-slav
vi-per-ous	void-ance	ward-er	wick-ered	xan-thine	
vi-ra-go	vol-a-til-i-ty	war-fa-rin	wick-et	xan-tho-gen-ate	
vi-ral	vol-a-til-i-za-tion	war-i-ness	wick-i-up	xan-tho-ma	**Z**
vi-re-mi-a	vol-can-ic	warm-er	wid-en	xan-tho-ma-to-sis	
vi-res-cence	vol-ca-no	warp-age	widg-eon	xan-thom-a-tous	
vir-gin-al	vo-cod-er	war-rant-ee	widg-et	xan-thom-e-ter	Zach-a-ri-ah
Vir-gin-ian	vo-lem-i-tol	war-rant-er	wid-ow-er	xan-tho-phyll	Zam-bi-an
vir-gin-i-ty	vo-li-tion	war-ran-tor (law)	wie-ner schnit-zel	xan-thop-ter-in	za-ni-ness
vir-gin-i-um	volt-age	war-ran-ty	Wies-ba-den	xan-thous	za-pa-te-a-do
vir-i-al	vol-ta-ic	war-ri-or	wie-sen-bo-den	xan-thox-y-le-tin	zeal-ot
vi-ri-ci-dal	vol-tam-e-ter	wash-a-ble	wild-er	xan-thy-drol	zea-lot-i-cal
vi-rid-i-ty	volt-am-me-ter	Wash-ing-to-ni-an	wil-der-ness	Xa-ve-ri-an	zeal-ous
vir-ile	vol-u-bil-i-ty	wasp-ish	Wil-helms-ha-ven	xe-ni-al	ze-a-xan-thin
vi-ril-i-ty	vol-ume	was-sail	Wil-helm-stras-se	xen-o-lith	ze-bra
vi-rol-o-gy	vol-u-me-nom-e-ter	Was-ser-mann	Wil-lam-ette	xe-non	ze-nith
vi-ro-sis	vo-lu-me-ter	wast-age	will-ful-ness	xen-o-pho-bi-a	ze-nog-ra-phy
vir-tu-al	vol-u-met-ric	wast-er	Wil-liam	xen-yl	ze-o-lite
vir-tu-os-i-ty	vo-lu-mi-nous	was-trel	Wil-ton	Xe-res	ze-ol-i-tize
vir-tu-o-so	vol-un-tar-i-ly	wa-ter-me-ter	wind-age	xe-ric	zeph-yr
vir-tu-ous	vol-un-teered	watt-age	wind-er	xe-ro-gel	Zep-pe-lin
vir-u-lent	vo-lup-tu-ar-y	wave-me-ter	wind-i-ness	xe-ro-graph-ic	ze-ro-ize
vi-rus	vo-lup-tu-ous	wa-ver (sway)	win-dow	xe-rog-ra-phy	ze-ros
vis-aged	vo-lute	wav-er (waving)	wind-row	xe-ro-phyte	zib-el-ine
vis-cer-al	vol-u-tin	Wa-ver-ley	Wins-low	xe-ro-phyt-ic	zinc-ate
vis-cid-i-ty	vol-vu-lus	wax-en	win-some	xe-ro-sis	zinc-if-er-ous
Vis-co-liz-er	vo-mer-ine	weak-ened	win-ter-ize	xiph-oid	zin-cog-ra-phy
vis-com-e-ter	vom-it-er	weak-ling	win-try	xi-phop-a-gus	zinc-oid
vis-co-scope	vom-i-tus	weap-on-eer	wip-er	xy-lem	zin-ger-one
vis-cose	voo-doo	wear-a-ble	wir-i-ness	xy-lene	zin-gi-ber-ene
vis-co-sim-e-ter	vo-ra-cious	wea-ri-ness	Wis-con-sin-ite	xy-le-nol	Zi-on-ism
vis-cos-i-ty	vo-rac-i-ty	wea-ri-some	wise-a-cre	xy-le-nyl	zirc-ite
vis-cous	vor-tex	wea-seled	wis-tar-i-a	xy-lic	zir-con-ate
vis-i-bil-i-ty	vor-ti-ces	weath-ered	Wis-te-ri-a	xy-li-dine	zir-co-ni-um
vi-sion-ar-y	vor-tic-i-ty	weath-er-om-e-ter	witch-er-y	xy-lin-de-in	zir-co-nyl
vi-sioned	vot-a-ble	weav-er	with-al	xy-lo-graph-ic	zith-er
vis-it-ant	vo-ta-ry	Web-er	with-ered	xy-log-ra-phy	Ziz-i-phus
vis-it-a-tion	vot-er	Web-ste-ri-an	wit-ti-cism	xy-loid	zlo-ty
vis-i-tor	vo-tive	Wechs-ler	wiz-ard-ry	xy-lol-o-gy	zo-an-thro-py
vi-sor	vouch-er	wed-ding	wiz-ened	xy-lom-e-ter	zo-di-ac
vis-ta	vow-el	Wedg-wood	wob-bu-la-tor	xy-loph-a-gous	zo-di-a-cal
vis-u-al	vox po-pu-li	Wednes-day	woe-ful-ness	xy-lo-phone	Zo-is-i-a
vis-u-al-i-ty	voy-ag-er	weed-er	wolf-ra-min-i-um	xy-lo-side	zois-it-i-za-tion
vis-u-al-iz-er	voy-a-geur	weep-er	wolf-ram-ite	xy-lot-o-my	Zoll-ver-ein
vi-tal-i-ty	vul-can-ite	wee-viled	wol-las-ton-ite	xy-lo-yl	zon-al
vi-tal-ize	vul-can-i-za-tion	weight-i-ness	wol-ver-ine	xy-lu-lose	zon-ar-y
vi-ta-min-ol-o-gy	vul-can-iz-er	Weight-om-e-ter	wom-an	xy-lyl-ene	zon-ate
vi-ta-scope	vul-gar-i-an	Wei-mar-an-er	wom-bat	Xy-ris	zo-nif-er-ous
vi-tel-lin	vul-gar-ism	weld-er	wom-en		zo-og-a-my
vi-ti-at-ed	vul-gar-i-ty	wel-kin	won-dered		zo-o-gen-ic
vit-i-cul-ture	vul-ner-a-ble	welsh-er	won-drous		zo-ol-a-ter
vit-i-li-go	vul-pine	wel-ter	wood-en		zo-o-log-i-cal
vit-rain	vul-pin-ic	welt-er (worker on	woof-er	**Y**	zo-ol-o-gy
vit-re-ous	vul-tur-ous	shoes, etc.)	wool-en		zo-om-e-ter
vi-tres-cence	vul-vi-tis	Wes-ley-an	wool-ly		zo-on-o-sis
vi-tres-ci-ble		west-er-ly	Worces-ter	Yak-i-ma	zo-o-phyte
vit-ri-fi-a-ble		west-ern-er	word-ster	Yak-u-tat	zo-os-co-py
vit-ri-fi-ca-tion	**W**	West-min-ster	work-er	ya-men	zo-os-ter-ol
vit-ri-ol		West-pha-li-an	wor-ri-some	Yan-kee	zo-ot-o-my
vit-ri-o-lat-ed	wad-dled	weth-er	wor-shiped	Ya-qui	Zo-ro-as-tri-an
vit-ri-ol-ic	wad-er	whal-er-y	wor-ship-er	yard-age	Zou-ave
vi-tu-per-a-tive	wa-fer	wharf-age	wor-sted	yaw-me-ter	Zo-ys-i-a
vi-va-cious	waf-fle	wheat-en	wor-thi-ly	Ya-zoo	zu-mat-ic
vi-vac-i-ty	waft-age	whee-dled	wor-thy	year-ling	zun-yite
vi-van-dier	wa-ger (bet)	wheel-er	wo-ven	yeast-i-ness	zwie-back
vi-vant	wag-er (competitor)	wheez-i-ness	wran-gler	yelp-er	zwit-ter-i-on
vi-var-i-um	wag-es	wher-ev-er	wreck-age	Yem-en-ite	zyg-a-de-nine
vi-va vo-ce	Wag-ne-ri-an	wheth-er	wres-tler	yeo-man	zy-gal
viv-id	wag-on-er	whi-lom	wres-tling	yes-ter-day	zy-go-mat-ic
viv-id-i-ty	wag-on-ette	whim-pered	wretch-ed	yield-a-ble	zy-gote
viv-i-fi-ca-tion	wain-scot-ing	whim-si-cal	wring-er	yo-del-er	zy-got-ic
viv-i-par-i-ty	wait-er	whim-sy	wrin-kled	yo-gurt	zy-mase
vi-vip-a-rous	wait-ress	whirl-er	wrist-let	yo-him-bine	zy-min
viv-i-sec-tion	waiv-er	whirl-i-gig	writ-er	yo-kel	zy-mo-gen-ic
vix-en-ish	wak-en-er	whisk-ered	Wy-an-dotte	yon-der	zy-mog-e-nous
vi-zier	walk-er	whis-kies	Wyc-liffe	Yo-sem-i-te	zy-mo-hy-drol-y-sis
Vlad-i-vos-tok	wal-lop-er	whis-ky	Wy-o-ming-ite	young-ster	zy-mol-o-gy
vo-ca-ble	Wal-tham	whis-pered		y-per-ite	zy-mom-e-ter
vo-cab-u-lar-y	waltz-er	whis-tler		yp-sil-i-form	zy-mo-sis
vo-cal-ist	wam-pum	whis-tling		yt-ter-bi-um	zy-mos-ter-ol
vo-cal-iz-er	wan-der	whit-en-ing	**X**	yt-ter-bous	zy-mos-then-ic
vo-ca-tion	wan-gled	whith-er		yt-trif-er-ous	zy-mur-gy
voc-a-tive	wan-ton	whit-ish	xan-tha-mide	yt-tri-um	
	wap-i-ti	whit-tled			

German/English Dictionary

German is spoken by over 80 million people in Germany, Austria and parts of Switzerland and Czechoslovakia. There are a number of local variations of German and sometimes you will hear people speaking in a way that seems quite different from what is shown in this *Guide*. However, almost everybody also speaks, or at least understands, the form of German given here, which is the one taught in the German schools.

*How to Use the Records and Guide

This *Guide* is not intended to give you a complete command of the language. If you want to embark upon a somewhat extensive study of the spoken language you should obtain the USAFI course, Spoken German—see the current USAFI Catalog for instructions. This *Guide* will, however, enable you to carry on simple conversations in German.

The records that go with this *Guide* give you a number of the most important words and phrases in German. Read the section called *Hints on Pronunciation* and then listen to the records until you know the *Useful Words and Phrases* by heart. Repeat each word out loud right after you hear it and say it exactly the way the German speaker does. Imitate the pronunciation as closely as you can, just as you might mimic someone who has an unusual accent. Try to get every detail of the pronunciation, even the rhythm and the intonation. Follow the words in your *Guide* but use them only as a reminder; if you hear something different from what you see written, go by what you hear. Remember that you can't get the sound of a language from the printed word alone—you have to use your ears even more than your eyes. If you don't have the records and can't get a German speaker to read the words, you will have to rely on the *Hints on Pronunciation* alone.

By the time you have practiced the *Useful Words and Phrases* several times you will know what sound each letter stands for in the *Guide*. You will then be able to pronounce the *Additional Expressions* even though you have not actually heard them and you will be able to form sentences of your own by using the section called *Fill-In Sentences*.

**Hints on Pronunciation

If you have studied German before, you may not need additional practice in pronunciation. However,

unless you have had a chance to try out your German and know that you are understood without any difficulty, you had better do a little practicing.

All the words and phrases in this *Guide* are written both in German spelling and in a simplified spelling which you read like English. (Don't use the German spelling, the one given in parentheses, unless you have studied German before.) *Read the simplified spelling as though it were English*. Each letter or combination of letters is used for the sound it usually stands for in English and it *always* stands for that sound. Thus, *oo* is always pronounced as it is in *too, boot, tooth, roost*, never as anything else. Say these words and then pronounce the vowel sound by itself. That is the sound you must use every time you see *oo* in the *Pronunciation* column. If you should use some other sound—for example, the sound of *oo* in *blood*—you may be misunderstood.

Syllables that are accented, that is, pronounced louder than others, are written in capital letters. Curved lines (‿) are used to show sounds that are pronounced together without any break; for example, *P‿FEN-nik* meaning "pfennig," *P‿FEF-fer* meaning "pepper."

Special Points

Here are a few points to note as you listen to the records:

AY	as in *may, say, play* but don't drawl it the way we do in English. Example: *TAY* meaning "tea."
O or *OH*	as in *go, so, oh, note, joke* but don't drawl it the way we do in English. Example: *VO* meaning "where."
AI	as in *aisle* Example: *AINSS* meaning "one."
EW	stands for a sound we do not have in English. To make it you round your lips as though to say the *oo* in *boo* and at the same time say the *ee* in *bee*. Example: *guh-MEW-zuh* meaning "vegetables."
ER	stands for a sound somewhat like the one in *her* except that you round your lips as you make the sound. Example: *TSVERLF* meaning "twelve."
KH	stands for a sound something like the one you make when you clear your throat to spit. Example: *NAHKH* meaning "toward."

*Records no longer available.   ** *ow* as in *now*; *ai* as in *aisle*

361

Memory Key

AY	as in *day* but not so drawled.
O or OH	as in *go* but not so drawled.
AI	as in *aisle*
EW	for the sound in *bee* said with the lips rounded.
ER	for the sound in *her* said with the lips rounded.
KH	for a sound which is like the one you make when you clear your throat to spit.

USEFUL WORDS AND PHRASES

The following is the exact wording of the German Language Records issued with this *Guide:*

These records give you a few useful phrases in German. To learn to say these phrases so that you will be understood, imitate the sounds exactly as you hear them. You will hear the English first, followed by the German; then repeat the German out loud, and say it *good und loud.* Remember! Repeat every German phrase right after you hear it.

In the *German Language Guide* which should be used with these records, all the phrases you will hear are written both in German spelling and in a simplified spelling which you read like English. Don't use the German spelling unless you have studied German before.

Listen to the records six or seven times and you will know the phrases by heart.

GREETINGS AND GENERAL PHRASES

English	Pronunciation and German Spelling
Good morning	*GOO-ten MAWR-gen* (Guten Morgen)
Good day	*GOO-ten TAHK* (Guten Tag)
Good evening	*GOO-ten AH-bent* (Guten Abend)
How are you?	*vee GAYT ess ee-nen?* (Wie geht es Ihnen?)
Sir	*main HAYR* (mein Herr)
Madam	*G‿NAY-dig-uh FROW* (gnädige Frau)
Miss	*G‿NAY-dig-ess FROY-lain* (gnädiges Fräulein)

When you address a person by name you say:

Mr. Schmidt	*HAYR SHMIT* (Herr Schmidt)
Mrs. Schmidt	*FROW SHMIT* (Frau Schmidt)
Miss Schmidt	*FROY-lain SHMIT* (Fräulein Schmidt)
Please	*BIT-tuh* (Bitte)
Excuse me	*fayr-TSAI-oong* (Verzeihung)
Thank you	*DAN-kuh* (Danke)

When someone thanks you, you answer with the word for "please."

English	Pronunciation and German Spelling
Please	*BIT-tuh* (Bitte)
Yes	*YA* (Ja)
No	*NAIN* (Nein)
Do you understand?	*fer-SHTAY-en zee?* (Verstehen Sie?)
I understand	*ish fer-SHTAY-uh* (Ich verstehe)
I don't understand	*ish fer-SHTAY-uh nisht* (Ich verstehe nicht)
Speak slowly	*SHPRESH-en zee LAHNK-zahm* (Sprechen Sie langsam)
Please repeat	*BIT-tuh vee-der-HO-len zee* (Bitte wiederholen Sie)

LOCATION

When you need directions to get somewhere you use the phrase "Where is?" and then add the words you need.

English	Pronunciation and German Spelling
Where is	*VO IST* (Wo ist)
a restaurant	*ain ress-to-RAHNG* (ein Restaurant)
Where is a restaurant?	*VO ist ain ress-to-RAHNG?* (Wo ist ein Restaurant?)
a hotel	*ain ho-TEL* (ein Hotel)
Where is a hotel?	*VO ist ain ho-TEL?* (Wo ist ein Hotel?)
a railroad station	*ain BAHN-hohf* (ein Bahnhof)
Where is a railroad station?	*VO ist ain BAHN-hohf?* (Wo ist ein Bahnhof?)
a toilet	*ai-nuh twa-LET-tuh* (eine Toilette)
Where is a toilet?	*VO ist ai-nuh twa-LET-tuh?* (Wo ist eine Toilette?)

DIRECTIONS

The answer to your question "Where is such and such?" may be "To the right" or "To the left" or "Straight ahead," so you need to know these phrases.

To the right	*nahkh RESHTS* (nach rechts)
To the left	*nahkh LINKS* (nach links)

In the word *NAHKH* you heard a sound you must practice. It is written in your *Language Guide* as *kh.* Listen to the word again and repeat: *NAHKH, NAHKH.* It is like clearing your throat when you have to spit. Try just the sound again: *kh, kh*

Straight ahead	*guh-RA-duh-OWSS* (geradeaus)

It is sometimes useful to say "Please show me."

** *ow* as in *now; ai* as in *aisle*

English	Pronunciation and German Spelling
Please show me	BIT-tuh TSAI-gen zee meer (Bitte zeigen Sie mir)

If you are driving and ask the distance to another town, it will be given you in kilometers, not miles.

Kilometer	kee-lo-MAY-ter (Kilometer)

One kilometer equals ⅝ of a mile.

NUMBERS

You need to know the numbers.

One	AINSS	eins
Two	TSVAI	zwei
Three	DRAI	drei
Four	FEER	vier
Five	FEWNF	fünf
Six	ZEKS	sechs
Seven	ZEE-ben	sieben
Eight	AHKHT	acht
Nine	NOYN	neun
Ten	TSAYN	zehn
Eleven	ELF	elf
Twelve	TSVERLF	zwölf

Notice the sound of er in the last word. Listen to the word again and repeat: TSVERLF, TSVERLF. We don't have this sound in English, but the sound we have in "her" is close to it. Round your lips as though you were pronouncing the "o" in go, and at the same time say the er in her. Try just the sound again: er, er.

Thirteen	DRAI-tsayn	dreizehn
Fourteen	FEER-tsayn	vierzehn
Fifteen	FEWNF-tsayn	fünfzehn
Sixteen	ZESH-tsayn	sechzehn
Seventeen	ZEEP-tsayn	siebzehn
Eighteen	AHKH-tsayn	achtzehn
Nineteen	NOYN-tsayn	neunzehn
Twenty	TSVAHN-tsik	zwanzig

To say "twenty-one," "twenty-two," etc. you say in German "one and twenty," "two and twenty," etc.

English	Pronunciation and German Spelling	
Twenty-one	AIN-oont-tsvahn-tsik	einundzwanzig
Twenty-two	TSVAI-oont-tsvahn-tsik	zweiundzwanzig
Thirty	DRAI-sik	dreissig
Forty	FEER-tsik	vierzig
Fifty	FEWNF-tsik	fünfzig
Sixty	ZESH-tsik	sechzig

Seventy	ZEEP-tsik	siebzig
Eighty	AHKH-tsik	achtzig
Ninety	NOYN-tsik	neunzig
Hundred	HOON-dert	hundert
Thousand	TOW-zent	tausend

WHAT'S THIS ?

When you want to know the name of something you can say "What's this?" or "What's that?" and point to the thing you mean.

English	Pronunciation and German Spelling
What is	VAHSS IST (Was ist)
this	DEESS (dies)
What's this?	VAHSS ist DEESS? (Was ist dies?)
What's that?	VAHSS ist DAHSS? (Was ist das?)

ASKING FOR THINGS

When you want something, use the phrase "I want" and then add the name of the thing wanted. Always use "Please"—BIT-tuh.

I want	ish MERSH-tuh (Ich möchte)
cigarettes	tsee-ga-RET-ten (Zigaretten)
I want cigarettes	ish MERSH-tuh tsee-ga-RET-ten (Ich möchte Zigaretten)
to eat	ESS-sen (essen)
I want to eat	ish MERSH-tuh ESS-sen (Ich möchte essen)

Here are the words for some of the things you may require.

English	Pronunciation and German Spelling
drinking water	TRINK-vahss-ser (Trinkwasser)
bread	BROHT (Brot)
butter	BOOT-ter (Butter)
eggs	AI-er (Eier)
cheese	KAY-zuh (Käse)
meat	FLAISH (Fleisch)
pork	SHVAI-nuh-flaish (Schweinefleisch)
mutton	HAHM-mel-flaish (Hammelfleisch)
veal	KAHLP-flaish (Kalbfleisch)
beef	RINT-flaish (Rindfleisch)
chicken	HOON (Huhn)
fish	FISH (Fisch)
soup	ZOOP-puh (Suppe)
vegetables	guh-MEW-zuh (Gemüse)

* * ow as in now; ai as in aisle

You have just heard another sound you must practice. It is written in your *Guide* as *ew*. Listen to the word again and repeat: *guh-MEW-zuh, guh-MEW-zuh*. To make this sound you round your lips as though to say *oo* but say *ee* instead. Try just the sound again: *ew, ew*.

English	Pronunciation and German Spelling
potatoes	*kar-TAWF-feln* (Kartoffeln)
beets	*RO-tuh REW-ben* (rote Rüben)
beans	*BO-nen* (Bohnen)
cabbage	*KOHL* (Kohl)
salad	*za-LAHT* (Salat)
fruit	*OHPST* (Obst)
milk	*MILSH* (Milch)
salt	*ZAHLTS* (Salz)
pepper	*P_FEF-fer* (Pfeffer)
sugar	*TSOOK-ker* (Zucker)
chocolate	*sho-ko-LA-duh* (Schokolade)
tea	*TAY* (Tee)
coffee	*KAHF-fay* (Kaffee)
a cup of coffee	*ai-nuh TAHSS-suh KAHF-fay* (eine Tasse Kaffee)
wine	*VAIN* (Wein)
beer	*BEER* (Bier)
a glass of beer	*ain GLAHSS BEER* (ein Glas Bier)
tobacco	*TA-bahk* (Tabak)
matches	*SHTRAISH-herl-tser* (Streichhölzer)

MONEY

To find out how much things cost, you say

How much	*vee-FEEL*	Wieviel
costs	*KAWSS-tet*	kostet
that	*DAHSS*	das
How much does that cost?	*vee-feel KAWSS-tet DAHSS?*	(Wieviel kostet das?)

The answer will be given you in marks and pfennigs

mark	*MARK* (Mark)
pfennig	*P_FEN-nik* (Pfennig)

TIME

When you want to know what time it is, you say really "How late is it?"

English	Pronunciation and German Spelling
What time is it?	*vee SHPAYT ist ess?* (Wie spät ist es?)
Two o'clock	*TSVAI OOR* (zwei Uhr)
Ten past two	*TSAYN nahkh TSVAI* (zehn nach Zwei)

English	Pronunciation and German Spelling
Quarter past five	*FEER-tel nahkh FEWNF* (viertel nach Fünf)

"Half past six" is "six o'clock thirty" or "half seven."

Half past six	*ZEKS oor DRAI-sik* (sechs Uhr dreissig) or *HAHLP ZEE-ben* (halb Sieben).

"A quarter of eight" is "three quarters eight."

Quarter of eight	*DRAI-feer-tel AHKHT* (dreiviertel Acht)

"Five minutes to nine" is "five minutes before nine."

Five minutes to nine	*FEWNF mee-NOO-ten for NOYN* (fünf Minuten vor Neun)

For the hours after 12 noon it is customary to say "thirteen o'clock"—*DRAI-tsayn OOR*, and so on, just as we do in the Army.

If you want to know when a movie starts or when a train leaves, you say:

English	Pronunciation and German Spelling
When	*VAHN* (Wann)
begins	*buh-GINT* (beginnt)
the movie	*dahss KEE-no* (das Kino)
When does the movie start?	*VAHN buh-GINT dahss KEE-no?* (Wann beginnt das Kino?)
leaves	*GAYT* (geht)
the train	*dayr TSOOK* (der Zug)
When does the train leave?	*vahn GAYT dayr TSOOK?* (Wann geht der Zug?)
Yesterday	*GESS-tern* (gestern)
Today	*HOY-tuh* (heute)
Tomorrow	*MAWR-gen* (morgen)

The days of the week are:

Sunday	*ZAWN-tahk* (Sonntag)
Monday	*MOHN-tahk* (Montag)
Tuesday	*DEENSS-tahk* (Dienstag)
Wednesday	*MIT-vawkh* (Mittwoch)
Thursday	*DAWN-nerss-tahk* (Donnerstag)
Friday	*FRAI-tahk* (Freitag)
Saturday	*ZAMSS-tahk* (Samstag) or *ZAWN-ah-bent* (Sonnabend)

OTHER USEFUL PHRASES

The following phrases will be useful.

** *ow* as in *now; ai* as in *aisle*

English	Pronunciation and German Spelling
What is your name?	*VEE HAI-sen zee?* (Wie heissen Sie?)
My name is___	*ish HAI-suh___* (Ich heisse___)
How do you say table (or anything else) in German?	*vahss ZA-gen zee fewr table owf DOYTSH?* (Was sagen Sie für table auf Deutsch?)
I am an American	*ish bin ah-may-ree-KA-ner* (Ich bin Amerikaner)
Please help me	*BIT-tuh HEL-fen zee meer* (Bitte helfen Sie mir)
Where is the nearest town?	*VO ist dee NAYSH-stuh AWRT-shaft?* (Wo ist die nächste Ortschaft?)
Good-by	*owf VEE-der-zayn* (Auf Wiedersehen)

ADDITIONAL EXPRESSIONS

English	Pronunciation and German Spelling
I am hungry	*ish HA-buh HOONG-er* (Ich habe Hunger)
I am thirsty	*ish HA-buh DOORST* (Ich habe Durst)
Halt! or Stop!	*HAHLT!* (Halt!)
Come here!	*KAWM-men zee HAYR!* (Kommen Sie her!)
Quickly	*SHNEL* (schnell)
Come quickly!	*KAWM-men zee SHNEL!* (Kommen Sie schnell!)
Go quickly!	*GAY-en zee SHNEL!* (Gehen Sie schnell!)
Help!	*HIL-fuh!* (Hilfe!)
Bring help!	*HO-len zee HIL-fuh!* (Holen Sie Hilfe!)
I am lost	*ish HA-buh mish fayr-LOW-fen* (Ich habe mich verlaufen)
I will pay you	*ish VAYR-duh EE-nen GELT GAY-ben* (Ich werde Ihnen Geld geben)
Where are the American sailors?	*VO ZINT dee a-may-ree-KA-nee-shen mah-TROH-zen?* (Wo sind die amerikanischen Matrosen?)
Where is the town?	*VO IST dee SHTAHT?* (Wo ist die Stadt?)
Where is it?	*VO IST ess?* (Wo ist es?)
How far is it?	*vee VAIT ist ess?* (Wie weit ist es?)
Which way is north?	*VO ist NAWR-den?* (Wo ist Norden?)
Which is the road to___?	*VO ist dayr VAYK nahkh___?* (Wo ist der Weg nach___?)
Draw me a map	*TSAISH-nen zee meer ai-nuh KAR-tuh* (Zeichnen Sie mir eine Karte)
Take me there	*BRIN-gen zee mish dawrt HIN* (Bringen Sie mich dort hin)
Take me to a doctor	*BRIN-gen zee mish tsoo AI-nem ARTST* (Bringen Sie mich zu einem Arzt)
Take me to a hospital	*BRIN-gen zee mish tsoo AI-nem la-tsa-RET* (Bringen Sie mich zu einem Lazarett)
Danger!	*guh-FAR!* (Gefahr!)

English	Pronunciation and German Spelling
Watch out!	*OWF-pahss-sen!* (Aufpassen!)
Gas!	*GAHSS!* (Gas!)
Take cover!	*DEK-koong!* (Deckung!)
Wait a moment!	*VAR-ten zee ai-nen OW-gen-blik!* (Warten Sie einen Augenblick!)

FILL-IN SENTENCES

In this section you will find a number of sentences, each containing a blank space which can be filled in with any one of the words in the list that follows. For example, to say "Where can I get some soap?" look for the phrase "Where can I get___?" in the English column and find the German expression given beside it: *VO kahn ish___buh-KAWM-men.* Then look for "soap" in the list that follows; the German word is *ZAI-fuh.* Put the word for "soap" in the blank space and you get *VO kahn ish ZAI-fuh buh-KAWM-men?*

English	Pronunciation and German Spelling
I want___	*ish MERSH-tuh___* (Ich möchte___)
We want___	*veer MERSH-ten___* (Wir möchten___)
Give me___	*GAY-ben zee meer___* (Geben Sie mir___)
Bring me___	*BRIN-gen zee meer___* (Bringen Sie mir___)
Get me___	*HO-len zee meer___* (Holen Sie mir___)
Where can I get___?	*VO kahn ish___ buh-KAWM-men?* (Wo kann ich___ bekommen?)
I have___	*ish HA-buh___* (Ich habe___)
We have___	*veer HA-ben___* (Wir haben___)
Have you___?	*HA-ben zee___?* (Haben Sie___?)

EXAMPLE

I want___	*ish MERSH-tuh___* (Ich möchte___)
food	*ET-vahss tsoo ESS-sen* (etwas zu essen)
I want food	*ish MERSH-tuh ET-vahss tsoo ESS-sen* (Ich möchte etwas zu essen)

apples	*EP-fel* (Äpfel)
bacon	*SHPEK* (Speck)
beefsteak	*BEEF-shtayk* (Beefsteak)
boiled water	*AHP-guh-kawkh-tess VAHSS-ser* (abgekochtes Wasser)
carrots	*GEL-buh REW-ben* (gelbe Rüben)
cucumbers	*GOOR-ken* (Gurken)
grapes	*TROW-ben* (Trauben)
ham	*SHIN-ken* (Schinken)
a meal	*ai-nuh MAHL-tsait* (eine Mahlzeit)
onions	*TSVEE-beln* (Zwiebeln)
oranges	*ahp-fel-ZEE-nen* (Apfelsinen)
peas	*AYRP-sen* (Erbsen)
rice	*RAISS* (Reis)

* * *ow as in* now; *ai as in* aisle

English	Pronunciation and German Spelling
spinach	shpee-NAHT (Spinat)
tangerines	mahn-da-REE-nen (Mandarinen)
turnips	VAI-suh REW-ben (weisse Rüben)
a cup	ai-nuh TAHSS-suh (eine Tasse)
a fork	ai-nuh GA-bel (eine Gabel)
a glass	ain GLAHSS (ein Glas)
a knife	ain MESS-ser (ein Messer)
a plate	ai-nen TEL-ler (einen Teller)
a spoon	ai-nen LERF-fel (einen Löffel)
a bed	ain BET (ein Bett)
bedding	BET-tsoyk (Bettzeug)
blankets	DEK-ken (Decken)
a mattress	ai-nuh ma-TRA-tsuh (eine Matratze)
a pillow	ain KISS-sen (ein Kissen)
a room	ain TSIM-mer (ein Zimmer)
sheets	BET-la-ken (Bettlaken)
cigars	tsee-GAR-ren (Zigarren)
a pipe	ai-nuh P⌣FAI-fuh (eine Pfeife)
pipe tobacco	P⌣FAI-fen-ta-bahk (Pfeifentabak)
ink	TIN-tuh (Tinte)
a pen	ai-nen FAY-der-hahl-ter (einen Federhalter)
a pencil	ai-nen BLAI-shtift (einen Bleistift)
a comb	ai-nen KAHM (einen Kamm)
hot water	HAI-sess VAHSS-ser (heisses Wasser)
a razor	ai-nen ra-ZEER-ahp-pa-raht (einen Rasierapparat)
razor blades	ra-ZEER-kling-en (Rasierklingen)
a shaving brush	ai-nen ra-ZEER-pin-zel (einen Rasierpinsel)
shaving soap	ra-ZEER-zai-fuh (Rasierseife)
soap	ZAI-fuh (Seife)
a toothbrush	ai-nuh TSAHN-bewr-stuh (eine Zahnbürste)
tooth paste	TSAHN-kraym (Zahncreme)
a towel	ain HAHN-tookh (ein Handtuch)
a handkerchief	ain TA-shen-tookh (ein Taschentuch)
a raincoat	ai-nen RAY-gen-mahn-tel (einen Regenmantel)
a shirt	ain HEMT (ein Hemd)
shoe laces	SHNEWR-zen-kel (Schnürsenkel)
shoe polish	SHOO-kraym (Schuhcreme)

English	Pronunciation and German Spelling
shoes	SHOO-uh (Schuhe)
undershirt	OON-ter-hemt (Unterhemd)
undershorts	OON-ter-ho-zen (Unterhosen)
underwear	OON-ter-vesh-shuh (Unterwäsche)
buttons	KNERP-fuh (Knöpfe)
a needle	ai-nuh NA-del (eine Nadel)
pins	SHTEK-na-deln (Stecknadeln)
safety pins	ZISH-sher-haits-na-deln (Sicherheitsnadeln)
thread	FA-den (Faden)
aspirin	ah-spee-REEN (Aspirin)
a bandage	ai-nuh BIN-duh (eine Binde)
cotton	VAHT-tuh (Watte)
a disinfectant	ain dess-in-fekts-YOHNSS-mit-tel (ein Desinfektionsmittel)
iodine	YOHT (Jod)
a laxative	ain AHP-fewr-mit-tel (ein Abführmittel)

I want to___	ish MERSH-tuh___ (Ich möchte___)

EXAMPLE

I want to___ eat	ish MERSH-tuh___ (Ich möchte___) ESS-sen (essen)
I want to eat	ish MERSH-tuh ESS-sen (Ich möchte essen)
buy it	ess KOW-fen (es kaufen)
drink	TRIN-ken (trinken)
have my clothes washed	mai-nuh ZA-khen VA-shen lahss-sen (meine Sachen waschen lassen)
rest	mish OWSS-roo-en (mich ausruhen)
sleep	SHLA-fen (schlafen)
take a bath	BA-den (baden)
wash up	mish VA-shen (mich waschen)

When you want a haircut or shave you say:

Haircut, please! BIT-tuh HA-ruh-shnai-den! (Bitte, Haareschneiden!)

Shave, please! BIT-tuh ra-ZEE-ren! (Bitte, Rasieren!)

Where is___?	VO ist___? (Wo ist___?)

EXAMPLE

Where is___?	VO ist___? (Wo ist___?)
a barber	ain free-ZER (ein Friseur)
Where is a barber?	VO ist ain free-ZER? (Wo ist ein Friseur?)
a bridge	ai-nuh BREWK-kuh (eine Brücke)

** ow as in now; ai as in aisle

English	Pronunciation and German Spelling
a bus	*ain AWM-nee-booss* (ein Omnibus)
a church	*ai-nuh KEER-shuh* (eine Kirche)
a clothing store	*ain KLAI-der-la-den* (ein Kleiderladen)
a dentist	*ain TSAHN-artst* (ein Zahnarzt)
a doctor	*ain ARTST* (ein Arzt)
a drugstore	*ai-nuh dro-gay-REE* (eine Drogerie)
a fountain (or well)	*ain BROON-nen* (ein Brunnen)
a garage	*ai-nuh ga-RA-shuh* (eine Garage)
a grocery store	*ain LAY-benss-mit-tel-guh-SHEFT* (ein Lebensmittelgeschäft)
a hospital	*ain la-tsa-RET* (ein Lazarett)
a house	*ain HOWSS* (ein Haus)
a laundry	*ai-nuh vesh-shuh-RAI* (eine Wascherei)
a mechanic	*ain may-SHA-nee-ker* (ein Mechaniker)
a pharmacy	*ai-nuh ah-po-TAY-kuh* (eine Apotheke)
a policeman	*ain po-lee-TSIST* (ein Polizist)
a porter	*ain guh-PAYK-tray-ger* (ein Gepäckträger)
a shoemaker	*ain SHOO-ster* (ein Schuster)
a (natural) spring	*ai-nuh KVEL-luh* (eine Quelle)
a tailor	*ain SHNAI-der* (ein Schneider)
a telephone	*ain tay-lay-FOHN* (ein Telephon)
a workman	*ain AR-bai-ter* (ein Arbeiter)
the camp	*dahss TROOP-pen-la-ger* (das Truppenlager)
the city	*dee SHTAHT* (die Stadt)
the highway	*dee LAHNT-shtra-suh* (die Landstrasse)
the main street	*dee HOWPT-shtra-suh* (die Hauptstrasse)
the market	*dayr MARKT* (der Markt)
the nearest town	*dee NAYSH-stuh AWRT-shaft* (die nächste Ortschaft)
the police station	*dahss po-lee-TSAI-ahmt* (das Polizeiamt)
the post office	*dahss PAWST-ahmt* (das Postamt)
the railroad	*dee AI-zen-bahn* (die Eisenbahn)
the river	*dayr FLOOSS* (der Fluss)
the road	*dayr VAYK* (der Weg)
the telegraph window (in post office)	*dayr tay-lay-GRAHM-shahl-ter* (der Telegrammschalter)

I am___	*ish bin___* (Ich bin___)
He is___	*ayr ist___* (Er ist___)
We are___	*veer zint___* (Wir sind___)
They are___	*zee zint___* (Sie sind___)
Are you___?	*zint zee___?* (Sind Sie___?)

EXAMPLE

I am___	*ish bin___* (Ich bin___)
sick	*KRAHNK* (krank)
I am sick	*ish bin KRAHNK* (Ich bin krank)

English	Pronunciation and German Spelling
tired	*MEW-duh* (müde)
wounded	*fer-VOON-det* (verwundet)

Is it___?	*ist ess___?* (Ist es___?)
It is___	*ess ist___* (Es ist___)
It is not___	*ess ist nisht___* (Es ist nicht___)
That is___	*dahss ist___* (Das ist___)
This is___	*deess ist___* (Dies ist___)
That is too___	*dahss ist tsoo___* (Das ist zu___)
That is very___	*dahss ist zayr___* (Das ist sehr___)

EXAMPLE

It is not___ good	*ess ist nisht___* (Es ist nicht___ gut) *GOOT*
It is not good	*ess ist nisht GOOT* (Es ist nicht gut)
bad	*SHLESHT* (schlecht)
expensive	*TOY-er* (teuer)
large	*GROHSS* (gross)
small	*KLAIN* (klein)
clean	*ZOW-ber* (sauber)
dirty	*SHMOO-tsik* (schmutzig)
cold	*KAHLT* (kalt)
hot	*HAISS* (heiss)
few	*VAY-nik* (wenig)
much	*FEEL* (viel)
enough	*guh-NOOK* (genug)
far	*VAIT* (weit)
near	*NA-huh* (nahe)
here	*HEER* (hier)
there	*DAWRT* (dort)

IMPORTANT SIGNS

German	English
Halt!	Stop!
Langsam!	Go slow!
Gefahr!	Danger!
Einbahnstrasse	One Way Street
Einbahnverkehr	One Way Traffic
Keine Durchfahrt	No Thoroughfare
Rechts fahren	Keep To The Right
Strasse im Bau	Road Under Construction
Kurve	Dangerous Curve
Kreuzung	Dangerous Crossing
Bahnübergang	Grade Crossing
Parken verboten	No Parking
Kein Zutritt	No Admittance
Frauen *or* Damen	Women

** *ow* as in *now; ai* as in *aisle*

IMPORTANT SIGNS

German	English
Männer *or* Herren	Men
Nichtraucher *or* Rauchen verboten	No Smoking
Eingang	Entrance
Ausgang	Exit

ALPHABETICAL WORD LIST

English	Pronunciation and German Spelling

A

a	*ain* (ein)
	or ain-en (einen)
	or ain-uh (eine)
am	
I am___	*ish BIN___* (Ich bin___)
American	*ah-may-ree-KA-ner* (Amerikaner)
American sailors	*ah-may-ree-KA-nee-shuh mah-TROH-zen* (amerikanische Matrosen)
I am an American	*ish BIN ah-may-ree-KA-ner* (Ich bin Amerikaner)
and	*oont* (und)
apples	*EP-fel* (Äpfel)
are	*zint* (sind)
Are you___?	*zint zee___?* (Sind Sie___?)
They are___	*zee zint___* (Sie sind___)
We are___	*veer zint___* (Wir sind___)
aspirin	*ah-spee-REEN* (Aspirin)

B

bacon	*SHPEK* (Speck)
bad	*SHLESHT* (schlecht)
bandage	*BIN-duh* (Binde)
barber	*free-ZER* (Friseur)
bath	
take a bath	*BA-den* (baden)
beans	*BO-nen* (Bohnen)
bed	*BET* (Bett)
bedding	*BET-tsoyk* (Bettzeug)
beef	*RINT-flaish* (Rindfleisch)
beefsteak	*BEEF-shtayk* (Beefsteak)
beer	*BEER* (Bier)
a glass of beer	*ain GLAHSS BEER* (ein Glas Bier)
beets	*RO-tuh REW-ben* (rote Rüben)
begins	*buh-GINT* (beginnt)
blankets	*DEK-ken* (Decken)
boiled water	*AHP-guh-kawkh-tess VAHSS-ser* (abgekochtes Wasser)

English	Pronunciation and German Spelling
bread	*BROHT* (Brot)
bridge	*BREWK-kuh* (Brücke)
bring	
Bring help!	*HO-len zee HIL-fuh!* (Holen Sie Hilfe!)
Bring me___	*BRIN-gen zee meer___* (Bringen Sie mir___)
bus	*AWM-nee-booss* (Omnibus)
butter	*BOOT-ter* (Butter)
buttons	*KNERP-fuh* (Knöpfe)
buy	
buy it	*ess KOW-fen* (es kaufen)

C

cabbage	*KOHL* (Kohl)
camp	*TROOP-pen-la-ger* (Truppenlager)
can	
Where can I get___?	*VO kahn ish___ buh-KAWM-men?* (Wo kann ich___ bekommen?)
carrots	*GEL-buh REW-ben* (gelbe Rüben)
cheese	*KAY-zuh* (Käse)
chicken	*HOON* (Huhn)
chocolate	*sho-ko-LA-duh* (Schokolade)
church	*KEER-shuh* (Kirche)
cigarettes	*tsee-ga-RET-ten* (Zigaretten)
cigars	*tsee-GAR-ren* (Zigarren)
city	*SHTAHT* (Stadt)
clean	*ZOW-ber* (sauber)
clothing store	*KLAI-der-la-den* (Kleiderladen)
coffee	*KAHF-fay* (Kaffee)
a cup of coffee	*ai-nuh TAHSS-suh KAHF-fay* (eine Tasse Kaffee)
cold	*KAHLT* (kalt)
comb	*KAHM* (Kamm)
Come!	*KAWM-men zee!* (Kommen Sie!)
Come here!	*KAWM-men zee HAYR!* (Kommen Sie her!)
Come quickly!	*KAWM-men zee SHNEL!* (Kommen Sie schnell!)
cost	*KAWST-et* (kostet)
How much does that cost?	*vee-feel KAWSS-tet DAHSS?* (Wieviel kostet das?)
cotton	*VAHT-tuh* (Watte)
cover	
Take cover!	*DEK-koong!* (Deckung!)
cucumbers	*GOOR-ken* (Gurken)
cup	*TAHSS-suh* (Tasse)

** *ow* as in *now*; *ai* as in *aisle*

English	*Pronunciation and German Spelling*
a cup of___	*ai-nuh TAHSS-suh___* (eine Tasse___)

D

Danger!	*guh-FARl* (Gefahr!)
day	*TAHK* (Tag)
Good day	*GOO-ten TAHK* (Guten Tag)
dentist	*TSAHN-artst* (Zahnarzt)
dirty	*SHMOO-tsik* (schmutzig)
disinfectant	*dess-in-fekts-YOHNSS-mit-tel* (Desinfektionsmittel)
Do you under-stand?	*fer-SHTAY-en zee?* (Verstehen Sie?)
doctor	*ARTST* (Arzt)
Take me to a doctor	*BRIN-gen zee mish tsoo ai-nem ARTST* (Bringen Sie mich zu einem Arzt)
Draw me a map	*TSAISH-nen zee meer ai-nuh KAR-tuh* (Zeichnen Sie mir eine Karte)
drink	*TRIN-ken* (trinken)
drinking water	*TRINK-vahss-ser* (Trinkwasser)
drugstore	*dro-gay-REE* (Drogerie)

E

eat	*ESS-sen* (essen)
something to eat	*ET-vahss tsoo ESS-sen* (etwas zu essen)
I want to eat	*ish MERSH-tuh ESS-sen* (Ich möchte essen)
eggs	*AI-er* (Eier)
eight	*AHKHT* (acht)
eighteen	*AHKH-tsayn* (achtzehn)
eighty	*AHKH-tsik* (achtzig)
eleven	*ELF* (elf)
enough	*guh-NOOK* (genug)
Excuse me	*fayr-TSAI-oong* (Verzeihung)
evening	*AH-bent* (Abend)
Good evening	*GOO-ten AH-bent* (Guten Abend)
expensive	*TOY-er* (teuer)

F

far	*VAIT* (weit)
How far is it?	*vee VAIT ist ess?* (Wie weit ist es?)
Is it far?	*ist ess VAIT?* (Ist es weit?)
few	*VAY-nik* (wenig)
fifteen	*FEWNF-tsayn* (fünfzehn)
fifty	*FEWNF-tsik* (fünfzig)
fish	*FISH* (Fisch)
five	*FEWNF* (fünf)
food	*ET-vahss tsoo ESS-sen* (etwas zu essen)
fork	*GA-bel* (Gabel)
forty	*FEER-tsik* (vierzig)

English	*Pronunciation and German Spelling*
fountain (well)	*BROON-nen* (Brunnen)
four	*FEER* (vier)
fourteen	*FEER-tsayn* (vierzehn)
Friday	*FRAI-tahk* (Freitag)
fruit	*OHPST* (Obst)

G

garage	*ga-RA-shuh* (Garage)
Gas!	*GAHSS!* (Gas!)
German	*DOYTSH* (Deutsch)
in German	*owf DOYTSH* (auf Deutsch)
get	
Get me___	*HO-len zee meer___* (Holen Sie mir___)
Where can I get___?	*VO kahn ish___buh-KAWM-men?* (Wo kann ich bekommen?)
Give me___	*GAY-ben zee meer___* (Geben Sie mir___)
glass	*GLAHSS* (Glas)
a glass of___	*ain GLAHSS___* (ein Glas___)
Go!	*GAY-en zeel* (Gehen Sie!)
Go quickly!	*GAY-en zee SHNEL!* (Gehen Sie schnell!)
good	*GOOT* (gut)
Good day	*GOO-ten TAHK* (Guten Tag)
Good evening	*GOO-ten AH-bent* (Guten Abend)
Good morning	*GOO-ten MAWR-gen* (Guten Morgen)
Good-by	*owf VEE-der-zayn* (Auf Wiedersehen)
grapes	*TROW-ben* (Trauben)
grocery store	*LAY-benss-mit-tel-guh-SHEFT* (Lebensmittelgeschäft)

H

hair	*HAR* (Haar)
Haircut, please!	*BIT-tuh HA-ruh-shnai-den!* (Bitte, Haareschneiden!)
half	*HAHLP* (halb)
Halt!	*HAHLT!* (Halt!)
ham	*SHIN-ken* (Schinken)
handkerchief	*TA-shen-tookh* (Taschentuch)
have	
Have you___?	*HA-ben zee___?* (Haben Sie___?)
I have___	*ish HA-buh___* (Ich habe___)
We have___	*veer HA-ben___* (Wir haben___)
he	*ayr* (er)
He is___	*ayr ist___* (Er ist___)

** *ow* as in *now; ai* as in *aisle*

English	Pronunciation and German Spelling
Help!	*HIL-fuh!* (Hilfe!)
Bring help!	*HO-len zee HIL-fuh!* (Holen Sie Hilfe!)
Please help me	*BIT-tuh HEL-fen zee meer* (Bitte helfen Sie mir)
here	*HEER* (hier)
It is here	*ess ist HEER* (Es ist hier)
Come here!	*KAWM-men zee hayr!* (Kommen Sie her!)
highway	*LAHNT-shtra-suh* (Landstrasse)
hospital	*la-tsa-RET* (Lazarett)
Take me to a hospital	*BRIN-gen zee mish tsoo AI-nem la-tsa-RET* (Bringen Sie mich zu einem Lazarett)
hot	*HAISS* (heiss)
hot water	*HAI-sess VAHSS-ser* (heisses Wasser)
hotel	*ho-TEL* (Hotel)
Where is a hotel?	*VO ist ain ho-TEL?* (Wo ist ein Hotel?)
house	*HOWSS* (Haus)
how	*VEE* (wie)
How are you?	*vee GAYT ess ee-nen?* (Wie geht es Ihnen?)
How do you say *table* in German?	*vahss ZA-gen zee fewr* table *owf DOYTSH?* (Was sagen Sie für *table* auf Deutsch?)
How far is it?	*vee VAIT ist ess?* (Wie weit ist es?)
How much does that cost?	*vee-feel KAWSS-tet DAHSS?* (Wieviel kostet das?)
hundred	*HOON-dert* (hundert)
hungry	
I am hungry	*ish HA-buh HOONG-er* (Ich habe Hunger)

I

I	*ish* (ich)
I am___	*ish bin___* (Ich bin___)
I have___	*ish HA-buh___* (Ich habe___)
I want___ or I want to___	*ish MERSH-tuh___* (Ich möchte___)
in German	*owf DOYTSH* (auf Deutsch)
ink	*TIN-tuh* (Tinte)
iodine	*YOHT* (Jod)
is	*ist* (ist)
Is it___?	*IST ess___?* (Ist es___?)
It is___	*ess IST___* (Es ist___)
It is not___	*ess ist NISHT___* (Es ist nicht___)

K

kilometer	*kee-lo-MAY-ter* (Kilometer)
knife	*MESS-ser* (Messer)

L

large	*GROHSS* (gross)
laundry	*vesh-shuh-RAI* (Wäscherei)
laxative	*AHP-fewr-mit-tel* (Abführmittel)
leave	*GAYT* (geht)
When does the train leave?	*vahn GAYT dayr TSOOK?* (Wann geht der Zug?)
left	*LINKS* (links)
To the left	*nahkh LINKS* (nach links)
lost	
I am lost	*ish HA-buh mish fayr-LOW-fen* (Ich habe mich verlaufen)

M

madam	*G‿NAY-dig-uh FROW* (gnädige Frau)
main street	*HOWPT-shtra-suh* (Hauptstrasse)
map	*KAR-tuh* (Karte)
Draw me a map	*TSAISH-nen zee meer ai-nuh KAR-tuh* (Zeichnen Sie mir eine Karte)
mark	*MARK* (Mark)
market	*MARKT* (Markt)
matches	*SHTRAISH-herl-tser* (Streichhölzer)
mattress	*ma-TRA-tsuh* (Matratze)
me	*mish* (mich) or *meer* (mir)
meal	*MAHL-tsait* (Mahlzeit)
meat	*FLAISH* (Fleisch)
mechanic	*may-SHA-nee-ker* (Mechaniker)
milk	*MILSH* (Milch)
Miss	*FROY-lain* (Fräulein) or *G‿NAY-dig-ess FROY-lain* (gnädiges Fräulein)
Mister	*HAYR* (Herr)
Monday	*MOHN-tahk* (Montag)
morning	*MAWR-gen* (Morgen)
movie	*KEE-no* (Kino)
When does the movie start?	*VAHN buh-GINT dahss KEE-no?* (Wann beginnt das Kino?)
Mrs.	*FROW* (Frau)
much	*FEEL* (viel)
mutton	*HAHM-mel-flaish* (Hammelfleisch)

N

name	
My name is___	*ish HAI-suh___* (Ich heisse___)
What's your name?	*VEE HAI-sen zee?* (Wie heissen Sie?)

** *ow* as in *now; ai* as in *aisle*

English	Pronunciation and German Spelling
near	*NA-huh* (nahe)
the nearest town	*dee NAYSH-stuh AWRT-shaft* (die nächste Ortschaft)
needle	*NA-del* (Nadel)
nine	*NOYN* (neun)
nineteen	*NOYN-tsayn* (neunzehn)
ninety	*NOYN-tsık* (neunzig)
no	*NAIN* (nein)
north	*NAWR-den* (Norden)
Which way is north?	*VO ist NAWR-den?* (Wo ist Norden?)
not	*nisht* (nicht)

O

English	Pronunciation and German Spelling
one	*AINSS* (eins)
onions	*TSVEE-beln* (Zwiebeln)
oranges	*ahp-fel-ZEE-nen* (Apfelsinen)

P

English	Pronunciation and German Spelling
pay	
I will pay you	*ish VAYR-duh EE-nen GELT GAY-ben* (Ich werde Ihnen Geld geben)
peas	*AYRP-sen* (Erbsen)
pen	*FAY-der-hahl-ter* (Federhalter)
pencil	*BLAI-shtift* (Bleistift)
pepper	*P⌣FEF-fer* (Pfeffer)
pfennig	*P⌣FEN-nik* (Pfennig)
pharmacy	*ah-po-TAY-kuh* (Apotheke)
pillow	*KISS-sen* (Kissen)
pins	*SHTEK-na-deln* (Stecknadeln)
safety pins	*ZISH-sher-haits-na-deln* (Sicherheitsnadeln)
pipe	*P⌣FAI-fuh* (Pfeife)
pipe tobacco	*P⌣FAI-fen-ta-bahk* (Pfeifentabak)
plate	*TEL-ler* (Teller)
Please	*BIT-tuh* (Bitte)
police station	*po-lee-TSAI-ahmt* (Polizeiamt)
policeman	*po-lee-TSIST* (Polizist)
pork	*SHVAI-nuh-flaish* (Schweinefleisch)
porter	*guh-PAYK-tray-ger* (Gepäckträger)
post office	*PAWST-ahmt* (Postamt)
potatoes	*kar-TAWF-feln* (Kartoffeln)

Q

English	Pronunciation and German Spelling
quickly	*SHNEL* (schnell)
Come quickly!	*KAWM-men zee SHNEL!* (Kommen Sie schnell!)

English	Pronunciation and German Spelling
Go quickly!	*GAY-en zee SHNEL!* (Gehen Sie schnell!)

R

English	Pronunciation and German Spelling
railroad	*AI-zen-bahn* (Eisenbahn)
railroad station	*BAHN-hohf* (Bahnhof)
Where is a railroad station?	*VO ist ain BAHN-hohf?* (Wo ist ein Bahnhof?)
raincoat	*RAY-gen-mahn-tel* (Regenmantel)
razor	*ra-ZEER-ahp-pa-raht* (Rasierapparat)
razor blades	*ra-ZEER-kling-en* (Rasierklingen)
repeat	*vee-der-HO-len zee!* (Wiederholen Sie!)
Please repeat	*BIT-tuh vee-der-HO-len zee* (Bitte wiederholen Sie)
rest	
I want to rest	*ish MERSH-tuh mish OWSS-roo-en* (Ich möchte mich ausruhen)
restaurant	*ress-to-RAHNG* (Restaurant)
Where is a restaurant?	*VO ist ain ress-to-RAHNG?* (Wo ist ein Restaurant?)
rice	*RAISS* (Reis)
right	*RESHTS* (rechts)
To the right	*nahkh RESHTS* (nach rechts)
river	*FLOOSS* (Fluss)
road	*VAYK* (Weg)
Which is the road to___?	*VO ist dayr VAYK nahkh___?* (Wo ist der Weg nach___?)
room	*TSIM-mer* (Zimmer)

S

English	Pronunciation and German Spelling
safety pins	*ZISH-sher-haits-na-deln* (Sicherheitsnadeln)
sailors	*mah-TROH-zen* (Matrosen)
Where are the American sailors?	*VO ZINT dee a-may-ree-KA-nee-shen mah-TROH-zen?* (Wo sind die amerikanischen Matrosen?)
salad	*za-LAHT* (Salat)
salt	*ZAHLTS* (Salz)
Saturday	*ZAMSS-tahk* (Samstag) or *ZAWN-ah-bent* (Sonnabend)
(to) say	*ZA-gen* (sagen)
How do you say *table* in German?	*vahss ZA-gen zee fewr table owf DOYTSH?* (Was sagen Sie für *table* auf Deutsch?)
seven	*ZEE-ben* (sieben)
seventeen	*ZEEP-tsayn* (siebzehn)
seventy	*ZEEP-tsik* (siebzig)

** *ow* as in *now*; *ai* as in *aisle*

English	Pronunciation and German Spelling
shave	
Shave, please!	*BIT-tuh ra-ZEE-ren!* (Bitte, Rasieren!)
shaving brush	*ra-ZEER-pin-zel* (Rasierpinsel)
shaving soap	*ra-ZEER-zai-fuh* (Rasierseife)
she	*zee* (sie)
sheets	*BET-la-ken* (Bettlaken)
shirt	*HEMT* (Hemd)
undershirt	*OON-ter-hemt* (Unterhemd)
shoemaker	*SHOO-ster* (Schuster)
shoes	*SHOO-uh* (Schuhe)
shoe laces	*SHNEWR-zen-kel* (Schnürsenkel)
shoe polish	*SHOO-kraym* (Schuhcreme)
show	
Please show me	*BIT-tuh TSAI-gen zee meer* (Bitte zeigen Sie mir)
sick	*KRAHNK* (krank)
sir	*main HAYR* (mein Herr)
six	*ZEKS* (sechs)
sixteen	*ZESH-tsayn* (sechzehn)
sixty	*ZESH-tsik* (sechzig)
sleep	*SHLA-fen* (schlafen)
slowly	*LAHNK-zahm* (langsam)
Speak slowly	*SPRESH-en zee LAHNK-zahm* (Sprechen Sie langsam)
small	*KLAIN* (klein)
soap	*ZAI-fuh* (Seife)
shaving soap	*ra-ZEER-zai-fuh* (Rasierseife)
soup	*ZOOP-puh* (Suppe)
speak	*SPRESH-en zee!* (Sprechen Sie!)
Speak slowly	*SPRESH-en zee LAHNK-zahm* (Sprechen Sie langsam)
spinach	*shpee-NAHT* (Spinat)
spoon	*LERF-fel* (Löffel)
(natural) spring	*KVEL-luh* (Quelle)
start	*buh-GINT* (beginnt)
When does the movie start?	*VAHN buh-GINT dahss KEE-no?* (Wann beginnt das Kino?)
station	
police station	*po-lee-TSAI-ahmt* (Polizeiamt)
railroad station	*BAHN-hohf* (Bahnhof)
Stop!	*HAHLT!* (Halt!)

English	Pronunciation and German Spelling
store	
clothing store	*KLAI-der-la-den* (Kleiderladen)
drugstore	*dro-gay-REE* (Drogerie)
Straight ahead	*guh-RA-duh-OWSS* (geradeaus)
street	*SHTRA-suh* (Strasse)
main street	*HOWPT-shtra-suh* (Hauptstrasse)
sugar	*TSOOK-ker* (Zucker)
Sunday	*ZAWN-tahk* (Sonntag)
T	
tailor	*SHNAI-der* (Schneider)
take	
Take cover!	*DEK-koong!* (Deckung!)
Take me to a doctor	*BRIN-gen zee mish tsoo AI-nem ARTST* (Bringen Sie mich zu einem Arzt)
Take me to a hospital	*BRIN-gen zee mish tsoo AI-nem la-tsa-RET* (Bringen Sie mich zu einem Lazarett)
Take me there	*BRIN-gen zee mish dawrt HIN* (Bringen Sie mich dort hin)
tangerines	*mahn-da-REE-nen* (Mandarinen)
tea	*TAY* (Tee)
telegraph window (in post office)	*tay-lay-GRAHM-shahl-ter* (Telegrammschalter)
telephone	*tay-lay-FOHN* (Telephon)
ten	*TSAYN* (zehn)
Thank you	*DAN-kuh* (Danke)
that	*dahss* (das)
What's that?	*VAHSS ist DAHSS?* (Was ist das?)
the	*dayr* (der) or *dee* (die) or *dahss* (das)
there	*DAWRT* (dort)
Take me there	*BRIN-gen zee mish dawrt HIN* (Bringen Sie mich dort hin)
they	*zee* (sie)
They are___	*zee zint___* (Sie sind___)
thirsty	
I am thirsty	*ish HA-buh DOORST* (Ich habe Durst)
thirteen	*DRAI-tsayn* (dreizehn)
thirty	*DRAI-sik* (dreissig)
this	*DEESS* (dies)
What's this?	*VAHSS ist DEESS?* (Was ist dies?)
thousand	*TOW-zent* (tausend)

* * ow as in now; ai as in aisle

English	Pronunciation and German Spelling
thread	*FA-den* (Faden)
three	*DRAI* (drei)
Thursday	*DAWN-nerss-tahk* (Donnerstag)
time	
What time is it?	*vee SHPAYT ist ess?* (Wie spät ist es?)
tired	*MEW-duh* (müde)
tobacco	*TA-bahk* (Tabak)
today	*HOY-tuh* (heute)
toilet	*twa-LET-tuh* (Toilette)
Where is a toilet?	*VO ist ai-nuh twa-LET-tuh?* (Wo ist eine Toilette?)
tomorrow	*MAWR-gen* (morgen)
too	*tsoo* (zu)
toothbrush	*TSAHN-bewr-stuh* (Zahnbürste)
tooth paste	*TSAHN-kraym* (Zahncreme)
towel	*HAHN-tookh* (Handtuch)
town	*AWRT-shaft* (Ortschaft)
or	*SHTAHT* (Stadt)
the nearest town	*dee NAYSH-stuh AWRT-shaft* (die nächste Ortschaft)
train	*TSOOK* (Zug)
When does the train leave?	*vahn GAYT dayr TSOOK?* (Wann geht der Zug?)
Tuesday	*DEENSS-tahk* (Dienstag)
turnips	*VAI-suh REW-ben* (weisse Rüben)
twelve	*TSVERLF* (zwölf)
twenty	*TSVAHN-tsik* (zwanzig)
two	*TSVAI* (zwei)

U

English	Pronunciation and German Spelling
undershirt	*OON-ter-hemt* (Unterhemd)
undershorts	*OON-ter-ho-zen* (Unterhosen)
understand	
Do you understand?	*fer-SHTAY-en zee?* (Verstehen Sie?)
I understand	*ish fer-SHTAY-uh* (Ich verstehe)
I don't understand	*ish fer-SHTAY-uh nisht* (Ich verstehe nicht)
underwear	*OON-ter-vesh-shuh* (Unterwäsche)

V

English	Pronunciation and German Spelling
veal	*KAHLP-flaish* (Kalbfleisch)
vegetables	*guh-MEW-zuh* (Gemüse)
very	*zayr* (sehr)

W

English	Pronunciation and German Spelling
Wait!	*VAR-ten zee!* (Warten Sie!)
Wait a moment!	*VAR ten zee ai-nen OW-gen-blik!* (Warten Sie einen Augenblick!)
want	
I want___ or I want to___	*ish MERSH-tuh___* (Ich möchte___)
We want___	*veer MERSH-ten___* (Wir möchten___)
wash	*VA-shen* (waschen)
I want to wash up	*ish MERSH-tuh mish VA-shen* (Ich möchte mich waschen)
I want to have my clothes washed	*ish MERSH-tuh mai-nuh ZA-khen VA-shen lahss-sen* (Ich möchte meine Sachen waschen lassen)
Watch out!	*OWF-pahss-sen!* (Aufpassen!)
water	*VAHSS-ser* (Wasser)
boiled water	*AHP-guh-kawkh-tess VAHSS-ser* (abgekochtes Wasser)
drinking water	*TRINK-vahss-ser* (Trinkwasser)
hot water	*HAI-sess VAHSS-ser* (heisses Wasser)
we	*veer* (wir)
We are___	*veer zint___* (Wir sind___)
We have___	*veer HA-ben___* (Wir haben___)
We want___	*veer MERSH-ten___* (Wir möchten___)
Wednesday	*MIT-vawkh* (Mittwoch)
welcome	
You're welcome	*BIT-tuh* (Bitte)
well	
I am well	*es GAYT meer GOOT* (Es geht mir gut)
well (for water)	*BROON-nen* (Brunnen)
what	*VAHSS* (was)
What's that?	*VAHSS ist DAHSS?* (Was ist das?)
What's this?	*VAHSS ist DEESS?* (Was ist dies?)
What is your name?	*VEE HAI-sen zee?* (Wie heissen Sie?)
What time is it?	*vee SHPAYT ist ess?* (Wie spät ist es?)
when	*VAHN* (wann)
When does the movie start?	*VAHN buh-GINT dahss KEE-no?* (Wann beginnt das Kino?)
When does the train leave?	*vahn GAYT dayr TSOOK?* (Wann geht der Zug?)

** *ow* as in *now; ai* as in *aisle*

English	Pronunciation and German Spelling	English	Pronunciation and German Spelling
where	*VO* (wo)		**Y**
Where is___?	*vo ist___?* (Wo ist___?)	yes	*YA* (ja)
Where are___?	*vo zint___?* (Wo sind___?)	yesterday	*GESS-tern* (gestern)
Where can I get___?	*vo kahn ish___ buh-KAWM-men?* (Wo kann ich___ bekommen?)	you	
		Are you___?	*sint zee___?* (Sind Sie___?)
wine	*VAIN* (Wein)	Have you___?	*HA-ben zee___?* (Haben Sie___?)
workman	*AR-bai-ter* (Arbeiter)		
wounded	*fayr-VOON-det* (verwundet)		* * *ow* as in *now; ai* as in *aisle*

Spanish/English Dictionary

Spanish is one of the most widespread languages in the world. It is spoken by some 25 million people in Spain and Morocco and over 60 million in South and Central America, Mexico, and the Caribbean. It is also one of the languages of the Philippines.

This *Language Guide* will enable you to ask directions, buy things or order a meal in these Spanish-speaking regions. Knowing a little Spanish will also help you get along with the people, for they will naturally be pleased to see a stranger showing enough interest in them to try to learn their language.

How to Use the Record * and Guide

This Guide is obviously not intended to give you a complete command of the Spanish language. If you want to embark upon a somewhat extensive study of the spoken language you should obtain the USAFI course, *Spoken Spanish*—see the current USAFI Catalog for instructions. This Language Guide will, however, enable you to carry on simple conversations in Spanish.

The records that go with this *Guide* give you a number of the most important words and phrases in Spanish. Read the section called *Hints on Pronunciation* and then listen to the records until you know the *Useful Words and Phrases* by heart. Repeat each word out loud right after you hear it, and say it exactly the way the Spanish speaker does. Imitate the pronunciation as closely as you can, just as you might mimic someone who has an unusual accent. Try to get every detail of the pronunciation, even the rhythm and intonation. Follow the words in your *Guide* but use them only as a reminder; if you hear something different from what you see written, go by what you hear. Remember that you can't get the sound of a language from the printed word alone—you have to use your ears even more than your eyes. If you don't have the records and can't get a Spanish speaker to read the words, you will have to rely on the *Hints on Pronunciation* alone.

By the time you have practiced the *Useful Words and Phrases* several times, you will know what sound each letter stands for in the *Guide*. You will then be able to pronounce the *Additional Expressions* even though you have not actually heard them, and you will be able to form sentences of your own by using the section called *Fill-In Sentences*.

Hints on Pronunciation

If you have studied Spanish before, you may not

*Records no longer available

need any additional practice in pronunciation. However, unless you have had a chance to try out your Spanish and know that you are understood without any difficulty, you had better do a little practicing.

You will find all the words and phrases written in a spelling which you read like English. When you see the Spanish word for "one" spelled *OO-no*, give the *oo* the sound it has in the English words *too, boot*, etc. and not the sound it has in German or any other language you may happen to know.

Each letter or combination of letters is used for the sound it usually stands for in English and it *always* stands for that sound. Thus, *oo* is always pronounced as in *too, boot, tooth, roost*, never as anything else. Say these words and then pronounce the vowel sound by itself. That is the sound you must use every time you see *oo* in the *Pronunciation* column. If you should use some other sound—for example, the sound of *oo* in *blood*—you might be misunderstood.

Syllables that are accented, that is, pronounced louder than others, are written in capital letters. In Spanish, unaccented syllables are not skipped over quickly, as they are in English. Hyphens are used to divide words into syllables in order to make them easier to read. Curved lines (‿) are used to show sounds that are pronounced together without any break; for example, *K‿YAY-ro* meaning "I want," *D‿YESS* meaning "ten."

Special Points

Here are a few points to note as you listen to the records:

AY	as in *may, say, play* but don't drawl it as we do in English. Since it is not drawled it sounds a little like the *e* in *let*. Example: *ka-FAY* meaning "coffee."
O or OH	as in *go, so, oh, note, joke* but don't drawl it as we do in English. Since it is not drawled it sounds a little like the *aw* in *saw*. Example: *NO* meaning "no."
H	as in *house, hat, hall* but stronger. Example: *free-HO-less* meaning "beans."
RR	stands for a strongly rolled r-sound, like the telephone operator's "thuh-r-r-ree" for "three" or like the Scotchman's "burr" in pronouncing *very* as "ver-r-ry." This double *rr* differs from the single *r*, which is made by a quick tap of the tongue against the gums back of the teeth. Example of *rr*: *see-ga-RREE-yohss* meaning "cigarettes." Example of *r*: *ah la day-RECH-ah* meaning "to the right."

You will often hear Spanish speakers pronounce the *d* very much like our *th*-sound in "breathe" and "then," the *b* very much like our *v*, and the *v* at the beginning of a word like *b*. Thus, *guisado* meaning "stew" may sound like *ghee-SA-tho* (*th* as in *then*); *sábado* meaning "Saturday" like *SA-va-do;* and *veinte* meaning "twenty" like *BAYN-tay*. If you pronounce a *d* or *v* or *b* according to what you see written you will be understood, but it is of course best to try to imitate the sound you hear.

Regional Differences

If you follow the pronunciation on the records that go with this *Guide*, you will be understood wherever Spanish is spoken. However, if you find yourself in a region where the people have a slightly different pronunciation, it is well to try to speak the way they do. Here are a few of the differences you will find:

About three-fourths of all Spanish speakers pronounce an *s*-sound in words like *SEN-tro* (spelled *centro*) meaning "center," *s_yoo-DAHD* (*ciudad*) meaning "city" and *PLA-sa* (*plaza*) meaning "plaza." In Central and Northern Spain, however, people use the *th*-sound of *thin* or *breath* in words like these and say *THEN-tro*, *th_yoo-DAHD*, *PLA-tha*. The *th*-sound is used in words that are written with *c* or *z* in Spanish spelling but not in words spelled with *s;* for example, *SEE* (*sí*) meaning "yes," *sen-YOR* (*señor*) meaning "sir," or *SAHL* (*sal*) meaning "salt."

Most Spanish speakers use a *y*-sound in words that are spelled with *ll*. The word *llama*, for example, in the expression *¿Cómo se llama usted?* meaning "What is your name?" is pronounced *YA-ma*. In Central and Northern Spain, however, a combination sound like the *ly* in *schoolyard* is used instead. Thus, *llama* is pronounced as *L_YA-ma*. In Argentina and in some other regions the *ll* has a sound something like the *j* in *judge*.

In Southern Spain and much of Latin America, *s*-sounds at the end of syllables are often not pronounced; thus, *ESS-tohss DOHSS OHM-bress* meaning "these two men" may sound like *AY-to DO OHM-bray*.

USEFUL WORDS AND PHRASES

The following is the exact wording of the Spanish language records issued with this *Guide*.

These records give you a few useful phrases in Spanish as spoken in most of Latin America. The phrases and other words which you will need are found also in the pamphlet which should be used with these records.

To learn to imitate the sounds of Spanish you should listen to the records at least six or seven times.

The English will be given first, followed by the Spanish. Then repeat the Spanish out loud and say it good and loud! Remember! Repeat every Spanish phrase right after you hear it.

Words, greetings, and general phrases, which are useful and should be memorized, are given first.

GREETINGS AND GENERAL PHRASES

English	Pronunciation and Spanish Spelling
Good day	*BWEN-ohs DEE-ahss* (Buenos días)
Good evening	*BWEN-ahss TAR-dess* (Buenas tardes)
Sir	*sen-YOR* (señor)
Madam	*sen-YO-ra* (señora)
Miss	*sen-yo-REE-ta* (señorita)

Spanish speakers have several words for "please" and they use them often.

Please	*SEER-va-say___* (Sírvase___)
or	*por fa-VOR* (Por favor)
or	*TEN-ga la bohn-DAHD day___* (Tenga la bondad de___)
Excuse me	*payr-DO-nay-may* (Perdóneme)
Thank you	*GRAHSS-yahss* (Gracias)

If you have studied Spanish, you probably remember the *th*-sound for the letter *c*, as in *GRAHTH-yahss*, instead of *GRAHSS-yahss*, which you have just heard. Both *GRAHTH-yahss* and *GRAHSS-yahss* are absolutely correct. But *GRAHSS-yahss* with the *s*-sound is used almost entirely in South and Central America as well as in the Philippines and many other places where Spanish is spoken.

Yes	*SEE* (sí)
No	*NO* (no)
Understand me?	*may ent-YEN-day?* (¿Me entiende?)
I don't understand	*NO ent-YEN-do* (No entiendo)
Please speak slowly	*TEN-ga la bohn-DAHD day ah-BLAR dess-PAHSS-yo* (Tenga la bondad de hablar despacio)

LOCATION

When you need directions to get somewhere, you use the phrase "Where is" and add the word you need.

Where is	*DOHN-day ess-TA* (Dónde está)
the restaurant	*el rress-ta_oo-RAHN-tay* (el restaurante)

In many parts of the Spanish-speaking world, the *s*-sound is frequently left out. Such words as *ess-TA* are often pronounced *ay-TA*. This is particularly true in Cuba and Chile.

the hotel	*el o-TEL* (el hotel)
Where is the hotel?	*DOHN-day ess-TA el o-TEL?* (¿Dónde está el hotel?)
the railroad station	*la ess-tahss-YOHN* (la estación)
Where is the railroad station?	*DOHN-day ess-TA la ess-tahss-YOHN?* (¿Dónde está la estación?)
the toilet	*el rray-TRAY-tay* (el retrete)
Where is the toilet?	*DOHN-day ess-TA el rray-TRAY-tay?* (¿Dónde está el retrete?)

DIRECTIONS

The answer to your question "Where is such and such?" may be "To the right" or "To the left" or "Straight ahead," so you need to know these phrases.

English	Pronunciation and Spanish Spelling	
To the right	*ah la day-RECH-ah*	(a la derecha)
To the left	*ah la eesk-YAYR-da*	(a la izquierda)
Straight ahead	*ah-day-LAHN-tay*	(adelante)

It is sometimes useful to say "please point."

Please point	*SEER-va-say ah-poon-TAR*	(Sírvase apuntar)

If you are driving and ask the distance to another town it will be given to you in kilometers, not miles.

Kilometers	*kee-LO-met-rohss*	(kilómetros)

One kilometer equals ⅝ of a mile.

NUMBERS

You need to know the numbers.

One	*OO-no*	uno
Two	*DOHSS*	dos
Three	*TRESS*	tres

In rapid conversation you will frequently hear these without the s-sound: *DO, TRAY*, instead of *DOHSS, TRESS*.

Four	*KWA-tro*	cuatro
Five	*SEEN-ko*	cinco
Six	*SAYSS*	seis
Seven	*S_YAY-tay*	siete
Eight	*O-cho*	ocho
Nine	*NWEV-ay*	nueve
Ten	*D_YESS*	diez

For the numbers "eleven" through "fifteen" you add an ending which sounds like *say*.

Eleven	*OHN-say*	once
Twelve	*DO-say*	doce
Thirteen	*TRESS-ay*	trece
Fourteen	*ka-TOR-say*	catorce
Fifteen	*KEEN-say*	quince

For the numbers "sixteen" through "nineteen" you put the word *d_yess-ee* (diez y) "ten and—" and then add the words for "six" through "nine."

Sixteen	*d_yess-ee-SAYSS*	dieciséis
Seventeen	*d_yess-eess-YAY-tay*	diecisiete
Eighteen	*d_yess-YO-cho*	dieciocho
Nineteen	*d_yess-een-WEV-ay*	diecinueve
Twenty	*VAYN-tay*	veinte
Twenty-one	*vaynt-YOO-no*	veintiuno
Twenty-two	*vayn-tee-DOHSS*	veintidós
Thirty	*TRAYN-ta*	treinta
Forty	*kwa-REN-ta*	cuarenta
Fifty	*seen-KWEN-ta*	cincuenta

English	Pronunciation and Spanish Spelling	
Sixty	*say-SEN-ta*	sesenta
Seventy	*say-TEN-ta*	setenta
Eighty	*o-CHEN-ta*	ochenta
Ninety	*no-VEN-ta*	noventa
One hundred	*S_YEN*	cien
One thousand	*MEEL*	mil

WHAT'S THIS?

When you want to know the name of something you can say "What's this?" and point to the thing you mean.

What is	*KAY ESS*	(Qué es)
this	*ESS-to*	(esto)
What's this?	*KAY ess ESS-to?*	(¿Qué es esto?)

ASKING FOR THINGS

When you want something you say "I want" and add the name of the thing wanted. Always be sure to say "please"— *SEER-va-say* or *por fa-VOR*.

I want	*K_YAY-ro*	(Quiero)
cigarettes	*see-ga-RREE-yohss*	(cigarrillos)
I want cigarettes	*K_YAY-ro see-ga-RREE-yohss*	(Quiero cigarrillos)
to eat	*ko-MAYR*	(comer)
I want to eat	*K_VAY-ro ko-MAYR*	(Quiero comer)

Here are the words for some of the things you may require:

bread	*PAHN*	(pan)
fruit	*FROO-ta*	(fruta)
oranges	*na-RAHN-hahss*	(naranjas)
bananas	*PLA-ta-nohss*	(plátanos)
or	*ba-NA-nohss*	(bananos)
water	*AH-gwa*	(agua)
eggs	*WEV-ohss*	(huevos)
butter	*mahn-tay-KEE-ya*	(mantequilla)
meat	*KAR-nay*	(carne)
beefsteak	*beef-TEK*	(biftec)
chops	*ko-STEE-yahss*	(costillas)
lamb	*kar-NAY-ro*	(carnero)
pork	*PWAYR-ko*	(puerco)
lamb chops	*ko-STEE-yahss day kar-NAY-ro*	(costillas de carnero)
pork chops	*ko-STEE-yahss day PWAYR-ko*	(costillas de puerco)
stew	*ghee-SA-do*	(guisado)
soup	*SO-pa*	(sopa)
potatoes	*PA-pahss*	(papas)
or	*pa-TA-tahss*	(patatas)
rice	*ah-RROHSS*	(arroz)
beans	*free-HO-less*	(frijoles)

English	Pronunciation and Spanish Spelling
fish	*pess-KA-do* (pescado)
milk	*LECH-ay* (leche)
ice cream	*ay-LA-do* (helado)
salad	*en-sa-LA-da* (ensalada)
a match	*oon FO-sfo-ro* (un fósforo)
beer	*sayr-VESS-ah* (cerveza)
a glass of beer	*oon VA-so day sayr-VESS-ah* (un vaso de cerveza)
a cup of coffee	*oo-na TA-sa day ka-FAY* (una taza de café)

HOW MUCH?

To find out how much things cost you say:

How much	*KWAHN-to* (Cuánto)
costs	*KWESS-ta* (cuesta)
this	*ESS-to* (esto)
How much does this cost?	*KWAHN-to KWESS-ta ESS-to?* (¿Cuánto cuesta esto?)

KWAHN-to KWESS-ta ESS-to?

TIME

To find out what time it is you say really "What hour is it?"

What time is it? *KAY O-ra ESS?* (¿Qué hora es?)

Ten past one is "it is the one and ten."

Ten past one *ESS la OO-na ee D⏑YESS* (es la una y diez)

Quarter past five is "they are the five and a quarter."

Quarter past five *SOHN lahss SEEN-ko ee KWAR-to* (son las cinco y cuarto)

Twenty past seven is "they are the seven and twenty."

Twenty past seven *SOHN lahss S⏑YAY-tay ee VAYN-tay* (son las siete y veinte)

Half past six is "six and a half."

Half past six *SOHN lahss SAYSS ee MED-ya* (son las seis y media)

Twenty to eight is "they are the eight minus twenty."

Twenty to eight *SOHN lahss O-cho men-ohss VAYN-tay* (son las ocho menos veinte)

Quarter of two is "they are the two minus a quarter."

Quarter of two *SOHN lahss DOHSS men-ohss KWAR-to* (son las dos menos cuarto)

Ten minutes to three is "they are the three minus ten."

Ten minutes to three *SOHN lahss TRESS men-ohss D⏑YESS* (son las tres menos diez)

It is also possible to indicate time before the hour by saying "so many minutes until the hour."

Ten to three *D⏑YESS pa-ra lahss TRESS* (diez para las tres)

If you want to know when a movie starts or when a train leaves you say:

English	Pronunciation and Spanish Spelling
At what time	*ah KAY O-ra* (A qué hora)
starts	*emp-YESS-ah* (empieza)
the movie	*el SEE-nay* (el cine)
What time does the movie start?	*ah KAY O-ra emp-YESS-ah el SEE-nay?* (¿A qué hora empieza el cine?)
the train	*el TREN* (el tren)
leaves	*SA-lay* (sale)
What time does the train leave?	*ah KAY O-ra SA-lay el TREN?* (¿A qué hora sale el tren?)
Today	*OY* (hoy)
Tomorrow	*mahn-YA-na* (mañana)
Yesterday	*ah-YAYR* (ayer)

The days of the week are:

Sunday	*do-MEEN-go* (domingo)
Monday	*LOO-ness* (lunes)
Tuesday	*MAR-tess* (martes)
Wednesday	*M⏑YAYR-ko-less* (miércoles)
Thursday	*H⏑WEV-ess* (jueves)
Friday	*V⏑YAYR-ness* (viernes)
Saturday	*SA-ba-do* (sábado)

OTHER USEFUL PHRASES

The following phrases will be useful:

What is your name? *KO-mo say YA-ma oo-STED?* (¿Cómo se llama usted?)

If you have studied Spanish you may have been taught that the *ll* as in ¿Cómo se llama usted? is pronounced like *l⏑y—L⏑YA-ma*. In most parts of Latin America, it sounds like a simple *y-sound—YA-ma*. In Argentina they pronounce it like the *j*-sound of the English word "pleasure"—for example: ¿*KO-mo say JA-ma?* instead of ¿*KO-mo say YA-ma?*

My name is___ *may YA-mo___* (Me llamo___)

How do you say table (or anything else) in Spanish? *KO-mo say DEE-say table en ess-pahn-YOHL?* (¿Cómo se dice table en español?)

There are many ways of saying "Good-by" in Spanish. The most usual is:

ahd-YOHSS (Adiós)

For "So long" you say in Spanish:

ah-sta L⏑WEG-o (Hasta luego)

For "See you soon" you say in Spanish:

ah-sta l⏑way-GHEE-to (Hasta lueguito)

For "I'll see you later" you say in Spanish:

ah-sta la VEESS-ta (Hasta la vista)

For "Until tomorrow" you say in Spanish:

ah-sta mahn-YA-na (Hasta mañana)

For "Until tonight" you say in Spanish:

ah-sta la NO-chay (Hasta la noche)

NOTE

The expression given on the record for "please point" may not be understood in some Spanish-speaking regions. If people do not understand you when you say *SEER-va-say ah-poon-TAR*, try saying *SEER-va-say sen-ya-LAR-may-lo*.

ADDITIONAL EXPRESSIONS

English	Pronunciation and Spanish Spelling
I am hungry	*TEN-go AHM-bray* (Tengo hambre)
I am thirsty	*TEN-go SED* (Tengo sed)
Stop!	*PA-ray!* (¡Pare!)
Come here!	*VEN-ga ah-KA!* (¡Venga acá!)
Right away *or* Quickly	*PROHN-to* (Pronto)
Come quickly!	*VEN-ga PROHN-to!* (¡Venga pronto!)
Go quickly!	*VA-ya PROHN-to!* (¡Vaya pronto!)
Help!	*so-KO-rro!* (¡Socorro!)
Bring help!	*TRA ee-ga ah-YOO-da!* (¡Tráiga ayuda!)
You will be rewarded	*NO lo ah-RA day BAHL-day* (No lo hará de balde)
I am an American	*SOY nor-tay-ah-may-ree-KA-no* (Soy norteamericano)
I am your friend	*SOY soo ah-MEE-go* (Soy su amigo)
Where are the sailors?	*DOHN-day ess-TAHN lohss mah-REE-nohss?* (¿Dónde están los marinos?)
Where are the American sailors?	*DOHN-day ess-TAHN lohss mah-REE-nohss nor-tay-ah-may-ree-KA-nohss?* (¿Dónde están los marinos norteamericanos?)
Which way is north?	*DOHN-day ess-TA el NOR-tay?* (¿Dónde está el norte?)
Which is the road to___?	*KWAHL ess el ka-MEE-no pa-ra___?* (¿Cuál es el camino para___?)
Draw me a map	*dee-BOO-hay-may oon PLA-no* (Dibújeme un plano)
Take me there	*YEV-ay-may ah-YA* (Lléveme allá)
Take me to a doctor	*YEV-ay-may ah oon MED-ee-ko* (Lléveme a un médico)
Take me to the hospital	*YEV-ay-may ahl o-spee-TAHL* (Lléveme al hospital)
How far is it?	*ah KAY dee-STAHNSS-ya ess-TA?* (¿A qué distancia está?)
Where is it?	*DOHN-day ess-TA?* (¿Dónde está?)
Is it far?	*ess-TA LAY-hohss?* (¿Está lejos?)
It is near	*ess-TA SAYR-ka* (Está cerca)
Danger!	*pay-LEE-gro!* (¡Peligro!)
Careful! *or* Watch out!	*kwee-DA-do!* (¡Cuidado!)
Gas!	*GA-sess!* (¡Gases!)
Take cover!	*ahl ah-BREE-go!* (¡Al abrigo!)
Wait a minute!	*ess-PAY-ray oon mee-NOO-to!* (¡Espere un minuto.)
Good luck!	*BWEN-ah SWAYR-tay!* (¡Buena suerte!)

FILL-IN SENTENCES

In this section you will find a number of sentences, each containing a blank space which can be filled in with any one of the words in the list that follows. For example, in order to say "I want a room," look for the phrase "I want___" in the English column and find the Spanish expression given beside it: *K YAY-ro___*. Then look for "a room" in the list that follows; the Spanish is *oon KWAR-to*. Put the word for "a room" in the blank space and you get *K YAY-ro oon KWAR-to*.

English	Pronunciation and Spanish Spelling
I want___	*K YAY-ro___* (Quiero___)
We want___	*kay-REM-ohss___* (Queremos___)
I need___	*ness-ay-SEE-to___* (Necesito___)
Bring me___	*TRA ee-ga-may___* (Tráigame___)
Give me___	*DAY-may___* (Déme___)
Where can I get___?	*DOHN-day kohn-SEE-go___?* (¿Dónde consigo___?)
I have___	*TEN-go___* (Tengo___)
We have___	*tay-NEM-ohss___* (Tenemos___)
I don't have___	*NO TEN-go___* (No tengo___)
We don't have___	*NO tay-NEM-ohss___* (No tenemos___)
Have you___?	*T YEN-ay oo-STED___?* (¿Tiene usted___?)

EXAMPLE

I want___	*K YAY-ro___* (Quiero___)
drinking water	*AH-gwa po-TA-blay* (agua potable)
I want drinking water	*K YAY-ro AH-gwa po-TA-blay* (Quiero agua potable)
apples	*mahn-SA-nahss* (manzanas)
bacon *or* salt pork	*to-SEE-no* (tocino)
or	*to-see-NET-ah* (tocineta)
or	*MA-grahss* (magras)
boiled water	*AH-gwa ayr-VEE-da* (agua hervida)
carrots	*sa-na-O-ree-ahss* (zanahorias)
chicken	*PO-yo* (pollo)
chocolate	*cho-ko-LA-tay* (chocolate)
cucumbers	*pay-PEE-nohss* (pepinos)
grapes	*OO-vahss* (uvas)
ham	*ha-MOHN* (jamón)
onions	*say-BO-yahss* (cebollas)
pepper	*peem-YEN-ta* (pimienta)
salt	*SAHL* (sal)
sugar	*ah-SOO-kar* (azúcar)
tea	*TAY* (té)
veal	*KAR-nay day tayr-NAY-ra* (carne de ternera)
a cup	*oo-na TA-sa* (una taza)
a fork	*oon ten-ay-DOR* (un tenedor)
a glass	*oon VA-so* (un vaso)

English	Pronunciation and Spanish Spelling
a knife	*oon koo-CHEE-yo* (un cuchillo)
a plate	*oon PLA-to* (un plato)
a spoon	*oo-na koo-CHA-ra* (una cuchara)
a bed	*oo-na KA-ma* (una cama)
blankets	*fra-SA-dahss* (frazadas)

In some regions the word given for "blankets" may not be understood. In that case try one of the following words:
>   *MAHN-tahss* (mantas)
>   *ko-BEE-hahss* (cobijas)

a mattress	*oon kohl-CHOHN* (un colchón)
a mosquito net	*oon mo-skee-TAY-ro* (un mosquitero)
a pillow	*oo-na ahl-mo-AH-da* (una almohada)
a room	*oon KWAR-to* (un cuarto)
sheets	*SA-ba-nahss* (sábanas)
a towel	*oo-na to-AH-ya* (una toalla)
cigars	*see-GA-rrohss* (cigarros)

In some regions the word *see-GA-rrohss* means "cigarettes." If you don't get what you want try one of the following words for "cigars":

>   *POO-rohss* (puros)
>   *ta-BA-kohss* (tabacos)

a pipe	*oo-na PEE-pa* (una pipa)
tobacco	*ta-BA-ko* (tabaco)
ink	*TEEN-ta* (tinta)
paper	*pa-PEL* (papel)
a pen	*oo-na PLOO-ma* (una pluma)
a pencil	*oon LA-peess* (un lápiz)
a comb	*oon PAY‿ee-nay* (un peine)
hot water	*AH-gwa kahl-YEN-tay* (agua caliente)
a razor	*oo-na na-VA-ha* (una navaja)
razor blades	*O-hahss day ah-fay-TAR* (hojas de afeitar)
a shaving brush	*BRO-cha day ah-fay-TAR* (brocha de afeitar)
shaving soap	*ha-BOHN day ah-fay-TAR* (jabón de afeitar)
soap	*ha-BOHN* (jabón)
a toothbrush	*oon say-PEE-yo day D‿YEN-tess* (un cepillo de dientes)
tooth paste	*PA-sta day D‿YEN-tess* (pasta de dientes)
a handkerchief	*oon pahn-yoo‿AY-lo* (un pañuelo)
a raincoat	*oon eem-payr-may-AH-blay* (un impermeable)

English	Pronunciation and Spanish Spelling
a shirt	*oo-na ka-MEE-sa* (una camisa)
shoe laces	*kor-DO-ness day sa-PA-tohss* (cordones de zapatos)
shoe polish	*bay-TOON* (betún)
shoes	*sa-PA-tohss* (zapatos)
underwear	*RRO-pa een-tayr-YOR* (ropa interior)
buttons	*bo-TO-ness* (botones)
a needle	*oo-na ah-GOO-ha* (una aguja)
safety pins	*eem-payr-DEE-bless* (imperdibles)
thread	*EE-lo* (hilo)
adhesive tape	*ess-pa-ra-DRA-po* (esparadrapo)
an antiseptic	*oon ahn-tee-SEP-tee-ko* (un antiséptico)
aspirin	*ah-spee-REE-na* (aspirina)
a bandage	*oon ven-DA-hay* (un vendaje)
cotton	*ahl-go-DOHN* (algodón)
a disinfectant	*oon dess-een-fek-TAHN-tay* (un desinfectante)
iodine	*YO-do* (yodo)
a laxative	*oon lahk-SAHN-tay* (un laxante)
gasoline	*ga-so-LEE-na* (gasolina)

I want to___	*K‿YAY-ro___* (Quiero___)

I want to___	*K‿YAY-ro___* (Quiero___)
eat	*ko-MAYR* (comer)
I want to eat	*K‿YAY-ro ko-MAYR* (Quiero comer)
buy it	*kohm-PRAR-lo* (comprarlo)
eat	*ko-MAYR* (comer)
drink water	*to-MAR AH-gwa* (tomar agua)
wash up	*la-VAR-may* (lavarme)
take a bath	*bahn-YAR-may* (bañarme)
rest	*dess-kahn-SAR* (descansar)
sleep	*dor-MEER* (dormir)
have my hair cut	*kor-TAR-may el PEL-o* (cortarme el pelo)
be shaved	*ah-fay-TAR-may* (afeitarme)

Where can I find___?	*DOHN-day PWED-o ah-YAR___?* (¿Dónde puedo hallar___?)
Where is there___?	*DOHN-day A‿ee___?* (¿Dónde hay___?)

Where can I find___?	*DOHN-day PWED-o ah-YAR___?* (¿Dónde puedo hallar___?)

English	Pronunciation and Spanish Spelling	English	Pronunciation and Spanish Spelling
a barber	*oon bar-BAY-ro* (un barbero)	the nearest settlement	*el po-BLA-do MAHSS sayr-KA-no* (el poblado más cercano)
Where can I find a barber?	*DOHN-day PWED-o ah-YAR oon bar-BAY-ro?* (¿Dónde puedo hallar un barbero?)	the police station	*el kwar-TEL day la po-lee-SEE-ah* (el cuartel de la policía)
a barber	*oon bar-BAY-ro* (un barbero)	the post office	*el ko-RRAY-o* (el correo)
a dentist	*oon den-TEE-sta* (un dentista)	the railroad	*el fay-rro-ka-RREEL* (el ferrocarril)
a doctor	*oon MED-ee-ko* (un médico)	the road	*el ka-MEE-no* (el camino)
a mechanic	*oon may-KA-nee-ko* (un mecánico)	the river	*el RREE-o* (el río)
a policeman	*oon po-lee-SEE-ah* (un policía)	the ship	*el BOO-kay* (el buque)
a porter	*oon MO-so* (un mozo)	the telephone	*el tay-LEF-o-no* (el teléfono)
a servant	*oon seerv-YEN-tay* (un sirviente)	the telegraph office	*el tay-LEG-ra-fo* (el telégrafo)
a shoemaker	*oon sa-pa-TAY-ro* (un zapatero)		
a tailor	*oon SA-stray* (un sastre)	the town	*el PWEB-lo* (el pueblo)
a workman	*oon o-BRAY-ro* (un obrero)		———————
a house	*oo-na KA-sa* (una casa)	I am___	*ess-TOY___* (Estoy___)
a church	*oo-na ee-GLESS-ya* (una iglesia)	He is___	*ess-TA___* (Está___)
a clothing store	*oo-na T_YEN-da day RRO-pa* (una tienda de ropa)	Are you___?	*ess-TA oo-STED___?* (¿Está usted___?)
a drugstore	*oo-na bo-TEE-ka* (una botica)		
a filling station	*oo-na ga-so-lee-NAY-ra* (una gasolinera)	**EXAMPLE**	
or	*oo-na ess-tahss-YOHN day ay-SENSS-ya* (una estación de esencia)	I am___	*ess-TOY___* (Estoy___)
		sick	*en-FAYR-mo* (enfermo)
a garage	*oon ga-RA-hay* (un garaje)	I am sick	*ess-TOY en-FAYR-mo* (Estoy enfermo)
a grocery	*oo-na T_YEN-da day ko-mess-TEE-bless* (una tienda de comestibles)	sick	*en-FAYR-mo* (enfermo)
a laundry	*oo-na la-vahn-day-REE-ah* (una lavandería)	well	*B_YEN* (bien)
		wounded	*ay-REE-do* (herido)
a spring (for water)	*oon ma-nahnt-YAHL* (un manantial)	hurt	*less-yo-NA-do* (lesionado)
or	*oon O-ho day AH-gwa* (un ojo de agua)	lost	*payr-DEE-do* (perdido)
a well	*oon PO-so* (un pozo)	tired	*kahn-SA-do* (cansado)
	———————		———————
Where is___?	*DOHN-day ess-TA___?* (¿Dónde está___?)	We are___	*ess-TA-mohss___* (Estamos___)
How far is___?	*ah KAY dee-STAHNSS-ya ess-TA___?* (¿A qué distancia está___?)	They are___	*ess-TAHN___* (Están___)
EXAMPLE		**EXAMPLE**	
Where is___?	*DOHN-day ess-TA___?* (¿Dónde está___?)	We are___	*ess-TA-mohss___* (Estamos___)
the bridge	*el PWEN-tay* (el puente)	sick	*en-FAYR-mohss* (enfermos)
Where is the bridge?	*DOHN-day ess-TA el PWEN-tay?* (¿Dónde está el puente?)	We are sick	*ess-TA-mohss en-FAYR-mohss* (Estamos enfermos)
the bridge	*el PWEN-tay* (el puente)	sick	*en-FAYR-mohss* (enfermos)
the bus	*el a_oo-to-BOOSS* (el autobús)	well	*B_YEN* (bien)
the city	*la s_yoo-DAHD* (la ciudad)	wounded	*ay-REE-dohss* (heridos)
the highway	*la ka-rray-TAY-ra* (la carretera)	hurt	*less-yo-NA-dohss* (lesionados)
the hospital	*el o-spee-TAHL* (el hospital)	lost	*payr-DEE-dohss* (perdidos)
the main street	*la KA-yay ma-YOR* (la calle mayor)	tired	*kahn-SA-dohss* (cansados)
the market place	*la PLA-sa del mayr-KA-do* (la plaza del mercado)		———————
the nearest town	*el PWEB-lo MAHSS sayr-KA-no* (el pueblo más cercano)	Is it___?	*ess-TA___?* (¿Está___?)
		It is___	*ess-TA___* (Está___)
		This is___	*ESS-to ess-TA___* (Esto está___)

English	Pronunciation and Spanish Spelling
That is___	*a-KAY-yo ess-TA___* (Aquello está___)
It is not___	*NO ess-TA___* (No está___)
It is too___ } It is very___ }	*ess-TA MOO_ee___* (Está muy___)

EXAMPLE

It is___	*ess-TA___* (Está___)
clean	*LEEMP-yo* (limpio)
It is clean	*ess-TA LEEMP-yo* (Está limpio)
dirty	*SOOSS-yo* (sucio)
hot *or* warm	*kahl-YEN-tay* (caliente)
cold	*FREE-o* (frío)
here	*ah-KEE* (aquí)
there	*ah-YEE* (allí)
near	*SAYR-ka* (cerca)
far	*LAY-hohss* (lejos)

Is it___?	*ESS___?* (¿Es___?)
It is___	*ESS___* (Es___)
This is___	*ESS-to ess___* (Esto es___)
That is___	*a-KAY-yo ess___* (Aquello es___)
It is not___	*no ESS___* (No es___)
It is too___ } It is very___ }	*ess MOO_ee___* (Es muy___)

EXAMPLE

This is___	*ESS-to ess___* (Esto es___)
expensive	*KA-ro* (caro)
This is expensive	*ESS-to ess KA-ro* (Esto es caro)
cheap	*ba-RA-to* (barato)
good	*BWEN-o* (bueno)
bad	*MA-lo* (malo)
big	*GRAHN-day* (grande)
small	*pay-KEN-yo* (pequeño)
enough	*soo-feess-YEN-tay* (suficiente)
much	*MOO-cho* (mucho)

NOTE

The last two sets of Fill-In Sentences are listed separately because there are two different words for "is" in Spanish.

IMPORTANT SIGNS

Spanish	English
Alto	Stop
Despacio	Slow
Desviación	Detour
Cuidado *or* Atención	Caution
Dirección de marcha única	One Way
Circulación prohibida *or* No hay paso	No Thoroughfare
Paso a nivel	Grade Crossing
Vía muerta	Dead End
Circulación por la derecha *or* Conserve su derecha	Keep to the Right
Viraje rápido *or* Curva peligrosa	Dangerous Curve
Ferrocarril	Railroad
Puente	Bridge
Cruce	Crossroad
Alta tensión *or* Cables de alta tensión	High Tension Lines
Prohibido el paso	Keep Out
Se prohibe la entrada	No Admittance
Prohibido el estacionamiento	No Parking
Prohibido fumar	No Smoking
Prohibido escupir	No Spitting
Lavatorio *or* Retrete *or* Mingitorio	Lavatory
Caballeros *or* Hombres	Men
Damas *or* Señoras *or* Mujeres	Women
Abierto	Open
Cerrado	Closed
Entrada	Entrance
Salida	Exit

ALPHABETICAL WORD LIST

English	Pronunciation and Spanish Spelling
	A
a	*oon* (un)
or	*oo-na* (una)
adhesive tape	*ess-pa-ra-DRA-po* (esparadrapo)
am	
I am	*ess-TOY* (Estoy)
or	*SOY* (Soy)
American (North American)	*nor-tay-ah-may-ree-KA-no* (norteamericano)
Americans	*nor-tay-ah-may-ree-KA-nohss* (norteamericanos)
American sailors	*mah-REE-nohss nor-tay-ah-may-ree-KA-nohss* (marinos norteamericanos)
and	*ee* (y)

English	Pronunciation and Spanish Spelling
antiseptic	*ahn-tee-SEP-tee-KO* (antiséptico)
apples	*mahn-SA-nahss* (manzanas)
are	
Are you___?	*ess-TAHN oo-STED-ess___?* (¿Están ustedes___?)
They are___	*ess-TAHN___* (Están___)
We are___	*ess-TA-mohss___* (Estamos___)
aspirin	*ah-spee-REE-na* (aspirina)

B

bacon or salt pork	*to-SEE-no* (tocino)
or	*to-see-NET-ah* (tocineta)
or	*MA-grahss* (magras)
bad	*MA-lo* (malo)
bananas	*ba-NA-nohss* (bananos)
or	*PLA-ta-nohss* (plátanos)
bandage	*ven-DA-hay* (vendaje)
barber	*bar-BAY-ro* (barbero)
bath	
take a bath	*bahn-YAR-may* (bañarme)
be shaved	
I want to be shaved	*K_YAY-ro ah-fay-TAR-may* (Quiero afeitarme)
beans	*free-HO-less* (frijoles)
bed	*KA-ma* (cama)
beefsteak	*beef-TEK* (biftec)
beer	*sayr-VESS-ah* (cerveza)
a glass of beer	*oon VA-so day sayr-VESS-ah* (un vaso de cerveza)
big	*GRAHN-day* (grande)
blankets	*fra-SA-dahss* (frazadas)
or	*ko-BEE-hahss* (cobijas)
or	*MAHN-tahss* (mantas)
boiled water	*AH-gwa ayr-VEE-da* (agua hervida)
bread	*PAHN* (pan)
bridge	*PWEN-tay* (puente)
bring	
Bring help!	*TRA_ee-ga a-YOO-da!* (¡Tráiga ayuda!)
Bring me___	*TRA_ee-ga-may___* (Tráigame___)
brush	*BRO-cha* (brocha)
shaving brush	*BRO-cha day a-fay-TAR* (brocha de afeitar)
bus	*a_oo-to-BOOSS* (autobús)
butter	*mahn-tay-KEE-ya* (mantequilla)
buttons	*bo-TO-ness* (botones)
buy it	*kohm-PRAR-lo* (comprarlo)

C

can	
I can	*PWED-o* (puedo)
cheap	*ba-RA-to* (barato)
Careful!	*kwee-DA-dol* (¡Cuidado!)

English	Pronunciation and Spanish Spelling
carrots	*sa-na-O-ree-ahss* (zanahorias)
cheap	*ba-RA-to* (barato)
chicken	*PO-yo* (pollo)
chocolate	*cho-ko-LA-tay* (chocolate)
chops	*ko-STEE-yahss* (costillas)
lamb chops	*ko-STEE-yahss day kar-NAY-ro* (costillas de carnero)
pork chops	*ko-STEE-yahss day PWAYR-ko* (costillas de puerco)
church	*ee-GLESS-ya* (iglesia)
cigarettes	*see-ga-RREE-yohss* (cigarrillos)
cigars	*see-GA-rrohss* (cigarros)
or	*POO-rohss* (puros)
or	*ta-BA-kohss* (tabacos)
city	*s_yoo-DAHD* (ciudad)
clean	*LEEMP-yo* (limpio)
clothing store	*T_YEN-da day RRO-pa* (tienda de ropa)
coffee	*ka-FAY* (café)
a cup of coffee	*oo-na TA-sa day ka-FAY* (una taza de café)
cold	*FREE-o* (frío)
comb	*PAY_ee-nay* (peine)
Come!	*VEN-ga!* (¡Venga!)
Come here!	*VEN-ga a-KAI* (¡Venga acá!)
Come quickly!	*VEN-ga PROHN-tol* (¡Venga pronto!)
cost	
it costs	*KWESS-ta* (cuesta)
How much does it cost?	*KWAHN-to KWESS-ta?* (¿Cuánto cuesta?)
cotton	*ahl-go-DOHN* (algodón)
cover	
Take cover!	*ahl ah-BREE-gol* (¡Al abrigo!)
cucumbers	*pay-PEE-nohss* (pepinos)
cup	*TA-sa* (taza)
a cup of___	*oo-na TA-sa day___* (una taza de___)

D

Danger!	*pay-LEE-grol* (¡Peligro!)
day	
Good day	*BWEN-ohz DEE-ahss* (Buenos días)
dentist	*den-TEE-sta* (dentista)
dirty	*SOOSS-yo* (sucio)
disinfectant	*dess-een-fek-TAHN-tay* (desinfectante)
doctor	*MED-ee-ko* (médico)
Take me to a doctor	*YEV-ay-may a oon MED-ee-ko* (Lléveme a un médico)
Draw me a map	*dee-BOO-hay-may oon PLA-no* (Dibújeme un plano)
(to) drink	*to-MAR AH-gwa* (tomar agua)
drinking water	*AH-gwa po-TA-blay* (agua potable)

English	Pronunciation and Spanish Spelling
drugstore	bo-TEE-ka (botica)

E

English	Pronunciation and Spanish Spelling
(to) eat	ko-MAYR (comer)
eggs	WEV-ohss (huevos)
eight	O-cho (ocho)
eighteen	d⌣yess-YO-cho (dieciocho)
eighty	o-CHEN-ta (ochenta)
eleven	OHN-say (once)
enough	soo-feess-YEN-tay (suficiente)
evening	
Good evening	BWEN-ahss TAR-dess (Buenas tardes)
Excuse me	payr-DO-nay-may (Perdóneme)
expensive	KA-ro (caro)
too expensive	MOO⌣ee KA-ro (muy caro)

F

English	Pronunciation and Spanish Spelling
far	LAY-hohss (lejos)
How far is it?	a KAY dee-STAHNSS-ya ess-TA? (¿A qué distancia está?)
Is it far?	ess-TA LAY-hohss? (¿Está lejos?)
fifteen	KEEN-say (quince)
fifty	seen-KWEN-ta (cincuenta)
a filling station	oo-na ga-so-lee-NAY-ra (una gasolinera)
or	oo-na ess-tahss-YOHN day ay-SENSS-ya (una estación de esencia)
(to) find	ah-YAR (hallar)
Where can I find___?	DOHN-day PWED-o ah-YAR___? (¿Dónde puedo hallar___?)
fish	pess-KA-do (pescado)
five	SEEN-ko (cinco)
fork	ten-ay-DOR (tenedor)
forty	kwa-REN-ta (cuarenta)
four	KWA-tro (cuatro)
fourteen	ka-TOR-say (catorce)
Friday	V⌣YAYR-ness (viernes)
friend	ah-MEE-go (amigo)
I am your friend	SOY soo ah-MEE-go (Soy su amigo)
fruit	FROO-ta (fruta)

G

English	Pronunciation and Spanish Spelling
garage	ga-RA-hay (garaje)
Gas!	GA-sess! (¡Gases!)
gasoline	ga-so-LEE-na (gasolina)
get	
Where can I get___?	DOHN-day kohn-SEE-go___? (¿Dónde consigo___?)
Give me___	DAY-may___ (Déme___)
glass	VA-so (vaso)
a glass of___	oon VA-so day___ (un vaso de___)

English	Pronunciation and Spanish Spelling
Go!	VA-ya! (¡Vaya!)
Go quickly!	VA-ya PROHN-to! (¡Vaya pronto!)
good	BWEN-o (bueno)
Good day	BWEN-ohz DEE-ahss (Buenos días)
Good evening	BWEN-ahss TAR-dess (Buenas tardes)
Good luck	BWEN-ah SWAYR-tay (Buena suerte)
Good-by	ahd-YOHSS (Adiós)
grapes	OO-vahss (uvas)
grocery	T⌣YEN-da day ko-mess-TEE-bless (tienda de comestibles)

H

English	Pronunciation and Spanish Spelling
hair	PEL-o (pelo)
have my hair cut	kor-TAR-may el PEL-o (cortarme el pelo)
half	MED-ya (media)
half past six	SAYSS ee MED-ya (seis y media)
ham	ha-MOHN (jamón)
handkerchief	pahn-yoo⌣AY-lo (pañuelo)
have	
Have you___?	T⌣YEN-ay oo-STED___? (¿Tiene usted___?)
I have___	TEN-go___ (Tengo___)
I don't have___	NO TEN-go___ (No tengo___)
We have___	tay-NEM-ohss___ (Tenemos___)
We don't have___	NO tay-NEM-ohss___ (No tenemos___)
he	EL (él)
He is sick	ess-TA en-FAYR-mo (Está enfermo)
help	ah-YOO-da (ayuda)
or	so-KO-rro (socorro)
Bring help!	TRA⌣ee-ga ah-YOO-da! (¡Tráiga ayuda!)
here	
Come here!	VEN-ga ah-KA! (¡Venga acá!)
highway	ka-rray-TAY-ra (carretera)
hospital	o-spee-TAHL (hospital)
Take me to a hospital	YEV-ay-may ah oon o-spee-TAHL (Lléveme a un hospital)
hot or warm	kahl-YEN-tay (caliente)
hot water	AH-gwa kahl-YEN-tay (agua caliente)
hotel	o-TEL (hotel)
Where is the hotel?	DOHN-day ess-TA el o-TEL? (¿Dónde está el hotel?)
house	KA-sa (casa)
how	KO-mo (cómo)
How are you?	KO-mo ess-TA oo-STED? (¿Cómo está usted?)
How do you say___?	KO-mo say DEE-say___? (¿Cómo se dice___?)
How far is it?	a KAY dee-STAHNSS-ya ess-TA? (¿A qué distancia está?)

English	Pronunciation and Spanish Spelling
how much	KWAHN-to (cuánto)
How much does this cost?	KWAHN-to KWESS-ta ESS-to? (¿Cuánto cuesta esto?)
hundred	S_YEN (cien)
hungry	
I am hungry	TEN-go AHM-bray (Tengo hambre)
hurt	less-yo-NA-do (lesionado)

I

English	Pronunciation and Spanish Spelling
I	YO (yo)
I am an American	SOY nor-tay-ah-may-ree-KA-no (Soy norteamericano)
I am sick	ess-TOY en-FAYR-mo (Estoy enfermo)
I have___	TEN-go___ (Tengo___)
I don't have___	NO TEN-go___ (No tengo___)
I want___	K_YAY-ro___ (Quiero___)
ice cream	ay-LA-do (helado)
in Spanish	en ess-pahn-YOHL (en español)
ink	TEEN-ta (tinta)
iodine	YO-do (yodo)
is	
Is it expensive?	ess KA-ro? (¿Es caro?)
Is it far?	ess-TA LAY-hohss? (¿Está lejos?)
It is expensive	ess KA-ro (Es caro)
It is not___	NO ESS___ (No es___)
What is it?	KAY ESS? (¿Qué es?)
Where is it?	DOHN-day ess-TA? (¿Dónde está?)
Where is there___?	DOHN-day A_ee___? (¿Dónde hay___?)

K

English	Pronunciation and Spanish Spelling
kilometers	kee-LO-met-rohss (kilómetros)
knife	koo-CHEE-yo (cuchillo)

L

English	Pronunciation and Spanish Spelling
lamb	kar-NAY-ro (carnero)
lamb chops	ko-STEE-yahss day kar-NAY-ro (costillas de carnero)
laundry	la-vahn-day-REE-a (lavandería)
laxative	lahk-SAHN-tay (laxante)
leave	
it leaves	SA-lay (sale)

English	Pronunciation and Spanish Spelling
left	
to the left	ah la eesk-YAYR-da (a la izquierda)
lost	payr-DEE-do (perdido)
luck	SWAYR-tay (suerte)
Good luck	BWEN-ah SWAYR-tay (Buena suerte)

M

English	Pronunciation and Spanish Spelling
Madam	sen-YO-ra (señora)
main street	KA-yay ma-YOR (calle mayor)
or	KA-yay preen-see-PAHL (calle principal)
map	PLA-no (plano)
Draw me a map	dee-BOO-hay-may oon PLA-no (Dibújeme un plano)
market place	PLA-sa del mayr-KA-do (plaza del mercado)
matches	FO-sfo-ro (fósforo)
mattress	kohl-CHOHN (colchón)
me	may (me)
meat	KAR-nay (carne)
mechanic	may-KA-nee-ko (mecánico)
milk	LECH-ay (leche)
minus	men-ohss (menos)
minute	mee-NOO-to (minuto)
Wait a minute	ess-PAY-ray oon mee-NOO-to (Espere un minuto)
Miss	sen-yo-REE-ta (señorita)
Monday	LOO-ness (lunes)
mosquito net	mo-skee-TAY-ro (mosquitero)
movie	SEE-nay (cine)
What time does the movie start?	ah KAY O-ra emp-YESS-ah el SEE-nay? (¿A qué hora empieza el cine?)
much	MOO-cho (mucho)

N

English	Pronunciation and Spanish Spelling
name	
My name is___	may YA-mo___ (Me llamo___)
What's your name?	KO-mo say YA-ma oo-STED? (¿Cómo se llama usted?)
near	SAYR-ka (cerca)
or	sayr-KA-no (cercano)
It is near	ess-TA SAYR-ka (Está cerca)
the nearest town	el PWEB-lo MAHSS sayr KA-no (el pueblo más cercano)
the nearest settlement	el po-BLA-do MAHSS sayr-KA-no (el poblado más cercano)
need	
I need___	ness-ay-SEE-to___ (Necesito___)

English	Pronunciation and Spanish Spelling
needle	*ah-GOO-ha* (aguja)
night	*NO-chay* (noche)
until tonight	*ah-sta la NO-chay* (Hasta la noche)
nine	*NWEV-ay* (nueve)
nineteen	*d̲_yess-een-WEV-ay* (diecinueve)
ninety	*no-VEN-ta* (noventa)
no *or* not	*NO* (no)
north	*NOR-tay* (norte)
Which way is north?	*DOHN-day ess-TA el NOR-tay?* (¿Dónde está el norte?)

O

of	*day* (de)
a cup of coffee	*oo-na TA-sa day ka-FAY* (una taza de café)
a glass of beer	*oon VA-so day sayr-VESS-ah* (un vaso de cerveza)
quarter of two	*lahss DOHSS men-ohss KWAR-to* (las dos menos cuarto)
one	*OO-no* (uno)
onions	*say-BO-yahss* (cebollas)
oranges	*na-RAHN-hahss* (naranjas)

P

paper	*pa-PEL* (papel)
past	
half past six	*lahss SAYSS ee MED-ya* (las seis y media)
quarter past five	*lahss SEEN-ko ee KWAR-to* (las cinco y cuarto)
ten past one	*la OO-na ee D̲_YESS* (la una y diez)
twenty past seven	*S̲_YAY-tay ee VAYN-tay* (siete y veinte)
pen	*PLOO-ma* (pluma)
pencil	*LA-peess* (lápiz)
pepper	*peem-YEN-ta* (pimienta)
pillow	*ahl-mo-AH-da* (almohada)
pins	
safety pins	*eem-payr-DEE-bless* (imperdibles)
pipe	*PEE-pa* (pipa)
plate	*PLA-to* (plato)
please	*por fa-VOR* (por favor)
or	*SEER-va-say___* (Sírvase___)
or	*TEN-ga la bohn-DAHD day___* (Tenga la bondad de___)
Please point	*SEER-va-say ah-poon-TAR* (Sírvase apuntar)
Please point it out to me	*SEER-va-say sen-ya-LAR-may-lo* (Sírvase señalármelo)

English	Pronunciation and Spanish Spelling
Please speak slowly	*TEN-ga la bohn-DAHD day ah-BLAR dess-PAHSS-yo* (Tenga la bondad de hablar despacio)
(to) point	*ah-poon-TAR* (apuntar)
(to) point it out to me	*sen-ya-LAR-may-lo* (señalármelo)
policeman	*po-lee-SEE-ah* (policía)
police station	*kwar-TEL day la po-lee-SEE-ah* (cuartel de la policía)
pork	*KAR-nay day PWAYR-ko* (carne de puerco)
pork chops	*ko-STEE-yahss day PWAYR-ko* (costillas de puerco)
porter	*MO-so* (mozo)
post office	*ko-RRAY-o* (correo)
potatoes	*PA-pahss* (papas)
or	*pa-TA-tahss* (patatas)

Q

quarter	*KWAR-to* (cuarto)
quarter of two	*DOHSS men-ohss KWAR-to* (dos menos cuarto)
quarter past five	*SEEN-ko ee KWAR-to* (cinco y cuarto)
quickly	*PROHN-to* (pronto)
Come quickly!	*VEN-ga PROHN-to!* (¡Venga pronto!)
Go quickly!	*VA-ya PROHN-to!* (¡Vaya pronto!)

R

railroad	*fay-rro-ka-RREEL* (ferrocarril)
railroad station	*ess-tahss-YOHN* (estación)
raincoat	*eem-payr-may-AH-blay* (impermeable)
razor	*na-VA-ha* (navaja)
razor blades	*O-hahss day ah-fay-TAR* (hojas de afeitar)
(to) rest	*dess-kahn-SAR* (descansar)
restaurant	*rress-ta_oo-RAHN-tay* (restaurante)
Where is the restaurant?	*DOHN-day ess-TA el rress-ta_oo-RAHN-tay?* (¿Dónde está el restaurante?)
rewarded	
You will be rewarded	*NO lo ah-RA day BAHL-day* (No lo hará de balde)
rice	*ah-RROHSS* (arroz)
right	
to the right	*ah la day-RECH-ah* (a la derecha)
right away	*PROHN-to* (pronto)
river	*RREE-o* (río)
road	*ka-MEE-no* (camino)
room	*KWAR-to* (cuarto)

English	Pronunciation and Spanish Spelling

S

English	Pronunciation and Spanish Spelling
safety pins	*eem-payr-DEE-bless* (imperdibles)
sailors	*mah-REE-nohss* (marinos)
Where are the American sailors?	*DOHN-day ess-TAHN lohss mah-REE-nohss nor-tay-ah-may-ree-KA-nohss?* (¿Dónde están los marinos norteamericanos?)
Where are the sailors?	*DOHN-day ess-TAHN lohss mah-REE-nohss?* (¿Dónde están los marinos?)
salad	*en-sa-LA-da* (ensalada)
salt	*SAHL* (sal)
Saturday	*SA-ba-do* (sábado)
say	
How do you say___?	*KO-mo say DEE-say___?* (¿Cómo se dice___?)
see	
I'll see you later	*ah-sta la VEE-sta* (Hasta la vista)
See you soon	*ah-sta l_way-GHEE-to* (Hasta lueguito)
servant	*seerv-YEN-tay* (sirviente)
seven	*S_YAY-tay* (siete)
seventeen	*d_yess-eess-YAY-tay* (diecisiete)
seventy	*say-TEN-ta* (setenta)
(to) shave	*ah-fay-TAR* (afeitar)
I want to be shaved	*K_YAY-ro ah-fay-TAR-may* (Quiero afeitarme)
shaving brush	*BRO-cha day ah-fay-TAR* (brocha de afeitar)
shaving soap	*ha-BOHN day ah-fay-TAR* (jabón de afeitar)
she	*AY-ya* (ella)
sheets	*SA-ba-nahss* (sábanas)
ship	*BOO-kay* (buque)
shirt	*ka-MEE-sa* (camisa)
shoemaker	*sa-pa-TAY-ro* (zapatero)
shoes	*sa-PA-tohss* (zapatos)
shoe laces	*kor-DO-ness day sa-PA-tohss* (cordones de zapatos)
shoe polish	*bay-TOON* (betún)
sick	*en-FAYR-mo* (enfermo)
sir	*sen-YOR* (senor)
six	*SAYSS* (seis)
sixteen	*d_yess-ee-SAYSS* (dieciséis)
sixty	*say-SEN-ta* (sesenta)
(to) sleep	*dor-MEER* (dormir)
slowly	*dess-PAHSS-yo* (despacio)
small	*pay-KEN-yo* (pequeño)
So long	*ah-sta L_WEG-o* (Hasta luego)

English	Pronunciation and Spanish Spelling
soap	*ha-BOHN* (jabón)
shaving soap	*ha-BOHN day ah-fay-TAR* (jabón de afeitar)
soon	
See you soon	*ah-sta l_way-GHEE-to* (Hasta lueguito)
soup	*SO-pa* (sopa)
Spanish	*ess-pahn-YOHL* (español)
in Spanish	*en ess-pahn-YOHL* (en español)
(to) speak	*ah-BLAR* (hablar)
Please speak slowly	*SEER-va-say ah-BLAR dess-PAHSS-yo* (Sírvase hablar despacio)
spoon	*koo-CHA-ra* (cuchara)
spring (for water)	*ma-nahnt-YAHL* (manantial)
start	
it starts	*emp-YESS-ah*
What time does the movie start?	*ah KAY O-ra emp-YESS-ah el SEE-nay* (¿A qué hora empieza el cine?)
station	
police station	*kwar-TEL day la po-lee-SEE-ah* (cuartel de la policía)
railroad station	*ess-tahss-YOHN* (estación)
Where is the railroad station?	*DOHN-day ess-TA la ess-tahss-YOHN* (¿Dónde está la estación?)
steak	
beefsteak	*beef-TEK* (biftec)
stew	*ghee-SA-do* (guisado)
Stop!	*PA-ray!* (¡Pare!)
store	*T_YEN-da* (tienda)
clothing store	*T_YEN-da day RRO-pa* (tienda de ropa)
straight ahead	*ah-day-LAHN-tay* (adelante)
street	*KA-yay* (calle)
main street *or*	*KA-yay ma-YOR* (calle mayor) *KA-yay preen-see-PAHL* (calle principal)
sugar	*ah-SOO-kar* (azúcar)
Sunday	*do-MEEN-go* (domingo)

T

English	Pronunciation and Spanish Spelling
tailor	*SA-stray* (sastre)
take	
Take cover!	*ahl ah-BREE-go!* (¡Al abrigo!)
Take me to a doctor	*YEV-ay-may ah oon MED-ee-ko* (Lléveme a un médico)
Take me to the hospital	*YEV-ay-may ahl o-spee-TAHL* (Lléveme al hospital)

English	Pronunciation and Spanish Spelling
Take me there	*YEV-ay-may ah-YA* (Lléveme allá)
tea	*TAY* (té)
telegraph office	*tay-LEG-ra-fo* (telégrafo)
telephone	*tay-LEF-o-no* (teléfono)
ten	*D‿YESS* (diez)
Thank you	*GRAHSS-yahss* (Gracias)
the	*el* (el)
or	*la* (la)
or	*lohss* (los)
or	*lahss* (las)
there	
Take me there	*YEV-ay-may ah-YA* (Lléveme allá)
they	*AY-yohss* (ellos)
They are sick	*ess-TAHN en-FAYR-mohss* (Están enfermos)
thirsty	
I am thirsty	*TEN-go SED* (Tengo sed)
thirteen	*TRESS-ay* (trece)
thirty	*TRAYN-ta* (treinta)
this	*ESS-to* (esto)
What's this?	*KAY ess ESS-to?* (¿Qué es esto?)
thousand	*MEEL* (mil)
thread	*EE-lo* (hilo)
three	*TRESS* (tres)
Thursday	*H‿WEV-ess* (jueves)
time	
at what time	*ah KAY O-ra* (a qué hora)
What time is it?	*KAY O-ra ESS?* (¿Qué hora es?)
tired	*kahn-SA-do* (cansado)
to	*ah* (a)
to the right	*ah la day-RECH-ah* (a la derecha)
to the left	*ah la eesk-YAYR-da* (a la izquierda)
to a doctor	*ah oon MED-ee-ko* (a un médico)
to the hospital	*ahl o-spee-TAHL* (al hospital)
twenty to eight	*O-cho men-ohss VAYN-tay* (ocho menos veinte)
ten minutes to three	*TRESS men-ohss D‿YESS* (tres menos diez)
or	*D‿YESS pa-ra lahss TRESS* (diez para las tres)
tobacco	*ta-BA-ko* (tabaco)
today	*OY* (hoy)
toilet	*rray-TRAY-tay* (retrete)

English	Pronunciation and Spanish Spelling
Where is the toilet?	*DOHN-day ess-TA el rray-TRAY-tay?* (¿Dónde está el retrete?)
tomorrow	*mahn-YA-na* (mañana)
too expensive	*MOO‿ee KA-ro* (muy caro)
toothbrush	*say-PEE-yo day D‿YEN-tess* (cepillo de dientes)
tooth paste	*PA-sta day D‿YEN-tess* (pasta de dientes)
towel	*to-AH-ya* (toalla)
town	*PWEB-lo* (pueblo)
the nearest town	*el PWEB-lo MAHSS sayr-KA-no* (el pueblo más cercano)
train	*TREN* (tren)
What time does the train leave?	*ah KAY O-ra SA-lay el TREN* (¿A qué hora sale el tren?)
Tuesday	*MAR-tess* (martes)
twelve	*DO-say* (doce)
twenty	*VAYN-tay* (veinte)
twenty-one	*vaynt-YOO-no* (veintiuno)
twenty-two	*vayn-tee-DOHSS* (veintidós)
two	*DOHSS* (dos)

U

English	Pronunciation and Spanish Spelling
understand	
Understand me?	*may ent-YEN-day?* (¿Me entiende?)
I don't understand	*NO ent-YEN-do* (No entiendo)
underwear	*RRO-pa een-tayr-YOHR* (ropa interior)
until	*ah-sta* (hasta)
Until tomorrow	*ah-sta mahn-YA-na* (Hasta mañana)
Until tonight	*ah-sta la NO-chay* (Hasta la noche)

V

English	Pronunciation and Spanish Spelling
veal	*KAR-nay day tayr-NAY-ra* (carne de ternera)

W

English	Pronunciation and Spanish Spelling
Wait!	*ess-PAY-rayl* (¡Espere!)
Wait a minute!	*ess-PAY-ray oon mee-NOO-tol* (¡Espere un minuto!)
want	
I want___ or I want to___	*K‿YAY-ro___* (Quiero___)
We want___	*kay-REM-ohss___* (Queremos___)
warm *or* hot	*kahl-YEN-tay* (caliente)
wash up	
I want to wash up	*K‿YAY-ro la-VAR-may* (Quiero lavarme)

English	Pronunciation and Spanish Spelling	English	Pronunciation and Spanish Spelling
Watch out!	*kwee-DA-dol* (¡Cuidado!)	**Where is it?**	*DOHN-day ess-TA?* (¿Dónde está?)
water	*AH-gwa* (agua)	**Where are they?**	*DOHN-day ess-TAHN?* (¿Dónde están?)
boiled water	*AH-gwa ayr-VEE-da* (agua hervida)	**Where can I find___?**	*DOHN-day PWED-o ah-YAR___?* (¿Dónde puedo hallar___?)
drinking water	*AH-gwa po-TA-blay* (agua potable)	**Where can I get___?**	*DOHN-day kohn-SEE-go___?* (¿Dónde consigo___?)
hot water	*AH-gwa kahl-YEN-tay* (agua caliente)	**Where is there___?**	*DOHN-day A_ee___?* (¿Dónde hay___?)
we	*no-SO-trohss*	**which**	*KWAHL* (cuál)
We are sick	*ess-TA-mohss en-FAYR-mohss* (Estamos enfermos)	Which is the road to___?	*KWAHL ess el ka-MEE-no pa-ra___?* (¿Cuál es el camino para___?)
We have___	*tay-NEM-ohss___* (Tenemos___)	Which way is north?	*DOHN-day ess-TA el NOR-tay?* (¿Dónde está el norte?)
We don't have___	*NO tay-NEM-ohss___* (No tenemos___)	**workman**	*o-BRAY-ro* (obrero)
We want___	*kay-REM-ohss___* (Queremos___)	**wounded**	*ay-REE-do* (herido)
Wednesday	*M_YAYR-ko-less* (miércoles)		
well (in good health)	*B_YEN* (bien)		**Y**
well (for water)	*PO-so* (pozo)	**yes**	*SEE* (sí)
what	*KAY* (qué)	**yesterday**	*ah-YAYR* (ayer)
What is it?	*KAY ESS?* (¿Qué es?)	**you**	*oo-STED* (usted)
What is your name?	*KO-mo say YA-ma oo-STED?* (¿Cómo se llama usted?)	**You will be rewarded**	*NO lo ah-RA day BAHL-day* (No lo hará de balde)
What time is it?	*KAY O-ra ESS?* (¿Qué hora es?)	**Have you?**	*T_YEN-ay oo-STED?* (¿Tiene usted?)
What's this?	*KAY ess ESS-to?* (?Qué es esto?)	**Are you sick?**	*ess-TA oo-STED en-FAYR-mo?* (¿Está usted enfermo?)
at what time	*ah KAY O-ra* (a qué hora)		
where	*DOHN-day* (dónde)		

French/English Dictionary

French is spoken by over 60 million people—about 47 million in France, the rest principally in Belgium, Switzerland, Canada, and the French-speaking African countries.

This *Language Guide* will enable you to ask directions, buy things or order a meal in these French-speaking regions. Knowing a little French will also help you get along with the people, for they will naturally be pleased to see a stranger showing enough interest in them to try to learn their language.

How to Use the Records* and Guide

This *Guide* is not intended to give you a complete command of the French language. For a thorough course in French, write to the United States Armed Forces Institute, Madison, Wisconsin. Even without a thorough course, however, the instructions given in this handbook will enable you to carry on simple conversations in the language.

The records that go with this *Guide* give you a number of the most important words and phrases in French. Read the section called *Hints on Pronunciation* and then listen to the records until you know the *Useful Words and Phrases* by heart. Repeat each word out loud right after you hear it and say it exactly the way the French speaker does. Imitate the pronunciation as closely as you can, just as you might mimic someone who has an unusual accent. Try to get every detail of the pronunciation, even the rhythm and the inflection of the voice. Follow the words in your *Guide* but use them only as a reminder; if you hear something different from what you see written, go by what you hear. Remember that you can't get the sound of a language from the printed word alone—you have to use your ears even more than your eyes. If you don't have the records and can't get a French speaker to read the words, you will have to rely on the *Hints on Pronunciation* alone.

By the time you have practiced the *Useful Words and Phrases* several times you will know what sound each letter stands for in the *Guide*. You will then be able to pronounce the *Additional Expressions* even though you have not actually heard them, and you will be able to form sentences of your own by using the section called *Fill-In Sentences*.

Records no longer available.

Hints on Pronunciation

You will find all the words and phrases written both in French spelling and in a simplified spelling which you read like English. Don't use the French spelling, the one given in parentheses, unless you have studied French before. *Read the simplified spelling as though it were English.* When you see the French word for "where" spelled *oo*, give the *oo* the sound it has in the English words *too, boot*, etc. and not the sound it has in German or any other language you may happen to know.

Each letter or combination of letters is used for the sound it usually stands for in English and it *always* stands for that sound. Thus, *oo* is always pronounced as it is in *too, boo, boot, tooth, roost*, never as anything else. Say these words and then pronounce the vowel sound by itself. That is the sound you must use every time you see *oo* in the *Pronunciation* column. If you should use some other sound—for example, the sound of *oo* in *blood*—you might be misunderstood.

Syllables that are accented, that is, pronounced louder than others, are written in capital letters. In French, unaccented syllables are not skipped over quickly, as they are in English. The accent is generally on the last syllable in the phrase.

Hyphens are used to divide words into syllables in order to make them easier to pronounce. Curved lines (‿) are used to show sounds that are pronounced together without any break; for example, *day-z‿UH* meaning "some eggs," *kawm-B‿YANG* meaning "how much?"

Special Points

Here are a few points to note as you listen to the records:

AY	as in *may, say, play* but don't drawl it out as we do in English. Since it is not drawled it sounds almost like the *e* in *let*. Example: *ray-pay-TAY* meaning "repeat."
J	stands for a sound for which we have no single letter in English. It is the sound we have in *measure, leisure, usual, division, casualty, azure*. Example: *bawn-JOOR* meaning "Good day."
EW	is used for a sound like *ee* in *bee* made with the lips rounded as though about to say the *oo* in *boot*. Example: *ek-skew-zay MWA* meaning "Excuse me."
U or UH	as in *up, cut, rub, gun*. Examples: *nuf* meaning "nine," *juh* meaning "I."
U or UH	as in *up, cut*, etc. but made with the lips rounded. Example: *DUH* meaning "two."

The difference between these two sounds is not too important in French and you will be understood if you use the vowel in *up* in all cases. The *uh* which is pronounced like the vowel in *up* but with the lips rounded is underlined in the *Useful Words and Phrases* so that you can compare the two sounds as you listen to the record.

NG, N or M   are used to show that certain vowels are pronounced through the nose, very much in the way we generally say *huh, uh-uh, uh-huh.* Examples: *lahnt-MAHNG* meaning "slowly," *juh kawm-PRAHNG* meaning "I understand," *NAWNG* meaning "no," *PANG* meaning "bread."

Memory Key

AY   as in *day* but not so drawled.

U or UH   as in *up.*

EW   for the sound in *bee* said with the lips rounded.

J   for the sound in *measure, division.*

NG, N or M for vowels pronounced through the nose.

USEFUL WORDS AND PHRASES

The following is the exact wording of the French Language records issued with this *Guide.*

These records give you a few useful phrases in French. To learn to say these phrases so that you will be understood, imitate the sounds exactly as you hear them. You will hear the English first, followed by the French; then repeat the French out loud, and say it *good and loud.* Remember! Repeat every French phrase right after you hear it.

In the *French Language Guide* which should be used with these records, all the phrases you will hear are written both in French spelling and in a simplified spelling which you should read like English. Don't use the French spelling unless you have studied French before.

Listen to the records six or seven times and you will know the phrases by heart.

GREETINGS AND GENERAL PHRASES

English	Pronunciation and French Spelling
Hello *or* Good day	*bawn-JOOR* (Bonjour)

Notice the sound of *j* in the word *JOOR.* Listen again and repeat: *JOOR, JOOR.* It is the same sound we have in *measure, usual, division, azure,* etc. We have no single letter for this sound in English, so we write it in your *Language Guide* as *j.* But remember—always pronounce *j* as you heard it in *JOOR,* never as the *j* in *judge.* Try just the sound again: *j, j.*

English	Pronunciation and French Spelling
Good evening	*bawn-SWAR* (Bonsoir)
How are you?	*kaw-MAHN-T_ah-lay VOO?* (Comment allez-vous?)
Sir	*muss-YUH* (Monsieur)
Madam	*ma-DAHM* (Madame)
Miss	*mad-mwa-ZEL* (Mademoiselle)

English	Pronunciation and French Spelling
Please	*SEEL voo PLAY* (S'il vous plaît)
Excuse me	*ek-skew-zay MWA* (Excusez-moi)
You're welcome	*eel nee ah pa duh KWA* (Il n'y a pas de quoi)
Yes	*WEE* (oui)
No	*NAWNG* (non)

In the last word you heard a sound pronounced through the nose. Listen again and repeat: *NAWNG, NAWNG.* In English we often have a somewhat similar sound when we say *huh, uh-uh, uh-huh.* The vowel sounds that must be pronounced through the nose like this are written in your *Guide* with an *ng* or *n,* and in a few cases, *m* after them. Always remember, however, that these letters are there only to remind you to pronounce the vowels through the nose. Try just the sound again: *AWNG, AWNG.*

English	Pronunciation and French Spelling
Do you understand?	*KAWM-pruh-nay VOO?* (Comprenez-vous?)
I understand	*JUH kawm-PRAHNG* (Je comprends)
I don't understand	*juh nuh KAWM-prahng PA* (Je ne comprends pas)
Speak slowly, please	*par-lay LAHNT-mahng, seel voo PLAY* (Parlez lentement; s'il vous plaît)
Please repeat	*RAY-pay-tay, seel voo PLAY* (Répétez s'il vous plaît)

LOCATION

When you need directions to get somewhere you use the phrase "where is" and then add the words you need.

English	Pronunciation and French Spelling
Where is the restaurant	*oo AY* (Où est) *luh RESS-to-RAHNG* (le restaurant)
Where is the restaurant?	*oo AY luh RESS-to-RAHNG?* (Où est le restaurant?)
the hotel	*lo-TEL* (l'hôtel)
Where is the hotel?	*oo AY lo-TEL?* (Où est l'hôtel?)
the railroad station	*la GAR* (la gare)
Where is the railroad station?	*oo AY la GAR?* (Où est la gare?)
the toilet	*luh la-va-BO* (le lavabo)
Where is the toilet?	*oo AY luh la-va-BO?* (Où est le lavabo?)

DIRECTIONS

The answer to your question "Where is such and such?" may be "To the right" or "To the left" or "Straight ahead," so you need to know these phrases:

English	Pronunciation and French Spelling
To the right	*ah DRWAT* (à droite)
To the left	*ah GOHSH* (à gauche)
Straight ahead	*too DRWA* (tout droit)

It is sometimes useful to say "Please show me.

English	Pronunciation and French Spelling
Please show me	*seel voo PLAY, mawn-tray-MWA* (S'il vous plaît, montrez-moi)

English	Pronunciation and French Spelling

If you are driving and ask the distance to another town it will be given you in kilometers, not miles.

Kilometer	kee-lo-METR	(kilomètre)

One kilometer equals ⅝ of a mile.

NUMBERS

You need to know the numbers.

One	UNG	un
Two	DUH	deux

You have just heard a sound you should practice. It is like the u-sound in *up* or *but*, said with the lips rounded. Listen again and repeat: *DUH, DUH*. Try just the sound again: *UH, UH*.

Three	TRWA	trois
Four	KATR	quatre
Five	SANK	cinq
Six	SEESS	six
Seven	SET	sept
Eight	WEET	huit
Nine	NUF	neuf
Ten	DEESS	dix
Eleven	AWNZ	onze
Twelve	DOOZ	douze
Thirteen	TREZ	treize
Fourteen	KA-TAWRZ	quatorze
Fifteen	KANZ	quinze
Sixteen	SEZ	seize
Seventeen	DEESS-SET	dix-sept
Eighteen	DEEZ-WEET	dix-huit
Nineteen	DEEZ-NUF	dix-neuf
Twenty	VANG	vingt

Three other vowels that are pronounced through the nose have now been used several times. You heard them in *kaw-MAHNG, VANG, UNG*. Listen again and repeat: *kaw-MAHNG, VANG, UNG*. Try just the sounds again: *AHNG, ANG, UNG*.

For "twenty-one," "thirty-one" and so on, you say "twenty and one," "thirty and one," but for "twenty-two," "thirty-two" and so on, you just add the words for "two" and "three" after the words for "twenty" and "thirty," as we do in English.

Twenty-one	van-t_ay UNG	vingt-et-un
Twenty-two	vant-DUH	vingt-deux
Thirty	TRAHNT	trente
Forty	KA-RAHNT	quarante
Fifty	SAN-KAHNT	cinquante
Sixty	SWA-SAHNT	soixante

"Seventy," "eighty," "ninety" are said "sixty ten," "four twenties" and "four twenties ten."

Seventy	swa-sahnt-DEESS	soixante-dix
Eighty	kat-ruh-VANG	quatre-vingt
Ninety	kat-ruh-van-DEESS	quatre-vingt-dix

English	Pronunciation and French Spelling	
One hundred	SAHNG	cent
One thousand	MEEL	mille

WHAT'S THIS?

When you want to know the name of something you can say "What is it?" or "What's this?" and point to the thing you mean.

What is it?	kess kuh SAY?	(Qu'est-ce que c'est?)
What's this?	kess kuh suh-SEE?	(Qu'est-ce que ceci?)
What's that?	kess kuh say kuh SA?	(Qu'est-ce que c'est que çà?)

ASKING FOR THINGS

When you want something use the phrase "I want" and then add the name of the thing wanted. Always use "Please" —*seel voo PLAY*.

I want	juh voo-DRAY	(Je voudrais)
some cigarettes	day see-ga-RET	(des cigarettes)
I want some cigarettes	juh voo-DRAY day see-ga-RET	(Je voudrais des cigarettes)
to eat	mahn-JAY	(manger)
I want to eat	juh voo-DRAY mahn-JAY	(Je voudrais manger)

Here are the words for some of the things you may require. Each of them has the French word for "some" before it.

bread	dew PANG	(du pain)
butter	dew BUR	(du beurre)
soup	duh la SOOP	(de la soupe)
meat	duh la V_YAHND	(de la viande)
lamb	dew moo-TAWNG	(du mouton)
veal	dew VO	(du veau)
pork	dew PAWR	(du porc)
beef	dew BUF	(du boeuf)
eggs	day-z_UH	(des oeufs)
vegetables	day lay-GEWM	(des légumes)

In the last word you heard a sound you must practice. It is written in your *Guide* as *ew*. Listen to the word again: *lay-GEWM, lay-GEWM*. To pronounce the sound *ew*, you say *ee* but at the same time round your lips as though about to say *oo*. Try just the sound again: *ew, ew*.

potatoes	day PAWM duh TAYR	(des pommes de terre)
string beans	day ah-ree-ko VAYR	(des haricots verts)
cabbage	day SHOO	(des choux)
carrots	day ka-RAWT	(des carottes)
peas	day puh-tee PWA	(des petits pois)
salad	duh la sa-LAD	(de la salade)
sugar	dew SEWKR	(du sucre)

English	Pronunciation and French Spelling
salt	*dew SEL* (du sel)
pepper	*dew PWAVR* (du poivre)
milk	*dew LAY* (du lait)
drinking water	*duh LO paw-TABL* (de l'eau potable)
a cup of tea	*ewn TASS duh TAY* (une tasse de thé)
a cup of coffee	*ewn TASS duh ka-FAY* (une tasse de café)
a glass of beer	*ung VAYR duh B_YAYR* (un verre de bière)
a bottle of wine	*ewn boo-TAY_ee duh VANG* (une bouteille de vin)
some matches	*day-z_ah-lew-MET* (des allumettes)

MONEY

To find out how much things cost, you say:

How much? *kawm-B_YANG?* (Combien?)

The answer will be given in francs, sous, and centimes.

Five centimes equal one sou, twenty sous or one hundred centimes equal one franc.

centime	*sahn-TEEM* (centime)
sou	*SOO* (sou)
franc	*FRAHNG* (franc)

TIME

When you want to know what time it is you say really "What hour is it?"

What time is it? *kel UR ay-t_EEL?* (Quelle heure est-il?)

For "One o'clock" you say "It is one hour."

One o'clock *eel ay-t_EWN UR* (Il est une heure)

For "Two o'clock" you say "It is two hours."

Two o'clock *eel ay DUH-Z_UR* (Il est deux heures)

"Ten past two" is "Two hours ten."

Ten past two *duh-z_UR DEESS* (deux heures dix)

"Quarter past five" is "Five hours and quarter."

Quarter past five *sank UR ay KAR* (cinq heures et quart)

"Half past six" is "Six hours and half."

Half past six *see-z_UR ay duh-MEE* (six heures et demie)

"Quarter of eight" is "Eight hours less the quarter."

Quarter of eight *wee-t_UR mwang luh KAR* (huit heures moins le quart)

When you want to know when a movie starts or when a train leaves, you say:

At what hour	*ah KEL UR* (à quelle heure)
begins	*kaw-MAHNSS* (commence)
the movie	*luh see-nay-MA* (le cinéma)

English	Pronunciation and French Spelling
When does the movie start?	*ah KEL UR kaw-MAHNSS luh see-nay-MA?* (A quelle heure commence le cinéma?)
the train	*luh TRANG* (le train)
leaves	*PAR* (part)
When does the train leave?	*ah KEL UR par luh TRANG?* (A quelle heure part le train?)
Yesterday	*ee-YAYR* (hier)
Today	*o-joord-WEE* (aujourd'hui)
Tomorrow	*duh-MANG* (demain)

The days of the week are:

Sunday	*dee-MAHNSH* (dimanche)
Monday	*LUN-DEE* (lundi)
Tuesday	*MAR-DEE* (mardi)
Wednesday	*MAYR-kruh-DEE* (mercredi)
Thursday	*JUH-DEE* (jeudi)
Friday	*VAHN-druh-DEE* (vendredi)
Saturday	*SAM-DEE* (samedi)

OTHER USEFUL PHRASES

The following phrases will be useful:

What is your name?	*kaw-MAHNG voo-z_ah-puh-lay VOO?* (Comment vous appelez-vous?)
My name is___	*juh ma-PEL___* (Je m'appelle___)
How do you say *table* in French?	*kaw-MAHNG deet voo* table *ang frahn-SAY?* (Comment dites-vous *table* en français?)
I am an American	*juh SWEE-Z_ah-may-ree-KANG* (Je suis Américain)
I am your friend	*juh SWEE vawtr ah-MEE* (Je suis votre ami)
Please help me	*ay-day MWA seel voo PLAY* (Aidez-moi s'il vous plaît)
Where is the camp?	*oo ay luh KAHNG?* (Où est le camp?)
Take me there	*muh-nay-z_ee MWA* (Menez-y moi)
Good-by	*o ruh-VWAR* (Au revoir)

ADDITIONS AND NOTES

Thank you	*mayr-SEE* (merci)
I want	*juh VUH* (Je veux)

The expression given on the record—*juh voo-DRAY*—is a polite way of saying "I want"; it really means "I would like." *juh VUH* is much stronger and should be used only when making a strong request or demand.

ADDITIONAL EXPRESSIONS

I am hungry	*jay FANG* (J'ai faim)
I am thirsty	*jay SWAF* (J'ai soif)

English	Pronunciation and French Spelling
Stop!	*ALT!* (Halte!)
Come here!	*vuh-NAY-Z͜ee-SEE!* (Venez ici!)
Right away	*toot SWEET* (Tout de suite)
Come quickly!	*vuh-nay VEET!* (Venez vite!)
Go quickly!	*ah-lay VEET!* (Allez vite!)
Help!	*o suh-KOOR!* (Au secours!)
Help me!	*ay-day MWA!* (Aidez-moi!)
Bring help!	*ah-lay shayr-SHAY dew suh-KOOR!* (Allez chercher du secours!)
You will be rewarded	*voo suh-RAY ray-kawm-pahn-SAY* (Vous serez récompensé)
Where are the American sailors?	*oo SAWNG lay mah-RANG-Z͜ah-may-ree-KANG?* (Où sont les marins américains?)
Which way is north?	*duh kel ko-TAY ay luh NAWR?* (De quel côté est le nord?)
Which is the road to___?	*kel ay luh shuh-MANG poor___?* (Quel est le chemin pour___?)
Draw me a map	*fet MWA ung kraw-KEE* (Faites-moi un croquis)
Is it far?	*ess kuh say LWANG?* (Est-ce que c'est loin?)
Take me to a doctor	*kawn-dwee-zay-MWA shay-z͜ung dawk-TUR* (Conduisez-moi chez un docteur)
Take cover!	*met-ay VOO-Z͜ah la-BREE!* (Mettez-vous à l'abri!)
Gas!	*gahz!* (Gaz!)
Danger!	*dahr JAY!* (Danger!)
Watch out!	*pruh-nay GARD!* (Prenez garde!)
Be careful!	*fet ah-tahnss-YAWNG!* (Faites attention!)
Wait!	*ah-tahn-DAY!* (Attendez!)
Good luck	*bawn SHAHNSS* (Bonne chance)

FILL-IN SENTENCES

In this section you will find a number of sentences, each containing a blank space which can be filled in with any one of the words in the list that follows. For example, in order to say "I want a room," look for the phrase "I want___" in the English column and find the French expression given beside it: *juh VUH___*. Then look for "a room" in the list that follows; the French is *ewn SHAHMBR*. Put the word for "a room" in the blank space and you get *juh VUH ewn SHAHMBR*.

English	Pronunciation and French Spelling
I want___	*juh VUH___* (Je veux___)
We want___	*noo voo-LAWNG___* (Nous voulons___)
I'd like___	*juh voo-DRAY___* (Je voudrais___)
I need___	*eel muh FO___* (Il me faut___)
Bring me___	*ah-pawr-tay MWA___* (Apportez-moi___)
Give me___	*daw-nay MWA___* (Donnez-moi___)
Where can I get___?	*oo pweej troo-VAY___?* (Où puis-je trouver___?)

English	Pronunciation and French Spelling
I have___	*jay___* (J'ai___)
We have___	*noo-z͜ah-VAWNG___* (Nous avons___)
We don't have___	*noo na-vawng PA___* (Nous n'avons pas___)
Have you___?	*ah-vay VOO___?* (Avez-vous___?)

EXAMPLE

I want___	*juh VUH___* (Je veux___)
boiled water	*duh LO boo-YEE* (de l'eau bouillie)
I want boiled water	*juh VUH duh LO boo-YEE* (Je veux de l'eau bouillie)
bacon	*LAR* (lard)
beefsteak	*bif-TEK* (bifteck)
chicken	*poo-LAY* (poulet)
chops	*kawt-LET* (côtelettes)
lamb chops	*kawt-LET duh moo-TAWNG* (côtelettes de mouton)
pork chops	*kawt-LET duh PAWR* (côtelettes de porc)
beans	*ah-ree-KO* (haricots)
rice	*REE* (riz)
spinach	*ay-pee-NAR* (épinards)
turnips	*na-VAY* (navets)
apples	*PAWM* (pommes)
chocolate	*shaw-kaw-LA* (chocolat)
fruit	*frwee* (fruit)
grapes	*day ray-ZANG* (des raisins)
oranges	*o-RAHNJ* (oranges)
a cup	*ewn TASS* (une tasse)
a plate	*ewn ahss-YET* (une assiette)
a glass	*ung VAYR* (un verre)
a knife	*ung koo-TO* (un couteau)
a fork	*ewn foor-SHET* (une fourchette)
a spoon	*ewn kwee-YAYR* (une cuillère)
a room	*ewn SHAHMBR* (une chambre)
a bed	*ung LEE* (un lit)
blankets	*day koo-vayr-TEWR* (des couvertures)
sheets	*day DRA* (des draps)
a mattress	*ung mat-LA* (un matelas)
a pillow	*un͜aw-ray-YAY* (un oreiller)
a mosquito net	*ewn moo-stee-KAYR* (une moustiquaire)
cigars	*day see-GAR* (des cigares)

English	Pronunciation and French Spelling	English	Pronunciation and French Spelling

English	Pronunciation and French Spelling
a pipe	ewn PEEP (une pipe)
tobacco	dew ta-BA (du tabac)
a pen	ewn PLEWM (une plume)
a pencil	ung kray-YAWNG (un crayon)
ink	duh LAHNKR (de l'encre)
a comb	ung PEN-yuh (un peigne)
hot water	duh lo SHOHD (de l'eau chaude)
a razor	ung ra-ZWAR (un rasoir)
razor blades	day LAM duh ra-ZWAR (des lames de rasoir)
a shaving brush	ung blay-RO (un blaireau)
shaving soap	dew sa-VAWNG ah BARB (du savon à barbe)
soap	dew sa-VAWNG (du savon)
a tooth-brush	ewn BRAWSS ah DAHNG (une brosse à dents)
tooth paste	duh la PAHT dahn-tee-FREESS (de la pâte dentifrice)
a towel	ewn sayrv-YET (une serviette)
a handker-chief	ung moo-SHWAR (un mouchoir)
a raincoat	un am-payr-may-AHBL (un imperméable)
a shirt	ewn shuh-MEEZ (une chemise)
shoes	day sool-YAY (des souliers)
shoe laces	day la-SAY (des lacets)
shoe polish	dew see-RAJ (du cirage)
underwear	day soo-vet-MAHNG (des sous-vêtements)
buttons	day boo-TAWNG (des boutons)
needle	ewn ah-GWEE-yuh (une aiguille)
pins	day-z ay-PANGL (des épingles)
safety pins	day-z ay-PANGL duh sewr-TAY (des épingles de sûreté)
thread	dew FEEL (du fil)
aspirin	duh lah-spee-REEN (de l'aspirine)
a bandage	ung pahnss-MAHNG (un pansement)
cotton	dew kaw-TAWNG (du coton)
a disin-fectant	ung day-zan-fek-TAHNG (un désinfectant)
iodine	duh L Yawd (de l'iode)
a laxative	ung lak-sa-TEEF (un laxatif)

| I want to___ | juh VUH___ (Je veux___) |
| I'd like to___ | juh voo-DRAY___ (Je voudrais___) |

English	Pronunciation and French Spelling
EXAMPLE	
I want to___	juh VUH___ (Je veux___)
eat	mahn-JAY (manger)
I want to eat	juh VUH mahn-JAY (Je veux manger)
buy it	lash-TAY (l'acheter)
drink	BWAR (boire)
wash up	muh la-VAY (me laver)
take a bath	prahndr ung BANG (prendre un bain)
rest	muh ruh-po-ZAY (me reposer)
sleep	dawr-MEER (dormir)
have my hair cut	muh fayr koo-PAY lay shuh-VUH (me faire couper les cheveux)
be shaved	muh fayr ra-ZAY (me faire raser)
Where is there___?	oo ee-ah-t EEL___? (Où y a-t-il___?)
Where can I find___?	oo pweej troo-VAY___? (Où puis-je trouver___?)
EXAMPLE	
Where is there___?	oo ee-ah-t EEL___? (Où y a-t-il___?)
a barber	ung kwa-FUR (un coiffeur)
Where is there a barber?	oo ee-ah-t EEL ung kwa-FUR? (Où y a-t-il un coiffeur?)
a dentist	ung dahn-TEEST (un dentiste)
a doctor	ung dawk-TUR (un docteur)
a mechanic	ung may-ka-neess-YANG (un mécanicien)
a policeman	un ah-JAHNG duh paw-LEESS (un agent de police)
a porter	ung pawr-TUR (un porteur)
a servant	ung daw-mess-TEEK (un domestique)
a shoemaker	ung kawr-dawn-YAY (un cordonnier)
a tailor	ung ta-YUR (un tailleur)
a workman	un oov-R YAY (un ouvrier)
a church	ewn ay-GLEEZ (une église)
a clothing store	ung ma-ga-ZANG duh kawn-feks-YAWNG (un magasin de confection)
a drugstore	ewn far-ma-SEE (une pharmacie)
a garage	ung ga-RAJ (un garage)
a grocery	ewn ay-peess-REE (une épicerie)
a house	ewn may-ZAWNG (une maison)
a laundry	ewn blahn-sheess-REE (une blanchisserie)
a spring	ewn SOORSS (une source)
a well	ung PWEE (un puits)
Where is___?	oo AY___? (Où est___?)
How far is___?	ah kel deess-TAHNSS ay___? (A quelle distance est___?)
EXAMPLE	
Where is___?	oo AY___? (Où est___?)

English	Pronunciation and French Spelling
the bridge	*luh PAWNG* (le pont)
Where is the bridge?	*oo AY luh PAWNG?* (Où est le pont?)
the bus	*lo-to-BEWSS* (l'autobus)
the city	*la VEEL* (la ville)
the highway	*la grahnd ROOT* (la grande route)
the hospital	*lo-pee-TAL* (l'hôpital)
the main street	*la grahng REW* (la grand' rue)
the market	*luh mar-SHAY* (le marché)
the nearest town	*luh vee-LAJ luh plew PRAWSH* (le village le plus proche)
the police station	*luh PAWST duh paw-LEESS* (le poste de police)
the post office	*luh bew-RO duh PAWST* (le bureau de poste)
the railroad	*luh shuh-MANG duh FAYR* (le chemin de fer)
the river	*la reev-YAYR* (la rivière)
the road	*la ROOT* (la route)
the ship	*luh na-VEER* (le navire)
the telegraph office	*luh bew-RO dew tay-lay-GRAF* (le bureau du télégraphe)
the telephone	*luh tay-lay-FAWN* (le téléphone)
the town	*luh vee-LAJ* (le village)

English	Pronunciation and French Spelling
I am___	*juh SWEE___* (Je suis___)
He is___	*eel AY___* (Il est___)
We are___	*noo SAWM___* (Nous sommes___)
You are___	*voo-z_ET___* (Vous êtes___)
They are___	*eel SAWNG___* (Ils sont___)

EXAMPLE

I am___	*juh SWEE___* (Je suis___)
sick	*ma-LAD* (malade)
I am sick	*juh SWEE ma-LAD* (Je suis malade)
wounded	*blay-SAY* (blessé)
lost	*payr-DEW* (perdu)
tired	*fa-tee-GAY* (fatigué)

It is___	*SAY___* (C'est___)
Is it___?	*ess kuh SAY___?* (Est-ce que c'est___?)
It is not___	*suh nay PA___* (Ce n'est pas___)

EXAMPLE

It is not___	*suh nay PA___* (Ce n'est pas___)
good	*BAWNG* (bon)

English	Pronunciation and French Spelling
It is not good	*suh nay pa BAWNG* (Ce n'est pas bon)
bad	*mo-VAY* (mauvais)
expensive	*SHAYR* (cher)
too expensive	*tro SHAYR* (trop cher)
here	*ee-SEE* (ici)
there	*LA* (là)
near	*PRAY* (pres)
far	*LWANG* (loin)

IMPORTANT SIGNS

Stop *or* Halte	Stop
Ralentir	Go Slow
Détour	Detour
Attention	Caution
Sens Unique	One Way
Sens Interdit	No Thoroughfare
Passage à Niveau	Grade Crossing
Impasse	Dead End
Tenez votre Droite	Keep to the Right
Tournant Dangereux	Dangerous Curve
Chemin de Fer	Railroad
Lignes à haute tension	High Tension Lines
Défense d'entrer	Keep Out *or* No Admittance
Défense de Fumer	No Smoking
W.C.	Toilet
Hommes	Men
Dames	Women
Entrée	Entrance
Sortie	Exit

ALPHABETICAL WORD LIST

English	Pronunciation and French Spelling
A	
a	*ung* (un)
or	*ewn* (une)
am	
I am	*juh SWEE* (Je suis)
Americans	*ah-may-ree-KANG* (américains)
American sailors	*mah-RANG Z_ah-may-ree-KANG* (marins américains)
I am an American	*juh SWEE-Z_ah-may-ree-KANG* (Je suis américain)
and	*ay* (et)

English	Pronunciation and French Spelling
apples	*PAWM* (pommes)
are	
Are you____?	*et VOO____?* (Etes-vous____?)
They are____	*eel SAWNG____* (Ils sont____)
We are____	*noo SAWM____* (Nous sommes____)
aspirin	*ah-spee-REEN* (aspirine)

B

bacon	*LAR* (lard)
bad	*mo-VAY* (mauvais)
bandage	*pahnss-MAHNG* (pansement)
barber	*kwa-FUR* (coiffeur)
beans	*ah-ree-KO* (haricots)
string beans	*ah-ree-ko VAYR* (haricots verts)
bed	*LEE* (lit)
beef	*BUF* (boeuf)
beer	*b_yayr* (bière)
a glass of beer	*ung VAYR duh B_YAYR* (un verre de bière)
blankets	*koo-vayr-TEWR* (couvertures)
boiled water	*o boo-YEE* (eau bouillie)
bread	*PANG* (pain)
bridge	*PAWNG* (pont)
bring	
Bring help!	*ah-lay shayr-SHAY dew suh-KOOR!* (Allez chercher du secours!)
Bring me____	*ah-pawr-tay MWA____* (Apportez-moi____)
brush	
shaving brush	*blay-RO* (blaireau)
bus	*o-to-BEWSS* (autobus)
butter	*BUR* (beurre)
buttons	*boo-TAWNG* (boutons)
buy it	*lash-TAY* (l'acheter)

C

cabbage	*SHOO* (chou)
can	
Where can I find____?	*oo PWEEJ troo-VAY____?* (Où puis-je trouver____?)
careful	
Be careful!	*fet ah-tahnss-YAWNG!* (Faites attention!)
carrots	*ka-RAWT* (carottes)

English	Pronunciation and French Spelling
centime	*sahn-TEEM* (centime)
chicken	*poo-LAY* (poulet)
chocolate	*shaw-kaw-LA* (chocolat)
chops	*kawt-LET* (côtelettes)
lamb chops	*kawt-LET duh moo-TAWNG* (côtelettes de mouton)
pork chops	*kawt-LET duh PAWR* (côtelettes de porc)
church	*ay-GLEEZ* (église)
cigarettes	*see-ga-RET* (cigarettes)
cigars	*see-GAR* (cigares)
city	*VEEL* (ville)
clothing store	*ma-ga-ZANG duh kawn-feks-YAWNG* (magasin de confection)
coffee	*ka-FAY* (café)
a cup of coffee	*ewn TASS duh ka-FAY* (une tasse de café)
comb	*PEN-yuh* (peigne)
Come!	*vuh-NAY!* (Venez!)
Come here!	*vuh-NAY-Z_ee-SEE!* (Venez ici!)
Come quickly!	*vuh-nay VEET!* (Venez vite!)
cotton	*kaw-TAWNG* (coton)
cover	
Take cover!	*met-ay VOO-Z_ah la-BREE!* (Mettez-vous à l'abri!)
cup	*TAHSS* (tasse)
a cup of____	*ewn TAHSS duh____* (une tasse de____)

D

Danger!	*dahn-JAY!* (Danger!)
day	*JOOR* (jour)
Good day	*bawng JOOR* (Bonjour)
dentist	*dahn-TEEST* (dentiste)
disinfectant	*day-zan-fek-TAHNG* (désinfectant)
Do you understand?	*KAWM-pruh-nay VOO?* (Comprenez-vous?)
doctor	*dawk-TUR* (docteur)
Take me to a doctor	*kawn-dwee-zay-MWA shay-z_ung dawk-TUR* (Conduisez-moi chez un docteur)
Draw me a map	*fet-mwa ung kraw-KEE* (Faites-moi un croquis)
(to) drink	*BWAR* (boire)
drinking water	*o paw-TABL* (eau potable)
drugstore	*far-ma-SEE* (pharmacie)

E

(to) eat	*mahn-JAY* (manger)
eggs	*UH* (oeufs)

English	*Pronunciation and French Spelling*
eight	*WEET* (huit)
eighteen	*DEEZ-WEET* (dix-huit)
eighty	*kat-ruh-VANG* (quatre-vingt)
eleven	*AWNZ* (onze)
excuse me	*ek-skew-zay MWA* (excusez-moi)
evening	*SWAR* (soir)
Good evening	*bawn-SWAR* (Bonsoir)
expensive	*SHAYR* (cher)

F

far	*LWANG* (loin)
Is it far?	*ess kuh SAY LWANG?* (Est-ce que c'est loin?)
How far is it?	*ah kel dee-stahnss ESS?* (A quelle distance est-ce?)
fifteen	*KANZ* (quinze)
fifty	*san-KAHNT* (cinquante)
(to) find	*troo-VAY* (trouver)
Where can I find___?	*oo pweej troo-VAY___?* (Où puis-je trouver___?)
fish	*pwa-SAWNG* (poisson)
five	*SANK* (cinq)
fork	*foor-SHET* (fourchette)
forty	*ka-RAHNT* (quarante)
four	*KATR* (quatre)
fourteen	*ka-TAWRZ* (quatorze)
franc	*FRAHNG* (franc)
French	*frahn-SAY* (français)
in French	*ang frahn-SAY* (en français)
Friday	*VAHN-druh-DEE* (vendredi)
friend	*ah-MEE* (ami)
I am your friend	*juh SWEE vawtr a-MEE* (Je suis votre ami)
fruit	*frwee* (fruit)

G

garage	*ga-RAJ* (garage)
get	
Where can I get___?	*oo pweej troo-VAY___?* (Où puis-je trouver___?)
Give me___	*daw-nay MWA___* (Donnez-moi___)
glass	*VAYR* (verre)
a glass of___	*ung VAYR duh___* (un verre de___)
Go!	*ah-LAY!* (Allez!)
Go quickly!	*ah-lay VEET!* (Allez vite!)
good	*BAWNG* (bon)
Good day	*bawng-JOOR* (Bonjour)

English	*Pronunciation and French Spelling*
Good evening	*bawn-SWAR* (Bonsoir)
Good-by	*o ruh-VWAR* (Au revoir)
grapes	*ray-ZANG* (raisins)
grocery	*ay-peess-REE* (épicerie)

H

hair	*shuh-VUH* (cheveux)
have my hair cut	*muh fayr koo-PAY lay shuh-VUH* (me faire couper les cheveux)
half	*duh-MEE* (demi)
half past six	*see-z_UR ay duh-MEE* (six heures et demi)
ham	*jahm-BAWNG* (jambon)
handkerchief	*moo-SHWAR* (mouchoir)
(to) have	*av-WAR* (avoir)
Have you?	*ah-vay VOO?* (Avez-vous?)
I have	*JAY* (J'ai)
I don't have	*juh nay PA* (Je n'ai pas)
We have	*noo-z_ah-VAWNG* (Nous avons)
We don't have	*noo na-vawng PA* (Nous n'avons pas)
he	*eel* (il)
He is___	*eel AY___* (Il est___)
Help!	*o suh-KOOR!* (Au secours!)
Bring help!	*ah-lay shayr-SHAY dew suh-KOOR!* (Allez chercher du secours!)
Help me!	*ay-day MWA!* (Aidez-moi!)
here	*ee-SEE* (ici)
Come here!	*vuh-NAY-z_ee-see!* (Venez ici!)
highway	*grahn ROOT* (grande route)
hospital	*o-pee-TAL* (hôpital)
Take me to a hospital	*kawn-dwee-zay-MWA ah lo-pee-TAL* (Conduisez-moi à l'hôpital)
hot water	*o shohd* (eau chaude)
hotel	*o-TEL* (hôtel)
house	*may-ZAWNG* (maison)
how	*kaw-MAHNG* (comment)
How are you?	*kaw-MAHN-T_ah-lay VOO?* (Comment allez-vous?)
How do you say___?	*kaw-MAHNG deet voo___?* (Comment dites-vous___?)
How far is it?	*ah kel dee-stahnss ESS?* (A quelle distance est-ce?)
How much?	*kawm-B_YANG?* (Combien?)
hundred	*SAHNG* (cent)
hungry	
I am hungry	*jay FANG* (J'ai faim)

English	Pronunciation and French Spelling

I

I	*juh* (je)
I have___	*JAY___* (J'ai___)
I don't have___	*juh nay PA* (Je n'ai pas___)
I am hungry	*jay FANG* (J'ai faim)
I am thirsty	*jay SWAF* (J'ai soif)
I want___ *or* I want to___	*juh VUH___* (Je veux___)
I would like___	*juh voo-DRAY___* (Je voudrais___)
ink	*AHNKR* (encre)
iodine	*yawd* (iode)
is	
He is___	*eel AY___* (Il est___)
It is___	*SAY___* (C'est___)
It is not___	*suh nay PA___* (Ce n'est pas___)
Is it___?	*ess kuh SAY___?* (Est-ce que c'est___?)
Is it far?	*ess-kuh SAY LWANG?* (Est-ce que c'est loin?)
What is it?	*kess kuh SAY?* (Qu'est-ce que c'est?)
Where is___?	*oo AY___?* (Où est___?)
Where is there___?	*oo ee-ah-t␣EEL___* (Où y-a-t-il___?)

K

kilometer	*kee-lo-METR* (kilomètre)
knife	*koo-TO* (couteau)

L

lamb	*moo-TAWNG* (mouton)
lamb chops	*kawt-LET duh moo-TAWNG* (côtelettes de mouton)
laundry	*blahn-sheess-REE* (blanchisserie)
laxative	*lak-sa-TEEF* (laxatif)
leave	
When does the train leave?	*ah KEL UR par luh TRANG?* (A quelle heure part le train?)
left	
to the left	*ah GOHSH* (à gauche)
like	
I would like	*juh voo-DRAY* (Je voudrais)
lost	*payr-DEW* (perdu)
luck	*SHAHNSS* (chance)
Good luck	*bawn SHAHNSS* (Bonne chance)

English	Pronunciation and French Spelling

M

madam	*ma-DAHM* (madame)
main street	*grahng REW* (grand'rue)
map	*kraw-KEE* (croquis)
Draw me a map	*fet MWA ung kraw-KEE* (Faites-moi un croquis)
market	*mar-SHAY* (marché)
matches	*ah-lew-MET* (allumettes)
mattress	*mat-LA* (matelas)
me	*MWA* (moi)
meat	*V␣YAHND* (viande)
mechanic	*may-ka-neess-YANG* (mécanicien)
milk	*LAY* (lait)
miss	*mad-mwa-ZEL* (mademoiselle)
moment	*maw-MAHNG* (moment)
Monday	*LUN-DEE* (lundi)
mosquito net	*moo-stee-KAYR* (moustiquaire)
movie	*see-nay-MA* (cinéma)
When does the movie start?	*ah KEL UR kaw-MAHNSS luh see-nay-MA* (A quelle heure commence le cinéma?)

N

name	
My name is___	*juh ma-PEL___* (Je m'appelle___)
What's your name?	*kaw-MAHNG voo-z␣ah-puh-lay VOO?* (Comment vous appelez-vous?)
near	*pray* (près)
the nearest town	*luh vee-LAJ luh plew PRAWSH* (le village le plus proche)
I need___	*eel muh FO___* (Il me faut___)
needle	*ay-GWEE-yuh* (aiguille)
nine	*NUF* (neuf)
nineteen	*deez-NUF* (dix-neuf)
ninety	*kat-ruh-van-DEESS* (quatre-vingt-dix)
no	*NAWNG* (non)
north	*NAWR* (nord)
Which way is north?	*duh kel ko-TAY ay luh NAWR?* (De quel côté est le nord?)
not	*ne . . . pa* (ne . . . pas)
I do not understand	*juh nuh kawn-prahng PA* (Je ne comprends pas)

O

of	*duh* (de)
of the *or*	*dew* (du) / *duh la* (de la)

English	Pronunciation and French Spelling
one o'clock	*UNG* (un)
one o'clock	*eel ay-t⏝EWN UR* (il est une heure)
two o'clock	*eel ay DUH-Z⏝UR* (il est deux heures)
oranges	*aw-RAHNJ* (oranges)

P

English	Pronunciation and French Spelling
past	
half past six	*see-z⏝UR ay duh-MEE* (six heures et demi)
pears	*PWAR* (poires)
peas	*puh-tee PWA* (petits pois)
pen	*PLEWM* (plume)
pencil	*kray-YAWNG* (crayon)
pepper	*PWAVR* (poivre)
pillow	*aw-ray-YAY* (oreiller)
pins	*ay-PANGL* (épingles)
safety pins	*ay-PANGL duh sewr-TAY* (épingles de sûreté)
pipe	*PEEP* (pipe)
plate	*ah-SYET* (assiette)
please	*seel voo PLAY* (S'il vous plaît)
policeman	*ah-JAHNG duh paw-LEESS* (agent de police)
police station	*pawst duh paw-LEESS* (poste de police)
pork	*PAWR* (porc)
pork chops	*kawt-LET duh PAWR* (côtelettes de porc)
porter	*pawr-TUR* (porteur)
post office	*bew-RO duh PAWST* (bureau de poste)
potatoes	*PAWM duh TAYR* (pommes de terre)

Q

English	Pronunciation and French Spelling
quarter	
quarter of eight	*wee-t⏝UR mwang luh KAR* (huit heures moins le quart)
quarter past five	*sank UR ay KAR* (cinq heures et quart)
quickly	*VEET* (vite)
Come quickly!	*vuh-nay VEET!* (Venez vite!)
Go quickly!	*ah-lay VEET!* (Allez vite!)

R

English	Pronunciation and French Spelling
railroad	*shuh-MANG duh FAYR* (chemin de fer)
railroad station	*GAR* (gare)
Where is the railroad station?	*oo AY la GAR?* (Où est la gare?)

English	Pronunciation and French Spelling
raincoat	*am-payr-may-ABL* (imperméable)
razor	*ra-ZWAR* (rasoir)
razor blades	*LAM duh ra-ZWAR* (lames de rasoir)
Repeat!	*ray-pay-TAY!* (Répétez!)
rest	
I want to rest	*juh VUH muh ruh-po-ZAY* (Je veux me reposer)
restaurant	*ress-to-RAHNG* (restaurant)
Where is the restaurant?	*oo AY luh ress-to-RAHNG?* (Où est le restaurant?)
rewarded	*ray-kawm-pahn-SAY* (récompensé)
You will be rewarded	*voo suh-RAY ray-kawn-pahn-SAY* (Vous serez récompensé)
rice	*REE* (riz)
right	
to the right	*ah DRWAT* (à droite)
right away	*toot SWEET* (tout de suite)
river	*reev-YAYR* (rivière)
road	*root* (route)
room	*SHAHMBR* (chambre)

S

English	Pronunciation and French Spelling
safety pins	*ay-PANGL duh sewr-TAY* (épingles de sûreté)
sailors	*mah-RANG* (marins)
Where are the American sailors?	*oo SAWNG lay mah-RANG-Z⏝ah-may-ree-KANG?* (Où sont les marins américains?)
salad	*sa-LAD* (salade)
salt	*SEL* (sel)
Saturday	*SAM-DEE* (samedi)
say	
How do you say___?	*kaw-MAHNG deet voo___?* (Comment dites-vous___?)
servant	*daw-mess-TEEK* (domestique)
seven	*SET* (sept)
seventeen	*deess-SET* (dix-sept)
seventy	*swa-sahnt-DEESS* (soixante-dix)
shave	
I want to be shaved	*juh VUH muh fayr rah-ZAY* (Je veux me faire raser)
shaving brush	*blay-RO* (blaireau)
shaving soap	*sa-VAWNG ah BARB* (savon à barbe)
she	*el* (elle)
sheets	*DRA* (draps)

English	Pronunciation and French Spelling
shirt	*shuh-MEEZ* (chemise)
shoes	*sool-YAY* (souliers)
shoe laces	*la-SAY* (lacets)
shoe polish	*see-RAJ* (cirage)
shoemaker	*kawr-dawn-YAY* (cordonnier)
show	
Show me	*mawn-tray-MWA* (Montrez-moi)
sick	*ma-LAD* (malade)
sir	*muss-YUH* (monsieur)
six	*SEESS* (six)
sixteen	*SEZ* (seize)
sixty	*swa-SAHNT* (soixante)
ship	*na-VEER*
Where is the ship?	*oo AY luh na-VEER* (Où est le navire?)
(to) sleep	*dawr-MEER* (dormir)
slowly	*lahnt-MAHNG* (lentement)
soap	*sa-VAWNG* (savon)
shaving soap	*sa-VAWNG ah BARB* (savon à barbe)
sou	*SOO* (sou)
soup	*SOOP* (soupe)
Speak!	*par-LAY!* (Parlez!)
Speak slowly	*par-lay lahnt-MAHNG* (Parlez lentement)
spoon	*kwee-YAYR* (cuillère)
spring (for water)	*SOORSS* (source)
starts	*kaw-MAHNSS* (commence)
When does the movie start?	*ah KEL UR kaw-MAHNSS luh see-nay-MA?* (A quelle heure commence le cinéma?)
station	
police station	*PAWST duh paw-LEESS* (poste de police)
railroad station	*GAR* (gare)
Where is the railroad station?	*oo AY la GAR* (Où est la gare?)
steak	
beefsteak	*bif-TEK* (bifteck)
Stop!	*ALT!* (Halte!)
store	*ma-ga-ZANG* (magasin)
clothing store	*ma-ga-ZANG duh kawn-feks-YAWNG* (magasin de confection)
straight ahead	*too DRWA* (tout droit)
street	*rew* (rue)
main street	*grahng REW* (grand'rue)
string beans	*ah-ree-ko VAYR* (haricots verts)
sugar	*sewkr* (sucre)
Sunday	*dee-MAHNSH* (dimanche)

English	Pronunciation and French Spelling
T	
tailor	*ta-YUR* (tailleur)
take	
I want to take a bath	*juh VUH prahndr ung BANG* (Je veux prendre un bain)
Take me to a doctor	*kawn-dwee-zay-MWA shay-z ung dawk-TUR* (Conduisez-moi chez un docteur)
Take me to the hospital	*kawn-dwee-zay-MWA ah lo-pee-TAL* (Conduisez-moi à l'hôspital)
Take me there	*muh-nay-z ee MWA* (Menez-y-moi)
tea	*TAY* (thé)
telegraph office	*bew-ro dew tay-lay-GRAF* (bureau du télégraphe)
telephone	*tay-lay-FAWN* (téléphone)
ten	*DEESS* (dix)
Thank you	*mayr-SEE* (merci)
that	
What's that?	*KESS kuh say kuh SA?* (Qu'est-ce que c'est que ça?)
the	*luh* (le)
or	*lah* (la)
or	*lay* (les)
there	
Take me there	*muh-nay-z ee MWA* (Menez-y-moi)
they	*eel* (ils)
They are	*eel SAWNG* (Ils sont)
thirsty	
I am thirsty	*jay SWAF* (J'ai soif)
thirteen	*TREZ* (treize)
thirty	*TRAHNT* (trente)
this	*suh-SEE* (ceci)
What's this?	*KESS kuh suh-SEE?* (Qu'est-ce que ceci?)
thousand	*MEEL* (mil)
thread	*FEEL* (fil)
three	*TRWA* (trois)
Thursday	*JUH-DEE* (jeudi)
time	
at what time	*ah kel UR* (à quelle heure)
What time is it?	*kel UR ay-t EEL?* (Quelle heure est-il?)
tired	*fa-tee-GAY* (fatigué)
to	
to the right	*ah DRWAT* (à droite)
to the left	*ah GOHSH* (à gauche)

English	Pronunciation and French Spelling
to a doctor	o dawk-TUR (au docteur)
to the hospital	ah lo-pee-TAL (à l'hôpital)
tobacco	ta-BA (tabac)
today	o-joord-WEE (aujourd'hui)
toilet	la-va-BO (lavabo)
Where is the toilet?	oo AY luh la-va-BO? (Où est le lavabo?)
tomorrow	duh-MANG (demain)
too expensive	tro SHAYR (trop cher)
toothbrush	BRAWSS ah DAHNG (brosse à dents)
tooth paste	PAHT dahn-tee-FREESS (pâte dentifrice)
towel	sayrv-YET (serviette)
town	vee-LAJ (village)
the nearest town	luh vee-LAJ luh plew PRAWSH (le village le plus proche)
train	TRANG (train)
When does the train leave?	ah KEL UR par luh TRANG? (A quelle heure part le train?)
Tuesday	MAR-DEE (mardi)
twelve	DOOZ (douze)
twenty	VANG (vingt)
twenty-one	van-t_ay UNG (vingt-et-un)
twenty-two	vant-DUH (vingt-deux)
two	DUH (deux)

U

understand	
Do you understand?	KAWM-pruh-nay VOO? (Comprenez-vous?)
I understand	juh kawm-PRAHNG (Je comprends)
I don't understand	juh nuh KAWM-prahng PA (Je ne comprends pas)
underwear	soo-vet-MAHNG (sous-vêtements)

V

veal	vo (veau)
vegetables	lay-GEWM (légumes)

W

Wait!	ah-tahn-DAY! (Attendez!)
Wait a moment	ah-tahn-DAY-Z_ung mo-MAHNG (Attendez un moment)
want	
I want___ or I want to___	juh VUH___ (Je veux___)
We want___	noo voo-LAWNG___ (Nous voulons___)
wash up	

English	Pronunciation and French Spelling
I want to wash up	juh VUH muh la-VAY (Je veux me laver
Watch out!	pruh-nay GARD! (Prenez garde!)
water	O (eau)
boiled water	O boo-YEE (eau bouillie)
drinking water	O paw-TABL (eau potable)
hot water	o SHOHD (eau chaude)
we	NOO (nous)
We are___	noo SAWM___ (Nous sommes___)
We have___	noo-z_ah-VAWNG___ (Nous avons___)
We don't have___	noo na-vawng PA___ (Nous n'avons pas___)
We want___	noo voo-LAWNG___ (Nous voulons___)
Wednesday	MAYR-kruh-DEE (mercredi)
well (for water)	pwee (puits)
welcome	
You're welcome	eel nee ah pa duh KWA (Il n'y a pas de quoi)
what	
What is it?	kess kuh SAY? (Qu'est-ce que c'est?)
What's this?	KESS kuh suh-SEE? (Qu'est-ce que ceci?)
What's that?	KESS kuh say kuh SAH? (Qu'est-ce que c'est que çà?)
What is your name?	kaw-MAHNG voo-z_ah-puh-lay VOO? (Comment vous appelez-vous?)
What time is it?	kel UR ay-t_EEL? (Quelle heure est-il?)
when	KAHNG (quand)
When does the movie start?	ah KEL UR kaw-MAHNSS luh see-nay-MA? (A quelle heure commence le cinéma?)
When does the train leave?	ah KEL UR par luh TRANG? (A quelle heure part le train?)
where	oo (où)
Where is___?	oo AY___? (Où est___?)
Where are___?	oo SAWNG___? (Où sont___?)
Where is there___?	oo ee-ah-t_EEL___? (Où y a-t-il___?)
which	
Which is the road to___?	kel ay luh shuh-MANG poor___? (Quel est le chemin pour___?)
Which way is north?	duh kel ko-TAY ay luh NAWR? (De quel côté est le nord?)
wine	vang (vin)
a bottle of wine	ewn boo-TAY_ee duh VANG (une bouteille de vin)

English	Pronunciation and French Spelling	English	Pronunciation and French Spelling
workman	*oov-R͜YAY* (ouvrier)	**you**	*voo* (vous)
wounded	*blay-SAY* (blessé)	**You will be rewarded**	*voo suh-RAY ray-kawm-pahn-SAY* (Vous serez récompensé)
Y		**Have you?**	*ah-vay VOO?* (Avez-vous?)
yes	*wee* (oui)	**Are you?**	*et VOO?* (Etes-vous?)
yesterday	*ee-YAYR* (hier)		

Medical Dictionary

A

a *abbr.* accommodation; anterior; asymmetric; area; total acidity.

a- *or* **an-** *prefix* without; lacking; wanting: asexual, anesthesia.

Å *abbr.* Ångstrom; Ångstrom unit.

āā *abbr.* (in prescriptions) of each.

ab- *prefix* from; deviating from: *abnormal.*

abactio induced abortion.

abactus venter induced abortion.

abalienated mentally incapable.

abalienation the state of being mentally deranged or incapable.

abapical opposite the extremity or apex.

abaptiston a conical-shaped trephine, designed to minimize damage to the brain tissues while removing a section of the skull.

abarognosis inability to estimate the weight of something.

abarthrosis a movable joint; synovial joint.

abarticular not directly involving a joint; at some distance from a joint.

abarticulation 1. diarthrosis. 2. a dislocated joint.

abasia difficulty in walking owing to faulty motor control.

abaxial 1. not within the axis of any body or part. 2. located at the opposite extremity of some axis.

abdient tending to move away from the point of a stimulus.

abdomen the section of the front part of the body lying between the pelvis and the thorax and containing many major organs; belly. —**abdominal** *adj.*

abdominalgia pain in the abdomen; bellyache.

abdomino- *combining form* relating to or associated with the abdomen.

abdominoscopy examination of the abdominal contents.

abduce abduct.

abduct to draw away from a median or center line.

abduction the manipulation of a limb away from the middle line of the body.

abductor a muscle, as the deltoid, that draws a limb away from the middle line of the body.

aberration deviation from or variation of the normal condition or course.

abiogenesis spontaneous generation of a living organism.

abionarce lack of energy and drive due to chronic illness.

abiotic not compatible with life; nonliving.

abirritant an agent that soothes or relieves irritation.

ablastin an antibody that inhibits the multiplication or growth of certain microorganisms.

ablation the detachment or removal of a bodily part, esp. by cutting.

ablatio retinae detachment of the retina of the eye.

ablepsia blindness.

abluent any agent capable of cleansing.

abortifacient an agent, as a drug, for inducing abortion. —**abortifacient** *adj.*

abortion spontaneous or induced expulsion of a fetus from the uterus, esp. during the first 12 weeks of pregnancy. —**abortive** *adj.*

abortus an aborted fetus.

abrasion a superficial cut or scrape on the skin or mucous membrane.

abreaction the release of tension and anxiety by the reliving of repressed painful experiences and the understanding of their meaning through the psychoanalytic process.

abruptio a tearing away or premature detachment, especially of the placenta (abruptio placentae).

abscess a localized accumulation of pus in a tissue or organ that is surrounded by inflamed tissue.

absinthism a nerve disorder caused by the excessive consumption of absinthe.

absorbefacient 1. causing absorption. 2. an agent that causes absorption.

absorbent taking in or up by capillary action. —**absorbency** *n.*

acalculia the inability or loss of ability to solve even a simple mathematicial problem.

acampsia abnormal stiffness or rigidity of a joint; ankylosis.

acantha the spine or a spinous process of a vertebra.

acanthosis abnormal thickening of the outermost layer of the epidermis.

acapnia a diminished amount of carbon dioxide in the blood.

acardia absence of the heart from birth.

acariasis any disease caused by infestation with mites (acarids).

acaricide an agent that kills mites.

Acarus a genus of mites including those causing scabies.

acatalepsy absence of comprehension or understanding. —**acataleptic** *adj.*

acataphasia a speech disorder characterized by an inability to express thoughts in clear, logical sequence.

acataposis inability to swallow liquids or great difficulty in doing so.

acathexis a mental disorder characterized by the absence of normal emotional reactions towards objects or ideas, esp. those that are subconsiously significant to the patient.

accessorius relating to any of various muscles, glands, nerves, etc., that have an accessory or auxiliary function; assisting.

accommodation the ability of the eye to focus on near and far objects by contraction of the ciliary muscles to control the curvature of the lens.

accouchement childbirth; labor and delivery.

acephaly absence of the head from birth.

acescent slightly acid.

acetabuloplasty an operation on the acetabulum to correct a deformity or treat osteoarthritis.

acetabulum the cuplike socket of the hipbone.

acetic acid the acid contained in vinegar, used esp. in urine testing.

acetone a colorless, volatile solvent liquid produced synthetically and found in minute quantities naturally in the body and in larger amounts in the condition diabetes mellitus.

acetonemia abnormal presence of large amounts of acetone in the blood.

acetonuria abnormal presence of large amounts of acetone in the urine.

acetylcholine a chemical compound released at autonomic nerve endings to aid in the transmission of nerve impulses.

acetylsalicylic acid chemical name for aspirin.

achalasia failure of various visceral openings or sphincters, as the pylorus, to relax normally.

Achilles tendon the large strong tendon joining the muscles of the calf of the leg with the bone of the heel.

achillorrhaphy surgical repair of a ruptured Achilles tendon.

achillotomy surgical division of the Achilles tendon.

achiria 1. absence of the hands from birth. 2. loss of sensation in one or both hands.

achlorhydria lack of hydrochloric acid in the stomach.

achluophobia fear of being in the dark.

acholia a lack of bile secretions.

achondroplasia abnormal development of cartilage leading to dwarfism.

achromasia the absence of normal skin pigmentation.

achylia absence of chyle in the intestinal tract.

acid any of various water-soluble, sour compounds that combine with alkalis to form salts and turn blue litmus paper red.

acidemia an abnormally high acid level of the blood.

acid-fast not decolorized easily by acids.

acidity the quality or degree of being acid.

acidosis a condition of decreased alkalinity of the blood and body tissues below normal levels.

aciduria the condition of an acid urine.

acinus *pl.* **acini** one of the small, secreting, saclike structures lining a compound gland.

acmesthesia sensitivity to a sharp point on the skin, as a pinprick.

acne a disorder of the skin esp. of the face, shoulders, and back that occurs chiefly during adolescence, is marked by pustules and blackheads, and is caused by hyperactivity of the sebaceous glands.

acnemia 1. wasting of the calf muscles. 2. absence of the legs from birth.

acomia baldness.

acoprosis absence or virtual absence of waste matter in the large intestine.

acorea absence of the pupil of the eye at birth.

acoustic of or relating to sound or hearing.

acquired assumed or contracted after birth; not congenital or hereditary.

acriflavine a yellow dye used as an antiseptic esp. on wounds.

acrocentric having the centromere closer to one arm of the chromosome than to the other.

acrocephaly a malformation of the skull in which the crown is pointed.

acrocyanosis a severe form of chilblains, resulting from an inadequate blood supply to the hands and feet.

acrodynia painful inflammation of the nerves of the fingers or toes.

acrogeria premature wrinkling and aging of the skin of the hands and feet.

acromegaly abnormal enlargement of the facial features, hands, and feet owing to hypersecretion of growth hormone by the pituitary gland after puberty. Compare *gigantism*.

acromicria abnormal smallness of the bones of the skull and extremities, thought to be caused by a deficiency of growth hormone secreted by the pituitary gland.

acromion the outward projection of the spine of the scapula forming the high point of the shoulder.

acronyx an ingrown fingernail or toenail.

acroparesthesia an abnormal numbness or tingling sensation in the hands or feet.

acrophobia an abnormally severe dread of being at a great height.

acrosome part of the head of a sperm cell.

ACTH adrenocorticotrophic hormone.

actinism the property of radiant energy that produces chemical changes.

actinodermatitis dermatitis resulting from exposure to radiant energy, esp. sunlight.

Actinomyces a genus of rod-shaped bacteria including disease-producing parasites.

actinomycin an antibacterial agent esp. active against Gram-positive bacteria, obtained from a species of *Actinomyces*.

actinomycosis disease produced by bacteria of the genus *Actinomyces* and characterized chiefly by discharging abscesses.

actinomyoca a swelling caused by infection with bacteria of the genus *Actinomyces*.

actinoneuritis inflammation of nerves caused by chronic exposure to radium or X-rays.

actinophage a virus capable of destroying bacteria of the genus *Actinomyces*.

actinotherapy treatment with infra-red or ultra-violet radiation.

activator a substance serving to effect a physical or chemical change in another substance while remaining itself inactive.

actomyosin a complex of actin and myosin that with ATP is responsible for muscular contraction and relaxation.

acupuncture a technique of Chinese origin of puncturing the body with needles to relieve pain or cure disease.

acute (of a disease) having a sudden onset, swift rise, and brief course.

acystia absence of the bladder from birth.

adactylia absence of fingers or toes from birth. —**adactylous** *adj.*

adamantinoma a highly destructive tumour of the jaw.

Adam's apple a prominence at the front of the neck (esp. in men), formed by the largest laryngeal cartilage.

adaptation an adjustment to environmental conditions or to variations or intensity of stimulation.

addiction compulsive physical or psychological dependency on a habit-forming drug.

Addison's disease a disease resulting from deficient secretions of the adrenal cortical hormone and being typically characterized by weight loss, nausea, low blood pressure, malaise, and brownish pigmentation of the skin and mucous membranes, esp. of the mouth.

adduct to draw (a limb) toward or past the median axis of the body. —**adduction** *n.*

adductor a muscle serving to draw a bodily part toward the median line of the body or toward the axis of a bodily extremity.

adenalgia pain originating in a gland.

adenectomy the surgical removal of a gland.

adenectopia the presence of a gland in an abnormal site.

adenine a purine chemical base coding hereditary data in the genetic code in DNA and RNA.

adenitis inflammation of a gland or a lymph node.

adenocarcinoma a malignant tumor in or composed of glandular cells.

adenocyte one of the cells forming a gland.

adenofibroma a benign tumor of connective tissue composed largely of glandular tissue.

adenoidectomy surgical removal of the adenoids.

adenoids an enlarged mass of glandular tissue in the nasopharynx that can potentially inhibit breathing. —**adenoidal** *adj.*

adenoma a benign tumor of glandular tissue.

adenosine a nucleoside yielding adenine and ribose.

adenosine diphosphate ADP.

adenosine monophosphate AMP.

adenosine triphosphate ATP.

adenovirus any of various DNA-containing viruses that cause infections of the upper respiratory tract.

ADH antidiuretic hormone.

adhesion tissues joined abnormally by fibrous tissue chiefly as the result of inflammation.

adiaphoresis inadequate ability to perspire.

adipoma a lipoma.

adipometer a device for measuring skin thickness.

adiponecrosis necrosis of fatty tissues.

adiposalgia painful areas of fatty tissue beneath the skin.

adipose relating to animal fat; fatty.

adiposis an excessive accumulation of body fat; liposis.

adiposity fatness; obesity.

aditus an anatomical passage or opening for entry.

adjuvant an ingredient that adds to the effectiveness of a remedy.

ad lib. as much as required (of a drug, remedy, etc.).

admedial near the median plane.

adnexa associated anatomical parts; appendages.

adolescence the period of life between puberty and maturity.

ADP adenosine diphosphate; an ester of adenosine converted to ATP for storing energy in the form of a high-energy phosphate bond.

adrenal 1. adjacent to the kidneys. 2. relating to or derived from the adrenal glands.

adrenalectomy surgical removal of one or both adrenal glands.

adrenal glands a pair of endocrine glands adjacent to the anterior medial border of the kidney, consisting of a cortex and a medulla.

adrenaline epinephrine.

adrenalopathy any disease or disorder of the adrenal glands.

adrenergic activated or transmitted by epinephrine (adrenaline).

adrenocorticotrophic hormone a hormone that is secreted by the anterior lobe of the pituitary gland and stimulates the secretion of hormones by the adrenal cortex.

adrenolytic a substance that inhibits the action of epinephrine (adrenaline) or the function of the adrenal glands.

adrenomegaly abnormal enlargement of the adrenal glands.

adrenopause a supposed period of reduced activity of the adrenal glands.

adrenosterone an androgen secreted by the adrenal cortex.

adrenotoxin any substance that is poisonous to the adrenal glands.

adsorbent relating to or characterized by adsorption.

adsorption the adhesion of a thin molecular layer of a substance, as a gas or liquid, to the solid or liquid surface with which it is in contact.

adventitia the outermost covering or coat of a vein, artery or other structure, not forming an integral part of it.

aerogen a bacillus that produces intestinal gas.

afebrile lacking fever; having a normal body temperature.

affect the consciously apprehended aspect of an emotion regarded as distinct from bodily reactions.

afferent carrying toward; said of nerves carrying impulses to a nerve center and of blood and lymph vessels supplying a particular organ or part.

affinity a force of attraction between particles or substances that brings them into a chemical combination.

afterbirth the placenta, umbilical cord, and fetal membranes expelled from the uterus after the birth of the infant.

afterbrain the metencephalon.

aftercare treatment and supervision of a patient discharged from a hospital.

afterdischarge the extension or prolongation of a reflex response after removal of the original stimulus.

afterimage a visual impression that remains after the stimulation causing it has ceased.

afterpain pain arising from uterine contractions following expulsion of the placenta.

aftosa foot and mouth disease.

agalactia the absence of milk secretion following the birth of a child.

agalorrhea the sudden stopping of the flow of milk from the breast.

agamous relating to reproduction by budding, fission or other nonsexual means.

agar *or* **agaragar** a gelatinous, colloidal extractive of a red alga, used esp. in bacteriology as a culture medium.

agenesis failure or lack of development, esp. of a bodily part.

agenosomia the absence or severe malformation of the genital organs in a fetus.

agerasia youthful appearance of an elderly person.

ageusia loss of the sense of taste.

agglutination the clumping together of particles, as blood cells or bacteria, suspended in a liquid.

agglutinin a substance, as an antibody, causing agglutination.

agglutinogen an antigen stimulating the production of an agglutinin.

aggression hostile or destructive behavior or attitude arising chiefly from frustration or feelings of inadequacy.

agitophasia abnormally rapid but impaired speech.

aglutition an inability to swallow.

agnea the inability to recognize objects.

agnosia a disturbance in the ability to comprehend the nature of a sensory impression.

agonist relating to or describing a muscle in a state of contraction, compared with its opposing (antagonist) muscle.

agoraphobia a fear of open spaces or of crossing an open area.

agraffe a device for holding the edges of a wound together without the use of sutures.

agrammatism loss of the ability to use words in a normal or meaningful pattern as the result of brain damage or disease.

agranulocytosis a destructive condition characterized by severe reduction in the number of granulocytes in the blood.

agraphia the psychological loss of the ability to express oneself in writing.

ague a malaria-like condition marked by fever, chills, and sweating recurring in paroxysms at regular intervals.

agyria a congenital defect of the brain in which the normal cerebral folds are undeveloped or absent.

AHG antihemophilic globulin; a blood-coagulating protein factor in which hemophiliacs are deficient.

AID. artificial insemination with donor semen.

AIH. artificial insemination with the husband's semen.

air embolism embolism resulting from air entering the circulatory system.

akathisia a psychological condition marked by restlessness, hyperactivity, and anxiety.

akinesis loss or impairment of movement.

Al *symbol* aluminum.

ala a wing or winglike part or anatomical process.

alalia the inability to talk due to impairment, as by disease, of the organs of speech.

alba the white matter of the brain, composed mainly of the myelinated axons of nerve cells.

albinism congenital deficiency in skin pigment resulting typically in milky skin, white hair, and eyes with red pupils and pink or blue irises.

albino one affected with albinism.

albocinereous relating to both the white and the gray matter of which the brain and spinal cord are composed.

albumin any of various water-soluble proteins found in blood plasma or serum, muscle, and the whites of eggs and other animal substances.

albuminuria the abnormal presence of albumin (or other proteins) in the urine, usually a sign of some kidney disorder.

alcohol a colorless, flammable, volatile liquid constituting the intoxicating agent in distilled and fermented liquors; ethyl alcohol.

alcoholism an abnormal physiologic or psychological dependence on alcoholic drinks, commonly characterized by excessive solitary or secret drinking and various withdrawal symptoms should drinking cease abruptly; poisoning of the body with alcohol.

alcoholophilia an unnatural craving for alcohol.

alcoholuria the presence of alcohol in the urine.

aldehyde an oxidation product of alcohol, being intermediate in composition between an acid and an alcohol.

aldosterone a hormone of the adrenal cortex regulating the body's salt and water balance.

aldosteronism a condition characterized by weakness, tetany, high blood pressure, irregular heartbeat, and excessive secretion of urine, associated with the production by the adrenal cortex of abnormally large amounts of aldosterone.

aleukocytosis a condition of greatly diminished numbers of white blood cells in the circulation or, rarely, their absence.

alexia an inability to read.

alga *pl.* **algae** any of a group of aquatic plants, as seaweeds, containing chlorophyll often with a brown or red pigment.

algesia sensitivity to pain.

algogenic producing or causing pain.

alimentary of or relating to nutrition or nourishment.

alimentary canal a tubular passage from the mouth to the anus serving to digest and absorb food and eliminate bodily waste.

alimentation the process of giving nourishment; the state of being nourished.

alinasal relating to the flaring part of the nostrils (alae nasi).

alinjection the preservation of tissue specimens by hardening with an injection of alcohol.

aliphatic oily or fatty.

aliquot a measured portion of something.

alkalemia excessive alkalinity of the blood.

alkalescence mild alkalinity or the process of becoming alkaline.

alkali a substance that combines with acids to form salts and turns red litmus paper blue.

alkalimeter an instrument for measuring the alkalinity of a mixture or the strength of alkalis alone.

alkaline relating to or having the properties of an alkali.

alkalinity the amount of alkali in a given substance.

alkaloid any of various complex, bitter, nitrogen-containing organic bases, as morphine or quinine, that are derived from plants and have potent pharmacological activities.

alkalosis a condition in which the body fluids become abnormally alkaline due to the withdrawal of acid or chlorides from the blood or an excess of alkalis in the blood or other body fluids.

allele allelomorph.

allelomorph any of a group of genes occurring alternatively at a given locus.

allergen a substance that induces allergy.

allergic relating to, inducing, or showing allergy.

allergist a physician specializing in allergy.

allergy hypersensitive reaction to a substance (allergen), as by the swelling of mucous membranes or sneezing or itching.

allochromasia a change in the color of the skin or hair.

allocortex the part of the cerebral cortex that is phylogenetically oldest.

allopath one who practices allopathy.

allopathy a system of medicine characterized by treating diseases by the induction of a dissimilar morbid reaction in some part of the body.

alloplasty the surgical repair of the human body using nonhuman tissue.

alloy a mixture of two or more metals.

alopecia loss of hair; baldness.

altitude sickness the effects, as nausea or nosebleed, of reduced oxygen in the blood resulting from exposure to rarefied air at high altitudes.

alveolotomy the surgical incision into the socket of a tooth to drain an abscess or gain access for other treatment.

alveolus 1. the socket of a tooth. 2. an air sac in the lungs.

alvine relating to the abdomen or intestines.

alvus the abdomen and its contents.

alymphia lack or deficiency of lymph.

amalgam an alloy of mercury and another metal used esp. for filling dental cavities.

amarillic relating to yellow fever.

amaroidal having a slightly bitter taste.

amastia congenital absence of one or both breasts.

amathophobia fear of dirt, dust or filth.

amaurosis progressive degeneration of sight, esp. in the absence of any pathological change to the eye.

ambidextrous using both hands with equal skill and ease.

ambivalence simultaneous attraction toward and repulsion from a person, object, or goal.

amblyopia dimness of vision not of apparent organic origin and attributed esp. to dietary deficiency or toxic effects. —**amblyopic** *adj.*

ambulant ambulatory.

ambulatory (of a patient) able to walk about.

ameba amoeba.

amebiasis amoebiasis.

amebicide amoebicide.

ameburia the presence of amoebas in voided urine.

ameiosis cell division in which gametes are formed without a reduction in their chromosome number.

amelanotic relating to certain types of growths on the skin that do not contain the pigment melanin.

amelia absence of one or more limbs from birth.

amelification formation of tooth enamel.

amelioration improvement in the condition of a patient or symptom.

amenorrhea abnormal cessation or absence of menstruation.

amentia mental deficiency.

ametria congenital absence of the uterus.

ametropia a defective refractive condition of the eye in which the image received fails to focus on the retina.

amino acid an amphoteric organic acid; esp., any of such acids that are the chief components of proteins and are obtained as essential components of the diet or are synthesized by living cells.

amitosis cell division by simple cleavage of the nucleus and division of the cytoplasm.

ammonia a volatile alkali with an extremely pungent odor.

ammoniemia the abnormal presence in the blood of ammonia or its breakdown products, resulting in various symptoms including weak pulse and coma.

ammoniuria the presence of an excessive amount of ammonia in voided urine.

amnesia loss of memory esp. from shock, brain injury, psychological repression, illness, or fatigue.

amnesiac one who suffers from loss of memory.

amnestic an agent that induces amnesia.

amniocentesis the drawing off of amniotic fluid for diagnostic purposes.

amnioclepsis the unrecognized escape of small amounts of amniotic fluid.

amnion the thin, membranous sac enclosing an embryo.

amniotic fluid the serous fluid surrounding and cushioning the embryo inside the amnion.

amniotomy deliberate rupture of the amnion to induce or facilitate labor.

amobarbital a barbiturate drug used to depress the central nervous system, induce sleep, etc., given by injection or as capsules.

amoeba *also* **ameba** a unicellular microscopic protozoan that moves by extending its membranous walls. —**amoebic, amebic** *adj.*

amoebiasis *also* **amebiasis** disease caused by infection with amoebas.

amoebicide *also* **amebicide** a substance lethal to amoebas.

amor lesbicus lesbianism.

amorphous having no definite shape; formless.

amotio retinae detachment of the retina.

AMP adenosine monophosphate; adenosine containing only one phosphoric acid group.

amphetamine a synthetic drug that is a stimulant to the central nervous system and is potentially addictive, once widely used to suppress appetite.

amphiarthrosis a joint with surfaces connected by disks of fibrocartilage.

amphiblestritis inflammation of the retina; retinitis.

amphicrania neuralgia affecting both sides of the head.

amphigenetic produced by both male and female.

amphodiplopia double vision affecting both eyes simultaneously.

amphoteric capable of acting either as an acid or as a base.

ampule *also* **ampul, ampoule** a small, hermetically sealed glass vial for holding a solution, esp. for hypodermic injection.

ampulla a flask-shaped swelling or pouch esp. of a duct.

amputate to perform an amputation.

amputation the cutting off of a limb or other bodily appendage.

amusia loss of the ability to recognize musical tones.

amyelencephalia congenital absence of both the brain and spinal cord.

amyelia congenital absence of the spinal cord.

amyelination loss of the protective myelin sheath that covers the axon of a nerve.

amyelineuria paralysis of the spinal cord.

amygdaloid resembling a tonsil or an almond in shape.

amygdala a mass of gray matter in the front part of the brain's temporal lobe.

amylase any of the enzymes that aid in the hydrolysis of starch and glycogen.

amyloid 1. a waxy, translucent glycoprotein deposited in some organs under unnatural conditions. 2. resembling starch.

amyloidosis the deposition of amyloid in bodily tissues or organs.

ana (in prescriptions) of each in equal amount.

anabolism constructive metabolism in which an organism synthesizes complex molecules from simpler ones.

anaerobe an organism living, thriving, or occurring in the absence of free oxygen. —**anaerobic** *adj.*

anal relating to or situated near the anus.

analeptic 1. a medication that is restorative or stimulating to the central nervous system. 2. relating to such a medicine or remedy; invigorating.

analgesia insensitivity to pain without loss of consciousness.

analgesic 1. a drug that relieves pain, such as aspirin. 2. relating to analgesia.

analgia freedom from pain.

anallergic 1. not causing the production of hypersensitivity or anaphylaxis. 2. a serum, etc., that is not anaphylactic.

analogous similar or comparable in many respects.

analysand one who is undergoing psychoanalysis.

analysis 1. separation of a whole into its component parts; identification or separation of the ingredients of a substance. 2. psychoanalysis.

analyst 1. one who is skilled in making analyses. 2. psychoanalyst.

ananaphylaxis a condition in which anaphylaxis is neutralized.

anaphase a stage in cell division in which the chromosomes move toward the poles of the cell.

anaphoresis reduction in activity of the sweat glands.

anaphylaxis extreme and sometimes fatal allergic response to the injection of a drug or foreign protein resulting from previous sensitization to the substance; anaphylactic shock.

anaplasia reversion of cells to a more primitive or less differentiated form.

anastate any product or substance formed as the result of anabolism.

anastole the separation, shrinking back or retraction of the edges of a wound.

anastomosis the uniting of blood vessels or tubular internal organs so as to create communication between them.

anatherapeusis treatment characterized by the gradual increase in the dose of a drug.

anatomical snuff-box the natural depression or hollow formed between the index finger and the base of the thumb when the latter is abducted.

anatomy a branch of medical science dealing with the form and structure of organisms, esp. the human body.

ancipital having two edges or heads.

anconad in the direction of the elbow.

androgen a hormone producing male sex characteristics. —**androgenic** adj.

androsterone an androgenic hormone occurring in male urine.

anemia also **anaemia** a condition in which the blood has a deficiency in red blood cells, in hemoglobin, or in volume. —**anemic, anaemic** adj.

anencephaly impaired development of the brain with absence of neural tissue in the cranium.

anergic marked by an abnormal degree of inactivity; unenergetic.

anesthesia also **anaesthesia** loss of sensitivity to pain with or without loss of consciousness, achieved through any of various means.

anesthesiologist also **anaesthesiologist** a physician specializing in anesthesiology.

anesthesiology also **anaesthesiology** a branch of medicine concerned with anesthesia and anesthetics.

anesthetic also **anaesthetic** 1. a substance producing anesthesia. 2. relating to or capable of producing anesthesia.

anesthetist also **anaesthetist** one who administers anesthetics.

anetic relaxing or soothing.

anetus intermittent fever.

aneuria lack of energy and drive.

aneurine vitamin B_1; thiamine.

aneurysm a permanent, blood-filled, abnormal dilation of the wall of a blood vessel.

aneurysmectomy surgical removal of the sac formed by an aneurysm.

aneurysmotomy surgical incision into the sac of an aneurysm.

anfractuosity a fissure or sulcus in the cerebrum.

angel's wing a deformity in which the shoulder blades project posteriorly.

angialgia pain in a blood vessel.

angiasthenia vascular weakness or instability.

angiectasis dilation of a blood vessel.

angiectomy surgical removal of a section of a damaged or diseased blood vessel, usually followed by suturing together the remaining ends or (in larger vessels) replacement of the segment with a graft.

angiitis also **angitis** inflammation of a blood vessel or lymph vessel.

angina a condition marked by spasmodic attacks of suffocating pain.

angina pectoris a condition marked chiefly by brief paroxysmal attacks of chest pains resulting from an insufficient supply of blood to the heart.

angiocardiography X-ray photography of the heart and its blood vessels after injection of a radiopaque contrast medium.

angiocardiopathy any disease that involves both the heart and blood vessels.

angiocarditis inflammation of the heart and blood vessels.

angiocholecystitis inflammation of the gallbladder and bile vessels.

angioclast a surgical instrument for controlling arterial bleeding; arterial forceps.

angioedema angioneurotic edema.

angiofibrosis fibrous thickening of the walls of blood vessels.

angiography X-ray photography of the blood vessels after injection of a radiopaque contrast medium.

angiohypertonia spasm of the blood vessels; angiospasm.

angiology the branch of anatomy concerned with the study of the blood vessels and lymphatics.

angioma a tumor composed of blood vessels or lymph vessels.

angioplasty plastic repair of blood vessels or lymphatic glands.

angiotomy surgical separation of a blood vessel.

anhidrotic an agent that checks sweating.

anhydrase an enzyme that acts in the removal of water from a compound.

anhydrous free from water.

animalcule a minute or microscopic organism.

anion an ion with a negative electric charge.

anisocoria inequality in the pupils of both eyes.

anisogamous marked by the fusion of heterogamous gametes or of gametes differing chiefly in size. —**anisogamy** n.

anisometropia marked inequality in refractive power in the two eyes.

ankle 1. the joint between the foot and the leg. 2. the region surrounding this joint.

ankyloblepharon adhesion or fusion of the edges of the eyelids.

ankyloglossia restricted mobility of the tongue resulting from a foreshortened frenum.

ankylosis 1. abnormal stiffness or immobilization of a joint through disease or surgery. 2. fusion of separate bones to form a single bone. —**ankylose** vb.

annular also **anular** ring-shaped, as a muscle.

annulorrhaphy the closure of the circular opening around a hernia by suturing.

anode the positive pole of a primary cell or of a storage battery that is delivering current.

anodontia the absence of teeth.

anodyne 1. a drug that eases pain. 2. serving to lessen pain.

anomia loss of the ability to recognize objects or recognize names.

anoperineal relating to or situated near the anus and perineum.

Anopheles any member of a large genus of mosquitoes including all those that transmit malaria to man.

anophelicide any agent that kills *Anopheles* mosquitoes.

anophelifuge an insect repellent effective against *Anopheles* mosquitoes.

anophthalmus 1. congenital absence of the eyes. 2. one born without eyes.

anorectal relating to or situated within the anus and the rectum.

anorectic 1. relating to anorexia. 2. a drug that suppresses appetite; anorexiant.

anorexia loss of appetite.

anorexia nervosa prolonged loss of appetite esp. when of neurotic origin.

anorexiant a drug or agent that causes a loss of appetite; anorectic.

anoscope proctoscope.

anosigmoidoscopy medical examination of the anus, rectum and lower part of the large intestine.

anosmia impairment or loss of the sense of smell.

anotia absence of the ear from birth.

anotus one without ears.

anovulant a drug that suppresses ovulation.

anovular *also* **anovulatory** 1. not related to or accompanied by ovulation. 2. without ovulation.

anovulation cessation or suppression of ovulation.

anoxemia a condition of the blood marked by insufficient oxygenation.

anoxia severe lack of oxygen causing permanent damage.

ansa 1. (in bacteriology) a small wire loop used to pick up and transport bacteria, protozoa, etc., suspended in a liquid film. 2. any bodily structure or part shaped like or resembling a loop or arc.

ansate *also* **ansiform** loop-shaped.

ansotomy surgical division of a constricting loop.

antacid 1. neutralizing an acid. 2. a substance that counteracts acidity, such as sodium bicarbonate or aluminum hydroxide.

antagonist 1. a muscle that contracts with and limits the action of another muscle with which it is paired. 2. a drug that counteracts the action of another drug.

antalgesic a drug or agent that eases pain; anodyne.

antalkaline neutralizing or counteracting alkalinity.

antasthmatic 1. preventing asthma or relieving the symptoms of an asthmatic attack. 2. an agent that prevents asthma or relieves its symptoms.

antefebrile occurring before the onset of a fever.

antemortem preceding death.

antenatal of or relating to an unborn child or to pregnancy; prenatal.

antepartum before birth.

anterior situated before or toward the front; reverse from posterior.

anterograde proceeding or pointed forward.

antero-inferior lying or situated in front and below.

antero-interior lying or situated toward the front and internally.

anterolateral lying or situated in front and to the side.

anteromedian lying or situated in front and toward a mid-line.

anteroposterior lying or situated from front to back.

anterosuperior lying or situated in front and above.

anthelmintic *also* **anthelminthic** an agent for expelling or destroying parasitic intestinal worms.

anthema any skin eruption.

anthocyanin any of various blue to red pigments that color plants.

anthracosilicosis a disease of the lungs resulting from prolonged inhalation of carbon dust and fine particles of silica.

anthracosis a disease of the lungs resulting from prolonged inhalation of carbon dust alone.

anthrax an acute, infectious disease chiefly of cattle and sheep that is caused by a spore-forming bacterium, is transmissible to man, and is characterized by external ulcerating nodules or by lesions in the lungs.

anthropoid 1. resembling man. 2. resembling an ape.

anthropology the study of the physical, cultural, and environmental aspects of mankind.

anthropometry the branch of anthropology concerned with comparative physical measurements of the body.

anthropophobia a fear of human companionship or an aversion to people generally.

antiagglutinin a specific antibody that counteracts, inhibits or destroys the activity of an agglutinin.

antianaphylaxis desensitization to the potentially harmful effects of a specific antigen, as by a series of very small but progressively increased doses of the antigen.

antiasthmatic 1. preventing asthma or relieving the symptoms of an asthmatic attack. 2. an agent that prevents asthma or relieves its symptoms.

antibacterial killing or inhibiting the growth of bacteria.

antibiotic 1. tending to or capable of preventing or destroying life. 2. a substance, as penicillin, produced by a microorganism and able to inhibit the growth of or kill another microorganism.

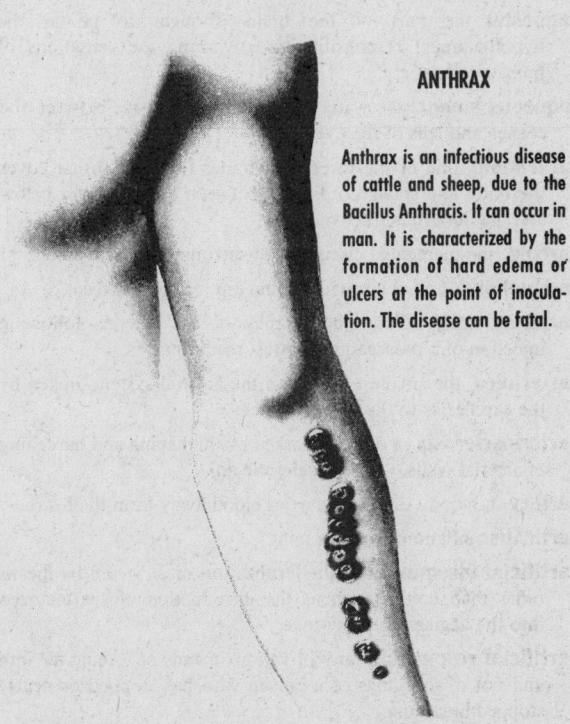

ANTHRAX

Anthrax is an infectious disease of cattle and sheep, due to the Bacillus Anthracis. It can occur in man. It is characterized by the formation of hard edema or ulcers at the point of inoculation. The disease can be fatal.

antibody a specific protein substance produced by the body to attack invading bacteria or other foreign matter.

anticholinergic repelling or annulling the physiologic action of acetylcholine.

antidiuretic 1. relating to the reduction of urinary excretion. 2. an agent that acts to reduce the excretion of urine.

antidote an agent that counteracts the effects of a poison or neutralizes the poison before it takes effect.

antiepileptic relating to a drug that prevents or relieves the severity of an epileptic seizure.

antifebrile reducing fever or relieving its symptoms.

antigen a substance, as a foreign protein or microorganism, that stimulates the production of an antibody when introduced into the body. —**antigenic** adj. —**antigenicity** n.

antihistamine any drug that counteracts the effects of histamine, used in the symptomatic treatment of various allergies.

antitoxin an antibody formed in response to the presence of a specific toxin and able to neutralize that toxin. —**antitoxic** adj.

aorta main artery of the trunk.

apastia failure to eat.

aphasia loss or impairment of the faculty of speech, due to some disease of or injury to the brain.

aphonia loss of the voice, esp. caused by laryngitis or some disease of the vocal cords or their nerve supply.

apnea breathlessness; inability to catch one's breath.

apneumia congenital absence of the lungs.

apodal without feet.

apodia congenital absence of the feet.

apoplexy stroke.

appendectomy surgical removal of the vermiform appendix.

appendicitis inflammation of the vermiform appendix.

appendix 1. any bodily appendage. 2. the wormlike (vermiform) appendage attached to the blind pouch at the beginning of the large intestine.

appestat the part of the brain (thought to be in the hypothalamus) responsible for governing the sensations of hunger and satiety.

aqueous humor the watery fluid filling the space between the cornea and lens of the eye.

arachnoid one of the three membranes (meninges) that cover the brain and spinal cord, lying between the pia mater below and the dura mater above.

areola the pigmented circular area surrounding the nipples.

arrhythmia any abnormal rhythm, esp. of the heartbeat.

arteriography X-ray photography of the arteries following injection of a radiopaque contrast medium.

arterioles the smallest vessels of the arterial system, linked by the capillaries to the venous system.

arteriosclerosis a disease marked by thickening and hardening of arterial walls. —**arteriosclerotic** adj.

artery a blood vessel that carries blood away from the heart.

arthritis inflammation of a joint.

artificial insemination the fertilization of an ovum by means other than coitus, such as the introduction of spermatozoa into the vagina with a syringe.

artificial respiration any of various means of forcing air into and out of the lungs of a person who has stopped or nearly stopped breathing.

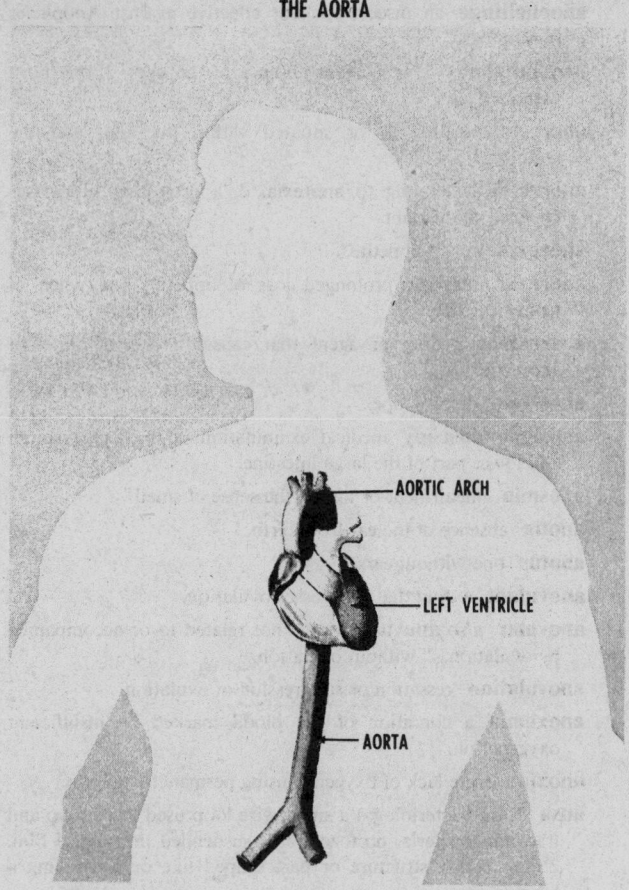

THE AORTA

AORTIC ARCH

LEFT VENTRICLE

AORTA

asbestosis a lung disease caused by chronic inhalation of tiny particles of asbestos.

ascariasis intestinal infestation with parasitic roundworms of the species *Ascaris lumbricoides*.

ascorbic acid vitamin C.

asepsis a germ-free condition.

Asian flu a severe epidemic of influenza that took place in 1957, caused by a virus strain that is thought to have originated in Singapore.

aspermia inability to produce or ejaculate semen.

asphyxia loss of consciousness from too little oxygen and overabundance of carbon dioxide in the blood.

aspirate to draw off fluid or gas (as from a body cavity) by means of suction.

aspirator an instrument for drawing off fluid or gas by means of suction.

aspirin a drug used to reduce pain and fever; acetylsalicylic acid.

astasia the inability to stand due to loss of motor coordination.

asteatosis loss of activity of the sebaceous glands or gross diminution of their secretions.

astereognosis loss of the ability to recognize shapes by the sense of touch.

asterixis involuntary jerking movements of various muscle groups caused by advanced liver disease or some disturbance of cerebral metabolism.

asternia absence of the breastbone (sternum).

asthenia loss of strength or stamina; debility. —**asthenic** adj.

asthenocoria retarded reaction of the pupil when stimulated by light, caused by a disorder of the adrenal glands.

asthenopia eyestrain; weak sight, caused by fatigue of the muscles that control the eyeball.

asthenospermia loss of movement or impaired motility of sperm cells.

asthma a condition that is marked by severely labored breathing, wheezing, and sensations of chest constriction along with periods of respite and is often thought to be of allergic origin.

astigmatism a defect of vision in which light rays entering the eye are abnormally bent before reaching the retina, thus producing a blurred image.

astatine a radioactive halogen element.

astomia congenital absence of the mouth.

astragalus former term for the ankle bone (talus).

astraphobia fear of lightning and thunder.

astringent 1. causing contraction of soft tissues. 2. an agent that causes contraction of tissues, used to check hemorrhage, arrest secretion, etc.

astrocyte a star-shaped cell of nervous tissues.

astrocytoma a tumor of nerve tissue composed of astrocytes.

asymmetry lack of symmetry; imbalance.

asystole cessation of the heartbeat; cardiac standstill.

atactilia loss of the sense of touch.

ataraxia calmness of mind; total relaxation; imperturbability.

atavism recurrence in an organism of a characteristic typical of its distant ancestors.

ataxia an inability to coordinate voluntary muscular movement.

ataxiophemia impaired coordination of the muscles concerned with speech production.

atelectasis 1. collapse or incomplete expansion of a lung. 2. defective expansion of the pulmonary alveoli at birth.

atelocardia incomplete development of the heart.

atelochilia harelip.

atelochiria incomplete or imperfect development of the hands.

athelia congenital absence of the nipples.

atherogenic of or relating to the production of degenerative changes in arterial walls.

atheroma degeneration of arterial walls resulting from the deposit of fatty esters.

atheromatosis widespread vascular disease characterized by atheroma.

atherosclerosis abnormal thickening of arterial walls resulting from fatty deposits and fibrosis. —**atherosclerotic** adj.

athetosis a nervous disorder chiefly of children that is usually the result of brain lesion and is characterized by continuous slow movements of the hands and feet. —**athetotic, athetosic** adj.

athlete's foot a fungus infection (ringworm) of the feet, typically of the areas between the toes, characterized by itching, cracking and scaling of the skin and the formation of watery blisters.

atlas the first vertebra of the neck, shaped like a ring and supporting the skull.

atom the smallest particle of an element existing either alone or in combination. —**atomic** adj.

atomizer an instrument for dispensing a liquid in a spray of fine droplets.

atony lack or insufficiency of muscular tone.

ATP adenosine triphosphate; an adenosine ester derivative supplying energy for many biochemical cellular processes.

atresia absence or closure of a natural bodily passage.

atrium pl. **atria** either of the two upper chambers of the heart. Also called auricle. —**atrial** adj.

atrophy the wasting away or decrease in size of a body part or tissue; degeneration.

atropine a white, poisonous, crystalline compound derived chiefly from belladonna and used to control spasms and dilate the pupil of the eye.

audiogram a graph tracing the relationship between frequency of vibration and the minimal level at which a person can hear.

audiometer an instrument for measuring keenness of hearing. —**audiometric** adj. —**audiometry** n.

auditory relating to or experienced through the sense of hearing.

aura a subjective sensation sometimes experienced before the onset of a neurological attack, as of epilepsy.

aural relating to the ear or the sense of hearing.

auricle 1. pinna. 2. atrium.

auricular 1. of or relating to the sense of hearing. 2. of or relating to the auricles (atria) of the heart.

auriscope an instrument for examining the ear; otoscope.

auscultation the diagnostic technique of listening to and analyzing sounds produced by organs within the body.

autism an emotional disorder found chiefly in young children and marked by alternating periods of extreme withdrawal and irrational violence. Also called infantile autism. —**autistic** adj.

autoclave 1. an electric appliance using superheated steam under pressure to sterilize dental or surgical instruments and other operating room equipment. 2. to subject to the action of an autoclave.

autoerotism also **autoeroticism** sexual desire and the seeking for its gratification directed toward oneself.

autogenous 1. originating within an organism. 2. produced independently of external influences or aid. —**autogenic** adj. —**autogeny** n.

autograft an organ or tissue transplanted from one part to another part of the same body.

autohypnosis hypnosis that is self-induced.

autoimmunity a condition in which the body is abnormally sensitive to some of its own tissues as the result of forming antibodies against them.

autoinfection reinfection resulting from the presence of pathogenic microorganisms already present in the body.

autointoxication poisoning resulting from toxins already within the body.

autolysis the disintegration of cells or tissues by enzymes produced within the body.

automatism repetitive, unconscious motor activity, as that sometimes following an epileptic seizure.

automyosophobia fear of being dirty or of smelling bad.

autonomic 1. acting independently: autonomic reflexes. 2. resulting from internal influences or causes.

autonomic nervous system the part of the nervous system that supplies smooth and cardiac muscle and glandular tissue and regulates involuntary actions.

autonomotropic acting on the autonomic nervous system, as a drug.

autophagia 1. the self-consumption of a cell. 2. the biting of one's own flesh.

autophilia love of self; narcissism.

autopsy a post-mortem examination; necropsy.

autoradiograph a photographic image produced by the radiation of a radioactive substance contained in a subject in close contact with the emulsion. —**autoradiography** *n.*

avascular 1. lacking blood vessels. 2. relating to an inadequate blood supply.

avirulent not virulent.

avitaminosis disease resulting from a dietary deficiency of any of various vitamins.

avulsion the tearing away or separation of a bodily structure or part either accidentally or surgically.

axanthopsia inability to see yellow hues or tints.

axenic (of a culture) free from contamination by foreign organisms.

axilla armpit.

axis *pl.* **axes** the second vertebra of the neck, serving as the pivot for turning the head.

axon a long nerve cell process that conducts impulses away from the cell body.

azoospermia inability to produce spermatozoa; absence of live sperm cells in the semen.

azotemia the abnormal accumulation of urea in the blood; uremia.

B

Babinski reflex *or* **Babinski's reflex** a reflex movement of the foot in which when the sole is tickled the great toe turns upward, indicative of organic lesion of the brain or spinal cord.

baccate resembling a berry; berrylike.

bacciform having the shape of a berry.

bacillary 1. rod-shaped. 2. relating to or produced by bacilli.

bacillemia the presence in the blood of rod-shaped bacteria.

bacilli *pl. of* bacillus.

bacillicide any agent capable of killing bacilli.

bacilliform rod-shaped; resembling a bacillus in form.

bacilliparous producing bacilli.

bacillogenic *or* **bacillogenous** 1. of bacillary origin; originating in bacilli. 2. producing bacilli; bacilliparous.

bacillophobia abnormal fear or dread of bacilli.

bacillosis a condition caused by infection with bacilli.

bacilluria the presence of bacilli in the urine.

bacillus *pl.* **bacilli** 1. any of a genus (*Bacillus*) of rod-shaped, aerobic bacteria including saprophytes and some parasites. 2. a disease-producing bacterium.

bacteremia the presence of bacteria in the blood.

bacteria *pl. of* bacterium.

bacterial relating to or caused by bacteria.

bactericholia the presence of bacilli in the bile.

bactericidal destructive of bacteria.

bactericide a drug or agent that destroys bacteria.

bacteriogenous 1. caused by bacteria or of bacterial origin. 2. producing bacteria.

bacteriology a science concerned with bacteria and their importance to medicine, agriculture, and industry.

bacteriolytic destroying or dissolving the cellular structure of bacteria.

bacteriopathology the study of diseases caused by bacteria or their toxic products.

bacteriophage a bacteriolytic virus.

bacteriophobia an abnormal fear of bacteria and other microorganisms.

bacteriosis widespread bacterial infection.

bacteriostasis prevention of the growth and multiplication of bacteria. —**bacteriostatic** *adj.*

bacteriostat any agent that inhibits the growth or multiplication of bacteria.

bacterium *pl.* **bacteria** any of a class of microscopic plantlike organisms lacking chlorophyll that have single-celled bodies, live in water, soil, organic matter, or in the bodies of animals and plants, and are significant as pathogens or for their chemical effects.

BAL British anti-lewisite; dimercaprol.

balanitis inflammation of the glans penis.

balanoplasty plastic surgery involving repair or reconstruction of the glans penis.

balanoposthitis inflammation of the glans penis and foreskin (prepuce).

balanorrhagia a constant discharge from the glans penis.

balanorrhea inflammation of the glans penis accompanied by the discharge or formation of pus.

balanus glans penis.

ball-and-socket joint enarthrosis.

balm 1. a soothing ointment or other application. 2. balsam.

balneology the branch of medical science concerned with balneotherapy.

balneotherapy the therapeutic use of baths, esp. using natural mineral waters, in treating disease or pain.

balsam 1. a fragrant, resinous exudate obtained from various trees. 2. balm.

bandage a strip of cloth or plastic fabric for binding and dressing wounds.

Band-Aid a trademark for a small adhesive bandage with a gauze pad affixed to the center of the adhesive side.

baragnosis inability to sense the weight of a hand-held object.

barbiturate any of various derivatives of barbituric acid used extensively as antispasmodics, sedatives, and hypnotics.

barbituric acid a synthetic crystalline acid that is derived from pyrimidine.

barbiturism chronic poisoning by derivatives of barbituric acid, characterized by fever, chills and headache.

barbula hirci the hairs that grow in the outer part of the external ear in men.

baresthesia the sense of pressure.

baresthesiometer a delicate instrument for measuring the sense of pressure.

barium a silver-white bivalent toxic metallic element.

barium enema a procedure for rendering the rectum and lower part of the large intestine visible on X-ray photographs by first introducing barium sulfate into the rectum under gentle pressure.

barium meal a procedure for rendering the esophagus and upper part of the digestive tract visible on X-ray photographs by first swallowing a quantity of barium sulfate.

barium sulfate a colorless insoluble compound used esp. as an opaque medium in X-ray photography of the alimentary canal.

baroreceptor a nerve ending, as in the arterial walls, responsive to changes in pressure.

bartholinitis inflammation of Bartholin's glands.

Bartholin's gland either of two glands, located one on each side of the vagina, that secrete a mucous lubricating fluid.

basad toward a base.

basal metabolic rate the rate at which an organism at rest releases heat.

base 1. the lowest or underlying part; foundation. 2. a chemical compound capable of reacting with an acid to form a salt.

basement membrane a thin single-layered membrane of connective tissue cells underlying the epithelium of many organs.

basic reacting as an alkali.

basiphobia fear of walking.

basophil or **basophile** a white blood cell with basophilic granules.

basophilia 1. an increased number of basophils in the blood. 2. a tendency to stain with basic dyes.

basophilic susceptible to staining with basic dyes.

bathmotropic affecting the excitability of nerves or muscles in response to stimuli.

bathophobia fear of looking down into deep places or a fear of being in a deep place.

bathycardia a condition in which the heart is located abnormally low in the thoracic cavity.

bathyesthesia sensation in muscles and other deep structures.

bathyhyperesthesia abnormal sensitivity of muscles and other deep structures.

bathyhypesthesia impairment or partial loss of sensation in muscles and deeper structures.

battered child syndrome the complex of severe physical harm to a child resulting from the brutality of a parent or other adult guardian.

BCG vaccine Bacillus Calmette-Guérin; a vaccine from living tubercle bacilli used to vaccinate against tuberculosis.

B complex vitamin B complex.

bdelygmia nausea.

bear down to contract the abdominal muscles and diaphragm during childbirth.

bedbug a wingless bloodsucking bug that feeds on human blood and sometimes infests houses.

bedpan a shallow receptacle used for urination or defecation by someone confined to bed.

bedsore an ulcerated lesion of tissue, esp. that overlying bony prominences, resulting from deprivation of nutrition through prolonged pressure.

behavior the conduct and response of an organism to outside stimuli.

behaviorism the psychological study of human behavior exclusive of the study of the mind and consciousness.

belch to raise gas or air from the stomach; eructate.

belladonna 1. a poisonous plant of the nightshade family that yields atropine. Also called *deadly nightshade*. 2. a medical extract, as atropine, of the belladonna plant.

belly 1. the thick central area of a muscle. 2. the abdomen.

belonephobia fear of sharp-pointed objects, such as needles or pins.

Benadryl a trademark for diphenhydramine hydrochloride (an antihistamine).

bends caisson disease; decompression sickness.

benign not malignant or a threat to life; innocent.

Benzadrine a trademark for amphetamine.

beriberi a vitamin deficiency disease affecting the nerves, heart, and digestive system and resulting from a lack of thiamine.

berylliosis poisoning from prolonged exposure to the element beryllium, as by direct contact or inhalation.

beryllium a white metallic bivalent element.

bestiality sexual intercourse between a human being and an animal.

betacism a relatively rare speech defect in which the sound of the letter B is given to other consonants.

beta globulin a globulin of plasma or serum with electrophoretic mobilities between alpha globulin and gamma globulin.

between-brain the diencephalon.

bhang a powdered preparation of cannabis which is smoked or chewed for its intoxicating effects in some Eastern countries.

bi- *prefix* 1. two. 2. twice. 3. double.

bicarbonate an acid salt of carbonic acid.

bicarbonate of soda sodium bicarbonate.

biceps either of two two-headed muscles, situated at the front of the upper arm or at the back of the upper leg.

bicornuate having two horn-shaped processes: *a bicornuate uterus.*

bicuspid 1. ending in or having two points: *bicuspid teeth.* 2. a premolar tooth.

bifid divided into two sections or parts by a median cleft: *a bifid chin.*

biforate having two openings.

bifurcate divided into two branches or parts. —**bifurcation** *n.*

bigeminal paired or consisting of two parts.

bilabe delicate forceps for removing calculi, as those lodged in the urethra.

bilateral having or affecting two sides.

bile a greenish or yellowish alkaline viscid fluid secreted by the liver and serving chiefly as an aid to digestion.

bilharziasis *pl.* **bilharziases** schistosomiasis.

biliary relating to bile.

bilious 1. of or relating to bile. 2. suffering from or marked by disordered liver function.

bilirachia the presence of bile in the spinal fluid.

bilirubin a reddish-yellow pigment found in bile, urine, and blood.

bilirubinemia the presence of abnormally large amounts of bilirubin in the blood.

bilirubinuria the presence of bile in the urine.

biliverdin a green pigment found in bile.

bimanual using or requiring both hands.

binary fission the division of a cell into two daughter cells.

binaural relating to or using both ears.

binocular relating to, using, or designed for use by both eyes.

binomial having two names, esp. for both genus and species.

bioassay analysis of the strength of a substance by comparing its effect on a test organism with the effect of a standard preparation.

bioastronautics the branch of science concerned with the effects of space travel on biological processes.

biochemistry chemistry that deals with life processes and compounds. —**biochemical** *adj.*

bioelectricity electrical activity in living organisms or tissues.

biogenesis the development of life from life already in existence. —**biogenetic** *adj.*

biogravics the branch of science concerned with studying the effects on living organisms of weightlessness and excessive gravitational force.

biology the scientific study of living organisms and their life processes. —**biologic, biological** *adj.*

biometry the statistical analysis of biological problems. —**biometric** *adj.*

biophage a parasite.

biophagous (of certain parasites) feeding on living organisms.

biophysics the application of the principles and methods of physics to biological problems. —**biophysical** *adj.*

biopsy the examination of tissues, fluids, or cells removed from the living body.

biosynthesis the production by a living organism of a chemical compound. —**biosynthetic** *adj.*

biotin a member of the vitamin B complex found in all forms of life.

biotoxicology the branch of science concerned with the study of toxins produced by living organisms.

biotoxin a toxin formed and shown to be present in the tissues of a living animal.

biparous having given birth to two young.

birth the emergence of a new individual from the body of its parent; parturition.

birthmark any skin blemish present at birth; nevus.

bisexual 1. having characteristics of both sexes; hermaphroditic. 2. erotically attracted to both sexes.

bisferious (of the pulse) beating twice.

bistoury a long knife-like instrument for draining abscesses, etc.

biventer (of a muscle) having two bellies.

blackhead comedo.

bladder a membranous sac functioning as a receptacle for a liquid, esp. the urinary bladder.

blain a sore or blister on the skin; blotch.

bland non-irritating; mild: *a bland diet.*

blastin a substance that stimulates the growth of cells.

blastogenesis 1. reproduction by budding. 2. embryonic development during cleavage and the formation of the germ layers.

blastoma a tumor composed mainly of undifferentiated or immature cells.

blastomere any of the cells into which the ovum divides after fertilization.

blastomycosis a skin disease caused by a yeast-like fungus.

blastula *pl.* **blastulas** *or* **blastulae** an early stage in the cleavage of a fertilized ovum.

bleeder a hemophiliac.

blennadenitis inflammation of the mucus-secreting glands.

blennemesis the vomiting of mucus.

blennogenic forming mucus.

blennoid resembling mucus; having a viscid consistency.

blennostatic relating to a reduction in mucus secretion.

blennothorax accumulation of mucus in the bronchi.

blennuria the presence of excessive amounts of mucus in the urine.

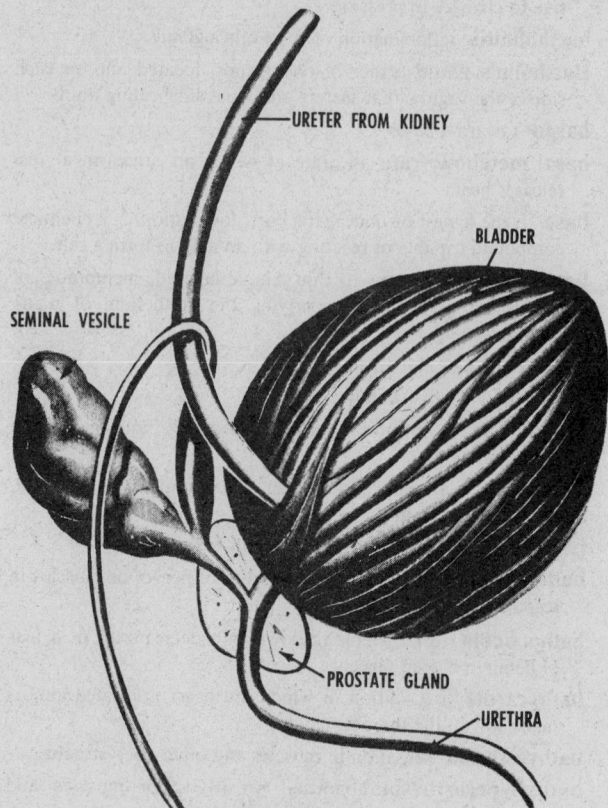

THE BLADDER AND THE PROSTATE GLAND

URETER FROM KIDNEY

BLADDER

SEMINAL VESICLE

PROSTATE GLAND

URETHRA

DUCTUS DEFERENS FROM TESTIS

blepharal relating to the eyelids.

blepharectomy surgical removal of part of the eyelid.

blepharedema swelling of the eyelids.

blepharism twitching of the eyelid.

blepharitis inflammation of the eyelid, esp. the margin.

blepharoadenoma a glandlike tumor of the eyelid.

blepharoatheroma a sebaceous cyst of the eyelid.

blindness lack of visual perception; loss of sight.

blind spot a point in the retina of the eye that is insensitive to light.

blister a usually circular elevation of the epidermis containing a watery liquid. —**blistery** *adj.*

blood the fluid circulating in the heart, arteries, veins and capillaries and carrying oxygen and nourishment to all parts of the body and bringing away waste products.

blood bank an establishment for storing blood or plasma.

blood cell a cell present normally in blood; a white blood cell, red blood cell or platelet.

blood count the determination of the number and type of blood cells present in a specific volume of blood.

blood group any of various classes into which human beings are grouped according to the presence or absence in their blood of certain antigens. Also called *blood type.*

blood poisoning septicemia.

blood pressure the pressure exerted by the blood flowing through the blood vessels, esp. the arteries.

blood sugar glucose present in the blood.

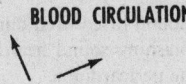

BLOOD CIRCULATION

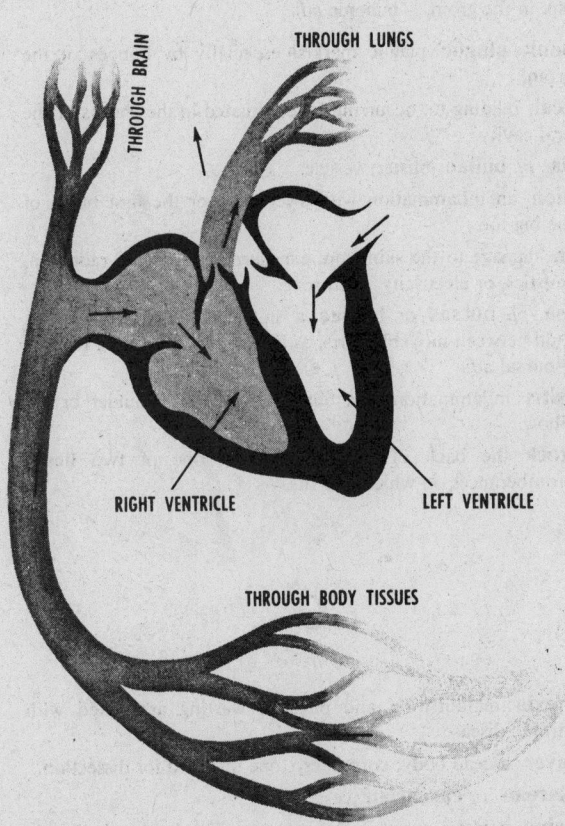

THROUGH BRAIN

THROUGH LUNGS

RIGHT VENTRICLE   LEFT VENTRICLE

THROUGH BODY TISSUES

blue baby an infant with a circulatory defect that imparts a bluish tint to the skin.

boil the common name for a furuncle.

bolus a soft, rounded mass of chewed food.

bone one of the hard structures forming the skeleton of a vertebrate. —**bony** or **boney** adj.

boric acid a white powder used in solution as a mild antiseptic.

boss a rounded swelling.

bosselated characterized by or having several rounded protuberances. —**bosselation** n.

botulin a toxin sometimes occurring in imperfectly canned food.

botulism acute food poisoning caused by the presence of botulin.

bougie a tapering surgical instrument for introduction into a bodily passage.

bougienage the use of a bougie in the examination or treatment of a bodily passage or canal.

bouton a knoblike swelling or structure.

bowel the intestine or one of its divisions.

bowleg a leg that bows outward at the knee. —**bowlegged** adj.

B.P. blood pressure.

brachialgia intense pain in the arm.

brachiocyllosis the condition of having a crooked arm.

brachiotomy incision into or removal of an arm.

brachium the upper part of the arm. —**brachial** adj.

brachycephalic having an abnormally short head or skull. —**brachicephaly** or **brachycephalia** n.

brachycnemic having abnormally short legs.

brachydactylic having abnormally short fingers.

brachydont having short teeth.

brachygnathia a receding lower jaw. —**brachygnathous** adj.

brachypodous having short feet.

bradycardia relatively slow heartbeat.

brain the part of the central nervous system located within the skull and serving as the organ of thought and neural and muscular coordination.

brain stem the part of the brain consisting of the pons, medulla oblongata and midbrain; all of the brain except the cerebrum and cerebellum.

breast either of two protuberant, glandular, milk-secreting organs on the front of the female chest; mammary gland.

bregma the point on the skull where the coronal and sagittal sutures meet.

Bright's disease a kidney disease marked by albumin in the urine; a form of nephritis.

Brill's disease an acute infectious disease similar to but milder than typhus.

broad-spectrum effective against many microorganisms or insects: broad-spectrum antibiotics; broad-spectrum insecticides.

Broca's area the speech center in the brain.

bromide a salt of hydrobromic acid, esp. one used as a depressant drug.

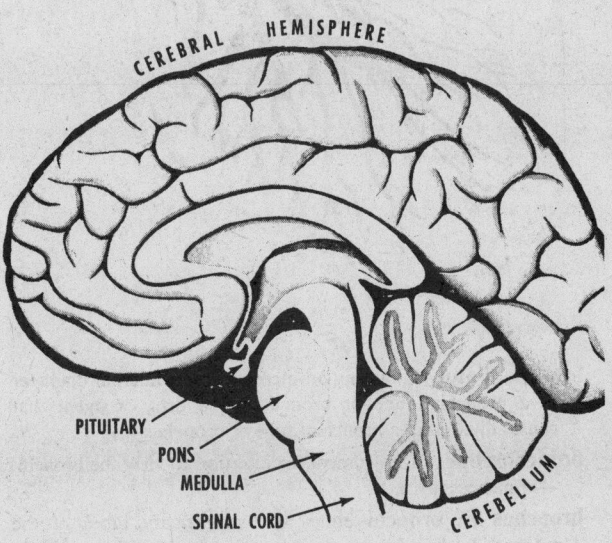

THE BRAIN
(CROSS SECTION)

CEREBRAL HEMISPHERE

PITUITARY

PONS

MEDULLA

SPINAL CORD

CEREBELLUM

bromine a liquid nonmetallic element obtained from sea water and natural brines, whose compounds are of medical use.

bromism *also* **brominism** poisoning caused by the chronic use of bromides.

bronchi *pl. of* bronchus.

bronchi- *or* **bronchio-** *prefix* bronchial tubes.

bronchiectasis *also* **bronchiectasia** dilation of a bronchus or of the bronchi.

bronchiogenic originating in or coming from the bronchi.

bronchiole *also* **bronchiolus** one of the smallest divisions of the bronchial tree, having no cartilaginous walls and being less than 1 mm in diameter.

bronchiostenosis the abnormal narrowing of a bronchial tube.

bronchitis inflammation of the bronchi.

BRONCHIAL TUBES

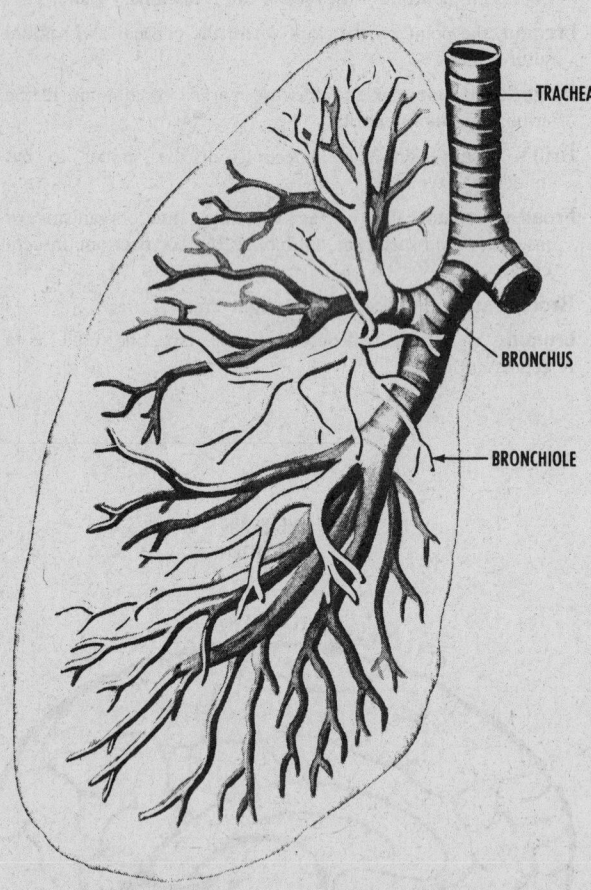

TRACHEA

BRONCHUS

BRONCHIOLE

bronchodilator 1. causing an increase in the internal diameter of a bronchial tube or bronchus. 2. a drug or agent that causes dilation of a bronchial tube or bronchus.

bronchoscope an instrument for insertion to view the bronchi. —**bronchoscopy** *n.*

bronchus *pl.* **bronchi** either of two primary tubes of the trachea leading to the right and left lung respectively. —**bronchial** *adj.*

brontophobia an abnormal fear of thunder.

brucellosis undulant fever.

bruise an epidermal injury with discoloration from ruptured blood vessels but without a break in the skin.

bruit any abnormal sound discovered during auscultation, such as a gurgling or splashing sound heard when both fluid and air are present in the pericardium.

bubo *pl.* **buboes** an inflammatory swelling of a lymph gland, esp. in the groin. —**bubonic** *adj.*

bubonic plague plague marked especially by buboes of the groin.

buccal relating to, occurring in, or situated in the cheeks or the oral cavity.

bulla *pl.* **bullae** blister; vesicle.

bunion an inflammation with swelling over the first bursa of the big toe.

burn damage to the skin from exposure to fire, heat, radiation, caustics, or electricity. —**burn** *vb.*

bursa *pl.* **bursas** *or* **bursae** a small sac filled with serous fluid between movable parts, as between a bone and a tendon. —**bursal** *adj.*

bursitis inflammation of a bursa, esp. of the shoulder or the elbow.

buttock the back of the hip forming one of two fleshy protuberances on which one sits.

C

cachexia malnutrition and physical wasting associated with chronic disease.

cadaver a dead body; corpse, esp. one intended for dissection.

caesarean *or* **caesarian** cesarean.

caffeine a bitter compound used as a stimulant and diuretic and found in coffee, tea, and kola nuts.

caffeinism chronic poisoning by caffeine, characterized by irritability, insomnia, and palpitations.

caisson disease a condition marked typically by pain, paralysis, asphyxia, and collapse, caused by too rapid a shift from a high-pressure atmospheric environment to a normal environment, which results in the release of nitrogen bubbles in the bloodstream and tissues. Also called *bends.*

calamine a pink powder used in lotions, ointments, etc., to relieve itching and as an astringent.

calcaneal *or* **calcanean** relating to the heel bone or calcaneus.

calcaneus a tarsal bone forming the major bone of the heel.

calcanodynia pain in the heel on walking or standing.

calcar a spurlike projection.

calcareous containing calcium or calcium carbonate.

calcarine spurlike.

calcariuria the presence of calcium salts in the urine.

calcaroid resembling lime salts.

calcemia the presence of abnormally large amounts of calcium in the blood.

calcicosis a lung disease caused by the inhalation of limestone dust.

calciferol vitamin D_2.

calcification the deposit of insoluble lime salts in tissue.

calciphilia a condition in which the tissues tend to absorb an abnormally large amount of calcium salts, leading to their calcification.

calciprivia lack of dietary calcium.

calciprivic deprived of calcium.

calcitonin a thyroid hormone important in the metabolism of calcium.

calcium a metallic element occurring only in combination, forming about 85 per cent of the mineral matter of bones.

calcium carbonate a compound used in medicine as an antacid.

calcodynia pain in the heel.

calcoid a tumor of the dental pulp.

calculary relating to a calculus or to the formation of calculi.

calculosis the tendency or predisposition to form calculi.

calculus *pl.* **calculi** *or* **calculuses** a concretion of mineral salts in a hollow organ or a duct; stone.

calicectomy surgical removal of a calyx.

caligo dimness of vision.

calipers an instrument with two adjustable legs for measuring the distance, diameter, or thickness between surfaces.

callosal relating to the corpus callosum.

callosity a callus.

callous thickened and hardened esp. from friction and pressure.

callus 1. a thickening of or hard thickened area of the skin; callosity. 2. a mass of tissue forming around a break in a bone and converted to bone during healing.

calor heat, one of the signs of inflammation.

Calorie a unit of heat; the amount of heat required to raise the temperature of one kilogram of water one degree centigrade: used to express heat- or energy-producing value of food oxidized in the body. Also called *kilocalorie*. —**caloric** *adj.*

calorifacient producing or generating heat.

calorimeter a device for the measurement of the amount of heat given off by a body.

calvarium the upper, domelike part of the skull.

calvities baldness; alopecia.

calyx one of the cuplike divisions of the renal pelvis.

canaliculus *pl.* **canaliculi** a small channel or passage.

cancer a malignant tumor of potentially limitless growth. —**cancerous** *adj.*

cancerocidal able to destroy cancer cells; cytotoxic.

cancerophobia an abnormal fear of getting cancer.

cancriform resembling cancer or the manifestations of a malignant growth.

cancroid 1. resembling a crab. 2. resembling a cancer.

candida any of a genus of yeast-like fungi that are the causative agents of thrush.

canine any of four pointed, conical teeth situated between the lateral incisors and first premolars in the upper and lower jaws.

canker a small ulcer of the lips, mouth, or tongue.

cannabis the dried flowering spikes of the hemp plant (*Cannabis sativa*), which yield hashish; marijuana.

cannabism severe hallucinations and other symptoms associated with cannabis poisoning.

cannula a small tube for insertion into a body cavity.

cannulation insertion of a cannula.

canthal relating to a canthus.

cantharides a counterirritant drug prepared from the dried bodies of the blister beetle (*Cantharis vesicatoria*), now no longer in use because of its dangerous irritant effects on the urinary tract; Spanish fly.

canthectomy surgical incision into a canthus to increase the width of the slit between the lids.

canthus *pl.* **canthi** either of the angular junctures of the eye formed by the meeting of the upper and lower eyelids.

capiat an instrument for removing foreign objects from the uterus or other body cavities.

capillarectasia dilation of the capillaries.

capillaritis inflammation of the capillaries.

capillarity the spontaneous rise or depression of liquids placed in very narrow tubes; an effect of surface tension.

capillary *pl.* **capillaries** any of the very small blood vessels forming a network throughout the body and connecting arterioles and venules.

capitate 1. having a round or head-shaped extremity. 2. one of the carpal bones.

capitium a special bandage made to fit the head.

capitopedal relating to both the head and feet.

capnogram a record of the amount of carbon dioxide in exhaled air.

caprizant denoting a bounding pulse beat.

capsule 1. an enveloping membrane around an organ, joint or other structure. 2. a small container made of soluble material, such as gelatin, for enclosing powdered drugs, medicated pellets, etc. 3. any bodily structure or part resembling a capsule.

capsulitis inflammation of an anatomical capsule.

caput *pl.* **capita** 1. the head. 2. any structure or part resembling a head; the rounded end of an organ or part.

carbohydrate any of various compounds of oxygen, hydrogen, and carbon, as sugars and starches, that are the principal energy-producing foods in the diet.

carbolic acid a disinfectant and poison derived from coal tar; phenol.

carbolize to mix with or add carbolic acid.

carboluria the presence of carbolic acid in the urine.

carbon dioxide a colorless, heavy gas, CO_2, that is noncombustible, is absorbed from the air by plants, and is formed in the tissues during respiration and expelled by the lungs.

carbon monoxide a colorless, odorless gas, CO, that is formed by incomplete combustion of carbon and is lethal in sustained amounts.

carbon monoxide poisoning poisoning by inhalation of carbon monoxide, marked by dizziness, headache, convulsions, paralysis, coma, and, eventually, death.

carbonuria the presence of carbon compounds, esp. carbon dioxide, in the urine.

carbophilic requiring carbon dioxide for efficient growth.

carbuncle a painful staphylococcal inflammation of the skin and subcutaneous tissue characterized by necrosis of the deeper tissues and multiple openings for the discharge of pus.

carbunculosis the presence of multiple carbuncles.

carcinectomy the surgical removal of a malignant tumor.

carcinogen an agent or substance producing or conducive to cancer. —**carcinogenesis** *n.* —**carcinogenic** *adj.* —**carcinogenicity** *n.*

carcinoma *pl.* **carcinomas** *or* **carcinomata** a malignant tumor of epithelial tissue. —**carcinomatous** *adj.*

carcinomatosis a condition marked by the spreading of carcinomas from a primary source.

carcinosarcoma a mixed malignant growth exhibiting features of both carcinoma and sarcoma.

carcinostatic 1. arresting the growth of a carcinoma. 2. an agent that arrests or inhibits the growth of a carcinoma.

cardi- or **cardio-** prefix heart; cardiac.

cardiac 1. of, near, or acting on the heart. 2. relating to the part of the stomach into which the esophagus opens.

cardialgia a burning sensation in the stomach or seeming to come from the region of the heart, usually caused by indigestion; heartburn.

cardiasthenia a condition in which the action of the heart is weak.

cardiataxia severe abnormalities or irregularities in the heart action.

cardiatelia failure of the heart to develop normally.

cardiectasia dilation of the heart.

cardiectopia abnormal location of the heart within the thoracic cavity.

cardioangiology the branch of science concerned with the heart and blood vessels.

cardioaortic relating to both the heart and aorta.

cardioarterial relating to the heart and the arteries.

cardiocele protrusion of the heart through a space in the diaphragm or other opening, such as a wound.

cardiocentesis a surgical procedure involving puncture of the heart.

cardiodynamics the forces, movements and actions of the beating heart.

cardiodynia pain originating in the heart.

cardiogenesis the embryonic formation of the heart.

cardiogenic originated by the heart; of cardiac origin.

cardiogram a tracing made by a cardiograph.

cardiograph an instrument that traces graphically the electrical events and movements taking place within the heart. —**cardiographer** n. —**cardiography** n.

cardiohepatomegaly abnormal enlargement of both the heart (cardiomegaly) and the liver (hepatomegaly).

cardioinhibitory slowing down or inhibiting the normal action of the heart.

cardiokinetic influencing the heart action.

cardiology the branch of medicine concerned with the heart and its disorders. —**cardiological** adj. —**cardiologist** n.

cardiomegaly abnormal enlargement of the heart.

cardiomuscular relating to the heart muscle.

cardiomyopathy a chronic disease of heart muscle.

cardiomyotomy surgical incision into the heart muscle.

cardionecrosis necrosis of part of the heart muscle, as in severe myocardial infarction.

cardiopalmus palpitation of the heart.

cardiopathy any disease of the heart.

cardiopericarditis inflammation of both the heart muscle and its surrounding sac (pericardium).

cardiophobia abnormal fear of heart disease.

cardiophone a specially adapted stethoscope for listening to heart sounds, usually consisting of a microphone and amplifier.

cardiospasm painful spasm of the stomach at its upper (cardiac) part or of the esophagus near the point where it joins the stomach, typically causing regurgitation.

cardiothrombus a blood clot within a heart chamber.

cardiotomy 1. surgical incision into the heart muscle. 2. surgical incision into the upper (cardiac) part of the stomach in the area of the esophageal opening.

cardiotoxic exerting a toxic or harmful effect on the action of the heart or its tissues.

cardiovalvulitis inflammation of the heart valves.

cardiovascular relating to or involving the heart and blood vessels.

caries 1. tooth decay (dental caries). 2. bone decay.

cariogenesis the process or mechanism of producing caries.

cariogenic (of certain dietary constituents, esp. sugar) producing tooth decay; causing caries.

carminative a substance, as oil of peppermint, aiding in the expulsion of gas from the alimentary canal.

carotene a yellow or red pigment occurring in some plants that is convertible to vitamin A.

carotenemia the presence in the blood of unusually large quantities of carotene, sometimes resulting in a yellowish-red pigmentation of the skin resembling jaundice; pseudo-jaundice.

carotenoid 1. any one of a group of plant pigments that includes carotene. 2. resembling carotene; yellowish.

carotid either of two great arteries passing up the neck and supplying the head with blood.

carpoptosia dropping of the wrist; wrist drop.

carpus the eight bones between the hand and the forearm; wrist.

carrier an agent who harbors pathogenic microorganisms transmittable to others while remaining personally immune to the disease.

cartilage translucent elastic tissue which, with bone, comprises the basic structure of the skeleton. —**cartilaginous** adj.

caruncle a small fleshy protuberance often of abnormal origin.

caseation necrosis in which damaged tissue is converted into a cheesy soft substance.

casein a phosphoprotein derived from milk.

cassette a special holder for photographic or X-ray film.

cast a mass of fibrous matter that takes the shape of the organ in which it is formed and is ejected from the body.

castration removal of the testes or the ovaries. —**castrate** vb.

catabolism a destructive phase of metabolism resulting in the breakdown of complex materials within the organism. —**catabolize** vb.

catalepsy a condition marked by suspended animation and a tendency for the limbs to remain in whatever position they are placed.

catalyst an agent or substance that speeds up a chemical reaction without itself taking part of it. —**catalysis** n.

catamenia menses. —**catamenial** adj.

catamnesis the medical history or follow-up of a patient after treatment of an illness.

cataphasia a speech disorder characterized by involuntary repetition of the same word.

cataphoresis electrophoresis.

cataplasm a poultice.

cataplexy a sudden loss of muscular strength following an emotional crisis.

cataract a clouding of the lens of the eye that obstructs the transmission of light.

catarrh inflammation of the mucous membranes and especially those of the nose and respiratory passages. —**catarrhal** adj.

catatonia a schizophrenic condition marked chiefly by stupor and immobility with occasional attacks of hyperactivity and excitability. —**catatonic** adj.

catgut a tough cord made from sheep intestines and used chiefly for absorbable sutures and ligatures.

catharsis 1. purgation. 2. the psychoanalytic resolution of an emotional conflict through verbal release.

cathartic 1. relating to catharsis. 2. an agent used to purge the bowels; purgative.

catheter a tubular instrument for introduction into a body cavity or passage esp. to permit withdrawal of fluids or maintain an opening.

catheterize to introduce a catheter into.

cat scratch fever also **cat scratch disease** a mild disease thought to be typically caused by the scratch of a cat and marked by malaise, fever, and swelling of the lymph glands.

cauda a structure or part resembling a tail or having a tapering extremity. —**caudal** adj.

cauda equina a bundle of nerve roots that extend downward from the spinal cord.

caudalis toward the tail; caudal.

caul the inner fetal membrane sometimes covering the head at birth.

caustic a chemical substance, as a strong acid or alkali, that has a corrosive action on other substances.

cauterization the application of a caustic agent to sear or destroy tissue and esp. to stop hemorrhage. —**cauterize** vb. —**cautery** n.

cavernous relating to or filled with hollow spaces: cavernous tissue.

cavitation the development of cavities in bodily tissue or organs esp. as a result of disease.

cavum a hole or hollow; cavity.

cecectomy surgical removal of the cecum of the large intestine.

cecitis inflammation of the cecum.

cecocolostomy the surgical formation of an artificial connection between the cecum and colon.

cecoptosis an abnormal downward displacement of the cecum.

cecotomy surgical incision into the cecum.

cecum the blind pouch forming the first part of the large intestine, to which the vermiform appendix is attached.

celiac also **coeliac** related to, situated in, or affecting the abdominal cavity.

celiac disease a chronic disease of young children marked by defective digestion and absorption of gluten and by persistent diarrhea.

celialgia abdominal pain; colic.

celiodynia celialgia; colic.

celiopathy the branch of pathology concerned with the study of abdominal diseases.

celiotomy laparotomy.

celitis peritonitis.

cell a microscopic mass of protoplasm containing a nucleus and other elements and constituting the basic reproducible structural unit of living organisms.

cellulitis a spreading inflammation of cellular or connective tissue, resulting from a failure of the body's immune mechanism to contain an originally localized infection.

celluloneuritis inflammation of nerve cells.

cellulose a polysaccharide that constitutes the chief structural part of the cell walls of plants.

celology the branch of surgery concerned with the study and repair of hernias.

celoscopy examination of any body cavity.

Celsius centigrade; relating to or having a thermometric scale divided into 100 degrees, with 0° representing freezing point and 100° representing boiling point. Abbreviated C

centesis surgical puncture of a body cavity, as for the draining off of contained fluid.

centigrade Celsius. Abbreviated C

central nervous system the part of the nervous system consisting of the brain and spinal cord and serving to coordinate the entire nervous system of the body.

centrifuge a machine that uses centrifugal force to separate substances, as the cellular components of blood from plasma, having different densities.

centriole either of a pair of cellular organelles near the nucleus and during mitosis forming the poles of the spindle.

centromere the clear cytoplasm containing a centriole.

centrum the center of any structure or part, as the body of a vertebra.

cephalalgia headache.

cephalic relating to or situated on or near the head.

cephalitis inflammation of the brain; encephalitis.

cephalogenesis the embryonic formation of the head.

cephalomegaly abnormal enlargement of the head.

cephalometry the science of measuring the head.

cephalomyitis inflammation of the muscles of the head and scalp.

cercus pl. **cerci** any stiff structure resembling a hair.

cerebellitis inflammation of the cerebellum.

cerebellospinal relating to both the cerebellum and spinal cord.

cerebellum one of the major divisions of the brain, situated underneath the rear part of the cerebrum and controlling muscular coordination and (together with the inner ear) bodily equilibrium. —**cerebellar** adj.

cerebral of or relating to the cerebrum.

cerebral accident sudden, severe injury within the cerebrum, esp. the rupture of a blood vessel.

cerebral cortex the topmost layer of gray matter that covers the cerebrum.

cerebral palsy a disorder resulting from brain damage before or during birth and marked typically by muscular incoordination and speech difficulties.

cerebration mental activity, conscious or subconscious.

cerebrifugal (of efferent nerve fibers or impulses) proceeding away from the cerebrum.

cerebripetal (of afferent nerve fibers or impulses) proceeding toward the cerebrum.

cerebritis a general, nonpurulent inflammation of the cerebrum or brain.

cerebromeningitis inflammation of both the brain and its covering membranes (meninges).

cerebropontile relating to the brain and pons.

cerebrospinal of or relating to the brain and spinal cord.

cerebrospinal fluid a watery, clear fluid surrounding the spinal cord and brain and filling the lateral ventricles of the brain.

cerebrovascular relating to or affecting the cerebrum and the blood vessels that supply it.

cerebrum the largest division of the brain, overlying the cerebellum and brain stem (medulla oblongata, midbrain and pons).

cerumen a yellowish waxy substance secreted by the glands of the external ear; earwax.

cervical relating to or affecting the neck or a cervix, esp. of the uterus.

cervicitis inflammation of the cervix of the uterus.

cestode any of a subclass of flatworms comprising the tapeworms.

chalk calcium carbonate.

chancre an initial lesion, esp. of the primary stage of syphilis. —**chancrous** adj.

chancroid a venereal disease characterized by an initial genital lesion resembling that of the primary stage of syphilis. —**chancroidal** adj.

change of life menopause; climacteric.

charas hashish.

cheilitis inflammation of the lips.

chem- or **chemo-** or **chemi-** prefix chemical; chemistry; chemically.

chemopallidectomy chemical destruction of part of a structure in the brain (globus pallidus), once widely used in the treatment of parkinsonism and related diseases.

chemoprophylaxis the prevention of disease by the administration of drugs.

chemoreceptor a sensory nerve-ending that receives chemical stimuli. —**chemoreception** n. —**chemoreceptive** adj.

chemotherapy the use of chemical agents in controlling or treating disease.

chest thorax.

chiasma a crossing of two tendons, nerves or other structures.

chickenpox an acute, contagious viral disease marked chiefly by low-grade fever and the formation of vesicles and occurring usually in children.

chilblain an inflammatory sore occurring esp. on the hands or feet as the result of exposure to cold.

chilitis also **cheilitis** inflammation of the lips.

chilophagia chronic biting of the lips.

chiropodist podiatrist. —**chiropody** n.

chiropractic a system of treating disease by manipulation, esp. of the spinal column.

chloramphenicol a broad-spectrum antibiotic.

chloroform a clear, volatile, toxic liquid that has an odor like ether and is used as a solvent and (esp. formerly) as a general anesthetic.

Chloromycetin a trademark for chloramphenicol.

chlorophyll also **chlorophyl** the green pigment of plants, preparations of which are used for their ability to soothe and remove odors.

chloropsia a rare visual defect in which everything appears to have a green or yellowish-green hue.

chlortetracycline a broad-spectrum antibiotic.

chloruretic relating to the action or effect of increasing the excretion of chloride in the urine.

cholagogue 1. an agent that causes contraction of the gallbladder, thereby stimulating the flow of bile into the duodenum. 2. relating to an agent that stimulates the flow of bile.

cholalic relating to bile.

cholangiography X-ray examination of the bile ducts. —**cholangiographic** adj.

cholangiotomy surgical incision into a bile duct.

cholangitis inflammation of a bile duct.

cholecyst a rare name for the gallbladder.

cholecystectomy surgical removal of the gallbladder.

cholecystitis inflammation of the gallbladder.

cholecystostomy surgical formation of an artificial opening into the gallbladder.

cholecystotomy surgical incision into the gallbladder.

cholelithiasis the presence or production of gallstones.

cholemesia the vomiting of bile.

cholemia the abnormal presence of bile salts in the bloodstream.

choleperitonitis inflammation of the peritoneum caused by the presence of bile in the abdominal cavity.

cholera an acute, infectious bacterial disease usually caused by drinking contaminated water and marked by vomiting and severe gastrointestinal disturbance.

choleriform resembling cholera; choleroid.

cholerrhagia the excessive flow of bile into the small intestine.

cholestasia also **cholestasis** cessation of the flow of bile.

cholesterol a steroid alcohol found in animal cells and body fluids and implicated as a contributing factor in arteriosclerosis and atherosclerosis.

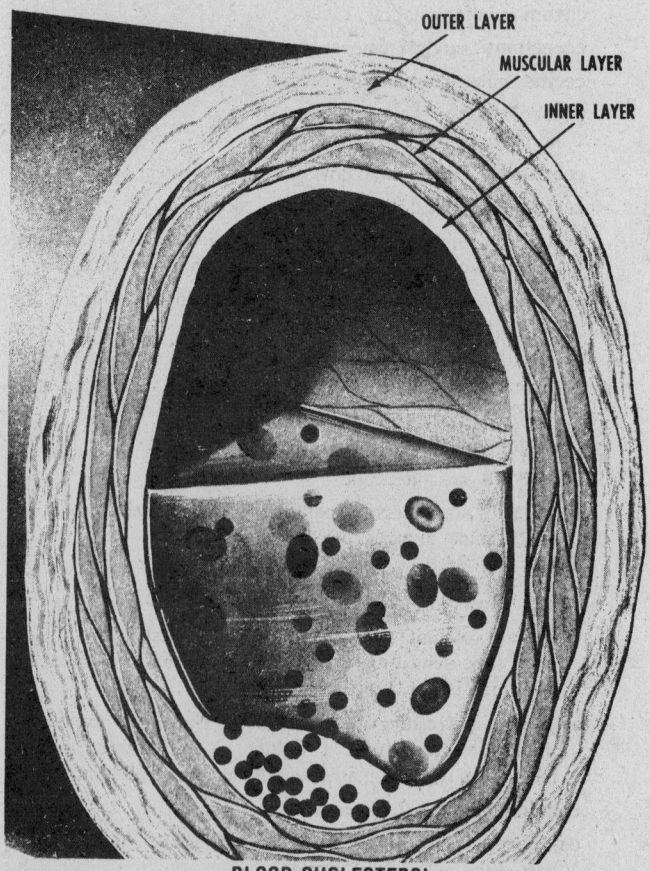

OUTER LAYER
MUSCULAR LAYER
INNER LAYER

BLOOD CHOLESTEROL

This is a cross section of a blood vessel showing the cholesterol (fat) particles invading the inner wall. A hard yellowish plaque forms which may eventually impede the blood flow.

ULCERATIVE COLITIS

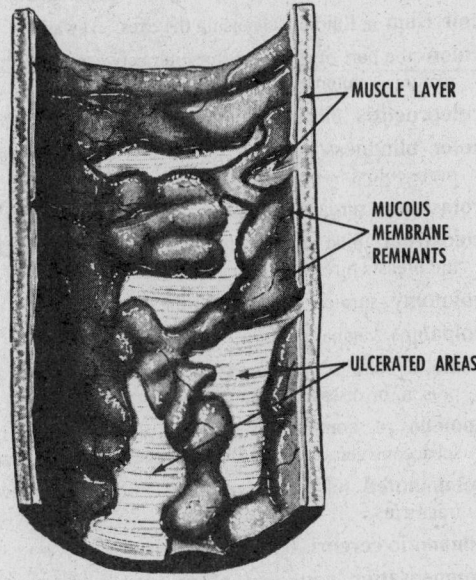

MUSCLE LAYER

MUCOUS MEMBRANE REMNANTS

ULCERATED AREAS

Colitis is an inflammation of the mucous membrane and walls of the large intestine, in the pathologic picture of which ulceration predominates. Ulceration generally begins in the rectum and spreads upward, eventually involving the entire colon. The symptoms are fever, malaise, prostration, persistent diarrhea, and the passage of blood, mucus, and pus.

cholesterolemia the presence in the bloodstream of unusually large amounts of cholesterol.

cholic relating to the bile.

choline an organic base that is a B-complex vitamin vital to liver function.

cholinergic relating to nerve endings that release acetylcholine.

choloplania the abnormal presence of bile salts in the tissues or bloodstream.

cholopoiesis the formation of bile.

cholorrhea excessive secretion of bile into the small intestine.

chondr- or **chondri-** or **chondro-** prefix cartilage.

chondral relating to cartilage.

chondrectomy surgical removal of a piece of cartilage.

chondritis inflammation of cartilage.

chondrodynia pain in cartilage.

chondrogenesis the formation of cartilage.

chondromalacia the abnormal softening of cartilage.

chondrosarcoma a malignant tumor derived from cartilage cells, usually near the extremities of long bones.

chondrotome a strong knife used to cut cartilage.

chondrotomy surgical separation or division of a cartilage.

chondrotrophic influencing the growth and development of cartilage.

chorda a tendon or tendinous structure or part.

chordee painful erection of the penis, often with a downward curvature, usually occurring as a symptom of gonorrhea.

chorditis inflammation of a cord, esp. a vocal cord.

chorea a disease marked by spastic movements of the muscles of the limbs and face and progressive mental deterioration.

chorioangioma a benign tumor of blood vessels, esp. those of the placenta.

chorion the outer embryonic membrane, part of which contributes to the placenta. —**chorionic** adj.

chorionitis inflammation of the outermost of the fetal membranes (chorion).

chorioretinitis inflammation of the choroid and retina of the eye.

choroid a vascular membrane between the retina and the sclerotic coat of the eye that contains pigment cells.

chromatid either of the paired complex strands of a chromosome.

chromaturia any abnormal discoloration of the urine.

chromesthesia 1. the stimulation of taste, smell, etc., by the perception of color. 2. color sense.

chromophobe also **chromophobic** (of certain tissues or cells) resistant to stain or incapable of receiving stains.

chromophobia an abnormal aversion to colors.

chromopsia incomplete or partial color blindness.

chromoscopy the procedure of testing for color perception.

chromosome one of the rod-shaped bodies of a cell nucleus containing the genes (each human cell has 46 chromosomes). —**chromosomal** adj. —**chromosomic** adj.

chromotrichial relating to colored hair.

chronognosis time sense; the ability to appreciate the passage of time.

chronotaraxis the inability to appreciate the passage of time; impaired time sense.

chyle a milky fluid found in lymph vessels and formed in the small intestine during the digestion of fats.

chyme a virtually liquid mass of partially digested food and secretions that is formed in the stomach and passes to the small intestine during the process of digestion.

cicatricial of or relating to a cicatrix.

cicatrix a scar remaining from a healed wound.

cilium pl. **cilia** a minute protoplasmic thread projecting from the surface of a cell and capable of lashing movements. —**ciliary** adj.

cimex pl. **cimices** a bedbug.

cinchona the dried bark of a tree (cinchona tree) from which quinine can be obtained, formerly used in the treatment of malaria; Peruvian bark.

cinchonism poisoning by cinchona, quinidine or quinine, characterized by headache, ringing in the ears or loss of hearing, and sometimes a severe allergic reaction.

circadian involving or based on 24-hour periods or intervals.

circinate (of certain structures or parts) shaped like a ring; circular.

circulation the movement of blood through the vessels resulting from the pumping action of the heart.

circulus a circular or ringlike structure or part.

circumcision the surgical removal of all or part of the foreskin. —**circumcise** vb.

cirrhosis disease of the liver marked by fibrosis and hardening.

cirsectomy surgical removal of a varicose vein.

cirsodesis the tying off or ligation of varicose veins.

cirsoid varicose.

cirsotome a surgical instrument for removing varicose veins.

clamp a device designed to constrict a vessel or to provide a secure hold on a structure.

clap (colloquial) gonorrhea.

claudication the condition of being lame; limping.

claustrophobia an abnormal fear of being in narrow or enclosed spaces.

clavicle a bone of the shoulder; collarbone.

cleft palate fissure of the roof of the mouth occurring congenitally.

climacteric 1. menopause. 2. a period in the male corresponding to the menopause in the female and marked by reduced sexual interest and activity.

climatotherapy treatment of a disease or disorder by moving to a different climate, as to a warm and dry climate in treating bronchitis.

clinic 1. medical instruction based on the examination and discussion of patients. 2. a medical facility supplementary to a hospital and specializing in the treatment of outpatients. 3. a group practice of several physicians working cooperatively. —**clinical** adj.

clinician a physician, psychiatrist, or psychologist specializing in clinical practice rather than in laboratory or research work.

clitoris a small organ homologous to the penis and located at the upper part of the vulva.

clitorism a rare, painful condition in which the clitoris remains erect for prolonged periods.

clonus a sequence of muscular spasms in which rigidity is followed by relaxation. —**clonic** adj.

club foot talipes; a deformed foot twisted out of normal position: a congenital defect.

coagulate to cause to become or to become thickened into a coherent mass; clot; curdle. —**coagulation** n.

coarctotomy surgical division of a stricture.

cobalt a hard, gray metallic element related to nickel and iron.

cocaine an alkaloid from coca leaves that is used as a local anesthetic and can become addictive.

coccus pl. **cocci** a spherical bacterium.

coccygectomy surgical removal of the coccyx.

coccygodynia pain in the coccyx.

coccyx the terminal bone of the spinal column formed by the fusion of four rudimentary vertebrae.

cochlea the spiral cavity of the internal ear that is the seat of the hearing organ. —**cochlear** adj.

coconsciousness two streams of consciousness existing simultaneously.

codeine a morphine derivative that is found in opium and is used as an analgesic and in cough suppressant remedies.

coition sexual intercourse.

coitus sexual intercourse.

colectasia distention of the colon.

colectomy surgical removal of a section of the colon or (rarely) its complete removal.

coleocele a vaginal hernia.

colic severe abdominal pains resulting from spasms of a hollow organ and chiefly affecting infants. —**colicky** adj.

colitis inflammation of the colon.

collagen an insoluble fibrous protein forming the major part of intercellular connective tissue.

collapse a state of acute prostration and physical depression.

collarbone clavicle.

colliculus any small anatomical elevation.

colloid a mucinous or gelatinous substance found in the thyroid and in certain other tissues. —**colloidal** adj.

collyrium a fluid for cleansing the eyes; eyewash.

colon the part of the large intestine between the cecum and the rectum. —**colonic** adj.

coloproctitis inflammation of both the colon and rectum.

color blindness inability to perceive or distinguish one or more colors. —**color-blind** adj.

colostomy surgical formation of an artificial anus.

colostrum milk, rich in protein and antibodies, secreted from the breasts directly after parturition.

colotomy surgical incision into the colon.

colpalgia vaginal pain.

coma a state of profound unconsciousness, as from injury, poison, or disease. —**comatose** adj.

comedo pl. **comedones** a small plug of sebum blocking a sebaceous gland esp. on the face, chest, or back; blackhead.

comminuted (of a fractured bone) broken into several small fragments.

commotio cerebri brain concussion.

compensation correction of an organic defect or loss by inceased functioning of another organ or part.

complement the substance in normal blood serum and plasma that combines with antibodies to combat bacteria and other antigens.

complex a group of repressed desires and memories that exert a powerful influence on a personality.

complication a secondary disorder or disease developing in consequence of a primary disease or injury.

compos mentis of sound mind, understanding, and memory.

compound a substance formed by the chemical union of two or more elements in strict proportion by weight.

compound fracture open fracture.

compress a folded pad or cloth, as of gauze, for applying local pressure to a bodily part.

conceive to become pregnant.

conception the act of becoming pregnant; the impregnation of an ovum.

concha pl. **conchae** 1. the largest and deepest cavity of the outer ear. 2. one of three thin bones in the nasal cavity.

concretion a hardened mass; calculus.

concussion a jarring injury to the brain that temporarily or permanently impairs its normal functioning.

condom a thin rubber sheath worn over the penis to prevent conception or venereal disease during sexual intercourse.

condyle a rounded prominence at the end of a bone.

condyloma a warty growth in the area of the anus and genitals.

confabulation the invention of events esp. to compensate for episodes of memory loss, as in chronic alcoholism.

confinement the state of preparing for childbirth; lying-in.

congenital existing at the time of birth: congenital deformity.

congestion an abnormal accumulation of blood in a bodily part.

conjunctiva pl. **conjunctivas** or **conjunctivae** the mucous membrane lining the inside of the eyelid and the forepart of the eyeball.

conjunctivitis inflammation of the conjunctiva.

connective tissue tissue that supports and binds together other tissues and forms ligaments and tendons.

consolidation an alteration in lung tissue in pneumonia in which air spaces become filled with exudate.

constipation abnormally delayed or difficult passage of feces.

consumption tuberculosis. —**consumptive** *adj.*

contact a person who has been exposed to or transmits an infectious disease.

contact lens a thin lens fitted over the cornea of the eye.

contagion the transmission of a disease by contact.

contagious communicable by direct or indirect contact; catching: *contagious disease.*

contraception the voluntary prevention of impregnation or conception.

contraceptive 1. relating to or used for contraception. 2. a contraceptive device or agent.

contraindication a caution against the advisability of using a particular medication or medical treatment. —**contraindicate** *vb.* —**contraindicative** *adj.*

contusion bruise. —**contuse** *vb.*

convalesce to regain one's health at a gradual pace. —**convalescence** *n.*

convolution any of the irregular ridges on the surface of the brain; gyrus.

convulsion an abnormal, violent muscular contraction or series of contractions. —**convulse** *vb.* —**convulsive** *adj.*

coprolalia a rare condition in which obscene or vulgar words are uttered involuntarily.

copulation sexual intercourse.

cordate heart-shaped.

cordectomy surgical removal of a cord.

corn a localized hardening and thickening of the skin, as on a toe, from pressure or friction.

cornea the transparent part of the eyeball coat that covers the pupil and iris and admits light.

coronary vessel any of the arteries and veins that carry the blood supply of the heart muscle.

corpulence *also* **corpulency** the state of being extremely fat. —**corpulent** *adj.*

corpuscle a cell, esp. a red or white blood cell.

cortex the outer layer of an organ or bodily structure. —**cortical** *adj.*

corticipetal (of nerve fibers) conveying nerve impulses toward the cerebral cortex.

corticothalamic relating to nerve fibers that connect the cerebral cortex with specific areas of the thalamus.

coryza an upper respiratory infection, esp. the common cold.

costal of or relating to the ribs.

costive affected with or causing constipation; constipated. —**costiveness** *n.*

costotome a surgical instrument for cutting through a rib.

costotomy surgical division of a rib.

cotyledon a nodule of the placenta.

counterdepressant 1. relating to the action of any drug or agent that prevents or inhibits the potential depressant action of another drug. 2. a drug or agent with this effect.

counterirritant an agent producing localized, superficial inflammation in order to reduce inflammation in adjacent, deeper structures or tissues. —**counterirritation** *n.*

courses menses.

couvercle a blood clot that forms outside of a vessel.

Cowper's gland either of two small glands that discharge into the male urethra.

coxalgia pain or inflammation involving the hip joint.

coxotomy surgical incision into the hip joint.

Coxsackie virus any of various viruses associated with human diseases.

c.p. *abbr.* chemically pure.

c.p.s. *abbr.* cycles per second; counts per second.

crab louse a louse that infests the pubic region of humans.

crabs infestation with crab lice.

cramp 1. a painful, spasmodic contraction of a muscle. 2. usually **cramps**, sharp abdominal pain.

crani- *or* **cranio-** *prefix* skull; cranial.

cranial of or relating to the skull.

cranial index the ratio of the maximum breadth of the skull to its maximum height, multiplied by 100.

cranialis toward the head; cranial; superior (in humans); anterior (in quadrupeds).

cranial nerve any of the twelve pairs of nerves arising from the brain to the periphery of the body.

craniectomy surgical removal of a piece of the skull, as in preparation for a brain operation.

craniology a science dealing with the variations in size and shape of the skulls of different races.

craniomalacia abnormal softening of the bones of the skull.

craniomeningocele the protrusion of the covering membranes of the brain (meninges) through a defect in the bones of the skull.

craniometry a science dealing with the measurement of skulls.

craniopathy any disease or disorder of the skull.

cranioplasty surgical repair of a skull defect or deformity.

craniopuncture surgical puncture of the skull.

craniosclerosis an abnormal thickening of the bones of the skull.

cranium the skull, esp. the part enclosing the brain.

crapulent *also* **crapulous** drunk; intoxicated with alcohol.

crater the depressed central portion of something, such as the recessed portion of an ulcer.

crateriform having a depressed center; hollowed.

c.r.d. *abbr.* chronic respiratory disease.

creatine a nitrogenous, energy-storing substance found in muscles.

crena a cleft or notch.

crena ani the cleft between the buttocks.

crenate *also* **crenated** indented or notched.

crepitant (of a sound heard from the lungs in pneumonia or certain other pulmonary diseases) crackling.

crepitation *also* **crepitus** 1. the fine grating sound heard when two ends of a broken bone rub together. 2. the crackling chest sound heard in pneumonia and other lung infections.

crest a bony ridge or prominence.

cretinism a congenital, abnormal condition caused by thyroid deficiency and marked by mental retardation and small stature. —**cretin** *n.* —**cretinous** *adj.*

cribriform pierced with small holes.

crisis the turning point in a disease or fever after which the patient either improves or declines rapidly.

croup inflammation of the larynx, esp. in infants, marked by periods of difficult breathing and hoarse cough. —**croupous** adj. —**croupy** adj.

crural relating to the thigh; femoral.

cry- or **cryo-** prefix cold; freezing.

cryalgesia pain caused by exposure to cold.

cryanesthesia the inability to sense or perceive cold.

cryesthesia the sensation of cold or the state of being especially sensitive to low temperatures.

cryohypophysectomy the surgical destruction of all or part of the pituitary gland (hypophysis cerebri) by cold.

cryotherapy the therapeutic use of cold, as that produced by liquid nitrogen.

crystalluria the presence of crystals in the urine.

cuneiform wedge-shaped: *cuneiform bone.*

cunnilingus or **cunnilinctus** oral stimulation of the vulva and clitoris. —**cunnilingual** adj.

cupula a cuplike or dome-shaped structure or part.

curare an extract of a vine used by South American Indians as an arrow poison and in medicine (in very small amounts) as a muscle relaxant.

curettage surgical cleaning or scraping using a curette.

curette or **curet** a surgical loop or scoop used in performing curettage. —**curette** or **curet** vb.

curie a unit of radioactive quantity.

cutaneous relating to or affecting the skin.

cuticle 1. the horny outer layer of the skin, esp. at the margins of the nail beds. 2. epidermis.

cyanocobalamin vitamin B_{12}.

cyanosis a bluish discoloration of the skin resulting from inadequate oxygenation of the blood.

cyclamate an artificially prepared sodium or calcium salt used as a sweetener.

cyst a fluid-filled, membranous sac developing abnormally in a bodily cavity or structure.

cystic fibrosis a hereditary disease of infants, children, and young adults that is attributable to dysfunction of the exocrine glands and is marked by pancreatic deficiency, respiratory problems, and loss of salt in the sweat.

cystine an amino acid that is a metabolic source of sulfur.

cystitis inflammation of the urinary bladder.

cystolith a calculus in the urinary bladder.

cystoscope an instrument for visual examination of the bladder and the introduction of exploratory instruments.

cyt- or **cyto-** prefix 1. cell: *cytology.* 2. cytoplasm.

cytochrome any of several iron-containing proteins that play an important role in cell oxidations.

cytogenetics the branch of biology dealing with the study of heredity (genetics) in relation to that of cells (cytology).

cytology the biological study of the structure, function, and life history of cells.

cytolysis the disintegration of cells.

cytoplasm the protoplasm of a cell excluding the nucleus.

cytotoxin a substance having a toxic effect on cells. —**cytotoxic** adj. —**cytotoxicity** n.

cytotropic attracted to cells.

D

dacryocystitis inflammation of the tear sac.

dacryocystotome a small knife for making incisions in the tear sac.

dacryolith a calculus in the tear duct.

dacryops the chronic presence of an accumulation of tears in the eye.

dacryopyorrhea the discharge of pus from the tear duct.

dacryopyosis the formation of pus in the tear sac or duct.

dacryorrhea the excessive flow of tears.

dactyl a finger or toe.

dactylalgia pain in a finger or toe.

dactyledema edema of the finger.

dactylology the science or practice of using the finger alphabet in communicating.

dactylomegaly abnormal enlargement of one or more fingers.

daltonism color blindness, esp. involving the color red.

dandruff small whitish flakes of desquamated cells forming chiefly on the scalp; scurf.

Darwinism a theory of the origin and evolution of new species of animals and plants stressing that natural selection favors the survival of some offspring over others; biological evolution.

DDT abbr. dichlorodiphenyltrichloroethane: a very powerful insecticide which can be poisonous if ingested with DDT-sprayed food that has not been properly washed.

deaf-mute a person who can neither hear nor speak.

deallergize desensitize.

deaminate to remove the amino group from (a compound). —**deamination** n.

deaquation dehydration.

debilitate to impair the strength of; enfeeble. —**debilitation** n.

debility loss of strength; feebleness; weakness.

debridement the surgical removal and cleansing of damaged or contaminated tissue.

decaffeinate to remove the caffeine from.

decalcify to remove calcium or calcium compounds from. —**decalcification** n.

decalvant making bald; removing the hair.

decapitate to sever the head of; behead. —**decapitation** n. —**decapitator** n.

decerebrate 1. having the cerebrum removed or rendered inactive. 2. to remove the cerebrum of or make incapable of cerebral activity.

decerebrize to remove the brain of.

dechloridation removal of salt (sodium chloride) from the body fluids and tissues by restricting the dietary intake of salt.

decidua pl. **deciduae** the mucous membrane lining the uterus that thickens and becomes modified in preparation for pregnancy and is cast off during parturition and menstruation. —**decidual** adj.

deciduitis inflammation of the decidua.

deciduoma a tumor of the uterus believed to arise from decidual tissue left behind following a miscarriage or abortion.

deciduous falling off or out at a certain stage in the life cycle: *deciduous teeth.*

deciliter one tenth of a liter.

decimeter one tenth of a meter.

decinormal (denoting the strength of a solution) one tenth that of normal or standard values.

decipara a woman who has given birth to ten children.

declinator a surgical instrument for retracting certain parts out of the immediate operative field.

decompensation failure of compensation, esp. inability of the heart to maintain adequate circulation.

decompose to undergo breakdown by hydrolytic enzymes; rot; putrify. —**decomposability** n. —**decomposable** adj. —**decomposition** n.

decompression the relieving of pressure or compression, esp. surgery to release internal bodily pressure. —**decompression** n.

decongestant a drug or agent that relieves congested blood vessels, esp. those of the mucous membrane of the nose.

decorticate to remove the outer covering or cortex from (an organ). —**decortication** n. —**decorticator** n.

decrudescence the lessening or easing of the symptoms of a disease or illness.

decubitus ulcer an ulcer formed by constant pressure on the skin over a bony prominence while lying in bed; bedsore; pressure sore.

decussate to intersect; cross, as nerve fibers. —**decussation** n.

defecation the discharge of feces from the bowels. —**defecate** vb.

defemination the loss of secondary sexual characteristics or femininity, esp. as the result of a hormonal disorder.

deferens a duct that conveys spermatozoa from each testicle; vas deferens; ductus deferens.

deferent downward; away from; carrying away.

deferentectomy vasectomy.

deferential relating to the vas deferens or ductus deferens.

deferentitis inflammation of the vas deferens.

defervescence the falling or lessening of a fever or the period during which this occurs.

defibrillate to restore the normal rhythm of (a fibrillating heart) with electrical shocks. —**defibrillation** n. —**defibrillator** n. —**defibrillatory** adj.

deficiency disease a disease, as rickets, beriberi, scurvy, resulting from a dietary deficiency, as of an essential vitamin or mineral.

deflorescence the disappearance of a skin eruption or the period during which a skin rash begins to abate.

defluxio sudden loss of hair.

deganglionate to deprive of ganglia.

degeneration progressive deterioration in the structure or function of organs or tissues. —**degenerate** vb.

deglutition the act or process of swallowing.

degustation the sense of taste; tasting.

dehiscence the bursting open of the edges of a wound, esp. after they have been sutured or sewn together.

dehydration loss of water; an abnormal depletion of body fluids. —**dehydrate** vb. —**dehydrator** n.

déjà vu the illusion of remembering events and scenes actually being experienced for the first time; paramnesia.

deleterious harmful; injurious.

deliquesce (of certain salts) to become liquid or damp as the result of atmospheric water absorption. —**deliquescence** n.

delirifacient 1. causing delirium. 2. a toxic agent capable of causing delirium.

delirium a mental condition characterized by hallucinations, disordered speech, and extreme confusion.

delirium tremens a violent psychotic delirium with tremors and hallucinations that is induced by prolonged and excessive

use of alcohol. Also called D.T.'s.

delivery parturition; childbirth.

delomorphous of definite shape and form.

deltoid a large triangular muscle covering the shoulder joint and serving to raise and lower the arm laterally.

delusion a false conviction about the self, other persons, or the environment that persists despite the demonstrable facts. —**delusional** adj.

dementia a condition of impaired or deteriorated mentality; insanity; madness.

dementia praecox an obsolete term for schizophrenia.

demilune a small body shaped like a crescent or half-moon, such as certain cells.

demineralization a loss or progressive diminution of mineral constituents, esp. of calcium from bone.

demorphinization 1. the process or technique of removing morphine from an opiate drug. 2. a method of curing morphine addiction by the gradual withdrawal of the drug.

demulcent a substance capable of soothing or protecting an irritated mucous membrane.

demyelination loss or destruction of the fatty insulating sheath (myelin) that surrounds most nerve fibers.

denarcotize to deprive an opitate drug of its narcotic properties; to remove narcotic properties from.

denature 1. to alter the structure of a protein molecule by physical or chemical action. 2. to make (alcohol) unfit for drinking without otherwise impairing its usefulness. —**denaturation** n.

dendriform branching out; tree-shaped.

dendrite any of the branching processes of a nerve cell that conveys impulses toward the cell body. —**dendritic** adj.

dendroid branching; like a tree.

dendron dendrite.

denematize deworm; free from infestation with nematodes.

denervate to deprive of a nerve supply. —**denervation** n.

dengue an acute viral disease chiefly of the tropics characterized by fever, headache, joint pains, and rash.

denitrify to remove nitrogen from. —**denitrification** n.

dens 1. a tooth. 2. a toothlike structure or part.

densimeter an instrument for measuring the density of a liquid.

dental of, relating to, affecting, or used for the teeth.

dentalgia toothache.

dentate notched; having teeth or cogs.

dentes teeth.

denticle 1. a small toothlike projection from a surface. 2. a small tooth.

denticulate notched; having fine teeth; serrated.

dentiform shaped like a tooth.

dentifrice any preparation used to clean the teeth, including toothpaste, tooth powder and special washes.

dentigerous having or containing teeth.

dentilabial relating to both the teeth and lips.

dentilingual relating to both the teeth and tongue.

dentinalgia pain or tenderness of the dentine.

dentine or **dentin** the calcareous substance that forms the body of a tooth.

dentiparous bearing teeth.

dentition 1. the development and cutting of teeth. 2. the form and arrangement of the teeth in the mouth.

dentoalveolar relating to the bony sockets surrounding the teeth.

dentulous containing teeth.

denture a partial or complete set of false teeth.

denucleated deprived of a nucleus.

deodorant a preparation that ameliorates or disguises unpleasant odors.

deodorize to eliminate or mask the unpleasant odor of.

deossification the removal of minerals from bone.

deoxidize to remove the oxygen from. —**deoxidation** n.

deoxyribonucleic acid a nucleic acid localized chiefly in cell nuclei that is the hereditary material of many organisms; DNA.

depigmentation partial or total loss of pigment or color.

depilate to remove hair. —**depilation** n.

depilatory 1. an agent for removing body hair. 2. able to remove hair.

deplumation loss or falling out of the eyelashes as the result of disease.

deprecusis loss of the ability to hear external sounds while eating, as the result of otosclerosis.

depressant an agent that reduces functional bodily activity esp. by inducing muscular relaxation.

depressed marked by or suffering from depression.

depression a condition marked by pessimism, inactivity, dejection, lack of concentration, and often insomnia.

depressomotor 1. inhibiting motor activity. 2. an agent that inhibits or slows motor activity.

depuration purification; removal of waste products.

deradenitis inflammation of the lymph nodes in the neck; cervical adenitis.

derma dermis.

dermatalgia pain restricted to the skin.

dermatitis any of various forms of inflammation of the skin.

dermatochalasis loose skin.

dermatoconiosis inflammation of the skin caused by the irritant effects of dust, usually affecting those who work in certain environments where an unusual amount of dust is generated.

dermatodynia pain restricted to the skin; dermatalgia.

dermatoid resembling skin.

dermatology a branch of medicine dealing with the structure, functions, and diseases of the skin. —**dermatologic, dermatological** adj. —**dermatologist** n.

dermatolysis a congenital defect in which the skin is abnormally loose.

dermatoma an overgrowth or thickening of the skin in a circumscribed area.

dermatome an instrument for removing very thin sections of skin, as in skin grafting.

dermatomegaly a congenital defect in which the skin hangs in heavy folds.

dermatoneurosis any skin eruption caused by emotional stimuli.

dermatopathology the microscopic study of skin lesions.

dermatopathy any disease or disorder of the skin.

dermatophobia an abnormal fear of skin diseases.

dermatophyte a fungus that is parasitic on the skin, hair, or nails. —**dermatophytic** adj.

dermatoplasty surgical repair of skin defects; skin grafting.

dermatosis any disease of the skin.

dermatozoon any skin parasite of the animal kingdom.

dermatozoonosis any skin eruption caused by an animal parasite.

dermatrophia also **dermatrophy** an abnormal wasting away or thinning of the skin.

dermis the inner mesodermic layer of the skin.

dermitis dermatitis; inflammation of the skin.

dermoid or **dermoidal** resembling or made up of skin.

dermoidectomy the surgical removal of a cyst on the skin.

dermology dermatology.

dermotropic attracted to or entering through the skin.

desensitize to render (a hypersensitive individual) insensitive to an aggravating agent. —**densensitization** n.

desiccant an agent that absorbs or dries, such as one placed in a bottle of tablets to prevent them from deteriorating in environmental moisture.

desiccate to dry up. —**desiccation** n. —**desiccative** adj.

desmitis inflammation of a ligament.

desmoenzymes enzymes that exist within cells; intracellular enzymes.

desmology the branch of anatomy concerned with the ligaments.

desmopathy any disease or disorder of the ligaments.

desmotomy the surgical separation of a ligament.

desquamate to peel off in scales. —**desquamation** n.

detoxicate detoxify.

detoxify to remove a poison or toxin or the effects of a poison or toxin from. —**detoxification** n.

deuteranopia color blindness limited to the inability to perceive green hues.

deviated septum a congenital or acquired (as by injury) deflection of the cartilaginous separation between the nostrils.

dexter relating to or located on the right.

dextroamphetamine amphetamine.

dextrose a glucose used esp. as an intravenously supplied nutrient replenisher.

diabetes any of various diseases marked esp. by excessive excretion of urine; (commonly) short for diabetes mellitus.

diabetes insipidus a metabolic disorder of the pituitary gland marked by intense thirst and the passage of large quantities of urine.

diabetes mellitus a metabolic disorder marked by insufficient secretion or utilization of insulin, polyuria, large amounts of sugar in the urine and blood, and by weight loss, thirst, and hunger.

diabetic 1. of, relating to, or affected with diabetes. 2. a person suffering from diabetes.

diacid an acid with two acid hydrogen atoms. —**diacid** or **diacidic** adj.

diagnosis the skill or act of identifying a disease from its symptoms and signs. —**diagnose** vb.

diagnostic of or relating to diagnosis.

diagnostics the branch of medicine dealing with the diagnosis of disease. —**diagnostician** n.

dialysis pl. **dialyses** the separation of substances in solution by means of their unequal diffusion through a semipermeable membrane.

dialyze to undergo dialysis. —**dialyzability** *n.* —**dialyzable** *adj.* —**dialyzer** *n.*

diapedesis the passage of blood or blood cells through vessel walls into the tissues. —**diapedetic** *adj.*

diaphanometer an instrument for measuring the relative transparency of fluids.

diaphoresis perspiration, esp. when profuse.

diaphoretic an agent that promotes diaphoresis.

diaphragm 1. the muscular partition separating the chest from the abdomen. 2. a circular cap usually of thin flexible rubber fitted over the cervix of the uterus as a barrier to conception.

diaphysectomy surgical removal of part of the shaft of a long bone.

diaphysis the shaft of a long bone.

diapiresis diapedesis.

diapyesis the formation of pus; suppuration.

diapyetic 1. relating to or causing suppuration. 2. anything that causes the production of pus.

diarrhea *also* **diarrhoea** frequent loose emptying of the bowels.

diarthric relating to two joints.

diarthrosis a joint that permits free movement, such as a ball-and-socket joint.

diastase an enzyme in plant cells and in digestive juice which acts in the conversion of starch into sugar.

diastasis *pl.* **diastases** 1. the rest period of the cardiac cycle occurring before systole. 2. separation of the epiphysis from the shaft of a long bone, as through injury.

diastole the dilation of the heart cavities during which they become filled with blood. —**diastolic** *adj.*

diathermy the therapeutic generation of heat in tissues by means of electric currents. —**diathermic** *adj.*

diathesis a constitutional predisposition toward a particular disease or abnormality.

diatomic having two atoms in the molecule.

dibromide a bromide (such as calcium bromide) that contains two bromine atoms in each molecule.

dichromasia a form of color blindness in which only two of the three primary colors are perceived, those usually perceived being red and blue or blue and green.

dichromat a person affected with dichromasia.

Dick test a test for susceptibility or immunity to scarlet fever by injection of scarlet fever toxin.

dicrotic of or relating to a pulse that beats twice for each single beat of the heart. —**dicrotism** *n.*

didelphic relating to or having a double uterus.

didymalgia pain in the testicles; orchialgia.

didymitis inflammation of the testicles; orchitis.

diencephalon the part of the brain that includes the thalamus, hypothalamus and related structures; between-brain.

dietetics the science of applying the principles of nutrition to balanced feeding.

diethylstilbestrol a synthetic preparation that is more powerful than natural estrogens, used to treat estrogen deficiencies and menopausal problems; stilbestrol.

dietician *or* **dietitian** a specialist in dietetics.

digest to convert (food) into absorbable form. —**digestibility** *n.* —**digestible** *adj.* —**digestion** *n.*

digestant 1. relating to or stimulating digestion. 2. something that aids or promotes digestion.

digestive 1. relating to or promoting digestion. 2. an agent that aids in or stimulates digestion.

digit a finger or toe. —**digital** *adj.*

digitalis the dried leaf of the common foxglove that when ground to powder acts as a powerful cardiac stimulant.

diiodide a compound that has two atoms of iodine in each molecule.

dilatation the condition of being stretched or expanded beyond normal dimensions: *dilatation of the abdomen.*

dilate to enlarge or widen in extent or degree. —**dilation** *n.*

dilator an instrument for enlarging a bodily opening, as the anus or urethra.

dilute to make thinner, more fluid, or less potent by addition of another substance. —**dilute** *adj.* —**dilution** *n.*

diopter *also* **dioptre** a unit of measurement of the refractive power of the lens.

dioptometer an instrument for measuring the refractive power of the eyes. —**dioptometry** *n.*

dioptroscopy the use of an ophthalmoscope to determine the degree of refraction.

diose the most simple sugar; glycolaldehyde.

diovulatory releasing two ova during one menstrual cycle.

dioxide an oxide containing two atoms of oxygen in the molecule.

diphtheria an acute infectious bacterial disease characterized by the formation of a false membrane in the throat or larynx.

diplacusis the hearing of two sounds from a single source due to a difference in perception by the two ears, either in pitch or time.

diplegia paralysis affecting both sides of the body in like areas. —**diplegic** *adj.*

diplococcus any of a genus of often pathogenic bacteria occurring chiefly in pairs.

diploë osseous tissue between the two layers of the skull. —**diploic** *adj.* —**diploetic** *adj.*

diploid having the basic (haploid) chromosome number doubled.

diplomyelia the abnormal presence of a longitudinal fissure in the spinal cord which divides it into distinct halves.

diplopia double vision.

dipsogen any agent that stimulates thirst.

dipsomania an uncontrollable craving for alcohol; alcoholism. —**dipsomaniac** *n.* —**dipsomaniacal** *adj.*

disaccharide a sugar that yields two monosaccharide molecules.

disarticulation the condition of being disjointed.

disc disk.

discharge the release of something contained, as of pus from a boil.

dischronation a disturbance in the ability to recognize the passage of time; loss of time sense.

discography X-ray of an intervertebral disk.

discoid resembling or shaped like a disk.

discopathy any disease involving an intervertebral disk.

disease a condition that impairs some function of the body or one of its parts. —**diseased** *adj.*

disinfectant an agent, as a chemical, that destroys certain harmful microorganisms: usually for external use only. —**disinfect** *vb.*

disk *or* **disc** any of various flattened and rounded anatomical structures, as one of the fibro-cartilaginous, articulating plates between vertebrae of the spinal column.

dislocation the displacement of a bone from its normal position in relation to another bone. —**dislocate** *vb.*

disorientation loss of a sense of time, identity, or place.

dispensary a place, as an outpatient clinic, providing medical and dental aid.

dispense to prepare and distribute (medication).

dispermy the penetration of an ovum by two sperm cells.

dissect to cut apart or open for scientific examination. —**dissection** *n.*

distal remote from the point of attachment or origin.

distemper any of certain specific infectious diseases of dogs, cats and horses, caused by infection with a virus (dogs and cats) or bacteria (horses).

districhiasis the growth of two hairs from a single hair follicle.

distrix the splitting of the ends of hairs.

diuresis an increased secretion of urine.

diuretic 1. relating to or tending to increase the flow of urine. 2. a drug or agent that increases the urinary output.

diurnal daily.

diverticulitis inflammation of a diverticulum.

diverticulosis an intestinal disorder marked by the presence of many diverticula.

diverticulum *pl.* **diverticula** a pouch or sac protruding abnormally from a hollow organ, as the bladder or intestine.

divulsion 1. the forcible dilation of the walls of a bodily cavity or passage. 2. the crude removal of a part by tearing or ripping it out.

divulsor an instrument used to force apart the walls of a bodily cavity or passage such as the urethra.

dizygotic *also* **dizygous** fraternal: *dizygotic twins.*

DNA deoxyribonucleic acid.

dolichocephalic having an unusually long head. —**dolichocephaly** *n.*

dolor pain, one of the signs of inflammation.

dolorific producing or causing pain.

dominant relating to or exerting genetic dominance.

donor a person used as the source of biological material, as for an organ transplant or blood transfusion.

dopa dihydroxyphenylalanine; an amino acid used in treating Parkinson's disease.

doraphobia an abnormal fear of petting animals or of touching their fur or skin.

dorsabdominal relating to both the back and the abdomen.

dorsad toward the back or posterior.

dorsal relating to or located near, on, or at the back.

dorsalgia pain in the back.

dorsiflexion an upward turning of the toes or foot.

dosage 1. the administration of drugs or other therapeutic agents in prescribed amounts. 2. the determination of the correct quantity of a drug to be administered or taken at one time.

dose the exact amount of a drug or therapeutic agent to be administered or taken at one time or at prescribed intervals.

double vision a disorder of vision in which two images of the same object are seen simultaneously because of unequal action of the eye muscles; diplopia.

douche 1. a stream of water, with or without medication or

other additives, directed so as to irrigate or cleanse a body cavity. 2. a device for giving a douche. —**douche** *vb.*

Down's syndrome mongolism.

drastic acting quickly and powerfully: *a drastic purgative.*

dropsy the excessive accumulation of clear fluid in body tissues or cavities; edema; ascites.

drug 1. a substance used in diagnosing, curing, mitigating, treating, or preventing disease. 2. a narcotic. —**drug** *vb.*

druggist a pharmacist.

D.T.'s delirium tremens.

duct a tube or vessel of the body esp. for the passage of secretions or excretions.

duodenum the first part of the small intestine extending from the pylorus to the jejunum. —**duodenal** *adj.*

dura mater the tough outer membrane enveloping the brain and spinal cord.

dwarf a person of unusually or abnormally small stature. —**dwarfish** *adj.* —**dwarfism** *n.*

dys- *prefix* abnormal; difficult.

dyscrasia an abnormal condition of the body: *blood dyscrasia.*

dysentery a disease that is characterized by intestinal inflammation, abdominal pain, and the passage of mucus and bloody stools and is caused by bacteria or protozoa.

dysfunction abnormal or impaired functioning. —**dysfunctional** *adj.*

dyslexia a disturbance in the ability to read; word blindness. —**dyslexic** *adj.*

dysmenorrhea difficult or painful menstruation. —**dysmenorrheal** *adj.* —**dysmenorrheic** *adj.*

dyspepsia indigestion. —**dispeptic** *adj.*

dysphagia difficulty in swallowing. —**dysphagic** *adj.*

dysphasia impairment of the ability to use or understand spoken language coherently owing to injury or brain disease. —**dysphasic** *adj.*

dysplasia abnormality of development, as of organs or cells. —**dysplasic** *adj.*

dyspnea difficult or labored respiration. —**dyspneic** *adj.*

dystrophy a disorder resulting from faulty nutrition. —**dystrophic** *adj.*

dysuria difficult or painful urination.

E

ear the organ of hearing and equilibrium, consisting of a sound-collecting outer ear separated by a membranous drum (tympanic membrane) from a sound-transmitting middle ear that is itself separated by a membranous fenestra from a sensory inner ear.

eardrum tympanic membrane.

earlobe the pendent part of the outer ear.

ebonation removal of bony fragments from a wound.

ebrietas *also* **ebriety** the state of being intoxicated with alcohol; drunkenness.

ebullism the formation at high altitudes of bubbles of water vapor in the tissues.

ebur tissue resembling ivory in appearance or consistency.

eburnation a degenerative change in bone in which it becomes hard and dense like ivory.

eburneous resembling ivory; having the color of ivory.

ecaudate without a tail; tailless.

ecbolic 1. hastening childbirth or accelerating the termination of pregnancy. 2. any agent that speeds up delivery or produces abortion; oxytocic.

eccdemic (of a disease) brought into a region or community; not epidemic or endemic.

eccentropiesis pressure exerted outwards.

ecchondroma a tumor formed as an outgrowth of cartilaginous tissue and usually protruding from the surface of a bone within a joint.

ecchymoma a small mass of clotted blood formed as the result of a bruise.

ecchymosis a bruise appearing on the skin or mucous membrane and resulting from the escape of blood into the tissues from ruptured blood vessels. —**ecchymotic** adj.

eccoprotic having the properties of a laxative; cathartic.

eccrine exocrine.

eccrisis 1. removal from the body of waste matter. 2. waste matter; excrement.

eccritic 1. acting to expel waste matter. 2. an agent that acts to excrete waste matter.

eccyesis the development of a fertilized ovum outside the uterus; extrauterine pregnancy.

ecdemomania an abnormal desire to wander.

ecdysiasm an abnormal erotic desire or tendency to remove one's clothes in the presence of strangers.

ECG electrocardiogram.

ecgonine an alkaloid derived from cocaine.

echeosis mental suffering and emotional upset caused by prolonged exposure to loud or disturbing noises.

echidnin snake venom.

echidnotoxin a toxic protein in snake venom.

echinococcus pl. **echinococci** any of a genus of tapeworms that in the larval stage invade tissues esp. of the liver and constitute a dangerous pathogen.

echinosis an abnormal condition of red blood cells characterized by the loss of their smooth outlines.

echis a highly poisonous snake occurring in parts of Africa and the Middle East; carpet viper.

echoacousia subjective impairment of hearing in which a sound seems to be repeated.

echoencephalography the diagnostic technique of using ultrasound in examining the cranial contents.

echokinesia the involuntary mimicking of a sign or gesture made by another person.

echolalia the often pathological echoing of the words spoken by other people. —**echolalic** adj.

echomatism the involuntary and automatic repetition of an observed act.

echophotony the phenomenon of mentally associating a musical tone or tones with a specific color or colors.

echophrasia echolalia.

echopraxia the involuntary repetition or imitation of movements made by someone else; echomatism.

eclabium the eversion of a lip.

eclampsia an attack of convulsions sometimes occurring during pregnancy. —**eclamptic** adj.

eclaptogenous convulsive or causing convulsions.

ecmnesia the failure to recall recent events; short-term loss of memory.

ecphoria the ability to remember; recall of memory.

ecphyma a wartlike growth or elevation.

ECT electroconvulsive therapy.

ectacolia dilation of the large intestine.

ectad toward the surface; outward or externally.

ectal outer or external.

ectasia also **ectasis** dilation of a tubular passage.

ecthyma a pus-generating bacterial infection of the skin caused by staphylococci or streptococci.

ectiris the outermost layer of the iris.

ecto- prefix on the outside; outer.

ectoderm the outermost germ layer of an embryo. —**ectodermal** adj. **ectodermic** adj.

ectoglobular not within a red blood cell or other globular body.

ectomorphic having a light, slender body. —**ectomorph** n.

-ectomy suffix surgical removal: mastectomy.

ectoparasite any parasite that lives on the outer surface of the body.

ectoperitonitis inflammation of the layer of peritoneum that lines the abdominal cavity.

ectopic occurring or appearing in an abnormal place, position, or manner.

ectopic pregnancy gestation occurring elsewhere than in the uterus, as a fallopian tube.

ectoplasm the outermost layer of the protoplasm of a living cell.

ectoplastic formed at the outside or periphery.

ectopotomy surgical removal of a fetus developing outside the uterus.

ectopy also **ectopia** abnormal displacement of an organ or part.

ectoretina the outermost layer of the retina.

ectosteal relating to the external surface of a bone.

ectotoxemia blood poisoning caused by the introduction of a poison into the body.

ectozoon an animal parasite that lives on the surface of the body.

ectrimma an ulcer caused by constant friction.

ectrogeny the congenital absence of any structure or part.

ectrotic preventing or inhibiting the development of a disease.

eczema inflammation of the skin characterized initially by redness, itching, and oozing vesicles and later by scaling and crusting. —**eczematous** adj.

ED effective dose.

ED$_{50}$ a dose which has the desired effect in half of the subjects or laboratory animals.

edeitis inflammation of the external genitals in the female; vulvitis.

edema any condition in which the tissues contain an excessive amount of fluid, such as the result of the inflammatory process, kidney disorders, or increased permeability of the capillary walls.

edematous characterized or marked by edema.

edentate without teeth; toothless.

edulcorate to make sweet or sweeter; sweeten. —**edulcorant** n.

EEG electroencephalogram.

effector 1. a muscle or gland that becomes active upon being stimulated. 2. a motor or secretory nerve ending in a muscle or gland.

efferent conveying impulses, blood, etc., outward: *efferent nerves.*

effuse (of the surface appearance of a bacterial culture) widely spreading; thin.

egersis the condition of being unusually alert or attentive; abnormal wakefulness.

egesta any waste matter discharged from the body, esp. feces.

egg the female sex cell; ovum.

eglandulous without glands.

ego (in psychoanalytic theory) the part of the mind or psyche that is conscious and serves to mediate between the id and the superego and react to the outside world.

egotropic self-centered.

egrotogenic (of an illness) induced by the patient.

eidetic 1. relating to or possessing a photographic memory; having total recall of what has been seen before. 2. a person with total recall of what he has seen.

eiloid resembling a loop, coil or roll.

ejaculate 1. to eject (semen) in orgasm. 2. the semen ejaculated in orgasm. —**ejaculation** n. —**ejaculatory** adj.

ejaculatio precox premature ejaculation of semen; extremely rapid male orgasm at the start of sexual intercourse.

EKG also **ECG** electrocardiogram.

elastosis degenerative changes in elastic tissue, esp. the skin.

elbow the joint of the arm between the upper arm and the forearm.

Electra complex the female equivalent of the Oedipus complex; symptoms caused by a daughter's suppressed sexual love for her father.

electroanesthesia anesthesia induced by means of an electric current.

electrobiology the branch of biology concerned with the study of electrical phenomena in living organisms.

electrocardiogram a tracing made by an electrocardiograph.

electrocardiograph an instrument for recording variations in the electrical current of the heartbeat and used esp. to diagnose abnormalities in heart function. —**electrocardiographic** adj. —**electrocardiography** n.

electrocatalysis the breakdown of compounds or chemical decomposition by means of electricity.

electrocauterization also **electrocautery** cauterization by means of an electrically heated wire.

electrochemistry the branch of science concerned with the study of chemical changes brought about by electricity.

electrocoagulation the use of high frequency currents to harden growths and diseased tissues.

electrocontractility the ability of a muscle to contract when stimulated electrically.

electroconvulsive therapy electroshock therapy.

electrode a conductor for establishing electrical contact with a nonmetallic part of a circuit.

electroencephalogram a tracing made by an electroencephalograph.

electroencephalograph an instrument for recording brain waves. —**electroencephalographic** adj. —**electroencephalography** n.

electrohemostasis the arrest of bleeding by the use of electrocauterization.

electrohysterograph an instrument for recording the electrical activity of the uterus.

electrolysis 1. the destruction of the roots of hair by means of an electric current. 2. chemical change, esp. ionization, of a substance when an electric current is passed through it.

electrolyte a solution or a substance in solution that is decomposed into ions by the passage through it of an electric current, such as certain acids, bases and salts.

electromyograph an instrument for recording the contraction of muscles following their electrical stimulation. —**electromyogram** n. —**electromyographic** adj. —**electromyography** n.

electronarcosis the use of electricity to produce sleep or loss of consciousness.

electroshock therapy the treatment of psychiatric disorders by use of short bursts of an electric current to induce a brief therapeutic coma.

electrosurgery the surgical use of electricity.

electrothanasia death by means of electricity; electrocution.

elephantiasis a chronic filarial disease caused by infestation of the lymphatics by nematodes and marked by gross enlargement of the limbs or scrotum and leathery hardening of the skin.

eliminate to expel (waste matter) from the body. —**elimination** n. —**eliminative** adj.

elinguation the surgical removal of the tongue.

elixir a usually alcohol-containing, sweetened liquid used as a vehicle for a medication, as a cough suppressant.

emaciation the condition of becoming very thin or of wasting away. —**emaciate** vb.

emaculation the removal of skin blemishes.

emasculation loss of masculinity by castration of the male. —**emasculate** vb.

embolectomy the surgical removal of an embolus.

embolism the sudden obstruction by an embolus of a blood vessel.

embololalia the periodic interjection of nonsense words in a sentence while talking.

embolus an abnormal body, as an air bubble or blood clot, floating in the blood.

embrocate to moisten and massage with a lotion. —**embrocation** n.

embryo pl. **embryos** the developing human being from the time of fertilization to the end of the eighth week after conception.

embryology the branch of biology dealing with embryos and their development. —**embryologist** n.

embryoplastic relating to the formation of an embryo.

emesis pl. **emeses** an act or instance of vomiting.

emetic an agent that induces vomiting. —**emetic** adj.

emetine hydrochloride a drug used in the treatment of amoebiasis.

emetology the scientific study of the causes and mechanisms responsible for vomiting.

EMF electromotive force; voltage.

-emia suffix blood.

emission a discharge of semen esp. when involuntary.

emmenagogic causing or increasing menstrual flow.

emmenia menses. —**emmenic** adj. .

emmenology the branch of medical science concerned with the study of normal and disordered menstruation.

emolient something that is soft and soothing to the skin or mucous membranes.

emotiovascular relating to vascular changes such as blushing and pallor induced by emotional stimuli.

emphysema a condition marked by air-filled expansion of tissues of the body esp. those of the lungs. —**emphysematous** *adj.*

empyema *pl.* **empyemata** the collection of pus in a body cavity. —**empyemic** *adj.*

emulsion a suspension of minute globules of one fluid within another. —**emulsive** *adj.*

enamel the hard thin calcareous substance forming the outer layer of a tooth.

enanthesis the skin eruption or rash associated with a specific internal disease, such as typhoid fever.

enarthrosis the ball-and-socket articulation of a joint in which the rounded extremity of one bone fits into the cuplike cavity of the other to permit movement in any direction.

encanthis a tiny growth at the inner angle of the eye.

encapsulated surrounded by a membranous capsule or sheath.

encarditis endocarditis; inflammation of the membrane that lines the chambers of the heart.

enceinte pregnant.

encelitis *also* **enceliitis** inflammation of any abdominal organ.

encephal- *or* **encephalo-** *prefix* brain: *encephalitis.*

encephalalgia headache.

encephalatrophy a wasting away of brain tissue; atrophy of the brain.

encephalic lying or situated within the cranial cavity.

encephalitis inflammation of the brain. —**encephalitic** *adj.*

encephalodialysis abnormal softening of the brain.

encephalodynia headache.

encephalogram an X-ray picture of the brain.

encephalography X-ray photography of the brain, esp. after air has been introduced into the lateral ventricles by lumbar puncture or directly into an area at the base of the brain.

encephalolith a calculus within the brain or one of its ventricles.

encephalomalacia softening of the brain.

encephalomeningitis inflammation of the brain and its covering membranes (meninges).

encephalomyelitis inflammation of the brain and spinal cord simultaneously.

encephalomyelopathy any disease involving both the brain and spinal cord.

encephalomyocarditis an acute febrile disease marked by inflammation, degeneration, and lesions of the skeletal and cardiac muscles and the central nervous system.

encephalon the brain of a vertebrate.

encephalopathy disease of the brain. —**encephalopathic** *adj.*

encephalospinal cerebrospinal.

encephalothlipsis brain compression.

encyst to form or become enclosed in a cyst. —**encystation** *n.*

end- *or* **endo-** *prefix* inside; within.

Endamoeba a genus of amoebas, usually distinguished from *Entamoeba,* that are parasitic in the intestines of invertebrates but do not affect man.

endangeitis *also* **endangiitis** inflammation of the inner coat of a blood vessel.

endangeitis obliterans inflammation of the inner coat of a blood vessel resulting in obstruction of the vessel.

endangium the inner coat of a blood vessel.

endaortitis inflammation of the inner coat of the aorta (the largest artery in the body).

endarterectomy the surgical removal of fatty deposits from the inner coat of a large artery.

endarterial within an artery or relating to its inner coat.

endarteritis inflammation of the inner coat of an artery.

endarterium the inner coat of an artery.

endaural within the ear.

endemia any endemic disease.

endemic peculiar or restricted to a particular area: *endemic diseases.*

endepidermis the inner layer of the epidermis.

endo- *prefix* within; inner.

endoangiitis inflammation of the inner coat of a blood vessel.

endocarditis inflammation of the lining of the heart.

endocardium *pl.* **endocardia** the thin membrane lining the inside of the heart.

endoceliac within a body cavity.

endocervicitis inflammation of the mucous membrane that lines the neck of the womb (cervix of the uterus).

endocolpitis inflammation of the mucous membrane that lines the vagina.

endocrine gland a gland, as the thyroid, producing secretions (hormones) that are circulated through the body in the bloodstream.

endocrinology a science dealing with endocrine glands and the hormones they secrete. —**endocrinologic** *or* **endocrinological** *adj.*

endocystitis inflammation of the mucous membrane that lines the urinary bladder.

endoderm the innermost layer of cells of an embryo. —**endodermal** *adj.*

endodontology the branch of dentistry concerned with the diagnosis and treatment of diseases that affect the dental pulp.

endoenteritis inflammation of the mucous membrane that lines the intestines.

endoenzyme any enzyme that is active within a cell.

endoesophagitis inflammation of the mucous membrane that lines the esophagus.

endogenous *or* **endogenic** growing from or produced within the body.

endolymph the fluid in the membranous labyrinth of the ear. —**endolymphatic** *adj.*

endometrium *pl.* **endometria** the mucous membrane lining the uterus.

endomorphic having a heavy rounded body with a tendency to become fat. —**endomorph** *n.*

end organ a structure forming the end of a neural path.

endoscope an instrument for viewing the inside of a hollow bodily organ. —**endoscopic** *adj.* —**endoscopy** *n.*

endothelium *pl.* **endothelia** the membrane lining blood vessels, serous cavities, and lymphatics.

endotracheal placed within or applied through the trachea.

enema introduction of a fluid into the rectum by way of the anus to help evacuate the lower bowel, introduce medicine, etc.

enervate 1. to lessen the strength or vitality of. 2. to remove or cut through a nerve.

engorge to congest with blood. —**engorgement** n.

engram (in the theory of memory mechanisms) a trace left in the brain following any experience, which is activated in the recall of that experience.

Entamoeba a genus of amoebas parasitic in the human digestive tract one species of which (*Entamoeba histolytica*) is responsible for causing amoebic dysentery. Compare *Endamoeba*.

enter- *or* **entero-** *prefix* intestine: *enterocolitis*.

enteralgia severe abdominal pain and cramps.

enterectasis dilation of the small intestine.

enterelcosis ulceration of the intestine.

enteric of or relating to the intestines.

enteric-coated (of tablets) having a coating unaffected by the digestive juices of the stomach but which dissolves to release the medication beneath on reaching the small intestine.

enteritis inflammation of the intestines, esp. of the small intestine.

enterobiasis infestation with pinworms (*Enterobius vermicularis*).

enterococcus streptococcus present normally in the intestine.

enterocolitis inflammation of both the large and small intestine.

enterohepatitis inflammation of both the intestine and liver.

enteromycosis any fungal disease of the intestines.

enteron the alimentary canal system esp. of the human embryo.

enteropathy any disease of the intestine. —**enteropathic** adj.

enterorrhagia bleeding into or from the intestines.

enterostomy surgical formation of an artificial opening into the intestine through the abdominal wall.

enterozoon any animal parasite inhabiting the intestine.

entoptic within the eyeball.

enuresis involuntary release of urine, esp. during sleep. —**enuretic** adj. & n.

enzyme a complex protein produced by living cells and capable of inducing chemical changes without itself being changed or destroyed in the process. —**enzymatic** or **enzymic** adj. —**enzymology** n.

enzymology the branch of science concerned with the study of the structure and function of enzymes.

eosin a red acid dye used for staining.

ephedrine an alkaloid used in the form of a salt to relieve asthma, hay fever, and nasal congestion.

epicanthic fold either of the extended folds of the skin of the upper eyelids over the inner or both angles of the eyes. Also called *Mongolian fold*.

epicardium the inner layer of the pericardium.

epicranium the muscles and skin that cover the cranium; the scalp.

epidemic affecting many individuals of the same community, region, or population simultaneously. —**epidemic** n. —**epidemical** adj.

epidemiology the scientific study of the distribution and occurrence of diseases. —**epidemiological** or **epidemiologic** adj. —**epidemiologist** n.

epidermis the outermost layer of the skin. —**epidermal** adj.

epidermitis inflammation of the outer layers of the skin.

epididymectomy surgical removal of the epididymis.

epididymis pl. **epididymides** an extended, convoluted mass of efferent tubes through which the sperm pass from the testis to the vas deferens. —**epididymal** adj.

epididymitis inflammation of the epididymis.

epigastric lying upon or over the stomach.

epiglottis the thin cartilaginous plate that folds back and protects the glottis during swallowing. —**epiglottal** adj.

epilepsy any of various diseases distinguished by disturbance of the electrical rhythms of the central nervous system with characteristic convulsive episodes and clouding of consciousness. —**epileptic** n. & adj.

epinephrine or **epinephrin** an adrenal hormone used medicinally as a bronchiole relaxant, heart stimulant, and vasoconstrictor. Also called *adrenaline*.

epiphysis pl. **epiphyses** the end of a long bone developing separately from the shaft (from which it is originally separated by an area of cartilage) with which it eventually unites.

episioplasty plastic surgery involving the vulva.

episiorrhagia bleeding from the vulva.

episiotomy surgical incision of the perineum to facilitate childbirth.

epispadias a congenital defect of the penis in which the urethra opens on the back surface.

epistaxis pl. **epistaxes** nosebleed.

epithelium pl. **epithelia** a membranous, protective tissue forming the outermost layer of the skin and lining tubes, cavities, and other free surfaces of the body. —**epithelial** adj.

erectile tissue tissue that becomes rigid when filled with blood, such as the penis, clitoris and nipples.

erection the condition of being rigid and elevated, as the penis or clitoris when filled with blood.

eremophobia the abnormal fear of being alone; fear of solitude.

ereuthophobia the abnormal fear of blushing.

ergasiophobia the abnormal fear of working or of work.

ergot 1. the dried sclerotium of a fungus replacing the seeds of a grass, as rye. 2. a disease of rye and other grasses caused by ergot fungus. 3. a derivative alkaloid of ergot used medicinally for its contractile action on smooth muscle.

ergotamine an alkaloid derivative from ergot, used esp. in treating migraine.

ergotism a toxic condition produced chiefly by eating grain or grain products infected with ergot fungus.

erogenous also **erogenic** producing or gratifying feelings of sexual excitement: *erogenous zones of the body*.

erosion the wearing away of the surface of a structure or part.

erotic of or arousing sexual desire.

erotophobia the abnormal fear of sexual intercourse or of physical contact associated with sexual arousal.

eruct to release stomach gas through the mouth; belch. —**eructation** n.

eruption the breaking out of a skin inflammation; rash. —**erupt** vb.

erysipelas an acute streptococcal inflammatory disease of the skin.

erythema acute, abnormal redness of the skin. —**erythematous** adj.

erythralgia a condition in which the skin is red and painful.

erythroblast an immature red blood cell.

erythroblastosis the abnormal presence in the bloodstream of large numbers of immature red blood cells.

erythrocyte a mature red blood cell.

erythrocytosis an abnormal increase in the number of circulating red blood cells; polycythemia.

erythropoiesis the production of red blood cells.

eschar a slough formed esp. after a burn.

esophagitis inflammation of the esophagus.

esophagus the part of the digestive tract between the pharynx and the stomach; gullet.

estrinase a liver enzyme that inactivates estrogens.

estrogen any of the female sex hormones, produced by the ovaries or prepared synthetically.

estrus the receptive phase of the sexual cycle of female animals; heat.

ethyl alcohol alcohol.

etiolate to make or become pale from lack of light. —**etiolation** *n.*

etiology the study of the causes of disease or the cause of a specific disease or abnormal condition. —**etiologic** or **etiological** *adj.*

eugenics a science dealing with methods to improve the hereditary qualities of a race or breed. —**eugeneticist** *n.* —**eugenic** *adj.*

eunuch a man or boy deprived of the testes; castrated male. —**eunuchoid** *adj.*

euphoria an exaggerated sense of elation and general well-being. —**euphoric** *adj.*

Eustachian tube the tube connecting the throat to the ear and serving to equalize air pressure on both sides of the eardrum.

eustachitis inflammation of the mucous membrane that lines a Eustachian tube.

euthanasia the act or practice of killing individuals considered hopelessly sick or injured or permitting them to die for reasons of mercy.

evacuate to discharge (waste products) from the body. —**evacuation** *n.*

evert to turn or fold outward or inside out. —**eversible** *adj.* —**eversion** *n.*

eviscerate to remove the bowels or entrails of. —**evisceration** *n.*

exacerbation an increase in the severity of a disease or an aggravation of its signs and symptoms.

exanthem any skin eruption associated with a general disease, such as measles.

exarteritis inflammation of the outer coat of an artery.

excipient an inert substance that is used as a vehicle for a drug.

excision the act of removing something by cutting; surgical removal. —**excise** *vb.*

excoriate to remove the skin of; abrade. —**excoriation** *n.*

excrement waste matter discharged from the alimentary canal; fecal matter.

excrescent forming an abnormal or useless outgrowth or enlargement. —**excrescence** *n.*

excreta waste matter.

excrete to discharge (waste matter) from the body. —**excretion** *n.*

exfoliate to cast off in flakes or scales. —**exfoliation** *n.*

exhale to breathe out.

exhibitionism an abnormal urge to expose one's body and

genitals to others without warning. —**exhibitionist** *n.* —**exhibitionistic** *adj.*

exhumation disinterment of a dead body. —**exhume** *vb.*

exobiology the branch of science concerned with examining evidence and investigating the possibility of life on other planets.

exogenous originating from or due to external causes.

exophthalmos also **exophthalmus** protrusion of the eyeballs, esp. as a consequence of overactivity of the thyroid gland (hyperthyroidism or thyrotoxicosis).

expectorant an agent that promotes the discharge of mucus from the respiratory tract. —**expectorant** *adj.*

expectorate to eject from the throat or lungs esp. by coughing; spit. —**expectoration** *n.*

extrasystole premature contraction of the heart.

extravasation the passage of a fluid, esp. blood, from its proper channel or vessels into surrounding tissues. —**extravasate** *vb.*

extravert or **extrovert** one whose interests are directed primarily outside the self. —**extraverted** or **extroverted** *adj.* —**extraversion** or **extroversion** *n.*

extremity a limb of the body; an arm or leg.

extrinsic originating or being on the outside; external.

extrovert extravert.

exudate 1. to exude matter; ooze. 2. matter exudated. —**exudation** *n.*

eye the organ of sight, consisting of a round structure with a clear outer covering (cornea) and a biconvex transparent lens to focus incoming light through the central gelatinous substance (vitreous humor) and onto the back light-sensitive surface (retina), situated as one of a pair in bony frontal orbits of the skull.

eyeball the approximately globular capsule of the vertebrate eye.

eyelid a movable lid of skin and muscle that can be lowered over the eye.

eyestrain fatigue or discomfort of vision esp. from overuse of the eyes.

THE EYE
(CROSS SECTION)

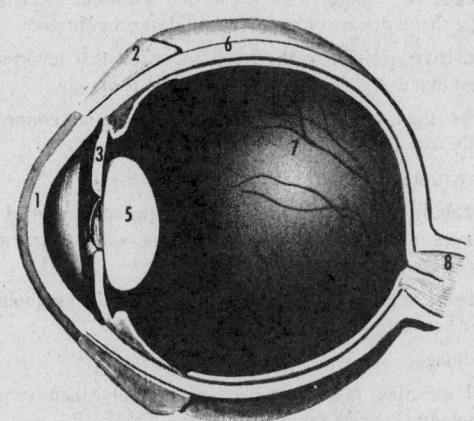

1	CORNEA	5	LENS
2	CONJUNCTIVA	6	SCLERA
3	IRIS	7	RETINA
4	PUPIL	8	OPTIC NERVE

F

face the front part of the human head that includes the forehead, eyes, nose, cheeks, mouth, and chin.

facial relating to the face or situated on the lower anterior part of the head.

facies *pl.* **facies** 1. an appearance or expression of the face indicating a particular condition; countenance. 2. the surface of a structure or part.

faciobrachial relating to or involving both the face and arm, as in the manifestations of juvenile muscular dystrophy.

faciocephalalgia pain in the face and head along the course of one or more nerves; neuralgia of this region.

faciocervical relating to or involving both the face and neck, as in a form of progressive muscular dystrophy.

faciolingual relating to or involving both the face and the tongue, as in a certain form of paralysis.

facioplasty plastic surgery involving the soft tissues of the face.

facioplegia palsy or paralysis of the facial muscles, usually with a loss of sensation in the skin of the face.

factitious fever fever produced artificially, as to fake an illness.

faecal fecal.

faeces feces.

falcial relating to a falx.

falcate *also* **falciform** shaped like a crescent or sickle.

fallacia an optical illusion or hallucination.

fallectomy surgical removal of a section of a fallopian tube; salpingectomy.

falling sickness a former popular term for epilepsy or an epileptic condition.

falling womb protrusion of the body of the uterus into the vagina.

fallopian tube either of a pair of tubes through which an ovum, released during ovulation, travels from the ovary to the uterus.

fallostomy surgical opening of a fallopian tube; salpingostomy.

fallotomy surgical separation of a fallopian tube; salpingotomy.

false-negative relating to the results of a test which incorrectly suggest that a disease or specific condition is not present.

false-positive relating to the results of a test that incorrectly suggest that a disease or specific condition is present.

false ribs the lower five pairs of ribs, which are not connected directly with the breastbone (sternum).

falx any structure or part shaped like a sickle.

falx cerebelli a fold or short process of the outermost of the meninges (dura mater) which forms a vertical partition between the two halves of the cerebellum.

falx cerebri a fold of dura mater that dips into the longitudinal fissure between the two halves of the cerebrum.

fames hunger.

familial affecting more members of a family than can be attributed to chance: *familial illnesses.*

family 1. parents and their children. 2. close blood relatives. 3. (in biologic classification) a division between order and genus.

fantasy mental images created in response to psychological need: *sexual fantasies of adolescence.*

faradic relating to induced electricity.

faradism the therapeutic use of an induced electric current. —**faradize** *vb.*

farinaceous starchy.

farsightedness the inability to focus on objects relatively close to the eye; hypermetropia; hyperopia.

fascia *pl.* **fasciae** a sheath of connective tissue enclosing muscle.

fascial relating to or resembling fascia.

fascicle fasciculus.

fascicular arranged in a bundle or rodlike collection.

fasciculation 1. the formation of fasciculi. 2. the involuntary twitching of groups of muscle fibers.

fasciculus *pl.* **fasciculi** a small bundle of fibers, esp. of muscles or nerves.

fasciectomy the surgical removal of strips of fascia.

fasciola a small group of fibers.

Fasciola a genus of flukes.

fascioplasty plastic surgery involving fascia.

fasciotomy surgical incision and separation of fascia.

fat animal tissue composed of cells enlarged with greasy or oily matter. —**fatty** *adj.*

fatigue 1. physical or emotional exhaustion. 2. to weary with labor or exertion.

fauces the passage between the soft palate and the base of the tongue that links the mouth and the pharynx.

faucitis inflammation of the fauces.

faveolus a small depression, esp. on the skin.

favus a contagious fungal disease of the skin, esp. of the scalp, characterized by the formation of round cup-shaped yellow crusts having a musty odor.

febrifacient causing or producing fever.

febrile of or relating to fever; feverish.

febrious conducive to the development of fever.

fecal *also* **faecal** of, relating to, or constituting feces.

feces *also* **faeces** solid waste matter formed in the large intestine and expelled through the anus.

fecund fruitful in offspring; prolific. —**fecundity** *n.*

feebleminded mentally incapable or deficient. —**feeblemindedly** *adv.* —**feeblemindedness** *n.*

fellatio *also* **fellation** oral stimulation of the penis.

felo de se 1. a person who commits suicide. 2. the act of suicide.

felon a whitlow.

feminism the abnormal development or condition in a male of feminine characteristics, usually as the result of a hormonal disorder.

femorotibial relating to both the femur and tibia.

femur *pl.* **femurs** *or* **femora** the bone extending from the pelvis to the knee; thighbone. —**femoral** *adj.*

fenestra *pl.* **fenestrae** an anatomical aperture, frequently one closed by a membrane.

fenestrated having openings suggestive of or resembling windows.

fenestration the presence of window-like openings in a structure or part.

ferment 1. to decompose or undergo fermentation. 2. a substance capable of bringing about fermentation.

fermentation the breakdown of complex substances by means of certain enzymes (ferments) produced by microorganisms such as bacteria, molds and yeasts, as in the production of alcohol.

fermentative causing or able to cause fermentation.

ferrous relating to iron or a salt containing iron (such as ferrous sulfate).

ferruginous relating to or containing iron.

fertile producing or capable of producing young; fecund. —**fertility** n.

fertilize to cause (a human egg) to become impregnated. —**fertilization** n.

fester to become inflamed and produce pus.

fetal also **foetal** of or relating to a fetus.

fetal position a resting position in which the body is curved with the legs drawn up, the arms are bent around the chest, and the head is inclined forward.

feticide the destruction of the fetus in induced abortion.

fetid having an offensive smell.

fetish or **fetich** an object or body part that becomes psychologically necessary for sexual gratification and may interfere with normal or complete sexual gratification.

fetishism also **fetichism** the pathological displacement of erotic interest to a fetish. —**fetishist** n.

fetor an extremely foul odor.

fetus also **foetus** a developing human being usually from three months after conception to birth.

fever an abnormal rise in body temperature. —**feverish** adj. —**feverishness** n.

fiber or **fibre** a threadlike structure, esp. a strand of nerve or muscle tissue. —**fibrous** adj. —**fibrousness** n.

FERTILIZATION

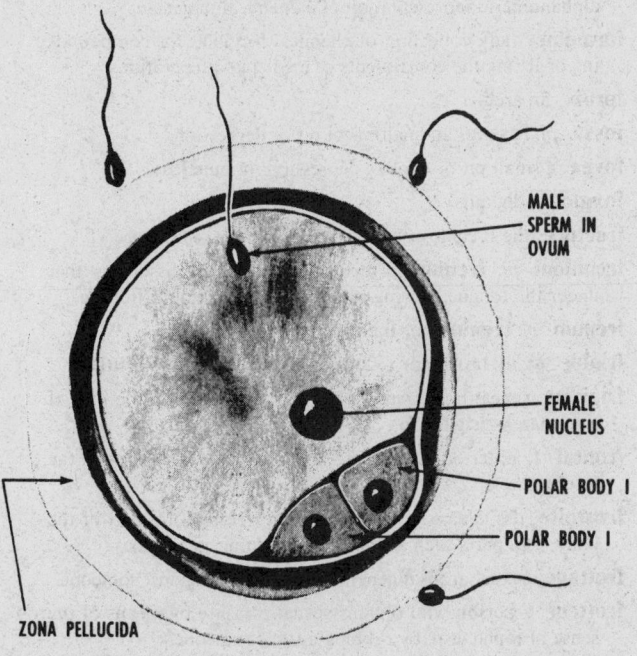

MALE
SPERM IN
OVUM

FEMALE
NUCLEUS

POLAR BODY I

POLAR BODY I

ZONA PELLUCIDA

THE EVENTS OF FERTILIZATION

The female ovum (egg), surrounded by a thick, transparent Zona Pellucida, divides unequally, producing Polar Body I. At this point, a single sperm penetrates the Zona. The ovum again divides, producing Polar Body II. The female nucleus migrates toward the male sperm. The union of the two completes fertilization.

fiberscope an instrument for examining body cavities and passages and composed of flexible bundles of glass fibers through which light is transmitted.

fibr- or **fibro-** prefix fiber; fibrous.

fibril a very small fiber.

fibrillation 1. irregular and uncoordinated contractions of the heart. 2. muscular twitching resulting from the spontaneous contraction of muscle fibers.

fibrin an insoluble component of blood, created by chemical conversion from fibrinogen, that forms the matrix of blood clots.

fibrinogen a clotting factor in solution in the bloodstream from which fibrin is made.

fibroblast a cell forming connective tissue. —**fibroblastic** adj.

fibroid 1. resembling or constituting fibrous tissue. 2. a benign tumor esp. when occurring in the uterine wall.

fibroma any fibrous tumor of connective tissue.

fibromatosis a condition characterized by the formation of many fibromas.

fibrosarcoma a malignant tumor derived from fibrous connective tissue.

fibrosis the reactive formation of fibrous tissue, as in the healing of a wound.

fibrositis rheumatic inflammation of fibrous tissue.

fibrotic relating to or characterized by fibrosis.

fibrous composed of or containing fibers.

fibula a slender bone that extends from the knee to the ankle on the outer side of the leg.

ficin an enzyme isolated from figs that is capable of dissolving proteins, used in the treatment of worm infestation.

field of vision visual field.

filaria pl. **filariae** any of various parasitic nematodes that infest the blood and tissues of mammals.

filariasis disease caused by infestation with filariae.

filariform resembling small threadlike worms or filariae.

filioparental relating to the relationships between parents and their children.

filterable virus a virus of such minute size that a fluid in which it is contained remains virulent even when passed through the pores of a special filter which can trap bacteria and the larger viruses.

filtrate the fluid that has been passed through a filter.

filtration the act or process of passing a fluid through a filter.

filum a threadlike structure; filament.

fimbria pl. **fimbriae** any structure or part resembling a fringe or having fringelike attachments, such as the upper part of the fallopian tubes nearest the ovaries.

fimbriate also **fimbriated** having fimbriae.

finger a digit of the hand, esp. any of the four digits of the hand other than the thumb.

fissure a cleft between two structures or parts; sulcus.

fissure of Rolando the central fissure of the cerebrum, dividing the parietal from the frontal lobe in each hemisphere; central sulcus.

fissure of Sylvius the lateral fissure of the cerebrum, dividing the temporal lobe from the frontal and parietal lobes in each hemisphere.

fistula pl. **fistulas** or **fistulae** an abnormal passage from an abscess to the surface of the body or from one organ to another. —**fistulous** adj.

flaccid lacking in firmness; soft; limp. —**flaccidity** *n.* —**flaccidly** *adv.*

flagellum *pl.* **flagella** a long, slender, tapering process providing the means of locomotion for certain cells, as spermatozoa and some protozoa.

flatfoot a condition of the feet in which the arches of the insteps are flattened so that the soles rest entirely on the ground.

flatulent marked by, affected with, or likely to cause gas within the stomach or intestinal tract. —**flatulence** *n.* —**flatulency** *n.*

flatus gas generated in the bowels or stomach.

flavedo yellowness of the skin; jaundice.

fletcherism a dietary system characterized by eating very small quantities of food each day which is to be excessively chewed before swallowing.

fletcherize to practice the dietary system (fletcherism) devised by the American dietician Horace Fletcher (1849-1919).

flexion 1. a bending of a joint between adjacent bones. 2. the condition or state of being bent.

flexor a muscle that produces flexion.

flooding profuse bleeding from the uterus, esp. following childbirth or in severe menstrual disorders.

fluke any of various species of parasitic flatworms (trematodes) which can infest the liver, blood, intestines or lungs.

fluor albus leukorrhea.

fluorescein a yellow or red dye that produces a vivid green fluorescence in solution, used in the diagnosis of disorders of the cornea and in intravenous injections for studying the rate of blood flow (circulation time).

fluorescent having the ability to become luminous when exposed to light rays, X-rays, or other forms of radiant energy.

fluoridate to add a fluoride to (as drinking water). —**fluoridation** *n.*

fluoride a compound of fluorine.

fluorine a nonmetallic, gaseous, halogenic element.

fluoroscope a device with a fluorescent screen for examining the movement and condition of deep structures of the body by means of X-rays. —**fluoroscopic** *adj.* —**fluoroscopy** *n.*

fluorosis a condition mainly characterized by discoloration of the teeth, caused by the chronic intake of excessive amounts of fluorine in the drinking water.

flutter 1. abnormal, spasmodic, muscular movement of a part of the body. 2. to move in irregular spasms. —**fluttery** *adj.*

focus *pl.* **focuses** *or* **foci** a point at which rays, as of light, converge.

folic acid a crystalline acid of the B complex found naturally in liver, yeast and green leafy vegetables and used in synthetic form to treat nutritional anemias and sprue.

folie à deux a condition in which two persons in an intimate relationship share the same delusional ideas.

follicle a small narrow-mouthed cavity or depression. —**follicular** *adj.* —**folliculate** *also* **folliculated** *adj.*

fomentation the application of a moist, hot substance to the skin to ease pain.

fomites articles, as items of clothing, that have been in contact with a person having a contagious disease and may themselves be agents of transmission.

fontanelle *or* **fontanel** a soft membrane-covered space at the top of an infant's skull before the bones have completely merged.

food poisoning acute gastrointestinal distress caused by ingestion of food containing toxic bacteria or chemical residues.

foot *pl.* **feet** the terminal part of a vertebrate leg that serves as support for standing; the part of the leg below the ankle.

foot-and-mouth disease an acute, contagious, febrile disease of viral origin affecting chiefly cloven-footed animals and marked by ulcerating vesicles in the mouth and about the hoofs. Also called *hoof-and-mouth disease.*

foramen *pl.* **foramina** a natural opening or hole, esp. in bone, for the passage of nerves, blood vessels, etc.

foramen magnum the large opening at the base of the skull for the passage of the spinal cord.

forceps *pl.* **forceps** any of various instruments used esp. in surgery for lifting, grasping, or holding.

forcipate resembling or shaped like forceps.

forebrain the part of the embryonic brain that develops into the cerebrum and closely related structures.

forensic medicine the branch of medicine concerned with the application of medical information to legal problems, as in proving criminal responsibility in a sudden death or death under unusual circumstances.

foreskin a retractable fold of skin that covers the glans of the penis; prepuce.

formaldehyde a pungent gas used in solution as a disinfectant and tissue preservative for anatomical specimens.

formalin an aqueous solution containing 37 per cent formaldehyde.

formication an abnormal sensation of insects creeping over the skin.

formula *pl.* **formulas** *or* **formulae** 1. prescription. 2. a nutritive mixture for feeding an infant. 3. the symbolic or alphanumeric representation of a chemical molecule.

formulary any collection of chemical formulas for compounding or listing the constituents of medicinal preparations.

fornix an arch.

fossa *pl.* **fossae** an anatomical pit or depression.

fovea a small pit or cuplike depression; minute fossa.

foxglove digitalis.

fracture the breaking of hard tissue, as bone. —**fracture** *vb.*

frenulum *pl.* **frenula** a membranous fold of tissue, as that under the tongue, serving as a support or restraint; frenum.

frenum *pl.* **frenums** *or* **frena** frenulum.

friable easily broken or reduced to powder; dry and brittle.

frigidity sexual unresponsiveness or indifference on the part of a woman. —**frigid** *adj.*

frontal 1. anterior. 2. relating to or situated on or near the forehead.

frostbite tissue damage resulting from freezing of a part of the body, esp. parts such as the ears, nose, fingers and toes.

frottage sexual arousal generated by rubbing against someone.

frotteur a person who obtains sexual pleasure by means of the sense of touch, esp. by rubbing against someone.

fructose a sugar occurring in honey and in many fruits.

full-term (of a fetus) retained in the uterus for the entire normal duration of pregnancy.

fulminating sudden and severe in onset: *fulminating infections.*

fundus *pl.* **fundi** the part or section of a hollow organ furthest from the natural opening.

fungicide an agent that destroys fungi. —**fungicidal** *adj.*

fungiform (of a structure or part) having a narrow base and a broad or branched upper free area; shaped like a mushroom.

fungus *pl.* **fungi** any of various primitive forms of plant life (including the mushrooms, molds and mildews) characterized by the absence of chlorophyll and living off organic matter.

funiculus any structure shaped like a cord; cordlike.

furuncle a swollen inflammation of the skin; boil.

fusiform spindle-shaped.

G

gag 1. a surgical device for holding the mouth open. 2. to hold (the mouth) open with a gag. 3. to retch.

gait a characteristic manner or style of walking.

galact- *or* **galacto-** *prefix* milk: *galactopoiesis.*

galactacrasia an abnormal composition of breast milk.

galactemia an abnormal condition in which the blood appears milky or cloudy.

galactophagous subsisting on milk.

galactophore a milk duct.

galactophoritis inflammation of a milk duct.

galactopoiesis the production and secretion of milk. —**galactopoietic** *adj.*

galactorrhea the excessive flow of milk.

galactoschesis the retention or inhibition of milk secretion.

galactostasis 1. the inhibition or suppression of milk secretion. 2. an abnormal accumulation of milk within the breast.

galacturia whiteness or milkiness of the urine due to the abnormal presence of chyle or lymph.

galea any structure or part shaped like or resembling a helmet.

galenical 1. relating to or resembling the philosophy and medical teaching of the Greek physician Galen (2nd century A.D.). 2. any therapeutic preparation derived from plants.

galeophilia the abnormal and excessive love of cats.

galeophobia the abnormal fear of cats.

gall secretion of the liver; bile.

gallbladder a pear-shaped membranous sac in which bile from the liver is stored until its release into the small intestine.

gallery the subcutaneous burrow occupied by some metazoan parasites.

galloping consumption a form of tuberculosis that has a rapid course ending in death.

gallop rhythm a sequence of three sounds heard on auscultation of the heart, usually caused by an excessively fast rate of contraction of the ventricles.

gallstone a calculus formed in the gallbladder or in a bile duct.

galvanic relating to or caused by galvanism.

galvanic battery a battery that produces electricity by means of chemical action.

galvanic current the direct current produced by a galvanic battery.

galvanism the therapeutic use of direct current produced by chemical energy in a galvanic battery. —**galvanization** *n.* —**galvanize** *vb.*

galvano- *prefix* direct current electricity.

galvanocautery electrocautery.

galvanochemical electrochemical.

galvanocontractility the ability of a muscle to contract when stimulated by a galvanic current.

galvanolysis electrolysis.

gamete a male or female reproductive cell; spermatozoon or ovum. —**gametic** *adj.*

gametogenesis the production of sperm or ova.

-gamic *suffix* relating to or resulting from sexual union.

gammacism a speech disorder characterized by difficulty in pronouncing correctly words or syllables that contain the letter g.

gamma globulin a globulin of serum or plasma that is involved in antibody production.

gamogenesis sexual reproduction.

gamophobia an abnormal fear of marriage.

gangliectomy *also* **ganglionectomy** the surgical removal of a ganglion or of ganglia.

gangliform resembling a ganglion; having the appearance or form of a ganglion or of ganglia.

ganglion *pl.* **ganglia** a mass of nerve tissue esp. if located outside the spinal cord or the brain. 2. a cystic swelling or tumor on a tendon. —**ganglial** *adj.* —**gangliate** *adj.*

ganglioneure a cell in a nerve ganglion.

ganglionitis inflammation of a ganglion or of ganglia.

gangrene necrosis of soft tissues of the body resulting from loss of blood supply.

gargle 1. a liquid for clearing or soothing the throat. 2. to rinse the throat with a gargle.

gas a basic state of matter characterized by free movement of its molecules, which permits it to expand indefinitely or to occupy the entire volume of a container holding it, or to be compressed until it assumes a liquid or eventually solid state.

gaseous relating to or having the properties or nature of gas.

gastr- *or* **gastro-** *or* **gastri-** *prefix* stomach; belly: *gastrectomy.*

gastralgia pain in the stomach; stomach ache.

gastrectomy surgical removal of part or all of the stomach, as in the treatment of severe gastric ulcers.

gastric of, relating to, or affecting the stomach.

gastric ulcer a peptic ulcer of the stomach.

gastritis inflammation of the mucous lining of the stomach.

gastroatonia loss of normal muscle tone in the stomach.

gastrocardiac relating to or involving both the stomach and the heart.

gastrocele a hernia of the stomach.

gastrocolitis inflammation of both the stomach and the colon.

gastrocolostomy the surgical formation of an artificial opening between the stomach and the colon.

gastrocolotomy surgical incision into the stomach and the colon.

gastroduodenal relating to or involving both the stomach and duodenum.

gastroenteritis inflammation of the stomach and intestines.

gastroenterology the branch of medical science concerned with the study and treatment of diseases of the stomach and intestines. —**gastroenterologist** *n.*

gastrointestinal of, relating to, or affecting the stomach and intestines.

gastrology the branch of medical science concerned with the study and treatment of diseases of the stomach (a part of gastroenterology).

gastromalacia abnormal softening of the walls of the stomach.

gastroscope an instrument for viewing and examining the interior of the stomach. —**gastroscopist** n. —**gastroscopy** n.

gastrosplenic relating to or involving both the stomach and the spleen.

gastrostomy the surgical formation of an artificial opening through the wall of the stomach.

gather (of a boil or furuncle) to form or ooze pus; come to a head.

gathering 1. the formation and accumulation of pus in a boil or abscess. 2. a localized collection of pus in a boil or abscess.

gauss a unit of the intensity of a magnetic field.

gauze a loosely woven fabric used for dressing wounds.

gavage feeding by means of a tube inserted through the nose and into the stomach; direct gastric feeding.

gene a tiny particle usually occurring in pairs on a chromosome and responsible for transmitting hereditary traits and characteristics from one generation to the next.

genetic also **genetical** of or relating to genetics.

genetics the branch of science concerned with the various aspects of heredity and the natural development of an organism. —**geneticist** n.

geniculate also **geniculated** (of a structure or part) bent like a knee.

geniculum any small structure bent like a knee or having a knotlike appearance.

genioplasty plastic surgery involving the chin or cheek.

genital relating to reproduction or the organs of reproduction: *genital organs.*

genitalia the reproductive organs; genitals.

genitals the reproductive organs: the penis and testes in the male and the vulva (external genitals), vagina, uterus, fallopian tubes and ovaries in the female.

genitourinary relating to reproduction and urination or to the organs responsible for these functions; urogenital.

genu 1. the knee. 2. any structure or part resembling a bent knee.

genu valgum knock knee (knees that bend inward).

genu varum bowleg (knees that bend outward).

genus pl. **genera** a group of related species, the distinct members of which are not usually able to interbreed.

geopathology the study of diseases in relation to different geographical characteristics, such as climate and terrain.

geriatric relating to old age or to the elderly.

geriatrician a physician who specializes in the practice of geriatrics.

geriatrics the branch of medical science concerned with the study and treatment of diseases in the elderly.

germ any microorganism, esp. one capable of causing disease; microbe.

German measles a viral infection common in children and accompanied by a typical skin eruption, milder than true measles (morbilli) but potentially dangerous to the developing fetus of a pregnant woman not previously exposed to the disease. Compare *measles.*

germ cell an ovum or spermatozoon.

germicide an agent capable of destroying germs. —**germicidal** adj.

gerontology the branch of medical science concerned with the

study of the process of aging and the social and health problems of the elderly.

gestation the developmental period within the womb from conception (fertilization of the ovum) until birth, averaging 266 days. Also called *gestation period.*

gigantism enlargement of the entire body or a limb as the result of overproduction of growth hormone by the pituitary gland before puberty, rarely producing a human giant up to eight feet tall. Compare *acromegaly.*

gingiva the gums.

gingivectomy surgical removal of some of the tissues of the gums, as in the management of severe infection (pyorrhea).

gingivitis inflammation of the gums.

gland a cell or collection of cells that produces specialized substances (secretions) from materials in the blood which are either used by the body or eliminated as waste matter.

glandular fever an acute infectious disease caused by a virus. Also called *infectious mononucleosis.*

glans pl. **glandes** the bulbous, vascular extremity of the penis or the clitoris.

glaucoma an eye disease marked by increased pressure within the eyeball and gradual loss of vision.

globulin any of a group of simple proteins occurring in animal and plant tissue, the best known of which is gamma globulin (important in the production of antibodies).

glossal of or relating to the tongue.

glossitis inflammation of the tongue.

glottis the two vocal cords and the space between them, concerned with sound production.

glucose a colorless, soluble sugar that occurs widely in nature and is produced naturally in the body by the breakdown of dietary starch.

gluteal of or relating to the buttocks or the gluteus muscles.

gluten a protein substance in cereals, responsible for a digestive disease (celiac disease) in children who are hypersensitive to it.

gluteus muscle any of the large muscles forming the buttocks.

glycerin also **glycerol** a sweet syrupy alcohol produced by the saponification of fats and used esp. as a solvent.

glycogen the carbohydrate that provides the body with a reserve of energy and heat, stored in the liver and converted into glucose on demand by active muscles.

glycosuria the abnormal presence of sugar in the urine, one sign of diabetes mellitus.

goiter also **goitre** abnormal enlargement of the thyroid gland.

gonad one of the sex glands; an ovary or testis. —**gonadal** adj.

gonadotrophin any of several hormones that stimulate the ovaries or testes.

gonococcus a bacterium that causes gonorrhea. —**gonococcal** *or* **gonococcic** adj.

gonorrhea a contagious bacterial disease typically characterized by inflammation of the urethra, urinary frequency, a burning sensation during urination and a discharge of pus from the penis or vagina, transmitted mainly during sexual intercourse with an infected partner (venereal disease). Also called *clap.*

gout a metabolic disorder characterized by excessive deposits of crystals of uric acid (urate) in the tissues and marked by painful swelling of the joints, esp. of the big toe. Also called *gouty arthritis.* —**gouty** adj.

Graafian follicle a small sac in an ovary that contains an ovum, one follicle rupturing each month during menstruation to release a mature ovum.

grand mal the most severe form of epilepsy.

granuloma a nodule or mass of chronically inflamed tissue.

gravel a mass of small concretions in the kidneys or bladder.

gravid pregnant.

gray matter or **grey matter** unmyelinated nerve cells and fibers of the brain and spinal cord, having a grayish color.

greenstick fracture a bone fracture in which the bone is partially fractured and partially bent.

grippe influenza. —**grippy** adj.

groin the area of the lower abdomen at the juncture of the legs with the trunk.

growing pains nonspecific pains often occurring in the legs of children.

gullet esophagus.

gumma a rubbery tumor that can appear anywhere on the body during the third stage of syphilis.

gut intestine.

gynecology the branch of medical science concerned with the diagnosis and treatment of diseases that affect women, esp. those involving the female reproductive system. —**gynecologist** n. —**gynecological** adj.

gynecomastia abnormal enlargement of the male breasts.

H

habena pl. **habenae** a restricting fibrous band. —**habenular** adj.

habit an act or response that has become virtually automatic and is thus difficult to break or interrupt. —**habitual** adj.

habituation a psychological dependence, esp. on drugs for which the user has an abnormal or compulsive craving or desire.

habitus the physical characteristics of an individual that are thought to play a role in the tendency to be affected by certain diseases or disorders.

hacking cough a short, frequent and usually dry (nonproductive) cough.

haem- or **haemo-** prefix hem-.

hagiotherapy therapy that depends on religious convictions, as when a sick person submits to religious rituals, goes on pilgrimages, touches sacred relics, etc.

hairball trichobezoar.

halation blurring of vision by strong light coming directly in front of or behind the viewed object or scene.

halethazole an antiseptic agent that is also effective against some species of fungus.

half-life the period of time taken for a radioactive isotope to lose half of its activity through disintegration.

half-way house a center or institution for housing patients who no longer require intensive medical or psychiatric care but who are not ready to resume normal social activities or employment within the community.

halide a salt or compound of a halogen.

haliphagia the ingestion of abnormally large quantities of a salt or salts, esp. of sodium chloride (common table salt) or sodium bicarbonate (a common antacid).

halisteresis a deficiency of calcium in the bones; osteomalacia. —**halisteretic** adj.

halitosis a condition of having foul breath.

halitus an expired breath; exhaled vapor.

hallex hallux.

hallucination 1. the perception of objects or sounds having no basis in reality and commonly arising from a nervous disorder, fatigue, or the use of a drug. 2. the objects or sounds so perceived. —**hallucinate** vb. —**hallucinatory** adj.

hallucinogen a drug, as LSD, inducing hallucinations. —**hallucinogenic** adj.

hallucinosis a severe mental disorder characterized by persistent or recurring hallucinations.

hallux pl. **halluces** the great toe; first digit of the foot. —**hallucal** adj.

hallux valgus a deformity of the big toe in which it bends over or beneath the adjacent toe.

hallux varus a deformity of the big toe in which it bends toward the inner side of the foot away from the adjacent toe.

haloderma a skin disorder caused by the ingestion of halides such as iodides and bromides.

halogen any of the elements fluorine, chlorine, bromine and iodine that combine with metals to form salts and with hydrogen to form acids. —**halogenous** adj.

halogenation the altering of the physical and therapeutic properties of a molecule by the incorporation of halogen atoms in its structure.

haloid resembling salt or a halogen.

halophil also **halophile** any microorganism that needs a high concentration of salt for enhanced growth. —**halophilic** adj.

haloprogin an antifungal agent.

halothane a general anesthetic developed by British chemists in the 1950s for its nonirritant and nonflammable properties.

ham the buttock and posterior part of the thigh.

hamartophobia an abnormal fear of error or of committing a sin.

hamate having a hook; hooked.

hammer malleus; one of the three small conducting bones of the middle ear.

hammertoe a deformity of a toe characterized by permanent angular flexion.

hamstring either of two groups of tendons at the back of the knee.

hamstring muscle any of the three muscles at the back of the thigh that extend the thigh when the leg is flexed.

hamular having the shape of a hook; hook-shaped.

hamulus any hooklike structure or part.

hangnail a small piece of partially detached skin at the base of a nail, esp. of a fingernail.

Hansen's disease leprosy.

hapalonychia lack of firmness or rigidity of the nails.

haphalgesia abnormal sensitivity of the skin to pain when touched lightly.

haphephobia abnormal dislike or fear of being touched by another person.

haplopia normal, single vision. Compare diplopia.

hapten also **haptene** an incomplete antigen capable of stimulating antibody formation only when covalently linked to protein.

haptodysphoria an unpleasant tactile sensation.

haptometer an instrument for measuring a person's sensitivity to touch.

harelip a congenital deformity in which the center of the upper lip is marked by a vertical fissure like that of a hare, often associated with cleft palate.

Hashimoto's disease chronic inflammation of the thyroid gland.

hashish resin obtained from the flowering tops of the female hemp plant (*Cannabis sativa*) and chewed or smoked for its hallucinogenic effect. Also called *charas, hash.*

haustus a medicinal potion.

hay fever acute allergic rhinitis and sometimes conjunctivitis caused typically by exposure of a hypersensitive person to pollens and dust.

headache pain or aching in the head. —**headachy** *adj.*

headshrinker *Slang* psychiatrist; psychoanalyst.

heal to make or become sound and whole.

health the condition of being sound in body and mind; freedom from pain or illness. —**healthy** *adj.*

health officer an official responsible for health and sanitation laws.

heart a hollow muscular organ that acts by rhythmic contraction to pump the blood through the circulatory system of the body.

heart attack an acute episode of dysfunctioning of the heart.

heart block irregularity in the rhythm of the heart resulting in decreased cardiac output.

heartburn a burning sensation at the lower end of the esophagus; pyrosis.

heart failure a condition in which the heart cannot pump blood at an adequate rate or in adequate volume to sustain life.

heart-lung machine a machine used for maintenance of oxygenation and circulation of the blood while the heart is stopped during heart surgery.

heart murmur an abnormal murmuring sound heard through the chest wall.

heat exhaustion a condition marked by nausea, weakness, dizziness, and sweating that results from exertion in a very warm climate and from the loss of sodium chloride from the body.

heat prostration heat exhaustion.

heatstroke heat exhaustion.

hebephrenia schizophrenia marked chiefly by childish behavior, hallucinations, and regressive response. —**hebephreniac** *n.* —**hebephrenic** *adj.*

hebetic relating to youth.

hebetude emotional disinterest; lethargy.

hebosteotomy surgical enlargement of the opening of the bony pelvis to facilitate childbirth.

hederiform (of specific sensory nerve endings in the skin) ivy-shaped.

hedonophobia an abnormal fear of pleasure or of having fun.

hedrocele prolapse of part of the intestine through the anus; proctocele.

helcoid resembling an ulcer.

helcoplasty the repair of ulcers by the use of skin grafts, being a form of dermatoplasty.

helcosis the development of an ulcer; ulceration.

helicine relating to a coil or helix; spiral.

helicoid resembling a helix or spiral.

heliencephalitis inflammation of the brain as a consequence of sunstroke.

helioaerotherapy treatment involving exposure to sunlight and fresh air.

heliopathy any injury incurred as a result of exposure to sunlight.

heliophobia an abnormal fear of being exposed to the rays of the sun.

heliosis sunstroke.

heliotherapy treatment by exposure to sunlight.

helix *pl.* **helices** *also* **helixes** 1. the inward-curving rim of the outer ear. 2. one of the two coiled strands forming the structure of DNA.

THE HEART

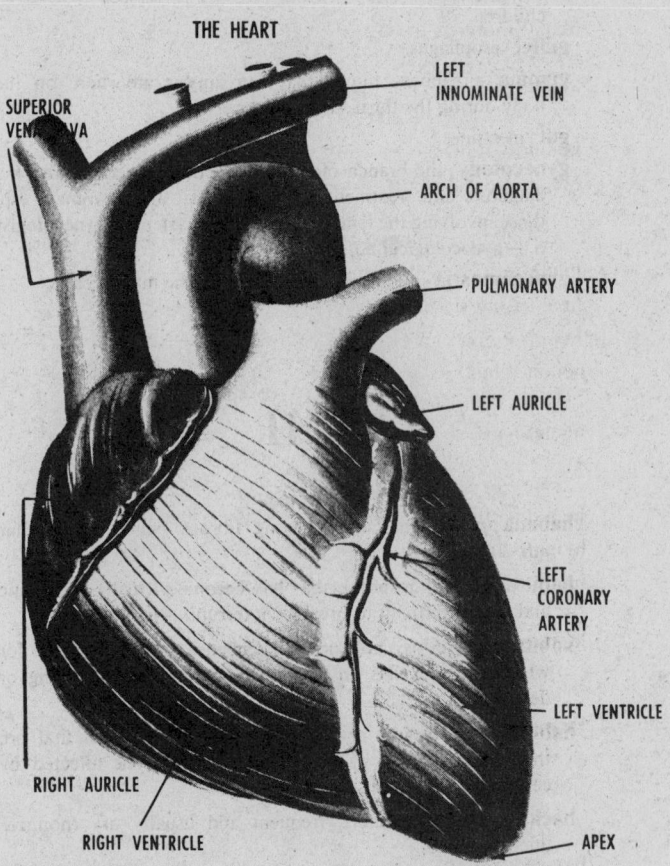

SUPERIOR VENA CAVA
LEFT INNOMINATE VEIN
ARCH OF AORTA
PULMONARY ARTERY
LEFT AURICLE
LEFT CORONARY ARTERY
LEFT VENTRICLE
RIGHT AURICLE
RIGHT VENTRICLE
APEX

helminth a parasitic worm esp. of the intestine. —**helminthic** *adj.*

helminthiasis infestation with parasitic worms.

helminthoid wormlike.

helminthology the study of parasitic worms.

heloma a corn.

helosis the condition of having corns on the feet or toes.

helotomy the surgical removal of a corn or corns.

hem- *or* **hemo-** *or* **haem-** *or* **haemo-** *prefix* blood.

hema- *or* **haema-** *prefix* blood.

hemachrosis unusual redness of the blood.

hemadostenosis a narrowing or contraction of the arteries.

hemagglutinate to cause agglutination of red blood cells. —**hemagglutination** *n.*

hemagglutinin an agent that causes hemagglutination.

hemagogue 1. promoting or enhancing the flow of blood. 2. an agent that promotes the flow of blood.

hemal relating to, involving, or affecting the blood or blood vessels.

hemanalysis laboratory examination or analysis of a sample of blood.

hemangio- *prefix* relating to or involving the blood vessels.

hemangioma a benign tumor made up of blood vessels.

hemarthrosis the abnormal presence of blood in a joint.

hematemesis the vomiting of blood or food mixed with blood.

hemathermal *also* **hemathermous** warm blooded.

hemathidrosis *also* **hematidrosis** an abnormal condition in which a person's sweat contains traces of blood.

hematic 1. relating to the blood. 2. any drug used in the treatment of anemia.

hematimeter a device used to count the number of blood cells in one cubic millimeter of blood.

hematin the portion of the hemoglobin molecule containing iron in the ferric state.

hematinemia the presence of heme in the circulating blood.

hematinic 1. relating to the blood. 2. any agent that increases the concentration of hemoglobin or the number of red blood cells in the circulating blood, used in the treatment of anemia.

hematinuria the abnormal presence of heme in the urine.

hematischesis the control or arrest of bleeding.

hematobium any parasite that lives in the blood.

hematoblast an immature or primitive cell from which all blood cells are derived. Also called *hemocytoblast*.

hematocele 1. a blood cyst. 2. the abnormal accumulation of blood within a bodily canal or cavity. 3. a swelling caused by effusion of blood into the sheath surrounding a testicle.

hematocelia bleeding into the peritoneal cavity.

hematochezia the passage of feces containing blood.

hematochyluria the abnormal presence of both blood and chyle in the urine.

hematocolpometra the accumulation of menstrual blood in the uterus and vagina, usually due to an obstruction of normal outflow by an intact hymen.

hematocrit 1. a centrifuge for separating the solid constituents of a blood sample from the plasma. 2. the percentage (by volume) of red blood cells in a sample of blood that has been centrifuged (which causes the cells to become packed in one end of the test tube or other container).

hematocystis an abnormal effusion of blood into the urinary bladder.

hematocyturia the presence of red blood cells (rather than just hemoglobin) in the urine. Compare *hemoglobinuria*.

hematogenesis the production of blood cells; hemopoiesis. —**hematogenic** *adj*. —**hematogenous** *adj*.

hematoglobin *also* **hematoglobulin** hemoglobin.

hematoid resembling blood; bloody; sanguineous.

hematology the study of the structure, functions, and diseases of blood and blood-forming tissues. —**hematologist** *n*.

hematoma *pl.* **hematomas** *or* **hematomata** a swelling or tumor composed of clotted blood.

hematometra an accumulation of blood within the cavity of the uterus.

hematomyelia bleeding into the substance of the spinal cord, usually as a response to injury.

hematopenia a deficiency in the size or number of the blood cells.

hematophagous (esp. of certain insects) surviving on a diet of blood.

hematophagia 1. (esp. of leeches or animals such as vampire bats) subsistence on the blood of other animals. 2. the drinking of blood as a supposed means of curing a disease or disorder.

hematopsia bleeding into the eye.

hematorrhachis bleeding of or into the spine; spinal hemorrhage.

hematosalpinx the abnormal accumulation of blood within a bodily tube, esp. a fallopian tube.

hematoscheocele the abnormal accumulation of blood within the cavity of the scrotum.

hematospectroscopy the examination of a sample of blood with the use of a spectroscope.

hematuria the presence of blood or blood cells in the urine.

heme the portion of hemoglobin that carries oxygen and gives the blood its characteristic color.

hemeralopia reduced visual capacity in the presence of bright light.

hemi- *prefix* one half.

hemiopalgia pain in one eye, usually associated with migraine.

hemiplegia paralysis of one side of the body. —**hemiplegic** *adj*.

hemochromatosis an iron metabolism disorder characterized by bronzing of the skin from iron-containing pigments deposited in the tissues.

hemodialysis purification or filtration of the blood, as with an artificial kidney, through dialysis.

hemoglobin an iron-containing respiratory pigment in the red blood cells.

hemoglobinemia the presence of free hemoglobin in the blood plasma.

hemoglobinuria the presence of free hemoglobin in the urine. —**hemoglobinuric** *adj*.

hemolysin a substance causing the breakdown of red blood cells.

hemolysis the breakdown or destruction of red blood cells. —**hemolytic** *adj*.

hemophilia a hereditary blood defect of males marked by delayed clotting of the blood and a tendency to hemorrhage after the slightest injury. —**hemophiliac** *n. & adj.* —**hemophilic** *adj*.

hemopoiesis the production of blood or blood cells in the body.

hemoptysis the coughing or spitting up of blood or sputum mixed with blood.

hemorrhage a heavy outpouring of blood from the blood vessels. —**hemorrhage** *vb.* —**hemorrhagic** *adj*.

hemorrhoids varicose dilation of veins near or at the anal sphincter. Also called *piles*. —**hemorrhoidal** *adj*.

hemostasis 1. the arresting of bleeding. 2. stagnation of the blood.

hemostat a surgical clamp for compressing a blood vessel that is bleeding.

hemostatic 1. stopping hemorrhage. 2. an agent that stops hemorrhage.

hemotoxin any substance, esp. one of biological origin, that causes destruction of red blood cells.

hemp a plant, *Cannabis sativa*, whose dried flower heads yield the drug hashish.

heparin a polysaccharide acid ester occurring esp. in the liver and useful in prolonging blood clotting time, as in the treatment of thrombosis and embolism.

hepat- *or* **hepato-** *prefix* 1. liver. 2. hepatic.

hepatalgia pain in the liver.

hepatatrophia *also* **hepatatrophy** a wasting away or atrophy of the liver.

hepatectomy surgical excision of part of the liver. —**hepatectomize** *vb.*

hepatic relating to, resembling, or affecting the liver.

hepatitis inflammation of the liver.

hepatocele herniation of part of the liver through the diaphragm or the abdominal wall.

hepatography X-ray photography of the liver.

hepatolithiasis the presence of calculi in the liver.

hepatologist an expert on the liver and the treatment of diseases that affect it.

hepatology the branch of medical science concerned with the liver and the diagnosis and treatment of diseases that affect it.

hepatoma a tumor of the liver.

hepatomegaly abnormal enlargement of the liver.

hepatopathy any disease of the liver.

hepatosplenomegaly abnormal enlargement of both the liver and spleen.

hepatotoxic capable of causing toxic damage to the liver. —**hepatotoxicity** *n.*

hereditary genetically transmittable or transmitted from generation to generation; inheritable or inherited.

heredity the sum of the genetic characteristics transmitted from one generation to the next chiefly through the chromosomes of the germ cells.

hermaphrodite one having sexual tissues or genitals of both sexes. —**hermaphroditic** *adj.* —**hermaphroditism** *n.*

hernia *pl.* **hernias** *or* **herniae** the protrusion of an organ or part through the wall or cavity within which it is normally contained. Also called *rupture.* —**hernial** *adj.*

herniate to develop a hernia.

heroin a narcotic drug obtained from morphine, formerly used as an antitussive but now rendered illegal in the U.S. because of its addictive properties and potential for abuse.

herpes any of various inflammatory viral diseases marked by clusters of vesicles. —**herpetic** *adj.*

herpes simplex a viral disease marked by clusters of watery vesicles on the mucous membranes chiefly of the lips, mouth, or genitals.

herpes zoster shingles.

hexachlorophene an antibacterial agent used in some soaps and detergents.

hexylresorcinol a broad-spectrum drug used in the treatment of worm infestations.

hiatus any gap, opening or fissure.

hiatus hernia *also* **hiatal hernia** an abnormal condition in which a portion of the top part of the stomach protrudes up through a gap in the diaphragm.

hiccup *also* **hiccough** repeated spasmodic inhalation of the breath accompanied by closure of the glottis and by a characteristic explosive sound. —**hiccup** *or* **hiccough** *vb.*

hidrosis the secretion of sweat; perspiration. —**hidrotic** *adj.*

high *Slang* intoxicated with drugs or alcohol. —**high** *n.*

hindbrain the division of the embryonic brain that develops into the cerebellum, pons, and medulla oblongata.

hip the upper part of the thigh.

hip joint the articulation between the innominate bone and the femur.

Hippocratic oath an oath traditionally taken by those entering medical practice that embraces a code of medical ethics attributed to the Greek physician Hippocrates, born about 460 B.C. and known as the "Father of Medicine".

hirsute 1. having hair; hairy. 2. relating to hirsutism.

hirsutism pronounced or excessive growth of hair esp. on the body.

histamine a compound found esp. in animal tissue and in ergot that causes dilation of the blood vessels in many allergic reactions. —**histaminic** *adj.*

histogenesis the formation and differentiation of animal tissues. —**histogenetic** *adj.*

histology a branch of anatomy dealing with the microscopic study of tissues. —**histological** *adj.*

histolysis the disintegration or degeneration of tissues.

hives urticaria.

Hodgkin's disease a neoplastic disease that is marked chiefly by enlargement of the lymph glands, liver, and spleen and by progressive anemia.

homeopath a practitioner of homeopathy.

homeopathy the treatment of a disease by administering minute doses of a substance or agent that in large doses in a healthy person would produce symptoms of the disease itself. —**homeopathic** *adj.*

homeostasis the automatic self-regulation of bodily functions under environmental variations, resulting in a basic balance or equilibrium of temperature, blood pressure, water content, blood sugar, etc.

homoerotic homosexual. —**homoeroticism** *n.*

homologous having the same relative position, structure, or function.

homosexual relating to or practicing homosexuality. —**homosexual** *n.*

homosexuality sexual desire toward or sexual activity practiced with members of one's own sex.

hookworm a parasitic nematode worm that attaches to the intestinal wall of the host and is a serious bloodsucking pest.

hormone a chemical substance secreted directly into the bloodstream by the endocrine glands which has a specific effect on cells remote from its point of origin. —**hormonal** *adj.*

housemaid's knee a swelling of the knee due to enlargement of the bursa in front of the patella and caused typically by prolonged kneeling on a hard surface or substance.

humerus the bone of the upper arm.

hydr- *or* **hydro-** *prefix* water.

hydrocephalus *also* **hydrocephaly** an abnormal increase in the amount of cerebrospinal fluid in the cranium resulting in enlargement of the skull and atrophy of the brain.

hydrophobia rabies.

hydrotherapy the scientific use of water in treating disease. —**hydrotherapeutic** *adj.*

hygiene the science and practice of maintaining good health. —**hygienic** *adj.*

hymen a membranous fold partially closing the entrance to the vagina; maidenhead. —**hymeneal** *adj.*

hyper- *prefix* excessive; above.

hyperacidity excessively acid. —**hyperacid** *adj.*

hypersensitive abnormally susceptible to a drug, antigen, or other agent. —**hypersensitivity** *n.*

hypertension blood pressure exceeding normal limits.

hypnosis a state resembling sleep that is induced by a hypnotist and in which the subject readily responds to suggestion. —**hypnotist** n. —**hypnotize** vb.

hypnotic 1. tending to induce sleep; soporific. 2. an agent that induces sleep.

hypo- or **hyp-** prefix 1. under; down. 2. less than normal.

hypochondria a depressed state of mind often centering on concern for imaginary illnesses. —**hypochondriac** n. & adj. —**hypochondriacal** adj.

hypochondriasis hypochondria.

hypodermic 1. relating to the parts beneath the skin. 2. adapted for injection beneath the skin: hypodermic needle.

hysterectomy surgical removal of the uterus.

hysteria a psychoneurotic disorder marked by extreme excitability and disturbances of various psychic and physical functions.

I

iatrology medical science.

ichthyoid shaped like a fish.

ichthyophagy the habit or practice of subsisting on fish.

ichthyophobia an abnormal fear of fish, whether living or dead.

ichthyosis a dry, scaly skin condition.

ichthyotoxin a toxic substance found in the roe of certain fishes.

ichthyotoxism poisoning caused by eating toxic fish roe, characterized by disorders of the nervous system and gastrointestinal tract.

ICSH abbr. interstitial cell-stimulating hormone.

ictal relating to or caused by a seizure or stroke.

icteric relating to or characterized by jaundice (icterus).

ictero- prefix relating to jaundice (icterus).

icterogenic causing jaundice.

icterohematuric relating to jaundice associated with blood in the urine.

icterohepatitis inflammation of the liver (hepatitis) marked by jaundice.

icterus jaundice.

id (in Freudian theory of psychoanalysis) one of the three basic divisions of the psyche, considered to be the most primitive part of the personality and accounting for simple drives and instinctive behaviour. Compare ego, superego.

identical twins monozygotic twins.

idiocy a condition of severely marked low intellectual capacity, typically with a functional IQ below 75.

idiopathic relating to any state or condition of unknown cause: idiopathic disease.

idiot one marked with idiocy.

ileitis inflammation of the ileum.

ileostomy the surgical construction of a communicating passage through the abdominal wall to the ileum.

ileum the distal section of the small intestine.

ilium the upper part of the innominate bone.

imbecility a condition of marked mental incapacity. —**imbecile** n.

immunity a condition of resistance to infection.

immunization the procedure or technique of bringing about or increasing a state of immunity in an individual, as by the injection of a vaccine or other agent into the body or taking an oral substance that provides protection against a specific disease.

immunosuppressive 1. relating to any of various drugs that act to suppress the body's natural immune response, used esp. to permit the surgical transplant of a foreign organ or tissue by inhibiting its biological rejection. 2. a drug with this action.

immunotherapy therapy aimed at the production of immunity in the patient.

immunotoxin any antitoxin.

impacted pressed or jammed together or against something else: impacted teeth.

impaction the state or condition of being impacted.

impalpable incapable of being detected by means of the sense of touch.

impaludism malaria.

imparidigitate possessing an odd number of toes or fingers.

impatent not open or patent; closed.

imperception the inability to form a mental image of an object subjected to the senses; inadequate or insufficient perception.

imperforate lacking an opening; closed. —**imperforation** n.

impermeable not capable of being penetrated; impervious to fluids.

impetigo a contagious skin rash.

implant 1. to graft or insert. 2. the material grafted or inserted. —**implantation** n.

impotence also **impotency** inability in the male to achieve erection of the penis. —**impotent** adj.

impotentia impotence.

impregnate 1. to cause to conceive. 2. to fill or permeate with some other substance; saturate. —**impregnation** n.

impressio pl. **impressiones** an indentation or impression apparently made by the pressure of one structure or part upon another.

impulsive relating to actions or behavior actuated by an impulse rather than conscious thought or reason.

imus (or a structure or part compared with a similar neighbor) lowermost; being most caudal or inferior.

inanition extreme weakness or lack of strength and drive due to dietary insufficiency or failure of the digestive system to assimilate food.

inappetence absence of craving or desire; lethargy.

inarticulate unable to speak or communicate clearly or intelligibly.

in articulo mortis at the time of death.

incise to cut with a knife or knife-like instrument.

incision 1. a separation or division of soft tissue with a scalpel or other knife-like instrument. 2. a cut or surgical wound.

incisura incision.

incisure a notch or incision.

incontinence inability of the body to control the elimination of urine (urinary incontinence) or feces (fecal incontinence). —**incontinent** adj.

incrustation the formation over a healing wound of a crust or scab.

incubation 1. the technique or practice of maintaining tissue cultures or microorganisms at a controlled temperature that favors their growth or development. 2. care of a premature baby in an incubator. 3. the period of time from exposure to an infecting microorganism to the first appearance of the signs or symptoms of the disease it causes.

incubator 1. an apparatus in which premature babies are placed and maintained at the optimum temperature and humidity. 2. any container or receptacle for the incubation of tissue cultures or microorganisms.

incubus a nightmare.

incus one of the three tiny conducting bones of the middle ear; anvil.

indigestion difficulty in digesting food or imperfect digestion, characterized by a burning sensation in the stomach or lower part of the esophagus (heartburn) and the formation of gas in the stomach, usually relieved by taking antacids; dyspepsia. —**indigestible** adj.

indomethacin a powerful anti-inflammatory drug used in the treatment of rheumatoid arthritis and other forms of joint inflammation.

indurated (of the normally soft tissues of the body) hardened; becoming firm or firmer. —**indurative** adj.

inebriant 1. intoxicating. 2. a drug or agent able to cause intoxication or drunkenness. —**inebriation** n.

inebriety the chronic consumption of excessive amounts of alcoholic beverages.

inert 1. slow; sluggish. 2. not active. 3. having no therapeutic or pharmacologic properties or action: an inert chemical.

in extremis at the point of death.

infant a baby, esp. one less than a year old. —**infancy** n.

infanticide the murder of a child.

infantile paralysis poliomyelitis.

infarct a necrotic area in an organ or tissue resulting from circulatory blockage. —**infarction** n. —**infarcted** adj.

infection invasion of the body by pathogenic organisms or the clinical signs and symptoms of such an invasion. —**infectious** adj.

infectious hepatitis an acute viral inflammation of the liver marked by fever, jaundice, and nausea.

infectious mononucleosis an acute infectious viral disease primarily affecting the lymph glands, which become swollen and tender. Also called glandular fever.

infecundity the inability of a woman to conceive; female sterility or barrenness.

inferior (of a structure or part) situated lower or below another structure or part; caudal.

inferiority complex acute feelings of lack of personal worth typically manifested in timidity or in overaggressiveness resulting from overcompensation.

infertility the inability to conceive or father offspring. —**infertile** adj.

infirm weak or feeble, esp. as the result of old age or a debilitating illness. —**infirmity** n.

infirmary a small hospital or medical center for the care and treatment of the ill or infirm, esp. one attached to a school or college.

inflammation the changes that take place in tissues in response to local damage, typically characterized by pain, heat, swelling, reddening and an interruption of function in the affected area.

inflammatory relating to or characterized by inflammation: inflammatory disease.

influenza an acute contagious viral disease affecting esp. the respiratory tract. —**influenzal** adj.

infraction also **infracture** a fracture, esp. one in which the broken bones are not displaced.

infrahyoid (of certain muscles) situated below the hyoid bone.

infundibulum any funnel-shaped structure or part, esp. the stalk-like extension by which the pituitary gland is attached to the base of the brain.

ingest to introduce food or drink into the stomach through the mouth. —**ingestion** n. —**ingestive** adj.

inguinal relating to or located near the groin.

inhale to breathe in; take air or gas into the lungs. —**inhalation** n.

inhalation therapy the therapeutic use of a nebulized solution of drugs or other therapeutic agents which the patient breathes in.

inject to introduce (fluid) into the body by means of a syringe. —**injection** n.

innervate to supply with nerves. —**innervation** n.

inquest a judicial inquiry into the causes of a death.

insanity a deranged state of the mind; madness. —**insane** adj.

inseminate to introduce semen into the vagina or uterus of.

insemination the deposition of semen within the vagina during sexual intercourse or introduced artificially (artificial insemination).

insensible 1. not appreciable by the senses. 2. not conscious.

insidious developing for a period before being detected: insidious disease.

in situ in a natural or original position.

insomnia inability to fall or stay asleep. —**insomniac** n.

inspiration the act of inhaling; inhalation.

insulin a hormone secreted by the islets of Langerhans in the pancreas and crucial to the metabolism of carbohydrates, also used in the treatment and control of diabetes mellitus.

insulinemia the presence of an abnormally large amount of insulin in the circulating blood.

insulin shock coma resulting from excessive amounts of insulin in the system.

insuloma a tumor of the islets of Langerhans of the pancreas (an adenoma).

integument an enveloping membrane or skin.

intelligence quotient a number indicating the apparent intelligence level of a person and arrived at by dividing the mental age by the chronological age and multiplying by 100. Also called IQ.

inter- prefix between; among.

intergyral between the convolutions (gyri) of the cerebral cortex.

intern a recent graduate of a medical school undergoing training at a hospital, usually for a period of one year, before becoming fully qualified to practice.

internal medicine a branch of medicine dealing with the diagnosis and treatment of diseases not requiring surgery, esp. those involving the internal organs of the chest and abdomen.

internist a physician specializing in internal medicine.

internuncial (of a neuron) connecting two other neurons.

interstitial situated between the cellular components of an organ or part.

intestinal relating to, affecting, or occurring in the intestine.

intestine the tubular section of the alimentary canal extending from the stomach to the anus.

intima *pl.* **intimae** *or* **intimas** the innermost coat of an organ or artery.

intimitis inflammation of an intima.

intolerance exceptional sensitivity, as to a drug or medication.

intra- *prefix* 1. between. 2. during. 3. inward; within.

intracardiac occurring or existing within the heart.

intracranial occurring or existing within the cranium.

intradermal occurring, accomplished, or situated within the layers of the skin.

intrauterine device a device, as a metal or plastic coil or loop, inserted and left in the uterus to prevent conception. Also called *intrauterine contraceptive device; IUCD; IUD.*

intravenous within a vein: *intravenous injection.*

introvert one whose interests and concerns center primarily on the self. —**introverted** *adj.* —**introversion** *n.*

intubation the insertion of a tube into a hollow organ, as the trachea. —**intubate** *vb.*

intussusception the abnormal infolding of one segment of the intestine within another segment. —**intussusceptive** *adj.*

in utero within the uterus.

involution 1. a turning inward or rolling over of a rim. 2. any backward or retrograde change. 3. the shrinking back to normal size of the uterus after childbirth. 4. a physical decline in bodily vigor, as that associated with menopause in women.

iodide a compound, as a salt, of iodine.

iodinate to combine or treat with iodine.

iodine a nonmetallic element of the halogen group, essential in minute amounts in the diet (as in iodized table salt) for the proper development and functioning of the thyroid gland.

iodize to impregnate or treat with iodine.

ion an atom or atom group containing a positive or negative charge of electricity.

IQ intelligence quotient.

iridectomy surgical removal of part of the iris of the eye.

iridemia bleeding from the iris.

iris the pigmented diaphragm surrounding the pupil of the eye.

iritis inflammation of the iris of the eye.

iron a metallic element essential in the diet for the prevention of iron-deficiency anemia, the production of hemoglobin, and as an essential component of certain enzymes.

irrigation the washing out or cleansing of a structure or part with water or other fluid. —**irrigate** *vb.*

irritant 1. tending to produce physical irritation. 2. something that irritates.

irritation a state of soreness or inflammation or irritability or overexcitation.

ischemia *also* **ischaemia** inadequate blood supply to an organ or part due to obstruction or constriction of the blood vessels. —**ischemic** *adj.*

ischium *pl.* **ischia** the posterior dorsal bone of the pelvis.

islets of Langerhans any of the groups of endocrine cells within the pancreas that secrete insulin.

isometrics a system of exercises stressing the contraction of opposing muscles in such a way that shortening is minimal but the increase in muscle fiber tone is great.

isthmus a contracted or restricted anatomical part connecting two larger bodily parts.

itching a persistent irritation of the cutaneous tissues that causes an urge to scratch and that is often held to result from mild stimulation of pain receptors. —**itch** *vb. & n.*

IUCD intrauterine contraceptive device.

IUD intrauterine device.

J

jactitation extreme restlessness; tossing from one side to the other.

jargon terms or expressions peculiar to a specific activity or field of interest: *medical jargon.*

jaundice yellowing of the skin, body fluids, and tissues resulting from the deposit of bile pigments. —**jaundiced** *adj.*

jaw either of the two bony structures within the mouth into which the teeth are set, forming an upper and immovable structure (maxilla) and a lower movable structure (mandible).

jejunectomy surgical removal of all or part of the jejunum.

jejunitis inflammation of the jejunum.

jejuno- *also* **jejun-** *prefix* relating to the jejunum.

jejunocolostomy the surgical formation of an artificial opening between the jejunum and the colon.

jejunoileal relating to both the jejunum and the ileum.

jejunoileitis inflammation of both the jejunum and the ileum; inflammation of the small intestine.

jejunojejunostomy the surgical formation of an artificial junction between two portions of the jejunum, as to bypass a diseased or permanently obstructed area.

jejunostomy the surgical formation of an artificial opening between the jejunum and the wall of the abdomen.

jejunotomy surgical incision into the jejunum.

jejunum the part of the small intestine between the duodenum and the ileum. —**jejunal** *adj.*

joint a point of articulation between two or more bones.

jugular 1. of or relating to the throat or the neck. 2. a jugular vein.

jugular vein either of two large veins in the neck that return blood from the head.

jugulum the neck or throat.

jugum *pl.* **juga** 1. a ridge connecting two points. 2. a type of surgical forceps.

junctura a joint; articulation.

K

kabure a form of schistosomiasis occurring in Asia, esp. in Japan.

kainophobia an abnormal fear of things unfamiliar or new; neophobia.

kala-azar a tropical or subtropical infectious disease caused by a species of protozoa (*Leishmania donovani*) and transmitted by the bite of infected sandflies (*Phlebotomus* species).

kaliemia the presence of potassium in the blood.

karyogenesis the formation and development of the nucleus of a cell.

karyokinesis equal division of the nucleus during cell division. —**karyokinetic** *adj.*

karyolysis the dissolution or destruction of the nucleus of a cell or its loss of ability to be stained by basic dyes. —**karyolytic** *adj.*

karyomitosis changes in the nucleus of a cell during cell division or mitosis.

karyomorphism the shape or form of the nucleus of a cell.

karyophage a parasitic protozoan within a cell that destroys its nucleus.

katabolism catabolism.

kathisophobia an abnormal fear of sitting down and remaining still.

kation cation.

keloid a dense scar resulting from growth of connective tissue.

kenophobia an abnormal fear of empty spaces.

keratectomy surgical removal of a portion of the cornea of the eye.

keratiasis the formation on the skin of horny warts.

keratic relating to horn or horny substances.

keratin a sulfur-containing fibrous protein constituting the basis of horny epidermal material, including the hair.

keratinize (of tissues) to make or become horny or hard.

keratitis inflammation of the cornea of the eye.

kerato- *also* **kerat-** *prefix* 1. the cornea. 2. a horny substance.

keratodermatitis inflammation of the horny layer of the skin.

keratogenous producing or causing the development of horny tissue.

keratohelcosis ulceration of the cornea.

keratoiritis inflammation of both the cornea and the iris.

keratolysis 1. periodic shedding of the skin. 2. a loosening of the skin's horny layer. —**keratolytic** *adj.*

keratoma a callus or horny growth.

keratomalacia a result of vitamin A deficiency of early childhood characterized by a softening of the cornea of the eye. Also called *xerotic keratitis.*

keratome a surgical knife for making incisions into the cornea of the eye.

keratometer a special instrument for measuring the curves of the cornea of the eye.

keratomycosis a fungal infection involving the cornea of the eye.

keratonyxis surgical puncture of the cornea.

keratoplasty surgical repair of the cornea.

keratosis any disorder characterized by overgrowth of horny material on the skin. —**keratotic** *adj.*

ketogenesis the generation of ketone bodies, as in diabetes.

ketone an organic compound having a carbonyl group linking two carbon atoms. —**ketonic** *adj.*

ketone body one of the three compounds acetoacetic acid, beta-hydroxybutyric acid, and acetone found in the urine and blood esp. in diabetes mellitus.

ketosis an abnormal increase of ketone bodies, as in diabetes mellitus.

ketosteroid a steroid containing a ketone group.

Kg *abbr.* kilogram.

kidney *pl.* **kidneys** either of a pair of bean-shaped organs, located near the spinal column behind the peritoneum, that excrete waste products of metabolism in the form of urine.

kilo- *prefix* one thousand.

kilogram one thousand grams. Abbr. *kg.*

kinaesthesia *or* **kinaesthesis** kinesthesia.

kinesia motion sickness.

kinesialgia pain caused by muscular activity.

kinesiology the branch of science concerned with the study of muscles, muscle groups, and muscular activity.

kinesioneurosis any functional disorder characterized by muscular spasms or tics.

-kinesis *suffix* movement.

kinesthesia *or* **kinesthesis** sensory awareness of bodily movements, as of muscles. —**kinesthetic** *adj.*

Klebsiella a genus of gram-negative bacteria associated with infections of the respiratory tract.

kleptomania a neurotic compulsion to steal without any economic need. —**kleptomaniac** *n.*

klieg eyes a condition of the eyes characterized by conjunctivitis and excessive watering and caused by prolonged exposure to very bright light.

knee a joint in the mid-part of the leg that connects the femur, tibia, and patella.

kneecap patella.

knee jerk an involuntary forward kick of the lower leg that results normally when the tendon below the patella is tapped lightly.

knock-knee a condition in which the legs turn inward at the knee. —**knock-kneed** *adj.*

knuckle a rounded prominence formed at the joining of two adjacent bones, esp. of a finger.

Koplik's spots a diagnostic sign of measles consisting of the development of tiny white spots on a red base on the inner surface of the cheeks, typically seen just before the appearance of the characteristic skin rash.

Korsakoff's syndrome *or* **Korsakoff's psychosis** an abnormal mental condition that is usually induced by chronic alcoholism and is marked chiefly by disorientation, hallucinations, and amnesia compensated for by confabulation.

kwashiorkor acute malnutrition in the young as the result of a diet low in protein and high in carbohydrates.

kyphosis abnormal curvature of the spine in a backward direction. —**kyphotic** *adj.*

L

labia *pl. of* labium.

labial of or relating to the lips or the labia.

labia majora the two fleshy, fatty outer lips that form the boundaries of the vulva.

labia minora the inner vascular lips of the vulva.

labio- *prefix* relating to lips.

labiochorea a chronic spasm of the lips, frequently presenting difficulty in producing clear speech sounds.

labioclination abnormal inclination of a tooth toward the lips.

labioglossolaryngeal relating to a paralysis affecting the lips, tongue and larynx.

labiomental relating to the lower lip and the extremity of the chin.

labiomycosis any fungal infection involving the lips.

labiopalatine relating to both the lips and the palate or roof of the mouth.

labioplacement (of a tooth or teeth) abnormal positioning toward the lips.

labor 1. the physiological activities that take place in the process of giving birth. 2. the period during which this takes place.

labrum *pl.* **labra** a lip or any structure or part shaped like or resembling a lip or lips.

labyrinth the bony and membranous structures that constitute the inner ear.

labyrinthectomy surgical removal of the labyrinth of the inner ear.

labyrinthitis inflammation of the labyrinth of the inner ear.

labyrinthotomy surgical incision into the labyrinth of the inner ear.

lacerate to tear roughly or jaggedly.

laceration a ragged, torn wound.

lacertus 1. any band of muscles or fibers. 2. the muscular part of the arm.

lachrymal *or* **lacrimal** of or relating to tears or to the glands that produce tears.

lacrimation the excessive formation and secretion of tears.

lacrimator any agent or substance that produces tears by its irritant effects on the eyes, such as tear gas.

lacrimatory causing the production of tears.

lacrimotomy surgical incision into the glands that produce tears.

lact- *or* **lacti-** *or* **lacto-** *prefix* milk.

lactate to secrete milk. —**lactation** *n.*

lacteal 1. relating to or like milk; milky. 2. a lymphatic vessel in which chyle is conveyed from the intestine.

lactescent resembling milk; milky.

lactic relating to milk.

lactiferous conveying or secreting milk: *lactiferous ducts.*

lactifuge any agent that arrests the flow of milk from the mammary glands.

lactigenous producing milk.

lactogen an agent that stimulates the production or secretion of milk.

lactogenesis milk production. —**lactogenic** *adj.*

lactovegetarian a vegetarian who includes dairy products in his diet, such as milk and cheese, as well as eggs.

lacus *pl.* **lacus** any very small collection or accumulation of fluid.

lacus lacrimalis a small space at the medial angle of the eye where tears collect after bathing the surface of the eyeball.

lagneia 1. sexual intercourse; coitus. 2. lust; sexual urge.

lagnesis *also* **lagnosis** excessive and persistent sexual desire in a man or woman; nymphomania or satyriasis.

lake (of blood in hemolysis) to change so that the hemoglobin is dissolved in the plasma.

-lalia *suffix* speech disorder.

laliophobia an abnormal fear of speaking or stuttering.

lallation a speech defect characterized by difficulty in enunciation of words that contain the letter *l.*

lalochezia psychological or emotional relief obtained by swearing or speaking obscene or vulgar words.

lalognosis the understanding of speech or spoken communication.

THE LACRIMAL APPARATUS

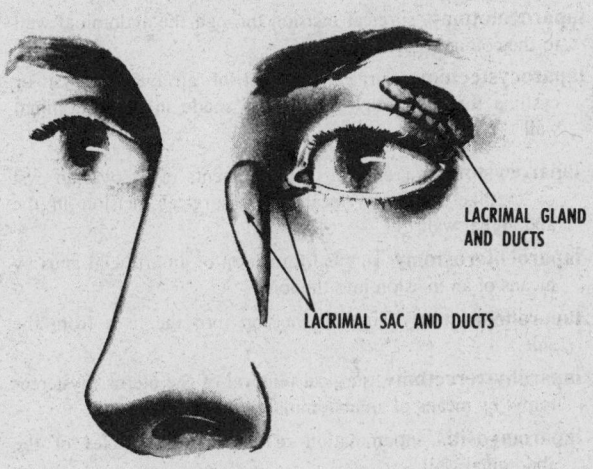

LACRIMAL GLAND AND DUCTS

LACRIMAL SAC AND DUCTS

The lacrimal gland secretes tears which are poured over the eyes through small ducts. The tears collect in the inner corner of the eye and pass through two small openings into the lacrimal ducts and into the lacrimal sac. The sac empties into the nose.

lalopathology a branch of science concerned with disorders of speech production and their treatment.

lalopathy any type of speech defect.

laloplegia paralysis of the muscles required in the production of speech sounds.

lalorrhea an excessive flow of words and phrases.

lambdacism 1. difficulty in or inability to pronounce or articulate the letter *l.* 2. pronunciation of the letter *l* as the letter *r.*

lamella *pl.* **lamellae** any thin layer or sheet. —**lamellar** *adj.*

lamina *pl.* **laminae** 1. any flat layer or thin plate. 2. the flattened part on either side of a vertebral arch. —**laminar** *adj.*

laminectomy surgical removal of a vertebral lamina, esp. the posterior arch of a vertebra.

laminitis inflammation of a lamina.

laminotomy surgical incision into a vertebral lamina.

lance 1. to incise an abscess, boil, etc., as to permit the release of pus. 2. a lancet.

lancet a small, pointed, two-edged knife used in surgery.

lancinating (of pain) piercing, cutting, or extremely sharp; tearing.

Langerhans' islets islets of Langerhans.

laniary (of the canine teeth) adapted for tearing.

lanolin wool grease refined esp. for use as the base of various ointments.

lanosterol a sterol found in wool fat.

lanthanides the rare earth elements.

lanthionine an amino acid obtained from wool.

lanuginous covered with soft hair; downy.

lanugo soft, downy hair covering the body.

lapactic laxative; purgative.

laparocele an abdominal hernia.

laparocolostomy the surgical formation of an artificial anus by creating a permanent opening between the colon and the abdominal wall.

laparocolotomy surgical incision through the abdominal wall to the colon; colotomy.

laparocystectomy surgical removal of an ovarian cyst or cystlike tumor through an incision made in the abdominal wall.

laparocystotomy removal of the contents of an ovarian cyst or cystlike tumor by means of a surgical incision in the abdominal wall.

laparoenterostomy surgical formation of an artificial anus by means of an incision into the loin.

laparohepatotomy surgical incision into the liver from the side.

laparohysterectomy surgical removal of the uterus (hysterectomy) by means of an abdominal incision.

laparomyositis inflammation of the lateral muscles of the abdominal wall.

laparonephrectomy surgical removal of the kidney by means of an incision in the loin.

laparosalpingectomy surgical removal of a fallopian tube by means of an abdominal incision.

laparosplenectomy surgical removal of the spleen by means of an incision in the abdominal wall.

laparosplenotomy surgical incision into the spleen through the abdominal wall.

laparotomize to subject (a patient) to laparotomy.

laparotomy *pl.* **laparotomies** surgical section of the abdominal wall.

laryngeal of or relating to the larynx.

laryngectomy *pl.* **laryngectomies** surgical removal of all or part of the larynx.

laryngitic relating to or caused by inflammation of the larynx.

laryngitis inflammation of the larynx.

laryngo- *also* **laryng-** *prefix* relating to the larynx.

laryngograph an instrument for measuring the movements of the larynx by means of a tracing (laryngogram).

laryngology a branch of medicine dealing with diseases of the larynx and nasopharynx.

laryngomalacia an abnormal softening of the cartilages of the larynx.

laryngoparalysis paralysis of the muscles of the larynx.

laryngopathy any disease or disorder affecting the larynx.

laryngopharyngectomy surgical removal of part of the larynx and pharynx, as in the treatment of cancer.

laryngopharyngitis inflammation of both the larynx and pharynx.

laryngoscope an instrument for visual examination of the larynx. —laryngoscopic *adj.* —laryngoscopist *n.* —laryngoscopy *n.*

laryngostenosis abnormal narrowing or stricture of the lumen of the larynx.

laryngostomy the surgical formation of a permanent opening from the neck into the larynx.

laryngotome a surgical knife for making incisions into the larynx.

larynx *pl.* **larynges** the upper part of the trachea that contains the vocal cords.

Lassa fever a viral disease first noted in Nigeria in 1969, characterized by high fever, headache, facial flushes, vomiting and bleeding from the skin and mucous membranes, thought to be transmitted by a species of rat.

lassitude a feeling of profound weakness; fatigue.

latent present but not active or visible: *latent infection.* —latency *n.*

lateral relating to, situated on, or coming from the side. —laterally *adv.*

lateralis lateral; at the side.

laudanum a tincture that contains opium, formerly widely used as a pain killer.

laughing gas nitrous oxide.

lavage the therapeutic irrigation of a hollow organ, such as the stomach or lower intestine.

laxative any agent serving to relieve constipation; cathartic.

L.E. *abbr.* 1. left eye. 2. lupus erythematosus.

lead poisoning chronic poisoning that is the result of ingestion or absorption of lead and is characterized by colic, a dark line along the gums, and muscular paralysis.

leg either of the lower limbs, used for standing and moving.

leiodermia the condition of having abnormally smooth or glossy skin.

leiomyoma a benign tumor derived from smooth or nonstriated muscle.

leiomyomatosis the condition of having several leiomyomas in different parts of the body.

leiomyosarcoma a malignant tumor derived from smooth or nonstriated muscle.

leiotrichous having hair that is straight; straight-haired.

Leishmania a genus of parasitic protozoa.

leishmaniasis infection with protozoa of the genus *Leishmania*, one species of which causes the disease kala-azar.

leishmaniosis leishmaniasis.

leishmanoid any pathological condition that resembles the signs of leishmaniasis.

lemic relating to any epidemic disease, esp. the plague.

lens a transparent, nearly spherical body in the eye that focuses light rays upon the retina.

lenticular having the shape of or resembling a lens.

lenticulopapular (of a skin eruption) having papules that are shaped like a tiny dome or convex lens.

lentiform lenticular; shaped like a lens.

leprology the branch of medical science concerned with the study and treatment of leprosy.

leprosy a chronic, communicable disease that is caused by a bacillus and is marked by the formation of granules on the skin that enlarge and spread, eventual paralysis of muscle, and the development of deformities. —leprous *adj.*

-lepsy *suffix* seizure: *catalepsy.*

lepto- *prefix* thin, slender or light; frail.

leptocephalous having an abnormally small head. —leptocephalus *n.*

leptochroa the condition of having skin that is abnormally delicate.

leptodermic characterized by or having abnormally thin skin.

leptomeninges the two inner membranes that envelop the brain and spinal cord; pia mater and arachnoid (as distinguished from the dura mater).

leptomeningitis inflammation of the pia mater and arachnoid; inflammation of the leptomeninges.

leptophonia the condition of having an abnormally weak

voice. —**leptophonic** *adj.*

leptopodia the condition of having unusually narrow or slender feet.

leptoprosopia the condition of having an unusually narrow face.

lesion an abnormal change in a part or tissue resulting from disease or injury.

Lesbian *or* **lesbian** a female homosexual. —**lesbianism** *n.*

lethal relating to or causing death; deadly; fatal. —**lethality** *n.* —**lethally** *adv.*

lethargy abnormal drowsiness, fatigue, or indifference. —**lethargic** *adj.*

lethe loss of memory; amnesia. —**letheral** *adj.*

leuk- *or* **leuko-** *or* **leuc-** *or* **leuco-** *prefix* white; colorless: *leukocyte.*

leukemia *also* **leukaemia** a malignant, progressive disease marked by an abnormal increase in the number of white blood cells in the tissues and in the blood. —**leukemic** *adj.*

leukocyte *or* **leucocyte** a white blood cell. —**leukocytic** *adj.*

leukocytoblast any immature cell that eventually develops into one of the white blood cells (leukocytes).

leukocytogenesis the formation and development of white blood cells; leukocytopoiesis.

leukocytoid resembling a white blood cell.

leukocytolysin any of various substances that cause the destruction or dissolution of white blood cells.

leukocytolysis the destruction or dissolution of white blood cells. —**leukocytolytic** *adj.*

leukocytoma the local accumulation of white blood cells in a dense mass.

leukocytopoiesis the formation and development of white blood cells; leukocytogenesis.

leukocytosis *or* **leucocytosis** an increased number of white blood cells in the circulating blood. —**leukocytotic** *adj.*

leukocytotoxin any toxic substance that causes the degeneration or destruction of white blood cells.

leukocyturia the presence of white blood cells in the urine.

leukoderma a partial or total absence of pigment in the skin. —**leukodermatous** *adj.*

leukodontia the desirable condition of having white teeth.

leukodystrophy the degeneration or destruction of the white matter of the brain, thought to be caused by a disorder of fat metabolism.

leukoencephalitis the inflammation of the white matter of the brain.

leukoma *or* **leucoma** a dense white opacity of the cornea of the eye.

leukopenia a condition in which there is an abnormally small number of white blood cells in the bloodstream. Also called *leukocytopenia.*

leukorrhea a whitish discharge from the vagina resulting from inflammation of its mucous membranes. —**leukorrheal** *adj.*

leukotomy the surgical division of nerve fiber tracts in the white matter of the frontal lobe of the cerebrum.

leukotrichia the state or condition of having white hair.

levator a muscle that raises a body part.

levulose fructose; fruit sugar.

libido, emotional or psychic energy, esp. sexual drive. —**libidinal** *adj.* —**libidinous** *adj.*

lichen any of various skin diseases marked by patches of small, firm papules.

lid eyelid.

life-span 1. an individual's duration of existence. 2. the average duration of existence of the members of a particular species.

ligament a tough band of tissue that connects bones together at the joints or supports an organ in place. —**ligamentary** *adj.* —**ligamentous** *adj.*

ligation ligature.

ligature any of various threads or wires used in surgery to tie off or constrict a vessel or part.

light adaptation adaptation of the eye to intensified light through contraction of the pupil and a decrease in visual purple.

limbus the region forming a margin between the cornea and sclera of the eye.

liminal of or relating to a sensory threshold; barely perceptible.

limitrophic (of the sympathetic nervous system) governing or controlling nutrition.

limosis abnormal and persistent hunger.

linea any long, narrow strip or mark anatomically distinguished from the surrounding areas by its elevation, color or texture.

lingua *pl.* **linguae** the tongue or a structure or part that resembles the tongue.

lingual of, relating to, or lying near the tongue.

lingually in the direction of the tongue; toward the tongue.

linguo- *prefix* relating to the tongue.

liniment a liquid preparation used for soothing irritated skin or as a counterirritant or cleansing agent.

linolenic acid a liquid, fatty acid held to be essential to nutrition.

lip 1. either of the two fleshy folds forming the margins of the mouth. 2. labium.

lip- *or* **lipo-** *prefix* fat; fatty.

lipase any of various enzymes that dissolve or split fat.

lipectomy the surgical removal of fatty tissue.

lipemia the presence in the bloodstream of an abnormally large amount of fatty material.

lipid any type of fat (such as fatty acids) or fatlike substance (such as cholesterol).

lipidosis any disorder of fat metabolism.

lipoarthritis inflammation of the fatty tissues of joints.

lipoblast an immature fat cell.

lipoblastoma a tumor of fatty tissue; lipoma.

lipocardiac 1. relating to fatty degeneration of the heart. 2. a person who suffers from fatty degeneration of the heart.

lipochondroma a tumor that contains both fat and cartilage.

lipoclasis lipolysis; the splitting up of fat.

lipocyte a fat cell.

lipodystrophy a disorder of metabolism of fat that affects chiefly women and is marked by obesity of the buttocks and legs.

lipofibroma a fatty tumor that contains a relatively large amount of fibrous tissue. Also called *fibrolipoma.*

lipogenesis the formation and development of fats or fatty tissue. —**lipogenetic** *adj.*

lipogenic fat producing; lipogenetic.

lipogenous producing fat.

lipoid 1. resembling fat. 2. a lipid.

lipoidemia the presence in the bloodstream of an abnormally large quantity of lipids; lipemia.

lipoiduria lipids in the urine.

lipolysis the decomposition or dissolution of fat. —**lipolytic** *adj.*

lipoma *pl.* **lipomas** *or* **lipomata** a tumor of fatty tissue. —**lipomatous** *adj.*

lipomatosis a condition characterized by the excessive deposition of fat in the tissues.

lipostomy congenital absence of the mouth.

Lippes loop an S-shaped plastic intrauterine device.

liquor an aqueous solution of a drug.

lithiasis *pl.* **lithiases** the formation of stony concretions in the body.

lithotomy *pl.* **lithotomies** surgical incision into the bladder to remove a stone.

liver a large vascular organ in the upper right part of the abdomen that secretes bile, maintains the composition of the blood, and regulates many important metabolic processes.

lobar of or relating to a lobe.

lobe a rounded protuberance of a bodily part or organ.

lobotomize to perform a lobotomy on.

lobotomy *pl.* **lobotomies** surgical incision of some or all of the fibers of a lobe of the brain performed for the relief of some mental disorders.

lobule a small lobe or a subsection of a lobe. —**lobular** *adj.*

localized restricted to a limited region or spot.

lockjaw 1. an initial symptom of tetanus in which spasms of the jaw muscles prevents opening of the jaws. 2. tetanus.

locomotor ataxia impairment in the coordination of bodily movements and irregularity of gait often occurring as a late symptom of syphilis.

locum tenens a person who substitutes for another, esp. a physician who temporarily takes over the responsibilities of another physician.

loin 1. the section on each side of the spinal column between the hipbone and the false ribs. 2. *pl.* the abdominal region about the hips including the pubic region. 3. *pl.* genitals.

long bone any of the large, elongated bones supporting a limb.

longevity a long duration of individual life.

lordosis abnormal curvature of the spine in a forward direction. —**lordotic** *adj.*

lotion a liquid preparation for cosmetic use or medicinal soothing of the skin.

louse *pl.* **lice** any of several small wingless insects that are parasitic on warm-blooded animals.

LSD lysergic acid diethylamide; an organic compound sometimes used experimentally in treating mental disorders and often having as side effects hallucinating and psychotic behavior.

lucid having full command of one's faculties; sane.

lues syphilis.

lumbago painful muscular rheumatism of the lumbar region.

lumbar of or relating to the loins or to the region of the back between the hipbone and the false ribs.

lumen *pl.* **lumina** *or* **lumens** the cavity within the tube of an organ or vessel.

lung either of two thoracic organs that are the chief functional organs of respiration.

lunule a crescent-shaped part of the body, as the light-colored area at the base of a nail.

lupus any of various diseases marked by skin lesions, as lupus erythematosus.

luxate to throw out of joint; dislocate. —**luxation** *n.*

lying-in the state or period attending childbirth; confinement.

lymph a transparent, slightly yellowish liquid occurring in the lymphatic vessels, bathing the tissues, and carrying away wastes.

lymphadenitis inflammation of the lymphatic glands.

M

maceration the softening of a solid by soaking it in a fluid substance. —**macerate** *vb.*

macies emaciation.

macrencephaly *also* **macrencephalia** extensive growth of the brain; the condition of having an unusually large brain.

macro- *or* **macr-** *prefix* large; long.

macrobiosis longevity; an unusually long span of life.

macrobiote any organism that is relatively long-lived.

macrobiotic 1. long-lived. 2. tending to extend or prolong life.

macrobiotics the scientific study of factors that influence the prolongation of life.

macroblast a large immature red blood cell (erythroblast).

macroblepharia the state or condition of having unusually large eyelids.

macrobrachia the condition of having unusually long or large arms.

macrocardia the state or condition of having an abnormally enlarged heart. Also called *cardiomegaly.*

macrocardius a person with an abnormally large heart.

macrocephalous *or* **macrocephalic** having an abnormally large head or cranium. —**macrocephaly** *n.*

macrocephalus a fetus with an abnormally large head.

macrocheilia abnormal enlargement of the lips. Also called *macrolabia.*

macrocyte an abnormally large red blood cell occurring in various forms of anemia. —**macrocytic** *adj.*

macroscopic *also* **macroscopical** sufficiently large to be visible to the naked eye.

macula *pl.* **maculae** *or* **maculas** macule. —**macular** *adj.*

macule a discolored but not elevated spot on the skin.

mal any disease or disorder.

mal- *prefix* bad; ill.

malabsorption ineffective or faulty absorption of nutrient materials from the alimentary canal.

malacia an abnormal softening of an organ, structure or part.

-malacia *suffix* abnormal softening.

malaco- *prefix* soft; softening.

malacoma malacia.

malacosis malacia.

malacosteon abnormal softening of the bones; osteomalacia.

malacotic relating to or characterized by an abnormal softening of an organ, structure or part; relating to malacia.

malacotomy surgical incision into soft structures or parts, esp. those of the abdominal wall.

maladie malady; illness; disease.

malady any illness or disease, esp. one of a potentially serious nature.

malaise a general feeling of ill health or torpor often accompanying the onset of a determinable illness.

malar of or relating to the cheek or to the side of the head.

malaria an infectious, febrile protozoal disease transmitted by female *Anopheles* mosquitoes and characterized chiefly by intermittent attacks of chills and fever. —**malarial** *also* **malarian** *adj.*

malariology the branch of medical science concerned with the study and treatment of malaria.

malarious relating to or characterized by the presence or prevalence of malaria.

malassimilation inadequate, incomplete or faulty assimilation of food.

mal comitial epilepsy. See *grand mal* and *petit mal.*

maldigestion inadequate or incomplete digestion.

malemission the failure of semen to be ejaculated from the penis during sexual intercourse.

maleruption imperfect or faulty eruption of a tooth or teeth.

malformation irregular or faulty structure or formation.

malignant tending to produce severe deterioration or death: *malignant disease.* —**malignancy** *n.*

malinger to feign illness so as to avoid duty or work. —**malingerer** *n.* —**malingering** *n.*

malleation a nervous disorder characterized by the repeating hammering or beating of the hands against the thighs.

malleolus *pl.* **malleoli** *or* **malleoluses** a rounded protuberance, as that on either side of the ankle joint.

malleotomy surgical division of the malleus.

malleus the largest of the three conducting bones of the middle ear; hammer.

malnutrition inadequate or faulty nutrition caused by a disorder of assimilation, insufficient dietary intake, or chronic imbalance of the diet.

malocclusion incorrect alignment of the teeth when the jaws are closed, as caused by loss of teeth, imperfect development, or abnormal growth and development of the jaw bones.

maloplasty plastic surgery involving the cheek or cheeks.

malpractice negligent, improper or careless treatment of a patient by physicians, nurses or other qualified medical personnel.

maltase an enzyme active in the hydrolysis of maltose to glucose.

maltose a sugar obtained by the hydrolysis of starch.

malum any disease.

malum caducum epilepsy.

malum cordis heart disease.

malus venereum syphilis.

mamma *pl.* **mammae** a mammary gland; breast. —**mammate** *adj.*

mammal any individual belonging to the class Mammalia, characterized by being warm-blooded vertebrates that suckle their offspring.

mammalogy the branch of biological science concerned with the study of mammals.

mammaplasty *also* **mammoplasty** plastic reconstruction of a breast.

mammary of, relating to, or located near the breasts.

mammary gland either of two large, compound glands situated on the chest of female mammals and modified to secrete milk for the feeding of young.

mammectomy *pl.* **mammectomies** mastectomy; surgical removal of the breast.

mammiform having the shape of a breast; breast-shaped; resembling a breast or mammary gland.

mammill- *or* **mammilli-** *prefix* 1. relating to the nipple or nipples. 2. relating to any small, rounded elevation resembling a nipple.

mammilla *pl.* **mammillae** 1. the nipple. 2. any structure or part that resembles a nipple.

mammillary relating to or resembling a nipple.

mammillated possessing projections or elevations that resemble a nipple.

mammillation 1. the condition of possessing projections or elevations that resemble a nipple. 2. any elevation or projection that resembles a nipple.

mammilliform shaped like a nipple.

mammillitis inflammation of a nipple.

mammitis inflammation of a breast or mammary gland; mastitis.

mammo- *prefix* relating to the breasts or mammary glands.

mammogram an X-ray photograph of the breast or mammary gland.

mammography X-ray examination of the breasts.

mammoplasty mammaplasty.

mammose 1. resembling or shaped like a breast or mammary gland. 2. possessing unusually large breasts.

mammotomy surgical incision into the breast or mammary gland. Also called *mastotomy.*

mammotropic having a direct effect on stimulating the formation, development or growth of the breasts.

mandible the lower jaw.

mandibula *also* **mandibulum** the lower jaw or mandible.

mandibular relating to the lower jaw or mandible.

mandibulectomy surgical removal of part or all of the lower jaw.

mandibulofacial relating to both the lower jaw and the face.

maneuver any specific procedure or movement, esp. in surgery or obstetrics.

mania an abnormal psychic state marked chiefly by elation, disorganized behavior, and physical hyperactivity.

maniac madman; lunatic. —**maniacal** *adj.*

manic affected with or resembling mania.

manic-depressive marked by psychotic alternation between seizures of mania and depression. —**manic-depressive** *n.*

manifestation (in medicine) the exhibition or development of specific diagnostic signs or symptoms of a disease or disorder.

maniphalanx any bony segment of a finger.

manometer any of various instruments for measuring gas or vapor pressure. —**manometric** *adj.* —**manometry** *n.*

mantle any layer that covers a structure or part.

manubrium *pl.* **manubria** an anatomical part or process shaped like a handle, esp. the upper part of the breastbone.

manus the hand.

manustupration masturbation.

marasmus progressive emaciation, esp. in the very young, resulting from malnutrition. —**marasmic** *adj.*

marcid wasting away or emaciating.

marcor marasmus.

margo margin or border; edge.

marihuana *or* **marijuana** cannabis.

mariposia the ingestion or drinking of sea water.

marmorated (of the skin) having a streaked or marble-like appearance.

marrow the soft, vascular substance that fills the cavities of most bones.

martial relating to or containing iron.

maschaladenitis inflammation of the axillary glands.

maschale axilla.

maschalephidrosis sweating in the armpits (axillae).

maschaloneus a tumor in the armpit or axilla.

maschalyperidrosis excessive sweating in the armpits.

masculine relating to or having male characteristics.

masculinity the sexual characteristics (primary and secondary) of the male.

masculinization the normal or (in women) abnormal development of male characteristics. —**masculinize** vb.

masculinus masculine.

masochism a form of sexual deviation in which pleasure is gained through being punished or humiliated. —**masochist** n. —**masochistic** adj.

masque mask.

massa a lump or mass; an accumulation of coherent material.

massage therapeutic stroking or kneading of the body, esp. to promote circulation of the blood or to relax muscles.

masseter a large, powerful muscle that raises the lower jaw and assists in chewing. —**masseteric** adj.

masseur a man skilled in massage and physiotherapy.

masseuse a woman skilled in massage and physiotherapy.

massotherapy the therapeutic use of massage.

mast- or **masto-** prefix breast; mammary gland.

mastadenitis inflammation of a breast or mammary gland; mastitis.

mastadenoma a benign tumor of the breast.

mastalgia pain in the breast. Also called mastodynia.

mastatrophy also **mastatrophia** a wasting away or atrophy of breast tissues; degeneration of the mammary glands.

mastauxe excessive growth of breast tissues; hypertrophy of the breasts.

mast cell a large cell occurring in connective tissue.

mastectomy pl. **mastectomies** surgical removal of a breast; mammectomy.

masthelcosis the formation of ulcers of the breasts; ulceration of the breast.

mastication the process of moving the jaws in chewing, esp. in preparation for swallowing food. —**masticate** vb. —**masticatory** n.

masticatus chewed or masticated.

mastitis inflammation of the breast or udder. —**mastitic** adj.

masto- or **mast-** prefix relating to or involving the breast.

mastodynia pain in the breast. Also called mastalgia.

mastoid 1. relating to or being a process of the temporal bone behind the ear. 2. resembling or shaped like a breast. —**mastoidal** adj.

mastoidectomy pl. **mastoidectomies** surgical removal of the mastoid process.

mastoiditis inflammation of the mastoid process.

mastoidotomy surgical incision into the mastoid process.

mastology the branch of medical science concerned with the anatomy, physiology and pathology of the breasts or mammary glands.

mastoncus a swelling or tumor of the breasts.

mastoparietal relating to the suture that unites the mastoid process and the parietal bone of the skull or to the bones themselves.

mastopathy any disease or disorder that involves the breasts or mammary glands.

mastopexy a surgical procedure for correcting excessively sagging breasts.

mastoplasia abnormal or excessive enlargement of the breasts.

mastoplasty any form of plastic surgery that involves the breasts.

mastoptosis a sagging of the breasts.

mastorrhagia bleeding from a breast or mammary gland.

mastosyrinx a fistula of the breast.

mastotomy surgical incision of the breast or mammary gland.

masturbation stimulation of the genitals exclusive of sexual intercourse and typically with the purpose of inducing orgasm. —**masturbate** vb. —**masturbatory** adj.

mater 1. anything that nourishes or forms. 2. mother.

materia substance; matter.

materia medica the branch of medical science dealing with drugs and medicines.

materies morbi any substance that is the direct cause of a disease.

maternal relating to or coming or derived from a mother.

maternity 1. relating to the obstetrical ward or department of a hospital or medical center. 2. the state or condition of being a mother; motherhood.

matrical relating to a matrix.

matricide 1. the murder of one's mother. 2. one who kills their own mother.

matrix 1. the intercellular substance of a tissue. 2. a mold in which something is cast. 3. the formative portion of a nail or a tooth. 4. the uterus or womb.

matter 1. any substance. 2. pus.

maturate (of a wound) to exude pus; suppurate.

maturation the process of becoming fully developed.

maxilla pl. **maxillae** or **maxillas** the upper jaw. —**maxillary** adj.

maxillitis inflammation of the upper jaw.

maxillodental relating to the upper jaw and the teeth it contains.

maxillofacial relating to the jaws and face.

maxillomandibular relating to both the upper and lower jaws.

maximus (in anatomical nomenclature) greatest.

mayidism pellagra.

MBC abbr. maximum breathing capacity.

M.C. abbr. 1. Medical Corps. 2. Master of Surgery (Magister Chirurgiae).

M.D. abbr. Doctor of Medicine (Medicinae Doctor).

M.D.S. abbr. Master of Dental Surgery.

measles a contagious viral disease, esp. of childhood, marked chiefly by the eruption of red circular spots on the skin and by infection of the respiratory tract.

meato- prefix relating to a meatus.

meatotomy surgical incision to enlarge the meatus of the urethra.

meatus pl. **meatuses** or **meatus** an opening to a body passage or organ. —**meatal** adj.

mechanophobia an abnormal fear of machines or machinery.

meconism addiction to or poisoning from the prolonged use of opium.

meconium 1. fecal matter accumulated in the bowel during fetal development and evacuated shortly after birth. 2. opium.

mediad toward the middle line.

medial relating to or located at or near the middle; median.

medialis medial.

median situated in the middle of the body or a part; central; medial.

medianum or **medianus** medial.

mediastinitis inflammation of the cellular components of the mediastinum.

mediastinography X-ray photography of the mediastinum.

mediastinum pl. **mediastina** a septum or space between two parts, esp. the space between the lungs containing the heart and other thoracic organs.

medic one who is engaged in medicine, esp. an assistant to a physician.

medicable capable of being treated; admitting of treatment and possible cure.

medical of, relating to, or involving the practice of medicine or physicians.

medical examiner a public official who performs post mortems to determine the cause of death.

medicament a substance or agent used to ease physical discomfort or treat disease.

medicate 1. to treat with medicine. 2. to infuse with a medication. —**medicated** adj.

medication 1. the process or act of medicating. 2. a substance or agent that promotes healing or soothes pain.

medicinal used to cure disease or relieve pain.

medicine 1. a preparation, substance, or drug used in treating disease. 2. the science of maintaining good health and of the alleviating, preventing, or curing of disease or injury.

medico pl. **medicos** a physician or medical student.

medico- or **medi-** prefix medical.

medicobiologic also **medicobiological** relating to the biological aspects of medicine or medical science.

medicochirurgical 1. relating to both medicine and surgery. 2. relating to both physicians and surgeons.

medicolegal relating to or concerning both medicine and the law.

medicomechanical (of therapy) relating to the use of both medical and mechanical measures.

medicus a physician or medical doctor.

mediocarpal relating to the central part of the wrist (carpus).

medulla pl. **medullas** or **medullae** 1. marrow. 2. the central part of an organ. 3. medulla oblongata.

medulla oblongata the lower portion of the brainstem continuous posteriorly with the spinal cord.

medullary also **medullar** of or relating to marrow or to a medulla.

mega- or **meg-** prefix large; great.

megabacterium a bacterium of unusually large size.

megacardia an abnormally enlarged heart. Also called cardiomegaly.

megacephaly the condition of having an abnormally large head.

megacolon a condition in which the colon is abnormally large and dilated.

megacycle one million cycles.

megadactyl having or characterized by unusually large fingers. —**megadactyly** n.

megadolichocolon a condition in which the colon is unusually long and dilated.

megakaryocyte a large cell found chiefly in bone marrow and regarded as being the source of blood platelets.

megal- or **megalo-** prefix large; giant; enormous.

megalgia extremely severe pain.

megalocardia an abnormally enlarged heart; megacardia. Also called cardiomegaly.

megaloencephalic relating to a brain of unusually large size. —**megaloencephaly** n.

megaloenteron the state or condition of having an unusually large intestine.

megalogastria the state or condition of having an unusually large stomach.

megalomania a delusional disorder marked by infantile convictions of one's own worth, importance, power, or greatness. —**megalomaniac** n. —**megalomaniacal** or **megalomanic** adj.

megalosplenia splenomegaly.

megalourethra a congenital dilation of the urethra.

megarectum extreme dilation of the rectum.

megavolt one million volts.

megohm one million ohms (a measure of electrical resistance).

megrim migraine.

meiosis the process of cell division resulting in the number of chromosomes in gamete-producing cells being reduced to one-half. —**meiotic** adj.

melalgia pain in an arm or leg, esp. pain that radiates from the foot to the upper leg or thigh (possibly caused by a disease related to vitamin deficiency).

melan- or **melano-** prefix dark; black.

melancholia an abnormal mental condition marked by extreme depression, impaired bodily and mental activity, loss of appetite, and insomnia. —**melancholiac** n. —**melancholic** adj.

melanin the dark brown pigment of the skin and hair.

melanism an excessive amount of dark pigmentation of the skin and hair. —**melanistic** adj.

melanoderma an abnormal deposition of melanin or metallic substances (such as iron or silver) in the skin causing severe darkening.

melanodermatitis the deposit of excessive amounts of melanin in an inflamed area of skin.

melanoid a dark pigment resembling melanin.

melanoma pl. **melanomas** or **melanomata** a dark-pigmented, usually malignant tumor.

melanomatosis a condition characterized by the widespread occurrence of melanomas.

melanonychia discoloration of the nails with a black pigment.

melanoplakia an abnormal condition characterized by the deposition of pigmented patches on the tongue and the inner surfaces of the cheeks.

melanosis a condition marked by abnormally intense dark pigmentation of the tissues of the body.

melanosity a dark complexion.

melanotic relating to or characterized by melanosis.

melanotrichous possessing black hair.

melanous having a dark complexion; brunette.

melanuria a condition in which the excreted urine has an abnormally dark color, caused by the presence of various pigments and the derivatives of products containing coal tar.

melasma gravidarum the unusual but often temporary discoloration of the skin during pregnancy.

melasma universale a patchy pigmentation of the skin occurring in old age.

melena the passage of dark, tarry stools as the result of traces of blood in the intestinal secretions and juices.

membrana *pl.* **membranae** a membrane.

membrana abdominis the peritoneum.

membranaceous membranous.

membrana cordis the pericardium.

membranate resembling a membrane; having the nature of a membrane.

membrane a thin, pliable layer of tissue. —**membranous** *adj.*

membraniform having the characteristics of appearance of a membrane.

membrum *pl.* **membra** a member or limb.

membrum muliebre the clitoris.

membrum virile the penis.

menarche the beginning of menstruation. —**menarcheal** *adj.*

mendelism the body of hereditary and genetic principles derived from Mendel's laws.

Mendel's laws laws of genetics stating that characteristics are determined by pairs of factors (genes); one member of each pair is dominant to the other; the members of each pair separate during gamete formation so that the gametes contain only one factor for each characteristic.

Menière's disease a dysfuntion of the membranous labyrinth of the inner ear marked by attacks of tinnitis, dizziness, and deafness. Also called *Menière's syndrome*.

meningeal of or relating to the meninges.

meninges the three membranes that surround the brain and spinal cord; the pia mater, arachnoid and dura mater.

meningioma *pl.* **meningiomas** *or* **meningiomata** a slow-growing tumor arising from the meninges and often exerting pressure on the brain.

meningism a condition that simulates meningitis but is characterized by irritation rather than true inflammation.

meningitis inflammation of the meninges. —**meningitic** *adj.*

meningo- *or* **mening-** *prefix* relating to the meninges.

meningocele protrusion of the covering membranes of the brain or spinal cord through a gap or defect in the skull or vertebral column.

meningocortical relating to both the meninges of the brain and the cerebral cortex.

meningoencephalitis inflammation of both the brain and its covering membranes (meninges). Also called *cerebro-meningitis*.

meningomyelocele protrusion through a defect in the vertebral column of a part of the spinal cord and its covering membranes.

meningopathy any disease or disorder of the covering membranes of the brain or spinal cord.

meningoradiculitis inflammation of both the spinal meninges and the roots of the spinal nerves.

meningorhachidian relating to both the spinal cord and its covering membranes.

meningorrhagia bleeding into or beneath the covering membranes of the brain or spinal cord.

meninx *pl.* **meninges** any of the three membranes surrounding the brain and spinal cord.

meniscectomy surgical removal of a meniscus, esp. one from the knee joint.

meniscotome a knife-like instrument used in the surgical removal of a meniscus.

meniscus any crescent-shaped structure or part, esp. the crescentic cartilage of the knee joint (*meniscus medialis*).

meno- *prefix* relating to menstruation or to the menses.

menolipsis a temporary interruption or cessation of menstruation.

menopause the period, usually occurring between the ages of 45 and 50, during which menstruation ceases. —**menopausal** *adj.*

menorrhagia abnormally heavy menstrual flow. —**menorrhagic** *adj.*

menosepsis a relatively rare form of blood poisoning caused by the absorption of septic material from retained menstrual blood.

menostasis *also* **menostasia** the absence of menstruation. Also called *amenorrhea*.

menostaxis an unusually prolonged flow of menstrual blood.

menothermal relating to hot flushes experienced as one symptom of the menopause.

menouria an abnormal condition in which some of the menstrual blood flows into the urinary bladder as a result of a fistula between the uterus and the bladder.

menoxenia any disorder or abnormality of menstruation.

menses the menstrual flow.

menstruant menstruating.

menstruation a discharge of tissue debris, secretions, and blood from the uterus in nonpregnant females from puberty occurring at approximately monthly intervals. —**menstrual** *adj.* —**menstruate** *vb.*

mental 1. of or relating to the mind. 2. of or relating to the chin.

mental defective one who has mental deficiency.

mental deficiency inadequate mental development usually attributed to a brain disorder or defect and thought to be incurable; feeblemindedness.

meprobamate a mild tranquilizer used in the relief of anxiety states and emotional tension.

meralgia pain in the upper part of the leg or thigh.

mes- *or* **meso-** *prefix* mid; middle; intermediate.

mesaortitis inflammation of the middle coat of the aorta.

mesarteritis inflammation of the middle coat of any artery.

mescaline a poisonous alkaloid derived from the dried tops of the mescal cactus and used as an antispasmodic and as a stimulant and hallucinogen. Also called *peyote*.

mescalism addiction to mescaline or psychological dependence on its effects (exotic or beautiful visions).

mesencephalon the middle part of the brain; midbrain. —**mesencephalic** *adj.*

mesencephalotomy surgical interruption of any of the fiber tracts or section of any of the tissues in the midbrain, as in the relief of intractable pain.

mesenteric of or relating to a mesentery.

mesenteritis inflammation of a mesentery.

mesenterium mesentery.

mesentery a membrane in the form of a double fold serving as attachment for various bodily organs, esp. the peritoneal fold connecting the small intestine to the back wall of the body.

mesmerism hypnotism. —**mesmeric** adj.

mesoderm the middle of the three primary germ layers of an embryo that develops into bone, muscle, connective tissue, and other structures. —**mesodermal** or **mesodermic** adj.

mesomorph one having a husky, muscular body build. —**mesomorphic** adj.

mesothelium pl. **mesothelia** epithelium derived from the mesoderm and lining serous body cavities. —**mesothelial** adj.

metabolism the chemical changes in living cells through which energy is provided for vital activities and processes by the breakdown of molecules and new molecules are synthesized to replace them. —**metabolic** adj.

metabolite any product of metabolism, such as an intermediate substance or waste product, esp. as produced during catabolism.

metabolize to subject to or perform metabolism.

metacarpal 1. of or relating to the metacarpus. 2. a bone of the metacarpus.

metacarpus the skeletal part of the hand between the carpus and the phalanges that is made up of the five elongated bones of the palm.

metaplasia the transformation of one kind of tissue into another form of tissue.

metastasis pl. **metastases** the transfer of a malignancy or a disease-producing agent from the original site to another part of the body. —**metastatic** adj. —**metastasize** vb.

metatarsal 1. of or relating to the metatarsus. 2. a bone of the metatarsus.

metatarsus the part of the foot between the tarsus and the phalanges.

methylcellulose a tasteless powder that swells when mixed with water, used in antiobesity therapy as a bulk substitute in foods.

metopodynia pain in the forehead, or toward the front of the head; frontal headache.

metra the uterus.

metra- or **metr-** prefix relating to or denoting the uterus.

metralgia pain in the uterus. Also called hysteralgia.

metratonia the lack of muscular tone in the walls of the uterus following childbirth.

metritis inflammation of the uterus.

metrocystosis the formation of cysts in the uterus.

metropathy any disease or disorder involving the uterus.

metrorrhagia profuse bleeding from the uterus at times other than during the normal menstrual period. —**metrorrhagic** adj.

mg. abbr. milligram.

mho the unit of electrical conductivity (the reciprocal of ohm, the unit of electrical resistance).

miasmology the branch of ecology concerned with the study and control of air pollution.

microbe germ; microorganism. —**microbial** or **microbic** adj.

microbicide any agent that kills microorganisms; an antiseptic.

microbiology a branch of biology concerned with microscopic forms of life. —**microbiological** also **microbiologic** adj. —**microbiologist** n.

microcephalic having an abnormally small head. —**microcephaly** n.

micrococcus pl. **micrococci** a small, rounded bacterium. —**micrococcal** adj.

microcyte a small red blood cell. —**microcytic** adj.

microorganism an organism of microscopic size.

microscope an optical instrument for viewing minute objects through magnification. —**microscopy** n.

microscopic also **microscopical** 1. of or relating to a microscope or to the use of a microscope. 2. invisible without the aid of a microscope.

microsome a minute structural part of a cell, consisting of ribosomes associated with endoplasmic reticulum. —**microsomal** adj.

microtome a special knife-like instrument for cutting sections of tissue for microscopic examination.

micturition the act or process of urinating; urination. —**micturate** vb.

midbrain the part of the vertebrate brain between the forebrain and hindbrain.

midgut the central part of the embryonic alimentary canal.

midline the median line or plane of the body or of some part of the body.

midriff the middle section of the human torso, esp. the diaphragm.

midwife a woman who assists another woman in childbirth. —**midwifery** n.

migraine severe headache often accompanied by nausea, vomiting, and distortion of vision. —**migrainous** adj.

miliaria an eruptive, itching inflammation of the skin, as prickly heat.

miliary consisting of a profusion of projecting lesions or tubercles.

milium pl. **milia** a small whitish protrusion of the skin resulting from blockage of the duct of an oil gland.

milk the fluid secreted by the mammary glands of females for the nourishment of their young.

milk tooth any of a set of initial, deciduous teeth replaced by permanent teeth.

miosis pl. **mioses** marked smallness or contraction of the eye pupil. —**miotic** adj.

miscarriage abortion, esp. when spontaneous.

mitochondrion pl. **mitochondria** a long, slender, membranous intracellular body producing energy for a cell. —**mitochondrial** adj.

mitosis pl. **mitoses** the process of division of the nucleus of a cell. —**mitotic** adj.

mitral valve the valve between the left ventricle and the left atrium of the heart. Also called biscupid valve.

molar a tooth with a flattened or rounded surface adapted for grinding food. —**molar** adj.

mole a pigmented protuberance or mark on the human skin.

molecule the smallest particle of a substance, composed of one or more atoms. —**molecular** adj.

mongolism also **mongolianism** a form of congenital idiocy marked by the formation of a broad, short skull, slanting eyes, and broad, short-fingered hands.

mongoloid or **mongolian** of or relating to mongolism.

moniliasis pl. **moniliases** thrush.

monocular of, relating to, or affecting a single eye.

monomania abnormally pronounced concentration on a single idea or object. —**monomaniac** n. —**monomaniac** or **monomaniacal** adj.

mononucleosis an acute, infectious, disease marked by fever, inflammation of the mucous membranes, and swelling of the lymph glands. Also called *infectious mononucleosis* and *glandular fever.*

monosaccharide the simplest form of a sugar, as glucose.

monozygotic twin one of two individuals developing originally from a single egg.

mons pubis the rounded, fleshy mound over the female pubic bones. Also called *mons veneris.*

monster one grotesquely malformed during fetal development.

morbid relating to, characteristic of, or affected with disease. —**morbidity** *n.*

morbus disease.

morgue a place where bodies of persons found dead are kept until they are identified or released for burial.

moribund being in a state approaching death; dying. —**moribundity** *n.*

morning sickness nausea and vomiting occurring during the early months of pregnancy, esp. on arising in the morning.

moron a mentally defective adult with a mental age of between 8 and 12 years.

morphine a bitter, addictive narcotic base that is the chief alkaloid of opium and is used as a sedative and painkiller.

morphinism a state of ill health resulting from the habitual use of morphine.

morphocytology the branch of biology concerned with the study of the size, shape, structure and other physical properties of cells.

morphology a branch of science dealing with the structure and shape of organisms. —**morphological** *adj.* —**morphologically** *adv.* —**morphologist** *n.*

mortality the ratio of the number of deaths to the total population; death rate.

mortuary *pl.* **mortuaries** a place in which dead bodies are kept until burial.

morula *pl.* **morulae** a solid mass of cells constituting an early stage of a fertilized ovum. —**morulation** *n.*

mosaic an organism composed of cells of different genetic types, caused by mutation or an anomaly of chromosome division. —**mosaicism** *n.*

motile capable of independent movement. —**motility** *n.*

motion sickness nausea induced by the movements of travel, as by plane, ship, or car.

motor 1. relating to a nerve that transmits impulses from a nerve center to a muscle or gland. 2. of or relating to movement of the muscles.

mountain sickness sickness resulting from insufficient oxygen at high altitudes.

mucoid resembling or constituting mucus.

mucous 1. secreting or containing mucus. 2. covered with mucus.

mucous membrane a bodily membrane that secretes and is protected by mucus.

mucus a slippery, viscous, glandular secretion produced by mucous membranes.

multiparous having undergone one or more previous childbirths.

multiple myeloma a disease of the bone marrow marked by many myelomas.

mumps a contagious viral disease marked chiefly by fever and swelling of the parotid glands.

mural relating to the wall of any bodily cavity.

murmur an abnormal sound heard on auscultation of the heart, lungs or blood vessels.

muscae volitantes cells and cell fragments in the vitreous humor and lens of the eye that appear as floating spots.

muscicide any agent that kills flies.

muscle body tissue that consists of long cells and expands or contracts a bodily part when stimulated. —**muscular** *adj.*

musculature the muscular structure of the body.

musculus *pl.* **musculi** a muscle.

mutation a change in hereditary genetic material or the resulting morphological or organic change transmitted to a subsequent generation.

mute a person who is unable to speak. —**mute** *adj.*

my- *or* **myo-** *prefix* muscle.

myalgia muscular pain. —**myalgic** *adj.*

myasthenia gravis a disease marked by progressive weakening of the muscles without atrophy.

mycosis *pl.* **mycoses** disease caused by a fungus. —**mycotic** *adj.*

mydriasis prolonged or marked dilation of the pupil of the eye.

mydriatic 1. causing dilation of the pupil. 2. an agent with this action.

myelitis inflammation of bone marrow or of the spinal cord.

myeloid of or relating to the spinal cord or to bone marrow.

myeloma a bone marrow tumor. —**myelomatous** *adj.*

myelopathy disease of the spinal cord or of the bone marrow. —**myelopathic** *adj.*

myocardiograph an instrument for making a traced recording of heart-muscle action. —**myocardiographic** *adj.*

myocarditis inflammation of the myocardium.

myocardium the muscular tissue of the heart.

myogenic relating to or originating from muscle tissue.

myoglobin an oxygen-binding protein in muscles, similar to hemoglobin in blood.

myology the study of muscles. —**myologic** *or* **myological** *adj.*

myoma *pl.* **myomas** *or* **myomata** a tumor composed of muscle tissue. —**myomatous** *adj.*

myopathy any abnormal condition of muscle or muscle tissue. —**myopathic** *adj.*

myope one having myopia.

myopia a condition of the eyes in which a visual image is focused in front of the retina, resulting in imperfect perception of distant objects; nearsightedness. —**myopic** *adj.* —**myopically** *adv.*

myotonia a tonic muscular spasm. —**myotonic** *adj.*

myxedema a hypothyroid condition marked by dry skin and hair, swelling of tissues, and decline of mental and physical vigor. —**myxedematous** *adj.*

myxoma *pl.* **myxomas** *or* **myxomata** a tumor of connective tissue cells. —**myxomatous** *adj.*

N

NAD *abbr.* no appreciable disease.

nail a horny sheath covering and protecting the outer end of each finger and toe.

nalorphine a drug used in the treatment of some types of overdose with narcotics and, since it induces severe withdrawal symptoms in morphine addicts, as a means of diagnosing morphine addiction.

nanism dwarfism.

nano- *prefix* (in the metric system of measurement) one-billionth (10^{-9}).

nanometer one-billionth of a meter; 10^{-9} meter.

nape the back of the neck.

narcissism 1. erotic interest in and attraction to one's own body. 2. egocentricity; egotism. —**narcissist** *n.* —**narcissistic** *adj.*

narcohypnosis deep sleep or unconsciousness induced by hypnosis.

narcolepsy an abnormal condition marked by frequent, sudden periods of deep sleep. —**narcoleptic** *n. & adj.*

narcomania 1. an intense desire or craving for narcotics. 2. severe mental disability caused by addiction to narcotic drugs.

narcosis a condition of unconsciousness or stupor induced by drugs or chemicals.

narcotic a drug, as opium or morphine, that is used in small amounts to ease pain or cause sleep but that in large amounts may cause addiction and death. —**narcotic** *adj.*

naris *pl.* **nares** either of the openings of the nose; nostril.

nasal of or relating to the nose or the nostrils.

THE NASAL CAVITY
(CROSS SECTION)

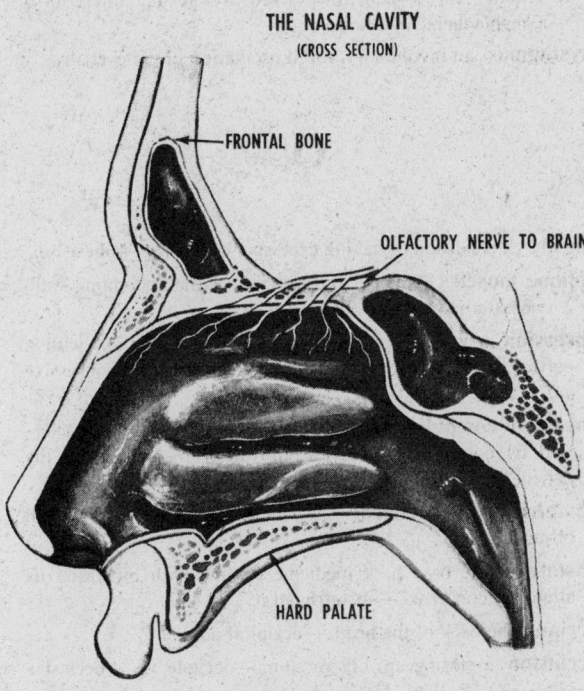

FRONTAL BONE

OLFACTORY NERVE TO BRAIN

HARD PALATE

OLFACTORY SENSE

Specialized sensory neurons, capable of being stimulated by airborne odor particles, are located in the roof of the nasal cavity. The neurons collect into numerous small nerves which form the olfactory nerve. The odors most recognized are floral, fruity, herbal or spicy, resinal, and smoky.

nasopharynx the nasal passages in continuation with the upper pharynx. —**nasopharyngeal** *adj.*

nates buttocks.

nausea a sensation of queasiness in the stomach, often associated with an urge to vomit. —**nauseate** *vb.*

navel a small depression in the center of the abdomen marking the former point of attachment of the umbilical cord; umbilicus.

ne- or **neo-** *prefix* 1. new; recent. 2. new and different in form.

neck 1. the part of an animal that connects the head with the body. 2. a necklike structure or part; cervix.

necrophilia obsessive and usually erotic interest in dead bodies. —**necrophilic** *adj.*

necrophobia an abnormal fear of dead bodies.

necropsy the detailed examination of a body and its organs and parts after death. Also called *post mortem, autopsy.*

necrosis *pl.* **necroses** the localized death of living tissue. —**necrotic** *adj.*

neisseria any of a genus of microorganisms including those causing gonorrhea.

nematode any of various cylindrical parasitic worms; esp. hookworm.

Nembutal a trademark for the sodium salt of pentobarbital.

neomycin a broad-spectrum antibiotic.

neonatal relating to or affecting a newborn infant, esp. during the first month after birth.

neonate a newborn child or one less than a month old.

neoplasia the formation of tumorous tissues. —**neoplastic** *adj.*

neoplasm new and abnormal tissue having no organic function; tumor. —**neoplastic** *adj.*

neph- or **nephro-** *prefix* kidney.

nephrectomy *pl.* **nephrectomies** the surgical removal of a kidney.

nephremorrhagia bleeding into or from the kidney.

nephritic renal; relating to the kidney.

nephritis inflammation of the kidney.

nephrogenic developing in the kidney or produced or originating in kidney tissue. —**nephrogenically** *adv.*

nephron the functional unit of the kidney which filters the blood of its waste products, numbering approximately one million in each kidney.

nephropathy an abnormal state of the kidney. —**nephropathic** *adj.*

nephrosis *pl.* **nephroses** degeneration of the kidneys without inflammation. —**nephrotic** *adj.*

nerve a filamentous band or bundle of nerve fibers outside the central nervous system that connects the brain and spinal cord with various organs and tissues of the body.

nerve gas a war gas that interrupts normal nerve transmission and induces intense respiratory spasm.

nervous 1. relating to or composed of neurons. 2. relating to or affecting the nerves. 3. easily excited or irritated; edgy.

nervous breakdown 1. neurasthenia, esp. when incapacitating. 2. emotional despair, esp. when intense and severe enough to require medical or psychiatric treatment.

nervous system the central nervous system or autonomic nervous system.

nervus *pl.* **nervi** nerve.

nervy excitable; irritable; nervous. —**nerviness** *n.*

nettle rash urticaria; hives.

neural of, relating to, or affecting the nerves or the nervous system. —**neurally** *adv.*

neuralgia acute pain radiating paroxysmally along the course of one or more nerves. —**neuralgic** *adj.*

neurasthenia a fundamentally neurotic condition marked chiefly by exhaustion, feelings of inadequacy, depression, loss of concentration and of appetite, insomnia, and often gastrointestinal disturbance. —**neurasthenic** adj. —**neurasthenically** adv.

neuritis pl. **neuritides** or **neuritises** painful inflammation of a nerve. —**neuritic** adj.

neuroblastoma pl. **neuroblastomas** or **neuroblastomata** a malignant tumor of nerve ganglia.

neurodynia neuralgia.

neuroleptanalgesia or **neuroleptoanalgesia** the administration of an analgesic agent and a tranquilizing drug jointly, esp. as an adjunct to surgery. —**neuroleptanalgesic** or **neuroleptoanalgesic** adj.

neuroleptic a drug used to alleviate mental disturbance; tranquilizer.

neurologist a physician specializing in the diagnosis and treatment of disease of the nervous system. —**neurology** n. —**neurologically** adv.

neuroma pl. **neuromas** or **neuromata** a tumor or new growth arising from a nerve or from nerve fibers.

neuromuscular relating to or involving the nervous system and muscles jointly.

neuron a nerve cell and its processes (axon and dendrites), being the chief unit of the nervous system. —**neuronal** adj. —**neuronic** adj.

neuropathy pl. **neuropathies** an abnormal and often degenerative condition of the nervous system. —**neuropathic** adj. —**neuropathically** adv.

neuropharmacology a branch of medicine concerned with the effects of drugs on the nervous system. —**neuropharmacologic** or **neuropharmacological** adj. —**neuropharmacologist** n.

neuropsychiatry a branch of medicine dealing with the relationships of mental and physical aspects of mental disorders. —**neuropsychiatric** adj. —**neuropsychiatrically** adv. —**neuropsychiatrist** n.

neurosis pl. **neuroses** any of various emotionally based, disabling, functional nervous disorders lacking a related physical lesion. —**neurotic** adj. & n. —**neurotically** adv.

neurosurgery surgery involving any part of the spinal cord, brain, or peripheral nerves. —**neurosurgeon** n. —**neurosurgical** adj. —**neurosurgically** adv.

neurotoxin a poisonous protein complex that acts on the nervous system. —**neurotoxic** adj.

nevus pl. **nevi** a pigmented area of the skin; mole; birthmark.

Newcastle disease a viral disease transmittable to humans that involves respiratory and nervous symptoms.

niacin nicotinic acid.

nicotine a poisonous alkaloid that is the active principle of tobacco.

nicotinic acid an acid of the vitamin B complex used in the treatment of pellagra. Also called niacin.

nictitate to blink the eyelids; wink. —**nictation** n. —**nictitation** n.

night blindness impaired visual capacity in faint light or in darkness. Also called nyctalopia.

nipple the pigmented protuberance in the center of each breast that in the female serves as the outlet for the secretion of milk in nursing.

nit the egg of a parasitic insect, esp. of a louse.

nitrate a salt of nitric acid.

nitric acid a chemical used as a local caustic agent, the fumes from which can be dangerous to health.

nitroglycerin a highly explosive oily liquid, the main constituent of dynamite, used medically as a vasodilator, esp. in the symptomatic relief of pain caused by angina pectoris.

nitrous oxide a colorless gas used chiefly as an anesthetic in dentistry and often producing laughter and exhilaration before the onset of insensibility. Also called laughing gas.

node a thickened or swollen enlargement of a part; a circumscribed mass of tissue: lymph node.

nodus pl. **nodi** node.

noetic relating to the mental processes.

nose the part of the face bearing the nostrils and constituting the chief vehicle for olfactory sensations.

nosology the branch of medical science concerned with the classification or description of diseases. —**nosologic** adj.

noxious physically harmful to living organisms: noxious gases.

nucleic acid an acid composed of sugar or a derivative of a sugar, a base, and phosphoric acid that is found chiefly in cell nuclei.

nucleolus pl. **nucleoli** a small spherical body within the nucleus of a cell, being occasionally one of two to five such bodies within a single cell nucleus.

nulliparous describing a female who has never borne offspring.

nutation the act of nodding the head, esp. involuntarily.

nyctalopia night blindness.

nymphomania abnormally intense sexual desire on the part of a female, esp. when unresolved by sexual intercourse. —**nymphomaniac** n. & adj.

nystagmus an involuntary, rapid oscillation of the eyeballs.

O

obesity a condition of having excessive bodily fat. —**obese** adj.

oblique muscles 1. two large muscles of the abdominal wall. 2. two external muscles of the eyeball.

obsession a persistent, often upsetting preoccupation with a particular idea, object, or person. —**obsess** vb. —**obsessive** adj. & n.

obsessive compulsive neurosis a mental disorder characterized by compulsive behavior known or recognized by the patient himself to be absurd.

obstetric or **obstetrical** of, relating to, or dealing with obstetrics.

obstetrics the branch of medicine dealing with birth and its attendant concerns. —**obstetrician** n.

occiput the back of the head. —**occipital** adj.

occlusion a closing up; obstruction. —**occlude** vb. —**occlusive** adj.

occult blood blood passed in the stools and detectable, because of the very small amounts, only by means of special laboratory tests.

occupational disease disease or disability arising from one's regular occupation.

ocular of or relating to the eyes or to sight. —**ocularly** adv.

oculomotor nerves the third pair of cranial nerves which act to help move the eyeball.

odontalgia toothache.

-odontia suffix of the teeth.

odontolith dental tartar; calcareous material deposited on a tooth.

odontology dentistry.

ohm the unit of electrical resistance. Compare *mho*.

oesophagus esophagus.

olfactory of or relating to the sense of smell.

olig- *or* **oligo-** *prefix* few; deficient; a little.

oligemia lack of blood.

oligospermia abnormally few spermatozoa in the semen.

omentum a free fold supporting or connecting structures within the abdominal cavity.

onychia inflammation of the matrix of a nail.

onychocryptosis an ingrowing nail.

onychomycosis a fungal infection of the nails or a nail.

oogenesis *pl.* **oogeneses** the production of ova within the ovary.

oophorectomy the surgical removal of an ovary.

ophthalm- *or* **ophthalmo-** *prefix* eyeball; eye.

ophthalmia inflammation of the eye and usually the conjunctiva.

ophthalmologist a physician or surgeon specializing in diseases of the eye. —**ophthalmological** *adj.* —**ophthalmology** *n.*

ophthalmoscope a small illuminated instrument for examining the interior of the eye, esp. the retina.

optic of or relating to the eyes or to sight. —**optically** *adv.*

optic disc the point at which the optic nerve enters the eye.

optician a maker of optical instruments and devices.

optometry the profession of examining the eyes for defects of structure and refraction and prescribing corrective lenses. —**optometrist** *n.*

oral of, relating to, or affecting the mouth. —**orally** *adv.*

THE ORAL CAVITY

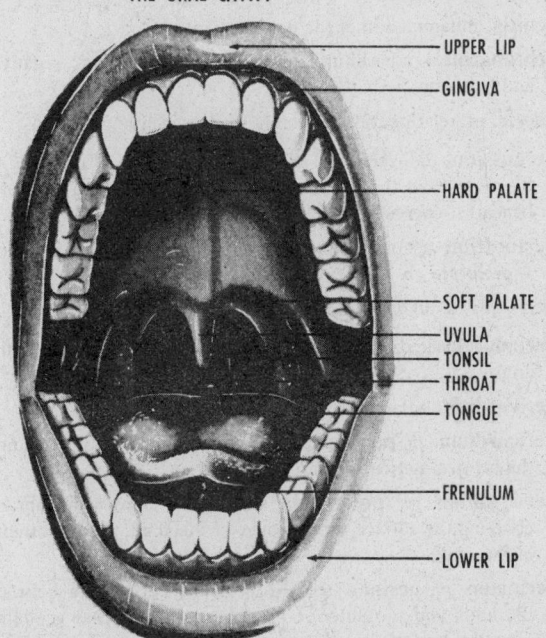

UPPER LIP
GINGIVA
HARD PALATE
SOFT PALATE
UVULA
TONSIL
THROAT
TONGUE
FRENULUM
LOWER LIP

orbit the bony cavity of the skull containing the eyeball.

orchis testicle.

orchitis inflammation of a testicle.

organ a differentiated bodily structure performing specific functions within the body.

organic relating to or affecting the organs of the body: *organic diseases.*

orgasm the climax of sexual excitement, which in the male leads to ejaculation of semen. —**orgasmic** *or* **orgastic** *adj.*

orifice an opening, esp. a natural opening of the body.

os *pl.* **oses** 1. bone. 2. mouth; orifice.

osseous resembling or composed of bone; bony.

ossicle a small bone or bony structure, esp. any of the three sound-conducting bones of the middle ear. —**ossicular** *adj.* —**ossiculate** *adj.*

ossification 1. the formation of bone. 2. the abnormal change into bone, as of connective tissues. —**ossify** *vb.*

oste- *or* **osteo-** *prefix* bone.

osteitis inflammation of bone.

osteoarthritis degenerative arthritis chiefly of the larger joints.

osteomyelitis inflammation of bone marrow.

osteopathy medical practice that ascribes the source of many diseases to be loss of structural integrity and uses the manipulation of joints as a healing technique. —**osteopath** *n.* —**osteopathic** *adj.*

otalgia earache.

otitis inflammation of the ear.

ovarian relating to or affecting the ovaries.

ovariectomy *pl.* **ovariectomies** the surgical removal of an ovary. —**ovariectomized** *adj.*

ovaritis inflammation of an ovary.

ovary *pl.* **ovaries** either of two female reproductive organs that produce eggs and female sex hormones.

ovulation the monthly development and discharge of a mature ovum from an ovary. —**ovulate** *vb.*

ovum *pl.* **ova** a female gamete; egg.

oxygenation to saturate or supply with oxygen. —**oxygenate** *vb.*

P

pacemaker 1. an area in the wall of the heart (sino-atrial node) where the impulse is generated that governs the rhythm of the heart's activity. 2. an electrical device for steadying or stimulating the action of the heart or for re-establishing the action of an arrested heart. Also called *artificial pacemaker.*

pachydermatous having an abnormal thickening of the skin.

pachydermia thickening of the skin.

pachylosis a condition characterized by an abnormally rough, dry and thick skin, esp. of the legs.

pachymeningitis inflammation and thickening of the outermost membrane (dura mater) that covers the brain and spinal cord.

paediatrics pediatrics.

pain a usually localized physical suffering associated with a bodily disorder, injury, or disease. —**painful** *adj.* —**painfully** *adv.* —**painfulness** *n.*

painter's colic lead poisoning.

palliative 1. a medicine or method of treatment that eases symptoms of a disease. 2. relating to the relief of symptoms; mitigating.

pallor deficiency of natural color of the skin, esp. of the face; paleness.

palm the flexible surface of the hand between the wrist and the base of the fingers.

palmar relating to or located on the palm.

palpation medical examination by means of the sense of touch. —**palpate** vb.

palpebra pl. **palpebrae** eyelid.

palpebral relating to an eyelid or to the eyelids.

palpebrate 1. having eyelids. 2. to open and close the eyelids very quickly; wink.

palpebration the act of winking.

palpitation a pronounced throbbing or pulsation of the heart that is perceptible to the patient. —**palpitate** vb.

palsy paralysis or partial paralysis; paresis.

paludism malaria.

panacea a remedy that is claimed to cure all ills.

pancreas a large gland that secretes digestive enzymes and insulin. —**pancreatic** adj.

pancreatic juice a clear, alkaline fluid produced by the pancreas and important to the digestive process.

pancreatitis, inflammation of the pancreas.

pandemic occurring over a large area and affecting large numbers of people: pandemic diseases.

papilla pl. **papillae** a small, nipple-shaped structure.

papilloma a benign tumor composed of epithelial tissue and characterized by one or more outward projections or outgrowths.

papule a small, conical elevation of the skin. —**papular** adj.

para- or **par-** prefix 1. alongside. 2. abnormal; faulty.

paracentesis withdrawal of fluid from a bodily cavity by means of surgical puncture and aspiration. —**paracentetic** adj.

paradenitis inflammation of the tissues that surround or are adjacent to a gland.

parageusia an impairment of the sense of taste.

paralysis pl. **paralyses** loss of function in part of the body, esp. when involving sensation or motion. —**paralytic** adj. —**paralyze** vb.

paramedian near the middle line of an organ, structure or part.

paramedical supplementing the work of professional medical personnel. —**paramedic** n. & adj.

paranoia a psychosis characterized chiefly by delusions of persecution or grandeur. —**paranoiac** adj. & n. —**paranoid** adj. & n.

paranoid schizophrenia a psychosis characterized by paranoia along with hallucinations and often characterized by mental deterioration.

paraplegia paralysis of the lower half of the torso and of both legs. —**paraplegic** adj. & n.

parasympathetic nervous system a part of the autonomic nervous system.

paresis partial or incomplete paralysis.

paresthesia an unaccountable numb, creeping, tingling, or prickling sensation of the skin.

parietal relating to the parietal bone of the skull.

parietal bone either of the two bones that together form the sides and roof of the skull.

Parkinson's disease a progressive disease, esp. of late life, marked by tremors and rigidity of resting muscles and by an shuffling gait when walking. Also called parkinsonism, Parkinson's syndrome.

parolfactory related to or associated with the sense of smell or the olfactory system.

parotid gland either of a pair of large salivary glands located below and in front of the ear.

parotitis 1. inflammation of a parotid gland. 2. mumps (properly, infectious parotitis).

paroxysm 1. the sudden flare-up of the symptoms of a disease. 2. a fit or convulsion. —**paroxysmal** adj.

pars pl. **partes** a part.

parturient giving or about to give birth.

parturition the act of giving birth to young; childbirth.

partus parturition; childbirth.

parvus small.

pasteurization exposure of a substance, as milk, to controlled heat to kill certain organisms without altering the chemical structure. —**pasteurize** vb.

patella pl. **patellae** or **patellias** a thick, triangular, movable bone at the front of the knee; kneecap.

pathogenic capable of causing disease: pathogenic bacteria. —**pathogenesis** n.

pathology the branch of medicine dealing with the nature of diseases and the bodily changes they cause. —**pathologic** or **pathological** adj. —**pathologist** n.

pathophobia an abnormal fear of disease.

pectoral of or relating to the chest or its muscles.

pediculosis the state or condition of being infested with lice.

pelvis pl. **pelvises** or **pelves** 1. the bony cavity outlined by the hips and lower bones of the spine and holding the lower intestine, bladder and (in females) the internal genital organs. 2. any bodily cavity resembling a basin or cup, such as that at the base of the kidney (renal pelvis). —**pelvic** adj.

penicillin any of several antibiotics produced by molds or synthetically and used esp. against cocci.

penile of or relating to the penis.

penis the male organ of copulation, composed of erectile tissue and containing the urethra.

penitis inflammation of the penis.

pentobarbital a barbiturate used as an antispasmodic, sedative, and hypnotic.

peptic of, relating to, or affecting the stomach or digestion.

percussion the technique of tapping the surface of the body to diagnose from the resultant sound the condition of the parts beneath. —**percuss** vb.

perforation a hole in an organ produced by disease or injury. —**perforate** vb.

peri- prefix all around; about.

perianal located around the area of the anus; surrounding the anus.

pericarditis inflammation of the pericardium.

pericardium pl. **pericardia** the membranous sac surrounding the heart. —**pericardial** adj.

pericranium pl. **pericrania** the thick, fibrous membrane covering the surface of the bones of the skull; the periosteum of the skull.

perineum pl. **perinea** the region of the pelvic floor between the anus and the anterior portion of the external genitalia. —**perineal** adj.

peristalsis the involuntary muscular waves of the intestine that move the contents onward. —**peristaltic** adj. —**peristaltically** adv.

peritoneum pl. **peritoneums** or **peritonea** the transparent membrane that lines the abdominal cavity. —**peritoneal** adj.

pernicious highly destructive or injurious; deadly: pernicious anemia.

PEPTIC ULCER

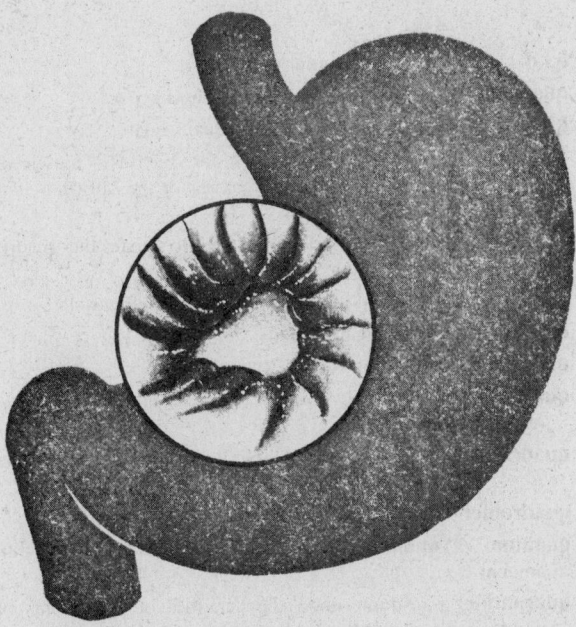

A peptic ulcer is a benign crater in the mucous membrane of the stomach or duodenum, caused by the action of the acid gastric juice.

peroral occurring through or taken by way of the mouth. —**perorally** adv.

pertussis whooping cough.

perversion an aberrant sexual practice.

pes pl. **pedes** foot.

pessary pl. **pessaries** 1. a device placed in the vagina to support the uterus or prevent conception. 2. a vaginal suppository.

pestilence an epidemic disease.

petit mal a mild form of epilepsy.

phagocyte a white blood corpuscle that typically consumes and destroys debris and foreign bodies.

phalanx pl. **phalanxes** or **phalanges** one of the digital bones of the hand or foot.

phallus pl. **phalluses** or **phalli** 1. the penis. 2. anything resembling or suggestive of a penis. —**phallic** adj.

phantom limb the sensation sometimes experienced after amputation of a limb that the limb is still there.

pharmaceutical 1. of or relating to pharmacy or to pharmacists. 2. of or relating to a drug or drugs. 3. a medicinal drug. —**pharmaceutically** adv.

pharmaco- prefix medicine; drug.

pharmacology the science dealing with medicinal drugs and their action on the body. —**pharmacological** adj. —**pharmacologist** n.

pharmacopoeia an official book describing drugs, medicinal preparations, and chemicals.

pharmacy pl. **pharmacies** 1. the practice of preparing, compounding, and dispensing drugs. 2. a place where drugs and medicines are compounded and dispensed. —**pharmacist** n.

pharyngeal of or relating to the pharynx.

pharyngitis inflammation of the pharynx.

pharynx the part of the alimentary canal between the mouth and the esophagus; the lower back part of the throat.

phimosis severe contraction of the foreskin usually requiring circumcision.

phlebectomy pl. **phlebectomies** excision of a vein.

phlebitis inflammation of a vein.

phlebotomy pl. **phlebotomies** the bleeding of a patient by the opening of a vein, as in the treatment of polycythemia.

phlegm a thick mucus produced in abnormal quantities by the respiratory passages.

phosphoprotein any of various proteins combined with a compound containing phosphorus.

phrenic 1. of or relating to the diaphragm. 2. relating to the mind.

phthisis an older name for tuberculosis of the lungs.

physiology a branch of biology dealing with the structure and function of living organisms. —**physiological** adj. —**physiologist** n.

physiotherapy therapy involving the use of heat, massage and exercise rather than medication. —**physiotherapist** n.

piles the informal name for hemorrhoids.

pimple a small, inflamed, pus-filled elevation of the skin; pustule. —**pimpled** adj. —**pimply** adj.

pink eye infectious conjunctivitis.

pituitary gland an endocrine gland at the base of the brain producing various essential hormones.

placebo a chemically inactive agent given to reassure a patient or used in the double-blind or single-blind evaluation of active drugs, where one group of patients receives the test drug and another the inactive agent.

placenta the vascular organ surrounding the fetus within the uterus. —**placental** adj.

plague an acute, infectious bacterial disease transmitted to man by rat fleas.

plantar relating to, affecting, or occurring on the sole of the foot: plantar wart.

plasma the liquid portion of the blood, in which the corpuscles are suspended.

plastic surgery surgical repair or restoration of damaged or deformed tissue. —**plastic surgeon.**

pleura pl. **pleurae** or **pleuras** a thin membrane lining the lungs and the inner surface of the chest cavity.

pleurisy inflammation of the pleura.

plexus a network of interlacing nerves or blood vessels.

pneumoconiosis fibrosis of the lungs from prolonged inhalation of irritant dust particles.

pneumonia a disease marked by severe inflammation of the lungs.

pockmark a cavity of the skin caused by a pustule, as from smallpox or acne.

podiatrist a physician specializing in the care and treatment of the feet. —**podiatry** n.

poliomyelitis a viral disease marked by inflammation of the nerve cells of the spinal cord, deformity, and paralysis. Also called infantile paralysis, polio.

polycythemia an abnormal increase in the total number of circulating red blood cells.

polyp a small projecting tumor, esp. in a body cavity or passage.

pons the bridge of tissue at the base of the brain that connects the medulla oblongata with the cerebral hemispheres and the cerebellum. Also called pons Varolii.

post mortem necropsy; autopsy.

postpartum following parturition.

postprandial following meals: *postprandial medication.*

poultice a moist bandage applied over a wound.

prepuce foreskin.

pressure point a point at which pressure may be applied to check hemorrhage.

prickly heat inflammation around the sweat ducts causing redness and itching.

primipara a woman who has borne only one child.

probe a slender instrument for exploring wounds.

proctology a branch of medicine dealing chiefly with the structure and diseases of the lower bowel. —**protological** *adj.* —**proctologist** *n.*

proctoscope an instrument for examining the interior of the rectum.

prostatectomy *pl.* **prostatectomies** surgical removal of the prostate gland.

prostate gland a muscular gland at the base of the male urethra that secretes the viscid fluid that is a major constituent of semen. —**prostatic** *adj.*

prostatitis inflammation of the prostate gland.

prosthesis replacement of an absent organ or limb with an artificial one. —**prosthetics** *n.*

pruritis an itching of the skin.

psittacosis a viral disease of birds, as parrots, transmittable to man.

psoriasis a skin disease marked by the formation of red scaly patches.

psychiatrist a physician who specializes in psychiatry.

psychiatry a branch of medicine that deals with mental, emotional, or behavioral disorders. —**psychiatric** *adj.* —**psychiatrically** *adv.*

psychoanalysis a method of treating emotional disorders in which the patient talks freely about himself and esp. about his dreams and childhood to an analyst. —**psychoanalytic** *adj.*

psychology the science concerned with the mind and human behavior. —**psychological** *adj.* —**psychologist** *n.*

psychopath a mentally deranged person. —**psychopathic** *adj.*

psychosis severe, disabling mental derangement marked esp. by a loss of contact with reality. —**psychotic** *n. & adj.*

psychosomatic relating to or involving both psychological and physical factors: *psychosomatic illness.*

puberty the age at which a person becomes capable of reproducing sexually and during which the genitals mature and the secondary sex characteristics appear; generally between the ages of 12 and 14.

pubes 1. the hair that appears just above the external genital organs at puberty. 2. the two bones forming the front of the pelvis. —**pubic** *adj.*

pupil the round, contractive area in the center of the eye.

purgative a medicine for inducing evacuation of the bowels.

pus a thick, opaque whitish fluid containing cellular debris and being a product of inflammation or infection.

pustule a small elevation of the skin containing pus. —**pustular** *adj.*

pyelitis inflammation of the pelvis of the kidney.

pylorus *pl.* **pylori** the valve-like opening of the stomach into the duodenum. —**pyloric** *adj.*

Q

q.i.d. *abbr.* quater in die: four times daily.

quack a pretender to medical skills. —**quackery** *n.*

quadrate having four sides that are equal; square.

quadriceps a muscle having four heads, such as a muscle of the thigh (*musculus quadriceps femoris*) or the calf (*musculus quadriceps surae*).

quadricepsplasty a surgical procedure to repair the quadriceps muscle of the thigh.

quadricuspid having four cusps. Also called *tetracuspid.*

quadridigitate having four digits.

quadriplegia paralysis of both legs and arms.

quadriplegic 1. relating to quadriplegia. 2. one with paralysis of all four limbs.

quadrisect to divide or separate into four parts. —**quadrisection** *n.*

quadruplet one of four children born at one birth.

quantum *pl.* **quanta** 1. a unit of radiant energy. 2. a definite amount.

quarantine a restraint upon the activities or movements of anyone with a communicable disease in order to inhibit its spread; detention and isolation from others for a given period of anyone with a contagious disease.

quartan recurring every fourth day.

quater in die (in prescription writing) four times daily.

quaternary 1. (of a chemical compound) containing four elements. 2. coming fourth in a series.

quick 1. pregnant with a child whose movement can be felt within the uterus. 2. any sensitive part that is particularly painful to touch. 3. the part of a finger or toe to which the nail is attached.

quickening the first indications of movement of the fetus within the uterus, usually noted within the first 16 to 20 weeks of pregnancy.

quicksilver mercury.

quin- *or* **quino-** *prefix* relating to or containing quinoline or quinine.

quinine a white, crystalline alkaloid derived from cinchona bark and used as an analgesic, antipyretic and antimalarial agent.

quinoline a substance derived from coal tar and used medically as an analgesic, antipyretic and in the treatment of amoebic dysentery and related infections.

quinsy inflammation of the throat with swelling and fever.

quintan recurring every fifth day.

quinti- *prefix* fifth.

quintipara a woman who has given birth five times.

quintuplet one of five children born at one birth.

quotidian occurring each day; recurring daily.

quotidian fever a malarial fever that flares up every day during the illness.

R

rabbit fever tularemia.

rabiate suffering from rabies.

rabic relating to or concerning rabies.

rabicidal destructive to the virus that causes rabies.

rabid affected with rabies.

rabies an acute and inevitably fatal viral disease transmitted by the bite of a rabid animal.

racemose (esp. of a gland) resembling a bunch of grapes.

rachi- or **rachio-** *prefix* relating to or indicating the spinal column.

rachialgia pain in the spine. Also called *rachiodynia*.

rachianalgesia spinal anesthesia.

rachidian relating to the spinal column.

rachiodynia pain in the spine. Also called *rachialgia*.

rachis *pl.* **rachises** *also* **rachides** spinal column.

rachitic relating to or affected with rickets; rickety.

radectomy surgical removal of all or part of the root of a tooth.

radiad in the direction of a radius or the radial side of a structure or part.

radical 1. (in chemistry) a group of atoms that act as a single unit, capable of passing unchanged from one chemical compound to another. 2. relating to or being anything that attacks or reaches an origin or root of something else.

radiobiology a branch of biology dealing with the effects on living organisms of radioactive materials or ionizing radiation. —**radiobiological** *adj.* —**radiobiologist** *n.*

radiograph a picture of internal structures of the body using X-rays or gamma rays on a sensitive photographic surface. —**radiographic** *adj.* —**radiography** *n.*

radiology the use of radiant energy, as X-rays, in the diagnosis and treatment of disease. —**radiological** *adj.* —**radiologist** *n.*

radiosensitive sensitive to the effects of radiant energy.

radiotherapy the treatment of disease by the use of radioactive substances or X-rays. —**radiotherapist** *n.*

radium a radioactive and fluorescent metallic element, used in the treatment of various tumors esp. by implantation or insertion into the tissues.

radium therapy the therapeutic use of radium, esp. in controlling the spread of tumors.

radius *pl.* **radii** *or* **radiuses** the outer and shorter bone of the forearm.

radix the root of anything, such as the root portion of a spinal or cranial nerve.

rale an abnormal respiratory sound.

ramus *pl.* **rami** a secondary branch of a bodily structure, as a nerve or vessel.

ranula a cyst formed in a mucous membrane, as that under the tongue. —**ranular** *adj.*

rape sexual intercourse with a female without her consent or when she is legally under age or mentally incapable of making moral decisions.

raphe a ridge, crease or fibrous junction uniting two parts of an organ or part.

rash a usually minor eruption on the skin.

rat-bite fever a febrile, bacterial disease transmitted by the bite of an infected rat.

reaction a bodily response to a stimulus. —**reactive** *adj.*

recalcitrant resistant to treatment: *a recalcitrant disease.*

receptor an organ that receives stimuli.

recessive tending to recede or be of minor importance.

recipient one who receives.

recrudescence a recurrence of symptoms after an abatement.

—**recrudesce** *vb.* —**recrudescent** *adj.*

rectal relating to, being near, or involving the rectum.

rectum *pl.* **rectums** *or* **recta** the part of the intestine from the sigmoid flexure to the anus.

rectus *pl.* **recti** a straight muscle, as one sustaining the abdomen.

recumbent lying down.

recuperate to recover health; become well. —**recuperative** *adj.* —**recuperation** *n.*

recurrent 1. turning back in an opposite direction. 2. repeated; returning after an intermission: *a recurrent head cold.*

red blood cell any of the hemoglobin-containing cells that carry oxygen to the tissues and give redness to the blood; erythrocyte.

reduction the correction of a hernia, fracture, or luxation.

reflex an automatic response to a stimulus that involves a nerve impulse passing to a nerve center and outward again, producing an automatic reaction. Also called *reflex act, reflex action.*

refractory resistant to cure or treatment: *a refractory wound.*

regeneration renewal or restoration of a structure or part of the body, esp. after injury. —**regenerate** *vb.*

regimen a strict plan of diet, medication, or exercise for the purpose of maintaining or restoring health.

regression 1. the decline of a symptom of a disease. 2. gradual loss of function of a body part, esp. as the result of the process of aging.

regurgitation 1. the casting up of incompletely digested food. 2. the backward flow of blood from a defective heart valve. —**regurgitate** *vb.*

Reiter's syndrome *or* **Reiter's disease** arthritis, conjunctivitis, and urethritis occurring simultaneously and of unknown cause.

rejection an immune reaction against grafted tissue or a transplanted organ.

relapse the recurrence of the symptoms of a disease after a period of recovery. —**relapse** *vb.*

relapsing fever any of various acute infectious diseases marked by recurrent high fever for periods of about a week and caused by various spirochetes.

remission a condition or period during which the symptoms of a disease subside.

renal relating to, affecting, or located in the area of the kidneys; nephritic.

resection the surgical excision of part of an organ or structure. —**resect** *vb.* —**resectable** *adj.*

resolution the diminution of inflammation.

resonance the sound produced by percussion of the chest.

respiration the intake of oxygen and expulsion of carbon dioxide from the lungs; breathing. —**respiratory** *adj.*

respirator 1. a device covering the mouth and nose for protecting the respiratory tract. 2. a device for aiding in artificial respiration.

respiratory system the system or organs, as the lungs, their circulatory and nervous supply, and their connecting channels, by which air is conducted to and from the body.

resuscitation the action of reviving a person from apparent death or from unconsciousness. —**resuscitate** *vb.*

retardation a less than normal degree of intellectual development. —**retard** *vb.* —**retardant** *adj* & *n.*

retch to strain in an effort to vomit. —**retch** *n.*

retention abnormal holding in of a secretion or fluid of the body.

reticular of or resembling a net or network: *reticular tissues.*

retina *pl.* **retinas** *or* **retinae** a sensory membrane that lines the interior of the eye, contains the light-sensitive receptors, receives the optical image formed by the lens, and is connected by the optic nerve to the brain. —**retinal** *adj.*

retinitis inflammation of the retina.

retinol vitamin A.

retinopathy any noninflammatory disorder of the retina.

retinoscopy the projection of a beam of light into the eye to observe abnormalities of the retina.

retractor 1. an instrument used in surgery to hold back the edges of a wound. 2. a muscle that draws back or in an organ or part.

retro- *prefix* back; behind.

retroflexion *or* **retroflection** the turning back of a bodily organ upon itself.

retroperitoneal located behind the peritoneum.

retroversion a bending backward of the cervix and uterus.

rheum a watery discharge from the eyes. —**rheumy** *adj.*

rheumatic relating to, affected with, or associated with rheumatism.

rheumatic fever an acute febrile disease marked chiefly by pain and inflammation of the joints and inflammation of the heart valves and the endocardium.

rheumatism inflammation or pain in joints, fibrous tissues, or muscles.

rheumatoid arthritis a progressive disease marked by inflammation, swelling, and sometimes deformation of the joints.

Rh factor a substance present in the red blood cells capable of producing antigenic reactions.

rhinal of, relating to, or affecting the nose; nasal.

rhinitis inflammation of the mucous membranes of the nose.

rhinopharyngitis inflammation of the nose and pharynx.

rhinoscope a speculum for examining the nasal passages.

rhinoscopy examination of the nasal passages.

rhodopsin a red photosensitive pigment in the rods of the retina of the eye.

rhonchus *pl.* **rhonchi** a hoarse whistling sound heard upon auscultation of the chest and caused by obstruction of the air passages.

rib any one of the twelve pairs of curved bones that enclose the lungs and protect the viscera of the chest.

riboflavin vitamin B.

ribonuclease an enzyme active in catalyzing the hydrolysis of RNA.

ribonucleic acid RNA.

ribosome any of the cytoplasmic granules that are rich in RNA and are central to protein synthesis. —**ribosomal** *adj.*

rickets a disease of childhood caused by insufficient assimilation of calcium and phosphorus from inadequate vitamin D and sunlight and marked by softening and deformation of the bones.

rickettsia *pl.* **rickettsias** *or* **rickettsiae** any of a family of microorganisms, intermediate in size between bacteria and viruses, that cause various diseases, as typhus and Rocky Mountain spotted fever. —**rickettsial** *adj.*

rigor mortis stiffening of the muscles in a dead body.

ringworm any of several diseases of the skin or scalp caused

by fungi and marked by ring-shaped, scaly, pigmented patches.

risus sardonicus a fixed, grinning expression caused by spasm of the facial muscles and associated chiefly with tetanus.

RNA ribonucleic acid; any of various nucleic acids found mainly in the nucleolus and mitochondria of cells and being important to the control of cellular chemical action, as protein synthesis.

rod any of the rod-shaped, photosensitive receptors in the retina of the eye.

roentgen 1. of or relating to X-rays. 2. the international unit of X-radiation or gamma radiation.

roentgenology a branch of radiology using X-rays for the diagnosis and treatment of disease. —**roentgenologic** *or* **roentgenological** *adj.* —**roentgenologist** *n.*

roentgenoscope fluoroscope. —**roentgenoscopic** *adj.* —**roentgenoscopy** *n.*

roentgen ray X-ray.

root 1. the basal, enlarged part of a hair within the skin. 2. the part of a tooth within the socket. 3. either of the two bundles of nerve fibers that emerge from the spinal cord, joining to form a single spinal nerve.

roseola a rose-colored rash, as that occurring as a symptom of German measles.

roughage food containing dietary fiber that is not readily digestible and therefore stimulates peristalsis and is considered essential to maintain the health of the intestinal tract.

rubefacient a substance that causes the skin to redden. —**rubefacient** *adj.*

rubella an infectious viral disease that is less severe than measles but is harmful to the fetus during pregnancy. Also called *German measles.*

ruga *pl.* **rugae** an anatomical wrinkle or fold, as one of the many folds of mucous membrane that lines the stomach.

rugose full of wrinkles; wrinkled.

rupture hernia.

S

Sabin vaccine an orally administered vaccine for protection against poliomyelitis, containing attenuated strains of live polio virus.

sabulous gritty or sandy; resembling coarse sand.

sac a small, internal, usually fluid-containing pouch. —**sacular** *adj.* —**saculated** *adj.*

saccharin a white crystalline compound that is much sweeter than cane sugar and is used in food and liquid as a calorie-free sweetener.

saccharine relating to sugar or sweetness; sweet.

saccharo- *or* **facchar-** *or* **facchari-** *prefix* relating to sugar.

saccus *pl.* **facci** a sac.

facrad in the direction of or toward the sacrum.

sacralgia pain in the region of the sacrum. Also called *sacrodynia.*

sacro- *or* **sacr-** *prefix* relating to the sacrum.

sacrococcygeal relating to both the sacrum and the coccyx.

sacrodynia pain in the region of the sacrum. Also called *sacralgia.*

sacroiliac 1. relating to both the sacrum and the ilium. 2.

(informal) the lower part of the back, including the base of the spine.

sacrolumbar relating to both the sacrum and the lumbar region. Also called *lumbosacral*.

sacrum *pl.* **sacra** the lower part of the vertebral column that connects with and forms part of the pelvis. —**sacral** *adj.*

sadism sexual pleasure derived from inflicting physical or mental pain on others; delight in cruelty. —**sadist** *adj.* & *n.* —**sadistic** *adj.* —**sadistically** *adv.*

sadomasochism sexual pleasure derived from both inflicting pain and cruelty on others and being the recipient of cruelty or physical pain.

sagittal relating to or located in the median plane of the body. —**sagittally** *adv.*

Saint Vitus's dance chorea.

sal *pl.* **sales** salt.

salify to convert or change into a salt.

saline consisting of or containing salt: *a saline solution.*

saliva the clear, alkaline, somewhat viscid liquid secretion of the salivary glands.

salivary of or relating to saliva or the salivary glands.

salivary gland any of the glands of the oral cavity that secrete saliva.

salivate to produce marked quantities of saliva.

salivation the production of saliva.

Salk vaccine a vaccine that contains three types of polio viruses that have been inactivated for inoculation against poliomyelitis.

salmonella *pl.* **salmonellae** *or* **salmonellas** any of a genus of microorganisms causing food poisoning, diseases of the genital tract, and inflammation of the gastrointestinal tract.

salmonellosis infection with salmonellae.

salpingectomy surgical removal of a fallopian tube.

salpingemphraxis obstruction of a eustachian or a fallopian tube.

salpingian relating to the eustachian or the fallopian tube.

salpingioma any tumor or growth developing in a fallopian tube.

salpingitis inflammation of a eustachian tube or a fallopian tube. —**salpingitic** *adj.*

salpingo- *or* **salping-** *prefix* relating to or denoting a tube, usually a fallopian or eustachian tube.

salpingocele hernia involving a fallopian tube.

salpingolysis the surgical or manual freeing from adhesions of a fallopian tube.

salpingo-oophor- *or* **salpingo-oophoro-** *prefix* relating to a fallopian tube and ovary.

salpingo-oophorectomy surgical removal of a fallopian tube and ovary.

salpingo-oophoritis inflammation of both a fallopian tube and ovary.

salpingoplasty plastic surgery involving the fallopian tubes.

salpingorrhagia bleeding from a fallopian tube.

salpingorrhaphy the procedure of suturing a fallopian tube.

salpinx *pl.* **salpinges** a eustachian or fallopian tube.

saltpeter potassium nitrate.

salubrious favoring health or healthy conditions; healthful. —**salubrity** *n.*

saluresis the excretion in the urine of sodium.

saluretic enhancing or favoring the excretion of sodium by the kidneys.

salutarium sanitarium.

salutary wholesome or healthful.

salve an adhesive, unctuous ointment for soothing wounds or sores.

sanative healing or curative.

sanatorium *pl.* **sanatoriums** *or* **sanatoria** an institution for the convalescent or for the chronically ill.

sandfly fever a febrile, viral disease transmitted by any of various biting, two-winged flies. Also called *phlebotomus fever.*

sanguine of, relating to, or filled with blood. —**sanguinary** *adj.* —**sanguineous** *adj.*

sanitarium *pl.* **sanitariums** *or* **sanitaria** sanatorium.

sanitary of or relating to health. —**sanitation** *n.*

sanitary napkin a soft, disposable, absorbent pad worn to absorb blood flow during the menstrual period.

sanitize to make sanitary.

sanity soundness of mind; rationality. —**sane** *adj.*

saphenous relating to or being either of the two chief superficial veins of the leg.

sapo- *or* **sapon-** *prefix* relating to soap.

saponaceous relating to or resembling soap; soapy.

saponify to convert into soap.

sapphic lesbian. —**sapphism** *n.*

sarapus one who has flatfoot.

sarcoid 1. relating to or resembling flesh; fleshy. 2. a tumor resembling a sarcoma.

sarcoidosis a chronic, progressive disease of unknown origin that is marked chiefly by the appearance of nodules on various bodily organs or tissues or on parts of the body.

sarcolemma a thin membrane enclosing a striated muscle fiber.

sarcoma *pl.* **sarcomas** *or* **sarcomata** an often malignant tumor of connective tissue, striated muscle, bone, or cartilage. —**sarcomatous** *adj.*

sarcomatosis *pl.* **sarcomatoses** a disease marked by the development and spreading of sarcomas.

sartorius a long muscle that crosses the front of the thigh.

sawbones *Slang.* physician; surgeon.

scab a crust over a wound formed of hardened blood, pus, and serum. —**scabby** *adj.*

scabies a contagious skin disease caused by mites and marked by intense itching. —**scabietic** *adj.*

scald a burn caused by hot liquid or steam. —**scald** *vb.*

scale a thin, dry aggregation of cells shed from the skin in some skin diseases. —**scale** *vb.*

scalp the skin covering the top of the head, normally covered with hair.

scapula *pl.* **scapulae** *or* **scapulas** either of the flat triangular bones forming the back of the shoulder; shoulder blade.

scar a mark on the skin remaining after the healing of a wound.

scarification the making of small incisions in the skin, as for a vaccination. —**scarify** *vb.*

scarlatina scarlet fever. —**scarlatinal** *adj.*

scarlet fever an acute, contagious disease marked by fever, extensive skin rash, tonsillitis, and generalized toxemia.

Schick test a test for susceptibility to diphtheria by skin injection of a dilution of diphtheria toxin.

schistosomiasis *pl.* **schistosomiases** a parasitic disease caused by infestation with blood flukes and marked by loss of blood and damage to tissues caused mainly by the deposition in the vessels and tissues of the worms' eggs. Also called *bilharzia*.

schizophrenia a psychotic condition marked chiefly by withdrawal from reality, hallucinations, delusions, and bizarre behavior. Also called (informal) *split personality*. —**schizophrenic** *adj. & n.*

sciatica pain radiating from the lower back to the buttocks and the lower extremities. —**sciatic** *adj.*

sciatic nerve either of a pair of large nerves of the posterior limb and pelvic region passing down the back of the thigh.

scissura 1. a fissure; cleft. 2. a splitting.

sclera the hard white outer coating of the eyeball excluding the cornea. —**scleral** *adj.*

scleradenitis inflammation and hardening of a gland.

sclerema a hardening of subcutaneous fat.

sclero- *or* **scler-** *prefix* 1. hard. 2. relating to the sclera.

scleroderma a skin disease marked by the hardening and thickening of the skin. —**sclerodermatous** *adj.*

sclerosis hardening of tissue. —**sclerotic** *adj.*

scolecoiditis appendicitis.

scolex *pl.* **scolices** the head of a tapeworm.

scoliosis *pl.* **scolioses** lateral curvature of the spine. —**scoliotic** *adj.*

scopolamine an alkaloid derived from the roots of plants of the nightshade family and used as a sedative and as a so-called truth serum.

scorbutic relating to or suffering from scurvy.

scorbutus scurvy.

scotoma *pl.* **scotomas** *or* **scotomata** a blind spot in the field of vision. —**scotomatous** *adj.*

scotophobia an abnormal fear of the dark.

scrotum *pl.* **scrotums** *or* **scrota** the external pouch that holds the testes. —**scrotal** *adj.*

scurf dry thin scales shed from the epidermis esp. in some skin diseases. —**scurfy** *adj.*

scurvy a disease caused by deficiency of ascorbic acid and marked chiefly by sponginess of the gums and loosening of the teeth.

sebaceous relating to, resembling, or secreting fatty material; fatty: *sebaceous glands*.

seborrhea abnormally profuse production and discharge of sebum. —**seborrheic** *adj.*

sebum a lubricant, fatty substance secreted by the sebaceous glands of the skin.

secondary sex characteristic a physical characteristic, as the appearance of facial hair in boys, that appears at the time of puberty but is not directly related to reproduction.

secondary syphilis the second stage of syphilis that appears from 2 to 6 months after the primary stage and is marked by lesions in the skin, organs, and tissues and has a duration of 3 to 12 weeks.

section 1. a surgical division of a structure or part; cut. 2. a cut surface. 3. an extremely thin slice of tissue taken for microscopic examination.

secundigravida a woman who is pregnant for the second time.

sedative 1. tending to calm or neutralize nervousness or excitement. 2. an agent or drug that has a sedative effect.

—**sedate** *vb.* —**sedation** *n.*

segmentum *pl.* **segmenta** 1. a section or part of a structure. 2. the part or region of an organ that has an independent function, separate nerve or vascular supply, etc.

semen a whitish, viscid fluid produced by the male reproductory tract that serves as the vehicle for spermatozoa.

semicircular canal a loop-shaped canal of the inner ear associated with maintenance of the sense of equilibrium.

seminal of, relating to, or consisting of semen.

senescence the condition or process of aging.

senility the loss of mental faculties owing to old age. —**senile** *adj.*

sensation a mental process, as seeing or smelling, that is a direct response to bodily stimulation.

sense organ a structure of the body, as an eye or ear, that receives stimuli and transmits the excitation to nerve fibers continuous with the central nervous system where the stimuli are interpreted as sensations.

sensitive highly susceptible; hypersensitive: *sensitive to ragweed pollen*.

sensitization the condition of being sensitive or hypersensitive to an antigen or drug. —**sensitize** *vb.*

sensory carrying nerve impulses from the sense organs to the nerve centers; afferent. —**sensorial** *adj.*

sepsis *pl.* **sepses** a toxic condition resulting from the spread of bacteria or the products of bacteria from an infection. —**septic** *adj.*

septicemia circulation of virulent microorganisms in the bloodstream. Also called *blood poisoning*.

septum *pl.* **septa** a dividing wall or membrane between two bodily cavities.

sequestrum *pl.* **sequestrums** *or* **sequestra** a fragment of dead bone; bony necrosis.

serosa a serous membrane. —**serosal** *adj.*

serous relating to or resembling serum; watery and thin.

serum *pl.* **serums** *or* **sera** the watery part of a fluid, as blood, remaining after coagulation or removal of the other parts.

serum sickness an allergic reaction following an injection of foreign serum and marked by skin rash, pain in the joints, swelling, fever, and prostration.

sesamoid of or relating to a mass of cartilage or bone at a joint or bony prominence. —**sesamoid** *n.*

sessile attached to a base; not free to move: *sessile polyps*.

sex 1. either of two divisions of living organisms distinguished as male or female respectively. 2. the functional, structural, and behavioral characteristics of the male or female sex. 3. sexual activity. 4. (informal) sexual intercourse.

sex chromosome a chromosome inherited differently in the two sexes and concerned with the determination of sex.

sexual 1. relating to or associated with sex or the sexes. 2. erotic in nature or character. —**sexually** *adv.*

sexual intercourse sexual connection esp. between human beings; penetration of the vagina by the penis, usually leading to orgasm; coitus.

sexuality sexual feelings and interests.

shinbone tibia.

shingles an acute viral inflammation of the spinal and cranial nerves marked by neuralgic pains and vesicular eruptions; herpes zoster.

shock severe circulatory disturbance with markedly reduced blood pressure and volume caused typically by a severe injury, burn, or the like.

show (informal) a discharge of bloodstained mucus from the vagina occurring chiefly at the beginning of labor.

sibling one of two or more individuals having the same parent.

sick bay an infirmary on a naval ship or at a naval station.

sick call a military formation at which individuals can report if in need of medical attention.

sickle to form into a crescent.

sickle-cell anemia an inherited anemia occurring chiefly among people of Negro ancestry and in which a large proportion or the majority of the red blood cells tend to sickle.

sigmoid curved like the letter *S*.

sigmoid flexure the contracted and crooked part of the colon just above the rectum.

silicon a nonmetallic element that is the most abundant element (25 per cent) next to oxygen in the earth's crust.

silicone an organic compound in which the carbon has been replaced by silicon.

silicosis a disease of the lungs marked by shortness of breath and caused by prolonged inhalation of silica dust.

simple fracture a bone fracture having no secondary complications.

sinciput the upper and fore part of the cranium. —**sinciputal** *adj.*

sinew a tendon connecting a muscle to a bone. —**sinewy** *adj.*

sinistral relating to or situated on the left side.

sinus 1. a passage leading from an abscess to an external opening of the body. 2. a dilated channel for venous blood. 3. an air-filled passage communicating from the bones of the skull to the nostrils.

sinusitis inflammation of a sinus of the skull.

sinusoid 1. resembling a sinus. 2. a blood channel in certain organs. —**sinusoidal** *adj.* —**sinusoidally** *adv.*

skeleton the rigid, supportive bony framework of the body. —**skeletal** *adj.* —**skeletally** *adv.*

skin the outer integument of the body.

skull the bony skeleton of the head protecting the brain and the major sense organs.

sleeping sickness an acute infectious protozoal disease chiefly of Africa that is marked by fever, tremors, intense lethargy and is transmitted by tsetse flies.

slough dead tissue cast off from the body or a bodily part.

smallpox a highly infectious viral disease marked by fever and scarring skin eruptions with pustules.

smegma a cheesy sebaceous substance collecting between the glans penis and the foreskin or around the labia minora and clitoris.

snare a surgical instrument consisting of a wire loop contracted by a mechanism in the handle and used for removing masses of tissue, such as the tonsils.

snow blindness inflammation and photophobia of the eyes resulting from exposure to ultraviolet light reflected from snow or ice. —**snow-blind** *adj.*

sodium pentobarbital a sodium salt of pentobarbital used esp. as a sedative and as an adjunct to other anesthesia.

solar plexus a nerve plexus in the abdomen.

soleus a muscle in the calf of the leg.

solvent a liquid capable of dissolving a substance.

somatic of, relating to, or affecting the body, esp. as distinct from the psyche.

somnambulism the habit of walking while asleep. —**somnambular** *adj.* —**somnambulist** *n.* —**somnambulistic** *adj.*

soporific an agent that tends to induce sleep; hypnotic. —**soporific** *adj.*

sore throat inflammation of the lining of the throat, esp. caused by a bacterial infection.

spasm an involuntary, abnormal muscular contraction. —**spasmodic** *adj.* —**spasmodically** *adv.*

spasmolytic capable of relieving spasms.

spastic 1. relating to or characterized by spasms. 2. marked by spastic paralysis. —**spastic** *n.*

spectroscope an instrument for forming and examining optical spectra. —**spectroscopy** *n.*

speculum *pl.* **specula** *or* **speculums** an instrument for insertion into a body passage for inspection or applying medication.

speech center the part of the brain controlling speech.

sperm 1. semen. 2. a spermatozoon; male sex cell.

spermatic cord a cord that suspends the testis within the scrotum and contains the vas deferens.

spermatozoon *pl.* **spermatozoa** a motile male gamete having a flagellum for propulsion and being the means for fertilizing the human egg.

spermicide *also* **spermatocide** a substance that destroys spermatozoa.

sphincter an annular muscle for contracting a body opening.

sphygmomanometer an instrument for measuring blood pressure. —**sphygmomanometry** *n.*

spinal column the backbone; vertebral column; spine.

spinal cord the cord of nerve tissue extending from the brain through the spinal column.

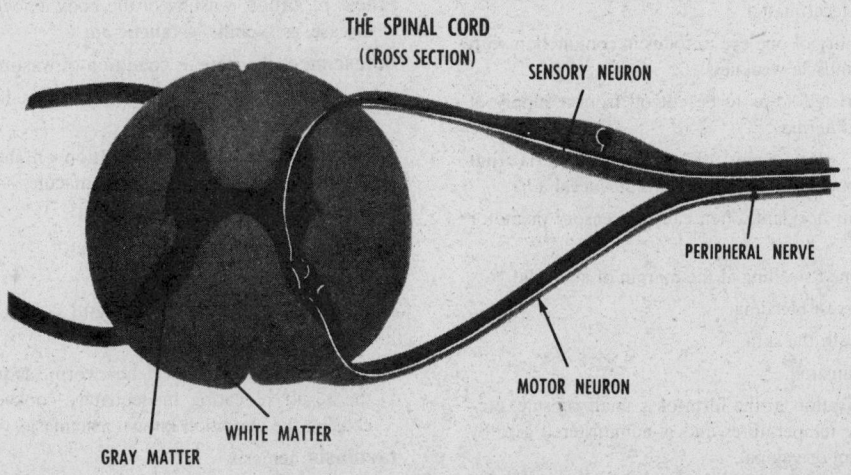

THE SPINAL CORD
(CROSS SECTION)

SENSORY NEURON

PERIPHERAL NERVE

MOTOR NEURON

WHITE MATTER

GRAY MATTER

spine the backbone; spinal column; vertebral column.

spirochete *also* **spirochaete** any slender, spirally undulating bacterium.

spleen a vascular organ involved with destruction of blood cells, storage of blood, and production of lymphocytes. —**splenic** *adj.*

splenectomy *pl.* **splenectomies** surgical removal of the spleen.

spotted fever any of various eruptive fevers, as typhus.

sprain a wrench of a joint with stretching or tearing of the ligaments.

sprue a chronic disease with chronic diarrhea, soreness of the tongue and mouth, and anemia.

sputum *pl.* **sputa** expectorated matter composed chiefly of mucus but sometimes also of discharge from the respiratory passages.

stapes *pl.* **stapes** *or* **stapedes** the innermost of the three conducting bones of the middle ear; stirrup.

staph staphylococcus.

staphylococcus *pl.* **staphylococci** any of various round (coccal) bacteria that include parasites of the skin and mucous membranes. —**staphylococcal** *adj.*

stasis *pl.* **stases** a slowing or stopping of the normal flow of body fluids.

steat- *or* **steato-** *prefix* fat.

steatopygia an abnormal development of fat on the buttocks. —**steatopygic** *or* **steatopygous** *adj.*

sterile unable to produce offspring. —**sterility** *n.*

sterilization deprivation of the ability to produce offspring, esp. by removal of the ovaries or by vasectomy. —**sterilize** *vb.*

sternum *pl.* **sternums** *or* **sterna** the breastbone.

stertor rasping, wheezing respiration during deep sleep; a snore. —**stertorous** *adj.*

stethoscope an instrument for listening to and diagnosing sounds produced within the body, esp. those of the heart and lungs.

stillborn dead at birth. —**stillborn** *n.*

stimulant a substance that produces alertness and a temporary increase in functional activity. —**stimulant** *adj.* —**stimulate** *vb.* —**stimulation** *n.*

stomach an expansion of the alimentary canal, extending from the esophagus to the duodenum, in which food is first digested before entering the small intestine.

stomachic an agent that stimulates the digestion of food in the stomach.

stool a discharge of fecal matter.

strabismus an inability of one eye to focus in conjunction with the other through muscle weakness.

strangulated constricted so as to be cut off from a supply of blood: *strangulated hernia.*

streptococcus any of a genus of parasitic bacteria that includes many important pathogens. —**streptococcal** *adj.*

stroke cardiovascular accident, often causing sensory or motor impairment.

sty *or* **stye** an inflamed swelling at the margin of an eyelid.

styptic tending to arrest bleeding.

subcutaneous beneath the skin.

sunstroke heat exhaustion.

suppository a medication in the form of a small capsule, etc., that melts at body temperatures and is administered esp. by means of the rectum or vagina.

suppuration the formation or discharge of pus. —**suppurate** *vb.* —**suppurative** *adj.*

surgery 1. the branch of medical science concerned with diseases and conditions requiring operations. 2. a specially equipped room where surgical operations are performed.

surgical of, relating to, or used in surgery. —**surgically** *adv.*

suspensory *pl.* **suspensories** a fabric supporter for the testicles.

suture a fiber or strand used to sew parts of the body that are wounded or have undergone surgery. —**suture** *vb.*

swab a wad of absorbent material, as cotton, used alone or wrapped around the end of a small stick to cleanse a wound or remove material from an area. —**swab** *vb.*

sweat to exude moisture through the skin, esp. profusely; perspire. —**sweat** *n.*

sycosis inflammation of the hair follicles esp. of the beard.

symphysis *pl.* **symphyses** an articulation of various bones joined together by fibrous cartilage.

symptom a bodily change experienced by a patient that is indicative of a disease or disorder. —**symptomatic** *adj.*

syncope temporary loss of consciousness; faint.

syndrome the aggregate of signs and symptoms characteristic of a particular disease.

synovia a transparent fluid secreted by a membrane of a joint or bursa. —**synovial** *adj.*

synovitis inflammation of the synovial membrane of a joint.

syphilis a chronic disease usually transmitted during sexual intercourse with an infected partner, caused by a spirochete and characteristically marked by three sequential degenerative stages occurring over the course of many years. —**syphilitic** *n* & *adj.*

syringe 1. an instrument for injecting a drug or medication and consisting of a hollow barrel with a plunger to hold the substance and a hollow needle. 2. an instrument with a nozzle and compressible bulb used for irrigation of a cavity.

systemic involving or affecting the entire body.

systole the contraction of the heart by which the blood is forced through the circulatory system.

T

tabella *pl.* **tabellae** a medicated mass of compressed material such as a tablet or lozenge.

tabes *pl.* **tabes** wasting of the body associated with a chronic disease, as syphilis. —**tabetic** *adj.*

tabescence the state or condition of wasting away.

tablespoon (as a unit of measure) one-half fluid ounce; 15 milliliters.

tache a small area of discoloration on the skin or a mucous membrane, such as a freckle or macule. —**tachetic** *adj.*

tachycardia increased heart beat.

tactile relating to the sense of touch.

tactus the sense of touch; touch.

taenia *also* **tenia** 1. any bandlike structure or part. 2. a tapeworm.

Taenia saginata the beef tapeworm, acquired by humans as the result of eating inadequately cooked infected beef and causing the condition known as teniasis.

taeniasis teniasis.

Taenia solium the pork tapeworm, acquired by humans as the result of eating inadequately cooked infected pork and causing the conditon known as cysticercosis.

talipes club foot.

tarsus 1. the seven bones that together constitute the articulation between the foot and leg; ankle. 2. the cartilaginous connective tissue supporting the eyelids. —**tarsal** *adj.*

tartar a calcium deposit forming on the teeth in combination with saliva and food particles.

taste bud an end organ lying chiefly on the surface of the tongue and conveying the sense of taste.

tear a drop of saline fluid secreted by the lacrimal glands. —**tear** *vb.* —**teary** *adj.*

teeth *pl. of* tooth.

tegument the skin; integument.

temperature degree of heat.

temple the flattened area on each side of the forehead. —**temporal** *adj.*

tendinitis inflammation of a tendon.

tendon a tough band or cord of dense connective tissue that joins a muscle with some other part. —**tendinous** *adj.*

tenesmus ineffectual, painful straining to evacuate the bowel or bladder.

teniasis *also* **taeniasis** the presence of tapeworms in the body; infestation with tapeworms.

tenorrhaphy suture of the cut ends of a tendon. Also called *tenosuture.*

tenosynovitis inflammation of both a tendon and its enclosing sheath. Also called *tendosynovitis.*

tenotomy surgical incision of a tendon, as in the treatment of a deformity caused by abnormal shortening of a muscle.

teratogenic tending to cause malformation of a fetus. —**teratogen** *n.* —**teratogenesis** *n.*

ter in die (in prescription writing) three times daily. Abbr. *t.i.d.*

tertiary syphilis the third degenerative and usually fatal stage of syphilis.

testicle testis.

testis *pl.* **testes** either of two male reproductive glands suspended in the scrotum.

testosterone a male hormone produced in the testes or synthetically and responsible for male secondary sex characteristics.

tetanus an acute infectious disease characterized by spasms of the muscles esp. of the jaw and caused by a bacillic toxin introduced through a wound.

tetany muscular spasms caused by mineral deficiency.

tetracycline a broad-spectrum antibiotic.

thalamus a mass of nerve cells at the base of the brain that is the main receptor for sensory impulses, which it transmits to the cerebral cortex.

thalidomide a hypnotic, sedative drug that was discovered in the early 1960s to produce malformation of the fetus when taken during pregnancy.

theca *pl.* **thecae** an enveloping sheath of a bodily part. —**thecal** *adj.*

therapeutics a branch of medical science dealing with methods of treating disease. —**therapeutic** *adj.*

thermography a technique for measuring the heat in various parts of the body and transforming the signals received into a diagnostic photographic record. —**thermograph** *n.* —**thermographic** *adj.*

thermometer an instrument, typically a liquid-filled glass tube with a numbered scale, used for recording variations in temperature. —**thermometric** *adj.*

thiamine *also* **thiamin** a B vitamin essential to metabolism and nerve function.

thigh the part of the leg between the pelvis and the knee.

thighbone femur.

thoracic relating to, involving, or located within the thorax.

thorax *pl.* **thoraxes** *or* **thoraces** the part of the body between the neck and the abdomen including the heart and lungs contained within it; chest.

thromb- *or* **thrombo-** *prefix* blood clot; relating to a blood clot or to clotting.

thromboembolism the blocking of a blood vessel by an embolus.

thrombophlebitis inflammation of a vein with thrombosis.

thrombosis *pl.* **thromboses** the formation of a clot within a blood vessel. —**thrombotic** *adj.*

thrombus *pl.* **thrombi** a blood clot formed within a blood vessel and remaining attached to its point of origin. Compare *embolus.*

thrush a fungus disease marked by the formation of white patches in the mucous membranes esp. of the mouth.

thymus a glandular structure of uncertain function that is present in the upper chest or base of the neck of the young and tends to atrophy with age.

thyroid 1. a large endocrine gland at the base of the neck producing the hormone thyroxine. Also called *thyroid gland.* 2. of or relating to the thyroid gland.

thyroidectomy *pl.* **thyroidectomies** surgical removal of tissue of the thyroid gland.

thyroiditis inflammation of the thyroid gland.

THE THYROID GLAND

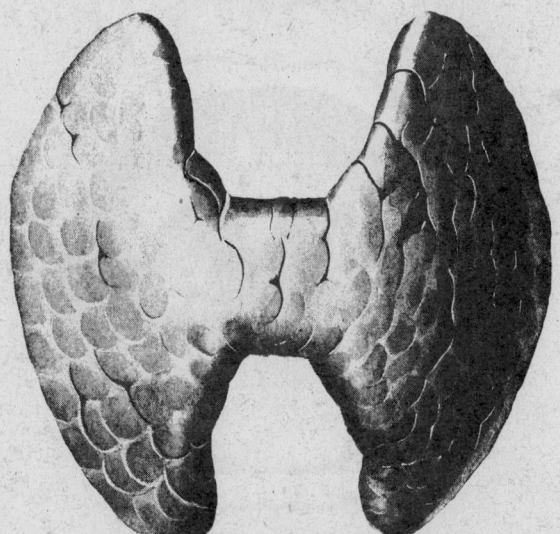

The thyroid is a large reddish, endocrine (ductless) gland located in front of, and on either side of, the trachea. It consists of two lateral lobes and a connecting isthmus.

tibia the larger of the two bones of the lower leg extending from the knee to the ankle; shin bone.

tic spasmodic, habitual twitching of a muscle, esp. of the face.

tic douloureux trigeminal neuralgia.

t.i.d. *abbr.* ter in die: three times daily.

tincture a medicinal substance diluted with alcohol. —**tincture** *vb.*

tinea any of various fungal skin diseases. Also called *ringworm.*

tinnitus a sensation of noise, as roaring or ringing, in the ears.

tissue an aggregate of cells of a particular kind together with its intercellular substance forming part of the body's structural material.

tissue culture the method of causing tissue to grow in a medium outside of the parent source.

tolerance 1. the ability to endure the effects of a drug, food, or other agent without adverse reaction. 2. the development of a decreased effect of a particular drug at a given dose, requiring that the dose be increased in order to achieve the original effect. —**tolerable** *adj.* —**tolerant** *adj.* —**tolerate** *vb.* —**toleration** *n.*

tone the condition of the body or any of its parts in relation to a standard of vigorous health.

tongue the muscular organ on the floor of the mouth equipped with the end organs providing the sense of taste and functioning as an organ of speech.

tongue-tie shortening of the frenum of the tongue resulting in restricted mobility. —**tongue-tied** *adj.*

tonic 1. any remedy that is considered to be invigorating. 2. relating to or characterized by tonus.

tonsil either of two masses of lymphoid tissue that lie one on each side of the throat.

tonsillectomy surgical removal of the tonsils.

tonsillitis inflammation of the tonsils.

TONSILLITIS

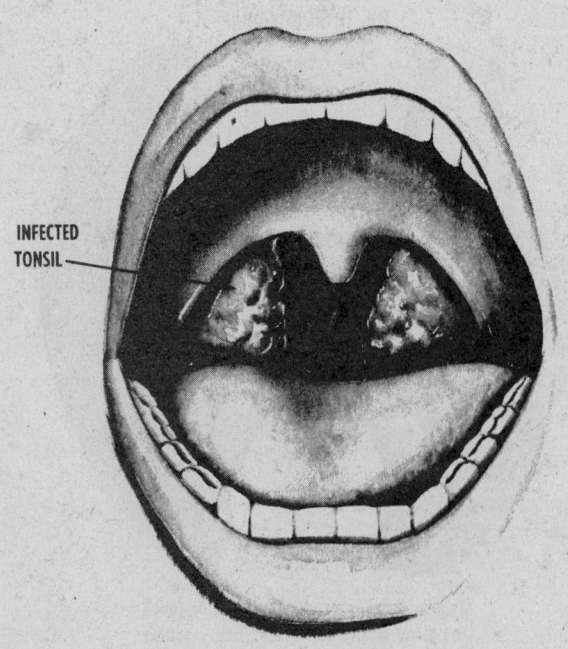

INFECTED
TONSIL

tonus a condition of mild contraction characteristic of normal muscle.

tooth *pl.* **teeth** one of the hard bony appendages lining the jaws and used in mastication.

tophus *pl.* **tophi** deposits of urate or crystals of uric acid in tissue characteristic of advanced or chronic gout, typically seen in the fleshy folds of the external ear.

topical intended for external application to a local area: *a topical anesthetic.*

torpor extreme sluggishness; lethargy.

torsion the act of twisting or the state of being twisted.

torso *pl.* **torsoes** *or* **torsi** the trunk of the body.

torticollis contraction of the neck muscles resulting in a twisted, unnatural carriage of the head. Also called *wryneck.*

tourniquet an instrument or device, as a bandage twisted and held fast with a stick, formerly recommended to check the flow of arterial bleeding.

toxemia the presence of a toxic substance in the blood. —**toxemic** *adj.*

toxic of, relating to, or caused by poison.

toxic- *or* **toxico-** *prefix* poison.

toxicant a toxic agent. —**toxicant** *adj.*

toxicology a branch of science dealing with poisons and their effects. —**toxicological** *or* **toxicologic** *adj.*

toxicosis *pl.* **toxicoses** a disease caused by poisoning.

toxigenic producing toxin. —**toxigenicity** *n.*

toxin a poisonous substance of bacterial or other origin that is capable of causing antibody formation.

toxoid a toxin that has had its toxicity neutralized so as to be functional as an antitoxin for injection.

toxoplasma any of a genus of parasitic protozoal microorganisms that are pathogens of vertebrate organisms. —**toxoplasmic** *adj.*

toxoplasmosis *pl.* **toxoplasmoses** a disease caused by infection with toxoplasmas and marked by severe damaging effects on the central nervous system.

trabecula *pl.* **trabeculae** *or* **trabeculas** a strand of connective tissue in the structure of a bodily part or organ.

trachea *pl.* **tracheae** *or* **tracheas** the main trunk of the air passages from the larynx to the bronchi. —**tracheal** *adj.*

tracheitis inflammation of the trachea.

tracheotomy *pl.* **tracheotomies** surgical incision of the trachea through the muscles and skin of the neck.

trachoma a chronic, contagious form of conjunctivitis.

traction a constant pulling force exerted on a skeletal part as a means of achieving proper alignment of bones.

tragus *pl.* **tragi** the cartilaginous prominence central to the opening of the outer ear.

trance an abnormal, profound state of sleep.

tranquilizer *also* **tranquillizer** a drug used to reduce or modify tension or anxiety. —**tranquilize** *also* **tranquillize** *vb.*

transfusion the transference of a fluid, as blood, into a vein.

transplant an organ or tissue used for transplantation. —**transplant** *vb.*

transplantation the transfer of an organ or tissue from one part of the body to another or from one individual to another.

transsexual one having a psychological urge to be a member of the opposite sex and often seeking surgical and hormonal remedy to alter gender. —**transsexualism** *n.*

transudation the passage of a fluid from a tissue or through a membrane. —**transude** *vb.*

transvestism the adoption of the attire and often the behavior of the opposite sex. —**transvestite** *n.*

trapezium *pl.* **trapeziums** *or* **trapezia** a wrist bone at the base of the thumb.

trapezius a large triangular muscle at each side of the back.

trauma *pl.* **traumas** *or* **traumata** physical or psychological injury. —**traumatic** *adj.* —**traumatically** *adv.*

treatment any of various means of curing or alleviating the signs and symptoms of a disease or disorder.

tremor a physical trembling caused typically by neurological disease, debility, or emotional stress. —**tremulous** *adj.*

trench mouth Vincent's angina.

trephine 1. a circular incision, as one made surgically on the skull or a cornea. 2. a surgical instrument for performing a trephine. —**trephination** *n.*

triceps a muscle arising from three heads, esp. the large muscle of the back of the upper arm.

tricuspid valve a valve of three flaps preventing the return of blood from the right ventricle to the right auricle of the heart.

trigeminal nerve either of two major nerves supplying motor and sensory fibers chiefly to the face.

trigeminal neuralgia intense paroxysmal pain of the trigeminal nerves. Also called: *tic douloureux.*

triplet any of three children born at one birth.

trismus a spasm of the muscles of the jaw; lockjaw.

trocar *also* **trochar** a sharp-pointed instrument used with a cannula for drawing off body fluids.

trochlear of, relating to, or affecting a trochlear nerve.

trochlear nerve a cranial nerve supplying motor fibers to the eye muscles.

trophic of, relating to, or involving nourishment. —**trophically** *adv.*

trunk the part of the body exclusive of the head or limbs; torso.

truss a device worn to retain a hernia by external pressure. —**truss** *vb.*

trypanosome any of a genus of parasitic protozoans that infest the blood, are usually transmitted by the bite of an insect, and cause serious disease, as sleeping sickness.

trypanosomiasis *pl.* **trypanosomiases** disease caused by trypanosomes.

tsetse fly a two-winged fly of Africa, south of the Sahara, that is a vector of trypanosomes. Also called *tsetse.*

tubal of or involving a tube, esp. a fallopian tube.

tubercle a small knobby excrescence or prominence; nodule.

tubercle bacillus a bacterium causing tuberculosis.

tubercul- *or* **tuberculo-** *prefix* tubercle; tubercle bacillus.

tubercular relating to or affected by tuberculosis.

tuberculin a sterile liquid extracted from the tubercle bacillus and used in the diagnosis of tuberculosis.

tuberculin test a test for hypersensitivity to tuberculin.

tuberculosis *pl.* **tuberculoses** a communicable disease caused by infection with the tubercle bacillus and characterized by toxic symptoms partly affecting the lungs. —**tuberculous** *adj.*

tubule a small, slender, anatomical channel.

tularemia an infectious plague-like disease transmitted by the bite of blood-sucking insects.

tumefaction the process or action of becoming swollen. —**tumefactive** *adj.*

tumescence the condition or process of becoming swollen. —**tumesce** *vb.* —**tumescent** *adj.*

tumor an abnormal growth or mass of tissue that is not inflammatory and may be either benign or malignant; neoplasm. —**tumorous** *adj.*

turgid marked by a state of swollenness; distended. —**turgidity** *n.* —**turgor** *n.*

tussive of, relating to, or involved in coughing.

twin either of two children born at one birth.

tympanic membrane a membrane that separates the external ear and the middle ear and serves in the reception and transmission of sound waves; eardrum.

tympanites distension of the abdomen caused by retention of abdominal gas.

tympanum *pl.* **tympana** *or* **tympanums** tympanic membrane; eardrum.

typhoid typhoid fever. —**typhoid** *adj.*

typhoid fever an acute, infectious bacterial disease marked by fever, headache, diarrhea and prostration.

typhus a severe febrile rickettsial disease marked by stupor and delirium in alternation, body rash, and violent headache and transmitted by body lice.

U

ulcer a break in mucous membrane or skin resulting in the development of an open sore. —**ulcerate** *vb.* —**ulceration** *n.* —**ulcerative** *adj.*

ulcerous relating to or marked by an ulcer.

ulcus *pl.* **ulcera** ulcer.

ulcus hypostaticum a bedsore; decubitus ulcer.

ulectomy surgical removal of scar tissue.

uletic relating to a scar; scarred.

uletomy surgical incision of a scar to relieve tension.

ulna the inner of two bones of the forearm between the elbow and the wrist. —**ulnar** *adj.*

ulnad toward the ulna.

ulo- *or* **ule-** *prefix* relating to or denoting a scar or scarring.

ulosis scar formation; cicatrization.

ultrafiltration filtration of a colloidal substance through a semipermeable membrane or other filter to separate it from its dispersion medium and crystalloids.

ultramicroscope a device using scattered light to make visible those particles too small for viewing by an ordinary microscope.

ultramicroscopic smaller than can be perceived with an ordinary microscope.

ultrasonics the diagnostic or therapeutic use of extremely high-frequency sound waves. —**ultrasonic** *adj.*

ultrasonogram a record obtained from the use of ultrasonography.

ultrasonography the diagnostic use of ultrasonic waves to locate, delineate or measure deep structures of the body by measuring their relative ability to reflect or transmit these extreme high-frequency sound waves.

ultraviolet ray a light ray beyond the visible spectrum at its violet end but having a wavelength longer than that of an X-ray.

umbilical of, relating to, or situated at the navel.

umbilical cord a cord from the navel of a fetus that connects with the mother's placenta.

umbilicus *pl.* **umbilici** *or* **umbilicuses** a small depression (or sometimes a slight elevation) in the center of the abdomen marking the original connective point of the umbilical cord.

uncinariasis infection with hookworms.

uncinate shaped like or resembling a hook; hook-shaped.

unconscious 1. not conscious; unable to perceive or respond to external stimuli. 2. (in psychoanalytic theory) the part of the mind that influences impulses, thoughts, desires, etc., but of which the individual is not aware.

undulant fever an acute, infectious, febrile disease marked by recurring attacks of fever and weakness; brucellosis.

unguent a healing or soothing ointment or salve.

unicellular consisting of a single cell: *unicellular microorganism.*

uniparous having borne only one child.

ur- *or* **uro-** *prefix* urine; urinary.

urea a white, crystalline substance found in urine, constituting the chief nitrogenous waste product of metabolism.

uremia a severe toxic condition caused by retention in the blood of high levels of the waste product urea, which is normally eliminated in the urine. —**uremic** *adj.*

ureter the long, narrow tube that carries the urine from the kidney to the bladder. —**ureteral** *adj.*

urethr- *or* **urethro-** *prefix* urethra: *urethritis.*

urethra *pl.* **urethras** *or* **urethrae** the canal that carries the urine from the bladder for excretion and in the male also serves as the conduit for semen. —**urethral** *adj.*

urethritis inflammation of the urethra.

urethroscope an instrument for viewing the interior of the urethra.

uric acid a waste product normally present in small quantities in urine, but which in larger amounts can form crystals of urate in the joints and give rise to the painful symptoms of gout or gouty arthritis.

urinalysis *pl.* **urinalyses** a chemical analysis of the constituents of urine.

urinary relating to or involving urine or the urinary bladder.

urinary bladder a membranous sac for retaining urine.

urination the act of excreting urine. —**urinate** *vb.*

urine fluid waste material secreted by the kidneys, temporarily stored in the urinary bladder, and eventually discharged from the body through the urethra.

urinometer a small hydrometer for determining the specific gravity of urine. —**urinometric** *adj.*

urogenital of, relating to, or involving the urinary and genital organs. —**urogenitally** *adv.*

urography X-ray examination of the urinary tract. —**urographologist** *n.*

urolith a calculus in the urinary tract.

urologist a specialist in urology.

urology a branch of medicine concerned with diseases or problems of the urinary or urogenital tracts. —**urologic** *or* **urological** *adj.*

urticaria an allergic reaction marked by an eruptive skin rash; nettle rash; hives.

uterus *pl.* **uteri** *or* **uteruses** an organ of the female for containing and nourishing the developing fetus; womb. —**uterine** *adj.*

uvea the posterior, pigmented layer of the iris of the eye.

uveitis inflammation of the uvea.

uvula *pl.* **uvulas** *or* **uvulae** a pendant lobe at the back of the soft palate. —**uvular** *adj.*

uvulectomy *pl.* **uvulectomies** surgical removal of the uvula.

uvulitis inflammation of the uvula.

V

vaccination 1. the inoculation with a vaccine to prevent smallpox. 2. inoculation with any bacterial vaccine. 3. the scar left by a vaccination. —**vaccinate** *vb.*

vaccine a suspension made from killed or attenuated organisms for inoculation to establish resistance to an infectious disease.

vaccinia cowpox.

vacciniform resembling cowpox (vaccinia).

vagal of or relating to the vagus nerve.

vagina a canal leading in the female from the external genital orifice to the uterus. —**vaginal** *adj.*

vaginectomy surgical removal of all or part of the vagina.

vaginismus painful contraction of the vaginal muscles, often associated with a psychological aversion to sexual intercourse and preventing insertion or withdrawal of the penis.

vaginitis inflammation of the vagina.

vaginopathy any disease or disorder of the vagina.

vaginoplasty plastic surgery involving the vagina.

vagus *pl.* **vagi** either one of the tenth pair of cranial nerves which supply chiefly the viscera with sensory and motor fibers.

valgus an abnormal outward turning or twisting of a joint.

valva *pl.* **valvae** valve. —**valval** *adj.* —**valvar** *adj.*

valve a fold of membranous tissue in a passage or channel that permits the flow of a fluid in just one direction. —**valvular** *adj.*

valvula *pl.* **valvulae** a small fold or valve.

valvulitis inflammation of the valves of the heart.

varicella chickenpox.

varicocele varicose enlargement of the veins of the spermatic cord.

varicose *also* **varicosed** abnormally swollen or dilated: *varicose veins.* —**varicosity** *n.*

variola smallpox. —**variolous** *adj.*

varioloid 1. resembling smallpox. 2. a mild form of smallpox occurring chiefly in persons who have previously had smallpox or who have been vaccinated.

varix *pl.* **varices** an abnormally dilated vein, artery or lymphatic vessel.

varus an abnormal condition of inward turning of a joint.

vas *pl.* **vasa** an anatomical duct.

vas- *or* **vaso-** *prefix* 1. vessel; blood vessel. 2. vas deferens.

vascular relating to or being a channel for the conveyance of a body fluid. —**vascularity** *n.*

vas deferens the excretory duct of the testis, through which semen is conveyed during ejaculation.

vasectomy *pl.* **vasectomies** surgical incision of the vas deferens chiefly as a permanent method of male contraception.

vasoconstriction narrowing of the diameter of blood vessels.

vasodilatation widening of the diameter of blood vessels.

vasomotor relating to or being nerves controlling the inner diameter of blood vessels.

vasoparalysis paralysis or lack of tone of blood vessels.

vasoparesis a slight degree of vasoparalysis.

vasopressin a hormone secreted by the posterior lobe of the pituitary gland that acts to elevate blood pressure and inhibit the excretion of urine.

vasospasm spasmodic contraction of a blood vessel. —**vasospastic** *adj.*

vastus one of three large muscles of the thigh.

vector an organism, as an insect, that transmits disease. —**vectorial** *adj.*

vegan a strict vegetarian who not only excludes meat but all animal products from the diet.

vegetation an abnormal concretion or outgrowth upon part of the body, as the valves of the heart.

vein any of the tubular vessels that branch throughout the body and carry oxygen-depleted blood to the heart (except the pulmonary veins, which convey oxygen-rich blood from the lungs to the heart).

vena cava *pl.* **venae cavae** either one of the two large veins (inferior and superior venae cavae) that carry the blood to the right atrium of the heart.

venepuncture venipuncture.

venereal 1. contracted or transmitted during sexual intercourse: *venereal disease.* 2. relating to or resulting from sexual intercourse.

venereal disease an infectious disease, esp. gonorrhea or syphilis, contracted through sexual intercourse or other sexual contact with an infected partner.

venereology *or* **venerology** a branch of medicine dealing with venereal diseases. —**venereological** *or* **venerological** *adj.* —**venereologist** *or* **venerologist** *n.*

venesection the opening of a vein for the letting of blood, as in the treatment of polycythemia.

venipuncture *also* **venepuncture** puncture of a vein, esp. for the withdrawal of a sample of blood for laboratory analysis.

venography X-ray examination of a vein after injection with a radiopaque substance.

venous relating to or affecting the veins.

ventral of or relating to the belly; abdominal. —**ventrally** *adv.*

ventricle 1. a chamber of the heart from which blood is forced into the arteries. 2. any one of the cavities of the brain that contain cerebrospinal fluid. —**ventricular** *adj.*

ventriculus *pl.* **ventriculi** a digestive cavity; stomach. —**ventricular** *adj.*

venule a small vein.

vermicide an agent for destroying intestinal worms. —**vermicidal** *adj.*

vermifuge causing worms to be expelled or destroyed. —**vermifuge** *n.*

verminosis *pl.* **verminoses** infestation with parasitic worms.

verruca *pl.* **verrucae** a wart.

version manual alteration in the uterine position of a fetus to achieve normal delivery.

vertebra *pl.* **vertebrae** *or* **vertebras** any of the thirty-three bony and cartilaginous segments that make up the spinal column. —**vertebral** *adj.*

vertex *pl.* **vertexes** *or* **vertices** the crown of the skull; top of the head.

vertigo *pl.* **vertigoes** *or* **vertigos** a state of disorientation in which an individual or his surroundings seem to be whirling; giddiness; dizziness. —**vertiginous** *adj.*

vesical of or relating to the urinary bladder.

vesicant an agent, as a gas, that induces blistering. —**vesicant** *adj.*

vesicate to blister.

vesicle a small, often painful elevation on the skin filled with watery fluid; blister. —**vesicular** *adj.*

vesiculate 1. covered with or containing vesicles. 2. to form or become covered with vesicles.

vestibule 1. the bony cavity of the labyrinth of the inner ear. 2. the opening between the labia minora of the vulva. —**vestibular** *adj.*

vestige the remnant of a bodily structure formerly having a functional purpose. —**vestigial** *adj.*

viable born in a fully normal and developed condition; fit for life: *viable fetus.* —**viability** *n.*

vibrio *pl.* **vibrios** any of a genus of bacteria in the form of an *S* or a comma, one of which causes cholera.

villus *pl.* **villi** a small, protruding, cellular process found on the surface of certain membranes. —**villous** *adj.*

Vincent's angina a mildly contagious bacterial disease marked chiefly by ulceration of the mucous membrane of the mouth and adjacent parts.

viremia the presence of viruses in the blood. —**viremic** *adj.*

viricide *or* **virucide** an agent that inactivates or destroys viruses. —**viricidal** *or* **virucidal** *adj.*

virilism 1. the development in a female of male secondary sex characteristics. 2. early development of secondary sex characteristics in a male.

virology a branch of science concerned with the study of viruses and the diagnosis and treatment of diseases they cause. —**virologic** *or* **virological** *adj.* —**virologically** *adv.* —**virologist** *n.*

virulence the ability of microorganisms to produce a disease with a rapid, severe, and malignant course. —**virulent** *adj.*

virus any of a large group of infective, submicroscopic agents that are capable of growing only in living cells and are the cause of many significant diseases.

viscera *pl.* of viscus.

viscid sticky in quality; adhesive; glutinous: *a viscid fluid.*

viscous viscid.

viscus *pl.* **viscera** an internal bodily organ.

vision the act or state of perceiving with the eyes.

visual of or relating to vision.

vital relating to life; essential to maintaining life: *the vital organs are the heart, lungs, brain, kidneys and liver.*

vital signs the body temperature, pulse and respiratory rates, and blood pressure, the existence of which indicates a person is alive.

vitamin any of various organic substances that are essential in the diet in very small quantities to maintain health; they act as metabolic regulators and are present chiefly in natural foodstuffs.

vitamin A any of various fat-soluble vitamins found typically in the oils of fish liver, in egg yolk, and in milk, deficiency of which results in impaired vision.

vitamin B complex a group of water-soluble vitamins that include niacin, riboflavin, thiamine, and niacinamide.

vitamin B$_1$ thiamine.

vitamin B$_2$ riboflavin; a vitamin of the B complex concerned with oxidative processes and found in kidney, liver, milk, grass, eggs, and other sources.

vitamin B$_6$ pyridoxine; a vitamin of the B complex that is necessary for protein metabolism.

vitamin B$_{12}$ a complex compound containing cobalt, found in liver, and essential to blood formation, growth, and the functioning of the nervous system.

vitamin C a vitamin found esp. in fruits and leafy vegetables and used in the prevention and treatment of scurvy and as a nutritional additive.

vitamin D a vitamin essential to the development of bones and teeth and found chiefly in milk, egg yolk, and the oil of fish liver.

vitamin E any of various vitamins important to the development of muscle and to fertility.

vitamin G riboflavin; vitamin B$_2$.

vitamin H biotin.

vitaminize to supplement with vitamins. —**vitaminization** n.

vitamin K either of two vitamins (vitamins K$_1$ and K$_2$) essential to the ability of the blood to clot.

vitiligo a skin condition marked by white, depigmented spots or patches on the body.

vitreous relating to or constituting the vitreous humor of the eye.

vitreous humor the transparent, clear, colorless substance between the lens and the retina of the eye.

vivisection surgery performed on living animals chiefly for purposes of research. —**vivisect** vb. —**vivisectionist** n.

vocal cords either of two pairs of folds of mucous membranes extending into the cavity of the larynx, which when vibrated by the passage of air act in the production of the voice.

voluntary functioning under conscious control: voluntary muscles.

volvulus a twisting of the intestine upon itself causing obstruction.

vomer a bone forming part of the septum of the nose.

vomit 1. to disgorge (the contents of the stomach) through the mouth. 2. the matter disgorged by vomiting.

vomiturition repeated, ineffectual attempts to vomit.

vomitus matter ejected by vomiting.

vulva pl. **vulvae** the external parts of the female genital organs; pudendum. —**vulval** or **vulvar** adj.

vulvitis inflammation of the vulva.

vulvovaginitis inflammation of the vulva and vagina.

W

wadding surgical dressing of carded cotton or sheets of wool.

waddle a swaying or side-to-side walk seen in some forms of muscular dystrophy or nervous disorders.

wale a linear weal, as one produced by the sharp blow of a stick or whip.

walk 1. the manner in which one moves; gait. 2. to move about on foot.

ward a room or area in a hospital equipped with beds for patients: surgical ward.

wart an epithelial tumor occurring typically as a horny projection on the skin of the extremities and caused by a virus. Also called verruca. —**warty** adj.

wash a lotion.

Wassermann reaction a test for the detection of syphilis. Also called Wassermann, Wassermann test.

waste 1. to lose tissue bulk; grow thin; emaciate. 2. excrement.

wasting emaciation.

waterborne carried by water: waterborne infections.

water brash a burning sensation in the stomach and esophagus with acid regurgitation; heartburn.

waters (colloquial) amniotic fluid.

Watson-Crick helix the double-stranded helical structure of deoxyribonucleic acid (DNA).

watt the unit of electrical power.

weal a lump or ridge raised on the skin, usually by a blow; welt.

wean to accustom (a child) to take nourishment other than by nursing. —**weaning** n.

webbing a congenital condition marked by the abnormal existence of a sheet or band of tissues joining two adjacent structures or parts.

welt a weal.

wen a cyst formed by obstruction of a sebaceous gland; a sebaceous cyst.

wheal a slightly elevated, reddened, itching patch on the skin typically associated with an insect bite or urticaria.

wheatgerm oil an oil rich in vitamin E, obtained from the germs of wheat seeds.

whiplash injury injury to the vertebrae and soft tissues of the neck produced by a sudden and violent jerking backward or forward of the head, as can occur to passengers involved in a rear-end collision of a motor vehicle.

whipworm a parasitic worm of the human intestine.

white blood cell leucocyte.

whitlow an abscess or purulent infection of the bed of a nail or the distal end of a finger. Also called felon.

whooping cough an infectious disease typically of children marked by paroxysms of violent coughing followed by a shrill, whooping drawing in of the breath. Also called pertussis.

Wilson's disease a rare hereditary disease marked by toxic deposits of copper in tissues, organs and the central nervous system and characterized esp. by symptoms of severe mental disorder.

windburn irritation and redness of the face caused by prolonged exposure to strong wind.

windpipe trachea.

wink 1. to open and close the eyelids very quickly, either as a conscious action or (usually) as an involuntary response. 2. the act or movement of opening and closing the eyelids quickly.

winter itch itching associated with exposure to cold, dry weather, thought to be caused by the drying of skin that is deficient in natural oils.

wisdom tooth the rearmost molar tooth in each half of each jaw, typically being the final teeth to erupt (as late as age 25 or so).

withdrawal 1. a pathological retreat from objective reality. 2. the complex of symptoms attending an addict following abstention from addictive drugs.

wolfram tungsten.

womb uterus.

wood alcohol an alcohol obtained from the distillation of wood, being poisonous and capable of causing blindness if ingested.

wood tick a species of tick occurring in North America and responsible for transmitting the micoorganisms that cause tularemia and Rocky Mountain spotted fever.

wool fat a fatty substance obtained from the wool of sheep, used as a base in the preparation of various ointments.

woolsorter's disease pulmonary anthrax caused by handling wool contaminated with the infecting microorganism *Bacillus anthrax.*

wound 1. an injury to the body involving piercing or laceration of the skin. 2. a surgical incision. 3. to injure; inflict a wound or wounds (on or upon).

W.r. *abbr.* Wassermann reaction.

wrinkle any crease or fold in the skin.

wrist the joint between the hand and the forearm; carpus.

writer's cramp muscular spasm of the hand induced by prolonged writing.

wryneck torticollis; stiff neck.

wuchereriasis infestation with threadlike worms of the genus *Wuchereria.* Also called *filariasis.*

X

xanthic 1. yellow or yellowish. 2. relating to xanthine.

xanthine a precursor of uric acid sometimes forming renal or urinary calculi.

xanthinuria the excretion of abnormally large quantities of xanthine in the urine.

xantho- *or* **xanth-** *prefix* yellow or yellowish.

xanthochromatic yellow-colored.

xanthochromia a condition characterized by the abnormal formation of yellow patches in the skin. Also called *xanthopathy.*

xanthochroous having a light or fair complexion; blond.

xanthocyanopsia a type of color blindness in which red and green are not distinguished but yellow and blue are; red-green blindness.

xanthoderma any yellowish discoloration of the skin. Also called *xanthoplasty.*

xanthodont a person with a yellowish discoloration of the teeth.

xanthoma a yellowish nodule or plaque in the skin caused by the deposition of certain lipids. —**xanthomatous** *adj.*

xanthomatosis a condition characterized by the multiple occurrence of xanthomas, esp. on the knees and elbows.

xanthone an agent that kills moth eggs.

xanthopathy xanthochromia.

xanthoplasty xanthoderma.

xanthopsia a visual defect in which all objects appear to be colored yellow.

xanthopsydracia a skin eruption characterized by the formation of small yellowish pustules.

xanthosis a yellowish discoloration seen in some malignant tumors and degenerating tissues.

xanthous yellow.

xanthylic relating to xanthine.

X chromosome a sex chromosome occurring paired in each female cell and zygote and singly in each male cell and zygote.

xenophobia an abnormal fear of meeting strangers.

xenophthalmia inflammation of the eye caused by the presence of a foreign particle.

Xenopsylla a genus of fleas, including the rat flea (*Xenopsylla cheopis*) which transmits the bacteria that cause the plague.

xenopus test a test for pregnancy in which the patient's urine is injected into the dorsal lymph sac of a toad.

xer- *or* **xero-** *prefix* dry.

xeransis a loss of moisture in the tissues.

xerantic causing dryness.

xerasia a condition characterized by abnormally dry and brittle hair.

xerochilia dryness of the lips.

xeroderma a dry, rough condition of the skin.

xeroma xeroph thalmia.

xeromycteria a condition characterized by abnormal dryness of the mucous membranes of the nose.

xeronosus xerosis.

xerophagia subsisting on a diet that is dry or lacking in moisture.

xerophthalmia a dry, thickened condition of the eyeball resulting from a deficiency of vitamin A.

xerosis severe dryness of the skin, mouth, or eye.

xerostomia excessive dryness of the mouth.

xerotes dryness.

xiphisternum *pl.* **xiphisterna** the posterior segment of the sternum.

xiphoid of, relating to or being the xiphisternum.

X ray a photon having a frequency distribution that is higher than the ultraviolet range of the electromagnetic spectrum and has the ability of penetrating various thicknesses of all solids.

x-ray to photograph, examine, or treat with X rays.

X-ray therapy treatment of a disease, as cancer, with the use of X rays.

Y

yaws an infectious tropical disease with symptoms resembling syphilis and caused by a spirochete. Also called *frambesia.*

Y chromosome a sex chromosome that is characteristic of male cells.

yeast any of various true fungi that are active fermenters of carbohydrates.

yellow fever an acute viral disease transmitted by a mosquito and marked by fever, prostration, jaundice, and occasionally bleeding. Also called *yellow jack.*

yerba a herb.

yolk the stored nutrient portion of an ovum.

yperite a type of mustard gas.

ytterbium a metallic element of the rare earth group.

yttrium a metallic element.

Z

zein a protein present in corn (maize).

zelotypia pathologically excessive zeal in the support or advocacy of a cause.

zero gravity *also* **zerogravity** the phenomenon or state of weightlessness resulting from the absence of the pull of gravity as occurs during flights into outer space.

zestocausis cautery achieved by the use of hot steam.

zinc a metallic element.

zincoid resembling or relating to zinc.

zingiber ginger.

zoanthropy a mental delusion of being a lower animal, such as a dog or cat.

zoetic relating to life.

zona *pl.* **zonae** an encircling area, as in shingles. —**zonal** *adj.*

zonula any small zone. —**zonular** *adj.*

zonula ciliaris suspensory ligament of the lens of the eye.

zoo- *prefix* relating to or denoting animal life or an animal.

zooblast any animal cell.

zooerastia human sexual gratification involving a lower animal.

zoograft a tissue graft obtained from a lower animal.

zoology the branch of science concerned with the study of animal life and its classifications. —**zoological** *adj.* —**zoologist** *n.*

zoomania an abnormal or exaggerated fondness or love of animals.

zoopathology the branch of pathology concerned with lower animals; veterinary pathology.

zoophagous eating the flesh of animals; carnivorous.

zoophobia an abnormal fear of animals.

zoster herpes zoster; shingles.

zygoma *pl.* **zygomata** *also* **zygomas** zygomatic arch.

zygomatic relating to or situated near the zygomatic arch.

zygomatic arch an arch of bone of the side of the face below the eyes; cheekbone. Also called *zygomatic bone.*

zygote a cell developing from the union of two gametes. —**zygotic** *adj.*

Heart Terms Dictionary

A

ADRENAL GLANDS *(ah-dre'nal)*
A pair of endocrine (hormone-secreting) glands that sit atop the kidneys. The inner portion of each—the adrenal medulla—secretes norepinephrine and epinephrine. Epinephrine is a heart stimulant and norepinephrine is a powerful blood vessel constrictor. The outer shell—the adrenal cortex—secretes aldosterone, cortisone, and other steroid hormones that influence the body's handling of salt, water, carbohydrates and other aspects of metabolism.

ADRENALIN *(ah-dren'ah-lin)*
See Epinephrine.

ADRENERGIC BLOCKING AGENTS *(ad"ren-er'jik)*
Drugs which block the normal response of an organ or tissue to nerve impulses transmitted by the adrenergic nervous system (more or less the same as the sympathetic nervous system). Blocking adrenergic nerves to the heart and blood vessels tends to decrease heart rate and the vigor of heart contraction and to suppress the constriction of blood vessels. Adrenergic blocking agents are often used to treat angina pectoris (since by reducing heart work they reduce its need for oxygen). Some are also used to treat arrhythmias and to control high blood pressure, especially when it is accompanied by a hyperactive heart.

There are two classes of these drugs, alpha- and beta-adrenergic blocking agents. Both can be used in cardiovascular disorders, although beta-adrenergic blocking agents are used more often; of these, propranolol is the most common.

AGE-ADJUSTED DEATH RATE
See Mortality Rate, Age-Adjusted.

AGE-SPECIFIC DEATH RATE
See Mortality Rate, Age-Specific.

ALDOSTERONE *(al-dos'ter-on OR al"do-ster'on)*
A hormone secreted by the adrenal cortex that promotes the retention of salt and water by the kidneys. Aldosteronism, or excessive secretion of this hormone, may cause an increase in blood pressure. In this case drugs known as aldosterone antagonists can be given; one example is spironolactone.

ALDOSTERONISM *(al"do-ster'on-izm")*
See Aldosterone.

AMINE *(ah-meen' OR am'in)*
An organic compound that may be derived from ammonia by the replacement of one or more of the hydrogen atoms by hydrocarbon fractions.

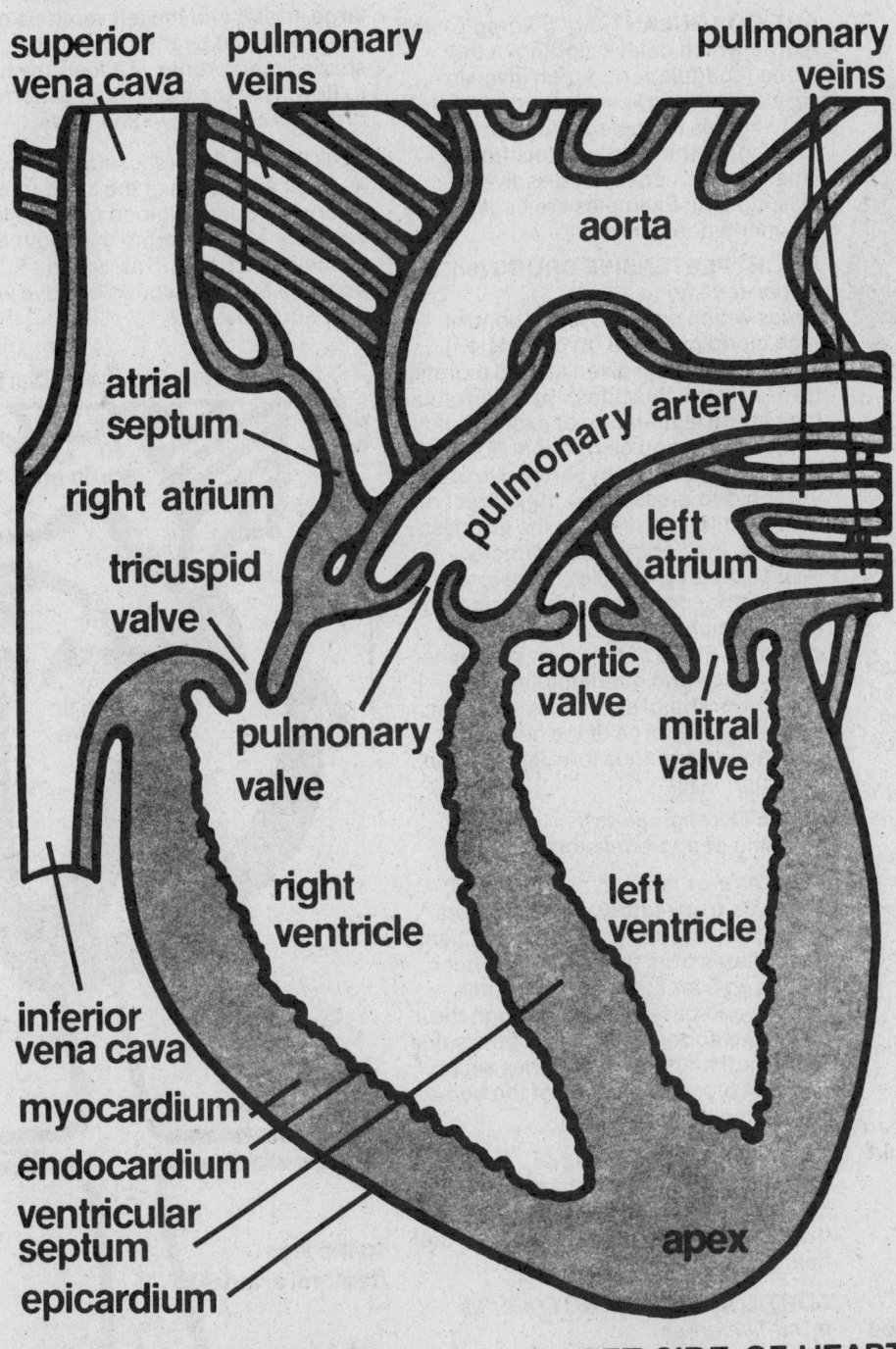

superior vena cava
pulmonary veins
pulmonary veins
aorta
atrial septum
right atrium
pulmonary artery
left atrium
tricuspid valve
aortic valve
mitral valve
pulmonary valve
right ventricle
left ventricle
inferior vena cava
myocardium
endocardium
ventricular septum
epicardium
apex

RIGHT SIDE OF HEART   **LEFT SIDE OF HEART**

ANEURYSM (an'u-rizm)
A ballooning-out of the wall of a vein, an artery or the heart due to weakening of the wall by disease, traumatic injury or an abnormality present at birth.

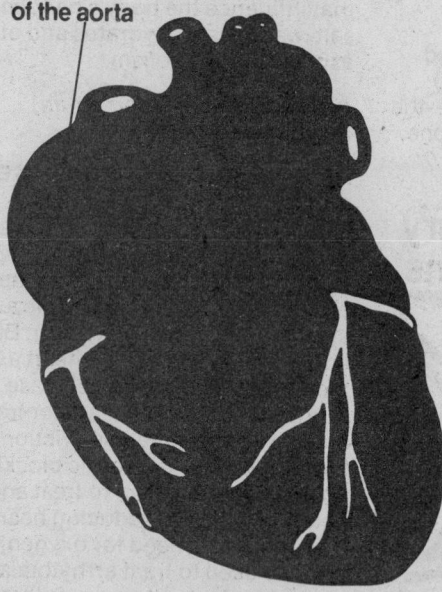

aneurysm of the ascending portion of the aorta

ANGINA PECTORIS (an-ji'nah OR an'ji-nah pek'tor-is)
An episode of chest pain due to a temporary discrepancy between the supply and demand of oxygen to the heart. This may be due to low oxygen levels in the blood (from smoking or respiratory disease), to a restricted bloodflow to the heart (coronary insufficiency) or to an increase in heart work beyond normal levels. Most often, angina pectoris is a chronic condition caused by a blood supply restricted by hardening and narrowing of the coronary arteries supplying the heart muscle (coronary atherosclerosis).

An angina attack is not to be confused with a heart attack (myocardial infarction), which results from a severe and prolonged lack of oxygenated blood to a part of the heart.

ANGIOCARDIOGRAPHY (an"je-o-kar"de-og'rah-fe)
A diagnostic method involving injection of an x-ray dye into the bloodstream. Chest x-rays taken after the injection show the inside dimensions of the heart and great vessels outlined by the liquid. **See Cineangiography.**

ANOREXIA (an"o-rek'se-ah)
Lack or loss of appetite for food.

ANOXIA (an-ok'se-ah)
Literally, no oxygen. This condition most frequently occurs when the blood supply (and hence the oxygen supply) to a part of the body is completely cut off. This results in the death of the affected tissue. For example, a specific area of the heart muscle may die when the blood supply has been blocked, as by a clot in the artery supplying that area.

ANTIARRHYTHMIC DRUGS (an"ti-ah-rith'mic)
Drugs which are used to treat disorders of the heart rate and rhythm. The drugs lidocaine, procaine amide, quinidine, digitalis, and propranolol are often given to correct arrhythmias. Atropine and isoproterenol are used in cases of abnormally slow heart rates.

ANTICOAGULANT (an"ti-ko-ag'u-lant)
A drug which delays clotting of the blood (coagulation). When given in cases of a blood vessel plugged up by a clot, it tends to prevent new clots from forming, or the existing clots from enlarging, but does not dissolve an existing clot. Examples are heparin and coumarin derivatives.

ANTIHYPERTENSIVE DRUGS (an"ti-hi"per-ten'siv)
Drugs which can be used to control high blood pressure (hypertension). Those most often given are the diuretics (primarily the thiazides), which promote the natural elimination of excess fluids in the tissues and circulation. Some of the other major antihypertensive drugs lower blood pressure by their direct or indirect dilating effect on the arteries. Hydralazine, for example, directly relaxes the tiny muscles in the artery walls. Other drugs block or damper the nerves which signal the arteries to constrict. Some of these are reserpine, methyldopa and guanethidine. The drug propranolol slows the heartbeat, decreases the force of the heart's contraction and thus lowers the blood pressure.

ANXIETY (ang-zi'e-te)
A feeling of apprehension.

AORTA (a-or'tah)
The main trunk artery which receives blood from the left ventricle of the heart. It originates from the base of the heart, arches up over the heart like a cane handle, and passes down through the chest and abdomen in front of the spine. It gives off many lesser arteries which conduct blood to all parts of the body except the lungs.

AORTIC ARCH (a-or'tik)
The part of the aorta, or large artery leaving the heart, which curves up like the handle of a cane over the top of the heart.

AORTIC INSUFFICIENCY (a-or'tik in"su-fish'en-se)
An improper closing of the valve between the aorta and the left ventricle of the heart permitting a backflow of blood.

AORTIC STENOSIS (a-or'tik ste-nos'sis)
A narrowing of the valve opening between the left ventricle of the heart and the large artery called the aorta. The narrowing may occur at the valve itself or slightly above or below the valve. Aortic stenosis may be the result of scar tissue forming after a rheumatic fever infection, or may have other causes.

AORTIC VALVE (a-or'tik)
Valve at the junction of the aorta, or large artery, and the left ventricle of the heart. Formed by three opposing cup-shaped membranes, it allows the blood to flow from the heart into the aorta and prevents a backflow. **See Valve.**

AORTOGRAPHY (a"or-tog'rah-fe)
X-ray examination of the aorta (main artery conducting blood from the left ventricle of the heart to the body) and its main branches. This is made possible by the injection of a dye which is opaque to x-rays.

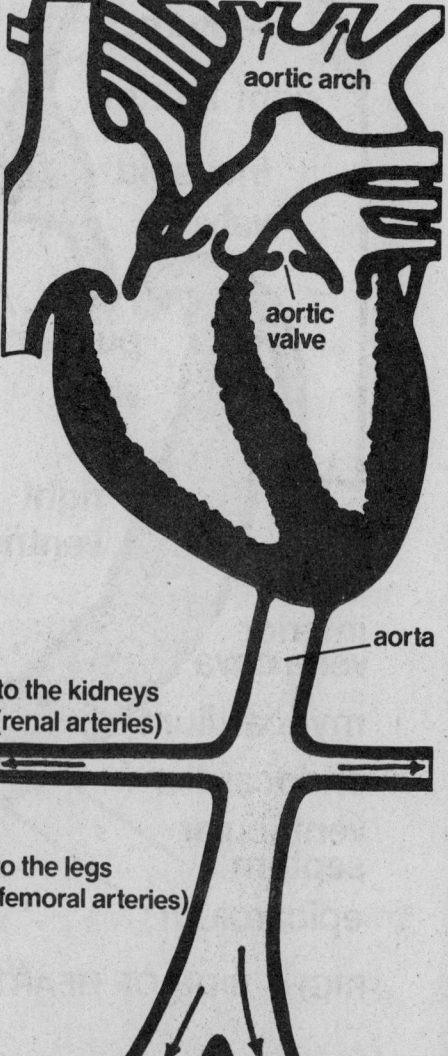

to the head (carotid arteries)

aortic arch

aortic valve

aorta

to the kidneys (renal arteries)

to the legs (femoral arteries)

APEX *(a'peks)*
The blunt rounded end of the heart, normally directed downward, forward, and to the left.

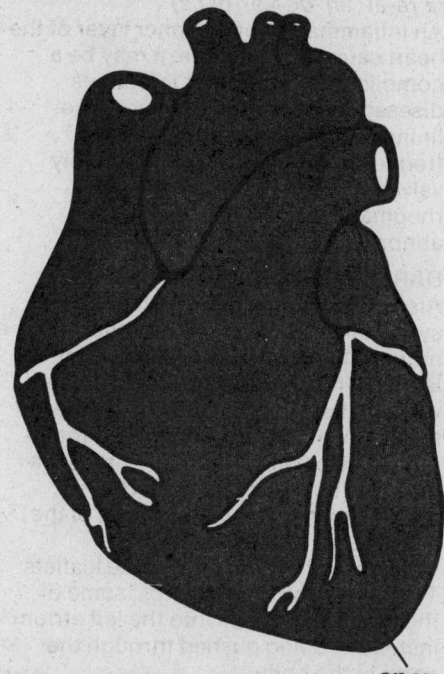

apex

ARCUS *(ar'kus)*
A curved or bowlike structure. **See Corneal Arcus.**

ARRHYTHMIA *(ah-rith'me-ah)*
Any variation from the normal rhythm of the heartbeat.

ARTERIAL BLOOD *(ar-te're-al)*
Oxygenated blood. The blood is oxygenated in the lungs and passes from the lungs to the left side of the heart via the pulmonary veins. It is then pumped by the left side of the heart into the arteries which carry it to all parts of the body. **See Venous Blood.**

ARTERIOLES *(ar-te're-ols)*
The smallest arterial vessels (about 0.2 mm. or 1/125 inch in diameter) resulting from repeated branching of the arteries. They conduct the blood from the arteries to the capillaries.

ARTERIOSCLEROSIS *(ar-te"re-o-skle-ro'sis)*
A group of diseases characterized by thickening and loss of elasticity of artery walls. This may be due to an accumulation of fibrous tissue, fatty substances (lipids) and/or minerals. **See Atherosclerosis.**

ARTERITIS *(ar"te-ri'tis)*
A general term for inflammation of arteries. This may be secondary to some underlying condition (such as an infectious disease) or it may be the primary phenomenon. Primary arteritis includes polyarteritis nodosa (which is disseminated throughout the body),

temporal arteritis (occurring at the temples) and aortitis (arteritis of the aorta and its major branches).

ARTERY *(ar'ter-e)*
Blood vessels which carry blood away from the heart to the various parts of the body. They usually carry oxygenated blood except for the pulmonary artery which carries unoxygenated blood from the heart to the lungs for oxygenation. **See Vein.**

ASCHOFF BODIES *(ash'of)*
Spindle-shaped nodules, occurring most frequently in the tissues of the heart, often formed during an attack of rheumatic fever. Named after Ludwig Aschoff (1866-1942), a German pathologist who described them.

ASSIST DEVICES
Special mechanical devices used to provide pumping assistance to a heart weakened by acute heart attack or heart failure.

ASYMMETRIC SEPTAL HYPERTROPHY (ASH) *(a"sim-met'rik sep'tal hi-per'tro-fe)*
Also called idiopathic hypertrophic sub-aortic stenosis (IHSS). A disease of the heart muscle (cardiomyopathy) in which there is an asymmetric enlargement (hypertrophy) of the walls of the left ventricle—the interventricular septum thickens more than the outer wall does. This makes the contraction of the left ventricle less effective and obstructs bloodflow to the aorta (and therefore to all parts of the body including the heart muscle itself). This condition is fairly common, is sometimes hereditary, and can create such symptoms as chest pain and dizziness. Treatment, when

abnormal, thickened septum (asymmetric septal hypertrophy)

necessary, includes surgery, drugs or reduced physical exertion.

ATHEROMA *(ath"er-o'mah)*
Also called plaque. A deposit of fatty (and other) substances in the inner lining of the artery wall, characteristic of atherosclerosis. Plural is **Atheromata** *(ath"er-o-mah'ta)*. **See Atherosclerosis.**

ATHEROSCLEROSIS *(ath"er-o"skle-ro'sis)*
A kind of arteriosclerosis in which the inner layer of the artery wall is made thick and irregular by deposits of a fatty substance. These deposits (called atheromata or plaques) project above the surface of the inner layer of the artery, and thus decrease the diameter of the internal channel of the vessel. **See Arteriosclerosis.**

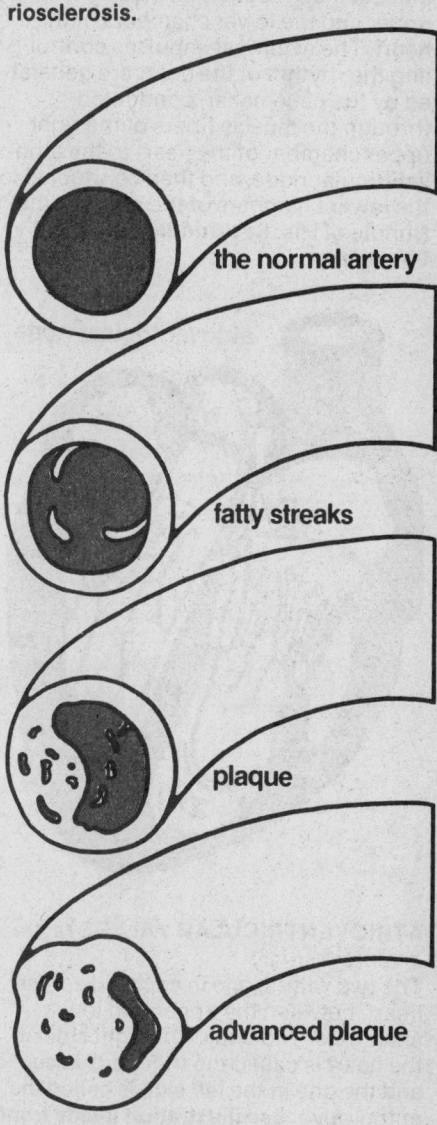

the normal artery

fatty streaks

plaque

advanced plaque

ATRIAL FIBRILLATION *(a"tre-al fi-bri-la'shun)*
See Fibrillation.

ATRIAL FLUTTER *(a'tre-al flut'er)*
An arrhythmia which occurs occasionally in healthy hearts, but more commonly in diseased hearts. It results in a

rapid regular heartbeat. Drugs are often used to slow the rate.

ATRIAL SEPTUM *(a'tre-al sep'tum)*
Sometimes called interatrial septum. Muscular wall dividing left and right upper chambers of the heart which are called atria. **See Septum.**

ATRIOVENTRICULAR BUNDLE *(a"tre-o-ven-trik'u-lar)*
See Bundle of His.

ATRIOVENTRICULAR NODE *(a"tre-o-ven-trik'u-lar)*
A small mass of special muscular fibers at the base of the wall between the two upper chambers of the heart. It forms the beginning of the Bundle of His which is the only known normal direct muscular connection between the upper and the lower chambers of the heart. The electrical impulses controlling the rhythm of the heart are generated by the pacemaker, conducted through the muscle fibers of the right upper chamber of the heart to the atrioventricular node, and then conducted to the lower chambers of the heart by the Bundle of His. **See Bundle of His and Pacemaker.**

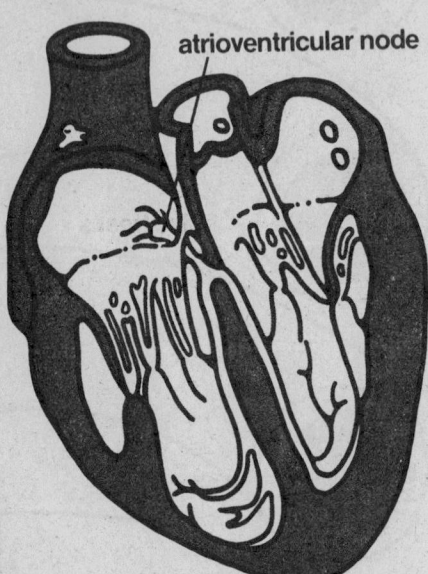

atrioventricular node

ATRIOVENTRICULAR VALVES *(a"tre-o-ven-trik'u-lar)*
The two valves, one in each side of the heart, between the upper and lower chambers. The one in the right side of the heart is called the tricuspid valve, and the one in the left side is called the mitral valve. **See illustration inside front cover.**

ATRIUM *(a'tre-um)*
Formerly "auricle." One of the two upper chambers of the heart. The right atrium receives unoxygenated blood from the body. The left atrium receives oxygenated blood from the lungs.

ATROPINE *(at'ro-peen)*
A drug used to treat, among other things, an abnormally slow heart rate; an antiarrhythmic drug.

AUENBRUGGER, LEOPOLD JOSEPH (1722-1809)
Austrian physician who invented the technique of tapping the surface of the body to determine the condition of organs beneath. The technique is called percussion.

AURICLE *(aw're-kl)*
Archaic term for atrium.

AUSCULTATION *(aws"kul-ta'shun)*
The act of listening to sounds within the body, usually with a stethoscope.

AUTONOMIC NERVOUS SYSTEM *(aw"to-nom'ik)*
Sometimes called the involuntary nervous system. The nerves of this system regulate tissues and functions not normally under conscious control (heartbeat, blood pressure, etc.). It consists of two divisions, the sympathetic and parasympathetic, which usually have opposing effects on the cardiovascular system: the sympathetic nerves, when stimulated, tend to increase heart rate, constrict blood vessels, and raise blood pressure; the parasympathetic tend to slow the heart rate, relax blood vessels, and lower blood pressure.

A-V BUNDLE
See Bundle of His.

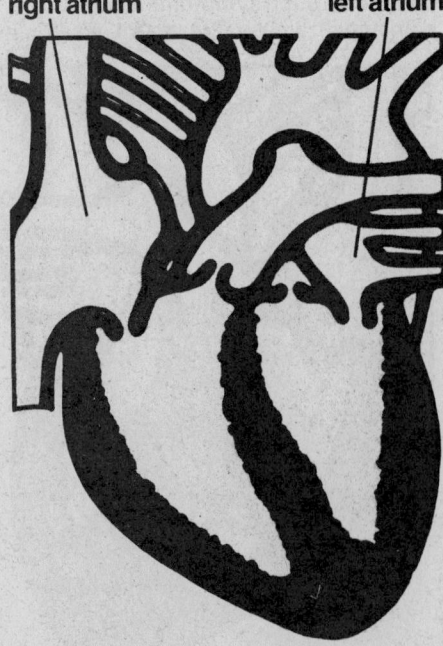

right atrium   left atrium

B

BACTERIAL ENDOCARDITIS *(bak-te're-al en"do-kar-di'tis)*
An inflammation of the inner layer of the heart caused by bacteria; it may be a complication of another infectious disease, an operation or injury. The lining of the heart valves is most frequently affected, most commonly valves with previous damage from rheumatic disease or congenital abnormality.

BARLOW'S SYNDROME *(bar'loz)*
Also called floppy mitral valve syndrome as well as systolic click-murmur syndrome, billowing mitral leaflet syndrome, and prolapsed mitral valve leaflet syndrome (among other terms). A structural alteration of the mitral valve (which normally permits a one-way flow of blood from the left atrium down to the left ventricle of the heart) leading to stretching and weakness of the cusps or valve leaflets. Thus when the heart pumps, some of the blood leaks back into the left atrium instead of being pushed through the aorta to the body.

This syndrome is associated with unusual chest discomfort and arrhythmias.

BARORECEPTORS *(bar"o-re-sep'torz)*
Sensory nerve endings which respond to changes in pressure, as those in the walls of blood vessels.

BEHAVIOR, TYPE A AND TYPE B
Two kinds of behavior patterns, as recognized in medicine. Type A behavior is characterized by high degrees of competitiveness, aggressiveness and feelings of the pressure of time. This type of behavior is thought by some cardiologists to be a risk factor in the development of coronary heart disease. Individuals with the converse Type B behavior are more easygoing and contemplative and more easily satisfied.

BENZOTHIADIAZIDES *(ben"zo-thi"ah-di'ah-sidz)*
See Thiazides.

BETA-BLOCKING AGENTS *(bay'tah)*
Also called beta-adrenergic blocking agents. **See Adrenergic Blocking Agents.**

BICUSPID VALVE *(bi-kus'pid)*
Usually called mitral valve. A valve of two cusps or triangular segments, located between the upper and lower chambers in the left side of the heart. However, in cardiology a "bicuspid valve" usually refers to the common congenital abnormality of the aortic valve's having two cusps instead of its usual three.

BIOFEEDBACK (bi"o-feed'bak)
A technique using instrumentation to provide moment-to-moment information about bodily processes which a person is not normally aware of, so that he or she can learn to control them. For example, one setup may include a blood pressure measuring device and colored lights to indicate whether the blood pressure is in the high or normal range. Evidence indicates that biofeedback may be used to teach a person to regulate his or her heart rate, blood pressure, bloodflow, skin temperature, and the activity of the gastrointestinal tract.

This term also refers to the normal and physiologic mechanisms the body uses to regulate myriad physiologic phenomena.

BLOOD PRESSURE
The force the flowing blood exerts against the artery walls. Two pressures are usually measured:
1. The upper, or **systolic**, pressure occurs each time the heart contracts (systole) and pumps blood into the aorta.
2. The lower, or **diastolic**, pressure occurs when the heart relaxes (diastole) and refills with blood flowing in from the large veins, the venae cavae.

The blood pressure is therefore expressed by two numbers, with the upper one over the lower one; for example, 120/80, which is spoken as "120 over 80."

BLUE BABIES
Babies having a blueness of skin (cyanosis)caused by insufficient oxygen in the arterial blood. This often indicates a heart defect, but may have other causes such as premature birth or impaired respiration.

BRADYCARDIA (brad-e-kar'de-ah)
Abnormally slow heart rate. Generally, anything below 60 beats per minute is considered bradycardia.

BRIGHT, RICHARD (1789-1858)
English physician who demonstrated the association of heart disease to kidney disease.

BUERGER'S DISEASE (ber'gerz)
A disease of the blood vessels which is more commonly called thromboangiitis obliterans. **See Thromboangiitis Obliterans.**

BUERGER'S SYMPTOM (ber'gerz)
In thromboangiitis obliterans (Buerger's disease), the pain in the affected leg when the patient is lying down is relieved only by letting the leg hang over the side of the bed. **See Thromboangiitis Obliterans.**

BUNDLE OF HIS (hiss)
Also called atrioventricular bundle or A-V bundle. A bundle of specialized muscle fibers running from a small mass of muscular fibers (atrioventricular node) between the atria of the heart down to the ventricles. It is the only known normal direct muscular connection between the atria and the ventricles, and serves to conduct impulses for the rhythmic heartbeat from the atrioventicular node to the heart muscle. Named after Wilhelm His, German anatomist.

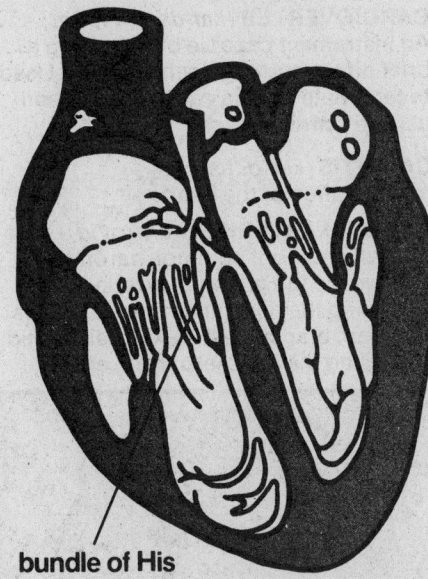

bundle of His

C

CAESALPINUS, ANDREAS (1519?-1603)
First to use the term "circulation" in connection with the movement of the blood. However, he still believed in many of the classical theories taught by Galen.

CALORIE (kal'o-re)
Sometimes called large or kilocalorie. Unit used to express food energy. The amount of heat required to raise the temperature of 1 kilogram of water 1 degree Centigrade.

A high caloric diet has a prescribed caloric value above the total daily energy requirement. A low caloric diet has a prescribed caloric value below the total energy requirement.

CAPILLARIES (kap'i-lar"ez)
The tiniest blood vessels. Capillary networks connect the arterioles and venules. Capillary walls are composed of a single layer of cells through which oxygen and nutritive materials pass out to the tissues, and carbon dioxide and waste products are admitted from the tissues into the bloodstream.

CARBON DIOXIDE (kar'bon di-ox'ide)
A waste product of chemical reactions in the cells. It passes from the cells to the blood which eventually releases it in the lungs to be breathed out.

CARDIAC (kar'de-ak)
Pertaining to the heart. Sometimes refers to a person who has heart disease.

CARDIAC ARREST
Cessation of the heartbeat. As a result, blood pressure drops abruptly and the circulation of the blood ceases. Until recently, this was always fatal. Today, the heart can be stimulated to start beating again and death averted under certain circumstances. **See Cardiopulmonary Resuscitation.**

CARDIAC CYCLE
A cardiac cycle is the series of mechanical and electrical events associated with one heartbeat. One cycle or beat lasts about 0.9 seconds and includes contraction and pumping, relaxation and filling actions.

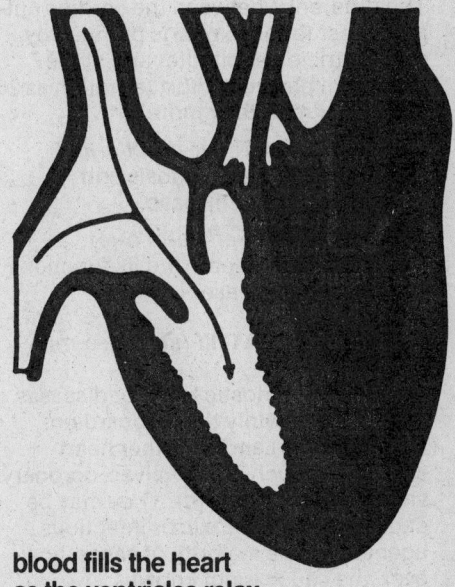

blood fills the heart as the ventricles relax

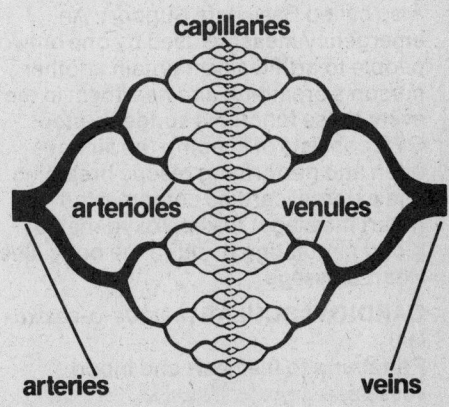

capillaries

arterioles   venules

arteries   veins

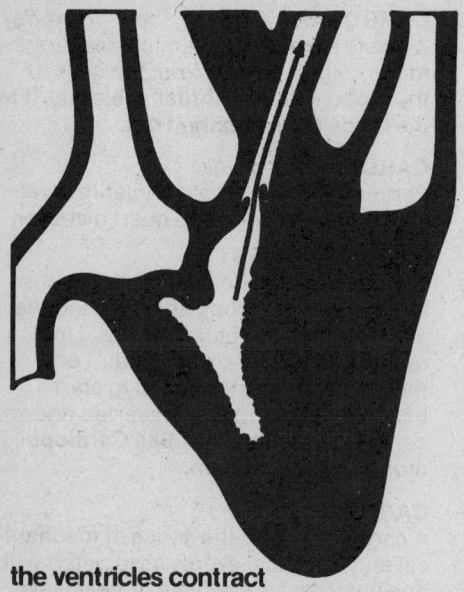

**the ventricles contract
and pump the blood out**

CARDIAC OUTPUT
The amount of blood pumped by the heart per minute.

CARDIAC RESERVE
The difference between the cardiac output at rest (about 5 quarts pumped by one ventricle per minute) and at the maximum physical effort (as much as 25 quarts per minute or more).

CARDIOLOGIST *(kar-de-ol'o-jist)*
A specialist in the diagnosis and treatment of heart disease.

CARDIOLOGY *(kar"de-ol'o-je)*
The study of the heart and its functions in health and disease.

CARDIOMYOPATHY *(kar"de-o-mi-op'ah-the)*
A general diagnostic term for diseases that involve mainly the myocardium (heart muscle) and not other heart structures (such as the valves, coronary vessels or pericardium). They may be caused by known toxic or infectious agents. For the majority of cases, however, the cause is not known.

CARDIOPULMONARY RESUSCITATION (CPR) *(kar"de-o-pul'mo-ner-e re-sus"i-ta'shun)*
Also called Basic Life Support. An emergency measure used by one or two people to artificially maintain another person's breathing and heartbeat in the event these functions suddenly stop. CPR consists of keeping the airway open and performing rescue breathing and external cardiac compression (heart massage) to keep oxygenated blood circulating through the body. **See Heart Massage.**

CARDIOVASCULAR *(kar"de-o-vas'ku-lar)*
Pertaining to the heart and blood vessels.

CARDIOVASCULAR-RENAL DISEASE *(kar"de-o-vas'ku-lar re'nal)*
Disease involving the heart, blood vessels, and kidneys.

CARDIOVERSION *(kar'de-o-ver"zhun)*
The application of very brief discharges of direct-current electricity across the intact chest and into the heart muscle in order to stop a cardiac arrhythmia (rhythm disorder) and allow the normal heart rhythm to take over. This technique is most often used as an emergency measure, but can also be used to correct chronic conditions.

CARDIOVERTER *(kar'de-o-ver"ter)*
An instrument capable of delivering a brief direct-current electric shock. Used to terminate certain cardiac arrhythmias. **See Cardioversion.**

CARDITIS *(kar-di'tis)*
Inflammation of the heart.

CAROTID ARTERIES *(kah-rot'id)*
The left and right common carotid arteries are the principal arteries supplying the head and neck. Each has two main branches, the external carotid artery and the internal carotid artery.

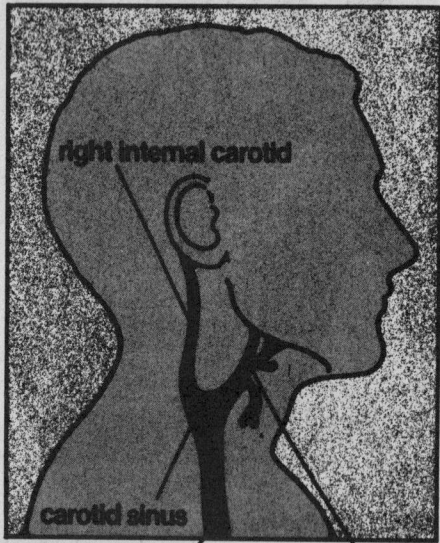

right common / **right external carotid**
carotid artery

CAROTID BODY *(kah-rot'id)*
A tiny (5 mm. or 1/5 inch) oval mass of cells located in each carotid sinus, that is, at the branching point in the arteries supplying the head and neck. The carotid bodies contain nerve endings known as chemoreceptors which are sensitive to oxygen and carbon dioxide content and to pH of the blood. For example, when the oxygen content of the blood is reduced, the carotid bodies cause an increase in respiration rate.

CAROTID SINUS *(kah-rot'id si'nus)*
On either side of the neck, a slight dilation at the point where the internal carotid artery branches from the common carotid artery. These arteries supply the head and neck with blood. The carotid sinus contains the carotid body and many baroreceptors, special nerve endings sensitive to changes in blood pressure to keep it relatively constant. For example, if blood pressure starts to rise, baroreceptors in the carotid sinuses are stimulated to reduce the rate and force of heart contraction and to dilate the arteries—thus lowering the blood pressure. **See Carotid Arteries and Carotid Body.**

CATHETER *(kath'e-ter)*
A thin, flexible tube which can be guided into body organs. A cardiac catheter is made of woven plastic, or other material to which blood will not adhere, and is inserted into a vein or artery (usually of an arm or a leg) and gently threaded into the heart. Its progress can be watched on a fluoroscope.

Cardiac catheters can be used for diagnosis (to take samples of blood or pressure readings in the chambers of the heart) or for treatment (to implant the electrodes of a pacemaker or to administer a drug).

catheter

CATHETERIZATION *(kath"e-ter-i-za'shun)*
In cardiology, the process of introducing a thin, flexible tube (a catheter) into a vein or artery and guiding it into the heart for purposes of examination or treatment.

CEREBRAL VASCULAR ACCIDENT *(ser'e-bral OR se-re'bral vas'ku-lar)*
Sometimes called cerebrovascular accident, apoplectic stroke, or simply stroke. An impeded blood supply to some part of the brain, generally caused by one of the following four conditions:
1. A blood clot forming in the vessel (cerebral thrombosis).

2. A rupture of the blood vessel wall (cerebral hemorrhage).

3. A piece of clot or other material from another part of the vascular system which flows to the brain and obstructs a cerebral vessel (cerebral embolism).

4. Pressure on a blood vessel as by a tumor.

For illustration see Stroke.

CEREBROVASCULAR *(ser"e-bro-vas'ku-lar)*
Pertaining to the blood vessels in the brain.

CHAGAS HEART DISEASE *(chag'as)*
A form of heart disease resulting from an infection by a microscopic parasite found in South America.

CHEMOTHERAPY *(ke"mo-ther'ah-pe)*
The treatment of disease by administering chemicals. Frequently used in the phrase "chemotherapy of hypertension," i.e., the treatment of high blood pressure by the use of drugs.

CHLOROTHIAZIDE *(klo"ro-thi'ah-zid)*
One of the thiazide diuretics (drugs which promote the excretion of urine). Sometimes used to treat high blood pressure and edema (waterlogged tissues).

CHOLESTEROL *(ko-les'ter-ol)*
A fat-like substance found in animal tissue. In blood tests the normal level for Americans is assumed to be between 180 and 230 milligrams per 100 cc. A higher level is often associated with high risk of coronary atherosclerosis.

CHOLESTYRAMINE *(ko"les-ti'rah-meen)*
A drug used to lower blood levels of the lipid cholesterol. **See Lipid-Lowering Drugs.**

CHORDAE TENDINEAE *(kor'di ten'dun-i)*
Fibrous chords which serve as guy ropes to hold the valves between the upper and lower chambers. They stretch from the cusps of the valves to muscles called papillary muscles in the walls of the lower heart chambers.

CHOREA *(ko-re'ah)*
Involuntary, irregular twitching of the muscles, sometimes associated wth rheumatic fever. Also called St. Vitus Dance, or Sydenham's Chorea.

CINEANGIOCARDIOGRAPHY *(sin"e-an"je-o-kar"de-og'rah-fe)*
A diagnostic method similar to angiocardiography except that instead of still x-ray pictures, motion pictures of the heart are made by fluoroscopy, as an injected opaque liquid is carried through the heart and blood vessels. **See Angiocardiography.**

CIRCULATORY *(ser'ku-lah-to"re)*
Pertaining to the heart, blood vessels, and the circulation of the blood.

CLAUDICATION *(klaw"di-ka'shun)*
Pain and lameness or limping. Can be caused by defective circulation of the blood in the vessels of the limbs. **See Intermittent Claudication.**

CLOFIBRATE *(klo-fi'brat)*
A drug generally used to lower elevated levels of triglyceride lipids in the blood. **See Lipid-Lowering Drugs.**

CLUBBED FINGERS *(klubd)*
Fingers with a short broad tip and overhanging nail, somewhat resembling a drumstick. This condition is sometimes seen in children born with certain kinds of heart defects and in adults with heart, lung or gastrointestinal diseases. It may also be familial and insignificant.

COAGULATION *(ko-ag"u-la'shun)*
Process of changing from a liquid to a thickened or solid state. The formation of a clot.

COARCTATION OF THE AORTA *(ko"ark-ta'shun of the a-or'ta)*
Literally a pressing together or narrowing of the aorta, the main trunk artery which conducts blood from the heart to the body. One of several types of congenital heart defects.

COLLATERAL CIRCULATION *(ko-lat'er-al ser"ku-la'shun)*
Circulation of the blood through nearby smaller vessels when a main vessel has been blocked up.

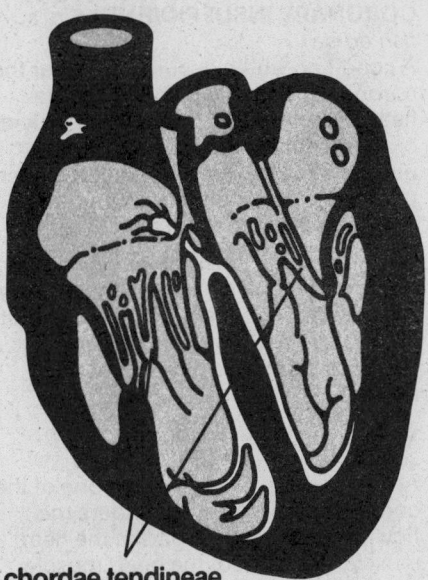

chordae tendineae

COMMISSUROTOMY *(kom"e-shur-ot'o-me)*
An operation to widen the opening in a heart valve which has become narrowed by scar tissue. The individual flaps of the valve are spread apart along the

natural lines of their closure by a blunt instrument. This operation was developed to correct rheumatic heart disease. **See Mitral Valvulotomy.**

CONGENITAL ANOMALY *(kon-jen'i-tal ah-nom'ah-le)*
An abnormality present at birth.

CONGESTIVE HEART FAILURE *(kon-jes'tiv)*
"Heart failure" is a condition in which the heart is unable to pump its required amount of blood.

Heart failure is often congestive because loss of pumping power by the heart leads to congestion in the body tissues; fluid accumulates in the abdomen and legs and/or in the lungs (pulmonary edema). Congestive heart failure often develops gradually over several years, although it can be acute (short and severe). It can be treated by drugs or in some cases by surgery. **See Heart Failure.**

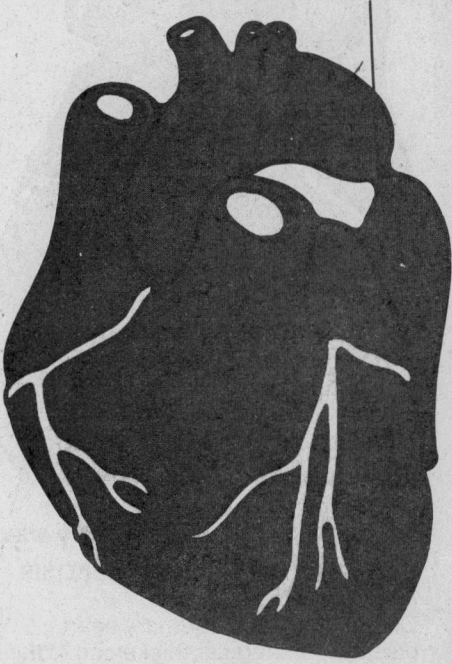

coarctation of the aorta

CONSTRICTIVE PERICARDITIS *(kon-strik'tiv per"i-kar-di'tis)*
A thickening of the outer sac of the heart which prevents the heart muscle from expanding and filling normally.

CONTRACTILE PROTEINS *(kon-trak'til pro'te-ins)*
Proteins which occur within all muscle fibers, including those of the heart muscle. Contractile proteins are responsible for shortening the muscle fibers and therefore causing the muscle to contract. There are several kinds of contractile proteins.

CORNEAL ARCUS *(kor'ne-al ar'kus)*
A hazy ring around the edge of the

cornea (the transparent covering over the front of the eye). It can have a variety of causes, including exposure to irritating chemicals, viral or bacterial infections, and old age. It can also be a normal finding in certain racial backgrounds.

In addition, corneal arcus can be a sign of Type II or Type IV hyperlipoproteinemia, blood-lipid disorders associated with premature development of atherosclerosis (hardening of the arteries).

CORONARY ARTERIES *(kor'o-na-re)*
Arteries, arising from the base of the aorta, which conduct blood to the heart muscle. These arteries, and the network of vessels branching off from them, come down over the top of the heart like a crown (corona).

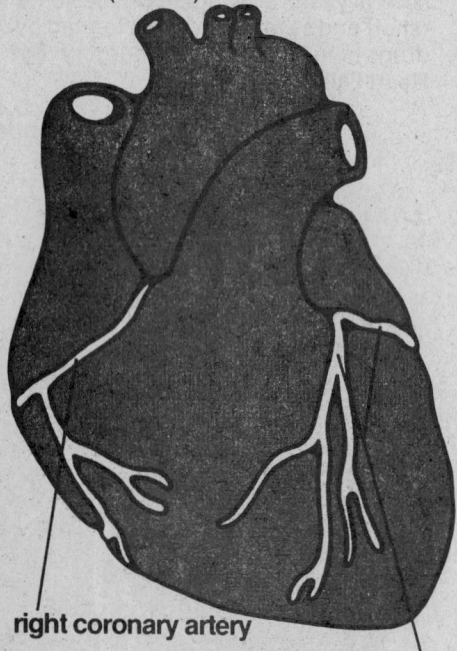

right coronary artery

left coronary artery

CORONARY ARTHEROSCLEROSIS *(ath"er-o"skle-ro'sis)*
Commonly called coronary heart disease. An irregular thickening of the inner layer of the walls of the arteries which conduct blood to the heart muscle. The internal channel of these arteries (the coronaries) becomes narrowed and the blood supply to the heart muscle is reduced. **See Atherosclerosis.**

CORONARY BYPASS SURGERY *(kor'o-na-re bi'pas)*
Surgery to improve the blood supply to the heart muscle when narrowed coronary arteries reduce flow of the oxygen-containing blood which is vital to the pumping heart. This reduction in bloodflow causes chest pain and leads to increased risk of heart attack. Thus coronary bypass surgery involves

constructing detours through which blood can bypass narrowed portions of coronary arteries to keep the heart muscle supplied. Veins or arteries taken from other parts of the body where they are not essential are grafted onto the heart to construct these detours.

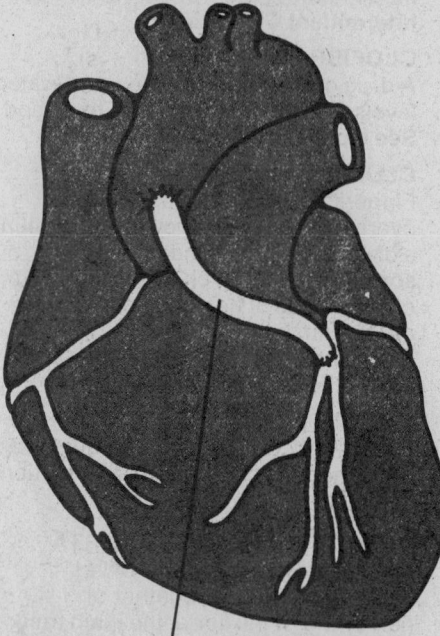

a bypass graft from the aorta to one of the coronary arteries

CORONARY HEART DISEASE
Also called coronary artery disease and ischemic heart disease. Heart ailments caused by narrowing of the coronary arteries and therefore a decreased blood supply to the heart (ischemia).

CORONARY INSUFFICIENCY *(in"su-fish'en-se)*
A condition which occurs whenever the coronary arteries (which supply the heart muscle with blood) do not provide oxygen adequate to the needs of the pumping heart. This may produce chest pain (angina pectoris) or a heart attack, or no pain may occur at all.

"*Acute* coronary insufficiency" is a term used to describe chest pain that is more severe than that of angina pectoris, but in which no heart muscle damage is done (as there would be in a heart attack).

CORONARY OCCLUSION *(o-kloo' zhun)*
An obstruction in a branch of one of the coronary arteries which hinders the flow of blood to some part of the heart muscle. This part of the heart muscle then dies because of lack of oxygen supply. Sometimes called a coronary heart attack or simply a heart attack. **See Heart Attack.**

CORONARY THROMBOSIS *(throm-bo'sis)*
Formation of a clot in a branch of one of

the arteries which conduct blood to the heart muscle (coronary arteries). A form of coronary occlusion. **See Coronary Occlusion.**

COR PULMONALE *(kor pul-mo-nal'e)*
Heart disease resulting from disease of the lungs or the blood vessels of the lungs. The lung problems cause high blood pressure in the pulmonary vessels (pulmonary hypertension). Thus the right ventricle enlarges because it must work harder to pump blood through the lungs.

CORVISART, JEAN NICOLAS (1755-1821)
One of the earliest of the modern cardiologists, and the first person to call him or herself a "heart specialist." Favorite physician to Napoleon.

COUMARIN *(koo'mah-rin)*
A class of chemical substances which delay clotting of the blood. An anticoagulant.

CPR
See Cardiopulmonary Resuscitation.

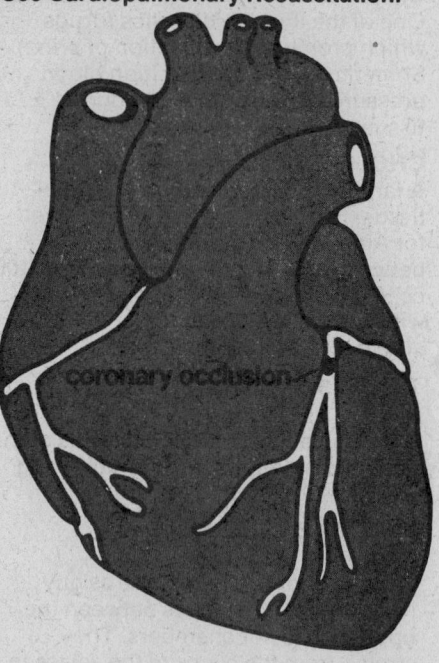

coronary occlusion

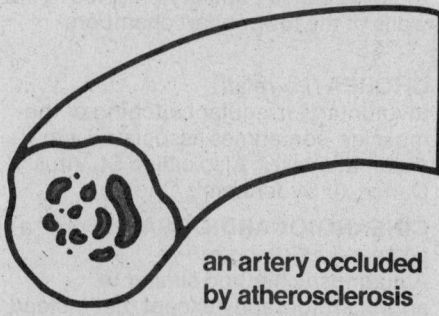

an artery occluded by atherosclerosis

CRUDE DEATH RATE
Also called crude mortality rate. The ratio of total deaths to total population during a given period of time, such as a

year. It is calculated by dividing the total number of deaths during the year by the mid-year population (estimated population on July 1) of the same year.

CYANOSIS *(si''ah-no'sis)*
Blueness of skin caused by insufficient oxygen in the blood. Oxygen is carried in the blood by hemoglobin, which is bright red when saturated with oxygen. When hemoglobin is not carrying oxygen, it is dark burgundy and is called reduced hemoglobin. The blueness of the skin occurs when the amount of reduced hemoglobin exceeds 5 grams per 100 cc. of blood.

D

DECOMPENSATION *(de''kom-pen-sa'shun)*
Inability of the heart to maintain adequate circulation, usually resulting in a waterlogging of tissues. A person whose heart is failing to maintain normal circulation is said to be "decompensated."

DEFIBRILLATION *(de-fib''ri-la'shun)*
Termination of atrial or ventricular fibrillation. Usually refers to treatment by the application of electric shock (cardioversion). **See Fibrillation and Cardioversion.**

DEPRESSANT *(de-pres'ant)*
Any drug which decreases functional activity.

DESCARTES, RENE (1596-1650)
Author of the first physiology textbook which accepted the theory of the circulation of the blood as described by William Harvey.

DEXTROCARDIA *(deks''tro-kar'de-ah)*
Two different types of congenital phenomena are often described as dextrocardia. The first is a condition more correctly termed "dextroversion" in which the heart is slightly rotated and lies almost entirely in the right (instead of the left) side of the chest. The second is a condition in which the left chambers of the heart are on the right side and the right chambers are on the left side, so that the heart and great vessels present a mirror image of the normal heart.

DIASTOLE *(di-as'to-le)*
In each heartbeat, the period of the relaxation of the heart. Atrial diastole is the period of relaxation of the atria, or upper heart chambers. Ventricular diastole is the period of relaxation of the ventricles, or lower heart chambers. **See Cardiac Cycle.**

DIET *(di'et)*
Daily allowance or intake of food and drink.

DIETETICS *(di-e-tet'iks)*
The science and art dealing with the application of principles of nutrition to the feeding of individuals or groups under different economic or health conditions.

DIETITIAN *(di-e-tish'an)*
One skilled in the scientific use of diet in health and disease.

DIGITALIS *(dij''e-tal'is)*
A drug prepared from leaves of the foxglove plant. Its main effect is cardiotonic, that is, it causes the heart muscle to pump more forcefully and effectively, thereby improving the circulation of the blood and promoting the normal elimination of excess fluid. Digitalis is often used to treat heart failure because it can relieve one of the early effects of the condition—buildup of fluid in the body tissues.

Digitalis is the most frequently used cardiotonic drug; other examples are ouabain and strophanthidin.

DILATION *(di-la'shun)*
A stretching or enlargement of the heart or blood vessels beyond the norm.

DIURESIS *(di''u-re'sis)*
Increased excretion of urine.

DIURETIC *(di''u-ret'ik)*
A medicine which promotes the excretion of urine. These drugs are often used to treat conditions involving excess body fluid such as hypertension and congestive heart failure. One important class of diuretics is the thiazides.

DUCTUS ARTERIOSUS *(duk'tus ar-te''re-o'sis)*
A small duct in the heart of the fetus between the artery leaving the right side of the heart (pulmonary artery) and the artery leaving the left side of the heart (aorta). Normally this duct closes soon after birth. If it does not close, the condition is known as patent or open ductus arteriosus. **See Patent Ductus Arteriosus.**

DYSPNEA *(disp'ne-ah)*
The uncomfortable sensation or awareness of shortness of breath.

E

ECG
See Electrocardiogram

ECHOCARDIOGRAPHY *(ek''o-kar''de-og'rah-fe)*
A diagnostic method by which pulses of sound (ultrasound) are transmitted into the body and the echoes returning from the surfaces of the heart and other structures are electronically plotted and recorded. Stop-action or real-time images of the heart can be made into a record of the heart's movements.

ECHOGRAM *(ek'o-gram)*
An image of the heart and great vessels, as would be produced by echocardiography.

ECTOMORPH *(ek'to-morf)*
Wiry body type.

EDEMA *(e-de'mah)*
Swelling due to abnormally large amounts of fluid in the tissues of the body.

EFFORT SYNDROME *(sin'drom)*
A group of symptoms (quick fatigue, rapid heartbeat, sighing breaths, dizziness) that do not result from disease of organs or tissues and that are out of proportion to the amount of exertion required. Often called functional heart disease.

EISENMENGER'S SYNDROME *(i'sen-meng''erz)*
A condition in which there is a large congenital shunting defect complicated by high blood pressure in the vessels of the lungs (pulmonary hypertension). A shunting defect is an abnormal opening between heart chambers (septal defect) or between the great vessels (such as patent ductus arteriosus) such that some oxygen-poor blood gets pumped to the body and some oxygen-rich blood gets pumped to the lungs.

The syndrome is also called Eisenmenger's Reaction. The term **Eisenmenger's Complex** is used only when the defect is in the ventricular septum.

EKG
See Electrocardiogram.

ELECTROCARDIOGRAM *(e-lek''tro-kar'de-o-gram'')*
Often referred to as ECG or EKG. A graphic record of the electric currents generated by the heart.

The word "electrocardiogram" most often refers to a resting electrocardiogram, that is, the patient is lying at rest while the recording is being made. The recording can also be made during exercise. **See Exercise Electrocardiogram.**

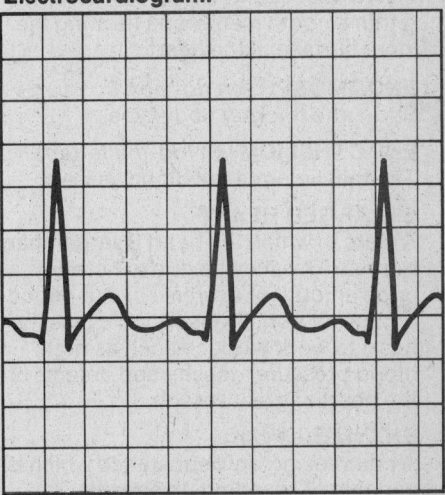

electrocardiogram

ELECTROLYTE (e-lek'tro-lit)
A substance which, when dissolved in a liquid, dissociates into ions (positively and negatively charged particles). A solution of electrolytes is capable of conducting an electrical current.

Electrolytes, especially sodium and potassium, occur naturally in the body fluids. Heart disease and medications to treat it can cause abnormal electrolyte concentrations in the body fluids. Physicians sometimes prescribe diet and medications to correct these disordered concentrations.

EMBOLISM (em'bo-lizm)
The blocking of a blood vessel by a clot or other substance carried in the bloodstream.

EMBOLUS (em'bo-lus)
A blood clot (or other substance such as an air bubble, fat or tumor) which drifts unattached in the bloodstream until it becomes lodged in a small vessel and obstructs circulation. **See Thrombus.**

ENDARTERECTOMY (end"ar-ter-ek'to-me)
Surgical removal of the innermost lining (intima) of an artery when it is thickened by fatty deposits (atheroma) and blood clots (thromboses).

ENDOCARDIAL FIBROELASTOSIS (en"do-kar'de-al fi"bro-e"las-to'sis)
A heart disease of unknown cause occurring in adults, but mostly in infants. It involves thickening of the lining of the heart chambers (endocardium) with elastic tissue. The thickening is most pronounced in the left ventricle and greatly impairs cardiac function.

ENDOCARDITIS (en"do-kar-di'tis)
Inflammation of the inner lining of the heart (endocardium) usually associated with acute rheumatic fever or some infectious agents.

ENDOCARDIUM (en"do-kar'de-um)
A thin smooth membrane forming the inner surface of the heart.

ENDOMORPH (en'do-morf)
Short and thickset body type.

ENDOTHELIUM (en"do-the'le-um)
The thin lining of the blood vessels.

ENLARGED HEART
A state in which the heart is larger than normal. This may be due to heredity, a large amount of exercise over a period of time, or conditions which cause the heart to work harder—such as high blood pressure, obesity and defects of the heart or great vessels.

ENZYME (en'zim)
A complex organic substance which is capable of speeding up specific biochemical processes in the body.

Enzymes are universally present in living organisms.

EPICARDIUM (ep"e-kar'de-um)
The outer layer of the heart wall. Also called the visceral pericardium.

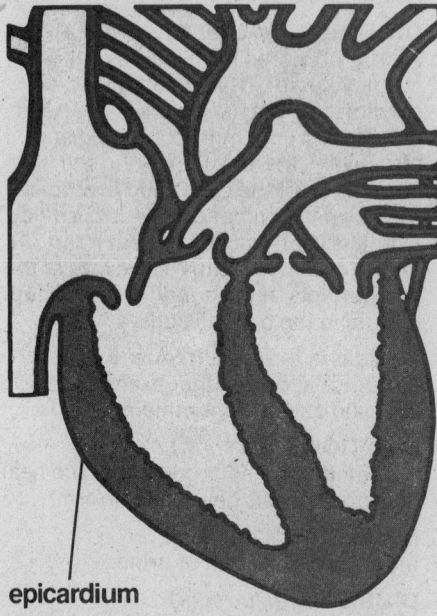

epicardium

EPIDEMIOLOGY (ep'e-de"me-ol'-o-je)
The science dealing with the factors which determine the frequency and distribution of a disease in a human community.

EPINEPHRINE (ep"e-nef'rin)
One of the secretions of two small glands, called adrenal glands, located just above the kidneys. This secretion, also called adrenalin, and sometimes prepared synthetically, constricts the small blood vessels (arterioles), increases the heart rate, and raises blood pressure. It is a vasoconstrictor or vasopressor substance.

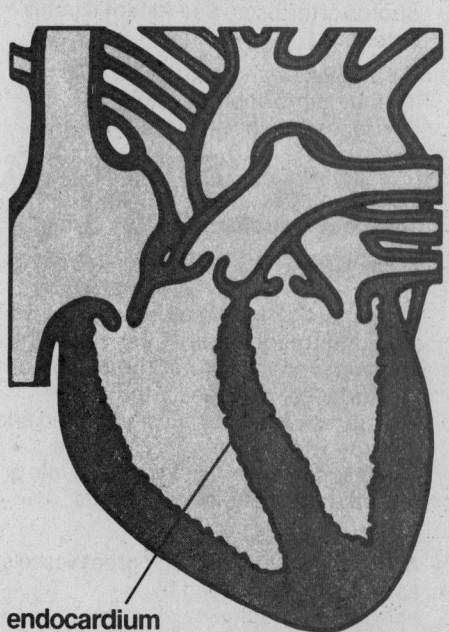

endocardium

ERYTHROCYTE (e-rith'ro-site)
Red blood cell.

ESOPHOGEAL VARICES (e-sof"ah-je'al var'i-seez)
Varicosed or swollen veins in the wall of the esophagus, the tube connecting the mouth and the stomach. These are dangerous because they may rupture and bleed profusely. Esophageal varices are often associated with cirrhosis of the liver. **See Varix.**

ESSENTIAL HYPERTENSION (e-sen'shal hi"per-ten'shun)
Sometimes called primary hypertension, and commonly known as high blood pressure. An elevated blood pressure of unknown cause.

ETIOLOGY (e"te-ol'o-je)
The sum of knowledge about the causes of a disease.

EXERCISE ELECTROCARDIOGRAM (e-lek"tro-kar'de-o-gram")
Often referred to as a "stress test." An electrocardiogram taken while the patient is exercising—usually jogging on a treadmill, walking up and down a short set of stairs, or pedaling on a stationary bicycle. **See Electrocardiogram.**

EXTRACORPOREAL CIRCULATION (eks"trah-kor-po're-al)
The circulation of the blood outside the body as by a mechanical pump or pump-oxygenator. This is often done while surgery is being performed on the heart.

EXTRASYSTOLE (eks"trah-sis'to-le)
A contraction of the heart which occurs prematurely and interrupts the normal rhythm.

EYEGROUND (i'ground)
The inside of the back part of the eye seen by looking through the pupil. Examining the eyeground is one means of assessing changes in the blood vessels. Also called fundus of the eye.

F

FABRICIUS AB AQUAPENDENTE, HIERONYMUS (1560-1634)
Italian anatomist, a teacher of William Harvey at Padua. He studied the valves of the veins. Harvey is reported to have credited the work of Fabricius with leading to his own concept of the circulation of the blood.

FALLOT, ETIENNE LOUIS ARTHUR (1850-1911) (fal-o')
French physician who gave an important description of a congenital heart defect known as the Tetralogy of Fallot (more accurately, Tetrad of Fallot). **See Tetralogy of Fallot.**

FEMORAL ARTERY *(fem'or-al ar'ter-e)*
Main blood vessel supplying blood to the leg.

FIBRILLATION *(fi-bri-la'shun)*
A kind of cardiac arrhythmia. Uncoordinated contraction of the heart muscle occurring when the individual muscle fibers take up independent irregular contractions. **Atrial fibrillation** involves very rapid, irregular contractions of the atria, followed irregularly by contractions of the ventricles. This may occur suddenly and for a short time, or, if there is an existing heart disease, can become chronic. Treatment is usually by drugs and sometimes by cardioversion (brief electric shock). **Ventricular fibrillation** involves contractions of the ventricles which are irregular, haphazard and ineffective, resulting in a rapid decline of blood circulation and death. Emergency treatment may include external cardiac massage (cardiopulmonary resuscitation—CPR), electrical defibrillation (cardioversion) or drugs. **See Cardiopulmonary Resuscitation and Cardioversion.**

FIBRIN *(fi'brin)*
An elastic, threadlike protein which forms the essential portion of a blood clot.

FIBRINOGEN *(fi-brin'o-jen)*
A protein dissolved in the blood which, by the action of certain enzymes, is converted into the insoluble threadlike protein of a blood clot (fibrin).

FIBRINOLYSIN *(fi"bri-no-li'sin)*
An enzyme which can cause coagulated blood to return to a liquid state.

FIBRINOLYTIC AGENTS *(fi"bri-no-lit'ik)*
Also called thrombolytic agents. Substances which dissolve blood clots. Two examples are streptokinase and urokinase.

FLOPPY MITRAL VALVE SYNDROME
See Barlow's Syndrome.

FLUORESCENT ANTIBODY TEST
(floo"o-res'ent an'te-bod"e)
A rapid and sensitive laboratory test. Among other things, it can be used to detect the disease-causing bacteria known as streptococci, especially those that cause rheumatic fever and therefore rheumatic heart disease. The test consists of "tagging" with a fluorescent dye the antibodies, i.e., substances in blood serum that have been built up to defend the body against bacteria. This dyed antibody is then mixed with a smear taken from the throat of the patient. If there are streptococci present in the smear, the glowing antibodies will attach to them, and they can be clearly seen through a

microscope. **See Rheumatic Fever and Rheumatic Heart Disease.**

FLUOROSCOPE *(floo'o-ro-skop)*
An instrument for observing the internal body organs at work. X-rays are passed through the body onto a fluorescent screen where the shadows of the beating heart and other organs can be seen and studied.

FLUOROSCOPY *(floo"or-os'ko-pe)*
The examination of structures within the body by means of a fluoroscope.

FLUTTER
See Atrial Flutter.

FORAMEN OVALE *(fo-ra'men o-va"le)*
An oval hole between the left and right upper chambers of the heart which normally closes shortly after birth. Its failure to close is one of the congenital defects of the heart, called a patent (open) foramen ovale.

FUNDUS OF THE EYE *(fun'dus)*
The inside of the back part of the eye seen by looking through the pupil. Examining the fundus of the eye is used as a means of assessing changes in the blood vessels. Also called the eyeground.

G

GALEN (CLAUDIUS GALENUS) (c. 130-200 A.D.)
Renowned Greek physician whose theory that life and health depended upon the balance of four "humors" in the body dominated medical practice for 1500 years. His concept of the ebb and flow of the blood (which transported the humors to various parts of the body) was not refuted until William Harvey's discovery of the circulation of the blood in 1628.

GALLOP RHYTHM
An extra heart sound which, when the heart rate is rapid enough, resembles a horse's gallop. It may or may not be significant.

GANGLION *(gang'gle-on)*
A mass of nerve cells which serves as a center of nervous influence.

GANGLIONIC BLOCKING AGENTS
(gang"gle-on'ik)
Drugs which block the transmission of a nerve impulse at the nerve centers (ganglia) rather than at the nerve endings (as would adrenergic blocking agents). Some of these drugs, such as hexamethonium and mecamylamine hydrochloride, may be used in the treatment of high blood pressure.

GENETICS *(je-net'iks)*
The study of heredity.

GUANETHIDINE *(gwa-ne'thi-deen)*
One of the drugs used to control high blood pressure. **See Antihypertensive Drugs.**

H

HARVEY, WILLIAM (1578-1657)
English physician who discovered the circulation of the blood and described his theory in 1628 in his classic work *De Motu Cordis.*

HEART ATTACK
The death of a portion of heart muscle which may result in disability or death of the individual, depending on how much of the heart is damaged. A heart attack occurs when an obstruction in one of the coronary arteries prevents an adequate oxygen supply to the heart. Symptoms may be none, mild or severe and may include chest pain (sometimes radiating to the shoulder, arm, neck or jaw), nausea, cold sweat, and shortness of breath.

Doctors often refer to a heart attack in terms of the obstruction (i.e., coronary occlusion, coronary thrombosis, or simply "coronary") or of the heart muscle damage (myocardial infarction, "infarct," or "M.I."). In common usage, the term "heart attack" often incorrectly refers to irregular heartbeats or attacks of angina pectoris.

HEART BLOCK
A condition in which the electrical impulse which travels through the heart's specialized conduction system to trigger the events of the heartbeat is slowed or blocked along its pathway. This can result in a dissociation of the rhythms of the upper and lower heart chambers, and is the major disorder for which artificial pacemakers are used. **See Sinoatrial Node and Pacemaker.**

HEART DISEASE
A general term used to mean ailments of the heart or blood vessels. Some of these are present at birth (congenital) and are either inherited or are the result of environmental influences on the embryo as it develops in the womb. The majority of cases of heart disease, however, are acquired later in life, for example, through the development of atherosclerosis.

HEART FAILURE
A condition in which the heart is unable to pump the amount of blood required to maintain a normal circulation. It can be isolated to either the left or the right side of the heart, or can involve the whole heart. Heart failure can develop from many heart and circulatory disorders, especially high blood pressure (an increased resistance to

bloodflow in the arteries), heart attack, rheumatic heart disease and birth defects.

Heart failure often leads to congestion in the body tissues; fluid accumulates in the abdomen and legs and/or in the lungs (pulmonary edema). Congestive heart failure often develops gradually over several years, although it can be acute (short and severe). It can be treated by drugs or in some cases by surgery.

HEART-LUNG MACHINE
A machine through which the bloodstream is diverted for pumping and oxygenation, for example, during heart surgery. **See Extracorporeal Circulation.**

HEART MASSAGE
Also called cardiac massage. An emergency technique using compression of the heart to keep the blood pumping through the body in the event the heart stops pumping effectively. **External heart massage** involves pressing on the chest to compress the heart between the breast-bone and the spine. Also, raising the pressure inside the chest by external compression may aid the heart's emptying as well. **Internal cardiac massage** is usually done in the operating room where the heart is directly compressed by the surgeon's hand through an incision in the chest.

HEMIPLEGIA *(hem"e-ple'je-ah)*
Paralysis of one side of the body caused by damage to the opposite side of the brain. Nerves cross in the brain, and one side of the brain controls the opposite side of the body. Such paralysis is sometimes caused by a blood clot or hemorrhage in a blood vessel in the brain. **See Stroke.**

HEMODYNAMICS *(he"mo-di-nam'iks)*
The study of the flow of blood and the forces involved.

HEMOGLOBIN *(he"mo-glo'bin)*
The oxygen-carrying red pigment of the red blood cells (corpuscles). When it has absorbed oxygen in the lungs, it is bright red and is called oxyhemoglobin. After it has given up some of its oxygen load in the tissues, it is dark burgundy in color and is called reduced hemoglobin.

HEMORRHAGE *(hem'or-ij)*
Loss of blood from a blood vessel. In external hemorrhage blood escapes from the body. In internal hemorrhage blood passes into tissues surrounding the ruptured blood vessel.

HEMORRHOIDS *(hem'o-roidz)*
Varices or excessively distended veins in the lower rectum and anus caused by a persistent increase in pressure within or against these veins. They are painful

and often complicated by inflammation, bleeding, and clotting blood. **See Varix.**

HEPARIN *(hep'ah-rin)*
A naturally occurring substance which tends to prevent blood from clotting. Sometimes used in cases of an existing clot in an artery or vein to prevent enlargement of the clot or the formation of new clots. An anticoagulant.

HIGH BLOOD PRESSURE
An unstable or persistent elevation of blood pressure above the normal range. Uncontrolled, chronic high blood pressure strains the heart, damages arteries, and creates a greater risk of heart attack, stroke, and kidney problems. Also known as hypertension. **See Primary Hypertension and Secondary Hypertension.**

HIS, WILHELM (1831-1904) *(hiss)*
German anatomist who discovered the bundle of specialized muscle fibers running from the upper to lower chambers of the heart. These fibers are known as the "Bundle of His."

HYDRALAZINE *(hi-dral'ah-zeen)*
One of the drugs used to control high blood pressure. **See Antihypertensive Drugs.**

HYDROGENATED *(hi'dro-jen-a"tid)*
Combined with more hydrogen; more saturated.

HYPERCHOLESTEREMIA *(hi"per-ko-les"ter-e'me-ah)*
An excess of a fatty substance called cholesterol in the blood. Sometimes called hypercholesterolemia or hypercholesterinemia. **See Cholesterol.**

HYPERLIPEMIA *(hi"per-li-pe'me-ah)*
An excess of fats or lipids in the blood. Also called hyperlipidemia.

HYPERLIPOPROTEINEMIA *(hi"per-lip"o-pro"te-in-e'me-ah)*
The name for several types of blood-lipid disorders involving high blood levels of lipoproteins (complexes of lipids—either cholesterol or triglycerides—and certain kinds of proteins). Some types of hyperlipoproteinemia (Type II and Type IV) are associated with the premature development of atherosclerosis (hardening of the arteries) and therefore with increased risk of heart attack and stroke.

HYPERTENSION *(hi"per-ten'shun)*
Commonly called high blood pressure. **See High Blood Pressure, Primary Hypertension, and Secondary Hypertension.**

HYPERTENSIVE *(hi"per-ten'siv)* .
A person with high blood pressure (hypertension).

HYPERTHYROIDISM *(hi"per-thi'roid-izm)*
A condition in which the thyroid gland is overly active. This may eventually result in a speeded up rate of heartbeat.

HYPERTROPHY *(hi-per'tro-fe)*
The enlargement of a tissue or organ due to increase in the size of its constituent cells. This may result from a demand for increased work.

HYPOCHOLESTEREMIC DRUGS *(hi"po-ko-les"te-re'mik)*
See Lipid-Lowering Drugs.

HYPOLIPEMIC DRUGS *(hi"po-li-pe'mik)*
Also called hypolipidemic drugs. **See Lipid-Lowering Drugs.**

HYPOTENSION *(hi"po-ten'shun)*
Commonly called low blood pressure. Blood pressure below the normal range. Most commonly used to describe an acute fall in blood pressure, as occurs in shock or syncope (fainting).

HYPOTHALAMUS *(hi"po-thal'ah-mus)*
A part of the brain which exerts control over activity of the abdominal organs, water balance, temperature, etc. Damage to the hypothalamus may cause abnormal gain in weight, among other things.

HYPOTHERMIA *(hy"po-ther'me-ah)*
Also called hypothermy. The state of low body temperature. Often induced (usually to 86-88 degrees F) during heart surgery in order to slow the metabolic processes. In this cooled state body tissues require less oxygen, and are therefore less likely to be damaged by oxygen deprivation.

HYPOTHYROIDISM *(hi"po-thi'roid-izm)*
A condition in which the thyroid gland is underactive, resulting in the slowing down of many of the body processes including the heart rate.

HYPOXIA *(hi-pok'se-ah)*
Less than normal content of oxygen in the organs and tissues of the body. At very high altitudes a healthy person experiences hypoxia because of insufficient oxygen in the air.

I

IATROGENIC HEART DISEASE *(i"at-ro-jen'ik)*
Literally means "caused by the doctor." A heart ailment inadvertently caused by the doctor or simply by the patient's belief that he has heart disease inferred from the manner and actions of his physician or other member of the medical team.

IDIOPATHIC HYPERTROPHIC SUBAORTIC STENOSIS (IHSS) *(id"e-o-path'ik hi"per-tro'fik sub"a-or'tik ste-no'sis)*
See Asymmetric Septal Hypertrophy.

ILIAC ARTERY *(il'e-ak ar'ter-e)*
A large artery which conducts blood to the pelvis and the legs.

INCIDENCE *(in'si-dens)*
The number of new cases of a disease developing in a given population during a specified period of time, such as a year.

INCOMPETENT VALVE *(in-kom'pe-tent)*
Any valve which does not close tight and leaks blood back in the wrong direction. Also called valvular insufficiency.

INFARCT *(in'farkt)*
The area of tissue which is damaged or dies as a result of receiving an insufficient blood supply. Frequently used in the phrase "myocardial infarct," referring to the area of heart muscle injury due to the interrupted flow of blood through the coronary artery which normally supplies it.

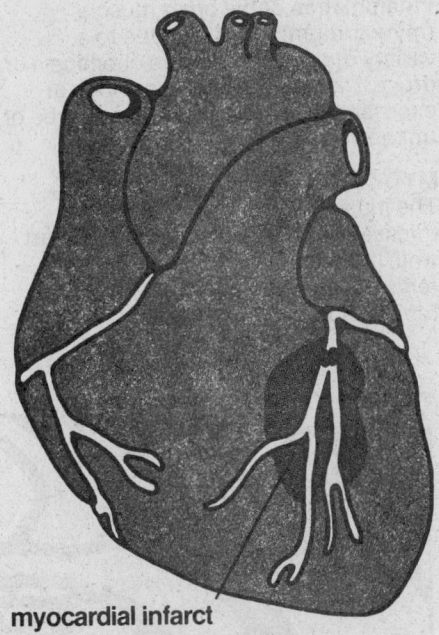

myocardial infarct

INFARCTION *(in-fark'shun)*
The occurrence of an infarct.

INNOMINATE ARTERY *(in-nom'i-nat)*
One of the largest branches of the aorta. It arises from the arch of the aorta and divides to form the right common carotid artery and the right subclavian artery.

INTERATRIAL SEPTUM *(in"ter-a'tre-al sep'tum)*
Sometimes called atrial septum. Muscular wall dividing left and right upper chambers (the atria) of the heart.
For illustration see Septum.

INTERMITTENT CLAUDICATION *(in"ter-mit'ent klaw"di-ka'shun)*
Pain in the muscles of a limb which, similar to angina pectoris, occurs intermittently—during stress but not at rest. This condition frequently accompanies diseases of the peripheral blood vessels, such as thromboangiitis obliterans. The resting muscle has an adequate blood supply, but when the need for blood increases (as during exercise), the disease impairs the circulation. An inadequate blood supply and the buildup of waste products of metabolism in the tissues cause pain. "Claudication" means lameness.

INTERVENTRICULAR SEPTUM *(in"ter-ven-trik'u-lar sep'tum)*
Sometimes called ventricular septum. Muscular wall, thinner at the top, dividing the left and right lower chambers of the heart which are called ventricles. **For illustration see Septum.**

INTIMA *(in'ti-mah)*
The innermost layer of a blood vessel (it includes the endothelium).

IN VITRO *(in vee'tro)*
Literally means "in glass," hence in a laboratory vessel. Describes a phenomenon studied outside a living body under laboratory conditions. **See In Vivo.**

IN VIVO *(in vee'vo)*
In a living organism. Describes a phenomenon studied in a living body. **See In Vitro.**

ISCHEMIA *(is-ke'me-ah)*
A local, usually temporary, deficiency of oxygen in some part of the body, often caused by a constriction or an obstruction in the blood vessel supplying that part.

ISCHEMIC HEART DISEASE *(is-kem'ik)*
Also called coronary artery disease and coronary heart disease. Heart ailments caused by narrowing of the coronary arteries and therefore a decreased blood supply to the heart (ischemia).

ISOPROTERENOL *(i"so-pro"te-re'nol)*
A drug which can be used as a cardiac stimulant to treat an abnormally slow heartbeat.

ISOTOPE *(i'so-top)*
Any of two or more species of a chemical element. The isotopes of one element are chemically identical, but differ by some physical property such as mass or radioactivity. Radioactive isotopes (radioisotopes) are often used in medicine to trace the fate of substances in the body. **See Radioisotopic Scanning.**

J

JUGULAR VEINS *(jug'u-lar)*
Veins which return blood from the head and neck to the heart.

L

LAENNEC, RENE THEOPHILE HYACINTHE (1781-1826)
French physician who invented the stethoscope.

LEEUWENHOEK, ANTONY VAN (1632-1723)
Dutch microscopist who, among other scientific contributions, discovered the interwoven structure of the muscle fibers of the heart.

LEUKOCYTES *(lu'ko-sitz)*
See White Blood Cells.

LIFESTYLE
An individual's typical way of life, including diet, kinds of recreation, job, home environment, location, temperament, and smoking, drinking and sleeping habits.

LINOLEIC ACID *(lin-o-lay'ik)*
An important component of many of the unsaturated fats. It is found widely in oils from plants. A diet with a high linoleic acid content tends to lower the amount of cholesterol in the blood.

LIPID *(lip'id)*
A fatty substance.

LIPID-LOWERING DRUGS
Drugs used to treat the various types of hyperlipoproteinemia, that is, abnormally high concentrations of lipids (fats) in the blood. Also called hypolipemic and hypolipidemic drugs; those drugs that lower blood levels of the lipid cholesterol are called hypocholesteremic.

The most common lipid-lowering drugs used are cholestyramine, clofibrate and nicotinic acid.

LIPOPROTEIN *(lip"o-pro'te-in)*
A complex consisting of lipid (fat) and protein molecules bound together. Lipids do not dissolve in the blood, but must circulate in the form of lipoproteins.

LUMEN *(lu'men)*
The passageway inside a tubular organ. The vascular lumen is the passageway inside a blood vessel.

M

MALIGNANT HYPERTENSION *(mah-lig'nant hi"per-ten'shun)*
Severe high blood pressure that may run a rapid course and cause damage to the blood vessel walls in the kidney,

eye, and other organs. Its cardinal feature is central nervous system impairment, for example, coma, seizures, etc.

MALPIGHI, MARCELLO (1628-1694) Italian anatomist who, among other discoveries, demonstrated the existence of capillary connections between the arteries and veins in the lungs.

MESOMORPH (mes'o-morf) Muscular body type.

METABOLISM (me-tab'o-lizm) A general term designating all chemical changes which occur to substances within the body.

METHYLDOPA (meth"il-do'pah) One of the drugs used to control high blood pressure. **See Antihypertensive Drugs.**

MITRAL INSUFFICIENCY (mi'tral in"su-fish'en-se) An incomplete closing of the mitral valve between the upper and lower chamber in the left side of the heart which permits a backflow of blood in the wrong direction. Sometimes the result of scar tissue forming after a rheumatic fever infection.

MITRAL STENOSIS (mi'tral ste-no'sis) A narrowing of the valve (called the mitral valve) opening between the upper and lower chamber in the left side of the heart. Sometimes the result of scar tissue forming after a rheumatic fever infection.

MITRAL VALVE (mi'tral) A valve of two cusps or triangular segments, located between the upper and lower chamber in the left side of the heart. **See Valve.**

MITRAL VALVULOTOMY (mi'tral val"vu-lot'o-me) An operation to widen the opening of the mitral valve by means of surgery with a knife. Usually performed when the valve opening is so narrowed as to obstruct bloodflow, which sometimes happens as a result of rheumatic fever. **See Commissurotomy.**

MONO-UNSATURATED FAT (mon"o-un-sat'u-rat-ed) A fat so constituted chemically that it is capable of absorbing additional hydrogen but not as much hydrogen as polyunsaturated fat. These fats in the diet have little effect on the amount of cholesterol in the blood. One example is olive oil. **See Polyunsaturated Fat.**

MORBIDITY RATE (mor-bid'i-te) The ratio of the number of cases of a disease to the number of well people in a given population during a specified period of time, such as a year. The term "morbidity" involves two separate concepts:
a. **Incidence** is the number of new cases of a disease developing in a given population during a specific period of time, such as a year.
b. **Prevalence** is the number of cases of a given disease existing in a given population at a specified moment of time.

MORTALITY RATE, AGE-ADJUSTED (mor-tal'i-te) Also called age-adjusted death rate. Death rates which have been standardized for age for the purpose of making comparisons between different populations or within the same population at various intervals of time. The age-specific death rates of the populations being compared are applied to a population that is arbitrarily selected as standard, to determine what would be the crude death rate in the standard population if it were exposed first to the rates of one population and then to the rates of the other.

MORTALITY RATE, AGE-SPECIFIC (mor-tal'i-te) Also called age-specific death rate. The ratio of deaths in a specific age group to the population of the same age group during a given period of time, such as a year. It is calculated by dividing the deaths that occurred among the specific age group during the year by the mid-year population in the same group (estimated population in the age group on July 1) of the same year.

MORTALITY RATE, CAUSE-SPECIFIC (mor-tal'i-te) The ratio of deaths from a specific cause to total population during a given period of time, such as a year.

MORTALITY RATE, CRUDE (mor-tal'i-te) The ratio of total deaths to total population during a given period of time, such as a year. Sometimes called crude death rate. It is calculated by dividing the total number of deaths during the year by the mid-year population (estimated population on July 1) of the same year.

MORTALITY RATE (SPECIFIC-CAUSE-OF-DEATH) (mor-tal'i-te) The number of deaths from a specific cause that occurred in a unit of population (such as per 100,000 or per 10,000 or per 1,000) in a specified time, such as a year.

MURMUR (mur'mur) An extra heart sound, sounding like fluid passing an obstruction, heard between the normal heart sounds.

MYOCARDIAL INFARCTION (mi"o-kar'de-al in-fark'shun) The damaging and death of an area of heart muscle (myocardium) resulting from an interruption in the blood supply reaching that area. **See Heart Attack.**

MYOCARDITIS (mi"o-kar-di'tis) Inflammation of the heart muscle (myocardium). It may be due to a variety of diseases, certain chemicals or drugs, trauma (e.g. electric shock or excessive x-ray treatment), or may be of unknown origin.

MYOCARDIUM (mi"o-kar'de-um) The muscular wall of the heart. The thickest of the three layers of the heart wall, it lies between the inner layer (endocardium) and the outer layer (epicardium).

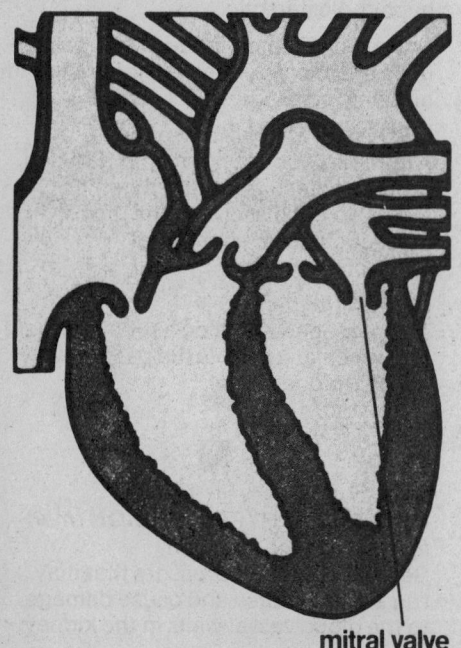
mitral valve

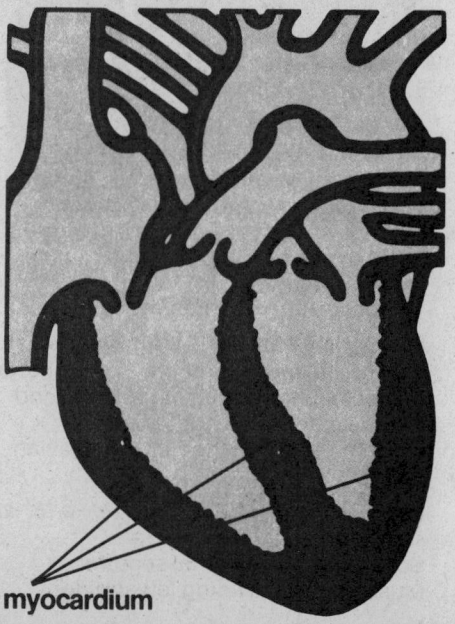
myocardium

N

NEUROCIRCULATORY ASTHENIA
(*nu"ro-cir'cu-lah-to"re as-the'na-ah*)
Sometimes called soldier's heart, effort syndrome, or functional heart disease. A complex of nervous and circulatory symptoms, often involving a sense of fatigue, dizziness, shortness of breath, rapid heartbeat, and nervousness. **See Effort Syndrome.**

NEUROGENIC (*nu"ro-jen'ik*)
Originating in the nervous system.

NICOTINIC ACID (*nik'o-tin"ik*)
A lipid-lowering drug which can be used to lower elevated levels of both cholesterol and triglycerides in the blood. **See Lipid-Lowering Drugs.**

NITRITES (*ni'trits*)
A group of chemical compounds, many of which cause dilation of the small blood vessels and thus lower blood pressure. Examples are amyl nitrite, sodium nitrite, nitroprusside and nitroglycerin.

NITROGLYCERIN (*ni-tro-glis'er-in*)
A drug (one of the nitrites) which relaxes the muscles in the blood vessels. Often used to relieve attacks of angina pectoris and spasm of coronary arteries. It is one of the vasodilators.

NORADRENALIN (*nor"ad-ren'ah-lin*)
See Norepinephrine.

NOREPINEPHRINE (*nor"ep-e-nef'rin*)
An organic compound which produces a rise in blood pressure by constricting the small blood vessels. Sometimes used in the treatment of shock. Also called noradrenalin.

NORMOTENSIVE (*nor"mo-ten'siv*)
Characterized by normal blood pressure.

NUTRITIONIST (*nu-trish'un-ist*)
One professionally engaged in investigating and solving problems of nutrition.

O

OBESITY (*o-bees'i-te*)
An increase in body weight beyond physical and skeletal requirements due to an accumulation of excess fat. This puts a strain on the heart and increases the chance of developing two major heart attack risk factors—high blood pressure and diabetes.

OCCLUSIVE (*o-kloo'siv*)
Closing or shutting off. A coronary occlusion is a closing off of a coronary artery (which supplies the heart muscle with blood).

OPEN-HEART SURGERY
Surgery performed on the opened heart. This phrase is also often used to refer to all heart surgery—whether or not the heart itself is opened.

ORGANIC HEART DISEASE
Heart disease caused by some structural abnormality in the heart or circulatory system.

OXYGEN (*ok'si-jen*)
A gas which is the most important component of the air we breathe. It is vital to energy-producing chemical reactions in the living cells of the body. Breathed into the lungs, it enters the bloodstream and is carried by the blood to the body tissues.

P

PACEMAKER (*pas'mak-er*)
A small mass of specialized cells in the right atrium of the heart which gives rise to the electrical impulses that initiate contractions of the heart. Also called sinoatrial node or S-A node of Keith-Flack. Under abnormal circumstances, other cardiac tissues may assume the pacemaker role by initiating electrical impulses which stimulate contraction.

The term "artifical pacemaker" is applied to an electrical device which can substitute for a defective natural pacemaker and control the beating of the heart by a series of rhythmic electrical discharges. If the electrodes which deliver the discharges to the heart are placed on the outside of the chest, it is called an "external pacemaker." If they are placed within the chest wall, it is called an "internal pacemaker."

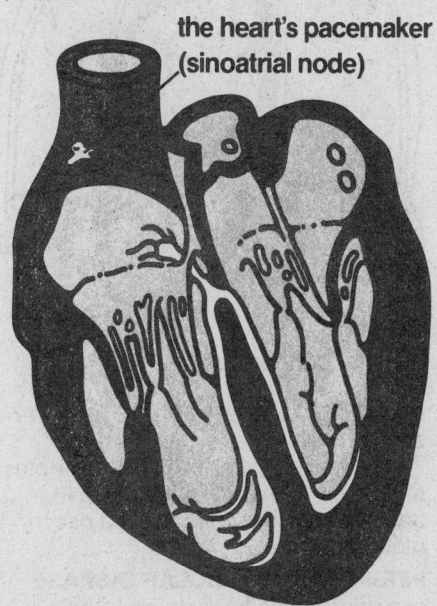

the heart's pacemaker (sinoatrial node)

PALPITATION (*pal"pi-ta'shun*)
A sensation of fluttering of the heart or abnormal rate or rhythm of the heart as experienced by the person.

PAPILLARY MUSCLES (*pap'i-ler"e*)
Small, cone-shaped muscles projecting from the walls of the lower heart chambers (the ventricles) to which are attached fibrous cords (chordae tendineae) stretching up to the flaps of the valves between upper and lower chambers. When the ventricles fill with blood and contract, the papillary muscles also contract and tighten the cords, allowing the valves to be pressed shut, but preventing them from being pushed back and open into the upper chambers (the atria) by the surging blood.

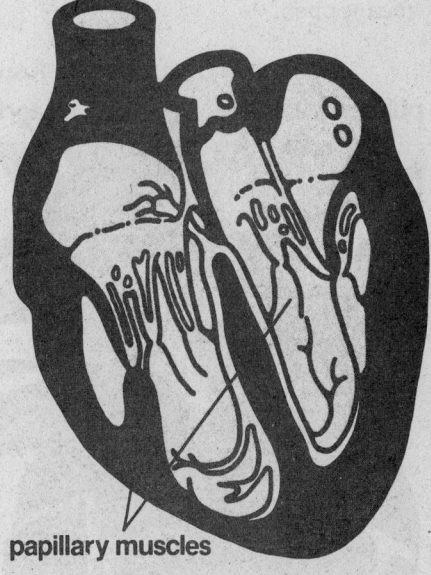

papillary muscles

PARASYMPATHETIC NERVOUS SYSTEM (*par"ah-sim"pah-thet'ik*)
One of the two divisions of the autonomic nervous system. **See Autonomic Nervous System.**

PARIETAL PERICARDIUM (*pah-ri'e-tal per"e-kar'de-um*)
A thickened protective membrane which is the outer wall of the pericardium, the double-walled sac surrounding the heart. **For illustration see Pericardium.**

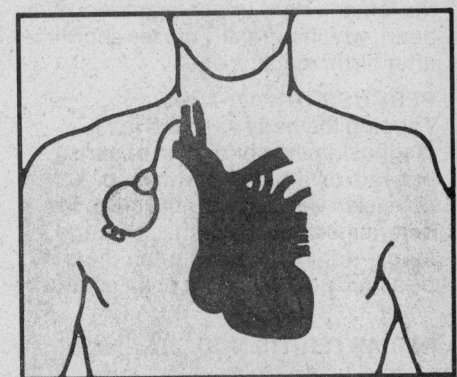

an implanted artificial pacemaker

PAROXYSMAL TACHYCARDIA
(par"ok-siz'mal tak"e-kar'de-ah)
A period of rapid heartbeats which
begins and ends suddenly.

PATENT DUCTUS ARTERIOSUS
(pa'tent duk'tus ar-te"re-o'sis)
A congenital heart defect in which a
small duct between the artery leaving
the left side of the heart (aorta) and the
artery leaving the right side of the heart
(pulmonary artery), which normally
closes soon after birth, remains open.
As a result of this duct's failure to close,
blood from both sides of the heart is
pumped into the pulmonary artery and
into the lungs. This defect is sometimes
called simply patent ductus. Patent
means open.

patent ductus arteriosus
pulmonary artery   aorta

PATENT FORAMEN OVALE *(pa'tent
fo-ra'men o-va'le)*
One type of congenital heart defect. An
oval hole (the foramen ovale) between
the left and right upper chambers of the
heart, which normally closes shortly
after birth, remains open.

PERCUSSION *(per-kush'un)*
Tapping the body as an aid in
diagnosing the conditions of parts
beneath by the sound obtained. A
physician will often tap the chest to
determine the state of the heart and
lungs—for instance, whether there may
be a fluid accumulation or an enlarged
heart.

PERIARTERITIS NODOSA *(per"e-
ar"te-ri'tis no-do'sa)*
See Polyarteritis Nodosa.

PERICARDIAL TAMPONADE *(per"i-
kar'de-al tam"pon-ad')*
An accumulation of excess fluid
between the two layers of the
membrane sac surrounding the heart
(the pericardium). This can happen
rapidly or gradually and impairs the
normal functioning of the heart. **See
Pericardium.**

PERICARDITIS *(per"e-kar-di'tis)*
Inflammation of the membrane sac
(pericardium) which surrounds the
heart.

PERICARDIUM *(per"e-kar'de-um)*
A closed sac surrounding the heart and
roots of the great vessels. The sac is
formed by two walls:
The **visceral pericardium** is on the
inside, closely adhering to the heart. It
forms the outermost layer of the heart
wall and is also called the epicardium.
The **parietal pericardium** is on the outer
side of the sac and is anchored to other
chest structures such as the
breastbone. It is a protective membrane.

The space inside the sac (the
pericardial cavity), between the two
walls, contains a fluid which provides
for smooth movements of the heart as it
beats.

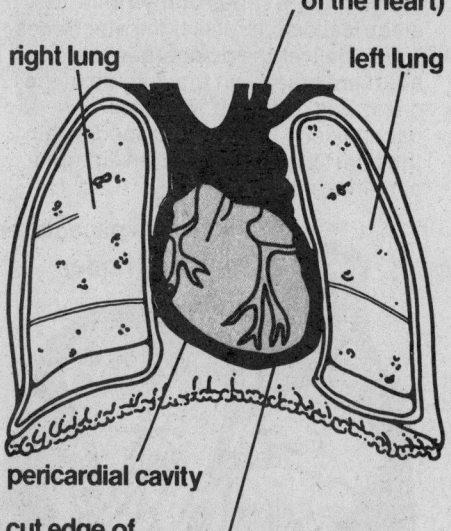

visceral pericardium
(epicardium or outer layer
of the heart)
right lung   left lung

pericardial cavity

cut edge of
parietal pericardium

PERIPHERAL RESISTANCE *(pe-rif'er-
al)*
The resistance offered by the arterioles
to the flow of blood. An increase in
peripheral resistance causes a rise in
blood pressure.

PERIPHERAL VASCULAR DISEASE
(pe-rif'er-al vas'cu-lar)
A term which, in its broadest sense,
refers to diseases of any of the blood
vessels outside of the heart and to
diseases of the lymph vessels. These

are circulation disorders caused by
changes in the caliber of the vessels.
Functional peripheral vascular diseases
are not structural or organic in cause,
but are transient and reversible. An
example is Raynaud's disease, which
can be triggered by cold temperatures,
emotional stress, work with vibrating
machinery or smoking. The term
organic describes circulation
disturbances which are caused by
structural changes in the vessels (such
as inflammation and tissue damage). An
example is Buerger's disease
(thromboangiitis obliterans).

PERSONALITY, TYPE A AND TYPE B
See Behavior, Type A and Type B.

PHEOCHROMOCYTOMA *(fe-o-
kro"mo-si-to'mah)*
A tumor which arises in the adrenal
glands. It produces and releases into
the bloodstream large quantities of
norepinephrine and epinephrine. These
powerful natural stimulants may then
create such symptoms as high blood
pressure, elevated heart rate,
headaches, anxiety, and excessive
sweating.

PHLEBITIS *(fle-bi'tis)*
Inflammation of a vein, often in the leg.
Sometimes a blood clot is formed in the
inflamed leg. **See also
Thrombophlebitis.**

PHOSPHOLIPIDS *(fos"fo-lip'idz)*
One of the three major classes of lipids
(fatty substances) in the blood. Unlike
the other two classes—cholesterol and
triglycerides—phospholipids are *not*
known to be associated with
atherosclerosis (hardening of the
arteries).

PLAQUE *(plak)*
See Atheroma.

PLASMA *(plaz'mah)*
The cell-free liquid portion of
uncoagulated blood. It is different from
serum which is the fluid portion of the
blood obtained after coagulation.

PLATELETS *(plat'letz)*
One of the three kinds of formed
elements found in the blood. Literally
"little plates," they are small, colorless,
disk-shaped bodies which are involved
in the formation of blood clots. Also
called thrombocytes. **See Red Blood
Cells and White Blood Cells.**

PLETHYSMOGRAPHY *(pleth"iz-
mog'rah-fe)*
The recording of changes in the size of
an organ, part, or limb as blood
circulates through it. However, lung
volumes can also be measured with the
technique.

POLYARTERITIS NODOSA *(pol"e-
ar"te-ri'tis no-do'sa)*
A disease of unknown cause

characterized by inflammation and destruction along segments of small and medium-sized arteries, creating lumps or nodes of scar tissue. This leads to functional impairment of the tissues supplied by the affected vessels.

POLYCYTHEMIA *(pol"e-si-the'me-ah)*
An abnormal condition of the blood characterized by an excessive number of red blood cells.

POLYUNSATURATED FAT *(pol"e-un-sat'u-rat-ed)*
A fat so constituted chemically that it is capable of absorbing additional hydrogen. These fats are usually liquid oils of vegetable origin, such as corn oil or safflower oil. A diet with a high polyunsaturated fat content tends to lower the amount of cholesterol in the blood. These fats are sometimes substituted for saturated fat in a diet in an effort to lessen the hazard of fatty deposits in the blood vessels. **See Mono-unsaturated Fat.**

PRESSOR *(pres'or)*
Tending to increase blood pressure, as a pressor substance.

PREVALENCE *(prev'ah-lens)*
The number of cases of a given disease existing in a given population at a specified moment of time.

PRIMARY HYPERTENSION *(hi"per-ten'shun)*
Also called essential hypertension. High blood pressure of unknown origin (as opposed to secondary hypertension, which is caused by some primary disease, such as kidney disease). Most people who have high blood pressure have primary hypertension. **See Secondary Hypertension.**

PROCAINE AMIDE *(pro'kane am'id)*
A drug sometimes used to treat abnormal rhythms of the heartbeat; an antiarrhythmic drug.

PROPRANOLOL *(pro-pran'o-lol)*
A member of the group of drugs known as beta-blocking agents. Propranolol is used to treat angina pectoris, cardiac arrhythmias, high blood pressure, and other disorders of the cardiovascular system. **See Adrenergic Blocking Agents.**

PROSTAGLANDINS *(pros"tah-glan'dinz)*
Hormone-like substances made from fatty acids which are found throughout the body tissues. They are thought to have important roles in tissue metabolism and bloodflow, among other things.

PROSTHESIS *(pros-the'sis)*
An artificial substitute for a body part, such as a leg, tooth, heart valve or blood vessel. The plural form is **Prostheses.**

PSYCHOSOMATIC *(si"ko-so-mat'ik)*
Pertaining to the influence of the mind, emotions, fears, etc., upon the functions of the body, especially in relation to disease.

PULMONARY *(pul'mo-ner"e)*
Pertaining to the lungs.

PULMONARY ARTERY
The large artery which conveys unoxygenated (venous) blood from the lower right chamber of the heart to the lungs. This is the only artery in the body which normally carries unoxygenated blood, all others carrying oxygenated blood to the body.

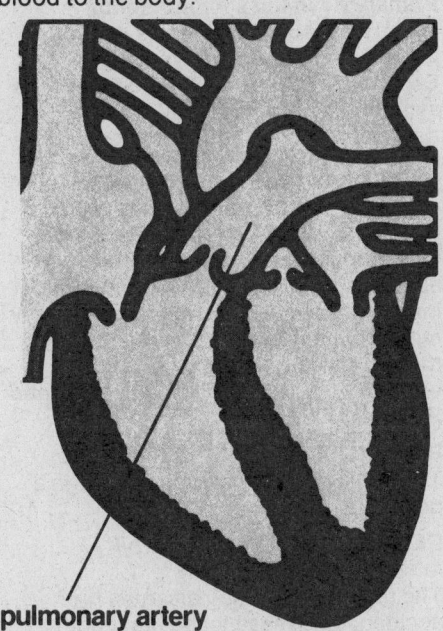

pulmonary artery

PULMONARY CIRCULATION
The circulation of the blood through the lungs, the flow being from the right lower chamber of the heart (right ventricle) through the lungs, back to the left upper chamber of the heart (left atrium). **See Systemic Circulation.**

PULMONARY EDEMA *(pul'mo-ner"e e-de'mah)*
A condition, usually acute (sudden and severe) but sometimes chronic, marked by an excess of fluid in the extravascular (outside the vessels) spaces in the lungs. It may be confined to the interstitial spaces or may appear in the alveoli (the millions of tiny air sacs in each lung). Pulmonary edema occurs most often as a complication of left ventricular failure due to ischemic heart disease, high blood pressure or disease of the aortic valve. **See Congestive Heart Failure and Heart Failure.**

PULMONARY EMBOLISM *(em'bo-lizm)*
A condition in which a blood clot (embolus), usually one formed in a vein of the leg or pelvis, breaks loose and becomes lodged in one of the arteries of

the lungs. This may produce no symptoms at all or may create very serious impairment of pulmonary circulation.

PULMONARY HYPERTENSION *(hi"per-ten'shun)*
High blood pressure (hypertension) in the blood vessels of the lungs. The two most common causes are chronic obstructive lung diseases (such as emphysema) and septal defects (holes in the wall which separates the left and right sides of the heart).

PULMONARY VALVE
Valve formed by three cup-shaped

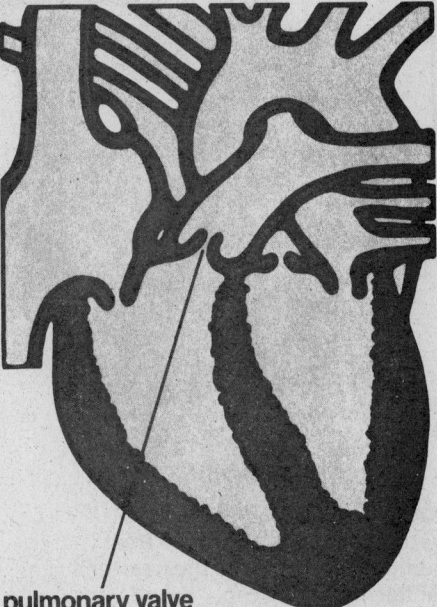

pulmonary valve

membranes at the junction of the pulmonary artery and the right lower chamber of the heart (right ventricle). When the right ventricle contracts, the pulmonary valve opens and the blood is forced into the artery leading to the lungs. When the chamber relaxes, the valve is closed and prevents a backflow of the blood. **See Valve.**

PULMONARY VEINS
The veins which conduct oxygenated blood from the lungs into the left upper chamber of the heart (left atrium).

PULSE *(puls)*
The expansion and contraction of an artery which may be felt with the finger.

PULSE PRESSURE
The difference between the blood pressure in the arteries when the heart is in contraction (systole) and when it is in relaxation (diastole).

PULSUS ALTERNANS *(pul'sus awl-ter'nanz)*
A pulse in which there is regular alternation of weak and strong beats.

PURKINJE FIBERS *(pur-kin'je)*
Specialized muscular fibers forming a

network in the walls of the lower chambers of the heart and believed to be involved in conducting electrical impulses to the muscular walls of the two lower chambers (ventricles). These electrical impulses are responsible for the contractions of the heart.

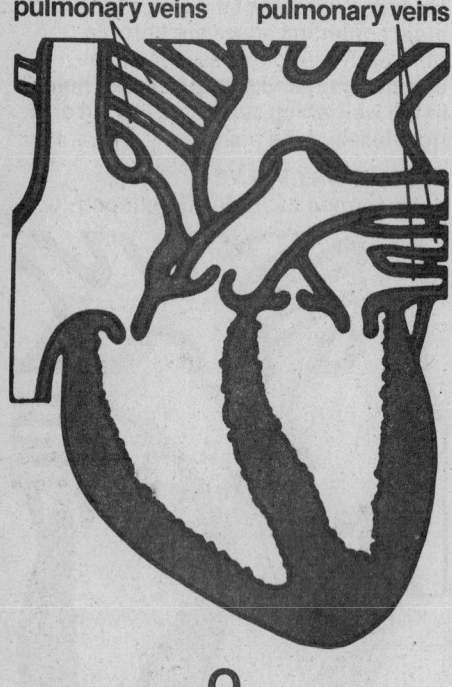

pulmonary veins   pulmonary veins

Q

QUINIDINE (kwin'i-deen)
A drug sometimes used to treat abnormal rhythms of the heartbeat; an antiarrhythmic drug.

R

RADIOISOTOPE (ray"de-o-i'so-top)
A radioactive form ("isotope") of an element. **See Isotope.**

RADIOISOTOPIC SCANNING (ray"de-o-i'so-top-ik skan'ning)
A diagnostic technique involving radioactive labelling of tissues and organs by the injection of radioisotopes into the bloodstream. The emitted radioactivity is detected by a scanner and a record or "scan" of the labelled area is made. Used by cardiologists to visualize the heart and great vessels, it can often reveal areas of heart damage. **See Isotope and Radioisotope.**

RAUWOLFIA (raw-wol'fe-ah)
A drug consisting of powdered whole root of a plant (Rauwolfia serpentina) which lowers blood pressure and slows the heart rate. Sometimes used in treatment of high blood pressure. An antihypertensive agent. **See Reserpine.**

RAYNAUD'S DISEASE (ray-noz')
Also called Primary Raynaud's Phenomenon. A disorder characterized

by occurrences of Raynaud's Phenomenon, but not known to have an underlying cause.

RAYNAUD'S PHENOMENON (ray-noz')
Short episodes of pallor and numbness in the fingers, toes and, rarely, the nose and ears, due to temporary constriction of the arterioles in the skin. Pallor in the affected area is followed by blueness (due to insufficient oxygen supply), then occasionally by redness as oxygenated blood rushes in. These episodes may be triggered by cold temperatures, emotional stress, working with vibrating machinery or cigarettes.

Primary Raynaud's Phenomenon is called **Raynaud's Disease**, is generally benign, and has no known cause. **Secondary Raynaud's Phenomenon** is a symptom of one of several serious disorders, which, if not detected and treated, may have serious consequences.

RED BLOOD CELLS (CORPUSCLES)
One of the three kinds of formed elements found in the blood. Their most important function is to carry oxygen by means of hemoglobin, the red pigment these cells contain. Also called erythrocytes. **See White Blood Cells and Platelets.**

REGURGITATION (re-gur"ji-ta'shun)
The backward flow of blood through a defective valve.

REHABILITATION (re"hah-bil"i-ta'shun)
The return of a person disabled by accident or disease to the maximum attainable physical, mental, emotional, social and economic usefulness, and, if employable, to an opportunity for gainful employment.

RENAL (re'nal)
Pertaining to the kidney.

RENAL CIRCULATION
The circulation of the blood through the kidneys. Important in heart disease because of its functon in the elimination of water, certain chemical elements, and waste products from the body.

RENAL HYPERTENSION (re'nal hi"per-ten'shun)
High blood pressure caused by damage to or disease of the kidneys or their blood vessels.

RESERPINE (res'er-peen OR re-ser'peen)
One of the organic substances found in the root of the Indian snake root plant (Rauwolfia serpentina) which lowers blood pressure, slows the heart rate, and has a sedative effect.

REVASCULARIZATION (re-vas"ku-lar-i-za'shun)
Restoration of sufficient bloodflow to

body tissues when supplying arteries are narrowed or blocked by injury or disease. Such surgery can be done on the legs, kidneys, brain, neck or (most commonly) the heart.

One procedure for cardiac revascularization is endarterectomy, removal of the thickened inner lining of a narrowed coronary artery. Other procedures may involve the use of additional blood vessels, either artificial ones or ones from elsewhere in the body. Vessels from other parts of the body may either be rerouted from nearby structures (for example, the internal mammary artery) or by grafting whole sections of vessels onto the heart (as is done with the saphenous vein in coronary bypass surgery). **See Endarterectomy and Coronary Bypass Surgery.**

RHEUMATIC FEVER (roo-mat'ik)
A disease, usually occurring in childhood, which may follow a few weeks after a streptococcal infection. It is sometimes characterized by one or more of the following: fever, sore swollen joints, a skin rash, occasionally by involuntary twitching of the muscles (called chorea or St. Vitus Dance) and small nodes under the skin. In some cases the infection affects the heart and may result in scarring the valves, weakening the heart muscle, or damaging the sac enclosing the heart. **See Rheumatic Heart Disease.**

RHEUMATIC HEART DISEASE (roo-mat'ik)
The damage done to the heart, particularly the heart valves, by one or more attacks of rheumatic fever. The valves are sometimes scarred so they do not open and close normally. **See Rheumatic Fever.**

RISK FACTORS
In cardiology, characteristics which are associated with an increased risk of developing coronary heart disease. These include high blood pressure (hypertension), elevated blood levels of cholesterol and other lipids (hyperlipoproteinemia), cigarette smoking, obesity, diabetes and a family history of heart disease. A competitive, aggressive lifestyle (Type A Behavior) is also thought to predispose a person to heart disease.

S

S-A NODE
See Sinoatrial Node.

SAPHENOUS VEIN (sah-fe'nus)
A large vein in the leg which can be removed and grafted onto the heart in coronary bypass surgery to provide adequate coronary circulation. **See Coronary Bypass Surgery.**

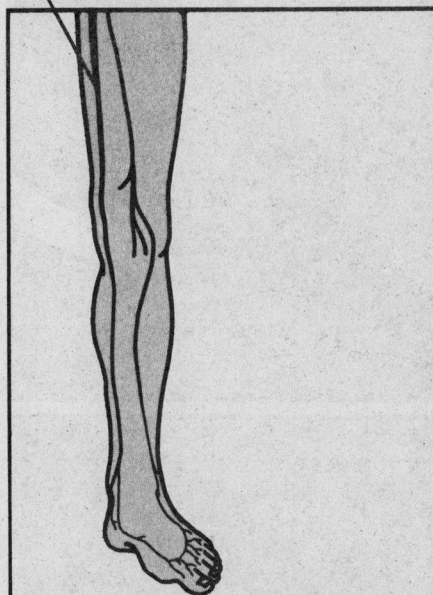

saphenous vein

SATURATED FAT (sat'u-rat"ed)
A fat so constituted chemically that it is not capable of absorbing any more hydrogen. These are usually the solid fats of animal origin such as the fats in milk, butter, meat, etc. A diet high in saturated fat content tends to increase the amount of cholesterol in the blood. Sometimes these fats are restricted in the diet in an effort to lessen the hazard of fatty deposits in the blood vessels.

SCLEROSIS (skle-ro'sis)
Hardening, as in the term "arteriosclerosis," hardening of the arteries.

SECONDARY HYPERTENSION (hi"per-ten'shun)
High blood pressure caused by (i.e.

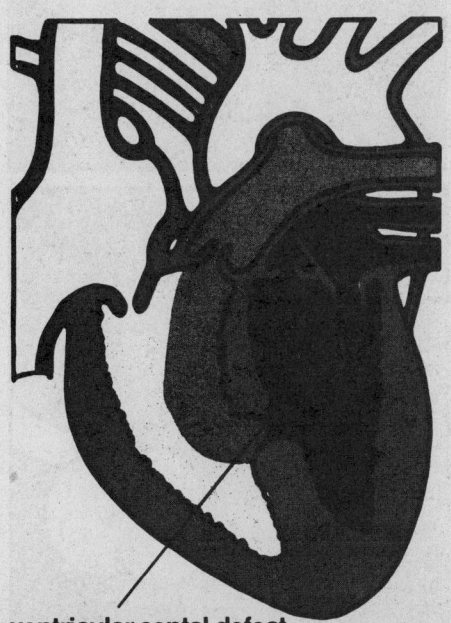

ventricular septal defect

secondary to) certain specific diseases or infections. **See Pheochromocytoma and Renal Hypertension.**

SEMILUNAR VALVES (sem"e-lu'nar)
Cup-shaped valves. The aortic valve at the entrance to the aorta and the pulmonary valve at the entrance to the pulmonary artery are semilunar valves. They consist of three cup-shaped flaps which prevent the backflow of blood.

SEPTAL DEFECT (sep'tal)
An abnormal opening in the wall (septum) that normally divides the right and left sides of the heart. There are both atrial and ventricular septal defects, depending on whether the upper or lower heart chambers are involved.

atrial septal defect

atrial septum

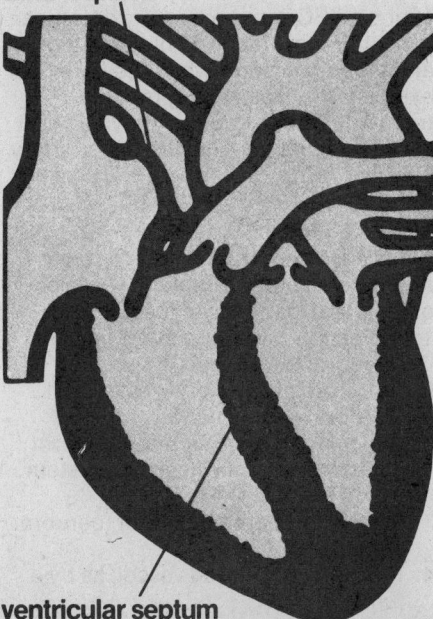

ventricular septum

SEPTUM (sep'tum)
A dividing wall.
1. Atrial or interatrial septum. Muscular wall dividing left and right upper chambers (atria) of the heart.
2. Ventricular or interventricular septum. Muscular wall, thinner at the top, dividing the left and right lower chambers (ventricles) of the heart.

SEROTONIN (ser"o-to'nin)
A naturally occurring compound, found mainly in the gastrointestinal tract and in lesser amounts in the blood, which has a stimulating effect on the circulatory system.

SERUM (se'rum)
The fluid portion of blood which remains after the cellular elements have been removed by coagulation. It is different from plasma which is the cell-free liquid portion of uncoagulated blood.

SERVETUS, MICHAEL (1509-1553)
Spanish physician who discovered the circulation of the blood through the lungs. Burned at the stake in Geneva for his religious doctrines.

SHOCK
The collection of symptoms resulting from an inadequate volume of fluid circulating through the body to maintain normal metabolism. This may be due to a large loss of blood or to some derangement of circulatory control. Shock is marked by hypotension (low blood pressure), pale, cold skin, usually tachycardia (weak, rapid pulse), and often anxiety. Cardiogenic shock is shock resulting from a greatly diminished cardiac output, such as may occur in a large heart attack.

SHUNT
A passage between two blood vessels or between the two sides of the heart, as in cases where an opening exists in the wall which normally separates them. In surgery, the operation of forming a passage between blood vessels to divert blood from one part of the body to another.

SIGN
Any objective evidence of a disease. **See Symptom.**

SINOATRIAL NODE (si"no-a'tre-al)
A small mass of specialized cells in the right upper chamber of the heart which give rise to the electrical impulses that initiate contractions of the heart. Also called S-A node or pacemaker. **For illustration see Pacemaker.**

SINUS RHYTHM (si'nus rith'm)
Normal heart rhythm as initiated by electrical impulses in the sinoatrial node or pacemaker. **See Pacemaker.**

SINUSES OF VALSALVA *(si'nus-sez of val-sal'vah)*
Three pouches in the wall of the aorta behind the three cup-shaped membranes of the aortic valve.

SODIUM *(so'de-um)*
A mineral essential to life, found in nearly all plant and animal tissue. Table salt (sodium chloride) is nearly half sodium. In some types of heart disease the body retains an excess of sodium and water, and therefore sodium intake is restricted.

SPHYGMOMANOMETER *(sfig"mo-mah-nom'e-ter)*
An instrument for measuring blood pressure in the arteries.

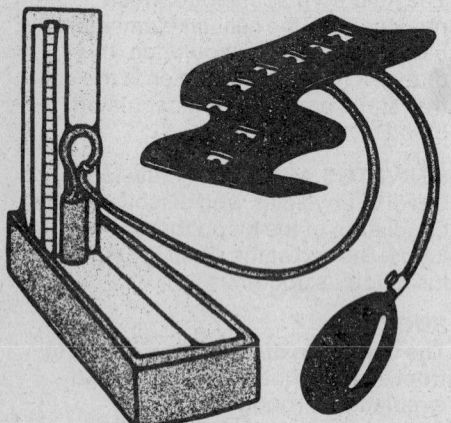

mercury column sphygmomanometer

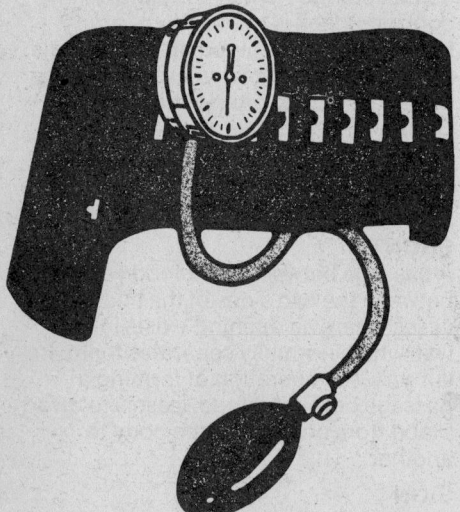

dial or aneroid sphygmomanometer

STARLING'S LAW OF THE HEART
A law which states that the more the heart muscle is stretched when an increased amount of blood fills the ventricles, the more vigorous its contraction will be, resulting in a greater amount of blood pumped out of the heart.

STASIS *(sta'sis)*
A stoppage or lessening of the flow of blood or other body fluid in any part.

STENOSIS *(ste-no'sis)*
A narrowing or stricture of an opening. Mitral stenosis, aortic stenosis, etc., mean that the valve indicated has become so narrowed that it does not function normally.

STETHOSCOPE *(steth'o-skop)*
An instrument for listening to sounds within the body.

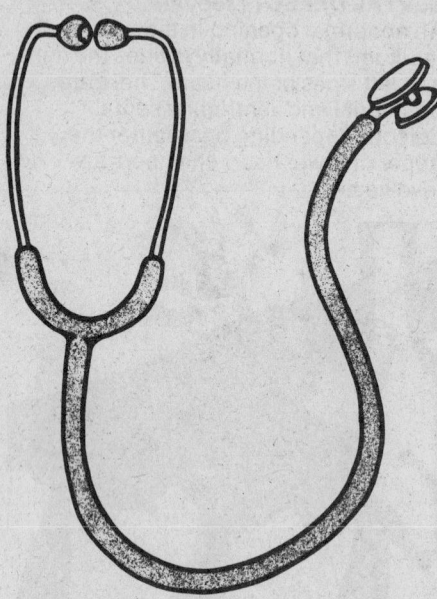

stethoscope

STRESS
Bodily or mental tension caused by physical, chemical or emotional factors. Stress can refer to physical exertion as well as mental anxiety.

STRESS TEST
A diagnostic method used to determine the body's response to physical exertion (stress). Usually involves taking an ECG and other physiological measurements (such as breathing rate and blood pressure) while the patient is exercising—usually jogging on a treadmill, walking up and down a short set of stairs, or pedaling on a stationary bicycle.

STROKE *(strok)*
Also called cerebral vascular accident. An impeded blood supply to some part of the brain, generally caused by:
1. A blood clot forming in the vessel (cerebral thrombosis).
2. A rupture of the blood vessel wall (cerebral hemorrhage).
3. A blood clot or other material from another part of the vascular system which flows to the brain and obstructs a cerebral vessel (cerebral embolism).
4. Pressure on a blood vessel, as by a tumor.

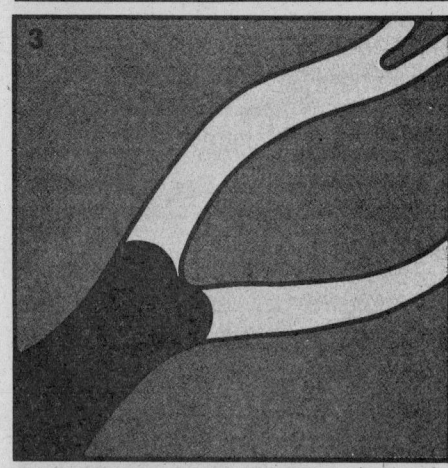

STROKE VOLUME (strok)
The amount of blood which is pumped out of the heart at each contraction of the heart.

SYMPATHECTOMY (sim"pah-thek'to-me)
An operation which interrupts some part of the sympathetic nervous system. The sympathetic nervous system is a part of the autonomic or involuntary nervous system which normally regulates tissues not under voluntary control, e.g., glands, heart, and smooth muscles. Sometimes the interruption is accomplished by drugs, in which case it is called a chemical sympathectomy.

SYMPATHETIC NERVOUS SYSTEM (sim"pah-thet'ik)
One of the two divisions of the autonomic nervous system. **See Autonomic Nervous System.**

SYMPTOM (simp'tum)
Any subjective evidence of a patient's condition. **See Sign.**

SYNCOPE (sin'ko-pe)
A faint. One cause for syncope can be an insufficient blood supply to the brain.

SYNDROME (sin'drom)
A set of symptoms which occur together and are therefore given a name to indicate that particular combination.

SYSTEMIC CIRCULATION (sis-tem'ik)
The circulation of the blood through all parts of the body except the lungs, the flow being from the left lower chamber of the heart (left ventricle) through the body, back to the right upper chamber of the heart (right atrium). **See Pulmonary Circulation.**

SYSTOLE (sis'to-le)
In each heartbeat, the period of contraction of the heart. Atrial systole is the period of the contraction of the upper chambers of the heart, called the atria.

Ventricular systole is the period of the contraction of the lower chambers of the heart, called the ventricles. **See Cardiac Cycle.**

T

TACHYCARDIA (tak"e-kar'de-ah)
Abnormally fast heart rate. Generally, anything over 100 beats per minute is considered a tachycardia.

TETRALOGY OF FALLOT (te-tral'o-je of fal-o')
A congenital malformation of the heart involving four distinct defects (hence tetralogy). Named for Etienne Fallot, French physician who described the condition in 1888. The four defects are:
1. An abnormal opening in the wall

between the lower chambers of the heart (ventricular septal defect).
2. Misplacement of the aorta, "overriding" the abnormal opening, so that is receives blood from both the right and left lower chambers instead of only the left.
3. Pulmonary outflow obstruction usually below or at the valve.
4. Enlargement of the right ventricle.

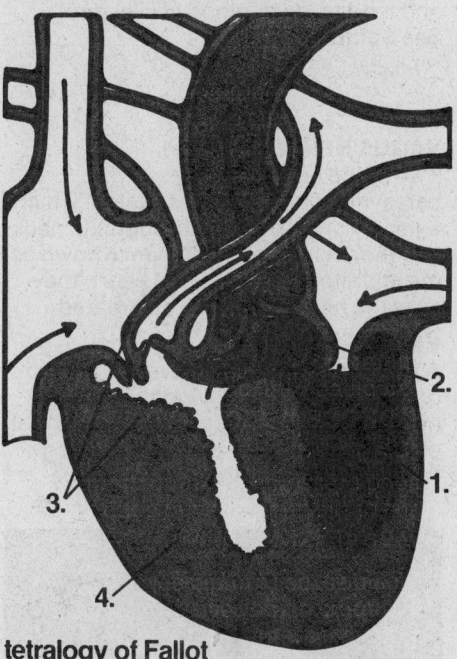

tetralogy of Fallot

THIAZIDES (thi'a-sidz)
Also called thiazide diuretics or benzothiadiazides. A class of diuretics (drugs which promote excretion of urine) which includes chlorothiazide. The thiazides are often used to treat high blood pressure and for the relief of edema, or waterlogged tissues. **See Antihypertensive Drugs.**

THORACIC (tho-ras'ik)
Pertaining to the chest (thorax).

THROMBECTOMY (throm-bek'to-me)
An operation to remove a blood clot from a blood vessel.

THROMBOANGIITIS OBLITERANS (throm"bo-an"je-i'tis ob-lit'er-anz)
Also called Buerger's disease. A disease of the blood vessels of the extremities, primarily the legs, which occurs most commonly in men and is associated with tobacco use. It is characterized by inflammation of the veins, arteries and nerves and by thrombosis in the vessels (blood clot formation). This leads to poor circulation and gangrene. **See Buerger's Syndrome.**

THROMBOEMBOLISM (throm"bo-em'bo-lizm)
Obstruction (embolism) of a blood vessel by a blood clot (thrombus) formed elsewhere in the circulatory system and carried along by the

bloodstream to plug a smaller vessel.

THROMBOLYTIC AGENTS (throm"bo-lit'ik)
Substances which dissolve blood clots. Also called fibrinolytic agents. Two examples are streptokinase and urokinase.

THROMBOPHLEBITIS (throm"bo-fle-bi'tis)
Inflammation and blood clotting in a vein.

THROMBOSIS (throm-bo'sis)
The formation or presence of a blood clot (thrombus) inside a blood vessel or cavity of the heart.

THROMBUS (throm'bus)
A blood clot which forms inside a blood vessel or cavity of the heart. **See Embolus.**

TOXIC (tok'sik)
Poisonous,

TRANSPLANTATION, HEART
The replacement of a healthy heart from a recently deceased donor into the chest of a person whose own heart can no longer function adequately. The donor's heart then replaces or assists the failing heart.

TRANSPOSITION OF THE GREAT VESSELS (trans"po-zish'un)
A congenital heart defect in which the two largest arteries occur in the wrong places: the aorta arises from the right (rather than left) ventricle and the pulmonary artery arises from the left (rather than right) ventricle. Thus the right heart pumps used blood from the body through the aorta and back to the body, and the left heart pumps oxygenated blood from the lungs back

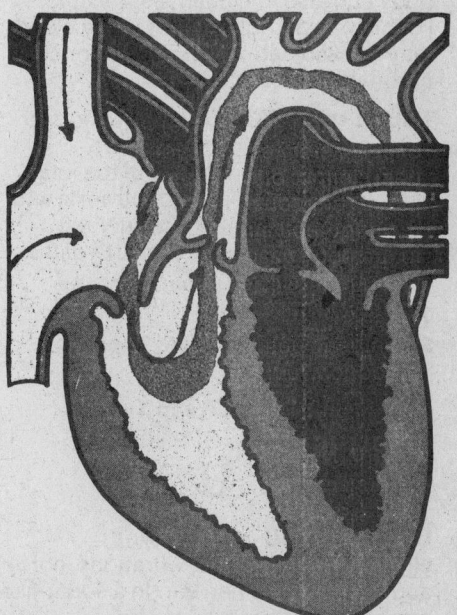

transposition of the great vessels with atrial septal defect

to the lungs. Only if there is a sizeable hole between right and left chambers (a septal defect) or a channel between the aorta and pulmonary artery (patent ductus arteriosus) will enough oxygenated blood get pumped to the body to sustain life for the infant.

TRICUSPID VALVE *(tri-kus'pid)*
A valve consisting of three cusps or triangular segments located between the upper and lower chamber in the right side of the heart. Its position corresponds to the mitral valve (which is bicuspid) in the left side of the heart. **See Valve.**

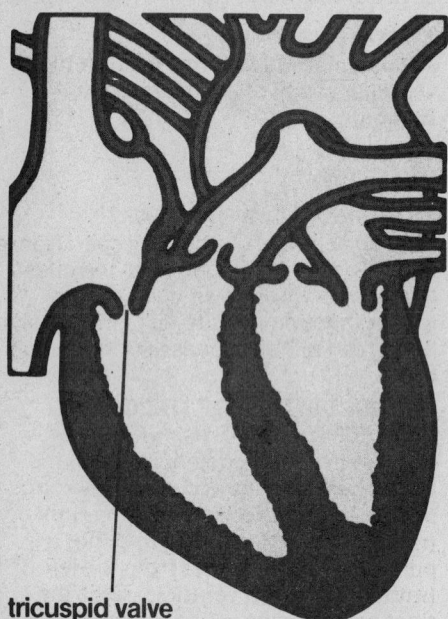

tricuspid valve

TRIGLYCERIDE *(tri-glis'er-id)*
The main type of lipid (fatty substance) found in the adipose (fat) tissue of the body and also the main dietary lipid. High levels of triglycerides in the blood may be associated with a greater risk of coronary atherosclerosis.

TRUNCUS ARTERIOSUS *(trun'kus ar-te"re-o'sus)*
An arterial trunk arising from the fetal heart which develops into the aorta and pulmonary artery. It is a congenital defect if it persists past the birth of the infant.

TYPE A BEHAVIOR
See Behavior, Type A and Type B.

TYPE B BEHAVIOR
See Behavior, Type A and Type B.

U

ULTRASOUND *(ul'tra-sownd)*
High frequency sound vibrations, not audible to the human ear. In a sonar-like application, it can be used by cardiologists for diagnosis. **See Echocardiography.**

UNSATURATED FAT *(un-sat'u-rat"ed)*
A fat whose molecules have one or more double bonds, so that it is capable of absorbing more hydrogen. **Mono-unsaturated fats**, such as olive oil, have only one double bond (the rest are single) and seem to have little effect on blood cholesterol. **Polyunsaturated fats**, such as corn oil and safflower oil, have two or more double bonds per molecule and tend to lower blood cholesterol. **See Saturated Fat.**

V

VAGUS NERVES *(va'gus)*
Two of the nerves of the parasympathetic nervous system which extend from the brain, through the neck and thorax into the abdomen. Known as the inhibitory nerves of the heart, they slow the heart rate when stimulated.

VALVE
A flap of tissue which prevents backflow of blood to keep it moving through the heart and circulatory system in the right direction. There are tiny valves along the inside of the veins and four large

how a one-way valve works

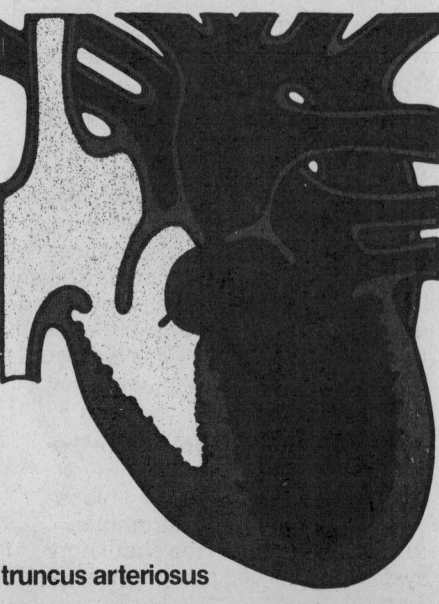

truncus arteriosus

valves at the entrances and exits of the ventricles in the heart. **See Aortic, Mitral, Pulmonary, and Tricuspid Valves.**

the heart valves seen from above (atria removed)

mitral valve (open)
tricuspid valve (open)

pulmonary (closed)
aortic valve (closed)

DIASTOLE (relaxation phase)

mitral valve (closed)
tricuspid valve (closed)

pulmonary valve (open)
aortic valve (open)

SYSTOLE (contraction phase)

right side　　　　left side

VALVULAR INSUFFICIENCY *(val'vu-lar)*
Valves which close improperly and permit a backflow of blood in the wrong direction. **See Incompetent Valve.**

VARICOSE VEINS *(var'i-kos)*
Also called "varicosities" and "varices," they are swollen veins found most frequently on the legs, especially the calves. **See Varix.**

VARIX *(var'iks)*
A varicosity or abnormally swollen vein, artery, or lymph vessel. The plural form is "varices." Varices can occur in such locations as the esophagus, the anus, or the legs (where they are more

commonly called "varicose veins"). **See Esophageal Varices, Hemorrhoids, and Varicose Veins.**

VASCULAR (vas'ku-lar)
Pertaining to the blood vessels.

VASO- (vas'o)
A combining form meaning vessel or duct.

VASOCONSTRICTOR (vas"o-kon-strik'tor)
Vasoconstrictor nerves are a part of the involuntary nervous system. When these nerves are stimulated, they cause the muscles of the arterioles to contract, narrowing the arteriole passage, increasing the resistance to bloodflow, and raising the blood pressure.

Vasoconstrictor agents (or vasopressors) are chemical substances which stimulate the muscles of the arterioles to contract. An example is norepinephrine (noradrenalin).

VASODILATOR (vas"o-di-lat'or)
Vasodilator nerves are certain nerve fibers of the involuntary nervous system which cause the muscle of the arterioles to relax, thus enlarging the arteriole passage, reducing resistance to the flow of blood, and lowering blood pressure.

Vasodilator agents are chemical compounds which cause a relaxation of the muscles of the arterioles. Examples

are nitroglycerin and other nitrites, hydralazine, and many others.

VASOINHIBITOR (vas"o-in-hib'i-tor)
An agent which inhibits the action of the vasomotor nerves, that is, an agent which prevents the blood vessels from a normal response (constriction or dilation) to stimuli.

VASOMOTOR (vas"o-mo'tor)
Any agent (nerve or substance) that affects the caliber of a vessel, especially of a blood vessel, that is, any agent that is either a vasoconstrictor or a vasodilator.

VASOPRESSOR (vas"o-pres'or)
A vasoconstrictor agent. **See Vasoconstrictor and also Pressor.**

VECTORCARDIOGRAPHY (vek"tor-kar"de-og'rah-fe)
Determination of the direction and magnitude of the electrical forces of the heart by using electrocardiography in three dimensions.

VEIN (vain)
Any one of a series of vessels of the vascular system which carries blood from various parts of the body back to the heart. All veins in the body conduct unoxygenated blood except the pulmonary veins which conduct freshly oxygenated blood from the lungs back to the heart.

VENA CAVA (ve'nah ka'vah)
One of the two great veins which conduct unoxygenated blood from the body to the right atrium of the heart. The superior vena cava brings blood from the upper part of the body (head, neck and chest). The inferior vena cava brings blood from the lower part of the body (legs and abdomen). Plural form is **Venae Cavae** (ve'ni ka'vi).

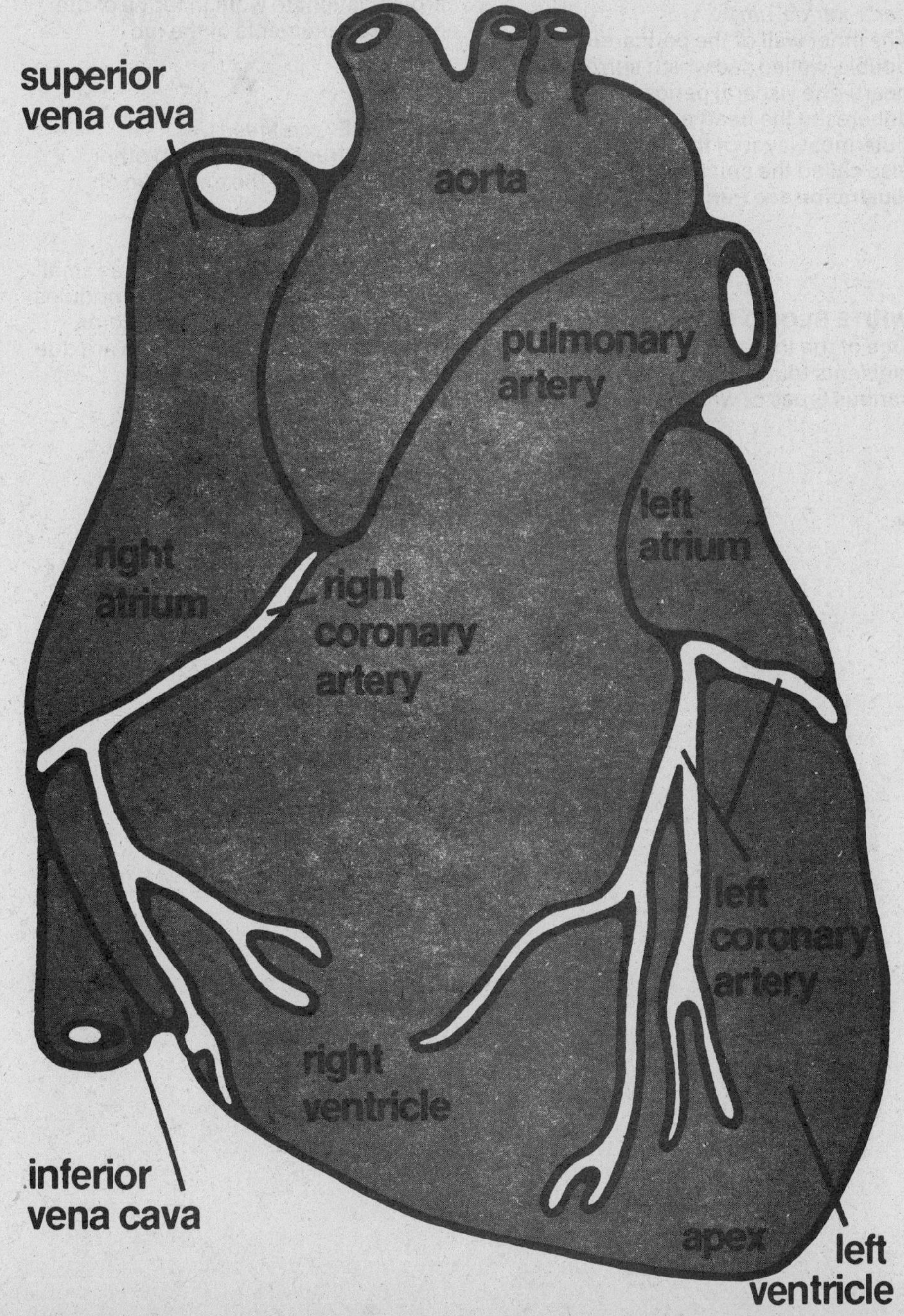

superior vena cava

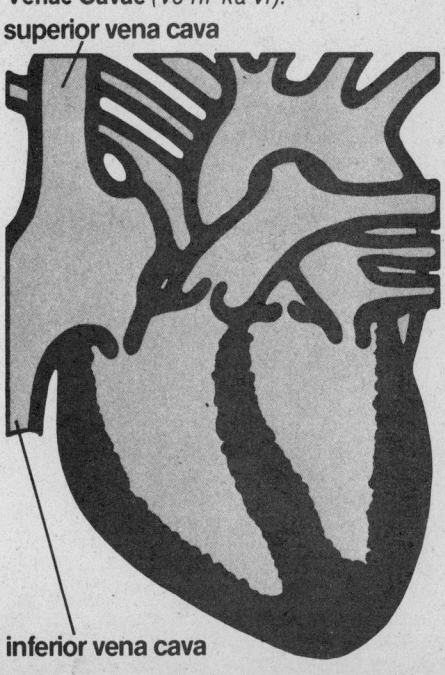

inferior vena cava

superior
vena cava

aorta

pulmonary
artery

left
atrium

right
atrium

right
coronary
artery

left
coronary
artery

inferior
vena cava

right
ventricle

apex

left
ventricle

VENOUS BLOOD *(ve'nus)*
Unoxygenated blood. The blood, with hemoglobin in the reduced state, is carried by the veins from all parts of the body back to the heart and then pumped by the right side of the heart through the pulmonary artery to the lungs where it is oxygenated.

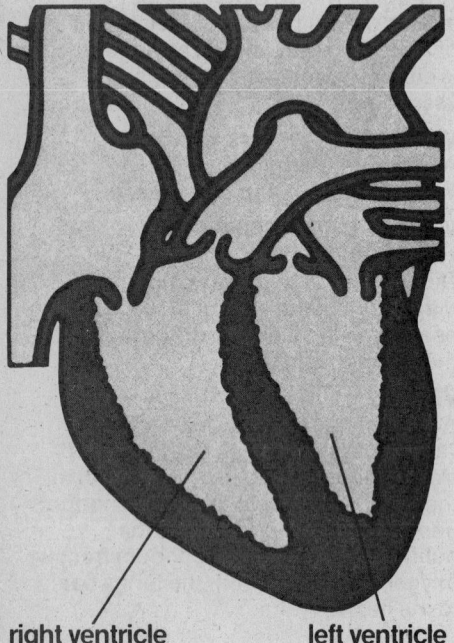

right ventricle　　　　　left ventricle

VENTRICLE *(ven'tre-kl)*
One of the two main pumping chambers of the heart. The left ventricle pumps oxygenated blood through the arteries to the body. The right ventricle pumps unoxygenated blood through the pulmonary artery to the lungs. Capacity of each ventricle in an adult averages 85 cc. or about 3 ounces.

VESALIUS, ANDREAS (1514-1564)
Belgian anatomist who questioned many of the then current theories of the circulatory system as taught by Galen, chiefly the existence of openings in the wall dividing the left from the right side of the heart through which blood was believed to pass.

VISCERAL PERICARDIUM *(vis'er-al per"i-kar'de-um)*
The inner wall of the pericardium, the double-walled sac which surrounds the heart. The visceral pericardium closely adheres to the heart and forms the outermost layer of the heart wall and is also called the epicardium. **For illustration see Pericardium.**

W

WHITE BLOOD CELLS
One of the three kinds of formed elements found in the blood. There are various types of white blood cells. Their best-known function is defense: they destroy foreign bodies, such as bacteria, in areas of infection. Also called leukocytes. **See Red Blood Cells and Platelets.**

WITHERING, WILLIAM (1741-1799)
Eminent English clinician who discovered the use and proper dosage of digitalis in the treatment of heart disease. By analyzing the effective herbal mixture used by an old woman in Shropshire, he identified foxglove leaves as the active ingredient which influenced the function of the heart and kidneys.

WORK CLASSIFICATION UNIT
A community facility involving a team approach to assessing the ability of the cardiac patient to work in terms of the energy requirements of the job.

X

XANTHINE *(zan'theen)*
A class of drugs used among other things to increase the excretion of urine. A diuretic.

XANTHOMA *(zan-tho'mah)*
A new growth of skin occurring as small flat or slightly raised patches or nodules which are yellowish-orange in color. The various types of xanthomas are due to blood lipid disorders (hyperlipoproteinemias).

Bible Dictionary

A

Aa'ron
The elder brother of and often the spokesman for Moses. From him descended, through his eldest son Eleazer, the hereditary class of priests in Israel.

Ab
The 5th month of the Hebrew year. *See* Calendar.

Ab'ba
A name addressed to God in Jewish and early Christian prayers. It occurs three times in the NT, with its Greek equivalent placed after it (Mk 14.36; Rom 8.15; Gal 4.6).

A·bed'ne·go
The Babylonian name of one of the companions of Daniel, his Hebrew name being Azariah. *See* Shadrach.

A'bel
(Heb. "vanity," "breath"; Akkad. "son") 1. The second son of Adam, who was murdered by his brother Cain (Gen 4.2ff). He was God-fearing and righteous, and in contrast with Cain is a pattern of a worshiper pleasing to God, who on that account has to suffer (1 Jn 3.12). He is described as righteous by our Lord (Mt 23.35), and in Heb 11.4 he stands at the head of the heroes of faith.

2. Part of the name of several places in Israel; it probably signifies "plain" or "meadow." *Abel of Beth-maacah*, a fortified city, identified with the mound Tell Abil, 12 mi. N of Lake Huleh, extreme north of Israel (2 Sam 20.14-19). *Abel-keramim*, the plain of the vineyards, in Ammonite territory, probably near modern Amman (Judg 11.29-33). *Abel-meholah*, probably east of the Jordan on Wadi el-Yabis, modern Tell el-Maqlub (Judg 7.22; 1 Kings 4.12; 19.16). *Abel-mizraim*, possibly between Jericho and the Dead Sea (Gen 50.11). *Abel-shittim*, in the plains of Moab NE of the Dead Sea; possibly the present Tell el Hammam. Early name for Shittim (Num 33.49).

A·bi'a·thar
(Heb. "the Father [God] gives abundantly") A priest who became the priest of David.

A'bib
(Heb. "young head of grain") The 1st month of the Hebrew year; Nisan. *See* Calendar.

Ab'i·gail
(Heb. "my father rejoices") Wife of Nabal and after Nabal's death the wife of David.

A·bim'e·lech
(Heb. "Melek is Father") 1. A king of Gerar who appears in similar accounts of Isaac and Rebecca and of Abraham and Sarah (Gen 20–21; 26).

2. Son of Jerubbaal (Gideon), king of Shechem (Judg 8.31; 9.1-57).

Ab'ner
(Heb. "father is Ner") Commander of the Israelite army under Saul.

a·bom·i·na'tion
Anything ritually or ethically repugnant or loathsome to God and men.

A'bra·ham, A'bram
(Heb. "Father of a multitude"; "exalted Father") One of the greatest OT characters, and possibly the story of two persons combined into one (Gen 11.27–25.8). Abraham was born in Ur of the Chaldees, in what is now Iraq. Terah, his father, migrated with Abraham and Sarah, Abraham's wife, and Lot, his nephew, as far as Haran, now Harran, in Turkey. There Terah died. The others, with flocks and herds, moved on to Palestine (Canaan).

Abraham stopped near ancient Shechem, a short distance E of Nablus and now extensively excavated; he moved on to Egypt for a time, then returned to Palestine for the remainder of his life. Lot settled at Sodom and became a Canaanite. When the Canaanites rebelled against Babylon and Lot was taken captive, Abraham recovered the captives and the booty.

Throughout his life, Abraham was in contact with the many peoples about him, carrying on various negotiations with them. He talked with God, to whom he was always faithful. And he doubted God when he and his wife Sarah were in their old age promised a son. This son was Isaac. However, Abraham's relationship with God was such that when he was called upon to sacrifice his only son he responded without question. God released him from the sacrifice and promised him many descendants and land, which promises were fulfilled.

At Sarah's death he arranged the purchase of a burial place at Machpelah, where he also was buried after a long life of constant activity and great drama.

Ab'sa·lom
(Heb. "father of peace") Son of David and Maachah, through popular arts alienating the people from his father, at length raised a revolt against him, but was defeated by Joab and slain by him, to the great sorrow of David (2 Sam 3.3, 13.20–19.10).

a·ca'cia
A tree providing a hard wood, useful in building.

Ac'cad
(Gen 10.10) One of the four cities of Nimrod in Shinar (Babylonia). Land of Sumer and Accad (or Akkad) is in the Assyrian inscriptions the common designation of Babylonia as a whole. *See* Akkad; Babylonia.

A·cel'da·ma, A·kel'da·ma
A burial ground outside the Jerusalem wall.

Acts of the A·pos'tles, The
Written by the author of the Gospel according to Luke, Acts is the account of what Jesus' disciples did after His resurrection. It tells about the early Christian church and its missionaries, the baptism of Cornelius, the Council in Jerusalem, and about the conversion of Paul and his journeys to establish churches and to teach. Acts emphasizes that the church is guided continually by the Holy Spirit.

Ad'am
("earthy," "a human") 1. The Hebrew word for man, specifically applied to the first man.

Created on the same day as the animals, he is not semi-divine but has the ability for spiritual growth.

2. A city east of the Jordan, now Tell ed-Damiyeh (Josh 3.9-17).

ad'a·mant

It is not known what is meant by this word; it is something impenetrably hard (Ezek 3.9; Jer 17.1; Zech 7.12).

A'dar, Ad'dar

The 12th Hebrew month. *See* Calendar.

Ad·on·i'

A Hebrew name for God.

Ad·o·ra'im

(Heb. "two threshing floors"?) A city identified with modern Dura, 5 mi. W-SW of Hebron (2 Chron 11.9).

A·dul'lam

(Heb. "retreat, refuge") Extensive ruins in the Wadi es-Sur, 9½ mi. ENE of Beit Jibrin, perhaps mark the site of Adullam, to which there are many biblical references.

a·ga'pe, the

(Gr. agape, "love") Love feasts, the common meals of the early Christians, which expressed the brotherly love that bound them together as one family, and culminated in the Lord's Supper. Gross abuses of this beautiful custom, such as are condemned in 1 Cor 11.17ff, and Jude 12, led to the separation of the Lord's Supper from the love feast in the post-apostolic church.

ag'ate

The agate is one of the many varieties of minutely crystalline silica, denoting those arranged more or less in bands of different tints. From a very early period it has been used as a gem, and was often engraved.

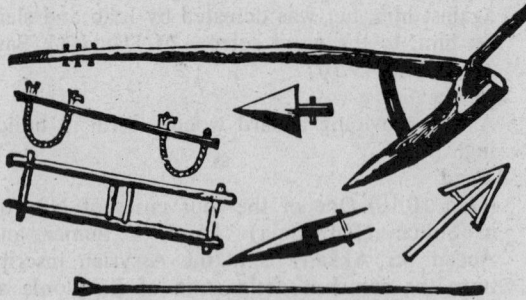

Plow and other implements

ag'ri·cul·ture

Excavations reveal a developed agriculture in Bible lands as early as 8000-7000 B.C.; flint sickles for harvesting and basalt mortars and pestles for grinding grain are found in abundance. The religious year of the Israelites was adjusted to the cultivation cycle, and many memorable passages of the Bible have reference to the life of seedtime and harvest.

The patriarchs and their descendants down to the conquest of Canaan were herdsmen of cattle (sheep, oxen, goats, asses, and camels). After the settlement, the western tribes learned agriculture, and the culture of the vine, olive, and fig tree, from the Canaanites. Among the crops raised were wheat, barley, rye, spelt, flax, cummin, fitches or vetch, beans, lentils, and millet.

A'hab

(Heb. "father's brother") Son of Omri, king of the northern kingdom of Israel in the time of Elijah, reigned 22 years. He defeated Benhadad, King of Damascus, twice, destroyed his capital, and shut him up in Aphek, afterward forming a treaty with him against Assyria. Shalmaneser II, King of Assyria, in his monolith inscription claims to have defeated Ahab and Benhadad with other kings at Karkar in 854 B.C. A year after this, Ahab met his death in a battle before Ramothgilead, in which Benhadad overcame both him and his ally, Jehoshaphat of Judah. The worship of Baal and Ashtoreth, introduced by his wife, the Tyrian princess, Jezebel, with the religious struggle this called forth in the country, and his robbery and judicial murder of Naboth, left in Israel a dark shadow on the memory of Ahab (1 Kings 16.29–22.40).

A·has·u·e'rus

The Persian king (485-465 B.C.?) in Ezra 4.6 and Esther. The Ahasuerus of Dan 9.1 is the father of Darius the Mede.

A'haz

(Heb. "possessor" or "he has grasped") Eleventh king of Judah, remembered for his wicked reign (2 Kings 16, 23.12; 2 Chron 28; Is 7,8,9).

A·ha·zi'ah

(Heb. "Yah has grasped") 1. Eighth king of Israel.

2. Sixth king of Judah.

A·hi'jah, A·hi'ah

(Heb. "brother of Yah") Name of 9 persons in the OT, one of whom was a priest in the time of Saul; another a prophet of Shiloh who foretold Jeroboam's kingship.

A·him'a·az

(Heb. "brother is counselor"?) Name of 3 persons in the OT, one of whom was a priest devoted to David.

A·hin'o·am

(Heb. "pleasantness") 1. Wife of Saul, daughter of Ahimaaz.

2. A wife of David, from Jezreel.

A·hith'o·phel

The royal counselor to David.

Ai'ja·lon, Aj'a·lon

(Heb. "place of the deer") 1. Modern Yalo, with remains of a fortified town.

2. A place in Zebulun, probably Tell el-Butneh in the Plain of Asochis.

Ak'kad, Ak·ka'di·an

The Akkadians were the first Semitic people to move into Mesopotamia; the first Akkadian names to appear among Babylonian rulers are found in the period 1200-1100 B.C. Their language had spread widely and had become the common usage for commerce and trade some 750 years earlier. Assyrian and Babylonian are considered dialects of Akkadian.

Alabaster vessels

Courtesy of *The Interpreter's Dictionary of the Bible*

Aloes

al'a·bas·ter

A soft stone, often veined; light cream in color. Much used for perfume flasks.

Al·ex·an'dri·a

The great seaport at the mouth of the Nile, founded by Alexander the Great about 332 B.C. He gave the Jews a quarter in it; in the early Christian age it was the chief trade center of East and West, and the home of literature and Greek philosophy.

al'gum

(2 Chron 2.8, 9.10, 11) or **al'mug** (1 Kings 2.8, 10.11, 12) A wood brought from Lebanon, as in 2 Chron 2.8, or from Ophir (1 Kings; 2 Chron 9.10, 11) Probably either pine or sandalwood.

Almond tree and blossoms

al'mond

(Heb. "waking") The common almond, whose beautiful pink-white flowers appear in January, the first of the year; hence its name. It grows wild on the higher lands of Palestine. There are frequent references to this tree in the Bible.

alms

(Gr. "pity"; "relief of the poor") Frequently mentioned and their giving practiced in many ways. Laws were written, tithes were taken with the poor in mind. Gleaning was usual. Passersby might gather as they walked. And the giving of alms meant merit for the donor.

al'mug

See Algum.

al'oes

1. An aromatic substance, probably an aromatic wood, such as white sandalwood, from which was made incense and perfume. It was an import, not native.

2. The true aloe, a succulent, provided a bitter and evil-smelling purgative and may have been used with myrrh in embalming.

al'pha and o·me'ga

The names of the first and last letters in the Greek alphabet. "Alpha and Omega" often indicates the whole extent, not merely the beginning and the end, of an act or a concept.

Al·phae'us

A Greek name appearing in the NT only. 1. The father of Levi, who may also have been called Matthew (Mk 2.14).

2. The father of James (the Less) (Mt 10.3; Mk 3.18; Lk 6.15; Acts 1.13).

al'tar

An artificial erection for the offering of sacrifices and prayers, originally of earth, turf, and unhewn stones. The law ordained that sacrifices should be offered only in the sanctuary; but the Hebrews continued to erect altars upon the high places until the Temple at Jerusalem, with its altar of incense in the sanctuary and its altar of burnt-offering in the forecourt, became under the reformation of Josiah universally recognized as the only place where sacrifices could be legitimately offered. The "horns" of the altar, placed at its four corners, were its most sacred parts. The blood of the sacrifices was smeared on them, and they were clasped by fugitives who claimed the right of asylum.

Am'a·lek·ites

A nomadic tribe, descendants of Esau, wandering from Sinai across the Negev, below the Sea of Galilee, as far as the Gulf of Aqabah. They warred with the Israelites over the centuries. Saul and David defeated them, but neither succeeded in exterminating them. At the time of Hezekiah they seem to have been completely defeated. In the Tell el-Amarna letters, they are classed as plunderers.

Am′a·sa
(Heb. "a burden") 1. A nephew of David.
2. An Ephraimite chief.

Am·a·zi′ah
(Heb. "Yah is strong") The name of 4 persons in the OT, one a king of Judah, presumably for 29 years.

am′ber
The word thus rendered is almost certainly not the familiar fossil resin of orange-yellow, which bears this name, but some metallic compound; possibly the mixture of gold and silver now called electrum, or bronze.

a′men′
A Hebrew word meaning "truth," used adverbially to express strong confirmation. It is used as a confirmatory response at the close of prayer ("May it be so").

am′e·thyst
A purplish variety of quartz (crystallized silica), often used for ornamental purposes. It looks like a pale purple glass, but is somewhat harder.

Am′mon·ites
A Semitic people settled NE of the Dead Sea. They warred with Israel, were vassals under David and Solomon, subsequently vassals of Assyria. Origen mentioned them in the 3rd century A.D., after which they seem to have disappeared among the Arabs. Excavations near Amman show a well-developed culture.

A′mon
(Heb. "reliable") Name of 3 persons in the OT, one a king of Judah; also the imperial god of Egypt.

Am′o·rites
An ancient people who may have occupied Syria and N Palestine; their language was probably the forerunner of Aramean. They refused the Israelites passage through their land. The Tell elAmarna letters give information of them at the period of a number of city states; excavations at Mori show a high state of civilization.

A′mos
(Heb. "burden bearer") One of the minor prophets, he was a shepherd of Tekoa, in Judah, and prophesied at Bethel in the reigns of Uzziah, King of Judah, and Jeroboam II, King of Israel. The priests accused him of treason, and expelled him from the northern kingdom, to which his prophecies mainly refer, and whose downfall he foretold.

A′mos, The Book of
The book of the herdsman from Tekoa. He received a direct call from God to prophesy against the unrighteousness of both Judah and Israel. Amos was the first prophet to proclaim that God was the ruler of the whole universe.

An′a·kim
(Heb. "people of the neck") A race of giants who, when driven from the mountains of He-

bron by Caleb or Joshua, found refuge in Philistia.

An·a·ni′as
(Heb. "Yah is gracious") Name of 3 NT persons, one of whom was the high priest before whom Paul was tried in Jerusalem. Another lost his life for attempting deceit regarding the price received for property he sold.

a·nath′e·ma
(Gr. "something set up") One form of the word developed a special meaning, "devoted to a divinity or to the lower world so as to be destroyed," and so came to mean accursed.

An′a·thoth
The birthplace of Jeremiah. The name is preserved in Anata, a town 3 mi. N of Jerusalem. The ancient city was at Ras el-Karrubeh, ½ mi. SW.

An′cient of Days
God Himself, of great dignity and wisdom.

an′cients
See Elders.

An′drew
(Gr. "manly") One of the 12 disciples of Jesus, brother of Simon Peter, son of Jonas or John, was born at Bethsaida on the Sea of Galilee. He was one of the first among the disciples of John the Baptist to become a follower of Jesus who called him, along with Peter, while fishing at the Sea of Galilee, to become a fisher of men. He appears to have been one of those disciples who, after Peter, James, and John, stood nearest to his Master. Acts mentions him only in 1.13. According to tradition, he suffered martyrdom in Achaia on a cross shaped in the form of the letter X (Mt 4:18, 10.2-4, 16.17; Mk 1.16-20, 29; 3.16-19, 13.3; Jn 1.35-42, 44; 6.5-9; 12.20-22; 21.15-17; Lk 5.10, 6.14-16; Acts 1.13).

an′gel
(Gr. "messenger") A messenger of God, with the evolving concept of a spiritual being.

an′ise
Seeds of this plant are used for flavoring, and have some use in medicine.

An′nas
See Caiaphas.

ant
Ants are proverbial for the marvelous instinct that guides them in the economy, work, and discipline of their communities. They are small insects, but have wonderful muscular strength. Harvester ants of Palestine store corn for winter (Prov 16.6-8; 30.25).

an′te·lope
The Hebrew word of the OT is also translated "wild bull," "wild ox." The gazelle, a species of antelope, lived in Palestine in biblical times. The antelope is often depicted on Egyptian monuments. It is a beautiful creature, standing about four feet high, very wild and fleet, and fierce when hard pressed by the hunter.

an′ti·christ
This word is used in the NT by John (1 Jn 2.18, 22; 4.3; 2 Jn 7) but the idea, variously expressed, appears as in Dan 7, Ezek 38 and 39, 2

Thess 2.3–10. As used in the NT the name may mean "one who usurps the place of Christ," or "one who sets himself up as a substitute for Christ." The principle of his opposition consists in the denial of the incarnation, which revealed the will of God to unite man with Himself through Christ, and in the assertion of man's divinity apart from God in Christ. St. Paul teaches that Antichrist will appear as a single adversary of Christ, "the man of sin," who, furnished by Satan "with all power, and signs, and wonders of falsehood," will sit "in the sanctuary of God, setting himself forth as God," and will be brought to nought by the manifestation of the coming of the Lord. As Moses was the type of Christ, so Balaam, the "Anti-Moses," was a type of Antichrist (2 Pet 2.15; Jude 11; Rev 2.14).

an·ti·mo·ny

Stibnite (antimony sulphide) was and still is in the East a pigment employed for darkening the outer part of the eye, as when Jezebel "painted" her eyes.

An'ti·och

1. In Syria, on the river Orontes, a great city, ranking next after Rome and Alexandria, where the name Christian was first used (Acts 11.26).

2. In Pisidia, visited by St. Paul and Barnabas (Acts 13.14-52).

An·tip'a·tris

A city 10 mi. NE of Jaffa (Joppa) named after Antipater, father of Herod the Great (Acts 23.31).

apes

Imported by Solomon (1 Kings 10.22). Baboons, apes, and monkeys are represented in the Assyrian and Egyptian monuments.

A'phek

(Heb. "fortress"?) The name of 4 places in the OT. Each location has been identified.

Ap·ol·lo'ni·a

A Greek city in Macedonia, S of Lake Balbe (Acts 17.1).

A·pol'los

An Alexandrian Jew who became a prominent teacher in the Apostolic ages. "Eloquent," "fervent in spirit," and "mighty in the Scriptures" (of the OT), he had been a disciple of John before Priscilla and Aquila at Ephesus "expounded to him the way of God more perfectly." After Paul's departure from Corinth he preached the gospel there. Though one of the parties in the Corinthian church named itself after him, he appears to have stood in a friendly relation to Paul, with whom he afterwards labored at Ephesus. He is last mentioned in Tit 3.13. Luther was the first to suggest that Apollos was the author of the Epistle to the Hebrews (Acts 18.24-28, 19.1; 1 Cor. 1.12, 3.3-10, 22; 4.6, 16.12).

a·pos'tle

(Gr. "to send off") The word appears about 80 times in the NT, limited to certain men of the first generation of the church and missionaries of the gospel. The first twelve apostles sent out by Jesus are named in Mk 3.14-19 and else-where. Others also are considered apostles, including Paul, James, Barnabas, Matthias, and in some groupings Junias, Andronicus, and Silvanus. Subsequently many claimed the title, which the church desired to limit to those who had seen Jesus and had firsthand knowledge of the Resurrection, who had the attributes called the signs of an apostle, and were fully committed to the church.

ap'ple

Since the apple grows poorly if at all in Bible lands, an attempt has been made to identify the fruit so called. The apricot seems best to fit the biblical text.

Aq'ui·la and Pris·cil'la

Friends in Corinth and Ephesus of the Apostle Paul, and his assistants in evangelism. In Ephesus they instructed the Alexandrian Apollos.

A·ra'bi·a, A·ra'bi·ans

(Gr. "desert") In biblical times there was no single name for the vast Arabian peninsula. Its peoples were nomads. They traded with Egypt and other countries, selling frankincense and other perfumes, and had camels, sheep, goats, and horses. They may have been dealers in the pet monkeys Solomon had brought from Ophir, of still unknown location. The peoples included Ishmaelites, Midianites, Dedanites, Sabeans, among others. At times they raided and plundered in Israel, at times carried on peaceful commerce. There was a marked difference in the peoples of the N and the S. Whether the Queen of Sheba came from N or S is not definite; more probably she was from the N. There was a certain amount of intermingling, too: for example, David's head camel keeper was an Ishmaelite, and his sister married an Ishmaelite. Moses had friendly contacts with them. Bible references to the peoples of what is now Arabia are plentiful.

A'ram

(Akkad. *Aramu*) The OT name of Syria and Mesopotamia (sometimes used of Syria alone).

Ar·a·ma'ic

The Aramaic language is properly the speech of the people of Aram, an area NE of Syria. They may have learned alphabetic writing from the Canaanites. After the Assyrian conquest Aramaic spread widely as a language of commerce and is found in conjunction with cuneiform on weights and clay tablets from distant regions of the empire. A form of Aramaic influenced the Greek alphabet, and other forms influenced scripts of Asia. It is noteworthy that Dan 2.4-7, 28; Ezra 4.8-6,18 and 7.12-26 are found originally in Aramaic. The language was used in Egypt, and it was spoken familiarly instead of Hebrew in Palestine; Jesus and his followers spoke one of its many dialects.

Eventually Aramaic was displaced by Arabic in much of the old Assyrian empire, even though in some regions it persisted for centuries.

Ar·a·me'ans

A Semitic people, traditionally descendants of Shem, they apparently were in early times

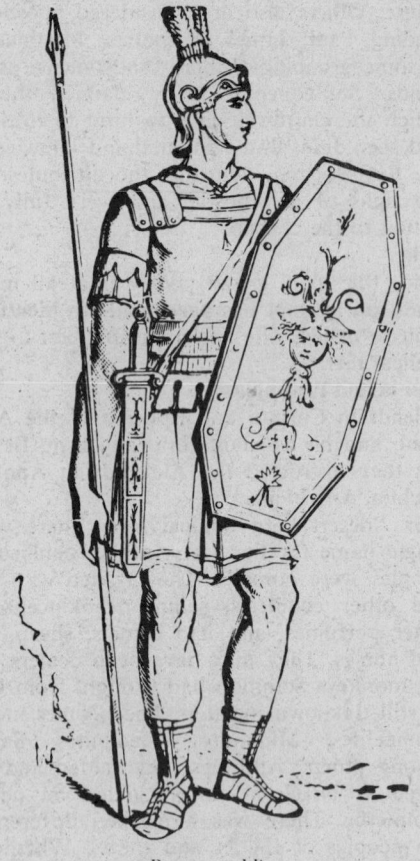

Roman soldier

among the nomads along the W side of the Syrian Desert. For a considerable time they were an active and expanding people, and their culture, particularly their language, spread over the Middle East. The Assyrians conquered and scattered them, and they vanished as a political power.

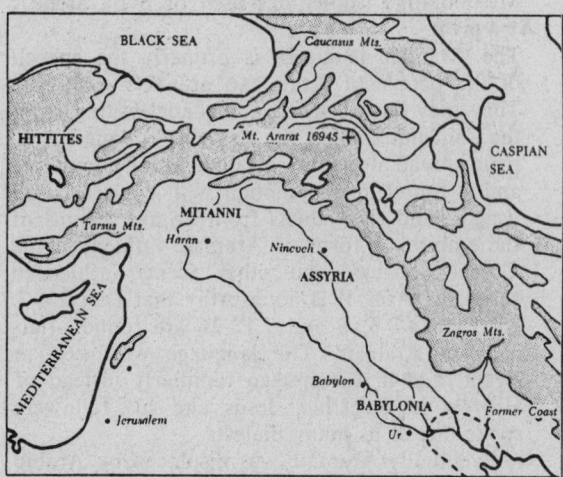

location of Mt. Ararat.

Ar·a·rat
The country of the river Aras in Armenia; also the mount of Ararat, on which the ark rested after the Flood (Gen 8.4), 16,900 ft. elevation.

Ar·is·tar'chus
A Macedonian Gentile arrested with Paul in Ephesus. He traveled with Paul and was a fellow prisoner in Rome.

Ark of the Cov'e·nant
The ark may have been a container for the Mosaic tablets and other sacred objects, or a throne for the invisible God; on it was a slab of gold to support the cherubim, the mercy seat. It probably goes back to the time of Moses, and was a focus for the religious life of the people. In Ex 25 are precise instructions for the construction of an ark. The OT has some 200 references to it: it was captured in battle, left in the homes of individuals, reverenced, sometimes ignored. After Solomon placed it in the sanctuary of the temple it dropped from history. A possibility is that it was destroyed during Nebuchadnezzar's invasion.

Ar·ma·ged'don
The place of the final great struggle between the forces of good and evil. It is linked to Megiddo.

arm'lets
See Frontlets.

arms, ar'mor
Down to the age of David the army of Israel consisted exclusively of foot soldiers. These were probably divided into two classes: the heavy-armed, wearing helmet, coat of mail, and greaves, and carrying a sword, one or two javelins, and a spear; and the light-armed, wearing helmet and corselet of leather, and carrying sword, bow, and sling. The metal earliest employed in the manufacture of weapons was probably an alloy of copper and tin. The use of imported iron followed later.

A sling

Ar′o·er

(Heb. "juniper"?) 1. A city on the N rim of the Arnon Gorge, 3 mi. SE of Dhiban. The ancient city is a mound beside modern 'Ara'ir.

2. A town of Gilead, possibly S of 'Amman near es-Sweiwina.

3. A town in S country of Judah, modern 'Ar'arah, 12 mi. SE of Beer-sheba.

Ar·tax·erx′es

The first Artaxerxes is mentioned in Ezra 7 and Neh 2 and 13. His grandson, Artaxerxes II, may have been the builder of the palace described in Esther 1.

Ar′te·mis

The virgin huntress of Greek classical mythology, called Diana by the Romans, was widely worshiped throughout the Greek world. Artemis or Diana of the Ephesians mentioned in Acts 19 was a fertility goddess, worship of whom was also widespread and elaborate.

As′ca·lon, Ash′ke·lon

One of the Philistine chief cities, on the seacoast. It may have been the birthplace of Herod the Great.

As·cents′, Songs of

See Degrees, Songs of.

Ash′dod

("fortress"?) A Philistine chief city, 10 mi. N of Ascalon (Ashkelon), and 3 mi. inland; now called Esdud. It was to Ashdod that the Ark was taken when captured by the Philistines.

A·she′rah

A Semitic fertility goddess and the goddess' cult object, a sacred tree (for which a pole was often substituted) which, with the Masseba or sacred stone pillar, stood near the altar on every Canaanite high place. The deity was believed to be present in the Asherah. There are many OT references to the trees and the groves on the high places.

Ash′ke·lon

See Ascalon.

Ash′to·reth, pl. Ash′ta·roth, Ash′to·roth

A Canaanite fertility goddess.

As·mo·de′us

The prince of demons, also called Abaddon, Apollyon, Beelzebul.

asp

A viper or adder; a poisonous snake.

ass

The domesticated ass, which is traced by Darwin to the wild ass of Abyssinia, is depicted in the earliest Egyptian records, and also on the oldest Assyrian monuments. The ass is much more highly prized in the East than in the West. From early times, white (albino) asses were reserved for dignitaries. The ass was the animal of peace as the horse was of war. It was forbidden to plough with an ass and an ox together. *Ass, Wild* Most of the Biblical references are to the wild ass of Syria, especially the descriptions in Job and the Prophets. The wild ass is untamable, and in fleetness far surpasses the horse. The allusions to its habits in Scripture are most accurate. The hunting of the wild ass is

Ashtoreth

frequently represented in the Assyrian sculptures.

as·sas′sin

(Arab, *hashashin* "those addicted to hashish, hemp") A numerous body of desperadoes that arose in Judea during the procuratorship of Felix, and afterward took a leading part in the Jewish war. Their name Sicarii was derived from the curved dagger (Lat. *sica*), which they carried under their clothes, and with which they stabbed their opponents secretly in the crowds at festivals.

As′shur, As′sur

See Assyria.

As·syr′i·a

After the decline of the great kingdom of Sumer, two Semitic-language peoples developed in its region. Babylonia gradually rose in the former Central Sumer area. To the N of it Assyria developed, early unstable and unaggressive, borrowing heavily from Babylonia, but with sharp distinctions in social and intellectual concepts. Several strong personalities built up successive Assyrian empires, which in turn broke up on the death of the particular person. This was the Assyrian history for hundreds of years. They gradually conquered the mountain peoples N and E of them, and turned to the W. From the time of Omri (876-869 B.C.) to Manasseh (687-642 B.C.) the people of Israel were under pressure from Assyria: paying tribute to, fighting against, being conquered by Assyria; Tiglath-pileser II (966-935 B.C.), a contemporary of Solomon, was known to Israel, as was Shalmaneser III (858-824 B.C.), the first Assyrian king to have contact with the kings of Israel. Tiglath-pileser III (745-727) B.C.) began large-scale deportations of the conquered. Esarheddon (680-669 B.C.) attacked Egypt. The over-extended Assyrian empire fell with the destruction of Asshur, its old capital, in 614 B.C. and of Nineveh in 612 B.C. by a coalition of Babylonia and the Medes. A vast quantity of historical, artistic, and literary material has been found in the excavations of the ancient Assyrian cities in what is now Iraq, Turkey, and Syria, and many previously unsuspected links between the ancient peoples have been revealed.

Ath′ens

The capital of Attica, the chief division of ancient Greece, and the seat of Greek literature, art, and civilization. Paul visited it in his second journey and delivered a famous address on the Areopagus, or Hill of Mars.

Ath′ter

See Molech.

A·tone′ment, Day of

This was the annual day of humiliation and expiation for the sins of the nation, when the high priest made atonement for the sanctuary, the priests, and the people. It was celebrated on the 10th day of Tishri, the 7th month, by abstinence from ordinary labor, by a holy convocation, and by fasting. It was the only fast enjoined by the Mosaic law, and hence was called "the fast." The high priest, laying aside his official ornaments, first offered a sin-offering for himself and for the priesthood, entering into the Holy of Holies with the blood. He afterwards took 2 he-goats for the nation. One was slain for Jehovah. On the head of the other the sins of the people were typically laid; it was made the sin-bearer of the nation; and, laden with guilt, was sent away into the wilderness. The idea of atonement was never at any time remote.

Sin offering

a·veng′er

Hebrew custom, like that of many other early peoples, authorized and even required the next of kin to avenge a murdered person by killing

his murderer. The Mosaic legislation aimed at mitigating its effects by providing cities of refuge to which a homicide might escape, and where he might claim a fair trial. Blood vengeance is mentioned often in the OT.

Az·a·ri′ah

(Heb. "Yah has helped") Name of 24 persons in the OT, one of whom was the prophet who encouraged Asa, king of Judah, to reform of religion. In 2 Chron 22.6, KJV, it is used instead of Ahaziah.

A·za′zel

The evil spirit of the wilderness to whom on the Day of Atonement the goat laden with the sins of the people is said to be sent.

B

Ba′al

The fertility gods of Canaan. There were many local Baals.

Ba′al·ze′bub

A god of the city of Ekron of the Philistines of whom King Ahaziah of Israel asked an oracle.

Ba′bel (Heb.), **Bab′y·lon** (Gr.)

Capital of Babylonia, or Shinar, also called Chaldea. Its ruins are near the present city of Hilla SW of Baghdad, on a small tributary of the Euphrates. Its temple of Bel (Marduk), the city God, a ziggurat or stepped tower, is the biblical Tower of Babel. It was a splendid and magnificent city, and became to the people of Israel a symbol of all that was wicked. In NT times it became the symbolic name for Rome.

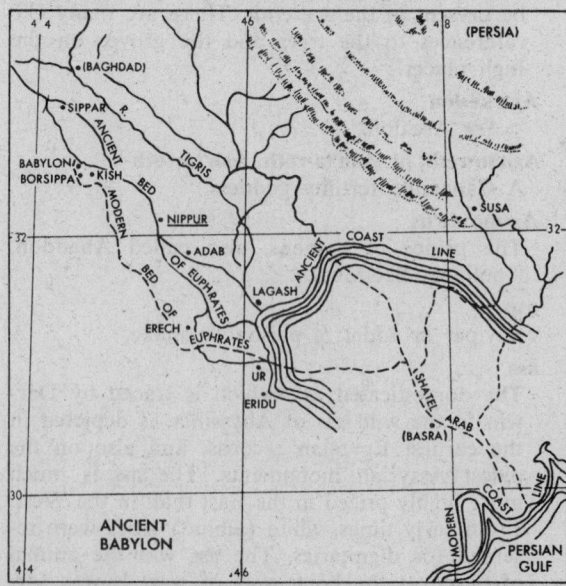

Bab·y·lo′ni·a

The downfall of Sumer brought Babylonia into being. The great Hammurabi (c. 1800-1750 B.C.) extended the power of his city-state, Babylon, making it a capital over other city-states. He was an effective administrator and established an enduring political plan; even so, the history of Babylonia is as that of Assyria, of war and destruction, advance and retreat. The complexities of the histories of both countries are slowly being resolved through excavations and subsequent interpretations of the records found. The aggressions of Babylon are woven through the history of the Israelites; there were the sorrowful days of the exiles, when thousands of the people of Israel were deported eastward, never to return. There were such happenings as the three young men in the fiery furnace (Dan 3). Lying as Israel did, between Egypt and the Tigris-Euphrates powers, Assyria and Babylonia, it was a buffer or a pawn in the multiple strife of the larger powers. But Babylon emerged as the most hated. Babylon was synonymous with all that was evil. It eventually became a part of the empire of the Medes and Persians.

Bab·y·lo'ni·an Cap·tiv'i·ty or Ex'ile

The period in Jewish history from the carrying away of the people to Babylon in 597 and 586 to their return in 538 B.C.

badg'er

A small mammal; a coney.

Ba'laam

("the clan brings forth"?) A seer, possibly from the neighborhood of Carchemish, summoned by the Moabite King Balak to pronounce a curse on Israel before its entrance into Canaan. Instead he spoke a series of blessings (Num 22–24). There are many references to Balaam in both OT and NT; in the NT he becomes the false prophet.

Baker, from an ancient marble

balm

An aromatic gum or resin used in healing and in cosmetics as well as for embalming. It is not fully identified.

bal'sam

See Mulberry.

bap'tism

(Gr. "dip" or "immerse") A rite using water as a symbol of religious purification.

Ba'rak

(Heb. "lightning-flash") Son of Abinoam, who, encouraged by the prophetess Deborah to take the lead in the struggle against the Canaanites, seized Mount Tabor with 10,000 men and, rushing down the mountain, defeated Sisera's army at its foot and along the right bank of the Kishon, near Megiddo. A splendid "song of Deborah and Barak" celebrates the victory (Judg 5).

bar'ley

Extensively cultivated in Palestine and neighboring countries from the earliest times.

Bar'na·bas

The surname given by the apostles to Joses or Joseph, a Levite of Cyprus, who was sent by them to Antioch to confirm the church there. From Antioch he "went forth to Tarsus to seek for Saul," whom he had introduced at Jerusalem to Peter and James as a new convert. When he had brought him to Antioch, they remained there together for a year, and "taught much people." Barnabas accompanied Paul on his first missionary journey, and on his journey to the council at Jerusalem, and afterward at Antioch. When Paul, starting on his second missionary journey, refused to take John Mark, the cousin of Barnabas, the two apostles separated, Barnabas taking Mark with him to Cyprus. Paul refers to him in 1 Cor 9.6; Gal 2.13; Col 4.10. The authorship of the Epistle to the Hebrews was attributed to Barnabas by Tertullian. The Codex Sinaiticus includes an "Epistle of Barnabas," which was regarded as canonical by many in the ancient church, but is held to date from the beginning of the 2nd century A.D. (Acts 4.36, 37; 8.1; 9.1, 27; 11.19-27, 30; 13.2, 3, 9, 13; 14.12, 14; 15).

Bar·thol'o·mew

(Aram. "son of Talmai"). One of the twelve apostles of Jesus (Mt 10.3; Mk 3.18; Lk 6.14; Acts 1.13). He is identified with Nathanael of Cana of Galilee (John 1.45-51; 21.2) on the ground that (1) Bartholomew is not mentioned in John, nor is Nathanael in the other three gospels; and (2) Philip in the first three gospels is associated with Bartholomew, and in John with Nathanael.

Ba'shan

A high tableland, 1600 to 2300 ft., sometimes considered coextensive with the Kingdom of Og.

bat

Classed among unclean winged creatures. It swarms in the numberless ravines, caves, and ruins of Palestine (Lev 11.19; Deut 14.19; Is 2.20).

bay tree

Does not refer to a particular kind of tree, but to a tree growing luxuriantly in its native soil, and is thus translated by the revisers (Ps 37.35). There is no ground for identifying the tree with the bay or noble laurel.

bdel'li·um

What is meant is uncertain, possibly a gem, but some have suggested a vegetable gum, others pearls (Gen 2.12; Num 11.7).

bean

Used both as a vegetable and as flour by the Jews.

bear

The Syrian brown bear was found in the N of Palestine as recently as the early 20th century. It is mentioned frequently in the OT.

beard

Full beards were common among Hebrews. Egyptians and Romans shaved the beard. Assyrians are portrayed with beards. Hebrews were forbidden to trim the beard; its removal or plucking was an insult, except in cases of leprosy.

Ancient types of beards

beat'en oil

Oil produced by crushing fully ripe olives, without pressing, was of the first quality, used for the lamp of the sanctuary.

bed

The poorer people in Palestine slept upon the bare floor, wrapped in their cloaks, or upon a mattress or quilt, which was rolled up and put away in the daytime. The wealthy used a wooden framework covered with cushions as a divan by day and a bed at night, and the more luxurious had bedsteads carved and inlaid with ivory. The bed of Og (Deut 3.11) was probably a sarcophagus of ironstone.

bee

Canaan was described as a land of milk and honey, which indicates that bees were plentiful. Honey entered into commerce with Tyre (Ezek 27.17).

Be·el'ze·bub, Be·el'ze·bul

The names used by Jesus and others for the chief or prince of devils.

bee'tle

Possibly the long-horned grasshopper.

be·he'moth

(Heb. "dumb beast") A name for the hippopotamus; sometimes, a mythical creature.

Bel

(Akkad. "he who possesses") The state god of Babylon (Marduk).

Be'li·al

(Heb. "worthless, useless") A liar; an iniquitous, wicked person.

Bel·shaz'zar

Babylonian prince, co-regent with his father Nabonidus.

Be·na'iah

(Heb. "Yah has built") The name of 9 persons in the OT, one of whom was a son of Jehaida, a valiant warrior under David, and commander of Solomon's army.

Ben'ja·min

The youngest son of Jacob; Rachel, his mother, died at his birth. Joseph, his brother, demanded that he be brought to Egypt before he would help his brothers. The tribe of Benjamin was the smallest of the tribes.

Ber'o·dach-bal'a·dan

See Merodach-Baladan.

ber'yl

A silicate of beryllium and aluminum; the crystals are usually green. The emerald is of the same type.

Beth'a·ny

A village on the E slope of the Mount of Olives. It is 1⅝ mi. E of Jerusalem, and is now called el-'Aziriyeh.

Beth·az'ma·veth

A town identified with modern Hizmeh, 5 mi. NNE of Jerusalem.

Beth'el

(Heb. "house of God") More frequently mentioned than any city except Jerusalem, Bethel (now Beitin) lies 14 mi. N of Jerusalem. It was founded before 2000 B.C., has been destroyed several times despite being heavily fortified, and has been excavated. Near here Abraham built his altar. The Ark of the Covenant rested here, and the place is associated with Jacob and Elijah and with the tabernacle. Jeroboam made it a place of idolatry.

Be·thes'da, Beth·za'tha

A spring, possibly with medicinal properties, near the sheep gate or market in Jerusalem. The precise location is not now known.

Beth'le·hem

(Heb. "house of bread"?) A very old town, about 6 mi. SSW of Jerusalem, associated with David, Ruth, and many other persons of the OT, and the birthplace of Jesus.

Beth'shan, Beth·she'an

(Heb. "house of safety") A fortress city at the N end of the Jordan Valley, dating back to the 4th millennium B.C. It was along the route between Egypt, Damascus, and Arabia. Excavations there have provided much information on life in Bible times.

Beth·she'mesh

(Heb. "house of the seen") The name of 4 places mentioned in the OT, one of which, 24 mi. W of Jerusalem, was first settled in the 3rd millennium B.C., as shown by excavations there.

Beth-za'tha

See Bethesda.

bier

The Israelites, like the later Jews, buried the bodies of their dead. The burial was within a few hours after death. Probably the wooden framework of a bed served for a bier, as the same word is used for both.

birds

There are in Palestine about 350 species of birds,

26 of which are peculiar to that country. In the Law, 19 or 20 species of birds, mostly carnivorous, are (with the addition of the bat) declared to be unclean. The birds caught for food were chiefly pigeon, partridge, and quail. The dove is mentioned in the Bible more than 50

Birds perched in a mimosa tree, from an Egyptian wall painting of about the time of Abraham

times, and was the bird with which the Israelites were most familiar. Turtledoves and young pigeons were the only birds used for sacrifices; hence there was a busy trade in them in the neighborhood of the Temple. There are many Scriptural allusions to the habits of pigeons. Dovecots made of pots imbedded in clay are numerous in Palestine. They are often placed inside the walls in the houses of the poor. At the present day partridges abound, and also wild ducks, especially near the Dead Sea. There is, on the whole, a deficiency of singing birds, though blackbirds, larks, finches, cuckoos, and Palestine nightingales are heard in spring. There are many birds of prey.

birth'right
A position of peculiar honor and privilege assigned to the eldest son. The birthright could be parted with or lost through misconduct.

bish'op
(Gr. "overseer") In the NT one of the overseers of a Christian congregation, synonymous with presbyter (elder).

bi·tu'men
("asphalt," "slime") The name includes several compounds of carbon and hydrogen, from which pitch, asphalt, etc., are obtained. Bitumen is often washed up on the shores of the Dead Sea. It is found near Nineveh and at the base of Hermon, and there are springs of it in the Euphrates Valley. This substance is not necessarily connected with volcanic disturbances. Also called *slime*.

boar, wild
Wild boars are especially numerous in the thickets and brakes of the Jordan Valley, whence, when the river rises just before harvest, they are driven out, and play havoc with the cornfields and cultivated ground of the uplands. They are equally common in the southern wilderness, where they plough the ground for the bulbs that abound there.

Bo'az
A virtuous and wealthy man of Bethlehem, who married the widow Ruth of Moab.

Booths, Feast of
An autumn festival, one of the 3 great annual festivals in Israel.

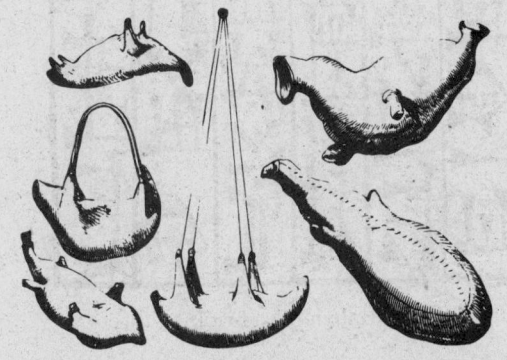

Leather bottles

box
The box shrub has been found in Palestine. *See* Pine.

bram'ble, bri'er, this'tle, thorn
About 20 biblical words imply thorny or spiny flora. Spine-bearing plants form a considerable portion of the flora of Palestine.

brass
Copper alloy. *See* copper.

bread
Commonly of wheat meal, sometimes of barley. The meal was kneaded in wooden troughs; the dough was then mixed with yeast or leaven, pressed or cut into thin, round cakes, then baked over hot stones or in an oven.

breth'ren of Jesus
Four in number (Mt 13.55; Mk 6.3), during His life unbelieving (Jn 7.3-7), were among the earliest members (Acts 1.14) and missionaries (1 Cor. 9.5) of the church. One of them, James the Lord's brother, had the authority of an Apostle (Gal 1.19; 2.9 and 12).

brick
Sun-dried brick made from muddy clay was widely used in the ancient world, but in Babylonia it was kiln dried. Often bricks were stamped with seals or names. Mortar in most areas was the same material as the bricks; in Assyria and Babylonia bitumen was used.

bri'er
See Bramble.

brim'stone
See Sulphur.

broom
A desert shrub.

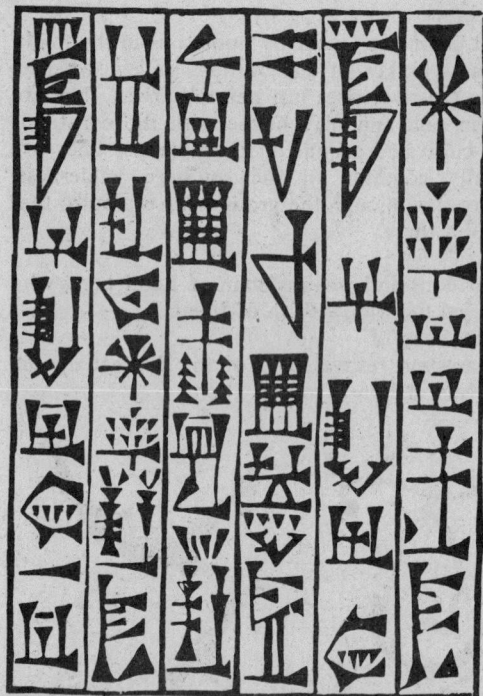

Babylonian brick

bronze

Copper alloy. *See* copper.

Bul

The 8th month in the Hebrew calendar.

bul'rush

The papyrus, which formerly grew in the Nile, rooting itself in the river mud. It is now extinct in Egypt, though still found higher up the Nile valley. It covers acres of the shallow water in Lake Merom. The papyrus has a triangular stem 8 to 10 feet high, terminating in a bush of slender leaves. Paper is made by pressing the pith into sheets.

bur'i·al

Probably, as it now is in Palestine, on the day of death, or next day. As soon as death had taken place, the eyes of the dead were closed. The body was washed, anointed, and swathed in linen. There is no mention of the Egyptian custom of embalming as having ever been followed by Israelites. In OT times the dead appear to have been buried in the clothes worn in life. The dead body was carried to the grave on an open bier, followed by the mourners and professional wailing-women. Burning of the dead was resorted to only in the case of criminals guilty of the most hateful of crimes and was regarded with horror. It was the greatest calamity to be deprived of burial. Many passages of the OT prove the desire of Israelites to be buried in the family burying-place ("with their fathers"), an evidence of their belief that the communion of kindred subsisted after death. The burial places were graves dug in the earth, caves, or chambers hewn in the rock, and closed with large stones to secure them from wild beasts. Such rock sepulchers abound in the neighbor-

hood of Jerusalem. In later times the custom arose of whitewashing every year after the rainy season the stones enclosing the sepulchers, to prevent passersby from being accidentally defiled by touching them.

burnt of'fer·ings

Sacrifices in which the victim was wholly burnt with fire, to express the entire surrender of the offerer to God.

bush, burn'ing

The bush that flamed as the angel called Moses may have been an acacia or a thorn bush. It has not been identified.

C

Caes·a·re'a

A city founded as Straton in the 4th century B.C., on the coast of Palestine 23 mi. S of Mt. Carmel. It was given to Herod by Augustus; Herod renamed it Caesarea in honor of Augustus and rebuilt it as a seaport.

Caes·a·re'a Phi·lip'pi

The name given by Philip the Tetrarch to Paneas, at the main Jordan source, and at the foot of Hermon; now the village of Banias.

Ca'ia·phas

Jewish high priest in the time of Jesus. His proper name was Joseph, Caiaphas being his surname. He was a son-in-law of Annas, high priest (A.D. 7-14). Under the Roman dominion the high priests were frequently changed; but Caiaphas held the office long. He was appointed by Pilate's predecessor, Valerius Gratus, probably about A.D. 18, and not removed till after the deposition of Pilate by Vitellius, governor of Syria, in A.D. 36. The statement (John 11.49; 18.13) that Caiaphas was "high priest that year" has led some to suppose wrongly that the high priests were at that time changed every year. The usage of Josephus in extending the title high priest to all those still living who had held the office explains how Annas is so styled in Acts 4.6 and probably John 18.19, 22.

cal'a·mus

Sweet flag was imported from a far country, possibly India, and sold in the markets of Tyre, and is still brought to the Damascus market from Arabia. Its root stock is aromatic. It was a chief ingredient of the holy anointing oil.

cal'en·dar

The Hebrews early used the equinox as the beginning of the new year, the agricultural year beginning in the spring and the civil or religious year in the autumn. The month was related to the lunar month, and seems to have been counted from the spring new year even when the autumnal new year was used; the use of the lunar month provided only 354¼ days instead of the necessary 365¼ between successive spring equinoxes, so that every few years an extra month had to be provided. The months were first given Canaanite names; then they came to be known by number and eventually, after the Exile, some of the Babylonian names were adopted. Various ways of adjusting the year were suggested by various persons, the added days sometimes early in the year, sometimes late. The 12-month sequence was not otherwise disturbed, and corresponded roughly with our contemporary calendar as follows: *Abib* or *Nisan*, April; *Ziv* or *Iyyar*, May; *Sivan*, June; *Tammuz*, July; *Ab*, August; *Elul*, September; *Ethanim* or *Tishri*, October; *Bul* or *Marchewan*, November; *Chislev*, December; *Tebeth*, January; *Shebat*, February; *Adar*, March.

Cal′va·ry

The place of the Crucifixion. Tradition places it where the Church of the Holy Sepulchre now stands. Other places in Jerusalem have been suggested.

Camels

cam′el

The camel, usually the Arabian, single-humped, has been the beast of burden and means of travel in the Near and Middle East for more than 3 millenniums. There is the slower burden-bearing camel and the swifter dromedary. The two-humped camel appears less often. The camel can go without water for several days, and its flat feet make it capable of traveling over sand. In biblical times, trade caravan travel across the deserts was commonplace; during warfare the camels carried supplies. Camel's milk was used, and the hair was woven into cloth used for tents and coarse robes such as that worn by John the Baptist.

cam′phire, cam′phor

See Henna.

Ca′naan, Ca′naan·ites

(Hurrian? "reeds"? "red purple"?) Canaan included the land between the Jordan River and the sea and the portion of Syria along the coast. The Canaanites were an advanced people, with a written language of 80 characters by 2000 B.C. It was an agricultural society, probably including merchants and seamen. The Hebrews learned writing from them, were sometimes attracted by their gods, intermarried with them, warred with them, and merged with them, seemingly in the 14th century B.C.

can′dle·stick

The candlestick of biblical times is properly called a *lampstand*. Many have been found in excavations. The earliest lamps were pottery saucers of olive oil, into which was laid a twisted thread as a wick. As early as 3000 B.C. the rims were pinched into lips to hold the thread wicks. Herod's temple had a seven-branched lampstand, called the Menorah, with a cup of oil at the top of each branch.

Ca·per′na·um

Excavations have shown Capernaum to be the

The seven-branched candlestick, representing that taken from the temple of Herod in the sack of Jerusalem in A.D. 69-70.

present Tell Hum, on the NNW coast of the Sea of Galilee.

Caph′tor

The traditional homeland of the Philistines; Caphtor has been identified as Crete. It has also been considered possible that the Philistines originated in the Aegean area and had sufficient contact with Cretans to have adopted dress and customs from them.

Cap·pa·do′ci·a

The area W of the Euphrates, S of the Black Sea, N of the Taurus Mountains, E of Galatia.

cap·tiv′i·ty

See Exile.

car′bun·cle

A red stone, garnet or ruby. Error in translation has in a few instances made it a green stone, such as emerald or beryl.

Car′che·mish, Char′che·mish

An ancient and important city on the Euphrates, an objective in warfare between Assyria and Egypt. Excavation has revealed its great antiquity. The present name is Jerablus.

Car′mel

(Heb. "garden," "orchard") A high headland on the coast of Palestine. The modern city of Haifa lies below.

cart

Goods were transported for the most part on the backs of men or of animals; but a cart, probably with 2 solid wheels, was also in use for carrying grain or other produce.

Courtesy of *The Interpreter's Dictionary of the Bible*

Upper: an ancient Egyptian cart; lower: a cart with captured women; from Lachish

cas′sia
A coarser kind of cinnamon.

cat
Apparently not commonly known in W Asia in biblical times. The cat was domesticated in Egypt 13 centuries before Christ. It was there a sacred animal, and thousands of mummified cats have been found.

cat′er·pil·lar
(Heb. "to peel off," "finish") Also translated as "destroying locust," "destroyer."

cat′tle
Words meaning cattle appear in the oldest languages. The Hebrews had oxen, asses, horses, sheep, and goats, and were familiar with camels.

ce′dar
Lebanon cedar grows also on the Taurus and Atlas Mountains. It was the king of trees, the symbol of grandeur, might, loftiness, and continuous expansion. Its wood was used in the successive temples at Jerusalem and in the palace of Nebuchadnezzar.

Ce′dron
See Kidron.

Cen′chre·a
Seaport 7 mi. E of Corinth.

chal·ced′o·ny
(Gr. *chalkedon*) One of the many varieties of minutely crystalline silica, of a light, translucent color, related to agate.

Chal·de′a, Chal·de·a′a
The plain of Babylon, or lower Mesopotamia; a region of swamps and lakes. One of its great cities was Ur of the Chaldees.

Chal·de′ans
The early people of Chaldea were fishermen and small-scale herdsmen and farmers, opposed to urbanized life. They were not willing to perform any kind of military service and avoided taxes.

They were at times under the control of Babylonia or Assyria; later, Chaldea controlled Babylonia and a wide empire, gradually changing the name from Babylonia to Chaldea. During this period Chaldea assisted in the conquest of Nineveh, the capital of Assyria. Thereafter Chaldea declined, and the Chaldeans went into the world as astrologers, magicians, fortune tellers, and diviners. As such they were famous throughout the Egyptian, Greek, and Roman worlds. The name is still associated with magic.

cha·me′le·on
A lizardlike creature.

cham′ois
A mountain sheep; a small, goat-like antelope.

Char′che·mish
See Carchemish.

char′i·ot
There were disk-wheeled vehicles drawn by asses in the 4th millennium B.C. in Mesopotamia. The first spoked wheels appeared about the time of Hammurabi. The vehicle was two-wheeled, closed in front and open behind, arranged to carry arrows and battle axes, and had a crew of 2, warrior and driver. Usually 2 horses were used. Around 1800 B.C. the chariot was the most powerful of weapons. With it, the Hyksos conquered most of Syria and Egypt. There were also gold and silver chariots and others painted and decorated for pleasure and display by royalty and the wealthy. When the Hebrews first entered Canaan, the Canaanites were using iron chariots; the Hebrews themselves apparently did not have chariots until the time of David. They traded grain to the Egyptians for horses.

Courtesy of *The Interpreter's Dictionary of the Bible*

Assyrian relief of a royal chariot

Ched·or·la′o·mer
An Elamite king with whom Abraham contended.

Che′mosh
God of the Moabites.

che′rub (pl. cher′u·bim)
A symbolical winged creature with a human face. Two cherubim were placed on the mercy seat or covering of the Ark of the Covenant in the Tabernacle and in the Temple, and figures representing cherubim were wrought into the hangings of the Holy of Holies.

chest′nut tree
A tall and majestic tree, growing near water in Palestine. From the globular form of the flow-

ers and fruits it is often called button-tree. *See* Plane tree.

Chin'ne·roth, Cin'ne·roth

An early name of the Sea of Galilee. Also the name of a district in Naphtali and of a fortified city in the district, now Tell el-'Oreimeh. Some excavation has been carried on at this site.

Chis'lev

The 9th month in the Hebrew calendar.

Chit'tim, Kit'tim

Greek Kition, the Phoenician port of Cyprus; the modern Larnaka. *See* Cyprus.

Christ

The coming of a Christ (Messiah) was foretold often in the OT, perhaps the most notable prophecy being in Is 9–11. He was to be of the House of David; justice and righteousness never ending would be established on His coming. This was not universally accepted; there were many unbelievers when Jesus was born, who remained unbelievers throughout His life. The believers accepted Him as God the Son, the second member of the Trinity, Christ (meaning the Anointed One), the Messiah, the One foretold: Jesus the Christ, Christ Jesus. His complete acceptance of Himself as the Son of God had its influence in winning many doubters, and the incomparable beauty and power of His preaching influence constantly increasing numbers of mankind.

Chron'i·cles

The two *Books of Chronicles* have much in common with the books of Samuel and Kings. They contain genealogical tables from Adam to the death of Saul, the reign of Solomon, the division of the kingdom, the exile, and the proclamation of Cyrus.

chro·nol'o·gy

It is doubtful that the authors of the books of the Bible were in any way conscious of writing history as history is known today. The calendar developed as they developed. They knew seasons rather than days, and periods of war or of peace or succession of rulers rather than years. Consequently a tidy arrangement by years is difficult for either OT or NT. Records of then contemporary governments, which have been and still are being revealed through excavations in the Near and Middle East, are constantly being checked against the gaps and uncertainties of the biblical record. It is possible that in time a complete chronology can be determined.

chrys'o·lite

(Gr. "chrysolithus") Properly this is a greenish-yellow gem, a variety of olivine, a ferromagnesian silicate. In early times the name was usually applied to the Oriental topaz, a yellow variety of corundum.

chrys'o·prase

(Gr. "chrysoprasos") An apple-green variety of chalcedony.

church

(Gr. *Ekklesia*, "an assembly") In the NT it is used in the following senses:

1. An ordinary public meeting (Acts 19.32, 39, 41).

2. The congregation of the Israelites under the Old Testament.

3. A meeting of Christians for worship.

4. The company of Christians associated for the worship and service of God in a particular locality or region.

5. The whole body of Christians throughout the world.

6. In the widest sense, the whole body of the redeemed.

Cin'ner·roth

See Chinneroth.

cir·cum·cis'ion

Removal of the foreskin. Circumcision was widely practiced; of the neighbors of the Hebrews, only the Philistines did not practice it.

cith'ern

A lyre-like instrument with 11 or 12 strings.

cit'ies

There were many ancient cities. Carbon-14 dating shows a wall and fortification at Jericho before 7000 or 8000 B.C. Cities had surrounding villages, whose inhabitants went inside the city walls in times of danger. The population of Ur of the Chaldees, where Abraham was born, has been estimated at a quarter to a half million.

cit'y of ref'uge

Crimes of violence were in ancient civilizations often avenged by the injured person himself or by a relative. But the accused person could be sure of trial according to the laws of the time and country if he could get to a city of refuge. In Palestine there were 6, 3 of them across the Jordan. The cities in Canaan were Kedesh, Shechem, and Hebron. The trans-Jordan cities were Bezer, Ramoth-Gilead, and Golan. Biblical law restricted refuge to the accidental homicide.

cloke, cloak

Originally a long strip of coarse cloth thrown over the shoulders. Later it became elaborated, of finer material, fitted, even embroidered. A creditor might seize this garment, but not the inner one. Sometimes called a *robe*, a *mantle*, a *garment*.

cloud

See Pillar of cloud and of fire.

coat

A garment worn under the mantle, usually tied by a girdle.

coat of mail

A sleeveless armor made (1) of skin or leather; or (2) of small plates of bronze or iron, sewn on leather or fastened together in rows.

coins

See Money.

Co·los'si·ans

The Letter (Epistle) of Paul to the Colossians was written by Paul, while he was a prisoner in Rome, to the Christians at Colossae in Asia Minor. Paul writes to encourage them with real truth—that through Christ they have the everlasting love of God.

com'fort·er

A paraclete. One who stands by to aid, to counsel, to strengthen; an advocate.

com·mand'ments
See Ten Commandments.

co'ney
(Heb. "the hider") A small animal, sometimes called a rock rabbit or rock badger. It is forbidden as food.

cop'per, brass, bronze
The name copper derives ultimately from Cyprus, the famous copper source of the ancient world. Egyptians, Edomites, and others mined copper in the Arabah, the area between the Dead Sea and the Gulf of Aqabah; Solomon's copper mines have been identified. Some articles made of copper have been found in excavations in the Holy Land. More bronze articles have been found; bronze is an alloy of copper and tin. The Phoenicians brought in tin ore as an article of commerce, and the Hebrews knew smelting and metallurgy. Brass, made of copper and zinc, has not been found, and seems not to have been made, nor have zinc deposits or worked-out mines been found.

cor'al
The red coral of the Mediterranean, used for beads and ornaments, was an article of commerce, and was considered a precious stone.

cor'ban
A Hebrew word, which is translated "offering" or "oblation," hence referring to any article or possession solemnly dedicated to God. Our Lord rebuked those who adopted this device to escape the necessity of supporting their parents.

co·ri·an'der
An annual plant, with seeds used as a spice.

Cor'inth
A city of Southern Greece, 40 mi. SW of Athens. Cenchreae was its eastern harbor. Destroyed by the Romans in 146 B.C., it was rebuilt by Julius Caesar in 46 B.C., and peopled by a colony of veterans and others. Situated on the isthmus which had always formed the highway of commerce between Asia and Italy, it became the metropolis of the Roman province of Achaia, the meeting-place of all the social forces of the age, and a center of licentiousness, much of it in the form of pagan religion and rites. The city was the home of Aquila and Priscilla, who became great friends of Paul and his assistants in evangelism in both Corinth and Ephesus; Paul was their frequent visitor.

Co·rin'thi·ans
The *Letters of Paul to the Corinthians* were written from Ephesus about 57 A.D. The Christians of Corinth found it hard to live as they knew they should and questioned Paul about their difficulties. In *First Corinthians* Paul answers their question, points out to them what they have done wrong, and encourages them with his message. "You are Christ's." *Second Corinthians* contains Paul's message of thanksgiving and love. Then he goes on to describe his tribulations as he went about preaching the gospel of Christ.

cor'mo·rant
A bird not positively identified.

corn
This is a general term, meaning grain. The grains grown in Palestine are wheat, barley, millet, and spelt. *See* Wheat.

cor'net
(Lat. *cornu*) A horn, a wind instrument made of horn, wood, or metal.

cos·met'ics
Ointments were used to counteract the dry heat of the climate, and perfumes were added to the ointments. Eye paint, usually black, was also used, and there is doubtful reference to henna, used in some cultures not only as a perfume but as a dye for hair, palms, soles of the feet, and nails.

cot'ton, hang'ings, net'work
Cotton was used in the Middle East from very early times. It is probable that the colored hangings in the palace of Susa (Esther 1.6) and the networks woven in Egypt (Is 19.9) were of cotton.

court
See Temple.

cov'e·nant
The religion of Israel rested on a covenant between Jehovah and that people. God founded the covenant by His promise, and His people's part in it was the fulfillment of the divine command. Entrance into it was marked by the sign of circumcision. A New Covenant was promised by the prophets; and this is established in Christ.

Cov'e·nant, Ark of the
See Ark of the Covenant.

Cov'e·nant, the Book of the
This is taken to refer to Ex 20.23–23.33.

crafts, crafts'men
Many craftsmen worked in their homes or had shops; sometimes a single craft occupied a special area in a town. Their number and diversity were increased notably by contact with the Canaanites and with the Babylonians during the Exile. Crafts included boatbuilders, netmakers, carpenters, wood carvers, furniture makers, carvers of ivory and alabaster, weavers, tanners, goldsmiths, silversmiths, bronzesmiths, leatherworkers, tentmakers, carpetmakers, ropemakers, basketmakers, fullers, dyers, jewelers, glassworkers, lampmakers, potters.

cre·a'tion
Cuneiform tablets have been discovered that give the different accounts of the creation current in Babylonia. One of them, in the form of a long poem, resembles in many respects the account in Gen 1. It commences with the statement that "in the beginning" all was chaos of waters. Then the Upper and Lower Firmaments were created, and the gods came into existence. After that comes a long account of the struggle between Bel-Marduk and the "Dragon" of Chaos, "the serpent of evil," with her allies, the forces of anarchy and darkness. It ended in the victory of the god of light, who thereupon created the present world by the power of his "word." The fifth tablet or book of the poem

describes the appointment of the heavenly bodies for signs and seasons, and the sixth (or perhaps the seventh) the creation of animals and reptiles.

Crete
An island in the Mediterranean SE of Greece. Center of Minoan civilization in the time of Abraham. Paul passed along the coast on his way to Rome. There was a Jewish colony on Crete; a Christian group was also established there. The people of the island were not well regarded (Tit 1.12).

crick'et
This may be the long-horned grasshopper.

crim'son, scar'let
Red coloring matter of many shades, extracted from cochineal insects; used for dyeing.

cross
The cross as a means of inflicting death in the most cruel and shameful way was used by the

Crosses

Phoenicians, from whom it passed to the Greeks and the Romans. It consisted of two beams of wood nailed one to the other in the form of X, or T, or +. The last, which is most familiar to us in art, was in all probability the shape of Christ's cross.

cu'cum·ber
Long cultivated in Syria and Egypt.

cum'min
The aromatic seed of an umbelliferous plant, used as a condiment.

curse
In the ancient warfare of the Israelites, as of the neighboring nations, the enemy and all his belongings were placed under a ban or curse. Thus on the Moabite stone we read, "I destroyed all the people of the city to delight the eyes of Chemosh and Moab."

Cush, Cu'shan, Cu'san
1. The Cushites in Ethiopia, the Kassites of Babylonia, or a Midianite tribe near Edom.
2. A king of Aram.

cut'ter
See Locust.

cym'bals
These were used in pairs, only by men, as signaling instruments and as accompaniments to the trumpet and lyre.

cy'press
The Hebrew word has been variously translated as pine or larch, box (box shrub), or holm (a form of oak; holly). *See* Holm tree; Pine.

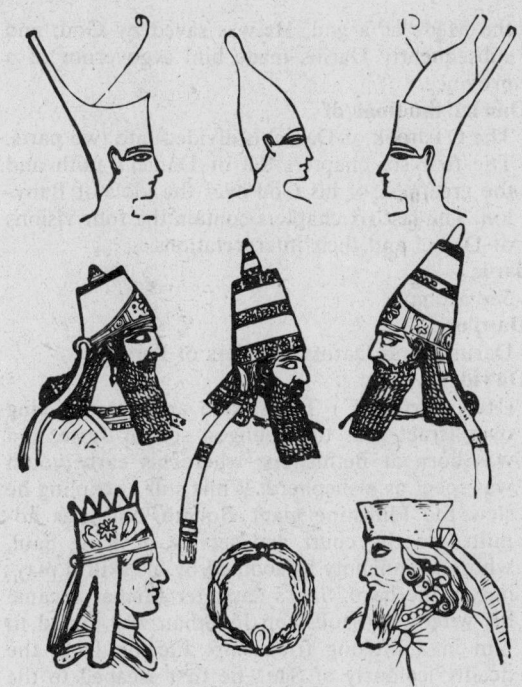

Ancient crowns

Cy'prus
A large island in the Mediterranean, 41 mi. from the Coast of Asia Minor and 60 mi. from Syria, also called Chittim or Kittim. In ancient times it was famous as a source of copper, and a particular pottery made there has been found in widely scattered excavations. It was the home of Barnabas, and was visited by Paul.

Cy'rus
A Persian king, founder of the Achaemenian dynasty.

D

Da·mas'cus
The first mention of Damascus in an inscription is dated in the 16th century B.C. It claims to be the oldest continuously occupied city site in the world, and is now the capital of Syria. In ancient times it was a widely known caravan center. The city was captured and plundered many times, by Assyria, Babylonia, David of Israel, Persia, Alexander the Great, and Rome.

Dan
1. The fifth son of Jacob.
2. A city in the N of Palestine, identified with Tell el-Qadi, to which the Danites migrated. Jeroboam established idolatry there.

Dan'iel
(Heb. "God has judged") The name of 3 persons in the OT, one of whom is the author of the 4th of the prophetic books. He was taken as a captive to Babylon, where he was trained in the king's palace. Among other triumphs he interpreted the king's dreams and the handwriting on the wall, looked after his own friends, Shadrach, Meshach, and Abednego, and then was cast into a den of lions for refusing to acknowledge Darius

the Mede as a god. He was saved by God, and subsequently Darius made him a governor of a province.

Dan'iel, the Book of

The OT book of Daniel is divided into two parts. The first six chapters tell of Daniel's faith and the greatness of his God over the idols of Babylon. The last six chapters contain the four visions of Daniel and their interpretations.

dar'ic

See Money.

Da·ri'us

Darius I and Darius II, rulers of Persia.

Da'vid

(Heb. "beloved") The second and greatest king over Israel, was the youngest son of Jesse, and was born at Bethlehem, where his early youth was spent as a shepherd. While still a stripling he slew the Philistine giant Goliath, and was admitted to the court and service of King Saul, whose melancholy he soothed by his skilful playing on the harp. Saul's daughter Michal became his wife, and Saul's son Jonathan was united to him in a lifelong friendship. Fleeing from the deadly jealously of Saul, he first escaped to the country of the Philistines. Then, gathering at the cave of Adullam a band of 400 (afterward 600) men, he contrived to avoid Saul by moving hither and thither in the S country. For 16 months he lived at Ziklag, as a vassal of the king of Gath. After the death of Saul and Jonathan at Gilboa, David reigned over Judah at Hebron for 7½ years, and after the death of Saul's son Ishbosheth he became king over all Israel. He took the stronghold Jebus, on the hill of Zion (the "city of David"), from the Jebusites, and built a palace there, with a tent beside it, in which the Ark of the Covenant was placed until a temple should be built for it by his successor. In addition to his old guard of 600 gibborim (or "heroes"), now largely recruited from foreigners, especially "Cherethites and Pelethites" (most probably Cretans and Philistines), he had, according to Chronicles, 288,000 fighting men, of whom 24,000 were under arms each month in the year. Several years of successful war made David master of the whole territory from the Euphrates to the Egyptian frontier. In the latter part of his reign of 32 years in Jerusalem, his favorite son Absalom rebelled against him and was slain, to his father's great sorrow; and shortly before his death, which has been variously dated 1015, 980, and 977 B.C., another son, Adonijah, attempted by means of a revolt to frustrate his father's choice of Solomon as successor.

David, while he was the hero of the people, refused to lift his hand against "the Lord's anointed," even in his own defense, contenting himself with an appeal to the Divine judgment. In contrast to Saul, he is "the man after God's own heart." Heroic confidence in God sustained him in all the difficulties of his life and of his reign. "He executed judgment and justice unto all his people," and established the monarchy on a sound civil and religious basis. The greatest

stain upon his character was his foul wrong done to Uriah, whose wife he wanted, followed by his indirect murder, by sending him into battle and arranging to have him deserted, sins of which he bitterly repented. The last song of "the sweet psalmist of Israel" expresses the spirit of his life and of his rule. In the darkest days of the nation's history, men felt that the promises of God could only be fulfilled under another David. The memory of the "sure mercies of David" and the "everlasting covenant" God made with him quickened their Messianic hope of One who should be given "for a witness to the people, a leader and commander to the people."

day

The word may mean the time from sunrise to sunset; or the civil day of 24 hours, from sunrise to sunrise or from sunset to sunset; or in a poetic sense of "in the time of" as in the phrase "in the day of . . ."

Day of A·tone'ment

See Atonement, Day of.

day star

See Lucifer.

dea'con

(Gr. "servant") In the NT, the name of a class of congregational office-bearers, first mentioned about A.D. 63. Their work seems chiefly to have been the visiting and relief of the poor. The early church appointed 7 in every church, and assigned to them the special care of the sick and of the poor.

dea'con·ess, serv'ant

Women especially charged with the care of the poor and sick women. Widows may have constituted a special case.

Dead Sea

This body of water at the mouth of the Jordan River is called in the Bible the Salt Sea, the Sea of the Arabah, the Sea of the Plain. It is about 53 mi. long and 10 mi. wide, 1500 ft. deep, and its surface is 1292 ft. below sea level. It is about 25 per cent salt, 5 times as salty as the ocean. Its mineral compounds are chlorides of magnesium, sodium, calcium, and potassium, as well as magnesium bromide.

Deb'o·rah

1. Rebekah's nurse and her lifelong companion.

2. An early judge of Israel. She roused opposition to Canaanite oppression of Israel, and Judg 5.2-31 is her Song of Victory over Canaan. It is one of the oldest Hebrew poems in existence, dating from the 12th century B.C., and it has been described as one of the most magnificent.

De·cap'o·lis

A federation of 10 Greek cities in Palestine, some of which lay along the trade routes of the day, and several of which were founded by soldiers from the armies of Alexander the Great. Most of them have been identified, and some have been extensively excavated.

Ded·i·ca'tion, Feast of

The principal feast of Dedication was that of the reconsecration of the temple after its desecration by the Greeks, an 8-day celebration today called Hanukkah, in mid-December. Sometimes it is called the Feast of Lights.

De·grees', Songs of, or As·cents', Songs of
The titles of 15 psalms. The degrees or ascents are believed to be the steps between the men's and women's courts of the temple. The Levites stood on these steps to sing these psalms.

De·li'lah
Samson's beloved. She was bribed by the Philistines to get for them the secret of his strength, which she did.

del'uge
See flood.

De·struc'tion, Cit'y of
See City of the Sun.

Deu·ter·on'o·my
A sequel to Numbers. Narrated in it are three speeches and two poems, supposedly spoken by Moses in Moab before the crossing of Jordan, in which he gives the Ten Commandments to the chosen people. A minor narrative in three of the chapters tells of the last days of Moses.

Di·a'na of the E·phe'si·ans
This is the Latin name of the ancient goddess of the region of Ephesus; some 300 years after the first Greek settlers had arrived in the area they had adopted this local mother-goddess or fertility goddess as their own, calling her Artemis. By 800 B.C., they had begun to build a magnificent temple for her. Worship of her was widespread and conducted in magnificent rituals and surroundings. The primary image, probably a meteorite, is believed to have been placed in the temple at Ephesus.

Di·as'po·ra, Dis·per'sion
At the time of the Exile the Jewish people scattered widely and settled permanently in Mesopotamia, particularly in Babylonia, and in Alexandria, Asia Minor, and as far away as Cyrenaica.

Di'bon
A Moabite city 13 mi. E of the Dead Sea, 3 mi. N of the Arnon River. The famous Moabite Stone was found in Dibon. It tells of a Moabite victory over Israel at the time of Omri.

dill
Both the plant and the seeds are used as flavoring and have some use in medicine.

Dis·per'sion
See Diaspora.

di·vorce'
The Hebrew name for husband, baal, meant "owner," and in primitive Israel dissolution of marriage might take place at the husband's will. The Book of the Covenant shows that the wife so put away retained the right to be fed and clothed by the husband (Ex. 21.7-11), unless she was redeemed by her own relatives, and thus set free to marry another man. In Deut. 24.1–4 it is enacted that the husband must give a dismissed wife a "bill of divorcement," a document releasing her from all claims on his part and setting her free to marry again.

Our Lord teaches that marriage rests on the original creative ordinance of God, making the bond between man and wife indissoluble, and that the Mosaic legislation with regard to divorce was a concession to natural hardness of heart, and did not correspond to its divine idea (Mt 19.4-9; 5.31 ff). Divorce was permissible only in the case of unfaithfulness (Mt 5.32; 19.9).

dog
Mentioned about 40 times in Scripture, almost always in a tone of contempt. The Jews, not being a hunting people, did not train the dog, except to guard their flocks (Job 30.1). They had not the noble mastiffs and wolfhounds we find carved on Assyrian monuments, nor the varied breeds of hunting dogs portrayed on the Egyptian walls. Their dogs were, doubtless, as they are still in Palestine, pariah or ownerless dogs, of a type not unlike the Scottish collie. Their nocturnal habits are referred to in Ps 59.14, 15. In the East they are the scavengers of the towns. The term dog is still hurled in reproach by the Jew at the Gentile and by the Moslem at the Christian. Christians also use it.

Do'than
The place where Joseph found his brothers. Now called Tell Dotha, excavations show it to have been a city from about 3000 B.C. to A.D. 300 or 400.

drach'ma
The unit of silver coinage of Greece; spoken of as a piece of silver.

drag'on
This seems to have been a fabulous monster of tremendous strength. It is called leviathan, sea monster, Rahab (in poetic passages only) and sea serpent. *See* Whale.

dress
The outermost garment of men may have been a rectangular piece of cloth, a mantle, cloak, cloke, wrapped about the body. Under that was a garment called a coat, tunic, robe or chiton (Greek), which might have been baglike, with openings for arms and head and of various lengths. A loincloth or girdle might be worn; the priests had breeches. The girdle and the tunic might be made of skins of animals. Cloth woven of wool, linen, animal hair, or fine linen (probably cotton) was used, of varying degrees of beauty and elegance. The draped or wrapped garments were tied around by a girdle, a long folded wool cloth, through which a sword might be thrust; also, it might be folded in such a way as to provide a money belt. Sandals were worn, fastened by leather straps. Men of importance wore a ring or rings. There was elaborate jewelry for men of rank or wealth. Women's clothing was similar, sometimes more elaborate, being decorated with fringe or other ornamentation. Women had more head dresses, veils, and ornaments than men. A number of dyes were used.

drom'e·da·ry
A finer and swifter race of camel, differing from the ordinary camel as a race horse does from a cart horse. According to an Arabic proverb, "Men are like camels—not one in a hundred is a dromedary."

E

ea'gle, gier, vul'ture

The largest flying birds of Palestine, all unclean for food. The vulture is a carrion-eating bird. The same Heb. word has been thus variously translated.

ear of grain

The individual head of grain.

ear'ring

These ornaments seem usually to have been circular in shape, made of gold. Men may have worn a single earring.

E'bal

A mountain N of Mount Gerizim and forming the N side of an E to W pass with Gerizim on the S.

eb'on·y

The core wood of several varieties of ebony, imported from Ceylon, S India, and possibly from Ethiopia. Egyptians, Babylonians, Greeks, Romans, and Phoenicians made furniture of ebony inlaid with ivory. Idols were also carved from ebony.

Ec·cle·si·as'tes

The book of *Ecclesiastes* contains the writings of a wealthy Jew who suffered from the sorrows and disappointments of life and now tries to discover the true value and meaning of life through God. The author of this book calls himself "The Preacher," "The son of David," and "king in Jerusalem." But whether this was Solomon or a later "son of David" is uncertain.

E'den

The root of the Hebrew word is uncertain, and the location of Eden has not been determined. The plain of the Tigris-Euphrates rivers has been most favored.

E'dom

(Heb. "the red region") Edom extended from the Brook Zered about 70 mi. toward the Gulf of Aqabah, with an approximate 15-mi. width. Excavations show a busy civilization there between the 23rd and 20th centuries, after which the only inhabitants were wandering Bedouins. In the 13th century the Edomites, a Semitic people, arrived. They were at war much of the time with the Israelites; David conquered them, making possible trade with Arabia and access to the copper mines of Edom. Later, Amaziah and his successor Azariah again conquered the country. After the Exile, the Edomites moved into Palestine. Eventually, Rome conquered the entire area.

E'gypt

The name applied since the time of Homer to the land of the Nile, in the NE of Africa. Egypt consists geographically of 2 halves, the N being the Delta, and the S, Upper Egypt, between Cairo and the First Cataract. The Hebrews called it Mizraim, the land of Ham, or Rahab. The Egyptians belonged to the Mediterranean race and their original home is still a matter of dispute. The ancient Egyptian language, of which the latest form is Coptic, is distantly connected with the Semitic family of speech.

The civilization of Egypt goes back to a remote antiquity. The two kingdoms, the north and the south, were united by Menes, founder of the first historical dynasty of kings. The first 6 dynasties, lasting until 2200 B.C., constitute what is known as the Old Kingdom, which had its capital at Memphis, S of Cairo (the Old Testament Moph or Noph). The native name was Mennofer, "the good place." The Pyramids were tombs of the monarchs of the Old Kingdom, those of Gizeh being erected in the time of the Fourth Dynasty.

After the fall of the Old Kingdom came a period of decline and obscurity, followed by the Middle Kingdom, the most powerful dynasty of which was the Twelfth. The Faiyum was rescued for agriculture by the kings of the Twelfth Dynasty, and 2 obelisks were erected in front of the temple of the Sun-god at On or Heliopolis (near Cairo), one of which is still standing. The capital of the Middle Kingdom was Thebes, in Upper Egypt.

The Middle Kingdom was overthrown by the Hyksos (*haq schas,* Bedouin chieftains) or Shepherd princes from Asia, whose three dynasties ruled over Northern Egypt for several centuries. They had their capital at Zoan or Tunis (now San), in the NE part of the Delta. In their time Abraham, Jacob, and Joseph entered Egypt. The Hyksos were finally expelled about 1600 B.C. by the hereditary princes of Thebes, who founded the Eighteenth Dynasty, and carried the war into Asia. Canaan, Syria, and Cyprus were subdued, and the boundaries of the Egyptian Kingdom were fixed at the Euphrates. The Sudan, which had been conquered by the kings of the Twelfth Dynasty, was again annexed to Egypt, and the eldest son of the Pharaoh took the title of prince of Cush. One of the later kings of the dynasty, Amen-hotep IV (1369-1353 B.C.), taking the name Akh-en-Aton (spirit of the sun), endeavored to supplant the ancient state religion of Egypt by a pantheistic monotheism derived from Asia, the one supreme god being adored under the image of the solar disk. The attempt led to religious and civil war, and the Pharaoh retreated from Thebes to Central Egypt, where he built a new capital, on the site of the present Tel el-Amarna. The cuneiform tablets that were found here in 1887 represent his foreign correspondence. He surrounded himself with officials and courtiers of Asiatic and more especially Canaanitish extraction; but the native party succeeded eventually in overthrowing the government; the capital of Amenhotep was destroyed, and the foreigners were driven out of the country—those that remained being reduced to serfdom.

The national triumph was marked by the rise of the Nineteenth Dynasty, in the founder of which, Ramses I, we must see the "new king, who knew not Joseph." His grandson, Ramses II. reigned 67 years (1290-1224 B.C.), and was an indefatigable builder. Pithom, excavated by Naville in 1883, was one of the cities he built; he may have been the Pharaoh of the Oppres-

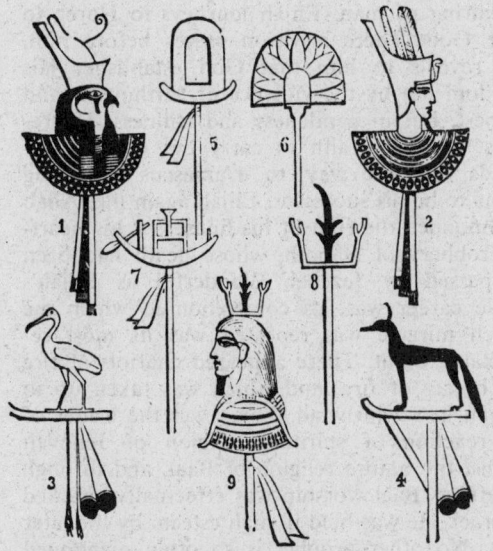

Egyptian standards

sion. The Pharaoh of the Exodus may have been one of his immediate successors, whose reigns were short. Under them Egypt lost its empire in Asia, and was itself attacked by barbarians from Libya and the north.

The Nineteenth Dynasty soon afterward came to an end, Egypt was distracted by civil war, and for a short time a Syrian, Irsu, ruled over it.

Then came the Twentieth Dynasty, the 2nd Pharaoh of which, Ramses III (1195-1164 B.C.), restored the power of his country. In one of his campaigns he overran the S part of Palestine, where the Israelites had not yet settled. They must at the time have been still in the wilderness. But it was during the reign of Ramses III that Egypt finally lost Gaza and the adjoining cities to the Philistines.

After Ramses III, Egypt fell into decay. Solomon married the daughter of one of the last kings of the Twenty-first Dynasty, which was overthrown by Sheshonk or Shishak I, the general of the Libyan mercenaries, who founded the Twenty-second Dynasty (940-745 B.C.). A list of the places he captured in Palestine is engraved on the outside of the S wall of the temple of Karnak.

In the age of Hezekiah, Egypt was conquered by Ethiopians from the Sudan, who constituted the Twenty-fifth Dynasty. The 3rd of them was Tirhakah (689-664 B.C.). In 671 B.C. it was conquered by the Assyrians, who divided it into 20 satrapies, and Tirhakah was driven back to his ancestral dominions. Fourteen years later it successfully revolted under Psamtik or Psammetichus I (663-609 B.C.) of Sais, the founder of the Twenty-sixth Dynasty. Among his successors were Neco of Necho and Hophra, or Apries. The dynasty came to an end in 525 B.C. when the country was subjugated by Cambyses. Soon afterward it became a Persian satrapy.

The title of Pharaoh, given to the Egyptian king, is the Egyptian for Great House. The name is found in very early Egyptian texts.

Egyptian religion was a strange mixture of pantheism and animal worship, the gods being adored in the form of animals. While the educated classes resolved their many deities into manifestations of one omnipresent and omnipotent divine power, the lower classes regarded the animals as incarnations of the gods. Under the Old Kingdom, Ptah, the Creator, the god of Memphis, was at the head of the Pantheon; afterward Amon, the god of Thebes, took his place. Amon, like most of the other gods, was identified with Re, the sun god of Heliopolis.

The Egyptians believed in a resurrection and a future state of rewards and punishments. The judge of the dead was Osiris, who had been slain by Set, the representative of evil, and afterward restored to life. His death was avenged by his son Horus, whom the Egyptians invoked as their Redeemer. Osiris and Horus, along with Isis, formed a trinity, representing the sun god under different forms.

The Pyramids, the temples, and the obelisks of Egypt have been described in all ages, but it was not until early in the 19th century, through the finding of the Rosetta stone, that the key to reading the hieroglyphic texts was discovered by the French scholar Champollion. The work of Brugsch and Birch then led to the recovery of history contained on the monuments or in papyri. The excavations of Mariette followed; and those of Petrie and De Morgan further increased our information about the religion, social customs, and history of Egypt. In 1896, among the ruins of a temple of Mer-ne-Ptah at Thebes, Petrie found a large granite stele, on which is engraved a hymn of victory commemorating the defeat of Libyan invaders who had overrun the Delta. At the end other victories of Mer-ne-Ptah are glanced at, and it is said that "the Israelites (I-s-y-r-a-e-l-u) are minished (?) so that they have no seed." This statement of an Egyptian poet is a remarkable parallel to Ex 1.10-22.

E′lah, Val′ley of

(Heb. "valley of the terebinth"?) A valley identified as Wadi es-Sant, 14 mi. WSW of Bethlehem.

E′lam, E′lam·ites

Elam occupied the area of the Zagros Mountains and present-day Luristan and Khuzistan. Its capital was Susa. Its history through about 2 millennia was warfare first with Sumer and subsequently with Babylonia and Assyria. Darius completed the conquest of the country.

el′ders, an′cients

Heads of families and tribes, among the early Hebrews as among other primitive peoples, administered justice within their own circles in time of peace and were the leaders in time of war (cf. the Arabian sheikh, or elder). The "elders of the city" afterward took the place of the elders of tribes and families, retaining their judicial functions. The "judges" and "officers" were probably those among the elders who acted respectively as administrators and executors of justice. When the synagogue became an established institution, the elders who were the civil authorities of a place were also the elders of its synagogue.

The elders or presbyters (Gr. "elders") of Christian churches were local overseers chosen after the model of the synagogue. They appear from the first to have been elected by the people, and, on their being approved by the apostles, to have been instituted to their office by prayer and the laying on of hands. Their duties were to exercise spiritual oversight over the people as pastors, visiting the sick and caring for the poor and for strangers, to maintain order in the religious assemblies, to teach, and to administer the affairs of the congregation, in concurrence with the deacons. The word elder or presbyter was interchangeable with the word bishop in NT times, and the offices were one and the same till about A.D. 150, when the presbyters first became subordinate to the bishops.

el'e·phant

The elephant is not mentioned in the OT, but Solomon imported ivory (1 Kings 10.22; 2 Chron 9.21) so there must have been knowledge of the animal. The Persians used elephants in warfare in the 4th century B.C., and they were used in war against Palestine by the Seleucids in 163 B.C.

E'li

(Heb. "exalted") A judge in Israel, he held that office and the high-priesthood for 40 years at Shiloh. His sons, Hophni and Phinehas, through gross misconduct, disgraced their priestly descent and position; and a great defeat, in which they and many Israelites were slain by the Philistines and the Ark of the Covenant was captured, was regarded as a divine judgment. Eli died of horror at the news and was succeeded by Samuel (1 Sam 1–4).

E·li'hu

(Heb. "he is my God") The name of 5 persons in the OT, one of whom argued with Job and his friends (Job 32–37).

E·li'jah, E·li'as

(Heb. "Yah is God") Elijah the Tishbite was of the inhabitants or sojourners of Gilead. His prophetic ministry belongs to the Northern Kingdom, in the reigns of Ahab and Ahaziah. When Ahab, under the influence of his Tyrian wife Jezebel, threatened to suppress the worship of Jehovah, and made Baal worship the court religion, Elijah suddenly appeared before the king to announce a long drought, in punishment of the apostasy of the covenant nation. While this lasted (3 years) he was at first miraculously fed by ravens at the brook Cherith and afterward lived at Zarephath, a Tyrian city, in the house of a widow, whose son he restored to life. Elijah now appears before Ahab, and challenges the prophets of Baal to a contest between Baal and Jehovah, in which it shall be shown by fire from heaven which is the true God. The fire consumes the sacrifice and altar of Jehovah; the people acknowledge that Jehovah is God, and fall upon the priests of Baal and slay them; and before evening there is a tempest of rain. But this victory is soon followed by defeat; and, despairing of man, Elijah journeys to Horeb to meet God. There a vision passes before him, and reveals to him that God establishes His kingdom not by the violence of earthquake and tempest, but in gentleness and stillness. He returns with new faith to carry out God's commands, on his way to Damascus anointing Elisha to be his successor. Elijah again met Ahab to announce the ruin of his house for his heartless robbery of Naboth, whose death had been compassed by Jezebel. Wonderful as Elijah's whole career was, its completion in which the Enoch miracle was repeated was its most remarkable event. There appeared chariots of fire and horses of fire, and Elijah was taken up to heaven in a whirlwind. Elijah was the leader of the reaction of spiritual religion of Jehovah against the nature religion of Baal, and through his efforts Baal worship was effectually checked in Israel. He was held in high esteem by the later Jews. No other prophet is so often mentioned in the NT. The last prophet, Malachi, prophesies his return before the day of the Lord. This prophecy was literally interpreted in Israel. The evangelists and Jesus show that it was fulfilled in John the Baptist. In the transfiguration of our Lord, Elijah appears as the representative of the prophets, beside Moses, the representative of the law (1 Kings 17–19, 21; 2 Kings 1, 2).

E·li'phaz

(Heb. "God crushes"?) One of Job's friends.

E·li'sha

(Heb. "God is salvation") The son of Shaphat of Abel-Mehclah, Elisha was the disciple and successor of Elijah, to whom he is related much as Joshua is to Moses. His prophetic work belonged to the reigns of Jehoram, Jehu, and Jehoahaz. As the spiritual guide of the people, he showed the same spirit of opposition to the idolatrous court and priesthood that had inspired Elijah, and was to the faithful servants of Jehovah what his great teacher had been before him, "the chariot of Israel, and the horsemen thereof," Israel's strength and protection. Many miracles are recorded as having been wrought by him. He died early in the reign of Joash, at an extreme old age (2 Kings 2-9, 12).

elm

An erroneous translation of ela (Hos 4.13), elsewhere rendered oak, teil tree, or terebinth. The elm is not found in Palestine.

E'lul

The 6th month in the Hebrew calendar.

em·balm'ing

A mode of preserving a dead body from decay by the use of aromatic spices. The art was practiced by the Egyptians from the very earliest times, and was by them brought to great perfection. It probably originated in the belief in the future reunion of the soul and the body. It was rarely practiced by the Jews. The Jewish process required 40 days, and that of the Egyptians 70 days. An embalmed body is a mummy.

em'er·ald

A variety of beryl of rich green color.

Em·ma'us

(Gr. "warm wells") A Judean town, not definitely identified. Four modern towns have been suggested.

En'dor

(Heb. "spring of *dor*") A city in Manasseh, home of a medium or witch consulted by King Saul. Near Endor, Sisera and Jabin were destroyed. Located at the modern Endor.

En·ro'gel

(Heb. "spring of the fuller") A spring in the valley of the Kidron, near Jerusalem.

E·phe'sians

The Letter of Paul to the Ephesians, written about A.D. 62, seems to be a general letter to the churches of Asia Minor. Paul presents God's eternal purpose to save men through faith in Christ; "the dividing wall of hostility" between Jews and Gentiles has been broken down through the cross of Christ. Paul exhorts us to live as worthy, true Christians.

Eph'e·sus

A famous city of Lydia, in Asia Minor, and the capital of Proconsular Asia, it is noted for its Temple of Artemis or Diana and its great theater. It was visited by Paul in his second journey when he left Aquila and Priscilla there to carry on the work; and in his third journey, when Demetrius raised an uproar against him.

eph'od

A priestly garment.

E'phra·im

(Heb. "fruitful") The most powerful of the tribes of Northern Israel, extended from Benjamin to Manasseh W of Jordan.

E'phra·im, Mount

The tribe of Ephraim lived in hill country; Joshua (an Ephraimite) was buried on Mount Ephraim, but which hill is intended is not known.

E·sar·had'don

King of Assyria and Babylonia (681-669 B.C.).

Es·dra·e'lon

Greek name for the W portion of the Valley of Jezreel, including the Valley of Megiddo. It is a well-watered and fertile valley, which separates Galilee from Samaria. The River Kishon drains it.

Es'dras, First and Sec'ond Books of

In the Vulgate these books appear as 3 and 4 Esdras, because Ezra and Neh have been counted as two books of Ezra. Counting them in this way, *Third Esdras* is a new version of the events relating to the return from the Captivity, the chief incident being a contest before the king by the young wits of the court. Zerubbabel wins with the well-known maxim, *Magna est veritas, et praevalebit*, "Truth is great, and will prevail." In consequence, he obtains concessions for the Jewish captives.

Fourth Esdras has perished in the Greek, but is extant in other versions. Its major part is a series of revelations to Ezra regarding the fortunes of Israel and of Jerusalem. Its date is probably after A.D. 70.

Es·senes'

An ascetic order, known to have existed from about 150 B.C. In the time of our Lord they were settled in monastic communities near the Dead Sea and in villages throughout the country. The Dead Sea Scrolls (found in 1947 and after) constitute a major part of the literature of the Qumran monastery. The name is probably from the root of a Hebrew word meaning "pious." The Essenes endeavored to reach absolute religious purity through strict abstemiousness and cleanliness. Their common meals were regarded as sacrificial feasts. Their lives were divided between religious exercises, lustrations (purification ceremonies), and labor at tillage and handicrafts. They had a community of goods and disapproved of marriage. They forbade trading, swearing of oaths, and anointing with oil. They sent gifts of incense to the Temple at Jerusalem, but differed from orthodox Judaism in their rejection of all animal sacrifices, in praying daily at sunrise, and in their view of the body as essentially evil and incapable of resurrection. The principles in which they differed from Judaism may have been derived from the East. They are not mentioned in the NT, and by the time of our Lord appear to have had little or no influence on the life of their nation.

Es'ther

A Jewess of Susa who became the queen of Ahasuerus, and frustrated a plot to destroy all Jews. This is commemorated in the Jewish festival of Purim.

Es'ther, the Book of

The last of the OT historical books, it contains an early example of pre-Christian anti-Semitism. Esther, a Jewess, was chosen as the new queen for Ahasuerus, the king of Persia. Her uncle Mordecai had incurred the enmity of Haman, the evil court favorite, and so brought the threat of death to his people. Esther, through her position, was able to avert the tragedy and save her people.

Eth'a·nim

The 7th month in the Hebrew calendar, later called Tishri.

E·thi·o'pi·a

An ancient name of the territory S of Egypt, also called Cush, and including what was subsequently called Sudan. From about 2000 B.C. there was sporadic warfare with Egypt. For some hundreds of years the area was independent of Egypt as the Kingdom of Nubia, with Napata as its capital. Later it was subdued in the expansion of the Assyrian empire.

Eu·phra'tes

The largest river in W Asia, called "the river" and "the great river." It flows from the mountains of Armenia to the Persian Gulf, 1700 mi.; 140 mi. above the Gulf, it is joined by the Tigris. The region between the rivers is thence called Mesopotamia.

ex'ile

Israel's geographical position made the country a buffer between Egypt to the W and the Assyrians and Babylonians to the E, involved in their almost constant warfare. In 721 B.C. the Assyrian Sargon II captured Samaria, the capital of the Northern Kingdom, and recorded in his inscriptions that he deported 27,290 Israelites to the E. With this deportation the identity of the N ten tribes disappeared; they were assimilated into the Assyrian population. People from the E were moved into Palestine. A century and a half later, after Babylonia had defeated Assyria, Jerusalem was captured; in 578 B.C. King Jehoiachin and some 10,000 of the population were deported to Babylon. An abortive rebellion led to further deportations in 587 B.C., and a reprisal deportation as a penalty for the assassination of the Babylon-appointed governor of Judah occurred in 582 B.C. Many of those deported were absorbed into the population of Babylonia, but following 538 B.C., the return from exile began, and with it the rebuilding of the temple.

Ex'o·dus

The return of the Hebrew people from Egypt to Israel is called the exodus from Egypt. The easy route had Egyptian fortifications scattered along the way, hence was avoided. It was for them, as a consequence, a journey of immense difficulty through wilderness and wild terrain, related in the Book of Exodus.

Ex'o·dus, the Book of

The second book of the OT relates the history of the Israelites from after the death of Joseph to the erection of the Tabernacle by Moses. It includes an account of the wanderings in the wilderness of Sinai and the giving of the law to the nation.

ex'or·cists

Persons who professed to expel evil spirits by adjuration or the performance of certain rites. Strolling exorcists were very numerous in the first century, especially in Asia Minor. Some of them undertook, instead of their usual formulas, to employ the name of Jesus (Acts 19.13).

E·ze'ki·el

(Heb. "God strengthens") A Jewish prophet, some of a priest Buzi, was among the captives whom Nebuchadnezzar carried with king Jehoiachin in 598 B.C. to Babylonia, where he settled near the river Chebar. His prophetic work extended over not less than 22 years (592-570).

E·ze'ki·el, the Book of

This OT book is written by the prophet of the exile. It is divided into two sections; the first denounces the sins and abominations of Jerusalem and the second looks to the future with the hope that the city will be restored after it has been cleansed. This latter section contains passages strongly messianic in nature.

Ez'ra, Ez'rah

(Heb. "Yahweh helps") The name of 3 persons in the OT, one of whom, a priest and scribe, was the organizer of the post-Exilic community. With the favor and support of Artaxerxes Longimanus, he led a band of 1800 male Israelites from Persia to Palestine in 458 B.C. to strengthen Zerubbabel's colony. He carried out a drastic reform by casting out the foreign wives and their children, and established a regular synagogue service, in which the chief place was given to reading and exposition of the Law. For this service he founded the special class of Scribes. Ezra exercised a most powerful influence on the development of Judaism. The complete subjection of the people under the Law was the fruit of his work (Ezra 7–10; Neh 8–10, and 12).

Ez'ra, the Book of

Ezra and Nehemiah are companion OT books, continuing the narration of Chronicles. Ezra details the first return of the Jews from their captivity in Babylon and the rebuilding of the Temple.

F

fal'low deer, roe'buck

More than one variety of deer can be found in the Near and Middle East, but the precise species to which reference is made has not been identified (Deut 4.5; 1 Kings 4.23).

fast'ing

Complete or partial abstinence from food is an expression of religious humiliation in the OT, often described by the phrase, "to afflict the soul." It was regarded as the natural sign of sorrow, especially of penitence; and where this mood, which gives fasting its value, is wanting, the prophets condemn it as displeasing to God (Jer 14.12). The only regularly recurring fast prescribed by the law is "from even till even" on the great Day of Atonement. After the Exile the days of national calamity were commemorated with fasting: the 10th day of the 10th month (Tebeth), the day of the beginning of the siege by Nebuchadnezzar; the 9th day of the 4th month (Tammuz), when the city was taken: the 7th day of the 5th month (Ab), when the Temple was destroyed, and in the 7th month (Tishri), the day of Gedaliah's murder. Fasting came to be regarded as meritorious in itself. The Pharisees fasted twice a week; on the 5th day of the week, when Moses was believed to have gone up to Mount Sinai and on the 2nd, when he was supposed to have descended. John's disciples fasted often. Our Lord imposed no fasting on His disciples while He was with them, but did not condemn the practice when followed in a right spirit, and He fasted before the beginning of His ministry. The first Christians fasted, in particular before the mission of Apostles and the appointment of elders. Paul's fastings appear to have been involuntary. The RSV excludes, on the evidence of the MSS, the references to fasting in Mt 17.21; Mk 9.29; Acts 10.30; 1 Cor 7.5.

fa'ther

The title of the First Person in the Godhead. God was revealed and known as the Father of His chosen people under the Old Testament dispensation and in a fatherly relation to individuals; but it was peculiarly the function of Christ to reveal the Fatherhood of God, and to bring men back to this relationship, as it is the function of the Spirit to seal and testify to this relationship of God and the believer.

feasts

The 3 annual festivals of the sanctuary were: (1) the Passover, (2) The Feast of Weeks, (3) the Feast of Tabernacles.

1. *The Passover* commemorated the deliverance of the Israelites from Egypt. It began on the 14th of Abib or Nisan in the evening, i.e. in the beginning of the 15th day, with a sacrificial meal, when a lamb or kid was roasted whole, and was eaten with bitter herbs and unleavened bread by the members of every family, and the head of the household recited the history of the redemption from Egypt. The sacrifices denoted expiation and dedication; the bitter herbs recalled the bitterness of the Egyptian bondage; unleavened bread was an emblem of purity.

2. *The Feast of Weeks* or of Harvest, or Day of Firstfruits or Pentecost (Gr. "fiftieth"), held on the 50th day or 7 weeks after the second day of the Passover, was the 2nd of the 3 annual festivals of the Sanctuary. It was limited to a single day, for only a portion of the products of the year had been garnered. Two loaves of leavened bread, representing the firstfruits of the grain harvest, were offered to the Lord. Ten suitable animals were sacrificed as a burnt offering, a kid for a sin offering, and 2 lambs for a peace offering.

3. *The Feast of Tabernacles,* or Ingathering, was the last of the 3 annual festivals. It was appointed to take place in the 7th month, at the close of the agricultural season, when all the products of the year had been gathered. It was celebrated during 7 days: The daily burnt offering included a total of 70 bullocks, distributed by a decreasing scale over the 7 days, and in addition 2 rams and 14 lambs daily, and as a sin offering a he-goat was daily sacrificed. During its celebration the people dwelt in booths made of the boughs of trees.

fer'ret, geck'o

A lizard such as the gecko is probably intended. A ferret is related to the weasel.

fig

This fruit is frequently mentioned in Scriptures, and indigenous to Palestine. These figs appear in February before the leaves, which do not cover the tree until a month or six weeks later. When the leaves are fully out, the fruits should be ripe.

fir

See Pine.

fish'es

The fishes of Palestine include several different species. The fishes of the Jordan and Lake Tiberias are extremely like those of the Nile. They are carplike, large-scaled fishes, barbels, dace and bleak, loaches, etc. The Phoenicians engaged in sea-fishing.

fitch'es

An archaic spelling for vetch, a legume. It probably should be translated as the word *spelt* rather than as any variety of vetch.

flax

This fiber was grown in Egypt and Palestine from very early times. The tabernacle hangings and the high priest's dress were of linen (Ex 27–29).

flea

This insect is only twice mentioned in the Bible, where David compares himself to a flea, a thing too insignificant for Saul to pursue. Fleas are, however, a real pest in the Holy Land, as in most other Mediterranean countries, the huts and camps of the natives swarming with them (1 Sam 24.16; 26.20).

flood

There are among native tribes of the Americas, the Pacific Islands and Australia and the early peoples of Mesopotamia, many stories of floods resembling that of the time of Noah. As re-

Coin of Apamea depicting Noah and ark.

lated in Gen 6–9, God found the mankind He had created to be wicked, and decided upon its destruction. Noah was a righteous man and was to be spared, he was instructed to build an ark, and to take into it 2 of every species of animal, with provisions, and with his wife, their 3 sons, and the sons' wives. God closed the ark and the rains came, flooding the entire earth. Some time after the rains stopped, Noah sent forth successively a raven and a dove to learn whether or not the waters had gone down. When on its 3rd flight the dove did not return, Noah knew that the bird had found a resting

Flood tablet from Nippur, Babylonia, bearing one of the earliest stories of the flood, and the fall of man. The language is Sumerian.

place, and the ark was again opened. The biblical statement is that the ark rested on Ararat. Archaeologists have been refused permission to search for it, as Ararat overlooks Soviet territory.

fly

Two Hebrew words are taken to mean fly, one the ordinary housefly, the other the large horsefly. The stinging fly, the 4th of the plagues visited on the Egyptians, is a separate word in the Hebrew.

food, laws regarding

In the law all animals are divided into the clean, which might be eaten, and the unclean, which are forbidden. It distinguishes as clean the beasts which both chew the cud and have parted hooves; fishes with fins and scales; all birds except 19 or 20, mostly carnivorous; and among creeping things, the locust. Laws more or less similar are found among the Egyptians, Hindus, Persians, and Muslims. The distinction between clean and unclean food before it was established in God's name in the law was a settled custom and tradition among the Jews, perhaps originally derived from the natural repugnance and loathing at the sight, or touch, or smell of many animals, from ill effects on health traced to various meats, and from the place which, e.g., swine's flesh, had in the customs of heathen idolatry. The purpose for which this traditional distinction of clean from unclean meats was elevated into a formal law is distinctly expressed; it was to form a part of the partition wall that should separate from the Gentiles the people chosen by Jehovah for His own possession. All those parts of animals which, according to the sacrificial ritual, were consecrated to the altar, were forbidden under severe penalties; especially blood, for (1) "the life of all flesh is the blood thereof," and must be given back to the Lord of life; and (2) blood was set apart to make atonement for the soul. Contrast the practice of the heathen, e.g., the Philistines, who in their idolatry drank the blood reeking in the sacrificial basin. Certain pieces of the fat of such animals as were suitable for sacrifices (oxen, sheep, and goats) were not to be eaten, but were consecrated to the Lord. It was forbidden also "to seethe a kid in his mother's milk," which might possibly be taken as equivalent to eating flesh with the blood, and thus forbidden to the Hebrews along with the blood sacraments of the heathen; present-day Arabs sometimes stew a lamb or kid in milk. The flesh of animals that had been strangled or killed without being bled in the regular manner and flesh that had been sacrificed to heathen idols were likewise forbidden. Except in times of great distress or of religious decline these laws were well observed. The scrupulousness of the Jews in regard to these laws of food rendered it difficult for Jewish Christians and Gentile Christians to eat together and enjoy full religious fellowship; a compromise was therefore agreed to by the Gentile Christians to meet the Jewish Christians on this point. Christ declared the whole of this legislation to be morally indifferent.

fox

In Ps 63.10 and Lam 5.18 the translation should be jackal rather than fox.

frank'in·cense

A fragrant gum resin imported into Palestine from Arabia.

freed'men

See Libertines.

frog

Frogs are mentioned in the OT only in connection with the second Egyptian plague.

front'lets and arm'lets

The same as phylacteries (Ex 13.16; Deut 6.8). To carry out the injunction of the Law literally, four passages (Ex 13.1-10, 11-16; Deut 6.4-9; 11.13-21) were copied on strips of parchment, enclosed in a leather case, and bound by a strap around the head or around the left arm.

G

Ga·la'tia

A Roman province in central Asia Minor. Its S portion was in Paul's missionary field.

Ga·la'tians

The Letter of Paul to the Galatians, written in A.D. 57 or 58, probably from Antioch, is the cornerstone of Christian freedom. In Galatians Paul tells of his own conversion and of how he stood firm in his belief that Christ was the Savior of people everywhere, not just those who observed every detail of the Jewish law.

gal'ba·num

A resinous juice used for the sacred incense.

Gal·i·le'ans

The people of Galilee being little under the influence of Jerusalem, the center of Jewish piety and culture, were looked down upon as ignorant rustics. They bitterly resented, however, the Roman yoke and supplied a large proportion of the Zealots.

Gal'i·lee

The region between Samaria on the W, the river Leontes on the S, the maritime plain on the N, and the Sea of Galilee, including its E coast, on the E. Exclusive of the lake, it measured about 50 mi. N and S, by 25 to 35 E and W. It included the plain of Esdraelon; Lower Galilee, a series of parallel ranges, none over 1,850 ft.; and Upper Galilee in the N, a series of plateaus surrounded by hills from 2,000 to 4,000 ft. high. The line between the two Galilees ran from the N end of the lake, W to Acre. Galilee is well watered and wooded, with stretches of good grain land. Earthquakes are frequent. The greatest thoroughfare is the so-called Way of the Sea, connecting Damascus with the Levant.

Gal'i·lee, the Sea of

In a great ditch 680 ft. below the level of the sea is the Sea of Galilee, 13 mi. long by 8 broad. On the W lay Tiberias; Magdala and Taricheae, where the fish were cured, were probably to the S. On the NW are Capernaum and Chorazin. Bethsaida is on the E of Jordan. On the eastern shore lay Gergesa. Gadara was about 5 mi. from the SE corner of the lake, about 2300 ft. above it.

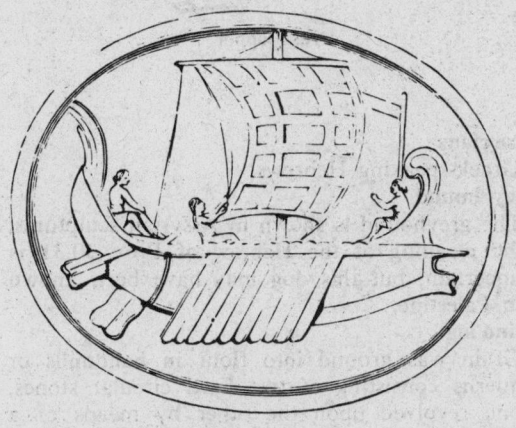

Roman galley

gall
A bitter, poisonous herb, possibly the same as the hemlock of Socrates.

gar'lic, gar'lick
A bulb of the lily family. Egyptian inscriptions list it, and during their wandering in the wilderness the Hebrews longed for it.

gate
In most Hebrew towns the only open space was just within the gate or gates. There the market was held, disputes were decided, and business of all kinds was transacted. The gate was the center of the social life of the place.

Ga'za
A famous Philistine city in SW Palestine, close to the sea. It retained its importance as a caravan depot in all ages. Little excavating has been done because of the modern city on the site of the old. *See also* Gezer.

geck'o
A lizard. *See* Ferret.

gems
Three lists of gems occur in the Bible: the high priest's breastplate (Ex 28); the ornaments of the king of Tyre (Ezek 28); the foundations of the heavenly Jerusalem (Rev 21).

Gems do not occur naturally in Palestine, and no great numbers have been found in excavations there, as compared with Egypt and Mesopotamia where many jewels have been found in tombs and temples. Faceted cutting was not understood, or at least not practiced, in the ancient world, but their engraving of jewels was fully as expert as anything done today.

Gen'e·sis
The first book of the OT; a collection of the earliest Israelite traditions concerning the origin of things. The book has two main divisions. The first is the history of early mankind, narrating the events of the Creation, the Fall, the Flood, and the Dispersion. The second section concerns the lives of Abraham, Isaac, Jacob, and Joseph.

Gen·nes'a·ret
A fertile plain on the shore of the Sea of Galilee. Also, an early name for the Sea of Galilee.

Ger'i·zim, Mount
Modern Jebel el-Tor, 2900 ft., directly S of Mount Ebal.

Geth·sem'a·ne
A garden at the foot of the Mount of Olives, where Judas betrayed Jesus. Its exact position is not known.

Ge'zer, Ga'zer, Ga·za'ra, Ga·ze'ra, Ga'za
Now called Tell el-Jazari, this site was excavated at the beginning of the 20th century. It had been a settlement at least since 4000 B.C.

Gid'e·on
(Heb. "hewer," "slasher") He tore down the Baal altar of his family and destroyed the Asherah. He was answered regarding his fitness to save Israel by having his fleece remain dry while the floor around it was wet with dew, and vice versa; he had other miraculous experiences. By a ruse he routed the Midianites. He was liberator and reformer but refused to be made king.

gier
See Eagle.

Gi'hon
An intermittent spring in the Kidron Valley beneath the City of David.

Gil·bo'a, Mount
Modern Jebel Fuqu'ah, at the E end of the Valley of Jezreel 6 mi. W of Beth-shean; elevation 1737 ft.

Gil'e·ad
(Heb. "monument of stones") 1. The name of 2 persons and a family in the OT.

2. A region E of the Jordan between the Yarmuk and Arnon rivers. It is a well-watered and fertile region, suitable for grapes and olives. Well forested, it is the source of balm of Gilead, an aromatic resin regarded as having medicinal properties and exported to Egypt and Phoenicia.

Gil'e·ad, Mount
There is no single Mount Gilead; the entire area is rugged, above the Jordan Valley, at this point 700 ft. below sea level.

Gil'gal
(Heb. "circle of stones") The name of several places in the OT. One lies E of Jericho, in the Jordan Valley. Possibly it is the modern Khirbet Mefjir. Another is probably the modern Jiljulieh, on the top of a high hill 7 mi. N of Bethel. This is the Gilgal of Elijah and Elisha. Another Gilgal has been compared with Harosheth-ha-Goiim but has not been definitely identified. It has been placed in Samaria, in Sharon, and elsewhere. One Gilgal near Shechem has been suggested and another is said to be on the road from Jericho to Jerusalem.

gnats, lice
Being among the smallest of insects they are used in metaphors to emphasize contrast, for example, to a bulky animal such as the camel.

goats
An important item in the pastoral wealth of the Near East since biblical times. They are

reared alongside of but not with the sheep. The sheep close graze the tender herbage; the goats browse on the twigs of the bushes. Goats' milk is preferred to any other.

goat, wild

The Sinaitic ibex. The Hebrew is translated always by "wild goat," except in Prov 5.19, where the feminine form is rendered "roe." Another word, akko, occurs only in Deut 14.5, where it is translated "wild goat." The Sinaitic ibex is a very beautiful creature, of a light fawn color, with very long recurved and regularly knotted horns, smaller and more slender than the Alpine and Himalayan species.

Gog and Ma'gog

Gog, prince of Meshech, who came from a land called Magog, is in Ezek 38–39 the leader of the forces of evil in a battle with Yahweh. In Rev 20.8 Magog is a leader with Gog of the forces of Satan in the battle of Armageddon.

gold

This metal apparently was not obtained in Palestine; some was imported from Sheba (part of Arabia), some from Ophir. The last district has been identified both with the W coast of India and with some part of the E coast of Africa. Some came from Nubia by way of Egypt. Gold, as we know from the contents of ancient graves, was in use for ornamental purposes at a very early date, even when stone held the place of metal for weapons and tools. It was no doubt obtained (and this is still a source of supply) by washing the river sands and other alluvial deposits.

Gol'go·tha

(Heb. "skull") The place of the crucifixion of Jesus.

Go·mor'rah

One of the 5 cities of the Valley mentioned with Sodom, Admah, Zeboim, and Zoar. Believed to be under the water of the S end of the Dead Sea.

go'pher wood

Not definitely identified.

Go'shen

The name of 3 places in the OT. One is presumably the area between Hebron and the Negev. Another is sometimes identified with modern Zahariyeh, 12 mi. SW of Hebron. The 3rd is the area of Egypt where the Israelites were from the time of Joseph until the Exodus.

gourd

The bottle gourd is used for booths and trellises in the Near East, and may be the plant mentioned in Jonah 4. The castor bean has also been suggested. The wild gourd has a poisonous fruit. At Gilgal during a famine, men were poisoned by it and appealed to Elisha for help. The vine of Sodom was probably the wild gourd.

grass' hop·per, lo'cust

"Locust" is sometimes used for the gregarious phase of certain short-horned grasshoppers. The grasshopper destroys vegetation at all stages of its life.

Grasshopper

Gre'cians

Greek-speaking Hebrews.

grey' hound

The greyhound is shown in Assyrian sculptures; the meaning of the Hebrew of Prov 30.31 is uncertain, but this dog may have been known in Palestine.

grind'ing

Grain was ground into flour in handmills or querns consisting of two hard circular stones, one revolved upon the other by means of a peg or handle. The labor was commonly performed by women. The Law forbade any one to take another's millstone in pledge.

grove

See Asherah.

H

Ha·bak'kuk

A prophet of Judah in the last days of Josiah (640-609 B.C.) and the reign of Jehoiakim (609-598 B.C.).

Ha·bak'kuk, the Book of

An OT book of prophecy concerned with the problem of unpunished evil in the world. It was revealed to Habakkuk that the Chaldean armies were to be God's means of punishing the wicked and that evil would destroy itself. The book concludes with a poem of thanksgiving and great faith.

Hag·ga'da, Hag·ga'dah

(Heb. "narration") The name for that part of the traditions of the Jewish scribes consisting of the elaboration of the historical and didactic portions of Scripture. As contrasted with the Halacha, which confined itself to the exposition and application of the text, its handling of the Scripture is unrestrained. It freely admits additions and interpolations, including legends.

Hag'ga·i

A Jewish prophet who came forward at Jerusalem, in 529 B.C., to urge the rebuilding of the Temple.

Hag'ga·i, the Book of

This OT book is a report on the utterances of the prophet Haggai during the second year of the reign of Darius, king of the Persian Empire, in the post-exilic period. The prophet is singularly concerned with the rebuilding of the Temple, which was essential to restoring the nation's religious purity. Haggai also believed that a great messianic age was at hand.

Hag·i·og'ra·pha

(Heb. "writings") The third division of the books included in the Hebrew Canon have a more diversified character than either Law or Prophecy, and they have never received a more definite designation.

hair

The Hebrews regarded a strong growth of hair both on the head and on the chin as an ornament to a man. By many it was worn hanging down to the shoulder. To cut off a man's beard was to offer him the grossest insult. Only in times of mourning was the head shaved. That the hair was also worn in locks or ringlets is shown by the case of Samson.

Ha·la·cha'

(Heb. "that which is current") The Rabbinical law of custom, which was developed beside the written Torah or Law of Moses. It was distinguished from the Haggada as being the legal part of the oral tradition of the scribes, including their expositions of the Torah, and all the additional laws which were recognized as binding by the Jews after the Exile.

Hal·lel', Hal·le·lu'jah

(Heb. "praise ye the Lord") Probably sung in unison by the Temple choir.

Ham

1. The name of Noah's second son.

2. A city E of the Jordan, attacked by Chedorlaomer. Tell Ham, the ruin of the ancient city, is near modern Ham on the Wadi er-Rejeilah.

3. A poetic synonym for Egypt, used several times in the Psalms.

Ha'math

A town on the Orontes in Syria, the modern Nahr el-Asi. Excavation revealed 12 layers, going back to Neolithic times. It is one of the important centers of Hittite inscriptions. It made alliance with David, and in 740 B.C. with Azariah (against Assyria). Conquered by the Assyrians in 720 B.C., the people of Hamath were transported to Samaria.

hang'ings

See Cotton.

Ha'ran

Now Harran, in Turkey, a city devoted to the moon cult, where Abraham stopped on his journey from Ur to Canaan.

hare

Though the name occurs only in the lists of Leviticus and Deuteronomy, there is no question about the translation, the hare being very common, and the Arabic name the same as the Hebrew. It was forbidden as food to the Israelites because it does not divide the hoof, even though (Moses parenthetically adds) it chews the cud, i.e., re-chews.

harp

A 10-string harp has been found in an Egyptian tomb of 1000 B.C., an earlier wooden one of 1550 B.C., and a golden lyre at Ur. The harp, lute and cithern are similar; David's harp, however, seems to have been more properly a lyre.

hart, hind

Fallow deer, habitat Syria, now almost if not altogether extinct in Palestine, must have been very common in ancient times. Deer are often depicted on the monuments both of Egypt and Assyria. The bones of the red deer have been found in caverns in Lebanon.

Har'vest, Feast of

One of the 3 great annual festivals, held at the end of the agricultural year. Also called the *Feast of Ingathering. See* Feasts.

hawk

The bird mentioned is not positively identified.

head-dress

The common head-dress of the people was probably like that of the modern Bedouin—a colored handkerchief bound round the head with a cord so as to shade both neck and ears from the sun. In later times the rich wore a turban formed of a long strip of fine linen rolled many times round the head. Yet another "headtire" was worn on festive occasions, especially by brides or bridegrooms.

heath

See Juniper.

He'brews

The descendants of Eber (Gen 10.21). They may have been a separate ethnic group, but were closely related to the Israelites; the names in some circumstances became interchangeable.

He'brews, the Let'ter to the

An anonymous NT book which urges the Hebrew Christian community not to fall back into Judaism and argues for Christian superiority.

He'bron

An ancient city in the high mountains of Judah, 19 mi. S of Jerusalem. The modern town, el-Khalil, surrounds the cave of Machpelah.

hedge'hog

The Hebrew word has also been translated "bittern" and "porcupine." Porcupines are found in modern Palestine.

Hel'len·ists

Greek-speaking Jews, in Judea or abroad, many of whom had adopted a measure of Greek (Hellenic) culture and manners.

hem'lock

A poisonous plant or one with a bitter root, also translated gall or wormwood. The plant most probably meant grows in waste places in Palestine, a perennial 3 to 4 ft. tall, with leaves resembling a carrot's.

hen'na, cam'phire

A fragrant flowering shrub. A dye prepared from the crushed leaves mixed with water is used to color the soles of the feet, palms, and nails.

Her'mon, Mount

The S spur of the anti-Lebanon, elevation 9100 ft., and frequently snow-covered. It is visible from many places in Palestine.

Her'od the Great

The founder of the dynasty that ruled Palestine 37 B.C.-A.D. 70, was the son of Antipater, an Idumaean, who had been Asmonaean governor in Edom, and who rose to a position of great influence as the minister of Hyrcanus II, the last Asmonaean king and high-priest. Antipater saw that the future of Judaea was in the hands of Rome and cunningly ingratiated himself first with Pompey, then, after his death, with Julius Caesar (who rewarded his assistance with men and money in Egypt in 48 B.C. by making him governor of Judaea, Samaria, and Galilee, under the nominal sovereignty of Hyrcanus), and after Caesar's assassination in 44 B.C., with Cassius, Antonius and Augustus. Herod consistently followed his father's policy and took advantage of all the vicissitudes of Roman affairs. He saw himself at last the "confederate king" (*rex socius*) of the Roman emperor. A decree of the Roman senate made him king of Judaea in 40 B.C. In 37 B.C. he married Mariamne, granddaughter of Hyrcanus, and with the help of two Roman legions, captured Jerusalem. The next 9 years he spent in strengthening his position. He executed 45 members (the Sadducee majority) of the Sanhedrin and murdered every member of the Asmonaean house, including his wife Mariamne. The next 14 years (28-14 B.C.) were chiefly devoted to the erection of public buildings, including a theater in Jerusalem and a great amphitheater outside the gates, as well as numerous heathen temples and new cities, the chief of which was Caesarea, named after the emperor. His greatest work was the rebuilding of the Temple. But the golden eagle, the symbol of Roman supremacy, which he placed over its chief entrance, was to the people a continual reminder of his subservience to Rome. All the material advantages of his despotic rule, the tranquility of the country, his remissions of taxation and encouragement of trade and agriculture, his provision for the poor in time of scarcity, were forgotten. His life was constantly threatened by conspiracies, which he fought with secret police and the most cruel torture. In the year 7 B.C. he caused Alexander and Aristobulus, his 2 sons by Mariamne, to be strangled at Samaria, a crime which led Augustus to remark that he would rather be one of Herod's swine than one of his sons. Another son, Antipater, who had tried to assassinate his father, was executed 5 days before the death of Herod in 4 B.C. His sons shared his dominions according to his will. The elder, Archelaus, ethnarch of Judaea, Samaria, and Idumaea, was deposed by Augustus for misgovernment in A.D. 6, and died in Gaul. The eastern and northern provinces fell to Philip, who died in A.D. 34. Herod Antipas, who received Galilee and Peraea, was deposed by Caligula in A.D. 39. The Herod of Acts 12 was a grandson of Herod "the Great," and was surnamed Agrippa. He obtained from Caligula the inheritance of Philip, and also that of Antipas, to which Claudius added Judaea and Samaria, so that from A.D. 41 to 44, he ruled over the whole of Palestine. He succeeded by cunning and hypocrisy in gaining the confidence of the people. His son, Herod Agrippa II (Acts 25, 26), after doing all in his power to dissuade the Jews from making war against the Romans, took their side against his countrymen, and after Jerusalem was taken, lived chiefly at Tiberias as a Roman vassal prince till he died childless in A.D. 100.

He·ro'di·ans

A political and nonpatriotic minority, in the main a court party, which stood to the Idumaean dynasty of the Herods in Galilee much as the Sadduceean nobility stood to the Roman procurator in Judaea. They made less pretense, however, of aiming higher than at worldly prosperity. Their natural enemies were the strict Pharisees; and it is a mark of the shifts to which both parties were driven in their hatred of Jesus that they united to work His ruin. The "leaven of Herod" (Mk 8.15) was worldly wisdom.

Hez·e·ki'ah

(Heb. "Yah is my strength") The name of 4 persons in the OT, one of whom was King of Judah 715–687 B.C.

Hid'de·kel

The Hebrew name of the Tigris River.

high place, sanc'tu·ar·y

The Canaanites were worshiping their gods on high places when Abraham appeared in their country. Usually there were groves of trees associated with these hilltops and other sites. The sanctuary was a temple with an altar or an altar alone, with the altar often elevated. The Israelites were instructed by God to destroy the Canaanite high places and the groves and the altars, usually dedicated to a local god, but in this they were frequently remiss. At times the high places were simply taken over. Hezekiah was diligent in their destruction, but many of the kings were indifferent. The sanctuary won recognition only after a long period.

high priest

The chief in the priestly hierarchy. At times in Israel's history, the chief priest shared full honors with the king.

hind

See Hart.

Hin'nom

A deep valley S of Jerusalem, called variously the Valley of the Sons of Hinnom, Valley of the Children of Hinnom, Valley of Ben-Hinnom, and usually identified with the modern Wadi er-Rababi.

Hit'tites

First mentioned by Sargon of Agade about the end of the 3rd millennium, the Hittites came from N of the Taurus Mountains, and at an early date conquered part of N Syria. They made Carchemish on the Euphrates one of their capitals, and established themselves in Kadesh near Emesa. After years of war, Ramses II of Egypt made a treaty of peace with the Hittite king, probably between 1290 and 1280 B.C. Hittites had previously settled in the south of Palestine, at Hebron, and at Jerusalem. They had a number of small kingdoms, and seem to have extended over the greater part of Asia Minor as well as over N Syria. The westward conquest by the Assyrians overcame the Hittite kingdoms and their independent history ended with the capture of Carchemish by Sargon in 717 B.C. The Hittites used a peculiar hieroglyphic writing, not deciphered until after 1925. The Egyptian monuments agree with their own in representing them as short, thick-limbed, with protrusive jaw and nose, beardless face, high cheekbones, yellow skin, and black hair and eyes. Their language was of the Indo-European group.

Hi'vites

A nation in Canaan before the Israelites.

holm tree, cy'press

Sometimes identified with the evergreen holm oak; since the root of the word means "to be lean," sometimes translated "cypress."

Ho·ly Ghost', Ho·ly Spir'it

The third person of the Trinity, through whom the entire Godhead works with man.

Hor, Mount

This may be a mountain on the border of Edom, or a mountain near Petra, now called Jebel Harun, elevation 4800 ft.

hor'net

(Heb. "depression") Hornets belong to the same order of insects as bees and wasps and are closely allied to the latter. All these insects have four wings; they wound by a sting lodged in the end of the abdomen, and inject a poisonous fluid into the wound.

horse

The horse was introduced in the Near East about the middle of the 2nd millennium B.C. Solomon brought the horse to Israel. The principal use was in warfare; the Israelites looked upon horses as a pagan luxury and a symbol of dependence on physical power rather than upon God. Nevertheless the use of the horse did increase, not only for war chariots but for transport. Israel's horses came from Egypt.

horse'leech

The horseleech (*haemopis sanguisuga*) and the medicinal leech (*hirudo medicinalis*) are both common in Palestine, as are several other kinds of leeches. The leeches abound in waters and damp places of hot countries and frequently become a regular pest, attacking men and animals alike.

Ho·se'a

(Heb. "salvation") The last of the great prophets of the Northern Kingdom.

Ho·se'a, the Book of

The first book of the twelve minor prophets in the OT. Because the times were outwardly prosperous, idolatry prevailed and immorality was rampant. Hosea urges a return to God in order that He may show mercy and forgiveness.

Ho·she'a

(Heb. "may Yah save") The name of 4 persons in the OT, one of whom was the last king of Israel.

house

(Heb. beth, common in compound names of places, as Beth-el) The nomad's house was his tent. The settled Hebrew dwelt generally in a one-story building with few and small windows, built of mud bricks or sun-dried brick, and flat-roofed. Here both the family and the animals found shelter, a raised dais separating the two.

But, except in bad weather, the family spent their day either in the open field or on the roof, where they also slept.

Hur'ri·ans

The name of an ancient people referred to variously as Horites, Hivites, Jebusites.

hy·e'na

The Hebrew word has also been translated "wild beast" and "speckled bird." The hyena has been the commonest of the carnivores of Palestine.

Hyk'sos kings

The Egyptian word for "rulers of foreign countries" was applied to the 15th and 16th dynasties in the Egyptian Delta. These foreigners, sometimes called the Shepherd Kings, had entered from the NE. The last ruler of the 17th dynasty at Thebes drove the Hyksos northward, and the first of the 18th dynasty expelled them from Egypt entirely in about 1550 B.C.

hys'sop

A bushy small plant, probably orégano or Syrian marjoram. The entire plant was used as a brush to sprinkle sacrificial blood. This use of the plant seems to have followed upon its use to mark the lintels of Hebrew homes at the 1st Passover.

I

i'bex

See Pygarg.

i'bis

The ibis is found in Egypt, but not in Palestine; it may have been native to Palestine in biblical times. The translation may be erroneous; the word has also been translated "great owl."

Im·man'u·el

(Heb. "God is with us") The name of the child whose birth was prophesied by Isaiah; in the NT it becomes a prophecy of the birth of Jesus.

In'gath·er·ing, Feast of

The Feast of Harvest. *See under* Feasts.

i'ron

It is probable that smelting iron ore and working iron began with the Hittites in the middle of the 2nd millennium B.C. The Philistines may have brought it to Palestine, but they permitted no Hebrew smiths. All iron work had to be taken to the Philistines. But gradually a supply of iron was imported, and iron slag is found in the Arabah, indicating that there was some native iron industry.

I'saac

(Heb. "he laughs") The son of Abraham and Sarah and half-brother of Ishmael was born when his parents were advanced in age. By his wife Rebekah he was the father of Jacob and Esau. He died at Hebron at the age of 180.

I·sa'iah

(Heb. "Yahweh is salvation") The son of Amoz, he prophesied in the reigns of Uzziah, Jotham, Ahaz, and Hezekiah, kings of Judah. Tradition says that he survived into the reign of Manasseh and was martyred by him. He advocated the policy of the separateness of Israel, opposing the Assyrian alliance of Ahaz and equally opposing all alliances with the neighboring peoples, with Egypt, or with the Babylonian-Elamitic combination against Assyria. During his life, the Assyrian and Babylonian empires were part of the time identical, the great oppressing power; and part of the time Babylon was a dangerous seducer, striving to lead the chosen people into disastrous hostilities with Assyria.

I·sa'iah, the Book of

This OT book is the first collection of prophecy of the five major Hebrew prophets. Judgment to come is fundamental to Isaiah's teaching. Israel and Judah are to perish but a remnant will survive and a new Jerusalem will rise up as a city of the faithful. It is also in Isaiah that memorable prophecies of Christ's coming are found.

Ish'ma·el

(Heb. "may God hear") The name of 6 persons in the OT, one of whom is Abraham's son, by Hagar. He is Isaac's half brother.

Ish'ma·el·ite

The wandering people of N Arabia, descendants of Ishmael, who were found in that region from the early 2nd millennium B.C. to the 7th century B.C.

Ish'tar

The Babylonian fertility goddess, Ashtoreth, in Palestine.

Is'ra·el

(Heb. "he who striveth with God," or "God striveth") The new name that Jacob received after his mysterious struggle at the Jabbok and hence the name of the whole people descended from him. The name "Hebrews" was mostly applied to them by foreigners, as was also the name "Jews," which arose at the time when Judah, after the fall of the Northern Kingdom, represented the entire people. After the separation under Jeroboam, the name Israel was con-

| JUDAH | DAN | ISSACHAR | ZEBULUN |
| 76,500 | 64,400 | 64,300 | 60,500 |

| ASHER | MANASSEH | BENJAMIN | NAPHTALI |
| 53,400 | 52,700 | 45,600 | 45,400 |

| | | | LEVI |
| | | | 23,000 |

| REUBEN | GAD | EPHRAIM | SIMEON |
| 43,730 | 40,500 | 32,500 | 22,200 |

Relative size of the 12 tribes of Israel, based on the number of men of military age

fined to the kingdom of the ten tribes, also called Ephraim after the chief of these. Moral and religious degeneracy, with frequent revolutions and changes of rulers, prepared its fall (722 B.C.). The Assyrians led the best of the people into exile, from which they never returned, and the remnant left was included in the mixed people known as the Samaritans.

It'a·ly

The peninsula in the middle of Southern Europe. The name was applied at different periods to the whole peninsula and to the southern part.

Iy'yar

A name of the 2nd month of the Hebrew year. It is also called Ziv.

J

ja'cinth, lig'ure

A variety of zircon, a reddish-orange stone.

Ja'cob

(Heb. "he overreaches") The son of Isaac and Rebekah and father of the people of Israel, he gained by craft the birthright and blessing that his father meant for his brother Esau. He fled to his uncle Laban, who treated him with cunning equal to his own. Yet he enriched himself in Laban's service and Laban's daughters, Leah and Rachel, became his wives. On his return, after a mysterious struggle in the darkness of night at the Jabbok, his name was changed to Israel and he was reconciled to Esau. His old age was made sorrowful by evil deeds of his sons, till at last he found a refuge in Egypt with his favorite, Joseph.

James

The name of 5 persons in the NT.

1. "The elder," son of Zebedee and brother of John, one of the Twelve, was martyred under Herod Agrippa.

2. James "the younger," son of Alphaeus, was also an Apostle.

3. James "the brother of the Lord" was a pillar in the church at Jerusalem and had probably been led to believe by a special appearance of our Lord to him. His judgment prevailed in the council at Jerusalem. For his piety he was called James the Just. According to Josephus, he was stoned to death by order of Ananus the high priest, between the departure of Festus and the arrival of the new procurator Albinus.

4. A son of Mary.

5. The father of Judas.

James, the Let'ter of

This NT book, according to tradition written by the brother of our Lord, provides ethical instruction for all Jewish people who have become Christians. It is clear and practical in its dealing with Christian behavior.

Ja'pho

See Joppa.

jas'per

A green chalcedony.

Jeb'u·sites

The tribe that occupied Jerusalem at the time

of the Israelitish conquest of Canaan. They seem to have been of the Amorite race.

Je·ho′a·haz

(Heb. "Yah has grasped") The name of 3 persons in the OT, one the King of Israel (815-801 B.C.) and one King of Judah (609-608 B.C.).

Je·ho′ram

See Joram.

Je·hosh′a·phat

(Heb. "Yah judges") The name of 4 persons in the OT, one of whom was King of Judah for 25 years, c. 850 B.C.

Je·ho′vah

The Hebrews did not commonly use the sacred name, in the fear that it might be profaned. The consonants of the name are four, called the tetragrammaton. To these vowels may be added, with the result that for a period of their history the spoken name was Adoni, Lord, arrived at by adding the vowels of that name to the consonants YHWH (JHVH). Misinterpretation of this eventually led to Jehovah.

Je′hu

(Heb. "he is Yah") The name of 4 persons in the OT, one of whom was King of Israel 842-815 B.C.

Jeph′thah

(Heb. "he opens") A warrior of Gilead, a judge in Israel and an illegitimate son, he was driven from home by his father's heirs. He lived the life of a freebooter in the land of Tob, east of Jordan, until the elders of the tribes summoned him to their help against the Amorites, who had oppressed them for 18 years. Returning a conquerer, he sacrificed his daughter, his only child, in fulfilment of a thoughtless vow.

Jer·e·mi′ah

(Heb. "may Yah lift up") The name of 10 persons in the OT, one of whom was Jeremiah the Prophet. Jeremiah's prophesying began in the 13th year of Josiah, 626 B.C., and covered the time following to the Exile. He was of priestly descent. His prophetic career began at an early age. In later years he was the leader of a small minority in Judah against 3 great wrongs: the religious apostasies of his people, their neglect of justice, and the false patriotism that led them to break faith by repeated revolts against Babylon. His services in this last matter were recognized by the Babylonian authorities.

Jer·e·mi′ah, the Book of

An OT account of the writing of certain of Jeremiah's prophecies, from dictation, by his friend Baruch. This seems to imply that these prophecies had been originally uttered without writing. As the roll of Baruch included "all" the prophecies for 23 years, besides "many like words," we are compelled to infer that most of the prophecies it contained were very briefly sketched. Jeremiah's mission was to testify to a doomed people, and then to witness their obduracy and their doom; but common opinion probably exaggerates the sorrowful element in the career of the "weeping prophet." It should be noticed that he prophesied concerning the return from the Exile, as well as concerning the Exile itself. It was especially his prophecies that actually led the exiles to the movement for return. Jeremiah insists especially upon the Lord's unfailing covenant with Israel and with David. He gives shape to the doctrine of a righteous "Branch" to grow up unto David. Like the other prophets, Jeremiah is a prophet not merely of rebuke and warning, but also of the Messianic promise and hope.

Jer′i·cho

An ancient city at the S end of the Jordan Valley, famous for its palms and gardens of balsam, which have now disappeared. It has been extensively excavated; carbon dating shows its oldest walls to date from 8000 to 7000 B.C.

Jer·o·bo′am

(Heb. "may the people grow numerous") The name of 2 kings of Israel, one of them Israel's 1st king, the son of Nebat, the founder of the N kingdom of Israel. He took advantage of the other tribes' envy of Judah and Jerusalem, and the general discontent with Solomon's oppressive taxation, to revolt against him. After the death of Solomon, on his son Rehoboam's blunt refusal to lighten the people's burdens, Jeroboam became the leader of the 10 northern tribes in their separation (922 B.C.). The reestablishment of the high places served to lend the political change a religious consecration. Golden calves and ox images, similar to those Aaron made in the wilderness, were set up at Dan in the north and Bethel on the southern frontier of Jeroboam's kingdom, to win the people away from the Temple at Jerusalem, where God was worshiped without images.

Jeroboam II ruled the kingdom of Israel from 786 to 746 B.C. He conquered in the N and E all the lands that had belonged to David and Solomon, and encouraged trade with the Phoenicians; but in his reign the Baal worship that Jehu had extirpated again arose, bringing with it the moral corruption in which Amos and Hosea foresaw the ruin of the king's house and of the nation.

Je·ru′sa·lem

(Heb. "foundation of Shalem") The chief city of Palestine, mentioned in Egyptian texts as early as the 19th and 18th centuries B.C., the 3rd most holy city of the Muslims and the most important to the Christians and Jews, the name of Jerusalem appears in more than 25 of the

Damascus Gate, the principal entry through the north wall of Jerusalem

Sketch of a Roman medal commemorating the capture of Jerusalem.

books of the OT and in more than a dozen books of the NT.

Flints found in excavations in the area indicate very early inhabitants, and pottery from the 4th millennium B.C. has been found at Jerusalem itself. Abraham was once and quite possibly twice at Jerusalem, then called Salem or Shalem. The Jebusites were there before Abraham had entered Palestine; David captured the city and made it his capital, and Solomon built the Temple and made the city splendid.

In the almost incessant warfare of the last 2 millennia B.C., Jerusalem was often besieged and captured. It was at various times possessed by Assyria, Egypt, Babylonia, Persia, and Greece. Nebuchadnezzar sacked and destroyed the city, and took its people into exile. When they returned, they rebuilt the Temple and much of the city, but in A.D. 70 the Romans captured Jerusalem and devastated it so thoroughly that almost nothing of the time of Jesus remained. However, a city grew again on the ruins. The Crusaders held it for a time, as did the Turks. At present, Jerusalem is divided between Jordan and the State of Israel.

Excavation has not been complete or thorough, because of the impossibility of carrying on such work in a densely populated area. Even so, a great number of the locations mentioned in the Bible have been identified and the life of Jerusalem in biblical times can be reconstructed.

Je·ru′sa·lem, the New

The principal city of God's new world that is to come, its spiritual capital, beautiful and adorned; an expression of the church of those who are of the people of God.

Jesh′u·a

See Joshua.

Je′sus

The coming of Jesus, the Christ, the .Messiah, was anticipated in the OT; of His life on earth the Gospels are the source of what we know. Secular contemporary accounts are fragmentary. Calendars were not stabilized as today, and the precise date of His birth is not recorded. The earliest Church did not concern itself with the facts of His physical life on earth. He was Jesus, the man, and Christ, the Anointed One, a person of the Triune God. But by the 5th century the Church had concerned itself sufficiently to have set December 25 as the date of His birth. This had been the date of the festival of the sun god Mithra, and to the Christians a

greater light was come, Jesus Christ, the true Light of the World.

Jesus was born in Bethlehem to Mary, the betrothed wife of Joseph, a carpenter. The genealogy is traced in the Gospels to David and to Abraham. The Gospels further· tell of the flight of the family to Egypt to avoid the slaughter of the Innocents by Herod the King, but say little of His early boyhood. The family lived the life of consecrated and pious Jews; Jesus must have had careful education and training, for at age 12 he talked on fully equal terms with the rabbis in the Temple.

Then follows another unrecorded period in His life. When a man of about 30 He was baptized by John the Baptist, who testified that this Jesus was the Son of God. After a great temptation to which He did not yield, He began His ministry, first calling His disciples. He was known by His works throughout Galilee and in adjacent areas, and attracted many followers, Jews and Greeks. But He disturbed many. He was arrested, tried, and crucified. There followed the Resurrection, the triumph over death. *See also* Christ.

Jew

The Bible provides definitions: 1. The members of the State of Judah (Neh 1.2; Jer 32.12; 40.11).

2. The post-exilic people of Israel in contrast to the Gentiles (Esther 9.15-19; Dan 3.8; Zech 8.23; John 4.9; Acts 14.1).

3. The adherents of worship of Yahweh as done at Jerusalem after the Exile (Esther 3.4-6; Dan 3.8). In contrast to Gentiles, Samaritans, proselytes (John 2.6, 4.9, 22; Acts 2.10, 14.1). The term is now highly fluid. It covers religion and birth, religion only, or birth only.

Jewish history between the Testaments

The whole period falls into four epochs.

1. *Persian Period* (537-330 B.C.). Nehemiah (444 B.C.) had been a favorite at the court to which, 90 years before, the Jews had owed their return from Exile; and, on the whole, the restored remnant remained loyal to the "great king," in spite of the tribute and other galling features of their subjection. Many Jews, however, were removed to Babylonia and elsewhere by Artaxerxes Ochus, about 350 B.C., for taking part in a revolt. To the last century of Persian rule belong the final breach between the Jews and the Samaritans, the gradual replacement among the Jews of Hebrew by the widespread Aramaic dialect, and the beginning of the recovery of Galilee to the faith of Jehovah.

2. *Greek Period* (330-167 B.C.). Alexander the Great, who ushers in this period, besides granting special· privileges to Jerusalem, bestowed marks of favor upon the Jews settled by him in his new city, Alexandria. It was here that Judaism entered into its most intimate relations with the Greek world of thought and literature. On Alexander's death (323 B.C.) his conquests passed into the hands of his generals and, during the struggles that ensued, Palestine shared in the confusion, until the battle of Ipsus (301

B.C.) made the kings of Egypt (the Ptolemies) its overlords for a full century, in spite of several attempts on the part of the rival kings of Syria (the Seleucids) to overthrow them. The new sovereign power was both stronger and juster than the Persian; and under it the government at Jerusalem in the hands of the high-priestly dynasty, assisted by a sort of senate including the higher ranks of the priesthood, grew and consolidated. Outside Palestine, too, the Jews waxed influential, not only in Alexandria, but also in Libya, Cyrene, Asia Minor, and all parts of Syria, where they settled either by the compulsion or favor of Ptolemies and Seleucids. From the other side also foreign intercourse was fostered by Greek settlements in Northern Palestine, especially about the Sea of Galilee.

The most momentous outcome of all this was the Greek version of the Hebrew Scriptures, called the Septuagint, which did much to break down Jewish isolation, and fixed the type of language in which the NT is written. The influence of Hellenic culture was at work in both the life and the literature of the Jews during the Ptolemaic supremacy (320-198 B.C.), but its effects became clearer after 198 B.C., when Antiochus the Great brought Judea under Seleucid or Syrian sway.

The priestly nobility grew more worldly in spirit as Hellenism advanced. The high-priesthood became an object of base intrigue. Under Antiochus Epiphanes it became the fashion among the upper classes to turn their names into Greek forms, e.g., Menelaus for Menahem, and in other ways to obscure their Jewish origin. At length the folly of Antiochus and his high-priestly tools led to a violent crisis and revolt.

3. *Maccabean or Asmonaean Period* (167-63 B.C.). The outrages upon the national religion which stung the Maccabees into revolt stirred the people to realize the value of their distinctive faith. From their ranks had arisen a party called the Chasidim, distinguished for piety. The Maccabean movement carried these with it, and became a rally of the whole nation to the faith of its fathers. By the wars of liberation from the yoke of Syria the religious end was attained. The Temple was restored and solemnly rededicated (165 B.C.), the rival temple on Mount Gerizim razed along with the Samaritan capital itself (129 B.C.), and the Maccabean leader recognized as "Governor and High Priest for ever, until there should arise a faithful prophet."

But the mass of the nation was now possessed by the spirit of foreign aggression; and against this the successors of the quiet Chasidim, whose expectation was from God and not from human agency, constantly protested. "The idea of Judaism" was in danger in the eyes of this growing party of religious protest, which in the last years of Hyrcanus (135-106 B.C.) became known as Pharisees (Perushim, or "Separatists"). These men, whose stronghold was among the Scribes or professed students of the

Law, by degrees gained the ear of the people. They indeed suffered a severe check under Alexander Jannaeus (105-78 B.C.), in whose favor a revulsion of popular feeling took place. But the lost ground was more than made up under his widow Salome (78-69 B.C.), who separated the secular and sacred headship (her son Hyrcanus II was high-priest). About this time the Sanhedrin came more under the influence of the Scribes than heretofore; and so it remained henceforth. On the death of Salome, internal dissensions, centering round Hyrcanus and his brother Aristobulus, gave the Romans their chance. Under Pompey they occupied Jerusalem, abolished the kingship, and restored the high-priestly dignity to Hyrcanus.

4. *Roman Period.* While the Pharisees gained by the change, which robbed the Sadducees of political power, it sharpened the contrast between the Pharisaic ideal and the popular hope of the restoration of the kingdom. It was especially galling when Antipater, of the hated Idumaean race, became the real power in the state under Rome till his death in 43 B.C., and when in 37 B.C. his son Herod the Great became by Rome's aid king of Judea.

"By birth an Idumaean, by profession a Jew, by necessity a Roman, by culture and by choice a Greek," this unscrupulous monarch maintained himself only by inspiring fear. He filled the chief offices with obscure men of priestly descent from Babylon and Alexandria and abolished the life tenure of the high-priesthood. He tried to overcome the national feeling against him by diverting attention to a great national object, the building of a new Temple, begun in 18 B.C. His death in 4 B.C. was the signal for an insurrection, which the Romans sternly repressed, handing over the country to 3 sons of Herod. Of these, Philip had the land east of Jordan; Antipas, Galilee and Perea; Archelaus, Judea and Samaria. After A.D. 6, Archelaus' kingdom passed under the direct rule of Rome, Pontius Pilate being procurator from A.D. 26 to 36.

Jo'ab
(Heb. "Yah is father") The name of 3 persons in the OT, one of whom was commander of David's army.

Jo'ash, Je·ho'ash
(Heb. "Yah gives") The name of 8 persons in the OT, one of whom was king of Judah (837-800 B.C.).

Job
1. The author of the Book of Job; unknown otherwise.

2. The name of the third son of Issachar, Iob, is sometimes written Job.

Job, the Book of
The first of the OT poetical books deals with the problem of suffering. God allows Satan to afflict Job, a prosperous and pious Jew, with many hardships in order to test his faith. Job loses his children and his worldly goods, and is afflicted by a terrible disease. Finally when God questions Job, he is forced to admit to the

limits of human wisdom, and bows humbly before the will of God. With this new humility his faith is strengthened and Job finds peace.

Jo'el
(Heb. "Yah is God") The name of 13 persons in the OT, one of whom is the author of the Book of Joel. Nothing is known of him.

Jo'el, the Book of
This OT prophetical book was written during a locust plague, a time of great distress for the people. The prophet sees in the devastation of the locusts an indication of the coming day of the Lord. Therefore all must repent with fasting and mourning. With repentance, however, there is a promise for relief and God's blessing for Israel.

John
The name of 5 persons in the NT; one is John the Baptist, another John the Apostle.

John the A·pos'tle
A son of Zebedee and brother of James, a fisherman, he has been called the Beloved Disciple. At the time of the Crucifixion, Jesus committed His mother to John's care. There is tradition that he was banished to Patmos, and that he was bishop at Ephesus for many years. He is considered the author of the Fourth Gospel, the Letters of John, and the book of Revelation.

John the Bap'tist
The son of Elizabeth, who was related to Mary, the Mother of Jesus, a prophet and descended from priests. He has been called the forerunner of Jesus, and was heeded by many for his own message of the need for repentance. He was arrested by Herod and beheaded in prison.

John Mark
See Mark.

John, the Gos'pel according to
The Fourth Gospel, written by "the disciple whom Jesus loved," tells us who Jesus was and what He is; what He can always mean to those who love Him. This Gospel contains more than the other Gospels about the stories of Lazarus and Nicodemus and Jesus' trial, crucifixion, and resurrection, and about the disciples Andrew, Philip, and Thomas.

John, the Let'ters of
These three NT epistles, traditionally assigned to the writer of the Fourth Gospel and Revelation, testify that God is love and that love is the test of religion. *Second John* is written to "the elect lady and her children," probably a church; *Third John* is addressed "to the beloved Gaius."

Jo'nah, Jo'nas
(Heb. "dove") The name of 2 persons in the OT, one of whom is the central figure of the Book of Jonah.

Jo'nah, the Book of
This OT book is the story of a prophet sent by God to Nineveh. Jonah was fearful of the call and tried to flee by sea to Tarshish. During the sea voyage he was thrown overboard by his fellow passengers and swallowed by a great fish sent by God. The prophet was saved and went on to Nineveh to successfully convert the people of that city.

Jon'a·than
(Heb. "Yah has given") The name of 15 persons in the OT, one of whom was the eldest son of Saul and David's friend. To David he gave his own robe and armor. He was a man of great strength and courage. He fell, with his father and 2 brothers, at the battle of Gilboa, leaving a son 5 years old, Meribbaal or Mephibosheth. He was lamented by David in the elegy called the Song of the Bow (2 Sam. 1.17-27).

Jop'pa, Ja'pho
(Heb. "beautiful") At this seaport for Jerusalem little excavation has been possible, because the site is a rock hill on which one city after another has been built. It first appears as a city in about 1500 B.C. when it was captured by Egyptians. Rafts of cedar logs for the Temple were floated to Joppa from Lebanon. Now it has become a part of the city of Tel Aviv.

Jo'ram, Je·ho'ram
(Heb. "Yah is high") The name of 5 persons in the OT, one of whom, Jehoram, was king of Judah (849-842 B.C.).

Jor'dan
The chief river of Palestine, flowing S for 100 miles through a deep valley. Its 3 sources are at the foot of Hermon. In its course are 2 lakes, Lake Huleh and the Sea of Galilee. From the Sea of Galilee to the Dead Sea the Jordan Valley (Ghor) is 65 mi. falling from 682 to 1292 ft. below sea level. The average width of the river is not more than 30 yds., and it varies in depth from 3 ft. at the fords to 7, 8, and 10 ft. The current is very rapid. The river was miraculously crossed by the Israelites and by Elijah and Elisha. In its waters Jesus was baptized by John the Baptist.

Jo'sech
See Joseph.

Jo'seph, Jo'se·phus, Jo'sech, Jo'ses
(Heb. "may Yah add") The name of 14 persons in the Bible. Included are Joseph the son of Jacob, Joseph the husband of Mary the mother of Jesus, and Joseph of Arimathea.

1. *Joseph, husband of Mary.* A carpenter, resident of Nazareth, descended from David. It is presumed that he died in Jesus' youth because there is little mention of him after Jesus was 12.

2. *Joseph, the son of Jacob and Rachel.* He was father of Ephraim and Manasseh, and thus ancestor of the people of the Northern Kingdom. Sold into Egypt by his brothers, he was imprisoned on a false accusation by his master's wife. (A similar incident occurs in a story, written in the time of Ramses II, preserved in a papyrus now in the British Museum.) Yet his skill in interpreting dreams brought him Pharaoh's favor and the first place next to the throne. Gen 42–47 relates how, during a famine, his father and brothers came to settle in Goshen.

3. *Joseph of Arimathea.* A member of the Sanhedrin. He buried the body of Jesus in a tomb on his own property.

Josh'u·a, Jesh'u·a

(Heb. "Yah is salvation") The name of 11 persons in the OT, one of whom is Joshua, son of Nun. Of the tribe of Ephraim, he led the people into the Promised Land. He died at age 110.

Josh'u·a, the Book of

This OT book tells the story of Moses' successor as leader of the Israelites, Joshua, son of Nun, and narrates the conquest of Canaan and the division of the country among the twelve tribes of Israel.

Jo·si'ah

(Heb. "let Yah give") The son of Amon, king of Judah from 639 to 608 B.C. In the 18th year of his reign the Book of the Law was discovered and thereafter the high places throughout the country were suppressed. He was defeated and slain by Pharaoh-Neco at Megiddo. Under his sons Jehoahaz (609), Jehoiachim (608-598) and Zedekiah (597-586) the kingdom of Judah was by turns under Egyptian and Babylonian domination, till its extinction in 586 B.C.

jot

A transliteration of iota, the name of the smallest letter in the Greek alphabet; used metaphorically for the smallest thing.

Jo'tham

(Heb. "may Yah complete") The name of 3 persons in the OT, one of whom was king of Judah 742-735 B.C.

Ju'bi·lee

The final year in a cycle of 50 years.

Ju·dae'a, Ju'dah

See Judea.

Ju'da·iz·ers

A name given to those among the early Jewish Christians who could not believe that all that had once been conveyed to man through the Law was now made available in far greater fullness in the Gospel. Thus they insisted on circumcision as giving a man the right to believe on Jesus as Israel's Savior. The Judaizers were a dwindling body among Palestinian Christians, and they have left no real record of themselves in the New Testament. When they appear in history later on, it is under the title of Ebionites, representing, as their predecessors had done, the "poor" (Heb. *ebion*) and oppressed classes in Jewish society.

Ju'das

The name of 6 persons in the NT, one of whom was Judas Iscariot, the betrayer of Jesus.

Ju'das Mac·ca·be'us

See Maccabees.

Jude, the Let'ter of

This NT epistle designates its author as "a servant of Jesus Christ and brother of James." Its message was for Christians wherever unity was threatened by heretical teaching and where Christian doctrinal and moral standards were questioned.

Ju·de'a, Ju'dah, Ju·dae'a

The land of the Jews, a name applied sometimes to the whole land of Palestine, sometimes to the S division only. It was used in the wider sense at the close of the Captivity, most of those who returned having belonged to the ancient kingdom of Judah. Under the Romans, and in the time of Christ, the name was restricted to the S division; the N being Galilee, and the middle, Samaria; but even then it sometimes denoted the whole country. In its limited sense, it formed part of the kingdom of Herod the Great, and included part of Idumaea, or the land of Edom. As a Roman province, it was annexed to the proconsulate of Syria, and was governed by a procurator. "The wilderness of Judea," in which John began his preaching, and where the temptation of Christ took place, was the E part of Judah, near the Dead Sea, and stretching toward Jericho. It was, and is still, a dreary and desolate region.

Judg'es, the Book of

This OT book is so called because it relates of the times of various rulers, or judges, of Israel from the possession of Canaan until the time of Samuel. Also found in Judges is the recounting of the adventures of Samson.

Ju'dith

1. This Apocryphal book is a story that was originally in Hebrew, but is not now extant in that language. It relates that when Nebuchadnezzar's general, Holofernes, was besieging the Jewish fortress of Bethulia, the besieged were rescued from their peril by the self-sacrifice of Judith, a Jewish woman, who surrendered herself to the camp of Holofernes, and by a stratagem succeeded in cutting off Holofernes' head. The story was probably written to inflame patriotic feeling at the time of some invasion.

2. Esau had a foreign wife named Judith.

ju'ni·per, heath

An almost leafless broom found in the Jordan Valley and the wilderness of Sinai. The Lebanon juniper is a timber-producing tree.

K

Ka'desh, Ka·desh-bar'ne·a, Mer·i·bah-ka'desh

Ancient Canaanite cities with the name Kadesh were sanctuaries. Two of them have been identified.

Kad'mon·ites

(Heb. "easterners") The people inhabiting the Syro-Arabian Desert between Palestine and the Euphrates.

Ke'nites

(Heb. "belonging to the smiths") A gypsylike nomadic or seminomadic tribe. As early as 1300 B.C., they were doing metal work in the areas they roamed over. They lost their identity shortly after 1000 B.C.

Ke'ri·oth

(Heb. "cities") The name of 2 cities in the OT. One of them, Kerioth-Hezron, has been identified with Khirbet el-Qaryatein.

Kid'ron, Ce'dron

A valley E of Jerusalem, through which an intermittent brook still flows. At one time the waters of a spring, Gihon, were allowed to flow through this valley. The stream was often used for irrigation.

Kings, First and Sec'ond

The two OT books follow the monarchy to its summit under Solomon and the nation's division, decline, and fall under Jeroboam and Rehoboam. Kings also gives an outline of the double captivity of Israel under the Assyrians and Judah under the Chaldeans.

Kir

(Heb. "wall") The name of 2 places in the OT, one of which is identified as Kerak, 11 mi. E of the Dead Sea, 17 mi. S of the Arnon.

Kir·i·ath-se'pher, Kir·jath-se'pher

(Heb. "city of the Scribe") An older name for Debir, the modern Tell Beit Mirsin, which has been partially excavated. It is possible that Abraham visited here.

Ki'shon, Ki'son

A river draining the Valley of Jezreel and the Plain of Acco, and emptying into the Mediterranean.

Kit'tim

See Chittim.

L

Lam·en·ta'tions

This OT book consists of five poems occasioned by the fall of Jerusalem and the Babylonian captivity. The first three elegies describe the terrible plight of the nation, the fourth compares the past history of Zion with her present state, and the last is a prayer for compassion and deliverance.

lamp'stand

See candlestick.

Ancient lamps used in the Near East.

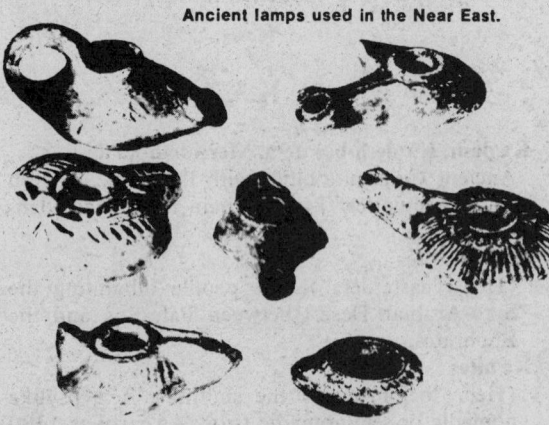

La·od·i·ce'a

A city on the Lycus River in Phrygia, one of the richest in Asia. It struck its own coins, traded wisely, and was an early Christian center. When destroyed by an earthquake in A.D. 60, it was affluent enough to arrange its own reconstruction.

lap'is laz'u·li, sap'phire

Both are blue stones, lapis being semiprecious and sometimes substituted for sapphire. *See* Sapphire.

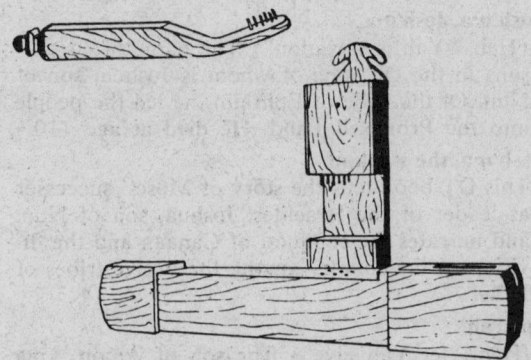

Ancient wooden lock, showing the bolt with its pins, and also the lift key to release it

la'ver

A vessel used in ceremonial rites of purification in the tabernacles and temples, and particularly in Solomon's Temple at Jerusalem. The concept is carried over to the container for the water of baptism.

law, the

The earliest collection of laws so far discovered is that of Ur, earlier than 2000 B.C. Several almost equally early codes have been found, including the code of Hammurabi. All these show evidence of being much earlier in actuality than the incised inscriptions found and translated. What has been called the law of Moses, found in the Pentateuch, may also be much earlier than its actual date of transcription. It is instruction and direction for moral, judicial, and ceremonial conduct, called the Torah by the Jewish people. The code of the Pentateuch is more humane in its judicial sections than other early codes, and much finer in its moral sections. In NT times Jesus recognized and accepted the divine origin and authority of these phases of the law. Though discussion of their extension and interpretation still continues, they are the basis of much of the code of the civilized world today. *See* Torah.

law'yers, scribes

Those skilled in the interpretation of the laws set down by Moses. *See* Scribes.

Laz'a·rus

1. Lazarus, the beggar in the parable of the beggar and the rich man, was taken to Abraham's bosom when he died. But the rich man was in torment after death and he wanted his brothers to be warned of what might befall them. He was denied.

2. Lazarus of Bethany, brother of Mary and Martha, was raised to life after being four days dead. This may have been a major factor in the decision to kill Jesus: their inability to explain the raising of Lazarus was infuriating to the high priests and the Pharisees.

lead

The metal was imported into Palestine, apparently from Tyre. There are, however, mines in the Lebanon, as well as in Sinai and parts of Egypt.

Leb'a·non

(Heb. "white") A mountain range to the N of Palestine, with summits of more than 11,000 ft. For a part of the year they are snow-capped.

leeks

These are included with onions and garlic as among the good things of Egypt for which the Israelites lusted in the wilderness.

len'tils

A legume used for food; a member of the pea family.

leop'ard

A large carnivorous animal found in Palestine as late as the 20th century. The Cheetah, a hunting leopard, was also widely familiar and is found in ancient sculptures.

lep'ro·sy

The Hebrew name means "a stroke," the disease being regarded as the sorest affliction by the hand of God. Its description is given in Lev 13, 14, along with the regulations connected with it. The "botch of Egypt" was probably elephantiasis, which, it is generally agreed, was the disease that afflicted Job, and which is quite distinct from leprosy. Lepers were required to live outside the camp or city and to warn passersby with cries of "Unclean! Unclean!"

le·vi'a·than

(Heb. "coiled one") The primeval dragon, and by extension a sea monster; the crocodile. *See* Whale.

Le'vites

The persons charged with the care of the Tabernacle and the Temple. They embraced all the men of the tribe of Levi, exclusive of the sons of Aaron, though the latter were also Levites and could perform any Levitical service. They were set apart for this service on behalf of the children of Israel. On the settlement of Canaan they were assigned to 48 cities, scattered over the whole country, and were provided with fields for the pasture of their cattle. In David's reign they were divided into 4 classes: (1) Assistants of the priests in the work of the sanctuary; (2) Judges and Scribes; (3) Gate-keepers; (4) Musicians. Each of these classes, with the possible exception of the 2nd, was subdivided into 24 courses, or families, to serve in rotation.

Le·vit'i·cus, the Book of

This 3rd book of the OT can also be called "The Book of the Law of the Priests" as it contains very little historical matter, concerning itself with priestly legislation and the practice of the law among the people. In Leviticus much importance is placed upon Israel's separation from all heathen influences so that the nation may retain its religious purity.

Lib'er·tines, freed'men

(Lat. "freedmen") These were probably descendants of Jews who had been taken to Rome or elsewhere by Pompey as prisoners of war, and had afterward received their freedom there. They did not speak Aramaic, then the language of Jerusalem, and separate synagogues for them were established.

lice

Lice were sent upon the Egyptians as the third plague.

lign·al'oe, al'oes

Lignum aloes, or wood of aloes. *See* aloes.

lig'ure, ja'cinth

This is the gem generally called in Greek lyncurion, from a singular notion as to its origin, which is identified with the true jacinth.

lil'y

This may have meant the scarlet martegon lily or the scarlet anemone, or have been used poetically for the lion; a beautiful flower.

li'on

Mentioned in the OT about 130 times, the animal was well known throughout W Asia as late as 500 B.C. The lion, Judah's emblem, was in all lands the symbol of royal power and strength. It was taken by pitfalls in its tracks, or by nets.

liz'ard

(Heb. "clinger"?) A reptile with scaly body, long tail, and usually 4 legs. A number of species occur in Palestine, including geckoes, skinks, and chameleons, and larger spiny lizards.

lo'custs

These insects are often referred to, and under 9 different names:

1. *Arbeh*, generally and rightly translated "locust." The record of the 8th plague in Egypt gives a true account of a typical severe invasion of locusts; an E wind brought them from the other side of the isthmus of Suez, and a W wind hurled them back into the Red Sea, where they perished. They are placed among the clean creatures.

2. *Sal'am*, occurring once only, and translated "bald locust." The word seems to have the same root as *sela*, which means rock; hence we may think of certain species of grasshoppers, which delight in basking on sun-exposed rocks, and translate the word "rock locust."

3. *Chargol*. In the vernacular, these are called katydids or long-horned grasshoppers.

4. *Chagab*, generally used for and translated "grasshoppers," many of which are much smaller than locusts.

5. *Gazam*, translated "palmerworm," is interpreted either as the locust in its larval stage or as the larva of butterflies or moths. "Palmerworm" should not apply to locusts.

6. *Yelek*, very difficult to interpret, the more so since there is no evidence that the different authors meant the same creature. It is translated "cankerworm" and caterpillar." Etymologically, the word means a creature that licks up the grass. It is evidently intended to express some insect pest.

7. *Tzelatzal*. The word *tzelatzal* means a tinkling, musical instrument, and is hence applied to a creature able to produce musical sounds. Thus the author may have used it as the name of one of the grasshoppers, the chirping notes of which are frequently loud enough to be heard at some distance, or for the well-

known cicada, which is found in abundance all around the Mediterranean.

8. *Gob* appears several times, and is translated "grasshoppers"; it cannot be referred to any particular kind.

9. *Chasil*, generally mentioned together with the locust, and therefore believed to signify the locust in its larval stage. But in some versions it is translated "caterpillar." *See* grasshopper.

Egyptian locust

Lord's Prayer

The model prayer which our Lord taught His disciples. According to the text of Luke it consists of 5 petitions, according to that of Matthew of 6 (or 7). The Reformed churches count 6; 3 with "Thy," and 3 with "our"; the Roman Catholics and Lutherans 7, regarding "Lead us not into temptation" and "Deliver us from evil" as separate petitions. The concluding doxology (occurring only in Matthew, and omitted in some versions), is wanting in the best MSS., and is a later addition, based on 1 Chron 29.11, and 2 Tim 4.18. It accords with the first 3 petitions.

Lord's Sup'per

(Cor 11.20), called also "breaking of bread" (Acts 2.42), "cup of blessing," "communion of the blood of Christ," and "of the body of Christ" (1 Cor 10.16), and "the Lord's table" (10.21). It is a holy ordinance, which Christ initiated as the last meal (the Passover) with His disciples, on the night before His death, and appointed to be observed in remembrance of Him. In it, by the giving and receiving of bread and wine, Christ's death is showed forth "till He come." As the Passover commemorated Israel's deliverance from the "house of bondage," and election to be a covenant-people, the Lord's Supper marks the establishment of a new covenant in His blood, His death being the foundation of a new relation of His church to God, and of the communion of His people with one another.

Lot

The nephew of Abraham, who came with Abraham to Canaan. The story of Lot is found in Gen 11.27–14.29; 19.

love ap'ple

The mandrake, a perennial herb, related to the poisonous nightshade. It is superstitiously considered an aphrodisiac.

Lu'ci·fer, day star

(Lat. "light bringer") The day star was a name applied by the prophet to the king of Babylon in his pride and splendor and glory before his fall, when he said, "I will ascend into heaven, I will exalt my throne above the stars of God" (Is 14.12-13).

Luke

A Gentile, a physician, an educated man, familiar with the E Mediterranean and adjacent countries, who in Acts appears as the companion of Paul from Troas to Philippi, where he probably remained from A.D. 52 to 58, rejoining the Apostle at that place, and continuing with him to the time when the narration closes (A.D. 58-63). In 2 Tim. 4.11 he is referred to as being with Paul. Hence the evangelist must have been in Palestine during the 2 years of Paul's imprisonment at Caesarea (A.D. 58-60).

Luke, the Gos'pel according to

This NT book, the 3rd Gospel, was written by "The beloved physician," the companion of the apostle Paul. Only in Luke are found the Magnificat, the story of the birth of John the Baptist, the Christmas story of the shepherds, the parables of the good Samaritan, the lost sheep, and the prodigal son, and the great hymns—the *Gloria in Excelsis* and *Nunc Dimittis*. Jesus is presented as the compassionate Savior, healer, redeemer, and friend of the weak. From this Gospel comes a special feeling of the mercy of God as Jesus made men understand it.

lute

An instrument resembling the harp and the cithern; examples have been found of the period of 1500 B.C.

LXX

See Septuagint.

lye

See Nitre.

lyre

An early stringed instrument found in Egyptian and Assyrian relief, the "harp" played by David. Played especially in the Temple by the Levites.

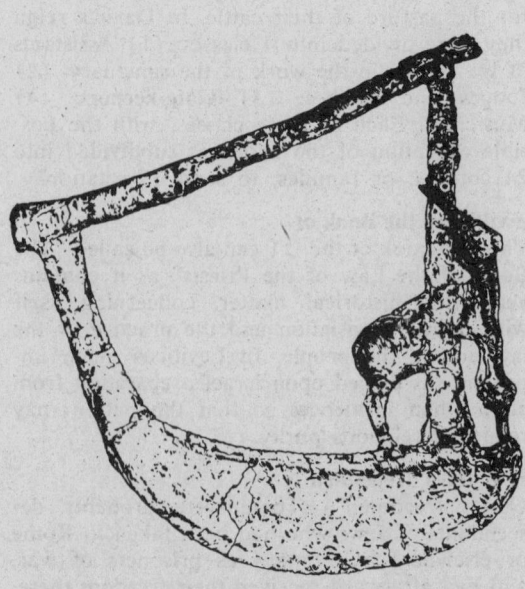

Lyre frame of silver, from Ur, dated previous to the time of Abraham

M

Mac'ca·bees

The family of priestly descent that freed the Jewish people from the Syrian yoke. The name Makkaba ("hammer") belongs properly to Judas, the third of the five sons of Mattathias, who from his father's death in 166 B.C. to his own death at the battle of Elasa or Adasa in 161 led the defenders of their country and faith in one of the most heroic struggles in history. His work was completed by his brothers, who founded the Asmonaean Dynasty. The Maccabees are included among the heroes of faith in Heb 11.

Mac·e·do'ni·a

In NT times, the northern Roman province of Greece, the southern being Achaia. Paul was summoned thither by the vision of the "man of Macedonia" and he visited it a 2nd time. Philippi was one of its chief cities, and there Lydia was converted.

Ma'gi

In the NT, the wise men from the East who came to worship the infant Christ. The name Magos is also given to Elymas in Acts 13.6, 8, and is there translated "sorcerer"; and to Simon who "used sorcery" (Acts 8.9).

Mal'a·chi

(Heb. "My messenger") An OT prophet.

Mal'a·chi, the Book of

The last book of the OT belongs to the period of Nehemiah. The prophet's message is to the priests and the people, charging them with indifference, doubt, and immorality. Malachi tells of the coming day of the Lord and closes the book with a prophecy of John the Baptist.

mal'low

Probably the shrubby orache, eaten only when nothing else is available.

Ma·nas'seh

(Heb. "one who causes to forget") The name of 2 persons in the OT, one the eldest son of Joseph and ancestor of one of the 12 tribes; the other was Judah's king (687-642 B.C.).

Ma·nas'seh, Prayer of

It is mentioned in the statement by the Chronicler, 2 Chron 33.18, 19. The extant Prayer of Manasseh found in the Apocrypha is a noble monument of devotion. The early Christian church placed it as one of the 9 canticles at the head of the Psalter.

man'drake

See Love apple.

man'na

(Heb. "What is that?") The food supplied to the Israelites in the wilderness. Studies in the Sinai region indicate that it is the honeydew secretion of two scale insects on the tamarisk bushes abundant there, very sweet and high in carbohydrates.

mar'ble

The name is properly applied to a completely crystalline limestone, such as is used for statuary, but is commonly extended to any ornamental limestone that can be polished. In Palestine, probably the latter was meant.

Mar'che·wan

A name of the 8th month of the Hebrew year. It is also called Bul.

Mark, John Mark

He was the son of Mary, at whose house in Jerusalem the early Christians seem to have found a home. He was a cousin of Barnabas, and the attendant of the 2 Christian preachers in Paul's first missionary journey. But he became the occasion of sharp contention between Paul and Barnabas in consequence of his leaving them at Perga. Afterward, however, he was with the Apostle Paul during his first imprisonment at Rome. The Apostle Peter refers to Mark as with him when he wrote his 1st epistle, probably at Babylon. Evidently the evangelist made a journey to the E about A.D. 63, and he was at Ephesus with Timothy shortly before the death of Paul. Reliable details of his later life are wanting. He is spoken of as the interpreter of Peter, and, according to tradition, was the founder of the church at Alexandria. His Gospel may have been written at Rome, between A.D. 63 and 66.

Mark, the Gos'pel according to

The earliest of the Gospels, this NT book contains much of the teaching of Peter. This Gospel presents Jesus as the man of power, the strong and active Son of God; its climax is reached when Peter makes his great confession, "You are the Christ."

Ma'ry

The name of 7 persons in the NT, one of them the mother of Jesus. Another Mary was the sister of Lazarus; a third is the mother of James the Younger; and a fourth, Mary Magdalene.

Mas'o·retes

Down to the close of the 5th century A.D., the tradition of the accepted pronunciation of the bare consonantal text of the OT was kept alive by the oral teaching of the Rabbis and by the recitation of the Scriptures in the synagogues. The reduction to writing of this exegetical tradition was the work of the scholars called the Masoretes, (from Masora, "tradition"), whose chief center was the Rabbinical school of Tiberias. They took great pains that the texts should be kept entire, for this purpose counting up the number of words, and even the number of letters in the different books, noting expressions that occurred but once or rarely, drawing attention to peculiar modes of writing, and the like. One great service rendered by the Masoretes was their devising a system of dots and strokes (vowel points), which are placed above, below, or in the heart of the consonants, and denote precisely how the words were read by the scholars of the time. These are regarded as forming no part of the sacred text, and the Pentateuch rolls used in the Synagogue are written in the bare consonants as originally received. Closely connected with the vowel system is the system of accents, which indicate the manner in which the words and clauses were separated or conjoined, and also form a kind of musical notation, according to which the Scriptures are to be melodiously recited. The text, with this array of symbols, is called the Masoretic text; and it gives us what was the traditional reading at the time the work was accomplished.

The Masoretic text, with its complete equipment, cannot be placed earlier than the 7th century of the Christian era. But it gives us a tradition reaching back to a much earlier time; and it is a cause of thankfulness that, in the handing down of the text, the Masoretes did not allow themselves to deviate in the smallest details from what they had received. There remain in the text, as they have handed it down, evident indications of what had been slips of the pen or mistakes of the eye of the transcribers, but the Masoretes allowed even these to stand, contenting themselves with drawing attention to their presence.

mas·se'ba

A sacred pillar.

Mat'thew

(Heb. "gift of Yah") Also called "Levi the son of Alphaeus." When called to become a disciple he was a publican, or tax gatherer, probably a collector of tolls and custom duties at the Sea of Galilee. His call is narrated in the 3 Gospels, but while he refers to the feast that Mark and Luke distinctly place at his house, he makes no allusion to that fact. Papias and Irenaeus, writing in the 2nd century, state that Matthew wrote in Hebrew (Aramaic). The earliest citations, some of them in works of the earlier half of the 2nd century, give the exact words of the Greek Gospel we now have, and no certain traces of a previous Aramaic Gospel have been discovered. If there was an Aramaic original, it was superseded very soon by a Greek version. The very early date often assigned (A.D. 45) may be correct if applied to an Aramaic original; but the Greek Gospel we have may have been written about A.D. 60.

Mat'thew, the Gos'pel according to

This first NT book has been pre-eminently the Gospel of the church. It tells us of God's love for Israel and of the fulfillment in Christ of God's promise to the nation. It gives the complete story of Jesus' ministry, death, and resurrection. The Sermon on the Mount, and some of the most precious of Jesus' parables are contained in this Gospel.

meals

In Palestine there were two meals, one late in the morning and the other, the chief one, in the evening.

meas'ures

Bath (liquid) = 5½ gallons.

Cor (liquid or dry) = 10 baths (liquid) = 55 gals. (dry).

Cubit (length) = 21.8 inches English (or 20.24 inches for the ordinary cubit).

Ephah (dry) = ½ bushel.

Hin (liquid) = 4 quarts.

Homer (dry) = 5.16 bushels.

Kab (dry) = 1.16 quarts.

Log (liquid or dry) = 0.67 pint.

Omer (dry) = 2.09 quarts.

Seah (dry) = ⅔ peck.

Medes

An Aryan or Indo-European people who inhabitated the country to the SW of the Caspian, whence they extended S to the Persian Gulf. One of the offshoots was the tribe of Persians. Called also Madai.

Me·gid'do, Me·gid'don, Ar·ma·ged'don

A Canaanite and later Israelite city identified as the modern Tell el-Mutesellim, overlooking the Plain of Esdraelon, 20 mi. SSE of Haifa. As an inhabited area it has a history of more than 3500 years. Both Egyptians and people from the E destroyed it. Thut-mose III of Egypt about 1450 B.C., Tiglath-pileser III the Assyrian in 733 B.C., and Neco of Egypt in 609 B.C. destroyed it completely. During its long history it has been a walled city, a royal chariot city, a city of great splendor, the site of many battles. It is believed to be the place of Armageddon, the final struggle. *See* Armageddon.

Mel·chiz'e·dek

(trad. "King of righteousness") A worshiper of the Supreme God, to whom, as priest and king of Salem or Jerusalem, Abraham gave tithes. In Heb 7 he is shown to be a type of Christ.

mel'on

A fruit known to them in Egypt for which the Israelites longed when in the wilderness. Both muskmelons and watermelons are common in Egypt.

Mer·i·bah-ka'desh

See Kadesh.

Mer'o·dach-bal'a·dan, Ber'o·dach-bal'a·dan

Ruler of a Chaldean tribe and twice (721-710, 704 B.C.) king of Babylon (Jer 50.2).

Me'sha

The name of 2 persons and a place in the OT, and of the king of Moab who erected the Moabite Stone, which chronicled his story.

Me'shach

The Babylonian name of one of the friends of Daniel. *See* Shadrach.

Mes·o·po·ta'mi·a

The land between the rivers, the Tigris and the Euphrates.

Mes·si'ah, Mes·si'as

(Heb. the "Anointed," same as Gr. *Christos*) Though in the OT sometimes applied to such divinely appointed agents as the high priest, the prophets, and even King Cyrus (Is 45.1), chiefly designates the promised Deliverer and Saviour whom prophecy foretold, and in whom all the promises of God are fulfilled.

Mi'cah

(Heb. "who is like Yah?") Micah the prophet, a contemporary of Isaiah.

Mi'cah, the Book of

The prophecy of the fourth in the great quartet of eighth-century B.C. prophets, with Amos, Hosea, and Isaiah, who preached against the idolatrous and unjust nations of their generation. Micah's message was stern and uncompromising; judgment was to come soon for Judah.

Mi'chael

(Heb. "who is like God?") One of the archangels.

Mid'i·an·ites

A tribe living in NW Arabia, descendants of Keturah and Abraham. They were nomads and traders with Egypt, and pillaged the Israelites until conquered by Gideon.

Mil'com

See Molech.

mill

The handmill consisted of 2 stones, between which the grain was ground. A rectangular and slightly concave stone might be rubbed over a larger stone, or 2 round stones, the lower convex and the upper concave, might have grain for grinding poured through a hole in the center of the top stone. These mills were used by women in the home. Larger round millstones turned on a flat lower stone by animal power were community enterprises. No part of a handmill could be taken for debt.

mil'let

The smallest of the grass seeds grown for food; usually mixed with other seeds or grains.

mil'lo

A part of the fortification of Jerusalem, erected by David.

mi'na

See Weights.

Mi'nor Proph'ets

The last 12 books of the OT. Because of their brevity, they are frequently called the minor prophets.

mint

(Gr. "sweet odor") An herb, the oil of which was used as a condiment and as medicine. Several species are found in Palestine. The Pharisees required the tithing even of mint, but neglected law and justice, mercy and faith.

Mint

mir'a·cle

(Lat. "wonderful thing") Defined as an event, whether natural or supernatural, in which one sees an act or revelation of God.

mite

See Money.

Miz'pah, Miz'peh

(Heb. "watchtower") The name of 4 towns and 1 region in the OT; 2 towns and the region have been tentatively identified.

Miz'ra·im

The Hebrew word for Egypt; it also applies to a land of Musri, from which Shalmaneser III got double-humped camels. Solomon imported horses from a place of this name.

Mo'ab·ites

A people allied to the Israelites, settled from before the time of Moses SE of the Dead Sea. Like the Ammonites, from whom they were separated by the river Arnon, they were descendants of Lot, and mortal enemies of Israel. They were subdued by Saul and David, and after Ahab's death cast off the yoke of the N kingdom. To this period belongs the Moabite Stone. Jeroboam II again made them tributary.

Mo'ab·ite Stone

In 1868 an inscription was found among the ruins of Dibon, giving an account by the Moabite king Mesha of his successful revolt from Samaria, and of his buildings in Moab. "Omri, king of Israel, oppressed Moab many days, for Chemosh was angry with his land." Then Mesha revolted in the time of Ahab. He overthrew the Israelites, took Medeba, Ataroth, Jahaz, and Nebo, where there had been an altar to "Yahweh" (Jehovah), and he rebuilt Korkhah, Aroer, Bezer, and other fortresses. It is clear from 2 Kings 3.5 that the chief successes of Mesha were gained after Ahab's death. The language of the inscription hardly differs from Hebrew.

mole

(Heb. "digger"?) The moles of Is 2.20 perhaps included the rat, ground squirrel, and similar animals. The U. S. mole is unknown in Palestine, but the mole-rat is very abundant.

Mo'lech, Mo'loch, Mil'com, Ath'ter

A deity to whom human sacrifices were made, and worshiped by Ammonites, Edomites, Moabites, and others. The Valley of Hinnom, outside Jerusalem, was a place of sacrifice to this god.

mon'ey

In the sense of stamped coin, money did not exist in Israel before the Exile. Of coined money, an invention of the Greeks, there is some trace in Western Asia in the 7th century B.C. in the Greek colonies and in Lydia. Gold and silver earlier were "weighed to" the seller by the buyer. The name of the common unit, the shekel, means "weight" (cf. English pound sterling; also Old French livre, and Italian lira, from Latin libra, "a pound"). The pieces of metal were in the form of bars (cf. the "wedge" of 50 shekels' weight in Josh 7.21), larger pieces in that of rings, as the Hebrew name for talent

Silver quarter-shekel

Mite of Herod the Great

Copper coin of Cyprus

Shekel of the sanctuary

Daric

Copper coin of Herod Agrippa II.

("circle") shows. The weighing of ring money is represented on the Egyptian monuments. The balance and the weights (of stone) were carried along with the precious metal in a bag attached to the girdle.

Recent investigations have proved that the ratio of the value of gold to that of silver fixed in Babylon and Assyria, 1:13½, prevailed over all Western Asia (in Greece it was 1:12). The whole monetary system of the Hebrews, as of their neighbors, was based on the Babylonian system of weights. The Babylonian weight-talent was equal to 60 minas of 60 shekels each; but the Babylonian money-talent was equal to 60 minas of 50 shekels each, or 3000 shekels. The unit, the shekel, was the same in both.

Darius I, Darius Hystaspes, extended the circulation of coins, but a gold coin called the daric was used earlier by King Cyrus (550-530 B.C.). After the Exile, Persian money was current. After the fall of the Persian monarchy, talents and drachmas came in. Simon Maccabaeus struck (141 B.C.) silver and bronze coins, of which a number are still extant, but the Greek money was still current, and in the time of our Lord they counted by drachmas and staters. The smallest copper coin in use is translated mite.

COINS OF THE BIBLE

Assarion, a Roman bronze coin, 1/10 denarius to 1/20 denarius. *See penny.*

Aureus, a Roman gold coin. Its weight was changed several times.

Beka, Bekah, half a shekel, 0.201 ounce.

Daric or *Dram,* a Persian gold coin, 8.424 grams.

Denarius, a Roman silver coin, 3.8 grams.

Drachma, a Greek silver coin, nearly equal to the Roman denarius.

Dram. See daric.

Gerah, 1/20 shekel, 8.71 grams.

Gold, the Roman aureus = 25 denarii, was of pure gold, and weighed 126¼ grains.

Lepton, the smallest Greek bronze coin; possibly 1/100 drachma. *See mite.*

Mite, the smallest Jewish coin.

Money, pieces of, in Gen 33.19; Job 42.11; Josh 24.32, are of unknown value. In the NT, piece of money, Gr. stater (only in Mt 17.27; R. V. shekel), a silver coin, the Attic silver tetradrachma (four drachmas), officially tariffed by Pompey 63 B.C. for purposes of exchange, at 4 denarii.

Penny in the NT represents a Roman silver coin, the denarius. It was the daily wage of a laborer or of a common soldier in the time of our Lord.

Pound (only occurring in Lk 19.13-25) is the mina = 100 drachmas.

Shekel (Heb. "weight," only in OT), 0.403 ounce. The "holy" shekel, mentioned in parts of Exodus, Leviticus, and Numbers, means the full weight shekel, as contrasted with that which had deteriorated in weight.

Denarius with image and superscription of Tiberius Caesar.

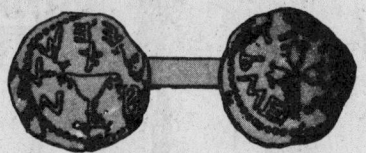

Silver half shekel of Year 1.

Procurator's copper coin.

Silver coin of Vespasian, commemorating the capture of Jerusalem.

Silver, piece of. Here probably shekels are meant. In the NT "piece of silver" represents the Gr. drachma or the silver shekel.

Silverlings. Silver shekels.

Talent, about 75 pounds.

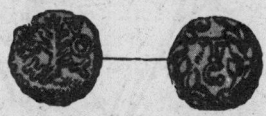

Copper coin of Herod Antipas, Tetrarch of Galilee.

Silver Drachma of Alexander the Great found at the Treasury, Persepolis, Iran.

mon'ey chang'ers

The money changers at the Temple sat in the court of the Gentiles, and were not allowed within the inner precincts or naos. Here they acted as bankers, and gave Jewish money in exchange for foreign, as only Jewish money could be used to pay the Temple tax. The practices of the money changers must have been so bad as to warrant their expulsion by our Lord, who "overthrew the tables of the money changers."

Weighing money

Mor'de·cai

The name of 2 persons in the OT, one of them the important character of the Book of Esther.

Mo·ri'ah

A region near Beer-Sheba, mentioned in the OT. Also, a rocky hill of Jerusalem N of the City of David, and the site of the Temple.

Mo'ses

The great deliverer and law-giver of Israel was the son of Amram and Jochebed, of the tribe of Levi, and younger brother of Miriam and Aaron. Born during the oppression of the Israelites in Egypt, he was placed while an infant child in an ark of bulrushes among the reeds of the river Nile, where he was found by the daughter of Pharaoh. Brought up in Pharaoh's house, he became learned in "all the wisdom of the Egyptians." In his 40th year he fled to Midian, "fearing the wrath of the king" for his killing an Egyptian whom he had found ill-treating a Hebrew. In Midian he married Zipporah, daughter of a priest and sheikh, and lived 40 years. Then God revealed Himself to Moses as Jehovah in a bush that burned and was not consumed, and commissioned him to return to Egypt and be the deliverer of Israel. After 10 miracles of judgment or "plagues" wrought by Moses, the greatest and last of these being the death of the first-born, Pharaoh consented, and the children of Israel set forth for Canaan. Thenceforward for 40 years he was their leader through the wilderness; at Sinai, where he received the law from Heaven; at Kadesh; and in the land of Moab, where he died, after viewing the promised land from the top of Pisgah. Moses, "the mediator of the old covenant," is one of the greatest figures in history. He made the children of Israel a nation, and established the national life of Israel on the basis of a religious covenant that determined the whole future of that people and of the world.

moth

(Heb. "consumer") The moth mentioned in the Bible is the clothes moth, of which several species are very destructive to fur and wool and the garments made of them. It is only the larvae that feed upon the hairs. In Is 51.8 we read, "For the moth shall eat them up like a garment, and the worm (Heb. sas) shall eat them like wool"; the word sas, translated "worm," is interpreted as the larva.

mourn'ing

Signs of mourning were: rending the outer garments, wearing sackcloth, strewing earth or ashes, cutting or shaving beard or hair, fasting, and in some cases, even cutting the hands and the body.

mouse

Doubtless a generic term, including all the small rodents. The mouse was forbidden as food by the Mosaic law.

mul'ber·ry, syc'a·mine, bal'sam

The black mulberry is common in Palestine. The Heb. word has also been translated as sycamine and as balsam.

A bough of the mulberry tree.

mur'der·ers

See Assassins.

mur'rain

An infectious disease of animals.

mu'sic

According to 1 Chron 15.17, David, credited as the originator of liturgical music, instituted an orchestra, with 3 leaders: Heman, Asaph, Ethan or Jeduthun, all of them Levites. These pioneers founded schools of musical performance. The instruments played were percussion, cymbals and timbrels or tambourines; stringed psalteries and harps; wind instruments, the pipe and the trumpet or cornet. There was antiphonal singing by Temple choirs and singing by the congregations.

Ancient musical instruments

The Temple priests used trumpets and cornets on special occasions, and the priestly family made up an orchestra as well.

mus'tard

An annual plant with very small seeds. It grows to a considerable size in Palestine.

Courtesy of *The Interpreter's Dictionary of the Bible*

Mustard

myrrh, per'fume
A general term for fragrant gums or resins from various trees and shrubs, most frequently the rockrose, the ladanum. It was an article of commerce as early as the 2nd millennium B.C.

myr'tle
A shrub indigenous to Western Asia and common on hillsides in Palestine, flourishing especially by watercourses. It has dark glossy leaves, marked with transparent dots, the result of the presence of a volatile aromatic oil. The flowers are small, white, and fragrant, and when dried are used as a perfume.

N

Na'a·man
(Heb. "pleasantness") A Syrian army commander, healed of leprosy by Elisha.

Na'hum, Na'um
The name of a person of the OT and one of the NT. Nahum of the OT and prophet of the Book of Nahum was born at Elkosh in SW Judah and prophesied in the period between 633 and 612 B.C.

Na'hum, the Book of
This OT book consists of two poems. The prophet tells of the fall of Nineveh, the capital of the Assyrian nation. God is depicted as revengeful to those who conspire against Him. The book of Nahum also contains a classic rebuke against warfare and militarism.

Na'in
(Heb. "pleasant") A town of SW Galilee, now called Nein, on the NW side of Nebi Dahi and 2 mi. SW of Endor.

nard
See Spikenard.

Na'than
(Heb. "gift") The court prophet who denounced David for planning Uriah's death and stealing his wife; he also assisted in securing the throne for Solomon.

Na·than'a·el
(Heb. "gift of God") A man of Cana of Galilee, often identified with Bartholomew.

Naz'a·reth
(Heb. "watchtower") The village in Lower Galilee where Jesus was brought up. It is not mentioned in the OT. It is now a flourishing town. The "brow of the hill" is probably the cliff to the N.

Naz'i·rites
(Heb. "one consecrated") These were not members of a party or brotherhood, but individuals "separated" to God's special service by a personal vow of longer or shorter duration. Of this nature was probably the vow of the men named in Acts 21.23-26, and even of Paul (Acts 18.18). The typical Nazirite of the NT is John the Baptist.

Ne'bo
The name of a Babylonian deity, and of 2 towns mentioned in the OT, one probably Kir-

beh Mekhayyet, 5 mi. SW of Heshbon, and the other Nuba, 15 mi. SW of Jerusalem.

Ne'bo, Mount
Probably a mountain of the Abarim range, modern Jebel en-Neba, 2740 ft. above sea level, 12 mi. E of the mouth of the Jordan River.

Neb·u·chad·nez'zar, Neb·u·chad·rez'zar
(Akkad. "Nabu protect my boundary stone") King of Babylonia for 43 years, he records in an inscription his defeat of the Pharaoh Amasis in 567 B.C., verifying the prophecy of Jeremiah (43.10-13); and a contract tablet, dated in his 40th year, proves that he had by that time conquered Tyre, confirming Ezek (28.7-14).

Ne·he·mi'ah
(Heb. "Yah has comforted") The name of 3 persons in the OT, one of whom was the restorer (with Ezra) of Judaism after the Babylonian exile and cupbearer to the Persian king Artaxerxes I, who gave him permission to return with a colony to Jerusalem in 445 B.C. Appointed governor of Judea, he rebuilt the city walls in spite of the opposition of the Samaritans and others, and organized the service of God, returning to Persia in 430.

Ne·he·mi'ah, the Book of
Ezra and Nehemiah are companion OT books. *Nehemiah* (or *Second Book of Ezra*) gives an account of the rebuilding of Jerusalem and of the efforts to bring religious reform to the people, covering the history of the Jews from the Exile to the time of Darius II.

net'works
See cotton.

New Je·ru'sa·lem
See Jerusalem, New.

Nic·o·de'mus
(Gr. "conqueror of the people") A member of the Sanhedrin, who came at night to talk with Jesus; he provided the spices for and helped to embalm the body of Jesus.

Nic·o·la'i·tans, Nic·o·la'i·tanes
The name of a sect of Gentile Christians in Ephesus and Pergamum, who rejected the decision of the Jerusalem council with regard to food, and its prohibition of unchastity.

Nile
The great fertilizing river of Egypt. The name, which means "dark" or "blue," is not found in the Bible, but it is understood to be referred to as Shihor or the black stream and as "the river." It is formed by 2 rivers: the White Nile, which flows from the Victoria Nyanza; and the Blue Nile, which flows from the Abyssinian Mountains. These streams unite at Khartoum. To the annual overflowing of the Nile, caused by periodic rains in the southern regions around its sources, Egypt owes its fertility. Below Cairo the river is divided into channels through the Deltas. The names and locations of these shift and the precise patterns in antiquity are not known.

Nim'rod
A legendary hero of the Mesopotamian region. The legends may have grown around the Baby-

lonian war god Ninurta, or a historical figure, the Assyrian king Tukulti-Ninurta (1246-1206 B.C.), the first Assyrian to rule over all Babylonia. Nimrod son of Cush has the legendary greatness.

Nin'e·veh

The later capital of Assyria after the kingdom had been extended north along the Tigris from Assur, the great city on the Upper Tigris, which has yielded almost a complete monumental history of Assyria. An inscription of the Akkad Dynasty (23rd to 21st century B.C.) has been found

Winged bull from the palace of Sargon near Nineveh

in the excavations. It was destroyed about 612 B.C. by the allied Medes, Persians, and Babylonians, after having been ruined by the Scythians.

Nip'pur

A city about 100 mi. S of Baghdad, founded around 4000 B.C.

Ni'san

The 1st month of the Hebrew year. Also called Abib. It falls in March-April.

ni'tre, lye

Native sodium carbonate, nitre, is found in Egypt about 50 mi. W of Cairo. The reference in Prov 25.20 and Jer 2.22, a substance used for cleaning, may be potassium carbonate, which in Palestine could be made from wood ashes. The addition of vinegar would destroy its action.

No'ah, No'e

Tenth generation from Adam, son of Lamech, and a righteous man, whose story is told in Gen 6–9. To Noah God gave the promise after the Flood that never again would he send such a catastrophe, and the rainbow was declared the reminder of His promise. *See* Flood.

Noph

The city of Memphis in Egypt.

Num'bers, the Book of

The 4th book of the OT, it is a continuation of Exodus, recording the stay of the Israelites in the wilderness of Sinai until their arrival at Moab. The title of the book is derived from the two numberings of the people recorded here.

O

oak, ter'e·binth

Three species of oak are found in Palestine. The terebinth is now identified as distinct from the oak. Symbolism of the oak includes long life and grandeur.

O·ba·di'ah

The name of 11 persons in the OT.

O·ba·di'ah, the Book of

This is the shortest book of the OT, containing only one chapter. In it is given a prophetic interpretation of a great calamity that has already occurred in Edom and a prediction of a universal judgment.

oil tree

This term can include the olive, wild olive, oleaster, and some pines.

ol'ive

Grafted on wild stock, the olive is extensively cultivated in Palestine for its valuable fruit and oil. The cherubim, the doors of the oracle, and the doorposts of the Temple were made of its finely grained wood.

Ol'ives, Mount of; Ol'i·vet, the Mount called

A mountain with 3 summits E of Jerusalem; the highest summit, sometimes called Mount Scopus, is 2963 ft. Gethsemane is on its lower slope. The Mount of Olives is closely associated with the last days of the life of Jesus.

o·me'ga

The last letter in the Greek alphabet, used in Revelation as a title for Christ as the One in whom all things find their consummation.

Om'ri

(Heb. "worshiper of Yah") The name of 4 persons in the OT, one of whom was king of Israel 876-968 B.C.

O·ni'as

The name of 5 priests, 2 of whom were high priests. The family descended from Zadok, appointed high priest by Solomon.

on'y·cha

An ingredient, possibly obtained from marine mollusks, of incense to be burned on the altar.

o'nyx

A chalcedony with bands of alternate milk-white and black. It is sometimes translated as a color rather than black.

O'phir

A place from which gold was obtained. The location has been placed in India, Africa, and Arabia; it seems probable that it was on the coast of Somaliland. The imports from Ophir, other than gold, seem characteristically African, such as monkeys and ivory.

or'gan, pipe

A pipe or perforated wind instrument, perhaps in a group or cluster.

or'na·ments

A list of feminine ornaments is given in Is 3.18-24. They included rings for the fingers, the ears, and the nose; bangles round the arms and the ankles; bracelets and necklaces; pomander boxes, and mirrors. Cosmetics were also used, both to blacken the nails and the eyelids, and to color the cheeks (2 Kings 9.30; Ezek 23.40).

Egyptian bracelets.

ouch'es
Settings for jewels.

P

Pa·dan-a'ram, Pad·dan-a'ram
The area in what is now S central Turkey, including the city of Haran, now Harran.

Pal'es·tine
The Greek and Roman name for Canaan, together with the country of Jordan occupied by the Jews (the Bible itself confines this name to the territory of the Philistines). Palestine is 140 mi. long, 40 to 50 mi. broad, some 8500 sq. mi. in area: about the size of Massachusetts or of Wales. It is shut off from Egypt by 100 mi. of desert; has the Arabian desert on the E, and the Mediterranean on the W; and is bounded on the N by the mountain chains of Lebanon and Anti-Lebanon. Palestine lies midway between the valleys of the Euphrates and the Nile, two of the earliest seats of civilization and of empire. The traffic between Mesopotamia and Egypt passed through it. Of these empires Palestine was the battlefield down to 500 B.C. Then others followed: the Persians under Cambyses, Greeks under Alexander, Seleucus and the Ptolemies, the Romans under Pompey, the Parthians, the Romans again and again, then in A.D. 634 the Arabs, in the 11th century the Turks and Crusaders, in the 13th and 14th, the Mongols, and in the 19th, Napoleon.

Israel came originally from the desert, and Midianites, Ishmaelites, Amalekites, Arabs, and other Semitic tribes kept pouring into the land; hence the population is in the main Semitic to this day.

The kingdom of Herod the Great embraced all the country won by the tribes under Joshua, except the tribe of Asher in the N, and a small part in the SW. It included: (1) W of Jordan, Galilee, Samaria, Judea, and Idumea; (2) E of Jordan, Perea, Gaulanitis, Auranitis, and Trachonitis, with Decapolis (part in Perea, part in Gaulanitis). The part E of Jordan thus comprehended the ancient kingdoms of Moab and Ammon; the earlier divisions of Gilead (from the Dead Sea to the Yarmuk), and Bashan (a volcanic plateau 2000 ft. above the sea), extending from the Yarmuk to Hermon; and the regions of Golan, E of the Sea of Galilee, and Hauran, still farther E.

Palestine is laid down from N to E in 4 long lines: the Maritime Plain, the Western (or Central) Range, the Jordan Valley, and the Eastern Range. Palestine W of Jordan is an upland carved out of masses of limestone, 2000 to 3000 ft. above the sea. The Ghor, or great trench of the Jordan Valley, descends from ocean level at Huleh to 682 ft. lower at the Sea of Galilee, and to 1292 ft. at the Dead Sea. The Western Range is broken by the Plain of Esdraelon, which opens a way from the Maritime Plain to the Jordan Valley. At its S end it declines into a broad plateau named the Negev, or Parched Land. The lower hills, known as the Shephelah, are between Judea and the Maritime Plain, which, farther N, is broken by Carmel. Thus the leading features of the country are: (1) the Maritime Plain, interrupted by (2) Carmel; (3) the Low Hills or Shephelah; (4) the Western Range, cut in two by (5) Esdraelon, and running S into the (6) Negev; (7) the Jordan Valley; (8) the Eastern Range.

The rivers of Palestine are the Jordan with its lakes, Huleh (Waters of Merom) and Gennesaret (Sea of Galilee), and its E tributaries, the Yarmuk and the Jabbok; the Arnon, flowing into the Dead Sea; and the Kishon, into the Mediterranean.

N of Carmel are natural harbors, large enough for the ships of the Phoenicians, whose chief seats were Accho (Ptolemais), and (farther N) Tyre, Sarepta, Sidon, and Byblus (Beirut); S of Carmel the shores are level to the mouths of the Nile. The seaports Caesarea, Joppa, Ascalon, and Gaza have no natural harbors.

The 4 long lines above described, with their breaks and additions, render Palestine a marvelous mixture of hilly and level country, with all kinds of climate from the tropical oasis of the Jordan plain to the sub-Alpine slopes of Hermon (9150 ft.). The subtropical coastland has a mean annual temperature of 69° F. In the Ghor in May a temperature has been observed of 110° F. in the shade at noon, and 88° F. in the shade at 8 A.M. Jerusalem (3167 ft. above the sea) has an average temperature of 63° F., ranging from 39° in January to 102° in August (the greatest extremes observed since 1860); the average variation of temperature within 24 hours being no less than 51° F. These changes are characteristics of the whole of Syria.

The brokenness of the land, and especially the mixture of hill and plain, predisposed Palestine to be a land of tribes and clans. The Western Range, both S and N of Esdraelon, with Gilead on the Eastern Range, comprised Israel's proper territory. This confinement to the hills secured Israel's independence and purity. The plains and the valleys were the portions of the country open to the traffic and the war of foreign empires. Though the ancient highways of trade between the Euphrates and the Nile, and from Tyre to the Arabian Gulf, passed through the entire length of Palestine, Israel was planted aloof from all these in mountain isolation; long after her neighbors had succumbed to Assyrian war or Greek culture, Judah preserved her independence and her loyalty to the law of her God.

palm′er·worm

A name more properly applied to certain insects other than the locust (particularly butterflies and moths), but the locust is intended where the translation is used.

palm tree

The date palm. Phoenicia means "land of palm"; Bethany "house of dates."

pan′nag

Possibly a place name; other possible translations are early figs; a kind of confection.

pa·py′rus

An aquatic reed, used as a writing material in Egypt from the early 3rd millennium B.C.

par′a·ble

(Gr. "comparison") The statement of a spiritual truth, a law or principle of the kingdom of God, by means of a description or narration of facts in the world of nature or in human experience, which are represented in such a way as to illuminate facts in the world of spirit.

par′a·clete

A Greek word, applied to Jesus Christ to indicate His function in making intercession for the people with God the Father. It implies one who pleads for, counsels, strengthens, comforts.

Par′thi·a

A country on the SE of the Caspian Sea. The kingdom of Parthia, founded 248 B.C. by Ar-

The papyrus, or paper reed, from the pith of which one of the principal writing materials of ancient time was made

saces II, grew into an empire, and contended on equal terms with Rome.

Pass′o·ver

The feast commemorating the deliverance from Egypt. It is one of the 3 annual great festivals, and occurs in the spring; also called the Feast of Unleavened Bread. *See* Feasts.

pas′to·ral let′ters, pas′to·ral e·pis′tles

The 3 epistles of Paul in which he gives instructions to Timothy and Titus for their ministry. It is believed that 1 Tim and Tit were written after the imprisonment mentioned in Acts 28, 30, 31, and 2 Tim during a 2nd imprisonment at Rome.

Pat′mos

A very rugged island south of Samos, where John wrote the Apocalypse, having, according to tradition, been banished to it during the reign of Domitian.

pa′tri·archs

The forefathers of the Israelites. Its strictest application is to the forefathers mentioned in Genesis. A few later names are added, such as David and Daniel.

Paul

Saul of Tarsus was the son of Hebrew parents, and belonged to the tribe of Benjamin. He was above his brethren in intellect and influence, as his namesake, the king, had been in mere physique. He was born to the privilege of Roman citizenship, and is best known by his Roman name of Paul; and he used his birthright for his own protection when persecuted as a

Palm tree

Christian (Acts 22.25-29). He thought highly of Tarsus, his birthplace, where he was brought up as a strictly Jewish child, getting possibly some insight into pagan literature, but mainly occupied with the Hebrew Canon. At the age of 13 he was most likely transferred to Jerusalem, where his sister was, and there put under the charge of Gamaliel, the son of Simeon, and grandson of the renowned Hillel.

Saul seems to have been led into deep antagonism to Christ and His cause and stood ready to undertake a crusade against the Christian cause. Accordingly, when Stephen earned the crown of martyrdom, the young Saul did not hesitate to hold the raiment of the witnesses who secured his condemnation and stoned him; he obtained authority from the chief priests to hunt down the Christians, and prosecuted his work of extermination. As he approached Damascus on his mission of persecution, he was overwhelmed by a dazzling splendor such as outshone the Syrian sun, and heard a voice saying to him, "Saul, Saul, why persecutest thou me?" Most probably the stricken persecutor recognized the voice; but to make sure, he cried, "Who art thou, Lord?" and received an answer, "I am Jesus, whom thou persecutest." He is directed to go on to Damascus, where he will receive further light. Here his lost sight is restored, he is baptized by Ananias, and receives the gift of the Holy Ghost.

He is now driven by the Spirit, as Christ had been before him, into the wilderness, and in Arabia he spends a considerable season in meditation. Three years enabled him to elaborate that view of Christianity now usually called Paulinism. The young rabbi at Gamaliel's feet becomes, at the feet of Christ, the great teacher of the church, translating Christianity into a universal religion.

On his 1st missionary journey he went to Antioch, where he and Barnabas were "set apart" for the work. They went then with John Mark to Salamis and Paphos on Cyprus, then to the mainland to Perga, where John Mark left them, and to Antioch in Pisidia; Iconium, Lystra, and Derbe. They reversed the route to return, and sailed from Atalia to Seleucia, the seaport of Antioch in Syria.

After a journey to Jerusalem and a conference there, Paul set off on his 2nd journey, which took him, with Silas and later with Timothy, into Syria and Cilicia, Derbe and Lystra, into Phrygia and Galatia, and into Macedonia, where new churches were established at Philippi, Thessalonica, and Beroea. There had been many stops along the way. Then he went into Athens, where he spoke in the market place, the Agora. From there he went to Corinth and Ephesus, and continued by boat to Caesarea in Palestine.

He went to Jerusalem and from there to Antioch where he lingered for some time, writing and resting. Then he set out on a 3rd journey, going again to Galatia and Phrygia, then on to Ephesus, where he stayed for more than 2 years. It was at Ephesus that there was a great riot against the new religion that Paul was preaching, instigated by those whose living was threatened, as they felt, by the threat to the great temple of Artemis, visited by worshipers from far and near. From Ephesus Paul went to Macedonia and Achaia, then to Troas to take ship for Caesarea, again with many stops along the way. He then went to Jerusalem.

In Jerusalem he was accused of taking Greeks into the inner Temple, and soldiers broke up the crowd that attacked him. His statement of Roman citizenship prevented his being scourged. He was turned over to Felix the procurator, who kept him imprisoned for 2 years. His successor, Festus, also found himself embarrassed by his prisoner, but Paul's appeal to Caesar, the right of a Roman citizen, led to his being sent to Rome. This too was an eventful voyage. Paul was allowed to visit friends along the way, and was not chained when the ship was wrecked at Malta. At Rome he was detained for 2 years under a sort of house arrest, then freed. He visited a number of the churches, but was again arrested and returned to Rome. The former tolerance was gone, and Christians were being prosecuted, having been blamed for the great fire in Rome. It is presumed that Paul was beheaded, following this 2nd trial.

Paul, the E·pis'tles (Let'ters) of

Of these we possess thirteen. They were written by amanuenses, and authenticated by the addition of a paragraph in Paul's own writing or by his signature. With the exception of the letters to Timothy and Titus, which are still questioned by some critics, those ascribed to Paul are generally received as his.

These 13 letters all belong to the later half of Paul's ministry. In A.D. 52 or 53, the 2 letters to the Thessalonians were written. Then follows another blank period till 57 or 58, when, within the space of a year, the 4 great epistles to the Corinthians, Galatians, and Romans were produced. Again there occurs an interval of 5 years till 63, when the 4 "prison epistles" appeared; and finally, yet another gap, until 66-68, when he sent the pastoral letters to Timothy and Titus.

In the earliest group the second coming and the kingdom of Christ are in the foreground. The 2nd group exhibits the doctrines of grace in conflict with Judaism, and also shows us in detail the difficulties Christianity had to overcome in the social ideas and customs of the Roman world. The 3rd group is characterized by a calmer spirit, a higher reach of Christian thought, more constructive statements regarding Christ's person. In the 4th group we have chiefly instructions regarding church order, interspersed with passages of remarkable beauty and richness.

pearl

Also translated ruby, crystal. Pearls were found in the Red Sea.

pel'i·can, vul'ture

Identification of the bird intended is not definite.

Pen·ta·teuch

(Gr. "five books") The 5 books of Moses in the OT. The Jews named these, from their chief contents, Torah Law; and the Greek translators gave each book its distinctive title; hence the names in our Bible: Genesis, origin, of the world and of men; Exodus, departure of the Israelites from Egypt; Leviticus, the book of the law of the priests; Numbers, from the numbering of the people related in it; Deuteronomy, second Law. The authorship of the Pentateuch has been the subject of much controversy.

Pen·te·cost

(Gr. "fiftieth") The 50th day after the ceremony of the barley sheaf in the Passover observances. On this day occurred the gift of the Holy Spirit to the church, and for this is observed by the Christian church.

per·fume

Perfume was important in the rites of worship and as a luxury item. Moreover, perfumes were important articles of commerce, originating as they did in India, Somaliland, Persia, Ceylon, Palestine, and the Red Sea. They were manufactured and blended, and in addition to Temple incense were used in spicing wine, on clothing and furniture, and in embalming.

Per·ga·mos, Per·ga·mum

A town of Mysia in Asia Minor, in the valley of the Caicus. Near the top of its acropolis hill, 1,000 ft. above the valley, are the ruins of many temples and a great theater. It is called the most spectacular Hellenistic city in Asia Minor.

Per·iz·zite, Pher·ez·ite

(Heb. "dweller of the open country"?) One of the peoples found in Canaan when the Israelites arrived.

Per·sians

The Persians were originally a Median tribe which settled in Persia, on the E side of the Persian Gulf. They were Aryans, their language belonging to the eastern division of the Indo-European group. One of their chiefs, Teispes, conquered Elam in the time of the decay of the Assyrian Empire, and established himself in the district of Anshan. His descendants branched off into 2 lines, one line ruling in Anshan, while the other remained in Persia. Cyrus II, king of Anshan, finally united the divided power, conquered Media, Lydia, and Babylonia, and carried his arms into the far E. His son, Cambyses, added Egypt to the empire, which, however, fell to pieces after his death. It was reconquered and thoroughly organized by Darius, son of Hystaspes, whose dominions extended from India to the Danube. Scripture mentions Cyrus, who released the captive Jews (Ezra 1.1); Darius, who confirmed the decree of Cyrus (Ezra 6.1); and Artaxerxes (Ezra 4.7; 7.1).

Pe·shit·ta

The Syriac version of the Bible, otherwise called the Peshitta (which means either simple or vulgate), belongs to the 3rd century. The OT part was made direct from the Hebrew, with occasional reference to the Septuagint, as early as the 1st century. It was very likely made in the first instance for Jewish proselytes. There is another Syriac version made directly from the Septuagint as it stood in the Hexapla.

Pe·ter

(Gr. "rock") Surname of that Simon, son of John, and brother of Andrew, who, originally a fisherman near Capernaum, became the first apostle of Jesus. His character vacillates between obstinate resolution and momentary cowardice, as is shown in the story of his denial of his Master. In Paul's letters he appears as a "pillar" of the primitive church and the "Apostle of the Circumcision." He was married and was accompanied by his wife on his journeys. Papal claims of primacy for Peter have appealed for support to Mt 16.17-19; Lk 22.32; and Jn 21.15-17; but are set aside by such passages as Mt 20.20-28; Mk 9.35; 10.35-45; Lk 9.48; 22.26.

Peter is not mentioned in Acts after the council of Jerusalem, A.D. 50, but Gal 2.11 refers to a subsequent visit by him to Antioch. His history after that incident has been overlaid with legends. It is impossible for him to have spent 25 years in Rome, though it is probable that his last years were passed there, and that he there suffered martyrdom. It is less probable that he and Paul were put to death at the same time. If "Babylon" is not, as some suppose, a mystical name for Rome, Babylon was the scene of his labor at some period after the visit to Antioch.

Pe·ter, the First and Sec·ond Let·ters of

Two NT epistles. *The First Letter of Peter* was probably written by the apostle Peter from Rome between A.D. 64 and 67 to Christians who had fled Asia Minor. It admonishes the pilgrims to have hope and courage and to trust in the power of God. *The Second Letter of Peter* was written by an unknown Christian leader, perhaps a disciple of Peter's, in the middle of the 2nd century. It warns of false teachers who had come into the early church and urges Christians to be brave and patient.

Pe·tra

The Roman name of the Nabataean city close to Mount Hor. No evidence of an Edomite settlement has been found. It seems to have been begun about the 4th century B.C.

pha·raoh

(Egyp. "the great house") One of the designations of the royal palace was "the Great House," as early as 2500 B.C. By 1500 B.C. it had become the designation or title of the ruler who lived in the palace.

Phar·i·sees

(Heb. "separated") The name given by their opponents to the party that arose among the Jewish scribes after the victory of the Maccabees, and devoted themselves to the most scrupulous fulfilment of the Law as expounded by the scribes.

Phe·ni·ce, Phe·ni·ci·a

See Phoenicia.

Pharaoh Ramses II, thought to have been the pharaoh of the oppression of Israel

Phi·le'mon

The receiver of the short letter of Paul which bears his name. He lived at Colossae, where his house was the meeting place of the Christian community.

Phi·le'mon, the Let'ter of Paul to

This NT epistle is a personal letter in which the apostle beseeches Philemon to take back a runaway slave, Onesimus. The slave had come to Rome, where Paul was being held prisoner, and there had been converted by Paul.

Phil'ip

(Gr. "lover of horses") The name of 4 persons in the NT.

1. Philip the Apostle, born in Bethsaida, one of the first to be called, and mentioned in the feeding of the 5000 from 5 loaves and 2 fishes, which Jesus blessed and broke.

2. Philip the Evangelist, a Greek-speaking Christian in Jerusalem, who following the martyrdom of Stephen fled to Samaria, where he became a successful missionary.

3. Philip the Tetrarch, son of Herod the Great and Cleopatra of Jerusalem, who ruled Batanea, Trachonitis, Auranitis, Gaulanitis, and Panias with justness and benevolence. He founded and built the city of Caesarea.

4. Herod, a half-brother of Philip the Tetrarch, son of Herod the Great and Mariamne, first husband of Herodias, who in Mk 6.17 and elsewhere is also called Philip.

Other persons of this name important in the history of biblical times are Philip II, king of Macedonia, 359-336 B.C., father of Alexander the Great; Philip V, king of Macedonia 220-179 B.C.; a Phrygian appointed, probably in 169 B.C., to be governor of Jerusalem; a regent of the Seleucid state appointed by Antiochus Epiphanes at his death (164 B.C.) and quickly overthrown by Lycias.

Phi·lip'pi·ans, the Let'ter of Paul to the

Written while Paul was in prison in Rome. Philippi was an important town of Macedonia on the great highway from E to W. Philip II of Macedonia had named it after himself. In Paul's time it was a Roman "colony," a settlement of veteran soldiers. From Philippi, where he had been at first grievously maltreated, he "once and again" received pecuniary aid. The letter was written to acknowledge the receipt of such a gift. It is the most "epistolary of all the epistles;" in it the apostle pours out his heart to his friends, and entreats them to be "of one accord, one mind."

Phi·lis'tines

One of the "People of the Sea," the possessors of Philistia, the coastland from Joppa to the Wadi Ghazzeh, with its 5 cities, Gaza, Ashkelon, Ashdod, Ekron, and Gath. Though not of the Semitic race, they adopted the Semitic language of Canaan. They came from Caphtor (Crete). They were repulsed by Ramses III of Egypt after their arrival at the coast and capture of the 5 cities, until then controlled by Egypt. The Israelites warred with and defeated them, and they disappeared as a separate people.

Phoe·ni'ci·a, Phe·ni'ci·a, Phe·ni'ce

A country stretching 120 mi. along the coast N of Palestine, averaging 20 mi. E to W. It was the great trading nation of its time, its sailors going to distant lands and often establishing colonies such as Carthage. The most valuable and profitable of many items of commerce was purple dye made from the sea snail murex. As cities were rebuilt in the same site after destruction and the sites are still occupied, excavation has been difficult. However, Egyptian objects of 3000 B.C. have been found, indicating active trade at that date. The country was prosperous at the time of Christ.

The Phoenicians are closely linked with the development of writing and the alphabet.

Phryg'i·a, Phryg'i·ans

An area and people of Asia Minor. Their boundaries shifted constantly under pressure of aggressive neighbors.

phy·lac'te·ries

Small containers, in which were placed quotations from Scripture, bound on the arm and forehead during prayer, and sometimes called amulets.

Pi'late, Pon'ti·us

Procurator of Judea from A.D. 26 to 36. Jesus was taken before him, accused of stirring up the people, but Pilate was not impressed and tried to avoid action by referring the matter to Herod Antipas. Herod also failed to act, and Jesus was returned to Pilate. Again Pilate found no fault with Him, washed his hands, and turned Jesus over to the mob to be crucified, after having Him scourged.

Unverified reports exist to the effect that Pilate himself became a Christian, and Eusebius quoted earlier reports that Pilate committed suicide.

pil'lar of cloud and fire

The cloud by day and the fire by night led the Israelites through the wilderness. The image may be that of cressets such as were used in Solomon's temple, which burned with flame and smoke.

pine, pine tree, cy'press, fir, wild ol'ive, box

The identification of evergreens and cone-bearing trees is uncertain. It is probable that authors of the Bible were not interested in precise botanical classification, and may not have been able to make such classifications.

Pis'gah, Mount

This is probably the present Ras es-Siyaghah, in the Abarim mountain range, and stands opposite Jericho.

Plowing with cattle, and with a camel

plane tree, chest'nut

As the chesnut or chestnut is very rare in the countries of the Bible, this is probably an error of translation. The plane tree does grow there.

Ple'ia·des, sev'en stars

A configuration of 7 stars in the constellation Taurus (Job 9.9; 38.31).

pome'gran·ate

A fruit found in Palestine. It is prominent in ancient art and in mythology.

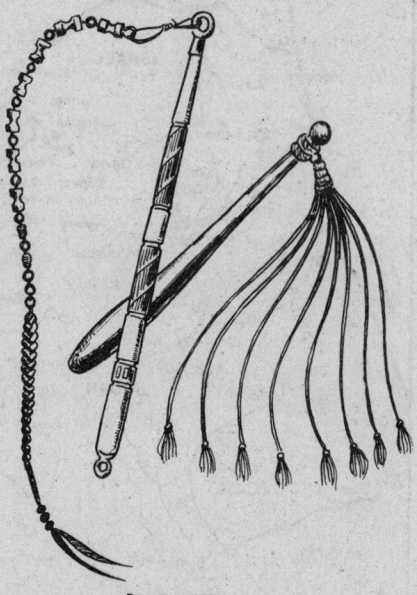

Roman scourges.

Pomegranate

pound, mi'na

Greek measures, mina and lipta, and the Latin libra apparently were measures of capacity and also of weight, 12 ounces, as is the Troy pound. *See* Weights.

priests

Ministers at the altar, descendants of Aaron, to whose family the priestly office was restricted by the Levitical legislation. In later times they traced their descent from the priestly family of Zadok, the contemporary of David. The priest was subject to special laws. His duties were mainly three: to minister at the Sanctuary, to teach the people, and to communicate the divine will. His dress, of white linen, consisted of short breeches; a coat without seam, reaching to the ankles; a girdle; a cap shaped like a cup. The priests were divided by David into 24 courses, each course usually officiating for a week at a time. The "second priest" was probably the same as the "ruler of the house of God" and the "captain of the Temple." As teachers of the people the priests were superseded, first by the prophets, afterward by the scribes. The "chief priests" of the NT were the acting high priest, former high priests still living, and members of these privileged families.

The High Priest was the spiritual chief of the nation. The head of the house of Aaron held this office. He was subject to special laws. His special duties were to oversee the Sanctuary, its service, and its treasures; to perform the service of the Day of Atonement, when he was required to enter the Holy of Holies; and to consult God by Urim and Thummim. It was after the Exile, and when Israel was under foreign domination, that the High Priest became also the political representative of the nation. His official garments, besides those common to the priests, were: the ephod, of blue, purple, scarlet, and fine linen, interwoven with gold thread, not otherwise identified; the breastplate, of the same material, which had, outside, twelve precious stones set in gold in four rows, each bearing the name of a tribe of Israel, and, inside, in a pocket, the Urim and Thummim; the sleeveless robe of the ephod, of dark blue, with a fringe of pomegranates and bells; the miter, a turban.

Pris·cil'la

See Aquila.

prod'i·gal son

A dramatic and vivid parable of repentance (Lk 15.11-32).

proph'ets

The books which, in the Hebrew Bible, immediately follow the Pentateuch, are Joshua, Judges, Ruth (by some considered an adjunct of Judges), Samuel, and Kings, which give a connected history of the nation from the death of Moses to the Babylonian Captivity, and all the books that we call prophetical, with the exception of Daniel.

The "former prophets" are so called simply from their position.

Among the latter prophets, the "Twelve," often termed minor prophets, have been placed together and reckoned as one book, owing to their being written on one roll.

Daniel, though a prophetical or rather apocalyptical book, is not put along with the other prophets; the most probable explanation being that it did not exist, at least in its present form, when the other prophetical books were included in the OT Canon.

Pottery from Tell-el-Obeid, near Ur, an ancient settlement in Babylonia

pros'e·lyte

(Gr. "newcomer, visitor") This word in OT times meant a person in a community not his own; perhaps a refugee, a stranger, an alien. In NT times it had come to mean a convert. Some of these embraced Judaism completely, accepting circumcision, the rite of baptism, and sacrifice. Others were of the persuasion of the Hellenists: they were admitted to worship without circumcision or acceptance of the Jewish law.

Prov'erbs, the Book of

The Book of Proverbs is included with the OT Wisdom literature, and it has customarily been attributed to Solomon. Contained in the book are short, pithy sayings of common sense and sound advice that relate to all ways of life; in short, a practical, everyday philosophy of living.

Psalms, the Book of

The first book in the group known as the Writings. These are hymns of both Judaism and Christianity. Psalms is a collection of poems written over a long period of time by various authors. They express the heart of humanity in all generations through a variety of religious experiences. Originally the poems were chanted or sung to the accompaniment of a stringed instrument. One of the characteristics of this Hebrew poetry is parallelism; that is, the second line reiterates the idea of the first line.

psal'ter·y

This instrument is found on Assyrian reliefs. Strings are drawn over a box resonator and struck with a rod.

pub'li·cans, tax col·lec'tors

The alien government, whether of Rome or of its deputy princes, the Herods, collected its taxes and customs through speculators, who bought up the right of collecting the revenue (publicum) for their own advantage. These men were called *publicani* by the Romans. The corresponding word in the NT covers not only the tax-farmer but also his collectors. These were often natives and were classed by the Jews not only with the social outcasts but also with the heathen, as if outside Israel altogether. Christ's gracious attitude to them was therefore specially criticized and his hopeful sympathy went to their hearts.

Pul, Put

King of Assyria, Tiglath-pileser III. Also an unidentified region.

pulse, veg′e·ta·ble

Things sown.

pur′ple

This dye was obtained from a species of mollusk abundant on the Phoenician coast and produced colors in the red-purple field. Garments so dyed were of great price.

py′garg, i′bex

A white-rumped antelope.

Q

Queen of Heav′en

Jeremiah censured the Jews for burning incense to and worshiping the Queen of Heaven. Precisely what goddess was so called by Jeremiah is not clear. Ishtar, goddess of love and fertility, was so designated as was Ashtoreth, the Canaanite fertility goddess. The Egyptians had a goddess Antit, called in Canaan Anat, also a fertility goddess, and all were called Queen of Heaven.

R

Ra′hab

(Heb. "wide, broad") 1. In the OT, the name of the woman who sheltered Joshua's men sent out as spies to Jericho.

2. A mythological dragon conquered by Yahweh, as mentioned in several poetic passages of the OT. The dragon Rahab was used figuratively to designate Egypt.

3. In the NT a woman in the genealogy of Jesus.

rain

Rain falls in Palestine from December to March. The beginning of the rainy season is called the "early," the end of it the "latter" rain. The summers are almost rainless.

reap′ing

Harvesting grain by hand. Barley ripened in April and May. The grain was cut halfway down the stalk by a sickle made of flints and tied in sheaves, or cut close to the head. After the 10th century B.C. the sickle blade was curved. The harvesting of all the grains required 6 or 7 weeks and the law forbade careful gleaning so there might be a share for the poor.

Re′chab, Re′chab·ites

(Heb. "rider"?) The Rechabites were a seminomadic people, roaming in the wilderness.

Red Sea

A body of water between Arabia and Africa, about 1200 mi. in length and from 130 to 250 mi. in width. The water has depths of 7200 ft. The Israelite crossing must have been at the bend of the Red Sea or through the lakes between it and the Nile Delta and the Mediterranean; there are several possible routes, but that used has not been determined.

ref′uge

See City of Refuge.

Reph′a·im

1. The dead, the Shades.

2. The pre-Israelite people in Palestine, reputed to be giants.

3. A valley near Jerusalem.

Rev·e·la′tion to John, the

This is the only prophetic book in the NT. Generally presumed to have been written by John, one of the apostles of Christ, about A.D. 95 or 96, the book is addressed to the seven Christian churches in Asia Minor, whose members were being persecuted by Roman officials. The images and illusions of Revelation are difficult for us to understand today, but to the persecuted members of the seven churches John's message was clearly one of hope, courage, and faith in times of trouble; and that on the Lord's day the faithful would be greatly rewarded. It is characterized by the use of symbolical visions as the vehicle of prophecy. The model for this mode of prophecy was set by the Book of Daniel. The theme of the Book is the gradual triumph of the kingdom of God, culminating in the Second Advent.

rie, rye

This is a grain of colder climates than Palestine. It is now believed that spelt is the grain to which this word refers.

riv′ers

In Mesopotamia the Euphrates and the Tigris and in Egypt the Nile were important to the agriculture and commercial life of the countries. Palestine had the Jordan, the Sea of Galilee, and the Dead Sea, but the people were not dependent on their river to the same degree as were the Egyptians and Mesopotamians. Palestine also had smaller streams, some of which at least ceased to flow in the dry season.

rocks

Clay, dust, earth, flint, lime, stone, and sand are words of more or less frequent occurrence in the Bible; but, as they are employed in their ordinary sense, they require no comment. It may, however, be observed that the firstnamed was used in making bricks, which very commonly, as in Egypt and in Assyria, were not burnt but sun-dried. In this case, straw was often added to increase the tenacity of the material. Some of the limestones of Palestine and the adjacent regions, as well as those of Egypt, afford excellent building stones, and certain varieties can be polished. The former are generally of a very pale cream-color.

rod, staff

The "rod and staff" of Ps 23.4 probably refer

to two instruments still used by Eastern shepherds, the first a heavy-headed club for driving off wild animals, the second a curved stick for guiding the sheep.

roe'buck

See fallow deer.

roll

Long strips of leather or papyrus that were written upon and then wound upon a spindle from which they could be wound off onto a second spindle as read (Ezek 2.9).

Ro'man cit'i·zen·ship

A prized possession in the time of Christ, conferring certain privileges; obtained by birth, grant, reward, or purchase. Since Paul was free born, he must have inherited his citizenship (Acts 22.27, 28).

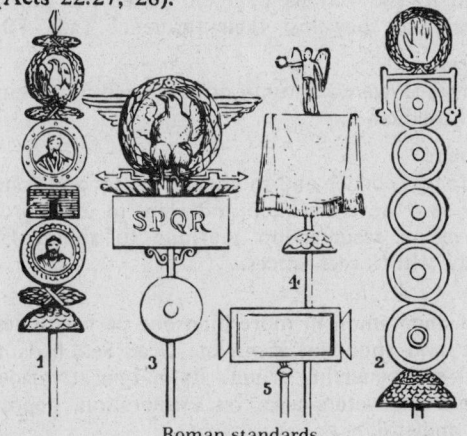

Roman standards

Ro'mans, the Let'ter of Paul to the

This book stands first among the Pauline letters, partly owing to its doctrinal importance, partly on account of its being addressed to the metropolis of the world. It was written from Corinth about 58 A.D. The purpose of the letter is to secure the active support of the church in Rome for his missionary program. Paul stresses the universality of man's sin but that God saves all men through faith in Christ. He discusses the place of Israel in God's plan of salvation and how Christians should conduct themselves.

Roman soldiers

Rome

A city in Italy, founded some 700 years after the entrance of Israel into the Promised Land, and at about the beginning of the ministry of Isaiah. By the time of Christ it had become the capital of an empire reaching from Britain to the Euphrates, and from the Black Sea into Africa. Christianity had reached to Rome, and there was a thriving church there previous to Paul's visit. The Jews were expelled from Rome about A.D. 50, but were soon allowed to return. It was here that Paul and Peter presumably suffered martyrdom about A.D. 64.

roof

In the East the roof is flat and usually surfaced with a 10-inch layer of tamped clay, in which grass grows in the rainy season (Ps 129.6). It is extensively used for drying, storage, and even for sleeping in the warmer months, thus needing a protecting wall about its edges (Deut 22.8).

rose

The context indicates that the true rose is not always intended; probably the word is at times used figuratively as well. The crocus may have been intended in some cases, and the oleander, the rose of Sharon. The rose of Jericho is a dried weed, which opens when put in water.

Ro·set'ta Stone

Found in 1799 in the Nile Delta, this stone had inscribed upon it the same decree in 3 languages: hieroglyphic Egyptian, Demotic, and Greek. With this key the hieroglyphic and Demotic scripts were deciphered within 35 years.

ru'by

The true ruby has not been found in excavated sites in the Near East. The red stone may possibly be red coral, or of the nature of the garnet.

rue, dill

Rue is a heavily scented perennial shrub widely used as a condiment and in medicines. Some early manuscripts have in Lk 11.42 dill instead of rue, and dill may have been intended.

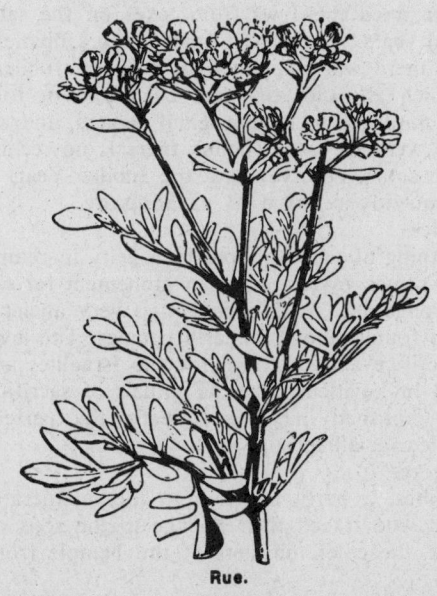

Rue.

rush

Reedlike plants, found in swampy areas and along river banks.

Ruth, the Book of

The story of Ruth, a Moabitess who, after her husband's death, accompanied her mother-in-law Naomi to Bethlehem, there married Boaz, and was thereby an ancestress of David. The book is an idyll of family life, often regarded as a supplement to the book of Judges, but possibly of a later date.

rye

See rie.

S

Sab'bath

(Heb. "cessation") The Israelites apparently adopted the calendar of the Canaanites about them, related to the Babylonian Calendar described below, before the giving of the Ten Commandments established the Sabbath as an ordinance forever. After the resurrection of Christ on the 1st day of the week, that day came to replace the 7th as the Christian Sabbath. The Babylonians observed a day of rest, called Sabattu, described as "a day of rest for the heart." On that day it was forbidden to eat cooked meat, to put on fresh clothes, to offer sacrifices, to ride in a chariot, and the like. It fell on the 7th, 14th, 19th, 21st, and 28th days of the lunar month, the 19th day being the 49th day, or 7th week, from the 1st of the preceding month. The Babylonian account of the Creation makes the Creator say to the moon: "On the 7th day halve thy disk; stand upright with its first half on the Sabbath (Sabattu)."

sab·bat'i·cal year

Every seventh year, during which, according to the law, the fields and vineyards were to be uncultivated, and their produce to be shared with the poor and the stranger and the beasts of the field. Debts of Israelites to Israelites, were to be remitted. Alexander the Great and Julius Caesar freed the Jews from taxes on the sabbatical years. After seven times seven sabbatical years there was appointed a Year of Jubilee, in which all lands that had been sold or forfeited returned to their original owners, and all slaves were set free. Though there is no record of the actual observance of the Jubilee Year, it is frequently referred to in Scripture.

sac'ri·fice

Something of value offered to a deity in return for expected favors, or as an atonement for sin or wrongdoing. Such a custom is very ancient, and is found among all early peoples. The laws of sacrifice and offerings for the Israelites are found in Leviticus. The OT rituals of sacrifice were abolished in Christ's death, the perfect sacrifice for all through all time.

Sad'du·cees

Zadokites, a party attached to the aristocratic priests who traced their lineage to the sons of Zadok, the chief ministers of the Temple from the time of Solomon. They were an exclusive caste, drawn from men of wealth and position. While the Pharisees found their strongholds in the synagogues and schools of the towns and villages, the Sadducees had their center in the Temple at Jerusalem. They were open to worldly influences of all kinds, including in later times Greek culture and Roman statecraft. Their main interest was political, and their guiding principle was to keep in with any power that secured to them their monopoly of office. They acknowledged as binding only the written Law, rejecting the traditions of the scribes; ignored the Messianic hope and the doctrine of the resurrection; and denied alike the existence of angels and spirits and the overruling or cooperating hand of God in the actions of men. After the fall of Jerusalem they lost their influence (A.D. 70).

saf'fron

Purple-flowered autumn crocus, used in cooking and medicines.

Sa·lo'me

Wife of Zebedee and mother of James and John. She saw the crucifixion and went to our Lord's grave on resurrection morning to anoint His body with sweet spices.

salt

Not uncommon in more than one part of Palestine, and abundant about the Dead Sea, beds of rock-salt occurring around its margin at various levels. Its waters also, on evaporation, deposit the mineral.

sal·u·ta'tions

Among the Jews the salutation was "Peace be with thee" and the like. The reply was, "The Lord bless thee." It was only in great haste or intense absorption that they were omitted.

Sa·ma'ri·a

A city in Palestine 42 mi. N of Jerusalem and 25 mi. E of the Mediterranean, founded by Omri about 920 B.C. as his capital. It was taken by Sargon in 722 B.C., and rebuilt by Herod the Great, who named it Sebaste. Excavation has revealed a magnificently built city, beautifully designed. The province of Samaria, the central part of Palestine, stretched from the sea to the Jordan Valley, coinciding with the land of the half-tribe of Manasseh.

Sa·mar'i·tans

The mixed population, partly of Israelitish descent, which the restored exiles found in Northern Israel. They were the hated neighbors and rivals of the Jewish theocracy. "Samaritan" was to the Jew a name of contempt and reproach (John 8.48).

Sa·mar'i·tan Pen'ta·teuch

A Qumran MS (Dead Sea Scrolls) verifies its antiquity and faithfulness of transmission, and other ancient scrolls indicate its antiquity. It is extant in MSS of very nearly as great age as the Hebrew.

Sam'son

(Heb. "sun's man") A judge or hero of the tribe of Dan, the son of Manoah, a native of Zorah, which belonged to Dan. He was a "Nazarite unto God" from his birth, the first Nazarite mentioned in Scripture. The narrative does not represent him as a leader of the people, either in war or peace; it consists of personal exploits against the Philistines.

Sam'u·el

The last of the Judges, an Ephraimite, a prophet of the 11th century B.C., who by wise administration in war and peace gained great authority in Israel, but had at last to yield to the popular wish, and resign his leadership to a king. He spent his later years at Ramah, founding and directing schools of the prophets.

Sam'u·el, the First and Sec'ond Books of

The two books of Samuel are one in the Hebrew. First and Second Samuel contain the history of Israel from Eli to the old age of David, particularly material concerning the religious and moral conditions of the period. Samuel is the great prophet-judge who helps to unite the scattered tribes under one king, Saul. The history of the reigns of Saul and David is also recorded.

san'dal

A sole of leather fastened to the foot by a strap or thong, a latchet. On the ancient monuments many types are shown, but most persons are usually depicted barefoot.

San'he·drin

The senate, or supreme Jewish court of justice for enforcing the Mosaic system of sacred law in national and civic life. It existed as early as the Grecian period. It sat under the presidency of the high priest, and consisted of some 71 members (chief priests, elders, scribes), among whom the priestly aristocracy generally had the upper hand, or a lower council of 23 members. It lost the power of life and death under the Romans though in moments of special excitement this limit was not always respected.

sap'phire, lap'is laz'u·li

Properly a blue variety of corundum but in ancient times the name may have denoted the beautifully mottled blue stone now called lapis lazuli. This is a silicate of various bases, softer than steel and still much valued for ornaments. It was obtained in Ethiopia and Persia. *See* Jacinth.

Sar'dis

Capital of Lydia. It was a wealthy commercial town, with a strong citadel.

sar'di·us, sar'dine

A reddish translucent variety of chalcedony darker than carnelian.

sar'do·nyx

A banded form of chalcedony.

Sar'gon

(Akkad. "the king is legitimate") Sargon I (1850 B.C.?) was a king of Assyria, listed on tablets and monuments as the 27th. Sargon II (722-705 B.C.) ended the kingdom of Israel by the conquest and destruction of Samaria, and deported more than 27,000 of its people; they disappeared or were absorbed in Media. Other conquered peoples were moved into Samaria to replace them.

Sa'ron

See Sharon.

sa'tyrs

(Heb. "hairy ones") Elsewhere the word means he-goats; but in some passages it means demons in the shape of goats, to whom the heathen sacrificed. Such satyrs are depicted on the Egyptian monuments.

Saul

Son of Kish, of the tribe of Benjamin, the first king over Israel. He fought successfully against Moab, Ammon, Edom, Zobah, the Philistines, and the Amalekites. Wilfulness in preferring sacrifice to obedience to the divine command before entering on the war against the Philistines, and violation of the curse against the Amalekites, proofs of his failure in allegiance to Jehovah, the true king of Israel, led to his rejection from the kingship. In wild fury he sought to take the life of David and massacred the Gibeonites and the priests of Nob. In the disastrous battle of Gilboa, where the brave Jonathan and two other sons of Saul were slain by the Philistines, he fell in despair upon his sword, and perished.

Stately in presence and demeanor, generous in impulse, upright in character, heroic in action, he yet showed that one act of disobedience, one instance of unfaithfulness, may be the beginning of a fall from a divine call to the highest service.

Saul of Tar'sus

See Paul.

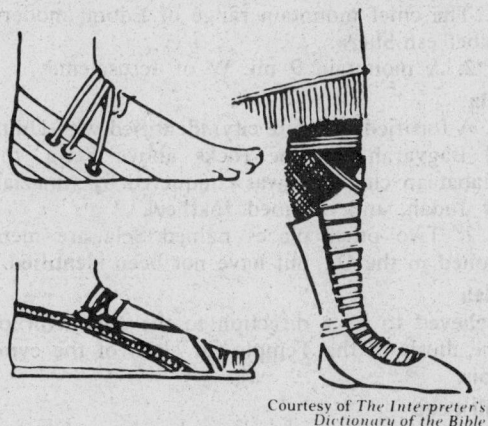

Courtesy of *The Interpreter's Dictionary of the Bible*

Assyrian sandals fastened to the foot by means of thongs (latchets)

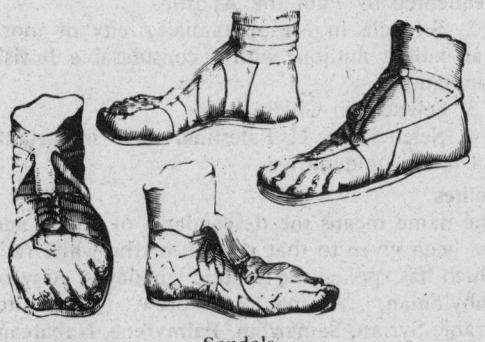

Sandals

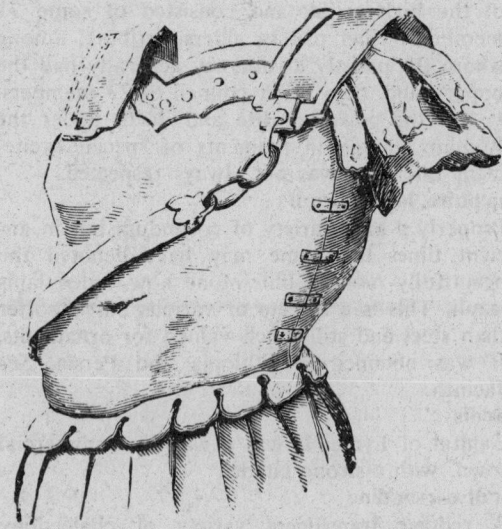

Saul's coat of mail

scape'goat
The goat laden with the sins of the people, and driven away into the wilderness on the Day of Atonement.

scar'let
A costly dye made from an insect similar to the cochineal and found in the Ararat valleys.

scor'pi·on
A lobster-shaped invertebrate with 8 legs, and a poisonous sting in the tail.

Scorpion

scribes
The "scholars" or men of letters to whom belonged the professional study of the Mosaic Law. This special class of non-priestly Jews, beginning in the time of Ezra, had by the Maccabaean period taken this duty under their own peculiar care, and formed a body of traditional law, which, though ever growing by discussion as fresh cases arose, was regarded as equally binding with the written Mosaic Law. Their work included a theoretic development of the Law to cover fresh cases; the teaching of it gratuitously to "disciples," its practical administration in the courts, in which they sat as judges or assessors. They were addressed as "master," "lord," "sir" (Rabbi or Rabboni), "father."

Scrip'ture, Scrip'tures
This first was a general term, meaning simply "writing" or "writings." Then came the more precise designation "The Scripture" or "The Scriptures," as we find these terms employed in the NT to denote what were the sacred books of the Jews at the time, and we now speak of Scripture, Scriptures, or Holy Scripture when we mean the collected writings held sacred by the Christian Church.

Scyth'i·a
The country N of the Euxine and Caspian.

Scyth'i·ans
The Scythians, also called Ashkenaz, moved through the Caucasus into Asia Minor, and made raids of extreme savagery until the Medes defeated and almost destroyed them.

seal, sig'net
Like other Eastern peoples (Babylonians, Egyptians), the Hebrews carried a ring or stamp, or in later times a cylinder engraved with certain figures or characters. This being impressed on a tablet of clay or soft wax served as a signature in a country where very few could write. Sealing with such a signet was also applied to the tomb of Jesus, and to the book in Revelation. Metaphorically, it is used of circumcision, of the Holy Spirit, and of converts as the attestation of Paul's ministry.

sea mon'ster
See Whale.

Se'ir, Mount
1. The chief mountain range of Edom; modern Jabel esh-Shera.

   2. A mountain 9 mi. W of Jerusalem.

Se'la
1. A fortified Edomite city, identified with Umm el Bagyarah, on the rocks above Petra, the Nabatean city. Sela was conquered by Amaziah of Judah, and renamed Joktheel.

   2. Two other places named Sela are mentioned in the OT but have not been identified.

se'lah
Believed to be a direction to the conductor of the music in the Temple for clash of the cymbals.

Se·leu'ci·a
The name of 9 ancient towns, 4 of them of interest to readers of the Bible.

   1. Seleucia in Syria, the port of Antioch, frequented by Paul the Apostle.

   2. Seleucia in Mesopotamia, a city of more than half a million, with a considerable Jewish population.

   3. Seleucia in Cilicia.

   4. Seleucia in N Palestine, once important, but today unidentified.

Sem'ites
The name means the descendants of Shem, and has been given to that portion of the white race which has spoken the Semitic languages: Assyro-Babylonian, Aramaic, Hebrew, Canaanite, Arabic Syrian, Samaritan, Palmyrene, Nabatean,

Phoenician, Moabite, Sabean, Minean, and Ethiopic.

Semitic man, possibly a Hebrew, from a wall painting in Egypt of about the time of Abraham. The man plucks his lyre; the donkey bears a pack, a spear, and a throwing stick

Sen·nach′e·rib
King of Assyria and Babylonia (705-681 B.C.).

Sep′tu·a·gint
The name of the oldest Greek version of the OT, made in Alexandria, which is called after the 70 interpreters who are supposed to have made it, the Septuagint (Lat. "seventy"), and commonly abbreviated by using the Roman numeral LXX. The legend of its formation is as follows. Ptolemy Philadelphus, king of Egypt, at the suggestion of his librarian, Demetrius Phalereus, sent an embassy to Eleazar, the high priest at Jerusalem, to obtain copies of the sacred books of the Jewish law, in order to translate them into Greek. Superb copies were sent, and a body of translators, 70 or 72 in number, were assigned quarters on the island of Pharos. A later tradition says that the translators were all shut up in separate cells, and that when they had finished their work, the translations were found to tally exactly.

There is no doubt that the Pentateuch was translated into Greek in Alexandria as early as the time of Ptolemy Philadelphus (284-246 B.C.). The true account of its origin is that, as there were in Alexandria many Jews who could not read the OT in the original, a Greek version was gradually produced for their use in the 3rd and 2nd centuries B.C.; probably the whole work was completed by 150 B.C. It is, as a translation, very unequal, and it has come down to us in a state of great corruption.

Ser′mon on the Mount
The address which in Mt 5–7 opens the public ministry of Jesus as the Messiah, while in Lk 6.17-49 it appears in a shorter form and at a later stage. The "mount of beatitudes," supposed to have been near the Sea of Galilee, has not been located. The Sermon on the Mount is an exposition of the nature of the kingdom of God and His righteousness. It sets forth in the beatitudes the character, and then, under the figures of the "salt of the earth" and "the light of the world," the duty to the world of the citizens of the Kingdom. After showing that the better righteousness of the Kingdom comes to fulfil and carry to perfection, not to destroy, what was good in the past, it proceeds to unfold the true righteousness with regard to the 6th, 7th, and 3rd commandments. Obedience should carry beyond the language of the commandments. Ch. 6 deals with the religious exercises of alms-giving, prayer, and fasting, and shows that the Christian's relation to his worldly property is to be without greed and avarice, without pursuit of by-ends, but with a single eye, and without anxiety. Ch. 7 forbids rash judgment and profanation of that which is holy, gives encouragement to prayer, lays down the "golden rule" of love, and enforces the necessity of religious decision; then, after describing the test which will distinguish false prophets from true, and false disciples from true, concludes with the double parable of the house and its foundation.

ser′pent
In Palestine more than 30 different kinds of serpents are known, of which some are poisonous. All snakes were considered unclean.

serv′ant
See Deaconess.

sev′en stars
See Pleiades.

Sha′drach, Me′shach, A·bed′ne·go
The Babylonian names of the 3 companions of Daniel, the Hebrew names being Hananiah, Michael, and Azariah. The 4 young men demonstrated the strength of Jewish faith at the hostile Babylonian court.

Shal·ma·ne′ser
(Akkad. "Salmanu is leader") The name of 5 kings of Assyria. The last Shalmaneser V (727-722 B.C.), besieged Samaria and died or was assassinated during the siege.

Shar′on, Sa′ron
(Heb. "plain or level country") From Carmel to some low hills S of Joppa extends the plain or level of Sharon, once covered in the N by a considerable forest, but more cultivated in its southern part.

She′ba
The name of 2 persons and a place, Beer-Sheba, mentioned in the OT, in addition to the queen of Sheba.

She′bat
The 11th month in the Hebrew calendar.

She′chem, Si′chem, Sy′chem
(Heb. "shoulder"?) An ancient Canaanite city near Mount Gerizim, 40 mi. N of Jerusalem. Abraham, Jacob, and Joshua visited Shechem, and Jereboam made it his capital. A small group of Samaritans lives in the modern town, with their synagogue on the S slope of Nablus. Excavations indicate the presence of a town as early as 4000 B.C.

sheep
The first animal mentioned in the Bible. The plains on the coast, the wilderness of the south, the rolling downs of Moab and eastern Bashan,

were and are pasture lands. Sheep were used for sacrifice; otherwise slain only for feasts, or to entertain guests. Ewe's milk was the most valued product of the flock; next in value was the wool. The common breed of today, with the enormous development of fat on the tail, seems to have been the ancient breed of Israel. The Eastern shepherd's life was one of ceaseless watchfulness. At evening the flocks are folded in caves, or in enclosures on the open plain.

shek'el
See Money.

She'lah, Si·lo'ah
(Heb. "pool of the aqueduct") A reservoir of the King's garden in Jerusalem; the lower pool. *See* Siloam.

She'ma
(Heb. "hear") "Hear, O Israel, the Lord our God is one. . . ." The central confession of Jewish faith (Deut 6.4-9; 11.13-21; Num 15.37-41).

She'ol
The abode of the dead.

shep'herd
The patriarchs lived a nomadic and pastoral life and the children of Israel to a large extent continued to be shepherds after their settlement in Canaan. Mount Carmel, Sharon, the hill country S of Hebron, Gilead and Bashan were noted for their pastures. The laborious life of the shepherd is referred to by Jacob. Its characteristic features

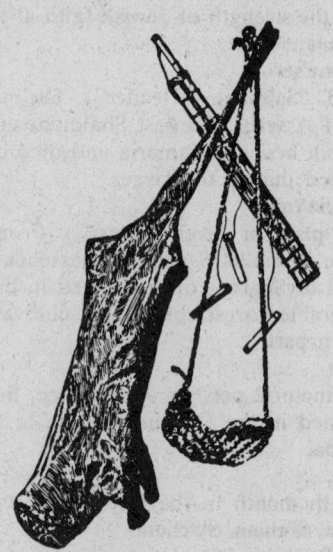

A shepherd's scrip, sling, and pipes

are the same to this day. The dress of a Syrian shepherd consists of a shirt of unbleached cotton, with a leathern girdle, and a large cloak of sheepskin, or wool, or hair, which also serves for a blanket at night. He carries a scrip or provision-pouch of kidskin, a gourd for holding water or milk, an oak staff six feet long, and a weapon in the form of an oak club two feet long, the thick end of which is studded with

nails. The shepherd stays with his sheep night and day. In the morning he counts them under his staff. Obedient to his call, they follow him to their pasture. At sunset they are led into caves or enclosures made of rough stones and the shepherd stays at night in a booth made of branches near the entrance, to be ready to protect his flock from thieves and from wild beasts.

shew'bread, Bread of the Pres'ence
The continual offering of bread in the Temple; 12 loaves, arranged in 2 rows.

shib'bo·leth
A Gilead password, mispronunciation of which by Ephraimites led to their detection.

Shi·lo'ah
An aqueduct in Jerusalem. *See* Siloam.

Shi'loh
A town of Ephraim, now Khirbet Seilum, 10 mi. NE of Bethel, the site of the Tabernacle from the time of Joshua to that of Samuel.

Shi'nar
A name for Babylonia.

Shi'shak
An Egyptian pharaoh (940-915 B.C.), the founder of the Egyptian Twenty-second Dynasty, has given, on the S wall of the temple of Karnak, a list of the places he captured in Palestine. Most of them were in Judah; a few, Megiddo and Taanach, belonged to the northern kingdom.

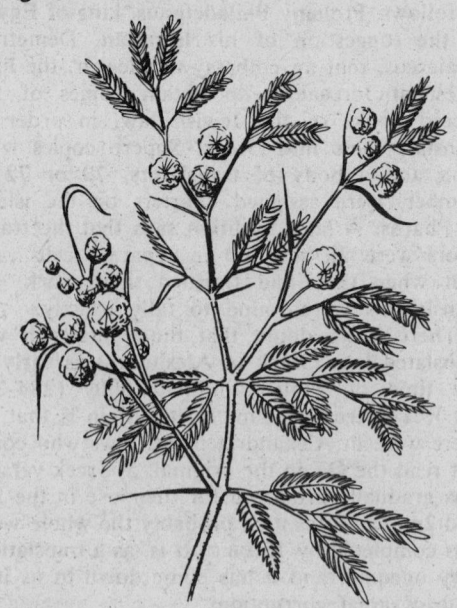

Shittah tree.

shit'tah tree, shit'tim wood
A kind of acacia tree.

Shu'nem
A village in Issachar, identified with modern Solem, first mentioned earlier than 1400 B.C. It lies 9 mi. N of Jenin. Saul fought the Philistines there, and Elijah revived the dead son of a woman of Shunem.

Shu'shan, Su'sa

The ancient capital of Elam, in SW Iran. Its history as a city for more than 5000 years has been revealed by excavation.

Si'chem

See Shechem.

Si'don

Now Saida, a very ancient Canaanite city with a good port, center of Phoenician trade, north of Tyre. Its name is set down on monuments as early as 1500 B.C. The sarcophagus of Esh-munazar, who ruled Phoenicia and Sharon in the 3rd century B.C., was found here.

sig'net

See Seal.

Si·lo'am, Si·lo'ah

A pool in Jerusalem, also called The Pool Between the Two Walls.

sil'ver

An imported metal in Palestine, though some may have been obtained in Lebanon from an ore of lead (the sulphide), which is frequently silver-bearing. Spain appears to have been one of the chief sources of supply in ancient times. Silver was used for money and for ornamental purposes, and was well known to the Egyptians in patriarchal ages.

Sim'e·on, Sym'e·on, Si'mon

(Heb. "[the deity] has heard") 1. The second son of Jacob, ancestor of one of the 12 tribes.

2. A devout man who blessed the infant Jesus when he was presented in the Temple.

Si'mon

(Heb. "[the deity] has heard")

1. Simon Peter. *See* Peter.

2. Simon the Zealot, also one of the Twelve.

3. Simon the Pharisee in whose house Jesus was anointed.

4. Simon of Cyrene, who carried the cross.

Si'mon Mac·ca·be'us

Brother of Judas Maccabeus. *See* Maccabees.

Si'mon Ma'gus

A Samaritan magician who, impressed by early Christian miracles, offered money to Peter and John for the power of the Holy Spirit.

Si'nai, Mount

Believed to be Jebel Musa, 7500 ft., near the S end of the Sinai Peninsula.

sing'ing

Singing and chanting were a part of the Temple service. The people had such folk music as work songs, songs for weddings and other festivities, and probably knew the fertility songs of the people among whom they lived.

Si'on

See Zion.

Si'van

The 3rd month in the Hebrew calendar.

slime

See Bitumen.

Smyr'na

The modern Izmir, originally a Greek colony. The old city was destroyed in the early 6th cen-
tury B.C., and refounded early in the 3rd century B.C. On the slope of Mount Pagus are the remains of the great theater and the stadium, close to which Polycarp, the first bishop, suffered martyrdom.

Sod'om

One of the Cities of the Plain. *See* Gomorrah.

Sol'o·mon

(Heb. "peaceful") Son of David and Bathsheba, the 3rd king of Israel. His history is narrated in 1 Kings 1–11 and 2 Chron 1–9. Under his brilliant reign the power of the kingdom reached its zenith. He stood on friendly terms with Egypt, and married a daughter of the Pharaoh. He maintained his authority over all the lands won by David and subjugated all the non-Israelite inhabitants of Palestine. His greatest achievement was the building of the Temple. He built a palace for himself, and another for his Egyptian queen; also the "House of the forest of Lebanon," an arsenal on Zion made of wood from Lebanon, and completed the fortification of Jerusalem. Not until all these works had been finished, in the 24th year of his reign, was the Temple consecrated. Solomon completed the transition of the kingdom which his father had consolidated into an Oriental despotism, establishing fortresses, increasing the army, introducing cavalry, and entering into great undertakings for the furtherance of trade with foreign nations. He formed an enormous harem, and was led away into idolatry under the influence of his heathen wives. The magnificence of his court was maintained by oppressive taxation, which, in the end, exasperated his subjects. The latter part of his reign did not fulfil the promise of its beginning, when, in the famous vision of Gibeon, he chose wisdom before long life, gold, or victory, and God gave him, besides riches and honor, "a wise and understanding heart." Along with an extraordinary power of discerning human motives, he had the gift of expressing his thoughts in pregnant sayings, which were famous even beyond his own country. There was nothing in the realm of nature of which he could not speak. He was pre-eminently skilled in that practical wisdom which, based on religion, embraced all the moral problems of life, and was the founder of the Wisdom Literature. Proverbs, Ecclesiastes, Song of Songs, the 72nd and 127th Psalms are ascribed to him. The collection of 18 poems called the Psalms of Solomon, also called the "Psalms of the Pharisees," were written in Hebrew in the 1st century B.C., and are now extant only in a Greek translation. The "Wisdom of Solomon" was also attributed to him.

Song of Sol'o·mon, the

The matchless poem of the OT is also called "Song of Songs" and "Canticles." This collection of love songs has long been an enigma and many interpretations have been offered for it. This love-relationship could signify the relation between God and His people, or that between Christ and the Church.

South Ra'moth

Ramoth of the Negev.

spelt

A coarse and inferior wheat.

spi'ces

Vegetable products used for fragrance or flavor. They were an important item of trade and of wealth, necessary for the worship in the Temple, and used in embalming.

spi'der

There are hundreds of species of spider in Palestine; that one mentioned in Prov 30.28 is more probably a lizard.

spike'nard, nard

A perennial herb with an aromatic root; a member of the Valerian family and native in India. The ointment was very expensive.

stac'te

Possibly an exudate from the storax tree or the opobalsamum; one of the aromatic ingredients of the Temple incense.

staff

See Rod.

Ste'phen

(Gr. "crown") The first Christian martyr, one of the Seven who were chosen for the special service of tables, the distribution of food to the poor. His gifts of inspired speech and miracle made him preeminent among the Seven. Accused of blasphemy against Moses and against God, he was condemned on the evidence of false witnesses. In his defense he showed by historical proof that the Jews had always resisted God's prophets, at last had murdered the Messiah, and that the Temple was not an indispensable and indestructible institution of the religion of revelation. He was stoned to death, and "fell asleep" with a prayer on his lips which was an echo of our Savior's upon the cross. Saul of Tarsus (later Paul) was standing by, consenting to the death, and he held the raiment of those who stoned him. The death of Stephen was the signal for the beginning of a general persecution of the Christians.

Suc'coth

A city of Gad, identified as Tell Deir'alla, 2 mi. N of the Jabbok. There is evidence of very early settlement. Succoth in Egypt has been identified with Tell el-Maskhutah.

sul'phur, brim'stone

Sulphur springs and encrustations of sulphur are not uncommon near the Dead Sea.

Su'mer, Su·me'ri·an

The Sumerians came into the Mesopotamian area about 3500 B.C., absorbing, driving out, or being absorbed by the Ubaid people, who had been there from 4000 B.C. Sumer developed elaborate irrigation systems, worked out rather complicated mathematical tables and algebraic problems, had a pharmacology, a pantheon, cylinder seals, and a system of cuneiform writing. Semitic nomads, the Amorites, gradually conquered the cities and introduced their language, Akkadian. Sumer was extinct as a people and a government, and Babylonia and Assyria arose in its place.

Sun, Cit'y of the; Cit'y of De·struc'tion

Probably a city in Egypt.

Su'sa

See Shushan.

swine

Regarded by Jews (and Muslims) as the most unclean and polluting of animals.

syc'a·mine

Possibly the mulberry tree.

syc'a·more, syc'o·more

A type of fig with a leaf like a mulberry leaf.

Sy'char

A village about a mile east of Shechem, near Joseph's tomb and Jacob's well, the modern Tell Balatah.

Sy'chem

See Shechem.

syn'a·gogue

(Gr. "a meeting") A Jewish meeting-house for worship. It served for church, law-court, and school, and was governed by local elders or "rulers" who had power to inflict various penalties, including scourging and excommunication (temporary and permanent). Meetings were held in the synagogue every Sabbath, and on the 2nd and 5th days of the week. Worship was conducted by any one selected by the ruler on each occasion. The synagogues, first instituted after the Exile, were the chief means by which religious knowledge and spiritual fellowship were maintained among the people. The organization of the early Christian communities was largely molded on the lines of the synagogue.

Syr'i·a

(Heb. "plain") The region extending from Mount Taurus to Tyre, and from the Mediterranean to the Tigris. In NT times Syria included Western Aram only. It was under a Roman proconsul.

T

tab'er·na·cle

The tabernacle and its furnishings, prepared according to the instructions of Ex 25–31 and carried by the Israelites during their wandering in the wilderness, and for a considerable period after that, was the place of the presence of God. It was a portable sanctuary, financed by voluntary gifts, that served until Solomon built the Temple. The materials to be used were available and in use for somewhat similar purposes in the lands round about; the colors to be used for the skins and hangings were also available. The tabernacle was designed to provide a suitable housing for the Ark of the Covenant and a meeting place for the rituals and worship of the people of Israel. It was surrounded by a court, also as specified, 150 x 75 ft., and enclosing in addition to the tabernacle an altar of burnt offering and a laver.

Tab'er·na·cles, Feast of

Also called the Feast of Booths, this is the celebration of the harvest. It begins on the day of the full moon of the 7th month; that is, in early October.

Ta'bor, Mount

In the NE corner of the Valley of Jezreel, 6 mi. ESE of Nazareth, Mount Tabor rises 1843 ft.

tal'ent

A weight used in Mesopotamia, Canaan, and Israel. Although it varied, it was in the neighborhood of 75 pounds. It was equivalent to 6000 drachmas (a silver coin) in NT times.

Tal'mud

(Heb. "to study, to learn") The fundamental code of the civil and canonical law of Rabbinical Judaism. It consists of the Mishna ("repetition"), i.e., the Halacha, or traditional law, as it was committed to writing by Rabbi Judah the Holy (who died A.D. 219) and his disciples, divided into 6 parts comprising 63 treatises, or 524 chapters. A supplementary work called Tosephta was completed about A.D. 400. The second part of the Talmud is the Gemara (completion), which originated in the school of Tiberias in Palestine about A.D. 250 and was completed about 400; and the Babylonian, which was developed in the school of Sura in Babylonia, and completed at 550. For the two methods of interpretation followed in the Talmud, *see* Halacha and Haggada.

Tam'muz

The 4th month in the Hebrew calendar.

Tam'muz, Tham'muz

The Sumerian god of spring vegetation.

Tares, left compared with wheat, right.

tares

Weeds.

Tar'gums

When the Biblical Hebrew was no longer understood by the Aramaic-speaking peoples, just as Wycliffe's English version would be unintelligible to a modern English congregation, it became necessary for a qualified translator to give the equivalent Aramaic when the Hebrew was read. This oral interpretation or Targum was at first of the simplest kind, but it gradually became more elaborate and was reduced to writing. The Targum of Onkelos on the Pentateuch, perhaps as old as the 2nd or 3rd century A.D., became official, as did the Targum of

Jonathan Ben Uzziel on the Prophets and Historical Books, which is of later date.

Tar'shish, Thar'shish

(Heb. "yellow jasper"?) The name of Taurus, a port, far off and not identified, a distant paradise, in the OT.

tax col·lec'tors

See Publicans.

tax'es

Every Hebrew who had reached the age of 20 had to pay a half shekel for the upkeep of the sanctuary. Under Nehemiah a third of a shekel was raised from every Israelite for the building of the temple. In later times the regular temple tax was a half shekel. Civil taxes were at first unknown, but Samuel shows that they would be exacted under the monarchy. Large contributions in kind were required by Solomon; the first cutting of grass is called "the king's mowing." Money taxes were demanded only in times of extraordinary necessity. Under the Persians the Jews were required to pay not only excise and land-tax, but also a capitation tax, a direct levy on each person; and their condition under the Egyptian and Syrian rule became still harder when Antiochus demanded 1000 talents. The taxes now began to be farmed, and this system was universal under the Roman domination, during which the Jews had to pay capitation and land taxes, as well as customs.

Te'beth

The 10th month of the Hebrew calendar.

teil

Obsolete name for lime or linden tree. *See* Terebinth.

Tell el-A·mar'na Tab'lets

A collection of 296 clay tablets found at Tell el-Amarna, in Egypt, in 1887. They consist of letters to Amen-hotep IV and his father, Amen-hotep III, from various kings of Western Asia, from Phoenician and Canaanite princes, written in cuneiform characters, and almost entirely in the Babylonian language, though only 1 or 2 of their writers were Babylonians. Their date is uncertain, but may be about 1400 B.C. and earlier. Israel is identified by some with the Khabiri of these letters, who invaded Egypt some 150 years before.

tem'ple

Solomon's Temple took its plan from the Tabernacle; but its general dimensions were double those of the Tabernacle, and its furniture and decorations were on a grander scale. The Temple proper was 90 x 30 ft., and 45 ft. high. It was built of stones dressed at the quarry, and roofed with cedar. The floors were of cypress overlaid with gold and the walls were lined with cedar overlaid with gold. No stone was seen. The Holy of Holies was a cube of 30 ft. In it were 2 cherubim of olive wood, overlaid with gold, each 15 ft. high, and with wings 7½ ft. long. It was separated from the Sanctuary by a curtain and by chains of gold and 2 doors of olive wood. The Holy Place, or Sanctuary, was 60 ft. long, 30 ft. wide, and 45 ft. high. There were windows in its walls, probably near the roof. It contained the altar of incense, which was of cedar overlaid with gold, 10 candlesticks, and 10 tables, and was entered from the vestibule by doors of cypress. Against the 2 sides and rear of the Temple were 3 stories of rooms for officials and for storage; in front was a portico 15 ft. wide before which stood the brass

Courtesy of *The Interpreter's Dictionary of the Bible*

Solomon's temple, front view, after Schick (1896)

pillars called Boaz and Jachin, 27 ft. high with lotus-shaped capitals, or column heads. The courts of the Temple were the great court for Israel, and the inner or upper court of the priests, walled off by a parapet, and containing a brass altar, a brass sea standing on 4 groups of 3 oxen each, and 10 lavers (vessels for ablutions) of brass. The Temple was burned by Nebuzar-adan, Nebuchadnezzar's general, 587 B.C.

Zerubbabel's Temple was erected by the Jews under Zerubbabel on their return from captivity. It had the same general plan as the old, though with different proportions, and on a scale of less magnificence. Begun September 24, 520, it was finished on March 3, 515 B.C.

Herod's Temple superseded Zerubbabel's. It was begun about 19 B.C., and was not finished till A.D. 63-64. The area was enlarged to twice the former dimensions. The Temple proper reproduced the old plan, except that the height was 60 instead of 45 ft. The Holy of Holies was separated from the Holy Place by a veil and was empty. The exterior eastern end was flanked by two wings, making the front 150 ft. long. Beyond the court of the priests lay a large court, of which the part nearest the Sanctuary was reserved for men of Israel, the E portion for women. These were enclosed by a strong wall. The grand portal in the E wall was probably the Beautiful Gate. Beyond these precincts was the large court of the Gentiles, where money changers sat and traders displayed cattle for sale.

Ten Com·mand'ments

The covenant requirements of Yahweh and the Israelites, covering prohibitions in man's relations with his God and his neighbor.

ter'a·phim

Small, portable household gods.

ter'e·binth

Also called the turpentine tree; a kind of sumac, yielding Chian turpentine. It has been translated as elm, but the elm does not occur in Palestine.

Tham'muz

See Tammuz.

thar'shish

See Tarshish.

Thes·sa·lo'ni·ans, the Let'ters of Paul to the

These two epistles written by Paul at Corinth in A.D. 50 or 51 are the earliest writings of the NT. They were occasioned by his interest in the church that he had founded within 18 months before at Thessalonica, and persecution had compelled him to leave. Paul tells these Christians what sort of persons they must be, and that they must do their duty every day and not stand idle, waiting for the Second Coming.

Thes·sa·lo·ni'ca

Now Salonika, in Macedonia, at the head of the Thermaic Gulf. It was in Paul's time a free city governed by 7 politarchs. Its public assembly of Demas is mentioned in Acts 17.5. It was rebuilt by Cassander (315 B.C.), and renamed after his wife, sister of Alexander the Great, and from 146 B.C. was the seat of the Roman governors of Macedonia. A great seaport and the center of the Via Egnatia (the great high road from the Adriatic to the Hellespont), it was, after Corinth, the second commercial city of the European Greeks, and it is now Salonika, or Thessaloniki in Greece.

this'tle

See Bramble.

Thom'as

One of the 12 disciples of Jesus, in the Gospel of John called Didymus ("twin"), which is the Greek rendering of the Aramaic name. The passages in John's Gospel, 11, 14, and 20, in which Thomas appears, reveal the intense love that bound him to his Master. The image of the crucifixion filled his mind, and his sorrow would not be comforted by others' testimony; he must himself see before he could believe that his Lord was risen. Jesus, tenderly reproving him, granted him all that he desired; "and Thomas answered and said unto Him 'My Lord and my God.'"

There is an early tradition that Thomas preached the gospel in Parthia and was buried at Edessa. The Christians of Malabar, the "Thomas-Christians," regarded him as the founder of their community.

thorn

See Bramble.

thresh'ing

Lighter grain, such as spelt and cummin, was beaten out with rods and flails; other kinds were threshed either by the feet of cattle or by a threshing instrument, made either of planks studded with stones or iron or of rollers spiked with iron teeth.

Thy·a·ti'ra

An important city of ancient Lydia, on the Lycus, with a large Greek population and a probable Jewish population, and noted for purple-dyeing and weaving. An inscription found there mentions its dyers' guild, among others.

thy'ine wood

The hard, fragrant wood of a North African cypress; also translated as scented wood.

Ti·be'ri·as

Built by Herod Antipas, on the W shore of the Sea of Galilee, and famous in the 2nd century A.D. for its schools of rabbis, and as the seat of the Sanhedrin, it is now a popular resort. It lies 700 ft. below sea level.

Tig·lath-pi·le'ser, Til·gath-pil·ne'ser III

King of Assyria (745-727 B.C.) and, with the name Pul, of Babylonia, 729-727 B.C. He invaded Palestine, and Hoshea, the king of Israel, paid him tribute.

tim'brel

A small drum or a tambourine.

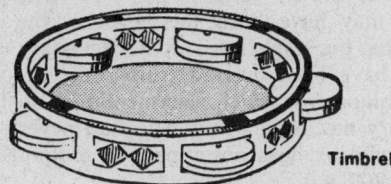

Timbrel.

time

Man early recognized the year, the seasons, and the lunar month, and the calendar, made with varying degrees of accuracy, is also ancient. It was easy to halve the lunar month into 14-day periods, and halve those into weeks. Then came the jockeying of time to make the week-and-lunar-month fit the cycle of the equinox. But the division of the single day into fixed segments of time was long in coming: the hour was of variable length until the 18th century. Hence the smaller divisions indicated for Bible times are approximations only. *See also* Calendar.

OLD TESTAMENT

Morning	until about 10 a.m.
Heat of the Day	until about 2 p.m.
Cool of the Day	until about 6 p.m.
First Night Watch	until midnight.
Second Night Watch	until 3 a.m.
Third Night Watch	until 6 a.m.

NEW TESTAMENT

Third Hour of the Day	6 to 9 a.m.
Sixth Hour of the Day	9 to 12 midday.
Ninth Hour of the Day	12 to 3 p.m.
Twelfth Hour of the Day	3 to 6 p.m.
First Watch, Evening	6 to 9 p.m.
Second Watch, Midnight	9 to 12 p.m.
Third Watch, Cockcrow	12 to 3 a.m.
Fourth Watch, Morning	3 to 6 a.m.

Tim'o·thy, Ti·mo'the·us

(Gk. "one who honors God") An assistant and companion of Paul who had been trained in piety by his Jewish-Christian mother Eunice and grandmother Lois. A convert of Paul's, he traveled in Macedonia and Greece, sometimes with the Apostle, sometimes commissioned by him. He appears afterward as the Apostle's representative at Ephesus and was at Rome while Paul was in prison there.

Tim'o·thy, the Let'ters of Paul to

Two epistles, written by the apostle to his friend Timothy at Lystra, tell of the conditions in the church and describe the qualifications and duties of church officers. *Second Timothy* contains Paul's request that Timothy come to Rome to see him. *First Timothy,* which has been compared with pearls of varied size and color loosely strung on one thread, must have been written between A.D. 64 and 67; *Second Timothy* was written about 67, and is the last of Paul's extant writings.

tin

The metal (obtained only from the oxide) has not been found in Palestine. It was, however, in use, chiefly as a constituent of bronze. It was brought to the Near East by the Phoenicians and was probably procured from the Caucasus.

Tir'ha·kah

A king of Ethiopia and Egypt (689-664 B.C.) who was defeated in the Nile Delta by the Assyrians and driven S. He set up his capital in Thebes.

tish'ri

The 7th month of the Hebrew calendar.

Ti'tus

As an assistant of Paul in his apostolic work, Titus accompanied him to the council at Jerusalem as a Gentile Christian who had remained uncircumcised. He afterward appears as Paul's commissioner in Corinth.

Ti'tus, the Let'ter of Paul to

This NT epistle mentions that Titus was left by Paul in Crete to organize the work there, and sets forth the duties of the pastoral office and the virtues of domestic and social life. It can scarcely have been written earlier than Nero's persecution (A.D. 64).

To'bit

The Book of Tobit may have been written in Aramaic about 200 B.C. It is the story of the reward of a good Jew and his son for their piety and good deeds. It is placed in the Apocrypha by Protestants.

tongues, speaking with

Glossolalia, which may range from unintelligible babbling to a possible higher language, opened to the Apostles in their ecstasy when, as it seemed, the Messianic age had come and they were the people of the New Covenant, with Jesus as the Anointed.

to'paz

The topaz is a fluosilicate of aluminum, generally of a resin-yellow color.

treas'ure, treas'ur·er, treas'u·ry

All wealth is treasure. The worldly wealth, the treasure of the Temple is listed in Ezra 1.9-11, 2.69-70. The royal treasures are listed in 2 Chron 32.27-29, and Solomon's in 1 Kings 10.10-29. But the teaching of Jesus was that worldly treasure was to be given up in order to have treasure in heaven. Treasuries, places where treasure might be kept, have been found in excavations, chests, grain pits in the rock, store-cities. Personal treasure might be carried on the body or buried in a secret place. The treasurer was the custodian of the treasure.

Fluted bowl and tumbler, and a spouted pitcher, all in gold, from Ur, and about the time of Abraham

trib'ute

A payment by one ruler or nation to another as acknowledgment of submission, for protection, or in fulfillment of a treaty. Some neighboring countries paid tribute to David and Solomon, and Omri also succeeded in exacting tribute, but during much of her history Israel was in the position of paying tribute to Syria and the Mesopotamian countries to the E and Egypt to the W.

The temple tax was sometimes called tribute, because of the covenant of God and the Israelites. Census of the population with a subsequent tax was also sometimes called tribute or civil tribute.

trump'et

The trumpets found are made of gold, silver, bronze, copper, bones, or shell, with an air column somewhat less than 2 ft. In the Dead Sea Scrolls are directions for blowing a number of complicated signals. The shofar or ram's horn is not a true trumpet.

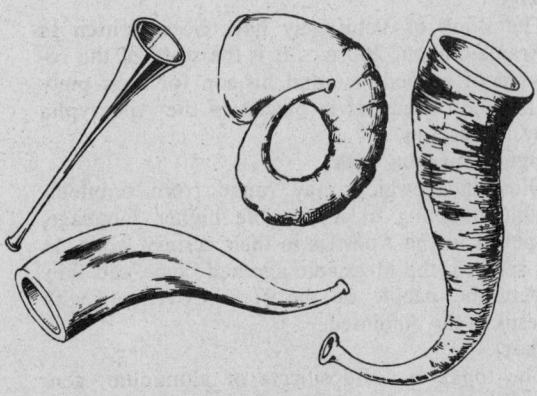

Ancient horns and trumpets.

Tyre

A famous Phoenician city which, according to Herodotus, dates to the 28th century B.C. It does appear as an already famous city in the 14th century, in the Tell el-Amarna Letters. King Hiram (981-947 B.C.), who traded with Solomon and sent workmen to help in the building of the Temple, built a great breakwater that gave Tyre one of the best harbors of the E Mediterranean; it can still be seen, now under 50 ft. of water. The city was famous for its purple dye, glassware, and other manufactures, and traded throughout the Mediterranean, founding many colonies; that at Carthage dates from 850 B.C. It was often attacked by Egypt and Assyria, and was at times forced to pay tribute to one or the other. It was Alexander who destroyed it, selling 30,000 of its people as slaves, and hanging 2000 of the leaders. Tyre never regained its former prestige, and is now a city of a few thousand, called Sur.

U

u'ni·corn, wild ox

This may have been the aurochs, the extinct wild ox; the single horn of the legendary unicorn may have been derived from some account of the rhinoceros, which was mentioned in the 4th century B.C. by a writer who had never seen it. The wild ox does not appear in sculptures later than 800 B.C.

Ur of the Chal·dees'

A city in present-day Iraq, now known as al-Mugayyer, some of which has been excavated. As early as 3000-2500 B.C. it was a magnificent city, with vast temples and palaces and fine works of art.

U'rim and Thum'mim

The sacred lots placed within the pocket of the breastplate of the high priest, used in question-and-answer communication with God. The answer was usually expected as "yes" or "no." The Urim and Thummim are not mentioned after the time of David.

Uz·zi'ah

(Heb. "Yah is my might") The name of 3 persons in the OT, one of whom was king of Judah (788-742 B.C.).

V

veg'e·ta·ble

Something sown.

ver·mil'ion

Red ocher, the hematite iron ore, was used for enamel and as a paint.

vine, vine'yard

The grapevine is one of the most characteristic plants of Palestine. Noah is credited with being the father of its culture; the manner of planting, usually on a hill, is described in Is 5.1-6. A watchman was maintained, and nonbearing vines were pruned away. The harvested crop of ripe grapes were eaten at once, dried as raisins, boiled into a thick syrup, or made into wine. Gleanings in the vineyard were left for widows and orphans, and for strangers. *See* Wine.

vows

In the OT, vows are solemn promises to offer sacrifices, etc., to God in return for His help, or to abstain from some legitimate enjoyment for His sake. Such vows are voluntary and are not to be lightly made; once made, they are to be inviolate. Our Lord only once mentions vows (Mt 15.5-9; Mk 7.11-13), condemning those who give to God what should go to support their parents. Paul, at Jerusalem, took part in a Nazarite vow (Acts 21.24-26), and made or fulfilled a similar vow at Cenchreae (Acts 18.18).

Vul'gate

(Lat. *versio vulgata,* "common version") The great work of Jerome, who about A.D. 382 was commissioned by Pope Damasus to revise the Latin Bible. The result of his labors is the Latin Vulgate, of which a vast number of MSS. are extant. Probably the best text of all for determining the text of the Vulgate as Jerome left it is the Codex Amiatinus, which was written shortly before A.D. 716 either at Wearmouth or at Jarrow in Northumberland, by the command of Ceolfrid the Abbot, as a votive offering for the Pope of Rome. Ceolfrid died on the journey to Rome, and the fortunes of the book after his death are unknown; it was probably presented to the Pope in due course, and ultimately found its way to the monastery of Monte Amiata, after which it is named. It is now in Florence.

The revision of the OT was made by Jerome in Palestine between 392 and 404, by direct reference to the Hebrew, of which language he had made himself master somewhat late in life. The work of revision is very unequally done; some books underwent very little change, others were much more carefully treated. In particular, the Psalter, which Jerome translated afresh from the Hebrew, had already been twice revised by him on the basis of the Septuagint; these revisions are known as the Roman and Gallican Psalters. The new Hebrew translation found very slow acceptance, and the old Psalter from the Septuagint was not displaced from ecclesiastical use until the 16th century. A curious parallel to the Roman conservatism over the Psalter will be found in the Psalter of the English Prayerbook, which does not follow the text of the Authorized Version, but that of the Great Bible of 1539-1541, though frequent efforts have been made to change it.

vul'ture

See Eagle.

W

wea'sel

(Heb. "to crawl, creep, burrow") Weasels, and also polecats, are common in Palestine, and perhaps others of the genus. The weasel is included in the list of unclean beasts.

Weeks, Feast of

The Day of First Fruits, the 2nd of the 3 great festivals of the year. It is also called the Feast of Pentecost. *See* Feasts.

weights, meas'ures of ca·pac'i·ty

Weights are notable for their inexactness. Excavations have yielded some inscribed weights, and the figures offered are averages only. As throughout Western Asia, the shekel is the basic weight; there are light and heavy shekels, common and royal. A light royal shekel is heavier than a light common shekel: this in addition to the variations in weights identically marked. The averages follow.

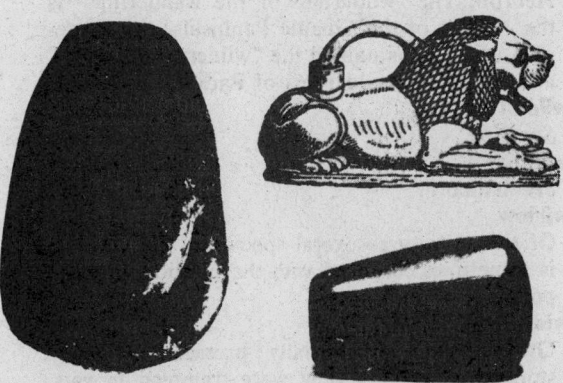

Stone weights used by ancient tradesmen in Nineveh. Often weights were made in the shape of a duck or a lion.

gerah, 1/20 shekel	8.71 grains
1/3 shekel	0.134 ounce
beka, 1/2 shekel	0.201 ounce
pim, 2/3 shekel	0.268 ounce
shekel	0.403 ounce
mina, 50 shekels	1.26 pounds
talent, 3000 shekels	75.6 pounds

Measures of capacity were never finally fixed and discrepancies are greater than with weights. The averages:

DRY MEASURES

kah	1.16 quarts
omer, issaron, 1/10 ephah	2.09 quarts
seah 1/3 ephah	2/3 peck
lethech, 1/2 homer	2.58 bushels
homer, cor	5.16 bushels

LIQUID MEASURES

log	0.67 pint
hin	1 gallon
bath	5½ gallons
cor, homer	55 gallons

wells

In a land of few rivers, where rain fell only at certain seasons, wells were of the utmost importance. They were artificial ponds or pits sunk in the ground, in which the rainwater collected and was stored. Springs were often supplemented with wells.

whale, sea mon'ster, drag'on, le·vi'a·than

The whale is an air-breathing, warm-blooded sea mammal. The great fish of Jonah is not otherwise identified. Large sharks are found, as well as dolphins and whales, in the Red Sea and the

Mediterranean. The mythological dragon and the leviathan, or sea monster, persisted in the folk lore.

wheat, corn

Wheat has been cultivated for food in the Near East since Neolithic times or longer. "Corn" as a name for a grain has in modern times been used for maize, discovered in the Western Hemisphere.

wil'der·ness

In Scripture wilderness generally denotes open, uncultivated ground, suitable for pasture, as well as desert, arid areas, and wild and rocky terrain. The wilderness of Judea, the Jeshimon, lies between the Dead Sea and the district of Hebron. The "wilderness of the wanderings" is the N part of the Sinaitic Peninsula, the W region of which is named the "wilderness of Shur" and the E the "wilderness of Paran."

wild ol'ive

See Pine.

wild ox

See Unicorn.

wil'low

Of this there are several species in Palestine. It is sometimes confused with the oleander and the poplar.

wine

Grapes were occasionally pressed by heavy stones, but usually they were trampled in vats. The quickly fermenting juice was put into jars or new skins. Water was scarce in Palestine, and the use of wine increased accordingly. It was abundant in the country, and was drunk, partly as sweet must, partly after fermenting and settling on the lees. It was an old custom to add spices. Wine before being drunk was commonly filtered, to remove dregs and insects. The vice of drunkenness is frequently referred to, and there are many emphatic warnings against it in Scripture. The Rechabites and Nazarites abstained from wine. The priests were forbidden to use it when engaged in their sacred duties. A drink-offering of wine was presented with the daily sacrifice, with the offering of the first fruits, and with various other sacrifices.

win'now·ing

After the grain was threshed, it was winnowed by being tossed in the air with shovels or forks after the nightwind had begun to blow. The grain then fell to the ground and the chaff was blown away.

wis'dom

The Book of Proverbs is the earliest extensive wisdom document. Many strains of source material can be traced in it, and it expresses a wisdom accumulated from all. It contains a number of short homilies, many similies, and balanced-line proverbs. The structure is poetic and impressive.

Wis'dom of Sol'o·mon

This book, together with the Wisdom of the Son of Sirach, or Ecclesiasticus, belongs to the class of what are called the sapiential books, represented within the limits of the Canon by Job, Proverbs, and Ecclesiastes.

The Wisdom of Solomon has nothing to do with Solomon, and is not older than the first (or perhaps second) century B.C. It was probably written in Greek by an Alexandrian Jew. It is a noble work, and was so highly esteemed by the Christian church that it came nearer to canonical acceptance than any other part of the Apocrypha. Some portions of it, which discuss the praise of wisdom, and the rewards and punishments attached respectively to the just and the unjust, have always been much admired, and some of its sentences have become proverbial: "In all ages wisdom entereth into holy souls, and maketh them friends of God and prophets"; "The souls of the righteous are in the hands of God, and there shall no torment touch them."

wolf

The wolf is everywhere known as the terror of the sheepfold. The wolf of Syria is the same as that of Europe, and formerly of Britain. The wolf is often spoken of in Scripture as the emblem of ferocity and bloodthirstiness.

worm

Included among the worms of the Bible are earthworms, larvae of moths, leaf-eating insects, maggots, beetles.

worm'wood

Several species of Artemesia are found in Palestine, all with a bitter taste.

writ'ing (He'brew)

From notices in the OT we learn that the Jews wrote their books with ink on rolls of smoothed sheepskin or goatskin, with a staff attached to each end. The rolls were not written across, but from end to end, the writing being arranged in columns. When a roll was read, the beginning of it was at the reader's right hand, the end at his left. When a column had been read, it was rolled round the right-hand staff, and a new column was unrolled from the left-hand one. According to Jewish tradition, the square character now in use was introduced by Ezra. Subsequent to the Restoration, the scribes transcribed from the old character to the new such books as were written in the former. This was a task of great delicacy, because of the condition of the texts and the dangers of error. In Hebrew writing originally only the consonants of the words were written, the vowels being supplied by the reader. In such a mode of writing, the same combination of consonants may be pronounced differently. Thus, to take an English example, the consonants BRD may be read bird, bard, broad, bread, etc., and the appropriate pronunciation must in each case be determined by the context. The danger in copying such a text was that the mind of the scribe would be continually engaged on the sense while his hand and eye were engaged on the form, or else that he would slavishly copy the letters without regarding the sense; and on either hand there was the risk of mistake, all the more that several letters in both scripts closely resembled one another, and that there was no system of punctuation, nor clear spacing between words. There are many readings in the Septuagint which appear to be due to variations in the Hebrew original from which it was translated.

Y

yoke
Animals engaged in ploughing were united to one another and to the shaft of the plough by a yoke, which was a framework of wood, or wood and leather, passing round the breast of each. The yoke was always double.

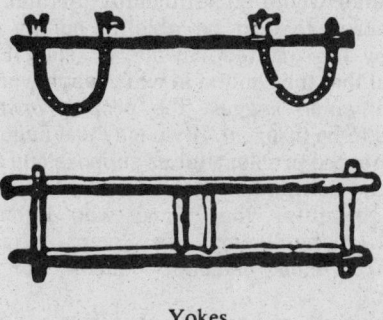

Yokes

Z

Zeal'ots
The extreme wing of the national party, in which the Pharisees represented the policy of passive resistance. From Herod the Great's time to the fall of Jerusalem in A.D. 70 they were in a constant state of ferment. Their headquarters were in Galilee. "Cananaean" is the Hebrew equivalent of Zealot.

Zech·a·ri'ah, Zach·a·ri'ah, Zach·a·ri'as, Ze'cher, Za'cher
(Heb. "Yah has remembered") The name of 33 persons in the Bible, one of whom was the son of Berechiah, a coadjutor of Haggai in promoting the rebuilding of the Temple, who prophesied in 520 and 518 B.C.

Zech·a·ri'ah, the Book of
This OT book of prophecy consists chiefly of visions presenting motives for confidence and effort. Chs. 9–14 have a different historical setting, and refer to conquests of Tiglath-pileser III (745-727 B.C.), and may have been written by the Zechariah of Is 8.2.

Zed·e·ki'ah, Zid·ki'jah
(Heb. "Yah is my righteousness") The name of 4 persons in the OT, one of whom was the last king of Judah.

Zeph·a·ni'ah
(Heb. "Yah has sheltered") The name of 4 persons in the OT, one of whom prophesied in the time of Josiah and before the fall of Nineveh (606 B.C.).

Zeph·a·ni'ah, the Book of
In this OT book the prophet Zephaniah warned Judah and Jerusalem that the great day of the Lord's judgment is near, the neighboring nations are about to fall. He urged Jerusalem to repent, prophesied that the faithful remnant will be gathered, and the peoples will serve Jehovah with one consent. The hymn of the world's judgment, *Dies irae, dies illa* ("That day of wrath, that dreadful day"), was taken by Thomas of Celano (13th century) from Zephaniah 1.14-18.

Ze·rub'ba·bel
(Akkad. "scion of Babylon) A descendant of the kings of Judah, who was permitted by Cyrus to lead back the Jews from exile in 538 B.C. He saw the completion of the new Temple in 515 B.C.

Zi'on, Si'on
Originally the name of the fortified hill of pre-Israelite Jerusalem and poetically extended to become the religious capital of Israel.

Ziv
Second month in the Hebrew calendar.

Zo'an
A city in NE Egypt, the capital of the Hyksos and now San el-Hajar. It was once called per-Ramses, and is the area from which the Exodus began.

Zo'phar
One of Job's friends.

WHAT IS THE BIBLE?

The name "Bible" is derived from the Greek word *biblos*, meaning "book." This "Book," actually composed of sixty-six separate books, is a collection of ancient Hebrew and Christian writings, each complete in itself. The order of these sixty-six books in the Old Testament and New Testament is a logical one, giving, in general, a consecutive history of mankind—from the story of creation in the first chapter of Genesis to the visionary future of the book of Revelation.

The order of Old Testament books in the English Bible differs somewhat from the order of the books of Hebrew Scriptures. The sacred writings of the Jews were divided into three parts: (1) the Law, five books setting forth the laws which God gave through Moses; (2) the Prophets, including the four "Former Prophets," Joshua, Judges, Samuel, and Kings, and the four "Latter Prophets," Isaiah, Jeremiah, Ezekiel, and the Twelve (the Twelve consisting of twelve brief prophetical books contained in a single scroll, thus looked upon as a single book); and (3) the Writings, which are divided into four sections: (a) Psalms, Proverbs, Job; (b) Song of Solomon, Ruth, Lamentations, Ecclesiastes, Esther; (c) Daniel; and (d) Ezra, Nehemiah, Chronicles. The relative importance of the scriptural writings according to Jewish thinking is shown by this order: The Law, standing first, was considered the most important; second, the Prophets; and third, the Writings, which were truly inspired and to be treasured but were not as important as the Law and the Prophets.

In English translations of the Old Testament, the thirty-nine books may be regarded as falling into four categories: (1) History, the books from Genesis to Esther, including the Pentateuch; (2) Poetry, the books from Job to the Song of Solomon; (3) the Major Prophets, the books of Isaiah, Jeremiah, Ezekiel, and Daniel (with Lamentations, a brief and largely poetical book, regarded as an appendix to the book of Jeremiah); and (4) the Minor Prophets, the same brief prophetical books spoken of by the Jews as "The Twelve."

The word "pentateuch," derived from the Greek, means "five books," and is used to designate the first five books of the Old Testament. This section is also called "The Law" or "The Books of Moses," following the Jewish tradition that these five books were written by Moses.

The twenty-seven New Testament books are also divided into four categories: (1) History, including the four Gospels (i.e. books proclaiming the good news) and the book of Acts; (2) Paul's Epistles, the books of Romans through Philemon; (3) the General Epistles, the books of Hebrews through Jude; and (4) the Apocalypse, the book of Revelation.

ORIGINAL LANGUAGES OF THE BIBLE

Nearly all the Old Testament was originally written in Hebrew; the small remaining portion was written Aramaic, sometimes called Syriac. The Aramaic section comprises three passages (Ezra 4:8—6:18; 7:12—26; Dan. 2:4—7:28), one verse of Jeremiah (10:11), and two words in Genesis (31:47, a place name meaning "heap of witness"). Aramaic was the language spoken by the people and was the language spoken by Jesus during His public ministry. However, the New Testament was written in Greek, the language used in letters and other writings. Greek was the language understood practically everywhere throughout the Roman Empire, even in the remote provinces, and was recognized as the language of culture.

Since few persons can easily read the ancient languages of the Scriptures, many versions and translations of the Bible have been made. It has been translated, either in whole or in part, into nearly every language of the world today; but, because the spoken languages change from generation to generation, the work of translation continues.

Hebrew.—All of the Old Testament manuscripts which have been found are written in square, black letters which resemble the printed Hebrew of today. These square characters came into use some years prior to the birth of Christ.

Two facts made the translator's task difficult. First, Hebrew then was written without any spaces separating the words. For this reason, the translator sometimes was puzzled to know where one word ended and the next began. Second, the Hebrew alphabet consisted of twenty-two letters, all of them consonants. (Four of these consonants, however, were sometimes used to represent vowels.) In writing, only the consonants were put down. The reader was expected to know what vowels should be added. Evidently it was believed that the reader would be sufficiently familiar with the sacred text to be able to supply from memory the omitted vowels, or else it was thought that the context in which each word occurred would suggest the proper vowel or vowels to be inserted. If we may use English to illustrate the problem, let us suppose one came upon the consonants m and n. Could one tell with certainty what word was intended? Would it be "man" or "men," "main," "mean," "mien," "moan," "moon," or even "omen."

In the sixth and seventh centuries A.D., when Hebrew as a spoken language was beginning to die out, it was observed that the rabbis were not always agreed as to the proper reading of passages in the synagogue scrolls. As a result, there was danger of confusion and misunderstanding. Accordingly, Jewish scholars of that period, who became known as the Massoretes, undertook to determine and to indicate the proper vowel or vowels for every word in the Hebrew Scriptures. They indicated these vowels by means of small marks above, within, or below the consonants. They did not regard these vowel points as a part of the sacred text, and for that reason they refrained from marking them on the synagogue scrolls. They did insert them, however, on other scrolls and in their commentaries on the Scriptures.

Furthermore, in Hebrew there are no capital letters to distinguish proper nouns from common nouns and to mark the beginning of each new sentence. Finally, Hebrew is read from right to left, rather than from left to right as in English. The lines of Hebrew follow naturally down the page, from top to bottom. In the case of a scroll or book, one begins to read at what we would consider the end or back, and continues his reading till he reaches what we would consider the beginning or front.

Greek.—The Greek in which the New Testament books were written differs somewhat from the classical Greek of a few centuries earlier. It is the *koine*, that is to say, the everyday speech of the common people (and of the aristocrats also) in the first century A.D. Greek is like English in that it is read from left to right. The vowels are included in the Greek alphabet, and they appear in all Greek words except a few frequently used abbreviations. The oldest and most important New Testament manuscripts are written entirely in capital letters, and for this reason are called uncials. As a rule, there are no spaces separating the words.

Later Greek manuscripts are written in a running hand (cursives). Both capital letters and small letters are employed. The latter frequently are joined together, much as in handwriting today. In the later manuscripts there are spaces between the words and some punctuation is employed. These manuscripts come from the ninth to fifteenth century A.D., and they are called miniscules. The name means "rather small"; they take that name from the fact that they are written in small letters rather than in capitals.

Although much writing in Old Testament times was done on papyrus (a kind of paper), important documents were written on carefully prepared skins (vellum or parchment), because of their greater durability and permanence. In the case of a long roll, the skins were stitched together. The New Testament manuscripts doubtless were written originally on papyrus. Later, when their great value had been perceived, they were copied on vellum. It is not possible to state precisely when the change from scrolls to books took place. It did not happen all at once. It is now known that there were papyrus books much earlier than had been supposed. For several centuries both scrolls and books were in common use. Important books were made of vellum rather than the more fragile papyrus. A manuscript which is in the form of a book, rather than a roll, is called a codex. The word codex means "book."

The History of the Chapter Divisions

In the Hebrew manuscripts there were some indications of where the major divisions of the text began and ended. Because these sections sometimes were rather long, it was inevitable that someone eventually would make marks of one sort or another in the margins. Perhaps these marks at first merely indicated the point at which he had stopped reading. Later, they may have been added for the guidance of the reader in the synagogue, and were meant to show him appropriate points at which his reading might begin and end.

In the case of the New Testament, sections were marked off at an early date. These sections were shorter than the present day chapter divisions.

The chapter divisions usually are attributed to Stephen Langton, Archbishop of Canterbury, in England. Langton died in 1228. Cardinal Hugo, who died in 1263, used these chapter divisions in a concordance which he prepared for use with the Latin Vulgate. Chapter divisions are found in Wyclif's versions of the New Testament (1382), and all subsequent English versions.

These chapter divisions proved so convenient when referring to passages of Scripture that Jewish scholars borrowed the idea and employed it in editions of the Hebrew Scriptures. Thus, the present-day Hebrew Old Testament has the same chapter divisions as does our English Old Testament.

The Origin of the Verse Divisions

The material within each chapter is further divided into verses, numbered in regular order throughout each chapter. Although these verse divisions are helpful, they should not be emphasized, for they are not properly a part of the Holy Scriptures. They should not be permitted to interrupt the connected reading of the Scriptures, especially when the passage is of a narrative or poetical character.

Most authorities hold that the verse divisions for the Old Testament were first worked out by Rabbi Nathan in 1448. A Greek New Testament, which was published in 1551 by Robert Stephanus, a printer of Paris, contains the same verse divisions and numbers which we have now in the New Testament. His Latin Vulgate, published in 1551, was the first complete Bible to contain the verse numbers with which we are familiar. The first English Bible to contain them was the Geneva Bible, published in 1560. Since then, all English Bibles have contained the verse numbers.

The Words in Italics

Readers of the King James Version now and again come upon words printed in italics; that is to say, with slanting letters. Some have supposed, mistakenly, that these words were printed in this fashion for emphasis. This is not the case. The explanation, really, is quite simple. The words in italics are words which do not have any equivalents in the Hebrew or Greek text. They are words which have been supplied by the translators in order to make the meaning of the sentence clearer, or in order to make the passage read more smoothly in English. Numerous italicized words are found in the fifth chapter of Matthew, and they occur with almost equal frequency in other parts of the Scriptures.

The Geneva Bible, which was a pioneer version in many different ways, was the first to use italics in this fashion.

HOW TO STUDY THE BIBLE

The Bible is the greatest book that has ever been written. In it God Himself speaks to men. It is a book of divine instruction. It offers comfort in sorrow, guidance in perplexity, advice for our problems, rebuke for our sins, and daily inspiration for our every need.

The Bible is not simply one book. It is an entire library of books covering the whole range of literature. It includes history, poetry, drama, biography, prophecy, philosophy, science, and inspirational reading. Little wonder, then, that all or part of the Bible has been translated into more than 1,200 languages, and every year more copies of the Bible are sold than any other single book.

The Bible alone truly answers the greatest questions that men of all ages have asked: "Where have I come from?" "Where am I going?" "Why am I here?" "How can I know the truth?" For the Bible alone reveals the truth about God, explains the origin of man, points out the only way to salvation and eternal life, and explains the age-old problem of sin and suffering.

The great subject of all the Bible is the Lord Jesus Christ and His work of redemption for mankind. The person and work of Jesus Christ are promised, prophesied, and pictured in the types and symbols of the Old Testament. In all of His truth and beauty, the Lord Jesus Christ is revealed in the gospels; and the full meanings of His life, His death, and His resurrection are explained in the epistles. His glorious coming again to this earth in the future is unmistakably foretold in the book of Revelation. The great purpose of the written Word of God, the Bible, is to reveal the living Word of God, the Lord Jesus Christ (read John 1:1-18).

Dr. Wilbur M. Smith relates seven great things that the study of the Bible will do for us:

1. **The Bible discovers and convicts us of sin.**
2. **The Bible helps cleanse us from the pollutions of sin.**
3. **The Bible imparts strength.**
4. **The Bible instructs us in what we are to do.**
5. **The Bible provides us with a sword for victory over sin.**
6. **The Bible makes our lives fruitful.**
7. **The Bible gives us power to pray.**

You do not need a whole library of books to study the Bible. The Bible itself is its own best commentator and explanation.

I. PERSONAL BIBLE STUDY

A. Devotional Bible Study

The Bible is not an end in itself but it is a means to the end of knowing God and doing His will. God has given us the Bible in order that we might know Him and that we might do His will here on earth.

Therefore devotional Bible study is the most important kind of Bible study. Devotional Bible study means reading and studying the Word of God in order that we may hear God's voice personally and that we may know how to do His will and to live a better Christian life.

For your devotional reading and study of the Bible, here are several important, practical suggestions:

1. Begin your Bible reading with prayer. **(Ps. 119:18; John 16:13, 14, 15).**
2. Take brief notes on what you read. Keep a small notebook for your Bible study (see no. 4).
3. Read slowly through one chapter, or perhaps two or three chapters, or perhaps just one paragraph at a time. After reading, ask yourself what this passage is about. Then reread it.
4. It is often very helpful in finding out the true meaning of a chapter or passage to ask yourself the following questions, and then write the answers simply in your notebook:
   a. What is the main subject of this passage?
   b. Who are the persons revealed in this passage: Who is speaking? About whom is he speaking? Who is acting?
   c. What is the key verse of this passage?
   d. What does this passage teach me about the Lord Jesus Christ?
   e. Is there any sin for me to confess and forsake in this passage?
   f. Is there any command for me to obey in this passage?
   g. Is there any promise for me to claim?
   h. Is there any instruction for me to follow?
   i. Is there any prayer that I should pray?

Not all of these questions may be answered in every passage.

5. Keep a spiritual diary. Either in your Bible study notebook mentioned above (no. 2), or in a separate notebook entitled, "My Spiritual Diary," write down daily what God says to you through the Bible. Write down the sins that you confess or the commands you should obey that are mentioned above.
6. Memorize passages of the Word of God. Write verses on cards with the reference on one side and the verse on the other. Carry these cards in your pocket and review them while you're waiting for a train, standing in lunch line, etc.

Other person prefer to memorize whole passages or chapters of the Bible. A small pocket Bible will help you to review these passages when you have spare moments. One of the best ways is to spend a few minutes every night before going to sleep, in order that your subconscious mind may help you fix these passages of God's Word in your mind while you're asleep. (Ps. 119:11).

To meditate means "to reflect, to ponder, to consider, to dwell in thought,"

Through meditation the Word of God will become meaningful and real to you, and the Holy Spirit will use this time to apply the Word of God to your own life and its problems.

7. Obey the Word of God. As Paul said to Timothy in 2 Tim. 3:16, "All scripture is inspired of God and profitable for teaching, for reproof, for correction, and for training in righteousness." The Bible has been given to us that we may live a holy life, well-pleasing unto God.

8. The Navigators, a group of men banded together just before World War II to encourage. Bible study among Christian servicemen, has developed a splendid plan for a personal, devotional study.

   a. After prayer, read the Bible passage through slowly once silently, and then read it again aloud.

   b. In a large notebook divide the paper into columns and head each column as follows: Chapter title, Key verse, Significant truth, Cross-references, Difficulties in this passage (personal or possible), Application to me, and Summary or outline of the passage. In each of these columns write the information desired.

Do not try to adopt all of these methods at once, but start out slowly, selecting those methods and suggestions which appeal to you. You will find, as millions of others have done before you, that the more you read and study the Word of God, the more you'll want to read it. Therefore the following suggestions of Bible study are made for those who wish to make a more intensive study of the Bible truths.

B. Study for Bible Knowledge

There are many valuable methods of Bible study. One may study the Bible to see the great truths which stand out in every book. Or one may study the Bible to find all of the marvelous details which are in this mine of spiritual riches. In this section there are several proven methods by which a person may do more intensive Bible study. The most important thing is to follow faithfully some systematic method of Bible study.

1. *Bible Study by Chapters.*

In the Bible there are 1,189 chapters in the Old and New Testaments. In a little over three years a person could make an intensive study of the whole Bible, just taking a chapter a day. It is usually a good practice to start your Bible study in the New Testament.

   a. Read through the chapter carefully, seeking to find its main subject or subjects.

   b. As you read each chapter, give it a title which suggests its main content.

   c. Reread the chapter again and make a simple outline of it which will include its main thoughts.

   d. Concerning each chapter, ask and answer the questions suggested in item number 4 of devotional Bible study hints above. Especially take note of any practical or theological problems in this chapter. Then using your concordance look up the key words in those verses and find out what other portions of the Bible will have to say about this question or problem. Compare Scripture with Scripture to find its true meaning. Very often to understand an important Bible chapter, one must study it together with the preceding or following chapters.

2. *Bible Study by Paragraphs.* A paragraph is a unit of thought in writing, usually containing several sentences. When an author changes his subject of emphasis in his writing, he usually begins a new paragraph. Studying the Bible by paragraphs like this is often called analytic Bible study.

   a. Read the paragraph carefully for its main thought or subject.

   b. In order to find the relation of the important words and sentences in this paragraph, it is often helpful to rewrite the text in paragraph form.

   c. From the text which you've now rewritten so that you can see the relationship of the various parts of the paragraph, it is easy to make a simple outline

   d. It is helpful also to look up important words in the concordance that occur in this paragraph.

3. *Bible Study by Verses.* In studying the historical passages of the Bible, such as much of the Old Testament or parts of the gospels, each verse may have only one simple meaning.

But many verses in both the Old and New Testaments are rich with many great Bible truths which will demand more detailed study. There are many ways that you can study a single Bible verse.

   a. Study it by the verbs in the verse. For example, if you were studying **John 3:16**, you would find the following verbs: "loved, gave . . . should not perish . . . hath . . ."
Or simply take the nouns in this wonderful verse: "God . . . world . . . only begotten Son . . . whosoever . . . everlasting life."

   b. Study a verse through the personalities revealed. For example, once again taking John 3:16, these very simple but significant points are brought to light: "God . . . only begotten Son . . . whosoever . . . Him."

   c. Study a verse by looking for the great ideas revealed in it.

d. Sometimes a combination of these various ideas applied to a verse will bring the richest results.

4. *Bible Study by Books.* After you have begun to study the Bible by chapters or paragraphs or verses, you will be ready to study the Bible by books.

a. There are several methods of Bible book study.

(1) One is called the inductive method of studying in detail the contents of a Bible book and then drawing from these details general conclusions or principles concerning the contents and purpose of the book.

(2) Another method of book study is called the synthetic method. By this method, one reads the Bible book over several times to receive the general impressions of the main ideas and purpose of the book without attention to the details. (It is sometimes hard to distinguish these two methods.)

(3) In some case the study of a Bible book becomes a historical study, if that book relates the history of a nation or a man in a particular period of time. For example, the book of Exodus tells the history of the children of Israel from the death of Joseph in Egypt until the erection of the tabernacle in the wilderness under Moses. This covers approximately 400 years.

The principles for Bible book study, whether inductive or synthetic, are very similar. Such study will require more time than the previous methods mentioned, but it will be amply rewarding to you.

b. Here are some methods for Bible study by books:

(1) Read the book through to get the mood, the sweep, and the general emphasis of the book.

(2) Reread the book many times, each time asking yourself one main question and jotting down the answers you find as you read. Here are the most important questions to ask:

First Reading
What is the central theme or emphasis of this book? What is the key verse in this book?

Second Reading
Remembering the theme of the book, see how it is emphasized and developed in the book. Look for any special problems or applications to this theme.

Third Reading
What does this book tell me about the author and his circumstances when he wrote?

Fourth Reading
What does the book tell me about the people to whom the book was written and their circumstances, need, or problems?

Fifth Reading
What are the main divisions of the book? Is there any outline apparent in the logical organization and development of the book? During this reading, it is now time to divide the text into the paragraphs as you see them and then give a title to each paragraph.

Sixth and Successive Readings
Look for other facts and/or information that your earlier reading has suggested. By now certain words will stand out in the book. See how often they recur.

As you read and reread a book, you'll find soon that you begin to see its structure and its outline very clearly. It is true, however, that there are many more than one possible outline for any given book. It depends on the principle of division that you select.

5. *Bible Study by Words.* There are two profitable and helpful ways of studying great words or subjects in the Word of God.

a. Word study by Bible books. Certain words have special significance in certain Bible books. For example, after studying the Gospel of John as a book and by chapters, you'll find it instructive and inspiring to trace the word "believe" or "belief." It occurs almost 100 times.

b. General word study. The fine index and concordance which you'll find in this Bible will be a great help. By the study of great Bible words anyone can soon become familiar with the great doctrines of the Bible and understand the great theological principles which the Bible reveals.

6. *Bible Study by Topics.* Closely related to the method of study by words, is the study according to great topics or subjects: Bible prayers, Bible promises, Bible sermons, Bible songs, Bible poems, etc.

Or one might study Bible geography by reading rapidly through and looking for rivers, seas, mountains, etc., highlighted in Scripture. For example, the mountain top experiences in the life of Abraham are a thrilling study.

Another challenging study is to read rapidly through the Gospels and epistles looking for the commands of the Lord to us. The list of Bible topics is unlimited.

First, for a topical study on prayer, look up the word "prayer," "pray," etc., in your concordance. Look up every form of these words and such related words as "ask," "intercession," etc. After you have looked up these verses, study them and bring together all the teaching on prayer that you find. You will find: conditions of prayer, words to be used in prayer, results to expect from prayer, when to pray, where to pray, etc.

7. *Bible Study Through Biography.* The Bible is a record of God's revealing Himself to men and through men. The Old Testament as well as the New is rich in such biographical studies.

Let us summarize various methods for studying the great Bible biographies:

a. Read the Bible book or passages in which this person's life is prominent, e.g., Abraham in **Gen. 12-25,** plus references to Abraham in **Heb. 11** and **Rom. 4.**

b. Trace character with your concordance.

c. Be careful to note indirect references to the man or his life in other portions of Scripture.

8. *Conclusion.* There are many other methods of studying the Bible: the psychological method, the sociological method, the cultural method, the philosophical method, etc. However, the methods given above largely include all these other methods.

Use all the Bible study methods suggested above. From time to time change your method so that you'll not become too accustomed to any one method, or tired from delving too deeply into one type of study.

The great thrill of Bible study is discovering these eternal truths of God's Word for yourself and embarking on the adventure of obeying them and experiencing the blessing in your personal life.

II. FAMILY BIBLE STUDY

Nothing is more important in a Christian home than the family altar. At a convenient time when all members of the family are home, father or mother should lead them in worship of God and in reading His Word. A simple program for family worship includes singing a hymn, an opening prayer by a family member, a brief Bible study and a concluding period of prayer in which all members take part.

The family altar and Bible study will bind the family togetrher, eliminate juvenile delinquency, foster deeper love, and enable each member to become a stronger, better Christian.

Since family Bible study usually includes small children, it is wise to avoid deep, difficult topics and study something of interest and help to all. Such subjects might be Bible biographies as outlined above, stories of miracles and deeds of Jesus as revealed in the Gospels, miracles in the Old Testament, and other narrative portions of the Bible. It is wise to keep the study brief and concentrate on a short passage of Scripture. For example, if the family is going to study the life of Moses, it could be divided into units like this:

First day: The birth of Moses: Exodus 2:1-10
Second day: Moses' great choice and great mistake: Heb. 11:24-27; Ex. 2:11-15
Third day: Moses' wilderness training: Ex. 2:16-25
Fourth day: Moses' call to serve God: Ex. 3:1-22
Fifth day: Moses' argument with God: Ex. 4:1-17
Sixth day: Moses' return to Egypt: Ex. 4:18-31, etc.

Here are several practical hints on how to make your family Bible study interesting and profitable to all:

1. Keep your family Bible study reasonably short: one brief chapter or several paragraphs a day.

2. Have each member read a verse.

3. Appoint one family member to lead in worship each day and select the passage to read. This one may appoint others to help in the family worship.

4. Read through a Bible book, a chapter or several paragraphs each day. As you read, together decide on a name or a title for each chapter and memorize this.

5. After reading the passage, have each member in the family explain one verse or one paragraph.

6. Let the leader (or the father or mother) prepare five or ten questions on the Bible passage and ask various members of the family to answer these questions after the passage has been read.

7. Study the maps in your Bible together and trace Paul's journeys, or the wandering of the children of Israel in Egypt.

8. Study Bible topics together. Assign verses concerning a topic or great word to each member of the family. Let each read this verse and tell what his verse teaches about his topic or word.

9. After the Bible reading, have each member tell what this verse means to him or how he believes it can be applied to his life.

10. Make up Bible games by having each member make up questions to try to stump the others.

11. Study a Bible book together, using the hints given above. There are many wonderful ways to make the Bible the heart of your home.

III. PRINCIPLES OF BIBLE INTERPRETATION

Since the Bible was written by many men over a period covering 1,500 years; and since the last author of the Bible has been dead 1,900 years, there are definite problems in understanding the exact meaning of certain passages of the Bible.

There is a need to interpret clearly certain passages of the Bible because there is a gap between the way we think and the words we use today and the way of thinking and the words that these Bible writers used thousands of years ago. Bible scholars have pointed out that there are language gaps—differences in words that we use; there are cultural gaps—different customs were in vogue then. There are geographical gaps—certain rivers that are spoken of in the Bible have long since dried up. Some places that are spoken of frequently in the Bible are not on our modern maps. And then there are historical gaps—the Bible speaks of kings and empires which existed years ago.

Therefore there is a need for Bible interpretation. This is a fascinating study in itself, but I want to give you just a few principles of interpretation of the Bible that will keep you from error and help you to understand the difficult passages of the Word of God.

1. Always remember that the Bible is God's infallible, inerrantly inspired word. There are no mistakes in the Bible. God has included everything in the Bible that He wants you to know and that is necessary for you to know concerning salvation and your Christian life.
2. The second principle of interpretation is to interpret the Bible in the light of its historical background. There are three aspects of this:
   a. Study the personal circumstances of the writer.
   b. Study the culture and customs of the country at the time that the writing or story was taking place.
   c. Study and interpret the Bible in the light of the actual historical situation and events that were taking place at the time of the story.
3. Interpret the Bible according to the purpose and plan of each book.
   Every Bible book has its specific purpose intended by the Holy Spirit to bring some special message to man.
4. One of the most important principles of interpretation is always to interpret according to the context of a verse.
   The "context" is the verses immedi-

ately preceding and immediately following the verse you are studying. If you do not take care to interpret the verse according to the context, you could make the Bible teach atheism. For the Bible itself says, "there is no God" (**Psalms 14:1**). But the context makes very clear what this verse means: The immediately preceding sentence says, "the *fool* hath said in his heart, 'there is not God.' "

Always study the passage immediately preceding and immediately following any verse, word, or topic to make sure that you see this truth in the setting which God intended.

5. Interpret always according to the correct meaning of words. You can find the correct meaning of a word in several ways. First of all look up the usage of the word in other parts of the Bible to find how it was used in that generation. Another way is to look up its background or its root. You could do this with the use of a dictionary. Still another way is to look up the synonyms—words that are similar in meaning but slightly different: for example, "prayer," "intercession," "supplication."
6. Interpret the Bible also according to all of the parallel passages which deal with the subject, and according to the message of the entire Bible.
   The more you read the Bible, the more you will understand that in it God is revealing His way of salvation to men from beginning to end. And when you come to a difficult passage, think of it in the light of the overall purpose of the Bible. For example, the animal sacrifices of the Old Testament are meant to be a picture of the perfect sacrifice of Jesus Christ on the cross.

If you will follow these simple rules, you will be kept from error and extremes, and you will be helped to understand correctly the teachings of even the more difficult passages in God's Word.

Business Terms Dictionary

BUSINESS AND INVESTMENT

ASSETS—those items, property, and services that reflect the total financial value of a person, business, or estate. Assets include the value of all real property and personal property you own.

BALANCE SHEET—a statement of the financial condition of an individual or business at any given time.

BETTER BUSINESS BUREAU—a nonprofit organization that gives information about companies and corporations to the public. In many instances, it provides information you will need when purchasing or using these specific products. The bureau patrols the advertising and marketing methods used by various companies. It may also provide business speakers for different school and civic groups.

BOND—a certificate evidencing a debt of a corporation. In other words, it is the corporation's promise to repay an amount of money that it has borrowed, usually with added interest; the bond holder simply lends his money to the corporation for repayment at a later date. When a corporation issues a bond without any security behind it, the bond is called a *debenture*. When there is security, it is called a *secured bond.*

BOOK VALUE—the assets of a business as shown on its account books. As used in the stock market, the term generally refers to a company's book value for each share of common stock. This value is obtained by dividing the company's total book value by the number of outstanding shares.

BROKER'S COMMISSION—a fee paid to a person for acting as an agent in a contract of sale. This fee is generally decided prior to the transaction and confirmed in writing.

CAPITAL—the total amount of property or assets an individual or business owns.

CAPITAL GAINS/LOSSES—In general, a *capital gain* is the excess of capital assets over the appraised value or cost of an asset. For example, if you've sold a share of stock at a higher price than what you paid for it, the excess is called a capital gain. A *capital loss* exists when an asset costs more than its appraised value, or if the asset is sold at a price less than it originally costs.

Under present tax laws, if an asset is held at least six months and then sold, the gain is considered to be a long-term capital gain and is charged at a lower tax rate.

CHARITABLE CONTRIBUTIONS—An individual or a corporation is allowed to give away a limited amount of money or property and deduct it from taxable income. Many organizations are allowed to receive these contributions.

COMMERCIAL PAPER—a piece of paper used to convey value in a business transaction.

COMMON STOCK—shares of stock that receive equal dividends from a corporation. When a company issues different classes of stock, the shares without special rights are *common*. Most of the stock issued by corporations is common.

COMPOUND INTEREST—interest paid upon interest, as well as upon principal. That is, the interest earned upon the principal is added to the principal, thereby raising the amount of the return to the lender. For example, D promises to repay $100 to C at the end of the year with interest at six percent per annum, compounded quarterly. At the end of the first quarter, the interest earned would be added to the principal. At the end of the second quarter, interest would be computed on the principal plus the preceding quarter's interest. This pattern would continue for the last two quarters as well. Thus, interest would be paid upon interest, as well as upon principal.

CONSUMER PROTECTION AGENCY—an organization created by the federal government to insure a customer's rights in business transactions. This agency offers information about truth in advertising, franchises, business rights, fair debt collection, label information, credit reporting, equal credit opportunity, and truth in lending.

CONVERTIBLE BOND—a bond that may be exchanged for stock in the corporation, under the conditions stated in the bond.

CORPORATION—an association of individuals that has its own distinct legal identity. A corporation has certain legal advantages for carrying on commercial activities. Among these advantages are: (1) continuity of the business. Its work will not be stopped if a member dies or withdraws from the corporation. (2) transferability of its property interest. This is done when the corporation sells stock. In this way, the corporation shares its financial obligations with people outside the corporation. (3) centralization of business control in the hands of its board of directors. (4) little or no individual liability for the debts of the corporation.

A corporation is a separate entity in the eyes of the law. Individuals who own an interest in the corporation (evidenced by their shares or certificates of stock) are called *stockholders.* By owning a share of stock, the stockholder generally enjoys three basic rights: (1) a right to share in the profits, (2) a right to vote upon major business decisions of the corporation, and (3) a right to share in the remaining assets if the corporation is dissolved.

The shares of stock may be given away, traded, or sold. This is generally done at a stock exchange. The exchange simply acts as a place where the various shares of stock can be traded.

DEPRECIATION—the decrease in the value of an asset or property due to wear and tear, obsolescence, and so on.

EX-DIVIDEND—A corporation may declare that it will pay a dividend to everyone who owns shares of its stock at a given date, and pay the dividends at a future date. The shares traded between the given dates will be marked *Ex-Dividend,* meaning they do not entitle the buyer to the new dividend.

FAIR MARKET VALUE—the price arrived at by a buyer and seller who are ready, willing, and able to buy and sell an asset.

FIRST-IN, FIRST-OUT—a method of pricing goods, based on the assumption that a merchant sells or uses goods in the same order in which they are received.

GIFT TAX—a tax upon the transfer of property, rather than on the property itself. This tax is levied during the lifetime of the person making the gift, rather than after his death. The federal gift tax applies only to the transfer of property by individuals, and not to transfers by corporations.

The gift must be made by a taxpayer, and it may be deducted only in the year the gift was made. The Internal Revenue Service has many lengthy rules governing this type of charitable contribution, especially gifts to corporations.

GOOD WILL—an intangible asset of every successful business. A business is said to have "good will" if its customers will probably return to make additional purchases.

INTANGIBLE ASSETS—the powers of a person or business that will allow continuing business success. Intangible assets would include a variety of privileges such as good will, secret processes, patents, and copyrights.

INTEREST—payment that a lender receives for the use of his money. It is usually a fixed percentage of the amount loaned (called *principal*), and it is to be paid at an agreed time.

INVENTORY—a list of the goods or property held by an individual or business.

INVESTMENT TRUST—an organization that accepts money from subscribers and invests it for them. The organization attempts to earn profits that can be distributed to the various subscribers.

LAST-IN, FIRST-OUT—a method of pricing goods, based on the assumption that the goods last received are the goods first sold or used.

LIABILITIES—the debts and obligations of an individual, business, or state.

LISTED STOCK—a stock of a corporation that is listed on the national stock exchange, such as the New York Stock Exchange or the American Stock Exchange. A stock that is not listed on one of the national exchanges is known as *unlisted.* It is sometimes referred to as stock "sold over the counter," or *over-the-counter* stock.

LOAN SHARK—a person who lends money at an exorbitant or illegal rate of interest. This is often called a "shirt-pocket loan." Usually it is for a short time (30 days or less) and its interest rate will be very high—perhaps 40 or 50 percent. Loan sharks often use severe techniques for making loans and collecting them, sometimes resorting to violence.

MONTHLY INVESTMENT PLAN—a plan in which an investor makes monthly payments to his stock broker. With this money, the broker buys as many shares as possible of certain stocks for the investor. If stock prices are low, the investor receives more stocks; if prices are high, he receives less stock. The investor may discontinue his monthly payment at any time.

MUNICIPAL BOND—a city's promise to repay a certain amount of money at a predetermined date and at a stated rate of interest. Federal and state governments levy no income tax on the interest paid by municipal bonds, so this is a very popular source of financing. A city or a county often uses this type of bond to finance large capital improvements.

MUTUAL FUND—an investment company that sells shares to the public, usually at a price determined by supply and demand. The proceeds of the sale are invested to make a profit. As the fund earns higher profits, its shares become more valuable.

NET WORTH—what remains after liabilities or obligations are subtracted from assets. As used in stock-market trading, the term means the net worth of each outstanding share of a company. It is obtained by dividing a company's total net worth by the number of its outstanding shares (i.e., the shares owned by persons outside the corporation).

NO-LOAD MUTUAL FUND—a mutual fund that charges no commission for the shares you buy. It may be hard to purchase shares of a no-load fund; most brokers do not like to sell them because they do not make any money on the sale. Investors usually buy these shares directly from the company that manages the no-load fund.

PREFERRED STOCK—stock that is given priority in the sharing of profits (called *dividends*). The holder of preferred stock is entitled to receive dividends out of the profits of a company at a fixed annual rate, before any profits are distributed to the common stockholders. With some preferred stocks, the fixed dividend is *cumulative*. In that case, if the fixed dividend is not paid within a given year, it must be paid the following year before any profits are distributed to common stockholders. If the preferred stock is *noncumulative,* no such accumulations take place.

PRICE-EARNINGS RATIO—the earnings of a corporation, divided by the number of shares. This ratio is a handy index to the financial condition of the corporation. Generally, as the company becomes more profitable, its price-earnings ratio increases.

PROBATE—official proof that a certain document is valid. For example, a probate court must determine whether a will is valid before the will can take legal effect. Witnesses who have signed the will are usually asked to appear; but it can be probated without their presence. After the court probates a will, it issues a certificate that declares the will legal and official.

PUTS and CALLS—A *put* is an option to sell a fixed amount of a certain stock or commodity at a specified price within a limited amount of time. A *call* is the privilege to buy a stock or commodity at a fixed price within a limited amount of time.

RECEIVABLES—the unpaid claims, bills, and notes of services or merchandise that other merchants have received from a company. These are carried on the company's books as being "due."

RULE OF 78's—the method for computing a refund of interest when a loan contract is paid before maturity. Another name for the Rule of 78's is the *Sum of the Digits*. The number *78* is the sum of the digits 1–12, which stand for the months of the year.

For example, let's say a person borrows $1,000 for 12 months. After two months, he decides to repay the loan. He should be charged only for the amount of time he used the money, so the rule of 78's says this figure would be 24/78 of the interest that would have been charged for the entire year. The borrower can get back 54/78 of the finance charge. *Note:* The rule of 78's applies only to a 12-month contract period.

SAVINGS BOND—a borrowing device that the federal government originated after World War II. The government was heavily in debt and needed a way to raise large amounts of money in a hurry. So it issued savings bonds to attract small loans from private citizens.

Today you can buy a Savings Bond for an amount smaller than its face value and turn it in for the full amount in cash at the end of a seven-year period. The savings bond earns about six percent interest during that time. Savings bonds are not as popular today as they were several years ago, because most banks and savings-and-loan companies pay a higher rate of return.

SECURITY—something given as a promise of repayment. A security may be any note, stock, treasury stock, bond, or debenture. It also includes any document that shows a person's membership or ownership in an organization that has borrowed money from him.

SHORT SALE—a contract to sell shares of stock that the seller does not own, or that are not under his control. The seller hopes that when he has to deliver the stock to the purchaser, its price will be lower than when he made the contract. If it is, he can buy the stock on the open market, deliver it, and make a profit.

SIMPLE INTEREST—interest paid only on the principal balance, and not figured on the accumulated interest. Simple interest is paid simply for the use of the money borrowed.

STOCK SPLIT—A corporation with 100,000 shares outstanding (i.e., owned by private investors) may decide to recall them and issue 200,000 shares, giving each shareholder two shares for one. This is known as a *stock split*. It does not increase or reduce the value of the shareholder's assets; his interest in the corporation remains the same. But if the price of the stock rises after a split, the value of the investor's holdings will increase more rapidly.

STRAIGHT-LINE METHOD—the most common way of figuring depreciation of an asset for tax purposes. Another name for it is *fixed percentage*. It is based on the theory that an asset will loose value at the same rate each year.

To use the straight-line method, estimate the ultimate salvage value of the item and subtract this from its original cost. Divide the result by the number of years you expect to use the item. This will give you the amount of straight-line depreciation for each year.

TREASURY BILL—an obligation of the United States Government to pay the bearer a fixed amount of money after a certain number of days. The Treasury Bill is the most important investment in today's money market. The most common Treasury Bills are the three- and six-month bills; they can be purchased at any Federal Reserve Bank. These bills raise new cash for the federal government. The biggest buyers of Treasury Bills are banks, corporations, and state and local government.

UNIFORM GIFT TO MINORS ACT—a federal law that allows an adult to make a gift to a minor without the minor's having to pay a gift tax. This gift may be in the form of money, security, proceeds from a life insurance policy, or annuities.

The gift can only be made to one minor, and only one person can act as custodian of the gift for the minor. The gift must be final, and the person who gives it must convey its legal title to the minor.

USURY—the act of lending money at an illegally high rate of interest. Usury laws vary from state to state. In some states, a violator of the usury law is required to refund the entire amount of interest paid; in other states, only the amount of excess interest is given back.

WARRANTS AND OPTIONS—A *warrant* confers the right to purchase stock in a corporation at a later date, under stated terms and conditions. A corporation may sell warrants much like it sells common stock. An *option* is similar, except that it is not necessarily sold. The corporation may give an option to a stockholder or friend of the company as a special privilege.

BANKING

BANKER'S ACCEPTANCE—a bank's agreement to accept a bill of exchange or bank draft. Since the bank becomes responsible to pay on the instrument, a person would prefer to exchange a bill or draft for an acceptance.

BILL OF EXCHANGE—a written order to pay a stated amount out of a bank account. A bill of exchange must conform to the following requirements: (1) It must be in writing and signed by the *drawer*—the person issuing the order; (2) It must contain an unconditional order to pay a certain sum in money; (3) It must be payable on demand or at a fixed time; (4) It must state that the amount is payable to a designated person or company, or to the person who holds the bill.

A bank will not honor a bill that does not conform to these requirements. If the bill does conform, it can move about quite freely in business transactions. There is an obvious risk involved in purchasing a bill of exchange that does not conform to any of these requirements, because it may not be honored by the bank that holds the drawer's account. Such a bill would be called a *non-negotiable* instrument.

Many of the common bills of exchange are checks, drafts, trade acceptances, and banker's acceptances. They involve a *drawer* (the person who draws up the bill), a *drawee* (the person who keeps the drawer's account), and a *payee* (a person to whom the bill is paid); so bills of exchange are referred to as *three-party* instruments. Promissory notes are known as *two-party* instruments, since they involve a *maker* (the person who makes the promise to pay) and a *payee* (the person to whom the note is payable).

The drawee is not responsible for the document until he accepts it. He may do this by writing the word *accepted* on the face of the document, followed by his name or initials.

CERTIFICATE OF DEPOSIT—a certificate issued by a bank to acknowledge the deposit of a specific sum of money. The bank promises to pay the depositor the face amount, along with an agreed amount of interest. Most certificates of deposit have an established expiration date; in all cases, the full payment is made only when the depositor gives the certificate back to the bank.

CERTIFIED CHECK—a bank's written promise to pay a specific amount of money on behalf of one of the bank's account holders. In effect, the bank takes funds out of the account and assumes the duty of paying the check when it is negotiated. Thus, it has been said that "a certified check is as good as cash."

CHECK—a bill of exchange drawn on a bank and payable on demand. It is the most common negotiable instrument.

When a depositor opens up a deposit account with a bank, he becomes a lender and a bank becomes his borrower. Under their contract, the bank must surrender the funds of a depositor whenever the depositor gives an order in the form of a check. The check must be presented to the bank within a reasonable time after it is issued.

A bank is not primarily responsible to pay the check; the person who wrote the check is. Therefore, a bank may refuse to honor a check. But if it refuses to pay a valid check, the bank has breached its contract with the depositor, and may be held liable for any losses the depositor incurs because the check was not honored.

COLLATERAL—a pledge of real or personal property to secure the payment of a loan or the extension of credit. Collateral can be in many forms, but it should have enough value to secure the loan. Also, it should be in a form that the lender can convert to cash, if the need arises. Many banks use only the borrower's signature as collateral for small loans. But each lending institution must decide the amount and type of collateral it will accept.

DISCOUNTING—a bank's practice of charging a fee for converting credit instruments into cash. A bank may advance money to the person who holds the instrument and charge him its usual discount rate. Then the bank holds the documents until maturity. If the person or institution that issued the document pays the bank, the transaction is closed. If not, the bank will expect the depositor to return its money.

FEDERAL RESERVE BANK—The Federal Reserve System was established in 1913 by President Woodrow Wilson when he signed the Federal Reserve Act. This act created 12 regional banks across the nation, controlled by the Federal Reserve Board of governors in Washington, D.C. These banks regulate the flow of credit and money. Any bank that wants to use money from the Federal Reserve Bank in its region must become a member of the Federal Reserve System. The Federal Reserve Bank provides many services for its member banks; it handles their reserve accounts, furnishes currency and coins, clears and collects checks, transfers funds by wire, and acts as a depository for the funds handled by government agencies.

INDEPENDENT RETIREMENT ACCOUNT—a bank account for accumulating money that a person will use during retirement. Each year the depositor can put up to fifteen percent of his earned income in the account, up to a maximum of $1,750 each year. This money is not charged Federal income taxes during the current year; it is taxed only when an individual starts

withdrawing money. He can do this as early as age 59½, and he must begin withdrawing the money by age 70½. He can take out the deposit in one lump sum or in a certain amount per month.

If both husband and wife are working, each of them can have an Individual Retirement Account. They can set aside a maximum total of $3,000 for these accounts each year. The bank pays interest to these accounts while the money is on deposit; the rate of interest varies from bank to bank.

INTEREST PENALTY—an amount of interest that you forfeit to the bank if you withdraw the money in a time certificate of deposit before it matures. The federal law states that when you cash a certificate of deposit before maturity, you will earn the regular passbook savings rate *minus* 90 days' interest. This means that if you cash a time certificate of deposit early, the bank will not pay interest for 90 days of the time you had the certificate in effect. The bank would pay you the regular passbook rate for the rest of the time you had the money on deposit.

JOINT TENANTS—the partners who jointly own an asset. In banking, this term usually refers to two or more people who jointly own a bank account. If one of the partners dies, his interest or ownership is automatically transferred to the remaining owner(s). Married couples often establish bank accounts as joint tenants.

LINE OF CREDIT—the amount of money that any one person, corporation, or organization can borrow with a certain amount of collateral. Different lending institutions have different ways of arriving at this figure.

For example, let us say that a certain bank has a policy of financing only 75 percent of the value of an automobile. A certain vehicle is valued at $10,000. The bank would loan up to $7,500 for this car; that's the line of credit available.

NONTAXABLE TRUST—an account that an employer uses to provide a stock bonus, pension, or profit-sharing plan for the benefit of his employees. The money deposited in this trust account will not be taxed if it meets all the requirements imposed by federal and state governments.

PRINCIPAL—the original amount of debt, or the initial amount a person owes to another. A bank charges interest only on the principal.

PROMISSORY NOTE—a written promise to pay. A promissory note must conform to the following: (1) It must be in writing and signed by the maker; (2) It must contain an unconditional promise to pay a certain sum of money; (3) It must be payable on demand or at a fixed future time; (4) It must be payable to a designated person or to the bearer.

The payee does not need to hold the note until the maturity date. He may decide to sell it to someone else; in that case, if the instrument is *order paper* (i.e., written to pay a designated person), he endorses the instrument and gives it to the buyer. If it is *bearer paper* (i.e., written to pay the bearer), he simply gives it to the buyer.

PROXY—authorization to allow another person to vote in your absence at a business meeting. In banking, this term usually refers to the proxies that an account holder in a savings-and-loan company may give to the officers of his company.

REDISCOUNTING—If a bank wants to convert some of its holdings into cash, it would submit its bills and notes to its local Federal Reserve Bank for rediscounting. After charging a *rediscount fee,* the Federal Reserve Bank would dispense the cash and hold the instruments until maturity. If all of the debtors pay their notes, the transaction is completed. If not, the Federal Reserve Bank will demand payment from the borrowing bank, which in turn will demand payment from the debtor(s).

SECURED LOAN—a loan that requires the borrower to make a pledge of collateral. Many institutions make only this type of loan. The greater the risk that the loan will not be repaid, the more security the lending institution will require. A good example might be an automobile loan. The bank will hold the title to the car as collateral until the debt has been paid. If the debt isn't paid, the bank may sell the car and recover the money it lended.

SIGNATURE LOAN—a loan that requires only the signature of the borrower as collateral. The lending institution relies on the integrity of the person who borrows the money. In most cases, this type of loan is for a short term and for a low amount.

TENANTS IN COMMON—ownership of an asset by two or more persons, in which each person has an individual interest. In banking, this term usually refers to the common ownership of a bank account. When one of the owners dies, his ownership passes to his heirs or to whomever he has named in his will; the surviving owners do not automatically inherit the account. Tenants in common do not necessarily have equal interests in the account. If one member wishes to dispose of his portion of the account and the others do not, he

may force them to convert the account to cash so that he can receive his share.

TRADE ACCEPTANCE—a bill of exchange that arises out of a merchant's purchase of goods. The seller of goods *(drawer)* signs over the debt of the buyer *(drawee),* to a designated agent *(payee).* When the buyer accepts this document, he agrees to pay his debt to the agent.

Let us say that ABC Company has purchased a shipment of goods on credit. The company that sold the goods to ABC issues a trade acceptance. When ABC Company receives the trade acceptance, one of its officers will write the word *accepted* across the face of the document with the date and place of payment, followed by his signature. ABC Company then becomes liable to pay the bill as stated.

TRUST OFFICER—one who manages a trust for someone else. The trust officer may also be called *trustee.*

INSURANCE

ACCIDENT INSURANCE—insurance covering such risks as death, dismemberment, loss of eyesight, or loss of time as a result of accidents. An *accident* is generally defined as an unlooked-for mishap; if someone intentionally cuts off his arm or leg, it would not be an accident. Accident insurance would cover death from accidental means, but no other kind of death.

DOUBLE INDEMNITY—an insurance company's practice of giving twice the amount of insurance benefits when an insured person dies. Double indemnity is most commonly given when the insured person dies in an accident. Many insurance companies do not give double indemnity if the death occurred through suicide, service in time of war, air travel, or disease.

FIRE INSURANCE—insurance that guards against the loss of property by fire. The person who owns a fire insurance policy must have an *insurable interest* in the property involved. In other words, the insured must have a lawful, economic interest in the safety or preservation of the property from loss or destruction. (For example, the average citizen couldn't buy fire insurance on the White House.)

FLOOD INSURANCE—insurance against loss caused by cloudbursts and floods, tidal waves or overflowing streams and rivers. This type of insurance is usually available in low-lying areas and in the vicinity of rivers and dams.

HEALTH INSURANCE—insurance to cover losses caused by illness or sickness.

INCONTESTABILITY—protection against having a life insurance policy cancelled by the insurance company. Most policies state that they are incontestable after two years, unless you fail to pay your premium.

INCREASE OF HAZARD—taking unnecessary or unusual risks. Usually a fire insurance policy will state that the insurance company is not liable for loss or damage if the likelihood of fire is increased by any means within your control. For example, the company may not pay for a fire if you keep fireworks, explosives, gasoline, kerosene, or other highly flammable materials on your property.

INDUSTRIAL LIFE INSURANCE—a fairly small amount of life insurance, for which you pay premiums at weekly or other frequent intervals. Generally, this kind of life insurance policy offers the least amount of protection for the dollars you spend.

INSURABLE INTEREST—Usually a person takes out a life insurance policy on himself. However, you can take out a life insurance policy on someone else and make yourself the beneficiary, if you have an insurable interest in the life of that person. The term *insurable interest* generally means: (1) In the case of persons related by blood or law, an interest that arises from love and affection, or (2) In the case of other persons, a lawful economic interest in protecting the life of the insured person.

LIFE INSURANCE—a form of insurance that pays benefits in the event of death. An insurance company will pay an agreed sum of money to a designated person (called a *beneficiary*) when the insured person dies. The beneficiary may be the estate of the insured, a member of his family, a business associate, or even a stranger. The policy will state whether you can change the name of the beneficiary. If you can't, the beneficiary has what is called a *vested interest*—that is, his interest in the policy may not be stripped from him without his consent. Thus, you may take out a life insurance policy on a member of your family or upon the life of another person who owes you a debt. A business partnership may take out a policy on the lives of its partners. Likewise, a corporation may obtain a life insurance policy for each of its corporate officers. But if you have no insurable interest in the life of the person insured, the law considers it to be a *contract of wager*. Even if an insurance company issues a policy under these circumstances, it is illegal and unenforceable.

MARINE INSURANCE—insurance that covers losses connected with marine activities. This contract may also protect against losses on inland waters or on land, if the losses are connected with a sea voyage. The person or firm obtaining this kind of insurance must have an insurable interest in the subject of the policy (e.g., the boat or the cargo carried by the boat).

MUTUAL INSURANCE—a form of insurance in which the policyholders make up the insurance company. (The *policyholders* are those who buy insurance policies.) Mutual insurance companies only insure the lives and property of their members. When the annual premiums that members pay exceed the amount of losses covered by the company, the company often pays a *dividend* (i.e., a small refund) to the policyholders.

PAID-UP and ENDOWMENT OPTIONS—the opportunity to convert a life insurance policy to another form of insurance, so that you do not have to pay premiums. The original policy may state that when you do this you can keep the same amount of insurance in force *(paid-up option)*, or that you will have a declining amount of insurance *(endowment option)*. Usually these options require that: (1) The money you've invested in the policy must be earning interest equal to the amount of your premium. (2) You must ask the company to convert the policy. (3) Your request will be subject to the company's approval. (4) The company will determine how much insurance you can buy under the new plan. (5) If you've borrowed money against your present policy, your new policy will become the collateral for the loan. Not all life insurance policies carry these options.

UNOCCUPANCY—a clause that states that the insurance company will not pay for loss or damage that occurs while an insured building is vacant or unoccupied beyond a certain period of time—usually ten days.

WAIVER OF PREMIUM—a provision that allows you to stop paying premiums on a life insurance policy if you become disabled. Your policy would remain in force, and when your disability ends you resume making the payments.

REAL ESTATE

ABSTRACT OF TITLE—a legal document that shows the history of ownership for a certain piece of property. In most states, the abstract of title passes from the seller to the buyer with each sale of property, and the buyer's name is added to the permanent record. The seller must pay the expense of bringing the abstract up to date. The buyer must have an attorney check the abstract to be sure it is complete.

APPRECIATION—a property's increase in value over a length of time. It is the opposite of *depreciation*. For example, let us say that a tract of land was purchased for $500 per acre five years ago. Today the same land would probably be worth at least $1,000 per acre.

ASSESSMENT—a government's charge against a certain parcel of real estate. This charge is usually made to cover the property owner's share of the cost of a public improvement such as a street or sewer.

BREACH OF CONTRACT—a situation in which one or both parties fail to perform a legal contract. Both parties must accept the breach. If one doesn't accept it for any reason, he may sue the other party to regain what was lost.

EARNEST MONEY—a down payment that a purchaser of real estate makes to show his good faith in the transaction. Earnest money shows the seller that the buyer really means to follow through with the agreement. Sometimes the seller refunds the money if the transaction fails to go through; sometimes he doesn't. This decision is up to the seller.

ESCROW—an account where money is held until a contract has been fulfilled. This type of arrangement is most often used in the sale of real estate. An escrow agent holds the buyer's down payment until the title search is completed and the transaction is closed. The seller receives none of the money until all the legalities are in order. Banks and lawyers are the most common escrow agents.

FEE SIMPLE—the transfer of property to someone and his heirs without limitations. An estate or inheritance that you own completely and without restrictions is called an estate in *fee simple*. You may use it in any way you choose during your life time or after your death (through your will). If you have not made any plans for the distribution of this estate, it must pass to your heirs without any future limitations.

FIRST/SECOND MORTGAGE—a lender's claim to a piece of property that the owner has used as collateral on a loan. If the property owner fails to repay his loan, the lender can force him to sell the property to repay the debt. The only difference between a first and second mortgage is the order in which the lenders file their claim on the property. A second mortgage would only be good after the first mortgage had been satisfied. A lender would prefer to have a first mortgage rather than a second mortgage, since he would be more likely to get his money back.

LIEN—a claim that a person or institution has upon the property of another. The borrower must keep the property as security for the debts. In other words, a lien puts a "hold" on a certain item until its borrower has paid the debt. A lender may hold a lien on real estate, an automobile, or any other item of personal property.

PRORATED TAXES—taxes that are split between the buyer and the seller of a piece of property. When property is sold, the taxes are usually divided according to the time the sale takes place. The buyer should only be expected to pay taxes for the time after he receives title to the property, and not for the entire year.

QUIT-CLAIM DEED—a deed that gives a buyer whatever right, title, or interest that the seller has in a piece of property. It does not indicate whether other persons have an interest in the property, too.

SURVEYOR'S REPORT—a report from a licensed surveyor, which is used to determine limits and boundaries of a piece of property. The surveyor checks legal descriptions of the tract and usually drives stakes at the corners of the property to aid anyone else determining the boundaries at a later time. A surveyor's report should include the measurements of the land in terms of acres, square miles, or square feet. It should also give definite boundaries, the corner locations, and a definite point of beginning the measurement.

The cost of this report varies upon the time required for the research. This fee is customarily paid by a person who is purchasing the property.

TITLE INSURANCE—a contract to protect the owner of real estate against loss arising from defective property titles, hidden liens, or other encumbrances.

Usually title insurance losses are very small, because title insurance companies examine all legal papers very carefully before they will insure them. The premiums paid for title insurance are quite high, because of the amount of time it takes to research the documents. The title company must examine many records of land titles involving many previous owners, deeds, mortgages, and so on. A title insurance policy remains in effect until some further change of ownership takes place, or until a claim is made against a property.

WARRANTY DEED WITH FULL COVE-NANTS—the most complete form of property title that a seller can give. In this type of deed, a seller guarantees: (1) that he has the right to give the purchaser the title as designated in the contract; (2) that the buyer shall enjoy the premises without having to dispute claims from others; (3) that the premises are free from encumbrances such as tax debts; (4) that the seller will provide any further necessary assurances of the title; and (5) that the seller will forever guarantee the buyer's title to the premises. This is the most valuable form of protection, from the purchaser's viewpoint.

Of course, a buyer can obtain title insurance from a title insurance company for even more protection.

BIOGRAPHICAL DICTIONARY

It would be impossible to name all of the people who have played an important role in the history of the United States. But in this chapter we list some of the leading Americans from all walks of life, both living and dead, who have left their mark on American society.

AARON, HENRY L. "HANK" (1934–   ), baseball player. Born in Mobile, Alabama, Aaron began playing for the Indianapolis Clowns of the Negro League in 1952. He joined the Milwaukee Braves as shortstop in 1954 and soon moved to an outfield position. The next year he emerged as top batter of the National League with a .328 average. When the Braves won the World Series in 1957, Aaron was voted the league's Most Valuable Player. He moved with the Braves to Atlanta in 1966, and broke Babe Ruth's home-run record when he hit run number 715 on April 8, 1974 in Atlanta.

ABBOTT, BUD (1896–1974), associated in comedy with Lou Costello. A son of Harry Abbott who served with Ringling Brothers' Circus, he organized a network of burlesque houses in the generation of the Ziegfeld Follies. Abbott starred in several movies, including *One Night in the Tropics, Hold That Ghost,* and *Abbott and Costello Meet Frankenstein.* He promoted the sale of millions of war bonds in World War II and entertained troops during the war. His efforts on behalf of radio, stage, and screen performance made him a well-known entertainer in an age that placed a premium on slapstick.

ABBOTT, LYMAN (1835–1922), an ordained minister of the Congregational Church; prominent journalist and exponent of the "social gospel." Abbott was associated with *Harper's Magazine* and *The Christian Union* (also known as *The Outlook*). He authored *The Life and Literature of the Ancient Hebrews* and other titles that sought to integrate religion and science. After the publication of Charles Darwin's theories of evolution, he became involved with liberal writers and thinkers. Abbott rarely opposed the theological trends of his day. He believed that man was constantly improving, and he affirmed the essential goodness of man. Ira Brown has written an excellent biography titled *Lyman Abbott* (1953).

ABERNATHY, RALPH DAVID (1926–   ), civil rights leader of the Southern Christian Leadership Conference. Abernathy was closely identified with Dr. Martin Luther King and the human rights revolution of the 1960s. A deliberative preacher committed to nonviolence, he was a member of the Atlantic Ministers Union and Operation Breadbasket. This gave him a unique sensitivity to the religious applications of human needs. During the Montgomery (Alabama) bus boycott he demonstrated strength of purpose and determination that helped to change the social order. He was ordained into the Baptist ministry in 1948.

ACHESON, DEAN (1893–1971), Secretary of State under President Truman; a diplomat in the early stages of the Cold War between the United

States and the Soviet Union. Acheson wrote *Power and Diplomacy,* among other titles. He was largely responsible for the establishment of the North Atlantic Treaty Organization (NATO). During the period of McCarthyism, Acheson refused to testify against his friend Alger Hiss, who had been charged with espionage. He received many honors during his lifetime, including honorary degrees from Yale University and Wesleyan University. He was affiliated with the Democratic Party.

ACUFF, ROY (1903–), born Maynardsville, Tennessee, a noted country-music singer and bandleader. Acuff organized the Smokey Mountain Boys and has been closely associated with Nashville's Grand Ole Opry. He has achieved international fame for his songs, "Wabash Cannon Ball," "That Lonely Mountain of Clay," and "The Great Judgment Morning." He produced a succession of recording classics for Columbia Records and was elected to the Country Music Hall of Fame. An automobile accident in 1965 left him severely injured, but he recovered sufficiently to record "Roy Acuff Sings Famous Opry Favorites" in 1967. He toured college campuses and received considerable recognition for his courage and determination in the face of his injuries.

ADDAMS, JANE (1860–1935), with Ellen Gates Starr organized Hull House in Chicago, Illinois, as a social and humanitarian center. Miss Addams was an early feminist and shared a Nobel Peace Prize. She authored *The Spirit of Youth* and *The City Streets.* Miss Addams was a leader of the Progressive Party and the Women's International Peace and Freedom. She sought legislation to end the corruption of political life in Chicago, and she served as an adviser to several Presidents.

ALI, MUHAMMAD (1942–), a significant figure in American boxing history, known for his colorful and poetic use of language. Born as Cassius M. Clay, he became associated with the Black Muslims and adopted his Muslim name. He refused to be drafted into the military in 1967 and became the center of legal controversies. He won numerous Golden Gloves awards, the Olympic Championship, and the Heavyweight Championship of the world. He has engaged in limited screen roles and frequently appears on television. Leon Spinks won the Heavyweight championship from Ali at Las Vegas, Nevada on February 15, 1978.

ALLEN, ETHAN (1738–1789), author and military figure from the Revolutionary period. During the American Revolution, Allen was captured by the British and was held as a prisoner of war. He organized a militia group in Vermont known as the Green Mountain Boys, and he asked the Continental Congress to raise similar units among the other colonies. He authored a book titled *Reason the Only Grade of Man* (1784), an apology for deism.

ALLPORT, GORDON (1897–1967), outstanding psychologist and teacher. Allport wrote *The Individual and His Religion.* He was associated with Harvard University and produced several new theories of personality and social psychology. Allport was involved in many different organizations, including the British Psychological Society and the National Research Council. He received numerous honors and recognitions, and served as editor of the *Journal for Abnormal and Social Psychology* from 1937 to 1949.

ANDERSON, MARIAN (1902–), black contralto recognized as an outstanding singer within concert and operatic circles. Honored in many countries for her musical excellence, she is a native of South Philadelphia. Miss Anderson authored *My Lord, What a Morning* and has travelled extensively, giving concerts in Great Britain, Scandinavia, Germany, and the Soviet Union. She has worked with Paul Robeson and others to achieve greater freedoms for black Americans. Miss Anderson has received special recognition from the National Association for the Advancement of Colored People (NAACP) and was honored by Howard University and 20 other colleges and universities with honorary doctorates.

Muhammad Ali lands a right to George Foreman during their title bout in Kinshasa, Zaire, on Oct. 29, 1976.

ANTHONY, SUSAN B. (1820–1906), an early proponent of women's rights, identified with the leadership of the American Suffrage Association and several temperance associations. Miss Anthony organized support for the enactment of the fourteenth and fifteenth amendments to the United States Constitution. She was involved in the publication of *The History of Woman's Suffrage* and worked with Ida Harper on *The Life and Work of Susan B. Anthony*.

ARBUCKLE, ROSCOE "FATTY" (1887–1933), American actor and producer born in Smith Center, Kansas. Mr. Arbuckle was identified with numerous motion picture roles in *Moonshine, The Bell Boy,* and *The Sheriff,* among others. He organized the Comique Film Corporation.

ARMSTRONG, LOUIS (1900–1971), jazz trumpeter and vocalist, also known as "Satchmo." Mr. Armstrong appeared in numerous movies, including *Pennies from Heaven, New Orleans, The Glenn Miller Story,* and *Hello Dolly.* Born in New Orleans, he revolutionized American Jazz. After touring the United States with his band, he played at the London Palladium and made numerous appearances before royalty in Sweden, Belgium, Holland, and Denmark. Mr. Armstrong's performance in *High Society* and numerous other recordings have made him an enduring part of the American scene.

ARMSTRONG, NEIL (1930–   ), veteran astronaut; the first man to set foot on the moon. Born near Wapakoneta, Ohio, he graduated from Purdue University. As a test pilot he was chosen to serve with Edwin Aldrin and Michael Collins on the historic moon flight of July 16, 1969. He also served as the command pilot for the later Gemini 8 program. Mr. Armstrong was an aviator for the United States Naval Reserve from 1949 to 1950. His name will always be associated with the famous words he spoke as he set foot on the moon: "One small step for man; one giant step for mankind."

ARNAZ, DESI (1917–1986), Latin American musician, comedian, and television producer. Born in Santiago, Cuba, he was associated in comedy with Lucille Ball during the early stages of television. Mr. Arnaz starred in several lesser-known movie musicals until he organized Desilu Productions with his wife, Lucille Ball. He co-starred with

Lucille Ball in other movie productions, such as *The Long, Long, Trailer* and *Forever Darling*. He hosted *Desilu Playhouse.* After 1962, he became an independent producer and president of Desi Arnaz Productions. He served during World War II in the United States Army.

ARNOLD, BENEDICT (1741–1801), a patriot and traitor from the Revolutionary period. Arnold organized an army early in the Revolutionary War, but escaped to the British in 1781. His name is synonymous with treachery. In the winter of 1776–1777, he was accused of misconduct and of stealing property from merchants in Montreal during the Canadian campaign. In anger, he resigned his commission in 1777. He conceived the idea of turning over the command of West Point to the English for a ransom; the plot was uncovered and he was forced to seek sanctuary with the English army.

ASBURY, FRANCIS (1745–1816), an early bishop in the Methodist Episcopal Church, associated with John Wesley. Asbury came to America as a missionary and remained to become a leading spokesman for the Independent Methodist Episcopal Church of America. He preached in the Pennsylvania, Maryland, Delaware, and Virginia colonies with a vigor and effectiveness that attracted popular notice. He developed a feud with rival church leader, Thomas Rankin, and during the American Revolution, they were asked to return to England. Rankin left but Asbury remained and became a leading force in the development of religious independence. He authored *Journals and Letters,* edited by Elmer T. Clark (1958).

ASTAIRE, FRED (1899–1987), American dancer and entertainer. His more famous screen performances include *Easter Parade* (1948), *On the Beach* (1959), and *The Pleasure of His Company* (1961). Mr. Astaire authored *Steps in Time.* His dancing abilities were emphasized in most of his screen performances, such as *The Ziegfeld Follies.* He starred on numerous television specials and occasionally appeared on *The Alcoa Premier.*

ASTOR, JOHN JACOB (1763–1848), American capitalist and entrepreneur. Born in Germany, he immigrated to America and became involved in fur-trading. He organized the American

Fur Company. Mr. Astor's life was characterized by the amassing of incredible wealth. Following the Louisiana Purchase, his trading activities penetrated the Northwest Territories; his traders would collect furs and sell them in the Far East. The town of Astoria was named after the family. After 1800, he became more interested in New York City real estate.

ATTUCKS, CRISPUS (1723-1770), among the group that precipitated the Boston Massacre. Attucks was among the first to die in the struggle that led to the American Revolution. Attucks has been described as a mulatto owned by Deacon William Browne of Framingham, Massachusetts. Although little is known about his life before the Boston Massacre, he has achieved stature as a martyr and patriot. J. B. Fisher, in the *American Historical Record,* Volume I (1872), sought to analyze the deeper meaning of Crispus Attucks' life.

AUDUBON, JOHN J. (1785-1851), a popular naturalist and *ornithologist* (one who studies birds). A man of science, he was responsible for the classification of numerous bird species. Audubon authored *Birds of America,* a classic in the study of birds. His fame extended to Europe. Audubon's earliest research was completed in the wilderness of Kentucky; he travelled to Henderson, Kentucky, to study rare birds. His famous bird drawings evolve from this period. His work is judged as excellent art and science.

AUTRY, GENE (1907-   ), singer, actor, and entertainer born in Tioga, Texas. Autry made his first record in 1929, singing cowboy songs. He starred in over eighty movies and owns several radio stations in the Southwest and on the West Coast. He has written many songs, including "You're the Only Star in My Blue Heaven" and "Here Comes Santa Claus." He has also produced several television specials.

BAEZ, JOAN (1941-   ), folk singer and political activist identified with the anti-war protests of the 1960s. Her musical style reflects melancholy and sadness. Miss Baez was a student at Boston University Fine Arts School. Early in her career, she appeared in Ballard Room and Club 47, and she attracted attention at the Newport (R.I.) Folk Festival. She toured college campuses and in 1962 had a successful Carnegie Hall con-

cert. She established the Institute for the Study of Non-violence in Carmel, California.

BAILEY, F. LEE (1933-   ), defense attorney born in Waltham, Massachusetts. Bailey achieved early fame in the second murder trial of Dr. Sam Sheppard, in which he won Dr. Sheppard's acquittal. He has been described as the most significant criminal lawyer in contemporary America. After Albert DeSalvo's revelations regarding the Boston Strangler Case, he fought for DeSalvo's acquittal but lost. The DeSalvo trial has been regarded as a classic episode in American legal history.

BAILEY, PEARL (1918-   ), female singer born in Newport News, Virginia. Miss Bailey attended various public schools until she achieved early fame as a popular vocalist with stage bands in New York. She has performed in several Broadway musicals, including *The House of Flowers.* She played significant roles in several screen plays, including *Carmen Jones* and *Variety Girl.*

BALL, LUCILLE (1911-   ), actress, television personality, producer, and director. Born in Jamestown, New York, she achieved early fame with her first husband, Desi Arnaz, in the successful television comedy series, *I Love Lucy.* She organized the Desilu Production Company and achieved additional successes in several film productions, including *Forever Darling* and *Love From a Stranger.* Miss Ball has been regarded as the most significant personality from the "situation comedy" programs of American television. Her programs have been syndicated around the world.

BALL, THOMAS (1819-1911), sculptor born in Boston, Massachusetts. Ball achieved early fame at the New England Museum. He travelled to Florence, Italy, at the end of the American Civil War, and received several significant commissions. His more famous creations include *Christmas Morning, St. John the Evangelist* and *Love Memories.* He authored an autobiography titled *My Threescore Years and Ten.* He returned to America in 1897. His most famous work done in the United States is the statue of President Washington.

BARNUM, PHINEAS T. (1810-1891), showman and organizer of circus performances. In 1844, Barnum engaged the services of Tom

Thumb, a dwarf, and travelled to Europe for a series of shows. Barnum was responsible for the early and successful appearances of Jenny Lind in America. He ran for Congress and was defeated. He then organized what came to be called "The Greatest Show on Earth," launching the circus firm of Barnum and Bailey in 1881. Barnum authored the *Life of P. T. Barnum Written by Himself* in 1855.

BASIE, WILLIAM "COUNT" (1904–1984), jazz musician, band leader, and composer. Born in Red Bank, New Jersey, Basie has been featured in concerts at Carnegie Hall and Lincoln Center. He has given command performances before the Queen of England and was featured at the Kennedy Inaugural Ball. Basie has also performed on numerous television programs. His new jazz styles and themes have achieved distinction.

BEAN, ROY (1825–1904), rough-and-ready judge of the American frontier. Born in Mason County, Kentucky, Bean worked as teamster and saloonkeeper in the Southwest until he settled in San Antonio, Texas. In 1882, he moved up the Pecos River and established a saloon for workers who were building the Southern Pacific Railroad. Appointed justice of the peace, he made his saloon in Vinegaroon, Texas his courtroom. Bean was noted for his humor. He became known as "the law west of the Pecos."

BEECHER, HENRY WARD (1813–1887), clergyman and public figure born in Litchfield, Connecticut. Beecher attended Amherst College and became a minister. He sought to effect a moral change in the lives of his audience. He edited the *Western Farmer and Gardener,* based in Indianapolis. In 1847, he was called to Park Street Church as minister; he rejected the invitation and launched a public speaking campaign against slavery in the United States.

BEECHER, LYMAN (1775–1863), clergyman and father of Henry Ward Beecher. Born in New Haven, Connecticut, the elder Beecher was instrumental in organizing the American Bible Society. He served as president of Lane Theological Seminary in Cincinnati, and became embroiled in controversies of the General Assembly of the Presbyterian Church in Ohio.

BELL, ALEXANDER GRAHAM (1847–1922), prolific American inventor born in Edinburgh, Scotland. Although the telephone is his most famous invention, Bell developed many early electronic devices for the deaf. His long-time assistant was Thomas Watson. The first words transmitted by telephone on April 3, 1877 were "Mr. Watson, come here; I want you." Bell received many honors, including the Volta Prize awarded by the French Government. He wrote *Duration of Life* and *Condition Associated with Longevity* (1918).

BENNY, JACK (1894–1974), violinist, vaudeville star, radio and motion-picture personality. Born in Waukegan, Illinois, as Benjamin Kubelsky, he took the stage name of Jack Benny. He achieved significant fame through his television program, *The Jack Benny Show*. He entertained the troops during World War II, and was honored by the National Academy of Television Arts and Science in 1957 for his contributions to the world of entertainment.

BERLIN, IRVING (1888–   ), composer and musician. Born in Russia and migrated to the United States in 1893, Berlin transformed American popular music with his relaxing themes and topical lyrics. Among his famous song titles are: "All Alone," "Remember Reaching for the Moon," and "When I Lost You." His most famous composition was "God Bless America." Berlin composed the stage musicals *Annie Get Your Gun, Call Me Madam,* and *Mr. President.*

BERNSTEIN, LEONARD (1918–   ), conductor, pianist, and composer. Born in Lawrence, Massachusetts, he became a student of Fritz Reiner and Serge Koussevitsky. He was appointed musical director of the New York Philharmonic, where he achieved worldwide recognition. Among his more famous musical creations have been *West Side Story* (1957) and music for *On the Waterfront* (1954). Bernstein wrote *The Joy of Music* (1959) and *Leonard Bernstein's Young People's Concerts for Reading and Listening* (1962).

BETHUNE, MARY MCLEOD (1875–1955), black educator. Born in Mayesville, South Carolina, she studied at Moody Bible Institute of Chicago and later served as president of Bethune-Cookman College. She was appointed as special adviser for minority affairs to President

Franklin Roosevelt and was associated with the National Association for the Advancement of Colored People (NAACP). For a time, she was president of the Central Life Insurance Company and served with the United Negro College Fund. Mrs. Bethune received many honors and degrees from colleges and universities, including Howard University, Wilberforce University, Atlanta University, and the Tuskegee Institute.

BLACK HAWK (1767–1838), Indian war chief. Born in a Sauk village on the Rock River in Illinois, Black Hawk opposed a treaty negotiated by William Henry Harrison with the Sauk nation in 1804; the treaty gave the United States all Sauk country east of the Mississippi River. Black Hawk assisted the British forces in the War of 1812. During the Black Hawk War, he was taken prisoner and jailed at Fort Armstrong in 1832. In 1833, he dictated the *Autobiography of Black Hawk* to a journalist, J. B. Patterson.

BLACK, HUGO L. (1886–1971), jurist and United States Senator. Born in Harlan County, Alabama, Black attended law school at the University of Alabama. He served as prosecuting attorney for Jefferson County from 1915 to 1917, and was in general law practice from 1919 to 1927. He was elected the United States Senator from Alabama for 1927–1931. He served as an associate justice on the United States Supreme Court from 1937 until his death in 1971. Black favored a liberal interpretation of the United States Constitution. He aided the Earl Warren court rulings in the area of civil rights.

BLOCK, HERBERT "HERBLOCK" (1909–　　), editorial cartoonist born in Chicago, Illinois. Block has served as a cartoonist with the *Washington Post* and the *Chicago Daily News*. He received the Pulitzer Prize, 1942 and 1954. He has been associated with various civil-liberty causes. Block wrote *The Herblock Book* (1952) and *Straight Herblock* (1964), among others. He was commissioned to design the United States postage stamp to commemorate the 175th anniversary of the Bill of Rights.

BOGART, HUMPHREY (1899–1957), actor and film producer. Born in New York City, Bogart portrayed outstanding screen roles without sentimentality. Among his best-known films were *Afri-*

can Queen, Caine Mutiny, and *Casablanca.* He was married to Lauren Bacall. Bogart's characterization of Captain Queeg in *Caine Mutiny* received an Academy Award.

BOONE, DANIEL (1734–1820), frontier explorer and Indian fighter. Born near Reading, Pennsylvania, Boone moved to Kentucky in 1767. There he was involved with several expeditions against the Shawnee Indians, and served as captain of the local militia when Kentucky became organized as part of Virginia. Stuart Edward White's *Daniel Boone, Wilderness Scout* (1922) is regarded as the best biography of Boone.

BOOTH, EDWIN T. (1833–1893), actor of international fame. Born in Bel Air, Maryland, Booth played minor roles in *Richard III* (1849) and *The Iron Chest* (1851). Then he travelled west to California, settled in San Francisco, and appeared in leading roles as Richard III, Macbeth, and Hamlet. He went to Australia on tour in 1854 and then to New York, where he obtained a major role in *The Fool's Revenge* in 1864. His younger brother John Wilkes Booth assassinated President Abraham Lincoln.

BOOTH, JOHN WILKES (1838–1865), actor and assassin of President Abraham Lincoln. Born in Bel Air, Maryland, Booth had considerable promise as an actor. He performed with great success at the Boston Museum in 1863. His sympathies were with the South during the Civil War, and he served as a member of the Virginia militia that arrested and executed John Brown. Booth organized the conspiracy that led to the assassination of President Lincoln on April 14, 1865.

BRADY, MATTHEW B. (1823–1896), pioneer photographer. Born in Warren County, New York, Brady began making portraits with the daguerreotype, an early photographic technique developed by S.F.B. Morse and J.W. Draper. Brady published *The Gallery of Illustrious Americans* in 1850. With the approval of President Lincoln, he photographed many historic scenes during the Civil War. His innovations had far-reaching significance in the development of photography.

BRINKLEY, DAVID (1920–　　), broadcast journalist. Born in Wilmington, North Carolina, Brinkley served as a reporter with Wilmington *Star-News* and then as Washington correspondent for the National Broadcasting Company (NBC). With Chet Huntley, he established a reputation as news analyst and co-anchor for *The NBC News.* Brinkley has received the du Pont and Peabody Awards for outstanding journalism.

BROOKS, PHILLIPS (1835–1893), clergyman, author, and composer. Born in Boston, Massachusetts, Brooks became an outstanding leader in American Protestantism. He came from a family that treasured piety and learning; scholarship and eloquence in preaching were the characteristics of his ministry in Boston. Brooks was a leading voice in the Episcopal Church in America. He delivered several noted lectures on preaching before the Divinity School of Yale College in 1877. Alexander U.G. Allen's *Life and Letters of Phillips Brooks* is the most useful biography.

BROWN, JOHN (1800–1859), abolitionist leader. Brown was born in Tourington, Connecticut. He is remembered for his attack on Harpers Ferry, Virginia before the Civil War. Brown hoped to start a wider revolt among black people by seizing the arsenal and distributing arms among the blacks. But the attack failed; John Brown was indicted on three counts of treason and executed.

BRYAN, WILLIAM JENNINGS (1860–1925), lawyer, editor, orator, and political figure. Born in Salem, Illinois, Bryan ran unsuccessfully for President on three occasions. He was described as "The Great Commoner" because of his policies that favored farmers and common laborers. In 1913, he was named Secretary of State by President Woodrow Wilson. He opposed the United States' entry into World War. Later Bryan defended the anti-evolution educational laws passed by the State of Tennessee. He successfully prosecuted a teacher named Thomas Scopes for violating the anti-evolution statutes.

BUNCHE, RALPH (1904–1971), diplomat and human rights leader. Bunche was born in Detroit, Michigan. He attended the University of California and Harvard University, as well as the London School of Economics. He studied anthropology and colonial policy. Bunche participated in several study projects on race relations and international understanding. He attended the San Francisco Conference of the United Nations as a member of the United States delegation. Later he served as a

member of the United Nations' Palestine Commission. He received the Nobel Prize, the Presidential Medal of Freedom, and the Spingarn Medal awarded by the National Association for the Advancement of Colored People (NAACP).

BURBANK, LUTHER (1849–1926), plant breeder and agricultural innovator. Burbank was born in Lancaster, Massachusetts. He was deeply influenced by Charles Darwin's views regarding plants and animal life. With an inheritance of 17 acres, he began a series of experiments that developed the "Burbank potato." He authored a significant publication titled *The Training of the Human Plant.* Burbank received an honorary degree from Tufts University. He was a fellow of the American Association for the Advancement of Science and the Royal Horticultural Society.

BURGER, WARREN (1907–   ), lawyer and Chief Justice of the United States. Born in St. Paul, Minnesota, Burger was appointed to the Supreme Court by President Nixon. Under his leadership, the Supreme Court has been less activist in legal sentiments than was the Earl Warren court. Burger has been involved with the Mayo Foundation. Prior to his appointment to the Supreme Court, he was a law partner in the firm Fairicy, Burger, Moore, & Costello.

BURR, AARON (1756–1836), lawyer and political figure, Vice-President under Thomas

Aaron Burr

Jefferson. Burr was born in Newark, New Jersey. After his term as Vice-President, he conspired to invade Spanish Territories in the Southwest and organize a separate nation. He killed Alexander Hamilton in a duel, which ended Burr's active involvement in politics until the conspiracy was discovered. He was tried for treason and acquitted on a legal technicality.

BURROWS, ABE (1910–1985), playwright and director born in New York City. Burrows wrote for the CBS and NBC radio networks. He was writer and star of *The Abe Burrows Show.* He co-authored *Guys and Dolls, Three Wishes for James,* and *How to Succeed in Business without Really Trying,* and he received a Pulitzer Prize for the last. Burrows' music achieved significance in recording with Decca Records.

BUSHNELL, HORACE (1802–1876), Congregational clergyman, author, and educator. Bushnell was born in Bantam, Connecticut. He rejected rigid Puritanism for liberal religious views. He authored *Christian Nurture* (1847), *God in Christ* (1848), and *Nature and the Supernatural* (1858). More conservative Christian thinkers regarded his views as heretical. He denied that religious conversion was necessary.

CAESAR, SID (1922–   ), actor and comedian born in Yonkers, New York. With the emergence of television, Sid Caesar achieved wide recognition. *Caesar's Hour* and *Sid Caesar Invites You* became popular TV programs. Mr. Caesar often appeared on *The Jackie Gleason Show* and *The Carol Burnett Show.* He starred in the motion picture, *It's a Mad, Mad, Mad, Mad World.* For his work in television, he received the Emmy Award and was named to the United States Hall of Fame.

CALDER, ALEXANDER (1898–1976), sculptor and illustrator. Born in Philadelphia, Pennsylvania, Calder studied at the Stevens Institute of Technology. He built animated wire performers called "the miniature circus" and travelled to Europe with the exhibit. As a result, he developed kinetic sculptures, or mobiles. His designs can be seen at the Lincoln Center, New York, Massachusetts Institute of Technology in Cambridge, and at the UNESCO Gardens in Paris.

CALHOUN, JOHN C. (1782–1850), American statesman and political theorist. Born in South Carolina, he served as a member of both houses of Congress and as Secretary of War in the administration of James Monroe. He served as Vice-President in 1825–1829. Calhoun authored the *South Carolina Exposition* that was a response to the so-called Tariff of Abominations. By 1830, Calhoun was promoting the theory of states' rights embraced in the Nullification Doctrine, which held that states could nullify acts of Congress. Calhoun also wrote *Disquisition on Government* and *Government of the United States,* both published posthumously.

CANTOR, EDDIE (1892–1964), comedian and humanitarian leader. Born in New York City, Mr. Cantor began his career in vaudeville and was later associated with burlesque. He toured as Sam Beverly Moon and starred in the stage productions *Broadway Brevities* (1920), *Make It Snappy* (1922), and *Whoopee* (1929). His first motion picture appearance was in 1926. Mr. Cantor was active in Jewish and Christian charities. He authored *Take My Life: The Way I See It* (1959). He received numerous recognitions for his charity work; Temple University honored him with a Doctor of Humane Letters degree.

CAPONE, ALPHONSE "AL" (1899–1947), gangster; perhaps the most notorious criminal in American history. Born in Naples, Italy, he came

Al Capone is led aboard a train to start his journey to the federal penitentiary in Atlanta, Georgia.

to the United States with his family and settled in Brooklyn, New York. In high school, he took charge of the Five Points gang. In a gang fight, he was slashed across the face with a razor blade, and carried the nickname of "Scarface Al" ever after. In 1920, gang leader Johnny Torrio summoned Capone to Chicago to supervise the sale of bootleg whiskey. Torrio retired in 1925, leaving Capone in charge of Chicago's largest crime racket. "Scarface Al" used murder, bombings, and torture to drive out his competitors. In 1927, he exerted his powers to elect "Big Bill" Thompson as mayor of the city. Capone's henchmen executed seven members of a rival gang in the infamous St. Valentine's Day Massacre of 1929. The United States Treasury Department arrested Capone in 1933 on charges of income-tax evasion. After serving 11 years in Alcatraz Prison, he retired to his Miami Beach estate.

CAPP, AL (1909–1979), newspaper cartoonist. Born in New Haven, Connecticut, Capp attended the Pennsylvania Academy of Fine Arts and the Museum of Fine Arts in Boston. He created the comic strip titled "Li'l Abner," which was widely syndicated throughout the United States. United Feature Syndicate distributed "Li'l Abner." He also served as columnist for the *New York Herald Tribune.* Capp was associated with the People to People program of the United Nations.

CARNEGIE, ANDREW (1835–1919), American industrialist, businessman, and philanthropist. Carnegie was born in Scotland. He became one of the so-called "Captains of Industry" at the turn of the century. In 1848, his family settled in the Allegheny region of Pittsburg. Carnegie was a self-educated lover of books, theater, and classical music. In the 1850s, he took advantage of the rising importance of steel. With his capital, Carnegie constructed the Bessemer Steel Rail Company. Toward the close of the century, he completely dominated the United States steel industry. He authored the article entitled "Wealth," which became the core of what sociologists called the Gospel of Wealth. He believed the rich should spend their fortunes for the welfare of the community. He supported the extensive construction of libraries that bear his name.

CARROLL, JOHN (1735–1815), first bishop of the Roman Catholic Church in America. Born in Upper Marlborough, Maryland, he supported the educational and political integration of the Roman Catholic Church with early America. Carroll sought to unify the several Catholic groups in America, and he obtained religious toleration for Catholics. Regulations developed by his associates became the first canon law in America. Carroll encouraged the establishment of parochial education, secular schools, and colleges at Georgetown (1788) and Baltimore (1799).

CARSON, KIT (1809–1868), soldier, Indian agent, and hunter. Born in Madison County, Kentucky, Carson had no formal education and remained illiterate all his life. He travelled to Arizona and southern California and married an Arapaho woman. He served as John C. Frémont's guide and helped Frémont plan expeditions to Wind River Mountains, the Oregon Trail, the Dalles River, and Klamath Lake. He guided Frémont through the Sierra Nevadas to the Great Salt Lake. Carson served in the Office of Indian Affairs and died in Fort Lyon, Colorado.

CARVER, GEORGE WASHINGTON (1861–1943), black botanist, chemist, and educator. Carver was born in Kansas Territory and attended school in Minneapolis, Kansas, and San Francisco. At Booker T. Washington's invitation, he came to the Tuskegee Institute, where he established an international reputation in horticulture and farming. He became a close friend of Henry A. Wallace, who ran for the United States Presidency. He also developed enduring friendships with Thomas Edison, Luther Burbank, and Harvey Firestone.

CHAMBERLAIN, WILT (1936–), professional basketball player. Born in Philadelphia, Pennsylvania, Chamberlain attended Kansas State University. He then served as star center for the Los Angeles Lakers, the Philadelphia 76ers, and the Philadelphia Warriors. In 1967, he led the National Basketball Association in points scored per season. He has achieved stature as an all-time great in the National Basketball Association.

CHANCELLOR, JOHN (1927–), broadcast journalist. Born in Chicago, Illinois, he attended DePaul Academy and became a reporter with the *Chicago Sun-Times.* From 1950 to 1965, he was on the staff of NBC News as a newswriter and served as a correspondent in Vienna, London, and Moscow. He served briefly on the NBC *Today* program. Under President Kennedy, Chancellor served as director of the Voice of America. In recent years, he has been anchorman with David Brinkley on the *NBC Nightly News*.

CHANNING, WILLIAM ELLERY (1780–1842), Unitarian theologian and minister. Channing was born in Newport, Rhode Island. He served as minister to the Federal Street Church in Boston most of his life. He held the view that God was merciful and would save all mankind; thus Channing established the basic tenets of Unitarianism and fathered the American Unitarian Association. Through his writings, he sponsored the movement for cultural independence from England. *The Importance and Means of a National Literature* (1830) is the most significant of his writings.

CHAPMAN, JOHN "JOHNNY APPLE-SEED" (1774-1845), planter of apple orchards on the American frontier. We cannot determine his parentage and place of birth; he was simply known as "Johnny Appleseed." He enjoyed long trips for the study of birds. Chapman's orchards of apple trees became legendary, particularly around Ashland County near Mansfield, Ohio. He said he was a primitive Christian. In 1838, he travelled into Allen County, Indiana. The legend of Johnny Appleseed is closely identified with the Westward expansion.

CHAVEZ, CESAR (1927–   ), union organizer among migrant farm workers. Chavez was born near Yuma, Arizona. His early activities in the California Community Service Organization established his abilities as an activist and organizer. He became director of the Organized National Farm Workers Association, which then merged with the Agricultural Workers Organizing Committee of the AFL-CIO. Chavez' ability to organize boycotts and strikes made the growers in the Modesto and Sacramento Valleys of California hostile toward his work. Chavez served in the United States Navy Reserve during World War II.

CHISHOLM, SHIRLEY (1924–   ), black Congresswoman and outspoken political leader born in Brooklyn, New York. She attended Brooklyn College and Columbia University; she has received honorary degrees from Pratt Institute, Hampton Institute, William Patterson College, and Capital University, among others. The Congresswoman has served in numerous organiza-

tions that deal with social programs and public policy. In 1972, she made an unsuccessful bid for the United States Presidency. She has written numerous books and pamphlets, including *Unbought and Unbossed* (1970) and *The Good Fight* (1973).

CLARK, WILLIAM (1770–1838), frontier explorer and Indian fighter born in Caroline County, Virginia. Clark served with "Mad" Anthony Wayne in his campaign against the Indians. He joined Meriwether Lewis for expeditions to the Pacific Northwest. Clark was skilled in dealing with Indians and making maps. His diaries of the Lewis and Clark expeditions are essential to our early knowledge of the Northwest Territories. Clark was appointed as superintendent of Indian affairs for the Louisiana Territories. He was a highly regarded soldier and explorer.

CLAY, HENRY (1777–1852), Secretary of State and political leader for a generation (1812–1852). Born in Hanover County, Virginia, Clay fathered the "American System"—a legislative program to unite the industrial East with the farming West. Clay's plan established protective tariffs and provided federal money for public improvements. Clay ran for the Presidency in 1844 as candidate of the Whig Party and lost. He was the

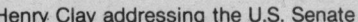

Henry Clay addressing the U.S. Senate

architect of the Compromise of 1850, which delayed the controversies that erupted in Civil War a decade later.

COBB, TY (1886–1961), regarded by many as the greatest offensive player in baseball history; called "the Georgia Peach." He was born in Narros, Georgia. Cobb was a fierce competitor; he appeared in more games (3,033), batted more times (11,429), with more hits (4,191), finished with a higher lifetime average (.367) than any other major league player. Cobb achieved his reputation with the Detroit Tigers, with which he spent 22 seasons. He was elected into the Baseball Hall of Fame in 1936.

CODY, WILLIAM F. "BUFFALO BILL" (1846–1917), Indian fighter whose fame became part of literature and legend; he established a Wild West show that achieved international standing. Cody was born in Scott County, Iowa. After serving in the Civil War, he worked as a civilian scout for the United States Army. He is said to have slaughtered 4,280 buffalo in an eight-month period to provide food for the Army. His reputation in marksmanship was equalled only by his memory of terrain and geography. Cody engaged in over sixteen Indian battles; his popularity as a showman developed later in life.

COFFIN, HENRY SLOANE (1877–1954), clergyman, author and educator. Born in New York City, Coffin became a leader of liberal evangelicalism. He served as president of Union Theological Seminary and was an effective preacher. Coffin sought to apply Christianity to social problems and tried to improve theological education. He served as a fellow of the Corporation of Yale University. He was moderator of the General Assembly of the Presbyterian Church in the U.S.A. Coffin wrote numerous books, including the *Meaning of the Cross* (1931).

COLE, NAT "KING" (1919–1965), singer, entertainer, and jazz pianist. Cole was born in Montgomery, Alabama. He organized the King Cole Trio and later he achieved prominence as a singer. His musical style was relaxed. Cole's most successful recordings included "Nature Boy" and "Walking My Baby Back Home." His name and voice are associated with the song "Unforgettable." He appeared in several motion pictures without distinction.

COPLEY, JOHN SINGLETON (1738–1815), American painter in the realist tradition, born in Boston, Massachusetts. Copley completed several portraits of outstanding Americans, including Paul Revere and Samuel Adams. In 1774, he travelled to Europe to avoid problems of the Revolutionary era. He was elected to the Royal Academy and painted several massive historical scenes, including *Siege of Gibraltar* (1791) and *The Death of the Earl of Chatham* (1781). Copley died in London.

COSTELLO, LOU (1906–1959), film and radio comedian associated with Bud Abbott in comedy. Born in Paterson, New Jersey, Costello worked as a common laborer at Metro-Goldwyn-Mayer Studios and then as a stunt man. After his comic talents emerged, he appeared on the *Kate Smith Hour.* Costello starred in several movies, including *Hold That Ghost, Abbott and Costello in Hollywood,* and *Abbott and Costello Meet the Mummy.* He is best known for his work in the comedy of errors.

CROCKETT, DAVID (1786–1836), political figure, Indian fighter, and celebrity of the American frontier. Born in Hawkins County, Tennessee, Crockett was involved with the so-called Creek War against Creek Indians in Alabama. He was elected to the Tennessee legislature and later won a seat in the United States House of Representatives. After three terms in Congress, he returned to Tennessee to organize an expedition to Texas, looking for new land and challenge. He died in the Battle of the Alamo.

CRONKITE, WALTER (1916–), broadcast journalist. Born in St. Joseph, Missouri, Cronkite began his career with the *Houston Post,* where he served as reporter. After a succession of assignments, he became a news correspondent with the American forces in World War II. He began his association with Columbia Broadcasting System (CBS) in 1950 and was assigned to develop the news department. In 1953, he began the narration of a series titled *You Are There;* in 1952, he inaugurated national television coverage of the political conventions; and in 1962, he became anchorman for the *CBS Evening News.* His name is synonymous with television news.

CROSBY, FRANCES J. "FANNY" (1820–1915), Christian composer born in New York City.

She wrote over five thousand hymns, including "Safe in the Arms of Jesus" and "There's Music in the Air." When six weeks old, she lost her eyesight. She entered an institution for the blind at age 15, and taught there from 1847 to 1858. She authored numerous publications that included *The Blind Girl and Other Poems* (1844), *A Wreath of Columbia's Flowers* (1859), and *Autobiography* (1906).

CROSBY, HARRY "BING" (1904–1977), singer, songwriter, and actor. Born in Tacoma, Washington, Crosby's easygoing manner suited the emerging style of popular music. He studied law for a period of time, then entered show business. The songs "Ghost of a Chance" and "When the Blue of the Night" became associated with his voice. He appeared in a series of filmed musical comedies with Bob Hope and Dorothy Lamour. He received an Academy Award for his performance in the film, *Going My Way* (1944). "I'm Dreaming of a White Christmas" is the song commonly associated with Crosby. His autobiography was entitled *Call Me Lucky.*

CURTIS, CYRUS H. K. (1850–1933), magazine publisher. Born in Portland, Maine, Curtis was educated in the public schools. He moved to Philadelphia, where he joined the staff of the *Tribune.* His success in publishing the *Ladies' Home Journal* achieved national recognition, and he became president of the newly organized Curtis Publishing Company. There he pursued other magazine enterprises, including *Country Gentleman* and the *Saturday Evening Post.* Under Curtis' direction, the *Post* achieved a national audience. He acquired the *New York Evening Post* in 1923 in an effort to compete with the Hearst papers and the *New York Times.*

CUSTER, GEORGE (1839–1876), soldier commonly known for his military operations against hostile Sioux and Cheyenne Indians. Custer was born in New Rumley, Ohio. In 1876, he was defeated in an epochal battle at the Little Big Horn in Wyoming. He and his entire army of 655 men were killed by a far superior force of Indians. Custer wrote an interesting commentary titled *My Life on the Plains;* his *War Memoirs* give a useful recollection of the Civil War.

DALEY, RICHARD (1902–1976), leading political figure of the Democratic Party. Born in the Bridgeport district of Chicago, Mr. Daley studied law at De Paul University. He was admitted to the bar in 1933. Through patronage and appointment power, he organized the Illinois Democratic Party with ultimate loyalty to himself. In 1955, he became mayor of Chicago and retained that post until his death, directing one of the most powerful political structures in American history. In 1960, he supported John F. Kennedy's bid for the Presidency and delivered his state for the Democratic presidential contender. In 1968, he was criticized for his treatment of anti-war protesters during the Democratic National Convention in Chicago. In spite of the criticism, political writers considered him the most effective mayor of a large metropolitan city.

DANA, CHARLES A. (1819–1897), newspaper editor and publisher. Dana was born at Hinsdale, New Hampshire. After a series of newspaper jobs, Dana used his friendship with Horace Greeley to secure the position of city editor at the *New York Tribune.* After the Civil War, he acquired the *New York Sun,* which he built into one of New York's greatest daily papers. He was described as a man of wide intellectual interests. Dana wrote *Recollections of the Civil War* (1898), *The Art of Newspaper Making* (1899), and other books.

DANIELS, JOSEPHUS (1862–1948), journalist and statesman, ambassador to Mexico, and Secretary of the Navy under President Woodrow Wilson. Daniels was born in Washington, North Carolina. He became a close friend of William Jennings Bryan and devoted his energies to the Democratic Party. Daniels used considerable restraint in his dealings with the Mexican government; he was a man of great diplomacy and political skill. Daniels authored several books, including *Tar Heel Editor, The Wilson Era: Years of War and After,* and *The Cabinet Diaries of Josephus Daniels.*

DAVIS, JEFFERSON (1808–1889), President of the Confederate States of America. Born in Todd County, Kentucky, Davis attended West Point Military Academy and graduated in 1828. He served with distinction in the Black Hawk Indian War of 1832. He then served as Secretary of War and as a Senator before the outbreak of the Civil War. After the Civil War broke the Confederacy, he lived a sad and helpless existence. Davis wrote *The Rise and Fall of the Confederate Government.*

DE FOREST, LEE (1873–1961), an inventor who pioneered in radio and broadcasting. De Forest was born at Council Bluffs, Iowa. He worked with the Western Electric Company in Chicago, where he invented the audio amplifier. This was the single most significant contribution to the advance of radio, and De Forest is often regarded as the father of radio. He held major responsibilities in the De Forest Wireless Telegraph Company and the Radio Telephone Company. He wrote *Father of Radio* (1950). William R. Maclaurin's *Invention and Innovation in the Radio Industry* explains De Forest's contributions.

DeMILLE, CECIL B. (1881–1959), motion picture producer and director who established a reputation for his spectacular portrayals of biblical themes. DeMille was born in Ashfield, Massachusetts. *The Ten Commandments, The King of Kings, The Sign of the Cross,* and *Samson and Delilah* were some of his best-known films. His screen productions cost millions, yet he was able to produce films that were highly profitable. DeMille rejected criticism that his productions were garish and unartistic by saying that public taste determines the standards of artistry. In later years, he developed movies that reflected historical themes, including *The Greatest Show on Earth, Union Pacific,* and *The Plainsman.*

DEMPSEY, JACK (1895–   ), champion heavyweight boxer. Because Dempsey was born in Manassa, Colorado, he was called the "Manassa Mauler." Initially he won the heavyweight championship from Jess Willard in 1919. The most controversial aspect of his career was the "long count" during the second fight between Dempsey and Gene Tunney. In the seventh round, Dempsey floored Tunney but failed to go to a neutral corner. The count was delayed; Tunney recovered and subsequently won the fight. After retirement, he became a restauranteur in New York City. With Bob Considine and Bill Slocum he co-authored the book, *Dempsey.*

DEWEY, GEORGE (1837–1917), first Admiral of the Navy; hero of the Spanish-American War. Dewey served under Admiral David G. Farragut during the Civil War. In 1897, he requested sea duty in the Pacific as commodore of the new American fleet. He led his six boats into Manila Bay on May 1, 1898, and destroyed the Spanish fleet of 10 ships. In August, he used the American navy to assist General Wesley Merritt's capture of Manila. He returned to a hero's welcome in the United States, where Congress named him Admiral of the Navy. Dewey published his autobiography in 1913.

DEWEY, JOHN (1859–1952), educator and pragmatic philosopher who advocated traditional values of education. Dewey was born in Burlington, Vermont. He believed that science was the highest manifestation of human intelligence. He established his reputation through articles in the *Journal of Speculative Philosophy.* Dewey studied at the University of Vermont, Johns Hopkins, the University of Michigan, and the University of Chicago. At Chicago, he turned to pedagogy and educational philosophy. He authored many books, including *Democracy and Education* (1916) and *Reconstruction in Philosophy* (1920).

DIMAGGIO, JOE (1914–   ), noted baseball player born in Martinez, California. DiMaggio played as an outfielder with the San Francisco Seals until 1934, when he was purchased by the New York Yankees. In his first year the Yankees recognized him as a potential star; he batted an average of .323, fielded .978, and established the

Admiral Dewey with President McKinley and Cardinal Gibbons, 1899

longest consecutive hitting record by hitting safely in 56 consecutive games. Fans called DiMaggio the "Yankee Clipper." On December 11, 1951, he announced his retirement from baseball. His subsequent marriage to actress Marilyn Monroe drew national attention.

DISNEY, WALTER E. "WALT" (1901–1966), filmmaker, cartoonist, and entertainment entrepreneur. A native of Chicago, Disney developed the cartoon characters Mickey Mouse and Donald Duck in the 1920s. He developed the first feature-length animated cartoons in *Snow White* (1938). Disney's later films *Pinocchio, Bambi, Fantasia,* and *Mary Poppins* achieved spectacular success. The amusement parks named Disneyland and Disney World bear his genius. *The Disney Version: The Life, Times, Art, and Commerce of Walt Disney,* by Richard Schickel (1968) is the most comprehensive study on Disney.

DIX, DOROTHEA L. (1802–1887), humanitarian associated with Dr. William Ellery Channing. Born in Hampden, Maine, Miss Dix became the tutor to Dr. Channing's children. Under Channing's influence, she initiated significant reforms in mental institutions. During the Civil War, she served as a superintendent of nurses; after the war, she continued her efforts on behalf of the mentally ill. Her reforms attracted international attention, particularly in Europe. Francis Tiffany's *The Life of Dorothea Lynde Dix* (1890) is the most definitive biography.

DOOLITTLE, JAMES H. "JIMMY" (1896–), aviator, oil company executive, and war hero. A native of Alameda, California, Doolittle became one of the most famous of American heroes during World War II. He led the first bombing of Japan and commanded thousands of planes in attacks on North Africa, Italy, and Germany. He commanded attacks upon German cities from 1944 to the end of the war in Europe. Doolittle then joined General Douglas MacArthur's command in the Far East until the end of the war in the Pacific. He became an executive of the Shell Oil Company after the war. In the 1950s, he became involved with NACA, which later became the National Aeronautics and Space Administration.

DOUGLAS, STEPHEN A. (1813–1861), United States Senator and candidate for the Presidency, identified with the Democratic Party. Born in Brandon, Vermont, Douglas spearheaded the new Democratic Party in Chicago. He sponsored efforts to make Chicago a significant rail center. The senatorial campaign of 1858 between Douglas and Abraham Lincoln was a rehearsal for the 1860 presidential campaign, even though Lincoln lost. In the famous Lincoln-Douglas debates, Lincoln established his national reputation. Many argue that if Douglas had become President, he could have prevented a Civil War. For a review of this argument, see Gerald M. Capers, *Stephen A. Douglas, Defender of the Union,* edited by Oscar Handlin (1959).

DOUGLAS, WILLIAM O. (1898–1980), liberal justice of the United States Supreme Court. Douglas was born in Yakima, Washington, and attended Columbia Law School. He served briefly as a professor at the Yale Law School, worked on legal matters for the Securities and Exchange Commission. In 1939, he was appointed to the Supreme Court and became the leader of the liberal wing of the court. He challenged tradition in his opinions on obscenity, religion, desegregation, and the rights of criminals. He wrote several books, including *Points of Revolution* (1970). The best study of Douglas' career is *Douglas of the Supreme Court: A Selection of His Opinions,* edited by Vern Countryman (1959).

DOUGLASS, FREDERICK (1817–1895), abolitionist, journalist, and orator. He was born at Tuckahoe, Maryland with the name of Frederick Augustus Washington Bailey. After he escaped from slavery he changed his name to Frederick Douglass. Greatly influenced by William Lloyd Garrison's *The Liberator,* Douglass joined the Massachusetts Anti-Slavery Society. He wrote *The Narrative of the Life of Frederick Douglass, an American Slave* (1845), which some abolitionists thought was too inflammatory. Douglass disagreed with William Lloyd Garrison on proper abolitionist procedures.

DREW, CHARLES RICHARD (1904–1950), a black surgeon who developed the blood bank and new methods for training surgeons. A native of Washington, D.C., Dr. Drew implemented the blood bank in World War II as director of the American Red Cross Bank. He chaired the department of surgery at Howard University and recommended new surgical standards to the National Medical Association. Dr. Drew received the

Spingarn Medal of the National Association for the Advancement of Colored People. He was awarded numerous honorary degrees from colleges and universities.

DU BOIS, WILLIAM E. B. (1868–1963), major black scholar and leader of black protest and panafricanism. Born in Great Barrington, Massachusetts, he received the Master of Arts degree and a doctorate from Harvard University. Dr. Du Bois organized the Niagara group, an all-black protest organization of scholars and professionals. He was one of the founders of the National Association for the Advancement of Colored People (NAACP) in 1909. He edited *Crisis,* a publication of the NAACP, and regarded himself as a Socialist. Dr. Du Bois authored numerous books and pamphlets.

DULLES, JOHN FOSTER (1888–1959), foreign diplomat and Secretary of State under President Dwight D. Eisenhower. Born in the nation's capital, Dulles served at the Paris Peace Conference in 1919. He was legal adviser to the United States delegation at the San Francisco conference on the United Nations. He supported General Eisenhower during the 1952 election. As Secretary of State, Dulles developed the broader aspects of North Atlantic Treaty Organization (NATO). He dealt courageously with the Suez Crisis of 1956 by compelling President Nasser of Egypt to withdraw. Louis L. Gerson's *John Foster Dulles* (1967) is a good biography of Dulles.

DURANTE, JIMMY (1893–1980), entertainer and songwriter born in New York City. Durante began his career in the Bowery district of New York, where he organized a five-piece jazz band for Club Alamo in Harlem. At this time, he was only known as a pianist. In 1923, he opened Club Durante. Other entertainers were attracted to his comedy and musical routines. He wrote many songs after 1923, including "I'm Jimmy, That Well-Dressed Man" and "Did You Ever Have the Feeling That You Wanted to Go?" He appeared in several Broadway musicals, including *Red, Hot and Blue* with Ethel Merman, *Keep off the Grass, Stars in Your Eyes.* He was nicknamed the "Schnozzle" for the generous proportions of his nose. Durante was regarded with great affection as an entertainer.

DUROCHER, LEO (1906–   ), professional baseball manager. Born in West Springfield, Massachusetts, he played for a time as a second baseman for the New York Yankees. Then he was shortstop for the Cincinnati Reds and St. Louis Cardinals. His fame comes from his management of the Brooklyn Dodgers, who won the National League pennant in 1951 and 1954. He became a television announcer for a short time, then returned as a manager for the Chicago Cubs 1966-1972 and the Houston Astros in 1972-1973. He co-authored a book entitled, *Nice Guys Finish Last* with Ed Linn. That phrase became synonymous with his name.

DWIGHT, TIMOTHY (1752–1817), Congregationalist minister and president of Yale College. Dwight was born in Northhampton, Massachusetts, and received his education at Hopkins Grammar School in New Haven, Connecticut. Dwight served in the Massachusetts Legislature, then taught Latin and Greek. He wrote "The Conquest of Canaan," an epic poem. In 1795, he became the president of Yale College; he administered the affairs of the college, taught moral philosophy, and served in the college pulpit on Sundays. Kenneth Silverman's *Timothy Dwight* is a significant study of his life.

EARHART, AMELIA (1898–1937), aviatrix. A native of Atchison, Kansas, Miss Earhart attended Columbia University and taught extension courses for the Commonwealth of Massachusetts. She was the first woman to cross the Atlantic in an airplane. Miss Earhart became the aviation editor of *Cosmopolitan Magazine* and vice-president of National Airways. She received numerous honors and recognitions, including the Distinguished Flying Cross and the gold medal of the National Geographic Society. She wrote *20 Hours, 40 Minutes* (1928) and *The Fun of It* (1931). Miss Earhart's plane went down in the Pacific Ocean as she was completing a round-the-world flight.

EASTMAN, GEORGE (1854–1932), inventor, industrialist, and mass producer of photographic equipment. Eastman was born in Waterville, New York. He made photography available to the general public. Eastman's discoveries in chemical processing were essential to the United States war effort during World War I. He developed an innovative system of profit-sharing that allowed his employees to enjoy the Eastman Company's profits. Eastman was a lonely man who took his own life. The best single work on Eastman is Carl W. Ackerman's *George Eastman* (1930).

EDDY, MARY BAKER (1821–1910), established the Church of Christ—Scientist in an effort to apply religion to health. She was born at Bow, New Hampshire. Her nervous condition in early life brought several illnesses, which led to her study of science and health. In 1908, she established the *Christian Science Monitor*. Her book, *Science and Health,* became the basis for her religious and scientific theories. Her most significant impact remained in Boston and the East Coast. *The Life of Mary Baker Eddy* by Sibyl Wilbur is the official biography.

EDDY, NELSON (1901–1967), screen star and entertainer, a native of Providence, Rhode Island. Mr. Eddy's baritone voice was matched with the soprano voice of Jeanette MacDonald for several filmed musicals. He starred in popular stage musicals during the 1930s and 1940s, including *Naughty Marietta* (1935), *Rose Marie* (1936), *Girl of the Golden West* (1938), and *Bittersweet* (1940). After his screen career, he entered radio and nightclub entertaining. Eddy made famous the songs, "Ah, Sweet Mystery of Life" and "Indian Love Call." His rich voice singing "Stouthearted Men" was his radio trademark.

EDISON, THOMAS A. (1847-1931), inventor who made outstanding contributions in electric light and electrical devices; his greatest contribution is the incandescent lamp. Born in Milan, Ohio, Edison made significant advances in organized research. Because of deafness, he was exempt from military service. Edison made major contributions to the development of the phonograph, lighting, electric-powered plant, and the movie industry. The Edison Company produced hundreds of movies, and Edison laid the basis for "talking" movies. He also contributed to the development of synthetic rubber. Edison sponsored the early work of Charles Steinmetz and other budding inventors. The best biography of Thomas A. Edison is Matthew Josephson's *Edison: A Biography* (1959).

EDWARDS, JONATHAN (1703–1758), New England minister and missionary, commonly regarded as America's finest preacher and theologian of the eighteenth century. He was born in East Windsor, Connecticut, the son and grandson of clergymen. Edwards' *Personal Narrative* (1740) reflects a close affection for God. He is associated with the Great Awakening, an intense period of revivalism in colonial America. He wrote the influential book entitled, *The Great Christian Doctrine of Original Sin Defended* (1758). His writings and sermons changed the outlook of his entire generation. He became president of the College of New Jersey, now Princeton University.

EINSTEIN, ALBERT (1879–1955), physicist, born in Ulm, Germany, and known for his theory of relativity. Einstein's general and special theories of relativity revolutionized the world of science. He approached President Roosevelt with his theories regarding the development of atomic energy for military purposes. This resulted in the "Manhattan Project" for the development of an atomic bomb. He was expelled from Nazi Germany because of his Jewish heritage, and this had a profound impact on his life. Einstein regarded himself a pacifist and humanitarian. Carl Seelig's biography, *Albert Einstein: A Documentary Biography* (1956), is one of the best portraits of Einstein.

Albert Einstein
This photograph is considered to be the last one made of the physicist. The occasion was Professor Einstein's 76th birthday on Mar. 14, 1955.

Douglas Fairbanks, Sr. (right) and son Douglas, (ca.) 1933

FAIRBANKS, DOUGLAS SR. (1883–1939), distinguished American actor born in Denver, Colorado. His marriages attracted national attention, particularly to Mary Pickford (divorced in 1935) and Lady Ashley. He made his first stage appearance in New York City; among other plays, he appeared in *All For a Girl, The Cub,* and *Show Shop.* He also appeared in motion pictures, such as *His Majesty the American, When the Clouds Roll By, The Mark of Zorro, Robin Hood,* and *The Taming of the Shrew.* He organized his own production company and achieved national attention for his somber portrayals.

FARRAGUT, DAVID G. (1801–1870), naval officer who carried significant assignments during the American Civil War. Born at Campbells Station, Tennessee, he opposed the Southern cause and migrated north to Hastings-on-the-Hudson. His initial assignment was to open the Mississippi to Union battleships. He stationed his gunboats in the Gulf of Mexico, which gave him a more direct striking capability between 1861 to 1864. In 1864, he was assigned to strike at Confederate defenses in Mobile Bay. His success led to the command to strike defenses at Wilmington, North Carolina, which he also accomplished. Farragut was regarded as among the outstanding heroes of the Civil War. A. T. Mahan's *Admiral Farragut* (1892) is still a classic.

FIELD, MARSHALL (1834–1906), merchant and chain-store retailer. Born near Conway, Mas-

sachusetts, Field served as a travelling salesman before he was admitted to partnership in the retail firm of Farwell, Field and Company. Unlike A. T. Stewart, John Wanamaker, and other leading retailers of his day, Field was not interested in political activity nor philanthropy; but he did give money to the newly established University of Chicago and fostered the establishment of the Chicago Manual Training School. He was also associated with the establishment of the Field Museum of Natural History in Chicago, and his will provided for the construction of the building in Chicago, and that houses the Field Museum.

FIELDS, W. C. (1879–1946), comedian of the stage, motion pictures, and radio. Fields was born in Philadelphia, Pennsylvania. His first appearances were in vaudeville productions and the Ziegfeld Follies. His fame developed from his movie appearances, in films such as *So's Your Old Man, It's the Old Army Game, One in a Million, David Copperfield, Never Give a Sucker an Even Break,* and his most popular *My Little Chickadee.* He also reached a national audience through his radio broadcast, *The Chase and Sanborn Hour.* Fields was highly regarded for his wry humor.

FINNEY, CHARLES G. (1792–1875), revivalist and educator. Finney was born in Warren, Connecticut. His term as president of Oberlin College gave Presbyterianism a significant voice in educating the ministry. His preaching style contained substance and eloquence. Finney was a strong advocate of temperance; he opposed the use of tobacco, tea, and coffee. Although a Mason, he opposed masonry. Among his more significant book titles: *Sermons on Important Subjects* (1836), *Lectures to Professing Christians* (1837), and *Lectures on Systematic Theology* (1846, 1847). His revivals reached wide audiences and had significant impact on the religious patterns of nineteenth-century America.

FITZGERALD, ELLA (1918–   ), jazz vocalist with an international reputation. Born in Newport News, Virginia, at age fifteen she entered an amateur contest at the Apollo Theatre in New York City. She was hired by Chick Webb for his band. In 1938, she gained worldwide fame with her recording of "A Tisket, a Tasket." Among her more famous recordings are "Love You Madly," "Hard-Hearted Hannah," and "He's My Guy."

Miss Fitzgerald is recognized as an outstanding performer and recording artist. She has received considerable respect in the black community for her civil rights concerns.

FORD, HENRY (1863–1947), automobile manufacturer born in Dearborn Township, Michigan. Ford learned the machinist trade and was the chief engineer for the Edison Illuminating Company. In 1903, he organized the world's largest automobile corporation. In 1914, he announced plans to involve all his workers in a profit-sharing plan, distributing millions of dollars back to his workers. His plan to mass-produce the Model T and Model A made the automobile readily available to the American public at competitive prices. He constructed assembly plants at Highland Park, Michigan, and River Rouge, Michigan; the latter was regarded as the largest single factory in the world. Ford was also active in political and humanitarian efforts. He built the Henry Ford Hospital; in 1918, he ran for the Senate and lost. Ford authored *My Life and Work* (1925) among other titles.

FOSDICK, HARRY EMERSON (1878–1969), clergyman and author who established the Riverside Church in New York, which was distinctive for its interdenominational character. Fosdick was born in Buffalo, New York. His *National Vespers* radio program brought his ideas into the national arena. He was ordained as a Baptist minister, but his theological perspective is associated with a liberal interpretation. Fosdick wrote numerous books, including *The Modern Use of the Bible* (1924) and *A Faith for Tough Times* (1952). His autobiography is contained in *The Living of These Days* (1956). He also wrote numerous hymns.

FOSTER, STEPHEN C. (1826–1864), composer of musical sketches and minstrel songs. At Jefferson College, Foster's musical capacities became evident to his teachers; he continued his education under tutors; his Negro ballads, "O Susanna" and "Away Down South," achieved instant success. In 1851, he began his work with E. P. Christy, who would sing Foster's songs. Each assisted the other. Foster's more famous songs were "The Old Folks at Home," "My Old Kentucky Home," and "Massa's in the Cold, Cold Ground." He remained in Pittsburgh, Pennsylvania most of his life; but his music gave a nostalgic reflection of Negro life in the Old South.

Benjamin Franklin
Signer of the Declaration of Independence

FRANKLIN, BENJAMIN (1706–1790), author, printer, inventor, diplomat, and scientist. Born in Boston, Massachusetts, he began a writing sequence on self-improvement at an early age. These efforts are best reflected in *Poor Richard's Almanack,* which contained slogans on personal improvement, such as: "Necessity never made a good bargain" and "It is hard for an empty sack to stand upright." Franklin became interested in electricity; he initiated projects for community improvement that included the lighting of streets with natural gas. He established police forces and circulating libraries. He also established the American Philosophical Association. Franklin served in the second Continental Congress. He travelled to France in 1776 to negotiate a treaty with the French Government, and negotiated the peace treaty with Great Britain. He served as a member of the Constitutional Convention. The best biography of Franklin is Carl Van Doren's *Benjamin Franklin* (1938).

FREMONT, JOHN C. (1813–1890), soldier and politician born in Savannah, Georgia. His explorations of Minnesota and Dakotas added to his knowledge of science and topography. He travelled the Oregon Trail with Kit Carson and explored the Columbia River. Fremont was regarded as the "Great Pathfinder." He travelled to California and wintered (1845) in Oregon. He then returned to California and served a short term as United

States Senator from California. He ran as a Presidential candidate of the newly formed Republican Party. His autobiographical sketch titled, *My Life* (1887), is a useful overview of the era.

FRIEDMAN, MILTON (1912–   ), foremost economist in the United States reflecting the conservative perspective. A native of Brooklyn, New York, he served as economic adviser to President Richard Nixon. He wrote *A Monetary History of the United States, 1867–1960* (1963). Friedman advocates the competitive free-market economy, and he originated the negative tax-credit idea. He is a professor at the University of Chicago; his economic theories are commonly associated with the Chicago School. Friedman has received numerous honors and awards, including the Nobel Prize for economics.

FULBRIGHT, J. WILLIAM (1905–   ), distinguished American political figure. Born in Sumner, Missouri, he attended the University of Arkansas and won a Rhodes scholarship to Oxford University. Fulbright received his law degree from George Washington University. From 1939 to 1941, he served as president of the University of Arkansas. In 1942, he began a political career as Representative to the United States House from the Third District. He called for the creation of the United Nations during World War II. In 1944, he was elected to the United States Senate; he sponsored laws that established an educational exchange program known as the Fulbright-Hays program. Fulbright served on the Senate Banking Committee. He criticized the war in Vietnam from his position as chairman of the Senate Foreign Relations Committee.

FULLER, R. BUCKMINSTER (1895–1983), architect, designer, and inventor. Born in Milton, Massachusetts, his earliest work was the Dymaxion House, a design that blends "dynamism" and "maximum utilization." Dymaxion House, like Fuller's Dymaxion Car, had interest but little direct use in production. He is described as a "catalyst to change." By mid-century some of his more enduring creations were taking form. The United States Pavilion at the Montreal Expo in 1967 was designed by Fuller; he was responsible for the geodesic dome that was built in Dearborn, Michigan for the Ford Motor Company. Fuller's influence is discussed by Roystan Landau, *New Directions in British Architecture* (1968).

FULTON, ROBERT (1765–1815), inventor and engineer born in Lancaster County, Pennsylvania. He built the first successful steamboat. Fulton and Robert R. Livingston designed the steamboat, which came to be called the *Clermont*. In 1807, the *Clermont* made its first trip. H. W. Dickinson's *Robert Fulton: Engineer and Artist: His Life and Works* (1913) is still a classic biography.

GALLUP, GEORGE H. (1901–   ), public opinion researcher. Born in Jefferson, Iowa, Gallup established his reputation as director of the American Institute of Public Opinion. He graduated from State University of Iowa, then served as a professor of journalism at Drake University and Northwestern University. His work in public opinion surveys evolved from reader-interest surveys that Gallup developed for the Des Moines *Register & Tribune,* the Cleveland *Plain Dealer* and the St. Louis *Post-Dispatch*. He established the American Institute of Public Opinion "impartially to measure and report public opinion." His surveys have become standards for political action or popularity. He has received honorary degrees from many universities, including Northwestern University and Tufts University.

GARFUNKEL, ART (1941–   ), singer and actor, associated in his early career with Paul Simon. Simon's acoustic guitar and Garfunkel's voice became a national standard of music during the 1960s. In 1964 they cut their first album titled, *Wednesday Morning*. One song that appeared on that album achieved national attention—"The Sound of Silence"; it eventually sold over one million copies. A succession of musical hits brought them international recognition. They composed and performed the music for the film entitled, *The Graduate*. "Bridge Over Troubled Waters" was another significant music success; in 1970, the two parted to pursue their separate careers. Garfunkel was born in Forest Hills, New York.

GARLAND, JUDY (1922–1969), actress and singer. Born in Grand Rapids, Michigan, she achieved instant success in her early portrayal of Dorothy in the film, *The Wizard of Oz*. Her singing of "Somewhere over the Rainbow" in that movie has become an American classic. She was also associated with Mickey Rooney in the Andy Hardy series of films. Her musical successes were highlighted by her performance in the film, *Easter*

Parade (with Fred Astaire); her performance in *A Star Is Born* was also widely acclaimed. In the 1960s, she made a spectacular return by appearances at the London Palladium and Carnegie Hall in New York. She received an Oscar nomination for her dramatic role in *Judgment at Nuremburg.*

GARRISON, WILLIAM L. (1805–1879),

editor, reformer, and leader of abolition. In Garrison's day, the anti-slavery movement was split into two camps: those who sought gradual elimination of slavery and those who wanted immediate reform and abolition. Garrison called for the more immediate formula through his newspaper, *The Liberator*. He opposed slaveholders in his book, *Thoughts on Colonization* (1832). He criticized the New England clergy for their reluctance to condemn the broader aspects of slavery. He viewed the Civil War as a means of destroying the institution of slavery, and he wanted to disband the American Anti-Slavery Society after the Civil War. George M. Frederickson's *William Lloyd Garrison* (1969) is an excellent study of his life. Garrison was born in Newburyport, Massachusetts.

GERONIMO (1829–1909), leader of the

Apache Indians. He was born with the name *Goyathlay,* and saw his family killed by Mexican troops in 1859. Taking the name *Geronimo* ("Jerome"), he led raids of revenge against white settlements in Arizona and New Mexico until he was confined to a reservation. In 1876, he led his warriors into Mexico, where he plundered white settlers for the next 10 years. He finally agreed to move to a reservation in Florida, but escaped en route. General Nelson A. Miles captured him after 18 months of pursuit. Later, Geronimo was converted to Christianity and lived peaceably with white people. He appeared in President Theodore Roosevelt's inaugural parade in 1905. *Geronimo's Story of His Life* (1906), by S. M. Barrett, gives Geronimo's own account of his experiences.

GERSHWIN, GEORGE (1898–1937), musical

composer, distinguished in classical and popular fields. He was born in Brooklyn, New York. With lyricist Irving Caesar, Gershwin composed "Swanee," made famous by Al Jolson in *Sinbad*. In the 1920s he established many successes with his brother Ira: "Oh Kay," "Funny Face," "Rosalie," and "Strike Up the Band." His most distinguished efforts included *Rhapsody in Blue* (1924) for piano and jazz, and *An American in Paris* (1928). He had a fondness for jazz forms and black musical expression, and Gershwin's music reflected the current American scene. The most outstanding biography is David Ewen's *George Gershwin: His Journey to Greatness*. Gershwin's opera, *Porgy and Bess* (1935), was a stinging social commentary on racial prejudice.

Geronimo (center) and his braves shortly before surrendering.

GIBBONS, JAMES (1834–1921), Roman Catholic Cardinal born in Baltimore, Maryland. Gibbons supported the Catholic Church in a generation of change. He wrote *The Faith of Our Fathers* (1875), in which he underscored the practical applications of Catholicism. Known for his religious toleration, Gibbons supported labor organizations such as the Knights of Labor. He had considerable administrative skills, and he blended a profound affection for the church with his deep regard for America. Robert D. Cross gives a masterful summary of his contributions in *The Emergence of Liberal Catholicism in America* (1958).

GLADDEN, WASHINGTON (1836–1918), Congregationalist clergyman who sought to apply Christian principles to social problems. Gladden was born in Norwich, Connecticut. In 1866, he accepted the parish in North Adams, Massachusetts. His writings appeared in the *New York Independent* and *Scribner's Monthly,* usually on ethical themes of everyday living. He served as moderator to the National Council of Congregational Churches, where his scholarship reflected less depth and more of the conventional. He wrote several books on biblical criticism, including *Who Wrote the Bible* (1891), *How Much Is Left of the Old Doctrines* (1899), and *Social Salvation* (1902). Gladden addressed his later writings to municipal reform; he served with some distinction in interchurch associations.

GLENN, JOHN (1921–   ), aviator, astronaut, and United States Senator. Born in Cambridge, Ohio, he attended Muskingum College and trained as a naval air cadet. During World War II he flew 59 fighter bomber missions in the Pacific; he flew 90 missions in the Korean War. Glenn received the Flying Cross on five occasions and was awarded the Air Medal 19 times. He was the oldest of seven astronauts selected in April 1959 for Project Mercury program; but he was selected to make the first orbital flight in 1961. He was the first man to fly at supersonic speeds from Los Angeles to New York. In more recent years, Glenn has distinguished himself in political life as a United States Senator from Ohio.

GODDARD, ROBERT H. (1882–1945), established rocketry and the science of astronautics. Goddard's reputation was established while he was at Clark University, where the focus of his study was rocketry. He was able to perfect a system for liquid-propelled rockets. During World War II he addressed his attention to the potential of rockets in war; he concluded his life as a researcher in the employ of the Curtiss-Wright Corporation. Goddard's importance to the development of aerospace technology and interplanetary travel is great. Milton Lehman's *This High Man: The Life of Robert H. Goddard* is the only definitive biography available. *The Papers of Robert H. Goddard,* edited by Esther C. Goddard and G. Edward Pendray, is a collection of his writings.

GOLDBERG, RUBE (1883–1970), newspaper cartoonist whose funny drawings became world famous. Goldberg's political cartoons reached a wide audience through syndication. He worked for the *San Francisco Chronicle,* the *San Francisco Bulletin,* and the *New York Evening Mail.* He created the characters Lala Palooza, Mike, and Ike before he was offered the position of political cartoonist for the *New York Sun.* His reputation was established from that perspective. His cartoon, "Peace Today," was awarded a Pulitzer Prize in 1948.

GOLDWATER, BARRY M. (1909–   ), United States Senator and candidate for the Presidency in 1964. He suffered a heavy defeat in his quest for the Presidency against President Lyndon Johnson. Born in Phoenix, Arizona, Goldwater attended the University of Arizona but left to manage his family's department stores. During World War II, he served in the Army Air Forces; he helped to organize the Arizona Air National Guard. He was first elected to the Senate in 1952 and was reelected in 1958. After his defeat in 1964, he returned to Arizona for a brief period away from the Senate. The voters sent him back to the Senate in 1966. He has written numerous articles and books on his political philosophy and issues of national importance.

GOODSPEED, EDGAR J. (1871–1962), Greek scholar and Bible translator. Goodspeed studied at Denison, Ohio, Yale, and Chicago universities. In 1898, he came to the University of Chicago as a lecturer, then professor of Patristic Greek. He served as secretary to the president of the university. He devoted considerable work to developing a more readable version of the Bible. He wrote *The Conflict of Severus, The Story of the New Testament, The New Testament—an Ameri-*

can Version, *The Complete Bible–an American Version.* He was born in Quincy, Illinois.

GOODYEAR, CHARLES (1800–1860), inventor and noted rubber manufacturer. Goodyear was born in New Haven, Connecticut. His father was a hardware manufacturer, and Charles became associated with his father's hardware store in Philadelphia. When the store went bankrupt, he began experiments with rubber products. His fascination with inflated rubber life preservers led to his acquaintance with the American Indian Rubber Company. Goodyear wrote *Gum-Elastic and Its Varieties* and began experiments of treating rubber with sulfur and turpentine. By mid-century, the rubber industry was established in the United States and he migrated to Europe. He was honored by Napoleon III of France for his contributions to the Paris Exposition of 1855.

GOULD, CHESTER (1900–　　), cartoonist famous for his "Dick Tracy" series. Born in Pawnee, Oklahoma, Gould attended Oklahoma A & M and graduated from Northwestern University. He served as cartoonist for the Hearst Newspapers from 1924 to 1929; in 1931, he began working with the *Chicago Tribune* and created the cartoon character Dick Tracy. The character was a serious detective whose primary task was to reckon with criminal elements. "Dick Tracy" reached wide circulation through the Chicago Tribune-New York News Syndicate. The cartoon strip reached hundreds of newspapers throughout the country.

GOULD, JAY (1836–1892), builder of railroads, stock manipulator, and industrial capitalist. Born in Roxbury, New York, Gould began his career as a leather merchant. He established himself as a stock market speculator and helped the Erie Railroad compete against railroad baron Cornelius Vanderbilt. Through unscrupulous practices, he accumulated wealth at the expense of Erie Railroad and many unsuspecting investors. Later he bought an interest in the Wabash and Union Pacific Railroads. His influence extended to Manhattan's rapid transit system and the Western Union Telegraph Company. Louis M. Hacker's *The World of Andrew Carnegie* places Gould and this era into perspective.

GRAHAM, WILLIAM F. "BILLY" (1918–　　), evangelist and religious thinker. Born in Charlotte, North Carolina, he studied at Wheaton College. After a brief tenure as a pastor in Western Springs, Illinois, Graham became an evangelist. He served with Youth for Christ, then as president of Northwestern College in Minneapolis. He organized the Billy Graham Evangelistic Association for massive evangelism efforts. Through the radio program *Hour of Decision,* he is heard worldwide. He has written *My Answer, World Aflame,* and *Angels,* among many other titles. He has spoken to millions through crusades and television. John C. Pollock's *Billy Graham: The Authorized Biography* is a helpful view of Billy Graham's life.

GREELEY, HORACE (1811–1872), journalist, reformer, and editor. He was an early partner with the *New Yorker,* but the paper lacked profitability. In 1841, he began a more successful experiment known as the *New York Tribune.* Greeley urged social reform and resisted revolutionary approaches. He opposed the pro-slavery Compromise of 1850. Greeley was instrumental in the establishing of the Republican Party; after the Civil War, he became identified with the Radical Republicans. Soon frustrated with that group, he established the Liberal Republican Party. He wrote *Recollections of a Busy Life.* G.G. Van Deusen's *Horace Greeley: Voice of the People* places the man within the context of his generation.

GUGGENHEIM, MEYER (1828–1905), industrialist who established a mining empire. Born in Lengnau, Switzerland, he came to the United States in 1848. He obtained interests in silver-mining in Colorado. Guggenheim later expanded his smelting and mine acquisitions to Mexico. With the establishment of the Guggenheim Exploration Company and the American Smelting Company, his family obtained control of the broader aspects of mining and smelting in the United States. With his seven sons he was able to establish a force that dominated the American industrial scene for generations. The dated but authoritative *The Guggenheims: The Making of an American Dynasty* (1937) by Harvey O'Conner is still an outstanding overview.

HALE, GEORGE ELLERY (1868–1938), noted astronomer and astro-physicist. Born at Chicago, Illinois, Hale attended the Massachusetts Institute of Technology, the Harvard College Observatory, and the University of Berlin. He served as director of the Kenwood Astro-Physical Observatory in Chicago from 1890 to

1896. He invented the spectroheliograph, which was first used in 1892 to discover solar vortices and magnetic fields of sun spots. Hale achieved an international reputation among scientists. He wrote many books, including *The Study of Stellar Evolution, Beyond the Milky Way,* and *The New Heavens.*

HAMILTON, ALEXANDER (1757–1804), political leader and financial advisor. He was born on the island of Nevis in the British West Indies, the illegitimate son of James Hamilton and Rachel Fawcett Lavien. During the early stages of the American Revolution, Hamilton served as a close confidante of General George Washington. He became a member of the Federalist Party after the Revolution and was a co-author of the Federalist Papers. Hamilton served as Secretary of the Treasury under President Washington. He supported the concept of a central banking authority as the United States Bank and authored numerous studies on banking. Hamilton drafted the basic text of Washington's "Farewell Address." He died in a duel with Aaron Burr.

HAMMERSTEIN, OSCAR II (1895–1960), lyricist, theatrical producer, and songwriter. Born in New York City, Hammerstein was a student at Columbia University and received a law degree in 1918. His first musical success was as lyricist with "Wildflower" (1923). He then wrote "Rose Marie" (1924), "Sunny" (1925) and "Desert Song" (1926). With Jerome Kern, he achieved success with *Showboat* (1927). With Richard Rodgers his success became phenomenal. Together they wrote *Oklahoma* (1943), *Carousel* (1945), and *South Pacific* (1949), which received a Pulitzer award. Other successes included *The King and I* (1951), *Flower Drum Song* (1958), and *The Sound of Music* (1959). His more famous musical themes include "The Last Time I Saw Paris," which received an Academy Award, and "Ol' Man River."

HANCOCK, JOHN (1737–1793), first signer of the Declaration of Independence. A Colonial merchant and patriot, Hancock opposed Great Britain's efforts to restrict colonial trade. He resisted the Stamp Act by engaging in smuggling; by 1773, his name was identified with rebellion. Hancock was disappointed when the Continental Congress appointed George Washington to command the armies around Boston as the Revolution mounted. As an accountant for Harvard College, he engaged

John Hancock
Signer of the Declaration of Independence

in erratic bookkeeping that brought embarrassment to him and his family. Hancock later served as president of the States Convention where Massachusetts ratified the United States Constitution. He also served as governor of Massachusetts.

HANDY, W. C. (1873–1958), black songwriter regarded as the "Father of the Blues." Born in Florence, Alabama, Handy grew up in a home where both parents were ministers and secular music was regarded with disdain. Yet he organized tours and minstrel performances. His fame grew out of the Mahara Minstrels, a group he led. He travelled to Memphis, Tennessee, where his "Memphis Blues" became famous among musical circles. He also published the classic "St. Louis Blues." Handy was accused of plagiarism on certain musical themes, but he resisted those claims. He organized the W. C. Handy Foundation for the Blind. His book entitled, *Blues: An Anthology* contains some material about his life. He also wrote his autobiography titled *Father of the Blues,* published in 1941.

HARDY, OLIVER (1892–1957), actor and comedian. He was the senior member of a comic team with Stan Laurel. Laurel and Hardy made their first movie in 1926; in their career they were responsible for over two hundred movie features. In the 1950s, they expanded their comedy to the medium of television. The overweight Hardy and the lean Laurel developed a comedy style that reflected the anxieties of life situations. Their slapstick humor was popular in America at the time. Hardy's line, "Another fine mess that you got us into," became associated with the routine.

HATFIELD, MARK O. (1922–), modern political figure. Born in The Dalles, Oregon, Hatfield graduated from Stanford University. He served as instructor and dean of students at Willamette University. From 1950 to 1956, he served as the Secretary of State for Oregon, and as governor from 1959 to 1967. He won election as United States Senator in 1967. Hatfield's involvement in the anti-war movement during the 1960s generated discontent within the Republican Party; he has been identified with the liberal Republicans. Hatfield is a significant leader in evangelical Protestantism. He has written several books, including *Between a Rock and a Hard Place.*

HEARST, WILLIAM RANDOLPH (1863–1951), newspaper publisher and editor. Born in San Francisco, California, Hearst grew up in a wealthy family. He was expelled from Harvard College in 1885, and received permission from his father to work with *The Daily Examiner*. There he sensationalized and fabricated the news in irresponsible fashion. After his father's death, he moved to New York where he used the *New York Morning Journal* to compete against Joseph Pulitzer's *New York World*. In an era of "yellow journalism," Hearst's irresponsible reporting generated a newspaper boom. He established the *Chicago American* in 1900, along with other newspapers in Boston and Los Angeles. Eventually he retired on the Hearst estate at San Simeon in southern California. Ferdinand Lundberg's *Imperial Hearst: A Social Biography* (1936) is an unflattering portrait.

HENRY, CARL F. H. (1913–), minister and educator. Henry was born in New York City. He received the Ph.D. from Boston University and the Th.D. from Northern Baptist Theological Seminary. He established *Christianity Today,* a journal for evangelical Protestantism. Dr. Henry has held faculty positions with Gordon, Fuller, Wheaton Colleges, and numerous other colleges and universities as visiting lecturer. He has authored a number of publications in systematic theology; but his most significant views were shared through his editorials for *Christianity Today,* which he edited from 1956 to 1968.

HENRY, PATRICK (1736–1799), orator and noted political figure born in Hanover County, Virginia. As a member of the Virginia House of Burgesses, Henry spoke against the Stamp Act and opposed the power of Parliament to tax Virginians. He was described as the "Demosthenes of America." His name is synonymous with rebellion, through his impassioned cry, "I know not what course others may take; but as for me, give me liberty or give me death." After the Revolution, he served as governor of Virginia. He opposed the American Constitution because he believed it would concentrate too much power in the central government.

HOFMAN, HANS (1880–1966), cubist and abstract painter. Born in Weissenberg, Germany, Hofman suffered under the political difficulties of postwar Germany. He decided to emigrate to America and accept an appointment at the University of California. During the 1940s, he exhibited his paintings in New York, where his work received wide attention. With exhibitions at the Whitney Museum during the decade of the 1960s, his reputation as a German-American master was assured. His more famous paintings are *Fantasia* (1943), *Liberation* (1947), *The Gate* (1959), and *Agrigento* (1961).

HOGAN, BEN (1912–), an outstanding golfer. Born in Dublin, Texas, Hogan attended Fort Worth public schools. In his professional career as a golfer, he won the United States Open championship on four occasions; the United States Masters twice; won the British Open once. In 1946 and 1948, he won the Professional Golfers Association championship. He has received numerous awards including the Ryder Cup. Hogan was named Golfer of the Year in 1948, 1950, 1951, and 1953. He has written several books on the game of golf, including *Power Golf.*

HOMER, WINSLOW (1836–1910), a well-known American painter in the naturalist tradition. A native of Boston, Massachusetts, Homer began his career by working for *Harper's Weekly* as an illustrator. He proceeded to painting adult subjects in their natural settings; and in 1873, he began his work with watercolors in a graphic style. He moved from New York to the coast of Maine, where he sought a balance in his perspective. Late in life, he moved to the Bahamas, Bermuda, and Florida. At his death, he was regarded as the most significant American painter. *The World of Winslow Homer,* by James Thomas Flexner (1966) gives a good analysis of the man and his generation.

HOOVER, J. EDGAR (1895–1972), first director of the Federal Bureau of Investigation. Upon his initial appointment as acting director in 1924, Hoover established a fingerprint collection and national crime laboratory. The bureau was the center of Prohibition controversies and organized crime. Hoover opposed the emerging menace of Communism, particularly after World War II; he became involved in the McCarthy campaigns, writing books and articles that dealt with the themes of organized crime and Communism. *Masters of Deceit* (1958) is his most famous publication. Hoover was born in Washington, D.C.

HOPE, BOB (1903–   ), comedian and film star. Born in Eltham, England, Hope developed an instinct for comedy during his early days in vaudeville. He appeared in 1935 in the Ziegfeld Follies with Fanny Brice. He starred in the musical, *Red, Hot, and Blue* with Jimmy Durante and Ethel Merman; he developed a close partnership with Bing Crosby and Dorothy Lamour in a series of films titled *Road to. . . .* During World War II, he entertained troops, particularly during the Christmas holiday season. In 1950, he appeared on the television show, *Star Spangled Revue,* and in October of 1950, he embarked on an entertainment tour for the United States Armed Forces in the Pacific. These tours were continued for over twenty-five years. His television specials draw large audiences. He authored *They've Got Me Covered* (1941), *I Never Left Home* (1944), and *So This Is Peace* (1946).

HOPKINS, JOHNS (1795–1873), merchant and philanthropist. He entered business in partnership with his brothers. In exchange for groceries, the Hopkins Brothers would receive whiskey; then they would sell the whiskey as "Hopkins Best" brand. He developed banking interests by buying up overdue notes. His primary investment was the Baltimore & Ohio Railroad; he became director of it in 1847. He advanced money to the City of Baltimore during periods of financial crisis; he established a hospital and a university that later adopted his name. His biographies have suggested that "he knew how to be generous in large matters."

HOUDINI, HARRY (1874–1926), circus entertainer and escape artist. His real name was Robert Housini. He was born soon after his parents left Budapest, Hungary for Appleton, Wisconsin. In his career as a magician, he took the name Harry Houdini; he learned his magic tricks from a variety of sources—sideshows, circuses, books. His wife Beatrice assisted him in magical routines; they worked the Orpheum circuit. After a sensational escape from Scotland Yard as a publicity stunt, he attracted great attention. Houdini toured the European continent, where he was able to extricate himself from many difficult situations. His return to America was received enthusiastically. He wrote *The Unmasking of Robert Housini* (1908) and starred in three motion pictures after World War I.

HOUSTON, SAMUEL (1793–1863), American statesman and soldier born in Rockbridge County, Virginia. Houston was a Jacksonian Democrat with great oratorical skills and military abilities. He was a lawyer with political ambitions. As a member of Congress and then governor of Tennessee, he became involved with the westward expansion. President Jackson asked Houston to negotiate treaties with various Indian tribes in the Southwest. He moved to Texas, where he advocated statehood for the territory. Houston directed military operations against Mexican president Antonio Lopez dé Santa Anna; from 1845–1859, he served as Senator from Texas. A good biography of Houston was written by Marquis James, *The Raven: A Biography of Sam Houston* (1929).

HOWARD, ROY W. (1883–1964), newspaper publisher who served as director of the Scripps-Howard newspaper chain from 1953 to 1964. Born in Gano, Ohio, his newspaper career began with the *Indianapolis News* in 1902. After he was appointed as general news manager for the United Press, he achieved a broader recognition among publishing circles. While covering World War I, he prematurely reported the signing of the Armistice. Howard negotiated the purchase of the *New York Telegram,* the *New York World,* and the *New York Sun.*

HOWE, ELIAS (1819–1867), inventor who designed the first sewing machine, which revolutionized the garment industry. With ingenuity and persistence, Howe developed a workable sewing machine by 1845 and applied for the appropriate patents. He travelled to England to sell his machine, fell into difficult times, and sold his patents. He returned to America nearly penniless. Through legal proceedings, he was able to get the appropriate license fees on machines that had been produced from 1849 to 1854 in violation of his valid patents. With this newfound wealth, his personal life was stabilized. After the Civil War, sewing machines became major items for mass production.

HUBBLE, EDWIN P. (1889–1953), noted astronomer. Hubble was born in Marshfield, Massachusetts, and pursued a doctorate at the Yerhes Observatory near Pasadena, California. He determined the distances to several galaxies and studied their composition. He led in the development of Mount Palomar's telescope. Hubble wrote an autobiograpical sketch in *The Realm of Nebulae* and *Observational Approach to Cosmology* (both published in 1937). Harlow Shapley's *Through Rugged Ways to the Stars* places Hubble in the context of modern astronomy.

HUGHES, CHARLES EVANS (1862–1948), statesman and chief justice of the United States. After a 20-year period as a lawyer, Hughes became governor of New York State. As governor, he introduced historic reform legislation. President William Taft appointed him to the Supreme Court. In 1916, he was the Presidential candidate for the Republican Party; but he lost to Woodrow Wilson. After World War I, he supported President Wilson's proposal to join the League of Nations. He served as Secretary of State in the scandal-ridden Harding Administration, and gave excellent service. He called the Washington Conference on the limitation of Armaments and dealt with German war reparations. President Herbert Hoover appointed him as Chief Justice of the United States, where his progressive rulings foreshadowed those of the Earl Warren court.

HUGHES, HOWARD R. (1905–1976), business tycoon who achieved great renown through his efforts in aviation technology. After the death of his parents, he took control of the Hughes Tool Company. There he established his reputation and his wealth. Hughes produced motion pictures, and owned hotels, gambling casinos, an airline, television networks, and mines for precious metals. His complex personality contributed to his problems. He required privacy and developed a secretive manner. When Clifford Irving wrote a fraudulent biography on Hughes, the recluse telephoned news reporters to expose the hoax. At his death, many acquaintances of Hughes produced documents that claimed to be his will.

HULL, CORDELL (1871–1955), Congressman, Secretary of State under President Franklin D. Roosevelt. Hull generated the "Good Neighbor" policy toward Latin America. He signed the far-reaching agreement of Montevideo that made it illegal for military powers to intervene in the affairs of nations in the New World. He called for lower tariffs and opposed the expansionism of Japan that preceded World War II. He worked toward the establishment of the United Nations and earned a Nobel Peace Prize in 1945. *The Memoirs of Cordell Hull* (2 vols., 1948) provide a useful overview of the man and his era.

HUMPHREY, HUBERT H. (1911–1978), political figure, United States Senator, and Vice-President of the United States under President Lyndon Johnson. Humphrey was recognized as a spokesman for liberal political views. He was born in Wallace, South Dakota, and attended the University of Minnesota, graduating as a pharmacist from the Denver (Colorado) School of Pharmacy. His father served in the South Dakota state legislature. Hubert studied political science at the University of Minnesota while he served as pharmacist in the family drugstore. He became fascinated by the New Deal of President Franklin Roosevelt. He campaigned for mayor of Minneapolis in 1945 and won. He pursued vigorous reform of urban politics in Minneapolis, and advocated civil rights. Humphrey favored medical insurance through Social Security, the National Defense Education Act, the Peace Corps, and countless other programs of Lyndon Johnson's "Great Society."

HUNTLEY, CHET (1911–1974), television newscaster who achieved national recognition as co-anchorman with David Brinkley on the *Huntley-Brinkley Report,* featured by the National Broadcasting Company. He served as a correspondent on the West Coast for all three television networks. In 1956, he was brought to New York to co-anchor the national political conventions with Brinkley. Their partnership continued until 1970, and their news reporting received every award in broadcasting. Their famous sign-off—"Good night, Chet; Good night, David"—was immediately associated with the report. Huntley returned to Big Sky, Montana, after 1970.

IVES, BURL (1909–   ), singer and actor. Ives worked with the Columbia Broadcasting System as a folk song artist on radio and travelled throughout the states as a troubadour. He has appeared on numerous television programs. Ives' appearances on stage and film reflect a form of character acting. He has been featured in several films, including *East of Eden, Our Man in Havanna,* and *Cat On A Hot Tin Roof.* His television appearances on *The Bold Ones* from 1970 to 1972 developed a new character form—the lawyer. He has received numerous awards and recognitions. His autobiography is titled *Wayfaring Stranger* (1948).

IVES, CHARLES E. (1874–1954), pioneer in musical expression. Born in Danbury, Connecticut, Ives received initial musical training from his father. He graduated from Yale College in 1898 as a skilled musician and organist. He sold insurance for a time, but continued to compose music. He blended opposite musical forms, using familiar themes within his compositions. He wrote four symphonies, four separate theme works, chamber works, piano sonatas, violin sonatas, hundreds of songs, as well as piano and organ works. Peter Yates' *Twentieth Century Music* (1967) gives particular reference to Ives.

JACKSON, JESSE (1941–   ), clergyman and civic leader. Born in Greenville, North Carolina, he attended the University of Illinois and did postgraduate work at the Chicago Theological Seminary. He was ordained to the ministry of the Baptist Church and worked with Dr. Martin Luther King and the Southern Christian Leadership Conference in civil rights efforts. Jackson established Operation Breadbasket and Operation PUSH (People United to Save Humanity). He has been active in the Coalition for United Community Action, and is recognized as a fiery speaker.

JACKSON, MAHALIA (1911–1972), black singer and civil rights activist born in New Orleans, Lousiana. Miss Jackson symbolized black protest by associating with the civil rights movement. She became famous through her singing of "He's Got the Whole World in His Hands" and other popular songs. She achieved recognition in the white community after a widely acclaimed concert at Carnegie Hall in 1950. She was regularly featured in the Newport Jazz Festival after 1958.

JACKSON, THOMAS "STONEWALL" (1824–1863), Civil War general and Confederate hero. Jackson attended the United States Military Academy and served in the Mexican War. In the 1860 election, he supported John C. Breckinridge for the Presidency. After Virginia seceded from the Union he was commissioned to defend Harpers Ferry. At the First Battle of Bull Run, he earned the name "Stonewall" through his determined strategy. He was less successful in the battle to protect Richmond from Union Forces under General McClellan, but he scored a great victory for the South at the Second Battle of Bull Run. At the Battle of Fredericksburg, he was mistaken for a Union soldier and accidentally shot. This proved fatal. In strategy and audacity, Jackson remained unequalled in the Confederate ranks.

JAMES, WILLIAM (1842–1910), philosopher and psychologist. James was educated at Harvard, and his educational interests reflected a composite of the Renaissance mind. He was a determined advocate of the evolutionary theories of Charles Darwin. He wrote *Principles of Psychology* (1890), in which he underscored the human qualities of habit, emotion, consciousness of self, stream of thought, and will. His concern for individual freedom was reflected in his lectures on "The Will to Believe." His book, *Varieties of Religious Experience,* remains a classic study of the psychology of religion. Bernard P. Brennan's *William James* (1968) is a useful biography.

JAY, JOHN (1745–1829), diplomat, politician, Chief Justice of the United States. Jay served as President of the Continental Congress in 1778; after the American Revolution, he served as the new nation's Secretary for Foreign Affairs. He was a co-author of the *Federalist Papers,* which made him an advocate of the American Constitution. With James Madison and Alexander Hamilton, he called for a more centralized authority. Jay proposed the early outlines of a national judiciary. The treaty that ended the war with Great Britain bears his name; although it was written by Alexander Hamilton, it bore the diplomatic skills of John Jay.

JOLSON, AL (1886-1950), singer and star of motion pictures and radio. Born in St. Petersburg, Russia, his real name was Asa Yoelson and he was the son of a Jewish cantor. In 1909, he joined a minstrel group and entertained in the New York Garden. His role in the motion picture entitled *The Jazz Singer* (1927) is regarded as the first talking

Al Jolson in a scene from the *Jazz Singer* (ca.) 1927

picture. In 1928, he appeared in the film, *The Singing Fool*. His renditions of such songs as "Mammy" and "April Showers" became a permanent part of the American musical scene. He produced George Gershwin's *Rhapsody in Blue,* and the film entitled *The Al Jolson Story* was a phenomenal success.

JONES, E. STANLEY (1884–1973), missionary, author, and spiritual leader. Jones served as a missionary to India. His writings give a balanced, positive expression of Christian experience. He wrote several books, including *A Song of Ascents* (1968), which is his spiritual autobiography. He worked with the Ashram movement in India to communicate a religious message of love and understanding. Jones stressed the need for conversion, transformation, and the abundant life.

JONES, JOHN PAUL (1747–1792), distinguished American Revolutionary officer. His naval operations during the Revolution contributed greatly to the American victory. Historians believe the duel between Jones' ship, the *Bon Homme Richard,* and the British ship *Serapis,* was a significant episode of the war. He managed to seize the copper-bottom ship from the British. Jones received a gold medal and numerous honors for his naval successes. He served a brief period in the Russian navy, and most of his later years were spent in Paris. Alfred Thayer Mahan's book, *The Major Operations of the Navies in the American War of Independence* (1913), remains the classic on John Paul Jones and the Revolution.

JONES, RUFUS M. (1863–1948), college professor and religious leader. Born in South China, Maine, Jones attended Haverford College and the University of Heidelberg. He received his graduate degrees from Harvard and Oxford universities. In 1889, he became instructor at the Oak Grove Seminary in Maine; he taught at Haverford College from 1904 to 1934. Jones served as chairman of the American Friends Service Committee and of the European Relief in 1917–1927 and 1934–1944. He wrote numerous books, including *Autobiography of George Fox: The Story of George Fox* (1919); *The Faith and Practise of the Quakers* (1927); *Re-thinking Religious Liberalism* (1936); and *The Radiant Life* (1944).

JUDSON, ADONIRAM (1788–1850), Baptist missionary to Burma and founder of the American Board of Commissioners for Foreign Missions (1810). Judson was a Congregationalist when he travelled to India under the sponsorship of the board. There he adopted Baptist beliefs and received support from the American Baptist Missionary Union. He then went to Rangoon, Burma, to begin the translation of Scripture into Burmese. His linguistic abilities brought him into contact with broader levels of Burmese royalty. He completed an English-Burmese dictionary.

KEATON, BUSTER (1895–1966), comedian and film star. Born in Piqua, Kansas, Keaton performed in vaudeville before his appearances in Hollywood. He made comic use of pantomime, his portrayals in silent movies established his reputation as a classic performer. Keaton achieved fame in television and as a motion picture actor and director. His performances in *A Funny Thing Happened on the Way to the Forum, Around the World in 80 Days,* and *It's a Mad, Mad, Mad, Mad World* were received with acclaim. He achieved a new standard of excellence in the film, *When Comedy was King*.

KELLER, HELEN (1880–1968), author and humanitarian. Miss Keller was born in Tuscumbia, Alabama. An early illness left her blind and deaf by the age of 18 months. Her tutor Anne Sullivan helped her gain an education; and by age 16, she matriculated at Radcliffe College. She graduated *cum laude*. Her life was dedicated to the broader aspects of education and assistance to the blind and deaf. Miss Keller knew Alexander Graham Bell, whose experiments became essential to her work with the deaf and blind. She authored *Helen Keller's Journal, Out of the Dark,* and *The Story of My Life,* among other works.

KELLY, EMMETT (1898–1979), renowned pantomime clown. Born in Sedan, Kansas, he served as cartoonist for the Advertizing Film Company, where he created the "Wearie Willie" pen-and-ink cartoon. In 1921, he joined the circus as a clown; he worked as a trapeze artist and clown from 1924 to 1931. He appeared in several pictures, including *The Fat Man, The Greatest Show on Earth,* and others. He appeared on television with Ed Sullivan, Garry Moore, Jackie Gleason, Captain Kangaroo, and others.

KELLY, GENE (1912–   ), dancer, actor, and motion-picture celebrity. Born in Pittsburg, Pennsylvania, he appeared in the New York productions *Leave It To Me* (1938), *Time of Your Life* (1940), *Pal Joey* (1941), and others. Kelly directed the dancers for several movies: *Anchors Aweigh* (1944), *The Pirate* (1948), *An American in Paris* (1950), and *Brigadoon* (1954). Between 1944 and 1946, he served in the United States Naval Reserve. He authored *Take Me Out to the Ballgame* (1948).

KELLY, GRACE (1929–1982), actress, model, and (since 1956) princess of Monaco. Born in Philadelphia, Pennsylvania, she attended the Raven Hall Academy and Stevens School in that city. After early stage productions, she appeared in several motion pictures: *High Noon, Dial M For Murder, Rear Window, The Country Girl, To Catch A Thief,* and *High Society.* She received the Academy award for her role in *Country Girl.* Her marriage to Prince Rainier III of Monaco received considerable attention in America and Europe.

KELLY, WALT (1913–1973), newspaper cartoonist. His fame grew out of the comic strip "Pogo," with the classic line: "We have seen the enemy, and he is us." Kelly's characters reflected an innocent satire on society. Pogo was an opossum who spoke garbled language and had a community of animal friends, such as Howland Owl and the other inhabitants of Okefenokee Swamp. Kelly first worked as an animator for Walt Disney Productions. His comic strip appeared first in the *New York Star;* it reached syndication in over four hundred newspapers. Kelly was named Cartoonist of the Year in 1952.

KENNEDY, EDWARD M. (1932–   ), United States Senator born in Brookline, Massachusetts. Educated at Harvard and the Univer-

sity of Virginia Law School, he won election to the Senate in 1962 to complete the unexpired term of his brother, John F. Kennedy. In 1964, he was reelected. Mary Jo Kopechne, a campaign worker, died in an automobile accident at Chappaquiddick, Massachusetts that cast shadows on Kennedy's personal integrity. Yet he won reelection in 1970 and 1976. In the Senate, he has established a national health insurance program and favored tax reform. During the 1960s, he loudly opposed the war in Vietnam.

KENNEDY, ROBERT F. (1925–1968), United States Senator assassinated in a Los Angeles hotel after he won the 1968 California Democratic Presidential primary. Kennedy served in the United States Navy during World War II. He graduated from Harvard and received his law degree from the University of Virginia Law School in 1951. He served as assistant counsel to Senator Joseph McCarthy's Permanent Subcommittee on Investigations; and in 1957, he was chief counsel to the Senate Select Committee conducting investigations into labor racketeering. In 1960, he conducted the campaign of his brother, John F. Kennedy, for the Presidency. From 1961 to 1964, he served as Attorney General. From 1965 to his death, he was Senator from New York. Kennedy authored *The Enemy Within* (1960), *Just Friends and Brave Enemies* (1962), and *Pursuit of Justice* (1964).

KETCHAM, HANK (1920–   ), cartoonist. Born in Seattle, Washington, his real name is Henry King. He worked with Universal Studios and Walt Disney Productions from 1938 to 1942. He created Dennis the Menace and related cartoon characters after 1951. His "Dennis the Menace" cartoon strip was distributed through Field Newspaper Syndicate. He has received numerous awards, including the Billy de Beck Award for Outstanding Cartoonist (1952). He wrote several *Dennis the Menace* cartoon book collections, beginning in 1954, and *I Wanna Go Home* (1965).

KING, MARTIN LUTHER, JR. (1929–1968), civil rights leader who developed and practiced nonviolence as a strategy in dealing with racial prejudice and segregation. King organized a bus boycott to deal with segregation on transportation facilities. He was active in the National Association for the Advancement of Colored Peoples (NAACP); later he organized the Southern Christian Leadership Conference. King participated in the "sit-ins" to integrate lunch counters. The apex of the civil rights movement was achieved in a rally in Washington, D.C., where King delivered his speech, "Let Freedom Ring." In December of 1964, King was nominated for the Nobel Prize. He became involved in the anti-war movement shortly before he was assassinated in Memphis, Tennessee. He authored numerous publications; his most famous was, *I Have a Dream* (1968).

KISSINGER, HENRY (1923–　）， diplomat and Secretary of State. Born in Furth, Germany, he emigrated to the United States in 1938. Kissinger served during World War II. He received his doctorate from Harvard in 1954. Kissinger received national attention through publication of *Nuclear Weapons and Foreign Policy* (1957). He became a political advisor to Nelson Rockefeller in 1957. In 1968, Richard Nixon named him Presidential Assistant for National Security. Kissinger arranged the visits made by President Nixon to China and the Soviet Union. He was the architect of the treaty that ended the United States involvement in Vietnam. He also began *détente* with the Soviet Union and limited disengagement in the Middle East. Kissinger was recognized as an outstanding Secretary of State.

KOUFAX, SANDY (1935–　）， baseball pitcher and sportscaster. Born in Brooklyn, New York, he attended the University of Cincinnati. In 1955, he began his professional baseball career with the Brooklyn Dodgers (later the Los Angeles Dodgers). He appeared in World Series championships in 1959, 1963, 1965, and 1966. From 1963 to 1966, he was named to the National League All-Star Team. He was named Major League Player of the Year in 1963 and 1965. In 1963, 1965, and 1966, he received the Cy Young Award. From 1966 to 1972, he was associated with the National Broadcasting Company (NBC) as a sportscaster.

KRESGE, S. S. (1867–1966), merchandiser and businessman who established a network of "five and dime" stores throughout the country to make less expensive merchandise available to a broader market. Kresge was the founder of the S. S. Kresge stores; and from 1907 to 1925, he served as president of the company. From 1913 to 1966, he was chairman of the board; at its peak, over nine hundred thirty general merchandise stores throughout the country bore his name.

KUIPER, GERARD (1905–1973), astronomer. Born in Harencarspel, Netherlands, he analyzed early lunar photos and determined the exact sites where Apollo space craft would land. As chief scientist for the Ranger spacecraft program, he augmented United States efforts in the NASA space projects. The lunar landing of 1969 would not have been possible without his efforts.

LaFARGE, CHRISTOPHER GRANT (1862–1938), modern architect. Born in New York City, LaFarge studied at the Massachusetts Institute of Technology, 1880–1881. He obtained the Master of Fine Arts degree from Princeton University and became a partner in the firm Heins & LaFarge. LaFarge was the architect for the Cathedral of St. John the Divine in New York; St. Matthew's in Washington, D.C.; St. Patrick's in Philadelphia; as well as numerous other churches, hospitals, and governmental structures. He served as general manager of the United States Housing Corporation; also, director of the American Institute of Architects.

LaFOLLETTE, ROBERT M. (1855–1925), political reformer. LaFollette graduated from the University of Wisconsin in 1879 and was admitted to the bar one year later. He served as a member of the United States House of Representatives from

Senator Robert La Follette (left) and Senator Burton K. Wheeler, presidential and vice-presidential candidates of the League for Progressive Political Action

1885 to 1891. He campaigned against political corruption in his own state and was elected governor of Wisconsin in 1900. During his two terms there, he enacted new laws enabling voters to nominate candidates by direct primary elections, regulating government employment, and levying more reasonable taxes on business. LaFollette won election to the United States Senate in 1906 and was reelected twice thereafter. He ran for the Presidency on three occasions—the most successful being in 1924, when he and his running mate Burton K. Wheeler polled five million votes for the League for Progressive Political Action. LaFollette's ideas influenced national policy. He published his *Autobiography: A Personal Narrative of Political Experiences,* in 1913.

LANDON, ALFRED "ALF" (1887–1987), political leader and presidential candidate. Born in West Middlesex, Pennsylvania, Landon graduated from the University of Kansas in 1908. In 1912 and 1914, he worked for the Progressive Party; in 1932, he was elected governor of Kansas. He brought major governmental reform in state finance, water conservation, and utility rate regulation. In 1936 he won the Republican nomination for President, but he carried only Maine and Vermont. He opposed the United States' entry into World War II; after the war, he assumed an independent position and sought recognition of Communist China.

LAUREL, STAN (1890–1965), motion picture comedian. Born in Ulverson, England, he was part of the famous comedy team with Oliver Hardy. The Laurel and Hardy duo made slapstick comedy popular in the 1920s and 1930s. After 1926, he starred with Hardy in a succession of comedies, including *Air Raid Wardens* (1943), *Jitterbugs* (1943), *The Dancing Masters* (1943), *The Big Noise* (1944), *Nothing But Trouble,* and *The Bullfighters* (1945). He also appeared in numerous television roles after 1950; with his partner, he became an enduring part of America.

LAWRENCE, DAVID (1888–1973), editor and columnist. Born in Philadelphia, Pennsylvania, Lawrence began his career as a columnist with the *New York Evening Post* in 1916. His columns were syndicated in over three hundred daily newspapers. In 1947, he became editor of the *U.S. News and World Report.* He wrote numerous books, including *Diary of a Washington Correspondent.* He received the Presidential Medal of Freedom in 1970.

LEE, ROBERT E. (1807–1870), general of the Confederate armies and one of the greatest military strategists of history. Lee was born in

Jefferson Davis and his Cabinet with General Lee in the Council Chamber at Richmond.

Westmoreland County, Virginia, and graduated from the United States Military Academy. He fought in the Mexican War. When the Civil War began, his blood ties in Virginia affirmed his allegiance to the South. He accepted a commission as colonel in the Confederate army; within a month, he was given command of all the Southern armies. The battles of the war revealed his abilities as a strategist and diplomat—from Manassas where he achieved victory, to Fredericksburg where Stonewall Jackson fell. Gettysburg and Vicksburg were overwhelming losses for Lee. Historians of war agree that Lee had better strategic than tactical sense. *Lee's Dispatches,* revised by Grady McWhiney (1957), gives a useful perspective.

LEWIS, JERRY (1926–   ), comedian and television personality. Educated in the public schools of Irvington, New Jersey, Lewis began his career as an entertainer by appearing in the hotels and clubs of the Catskills. He formed a highly successful comedy routine with Dean Martin from 1946–1956. The Martin-Lewis comedy routine appeared on television until an embittered quarrel terminated the association. Lewis appeared in zany roles on screen, including *Sad Sack* (1957), *The Nutty Professor, Big Mouth,* and others. He has appeared on television and has developed a national relationship with the Muscular Dystrophy Association. His yearly telethons have raised millions of dollars for medical research in muscular dystrophy.

LEWIS, JOHN L. (1880–1969), labor leader who organized the Congress of Industrial Organizations (CIO) and was head of the United Mine Workers of America (UMWA). Born in Lucas, Iowa, Lewis worked as a miner in Montana and Utah. After a mine disaster in Wyoming, he dedicated his life to mine safety and defending miner's causes. He used the UMWA as a political base to launch his labor programs in Congress. During the Great Depression and Franklin Roosevelt's New Deal, he differed with the leadership of the American Federation of Labor and organized the CIO. He confronted the steel industry and the automobile industry and gained political leverage. In the 1940 election, he supported the Republican Wendell Willkie in preference to Roosevelt. Saul Alinsky's *John L. Lewis* (1949) is a useful biography.

LEWIS, MERIWETHER (1774–1809), frontier explorer. Born in Albemarle County, Virginia, he explored the territories of the Northwest with William Clark. President Thomas Jefferson, a friend and associate, commissioned their westward expedition. With considerable difficulty, they moved westward into territories inhabited by Indians and wildlife. Lewis' skills in dealing with the Indians proved essential to avoiding war. Upon his return, he was made governor of the Upper Louisiana Territory. However, his journals about the expedition were less persuasive than were those of William Clark, and it is agreed that Clark was an essential component of the expedition. See Bernard DeVoto, *The Journals of Lewis and Clark* (1953).

LINDBERGH, CHARLES A. (1902–1974), aviator who made the first solo non-stop flight across the Atlantic Ocean. Lindbergh was competing for a $25,000 prize posted by Raymond Orteig. He assembled the necessary financial backing to construct the plane he called *Spirit of St. Louis.* On May 20, 1927, he left New York, and in 33½ hours he arrived in Paris. He received numerous awards for the feat. In 1932, he and his wife were horrified at the kidnapping of their infant son; they paid a ranson of $50,000, but the baby was found dead. Lindbergh organized the America First Organization to prevent United States' entry into World War II; after the Japanese attack on Pearl Harbor, he joined the war effort. He wrote *We* (1927) and *The Spirit of St. Louis* (1953); he received a Pulitzer Prize for the latter.

Lindbergh stands under the wing of his plane, the *Spirit of St. Louis,* before taking off on his transatlantic flight.

LINDSAY, JOHN V. (1921–　　), political leader and news commentator. Born in New York City, Lindsay graduated from Yale in 1944 and served in the Navy during World War II. He represented New York's seventeenth Congressional District in the House of Representatives from 1959 until his election as mayor of New York in 1965. He began his political career as a Republican, but later changed his party affiliation to Democrat. His years as mayor of New York saw a succession of labor difficulties and conflicts. After leaving office, he turned his attention to television and broadcast interests; he has appeared on ABC's *Good Morning, America* program as political and public affairs commentator.

LODGE, HENRY CABOT, JR. (1902–　　), Senator, government official, author, and lecturer. Lodge graduated from Harvard and Northwestern University, and was elected to the U.S. Senate from Massachusetts in 1936. He resigned the Senate for military service during World War II; he was reelected in 1946. In 1960, he ran with Richard Nixon as the Vice-Presidential candidate for the Republican Party. From 1953 to 1960, he served as the United States representative to the United Nations. He was United States Ambassador to South Vietnam from 1963 to 1964 and 1965 to 1967; there he served a significant diplomatic function. Lodge authored *The Storm Has Many Eyes;* he has received numerous honors and recognitions.

LOUIS, JOE (1914–1981), American boxer and world heavyweight champion. Louis demonstrated his boxing abilities by his successes in the Golden Gloves competition of 1933. Also called the "Brown Bomber," his successes became legendary—particularly over boxers like Billy Conn, Rocky Marciano, and "Jersey Joe" Walcott. During World War II, he boxed on behalf of Army and Navy Relief. He authored *My Life Story* (1947). Jack Olsen's *The Black Athlete: A Shameful Story* (1968) places Louis within the generation of black athletes and racial discrimination.

LUCE, HENRY R. (1898–1967), magazine publisher. Born in Tenchow, China of Presbyterian missionary parents, Luce graduated *summa cum laude* from Yale University. With Briton Hadden, he founded *Time* magazine in 1922; the success of *Time* ushered in a new form of magazine journalism. In 1930, he launched *Fortune,* designed for the business executive. His marriage to playwright Clare Boothe Brokaw was much publicized. In this same period was launched *Life,* a venture into photographic journalism. At the time of his death, the combined circulation of *Life* and *Time* was in the millions. The most definitive study on the man and his ventures is John Kobler's *Luce: His Time, Life, and Fortune* (1968).

MacARTHUR, DOUGLAS (1880–1964), American general with distinguished service in the Far East during the occupation and reconstruction of Japan after World War II. MacArthur graduated from West Point with the highest scholastic average in the history of the academy. His rise within the military was spectacular. In 1936, he was dispatched to the Philippines by President Roosevelt to devise a strategy of defense; MacArthur mistakenly thought that the Japanese

Max Schmeling hangs on the ropes as he is pummeled by Joe Louis in their championship fight on June 22, 1938.

General Douglas MacArthur strides ashore during the landing on Leyte on Oct. 20, 1944.

wouldn't engage in such an attack. During World War II, he reclaimed the Philippines. After the war, he sought to expand American military efforts in the Korean War; because this strategy disagreed with President Truman's, he was dismissed. MacArthur returned to the United States in the midst of sympathy for the military hero. He authored *Reminiscences* (1964), an autobiography.

McCORMICK, CYRUS H. (1809–1884), inventor and manufacturer. He was primarily interested in farm machinery. In 1832, he took out a patent for a horizontal plow. He built a factory in Chicago for manufacturing reapers, and by midcentury he had a national market for reapers. Throughout his life, he competed with Obed Hussey for advantage in the farm machinery market. A contest in London pitted the McCormick reaper against the Hussey, and McCormick won. He expanded his factories in the United States; he developed steam-powered, self-propelled combines. He gave large sums of money to religious causes, and he received numerous honors from governments and organizations. William T. Hutchinson's *Cyrus Hall McCormick* is the standard biography.

MacDONALD, JEANETTE (1907–1965), actress and singer. With Nelson Eddy, she starred in several outstanding musical productions, including *Naughty Marietta* (1935), *Rose Marie* (1936), *Maytime* (1937), *Sweethearts* (1938), and *New Moon* (1940). She appeared in Broadway musicals such as *Love Me Tonight* (1932) and *One Hour With You* (1932). She starred with Clark Gable in *San Francisco* (1936).

McGUFFEY, WILLIAM H. (1800–1873), author of early elementary-school readers. McGuffey served as president of Cincinnati College and sought to promote public education. In 1836, he wrote the *Eclectic Readers;* the last of the now-famous *McGuffey Readers* was completed in 1854. Each of his books contained readings, aphorisms, messages on thrift and initiative. Within the emerging public schools, the readers were popular for several generations. McGuffey became president of Ohio University, and later professor of natural and moral philosophy at the University of Virginia. Richard D. Mosier's *Making the American Mind: Social and Moral Ideas in the McGuffey Readers* (1947) describes the impact of McGuffey's books.

MACHEN, J. GRESHAM (1881–1937), theologian and Bible scholar. Born in Baltimore, Maryland, Machen studied at Johns Hopkins University, Princeton University, and Princeton Theological Seminary. He then became professor and lecturer at Princeton. Machen was ordained as a Presbyterian minister; he became a leading voice of orthodox Protestantism in the early twentieth century. His books include *The Origin of Paul's Religion* (1921), *Christianity and Liberalism* (1923), *New Testament Greek for Beginners* (1923), and *The Virgin Birth of Christ* (1930).

McNAMARA, ROBERT S. (1916–   ), banker, automobile executive, public servant. McNamara was born in San Francisco, California, and received his undergraduate education at the University of California. He received his graduate degree in business administration from Harvard University. McNamara served for a brief period as a professor at Harvard. He became an executive with the Ford Motor Company in 1946 and president of that firm in 1960. President John Kennedy named him as Secretary of Defense in 1961. His eight years in that office were the most difficult years of the war in Vietnam. In 1968, he became president of the World Bank. McNamara has received numerous honors and recognitions. He authored *The Essense of Security* (1968) and other titles.

MADDOX, LESTER (1915–   ), segregationist leader and Georgia politician. Born in Atlanta, Georgia, he engaged in various business relationships—real estate, furniture, and a restaurant. As owner of a restaurant, he was told to comply with an integration order. He refused to comply and the restaurant was closed. He subsequently ran for political office and was elected governor of Georgia from 1967 to 1971. He served as lieutenant-governor under Governor Jimmy Carter in 1971–1975.

MALCOLM X (1925–1965), black religious leader. He was born as Malcolm Little in Omaha, Nebraska. Influenced by his father and the "back to Africa" ideas of Marcus Garvey, he resolved to defend the cause of black people. As a child, he saw his father murdered. In Boston, he worked in various menial jobs and was arrested for burglary. While in prison, he was converted to the Black Muslim religion; this provided a new forum for his ideas on race. He became an assistant minister of the Detroit Mosque. After the Kennedy assassination he made certain remarks that caused his suspension from the Black Muslims. He left the Nation of Islam to join the Organization of Afro-American Unity, and was assassinated at a public rally. His experiences were included in *The Autobiography of Malcolm X* by Alexander Haley.

MANCINI, HENRY (1924–), popular composer. Born in Cleveland, Ohio, Mancini attended the Juilliard Institute of Music. He served as pianist and arranger for the Tex Beneke Orchestra. As staff composer for Universal Pictures, he wrote scores for *The Glenn Miller Story, The Benny Goodman Story, The Great Waldo Pepper,* and other films. His recordings have achieved national attention. Among them are "Days of Wine and Roses" and "Moon River" (with Johnny Mercer). Mancini has received over twenty Grammy awards; he received Academy Awards for his music in *Breakfast at Tiffany's, Moon River,* and *Days of Wine and Roses.*

MANN, HORACE (1796–1859), educational reformer who promoted education throughout the United States. After graduating as valedictorian from Brown University, he pursued the study of law. His legal studies were interrupted by an interest in tutoring Latin and Greek; but later he returned to his legal studies, graduated from Tapping Reeve, and was admitted to the bar in 1823. He regarded education as "the great equalizer" of society. He abandoned a political career for a position as First Secretary of the State Board of Education. His admiration for Prussian education and non-sectarian study made his views controversial. Mann served as a member of the United States House of Representatives and president of Antioch College. *The Republic and the School: The Education of Free Men* (1957) is the most comprehensive collection of his writings.

MANTLE, MICKEY (1931–), baseball player born in Spavinaw, Oklahoma. In 1949, he signed with the New York Yankees. He has appeared with the New York Yankees in numerous World Series and All-Star games. Mantle is regarded as an outstanding baseball player. He was inducted into the Baseball Hall of Fame in 1974.

MARSHALL, GEORGE C. (1880–1959), soldier, statesman, architect of United States foreign policies after World War II. Marshall graduated from Virginia Military Institute and served in World War I under General John Pershing. Appointed Chief of Staff of the Army, he helped to prepare the United States for World War II. He received criticism for his failure to alert our Far East bases of the impending attack by the Japanese; but he directed military operations throughout the war and served as advisor to President Roosevelt. After the war he was named Secretary of State. The Marshall Plan set up a framework for the reconstruction of war-devastated Europe; actually, the plan combined the wisdom of George Kennan and Dean Acheson. Marshall encouraged the formation of the North Atlantic Treaty Organization (NATO). He was Secretary of Defense during the Korean War. The best work on Marshall is Forrest C. Pogue's *George C. Marshall* (2 vols., 1963, 1967).

MARSHALL, JOHN (1755–1835), the fourth Chief Justice of the United States. Marshall consolidated the principle of judicial review and strengthened the powers of the Supreme Court. Marshall was named to the court in 1801; he authored a definitive five-volume biography of George Washington. In 1803, his ruling in the celebrated case of *Marbury* vs. *Madison* established the principle of declaring acts of Congress unconstitutional. In *United States* vs. *Peters* he established the Supreme Court as the final interpreter of Federal law. In *McCulloch* vs. *Maryland* and *Gibbons* vs. *Ogden,* he upheld the principle that allowed the chartering of the Second Bank of the United States and the credit structure for interstate currency. Marshall was one of the truly outstanding Chief Justices in American history. *The Life of John Marshall,* by Albert J. Beveridge (2 vols., rev. ed. 1947) is a significant biography.

MARSHALL, THURGOOD (1908–), civil rights lawyer, Associate Justice of the United States Supreme Court. A native of Baltimore, Maryland, Marshall developed techniques for civils rights litigation during his early career as a lawyer. He served as counsel for the Baltimore chapter of the National Association for the Advancement of Colored People (NAACP). In 1938, he was admitted to practice before the United States Supreme Court. He achieved a phenomenal success ratio in his cases before the high court. For example, he argued the successful *Brown* vs.

Board of Education, which overturned segregation in public education. In 1964, President Johnson appointed him Solicitor General; in 1967, he was named to the Supreme Court. He has received numerous honors. An excellent biography is Lewis H. Fenderson's *Thurgood Marshall* (1969).

MARTIN, DEAN (1917–   ), actor, singer, and comedian. Born in Steubenville, Ohio, Martin became associated with Jerry Lewis in a successful comedy routine. The television series titled *The Martin-Lewis Comedy Hour* achieved considerable attention. His disagreement with Lewis resulted in the break-up of the comedy team. His screen roles have varied from the *Matt Helm* series to *The Bells Are Ringing* (1960), *Oceans II* (1960), *Silences* (1970), and *Airport*. His weekly television program on the National Broadcasting Company was widely received.

MARTIN, MARY (1913–   ), actress and singer born in Weatherford, Texas. Miss Martin was the singer in *Leave It to Me* (1938). She then starred in numerous musical productions, including *The Great Victor Herbert, Kiss the Boys Goodbye, Birth of the Blues,* and *Night and Day.* She starred in Noel Coward's *Pacific 1860.* Her role as entertainer in tours of United States military forces received acclaim. Her roles in *Annie Get Your Gun* (1948), the stage production of *South Pacific* (1949–1952), *Peter Pan* (1954–1955), and *The Sound of Music* (1959–1961) were widely acclaimed.

MARX, JULIUS "GROUCHO" (1890–1977), comedian and entertainer. In his early days, he joined his brothers Harpo and Chico in comic routines; the vaudeville circuit became the arena for the Marx comedy. With a cigar in hand, Groucho perfected comedy of the lunatic fringe. His scandalous humor was in comedy revues such as *Monkey Business* (1929), *Horsefeathers* (1932), and *Duck Soup* (1933). After the war, he became the host of a radio quiz show, *You Bet Your Life,* which achieved remarkable television success. The last movie effort starring Harpo and Chico was *The Incredible Jewel Robbery* (1959). A useful study of Groucho and his brothers is by Allen Eyles: *The Marx Brothers: Their World of Comedy* (second edition, 1969).

MATHER, COTTON (1663–1728), a leading author from the Puritan era, associated with the Salem witchcraft trials. Mather's youth was as remarkable as his life. At twelve, he was a student at Harvard College. He studied medicine, philosophy, and science in his teens. With his father, Increase Mather, he became a guiding force in the emerging Puritan society. The Salem witchcraft mentality was generated by Cotton Mather; his ill-fated efforts to become president of Harvard College or Yale brought serious disappointments in his later life. He was honored by other means—through election to the Royal Society of London. The best biography on Cotton Mather is Barrett Wendell's *Cotton Mather: The Puritan Priest* (rev. ed., 1963).

MAULDIN, BILL (1921–   ), editorial cartoonist. Born in Mountain Park, New Mexico, he studied at the Chicago Academy of Fine Arts. Mauldin served as cartoonist for the *St. Louis Post-Dispatch* until 1962, when he joined the staff of the *Chicago Sun-Times.* During World War II, he served with the United States Army; his military service earned him The Purple Heart and Legion of Merit award. Mauldin received the Pulitzer Prize for cartoons in 1944 and 1958. He authored numerous books, including *Bill Mauldin's Army* (1951), *Bill Mauldin in Korea* (1953), and *The Brass Ring* (1972).

MAYS, WILLIE (1931–   ), professional baseball player born in Westfield, Alabama. In 1950, he joined the New York Giants, which later moved to San Francisco. From 1951 to 1972, he was characterized as a "superstar" of baseball because he held numerous records: National League home run record; National League's Most Valuable Player of 1954 and 1965; and the Sporting News Player of the Year 1954. He wrote *Willie Mays: My Life In and Out of Baseball* (1966).

MEAD, MARGARET (1901–1978), anthropologist and author. Her early studies in Samoa provided new insights into tension, social organization, and adulthood; she authored *Coming of Age in Samoa.* She served as curator of ethnology at the American Museum of National History, then returned to her anthropological studies in New Guinea and wrote *Growing up in New Guinea* (1930). In later writings, she applied her findings to issues of public policy. After World War II, she authored *The Study of Cultures at a Distance* (1953) on cultural integration and analysis. In the 1960s and 1970s, her studies concerned the need for population control.

MEANY, GEORGE (1894–1980), labor leader associated with the American Federation of Labor (AFL). In his early career, Meany was associated with the building trades unions in New York. He promoted the pro-labor legislation of the New Deal; and during World War II, he served on the War Labor Board. In 1952, he was chosen as president of the AFL; later, he became president of the combined AFL and Congress of Industrial Organizations (CIO). Meany committed the organization to social reform and civil rights. Most Presidents since Eisenhower have had to reckon with the labor movement led by George Meany.

MELLON, ANDREW W. (1855–1937), businessman and United States Secretary of the Treasury. While associated with T. Mellon & Sons, he assisted in forming the Aluminum Corporation of America and organized the Gulf Oil Corporation. He then formed the Mellon National Bank of Pittsburgh, which identified him with significant banking and investment leaders. During the 1920s, he assisted the Harding, Coolidge, and Hoover Administrations in planning their monetary policies. His tax policies contributed to the unequal distribution of income that culminated with the Great Depression. Mellon wrote *Taxation: The People's Business* (1924).

MENNINGER, KARL (1893–   ), psychiatrist and author. Born in Topeka, Kansas, Menninger attended the University of Wisconsin and Harvard, receiving his medical degree *cum laude* from Harvard University. In 1946, he established the Menninger School of Psychiatry; he has been involved in the treatment, education, and rehabilitation of mental disorders. Menninger's books include *The Vital Balance* and *Love Against Hate.*

MILLER, GLENN (1904–1944), band leader of the "swing" era. Born in Chicago, Miller attended schools in Colorado and graduated from the University of Colorado. He began his musical career as a trombone player and as arranger for various orchestras. In 1933, he organized the Glenn Miller Band. The band played on several radio programs, but regularly appeared on the *Chesterfield Radio Program.* He composed many songs that achieved national popularity, including "Moonlight Serenade." Miller died in a plane crash over Holland shortly before the end of World War II.

MONDALE, WALTER (1928–   ), Vice-President of the United States and former United States Senator. In 1948, he worked in Hubert Humphrey's campaign for the Senate. He left Minnesota to work in Washington, D.C., for the student wing of Americans for Democratic Action; then he returned to Minnesota and graduated from college in 1951. In 1956, he obtained his law degree. In 1964, while serving as attorney general for Minnesota, he was appointed to finish Humphrey's Senate term when Humphrey became Vice-President; he was reelected in 1966 and 1972. On January 20, 1977, he became the forty-second Vice-President of the United States. Mondale has projected the image of a political liberal.

MONROE, MARILYN (1926–1962), motion picture star who built her reputation on a frivolous and sexual image. She was an illegitimate child with the name of Norma Jean Mortenson. Raised by foster parents, she had an unsuccessful marriage to an aircraft worker named James Dougherty. Then she became a photographer's model. In 1954, she married baseball star Joe DiMaggio, but the marriage lasted less than a year. She married playwright Arthur Miller but again was divorced in four years. Her most famous screen roles were in *Gentlemen Prefer Blondes* (1953), *How to Marry a Millionaire* (1953), *The Seven-Year Itch* (1955), *Some Like It Hot* (1959), and *The Misfits* (1961).

MOODY, DWIGHT L. (1837–1899), revivalist and evangelist. While Moody worked as a shoe salesman in Chicago, he became interested in the Young Men's Christian Association (YMCA). He organized "Sunday Schools" for slum families, supported through the YMCA. In 1872, he teamed up with Ira D. Sankey to hold revivals throughout England and Scotland; he then returned to America where he conducted revivals in New York, Philadelphia, Chicago, and Boston. Moody established schools for ministers in Northfield, Massachusetts, and Chicago. Chicago Bible Institute (named after Moody upon his death) achieved a great reputation. James Findlay's *Dwight L. Moody; American Evangelist* (1969) is a good biography.

MORGAN, J. PIERPONT (1837–1913), banker and financier who was instrumental in the financial reorganization of the railroads. During a severe economic crisis in 1893, Morgan managed to sell government bonds for gold. He organized the House of Morgan investment and banking corporation; established United States Steel as the largest corporation of its day; and gained control of major rail routes to the West. He was an avid collector of art; through a personal interest, he provided the funds to make the Metropolitan Museum of Art in New York among the finest museums in the world. Frederick Lewis Allen's *The Great Pierpont Morgan* (1949) is the most readable biography on the man.

MORRIS, GOUVERNEUR (1752–1816), statesman and diplomat. Born in Morisania, New York, he served in the New York provisional congress during the early stages of the American Revolution. He was elected in 1778 as a delegate to the Continental Congress and served as an assistant to Robert Morris, who was Superintendent of Finance. Morris was a significant delegate to the Constitutional Convention in 1787; he helped to draft the American Constitution, which he also signed. Morris served as foreign minister to France from 1792 to 1794. He also served as Senator from New York, and was critical of Jeffersonian Democrats. The diary of Morris is contained in *A Diary of the French Revolution* (2 vols., 1939) edited by B. C. Davenport.

MORSE, SAMUEL F. B. (1791–1872), inventor and designer of the first telegraph system. Morse was born in Charlestown, Massachusetts, the son of a clergyman. He graduated from Yale College. As an artist and painter, his work attracted little attention. Then he developed an interest in electricity. He combined the existing technology of sender, receiver, and code to invent telegraphy. Congress authorized the construction and development of a telegraphic line between Washington, D.C., and Baltimore, Maryland. By 1844, he was able to send the message "What hath God wrought" over this line. Robert L. Thompson's book, *Wiring a Continent* (1947) places Morse within the broader framework of technology.

MOSES, ANNA MARY ROBERTSON "GRANDMA" (1860–1961), painter of the primitive style. Born in Greenwich, New York, she held her first show in New York City in 1940. Subsequently her paintings were exhibited in shows throughout the United States, including the Museum of Modern Art in New York, the Metropolitan Museum in New York, and the Carnegie Institute. From 1950 to 1957, her paintings were exhibited in Europe. She received the Certificate of Merit (1956), the Woman's National Press Club Award (1949), and others. She wrote *My Life's History: Autobiography of Grandma Moses* (1952).

MUHAMMAD, ELIJAH (1897–1975), leader of the black Nation of Islam. Born in Sandersville, Georgia, he became Minister to the Nation of Islam in 1934. He molded the Nation of Islam into an organization of social, economic, and religious importance. Muhammad preached a message of black nationalism and imposed a standard of strict morality. He called for separation from white America and rejected the notion of racial integration. Malcolm X and boxer Muhammad Ali were among the more influential converts to the Nation of Islam.

MURROW, EDWARD R. (1908–1965), broadcast journalist. Born near Greensboro, North Carolina, Murrow spent his early youth in Washington State. He worked in logging camps as he attended Washington State College. In 1935, he joined the Columbia Broadcasting System. He travelled to London in 1937, and there he developed the dramatic "on the spot" style of radio news journalism. He won renown for his broadcasts describing the bombing raids on the city of London. After the war he developed television news journalism through the *See It Now* program; his most famous program was *Person to Person*. In 1961, he was appointed director of the United States Information Agency. Alexander Kendrick's *Prime Time* (1969) is a biography of Murrow.

NADER, RALPH (1934–   ), consumer advocate. Born in Winsted, Connecticut, Nader graduated *magna cum laude* from Princeton University. He later graduated from Harvard Law School. He was appointed as a consultant to the Department of Labor in his initial work on auto safety; served with Senator Abraham A. Ribicoff's Government Operations Subcommittee as a resource expert on safety. Nader wrote *Unsafe at Any Speed: The Designed-In-Dangers of the American Automobile* (1965) and became a bitter foe of the automobile industry. General Motors admitted spying on him, and he sued the company for $26 million in 1966. Nader organized the Center for the Study of Responsive Law in 1969. He has become identified with the consumer protection movement.

The Third-Term Panic, by Thomas Nast.
(The first use of the elephant as the symbol of the Republican Party.)

NAST, THOMAS (1840–1902), caricaturist, painter, and political cartoonist. Nast was born in Ludwig, Bavaria. As a youth he emigrated to the United States. In 1862, he began working for the *Harper's Weekly;* his initial cartoon attacks dealt with the Andrew Johnson Administration. His caricatures of Boss Tweed and the Tammany Hall political machine of New York City achieved national attention. He was offered a $200,000 bribe to stop the series, but he refused the bribe. Nast invented the symbols now associated with the Democratic and Republican parties—the donkey and elephant.

NATION, CARRY (1846–1911), temperance reformer, agitator, and an early leader in the Prohibition movement. Born in Garrard County, Kentucky, she married Dr. Charles Gloyd in 1867. He became an alcoholic and brought considerable hardship to his wife. In 1877, she married David Nation; and in 1890, she began her work with the Women's Christian Temperance Union (WCTU). Mrs. Nation and her associates organized prayer groups outside saloons and bars. In her campaign on behalf the WCTU, she carried a hatchet for breaking up saloon furniture. She displayed an aggressive character in achieving her moral ends.

NEUMANN, JOHN N. (1811–1860), religious leader; first male American saint of the Roman Catholic church. Born in Prachatice (now in Czechoslovakia), Neumann studied at the University of Prague and came to the United States as a Catholic missionary in 1836. After several years of missionary and pastoral work, he was named Bishop of Philadelphia in 1852. Neumann established about one hundred parochial schools and a Catholic seminary; he was well known for his deep personal faith in God. He was declared venerable in 1896, beatified in 1963, and canonized as a saint in 1977.

NICKLAUS, JACK (1940–   ), professional golfer born in Columbus, Ohio. Nicklaus attended Ohio State University. His career as a professional golfer included winning these major tournaments: United States Open 1962, 1967, 1972; United States Masters 1963, 1965, 1966, 1972, 1975; the British Open 1968, 1970; the Professional Golfer's Association (PGA) 1963, 1971, 1973, 1974. He has won more tournament championships than any other person in the history of professional golf. Nicklaus has authored numerous publications, such as *Ways to Lower Your Golf Score* (1962) and *The Best Way to Better Golf* (1974).

NIEBUHR, H. RICHARD (1894–1962), theologian and sociologist of religion. Born in Wright City, Missouri, Niebuhr graduated from Elmhurst College (1912) and Eden Theological Seminary (1915). He received his Bachelor of Divinity degree and doctorate from Yale University. Niebuhr authored *The Social Sources of Denominationalism* (1929), in which he discusses the relationships of social groups to denominations. His *Kingdom of God in America* (1937) discusses the concept of "Kingdom" in the transformation of Puritan thought to Protestant ideas in American history. He participated in study groups that led to the major assemblies of the World Council of Churches. He was instrumental in the merger between the United Church of Christ, Congregational, and Evangelical and Reformed Churches.

NIEBUHR, REINHOLD (1892–1971), distinguished theologian within the Neo-Orthodox movement. Born in Wright City, Missouri, Niebuhr attended Elmhurst College and Eden Theological Seminary. He received his master's degree from Yale University. Niebuhr pastored a church in Detroit, Michigan, from 1915 to 1928. In 1927, he wrote *Does Civilization Need Religion?* This book criticized the capitalistic values of the American industrial order. In 1928, he joined the faculty of Union Theological Seminary in New York City. There he wrote an attack on liberal Protestantism titled *Moral Man in Immoral Society* (1932). His many books and articles underscored the social and cultural applications of theology. He opposed the expansion of United States military power in Asia during the 1960s.

OAKLEY, ANNIE (1860–1926), an outstanding figure from America's Wild West. Born in Drake County, Ohio, she teamed up with Frank E. Butler in vaudeville and later married him. In spite of her abilities in marksmanship, she was a modest woman. Her exploits inspired the modern musical, *Annie Get Your Gun.* Miss Oakley's religious views were fundamentalist. She was generous with her wealth, and many legends grew out of her reputation after she died. Annie Fern Swarthout's *Missie: An Historical Biography of Annie Oakley* (1947) is a very interesting study.

OCHS, ADOLPH S. (1858–1935), newspaper publisher and philanthropist. Born in Cincinnati, Ohio, Ochs bought and published the *Chattanooga Dispatch* and the *Chattanooga Times.* Then he moved to New York City where, in 1896, he acquired control of the *New York Times.* In an age of "yellow journalism," he sought to establish a newspaper that reflected dignity and trust. He established the *New York Times Index of Current History* (a topical journal) and funded the de-

President John F. Kennedy, Governor Connally, and Mrs. Jacqueline Kennedy stand under the wing of the presidential plane moments after arriving in Dallas, Texas, on Nov. 22, 1963.

velopment of the *Dictionary of American Biography.* Ochs tried to make editorial opinion more objective. Gay Talese's, *The Kingdom and the Power* (1969) is a massive overview of Ochs and the *New York Times.*

ONASSIS, JACQUELINE KENNEDY (1929–   ), former wife of John F. Kennedy, the thirty-fifth President of the United States. Born in Southampton, New York, she attended Vassar College and The Sorbonne in Paris, France. After the assassination of President Kennedy, she received national consolation and regard. In 1968, she married Aristotle Onassis, wealthy Greek shipbuilder; the marriage attracted considerable notice. Since Onassis' death she has served as a publishing consultant. In earlier years, she was photographer for the *Washington Times-Herald.* Mrs. Onassis is a trustee of the Whitney Museum of American Art; she has received an Emmy Award for public service.

OPPENHEIMER, J. ROBERT (1904–1967), physicist; director of the atomic energy research project at Los Alamos, New Mexico. Born in New York City, Oppenheimer attended Harvard University and Cambridge University. He joined the staff of the California Institute of Technology in Pasadena, where he established a reputation in quantum mechanics and research in the continuous spectrum. Oppenheimer served as director of the project to develop the atomic bomb. After the development of the bomb, he regretted its devastation. He became the focus of attacks by Senator Joseph McCarthy, who alleged that Oppenheimer had communist sympathies; the allegations were unfounded. In the 1960s, he received the Fermi Award and was appointed director of the Institute for Advanced Study at Princeton University.

OWENS, JESSE (1913–1980), Olympic track star. He was born in Oakville, Alabama, the son of a sharecropper. He soon became an outstanding athlete. In 1935, he competed in the National Intercollegiate Track and Field Championships, where he established new records in broad jump and track. As a member of the United States Olympic team, he won four gold medals and served to refute Adolf Hitler's concept of "Aryan superiority." After several unsuccessful enterprises, Owens was appointed national director of physical education for blacks by the Office of Civilian Defense. He served as director of personnel for Ford Motor Company in Detroit from 1942 to 1946. He has received numerous recognitions and appointments. His autobiography is entitled, *Blackthink: My Life as a Black Man and White Man* (1970).

PALEY, WILLIAM S. (1901–   ), television network executive. Born in Chicago, Illinois, he attended the University of Chicago and the University of Pennsylvania. In 1928, he joined the staff of the Columbia Broadcasting System, where he rose from president to chairman of the board. He has served on numerous federal commissions, including the White House Conference on Education, Resources for Freedom, and others. He served in the military in World War II and was decorated with the Legion of Honor and Legion of Merit.

PALMER, ARNOLD (1929–   ), professional golfer born in Youngstown, Pennsylvania. Palmer attended Wake Forest College. As a golfer, he won the Masters Tournament in 1958, 1960, 1962, and 1964; the United States Open in 1960; the British Open in 1961 and 1962; and others. His friendship with President Dwight Eisenhower (and the President's affection for golf) established Palmer as a national celebrity. He is the president of Arnold Palmer Enterprises.

PATTERSON, FLOYD (1935–   ), boxer and former heavyweight champion, born in Waco, North Carolina. In 1952, Patterson began his boxing career as an Olympic middleweight champion; later in 1952, he fought his first professional fight. In 1956, he won the World Heavyweight Championship by defeating Archie Moore (the title had been vacated by the retirement of Rocky Mar-

ciano). After several defenses of the title, he lost it to Ingemar Johansson in 1959. He regained the title from Johansson in 1960, then lost it to Sonny Liston in 1962.

PATTERSON, JOSEPH MEDILL (1879–1946), newspaper publisher. Born in Chicago, Patterson attended the Groton School and Yale University. He began a journalistic career with the *Chicago Tribune* in 1901. In 1919, he founded the *New York Daily News* and remained as editor and publisher of that newspaper from 1919 to 1946. He served during World War I and wrote several books, including *The Fourth Estate* (with J. Keeley and Harriet Ford), *By-Products,* and *Rebellion.* His *New York Daily News* emphasized sensationalism, sex, and crime. After the financial crash of 1929, he addressed the newspaper to social reform and New Deal legislation. Although he supported President Franklin Roosevelt on most items, he felt that the United States should not enter World War II.

PATTON, GEORGE S. (1885–1945), general and military strategist. Born in San Gabriel, California, Patton graduated from the United States Military Academy at West Point. He distinguished himself as a tactician and commander of mobile tank warfare. His strict discipline and colorful language earned him the nickname "Old Blood and Guts." Patton was a student of United States Civil War strategy. Between World Wars, he learned tank warfare. He established his reputation in the North African campaign and the capture of Palermo. His sweep across France with the Third Army was marked by ruthlessness and drive. Patton was strategically involved in the Battle of the Bulge. He authored *War as I Knew It.*

PAULING, LINUS (1901–   ), atomic chemist. Born in Portland, Oregon, Pauling studied at Oregon State University and California Institute of Technology. He headed the Gates and Crellin Laboratories. His studies involved hemoglobin and protein structures. He is a member of the National Academy of Sciences and numerous other associations. In 1954, he received the Nobel Prize in Chemistry and the Nobel Peace Prize in 1962. Pauling has written numerous articles; his most famous appeared in 1931 and was entitled "The Nature of the Chemical Bond." Pauling advocated military disarmament, as described in *Quest for Peace* (1966) by Mortimer Lipsky.

PEABODY, GEORGE (1795–1869), merchant, financier, and philanthropist. Peabody dealt in securities in London after 1837; he generated capital for American industries. His firm, George Peabody and Company, specialized in foreign exchange. Peabody's international banking earned him a considerable personal fortune. After the Panic of 1837, he purchased several securities that were depressed. His company brought large supplies of capital investment to the United States. His wealth was distributed in various programs of educational reconstruction and poor relief. Franklin Parker's *George Peabody: A Biography* (1971) is highly informative and readable.

PEALE, NORMAN VINCENT (1898–   ), influential Protestant clergyman. Peale obtained his undergraduate degree from Ohio Wesleyan College in 1920. He was torn between a career in journalism or the ministry; he worked for the *Morning Republican* in Findlay, Ohio, and the *Detroit Journal*. He returned to study at Boston University and was ordained into the Methodist Episcopal Church in 1921. In 1932, he became pastor of the Marble Collegiate Church in New York. He has written numerous books, including *The Art of Living* (1932), *A Guide to Confident Living* (1948), *The Art of Real Happiness* (1950), and his phenomenally successful book, *The Power of Positive Thinking* (1952). Peale also began a radio program titled *The Art of Living,* which began in 1935 on NBC. He has been criticized for his moral pragmatism.

PEALE, REMBRANDT (1778–1860), painter best known for his portraits of Revolutionary heroes. Born in Bucks County, Pennsylvania, Peale was a son of the renowned painter, Charles Willson Peale. He made several trips to France, where he met Jacques Louis David and other leading artists. Peale established the Pennsylvania Academy of Fine Arts. His portrait of George Washington (1822) achieved considerable fame. He was elected president of the American Academy of the Fine Arts in 1825. Peale wrote *Graphics: The Art of Accurate Delineation* (1835). He developed a massive series of paintings on death that reflected several allegorical figures. In an era that emphasized romanticism, Peale's realistic work achieved considerable fame, particularly in Europe.

PEARSON, DREW (1897–1969), controversial newspaper columnist. His syndicated news column "Washington Merry-Go-Round" first appeared in 1932; he shared the writing with Jack Anderson after 1959. Pearson reported President Franklin Roosevelt's plan to pack the Supreme Court; he was generally disliked among Presidents and other public officials. He sponsored humanitarian causes; for example, he organized the Friendship Train to collect food for the people of Europe. He authored several books, including *Washington Merry-Go-Round* (1931) and (with Jack Anderson) *The Case Against Congress* (1968).

PEARY, ROBERT E. (1856–1920), Arctic explorer, famous for his discovery of the North Pole. Peary was born in Cresson, Pennsylvania. After his studies in civil engineering, he served as a county surveyor and draftsman. He was commissioned in the United States Navy in 1881. His early travels to Greenland were a prelude to his subsequent discovery of the North Pole. He reached the North Pole on April 6, 1909; but controversy surrounded Frederick A. Cook's claims that he reached the North Pole in 1908. In later life, Peary became identified with the development and expansion of aviation. John Edward Weems *Race to the Pole* (1960) details the controversy between Cook and Peary.

PENN, WILLIAM (1644–1718), Quaker leader and founder of Pennsylvania. Penn was born in London, where he became associated with the development of Quakerism and the Society of Friends. At Oxford, he was influenced by Puritanism and was expelled from the university. In 1672, he became a Quaker advocate. After the Glorious Revolution of 1688, he came to establish the colony of Pennsylvania. In 1712, he sold the colony to England. His last years were filled with disappointment. Mary M. Dunn's *William Penn: Politics and Conscience* (1967) is a useful analysis of the man.

PENNEY, JAMES C. (1875–1971), business executive and philanthropist born in Hamilton, Ohio. In 1902, he established the J.C. Penney Company, which operated on the principle of the Golden Rule and Christian morality. The department stores that he opened were called Golden Rule Stores; his first store was in Kemmerer, Wyoming. By 1971, his chain of stores numbered 1,660 outlets with gross sales of $4.1 billion. Penney exhibited a deep religious perspective in his personal manner and corporate leadership.

PERRY, OLIVER H. (1785–1819), naval officer and hero of the War of 1812. Born in South Kingston, Rhode Island, Perry held the command of a flotilla at Newport, Virginia, at the outbreak of the War of 1812. Commander Robert H. Barclay challenged Perry on September 10, 1813 in a battle between Perry's *Niagra* and Barclay's *Detroit*. Barclay was defeated, and Perry sent his superiors the famous message: "We have met the enemy and they are ours." This decisive victory strengthened United States claims in the Northwest. Perry retired and received honors from Congress. He later travelled to the Mediterranean, where he died of yellow fever.

PERSHING, JOHN J. (1860–1948), distinguished American commander during World War I. After graduation from West Point in 1886, Pershing was assigned to the campaign against the Apache Indians in the Southwest United States. He was also involved in the Spanish-American War and served as military attache in Tokyo during the Russo-Japanese War (1904–1905). Pershing's most significant service came during World War I, when he called for an independent American army. The Allies questioned his strategy during the last years of the war. Congress awarded him the title General of the Armies, a title given previously to George Washington. He authored *My Experiences in the World War* (1948), which was awarded the Pulitzer Prize.

PICKFORD, MARY (1893–1979), actress and movie star born in Toronto, Canada. Her acting career began at age eight, when she appeared in various melodramas and as a child actress on Broadway. At age 13, she took the name Mary Pickford. She appeared in various roles between 1910 and 1916, when she established the Mary Pickford Film Company. She joined Douglas Fairbanks, Charlie Chaplin, and the United Artists Corporation in 1919. She starred in numerous productions on the silent screen. She aided the work of numerous philanthropic and charity organizations.

PINKERTON, ALLAN (1819–1884), founder of a famous detective agency that bears his name; prototype of the modern crime investigator. Born in Glasgow, Scotland, he migrated to Dundee, Illinois. He supported abolitionists and the Underground Railroad in the years leading up to the Civil War. In 1850, he served as the director of police in Chicago; he then organized his private agency. He worked with the United States Post Office and the Illinois Central Railroad to solve robberies. He prevented an assassination of President Lincoln during the first inaugural. He organized the framework of the most comprehensive detective agency.

POCAHONTAS (ca. 1595–1617), early symbol of the American Indians. The daughter of an Indian chief, her real name was Matoaka; *Pocahontas* means "playful one." According to tradition, she played at the fort at Jamestown. She was taken as a prisoner by Captain Samuel Argall to guarantee the safety of Englishmen who had fallen into Indian hands. She was brought to Jamestown, instructed in Christianity, and baptized. She married colonial leader John Rolfe, and the marriage brought a period of peace between the colonists and the Indians. During a trip to England, she contracted smallpox and died in 1617.

POLLOCK, JACKSON (1912–1956), painter within the abstract, expressionist tradition. Born in Cody, Wyoming, he studied with Thomas Hart Benton between 1929 and 1931. He worked with the Depression-inspired Federal Arts Project from 1938 to 1942. During World War II, his art was influenced by European developments in cubism and surrealism. His paintings attracted the attention of Peggy Guggenheim; and under the Guggenheim influence, his art was shown throughout Europe. Pollock's international reputation became established in this period. During the last years of his life, his work was seen at the Sidney Janis Gallery in New York. In 1956, he was honored by a special exhibition at the New York Museum of Modern Art.

POPE, JOHN RUSSELL (1874–1937), architect; best known for designing the National Gallery of Art in Washington, D.C. Pope was born in New York City and trained at the American Academy at Rome. He was able to duplicate historic architectural styles through his studies. Pope began his architectural career in New York. He designed the Scottish Rite Temple in Washington, D.C., and was chosen to design memorials for Theodore Roosevelt in Washington and Abraham Lincoln in Hodgenville, Kentucky.

POST, ELIZABETH L. "EMILY" (1872–1960), well-known authority on social manners.

Born in Baltimore, Maryland, she began writing short stories and novels in 1904. Her book, *Etiquette,* appeared in 1922 and went through 10 revisions and 89 printings. It served as a guide to proper behavior and manners for ordinary people. Miss Post regarded etiquette as the science of proper living. She also wrote a nationally syndicated newspaper article on etiquette and authored numerous other publications, including *The Personality of a House* (1930), *Children Are People* (1940), and the *Emily Post Cook Book* (1949).

PRESLEY, ELVIS (1935–1977), singer commonly recognized as the father of "rock and roll" music. Presley's performances were filled with emotion and intensity. His gyrating hips and suggestive stage movements became a trademark, and he was idolized by teenagers throughout the world. He signed a recording contract with RCA Victor in 1956; he then recorded success after success. His first 45 records sold over a million copies each. Presley appeared in *Love Me Tender* and a succession of movies. He grossed over $4.3 billion in his 21-year career. His more famous musical titles included "Love Me Tender," "All Shook Up," and "Are You Lonesome Tonight?" His Graceland Mansion in Memphis, Tennessee, was a mecca for his fans.

PULITZER, JOSEPH, SR. (1847–1911), newspaper publisher and editor. Born in Mako, Hungary, he grew up in Budapest and pursued an active interest in military affairs. After being rejected by the French Foreign Legion, he was recruited by the Union forces for the Civil War and obtained passage to Boston. He quickly became identified with journalism through the *Westliche Post* in 1871. He purchased the *St. Louis Post-Dispatch,* which had shaky finances until about 1881. He served as a delegate to the National Democratic Convention and was elected as a member of Congress from New York in 1885. He then purchased the *New York World,* which added strength to his emerging influence. He used the *World* to promote sensational journalism and scandal. Its fiery reports from Cuba drew the United States into the Spanish-American War.

PYLE, ERNEST T. "ERNIE" (1900–1945), outstanding newspaper correspondent of World War II. Born near Dana, Indiana, Pyle studied journalism at Indiana University. After varied assignments, he received permanent appointment with the Scripps-Howard newspaper chain. Pyle developed a column that was syndicated through two hundred daily newspapers. He received a Pulitzer Prize for his coverage of the campaigns in North Africa, Sicily, Italy, and France. Pyle was with United States forces in Iwo Jima, where he died. He authored *Ernie Pyle in England* (1941), *Here Is Your War* (1943), *Brave Men* (1944), and *Last Chapter* (1946).

REAGAN, RONALD WILSON (1911–　　) In 1980, former Hollywood actor and governor of California, Ronald Reagan was elected President of the United States. At age 69, he was the oldest person ever elected President. After only 70 days in office he survived an assassin's bullet. Born in Tampico, Ill., February 6, 1911, he dreamed of becoming a movie star. After graduating from Eureka (Ill.) College he worked as a sports announcer for a radio station in Des Moines, Iowa. In 1937, he signed his first movie contract. During World War II, Reagan served as a captain in the United States Army. Afterward, he resumed acting and became president of the Screen Actors Guild. He married Jane Wyman in 1940 and had a daughter, Maureen, and adopted a son, Michael. They divorced in 1948, and in 1952 he married actress Nancy Davis. They had two children, Patricia and Ronald. In 1964, this Republican began campaigning for Barry Goldwater for President. Encouraged by his oratorical skills he ran for governor of California in 1966 and won. In 1980, after a nationally televised debate with Jimmy Carter he won a landslide victory for President and had another landslide victory for reelection in 1984. His presidency faced high unemployment, a recession, high interest rates and a stock market crash in 1987. He also faced terrorism in Lebanon, Israel's invasion of Lebanon and the Argentine invasion of the Falkland Islands. On the home front the Iran-Contra crisis shook the Presidency and U.S. credibility. He introduced tax cuts and sharp cuts in government spending. He won high marks for nominating Sandra Day O'Connor as the first woman on the Supreme Court and for his handling of the hijacking of an American plane in Beirut by Moslem extremists, the attack on Libya in 1986 and the successful invasion in Grenada. He worked hard to reach agreement with the Soviet Union to abolish intermediate long-range missiles during Summit meetings in Iceland with Soviet Premier Gorbachev and again in the United States in 1987. Reagan enjoys horseback riding and life on his ranch in California.

Presidential candidate Ronald Reagan waves to an enthusiastic crowd on his arrival on Aug. 15, 1976, in Kansas City.

**REASONER, HARRY (1923–   ), broadcast journalist. Born in Dakota City, Iowa, Reasoner began a writing career in 1946 with the *Minneapolis Times*. In 1948, he began an association with radio station WCCO in Minneapolis, a CBS radio affiliate. After a period of time with the United States Information Agency in the Far East, he returned to CBS with a television assignment in New York. He covered the racial crisis in Little Rock, Arkansas, in 1958. During the 1960s, he had numerous assignments with *CBS Reports* and narrated special documentaries on smoking, taxation, and federal aid to schools. He was seen as the weekly anchorman for *CBS Sunday News* until 1970, when he left CBS to join ABC News. He co-anchored news broadcasts at ABC with Howard K. Smith and Barbara Walters, then returned to the staff of CBS News in 1978.

REED, WALTER S. (1851–1902), military surgeon who is credited with having conquered yellow fever. Reed received two medical degrees, one from the University of Virginia and another from Bellevue Hospital Medical College. He served as a professor at the Army Medical School in Washington. He was able to determine the mode of transmission of yellow fever through many controlled experiments. He developed a way to immunize soldiers against the disease. In 1901, he resumed his teaching responsibilities at the Army Medical School. Reed received many honors, including honorary degrees from Harvard University and the University of Michigan. For more information about his life and times, read Albert E. Truby's, *Memorial of Walter Reed: The Yellow Fever Episode* (1943).

REMINGTON, FREDERIC (1861–1909), author and sculptor; painter and illustrator. Remington attended several schools, including Yale School of Fine Arts. His early work reflected his fascination with the West. He often painted horses in action. His work contained a high degree of realism. He represented the cowboy, Indian, and the Western landscape with native color. Remington wrote many significant books, including *Pony Tracks* (1895), *Stories of War and Peace* (1899), and *The Way of an Indian* (1906). A significant collection of his work can be found in the New York Public Library.

RENWICK, JAMES, JR. (1818–1895), architect most famous for St. Patrick's Cathedral in New York City. Born in the Bloomingdale section of New York, Renwick got his abilities in design from his father, James Renwick. He graduated from Columbia College. His designs for several churches brought him to national prominence— Grace Church, Church of the Puritans on Union Square, Church of the Covenant, and St. Patrick's Cathedral. Renwick also designed the New Smithsonian Institution in Washington. He taught a generation of apprentices and draftsmen and was a collector of art objects from his trips abroad.

RESTON, JAMES (1909–   ), author and journalist born in Clyde-Bank, Scotland. Reston attended the University of Illinois and began his journalistic career with the *Springfield Daily News*. In 1934, he joined the staff of the Associated Press in London. In 1939, he came back to the United States to work with the *New York Times*— first as reporter for the London bureau, then with the Washington bureau, finally as Chief Washington Correspondent (1953–1964). From 1964 to 1968, he was associate editor of the *Times*. He received the Pulitzer Prize in 1945 and 1957. Reston has received numerous other awards, recognitions, and honorary degrees.

RICKENBACKER, EDWARD "EDDIE" (1890–1973), World War I flying ace, racing driver, and executive of a major airline. Rickenbacker worked with the Frayer-Miller company as a race driver and he achieved numerous records. During World War I, he shot down more than twenty-two enemy planes, and became the most decorated pilot of the war. As general manager and later president of Eastern Airlines, he brought innovative promotions to the industry. After World War

II, he supported conservative McCarthyism and the anti-communist crusade. His autobiography is titled, *Rickenbacker—An Autobiography.*

RIDDLE, NELSON (1921–1985), composer, conductor, and arranger of popular musical themes. He was associated with numerous bands early in his career, including the Tommy Dorsey Band. He served as staff arranger for the National Broadcasting Company in Hollywood, 1947–1950; then he was musical director for Capitol Records, 1951–1962. Riddle has been guest conductor with the Hollywood Bowl and the Atlanta Symphony. He received the Emmy nomination in 1954, 1955, 1956, and 1957, and an Oscar nomination in 1960. Riddle received a Grammy award for *Come Blow Your Horn* and other musical scores. He composed theme music for the television series *Untouchables, Naked City, Route 66,* and others.

ROCKEFELLER, JOHN D., JR. (1874–1960), business entrepreneur and philanthropist. Born in Cleveland, Ohio, Rockefeller was educated at Brown University. After graduation, he became involved in the business affairs of Standard Oil Company, which his father had founded. He disliked the world of business and became involved in philanthrophy. He established the Rockefeller Institute for Medical Research and the Rockefeller Foundation. He supported the education of black people in the South. The last quarter-century of his life was devoted to conservation, the national parks system, and the restoration of Williamsburg. His modesty was in direct contrast to the image that his father projected.

ROCKEFELLER, NELSON A. (1908–1979), former governor of New York and Vice-President of the United States under President Gerald R. Ford. He was a son of John D. Rockefeller, Jr. His government service began as Assistant Secretary of State in 1944–1945. After the war, he chaired the Development Advisory Board. From 1958 to 1973, he was governor of New York, where he inaugurated a major construction program in the state capital of Albany. After President Richard Nixon's resignation, he was named by President Ford to become Vice-President. He was a trustee of the Rockefeller Brothers fund.

ROCKWELL, NORMAN (1894–1978), painter and illustrator of covers for the *Saturday Evening Post* and numerous other magazines, including the *Ladies' Home Journal, Look,* and *McCall's.* Rockwell's *Paintings of Four Freedoms* is represented in the Metropolitan Museum of Art in New York City. During World War I, he served as a first-class painter with the United States Navy. He received numerous recognitions and honorary degrees, and wrote *Norman Rockwell: My Adventures as an Illustrator* (1959), *The Norman Rockwell Album* (1961), *Norman Rockwell: Artist and Illustrator* (1970), and *Norman Rockwell's America* (1975).

RODGERS, RICHARD (1902–1979), noted composer of music. Born near Arverne, New York, Rodgers worked with Lorenze Hart and Jerome Kern in his early years. With Lorenze Hart, he produced a succession of musicals that captured national attention; among their more successful productions were: *On Your Toes* (1936), *Babes in Arms* (1937), and *Pal Joey* (1940). His more popular music with Hart included *My Funny Valentine, With a Song in My Heart, This Can't Be Love,* and *The Lady Is a Tramp.* His association with Oscar Hammerstein resulted in such musical successes as *Carousel* (1945), *South Pacific* (1949), *The King and I* (1951), and *The Sound of Music* (1959). Rodgers' most popular songs include "If I Loved You," "Hello Young Lovers," and "Climb Every Mountain."

ROGERS, WILL (1879–1935), entertainer and newspaper columnist. Rogers was born in Cologah, Oklahoma, of Indian descent; as a young man he was a cowboy—panhandling, twirling rope, and herding steers. In 1902, he joined a Wild West show in Australia. In 1912, he played in his first Broadway musical, *The Wall Street Girl,* and in 1922, he appeared in the Ziegfeld Follies. That same year, he began writing a column that wedded political humor with wit; the column appeared daily in 1926 and was widely syndicated. He authored *Letters of a Self-Made Diplomat to His President* (1926) and *There's Not a Bathing Suit in Russia* (1927). He was an early enthusiast of air travel and was killed in a plane crash en route to Alaska.

ROONEY, MICKEY (1920–), actor and star of films. Born in Brooklyn, New York, he first appeared in vaudeville with his parents. Rooney starred in numerous television and film productions, including *Hold That Kiss, Babes in Arms, National Velvet, Breakfast at Tiffany's, Requiem* *for a Heavyweight,* and the entire *Andy Hardy* series. He starred in the television spectacular *Pinocchio* (1957). Rooney wrote *An Autobiography* (1965).

ROOSEVELT, ELEANOR (1884–1962), author, diplomat, and wife of President Franklin Delano Roosevelt, thirty-second President of the United States. After her husband contracted polio in 1921, she became increasingly involved with his career. She rejected her mother-in-law's notion that Franklin should surrender to his condition. During the Great Depression, she led several New Deal programs for work relief. During World War II, she became involved with several efforts on behalf of the Red Cross and war relief. After the death of her husband in 1945, she assumed international stature in connection with her work on the United Nations. She was a leading voice in the Democratic Party, particularly on behalf of Adlai Stevenson's campaigns for the Presidency. Mrs. Roosevelt authored numerous books, including *On My Own* (1958).

ROOT, ELIHU (1845–1937), Secretary of War and Secretary of State; Senator from New York. Mr. Root attended Hamilton College and graduated from New York University with a law degree. He served as Secretary of War under President William McKinley during the Spanish-American War, and created the Army War College. He was highly regarded by President Theodore Roosevelt; and in 1905, he was named Secretary of State. He was awarded the Nobel Peace Prize in 1912. As Senator from New York (1909–1915), he opposed the progressive program of the Taft Administration, Root authored numerous titles. Richard Jessup's *Elihu Root* (2 vols., 1938) is the official biography.

ROSS, BETSY (1752–1836), legendary maker of the first American flag. Born in Philadelphia, Pennslyvania, she attended the Friends School in Philadelphia and demonstrated a great skill for needlework. In 1773, she eloped with John Ross, whom she married. She was a loyal member of the Society of Free Quakers. The story that George Washington commissioned her to make the first Stars and Stripes is based on tradition; but the flag was adopted as the national flag on June 14, 1777. There is considerable romance and legend associated with her making of the flag.

ROZELLE, PETE (1927–   ), football figure, flamboyant commissioner of the National Football league. Born in South Gate, California, Rozelle, was educated at the University of San Francisco. From 1948 to 1950, he served as the news director of the University of San Francisco; from 1952 to 1955, he was the public relations director for the Los Angeles Rams. Rozelle was general manager of the Los Angeles Rams from 1955 to 1957. In 1960, he was appointed commissioner of the National Football League.

RUBINSTEIN, ARTUR (1887–1982), concert pianist. Born in Lodz, Poland, he made his concert debut in Berlin at the age of twelve. He studied under I. J. Paderewski and began his concert tours with appearances in Paris, London, and the United States in 1905–1906. After World War II, Rubinstein came to live in the United States and continued a hectic pace of concert playing. He is noted for his stirring renditions of classical and patriotic themes.

RUSK, DEAN (1909–   ), Secretary of State during a turbulent era of American-Soviet relations. Appointed by President John Kennedy, he was loyal to the Kennedy-Johnson program of war in Vietnam. He personally confronted the Senate with the Administration's policies in Southeast Asia. Rusk had been president of the Rockefeller Foundation and became identified with foreign policy during the post-World War II period. However, he was unable to chart a course different from the John Foster Dulles policies of the 1950s.

RUTH, GEORGE HERMAN "BABE" (1895–1948), legendary sports figure called the

Babe Ruth hits his 60th home run.

"sultan of swat" for his ability to hit home runs. Ruth began his baseball career as a pitcher for the Boston Red Sox. Because of his reputation as a hitter, he was transferred to the outfield. He became a national celebrity and the perennial home-run king. In 1927, he hit 60 home runs, a record that remained until Roger Maris hit 61 in an extended game. His 714 lifetime home runs remained the record until Hank Aaron surpassed that mark. He is regarded as the game's greatest player. He died of cancer in 1948.

SALK, JONAS (1914–　), developed the first vaccine to combat polio. After his study at the College of Medicine of New York, Salk interned at New York's Mount Sinai Hospital. During his stay at the University of Michigan he developed a vaccine for influenza. Working with the National Foundation for Infantile Paralysis, he developed the successful vaccine for polio. Controversies surrounded his achievements; the Sabin oral vaccine competed with his. In 1963, he established the Salk Institute for Biological Studies. For more information, see Richard Carter's *Breakthrough: The Saga of Jonas Salk* (1966).

SALOMON, HAYM (1740–1785), financier, merchant, and banker of the Revolutionary period. Salomon was born in Poland and emigrated to New York in the early 1770s. During the British occupation of New York in 1776, he was arrested as a spy. He induced Hessians to desert the British army, which established his identity among the revolutionaries. Salomon's business and commercial dealings brought him unusual successes in the area of securities. He worked with Robert Morris to maintain a flow of finance and credit during the crucial "last days" of the American Revolution. Following the war, he suffered heavy financial losses.

SARNOFF, DAVID (1891–1971), pioneer radio technician and chairman of the Radio Corporation of America. His early work with John Wanamaker's station in New York allowed him to develop his interests in radio; he was the first to receive the distress call of the S.S. *Titanic* in 1912. Sarnoff became inspector and instructor for the Marconi Institute, which was then merged with the Radio Corporation of America owned by Owen D. Young. Sarnoff supervised the manufacture of radio sets and the expansion of radio programming. RCA became a leader in radio and television

broadcast and electronics manufacture. Sarnoff served as communications consultant to President Dwight Eisenhower. He received numerous honors.

SCHECHTER, SOLOMON (1847–1915), a leading voice in Judaism in the United States. Born in Focsani, Romania, his career began as a reader in rabbinics at Cambridge University. During this period, he wrote several books on rabbinic theology. In 1902, he became president of the Jewish Theological Seminary of America in New York and emerged as the leader of conservative Judaism. He became a spokesman for American Zionism. Schechter's numerous writings are contained in his *Seminary Addresses and Other Papers* (1969). He served as co-editor of the *Jewish Quarterly Review*.

SCHLESINGER, ARTHUR, JR. (1917–　), distinguished historian and author. His father, Arthur Schlesinger, Sr. was also a historian and professor. The younger Schlesinger graduated from Harvard in 1938, and the following year his thesis was published under the title *Orestes Brownson: A Pilgrim's Progress*. During World War II, he served as a member of the Office of Strategic Services. His book entitled *The Age of Jackson* brought him into national prominence. *The Vital Center* (1949) was his third book. His study of the Roosevelt Presidency resulted in three volumes: *The Crisis of the Old Order, The Coming of the New Deal,* and *The Politics of Upheaval.* He was appointed special adviser to President John Kennedy. His study of the Kennedy Presidency, titled *A Thousand Days,* received national attention.

SCHULLER, ROBERT (1926–　), popular clergyman, proponent of "church growth." Born in Alton, Iowa, Schuller attended Hope College and Western Theological Seminary. He established the Garden Grove (California) Community Church in 1955 and began a television and radio ministry. In 1970, he established the Robert H. Schuller Institute for Successful Church Leadership. His leadership has made a national impact. He has authored numerous titles, including *God's Way to the Good Life* (1963), *Your Future Is Your Friend* (1964), *You Can Become the Person You Want to Be* (1973), and others. Dr. Schuller's weekly television broadcast is entitled *The Hour of Power*.

SCHULZ, CHARLES (1922–   ), newspaper cartoonist, famous for his "Peanuts" series. Born in Minneapolis, Minnesota, he served as cartoonist for the *St. Paul Pioneer Press* and the *Saturday Evening Post* (1948–1949). In 1950, he created the comic strip "Peanuts," with characters Charlie Brown, Lucy, Linus, and Snoopy. Schulz has received the Outstanding Cartoonist Award from the National Cartoonist Association (1956) and an Emmy Award for the television special, *A Charlie Brown Christmas* (1966). His collected cartoons have appeared in books under numerous titles: *Peanuts; More Peanuts; Good Grief, More Peanuts; A Charlie Brown Christmas,* and others.

SCOTT, GEORGE C. (1927–   ), actor and star of motion pictures. Born in Wise, Virginia, Scott attended Redford High School in Detroit. During World War II, he enlisted in the Marines. Later he entered the School of Journalism of the University of Missouri; there he appeared in several dramatic performances. During the 1950s, he achieved very little. But during his performance in *Comes the Day* on Broadway, Otto Preminger observed Scott's abilities and offered him the lead in the film, *Anatomy of a Murder.* He received an Academy nomination for that role. *The Hustler* (1961) was his next role, followed by *Patton* (1970). Scott has made numerous television appearances in *Playhouse 90, Armstrong Theatre,* and *Hallmark Hall of Fame,* among others.

SEABURY, SAMUEL (1729–1796), the first bishop of the Episcopal Church in America. He was born in Groton, Connecticut as the son of a Congregational minister. He attended Yale College. Seabury worked diligently to maintain union with the British crown; he called for orderly change and petition. His pamphlets were answered by Alexander Hamilton and others who called for revolution. After the Revolution, Anglican officials in Great Britain consecrated him to serve the church in the now-independent colonies. Seabury's sermons and writings were published in *Discourses on Several Subjects* (1793) and *Discourses on Several Important Subjects* (1798).

SELZNICK, DAVID O. (1902–1965), motion picture producer, whose greatest work was the epic *Gone with the Wind* (1939). Selznick's name is associated with other outstanding screen productions, including *A Star is Born* (1937) and *A Farewell to Arms* (1957). He was rated Outstand-

ing Producer for 22 consecutive years. Selznick received Academy Awards for the best production of the year in 1939 and 1940.

SENNETT, MACK (1884–1960), producer of silent movies. In 1912, he organized the Keystone Company; and within the first year, he produced over one hundred forty comedies under the *Keystone* label. Sennett's movies lacked logic or cohesion; they offered a succession of "slapstick" episodes instead. Gloria Swanson added a sexual delight to the Keystone series. In 1928, Sennett was awarded an honor by the Academy of Motion Picture Arts and Sciences for his "contributions to comedy techniques of the screen."

SETON, ELIZABETH B. (1774–1821), first American to be named a saint by the Roman Catholic church. The Seton family travelled to Italy in 1803 to visit the Filicchi family, prominent in banking. There Miss Seton was converted to Catholicism. Upon returning to the United States, she established a boarding school in Baltimore called Sisters of the Charity of St. Joseph. After 1814, she opened orphanages and schools under the same order in New York and Philadelphia. She was declared venerable in 1959, beatified in 1963, and canonized as a saint in 1975.

SEVAREID, ERIC (1912–   ), broadcaster, news commentator, and author. Born in Velva, North Dakota, Sevareid studied at the University of Minnesota and then travelled to France and enrolled at the Alliance Francaise. After a brief period as a reporter for the *Minneapolis Star,* he joined the staff of the *New York Herald Tribune* in Paris. In 1939, he became a European correspondent for the Columbia Broadcasting System, and broadcast the fall of France to the Nazis. After the war, he became a national correspondent for CBS News. In the 1960s, his editorial commentaries appeared on the *CBS Evening News with Walter Cronkite.* Sevareid received numerous awards, including the George Foster Peabody award in 1949, 1964, and 1968. He authored *Not So Wild a Dream* (1946) and *This Is Eric Sevareid* (1964), among others.

DeSEVERSKY, ALEXANDER P. (1894–1974), aeronautic engineer born in Tiflis (now a part of the U.S.S.R.). DeSeversky served as an aviator for Tzarist Russia and engaged in combat action during World War I. He then served as a lower-level diplomat in America. When Russia closed its Washington embassy in 1918, he decided to remain in the United States. After World War I, he became a strong advocate of strategic air power. He contributed greatly to modern aircraft technology, and developed the first automatic bombsight.

SEWARD, WILLIAM HENRY (1801–1872), Secretary of State under President Abraham Lincoln. Seward graduated from Union College and was admitted to the bar in 1822. He was elected as the Whig candidate for governor of New York; as a two-term governor, he came into conflict with governors from Southern states. Seward wrote *Argument in Defense of William Freeman,* the account of his legal defense of two Negroes. As Secretary of State, Seward was a strong defender of Lincoln. He is considered to be among the greatest Secretaries of State; his most famous action was the purchase of Alaska from Russia.

SHEPARD, ALAN B., JR. (1923–   ), the first American to travel in space. Born in East Derry, New Hampshire, Shepard graduated from the United States Naval Academy and the Naval War College. He served as a test pilot with the United States Navy Test Pilot School and joined the Project Mercury space program of NASA in 1959. He was the first American in space with a sub-orbital flight on May 5, 1961. He was selected to command the Apollo 14 Lunar Landing Mission in 1971 and became the fifth man to walk on the

Apollo 14 astronauts (left to right) Stuart Roosa, Alan Shepard, and Edgar Mitchell

moon. Shepard has received numerous honors and awards, including a Presidential Citation, the NASA Distinguished Service Award, and the Lungley Award of the Smithsonian Institution.

SHRIVER, R. SARGENT (1915–   ), lawyer and public figure, candidate for the Vice-Presidency with George McGovern in 1972. Shriver graduated from Yale College, *cum laude,* in 1938. He married Eunice Kennedy, sister of the future President John Kennedy. His work as the first director of the Peace Corps in the Kennedy Administration drew international attention. Shriver served as director of the Office of Economic Opportunity under President Johnson and was appointed Ambassador to France. Presently he practices law in Washington, D.C.; he has received numerous honors and awards. His efforts on behalf of the Peace Corps brought him into contact with world leaders in developing countries.

SIKORSKY, IGOR (1889–1972), aeronautical engineer who designed the first multi-motored airplane and the first practical helicopter (in 1939). Sikorsky served as engineering manager and consultant to the Sikorsky Aircraft Division of the United Aircraft Corporation. He designed the S-42 Clipper Ship for Pan American Airlines. United Aircraft developed Sikorsky's helicopter designs, and the V5-300 was the first helicopter to go into mass production. Although helicopters were not used in World War II, they became vital military tools in Korea and Vietnam. Frank J. Delear's *Igor Sikorsky: His Careers in Aviation* is a useful biography.

SIMON, PAUL (1941–   ), musician and composer who became famous for his compositions with Art Garfunkel. Born in Newark, New Jersey, Simon met Garfunkel in the sixth grade. They began singing together in the mid-1950s as teen-agers. Simon entered Queens College to study literature and then went to law school. He and Garfunkel continued singing together, and recorded an album titled, *Wednesday Morning, 3 A.M.* The album achieved success through a song titled "The Sounds of Silence." Simon's success is evident in his musical score for *The Graduate,* for "Bridge Over Troubled Water" and other titles. In 1970, the two singers parted company. On his own, Simon has composed and performed numerous musical selections.

SINATRA, FRANK (1915–   ), singer and actor. Born in Hoboken, New Jersey, Sinatra began his career by touring with the Henry James and Tommy Dorsey Bands. He played leading roles in the movies, *Guys and Dolls, The Tender Trap, Pal Joey, Can Can*, and *Oceans II*. Sinatra received an Academy Award for best supporting role in *From Here to Eternity* (1953). He has received numerous additional awards, including the Peabody and Emmy Awards in 1965, and the Sylvania TV Award.

SIRICA, JOHN (1904–   ), judge who presided over the trials of Watergate scandal, which ousted President Richard Nixon from office. Born in Waterbury, Connecticut, he attended George Washington University Law School. Sirica found the work difficult and had to drop his studies. Later he enrolled at Georgetown University Law School. He graduated and was admitted to the bar in 1926. In 1930, he became Assistant United States Attorney for the District of Columbia; he later built a private law practice and entered Republican politics. In 1957, President Dwight Eisenhower appointed him to the United States District Court for the District of Columbia. By virtue of seniority, he became the chief judge of the District Court. He presided over the case that involved the seven Watergate defendants, including Presidential aides H. R. Haldeman and John Erlichman.

SITTING BULL (1831–1890), a Hunkpapa Sioux medicine man and Indian chief, leader of his tribe at the time of George Custer's massacre. The battle at the Little Bighorn River wiped out Custer and 265 men at the hands of Crazy Horse and his warriors. After 1879, the United States government offered amnesty to Indians who would surrender. Sitting Bull had left for Canada after the episode at Little Bighorn, so he accepted government amnesty. He was placed on a reservation in the Dakota Territory. In 1890, he was arrested on rumors that he would lead the Sioux on the warpath again; he was fatally shot in a struggle that ensued. Robert M. Utley's *The Last Days of The Sioux Nation* (1963) contains a scholarly analysis of Sitting Bull's life.

SLOAN, ALFRED P., JR. (1875–1966), business executive; first president of General Motors. Born in New Haven, Connecticut, Sloan attended public schools and the Polytechnic Institute. He graduated from the Massachusetts Institute of Technology with a bachelor's degree in 1895. His work with the Hyatt Rolling Bearing Company provided steel roller bearings for the automobile industry. Sloane's work came to the attention of William C. Durant, the builder of General Motors. Durant made Sloan the president of United Motors Corporation, which was eventually merged with General Motors. When the control of General Motors passed to the Dupont family, Sloan assumed greater influence. At his retirement, GM controlled 52 percent of the automobile market. He endowed the Alfred P. Sloan Foundation, whose primary contributions have been to the Sloan-Kettering Cancer Research.

SMITH, JOSEPH (1805–1844), religious leader; founder of the Church of Jesus Christ of Latter Day Saints (Mormons). In 1830, he published the *Book of Mormon*. Smith stressed the need for a restored church, and he suggested that he had special revelations from God. He organized a Utopian community of followers and led them westward to Nauvoo, Illinois. Smith admonished his followers against the use of tobacco, alcohol, and hot drinks. Through the theory of the "Hamitic Curse," Smith excluded blacks from the Mormon faith. Smith was murdered on June 27, 1844, while in jail, awaiting trial.

SMITH, HOWARD K. (1914–   ), newscaster and commentator. Born in Louisiana, he attended Tulane University and travelled in Europe after graduation. There Smith accepted a Rhodes scholarship to study at Merton College, Oxford University. During World War II, he served as a reporter with United Press. In 1940, he joined the CBS editorial team. In 1942, Smith wrote *Last Train from Berlin*. After the war, he served as the chief European correspondent for CBS and worked with Edward R. Murrow on the television series, *See It Now*. In 1957, he returned to America, where he became moderator for *The Great Challenge, Face the Nation*, and other programs of public policy. Smith also moderated the first of the Kennedy-Nixon Presidential debates. In October 1961, he resigned his position with CBS over a policy dispute. He moderated ABC's *Issues and Answers* program, and later he was co-anchor with Harry Reasoner on the *ABC Evening News*.

SNEAD, SAM (1912–   ), professional golfer born in Hot Springs, Virginia. Snead became a golfing professional in 1935. He won the Professional Golfer's Association (PGA) Championship in 1942, 1949, and 1951; the British Open in 1946; and the Master's Golf Tournament in 1949, 1952, and 1954. He was inducted into the Professional Golfer's Association Hall of Fame. Snead has written several books, including *How to Hit a Golf Ball* (1940), *How to Play Golf* (1946), and (with Al Stump) *Education of a Golfer* (1962).

SOUSA, JOHN PHILIP (1854–1932), America's foremost composer of music for marching bands. Born in Washington, D.C., he enlisted in the Marine Band. During the Centennial Exposition in Philadelphia, he played in the orchestra conducted by Jacques Offenbach. In 1880, he became the Director of the Marine Band; and in 1892, he organized what he called the New Marine Band. Sousa made several trips to Europe and was widely acclaimed. Some of his compositions achieved an international reputation: "The Stars and Stripes Forever," "The High School Cadets," "The Washington Post," and "The Gladiator." Sousa also wrote comic operas, including *The Bridge Elect*.

SPOCK, BENJAMIN (1903–   ), physician and educator, noted for his principles of child-rearing. Born in New Haven, Connecticut, Spock received his medical degree from the College of Physicians and Surgeons of Columbia University. As a pediatrician, he authored the *Common Sense Book of Baby and Child Care* (1946), which has gone through numerous printings. Spock's views on child-rearing influenced a generation of parents. In the decade of the 1960s, his opposition to the war in Vietnam brought prestige to the movement of protest and dissent. He authored other books, including *Decent and Indecent* (1970) and *A Teenagers' Guide to Life and Love* (1970). Spock has served on the faculty of the University of Pittsburg and Case Western Reserve, and on the staff of the Mayo Clinic.

STASSEN, HAROLD (1907–   ), lawyer and controversial candidate for President. A native of West St. Paul, Minnesota, Stassen attended the University of Minnesota and Hamlin University. From 1938 to 1945, he was the governor of Minnesota; and in 1948, he became president of the University of Pennsylvania. In 1953, he left the university to take assignments with the Disarmament Commission and as Special Assistant to the President. During World War II, he served in

Charles Steinmetz

the South Pacific, where he earned the Legion of Merit and the Bronze Star. He authored *Where I Stand* (1947). Stassen's liberal views made him an unsuccessful contender for the Republican Presidential nomination in 1948, 1964, and 1968. But his ideas affected Republican foreign policy.

STEINMETZ, CHARLES (1865–1923), mathematician and electrical engineer. Born in Breslau, he came to Yonkers, New York, to work with the electrical inventor Rudolph Eickemeyer in developing alternating-current devices. General Electric hired Steinmetz to do industrial research, and he gave GE a reputation for research and development. Steinmetz perfected the incandescent and arc lights. He also worked on new batteries and other electrical problems. As a consulting engineer with GE, he had freedom to explore projects and problems that were to his liking.

STEVENSON, ADLAI E. (1900–1965), diplomat, governor, and candidate for the United States Presidency. He was the grandson of Adlai E. Stevenson, who served as Vice-President in 1893–1897. He graduated from Princeton University, attended Harvard Law School, and graduated from the Northwestern Law School in 1926. During World War II, he was assistant to the Secretary of the Navy. He served as an adviser to the United States delegation at the San Francisco Conference, which chartered the United Nations. In 1948, he was elected governor of Illinois. He ran for President in 1952 and 1956 and lost. In 1960, President John Kennedy named Stevenson as United States Ambassador to the United Nations.

STOKES, CARL (1927–   ), the first black mayor of a major American city. Born in Cleveland, Ohio, he passed the bar examination in 1957 and established a law firm with his brother.

Elected to the Ohio House of Representatives in 1962, he became mayor of Cleveland in 1967. *The Cleveland Plain Dealer* lauded his election; he showed a balance in his administration. In 1969, he won reelection; but chose to enter broadcasting instead of attempting another campaign in 1971.

STONE, MELVILLE E. (1848–1929), newspaper executive. Born in Hudson, Illinois, Stone became a newspaper reporter for the *Chicago Republican* in 1867. In 1875, he organized the first penny daily in the United States, the Chicago *Daily News*. He sold out his interests in 1888 and became associated with the Globe National Bank. In 1893, he became the general manager of the Associated Press and moved the AP to New York to compete with the United Press. Stone developed a close relationship between the AP and Reuter Telegram Company of Great Britain for sharing foreign news. His autobiography is titled *Fifty Years a Journalist* (1921).

STRAUS, ISIDOR (1845–1912), merchant and chain-store president born in Otterburg, Bavaria. Educated in public schools, Straus was not able to attend West Point, due to the American Civil War. After the war, he established the enterprise of L. Straus & Son. In 1874, the basement of R. H. Macy and company became the center of Straus merchandising. Throughout Boston, Chicago, and Philadelphia, the Straus family established department stores. Isidor and brother Nathan made R. H. Macy the largest department store in the world. Through underselling, advertising and odd pricing, they controlled the merchandising market. Straus described himself as a Gold Democrat and a friend of President Grover Cleveland. He served as a United States Congressman from 1893 to 1895.

STREISAND, BARBRA (1942–   ), singer, actress, and film producer. A native of Brooklyn, New York, she began her career playing in summer stock theater. She appeared in numerous clubs, including Bon Soir and The Blue Angel. Miss Streisand starred in the Broadway roles of *I Can Get It For You Wholesale* (1962) and *Funny Girl* (1964–65). As a recording artist for Columbia Records, she became nationally popular. Miss Streisand has appeared in numerous screen roles, including *Funny Girl, Hello Dolly, On a Clear Day You Can See Forever, The Owl and the Pussycat, What's Up Doc? The Way We Were, A Star Is Born*

(which she produced), and others. She received the Academy Award as best actress for her role in *Funny Girl* (1968).

STUART, GILBERT (1755–1828), painter and portraitist of the early Republic. During the Revolutionary period, his family moved to London, where he met fellow American exile, Benjamin West. During his London period, Stuart was regarded among the great artists, equal with Joshua Reynolds and Thomas Gainsborough. In 1792, he returned to America and achieved fame through his portraits of Washington. Although Stuart painted President Washington during the later years of his life, little of age is reflected in the portrait of the man. Stuart's portraits of other Revolutionary figures reveal a style that transcends age. He used few colors, but his mixtures reflected shadows and illusions. He set the standard for American portrait painting that prevailed in the nineteenth century.

SUNDAY, WILLIAM A. "BILLY" (1863–1935), preacher and revivalist who introduced America to the "sawdust trail." Born in Ames, Iowa, Sunday began his career as a baseball player with the Chicago White Sox in 1883. He later played with teams in Pittsburgh and Philadelphia. He embraced Christianity and left baseball in 1891 to begin working with the Young Men's Christian Organization. Sunday's preaching reflected the fundamentalist tradition. He opposed Sabbath-breaking and the use of alcohol, and he stirred religious enthusiasm. Sunday wrote several books that coincided with his athletic integration of Christianity, such as *Burning Truths from Billy's Bat* (1914).

SUSSKIND, DAVID (1920–1987), producer for television, motion pictures, and theatre. Susskind was born in New York City and graduated from Harvard University. He worked with the publicity department of Warner Brothers and Universal Pictures from 1946 to 1948. From 1952, he produced several Broadway plays, including *A Very Special Baby* (1956) and *Brief Lives* (1967). He produced a number of motion pictures: *Raisin in the Sun* (1960), *Requiem for a Heavyweight* (1961), *All Things Bright and Beautiful* (1976), and others. Susskind has been involved in producing several television programs, such as *The du Pont Show of the Month, Kaiser Aluminum Hour, Hallmark Hall of Fame*, and *Kraft Theatre*. He has received the Peabody Award, Academy Awards, and numerous other recognitions and honors.

SWANSON, GLORIA (1899–1983), actress and film celebrity. Born in Chicago, Illinois, she began working with Essanay Studios in Chicago. She later formed her own production company, called Gloria Swanson Productions. From 1971, she organized the Facial Fitness Clinics. Miss Swanson starred in numerous screen productions, including *Airport 1975* and *Sunset Boulevard* (1950). The first picture that recorded her speaking and singing was *The Trespasser* (1929). She appeared in the Broadway production, *Butterflies Are Free* (1970–1972). Miss Swanson is recognized for her acting abilities and business perception.

TAYLOR, ELIZABETH (1932–   ), actress and movie personality born in London, England. Miss Taylor's first major screen role was in *National Velvet* (1944). She also starred in *A Place in the Sun* (1950), *The Last Time I Saw Paris, Cat on a Hot Tin Roof, Butterfield 8, Cleopatra, The Sand Piper,* and *Who's Afraid of Virginia Wolf?* She received Academy Awards for her roles in *Butterfield 8* and *Who's Afraid of Virginia Wolf?* She has authored *Nibbles and Me* (with Richard Burton) and *World Enough and Time.* She has become notorious for her numerous marriages—to Conrad Nicholas Hilton, Jr.; to Michael Wilding; to Mike Todd; to Eddie Fisher; to Richard Burton (twice); and to John Warner.

TAYLOR, KENNETH (1917–   ), religious publishing executive. Taylor attended Wheaton (Illinois) College and began his publishing career with Moody Press. In 1963, he became president of his own company, Tyndale Press. He has served as an officer with numerous other organizations, including Living Bibles International and Coverdale Publishers. He has authored numerous titles, including *Is Christianity Credible?* (1946), *Living Letters: The Paraphrased Epistles* (1962), and *The Living Bible* (1971).

TEMPLE, SHIRLEY (1928–   ), actress, popular child star of movies in the 1930s, and politician. At the age of seven, she was Hollywood's greatest box-office attraction. She is remembered for her singing of "The Good Ship Lollipop." She portrayed a child who was capable of dealing with adult ego and hatred. Her films in-

cluded *Baby Burlesks, Stand Up and Cheer, Little Miss Marker, Wee Willie Winkie,* and *The Little Princess.* In later life, she married a civic leader in San Francisco and became affiliated with the Republican Party. She ran unsuccessfully for the office of United States Representative to Congress. In 1969, President Nixon appointed her a member of the United States delegation to the United Nations General Assembly.

TESLA, NIKOLA (1856–1943), electrical engineer and inventor born in Smiljan, Croatia (now Yugoslavia). He devised an electrical transformer known as the Tesla coil. He worked briefly with Thomas Edison, designing electrical dynamos; in 1887, he established his own laboratory in New York. Tesla sided with engineers who favored alternating electrical current, rather than direct current (which Edison advocated). The alternating current system was adopted by George Westinghouse and became the basis for power generation from the Niagara Falls to Chicago's Columbian Exposition. Tesla produced motors, transformers, electrical coils, and other devices that contributed greatly to the emerging world of electrical technology.

THOMAS, LOWELL (1892–   ), radio news commentator, born in Woodington, Ohio. Thomas attended the University of Northern Indiana, University of Denver, Kent College, and Princeton University. In 1915, he made the first of a series of filmed travelogues; he toured extensively and lectured on his travels. President Woodrow Wilson appointed him to the civilian commission on World War I. In 1930, he made his debut on CBS radio; he would regularly conclude his nightly news broadcasts with the words, "So long until tomorrow." He continued producing *Lowell Thomas and the News* until 1976. He was the voice of Movietone News and served in the development of Cinerama movie features. Among his numerous publications are *Beyond the Khyber Pass* (1925), *The Untold Story of Exploration* (1936), and *With Allenby in the Holy Land* (1938).

THURMOND, STROM (1902–   ), former governor of South Carolina, Presidential candidate, and United States Senator. In 1948, Thurmond launched a Presidential campaign under the "states' rights" banner of the Dixiecrats. He attended Clemson College and was admitted to the bar in 1930. His public career has been identified with the concept of "states' rights" and racial segregation. In 1964, he broke with the Democratic Party and became a Republican. He has served in the United States Senate for over two decades. During World War II, he served in the United States Army during the invasion of Europe. He received the Bronze Star, the Purple Heart, and the Legion of Merit.

TILLICH, PAUL (1886–1965), theologian, religious scholar, and author. Born in Starzeddel, Prussia, Tillich attended the Universities of Berlin, Tübingen, and Halle. He received the Ph.D. from the University of Breslau. Ordained a minister in the Evangelican Lutheran Church, he taught at Marburg, Dresden, and Leipzig before becoming professor at the University of Frankfurt am-Main in 1929. He opposed the Nazis and was dismissed from the university, so he emigrated to the United States. Tillich taught at Union Theological Seminary (1933–1955), Harvard University (1955–1962), and the University of Chicago (1962–1965). He wrote numerous books, including a three-volume *Systematic Theology* (1951–1963).

TRUMBULL, JOHN (1756–1843), painter of historic scenes from the Revolutionary War. Trumbull was born in the Connecticut colony, where his father was governor. He took private painting lessons from John Singleton Copley and graduated from Harvard at age 17. During the Revolution, he served as aide-de-camp to General Washington. In 1780, he sailed to London, where he studied with Benjamin West. A controversy with Thomas Jefferson in 1793 damaged his later career. His art is in the tradition of Peter Paul Rubens; it deals exclusively with the American Revolution. Trumbull's works include the famous *Battle of Bunker Hill* and *Capture of the Hessians at Trenton.* He achieved fame in later life with commissions from Congress for paintings of the *Signing of the Declaration of Independence, Surrender of Cornwallis at Yorktown,* and others that decorate the rotunda of the Capitol in Washington.

TRUTH, SOJOURNER (1797–1883), abolitionist leader whose real name was Isabella Baumfree. Born in Ulster County, New York, she was the daughter of an African couple. After New York had passed an emancipation act, she asked for freedom from her master John J. Dumont. He re-fused and she ran away with one of her five children. She worked menial jobs and came under the influence of a religious fanatic named Mathias. Eventually she left Mathias and travelled to speak on her own, with the name of Sojourner Truth. She was the first person to test the legality of segregation on Washington, D.C., street cars.

TUBMAN, HARRIET (ca. 1820–1913), black agent for the Underground Railroad. Tubman helped hundreds of slaves flee captivity. She was born a slave herself, in Dorcester County, Maryland. In 1848, she ran away with her two brothers, leaving her husband John Tubman behind. A bounty of $40,000 was placed on her. Before the Civil War, she returned to the South 20 times to help over three hundred slaves to escape. She supported John Brown's insurrection at Harpers Ferry, Virginia. Tubman spoke against slavery and in support of women's rights. During the war, she served as a scout and nurse for the Union forces.

TUNNEY, JAMES J. "GENE" (1898–1978), professional boxer; corporation director. Born in New York City, Tunney won the light heavyweight championship at Paris in 1919. In 1926, he won the heavyweight championship from Jack Dempsey. He retained that title in a return engagement at Chicago in 1927. He retired from boxing in 1928 undefeated. He has served as director to many corporations, including the Bank of Commerce of New York and the Penobscot Building in Detroit. He wrote *A Man Must Fight* (1932) and *Arms for Living* (1941). In later years, Jack Dempsey became Tunney's close personal friend.

TURNER, NAT (1800–1831), black slave leader born in Southampton County, Virginia. He was a restless young man who turned to the Bible for guidance on slavery and freedom. He believed he was appointed of God to deliver his people from slavery, and he understood a solar eclipse to be a sign from God that he was supposed to lead a rebellion. Turner and his friends killed many whites in the rebellion that bears his name. By August of 1831, the tide had turned, and blacks were executed in large numbers. After a brief escape, Turner was caught, tried, and executed. His rebellion galvanized the abolitionist movement. William Styron's *Confessions of Nat Turner* (1968) is an analysis of the man and the movement.

VALENTINO, RUDOLPH (1895–1926), actor and matinee idol of the silent-film era. Born in Castellanetz, Italy, he attended the Dante Alighieri College and the Royal Academy. He came to the United States in 1913 and began his career as a dancer. Valentino joined the Musical Comedy Company and travelled to San Francisco. He entered motion pictures during a stay in Los Angeles, and scored a remarkable triumph as Julio in *The Four Horsemen.* His other performances included *The Conquering Power, Blood and Sand, The Sainted Devil,* and others.

VALLEE, RUDY (1901–1986), orchestra leader, vocalist, and popular radio personality. In 1929 he starred in the film, *Vagabond Lover;* a succession of screen performances followed: *George White's Scandals* (1934), *Sweet Music* (1935), *Gold Diggers in Paris* (1938), and *Too Many Blondes* (1941). Vallee had a weekly radio program for Standard Brands from 1929 to 1939. He has made frequent nightclub appearances and starred in the musical comedy *How to Succeed in Business Without Really Trying* (1961). During World War I, he served in the United States Navy.

VAN BUREN, ABIGAIL (1918–   ), writer, lecturer, and newspaper columnist. Born in Sioux City, Iowa, she attended Morningside College. Miss Van Buren has engaged in volunteer activities on behalf of better mental health and the National Foundation for Infantile Paralysis. In 1956, she began writing a column for the *San Francisco Chronicle* titled "Dear Abby." Her column was syndicated through the *Chicago Tribune-New York News Syndicete.* It now appears in foreign press as well, including Brazil, Australia, Japan, Germany, and Holland. In 1963, she established a *Dear Abby* radio program on CBS. She authored *Dear Abby* (1957), *Dear Teen Ager* (1959), and *Dear Abby on Marriage* (1962).

VANDERBILT, CORNELIUS (1794–1877), wealthy builder of railroads and steamship companies. After the success of Robert Fulton and Robert Livingston with steamboats, Vanderbilt became involved with steamboat operations. In a competitive war against Daniel Drew, Vanderbilt was able to establish steamship service between New York and Peekskill. He then opened service between New York, Providence, and Boston. His primary success was achieved in connection with the expansion of railroads after the Civil War.

Commodore Vanderbilt again challenged Daniel Drew in pursuit of the Erie Railroad. Illegal maneuvers by Drew, Jay Gould, and James Fisk almost destroyed Vanderbilt in his pursuit of the Erie. He turned his attention to acquiring the Lake Shore, Illinois, and Michigan Central rail companies, which he did.

VAUGHN, SARAH (1924–   ), jazz vocalist born in Newark, New Jersey. In 1942, she joined the Earl Hines Orchestra; and in 1943, she sang with the Billy Eckstein Band. She has served as vocalist for Mercury Records. In 1942, she won the Apollo Theatre amateur contest. She received the annual Vocalist Award from *Down Beat,* 1946 to 1952; and she has appeared on numerous television programs.

WALLACE, GEORGE (1919–   ), political leader, governor, and candidate for President. Born at Clio, Alabama, Wallace studied law at the University of Alabama. As governor, he defied a Supreme Court integration order at the University of Alabama. In 1968, his challenge to the Democratic Party resulted in the formation of the American Independent Party. He captured much of the South and nationally obtained 14 percent of the popular vote in that election. In 1972, he became the object of an assassination attempt, which left him paralyzed. He was reelected governor of Alabama, but declining health made him discard plans for another term.

WARHOL, ANDY (1931–1987), pioneer in pop art and filmmaking. Warhol attended the Carnegie Institute of Technology and received a degree in pictorial design. He began work as a designer with *Glamour* magazine, then *Vogue* and *Harper's Bazaar.* He used the comic-strip characters Dick Tracy, Popeye, and Superman for colorful effects, and he painted Campbell Soup cans in endless rows to show the monotony of American society. After 1965, he concentrated on filmmaking. *The Chelsea Girls* (1966) and *Trash* (1970) received considerable public notice.

WARING, FRED (1900–1984), musical conductor and entertainer born in Tyrone, Pennsylvania. Waring attended Pennsylvania State College. He composed numerous songs and appeared in several musical shows on Broadway and in motion pictures. He organized an ensemble called "The Pennsylvanians" and began a radio program of the same title in 1933. In 1948, he organized the Fred Waring Music Workshops for Choral Directors. He conducted musical groups for *The Fred Waring Show* on television and produced numerous television programs.

WASHINGTON, BOOKER T. (1856–1915), black educator who was born a slave in Franklin County, Virginia. Booker overheard talk about a school for blacks called the Hampton Institute; the institute had been founded by a Union general and emphasized trades and manual training. In 1881, he was invited to go to Tuskegee to head up the institute, which he discovered had no buildings or program. Under his leadership, the institute became a vital force in education of black youth. In 1895, he delivered the famous "Atlanta Compromise" speech, in which he renounced protest and agitation as a means of achieving educational reform. His views were in contrast to those of Frederick Douglass, who called for racial agitation.

WAYNE, ANTHONY (1745–1796), military hero of early America. Born at Easttown, Pennsylvania, he attended local schools and learned surveying. When the Revolution began, Wayne organized a regiment of infantry and joined General George Washington at Morristown, New Jersey. He gave distinguished service in several battles; he also served with Marquis de Lafayette in Virginia until the British surrender at Yorktown. In 1792, Wayne was asked to serve as Commander-in-Chief of the Army. At Full Timbers, Ohio, he defeated Indians in the first of several battles. Indian tribes recognized his military superiority and signed the treaty of Greenville in 1795.

WAYNE, JOHN (1907–1979), actor and movie personality, noted for his character portrayals from the Old West. Born in Winterset, Iowa, his name was Marian Michael Morrison; but early in life he received the nickname "Duke." On an athletic scholarship, he studied at the University of Southern California. His career as a screen actor began as a stunt man and with bit parts in Westerns. He made two Westerns with Columbia: *Girls Demand Excitement* (1931) and *Three Girls Lost.* Over the next few years he made low-budget Westerns. During and after World War II, he emerged as an actor of some renown; his role in *True Grit* won an Academy Award nomination. During the

War in Vietnam, he projected the image of a loyalist to the Administration's expanding of the war. Mike Tomkies' *Duke* (1971) is a useful biography.

WEBSTER, DANIEL (1782–1852), celebrated lawyer and politician. Webster was born in Salisbury, New Hampshire. He graduated from Dartmouth College and then studied law. Identified as a leading spokesman for the Federalists, he was elected to the House of Representatives in 1813. In 1816, his political career temporarily ended, but he achieved prominence in arguing several significant cases before the Supreme Court. For example, Webster defended the Bank of the United States in *McCulloch* vs. *Maryland.* In 1823, he returned to the House of Representatives; and from 1825 to 1829, he supported the Federalist President John Quincy Adams. Webster's Senate record achieved historic importance. He supported President Andrew Jackson on the nullification controversy. His last debate was on behalf of the unpopular Fugitive Slave Law in 1850. He served as Secretary of State in Millard Fillmore's administration.

WEBSTER, NOAH (1758–1843), lexicographer who compiled a dictionary of American usage. Webster was an active literary man; he read widely and was admitted to the bar in 1781. He authored *A Grammatical Institute of the English Language: Part I* in 1783. His grammar book sold over seventy million copies. Webster toured the United States selling his textbooks. As a Federalist, he wrote *Sketches on American Policy* (1785); he authored numerous books and pamphlets, his most famous being *The Effects of Slavery on Morals and Industry* (1793). His dictionaries became his most enduring contribution to American thought and learning.

WEISSMULLER, JOHNNY (1904–1984), Olympic swimmer and movie star as "Tarzan." Born in Windber, Pennsylvania, Weissmuller became a skilled free-style swimmer. In the 1920s, he established world records in over sixty-seven events. Weissmuller was trained as a swimmer at the Illinois Athletic Club in Chicago. In the 1924 and 1928 Olympic games, he won five gold medals; he also won a bronze medal as a member of the United States water polo team. In his acting role as "Tarzan," his abilities as a free-style swimmer made him world famous.

**WELCH, RAQUEL (1942–   ), model, movie actress, and renowned sex symbol. She was born Raquel Tejada in Chicago, Illinois, of Castilian Spanish parents. The family moved to LaJolla, California, where her father worked for General Dynamics. After graduating from high school, she served temporarily as a weather girl for a San Diego television station while attending San Diego State College. After marriage in 1959, she had two children and became a householder. Divorced in 1964, she travelled to Texas where she modeled for Neiman-Marcus department stores. She then returned to Hollywood, where she received minor roles until she appeared in *Life* magazine (October 2, 1964). She soon obtained a contract with Twentieth Century-Fox. She then appeared in *Fantastic Voyage, Bandolero, Lady in Cement, The Magic Christian,* and *Myra Breckinridge,* among others.

WEST, BENJAMIN (1738–1820), noted painter of the Revolutionary era. Born in Springfield Township, Pennsylvania, West was among the most outstanding of America's new artists. He reflected the neo-classical tradition. He lived for a time in Italy, where he attracted numerous patrons. West received encouragement from Joshua Reynolds and won numerous portrait commissions. He became a close friend of King George III; and after the death of Reynolds, he was named president of the Royal Academy. West's more famous paintings include *Death on the Pale Horse* (1802) and *Christ Healing the Sick* (1811). West helped many young artists who visited his studio.

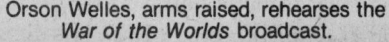

Orson Welles, arms raised, rehearses the
War of the Worlds broadcast.

WEST, MAE (1892–1980), stage and film actress; her sensuality established her stage presence in early vaudeville days. Miss West made her debut with the Keith vaudeville circuit. When she starred in a sensational Broadway play titled *Sex* (1926), she was jailed for her role and attracted national publicity. She starred in several movies, including *Diamond Lil* (1928); *The Constant Sinner* (1931) and *Night after Night* (1932). During World War II, her name was attached to the inflatable life jackets that were used by Allied soldiers. Her autobiography was titled *Goodness Had Nothing to Do With It* (1959). In 1970, she starred in the screen production of *Myra Breckinridge.*

WELK, LAWRENCE (1903–   ), famed orchestra leader of the "big band" era. Born in Strasburg, North Dakota, he appeared on radio station WNAX of Yankton, South Dakota in 1920. In 1927, he organized an orchestra that appeared throughout the country. Welk's orchestra appeared on television in Los Angeles from 1950 to 1955, when the American Broadcasting Company syndicated the Lawrence Welk show nationally. The program achieved considerable popularity until it was cancelled in 1971. Welk was a recording artist for Ranwood Records; he has received numerous awards and recognitions, including the Top Dance Band of America award in 1955. His program is now syndicated by the National Broadcasting Company.

WELLES, ORSON (1915–1985), motion picture actor, director, producer, writer, and photographer. His various theatrical roles have placed him among the outstanding actors of his generation. Born in Kenosha, Wisconsin, he studied at the Art Institute of Chicago. Welles' acting debut was made at Gate Theatre, Dublin, in the fall of 1931. He made his Broadway debut in Shakespeare's *Romeo and Juliet* (1934); he had toured with the Katherine Cornell Company in *Candida* (1933) and *The Barretts of Wimpole Street.* His radio career began with narrating the series, *The March of Time.* His simulation of a Martian invasion in 1938 created a panic among his radio listeners. He has directed numerous Shakespearean plays and has appeared on television.

WESTINGHOUSE, GEORGE (1846–1914), distinguished American inventor and manufacturer; developed the transmission of electrical power. He served with the Union Army in the Civil

War and attended Union College. His fortune came from the patents on his air-brake invention. In 1882, he formed the Union Switch and Signal Company and directed his attention to the orderly transmission of natural gas. In 1886, he formed the Westinghouse Electric Company. In the 1890s, Westinghouse received contracts to develop power from the Niagara Falls. During the 1880s, he received an average of one patent per month for his inventions; his truly significant inventions include the geared turbine and air springs.

WESTMORELAND, WILLIAM C. (1914–), commander of American forces in Vietnam and chief military adviser to President Lyndon Johnson. Westmoreland was born in Spartanburg County, South Carolina, and graduated from West Point in 1936. He commanded the Thirty-Fourth Field Artillery Battalion of the Ninth Infantry Division in Europe during World War II. He served as an instructor at the Command and General Staff College and the Army War College. Between 1960 and 1963, he was superintendent of the U.S. Military Academy, where his effectiveness contributed to his elevation to general. He was assigned to the Military Assistance Program in Vietnam, where he advocated increased bombing and "search and destroy" missions. By 1967, he had over 500,000 men under his command. In 1968, he became Army Chief of Staff. He ran unsuccessfully for governor of South Carolina.

WHISTLER, JAMES A. McNEILL (1834– 1903), lithographer and painter; emphasized "art for art's sake." Born in Lowell, Massachusetts, Whistler moved to St. Petersburg, Russia, early in his life when his father worked on a Russian rail project commissioned by Tsar Nicholas I. He returned to America in 1849 and studied at the United States Military Academy. Because he could not conform to the rules, he was dismissed in 1854. He travelled to Europe and studied for a time at the Louvre. In 1859, his first painting appeared; it was titled *At the Piano*. In 1871, he began certain themes titled *Nocturnes* in etchings, including *The Artist's Mother* (1872). His views on aesthetics were summarized in "Ten O'Clock," a lecture delivered at Prince's Hall.

WHITE, WILLIAM ALLEN (1868–1944), prize-winning journalist and author. Born in Emporia, Kansas, he attended Emporia College. He began his journalistic career with work on various newspapers. He purchased the *Emporia Gazette* in 1895 and continued working with that paper until his death. His progressive views ran contrary to conservative political trends. He backed Teddy Roosevelt and the Bull Moose party in 1912; in the 1930s he supported the New Deal of Roosevelt. White worked enthusiastically with "The Committee to Defend America by Aiding the Allies" in generating hostility for Nazism. He received the Pulitzer Prize for *The Autobiography of William Allen White*.

WHITNEY, ELI (1765–1825), inventor who perfected the cotton gin. Whitney was born in Westboro, Massachusetts, and graduated from Yale college. Although a number of cotton gins were in operation in the 1790s, only Whitney's design made practical sense. He manufactured small arms for the federal government, but his delivery of these small arms was hopelessly behind schedule. He substituted machines for hand labor, made uniform parts, and accelerated production. Whitney gave substance to the concept of mass production.

WILKINS, ROY (1901–1981), important civil rights leader. Wilkins was born in St. Louis, Missouri, and attended the University of Minnesota. He served in the local chapters of the National Association for the Advancement of Colored People (NAACP) and edited *Call*, a militant weekly newspaper. In 1931, he joined the executive staff of the NAACP at its national headquarters. He worked on numerous internal studies for the NAACP, and in 1955, became the Executive Director of the organization. He enthusiastically supported the Kennedy Civil Rights program. His organizing abilities, articulate speech, and incisive writing made him a significant leader in the black community. He received the Medal of Freedom from President Nixon in 1969, the Spingarm Award from the NAACP, as well as many other honors and awards.

WILLARD, FRANCES E. (1839–1898), prominent temperance leader. Born in Churchville, New York, she sought independence from her parents at an early age. She attended Northwestern Female College and graduated as class valedictorian. After a brief teaching career, she authored a book titled, *Nineteen Beautiful Years* (1864). Miss Willard toured Europe from 1869 to 1870 and studied at the Sorbonne. She was appointed president of Northwestern Female College in 1871. After 1874, she resigned and accepted the presidency of the Women's Christian Temperance Union (WCTU). She is best known for her work with the WCTU. Miss Willard helped establish the Prohibition Party in 1884; she became president of the World Women's Temperance Union in 1891.

WILLIAMS, ROGER (1603–1683), Puritan clergyman; spokesman for religious toleration and separation of church and state. Williams believed that sinful mankind was hopeless until Christ's return. He refused to serve the Massachusetts Church because it maintained close ties with civil authority. He was banished to Rhode Island in 1635, and there he authored a dictionary titled *A Key into the Language of America* (1643). His quest for perfection made him first a Baptist and then a Seeker. In 1643, he travelled to England and wrote *Queries of Highest Consideration* (1644). Williams opposed the Christian persecution of other Christian groups. He returned to Providence and sought to unify the colony; he disagreed with the local Quakers but granted them toleration nonetheless.

WILLIAMS, TED (1918–   ), baseball player born in San Diego, California. Williams was professionally associated with the Boston Red Sox of the American League; he compiled a lifetime batting average of .344. Williams' career spanned the years 1939 to 1960. He hit a total of 521 homeruns and won the triple crown of baseball (best average, most home runs, most runs batted in) twice. He was elected to the Baseball Hall of Fame in 1966. He managed the Washington Senators; in his initial year as manager he received the American League Manager of the Year Award.

WINCHELL, WALTER (1897–1972), newspaper columnist and newscaster. Winchell began his radio program with the familiar words, "Good evening, Mr. and Mrs. America and all ships at sea; let's go to press." At first he was a performer in vaudeville. His journalistic career began in 1920 with the *New York Evening Graphic;* later he was associated with the Hearst *New York Mirror.* Winchell introduced a variety of items—political and theatrical—in his column "On Broadway." His column was syndicated in over eight hundred newspapers; his radio career began in 1932. His easily recognized voice narrated the popular tele-

vision series *The Untouchables.* Later in life, he wrote for the *New York Journal Tribune.*

WINTHROP, JOHN (1588–1649), political leader and historian; a dominant figure in the early development of the Massachusetts Bay Colony. Born in Suffolk County, England, he agreed to go to America in 1629. Winthrop called for a covenant Christian community in his famous sermon, "A Model of Christian Charity." He was the political leader of the colony. New England society in the seventeenth century bore the enduring stamp of John Winthrop.

WOOD, GRANT (1892–1942), regional painter of the 1930s. A native of Anamosa, Iowa, Wood took painting lessons during the family stay at Cedar Rapids, Iowa. During World War I, he took classes in fresco painting at the Chicago Art Institute. He left for Europe in 1923 and spent time at the Academie Julian in Paris. On his return to America, he worked at a factory in Cedar Rapids while painting various subjects. In 1927, he received a commission for a stained-glass window for the Cedar Rapids City Hall. Wood was most famous for his homespun themes. His painting titled *American Gothic* (1930) attracted widespread notice; his satiric sense was evident in *Daughters of the American Revolution.* He opposed conservative political tendencies and directed several projects for the Works Project Administration (WPA).

WOOLWORTH, FRANK (1852–1919), chain-store executive; originator of the "five and dime" store concept. Born in upstate New York, Woolworth opened his first store with a modest three hundred dollars inventory. The growth of his chain stores was spectacular; he derived capital for new stores from profits. He relocated his headquarters in Brooklyn, New York, which brought him into close contact with suppliers and wholesalers. Woolworth emphasized window and counter displays. His enterprises grew rapidly between 1890 and 1910, until his gross business revenue exceeded sixty million dollars annually. In 1913, he began erecting the structure in New York that became the Woolworth Building. At his death, there were over one thousand stores nationwide.

WRIGHT, FRANK LLOYD (1867–1959), the most innovative architect of the twentieth century. Wright's work reflects his fertile imagination. He worked at the firm of Dankmar Adler and Louis Sullivan of Chicago in 1887. He was greatly influenced by Louis Sullivan; and in 1893, he opened his own office. The houses Wright built in Chicago and elsewhere gained particular attention for their innovative spirit. His international fame brought him Japanese and European projects; for example, he designed the Imperial Hotel in Tokyo. Wright blended radical and traditional concepts of architecture. His most famous creations are the Guggenheim Museum in New York, the Administration Building for the Johnson Wax Company, and the Greek Orthodox Church in Milwaukee. Wright was an authentic giant in American architecture and design.

WRIGHT BROTHERS, ORVILLE (1871–1948); WILBUR (1867–1912), aviation pioneers born in Millville, Indiana. In 1892, they opened the Wright Cycle Shop in Dayton, Ohio. The efforts of Otto Lilienthal, glider pilot, attracted the interest of the Wright Brothers. The Wrights were acquainted with the combustion engine, aerodynamics, and basic engineering. Together they developed double-winged gliders and applied motor techniques to the glider. On December 17, 1903, they made the first "heavier-than-air craft" flight (which lasted twelve seconds) at Kitty Hawk, North Carolina. On May 22, 1906, they received a patent for their machine. The federal government demonstrated an interest in the machine, and they received bids for construction and development. The brothers formed the American Wright Company to produce aircraft. The death of Wilbur Wright greatly affected Orville; in 1915, he sold his rights to the company and left manufacturing. He served as a member of the National Advisory Committee for Aeronautics (NACA), the predecessor to NASA. His efforts contributed greatly to the subsequent advances made in aerospace technology.

WYETH, ANDREW (1917–   ), the most significant American painter of his generation. His father was the book illustrator for great American classics such as *Treasure Island.* The most famous of his paintings is *Christina's World.* Wyeth used his neighbors as his subjects; he utilized high and low points of emphasis. He received numerous awards, including the Medal of Freedom. In 1970, Wyeth held a one-man exhibit at the White House. His professional technique and graphic ability have become his legacy to American art.

Flight of the Wright Brothers' first airplane.

YOUNG, BRIGHAM (1801–1877), pioneer leader of the Mormons. In 1832, he read Joseph Smith's *Book of Mormon* and was baptized into the new faith. He formed a Mormon church in Kirkland, Ohio, in 1833. In 1835, he was selected as a member of the Quorum of Twelve Apostles to assist Joseph Smith; he became the fiscal agent for the emerging church in 1841. On December 5, 1847, he was elected president of the Quorum of Twelve Apostles, a position he retained until his death. After Smith was murdered, Young led the Mormons to Utah and established Mormon communities around the Great Salt Lake. He encouraged polygamy and opposed the use of liquor, stimulants, and tobacco. Young established the University of Deseret (now the University of Utah) in 1850.

YOUNG, CHIC (1901–1973), newspaper cartoonist who created the popular feature, "Blondie." Born in Chicago, Illinois, his real name was Murat Bernard. He developed "Blondie," her husband Dagwood, and associated characters. The comic strip was syndicated nationally through King Features. At the time of his death, it was appearing in over sixteen hundred newspapers in 60 countries.

YOUNG, DENTON T. "CY" (1867–1955), baseball player from Gilmore, Ohio. Young began playing for the Cleveland team of the National League in 1890. During his career, he pitched for the St. Louis Cardinals, the Boston Red Sox, the Cleveland Indians, and the Boston Braves. He pitched 751 complete games, winning 511 of them. He also pitched baseball's first "perfect" game (in which no batters reached base) on May 5, 1904. After his death, the major baseball leagues established the Cy Young Award for the best pitcher of the year.

YOUNG, WHITNEY M. (1921–1971), civil rights leader. Born in Lincoln Ridge, Kentucky, he graduated from Kentucky State College and the University of Minnesota. Young was associated with the Urban League in St. Paul, Minnesota, and Omaha, Nebraska. He became dean of the school of Social Work at Atlanta University in 1954. After a period of study at Harvard University, he was named executive director of the Urban League; there he introduced the concept of preferential treatment of blacks in jobs and educational facilities. He tried to mediate between militant civil rights groups and those who advocated more orderly processes. President Richard Nixon awarded him the Medal of Freedom in 1969. Young authored *To Be Equal* (1964) and *Beyond Racism* (1969).

ZAHARIAS, MILDRED DIDRIKSON "BABE" (1914–1956), Olympic athlete; regarded as the greatest woman golfer of all time. She appeared in the Olympic Games at Los Angeles in 1932, where she was the top performer in the 80-meter hurdle and the javelin throw. She excelled in athletic endeavors such as baseball, basketball, swimming, and diving. But her greatest achievements were in golf. From 1935 to 1950, she won every major women's golf championship—the United States National Open in 1948, 1950, and 1954; the national amateur tournament in 1946; and the World Championship four times. In 1947, she became a professional golfer. Stricken with cancer in 1953, she waged a battle to overcome the disease. She continued her athletic successes until her death in 1956. She wrote *This Life I've Led,* her autobiography.

"Babe" Didrikson Zaharias won The AP Award six times, once for starring in track and field and the five others for golfing brilliance. Later, the award was named in her honor.

ZENGER, JOHN PETER (1697–1746), colonial newspaper publisher. Born in the Rhine Country of Germany, he became an apprentice printer to William Bradford. He moved to Chestertown, Pennsylvania, to establish his reputation. Zenger became involved in New York political controversies after he arrived there in 1732. He used his *New York Weekly Journal* to support the political faction of Lewis Morris. Zenger was arrested in 1734 and charged with printing seditious and libelous material. His lawyers were disbarred, so Alexander Hamilton came from Philadelphia to defend Zenger. He was acquitted, and the case became a classic in constitutional law.

ZIEGFELD, FLORENZ (1869–1932), theatrical manager who made burlesque famous. Ziegfeld was born in Chicago, Illinois. In 1906, he developed "The Parisian Model," a revue that attracted popular notice. After viewing the Follies Bergere in Paris, he returned to the United States to assemble the Ziegfeld Follies. He developed several stars; Fanny Brice, Marilyn Miller, W. C. Fields, Eddie Cantor, and Will Rogers were under contract to Ziegfeld. He attempted musical comedy with such productions as *Show Boat, Rio Rita,* and *Bittersweet.* But in 1927, he abandoned the Follies because the Great Depression made it seem inappropriate.

Roget's Thesaurus

Plan of Classification
(following the original Roget plan)

Tabular Synopsis of Categories

Class I. ABSTRACT RELATIONS
I. EXISTENCE
1. existence
2. nonexistence
3. substantiality
4. unsubstantiality
5. intrinsicality
6. extrinsicality
7. state
8. circumstance

II. RELATION
9. relation
10. nonrelation
11. consanguinity
12. correlation
13. identity
14. contrariety
15. difference
16. uniformity
16a. lack of uniformity
17. similarity
18. dissimilarity
19. imitation
20. nonimitation
20a. variation
21. copy
22. prototype
23. agreement
24. disagreement

III. QUANTITY
25. quantity
26. degree
27. equality
28. inequality
29. mean
30. compensation
31. greatness
32. smallness
33. superiority
34. inferiority
35. increase
36. decrease
37. addition
38. deduction
39. adjunct
40. remainder
40a. decrement
41. mixture
42. simpleness
43. junction
44. disjunction
45. link
46. coherence
47. incoherence
48. combination
49. decomposition
50. whole
51. part
52. completeness
53. incompleteness
54. composition
55. exclusion
56. component
57. extraneousness

IV. ORDER
58. order
59. disorder
60. arrangement
61. derangement
62. precedence
63. sequence
64. precursor
65. sequel
66. beginning
67. end
68. middle
69. continuity
70. discontinuity
71. term
72. assemblage
73. dispersion
74. focus
75. class
76. inclusion
77. exclusion
78. generality
79. specialty
80. regulation
81. multiformity
82. conformity
83. unconformity

V. NUMBER
84. number
85. numeration
86. list
87. unity
88. accompaniment
89. duality
90. duplication
91. bisection
92. triality
93. triplication
94. trisection
95. quaternity
96. quadruplication
97. quadrisection
98. five, etc.
99. quinquesection
100. plurality
100a. fraction
101. zero
102. multitude
103. fewness
104. repetition
105. infinity

VI. TIME
106. time
107. absence of time
108. period
109. course
110. durability
111. transience
112. perpetuity
113. instantaneousness
114. chronometry
115. anachronism
116. antecedence
117. posteriority
118. present time
119. different time
120. contemporaneousness
121. the future
122. the past
123. newness
124. oldness
125. morning; noon
126. evening; midnight
127. youth
128. age
129. infant
130. veteran
131. adolescence
132. earliness
133. lateness
134. opportuneness
135. unopportuneness
136. frequency
137. infrequency
138. regularity
139. irregularity

VII. CHANGE
140. change
141. permanence
142. cessation
143. continuance
144. conversion
145. reversion
146. revolution
147. substitution
148. interchange
149. changeableness
150. stability
151. present events
152. future events

613. habit
615. motive

617. plea
618. good
620. intention
622. pursuit

625. business
626. plan
627. method
628. mid-course
630. requirement
631. instrumentality
632. means
633. instrument
634. substitute
635. materials
636. store
637. provision

640. insufficiency
642. importance
644. utility
646. expedience
648. goodness
650. perfection
652. cleanness
654. health
656. salubrity
658. improvement
660. restoration
662. remedy
664. safety
666. refuge
668. warning
669. alarm
670. preservation
671. escape
672. deliverance
673. preparation
675. essay
676. undertaking
677. use

680. action
682. activity
684. haste
686. exertion
688. fatigue
690. agent
691. workshop
692. conduct
693. direction
694. director
695. advice
696. council
697. precept
698. skill
700. expert
702. cunning
704. difficulty
706. hindrance
708. opposition
710. opponent
712. party
713. discord
715. defiance
716. attack
718. retaliation
720. contention
722. warfare
724. mediation
725. submission

614. disuse
615a. absence of motive
616. dissuasion

619. evil
621. chance
623. avoidance
624. relinquishment

629. circuit

638. waste
639. sufficiency
641. redundance
643. unimportance
645. inutility
647. inexpedience
649. badness
651. imperfection
653. uncleanness
655. disease
657. insalubrity
659. deterioration
661. relapse
663. bane
665. danger
667. pitfall

674. nonpreparation

678. disuse
679. misuse
681. inaction
683. inactivity
685. leisure
687. repose
689. refreshment

699. unskillfulness
701. bungler
703. artlessness
705. facility
707. aid
709. cooperation
711. auxiliary

714. concord

717. defense
719. resistance
721. peace
723. pacification

726. combatant
727. arms
728. arena
729. completion
731. success
733. trophy
734. prosperity

730. noncompletion
732. failure

735. adversity
736. mediocrity

II. INTERSOCIAL VOLITION

737. authority
739. severity
741. command
742. disobedience
744. compulsion
745. master
747. scepter
748. freedom
750. liberation

753. keeper
755. commission

758. consignee
759. deputy
760. permission
762. consent
763. offer
765. request
767. petitioner
768. promise
769. compact
770. conditions
771. security
772. observance

738. laxity
740. lenience

743. obedience

746. servant

749. subjection
751. restraint
752. prison
754. prisoner
756. abrogation
757. resignation

761. prohibition

764. refusal
766. deprecation

773. nonobservance
774. compromise

775. acquisition
777. possession
778. participation
779. possessor
780. property
781. retention
783. transfer
784. giving
786. apportionment
787. lending
789. taking
791. stealing
792. thief
793. booty
794. barter
795. purchase
797. merchant
798. merchandise
799. market
800. money
801. treasurer
802. treasury
803. wealth
805. credit
807. payment
809. expenditure
811. accounts
812. price
814. dearness
816. liberality
818. prodigality

776. loss
777a. exemption

782. relinquishment

785. receiving

788. borrowing
790. restitution

796. sale

804. poverty
806. debt
808. nonpayment
810. receipt

813. discount
815. cheapness
817. economy
819. parsimony

Class VI. AFFECTIONS
I. AFFECTIONS IN GENERAL

820. affections
821. feelings
822. sensibility
824. excitation
825. excitability

823. insensibility

826. inexcitability

II. PERSONAL AFFECTIONS

827. pleasure
828. pain
829. pleasurableness
830. painfulness
831. content
832. discontent
833. regret
834. relief
835. aggravation
836. cheerfulness
837. dejection
838. rejoicing
839. lamentation
840. amusement
841. weariness
842. wit
843. dullness
844. humorist
845. beauty
846. ugliness
847. ornament
848. blemish
849. simplicity
850. taste
851. vulgarity
852. fashion
853. ridiculousness
854. fop
855. affectation
856. ridicule
857. laughing-stock
858. hope
859. hopelessness
860. fear
861. courage
862. cowardice
863. rashness
864. caution
865. desire
867. dislike
866. indifference
868. fastidiousness
869. satiety
870. wonder
871. expectance
872. prodigy
873. repute
874. disrepute
875. nobility
876. commonalty
877. title
878. pride
879. humility
880. vanity
881. modesty
882. ostentation
883. celebration
884. boasting
885. insolence
886. servility
887. blusterer

III. SYMPATHETIC AFFECTIONS

888. friendship
889. enmity
890. friend
891. enemy
892. sociality
893. seclusion, exclusion
894. courtesy
895. discourtesy
896. congratulations
897. love
898. hate
899. favorite
900. resentment
901. irascibility
901a. sullenness
902. endearment
903. marriage
904. celibacy
905. divorce
906. benevolence
907. malevolence
908. malediction
909. threat
910. philanthropy
911. misanthropy
912. benefactor
913. evildoer
914. pity
914a. pitilessness

915. condolence
916. gratitude
917. ingratitude
918. forgiveness
919. revenge
920. jealousy
921. envy

IV. MORAL AFFECTIONS

922. right
923. wrong
924. claim
925. unrightfulness
926. duty
927. dereliction of duty
927a. exemption
928. respect
929. disrespect
930. contempt
931. approbation
932. disapprobation
933. flattery
934. detraction
935. flatterer
936. detractor
937. vindication
938. accusation
939. probity
940. improbity
941. knave
942. disinterestedness
943. selfishness
944. virtue
945. vice
946. innocence
947. guilt
948. good man
949. bad man
950. penitence
951. impenitence
952. atonement
953. temperance
954. intemperance
954a. sensualist
955. asceticism
956. fasting
957. gluttony
958. sobriety
959. drunkenness
960. purity
961. impurity
962. libertine
963. legality
964. illegality
965. jurisdiction
966. tribunal
967. judge
968. lawyer
969. lawsuit
970. acquittal
971. condemnation
972. punishment
973. reward
974. penalty
975. scourge

V. RELIGIOUS AFFECTIONS

976. deity
977. angel
978. devil
979. fabulous spirit
980. demon
981. heaven
982. hell
983. theology
983a. orthodoxy
984. heterodoxy
985. revelation
986. religious writings
987. piety
988. impiety
989. irreligion
990. worship
991. idolatry
992. sorcery
993. spell
994. sorcerer
995. churchdom
996. clergy
997. laity
998. rite
999. canonicals
1000. temple

Thesaurus

Class I

Words Expressing Abstract Relations

I. Existence

1 existence *n* being, entity, subsistence, reality, actuality, presence, fact, matter of fact, truth. science of existence: ontology.

v exist, be, subsist, live, breathe; occur, happen, take place; consist in, lie in; endure, remain, abide, survive, last, stay, continue.

adj existent, extant; prevalent, current, afloat; real, actual, true, positive, absolute; substantial, substantive; well founded, well grounded.

adv actually, in fact, in reality.

2 nonexistence *n* inexistence; insubstantiality, nonentity; blank, *tabula rasa*, void, emptiness, nothingness; potential, possibility; annihilation, extinction, obliteration, total destruction.

v not exist; pass away, perish, die, die out, disappear, dissolve; annihilate, destroy, obliterate, wipe off the face of the earth; nullify, void; take away, remove.

adj nonexistent, inexistent; blank, void, empty; unreal, baseless, unsubstantial, intangible, ineffable, spiritual, spectral; unborn, uncreated, unbegotten, unconceived; potential, possible; exhausted, gone, lost, departed, extinct, defunct; fabulous, visionary, imaginative, ideal, conceptual, abstract.

3 substantiality *n* materiality, corporality, tangibility, material existence, bodiliness, matter, stuff; creature, being, person, body, flesh and blood, substance; thing, object, article.

adj substantive, substantial, corporeal, material, bodily, physical, concrete, tangible, palpable, corporal, materialistic.

4 unsubstantiality *n* nothingness; nothing, naught, nil, nullity, zero; shadow, phantom, apparition, dream, illusion; fallacy, inanity, frivolity; hollowness, blank, void; flimsiness, thinness, slightness.

v vanish, evaporate, fade, dissolve, melt away, disappear.

adj unsubstantial, baseless, groundless, ungrounded, without foundation, fallacious, erroneous, untenable; insignificant, slight, thin, trifling, frivolous; imaginary, visionary, dreamy, shadowy, ethereal, airy, immaterial, spectral, illusory, incorporeal, intangible, bodiless, abstract; vacant, vacuous, empty, blank, hollow.

5 intrinsicality *n* ego, essence, quintessence, gist, pith, marrow, sap, lifeblood, backbone, heart, soul, core; principle, nature, constitution, construction, character, type, quality; habit, temper, temperament, personality, spirit, humor, grain, moods, features, peculiarities, aspects, idiosyncrasies, tendencies, bents; inbeing, inherence, essentiality.

v be intrinsic, be inherent.

adj intrinsic, inherent, implanted, innate, inborn, inbred, ingrained; essential, fundamental, basic, normal; inherited, congenital, hereditary, indigenous, in the blood, in the genes; instinctive, instinctual, internal, personal, subjective; characteristic, peculiar, idiosyncratic; fixed, set in one's ways, invariable, unchangeable, incurable, ineradicable.

adv intrinsically, at bottom, in effect, practically, virtually, substantially.

6 extrinsicality *n* extraneousness, externals.

adj extrinsic, extraneous, external, adventitious; collateral, accidental, incidental, objective.

adv extrinsically.

7 state *n* condition, case, circumstances, situation, status, surroundings, pass, plight, pickle; mood, temper, frame; constitution, structure, form, phase, frame, fabric, stamp, set, fit, mold; mode, style, fashion, light, complexion, character; tone, tenor, turn.

v be in a state.

8 circumstance *n* situation, phase, position, condition, posture, attitude, place, point; footing, standing, status; occasion, happening, event, juncture, conjunction; predicament, exigency, emergency, crisis, pinch, plight, pass; climax, apex, turning point.

adj circumstantial, conditional, provisional; contingent, incidental, adventitious; critical, climactic.

adv under the circumstances, under the conditions; thus, in such wise; accordingly, that being the case, since, seeing that, as matters stand; conditionally, provided, if, in case; if so, if it so happen, in the event of, provisionally, unless.

II. Absolute Relation

9 relation *n* connection, concern, bearing, reference; correlation, analogy; similarity, affinity, homogeneity, alliance, association, nearness; approximation, relationship; comparison, ratio, proportion; link, tie, bond.

v relate to, refer to; bear upon, regard, concern, touch, affect, have to do with, pertain to, appertain to, belong to; bring into relation with, associate, connect, parallel; link, bind, tie.

adj relative, relative to, relating to, referable to, with reference to; belonging to; related, connected, associated, affiliated, allied; in the same category, relevant.

adv as regards, about, concerning, with relation to, with reference to, with regard to, with respect to, in connection with, under the head of, in the matter of.

10 [absence of relation] **non-relation** *n* irrelation, dissociation, lack of connection; disconnection, disjunction; inconsequence, irreconcilability, disagreement, heterogeneity; independence.

v have no relation to, have no bearing upon, have nothing to do with, have no connection with.

adj unrelated, irrespective, unallied, unconnected, disconnected, heterogeneous, independent; adrift, insular, isolated; extraneous, strange, alien, foreign, outlandish, exotic; irrelevant, inapplicable, not pertinent, beside the mark, off base; remote, farfetched, out-of-the-way, forced, detached, distanced; incidental, parenthetical.

adv parenthetically, by the way, by the by; incidentally.

11 [relations of kindred] **consanguinity** *n* relationship, kindred, blood; parentage, paternity, maternity, lineage, heritage; filiation, affiliation, connection, alliance, tie; family, blood relation, ties of blood, kinsman, kinfolk, kith and kin, relation, relative, one's own, one's own flesh and blood; fraternity, sorority, brotherhood, sisterhood; race, stock, generation.

v be related to, claim relationship with.

adj related, akin, consanguineous, allied, affiliated, connected; kindred, familial.

12 [double or reciprocal relation] **correlation** *n* correspondence, reciprocity, reciprocation, interdependence, mutuality, interchange, exchange.

v reciprocate, alternate, interchange, interact, interdepend; interchange, exchange; correlate, correspond, relate.

adj reciprocal, mutual, correlative, corresponding, analogous, complementary; equivalent, interchangeable, alternate.

adv reciprocally.

13 identity *n* sameness, exactness, equality, correspondence, parallelism, unity, convertibility, resemblance, similarity; self, oneself, name, personality; facsimile, duplicate, replica, copy, reproduction.

v be identical, coincide, coalesce.

adj identical, self, the same, selfsame; coincident, coinciding, coalescent, indistinguishable; one, equal, equivalent.

adv identically.

14 contrariety *n* contrast, foil, antithesis, oppositeness, opposition, contradiction, antipathy, antagonism; the reverse, the inverse, the converse, inversion, subversion, reversal, the opposite, antipodes.

v be contrary, contrast with, differ from, oppose; invert, revert, turn upside down; contradict, contravene; antagonize.

adj contrary, opposite, counter, converse, reverse; opposed, antithetical, contrasted, antipodean, antagonistic, opposing; conflicting, inconsistent, contradictory; negative, hostile.

15 difference *n* discrepancy, disparity, dissimilarity, inconsistency, variance, variation, diversity, imbalance, disagreement, inequality, inequity, divergence, contrast, contrariety; discrimination, distinction, nice distinction, shade, nuance, subtlety.

v differ, vary; diversify, modify, change, alter; contrast, mismatch; discriminate, distinguish.

adj different, diverse, heterogeneous, unlike, divergent, altered, changed, deviant, deviating, variant, varied, modified; diversified, various, divers, miscellaneous, manifold; other, another, not the same, unequal, unmatched, wide apart; distinctive, characteristic, discriminative.

16 uniformity *n* homogeneity, permanence, continuity, consistency, stability, accordance, standardization, conformity, agreement; regularity, constancy, evenness, sameness; monotony, routine, invariability.

v be uniform, accord with; conform to, assimilate; level, smooth, even.

adj uniform, homogeneous, of a piece, consistent; consistent, regular, constant, even, level; invariable, unchanging, unvarying, unvaried, unchanged, constant, regular; undiversified, solid, plain, dreary, monotonous, routine.

adv uniformly; always, invariably, without exception; ever, forever.

16a lack of uniformity *n* diversity, irregularity, unevenness, inconsistency, nonconformity, heterogeneity.

adj diversified, varied, irregular, inconsistent, motley, patchwork, uneven, rough; multifarious, of various kinds.

17 similarity *n* resemblance, likeness, similitude, semblance, affinity, approximation, parallelism; agreement, correspondence, analogy; brotherhood, family likeness; repetition, sameness, uniformity, identity; the like, fellow, match, pair, mate, twin, double, counterpart; alter ego, chip off the old block, birds of a feather, like two peas in a pod; simile, parallel, type, image, representation.

v be similar, resemble, look like, bear a resemblance, take after, approximate, parallel, match, rhyme with.

adj similar, resembling, like, alike; twin; analogous, parallel, of a piece; allied to, akin to, corresponding; approximate, much the same, near, close, something like; imitative, mock, pseudo, simulating, representing, representative; exact, true, lifelike, faithful, true to life, identical.

adv as if, so to speak; as it were, as if it were; quasi, just as.

18 dissimilarity *n* dissimilitude, unlikeness, difference; diversity, disparity, divergence; novelty, originality, uniqueness.

v be unlike, differ from, bear no resemblance; vary, diversify, differentiate.

adj dissimilar, unlike, different, disparate; unique, new, novel, unprecedented, unmatched, unequaled; diversified.

19 imitation *n* copying; copy, duplication, reproduction, replica; mocking, mimicry, aping; simulation, impersonation, representation, semblance, approximation, paraphrase, parody; plagiarism, forgery.

v imitate, copy, mirror, reflect, impersonate, duplicate, reproduce, simulate, counterfeit; mock, take off, mimic, ape, personate, parody, caricature, travesty; follow, emulate, pattern after, model oneself on, parallel, follow, take after.

adj imitative, modeled after, modeled on, based on; fake, phony, counterfeit, false, imitation, mock; duplicate, second hand.

adv literally, word for word, to the letter.

20 nonimitation *n* originality, uniqueness.

adj unimitated, uncopied; unmatched, unparalleled; inimitable, original, unique, special, one of a kind, rare, exceptional.

20a variation *n* alteration, change, modification; divergency, deviation, aberration, innovation.

v vary, change; deviate, diverge, alternate, modify.

adj varied, modified, diversified, altered, changed.

21 [result of imitation] **copy** *n* facsimile, counterpart, effigy, form, likeness, similitude, semblance, cast, mold, model, representation, image, portrait; reflexion, shadow, echo; transcript, transcription, reproduction, imitation, carbon, ditto, stencil, duplicate, reprint, transfer, replica; parody, caricature, burlesque, travesty, paraphrase; counterfeit, forgery, deception.

adj faithful, lifelike, exact, similar.

22 [thing copied] **prototype** *n* original, model, pattern, precedent, standard; type, archetype, exemplar, paradigm, module, example; text, copy, design; die, mold; matrix, mint, seal, punch, intaglio, negative, plate, stamp.

v be an example, set an example.

23 agreement *n* unanimity, harmony, accord, accordance, concord, union, unity, understanding, settlement, treaty, pact; uniformity, conformity, consistency, congruity, logic, correspondence, parallelism, apposition; consent, assent, concurrence, cooperation.

v agree, accord, harmonize; correspond, tally, (*informal*) jibe; meet, suit, fit, befit, square with, dovetail, match; adapt, fit, accommodate, adjust.

adj agreeing, accordant, correspondent, congenial, harmonious; reconcilable, comfortable, compatible, congruous, consistent, logical, consonant, commensurate; in accordance with, in harmony with, in keeping with; apt, apposite, pat, pertinent; agreeable, happy, felicitous.

24 disagreement *n* discord, dissonance, dissidence, disunion, discrepancy, nonconformity, incongruity, dissension, conflict, opposition, antagonism, difference; disparity, disproportion, mismatch, variance, divergence, inequity, inequality.

v disagree, clash, jar, argue, quarrel, dispute.

adj disagreeing, discordant, dissonant, inharmonious; at variance, hostile, conflicting, antagonistic, clashing, disputing, factious, dissenting, irreconcilable, incompatible, inconsistent with; incongruous, disproportionate, disparate, divergent; disagreeable, uncongenial, mismatched; out of joint, out of step, out of tune.

III. Simple Quantity

25 [absolute quantity] **quantity** *n* size, mass, volume, amount, measure, measurement, substance, strength; mouthful, spoonful, handful; stock, batch, lot, dose.

adj quantitative, some, any, more or less.

26 [relative quantity] **degree** *n* grade, extent, measure, amount, ratio, standard, height, pitch; reach, range, scope, rate, caliber; gradation, shade, tint; tenor, tone, compass; sphere, station, rank, standing; point, mark, stage, level; intensity, strength.

adj comparative, gradual, shading off.

adv by degrees, gradually, step by step, bit by bit, little by little, inch by inch, drop by drop; in some degree, to some extent; up to a point.

27 [sameness of quantity or degree] **equality** *n* parity, symmetry, balance, counterbalance; evenness, monotony, level; equivalence, equipose, equilibrium; par, even keel, quits; identity, similarity; tie, dead heat, draw, drawn game, neck and neck race; match, peer, equal, mate, fellow, brother; equivalent.

v equal, match, reach, keep pace with, run abreast; come up to; balance, even the score; equalize, level, trim, adjust; strike a balance; restore equilibrium.

adj equal, even, level, monotonous, coequal, symmetrical, balanced; on a par with, on a level with, on an equal footing with, up to the mark; equivalent, tantamount, synonymous, quits, even, much the same, all one, one and the same; drawn, half and half, six of one and half a dozen of another.

adv equally, to all intents and purposes.

28 [difference of quantity or degree] **inequality** *n* disparity, dissimilarity, difference, odds; unevenness, imbalance; inferiority, shortcoming, deficiency, imperfection, inadequacy; mediocrity; superiority.

v be unequal, have the advantage, turn the scale, turn the tide; topple, overmatch; not come up to, fall short of, not come up to snuff.

adj unequal, uneven, imbalanced; disparate, partial, inferior, insufficient, deficient, inadequate, mediocre, short.

29 mean *n* medium, average, balance, middle, mid-point, center, median, golden mean; compromise, neutrality.

v split the difference, take the average, move to the center.

adj mean, intermediate, middle, average, standard, normal, neutral; mediocre, middle class, bourgeois, commonplace, run of the mill, egalitarian.

adv on the average, in the long run.

30 compensation *n* equation; indemnification, requital; compromise, measure for measure, tit for tat, eye for an eye, retaliation, equalization; setoff, off-set, counterpoise, ballast; indemnity, equivalent, *quid pro quo*, amends, reparation.

v compensate, indemnify, recompense, remunerate; counterbalance, counterpoise, countervail, offset, counteract, balance, balance out, make up for, square, even out, equalize; cover, neutralize, nullify; redeem, atone, make amends.

adj compensatory, compensating, equivalent, equal.

adv but, however, yet, still, notwithstanding, nevertheless, although, though, nonetheless; howbeit, albeit; at all events, at any rate, be that as may, even so, on the other hand, at the same time.

31 greatness *n* magnitude, size, bulk, dimensions, vastness; multitude; enormousness, immensity, might, strength, intensity, fullness; importance, distinction, eminence, renown; quantity, store, volume, mass, bulk, heap; abundance, sufficiency.

v be great, soar, tower, rise above, transcend; enlarge, increase, expand.

adj great, large, considerable, big, huge, mammoth, gigantic; ample, abundant, sufficient; full, intense, strong; widespread, extensive, wholesale; goodly, noble, precious, mighty; utter, uttermost, arch, profound, intense, consummate; extraordinary, important, unsurpassed, supreme; complete, total; vast, immense, enormous, extreme, inordinate, excessive, extravagant, exorbitant, outrageous, monstrous; towering, stupendous, prodigious, marvelous; unlimited, infinite; absolute, positive, stark, decided, unequivocal, essential, perfect; remarkable, notable, noteworthy.

adv [in a positive degree] truly; decidedly, unequivocally, absolutely, essentially, fundamentally, downright; [in a complete degree] entirely, completely, totally, wholly; abundantly, fully, amply, widely; [in a great or high degree] greatly, much, indeed, very, very much, most, pretty, pretty well, enough, in a great measure, to a large extent; richly, on a large scale, ever so much; mightily, powerfully; extremely, exceedingly, intensely, exquisitely, consummately, acutely, indefinitely, immeasurably, beyond compare, beyond measure, beyond all bounds, incalculably, infinitely; [in a supreme degree] pre-eminently, superlatively, supremely, incomparably; [in a too great degree] immoderately, inordinately, exorbitantly, excessively, enormously, preposterously, monstrously, out of all proportion, with a vengeance; [in a marked degree] particularly, remarkably, singularly, curiously, uncommonly, unusually, peculiarly, notably, signally, strikingly, pointedly, mainly, chiefly; famously, egregiously, prominently, glaringly, emphatically, strangely, wonderfully, amazingly, surprisingly, astonishingly, incredibly, marvelously, stupendously; [in a violent degree] violently, furiously, severely, desperately, tremendously, extravagantly; [in a painful degree] painfully, sadly, sorely, bitterly, piteously, grievously, miserably, cruelly, woefully, lamentably, shockingly, frightfully, fearfully, dreadfully, terribly, horribly.

32 smallness *n* littleness, tininess, diminutiveness; slenderness, thinness, paltriness, slightness; paucity, fewness, sparseness, scarcity; unimportance, triviality, inconsequentiality, pettiness, insignificance; meanness, sordidness, selfishness, narrow-mindedness; small quantity, modicum, atom, particle, molecule, point, speck, dot, dab, mote, jot, iota; minutiae, details, *soupçon*, scintilla, granule; drop, droplet, drizzle, sprinkling, dash, smack, tinge; dole, scrap, shred, splinter; mite, bit, morsel, crumb, seed; snippet, snatch, slip; chip, sliver; nutshell, thimbleful, spoonful, handful, mouthful; fragment, fraction, drop in the ocean; trifle.

v be small.

adj small, little, tiny, diminutive, petite, miniature, minuscule, minute, microscopic, infinitesimal, fine; unimportant, trivial, minor, secondary, trifling, inconsequential, petty, paltry, insignificant; slender, thin, slight, scanty, scant, meager, insufficient; few, sparse, scarce; low, so-so, middling, tolerable, inconsiderable, inappreciable; mean, sordid, selfish, narrow, narrow-minded, illiberal, ungenerous; feeble, weak, faint.

adv [in a small degree] to a small extent; a wee bit; slightly, imperceptibly, faintly; miserably, wretchedly;

insufficiently, imperfectly; passably, pretty well, well enough; [in a certain or limited degree] partially, in part, to a certain degree; some, rather, to some degree; simply, only, purely, merely, at the least; ever so little; almost, nearly, well nigh, short of, not quite, all but, near the mark; scarcely, hardly, barely, only just, no more than; [in an uncertain degree] about, thereabouts, somewhere about; [in no degree] noway, nowise, not at all, not in the least, not a bit, not a jot, not a whit, in no respect, by no means, on no account.

33 superiority n supremacy, pre-eminence, ascendancy, transcendence; excellence, greatness, nobility, eminence, worthiness, preponderance; predominance, prevalence, advantage; majority; quality, high caliber.

v be superior, exceed, excel, transcend, outdo, outweigh, outrival, outrank; pass, surpass; top, cap, outstrip, eclipse, predominate, prevail; take precedence, come first.

adj superior, greater, major, higher, exceeding; supreme, greatest, utmost, paramount, pre-eminent, foremost, crowning; first-rate, important, excellent, unrivaled, matchless, priceless, unparalleled, unequaled, unsurpassed, inimitable, incomparable, superlative, beyond compare, transcendent.

adv beyond, more, over, over and above, at its height; [in a superior or supreme degree] eminently, pre-eminently, prominently, surpassingly, superlatively, supremely, above all, to crown all, par excellence; principally, especially, particularly, peculiarly.

34 inferiority n low quality, deficiency, imperfection, shortcoming, inadequacy; mediocrity, commonalty, commonness, poorness, meanness; minority, subordination, subjection.

v be inferior, fall short of, come short of, not come up to, not pass muster; want, lack.

adj inferior, minor, less, lesser, deficient; poor, indifferent, mean, base, bad, shabby, paltry, humble, imperfect, mediocre, common, commonplace, second-rate; poorer; secondary, minor, subordinate, lower; diminished, reduced, unimportant.

adv less, subpar; short of, under.

35 increase n growth, augmentation, enlargement, extension, expansion, addition, increment, accretion, aggrandizement; development, rise, ascent.

v increase, grow, dilate, enlarge, expand, multiply; augment, add to, enlarge, greaten; extend, spread out, prolong; advance, rise, sprout, ascend; raise, exalt, deepen, heighten, intensify, magnify, redouble; aggrandize.

adj increasing, growing; additional, incremental; developmental.

36 decrease n diminution, abatement, decline, reduction, wane, falling-off, contraction, dwindling, shrinking, lessening, ebb, ebbing; subtraction, abridgment, shortening; depreciation, deterioration.

v decrease, lessen, abate, fall off, decline, contract, shrink, dwindle, wane, ebb, subside; diminish, deteriorate, depreciate, languish, decay; abridge, shorten, subtract.

adj decreased, decreasing, on the wane.

37 addition n increment, increase, enlargement, aggrandizement, accession; supplement, adjunct, attachment, addendum; annexation, interposition, insertion; uniting, joining.

v add, annex, affix, subjoin, tack on, append, attach, join, supplement, increase, augment, make an addition to; accrue, accumulate, pile up; total, sum, add up; reinforce.

adj additional, supplemental, supplementary; extra, accessory, auxiliary.

adv in addition, more, plus; and, also, likewise, too, further, furthermore, besides, to boot, etc., and so on, and so forth; over and above, moreover; with, as well as, together with, along with, in conjunction with.

38 deduction n subtraction, retrenchment, withdrawal, removal; mutilation, amputation, curtailment; shortening, abbreviation; decrease, cutback.

v deduct, subtract, retrench, withdraw, remove; take from, take away; shorten, abbreviate, cut back, pare down, reduce, decrease, diminish, curtail, eliminate, deprive of; mutilate, amputate, cut off, cut away, excise; pare, thin, thin out, prune, scrape, file.

adj subtracted, subtracting; removable, reducible; deductible.

adv less, short of; minus, without, excepting, except, with the exception

of, save, exclusive of.

39 [thing added] adjunct n addition, affix, suffix, appendage, annex, augmentation, increment, reinforcement, accessory, accompaniment, sequel; addendum, complement, supplement, appendix, attachment; rider, offshoot, episode, corollary.

adj additional.

40 [thing remaining] remainder n residue, remains, remnant, leftover, excess, superfluity, balance, surplus, rest, relic; leavings, odds and ends, residuum, dregs, refuse, crumbs, stubble, ruins, skeleton, stump.

v remain, survive, be left; be left over.

adj remaining, left, left over, residual; over, odd, spare, unused; superfluous; surviving.

40a [thing deducted] decrement n discount, defect, loss, deduction.

41 mixture n admixture, mix, combination, mingling, amalgamation, junction; infusion, suffusion, transfusion; infiltration, interlarding, interpolation; adulteration. thing mixed: tinge, tincture, touch, dash, sprinkling, spice, seasoning, infusion. compounds: alloy, amalgam, mélange, pastiche, miscellany, medley, patchwork, hotchpotch, gallimaufry, conglomeration, jumble, potpourri, farrago; cross, hybrid, mongrel.

v mix, join; combine, blend, mingle, commingle, confuse, jumble, unite, compound, amalgamate, adulterate; interlard, interlace, intertwine, interweave, interpolate; conjoin, associate, consort; instill, imbue, infuse, suffuse, transfuse, infiltrate, dash, tinge, tincture, season, blend, cross.

adj mixed, composite, half-and-half, hybrid, cross, mongrel, heterogeneous; motley, variegated, miscellaneous, promiscuous, indiscriminate.

adv among, amongst, amid, amidst, with; in the midst of.

42 [freedom from mixture] simpleness n purity, homogeneity; elimination, sifting, purification.

v simplify; sift, winnow, eliminate, strain, clean, purify; disentangle.

adj simple, uniform, homogeneous, single, pure, clear; unmixed, unadulterated, elemental, elementary, basic.

43 junction n joining, union; connection, conjunction, annexation, attachment; coupling, marriage, wedlock; confluence, communication, concatenation; meeting, assemblage, assembly, reunion; joint, joining, juncture, pivot, hinge, articulation; seam, stitch, linkage, link.

v join, unite, connect, link up, link; associate; put together, piece together, bind together; attach, fix, affix, fasten, bind, secure, clinch, twist, tie, string, strap, sew, lace, stitch, hem, knit, button, buckle, hitch, lash, splice, gird, tether, picket, moor, harness, leash; chain; fetter, lock, hook, couple, link, yoke, bracket; marry, wed, bridge over, span; pin, bolt, clasp, clamp, screw, rivet; solder, weld, fuse; entwine, interlace, intertwine, interweave; entangle.

adj joined, joint; corporate, compact; firm, fast, close, tight, taut, secure, set, inseparable, indissoluble.

adv jointly, in conjunction with; fast, firmly; intimately.

44 disjunction n disconnection, disunion, disengagement, dissociation, discontinuity; isolation, insularity, insulation, separateness; dispersion; separation, parting; detachment, segregation; divorce; division, subdivision, break, fracture, rupture; dismemberment, dislocation, severance; fissure, breach, rent, split, rift, crack, cut, slit, incision.

v disjoin, disconnect, disengage, disunite, dissociate, divorce, part, detach, separate, disentangle, cut off, rescind, discontinue; segregate, set apart, keep apart, isolate, insulate; cut adrift, loose, set free, liberate; divide, subdivide, sever, dissever, cut, saw, snip, chop, ax, cleave, rive, rend, slit, split, splinter, chip, crack, snap, break, tear, burst, rend; wrench, rupture, shatter; hack, hew, slash, slice, cut up, carve, dissect, tear to pieces; disband, disperse, dislocate, break up, apportion, divide; part, part company, separate, leave.

adj disjoined, discontinuous, disjunctive; isolated, insular; separate, apart, asunder, loose, adrift, free; unattached, unconnected.

adv separately, one by one, severally, apart, adrift, asunder.

45 link n connective, connection, vinculum, copula, tie, bond, bridge; junction, bracket.

v link, bond, join, connect, conjoin, fasten, pin, bind, tie; bridge, span.

46 coherence n cohesion, cohesiveness, adherence, adhesion, adhesiveness; connection, union, conglomeration, aggregation, consolidation; stickiness, inseparability.

v cohere, adhere, stick, cling, cleave, hold, take hold, clasp, hug; hang together, stay together; glue, cement, paste, solder, weld; consolidate, solidify, agglomerate.

adj cohesive, adhesive, adhering, sticky; tenacious, tough; united, unified, inseparable, inextricable, (informal) together, (informal) tight.

47 incoherence n looseness, laxity, relaxation, nonadhesion; loosening, disjunction, disconnection; disagreement, inconsistency, incongruity.

v loosen, make loose, slacken, relax; detach, disjoin.

adj nonadhesive, noncohesive, detached, loose, slack, lax, relaxed, segregated, unconsolidated; inconsistent, incongruous, illogical, absurd, rambling.

48 combination n mixture; junction; union, unification, synthesis, incorporation, amalgamation, coalescence, fusion, blend, blending, mix, centralization; compound, alloy, amalgam, composition, composite.

v combine, unite, incorporate, amalgamate, absorb, blend, mix, merge, fuse, marry, consolidate, coalesce, centralize, cement, harden, solidify.

adj combined, unified.

49 decomposition n analysis, dissection, dissolution, breaking down; disjunction; corruption, decay, rot, putrefaction.

v decompose, analyze, dissolve; resolve into its elements, dissect, disperse, crumble; decay, rot, turn.

adj decomposed.

50 [principal part] whole n totality, entirety, total, sum, aggregate; unity, completeness, integrity, indivisibility; bulk, mass, lump; body, trunk.

v form a whole, integrate, embody, amass, aggregate, assemble; amount to, come to, add up to.

adj whole, total, full, entire, undiminished, undivided, integral, complete, unimpaired, unbroken, faultless, sound, intact; indivisible, indissoluble.

adv wholly, altogether; totally, completely, entirely, all, all in all, wholesale, in a body, collectively, in the main, on the whole.

51 part n division, portion, piece, fragment, fraction, lump, bit, component, constituent, ingredient, element, section, segment, subdivision; member, limb, branch, bough, offshoot, ramification; compartment, department, class.

v part, divide, break, disjoin; partition, apportion, allot.

adj fractional, fragmentary, sectional; divided, split up.

adv partly, in part, partially; piecemeal, bit by bit, by installments, in dribs and drabs, in drips and snatches; in detail.

52 completeness n wholeness, entirety, totality, solidarity, fullness, intactness, unity, perfection; thoroughness.

v complete, accomplish, fulfill, finish; fill, charge, load, replenish; fill up, fill in; saturate.

adj complete, entire, whole, full, intact, undivided, one, perfect, fulfilled; full, good, absolute, thorough, solid; exhaustive, radical, sweeping, thoroughgoing; consummate, unmitigated, sheer, unqualified, unconditional; brimming, brimful, chock-full, saturated, crammed, replete, fraught.

adv completely, altogether, outright, wholly, totally, quite, utterly; fully, thoroughly, in all aspects, in every respect, out and out, to all intents and purposes; throughout, from first to last, from beginning to end, from top to bottom, from head to foot, every whit, every inch.

53 incompleteness n deficiency, shortcoming, insufficiency, imperfection; immaturity; noncompletion.

[part wanting] defect, deficit, omission, interval, break; discontinuity, missing link.

v be incomplete, fall short of; lack; neglect.

adj incomplete, imperfect, unfinished, uncompleted, defective, deficient, wanting, lacking, failing, short, short of; meager, lame, limp, perfunctory, sketchy, crude, immature; in progress, in preparation, going on, ongoing, proceeding.

adv incompletely.

54 composition n constitution, make-up, form; combination, compilation, incorporation, inclusion, synthesis.

v be composed of, be made up of, consist of; include, contain, hold, comprehend, take in, admit, embrace, embody; compose, constitute, form, make.

adj constituting.

55 exclusion n omission, exception, rejection, repudiation; exile, seclusion, segregation, separation, elimination, prohibition; restraint, keeping out.

v exclude, bar, leave out, shut out, keep out; reject, repudiate, blackball, throw out; lay aside, put aside, set aside; relegate, segregate, separate, seclude, banish, exile; pass over, omit, eliminate, weed out, winnow.

adj exclusive, not included in; inadmissible.

56 component n component part, integral part, element, constituent, ingredient; contents, feature, member, part; personnel.

v enter into, be part of, form part of; merge in, share in, participate; belong to, appertain to; form, make, constitute.

adj inclusive, comprehensive.

57 extraneousness n extrinsicality, externality; superfluousness; foreign body, foreign substance; intrusion.

v be extraneous, be unnecessary.

adj extraneous, foreign, alien, extrinsic, external; not germane, nonessential, superfluous; excluded.

IV. Order

58 order n regularity, uniformity, arrangement, harmony, symmetry; course, routine, method, methodology; disposition, array, arrangement, system, economy, discipline, orderliness; gradation, progression, series, sequence, continuity; rank, place, grade, class, degree.

v order, regulate, manage, adjust, arrange, systematize, standardize, rank.

adj orderly, regular, systematic, methodical; in order, neat, tidy, well-regulated, well-organized, organized, uniform, symmetrical, businesslike, shipshape.

adv in order, methodically, in turn, in its turn; step by step, at regular intervals, systematically.

59 disorder n derangement, disarray, untidiness, irregularity, anomaly; anarchy, anarchism, disunion, discord; confusion; jumble, mess, muddle, hash, hodgepodge, chaos; perplexity, labyrinth, wilderness, jungle; raveling, entanglement, complication, convolution; turmoil, ferment, agitation, trouble, row, disturbance, convulsion, tumult, uproar, riot, rumpus, ruckus, scramble, fracas, melee, pandemonium.

v disorder, put out of order, derange, ruffle, rumble; confuse, jumble, mess up.

adj disorderly, out of order, out of place, irregular, desultory; anomalous, disorganized, straggling, unsystematic, untidy, slovenly, messy; indiscriminate, chaotic, confused, deranged; anarchic, inverted, convoluted, topsy-turvy; complex, complicated, perplexed, involved, raveled, entangled, knotted, tangled; troublesome, problematical; riotous, violent, turbulent, tumultuous.

adv irregularly, helter skelter; at cross purposes, (informal) after the flood.

60 [reduction to order] arrangement n plan, method, organization; preparation, groundwork, planning; sorting, disposal, disposition, distribution, assortment, allotment, apportionment, graduation, groupings; analysis, classification, division, ordering, systematization.

v arrange, dispose, place, form; set out, marshal, range, array, rank, group, parcel out, allot, apportion, assign, dole out, distribute; sort, sift, put into shape; plan, prepare, organize, lay the groundwork; classify, divide, file, register, catalog, record, tabulate, index, graduate, rank; regulate, systematize, coordinate, organize, settle, fix; unravel, disentangle, straighten out.

adj arranged, ordered; methodical, orderly, regular, systematic.

61 [subversion of order] derangement n disorder, mess, disarray, disorganization; discomposure, disturbance, dislocation, perturbation, interruption.

v derange, disarrange, discompose, displace, misplace; mislay, disorder,

disorganize; embroil, disconcert, convulse, unsettle, disturb, confuse, trouble, perturb, jumble, muddle, fumble; unhinge, dislocate, throw out of gear, throw out of whack; invert, turn upside down, turn topsy-turvy; complicate, confound, tangle, entangle; litter, scatter, mix.

62 precedence n coming before, the lead, superiority; precursor, antecedence; importance, consequence; priority, preference.

v precede, come before, forerun, come first; head, lead the way, usher in, introduce; set the fashion, influence, establish; have precedence, take precedence; place before, prefix, preface.

adj preceding, precedent, antecedent, anterior, prior, before; former, foregoing; preliminary, prefatory, introductory; preparatory.

adv before; in advance.

63 sequence n coming after, following, succession, order, series; posteriority; continuation; order of succession; outcome, consequence, result, sequel.

v succeed, come after, follow, ensue; replace.

adj succeeding, following; consequent, subsequent; proximate, next; sequential, consecutive.

adv after, subsequently; behind.

64 precursor n antecedent, precedent, predecessor, forerunner, pioneer, leader, bellwether; herald, harbinger; prelude, preamble, preface, prolog, proem, prefix, foreword, introduction; heading, frontispiece, groundwork; preparation.

adj prefatory, introductory, preliminary, precursory.

65 sequel n continuation, extension, supplement, outgrowth, offshoot, result, consequence, inference, deduction; result, consequence, aftermath, outcome, effect; conclusion, end, culmination, dénouement, finale, finish; appendage, suffix, epilog, postscript, tag, train, trail, wake; afterthought, afterpiece, second thoughts.

66 beginning n commencement, opening, outset, start, initiation, inauguration; introduction, prelude; outbreak, onset, brunt; initiative, first move; origin, cause, source, bud, germ, genesis, birth, nativity, cradle; starting point, first step, square one; title page, head, heading; rudiments, basics, elements.

v begin, commence, open, start, initiate, inaugurate; conceive; set out, embark, depart; usher in, lead the way, take the lead, take the initiative, head, stand at the head, launch, set in motion, get going, take the first step, break ground; burst forth, break out; begin at the beginning, start again, start over, make a fresh start; originate, conceive, think up.

adj initial, introductory, inaugural; incipient; embryonic, rudimental, primal, essential, natal, nascent; first, foremost, leading; maiden, virgin.

adv first, in the first place, first and foremost; in the bud, in its infancy; from the beginning.

67 end n close, termination, conclusion, finale, finish, last word; consummation, climax, apex, dénouement; goal, destination; expiration, death, finality; limit, extreme, extremity; breakup, last stage, final stage, turning point, death blow.

v end, close, finish, terminate, conclude; expire, die, come to a close, draw to a close, run its course, run out, pass away; bring to an end, put an end to, make an end of, wrap up; get through, complete, consummate; stop, desist, call it quits.

adj final, terminal, concluding; conclusive, crowning, definitive, last, ultimate, consummate; ended, settled, decided, over, concluded, played out.

adv finally, at last, once and for all, over and done with.

68 middle n center, midpoint, midst; mean, midcourse, middle ground, compromise; core, kernel, heart, nucleus, nub; equidistance, bisection; equator, diaphragm, midriff.

adj middle, medial, mean, mid, median, midmost; intermediate, equidistant, central, halfway.

adv midway, halfway, in the middle.

69 [uninterrupted sequence] continuity n continuousness, consecutiveness, progression, constant flow, succession, train, series, chain, string, scale, gradation; round, suite; procession, column, retinue; pedigree, genealogy, lineage; rank, file, line, row, range, tier.

v follow in a line; arrange in a series, string together, file, thread, graduate, tabulate.
adj continuous, progressive, successive, serial, consecutive, unbroken, uninterrupted, gradual; linear, in a line; perennial, constant.
adv continuously, in succession, consecutively; gradually, step by step, in a column.

70 [interrupted sequence] **discontinuity** *n* disjunction, disconnectedness; interruption, break, fracture, fault, flaw, crack, cut; gap, interval, caesura, pause, (*informal*) breather, rest, intermission, parenthesis, episode.
v alternate; discontinue, break, interrupt, intervene; pause, rest, take a breather, stop; break in upon, interpose; disconnect.
adj discontinuous, disconnected, unconnected, broken, interrupted; fitful, spasmodic, desultory, intermittent, irregular; alternate, recurrent, periodic.
adv at intervals, in snatches, by fits and starts.

71 term *n* rank, station, stage, step, phase; scale, grade, degree, status, position, place, point, mark, period, limit; stand, standing, footing.

72 assemblage *n* collection, levee, gathering, ingathering, muster; concourse, conflux, congregation; meeting, reunion; assembly, congress, convention, conclave, council; miscellany, compilation, menagerie; crowd, throng, mob, flood, rush, rash, deluge, press, crush, horde, body, tribe, crew, gang, squad, band, party, swarm, flock, bevy; company, troop, regiment, squadron, army; host, multitude, populace, clan, brotherhood, sisterhood, association; group, cluster, clump, batch, pack, assortment; accumulation, heap, lump, pile, mass, conglomeration, conglomerate, aggregation, aggregate; quantity.
v assemble, come together, collect, gather, muster; meet, unite, join, rejoin; cluster, flock, swarm, surge, stream, herd, crowd, throng, associate; congregate, concentrate, huddle; bring together, draw together, place together, lump together; convene, invoke; compile, group, assemble, unite; amass, accumulate, store.
adj assembled; closely packed, dense, crowded, teeming, swarming, populous.

73 dispersion *n* divergence, spreading, radiation, dissemination, diffusion, dissipation, distribution, apportionment, division.
v disperse, scatter, sow, disseminate, diffuse, shed, spread, dispense, disband, distribute, apportion, divide; break up, dispel, cast forth, strew, cast, sprinkle; issue, deal out, dole out.
adj dispersed, spread, scattered, strewn, diffuse, diffusive; sparse, widespread, broadcast; adrift, stray, disheveled.

74 [place of meeting] **focus** *n* center, gathering place, haunt, rendezvous, rallying point, headquarters, club, retreat.
v focus, bring to a point, bring to a focus; center on, bring out, clarify, elucidate.

75 class *n* division, subdivision, category, heading, order, section; department, province, domain; type, kind, sort, genus, species, variety, family, race, tribe, cast, clan, breed, sect.

76 inclusion *n* admission, acceptance into, incorporation, comprehension, reception.
v include, comprise, comprehend, contain, admit, embrace, receive, accept; inclose, circumscribe, encircle, encompass, embody, incorporate; number among, count among, fall under.
adj inclusive, comprehensive, extensive, all-embracing, compendious, sweeping; including, incorporating.

77 exclusion *n* (see 55).

78 generality *n* universality, catholicity, miscellany, miscellaneousness; generalization, simplification, oversimplification; prevalence, common run.
v be general, be universal, prevail, be true for everyone; render general, generalize, universalize; make a generalization, abstract, simplify.
adj general, universal, catholic, common, ecumenical, egalitarian, worldwide; prevalent, prevailing, rife, current; generic, collective, all-encompassing, comprehensive, all-inclusive, broad, widespread.

79 specialty *n* speciality, skill, ability, talent; individuality, singularity, distinctive feature, particularity, personality, characteristic, mannerism, idiosyncrasy, nonconformity; particulars, details, items; special feature.
v specify, particularize, individualize, specialize; designate, determine, single out, isolate, differentiate; be specific, come to the point, detail, get down to particulars.
adj special, particular, especial, individual, specific, proper, personal, original, private, respective, definite, certain, endemic, peculiar, characteristic, marked, appropriate, exclusive, singular, exceptional, idiomatic, unique.
adv specially, especially, in particular; each, apiece, severally, respectively, each to each, each to his own; in detail.

80 regulation *n* regularity, uniformity, constancy, clockwork, precision, exactness; routine, custom, formula, rule, form, procedure; standard, model, precedent, prototype; conformity, convention; nature, law, principle; normal state, ordinary condition, normalcy; hard and fast law.
adj regular, uniform, constant, steady; customary, conventional, formal, formulaic, procedural.

81 multiformity *n* variety, diversity.
adj multifold, multifarious, manifold, many-sided; heterogeneous, motley, mosaic; indiscriminate, irregular, diversified, diverse; of every description, all manner of kinds.

82 conformity *n* observance, compliance, assent; conventionality, customariness, agreement; example, instance, specimen, sample, illustration, exemplification, case in point.
v conform to, accommodate oneself to, adapt to; be regular, conform, follow the rules, obey the rules, go by the rules, comply, assent, agree, yield, give in, accept, harmonize; illustrate, stand as an example, embody.
adj conformable to rule, adaptable, agreeable, compliant, malleable; conventional, customary, standard, ordinary, common, habitual, usual, natural, normal, typical; formal, orthodox, strict, rigid, uncompromising; exemplary, illustrative.
adv by rule, in conformity with, in accordance with, in keeping with, consistent with; for the sake of conformity, as a matter of course, for form's sake; invariably, uniformly.

83 unconformity *n* nonconformity, unconventionality, nonobservance, informality; anomaly, variation, inconsistency, irregularity, incongruity, oddity, eccentricity, peculiarity, aberration, abnormality, exception; violation of custom, infraction, infringement; individuality, originality, mannerism, idiosyncrasy, quirk.
v be unconformable.
adj unconformable, unconventional; unnatural, odd, eccentric, peculiar, aberrant, abnormal, exceptional; anomalous, inconsistent, irregular, incongruous, arbitrary, whimsical, wanton; unusual, uncustomary, uncommon, rare, singular, unique, extraordinary; queer, quaint, strange; original, fantastic, newfangled, bizarre, outlandish, exotic, esoteric.
adv unless, except, save, beside.

V. Number

84 number *n* numeral, symbol, figure, cipher, digit, integer, round number, whole number, fraction; sum, total, product.
adj numeral; prime, fractional, decimal; positive, negative.

85 numeration *n* numbering; tallying, enumeration, reckoning, computation, calculation; arithmetic, calculus, algebra; statistics, poll, census, roll call; arithmetic operations.
v number, count, tell, tally, enumerate, add up, sum, reckon, compute, calculate, take account; muster, poll, recite; add, subtract, multiply, divide.
adj numeral, numerical; arithmetical, analytic, algebraic, statistical, numerable, computable, calculable.

86 list *n* catalog, index, listing, inventory, schedule, register, record, ledger, tally, file, table, calendar; directory, gazette, atlas, dictionary, thesaurus; roll, checklist.

87 unity *n* oneness, singleness, singularity, individuality; unification, unison, uniformity.
v unite, join, combine; isolate, insulate, seclude.
adj one, sole, single, solitary, lone; individual, apart, alone; unaccompanied, unattended, singlehanded, solo; singular, odd, unique; isolated, insular.
adv singly.

88 accompaniment *n* association, partnership, company; accessory, adjunct, concomitant, attachment, complement, attendant, fellow, associate, coexistence.
v accompany, join, escort, convoy, wait on; coexist with, consort with; associate with, couple with.
adj accompanying, fellow, twin, joint; associated with, coupled with; accessory, concomitant, attendant.
adv with, together with, along with, in company with, hand in hand, side by side; therewith, herewith.

89 duality *n* dualism, doubleness, polarity, biformity, duplexity; two, deuce, couple, brace, pair, twins.
v pair, mate, couple, bracket, pair off, yoke.
adj two, twain; dual, twin, two-sided, binary, binomial, duplex; coupled, both.

90 duplication *n* doubling, reduplication; iteration, repetition; renewal.
duplicate, double, copy, carbon, facsimile.
v double; redouble, reduplicate; repeat, renew; duplicate.
adj double; doubled, duplicated; twin, duplicate, second.
adv twice, once more, over again.

91 bisection *n* halving, bifurcation, twofold division, forking, dichotomy, (*informal*) fifty-fifty split.
v bisect, divide in two, halve, divide, split, cut in two, cleave, fork, bifurcate; split down the middle, (*informal*) go halves.
adj bisected, cloven, cleft, halved; bipartite; bifurcated; semi-, demi-, hemi-.

92 triality *n* trinity; three, triad, triplet, trio.
adj three, threefold, triform, tertiary.

93 triplication *n* tripling; triplicity.
v triple, treble, cube.
adj triple, treble; threefold, triplicate; third.
adv three times, thrice; in the third place, thirdly; triply, trebly.

94 trisection *n* tripartition, threefold division, third, third part.
v trisect, divide into three parts.

95 quaternity *n* four, tetrad, quartet, quarter.
v square, reduce to a square.
adj four, fourfold, quadrilateral.

96 quadruplication *n* quadrupling, multiplying by four.
v multiply by four, quadruplicate.
adj four, fourfold, quadruple; fourth.
adv four times, in the fourth place, fourthly.

97 quadrisection *n* quartering, quadripartition, fourfold division; fourth part, quarter.
v quarter, divide into four parts.
adj quartered, quadripartite.

98 five, etc. *n* five; six, half a dozen; seven; eight; nine; ten, decade; eleven; twelve, dozen; thirteen, baker's dozen, long dozen; twenty, score; twenty-five, quarter of a hundred; fifty, half a hundred; hundred, century, centenary; thousand.

99 quinquesection *n* fivefold division.
adj quinquepartite.

100 [more than one] **plurality** *n* two or more, couple, few, several; majority, multitude.
adj plural, more than one, upwards of, some, several, many, numerous.

100a [less than one] **fraction** *n* fractional part, segment, subdivision, part, portion.

101 zero *n* nothing, naught, (*informal*) zip; none, shutout; nobody.

102 multitude *n* multitudinous, multiplicity, profusion, mass, quantity, volume, abundance, amplitude, enormity; numbers, array, scores, droves, host, throng, collection; mob, crowd, assemblage.
v be numerous, swarm with, teem with, crowd, swarm, outnumber, multiply; people, populate.
adj multitudinous, manifold, profuse, multiple, teeming, populous, crowded, thick; many, several, sundry, various, numerous; endless, infinite.

103 fewness *n* paucity, scarcity, sparseness, scantiness; small number, small quantity; infrequency.
diminution of number: reduction, weeding, elimination.
v render few, reduce, diminish, weed, thin, eliminate, eradicate.
adj few, not many, scanty, scarce, sparse, rare, few and far between, limited, meager; sporadic, occasional, infrequent; reduced, diminished, pared back.

104 repetition *n* iteration, reiteration, recapitulation, restatement; sameness, monotony, harping, recurrence, tautology; redundance; rhythm, beat, echo, reverberation; reappearance, reproduction, duplication.
v repeat, iterate, reiterate, recapitulate, restate, rehash, go over again, harp on, hammer; reproduce, duplicate, echo; recur, revert, return, reappear; resume, return to, go back to; rehearse, go over the same ground.
adj repeated, repetitious, recurrent, recurring, frequent, incessant, never-ending, unceasing; repetitive, redundant, tautological; rhythmic, reverberant, reverberating; monotonous, harping, iterative; habitual.
adv repeatedly, often, again, anew, afresh, over again, once more; over and over, again and again, year after year; ditto, encore.

105 infinity *n* infinitude, infiniteness, perpetuity, endlessness, boundlessness, inexhaustibility, immeasurability, limitlessness, vastness, expanse.
v be infinite, have no limits, know no bounds, go on forever.
adj infinite, countless, numberless, limitless, boundless, measureless, unlimited, interminable, inexhaustible, incalculable; immense, vast, endless, perpetual; incomprehensible; eternal, perfect, omnipotent, absolute.
adv infinitely, *ad infinitum*.

VI. Time

106 time *n* duration, extent; period, interval, spell, term, space, span, season, stage; course; interim, interlude; interregnum, intermission; respite, break, timeout; era, epoch, season, age, year, date.
v time, measure, pace; continue, last, endure, go on, remain, persist, stand; pass time, spend time, while away the time, waste time, kill time, fill up the time.
adj permanent, lasting, durable; timely.
adv while, whilst, during, in the course of, for the time being, in due time; meantime, meanwhile, in the meantime, in the interim; till, until, up to, yet; the whole time, all the time, throughout, for good, (*informal*) for keeps.

107 absence of time *n* no time; outside time.
adv never, at no time; on no occasion, nevermore.

108 [definite duration or period of time] **period** *n* interval, age, era, eon, epoch, term, time; year, decade, century, millennium; lifetime, generation.

109 [indefinite duration] **course** *n* march of time,
course of time, flux, passing time.
v elapse, lapse, flow, run, proceed, advance, pass, flit, fly, slip, slide, drag, creep, crawl; run its course; expire, go by, pass by.
adv in due time, in due course, in due season, in time.

110 [long duration] **durability** *n* permanence, persistence, continuance, lastingness, standing, stability; survival, longevity; protraction, prolongation.
v last, remain, stand, endure, abide, continue, persist; tarry, drag on, drag out, prolong, protract, eke out, draw out, lengthen; outlive, outlast, survive.
adj permanent, durable, lasting, longstanding, stable, immutable, invariable, constant; enduring, abiding, perpetual; lingering, protracted, prolonged, spun-out.
adv long, for a long time, ever so long; long ago; all day long, all the livelong day.

111 [short duration] **transience** *n* imperma-
nence, evanescence, ephemerality, transitoriness, mortality; suddenness, swiftness, changeableness, vicissitude, uncertainty.
v be transient, flit, pass away, fly, gallop, vanish, fade, evaporate, melt.
adj transient, transitory, evanescent, ephemeral, fleeting, flitting, flying, passing; impermanent, temporal, temporary, provisional, short-lived; perishable, precarious, vulnerable, mortal; brief, quick, brisk; sudden, momentary, instantaneous.
adv temporarily, for the moment, for a time; awhile, soon; briefly.

112 [endless duration] **perpetuity** *n* eternity, tim-
elessness, everlastingness, endlessness, infinity; constancy, endurance, durability, ceaselessness.
v last forever, endure, go on forever; perpetuate, immortalize, eternalize.
adj perpetual, eternal, timeless, everlasting, endless; unceasing, ceaseless, interminable, neverending, continuous, incessant, uninterrupted; unfading, imperishable, unvulnerable, immortal.
adv perpetually, always, ever, evermore, forever; constantly, continuously.

113 [point of time] **instantaneousness** *n* suddenness, abruptness; moment, instant, second, twinkling, trice, flash, crack, burst.
v be instantaneous, twinkle, flash.
adj instantaneous, momentary, sudden, instant, abrupt.
adv instantaneously, in no time, (*informal*) in two shakes (of a lamb's tail), presto, suddenly, like a shot, in a moment, all of a sudden, in a jiffy; immediately, on the spur of the moment, on a moment's notice.

114 [estimation, measurement and record of time] **chronometry** *n* chronology, timetable; almanac, calendar, register, chronicle, log, annal(s), journal, diary; clock, watch, stopwatch, timepiece, chronometer.
v fix the time, mark the time; date, register, chronicle; measure time, mark time, beat time.
adj chronological.

115 [false estimate of time] **anachronism** *n* misdate, misplacement, chronological error; disregard of time.
v misdate, antedate, postdate, anticipate; take no note of time.
adj misdated; undated, overdue; anachronistic, out of place, misplaced.

116 antecedence *n* priority, anteriority, precedence, pre-existence; antecedent, predecessor, precursor, forerunner.
v precede, antedate, come before; go before, lead, forerun; dawn, presage, herald, break the ground.
adj antecedent, prior, previous, anterior, preceding, pre-existent; former, foregoing, aforementioned; precursory, introductory.
adv before, prior to; earlier, previously, ere, already, yet, beforehand.

117 posteriority *n* succession, sequence; subsequence, following, continuance; successor, sequel, follower; future, futurity.
v follow after, come after, go after, succeed, be subsequent to.
adj posterior, subsequent, following, after, later, succeeding, successive, ensuing, resulting; posthumous.
adv subsequently, after, afterwards, since, later; next, close upon, thereafter, thereupon; ultimately.

118 present time *n* the present juncture, the present day; the times, the time being, right now.
adj present, actual, instant, current, existing.
adv at this time, at this moment; at the present time, now, at present, nowadays.

119 different time *n* other time; another time.
adv at that time, at that instant; then, on that occasion; when, whenever, whensoever; at some other time, at a different time, at some time or other.

120 contemporaneousness *n* simultaneousness, synchronism, simultaneity, coincidence, concurrence, coexistence, concomitance.
v coexist, concur, accompany, go side by side, keep pace with; synchronize.
adj simultaneous, coincident, concurrent, concomitant, coexisting; contemporary, contemporaneous, coeval.
adv simultaneously, concurrently, together, at the same time.

121 the future *n* futurity, hereafter, time to come, tomorrow, morrow; millennium, doomsday, day of judgment, crack of doom, flood; advent, eventuality; destiny, fate; heritage, heirs, posterity; prospect, expectation, anticipation.
v look forward, anticipate, expect, foresee; approach, await, threaten, impend, come near, draw near, come on.
adj future, to come; coming, impending, near, close at hand, in

prospect; eventual, ulterior.

adv prospectively, hereafter, in future, in course of time, tomorrow; eventually, ultimately, sooner or later; henceforth, from this time; soon, early, on the eve of, on the point of, on the brink of.

122 the past *n* past time, days of old, days of yore, days gone by, yesterday, yesteryear, former times, ancient times; retrospection, memory; antiquity, history, time immemorial, remote past; ancestry, lineage, forbears; heritage.

v run its course, pass away, pass, lapse, blow over.

adj past, gone, gone by, passed away, bygone, elapsed, lapsed, expired, extinct, forgotten, irrecoverable, obsolete; former, pristine, late; foregoing, last, latter, recent; looking back, retrospective; retroactive.

adv formerly, of old, of yore, ago, over; long ago, years ago, a long while back, some time ago; lately, of late; retrospectively, ere now, before now, hitherto, heretofore; already, yet, up to this time.

123 newness *n* novelty, recentness, freshness; immaturity, greenness, youth, juvenility; innovation, uniqueness, originality; renovation, restoration; modernity, modernism, stylishness, fashionableness, newfangledness, fashion, faddishness, the latest thing, futurism, trendiness.

v renew, renovate, restore; modernize.

adj new, novel, recent, fresh; green, immature, unripe, young, youthful, untried, untested, virgin, virginal; modern, late, new, newfangled, stylish, fashionable, faddish, trendy, brand-new, up-to-date; renovated, restored, spick and span.

adv newly, afresh, anew, lately, just now, of late.

124 oldness *n* age, antiquity; maturity, ripeness; decline, decay, old age, senility, superannuation; archaism, antiquarianism, relic, thing of the past; tradition, custom, common law.

v be old, have had its day, have seen its day; become old, age, fade.

adj old, ancient, antique; time-honored, venerable, traditional, vintage, of long standing; elderly, aged, hoary, decayed, senile, decrepit; primeval, primitive, aboriginal, primordial, antediluvian, prehistoric, archaic; traditional, prescriptive, customary, immemorial, inveterate, rooted; antiquated, outdated, outmoded, of other times; out of date, obsolete, out-of-fashion, out-of-style, gone by, stale, old-fashioned, timeworn, crumbling, ramshackle, run-down, wasted.

125 morning. noon *n* morning, morn, dawn, daybreak, sunrise, sunup, forenoon, break of day, peep of day, prime of day, morningtide, matins, cockcrow, first blush, antemeridian, A.M.

noon, midday, noonday, noontide, meridian, prime, height, noontime.

spring, springtime; summer, summertime, midsummer.

126 evening. midnight *n* evening, eve, eventide, dusk, vespers, nightfall, sundown, sunset, twilight, curfew, bedtime; afternoon, post meridian, P.M.

midnight, end of the day, close of the day, witching hour, dead of night.

autumn, fall, harvest time; winter.

127 youth *n* juvenility, infancy, childhood, boyhood, girlhood; minority, tender years, young years, formative years, next generation, tender age; cradle, nursery; puberty.

adj young, youthful, juvenile, green, callow, budding, immature, developing, underage, formative; younger, junior.

128 age *n* old age, advanced age, senility, years, gray hairs, declining years, golden years, mature years, decrepitude, anility, superannuation, longevity, ripe age, ripe old age; maturity, seniority, eldership.

adj aged, old, advanced, gray, elderly; senile, decline, failing, waning, ripe, overripe, mellow, venerable, wrinkled, wizened; older, elder, eldest.

129 infant *n* baby, babe, babe in arms, nursling, little one, tot, toddler, chick, kid, lamb, cherub; youth, youngster, child, minor; girl, lass, maiden, miss, schoolgirl; boy, lad, stripling, master, schoolboy.

adj infantile, infantlike, puerile, girlish, boyish, childish, babyish; newborn, young.

130 veteran *n* old man, old woman, patriarch, matriarch, grandmother, grandfather, grandsire, seer, graybeard, forefather, elder.

adj aged, old.

131 adolescence *n* majority, adulthood, manhood, womanhood, maturity, ripeness, fullness, puberty, pubescence; teenage years, prepubescence.

v come of age, grow up, attain majority.

adj adolescent, teenage, pubescent, of age, grown up, full grown, adult, womanly, manly, marriageable, nubile.

132 earliness *n* punctuality, promptitude, speediness, readiness, expedition, alacrity, quickness, haste; suddenness; prematurity, precocity, precipitation, anticipation.

v be early, be beforehand; anticipate, forestall, steal a march on, get a head start; bespeak, secure, engage, pre-engage; accelerate, expedite, quicken, hasten, make haste, make time, hurry.

adj early, timely, punctual, on time, prompt; premature, precipitate, precocious, anticipatory; sudden, instantaneous, immediate, expeditious; unexpected.

adv early, soon, anon, betimes, before long; punctually, to the minute, on time, on the dot; beforehand, prematurely, precipitately, too soon, hastily, in anticipation, unexpectedly; suddenly, instantaneously, at short notice, on the spur of the moment; at once, on the spot, on the instant, at sight, straight, offhand, straightway; forthwith, summarily, immediately, shortly, quickly, speedily; presently, by and by, directly.

133 lateness *n* tardiness, slowness, sloth, tarrying, dilly-dallying, loitering; delay, procrastination, postponement, adjournment, retardation, protraction, prolongation; respite, reprieve; suspension, moratorium, stop, stay.

v be late, tarry, wait, stay, bide, take time, linger, loiter, dawdle, shilly-shally, dilly-dally; put off, defer, delay, lay over, suspend; retard, postpone, adjourn; procrastinate, prolong, protract, drag out, draw out; lengthen, table, shelve, stall.

adj late, tardy, slow, dilatory, backward, unpunctual; delayed, overdue, belated.

adv late; backward, at the eleventh hour, at length, at last; ultimately, behind time; too late; slowly, leisurely, deliberately, at one's leisure, on one's own time.

134 opportuneness *n* timeliness, opportunity, occasion, suitable time, proper time, suitability, high time; crisis, turn, juncture; turning point, given time; nick of time, golden opportunity; clear stage, open field.

v be opportune, be suitable; seize the opportunity, seize the time, seize the day, *carpe diem*, use the occasion; suit the occasion, be expeditious, strike while the iron is hot.

adj opportune, timely, well-timed, seasonable, suitable, appropriate; providential, lucky, fortunate, happy, favorable, fortuitous, propitious, auspicious.

adv opportunely, in due time, in the nick of time, just in time, now or never; by the way, by the by, speaking of, while on the subject; on the spot, on the spur of the moment, since the occasion presents itself.

135 inopportuneness *n* untimeliness, unseasonableness, improper time, unsuitable time; (*informal*) bad timing; intrusion; anachronism.

v be ill timed, mistime, intrude, break in upon, (*informal*) butt in; lose an opportunity, waste an occasion, (*informal*) blow one's chance, let the opportunity slip by; waste time.

adj inopportune, untimely, unpropitious, unseasonable, unsuitable, inauspicious, unfavorable, unfortunate, unsuited, untoward, unlucky; ill-timed, mistimed, poorly timed; unpunctual, premature.

136 frequency *n* repetition, recurrence, iteration, reiteration.

v recur, repeat, reiterate; keep on, continue; attend regularly, visit often, patronize.

adj frequent, oft-repeated, recurring, incessant, constant, continual, perpetual; habitual, customary.

adv often, oft, oftentimes, frequently, repeatedly, day after day; daily, hourly, every day; perpetually, continually, constantly, incessantly, at all times; commonly, habitually, customarily; sometimes, occasionally, at times, now and then, every once in a while, from time to time.

137 infrequency *n* rarity, rare occurrence; long shot, surprise, (*informal*) mindblower.

v be rare, be infrequent.

adj infrequent, occasional, sporadic, rare, uncommon, unusual, unheard of, unprecedented; few, scant, scarce.

adv infrequently, rarely, seldom, scarcely, hardly; not often, hardly ever.

138 regularity [of recurrence] *n* periodicity, intermittence; beat, pulse, pulsation, rhythm; alternation, oscillation, vibration; bout, round, turn, revolution, rotation, rpm; cycle, period, routine; punctuality, regularity, steadiness.

v recur, revolve, return, come in its turn, come round again; beat, pulsate, alternate.

adj regular, periodic, periodical; serial, recurrent, cyclical, cyclic, recurring, rhythmical, rhythmic; intermittent, alternate, every other; regular, steady, punctual, continual, constant, regular as clockwork.

adv regularly, periodically, serially, cyclically; intermittently, alternately; by turns, in turn, in rotation, off and on, round and round.

139 irregularity [of recurrence] *n* uncertainty, unpredictability, haphazardness, fitfulness, capriciousness.

v be irregular, be haphazard.

adj irregular, uncertain, unpredictable, haphazard, fitful, capricious, flickering; spasmodic, sporadic.

adv irregularly, fitfully, capriciously, by fits and starts.

VII. Change

140 change *n* alteration, modulation, modification, variation, mutation, permutation, qualification, deviation, turn, shift, innovation; diversion, break; transformation, transfiguration, transmutation, metamorphosis; conversion, revolution, inversion, reversal; displacement, transference, transposition; changeableness.

v change, alter, vary, modulate, qualify, diversify, tamper with, play with, experiment with; turn, shift, veer, tack, swerve, warp, deviate, turn aside; turn, take a turn, (*informal*) hang a turn; modify, revamp, transform, transfigure, transmute, metamorphose, convert; innovate, restructure, give a new turn to, recast, redesign, remodel.

adj changed, newfangled; changeable, variable, transformable; innovative.

141 permanence *n* stability, invariability, unalterability, immutability, constancy; endurance, durability, persistence; maintenance, preservation, conservation; obstinacy, immovability, inflexibility, immobility, rigidity.

v endure, bide, abide, stay, remain, last, persist, stand, stand fast; maintain, keep, keep up, preserve; subsist, live, outlive, survive.

adj permanent, lasting, unchanged, unchanging, fixed, stable, invariable, constant; enduring, durable, abiding, everlasting; intact, inviolate; persistent.

adv permanently, for good, for good and all.

142 cessation *n* discontinuation, discontinuance, halt, stoppage, termination, suspension, interruption, stopping; pause, rest, lull, respite, truce, break; interregnum, abeyance; completion, end, finish; stop, death.

v cease, discontinue, terminate, desist, stay; break off, leave off, hold, stop, pull up, stop short, halt, pause, rest; suspend, interrupt, delay, cut short, arrest, bring to a standstill; complete, end, finish, close up shop; wear away, go out, die out, pass away, die.

143 continuance [in action] *n* continuation, continuity, protraction, prolongation, maintenance, perpetuation; persistence, perseverance, repetition.

v continue, persist, go on, keep on, hold on; abide, keep, pursue, stick to; maintain course, carry on, keep up; sustain, uphold, hold up, keep going, maintain, preserve, perpetuate, prolong.

adj continuing, uninterrupted, unvarying; continuous, persistent, perpetual.

144 conversion *n* transformation, transmutation, reduction, change, changeover, resolution, assimilation; passage, transit, transition, shifting, flux; growth, progress, development; chemistry, alchemy.

v be converted into, become, turn into, lapse, shift; pass into, grow into, ripen into, merge into; melt, grow, ripen, mature, mellow; convert into, resolve into; make, render; mold, form, model, remodel, remake, do over, reform, reorganize; assimilate, bring into, reduce to.

adj convertible, transmutable, changeable.

145 reversion *n* return, revulsion, reverting, returning; alternation, rotation; inversion; recoil, reaction, reflex, repercussion, rebound, boomerang, ricochet, backlash, repulse; retrospection, retrogression, retrogradation, falling back; restoration, going back; turning point, turn of the tide.

v revert, return, turn back, reverse; relapse, regress, fall back; recoil, rebound; retreat; restore; undo, unmake; turn the tide.

146 [sudden or violent change] **revolution** *n* revolt, rebellion, overthrow, overturn, coup, *coup d'état*, rising, uprising, mutiny, counterrevolution; breakup, destruction, subversion, clean sweep; spasm, convulsion, throe, revulsion.

v revolt, rebel, rise, rise up; revolutionize, remodel, recast, change.

adj revolutionary, rebellious; new.

147 substitution *n* replacement, supplanting, commutation, exchange, change, shift.

substitute, expedient, makeshift, stopgap, equivalent, double, alternative, representative.

v substitute, put in the place of, change, exchange, interchange; replace, supplant, supersede, take the place of, stand for, represent, pinch hit, substitute for, sub; redeem, commute, alternate.

adv instead, in place of, in lieu of.

148 [double or mutual change] **interchange** *n* exchange, commutation, permutation, transposition; reciprocation, reciprocity, intercourse; barter, swap, trade; interchangeability; retaliation, reprisal, requital, retort, cross-fire.

v interchange, exchange, barter, trade, swap, bandy, transpose, commute, reciprocate; give and take, battle with words; retort, requite, retaliate.

adj interchangeable, all-purpose, multi-purpose; reciprocal; mutual.

adv in exchange, vice versa, turn and turn about.

149 changeableness *n* mutability, inconstancy, volatility, instability; malleability, adaptability, versatility, mobility; vacillation, irresolution, indecision, capriciousness, oscillation, alternation, fluctuation, vicissitude; restlessness, fidgetiness, disquiet, disquietude; unrest, agitation.

v fluctuate, oscillate, vary, waver, flounder, shuffle, hem and haw, vacillate, tremble, alternate.

adj changeable, mutable, variable, malleable, adaptable, adjustable, versatile, mobile, transformable, convertible; inconstant, unsteady, unstable, unreliable, vacillating, oscillating, fluctuating; volatile, fitful, fickle, capricious, mercurial, indecisive, irresolute, flighty, impulsive, fanciful, erratic, wayward, wanton; restless, fidgety, tremulous, agitated; unfixed, unsettled.

150 stability *n* immutability, unchangeableness, constancy; firmness, fixity, solidity, steadiness, soundness, balance, stabilization, equilibrium, quiescence; immobility, immovability, fixedness; steadfastness, reliability, resolution, determination, obstinacy, stubbornness, pertinacity, tenacity, doggedness, will, pluck, resoluteness; permanence, endurance, perseverance, durability; continuity, uniformity, changelessness.

v be firm, stick fast, stand firm; settle, establish, fix, set, stabilize; retain, keep hold; make sure, fasten, make solid.

adj stable, fixed, rigid, firm, steady, established, strong, sturdy, immovable, invariable, unvarying, permanent, unchangeable, unchanging, unalterable, immutable; enduring, constant, durable, lasting, abiding, secure, fast, perpetual; unwavering, steadfast, staunch, reliable, steady, solid, sound, balanced; resolute, obstinate, dogged, willful, stubborn, pertinacious, tenacious.

151 present events *n* event, occurrence, incident, affair, eventuality, happening, proceeding, transaction, fact; phenomenon; circumstance, situation, particular; adventure, episode, thrill; crisis, pass, emergency, contingency, impasse; things, doings, affairs, matters, issues; the world, life, the times.

v happen, occur, take place, come to pass, take place, come about, come round; fall out, turn out, befall, chance, prove, eventuate; turn up, crop up, arise, arrive, issue, ensue, start, hold; take its course, pass off; experience, meet with, meet up with, fall to, be one's lot, be one's fortune, find, encounter, undergo, go through, live through, endure, put up with.

adj happening, going on, doing, current; eventful, stirring, bustling, busy, full of incident.

adv eventually, finally; as things go, in the course of things, as it happens.

152 future events *n* destiny, luck, lot, chance, fortune, karma, doom, end; future, futurity, next world, hereafter; prospects, expectations, tomorrow.

v impend, hang over, hover, threaten, loom, await, come on, approach; foreordain, preordain; destine, predestine, doom, have in store for.

adj impending, destined; coming, in store, to come, at hand, near, close by, imminent, brewing, forthcoming; in the wind, in the cards, in prospect, looming, on the horizon.

adv in time, in the long run, in good time, in its own sweet time, eventually.

VIII. Causation

153 cause *n* origin, source, principle, element; prime mover, first cause; author, producer, creator; mainspring, agent, catalyst; groundwork, foundation, support; spring, fountain, well, fount, font; genesis, descent, remote cause, influence; pivot, hinge, axis, turning point; egg, germ, embryo, root, nucleus, seed; causality, causation, origination, production.

v cause, originate, give rise to, occasion, sow the seeds of, kindle, bring to pass, bring about; produce, create, set up, develop; found, broach, institute; induce, evoke, elicit, draw, provoke; determine, decide; conduce to, contribute, have a hand in, influence, effect.

adj causal, generative, productive, formative, creative; primal, primary, original, embryonic.

adv because.

154 effect *n* consequence, issue, derivation, upshot, outgrowth, development, fruit, crop, harvest, product, outcome, end, conclusion; offspring, offshoot; complications, concomitants, side effects.

v be the effect of, be due to, be owing to; originate in, originate from, rise from, spring from, proceed from, emanate from, come from, grow from, issue from, flow from, result from; depend upon, hinge upon.

adj owing to, resulting from, due to, derivable from, caused by; derived from, evolved from; derivative, hereditary.

adv consequently, as a consequence, necessarily.

155 [assignment of cause] **attribution** *n* theory, ascription, assignment, rationale, reference to, accounting for; imputation, derivation; explanation, interpretation, reason why.

v attribute to, ascribe to, impute to, refer to, point to, trace to, assign to; account for, derive from; theorize, speculate.

adj attributed, attributable, referable, due to, owing to.

adv hence, thence, therefore, *ergo*, for, since, on account of, because; why? wherefore? whence? how come? how so?

156 [absence of assignable cause] **chance** *n* fortune, fate, accident, hap, hazard, luck, fluke, (*informal*) freak; gamble, lottery, tossup, fifty-fifty chance, throw of the dice, heads or tails; probability, possibility, contingency, odds; speculation, gaming, gambling.

v chance, hap, turn up; fall to one's lot; stumble on, light on; take one's chances.

adj chancy, causal, fortuitous, accidental, (*informal*) iffy, adventitious, haphazard, random, indeterminate, flukey, (*informal*) freaky.

adv by chance, by accident; at random; perchance, as chance will have it.

157 power *n* potency, strength, puissance, might, force, energy, vigor; control, command, dominion, authority, rule, sway, ascendancy, sovereignty, omnipotence; ability, capability, capacity, facility, competence, competency, efficacy; validity, cogency.

v be powerful, control, command, rule; confer power, empower, invest, endow; arm, strengthen, authorize; compel, force.

adj powerful, potent, strong, mighty, energetic; able, capable, competent, efficacious, equal to, up to, effective, efficient, adequate; omnipotent, almighty; influential, forceful.

adv powerfully.

prep by virtue of, by dint of.

158 impotence *n* inability, incapability, incapacity, infirmity, debility, disability; inefficacy, inefficiency, incompetence, ineptitude. feebleness, weakness, frailty, powerlessness; helplessness, prostration, paralysis, collapse, exhaustion; decrepitude, senility; sexual failure, barrenness.

v be impotent; collapse, faint, swoon, drop; render powerless, disable, disarm, incapacitate, disqualify, invalidate; cramp, tie the hands, paralyze, muzzle, cripple, maim, laim, hamstring, throttle, strangle, tie up in knots; unman, unnerve, enervate; shatter, exhaust, weaken; emasculate.

adj impotent, powerless, incapable, unable, incompetent, ineffective, inefficient, ineffectual, inept, unfit, unfitted, unqualified; disabled, incapacitated, crippled, paralyzed, paralytic; decrepit, senile, exhausted, worn out, used up, limp, spent; weak, frail, infirm, feeble, helpless; harmless; sterile, barren, frigid; emasculated, inadequate, inoperative; futile, fruitless, bootless, vain.

159 strength *n* power, force, might, vigor, health, stoutness, hardiness, lustihood, stamina, energy, potency, capacity; spring, bounce, tone, elasticity, tension; virility, vitality, nerve, verve; strengthening, invigoration, refreshment.

v strengthen, invigorate, brace, nerve, fortify, sustain, harden, steel; vivify, revivify, refresh, reinforce, restore.

adj strong, mighty, vigorous, forceful, hard, stout, robust, sturdy, hardy, powerful, potent, puissant; irresistible, invincible, indomitable, unconquerable, impregnable, inextinguishable incontestable; able-bodied, athletic, muscular, sinewy, strapping, gigantic, Herculean.

adv strongly, by force.

160 weakness *n* debility, relaxation, languor, enervation; impotence, infirmity, fragility, flaccidity; frailty, delicacy, softness; senility, decrepitude.

v be weak, drop, crumble, give way, teeter, totter, tremble, shake, halt, limp, fade, languish, decline, flag, fail; weaken, enfeeble, cramp, debilitate, shake, enervate, unnerve; relax; dilute, water down.

adj weak, feeble, infirm, sickly; languid, faint, dull, slack, spent; limp, flaccid, powerless, impotent; relaxed, unstrung, unnerved; frail, fragile, delicate, flimsy; rickety, drooping, teetering, tottering, withered, shaky, shattered; palsied, decrepit, lame; decayed, rotten, worn, seedy, wasted, laid low.

161 production *n* creation, formation, fabrication, construction, manufacture; building, architecture, erection; organization, establishment, workmanship, craftsmanship, performance; achievement, product, end result; flowering, fructification, fruition, fulfillment; gestation, evolution, development, growth; genesis, generation, procreation; authorship, publication, works, *oeuvre*.

v produce, perform, operate, do, make, form, construct, fabricate, frame, contrive, manufacture; build, raise, rear, erect, put up; set up, establish, constitute, compose, organize, institute; achieve, accomplish, fulfill; bud, flower, blossom, bloom, bear fruit, bring forth; propagate, beget, generate, procreate, engender; breed, hatch, develop, bring up; induce, cause.

adj productive, constructive, formative, creative; generative; prolific, blooming.

162 [nonproduction] **destruction** *n* waste, dissolution, breaking up, disruption; consumption; fall, downfall, ruin, perdition; breakdown, wreck, wrack, havoc, mess, chaos, cataclysm; desolation, extinction, annihilation, demolition; overthrow, subversion, suppression; dilapidation, devastation, road to ruin.

v perish, fall, tumble, topple, fall to pieces, break up, crumble, go to the dogs, go to wrack and ruin; destroy, do away with, demolish, tear up, overturn, overthrow, wipe out, (*informal*) waste; upset, subvert, undo; waste, squander, dissipate, dispel, dissolve; smash, squash, squelch, shatter, crumble, batter, crush, pull to pieces; fell, sink, scuttle, wreck, swamp, ruin, raze, level, expunge, erase, sweep away; lay waste, ravage, gut; disorganize, dismantle, take apart; devour, devastate,

desolate, sap, exterminate, extinguish, stamp out, trample out, crush out, eradicate.

adj destructive, subversive, ruinous, incendiary, deadly, lethal, fatal; destroyed, wiped out, extinct.

163 reproduction *n* renovation, restoration, renewal, revival, regeneration, revivification, resuscitation, reanimation, resurrection; reappearance; generation, childbirth.

v reproduce, renovate, restore, renew, revive, regenerate, revivify, resuscitate, breathe new life into, reanimate, refashion, resurrect, bring back to life; give birth to, multiply, people the world.

adj reproductive; regenerative, restorative; renascent, reappearing, resurgent.

164 producer *n* originator, inventor, author, founder, generator, mover, creator, maker, architect; backer, angel.

165 destroyer *n* spoiler, waster, ravager, wrecker, killer, assassin, executioner; cankerworm, bane; iconoclast, rebel, pessimist, cynic, nihilist, misanthrope.

166 parentage *n* family, ancestry, lineage, genealogy; procreator, progenitor.

paternity: fatherhood, fathership; father, dad, pop, sire, papa, (*informal*) old man; grandfather, grandsire.

maternity: motherhood; mother, mom, ma, mamma, mummy, mum, (*informal*) old lady; grandmother.

adj parental, familial, ancestral, lineal, paternal, maternal; patriarchal, matriarchal.

167 posterity *n* progeny, breed, issue, offspring, brood, litter, family, children, grandchildren, heirs; child, son, daughter; descendant, heir, scion, (*informal*) chip off the old block; heredity.

adj filial.

168 productiveness *n* fecundity, fertility, fruitfulness, productivity; multiplication, propagation, procreation; creativity, inventiveness, originality.

v make productive, fructify, fulfill; procreate, generate, conceive, impregnate, fertilize; teem, multiply, produce, reproduce.

adj productive, prolific, fruitful, copious; teeming, fertile, fecund; procreative, generative, life-giving.

169 unproductiveness *n* infertility, sterility, barrenness, unfruitfulness, impotence; unprofitableness, wastefulness.

v be unproductive, do nothing, produce nothing, come to nothing.

adj unproductive, unfruitful, infertile, barren, sterile, arid; unprofitable, useless.

170 agency *n* operation, force, working, function, office, maintenance, exercise, work, play; causation, instigation, instrumentality, influence.

v operate, work, do; act, perform, play, support, sustain, maintain, take effect, quicken, strike; come into play, have free play; bring to bear upon, influence.

adj operative, efficient, efficacious, effectual, practical; at work, on foot, in operation, in force, in play, in action.

adv through the agency of, by means of.

171 energy *n* force, power, strength, intensity, vigor, zeal, dynamism, pep, fire, spirit, ebullience, life; activity, agitation, exertion, effervescence, ferment, fermentation, ebullition, bustle.

v give energy, energize, stimulate, kindle, excite, inflame, exert; strengthen, invigorate; sharpen, intensify.

adj energetic, strong, forcible, potent, forceful, active, powerful, intense, vigorous, zealous, dynamic, ebullient, spirited, animated, keen, vivid, sharp, acute, incisive, trenchant, biting; invigorating, rousing, stimulating; energized.

172 inertness *n* inertia, inactivity, torpor, languor, dullness, immobility, passivity, passiveness, lifelessness; quiescence, latency; inexcitability, sloth, indolence, irresolution, indecisiveness, cowardice, spinelessness.

v be inert, be inactive.

adj inert, inactive, immobile, unmoving, motionless, lifeless, passive, dead; sluggish, dull, heavy, flat, slack, tame, slow, blunt, torpid, languid; latent, dormant, sleeping, smoldering, quiescent.

adv in suspense, in abeyance.

173 violence *n* vehemence, fury, ferocity, impetuosity, boisterousness, turbulence, ebullition, effervescence,

intensity, severity, acuteness; energy, force, might; fit, paroxysm, orgasm, spasm, convulsion, throe; exacerbation, exasperation, hysterics, excitability, passion; outbreak, outburst, uproar, riot, explosion, blow-up, blast, eruption; turmoil, disorder, ferment, agitation, storm, tempest; destruction, brutality, fighting, combat, warfare, hostilities; injury, wrong, outrage, injustice.

v be violent, ferment, effervesce; romp, rampage, run wild, run riot, rush, tear, run headlong, run amuck, go wild, kick up a row, (*informal*) flip out, go beserk; bluster, rage, roar, riot, storm, boil, boil over, fume, foam; explode, go off, detonate, thunder, blow up, flare, burst; render violent, sharpen, stir up, quicken, excite, incite, urge, lash, whip up, stimulate; irritate, inflame, kindle, accelerate, aggravate, exasperate, exacerbate, convulse, infuriate, madden, fan the fire, whip into a frenzy.

adj violent, vehement, acute, sharp; rough, rude, bluff, boisterous, brusque, abrupt, wild, impetuous, rampant; disorderly, turbulent, blustering, raging, riotous, tumultuous, obstreperous; raving, frenzied, (*informal*) freaked, mad, unhinged, insane; desperate, furious, frantic, hysterical; savage, fierce, ferocious, physical, brutal, combative; uncontrollable, ungovernable, irrepressible, excited; spasmodic, convulsive, orgasmic; explosive, volcanic, stormy.

adv violently; by storm, by force.

174 moderation *n* temperateness, temperance, reasonableness, judiciousness, deliberateness, fairness; gentleness, mildness, calmness, peacefulness; quiet, calm, composure; lenity, lenience; relaxation, assuagement, tranquilization, pacification, mitigation; measure, middle ground, middle of the road.

v moderate, ally, meliorate, calm, pacify, assuage, lull, smooth, compose, still, calm, quiet, hush, sober, mitigate, soften, mollify, temper, qualify, alleviate, appease, lessen, abate, diminish; slake, curb, tame; arbitrate, referee, umpire, regulate.

adj moderate, temperate, reasonable, judicious, deliberate, fair, gentle, mild, calm, cool, sober, measured, unruffled, quiet, tranquil, still, peaceful, pacific; unexciting, even, smooth, bland, palliative; lenient, relaxed, easy going.

adv moderately, in moderation, within reason.

175 influence *n* importance, weight, pressure, preponderance, prevalence, sway; predominance, ascendancy; dominance, reign, rule, authority, power, control, capability; input, (*informal*) say, persuasion, play, leverage, vantage ground; patronage, protection, auspices.

v be influential, have a say, have input, carry weight, affect, sway, impress, bias, direct, control; move, activate, incite, impel, rouse, arouse, induce, persuade; dominate, predominate, outweigh, override, prevail.

adj influential, important, weighty; prevalent, rife, rampant, dominant, predominant; potent, powerful, effective, authoritative.

175a absence of influence *n* impotence, powerlessness; unimportance, irrelevancy.

adj uninfluential, unpersuasive, weak, impotent, (*informal*) wishy-washy.

176 tendency *n* aptness, aptitude, disposition, predisposition, proclivity, proneness, propensity, susceptibility, inclination, leaning, bias, drift, trend, bent, turn; quality, nature, temperament; idiosyncrasy, cast, vein, mood, humor.

v tend, contribute, conduce, lead, dispose, incline, verge, bend to, gravitate toward, lean, drift, tend, affect; promote, influence.

adj tending, leaning, conducive, working toward, in a fair way to; liable, likely; influential, instrumental, useful, subsidiary, subservient.

177 liability *n* susceptibility, penchant, vulnerability, predilection, propensity, tendency, drawback, hindrance, obstacle, difficulty, impediment; responsibility, obligation, debt, debit, indebtedness, pledge.

v be liable, incur, lay oneself open to, run the risk of, stand a chance, expose oneself to.

adj liable, subject, exposed, likely, open, in danger of; obliged, responsible, accountable, answerable; contingent, incidental, possible.

178 concurrence *n* accordance, accord, agreement, consent, assent; cooperation, collaboration, partnership;

alliance, concert, union.

v concur, conduce, conspire, contribute; agree, unite, combine, hang together, pull together, cooperate, collaborate; keep pace with, run parallel, go hand in hand with.

adj concurrent, cooperative, collaborative, joint, allied with, of one mind, at one with, in concert with.

179 counteraction *n* opposition, antagonism, contrariety, polarity; clashing, collision, interference, resistance, friction; reaction, response, counterblast, counter maneuver; neutralization, check, curb, hindrance; repression, restraint.

v counteract, run counter to, clash, cross, interfere with, conflict with; jostle, run up against, oppose, antagonize, withstand, resist, hinder, impede, check, curb, repress, restrain; recoil, react; neutralize, nullify, cancel out, undercut, undermine, undo; counterpoise, offset, balance out, compensate.

adj counteracting, antagonistic, conflicting, contrary, reactionary.

adv although.

prep in spite of, against.

Class II
Words Relating to Space
I. Space in General

180 [indefinite space] **space** *n* extension, extent, expanse, span, stretch, scope, range, latitude, spread, proportions, sweep, capacity, play, swing, expansion; elbowroom, room, breathing space, leeway; open space(s), free space, waste, desert, wild, wilderness; unlimited space, wide world, heavens, universe, solar system, outer space, abyss, the void, infinity.

adj spacious, roomy, extensive, expansive, capacious, ample; widespread, vast, worldwide, boundless, limitless, unlimited, infinite.

adv extensively, far and wide, right and left, from the four corners of the world, all over, from pole to pole, under the sun, on the face of the earth, from all points of the compass, to the four winds.

180a inextension *n* nonextension, point, atom.

181 [definite space] **region** *n* sphere, ground, soil, area, realm, quarter, orb, hemisphere, circuit, circle; domain, tract, territory, country, county, province; clime, climate, zone, meridian, latitude.

adj regional, provincial, territorial.

182 [limited space] **place** *n* spot, point; niche, nook, hole, pigeonhole; locality; locale, situation.

adv somewhere, in some place, here and there, in various places.

183 situation *n* position, locality, locale, latitude and longitude, location; footing, standing, standpoint; aspect, attitude, posture, perspective, pose; place, site, station, post, predicament, whereabouts; bearings, direction; topography, geography; map, chart.

v be situated, be located, lie, have its seat in; situate, locate.

adj situated, located; local, topical, topographical.

adv here and there, hereabouts, thereabouts, in such and such a place.

184 location *n* place, situation; establishment, settlement, installation; anchorage, mooring, encampment.

v locate, place, situate, put, lay, set, make a place for, seat; station, lodge, quarter, house, post, install; establish, fix, settle, root; graft, plant; inhabit, domesticate, colonize, take root, establish roots, come to rest, settle down, take up quarters, locate oneself, relocate; squat, perch, bivouac, burrow, get a footing, encamp.

adj located, placed, ensconced, rooted, settled, moored.

185 displacement *n* dislocation, misplacement, derangement, transposition; ejection, expulsion, banishment, removal, exile.

v displace, dislodge, disestablish; misplace, disturb, disorder, unsettle, derange, confuse; transpose, set aside, transfer, remove, unload, empty, eject, expel, banish, exile; vacate, depart, leave.

adj displaced; unplaced, unhoused, unsettled, unestablished; homeless, out of place, misplaced, out of its element.

186 presence *n* attendance, company; occupancy, occupation; ubiquity, omnipresence, permeation, pervasion, pervasiveness, diffusion, dispersion; nearness, vicinity, proximity, closeness.

v be present; look on, attend, stand by, remain, find oneself, occupy, inhabit, dwell, stay, sojourn, live, abide, lodge, nestle, roost, perch, tenant; fill, pervade, permeate, run through.

adj present, attending; occupying, inhabiting, resident, moored; ubiquitous, omnipresent, pervasive, diffused; near, close, in proximity.

adv here, there, and everywhere; in presence of.

187 absence *n* nonappearance, nonattendance, absenteeism, nonresidence; emptiness, void, vacuum, vacancy, vacuity.

v be absent; keep away, play truant, absent oneself, stay away.

adj absent, not present, away, out, not here, not in, not present, off; wanting, lacking, missing, nonexistent; vacant, empty, void, vacuous, devoid.

adv without, minus, nowhere, *sans*; elsewhere.

188 inhabitant *n* resident, dweller, occupant, tenant, inmate, boarder, lodger; native, townsman, villager, citizen; population, community, society, state, people, race, nation.

v inhabit, live, reside, dwell.

adj indigenous, native, domestic.

189 habitation *n* abode, residence, domicile, lodging, dwelling, address, habitation, housing, quarters; home, homestead, motherland, fatherland, country; nest, lair, den, cave, hole, hiding place, cell, hive, haunt, habitat, perch, roost, retreat, (*informal*) pad, (*informal*) crashpad.

v inhabit, take up one's abode.

190 [things contained] **contents** *n* stuffing, cargo, lading, freight, shipment, haul, load, bale, burden.

v load, lade, ship, haul, charge, fill, stuff.

191 receptacle *n* container, holder, repository, vessel, receiver, depository, reservoir; storage areas; bulk containers; liquid containers; wrapping.

II. Dimensions

192 size *n* proportions, dimensions, magnitude, bulk, volume; largeness, greatness, expanse, amplitude, mass; capacity, tonnage; corpulence, obesity, plumpness, hugeness, enormousness, immensity; monstrosity, enormity; giant, monster, mammoth, behemoth, leviathan, elephant; lump, bulk, block, mass, clod, thumper, whopper, strapper, (*informal*) mother, mountain, mound, heap.

v be large, become large, expand.

adj sizable, large, big, great, considerable, bulky, voluminous, ample, massive, massy, capacious, comprehensive, spacious, mighty, towering, magnificent; corpulent, stout, fat, plump, obese, portly, full-grown, stalwart, brawny, hulky, unwieldy, bulky, lumpish, whopping, thundering, thumping, overgrown; huge, immense, enormous, mighty, vast, amplitudinous, stupendous, monstrous, gigantic, colossal.

193 littleness *n* smallness, diminutiveness, tininess; epitome, microcosm; vanishing point.

v be little, become little, decrease.

adj little, small, minute, diminutive, microscopic, submicroscopic; tiny, puny, wee, miniature, pigmy, dwarf, undersized, underdeveloped, dwarfish, stunted, dumpy, squat; imperceptible, invisible, infinitesimal.

194 expansion *n* increase, enlargement, extension, growth, development; augmentation, aggrandizement, increment, amplification; spreading, swelling, distention, puffiness, dropsy.

v expand, widen, enlarge, extend, grow, increase, swell, fill out; dilate, stretch, spread; bud, sprout, shoot, germinate, open, burst forth; outgrow, overrun; spread, extend, aggrandize; distend, develop, amplify, spread out, magnify; inflate, puff up, blow up, stuff, pad, cram, fatten, exaggerate.

adj expanded, larger; swollen, expansive, widespread, overgrown, exaggerated, bloated, fat, turgid, tumid, dropsical; pot-bellied, chubby, corpulent, obese, heavy; full-blown, full-grown.

195 contraction *n* reduction, diminution; decrease, lessening, shrinking; collapse; emancipation, attenuation, atrophy; condensation, compression, compactness, compendium, squeezing.

v contract, become small, lessen, decrease, dwindle, shrink, narrow, shrivel, collapse, wither, wizen, fall away, waste, wane, ebb, decay, deteriorate; diminish, contract, draw in, constrict, condense, compress, sque-

eze, crush, crumple up, pinch, squash, cramp; pare, reduce, attenuate, scrape, file, grind, chip, shave, shear, cut down; circumscribe, limit, restrain, confine.
adj contracting, astringent; shrunk, shrunken, contracted; wizened, stunted, waning; compact.

196 distance *n* remoteness, farness, background, offing, far cry to, horizon, elongation; interval, remove, gap, span, reach, range; outpost, outskirts, foreign parts.
v be distant; extend to, stretch to, reach to, spread to; range.
adj distant, far off, far away, remote, far, afar, outlying, removed, at a distance, away, yonder, yon; inaccessible, out of the way, unapproachable.
adv far off, far away, afar, away, a long way off.

197 nearness *n* closeness, propinquity, proximity, proximation; vicinity, neighborhood, contiguity; short distance, earshot, close quarters, stone's throw, gunshot, hair's breadth; approach, access.
v be near, adjoin, neighbor, border upon, touch, stand next to; approximate, come close to, resemble; converge, crowd.
adj near, nigh, close, neighboring, adjoining, adjacent, bordering; proximate, approximate; at hand, handy; intimate.
adv near, nigh, hard by, close to, close upon, within reach, at one's fingertips.

198 interval *n* separation, space, break, gap, caesura, interspace, interstice, distance; hiatus, skip, division, opening; pause, recess, interim, respite, interlude, interregnum, interruption, term, spell, period; cleft, crevice, chink, cranny, crack, slit, fissure, rift, flaw, breach, rent, gash, cut, leak; ditch, dike, gorge, ravine, abyss, gulf.
v gape, open; intervene, interrupt.

199 contiguity *n* contact, contiguousness, proximity, apposition, juxtaposition, touching, abutment, meeting.
v be contiguous, join, adjoin, abut on, border, touch, meet, graze, adhere; coincide, coexist.
adj contiguous, touching, in contact, end to end; close, near.

200 length *n* distance, extent, longitude, span, reach, range; lengthiness, elongation, size; duration, continuance, term, period.
v be long, stretch out, sprawl; extend to, reach to, stretch to; lengthen, stretch, elongate, extend; prolong, protract, draw out, spin out.
adj long, lengthy, extended, outstretched; lengthened, interminable; linear, lineal, longitudinal; tall, stringy, protracted, lanky.
adv lengthwise, at length, longitudinally.

201 shortness *n* brevity, littleness; shortening, abridgment, abbreviation, conciseness, condensation; retrenchment, curtailment, reduction.
v be short; shorten, abridge, abbreviate, condense, compact, compress, epitomize; retrench, cut short, reduce, pare down, clip back, cut back, prune, shear, shave, crop, chop up, hack up, truncate.
adj short, brief, curt; compendious, compact, compressed, condensed; stubby, stunted, stumpy, squat, dumpy; concise, pointed; curtailed, cut back, reduced, shortened, abbreviated, abridged.

202 breadth. thickness *n* breadth, width, latitude, amplitude, extent, diameter.
thickness, density, denseness, heaviness, bulk, body.
v be broad; expand, widen. be thick; thicken.
adj broad, wide, ample, extended, expansive, large; outspread, outstretched.
thick, dense, heavy, bulky, solid, compact; dumpy, squat, thickset.

203 narrowness. thinness *n* narrowness, slenderness, exiguity, closeness, straitness, scantiness, slightness, slimness.
thinness, slenderness, slimness, leanness, lankness, meagerness, skinniness.
v be narrow; narrow, taper. be thin; thin, slenderize, slim; dilute, water down.
adj narrow, close, slender, thin, fine, threadlike, slim, delicate; restricted, confined, limited; thin, emaciated, lean, skinny, meager, gaunt, spindly, lanky, scrawny, haggard, pinched, skeletal, wasted; frail, unsound, fragile; weak, shrill, faint, feeble; watery, waterish, diluted, unsubstantial.

204 layer *n* stratum, substratum, bed, zone, floor, stage, story, tier, slab, tablet, board, sheet, platter; scale, coat, peel, membrane, film, leaf, slice.
v slice, shave, pare, peel; plate, coat, veneer; cover; layer.
adj layered, stratified, tiered; scaly, filmy, membranous, flaky.

205 filament *n* thread, fiber, strand, hair, cilia, tendril, gossamer, wire, strand, vein.
adj fibrous, threadlike, wiry, stringy, ropy; capillary.

206 height *n* altitude, stature, elevation, tallness; prominence, eminence, pre-eminence, loftiness, sublimity; top, peak, pinnacle, acme, summit, zenith, culmination.
v tower, soar, hover, cap, command; mount, bestride, surmount, overhang; heighten, elevate, raise up, rise up.
adj high, tall, elevated, towering, skyscraping, gigantic, huge, colossal; distinguished, prominent, eminent, pre-eminent, exalted, lofty, sublime; overhanging, overlying.

207 lowness *n* depression, debasement, prostration; flatness, proneness; lowlands, flatlands.
v be low; lie low, lie flat, crouch, slouch, wallow, grovel; underlie; lower, depress.
adj low, flat, level, low-lying; crouched, squat, prone, supine, prostrate, depressed; groveling, abject, sordid, mean, base, lowly, degraded, debased, ignoble, vile.
adv under, beneath, underneath, below, down, downward; underfoot, underground; downstairs, belowstairs.

208 depth *n* deepness, profundity, obscurity; depression, bottom, unfathomable space; pit, hollow, shaft, well, crater, chasm, abyss, bottomless pit; central part, midst, middle, bosom, womb, base, heart, core; soundings, draft, submersion, dive.
v deepen, hollow, plunge, sink, dig, excavate; sound, have the lead, take soundings.
adj deep, deep-seated, profound, mysterious, obscure, unfathomable; sunk, buried, submerged; bottomless, soundless, fathomless, unfathomed, abysmal, yawning, gaping.
adv beyond one's depth, out of one's depth, over one's head.

209 shallowness *n* superficiality, banality, triviality, frivolity, flimsiness, emptiness, vacancy; shallow, shoal, sand bar.
adj shallow, superficial, slight, cursory, trivial, banal, trashy, flimsy, substanceless, empty, vacuous, vacant; skin-deep, ankle-deep, knee-deep.

210 summit *n* top, peak, apex, pinnacle, vertex, acme, culmination, zenith; height, pitch, maximum, climax; crowning point, turning point, watershed.
v culminate, climax, crown, top.
adj highest, top, topmost, uppermost, tiptop; capital, head, polar; supreme, supernal.

211 base *n* bottom, stand, rest, pedestal, dado, understructure, substructure, foot, basis, foundation, ground, groundwork; principle, touchstone, fundamental part, element, ingredient; bottom, nadir, foot, sole, heel.
adj bottom, undermost, nethermost; fundamental, basic, elemental; based on, founded on, grounded on, built on; base, vile, venal.

212 verticality *n* perpendicularity, erectness; wall, precipice, cliff.
v be vertical, stand up straight, stand upright, stand erect, stand straight and tall.
adj vertical, upright, erect, perpendicular, straight, bolt upright, plumb.
adv vertically, on end, endwise.

213 horizontality *n* flatness; level, plane, stratum; horizon; recumbency, lying down, reclination, proneness, supination, prostration.
v be horizontal, lie, recline, lie down, lie flat, sprawl; render horizontal, flatten, level, prostrate, knock down, floor, fell.
adj horizontal, level, even, plane, flat, smooth; prone, supine, prostrate.
adv horizontally, on one's back.

214 suspension *n* hanging down, free swinging; pendant, tail, train, flap, pendulum.
v suspend, hang, swing, dangle; flap, trail, flow; depend.
adj suspended, pendent, hanging, swinging, dangling, pendulous; dependent.

215 support *n* foundation, base, basis, ground, footing, hold; supporter, prop, brace, stay, rib, truss, stalk, stilts, splint; bar, rod, boom, outrigger; staff, stick, crutch; bracket, ledge, shelf, trestle, buttress.
v support, bear, carry, hold, sustain, shoulder, bolster; shore up, hold up, prop up, brace; help, aid, maintain, sustain; base, found, ground.
adj supporting, supported; fundamental.

216 parallelism *n* coextension; comparison, affinity, correspondence, semblance, likeness, resemblance, analogy, equation.
v parallel, compare, relate, associate, connect, correspond to, equate.
adj parallel, coextensive, collateral, aligned, equal; like, similar, allied, corresponding, correlative, analogous, equivalent.

217 obliquity *n* incline, inclination, slope, slant, leaning, tilt, list, bend, curve; acclivity, rise, ascent, grade, rising ground, hill, bank; declivity, decline, downhill, dip, fall; steepness.
v be oblique, slope, slant, lean, incline, stoop, decline, descend; bend, careen, slouch, sidle; render oblique, sway, bias, slant, warp, incline, bend, crook, tilt, distort.
adj oblique, inclined; sloping, tilted; askew, asquint, awry, crooked; uphill, rising, ascending; downhill, falling, descending; declining, declivitous; steep, abrupt, sharp, precipitous; diagonal, transverse.
adv obliquely, on one side; askew, askance, edgewise, at an angle; sidelong, sideways, slantwise.

218 inversion *n* subversion, reversion, contraposition, transposition, transposal, conversion; contrariety, contradiction, opposition, polarity, antithesis; reversal, overturn, somersault, turn of the tide, revulsion, revolution.
v be inverted, turn about, wheel about, go about, turn over, go over, tilt over; invert, subvert, reverse, overturn, upturn, upset, turn topsy-turvy; transpose.
adj inverted, inside out, wrong side out, upside down, topsy-turvy; inverse, reverse, obverse, opposite.
adv inversely.

219 crossing *n* intersection, grade crossing, crossroad, interchange; network, reticulation; net, netting, network, web, mesh, wicker, lace; mat, matting, plait, trellis, lattice, grating, grille, gridiron, tracery, fretwork, filigree; knot, entanglement.
v cross, intersect, interlace, intertwine, interweave, interlink, crisscross; twine, intwine, weave, twist, wreathe; dovetail, splice, link, link up; mat, plait, plat, braid; tangle, entangle, ravel; net, knot, twist.
adj crossing; crossed, matted, transverse; weaved, woven, intertwined, interlaced.

220 exteriority *n* outside, exterior; surface, superficies; covering, skin, face, appearance, façade, aspect, facet.
v be exterior, lie around, encircle.
adj exterior, external, outer, outside, outward, superficial; outlying, extraneous, foreign, extrinsic.
adv externally, out, over, outwards.

221 interiority *n* interior, inside, inner part, center, interspace; subsoil, substratum, contents, substance, pith, marrow, backbone, heart, bowels, belly, guts, lap, womb; recesses, innermost recesses, hollows, nook, niche, cave.
v be interior, be inside; inclose, circumscribe; intern; embed, insert.
adj interior, internal, inside, inner, inward, inmost, innermost; deep-seated, inlaid, embedded, ingrained, innate, inherent, intrinsic, inborn; private, secret, intimate, confidential; home, domestic.
adv internally; inward, within, indoors, withindoors.

222 centrality *n* center, middle, midst; core, kernel, nucleus, heart, pole, axis, pivot, navel, nub, hub; centralization; center of gravity.
v be central; centralize, concentrate; focus on, bring into focus, get to the heart of.
adj central, middle, pivotal, focal, concentric; middlemost.
adv centrally; middle, midst.

223 covering *n* cover; canopy, awning, tent, marquee; umbrella, parasol, sunshade; shade, screen, shield; roof, ceiling, thatch, shed; top, lid; bandage, wrappings; coverlet, blanket, sheet, quilt, tarpaulin; skin, fleece, fur, hide; clothing, mask; peel, crust, bark, rind; veneer, coating, facing, varnish.
v cover, superimpose, overlay, overspread; wrap, encase, face, case, veneer, paper; conceal, cover over.
adj covered, clothed, wrapped; protected.

224 lining *n* inner coating, coating; filling, stuffing, padding, wadding.
v line, stuff, wad, pad, fill; coat, incrust, face, cover.
adj lined.

225 dress *n* clothing, covering, raiment, drapery, costume, attire, garb, apparel, wardrobe, outfit, clothes; equipment, livery, gear, rigging, trappings, togs, accouterments; uniforms, regimentals, suit.
v dress, clothe, drape, robe, array, fit out, deck out, garb, rig out, apparel; equip, harness, outfit, uniform; cover, wrap, wrap up, sheathe, swathe, swaddle.
adj dressed, clothed, clad, invested.

226 undress *n* nudity, nakedness, bareness, dishabille.
v undress, uncover, divest, expose, disrobe, strip, bare, doff, peel, take off, put off, lay open.
adj undressed, nude, naked, bare, stark-naked, exposed, in the buff, *au naturel*, in the altogether, in one's birthday suit; undressed, unclad, undraped, disrobed.

227 environment *n* environs, surroundings, outskirts, suburbs, purlieus, precincts, neighborhood.
v environ, surround, encompass, compass, inclose, enclose, circle, encircle, gird, twine round, hem in.
adj surrounding, circumjacent.
adv around, about; without; on every side, on all sides, right and left, every which way.

228 interspersion *n* interjacence, interlocation, interpenetration, permeation; interjection, interpolation, interlineation, intercalation; intervention, interference, interposition, intrusion; insinuation; insertion.
v intervene, come between, get between, interpenetrate; intersperse, permeate, introduce, throw in, work in, interpose, interject, interpolate, insert; interfere, intrude, obtrude.
adj intervening, interjacent; parenthetical, episodic; intrusive.
adv between, betwixt, among, amid, amongst; in the thick of, betwixt and between; parenthetically.

229 circumscription *n* limitation, enclosure; confinement, restraint.
v circumscribe, limit, bound, confine, inclose; surround, hedge in, fence in, wall in; imprison, restrain; enfold, bury, incase.
adj circumscribed, confined, restrained, imprisoned; buried in, immersed in, embosomed, embedded.

230 outline *n* circumference, perimeter, periphery; circuit, lines, contour, profile, silhouette.
v outline, draw, sketch, trace, profile.

231 edge *n* frame, fringe, trimming, trim, edging, skirting, hem; verge, brink, brim, lip, margin, border, skirt, rim, mouth; threshold, door, porch, portal; coast, shore.
v edge, skirt, border; trim, hem.

232 enclosure *n* envelope, case, wrapper; girdle; pen, fence, fold, cote, corral, stockyard, paddock, yard, pound, compound; fence, pale, paling, balustrade, rail, railing; hedge; wall, barrier, barricade; gate, gateway, door, doorway; boundary, border.
v enclose, circumscribe.

233 limit *n* boundary, bounds, extent, confine, term, pale, verge; termination, terminus; frontier, marches, outer edges, unknown; boundary line, border, edge; turning point, flood gate.
v limit, restrain, restrict, confine, check, hinder, bound, circumscribe, define.
adj limited, definite; terminal.
adv thus far, only so far, thus far and no further.

234 front *n* forefront, foreground, lead; face, frontage, façade, frontispiece, proscenium; vanguard, front rank, first rank, head of the column, advanced guard.
v front, face, confront; be in front, stand in front; come to the front.
adj fore, foremost; front, frontal, anterior, forward.
adv before, in front, in advance; ahead, right ahead, in the foreground; in the lead.

235 rear *n* back, background, rearguard, rear rank; distance, hinterland; rump, buttocks, posterior, rear, backside, hindquarters; wake, train; reverse, other side of the coin, (*informal*) flipside.
v be behind, bring up the rear; rear, bring up, nurture, raise; elevate, lift, loft, lift up, hold up; build, put up, erect.
adj rear, back, hindmost; posterior.
adv behind, in the rear, in the background, at the heels; after, aft, rearward.

236 side *n* laterality, flank, quarter, lee, hand; cheek, jowl, shoulder; profile, lee side, broadside.
v be on the side; be side by side, be cheek to cheek; flank, skirt, outflank, sidle.
adj sidelong, lateral; flanking, skirting; flanked.
adv sideways, sidelong; broadside, on one side, abreast, alongside, beside, side by side, cheek by jowl; laterally.

237 opposition *n* opposite, contraposition, opposite side, opposite poles, polarity, antithesis, reverse, inverse; counterpart, companion piece, complement.
v be opposite; stand as opposites, oppose.
adj opposite, reverse, inverse, converse; antipodal, antithetical, countering, opposing; fronting, facing, diametrically opposite; complementary.
adv over, over the way, over against; poles apart; face to face.

238 right *n* right hand, right side; offside, starboard.
adj right-handed, dextral.

239 left *n* left hand, left side; near side, port.
adj left-handed, sinistral.

III. Form

240 form *n* shape, outline, mold, appearance, cast, cut, configuration; make, formation, frame, construction, cut, set, build, trim; mold, model, pattern; posture, attitude, convention, rule, formality, formula, ceremony, conformity.
v form, shape, figure, fashion, carve, cut, chisel, hew, cast; shape, model, mold, fashion, cast, construct, build; stamp, cast, type.
adj formal, ceremonial, ceremonious, conventional; regular, set, fixed, stiff, rigid.

241 formlessness *n* shapelessness, amorphism, asymmetry; disorder, chaos; misproportion, deformity, disfigurement, defacement, mutilation, truncation.
v deface, disfigure, deform, mutilate, truncate.
adj formless, shapeless, amorphous, asymmetrical, unformed, unshaped, unfashioned, unshapely, misshapen, out of proportion, disordered, chaotic; rough, rude, coarse, barbarous, rugged.

242 [regularity of form] **symmetry** *n* shapeliness, finish, comeliness, gracefulness, grace, beauty; proportion, uniformity, parallelism; regularity, evenness, balance, order, harmony, agreement.
adj symmetrical, shapely, well set, finished; beautiful, lovely; classic, classical, formal, chaste, severe; regular, uniform, balanced, harmonious, ordered; even, parallel, equal.

243 [irregularity of form] **distortion** *n* contortion, warp, buckle, screw, twist; crookedness, obliquity; deformity, malformation, misproportion, disfigurement, monstrosity, ugliness; asymmetry.
v distort, contort, warp, buckle, screw, twist, wrest; writhe, grimace, make faces; deform, disfigure, misshape.
adj distorted, out of shape, irregular, unsymmetrical, awry, askew, crooked; not true, not straight, uneven; misshapen, ill-made, ill-fashioned, ill-proportioned, malformed, deformed.

244 angularity *n* bifurcation, bend, fork, crook, notch, angle; elbow, knee, knuckle, crotch; right angle, acute angle, obtuse angle; corner, nook, niche, recess.
v angle, tilt, bend, fork, bifurcate.
adj angular, bent, crooked, jagged, serrated; forked, bifurcate, cornered, V-shaped, hooked; akimbo.

245 curvature *n* curve, incurvature, bend; flexure, bending, crook, hook;

deflection, turn, deviation, detour, sweep, curl, winding; curve, arc, arch, arcade, vault, bow, crescent, half-moon, horse-shoe, loop; parabola, hyperbola.

v be curved, sweep, sag; deviate, turn; render curved, bend, curve, deflect, inflect, crook; turn, round, arch, arch over, bow, curl, coil, recurve.

adj curved, bowed, vaulted, hooked, arched, arced; circular, nonlinear, semi-circular, rounded, crescent, crescent-shaped, lunar, demi-lune.

246 straightness *n* directness; inflexibility, stiffness; straight line, direct line, bee line.

v be straight, go straight; render straight, straighten, rectify, correct, right; put right, put straight, unbend, unfold, uncurl, unravel.

adj straight, even, true, unbent, direct, rectilinear, linear, not curved, uncurved; square, erect, perpendicular, vertical, upright; candid, forthright, definite, reliable, plain, blunt, frank, sure, positive, irrefutable, certain, unequivocal, inescapable; honest, honorable, fair, just, equitable, impartial, aboveboard, reputable, scrupulous, worthy, lawful, licit, conscientious, decent, ethical; correct, sound, sane, accurate, true; sober, conventional, provincial, (*informal*) unhip, (*informal*) square, (*informal*) not with it.

247 [simple circularity] **circularity** *n* roundness, rotundity; circle, ring, hoop, areola; bracelet, armlet; eye, loop, wheel, cycle, orb, orbit; zone, belt, cord, band, sash, girdle, circuit; wreath, garland, crown, corona, coronet; necklace, collar; ellipse, oval.

v round; go around, encircle, circle.

adj round, rounded, circular, oval, elliptic, elliptical, egg-shaped.

248 [complex circularity] **convolution** *n* involution, winding, wave, undulation, sinuosity, meandering, twist, twirl; coil, roll, curl, buckle, spiral, corkscrew, worm, tendril; serpent, snake, eel; maze, labyrinth.

v wind, twine, entwine, twirl, wave, undulate, meander, turn; twist, coil, roll; wrinkle, curl, frizz, frizzle; wring, contort.

adj convoluted, winding, twisted; wavy, undulating, circling, snaky, serpentine; involved, intricate, complex, complicated, labyrinthine, tortuous, mazy; spiral, coiled.

adv in and out, round and round.

249 rotundity *n* roundness, cylindricality, sphericity, globularity; cylinder, barrel, drum; roll, roller, rolling pin; sphere, globe, ball, spheroid, globule; bulb, pellet, pill, marble, pea, knob, pommel.

v sphere, form into a sphere, roll into a ball, round.

adj rotund, round, circular, ball-shaped; cylindrical, spherical, globular; egg-shaped, pear-shaped, ovoid.

250 convexity *n* prominence, projection, swelling, bulge, protuberance, protrusion; hump, hunch, bunch; knob, node, nodule, bump, clump; pimple, pustule, pock, growth, polyp, blister, boil; nipple, teat, pap, breast; nose, beak, snout, nozzle; peg, button, stud, ridge; cupola, dome, arch; relief, high relief, low relief; hill, mountain, cape, ness, promontory, headland; jetty, ledge, spur.

v project, bulge, protrude, jut out, stand out, stick out, stick up, start up, shoot up, swell up; raise; emboss.

adj convex, prominent, protuberant; bossed, nodular, bunchy, hummocky, bulbous, swollen, swelling, bloated, bowed, arched, bellied; salient, in relief, raised.

251 flatness *n* smoothness, evenness; plane, level; plate, platter, table, tablet, slab.

v flatten, level, even off.

adj flat, plane, even, smooth; level, smooth, horizontal; flat as a pancake.

252 concavity *n* depression, dip, hollow, indentation, dent, cavity, dint, dimple; excavation, pit, trough; cup, basin, crater; valley, vale, dale, dell, glade, grove, glen, cave, cavern.

v render concave, depress, hollow, scoop, scoop out, gouge; dig, delve, excavate, mine, stave in, tunnel.

adj concave, hollow, hollowed out; indented, dented, sunken, cupped; cavernous, rounded inward, incurved.

253 sharpness *n* acuteness, pointedness; point, spike, spine, needle, pin, prick, prickle, spur, barb, thorn; knife edge, cutting edge, razor edge.

v be sharp, taper to a point; sharpen, point, whet, barb, strop, grind, whittle.

adj sharp, keen, acute, trenchant; pointed, peaked, conical, spiked, spiky, tapering; studded, prickly, barbed, spiny, thorny, bristling, thistly; craggy, snaggy; cutting, sharp edged, razor sharp.

254 bluntness *n* dullness; obtuseness, roughness.

v be blunt; render blunt, dull, take off the point, round the edge.

adj blunt, dull, obtuse, dimwitted; rough, gruff; rounded, round, unsharpened, unpointed.

255 smoothness *n* polish, gloss; lubrication, lubricity.

v smooth, plane, file, scrape, shave, sand, sandpaper; level, press, flatten, roll; iron, steam press; polish, burnish, rub, wax, sleek, buff, glaze; lubricate, oil, grease.

adj smooth, polished, glossy, shiny, sleek, silken, silky; even, level, sanded; soft, downy, velvety; slippery, glassy, oily.

256 roughness *n* asperity, irregularity, corrugation, nodulation; grain, texture, pile, nap.

v roughen, rough up, crinkle, ruffle, rumple, crumple.

adj rough, uneven, irregular, rugged, scabrous, knotted, craggy, gnarled; shaggy, coarse, hairy, bristly, hirsute; scraggly, prickly, bushy; unpolished, unsmooth, rough-hewn, textured; downy, velvety, fluffy, wooly.

adv against the grain.

257 notch *n* dent, nick, cut, scratch, indentation; saw, tooth, scallop.

v notch, nick, cut, scratch, indent, jag, scarify, scallop.

adj notched, toothed, serrated.

258 fold *n* plait, ply, crease, pleat, tuck; wrinkle, ripple, rimple, pucker, ruffle.

v fold, double, plait, crumple, crease, pleat, wrinkle, crinkle, ripple, curl, rumple, frizzle, rimple, ruffle, pucker, corrugate; tuck, hem, gather.

adj folded.

259 furrow *n* groove, rut, scratch, streak, cut, crack, score, incision, slit; channel, gutter, trench, gulley, ditch, dike, moat, trough; ravine, valley.

v furrow, dig, plow; channel, flute, groove, incise, cut, engrave, etch, seam, cleave, score; wrinkle, knit, pucker.

adj furrowed, ribbed, striated, fluted.

260 opening *n* hole, gap, aperture, orifice, perforation, pinhole, peephole, keyhole; slot, slit, rift, breach, cleft, chasm, fissure, rent; outlet, inlet, vent; portal, porch, gate, hatch, door, doorway, gateway; way, path, channel, passage.

v open, ope, gape, yawn; perforate, pierce, tap, bore, drill; mine, tunnel, dig to daylight; impale, spike, spear, gore, spit, stab, puncture, lance, stick, prick, riddle; uncover, unclose, lay bare, expose, bare, reveal; lay open, cut open, rip open, throw open.

adj open, unclosed, uncovered, exposed; ajar, wide-open, gaping, yawning; perforated, porous, reticulated, permeable; accessible, available, public.

261 closure *n* blockade, shutting up, obstruction, stoppage, clogging, sealing, plugging; contraction; constipation; culmination; cessation, completion, termination, windup; lid, top, cap, stopper, plug, barrier.

v close, plug, block up, stop up, fill up, cork up, cork, button up, stuff up, shut up, dam up; blockade, obstruct, hinder; bar, bolt, stop, seal, choke, throttle, shut.

adj closed, shut, unopened; unpierced, impervious, impermeable; impenetrable, impassable, pathless; tight, snug, airtight, unventilated, watertight, hermetically sealed.

262 perforator *n* piercer, borer, auger, drill, awl, scoop, corkscrew, probe, lancet, scalpel, needle, pin, stiletto, puncher, hole puncher, gouge; knife, spear, bayonet.

263 stopper *n* lid, cap, cover; cork, spike, stopcock, pin, plug, tap, faucet, valve, spigot, rammer, ramrod; wadding, stuffing, padding, stopping, bandage, tourniquet.

IV. Motion

264 motion *n* movement, action, activity, move, going; progress, locomotion; mobilization, mobility, movableness, motive power; unrest, restlessness; stream, flow, flux, run, course, stir; rate, pace, step, tread, stride, gait; velocity, speed.

v move, go, hie, budge, stir, pass, flit; hover around, hover about; shift, slide, glide, roll, roll on, flow, drift, stream, run, sweep along; wander, meander, browse, stroll, walk, perambulate; dodge, keep on one's toes, keep moving, hit the road, (*informal*) truck; move, impel, propel; mobilize.

adj moving, in motion, traveling, on the road; transitional, shifting, mobile, movable; mercurial, restless, unquiet, nomadic, transient.

adv under way; on the move, on the go, on the march.

265 rest *n* quiescence, stillness, quietude, calm, calmness, tranquillity, repose, serenity, peace, silence; pause, lull, cessation; stagnation, immobility, fixity.

v rest, be still, stand still, lie still, stand immobile, keep quiet, repose; remain, stay, pause, wait, mark time, hold, halt, stop short, cease, desist, discontinue, stop; stagnate, be inactive, immobilize; dwell, settle, settle down, establish roots; alight, arrive; stand fast, stand firm, stick fast; quell, becalm, hush, stay, lull, lull to sleep, tranquilize.

adj restful, quiescent, still, calm, tranquil, peaceful, undisturbed, unruffled, serene, silent; motionless, fixed, stationary; unmoved, stable, at rest, at a standstill, stock-still, sleeping, dormant, inactive, stagnant.

266 [locomotion by land] **journey** *n* traveling, travel, excursion, tour, trip, expedition, jaunt, pilgrimage; wayfaring, roving, gadding about, (*informal*) bumming around, nomadism, vagabondism; migration, immigration, moving; walk, promenade, constitutional, stroll, peregrination, perambulation, march, stroll, saunter, jaunt, outing, hike, airing; horsemanship, horseback riding; drive, driving, motoring, ride, spin; cycling, biking; procession, cavalcade, caravan, file, cortege, column.

v journey, travel, tour, take a trip; flit, take wing, (*informal*) hit the road, rove, ramble, roam, prowl, (*informal*) bum, (*informal*) bum around, range, traverse, scour the country, wander, meander, saunter, gad about; move, migrate, immigrate.

adj journeying, traveling, on the road; itinerant, peripatetic, rambling, roving, gadding, flitting, vagrant, nomadic, migratory, wayfaring.

267 [locomotion by water or air] **navigation** *n* voyage, sail, cruise, passage, boat ride; aquatics, boating, yachting, sailing, shipping.

flight, air travel, flying, gliding; aeronautics, aviation.

v navigate; sail, put to sea, embark, shove off, spread the sails, make sail, take oar; go boating, cruise, float, drift, coast; row, paddle, pull, scull, punt, steam; ride the waves.

fly, take off, take wing, take to the skies; aviate, soar, glide, fly over, plane, jet.

adj sailing, nautical, naval, maritime, seagoing, seafaring, ocean-going; afloat; navigable.

flying, jetting; aloft, in flight; aviational, aeronautical, aerial.

268 traveler *n* wayfarer, journeyer, rover, rambler, wanderer, free spirit, nomad, vagabond, bohemian, gypsy, itinerant, vagrant, tramp, hobo, straggler, waif; pilgrim, palmer, seeker, quester; voyager, passenger, tourist, sightseer, excursionist, vacationer, globe-trotter, jet-setter; immigrant, emigrant, refugee, fugitive; pedestrian, walker, cyclist, biker, rider, horsewoman, horseman, equestrian, driver.

269 mariner, flier *n* mariner, sailor, seaman, seafaring man, sea dog; pilot, skipper, captain, commander, helmsman, steersman; crew, hands, mates; navigator, flier, airman, aviator, aviatrix, pilot, skipper; astronaut, cosmonaut, spaceman.

270 transference *n* transfer, move, shift, transit, transition, passage, transmission, transport, transplantation, transposition; removal, relegation, deportation, extradition.

v transfer, transmit, transport, convey, carry, bear, pass; move, shift, conduct, convey, bring, fetch, reach; send, delegate, consign, turn over, hand over, deliver; transpose, transplant, displace, remove, relegate, deport, extradite; shovel, ladle.

adj transferable, transmittable, transmissible, transportable, movable, portable.

271 carrier *n* porter, bearer, messenger, runner, courier; postman, letter carrier; conductor, conveyor, transporter; freighter, ship, barge; train, locomotive; truck, vehicle, carriage; beast of burden.

272 vehicle *n* conveyance, carriage, transportation, rig; car, motorcar, automobile, (*informal*) wheels, truck; wagon, cart, coach, chaise, buggy; bicycle, bike, motorcycle, motor-scooter; train, sleeping car, cattle car, boxcar.

273 ship *n* vessel, boat, liner, freighter, steamer, schooner, sailboat, motorboat, merchant ship, barge, tugboat, tanker, trawler, yacht, cruiser, yawl, ketch, brig, brigantine, square-rigger, sloop, cutter, launch; navy, fleet.

airplane, plane, jet, jumbo jet, aircraft, glider, helicopter, dirigible, blimp, balloon, spaceship, capsule, module, space station.

274 velocity *n* rapidity, quickness, swiftness, celerity, speed, alacrity; acceleration, pickup; spurt, rush, dash, race, flying, flight.

v move quickly, speed, hie, hasten, post, scamper, run, race, shoot, tear, whisk, sweep, rush, dash, dash off; bolt, bound, spring, dart, flit; hurry, hasten, haste, accelerate, (*informal*) turn on the juice, quicken, speed up, take off like a shot.

adj fast, speedy, swift, rapid, quick, brisk, fleet; nimble, agile, expeditious, light-footed, fast as a bullet, quick as lightning.

adv swiftly, apace, at full speed, at full gallop, posthaste.

275 slowness *n* languor, sluggishness, slackness, sloth, indolence; deliberateness, moderation, leisureliness; tardiness.

v move slowly, creep, crawl, lag, drawl, linger, loiter, saunter, trail, drag, dawdle; plod, trudge, lumber; grovel, sneak, steal, worm one's way, inch; waddle, wobble, shuffle, hobble, limp, shamble, amble, traipse, slouch, mince, mince steps, halt; flag, totter, teeter, stagger; retard, hinder, impede, obstruct; slacken, check, relax, moderate; brake, curb, slow, put on the brakes.

adj slow, slack, late, tardy; gentle, easy, unhurried, deliberate, gradual, moderate, leisurely; languid, sluggish, indolent, lazy; tedious, humdrum, dull, boring; dense, stupid.

adv slowly, leisurely; at half speed, at a snail's pace; gradually, little by little, step by step, inch by inch, bit by bit, one step at a time.

276 impulse *n* impetus, implosion, push, thrust, shove; propulsion; sudden impulse, yearning, craving; reaction, response, reflex; collision, clash, encounter, shock, bump, crash; impact; blow, stroke, knock, rap, tap, slap, smack, pat, dab; hit, whack, thwack, slam, punch, belt, kick, thump, cut, thrust, lunge.

v impel, push, urge, thrust, shove, heave, prod, shoulder, jostle, hustle, hurtle, jog, jolt; start, give a start to, set going, get going, drive; run against, bump against, butt against; collide with, run into, bang into, butt; strike, knock, bang, hit, thump, beat, slam, dash, punch, thwack, whack; batter, pelt, buffet, butt; hit, rap, slap, tap, pat, dab.

277 recoil *n* reflex, rebound, ricochet, boomerang, backfire, backlash; snap, elasticity; reverberation, resonance; reaction, response, rebuff, repulse, revulsion.

v recoil, rebound, ricochet, boomerang, snap back, spring back, fly back; react, respond; reverberate, echo, quiver.

adj reactionary; elastic, backfiring.

278 direction *n* bearing, course, set, drift, tenor, trend, tendency, inclination; tack, aim, determination, intention; points of the compass, cardinal points; line, path, road, range, line of march; alignment.

v direct, point, aim; tend toward, point toward, conduct to, go to; bend, tend, verge, incline, determine; steer for, make for, aim at, level at, set one's sights on, take aim, hold a course for, be bound for.

adj direct, straight; bound for; undeviating, unswerving.

adv toward, on the road to; hither, thither, whither; directly, straight, straightforward, point-blank, on a line with.

279 deviation *n* diversion, digression, departure from, aberration; divergence, zigzag, detour, circuit; warp, refraction; swerving.

v deviate, alter one's course, turn, bend, curve, swerve, heel, bear off; divert, deflect, shift, shunt, draw aside, crook, warp; stray, straggle, digress, ramble, rove, drift, go astray, go adrift; wander, wind, twist, meander; veer, turn aside, change direction, steer clear of, dodge.

adj deviating, errant, aberrant; discursive, desultory, loose, rambling, digressive, stray, erratic, undirected; circuitous, indirect, zigzag, roundabout, crooked.

adv astray, roundabout, wide of the mark; circuitously.

280 [going before] **precedence** *n* priority; leading, heading, the lead, van, vanguard; precursor, coming beforehand.

v precede, go before, forerun; usher in, introduce, herald; head, take the lead, lead the way; take precedence, have priority, come first, come before.

adv in advance, before, ahead, in the vanguard, in front.

281 [going after] **sequence** *n* coming after, following, sequel; shadow, dangler, train.

v follow, come in sequence, go after; attend, be attendant on, follow in the steps of, follow in the wake of, trail, shadow; pursue; lag, fall behind.

adj following; sequential.

adv behind, after; in the rear.

282 [motion forward **progression** *n* progress, improvement, proceeding, advance, advancement, headway; growth, rise, increase, development.

v proceed, advance, progress, get on, get along, gain ground, press onward, forge ahead, make headway, make progress, make strides, stride forward; grow, develop, increase, improve.

adj advancing; progressive, advanced.

adv forward, onward; forth, on, ahead.

283 [motion backward] **regression** *n* retrogression, retreat, recession, retirement, withdrawal; reflux, backwater, return, recoil; backsliding; deterioration, decrease, fall.

v regress, recede, return, revert, retreat, back out, back down, turn back, fall back, drop out, retire, withdraw; lose ground, drop off, fall behind; ebb, shrink, shy.

adj retrograde, retrogressive; regressive, refluent, reflex.

adv backwards; aboutface.

284 propulsion *n* propulsive force, impulse, push, projection, thrust, drive, impulsion, impetus; throw, fling, toss, shot, discharge.

v propel, project, throw, fling, cast, pitch, chuck, toss, heave, hurl; drive, sling, push, shove; send off, fire off, discharge, shoot, launch, let fly; put in motion, set in motion, start, get going, impel; expel.

adj propulsive.

285 traction *n* drawing, hauling, pulling, towing, towage; yank, tug, drag, jerk.

v draw, pull, haul, lug, drag, tug, tow, trail, train, take in tow; wrench, jerk, yank.

adj tractile; in tow.

286 [motion towards] **approach** *n* access, advent, advance; nearness, approximation.

v approach, near, draw near, move towards, get close to; gain on, get closer to; pursue, trail.

adj approaching; approximate; impending, imminent.

287 [motion from] **recession** *n* retirement, withdrawal; flight, removal, retreat; regression, return, falling back, regress; reaction, reversal, recoil; departure, leave-taking.

v recede, move back, go back, move away from, retire, withdraw; drift, abate, fade, wane, ebb, subside, drift away, fall back, shrink; react, revert, relapse, recoil, regress; run away, fly, avoid.

288 attraction *n* attractiveness, inclination, affinity; pull, magnetism, gravity.

v attract, draw, drag, pull, magnetize, exert force; interest, invite, engage, fascinate, lure, allure, charm, decoy, bait.

adj attractive, attracting, enticing, seductive, alluring; have pull, magnetic, gravitational.

289 repulsion *n* aversion, antipathy, dislike; repulse, rebuff.

v repel, push back, drive away, chase away, rebuff, beat back; repulse, revolt, offend, sicken, disgust, displease, irritate.

adj repulsive, repellent, averse, repelling.

290 convergence *n* confluence, conflux, concurrence, concourse, congress, coming together, meeting, joining.

v converge, concur, come together, meet, join, unite; gather together, concentrate, center.

adj convergent, confluent, concurrent.

291 divergence *n* division, radiation, spread, severance, separation, refraction, deflection; ramification, furcation, branching, forking, detachment; deviation, aberration, disparity, difference, variance, heterogeneity.

v diverge, ramify, radiate, branch off, fork, spread, swerve, scatter, disperse; divide, separate, part, sever; vary, deviate, dissent, disagree.

adj divergent, radial, radiant, centrifugal.

292 arrival *n* advent, coming; reaching, attainment, landing, debarkation, disembarkation; reception, welcome, welcoming.

v arrive, get to, come to, reach a point, attain, complete; light, alight, dismount; land, disembark, debark, deplane, detrain.

293 departure *n* embarkation; outset, start, starting point, place of departure, point of departure; removal, exit; exodus, flight; leave-taking, valediction, *adieu*, farewell, goodbye.

v depart, go away, take one's leave, start, set out, leave, retire, quit, withdraw, absent, go, (*informal*) split, take off, (*informal*) cut out, move off, move out, ship out, pack it up; vacate, evacuate, abandon; sally, set forth, set forward, go forth; embark, set sail, put out to sea, shove off, get under way, enplane, entrain.

294[motion into] **ingress** *n* entrance, entry; influx, intrusion, inroad, incursion, invasion, irruption, penetration, infiltration; insinuation, insertion.

v enter, come in, pour in, flow in; burst in, break in, invade, intrude; penetrate, infiltrate, insinuate oneself.

adj incoming, inbound.

295 [motion out of] **egress** *n* exit, issue; emergence, emanation; outbreak, outburst, eruption; evacuation, leakage, percolation, oozing, drainage, drain; outpouring, gush, effluence, effusion, discharge.

v emerge, emanate, issue; pass out of, come out of, pour out of, flow out of; exude, leak, ooze, drain, drip, trickle, dribble; gush, gush out, pour out, spout, flow out, discharge; escape, find vent.

adj outgoing, outward, outbound.

296 [motion into, actively] **reception** *n* admission, admittance, entry, entrée; importation, introduction, initiation, induction, absorption; ingestion, eating, drinking; suction, sucking; insertion, injection.

v give entrance to, admit, introduce, usher, initiate, induct; receive, import, bring in, ingest, absorb, imbibe.

297 [motion out of, actively] **ejection** *n* rejection, expulsion, eviction, dislodgment, banishment, exile; emission, effusion, discharge, evacuation, regurgitation, elimination.

v reject, eject, expel, evict, dislodge, banish, exile; push aside, push away, turn away, brush aside; empty, drain, clear out, clean out, purge, void, evacuate; vomit, spew, regurgitate, throw up, (*informal*) puke, retch, (*informal*) barf, belch out, burp out; discharge, eliminate, discard, get rid of, do away with, cast off, cut adrift, turn out, throw out, oust.

298 eating *n* dining, supping, taking nourishment; ingestion, chewing, mastication; imbibition, drinking, food, nourishment, nutrition, nutriment, sustenance, subsistence, provender, provisions, rations, keep, board, fare; drink, beverage, potion, draught.

v eat, feed, breakfast, lunch, dine, sup, break bread; taste, devour, wolf, swallow, gulp, bolt, gulp down, fall to, dig in; chew, masticate, bite, bite into, chomp, munch, crunch, gnaw, nibble, peck at; live on, live off, fatten, feast on.

drink, drink up, drink one's fill, quaff, (*informal*) down, chug, empty, sip.

adj eatable, edible, digestible; drinkable, potable; nutritious, nutritive.

299 excretion *n* discharge, emanation, exhalation, secretion, effusion, perspiration, sweat; evacuation, elimination, urination; hemorrhage, bleeding.

v excrete; emanate, exhale; secrete, perspire, sweat; eliminate, evacuate; urinate.

300 [forcible ingress] **insertion** *n* implantation, injection, inoculation, infusion, importation, insinuation, interpolation; immersion, submersion, dip, plunge.

v insert, introduce, put in; inject, infuse, instill, inoculate, impregnate, imbue; graft, ingraft, implant, plant, bud; thrust in, stick in, shove in, ram in, stuff in, tuck in, press in, drive in; immerse, merge; dip, plunge.

301 [egress] **extraction** *n* removal, elimination, extrication, eradication, extirpation, extermination, ejection; wrench, squeezing, pulling.

v extract, draw, draw out, take out, pull out, tear out, rip out, pluck out; wring from, wrench, pull; root out, weed out, rake out, eradicate, uproot, pull up, extirpate; evolve, elicit, draw forth; extricate, remove, eliminate; squeeze out.

302 [motion through] **passage** *n* transmission; permeation, penetration, infiltration; ingress, egress; voyage, trip, tour, excursion, journey; way, route, channel, avenue, road, path, way, thoroughfare, conduit.

v pass, pass through; penetrate, permeate, thread, go through, cut across; ford, traverse, cross; go, move, proceed; leave, go away, depart.

303 [motion beyond] **infringement** *n* transgression, trespass, encroachment, infraction.

v infringe, transgress, trespass, encroach; surpass, go beyond, shoot ahead of, overrun; overstep, overreach, overshoot; outstrip, outrun, outride, outdo; exceed, surmount, transcend, soar.

adv beyond the mark, ahead.

304 [motion short of] **shortcoming** *n* failure, falling short; default, defalcation; incompleteness, imperfection, deficiency, insufficiency, noncompletion.

v fall short, come up short, come short of, not reach; want, lack; fail, break down, collapse, come to nothing; fall through, cave in.

adj deficient, lacking, insufficient; incomplete, imperfect.

305 ascent *n* ascension; rising, rise, upgrowth; leap, jump; acclivity, hill, grade.

v ascend, rise, mount, climb upward, climb, arise; clamber, mount, scale, go up, get up; tower, soar, hover, surmount, scale the heights.

adj ascendant; rising, acclivitous.

306 descent *n* declension, inclination, declination, slope, declivity, grade, decline, drop, cliff, precipice, dip, hill; fall, falling, descending, sinking; downfall, tumble, slip, tilt, trip, lurch.

v descend, go down, drop down, come down, drop, fall, gravitate, slip, slide, settle; decline, set, sink, droop, wilt, slump; dismount, alight, get down; swoop down, stoop; tumble, trip, stumble, lurch, pitch, topple, tilt, sprawl.

adj declivitous, sloping, precipitous, steep; descending.

307 elevation *n* raising; erection, lift; upheaval; sublimation, exaltation; prominence, height.

v elevate, heighten, raise, lift, lift up, erect; set up, tilt up, rear, hoist, heave; uplift, upraise, uprear; exalt, enhance, advance; take up, drag up, fish up, drag, dredge.

adj elevated, stilted, rampant.

308 depression *n* lowering; dip, concavity; upset, overturn, overthrow; prostration, abasement, debasement, degradation; bow, curtsy, genuflection, kowtow, obeisance.

v depress, lower, let down, take down, cast down, let drop, let fall; sink, debase, bring low, abase, degrade, reduce; overthrow, overturn, upset, prostrate, level, fell; bow, curtsy, genuflect, kowtow, kneel, bend over, make obeisance.

adj depressed; at a low ebb; prostrate, horizontal.

309 leap *n* jump, hop, spring, bound, vault; dance, caper, frisk, buck.

v leap, jump, hop, spring, bound, vault, hurtle, hurdle; dance, caper, trip, skip, frisk, bob, flounce, start; trip the light fantastic toe, dance all night.

adj leaping; frisky, lively, springy.

310 plunge *n* dip, dash, rush, dive, leap; ducking, dunking, submersion, immersion.

v plunge, immerse, submerge, douse, souse, dunk, dip; dash, rush, hasten, hurry; dive, leap, jump; descend, drop, fall, hurtle over.

311 circular motion *n* circulation, circularity; turn, excursion; circumvention, circumnavigation, circling; turning; coil, corkscrew, spiral; full circle, full turn, turn, circuit, lap.

v turn, bend, wheel, turn a circle, turn around, make a U-turn, put about, make a complete circle; circle, go around, circuit, circumnavigate; whisk, twirl, twist.

adj circuitous, roundabout; circular.

312 rotation *n* revolution, gyration, circulation, roll; spinning, pirouette, convolution; whir, whirl, eddy, vortex, whirlpool, maelstrom; cyclone, tornado.

v rotate, turn, spin, revolve, wheel, whirl, twirl, spin around; pivot, swivel, circle around.

adj rotating, rotary, gyratory, revolving.

313 evolution *n* evolvement, unfolding, development.

v evolve, unfold, unfurl, unroll, unwind, develop.

adj evolutionary, evolutional.

314 [motion to and fro] **oscillation** *n* vibration, pulsation, undulation; pulse, beat, (*informal*) vibes, ripple, wave; alternation, coming and going, ebb and flow, ups and downs, flux and reflux; fluctuation, vacillation, irresolution.

v oscillate, vibrate, vacillate, swing, fluctuate, vary; undulate, wave; pulsate, beat, throb, ripple; reel, quake, quiver, quaver, shake; roll, toss, pitch; flounder, stagger, totter.

adj oscillating; undulatory; pulsating.

adv to and fro, up and down, back and forth, seesaw, zigzag, in and out, from side to side.

315 [irregular motion] **agitation** *n* stir, ripple, tremor, shake, jog, jolt, jar, jerk, shock, quiver, quaver, twitter, flicker, flutter; disquiet, perturbation, commotion, turbulence, turmoil, tumult; hubbub, bustle, fuss, ado, racket, fits; spasm, throe, throb, palpitation, convulsion, fit; disturbance, disorder, restlessness, hypertension; ferment, fermentation, ebullition, effervescence, hurly-burly; tempest, storm, groundswell, whirlpool, vortex; whirlwind, tornado, cyclone, twister.

v be agitated, shake, tremble, quiver, quaver, quake, shiver, twitter, writhe, toss, shuffle, tumble, stagger, bob, reel, sway; waggle, wriggle, dance, prance, stumble, shamble, flounder, totter, teeter, flounce, flop; throb, pulsate, beat, palpitate, go pit-a-pat; flutter, flicker, bicker, bustle; ferment, effervesce, foam, boil, bubble, simmer; agitate, shake, convulse, toss, tumble, bandy, flap, whisk, jerk, hitch, jolt, joggle, jostle, buffet, hustle, disturb, stir, shake up, churn, jounce, wallop, whip.

adj agitated, shaking, pulsating, tremulous, convulsive, jerky, shaky, throbbing.

adv by fits and starts; in convulsions, in fits.

Class III

Words Relating to Matter

I. Matter in General

316 materiality *n* corporeality, substantiality, flesh and blood, physicality; matter, body, substance, brute matter, physical elements, material; object, article, thing, materials.

science of matter: physics, natural philosophy, physical science, materialism.

materialist, physicist.

v materialize, embody, body in.

adj material, bodily, corporeal, physical, somatic; sensible, tangible, palpable, touchable, substantial, unspiritual, materialistic.

317 immateriality *n* incorporeality, insubstantiality, spirituality, ineffability.

adj immaterial, incorporeal, unsubstantial, intangible, ineffable, untouchable, bodiless, unreal, unearthly, spiritual, psychical, otherworldly.

318 world *n* creation, nature, universe, solar system, galaxy, globe, earth, wide world, sphere, macrocosm; heavens, firmament, vault, celestial spaces, space, sky; heavenly bodies, planets, asteroids, comets, meteors, constellations.

adj worldly, mundane, terrestrial, earthly, sublunary; cosmic, celestial, heavenly, astral, solar, lunar.

adv in all creation, on the face of the earth, under the sun, here below.

319 gravity *n* gravitation, weight, heaviness, pull, pressure, load, burden.

v gravitate, weigh, pull, press, encumber, load, be heavy.

adj weighty, heavy, heavy as lead, ponderous, lumpish, cumbersome, burdensome, cumbrous, massive, unwieldy, like a ton of bricks.

320 levity *n* lightness, buoyancy, volatility; ferment, leaven, yeast.

v be light, float, swim, waft; lighten, leaven.

adj light, subtle, airy, weightless, ethereal, volatile, buoyant, feathery.

II. Inorganic Matter

321 density *n* solidity, solidness, impenetrability, impermeability; condensation, solidification, consolidation, concretion, coagulation, petrification, hardening, crystallization, thickening; solid body, mass, block, knot, lump, conglomerate.

v be dense; solidify, condense, consolidate, coagulate, congeal, set, cohere, crystallize, petrify, harden; condense, compress, thicken.

adj dense, solid, compact, close, thick, substantial, massive; impenetrable, impermeable, coherent, cohesive; indivisible, indissoluble, insoluble.

322 thinness *n* rarity, tenuity; rarefaction, expansion, dilation, inflation.

v thin, rarefy, expand, dilate, inflate.

adj thin, rare, fine, tenuous, compressible, flimsy, slight, light; unsubstantial.

323 hardness *n* rigidity, firmness, inflexibility, temper; induration, petrification, ossification, crystallization.

v harden, stiffen, cement, petrify, temper, ossify.

adj hard, solid, firm, inflexible, rigid, resistant, adamantine, impenetrable, strong, hard as a rock, hard as nails, tough.

324 softness *n* pliability, flexibility, pliancy, malleability, ductility, tractility, plasticity, flaccidity, elasticity; mollification, softening.

v soften, mollify, mash, knead, temper, bend, yield, give, relent, relax.

adj soft, tender, supple, pliant, pliable, flexible, limber, plastic, ductile, tractile, tractable, plastic, malleable, moldable, impressible, elastic; flabby, limp, flimsy, flaccid, doughy, mushy, squishy, waxy, soft as butter.

325 elasticity *n* springiness, spring, resilience, resiliency, give.

v be elastic, spring, give, bend, stretch; spring back, recoil.

adj elastic, tensile, springy, resilient, buoyant, rubbery.

326 inelasticity *n* want of elasticity, flaccidity, limpness, softness, mushiness.

adj inelastic, flaccid, limp.

327 tenacity *n* toughness, strength, cohesiveness, cohesion; stubbornness, obstinacy, grit.

adj tenacious, cohesive, tough, strong, resistant, gristly, stringy, gummy, adhesive, sticky, viscous, glutinous; stubborn, obstinate.

328 brittleness *n* fragility, frailty, breakability.

v be brittle; break, crack, snap, split, shiver, splinter, crumble, burst, fly, fly to pieces, shatter, give way.

adj brittle, fragile, breakable, frangible, delicate, frail, splintery, crisp.

329 structure *n* organization, constitution, anatomy, frame, framework, mold, form, architecture, construction. texture: tissue, grain, web, surface; coarseness; fineness.

adj structural, organizational, anatomical, anatomic, architectural textural: fine, delicate, subtle, gossamery, filmy; coarse, homespun, rough, woolly.

330 granularity *n* pulverulence, sandiness, graininess, friability; powder, dust, sand, grit, grain, particle, crumb, fine powder.

reduction to powder; pulverization, granulation, disintegration, abrasion, attenuation, filing.

tools for pulverization: mill, grater rasp, file, mortar and pestle, grinder, grindstone.

v grind, pulverize, granulate, grate, scrape, file, abrade, rasp, pound, beat, crush, crumble, disintegrate.

adj granular, powdery, mealy, floury, branny, dusty, sandy, arenose, gritty, crumbly.

331 friction *n* attrition, rubbing, abrasion, elbow-grease.

v rub, scratch, scrape, scrub, fray, rasp, curry, scour, polish, rub out, erase, grind.

332 [absence or prevention of friction] **lubrication** *n* anointment, oiling, greasing, coating, lathering.

v lubricate, oil, grease, lather; anoint.

333 fluidity *n* liquidity, liquefaction, solubility, fluency.

v be fluid, flow, run, pour, stream; liquefy.

adj fluid, liquid, watery, serous, sappy, juicy, soluble; fluent, unstable.

334 gaseity *n* gaseousness, vaporousness, volatility.

adj gaseous, vaporous, airy, etheric, voluble, evaporable; flatulent, windy.

335 liquefaction *n* liquefying, deliquescence, melting, thawing, solubleness, dissolution.

v liquefy, melt, thaw, dissolve.

adj deliquescent, soluble, dissolvable, solvent.

336 vaporization *n* atomization, steaming, boiling, distillation, gasification, evaporation.

v vaporize, atomize, distill, evaporate, gasify, boil, steam.

adj vapory, vaporous, volatile, evaporable, gaseous.

337 water *n* liquid, serum, lymph, fluid, aqua.

v add water, water, wet, moisten, dip, immerse, submerge, plunge, douse, dunk, drown, soak, steep, wash, sprinkle, splash, souse, drench; dilute; deluge, inundate.

adj watery, aqueous, liquid, fluid, wet, moist, humid, soggy, sodden, rheumy, hydrous, juicy, lush, succulent; waterish, adulterated, transparent, thin, weak, tasteless, insipid, vapid, flat, feeble, dull.

338 air *n* atmosphere, stratosphere, the open, open air, blue sky, sky; weather, climate, clime; ventilation, current, breath of air, wind, breeze.

v air, ventilate, fan, aerate, freshen, refresh, cool.

adj airy, open, exposed, breezy, windy; flatulent; effervescent; atmospheric, aerial, ethereal, aeriform.

adv in the open air, out in the open, out of doors, in the wide open spaces, under the stars.

339 moisture *n* dampness, humidity, dankness, dew, wetness, condensation; perspiration.

v moisten, sponge, damp, bedew, wet, soak, saturate, sodden, sop, drench; perspire.

adj moist, damp, watery, humid, dank, dewy, muggy, juicy, wet; soggy, mushy, marshy, muddy.

340 dryness *n* drought, aridity; dessication, drainage, evaporation.

v dry, dry up, soak up, sponge, swab, wipe; drain, parch, evaporate.

adj dry, arid, parched, juiceless, sapless, dry as a bone.

341 ocean *n* sea, main, deep, brine, salt water, waters, high seas, waves, billows, great waters, tides.

adj oceanic, marine, maritime, seagoing, oceanographic.

342 land *n* earth, ground, dry land, mother earth, *terra firma*; continent, inlands, interior, shore, coast, terrain, dirt, soil, rock, chalk; real estate, lands, grounds, acres, acreage.

v land, alight, arrive, disembark, come ashore, go ashore, tie up, set foot on dry land.

adj earthy, terrestrial, earthly, alluvial, landed, territorial, continental.

adv ashore, on land, on dry land.

343 gulf, lake *n* gulf, bay, inlet, estuary, bayou, arm, fjord, firth, lagoon, cove, mouth, natural harbor, sound, straits.

lake, loch, lough, mere, tarn, basin, reservoir, lagoon, pond, pool.

344 plain *n* plateau, champaign, grassland, pasture, pasturage, meadow, flat, moor, heath, tundra, prairie, lowland, steppe, field, desert, basin, fields, grounds.

345 marsh *n* swamp, morass, moss, fen, bog, quagmire, slough, wash, mud.

adj marshy, swampy, boggy, quaggy, soft, muddy, sloppy, squashy.

346 island *n* isle, islet, atoll, reef, ait, key, bar, holm, ridge, eyot, archipelago.

adj insular, sea-girt.

347 [fluid in motion] **stream** *n* stream, etc. (of water) **348**; (of air) **249**.

v flow, etc., 348; blow, etc., **349**.

348 [water in motion] **river** *n* running water, jet, spurt, squirt, spout, splash, rush, gush, torrent; fall, cascade, inundation, deluge; rain, rainfall, storm; trickle, drizzle, shower; stream, course, flux, flow, flowing, current, tide, race; spring, rill, rivulet, stream, river, tributary; rapids, flood, whirlpool, maelstrom, vortex, eddy; wave, billow, surge, swell, ripple, surf, breaker, white caps, rough seas, rolling seas, choppy seas; irrigation, pump, hose.

v flow, run, gush, pour, spout, roll, jet, well issue; drop, drip, dribble, drizzle, trickle, stream, overflow, inundate, deluge, flow over, splash, swash; gurgle, murmur, babble, bubble, sputter, spurt, regurgitate; ooze, flow out, squeeze; rain, rain hard, rain cats and dogs, rain in torrents, rain in buckets; flow into, open into, drain into; pour, pour out, shower down, irrigate, drench, spill.

adj fluent, tidal, streamy, showery, rainy, trickly, drizzly, bubbly.

349 [air in motion] **wind** *n* draft, air, breath of air, puff, whiff, zephyr, drift, blow; fresh wind, stiff breeze, keen blast, trade wind, gust, blast, breeze, squall, gale, storm, tempest, hurricane, whirlwind, tornado, twister, cyclone, monsoon.

v blow, waft, blow hard, blow great guns, stream, gust, blast, storm; respire, breathe, pant, puff, gasp, wheeze, cough; fan, ventilate, inflate, pump, blow up.

adj windy, drafty, breezy, stormy, tempestuous, cyclonic.

350 [channel for the passage of water] **conduit** *n* channel, duct, aqueduct, canal, trough, gutter, dike, main, gully, moat, ditch, drain, sewer, culvert, sough, siphon, pipe, tube, hose, funnel, tunnel, artery, spout, floodgate, watergate, sluice, lock, valve.

351 [channel for the passage of air] **air-pipe** *n* tube, shaft, flue, chimney, funnel, vent, hole, windpipe, duct.

352 **semiliquidity** *n* viscosity, adhesiveness, stickiness, glutinosity, pastiness.

v thicken, mash, squash, churn, beat up, blend.

adj semiliquid, semifluid; milky, muddy, creamy, slushy, starchy, gummy, gluey, sticky, slimy, oozy, thick, succulent, viscous, viscid, glutinous, adhesive, clammy.

353 [mixture of air and water] **bubble, cloud** *n* bubble, foam, froth, head, lather, suds, spray, surf, yeast; effervescence, fermentation, bubbling, boiling, gurgling, foaming.

cloud, vapor, fog, mist, haze, steam; nebula, nebulosity, cloudiness, opacity, dimness.

v bubble, boil, foam, froth, gurgle, lather, effervesce, ferment, fizzle.

cloud, fog, mist, steam, shadow, darken, cast over, steam up.

adj bubbly, foamy, frothy; effervescent.

cloudy, foggy, misty, hazy, steamy.

354 **pulpiness** *n* pulp, paste, dough, curd; fleshiness, fattiness, sponginess.

v pulp, mash, squeeze, juice, squash.

adj pulpy, pasty, doughy, fleshy, meaty, fatty.

355 **unctuousness** *n* unctuosity, oiliness, greasiness, lubricity; lubrication, ointment, grease, oil, anointment.

v oil, grease, lubricate.

adj unctuous, oily, greasy, oleaginous, slippery, slimy, slick.

356 **oil** *n* fat, butter, cream, grease, tallow, suet, lard, dripping, blubber; soap, wax; petroleum, gasoline, kerosene, propane, naphtha; vegetable oil, salad oil, olive oil, linseed oil; ointment, unguent, liniment, salve, balm.

356a **resin** *n* rosin, gum, wax, amber, ambergris, bitumen, pitch, tar, asphalt; varnish, lacquer, shellac, mastic, sealing wax, putty.

v resin, rosin; varnish, shellac, lacquer, overlay.

adj resinous, gummy, waxy.

III. Organic Matter

357 **animate matter** *n* nature, natural world, animated nature, living beings, organisms, organic remains, animal life, plant life, fauna, flora; protoplasm, cell.

science of living beings: biology, natural history, zoology, botany, anatomy, physiology, organic chemistry.

naturalist, biologist, zoologist, botanist.

adj animate, organic.

358 **inanimate matter** *n* mineral world, mineral kingdom, inorganic matter, brute matter.

science of the mineral kingdom: mineralogy, geology, metallurgy.

adj inanimate, inorganic, mineral.

359 **life** *n* existence, being; animation, vigor, vivacity, vitality, energy, vital spark, vital flame, lifeblood, spirit, soul; respiration, breath, breath of life; nourishment, nutriment, staff of life.

v be alive, live, breathe, respire, exist, subsist; be born, come into the world, see the light; quicken, revive, come to; give birth to, bring to life, vitalize; vivify, reanimate; keep alive, *(informal)* keep going, *(informal)* hang in there.

adj alive, live, vigorous, vivacious, vital, energetic, lively, alive and kicking, active.

360 **death** *n* decease, demise, expiration, passing, dissolution, departure, release, rest, quietus, fall; end, cessation, loss of life, extinction, dying, mortality, doom, finale, stop; last breath, final gasp, death rattle, death agonies, hand of death, dying day, *rigor mortis;* decay, fatality, natural causes, death blow.

v die, decease, pass away, pass on, perish, expire, depart, dissolve; cease, end, vanish, disappear; fail, subside, fade, sink, fall, decline, wither, decay; be taken, yield, give in, breathe one's last, end one's days, depart this life, be no more, drop off, pop off, drop dead, drop down dead, break one's neck, give up the ghost, shuffle off the mortal coil, go the way of all flesh, turn to dust, *(informal)* kick the bucket, *(informal)* go out like a light, *(informal)* croak.

adj dead, lifeless, extinct, defunct, late, gone, no more, dead and gone, dead as a door nail; deadly, fatal, lethal.

361 [destruction of life; violent death] **killing** *n* murder, homicide, assassination, slaughter, bloodshed, carnage, butchery, massacre, holocaust; suffocation, strangulation, garrote, hanging, electrocution, gassing, drawing and quartering; suicide, regicide, parricide, matricide, fratricide, infanticide; death blow, finishing stroke, *coup de grace*, execution; suicide; slaughtering, hunting, coursing, shooting, fishing; butcher, slayer, murderer, executioner, assassin, cutthroat, thug, guerilla, saboteur, garroter.

v kill, put to death, murder, slaughter, butcher, massacre, execute, behead, decapitate, guillotine, dispatch, *(informal)* waste; *(informal)* wipe out, strangle, garrote, hang, throttle, choke, stifle, suffocate, smother, asphyxiate, drown, gas, electrocute, stab, bayonet, cut, cut to pieces, cut to ribbons, mutilate, run through, put to the sword, shoot, gun down, do away with, *(informal)* blow away; hunt, spear; cut off, nip in the bud, cut down, give no quarter, decimate; commit suicide, destroy oneself, blow one's brains out, put an end to oneself.

adj murderous, homicidal, bloodthirsty, bloody, gory; mortal, fatal, lethal, deadly, deathly; suicidal.

362 **corpse** *n* body, remains, carcass, corse, cadaver, empty vessel, bones, skeleton, relics, mortal remains, mortal coil, clay, dust, ashes, earth, carrion, fodder, food for worms, shade, ghost.

adj corpselike, cadaverous.

363 **interment** *n* burial, sepulture, entombment, inhumation; cremation; funeral, funeral rites, obsequies, wake; knell, death bell, dirge, elegy; shroud, winding sheet, grave clothes; coffin, shell, sarcophagous, urn, pall, bier, catafalque, hearse; grave, pit, sepulchre, tomb, vault, crypt, catacomb, mausoleum, cemetery, burial ground, mortuary, graveyard, charnel house, morgue; monument, gravestone, tombstone, headstone, *memento mori;* exhumation, disinterment, autopsy, post mortem examination.

v inter, bury, lay in the grave, lay to rest, lay in the ground, consign to the grave, entomb; lay out, mummify, embalm; cremate; exhume, disinter, unearth.

adj burial, funereal, funeral, mortuary, sepulchral, cinerary.

364 **animality** *n* corporality, animal life, living being, flesh, flesh and blood; physique, strength, vigor, vitality.

adj animalistic, bodily, corporeal, fleshly.

365 **vegetation** *n* vegetable life, growth, plant life.

adj vegetative; rank, dense, lush, fecund.

366 **animal** *n* animal kingdom, brute creation, fauna; beast, brute, creature, living thing, creeping thing, dumb animal; mammal, quadruped, bird, reptile, fish, crustacean, shellfish, mollusk, worm, insect; flocks and herds, wild animals, domestic animals, livestock, game, beasts of the field, fowls of the air.

adj animal, animalistic, zoological.

367 **vegetable** *n* vegetable kingdom, flora, plant life, flowerage, herbage, shrubbery, foliage, leafage, leaves, foliation, verdure, greens; tree, shrub, bush, creeper, herb, fruit, grass.

v vegetate, germinate, shoot, sprout, shoot up, grow, swell, spring up, develop, increase, flourish, blossom, bloom.

adj vegetable, vegetal, vegetative, leguminous, herbal, herbaceous, botanic, verdant.

368 [science of animals] **zoology** *n* morphology, zoography, embryology, anatomy; comparative anatomy, animal physiology, comparative physiology, anthropology, ornithology, icthyology, paleontology, entomology.

adj zoological.

369 [science of plants] **botany** *n* phytology, vegetable physiology, dendrology; flora, botanic garden.

adj botanical, herbal, horticultural.

370 [management of animals] **ranching** *n* breeding, raising; taming, domestication; veterinary science

v ranch, raise, breed; tame, domesticate, train, housebreak; cage, bridle, restrain.

adj bred; tame, domestic, domesticated, housebroken.

371 [management of plants] **agriculture** *n* farming, cultivation, husbandry, tillage; agronomy, agrobiology, agrology, agronomics; gardening, horticulture, floriculture, landscaping, arboriculture; forestry.

v cultivate, till, till the soil, work the land, farm, garden, sow, seed, plant; reap, mow, cut; plow, plough, harrow, rake, weed, hoe, lop; garden, landscape.

adj agricultural, agrarian; arable, fertile.

372 **mankind** *n* human race, man, woman, humankind, human species, humanity, mortality, people, human being, person, personage, individual, creature, fellow creature, fellow man, mortal, body, soul, somebody, someone, one, party, head, hand, heart.

people, persons, folk, public, society, community, group, general public, society of men, civilization, commonwealth, commonweal, body politic, human community, population, millions, multitudes.

adj human, mortal, personal, individual; social, national, civic, public; cosmopolitan, humanitarian.

373 **man** *n* male, manhood, masculinity, he him; gentleman, sir, mister, Mr., master, swain, fellow, chap, boy.

male animal: cock, drake, gander, dog, boar, stag, hart, buck, stallion, tomcat, billygoat, ram, bull, ox; gelding, steer.

adj male, masculine, manly.

374 **woman** *n* female, womanhood, femininity, she, her; lady, gentlewoman, madam, madame, miss, *(informal)* ma'am, Ms., Mrs., matron, girl.

female animal: hen, bitch, sow, doe, roe, mare, nannygoat, ewe, cow.

adj female, feminine, womanly.

375 **sensibility** *n* sensation, sensitiveness, feeling, responsiveness, impressibility; sensation, impression, touch; consciousness.

v be sensible, be sensitive to, feel, touch, perceive; render sensible, sharpen, cultivate, stir, excite, sensitize; cause sensation, impress, excite an impression, stir.

adj sensitive, sensible, sensuous; perceptive, sentient, responsive, susceptible, conscious, aware, alive, acute, sharp, keen, vivid, lively.

adv to the quick.

376 **insensibility** *n* lack of feeling, obtuseness, paralysis, numbness, anesthesia; insusceptibility, unresponsiveness, unconsciousness.

v be insensible; render insensible, blunt, pall, numb, benumb, paralyze, deaden, freeze, anesthetize; cloy, stuff, satiate, drown; stupefy, stun.

adj insensible, senseless, unsusceptible, unresponsive, insensitive, numb, hard, dead; dull, dense, thick, obtuse, unperceptive; anesthetic, paralytic.

377 **pleasure** *n* bodily pleasure, sensuality, sensuousness, physical gratification, sex, sexuality, sensual delight, ecstasy, orgasm, climax; titillation, teasing; comfort, ease, relish, delight, joy, luxury, luxuriousness, pleasure, lap of luxury.

v feel pleasure, receive pleasure, enjoy, relish, revel in, bask in, swim in, luxuriate, feast on, wallow in, gloat over, *(informal)* dig, *(informal)* get off on, *(informal)* be turned on, *(informal)* get into; give pleasure, *(informal)* turn on, thrill, excite.

adj pleasurable, sensual, sensuous, sexual, voluptuous, luxurious, ecstatic, orgasmic, climactic; agreeable, comfortable, cordial, delightful, joyful; palatable, sweet, tasty; fragrant; melodious, lovely.

adv in comfort, in ecstasy, on a bed of roses.

378 **pain** *n* suffering, dolor, ache, aching, smart, shoot, shooting, twinge, twitch, gripe, grip, hurt, cut, sore, soreness, tenderness, discomfort, malaise, disease; spasm, cramp, crick, stitch, convulsion, throe, throb, pang; torment, torture, rack, anguish, agony.

v feel pain, suffer, undergo pain, ache, smart, bleed, tingle, shoot, twinge, twitch, writhe, wince, hurt; inflict pain, hurt, chafe, sting, bite, gnaw, gripe, pinch, tweak, grate, gall, fret, prick, pierce, wring, convulse; torment, torture, wrack, agonize.

adj painful, dolorous, sore, tender, raw, uncomfortable; convulsive, torturous.

379 **touch** *n* contact, feeling, tactility, palpability, impact, feel, sensation; manipulation, handling, rubbing, massaging, fondling, fingering, kneading, stroking, brushing, grazing over.

v touch, feel, handle, finger, fondle, thumb, paw, grab, rub, massage, knead, stroke, brush, manipulate, run the fingers over, graze over.

adj tactual, tactile, palpable.

380 **sensations of touch** *n* itching, tickling, titillation, scratching, pricking, stinging.

v itch, tingle, creep, thrill, prick, scratch, sting.

adj itching; ticklish, scratchy, itchy.

381 **numbness** *n* physical insensibility, lack of feeling, deadness.

v benumb, anesthetize, deaden, dull, drug.

adj numb, dull, benumbed, insensible, unfeeling, frozen, drugged, dead, deadened, dulled.

382 **heat** *n* warmth, caloricity, caloric, temperature; glow, flush, warmth, intensity, ardor, passion, fever, fervor, zeal; fire, spark, flame, blaze.

v be hot, glow, flush, sweat, swelter, smoke, stew, simmer, seethe, boil, burn, broil, blaze, flame; smolder, parch, fume, pant; heat, warm, thaw, defrost; stimulate, stir, animate, arouse.

adj hot, warm, mild, genial, tepid, lukewarm, unfrozen; heated, torrid, sultry, burning, fiery; sunny, tropical, suffocating, stifling, sweltering, oppressive, reeking, baking; fiery, incandescent, ebullient, glowing, smoking, blazing, on fire, afire, in flames, aflame, ablaze; ardent, fervent, fervid, angry, furious, vehement, intense, excited, excitable, irascible, animated, violent, passionate.

383 **cold** *n* coldness, iciness, frigidity, chilliness, coolness.

v be cold, shiver, quake, shake, tremble, shudder, quiver; chill, freeze, refrigerate.

adj cold, chilly, chill, cool, frigid, gelid, frozen, freezing, bitter, bitter cold, numbing, nipping, cutting, shivering, bleak, raw, frost-bitten, icy, glacial, frosty, wintry, hibernal, arctic, polar; impassionate, unemotional, apathetic, unresponsive, unsympathetic, stoical, unfeeling, indifferent, cold-blooded, heartless, imperturbable; polite, formal, reserved, hostile; deliberate, depressing, dispiriting, disheartening.

adv coldly, bitterly.

384 **calefaction** *n* heating, melting, fusion, liquefaction, combustion; cauterization; calcination; incineration, cremation; carbonization.

v heat, warm, chafe; fire, set fire to, set on fire, kindle, light, ignite, rekindle; melt, thaw, fuse, liquefy; burn, inflame, roast, broil, toast, cook, fry, grill, singe, parch, bake, scorch; brand, cauterize, sear, burn in; boil, digest, stew, sauté, cook, scald, parboil, simmer; take fire, catch fire.

adj heated, warmed, fired, burnt, scorched; molten; flammable, combustible, volcanic.

385 **refrigeration** *n* cooling, congelation, glaciation, icing; solidification, hardening.

v refrigerate, keep cold, chill, ice, congeal, freeze; cool, fan, refresh; benumb, starve, pinch, nip, cut, pierce, bite; quench, put out, stamp out, extinguish.

adj cooled, frozen, chilled; incombustible, inflammable, fireproof.

386 **furnace** *n* oven, stove, range; hearth, heater, kiln, oil burner, space heater, blast furnace, forge, fire place, fiery furnace.

387 **refrigerator** *n* ice box, fridge, ice chest, frigidaire, cold storage, freezer, ice house.

388 **fuel** *n* firing, combustible; coal, hard coal, anthracite, bituminous coal, soft coal, carbon, coke, charcoal; wood, firewood, kindling, brushwood, log, cinder, ember, ash; turf, peat, fuel oil, fossil fuel, petroleum, gasoline, kerosene; gas, natural gas, propane; electricity; nuclear power; solar energy; waterpower; windpower.

v fuel, feed, stoke, fire; power.

adj carbonaceous; combustible, flammable, burnable.

389 **thermometer** *n* thermometograph, thermoscope, thermostat, telethermometer, pyrometer, calorimeter, glass, mercury.

390 **taste** *n* flavor, savor, sensation, gusto, relish; smack, smatch, tang, aftertaste; morsel, bit, sip.

v taste, flavor, savor, smatch, smack; tickle the palate, tickle the tastebuds; smack the lips.

adj tasty, savory, flavory, flavorful, flavored; palatable, digestible, *(informal)* edible.

391 **tastelessness** *n* insipidity, blandness, flatness, unsavoriness.

v be tasteless.

adj tasteless, insipid, bland, flat, weak, mild, vapid, wishy-washy, *(informal)* plastic, pasty.

392 **pungency** *n* piquancy, poignancy, tang, bite, nip, sharpness, acridity, bitterness, hotness, sourness, unsavoriness.

v be pungent; make pungent, season, spice, salt, pepper, pickle, brine, devil, smoke, curry.

adj pungent, strong, full-flavored, seasoned, highly seasoned, spiced; sharp, biting, nippy, acrid, bitter, sour, stinging, spicy, salty, peppery, piquant, hot; unsavory.

393 **condiment** *n* seasoning, flavoring, sauce, spice, relish; salt, pepper.

v season.

394 **savoriness** *n* flavor, flavorfulness, taste, tastiness, relish, piquancy, zest, tang, delectability, palatability.

v be savory, tickle the palate, taste good, taste great; savor, enjoy, appreciate, relish, like, taste.

adj savory, good, tasty, palatable, nice, dainty, delectable, flavorful, appetizing, delicate, delicious, exquisite, rich, luscious, full-flavored, pungent, ambrosial.

395 **unsavoriness** *n* tastelessness, flavorlessness, blandness; acridness, sourness.

v be unsavory, be unpalatable, taste bad, sicken, disgust, pall, nauseate, turn the stomach, make one sick.

adj unsavory, tasteless, flavorless, bland, flat; bad tasting, ill-flavored, acrid, bitter, sour, unpalatable, inedible, offensive, repulsive, nasty, vile, sickening, nauseous, loathsome, unpleasant, awful.

396 **sweetness** *n* sugariness, saccharinity, syrupiness, stickiness.

v sweeten, sugar, candy.

adj sweet, sugary, syrupy, honeyed, saccharine, candied, sticky, gooey, luscious, lush, cloying; sweetened.

397 **sourness** *n* acridity, tartness, sharpness, vinegariness, acerbity, acidity.

v sour, acidify, acerbate, curdle, acidulate, ferment, spoil.

adj sour, acid, bitter, tart, sharp, vinegary, acidulous, astringent, acerbic, acrid; fermented, rancid, bad, spoiled, turned, curdled, gone bad; styptic, hard, rough.

398 **odor** *n* smell, scent; effluvium; exhalation, emanation; fume, essence, redolence.

v have an odor, smell, smell of, give out a smell; smell, scent, sniff, snuff, inhale.

adj odorous, odoriferous, smelly, strong smelling, redolent, pungent.

399 **inodorousness** *n* absence of

smell, odorlessness.

v be inodorous, not smell, have no odor, be odorless.

adj odorless, scentless, unsmelling.

400 fragrance *n* aroma, redolence, perfume, sweet smell, sweet scent, smell.

v be fragrant, smell sweet, have a perfume, scent, perfume.

adj fragrant, aromatic, redolent, spicy, scented, perfumed, sweet scented, sweet smelling, odoriferous, odorific.

401 fetor *n* bad smell, bad odor, foul smell, offensive smell, stink, stench, fume, foulness, fetidness, rancidity, rankness, fustiness, mustiness.

v have a bad smell, smell bad, smell rotten, smell, stink, reek.

adj fetid, strong smelling, bad, strong, fulsome, offensive, rank, rancid, noisome, mephitic, miasmic, musty, fusty, foul, rotten, putrid, reeking, stinking, stinky, suffocating, nauseating, nauseous, *(informal)* gross.

402 sound *n* noise, tone, pitch, sound vibrations, strain, sonority, sonorousness, twang, intonation, cadence; audibility, resonance, voice.

science of sound: acoustics, phonology, phonetics, electronic sound reproduction.

v sound, make a noise; give out sound, emit sound; resound, echo.

adj sounding, sonorous, resonant, audible, distinct.

403 silence *n* stillness, quiet, peace, hush, lull, quiescence, dead silence; muteness, speechlessness, taciturnity.

v silence, still, hush, stifle, muffle, stop, muzzle, gag; be silent, hold one's tongue, shut up, keep quiet, be still.

adj silent, quiet, still, calm, noiseless, soundless, hushed, quiescent; mute, speechless, taciturn; solemn, soft, deathlike, awful, silent as the grave.

adv silently.

404 loudness *n* loud noise, power, resonance, thunderousness, roaring, vociferousness, clamorousness; din, clang, clangor, clamor, noise, roar, uproar, hubbub, boom, racket, outcry; blast, peal, swell, flourish of trumpets, boom; thunder, explosion.

v be loud, peal, swell, clang, boom, thunder, fulminate, roar, resound, bellow, scream, holler, shout; ring in the ears, pierce the ears, split the eardrums, stun, deafen; shake, awake.

adj loud, noisy, vociferous, resounding, clamorous, deafening, stentorian, boisterous, tumultuous, sonorous, deep, full, powerful, thundering, ear-splitting, piercing, uproarious, obstreperous, shrill, sharp.

adv loudly, noisily, at the top of one's voice, at the top of one's lungs, aloud.

405 faintness *n* faint sound, whisper, breath, undertone, murmur, hum; inaudibility; hoarseness.

v whisper, breathe, murmur, hum, mutter, speak softly, speak in low tones.

adj faint, whispered, indistinct, dim, inaudible, barely audible, low, stifled, muffled, murmured, muted; gentle, soft, languid, floating, flowing; hoarse, husky.

406 [sudden and violent sounds] **snap** *n* rap, thud, burst, explosion, detonation, discharge, firing, salvo, pop, bang, blast.

v rap, snap, tap, knock, click, clash, crack, crackle, crash, beat.

407 [repeated and protracted sounds] **roll** *n* drumming, tapping, rumbling, grumbling; dingdong, whirring, droning; ratatat, rubadub, pitapat; quaver, quiver, clutter, racket; peal of bells; reverberation.

v roll, drum, rumble, grumble, rattle, clatter, patter, clack; hum, trill, shake; chime, peal, toll; tick, beat.

408 resonance *n* ring, ringing, chime, clang, clangor, boom, roll, roar, rumble, thunder, vibrato, timbre, twang, vibration, reverberation, tintinnabulation, booming, quaver, dingdong, echoing, sonorousness.

v resound, reverberate, re-echo; ring, jingle, chink, clink; gurgle, echo, ring in the ear.

adj resonant, resounding, reverberant, reverberating; deep-toned, deep-sounding.

408a nonresonance *n* dead sound, thud, thump, muffled drums, cracked bell; damper, mute, muffler.

v sound dead, thud, thump; muffle, dampen, mute.

adj nonresonant, dampened, muted, muffled, deadened; dead.

409 [hissing sounds] **sibilation** *n* hissing, wheezing, buzzing, zipping, whooshing; high note.

v hiss, buzz, whiz, wheeze, whoosh, zip, rustle, whistle, fizzle; squash, sneeze.

adj sibilant; hissing, wheezy.

410 [harsh sounds] **stridency** *n* discord, dissonance, harshness, raucousness, atonality, clashing, grinding, grating, rasping, sharpness, creaking, shrillness.

v creak, grate, jar, jangle, clank, clink, grind, grate; scream, yelp.

adj strident, sharp, high, acute, shrill, atonal, unharmonious, unmusical, dissonant, discordant, cacophonous; piercing, ear-piercing, cracked; creaking, harsh, coarse, hoarse, rough, gruff, grating, jarring, guttural, squawking, acute, scratching, croaking, rasping, sour, clashing.

411 cry *n* shout, scream, yell, shriek, roar, howl, wail; exclamation, outcry, clamor, vociferation; hubbub, hullabaloo, chorus, hue and cry; entreaty, appeal, solicitation, plea, plaint, prayer, crying, weeping, wailing, sobbing, lament, whimper, whimpering, tears, moaning.

v cry, roar, shout, bawl, brawl, hoop, whoop, yell, bellow, howl, scream, screech, shriek, squeak, squeal, whine, whimper, wail, weep, sob, moan, lament; cheer, hoot; grumble, groan, complain; vociferate, raise one's voice, sing out, cry out, yell out, exclaim, holler, shout at the top of one's lungs.

adj crying, clamorous; vociferous; solicitous; stentorian.

412 [animal sounds] **ululation** *n* howling, crying, belling, screeching, singing, growling, purring.

v cry, roar, bellow, bark, yelp, yap, growl, snarl, howl, bay, grunt, snort, neigh, bray, mew, purr, caterwaul, bleat, low, moo, squeak, oink, baa, crow, croak, screech, caw, coo, gobble, quack, cackle, gaggle, chuck, cluck, clack, chirp, chirrup, twitter, cuckoo, hum, buzz, hiss, blatter.

413 melody, concord *n* melodiousness, tunefulness, sweet sounds, mellifluence, musicalness, euphony; timbre, tone color, pitch; tune, song, aria, theme, measure, plainsong, canticle, strain, lay.

harmony, harmoniousness; rhythm, meter; symphony, euphony, consonance, attunement, modulation, syncopation; counterpoint, polyphony; concordance, pleasing combination.

v harmonize, chime, symphonize, blend; tune, accord.

adj melodious, musical, tuneful, melodic, lyrical, euphonious, singing, ringing, sweet-sounding, euphonic, mellifluous, dulcet, mellow, clear, sweet, rich, soft, silvery, agreeable, pleasing.

concordant, harmonious, agreeing, symphonious, suiting, congenial, blending, synchronized, consistent, in rapport, in unison, confluent, conjoined, symmetrical, proportionate, consonant, compatible.

414 discord *n* dissonance, atonality; harshness; racket, noise, inharmoniousness.

v be discordant; jar, grate.

adj discordant, dissonant, atonal, harsh; out of tune, tuneless, unmelodious, inharmonious, unmusical; jarring, grating, cacophonous, screeching.

415 music *n* sweet sounds, pleasing sounds, harmonious sounds, melody, song, tune, strain, air, harmony; classical music, popular music, folk music, jazz, electronic music; orchestral music, instrumental music, symphonic music, chamber music; ragtime, reggae, swing, bebop, bop, barrelhouse, rock; pop music, vocal music, choral music, solo, duet, duo, sonata, trio, quartet, quintet, sextet, septet, octet.

v make music, perform; compose.

adj musical, lyrical; instrumental, orchestral, symphonic, vocal, choral, operatic.

416 musician [performance of music] *n* artist, performer, concert artist, player, soloist, instrumentalist, vocalist, accompanist, singer, minstrel; symphony orchestra, orchestra, chamber orchestra, band, rock and roll band, group, combo, ensemble, chamber group, quartet, trio; chorus, choir, vocal group.

v make music, play, perform, strike up, concertize, execute, accompany, present the music, solo, improvise, play the notes; sing, croon, warble, vocalize, spin a melody.

adj musical, instrumental, vocal, choral, operatic; lyrical, harmonious, brilliant, sharp, incisive.

417 musical instruments *n* orchestra, band, brass band, marching band, military band, ensemble, group; strings, plucked instruments, bowed instruments, hammered instruments; woodwinds, winds, tubed instruments, reed instruments, brass instruments; percussion; synthesizer.

418 hearing *n* audition, auscultation, listening, perception, audibility, ear; regarding, attending, heeding.

hearer, auditor, listener; eavesdropper.

v hear, listen, attend, lend an ear, bend an ear, *(informal)* tune in, give a hearing to, give audience to, prick up one's ears, be all ears; overhear, eavesdrop; heed, regard.

adj hearing, auditory, auricular.

419 deafness *n* hardness of hearing, inaudibility.

v be deaf, not hear; turn a deaf ear to, plug up one's ears; deafen, stun, split the eardrums.

adj deaf, stone-deaf, hard of hearing; deafened, stunned; unheeding, inattentive.

420 light *n* ray, beam, stream, gleam, streak; sunbeam, moonbeam, aurora, dawn, sunrise, day-break, day, daylight, light of day, sunshine, broad daylight, glow, glint, glimmering; sun, moon; flush, halo, glory, aureole; spark, scintilla, scintillation, flash, blaze, coruscation; flame, lightening, flare; luster, sheen, shimmer, reflection, refraction; brightness, brilliancy, splendor, effulgence, radiance, illumination, radiation; luminosity, lucidity.

science of light: optics, photography, radioactivity.

v shine, glow, glitter, glisten, gleam, beam, flare, flare up, glare, flash, glimmer, shimmer, flicker, sparkle, scintillate, coruscate, flash, blaze; light, reflect, dazzle, bedazzle, daze, radiate; lighten, enlighten, light, irradiate, shed light upon, cast light upon, illuminate, illumine, kindle, fire.

adj luminous, lucent; light, bright, vivid, splendid, resplendent, lustrous, shiny, radiant; sheeny, glossy, glassy, sunny, burnished; cloudless, clear, unclouded; effulgent, blazing, ablaze, phosphorescent, aglow; iridescent.

421 darkness *n* blackness; obscurity, doom, murkiness, murk; duskiness, dusk, dimness; night, midnight, dead of night; shade, shadow, umbra, penumbra; obscuration; adumbration, extinction, eclipse, total eclipse.

v be dark; darken, obscure, shade, dim, shadow, overcast, cloud, becloud; extinguish, put out, blow out, snuff out.

adj dark, obscure, black, pitch black, nocturnal, overcast, cloudy, darkened; dingy, lurid, murky, gloomy, oppressive; shadowy, shady, umbrageous.

422 dimness *n* duskiness, shadowiness, gloominess, cloudiness, mist, mistiness, haze, haziness, fogginess, paleness, shade, nebulosity, gray, grayness.

v be dim, grow dim, darken, obscure, adumbrate, becloud, cloud, shadow, shade, eclipse, cloud over; blur, dull, fade, pale; glimmer, twinkle, flutter, flicker, waver.

adj dim, dull, dingy, lackluster, darkish, darkened, gray, dark, faint, pale, cloudy, misty, murky, overcast, nebulous, shadowy, umbrageous, blurry, hazy, opaque, foggy, bleary, gloomy, lurid, leaden.

423 [source of light] **luminary** *n* natural light, sun, moon, stars, flame, fire, spark, phosphorescence; artificial light, lamp, gas lamp, oil lamp, kerosene lamp, electric light, lantern, torch, candle, taper, light bulb.

v light, illuminate.

adj self-luminous; phosphorescent, radiant.

424 shade *n* cover, awning, umbrella, parasol, sunshade; screen, curtain, shutter, blind, gauze, veil, mantle, mask, sunglasses, *(informal)* shades; cloud, mist, fog, shadow.

v shade, veil, cover, screen, curtain, veil, draw a curtain, pull the shade, cast a shadow.

adj shady, shadowy, cloudy.

425 transparency *n* transparence, transluscence, diaphanousness, clearness, lucidity, limpidity, thinness, sheerness, gauziness, flimsiness.

v be transparent, transmit light.

adj transparent, pellucid, lucid, diaphanous, translucent, limpid, clear, crystalline, see-through, sheer, gauzy, flimsy.

426 opacity *n* opaqueness, darkness, cloudiness, filminess, haziness, mistiness, nontransparency.

v be opaque, obstruct the passage of light.

adj opaque, impervious to light, impenetrable to light, dim, filmy, thick, smoky, misty, smoggy, shady, murky, cloudy, hazy, obscure, clouded, foggy, unclear, frosted, nontransparent, nontranslucent.

427 semitransparency *n* opalescence, milkiness, pearliness; film, mist.

v let in partial light.

adj semitransparent, semipellucid, semiopaque, opalescent, pearly, nacreous, milky.

428 color *n* hue, tint, tinge, dye, complexion, shade, tincture, cast, coloration, tone, key; primary color, secondary color, complementary color; coloring; spectrum, prism, spectroscope; pigment, paint, dye, wash, stain.

v color, dye, tinge, stain, tint, paint, wash; illuminate, emblazon.

adj colored, dyed, tinted; prismatic, chromatic; bright, vivid, intense, deep, rich, gorgeous; fresh, unfaded; gaudy, florid, garish, showy, flashy, glaring; mellow, harmonious, pearly, sweet, delicate, tender, refined; dull, gray.

429 [absence of color] **colorlessness** *n* neutral tint, black and white, chiaroscuro, monochrome; etiolation, pallor, paleness, discoloration.

v lose color, fade, turn pale, become colorless, pale; deprive of color, bleach, wash out, blanch, tarnish, etiolate, tone down, whiten.

adj uncolored, colorless, hueless, pale, pallid, faint, dull, dun, wan, sallow, dingy, ashy, gray, ashen, lackluster; discolored; light-colored, fair, blond, white.

430 whiteness *n* milkiness, frostiness, silveriness, pearliness; etiolation, albification, decoloration, colorlessness; albinism.

v whiten, bleach, blanch, etiolate, whitewash.

adj white, snowy, frosted, snow-white, milk-white, milky, chalky, pearly, ivory, silver, silvery, opaline, whitish, albinistic, etiolated, bleached, blanched, fair, light, wan, pallid, pale, lackluster, colorless, anemic, sallow, faint.

431 blackness *n* darkness, swarthiness, lividness; ink, ebony, coal, charcoal, pitch; obscurity.

v black, blacken, darken; blot, smutch, smut, smirch.

adj black, sable, somber, livid, dark, inky, ebony, pitchy, swarthy, sooty, dingy, dusky, murky; jet-black, pitch-black, black as coal, coal-black, kohl-black, black as night.

432 gray *n* grayness, neutral tint, silver, salt and pepper, dove color.

adj gray, iron-gray, silver, silvery, silverish, grayish, dun, drab, ashy, ashen, dove-colored, dapple-gray; grizzly, grizzled, hoary.

433 brown *n* brownness, beige, khaki.

adj brown, bay, dapple, auburn, nutbrown, chocolate, chestnut, cinnamon, russet, tawny, tan, brunette, mahogany, khaki, beige, ochre, sepia, hazel, brownish, coffee, cocoa, rust, roan, sorrel.

434 red *n* redness; blush, color.

v redden, blush, flush, get red in the face, turn color.

adj red, reddish, scarlet, crimson, blood red, bloody, cherry-colored, vermilion, carmine, maroon, pink, hot pink, rosy, ruby, salmon, wine-colored; red-faced, blushing, embarrassed, red as beet, red as a lobster, flushed, burning, fuming, flaming, inflamed; ruddy, glowing, blooming, warm, hot.

435 green *n* greenness, verdure, blue and yellow.

adj green, greenish, verdant, olive, pea-green, emerald, apple, Kelly green, blue-green, aquamarine, sea-green; grassy, verdurous; fresh, new, recent, young, innocent, naive, raw, unseasoned, immature, inexperienced, ignorant; sickly, wan, pale, livid; jealous, envious.

436 yellow *n* yellowness, jaundice.

v yellow, age, turn color, dry up.

adj yellow, yellowish, gold, golden, ocher, lemon, citrine, saffron, aureate, creamy, straw-colored, flaxen, blond, tawny, sallow; sordid, cheap; cowardly, *(informal)* chicken, craven, lily-livered, contemptible, despicable, mean, cringing, groveling; jaundiced.

437 purple *n* blue and red.

adj purple, purplish, lavender, lilac, magenta, orchid, violet, plum-colored, mauve.

438 blue *n* blueness.

adj blue, bluish, azure, marine blue, navy, aquamarine, greenish blue, sapphire, turquoise, cobalt, baby blue; depressed, down in the dumps, *(informal)* in the pits, *(informal)* down, low.

439 orange *n* red and yellow; flame.

adj orange, orangy, orangish, brass, copper, apricot, tangerine, gold, flame-colored.

440 variegation *n* striation, spottiness, streakiness, iridescence, play of colors.

v variegate, diversify, streak, stripe, checker, speckle, bespeckle, fleck, dapple; dot, striate, tattoo, inlay; embroider, quilt.

adj variegated, multi-colored, many-colored, kaleidoscopic; iridescent, prismatic, opaline, nacreous, pearly; pied, piebald, mottled; dappled, salt and pepper, marbled, flecked, speckled, spotty, studded, freckled, flecky, spotted, diversified; striped, veined, lined, striated, streaked, brindled, banded, checked, checkered, plaid, mosaic, inlaid.

441 vision *n* sight, optics, eyesight; view, look, glance, ken, glimpse, peep, peek, gaze, stare, leer; contemplation, regard, survey; point of view, outlook, viewpoint, perspective, standpoint; perspicacity, discernment, perception, penetration.

v see, behold, discern, perceive, have in sight, descry, sight, make out, discover, distinguish, recognize, spy, espy, catch a glimpse of, command a view of, witness; envision, contemplate; look, view, eye, survey, scan, inspect, run the eye over, glance around; observe, watch, watch for, peep, peer, peek, pry, take a peep, leer, ogle, glare.

adj visual, ocular, optic; clear-sighted, eagle-eyed, discerning; visionary, farsighted.

adv on sight, at first sight, at a glance.

442 blindness *n* sightlessness; cataract; ignorance.

v be blind, not see; grope in the dark; blind, hoodwink, dazzle; screen, hide, mask.

adj blind, eyeless, sightless, unseeing, dark, purblind, stone-blind; dimsighted, undiscerning, ignorant.

adv blindly, blindfold, darkly.

443 [imperfect vision] **dimsightedness** *n* nearsightedness, farsightedness, purblindness, presbyopia, myopia, astigmatism, color blindness, cataract, ophthalmia; squint, cross-eye, strabismus, lazy eye, cockeye, swivel eye, goggle eyes.

fallacies of vision: refraction, distortion, illusion, mirage, phantasm, vision, specter, apparition, ghost; mirror, lens.

v be dimsighted, see double, wink, blink, squint, look askance, screw up the eyes.

adj dimsighted, purblind, myopic, astigmatic, nearsighted, farsighted, colorblind; blear-eyed, goggle-eyed, cockeyed, crosseyed.

444 spectator *n* beholder, observer, looker-on, onlooker, witness, eyewitness, bystander, passerby; sightseer, audience, crowd; spy, sentinel.

v witness, behold, look on.

445 optical instruments *n* lens, magnifying glass, microscope; spectacles, monocle, eyeglasses, glasses, contact lens, goggles, pince-nez; telescope, lorgnette, binoculars, spyglass, opera glasses; mirror, looking glass, reflector; prism, kaleidoscope, stereoscope.

446 visibility *n* perceptibility, discernibleness, distinctness, clearness, clarity, perceivability, conspicuousness, definition, sharp outline; appearance, manifestation.

v be visible, appear, open to the view, present itself, show itself, reveal itself, peep up, show up, turn up, start up, pop up, crop up; glimmer, loom; burst forth, burst upon the view, come into sight, come into view, come forth, come forward, attract attention.

adj visible, perceptible, discernible, perceivable, apparent, obvious, manifest, plain, clear, distinct, definite, well-defined, outlined, well-marked; recognizable, palpable, glaring, conspicuous, in full view, in full sight, in front of one's nose, under one's nose, before one's eyes.

447 invisibility *n* indistinctness, imperceptibility, invisibleness, indefiniteness; mystery, obscurity, delitescence, haziness, cloudiness; concealment; latency.

v be invisible; be hidden; escape notice; render invisible, conceal, hide.

adj invisible, imperceptible; not in sight, out of sight, out of view, unseen; inconspicuous, covert; dim, faint, mysterious, dark, obscure, confused, indistinct, indistinguishable, shadowy, indefinite, undefined, unmarked, blurry, blurred, unfocused, out of focus, misty, veiled; concealed, hidden.

448 appearance *n* phenomenon, sight, show, scene, view; prospect, vista, perspective, lookout, outlook, bird's-eye view, scenery, landscape, picture, tableau; display, exposure; pageant, spectacle; aspect, phase, seeming, shape, form, manifestation, guise, look, complexion, color, image, mien, air, cast, carriage, comportment, demeanor; presence; feature, trait, lines, outline, contour, face, countenance, physiognomy, visage, profile, outsides.

v appear, be visible, seem, look, show, present; figure, cut a figure; present to the view.

adj apparent, seeming, ostensible.

adv apparently, to all appearance, ostensibly, seemingly, on the face of it, at first sight, to the eye.

449 disappearance *n* evanescence, eclipse; departure, exit; loss.

v disappear, vanish, dissolve, melt, melt away, fade, pass, pass out, go, depart, leave no trace, be gone.

adj disappearing, evanescent; departed, left; missing, lost, vanished.

Class IV

Intellectual Faculties

I. Formation of Ideas

450 intellect *n* rationality, mind, understanding, reason, faculties, judgment, sense, common sense, wits, brains, (*informal*) smarts; brain, head, pate, (*informal*) noodle, skull, (*informal*) upstairs.

v intellectualize, reason, understand, realize, ruminate; note, notice, mark, be aware of, take cognizance of.

adj intellectual, mental, cerebral, rational, sensical, commonsensical.

450a absence of intellect *n* want of intellect; inanity, imbecility, brutishness, brute instinct.

adj unintellectual, unintelligent, unrational, nonrational, empty-headed.

451 thought *n* abstraction, concept, conception, opinion, judgment, belief, idea, notion, tenet, conviction, speculation, consideration, contemplation; meditation, pondering, reflection, musing, cogitation, thinking; intention, design, purpose, intent; anticipation, expectation; consideration, attention, care, regard; trifle, mote.

v think, cogitate, meditate, reflect, muse, ponder, ruminate, contemplate; consider, regard, suppose, look upon, judge, esteem, deem, count, account; bear in mind, recollect, recall, remember; intend, mean, design, purpose; believe, suppose; anticipate, expect.

adj thoughtful, contemplative, meditative, reflective, pensive, deliberate; lost in thought, absorbed, engrossed in; careful, heedful, mindful, regardful, considerate, attentive; discreet, prudent, wary, cautious, circumspect.

452 absence of thought *n* incogitancy, vacancy of mind, thoughtlessness, fatuity, vacuity, emptiness; inattention.

v not think, make the mind a blank, (*informal*) turn off the brain, (*informal*) tune out.

adj vacant, unoccupied, empty; unthinking; inattentive, absent, (*informal*) turned off, (*informal*) tuned out; thoughtless, inconsiderate, unmindful, unheedful, imprudent; unreflective.

453 idea *n* thought, conception, theory, notion; observation, impression, apprehension, perception, brainstorm, brainchild, fancy, (*informal*) flash; opinion, view, belief, sentiment, judgment, supposition; plan, object, objective, aim.

adj ideational.

454 topic *n* subject, theme, thesis, subject-matter, food for thought; business, affair, argument.

adj topical, thematic.

adv under consideration, in question.

455 curiosity *n* interest, inquisitiveness, inquiring mind, thirst for knowledge; spying, prying, meddlesomeness, spy, eavesdropper, gossip.

v be curious, take an interest in, stare, gape, spy, pry.

adj curious, inquisitive, inquiring, prying, spying, peeping, meddlesome, interested.

456 incuriosity *n* lack of interest, incuriousness, indifference, unconcern.

v have no curiosity, take no interest in.

adj incurious, uninquisitive, uninquiring, uninterested, indifferent, impassive, bored, apathetic.

457 attention *n* attending to, attentiveness, intentiveness, care, consideration, observation, heed, regard, mindfulness, notice, watchfulness, alertness; study, scrutiny; civility, courtesy, respect, politeness.

v be attentive, attend, observe, look, see, notice, remark, regard, pay attention, heed; examine, study, scrutinize.

adj attentive, observant, mindful, heedful, thoughtful, alive, alert, awake, on the watch, wary, circumspectful, watchful, careful; polite, courteous, respectful, deferential.

458 inattention *n* inattentiveness, inconsideration, heedlessness, unmindfulness, disregard, unconcern.

v be inattentive, overlook, disregard, pay no attention to, gloss over.

adj inattentive, unobservant, unmindful, unheeding, thoughtless, blind to, deaf to, napping, asleep, lost.

459 care *n* heed, caution, prudence, pains, anxiety, regard, attention, vigilance, carefulness, solicitude, circumspection, alertness, watchfulness, wakefulness; accuracy, exactness.

v be careful, take care.

adj careful, cautious, circumspect, watchful, vigilant, guarded, wary, prudent, tactful; painstaking, meticulous, discerning, exact, thorough, concerned, scrupulous, particular, finical, conscientious, attentive, heedful, thoughtful.

460 neglect *n* disregard, dereliction, negligence, remissness, carelessness, failure, omission, default, inattention, heedlessness, recklessness.

v neglect, disregard, ignore, slight, overlook, omit, be remiss, be negligent.

adj neglectful, disregardful, remiss, careless, negligent, unmindful, inattentive, indifferent, heedless, inconsiderate, thoughtless, imprudent; unwary, unguarded; neglecting, neglected, unheeded, uncared for, unobserved, unnoticed, unattended to.

461 inquiry *n* investigation, examination, study, scrutiny, exploration, research, search, pursuit; inquiring, questioning, interrogation; query, question.

inquirer, investigator, inquisitor, inspector.

v inquire, ask, question, interrogate, query, investigate, examine, seek, search, look for, study, consider.

adj inquiring, inquisitive, curious, scrutinizing, questioning, exploring; inquisitorial, exploratory, interrogative.

462 answer *n* reply, response, retort, rejoinder; discovery, solution; rationale.

v answer, reply, respond, rebut, retort, rejoin; explain, interpret, discover, solve; satisfy, set at rest, atone for.

adj responsive; answerable, discoverable, soluble.

463 experiment *n* test, trial, examination, proof, assay, procedure; experimentation, research, investigation, analysis.

experimenter, analyzer, adventurer.

v experiment, try, test, examine, analyze, prove, assay, essay.

adj experimental, probative, analytic.

464 comparison *n* collation, association, relating, likening, correlation, comparative relation, setting side by side, juxtaposition.

v compare, collate, confront, place side by side, pit one against another, juxtapose, relate, correlate.

adj comparative, metaphorical, compared with; comparable.

465 discrimination *n* distinction, differentiation, diagnosis; appreciation, estimation, discernment, critique, judgment; nicety, refinement, taste.

v discriminate, distinguish, set apart, differentiate.

adj discriminating, critical, distinguishing, discriminative, discriminatory, choosy, picky; discerning, perceptive; tasteful, refined.

465a indiscrimination *n* indistinction, indistinctness, lack of discernment.

v be indiscriminate, not discriminate, confound, confuse.

adj indiscriminate, miscellaneous, undiscriminating.

466 measurement *n* survey, valuation, appraisement, assessment, estimate, estimation, reckoning, gauging; measure, standard, rule, gauge, scale.

v measure, survey, assess, rate, value, appraise, estimate.

adj measurable.

467 [on one side] **evidence** *n* facts, indication, sign, signal; ground, grounds, proof, testimony; information, deposition, affidavit, exhibit, citation, reference, confirmation, corroboration.

v be evident, evince, show, tell, cite, signal, indicate, imply, argue, bespeak; give evidence, testify, depose, witness.

adj evident, evidential, indicative, inferential, referential, corroborative, confirmatory.

468 counter-evidence *n* disproof, refutation, rebuttal, conflicting evidence, negation.

v rebut, refute, check, weaken, contravene, contradict, deny.

adj countervailing, contradictory, conflicting, unsupportive, uncorroborative.

469 qualification *n* modification, limitation, mitigation, narrowing, restriction, coloring, allowance, consideration, extenuation, extenuating circumstances, condition, proviso, exception.

v qualify, modify, limit, mitigate, restrain, narrow, restrict, color, allow, allow for, make allowance for, consider, extenuate, except, make an exception, take into account, take into consideration.

adj qualified, qualifying, provided, conditional, extenuating, mitigating, admitting, supposing, with the proviso, provided that.

470 possibility *n* feasibility, practicality, likelihood, potentiality; contingency, chance.

v be possible, stand a chance, admit of, (*informal*) could be.

adj possible, imaginable, conceivable, credible, feasible, practical, performable, achievable, within reach, within the bounds of possibility, potential.

adv possibly, perhaps, perchance, peradventure, maybe.

471 impossibility *n* impracticality, unfeasibility, hopelessness.

v be impossible, have no chance.

adj impossible, not possible, inconceivable, incredible, unimaginable, unreasonable, unfeasible, impractical, unobtainable, unperformable, unachievable, beyond the bounds of reason, absurd, (*informal*) fat chance, (*informal*) no way.

472 probability *n* likelihood, likeliness, plausibility, tendency, prospect, good chance, reasonable chance, expectation.

v be probable, point to, tend, imply, bid fair.

adj probable, likely, plausible, reasonable, presumable, well-founded, hopeful.

adv probably, in all probability, in all likelihood, most likely, presumably.

473 improbability *n* unlikelihood, bare possibility, implausibility, doubtfulness, questionableness.

v be improbable, not have much of a chance.

adj improbable, unlikely, implausible, doubtful, questionable, beyond all reasonable expectation.

474 certainty *n* fact, truth; infallibility, reliability, unquestionableness, inevitability, certitude, assurance, confidence, conviction.

v be certain, stand to reason, render certain, clinch, make sure; know.

adj certain, confident, sure, assured, convinced, satisfied, indubitable, indisputable, unquestionable, undeniable, incontestable, unimpeachable, irrefutable, unquestioned, incontrovertible, absolute, positive, plain, patent, obvious, clear; sure, inevitable, infallible, unfailing; fixed, agreed upon, settled, prescribed, determined, determinate, constant, stated, given; definite, particular, special, especial; reliable, trustworthy, dependable, trusty.

adv certainly, for certain, no doubt, doubtless, undoubtedly, (*informal*) sure enough.

475 uncertainty *n* insecurity, instability, unreliability, fallibility, danger; incertitude, doubt, doubtfulness, ambiguity, vagueness, questionableness, dubiousness; haziness, fogginess, obscurity; undependability, changeableness, variability, capriciousness, irregularity, fitfulness, chanciness.

v be uncertain, hesitate, flounder, waver; render uncertain, pose, puzzle, perplex, confuse, confound, bewilder; doubt, question.

adj uncertain, insecure, precarious, unsure, doubtful, unpredictable, problematical, unstable, unreliable, unsafe, fallible, perilous, dangerous; unassured, undecided, indeterminate, undetermined, unfixed, unsettled, indefinite, ambiguous, questionable, dubious; doubtful, vague, indistinct; undependable, changeable, variable, capricious, unsteady, irregular, fitful, desultory, chance, (*informal*) chancy.

476 reasoning *n* ratiocination, rationalism, dialectics; discussion, comment, argumentation, debate, disputation.

logic, induction, deduction, chain of thought, analysis, synthesis, syllogistic reasoning.

argument, case, proposition, terms, premises, postulate, data; inference, *argumentum ad hominem*, *paralipsis*, *a priori*, *a posteriori*, *reductio ad absurdum*, enthymeme, dilemma, on the horns of a dilemma.

reasoner, logician, dialectician, disputant, wrangler, arguer, debater, polemicist, casuist, rationalist.

arguments, reasons, pros and cons.

v to reason, discuss, argue, debate, dispute, wrangle; deduce, induce, infer, analyze, synthesize, postulate, propose, contend, demonstrate.

adj reasoning, rationalistic, dialectical, dialectic, argumentative, disputatious; logical, inductive, deductive, analytical, synthetic, syllogistic, inferential; demonstrable.

477 [the absence of reasoning] **intuition**.

[false reasoning] **sophistry** *n* intuition, instinct, hunch, presentiment; insight, discernment, inspiration.

casuistry, jesuitry, perversion, equivocation, evasion, chicanery, quiddity, speciousness, (*informal*) bull, (*informal*) malarkey, bunk; false statement; fallacy, sophism.

sophist.

v intuit; reason falsely, pervert, quibble, equivocate, evade, mislead, gloss over, cavil, refine, subtilize, misrepresent, fence, beg the question.

adj intuitive, instinctive, instinctual, sophistical, equivocal, evasive, specious, fallacious, illogical, unsound, false, incorrect, untenable; inconsequential, weak, feeble, poor, flimsy, vague, nonsensical, absurd, foolish; frivolous, pettifogging, trifling, quibbling, nit-picking, subtle, over-refined.

adv intuitively, by intuition; illogically.

478 demonstration *n* proof, conclusiveness, example, verification, explanation.

v demonstrate, prove, establish, verify; evince, show, explain.

adj demonstrative, demonstrable, probative, conclusive, convincing; demonstrated, proven, proved, shown.

479 confutation *n* refutation, answer, disproof, invalidation, exposure.

v confute, refute, disprove, expose the error, overturn, invalidate.

adj confutable, refutable.

480 judgment *n* verdict, decree, decision, determination, conclusion, result, upshot, deduction, inference, assessment, opinion, estimate, criticism, critique; understanding, discrimination, discernment, perspicacity, sagacity, wisdom, intelligence, prudence, brains, taste, penetration, discretion, common sense.

judge, assessor, reviewer, critic, commentator; connoisseur.

v judge, estimate, consider, regard, esteem, appreciate, appraise, reckon, value; decide, determine, conclude, form an opinion, pass judgment; criticize, rate, rank; try, pass sentence upon, rule.

adj judicious, judicial, judgmental, determinate, conclusive; critical, discriminating, penetrating, perspicacious.

480a discovery *n* detection, determination, disclosure, trove, find.

v discover, learn of, ascertain, unearth, uncover, determine, ferret out, flush out, dig up; find out, detect, espy, descry, discern, see, notice, hit upon, stumble onto.

481 misjudgment *n* miscalculation, miscomputation, misconception, misinterpretation, misapprehension.

v misjudge, misconjecture, misconceive, misunderstand, misconstrue, misinterpret; overestimate, underestimate.

adj misjudging, ill-judging, wrongheaded, (*informal*) off base, wrong, in error.

482 overestimation *n* exaggeration, overvaluation, optimism; miscalculation.

v overestimate, overrate, overprize, overpraise, exaggerate, magnify, attach too much importance to, set too high a value on; miscalculate.

adj overestimated, overrated, inflated, pompous, pretentious.

483 underestimation *n* undervaluation, depreciation, detraction; modesty, self-depreciation; pessimism.

v underestimate, undervalue, underrate, depreciate, disparage, detract, slight, minimize, make light of, make little of, disregard.

adj underestimating, depreciating, depreciative, deprecatory; underestimated, depreciated, unvalued, unprized; modest, pessimistic.

484 belief *n* opinion, view, tenet, doctrine, dogma, creed; certainty, conviction, assurance, confidence, persuasion, believing, trust, reliance; credence, credit, acceptance, faith, assent.

believe, credit, give credence to, accept, have faith in, give assent, accept; know, see, realize, assume, presume; think, opine, hold, conceive, consider; rely on, put one's trust on, have confidence in.

adj certain, sure, assured, positive, cocksure, satisfied, confident, convinced, secure; believing, trusting, confiding, credulous; believed, accredited, trusted, accepted; believable, credible, trustworthy.

485 disbelief, doubt *n* disbelief, incredulity; dissent, change of mind, retraction.

uncertainty, irresolution, hesitation, hesitancy, vacillation, misgiving, suspense; scruple, qualm, mistrust, distrust, suspicion, skepticism.

unbeliever, nonbeliever; skeptic.

v disbelieve, discredit, dissent, doubt, distrust, mistrust, suspect, have qualms; hesitate, waver, demur.

adj unbelieving, incredulous, doubtful, disputable, questionable, suspicious; uncertain, unsure; doubting, hesitating, hesitant, wavering, irresolute, dubious, skeptical.

486 credulity *n* credulousness, gullibility, infatuation, superstition, self-deception, self-delusion.

gull, dupe, (*informal*) sucker.

v be credulous, swallow.

adj credulous, believing, trusting, unsuspecting, gullible; simple, silly, childish, stupid; infatuated, superstitious.

487 incredulity *n* incredulousness, caution, wariness, suspicion, doubt, skepticism, disbelief.

nonbeliever, skeptic, heretic.

v be incredulous, distrust, doubt, suspect.

adj incredulous, cautious, wary, suspicious, dubious, doubtful, skeptical, unbelieving.

488 assent *n* acknowledgment, agreement, concurrence, acquiescence, consent, allowance, approval, concord, accord, approbation.

v assent, acquiesce, accede, concur, agree, fall in, acknowledge, admit, yield, allow; own, avow, confess.

adj assenting, agreeing, concurring, consenting, of one accord, of the same mind; agreed, acquiescent.

489 dissent *n* difference, discordance, dissension, disagreement, dissatisfaction; opposition, protest; nonconformity, separation.

dissenter, protester, rebel, radical, dissident, nonconformist.

v dissent, differ, disagree, protest, contradict; repudiate.

adj dissenting, negative; dissident, contradictory, disagreeing, opposing; nonconformist.

490 knowledge *n* enlightenment, erudition, wisdom, science, letters, information, learning, scholarship, lore; understanding, discernment, perception, apprehension, comprehension, judgment.

v know, be aware of; understand, discern, perceive, realize, fathom, apprehend, comprehend, (*informal*) dig; (*informal*) be hip; learn, discover.

adj knowing, aware of, cognizant of, acquainted with, privy to; discerning, perceptive, (*informal*) sharp, shrewd; knowledgeable, educated, enlightened, erudite, wise, instructed, learned, well-educated, bookish, well-read; known, recognized, received.

491 ignorance *n* illiteracy, unenlightenment, unawareness, unlearnedness, unacquaintance, unconsciousness, inexperience, darkness, blindness, incomprehension, simplicity, stupidity.

v be ignorant, know nothing, have no idea, be blind to.

adj ignorant, illiterate, unlettered, uneducated, uninstructed, untaught, untutored, uninformed, unenlightened, nescient; shallow, superficial; stupid, dumb, thick, dull.

492 scholar *n* savant, wise man, sage, academician, thinker, intellectual, bibliomaniac, bookworm, pedant; student, pupil, disciple, learner.

493 ignoramus *n* illiterate, know-nothing, blockhead, numskull, dullard, simpleton, dunce, ass, fool, bonehead, duffer, dolt, turkey, twerp, idiot, imbecile, cretin, moron, dimwit, (*informal*) jerk.

494 truth *n* fact, reality, verity, veracity; accuracy, precision, exactness.

v be true, be the case, have a true ring.

adj true, factual, actual, real, authentic, genuine, veracious, truthful, veritable; pure, natural; accurate, exact, faithful, correct, precise; agreeing; right, proper; legitimate, rightful; to the point, (*informal*) right on, (*informal*) where it's at, (*informal*) on target.

495 error *n* fallacy, misconception, misapprehension, misunderstanding, misinterpretation, misjudgment; aberration, inexactness, laxity; mistake, fault, blunder, slip, oversight, flaw, stumble, bungle; delusion, false impression.

v err, be in error, mistake, blunder, slip, go astray, trip up; misconceive, misapprehend, misunderstand, misinterpret, miscalculate, misjudge.

adj erroneous, in error, fallacious, mistaken, incorrect, inaccurate, false, wrong, untrue, (*informal*) off base, (*informal*) off the mark.

496 maxim *n* proverb, aphorism, dictum, saying, adage, apothegm, motto, epigram, *mot juste*, truism, words of wisdom, axiom.

adj proverbial, aphoristic, axiomatic, truistic, (*informal*) corny, trite.

adv as they say, as the saying goes.

497 absurdity *n* nonsense, imbecility, foolishness, silliness, inanity, stupidity; farce, rhapsody, farrago, blunder, bathos; inconsistency, paradox, *non sequitur*, jargon, extravagance, exaggeration.

v be absurd, talk nonsense, play the fool.

adj absurd, nonsensical, ridiculous, silly, preposterous, foolish, inane, asinine, stupid, senseless, unreasonable, irrational, incongruous, self-contradictory, paradoxical; farcical, rhapsodic, bathetic, extravagant, exaggerated, bombastic, fantastic, meaningless.

498 intelligence. wisdom *n* intelligence, intellect, mind, capacity, understanding, discernment, reason, acumen, aptitude, penetration, brains, (*informal*) smarts; knowledge, news, information, tidings.

discretion, reasonableness, judgment, discernment, insight, sense, common sense, sagacity, insight, understanding, prudence; knowledge, information, learning, sapience, erudition, enlightenment.

v be intelligent; understand, discern, reason; be wise, discriminate.

adj intelligent, understanding, intellectual, quick, bright; astute, clever, sharp, alert, bright, apt, discerning, canny, shrewd, nimble, penetrating, piercing, on the ball.

wise, discerning, judicious, sage, sapient, sensible, sound, penetrating, sagacious, intelligent, perspicacious, profound, rational, prudent, cautious, politic, reasonable, thoughtful, reflective; learned, educated, erudite, schooled.

499 imbecility. folly *n* imbecility, want of intelligence, incompetence, incapacity, vacancy, dull understanding, meanness, simplicity, shallowness, stolidity, hebetude, puerility, fatuity, silliness, foolishness, driveling, stupidity, idiocy.

frivolity, irrationality, trifling, ineptitude, silliness, eccentricity, extravagance; rashness.

v be imbecilic,

be foolish, trifle, drivel, dote, ramble.

adj imbecile, imbecilic, idiotic, fatuous, driveling; vacant, mindless, witless, brainless, weak-headed, addle-brained, muddle-headed, dull-witted, feeble-minded, half-witted, dull, shallow, stolid, dim-witted, thick-skulled; shallow, weak, wanting, soft, sappy, stupid, obtuse, blunt, stolid, doltish, thick as a brick, asinine; childish, childlike, infantile, puerile, simple.

foolish, silly, senseless, irrational, insensate, nonsensical, inept, frivolous, trifling; eccentric, crazed, rash, thoughtless, giddy, obstinate, bigoted, narrow-minded; foolish, unwise, injudicious, improper, unreasonable, ridiculous, stupid, asinine; ill-conceived, ill-advised, ill-judged, inexpedient, extravagant, frivolous, trivial, useless.

500 sage *n* wise man, master mind, thinker, philosopher, oracle, luminary, man of learning, expert, authority.

501 fool *n* simpleton, dolt, dunce, blockhead, nincompoop, ninny, numskull, ignoramus, booby, sap, dunderhead, dunderpate, idiot, natural, oaf, lout, loon, dullard; jester, buffoon, droll, zany, harlequin, clown; imbecile, moron, idiot, cretin.

502 sanity *n* soundness, mental balance, rationality, reason, sense, clear-headedness, lucidity, coherence, normality, sobriety, (*informal*) good head.

v be sane, (*informal*) have one's act together.

adj sane, rational, reasonable, sensible, clearheaded, level-headed, logical, sober, lucid, self-possessed, (*informal*) together.

503 insanity *n* disorder, imbalance, derangement, dementia, lunacy, madness, craziness, aberration; frenzy, raving, incoherence, delirium, delusion; (*informal*) oddity, eccentricity, twist, mania.

v be insane, become insane, lose one's senses, go mad, rave, rant, (*informal*) lose it.

adj insane, deranged, demented, lunatic, crazed, crazy, maniacal, mad, touched, cracked, unhinged, unsettled, daft, frenzied, possessed, delirious, far gone, wild, flighty, distracted, frantic, mad as a hatter, (*informal*) crackers, (*informal*) zonkers, (*informal*) nuts, (*informal*) zonko, (*informal*) weird, (*informal*) bananas, (*informal*) kaput.

504 madman *n* lunatic, maniac, bedlamite, raver, (*informal*) nut, (*informal*) weirdo, (*informal*) crazy; dreamer, romantic, rhapsodist, enthusiast, visionary, seer, fanatic.

505 memory *n* retention, retentiveness, remembrance, recollection, reminiscence, retrospect; recognition; reminder, hint, suggestion, keepsake, souvenir, memento, token, memorial.

v remember, recall, recollect, call up, call to mind, bring to mind, think back upon, haunt one's thoughts, (*informal*) flash on; remind, suggest, hint, prompt, summon up, reminisce; retain, keep in mind, bear in mind, memorize, engrave in the mind, learn by heart; keep the memory alive.

adj reminiscent (of), mindful (of); fresh, alive, vivid; unforgotten, enduring, indelible, memorable, never to be forgotten, unforgettable, stirring, eventful.

506 oblivion *n* forgetfulness, short memory, slippery memory, untrustworthy memory, obliteration of the past, amnesia.

v forget, be forgetful, have a short memory, lose sight of, sink into oblivion; unlearn, efface from the memory, think no more of, consign to oblivion, banish from one's thoughts.

adj oblivious, forgetful, heedless, deaf to the past, insensible; out of mind, unremembered, forgotten, past recollection, buried, sunk into oblivion.

507 expectation *n* expectancy, anticipation, prospect, reckoning, calculation; suspense, waiting; hope, trust, assurance, confidence, reliance, presumption.

v expect, look for, look out for, look forward to, anticipate, await, hope for, wait for, foresee, prepare for, count on, rely on; predict, prognosticate, forecast.

adj expectant, watchful, vigilant, open-eyed, on tenterhooks, on one's toes, ready, in readiness, prepared, (*informal*) all set for; foreseen, long expected, prospective, in view, in sight, on the horizon, impending.

adv expectantly, on the watch, on edge, with bated breath.

508 nonexpectation *n* unforeseen occurrence, surprise, shock, blow, wonder, bolt out of the blue, astonishment; miscalculation, false expectation.

v not expect, be taken by surprise, catch unawares; burst upon, come out of nowhere, drop from the clouds; surprise, startle, stun, stagger, throw off one's guard, astonish.

adj nonexpectant, surprised, unwarned, unaware, off one's guard; unanticipated, unexpected, unlooked for, unforeseen; unheard of, startling; sudden.

adv unexpectedly, abruptly, suddenly, without warning.

509 [failure of expectation] **disappointment** *n* failure, defeat, frustration, unfulfillment, blighted hope, vain expectation, disillusion, (*informal*) come-down.

v be disappointed; disappoint, dash one's hopes, dash one's expectations, balk, jilt, tantalize; dumfound, disillusion, let down.

adj disappointed; disgruntled, disconcerted, aghast.

510 foresight *n* prudence, forethought, prevision, anticipation, precaution; forecast; prescience, fore-knowledge, prospect.

v foresee; look forward to, look ahead, look beyond; look into the future; see one's future, catch the lay of the land; anticipate, expect, assume, surmise, predict, forewarn.

adj anticipatory, prescient; far-sighted, prudent, provident; prospective, expectant.

511 prediction *n* prophecy, forecast, augury, prognostication, foretoken, portent, divination, soothsaying, presage.

v predict, foretell, prophesy, foresee, forecast, presage, augur, prognosticate, foretoken, portend, divine.

adj prophetic, oracular, portentous, premonitory.

512 omen *n* portent, foreboding, augury, sign, harbinger; sign of the times, symbol, warning.

513 oracle *n* prophet, prophetess, seer, soothsayer, augur, fortune-teller, witch, sibyl, necromancer, sorcerer, clairvoyant, interpreter.

514 supposition *n* assumption, presumption, condition, hypothesis, theory, postulate, proposition, thesis, theorem; conjecture, suggestion, guess, guesswork, suspicion, inkling, speculation.

v suppose, conjecture, surmise, suspect, guess, divine; theorize, speculate, presume, presuppose, assume, predicate; believe, take for granted; propound, put forth, propose, advance, hazard a suggestion, suggest.

adj assumed, given; conjectural, hypothetical, presumptive, theoretical, speculative, suggestive.

515 imagination *n* imaginativeness, fancy, invention, inspiration, creativity, originality, fiction, vision, fantasy, illusion, ideality, castles in the air, dreaming, dream, golden dreams; mental image, conception, idea, notion, thought, conceit, fancy, whim, figment, romance, vision, dream, chimera, shadow, illusion, phantasm, supposition, delusion; verve, vivacity, liveliness, animation.

v imagine, fancy, conceive, dream, idealize; create, originate, think up, devise, invent, coin, fabricate.

adj imaginative, fanciful, original, inventive, creative, visionary, ideal, unreal, illusory, unsubstantial, dreamy, dreamlike, romantic, fantastic, fabulous, chimerical, fantastical; vivacious, lively, animated; imaginable, conceivable, possible, believable; imagined.

II. Communication of Ideas

516 [idea to be conveyed] **meaning** *n* tenor, spirit, gist, trend, idea, purport, significance, signification, sense, import, denotation, conotation, interpretation; intent, intention, aim, object, purpose, design.

thing signified: matter, subject matter, substance, gist, argument.

v mean, signify, denote, conote, express, import, purport; convey, imply, indicate, point to, allude to, touch on, drive at, involve; declare, affirm, state; intend, aim, design, purpose.

adj meaning; meaningful, pointed, poignant, significant, expressive.

517 meaninglessness *n* unmeaningness, absence of meaning, senselessness, emptiness, empty words, rhetoric, platitude, nonsense, jargon, gibberish, jabber, rant, bombast, (*informal*) hot air; inanity, rigmarole, absurdity, ambiguity.

v mean nothing, jabber, rant, say nothing.

adj meaningless, senseless, nonsensical, inexpressive, vague, trivial, insignificant.

518 intelligibility *n* comprehensibility, clarity, clearness, lucidity, coherence, explicitness, persicuity, precision, plain-speaking.

v be intelligible; render intelligible, clear up, simplify, elucidate, explain; understand, comprehend, take in, catch on, grasp, follow, master.

adj intelligible, understandable, comprehensible, clear, clear as day, lucid, luminous, transparent; plain, distinct, pointed, clear-cut, obvious, explicit, precise; graphic, illustrative, expressive.

519 unintelligibility *n* incomprehensibility, vagueness, obscurity, ambiguity, uncertainty, confusion.

v be unintelligible; render unintelligible, conceal, darken, confuse, perplex, mystify, bewilder.

adj unintelligible, incomprehensible, indecipherable, unfathomable, inexplicable, inscrutable, insoluble, impenetrable; puzzling, enigmatic, obscure, muddy, dim, nebulous, mysterious, (*informal*) strange, (*informal*) weird; inexpressible, incommunicable, ineffable, unutterable.

520 equivocalness *n* ambiguity, uncertainty, questionableness, dubiousness, indeterminateness; double-meaning, word-play, double entendre, pun, play on words, conundrum, riddle, quibble; equivocation, duplicity, prevarication, white lie.

v be equivocal; have two meanings; equivocate, prevaricate.

adj equivocal, ambiguous, uncertain, doubtful, questionable, dubious, indeterminate; duplicitous, enigmatic, double-edged, deceptive, misleading.

521 figure of speech *n* phrase, expression, euphemism, manner of speaking, colloquialism, idiom, image; metaphor, simile, imagery, poetic device, poetics, figures of beauty.

v employ figures of speech; image, speak prettily.

adj figurative, idiomatic, colloquial, colorful, imagistic, poetic, expressive, allusive.

522 interpretation *n* definition, explanation, explication, elucidation, translation; exegesis, exposition, comment, commentary, gloss; solution, answer, meaning.

v interpret, define, explain, explicate, elucidate, translate, shed light on, cast light on, decipher, decode, unravel, disentangle, gloss, annotate, expound, comment upon; construe, understand.

adj explanatory, expository, exegetical, interpretative, interpretive; interpretable, explicable, intelligible.

adv in explanation, that is to say, namely.

523 misinterpretation *n* misapprehension, misconception, misunderstanding, misreading, misconstruction, mistake; misrepresentation, perversion, exaggeration, false coloration, falsification, travesty.

v misinterpret, misapprehend, misconceive, misunderstand, misread, misconstrue, misapply, mistake; misrepresent, pervert, misstate, garble, falsify, distort, travesty, stretch the meaning, twist the meaning.

524 interpreter *n* translator, explainer, expounder, expositor, commentator, annotator, guide, critic; spokesman, speaker, representative.

525 manifestation *n* indication, expression, exposition, demonstration, showing, display, exhibition, declaration; materialization; openness, candor.

v make manifest, show, display, reveal, disclose, open, exhibit, evince, evidence, demonstrate, declare, express, make known; appear, be plain, come to light, materialize; indicate, point out.

adj manifest, evident, obvious, apparent, plain, clear, distinct, patent, open, palpable, visible, unmistakable, conspicuous, explicit; unreserved, downright, frank, plain spoken; barefaced, bold; manifested.

adv manifestly, openly, plainly, above board, in broad daylight, in plain sight.

526 latency *n* dormancy, latentness, quiescence, obscurity, darkness, hidden meaning, obscure meaning, undercurrent, suggestion, concealment; potentiality.

v be latent, lurk, smolder, underlie.

adj latent, dormant; lurking, secret, cryptic, veiled, hidden; potential; implied, implicit; allusive.

527 information *n* enlightenment, knowledge, news, data, facts, circumstances, situations, intelligence, advice; communication, notification, announcement, record; hint, suggestion, innuendo, inkling, whisper, insinuation.

informant, authority, intelligencer, reporter; informer, eavesdropper, detective, newsmonger; messenger.

guide, guidebook, handbook, manual, map, chart.

v inform, tell, acquaint with, impart to, make acquainted with, apprize, advise, enlighten; communicate, make known, express, mention, let fall, intimate, hint, insinuate, allude to, suggest; announce, report, give an account, disclose; know, learn, find out, get the scent of.

adj informed, communicated, reported, advised, apprized of, acquainted with, enlightened, published, (*informal*) filled in; declarative, expository, communicative.

528 concealment *n* hiding, secretion, ensconcing, sheltering, covering, burying, screening; keeping secret, secrecy, hiding, disguising, veiling, camouflaging, obscuring, dissembling, obfuscation, evasiveness; reticence, reserve, reservation, suppression, silence, secretiveness.

v conceal, hide, secrete, cover, put away, ensconce, bury, screen, shelter, keep out of sight, stow away; keep secret, hide, disguise, veil, cloak, mask, camouflage, obscure, obfuscate, dissemble, be evasive.

adj concealed, hidden, secret, private, privy, confidential, in secret, close, undercover, in hiding, in disguise, covert, mysterious; furtive, stealthy, surreptitious, secretive, evasive, clandestine; reserved, reticent, suppressed, uncommunicative.

adv secretly, in secret, in private, behind closed doors, on the sly; confidentially; stealthily.

529 disclosure *n* revelation, divulgence, exposition, exposure; exposé, uncovering, muckraking; acknowledgment, avowal, confession.

v disclose, discover, uncover, lay open, expose, bring to light, unmask; reveal, make known, divulge, show, tell, unveil, unmask, communicate; let slip, let drop, betray, blurt out; acknowledge, allow, concede, grant, admit, own up, confess.

adj disclosed, revealed.

530 [means of concealment] **ambush** *n* ambuscade, lurking place, trap, snare, pitfall; hiding place, secret place, recess, hole, cubbyhole; screen, cover, shade, blinker, veil, curtain, cloak, cloud; mask, visor, disguise, masquerade.

v ambush, lie in wait for, set a trap for.

531 publication *n* issuance, distribution; announcement, proclamation, promulgation, propagation, pronouncement, declaration, disclosure, divulgence, advertisement, publicity; edition.

v publish, issue, distribute, print; make public, make known, announce, proclaim, promulgate, propagate, circulate, spread, disseminate, declare, disclose, divulge, advertise, publicize, get into print.

adj published; current, public, in circulation, in print, in black and white.

532 news *n* information, intelligence, tidings, report, rumor, scuttlebutt, hearsay, gossip, (*informal*) the word; newsstory, headlines, copy.

reporter, newsmonger, talebearer, gossip, tattler, informer.

v transpire, make news, make headlines; be rumored.

adj in the news, in the headlines, current, in circulation, in print.

533 secret *n* mystery; problem, question, difficulty, a confidence; unintelligibility.

adj secret, hidden, concealed, unrevealed, unknown, mysterious; reticent, secretive; private.

534 messenger *n* envoy, emissary, representative, intermediary, go-between, delegate, courier, runner, errand boy; intelligencer, reporter, newsmonger, spokesman, informant; forerunner, harbinger, herald, precursor.

535 affirmation *n* statement, profession, pronouncement, deposition, assertion, declaration; confirmation, ratification, endorsement; swearing, oath, affidavit; emphasis, dogmatism.

v affirm, state, assert, aver, avow, maintain, declare, swear, asseverate, depose, testify, say, pronounce; establish, confirm, ratify, approve, endorse, assent, acknowledge; swear, emphasize.

adj affirmative, declaratory, declarative, positive, assertive, emphatic, dogmatic; confirmative, corroborative, affirming, acquiescent.

536 negation. denial *n* nullification, invalidation.

disputation, confutation, contradiction, qualification; repudiation, rejection, abjuration, disavowal, disclaimer, recantation, retraction, rebuttal.

v negate, nullify, cancel, invalidate.

deny, dispute, controvert, contravene, oppose, gainsay, contradict, rebut; reject, renounce, abjure, disclaim, disavow; recant, revoke; refuse, repudiate, disown.

adj contradictory; negative.

537 teaching *n* instruction, education, pedagogy, pedagogics, edification, tutelage, tutorship; guidance, direction, preparation, schooling, learning, discipline; lesson, lecture, disquisition, discourse, explanation, harangue, homily, sermon, lore; doctrine, dogma, tenet, principle, rule, maxim, article of faith, creed, credo, belief, opinion.

v teach, instruct, edify, educate, inform, enlighten, prepare, discipline, train, drill, tutor, prime, coach, guide, direct, school, indoctrinate, inculcate, infuse, instill, imbue; expound, interpret, lecture, discourse, hold forth, sermonize, moralize.

adj educational, scholastic, academic, pedagogic, pedagogical, didactic; edifying, instructive.

538 misteaching *n* misinformation, misdirection, misguidance, perversion, sophistry, error.

v misteach, misinform, misinstruct, misdirect, misguide, pervert, mislead, misrepresent, confuse, bewilder, lie.

539 learning *n* acquisition of knowledge, acquirements, attainment, mental cultivation, scholarship, erudition, study, inquiry, questioning, search, pursuit of knowledge.

apprenticeship, tutelage, matriculation.

v learn, acquire, gain knowledge, memorize, master, study, grind, cram, (*informal*) book, read, peruse, pore over, wade through, ingest, burn the midnight oil, (*informal*) pull an all-nighter.

adj studious, industrious; scholarly, scholastic, well-read, learned, erudite.

540 teacher *n* instructor, tutor, lecturer, professor, don, master, schoolmaster, guide, counselor, adviser, mentor; preacher, missionary, propagandist.

541 learner *n* scholar, student, pupil, apprentice, novice, neophyte, beginner; disciple, acolyte, follower.

542 school *n* academy, educational institution, college, university, institute, seminary, place of learning.

schoolbook, textbook, text, primer, grammar, reader, workbook.

adj scholastic, academic, collegiate.

543 veracity *n* truthfulness, frankness, truth, sincerity, candor, honesty, probity, fidelity, accuracy.

v speak the truth, (*informal*) level with, (*informal*) be straight with.

adj veracious, true, truthful, sincere, honest, honorable, candid, frank, open, straightforward, honest, scrupulous, punctilious, trustworthy.

544 falsehood *n* falsification, lie, fib, untruth, distortion, deception, misrepresentation, fabrication, fiction, sham; untruthfulness, lying, prevarication, duplicity, double dealing, deceitfulness, equivocation, dissembling, cunning, guile, insincerity, dishonesty, inaccuracy.

v lie, fib, falsify, prevaricate, misrepresent, deceive, (*informal*) come on to, doctor, feign, pretend, play false, dissemble, counterfeit, fabricate.

adj false, untrue, wrong, mistaken, incorrect, erroneous; untruthful, lying, mendacious, dishonest, deceitful, treacherous, faithless, insincere, hypocritical, disingenuous, unfaithful, cunning, perfidious, two-faced, recreant; deceptive, misleading, fallacious, spurious, fraudulent, bogus, phony, sham, counterfeit.

545 deception *n* deceiving, guiling, falseness, untruthfulness; artifice, sham, cheat, imposture, deceit, treachery, subterfuge, stratagem, ruse, hoax, fraud, trick, wile, snare, trap, illusion, delusion.

v deceive, mislead, lead astray, take in, delude, cheat, cozen, dupe, gull, fool, bamboozle, hoodwink, (*informal*) con, trick, double-cross, defraud, outwit; entrap, ensnare, betray.

adj deceptive, misleading, delusive, illusory, fallacious, specious, untrue, false, deceitful; tricky, cunning, insidious.

546 untruth *n* falsehood, fib, lie, fiction, story, tale, tall tale, fabrication, fable, forgery, invention.

v make believe, pretend, feign, sham, fib, lie.

adj untrue, false, trumped up, unfounded, invented, fictitious, fabulous.

547 dupe *n* gull, pigeon, laughingstock, greenhorn, fool, sucker, puppet, (*informal*) nebbish.

v be deceived, be the dupe of, fall into a trap, go for the bait, bite, swallow.

adj credulous, gullible, unsuspecting, trusting.

548 deceiver *n* dissembler, hypocrite, sophist, liar, (*informal*) fast talker, storyteller, (*informal*) faker, (*informal*) phony, fraud, (*informal*) four-flusher, (*informal*) shyster, confidence man, con man, cheat, swindler, imposter, pretender, humbug, adventurer, adventuress, serpent, snake in the grass.

549 exaggeration *n* overstatement, hyperbole, extravagance, coloring, coloration, embroidery; yarn, tale, (*informal*) shaggy dog story, (*informal*) fish story; tempest in a teacup, much ado about nothing, puffery, rant.

v exaggerate, magnify, amplify, expand, overestimate, overstate; heighten, color, embroider, puff up, fill out.

adj exaggerated, overwrought, bombastic, magniloquent, hyperbolic, fabulous, extravagant, preposterous.

550 [means of communication] **indication** *n* symbolism, semiology; sign, symbol, index, indicator, pointer, note, token, symptom; type, mark, figure, emblem, insigne, cipher, device, representation; signal, beacon, alarm; feature, trait, characteristic, peculiarity, quality, earmark, cast; gesture, gesticulation, motion, cue, hint, clue, scent.

v indicate, denote, betoken, designate, signify, represent, stand for, typify, symbolize; note, mark, stamp; label, ticket; make a sign, signalize, signal, gesture, gesticulate; sign, seal, attest, underline, underscore, call attention to.

adj indicative, indicatory; connotative, denotative, typical, representative, symbolic, symbolical, characteristic, significant, emblematic.

551 record *n* trace, vestige, relic, remains; monument, achievement; account, chronicles, annals, history, note, register, memorandum, document, diary, log, journal, ledger.

v record, set down, place in the record, chronicle, enter, register, enter, list, enroll; commemorate, celebrate.

552 [suppression of sign] **obliteration** *n* erasure, cancelation, deletion, blot, effacement, extinction.

v obliterate, efface, expunge, erase, cancel, delete, blot out, rub out, strike out, wipe out, leave no trace.

adj obliterated, erased, blotted out; unrecorded.

553 recorder *n* notary, clerk, registrar, register, secretary, scribe, bookkeeper; annalist, historian, historiographer, chronicler, biographer, journalist, antiquarian, memorialist.

554 representation *n* depiction, imitation, illustration, delineation, expression, imagery, portraiture, figuration.

v represent, delineate, depict, portray, picture, figure, describe, trace, copy, illustrate, symbolize; personate, personify, play, mimic.

adj representative, imitative, illustrative, figurative, symbolic, descriptive.

555 misrepresentation *n* distortion, exaggeration, misfiguration, falsification; bad likeness, caricature.

v misrepresent, distort, overdraw, exaggerate, falsify, caricature, daub.

556 painting *n* fine art, picture, depiction, representation, pictorialization, delineation, design, drawing, likeness, copy, imitation, fake, image.

art gallery, picture gallery, studio.

v paint, design, limn, draw, sketch, pencil, color; depict, represent.

adj pictorial, picturesque.

557 sculpture *n* carving, modeling, statuary; ceramics, potting.

statue, statuette, bust; cast, mold.

v sculpt, fashion, cast, mold, model, chisel, carve, cut, shape, form, figure, hew.

558 engraving *n* etching, chiseling, incising, plate engraving, photo-engraving.

v engrave, grave, carve, incise, chisel, hatch, etch, stipple, print.

559 artist *n* painter, drawer, sketcher, designer, draftsman, cartoonist, caricaturist, sculptor, engraver.

560 language *n* speech, phraseology, style, expression, diction, jargon, dialect, terminology, vernacular, lingo, tongue.

literature, letters, belles lettres, humanities, classics, dead language.

linguist.

v express, say, express by words.

adj lingual, linguistic; dialectic, vernacular, current, colloquial, slangy, polyglot, literary.

561 letter *n* character, hieroglyph, symbol, alphabet, consonant, vowel.

syllable, monosyllable, dissyllable, polysyllable.

spelling, orthography; phonetics; cipher, code; monogram, anagram.

v spell.

adj literal; alphabetical; syllabic; phonetic.

562 word *n* term, symbol, name, part of speech.

dictionary, vocabulary, lexicon, index, thesaurus, glossary.

etymology, derivation, philology, terminology, lexicography.

adj literal, verbal.

563 neology *n* neologism, new-fangled expression, (*informal*) hip expression, barbarism, corruption.

neologist, word coiner.

v coin words.

adj neologic, neological; colloquial, slang, (*informal*) hip, cant, barbarous.

564 nomenclature *n* naming; name, appellation, designation, epithet, nickname, (*informal*) moniker, (*informal*) handle, label, title, head, heading; style, proper name, surname, namesake.

v name, call, term, designate, denominate, style, entitle, dub, christen, baptize, nickname, characterize, specify, label.

adj titular, nominal.

565 misnomer *n* misnaming, malapropism; sobriquet, nickname, assumed name, alias, pen name, stage name, pseudonym, nom de plume, nom de guerre.

v misname, miscall, misterm; take an assumed name.

adj misnamed; soi-disant, self-styled; so-called.

566 phrase *n* expression, set phrase, turn of speech, idiom, tag phrase, figure of speech, euphemism, motto; phraseology.

v phrase, express, put into words, find the right words, arrange in words, voice, vocalize.

567 grammar *n* rules of language, usage, forms, style, formal features, constructions, parts of speech; accidence, syntax, inflection, case, declension, conjugation; grammar book, primer, rulebook.

grammarian.

adj grammatical, syntactic, syntactical.

568 solecism *n* ungrammatical usage, bad grammar, faulty grammar, error, slip, inconsistency, impropriety.

v solecize.

adj ungrammatical, incorrect, inaccurate, faulty, inconsistent, improper.

569 style *n* diction, phraseology, wording; composition, mode of expression, choice of words, command of language, mode, manner, method, approach; kind, form, appearance, character, touch, characteristic, mark, signature, imprint, (*informal*) name.

v style, compose, express by words; write.

adj stylistic; characteristic; expressive.

570 perspicuity *n* clearness, clarity, lucidity, plainness, plain-speaking, distinctness, explicitness, exactness, intelligibility.

adj perspicuous, pellucid, clear, lucid, intelligible, plain, distinct, explicit, exact, definite, unequivocal.

571 obscurity *n* unintelligibility, involution, confusion, indistinctness, indefiniteness, ambiguity, vagueness, inexactness, impenetrability.

adj obscure, involved, confused, unintelligible, impenetrable, indefinite, vague, inexact, hidden, dark.

572 conciseness *n* brevity, summary, abridgment, terseness, pithiness, compression, tightness.

v be concise, condense, abridge, abstract, compress, tighten; come to the point.

adj concise, brief, compendious, short, terse, laconic, pithy, trenchant, succinct, compact, tight.

adv concisely, briefly, summarily, in short.

573 diffuseness *n* long-windedness, verbosity, wordiness, verbiage, looseness, exuberance, redundancy, profuseness, richness.

v be diffuse, enlarge, amplify, expand, inflate; meander, digress, ramble, run on and on.

adj diffuse, profuse, wordy, verbose, copious, exuberant; lengthy, long-winded, protracted, prolix, diffusive, roundabout; digressive, discursive, loose.

574 vigor *n* power, force, boldness, spirit, verve, heart, ardor, enthusiasm, raciness, glow, fire, warmth; loftiness, elevation, gravity, sublimity; eloquence, strong language.

adj vigorous, nervous, powerful, forcible, forceful, trenchant, biting, incisive, impressive; spirited, lively, glowing, sparkling, racy, bold, pungent, pithy; lofty, elevated, sublime, grand, weighty; eloquent, vehement, impassioned, passionate.

575 feebleness *n* weakness, enervation, frailty, faintness.

adj feeble, tame, weak, meager, vapid, insipid; trashy, poor, dull, dry, languid; prosy, prosaic, slight; careless, loose, slip-shod, wishy-washy, sloppy, slovenly; puerile, childish.

576 plainness *n* simplicity, homeliness, restraint, severity.

v speak plainly, speak directly, come straight to the point, be straightforward, not beat around the bush.

adj plain, simple, homely, homey, unadorned, unvarnished, neat, homespun; severe, chaste, pure.

adv in plain terms, in plain English; point-blank.

577 ornament *n* floridness, ornateness, elegance, grandiloquence, magniloquence, rhetorical flourish, declamation, rhetoric, flourish, fancy talk, (*informal*) big words; pretention, inflation, bombast, fustian, rant, fine writing, fine speaking.

v ornament, overcharge, talk big, talk fancy.

adj ornate, ornamented, beautified, florid, rich, flowery, fancy; euphuistic, euphemistic; sonorous, high sounding, inflated, swelling, turgid, pompous, pedantic, stilted, high-flown, sententious, rhetorical, declamatory, grandiose, grandiloquent, magniloquent, bombastic, flashy.

578 elegance *n* taste, good taste, propriety, correctness; lucidity, purity, grace, ease; gracefulness, euphony, gentility, cultivation, polish, refinement.

purist, classicist.

adj elegant, polished, classic, classical, fine, tasteful, proper, correct; chaste, pure, graceful, easy, readable, fluent, flowing, unaffected, natural, mellifluous, euphonious, felicitous, neat, well put.

579 inelegance *n* tastelessness, vulgarity, impropriety; bad diction, awkwardness, stiffness, turgidity, abruptness; barbarism, solecism, slang, mannerism, affectation, formality.

adj inelegant, graceless, ungraceful, harsh, abrupt, dry, stiff, cramped, formal, forced, labored, awkward, ponderous, turgid; artificial, mannered, affected, euphuistic; tasteless, barbarous, uncouth, rude, crude, vulgar.

580 voice *n* vocality, intonation, articulation, enunciation, distinctness, clearness, delivery; accent, accentuation, emphasis, stress; utterance, vocalization.

v voice, speak, utter; articulate, enunciate, vocalize, intone, pronounce, accent, accentuate, deliver.

adj vocal, oral; articulate, distinct, euphonious, melodious.

581 muteness *n* dumbness, silence, speechlessness; aphasia.

v be mute, be silent, be dumb; silence, muzzle, muffle, suppress, smother gag, strike dumb, dumfound.

adj mute, silent, dumb, mum, tongue-tied; voiceless, speechless.

582 speech *n* talk, parlance, locution, conversation, parley, communication, prattle; talk, oration, address, discourse, lecture, recitation, sermon, harangue, tirade; oratory, eloquence, rhetoric, declamation.

speaker, spokesman, mouthpiece, orator, rhetorician.

v speak, utter, talk, voice, converse, communicate, pronounce, say, articulate; declaim, harangue, stump, spout, rant, lecture, sermonize, discourse, expatiate, soliloquize, address.

adj oral; talkative, conversational; declamatory.

583 [imperfect speech] **inarticulateness** *n* stammering, hesitation, muttering, mumbling, stuttering; reticence, taciturnity; speech impediment, aphasia.

v be inarticulate, stammer, hesitate, mutter, mumble, slur one's words, garble, sputter, hem and haw, whisper, croak, crack.

adj inarticulate, tongue-tied, speechless, voiceless, hesitant, reticent, taciturn.

584 loquacity *n* loquaciousness, volubility, talkativeness, verbosity, garrulity, volubility; chatter, jabber, prattle, twaddle.

talker, chatterer, chatterbox, babbler, ranter.

v be loquacious, talk a mile a minute, pour forth, prate, chatter, babble, gab, run off at the mouth, jabber, jaw, gush.

adj loquacious, voluble, talkative, verbose, wordy, garrulous, chatty, chattering, glib, fluent, effusive.

585 taciturnity *n* silence, muteness, reserve, reticence, uncommunicativeness.

v be silent, keep silence, keep quiet, hold one's tongue, say nothing.

adj taciturn, silent, mute, mum, reserved, reticent, guarded, uncommunicative, close-mouthed, quiet.

586 public address *n* allocution, speech, formal speech, address, invocation.

v speak to, address; invoke, hail, salute; lecture, pronounce.

587 response *n*. See **answer 462**.

588 conversation *n* interlocution, colloquy, confabulation, talk, (*informal*) rap, discourse, verbal interchange, dialog, oral communication; chat, chit, chit-chat, small talk, table talk, idle talk, prattle, gossip; conference, parley, interview, audience, *tête-à-tête*, council, congress; palaver, debate, discussion.

v converse, confabulate, talk together, hold a conversation, carry on a conversation, engage in a discussion; bandy words, chat, chit-chat, gossip, tattle, prate; discourse with, confer with; talk it over, (*informal*) rap, (*informal*) chew the fat.

adj conversational, conversable; chatty, gossipy.

589 soliloquy *n* monolog, apostrophe, aside.

v soliloquize, talk to oneself, think out loud, apostrophize.

590 writing *n* chirography, penmanship, calligraphy, hand, script, longhand, shorthand, stenography; handwriting, signature, mark, hand; manuscript, MS., document, script, writ, author's copy, copy, original; composition, authorship, work, opus, book, volume, tome, publication, article, poetry, verse, literature.

writer, author, scribe, scrivener, clerk, copyist, secretary.

v write, pen, copy, transcribe; print, scribble, scrawl, scratch; compose, draw out, write down, set down, put pen to paper, take up the pen, take pen in hand.

adj written, in writing, in black and white.

591 printing *n* lettering, typography; type; composition, print, letterpress, text, matter; copy, impression, proof.

printer, compositor, reader, proofreader, copyeditor.

v print, compose; go to press, publish, bring out, issue.

adj typographical, printed.

592 correspondence *n* letter, epistle, missive, note, post card; communication, dispatch, bulletin, circular.

v correspond, communicate, write to, send a letter.

adj epistolary; in touch with, in communication with.

593 book *n* booklet; writing, work, volume, tome, opus, tract, treatise, brochure, handbook; novel, story; script, libretto; publication.
writer, author, essayist, editor; bookseller, publisher; librarian, bibliophile, bookworm.

594 description *n* narration, account, recounting, telling, recital, relation, statement, report, record; delineation, portrayal, characterization, representation, depiction, sketch, vignette.
v describe, set forth, narrate, account, recount, recite, rehearse, tell, relate, detail; picture, delineate, portray, characterize, limn, represent, depict.

595 dissertation *n* treatise, essay, thesis, theme, tract, discourse, disquisition, investigation, study, discussion, exposition; commentary, critique, criticism, review, article, commentator, critic, essayist, reviewer.
v discuss a subject, treat, examine, comment, criticize, explain.

596 compendium *n* abstract, précis, epitome, analysis, digest, compendium, brief, abridgment, abbreviation, condensation, summary; draft, note, synopsis, outline, syllabus, contents, prospectus; compilation, collection, album, anthology; extracts, cuttings, fragments, pieces; list, inventory, survey.
v abridge, abstract, précis, epitomize, summarize; abbreviate, shorten, condense, compress; compile, collect, note; list, inventory, survey.
adj compendious, synoptic, analytic, analytical.

597 poetry *n* poetics; verse, poesy, versification, rhyming, rhymes, making verses, metrics; doggerel.
poet, laureate, bard, troubadour, minstrel, versifier, rhymer, sonneteer, rhapsodist, poetaster.
v poeticize, sing, versify, rhyme, make verses, compose.
adj poetic, poetical, rhythmic, metrical, lyrical, tuneful, musical; beautiful, lovely, tender, sensitive.

598 prose *n* writing, fiction, imaginative writing, narrative prose.
v write prose.
adj prosy, unpoetic, rhymeless; prosaic, dull, flat, matter-of-fact, unimaginative, commonplace, humdrum, pedestrian, trite, hackneyed, mediocre, stock, ordinary; fictional.

599 the drama *n* the stage, the theater; theatricals, dramaturgy, playwriting; play, drama, stage-play, opera.
performance, acting, representation, impersonation, stage business, actor, actress, player, performer, thespian.
theater, playhouse, operahouse, amphitheater.
dramatist, playwriter, playwright.
v dramatize, act, play, perform, personate, act a part, put on the stage, enact.
adj dramatic, theatrical, histrionic, stagy.

Class V

Voluntary Powers

I. Individual Volition

600 will *n* volition, free will, freedom; choice, wish, desire, pleasure, disposition, inclination; intent, purpose, option; determination, resolution, resoluteness, decision, forcefulness; force of will, will power, self-control.
v will, see fit, think fit, decide, decree, determine, direct, command, bid.
adj willful, voluntary, volitional, intentional; free, optional, discretionary; autocratic, obdurate, adamant.
adv willfully, voluntarily, at will; of one's own accord, intentionally, deliberately.

601 necessity *n* obligation, compulsion, subjection; fate, destiny, fatality; inevitability, inevitableness, unavoidability, unavoidableness, irresistibility; requirement, requisite, demand; instinct, impulse.
v be obligated, be obliged, be fated; necessitate, compel, subject; require.
adj necessary, essential, requisite, needful; inevitable, unavoidable, ineluctable, irresistible, inexorable; compulsory; involuntary, instinctive, automatic, blind, mechanical.
adv necessarily, of necessity, willy nilly.

602 willingness *n* disposition, inclination, leaning, propensity, frame of mind, liking, humor, mood, vein, bent, penchant, aptitude; geniality, cordiality, good will; alacrity, readiness, eagerness, enthusiasm; assent, compliance, agreement.
v be willing, incline, lean to, mind, hold to, cling to; desire; acquiesce, assent, comply; find one's way to, give it a shot, *(informal)* take a swing at, *(informal)* lay into.
adj willing, fain, favorable, content, well disposed; ready, earnest, eager, desirous; genial, cordial.
adv willingly, freely, with pleasure, with all one's heart, graciously.

603 unwillingness *n* indisposition, disinclination, reluctance, dislike; aversion, indifference, slowness, lack of readiness, obstinacy; scrupulousness, hesitation, qualm, shrinking, holding back, recoil; averseness, dissent, refusal.
v be unwilling, dislike; demur, hesitate, shrink from, swerve, recoil; dissent, refuse.
adj unwilling, loath, reluctant, averse; laggard, backward, slow, slack, indifferent; scrupulous, hesitant.
adv unwillingly, grudgingly, against one's will, under protest.

604 resolution *n* determination, will, decision, strength of mind, resolve, firmness, energy, manliness, vigor, resoluteness; pluck, zeal, devotion; self-control, self-command, self-possession, self-reliance, self-restraint, self-denial; tenacity, perseverance, obstinacy, *(informal)* gumption.
v be resolute, resolve, will, determine, decide, make a resolution, conclude, fix, bring to a crisis, take a decisive step; stand firm, insist upon, make a point of, not give an inch.
adj resolute, firm, steadfast, resolved, purposeful, fixed, inflexible, bold, game, indomitable, relentless, tenacious, gritty, stern, irrevocable, obstinate.
adv resolutely, in earnest, earnestly, manfully.

604a perseverance *n* persistence, tenacity, resolution, doggedness, determination, steadfastness, indefatigability, pluck, stamina, backbone.
v persevere, persist, continue, keep on, last, stick it out, hang in there.
adj persevering, constant, steady, steadfast, persistent, tenacious, resolute, dogged, indefatigable, indomitable, staunch, true, game, *(informal)* tough.

605 irresolution *n* indecision, indetermination, instability, uncertainty; hesitation, hesitancy, vacillation, oscillation, changeableness, fluctuation, fickleness, weakness, frailty, timidity, cowardice.
v be irresolute, dawdle, dilly-dally, shilly-shally, hesitate, falter, waver, vacillate, change, fluctuate, blow hot and cold.
adj irresolute, indecisive, indeterminate, unstable, uncertain; hesitant, changeable, capricious, fickle, frail, feeble, weak, timid, *(informal)* soft, cowardly.

606 obstinacy *n* doggedness, persistence, pertinacity, resolution, intractability, firmness, immovability, inflexibility, obduracy, willfulness, perversity, stubborness, mulishness; uncontrollability, wildness.
fixed idea, *idée fixe,* fanaticism, zealotry, infatuation, monomania; bigotry, intolerance, dogmatism.
bigot, dogmatist, zealot, fanatic.
v be obstinate, persist, die hard, fight, stick to an idea.
adj obstinate, dogged, persistent, pertinacious, resolute, intractable, firm, refractory, headstrong, willful, inflexible, immovable, perverse, stubborn, mulish, pig-headed; wayward, unruly, incorrigible, uncontrollable, wild; fanatic, zealous, monomaniacal; intolerant, dogmatic, arbitrary.

607 recantation *n* tergiversation, renunciation, abjuration, retraction, defection, apostasy, disavowal, revocation, reversal.
turncoat, apostate, renegade, deserter.
v recant, change one's mind, abjure, retract, renounce, disavow, revoke, defect, change sides.
adj changeful, irresolute, slippery, timeserving.

608 caprice *n* fancy, humor, whim, quirk, freak, fad, vagary, prank.
v be capricious.
adj capricious, erratic, eccentric, fitful, inconsistent, fanciful, whimsical, crotchety, freakish, wayward, wanton; contrary, captious, unreasonable, arbitrary, fickle; frivolous.

609 choice *n* selection, decision, pick, choosing, election, option, alternative, preference, predilection, desire.
v choose, select, elect, make a choice, prefer, pick, cull, decide.
adj optional, discretional, preferential.

609a neutrality, absence of choice *n* neutrality, indifference; indecision, irresolution.
no choice, first come first served.
v be neutral, have no preference, waive, abstain.
take what's offered.
adj neutral, indifferent; indecisive, irresolute.

610 rejection *n* refusal, repudiation, renunciation; exclusion, elimination.
v reject, refuse, repudiate, decline, deny, rebuff, repel, renounce; discard, throw away, exclude, eliminate; jettison.

611 predetermination *n* premeditation, predeliberation, foregone conclusion; resolve, intention; fate, predestination, destiny.
v predetermine, predestine, premeditate, resolve beforehand, calculate.
adj aforethought; foregone.
adv advisedly, deliberately, intentionally.

612 impulse *n* sudden thought, flash, spurt, inspiration, improvisation.
v improvise, extemporize; flash on, hit on, come up with, pull out of a hat, pull out of the air; say what comes to mind.
adj impulsive, impromptu, spontaneous; extemporaneous.
adv extempore, extemporaneously; impromptu, offhand, impulsively.

613 habit *n* addiction, disposition, tendency, bent, wont; custom, prescription, practice, way, usage, wont, manner; prevalence, observance; conventionalism, conventionality, mode, fashion, vogue, conformity; rule, precedent, routine, rut, groove.
v habituate, inure, harden, season; accustom, familiarize; acclimate, accommodate; cling to, adhere to, acquire a habit, fall into a rut; be habitual, come into use, become a habit, take root.
adj habitual, customary, prescriptive, usual, general, ordinary, common, frequent, everyday, familiar, trite, commonplace, conventional, regular, set, stock, fixed, permanent; prevalent, current, fashionable; addictive.
adv habitually, as usual, as things go, as the world goes; as a rule, for the most part, generally.

614 disuse *n* desuetude, disusage, lack of practice.
v be unaccustomed, break a habit; disuse.
adj unaccustomed; unusual, original.

615 motive *n* reason, ground, principle, mainspring, purpose, cause, occasion, influence, impulse, instigation, spur, stimulus, incitement, incentive, inducement, consideration, temptation, motivation; intention, ulterior motive.
v motivate, induce, move, inspire, put up to, prompt, stimulate, spur, excite, arouse, rouse, incite, instigate; influence, sway, incline, dispose, lead, persuade, prevail upon, enlist, engage, invite, court, tempt, charm.
adj suasive, persuasive, seductive, attractive, provocative.

615a absence of motive *n* caprice, chance, absence of design.
v have no motive.
adj capricious, without rhyme or reason.
adv capriciously.

616 dissuasion *n* expostulation, remonstrance, deprecation, discouragement, damper, restraint, curb, check.
v dissuade, cry out against, remonstrate, expostulate, warn, disincline, indispose, shake, discourage, dishearten, disenchant; deter, hold back, restrain, repel, turn aside, wean from, damp, cool, chill, blunt.
adj dissuasive.

617 [ostensible motive, ground, or reason] **plea** *n* pretext, allegation, excuse; pretense, shallow excuse, lame excuse, makeshift.
v plead, allege, excuse, make a pretext of, pretend.
adj ostensible, alleged.
adv ostensibly, under the pretense of.

618 good *n* benefit, interest, service, behalf, advantage, improvement, gain, boot, profit, harvest; boon, blessing, good luck, prize, good fortune, windfall, godsend; prosperity, happiness, goodness.
v benefit, serve, profit, advantage.
adj commendable; useful, good, beneficial, advantageous.

619 evil *n* ill, harm, hurt, mischief, nuisance; damage, loss; disadvantage, drawback; disaster, accident, casualty, mishap, misfortune; calamity, catastrophe, tragedy, ruin, destruction, adversity; mental suffering, pain, anguish; outrage, wrong, injury, foul play.
v be in trouble; harm, hurt, injure, ruin, destroy, torture.
adj evil, hurtful, injurious, harmful; disastrous, catastrophic, cataclysmic, tragic, ruinous.

620 intention *n* intent, purpose, project, undertaking, design, ambition, contemplation, view, proposal, meaning; object, aim, end, destination, mark, point, goal, target, prey, quarry, game; decision, determination, resolve, resolution, settled purpose.
v intend, mean, design, purpose, propose, contemplate, plan, expect, mediate, calculate, project, aim for, aim at, aspire at.
adj intentional, advised, express, determinate, bound for, bent upon, in view, in prospect.
adv intentionally, advisedly, wittingly, knowingly, purposely, on purpose, by design, pointedly; deliberately.

621 [absence of design] **chance** *n* destiny, lot, fate, luck, good luck, turn, *(informal)* break, *(informal)* jinx, fortune; speculation, venture, stake, shot in the dark, fluke; wager, gambling, betting.
gambler, gamester, adventurer.
v chance, chance it, tempt fate, speculate, risk, venture, hazard, stake, wager, bet, place a bet, gamble, play for.
adj unintentional, accidental, random; fortuitous, lucky; speculative, venturesome.
adv unintentionally, unwittingly.

622 pursuit *n* pursuance, enterprise, undertaking, business, adventure, essay, quest, search.
v pursue, prosecute, follow, do, engage in, undertake, endeavor, seek, aim at, fish for, press on, go after, chase.
adj in quest of, in pursuit of.

623 avoidance *n* evasion, flight, escape, retreat, recoil, departure; abstention, abstinence, forbearance, inaction.
avoider, shirker, quitter, truant; fugitive, refugee, runaway, deserter.
v avoid, shun, steer clear of, keep clear of, evade, elude, shirk, fly from, turn away from; abstain, refrain, eschew, leave alone, not get involved; shrink, hold back, retire, recoil, flinch, blink, shy, dodge, beat a retreat, turn tail, run for one's life, head for the hills, take flight, beat it out; desert, sneak off, shuffle off, slink away, steal away, slip, sneak, bolt, abscond.
adj elusive, evasive, escapist, fugitive.

624 relinquishment *n* surrender, resignation, yielding, waiver, waiving, abdication, leaving, desertion, withdrawal, secession, abandonment, renunciation.
v relinquish, surrender, give up, resign, yield, cede, waive, forswear, forgo, abdicate, leave, forsake, desert, renounce, quit, abandon, let go, resign, *(informal)* throw in the towel, call it quits, *(informal)* hang it up.

625 business *n* occupation, trade, craft, profession, calling, employment, vocation, pursuit; affair, matter, concern, transaction, undertaking; function, duty, office, position, part, role, capacity.
v employ oneself, undertake, turn one's hand to; be at work on, be engaged in, be occupied with.
adj businesslike; workaday, professional, official, functional; busy.

626 plan *n* scheme, plot, stratagem, policy, procedure, project, formula, method, system, organization, design, contrivance, device; drawing, sketch, draft, map, chart, diagram, representation; intrigue, cabal, conspiracy.
planner, designer, organizer, schemer, strategist, intriguer.
v plan, arrange, frame, scheme, plot, design, devise, contrive, invent, concoct, hatch; project; forecast; systematize, organize, cast, recast, lay groundwork.
adj procedural, formulaic, methodological, systematic, organizational; conspiratorial; strategic.

627 [path] **method** *n* road, procedure, way, means, manner, fashion, technique, process, course, route, track, beat, tack; door, gateway, channel, passage, avenue, means of access, approach.
adv how, in what way, in what manner; by what mode; one way or another, after this fashion.

628 mid-course *n* middle way, middle course, mean, golden mean; compromise, *(informal)* six of one and half a dozen of another, half measures, neutrality.
v steer a middle course, go straight; compromise, go half way, make a compromise.
adj moderate, midway; neutral, impartial.

629 circuit *n* roundabout way, digression, detour, loop, winding.
v go round about, make a circuit, detour, wind around, circle around; deviate, digress.
adj circuitous, indirect, roundabout; zigzag.
adv in a roundabout way, by an indirect course, indirectly.

630 requirement *n* requisite, requisition, need, necessity, wants, claim, demand, prerequisite; mandate, order, command, directive, injunction, charge, claim, precept.
v require, need, call for, have occasion for, necessitate, obligate; demand, request, need, order, enjoin, direct, ask.
adj requisite, necessary, essential, indispensable, needful; urgent, exigent, instant, crying.
adv of necessity.

631 instrumentality *n* mediation, intervention, medium, intermedium, vehicle, hand; aid; subservience.
go-between, intermediary, minister.
v mediate, minister, intervene; be instrumental, aid.
adj instrumental, useful, serviceable; intermediary, intermediate.
adv through, by, whereby, thereby, by the agency of, by dint of, by means of.

632 means *n* resources, wherewithal, way, ways and means, know how, ability; agency, method, approach; capital, provisions.
v have the means, find the means, possess the means.
adj instrumental.
adv by means of; herewith, therewith; wherewithal.

633 instrument *n* tool, implement, utensil, machinery, equipment.
adj instrumental; mechanical.

634 substitute *n* deputy, alternate, understudy, stand-in, proxy, *(informal)* sub, replacement.
v to substitute for, sub.

635 materials *n* raw materials, resources, stuff, stock, staples, supplies.

636 store *n* stock, fund, mine, supply, reserve, reservoir, *(informal)* stash; accumulation, hoard, storing, storage.
v store, put aside, lay away; store up, put up, hoard away, accumulate, amass, garner; reserve, husband, *(informal)* stash, hold back.
adj in store, in reserve, spare.

637 provision *n* supply, grist, resources, store, provender, stock, food; catering, providing, purveying, purveyance, supplying.
v make provision, provide, lay in, lay in a stock, lay in a store; supply, furnish, purvey, provision, cater, stock, store, replenish.

638 waste *n* consumption, expenditure, dissipation, diminution, decline, emaciation, exhaustion, loss, destruction, decay, impairment; misuse, prodigality, wasting; ruin, devastation, spoilation, desolation.
v waste, consume, spend, throw out, expend, squander, misuse, misspend, dissipate; destroy, wear away, erode, eat away, reduce, wear down, exhaust, enfeeble, wear out.
adj wasteful, prodigal, spendthrift; destructive; wasted, gone to waste.

639 sufficiency *n* adequacy, enough, competence.
v be sufficient, suffice, do, just do, satisfy; have enough.
adj sufficient, enough, adequate, ample, up to the mark, competent, commensurate, satisfactory.
adv sufficiently, amply.

640 insufficiency *n* inadequacy, incompetence, incompleteness, deficiency, imperfection, shortcoming; paucity, scarcity, dearth; dole, pittance; emptiness, poorness, depletion, flaccidity.

v be insufficient, not suffice, not do, fall short of, (*informal*) not cut it; want, lack, need, require, be in want.

adj insufficient, inadequate, too little, not enough, incomplete, deficient, imperfect, wanting, short, scarce, meager, poor, thin, sparse, scant; incompetent, perfunctory.

641 redundance *n* superfluity, superabundance, too much, too many, exuberance, profuseness, profusion, plenty, repletion, plethora, congestion, surfeit, overdose, overflow; excess, surplus; repetition, verbosity.

v superabound, overabound, swarm, overflow, run over, run riot, overrun, overdose, overload, overdo, overwhelm; supersaturate, gorge, glut, load, drench, inundate, deluge, flood; choke, cloy, suffocate, pile on, lay on thick, lavish.

adj redundant, exuberant, inordinate, superabundant, excessive, overmuch, replete, profuse, lavish; exorbitant, extravagant, overweening, (*informal*) much; superfluous, unnecessary, needless, over and above, spare, duplicate; repetitious, verbose.

adv over and above, over much, out of proportion, beyond bounds, over one's head.

642 importance *n* consequence, substance, weight, moment, prominence, consideration, significance, import, concern, emphasis, interest, momentousness, weightiness; gravity, seriousness, solemnity; pressure, urgency, stress.

v be important, deserve consideration, be worthy of notice, merit attention; attach importance, ascribe importance, value, care for, set store by; import, signify, matter, boot, carry weight; accentuate, emphasize, lay stress on; mark, underline, underscore.

adj important, consequential, weighty, momentous, prominent, considerable, significant, notable, salient; grave, serious, earnest, grand, solemn, impressive, commanding, imposing; urgent, pressing, critical, crucial, paramount, essential, vital, prime, primary, principal, all-important, capital, foremost, of vital importance; superior, considerable; significant, telling, trenchant, emphatic.

643 unimportance *n* insignificance, immateriality, triviality, paltriness, indifference, nothing, trifling; trumpery, trash, rubbish, frippery, chaff, bauble, trifle.

v be unimportant, not matter, matter little, signify little; make light of.

adj unimportant, of little account, of small importance, immaterial, unessential, nonessential, inconsequential, insignificant, inconsiderable, so-so; commonplace, ordinary, uneventful, mere, common; trifling, trivial, slight, slender, light, flimsy, shallow; frivolous, petty, niggling, piddling; poor, paltry, pitiful, sorry, mean, meager, shabby, beggarly, worthless, cheap, tawdry, trashy, gimmicky; unworthy of consideration, unworthy of notice; useless, of no account.

644 utility *n* usefulness, efficacy, helpfulness, service, use, stead, avail, help, aid; applicability, value, worth, productiveness.

v be useful, avail, serve, perform, help, aid, benefit; act a part, discharge a function, stand one in good stead.

adj useful, serviceable, functional, advantageous, valuable, productive, profitable, helpful, effectual, effective, efficacious, beneficial, salutary; applicable, available, practical, practicable, workable.

645 inutility *n* uselessness, inefficacy, ineptitude, inaptitude, inadequacy, inefficiency, unfruitfulness, futility, worthlessness, hopelessness.

v be useless, be of no help.

adj useless, unavailing, futile, inutile, fruitless, vain, ineffectual, profitless, bootless, valueless, worthless, hopeless; unserviceable, unusable, inoperative.

646 expedience *n* expediency, fitness, utility, suitability, profitability, advisability, propriety, appropriateness, desirability; opportunism, pragmatism, realism.

v be expedient, suit, befit, suit the occasion.

adj expedient, advantageous, opportune, fit, suitable, convenient, profitable, worthwhile, advisable, meet, proper, becoming, appropriate, desirable.

647 inexpedience *n* inexpediency, impropriety, unfitness, unsuitability, inappropriateness, undesirability; inconvenience, impracticality.

v be inexpedient, be inconvenient, hinder.

adj inexpedient, inopportune, unfit, unsuitable, disadvantageous, discommodious, unadvisable, unseemly, improper, unworkable, impractical, inconvenient, unprofitable, useless, worthless.

648 [good qualities] **goodness** *n* virtue, excellence, merit, value, worth; perfection, eminence, superiority, masterpiece, *chef d'oeuvre*, prime, flower, cream, elite, pick, pick of the litter, salt of the earth, (*informal*) A-1, (*informal*) tops, second to none; gem, jewel, treasure, one in a million; beneficence.

v be good, excel, transcend, stand the test, pass muster, challenge comparison, vie, emulate, rival, (*informal*) dwarf the competition; be beneficial, do good, profit, benefit, improve, be the making of, do a world of good, produce a good effect, do a good turn.

adj good, excellent, better, superior, above par, fine, genuine, true; best, choice, select, rare, invaluable, priceless, inestimable, superlative, perfect, inimitable, first-rate, first-class, very best, crack, prime, tip-top, capital, (*informal*) tops; beneficial, valuable, advantageous, profitable, edifying, salutary, serviceable; favorable, propitious.

649 [bad qualities] **badness** *n* harmfulness, hurtfulness, virulence, painfulness, abomination, pestilence, guilt, depravity, vice, evil, malignity, malevolence; bane, plague, evil star, ill wind, bad omen, (*informal*) jinx, (*informal*) whammy; snake in the grass, skeleton in the closet, (*informal*) ghosts, (*informal*) demons; ill-treatment, annoyance, molestation, abuse, oppression, persecution, outrage, misusage, injury, damage.

v hurt, harm, injure, damage, pain; wrong, aggrieve, oppress, persecute, trample upon, tread upon, walk over, overburden, weigh down, run down; victimize, maltreat, molest, abuse, ill-use, bruise, scratch, maul, smite, do violence, do harm, stab, pierce.

adj hurtful, harmful, baleful, injurious, deleterious, detrimental, noxious, pernicious, mischievous; oppressive, burdensome, onerous, malign, malevolent; virulent, venomous, corrosive, poisonous, deadly, destructive; bad, ill, dreadful, horrid, horrible, dire, rank, foul, rotten, as low as one can go, (*informal*) the pits; evil, wrong, reprehensible, hateful, abominable, detestable, execrable, damnable, infernal, diabolical; vile, base, villainous, cruel, mean, low; deplorable, wretched, sad, grievous, lamentable, pitiable, pitiful, woeful, painful.

650 perfection *n* ideal, summit, paragon, model, standard, pattern, mirror; impeccability, faultlessness, excellence; masterpiece, master stroke; transcendence, superiority.

v perfect, bring to perfection, ripen, mature, complete, finish; be perfect, transcend.

adj perfect, faultless, immaculate, spotless, unblemished, impeccable, exquisite, consummate; in perfect condition, sound, intact; best, model, standard, inimitable, beyond all praise.

651 imperfection *n* deficiency, inadequacy, insufficiency, immaturity; fault, defect, weak point, weak spot, flaw, taint, blemish, weakness, shortcoming, drawback.

v be imperfect, have a defect, not pass muster, fall short.

adj imperfect, deficient, inadequate, insufficient, immature, defective, faulty, unsound, out of order, out of tune, warped, lame, frail, weak, crude, incomplete, below par, found wanting; indifferent, middling, ordinary, mediocre, average, so-so, tolerable, fair, passable, decent, not bad, bearable, better than nothing; inferior, secondary, second-rate, poor substitute.

652 cleanness *n* purity, purification, purgation, cleanliness; ablution, lavation; neatness, tidiness, orderliness; cathartic, purgative, laxative; detergent, disinfectant.

v clean, cleanse, purify, purge, expurgate, clarify, refine; wash, launder, scour, scrub, disinfect, fumigate, deodorize, ventilate; rout out, clear out, sweep out, make a clean sweep of, start fresh; neaten, tidy up, order, put things in order.

adj clean, pure, immaculate, spotless, stainless, unsullied, sweet; neat, spruce, tidy, trim, kempt.

653 uncleanness *n* impurity, defilement, contamination, taint; decay, putrefaction, corruption, mold, mildew, rot, dry rot; squalor, slovenliness, filth, dirt, smut, grime, mud, mire, muck, quagmire, slime.

v be unclean, rot, putrefy, fester, rankle, reek, stink, mold, go bad; dirty, soil, tarnish, spot, smear, blot, blur, smudge, smirch; besmear, befoul, splash, stain, sully, pollute, defile, debase, contaminate, taint, corrupt.

adj unclean, dirty, filthy, grimy, soiled; dusty, smutty, sooty, slimy; slovenly, untidy, sluttish, dowdy, unkempt, unscoured, squalid; nasty, coarse, foul, impure, offensive, abominable, beastly, reeky, fetid; moldy, musty, moth-eaten, bad, gone bad, rancid, rotten, corrupt, putrid, carious, fecal; gory, bloody; gross.

654 health *n* soundness, well-being, vigor, good health, bloom, color, vitality, robust health.

v be in health, be healthy, bloom, flourish, feel fine, feel good.

adj healthy, healthful, in health, well, sound, hearty, hale, strong, hardy, robust, vigorous, fit as a fiddle, in top shape, chipper, (*informal*) all together.

655 disease *n* illness, sickness, ill health, ailment, infirmity, indisposition, complaint, disorder, malady; delicacy, delicate condition, decline, deterioration, decay.

v ail, suffer, be affected with, droop, flag, languish, sicken, pine, gasp, waste away, fail; take sick, take ill, come down with, contract a disease, catch a bug.

adj ill, sick, indisposed, not well, unwell, in poor health, in bad health, ailing, poorly, laid up, bed-ridden, out of sorts, under the weather, (*informal*) in bad shape; sickly, infirm, unsound, unhealthy, (*informal*) falling apart, weak, lame, decrepit; diseased, morbid, mangy, corrupt, contaminated, leprous.

656 salubrity *n* healthiness, healthfulness, wholesomeness.

v be salubrious, be good for, agree with.

adj salubrious, healthy, healthful, salutary, wholesome, sanitary, bracing, invigorating, benign, nutritious, tonic, hygienic.

657 insalubrity *n* unhealthiness, unsoundness.

v be unhealthy, not be good for, disagree with.

adj insalubrious, unhealthy, unwholesome, noxious, noisome, deleterious, pestilential, bad, harmful, virulent, venomous, poisonous, septic, toxic, deadly.

658 improvement *n* amelioration, amendment, emendation, correction, revision, reformation, restoration, repair, betterment, gain, advancement, elevation, increase, refinement, elaboration; acculturation, cultivation, civilization.

reformer, radical.

v improve, mend, amend, get better; ameliorate, better, amend, emend, correct, right, rectify, revise, reform, restore, repair; advance, progress, ascend, increase, fructify, ripen, mature; refine, enrich, elaborate; promote, cultivate, foster, enhance.

adj better, better off, all for the better; emendatory, corrective, reformative, restorative, improving, progressive, improved.

659 deterioration *n* debasement, recession, retrogradation, degeneracy, degeneration, degradation, deprivation, depravity, retrogression; detriment, damage, loss, injury, impairment, contamination, spoilage, corruption, adulteration; decline, declension, senility, decrepitude; decadence, decay, dilapidation, falling off, wear and tear, erosion, corrosion, rottenness, blight, atrophy, collapse.

v deteriorate, degenerate, fall off, wane, ebb, decline, droop, go down, go downhill, sink, go to seed, go to waste, lapse, break down, crack, shrivel, fade, wither, molder, rot, rankle, decay, go bad, rust, crumble, shake, totter, perish, die; taint, infect, contaminate, poison, canker, corrupt, pollute, vitiate, debase, degrade, adulterate; injure, impair, damage, harm, hurt, spoil, mar, despoil, dilapidate, waste, ravage; wound, maim, cripple, scotch, mangle, mutilate, disfigure, blemish, deface, warp; blight, rot, corrode, erode, wear away, wear out, sap, mine, undermine, shake the foundations of, break up, destroy, decimate.

adj deteriorated, unimproved, injured, degenerate, imperfect; battered, weathered, weather-beaten, all the worse for wear, stale, dilapidated, faded, shabby, threadbare, worn, far gone, (*informal*) had it; decayed, moth-eaten, worm-eaten, mildewed, rusty, moldy, seedy, time-worn, wasted, crumbling, moldering, rotten, blighted, tainted; decrepit, broken down, worn-out, used up, out of commission, in a bad way, past cure, past hope, (*informal*) long gone.

660 restoration *n* reestablishment, replacement, reinstatement, renewal, rehabilitation, reconstruction, reproduction, rebuilding, renovation, revival; refreshment, resuscitation, revivification; renaissance, renascence, new birth, regeneration, reconversion; redress, retrieval, reclamation, recovery, resumption; repair, reparation, restitution, relief, deliverance, rectification, cure, healing; redemption.

v restore, recover, rally, revive, come round, pull through, get well, get over; reestablish, replace, rehabilitate, reinstate; reconstruct, rebuild, reproduce, reorganize, reconstitute, renew, renovate; redeem, reclaim, recover, retrieve, rescue, deliver; redress, recure; cure, heal, remedy, doctor, bring round; resuscitate, revive, reanimate, revivify, reinvigorate, refresh; recoup, make good, square, set to rights, correct, put in order; repair, retouch, patch up, fix.

adj restorative, recuperative, curative, remedial; restorable, remediable, retrievable, curable; restored, convalescent, renascent, reborn.

661 relapse *n* lapse, falling back, retrogradation, deterioration, backsliding.

v relapse, lapse, fall back, slip back, sink back, suffer a relapse, fall again.

adj retrograde.

662 remedy *n* help, redress, solution, answer, panacea; cure, relief, medicine, treatment, restorative, specific, medication, ointment, balm; antidote, corrective, antitoxin, counteractive.

doctor, physician, surgeon.

v remedy, cure, heal, set right, put right, doctor, nurse, restore, recondition, repair, redress; counteract, remove, correct, right, solve.

adj remedial, restorative, corrective, palliative; medicinal, therapeutic, curative; soluble.

663 bane *n* curse, evil, plague, scourge, pain, nuisance, thorn in the side, pain in the neck; poison, virus, venom; fungus, mildew, dry rot, canker, cancer; sting, fang, thorn, bramble, briar, nettle.

adj baneful, bad, sinister, pernicious, evil, baleful, poisonous, venomous, ruinous, unwholesome, harmful, deadly.

664 safety *n* security, surety, impregnability, invulnerability; safeguard, safety valve, precaution, custody, safe keeping, preservation, protection.

protector, guardian, warden, preserver, custodian, watchdog, sentinel, scout.

v be safe; protect, take care of, care for, preserve, cover, screen, shelter, shroud, guard, defend, secure, house, garrison; watch, patrol, look out, take precautions.

adj safe, secure, snug, warm, sure, sound, on the safe side, out of danger; dependable, trustworthy, sure, reliable; cautious, wary, careful; defensible, tenable, invulnerable, impregnable, unassailable, safe and sound.

665 danger *n* hazard, insecurity, instability, precariousness, slipperiness, risk, peril, jeopardy, liability, exposure; injury, evil, suil; warning, alarm, apprehension.

v be in danger, run into trouble, lay oneself open to, hang by a thread, totter; endanger, expose to danger, imperil, jeopardize, adventure, venture, risk, hazard, threaten.

adj dangerous, hazardous, risky, perilous, precarious, unsafe, insecure, unstable, untrustworthy, unsteady, shaky, slippery, ominous, fearful, explosive, fraught with danger; defenseless, vulnerable, open, liable.

666 refuge *n* sanctuary, retreat, asylum, hiding place, stronghold, fortress, shelter, cover; anchor, mainstay, support, check, last resort, safeguard.

v seek refuge, take refuge, find refuge, take shelter, find safety.

667 pitfall *n* snare, trap, snag, ambush, snake in the grass, wolf in sheep's clothing, menace, complication, danger; slippery ground, weak foundation, rocks, reefs, sunken rocks, sand, quicksand, breakers, shoals, shallows, precipice, maelstrom.

668 warning *n* caution, notice, premonition, prediction, admonition, advice, lesson; alarm, omen, sign, signal, augury, portent, presage.

sentinel, sentry, watch, watchman, watchdog, patrol, scout, spy.

v warn, caution, admonish, forewarn; give notice, notify, appraise, inform; menace, threaten, portend.

adj premonitory, cautionary, advisory; ominous, portentous.

669 [indication of danger] **alarm** *n* alarum, alarm bell, tocsin, distress signal, siren, danger signal, hue and cry, SOS, cry, scream.

v alarm, sound the alarm, warn, cry out.

670 preservation *n* safekeeping, conservation; guarding, safeguard, shelter, protection, defense; maintenance, support, sustenance, continuance, retention, salvation.

v preserve, keep, conserve; guard, safeguard, shelter, shield, protect, defend, rescue; keep up, maintain, continue, support, uphold, sustain; retain: store, husband; cure, pickle, bottle, can.

adj preserved, unimpaired, uninjured, unhurt, safe, sound, intact; conservative, preservative.

671 escape *n* flight, evasion, loophole, retreat; reprieve, release, liberation; narrow escape, close call, near miss.

v escape, flee, abscond, fly, steal away, run away, (*informal*) take off, (*informal*) split; shun, fly, elude, evade, avoid.

adj stolen away, fled, (*informal*) cut out.

672 deliverance *n* extrication, disentanglement, rescue, reprieve, respite; liberation, release, emancipation, freedom; redemption, salvation.

v deliver, extricate, disentangle, rescue, reprieve, save, redeem; set free, liberate, release, emancipate, free; come to the rescue.

673 preparation *n* provision, plan, arrangement, anticipation, precaution, forecast, rehearsal; groundwork, homework, foundation, scaffolding; training, education, dissemination; readiness, ripeness, maturity.

v prepare, get ready, make ready, prime, arrange, make preparations, plan, devise, anticipate, lay the foundations, provide, order; mature, ripen, mellow, season, nurture; equip, arm, fit out, furnish; train, teach, prepare for, rehearse, make provision for, take steps, provide against.

adj prepatory, precautionary, provident, preparative, preparatory; provisional, preliminary; prepared, ready, available, all ready, handy; ripe, mature, mellow.

674 nonpreparation *n* unpreparedness, unreadiness; improvidence.

v be unprepared; extemporize, improvise.

adj unprepared, incomplete, premature, rudimental, embryonic, immature, unripe, raw, green, coarse, crude, rough, unhewn, untaught, fallow, unready; out of order, nonfunctional, (*informal*) on the fritz, in disrepair, (*informal*) out of whack; shiftless, improvident, thoughtless, careless, slack, remiss, happy-go-lucky.

675 essay *n* trial, endeavor, effort, attempt, struggle, venture, adventure, speculation, experiment.

v essay, try, experiment; endeavor, strive, tempt, attempt, venture, adventure, speculate, tempt fortune, (*informal*) give it a go, (*informal*) take a shot at.

adj experimental, tentative, probationary; venturesome, adventurous, speculative.

adv experimentally, on trial.

676 undertaking *n* task, job, venture, engagement, compact, contract, enterprise; pilgrimage, quest.

v undertake, engage in, embark on, launch into, plunge into, volunteer; engage, promise, contract, take upon onself, devote onself to, determine, take up, take in hand; tackle, set about, fall to, begin, broach.

677 use *n* employ, exercise, application, appliance; disposal; consumption; agency, usefulness; benefit, recourse, resort, avail; utilization, utility, service, wear; usage.

v use, make use of, employ, put to use, put into operation, apply, set in motion, set to work; ply, work, wield, handle, manipulate; exert, exercise, practice, avail oneself of, profit by; resort to, have recourse to, recur to, take up, try; utilize, bring into play, press into service; use up, consume, expend, tax, task, wear.

adj useful, instrumental, utilitarian, subservient, employable, applicable, beneficial.

678 disuse *n* forbearance, abstinence; relinquishment, abandonment; desuetude.
v not use, do without, dispense with, let alone, forbear, abstain, spare, waive, neglect; keep back, reserve; disuse, lay up, shelve, set aside, put aside, leave off, have done with; supersede, discard, throw aside, relinquish, dismantle.
adj not in use, unemployed, unapplied; disused, unused, done with.

679 misuse *n* misusage, misemployment, misapplication, misappropriation; abuse, profanation, prostitution, desecration; waste.
v misuse, misemploy, misapply, misappropriate; abuse, profane, prostitute, desecrate; waste, squander, destroy; overwork, overtask, overtax.

680 action *n* movement, work, labor, performance, moving, working, performing, operation; deed, act, feat, exploit; conduct, behavior, procedure, execution; energetic activity, exercise, exertion, energy, effort; affair, encounter, meeting, engagement, conflict, combat, fight, battle.
actor, doer, worker.
v act, do, perform, execute, achieve, transact, enact; commit, perpetrate, inflict; exercise, prosecute, carry on, work, function, labor, operate, exert energy, be active; behave, conduct oneself, comport oneself; play, feign, fake, imitate.
adj in action, in operation, operative.

681 inaction *n* passivity, inactivity, idleness, slothfulness; waiting, mulling around, killing time; rest, repose.
v not act, not do, be inactive, abstain from doing, do nothing, let alone, let things take their course; stand aloof, refrain, pause, wait, bide one's time, cool one's heels, waste time, lie idle.
adj inactive, passive, idle, slothful; out of work.

682 activity *n* movement, hustle, bustle, stir, fuss, flurry, action, business; industry, assiduity, assiduousness, laboriousness, drudgery; diligence, perseverance, vigilance, wakefulness, restlessness, fidgetiness; briskness, liveliness, animation, life, vivacity, spirit, dash, energy; eagerness, zeal, ardor, vigor, abandon, exertion; earnestness, intentness, devotion.
v be active, busy oneself in, stir about, rouse oneself, speed, hasten, bustle, fuss, *(informal)* raise a ruckus; push, push ahead, *(informal)* step on it, *(informal)* move it, make progress; toil, plod, persist, persevere, hustle, *(informal)* hustle it, *(informal)* push; look sharp, keep moving, seize the opportunity, *carpe diem*, lose no time, dash off, make haste; have a hand in, trouble oneself about.
adj active, brisk, lively, busy as a bee, vivacious, alive, frisky; quick, prompt, ready, alert, spry, sharp, smart, awake, wide awake, eager, zealous; industrious, assiduous, diligent, vigilant; businesslike; restless, fussy, fidgety, busy.

683 inactivity *n* inaction, inertness, lull, quiescence; idleness, remissness, sloth, indolence, dawdling, laziness; dullness, languor, sluggishness, torpor, stupor, lethargy; procrastination.
idler, drone, dawdler, moper, lounger, loafer, sluggard, laggard, slumberer.
v be inactive, do nothing, dawdle, lag, hang back, slouch, loll, lounge, loaf, loiter, take it easy; fritter away time, idle, piddle, putter, dabble, dally, dilly-dally; languish, flag, relax; kill time, waste time.
adj inactive, motionless; indolent, lazy, slothful, idle, remiss, slack, inert, torpid, sluggish, languid, supine, heavy, dull, listless; laggard, slow, rusty, lackadaisical, irresolute; drowsy, lethargic, soporific, dreamy, dreamy-eyed.

684 haste *n* urgency, need, hurry, flurry, bustle, spurt, rush, dash, scramble, bustle, ado, precipitancy, precipitation; swiftness, celerity, alacrity, quickness, rapidity, dispatch, speed, expedition, promptitude, timeliness, promptness.
v haste, hasten, make haste, hurry, dash, push on, press on, press forward, scurry, bustle, scramble, rush, accelerate, urge, expedite, quicken, speed, precipitate, dispatch.
adj hasty, speedy, quick, hurried, swift, rapid, fast, fleet, brisk; precipitate, rash, foolhardy, reckless, indiscreet, thoughtless, headlong; testy, touchy, irascible, petulant, waspish, fretful, fiery, excitable, irritable, peevish.

685 leisure *n* spare time, free time, convenience, liberty, pause, stay, halt, lull, breather, *(informal)* letup, breathing spell, break, *(informal)* time out; interlude, vacation, holiday.
v have leisure, take one's time; rest, relax, repose.
adj leisure, spare, free; leisurely, slow, deliberate, quiet, calm, restful, peaceful, languid, easy, gradual.

686 exertion *n* effort, action, activity, endeavor, struggle, attempt, strain, trial, stress; labor, work, toil, travail; trouble, pain; energy.
v exert, exert oneself, labor, work, toil, sweat, drudge, strive, strain; work hard, rough it, buckle to, take pains, concentrate, spare no effort.
adj laborious, wearisome, burdensome, *(informal)* tough, *(informal)* rough, strenuous, herculean, Sisyphean.

687 repose *n* rest, sleep, slumber; relaxation, breathing spell; halt, pause, respite, cessation; day of rest, Sabbath; holiday, vacation, recess.
v repose, rest; relax, unbend, slacken, catch one's breath, get one's wind, take a breather, pause; recline, lie down, go to bed, take a nap, go to sleep; take a holiday, go on vacation, shut up shop.
adj reposing, resting.
adv at rest.

688 fatigue *n* weariness, lassitude, tiredness, exhaustion, faintness; ennui, boredom, tedium, languor, yawning, drowsiness.
v be fatigued, yawn, droop, sink, flag, *(informal)* give out; gasp, pant, puff, blow, drop, swoon, faint; fatigue, tire, weary, exhaust, wear out; tax, task, strain; bore, tire, irritate, annoy.
adj fatigued, weary, drowsy, haggard, faint, exhausted, spent, tired, tired to death, worn out, *(informal)* gone; breathless.

689 refreshment *n* recovery of strength, restoration, revival, repair, relief.
v refresh, brace, strengthen, reinvigorate, revive, stimulate, freshen, cheer, enliven, reanimate; restore, repair, renew.
adj refreshing, restoring.

690 agent *n* doer, actor, performer, perpetrator, operator; practitioner, executioner, executor, executrix, minister, representative, deputy, servant, worker; participant, party to.

691 workshop *n* laboratory, factory, mill, mint, forge, studio; hive, beehive, seat of activity.

692 conduct *n* behavior, demeanor, action, actions, deportment, bearing, carriage, mien, manners; process, ways, practice, procedure, method; policy, tactics, strategy, plan; direction, management, execution, guidance, leadership, administration.
v conduct, behave, deport, act, bear; transact, execute, dispatch, discharge, proceed with, enact; direct, manage, carry on, supervise, regulate, administer, guide, lead.
adj procedural, practical, methodical, tactical, strategical, businesslike; directive, managerial, administrative, executive.

693 direction *n* guidance, advice, regulation, conduct, management, disposition, supervision, auspices, steerage, stewardship, ministration, administration, control, leadership, government, rule, command; order, command, instruction.
v direct, guide, advise, regulate, conduct, manage, control, dispose, supervise, overlook, steer, steward, pilot, minister, administer, legislate, lead, rule, govern, have charge of, command; order, instruct, prescribe.
adj directing, guiding, supervisory, managing, administering.

694 director *n* manager, governor, controller, superintendent, supervisor, overseer, inspector, foreman, surveyor, taskmaster, master, leader, boss; adviser, guide, pilot, captain, helmsman, driver; head, chief, principal, president, minister, official, functionary.

695 advice *n* counsel, opinion, recommendation, guidance, suggestion, persuasion, urging, exhortation; instruction, charge, injunction; admonition, warning, caution.
adviser, council, counselor, mentor.
v advise, give counsel to, suggest, recommend, prescribe, advocate, exhort, persuade; enjoin, enforce, charge, instruct; admonish, caution, warn; take counsel, confer, deliberate, discuss, consult, refer to; give counsel, offer counsel.
adj advisory, suggestive, persuasive, suasive; admonitory.

696 council *n* committee, court, chamber, cabinet, board, board of directors, advisory board, staff, syndicate, chapter; assembly, caucus, conclave, meeting, conference, session.

697 precept *n* direction, instruction, charge, prescript, prescription; golden rule, maxim, canon, law, code, act, statute, regulation, formula, form, technicality, rubric; order, command.

698 skill *n* skillfulness, dexterity, adroitness, expertness, proficiency, competence, facility, knack, mastery; accomplishment, acquirement, attainment, ability, craft; knowledge, wisdom, *savoir faire*, tact, wit, sagacity, discretion, finesse, craftiness, cunning, management; cleverness, ingenuity, capacity, talent, talents, faculty, endowment, *forte*, turn, gift, genius; intelligence, sharpness, readiness, invention, inventiveness, aptness, aptitude, proclivity, capacity for, genius for, felicity, capability, qualification.
v be skillful, excel in, be master of, have a knack for; take advantage of.
adj skillful, dextrous, adroit, adept, expert, apt, handy, quick, deft, proficient, masterly, crack, first-rate, conversant; skilled, experienced, practiced, competent, efficient, qualified, capable, fit, fit for, trained, prepared, finished; clever, able, ingenious, felicitous, inventive; shrewd, sharp, smart, intelligent, cunning, tactful, discreet, wise, knowledgeable.
adv skillfully, artistically, with consummate skill.

699 unskillfulness *n* want of skill, incompetence, inability, inexpertness, maladroitness, ineptitude, clumsiness, awkwardness, carelessness, bumbling, bungling; indiscretion.
v be unskillful, blunder, bungle, boggle, fumble, botch, stumble.
adj unskillful, unskilled, inexpert, incompetent, unable, inapt, bungling, inept, maladroit, awkward, clumsy, gawky; unfit, ill-qualified, unhandy, not conversant; raw, rusty, out of practice.

700 expert *n* specialist, authority, master, professional, connoisseur, veteran, old hand, old soldier; genius, mastermind, wizard, prodigy, *(informal)* pro.

701 bungler *n* blunderer, blunderhead, fumbler, duffer, clown, *(informal)* turkey, butter-fingers, greenhorn, amateur, rookie, novice, *(informal)* Sunday driver, *(informal)* armchair quarterback.

702 cunning *n* craftiness, skillfulness, shrewdness, artfulness, wiliness, subtlety, finesse, artifice, device, stratagem, intrigue, craft, guile, chicanery, duplicity, subterfuge, deceit, deceitfulness, slyness, deception; ability, skill, adroitness, expertness.
v be cunning, maneuver, contrive, manipulate, intrigue, finesse, surprise.
adj crafty, shrewd, artful, wily, subtle, tricky, foxy, politic, insidious, stealthy, Machiavellian, deceitful, duplicitous, sly, deceptive; canny, astute; ingenious, clever, skillful, sharp.

703 artlessness *n* simplicity, innocence, naivete, unworldliness, inexperience, inexposure, plainness, plain speaking, sincerity, honesty, openness, candor, matter of factness, bluntness.
v be artless, speak one's mind, come to the point, pull no punches.
adj artless, natural, simple, innocent, naive, childlike, unsuspicious, unworldly, unartificial, plain; sincere, frank, open, candid, honest, ingenuous, guileless, straightforward, aboveboard, point-blank, plain spoken, outspoken, blunt, direct, matter of fact.
adv in plain English, in simple words, without mincing words.

704 difficulty *n* dilemma, predicament, quandary, fix, exigency, emergency, crisis, trouble, problem, scrape, entanglement, strait, pass, pinch; reluctance, unwillingness, obstinacy, stubbornness; demur, objection, obstacle; labor, task, hard task, herculean task.
v be difficult, pose, perplex, bother, nonplus, hinder; encumber, embarrass, entangle.
adj difficult, hard, arduous, troublesome, irksome, laborious, formidable; awkward, unwieldy, unmanageable; fastidious, particular, stubborn, intractable, perverse; obscure, complex, intricate, delicate, uncertain, ticklish, critical; unfeasible, impractical, impossible, hopeless; austere, rigid.

705 facility *n* ease, easiness, capability, feasibility, practicability; flexibility, pliancy, smoothness, child's play.
v be easy, run smoothly, work well; facilitate, smooth, ease, lighten, free, clear, disencumber, disentangle, extricate, unravel.
adj easy, facile; feasible, practicable, within reach, accessible; manageable, tractable, pliant, smooth.
adv easily, readily, smoothly.

706 hindrance *n* impediment, deterrent, hitch, encumbrance, obstruction, check, stricture, restraint, hobble, obstacle, stumbling block; interruption, interference; impeding, stopping, stoppage, preventing.
v hinder, interrupt, check, impede, retard, encumber, delay, hamper, obstruct, trammel, cramp, handicap; block, thwart, frustrate, disconcert, prevent.
adj obstructive, intrusive; onerous, burdensome, cumbersome, obtrusive.

707 aid *n* help, support, succor, assistance, service, furtherance; relief, rescue, charity; assistant, helper, supporter, servant; patronage, championship, advocacy, favor, interest.
v aid, support, help, succor, assist, serve, abet, back, second; spell, relieve, rescue; sustain, uphold, prop, hold up, bolster; promote, facilitate, ease, advocate; be of help, give help, give assistance, oblige, accommodate, humor, encourage.
adj aiding, auxiliary, helpful, supportive; charitable; friendly, amicable, well-disposed, neighborly.

708 opposition *n* antagonism, hostility, resistance, counteraction; competitition, enemy, foe, adversary, antagonist; opposing, resisting, combating.
v oppose, resist, combat, withstand, thwart, confront, contravene, interfere, hinder, obstruct, prevent, check; contradict, gainsay, deny, refuse, dissent.
adj adverse, antagonistic, contrary, at var[illegible], at odds, anti, at issue, in opposition; unfavorable, unfriendly, hostile, inimical, resistant.
adv against, versus, counter to, in conflict with, at cross purposes; in spite, in defiance.

709 cooperation *n* concert, concurrence, agreement, concord, togetherness, harmony, unanimity; complicity, collusion, participation, combination, union, team-work; association, partnership, alliance, pool, coalition, confederation, fusion, fellowship, fraternity; unanimity, partisanship, spirit, party spirit, *esprit de corps*.
v cooperate, concur, combine, unite, pool, share, band together, pull together; act in concert, join forces, fraternize; conspire, be in league with; side with, go along with, join hands with, throw in one's lot with, rally round; participate, have a hand i[illegible].
adj cooperating, cooperative, participatory; in league, party to.
adv cooperatively, unanimously, shoulder to shoulder.

710 opponent *n* adversary, antagonist, competitor, rival, opposition; enemy, foe.

711 auxiliary *n* helper, aid, ally, assistant, confederate, collaborator, colleague, associate, partner, mate, friend.

712 party *n* group, gathering, assembly, assemblage, company, crew, band; clan, family, fellowship, community; body, faction, side, circle, clique, set, gang, claque, coterie, combination, ring, league, alliance, association.
v unite, join, band together, cooperate, assemble.
adj clannish, cliquish, communal, familial, fraternal.

713 discord *n* dissidence, dissonance, disagreement, clash, shock; variance, difference, dissension, misunderstanding, cross-purposes, odds, division, split, rupture, disruption, breach, schism, feud, conflict, struggle, argument, contention, quarrel, dispute, tiff, squabble, altercation, words; strife, outbreak.
v be discordant, disagree, clash, jar, conflict, differ, dissent, fall out, quarrel, dispute, squabble, wrangle, bicker, have words with; split, break, disunite, feud.
adj discordant, dissident, dissonant; divisive, disruptive; contentious, argumentative, quarrelsome, disputatious, fractious; at variance, at cross purposes.

714 concord *n* accord, harmony, sympathy, agreement, union, unison, unity, peace; amity, friendship, alliance, *detente*, understanding, togetherness, conciliation.
v agree, accord, harmonize with, fraternize, understand one another, concur, pull together; side with, sympathize with.
adj concordant, congenial, in accord; harmonious, sympathetic, friendly, fraternal, conciliatory.
adv with one voice, unanimously, in concert with.

715 defiance *n* daring, courage, courageousness, bravery, boldness; assertiveness, aggressiveness; antagonism, insubordination, recalcitrance, rebelliousness, insolence, resistance.
v defy, challenge, resist, dare, brave, flout, scorn, despise.
adj defiant, daring, courageous, brave, bold; resistant, insolent, rebellious, recalcitrant, contumacious, insubordinate, antagonistic.
adv in the face of, under one's very nose.

716 attack *n* onslaught, assault, offense, battery, onset, charge, encounter, aggression, incursion, invasion, sally, sortie, raid, foray; criticism, blame, censure, abuse.
assailant, aggressor, invader, attacker.
v assail, assault, molest, threaten, storm, charge, set upon, invade, bombard, beset, besiege, lay siege, storm; criticize, impugn, blame, censure, abuse; declare war, begin hostilities.
adj aggressive, offensive; critical, abusive.
adv on the offensive.

717 defense *n* guard, garrison, fortification, shield, shelter, screen, preservation, protection, guardianship, safeguard, security; justification, pleading, vindication.
v defend, guard, fortify, shield, shelter, screen, preserve, protect, keep safe, guard against, watch over, safeguard, secure; parry, repel, put to flight; uphold, maintain, justify, vindicate.
adj defensive, protective.

718 retaliation *n* reprisal, requital, retort, counterstroke, counterattack, retribution, reciprocation, reciprocity, recrimination, revenge, vengeance, reaction.
v retaliate, requite, retort, counterattack, revenge, repay, return, avenge.
adj retaliatory, vengeful, revengeful, retributive, reciprocal, reactive.
adv in retaliation.

719 resistance *n* opposition, withstanding, front, stand, oppugnance, reluctance, repulsion; interference, friction; insurrection, insurgence, rebellion.
v resist, withstand, stand up, stand; confront, oppose, grapple with, rise up, revolt, rebel, repel, repulse.
adj resistant, refractory, recalcitrant, repulsive, repellent; stubborn, indomitable, obstinate.

720 contention *n* struggling, struggle, strife, discord, dissention, quarrel, disagreement, squabble, feud; rupture, break, falling out; opposition, belligerency, combat, conflict, competition, rivalry, contest; disagreement, dissension, debate, wrangle, altercation, dispute, argument, controversy.
v contend, struggle, strive, fight, battle, combat, vie, compete, rival; debate, dispute, argue, wrangle; assert, maintain, claim.
adj contentious, combative, belligerent, bellicose, warlike, quarrelsome, pugnacious; competitive.

721 peace *n* treaty, truce, accord, amity, harmony, concord; calm, quiet, tranquillity, peacefulness, calmness; order, security.
v be at peace; keep the peace; make peace.
adj peaceful, tranquil, placid, serene, calm, complacent; mellow, halcyon, pacific; peaceable, amicable, friendly, amiable, mild, gentle.

722 warfare *n* fighting, hostilities, war, combat, battle, ordeal; tactics, strategy, generalship.
v war, make war, wage war, fight, give fight, battle, do battle, combat, contend, cross swords.
adj warlike, contentious, belligerent, combative, bellicose, martial, military, militant.
adv to arms.

723 pacification *n* conciliation, reconciliation, accommodation, arrangement, adjustment, compromise; amnesty, peace offering, truce, armistice, suspension of hostilities.

v pacify, reconcile, propitiate, placate, conciliate, accommodate, appease, make peace; quiet, calm, tranquilize, assuage, still, smooth, moderate, ameliorate, mollify, meliorate, soothe, bury the hatchet.

adj pacific, concilatory.

724 mediation *n* negotiation, arbitration, parley; intervention, intercession, interposition.

mediator, arbiter, arbitrator, peacemaker, go-between, negotiator, moderator, diplomat.

v mediate, intercede, intervene, interpose, interfere; step in, negotiate, arbitrate.

adj mediatory.

725 submission *n* nonresistance, obedience, compliance, acquiescence, yielding, submissiveness, pliancy; surrender, cessation, capitulation; resignation, passivity, docility.

v succumb, submit, yield, bend, acquiesce, resign, agree, obey, comply, bow, surrender, capitulate.

adj submissive, obedient, compliant, acquiescent, passive, docile, tame, humble.

726 combatant *n* fighter, contestant, disputant, battler, litigant, contender, competitor, militarist, soldier, warrior, polemic, candidate; antagonist, foe, enemy, opponent, rival, adversary, assailant, opposition, assailer, assailant, assaulter, opposer, opponent.

727 arms *n* weapons, weaponry, armaments, armor, ammunition, munitions, deadly weapons.

v arm, outfit, ready for battle, prepare for battle.

728 arena *n* battleground, battlefield, field of battle, theater, ring, lists; playhouse, amphitheater, stage, boards; Colosseum, gymnasium, playing field.

729 completion *n* culmination, finish, conclusion, close, termination, end, finale; upshot, result; final touch, crowning touch; consummation, accomplishment, achievement, fulfillment; performance, execution; perfection, thoroughness.

v complete, finish, end, conclude, close, terminate, finalize; consummate, perfect, accomplish, do, fulfill, achieve, effect, execute, enact, dispatch, discharge.

adj whole, entire, full, intact, unbroken, one, perfect; done, consummate, perfect, thorough, through-and-through.

adv completely, thoroughly; perfectly.

730 noncompletion *n* incompleteness, nonfulfillment, nonperformance; neglect, shortcoming.

v not complete, leave unfinished, leave undone; neglect, let alone, let slip; fall short of.

adj incomplete, unfinished, sketchy.

731 success *n* progress, advance; hit, stroke, trump card; good fortune, good luck, luck, break; prosperity, achievement, fulfillment, accomplishment; ascendancy, mastery, conquest, victory, triumph; proficiency, skill, mastery.

v succeed, attain an end, secure an objective; progress, advance; accomplish, achieve, effect, complete; prosper, find fulfillment, fulfill oneself; master, conquer, triumph, surmount, overcome.

adj successful, prosperous, well-to-do; victorious, triumphant; masterful, proficient.

adv successfully, with flying colors, in triumph.

732 failure *n* unsuccessfulness, miscarriage, abortion, failing; neglect, omission, dereliction, non-performance; deficiency, insufficiency, defectiveness; blunder, mistake, fault, slip, mishap, scrape, mess, fiasco, breakdown; decline, decay, deterioration, loss; bankruptcy, insolvency, bust, dud.

v fail, come short, fall short, disappoint, miss the mark, miscarry, abort, blunder, botch, make a mess of, *(informal)* blow it, founder, flounder, sink, go amiss, go wrong, go hard with; fall off, dwindle, decline, fade, weaken, wane, give out, cease; desert, forsake.

adj unsuccessful, abortive, stillborn, fruitless, bootless, ineffectual, inefficient, insufficient, useless; lost, undone, bankrupt; wide of the mark, erroneous; frustrated, thwarted, foiled, defeated; defective, faulty.

adv unsuccessfully, in vain, to little purpose.

733 trophy *n* medal, prize, palm, laurel, honor, accolade, decoration, reward, recognition, triumph, celebration.

734 prosperity *n* well-being, success, fortune, wealth, affluence.

v prosper, thrive, flourish, rise, make one's way, flower, grow, blossom, bloom, fructify, succeed, *(informal)* make it.

adj prosperous, successful, wealthy, rich, well-to-do, well-off; favorable, propitious, fortunate, lucky, auspicious, golden, bright.

735 adversity *n* calamity, distress, catastrophe, crisis, disaster, failure; bad luck, hard times, misfortune, *(informal)* downers, *(informal)* bummers, trouble, hardship, pressure, affliction, wretchedness.

v go downhill, go to the dogs, decay, sink, decline, come to grief, *(informal)* hit the pits, fall on evil days.

adj adverse, unfavorable, unlucky, unfortunate; calamitous, disastrous, critical, dire, catastrophic; unprosperous, hapless, in a bad way, under a cloud, in adverse circumstances, down in the mouth.

adv adversely; if worst comes to worst.

736 mediocrity *n* average capacity, ordinariness, commonplaceness, insignificance, passableness, tolerableness, indifference, inferiority, paltriness, triviality; moderation, golden mean.

v jog on, get along.

adj mediocre, average, normal, ordinary, commonplace, run-of-the-mill, insignificant, tolerable, unimportant, indifferent, inferior, poor, slight, paltry; moderate, reasonable, temperate, respectable.

II. Intersocial Volition

737 authority *n* control, influence, jurisdiction, command, rule, sway, power, dominion, supremacy; expert, adjudicator, arbiter, judge, sovereign, ruler; warrant, justification, permit, permission, sanction, liberty, authorization.

v authorize, empower, commission, allow, permit, sanction, approve; warrant, justify, legalize, support, back; rule, sway, control, administer, govern.

adj authoritative, peremptory, magisterial, imperative, dogmatic, masterful; executive, administrative, sovereign, regnant, supreme, dominant, paramount, predominant, preponderant, influential, official, decisive, valid, absolute.

738 [absence of authority] **laxity** *n* laxness, looseness, slackness, lenience, toleration, relaxation, loosening, licence, freedom.

v be lax, tolerate, relax, give a free rein.

adj lax, loose, slack, remiss, lenient, negligent, careless, weak.

739 severity *n* seriousness, gravity, sternness, harshness, austerity, rigidity, rigorousness, strictness, stringency, relentlessness, abruptness, curtness; arbitrariness, absolutism, despotism, dictatorship, autocracy, tyranny, oppression; strength, force, brute force, coercion.

tyrant, disciplinarian, despot, taskmaster, oppressor, inquisitor.

v be severe, tyrannize, domineer, dominate, bully, inflict, wreak, be hard on, ill-treat, maltreat, oppress, trample on, crush, coerce.

adj severe, serious, grave, stern, harsh, austere, rigid, stiff, dour, rigorous, strict, strait-laced, stringent, relentless, hard, inexorable, abrupt, peremptory, curt, short; arbitrary, absolute, despotic, dictatorial, autocratic, tyrannical, oppressive, coercive, inquisitorial, ruthless, cruel, malevolent, arrogant.

adv severely, with a high hand, with a heavy hand.

740 lenience *n* leniency, tolerance, toleration, moderation, mildness, gentleness, favor, indulgence, forbearance, quarter, compassion, clemency, mercy.

v be lenient, tolerate, bear with, favor, indulge, allow.

adj lenient, tolerant, mild, easy, easy-going, gentle, tender, indulgent, compassionate, sympathetic, merciful.

741 command *n* order, ordinance, direction, bidding, injunction, charge, mandate, behest, ukase, commandment, requisition, requirement, instruction, dictum, act, fiat; demand, exaction, claim, request; control, mastery, disposal, rule, sway, power, domination.

v command, order, direct, bid, demand, charge, instruct, enjoin, require, impose; decree, enact, ordain, dictate, prescribe, appoint; claim, lay claim to.

adj commanding, authoritative.

742 disobedience *n* noncompliance, nonobservance, insubordination, contumacy, infraction, infringement, defiance, unruliness, rebelliousness, obstinacy, stubbornness, resistance, mutinousness, mutiny, rebellion.

insurgent, mutineer, rebel, revolutionary, rioter, traitor, *(informal)* radical.

v disobey, transgress, violate, disregard, defy, infringe, shirk, resist, mutiny, rebel, revolt.

adj disobedient, insubordinate, contumacious, defiant, refractory, unruly, fractious, rebellious, mutinous, obstinate, stubborn, unsubmissive, uncompliant, recalcitrant, insurgent, riotous.

743 obedience *n* observance, compliance, docility, tractability, deference, respect, duty, subservience, submissiveness, obsequiousness; allegiance, loyalty, fealty, homage, devotion.

v obey, comply, submit, follow, attend to, serve.

adj obedient, submissive, compliant, tractable, docile, deferential, respectful, dutiful, loyal, subservient.

adv obediently, in compliance with, in obedience to.

744 compulsion *n* coercion, constraint, duress, enforcement, conscription, force; impulse, necessity.

v compel, force, make, drive, coerce, constrain, enforce, impel, require, necessitate, oblige, motivate; subdue, subject, bend, bow, overpower.

adj compelling, compulsory, coercive, forcible, constraining; obligatory, necessary, unavoidable, inescapable, ineluctable, irresistible, inexorable.

adv by force, forcibly, on compulsion.

745 master *n* lord, commander, commandant, chief, head, leader, director, ruler, boss, authority.

746 servant *n* subject, retainer, follower, henchman, domestic, menial, help, helper, employee, worker, laborer.

v serve, function, answer, assist, help, aid, provide, cater, satisfy; wait on, attend.

747 [insignia of authority] **scepter** *n* regalia, staff, symbol, emblem, flag, badge; title.

748 freedom *n* liberty, independence, autonomy, noninterference; immunity, franchisement, franchise, privilege, latitude, scope; ease, facility; frankness, openness; familiarity, license, looseness, laxity.

v be free, have scope, do as one likes, do what one wants; free, liberate, permit, allow, set free.

adj free, independent, at large, loose, scot free; unconstrained, unconfined, unchecked, unhindered, unobstructed, unbound, uncontrolled, ungoverned, unchained, unfettered, unshackled, uncurbed, unbridled, unmuzzled; unrestricted, unlimited, unconditional; absolute; discretionary; wanton, rampant, irrepressible, unvanquished; immune, exempt, freed; autonomous.

adv freely.

749 subjection *n* dependence, subordination, thrall, thralldom, subjugation, bondage, serfdom, slavery, servitude, enslavement; service, employ, tutelage, constraint, yoke, submission, obedience.

v be subject, be at the mercy of, depend upon, fall prey to, play second fiddle to, serve, submit; subject, subjugate, master, tame, tread down, weigh down, enslave, enthral, rule.

adj subject, dependent, subordinate; under control, in harness.

750 liberation *n* disengagement, release, enlargement, emancipation, enfranchisement, deliverance, extrication, discharge, dismissal, acquittal, absolution.

v liberate, set free, free, disengage, release, emancipate, enfranchise, deliver, extricate, discharge, dismiss, unfetter, disenthrall, set loose, loose, let out, acquit, absolve.

adj liberated, freed.

751 restraint *n* restriction, circumscription, limitation, control, confinement, curb, check, suppression, constraint, repression.

v restrain, check, keep down, repress, curb, bridle, suppress, compel, hold, keep, constrain; restrict, circumscribe, confine, hinder.

adj restrained, constrained, restrictive, suppressive, repressive; imprisoned, pent up, under restraint.

752 prison *n* jail, gaol, cage, coop, pen, penitentiary, jailhouse, cell, block, dungeon, lock-up, stir, irons, *(informal)* calaboose, *(informal)* hoosegow, *(informal)* the joint, *(informal)* the big house.

753 keeper *n* custodian, guard, *(informal)* screw, jailer, gaoler, warder; escort, body-guard; protector, guardian, governor, governess, teacher, tutor, nurse.

754 prisoner *n* captive, convict, con, jailbird.

v be imprisoned, stand convicted.

adj in prison, in custody, in chains, under wraps, in stir.

755 [vicarious authority] **commission** *n* delegation, consignment, assignment, deputation, legation, mission, embassy, agency, special committee; errand, charge, permit; appointment, nomination, charter.

v commission, delegate, consign, assign, charge, entrust, authorize; appoint, name, nominate, ordain; install, induct, invest, employ, empower.

756 abrogation *n* abolition, cancelation, annulment, repeal, retraction, revocation, remission, recision, nullification, invalidation.

v abrogate, abolish, cancel, annul, repeal, retract, revoke, rescind, nullify, void, invalidate.

adj null and void.

757 resignation *n* abjuration, renunciation, abdication, abandonment, desertion, relinquishment, retirement.

v resign, quit, give up, abjure, renounce, forgo, disclaim, abrogate, abandon, desert, relinquish, retire.

758 consignee *n* trustee, nominee, committee, delegation, delegate, commission; functionary, agent, representative, messenger.

759 deputy *n* substitute, proxy, delegate, representative, surrogate, alternate, second, assistant.

v stand for, represent, answer for.

760 permission *n* authorization, warrant, sanction, liberty, license, enfranchisement, franchise, leave, permit, liberty, freedom, allowance, consent, concession, tolerance, sufferance, indulgence, favor.

v permit, allow, let, tolerate, bear with, agree to, suffer, concede, accord, favor, humor, indulge; grant, empower, franchise, charter, confer, license, authorize, warrant, sanction.

adj permitted, permissive, indulgent, libertarian, tolerant; permissible, allowable, legal, legalized, lawful, legitimate.

761 prohibition *n* interdiction, injunction, prevention, embargo, ban, restriction, disallowance.

v prohibit, forbid, interdict, veto, disallow, bar, restrict, limit; prevent, hinder, preclude, obstruct.

adj prohibitive, proscriptive, restrictive; preventive.

762 consent *n* assent, acquiescence, acceptance, acknowledgment, permission, compliance, concurrence, agreement, approval; accord, concord, consensus, settlement, ratification, confirmation.

v consent, assent, agree, concur, permit, allow, let, yield, grant, comply, accede, acquiesce.

adj compliant, agreeable, amenable.

763 offer *n* proposal, proposition, overture, tender, bid; offering, gift.

v offer, present, proffer, tender; propose, give, move, put forward, advance, invite, hold out, make a motion; hawk, merchandise, offer for sale.

adj for sale, in the open market.

764 refusal *n* rejection, spurning, denial, rebuff, repulse, repudiation; abnegation, protest, renunciation, disclaimer.

v refuse, decline, reject, spurn, turn down, deny, rebuff, repulse, repudiate; resist, repel, repudiate, renounce, disclaim, rescind, revoke.

adj noncompliant, dissident, recalcitrant, reluctant.

765 request *n* claim, demand, application, appeal, solicitation, petition, suit, entreaty, supplication, prayer.

v request, ask, ask for, beg, sue, petition, entreat, supplicate, solicit, beseech, plead, implore, require, demand, importune, clamor for.

adj importunate, clamorous, solicitous.

766 [negative request] **deprecation** *n* expostulation, intercession, mediation, protest, disapproval, remonstrance.

v deprecate, protest, expostulate, enter a protest, disapprove, remonstrate.

adj deprecatory, expostulatory, remonstrative; unsought.

767 petitioner *n* claimant, aspirant, postulant, seeker, solicitor, suitor, applicant, suppliant, supplicant; competitor, bidder; beggar, mendicant, panhandler, *(informal)* bum, *(informal)* streetwalker.

768 promise *n* undertaking, word, covenant, commitment, pledge, assurance, profession, vow, oath, guarantee, warranty, obligation, contract.

v promise, undertake, engage, enter into, bind oneself, commit oneself, pledge, agree, assure, warrant, guarantee, covenant, swear, give one's word; secure, give security, underwrite.

adj promissory, upon one's oath, on one's honor; promised, pledged, committed, bound, sworn.

769 compact *n* covenant, pact, contract, treaty, agreement, negotiation, bargain, arrangement, *(informal)* deal.

v contract, negotiate, bargain, stipulate, make terms; agree, engage, promise; complete, settle, confirm, subscribe, endorse.

adj compactual, contractual, promissory.

770 conditions *n* terms, articles, clauses, provisions, provisos, stipulations, promises, obligations, covenants.

v condition, stipulate, insist upon, contract, provide, bind, tie, oblige.

adj conditional, provisional.

adv conditionally, provisionally, on condition.

771 security *n* guarantee, warranty, bond, tie, pledge, promise, contract; mortgage, lien, pawn; stake, deposit, collateral, *(informal)* IOU, *(informal)* mark, promissory note; deed, bill of sale, receipt, certificate, title; sponsorship, surety, bail.

v give security, post bail, pawn, mortgage; guarantee, warrant, assure, promise; accept, endorse, underwrite, sponsor, stand for.

772 observance *n* performance, compliance, obedience, execution, discharge, acquittance, fulfillment, satisfaction; adhesion, acknowledgment, fidelity, faithfulness.

v observe, comply with, respect, abide by, acknowledge, adhere to, be faithful to, obey, act up to; meet, fulfill; carry out, execute, perform, satisfy, discharge.

adj observant, compliant, faithful, obedient, true, honorable; punctilious, scrupulous, as good as one's word.

adv faithfully.

773 nonobservance *n* evasion, failure, omission, noncompliance, neglect, negligence, laxity, laxness, carelessness, irresponsibility, disobedience; infringement, infraction, violation, transgression.

v fail, neglect, evade, omit, elude, ignore, disregard, discard, set at naught; infringe, transgress, violate, break.

adj nonobservant, lax, loose, disdainful, evasive, elusive, negligent, irresponsible, disobedient.

774 compromise *n* adjustment, negotiation, concession; compensation.

v compromise, bend, give and take, split the differences, come to an agreement, opt for the mean, adjust, arrange, settle.

775 acquisition *n* procurement, appropriation, gain, attainment, purchase, gift, find; profit, earnings, wages, winnings, income, proceeds, produce, crop, harvest, benefit.

v acquire, appropriate, gain, win, earn, attain, gather, collect; take over, take possession of, procure, secure, obtain, get, come into, receive, get hold of; profit, turn to profit.

adj profitable, advantageous, gainful, remunerative.

776 loss *n* damage, injury, privation, lapse, forfeiture, deprivation.

v lose, incur a loss, miss, mislay, let slip, forfeit; waste, get rid of.

adj lost, bereft, minus, deprived of, cut off, rid of; long lost, irretrievable.

777 possession *n* ownership, occupancy, holding, proprietorship, tenure, tenancy, control, custody; belonging.

v possess, own, have, hold, occupy, control, command, have to oneself, have in hand, belong to.

adj possessing, possessed of, in possession of, master of, in hand, at one's disposal; possessive, custodial.

777a exemption *n* exception, immunity, impunity, release.

v exempt, excuse, release; not have, be without.

adj exempt from, immune from, devoid of, without.

778 [joint possession] **participation** *n* partnership, co-ownership, joint tenancy, common holding, communion, community of possessions; communism, socialism, collectivism; cooperation.

participant, sharer, partner, copartner, shareholder; communist, socialist.

v participate, partake, share, share in, go halves, split up, divide, have in common, own in common.

adj participatory, joint, common, collective, communal, communist, communistic, socialist, socialistic.

779 possessor *n* holder, occupant, tenant, lessee; proprietor, proprietress, master, mistress, owner.

780 property *n* possession, possessions, goods, effects, chattels, estate, belongings, assets, means, resources, land, real estate, acreage; ownership, right; attribute, quality, characteristic, feature.

781 retention *n* keeping, holding, detention, custody, preservation, maintenance.

v retain, keep, hold, hold fast, secure, withhold, preserve, detain, reserve, maintain.

adj retentive.

782 relinquishment *n* renunciation, surrender, resignation, yielding, waiver, abdication, desertion, abandonment, quitting.

v relinquish, renounce, surrender, give up, resign, yield, cede, waive, forswear, forgo, abdicate, leave, forsake, desert, quit, abandon, let go, discard, cast off, dismiss, divest oneself.

adj cast off, done away with, left, forsworn, given up, left behind.

783 transfer *n* sale, lease, release, exchange, interchange; transference, transmission, changing hands.

v transfer, convey, assign, grant, consign, make over, hand over, pass, transmit, change, exchange, interchange, change hands; devolve, succeed.

adj transferable, conveyable, transmissive, exchangeable.

784 giving *n* bestowal, presentation, concession, delivery, consignment, dispensation, endowment, investiture, award; charity, almsgiving, liberality, generosity, philanthropy; gift, donation, present, boon, favor, grant, offering; allowance, contribution, donation, bequest, legacy; alms, largesse, bounty, help, gratuity; bribe, bait.

giver, granter, donor.

v give, bestow, confer, grant, accord, award, assign, entrust, consign; invest, allow, settle upon, donate, bequeath, leave; furnish, supply, help; afford, spare, favor with, lavish; deliver, hand, pass, turn over, present, give away, dispense, dispose of, give out, deal out, dole out, mete out, fork out; pay, render, impart.

adj charitable, beneficent, tributary, liberal, generous, philanthropic.

785 receiving *n* acquisition, reception, acceptance, admission, recipient, receiver, legatee, grantee, donee, beneficiary, pensioner.

v receive, take, acquire, admit, take in, accept; come into, fall to one, accrue.

adj receiving; received.

786 apportionment *n* allotment, consignment, assignment, allocation, distribution, dispensation, division, partition; portion, lot, share, measure, dose, dole, ration, ratio, proportion, quota, allowance.

v apportion, divide, distribute, dispense, allot, share, mete, portion out, parcel out, dole out, deal, carve, administer; partition, assign, appropriate, appoint.

adj distributive; respective.

787 lending *n* loan, advance, accommodation, mortgage, investment.

v lend, loan, advance, accommodate, lend on security, pawn; let, lease.

788 borrowing *n* pledging, pawning; appropriating, stealing, theft.

v borrow, pledge, pawn, borrow money; hire, rent, lease; appropriate, use, steal from, imitate.

789 taking *n* appropriation, capture, apprehension, seizure, abduction, dispossession, deprivation, expropriation, divestment, confiscation, eviction; extortion, theft; reprisal, recovery.

v take, catch, hook, nab, bag, pocket, receive, accept; reap, cull, pluck, gather; appropriate, assume, possess oneself of, help oneself to, commandeer, make free with; take away, abduct, steal, seize, snatch, snap up, capture, get hold of, take from, take away from, dispossess, expropriate, oust, eject, divest, confiscate, usurp, strip, fleece; retake, resume, recover.

adj predatory, rapacious, parasitic, greedy, ravenous.

790 restitution *n* return, restoration, reinvestment, rehabilitation, reparation, atonement, compensation, recovery.

v return, restore, give back, render, give up, let go; recoup, reimburse, compensate, reinvest, remit, rehabilitate, repair, make good, settle up; recover, get back, redeem, take back again.

adj compensatory, redemptive, recouperative.

791 stealing *n* theft, thievery, robbery, swindling, fraud, appropriation.

v steal, take, thieve, rob, pilfer, purloin, *(informal)* swipe, filch, embezzle, swindle, appropriate, fleece, defraud, *(informal)* rip off, *(informal)* screw.

adj thievish, light-fingered, piratical, predatory.

792 thief *n* robber, pilferer, filcher, rifler, crook, *(informal)* rip-off artist, cheat; burglar, house-breaker, second-story man, safecracker.

793 booty *n* spoils, plunder, prize, loot, catch, pickings, stolen goods, *(informal)* haul.

794 barter *n* exchange, trade, traffic, commerce, business, bargain; dealing, transaction, negotiation.

v barter, trade, exchange, traffic, bargain, swap, buy and sell, give and take, deal, haggle, negotiate, drive a bargain, transact.

adj commercial, mercantile; interchangeable, in trade, for sale, marketable.

795 purchase *n* buying, purchasing, acquisition; bargain, buy.

buyer, purchaser, shopper, customer, client, patron, clientele.

v purchase, buy, acquire, get, obtain, procure; shop, market, go shopping.

796 sale *n* selling, vendition, commerce, mercantilism, transaction, exchange, auction, trade.

seller, vendor, merchant.

v sell, trade, barter, vend, exchange, deal in, dispose, merchandise, hawk.

adj salable, marketable, vendible, for sale.

797 merchant *n* trader, dealer, seller, salesman, saleswoman, tradesman, shopkeeper, retailer, hawker, huckster, peddler, broker.

798 merchandise *n* goods, wares, commodity, articles, stock, produce, product, staple commodity, store, cargo.

v merchandise, sell.

799 market *n* mart, marketplace, fair, bazaar, business district, mall, shopping center, store, department store, establishment, place of business, office.

800 money *n* finance, accounts, funds, assets, wealth, supplies, ways and means, wherewithal, capital, almighty dollar, cash, currency, hard cash, *(informal)* bucks, change, small change, *(informal)* green, greenbacks; sum, amount, balance.

adj monetary, pecuniary, financial, fiscal.

801 treasurer *n* bursar, banker, purser, receiver, steward, trustee, accountant, paymaster, cashier, teller, financier.

802 treasury *n* bank, exchequer, strongbox, stronghold, coffer, chest, depository, purse, moneybag, safe, vault, cash box, cash register, till; securities, stocks, bonds, notes.

803 wealth *n* riches, fortune, opulence, affluence, easy circumstance, *(informal)* silver spoon, independence, competence, sufficiency, solvency; provision, livelihood, maintenance, means, resources, substance; income, capital, money.

v be wealthy, be rich.

adj wealthy, rich, affluent, well-off, well-to-do, comfortable.

804 poverty *n* indigence, penury, pauperism, destitution, want, need, neediness, lack, privation, distress, difficulties, straits, bad straits.

v be poor, want, lack, starve, live from hand to mouth, go to the dogs.

adj poor, indigent, destitute, poverty-stricken, needy, penniless, broke, *(informal)* bust, hard up, insolvent, seedy, beggarly.

805 credit *n* trust, score, tally, account, *(informal)* tab, bill.

creditor, lender, usurer.

v credit, accredit, entrust, keep an account with.

806 debt *n* obligation, liability, debit, score, duty, due.

debtor, borrower.

adj liable, answerable for, in debt; unpaid, in arrear.

807 payment *n* discharge, settlement, clearance, liquidation, satisfaction, reckoning, arrangment; acknowledgment, release, receipt, voucher; installment, remittance.

v pay, settle, liquidate, discharge, quit, acquit oneself of, reckon up, satisfy, compensate, reimburse, remunerate, recompense, make payment, square accounts, balance accounts, pay in full.

adj out of debt, solvent; straight, clear.

808 nonpayment *n* default, protest, repudiation; insolvency, bankruptcy, failure.

v not pay, default, fail, stop payment; run up bills.

adj in debt.

809 expenditure *n* outlay, expenses, disbursement, payment, costs, fees.

v expend, spend, pay out, disburse, *(informal)* fork out, lay out.

810 receipt *n* value received, acknowledgment of payment.

v receive, take, get, bring in.

adj profitable, remunerative.

811 accounts *n* money matters, finance, budget, bill, score, reckoning, account; statement, ledger, inventory, register, book, books, sheet; balance.

accountant, auditor, bookkeeper, financier.

v keep accounts, enter, post, book, credit, debit, balance.

812 price *n* amount, cost, expense, charge, figure, demand, damage, fare, hire, wages; worth, rate, value, valuation, appraisal; market price, quotation; bill, invoice.

v price, set a price, fix a price, appraise, assess, charge, demand, ask, require, exact; fetch, sell for, bring in, yield, accord.

813 discount *n* abatement, reduction, depreciation, allowance, qualification, rebate, sale.

v discount, put on sale, reduce, take off, allow, deduct, abate, rebate.

814 dearness *n* expensiveness, costliness, high price; overcharge, extravagance, exorbitance.

v be expensive, cost a lot; overcharge, bleed, fleece, extort.

adj dear, expensive, costly, precious; extravagant, exorbitant, unreasonable; priceless.

815 cheapness *n* low price, depreciation, bargain, value, *(informal)* steal, *(informal)* great buy.

v be cheap, cost little.

adj cheap, moderate, reasonable, inexpensive, dirt cheap.

816 liberality *n* generosity, munificence, bounty, bounteousness, hospitality, charity.

v be liberal, spend freely, give, spare no expense.

adj liberal, free, generous, bountiful, hospitable, munificent, beneficient, princely, charitable.

817 economy *n* frugality, thrift, thriftiness, saving, care, husbandry, retrenchment, parsimony.

v economize, save, retrench, husband.

adj economical, frugal, careful, thrifty, chary, parsimonious.

818 prodigality *n* unthriftiness, waste, wastefulness, profusion, profuseness, extravagance, profligacy, lavishness, squandering.

prodigal, spendthrift, squanderer.

v be prodigal, squander, lavish, misspend, waste, dissipate, fritter one's money.

adj prodigal, profuse, unthrifty, improvident, wasteful, profligate, extravagant, lavish.

819 parsimony *n* stinginess, illiberality, avarice, rapidity, rapacity, venality, cupidity, selfishness.

miser, niggard, churl, skinflint, codger, scrimp, *(informal)* tightwad, usurer, Scrooge.

v be parsimonious, grudge, begrudge, stint, pinch, hold back, withhold, starve, famish.

adj parsimonious, penurious, stingy, cheap, miserly, mean, pennywise, niggardly, tight, ungenerous, churlish, mercenary, venal, covetous, usurious, avaricious, greedy, rapacious, selfish.

Class VI

Words relating to the Sentient and Moral Powers

I. Affections in General

820 affections *n* character, qualities, disposition, nature, spirit, temper, temperament, idiosyncracy, habit, bent, bias, predisposition, proclivity, propensity, humor, mood, sympathy; soul, heart, inner man, essence; passion, driving spirit, ruling passion.

adj affected, characterized, formed, cast, molded, tempered, predisposed, prone, inclined, imbued; inborn, ingrained, deep-rooted.

adv at heart.

821 feeling *n* consciousness, impression; emotion, passion, sentiment, sensibility; sympathy, empathy; fervor, ardor, zeal, warmth, tenderness, sensitivity, sentimentality, susceptibility, pity; sentiment, opinion.

v feel, receive an impression, respond to.

adj feeling, emotional, sensitive, tender; sympathetic; emotional, impassioned, passionate, fervent, tender, sensitive, heart-felt, thrilling, rapturous, soul-stirring; moved, touched, affected.

adv heart and soul, from the bottom of one's heart.

822 sensibility *n* responsiveness, sensitiveness, awareness, susceptibility, impressibility, tenderness, sentimentality, sentimentalism; excitability; appreciation, understanding, moral sensibility.

v be sensitive, have a soft spot in one's heart.

adj sensitive, impressionable, susceptible, tender, warm-hearted, sentimental; excitable; aware, understanding, appreciative.

823 insensibility *n* insensitiveness, impassivity, apathy, coldness, callousness; imperturbable; dullness, boorishness.

v be insensitive, not care, be unaffected, have no interest in.

adj insensitive, unconscious, unaware; inattentive, indifferent, lukewarm; apathetic, impassive, unimpressionable; cold-blooded, cold-hearted, unmoved, unaffected, callous, thick-skinned, uncaring.

adv in cold blood.

824 excitation *n* excitation of feeling; mental excitation; galvanism, stimulation, provocation, inspiration, infection; animation, agitation, perturbation; fascination, intoxication, ravishment; irritation, anger, passion, thrill.

v excite, affect, touch, move, impress, interest, animate, inspire, infect, awake; evoke, provoke; stir up, wake up, light up; rouse, arouse, stir, fire, kindle, inflame; stimulate, quicken, sharpen, whet, wet the appetite, fan the fire, raise to a fervor; absorb, rivet, intoxicate, fascinate, enrapture; agitate, perturb, ruffle, fluster, disturb, startle, shock, stagger, astound, electrify, galvanize; irritate.

adj excited, excitable, wrought up, overwrought, upset, hysterical, hot, red-hot, flushed, feverish, boiling, ebullient, seething, fuming, raging, raving, frantic, mad, distracted, beside oneself; exciting, warm, glowing, fervid, soul-stirring, thrilling, overwhelming, overpowering, sensational.

825 [excess of sensitiveness] **excitability** *n* impetuosity, vehemence, boisterousness, impatience, intolerance, irritability, restlessness, agitation; passion, excitement, fever, tumult, ebullition, tempest, fit, paroxysm, explosion, outburst, agony; violence, rage, fury, furor, desperation, madness, distraction, delirium, frenzy, hysterics.

v be impatient, lose patience, fuss, fidget; lose one's temper, flare up, burn, boil over, foam, fume, rage, rant, run wild, go mad, go into hysterics.

adj excitable, high-strung, nervous, irritable, impatient, intolerant; feverish, hysterical, delirious, mad; hurried, restless, fidgety, fussy; vehement, violent, wild, furious, fierce, fiery, hotheaded; overzealous, enthusiastic, impassioned, fanatical; rabid, clamorous, turbulent, tumultuous, boisterous; impulsive, impetuous, passionate, uncontrolled, uncontrollable, ungovernable, irrepressible, volcanic.

826 inexcitability *n* imperturbability, even temper, dispassion, patience, impassivity; coolness, calmness, composure, placidity, serenity, quietude; self-possession, self-restraint, stoicism; resignation, submission, sufferance, endurance, forbearance, fortitude, moderation, restraint.

v bear, endure, tolerate, suffer, put up with, reconcile oneself to, resign oneself to, brook, swallow, make the best of, stomach; compose, appease, propitiate, repress, calm down, cool down.

adj inexcitable, imperturbable, unsusceptible, dispassionate, enduring, stoical, staid, sober, sedate; easygoing, peaceful, placid, calm, cool; composed, collected, unruffled, content, resigned, subdued.

II. Personal Affections

827 pleasure *n* happiness, gladness, delectation, enjoyment, delight, joy, glee, cheer, cheerfulness, well-being, satisfaction, gratification, comfort, ease; felicity, bliss, enchantment, transport, rapture, ravishment, ecstasy, luxury, sensuality, voluptuousness.

v be pleased, joy, enjoy oneself, have one's head in the clouds, fall into raptures; be pleased with, derive pleasure from, take pleasure in, *(informal)* get into, delight in, rejoice in, indulge in, luxuriate in, relish, love, enjoy, like, *(informal)* dig, take a fancy to, take a shine to.

adj happy, blissful, joyful, gladsome, cheerful; comfortable, at ease, content; ecstatic.

adv happily, with pleasure.

828 pain *n* suffering, distress, torture, misery, dolor, anguish, agony, torment, throe, pang, ache, smart, twinge, stitch; displeasure, dissatisfaction, discomfort, discomposure, disquiet, malaise, inquietude, uneasiness, vexation, discontent, dejection, weariness; annoyance, irritation, worry, affliction, bore, bother, mortification, plague; care, solicitude, trouble, trial, ordeal, burden, load, fret; prostration, desolation, despair.

v suffer, afflict, torture, torment, distress, despair; hurt, harm, injure, trouble, grieve, disquiet, discomfort, discompose, worry, irritate, vex, mortify, plague.

adj uncomfortable, uneasy, weary; unhappy, infelicitous, poor, wretched, miserable, woebegone, careworn, cheerless, sorry, sorrowful, stricken, in tears, in despair.

829 pleasurableness *n* pleasantness, agreeableness, delectability, delight, congeniality; sprightliness, cheer, cheerfulness, liveliness; attraction, attractiveness, charm, fascination, enchantment, witchery, seduction, winning ways, amenity, amiability; loveliness, beauty, brightness; goodness.

v be pleasurable, afford pleasure, offer pleasure, please, charm, delight, gladden, cheer; attract, invite, allure, stimulate, interest, captivate, fascinate, enchant, entrance, enrapture, bewitch, ravish, enravish, transport; agree with, satisfy, gratify; slake, satiate, quench; regale, refresh, treat, amuse.

adj pleasurable, pleasant, agreeable, enjoyable, delightful, congenial, amiable; comfortable, cordial, genial, gladsome, sweet, delectable, nice, dainty, delicate, delicious, luscious, luxurious, voluptuous, sensual; attractive, lovely, beautiful, seductive, rapturous, ecstatic, beatific, heavenly; fair, sunny, bright; gay, sprightly, merry, cheery, cheerful, lively, vivacious.

830 painfulness *n* trouble, care, trial, affliction, blow, burden, curse, mishap, misfortune, adversity; annoyance, nuisance, grievance, bore, bother, vexation, mortification; wound, sore, sore subject, thorn in the side, skeleton in the closet; sorry sight, heavy news, bad news; affront, insult, offense.

v pain, hurt, wound, sadden, displease, annoy, trouble, disturb, cross, perplex, irk, vex, mortify, worry, plague, bother, pester, harass, badger, bait, heckle, irritate, anger, persecute, provoke; harrow, torment, torture; affront, insult, give offense, offend.

maltreat, mistreat; sicken, disgust, revolt, nauseate, repel, shock, horrify, appal.

adj painful, hurtful, dolorous; unpleasant, disagreeable, unpalatable, bitter, distasteful; unwelcome, undesirable, obnoxious; dismal, dreary, melancholy, grievous, piteous, woeful, rueful, mournful, deplorable, pitiable, lamentable, pathetic; invidious, vexatious, troublesome, irksome, wearisome, worrisome; intolerable, insufferable, unsupportable, unbearable, unendurable, grim, dreadful, fearful, frightful, dire, odious, hateful, repulsive, repellant, abhorrent, horrid, horrible, offensive, nauseous, loathsome, vile, hideous; sore, severe, grave, hard, harsh, cruel; ruinous, disastrous, calamitous, tragic; burdensome, onerous, oppressive, cumbersome.

adv painfully.

831 content *n* contentment, complacency, satisfaction, ease, serenity, comfort; conciliation, resignation.

v gratify, satisfy, set at ease, comfort, appease, conciliate, reconcile.

adj contented, complacent, satisfied, sanguine, comfortable; assenting, acceding, resigned, willing, agreeable.

adv to one's heart's content.

832 discontent *n* discontentment, dissatisfaction, uneasiness, disquietude, restlessness, displeasure.

v be discontented, repine, regret, fret, chafe, grumble; dissatisfy, disappoint, disconcert.

adj discontented, dissatisfied, displeased, uneasy, restless, dejected, malcontent, regretful, down in the dumps.

833 regret *n* sorrow, lamentation, grief; remorse, penitence, contrition, repentance.

v regret, deplore, lament, feel sorry about, grieve at, bemoan, bewail, rue, mourn for, repent.

adj regretful, sorry, lamentable, rueful; penitent, contrite.

834 relief *n* deliverance, alleviation, ease, assuagement, mitigation, comfort, solace, consolation; help, assistance, aid.

v relieve, ease, alleviate, assuage, mitigate, allay, comfort, soothe, lessen, abate, diminish; cheer, comfort, console; aid, help, assist, succor, refresh, remedy, support.

adj soothing, consoling, assuaging, comforting, palliative, curative.

835 aggravation *n* worsening, heightening, intensification, exaggeration; (*informal*) annoyance, irritation, vexation.

v aggravate, worsen, intensify, heighten, increase, make serious, make grave.

adj worse, intensified, irritated.

adv from bad to worse, out of the frying pan and into the fire.

836 cheerfulness *n* geniality, high spirits, liveliness, vivacity, joviality, jocularity, mirth, merriment, exhilaration.

v cheer, gladden, enliven, inspirit, delight, rejoice, exhilarate, animate, encourage; shout, applaud, acclaim, salute.

adj cheery, gay, blithe, happy, lively, spirited, sprightly, joyful, joyous, mirthful, buoyant, sparkling, vivacious, gleeful, sunny, jolly; pleasant, bright, gay, winsome, gladdening, cheery, cheering, inspiring, animating, hearty, robust.

adv cheerfully.

837 dejection *n* depression, heaviness, heavy heart, melancholy, sadness, dumps, doldrums, despondency, gloom, weariness, disgust, despair, hopelessness.

v be dejected, lose heart, frown, mope, droop, despond, brood over, sink, despair.

adj unhappy, depressed, dispirited, disheartened, discouraged, despondent, (*informal*) down, downhearted, sad, melancholy, lugubrious, heartsick, dismal, gloomy, miserable, desolate; pessimistic, cynical.

adv with a long face, with tears in one's eyes.

838 rejoicing *n* exaltation, triumph, jubilation, reveling, merrymaking, celebration, paean; smile, smirk, grin, giggle, titter, laughter, guffaw, shout, peal of laughter.

v rejoice, congratulate oneself, clap one's hands, dance, skip, sing, hurrah, cry for joy, leap with joy, exalt, triumph; smile, smirk, grin, giggle, titter, chuckle, cackle, laugh, crow, burst out, shout, split, roar, shake one's sides, split one's sides.

adj jubilant, exultant, triumphant, flushed, (*informal*) high, elated, laughing, convulsed with laughter.

839 lamentation *n* lament, howl, wail, wailing, complaint, moan, moaning, groan, sob, sigh; dirge, elegy, monody, threnody.

v lament, bewail, bemoan, deplore, grieve, scream, sob, cry, weep, mourn over, sorrow over.

adj lamenting, in mourning, sorrowful, mournful, lamentable, tearful, plaintive.

840 amusement *n* enjoyment, entertainment, recreation, diversion, relaxation, pastime, pleasure, playing, festivity.

v amuse, entertain, cheer, divert, enliven, interest; amuse oneself, play, sport, make merry.

adj amusing, entertaining, diverting, relaxing, pleasant, witty, jovial, jolly, playful.

841 weariness *n* ennui, lassitude, fatigue, exhaustion, boredom; tedium, monotony, dullness.

v weary, tire, fatigue, bore, exhaust.

adj wearisome, tiresome, boring, tedious, irksome, monotonous, humdrum, dull, prosaic, trying; weary, drowsy, exhausted, tired, wearied, fatigued; uninterested, impatient, dissatisfied.

842 wit *n* drollery, facetiousness, pleasantry, repartee, cleverness, humor, fun; understanding, intelligence, sagacity, wisdom, intellect, mind, sense.

v joke, jest, banter, pun.

adj witty, quick, quick-witted, nimble, sharp, clever, facetious, whimsical, pleasant, humorous, playful, sparkling, scintillating; intelligent, sagacious, wise, perceptive, insightful.

843 dullness *n* heaviness, flatness, stupidity, obtuseness, lack of originality, banality.

v be dull, blunt, deaden, benumb.

adj dull, uninteresting, unimaginative, dry, prosaic, matter-of-fact, commonplace, boring, tedious, dreary, vapid; stupid, stolid, slow, flat.

844 humorist *n* wit, wag, comedian, comedienne, joker, jester, wisecracker, epigrammatist, punster, buffoon, clown, fool, satirist, lampooner, cutup, funnyman.

845 beauty *n* loveliness, pulchritude, elegance, grace, gracefulness, comeliness, seemliness, fairness, attractiveness, brilliance, radiance, splendor, gorgeousness, magnificence, sublimity.

v beautify.

adj beautiful, handsome, comely, seemly, attractive, lovely, pretty, fair, fine, elegant, beauteous, graceful, pulchritudinous, brilliant, radiant, gorgeous, magnificent; artistic, aesthetic, picturesque.

846 ugliness *n* homeliness, inelegance, unsightliness, distortion, disfigurement, deformity, frightfulness.

v deface, disfigure, distort.

adj ugly, displeasing, hard-featured, unlovely, unsightly, unseemly, homely; hideous, gruesome, repulsive, offensive, revolting, terrible, base, vile, squalid, gross, monstrous, heinous; disagreeable, unpleasant, objectionable.

847 ornament *n* ornamentation, adornment, decoration, embellishment, frills, finery.

v ornament, embellish, adorn, decorate, beautify.

adj ornamental, decorative; ornamented, ornate, embellished, beautified.

848 blemish *n* disfigurement, deformity, defect, flaw, fault, taint, blot, spot, speck.

v stain, sully, spot, taint, tarnish, injur, mar, damage, deface, impair.

adj disfigured, injured, imperfect, discolored, freckled, pitted.

849 simplicity *n* plainness, homeliness; clarity, chasteness, restraint, severity, lack of adornment, lack of affectation.

v simplify, uncomplicate, clarify, strip to essentials, get back to basics.

adj simple, plain, homely, natural, unadorned, unaffected, unembellished, neat, unassuming, unpretentious; chaste, severe; clear, straightforward, lucid.

850 [good taste] **taste** *n* good taste, delicacy, refinement, polish, elegance, grace, discrimination, culture, cultivation.

v show taste, appreciate, judge, criticize, discriminate.

adj tasteful, in good taste, decorous, attractive, cultivated, cultured, refined, discriminative, polished, felicitous, appropriate, suitable, apt, becoming, pleasing.

adv tastefully, elegantly.

851 [bad taste] **vulgarity** *n* bad taste, barbarism, coarseness, lack of decorum, ill-breeding, boorishness; gaudiness, tawdriness, finery, frippery, tinsel.

v be vulgar; vulgarize.

adj vulgar, in bad taste, unrefined, boorish, common, coarse, ill-bred, ill-mannered, ignoble, mean, plebeian, crude, rude, shabby; gaudy, tawdry, flashy, garish, crass, showy, (*informal*) tacky.

852 fashion *n* custom, style, vogue, mode, rage, craze; conventionality, conformity; society, polite society, beau monde; manners, breeding, air, demeanor, savoir-faire, gentility, decorum, propriety, etiquette.

v be fashionable, be the rage; fashion, adapt, suit, fit, adjust; make, shape, frame, form, mold.

adj fashionable, in vogue, à la mode, all the rage; modish, stylish, conventional, customary; well-bred, well-mannered, civil, polite, courteous, polished, refined, genteel, decorous.

853 ridiculousness *n* outrageousness, silliness, absurdity.

v be ridiculous, make a fool of oneself, play the fool.

adj absurd, preposterous, extravagant, asinine, laughable, nonsensical, silly, funny, ludicrous, droll, comical, farcical, outlandish, outrageous, fantastic.

854 fop *n* fine gentleman, dandy, (*informal*) dude, coxcomb, beau, man about town, prig, jackanapes.

855 affectation *n* affectedness, pretense, pretention, airs, mannerisms, unnaturalness, display, show, sham, feigning, simulation, foppery.

v affect, act a part, put on airs, pretend, assume, feign, counterfeit, simulate, pose, attitudinize.

adj affected, pretentious, ostentatious, feigned, artificial, stilted, mannered, stagey, theatrical, modish, unnatural.

856 ridicule *n* derision, scoffing, mockery, gibes, jeers, taunts, raillery; satire, burlesque, sneer, banter, wit, irony.

v ridicule, deride, banter, chaff, twit, mock, taunt, make fun of, sneer at, burlesque, satirize, rail at, lampoon, jeer at, scoff at, (*informal*) put down.

adj derisory, derisive, sarcastic, ironic, ironical, burlesque, mocking.

857 [object and cause of ridicule] **laughing-stock** *n* butt, game, fair game, fool, dupe, original, oddity, queer fish, square, straight, buffoon.

858 hope *n* confidence, trust, reliance, faith, assurance; expectation, expectancy, anticipation, aspiration, longing, desire, dream, wish.

v hope, trust, rely on, lean on, have faith in; hope for, expect, presume, anticipate; long for, desire.

adj hopeful, expectant, sanguine, optimistic, confident; probable, promising, propitious, reassuring, encouraging, cheering, inspiriting.

859 hopelessness *n* despair, desperation, despondency, dejection, pessimism.

v despair, give up hope, despond.

adj hopeless, despairing, desperate, despondent, forlorn, disconsolate; irremediable, remediless, unremedial, incurable.

860 fear *n* apprehension, consternation, dismay, alarm, trepidation, dread, terror, fright, horror, panic; anxiety, solicitude, suspicion, misgiving, concern; awe, reverence, veneration.

v fear, be afraid of, apprehend, distrust, dread; revere, venerate, reverence.

adj fearful, afraid, apprehensive, dismayed, alarmed, frightened, terrified, horrified, aghast, terror-stricken, horror-stricken, panic-stricken; anxious, concerned, solicitous, suspicious; fearful, awesome, awe-inspiring; awful, dreadful, terrible.

861 courage *n* fearlessness, dauntlessness, intrepidity, guts, fortitude, pluck, spirit, nerve, heroism, daring, audacity, bravery, mettle, valor, hardihood, bravado, gallantry.

v dare, venture, look danger in the face, take heart, take the bull by the horns.

adj courageous, fearless, dauntless, intrepid, (*informal*) gutsy, spirited, stout-hearted, resolute, bold, heroic, daring, audacious, brave, valorous, enterprising, adventurous, gallant.

862 cowardice *n* fear, poltroonery, dastardliness, faint-heartedness, yellow streak, dread, timidity, baseness, abject fear.

coward, poltroon, craven, sneak, lily-liver, (*informal*) chicken.

v be cowardly, cower, skulk, quail, hide.

adj cowardly, fearful, craven, dastardly, pusillanimous, recreant, timid, timorous, faint-hearted, lily-livered, chicken-hearted, fearful, afraid, scared, spineless, (*informal*) chicken.

863 rashness *n* haste, impetuosity, recklessness, impulsiveness, heedlessness, thoughtlessness, imprudence, indiscretion, audacity, carelessness, foolhardiness.

v be rash, plunge.

adj rash, hasty, impetuous, reckless, headlong, precipitate, impulsive, thoughtless, heedless, imprudent, indiscreet, careless, unwary, foolhardy, presumptuous, audacious.

864 caution *n* prudence, discretion, circumspection, heed, care, wariness, heedfulness, vigilance, forethought; warning, admonition, advice, injunction, counsel.

v be cautious, take care; warn, admonish, advise, counsel.

adj cautious, prudent, heedful, careful, watchful, discreet, wary, vigilant, alert, provident, chary, circumspect, guarded.

865 desire *n* longing, fancy, craving, yearning, wish, want, need, hunger, appetite, thirst; request, wish, ambition, aspiration; love, passion, lust.

v desire, wish for, long for, crave, want, wish, covet, fancy; ask, request, solicit; lust for.

adj desirous, desiring, craving, wishful, hungry, thirsty, covetous, fervent, ardent, lustful.

866 indifference *n* unconcern, listlessness, apathy, insensibility, coolness, insensitiveness, inattention.

v be indifferent, take no interest in, have no heart for, spurn, disdain.

adj indifferent, unconcerned, listless, apathetic, cool, cold, lukewarm, insensitive, inattentive.

867 dislike *n* disinclination, disrelish, distaste, disgust, repugnance, antipathy, antagonism, aversion, hatred, horror, loathing.

v dislike, disrelish, be averse to, be disinclined, be reluctant, have no taste for; disgust, repel, nauseate, hate, loathe.

adj disliking, disinclined, averse, loath; dislikable, distasteful, disagreeable, offensive, repulsive, repugnant, repellent, abhorrent, nauseating, disgusting, loathsome.

868 fastidiousness *n* nicety; hypercriticism; discernment, discrimination, judiciousness, keenness, perspicacity.

v be fastidious, split hairs.

adj fastidious, nice, dainty, delicate; hard to please, finicky, hypercritical, fussy, querulous, meticulous, exacting, scrupulous, proper, priggish, prim; discerning, discriminative, judicious, keen, sharp, perspicacious, sagacious.

869 satiety *n* repletion, saturation, glut, surfeit; disgust, weariness.

v sate, satiate, saturate, cloy, glut, stuff, gorge, surfeit; gall, disgust, bore, tire, weary.

adj satiated, glutted, stuffed, gorged, surfeited; disgusted, bored, tired, weary.

870 wonder *n* surprise, marvel, astonishment, stupefaction, amazement, awe, admiration, bewilderment, puzzlement.

v wonder, think, speculate, conjecture, meditate, ponder, question; marvel, admire, be surprised, start, stare, startle, astonish, amaze, astound, stagger, stupefy, bewilder, dumfound.

adj marvelous, wonderful, extraordinary, remarkable, awesome, startling, wondrous, miraculous, astonishing, amazing, astounding, unique, curious, strange, odd, peculiar; astonished, surprised, aghast, agog, startled, breathless, awe-struck, spell-bound, lost in wonder, amazed, fascinated, bewildered.

871 expectance *n* expectancy, expectation.

v expect, foresee, assume, not be surprised, make nothing of.

adj expecting, expectant, relied on, expected, figured on, foreseen.

872 prodigy *n* phenomenon, wonder, marvel, miracle; freak, monstrosity, spectacle, curiosity; genius, intellectual giant, wizard, mastermind, expert, sage, child genius, wunderkind.

873 repute *n* estimation, reputation, account, regard, report; name, standing, distinction, credit, respect, respectability, dignity, greatness, eminence, honor, renown.

v consider, esteem, account, hold, regard, deem, reckon; be held in high repute, be distinguished.

adj reputed, regarded, accounted; reputable, respected, respectable, esteemed, celebrated, distinguished, dignified, honored, renowned, eminent.

874 disrepute *n* disgrace, dishonor, disfavor, discredit, ill repute, low repute, bad name, shame, degradation, obloquy, debasement, ignominy, infamy, stain, spot, blot, tarnish, taint.

v disgrace oneself, have a bad name, shame, disgrace, dishonor, tarnish, stain, taint, blot.

adj disreputable, base, low, unsavory, shady, unworthy, disgraced, vile, ignominious, dishonorable, opprobrious, shameful, disgraceful, infamous, tainted, tarnished.

875 nobility *n* distinction, eminence, stateliness, majesty, grandeur, dignity, loftiness, profundity, highmindedness; rank, condition, high birth, gentility, quality, royalty, aristocracy, lord, lady.

v be noble; ennoble.

adj noble, exalted, honorable, dignified, imposing, stately; titled, aristocratic, patrician, high-born.

876 commonalty *n* the common people, the lower classes, commoners, multitude, proletariat, populace, rank and file, bourgeoisie, general public, citizenry, peasantry, crowd, herd, rabble.

adj common, mean, low, base, ignoble, vulgar, homely, plebeian, proletarian, low-born, obscure, rustic, boorish, uncivilized.

877 title *n* honor, name, designation, decoration.

adj titled.

878 pride *n* self-respect, self-assurance, self-esteem, conceit, vanity, egotism, arrogance, vainglory, self-importance; insolence, haughtiness, superciliousness, presumption.

v be proud, presume, swagger, give oneself airs.

adj proud, high-minded, dignified, stately, noble, imposing, honorable, creditable; self-assured, self-satisfied, contented, egotistical, vain, conceited, arrogant, haughty, smug, overbearing, over-confident, snobbish, supercilious, presumptuous.

879 humility *n* modesty, humbleness, meekness, lowliness, submissiveness.

v lower, abase, debase, degrade, humiliate, mortify, shame, subdue, crush, break.

adj humble, low, lowly, unassuming, plain, common, poor, meek, modest, submissive, unpretentious; respectful, polite, courteous.

adv with downcast eyes, on bended knee.

880 vanity *n* pride, conceit, self-esteem, self-complacency, egotism, self-admiration, self-love, self-glorification; hollowness, emptiness, sham, triviality.

v be vain, have too high an opinion of oneself, inflate, puff up.

adj vain, conceited, egotistical, self-complacent, proud, vainglorious, arrogant, overweening, inflated; useless, hollow, trifling, trivial.

881 modesty *n* humility, diffidence, timidity, bashfulness; moderation, decency, propriety, simplicity, chastity, prudery, prudishness.

v be modest, retire, give way to, stay in the background.

adj modest, humble, diffident, timid, timorous, bashful, sheepish, shy; moderate, humble, unpretentious, decent, becoming, proper, inextravagant, unostentatious, retiring, unassuming, unobtrusive; demure, prudish, chaste, pure, virtuous.

adv modestly, humbly, quietly, privately, without ceremony.

882 ostentation *n* pretention, pretentiousness, semblance, show, showiness, pretense, display, pageantry, pomp, pompousness, flourish, splendor.

v show off, parade, display, exhibit, blazon forth, emblazon, flaunt.

adj ostentatious, pretentious, showy, flashy, grand, pompous, garish, gaudy, flaunting, high-sounding, sumptuous, theatrical, dramatic, solemn, majestic, ceremonious, punctilious, over-blown.

adv with a flourish.

883 celebration *n* ceremony, ceremonial, commemoration, solemnization, observance, memorialization, festival, festivity.

v celebrate, commemorate, observe, keep; proclaim, announce; praise, extol, laud, glorify, honor, applaud, commend; solemnize, ritualize.

adj celebrational, commemorative, honorific, commendatory; celebrated, famous, renowned, illustrious, eminent, famed.

adv in honor of, in commemoration of, in celebration of.

884 boasting *n* bragging, swaggering, braggadocio, bravado.

boaster, braggart, blusterer, *(informal)* windbag.

v exaggerate, brag, vaunt, swagger, crow, strut, talk big.

adj boasting, boastful, pretentious, vainglorious, elated, exultant, jubilant, triumphant.

885 [undue assumption of superiority] **insolence** *n* boldness, rudeness, disrespect, impertinence, impudence, haughtiness, arrogance, audacity, abusiveness, contemptuousness.

v be insolent, swagger, assume, presume, take liberties, ride roughshod over.

adj insolent, bold, rude, disrespectful, impertinent, impudent, brazen, brassy, haughty, arrogant, audacious, presumptuous, overbearing, abusive, contemptuous, insulting.

886 servility *n* submissiveness, obsequiousness, abasement, slavishness, cringing, fawning, meanness, baseness, groveling, sycophancy, slavery.

toady, sycophant, boot-licker, *(informal)* apple-polisher, *(informal)* brown-noser.

v be servile, cringe, bow, stoop, kneel, toady, fawn, lick the boots of; sneak, crawl, crouch, cower.

adj servile, obsequious, slavish, cringing, fawning, sycophantic, groveling, sniveling, mealy-mouthed, abject, base, mean.

887 blusterer *n* swaggerer, braggart, boaster, windbag, bully, ruffian, rowdy, redneck.

III. Sympathetic Affections

888 friendship *n* amity, friendliness, harmony, concord, fellow-feeling, sympathy, good will, affection; companionship, comradeship, fellowship, fraternity, intimacy.

v be friendly, have an acquaintance with, keep company with, know, sympathize with, befriend, make friends with.

adj friendly, kind, kindly, amiable, neighborly, brotherly, cordial, genial, well-disposed, benevolent, kind-hearted, affectionate; helpful, advantageous, propitious; acquainted, familiar, intimate.

adv amicably, with open arms.

889 enmity *n* unfriendliness, dislike, discord, ill will, antagonism, animosity, hostility, malevolence, hatred.

v be at odds with.

adj inimical, unfriendly, alienated, estranged, hostile.

890 friend *n* companion, acquaintance, crony, chum, pal, mate, fellow, bosom buddy, intimate, confidant; well-wisher, patron, supporter, backer, advocate, partisan, defender, sympathizer; ally, associate.

891 enemy *n* foe, adversary, opponent, antagonist, attacker.

892 sociality *n* sociableness, gregariousness, social interaction, social intercourse, comradeship, camaraderie, companionship, cordiality, good fellowship, conviviality.

v be sociable, consort with, fraternize, welcome.

adj sociable, gregarious, social, warm, genial, cordial, friendly, convivial, amicable, clubbish, chummy, neighborly, hospitable.

893 seclusion, exclusion *n* privacy, retirement, withdrawal, solitude, sequestration, retreat, isolation, hiding, secrecy, elimination, prohibition, exception, omission, preclusion, rejection, ejection, expulsion, banishment, ostracism, exile.

recluse, hermit, cenobite, outcast, castaway, pariah, wastrel, foundling.

v seclude oneself, retire, withdraw, retreat, sequester, isolate, hide, exclude, eliminate, prohibit, reject, eject,

expel.

adj secluded, retired, withdrawn, sequestered, private, isolated, solitary, excluded, eliminated, prohibited, omitted, precluded, rejected, ejected, repulsed, banished, ostracized, exiled.

894 courtesy *n* civility, sociability, politeness, good manners, good behavior, affability, gentility, graciousness, courtliness, respect.

v be courteous, behave well.

adj courteous, civil, polite, well-mannered, well-bred, gentlemanly, gallant, urbane, debonair, affable, gracious, courtly, respectful, obliging.

895 discourtesy *n* disrespect, ill-breeding, bad manners, tactlessness, rudeness, impudence, vulgarity.

v be discourteous.

adj discourteous, ill-bred, ill-mannered, ill-behaved, ungentlemanly, uncivil, impolite, ungracious, vulgar, crude, disrespectful, rude.

896 congratulations *n* felicitation, compliment, salute, salutation.

v congratulate, offer congratulations, salute.

adj congratulatory; complimentary.

897 love *n* affection, liking, regard, friendliness, kindness, kindliness, tenderness, fondness, devotion, warmth, attachment, yearning, passion, rapture, adoration, idolatry.

lover, admirer, suitor, adorer, wooer; beau, sweetheart, flame, love, truelove, paramour, boyfriend, girlfriend, ladylove, idol, darling, angel, beloved.

v love, like, be fond of, have affection for, be enamored of, be in love with, cherish, adore, revere, adulate, idolize.

adj loving, smitten, affectionate, tender, fond, attached, enamored, devoted, amorous, passionate, adoring; lovable, adorable, winning, enchanting, bewitching.

898 hate *n* dislike, aversion, animosity, hatred, antipathy, detestation, loathing, abhorrence, odium, horror, repugnance.

v hate, dislike, detest, abhor, loathe, despise, execrate, abominate.

adj hateful, detestable, odious, abominable, loathsome, abhorrent, repugnant, invidious, obnoxious, offensive, disgusting, nauseating, revolting, vile, repulsive; hating, averse from, set against, bitter, spiteful, malicious.

899 favorite *n* pet, minion, idol, jewel, spoiled child, apple of one's eye, man after one's own heart; love, dear, darling, honey, sweetheart.

900 resentment *n* displeasure, pique, umbrage, animosity, bitterness, envy, jealousy, anger, wrath, indignation.

v resent, take offense, bristle over, chafe, fume, frown, pout, snarl, gnash, growl, scowl, glower, grouch, bear a grudge.

adj resentful, offended, bitter, worked up, angry, wrathful, irate, indignant; envious, jealous.

901 irascibility *n* irritability, excitability, sensitivity.

v be irascible, quick to fly off the handle, have a temper.

adj irascible, testy, short-tempered, hot-tempered, quick-tempered, touchy, temperamental, irritable, snappish, petulant, overly sensitive, choleric.

901a sullenness *n* moodiness, moroseness, churlishness, sluggishness.

v be sullen, frown, scowl, sulk, pout.

adj silent, reserved, sulky, morose, moody, ill-humored, sour, vexatious, bad-tempered, surly, cross, grumpy, peevish, perverse; gloomy, dismal, cheerless, overcast, somber, mournful, dark; slow, sluggish, dull, stagnant.

902 [expression of affection or love] **endearment** *n* embrace, caress, hug, kiss, blandishment, dalliance, love token.

v endear, embrace, caress, blandish, flirt, dally.

adj endearing.

903 marriage *n* wedding, nuptials, matrimony, wedlock; union, alliance, association, confederation.

married man, married woman, husband, wife, spouse, mate, partner, consort, better half, *(informal)* old man, *(informal)* old lady.

v marry, tie the knot, take to the altar, wive, couple.

adj married, wed, united.

904 celibacy *n* sexual abstinence; bachelorhood.

celibate, unmarried man, bachelor, unmarried woman, spinster, old maid, virgin, maiden; priest.

adj celibate, unmarried.

905 divorce *n* marital separation, legal separation; separation, disunion, isolation.

v divorce, *(informal)* split up, separate, isolate.

adj divorced, separated, *(informal)* split up.

906 benevolence *n* kindness, kindliness, humanity, tenderness, kindheartedness, unselfishness, generosity, liberality, charity, philanthropy, altruism.

good Samaritan, sympathizer, altruist.

v wish well, take an interest in, treat well, comfort, benefit, assist, aid.

adj benevolent, kind, kindly, well-disposed, kind-hearted, humane, tender, tender-hearted, unselfish, generous, liberal, benevolent, obliging, charitable, philanthropic, altruistic.

907 malevolence *n* ill will, enmity, rancor, resentment, malice, maliciousness, spite, spitefulness, grudge, hate, hatred, venom.

v bear ill will.

adj malevolent, malicious, resentful, spiteful, begrudging, hateful, venomous, vicious, hostile, ill-natured, evil-minded, rancorous.

908 malediction *n* curse, swear, imprecation, denunciation, cursing, damning, damnation, execration; slander.

v curse, swear, imprecate, denounce, damn, execrate; slander.

909 threat *n* menace, danger, indication, portent, foreboding, prognostication; intimidation.

v threaten, menace, endanger, indicate, presage, impend, portend, augur, forebode, foreshadow, prognosticate; frighten, denounce, intimidate, cow, badger.

adj threatening, menacing, endangering, impending, auguring, foreshadowing, foreboding, ominous, inauspicious, sinister, frightening, intimidating.

910 philanthropy *n* humaneness, compassion, humanitarianism, benevolence, helpfulness, munificence, public spirit, charity.

philanthropist, humanitarian, patriot.

adj philanthropic, humanitarian, benevolent, munificent, altruistic, public spirited, civic minded, charitable.

911 misanthropy *n* hatred of mankind, incivism.

misanthrope, man-hater; misogynist, woman-hater.

adj misanthropic, antisocial, uncivil.

912 benefactor *n* succorer, patron, supporter, contributor, friend.

913 evildoer *n* wrongdoer, troublemaker, subversive, oppressor, destroyer.

914 pity *n* sympathy, compassion, commiseration, condolence, mercy.

v pity, commiserate, feel sorry for, be sorry for, sympathize with, feel for.

adj pitying, compassionate, sympathetic, touched, moved, affected, feeling.

914a pitilessness *n* cruelty, meanness, ruthlessness, hard-heartedness.

v have no pity for.

adj pitiless, merciless, cruel, mean, unmerciful, ruthless, implacable, relentless, inexorable, hard-hearted, stony.

915 condolence *n* lamentation, sympathy, consolation.

v condole with, console, sympathize, lament.

916 gratitude *n* thanks, thankfulness, appreciation, indebtedness.

v be grateful, thank, appreciate.

adj grateful, appreciative, thankful, obliged, beholding, indebted, in one's debt.

917 ingratitude *n* thanklessness, unthankfulness.

ingrate.

v be ungrateful.

adj ungrateful, unthankful, unmindful, thankless.

918 forgiveness *n* pardon, excuse, indulgence, remission, reprieve, amnesty, grace, absolution.

v forgive, pardon, excuse, absolve, reprieve, acquit.

adj forgiving.

919 revenge *n* vengeance, retaliation, requital, reprisal, retribution, vindictiveness, vengefulness.

avenger, vindicator, nemesis.

v revenge, avenge, retaliate, requite, vindicate.

adj revengeful, vengeful, vindictive, spiteful, malevolent, resentful, malicious, malignant, unforgiving, implacable.

920 jealousy *n* envy, resentment; suspicion; watchfulness, vigilance.

v be jealous.

adj jealous, envious, resentful; suspicious; solicitous, watchful, vigilant.

921 envy *n* jealousy, enviousness, grudge, covetousness.

v envy, covet, begrudge, resent.

adj envious, covetous, jealous, begrudging.

IV. Moral Affections

922 right *n* virtue, justice, fairness, integrity, equity, equitableness, uprightness, rectitude, morality, morals, goodness, honor, lawfulness; accuracy, truth.

v be right; do right.

adj right, just, good, equitable, moral, fair, upright, honest, lawful; correct, proper, suitable, fit; correct, true, accurate; genuine, legitimate, rightful.

adv righteously, rightfully, lawfully, rightly, justly, fairly, equitably.

923 wrong *n* evil, wickedness, misdeed, sin, vice, immorality, iniquity, inequity, injustice, unlawfulness.

v wrong, injure, harm, maltreat, abuse, oppress, cheat, defraud, dishonor.

adj wrong, bad, evil, wicked, sinful, immoral, iniquitous, reprehensible, unjust, crooked, dishonest; erroneous, inaccurate, incorrect, false, untrue, mistaken; improper, unappropriate, unfit; awry, amiss, out of order.

adv wrongly, wickedly, sinfully.

924 claim *n* due, right, privilege, prerogative, prescription, demand, sanction, warrant, license.

claimant, appellant.

v claim, deserve, have the right, be entitled.

adj claiming, having a right to, privileged, prescribed, sanctioned, allowed, licensed, authorized, due.

925 [absence of right] **unrightfulness** *n* impropriety, illegitimacy, presumption.

usurper, pretender.

v be unentitled.

adj unrightful, having no right to, unentitled, unauthorized, unwarranted, illegitimate, not licensed.

926 duty *n* obligation, function, responsibility, onus, burden, business; conscience, moral imperative, sense of duty; homage, respect, reverence.

v do one's duty, behoove, become, befit, beseem; observe, perform, fulfill, discharge.

adj obligatory, binding, imperative, incumbent, under obligation, obliged, bound, tied, duty bound; dutiful, respectful, docile, submissive, deferential, reverential, obedient.

927 dereliction of duty *n* nonobservance, nonperformance, neglect, failure, carelessness, fault, infraction, violation, transgression.

v neglect, slight, fail, violate.

adj undutiful, negligent, careless, at fault, failing, in violation.

927a exemption *n* immunity, impunity, privilege, freedom, exception, excuse, dispensation.

v exempt, excuse, release, acquit, discharge, free.

adj exempt, immune, privileged, freed, excepted, excused, unbound.

928 respect *n* esteem, deference, regard, consideration, estimation, veneration, reverence, homage, honor, admiration, approbation, approval, affection, feeling; respects, regards, duty; regard, consideration, attention, devotion.

v honor, revere, reverence, esteem, venerate, regard, consider, defer to, admire, adulate, adore, love; regard, heed, attend, notice, consider.

adj respectful, courteous, polite, well-mannered, well-bred, civil, deferential; respected, estimable, venerable, admirable; respecting, heeding, considering, regarding, attending.

929 disrespect *n* discourtesy, impoliteness, rudeness, crudeness, incivility, impudence, impertinence, irreverence, derision.

v hold in disrespect, be disrespectful, insult, deride, scoff, mock, sneer, jeer, deride, ridicule, scorn.

adj disrespectful, discourteous, impolite, rude, crude, uncivil, impudent, impertinent, irreverent, insulting, derisive, scornful.

930 contempt *n* scorn, disdain, derision, contumely; dishonor, disgrace, shame.

v feel contempt for, contemn, scorn, disdain, deride, despise.

adj contemptible, despicable, mean, low, miserable, abject, base, vile; contemptuous, scornful, disdainful, derisive; dishonorable, disgraceful, shameful.

931 approbation *n* approval, sanction, esteem, admiration, commendation.

v approbate, approve, esteem, value, honor, admire, appreciate, sanction, endorse, commend, praise.

adj commendatory, complimentary, laudatory; approved, praised, in high esteem, in favour; praiseworthy, commendable, good, meritorious, estimable, creditable.

932 disapprobation *n* disapproval, dislike, disesteem, odium, disparagement, deprecation, denunciation, censure.

v disapprove, dislike, object to, frown upon, censure, blame, reproach, reprove, admonish, berate.

adj disapproving, disparaging, reproachful, defamatory, denunciatory, condemnatory.

933 flattery *n* adulation, charming, lip-service, *(informal)* brown-nosing, fawning, flunkeyism, sycophancy.

v flatter, curry favor, slobber over, *(informal)* lay it on thick, wheedle, fawn, court, *(informal)* brown-nose, pander to, overpraise.

adj flattering, adulatory, honey-mouthed, smooth-tongued, servile, sycophantic.

934 detraction *n* detracting, disparagement, belittling, defamation, vilification, calumny, abuse, slander, aspersion, deprecation.

v detract, run down, criticize, decry, disparage, blacken, belittle, depreciate, cast aspersions, defame, malign, abuse, slander, vilify.

adj detracting, disparaging, belittling, derogatory, depreciating, calumnious, abusive, slanderous, vilifying, scurrilous.

935 flatterer *n* adulator, toady, flunkey, *(informal)* apple-polisher, fawner, sycophant, *(informal)* brown-noser, bootlicker, opportunist, courtier.

936 detractor *n* reprover, critic, carper, slanderer, *(informal)* hatchet man, backbiter, defamer, castigator, satirist, cynic, reviler.

937 vindication *n* exoneration, exculpation, acquittal; justification, warrant, support, defense.

apologist, vindicator, defender.

v vindicate, exonerate, acquit, clear; uphold, justify, maintain, defend, support.

adj vindicating, vindicated, exonerated, exonerating, exculpatory, acquitted; justified, warranted, supported.

938 accusation *n* arraignment, indictment, charge, incrimination, impeachment; accusal, blaming, inculpation, charging, imputation.

accuser, prosecutor, plaintiff; relator, informer; appellant.

v charge, arraign, indict, charge, incriminate, impeach; blame, inculpate, charge, involve, point to, impute.

adj accused, accusing, accusatory, accusative, incriminatory, imputative.

939 probity *n* honesty, uprightness, virtue, rectitude, integrity.

v be honorable.

adj honest, honorable, virtuous, upright, scrupulous, high-principled.

940 improbity *n* dishonesty, wickedness, immorality, evil.

v be dishonest, play false.

adj dishonest, dishonorable, unscrupulous, immoral, wicked, evil.

941 knave *n* rogue, rascal, blackguard, sneak, villain, scoundrel.

942 disinterestedness *n* impartiality, fairness, lack of bias, unselfishness, generosity, liberality.

v be disinterested.

adj disinterested, unbiased, unprejudiced, unselfish, impartial, fair, generous, liberal.

943 selfishness *n* self-interest, self-seeking, self-love, egoism, egotism, solipsism, illiberality, parsimony, stinginess, meanness.

v be selfish, cultivate one's own garden, look after oneself, feather one's own nest.

adj selfish, self-centered, self-indulgent, self-interested, self-seeking, egotistical, solipsistic, illiberal, parsimonious, stingy, cheap, mean.

944 virtue *n* virtuousness, goodness, uprightness, morality, ethics, probity, rectitude, integrity; excellence, merit, quality, asset; innocence, chastity, purity.
v be virtuous, have the virtue of.
adj virtuous, right, upright, moral, righteous, good, chaste, pure.

945 vice *n* fault, sin, depravity, iniquity, immorality, wickedness; blemish, blot, imperfection, defect.
v sin, err, transgress, trespass.
adj vicious, immoral, depraved, profligate, wicked, sinful, sinning, corrupt, bad, iniquitous; reprehensible, blameworthy, censurable, wrong, improper; spiteful, malignant, malicious, malevolent; faulty, defective; ill-tempered, bad-tempered, refractory.

946 innocence *n* purity, virtue, virtuousness, faultlessness, spotlessness; guiltlessness, blamelessness; uprightness, honesty; naïveté, simplicity, artlessness, guilelessness, ingenuousness.
v be innocent.
adj innocent, pure, untainted, sinless, virtuous, virginal, blameless, faultless, impeccable, spotless, immaculate; guiltless, blameless; upright, honest, forthright; naïve, simple, unsophisticated, artless, guileless, ingenuous.

947 guilt *n* guiltiness, culpability, criminality; sinfulness.
v be guilty.
adj guilty, culpable, to blame, in fault.

948 good man *n* model, paragon, hero, soldier, saint, salt of the earth, (*informal*) ace.

949 bad man *n* wrong-doer, evildoer, sinner, scoundrel, miscreant, villain, wretch, monster, devil, demon, scum of the earth.

950 penitence *n* contrition, atonement, compunction, repentance, remorse, regret.
penitent, prodigal son.
v be penitent, repent, rue, regret.
adj penitent, sorry, contrite, repenting; repentant, atoning, amending, remorseful, regretful; penitential.

951 impenitence *n* irrepentance, obduracy, hardness of heart.
v be impenitent, show no remorse.
adj impenitent, uncontrite, not sorry, obdurate, unrepentant, remorseless; unrepenting, unrepented, unatoned; irreclaimable.

952 atonement *n* satisfaction, reparation, compensation, amends, quittance; redemption, expiation, reclamation, conciliation, propitiation.
v atone, atone for; give satisfaction, satisfy, make amends; expiate, propitiate, reclaim, redeem, repair, absolve, purge, shrive, do penance, repent.
adj atoning, propitiating, propitiatory, redemptive, expiating, expiatory.

953 temperance *n* moderation, self-restraint, self-control, continence; sobriety, even-temperedness, calmness, coolness, detachment, dispassion.
vegetarian; teetotaler; abstainer.
v be temperate, abstain, forbear, restrain.
adj temperate, moderate, self-controlled, self-restrained, frugal, sparing; sober, calm, cool, detached, dispassionate.

954 intemperance *n* excess, exorbitance, inordinateness, extravagance; indulgence, high living, self-indulgence, epicurism, epicureanism, sybaritism; inabstinence, alcoholism.
v be intemperate, indulge, wallow in.
adj intemperate, excessive, exorbitant, inordinate, extravagant; indulgent, self-indulgent, epicurean.

954a sensualist *n* sybarite, voluptuary, pleasure-seeker, epicure, epicurean, libertine, hedonist.

955 asceticism *n* puritanism, austerity, abstemiousness, self-abnegation, self-denial, total abstinence, self-motification.
ascetic, anchorite, puritan, martyr; hermit, recluse.
v abstain, deny oneself, fast, starve.
adj ascetic, puritanical, austere, abstemious, rigorous, rigid, stern, severe, harsh, strict, self-denying, self-mortifying.

956 fasting *n* day of fasting; going hungry, starving oneself, starvation.
v fast, starve, famish.
adj fasting, starving, unfed; starved, half-starved, hungry.

957 gluttony *n* greed, greediness, voracity; epicurism, gormandizing, gulosity, crapulence, over-eating, (*informal*) piggishness.
glutton, epicure, cormorant, hog, (*informal*) pig.
v be gluttonous, hog; overeat, gorge, stuff oneself, make a pig of oneself, guzzle, bolt, devour, engorge, gobble up.
adj gluttonous, greedy, voracious; epicurean, gormandizing, crapulent, swinish, (*informal*) piggish.

958 sobriety *n* abstinence, teetotalism.
teetotaler, abstainer.
v be sober, abstain, take the pledge.
adj sober, unintoxicated, on the wagon, (*informal*) straight, (*informal*) dry, dry as a bone.

959 drunkenness *n* intemperance, drinking, inebriety, insobriety, intoxication, alcoholism.
drunkard, sot, tippler, drinker, inebriate, dipsomaniac, alcoholic, (*informal*) boozer, (*informal*) lush, (*informal*) juicer.
v be drunk, drink, imbibe, booze, guzzle, swill, soak, sot, lush, drink like a fish, hit the bottle.
adj drunk, drunken, sotted, intoxicated, inebriated, tipsy, tight, (*informal*) potted, (*informal*) stewed, (*informal*) stewed to the gills, dead drunk, (*informal*) plowed, (*informal*) plastered, (*informal*) tanked, (*informal*) wasted, (*informal*) juiced, (*informal*) blown away, (*informal*) high, (*informal*) flying, (*informal*) feeling no pain.

960 purity *n* cleanness; decency, decorum, delicacy; continence, chastity, innocence, modesty, virtue, virginity; simplicity, genuineness, faultlessness, perfection; guiltlessness, honesty, uprightness.
virgin, vestal virgin.
v be pure.
adj pure, decent, delicate; innocent, continent, chaste, viginal, modest, virtuous, undefiled, unsullied, unstained, untainted, uncorrupted, clean, spotless, immaculate; simple, genuine, faultless, perfect; honest, upright; unmixed, unadulterated, uncontaminated.

961 impurity *n* indecency, indelicacy; incontinence, immodesty, lewdness, concupiscence, prurience, lechery; grossness, obscenity, ribaldry, smut, bawdry; uncleanness, adulteration, contamination, defilement; fault, flaw, imperfection; guilt, sin, sinfulness.
v be impure.
adj impure, indecent, indelicate; incontinent, immodest, unchaste, concupiscent, lewd, prurient, lecherous; gross, obscene, ribald, dirty, smutty, bawdy; unclean, sullied, defiled, contaminated, adulterated, tainted, stained, corrupted, jaded; faulty, flawed, imperfect; guilty, sinning, sinful, wicked.

962 libertine *n* rake, roué, debauchee, lecher, sensualist, voluptuary, profligate, seducer, deceiver, courtesan, prostitute, strumpet, harlot, whore, street-walker, trollop, hussy, bitch, slut, minx.

963 legality *n* legitimacy, legitimateness, lawfulness; duty, obligation.
law, code, constitution, charter, statute, regulation, decree, order.
v legalize; legislate, enact, ordain, decree, codify, formulate, pass a law.
adj legal, legitimate, authorized, licit, lawful, legalized, legislated; constitutional.

964 illegality *n* illegitimacy, unlawfulness, illicitness, lawlessness.
v be illegal, offend against the law, violate the law.
adj illegal, unlawful, illegitimate, illicit, contraband, unconstitutional, unchartered, unwarranted, unauthorized, unlicensed, proscribed, prohibited, outlawed, criminal; lawless, arbitrary, despotic, unanswerable, unaccountable.

965 [executive] **jurisdiction** *n* judicature, authority, power, right, control; territory, range, magistracy.
v judge, sit in judgment; administer.
adj jurisdictive, judicial, administrative; inquisitorial.

966 tribunal *n* court, courtroom, board, bench, court of law, court of justice, bar of justice, judgment seat, dock, forum, witness-chair.

967 judge *n* justice, judiciary, magistrate, judicator, adjudicator, jurist, juror; moderator, arbiter, arbitrator, umpire, referee.
v judge, adjudge, determine, hear a cause, try a case, pass sentence.
adj judicial, judicious, juridical, legal, juristic, judicatory, jurisdictive.

968 lawyer *n* attorney, attorney-at-law, counselor, barrister, solicitor, pleader, counsel, advocate, counselor-at-law, legal adviser; prosecutor, prosecuting attorney, district attorney, public prosecutor, attorney general.
bar, legal profession.
v practice law, be called to the bar, plead, read the law.
adj learned in the law.

969 lawsuit *n* suit, action, cause, dispute, contention; case, debate, litigation, legal proceedings, legal action, legal process, trial, debate, pleadings, argument, argumentation, disputation, prosecution; writ, summons, subpoena, affidavit, suitor, party to a suit, litigant, verdict, decision; precedent.
v go to the law, sue, file a claim, bring to trial, put on trial, serve, serve with a writ, cite, arraign, prosecute, bring an action against, indict, impeach, attach, summon.
adj litigious.

970 acquittal *n* clearance, exculpation, exoneration, absolution, discharge, pardon; impunity, immunity.
v acquit, exculpate, exonerate, clear, absolve, pardon; discharge, release, liberate, set free.
adj acquitted, cleared, exculpated, exonerated; discharged, released, set free.

971 condemnation *n* conviction, guilty verdict, proscription.
v condemn, convict, find guilty, damn, doom, proscribe; stand condemned.
adj condemned, condemnatory, convicted.

972 punishment *n* sentence, judgment, penalty, retribution, discipline, chastisement, castigation, reproof, correction.
v punish, inflict punishment, correct, discipline, penalize, reprove, castigate, chasten, administer correction, scold, berate, jail, incarcerate, execute, torture, banish, flog, whip, lash, scourge.
adj punishing, punitive, castigatory, penalized, penalizing; punished, castigated.

973 reward *n* recompense, prize, desert, compensation, pay, remuneration, requital, merit; bounty, premium, bonus; reparation, redress; retribution, reckoning, amends.
v reward, recompense, requite, compensate, pay, remunerate.
adj rewarding, remunerative, compensatory, retributive, reparatory; rewarded.

974 penalty *n* punishment, retribution, pain, pains, penance; fine, forfeit, damages, sequestration, incarceration, confiscation.
v penalize, punish; fine, confiscate, sequester; penalized, punished.

975 scourge *n* punishment, flogging; affliction, calamity, plague, bane, pest, nuisance; whip, lash, strap, throng, rod, cane, stick; prison, house of correction.
gaoler, jailer, executioner, hangman.

976 deity *n* divinity, god, godhead, omnipotence, providence, lord, the almighty, supreme being, first cause, prime mover, author, creator, the infinite, the eternal, the all-powerful, the all-merciful, omnipresence.
adj divine, godly, almighty, holy, hallowed, sacred, heavenly, celestial, sacrosanct; superhuman, supernatural, spiritual, ghostly, unearthly.

977 angel *n* glorified spirit, beneficent spirit, ministering spirit, heavenly spirit, winged being, seraph, cherub, archangel, helper, spirit, guardian; (*informal*) friend, patron, protector, guardian angel, love.
adj angelic, seraphic, cherubic, spiritual, ethereal; pure, good, righteous, ideal, beautiful; (*informal*) adorable, entrancing, transporting, rapturous, lovely, enrapturing.

978 devil *n* Satan, Lucifer, Beelzebub; tempter, evil one, evil spirit, serpent, prince of darkness, demon, evil incarnate.
diabolism, satanism.
adj devilish, satanic, diabolic, infernal, hellish.

979 fabulous spirit *n* god, goddess, fairy, fay, sylph, faun, nymph, nereid, dryad, sea-maid, oread, naiad, mermaid, kelpie, nixie, sprite, pixie, elf.
adj fabulous, mythological, imaginary, sylphic.

980 demon *n* demonology; devil, fiend, evil spirit, incubus, monster, succubus, succuba, fury, harpy, ghoul, vampire, ogre, gnome, imp, kobold, dwarf, urchin, troll, sprite, bad fairy, leprechaun; ghost, specter, apparition, spirit, shade, shadow, vision, hobgoblin, wraith, spook, banshee, siren, satyr.
adj demonic, supernatural, weird, uncanny, unearthly, spectral, ghostly, ghostlike, elfin, fiendish, impish, haunted.

981 heaven *n* kingdom of heaven, kingdom of god, heavenly kingdom, paradise, nirvana; celestial bliss, glory.
adj heavenly, celestial, supernal, unearthly, paradisaic, paradisical, beatific, elysian, blissful, beautiful, divine, blessed, beatified, glorified.

982 hell *n* Gehenna, inferno, Hades, Erebus, pandemonium, abyss, limbo; [*informal*] torment, torture, pain, agony, suffering.
adj hellish, infernal, stygian, satanic, diabolic, devilish; [*informal*] painful, agonizing, excruciating, horrifying, unendurable.

983 theology *n* theosophy, divinity, hagiography, theologics, theism, monotheism, religion, religious persuasion, dogma, creed, credo, doctrine, tenet, articles of faith.
theologian, theologue, divine.
adj theological, religious, theosophical, hagiological.

983a orthodoxy *n* soundness; strictness, faithfulness, adherence, observance; truth, true faith, religious truth.
adj orthodox, sound, strict, faithful, catholic, doctrinal, authoritative, official, traditional; scriptural, divine, Christian; conventional, established, approved, prescriptive, prevailing, customary.

984 heterodoxy *n* unorthodoxy, nonconformity, iconoclasm, doubt, skepticism, recusancy, dissent, misbelief, error, heresy, schism, apostasy.
pagan, heathen, dissenter, nonconformist, skeptic, heretic, atheist.
adj heterodox, nonconformist, nonconforming, iconoclastic, doubting, skeptical, unscriptural, unorthodox, uncanonical, recusant, dissenting, misbelieving, heretical, schismatic.

985 revelation *n* disclosure, discovery, expression, declaration, expression, utterance, publication, admission, confession, acknowledgment; enlightenment, proclamation, announcement; Christian Revelation, Scriptures, word of god.
adj revelatory; instructive; confessional.

986 religious writings *n* Scriptures, *Bible*, Old Testament, New Testament, The Vedas, Upanishads, Bhagavad Gita, Koran, Alcoran, Avesta.

987 piety *n* godliness, devoutness, devotion, humility, veneration, sanctity, grace, holiness; reverence, regard, respect.
believer, devotee, pietist, righteous man.
v be pious, have faith; believe, revere, venerate, sanctify, consecrate.
adj pious, devout, godly, reverent, religious, holy, sacred, pietistic, saintly; devoted, humble, reverential.

988 impiety *n* irreverence, irreligion, scoffing, profaneness, profanity, blasphemy, desecration, sacrilege, sin, sinfulness; hypocrisy, cant, sanctimony, sanctimoniousness.
sinner, scoffer, blasphemer, sacrilegist, hypocrite.
v be impious, scoff, swear, profane, blaspheme, desecrate, revile, commit sacrilege.

989 irreligion *n* ungodliness, laxity, impiety, indifference, apathy, skepticism, doubt, disbelief, incredulity, agnosticism, freethinking, atheism, infidelity.
skeptic, doubter, nonbeliever, agnostic, cynic, freethinker, atheist, infidel, heathen.
v be irreligious, doubt, disbelieve, lack faith, question.
adj irreligious, godless, ungodly, unholy, unhallowed, undevout; skeptical, doubting, unbelieving, indifferent, apathetic, incredulous, freethinking, agnostic, atheistic, faithless; worldly, earthly, unspiritual.

990 worship *n* reverence, homage, adoration, honor; regard, idolizing, idolatry, deification; prayer, supplication, petition; service, celebration, rites.
worshiper, congregation, suppliant, communicant, celebrant.
v worship, adore, adulate, idolize, deify, love, like; pray, kneel, bow, fall on one's knees; invoke, supplicate, offer prayers, petition; praise, bless, laud, glorify, magnify, sing praises.
adj worshiping, revering, adoring, honoring; worshipful, reverential, honorific, celebrational.

991 idolatry *n* idolism, idolatrousness, idolization, fetishism, idol-worship, deification, demonology; blind adoration, extravagant love, fervor, ardency, enchantment, hero worship.
idol, image, icon, symbol, statue, false god, pagan deity.
v idolize, worship idols, idolatrize, worship, glorify, put on a pedestal, canonize, deify, apotheosize; dote upon, treasure, prize.
adj idolatrous, idol-worshiping, pagan, fetishistic; adoring, impassioned, lovesick.

992 sorcery *n* occultism, magic, witchery, enchantment, witchcraft, spell, necromancy, divination, charm, conjuration, bewitchery, spiritualism.
v practice sorcery, conjure, charm, enchant, bewitch, divine, entrance, mesmerize, cast a spell, call up spirits, raise spirits.
adj magic, magical, bewitching, enchanting, charming, incantory, weird, cabalistic, talismanic; charmed, bewitched, enchanted.

993 spell *n* charm, incantation, exorcism, voodoo, trance, rapture, suggestion, jinx, hocus-pocus, mumbo-jumbo, abracadabra.

994 sorcerer *n* magician, conjuror, necromancer, wizard, witch, exorcist, charmer, medicine man, shaman, medium, clairvoyant, mesmerist, soothsayer, guru.

995 churchdom *n* church, ministry, priesthood, sisterhood, prelacy, hierarchy.
v call, ordain, consecrate, bestow, elect.
adj ecclesiastical, clerical, priestly, pastoral, ministerial, hierarchical.

996 clergy *n* clerical, ministry, priesthood, the cloth, clergyman, divine, ecclesiastic, churchman, pastor, shepherd, minister, preacher, parson, father, reverend, priest, rabbi.
v receive the call, take orders.
adj clerical; ordained.

997 laity *n* fold, flock, congregation, assembly, brethren, people; layman, parishioner.
v secularize.
adj lay, laical, secular, civil, temporal.

998 rite *n* ceremony, observance, function, service, procedure, form, usage.
v perform a rite.
adj ritualistic, ceremonial.

999 canonicals *n* religious garments, vestments, robe, gown, surplice.

1000 temple *n* place of worship, house of god, cathedral, church, chapel, meetinghouse, synagogue, tabernacle, mosque, shrine, pantheon; monastery, priory, abbey, friary, convent, nunnery, cloister; parsonage, rectory, vicarage.
adj churchly, cloistered, monastic.

atheistic adj 989
athletic adj 159
at intervals adv 70
at issue adj 708
at its height adv 33
at large adj 748
atlas n 86
at last adv 67, 133
at length adv 133, 200
atmosphere n 338
atmospheric adj 338
at no time adv 107
at odds adj 708
atoll n 346
atom n 32, 180a
atomization n 336
atomize v 336
atonal adj 410, 414
atonality n 410, 414
at once adv 132
atone v 30, 952
atone for v 462, 952
atonement n 952
atonement n 790, 950
at one's disposal adj 777
at one's fingertips adv 197
at one's leisure adv 133
at one with adj 178
atoning adj 950, 952
at present adv 118
at random adv 156
at regular intervals adv 58
at rest adj 265; adv 687
atrophy n 195, 659
at short notice adv 132
at sight adv 132
at some other time adv 119
at some time or other adv 119
attach n 37, 43, 969
attached adj 897
attach importance v 642
attachment n 37, 39, 43, 88, 897
attach too much importance to v 482
attack n 716
attacker n 716, 891
attain v 292, 775
attain an end v 731
attain majority v 131
attainment n 292, 539, 698, 775
attempt n 675, 686; v 675
attend v 186, 281, 418, 457, 746, 928
attendance n 186
attendant n 88; adj 88
attending n 418; adj 186, 928
attending to n 457
attend regularly v 136
attend to v 743
attention n 457
attention n 451, 459, 928
attentive adj 451, 457, 459
attentiveness n 457
attenuate v 195
attenuation n 195, 330
attest v 550
at that instant adv 119
at that time adv 119
at the eleventh hour adv 133
at the heels adv 235
at the least adv 32
at the present time adv 118
at the same time adv 30, 120
at the top of one's lungs adv 404
at the top of one's voice adv 404
at this moment adv 118
at this time adv 118
at times adv 136
attire n 225
attitude n 8, 183, 240

attitudinize v 855
attorney n 968
attorney-at-law n 968
attorney general n 968
attract v 288, 829
attract attention v 446
attracting adj 288
attraction n 288
attraction n 829
attractive adj 288, 615, 829, 845, 850
attractiveness n 288, 829, 845
attributable adj 155
attribute n 780
attributed adj 155
attribute to v 155
attribution n 155
attrition n 331
attunement n 413
at variance adj 24, 708, 713
at will adv 600
at work adj 170
auburn adj 433
auction n 796
audacious adj 861, 863, 885
audacity n 861, 863, 885
audibility n 402, 418
audible adj 402
audience n 444, 588
audition n 418
auditor n 418, 811
auditory adj 418
auger n 262
augment v 35, 37
augmentation n 35, 39, 194
augur n 513; v 511, 909
auguring adj 909
augury n 511, 512, 668
au naturel adj 226
aureate adj 435
aureole n 420
auricular adj 418
aurora n 420
auscultation n 418
auspices n 175, 693
auspicious adj 134, 734
austere adj 704, 739, 955
austerity n 739, 955
authentic adj 494
author n 153, 164, 590, 593, 976
authoritative adj 175, 737, 741, 983a
authority n 737
authority n 157, 175, 500, 527, 700, 745, 965
authorization n 737, 760
authorize v 157, 737, 755, 760
authorized adj 924, 963
author's copy n 590
authorship n 161, 590
autocracy n 739
autocratic adj 600, 739
automatic adj 601
automobile n 272
autonomous adj 748
autonomy n 748
autopsy n 363
autumn n 126
auxiliary n 711
auxiliary adj 37, 707
avail n 644, 677; v 644
available adj 260, 644, 673
avail oneself of v 677
avarice n 819
avaricious adj 819
avenge v 718, 919
avenger n 919
avenue n 302, 627
aver v 535
average n 29; adj 29, 651, 736
average capacity n 736
averse adj 289, 603, 867
averse from adj 898
averseness n 603

aversion n 289, 603, 867, 898
Avesta n 986
aviate v 267
aviation n 267
aviational adj 267
aviator n 269
aviatrix n 269
avoid v 287, 623, 671
avoidance n 623
avoider n 623
avow v 488, 535
avowal n 529
await v 121, 152, 507
awake v 404, 824; adj 457, 682
award n 784; v 784
aware adj 375, 822
awareness n 822
aware of adj 490
away adj 187, 196; adv 196
awe n 860, 870
a wee bit adv 32
awe-inspiring adj 860
awesome adj 860, 870
awe-struck adj 870
awful adj 395, 403, 860
awhile adv 111
awkward adj 579, 699, 704
awkwardness n 579, 699
awl n 262
awning n 223, 424
awry adj 217, 243, 923
ax v 44
axiom n 496
axiomatic adj 496
axis n 153, 222

B

baa v 412
babble v 348, 584
babbler n 584
babe n 129
babe in arms n 129
baby n 129
baby blue adj 438
babyish adj 129
bachelor n 904
bachelorhood n 904
back n 235; v 707, 737; adj 235
back and forth adv 314
backbiter n 936
backbone n 5, 221, 604a
back down v 283
backer n 164, 890
backfire v 277
backfiring adj 277
background n 196, 235
backlash n 145, 277
back out v 283
backside n 235
backsliding n 283, 661
backward adj 133, 603; adv 133
backwards adv 283
backwater n 283
bad adj 34, 397, 401, 649, 653, 657, 663, 923, 945
bad diction n 579
bad fairy n 980
badge n 747
badger v 830, 909
bad grammar n 568
bad likeness n 555
bad luck n 735
bad man n 949
bad manners n 895
bad name n 874
badness n 649
bad news n 830
bad odor n 401
bad omen n 649
bad smell n 401
bad straits n 804
bad taste n 851
bad tasting adj 395
bad-tempered adj 901a, 945
bad timing n 135
bag n 789
bail n 771
bait n 784; v 288, 830
bake v 384
baker's dozen n 98

baking adj 382
balance n 27, 29, 40, 150, 242, 800, 811; v 27, 30, 811
balance accounts v 807
balanced adj 27, 150, 242
balance out v 30, 179
bale n 190
baleful adj 649, 663
balk v 509
ball n 249
ballast n 30
balloon n 273
ball-shaped adj 249
balm n 356, 662
balustrade n 232
bamboozle v 545
ban n 761
banal adj 209
banality n 209, 843
bananas adj 503
band n 72, 247, 416, 417, 712
bandage n 223, 263
banded adj 440
band together v 709, 712
bandy v 148, 315
bandy words v 588
bane n 663
bane n 165, 649, 975
baneful adj 663
bang n 406; v 276
bang into v 276
banish v 55, 185, 297, 972
banished adj 893
banish from one's thoughts v 506
banishment n 185, 297, 893
bank n 217, 802
banker n 801
bankrupt adj 732
bankruptcy n 732, 808
banshee n 980
banter n 856; v 842, 856
baptize v 564
bar n 215, 346, 968; v 55, 261, 761
barb n 253; v 253
barbarism n 563, 579, 851
barbarous adj 241, 563, 579
barbed adj 253
bard n 597
bare v 226, 260; adj 226
barefaced adj 525
barely adv 32
barely audible adj 405
bareness n 226
bare possibility n 473
barf v 297
bargain n 769, 794, 795, 815; v 769, 794
barge n 271, 273
bark n 223; v 412
barrelhouse n 415
barren adj 158, 169
barrenness n 158, 169
barricade n 232
barrier n 232, 261
barrister n 968
barter n 794
barter n 148; v 148, 794, 796
base n 211
base n 208, 215; v 215; adj 34, 207, 211, 649, 846, 874, 876, 886, 930
based on adj 19, 211
baseless adj 2, 4
baseness n 862, 886
bashful adj 881
bashfulness n 881
basic adj 5, 42, 211
basics n 66
basin n 252, 343, 344
basis n 211, 215
bask in v 377
batch n 25, 72
bathetic adj 497

bathos n 497
batter v 162, 276
battered adj 659
battery n 716
battle n 680, 722; v 720, 722
battlefield n 728
battleground n 728
battler n 726
battle with words v 148
bauble n 643
bawdry n 961
bawdy adj 961
bawl v 411
bay n 343; v 412; adj 433
bayonet n 262; v 361
bayou n 343
bazaar n 799
be v 1
be absent v 187
be absurd v 497
beacon n 550
be active v 459, 682
be affected with v 655
be afraid of v 860
be agitated v 315
beak n 250
beam n 420; v 420
bear n 215, 270, 692, 826
bearable adj 651
bear a grudge v 900
bear a resemblance v 17
bearer n 271
bear fruit v 161
bear ill will v 907
bearing n 9, 278, 692
bearings n 183
bear in mind v 451, 505
bear no resemblance v 18
bear off v 279
be artless v 703
bear upon v 9
bear with v 740, 760
beast n 366
beastly adj 653
beast of burden n 271
beasts of the field n 366
beat n 104, 138, 314, 627; v 138, 276, 314, 315, 330, 406, 407
beat a retreat v 623
beat back v 289
beatific adj 829, 981
beatified adj 981
beat it out v 623
be at odds with v 889
be at peace v 721
be attendant on v 281
be attentive v 457
be at the mercy of v 749
beat time v 114
beat up v 352
be at work on v 625
beau n 897, 854
beau monde n 852
beauteous adj 845
beautified adj 577, 847
beautiful adj 242, 597, 829, 845, 977, 981
beautify v 845, 847
beauty n 845
beauty n 242, 829
be averse to v 867
be aware of v 450, 490
be beforehand v 132
be behind v 235
be beneficial v 648
be blind v 442
be blind to v 491
be blunt v 254
bebop n 415
be born v 359
be bound for v 278
be brittle v 328
be broad v 202
be called to the bar v 968
becalm v 265
be capricious v 608
be careful v 459

because adv 153, 155
be cautious v 864
be central v 222
be certain v 474
be cheap v 815
be cheek to cheek v 236
becloud v 421, 422
be cold v 383
become v 144, 926
become a habit v 613
become colorless v 429
become insane v 503
become large v 192
become little v 193
become old v 124
become small v 195
becoming adj 646, 850, 881
be composed of v 54
be concise v 572
be contiguous v 199
be contrary v 14
be converted into v 144
be courteous v 894
be cowardly v 862
be credulous v 486
be cunning v 702
be curious v 455
be curved v 245
bed n 204
be dark v 421
bedazzle v 420
be deaf v 419
be deceived v 547
be degrees adv 26
bedew v 339
be dejected v 837
be dense v 321
be difficult v 704
be diffuse v 573
be dim v 422
be dimsighted v 443
be disappointed v 509
be discontented v 832
be discordant v 414, 713
be discourteous v 895
be dishonest v 940
be disinclined v 867
be disinterested v 942
be disrespectful v 929
be distant v 196
be distinguished v 873
bedlamite n 504
bed-ridden adj 655
be drunk v 959
bedtime n 126
be due to v 154
be dull v 843
be dumb v 581
be early v 132
be easy v 705
be elastic v 325
bee-line n 246
Beelzebub n 978
be enamored of v 897
be engaged in v 625
be entitled v 924
be equivocal v 520
be evasive v 528
be evident v 467
be expedient v 646
be expeditious v 134
be expensive v 814
be exterior v 220
be extraneous v 57
be faithful to v 772
befall v 151
be fashionable v 852
be fastidious v 868
be fated v 601
be fatigued v 688
befit v 23, 646, 926
be firm v 150
be fluid v 333
be fond of v 897
be foolish v 499
before adj 62; adv 62, 116, 234, 280
being n 1, 3, 359
beforehand adv 116, 132
before long adv 132
before now adv 122
before one's eyes adj 446
be forgetful v 506
befoul v 653

be fragrant v 400
be free v 748
befriend v 888
be friendly v 888
beg v 765
be general v 78
beget v 161
beggar n 767
beggarly adj 643, 804
begin v 66, 676
begin at the beginning v 66
begin hostilities v 716
beginner n 541
beginning n 66
be gluttonous v 957
be gone v 449
be good v 648
be good for v 656
be grateful v 916
be great v 31
begrudge v 819, 921
begrudging adj 907, 921
beg the question v 277, 477
be guilty v 947
be habitual v 613
behalf n 618
be haphazard v 139
be hard on v 739
behave v 680, 692
behave well v 894
behavior n 680, 692
behead v 361
be healthy v 654
be heavy v 319
be held in high repute v 873
behemoth n 192
behest n 741
be hidden v 447
behind adv 63, 235, 281
behind closed doors adv 528
behind time adv 133
be hip v 490
behold v 441, 444
beholder n 444
beholding adj 916
be honorable v 939
behoove v 926
be horizontal v 213
be hot v 382
be identical v 13
beige n 433; adj 433
be ignorant v 491
be illegal v 964
be ill timed v 135
be imbecilic v 499
be impatient v 825
be impenitent v 951
be imperfect v 651
be impious v 988
be important v 642
be impossible v 471
be impotent v 158
be imprisoned v 754
be improbable v 473
be impure v 961
be inactive v 172, 265, 681, 683
be inarticulate v 583
be in a state v 7
be inattentive v 458
be incomplete v 53
be inconvenient v 647
be incredulous v 487
be in danger v 665
be indifferent v 866
be indiscriminate v 465a
be in error v 495
be inert v 172
be inexpedient v 647
be inferior v 34
be infinite v 104
be influential v 175
be infrequent v 137
be in front v 234
be inherent v 5
be in health v 654
be in league with v 709
be in love with v 897
be innocent v 946
be inodorous v 399
be insane v 503
be insensible v 376

compendious adj 76, 201, 572, 596
compendium n 596
compendium n 195, 596
compensate v 30, 179, 790, 807, 973
compensating adj 30
compensation n 30
compensation n 774, 790, 952, 973
compensatory adj 30, 790, 973
compete v 720
competence n 157, 639, 698, 803
competency n 157
competent adj 157, 639, 698
competition n 720
competitition n 708
competitive adj 720
competitor n 710, 726, 767
compilation n 54, 72, 596
compile v 72, 596
complacency n 831
complacent adj 721, 831
complain v 411
complaint n 655, 839
complement n 39, 88, 237
complementary adj 12, 237
complementary color n 428
complete v 52, 67, 142, 292, 650, 729, 731, 769; adj 31, 50, 52
completely adv 31, 50, 52, 729
completeness n 52
completeness n 50
completion n 729
completion n 142, 261
complex adj 59, 248, 704
complexion n 7, 428, 448
compliance n 82, 602, 725, 743, 762, 772
compliant adj 82, 725, 743, 762, 772
complicate v 61
complicated adj 59, 248
complication n 59, 667
complications n 154
complicity n 709
compliment n 896
complimentary adj 896, 931
comply v 82, 602, 725, 743, 762
comply with v 772
component n 56
component n 51
component part n 56
comportment n 448
comport oneself v 680
compose v 54, 161, 174, 415, 569, 590, 591, 597, 826
composed adj 826
composite n 48; adj 41
composition n 54
composition n 48, 569, 590, 591
compositor n 591
composure n 174, 826
compound n 48, 232; v 41
comprehend v 54, 76, 490, 518
comprehensibility n 518
comprehensible adj 518
comprehension n 76, 490
comprehensive adj 56, 76, 78, 192
compress v 195, 201, 321, 572, 596
compressed adj 201
compressible adj 322

compression n 195, 572
comprise v 76
compromise n 774
compromise n 29, 30, 68, 628, 723; v 628, 774
compulsion n 744
compulsion n 601
compulsory adj 601, 744
compunction n 950
computable adj 85
computation n 85
compute v 85
comradeship n 888, 892
con n 754; v 545
concatenation n 43
concave adj 252
concavity n 252
concavity n 308
conceal v 223, 447, 519, 528
concealed adj 447, 528, 533
concealment n 528
concealment n 447, 526
concede v 529, 760
conceit n 515, 878, 880
conceited adj 878, 880
conceivable adj 470, 515
conceive v 66, 168, 484, 515
concentrate v 72, 222, 290, 686
concentric adj 222
concept n 451
conception n 451, 453, 515
conceptual adj 2
concern n 9, 625, 642, 860; v 9
concerned adj 459, 860
concerning adv 9
concert n 178, 709
concert artist n 416
concertize v 416
concession n 760, 774, 784
conciliatory adj 723
conciliate v 723, 831
conciliation n 714, 723, 831, 952
conciliatory adj 714
concise adj 201, 572
concisely adv 572
conciseness n 572
conciseness n 201
conclave n 72, 696
conclude v 67, 480, 604, 729
concluded adj 67
concluding adj 67
conclusion n 65, 67, 154, 480, 729
conclusive adj 67, 478, 480
conclusiveness n 478
concoct v 626
concomitance n 120
concomitant n 88; adj 88, 120
concomitants n 154
concord n 413, 714
concord n 23, 413, 488, 709, 721, 762, 888
concordance n 413
concordant adj 413, 714
concourse n 72, 290
concrete adj 3
concretion n 321
concupiscence n 961
concupiscent adj 961
concur v 120, 178, 290, 488, 709, 714, 762
concurrence n 178
concurrence n 23, 120, 290, 488, 709, 762
concurrent adj 120, 178, 290
concurrently adv 120
concurring adj 488

condemned adj 971
condensation n 195, 201, 321, 339, 596
condense v 195, 201, 321, 572, 596
condensed adj 201
condiment n 393
condition n 7, 8, 469, 514, 875; v 770
conditional adj 8, 469, 770
conditionally adv 8, 770
conditions n 770
condolence n 915
condolence n 914
condole with v 915
conduce v 176, 178
conduce to v 153
conducive adj 176
conduct n 692
conduct n 680, 693; v 270, 692, 693
conduct oneself v 680
conductor n 271
conduct to v 278
conduit n 350
conduit n 302
confabulate v 588
confabulation n 588
confederate n 711
confederation n 709, 903
confer v 695, 760, 784
conference n 588, 696
confer power v 157
confer with v 588
confess v 488, 529
confession n 529, 985
confessional adj 985
confidant n 890
confidence n 474, 484, 507, 533, 858
confidence man n 548
confident adj 474, 484, 858
confidential adj 221, 528
confidentially adv 528
confiding adj 484
configuration n 240
confine n 233; v 195, 229, 233, 751
confined adj 203, 229
confinement n 229, 751
confirm v 535, 769
confirmation n 467, 535, 762
confirmative adj 535
confirmatory adj 467
confiscate v 789, 974
confiscation n 789, 974
conflict n 24, 680, 713, 720; v 713
conflicting adj 14, 24, 179, 468
conflicting evidence n 468
conflict with v 179
confluence n 43, 290
confluent adj 290, 413
conflux n 72, 290
conform v 82
conformable to rule adj 82
conformity n 82
conformity n 16, 23, 80, 240, 613, 852
conform to v 16, 82
confound v 61, 465a, 475
confront v 234, 464, 708, 719
confuse v 41, 59, 61, 185, 465a, 475, 519, 538
confused adj 59, 447, 571
confusion n 59, 519, 571
confutable adj 479
confutation n 479
confutation n 536
confute v 479
congeal v 321, 385
congelation n 385

congenial adj 23, 413, 714, 829
congeniality n 829
congenital adj 5
congestion n 641
conglomerate n 72, 321
conglomeration n 41, 46, 72
congratulate v 896
congratulate oneself v 838
congratulations n 896
congratulatory adj 896
congregate v 72
congregation n 72, 990, 997
congress n 72, 290, 588
congruity n 23
congruous adj 23
conical adj 253
conjectural adj 514
conjecture n 514; v 514, 870
conjoin v 41, 45
conjoined adj 413
conjugation n 567
conjunction n 8, 43
conjuration n 992
conjure v 992
conjurer n 994
con man n 548
connect v 9, 43, 45, 216
connected adj 9, 11
connection n 9, 11, 43, 45, 46
connective n 45
connective adj 45
connoisseur n 480, 700
connotative adj 550
conotation n 516
conote v 516
conquer v 731
conquest n 731
consanguineous adj 11
consanguinity n 11
conscience n 926
conscientious adj 246, 459
conscious adj 375
consciousness n 375, 821
conscription n 744
consecrate v 987, 995
consecutive adj 63, 69
consecutively adv 69
consecutiveness n 69
consensus n 762
consent n 762
consent n 23, 178, 488, 760; v 762
consenting adj 488
consequence n 62, 63, 65, 154, 642
consequent adj 63
consequential adj 642
consequently adv 154
conservation n 141, 670
conservative adj 670
conserve v 670
consider v 451, 461, 469, 480, 484, 873, 928
considerable adj 31, 192, 642
considerate adj 451
consideration n 451, 457, 469, 615, 642, 928
considering adj 928
consign v 270, 755, 783, 784
consignee n 758
consignment n 755, 784, 786
consign to oblivion v 506
consign to the grave v 363
consistency n 16, 23
consistent adj 16, 23, 413
consistent with adv 82
consist in v 1
consist of v 54
consolation n 834, 915
console v 834, 915
consolidate v 46, 48, 321
consolidation n 46, 321

consoling adj 834
consonance n 413
consonant n 561; adj 23, 413
consort n 903; v 41
consort with v 88, 892
conspicuous adj 446, 525
conspicuousness n 446
conspiracy n 626
conspiratorial adj 626
conspire v 178, 709
constancy n 16, 80, 112, 141, 150
constant adj 16, 69, 80, 110, 136, 138, 141, 150, 474, 604a
constant flow n 69
constantly adv 112, 136
constellations n 318
consternation n 860
constipation n 261
constituent n 51, 56
constitute v 54, 56, 161
constituting adj 54
constitution n 5, 7, 54, 329, 963
constitutional n 266; adj 963
constrain v 744, 751
constrained adj 751
constraining adj 744
constraint n 744, 749, 751
constrict v 195
constricted adj 195
constricting adj 195
construct v 161, 240
construction n 5, 161, 240, 329
constructions n 567
constructive adj 161
construe v 522
consult v 695
consume v 638, 677
consummate v 67, 729; adj 31, 52, 67, 650, 729
consummately adv 31
consummation n 67, 729
consumption n 162, 638, 677
contact n 199, 379
contact lens n 445
contain v 54, 76
container n 191
contaminate v 653, 659
contaminated adj 655, 961
contamination n 653, 659, 961
contemn v 930
contemplate v 441, 451, 620
contemplation n 441, 451, 620
contemplative adj 451
contemporaneousness n 120
contemporaneous adj 120
contemporary adj 120
contempt n 930
contemptible adj 435, 930
contemptuous adj 885, 930
contemptuousness n 885
contend v 476, 720, 722
contender n 726
content n 831
content n 602, 826, 827
contented adj 831, 878
contention n 720
contention n 713, 969
contentious adj 713, 720, 722
contentment n 831
contents n 190
contents n 56, 221, 596
contest n 720
contestant n 726
contiguity n 199
contiguity n 197
contiguous adj 199

contiguousness n 199
continence n 953, 960
continent n 342; adj 960
continental adj 342
contingency n 151, 156, 470
contingent adj 8, 177
continual adj 136, 138
continually adv 136
continuance n 143
continuance n 110, 117, 200, 670
continuation n 63, 65, 143
continue v 1, 106, 110, 136, 143, 604a, 670
continuing adj 143
continuity n 69
continuity n 16, 58, 143, 150
continuous adj 69, 112, 143
continuously adv 69, 112
continuousness n 69
contort v 243, 248
contortion n 243
contour n 230, 448
contraband adj 964
contract n 676, 768, 769, 771; v 36, 195, 676, 769, 770
contract a disease v 655
contracted adj 195
contracting adj 195
contraction n 195
contraction n 36, 261
contractual adj 769
contradict v 14, 468, 489, 536, 708
contradiction n 14, 218, 536
contradictory adj 14, 468, 489, 536
contraposition n 218, 237
contrariety n 14
contrariety n 15, 179, 218
contrary adj 14, 179, 608, 708
contrast n 14, 15; v 15
contrasted adj 14
contrast with v 14
contravene v 14, 468, 536, 708
contribute v 153, 176, 178
contribution n 784
contributor n 912
contrite adj 833, 950
contrition n 833, 950
contrivance n 626
contrive v 161, 626, 702
control n 157, 175, 693, 737, 741, 751, 777, 965; v 157, 175, 693, 737, 777
controller n 694
controversy n 720
controvert v 536
contumacious adj 715, 742
contumacy n 742
contumely n 930
conundrum n 520
convalescent adj 660
convene v 72
convenience n 685
convenient adj 646
convention n 72, 80, 240
conventional adj 80, 82, 240, 246, 613, 852, 983a
conventionalism n 613
conventionality n 82, 613, 852
converge v 197, 290
convergence n 290
convergent adj 290
conversable adj 588
conversant adj 698
conversation n 588
conversation n 582
conversational adj 582, 588

converse v 582, 588; adj 14, 237
conversion n 144
conversion n 140, 218
convert v 140
convertibility n 13
convertible adj 144, 149
convert into v 144
convex adj 250
convexity n 250
convey v 270, 516, 783
conveyable adj 783
conveyance n 272
conveyor n 271
convict n 754; v 971
convicted adj 971
conviction n 451, 474, 484, 971
convinced adj 474, 484
convincing adj 478
convivial adj 892
conviviality n 892
convoluted adj 59, 248
convolution n 248
convolution n 59, 312
convoy n 88
convulse v 61, 173, 315, 378
convulsed with laughter adj 838
convulsion n 59, 146, 173, 315, 378
convulsive adj 173, 315, 378
coo v 412
cook n 384, 384
cool v 338, 385, 616; adj 174, 383, 826, 866, 953
cool down v 826
cooled adj 385
cooling n 385
coolness n 383, 826, 866, 953
cool one's heels v 681
coop n 752
cooperate v 178, 709, 712
cooperating adj 709
cooperation n 709
cooperation n 23, 178, 778
cooperative adj 178, 709
cooperatively adv 709
coordinate v 60
co-ownership n 778
co-partner n 778
copious adj 168, 573
copper n 439
copula n 45
copy n 21
copy n 13, 19, 22, 90, 532, 556, 590, 591; v 19, 554, 590
copyeditor n 591
copying n 19
copyist n 590
cord n 247
cordial adj 377, 602, 829, 888, 892
cordiality n 602, 892
core n 5, 68, 208, 222
cork n 263; v 261
corkscrew n 248, 262, 311
cork up v 261
cormorant n 957
corner n 244
cornered adj 244
corny adj 496
corolla n 247
corollary n 39
corona n 247
coronet n 247
corporal adj 3
corporality n 3, 364
corporate adj 43
corporeal adj 3, 316, 364
corporeality n 316
corpse n 362
corpselike adj 362
corpulence n 192
corpulent adj 192, 194
corral n 232
correct v 246, 658, 660, 662, 972; adj 246, 494, 578, 922, 922

correction n 658, 972
corrective n 662; adj 658, 662
correctness n 578
correlate v 12, 464
correlation n 12
correlation n 9, 464
correlative adj 12, 216
correspond v 12, 23, 592
correspondence n 592
correspondence n 12, 13, 17, 23, 216
correspondent adj 23
corresponding adj 12, 17, 216
correspond to v 216
corroboration n 467
corroborative adj 467, 535
corrode v 659
corrosion n 659
corrosive adj 649
corrugate v 258
corrugation n 256
corrupt v 653, 659; adj 653, 655, 945
corrupted adj 961
corruption n 49, 563, 653, 659
corse n 362
cortege n 266
coruscate v 420
coruscation n 420
cosmic adj 318
cosmonaut n 269
cosmopolitan adj 372
cost n 812
cost a lot v 814
costliness n 814
cost little v 815
costly adj 814
costs n 809
costume n 225
cote n 232
coterie n 712
cough v 349
could be v 470
council n 696
council n 72, 588, 695
counsel n 695, 864, 968; v 864
counselor n 540, 695, 968
counselor-at-law n 968
count v 85, 451
count among v 76
countenance n 448
counter adj 14
counteract v 30, 179, 662
counteracting adj 179
counteraction n 179
counteraction n 708
counteractive n 662
counterattack n 718; v 718
counterbalance n 27; v 30
counterblast n 179
counter-evidence n 468
counterfeit n 21; v 19, 544, 855; adj 19, 544
countering adj 237
counter maneuver n 179
counterpart n 17, 21, 237
counterpoint n 413
counterpoise n 30; v 30, 179
counterrevolution n 146
counterstroke n 718
counter to adv 708
countervail v 30
countervailing adj 468
countless adj 104
count on v 507
country n 181, 189
county n 181
coup n 146
coup d'état n 146
coup de grace n 361
couple n 89, 100; v 43, 89, 903
coupled adj 89
coupled with adj 88

couple with v 88
coupling n 43
courage n 861
courage n 715
courageous adj 715, 861
courageousness n 715
courier n 271, 534
course n 109
course n 58, 106, 264, 278, 348, 627
course of time n 109
coursing n 361
court n 696, 966; v 615, 933
courteous adj 457, 852, 879, 894, 928
courtesan n 962
courtesy n 894
courtesy n 457
courtier n 935
courtliness n 894
courtly adj 894
court of justice n 966
court of law n 966
courtroom n 966
cove n 343
covenant n 768, 769; v 768
covenants n 770
cover n 223, 263, 424, 530, 666; v 30, 204, 223, 224, 225, 424, 528, 664
covered adj 223
covering n 223
covering n 220, 225, 528
coverlet n 223
cover over v 223
covert adj 447, 528
covet v 865, 921
covetous adj 819, 865, 921
covetousness n 921
cow n 374; v 909
coward n 862
cowardice n 862
cowardice n 172, 605
cowardly adj 435, 605, 862
cower v 862, 886
coxcomb n 854
cozen v 545
crack n 44, 70, 113, 198, 259; v 44, 328, 406, 583, 659; adj 648, 698
cracked adj 410, 503
cracked bell n 408a
crackers adj 503
crackle v 406
crack of doom n 121
cradle n 66, 127
craft n 625, 698, 702
craftiness n 698, 702
craftsmanship n 161
crafty adj 702
craggy adj 253, 256
cram v 194, 539
crammed adj 52
cramp n 378; v 158, 160, 195, 706
cramped adj 579
cranny n 198
crapulence n 957
crapulent adj 957
crash n 276; v 406
crashpad n 189
crass adj 851
crater n 208, 252
crave v 865
craven n 862; adj 435, 862
craving n 276, 865; adj 865
crawl v 109, 275, 886
craze n 852
crazed adj 499, 503
craziness n 503
crazy n 504; adj 503
creak v 410
creaking n 410; adj 410
cream n 356, 648
creamy adj 352, 435
crease n 258; v 258
create v 153, 515
creation n 161, 318
creative adj 153, 161, 515

creativity n 168, 515
creator n 153, 164, 976
creature n 3, 366, 372
credence n 484
credible adj 470, 484
credit n 805
credit n 484, 873; v 805, 811; 484
creditable adj 878, 931
credo n 537, 983
credulity n 486
credulous adj 484, 486, 547
credulousness n 486
creed n 484, 537, 983
creep v 109, 275, 380
creeper n 367
creeping thing n 366
cremate v 363
cremation n 363, 384
crescent n 245; adj 245
crescent-shaped adj 245
cretin n 493, 501
crevice n 198
crew n 72, 269, 712
crick n 378
criminal adj 964
criminality n 947
crimson adj 434
cringe v 886
cringing n 886; adj 435, 886
crinkle n 256, 258
cripple v 158, 659
crippled adj 158
crisis n 8, 134, 151, 704, 735
crisp adj 328
criss-cross v 219
critic n 480, 524, 595, 936
critical adj 8, 465, 480, 642, 704, 716, 735
criticism n 480, 595, 716
criticize v 480, 595, 716, 850, 934
critique n 465, 480, 595
croak v 412, 583
croaking adj 410
crony n 890
crook n 244, 245, 792; v 217, 245, 279
crooked adj 217, 243, 244, 279, 923
crookedness n 243
croon v 416
crop n 154, 775; v 201
crop up v 151, 446
cross n 41; v 41, 179, 219, 302, 830; adj 41, 901a
crossed adj 219
cross-eye n 443
crosseyed adj 443
cross-fire n 148
crossing n 219
crossing adj 219
cross-purposes n 713
crossroad n 219
cross swords v 722
crotch n 244
crotchety adj 608
crouch v 207, 886
crouched adj 207
crow v 412, 838, 884
crowd n 72, 102, 444, 876; v 72, 102, 197
crowded adj 72, 102
crown n 247; v 210
crowning adj 33, 67
crowning point n 210
crowning touch n 729
crucial adj 642
crude adj 53, 579, 651, 674, 851, 895, 929
crudeness n 929
cruel adj 649, 739, 830, 914a
cruelly adv 31
cruelty n 914a
cruise n 267; v 267
cruiser n 273
crumb n 32, 330
crumble v 49, 160, 162, 328, 330, 659
crumbling adj 124, 659
crumbly adj 330
crumbs n 40

crumple v 256, 258
crumple up v 195
crunch v 298
crush n 72; v 162, 195, 330, 739, 879
crush out v 162
crust n 223
crustacean n 366
crutch n 215
cry n 411
cry n 669; v 411, 412, 839
cry for joy v 838
crying n 411, 412; adj 411, 630
cry out v 411, 669
cry out against v 616
crypt n 363
cryptic adj 528
crystalline adj 425
crystallization n 321, 323
crystallize v 321
cubbyhole n 530
cube v 93
cuckoo v 412
cue n 550
cull v 609, 789
culminate v 210
culmination n 65, 206, 210, 261, 729
culpability n 947
culpable adj 947
cultivate v 371, 375, 658
cultivated adj 850
cultivate one's own garden v 943
cultivation n 371, 578, 658, 850
culture n 850
cultured adj 850
culvert n 350
cumbersome adj 319, 706, 830
cumbrous adj 319
cumulation n 702
cunning n 544, 698; adj 544, 545, 698
cup n 252
cupidity n 819
cupola n 250
cupped adj 252
curable adj 660
curative adj 660, 662, 834
curb n 179, 616, 751; v 174, 179, 275, 751
curd n 354
curdle v 397
curdled adj 397
cure n 660, 662; v 660, 670
curfew n 126
curiosity n 455
curiosity n 872
curious adj 455, 461, 870
curiously adv 31
curl n 245, 248; v 245, 248, 258
currency n 800
current n 338, 348; adj 1, 78, 118, 151, 531, 532, 560, 613
curry v 331, 392
curry favor v 933
curse n 663, 830, 908; v 908
cursing n 908
cursory adj 209
curt adj 201, 739
curtail v 38
curtailed adj 201
curtailment n 38, 201
curtain n 424, 530; v 424
curtness n 739
curtsy n 308; v 308
curvature n 245
curve n 217, 245, 245; v 245, 279
curved adj 245
custodial adj 777
custodian n 664, 753
custody n 664, 777, 781
custom n 80, 124, 613, 852
customarily adv 136
customariness n 82

customary adj 80, 82, 124, 136, 613, 852, 983a
customer n 795
cut n 44, 70, 198, 240, 257, 259, 276, 378; v 44, 240, 257, 259, 361, 371, 385, 557
cut across v 302
cut adrift v 44, 297
cut a figure v 448
cut away v 38
cutback n 38; v 38, 201; adj 201
cut down v 195, 361
cut in two v 91
cut off v 38, 44, 361; adj 776
cut open v 260
cut out v 293
cut short v 142, 201
cutter n 273
cutthroat n 361
cutting adj 253, 383
cutting edge n 253
cuttings n 596
cut to pieces v 361
cut to ribbons v 361
cutup n 844; v 44
cycle n 138, 247
cyclic adj 138
cyclical adj 138
cyclically adv 138
cycling n 266
cyclist n 268
cyclone n 312, 315, 349
cyclonic adj 349
cylinder n 249
cylindrical adj 249
cylindricality n 249
cynic n 165, 936, 989

D

dab n 32, 276; v 276
dabble v 683
dad n 166
dado n 211
daft adj 503
daily adv 136
dainty adj 394, 829, 868
dale n 252
dalliance n 902
dally v 683, 902
damage n 619, 649, 659, 776, 812; v 649, 659, 848
damages n 974
damn v 908, 971
damnable adj 649
damnation n 908
damning n 908
damp v 339, 616; adj 339
dampen v 408a
dampened adj 408a
damper n 408a, 616
dampness n 339
dam up v 261
dance n 309; v 309, 315, 838
dance all night v 309
dandy n 854
danger n 665
danger n 475, 667, 909
dangerous adj 475, 665
danger signal n 669
dangle v 214
dangler n 281
dangling adj 214
dank adj 339
dankness n 339
dapple v 440; adj 433
dappled adj 440
dapple-gray adj 432
dare v 715, 861
daring n 715, 861; adj 715, 861
dark adj 421, 422, 431, 442, 447, 571, 901a
darken v 353, 421, 422, 431, 519
darkened adj 421, 422
darkish adj 422
darkly adv 442
darkness n 421
darkness n 426, 431, 491, 526

darling n 897, 899
dart v 274
dash n 32, 41, 274, 310, 682, 684; v 41, 274, 276, 310, 684
dash off v 274, 682
dash one's expectations v 509
dash one's hopes v 509
dastardliness n 862
dastardly adj 862
data n 476, 527
date n 106; v 114
dauntless adj 861
dauntlessness n 861
dawdle v 133, 275, 605, 683
dawdler n 683
dawdling n 683
dawn n 125, 420; v 116
day n 420
day after day adv 136
daybreak n 125, 420
daylight n 420
day of fasting n 956
day of judgment n 121
day of rest n 687
days gone by n 122
days of old n 122
days of yore n 122
daze v 420
dazzle v 420, 442
de n 220, 234
dead adj 172, 360, 376, 381, 408a
dead and gone adj 360
dead as a door nail adj 360
dead drunk adj 959
deaden v 376, 381, 843
deadened adj 381, 408a
dead heat n 27
dead language n 560
deadly adj 162, 360, 361, 649, 657, 663
deadly weapons n 727
deadness n 381
dead of night n 126, 421
dead silence n 403
dead sound n 408a
deaf adj 419
deafen v 404, 419
deafened adj 419
deafening adj 404
deafness n 419
deaf to adj 458
deaf to the past adj 506
deal n 786, 794
dealer n 797
deal in v 796
dealing n 794
deal out v 73, 784
dear n 899; adj 814
dearness n 814
dearth n 640
death n 360
death n 67, 142
death agonies n 360
death bell n 363
death blow n 67, 360, 361
deathlike adj 403
deathly adj 361
death rattle n 360
debark v 292
debarkation n 292
debase v 308, 653, 659, 879
debased adj 207
debasement n 207, 308, 659, 874
debate n 476, 588, 720, 969; v 476, 720
debater n 476
debauchee n 962
debilitate v 160
debility n 158, 160
debit n 177, 806; v 811
debonair adj 894
debt n 806
debt n 177
debtor n 806
decade n 98, 108
decadence n 659
decapitate v 361

decay n 49, 124, 360, 638, 653, 655, 659, 732; v 36, 49, 195, 360, 659, 735
decayed adj 124, 160, 659
decease n 360; v 360
deceit n 545, 702
deceitful adj 544, 545, 702
deceitfulness n 544, 702
deceive v 544, 545
deceiver n 548
deceiver n 962
deceiving n 545
decency n 881, 960
decent adj 246, 651, 881, 960
deception n 545
deception n 21, 544, 702
deceptive adj 520, 544, 545, 702
decide v 153, 480, 600, 604, 609
decided adj 31, 67
decidedly adv 31
decimal adj 84
decimate v 361, 659
decipher v 522
decision n 480, 600, 604, 609, 620, 969
decisive adj 737
deck out v 225
declaim v 582
declamation n 577, 582
declamatory adj 577, 582
declaration n 525, 531, 535, 985
declarative adj 527, 535
declaratory adj 535
declare v 516, 525, 531, 535
declare war v 716
declension n 306, 567, 659
declination n 306
decline n 36, 124, 217, 306, 638, 655, 659, 732; v 36, 160, 217, 306, 360, 610, 659, 732, 735, 764; adj 128
declining adj 217
declining years n 128
declivitous adj 217, 306
declivity n 217, 306
decode v 522
decoloration n 430
decompose v 49
decomposed adj 49
decomposition n 49
decorate v 847
decoration n 733, 847, 877
decorative adj 847
decorous adj 850, 852
decorum n 852, 960
decoy v 288
decrease n 36
decrease n 38, 195, 283; v 36, 38, 193, 195
decreased adj 36
decreasing adj 36
decree n 480, 963; v 600, 741, 963
decrement n 40a
decrepit adj 124, 158, 160, 655, 659
decrepitude n 128, 158, 160, 659
decry v 934
deduce v 476
deduct v 38, 813
deductible adj 38
deduction n 38
deduction n 40a, 65, 476, 480
deductive adj 476
deed n 680, 771
deem v 451, 873
deep n 341; adj 208, 404, 428
deepen v 35, 208

favorable adj 134, 602, 648, 734
favorite n 899
favor with v 784
fawn n 886, 933
fawner n 935
fawning n 886, 933; adj 886
fay n 979
fealty n 743
fear n 860
fear n 862; v 860
fearful adj 665, 830, 860, 862
fearfully adv 31
fearless adj 861
fearlessness n 861
feasibility n 470, 705
feasible adj 470, 705
feast on v 298, 377
feat n 680
feather one's own nest v 943
feathery adj 320
feature n 56, 79, 448, 550, 780
features n 5
fecal adj 653
fecund adj 168, 365
fecundity n 168
feeble adj 32, 158, 160, 203, 337, 477, 575, 605
feeble-minded adj 499
feebleness n 575
feebleness n 158
feed v 298, 388
feel n 379; v 375, 379, 821
feel contempt for v 930
feel fine v 654
feel for v 914
feel good v 654
feeling n 821
feeling n 375, 379, 928; adj 821, 914
feel pain v 378
feeling no pain adj 959
feel pleasure v 377
feel sorry about v 833
feel sorry for v 914
fees n 809
feign v 544, 546, 680, 855
feigned adj 855
feigning n 855
felicitation n 896
felicitous adj 23, 578, 698, 850
felicity n 698, 827
fell v 162, 213, 308
fellow n 17, 27, 88, 373, 890; adj 88
fellow creature n 372
fellow-feeling n 888
fellow man n 372
fellowship n 709, 712, 888
female n 374; adj 374
female animal n 374
feminine adj 374
femininity n 374
fen n 345
fence n 232; v 277, 477
fence in v 229
ferment n 59, 171, 173, 315, 320; v 173, 315, 353, 397
fermentation n 171, 315, 353
fermented adj 397
ferocious adj 173
ferocity n 173
ferret out v 480a
fertile adj 168, 371
fertility n 168
fertilize v 168
fervent adj 382, 821, 865
fervid adj 382, 824
fervor n 382, 821, 991
fester n 653
festival n 883
festivity n 840, 883
fetch v 270, 812
fetid adj 401, 653
fetidness n 401
fetishism n 991
fetishistic adj 991

fetor n 401
fetter v 43
feud n 713, 720; v 713
fever n 382, 825
feverish adj 824, 825
few n 100; adj 32, 103, 137
few and far between adj 103
fewness n 103
fewness n 32
fiasco n 732
fiat n 741
fib n 544, 546; v 544, 546
fiber n 205
fibrous adj 205
fickle adj 149, 605, 608
fickleness n 605
fiction n 515, 544, 546, 598
fictional adj 598
fictitious adj 546
fidelity n 543, 772
fidget v 825
fidgetiness n 149, 682
fidgety adj 149, 682, 825
field n 344
field of battle n 728
fields n 344
fiend n 980
fiendish adj 980
fierce adj 173, 825
fiery adj 382, 684, 825
fiery furnace n 386
fifty n 98
fifty-fifty chance n 156
fifty-fifty split n 91
fight n 680; v 606, 720, 722
fighter n 726
fighting n 173, 722
figment n 515
figuration n 554
figurative adj 521, 554
figure n 84, 550, 812; v 240, 448, 554, 557
figured on adj 871
figure of speech n 521
figure of speech n 566
figures of beauty n 521
filament n 205
filch v 791
filcher n 792
file n 69, 86, 266, 330; v 38, 60, 69, 195, 255, 330
file a claim v 969
filial adj 167
filiation n 11
filigree n 219
filing n 330
fill v 52, 186, 190, 224
filled in adj 527
fill in v 52
filling n 224
fill out v 194, 549
fill up v 52, 261
fill up the time v 106
film n 204, 427
filminess n 4
filmy adj 204, 329, 426
filth n 653
filthy adj 653
final adj 67
finale n 65, 67, 360, 729
final gasp n 360
finality n 67
finalize v 729
finally adv 67, 151
final stage n 67
final touch n 729
finance n 800, 811
financial adj 800
financier n 801, 811
find v 480a, 775; v 151
find fulfillment v 731
find guilty v 971
find oneself v 186
find one's way to v 602
find out v 480a, 527
find refuge v 666
find safety v 666
find the means v 632
find the right words v 566
find vent v 295

fine n 974; v 974; adj 32, 203, 322, 329, 578, 648, 845
fine art n 556
fine gentleman n 854
fineness n 329
fine powder n 330
finery n 847, 851
fine speaking n 577
finesse n 698, 702; v 702
fine writing n 577
finger v 379
fingering n 379
finical adj 459
finicky adj 868
finish n 65, 67, 142, 242, 729; v 52, 67, 142, 650, 729
finished adj 242, 698
finishing stroke n 361
fire n 171, 382, 423, 574; v 384, 388, 420, 824
fired adj 384
fire off v 284
fire place n 386
fireproof adj 385
firewood n 388
firing n 388, 406
firm adj 43, 150, 323, 604, 606
firmament n 318
firmly adv 43
firmness n 150, 323, 604, 606
first adj 66; adv 66
first and foremost adv 66
first blush n 125
first cause n 153, 976
first-class adj 648
first come first served v 607, 609a
first move n 66
first rank n 234
first-rate adj 33, 648, 698
first step n 66
firth n 343
fiscal adj 800
fish n 366
fish for v 622
fishing n 361
fish story n 549
fish up v 307
fissure n 44, 198, 260
fit n 7, 173, 315, 825; v 23, 852; adj 646, 698, 922
fit as a fiddle adj 654
fit for adj 698
fitful adj 70, 139, 149, 475, 608
fitfully adv 139
fitfulness n 139, 475
fitness n 646
fit out v 225, 673
fits n 315
five, etc. n 98
five n 98
fivefold division n 99
fix n 704; v 43, 60, 150, 184, 604, 660
fix a price v 812
fixed adj 5, 141, 150, 240, 265, 474, 604, 613
fixed idea n 606
fixedness n 150
fixity n 150, 265
fix the time v 114
fizzle v 353, 409
fjord n 343
flabby adj 324
flaccid adj 160, 324, 326
flaccidity n 160, 324, 326, 640
flag n 747; v 160, 275, 655, 683, 688
flaky adj 204
flame n 382, 420, 423, 439, 897; v 382, 897
flame-colored adj 439
flaming adj 434
flammable adj 384, 388
flank n 236; v 236

flanked adj 236
flanking adj 236
flap n 214; v 214, 315
flare n 420; v 173, 420
flare up v 420, 825
flash n 113, 420, 453, 612; v 113, 420
flash on v 505; v 612
flashy adj 428, 577, 851, 882
flat n 344; adj 172, 207, 213, 251, 337, 391, 395, 598, 843
flat as a pancake adj 251
flatlands n 207
flatness n 251
flatness n 207, 213, 391, 843
flatten v 213, 251, 255
flatter v 933
flatterer n 935
flattering adj 933
flattery n 933
flatulent adj 334, 338
flaunt v 882
flaunting adj 882
flavor n 390, 394; v 390
flavored adj 390
flavorful adj 390, 394
flavorfulness n 394
flavoring n 393
flavorless adj 395
flavorlessness n 395
flavory adj 390
flaw n 70, 198, 495, 651, 848, 961
flawed adj 961
flaxen adj 435
fleck v 440
flecked adj 440
flecky adj 440
fled adj 671
flee v 671
fleece n 223; v 789, 791, 814
fleet n 273; adj 274, 684
fleeting adj 111
flesh n 364
flesh and blood n 3, 316, 364
fleshiness n 354
fleshly adj 364
fleshy adj 354
flexibility n 324, 705
flexible adj 324
flexure n 245
flicker n 315; v 315, 420, 422
flickering adj 139
flier n 269
flier n 269
flight n 267, 274, 287, 293, 623, 671
flighty adj 149, 503
flimsiness n 4, 209, 425
flimsy adj 160, 209, 322, 324, 425, 477, 643
flinch v 623
fling n 284; v 284
flip out v 173
flipside n 235
flirt v 902
flit v 109, 111, 264, 266, 274
flitting adj 111, 266
float v 267, 320
floating adj 405
flock n 72, 997; v 72
flocks and herds n 366
flog v 972
flogging n 975
flood n 72, 121, 348; v 641
flood gate n 233, 350
floor n 204; v 213
flop v 315
flora n 357, 367, 369
floriculture n 371
florid adj 428, 577
floridness n 577
flounce v 309, 315
flounder v 149, 314, 315, 475, 732
flourish n 577, 882; v 367, 654, 734

flourish of trumpets n 404
floury adj 330
flout v 715
flow n 264, 348; v 109, 214, 264, 333, 347, 348
flower n 648; v 161, 734
flowerage n 367
flowering n 161
flowery adj 577
flow from v 154
flow in v 294
flowing n 348; adj 405, 578
flow into v 348
flow out v 295, 348
flow out of v 295
flow over v 348
fluctuate v 149, 314, 605
fluctuating adj 149
fluctuation n 149, 314, 605
flue n 351
fluency n 333
fluent adj 333, 348, 578, 584
fluffy adj 256
fluid n 337; adj 333, 337
fluidity n 333
fluke n 156, 621
flukey adj 156
flunkey n 935
flunkeyism n 933
flurry n 682, 684
flush n 382, 420; v 382, 434
flushed adj 434, 824, 838
flush out v 480a
fluster v 824
flute v 259
fluted adj 259
flutter n 315; v 315, 422
flux n 109, 144, 264, 348
flux and reflux n 314
fly v 109, 111, 267, 287, 328, 671
fly back v 277
fly from v 623
flying n 274, 267; adj 111, 267, 959
fly over v 267
fly to pieces v 328
foam n 353; v 173, 315, 353, 825
foaming n 353
foamy adj 353
focal adj 222
focus n 74
focus v 74
focus on v 222
fodder n 362
foe n 708, 710, 726, 891
fog n 353, 424
fogginess n 422, 475
foggy adj 422, 426, 353
foil n 14
foiled adj 732
fold n 258
fold n 232, 997; v 258
folded adj 258
foliage n 367
foliation n 367
folk n 372
folk music n 415
follow v 19, 63, 281, 518, 622, 743
follow after v 117
follower n 117, 541, 746
follow in a line v 69
following n 63, 117, 281; adj 63, 117, 281
follow in the steps of v 281
follow in the wake of v 281
follow the rules v 82
folly n 499
fond adj 897
fondle v 379
fondling n 379
fondness n 897

font n 153
food n 298, 637
food for thought n 454
food for worms n 362
fool n 501
fool n 493, 547, 844, 857; v 545
foolhardiness n 863
foolhardy adj 684, 863
foolish adj 477, 497, 499
foolishness n 497, 499
foot n 211
footing n 8, 71, 183, 215
fop n 854
foppery n 855
for adv 155
for a long time adv 110
for a time adv 111
forbear v 678, 953
forbearance n 623, 678, 740, 826
forbears n 122
forbid v 761
force n 157, 159, 170, 171, 173, 574, 739, 744; v 157, 744
forced adj 10, 579
forceful adj 157, 159, 171, 574
forcefulness n 600
force of will n 600
forcible adj 171, 574, 744
forcibly adv 744
ford v 302
fore adj 234
forebode v 909
foreboding n 512, 909; adj 909
forecast n 510, 511, 673; v 507, 511, 626
forefather n 130
forefront n 234
foregoing adj 62, 116, 122
foregone adj 611
foregone conclusion n 611
foreground n 234
foreign adj 10, 57, 220
foreign body n 57
foreign parts n 196
foreign substance n 57
fore-knowledge n 510
foreman n 694
foremost adj 33, 66, 234, 642
forenoon n 125
foreordain v 152
forerun v 62, 116, 280
forerunner n 64, 116, 534
foresee v 121, 507, 510, 511, 871
foreseen adj 507, 871
foreshadow v 909
foreshadowing adj 909
foresight n 510
forestall v 132
forestry n 371
foretell v 511
forethought n 510, 864
foretoken n 511; v 511
forever adv 16, 112
forewarn v 510, 668
foreword n 64
forfeit n 974; v 776
forfeiture n 776
for form's sake adv 82
forge n 298, 691
forge ahead v 282
forgery n 19, 21, 546
forget v 506
forgetful adj 506
forgetfulness n 506
forgive v 918
forgiveness n 918
forgiving adj 918
forgo v 624, 757, 782
forgotten adj 122, 506
fork n 244; v 91, 244, 291
forked adj 244

for keeps adv 106
forking n 91, 291
fork out v 784
forlorn adj 859
form n 240
form n 7, 21, 54, 80, 329, 448, 569, 697, 998; v 54, 56, 60, 144, 161, 240, 557, 852
formal adj 80, 82, 240, 242, 383, 579
formal features n 567
formality n 240, 579
formal speech n 586
form an opinion v 480
formation n 161, 240
formative adj 127, 153, 161
formative years n 127
form a whole v 50
formed adj 820
former adj 62, 116, 122
formerly adv 122
former times n 122
formidable adj 704
form into a sphere v 249
formless adj 241
formlessness n 241
form part of v 56
forms n 567
formula n 80, 240, 626, 697
formulaic adj 80, 626
formulate v 963
forsake v 624, 732, 782
for sale adj 763, 794, 796
forswear v 624, 782
forsworn adj 782
forte n 698
forth adv 282
forthcoming adj 152
for the moment adv 111
for the most part adv 613
for the sake of conformity adv 82
for the time being adv 106
forthright adj 246, 946
forthwith adv 132
fortification n 717
fortify v 159, 717
fortitude n 826, 861
fortress n 666
fortuitous adj 134, 156, 621
fortunate adj 134, 734
fortune n 152, 156, 621, 734, 803
fortune-teller n 513
forum n 966
forward adj 234; adv 282
fossil fuel n 388
foster v 658
foul adj 401, 649, 653
foulness n 401
foul play n 619
foul smell n 401
found v 153, 215
foundation n 153, 211, 215, 673
founded on adj 211
founder n 164; v 732
foundling n 893
found wanting adj 651
fount n 153
fountain n 153
four n 95; adj 95, 96
four-flusher n 548
fourfold adj 95, 96
fourfold division n 97
fourth n 96
fourthly adv 96
fourth part n 97
four times adv 96
fowls of the air n 366
foxy adj 702
fracas n 59
fraction n 100a
fraction n 32, 51, 84
fractional adj 51, 84
fractional part n 100a
fractious adj 713, 742
fracture n 44, 70

light of day n 420
light on v 156
light up v 824
like v 394, 827, 897, 990; adj 17, 216
like a shot adv 113
like a ton of bricks adj 319
likelihood n 470, 472
likeliness n 472
likely adj 176, 177, 472
likeness n 17, 21, 216, 556
likening n 464
like two peas in a pod n 17
likewise adv 37
liking n 602, 897
lilac 437
lily-liver n 862
lily-livered adj 435, 862
limb n 51
limber adj 324
limbo n 982
limit n 233
limit n 67, 71; v 195, 229, 233, 469, 761
limitation n 229, 469, 751
limited adj 103, 203, 233
limitless adj 104, 180
limitlessness n 105
limn n 556, 594
limp v 160, 275; adj 53, 158, 160, 324, 326
limpid adj 425
limpidity n 425
limpness n 326
line n 69, 278; v 224
lineage n 11, 69, 122, 166
lineal adj 166, 200
linear adj 69, 200, 246
lined adj 224, 440
line of march n 278
liner n 273
lines n 230, 448
linger v 133, 275
lingering adj 110
lingo n 560
lingual adj 560
linguist n 560
linguistic adj 560
liniment n 356
lining n 224
link n 45
link n 9, 43; v 9, 43, 45, 219
linkage n 43
link up v 43, 219
linseed oil n 356
lip n 231
lip-service n 933
liquefaction n 335
liquefaction n 333, 384
liquefy v 333, 335, 384
liquefying n 335
liquid n 337; adj 333, 337
liquidate v 807
liquidation n 807
liquid containers n 191
liquidity n 333
list n 86
list n 217, 596; v 551, 596
listen v 418
listener n 418
listening n 418
listing n 86
listless adj 683, 866
listlessness n 866
lists n 728
literal adj 561, 562
literally adv 19
literary adj 560
literature n 560, 590
litigant n 726, 969
litigation n 969
litigious adj 969
litter n 167; v 61
little adj 32, 193
little by little adv 26, 275
littleness n 193
littleness n 32, 201
little one n 129

live n 374; v 1, 141, 186, 188, 359; adj 359
live from hand to mouth v 804
livelihood n 803
liveliness n 515, 682, 829, 836
lively adj 309, 359, 375, 515, 574, 682, 829, 836
live off v 298
live on v 298
livery n 225
livestock n 366
live through v 151
livid adj 431, 435
lividness n 431
living being n 364
living beings n 357
living thing n 366
load n 190, 319, 828; v 52, 190, 319, 641
loaf v 683
loafer n 683
loan n 787; v 787
loath adj 603, 867
loathe v 867, 898
loathing n 867, 898
loathsome adj 395, 830, 867, 898
local adj 183
locale n 182, 183
locality n 182, 183
locate v 183, 184
located adj 183, 184
locate oneself v 184
location n 184
location n 183
loch n 343
lock n 350; v 43
lock-up n 752
locomotion n 264
locomotive n 271
locution n 582
lodge v 184, 186
lodger n 188
lodging n 189
loft v 235
loftiness n 206, 574, 875
lofty adj 206, 574
log n 114, 388, 551
logic n 23, 476
logical adj 23, 476, 502
logician n 476
loiter v 133, 275, 683
loitering n 133
loll v 683
lone adj 87
long adj 200; adv 110
long ago adv 110, 122
long dozen n 98
longevity n 110, 128
long expected adj 507
long for v 858, 865
longhand n 590
longing n 858, 865
longitude n 200
longitudinal adj 200
longitudinally adv 200
long lost adj 776
long shot n 137
longstanding adj 110
long-winded adj 573
long-windedness n 573
look n 441, 448; v 441, 448, 457
look after oneself v 943
look ahead v 510
look askance v 443
look beyond v 510
look danger in the face v 861
looker-on n 444
look for v 461, 507
look forward v 121
look forward to v 507, 510
looking back adj 122
looking glass n 445
look into the future v 510
look like v 17
look on v 186, 444
lookout n 448; v bane
look out for v 507
look sharp v 682
look upon v 451

loom v 152, 446
looming adj 152
loon n 501
loop n 245, 247, 629
loophole n 671
loose v 44, 750; adj 44, 47, 279, 573, 575, 738, 748, 773
loosen v 47
looseness n 47, 573, 738, 748
loosening n 47, 738
loot n 793
lop v 371
loquacious adj 584
loquaciousness n 584
loquacity n 584
lord n 745, 875, 976
lore n 490, 537
lorgnette n 445
lose v 776
lose an opportunity v 135
lose color v 429
lose ground v 283
lose heart v 837
lose it v 503
lose no time v 682
lose one's senses v 503
lose one's temper v 825
lose patience v 825
lose sight of v 506
loss n 776
loss n 40a, 449, 619, 638, 659, 732
loss of life n 360
lost adj 2, 449, 458, 732, 776
lost in thought adj 451
lost in wonder adj 870
lot n 25, 152, 621, 786
lottery n 156
loud adj 404
loudly adv 404
loudness n 404
loud noise n 404
lough n 343
lounge n 683
lounger n 683
lout n 501
lovable adj 897
love n 897
love n 865, 897, 899, 977; v 827, 928, 990
loveliness n 829, 845
lovely adj 242, 377, 597, 829, 845, 977
lover n 897
lovesick adj 991
love token n 902
loving adj 897
low v 412; adj 32, 207, 405, 438, 649, 874, 876, 879, 930
low-born adj 876
lower v 207, 308, 879; adj 34
lowering n 308
lowland n 344
lowlands n 207
lowliness n 879
lowly adj 207, 879
low-lying adj 207
lowness n 207
low price n 815
low quality n 34
low relief n 250
low repute n 874
loyal adj 743
loyalty n 743
lubricate v 255, 332, 355
lubrication n 332
lubrication n 255, 355
lubricity n 255, 355
lucent adj 420
lucid adj 425, 502, 518, 570, 849
lucidity n 420, 425, 502, 518, 570, 578
Lucifer n 978
luck n 152, 156, 621, 731
lucky adj 134, 621, 734
ludicrous adj 853
lug v 285
lugubrious adj 837
lukewarm adj 382, 823, 866

lull n 142, 265, 403, 683, 685; v 174, 265
lull to sleep v 265
lumber v 275
luminary n 423
luminary n 500
luminosity n 420
luminous adj 420, 518
lump n 50, 51, 72, 192, 321
lumpish adj 192, 319
lump together v 72
lunacy n 503
lunar adj 245, 318
lunatic n 504; adj 503
lunch v 298
lunge n 276
lurch n 306; v 306
lure v 288
lurid adj 421, 422
lurk v 526
lurking adj 526
lurking place n 530
luscious adj 394, 396, 829
lush n 959; v 959; adj 337, 365, 396
lust n 865
luster n 420
lust for v 865
lustful adj 865
lustihood n 159
lustrous adj 420
luxuriate v 377
luxuriate in v 827
luxurious adj 377, 829
luxuriousness n 377
luxury n 377, 827
lying n 544; adj 544
lying down n 213
lymph n 337

M

ma n 166
Machiavellian adj 702
machinery n 633
macrocosm n 318
mad adj 173, 503, 824, 825
madam n 374
madame n 374
mad as a hatter adj 503
madden v 173
madman n 504
madness n 503, 825
maelstrom n 312, 348, 667
magenta adj 437
magic n 992; adj 992
magical adj 992
magician n 994
magisterial adj 737
magistracy n 965
magistrate n 967
magnetic adj 288
magnetism n 288
magnetize v 288
magnificence n 845
magnificent adj 192, 845
magnify v 35, 194, 482, 549, 990
magnifying glass n 445
magniloquence n 577
magniloquent adj 549, 577
magnitude n 25, 31, 192
mahogany adj 433
maiden n 129, 904; adj 66
maim v 158, 659
main n 341, 350
mainly adv 31
mainspring n 153, 615
mainstay n 666
maintain v 141, 143, 170, 215, 535, 670, 717, 720, 781, 937
maintain course v 143
maintenance n 141, 143, 170, 670, 781, 803
majestic adj 882
majesty n 875
major adj 33
majority n 33, 100, 131
make n 240; v 54, 56, 144, 161, 744, 852
make a choice v 609

make a circuit v 629
make a clean sweep of v 652
make a complete circle v 311
make a compromise v 628
make acquainted with v 527
make a fool of oneself v 853
make a fresh start v 66
make a generalization v 78
make allowance for v 469
make amends v 30, 952
make a mess of v 732
make a motion v 763
make an addition to v 37
make an end of v 67
make an exception v 469
make a noise v 402
make a pig of oneself v 957
make a place for v 184
make a point of v 604
make a pretext of v 617
make a resolution v 604
make a sign v 550
make a U-turn v 311
make believe v 546
make faces v 243
make for v 278
make free with v 789
make friends with v 888
make fun of v 856
make good v 660, 790
make grave v 835
make haste v 132, 682, 684
make headlines v 532
make headway v 282
make known v 525, 527, 529, 531
make light of v 483, 643
make little of v 483
make loose v 47
make manifest v 525
make merry v 840
make music v 415, 416
make news v 532
make nothing of v 871
make obeisance v 308
make one sick v 395
make one's way v 734
make out v 441
make over v 783
make payment v 807
make peace v 721, 723
make preparations v 673
make productive v 168
make progress v 282, 682
make provision v 637
make provision for v 673
make public v 531
make pungent v 392
maker n 164
make ready v 673
make sail v 267
make serious v 835
makeshift n 147, 617
make solid v 150
make strides v 282
make sure v 150, 474
make terms v 769
make the best of v 826
make the mind a blank v 452
make time v 132
make-up n 54
make up for v 30
make use of v 677
make verses v 597
make war v 722
making verses n 597
maladroit adj 699
maladroitness n 699
malady n 655
malaise n 378, 828

make a circuit v 629
malapropism n 565
malarkey n 477
malcontent adj 832
male n 373; adj 373
male animal n 373, 374
malediction n 908
malevolence n 907
malevolence n 649, 889
malevolent adj 649, 739, 907, 919, 945
malice n 907
malicious adj 898, 907, 919, 945
maliciousness n 907
malign v 934; adj 649
malignant adj 919, 945
malignity n 649
mall n 799
malleability n 149, 324
malleable adj 82, 149, 324
maltreat v 649, 739, 830, 923
mamma n 166
mammal n 366
mammoth n 192; adj 31
man n 373
man n 372
man about town n 854
man after one's own heart n 899
manage v 58, 692, 693
manageable adj 705
management n 692, 693, 698
manager n 694
managerial adj 692
managing adj 693
mandate n 630, 741
maneuver v 702
manfully adv 604
mangle v 659
mangy adj 655
man-hater n 911
manhood n 131, 373
mania n 503
maniac n 504
maniacal adj 503
manifest adj 446, 525
manifestation n 525
manifestation n 446, 448
manifested adj 525
manifestly adv 525
manifold adj 15, 81, 102
manipulate v 379, 677, 702
manipulation n 379
mankind n 372
mankind n 372
manliness n 604
manly adj 131, 373
manner n 569, 613, 627
mannered adj 579, 855
mannerism n 79, 83, 579
mannerisms n 855
manner of speaking n 521
manners n 692, 852
man of learning n 500
mantle n 424
manual n 527
manufacture n 161; v 161
manuscript n 590
many adj 100, 102
many-colored adj 440
many-sided adj 81
map n 183, 527, 626
mar v 659, 848
marble n 249
marbled adj 440
march n 266
marches n 233
marching band n 417
march of time n 109
mare n 374
margin n 231
marine adj 341
marine blue adj 438
mariner n 269
mariner n 269

marital separation n 905
maritime adj 267, 341
mark n 26, 71, 550, 569, 590, 620; v 450, 550, 642
marked adj 79
market n 799
market v 795
marketable adj 794, 796
marketplace n 799
market price n 812
mark the time v 114
mark time v 114, 265
maroon adj 434
marquee n 223
marriage n 903
marriage n 43
marriageable adj 131
married adj 903
married man n 903
married woman n 903
marrow n 5, 221
marry v 43, 48, 903
marsh n 345
marshal v 60
marshy adj 339, 345
mart n 799
martial adj 722
martyr n 955
marvel n 870, 872; v 870
marvelous adj 31, 870
marvelously adv 31
masculine adj 373
masculinity n 373
mash v 324, 352, 354
mask n 223, 424, 530; v 442, 528
masquerade n 530
mass n 25, 31, 50, 72, 102, 192, 321
massacre n 361; v 361
massage n 379
massaging n 379
massive adj 192, 319, 321
massy adj 192
master n 745
master n 129, 540, 694, 700, 779; v 518, 539, 731, 749
masterful adj 731, 737
masterly adj 698
master mind n 500, 700, 872
master of adj 777
masterpiece n 648, 650
master stroke n 650
mastery n 698, 731, 741
mastic n 356a
masticate v 298
mastication n 298
mat n 219; v 219
match n 17, 27; v 17, 23, 27
matchless adj 33
mate n 17, 27, 711, 890, 903; v 89
material n 316; adj 3, 316
material existence n 3
materialism n 316
materialist n 316
materialistic adj 3, 316
materiality n 316
materiality n 3
materialization n 525
materialize v 316, 525
materials n 635
materials n 316
maternal adj 166
maternity n 11, 166
mates n 269
matins n 125
matriarch n 130
matriarchal adj 166
matricide n 361
matriculation n 539
matrimony n 903
matrix n 22
matted adj 219
matter n 3, 316, 516, 591, 625; v 642
matter little v 643
matter-of-fact n 1; adj 598, 703, 843

701 ROGET'S THESAURUS muggy

matter of factness n 703
matters n 151
matting n 219
mature v 144, 650, 658, 673; adj 673
mature years n 128
maturity n 124, 128, 131, 673
maul v 649
mausoleum n 363
mauve adj 437
maxim n 496
maxim n 537, 697
maximum n 210
maybe adv 470
maze n 248
mazy adj 248
meadow n 344
meager adj 32, 53, 103, 203, 575, 640, 643
meagerness n 203
mealy adj 330
mealy-mouthed adj 886
mean n 29
mean n 68, 628; v 451, 516, 620; adj 29, 32, 34, 68, 207, 435, 643, 649, 819, 851, 876, 886, 914a, 930, 943
meander v 248, 264, 266, 279, 573
meandering n 248
mélange n 41
meaning n 516
meaning n 522, 620; adj 516
meaningful adj 516
meaningless adj 497, 517
meaninglessness n 517
meanness n 32, 34, 499, 886, 914a, 943
mean nothing v 517
means n 632
means n 627, 780, 803
means of access n 627
meantime adv 106
meanwhile adv 106
measurable adj 466
measure n 25, 26, 174, 413, 466, 786; v 106, 466
measured adj 174
measure for measure n 30
measureless adj 104
measurement n 466
measurement n 25
measure time v 114
meaty adj 354
mechanical adj 601, 633
medal n 733
meddlesome adj 455
meddlesomeness n 455
medial adj 68
median n 29; adj 68
mediate v 620, 631, 724
mediation n 724
mediation n 631, 766
mediator n 724
mediatory adj 724
medication n 662
medicinal adj 662
medicine n 662
medicine man n 994
mediocre adj 28, 29, 34, 598, 651, 736
mediocrity n 736
mediocrity n 28, 34
meditate v 451, 870
meditation n 451
meditative adj 451
medium n 29, 631, 994
medley n 41
meek adj 879
meekness n 879
meet v 23, 72, 199, 290, 772; adj 646
meeting n 43, 72, 199, 290, 680, 696
meetinghouse n 1000
meet up with v 151
meet with v 151
melancholy n 837; adj 830, 837
melee n 59
meliorate v 174, 723
mellifluence n 413
mellifluous adj 413, 578
mellow v 144, 673; adj 128, 413, 428, 673, 721
melodic adj 413
melodious adj 377, 413, 580
melodiousness n 413
melody n 413
melody n 415
melt v 111, 144, 335, 384, 449
melt away v 4, 449
melting n 335, 384
member n 51, 56
membrane n 204
membranous adj 204
memento n 505
memento mori n 363
memorable adj 505
memorandum n 551
memorial n 505
memorialist n 553
memorialization n 883
memorize v 505, 539
memory n 505
memory n 122
menace n 667, 909; v 668, 909
menacing adj 909
menagerie n 72
mend v 658
mendacious adj 544
mendicant n 767
menial n 746
mental adj 450
mental balance n 502
mental cultivation n 539
mental excitation n 824
mental image n 515
mental suffering n 619
mention v 527
mentor n 540, 695
mephitic adj 401
mercantile adj 794
mercantilism n 796
mercenary adj 819
merchandise n 798
merchandise v 763, 796, 798
merchant n 797
merchant n 796
merchant ship n 273
merciful adj 740
merciless adj 914a
mercurial adj 149, 264
mercury n 389
mercy n 740, 914
mere n 343; adj 643
merely adv 32
merge v 48, 300
merge in v 56
merge into v 144
meridian n 125, 181
merit n 648, 944, 973
merit attention v 642
meritorious adj 931
mermaid n 979
merriment n 836
merry adj 829
merrymaking n 838
mesh n 219
mesmerist n 994
mesmerize v 992
mess n 59, 61, 162, 732
messenger n 534
messenger n 271, 527, 758
mess up v 59
messy adj 59
metallurgy n 358
metamorphose v 140
metamorphosis n 140
metaphor n 521
metaphorical adj 464
mete v 786
meteors n 318
mete out v 784
meter n 413
method n 627
method n 58, 60, 569, 626, 632, 692
methodical adj 58, 60, 692
methodically adv 58
methodological adj 626
methodology n 58
meticulous adj 459, 868
metrical adj 597
metrics n 597
mettle n 861
mew v 412
miasmic adj 401
microcosm n 193
microscope n 445
microscopic adj 32, 193
mid adj 68
mid-course n 628
midcourse n 68
midday n 125
middle n 68
middle n 29, 208, 222; adj 29, 68, 222; adv 222
middle class adj 29
middle course n 628
middle ground n 68, 174
middlemost adj 222
middle of the road n 174
middle way n 628
middling adj 32, 651
midmost adj 68
midnight n 126
midnight n 421
mid-point n 29, 68
midriff n 68
midst n 68, 208, 222; adv 222
midsummer 125
midway adj 628; adv 68
mien n 448, 692
might n 31, 157, 159, 173
mightily adv 31
mighty adj 31, 157, 159, 192, 192
migrate v 266
migration n 266
migratory adj 266
mild adj 174, 382, 391, 721, 740
mildew n 653, 663
mildewed adj 659
mildness n 174, 740
militant adj 722
militarist n 726
military adj 722
military band n 417
milkiness n 427, 430
milk-white adj 430
milky adj 352, 427, 430
mill n 330, 691
millennium n 108, 121
millions n 372
mimic v 19, 554
mimicry n 19
mince v 275
mince steps v 275
mind n 450, 498, 842; v 602
mindblower n 137
mindful adj 451, 457
mindfulness n 457
mindful (of) adj 505
mindless adj 499
mine n 636; v 252, 260, 659
mineral adj 358
mineral kingdom n 358
mineralogy n 358
mineral world n 358
mingle v 41
mingling n 41
miniature adj 32, 193
minimize v 483
minion n 899
minister n 631, 69 694, 996; v 631, 693
ministerial adj 995
ministering spirit n 977
ministration n 693
ministry n 995, 996
minor n 129; adj 32, 34
minority n 34, 127
minstrel n 416, 597
mint n 22, 691
minus adj 776; adv 38, 187
minuscule adj 32
minute adj 32, 193
minutiae n 32
minx n 962
miracle n 872
miraculous adj 870
mirage 443
mire n 653
mirror n 445, 650; v 19; 443
mirth n 836
mirthful adj 836
misanthrope n 165
misanthropic adj 911
misanthropy n 911
misapplication n 679
misapply v 523, 679
misapprehend v 495, 523
misapprehension n 481, 495, 523
misappropriate v 679
misappropriation n 679
misbelief n 984
misbelieving adj 984
miscalculate v 482, 495
miscalculation n 481, 482, 508
miscall v 565
miscarriage n 732
miscarry v 732
miscellaneous adj 15, 41, 465a
miscellaneousness n 78
miscellany n 41, 72, 78
mischief n 619
mischievous adj 649
miscomputation n 481
misconceive v 481, 495, 523
misconception n 481, 495, 523
misconjecture v 481
misconstruction n 523
misconstrue v 481, 523
miscreant n 949
misdate n 115; v 115
misdated adj 115
misdeed n 923
misdirect v 538
misdirection n 538
misemploy v 679
misemployment n 679
miser n 819
miserable adj 828, 837, 930
miserably adv 31, 32
miserly adj 819
misery n 828
misfiguration n 555
misfortune n 619, 735, 830
misgiving n 485, 860
misguidance n 538
misguide v 538
mishap n 619, 732, 830
misinform v 538
misinformation n 538
misinstruct v 538
misinterpret v 481, 495, 523
misinterpretation n 523
misinterpretation n 481, 495
misjudge v 481, 495
misjudging adj 481
misjudgment n 481
misjudgment n 495
mislay v 61, 776
mislead v 477, 538, 545
misleading adj 520, 544, 545
mismatch n 24; v 15
mismatched adj 24
misname v 565
misnamed adj 565
misnaming n 565
misnomer n 565
misogynist 911
misplace v 61, 185
misplaced adj 115, 185
misplacement n 115, 185
misproportion n 241, 243
misread v 523
misreading n 523
misrepresent v 277, 477, 523, 538, 544, 555
misrepresentation n 555
misrepresentation n 523, 544
miss n 129, 374; v 776
misshape v 243
misshapen adj 241, 243
missing adj 187, 449
missing link n 53
mission n 755
missionary n 540
missive n 592
misspend v 638, 818
misstate v 523
miss the mark v 732
mist n 353, 422, 424, 427; v 353
mistake n 495, 523, 732; v 495, 523
mistaken adj 495, 544, 923
misteach v 538
misteaching n 538
mister n 373
misterm v 565
mistime v 135
mistimed adj 135
mistiness n 422, 426
mistreat v 830
mistress n 779
mistrust n 485; v 485
misty adj 353, 422, 426, 447
misunderstand v 481, 495, 523
misunderstanding n 495, 523, 713
misusage n 649, 679
misuse n 679
misuse n 638; v 638, 679
mite n 32
mitigate v 174, 469, 834
mitigating adj 469
mitigation n 174, 469, 834
mix n 41, 48; v 41, 48, 61
mixed adj 41
mixture n 41
mixture n 48
moan n 839; v 411
moaning n 411, 839
moat n 259, 350
mob n 72, 102
mobile adj 149, 264
mobility n 149, 264
mobilization n 264
mobilize v 264
mock v 19, 856, 929; adj 17, 19
mockery n 856
mocking n 19; adj 856
mode n 7, 569, 613, 852
model n 21, 22, 80, 240, 650, 948; v 144, 240, 557; adj 650
modeled after adj 19
modeled on adj 19
modeling n 557
model oneself on v 19
mode of expression n 569
moderate v 174, 275, 723; adj 174, 275, 628, 736, 815, 881, 953
moderately adv 174
moderation n 174
moderation n 275, 736, 740, 826, 881, 953
moderator n 724, 967
modern adj 123
modernism n 123
modernity n 123
modernize v 123
modest adj 483, 879, 881, 960
modestly adv 881
modesty n 881
modesty n 483, 879, 960
modicum n 32
modification n 20a, 140, 469
modified adj 15, 20a
modify v 15, 20a, 140, 469
modish adj 852, 855
modulate v 140
modulation n 140, 413
module n 22, 273
moist adj 337, 339
moisten v 337, 339
moisture n 339
mold n 7, 21, 22, 240, 329, 557, 653; v 144, 240, 557, 653, 852
moldable adj 324
molded adj 820
molder v 659
moldering adj 659
moldy adj 653, 659
molecule n 32
molest v 649, 716
molestation n 649
mollification n 324
mollify v 174, 324, 723
mollusk n 366
molten adj 384
mom n 166
moment n 113, 642
momentary adj 111, 113
momentous adj 642
momentousness n 642
monetary adj 800
money n 800
money n 803
moneybag n 802
money matters n 811
mongrel n 41; adj 41
moniker n 564
monochrome n 429
monocle n 445
monody n 839
monogram n 561
monolog n 589
monomania n 606
monomaniacal adj 606
monosyllable n 561
monotheism n 983
monotonous adj 16, 27, 104, 841
monotony n 16, 27, 104, 841
monsoon n 349
monster n 192, 949, 980
monstrosity n 192, 243, 872
monstrous adj 31, 192, 846
monstrously adv 31
monument n 363, 551
moo v 412
mood n 7, 176, 602, 820
moodiness n 901a
moods n 5
moody adj 901a
moon n 420, 423
moonbeam n 420
moor n 344; v 43
moored adj 184, 186
mooring n 184
mope v 837
moper n 683
moral adj 922, 944
moral imperative n 926
morality n 922, 944
moralize v 537
morals n 922
moral sensibility n 822
morass n 345
moratorium n 133
morbid adj 655
more adv 33, 37
more or less adj 25
moreover adv 37
more than one adj 100
morgue n 363
morn n 125
morning n 125
morning n 125
morningtide n 125
moron n 493, 501
morose adj 901a
moroseness n 901a
morphology n 368
morrow n 121
morsel n 32, 390
mortal n 372; adj 111, 361, 372
mortal coil n 362
mortality n 111, 360, 372
mortal remains n 362
mortar and pestle n 330
mortgage n 771, 787; v 771
mortification n 828, 830
mortify v 828, 830, 879
mortuary n 363; adj 363
mosaic adj 81, 440
moss n 345
most adv 31
most likely adv 472
mote n 32, 451
moth-eaten adj 653, 659
mother n 166, 192
mother earth n 342
motherhood n 166
motherland n 189
motion n 264
motion n 550
motionless adj 172, 265, 683
motivate v 615, 744
motivation n 615
motive n 615
motive power n 264
mot juste n 496
motley adj 16a, 41, 81
motorboat n 273
motorcar n 272
motorcycle n 272
motoring n 266
motorscooter n 272
mottled adj 440
motto n 496, 566
mound n 192
mount v 206, 305
mountain n 192, 250
mourn for v 833
mournful adj 830, 839, 901a
mourn over v 839
mouth n 231, 343
mouthful n 25, 32
mouthpiece n 582
movable adj 264, 270
movableness n 264
move n 264, 270; v 175, 264, 266, 270, 302, 615, 763, 824
move away from v 287
move back v 287
moved adj 821, 914
movement n 264, 680, 682
move off v 293
move out v 293
move quickly v 274
mover n 164
move slowly v 275
move to the center v 29
move towards v 286
moving n 266, 680; adj 264
mow v 371
Mr n 373
Ms n 374, 590
much adj 641; adv 31
much ado about nothing n 549
much the same adj 17, 27
muck n 653
muckraking n 529
mud n 345, 653
muddle n 59; v 61
muddle-headed adj 499
muddy adj 339, 345, 352, 519
muffle v 403, 408a, 590
muffled adj 405, 408a
muffled drums n 408a
muffler n 408a
muggy adj 339

703 ROGET'S THESAURUS paramount

off adj 187
off and on adv 138
off base adj 10, 481, 495
offend v 289, 830
offend against the law v 964
offended adj 900
offense n 716, 830
offensive adj 395, 401, 653, 716, 830, 846, 867, 898
offensive smell n 401
offer n 763
offer v 763
offer congratulations v 896
offer counsel v 695
offer for sale v 763
offering n 763, 784
offer pleasure v 829
offer prayers v 990
offhand adv 132, 612
office n 170, 625, 799
official n 694; adj 625, 737, 983a
offing n 196
off one's guard adj 508
off-set n 30; v 30, 179
offshoot n 39, 51, 65, 154
offside n 238
offspring n 154, 167
off the mark adj 495
of late adv 122, 123
of little account adj 643
of long standing adj 124
of necessity adv 601, 630
of no account adj 643
of old adv 122
of one accord adj 488
of one mind adj 178
of one's own accord adv 600
of other times adj 124
of small importance adj 643
oft adv 136
often adv 104, 136
oftentimes adv 136
of the same mind adj 488
oft-repeated adj 136
of various kinds adj 16a
of vital importance adj 642
of yore adv 122
ogle v 441
ogre n 980
oil n 356
oil n 355; v 255, 332, 355
oil burner n 386
oiliness n 355
oiling n 332
oil lamp n 423
oily adj 255, 355
oink v 412
ointment n 355, 356, 662
old adj 124, 128, 130
old age n 124, 128
older adj 128
old-fashioned adj 124
old hand n 700
old lady n 166, 903
old maid n 904
old man n 130, 166, 903
oldness n 124
old soldier n 700
Old Testament n 986
old woman n 130
oleaginous adj 355
olive adj 435
olive oil n 356
omen n 512
omen n 668
ominous adj 665, 668, 909
omission n 53, 55, 460, 732, 773, 893
omit v 55, 460, 773
omitted adj 893
omnipotence n 157, 976
omnipotent adj 104, 157
omnipresence n 186, 976
omnipresent adj 186
on adv 125, 282
on a bed of roses adv 377
on account of adv 155
on a large scale adv 31
on a level with adj 27
on a line with adv 278
on all sides adv 227
on a moment's notice adv 113
on an equal footing with adj 27
on a par with adj 27
on bended knee adv 879
once and for all adv 67
once more adv 90, 104
on compulsion adv 744
on condition adv 770
on dry land adv 342
one n 372; adj 13, 52, 87, 729
one and the same adj 27
one by one adv 44
on edge adv 507
one in a million n 648
on end adv 212
oneness n 87
one of a kind adj 20
onerous adj 649, 706, 830
oneself n 13
one's own n 11
one's own flesh and blood n 11
one step at a time a 275
on every side adv 2
one way or another adv 627
on fire adj 382
on foot adj 170
ongoing adj 53
on land adv 342
onlooker n 444
only adv 32
only just adv 32
only so far adv 233
on no account adv 32
on no occasion adv 107
on one's back adv 213
on one's honor adj 768
on one side adv 217, 236
on one's own time adv 133
on one's toes adj 507
on purpose adv 620
onset n 66, 716
on sight adv 441
onslaught n 716
on target adj 494
on tenterhooks adj 507
on that occasion adv 119
on the average adv 29
on the ball adj 498
on the brink of adv 121
on the dot adv 132
on the eve of adv 121
on the face of it adv 448
on the face of the earth adv 180, 318
on the go adv 264
on the horizon adj 152, 507
on the horns of a dilemma n 476
on the instant adv 132
on the march adv 264
on the move adv 264
on the offensive adv 716
on the other hand adv 30
on the point of adv 121
on the road adj 264, 266
on the road to adv 278
on the safe side adj 664
on the sly adv 528
on the spot adv 132, 134
on the spur of the moment adv 113, 132, 134
on the wagon adj 958
on the wane adj 36
on the watch adj 457; adv 507
on the whole adv 50
on time adj 132; adv 132
ontology n 1
on trial adv 675
onus n 926
onward adv 282
ooze v 295, 348
oozing n 295
oozy adj 352
opacity n 426
opacity n 353
opalescence n 427
opalescent adj 427
opaline adj 430, 440
opaque adj 422, 426
opaqueness n 426
ope v 260
open v 66, 194, 198, 260, 525; adj 177, 260, 338, 525, 543, 665, 703
open air n 338
open-eyed adj 507
open field n 134
opening n 260
opening n 66, 198, 260
open into v 348
openly adv 525
openness n 525, 703, 748
open space(s) n 180
open to the view v 446
opera n 599
opera glasses n 445
operahouse n 599
operate v 161, 170, 680
operatic adj 415, 416
operation n 170, 680
operative adj 170, 680
operator n 690
ophthalmia n 443
opine 484
opinion n 451, 453, 480, 484, 537, 695, 821
opponent n 710
opponent n 726, 891
opportune adj 134, 646
opportunely adv 134
opportuneness n 134
opportunism n 646
opportunist n 935
opportunity n 134
oppose v 14, 179, 237, 536, 708, 719
opposed adj 14
opposer n 726
opposing n 708; adj 14, 237, 489
opposite n 237; adj 14, 218, 237
oppositeness n 14
opposite poles n 237
opposite side n 237
opposition n 237, 708
opposition n 14, 24, 218, 489, 710, 719, 720, 726
oppostion n 179
oppress v 649, 739, 923
oppression n 649, 739
oppressive adj 382, 421, 649, 739, 830
oppressor n 739, 913
opprobrious adj 874
oppugnance n 719
opt for the mean v 774
optic adj 441
optical instruments n 445
optics n 420, 441
optimism n 482
optimistic adj 858
option n 600, 609
optional adj 600, 609
opulence n 803
opus n 590, 593
oracle n 513
oracle n 500
oracular adj 511
oral adj 580, 582
oral communication n 588
orange n 439
orange adj 439
orangish adj 439
orangy adj 439
oration n 582
orator n 582
oratory n 582
orb n 181, 247
orbit n 247
orchestra n 416, 417
orchestral adj 415
orchestral music n 415
orchid adj 437
ordain v 741, 755, 963, 995
ordained adj 996
ordeal n 722, 828
order n 58
order n 63, 75, 242, 630, 693, 697, 721, 741, 963; v 58, 630, 652, 673, 693, 741
ordered adj 60, 242
ordering n 60
orderliness n 58, 652
orderly adj 58, 60
order of succession n 63
ordinance n 741
ordinariness n 736
ordinary adj 82, 598, 613, 643, 651, 736
ordinary condition n 80
oread n 979
organic adj 357
organic chemistry n 357
organic remains n 357
organisms n 357
organization n 60, 161, 329, 626
organizational adj 329, 626
organize v 60, 161, 626
organized adj 58
organizer n 626
orgasm n 173, 377
orgasmic adj 173, 377
orifice n 260
origin n 66, 153
original n 22, 590, 857; adj 20, 79, 83, 153, 515, 614
originality n 18, 20, 83, 123, 168, 515
originate v 66, 153, 515
originate from v 154
originate in v 154
origination n 153
originator n 164
ornament n 577, 847
ornament v 577, 847
ornamental adj 847
ornamentation n 847
ornamented adj 577, 847
ornate adj 577, 847
ornateness n 577
ornithology n 368
orthodox adj 82, 983a
orthodoxy n 983a
orthography n 561
oscillate v 149, 314
oscillating adj 149, 314
oscillation n 314
oscillation n 138, 149, 605
ossification n 323
ossify v 323
ostensible adj 448, 617
ostensibly adv 448, 617
ostentation n 882
ostentatious adj 855, 882
ostracism n 893
ostracized adj 893
other adj 15
other side of the coin n 235
other time n 119
otherworldly adj 317
oust v 297, 789
out adj 187; adv 220
out and out adv 52
outbound adj 295
outbreak n 66, 173, 295, 713
outburst n 173, 295, 825
outcast n 893
outcome n 63, 65, 154
outcry n 404, 411
outdated adj 124
outdo v 33, 303
outer adj 220
outer edges n 233
outer space n 180
outfit n 225; v 225, 727
outflank v 236
outgoing adj 295
outgrow v 194
outgrowth n 65, 154
outing n 266
out in the open adv 338
outlandish adj 10, 83, 853
outlast v 110
outlawed adj 964
outlay n 809
outlet n 260
outline n 230
outline n 240, 448, 596; v 230
outlined adj 446
outlive v 110, 141
outlook n 441, 448
outlying adj 196, 220
outmoded adj 124
outnumber v 102
out of all proportion adv 31
out of commission adj 659
out of danger adj 664
out of date adj 124
out of debt adj 807
out of doors adv 338
out-of-fashion adj 124
out of focus adj 447
out of its element adj 185
out of joint adj 24
out of mind adj 506
out of one's depth adv 208
out of order adj 59, 651, 674, 923
out of place adj 59, 115, 185
out of practice adj 699
out of proportion adj 241; adv 641
out of shape adj 243
out of sight adj 447
out of sorts adj 655
out of step adj 24
out-of-style adj 124
out of the frying pan and into the fire adv 835
out-of-the-way adj 10, 196
out of tune adj 24, 414, 651
out of view adj 447
out of work adj 681
outpost n 196
outpouring n 295
outrage n 173, 619, 649
outrageous adj 31, 853
outrageousness n 853
outrank v 33
outride v 303
outrigger n 215
outright adv 52
outrival v 33
outrun v 303
outset n 66, 293
outside n 220; adj 220
outsides n 448
outside time n 107
outskirts n 196, 227
outspoken adj 703
outspread adj 202
outstretched adj 200, 202
outstrip v 33, 303
outward adj 220, 295
outwards adv 220
outweigh v 33, 175
outwit v 545
oval n 247; adj 247
oven n 386
over adj 40, 67; adv 33, 122, 220, 237
overabound v 641
over again adv 90, 104
over against adv 237
over and above adj 641; adv 33, 37, 641
over and done with adv 67
over and over adv 104
overbearing adj 878, 885
over-blown adj 882
overburden v 649
overcast v 421; adj 421, 422, 901a
overcharge n 814; v 577, 814
overcome v 731
over-confident adj 878
overdo v 641
overdose n 641; v 641
overdraw v 555
overdue adj 115, 133
overeat v 957
over-eating n 957
overestimate v 481, 482, 549
overestimated adj 482
overestimation n 482
overflow n 641; v 348, 641
overgrown adj 192, 194
overhang v 206
overhanging adj 206
overhear v 418
overlay v 223, 356a
overload v 641
overlook v 458, 460, 693
overlying adj 206
overly sensitive adj 901
overmatch v 28
overmuch adj 641; adv 641
over one's head adv 208, 641
overpower v 744
overpowering adj 824
overpraise v 482, 933
overprize v 482
overrate v 482
overrated adj 482
overreach v 303
over-refined adj 477
override v 175
overripe adj 128
overrun v 194, 303, 641
overseer n 694
overshoot v 303
oversight n 495
oversimplification n 78
overspread v 223
overstate v 549
overstatement n 549
overstep v 303
overtask v 679
overtax v 679
over the way adv 237
overthrow n 146, 162, 308; v 162, 308
overture n 763
overturn n 146, 218, 308; v 162, 218, 308, 479
overvaluation n 482
overweening adj 641, 880
overwhelm v 641
overwhelming adj 824
overwork v 679
overwrought adj 549, 824
overzealous adj 825
ovoid adj 249
owing to adj 154, 155
own v 488, 777
owner n 779
ownership n 777, 780
own in common v 778
own up v 529

P

P n 126
pace n 264; v 106
pacific adj 174, 721, 723
pacification n 723
pacification n 174
pacify v 174, 723
pack n 72
pack it up v 293
pact n 23, 769
pad n 189; v 194, 224
padding n 224, 263
paddle v 267
paddock n 232
paean n 838
pagan n 984; adj 991
pagan deity n 991
pageant n 448
pageantry n 882
pain n 378, 828
pain n 619, 663, 686, 974, 982; v 649, 830
painful adj 378, 649, 830, 982
painfully adv 31, 830
painfulness n 830
painfulness n 649
pain in the neck n 663
pains n 459, 974
painstaking adj 459
paint n 428; v 428, 556
painter n 559
painting n 556
pair n 17, 89; v 89
pair off v 89
pal n 890
palatability n 394
palatable adj 377, 390, 394
palaver n 588
pale n 232, 233; v 422, 429; adj 422, 429, 430, 435
paleness n 422, 429
paleontology n 368
paling n 232
pall n 363; v 376, 395
palliative adj 174, 662, 834
pallid adj 429, 430
pallor n 429
palm n 733
palmer n 268
palpability n 379
palpable adj 3, 316, 379, 446, 525
palpitate v 315
palpitation n 315
palsied adj 160
paltriness n 32, 643, 736
paltry adj 32, 34, 643, 736
panacea n 662
pandemonium n 59, 982
pander to v 933
pang n 378, 828
panhandler n 767
panic n 860
panic-stricken adj 860
pant v 349, 382
pap n 250
papa n 166
paper v 223
par n 27
parabola n 245
parade v 882
paradigm n 22
paradisaic adj 981
paradise n 981
paradisical adj 981
paradox n 497
paradoxical adj 497
paragon n 650, 948
paralipsis n 476
parallel n 17; v 9, 17, 19, 216; adj 17, 216, 242
parallelism n 216
parallelism n 13, 17, 23, 242
paralysis n 158, 376
paralytic adj 158, 376
paralyze v 158, 376
paralyzed adj 158
paramount adj 33, 642, 737

pleasing *adj* 413, 850
pleasing combination *n* 413
pleasing sounds *n* 415
pleasurable *adj* 377, 829
pleasurableness *n* 829
pleasure *n* 377
pleasure *n* 827
pleasure *n* 377, 600, 840
pleasure-seeker *n* 954a
pleat *n* 258; *v* 258
plebeian *adj* 851, 876
pledge *n* 177, 768, 771; *v* 768, 788
pledged *adj* 768
pledging *n* 788
plenty *n* 641
plethora *n* 641
pliability *n* 324
pliable *adj* 324
pliancy *n* 324, 705, 725
pliant *adj* 324, 705
plight *n* 7, 8
plod *v* 275, 682
plot *n* 626; *v* 626
plough *v* 371
plow *v* 259, 371
plowed *adj* 959
pluck *n* 150, 604, 604a, 861; *v* 789
plucked instruments *n* 417
pluck out *v* 301
plug *n* 261, 263; *v* 261
plugging *n* 261
plug up one's ears *v* 419
plumb *adj* 212
plum-colored *adj* 437
plump *adj* 192
plumpness *n* 192
plunder *n* 793
plunge *n* 310
plunge *n* 300; *v* 208, 300, 310, 337, 863
plunge into *v* 676
plural *adj* 100
plurality *n* 100
plus *adv* 37
ply *n* 258; *v* 677
pock *n* 250
pocket *v* 789
poesy *n* 597
poet *n* 597
poetaster *n* 597
poetic *adj* 521, 597
poetical *adj* 597
poetic device *n* 521
poeticize *v* 597
poetics *n* 521, 597
poetry *n* 597
poetry *n* 590
poignancy *n* 392
poignant *adj* 516
point *n* 8, 26, 32, 71, 180a, 182, 253, 620; *v* 253, 278
point-blank *adj* 703; *adv* 278, 576
pointed *adj* 201, 253, 516, 518
pointedly *adv* 31, 620
pointedness *n* 253
pointer *n* 550
point of departure *n* 293
point of view *n* 441
point out *v* 525
points of the compass *n* 278
point to *v* 155, 472, 516, 938
point toward *v* 278
poison *v* 659, 663
poisonous *adj* 649, 657, 663
polar *adj* 210, 383
polarity *n* 89, 179, 218, 237
pole *n* 222
polemic *n* 726
polemicist *n* 476
poles apart *adv* 237
policy *n* 626, 692
polish *n* 255, 578, 850; *v* 255, 331
polished *adj* 255, 578, 850, 852
polite *adj* 383, 457, 852, 879, 894, 928
politeness *n* 457, 894
polite society *n* 852
politic *adj* 498, 702
poll *n* 85; *v* 85
pollute *v* 653, 659
poltroon *n* 862
poltroonery *n* 862
polyglot *adj* 560
polyp *n* 250
polyphony *n* 413
polysyllable *n* 561
pommel *n* 249
pomp *n* 882
pompous *adj* 482, 577, 882
pompousness *n* 882
pond *n* 343
ponder *v* 451, 870
pondering *n* 451
ponderous *adj* 319, 579
pool *n* 343, 709; *v* 709
poor *adj* 34, 477, 575, 640, 643, 736, 804, 828, 879
poorer *adj* 34
poorly *adj* 655
poorly timed *adj* 135
poorness *n* 34, 640
poor substitute *adj* 651
pop *n* 166, 406
pop music *n* 415
pop off *v* 360
populace *n* 72, 876
popular music *n* 415
populate *v* 102
population *n* 188, 372
populous *adj* 72, 102
pop up *v* 446
porch *n* 231, 260
pore over *v* 539
porous *adj* 260
port *n* 239
portable *adj* 270
portal *n* 231, 260
portend *v* 511, 668, 909
portent *n* 511, 512, 668, 909
portentous *adj* 511, 668
porter *n* 271; 532
portion *n* 51, 100a, 786
portion out *v* 786
portly *adj* 192
portrait *n* 21
portraiture *n* 554
portray *v* 554, 594
portrayal *n* 594
pose *n* 183; *v* 475, 704, 855
position *n* 8, 71, 183, 625
positive *adj* 1, 31, 84, 246, 474, 484, 535
possess *v* 777
possessed *adj* 503
possessed of *adj* 777
possessing *adj* 777
possession *n* 777
possession *n* 780
possessions *n* 780
possessive *adj* 777
possess oneself of *v* 789
possessor *n* 779
possess the means *v* 632
possibility *n* 470
possibility *n* 2, 156
possible *adj* 2, 177, 470, 515
possibly *adv* 470
post *n* 183; *v* 184, 274, 811
post bail *v* 771
post card *n* 592
postdate *v* 115
posterior *n* 235; *adj* 117, 235
posteriority *n* 117
posteriority *n* 63
posterity *n* 167
posterity *n* 121
posthaste *adv* 274
posthumous *adj* 117
postman *n* 271
post meridian *n* 126
post mortem examination *n* 363
postpone *v* 133
postponement *n* 133
postscript *n* 65
postulant *n* 767
postulate *n* 476, 514; *v* 476
posture *n* 8, 183, 240
potable *adj* 299
pot-bellied *adj* 194
potency *n* 157, 159
potent *adj* 157, 159, 171, 175
potential *n* 2; *adj* 2, 470, 526
potentiality *n* 470, 526
potion *n* 298
potpourri *n* 41
potted *adj* 959
potting *n* 557
pound *n* 232; *v* 330
pour *v* 333, 348
pour forth *v* 584
pour in *v* 294
pour out *v* 295, 348
pour out of *v* 295
pout *v* 900, 901a
poverty *n* 804
poverty-stricken *adj* 804
powder *n* 330
powdery *adj* 330
power *n* 157
power *n* 159, 171, 175, 404, 574, 737, 741, 965; *v* 388
powerful *adj* 157, 159, 171, 175, 404, 574
powerfully *adv* 31, 157
powerless *adj* 158, 160
powerlessness *n* 158, 175a
practicability *n* 705
practicable *adj* 644, 705
practical *adj* 170, 470, 644, 692
practicality *n* 470
practically *adv* 5
practice *n* 613, 692; *v* 677
practiced *adj* 698
practice law *v* 968
practice sorcery *v* 992
practitioner *n* 690
pragmatism *n* 646
prairie *n* 344
praise *v* 883, 931, 990
praised *adj* 931
praiseworthy *adj* 931
prance *v* 315
prank *n* 608
prate *v* 584, 588
prattle *n* 582, 584, 588
pray *v* 990
prayer *n* 411, 765, 990
preacher *n* 540, 996
preamble *n* 64
precarious *adj* 111, 475, 665
precariousness *n* 665
precaution *n* 510, 664, 673
precautionary *adj* 673
precede *v* 62, 116, 280
precedence *n* 62, 280
precedence *n* 116
precedent *n* 22, 64, 80, 613, 969; *adj* 62
preceding *adj* 62, 116
precept *n* 697
precept *n* 630
precincts *n* 227
precious *adj* 31, 814
precipice *n* 212, 306, 667
precipitancy *n* 684
precipitate *v* 684; *adj* 132, 684, 863
precipitately *adv* 132
precipitation *n* 132, 684
precipitous *adj* 217, 306
precise *adj* 494, 518
precision *n* 80, 494, 518
preclude *v* 761
precluded *adj* 893
preclusion *n* 893
precocious *adj* 132
precocity *n* 132
precursor *n* 64
precursor *n* 62, 116, 280, 534
precursory *adj* 64, 116
predatory *adj* 789, 791
predecessor *n* 64, 116
predeliberation *n* 611
predestination *n* 611
predestine *v* 152, 611
predetermination *n* 611
predetermine *v* 611
predicament *n* 8, 183, 704
predicate *v* 514
predict *v* 507, 510, 511
prediction *n* 511
prediction *n* 668
predilection *n* 177, 609
predisposed *adj* 820
predisposition *n* 176, 820
predominance *n* 33, 175
predominant *adj* 175, 737
predominate *v* 33, 175
pre-eminence *n* 33, 206
pre-eminent *adj* 33, 206
pre-eminently *adv* 31, 33
pre-engage *v* 132
pre-existence *n* 116
pre-existent *adj* 116
preface *n* 64; *v* 62
prefatory *adj* 62, 64
prefer *v* 609
preference *n* 62, 609
preferential *adj* 609
prefix *n* 64; *v* 62
prehistoric *adj* 124
précis *n* 596; *v* 596
prelacy *n* 995
preliminary *adj* 62, 64, 673
prelude *n* 64, 66
premature *adj* 132, 135, 674
prematurely *adv* 132
prematurity *n* 132
premeditate *v* 611
premeditation *n* 611
premises *n* 476
premium *n* 973
premonition *n* 668
premonitory *adj* 511, 668
preordain *v* 152
preparation *n* 673
preparation *n* 60, 64, 537
preparative *adj* 673
preparatory *adj* 62, 673
prepare *v* 60, 537, 673
prepared *adj* 507, 673, 698
prepare for *v* 507, 673
prepare for battle *v* 727
prepatory *adj* 673
preponderance *n* 33, 175
preponderant *adj* 737
preposterous *adj* 497, 549, 853
preposterously *adv* 31
prepubescence *n* 131
prerequisite *n* 630
prerogative *n* 924
presage *n* 511, 668; *v* 116, 511, 909
presbyopia *n* 443
prescience *n* 510
prescient *adj* 510
prescribe *v* 693, 695, 741
prescribed *adj* 474, 924
prescript *n* 697
prescription *n* 613, 697, 924
prescriptive *adj* 124, 613, 983a
presence *n* 186
presence *n* 1, 448
present *n* 784; *v* 448, 763, 784; *adj* 118, 186
presentation *n* 784
present events *n* 151
presentiment *n* 477
present itself *v* 446
presently *adv* 132
present the music *v* 416
present time *n* 118
present to the view *v* 448
preservation *n* 670
preservation *n* 141, 664, 717, 781
preservative *adj* 670
preserve *v* 141, 143, 664, 670, 717, 781
preserved *adj* 670
preserver *n* 664
president *n* 694
press *n* 72; *v* 255, 319
press forward *v* 684
press in *v* 300
pressing *adj* 642
press into service *v* 677
press on *v* 622, 684
press onward *v* 282
pressure *n* 175, 319, 642, 735
presto *adv* 113
presumable *adj* 472
presumably *adv* 472
presume *v* 514, 858, 878, 885; 484
presumption *n* 507, 514, 878, 925
presumptive *adj* 514
presumptuous *adj* 863, 878, 885
presuppose *v* 514
pretend *v* 544, 546, 617, 855
pretender *n* 548, 925
pretense *n* 617, 855, 882
pretention *n* 577, 855, 882
pretentious *adj* 482, 855, 882, 884
pretentiousness *n* 882
pretext *n* 617
pretty *adj* 845; *adv* 31
pretty well *adv* 31, 32
prevail *v* 33, 78, 175
prevailing *adj* 78, 983a
prevail upon *v* 615
prevalence *n* 33, 78, 175, 613
prevalent *adj* 1, 78, 175, 613
prevaricate *v* 520, 544
prevarication *n* 520, 544
prevent *v* 706, 708, 761
preventing *n* 706
prevention *n* 761
preventive *adj* 761
previous *adj* 116
previously *adv* 116
prevision *n* 510
prey *n* 620
price *n* 812
price *v* 812
priceless *adj* 33, 648, 814
prick *n* 253; *v* 260, 378, 380
pricking *n* 380
prickle *n* 253
prickly *adj* 253, 256
prick up one's ears *v* 418
pride *n* 878
pride *n* 880
priest *n* 904, 996
priesthood *n* 995, 996
priestly *adj* 995
prig *n* 854
priggish *adj* 868
prim *adj* 868
primal *adj* 66, 153
primary *adj* 153, 642
primary color *n* 428
prime *n* 125, 648; *v* 537, 673; *adj* 84, 642, 648
prime mover *n* 153, 976
prime of day *n* 125
primer *n* 542, 567
primeval *adj* 124
primitive *adj* 124
primordial *adj* 124
princely *adj* 816
prince of darkness *n* 978
principal *n* 694; *adj* 642
principally *adv* 33
principle *n* 5, 80, 153, 211, 537, 615
print *n* 591; *v* 531, 558, 590, 591
printed *adj* 591
printer *n* 591
printing *n* 591
prior *adj* 62, 116
priority *n* 62, 116, 280
prior to *adv* 116
prism *n* 428, 445
prismatic *adj* 428, 440
prison *n* 752
prison *n* 975
prisoner *n* 754
pristine *adj* 122
privacy *n* 893
private *adj* 79, 221, 528, 533, 893
privately *adv* 881
privation *n* 776, 804
privilege *n* 748, 924, 927a
privileged *adj* 924, 927a
privy *adj* 528
privy to *adj* 490
prize *n* 618, 733, 793, 973; *v* 991
probability *n* 472
probability *n* 156
probable *adj* 472, 858
probably *adv* 472
probationary *adj* 675
probative *adj* 463, 478
probe *n* 262
probity *n* 939
probity *n* 543, 944
problem *n* 533, 704
problematical *adj* 59, 475
procedural *adj* 80, 626, 692
procedure *n* 80, 463, 626, 627, 680, 692, 998
proceed *v* 109, 282, 302
proceed from *v* 154
proceeding *n* 151, 282; *adj* 53
proceeds *n* 775
proceed with *v* 692
process *n* 627, 692
procession *n* 69, 266
proclaim *v* 531, 883
proclamation *n* 531, 985
proclivity *n* 176, 698, 820
procrastinate *v* 133
procrastination *n* 133, 683
procreate *v* 161, 168
procreation *n* 161, 168
procreative *adj* 168
procreator *n* 166
procure *v* 775, 795
procurement *n* 775
prod *v* 276
prodigal *n* 818; *adj* 638, 818
prodigality *n* 818
prodigality *n* 638
prodigal son *n* 950
prodigious *adj* 31
prodigy *n* 872
prodigy *n* 700
produce *n* 775, 798; *v* 153, 161, 168
produce a good effect *v* 648
produce nothing *v* 169
producer *n* 164
producer *n* 153
product *n* 84, 154, 161, 798
production *n* 161
production *n* 153
productive *adj* 153, 161, 168, 644
productiveness *n* 168
productiveness *n* 644
productivity *n* 168
proem *n* 64
profanation *n* 679
profane *v* 679, 988
profaneness *n* 988
profanity *n* 988
profession *n* 535, 625, 768
professional *n* 700; *adj* 625
professor *n* 540
proffer *v* 763
proficiency *n* 698, 731
proficient *adj* 698, 731
profile *n* 230, 236, 448; *v* 230
profit *n* 618, 775; *v* 618, 648, 775
profitability *n* 646
profitable *adj* 644, 646, 648, 775, 810
profit by *v* 677
profitless *adj* 645
profligacy *n* 818
profligate *n* 962; *adj* 818, 945
profound *adj* 31, 208, 498
profundity *n* 208, 875
profuse *adj* 102, 573, 641, 818
profuseness *n* 573, 641, 818
profusion *n* 102, 641, 818
progenitor *n* 166
progeny *n* 167
prognosticate *v* 507, 511, 909
prognostication *n* 511, 909
progress *n* 144, 264, 282, 731; *v* 282, 658, 731
progression *n* 282
progression *n* 58, 69
progressive *adj* 69, 282, 658
prohibit *v* 761, 893
prohibited *adj* 893, 964
prohibition *n* 761
prohibition *n* 55, 893
prohibitive *adj* 761
project *n* 620, 626; *v* 250, 284, 620, 626
projection *n* 250, 284
proletarian *adj* 876
proletariat *n* 876
prolific *adj* 161, 168
prolix *adj* 573
prolog *n* 64
prolong *v* 35, 110, 133, 143, 200
prolongation *n* 110, 133, 143
prolonged *adj* 110
promenade *n* 266
prominence *n* 206, 250, 307, 642
prominent *adj* 206, 250, 642
prominently *adv* 31, 33
promiscuous *adj* 41
promise *n* 768
promise *n* 771; *v* 676, 768, 769, 771
promised *adj* 768
promises *n* 770
promising *adj* 858
promissory *adj* 768, 769
promissory note *n* 771
promontory *n* 250
promote *v* 176, 658, 707
prompt *v* 505, 615; *adj* 132, 682

scene n 448
scenery n 448
scent n 398, 550; v 398, 400
scented adj 400
scentless adj 399
scepter n 747
schedule n 86
scheme n 626; v 626
schemer n 626
schism n 713, 984
schismatic adj 984
scholar n 492
scholar n 541
scholarly adj 539
scholarship n 490, 539
scholastic adj 537, 539, 542
school n 542
school v 537
schoolbook n 542
schoolboy n 129
schooled adj 498
schoolgirl n 129
schooling n 537
schoolmaster n 540
schooner n 273
science n 490
science of existence n 1
science of light n 420
science of living beings n 357
science of matter n 316
science of sound n 402
science of the mineral kingdom n 358
scintilla n 32, 420
scintillate v 420
scintillating adj 842
scintillation n 420
scion n 167
scoff n 929, 988
scoff at v 856
scoffer n 988
scoffing n 856, 988
scold v 972
scoop n 262; v 252
scoop out v 252
scope n 26, 180, 748
scorch v 384
scorched adj 384
score n 98, 259, 805, 806, 811; v 259
scores n 102
scorn v 930; v 715, 929, 930
scornful adj 929, 930
scotch v 659
scot free v 748
scoundrel n 941, 949
scour v 331, 652
scourge n 975
scourge v 663, 972
scour the country v 266
scout n 664, 668
scowl v 900, 901a
scraggly adj 256
scramble n 59, 684; v 684
scrap n 32
scrape n 704, 732; v 38, 195, 255, 330, 331
scratch n 257, 259; v 257, 331, 380, 590, 649
scratching n 380; adj 410
scratchy adj 380
scrawl v 590
scrawny adj 203
scream n 411, 669; v 404, 410, 411, 839
screech v 411, 412
screeching v 412; adj 414
screen n 223, 424, 530, 717; v 424, 442, 528, 664, 717
screening n 528
screw n 243; v 43, 243
screw up the eyes v 443
scribble v 590
scribe n 553, 590
scrimp v 819
script n 590, 593
scriptural adj 983a

Scriptures n 985, 986
scrivener n 590
Scrooge n 819
scrub v 331, 652
scruple n 485
scrupulous adj 246, 459, 543, 603, 772, 868, 939
scrupulousness n 603
scrutinize v 457
scrutinizing adj 461
scrutiny n 457, 461
scull v 267
sculpt v 557
sculptor n 559
sculpture n 557
scum of the earth n 949
scurrilous adj 934
scurry n 684
scuttle v 162
scuttlebutt n 532
sea n 341
sea dog n 269
seafaring adj 267
seafaring man n 269
sea-girt adj 346
seagoing adj 267, 341
sea-green adj 435
seal n 22; v 261, 550
sealing n 261
sealing wax n 356a
seam n 43; v 259
sea-maid n 979
seaman n 269
sear v 384
search n 461, 539, 622; v 461
season n 106, 106; v 41, 392, 393, 613, 673
seasonable adj 134
seasoned adj 392
seasoning n 41, 393
seat v 184
seat of activity n 691
secession n 624
seclude v 55, 87
secluded adj 893
seclude oneself v 893
seclusion n 893
seclusion n 55
second n 113, 759; v 707; adj 90
secondary adj 32, 34, 651
secondary color n 428
second hand adj 19
second-rate adj 34, 651
second-story man n 792
second thoughts n 65
second to none n 648
secrecy n 528, 893
secret n 533
secret adj 221, 526, 528, 533
secretary n 553, 590
secrete v 299, 528
secretion n 299, 528
secretive adj 528, 533
secretiveness n 528
secretly adv 528
secret place n 530
sect n 75
section n 51, 75
sectional adj 51
secular adj 997
secularize v 997
secure v 43, 132, 664, 717, 768, 775, 781; adj 43, 150, 484, 664
secure an objective v 731
securities n 802
security n 771
security n 664, 717, 721
sedate adj 826
seducer n 962
seduction n 829
seductive adj 288, 615, 829
see v 441, 457, 480a; 484
see double v 443
seedy adj 160, 659, 804
see fit v 600
seeing that adv 8

seek v 461, 622
seeker n 268, 767
seek refuge v 666
seem v 448
seeming n 448; adj 448
seemingly adv 448
seemliness n 845
seemly adj 845
see one's future v 510
seer n 130, 504, 513
seesaw adv 314
seethe v 382
see the light v 359
seething adj 824
see-through adj 425
segment n 51, 100a
segregate v 44, 55
segregated adj 47
segregation n 44, 55
seize v 789
seize the day v 134
seize the opportunity v 134, 682
seize the time v 134
seizure n 789
seldom adv 137
select v 609; adj 648
selection n 609
self n 13; adj 13
self-abnegation n 955
self-admiration n 880
self-assurance n 878
self-assured adj 878
self-centered adj 943
self-command n 604
self-complacency n 880
self-complacent adj 880
self-contradictory adj 497
self-control n 600, 604, 953
self-controlled adj 953
self-deception n 486
self-delusion n 486
self-denial n 604, 955
self-denying adj 955
self-depreciation n 483
self-esteem n 878, 880
self-glorification n 880
self-importance n 878
self-indulgence n 954
self-indulgent adj 943, 954
self-interest n 943
self-interested adj 943
selfish adj 32, 819, 943
selfishness n 943
selfishness n 32, 819
self-love n 880, 943
self-luminous adj 423
self-mortifying adj 955
self-motivation n 955
self-possessed adj 502
self-possession n 604, 826
self-reliance n 604
self-respect n 878
self-restrained adj 953
self-restraint n 604, 826, 953
selfsame adj 13
self-satisfied adj 878
self-seeking n 943; adj 943
self-styled adj 565
sell v 796, 798
seller n 796, 797
sell for v 812
selling n 796
semblance n 17, 19, 21, 216, 882
semi- adj 91
semi-circular adj 245
semifluid adj 352
semiliquid adj 352
semiliquidity n 352
seminary n 542
semiology n 550
semiopaque adj 427
semipellucid adj 427
semitransparency n 427
semitransparent adj 427
send v 270
send a letter v 592
send off v 284
senile adj 124, 128, 158

senility n 124, 128, 158, 160, 659
seniority n 128
sensation n 375, 379, 390
sensational adj 824
sensations of touch n 380
sense n 450, 498, 502, 516, 842
senseless adj 376, 497, 499, 517
senselessness n 517
sense of duty n 926
sensibility n 375, 822
sensibility n 821
sensible adj 316, 375, 498, 502
sensical adj 450
sensitive adj 375, 597, 821, 822
sensitiveness n 375, 822
sensitivity n 821, 901
sensitize v 375
sensual adj 377, 829
sensual delight n 377
sensualist n 954a
sensualist n 962
sensuality n 377, 827
sensuous adj 375, 377
sensuousness n 377
sentence n 972
sententious adj 577
sentient adj 375
sentiment n 453, 821
sentimental adj 822
sentimentalism n 822
sentimentality n 821, 822
sentinel n 444, 664, 668
sentry n 668
separate v 44, 55, 291, 905; adj 44
separated adj 905
separately adv 44
separateness n 44
separation n 44, 55, 198, 291, 489, 905
sepia adj 433
septet n 415
septic adj 657
sepulchral adj 363
sepulchre n 363
sepulture n 363
sequel n 65
sequel n 39, 63, 117, 281
sequence n 63, 281
sequence n 58, 117, 281
sequential adj 63, 281
sequester v 893, 974
sequestered adj 893
sequestration n 893, 974
seraph n 977
seraphic adj 977
serene adj 265, 721
serenity n 265, 826, 831
serfdom n 749
serial adj 69, 138
serially adv 138
series n 58, 63, 69
serious adj 642, 739
seriousness n 642, 739
sermon n 537, 582
sermonize v 537, 582
serous adj 333
serpent n 248, 548, 978
serpentine adj 248
serrated adj 244, 257
serum n 337
servant n 746
servant n 690, 707
serve v 618, 644, 707, 743, 746, 749, 969
serve with a writ v 969
service n 618, 644, 677, 707, 749, 990, 998
serviceable adj 631, 644, 648
servile adj 886, 933
servility n 886
servitude n 749
session n 696
set n 7, 240, 278, 712; v 150, 184, 306, 321;

adj 43, 240, 613
set about v 676
set against adj 898
set an example v 22
set apart v 44, 465
set a price v 812
set aside v 55, 185, 678
set at ease v 831
set at naught v 773
set a trap for v 530
set at rest v 462
set down v 551, 590
set fire to v 384
set foot on dry land v 342
set forth v 293, 594
set forward v 293
set free v 44, 672, 748, 750, 970; adj 970
set going v 276
set in motion v 66, 284, 677
set in one's ways adj 5
set loose v 750
setoff n 30
set on fire v 384
set out v 60, 66, 293
set phrase n 566
set right v 662
set sail v 293
set store by v 642
settle v 60, 150, 184, 265, 306, 769, 774, 807
settled adj 67, 184, 474
settle down v 184, 265
settled purpose n 620
settlement n 23, 184, 762, 807
settle up v 790
settle upon v 784
set too high a value on v 482
set to rights v 660
set to work v 677
set up v 153, 161, 307
set upon v 716
seven n 98
sever v 44, 291
several n 100; adj 100, 102
severally adv 44, 79
severance n 44, 291
severe adj 242, 576, 739, 830, 849, 955
severely adv 31, 739
severity n 739
severity n 173, 576, 849
sew v 43
sewer n 350
sex n 377
sextet n 415
sexual adj 377
sexual abstinence n 904
sexual failure n 158
sexuality n 377
shabby adj 34, 643, 659, 851
shade n 424
shade n 15, 26, 223, 362, 421, 424, 428, 530, 980; v 421, 422, 424
shading off adj 26
shadow n 4, 21, 281, 421, 424, 515, 980; v 281, 353, 421, 422
shadowiness n 422
shadowy adj 4, 421, 422, 424, 447
shady adj 421, 424, 426, 874
shaft n 208, 351
shaggy adj 256
shaggy dog story n 549
shake n 315; v 160, 314, 315, 383, 404, 407, 616, 659
shake one's sides v 838
shake the foundations of v 659
shake up v 315
shaking adj 315

shaky adj 160, 315, 665
shallow n 209; adj 209, 491, 499, 643
shallow excuse n 617
shallowness n 209
shallowness n 499
shallows n 667
sham n 544, 545, 855, 880; v 546; adj 544
shaman n 994
shamble v 275, 315
shame n 874, 930; v 874, 879
shameful adj 874, 930
shape n 448; v 240, 557, 852
shapeless adj 241
shapelessness n 241
shapeliness n 242
shapely adj 242
share n 786; v 709, 778, 786
shareholder n 778
share in v 56, 778
sharer n 778
sharp adj 171, 173, 217, 253, 375, 392, 397, 404, 410, 416; adj 490, 498, 682, 698, 702, 842, 868
sharp edged adj 253
sharpen v 171, 173, 253, 375, 824
sharpness n 253
sharpness n 392, 397, 410, 698
sharp outline n 446
shatter v 44, 158, 162, 328
shattered adj 160
shave v 195, 201, 204, 255
she n 374
shear v 195, 201
sheathe v 225
shed n 223; v 73
shed light on v 522
shed light upon v 420
sheen n 420
sheeny adj 420
sheepish adj 881
sheer adj 52, 425
sheerness n 425
sheet n 204, 223, 811
shelf n 215
shell n 363
shellac n 356a; v 356a
shellfish n 366
shelter n 666, 670, 717; v 528, 664, 670, 717
sheltering n 528
shelve v 133, 678
shepherd n 996
shield n 223, 717; v 670, 717
shift n 140, 147, 270; v 140, 144, 264, 270, 279
shifting n 144; adj 264
shiftless adj 674
shilly-shally v 133, 605
shimmer n 420; v 420
shine v 420
shiny adj 255, 420
ship n 273
ship v 271; v 190
shipment n 190
ship out v 293
shipping n 267
shipshape adj 58
shirk v 623, 742
shirker n 623
shiver v 315, 328, 383
shivering adj 383
shoal n 209
shoals n 667
shock n 276, 315, 508, 713; v 824, 830
shockingly adv 31
shoot n 378; v 194, 274, 284, 361, 367, 378
shoot ahead of v 303
shooting n 361, 378
shoot up v 250, 367
shop v 795
shopkeeper n 797
shopper n 795
shopping center n 799

shore n 231, 342
shore up v 215
short adj 28, 53, 201, 572, 640, 739
shortcoming n 304
shortcoming n 28, 34, 53, 640, 651, 730
short distance n 197
shorten v 36, 38, 201, 596
shortened adj 201
shortening n 36, 38, 201
shorthand n 590
short-lived adj 111
shortly adv 132
short memory n 506
shortness n 201
short of adj 53; adv 32, 34, 38
short-tempered adj 901
shot n 284
shot in the dark n 621
shoulder n 236; v 215, 276
shoulder to shoulder adv 709
shout n 411, 838; v 404, 411, 836, 838
shout at the top of one's lungs v 411
shove v 276; v 276, 284
shove in v 300
shovel v 270
shove off v 267, 293
show n 448, 855, 882; v 448, 467, 478, 525, 529
shower n 348
shower down v 348
showery adj 348
showiness n 882
showing n 525
show itself v 446
shown adj 478
show no remorse v 951
show off v 882
show taste v 850
show up v 446
showy adj 428, 851, 882
shred n 32
shrewd adj 490, 498, 698, 702
shrewdness n 702
shriek n 411; v 411
shrill adj 203, 404, 410
shrillness n 410
shrink v 36, 195, 283, 287, 623
shrink from v 603
shrinking n 36, 195, 603
shrive v 952
shrivel v 195, 659
shroud n 363; v 664
shrub n 367
shrubbery n 367
shrunk adj 195
shrunken adj 195
shudder v 383
shuffle v 149, 275, 315
shuffle off v 623
shuffle off the mortal coil v 360
shun v 623, 671
shunt v 279
shut v 261; adj 261
shutout n 101; v 55
shutter n 424
shutting up n 261
shut up v 261, 403
shut up shop v 687
shy v 283, 623; adj 881
shyster n 548
sibilant adj 409
sibilation n 409
sibyl n 513
sick adj 655
sicken v 289, 395, 655, 830
sickening adj 395
sickly adj 160, 435, 655
sickness n 655
side n 236
side n 712
side by side adv 88, 236
side effects n 154

sidelong adj 236; adv 217, 236
sideways adv 217, 236
side with v 709, 714
sidle v 217, 236
sift v 42, 60
sifting n 42
sigh n 839
sight n 441, 448; v 441
sightless adj 442
sightlessness n 442
sightseer n 268, 444
sign n 467, 512, 550, 668; v 550
signal n 467, 550, 668; v 467, 550
signalize v 550
signally adv 31
signature n 569, 590
significance n 516, 642
significant adj 516, 550, 642
signification n 516
signify v 516, 550, 642
signify little v 643
sign of the times n 512
silence n 403
silence n 265, 528, 581, 585; v 403, 581
silent adj 265, 403, 581, 585, 901a
silent as the grave adj 403
silently adv 403
silken adj 255
silky adj 255
silliness n 497, 499, 853
silly adj 486, 497, 499, 853
silouette n 230
silver n 432; adj 430, 432
silveriness n 430
silverish adj 432
silvery adj 413, 430, 432
similar adj 17, 21, 216
similarity n 17
similarity n 9, 13, 27
simile n 17, 521
similitude n 17, 21
simmer v 315, 382, 384
simple adj 42, 486, 499, 576, 703, 849, 946, 960
simpleness n 42
simpleton n 493, 501
simplicity n 849
simplicity n 491, 499, 576, 703, 881, 946, 960
simplification n 78
simplify v 42, 78, 518, 849
simply adv 32
simulate v 19, 855
simulating adj 17
simulation n 19, 855
simultaneity n 120
simultaneous adj 120
simultaneously adv 120
simultaneousness n 120
sin n 923, 945, 961, 988; v 945
since adv 8, 117, 155
sincere adj 543, 703
sincerity n 543, 703
since the occasion presents itself adv 134
sinewy adj 159
sinful adj 923, 945, 961
sinfully adv 923
sinfulness n 947, 961, 988
sing v 416, 597, 838
singe v 384
singer n 416
singing n 412; adj 413
single adj 42, 87
singlehanded adj 87
singleness n 87
single out v 79
singly adv 87
sing out v 411
sing praises v 990
singular adj 79, 83, 87
singularity n 79, 87
singularly adv 31
sinister adj 663, 909
sinistral adj 239
sink v 162, 208, 306, 308, 360, 659, 688, 732, 735, 837
sink back v 661
sinking n 306
sink into oblivion v 506
sinless adj 946
sinner n 949, 988
sinning adj 945, 961
sinuosity n 248
sip n 298, 390
siphon n 350
sir n 373
sire n 166
siren n 669, 980
sisterhood n 11, 72, 995
Sisyphean adj 686
site n 183
sit in judgment v 965
situate v 183, 184
situated adj 183
situation n 183
situation n 7, 8, 151, 182, 184
situations n 527
six n 98
six of one and half a dozen of another n 628; adj 27
sizable adj 192
size n 192
size n 25, 31, 200
skeletal adj 203
skeleton n 40, 362
skeleton in the closet n 649, 830
skeptic n 485, 487, 984, 989
skeptical adj 485, 487, 984, 989
skepticism n 485, 487, 984, 989
sketch n 594, 626; v 230, 556
sketcher n 559
sketchy adj 53, 730
skill n 698
skill n 79, 702, 731
skilled adj 698
skillful adj 698, 702
skillfully adv 698
skillfulness n 698, 702
skin n 220, 223
skin-deep adj 209
skinflint n 819
skinniness n 203
skinny adj 203
skip n 198; v 309, 838
skipper n 269
skirt n 231; v 231, 236
skirting n 231; adj 236
skulk v 862
skull n 450
sky n 318, 338
skyscraping adj 206
slab n 204, 251
slack adj 47, 160, 172, 275, 603, 674, 683, 738
slacken v 47, 275, 687
slackness n 275, 738
slake v 174, 829
slam n 276; v 276
slander n 908, 934; v 908, 934
slanderer n 936
slanderous adj 934
slang n 579; adj 563
slangy adj 560
slant n 217; v 217
slantwise adv 217
slap n 276; v 276
slash v 44
slaughter n 361; v 361
slaughtering n 361
slavery n 749, 886
slavish adj 886
slavishness n 886
slayer n 361
sleek v 255; adj 255
sleep n 687
sleeping adj 172, 265
sleeping car n 272
slender adj 32, 203, 643
slenderize v 203
slenderness n 32, 203
slice n 204; v 44, 204
slick adj 355
slide v 109, 264, 306
slight v 460, 483, 927; adj 4, 32, 209, 322, 575, 643, 736
slightly adv 32
slightness n 4, 32, 203
slim v 203; adj 203
slime n 653
slimness n 203
slimy adj 352, 355, 653
sling v 284
slink away v 623
slip n 32, 306, 495, 568, 732; v 109, 306, 495, 623
slip back v 661
slipperiness n 665
slippery adj 255, 355, 607, 665
slippery ground n 667
slippery memory n 506
slip-shod adj 575
slit n 44, 198, 260, 259; v 44
sliver n 32
slobber over v 933
sloop n 273
slope n 217, 306; v 217
sloping adj 217, 306
sloppy adj 345, 575
slot n 260
sloth n 133, 172, 275, 683
slothful adj 681, 683
slothfulness n 681
slouch v 207, 217, 275, 683
slough n 345
slovenliness n 653
slovenly adj 59, 575, 653
slow v 275, 420; adj 133, 172, 275, 603, 683, 685, 843, 901a
slowly adv 133, 275
slowness n 275
slowness n 133, 603
sluggard n 683
sluggish adj 172, 275, 683, 901a
sluggishness n 275, 683, 901a
sluice n 350
slumber n 687
slumberer n 683
slump v 306
slur one's words v 583
slushy adj 352
slut n 962
sluttish adj 653
sly adj 702
slyness n 702
smack n 32, 276, 390; v 390
smack the lips v 390
small adj 32, 193
small change n 800
smallness n 32
smallness n 193
small number n 103
small quantity n 32, 103
small talk n 588
smart n 378, 828; v 378; adj 682, 698
smarts n 450, 498
smash v 162
smatch n 390; v 390
smear v 653
smell n 398, 400; v 398, 401
smell bad v 401
smell of v 398
smell rotten v 401
smell sweet v 400
smelly adj 398
smile n 838; v 838
smirch v 431, 653
smirk n 838; v 838
smite v 649
smitten adj 897
smoggy adj 426
smoke v 382, 392
smoking adj 382
smoky adj 426
smolder v 382, 526
smoldering adj 172
smooth v 16, 174, 255, 705, 723; adj 174, 213, 251, 255, 705
smoothly adv 705
smoothness n 255
smoothness n 251, 705
smooth-tongued adj 933
smother v 361, 581
smudge v 653
smug adj 878
smut n 653, 961; v 431
smutch v 431
smutty adj 653, 961
snag n 667
snaggy adj 253
snake n 248
snake in the grass n 548, 649, 667
snaky adj 248
snap n 406
snap n 277; v 44, 328, 406
snap back v 277
snappish adj 901
snap up v 789
snare n 530, 545, 667
snarl v 412, 900
snatch n 32; v 789
sneak n 941; v 275, 623, 862, 886
sneak off v 623
sneer n 856; v 929
sneer at v 856
sneeze v 409
sniff v 398
snip v 44
snippet n 32
sniveling adj 886
snobbish adj 878
snort v 412
snout n 250
snow-white adj 430
snowy adj 430
snuff v 398
snuff out v 421
snug adj 261, 664
soak v 337, 339, 959
soak up v 340
soap n 356
soar v 31, 206, 267, 303, 305
sob n 839; v 411, 839
sobbing n 411
sober v 174; adj 174, 246, 502, 826, 953, 958
sobriety n 958
sobriety n 502, 953
sobriquet n 565
so-called adj 565
sociability n 894
sociable adj 892
sociableness n 892
social adj 372, 892
social interaction n 892
social intercourse n 892
socialism n 778
socialist n 778; adj 778
socialistic adj 778
sociality n 892
society n 188, 372, 852
society of men n 372
sodden v 339; adj 337
soft adj 255, 324, 345, 403, 405, 413, 499
soft as butter adj 324
soft coal n 388
soften v 174, 324
softening n 324
softness n 324
softness n 160, 326
soggy adj 337, 339
soi-disant adj 565
soil n 181, 342; v 653
soiled adj 653
sojourn v 186
solace n 834
solar adj 318
solar energy n 388
solar system n 180, 318
solder v 43, 46
soldier n 726, 948
sole n 211; adj 87
solecism n 568
solecism n 579
solecize v 568
solemn adj 403, 642, 882
solemnity n 642
solemnization n 883
solemnize v 883
solicit v 765, 865
solicitation n 411, 765
solicitor n 767, 968
solicitous adj 411, 765, 860, 920
solicitude n 459, 828, 860
solid adj 16, 52, 150, 202, 321, 323
solidarity n 52
solid body n 321
solidification n 321, 385
solidify v 46, 48, 321
solidity n 150, 321
solidness n 321
soliloquize v 582, 589
soliloquy n 589
solipsism n 943
solipsistic adj 943
solitary adj 87, 893
solitude n 893
solo n 415; adj 87; v 416
soloist n 416
solubility n 333
soluble adj 333, 335, 462, 662
solubleness n 335
solution n 462, 522, 662
solve v 462, 662
solvency n 803
solvent adj 335, 807
somatic adj 316
somber adj 431, 901a
some adj 25, 100; adv 32
somebody n 372
someone n 372
somersault n 218
something like adj 17
some time ago adv 122
sometimes adv 136
somewhere adv 182
somewhere about adv 32
son n 167
sonata n 415
song n 413, 415
sonneteer n 597
sonority n 402
sonorous adj 402, 404, 577
sonorousness n 402, 408
soon adv 111, 121, 132
sooner or later adv 121
soothe v 723, 834
soothing adj 834
soothsayer n 513, 994
soothsaying n 511
sooty adj 431, 653
sop v 339
sophism n 477
sophist n 477, 548
sophistical adj 477
sophistry n 477
sophistry n 538
soporific adj 683
sorcerer n 994
sorcerer n 513
sorcery n 992
sordid adj 32, 207, 435
sordidness n 32
sore n 378, 830; adj 378, 830
sorely adv 31
soreness n 378
sore subject n 830
sorority n 11
sorrel adj 433
sorrow n 833
sorrowful adj 828, 839
sorrow over v 839
sorry adj 643, 828, 833, 950
sorry sight n 830
sort n 75; v 60
sortie n 716
sorting n 60
SOS n 669
so-so adj 32, 643, 651
sot n 959; v 959
so to speak adv 17
sotted adj 959
sough n 350
soul n 5, 359, 372, 820
soul-stirring adj 821, 824
sound n 402
sound n 343; v 208, 402; adj 50, 150, 246, 498, 650, 654, 664, 670, 983a
sound dead v 408a
sounding adj 402
soundings n 208
soundless adj 208, 403
soundness n 150, 502, 654, 983a
sound the alarm v 669
sound vibrations n 402
soupçon n 32
sour v 397; adj 392, 395, 397, 410, 901a
source n 66, 153
sourness n 397
sourness n 392, 395
souse v 310, 337
souvenir n 505
sovereign n 737; adj 737
sovereignty n 157
sow n 374; v 73, 371
sow the seeds of v 153
space n 180
space n 106, 198, 318
space heater n 386
spaceman n 269
spaceship n 273
space station n 273
spacious adj 180, 192
span n 106, 180, 196, 200; v 43, 45
spare v 678, 784; adj 40, 636, 641, 685
spare no effort v 686
spare no expense v 816
spare time n 685
sparing adj 953
spark n 382, 420, 423
sparkle v 420
sparkling adj 574, 836, 842
sparse adj 32, 73, 103, 640
sparseness n 32, 103
spasm n 146, 173, 315, 378
spasmodic adj 70, 139, 173
speak v 580, 582
speak directly v 576
speaker n 524, 582
speaking of adv 134
speak in low tones v 405
speak one's mind v 703
speak plainly v 576
speak prettily v 521
speak softly v 405
speak the truth v 543
speak to v 586
spear n 262; v 260, 361
special n 79; adj 20, 79, 474
special committee n 755
specialist n 700
speciality n 79
specialize v 79
specially adv 79
specialty n 79
species n 75
specific n 662; adj 79
specify v 79, 564
specimen n 82
specious adj 477, 545
speciousness n 477
speck n 32, 848
speckle v 440
speckled adj 440
spectacle n 448, 872
spectacles n 445
spectator n 444
specter n 980; 443
spectral adj 2, 4, 980
spectroscope n 428
spectrum n 428
speculate v 155, 514, 621, 675, 870
speculation n 156, 451, 514, 621, 675
speculative adj 514, 621, 675
speech n 582
speech n 560, 586
speech impediment n 583
speechless adj 403, 581, 583
speechlessness n 403, 590
speed n 264, 274, 684; v 274, 682, 684
speedily adv 132
speediness n 132
speed up v 274
speedy adj 274, 684
spell n 993
spell n 106, 198, 992; v 561, 707
spell-bound adj 870
spelling n 561
spend v 638, 809
spend freely v 816
spendthrift adj 638, 818
spend time v 106
spent adj 158, 160, 688
spew v 297
sphere n 26, 181, 249, 318; v 249
spherical adj 249
sphericity n 249
spheroid n 249
spice n 41, 393; v 392
spiced adj 392
spick and span adj 123
spicy adj 392, 400
spigot n 263
spike n 253, 263; v 260
spiked adj 253
spiky adj 253
spill v 348
spin n 266; v 312
spin a melody v 416
spin around v 312
spindly adj 203
spine n 253
spineless adj 862
spinelessness n 172
spinning n 312
spin out v 200
spinster n 904
spiny adj 253
spiral n 248, 311; adj 248
spirit n 5, 171, 359, 516, 574, 682, 709, 820, 861, 977, 980
spirited adj 171, 574, 836, 861
spiritual adj 2, 317, 976, 977
spiritualism n 992
spirituality n 317
spit v 260
spite n 907
spiteful adj 898, 907, 919, 945
spitefulness n 907
splash n 348; v 337, 348, 653
splendid adj 420
splendor n 420, 845, 882
splice v 43, 219
splint n 215
splinter n 32; v 44, 328
splintery adj 328
split n 44, 713; v 44, 91, 293, 328, 713, 838
split down the middle v 91
split hairs v 868
split one's sides v 838
split the difference v 29
split the differences v 774
split the eardrums v 404, 419
split up v 778, 905; adj 51, 905
spoil v 397, 659

713 ROGET'S THESAURUS trite

terminus n 233
terms n 476, 770
terrain n 342
terrestrial adj 318, 342
terrible adj 846, 860
terribly adv 31
terrified adj 860
territorial adj 181, 342
territory n 181, 965
terror n 860
terror-stricken adj 860
terse adj 572
terseness n 572
tertiary adj 92
test n 463; v 463
testify v 467, 535
testimony n 467
testy adj 684, 901
tête-à-tête n 588
tether v 43
tetrad n 95
text n 22, 542, 591
textbook n 542
texture n 256, 329
textured adj 256
thank v 916
thankful adj 916
thankfulness n 916
thankless adj 917
thanklessness n 917
thanks n 916
that being the case adv 8
thatch n 223
that is to say adv 522
thaw v 335, 382, 384
thawing n 335
the all-merciful n 976
the all-powerful n 976
the almighty n 976
theater n 599, 728
theatrical adj 599, 855, 882
theatricals n 599
the cloth n 996
the common people n 876
the converse n 14
the drama n 599
the eternal n 976
theft n 788, 789, 791
the future n 121
the infinite n 976
the inverse n 14
theism n 983
the latest thing n 123
the lead n 62, 280
the like n 17
the lower classes n 876
thematic adj 454
theme n 413, 454, 595
then adv 119
thence adv 155
theologian n 983
theological adj 983
theologics n 983
theologue n 983
theology n 983
the open n 338
the opposite n 14
theorem n 514
theoretical adj 514
theorize v 155, 514
theory n 155, 453, 514
theosophical adj 983
theosophy n 983
the past n 122
the present day n 118
the present juncture n 118
therapeutic adj 662
there adv 186
thereabouts adv 32, 183
thereafter adv 117
thereby adv 631
therefore adv 155
thereupon adv 117
the reverse n 14
therewith adv 88, 632
thermometer n 389
thermometograph n 389
thermoscope n 389
thermostat n 389
the same adj 13
thesaurus n 86; 562
thesis n 454, 514, 595
thespian n 599
the stage n 599
the theater n 599
the time being n 118
the times n 118, 151
The Vedas n 986
the void n 180
the whole time adv 106
the word n 532
the world n 151
thick n 202; adj 102, 321, 352, 376, 426, 491
thick as a brick adj 499
thicken v 202, 321, 352
thickening n 321
thickness n 202
thickness n 202
thickset n 202
thick-skinned adj 823
thick-skulled adj 499
thief n 792
thieve v 791
thievery n 791
thievish adj 791
thimbleful n 32
thin v 38, 103, 203, 322; adj 4, 32, 203, 322, 337, 640
thing n 3, 316
thing mixed n 41
thing of the past n 124
things n 151
thing signified n 516
think v 451, 870; 484
think back upon v 505
thinker n 492, 500
think fit v 600
thinking n 451
think no more of v 506
think out loud v 589
think up v 66, 515
thinness n 203, 322
thinness n 4, 32, 203, 425
thin out v 38
third n 94; adj 93
thirdly adv 93
third part n 94
thirst n 865
thirst for knowledge n 455
thirsty adj 865
thirteen n 98
thistly adj 253
thither adv 278
thorn n 253, 663
thorn in the side n 663, 830
thorny adj 253
thorough adj 52, 459, 729
thoroughfare n 302
thoroughgoing adj 52
thoroughly adv 52, 729
thoroughness n 52, 729
though adv 30
thought n 451
thought n 453, 515
thoughtful adj 451, 457, 459, 498
thoughtless adj 452, 458, 460, 499, 674, 684, 863
thoughtlessness n 452, 863
thousand n 98
thrall n 749
thralldom n 749
thread n 205; v 69, 302
threadbare adj 659
threadlike adj 203, 205
threat n 909
threaten v 121, 152, 665, 668, 716, 909
threatening adj 909
three n 92; adj 92
threefold adj 92, 93
threefold division n 94
three times adv 93
threnody n 839
threshold n 231
thrice adv 93
thrift n 817
thriftiness n 817
thrifty adj 817
thrill n 151, 824; v 377, 380
thrilling adj 821, 824
thrive v 734
throb n 315, 378; v 314, 315
throbbing adj 315
throe n 146, 173, 315, 378, 828
throng n 72, 102, 975; v 72
throttle v 158, 261, 361
through adv 631
through-and-through adj 729
throughout adv 52, 106
through the agency of adv 170
throw n 284; v 284
throw aside v 678
throw away v 610
throw in v 228
throw in one's lot with v 709
throw in the towel v 624
throw off one's guard v 508
throw of the dice n 156
throw open v 260
throw out v 55, 297, 638
throw out of gear v 61
throw out of whack v 61
throw up v 297
thrust n 276, 284; v 276
thrust in v 300
thud n 406, 408a; v 408a
thug n 361
thumb v 379
thump n 276, 408a; v 276, 408a
thumper n 192
thumping adj 192
thunder n 404, 408; v 173, 404
thundering adj 192, 404
thunderousness n 404
thus adv 8
thus far adv 233
thus far and no further adv 233
thwack n 276; v 276
thwart v 706, 708
thwarted adj 732
tick v 407
ticket v 550
tickle the palate v 390, 394
tickle the tastebuds v 390
tickling n 380
ticklish adj 380, 704
tidal adj 348
tide n 348
tides n 341
tidiness n 652
tidings n 498, 532
tidy adj 58, 652
tidy up v 652
tie n 9, 11, 27, 45, 771; v 9, 43, 45, 770
tied adj 926
tier n 69, 204
tiered adj 204
ties of blood n 11
tie the hands v 158
tie the knot v 903
tie up v 342
tie up in knots v 158
tiff n 713
tight adj 43, 46; adj 261, 572, 819, 959
tighten v 572
tightness n 572
till n 802; v 371; adv 106
tillage n 371
till the soil v 371
tilt n 217, 306; v 217, 244, 306
tilted adj 217
tilt over v 218
tilt up v 307
timber n 413
timbre n 408
time n 106
time n 108; v 106
time-honored adj 124
time immemorial n 122
timeless adj 112
timelessness n 112
timeliness n 134, 684
timely adj 106, 132, 134
timeout n 106
timepiece n 114
timeserving adj 607
timetable n 114
time to come n 121
timeworn adj 124, 659
timid adj 605, 862, 881
timidity n 605, 862, 881
timorous adj 862, 881
tincture n 41, 428; v 41
tinge n 32, 41, 428; v 41, 428
tingle v 378, 380
tininess n 32, 193
tinsel n 851
tint n 26, 428; v 428
tinted adj 428
tintinnabulation n 408
tiny adj 32, 193
tippler n 959
tipsy adj 959
tiptop adj 210, 648
tirade n 582
tire v 688, 841, 869
tired adj 688, 841, 869
tiredness n 688
tired to death adj 688
tiresome adj 841
tissue n 329
tit for tat n 30
titillation n 377, 380
title n 877
title n 564, 747, 771
titled adj 875, 877
title page n 66
titter n 838; v 838
titular adj 564
to a certain degree adv 32
toady n 886, 935; v 886
to a large extent adv 31
to all appearance adv 448
to all intents and purposes adv 27, 52
to and fro adv 314
to arms adv 722
to a small extent adv 32
toast v 384
to blame adj 947
to boot adv 37
to come adj 121, 152
to crown all adv 33
tocsin n 669
toddler n 129
together adj 46, 502; adv 120
togetherness n 709, 714
together with adv 37, 88
togs n 225
toil n 686; v 682, 686
token n 505, 550
tolerable adj 32, 651, 736
tolerableness n 736
tolerance n 740, 760
tolerant adj 740, 760
tolerate v 738, 740, 760, 826
toleration n 738, 740
to little purpose adv 732
toll v 407
tomb n 363
tombstone n 363
tomcat n 373
tome n 590, 593
tomorrow n 121, 152; adv 121
tone n 7, 26, 159, 402, 428
tone color n 413
tone down v 429
tongue n 560
tongue-tied adj 581, 583
tonic adj 656
tonnage n 192
too adv 37
tool n 633
too late adv 133
too little adj 640
tools for pulverization n 330
too many n 641
too much n 641
to one's heart's content adv 831
too soon adv 132
tooth n 257
toothed adj 257
top n 206, 210, 223, 261; v 33, 210; adj 210
topic n 454
topical adj 183, 454
topmost adj 210
topographical adj 183
topography n 183
topple v 28, 162, 306
topsy-turvy adj 59, 218
torch n 423
to reason v 476
torment n 378, 828; v 378, 828, 830
tornado n 312, 315, 349
torpid adj 172, 683
torpor n 172, 683
torrent n 348
torrid adj 382
tortuous adj 248
torture n 378, 828, 982; v 378, 619, 828, 830, 972
torturous adj 378
to some degree adv 32
to some extent adv 26
toss n 284; v 284, 314, 315
tossup n 156
to substitute for v 634
tot n 129
total n 50, 84; v 37; adj 31, 50
total abstinence n 955
total destruction n 2
total eclipse n 421
totality n 50, 52
totally adv 31, 50, 52
to the eye adv 448
to the four winds adv 180
to the letter adv 19
to the minute adv 132
to the point adj 494
to the quick adv 375
totter v 160, 275, 314, 315, 659, 665
tottering adj 160
touch n 379
touch n 41, 375, 569; v 9, 197, 199, 375, 379, 824
touchable adj 316
touched adj 503, 821, 914
touching n 199; adj 199
touch on v 516
touchstone n 211
touchy adj 684, 901
tough adj 46, 323, 327
toughness n 327
tour n 266, 302; v 266
tourist n 268
tourniquet n 263
tow v 285
towage n 285
toward adv 278
tower v 31, 206, 305
towering adj 31, 192, 206
towing n 285
townsman n 188
toxic adj 657
trace n 551; v 230, 554
tracery n 219
trace to v 155
track n 627
tract n 181, 593, 595
tractability n 743
tractable adj 324, 705, 743
tractile adj 285, 324
tractility n 324
traction n 285
trade n 148, 625, 794, 796; v 148, 794, 796
trader n 797
tradesman n 797
trade wind n 349
tradition n 124
traditional adj 124, 983a
traffic n 794; v 794
tragedy n 619
tragic adj 619, 830
trail n 65; v 214, 275, 285, 286, 281
train n 65, 69, 214, 235, 271, 272, 281; v 285, 370, 537, 673
trained adj 698
training n 673
traipse v 275
trait n 448, 550
traitor n 742
trammel v 706
tramp n 268
trample on v 739
trample out v 162
trample upon v 649
trance n 993
tranquil adj 174, 265, 721
tranquilization n 174
tranquilize v 265, 723
tranquillity n 265, 721
transact v 680, 692, 794
transaction n 151, 625, 794, 796
transcend v 31, 33, 303, 648, 650
transcendence n 33, 650
transcendent adj 33
transcribe v 590
transcript n 21
transcription n 21
transfer n 783
transfer n 21, 270; v 185, 270, 783
transferable adj 270, 783
transference n 270
transference n 140, 783
transfiguration n 140
transfigure v 140
transform v 140
transformable adj 140, 149
transformation n 140, 144
transfuse v 41
transfusion n 41
transgress v 303, 742, 773, 945
transgression n 303, 773, 927
transience n 111
transient adj 111, 264
transit n 144, 270
transition n 144, 270
transitional adj 264
transitoriness n 111
transitory adj 111
translate v 522
translation n 522
translator n 524
translucent adj 425
transluscence n 425
transmissible adj 270
transmission n 270, 302, 783
transmissive adj 783
transmit v 270, 783
transmit light v 425
transmittable adj 270
transmutable adj 144
transmutation n 140, 144
transmute v 140
transparence n 425
transparency n 425
transparent adj 337, 425, 518
transpire v 532
transplant v 270
transplantation n 270
transport n 270, 827; v 270, 829
transportable adj 270
transportation n 272
transporter n 271
transporting adj 977
transposal n 218
transpose v 148, 185, 218, 270
transposition n 140, 148, 185, 218, 270
transverse adj 217, 219
trap n 530, 545, 667
trappings n 225
trash n 643
trashy adj 209, 575, 643
travail n 686
travel n 266; v 266
traveler n 268
traveling n 266; adj 264, 266
traverse v 266, 302
travesty n 21, 523; v 19, 523
trawler n 273
treacherous adj 544
treachery n 545
tread n 264
tread down v 749
tread upon v 649
treasure n 648; v 991
treasurer n 801
treasury n 802
treat v 595, 829
treatise n 593, 595
treatment n 662
treat well v 906
treaty n 23, 721, 769
treble v 93; adj 93
trebly adv 93
tree n 367
trellis n 219
tremble v 149, 160, 315, 383
tremendously adv 31
tremor n 315
tremulous adj 149, 315
trench n 259
trenchant adj 171, 253, 572, 574, 642
trend n 176, 278, 516
trendiness n 123
trendy adj 123
trepidation n 860
trespass n 303; v 303, 945
trestle n 215
triad n 92
trial n 463, 675, 686, 828, 830, 969
triality n 92
tribe n 72, 75
tribunal n 966
tributary n 348; adj 784
trice n 113
trick n 545; v 545
trickle n 348; v 295, 348
trickly adj 348
tricky adj 545, 702
trifle n 32, 451, 643; v 499
trifling n 499, 643; adj 4, 32, 477, 499, 643, 880
triform adj 92
trill v 407
trim n 231, 240; v 27, 231; adj 652
trimming n 231
trinity n 92
trio n 92, 415, 416
trip n 266, 302, 306; v 306, 309
tripartition n 94
triple v 93; adj 93
triplet n 92
triplicate adj 93
triplication n 93
triplicity n 93
tripling n 93
triply adv 93
trip the light fantastic toe v 309
trip up v 495
trisect v 94
trisection n 94
trite adj 496, 598, 613

unnatural adj 83, 855
unnaturalness n 855
unnecessary adj 641
unnerve v 158, 160
unnerved adj 160
unnoticed adj 460
unobservant adj 458
unobserved adj 460
unobstructed adj 748
unobtainable adj 471
unobtrusive adj 881
unoccupied adj 452
unopened adj 261
unorthodox adj 984
unorthodoxy n 984
unostentatious adj 881
unpaid adj 806
unpalatable adj 395, 830
unparalleled adj 20, 33
unperceptive adj 376
unperformable adj 471
unpersuasive adj 175a
unpierced adj 261
unplaced adj 185
unpleasant adj 395, 830, 846
unpoetic adj 598
unpointed adj 254
unpolished adj 256
unprecedented adj 18, 137
unpredictability n 139
unpredictable adj 139, 475
unprejudiced adj 942
unprepared adj 674
unpreparedness n 674
unpretentious adj 849, 879, 881
unprized adj 483
unproductive adj 169
unproductiveness n 169
unprofitable adj 169, 647
unprofitableness n 169
unpropitious adj 135
unprosperous adj 735
unpunctual adj 133, 135
unqualified adj 52, 158
unquestionable adj 474
unquestionableness n 474
unquestioned adj 474
unquiet adj 264
unrational adj 450a
unravel v 60, 246, 522, 705
unreadiness n 674
unready adj 674
unreal adj 2, 317, 515
unreasonable adj 471, 497, 499, 608, 814
unrecorded adj 552
unrefined adj 851
unreflective adj 452
unrelated adj 10
unreliability n 475
unreliable adj 149, 475
unremedial adj 859
unremembered adj 506
unrepentant adj 951
unrepented adj 951
unrepenting adj 951
unreserved adj 525
unresponsive adj 376, 383
unresponsiveness n 376
unrest n 149, 264
unrestricted adj 748
unrevealed adj 533
unrightful adj 925
unrightfulness n 925
unripe adj 123, 674
unrivaled adj 33
unroll v 313
unruffled adj 174, 265, 826
unruliness n 742
unruly adj 606, 742
unsafe adj 475, 665
unsavoriness n 395
unsavoriness n 391, 392

unsavory adj 392, 395, 874
unscoured adj 653
unscriptural adj 984
unscrupulous adj 940
unseasonable adj 135
unseasonableness n 135
unseasoned adj 435
unseeing adj 442
unseemly adj 647, 846
unseen adj 447
unselfish adj 906, 942
unselfishness n 906, 942
unserviceable adj 645
unsettle v 61, 185
unsettled adj 149, 185, 475, 503
unshackled adj 748
unshaped adj 241
unshapely adj 241
unsharpened adj 254
unsightliness n 846
unsightly adj 846
unskilled adj 699
unskillful adj 699
unskillfulness n 699
unsmelling adj 399
unsmooth adj 256
unsophisticated adj 946
unsought adj 766
unsound adj 203, 477, 651, 655
unsoundness n 657
unspiritual adj 316, 989
unstable adj 149, 333, 475, 605, 665
unstained adj 960
unsteady adj 149, 475, 665
unstrung adj 160
unsubmissive adj 742
unsubstantial adj 2, 4, 203, 317, 322, 515
unsubstantiality n 4
unsuccessful adj 732
unsuccessfully adv 732
unsuccessfulness n 732
unsuitability n 647
unsuitable adj 135, 647
unsuitable time n 135
unsuited adj 135
unsullied adj 652, 960
unsupportable adj 830
unsupportive adj 468
unsure adj 475, 485
unsurpassed adj 31, 33
unsusceptible adj 376, 826
unsuspecting adj 486, 547
unsuspicious adj 703
unswerving adj 278
unsymmetrical adj 243
unsympathetic adj 383
unsystematic adj 59
untainted adj 946, 960
untaught adj 491, 674
untenable adj 4, 477
untested adj 123
unthankful adj 917
unthankfulness n 917
unthinking adj 452
unthriftiness n 818
unthrifty adj 818
untidiness n 59
untidy adj 59, 653
until adv 106
untimeliness n 135
untimely adj 135
untouchable adj 317
untoward adj 135
untried adj 123
untrue adj 495, 544, 545, 546, 923
untrustworthy adj 665
untrustworthy memory n 506
untruth n 546
untruth n 544
untruthful adj 544
untruthfulness n 544, 545
untutored adj 491
unusable adj 645

unused adj 40, 678
unusual adj 83, 137, 614
unusually adv 31
unutterable adj 519
unvalued adj 483
unvanquished adj 748
unvaried adj 16
unvarnished adj 576
unvarying adj 16, 143, 150
unveil v 529
unventilated adj 261
unvulnerable adj 112
unwarned adj 508
unwarranted adj 925, 964
unwary adj 460, 863
unwavering adj 150
unwelcome adj 830
unwell adj 655
unwholesome adj 657, 663
unwieldy adj 192, 319, 704
unwilling adj 603
unwillingly adv 603
unwillingness n 603
unwillingness n 704
unwind v 313
unwise adj 499
unwittingly adv 621
unworkable adj 647
unworldliness n 703
unworldly adj 703
unworthy adj 874
unworthy of consideration adj 643
unworthy of notice adj 643
up and down adv 314
Upanishads n 986
upgrowth n 305
upheaval n 307
uphill adj 217
uphold v 143, 670, 707, 717, 937
uplift v 307
upon one's oath adj 768
uppermost adj 210
upraise v 307
uprear v 307
upright adj 212, 246, 922, 939, 944, 946, 960
uprightness n 922, 939, 944, 946, 960
uprising n 146
uproar n 59, 173, 404
uproarious adj 404
uproot v 301
ups and downs n 314
upset n 308; v 162, 218, 308; adj 824
upshot n 154, 480, 729
upside down adj 218
upstairs n 450
up to adj 157; adv 106
up to a point adv 26
up-to-date adj 123
up to the mark adj 27, 639
up to this time adv 122
upturn n 218
upwards of adj 100
urbane adj 894
urchin n 980
urge v 173, 276, 684
urgency n 642, 684
urgent adj 630, 642
urging n 695
urinate v 299
urination n 299
urn n 363
usage n 567, 613, 677, 998
use n 677
use n 644; v 677, 788
used up adj 158, 659
useful adj 176, 618, 631, 644, 677
usefulness n 644, 677
useless adj 169, 499, 643, 645, 647, 732, 880
uselessness n 645
use the occasion v 134
use up v 677

usher v 296
usher in v 62, 66, 280
usual adj 82, 613
usurer n 805, 819
usurious adj 819
usurp v 789
usurper n 925
utensil n 633
utilitarian adj 677
utility n 644
utility n 646, 677
utilization n 677
utilize v 677
utmost adj 33
utter v 580, 582; adj 31
utterance n 580, 985
utterly adv 52
uttermost adj 31

V

vacancy n 187, 209, 499
vacancy of mind n 452
vacant adj 4, 187, 209, 452, 499
vacate v 185, 293
vacation n 685, 687
vacationer n 268
vacillate v 149, 314, 605
vacillating adj 149
vacillation n 149, 314, 485, 605
vacuity n 187, 452
vacuous adj 4, 187, 209
vacuum n 187
vagabond n 268
vagabondism n 266
vagary n 608
vagrant n 268; adj 266
vague adj 475, 477, 517, 571
vagueness n 475, 519, 571
vain adj 158, 645, 878, 880
vain expectation n 509
vainglorious adj 884, 880
vainglory n 878
vale n 252
valediction n 293
valid adj 737
validity n 157
valley n 252, 259
valor n 861
valorous adj 861
valuable adj 644, 648
valuation n 466, 812
value n 644, 648, 812, 815; v 466, 480, 642, 931
value received n 810
valueless adj 645
valve n 263, 350
vampire n 980
van n 280
vanguard n 234, 280
vanish v 4, 111, 360, 449
vanished adj 449
vanishing point n 193
vanity n 880
vanity n 878
vantage ground n 175
vapid adj 337, 391, 575, 843
vapor n 353
vaporization n 336
vaporize v 336
vaporous adj 334, 336
vaporousness n 334
vapory adj 336
variability n 475
variable adj 140, 149, 475
variance n 15, 24, 291, 713
variant adj 15
variation n 20a
variation n 15, 83, 140
varied adj 15, 16a, 20a
variegate v 440
variegated adj 41, 440
variegation n 440
variety n 75, 81
various adj 15, 102
varnish n 223, 356a; v 356a
vary v 15, 18, 20a, 140,

149, 291, 314
vast adj 31, 104, 180, 192
vastness n 31, 105
vault n 245, 309, 318, 363, 802; v 309
vaulted adj 245
vaunt v 884
veer v 140, 279
vegetable n 367
vegetable adj 367
vegetable kingdom n 367
vegetable life n 365
vegetable oil n 356
vegetable physiology n 369
vegetal adj 367
vegetarian n 953
vegetate v 367
vegetation n 365
vegetation n 365
vegetative adj 365, 367
vehemence n 173, 825
vehement adj 173, 382, 574, 825
vehicle n 272
vehicle n 271, 631
veil n 424, 530; v 424, 528
veiled adj 447, 526
veiling n 528
vein n 176, 205, 602
veined adj 440
velocity n 274
velocity n 264
velvety adj 255, 256
venal adj 211, 819
venality n 819
vend v 796
vendible adj 796
vendition n 796
vendor n 796
veneer n 223; v 204, 223
venerable adj 124, 128, 928
venerate v 860, 928, 987
veneration n 860, 928, 987
vengeance n 718, 919
vengeful adj 718, 919
vengefulness n 919
venom n 663, 907
venomous adj 649, 657, 663, 907
vent n 260, 351
ventilate v 338, 349, 652
ventilation n 338
venture n 621, 675, 676; v 621, 665, 675, 861
venturesome adj 621, 675
veracious adj 494, 543
veracity n 543
veracity n 494
verbal adj 562
verbal interchange n 588
verbiage n 573
verbose adj 573, 584, 641
verbosity n 573, 584, 641
verdant adj 367, 435
verdict n 480, 969
verdure n 367, 435
verdurous adj 435
verge n 231, 233; v 176, 278
verification n 478
verify v 478
veritable adj 494
verity n 494
vermilion adj 434
vernacular n 560; adj 560
versatile adj 149
versatility n 149
verse n 590, 597
versification n 597
versifier n 597
versify v 597
versus adv 708
vertex n 210
vertical adj 212, 246
verticality n 212

vertically adv 212
verve n 159, 515, 574
very adv 31
very best adj 648
very much adv 31
vespers n 126
vessel n 191, 273
vestal virgin n 960
vestige n 551
vestments n 999
veteran n 130
veteran n 700
veterinary science n 370
veto v 761
vex v 828, 830
vexation n 828, 830, 835
vexatious adj 830, 901a
vibes n 314
vibrate v 314
vibration n 138, 314, 408
vibrato n 408
vice n 945
vice n 649, 923
vice versa adv 148
vicinity n 186, 197
vicious adj 907, 945
vicissitude n 111, 149
victimize v 649
victorious adj 731
victory n 731
vie v 648, 720
view n 441, 448, 453, 484, 620; v 441
viewpoint n 441
vigilance n 459, 682, 864, 920
vigilant adj 459, 507, 682, 864, 920
viginal adj 960
vignette n 594
vigor n 574
vigor n 157, 159, 171, 359, 364, 604, 654, 682
vigorous adj 159, 171, 359, 574, 654
vile adj 207, 211, 395, 649, 830, 846, 874, 898, 930
vilification n 934
vilify v 934
vilifying adj 934
villa n 189
villager n 188
villain n 941, 949
villainous adj 649
vinculum n 45
vindicate v 717, 919, 937
vindicated adj 937
vindicating adj 937
vindication n 937
vindication n 717
vindicator n 919, 937
vindictive adj 919
vindictiveness n 919
vinegariness n 397
vinegary adj 397
vintage adj 124
violate v 742, 773, 927
violate the law v 964
violation n 773, 927
violation of custom n 83
violence n 173
violence n 825
violent adj 59, 173, 382, 825
violently adv 31, 173
violet adj 437
virgin n 904, 960; adj 66, 123
virginal adj 123, 946
virginity n 960
virility n 159
virtually adv 5
virtue n 944
virtue n 648, 922, 939, 946, 960
virtuoso adj 881, 939, 944, 946, 960
virtuousness n 944, 946
virulence n 649
virulent adj 649, 657
virus n 663
visage n 448

viscid adj 352
viscosity n 352
viscous adj 327, 352
visibility n 446
visible adj 446, 525
vision n 441
vision n 443, 515, 980
visionary n 504; adj 2, 4, 441, 515
visit often v 136
visor n 530
vista n 448
visual adj 441
vital adj 359, 642
vital flame n 359
vitality n 159, 359, 364, 654
vitalize v 359
vital spark n 359
vitiate v 659
vivacious adj 359, 515, 682, 829, 836
vivacity n 359, 515, 682, 836
vivid adj 171, 375, 420, 428, 505
vivify v 159, 359
vocabulary 562
vocal adj 415, 416, 580
vocal group n 416
vocalist n 416
vocality n 580
vocalization n 580
vocalize v 416, 566, 580
vocal music n 415
vocation n 625
vociferate v 411
vociferation n 411
vociferous adj 404, 411
vociferousness n 404
vogue n 613, 852
voice n 580
voice n 402; v 566, 580, 582
voiceless adj 581, 583
void n 2, 4, 187; v 2, 297, 756; adj 2, 187
volatile adj 149, 320, 336
volatility n 149, 320, 334
volcanic adj 173, 384, 825
volition n 600
volitional adj 600
volubility n 584
voluble adj 334, 584
volume n 25, 31, 102, 192, 590, 593
voluminous adj 192
voluntarily adv 600
voluntary adj 600
volunteer v 676
voluptuary n 954a, 962
voluptuous adj 377, 829
voluptuousness n 827
vomit v 297
voodoo n 993
voracious adj 957
voracity n 957
vortex n 312, 315, 348
voucher n 807
vow n 768
vowel n 561
voyage n 267, 302
voyager n 268
V-shaped adj 244
vulgar adj 579, 851, 876, 895
vulgarity n 851
vulgarity n 579, 895
vulgarize v 851
vulnerability n 177

W

wad v 224
wadding n 224, 263
waddle v 275
wade through v 539
waft v 320, 349
wag n 844
wager n 621; v 621
wages n 775, 812
wage war v 722
waggle v 315
wagon n 272
waif n 268

Dictionary of Occupational Titles

000.000-000 MUSEUM INTERN (museum)

A term applied to individuals who perform curatorial, administrative, educational, conservation, or research duties in museum or similar institution, to assist professional staff in utilization of institution's collections and other resources and to gain practical experience and knowledge to enhance personal qualifications for career. Classifications are made according to assignment which is usually based upon academic specialization as CRAFT DEMONSTRATOR (museum), PAINTINGS RESTORER (profess. & kin.), RESEARCH ASSISTANT (profess. & kin.), or RESEARCH ASSOCIATE (museum).

000.000-000 RESEARCH ASSOCIATE (profess. & kin.)

A term applied to persons who conduct independent research in scientific, legal, medical, political, academic, or other specialized fields. Individuals working at this level are required to have a graduate degree. Classifications are made according to field of specialization as AERODYNAMIST (aircraft-aerospace mfg.); METALLURGIST, PHYSICAL (profess. & kin.); MICROBIOLOGIST (profess. & kin.); PATHOLOGIST (medical ser.); POLITICAL SCIENTIST (profess. & kin.).

002.167-018 AERONAUTICAL PROJECT ENGINEER (aircraft-aerospace mfg.)

Directs and coordinates activities of personnel engaged in designing landing gear, flight control equipment, and armaments of military aircraft, applying knowledge of engineering theory and technology: Reviews request from military services or formulates idea for design and capability changes of aircraft. Analyzes proposals for engineering feasibility, design, production time, and advantages and disadvantages of proposals, using knowledge of engineering theory and technology. Discusses proposals with engineering and military personnel, and assigns and directs personnel to design proposals. Examines and reviews drawings, design specifications, reports, tests, photographs, and finished parts for accuracy and quality control. Coordinates production of parts by subcontractors. GOE 05.01.08 PD L56 EC I56 M6 L6 SVP 9 SOC 1622

003.281-018 DRAFTER, ELECTRO-MECHANICAL (profess. & kin.)

Drafts engineering details and plans of electrical components, assemblies, and systems, working from sketches, conceptual drawings, and notes, utilizing knowledge of standard drafting practices: Receives engineering notes, conceptual drawings, and sketches from engineer. Computes drafting specifications, such as spacing and configuration dimensions to determine drawing data for draft, using calculator and engineering notes and utilizing knowledge of specifications determined by standard manufacturing practices and routine arithmetic, algebraic, and geometric procedures. Drafts detailed documents, such as wiring diagrams, layout drawings, mechanical details, and intermediate and final assemblies of products. GOE 05.03.02 PD S46 EC I M4 L4 SVP 7 SOC 372

005.061-042 WASTE-MANAGEMENT ENGINEER, RADIOACTIVE MATERIALS (profess. & kin.)

Designs, implements, and tests systems and procedures to reduce volume and dispose of nuclear waste materials and contaminated objects: Identifies objects contaminated by exposure to radiation, such as trash, workers' clothing, and discarded tools and equipment. Analyzes samples of sludge and liquid effluents resulting from operation of nuclear reactors to determine level of radioactivity in substances and potential for retention of radioactivity, using radioactivity counters and chemical and electronic analyzers. Refers to State and Federal regulations and technical manuals to determine disposal method recommended for prevention of leakage or absorption of radioactive waste. Compares costs of transporting waste to designated nuclear waste disposal sites and reducing volume of waste and storing waste on plant site. Confers with equipment manufacturers' representatives and plant technical and management personnel to discuss alternatives and to choose most suitable plan on basis of safety, efficiency, and cost-effectiveness. Designs and draws plans for systems to reduce volume of waste by solidification, compaction, or incineration. Oversees construction, testing, and implementation of waste disposal systems, and resolves operational problems. Develops plans for modification of operating procedures to reduce volume and radioactive level of effluents, and writes manuals to instruct workers in changes in work procedures. Advises management on selection of lands suitable for use as nuclear waste disposal sites and on establishment of effective safety, operating, and closure procedures. GOE 05.01.03 PD L456 EC I6 M5 L5 SVP 8 SOC 1628

005.261-010 ENGINEERING TECHNICIAN (profess. & kin.)

Conducts surveys and studies and inspects existing water and wastewater treatment systems and those under construction to insure that pollution control requirements are met: Reviews plans and specifications for details concerning construction or repair of sewage systems, sewage and water treatment facilities, and water supply systems for conformance to pollution control requirements. Reviews information, such as size of unit, capacities, length of pipe, reinforcements, unit locations, and other data to insure adherence to requirements. Conducts stream surveys and comprehensive basin studies to gather data. Sets up and maintains water monitoring equipment to obtain samples, flow measurements, and other data. Tabulates data and prepares sketches, diagrams, and graphs for evaluation by engineering staff. Inspects existing systems and construction, in progress and upon completion, to insure pollution control requirements are met. Performs various other duties, such as filing plans and other doc-

uments, answering inquiries, and assisting engineering personnel, or assisting and training personnel operating equipment. GOE 05.03.08 PD L46 EC I M4 L4 SVP 7 SOC 3719

007.161-038 SOLAR-ENERGY-SYSTEMS DESIGNER (profess. & kin.)

Designs solar domestic hot water and space heating systems for new and existing structures, applying knowledge of energy requirements of structure, local climatological conditions, solar technology, and thermodynamics: Estimates energy requirements of new or existing structures, based on analysis of utility bills of structure, calculations of thermal efficiency of structure, and prevailing climatological conditions. Determines type of solar system, such as water, glycol, or silicone, which functions most efficiently under prevailing climatological conditions. Calculates onsite heat generating capacity of different solar panels to determine optimum size and type of panels which meet structure's energy requirements. Arranges location of solar system components, such as panel, pumps, and storage tanks, to minimize length and number of direction changes in pipes and reconstruction of existing structures. Studies engineering tables to determine size of pipes and pumps required to maintain specified flow rate through solar panels. Specifies types of electrical controls, such as differential thermostat, temperature sensors, and solenoid valves, compatible with other system components, using knowledge of control systems. Completes parts list, specifying components of system. Draws wiring, piping, and other diagrams, using drafting tools. May inspect structures to compile data used in solar system design, such as structure's angle of alinement with sun and temperature of incoming cold water. May inspect construction of system to insure adherence to design specifications. GOE 05.03.07 PD L46 EC I M4 L4 SVP 5 SOC 1635

007.267-010 DRAWINGS CHECKER, ENGINEERING (profess. & kin.)

Examines engineering drawings of military and commercial parts, assemblies, and installations to detect errors in design documents: Compares figures and lines on production drawing or diagram with production layout, examining angles, dimensions, bend allowances, and tolerances for accuracy. Determines practicality of design, material selection, available tooling, and fabrication process applying knowledge of drafting and manufacturing methods. Confers with design personnel to resolve drawing and design discrepancies. May specialize in checking specific types of designs, such as mechanical assemblies, microelectronic circuitry, or fluid-flow systems. GOE 05.03.02 PD S46 EC I M4 L4 SVP 6 SOC 1635

008.061-030 NUCLEAR-DECONTAMINATION RESEARCH SPECIALIST (profess. & kin.)

Conducts research into problems of decontaminating radioactive equipment and work areas in nuclear plants, laboratories, and other facilities: Examines and tests machinery and equipment to determine type and cause of radioactive contamination, using electron microscope, Geiger counter, and scintillation counter. Develops new decontamination processes, using knowledge of nuclear chemistry. Invents and constructs models of equipment to achieve specific objectives in decontamination processes, devising ways to minimize radiation risk to operative personnel. Devises wash and leach procedures and designs electropolishing equipment to clean and decontaminate metals. Invents regenerative-dilute decontamination process to reduce volume of radioactive liquid waste generated from wash and leach procedures. Prepares technical report to explain research and development of improved techniques and equipment for decontamination of radioactive equipment and work areas. GOE 05.01.01 PD L456 EC I M6 L6 SVP 8 SOC 1626

011.261-018 NONDESTRUCTIVE TESTER (bus. ser.)

Conducts radiographic, penetrant, ultrasonic, and magnetic particle tests on metal parts in commercial testing laboratory to determine if parts meet nondestructive specifications: Reviews test orders to determine type of tests requested, test procedures to follow, and part acceptability criteria. Applies agents such as cleaners, penetrants, developers, and couplant (light oil which acts as medium) to parts, or heats parts in oven, to prepare parts for testing. Determines test equipment settings according to type of metal, thickness, distance from test equipment, and related variables, using standard formulas. Calibrates test equipment, such as magnetic particle, X-ray, and ultrasonic contact machines, to standard settings, following manual instructions. Sets up equipment to perform tests, and conducts tests on parts, following procedures established for specified tests performed. Examines surface-treated materials when conducting penetrant and magnetic particle tests to locate and identify flaws, cracks, and related defects, using black light. Moves transducer probe across part when conducting ultrasonic tests and observes CRT (cathode ray tube) screen to detect and locate discontinuities in metal structure [ULTRASONIC TESTER (bus. ser.)]. Examines film when conducting radiographic tests to locate structural or welding flaws. Marks tested parts to indicate areas where flaws are detected. Evaluates test results against designated standards, utilizing knowledge of metals and testing experience. Prepares reports outlining findings and conclusions. May perform similar tests on parts or structures composed of materials other than metals. GOE 05.07.01 PD H346 EC B M3 L3 SVP 6 SOC 399

015.061-026 NUCLEAR-FUELS RECLAMATION ENGINEER (profess. & kin.)

Plans, designs, and oversees construction and operation of nuclear fuels reprocessing systems: Performs research and experiments to determine acceptable methods of reclaiming various types of nuclear fuels. Designs nuclear fuel reclamation systems and equipment for pilot plants. Communicates with vendors and contractors, and computes cost estimates of reclamation systems. Writes project proposals and submits them to company review board. Studies safety procedures, guidelines, and controls, and confers with safety officials to insure that safety limits are not violated in design, construction, or operation of systems and equipment. Oversees nuclear fuels reprocessing system construction and operation, conferring with construction supervisory and operating personnel. Tests system equipment and approves equipment for operation. Monitors operations to detect potential or inherent problems. Initiates corrective actions and orders plant shutdown in emergency situations. Identifies operational and processing problems and recommends solutions. Maintains log of plant operations, and prepares reports for review by plant officials. GOE 05.01.03 PD L456 EC I6 M5 L5 SVP 7 SOC 1627

015.061-030 NUCLEAR-FUELS RESEARCH ENGINEER (profess. & kin.)

Studies behavior of various fuels and fuel configurations in differentiated reactor environments to determine safest and most efficient usage of nuclear fuels, applying theoretical and experiential knowledge of reactor physics and thermal and metallurgical characteristics of nuclear fuels and fuel cell claddings: Analyzes available data and consults with other scientists to determine parameters of experimentation and suitability of analytical models. Designs fuels behavior tests and coordinates activities of experimental research team in performance and analysis of test operations. Monitors test reactor indicators of factors such as neutron power level, coolant level, and vital pressure, temperature and humidity readings, and changes or modifies procedures to meet test goals. Synthesizes analyses of test results and prepares technical reports to disseminate findings and recommendations. Formulates equations that describe phenomena occurring during fissioning of nuclear fuels and develops analytical models for nuclear fuels research. GOE 05.01.03 PD L456 EC I M6 L6 SVP 8 SOC 1627

015.067-010 NUCLEAR-CRITICALITY SAFETY ENGINEER (profess. & kin.)

Conducts research and analyzes and evaluates proposed and existing methods of transportation, handling, and storage of nuclear fuel to preclude accidental nuclear reaction at nuclear facilities: Reviews and evaluates fuel transfer and storage plans received from nuclear plants. Studies reports of nuclear fuel characteristics to determine potential or inherent problems. Reads blueprints of proposed storage facilities and visits storage sites to determine adequacy of storage plans. Forecasts nuclear fuel criticality (point at which nuclear chain reaction becomes self-sustaining), given various factors which may exist in fuel handling and storage, using knowledge of nuclear physics, calculator, and computer terminal. Determines potential hazards and accident conditions which may exist in fuel handling and storage and recommends preventive measures. Summarizes findings and writes reports. Confers with project officials to resolve situations where hazard is beyond acceptable levels. Prepares proposal reports for handling and storage of fuels to be submitted to government review board. Studies existing procedures and recommends changes or additions to guidelines and controls to insure prevention of self-sustaining nuclear chain reaction. GOE 05.01.02 PD L456 EC I67 M6 L5 SVP 8 SOC 1627

015.137-010 RADIATION-PROTECTION ENGINEER (gov. ser.)

Supervises and coordinates activities of workers engaged in monitoring radiation levels in water and detecting corrosion of equipment used to produce nuclear energy for generation of power: Evaluates data concerning chemical analysis of water in primary and supportive plant systems to determine compliance with regulations governing radiation content and corrosion control. Investigates problems concerning excessive radiation or corrosion of equipment, applying knowledge of radiation protection techniques and principles of chemistry and engineering to correct conditions. Confers with other supervisory personnel, representatives of equipment manufacturing firms, and regulatory agency staff members to discuss problems and develop plans for safe and efficient monitoring program. Supervises workers who test and analyze water samples and monitor operation of processing system. Prepares reports of environmental monitoring operation and radioactive waste release and shipment activities for review by administrative personnel and submission to regulatory agency. GOE 05.01.02 PD S5 EC I M4 L5 SVP 8 SOC 1627

015.167-010 NUCLEAR-PLANT TECHNICAL ADVISOR (light, heat, & power)

Monitors plant safety status, advises operations staff, and prepares technical reports for operation of thermal-nuclear reactor at electric-power generating station: Observes control-room instrumentation systems and confers with operating personnel to insure safe operation of plant. Walks throughout plant and observes machinery, equipment, and operating procedures to identify potential hazards. Examines locations of accidents and transients (sudden changes of voltage or load) and obtains data to formulate preventive measures. Implements changes in systems, procedures, structure, or equipment to improve safety. Compares critical parameters with plant transient predictions and accident analysis and determines

whether response of plant safety systems is sufficient. Formulates corrective actions, calculates critical parameters from raw data, and computes rate of control rod withdrawal during reactor startup. Confers with operating personnel to provide technical assistance and to discuss maintenance activities, abnormal conditions, and safe operation of plant. Prepares reports to inform management officials of any proposed changes or irregularities in plant operation or systems. GOE 05.01.02 PD L56 EC I M5 L5 SVP 8 SOC 1627

015.167-014 NUCLEAR-TEST-REACTOR PROGRAM COORDINATOR (profess. & kin.)

Evaluates, coordinates, and oversees testing of nuclear reactor equipment: Analyzes test proposal to insure that test is valid and feasible. Identifies and resolves problems, such as incompatibilities between proposal and nuclear test-reactor system. Coordinates technical and financial agreements involving feasibility, scope, purpose, and cost of project in nuclear test facility. Assists engineering personnel in interpretation of test language, mathematical formulas, and computer codes used in test. Writes operational instructions. Inspects general condition of nuclear test-reactor vessel and related systems. Verifies setup of nuclear test-reactor for compliance with specifications. Observes control room instrumentation to insure that performance factors such as neutron power level, chemical composition of coolant, and reactor temperatures and pressures are carried out as prescribed. Evaluates and resolves operational problems. Coordinates activities directed toward removal of test specimens from reactors and subsequent chemical, metallurgical, or mechanical analysis. Compiles report of test results. GOE 05.01.04 PD L456 EC I6 M5 L5 SVP 8 SOC 1627

015.261-010 CHEMICAL-RADIATION TECHNICIAN (gov. ser.)

Tests materials and monitors operations of nuclear-powered electric generating plant, using specialized laboratory equipment and chemical and radiation detection instruments: Collects samples of water, gases, and solids at specified intervals during production process, using automatic sampling equipment. Analyzes materials, according to specified procedures, to determine if chemical components and radiation levels are within established limits. Records test results and prepares reports for review by supervisor. Assists workers to set up equipment and monitors equipment that automatically detects deviations from standard operations. Notifies personnel to adjust processing equipment, quantity of additives, and rate of discharge of waste materials, when test results and monitoring of equipment indicate that radiation levels, chemical balance, and discharge of radionuclide materials are in excess of standards. Carries out decontamination procedures to insure safety of workers and continued operation of processing equipment in plant. Calibrates and maintains chemical instrumentation sensing elements and sampling system equipment, using handtools. Assists workers in diagnosis and correction of problems in instruments and processing equipment. Advises plant personnel of methods of protection from excessive exposure to radiation. GOE 11.10.03 PD L4 EC I M3 L3 SVP 6 SOC 389

017.261-042 DRAFTER, COMPUTER-ASSISTED (profess. & kin.)

Drafts layouts, drawings, and designs for application in such fields as aeronautics, architecture, or electronics, according to engineering specifications, using computer: Reviews engineering drawings and supporting documents to verify freedom of movement between parts and adherence to company or industry standard practices and adequacy of parts identification. Analyzes design and confers with engineering staff to resolve details not completely defined. Locates file relating to projection data base library and loads program into computer. Retrieves information from file and displays information on cathode-ray-tube (CRT) screen, using required computer language. Types commands to rotate or zoom-in on display to redesign, modify, or otherwise edit existing design. Traces over face of photosensitive screen to redraw details or rewrite text. Displays final drawing on screen to verify completeness, clarity, and accuracy of drawing. Types command to transfer drawing dimensions from computer onto hardcopy, using peripheral equipment, such as digitizer or plotter controlled by computer. Submits completed drawings to supervisor for review. GOE 05.03.02 PD S46 EC I M4 L4 SVP 7 SOC 372

019.167-018 RESOURCE-RECOVERY ENGINEER (gov. ser.)

Plans and participates in activities concerned with study, development, and inspection of solid-waste resource recovery systems and marketability of solid-waste recovery products: Conducts studies of chemical and mechanical solid-waste recovery processes and system designs to evaluate efficiency and cost-effectiveness of proposed operations. Inspects solid-waste resource recovery facilities to determine compliance with regulations governing construction and use. Collects data on resource recovery systems and analyzes alternate plans to determine most feasible systems for specific solid-waste recovery purposes. Prepares recommendations for development of resource recovery programs, based on analysis of alternate plans and knowledge of physical properties of various solid-waste materials. Confers with design engineers, management personnel, and others concerned with recovery of solid-waste resources to discuss problems and provide technical advice. Coordinates activities of workers engaged in study of potential markets for reclaimable materials. Lectures civic and professional organizations and provides information about practices to media representatives to promote interest and participation in solid-waste recovery practices. GOE 05.01.02 PD S56 EC I M6 L5 SVP 8 SOC 1628

020.224-010 CUSTOMER-SUPPORT SPECIALIST (whole. tr.)

Converts clients' manual accounting systems to computerized systems, trains clients' employees to program systems, and diagnoses computer hardware malfunctions: Reviews and evaluates client's manual accounting and bookkeeping systems, using established accounting procedures to convert from manual system to computerized system. Contacts computer software vendor to order initial supply of forms. Teaches client's employees to program computer, using standardized programing methods and observing hands-on practices. Reviews client's operational procedures to implement improvements. Troubleshoots computer hardware malfunctions, using electronic test meter and tools, and repairs simple malfunctions or writes service order for use of repair personnel. GOE 11.01.01 PD L456 EC I M4 L4 SVP 7 SOC 1719

020.262-010 SOFTWARE TECHNICIAN (profess. & kin.)

Analyzes problems, plans and develops software programs, transfers programs to memory chips, installs chips on printed circuit boards (PCB), and tests and corrects operation of chips and boards, using computer equipment: Assembles units into logical sequence and translates charts into programed computer language to develop detailed flow charts. Enters coded commands into computer, tests printer for system errors, and corrects errors by altering commands until desired results are attained, using keyboard. Transfers program data onto disk, using terminal keyboard, mounts disk onto cathode-ray-tube (CRT) unit, checks screen for errors, and corrects errors as necessary. Mounts disk and blank chips in device which imprints program onto erasable memory chip. Writes specifications and instructs operator how to input data to obtain required results. Installs chips on printed circuit board and connects lead wires to board circuitry, utilizing diagrams and knowledge of electric circuitry and electronics. Observes operation of chip in terminal, changes sequence of program commands if necessary, and submits data specifications on tested chip to engineering department. GOE 11.01.01 PD L456 EC I M4 L4 SVP 7 SOC 3971

022.081-010 TOXICOLOGIST (drug. prep. & rel. prod.)

Conducts research on toxic effects of cosmetic products and ingredients on laboratory animals for manufacturer of cosmetics: Applies cosmetic ingredient or cosmetic being developed to exposed shaved skin area of test animal and observes and examines skin periodically for possible development of abnormalities, inflammation, or irritation. Injects ingredient into test animal, using hypodermic needle and syringe, and periodically observes animal for signs of toxicity. Injects antidotes to determine which antidote best neutralizes toxic effects. Tests and analyzes blood samples for presence of toxic conditions, using microscope and laboratory test equipment. Dissects dead animals, using surgical instruments, and examines organs to determine effects of cosmetic ingredients being tested. Prepares formal reports of test results. GOE 02.04.02 PD L456 EC I M4 L5 SVP 8 SOC 382

022.261-018 CHEMIST, INSTRUMENTATION (profess. & kin.; sanitary ser.)

Conducts chemical analyses of wastewater discharges of industrial users of municipal wastewater treatment plant to determine industrial waste surcharge assessments and to insure that users meet pollution control requirements: Conducts chemical analyses of samples, using special instrumentation, such as gas chromatograph with electron capture, flame ionization, and thermal conductivity detectors, ultraviolet-visible recording spectrophotometer with photometry attachments, and infrared spectrophotometer. Compares findings with industry declared data and legal requirements and notes variations to be used in determining industrial waste surcharge assessments and to regulate industrial waste discharges. Develops new procedures in use of equipment and procedures for analyzing samples. Directs subordinate laboratory personnel in routine tests. GOE 02.01.01 PD L46 EC I7 M5 L4 SVP 7 SOC 3831

022.261-022 CHEMIST, WASTEWATER-TREATMENT PLANT (profess. & kin.; sanitary ser.)

Analyzes samples of streams, raw and treated wastewater, sludge, and other byproducts of wastewater treatment process to determine efficiency of plant processes and to insure that plant effluent meets water pollution control requirements, using standard laboratory equipment: Conducts tests for settleable solids, suspended solids, total solids, volatile solids, volatile acids, alkalinity, pH, dissolved oxygen demand, turbidity, and other substances. Initiates changes in laboratory procedures and equipment in order to increase efficiency of laboratory. Directs laboratory personnel in prescribed laboratory techniques and performance of routine tests. GOE 02.04.02 PD L46 EC I7 M5 L4 SVP 7 SOC 3831

024.267-010 GEOLOGICAL AIDE (petrol. production)

Examines and compiles geological information to provide technical data to GEOLOGIST, PETROLEUM (petrol. production), using surface and subsurface maps, oil and gas well activity reports, and sand and core analysis studies: Studies geological reports to extract well data and posts data to maps and logs. Draws subsurface formation contours on charts to lay out and prepare geological cross section charts. Compiles information regarding well tests, completions, and formation tops to prepare oil or gas well records. Records net sand and sand percentage counts and calculates

isopachous values to compile sand analysis data. Studies directional logs and surveys to calculate and plot formation tops. Reads well activity reports and records key well locations in drilling activity book. Assembles and distributes prepared charts, maps, and reports to geologist requesting material. Maintains file record systems and geological library. Attends SCOUT (petrol. production) meeting to compile information on well activity. Contacts competitors to acquire oil and gas samples from wells. Operates computer terminal for input and retrieval of geological data. GOE 02.04.01 PD L456 EC I M5 L5 SVP 8 SOC 3833

040.261-010 SOIL-CONSERVATION TECHNICIAN (profess. & kin.)

Provides technical assistance to land users in planning and applying soil and water conservation practices, utilizing basic engineering and surveying tools, instruments, and techniques and knowledge of agricultural and related sciences, such as agronomy, soil conservation, and hydrology: Analyzes conservation problems of land and discusses alternative solutions to problems with land users. Advises land users in developing plans for conservation practices, such as conservation cropping systems, woodlands management, pasture planning, and engineering systems, based on cost estimates of different practices, needs of land users, maintenance requirements, and life expectancy of practices. Computes design specification for particular practices to be installed, using survey and field information technical guides, engineering field manuals, and calculator. Submits copy of engineering design specifications to land users for implementation by land user or contractor. Surveys property to mark locations and measurements, using surveying instruments. Monitors projects during and after construction to insure projects conform to design specifications. Periodically revisits land users to view implemented land use practices and plans. GOE 02.02.02 PD L456 EC B M4 L4 SVP 7 SOC 1852

041.061-094 STAFF TOXICOLOGIST (gov. ser.)

Studies effects of toxic substances on physiological functions of human beings, animals, and plants to develop data for use in consumer protection and industrial safety programs: Designs and conducts studies to determine physiological effects of various substances on laboratory animals, plants, and human tissue, using biological and biochemical techniques. Interprets results of studies in terms of toxicological properties of substances and hazards associated with misuse of products containing substances. Provides information concerning toxicological properties of products and materials to regulatory agency personnel and industrial firms. Reviews toxicological data submitted by others for adequacy, and suggests amendment or expansion of data to clarify or correct information. Confers with governmental and industrial personnel to provide advice on precautionary labeling for hazardous materials and products and on nature and degree of hazard in cases of accidental exposure or ingestion. Prepares and maintains records of studies for use as toxicological resource material. Testifies as expert witness on toxicology in hearings and court proceedings. GOE 02.02.01 PD L456 EC I6 M6 L5 SVP 8 SOC 1854

041.067-010 MEDICAL COORDINATOR, PESTICIDE USE (gov. ser.)

Studies human health-and-safety aspects of pesticides and other agricultural chemicals: Studies long-term health implications of low-dose pesticide exposure and determines safe worker reentry intervals. Reviews and provides recommendations on medical regulations governing use of pesticides. Reviews information and recommendations pertaining to safe levels of pesticide residues on agricultural products. Recommends specifications for safe working conditions for workers exposed to pesticides or their residues, and makes recommendations on public safety aspects of pesticide exposure. Confers with health department personnel to develop programs to improve ability of physicians and other medical personnel to diagnose, treat, and report pesticide-related illnesses. Confers with government agency representatives, physicians, university staff members, and other research workers to develop health and safety standards related to pesticide exposure. Advises industry representatives on organization of adequate medical supervision programs for employers. Prepares reports on research studies. Addresses interested groups as requested. GOE 02.02.01 PD S5 EC I M5 L6 SVP 9 SOC 1855

041.167-010 ENVIRONMENTAL EPIDEMIOLOGIST (gov. ser.)

Plans, directs, and conducts studies concerned with incidence of disease in industrial settings and effects of industrial chemicals on health: Confers with industry representatives to select occupational groups for study and to arrange for collection of data concerning work history of individuals and disease concentration and mortality rates among groups. Plans methods of conducting epidemiological studies and provides detailed specifications for collecting data to personnel participating in studies. Develops codes to facilitate computer input of demographic and epidemiological data for use by data processing personnel engaged in programing epidemiological statistics. Compares statistics on causes of death among members of selected working populations with those among general population, using life-table analyses. Analyzes data collected to determine probable effects of work settings and activities on disease and mortality rates, using valid statistical techniques and knowledge of epidemiology. Presents data in designated statistical format to illustrate common patterns among workers in selected occupations. Initiates and maintains contacts with statistical and data processing managers in other agencies to maintain access to epidemiological source materials. Evaluates materials from all sources for addition to or amendment of epidemiological data bank. Plans and directs activities of clerical and statistical personnel engaged in tabulation and analysis of epidemiological information to insure accomplishment of objectives. GOE 02.02.01 PD L56 EC I M6 L5 SVP 8 SOC 1854

041.384-010 HERBARIUM WORKER (profess. & kin.)
Fumigates, presses, and mounts plant specimens, and maintains collection records of herbarium maintained by botanical garden, museum, or other institution: Records identification information concerning incoming plants. Places specimens in fumigation cabinet and turns valves to release toxic fumes that destroy insects, fungus, or parasites adhering to specimens. Arranges specimens between sheets of unsized paper so that upper and under portions of leaves, blossoms, and other components are visible, and pads paper with layers of felt and newsprint to protect specimens and form stacks. Places specified number of stacks in pressing frame and writes identification information on top layer of paper on each stack. Secures frame around stacks by tightening frame section with screws, fastening with leather straps, or tying with twine, to compress stacks and press and dry specimens in desired configuration. Mounts dried specimens on heavy paper, using glue, adhesive strips, or needle and thread, taking care to prevent distortion or breakage of specimens. Writes identification information on papers and inserts mounted specimens in labeled envelopes or folders. Files folders in drawers or cabinets according to standard botanical classification system. Maintains card files of specimens in herbarium collection and records of acquisitions, loans, exchanges, or sales of specimens. GOE 02.04.02 PD L46 EC I M3 L4 SVP 5 SOC 399

045.107-046 PSYCHOLOGIST, CHIEF (profess. & kin.)
Plans psychological service programs, and directs, coordinates, and participates in activities of personnel engaged in providing psychological services to clients in psychiatric center or hospital: Reviews reports, case management reviews, and psychiatric center's or hospital's procedural manual to assess need for psychological services. Plans psychological treatment programs that meet standards of accreditation. Plans utilization of available staff, assigns staff to treatment units, and recruits professional and nonprofessional psychological staff. Develops, directs, and participates in training programs. Directs testing and evaluation of new admissions and re-evaluation of present clients. Participates in staff conferences to evaluate and plan treatment programs. Interviews clients that present difficult and complex diagnostic problems and assesses their psychological status. Reviews management of cases, assignments, case problems, issues, and methods of treatment. Works with community agencies to develop effective corrective programs and to arrange to provide psychological services. Plans and supervises psychological research. Collaborates with psychiatrists and other professional staff to help develop comprehensive program of therapy, evaluation, and treatment. GOE 10.01.02 PD S56 EC I M5 L6 SVP 8 SOC 1915

049.364-014 VECTOR CONTROL ASSISTANT (gov. ser.)
Assists public health staff in activities concerned with identification, prevention, and control of vectors (disease-carrying insects and rodents): Carries and sets up field equipment to be used in surveys of number and type of vectors in area. Sets traps and cuts through brush and weeds to obtain specimens of vector population for use in laboratory tests, using sweep. Prepares, mounts, and stores specimens, following instructions of supervisor. Prepares reports of field surveys and laboratory tests based upon information obtained from personnel involved in specific activities, for use in planning and carrying out projects for prevention and control of vectors. GOE 02.04.02 PD L4 EC B M2 L3 SVP 5 SOC 382

054.107-010 CLINICAL SOCIOLOGIST (profess. & kin.)
Develops and implements corrective procedures to alleviate group dysfunctions: Confers with individuals and groups to determine nature of group dysfunction. Observes group interaction and interviews group members to identify problems related to factors such as group organization, authority relationships, and role conflicts. Develops approaches to solution of group's problems, based on findings and incorporating sociological research and study in related disciplines. Develops intervention procedures, utilizing techniques such as interviews, consultations, role playing, and participant observation of group interaction, to facilitate resolution of group problems. Monitors group interaction and role affiliations to evaluate progress and to determine need for additional change. GOE 11.03.02 PD S56 EC I M4 L5 SVP 6 SOC 1916

070.107-018 DIRECTOR, DIAGNOSTIC-AND-EVALUATION CLINIC (medical ser.)
Plans, coordinates, and participates in activities of diagnostic clinic serving suspected mental retardates: Establishes procedures for admitting and examining suspected retardates and providing related services, such as home visits, parent counseling, and followup evaluations. Directs and coordinates activities of staff engaged in clinical, maintenance, and clerical services. Arranges for treatment and specialized diagnostic services performed outside clinic. Conducts conferences with staff to arrive at diagnostic conclusions, resolve administrative problems, and inform staff of changes in responsibilities or procedures. Interprets clinic program to parents and visitors, and explains diagnostic findings and patient-care or rehabilitation recommendations to parents. Represents clinic at professional meetings and in contacts with other agencies. Prepares or directs preparation of records, recommendation, and reports for budgetary approval and for use by public health, welfare, and school officials. Examines patients

and provides emergency or inpatient treatment. Participates in research activities. Instructs clinic staff, medical and nursing students, residents, and interns in diagnosis and treatment of retarded persons. GOE 02.03.01 PD L56 EC I M5 L6 SVP 8 SOC 261

070.117-010 CHIEF OF NUCLEAR MEDICINE (medical ser.)
Directs activities of nuclear technology laboratory, performs nuclear medical research, determines treatment for patients, and instructs medical students in theory and techniques of nuclear medicine in hospital: Formulates policies and directs operation of nuclear laboratory. Coordinates activities of nuclear laboratory with other hospital departments and medical staff. Performs and directs research to develop new uses for nuclear medicine in diagnosis and treatment of patients. Examines patients, evaluates results of tests, confers with physicians, and recommends treatment for patients. Instructs medical students in theory and techniques of nuclear medicine. Attends conferences, seminars, and workshops, and and reads professional and technical journals to acquire knowledge of current information and research in nuclear medicine. GOE 02.03.01 PD L56 EC I M5 L6 SVP 9 SOC 261

070.117-014 DIRECTOR OF RADIOLOGY (medical ser.)
Administers radiology programs and directs and coordinates department activities in accordance with accepted national standards and administrative policies: Plans, organizes, and oversees radiology program in cooperation with hospital officials and other departments. Participates with personnel of other departments to plan joint administrative and technical programs and recommends methods and procedures to coordinate radiological services with other departments. Investigates and studies trends and developments in radiologic practices and techniques. Develops manuals to assist staff members to keep abreast of current methods, procedures, and techniques. Develops and oversees safety programs to insure safe and acceptable use of X-ray equipment and radioactive materials used in diagnosis and therapy. Prepares and submits budgets, reports, records, and statistical data to ADMINISTRATOR, HOSPITAL (medical ser.). Presents lectures, seminars, and on-the-job training to instruct students and interns in theory and practice of radiology. Recommends course of action following diagnosis to provide technical assistance and guidance. Oversees activities of subordinates and uses X-ray equipment to diagnose symptoms and conditions of patients. GOE 02.03.01 PD L56 EC I6 M5 L6 SVP 8 SOC 261

072.117-010 DIRECTOR, DENTAL SERVICES (medical ser.)
Administers dental program in hospital and directs departmental activities in accordance with accepted national standards and administrative policies: Confers with hospital administrators to formulate policies and recommend procedural changes. Establishes training program, using lectures and seminars, to advance skill levels of students and interns involved in dentistry practice. Implements procedures for hiring of professional staff and approves hiring and promotion of all staff members. Establishes work schedules and assigns staff members to duty stations to maximize efficient use of staff. Observes and assists staff members at work to insure safe and ethical practices and to solve problems and demonstrate techniques. Confers with ADMINISTRATOR, HOSPITAL (medical ser.) to submit budget and statistical reports used to justify expenditures for equipment, supplies, and personnel. GOE 02.03.02 PD S56 EC I M5 L5 SVP 8 SOC 262

073.101-018 ZOO VETERINARIAN (medical ser.)
Maintains zoo veterinary clinic and plans, supervises, and participates in all phases of health care program for zoo animal collection: Establishes and conducts effective quarantine and testing procedures for all incoming animals to insure health of collection, prevent spread of disease, and comply with government regulations. Conducts regularly scheduled immunization and preventive care programs to maintain health of animals and guard against spread of communicable diseases. Provides immediate medical attention to diseased or traumatized animals. Participates with other personnel in planning and executing zoo nutrition and reproduction programs for animals in collection. Develops special programs to encourage reproduction among animals designated as belonging to endangered species, based on knowledge of native habitats and instincts. Participates in employee training in handling and care of animals in collection. Conducts postmortem studies and analyses. Develops medical record system and supervises workers engaged in maintenance of records. GOE 02.03.03 PD M3456 EC I6 M5 L5 SVP 8 SOC 27

073.361-014 LABORATORY ASSISTANT, ZOO (medical ser.)
Assists professional veterinary workers in examination and treatment of animals and performance of research: Prepares treatment room for examination of animals and holds or restrains animals during examination, treatment, or innoculation. Hands instruments and materials to professional workers as directed. Sterilizes and cleans instruments. Administers immunization innoculations to animals to comply with quarantine regulations or assist in preventive medicine program. Performs routine laboratory tests, such as urinalyses and blood counts according to established procedures. Prepares vaccines and serums according to standard laboratory methods, and bottles and stores materials for future use. Assists professional workers in performance of autopsies. Maintains records of preventive and therapeutic treatment administered. Assists professional personnel in perform-

ance of tests and maintenance of records associated with various research projects. GOE 02.04.02 PD L46 EC I6 M3 L4 SVP 5 SOC 369

074.131-010 DIRECTOR, PHARMACY SERVICES (medical ser.)

Supervises and coordinates activities of personnel in hospital pharmacy: Plans, establishes, and implements procedures in hospital pharmacy according to standard practices, hospital policies, and legal requirements. Directs pharmacy personnel programs, such as hiring, training, and intern program. Establishes work schedules and assigns pharmacy personnel to work stations, such as research or dispensary. Supervises personnel engaged in maintenance of records, formularies, and reports of drugs and other supplies dispensed, for drug control and budgetary purposes. Analyzes records to indicate prescribing trends and excessive usage. Prepares pharmacy budget, newsletters, and other reports required by hospital administrators. Attends staff meetings to advise and inform hospital medical staff of various drug applications and characteristics. Supervises and assists pharmacy personnel to prepare and dispense drugs. Observes pharmacy personnel at work to insure safe, legal, and ethical practices. Maintains master files of formulas and procedures for stock drugs prepared in pharmacy. Oversees preparation and dispensation of experimental drugs which are in clinical stage of development. Contacts drug wholesalers to order drugs and chemicals to maintain adequate drug stock levels. GOE 02.04.01 PD S456 EC I M6 L6 SVP 8 SOC 301

074.161-014 RADIOPHARMACIST (medical ser.)

Prepares and dispenses radioactive pharmaceuticals used for patient diagnosis and therapy, applying principles and practices of pharmacy and radiochemistry: Receives radiopharmaceutical prescription from PHYSICIAN (medical ser.) and reviews prescription to determine suitability of radiopharmaceutical for intended use. Verifies that specified radioactive substance and reagent will give desired results in examination or treatment procedures, utilizing knowledge of radiopharmaceutical preparation and principles of drug biodistribution. Calculates volume of radioactive pharmaceutical required to provide patient with desired level of radioactivity at prescribed time, according to established rates of radioisotope decay. Compounds radioactive substances and reagents to prepare radiopharmaceutical, following radiopharmacy laboratory procedures. Assays prepared radiopharmaceutical, using measuring and analysis instruments and equipment, such as ionization chamber, pulse-height analyzer, and radioisotope dose calibrator, to verify rate of drug disintegration and to insure that patient receives required dose. Consults with PHYSICIAN (medical ser.) following patient treatment or procedure to review and evaluate quality and effectiveness of radiopharmaceutical. Conducts research to develop or improve radiopharmaceuticals. Prepares reports for regulatory agencies to obtain approval for testing and use of new radiopharmaceuticals. Maintains control records for receipt, storage, preparation, and disposal of radioactive nuclei. Occasionally conducts training for students and medical professionals concerning radiopharmacy use, characteristics, and compounding procedures. GOE 02.04.01 PD M456 EC I6 M5 L5 SVP 7 SOC 301

075.127-030 NURSE SUPERVISOR, EVENING-OR-NIGHT (medical ser.)

Plans, organizes, and directs activities for evening or night shift of hospital nursing department: Establishes policies and procedures for nursing department, following directions of hospital administrators. Observes techniques of and services rendered by nursing staff to insure adherence to hospital guidelines. Demonstrates techniques for nursing students and new personnel to provide training and direction. Identifies problem areas in nursing department, such as understaffing, absenteeism, and wastefulness, and takes corrective action. Monitors use of supplies and equipment to avoid abuses and requisitions supplies. Responds to various departments requesting emergency assistance and assigns staff accordingly during emergencies. Prepares work schedule and assigns duties to nursing staff in department for efficient use of personnel. GOE 10.02.01 PD L456 EC I M4 L5 SVP 8 SOC 29

076.124-018 HORTICULTURAL THERAPIST (medical ser.)

Plans, coordinates, and conducts therapeutic gardening program to facilitate rehabilitation of physically and mentally handicapped patients: Confers with medical staff and patients to determine patients' needs. Evaluates patients' disabilities to determine gardening programs. Conducts gardening sessions to rehabilitate, train, and provide recreation for patients. Revises gardening program, based on observations and evaluation of patients' progress. GOE 10.02.02 PD L3456 EC B M4 L5 SVP 7 SOC 3039

076.127-018 DANCE THERAPIST (medical ser.)

Plans, organizes, and leads dance and body movement activities to improve patients' mental outlooks and physical well-beings: Observes and evaluates patient's mental and physical disabilities to determine dance and body movement treatment. Confers with patient and medical personnel to develop dance therapy program. Conducts individual and group dance sessions to improve patient's mental and physical well-being. Makes changes in patient's program based on observation and evaluation of progress. Attends and participates in professional conferences and workshops to enhance efficiency and knowledge. GOE 10.02.02 PD L2456 EC I M3 L5 SVP 8 SOC 3039

076.264-010 PHYSICAL-INTEGRATION PRACTITIONER (per. ser.)

Conducts physical integration program to improve client's muscular function and flexibility: Determines client's medical history regarding acci-

dents, operations, or chronic health complaints to plan objectives of program, using questionnaire. Photographs client to obtain different views of client's posture to facilitate treatment, using camera. Instructs client to demonstrate arm and leg movement and flexion of spine to evaluate client against established program norms. Determines program treatment procedures and discusses goals of program with client. Applies skin lubricant to section of body specified for treatment and massages muscles to release subclinical adhesions either manually or using handheld tool, utilizing knowledge of anatomy. Demonstrates and directs client's participation in specific exercises designed to fatigue desired muscle groups and release tension. Observes client's progress during program through such factors as increased joint movement, improved posture, or coordination. Records client's treatment, response, and progress. GOE 10.02.02 PD L456 EC I M1 L2 SVP 6 SOC 3033

078.161-014 CARDIOPULMONARY TECHNOLOGIST, CHIEF (medical ser.)

Coordinates activities of CARDIOPULMONARY TECHNOLOGISTS (medical ser.) engaged in performing diagnostic testing and treatment of patients with heart, lung, and blood vessel disorders: Establishes methods for conducting tests and treatments, applying knowledge of medical requirements and laboratory procedures. Schedules patients for tests and treatment by staff members. Reviews reports to insure compliance with test and treatment procedures. Develops and modifies training program for assigned personnel. Evaluates worker performances and recommends promotions, transfers, and dismissals. GOE 02.04.02 PD L456 EC I M4 L5 SVP 7 SOC 369

078.161-018 CHIEF TECHNOLOGIST, NUCLEAR MEDICINE (medical ser.)

Supervises and coordinates activities of NUCLEAR MEDICAL TECHNOLOGISTS (medical ser.): Assigns workers to prepare radiopharmaceuticals, perform nuclear medicine studies, and conduct in vitro and ex vivo laboratory tests, and monitors activities to insure efficiency and accuracy of procedures. Develops protocols for new or revised procedures and trains department workers and other personnel in treatment theory, management of patient, and calibration and use of equipment. Administers radiopharmaceuticals under direction of PHYSICIAN (medical ser.) or other qualified medical personnel. Assists in coordinating activities with other departments and in resolving operating problems. GOE 02.04.02 PD L456 EC I6 M4 L5 SVP 8 SOC 365

078.221-010 IMMUNOHEMATOLOGIST (medical ser.)

Performs immunohematology tests, recommends blood problem solutions to doctors, and serves blood bank and community as consultant and instructor: Visually analyzes blood in specimen tubes to determine temperature and speed of centrifuge for starting hematology tests. Centrifuges blood specimen to separate red cells from serum and examines separated cells to detect presence of antibodies. Interprets evidence observed to devise experiments and suggest techniques that will resolve patient's blood problems. Combines known and unknown serums with red cells in test tubes and selects reagents, such as albumin, protolytic enzymes, and antihuman globulin, for individual tests to enhance and make visible reactions of agglutination and hemolysis. Processes various combinations in centrifuge and examines resulting samples under microscope to identify evidence of agglutination or hemolysis. Repeats and varies tests until normal suspension of reagents, serum, and red cells is attained. Writes blood specifications to meet patient's need, on basis of test results, and applies knowledge of blood classification system to locate donor's blood. Performs hematology tests on donor's blood to confirm matching blood types. Requisitions and sends blood to supply patient's need, and prepares written report to inform physician of test results and of required volume of blood to administer. Forwards copy of report to furnish data input for computer files. Studies worksheets to evaluate completeness of hematology tests and reads labels of related specimen tubes to identify known patients. Instructs MEDICAL LABORATORY TECHNICIANS (medical ser.) in classroom, in work situations, and over telephone to teach techniques of microscopic identification of precipitation, agglutination, or hemolysis in blood that leads to resolutions of problems. Writes notes on worksheets of MEDICAL LABORATORY TECHNICIANS (medical ser.) to suggest possible solutions for specific problems and returns worksheets and specimens to aid personnel in blood bank reference library. GOE 02.04.02 PD L3456 EC I M3 L5 SVP 8 SOC 369

078.262-010 PULMONARY-FUNCTION TECHNICIAN (medical ser.)

Performs pulmonary-function, lung-capacity, and blood-and-oxygen tests to gather data for medical evaluation, following instructions of supervisor: Confers with patient in treatment room to explain test procedures. Explains specified methods of breathing to patient and conducts pulmonary-function tests, such as helium dilution and gross spirometry tests, and lung-capacity tests, such as vital capacity and maximum breathing capacity tests, using spirometer. Activates co-oximeter and injects blood specimen into co-oximeter to perform blood analysis tests, such as oxygen saturation and red cell count. Collects and analyzes contents of expired air of patient, using oxygen analyzer. Observes and records readings on metering devices of analysis equipment, and conveys findings of tests and analyses to supervisor for evaluation. GOE 10.03.01 PD L456 EC I6 M4 L4 SVP 6 SOC 369

078.361-034 RADIATION-THERAPY TECHNOLOGIST (medical ser.)
Operates radiation therapy equipment to treat patients with prescribed doses of ionizing radiation: Positions patient under equipment to expose necessary areas to treatment and adjusts equipment according to instructions. Calculates exposure time and intensity required, using mechanical and electronic regulating controls. Turns controls to operate and adjust equipment and regulate application. Observes dials to monitor duration and intensity of treatment. Prepares and maintains records for review by medical staff. GOE 02.03.04 PD L46 EC I M4 L4 SVP 6 SOC 365

078.362-030 CARDIOPULMONARY TECHNOLOGIST (medical ser.)
Performs diagnostic tests of cardiovascular and pulmonary systems of patients in hospital, using variety of laboratory machines and other work devices, to aid physicians in diagnosis and treatment: Conducts electrocardiogram, phonocardiography, vectorcardiography, ultrasound, stress, cardiac catherization, blood pressure, and other vascular tests to diagnose disorders of cardiovascular system, using variety of laboratory equipment, such as electrocardiograph and phonocardiograph machines, stethoscope, and catheter. Conducts tests of pulmonary system to diagnose pulmonary disorders, using respiratory equipment. Analyzes and interprets test findings and furnishes results to physician. GOE 10.03.01 PD L456 EC I M4 L4 SVP 7 SOC 369

078.362-034 PERFUSIONIST (medical ser.)
Sets up and operates heart-lung machine in hospital to take over functions of patient's heart and lungs during surgery or respiratory failure: Consults with surgeon or physician to obtain patient information needed to set up heart-lung machine. Assembles, sets up, and tests heart-lung machine to insure that machine functions according to specifications. Operates heart-lung machine to regulate blood circulation and composition and oxygen and carbon dioxide levels, to administer drugs, and to control body temperature during surgery or respiratory failure of patient. Changes quantities administered at direction of physician, surgeon, or anesthesiologist. Cleans, repairs, and adjusts malfunctioning parts of heart-lung machine. GOE 10.03.02 PD L456 EC I M3 L4 SVP 7 SOC 369

079.131-010 DIRECTOR, SPEECH-AND-HEARING (medical ser.)
Directs and coordinates activities of personnel in hospital speech and hearing department engaged in research and in testing and treating patients according to established policies: Organizes and establishes personnel procedures, including hiring and training, counsels employees, and evaluates work performance. Confers with ADMINISTRATOR, HOSPITAL (medical ser.) and committee members to request expenditures for equipment, supplies, and personnel. Meets with ADMINISTRATOR, HOSPITAL (medical ser.), department officials, and staff members to explain new techniques and procedures or to demonstrate new and innovative equipment. Plans and directs research and treatment programs to provide direction and assistance to staff members. Conducts workshops and seminars to develop staff expertise and knowledge. Analyzes data and maintains records of research and treatment programs. GOE 11.07.02 PD S56 EC I M5 L5 SVP 8 SOC 131

079.137-010 UTILIZATION-REVIEW COORDINATOR (medical ser.)
Supervises and coordinates activities of utilization review staff and develops policies, standards, and procedures governing admissions and treatment of patients of health-care facility: Analyzes individual patient records to determine legitimacy of admission and continued stay in health-care facility, reviews patient treatment plans to insure adherence to established criteria and standards, and supervises activities of utilization review staff. Reviews and analyzes governmental and accrediting agency standards governing admissions, treatment, and continued stay of patients to develop policies, procedures, and criteria for facility center. Reviews application for patient admission and determines necessity of each admission, applying established admission criteria. Aproves admission or refers case to facility Utilization Review Committee for review and course of action when case fails to meet criteria. Reviews inpatient medical records to determine necessity of continued stay or discharge. Reviews physician treatment plans for inpatients to determine appropriateness of plan to patient manifested conditions and to insure consistency with standard medical practice and facility policies. Makes clinical judgment regarding correctness of physician directed care. Determines next review date in accordance with established diagnostic criteria. Abstracts data from records. Assists review committee in planning and holding federally mandated quality assurance reviews, periodic medical reviews, and professional reviews. Serves as review committee liaison with other committees within facility in development of policies and procedures. Participates in facility orientation and training programs. Supervises and coordinates activities of utilization review staff in maintenance of policy and procedure manuals, file, records, and correspondence. GOE 11.07.02 PD L56 EC I M4 L5 SVP 7 SOC 131

079.224-010 HOME HEALTH TECHNICIAN (medical ser.)
Provides patient care, assistance, and instructions in household management and inhome medical care techniques to patients and families in home or homelike environment: Assists ambulatory and bedridden patient with dressing, bathing, grooming, and elimination. Transfers patient to and from wheelchair, and helps patient to walk to and from bed, shower, tub, and lavatory. Performs procedures and treatments as directed by professional staff, such as massages, hot and cold applications, dressing changes, wound irrigation, enemas, douches, catheterizations, and ostomy care, utilizing knowledge of body structures and function and aseptic techniques. Administers oral medications and injections under medical supervision. Measures and records patient temperature, pulse, and respiration rates, blood pressure, fluid intake and output, and performs throat inspection and urine tests to provide data for health-care team assessment. Teaches patients and family members approved medical techniques, such as mobility training in use of walkers, crutches, and other range-of-motion and supportive devices, to enable continuing home care, utilizing knowledge of physical rehabilitation techniques. Demonstrates basic home management techniques, such as housekeeping, nutrition, meal planning and preparation, and adapts techniques to patient's physical limitations. Guides and encourages patient and family to obtain optimal adjustment to illness or disability. GOE 10.03.02 PD M456 EC I6 M3 L4 SVP 6 SOC 369

079.271-014 ACUPRESSURIST (medical ser.)
Examines patients and analyzes findings to diagnose and treat physical problems according to knowledge and techniques of acupressure: Directs patient to lie on treatment couch and positions patient's arms and legs in relaxed position to facilitate examination and treatment. Examines patient's muscular system visually and feels tissue around muscles, nerves, and blood vessels to locate knots and other blockages which indicate excessive accumulations of blood, water, and other substances in tissue. Determines cause of accumulations and treatment procedures, according to knowledge of acupressure and experience. Feels tissue around muscles, nerves, and blood vessels to locate pressure points and presses at pressure points, using thumbs, fingers, and elbows to redirect accumulated body fluids into normal channels according to acupressure knowledge, techniques, and experience. Discusses findings with patient and explains relationship to internal organs. Outlines course of treatment for patient and advises patient regarding methods and diet for prevention of problem recurrence. Uses specific method or combination of acupressure methods, such as Ghi Ahp, Jin Shin Do, or Shiatsu, and may be known accordingly. GOE 10.02.02 PD M45 EC I M3 L4 SVP 7 SOC 289

079.361-014 ANIMAL HEALTH TECHNICIAN (medical ser.)
Assists veterinary staff to diagnose and treat animals for injury and illness, applying knowledge of veterinary medical assisting procedures and techniques and following directions of veterinary staff: Soothes and quiets patients prior to examination or treatment and restrains patients during examination and treatment to facilitate procedures. Measures and records patient temperature, pulse rate, and respiration as directed. Applies bandages, dressings, and splints, and administers oxygen and oral and injected medications as prescribed. Administers treatments, cleans teeth, removes sutures, and inserts catheters, endotracheal tubes, and related devices as instructed. Draws patient blood and collects specimens as directed. Gathers and positions surgical packs and related instruments and materials for use by veterinary staff during surgery. Administers prescribed preanesthetic drugs to patient, and washes, shaves, and applies antiseptic solution to surgical site to prepare patient for surgery. Monitors patient's vital signs and reflexes during and after surgery and informs veterinary staff of changes. Observes patients in hospital to monitor eating and elimination and to detect abnormal conditions. Conducts test and microscopic examinations of specimens, following standard test and examination procedures and using various laboratory equipment and materials. Dispenses prescribed drugs, maintains prescription records, and inventories supplies of drugs, instruments, and related items. Cleans and sterilizes instruments and materials and maintains equipment and machines. Sets up and operates radiological equipment to conduct X-ray examinations of patients, utilizing knowledge of radiological techniques and procedures. GOE 02.03.03 PD M456 EC I M3 L4 SVP 6 SOC 27

079.364-022 PHLEBOTOMIST (medical ser.)
Draws blood from patients or donors in hospital, blood bank, or similar facility for analysis or other medical purposes: Assembles equipment, such as tourniquet, needles, blood collection devices, gauze, cotton, and alcohol on work tray, according to requirements for specified tests or procedures. Verifies or records identity of patient or donor and converses with patient or donor to allay fear of procedure. Applies tourniquet to arm, locates accessible vein, swabs puncture area with disinfectant, and inserts needle into vein to draw blood into collection tube or bag. Withdraws needle, applies treatment to puncture site, and labels and stores blood container for subsequent processing. May prick finger to draw blood. May conduct interviews, take vital signs, and draw and test blood samples to screen donors at blood bank. GOE 02.04.02 PD L456 EC I M2 L4 SVP 3 SOC 5233

079.374-026 PSYCHIATRIC TECHNICIAN (medical ser.)
Provides nursing care to mentally ill, emotionally disturbed, or mentally retarded patients in psychiatric hospital or mental health clinic and participates in rehabilitation and treatment programs: Helps patients with their personal hygiene, such as bathing and keeping beds, clothing, and living areas clean. Administers oral medications and hypodermic injections, following physician's prescriptions and hospital procedures. Takes and records measures of patient's general physical condition, such as pulse, temperature, and respiration, to provide daily information. Observes patients to detect behavior patterns and reports observations to medical staff. Intervenes to restrain violent or potentially violent or suicidal patients by verbal or physical means as required. Leads prescribed individual or

group therapy sessions as part of specific therapeutic procedures. May complete initial admittance forms for new patients. May contact patient's relatives by telephone to arrange family conferences. May issue medications from dispensary and maintain records in accordance with specified procedures. May be required to hold State license. GOE 10.02.02 PD M45 EC I6 M3 L4 SVP 6 SOC 366

090.222-010 INSTRUCTOR, BUSINESS EDUCATION (education)
Instructs students in commercial subjects, such as typing, filing, secretarial procedures, business mathematics, office equipment use, and personality development, in business schools, community colleges, or training programs: Instructs students in subject matter, utilizing various methods, such as lecture and demonstration, and uses audiovisual aids and other materials to supplement presentations. Prepares or follows teaching outline for course of study, assigns lessons, and corrects homework and classroom papers. Administers tests to evaluate students' progress, records results, and issues reports to inform students of their progress. Maintains discipline in classroom. GOE 11.02.01 PD M456 EC I M4 L5 SVP 8 SOC 2233

099.117-030 DIRECTOR, EDUCATION (museum)
Plans, develops, and administers educational program of museum, zoo, or similar institution: Confers with administrative personnel to decide scope of program to be offered. Prepares schedules of classes and rough drafts of course content to determine number and background of instructors needed. Interviews, hires, trains, and evaluates work performance of education department staff. Contacts and arranges for services of guest lecturers from academic institutions, industry, and other establishments to augment education staff members in presentation of classes. Assists instructors in preparation of course descriptions and informational materials for publicity or distribution to class members. Prepares budget for education programs and directs maintenance of records of expenditures, receipts, and public and school participation in programs. Works with other staff members to plan and present lecture series, film programs, field trips, and other special activities. May teach classes. May speak before school and community groups and appear on radio or television to promote institution programs. May coordinate institution educational activities with those of other area organizations to maximize utilization of resources. May train establishment volunteers to assist in presentation of classes or tours. May develop and submit program and activity grant proposals and applications and implement programs funded as result of successful applications. GOE 11.07.03 PD S56 EC I M4 L5 SVP 7 SOC 1283

099.167-030 EDUCATIONAL RESOURCE COORDINATOR (museum)
Directs operation of educational resource center of museum, zoo, or similar establishment: Maintains collections of slides, video tapes, programed texts, and other educational materials related to institution specialty, storing or filing materials according to subject matter, geographic or ethnic association, or historical period. Composes or directs others in composition of descriptions of materials, and prepares catalog listing materials for use of museum staff members, area school teachers, and others. Compiles list of books, periodicals, and other materials designed to augment items available in resource center. Explains storage and cataloging systems to teachers and others who visit center and suggests materials for various projects, such as preparing school classes for tour of institution or presentation of lecture for community group. Issues loan materials to teachers or lecturer, or schedules and coordinates delivery of materials to designated locations. Maintains records of loans and prepares circulation reports for review by administrative personnel. Conducts workshops to acquaint educators with use of institution's facilities and materials. Attends teacher meetings and conventions to promote use of institution services. GOE 11.07.03 PD L56 EC I M2 L5 SVP 7 SOC 1283

099.227-038 TEACHER (museum)
Teaches classes, presents lectures, conducts workshops, and participates in other activities to further educational program of museum, zoo, or similar institution: Plans course content and method of presentation, and prepares outline of material to be covered and submits it for approval. Selects and assembles materials to be used in teaching assignment, such as pieces of pottery or samples of plant life, and arranges use of audiovisual equipment or other teaching aids. Conducts classes for children in various scientific, history, or art subjects, utilizing museum displays to augment standard teaching methods and adapting course content and complexity to ages and interests of students. Teaches adult classes in such subjects as art, history, astronomy, or horticulture, using audiovisual aids, demonstration, or laboratory techniques appropriate to subject matter. Presents series of lectures on subjects related to institution collections, often incorporating films or slides into presentation. Conducts seminars or workshops for school system teachers or lay persons to demonstrate methods of using institution facilities and collections to enhance school programs or to enrich other activities. Conducts workshops or field trips for students or community groups and plans and directs activities associated with projects. Plans and presents vacation or weekend programs for elementary or preschool children, combining recreational activities with teaching methods geared to age groups. Conducts classes for academic credit in cooperation with area schools or universities. Teaches courses in museum work to participants in work-study programs. Works with adult leaders of youth groups to assist youths to earn merit badges or fulfill other group requirements. Maintains records of attendance. Evaluates success of courses, basing evaluation on number and enthusiasm of persons participating and recom-

mends retaining or dropping course in future plans. When course is offered for academic credit, evaluates class member performances, administers tests, and issues grades in accordance with methods used by cooperating educational institution. GOE 11.02.01 PD L456 EC I M4 L5 SVP 7 SOC 2216

100.117-014 LIBRARY CONSULTANT (library)
Advises administrators of public libraries: Analyzes administrative policies, observes work procedures, and reviews data relative to book collections to determine effectiveness of library service to public. Compares allocations for building funds, salaries, and book collections with statewide and national standards, to determine effectiveness of fiscal operations. Gathers statistical data, such as population and community growth rates, and analyzes building plans to determine adequacy of programs for expansion. Prepares evaluation of library systems based on observations and surveys, and recommends measures to improve organization and administration of systems. GOE 11.07.04 PD S5 EC I M4 L6 SVP 8 SOC 251

102.117-014 DIRECTOR, MUSEUM-OR-ZOO (museum)
Administers affairs of museum, zoo, or similar establishment: Confers with institution's board of directors to formulate policies and plan overall operations. Directs acquisition, education, research, public service, and development activities of institution, consulting with curatorial, administrative, and maintenance staff members to implement policies and initiate programs. Works with members of curatorial and administrative staffs to acquire additions to collections. Confers with administrative staff members to determine budget requirements, plan fund raising drives, prepare applications for grants from government agencies or private foundations, and solicit financial support for institution. Establishes and maintains contact with administrators of other institutions to exchange information concerning operations and plan, coordinate, or consolidate community service and education programs. Represents institution at professional and civic social events, conventions, and other gatherings to strengthen relationships with cultural and civic leaders, present lectures or participate in seminars, or explain institution's functions and seek financial support for projects. Reviews materials prepared by staff members, such as articles for journals, request for grants, and reports on institution programs, and approves materials or suggests changes. Instructs classes in institution's education program or as guest lecturer at university. Writes articles for technical journals or other publications. GOE 11.02.01 PD S56 EC I M4 L6 SVP 8 SOC 252

102.167-014 HISTORIC-SITE ADMINISTRATOR (museum)
Manages operation of historic structure or site: Discusses house or site operation with governing body representatives to form or change policies. Oversees activities of building and grounds maintenance staff and other employees. Maintains roster of volunteer guides, and contacts volunteers to conduct tours of premises according to schedule. Conducts tours, explaining points of interest and answers visitors' questions. Studies documents, books, and other materials to obtain information concerning history of site or structure. Conducts classes in tour presentation methods for volunteer guides. Accepts group reservations for house tours and special social events. Arranges for refreshments, entertainment, and decorations for special events. Collects admission and special event fees, and maintains records of receipts, expenses, and numbers of persons served. Assists in planning publicity, and arranges for printing of brochures or placement of information in media. Inspects premises for evidence of deterioration and need for repair, and notifies governing body of such need. GOE 11.02.01 PD L46 EC I M4 L5 SVP 5 SOC 252

102.167-018 REGISTRAR, MUSEUM (museum)
Maintains records of accession, condition, and location of objects in museum collection, and oversees movement, packing, and shipping of objects to conform to insurance regulations: Observes unpacking of objects acquired by museum through gift, purchase, or loan to determine that damage or deterioration to objects has not occurred. Registers and assigns accession and catalog numbers to all objects in collection, according to established registration system. Composes concise description of objects, and records descriptions on file cards and in collection catalogs. Oversees handling, packing, movement, and inspection of all objects entering or leaving establishment, including traveling exhibits, and confers with other personnel to develop and initiate most practical methods of packing and shipping fragile or valuable objects. Maintains records of storage, exhibit, and loan locations of all objects in collection for use of establishment personnel, insurance representatives, and other persons utilizing facilities. Prepares acquisition reports for review of curatorial and administrative staff. Periodically reviews and evaluates registration and catalog system to maintain applicability, consistency, and operation. Recommends changes in recordkeeping procedures to achieve maximum accessibility to and efficient retrieval of collection objects. Arranges for insurance of objects on loan or special exhibition, or recommends insurance coverage on parts of or entire collection. GOE 07.01.02 PD S56 EC I M4 L5 SVP 6 SOC 252

102.361-014 RESTORER, CERAMIC (museum)
Cleans, preserves, restores, and repairs objects made of glass, porcelain, china, fired clay, and other ceramic materials: Coats excavated objects with surface-active agents to loosen adhering mud or clay and washes objects with clear water. Places cleaned objects in dilute hydrocholoric acid

or other solution to remove remaining deposits of lime or chalk, basing choice of solution on knowledge of physical and chemical structure of objects and destructive qualities of solvents. Cleans glass, porcelain, or similar objects by such methods as soaking objects in lukewarm water with ammonia added, wiping gilded or enameled objects with solvent-saturated swab, or rubbing objects with paste cleanser. Rubs objects with jewelers' rouge or other mild cleanser, soaks objects in distilled water with bleach or solvent added, or applies paste or liquid solvent, such as magnesium silicate or acetone, basing choice of method and material on age, condition, and chemical structure of objects, to remove stains from objects. Recommends preservation measures, such as control of temperature, humidity, and exposure to light, to curatorial and building maintenance staff to prevent damage to or deterioration of object. Impregnates surfaces with diluted synthetic lacquers to reduce porosity of material to increase durability of ancient earthenware. Restores or simulates original appearance of objects by such methods as polishing surfaces to restore translucency, removing crackled glaze and applying soluble synthetic coating, grinding or cutting out chipped edges and repolishing surfaces, or applying matt paints, gold leaf, or other coating to object, basing methods and materials used on knowledge of original craft and condition of objects. Repairs broken objects, employing such techniques as bonding edges together with adhesive, inserting dowel pins in sections and cementing together, or affixing adhesive coated strips to inner portions of broken objects. Replaces missing sections of objects by constructing wire frames of missing sections, shaping plasticene or other materials over frames, affixing modeled sections to objects with dowels or adhesive, and painting attached sections to reproduce original appearance. Constructs replicas of archaeological artifacts or historically significant ceramic ware, basing construction design on size, curvature, and thickness of excavated shards or pieces of objects available and knowledge of techniques and designs characteristic of period. GOE 01.06.02 PD L46 EC I M5 L5 SVP 7 SOC 252

109.067-014   RESEARCH ASSOCIATE (museum)
Plans, organizes, and conducts research in scientific, cultural, historical, or artistic field for use in own work or in project of sponsoring institution: Develops plans for project or studies guidelines for project prepared by professional staff member to outline research procedures to be followed. Plans schedule according to variety of methods to be used, availability and quantity of resources, and number of subordinate personnel assigned to participate in project. Conducts research, utilizing institution library, archives, and collections, and other sources of information, to collect, record, analyze, and evaluate facts. Discusses findings with other personnel to evaluate validity of findings. Prepares reports of completed projects for publication in technical journals, for presentation to agency requesting project, or for use in further applied or theoretical research activities. GOE 11.03.03 PD S56 EC I M6 L6 SVP 7 SOC 252

109.361-010   RESTORER, PAPER-AND-PRINTS (library; museum)
Cleans, preserves, restores, and repairs books, documents, maps, prints, photographs, and other paper objects of historic or artistic significance: Examines or tests objects to determine physical condition and chemical structure of paper, ink, paint, or other coating, in order to identify problem and plan safest and most effective method of treating material. Cleans objects by such methods as sprinkling crumbled art gum or draft powder over surface and rotating soft cloth over cleaning agent to absorb soil (dry cleaning), immersing objects in circulating bath of water or mild chemical solution (wet cleaning), or applying solvent to remove rust, fly specks, mildew, or other stains, basing choice of method on knowledge of physical and chemical structure of objects and effects of various kinds of treatment. Preserves or directs preservation of objects by such methods as immersing paper in deacidification baths to remove acidity from papers and ink to prevent deterioration, sealing documents or other papers in cellulose cases and passing sealed objects through heated rollers to laminate them, spraying objects, storage containers, or areas with fungicides, insecticides, or pesticides, and controlling temperature, humidity, and exposure to natural or artificial light in areas where objects are displayed or stored. Restores objects to original appearance by such methods as immersing papers in mild bleach solution to brighten faded backgrounds, removing old varnish from such art works as engravings and mezzotints, or strengthening papers by resizing in bath of gelatin solution. Repairs objects by such methods as mending tears with adhesive and tissue, patching and filling worm holes, torn corners, or large tears by chamfering, inserting, affixing, and staining paper of similar weight and weave to simulate original appearance, or retouching stained, faded, or blurred watercolors, prints, or documents, using colors and strokes to reproduce those of original artist or writer. GOE 01.06.03 PD S46 EC I M5 L5 SVP 7 SOC 252

109.364-010   CRAFT DEMONSTRATOR (museum)
Demonstrates and explains techniques and purposes of handicraft or other activity, such as candle dipping, horseshoeing, or soap making, as part of display in history or folk museum, or restored or refurbished farm, village, or neighborhood: Studies historical and technical literature to acquire information about time period and lifestyle depicted in display and craft techniques associated with time and area, to devise plan for authentic presentation of craft. Drafts outline of talk, assisted by research personnel, to acquaint visitors with customs and crafts associated with folk life depicted. Practices techniques involved in handicraft to insure accurate and skillful demonstrations. Molds candles, shoes horses, operates looms, or

engages in other crafts or activities, working in appropriate period setting, to demonstrate craft to visitors. Explains techniques of craft, and points out relationship of craft to lifestyle depicted to assist visitors to comprehend traditional techniques of work and play peculiar to time and area. Answers visitor questions or refers visitor to other sources for information. GOE 09.01.02 PD L456 EC B M2 L4 SVP 4 SOC 252

109.367-010   MUSEUM ATTENDANT (museum)
Conducts operation of museum and provides information about regulations, facilities, and exhibits to visitors: Opens museum at designated hours, greets visitors, and invites visitors to sign guest register. Monitors visitors' viewing exhibits, cautions persons not complying with museum regulations, distributes promotional materials, and answers questions concerning exhibits, regulations, and facilities. Arranges tours of facility for schools or other groups, and schedules volunteers or other staff members to conduct tours. Examines exhibit facilities and collection objects periodically and notifies museum professional personnel or governing body when need for repair or replacement is observed. GOE 07.04.04 PD L56 EC I M3 L4 SVP 3 SOC 252

129.027-010   CANTOR (profess. & kin.)
Chants and reads portions of ritual during religious services, and directs congregants in musical activities: Arranges musical portion of religious services in consultation with leader of congregation. Chants or recites religious texts during worship services or other observances and trains and leads congregants in musical responses. May create variations of traditional music or compose music for services. May train and direct choir or teach vocal music to youth or other groups of congregants. GOE 11.07.03 PD L5 EC I M1 L4 SVP 8 SOC 2049

141.137-010   PRODUCTION MANAGER, ADVERTISING (profess. & kin.)
Coordinates activities of design, illustration, photography, paste-up, and typography personnel to prepare advertisements for publication, and supervises workers engaged in pasting-up advertising layouts in art department or studio: Determines arrangement of art work and photographs and selects style and size of type, considering factors such as size of advertisement, design, layout, sketches, and method or printing specified. Submits copy and typography instructions to printing firm or department for typesetting. Reviews proofs of printed copy for conformance to specifications. Assigns personnel to mount printed copy and illustration on final layouts, coordinating assignments with completion of art work to insure that schedules are maintained. Writes instructions for final margin widths and type sizes, and submits layout for printing. Examines layout proofs for quality of printing and conformance to layout. GOE 01.02.03 PD S456 EC I M3 L4 SVP 7 SOC 322

142.061-058   EXHIBIT DESIGNER (museum)
Plans, designs, and oversees construction and installation of permanent and temporary exhibits and displays: Confers with administrative, curatorial, and exhibit staff members to determine theme, content, interpretative or informational purpose, and planned location of exhibit, to discuss budget, promotion, and time limitations, and to plan production schedule for fabrication and installation of exhibit components. Prepares preliminary drawings of proposed exhibit, including detailed construction, layout, and special effect diagrams and material specifications, for final drawing rendition by other personnel, basing design and specifications on knowledge of artistic and technical concepts, principles, and techniques. Submits plan for approval, and adapts plan as needed to serve intended purpose or to conform to budget or fabrication restrictions. Oversees preparation of artwork and construction of exhibit components to insure intended interpretation of concepts and conformance to structural and material specifications. Arranges for acquisition of specimens or graphics or building of exhibit structures by outside contractors as needed to complete exhibit. Inspects installed exhibit for conformance to specifications and satisfactory operation of special effects components. Oversees placement of collection objects or informational materials in exhibit framework. GOE 01.02.03 PD S456 EC I M4 L5 SVP 7 SOC 322

143.260-010   OPTICAL-EFFECTS-CAMERA OPERATOR (motion pic.)
Sets up and operates optical printers and related equipment to produce fades, dissolves, superimpositions, and other optical effects required in motion pictures, applying knowledge of optical effects printing and photography: Reads work order and count sheet to ascertain optical effects specifications and location of subject material on original photography film. Analyzes specifications to determine work procedures, sequence of operations, and machine setup, using knowledge of optical effects techniques and procedures. Loads camera of optical effects printer with magazine of unexposed film stock. Mounts original photography film in transport and masking mechanism of optical-printer projector and moves film into designated position for optical effect, using counter and film markings to determine placement. Adjusts camera position, lens position, mask opening, lens aperture, focus, shutter angle, film transport speed, and related controls, using precision measuring instruments and knowledge of optical effects techniques to determine settings. Selects designated color and neutral density filters and mounts in filter holder to control light and intensity. Sets controls in automatic or manual mode, moves control to start camera, and observes printer operation and footage counter during film-

ing. Adjusts controls during filming operation when operating in manual mode, and stops camera when designated counter reading is observed. Moves controls to rewind camera film and original photography film and repeats select portions or entire operation number of times necessary to produce designated effect. Sets up and operates animation and matte cameras and related equipment to photograph artwork, such as titles and painted mattes. Sets up and operates single pass optical printers when enlarging or reducing film or performing related operations. Sets up and operates subtitle camera and related equipment to photograph film subtitles. Examines frames of film exposed with different combinations of color filters (wedges) to select optimum color balance based on experience and judgment. GOE 01.02.03 PD L46 EC I M3 L3 SVP 7 SOC 326

149.261-010 EXHIBIT ARTIST (museum)
Produces artwork for use in permanent or temporary exhibit settings of museum, zoo, or similar establishment, performing any combination of following duties to prepare exhibit setting and accessories for installation: Confers with professional museum personnel to discuss objectives of exhibits and type of artwork needed. Makes scale drawing of exhibit design, indicating size, position, and general outlines of artwork needed for use of installation and other fabrication personnel. Paints scenic, panoramic, or abstract composition on canvas, board, burlap, or other material to be used as background or component of exhibit, following layout prepared by designer. Paints or stencils exhibit titles and legends on boards, or cuts letters from plastic or plywood to form title and legend copy, and mounts letters on panel or board, using adhesives or handtools. Photographs persons, artifacts, scenes, plants, or other objects, and develops negatives to obtain prints to be used in exhibits. Enlarges, intensifies, or otherwise modifies prints, according to exhibit design specifications. Fashions exhibit accessories, such as human figures, tree parts, or relief maps, from clay, plastic, wood, fiberglass, papier mache, or other materials, using hands, handtools, or molding equipment to cut, carve, scrape, mold, or otherwise shape material to specified dimensions. Brushes or sprays protective or decorative finish on completed background panels, informational legends, and exhibit accessories. Maintains files of photographs, paintings, and accessories for use in exhibits. GOE 01.02.03 PD L46 EC I M3 L4 SVP 6 SOC 325

159.042-010 LASERIST (amuse. & rec.)
Creates optical designs-and-effects show for entertainment of audiences, using control console and related laser projection and recording equipment: Sets up and operates console to control laser projection, recording equipment, and house lights. Presses switches and turns dials to dim house lights, cue opening music, and begin programed laser sequence. Moves controls to orchestrate colors, patterns, and movements in concert with musical accompaniment. Tests, repairs, and adjusts laser and sound systems, using circuit schematics and test equipment. Examines, cleans, and maintains system cooling, optical, and sound equipment according to preventive maintenance schedule. Discusses show concepts and laser equipment operation with press representatives to promote public relations. GOE 05.03.05 PD L456 EC I M3 L4 SVP 6 SOC 328

161.267-030 BUDGET ANALYST (gov. ser.)
Analyzes current and past budgets, prepares and justifies budget requests, and allocates funds according to spending priorities in governmental service agency: Analyzes accounting records to determine financial resources required to implement program and submits recommendations for budget allocations. Recommends approval or disapproval of requests for funds. Advises staff on cost analysis and fiscal allocations. GOE 11.06.05 PD S45 EC I M3 L4 SVP 7 SOC 1419

164.117-018 MEDIA DIRECTOR (profess. & kin.)
Plans and administers media programs in advertising department of food corporation: Confers with representatives of advertising agencies, product managers, and corporate advertising staff to establish media goals, objectives, and strategies within corporate advertising budget. Confers with advertising agents or media representatives to select specific programs and negotiate advertising to insure optimum use of budgeted funds and long-term contracts. Adjusts broadcasting schedules due to program cancellations. Studies demographic data and consumer profiles to identify target audiences of media advertising. Reads trade journals and professional literature to stay informed of trends, innovations, and changes that affect media planning. GOE 11.09.01 PD S456 EC I M4 L5 SVP 8 SOC 125

165.117-014 DIRECTOR, FUNDS DEVELOPMENT (profess. & kin.)
Plans, organizes, directs, and coordinates ongoing and special project funding programs for museum, zoo, or similar institution: Prepares statement of planned activities and enlists support from members of institution staff and volunteer organizations. Develops public relations materials to enhance institution image and promote fundraising program. Identifies potential contributors to special project funds and supporters of institution ongoing operations through examination of past records, individual and corporate contracts, and knowledge of community. Plans and coordinates fund drives for special projects. Assigns responsibilities for personal solicitation to members of staff, volunteer organizations, and governing body according to special interests or capabilities. Organizes direct mail campaign to reach other potential contributors. Plans and coordinates benefit events, such as banquets, balls, or auctions. Organizes solicitation drives for pledges of ongoing support from individuals, corporations, and founda-

tions. Informs potential contributors of special needs of institution, and encourages individuals, corporations, and foundations to establish or contribute to special funds through endowments, trusts, donations of gifts-in-kind, or bequests, conferring with attorneys to establish methods of transferring funds to benefit both donors and institution. Researches public and private grant agencies and foundations to identify other sources of funding for research, community service, or other projects. Supervises and coordinates activities of workers engaged in maintaining records of contributors and grants and preparing letters of appreciation to be sent to contributors. GOE 11.09.02 PD S5 EC I M4 L5 SVP 7 SOC 139

166.167-050 PROGRAM SPECIALIST, EMPLOYEE-HEALTH MAINTENANCE (profess. & kin.)
Coordinates activities of area employers in setting up local government funded program within establishments to help employees who are not functioning at satisfactory levels of job performance due to alcoholism or other behavioral medical problems: Writes and prepares newspaper advertisements, newsletters, and questionnaires and speaks before community groups to promote employee assistance program within business community. Analyzes character and type of business establishments in area, and compiles list of prospective employers appropriate for implementing assistance program. Contacts prospective employers, explains program and fees, points out advantages of program, and reaches agreement with interested employers on extent of proposed program. Develops program within establishment. Establishes committee composed of company officials and workers to develop statement of employee assistance program and policy and procedures. Plans and conducts training sessions for company officials to develop skills in identifying and handling employees troubled by alcoholism or other personal problems. Assists employer in setting up in-plant educational program to prevent alcoholism, using posters, pamphlets, and films, and establishes referral network providing for in-plant and out-of-plant group or individual counseling for troubled employees. Confers with team member of assistance program who provides counseling regarding planning and progress of counseling components. Confers with staff of employee assistance program regarding progress and evaluation of current programs and proposals for developing new programs. GOE 11.05.02 PD S5 EC I M3 L5 SVP 6 SOC 123

166.257-010 EMPLOYER RELATIONS REPRESENTATIVE (profess. & kin.)
Establishes and maintains working relationships with local employers to promote use of public employment programs and services: Contacts employers new to area or company requiring revisit and arranges appointment to visit company representative or employer responsible for hiring workers. Establishes rapport between Employment Service and company to promote use of agency programs and services. Confers with employer to resolve problems, such as local employment office effectiveness, employer complaints, and alternative employer actions for recruiting qualified applicants. Answers employer questions concerning Employment Service programs or services available. Solicits employers to list job openings with Employment Service. Receives job orders from employers by phone or in person and records information to facilitate selection and referral process. GOE 11.09.03 PD L45 EC I M2 L4 SVP 6 SOC 332

166.267-034 JOB DEVELOPMENT SPECIALIST (profess. & kin.)
Promotes and develops employment and on-the-job training opportunities for disadvantaged applicants: Assists employers in revising standards which exclude applicants from jobs. Demonstrates to employers effectiveness and profitability of employing chronically unemployed by identifying jobs that workers could perform. Establishes relationships with employers regarding problems, complaints, and progress of recently placed disadvantaged applicants and recommends corrective action. Assists employers in establishing wage scales commensurate with prevailing rates. Promotes, develops, and terminates on-the-job training program opportunities with employers and assists in writing contracts. Identifies need for and assists in development of auxiliary services to facilitate bringing disadvantaged applicants into job-ready status. Informs business, labor, and public about training programs through various media. GOE 11.03.04 PD S5 EC I M3 L4 SVP 5 SOC 143

166.267-038 PERSONNEL RECRUITER (profess. & kin.)
Seeks out, interviews, screens, and recruits job applicants to fill existing company job openings: Discusses personnel needs with department supervisors to prepare and implement recruitment program. Contacts colleges to set up oncampus interviews. Provides information on company facilities and job opportunities to potential applicants. Interviews college applicants to obtain work history, education, training, job skills, and salary requirements. Screens and refers qualified applicants to company hiring personnel for followup interview. Arranges travel and lodging for selected applicants at company expense. Performs reference and background checks on applicants. Corresponds with job applicants to notify them of employment consideration. Files and maintains employment records for future references. Projects yearly recruitment expenditures for budgetary control. GOE 11.03.04 PD S5 EC I M3 L5 SVP 7 SOC 143

168.161-014 INDUSTRIAL-SAFETY-AND-HEALTH TECHNICIAN (any ind.)

Plans and directs safety and health activities in industrial plant to evaluate and control environmental hazards: Tests noise levels and measures air quality, using precision instruments. Maintains and calibrates instruments. Administers hearing tests to employees. Trains forklift operators to qualify for licensing. Enforces use of safety equipment. Lectures employees to obtain compliance with regulations. Develops and monitors emergency action plans. Investigates accidents and prepares accident reports. Assists management to prepare safety and health budget. Recommends changes in policies and procedures to prevent accidents and illness. GOE 11.10.03 PD L456 EC I M4 L4 SVP 6 SOC 1473

168.167-086 SAFETY MANAGER (medical ser.)

Plans, implements, coordinates, and assesses hospital accident, fire prevention, and occupational safety and health programs under general direction of hospital officials, utilizing knowledge of industrial safety-related engineering discipline and operating regulations: Develops and recommends new procedures and approaches to safety and loss prevention based on reports of incidents, accidents, and other data gathered from hospital personnel. Disseminates information to department heads and others regarding toxic substances, hazards, carcinogens, and other safety information. Assists department heads and administrators in enforcing safety regulations and codes. Measures and evaluates effectiveness of safety program, using established goals. Conducts building and grounds surveys on periodic and regular basis to detect code violations, hazards, and incorrect work practices and procedures. Develops and reviews safety training for hospital staff. Maintains administrative control of records related to safety and health programs. Prepares and disseminates memos and reports. Maintains required records. Assists personnel department in administering worker compensation program. GOE 11.10.03 PD L56 EC I M5 L5 SVP 7 SOC 1473

168.261-010 RADIATION-PROTECTION SPECIALIST (gov. ser.)

Tests X-ray equipment, inspects areas where equipment is used, and evaluates operating procedures to detect and control radiation hazards: Visits hospitals, medical offices, and other establishments to test X-ray machines and fluoroscopes and to inspect premises. Tests equipment to determine that kilovolt potential, alinement of components, and other elements of equipment meet standards for safe operation, using specialized instruments and procedures. Operates equipment to determine need for calibration, repair, or replacement of tubes or other parts. Measures density of lead shielding in walls, using radiometric equipment. Computes cumulative radiation levels and refers to regulations to determine if amount of shielding is sufficient to absorb radiation emissions. Examines license of equipment operator for authenticity and observes operating practices to determine competence of operator to use equipment. Confers with physicians, dentists, and X-ray personnel to explain procedures and legal requirements pertaining to use of equipment. Demonstrates exposure techniques to improve procedures and minimize amount of radiation delivered to patient and operator. Reviews plans and specifications for proposed X-ray installations for conformance to legal requirements and radiation safety practices. Contacts organizations submitting inadequate specifications to explain changes in shielding or layout needed to conform to regulations. GOE 11.10.03 PD L456 EC I M4 L5 SVP 8 SOC 1473

168.267-082 AGRICULTURAL-CHEMICALS INSPECTOR (gov. ser.)

Inspects establishments where agricultural service products, such as livestock feed and remedies, fertilizers, and pesticides, are manufactured, sold, or used to insure conformance to laws regulating product quality and labeling: Visits processing plants, distribution warehouses, sales outlets, agricultural pest control service organizations, and farmers to collect product samples for analysis and to examine fresh and dried produce for spray residue. Inspects product label information concerning ingredients and advertising claims for conformance to chemical analysis of ingredients and documented effects of use. Investigates suspected violations of product quality and labeling laws. Interviews farmers, merchants, and others to determine nature of suspected violations and to obtain documented evidence to be used in legal action against violators. Calls on dealers to determine that licensing requirements have been met, and calls on manufacturers and distributors to collect delinquent tonnage reports. Prepares reports of all inspections and investigations for review by supervisory personnel and for use as evidence in legal action initiated by others. GOE 11.10.03 PD L5 EC B M2 L3 SVP 7 SOC 1473

168.267-086 HAZARDOUS-WASTE MANAGEMENT SPECIALIST (gov. ser.)

Conducts studies on hazardous waste management projects and provides information on treatment and containment of hazardous waste: Participates in developing hazardous waste rules and regulations to protect people and environment. Surveys industries to determine type and magnitude of disposal problem. Assesses available hazardous waste treatment and disposal alternatives, and costs involved, to compare economic impact of alternative methods. Assists in developing comprehensive spill prevention programs and reviews facility plans for spill prevention. Participates in developing spill-reporting regulations and environmental damage assessment programs. Prepares reports of findings concerning spills and prepares material for use in legal actions. Answers inquiries and prepares informational literature to provide technical assistance to representatives of industry,

government agencies, and to general public. Provides technical assistance in event of hazardous chemical spill and identifies pollutant, determines hazardous impact, and recommends corrective action. GOE 11.10.03 PD S5 EC I M3 L5 SVP 7 SOC 1473

168.267-090 INSPECTOR, WATER-POLLUTION CONTROL (gov. ser.)

Inspects sites where discharges enter State waters and investigates complaints concerning water pollution problems: Inspects wastewater treatment facilities at sites, such as mobile home parks, sewage treatment plants, and other sources of pollution. Inspects lagoons and area where effluent enters State waters for such features as obvious discoloration of water, sludge, algae, rodents, and other conditions. Informs owner when unacceptable or questionable conditions are present and recommends corrective action. Notifies mobile laboratory technicians when sampling is required. Advises property owners, facility managers, and equipment operators concerning pollution control regulations. Investigates complaints concerning water pollution problems. Compiles information for pollution control discharge permits. Prepares technical reports of investigations. GOE 11.10.03 PD L5 EC I M4 L5 SVP 7 SOC 1473

168.267-094 MARINE-CARGO SURVEYOR (bus. ser.)

Inspects cargoes of seagoing vessels to certify compliance with national and international health and safety regulations in cargo handling and stowage: Reads vessel documents that set forth cargo loading and securing procedures, capacities, and stability factors to ascertain cargo capabilities according to design and cargo regulations. Advises crew in techniques of stowing dangerous and heavy cargo, such as use of extra support beams (deck bedding), shoring, and additional stronger lashings, according to knowledge of hazards present when shipping grain, explosives, logs, and heavy machinery. Inspects loaded, secured cargo in holds and lashed to decks to ascertain that pertinent cargo handling regulations have been observed. Issues certificate of compliance when violations are not detected. Recommends remedial procedures to correct deficiencies. Measures ship holds and depth of fuel and water in tanks, using sounding line and tape measure, and reads draft markings to ascertain depth of vessel in water. Times roll of ship, using stopwatch. Calculates hold capacities, volume of stored fuel and water, weight of cargo, and ship stability factors, using standard mathematical formulas and calculator. Analyzes data obtained from survey, formulates recommendations pertaining to vessel capacities, and writes report of findings. Inspects cargo handling devices, such as boom, hoists, and derricks, to identify need for maintenance. GOE 11.10.03 PD L456 EC B6 M4 L4 SVP 9 SOC 1473

168.267-098 PESTICIDE-CONTROL INSPECTOR (gov. ser.)

Inspects operations of distributors and commercial applicators of pesticides to determine compliance with government regulations on handling, sale, and use of pesticides: Inspects premises of wholesale and retail distributors to insure that registered pesticides are handled in accordance with State and Federal regulations. Determines that handlers possess permits and sell restricted pesticides only to authorized users. Evaluates pesticides for correct labeling, misbranding, misrepresentation, or adulteration, and confiscates or quarantines unacceptable pesticides. Inspects operations of commercial applicators of pesticides and observes application methods to insure correct use of equipment, application procedures, and that applicators possess valid permits. Determines that accurate records are kept to show pesticides used, dosage, times, places, and methods of applications. Inspects premises to insure that storage and disposal of pesticides conform to regulations. Investigates complaints concerning pesticides and uses. Identifies insect or disease, recommends treatment, and authorizes emergency use of suitable restricted pesticides to respond to emergency situations, such as insect infestations or outbreaks of plant disease. GOE 11.10.03 PD L5 EC I M2 L3 SVP 7 SOC 1473

168.267-102 PLAN CHECKER (gov. ser.)

Examines commercial and private building plans and inspects construction sites to insure compliance with building code regulations: Reviews building plans for completeness and accuracy. Examines individual plan components to insure that all code mandated items are included. Calculates footage between building components, such as doors, windows, and parking areas and amount of area occupied by components to insure compliance with code. Notes instances of noncompliance on plans and correction sheet and suggests modifications to bring plans into compliance. Approves and signs plans meeting code requirements. Inspects building sites and buildings to insure construction follows plans. Submits reports detailing items of noncompliance to builder for correction. Provides code information to individuals planning buildings. Issues occupancy certificates to building owners when completed buildings are in compliance with codes. Tours jurisdictional area to detect unapproved or noncompliance construction. Proposes studies to improve or update building codes. Testifies at appeal hearings regarding buildings alleged to be not in compliance with codes. GOE 05.03.06 PD L456 EC I M4 L4 SVP 7 SOC 1472

168.267-106 REGISTRATION SPECIALIST, AGRICULTURAL CHEMICALS (gov. ser.)

Reviews and evaluates information on applications for registration of products containing dangerous chemicals for compliance with statutory regulations: Reads registration applications from manufacturers and distributors of pesticides, fertilizers, and other products containing dangerous chemicals. Evaluates label information to determine that directions for use and claims for effectiveness of product are stated clearly and accurately. Reviews statements concerning product ingredients, effects of misuse, and administration of antidotes for adequacy of information and conformance to regulatory requirements for substances. Forwards approved applications to other personnel for registration. Contacts manufacturers and distributors of products not meeting standards to clarify regulations and to suggest changes in label information to permit registration. Prepares, organizes, and maintains records to document activities and provide reference materials. Conducts studies and investigations of faulty labeling or use of products as directed by agricultural agency personnel. GOE 11.10.03 PD S5 EC I M3 L4 SVP 7 SOC 1473

168.267-110 SANITATION INSPECTOR (gov. ser.)

Inspects community land areas and investigates complaints concerning neglect of property and illegal dumping of refuse to insure compliance with municipal code: Inspects designated areas periodically for evidence of neglect, excessive litter, and presence of unsightly or hazardous refuse. Interviews residents and inspects area to investigate reports of illegal dumping and neglected land. Locates property owners to explain nature of inspection and investigation findings and to encourage voluntary action to resolve problems. Studies laws and statutes in municipal code to determine specific nature of code violation and type of action to be taken. Issues notices of violation to land owners not complying with request for voluntary correction of problems. Issues notices of abatement to known violators of dumping regulations and informs other municipal agencies of need to post signs forbidding illegal dumping at designated sites. Prepares case materials when legal action is required to solve problems. Conducts informational meetings for residents, organizes neighborhood cleanup projects, and participates in campaigns to beautify city to promote community interest in eliminating dangerous and unsightly land use practices. GOE 11.10.03 PD L5 EC B M2 L3 SVP 5 SOC 1473

168.367-018 CODE INSPECTOR (gov. ser.)

Inspects existing residential buildings and dwelling units, visually, to determine compliance with city ordinance standards and explains ordinance requirements to concerned personnel: Obtains permission from owners and tenants to enter dwellings. Visually examines all areas to determine compliance with ordinance standards for heating, lighting, ventilating, and plumbing installations. Measures dwelling units and rooms to determine compliance with ordinance space requirements, using tape measure. Inspects premises for overall cleanliness, adequate disposal of garbage and rubbish, and for signs of vermin infestation. Prepares forms and letters advising property owners and tenants of possible violations and time allowed for correcting deficiencies. Consults file of violation reports and revisits dwellings at periodic intervals to verify correction of violations by property owners and tenants. Explains requirements of housing standards ordinance to property owners, building contractors, and other interested parties. GOE 05.03.06 PD L56 EC I6 M2 L3 SVP 5 SOC 1473

169.117-014 GRANT COORDINATOR (profess. & kin.)

Develops and coordinates grant-funded programs for agencies, institutions, local government, or units of local government, such as school systems or metropolitan police departments: Reviews literature dealing with funds available through grants from governmental agencies and private foundations to determine feasibility of developing programs to supplement local annual budget allocations. Discusses program requirements and sources of funds available with administrative personnel. Confers with personnel affected by proposed program to develop program goals and objectives, outline how funds are to be used, and explain procedures necessary to obtain funding. Works with fiscal officer in preparing narrative justification for purchase of new equipment and other budgetary expenditures. Submits proposal to officials for approval. Writes grant application, according to format required, and submits application to funding agency or foundation. Meets with representatives of funding sources to work out final details of proposal. Directs and coordinates evaluation and monitoring of grant-funded programs, or writes specifications for evaluation or monitoring of program by outside agency. Assists department personnel in writing periodic reports to comply with grant requirements. Maintains master files on all grants. Monitors all paper work connected with grant-funded programs. GOE 11.05.02 PD S456 EC I M4 L6 SVP 7 SOC 149

169.167-062 COORDINATOR, SKILL-TRAINING PROGRAM (gov. ser.)

Plans and arranges for cooperation with and participation in skill training program by private industry, agencies, and concerned individuals: Organizes and coordinates recruiting, training, and placement of participants. Contacts various service agencies on behalf of trainees with social problems and refers trainees to appropriate agencies to insure trainees receive maximum available assistance. Prepares periodic reports to monitor and evaluate progress of program. GOE 07.01.02 PD L5 EC B M4 L4 SVP 6 SOC 139

169.167-066 LEGISLATIVE ASSISTANT (gov. ser.)

Assists legislator in preparation of proposed legislation: Conducts research into subject of proposed legislation and develops preliminary draft of bill. Analyzes pending legislation and suggests to legislator action to be taken. Briefs legislator on policy issues. Attends committee meetings and prepares reports of proceedings. Speaks with lobbyists, constituents, and members of press to gather and provide information on behalf of legislator. Analyzes voting records of other legislators and political activity in legislator home district to derive data for legislator consideration. Maintains liaison with government agencies affected by proposed or pending legislation. Assists in campaign activities and drafts speeches for legislator. GOE 11.05.03 PD S5 EC I M3 L5 SVP 7 SOC 1139

169.262-010 CASEWORKER (gov. ser.)

Performs research into laws of United States and procedures of Federal agencies and prepares correspondence in office of Member of Congress to resolve problems or complaints of constituents: Confers with individuals who have requested assistance to determine nature and extent of problems. Analyzes U. S. Code to become familiar with laws relating to specific complaints of constituents. Researches procedures and systems of governmental agencies and contacts representatives of Federal agencies to obtain information on policies. Contacts Congressional Research Service to collect information relating to agency policies and laws. Contacts colleges and universities to obtain information relating to constituent problems. Determines action to facilitate resolution of constituent problems. Composes and types letters to Federal agencies and Congressional committees concerning resolution of problems of constituents. Prepares memoranda to inform Member of Congress of problems which require legislative attention. Confers with personnel assisting Member of Congress to discuss introduction of legislation to solve constituent problems. Calculates Social Security benefits, veterans' benefits, tax assessments, and other data concerning constituent complaints, using desk calculator. GOE 07.01.06 PD S456 EC I M3 L4 SVP 5 SOC 1139

169.267-030 PASSPORT-APPLICATION EXAMINER (gov. ser.)

Approves applications for United States passports and related privileges and services: Reviews information on applications, such as applicant's birthplace and birthplaces of applicant's parents, to determine eligibility according to nationality laws and governmental policies. Examines supporting documents, such as affidavits, records, newspaper files, and Bibles, to evaluate relevance and authenticity of documents. Queries applicants to obtain additional or clarifying data. Forwards approved applications to designated official, and prepares summaries for cases not approved indicating points of law. Answers questions of individuals concerning passport applications and related services. GOE 07.01.05 PD L56 EC I M3 L4 SVP 5 SOC 1473

180.161-014 SUPERINTENDENT, HORTICULTURE (museum)

Plans, coordinates, and directs activities concerned with breeding, growing, and displaying ornamental flowers, shrubs, and other plants in botanical garden, arboretum, park, or similar facility: Confers with administrative, technical, and maintenance staff members to plan activities for maintenance of growing stock and production of plants for display on grounds, installation in special exhibits, sale to public, or use in research projects. Discusses plans for renovation or additions to facility with administrative personnel and devises designs for floral exhibits to complement theme of new or renovated sections. Prepares scale drawings of outdoor or greenhouse exhibits for use of gardening staff members. Issues instructions to supervisory personnel in charge of plant growing, greenhouse, and display activities. Inspects greenhouse, hothouses, potting sheds, experimental growing areas, and other areas to determine need for repair and to observe activities of workers. Maintains inventory of propagation and growing equipment and supplies, and orders additional materials as needed. Arranges purchase, sale, or exchange of plants with representatives of similar institutions. Confers with research personnel to discuss development of new strains of plants and to devise methods to exhibit, publicize, or market new products. Represents establishment at civic or professional meetings. Participates in radio or television shows or prepares articles for newspapers to provide horticultural information to public. GOE 02.02.02 PD L456 EC I M4 L5 SVP 8 SOC 5525

187.117-058 DIRECTOR, OUTPATIENT SERVICES (medical ser.)

Supervises and directs activities of outpatient clinic and coordinates activities of clinic with those of other hospital departments: Establishes clinic policies and procedures in cooperation with other hospital officials. Interprets and administers personnel policies and provides for training program. Reviews clinic activities and recommends changes in, or better utilization of, facilities, services, and staff. Establishes and maintains work schedules and assignments of resident professional staff members. Authorizes purchase of supplies and equipment. Prepares and submits budget, records, reports, and statistical data to ADMINISTRATOR, HOSPITAL (medical ser.). Meets with personnel of other local institutions and organizations to promote public health and educational services. Oversees operation of clinic and recommends procedures, treatments, or other course of action to assist medical staff. GOE 11.07.02 PD S56 EC I M5 L6 SVP 8 SOC 131

187.117-062 RADIOLOGY ADMINISTRATOR (medical ser.)

Plans, directs, and coordinates administrative activities of radiology department of hospital medical center: Conducts studies and implements changes to improve internal operations of department. Advises staff and supervisors on administrative changes. Assists hospital officials in preparation of department budget. Conducts specified classes and provides training material to assist in student training program. Directs and coordinates personnel activities of department. Recommends cost saving methods and hospital supply changes to effect economy of department operations. Interprets, prepares, and distributes statistical data regarding department operations. GOE 11.07.02 PD S56 EC I M5 L5 SVP 7 SOC 137

187.134-010 SUPERVISOR, CONTRACT-SHELTERED WORKSHOP (nonprofit organ.)

Supervises and coordinates activities of handicapped individuals in sheltered workshop to train and improve vocational skills for gainful employment through productive work: Assigns individual to specific tasks, such as cleaning, sorting, assembling, repairing, or hand packing products or components. Demonstrates job duties to handicapped individual and observes worker performing tasks to insure understanding of job duties. Monitors work performance at each individual's work station to insure compliance with procedures and safety regulations and to note behavior deviations. Examines work piece visually to verify adherence to specifications. Confers with individuals to explain or to demonstrate task again to resolve work related difficulties. Reassigns individual to simpler tasks when worker cannot perform assigned tasks, or to tasks containing higher degrees of complexity as level of competence is reached. Performs other duties described under SUPERVISOR (any ind.). GOE 11.07.03 PD L45 EC I M2 L2 SVP 7 SOC 127

187.167-202 DIRECTOR, CRAFT CENTER (profess. & kin.)

Plans, organizes, and directs activities of craft center operated by folk or history museum, historic or ethnic area or community, or historic or regional theme park: Consults with administrative personnel to plan activities, such as craft classes, exhibits, and other projects conducted in cooperation with sponsoring institution. Orders supplies needed for basketry, leatherwork, candlemaking, macrame, tole painting, beadwork, or other crafts compatible with institution theme. Plans and writes publicity material for craft classes, and coordinates presentation of craft shows and exhibits, arranging for participants, and overseeing installation of exhibit booths, distribution of publicity materials, and scheduling of craft demonstrations. Maintains inventory, personnel, and accounting records. Arranges for consignment of craft items for sale, directs sales personnel, and maintains records of operation. Reports operational activities to institution administrative staff or governing body, and confers with staff to plan and implement changes in operation of facilities. GOE 11.07.04 PD L456 EC I M4 L5 SVP 7 SOC 1352

188.117-030 COURT ADMINISTRATOR (gov. ser.)

Administers nonjudicial functions of court: Coordinates activities such as jury selection, notification, and utilization, case scheduling and tracking, personnel assignment, and space and equipment allocation to accomplish orderly processing of court cases. Investigates problems that affect caseflow and recommends or implements corrective measures. Compiles and analyzes data on court activity to monitor management performance and prepare activity reports. Conducts research to analyze current and alternative personnel, facilities, and data management systems and consults with judicial staff of court to evaluate findings and recommendations. May oversee accounting of revenues and expenditures and prepare and justify budget. May resolve questions and complaints raised by court personnel, attorneys, and members of other organizations and public. GOE 11.05.03 PD L56 EC I M4 L5 SVP 8 SOC 1131

188.167-110 PLANNER, PROGRAM SERVICES (gov. ser.)

Conducts studies, prepares reports, and advises public and private sector administrators on feasibility, cost-effectiveness, and regulatory conformance of proposals for special projects or ongoing programs in such fields as transportation, conservation, or health care: Consults with administrators or planning councils to discuss overall intent of programs or projects, and determines broad guidelines for studies, utilizing knowledge of subject area, research techniques, and regulatory limitations. Reviews and evaluates materials provided with proposals, such as environmental impact statements, construction specifications, or budget or staffing estimates, to determine additional data requirements. Conducts field investigations, economic or public opinion surveys, demographic studies, or other appropriate research to gather required information. Organizes data from all sources, using appropriate statistical methods to insure validity of materials. Evaluates information to determine feasibility of proposals or to identify factors requiring amendment. Develops alternate plans for program or project, incorporating recommendations, for review of officials. Maintains collection of socioeconomic, environmental, and regulatory data related to agency functions, for use by planning and administrative personnel in government and private sectors. Reviews plans and proposals submitted by other governmental planning commissions or private organizations to assist in formulation of overall plans for region. GOE 11.03.02 PD L56 EC I M5 L6 SVP 7 SOC 192

189.117-038 USER REPRESENTATIVE, INTERNATIONAL ACCOUNTING (electronics)

Directs activities of information systems group engaged in designing, developing, implementing, and maintaining worldwide integrated finance and accounting system utilized by multi-national organization: Studies and analyzes general plan proposal, confers with corporate officials to obtain details of general plan, and obtains systems requirements from corporate and international accounting and management personnel to compile raw data for plan development. Develops methods and procedures for project

accomplishment, applying knowledge of foreign monetary and tax systems and international accounting conventions. Prepares specifications documenting systems and project requirements, including time frame, staffing, activity schedule, and methods and procedures. Interprets international finance and accounting policies and procedures to provide coding assistance to others engaged in systems design and coding. Oversees entering of base data and programs into computer, analyzes output to identify existence and nature of problems, and orders indicated corrections to design or program. Writes procedures manuals for users, reflecting and adapting individual accounting conventions and monetary and tax systems into overall integrated system. Prepares training plan and trains user staff prior to implementation of system. Edits and audits financial and accounting reports to identify problems in installed system and initiates corrective measures. GOE 11.05.02 PD S56 EC I M5 L5 SVP 8 SOC 139

189.167-054 SECURITY CONSULTANT (bus. ser.; per. ser.)

Plans, directs, and oversees implementation of comprehensive security systems for protection of individuals and homes, and business, commercial, and industrial organizations, and investigates various crimes against client: Inspects premises to determine security needs. Studies physical conditions, observes activities, and confers with client's staff to obtain data regarding internal operations. Analyzes compiled data and plans and directs installation of electronic security systems, such as closed circuit surveillance, entry controls, burglar alarms, ultrasonic motion detectors, electric eyes, and outdoor perimeter and microwave alarms. Directs installation and checks operation of electronic security equipment. Plans and directs personal security and safety of individual, family, or group for contracted period. Provides bulletproof limousine and bodyguards to insure client protection during trips and outings. Suggests wearing bulletproof vest when appropriate. Plans and reviews client travel itinerary, mode of transportation, and accommodations. Travels with client and directs security operations. Investigates crimes committed against client, such as fraud, robbery, arson, and patent infringement. Reviews personnel records of client staff and conducts background investigation of selected members to obtain personal histories, character references, and financial status. Conducts or directs surveillance of suspects and premises to apprehend culprits. Notifies client of security weaknesses and implements procedures for handling, storing, safekeeping, and destroying classified materials. Reports criminal information to authorities and testifies in court. GOE 04.02.02 PD L56 EC I6 M3 L5 SVP 7 SOC 5144

195.107-042 CORRECTIONAL-TREATMENT SPECIALIST (social ser.)

Provides casework services for inmates of penal or correctional institution: Interviews inmate and confers with attorneys, judges, and probation officers to compile social history reflecting such factors as nature and extent of inmate criminality and current and prospective social problems. Analyzes collected data and develops and initiates treatment plan. Interviews inmate and consults with employees of institution, such as supervisory personnel, PSYCHOLOGIST, CLINICAL (profess. & kin.), and CHAPLAIN (profess. & kin.), to evaluate inmate social progress, and counsels inmate concerning perceived problems. Reports inmate progress and makes recommendations to parole officials. Assists inmate with matters concerning detainers, sentences in other jurisdictions, and writs. Confers with inmate family to identify family needs prior to inmate release. Occasionally conducts collective counseling for small groups of inmates. Lectures groups of newly admitted inmates to inform them of institution rules and regulations. GOE 10.01.02 PD S5 EC I M3 L5 SVP 7 SOC 2032

195.107-046 PROBATION-AND-PAROLE OFFICER (profess. & kin.)

Counsels juvenile or adult offenders in activities related to legal conditions of probation or parole: Reviews social history of institutionalized offenders due for parole, and talks with offenders regarding development of release plans by parole commission. Determines which juvenile cases fall within jurisdiction of courts and which should be adjusted informally or referred to other agencies. Confers with legal representatives, family, and other concerned persons to conduct prehearing or presentencing investigations. Compiles reports and testifies in courts when requested. Reviews file folders on assigned offenders to determine violation committed and legal stipulation of release. Explains legal requirements to offender, such as visits to office, payment of restitution, and employment requirements to inform offender of release conditions. Interviews offender to formulate release plan and to identify specific problems that hinder probation or parole, such as family indifference, need of employment, and health conditions in need of attention, utilizing interviewing and counseling techniques. Refers offender to other agencies to correct problems, such as drug addiction, educational deficiency, and personality adjustments. Visits and telephones business firms to develop jobs for unemployed offenders. Evaluates offender progress during release with visits to home and place of work. Secures remedial action, or requests leniency by courts, if necessary, when offender behavior justifies such action. GOE 10.01.02 PD L456 EC I6 M3 L5 SVP 7 SOC 2032

195.167-042 ALCOHOL-AND-DRUG-ABUSE-ASSISTANCE PROGRAM ADMINISTRATOR (gov. ser.)

Coordinates government programs dealing with prevention and treatment of alcohol and drug abuse problems affecting work performance of employees in private and public sectors of work force: Studies composition of industrial and business communities and state agencies to determine methods of promoting information concerning alcohol and drug abuse prevention and treatment programs to executives and administrators in industry and government. Confers with management personnel to explain purpose and benefits of Employee Assistance Program, and attempts to establish programs in establishments, organizations, and agencies. Consults with representatives of Area Service Providers (professionals in health care, counseling, and other special services) to develop participation in prevention and treatment programs. Instructs personnel in methods of recognizing and identifying employee problems, referring employee to community Area Service Providers, and maintaining records of program-related activities. Consults with management and administrators of participating organizations and Area Service Providers to evaluate progress of program and identify administrative problems. Implements corrective action plan to solve problems. Develops training materials to be used by participating organizations and Area Service Providers. Prepares articles for newspaper and other media to explain purpose of program. Lectures and participates in workshops, radio and television interviews, community meetings, and other organizational functions to promote acceptance and support of program. Prepares grant proposals and reports for submission to department supervisor. GOE 11.07.01 PD L45 EC I M3 L5 SVP 7 SOC 1139

195.267-018 PATIENT-RESOURCES-AND-REIMBURSEMENT AGENT (gov. ser.)

Investigates financial assets, properties, and resources of hospitalized retarded and brain-damaged clients to protect financial interests and provide reimbursement of hospital costs: Visits and interviews or contacts by mail or telephone relatives, friends, former employers, pension funds, fraternal and veterans organizations and government agencies. Records documentation of financial resources in patient files. Analyzes data accumulated, such as disability allowances, medicare, medicaid, social security pension, dividends, interest, and insurance, and determines ability to pay for hospitalization. Determines additional sources from which reimbursements can be obtained. Prepares reports and enumerates amounts and sources of reimbursements, including public assistance from social agencies in behalf of patients and families. Reviews patients records to insure that reimbursements are maintained. Applies for appointment of conservators to financially protect patients with assets over statutory limits and submits names of appointees to courts. Occasionally attends court hearings to protect patient interests. GOE 10.01.02 PD L456 EC I M3 L5 SVP 7 SOC 2032

195.367-018 COMMUNITY WORKER (gov. ser.)

Investigates problems of residents of assigned neighborhood to determine needs of those disadvantaged because of income, age, or other economic or personal handicaps: Seeks out and assists persons in need of agency services, under direction of professional staff. Visits individuals and families, and addresses neighborhood groups to publicize supportive services available to the unemployed, parolees, or others needing special assistance. Follows-up all contacts and prepares and submits reports of activities. GOE 10.01.02 PD L5 EC B M4 L4 SVP 6 SOC 2032

195.367-022 FOOD-MANAGEMENT AIDE (gov. ser.) nutrition aide.

Advises low income family members how to plan, budget, shop, prepare balanced meals, and handle and store food, following prescribed standards: Advises clients of advantages of food stamps, how to obtain stamps, and use of stamps during shopping trips. Transports clients to shopping area, using automobile. Observes clients' food selections. Recommends alternate economical and nutritional food choices. Observes and discusses meal preparation. Suggests alternate methods of food preparation. Assists in planning of food budget, utilizing charts and sample budgets. Advises clients on preferred methods of sanitation. Consults with supervisor concerning programs for individual families. Maintains records concerning results of family visits. GOE 10.01.02 PD L5 EC I M2 L3 SVP 3 SOC 2032

195.367-026 PREPAROLE-COUNSELING AIDE (gov. ser.)

Provides individual and group guidance to inmates of correctional facility, who are eligible for parole, and assists in developing vocational and educational plans in preparing inmates for reentry into community life: Conducts inmate orientation sessions to explain programs and resources available to inmates and to induce inmates to join programs. Interviews inmates to record data on individual problems, needs, interests, and attitude. Holds individual and group counseling sessions to discuss programs available that affect inmate's reentry into community life, such as housing and financial aid, veteran's benefits, work release programs, vocational rehabilitation, and job search assistance. Prepares and maintains case folder for each inmate and discusses findings with supervisor to obtain assistance in establishing goals and plan of action for inmates. Conducts followup interview to ascertain inmate progress. Prepares correspondence and applications for medicare, medicaid, veteran benefits, food stamps, and housing. Telephones and corresponds with persons and agencies outside facility to insure that family and/or business matters are attended to. Meets with family members at facility to discuss and resolve problems prior to release of inmate. Develops and prepares informational packets for inmate, listing outside agencies and programs that could assist ex-offender upon release. GOE 10.01.02 PD S5 EC I M2 L4 SVP 6 SOC 5133

195.367-030 RECREATION AIDE (social ser.)

Assists RECREATION LEADER (social ser.) in conducting recreation activities in community center or other voluntary recreation facility: Arranges chairs, tables, and sporting or exercise equipment in designated rooms or other areas for scheduled group activities, such as banquets, wedding receptions, parties, group meetings, or sports events. Welcomes visitors and answers incoming telephone calls. Notifies patrons of activity schedules and registration requirements. Monitors spectators and participants at sports events to insure orderly conduct. Receives, stores, and issues sports equipment and supplies. May keep attendance records or scores at sporting events, operate audiovisual equipment, monitor activities of children during recreational trips or tours, or perform other duties as directed by RECREATION LEADER (social ser.). GOE 09.01.01 PD M456 EC I M2 L3 SVP 2 SOC 5269

195.367-034 SOCIAL-SERVICES AIDE (social ser.)

Assists professional staff of public social service agency, performing any combination of following tasks: Interviews individuals and family members to compile information on social, educational, criminal, institutional, or drug history. Visits individuals in homes or attends group meetings to provide information on agency services, requirements, and procedures. Provides rudimentary counseling to agency clients. Oversees day-to-day group activities of residents in institution. Meets with youth groups to acquaint them with consequences of delinquent acts. Refers individuals to various public or private agencies for assistance. May care for children in client's home during client's appointments. May accompany handicapped individuals to appointments. GOE 10.01.02 PD L5 EC I M3 L5 SVP 6 SOC 2032

199.167-018 ENERGY-CONTROL OFFICER (education)

Monitors energy use and develops, promotes, implements, and coordinates energy conservation program in county school district facilities: Compiles monthly energy report on consumption of electricity, fuel, oil, coal, LP gas, and water in school facilities, listing units consumed and costs. Sets up energy monitoring devices in school facilities that graphically plot energy usage and temperature changes during extended periods of time. Visits school facilities on regular basis to inspect monitoring devices and utilities usage. Determines areas in which energy conservation measures are needed, and compiles needs-assessment report of all school facilities. Monitors energy usage of extracurricular activities in school facilities. Coordinates energy conservation activities in areas with those of local, State, and Federal conservation groups. Recommends energy conservation policies to board of education. Presents lectures on resource conservation at teachers' meetings and to civic groups. GOE 05.03.08 PD L56 EC I M4 L4 SVP 7 SOC 399

199.167-022 ENVIRONMENTAL ANALYST (gov. ser.)

Directs, develops, and administers State governmental program for assessment of environmental impact of proposed recreational projects: Directs assessment of environmental impact and preparation of impact statements required for final evaluation of proposed actions. Directs identification and analysis of alternative proposals for handling projects in environmentally sensitive manner. Plans for enhancement of environmental setting for each proposed recreational project. Designs and directs special studies to obtain technical environmental information regarding planned projects, contacting and utilizing various sources, such as regional engineering offices, park region laboratories, and other governmental agencies. Prepares and controls budget for functions of impact-statement preparation program. Attends meetings and represents department on subjects related to program. GOE 11.05.03 PD S5 EC I M3 L4 SVP 8 SOC 1133

199.261-014 PARKING ANALYST (gov. ser.) engineering technician, parking.

Develops plans for construction and utilization of revenue-producing vehicle parking facilitites: Plans and conducts comprehensive field surveys to locate sites for new parking facilities. Analyzes factors such as capacity, turnover, rates, and required property changes relative to proposed sites, and prepares maps, graphs, tracings, and diagrams to illustrate findings. Designs parking lot facilities, including spaces, aisles, driveways, lighting, gates, landscaping, cashier booths, storm drains, grades, and paving details, and prepares cost estimates. Evaluates work performed by contractors to verify conformity to specifications. Keeps log of construction projects and prepares final reports. Reports maintenance problems occurring at facilities to supervisor. Prepares replies to public suggestions and complaints. GOE 05.03.06 PD L456 EC B M4 L5 SVP 7 SOC 399

199.267-034 RESEARCH ASSISTANT (profess. & kin.) II researcher.

Compiles and analyzes verbal or statistical data to prepare reports and studies for use by professional workers in variety of areas, such as science, social science, law, medicine, or politics: Searches sources, such as reference works, literature, documents, newspapers, and statistical records, to obtain data on assigned subject. Analyzes and evaluates applicability of collected data. Prepares statistical tabulations, using calculator or adding machine. Writes reports or presents data in formats, such as abstracts, bibliographies, graphs, or maps. May interview individuals to obtain data or draft correspondence to answer inquiries. When conducting studies to assist lawmakers may be designated LEGISLATIVE AIDE (gov. ser.). GOE 11.08.02 PD S56 EC I M3 L5 SVP 6 SOC 399

203.362-022 WORD-PROCESSING-MACHINE OPERATOR (clerical) word processor.

Operates word processing equipment to record, edit, store, and revise correspondence, reports, statistical tables, forms, and other materials, utilizing clerical skills and knowledge of word processing functions: Reads instructions to determine procedures to be followed regarding material to be prepared or revised and required format for finished copy. Depresses keys on word processing equipment to adjust controls for spacing, margins, and tabulation, and places tape cassette, diskette, or other magnetic recording medium in holder. Keyboards (types) original material into machine memory, typing from printed copy, machine dictation, or related sources. Reads proof copy of material entered into machine memory, and depresses keys to correct typographical errors, print out final copy, and record material onto magnetic medium. Locates medium in file when revisions are required, places medium in holder and presses keys to insert (type), delete, correct, reposition, or reformat designated material. May operate equipment that extends word processing capabilities, such as cathode ray tube displays (CRT's), single or multiple printers, or optical character recognition (OCR). Important variations are kinds (trade names) of word processing equipment operated. May operate electronic typewriters with limited editing capabilities. GOE 07.06.02 PD S456 EC I M1 L3 SVP 4 SOC 4624

203.582-074 ELECTRONIC-TYPESETTING-MACHINE OPERATOR (print. & pub.)

Operates terminal keyboard of electronic typesetting machine and auxiliary equipment, such as photocomposing and developing machines, to produce hard copy of text such as inhouse publications: Measures lines of copy and size of type to be input to determine machine settings required, using printer's rule. Loads disk or tape into electronic typesetting machine and depresses keys to set length and thickness of printed lines. Depresses keys to input material and scans video screen to monitor input. Depresses keys to move cursor (indicator) to point where error occurs and to delete or correct error. Loads completed disk or tape and magazine of photosensitive paper into photocopying machine. Sets font selector controls to select type of specified face and size and starts machine that automatically prints text from disk or tape onto photosensitive paper. Removes magazine of photosensitive paper from photocopying machine at end of cycle, inserts magazine in developing machine, and starts machine. Proofreads developed copy to detect additional errors. Corrects errors on disk or tape, using typesetting machine and video screen, to prepare disk or tape to produce error-free copy. GOE 07.06.02 PD S46 EC I M3 L4 SVP 6 SOC 4793

203.582-078 NOTEREADER (clerical)

Operates typewriter to transcribe stenotyped notes of court proceedings, following standard formats for type of material transcribed: Reads work order to obtain information, such as type of case, case number, number of copies required, and spelling of participant's names. Reviews form books to ascertain format required for specified document, and adjusts typewriter settings for indentation, line spacing, and other style requirements. Operates typewriter to transcribe contractions and symbols of stenotyped text into standard language form. Proofreads typed copy to identify and correct errors and to verify format specifications. Copies typed documents, using copying machines. May use automatic or manual stenotype noteholder. GOE 07.06.02 PD S46 EC I M1 L3 SVP 5 SOC 4624

205.367-062 REFERRAL CLERK, TEMPORARY-HELP AGENCY (clerical) staffing clerk.

Compiles and records information about temporary job openings and refers qualified applicants from register of temporary help agency: Receives call from hospital, business, or other type of organization requesting temporary workers and obtains and records information regarding job requirements. Reviews records to locate registered workers who match organization requirements and are available for scheduled work shift. Notifies selected workers of job availability and records referral information on agency records. Sorts mail, files records, and performs related clerical duties. May give employment applications to applicants, schedule interviews with agency registration interviewers, or administer standard agency skill tests. May specialize in referring specific types of workers, such as nurses. GOE 07.05.03 PD S56 EC I M3 L3 SVP 3 SOC 4692

209.362-030 CONGRESSIONAL-DISTRICT AIDE (gov. ser.)

Provides information and assistance to public and performs variety of clerical tasks in office of congressional legislator: Answers requests for information and assistance from constituents and other members of public, by phone or in person, using knowledge of governmental agencies and programs and source materials, such as agency listings and directories. Transcribes reports and types letters, using electric typewriter. Operates telecopier to receive and send messages, reports, and other documents. Opens and sorts mail according to addressee or type of assistance or information requested. Maintains record of telephone calls. Files correspondence, reports, and documents. Occasionally composes correspondence in response to written requests. Occasionally contacts other governmental or private agencies to act as liaison on behalf of constituents. GOE 07.04.04 PD S46 EC I M3 L4 SVP 5 SOC 463

209.567-022 OFFICE CLERK (clerical)

Performs any combination of following and similar clerical tasks in office where typing is not required: Copies information from one record

to another. Sorts, files, and retrieves records or other documents. Addresses and stuffs envelopes. Sorts and distributes mail. Proofreads records and reports. Duplicates records, using copying machine. Answers telephone and records or relays messages. GOE 07.07.03 PD L456 EC I M2 L3 SVP 2 SOC 463

213.582-010 DIGITIZER OPERATOR (bus. ser.; petrol. production)

Operates encoding machine to trace coordinates on documents, such as maps or drawings, and to encode document points into computer: Reads work order to determine document points to be digitized (encoded). Positions document on digitizer (encoding machine) table. Guides digitizer cursor over document to trace coordinates, stops at specified points, and punches cursor key to digitize points into computer memory unit. Observes monitor screen periodically to verify completeness of encoding. Types command on keyboard to transfer encoded data from memory unit to magnetic tape. Keeps record of work orders, time, and tape production. GOE 07.06.01 PD S46 EC I M3 L2 SVP 5 SOC 4613

214.362-042 BILLING CLERK (clerical)

Operates calculator and typewriter to compile and prepare customer charges, such as labor and material costs: Reads computer printout to ascertain monthly costs, schedule of work completed, and type of work performed for customer, such as plumbing, sheetmetal, and insulation. Computes costs and percentage of work completed, using calculator. Compiles data for billing personnel. Types invoices indicating total costs for project and cost amounts. GOE 07.02.04 PD S46 EC I M3 L3 SVP 4 SOC 4715

219.362-070 TAX PREPARER (bus. ser.) income-tax-return preparer; tax form preparer.

Prepares income tax return forms for individuals and small businesses: Reviews financial records, such as prior tax return forms, income statements, and documentation of expenditures to determine forms needed to prepare return. Interviews client to obtain additional information on taxable income and deductible expenses and allowances. Computes taxes owed, using adding machine, and completes entries on forms, following tax form instructions and tax tables. Consults tax law handbooks or bulletins to determine procedure for preparation of atypical returns. Occasionally verifies totals on forms prepared by others to detect errors of arithmetic or procedure. Calculates form preparation fee according to complexity of return and amount of time required to prepare forms. GOE 07.02.02 PD S56 EC I M4 L3 SVP 4 SOC 4712

221.387-054 BATCH-RECORDS CLERK (fabric. plastics prod.)

Compiles and maintains plastic-mixing and ingredient records, and prepares daily mixing instructions for use by MATERIAL MIXERS (fabric. plastics prod.): Compiles and maintains daily mixing and perpetual inventory records from work orders, mixing logs, and formula cards that indicate production information, such as type and quantity of plastic ingredients mixed, ingredient formulas, number of products molded, and identification numbers of molds and molding machines utilized. Copies formula for each plastic mixture from specified formula card onto display card for use by MATERIAL MIXER (fabric. plastics prod.). Determines and records amount of plastic mixture required for each molding machine in daily mixing log, based on amount of mixture stored at each machine and knowledge of machine's consumption rate. GOE 05.09.02 PD S46 EC I5 M2 L2 SVP 3 SOC 4752

222.387-066 SAMPLE CLERK (fabric. plastics prod.)

Receives and fills requisitions for samples of fabricated plastic products and inspects samples for conformance to company standards: Collects sample products from production lines and inspects samples for conformance to company standards, using specification sheets, gages, and color standard chart. Stores selected samples in sample room, pending requests for samples from sales representatives and customers. Wraps and packs samples, upon request, for shipment. Maintains records of requests received and filled. Maintains perpetual inventory of samples and replenishes sample stock to maintain required levels. GOE 05.09.01 PD L46 EC I M3 L3 SVP 5 SOC 4757

222.387-070 TYPE-LIBRARY CLERK (mach. mfg.)

Issues and stores prints of type characters used in type photography: Reads work order specifications to determine type character prints required and selects prints from files. Examines prints for clarity and sharpness of characters, and measures characters to insure correctness of size and accuracy of dimensions, using millimeter rule. Notifies SUPERVISOR, TYPE PHOTOGRAPHY (mach. mfg.) of prints needing correction or replacement. Sorts and collates prints in order indicated on work order and forwards prints to photographer for processing. Examines letters on prints returned from photographer and adds precut adhesive-backed corners to letters as necessary to compensate for shrinkage of photographed image. Refiles prints in designated files. GOE 05.09.01 PD S46 EC I M2 L2 SVP 3 SOC 4754

230.647-010 SINGING MESSENGER (bus. ser.)

Performs song and dance routines to deliver messages and entertain specified individuals for customers of message delivery service: Practices song and dance routines with experienced worker to become familiar with routines offered by service. Receives customer instructions from dispatcher, selects standard message supplied by service, or records customer's personalized message on form, using typewriter or pen. Applies theatrical makeup and dresses in costume, when necessary; and travels to destination, using vehicle, maps, and customer instructions. Locates recipient of message and performs routine, basing time frame of routine on recipient's reaction. May play musical instruments, such as kazoo or finger cymbals, during routine. May present gift items at conclusion of performance. GOE 07.07.02 PD L2456 EC I M2 L3 SVP 2 SOC 4745

238.367-034 SCHEDULER (museum) education department registrar; museum service scheduler.
Makes reservations and accepts payment for group tours, classes, field trips, and other educational activities offered by museum, zoo, or similar establishment: Provides information regarding tours for school, civic, or other groups, suggests tours on institution calendar, and contacts group leaders prior to scheduled dates to confirm reservations. Provides information regarding classes, workshops, field trips, and other educational programs designed for such special groups as school or college students, teachers, or handicapped persons. Registers groups and individuals for participation in programs, enters registration information in department records, and contacts participants prior to program dates to confirm registration and provide preparatory information. Prepares lists of groups scheduled for tours and persons registered for other activities for use of DIRECTOR, EDUCATION (museum) or other personnel. Collects and records receipts of fees for tours, classes, and other activities. Maintains records of participating groups, fees received, and other data related to educational programs for use in preparation of department reports. May take reservations and sell advance tickets to exhibits, concerts, and other events sponsored by institution, prepare periodic summaries of department activities for review by administrative personnel, or arrange for various support services to facilitate presentation of special activities. GOE 07.05.01 PD S456 EC I M3 L3 SVP 3 SOC 4649

239.367-030 DISPATCHER, STREET DEPARTMENT (gov. ser.)
Receives and records public requests for street maintenance services and relays work orders to maintenance crews, using telephone and two-way radio: Receives telephone requests from public for services, such as street repair, repair of traffic signals, erection of traffic barricades, and snow removal. Relays work orders, messages, and information to or from work crews, supervisors, and field inspectors. Answers routine questions from public and directs requests for other information to designated personnel. Maintains daily log of work orders, messages, or reports received and relayed. GOE 07.04.05 PD S5 EC I M1 L2 SVP 3 SOC 4751

241.367-038 INVESTIGATOR, DEALER ACCOUNTS (finan. inst.)
Visits dealers to verify purchases financed by bank against physical inventory of merchandise, using bank records: Reviews computer printouts listing customer names, addresses, and descriptions of merchandise financed through bank credit and chattel mortgage accounts to plan itinerary of unannounced visits to dealer premises. Explains purpose of visit and locates merchandise in areas, such as showroom, storage room, or car lot. Observes features of merchandise, such as size, color, model, and serial number, to verify item against computer printout. Examines records and questions dealer to determine disposition of items missing from inventory and to elicit information on dealer arrangement for payment to bank for merchandise sold. Records findings on printout and notifies supervisor of unusual findings. GOE 07.05.02 PD L56 EC I M3 L4 SVP 2 SOC 4783

241.367-042 PROPERTY-ASSESSMENT MONITOR (gov. ser.)
Gathers property assessment data at owner premises, verifies data against previously recorded data, and records discrepancies: Visits property, observes premises, and confers with owner to collect and verify property assessment data, using data cards (property assessment records) as guides. Measures and records size of land boundaries and house, using tape measure. Records type of exterior coverings and physical condition of exterior and interior of house. Counts and records number of bathrooms, stoves, and fireplaces. Verifies findings against recorded data and notes discrepancies. Occasionally attends town meetings to answer taxpayer questions regarding use of information contained on data cards. GOE 07.05.02 PD L456 EC I M4 L4 SVP 3 SOC 4799

249.366-010 COUNTER CLERK (photofinish.)
Receives film for processing, loads film into equipment that automatically processes film for subsequent photo printing, and collects payment from customers of photofinishing establishment: Answers customer's questions regarding prices and services. Receives film to be processed from customer and enters identification data and printing instructions on service log and customer order envelope. Loads film into equipment that automatically processes film, and routes processed film for subsequent photo printing. Files processed film and photographic prints according to customer's name. Locates processed film and prints for customer. Totals charges, using cash register, collects payment, and returns prints and processed film to customer. Sells photo supplies, such as film, batteries, and flashcubes. GOE 07.03.01 PD L456 EC I M2 L2 SVP 2 SOC 4363

249.367-082 PARK AIDE (gov. ser.) park technician; ranger aide.
Assists PARK RANGER (gov. ser.) or PARK SUPERINTENDENT (gov. ser.) in operation of State or national park, monument, historic site, or recreational area through performance of any combination of clerical and other duties: Greets visitors at facility entrance and explains regulations. Assigns campground or recreational vehicle sites and collects fees at park offering camping facilities. Monitors campgrounds, cautions visitors against infractions of rules, and notifies PARK RANGER (gov. ser.) of problems. Replenishes firewood and assists GROUNDSKEEPER, PARKS AND GROUNDS (gov. ser.) to maintain camping and recreational areas in clean and orderly condition. Conducts tours of premises and answers visitors' questions when stationed at historic park, site, or monument. Operates projection and sound equipment and assists PARK RANGER (gov. ser.) in presentation of interpretive programs. Provides simple first-aid treatment to visitors injured on premises and assists persons with more serious injuries to obtain appropriate medical care. Participates in carrying out fire-fighting or conservation activities. Assists other workers in activities concerned with restoration of buildings and other facilities, or excavation and preservation of artifacts when stationed at historic or archeological site. GOE 07.04.03 PD L56 EC B M3 L4 SVP 3 SOC 4645

249.367-086 SATELLITE-INSTRUCTION FACILITATOR (education) satellite-project site monitor.
Monitors training programs transmitted by communication satellite from institution of higher learning to remote educational institution or facility: Registers students for satellite communication courses and sells and distributes textbooks and other classroom materials. Activates audiovisual receiver and monitors classroom viewing of live or recorded courses transmitted by communication satellite. Stimulates classroom discussion immediately after broadcast, following standardized format. Monitors live seminar transmittals from institute of higher learning, elicits responses from classroom students, and consolidates and transmits students' questions by teletype or telephone to seminar participants for direct response via satellite. Distributes homework assignments and test blanks to students. Collects completed assignments and tests and mails them to institute of higher learning. Maintains class attendance records. GOE 07.01.02 PD S456 EC I M2 L3 SVP 3 SOC 4795

249.587-018 DOCUMENT PREPARER, MICROFILMING (bus. ser.)
Prepares documents, such as brochures, pamphlets, and catalogs, for microfilming, using paper cutter, photocopying machine, rubber stamps, and other work devices: Cuts documents into individual pages of standard microfilming size and format when allowed by margin space, using paper cutter or razor knife. Reproduces document pages as necessary to improve clarity or to reduce one or more pages into single page of standard microfilming size, using photocopying machine. Stamps standard symbols on pages or inserts instruction cards between pages of material to notify MICROFILM-CAMERA OPERATOR (bus. ser.) of special handling, such as manual repositioning, during microfilming. Prepares cover sheet and document folder for material and index card for company files indicating information, such as firm name and address, product category, and index code, to identify material. Inserts material to be filmed in document folder and files folder for processing according to index code and filming priority schedule. GOE 07.05.03 PD S46 EC I M1 L2 SVP 2 SOC 4759

251.157-014 SALES REPRESENTATIVE, DATA-PROCESSING SERVICES (bus. ser.)
Contacts representatives of government, business, and industrial organizations to solicit business for data-processing establishment: Calls on prospective clients to explain types of services provided by establishment, such as inventory control, payroll processing, data conversion, sales analysis, and financial reporting. Analyzes data-processing requirements of prospective client and draws up prospectus of data-processing plan designed specifically to serve client's needs. Consults SYSTEMS ANALYST, ELECTRONIC DATA PROCESSING (profess. & kin.) and SYSTEMS ENGINEER, ELECTRONIC DATA PROCESSING (profess. & kin.) employed by data-processing establishment to secure information concerning methodology for solving unusual problems. Quotes prices for services outlined in prospectus. Revises or expands prospectus to meet client's needs. Writes order and schedules initiation of services. Periodically confers with clients and establishment personnel to verify satisfaction with service or to resolve complaints. GOE 08.01.02 PD L56 EC I M5 L5 SVP 7 SOC 4152

261.357-074 SALESPERSON, LEATHER-AND-SUEDE APPAREL-AND-ACCESSORIES (ret. tr.)
Sells suede and leather apparel and accessories: Advises customer on selection of apparel and on coordination of accessories, such as handbags, belts, and boots. Answers questions regarding cleaning requirements, color fastness, and durability of article. Packs or wraps customer purchase. Checks merchandise deliveries against packing slips. Tickets merchandise, using ticket gun. Inventories stock. Posts daily sales from sales slips onto inventory sheet. Performs other duties as described under SALESPERSON (ret. tr.; whole. tr.). GOE 08.02.02 PD L456 EC I M3 L3 SVP 5 SOC 4346

295.357-018 FURNITURE-RENTAL CONSULTANT (ret. tr.) decorator consultant; rental clerk, furniture.
Rents furniture and accessories to customers: Talks to customer to determine furniture preferences and requirements. Guides or accompanies customer through showroom, answers questions, and advises customer on compatibility of various styles and colors of furniture items. Compiles list of customer-selected items. Computes rental fee, explains rental terms, and presents list to customer for approval. Prepares order form and lease agreement, explains terms of lease to customer, and obtains customer sig-

nature. Obtains credit information from customer. Forwards forms to credit office for verification of customer credit status and approval of order. Collects initial payment from customer. Contacts customers to encourage followup transactions. May visit commercial customer site to solicit rental contracts, or review floor plans of new construction and suggest suitable furnishings. May sell furniture or accessories [SALESPERSON, FURNITURE (ret. tr.)]. GOE 09.04.02 PD L456 EC I M2 L2 SVP 2 SOC 4363

295.367-026 STORAGE-FACILITY RENTAL CLERK (bus. ser.; ret. tr.)
Leases storage space to customers of rental storage facility: Informs customers of space availability, rental regulations, and rates. Assists customers in selection of storage unit size according to articles or material to be stored. Records terms of rental on rental agreement form and assists customer in completing form. Photographs completed form and customer to establish identification record, using security camera. Computes rental fee and collects payment. Maintains rental status record and waiting list for storage units. Notifies customers when rental term is about to expire or rent is overdue. Inspects storage area periodically to insure storage units are locked. Observes individuals entering storage area to prevent access to or tampering with storage units by unauthorized persons. Loads film into security and surveillance cameras, records dates of film changes, and monitors camera operations to insure performance as required. Cleans facility and maintains premises in orderly condition. GOE 09.04.02 PD L46 EC I M3 L3 SVP 2 SOC 4363

299.677-014 SALES ATTENDANT, BUILDING MATERIALS (ret. tr.) yard salesperson.
Assists customers and stocks merchandise in building materials and supplies department of self-service general store: Answers questions and advises customer in selection of building materials and supplies. Cuts lumber, screening, glass, and related materials to size requested by customer, using powersaws, holding fixtures, and various hand cutting tools. Assists customer in loading purchased materials into customer's vehicle. Moves materials and supplies from receiving area to display area, using forklift or handtruck. Marks prices on merchandise or price stickers, according to pricing guides, using marking devices. Straightens materials on display to maintain safe and orderly conditions in sales areas. Covers exposed materials when required to prevent weather damage. Counts materials and records totals on inventory sheets. GOE 09.04.02 PD H3456 EC I M2 L2 SVP 3 SOC 4362

309.367-010 HOUSE SITTER (dom. ser.)
Occupies and oversees house to maintain order and security of property and conduct necessary business transactions during temporary absence of owner, renter, or other occupant: Monitors entrances to property and secures locks and other devices to prevent access of unauthorized persons. Answers telephone and doorbell, takes messages, and forwards information to employer as requested. Forwards or files mail. Pays current bills from designated funds and makes deposits to accounts as required. Cleans, vacuums, and dusts house, using vacuum cleaner and other housecleaning aids. Feeds and waters pets and takes ill pets to veterinarian for treatment. Inspects utilities, such as plumbing and air conditioning, to detect problems requiring services of repairer and contacts repair establishment to arrange for necessary repairs. May care for swimming pool or grounds or perform other related duties. GOE 09.05.06 PD L46 EC I M2 L2 SVP 2 SOC 509

311.472-010 FAST-FOODS WORKER (hotel & rest.) cashier, fast foods restaurant.
Serves customer of fast food restaurant: Requests customer order and depresses keys of multi-counting machine to simultaneously record order and compute bill [FOOD TABULATOR, AUTOMATED SYSTEMS (hotel & rest.)]. Selects requested food items from serving or storage areas and assembles items on serving tray or in takeout bag. Notifies kitchen personnel of shortages or special orders. Serves cold drinks, using drink-dispensing machine, or frozen milk drinks or deserts, using milkshake or frozen custard machine. Makes and serves hot beverages, using automatic water heater or coffeemaker. Presses lids onto beverages and places beverages on serving tray or in takeout container. Receives payment. May cook or apportion french-fries or perform other minor duties to prepare food, serve customers, or maintain orderly eating or serving areas. GOE 09.04.01 PD L456 EC I M2 L2 SVP 2 SOC 5216

319.464-014 VENDING-MACHINE ATTENDANT (hotel & rest.)
Stocks machines and assists customers in facility where food is dispensed from coin-operated machines: Places food or drink items on shelves of vending machines and changes shelf labels as required to indicate selections. Makes change for customers and answers questions regarding selections. Adjusts temperature gages to maintain food items at specified temperatures. Performs minor repairs or adjustments on machines to correct jams or similar malfunctions, using handtools. Prepares requisitions for food and drink supplies. Cleans interior and exterior of machines, using damp cloth. Maintains eating area in orderly condition. May sell precooked foods from hot table. May remove money from vending machines and keep records of receipts. GOE 09.04.01 PD L56 EC I M2 L2 SVP 2 SOC 5219

331.674-014 FINGERNAIL FORMER (per. ser.)
Forms artificial fingernails on customer's fingers: Roughens surfaces of fingernails, using abrasive wheel. Attaches paper forms to tips of custom-

er's fingers to support and shape artificial nails. Brushes coats of powder and solvent onto nails and paper forms with handbrush to extend nails to desired length. Removes paper forms and shapes and smooths edges of nails, using rotary abrasive wheel. Brushes additional powder and solvent onto new growth between cuticles and nails to maintain nail appearance. May soften, trim, or cut cuticles, using oil, water, knife, or scissors, to prepare customer's nails for application of artificial nails. GOE 09.05.01 PD S46 EC I M1 L2 SVP 3 SOC 5253

349.477-010 JINRIKISHA DRIVER (amuse. & rec.) rickshaw driver.
Conveys passengers to destinations, using three-wheeled vehicle: Pumps pedals and turns handlebars to propel and steer vehicle along roadway to attract and convey passengers for novelty rides. Assists passengers into carriage of vehicle and asks their destination. Records time or odometer reading at start of trip. Conveys passengers to specified destination. Computes fare according to miles traveled or time expended and collects payment. GOE 01.07.03 PD M456 EC O M2 L2 SVP 1 SOC 5269

349.677-018 CHILDREN'S ATTENDANT (amuse. & rec.)
Monitors behavior of unaccompanied children in children's section of theater to maintain order: Escorts children who are unaccompanied by adult between theater entrance and children's section when children enter or leave theater. Maintains order among children and searches for lost articles. Notes when each child enters section and reminds child to go home after witnessing complete performance. GOE 09.05.08 PD L56 EC I M1 L1 SVP 2 SOC 5256

355.374-014 MEDICATION AIDE (medical ser.) pharmacy technician.
Administers prescribed medications to patients and maintains related medical records under supervision of NURSE, GENERAL DUTY (medical ser.), PHARMACIST, HOSPITAL (profess. & kin.), or similar personnel: Receives supply of ordered medications and apportions, mixes, or assembles drugs for administration to patients. Verifies identity of patient receiving medication and records name of drug, dosage, and time of administration on specified forms or records. Presents medication to patient and observes ingestion or other application, or administers medication, using specified procedures. Takes vital signs or observes patient to detect response to specified types of medications and prepares report or notifies designated personnel of unexpected reactions. Documents reasons, such as discharge of patient, prescribed drugs are not administered. May record and restock medication inventories. May give direct patient care such as bathing, dressing, and feeding patients, and assisting in examinations and treatments [NURSE AIDE (medical ser.)]. GOE 10.03.02 PD L456 EC I M3 L3 SVP 4 SOC 5233

355.377-018 MENTAL-RETARDATION AIDE (medical ser.) resident care aide.
Assists in providing self-care training and therapeutic treatments to residents of mental retardation center: Demonstrates activities such as bathing and dressing to train residents in daily self-care practices. Converses with residents to reinforce positive behaviors and to promote social interaction. Serves meals and eats with residents to act as role model. Accompanies residents on shopping trips and instructs and counsels residents in purchase of personal items. Aids staff in administering therapeutic activities, such as physical exercises, occupational arts and crafts, and recreational games, to residents. Restrains disruptive residents to prevent injury to themselves and others. Observes and documents residents' behaviors, such as speech production, feeding patterns, and toilet training, to facilitate assessment and development of treatment goals. Attends to routine health-care needs of residents under supervision of medical personnel. May give medications as prescribed by PHYSICIAN (medical ser.). May train parents or guardians in care of deinstitutionalized residents. GOE 10.03.02 PD M456 EC I M3 L3 SVP 6 SOC 5233

355.674-022 RESPIRATORY-THERAPY AIDE (medical ser.)
Assists personnel in Respiratory Therapy Department of hospital, performing any or all of following tasks: Cleans, disinfects, and sterilizes equipment and supplies used in administration of respiratory therapy, using sponges, brushes, and cleaning solutions, and placing items in sterilization chamber for designated time period to insure absence of contamination. Examines equipment to detect indications of disrepair, such as worn tubes or loose connections, and notifies supervisory staff when such indications are noted. Actuates equipment and observes gages measuring pressure, rate of flow, and continuity to test equipment, and notifies supervisor when malfunctions are observed. Assists supervisory personnel in maintenance of inventory records. Delivers oxygen tanks and other equipment and supplies to specified hospital locations. Answers phone and takes and relays messages regarding department operations. Assists in administration of gas or aerosol therapy to patients. GOE 10.03.02 PD M456 EC I M3 L3 SVP 4 SOC 5233

359.363-010 HEALTH-EQUIPMENT SERVICER (medical ser.)
Delivers, installs, demonstrates, and maintains rental medical equipment, such as respirator, oxygen equipment, hospital beds, and wheel chairs, for use in private residences: Loads medical equipment on truck and delivers equipment to renter's or patient's residence. Unloads, installs, and sets up equipment, using handtools. Inspects and maintains rental oxygen equipment, performing such tasks as inspecting hoses and water traps to detect leaks and condensation; observing gages of oxygen analyzer, pressure

gages, and other monitoring equipment to determine pressure and oxygen content of air output of compressors and concentrators; and changing filters. Maintains record on oxygen equipment by hours of usage to determine need for maintenance. GOE 10.03.02 PD H456 EC I6 M2 L3 SVP 5 SOC 5233

359.367-014 WEIGHT-REDUCTION SPECIALIST (per. ser.) nutrition educator.

Assist clients in devising and carrying out weight-loss plan, using established dietary programs and positive reinforcement procedures: Interviews client to obtain information on weight development history, eating habits, medical restrictions, and nutritional objectives. Weighs and measures client, using measuring instruments, and enters data on client record. Discusses eating habits with client to identify dispensable food items and to encourage increased consumption of high nutrition, low calorie food items, or selects established diet program which matches client goals and restrictions. Explains program and procedures which should be followed to lose desired amount of weight, and answers client questions. Reviews client food diary at regular intervals to identify eating habits which do not coincide with established or agreed upon dietary program, and reviews weight loss statistics to determine progress. Counsels client to promote established goals and to reinforce positive results. May photograph client during therapy to provide visual record of progress. May conduct aversion therapy, utilizing electric shock, rancid odors, and other physical or visual stimulus to promote negative association with food designated for elimination from diet. May conduct positive conditioning therapy sessions, utilizing physical and visual stimulus to promote positive association with foods designated for increase in diet. May give client weight-loss aids, such as calorie counters, or sell nutritional products to be used in conjunction with diet program. GOE 09.05.01 PD 456 EC I M2 L3 SVP 3 SOC 5269

359.677-030 RESEARCH SUBJECT (any ind.) subject, scientific research.

Submits to scientifically conducted research relating to such fields as medicine, psychology, or consumer-product testing: Participates in activities such as performing physical tasks, taking psychological tests, or using experimental products, following instructions of researcher. Replies verbally or records responses to questionnaire to provide researcher with data for evaluation. GOE 09.05.06 PD L5 EC I M2 L3 SVP 1 SOC 5269

377.267-010 DEPUTY UNITED STATES MARSHALL (gov. ser.)

Enforces law and order under jurisdiction of Federal courts: Receives prisoners into Federal custody. Escorts prisoners to and from jails and courts and guards prisoners during hospitalization. Provides protection to court personnel, jurors, and witnesses or their families. Serves civil and criminal writs. Reviews records, gathers information, and traces and arrests individuals named in criminal warrants. Assists Federal agencies in matters such as investigations, raids, and arrests as directed. Seizes property pursuant to court orders. GOE 04.01.02 PD M456 EC B6 M2 L3 SVP 5 SOC 5134

379.263-014 PUBLIC-SAFETY OFFICER (gov. ser.)

Patrols assigned beat and responds to emergency calls to protect persons or property from crimes, fires, or other hazards: Patrols assigned area on foot or horseback or using vehicle to regulate traffic, control crowds, prevent crime, or arrest violators. Responds to crimes in progress, initiating actions such as aid to victims and interrogation of suspects. Attends public gatherings to maintain order. Responds to fire alarms or other emergency calls. Forces openings in buildings for ventilation of fire or for entry, using ax or crowbar. Controls and extinguishes fires, using water and chemicals. Administers first aid and artificial respiration to injured persons. Participates in drills and emergency precautionary demonstrations. May inspect establishments for compliance with local regulations. May drive and operate firefighting and other emergency equipment. GOE 04.01.02 PD V2456 EC B4567 M3 L3 SVP 7 SOC 5149

379.364-014 BEACH LIFEGUARD (amuse. & rec.)

Patrols public beach area to monitor activities of swimmers and prevent illegal conduct: Observes activities in assigned area on foot, in vehicle, or from tower or headquarters building with binoculars to detect hazardous conditions, such as swimmers in distress, disturbances, or safety infractions. Cautions people against use of unsafe beach areas or illegal conduct, such as drinking or fighting, using megaphone. Rescues distressed persons from ocean or adjacent cliffs, using rescue techniques and equipment. Examines injured individuals, administers first aid, and monitors vital signs, utilizing training, antiseptics, bandages, and instruments, such as stethoscope and sphygmomanometer. Administers artificial respiration, utilizing cardiopulmonary or mouth-to-mouth methods or oxygen to revive persons. Compiles emergency and medical treatment report forms and maintains daily information on weather and beach conditions. Occasionally operates switchboard or two-way radio system to maintain contact and coordinate activities between emergency rescue units. GOE 04.02.03 PD V456 EC O M2 L2 SVP 4 SOC 5149

379.367-010 SURVEILLANCE-SYSTEM MONITOR (gov. ser.)

Monitors premises of public transportation terminals to detect crimes or disturbances, using closed circuit television monitors, and notifies authorities by telephone of need for corrective action: Observes television screens that transmit in sequence views of transportation facility sites. Pushes hold button to maintain surveillance of location where incident is developing, and telephones police or other designated agency to notify authorities of location of disruptive activity. Adjusts monitor controls when required to improve reception, and notifies repair service of equipment malfunctions. GOE 04.02.03 PD S56 EC I M1 L3 SVP 2 SOC 5149

383.684-010 EXTERMINATOR HELPER (any ind.) pest control worker helper.

Assists EXTERMINATOR (any ind.) in destroying and controlling field rodents, noxious weeds, or other pests in or around buildings, performing any combination of following tasks: Sets traps and places poisonous bait in rodent infested areas. Fumigates burrows, using toxic gas, or kills rodents, using firearms. Secures tarpaulins over building to be fumigated, using ladder. Applies insecticides to buildings and grounds, using spray pumps and other equipment. Digs up, sprays with herbicides, or burns noxious weeds. Identifies and reports evidence of pest infestation. May drive service vehicles or equipment. Performs other duties as described under HELPER (any ind.).. GOE 05.10.09 PD M234 EC B37 M2 L2 SVP 4 SOC 5246

406.684-018 GARDEN WORKER (agric.; museum) gardener-florist.

Cultivates and cares for ornamental plants and installs floral displays in indoor or outdoor settings through performance of any combination of following duties as directed by supervisory personnel: Conditions and prepares soils and plants seeds, seedlings, or bulbs in greenhouse or outdoor growing area, using spades, trowels, sprayers, sprinklers, cultivators, and other gardening handtools and equipment. Fertilizes, waters, weeds, transplants, or thins plants in growing areas. Mixes and applies pesticides to maintain health of plants and prepare plants for installation in greenhouse or outdoor display areas. Lays sod or artificial grass and builds framework for indoor floral displays, or prepares outdoor display beds according to work plan. Transplants plants from growing area to display beds, or places potted plants in beds according to work plans. Attends display beds to maintain health of plants and beauty of display. Maintains and repairs gardening handtools and equipment and structures, such as greenhouses and hot beds, using maintenance and carpentry tools. May mow lawns, prune trees, and perform other duties to maintain grounds. GOE 03.04.04 PD M346 EC B M2 L3 SVP 4 SOC 5622

408.364-010 PLANT-CARE WORKER (agric.) interior horticulturist; plant tender.

Cares for ornamental plants on various customer premises, applying knowledge of horticultural requirements, and using items such as insecticides, fertilizers, and gardening tools: Reads work orders and supply requisitions to determine job requirements, and confers with supervisor to clarify work procedures. Loads plants and supplies onto truck in order of scheduled stops, using handtruck. Drives truck to premises and carries needed supplies to work area. Examines plants and soil to determine moisture level, using water sensor gage, and waters plants according to requirements of species, using hose and watering can. Sponges plant leaves to apply moisture and remove dust. Observes plants under magnifying glass to detect insects and disease, and consults plant care books or confers with supervisor to identify problems and determine treatments. Selects and applies specified chemical solutions to feed plants, kill insects, and treat diseases, using hose or mist-sprayer. Transplants rootbound plants into larger containers. Pinches and prunes stems and leaves to remove dead and diseased leaves, to shape plants, and to induce growth, using shears. Removes diseased and dying plants from premises and replaces them with healthy plants. Informs customer of plant care needs. Enters record of actions taken at each stop in route book and prepares requisitions for materials needed on subsequent visit. Returns diseased, dying, and unused plants and supplies to employer premises. GOE 03.04.05 PD M456 EC I67 M2 L3 SVP 3 SOC 5619

410.161-022 HOG-CONFINEMENT-SYSTEM MANAGER (agric.)

Breeds and raises swine in confinement buildings for purpose of selling pork to meatpacking establishments: Selects and breeds swine according to knowledge of animals, genealogy, characteristics, and offspring desired. Regulates breeding of sow herd to produce maximum number of litters. Attends sows during farrowing and helps baby pigs to survive birth and infancy. Castrates and docks pigs. Notches ears to identify animals. Determines weaning dates for pigs based on factors such as condition of sows, cost of feed, and available space in nursery. Vaccinates swine for disease and administers antibiotics and iron supplements, using syringes and hypodermic needles. Formulates rations for swine according to nutritional needs of animals and cost and availability of feeds. Grinds and mixes feed and adds supplements to satisfy dietary requirements. Stores and periodically examines feeds to insure maintenance of appropriate temperatures and moisture levels. Operates water foggers, air conditioners, fans, and heaters to maintain optimal temperature in swine confinement buildings. Flushes hog wastes into holding pit. Repairs and maintains machinery, plumbing, physical structures, and electrical wiring and fixtures in swine farrowing, nursery, and finishing buildings. May hire and supervise worker to assist in swine production activities. GOE 03.01.01 PD M456 EC I M4 L4 SVP 7 SOC 5514

ENCYCLOPEDIA SECTION

- Communication Through Language
- Special Compositions
- Reading Skills
- Where to Write for Vital Records
- The Business World
- World History
- American History
- Authors and Their Works
- States and Countries
- Condensed World Gazetteer
- Quick Reference World Maps
- Math Formulas/Equivalent Measures
- Metric Conversions
- Cooking and Nutrition
- Four-Year Colleges and Universities
- Computer Science
- Computer Glossary
- Music Glossary
- Geology
- Astronomy
- Biology
- Physics
- Space Glossary
- The Shuttle Era

COMMUNICATION THROUGH LANGUAGE

BASIC TOOLS

Punctuation Marks

Many of us look on marks of punctuation as annoying inventions of English teachers to make the hard job of writing even harder. Consequently, we ignore punctuation whenever we can, which is most of the time, and turn over the job of inserting the proper marks to instructors, copy editors, or to anyone else likely to get a mysterious pleasure from the process.

Actually, punctuation is almost as essential to clear writing as words themselves are. It is the function of words to identify meanings, and it is the function of punctuation to package the meanings in usable clumps, like phrases, clauses, and sentences. Imagine trying to read this page if all the letters were run together (for spacing is punctuation, too) from top to bottom, with no capital letters, no breaks, no clumping of word groups. Punctuation really *says* things, just as words do, but it says them more economically. A period, for example, says "Pause here. A complete thought has been expressed." And so with all the other marks.

Punctuation also serves another vital function, that of stylistic effectiveness. When you speak, of course, you use physical means to achieve clarity and vigor. You raise and lower your voice; you emphasize a point with a gesture of your finger; you speak rapidly and then slowly to provide contrast; you say particular words with unusual stress. None of this could be passed on to your reader, however, if you did not use punctuation

marks. The reader of a well-punctuated page almost feels as if he were listening to you speak.

So do not underestimate the importance of punctuation. No writing is good if it is not clear, and no writing is clear if it is not well punctuated.

TERMINAL MARKS

Marks of punctuation that have the power to end a sentence are called "terminal marks." A sentence may be brought to an end without necessarily being complete; that is, it does not have to possess a full subject and predicate. The terminal mark may be used with a phrase, or even a single word. The following are examples of how terminal marks may be used:

Questions and Answers
    What are you doing? Not much.

Imperatives
    Do it now. Go. Don't.

Exclamations
    What luck! Bah! Humbug!

We generally think that the period, question mark, and exclamation mark are the only terminal marks. This is not so. Two other marks have the power to end a sentence. The dash can interrupt or summarily end a sentence before it is completed; and the colon–essentially a mark of introduction–can terminate an introductory statement when what follows it begins with a capital letter.

Dash as a Terminal Mark

"I swear I never again will drive a—" The mad honking of automobiles cut him short.

Colon as a Terminal Mark

In conclusion, I make this promise: If elected, I shall serve you to the best of my ability.

These are only incidental uses of the dash and colon, however. The three chief terminal marks are still the period, question mark, and exclamation mark.

Note: To avoid confusion with examples and quoted material, we will use block paragraphs in the following sections on punctuation and grammar.

Period

The period (.) is the most common terminal mark of punctuation. It presents few problems to students. The only difficulties ordinarily encountered are in distinguishing between abbreviations that take periods and abbreviations that are accepted as the shortened forms of proper names and do not take periods. The other difficulty with the period is its use in relation to other marks of punctuation. The rules for use of the period are given below.

A period is used at the end of a declarative sentence.

We have nothing to fear but fear itself. *–Franklin D. Roosevelt*

A period is used at the end of an imperative sentence.

Go at once.
She said, "Help me."

Do not use a period when an imperative sentence is so strong that it becomes an exclamation. Such a sentence is followed by an exclamation mark. Whether an imperative sentence is ended by a period or an exclamation mark depends entirely on the degree of emphasis desired.

"Go at once!" he shouted.
"Help!" she cried.

A period is used at the end of a sentence that is interrogative in form but to which an answer is not required.

Children, will you stop that noise at once.

A period is used to represent a decimal point.

17.4°   75.2% $1.75

A period is used after figures and letters to represent principal divisions of lists.

IV. Gross income
　A. Expenses
　　1. Net income
　　　a. Net earnings per share

Do not use a period when the figures or letters are in parentheses.

(IV) Gross income
　(A) Expenses
　　(1) Net income
　　　(a) Net earnings per share

A period is used with most abbreviations.

A.M.	P.M.	Mrs.	Ave.	etc.
Mon.	Jan.	treas.	i.e.	M.D.
F.D.R.	John F. Kennedy			L.B.J.

Do not use a period after a person's nickname, or after the shortened form of a person's name.

Sue   Hank   Doug   Bob

Do not use a period after letters of the alphabet used in place of a person's name.

Mr. A told Mr. B   X said to Y

Do not use a period after the call letters of radio and TV stations.

WPIX   KLOB   ABCTV

Do not use a period after familiar shortened forms of common words.

tab   ad   el   lab   electro

Do not use a period with abbreviations that are accepted as the shortened forms of proper names.

OWI	Pan Am	MiG
TWA	FBI	SAC

Do not use a period after Roman numerals except to represent principal divisions of lists.

Henry V   Act III   Vol. II
Ecclesiastes II   Matthew V

Do not use a period after ordinal endings of numbers.

3rd   6th   21st   92nd

Do not use a period with mathematical equations, trigonometrical terms, or chemical symbols.

$y \times 4 = y^2$ log   sin H_2O

Do not use a period with the abbreviated form of the words *manuscript* and *manuscripts*.

> MS   MSS

Do not use periods with the following miscellaneous abbreviations (notice the proper spacings):

> S O S (radio distress call)
> I O U (I owe you)
> A B C's (Know your A B C's)

Do not use a period after the initials of the writer and the secretary in business letters (which appear in the bottom left-hand corner).

> JRS:BS   HTB:fn   rmm:ns   tdc/al

In Relation to Other Marks of Punctuation

The period is not used in addition to a question mark or an exclamation mark at the end of a sentence. It is always placed inside closing quotation marks.

The period is placed outside the closing parenthesis when the parenthesis encloses the last word of a sentence. The period is placed inside the closing parenthesis only when what is enclosed in parentheses is a complete sentence and the first letter is capitalized.

> This is called the law of natural selection (Darwinism).

> This is called the law of natural selection. (This law cannot be too highly stressed in the study of biology.)

When a sentence ends with an abbreviation that requires a period of its own, no second period is added.

> For your first day in school, you must remember to take paper, pencils, erasers, etc.

Question Mark

The question mark (?) follows an interrogative word, phrase, clause, or sentence. It has the power to end a sentence, yet it may also punctuate a quotation within a sentence without ending the sentence. This mark is always used to indicate a question.

A question mark should follow every direct question.

> Have you done your homework?

> "What time is it?" he asked.

Do not use a question mark after an indirect question.

> I was asked if I had finished my homework.

> He asked what time it was.

Do not use a question mark at the end of an interrogative sentence to which no answer is required.

> Will you please enter my name on your mailing list.

Do not use a question mark after a question that is actually an exclamation.

> How could you!   How dare you!

A declarative expression may be transformed into a question by the mere addition of a question mark.

> The train was late.   The train was late?
> Really.   Really?

A question mark is enclosed in parentheses after a fact that is doubtful.

> America was first visited by a white man in A.D. 1000 (?).

> The crowd numbered 650 (?) cheering students.

A question mark in parentheses should not be used to indicate irony.

Poor   This is a great (?) book.

Better   This is hardly a great book.

When more than one question is asked in a sentence, a question mark may or may not be used depending upon the degree of emphasis desired. For emphasis, each separate question begins with a capital letter and terminates with its own question mark. A single question mark is used at the end of a sentence when the questions within the sentence are related and form a unified thought.

> The teacher asked, "How large is Berlin? What is its population? and In what country is it located?"

> How am I expected to know the size, population, and location of a city when I don't have an atlas?

More than one question mark placed for special emphasis does not conform to accepted usage. A period or a comma is never used in addition to the question mark.

Wrong   Did you really like that play?.

Right   Did you really like that play?

Wrong   "Will you come with us?," she asked.

Right   "Will you come with us?" she asked.

The question mark should be placed inside quotation marks if it belongs to the quotation (as shown in the example immediately above). It should be placed outside quotation marks if it does not belong to the quotation.

> Who first said, "Haste makes waste"?

Exclamation Mark

The exclamation mark (!) adds forceful emphasis to a declarative word, expression, or sentence. The exclamation mark is used after a strong command or exhortation.

> "Get out!" she screamed.

> "Don't shoot!" he pleaded.

The exclamation mark is used after an expression of strong emotion.

> What a stroke of luck!

> How the mighty are fallen!

An interjection is a word that expresses emotion. It may be strong enough on its own merit not to require an exclamation mark. The exclamation mark merely helps to strengthen it.

> Oh, what a beautiful day.

> Wow! What a blizzard.

The exclamation mark is placed either immediately after an interjection that begins a sentence, or at the end of the sentence introduced by an interjection.

> Whew! That was a close call.

> Oh, what a beautiful day!

COMMA

The comma is a comparatively weak but subtle mark of punctuation. It is used–and misused–more frequently than any other punctuation mark. This is because the comma has such varied functions. Chiefly, it introduces, separates, and encloses. In addition, it indicates omission. None of these functions is performed by the comma with the authority or finality of such marks as the colon, semicolon, or dash. All the comma indicates is a mild pause, hence its subtle, elusive nature. In the rules for comma usage that follow, the term "to separate" means that the comma separates a word, phrase, or clause from the rest of the sentence. A single comma is used to separate. The term "to enclose" means that an expression appearing within a sentence is enclosed in commas. Two commas are used to enclose: one comma is placed immediately preceding, and the other following, the expression. When an expression to be enclosed ends the sentence, a period is used instead of the second enclosing comma.

Quoted References

A comma is used to introduce a short quotation, maxim, or proverb.

> Helen said, "It's a lovely day."

> The saying is, "Time waits for no man."

Do not use a comma to introduce a formal quotation or a quotation that consists of two or more sentences. A colon is used instead of the comma (see page 9). Do not use a comma to introduce a quoted word or phrase that is the subject or object of a sentence.

> "Fourscore and seven years ago" is the most famous opening passage of any address ever made.

> The president spoke on "Our Relations with Latin America."

> Obey the "Slow down" signs.

> Must you always ask "Why?"

> Can't you say "Thank you" occasionally?

Do not use a comma preceding a quotation introduced by the conjunction *that*.

Wrong   The travel poster suggested that, "California is the land of sunshine."

Right   The travel poster suggested that "California is the land of sunshine."

A comma is used after a quotation to separate such expressions as *he said* and *she replied*. Commas are used to enclose such expressions when they break into or interrupt a quotation.

> "It's a grand day," Bill said.

> "The weather is perfect," she said, "for the Winter Carnival."

Do not use a comma in addition to a question mark or mark of exclamation following a quotation.

Wrong   "Do you think we can leave early?," she asked.

Right   "Do you think we can leave early?" she asked.

Series Separation

Commas are used to separate words, phrases, and clauses in a series. (In journalistic writing the comma is frequently omitted before the final conjunction in a series. This practice is not sanctioned in formal writing.)

> Our American professors like their literature clear, cold, pure, and very dead. *–Sinclair Lewis*

> All the things I really like to do are either immoral, illegal, or fattening.*–Alexander Woollcott*

Do not use commas when the conjunction is repeated before each item in a series.

Wrong   It rained, and thundered, and hailed.

Right   It rained and thundered and hailed.

Do not use a comma after the last item in a series.

Wrong   We planted roses, violets, and nasturtiums, in our garden.

Right   We planted roses, violets, and nasturtiums in our garden.

Commas are used to separate two or more coordinate adjectives modifying the same noun. Adjectives may be considered coordinate when they are in a series and the coordinating conjunction *and* can be readily substituted for the comma.

> Caroline is a comely, tow-headed girl.

> John is a short, stocky, powerful wrestler.

Do not use the comma to separate adjectives that appear as part of a compound noun, that is, if *and* cannot be readily substituted for the comma.

Wrong   She is a comely, little girl.

Right   She is a comely little girl.

Do not use the comma to separate one adjective that modifies another.

Wrong   He has a deep, tan sunburn.

Right   He has a deep tan sunburn.

Separation in Compound Sentences

A comma is used to separate the main (independent) clauses of a sentence joined by coordinating conjunctions like *and, but, or, nor, for,* and *yet.*

> It's better to give than to lend, and it costs about the same.*–Philip Gibbs*

> My folks didn't come over on the *Mayflower,* but they were there to meet the boat.*–Will Rogers*

We do not know what to do with this short life, yet we want another which will be eternal.*–Anatole France*

> Arguments are extremely vulgar, for everybody in good society holds exactly the same opinions.*–Oscar Wilde*

Do not use a comma to separate main clauses when the clauses already contain commas within them. A semicolon is used instead of the comma (see page 10).

Do not use a comma to separate main clauses when they are short and are closely connected in thought, provided that the omission of the comma will not lead to a misreading.

Wrong   Grace picked up the photo that stood on the table and walked away. (The omission of the comma in this sentence could be misread as referring to picking up a photo that walked away.)

Right   Grace picked up the photo that stood on the table, and walked away.

Do not use a comma to separate main clauses when the second clause has the same subject as the first clause and the subject is not repeated.

> She was a brunette by birth but a blonde by habit.*–Arthur Baer*

> Poverty is very good in poems but very bad in the house; very good in maxims and sermons but very bad in practical life.*–Henry Ward Beecher*

A comma is used to separate an introductory subordinate phrase or clause from a main clause. Such clauses often begin with subordinating conjunctions (*when, if, because, since, while, as,* etc.).

> Where all think alike, no one thinks very much.*–Walter Lippmann*

> When you get to the end of your rope, tie a knot and hang on.*–Franklin Delano Roosevelt*

> If you're there before it's over, you're on time.*–James J. Walker*

A comma is used to separate an introductory phrase containing a participle or an infinitive used as an adjective or an adverb.

> Drawing on my fine command of knowledge, I said nothing.*–Robert Benchley*

> To keep your friends, treat them kindly; to kill them, treat them often.*–George D. Prentice*

Do not use a comma to separate a gerund or an infinitive phrase that is the subject of the sentence.

Wrong   Writing carelessly, causes bad grades.

Right   Writing carelessly causes bad grades.

To profit from good advice requires more wisdom than to give it.–*John Churton Collins*

Parenthetical Expressions, Appositives

Commas are used to enclose such parenthetical expressions as the following: *to tell the truth, in the main, generally speaking, you must admit, I should say, I know, I believe, we may understand, in short, for one thing, in the long run, for the most part, in fact,* and *it is true.*

Opera in English is, in the main, just about as sensible as baseball in Italian.–*H. L. Mencken*

The greatest of faults, I should say, is to be conscious of none.–*Thomas Carlyle*

Thomas Carlyle

Commas are used to enclose the parenthetical expressions *for example, for instance,* and *that is.*

Take, for example, the poets we have been reading.

Consider the books we have been reading, for instance.

This is not an adequate map, that is, not from an artist's point of view.

Commas are used to enclose nonlimiting (also called "nonrestrictive") phrases and clauses within a sentence. Though it may add information and help clarify meaning, a nonlimiting phrase or clause is not necessary to identify the word or words it modifies. It can be omitted from the sentence without changing the meaning. A limiting (also called "restrictive") phrase or clause, however, is necessary to identify the word or words it modifies. An integral part of the sentence, a limiting phrase or clause is *not* enclosed in commas.

Nonlimiting: *The Spirit of St. Louis,* which Lindbergh flew across the Atlantic, was a single-engine airplane.

Limiting: The airplane that Lindbergh flew across the Atlantic was *The Spirit of St. Louis.*

Commas are used to enclose a parenthetical aside that interrupts the free flow, or thought, of a sentence and that can be omitted without changing the meaning of the sentence. An aside–like other parenthetical expressions–may add information, but the essential thought of the sentence is complete without it.

That, like it or not, is the way to learn to write; whether I have profited or not, that is the way.–*Robert Louis Stevenson*

Age carries all things, even the mind, away.–*Virgil*

Commas are used to enclose words in apposition. An appositive is a noun or a pronoun (or any group of words used as a noun or a pronoun) that is set beside another noun or pronoun having the same meaning. An appositive adds information, but it is not absolutely essential to the meaning or clarity of the sentence.

Helen, my sister, is coming to the prom.

Roger Martin Du Gard, the author, was a close friend of André Gide.

Do not use commas to enclose limiting or "restrictive" appositives. A limiting appositive is absolutely necessary to the meaning and clarity of the sentence, because it actually identifies a particular person or thing. A limiting appositive is frequently part of a name.

My sister Helen is coming to the prom. (My sister Helen is coming, not my sister Barbara.)

The author Roger Martin Du Gard was a close friend of André Gide.

Expressions Not in Normal Order

Commas are used to enclose an expression that does not appear in its normal order in the sentence.

Not normal order: A cynic is a man who, when he smells flowers, looks around for a coffin.–*H. L. Mencken*

Normal order: A cynic is a man who looks around for a coffin when he smells flowers.

Omissions

A comma is used to take the place of one or more omitted words. Usually the comma takes the place of a verb or verb phrase.

> To love and win is the best thing; to love and lose, the next best.–*William Makepeace Thackeray*

> To eat is human; to digest, divine.–*Mark Twain*

Direct Address

A comma is used to separate a word or words in direct address, either at the beginning or the end of a sentence. When an expression in direct address appears within the sentence, commas are used to enclose it.

> Sir, I wish to leave the room.

> I move, Mr. Chairman, that the motion be put to a vote.

Contrasts

A comma is used to separate letters, words, phrases, or clauses that are contrasted. Such contrasts are generally introduced by the word *not*.

> We live in deeds, not years; in thoughts, not breaths.–*Philip James Bailey*

> Genius is born, not paid.–*Oscar Wilde*

Direct Questions

A comma is used to separate a direct question from the rest of the sentence. The first word of the direct question may be capitalized or not, depending upon how much the writer wishes to emphasize the question.

> The question is, where do we go from here?

> Have you ever asked yourself the question, Why am I here?

> I wondered, what do I do next?

Interjections

A comma is used to separate mild interjections from the rest of the sentence. When the interjection appears within the sentence, commas are used to enclose it. (An interjection becomes an exclamation when it is followed by an exclamation mark [see page 4].)

> Well, let me see now.

> Oh, why, oh, why did I ever do that?

Do not use a comma when such words as *well* and *why* are used as adverbs.

> Well done, team.

> Why am I not good enough for you?

Do not use a comma immediately following the vocative *O* (that is, when *O* is used to emphasize the name of a person or persons being addressed).

> O ye Gods, grant us what is good, whether we pray for it or not, but keep evil from us, even though we pray for it.–*Plato*

However, you should use a comma after the interjection *O*.

> O, for a draught of vintage!–*John Keats*

Yes and No

A comma is used to separate the words *Yes* and *No* from the rest of the sentence.

> Yes, it was a wonderful book.

> No, you are not to leave.

> I have already given my answer and that is, no.

Do not use a comma when the word *Yes* or *No* is a direct object.

> Jane answered yes to the suggestion.

> I said to tell him no.

Emphasis

A comma may be used to separate a word or words strictly for emphasis, or to add an element of surprise. This is a subtle use of the comma. The dash is used more frequently for emphasis and surprise (see page 11).

> I spent a year in that town, one Sunday. –*Warwick Deeping*

> One would think that only a policeman would be safe in the subway, these days.

Ordinal Adverbs

Commas are used to separate ordinal adverbs (*first, second, third,* etc.) and ordinal adverb phrases such as *in the first place* and *in the second place.*

> First, I wish to announce that the library will be open during the Christmas recess; second, that all borrowed books must be returned on or before the first day of classes.

> In the first place, there isn't time; in the second, we don't have the facilities to do a proper job.

Figures

Commas are used to separate the digits in figures above 999. The comma is placed preceding every third digit, counting backward from the last digit. Note that in sums of money the digits denoting cents are not counted.

> 1,000   1,999   2,000   12,605
> $99.00 $999,000 $1,000,000
> $2,105,602,000.46

Do not use the comma in numbers denoting dates.

> The Trojan War began in 1194 B.C.

> George Orwell's *1984* is a remarkable book.

Do not use the comma in page numbers, telephone numbers, and street numbers. The comma is also not generally used in serial numbers.

> You will find the reference on page 1201.

> Please phone me at 212-8915.

Do not use the comma in decimals.

> .1329   .89641

Do not use the comma in numbers denoting dimensions, weights, and measures.

> 6 ft. 3 in.   10 feet 11 inches

> 11 hr. 38 min.   11 hours 38 minutes

Commas are used to enclose the year when the year immediately follows the name of the month.

> In December, 1964, John moved to Los Angeles.

> May 8, 1945, was the day Germany formally surrendered, ending World War II in Europe.

A comma is used to separate unrelated figures that appear next to each other.

> In 1960, 68,837,000 presidential votes were cast—an increase of 6,800,000 from the presidential election of 1956.

Addresses

Commas are used to enclose the name of a state when it immediately follows the name of a city or town.

> John moved from Denver, Colorado, to Los Angeles, California.

Do not use the comma in addresses to separate digits in street numbers, nor to separate the street number from the street itself.

> This is to notify you that I have moved my address from 1135 Biscayne Blvd., Miami, Florida, to 1060 Park Ave., New York, N.Y.

Titles and Degrees

Commas are used to enclose an abbreviation or phrase that denotes a person's title or degree, when it follows the person's name.

> Lyndon B. Johnson, President of the United States, will address the United Nations.

> Henry Nathan, M.D., and Lester Hawthorne, Ph.D., are the expert witnesses for the defense.

Initials

Commas are used to enclose a person's initials when the initials follow the person's name.

> The authors are Johnson, L. M., and Scott, N. R.

Letters

A comma is used to separate the salutation of a friendly, informal letter from the body of the letter.

> Dear Bill,   Dear Susan,   Dear Mother,

Do not use a comma after the salutation in a formal business letter. A colon is used instead.

> Dear Mr. Marks: Dear Sir:

A comma is used to separate the complimentary close of both informal and business letters from the writer's signature.

> Sincerely,   Yours truly,

COLON

The colon (:) is a formal mark of punctuation. It has two functions only: to introduce and to separate. As a mark of introduction, the colon introduces formal quotations, restatements or clarifying examples, and lists or enumerations. As a mark of separation, the colon separates the salutation in a formal letter from the main body of the letter, titles from subtitles, scenes of plays from acts, etc. A colon is used to introduce a formal quotation.

> Franklin D. Roosevelt said: "We have nothing to fear but fear itself."

> The first line of Franz Kafka's *The Trial* reads: "Someone must have been telling lies

about Joseph K., for without having done anything wrong he was arrested one fine morning."

Do not use a colon to introduce a maxim, a proverb, or a quotation of a single sentence in ordinary dialogue.

> The saying is, "A stitch in time saves nine."

> John said, "Let's go to the movies."

A colon is used to introduce all quotations longer than one sentence.

> As John left the theatre he said: "I liked the play. I must recommend it to my friends."

The colon may take the place of such expressions as *in effect, in other words,* and *namely* to introduce new statements, restatements, and clarifying examples.

> Readers are of two sorts: one who carefully goes through a book, and the other who as carefully lets the book go through him. –*Douglas Jerrold*

James Russell Lowell

> Whatever you may be sure of, be sure of this: that you are dreadfully like other people.– *James Russell Lowell*

The colon is used to introduce formal lists and enumerations.

> I have come to the following conclusions:

> Kindly forward the items listed:

> Mix the ingredients as follows:

The colon is used in reference to time to separate hours from minutes.

> 10:15 A.M.   6:50 P.M.

The colon is used to separate a subtitle from a main title.

> *Wheat: The Staff of Life*

> *My Father: A Memoir of Mark Twain*

The colon is used to separate a scene from an act in a play.

> Act III: scene ii

The colon is used to separate verse from chapter in the Bible.

> The Song of Solomon 2:1

> Ezekiel 10:6

In reference matter, the colon is used to separate the home office from the name of a publishing firm.

> Chapel Hill, N.C.: University of North Carolina Press

> New York: Basic Books

The colon is used following the salutation in a formal business letter.

> Dear Mr. Jones: Dear Sir: Gentlemen:

In Relations to Other Marks of Punctuation

The colon takes the place of the period after an abbreviation, such as *etc.*

> The following synthetic materials contain dacron, nylon, aquilon, etc:

When the colon appears together with closing quotation marks, the colon always follows the quotation marks.

> The teacher said, "Please answer the following questions":

The colon always follows a closing parenthesis.

> The librarian recommended the following books (all by Maugham):

The colon commonly used to be joined with the dash. This is no longer accepted usage.

Wrong   We must follow these rules:–

Right   We must follow these rules:

SEMICOLON

The semicolon, consisting of a period atop a comma (;), is strictly a mark of separation. Unlike a colon, it does not introduce; unlike a comma, it does not enclose; and, unlike a period, it does not terminate. Its sole function is to separate parts of sentences that cannot be separated by the comma. It marks a greater break or a longer pause than the comma, yet it does not carry the full authority of the period and other terminal marks to end a sentence.

A semicolon separates main (independent) clauses of a sentence when those clauses are not already joined by coordinating conjunctions like *and, but or, neither, nor, for,* and *yet.*

Abraham Lincoln

With educated people, I suppose, punctuation is a matter of rule; with me it is a matter of feeling. But I must say I have a great respect for the semicolon; it's a useful little chap.
–Abraham Lincoln

A semicolon separates the main (independent) clauses of a sentence when the clauses are joined by coordinating conjunctions but when one or more already contain commas.

Don't ever prophesy; for if you prophesy wrong, nobody will forget it; and if you prophesy right, nobody will remember it. *–Josh Billings*

If you have charm, you don't need to have anything else; and if you don't have it, it doesn't matter what else you have.*–James M. Barrie*

A semicolon separates main (independent) clauses of a sentence that are joined by conjunctive adverbs like *thus, however, consequently, therefore, accordingly, besides,* and *moreover.*

I do best in subjects that relate to science; consequently, I plan to major in science next year.

He is taking six courses this semester; however, he has given up his part-time job and will have more time to study.

A semicolon separates items in a series when parts of the items are already separated by commas. The reason is that without the semicolon, the main parts would be indistinguishable.

The winners were: John, first; Bill, second; Tom, third.

New York Central has railroad stations in Chicago, Illinois; Sante Fe, New Mexico; and Los Angeles, California.

In Relation to Other Marks of Punctuation

A semicolon is always placed outside quotation marks.

Play the "Appassionata Sonata"; play it with feeling this time.

A semicolon appearing next to words in par-entheses is always placed after the closing parenthesis.

The advanced math course intrigues me (with the possible exception of geometry); basketball practice, however, intrigues me more.

DASH

The dash (—) is roughly twice the length of a hyphen. On the typewriter it is indicated by two successive hyphens. The dash is extraordinarily versatile. It can perform any one of the four major functions of punctuation: introduction, separation, enclosure, and termination. In addition, the dash can indicate interruption and omission (of words, letters, figures). The dash is often used indiscriminately, especially by beginning writers, precisely because it is so versatile. It is, after all, a conspicuous, highly obtrusive mark of punctuation. Properly used, the dash is an ideal method of injecting an element of irony or surprise into a sentence, but to accomplish this it must be used sparingly. Other marks of punctuation can usually take the place of the dash, and they should be substituted for it whenever one of the rules given below does not completely justify its use.

In the past, other marks of punctuation–the colon, in particular–were commonly used with the dash. Proper usage now requires the dash to stand alone. Do not confuse the dash with the shorter hyphen (see page 14).

The dash indicates a sudden break or change of thought.

Where was I on the night of last July 10? I was in my home–no, let me think, maybe I was at the theater.

Are you–do you feel all right?

The dash is used following a direct quotation to indicate an interruption in discourse.

"Really, now you ask me," said Alice, very much confused, "I don't think—"

"Then you shouldn't talk," said the Hatter.*–Lewis Carroll*

Dashes may be used to set off a parenthetical thought to give it strong emphasis. Recourse to this use of the dash should be sparing.

Yesterday, December 7, 1941–a date which will live in infamy–the United States of America was suddenly and deliberately attacked by naval and air forces of the Empire of Japan.–*Franklin D. Roosevelt*

Sometimes a parenthetical expression already contains punctuation within it and the expression cannot be enclosed in parentheses because it properly belongs to the sentence. Then dashes are used to set it off. This use of the dash frequently takes the place of commas that might otherwise be misread as series commas.

His clothes–dirty, shabby, torn–belied his circumstances.

The dash may be used as a substitute for the expressions *that is; in other words*, and *namely*.

He admits that there are two sides to every question–his own and the wrong side. –*Channing Pollock*

The dash may be used to set off a word or group of words to add an element of surprise, to show an unexpected turn of thought.

Josh Billings

There are two things in life for which we are never fully prepared, and that is–twins. –*Josh Billings*

A pun is the lowest form of humor–when you don't think of it first. –*Oscar Levant*

The dash is used before a summarizing expression such as *all such, these,* and *all these.*

Barrymore, Gielgud, Evans–these were great Hamlets in their time.

The dash may be used to indicate a word, or part of a word, that has been omitted.

That fellow is a d—— fool.

A dash is used to indicate inclusion in dates, to take the place of the words *to* or *through.*

Vacation will be June–September.

I was in the Army 1963–1965.

Do not use the dash to indicate inclusion when the words *from* or *between* precede the date.

Wrong　Vacation will be from June–September.

Right　Vacation will be from June to [*or* through] September.

In Relation to Other Marks of Punctuation

When the dash ends a sentence, all other terminal marks (period, question mark, exclamation mark) are omitted.

PARENTHESES

When an expression cannot be sufficiently set off by commas or dashes, parentheses are used to enclose it. Generally, in order for a statement to be enclosed in parentheses, it must have no grammatical relationship to the rest of the sentence. Whatever is said in the parentheses should not be referred to again in the sentence. Statements within parentheses are completely independent of the rest of the sentence. Parentheses are used to set off a comment that may be only remotely connected to the meaning of the sentence itself.

The astronomer reported (as the result of too much star-gazing, I suppose) that the mean distance between the moon and the earth was 238 miles.

Parentheses are used to enclose references and directions.

The book was hailed by at least one critic (see *The Saturday Review*, Nov. 30, 1963, page 43).

Parentheses may be used to enclose figures or letters marking the order of a series.

(1) . . . . (2) . . . . (3) . . . .
(a) . . . . (b) . . . . (c) . . . .

BRACKETS

Brackets ([]), like parentheses, enclose statements that are independent of the rest of the sentence. Unlike parentheses, brackets enclose parenthetical material inserted by someone other than the author of the sentence. Brackets are generally used by editors to supply missing material to make an author's meaning clearer, or to draw attention to an author's error of fact. Brackets are used to enclose an explanatory comment in quoted material.

She [Gertrude Stein] used to counsel Hemingway at great length.

Brackets are used to enclose a correction of a quoted statement of fact.

Douglas Fairbanks Junior [Senior] was married to Mary Pickford.

Brackets are used to enclose the word *sic,* which is Latin for "thus," to call attention to the fact that some remarkable or inaccurate expression, misspelling, or error is being quoted literally.

In his speech he suggested that Li'l Abner was the most literate [sic] cartoon in America.

Brackets may be used to take the place of parentheses within parentheses.

An interesting comment on the Witches Sabbath is contained in the author's previous book (see *Medieval Europe,* pp. 204-229 [2d ed.]).

QUOTATION MARKS

A chief function of quotation marks (" ") is to identify words spoken in direct discourse. Another chief function is to identify words said or written by one person and quoted or reproduced by another. In addition, quotation marks may be used to distinguish words from other words that surround them in a sentence. Used this way, they approach–but not quite–the distinguishing function of italics. Modern journalistic practice is to use quotation marks as an actual substitute for italics. Newspapers and magazines often use quotation marks, for example, to set off the titles of books and plays–a practice not countenanced in formal writing. Formal writing limits the distinguishing strength of quotation marks to subdivisions, such as the titles of chapters of books and the titles of stories and articles appearing in books or magazines. Quotation marks are used at the beginning and end of every direct quotation. A direct quotation consists of the exact words of a speaker and the exact words used in reproducing a quoted passage.

"Speak for yourself, John," suggested Priscilla.

"Even when laws have been written down," said Aristotle, "they ought not always to remain unaltered."

Quotation marks are not used with an indirect quotation.

Aristotle suggested that even when laws are written down, they ought not always to remain unaltered.

When a quotation consists of more than one paragraph, place the quotation marks at the beginning of each new paragraph and at the end of the last paragraph only.

Quotation marks may be used to set off slang terms in formal writing, not generally, however, in informal writing, and almost never in dialogue.

The policeman was annoyed by a group of young men who said they did not "dig" his actions.

He has the job "sewed up."

Quotation marks are used to set off quoted references to chapter headings of a book, titles of articles, stories, poems, etc., appearing in magazines and other periodicals.

Chapter II: "My Early Years"

Have you read "Backstairs at the White House" in last month's *Digest?*

Quotation marks are used to set off the title of a book series.

"Great Art of Western Civilization" series.

Quotation marks are used to set off quoted references to the title of a lecture, sermon, or speech unless it has been established as virtually public domain.

Dr. Jones will speak on "The Meaning of Christmas."

the Sermon on the Mount

the Gettysburg Address

Quotation marks are used to set off quoted reference to the titles of songs and short musical works.

"Say It with Music"

"Slaughter on Tenth Avenue"

Quotation marks are used to set off quoted reference to the titles of paintings and sculpture.

"Nude Descending a Staircase" by Duchamp

"Bird in Flight" by Brancusi

A single quotation mark is used to enclose a quotation within a quotation. Double quotation marks are used to enclose an additional quotation within the second.

> He said: "John told me that Mary said, 'You know that Henry hasn't heard "Alexander's Rag Time Band" yet.' "

In Relation to Other Marks of Punctuation

The period and comma are always placed inside the quotation marks.

> Henry Ford said, "History is the bunk."

> Although Anne said, "That was a fine play," she did not meant it.

A colon or semicolon after a quotation always appears outside the quotation marks.

> "Television is taking the place of movies": This suggestion grows in truth each day.

> Mary said, "Of course not"; and she meant it.

All other marks of punctuation are placed inside the quotation marks if they refer specifically to the quotation. They are placed outside if they refer, not to the quotation, but to the sentence as a whole.

> "Has it occurred to you that your parents have been waiting all day?" he asked.

> Did you remember to say "Thank you"?

> She exclaimed, "My gosh, I forgot!"

Quotation marks may be omitted when a single word is used.

> What can we do if they all say yes?

APOSTROPHE

The apostrophe mark (') is essentially a spelling device used to indicate the possessive case of nouns and the plural of letters and figures. As a mark of punctuation, it is used to denote the omission of one or more letters or figures. The apostrophe also denotes the omission of letters in words.

> o'clock   shouldn't
> haven't   don't

Do not use the apostrophe in words that are accepted shortened forms. Generally, such words would otherwise have an apostrophe preceding their first letter.

> phone   cello
> Frisco   plane
> possum   copter

The apostrophe denotes the omission of figures.

> the Spirit of '76   the class of '63

POINTS OF ELLIPSIS

The points of ellipsis consist of three consecutive periods (. . .). They indicate an omission, a lapse of time, or a particularly long pause. When the points of ellipsis fall at the end of a sentence, a fourth–the terminal period–is added.

The points of ellipsis indicate the deliberate omission of one or more words from a quoted passage.

> The playbill quoted Wolcott Gibbs as saying "I couldn't leave the theatre . . ." when what he really said was "I couldn't leave the theatre soon enough."

A full line of points of ellipsis indicates the omission of one or more paragraphs from a quoted passage. It may also indicate the omission of one or more lines of poetry.

The points of ellipsis indicate passage of time.

> Three . . . two . . . one . . . zero.

The points of ellipsis may be used as a substitute for the expression *and so forth*.

> The glamor of motion pictures is usually represented by the *heroes*, Cary Grant, Troy Donohue, . . . , and the *heroines*, Audrey Hepburn, Tuesday Weld, ...

The points of ellipsis may be used to indicate that a statement is deliberately left unfinished.

> Even before the act was half over, I thought, "Well. . . ."

The points of ellipsis are often used in advertising writing between short groups of words for emphasis; but the practice is not acceptable in formal writing.

> Don't hesitate . . . send for your copy today.

The points of ellipsis are often used in textbooks, examinations, and commercial coupons to indicate words to be filled in.

> Four kinds of citrus fruit are . . . , . . . , . . . , ...

> Enclosed find $ . . . for . . . copies at . . . each.

> Name . . . .
> Address . . . .
> City . . . . State . . . . . . Zip . . . .

In Relation to Other Marks of Punctuation

The points of ellipsis are always placed inside quotation marks, whether they fall at the beginning or end of the sentence.

> Jean said, ". . . and, furthermore, I wouldn't have gone even if. . . ."

HYPHEN

The hyphen is both a word connector and a word separator. As a connector, it joins compound words. As a word separator, it marks the division of an uncompleted word at the end of a line when there is no room for all of it, so that part of the word must be carried over to the next line. Such division of words is known as *syllabication*. Below are presented other, minor uses of the hyphen.

The hyphen is used to indicate inclusion of numbers in street addresses, social security numbers, account numbers, etc.

> 38-14 Sunset Blvd.
>
> 032-16-1379
>
> Library of Congress Catalogue Card Number 64-20010

The hyphen is used between inclusive page numbers.

> For a discussion of the causes of the war, see pp. 29-138.

ASTERISK AND SUPERIOR FIGURE

The asterisk (*), once the universal mark of omission, is now little more than a reference mark. Even in this capacity it is rapidly being superseded by the superior figure. The asterisk may be used as a footnote reference when only a few such references are planned.

> Allergy diseases are often caused by psychogenic factors.*
>
> *William Nesbitt, *Psychosomatic Medicine* (Philadelphia: Saunders, 1959), pp. 26-49.

The superior figure is used when many footnote references are planned.

> "It is proper for an escort to precede a lady through a revolving door."[4]
>
> [4]Sophie Hadida, *Manners for Millions* (New York: Permabooks, 1934), p. 38.

BAR (VIRGULE)

The bar is a diagonal line. It has two principal functions: to serve as a mark of separation and to indicate the omission of words. The bar also appears in such expressions as *and/or*. This use of the bar, however, is not acceptable in formal writing. When running together lines of quoted poetry, use the bar to indicate the correct ending of lines.

> A thing of beauty is a joy forever;/Its loveliness increases; it will never/Pass into nothingness; but still will keep/A bower quiet for us, and a sleep/Full of sweet dreams, and health, and quiet breathing./–*John Keats*

Use the bar, in addresses, to separate the letters *c* and *o* to form the symbol meaning *in care of*.

> % Richard Watts   % Miss Helen
> Smith   Jones

The bar is sometimes used in informal notes and memoranda in the contractions of dates.

> January 8, 1964   1/8/64
>
> June 29, 1970   6/29/70

The bar is occasionally used in business reports and in technical writing to indicate the omission of such words as *per* and *as*. Note that when the bar is used in abbreviations, the period that ordinarily follows the abbreviation is omitted.

> barrels per day   barrels/day   bbls/day
> bill of lading   B/L

Use the bar on the typewriter in place of the caret.

> Into the street the Piper stept,
>
>   a
> Smiling first/little smile. . . .
>   –*Robert Browning*

CARET

The word *caret* is Latin and literally means "it is missing." The caret (ʌ) is used to indicate where letters or words are to be inserted in a written line, or between lines. Use the caret freely on rough drafts, sparingly–if at all–on the finished composition. A single page with more than one insertion should be rewritten or retyped.

The keyboards of standard typewriters do not carry the caret, and the current practice is to use the bar as follows:

find
Look before, or you'll / youself behind.
—*Poor Richard's Almanac*

The caret itself has to be written in by hand. Write the caret as an inverted *v*. Since it is such a conspicuous mark, the caret should be made small and in light, not heavy, lines.

s
We visited the capitol in Boston, Massachusetts.

upon
All experience is an arch, to build.—*Henry Brooks Adams*

Ditto marks ('') are pairs of inverted commas, used where considerable repetition occurs, to take the place of words and groups of words. Ditto itself is derived from the Latin *dicere* (to say) and means "the aforementioned thing." The marks are restricted chiefly to lists and tabulations.

The ditto is another mark that does not appear on standard typewriter keyboards. Quotation marks are the acceptable substitute.

Grammar

Few words can be classified absolutely as one or another of the eight parts of speech traditionally distinguished in our language. Most of us would automatically say that *swim* is a verb; yet in the sentence *He went for a swim,* it is clearly a noun. An even more confusing example is *up:*

> The proposal was on the *up* and up. (noun)
>
> The auctioneer encouraged us to *up* our bid. (verb)
>
> His time was *up.* (adjective, modifying *time*)
>
> We flew *up* and over the clouds. (adverb, modifying *flew*)
>
> He went *up* the stairs. (preposition)

It is clear that we may assign a word to a grammatical class only by considering its use, or *function,* in its context. Grammar is a way of talking about the relationship of words.

NOUNS

A *noun* is a name. It indicates a person, place, or thing.

> The *fireman* climbed to the *top* of the *ladder.*

Not all "things" are concrete objects. A noun may also name a quality, an action, or a concept.

> The *brutality* of the *murder* underlined its *injustice.*

Nouns may be further classified according to five types:

1. A *common* noun names a class or group of persons, places, or things. A title is ordinarily treated as a common noun.

   > My *father* is a *history professor.*

   But if it used as a specific name or as part of one it is considered a proper noun.

   > I introduced *Father* to *Professor White* of the *Department of History.*

2. A *concrete* noun names a particular or specific member of a class or group that can be seen, heard, touched, smelled, or tasted—one that can be perceived by the senses.

   > *Naomi Swift,* the famous contralto, sang a fourth *aria.* In her *hair* the *rose* glowed as red as *wine.*

3. An *abstract* noun names a quality or concept.

   > Continued *apathy* will compromise the *freedom* we enjoy under *democracy.*

4. A *proper* noun names a specific person, place, or thing; it is capitalized.

   > After *President Jefferson* returned from *Monticello* he addressed *Congress.*

5. A *collective* noun is a proper or common noun which names a group of persons or things.

   > group   crowd   pack

Note: Nouns can belong to more than one type.

Concrete, common, and collective: He joined a *brotherhood* to meet friends.

Concrete, proper, and collective: He was a member of the *Brotherhood* of RR Engineers.

Abstract, common, and collective: He believed in the *brotherhood* of man.

A noun may be a single word:

The *attorney* is Adams;

or a compound word:

Richard Adams became *attorney general;*

or a phrase:

Hunting the elusive fox was strenuous sport;

or a clause:

That he could have been lying was out of the question.

Gender

The *gender* of a noun presents no problem in English. *Masculine nouns* refer to males (boy, father), *feminine* to females (woman, girl). All others are *neuter*. A number of nouns have masculine and feminine forms clearly marked by differences of pronunciation or of spelling (aviator, aviatrix; alumnus, alumna; fiancé, fiancée). Except in the case of the last example, the tendency seems to be toward using masculine forms in place of the feminine (aviator, etc.).

Number

The *number* of a noun is a way of indicating how many persons, places, and things it refers to. A noun is *singular* if it names one, and *plural* if it names two or more.

Case

The *case* of a noun is determined by what it does in a sentence. If it is *doing* something, it is in the nominative (or subjective) case, as in "The *teacher* graded my paper." If something is *being done to it,* the noun is usually in the objective (or accusative) case, as in "The teacher graded my *paper*." If the noun is said to own something, it is in the possessive (or genitive) case, as in "the *dog's* tail."

Since the forms of nominative and objective nouns are identical, there is no problem in English of writing them correctly. Even the genitive case causes little difficulty in its grammatical relationships.

Use of Nouns

As *subject* (nominative case): The subject of a sentence is the person, place, or thing about which the statement is made or question asked.

The *girl* enjoyed dancing.

Didn't the *boy* know how to dance?

As *object* (objective, or accusative, case): The *direct object* of a sentence is the person, place, or thing directly affected by the action of a transitive verb.

The car crossed the *bridge*.

The college announced *that tuition would go up again*. (clause as object)

The *indirect object* is indirectly affected by the action of a transitive verb. It precedes the direct object, unless it is a prepositional phrase.

He sent *his mother* a birthday present.

He sent a birthday present *to his mother*.

As *subjective complement* (nominative case), also called the *predicate nominative*. The complement is a noun related directly to the subject, not the verb.

He is the heaviest *player* on the team.

Jenny seemed the last *person* you'd expect to get into trouble.

A linking verb (see page 21) connects subject and subjective complement.

As *objective complement* (objective case): Completes the sense of a transitive verb, related directly to the direct object, not the verb.

She called her best friend a green-eyed *monster*.

Linus considers Beethoven the only *composer*.

As *appositive:* An appositive is a noun that usually follows another noun with the same meaning. It takes the same case as the noun with which it is in apposition.

Our next-door neighbor, a *veteran* of World War II, refuses to join the American Legion. (*Veteran* is in apposition with *neighbor;* both are nominative.)

He finally joined the VFW, a livelier *organization*. (*Organization* is in apposition with *VFW,* both are objective.)

In *direct address:*

> *Darling,* I agree.
>
> Be good, my *dear,* and let who will be clever.

PRONOUNS

A *pronoun* refers to a person, place, or thing without naming it.

> *She* bit *his* arm. Wash *it* with *this.*
>
> *Everyone who* wants to come is welcome.
>
> There are *four,* you say?

The noun (or pronoun) for which a pronoun substitutes is called its *antecedent.* Thus, in the first example above, *arm* is the antecedent of *it.* The antecedents of *she, his,* and *this* are implied; both speaker and hearer (or writer and reader) know who *she* and *he* are, and *this* refers to an object physically present. The antecedent of *who* in the second example, is *Everyone.* Pronouns may be classified according to seven types:

1. *Personal* pronouns substitute for the name of the person speaking, the person spoken to, or the person or object spoken of. Personal pronouns can be troublesome because, unlike nouns (which rarely change their forms except in the possessive case), most pronouns take a different form for each of the three cases: nominative, objective, and possessive.

	NOMINATIVE	OBJECTIVE	POSSESSIVE
1ST PERSON			
singular	I	me	my, mine
plural	we	us	our, ours
2ND PERSON			
singular	you	you	your, yours
plural	you	you	your, yours
3RD PERSON			
singular			
masculine	he	him	his
feminine	she	her	her, hers
neuter	it	it	its, of it
either gender	one	one	one's
plural	they	them	their, theirs

2. *Relative* pronouns link a subordinate clause with an independent one, referring to a noun or pronoun in the independent clause.

> We smiled at the clerk *who* had been so pleasant.
>
> The batter hit a line drive *which* sent two men home.

There is no difficulty of declension with most rela-

tive pronouns; only *who* and *whom* (and their related compound forms) present problems. The distinction between these has virtually disappeared in speech, but is still maintained in writing.

NOMINATIVE	OBJECTIVE	POSSESSIVE
who	whom	whose
whoever	whomever	whosever
which	which	of which
that	that	whose
what	what	——
as	as	——

Who and its related forms refer to people, *which* to other living creatures and to things; *that* may be used for either persons or things. *What* is the equivalent of *that which* when used as a relative pronoun. *As* appears in a dependent clause, when *such* or *the same* has appeared in the independent clause.

> Ours is the same *as* yours.

Note: Except for the word *one's,* the possessive case of both personal and relative pronouns has no apostrophe.

3. *Interrogative* pronouns introduce questions. They include *who* (objective, *whom;* possessive, *whose*), *which,* and *what.*

> *Who* saw him leave?
> *Whom* do you mean?
> *Which* are the best roads from here?
> *What* is the direction you want to take?

Who (and its related forms) inquires about a person, *which* about a person or thing in a group, *what* about anything.

Note: Remember that the objective form *(whom):* is the object of a verb or a preposition.

> *Whom* did Petrarch love?
> *Whom* do you get them from?

Whose, which, and *what* also function as interrogative adjectives, when instead of substituting for a noun they modify it.

> *Which roads* are best?
> *What direction* are you taking?

4. *Demonstrative* pronouns point out specific persons or things. Principal ones are *this* (plural, *these*) and *that* (plural, *those*).

> *This* is the least flattering of all the photos. Have you seen *those?*

Note: Demonstrative pronouns may also function as demonstrative adjectives.

> *This photo* is more flattering than *those others.*

5. *Indefinite* pronouns point out persons or things, but less specifically than demonstrative pronouns. A great number in this classification include the following:

SINGULAR INDEFINITE PRONOUNS

another	everything
anyone	somebody
each	such
either	

PLURAL INDEFINITE PRONOUNS

both	many
few	several

SINGULAR OR PLURAL INDEFINITE PRONOUNS

all	most
any	none
more	some

The only problem likely to arise with the use of the indefinite pronoun is that of number; see *Agreement*, page 19.

Note: Except for the words *none* and *plenty*, indefinite pronouns can function as adjectives as well.

6. *Reflexive* pronouns refer back to the subject. A reflexive pronoun is usually the direct object of a verb.

> We dressed *ourselves* hastily.

Reflexive pronouns may also be used for emphasis.

> Many feared the Senate *itself* was discredited.

In formal English the reflexive form is not used as a substitute for either subject or object; this is likely to be a practical problem only in the first person.

> Myrna and I (not: *myself*) made all the arrangements.

> They asked Myrna and *me* (not: *myself*) to chaperone the dance.

7. *Reciprocal* pronouns are compound indefinite pronouns which indicate some mutual relationship between two or more persons and things.

> The lovers lived only for *each other*.

> All members of the company saw *one another* every day.

Case of Pronouns

The case rules that apply to nouns apply also to pronouns. Unlike nouns, however, pronouns frequently change their form according to whether they are in the nominative, objective, or possessive case. For this reason the case rules for pronouns are given separately below. A pronoun used as the subject of a verb takes the nominative case.

Right   John and *I* are invited, aren't *we*?

When a verb is omitted but understood, be sure to supply it mentally in order to determine whether the pronoun is used as its subject.

Wrong   John knows more than *her*.

   You are as good a player as *me*.

Right   John knows more than *she* (does). (*She* is the subject of the omitted verb *does*.).

Right   You are as good a player as *I* (am).

A pronoun used as a predicate nominative takes the nominative case. A predicate nominative is a noun or pronoun that follows *am, is, are, was, were, be, been*, and that refers back to the subject.

Wrong   Knock. Knock. Who's there? It's *me*.

   Could that be *her* already?

   It might have been *him*.

Right   Knock. Knock. Who's there? It's *I*. (*I* is the predicate nominative after the verb *is*.)

   Could that be *she* already?

   It might have been *he*.

Do not permit such interrupting expressions as *do you suppose, believe, think, say*, etc., to affect the case of *who* and *whom*.

Wrong   *Whom* do you believe was the guilty person?

Right   *Who* do you believe was the guilty person? (*Who* is the subject of *was*, not the object of *believe*.)

Be careful not to confuse the subject of a verb with the object of a preposition.

Wrong   I will vote for *whomever* is the best candidate.

Right   I will vote for *whoever* is the best candidate. (*Whoever* is the subject of *is*. The object of the preposition *for* is the whole clause *whoever is the best candidate*.)

A pronoun that is the subject of an infinitive takes the objective case. The infinitive is the form of the verb preceded by *to: to be, to dance*, etc.

Wrong   Do you expect John and *I* to be ready?

Right   Do you expect John and *me* to be ready? (*Me* is the subject together with *John* of the infinitive *to be*.)

A pronoun that follows the infinitive *to be* takes the objective case.

Wrong   Mary took John to be *I*.

Right   Mary took John to be *me*.

A pronoun used as the object of a verb, of an infinitive, or of a preposition, or as the indirect object, takes the objective case.

Wrong   *Who* did you ask to the party?

Right   *Whom* did you ask to the party? (*Whom* is the object of the verb *ask*.)

Wrong   The time has come for *we* students to get to work.

Right   The time has come for *us* students to get to work. (*Us* is the object of the preposition *for*.)

Wrong   The coach gave John and *I* a briefing.

Right   The coach gave John and *me* a briefing. (*John* and *me* are the indirect objects of the verb *gave*.)

A pronoun used in apposition with a noun takes the same case as the noun.

Wrong   The instructor wants us all–Harry, Sam, and *I*–to stay after class.

Right   The instructor wants us all–Harry, Sam, and *me*–to stay after class. (*Harry, Sam,* and *me* are in apposition with *us* and therefore take the same case.)

A pronoun used before a gerund takes the possessive case. A *gerund* is a verbal used as a noun. It has the same form as the verb's present or perfect participle.

Wrong   I was sure of *him* winning the prize.

Right   I was sure of *his* winning the prize. (*Winning* is the gerund. It is the object of the preposition *of*.)

The case form of the relative pronouns *who* and *whoever* depends upon how the pronoun is used in the clause it introduces.

Right   I already know *who* will come to the party. (*Who* is the subject of the verb *come* and is therefore in the nominative case.)

          The captain, *whom* I have never met, has asked to see me. (*Whom* is the direct object of the verb *met* and is therefore in the objective case.)

Agreement

Since pronouns are substitute words for other words, there must be agreement between them; otherwise the meaning of the substitute word will not be clear. The word for which a pronoun substitutes and to which it refers is its antecedent. A pronoun does not necessarily agree with its antecedent in case; but it must always agree with it in gender, number, and person.

The problem words are *each, either, neither, every, everyone, anybody, nobody, everybody, somebody*. In informal speech, we generally treat these words as collectives and we make the pronouns that refer to them singular or plural according to sound or whim. In formal writing, these words are treated as singular; therefore, a pronoun that has any one of these words as an antecedent should also be singular.

Informal   Each of us knew what *we* were doing.

Formal   Each of us knew what *he* was doing.

Informal   Everybody should know what *they* want out of life.

Formal   Everybody should know what *he* wants out of life.

Informal   Will everyone please open *their* book to page 56.

Formal   Will everyone please open *his* book to page 56.

Informal   Every city and town had a large increase in *their* population.

Formal   Every city and town had a large increase in *its* population.

When an antecedent includes mixed sexes and calls for a singular number, the use of *their* as an all-inclusive pronoun is wrong. The use of the double pronouns *he or she, his or her, him or her* is also undesirable. The pronoun that should be used for both sexes is *he, his, him*.

Wrong   Every man, woman, and child should wear *their* life jacket.

Undesirable   Every man, woman, and child should wear *his or her* life jacket.

Right   Every man, woman, and child should wear *his* life jacket.

Use the pronoun *who* to refer to people, *which* to animals other than humans and to things, and *that* for either persons or things.

Wrong   *Which* is that person?

Right   *Who* is that person?

There are two exceptions to the above rule. *Which* may be used to refer to persons considered as a group. Also, when a reference to an animal results in the awkward *of which* construction, the acceptable alternative is *whose.*

Right   Anthropologist believe that the race *which* gave America its first settlers was Mongoloid.

Awkward   I claim that the cheetah, the speed *of which* has been timed at seventy miles an hour, is the world's fastest four-legged animal.

Right   I claim that the cheetah, *whose* speed has been timed at seventy miles an hour, is the world's fastest four-legged animal.

When two antecedents are joined by *or* or *nor,* the pronoun should agree with the nearer antecedent.

Wrong   Neither the President nor the members of the Cabinet could foresee *his* fate.

Right   Neither the President nor the members of the Cabinet could foresee *their* fate.

Reference

A pronoun may be grammatically correct. It may agree in every way—in person, number, and gender—with its antecedent, and it may have just the right case form. Yet if the antecedent is not immediately clear, all the effort will be utterly wasted. The reader must be able to tell at a single glance exactly what your pronoun refers to. One of the worst writing sins you can commit is to force your reader to reread the sentence or refer back to a previous sentence to find your meaning. This sin is frequently caused by an ambiguous or misplaced pronoun. A pronoun should have a clearly defined antecedent and should be placed as near the antecedent as possible.

Indefinite   I had a fascinating time in Mexico. *They* are a colorful people. (The antecedent of the pronoun *They* may be obvious to the writer, but not to the reader. Who are *They?*)

Definite   I had a fascinating time on my trip to Mexico. Mexicans are a colorful people.

Definite   I had a fascinating time on my trip to Mexico. It is a colorful country.

Shun the indefinite use of the pronoun *it.* In certain idiomatic phrases the indefinite use of *it* is acceptable. (*It is a fine day. It is a fact. It is necessary. It is likely. It is true.*) But when *it* is not part of an accepted idiom, avoid the indefinite use altogether.

Indefinite   In the chapter on the second voyage, it reveals that Columbus sent five hundred Indian slaves as a gift to Queen Isabella.

Definite   The chapter on the second voyage reveals that Columbus sent five hundred Indian slaves as a gift to Queen Isabella.

Avoid the use of the impersonal *it* and the pronoun *it* in the same sentence.

Indefinite   The car is in rough shape, and it will probably cost more to repair it than the price of a new one.

Definite   The car is in rough shape, and the cost of repairing it will probably be more than the price of a new one.

Shun the indefinite use of the pronouns *you* and *they.* The indefinite use of these pronouns is acceptable in informal speech, but not in formal writing. In formal writing use *one* and *everyone.*

Informal   In this class *you* are not permitted to take notes.

Formal   In this class *one* (or *a student*) is not permitted to take notes.

Informal   *They* greet tourists warmly in Holland.

Formal   *Everyone* greets tourists warmly in Holland.

VERBS

A *verb* is a word or group of words that indicates action, condition (being), or process.

They *began* the boat race this morning; by six this evening they *will have sailed* halfway to the island.

He *was* a good dog. The house *seems* empty without him.

The rose *had become* an even deeper crimson.

Types of Verbs

Verbs may be classified according to four types:

1. A *transitive* verb requires a direct object to complete its meaning.

> Hilda *bathed* the *baby*. (The subject, *Hilda*, performs the action upon the direct object, *baby*.)

> Ulysses *plunged* the *stake* into the Cyclops' eye. (The verb *plunged* is transitive and the direct object is *stake*.)

2. An *intransitive* verb is complete within itself and does not require a direct object.

> Let us *pray*.
> We *felt* relieved.
> We *plunged* into the pool and *swam*. Then we *lay* in the sun.

Most verbs, like *plunge,* can be either transitive or intransitive. But *lie* is intransitive only. It is a troublesome verb because its past tense *lay* is frequently confused with the present tense of transitive *lay*.

	TRANSITIVE	INTRANSITIVE
PRESENT TENSE	lay (something down)	lie (on my bed)
PAST TENSE	laid (something down)	lay (on my bed)
PAST PARTICIPLE	have laid (something down)	have lain (on my bed)

3. A *linking* verb or *copula* joins the subject to its complement, which is a predicate noun or adjective. The more common ones are:

appear	look
be	seem
become	smell
feel	taste
grow	turn

Most of these verbs are not exclusively linking verbs.

USED AS LINKING VERBS	USED AS OTHER VERBS
It *grew* colder.	He *grew* a beard. (Transitive verb)
That *tasted* bad.	They *will taste* their soup. (Transitive verb)
He *turned* pirate.	She stopped and *turned*. (Intransitive verb)

4. An *auxiliary* verb helps the main verb of the sentence. It may be formed from *have, can, may, be, shall, will, might, must,* and *do,* and appears before the main verb in a verb phrase.

> We *can* go if we like.

> She *might have been* told earlier.

> I *am* finishing my letter.

Principal Parts

Verbs in English have three principal parts:

INFINITIVE OR BASIC FORM	to walk to sleep	to go to bite
PAST TENSE, USED IN THE SIMPLE PAST	walked slept	went bit
PAST PARTICIPLE, "USED TO" FORM COMPOUND TENSES	(has) walked (has) slept	(has) gone (has) bitten

Regular (or *weak*) verbs form their principal parts by adding *-ed, -d,* or *-t* to the infinitive.

> wanted   placed   dealt

Irregular (or *strong*) verbs change or retain the vowel of the infinitive and do not add *-ed, -d,* or *-t*.

> throw, threw, thrown

> choose, chose, chosen

Intransitive   sit, sat, sat

Transitive   set, set, set

Sometimes a verb may have more than one form:

> shine, shone (or shined), shone (or shined)

> dream, dreamed (or dreamt), dreamed (or dreamt)

Consult a recent dictionary if there is any question of a form's being nonstandard:

> see, saw (*not standard:* seen), have seen

Person and Number

Person and number present few problems in English verbs; the verb form usually changes only in the third person singular of the present tense, where an *s* is added (*I jump, he jumps; I cry, she cries*). A notable exception is the highly irregular verb *be,* but this is so frequently used it presents no practical difficulty.

Tense

The tense of a verb indicates the time of its action. There are six tenses in English:

1. The *present* tense uses three forms for positive statements.

SIMPLE PRESENT:	We *know,* you *say,* he *rides*
PROGRESSIVE:	I *am rushing,* you *are moving,* he *is standing* still
EMPHATIC:	I *do move,* he *does ride*

In questions or in negative statements, the progressive or emphatic form is generally used.

PROGRESSIVE:	*Are* you *coming?* She *is* not *coming*
EMPHATIC:	*Does* he *swim?* They *do* not *swim*

2. The *past* tense indicates past time not continuing to the present. It uses three forms for positive statements.

SIMPLE PAST: I *took,* you *jumped,* she *sank*

PROGRESSIVE: He *was flying,* we *were laughing*

EMPHATIC: You *did believe,* they *did prove*

In questions or in negative statements, the progressive or emphatic form is generally used.

3. The *perfect* (or *present perfect*) tense indicates past time continuing to the present. It is formed by adding the past participle to *have* or *has.*

> I *have shown* her the ring.
>
> *Have* you *been* here long?
>
> He *has filled* the tub.

4. The *past perfect* tense indicates past time occurring before a definite time in the past. It is formed by adding the past participle to *had.*

> We *had been* in the new house for a week.
>
> You *had come* to visit us.
>
> *Had* she *set* the table yet?

Note: In the examples immediately above, any subsequent actions would still be in the past (She *set* the table when I arrived). But an action subsequent to those in the examples for the present perfect would naturally be in the present (He has filled the tub. He *is washing* now).

5. The *future* tense indicates future time continuing from the present. It has three forms.

> We *will* not *leave.*
>
> You *will be having* dinner.
>
> *Is* he *going to tell* us?

The old distinction between *shall* (simple futurity) and *will* (future of determination) has virtually disappeared except in formal writing. It may also be used in the first person, to make clear an important difference in attitude.

> I *shall* do it. (compliance)
>
> I *will* do it. (desire)

6. The *future perfect* tense indicates future time occurring before a definite time in the future. It is formed by adding the past participle to the future tense of *have.*

> He *shall have seen* them before you do.
>
> *Will* they *have escaped* (before the house burns down)?

Note: The present tense may be used for future time (I *leave* for home tomorrow); past time, especially to add immediacy to a narrative (It *is* dark, this Christmas Eve, as Washington *approaches* Trenton); to make a statement that is presumably true at any time (Too many cooks *spoil* the broth); or to discuss a fictional past (When Huck *sneaks* ashore from the raft, we *see* intrepidity at its height).

Voice

A verb is in the *active voice* when its subject performs the action.

> Tennyson published *In Memoriam* in 1850. (*Tennyson* is the subject and the verb *published* is in the active voice.)

A verb is in the *passive voice* when its subject is acted upon.

> *In Memoriam* was published by Tennyson in 1850. (*In Memoriam* is the subject and the verb *published* is in the passive voice.)

Except for a reason of deliberate emphasis, choose the active voice in preference to the passive voice. It will make your writing more lively and vigorous. *Betty gave a party for all the children* is livelier than *A party was given by Betty for all the children.*

Mood

The *mood* of a verb refers to the manner in which a statement is expressed. There are three moods in English.

1. The *indicative* mood states a fact.

> I *spent* the holiday in New York.
>
> He *knew* you *had come.*

2. The *imperative* mood gives a command.

> *Stop!*
>
> *Try* and *make* me.

3. The *subjunctive* mood expresses a wish, a doubt, or a condition contrary to fact.

> I wish he *were* somewhere else.
>
> We wondered if we *were* going to get away with it.

Note: The past subjunctive of the verb *be,* which is *were* in all three persons and both numbers, is the only subjunctive of any real importance in English. In informal writing and in speech, the indicative *was* is an acceptable substitute. Other uses of the subjunctive are consciously formal (We request that this *be* omitted from the report; if this *prove* false I shall resign), or preserved in automatic phrases (*come* what may, whatever it *cost*). The subjunctive mood has largely disappeared.

Finite and Infinite Verbs (Verbals)

A *finite* verb is capable of making a complete and independent assertion.

> She *finished* the book.

> You *have done* a good job.

A finite verb is limited to a specific person, by a noun or a pronoun (the bear *roars;* he *climbs*). It is also limited in number, either singular or plural (she *laughs;* they *laugh*). And it is limited in time, by a tense form (we *sit;* we *sat*). A finite verb serves as a main verb in a sentence or clause.

> She *had eaten* before we *began.*

An *infinite* verb, or *verbal*, is not thus limited. It cannot be used to make a sentence of the typical subject-verb pattern, but is characteristically used in subordinate constructions. (A clear understanding of the difference between a finite verb and a verbal will eliminate most careless sentence fragments from your writing.) There are three classes of verbals:

1. The *infinitive* is one of the present forms of a verb, with *to* either present or understood.

	ACTIVE	PASSIVE
PRESENT	(to push)	(to) be pushed
PERFECT	(to) have pushed	(to) have been pushed

Most versatile of the verbals, the infinitive may be used as a noun:

> *To ride* is good sport. (subject)

> She wanted *to play* with the puppies. (object of a verb)

> They wanted nothing but *to be left* alone. (object of a preposition)

> His intention was *to have kissed* her. (subjective complement)

as an adjective:

> Ned Creeth is my choice *to represent* us. (modifies *choice*)

> It was courageous *to volunteer*. (modifies *courageous*)

as an adverb:

> I am sorry *to disappoint* you. (modifies *sorry*)

> *To find* work, he moved to the city. (modifies *moved*)

with an auxiliary as part of a finite verb:

> We must *find* a way. (*to* understood)

2. The *participle* is one of the present or past participle forms of a verb.

	ACTIVE	PASSIVE
PRESENT	trying	being tried
PAST	having tried	having been tried

It may be used as an adjective:

> He shot the *leaping* deer.

> The *broken* vase lay near the window.

> *Having paid* our respects, we left.

as part of a finite verb:

> We were *playing* leapfrog.

> I have *had* enough for now.

in an absolute construction (a phrase grammatically independent of any other part of the sentence):

> The city *having been taken,* Caesar moved on. (The entire phrase *The city having been taken* is the absolute construction.)

3. The *gerund* is one of the present participial forms of a verb, and is used as a noun.

> *Kissing* is pleasant, but *being kissed* is a perfect joy. (subject, active and passive)

> Many prefer *going* to the movies. (object of a verb)

> Others waste their time in *bowling*. (object of a preposition)

> Uncle Jack's favorite recreation is *sleeping*. (subjective complement)

Problems in Use

The following are some persistent problems in the use of verbs and verbals:

SHALL (SHOULD) and WILL (WOULD)
In questions, *will* is properly used in all persons. However, *shall* is often used to convey a sense of propriety or obligation. *Won't* is the regular negative form.

> *Shall* I write to thank her?

> What *shall* I do to avoid it?

> What *won't* you do?

Do not overuse *shall.* It is neither more correct nor more elegant than *will.*

Should and *would* suggest doubt or uncertainty.

> That *should* be all right. (contrast: That *will* be all right.)

In polite requests, *would* and *should* are used for the first person, *would* for the second.

> I *would* (or *should*) be very grateful for your help.

> *Would* you please pass the hominy grits?

CAN and MAY

Can and *may* are used to show ability and possibility, respectively.

> You *can* do it if you try.

> We *may* arrive in time.

Can is used increasingly to express permission.

> *Can* I come in?

> You *can* choose the one you want.

This use of *can* is still not considered formally correct. In writing, and even in speaking, it is preferable to use *may.*

> *May* I come in?

> You *may* choose the one you want.

LIE, SIT, RISE

Lie, sit, and *rise* are intransitive verbs. They should not be confused with their transitive counterparts *lay, set,* and *raise.* The best way to avoid difficulty with these troublesome pairs is simply to memorize their principal parts, and then to decide whether a construction calls for a transitive or intransitive verb.

	TRANSITIVE	INTRANSITIVE
PRESENT	lay, set, raise (something)	lie, sit, rise
PAST	laid, set, raised (something)	lay, sat, rose
PAST PARTICIPLE	(have) laid, set, raised (something)	(have) lain, sat, risen

Remember that a hen *sets* on her eggs, and the sun *sets* in the west.

GET

The past participle of the verb *get* is either *got* or *gotten.* The latter seems the more common. (The only past participle of *forget* is *forgotten.*) Avoid *have got* and *have got to* (meaning *must*) where *have* and *have to* are sufficient.

Wrong	I have got some here.
	I haven't got any more.
	I have got to leave soon.
Right	I have some here.
	I haven't any more.
	I have to leave soon.

AIN'T

Ain't is a contraction of *am not, are not,* and occasionally *have not;* despite its long history in English, it is a nonstandard form. Use the equally convenient contractions *I'm not, aren't,* and *haven't.* However, there is no completely satisfactory form for the first person singular negative interrogative: *am I not* is too formal for most speakers, and the clumsy *aren't I* is not everywhere accepted.

Misuse of Past Tense

One of the most common verb errors is to use the past tense instead of the past participle. Use the past participle whenever there is an auxiliary or helping verb.

Wrong	It wasn't until I left the house that I noticed I had *forgot* my books.
Right	It wasn't until I left the house that I noticed I had *forgotten* my books. (The auxiliary verb *had* demands the past participle.)

Sequence of Tenses

Avoid unnecessary shifts from one tense to another in the same sentence. Make a verb in a subordinate clause (or an infinitive or a participle) agree in time with the verb in the main clause.

Wrong	Whenever he *said* yes, she *says* no. (The verb *said* in the subordinate clause does not agree in time with the verb *says* in the main clause.)
Right	Whenever he *says* yes, she *says* no. (Both verbs agree.)
	Whenever he *said* yes, she *said* no. (Both verbs agree.)

An exception to the above rule applies when one states a universal truth (a statement that is true regardless of time).

> Sally *said* that it *is* better to be wise than virtuous. (Disagreement between verbs is acceptable because a universal truth requiring the present tense is stated.)

When two past actions are stated in the same sentence, use the past perfect tense for the earlier action.

Wrong   Fred realized just in time that he already *drank* too much.

Right   Fred realized just in time that he *had* already *drunk* too much. (The action of the second verb occurred before that of the first verb.)

After *if*, use the auxiliary verb *had* instead of *would have*.

Wrong   If you *would have* used your head, you wouldn't be in this mess.

Right   If you *had* used your head, you wouldn't be in this mess.

The past infinitive is often used to express action not yet completed at the time of the main or preceding verb. This is wrong. The present infinitive is demanded in such constructions.

Wrong   We wanted *to have finished* the job by tonight.

Right   We wanted *to finish* the job by tonight. (The present infinitive *to finish* is demanded because its action has not yet taken place at the time of the main verb *wanted*.)

Agreement of Subject and Verb

A verb must always agree with its subject in person and number. It is often difficult to tell which is the true subject, or whether a subject is considered singular or plural. The rules below govern the agreement of subject and verb.

The following pronouns, often taken to be plural, are singular and therefore require a singular verb: *each, everyone, everybody, either,* and *neither.*

Wrong   Each of the candidates *are* competent.

Neither of us *are* ready.

Right   Each of the candidates *is* competent.

Neither of us *is* ready.

The following nouns, plural in form, are considered singular in meaning and therefore require a singular verb: *news, economics, mathematics, politics, mumps,* and *measles. The United States* also takes a singular verb.

Wrong   The economics of the plan *are* hazardous.

Right   The economics of the plan *is* hazardous.

The United States *has* treated the American Indians abominably.

A collective noun generally takes a singular verb. However, when the individuals of the group are considered, the verb is plural.

Our team always *wins.*

The family *is* worried about my late hours. (Family regarded as a single unit–more usual.)

The family *have* gone about their chores. (Individuals of the family considered–less usual.)

The words *there* and *here* are not subjects. In constructions introduced by *there* and *here,* look for the true subject to ascertain the number of the verb.

Wrong   *There's* several ways to skin a cat.

Right   There *are* several ways to skin a cat.

Fractions take a singular verb when bulk or a total number or amount is considered, a plural verb when individuals are considered. This rule applies also to words such as *all, any, none, some, more,* and *most.*

Two-thirds of the student body *was* present.

Two-thirds of the students *were* present.

All the money *has* somehow vanished.

All the members of the team *are* on the honor list.

When the word *number* is preceded by the definite article *the,* it usually takes a singular verb. When it is preceded by the indefinite article *a,* it takes a plural verb.

The number on the team who can be counted on in a tight spot *is* small.

A number of the team *have* proved their worth.

When subjects are contrasted, the verb agrees with the affirmative subject.

Wrong   She, not I, *am* responsible.

Right   She, not I, *is* responsible.

When the subject is a relative pronoun, look for the pronoun's antecedent to determine whether the verb is singular or plural. Relative pronouns are *who, which,* and *that.*

Wrong   Joe is one of the few students who *has* maintained an A average.

Right   Joe is one of the few students who *have* maintained an A average. (The antecedent of the relative pronoun *who* is *students*, hence it takes a plural verb.)

Words joined to a subject by *as well as, in addition to, with, together with, including,* and *rather than* do not affect the verb.

Wrong The entire student body, as well as most of the members of the faculty, *have* denounced President Green's decision.

Right The entire student body, as well as most of the members of the faculty, *has* denounced President Green's decision.

A compound subject joined by *and* generally takes a plural verb.

Wrong Her arrival and departure *was* not even noticed.

Right Her arrival and departure *were* not even noticed.

Do not use a plural verb when the subject is a compound that is regarded as a single entity.

> The long and short of the matter *is* that our front line is weak.

> Spaghetti and meat balls *is* my favorite.

> Bread and butter *is* all that we have for supper.

Singular subjects joined by *and* but preceded by *every* take a singular verb.

Wrong Every man, woman, and child *are* accounted for.

Right Every man, woman, and child *is* accounted for.

Singular subjects joined by *or, either . . . or, nor,* or *neither . . . nor,* take a singular verb.

Wrong Neither Adams nor Williams *are* present.

Right Neither Adams nor Williams *is* present.

When a verb has two or more subjects differing in person or number and connected by *or, either . . . or, nor,* or *neither . . . nor,* the verb agrees with the subject nearer it.

Wrong Either he or you *is* wrong.

Right Either he or you *are* wrong. (The verb agrees in person with the pronoun nearer it.)

Wrong Either new players or a new play *are* needed.

Right Either new players or a new play *is* needed. (The verb agrees in number with the noun nearer it.)

Irregular Verbs

To find the proper form of irregular verbs, consult a reliable dictionary. It is important to know how dictionaries enter the forms of irregular verbs. The main entry for all verbs is the infinitive (without the *to*) or present tense form. Following the verb's phonetic respelling comes, first, the past tense form, next, the past participial form, and finally, the present participial form. Acceptable variant forms are given. However, if any one form is the same as the one immediately preceding it, that form is not repeated. For verbs that are not irregular, the past tense and the past participle, when not given, are assumed to be formed in the usual way by adding *-d* or *-ed*.

ADJECTIVES AND ADVERBS

Adjectives and adverbs are *modifiers,* words which change the meaning of other words to make them clearer, more exact, weaker, or stronger.

An *adjective* modifies a noun or pronoun. It may answer the questions How many? What kind? Which one?

HOW MANY?

three brothers   *one* dollar   *many* men

WHAT KIND?

early bird   *whole* truth   *beautiful* girl

WHICH ONE?

this visit   *whose* jug?   *her* book

Note that *this, whose,* and *her*–often used as pronouns–here function as *pronominal adjectives.* A pronominal adjective always accompanies a noun.

Also note that the indefinite article *a* (*an*) identifies something as one of its kind (*a* boy, *an* apple), or serves as a substitute for *each* or *every* (once *a* week). The definite article *the* identifies one or more persons or objects by separating them from all others of their kind. Both articles are therefore adjectives.

An *adverb* modifies a verb, adjective, or other adverb. It may answer the questions How? When? Where? How much?

HOW?

Come *quickly.*   It moves *clockwise.*

WHEN?

They arrived *yesterday.*

WHERE?

They went *home*.   *Here* it is.

HOW MUCH?

We are more active now, but *only partly* happy.

In addition, there are the conjunctive adverbs (*however, moreover, nevertheless, therefore*), and adverbs of assertion and concession (*yes, no, not, maybe, probably*).

Many adverbs may be distinguished from adjectives by their *-ly* ending (*happy, happily; hard, hardly; particular, particularly*). But some of the more common adverbs do not end in *-ly: now, quite, there, then, up, down, for*. The last four of these can also be adjectives; there is a long list of adjectives and adverbs with identical forms, including *better, early, fast, much, straight*, and *well*.

Some adverbs have two forms: *loud, loudly; slow, slowly; soft, softly; quick, quickly; wrong, wrongly*. Sometimes there is a clear difference of meaning between the two.

He tried *hard*.   He *hardly* tried.

She came *late*.   *Lately* she has been coming at dinner time.

With others, choice depends on sound or on level of usage. The *-ly* ending is more common in formal writing. It is almost invariably used when the adverb precedes the verb (*Tightly* he gripped the narrow ledge). The short form is used especially in commands (hold on *tight*; go *slow*). Do not drop the *-ly* from the adverbs *considerably, really, sincerely*, and the like. For any question of the standard form consult a dictionary.

Adjectives and adverbs in English do not change their forms to indicate person, number, or case. However, they do change their forms to indicate degrees of comparison. They are compared in three degrees, frequently by adding *-er* and *-est*.

	POSITIVE	COMPARATIVE	SUPERLATIVE
ADJECTIVE	long	longer	longest
ADVERB	far	farther	farthest

Some have irregular comparisons, but these rarely cause difficulty:

	POSITIVE	COMPARATIVE	SUPERLATIVE
ADJECTIVE	good	better	best
	bad	worse	worst
	many, much	more	most
ADVERB	well	better	best
	best	worse	worst

Words of two syllables may have comparisons in *-er* and *-est*, or may use *more (less)* and *most (least)*; the choice is determined by rhythm and emphasis. Words of three or more syllables are compared only with *more (less)* and *most (least)*.

	POSITIVE	COMPARATIVE	SUPERLATIVE
ADJECTIVE	lovely	lovelier; more (less) lovely	loveliest; most (least) lovely
	beautiful	more (less) beautiful	most (least) beautiful
ADVERB	beautifully	more (less) beautifully	most (least) beautifully

In informal speech, or for reasons of emphasis, the superlative is often used in place of the comparative. But the general rule in formal writing is to use the comparative in comparing two things, the superlative for three or more.

Informal   Put your *best* foot forward.
May the *best* team win.

Formal   The *better* team won decisively.
Rome is the *oldest* of European capitals.

Absolute adjectives cannot, strictly speaking, be compared; something is either *dead, possible, full, perfect, unique*, or it isn't. But in informal usage absolute adjectives are often modified by comparisons, either for emphasis ("*deader* than a doornail") or because some of them have virtually lost their absolute meaning ("this box is *emptier* than that"). In formal usage, "more nearly empty" would be preferable.

Things compared should be of the same kind.

Wrong   Marlowe's plays are not so highly regarded as Shakespeare.

Right   Marlowe's plays are not so highly regarded as those of Shakespeare (or *as Shakespeare's*).

Other is used only when the things compared are of the same class.

Wrong   Helen is more intelligent than any *other* boy.

Right   Helen is more intelligent than any boy.

She reads more widely than any *other* student.

Do not use *other* with superlative comparisons.

Wrong   Helen was the most intelligent of all the *other* students.

Right   Helen was the most intelligent of all the students.

An adjective may precede a noun (or pronoun), or follow one. Or an adjective may follow a linking verb (copula).

> The *tired* nations sought a peace, one *secure* and *permanent*. (*Tired* precedes and modifies the noun *nations*. *Secure* and *permanent* follow and modify the pronoun *one;* this word order is not common but completely acceptable.)

> They hoped it would not prove *illusory*. (*Illusory* follows the linking verb *prove* and modifies the pronoun *it*.)

Notice in the example immediately above that an adjective, like a noun, may serve as subjective complement. This is not true of adverbs:

Wrong   It seems *truly*.
Right   It seems *true*.

Through frequent use, *I feel badly* is now sometimes acceptable in informal speech; but to be formally correct, say:

> I feel *bad*.

> I feel *ill*.

> I feel *well*. (meaning: I do not feel ill.)

> I feel *good*. (meaning: I feel positively happy, *or* healthy.)

PREPOSITIONS

A *preposition* connects a noun or pronoun with another word in the sentence, and establishes the relationship between them.

> Peter walked *to* the store. (connecting *walked* and *store*)

> He returned *with* them. (connecting *returned* and *them*)

Since word relationships are more difficult concepts to handle than "plain facts," prepositions are probably the most difficult parts of speech to make satisfactory rules for. Many are used in expressions that are impossible to analyze logically, the meaning of which is usually clear to the native speaker of English: *compare with* and *compare to*, for instance, or *differ from* and *differ with*. Rules in such cases are cumbersome and possibly misleading. The best way to learn proper use of prepositions is by paying attention to the speech and writing of people who use English accurately. Some of the more common prepositions:

about	beneath	in
above	beside	of
along	between	on
among	by	over
at	during	to
before	except	with
behind	for	without
below	from	

The noun or pronoun introduced by the preposition is called *the object of the preposition* and must be in the objective case. This rule gives trouble only in the case of coordinated pronouns. Thus,

> The waiter brought some *for her and me*. (NOT: *she and I*)

A preposition with its object is called a *prepositional phrase* and is used as an adjective or an adverb.

> The boy *with the dog* is my brother. (adjective, modifying noun *boy*)

> They are all playing *with the dog*. (adverb, modifying verb *are playing*)

> He threw his hat *over the fence*. (adverb, modifying verb *threw*)

In informal conversation, prepositions are sometimes doubled, though this is not really necessary to the meaning of the sentence. Double prepositions are rarely used in writing.

Informal   We left *at about* nine o'clock.

Formal   We left *about* nine o'clock.

Never repeat the same preposition near the beginning and at the end of a sentence: She is the person *for* whom I took all that trouble *for*. This is a mark of carelessness. However, contrary to a frequent yet mistaken belief, a preposition may be used at the end of a sentence, whenever it sounds natural to the rhythm of the sentence.

> Where does she come *from?*

> Whom did she go *with?*

The first example below is obviously a much more natural (and effective) sentence, despite the two prepositions with which it ends, than the second example.

> That's the kind of stupidity I won't put *up with*.

> That's the kind of stupidity *up with which* I will not put.

One classic example ends with no fewer than five prepositions:

What did you put the book you were being read *to out of away for?*

This sentence, too clumsy for formal, written English, is perfectly clear (though not very elegant) as spoken language.

Problem Prepositions

As already stated, the major problem with most prepositions is their idiomatic use. The following prepositions often pose problems in general usage.

AMONG, BETWEEN

Among is used when more than two persons or things are considered. *Between* is used when only two are considered. This rule, which may be relaxed in informal conversation, must be rigidly followed in written English.

> Divide the money *among* Frank, John, and Bill.

> We must choose *between* Frank and John.

An exception to this rule occurs when a mutual or reciprocal relationship is indicated. In this event, *between* is used for more than two.

> A treaty was concluded *between* the three nations.

> Frank, John, and Bill agreed *between* them that they would divide the prize.

AT, IN

At and *in* may often be used interchangeably. However, certain rules govern their usage when they indicate place or locality.

In is used when the reference to the interior of a building is stressed; *at,* when the site itself is stressed.

> Please meet me *in* the reception room of the dean's office.

> Classes will be held *at* Judson Hall.

In is used before the names of countries; *at* before the names of business firms, office buildings, schools, universities, etc.

> The International Conference will be held next year *in* Switzerland.

> I was educated *at* Princeton.

In is used before the name of a city to give the impression of permanence; *at,* to indicate a temporary stay.

> John goes to school *at* Trenton, but he lives *in* Philadelphia.

> Following a brief stay *at* Mexico City, we spent a month *in* Oaxaca.

In is used before the name of a city in local addresses; *at,* before the street number.

> Bill lives *in* Newark *at* 562 Kensington Avenue.

BELOW, BENEATH, UNDER, UNDERNEATH

These prepositions are generally used interchangeably, and in most cases one will be as grammatically correct as the other. Choice is usually determined by courtesy. Thus, the use of *beneath* may imply inferiority or contempt where *below* would be more courteous. The example below implies inferiority:

> Mary is in the class *beneath* me.

To substitute the word *below* does not make the construction more grammatically correct; however, it does make it more courteous and more in accord with accepted usage.

> Mary is in the class *below* me.

BESIDE, BESIDES

Beside is used to mean *next to. Besides* (ordinarily an adverb) is used to mean *in addition to* or *moreover.*

> Please sit *beside* me.

> *Besides* a dog, I have three cats. (*Besides* modifies the verb *have.*)

IN, INTO

In refers to position. *Into* denotes motion from without to within.

> We ate a buffet supper *in* the living room.

> We marched *into* the dining room.

ON, ONTO, ON TO

On refers to position upon something; *onto* denotes motion toward the upper surface of something; the two-word form *on to* is used when *on* belongs to the verb.

> I rode *on* the horse.

> I got *onto* the horse.

> I hung *on to* the horse.

ITEMS IN A SERIES

Items in a series must always be parallel in form. This means that when a preposition is used to introduce a series, it should be either repeated before each ensuing item or dropped before each ensuing item.

Wrong   I shall send invitations to John, Bill, and to Mary.

Right   I shall send invitations to John, to Bill, and to Mary.

Right   I shall send invitations to John, Bill, and Mary.

CONJUNCTIONS

A *conjunction* connects words, phrases, or clauses.

> black *and* blue (words)
>
> with the group *but* not part of it (phrases)
>
> He agreed, *though* he had reservations. (clauses)

Conjunctions may be classified according to four types:

A *coordinating conjunction* connects equal words, phrases, or clauses. There are six coordinating conjunctions. These are: *and, but, for, nor, or, yet.*

> We didn't walk, *nor* did we drive.
>
> It rained, *yet* we enjoyed the farm.

A coordinating conjunction may occasionally introduce a sentence closely related in thought to the preceding one.

> We managed to win the first game. *But* we never had a chance for the championship.

Correlative conjunctions are used in pairs to connect equal elements that are parallel in form. They replace a coordinating conjunction for greater emphasis.

> We will go to Yellowstone Park *or* Yosemite. (coordinating conjunction)
>
> We will go *either* to Yellowstone Park *or* Yosemite. (correlative conjunctions)

The most common correlative conjunctions are *both . . . and, neither . . . nor, either . . . or, whether . . . or,* and *not only . . . but (also).*

> I didn't care *whether* we went *or* stayed home.
>
> At the party we met *not only* the Jacksons *but* the Blairs.
>
> *Not only* the husbands came *but also* the children.

A *conjunctive adverb* connects clauses in addition to modifying a verb (or clause). The most common are:

accordingly	however	nevertheless
also	indeed	still
besides	likewise	then
furthermore	meanwhile	therefore
hence	moreover	thus

A group of words may also serve as a conjunctive adverb:

> in fact   for that reason
> in the first place   on the contrary
> in the meantime   on the other hand

The conjunctive adverb always has a semicolon before it when it is used between independent clauses.

> I hadn't set the clock; *hence*, I was late.
>
> The search may have ended; *indeed*, it's likely.
>
> We tried the engine; but *in the meantime*, the tire had gone flat.

A *subordinating conjunction* introduces a dependent clause and subordinates it to an independent clause. It establishes the relation between the two clauses. This relation may be one of

CAUSE: *as, because, inasmuch as, since*

> We went indoors, *as* it had grown quite dark.
>
> *Since* he likes animals, they like him.

COMPARISON: *as . . . as, so . . . as, than*

> Chaucer's language is not *so* difficult *as* you may think.
>
> There was more smoke *than* (there was) fire.

CONCESSION: *although, though, while*

> *Although* he works hard, he's not very efficient.
>
> He doesn't write well, *though* he tries.

CONDITION: *if, provided that, unless*

> She'll come *provided that* you do.
>
> *Unless* you run you won't catch her.

MANNER: *as, as if, as though*

> Do *as* you would be done by.
>
> It seemed *as though* he would win.

PLACE: *where, wherever, whence, whither*

> *Where* one is good, two are better.

"And *whence* they come and *whither* they shall go

The dew upon their feet shall manifest."

PURPOSE: *in order that, so that, that*

So *that* there will be enough for all, take no more than you need.

They died *that* we may live.

RESULT: *so that, so . . . that, such . . . that*

He studied hard, *so that* finally he was the recognized expert in the field.

Such was his optimism *that* we all were prepared for success.

TIME: *after, as, before, since, till, until, when, while*

Ruth arrived *as* they were leaving.

Until you spoke I didn't know you were there.

Troublesome Conjunctions

The following are troublesome conjunctions:

AND, ALSO

Also should not be used in place of *and* to connect items in a series.

Wrong I study English, French, Spanish, *also* Russian.

Right I study English, French, Spanish, and Russian.

AND, ETC.

The abbreviation *etc.* means "and so forth." It is incorrect to use *and* to connect the last item in a series when the last item is followed by *etc.*

Wrong We need eggs, bacon, and bread, etc.

Right We need eggs, bacon, bread, *etc.*

AND WHICH, AND WHO

These should not be used unless preceded in the same sentence by *which* or *who*.

Wrong I am looking for a course with four credits *and which* holds classes on Wednesday mornings.

Right I am looking for a course *which* offers four credits *and which* holds classes on Wednesday mornings.

AND, BUT

And is used to show addition; *but*, to show contrast.

Wrong Mary and I have been invited to a party, *and* I have to take care of my younger brother.

Right Mary and I have been invited to a party, *but* I have to take care of my younger brother.

AS, AS IF, LIKE

As and *as if* are respectably used as conjunctions to introduce clauses of various kinds and to connect comparisons. *Like*, which is gaining respectability as a conjunction in informal usage, is treated only as a preposition in formal writing. Grammarians shudder when they see *like* usurping the role of *as* and *as if*.

Informal You act *like* you're hurt.

Formal You act *as if* you were hurt.

AS, BECAUSE, SINCE

Any one of these may be used to introduce clauses of cause or reason, that is, to connect the stated cause with a fact already given.

I came *because* I was worried.

As you won't go, I will stay.

Since I can, I will.

However, *because* is limited to introducing clauses of cause or reason. *As* and *since* are also used to introduce clauses involving time. To introduce duration of time, use *as*. To introduce sequence of time, use *since*.

I worked less and less *as* each day passed. (time duration)

I haven't done any work *since* last you were here. (time sequence)

BECAUSE, FOR

Because is used when the reason it introduces is based upon fact. *For* is used when the reason it introduces is based upon opinion or speculation.

Come inside, *because* it is raining. (The reason given is an established fact.)

We are going to have a storm, *for* there is a ring around the moon. (The reason given is based on speculation.)

IF, WHETHER

If introduces clauses of supposition or condition involving uncertainty or doubt.

If I had known you were coming, I would have prepared a feast. (implies uncertainty)

If may also stand for *even though* or *whenever*.

If I am wrong, you are not right. (implies *even though*)

If I do not know, I try to find out. (implies *whenever*)

On the other hand, *whether* introduces clauses which involve an alternative. The alternative may be stated or understood. (*Whether* is the conjunction most likely to be used when followed by *or*.)

It will not make any difference *whether* I know or not. (alternative stated)

Please let me know *whether* I am right. (alternative implied)

WHEN, WHERE

When should not be used to introduce a definition unless the definition involves a time element; *where* should not be used unless the definition involves place or location.

Wrong   A foul is *when* (or *where*) the ball leaves the court.

Right   A foul is made *when* the ball leaves the court during the playing period. (time involved)

Right   A foul is made at the place *where* the ball crosses the foul line. (place involved)

WHEN, WHILE

When refers to a fixed period of time; *while* to duration of time.

When you are willing to talk, I will listen. (fixed time: as soon as you are ready to talk)

While you talk, I will listen. (time duration: during the time that you talk)

WHILE, ALTHOUGH, BUT, WHEREAS

While is often used colloquially to mean *although, but,* and *whereas*.

Colloquial   I like Mary, *while* I like Jeanne better.

Formal   I like Mary, *but* I like Jeanne better.

Colloquial   Mary is fat, *while* Jeanne is slim.

Formal   Mary is fat, *whereas* Jeanne is slim.

INTERJECTIONS

An interjection is a word of exclamation which expresses emotion, but which has no grammatical relation to the rest of the sentence.

Oh! Hey! Whoa! Ouch! Ha, ha! Boo!

Many words that generally serve as other parts of speech may be used as interjections:

Well! Heavens! Nuts! Run! Good!

SENTENCES

The division of words into eight main parts of speech—a useful way to point out their individual characteristics—is technically termed *accidence*. But words are seldom used alone; how they are put together in sentences is termed *syntax*.

A *sentence* is a group of words expressing a complete thought. It may make a statement, ask a question, give a command, or express an exclamation.

Antarctica is the seventh continent.

Are Europe and Asia separate continents?

See America first!

So this is Africa!

However, a complete thought may be expressed by a single word: a man entering an elevator and saying, "Down"; the answers ("Are you going?") "No," ("Where is it?") "Here," or ("How do you feel?") "Happy." The concept of a *complete thought* is satisfied by such limited sentences as the telegraphic ARRIVING LAGUARDIA FRIDAY. HOME BEFORE SIX. LOVE STANLEY; or the journalistic headline LABOR UNIONS/HIT JOB LOSSES. But in addition, readers expect most sentences to be *grammatically complete*.

Grammatical Completion

The grammatically complete *simple sentence* consists of a subject and a predicate. The *subject* is a noun or a noun equivalent (pronoun in the nominative case, noun clause, gerund, infinitive) naming the person, place, or thing with which the sentence is chiefly concerned. The *predicate* is the verb or verb phrase asserting something about the subject.

Children (subject) *play* (predicate).

This simple sentence may be expanded and made more complicated (or significant) in various ways.

The subject may be modified:

Happy children play.

The predicate may be modified:

> Children play *hard*.

Or the verb may be given a complement:

> Children play *games*.

It becomes a *compound sentence* when two or more subjects attach to a single predicate:

> *Children* and *adults* play.

or when two or more predicates follow from a single subject:

> Children *play* and *sleep*.

or when two or more simple sentences closely related in thought are joined by commas, semicolons, or coordinating conjunctions:

> Children play, men work, and women manage.

However complicated it may become, the sentence rests on the solid base of subject and predicate. This is true in the *declarative sentence* (above), the *interrogative sentence:*

> Do children play?

the *exclamatory sentence:*

> How happily the children play!

and the *imperative sentence:*

> Play, children! (the subject, *you*, is understood)

The sentence may be made more flexible and expressive by the use of phrases and clauses.

Phrases

A *phrase* is a group of words used as a single part of speech (noun, adjective, adverb, or verb). It does not contain a subject and a predicate.

NOUN PHRASE: It is impossible *not to pity him; trying to help* him is a problem.

ADVERBIAL
PHRASE: *By Monday* they were gone.
               I hung it *on the wall*.

ADJECTIVE
PHRASE: A man *of honor*, a name *to admire*.

VERB PHRASE: He *has asked* for you; he *must have forgotten* already.

Phrases may also be classified by form:

A *prepositional phrase* consists of a preposition and its object, and any accompanying modifiers. It is used as an adjective or adverb.

> *At once* they left *for the big town*. (prepositional phrases used as adverbs)
>
> The man *with the hoe*. (used as adjective)
>
> He felt lost *in the impersonal clamor* (used as adverb) *of the advertising industry*. (used as adjective)

An *infinitive phrase* consists of an infinitive (and its object, if present), and any accompanying modifiers. It is used as a noun, adjective, or adverb.

> I want *to see* (infinitive) *the moon* (object). (infinitive phrase used as noun)
>
> Professor Thomson is the man *to know*. (used as adjective)
>
> A diplomat must be able *to make* (infinitive) *the most* (object) *of the existing situation*. (prepositional phrase, adjective modifying *the most*, used as adverb)

A *participial phrase* consists of a participle (and its object, if present), and any accompanying modifiers. It is used as an adjective.

> *Thinking quickly*, he regained his poise.
>
> The plane *carrying* (participle) *the serum* (object) arrived in time.
>
> Shirley, *earnestly* (adverb modifying the next word, *talking*) *talking* (participle) *to the group* (prepositional phrase, adverb modifying *talking*), signaled Carrie to wait.

A *gerund phrase* consists of a gerund (and its object, if present), and any accompanying modifiers. It is used as a noun.

> Daily *swimming* kept him in trim.
>
> *Flying* (gerund) *a kite* (object) can be hard work.
>
> His editor advised *writing* (gerund) *on a totally new subject*. (prepositional phrase, adjective modifying *writing*)

A *verb phrase* consists of a verb and its auxiliaries.

> I *will have seen* him by then.
>
> The Senate *could* hardly *have foreseen* the result of its action.

Clauses

A *clause* is a group of words containing a subject and a predicate. It may be independent or dependent. An *independent clause* is, essentially, a sentence; it differs only in its capitalization and/or punctuation. In the following example the independent clause can stand alone by capitalizing *he* and adding a period after *plotters*.

> Mindful of his honor, *he avoided every contact with the plotters* and refused to listen to their schemes.

A *dependent clause* cannot stand alone. It is connected to an independent clause by a relative pronoun, present or implied (*who, which, that*), or by a subordinating conjunction (*after, because, since, while,* etc.) and functions as a part of the sentence–as noun, adjective, or adverb.

> *That everyone was against him* was his constant complaint. (noun clause, subject)

> He estimated *which of the problems he could solve.* (noun clause, object of verb)

> In the afternoon we came to *what was evidently the main road.* (noun clause, object of preposition *to*)

> The man *who fails at everything he tries* may not be trying. (adjective clause, modifying *man*)

> He may succeed *if he tries a completely new approach.* (adverbial clause, modifying *succeed*)

A dependent clause need not be so complete as these examples. Often, especially in spoken language and informal writing, the connective between independent clause and dependent adjective clause is merely implied and not expressed.

> The man *he said was coming* never showed up. (*Who* or *that* is understood.)

Sometimes in informal speech or writing a dependent clause contains neither subject nor verb.

> *When crossing,* look both ways. (*When you are crossing* is understood.)

> His clothes were old *though clean.* (*Though they were clean* is understood.)

Constructions such as these are called *elliptical clauses.* When properly related to the main clause, an elliptical clause adds economy and punch to writing. The dependent clause used as an adjective (*adjective clause*) is called *restrictive* if it adds information necessary to identify the subject, or restricts it to a special case.

> The boy *you met last Friday* telephoned again.

> The man *who can plan ahead* is automatically at an advantage.

> Rebellions *that are successful* are recorded as revolutions.

If the subject requires no further identification after being named, the clause is *nonrestrictive,* and simply adds additional information.

> Jaspar, *who never gave up,* finally hit on a way to catch the chipmunk.

There is only one Jaspar being discussed, and the reader presumably knows who he is; the nonrestrictive clause is not essential to the meaning of the sentence, though it enriches it. Here are two more examples of nonrestrictive clauses.

> He sat on the table, *which could barely support him.*

> She was sure that the man, *whom she had not met,* must be her long-lost brother.

Who (whom) and *which* may introduce either restrictive or nonrestrictive clauses, but *that* introduces only restrictive clauses. Relative pronouns may be omitted only in restrictive clauses.

> The man *we hoped to see* has left. (Restrictive *who* is understood.)

> We all liked the pie *she baked.* (Restrictive *that* is understood.)

Nonrestrictive clauses are set off by commas, and often the various choices of punctuation can give the sentence radically different meanings.

RESTRICTIVE
CLAUSE: Engineers who have little understanding of theory are rarely put in charge of a program.

NON-
RESTRICTIVE
CLAUSE: Engineers, who have little understanding of theory, are rarely put in charge of a program.

The first is a warning; the second is a sneer. (For the specific rules on punctuating restrictive and nonrestrictive clauses, see page 6.)

Kinds of Sentences

A *simple sentence* contains only one independent clause, however modified.

> In times of economic expansion almost any investor may seem a financial wizard by his luck on the stock market.

Stripped of the adverbial prepositional phrases *in times of economic expansion* and *by his luck,* the adjective phrase *on the stock market,* the adverb *almost,* the adjective *financial,* this example reveals itself as basically the simple sentence *(almost any) investor may seem a wizard.*

A *compound sentence* contains two or more coordinate independent clauses, joined by a coordinating conjunction:

> He tried hard, but he simply had no talent.

or by a conjunctive adverb preceded by a semicolon:

> It had begun to rain; however, they had brought umbrellas.

or by a semicolon (or colon) alone:

> He was tired of life; he was afraid to die.

> The Greeks made their decision: They would resist the Persian invasion.

A *complex sentence* contains one independent clause and one or more dependent clauses.

> However fast we ran, the ball ran faster.

> He whispered that he was sure (that) he had recognized one of the men who had come in. (three dependent clauses, the second with *that* understood)

A *compound-complex* sentence contains two or more independent clauses, and one or more dependent clauses.

> Atlhough the weather forecast promised rain, the sky was cloudless, and the dry spell continued.

Spelling and Vocabulary

Spelling is not the horrendous problem that many students think it is. By the time they have reached senior high school, and certainly by the time they finish college, most people have learned most of the words they will ever use, and they spell most of them correctly. The problem is caused by those few words which are misspelled over and over again. Another, but quite separate, problem is the rapid rate at which new words are added to our vocabulary, notably those emerging from enlarging technology and from areas of professional specialization.

For the average person afflicted with habits of bad spelling, corrective measures are not difficult to determine or apply. If you fall in this category, you probably spell most words quite correctly, and only fall down, with depressing recurrence, on certain kinds of words. To improve, you need not relearn how to spell, but only ferret out and concentrate on those specific areas where you have trouble. You will probably find that your problems are confined to certain special areas. Perhaps you are confused by words with *-able* or *-ible* endings, or by the question of whether to double final consonants or not. Once you have a list of such troublesome words—and the real job is running them down—you can take effective curative measures. Brief but regular periods devoted to memorizing the correct spellings will quickly produce results, particularly if the memorizing period is just before you go to bed.

BUILDING A VOCABULARY

We tend to avoid words we do not know how to spell, and in so doing we forget them by nonuse. With the spelling handicap reduced we can explore the various ways of acquiring a large and useful vocabulary.

In school the teacher advises, "Look up in the

dictionary every word you don't know and write it, with its definition, in a notebook. Then examine the meaning of its root, or roots, also possible suffix and/or prefix. Pronounce the word over to yourself, and finally use it in speaking and writing." This remains the surest technique, but it is slow, and demands more conscientious application than most people are prepared to bring to it.

The best way to build a vocabulary is to broaden one's intellectual horizons. An interest and a delight in words and the ideas they convey will bring about attentive listening and wide and thorough reading. It can give impetus to frequent use of the dictionary, memorization of selected vocabulary lists, and the study of the origin and development of words (etymology).

We all possess three basic vocabularies—a speaking, a writing, and a reading vocabulary. Of the three, the reading vocabulary contains by far the largest number of words. As we read extensively, all three vocabularies will expand, but at surprisingly different rates. The reading vocabulary increases the fastest. Only relatively few words will seep down into the speaking and writing vocabularies. We recognize any number of words when we see them in print, but they are neither on the tips of our tongues nor on the points of our pens—ready for us to use when they are applicable.

The main problem is to make the newly learned words accessible when we are speaking—but more especially when we are writing. The words we have learned must become familiar friends; not only should they be recognizable when we see and hear them again, but they should be instantly available.

A much surer way than the list method for making a new word your very own is to use the word in a sentence of your own construction. Don't attempt to do this with every new word you come upon. Be selective. Take the words that appeal to and interest you—words that you think you may want to use again in the future. When a word does appeal to you, go to the dictionary for help in defining it precisely. When you have the definition (or, rather, definitions, for most words have a number of meanings), don't simply accept the dictionary example of how it is used. Compose your own illustrative sentence to fix the new-found word in your mind. Let the sentence express something that is essentially *you*—some interest of yours. Perhaps the word can be used in relation to some hobby or to a friend.

A few words of caution: Don't be too quick to flaunt the new words in public. Don't insist on forcing them into your very next composition or report. You may have a fair idea of the meaning of a word; you may have a good sentence in mind. At the same time, you may not be using the word in precisely its right context. A good idea is to wait a bit before exposing the word to public hearing or view. For example, if the word has to do with biology, try the sentence out on a friend who is at home in this field, and make sure from him that you are using it correctly. This is the most creative way of fixing new words in your mind. It can be guaranteed to work, and even more important, the new words will be ready for recall and use when the occasion arises.

PRONUNCIATION

Just as important as the written word is the spoken or sounded word. The sounded word precedes the written word by thousands of years, and of course without the one there could not be the other. And just as there are correct ways to use words in writing, so are there correct ways to sound them in speaking.

English is supposedly a phonetic language. That is, the letters of our alphabet stand for sounds, and the way words are spoken or pronounced is supposed to correspond to the way they are spelled. In practice it doesn't always work out that way. In the early years, English was more or less phonetic, but time has brought drastic changes in pronunciation, while changes in spelling have not kept pace. (It is an interesting paradox that the language has been remarkably liberal in the matter of pronunciation yet remarkably conservative in the matter of spelling.) It is the gulf that has been created between pronunciation and spelling—widened during the last several centuries by the invention of the printing press—that has transformed English from a phonetic to a most unphonetic language.

To fill this gulf, our dictionaries respell countless thousands of words according to the way they are actually sounded in practice, and they construct elaborate phonetic alphabets that correspond to the true sounds (see page 38). The dictionaries don't always succeed, however, since there is considerable difference in the way people speak. Still, the dictionaries are our only guide, and if you follow the phonetic respellings of a reputable dictionary, you will be sure of pronouncing words correctly in most instances.

In the United States, there are three more or less distinct types of pronunciation–the northeastern, the southern, and the northwestern. Even when pronunciation differs from the norm or standard as given in dictionaries, it is nevertheless considered correct and proper as long as the pronunciation is used by the educated people of any one of these regions.

Common Errors

Do not sound the *t* in most words ending in *-sten* and *stle*.

> fasten
> wrestle
> chasten

Do not sound the *t* in the following words:

> often
> soften

Beware of dropping the *g* in words that end in *-ing* and in *-ength*.

> believing *not* believin'
>
> thinking *not* thinkin'

Beware of dropping the letters *d, t,* and *l*. Even in the South, the practice of dropping these letters is regarded as vulgar by educated Southerners.

> old *not* ol'
>
> just *not* jus'
>
> self *not* se'f

Beware of dropping the letter *r*. In New England and the South, correct pronunciation sanctions the substitution of the short *a* for the letter *r* in certain words. But to drop the *r* altogether in these words is regarded as vulgar (not *do'* for *door* or *fo'* for *for*). In these same regions, on the other hand, it is perfectly proper to drop the *r* in words such as *car* and *farther*.

Beware of the so-called intrusive *r*. Do not insert an *r* in a word where it does not belong, nor between two words when one word ends with a vowel and the following word begins with a vowel.

> spoil *not* spurl
>
> law and order *not* lawr and order
>
> the idea (*not* idear) of it

Do you prize the dictionary as the most valuable tool in your possession to help you choose and use words properly? If you answer no, you are among a majority of students who feel the same way. If you answer yes, you are in a minority who understand what the dictionary is–and who also know how to use it. For the chief reason most people neglect the dictionary is that they just don't know what it's all about. The following pages show how to use the dictionary the way it should be used.

Meanings of Words

A word sometimes has as many as fifty or sixty different meanings or shades of meaning. This is not common, but the point to remember is that a word doesn't necessarily have just one meaning. Most words have several meanings, according to the ways they are used in a sentence. Moreover, the same word changes its form, usually its spelling, and often its pronunciation, according to the part of speech it takes. Therefore, never take the definition immediately following an entry as final. You must read–or at least scan–all its definitions. Different meanings are usually numbered.

Spelling

Occasionally an entry will have two or more different spellings of the same word. This means that all given spellings are in general use. All are acceptable, but the one given first is usually the preferred form. Irregular spellings of the plural form of a word are also given. Regular formations, however, are not given. Thus, when a plural spelling is omitted we can take it for granted that the word forms its plural in the regular way, by adding *s* to the singular and by adding *-es* to words ending in *s, x, z, ch,* and *sh*. Plurals of compound words are also generally omitted when they are formed in the same way as the plurals of the main word. British spelling variations are preceded by the abbreviation *Brit*. Such forms are acceptable in Great Britain, not in the United States.

Inflectional Forms

Often a word is spelled in various ways according to its use; we call these various spellings the *inflectional forms* of the word. For example, plurals of nouns are inflectional forms of the nouns, various tenses of verbs are inflectional forms of the verbs, while comparative and intensive forms of adjectives are their inflectional forms.

A good dictionary lists the inflectional forms that are irregular or that give trouble in spelling. When two inflected forms are listed for a verb, the first is the form for both the past tense and the past participle. When three forms are given, the first is the form for the past tense, the second the past participle, and the third the present participle.

Inflections formed in the regular way are seldom given, even in good dictionaries. In addition to the spelling of plurals, forms regarded as regular inflections include, for verbs, present tenses formed by adding -s or -es, past tenses and past participles formed by adding -ed, and present participles formed by adding -ing. Comparatives and superlatives formed in the regular way (by adding -er and -est to the positive form) are also omitted in most entries.

Usage Labels

Various labels signify a word's status in actual usage. These labels are extremely important. They indicate under what circumstances a word may properly be used. The conventional labels are: *colloquial* (used in conversation but not in formal writing), *slang* (restricted to rare occasions in informal conversation and informal writing), *obsolete* (no longer used), *archaic* (used only in special contexts, as in church ritual, but no longer in general use), *poetic* (restricted to poetry), *dialect* (restricted to special geographical areas), and *British* (characteristically British rather than American). Words that have more than one meaning are generally treated as follows: when the label follows the number introducing a definition, it applies to that definition only; when it precedes a number, it applies to all the definitions that follow.

Syllable Division

The division of all words into syllables is a universal practice of dictionaries. This is done partly as an aid to pronunciation and word derivation, and partly to show how a word is divided at the end of a line when there isn't enough space to write the full word on the same line. Syllable division is indicated by centered dots or small dashes. Some dictionaries divide the word's main entry into syllables, others indicate them in the phonetic respelling (see below) that immediately follows the entry. Many persons confuse the dot (·) or short dash (-) with the longer, heavier dash (–) that indicates a hyphen in compound words. The following is a sample compound word entry in Webster's

New World Dictionary (note the difference between the syllable dot and the hyphen):

hel·ter–skel·ter

Accent Marks

Dictionary entries also carry accent marks (′) to indicate which particular syllable or part of the word should be stressed. Some dictionaries place the accent marks in the entry itself, others in the respelling that follows the entry. The important thing to remember is that the accent mark appears immediately *after* the syllable to be stressed. When two syllables in a word are to be accented, the syllable that receives the lighter stress is marked by a light accent mark (′). It should be pronounced with less stress than syllables marked with the dark accent mark, but with more stress than syllables that carry no accent mark at all. Words of one syllable have no accent marks. Instead of light and dark marks, some dictionaries use single and double accent marks. The single mark indicates heavy stress; double marks, light stress.

Phonetic "Respelling"

A wide gulf often exists between how words are spelled and how they are pronounced (see page 36). For this reason, all good dictionaries give the phonetic spelling of troublesome words, in addition to the way they are conventionally spelled. The phonetic spelling indicates how to sound out the various parts of a word in actual speech. It is termed the "respelling." Surprisingly few people know how to handle a respelling, but it is very simple.

A word respelling may consist of a simple rearrangement or substitution of vowels and consonants. It may also consist of symbols called "diacritical marks," which appear over the vowels. These marks indicate when a vowel is to be pronounced long, short, etc. It is not necessary to know the names of these marks, and it is not even necessary to memorize how to make the sounds of any particular mark. For they appear in a key at the bottom (or top) of each page (or alternate page) of all good dictionaries. And next to each mark is a short word that anyone can readily pronounce and that shows just what sound is called for. Sometimes the mark is contained in the short word instead of appearing separately. The marks appear in alphabetical order for ready reference. All you need to pronounce a word is to refer to this key listing. You find the vowel with the diacritical mark that corresponds to the mark in the respelling of the word given in the main entry. You pronounce it just as it is sounded in the short word given in the key.

Suppose that we want to be sure of the proper pronunciation of the name of the composer Wagner. The entry in Webster's *New World Dictionary* (Compact Desk Edition) gives the following respelling after the main entry:

väg′nēr

Now we immediately know that the beginning letter *W* is pronounced as a *V*. But how about the *ä* and the *ē*? These are termed "two-dot *a*" and "tilde *e*" respectively, but we don't need to know this. At the bottom of the page is the following key list:

fat, āpe, bâre, cär; ten, ēven, ovēr; is, bīte; lot, gō, hôrn, tōōl, look; oil, out; up, ūse, fûr; ə for *a* in *ago*; *th*in, *th*en; zh, leisure; η, ring; ë, Fr. leur; ö, Fr. feu; Fr. mo*n;* ü, Fr. duc; kh, G. ich, doch. ‡ foreign; < derived from

We can see that the *a* with the two dots above it is in the short word *cär*, so we know that the *a* in *Wagner* is pronounced as the *a* in *car*. Similarly, the *e* is contained in the short word *ovēr*, which is how the *e* in *Wagner* should be sounded.

A comprehensive version of the phonetic key appears in the front pages of your dictionary. Ordinarily the simpler key on the pages with the entries is sufficient. Phonetic alphabets vary somewhat between dictionaries, but when you are acquainted with the markings of one, you will be able to interpret the others easily.

One mark that may give some trouble is the so-called *schwa*, or inverted *e* (ə). Not all dictionaries employ the schwa, but it is coming into increasing use, and you should know about it.

When the schwa (ə) appears in a respelling, it always takes the place of a vowel. It is a sign that the vowel is reduced in strength of stress. It has an enfeebled *uh* sound, as the *a* has in the words *ago* and *about*. The schwa can present difficulties, as you can't be sure just how to sound it in every case. You will soon get the knack of it, however, after you see it used a number of times in a dictionary. Its purpose, to repeat, is to reduce, almost to ignore, the vowel's stress. The schwa's importance will be apparent when you realize how dull and unpleasant English would sound if every vowel were clearly stressed and enunciated. To relieve the monotony of vowel enunciation, there are times when vowels should lose their force, and the schwa tells us just when to pass quickly over them.

Word Derivation

The chief languages upon which English is founded are Anglo-Saxon, Old Norse, Old French, Middle English, Latin, and Greek. The abbreviations used by dictionaries to specify the language (or languages) from which a word is derived are, in order of their appearance above: AS., ON., OF., ME., L., and Gk. Additional language abbreviations are listed in the front of the dictionary. The symbol > means "derived from." Generally, word derivation information appears in brackets, either at the beginning or at the end of the entry. A question mark following the derivation signifies that it is only a guess and at best is uncertain.

Frequently Misspelled Words

Words shown with an asterisk below also have an alternate correct spelling. See any good dictionary for the alternate spelling.

A

abominable
abridgment
absence
abundance
abundant
academic
academically
academy
accelerating
accentuation
acceptable
acceptance
accepting
accessible
accessory*
accidental
accidentally
acclaim
accommodate
accompanied
accompanies
accompaniment
accompanying
accomplish
accountant
accuracy
accurate
accurately
accuser
accuses
accusing
accustom
achievement
achieving
acknowledgment*
acquaintance
acquire
across
actuality
actually
acutely
adequately
adhering
admirable
admissible*
admission

admittance
adolescence
adolescent
advancement
advantageous
adversaries
advertisement*
advertiser*
advertising*
advice
advise
aerial
aesthetic
affect
affiliate
afraid
against
ageless
aging
aggravate
aggressive
alibis
allegedly
allergies
alleviate
allotment
allotted
allowed
allows
all right*
all together
already
altar
alter
alternate
alternative
altogether
amateur
amenable
amiable
amicably
among
amount
amplified
amusing
analogies
analysis

analyze
anarchy
anecdote
angrily
annihilate
announcing
annually
anonymous
another
anticipated
antique
anxieties
apiece
apologetically
apologized
apology
apostrophe
appall*
apparatus
apparent
appearance
applies
applying
appraise
appreciate
appreciation
apprehend
approaches
appropriate
approval
approximate
apropos
aptly
aquarium
arbitrary
arduous
area
aren't
arguing
argument
arise
arising
armies
arouse
arousing
arrangement
arrears

arriving
artfully
article
artificial
ascent
ascetic
asinine
asphalt
asphyxiation
aspiration
assassin
assemblies
assertiveness
assiduous
assignment
assimilate
assistance
associating
assortment
assuming
asthma
astonish
astronaut
astute
asylum
atheist
athlete
athletic
atrocious
atrocity
attachment
attack
attempts
attendance
attendant
attended
attirement
attitude
attractive
attribute
audacious
audacity
audience
augment
auspicious
authenticity
author

authoritarian
authoritative
authority
authorization
authorize
autumn
available
awareness
awesome
awfully

B

babbling
balancing
ballerina
balminess
bankruptcy
bare
barely
bargain
barrenness
barrier
barroom
bashfulness
basically
basis
battling
bawdiness
bazaar
bearable
beauteous
beautified
beautiful
beautifying
beauty
become
becoming
before
began
beggar
beginner
beginning
begrudging
beguile
behaving
behavior
belatedly

belief
believe
belittling
belligerence
beneath
benefactor
beneficent
beneficial
benefited*
benevolence
benign
biannual
bicycle
bicycling
bigamy
bigger
biggest
binoculars
biscuit
biting
bitten
blameless
bluing
blurred
blurry
boastfully
bohemian
boisterous
boloney
booby trap
boring
born
borne
bossiness
botanical
bottling
boulevard
bouncing
boundary
bounties
braggadocio
breath
breathe
breezier
brief
brilliance
brilliant
brimming
Britain
Britannica
brochure
bronchial
brutally
budget
bulging
bulletin

bumptious
buoy
buoyant
buried
bursar
bury
bushiness
business
busy

C
cabaret
cafeteria
caffeine
calamity
calculation
calendar
callous
callus
calves
camaraderie
canceled*
candescence
canniness
canning
canoeing
capably
capacity
capitalism
capital
capitol
capricious
captaincy
captivity
careen
career
careless
cargoes
caribou
caricature
caring
carnally
carousing
carpentry
carpeted
carried
carrier
carries
carrousel*
carrying
cascade
casserole
casually
cataclysmal
cataloged*
catalyst
catastrophe

category
caught
causally
causing
caustic
cautious
ceaseless
celibacy
celluloid
cemetery
centrifugal
centuries
ceramics
cerebellum
certainly
certificate
certified
cessation
chafe
chagrined
chalice
challenge
chancing
changeable
changing
chaotic
characteristic
characterized
charging
charlatan
chastise
chatty
chauffeur
chauvinism
cheerier
chief
children
chilliness
chiseling*
chivalry
choice
choose
choosing
chose
choreography*
Christianity
chronically
chronicle
cigarette
cinema
cipher
circling
circuit
circulating
circumstantial
cite
citizen

claimant
clairvoyance*
clamorous
clarify
classification
claustrophobia
cleanly
cleanness
cleanse
clemency
climactic
climatic
closely
clothes
cloudiest
coarse
cocoa
coerce
cognizance*
cohort
coincidence
collaborate
collectively
collegiate
collision
colloquial
colossal
combining
comfortable
coming
commentary
commercial
commiserate
commission
commitment
committee
commodities
commotion
communicate
companies
comparative
comparing
compassion
compatible
compel
compelled
competition
competitive
competitor
complacence
complement
completely
compliment
comprehendible
comprehensible
compromising

concede
conceit
conceive
conceivable
concentrate
concern
concession
condemn
condescend
conditionally
conferred
confidentially
confuse
confusion
congenial
conniving
connotation
connote
conquer
conscience
conscientious
conscious
consciousness
consequence
consequently
conservatively
considerably
considerately
consistency
consistent
conspicuous
constancy
consul
contagious
contemporary
contemptible
contemptuous
continuing
continuously
contrarily
contritely
contrivance
controlled
controlling
controversial
controversy
convalesce
convenience
convenient
conveyance
convincingly
coolly
cooperate
cooperative
coordinate
coordination

corporal
correlate
correspondent
corroborate
corruption
council
counsel
counselor*
countenance
countries
courtesy
cowardice
cozier
crazily
create
credibility
crescendo
crescent
crevice
criminally
cringing
criticism
criticize
crucially
crudely
cruelly
cruelty
crystal
cultivating
cultural
cunning
curing
curiosity
curious
curriculum
cycle
cynicism

D
dahlia
dallying
dauntless
dazedly
debatable*
deceased
deceitfully
deceive
decent
decided
decision
dedicating
deductible
defenseless
deferred
deficiency

define
definitely
definition
degeneracy
deliberating
delicately
delightfully
delinquency
demoralize
denied
denominational
denouncement
department
dependent*
deplorable
depreciate
depressant
depression
derangement
derisive
descend
describe
description
desert
deservedly
desirability
desire
desolately
despair
desperate
desperation
despising
despondency
desert
dessert
destitution
destruction
detach
deteriorate
determining
detriment
deuce
devastating
development*
deviation
device
devise
dexterity
diabolic
diagonally
dialogue
dictionary
difference
different
difficult
dilapidated

dilemma
diligence
diminutive
diner
dinghy
dining
dinner
dinosaur
diphthong
dipsomania
direness
disagreeable
disappear
disappoint
disapproval
disarray
disastrous
disbelief
discernible*
disciple
discipline
disconsolately
discourteous
discreditable
discrimination
discussion
disease
disguise
disgusted
dishevelment
disillusioned
disintegrate
dismally
dismissal
disparaging
disparity
dispersal
dispirited
dispossess
disprove
disqualified
disreputable
dissatisfied
dissension
dissoluteness
dissolve
dissuading
distraught
distressingly
disuse
diversely
divide
divine
divisible
docilely
doesn't

dolorous
dominant
dormitories
double
doubtfulness
drastically
dropped
drudgery
dually
during
duteous
dye
dyed
dyeing
dying

E
eager
easel
easily
eccentric
echelon
ecstasy*
eczema
edified
educating
eerily
effect
efficiency
efficient
effortlessly
egotistical
eighth
eightieth
either
elaborate
elapse
elegy
element
elementary
eligible
eliminate
emaciate
embarrass
embarrassment
embellish
embitter
emergencies
emerging
eminence
emperor
emphasize
employment
emptiness
emulate
enabling

enamel
enamored
encourage
encyclopedia
endeavor
energies
engaging
enjoy
enormous
enough
enrapture
enroute
ensconce
ensuing
enterprise
entertain
entertainment
enthusiastic
enthusiastically
enticement
entirely
entrance
enumerate
enunciate
envelop
envelope
enviable
environment
epitome
equable
equally
equipment
equipped
erratic
erroneous
escapade
escape
especially
essence
et cetera*
ethical
etiquette
eulogy
evacuate
evaporate
eventful
everything
evidently
exaggerate
exceed
excellence
excellent
except
excessive
excising
excitable

excruciating
excusing
exercise
existence
existent
expelled
expense
experience
experiment
explanation
expulsion
extensively
extenuate
extremely

F

fabricator
facetious
facility
facing
facsimile
factually
fallacy
falsely
falsified
familiar
families
fanatical
fancied
fantasies
fantasy
farewell
fascinate
fashions
fastidious
fatally
fatigue
favorable
favorite
feasible
ferocity
fertility
fetish
fiancé
fiancée
fickleness
fictitious
fidelity
field
fierce
fifteenth
figuring
finally
financially
financier
finesse
fitfully

flamboyant
flammable
flatterer
flexible
flimsiness
flippancy
flourish
fluidity
fluorescent
forbearance
forbidding
foreigners
forfeit
forgotten
formally
formerly
formidable
fortieth
fortitude
fortunately
forty
forward
fourth
freer
frequency
friendliness
frightfully
frivolous
fulfill
fundamentally
furrier
further

G

gaiety
galvanizing
gamble
gambol
garish
garnishee
garrulous
gaseous
gauche
gauging
gazette
generally
generating
generic
geniality
genius
gentlest
gesticulating
ghastliest
gladden
glamorous
glamour°
glorified

gluttony
government
governor
gradually
grammar
grammatically
grandeur
grandiloquence
grandiose
graphically
gratefully
gratification
gratuitous
greasing
grieving
grimacing
group
grudgingly
gruesome
guaranteed
guidance
guiding
guileless
guillotine
gullible
gutturally
gypped

H

habitable
hackneyed
hallucination
halving
hamster
handicapped
handled
handsomely
happen
happened
happiness
harangue
harassment
harmfully
harmonizing
hear
height
heinous
hemorrhage
hereditary
heresy
heretofore
heroes
heroic
heroine
hesitancy
heterogeneity
heuristic

hibernate
hierarchy
hilarity
hindrance
hirable
hoarsely
holocaust
homage
homely
homilies
homogeneous
hopeful
hopeless
hoping
horizontally
horrendous
horrified
hospitality
hospitalization
huge
human
humane
humanistic
humidified
humiliating
humorist
humorous
hundred
hundredth
hunger
hungrily
hungry
hydrophobia
hygiene
hygienic
hyphenation
hypnotizing
hypocrisy
hypocrite
hypothesis
hysterical

I

icicle
ideally
ideologies
idiocy
idiomatic
idiosyncrasy
ignoramus
ignorance
ignorant
illegible
illiteracy
illuminate
illusory

imagery
imaginary
imagination
imagine
imbibing
imitating
immaculate
immanent
immediately
immense
immigrant
imminent
immobilized
impartially
impasse
impeccable
impeding
imperceptible
impersonally
impinging
implausible
imploring
impoliteness
importance
impresario
impressionistic
improbability
improvement
inadequacy
inappeasable
inattentively
incalculable
incessantly
incidentally
incomparable
incomprehensible
inconceivable
inconsequential
inconstancy
incorrigible
increase
indefinite
independence
independent
indeterminate
indexes°
indispensable
individually
industries
inebriation
inefficiency
inevitable
inexcusable
inferred
infinitely
inflame

inflammation
inflammatory
influence
influential
informally
infringement
infuriating
ingenious
ingenuity
ingenuous
ingratiate
ingredient
inimitable
initiative
injurious
innervate
inoculate
inquiries
inscrutable
inseparable
insincere
insouciance
installment
instinctive
insuperable
insusceptible
intangible
intellect
intelligence
intelligent
interceding
interchanging
interest
interference
interim
interlining
intermediary
intermittent
internally
interpretation
interrogator
interrupt
intervening
intimately
intricately
intrigue
intuition
involve
invulnerability
irascible
ironical
irrationality
irrefutable
irrelevant
irreproachable
irresistible

irreverence
irreversible
irritable
irritating
irruptive
issuing
itinerary
its
it's

J

jauntily
jealousy
jeopardy
jettison
jocundity
jolliness
jovially
judgment°
judicially
juiciness
juvenile

K

kaleidoscope
keenness
khaki
kidnaped°
kindlier
kinescope
knowledge

L

laboratory
laborer
laboriously
labyrinth
laconic
laid
lamentable
languorous
largess°
laryngitis
lascivious
lassitude
lately
later
laureate
lazier
lead (v.)
lead (n.)
leafy
learnedly
legacy
legality
legibility
leisurely
lengthening

leniency
lenses
lesion
lethally
lethargy
letup
levying
libelous°
liberally
libidinous
license°
licentious
liege
likelihood
likely
likeness
limousine
linage
lineage
listener
literally
literary
literate
literature
litigation
liveliest
livelihood
liveliness
lives
lodging
loneliness
lonely
longitudinal
looniness
loose
lose
losing
loss
lugubrious
luminosity
lustfulness
luxury
lyricism

M

macabre°
macaroni
mademoiselle
magazine
magnanimity
magnificence
magnificent
maintenance
malefactor
malleable
manageability
management

maneuver
manful
manginess
maniacal
manifesto
manner
manning
manually
manufacturers
marauder
marionette
marriage
marveled
masquerade
massacre
massacring
material
maternally
mathematics
matriculating
matter
maturely
maturing
mausoleum
maybe
meant
measurement
mechanics
medallion
medical
medicine
medieval°
mediocrity
melancholia
melancholy
melee
meltable
memorability
memorizing
menacingly
mentally
merchandise
mere
merely
methods
microscopic
middling
mien
mightily
mileage
milieu
millennium
millionth
mimicker
mincingly
miniature

minority
minuscule
minutes
miraculous
mirrored
misalliance
misanthrope
miscalculation
miscellaneous
mischief
mischievous
misconstruing
mismanagement
misshapen
misspell
mistakable
moderately
moisturize
mollification
momentarily
monetary
monitor
monopolies
monosyllable
monotonous
monstrosity
moodily
moral
morale
morally
morbidity
morosely
mortally
mortifying
mosaic
mosquitoes
motif
mottoes°
mousiness
movable°
mucilage
multiplicity
multitudinous
mundanely
munificent
musically
musing
mutuality
mysterious

N

naïve°
naïveté°
namely
narcissus
narrative
natively

naturalistic
naturally
naughtily
nauseate
nearly
necessary
needlessly
nefarious
negativism
negligence
negligible
Negroes
neighbor
neither
neurotic
nevertheless
nicety
niggardly
nihilism
nimbly
nineteen
ninetieth
ninety
ninth
noble
noisily
nominally
noncombustible
normally
nostalgia
noticeable
noticing
notifying
notoriety
nourishment
nudity
nuisance
nullify
numerous
nuptial
O
obedience
objectively
obliging
obliquely
obliterate
obsequious
observance
obsess
obsolescent
obstacle
obstinately
obtuseness
occasion
occupancy
occupying

occur
occurred
occurrence
occurring
o'clock
oculist
oddly
odoriferous
odyssey
Oedipus
off
offense
offensively
officially
officiating
officious
omission
omit
omitted
oncoming
opaque
operate
opinion
opponent
opportunely
opportunity
oppose
opposite
oppression
optimism
optionally
oracular
orating
orderliness
ordinarily
ordinary
organization
original
ornamental
ornateness
orthodoxy
oscillate
ostentatious
ostracism
outrageous
outweigh
overdevelopment
overrun
P
pacified
pageant
paid
painstaking
palatable
palladium
palpitating

pamphlets
pancreas
panicky
pantomime
papier-mâché*
parable
parading
paradoxically
parallel
paralleled
paralyzed
parental
parentheses
parenthesis
parliament
paroxysm
parsimonious
partaking
partiality
participating
participial
participle
particular
passable
passed
passionately
passivity
past
pasteurize
pastime
pastoral
pastorale
pastries
pathetically
pathologist
patriarch
patriotically
patrolling
patronize
paunchy
pausing
peace
pealing
peculiar
pecuniary
pedagogue
pedagogy
pedantic
pedestrian
peeve
peignoir
penetrate
penicillin
penitent
penniless
penology

penury
perambulating
perceive
perceptible
percipience
peremptorily
perfidious
performance
perfunctory
perilous
periodic
permanent
permit
perpetually
persevering
persistent
personal
personally
personnel
perspicacity
persuade
pertain
perversely
pessimism
pestilence
petticoat
petulancy
pharmaceutical
phase
phenomenon
philosophy
phlegmatic
phobia
phonetically
phosphoric
photogenic
phraseology
phrasing
physical
physician
physique
pianos
picayune
piccolo
picnicked*
pictorially
piece
piecing
piling
pinnacle
piquancy
pirouette
piteous
pitifulness
placating
placidity

plagiary
plaintively
planetarium
planned
platitude
plausible
playwright
pleasant
pleasurable
plebeian
plenteous
pliability
poetically
poignant
politely
political
politician
polyethylene
pontifical
popularize
populous
pornographic
porosity
portable
portfolios
positively
possession
possibility
possible
postponement
potentiality
practicability
practical
practically
practice
precautionary
precede
precipice
precipitous
precisely
precursor
predecessor
predictable
predominant
preexistence
preferred
prejudice
prematurely
prepare
preposterous
presence
preservable
prestige
presumedly
pretension
prettily

prevalent
primitive
principal
principle
prisoners
privilege
probably
procedure
proceed
producible
profession
professor
proficient
prognosticating
progressively
prominent
promissory
pronounce
pronunciation
pronouncing
propaganda
propagate
prophecy*
prophesy*
psychoanalysis
psychology
psychopathic
psychosomatic
ptomaine
puerile
pugnacity
punctilious
purposeless
pursue

Q
quadruplicate
quantity
quarreled*
queasiness
querulous
questionnaire
queue
quiescent
quintessence
quipster
quixotic
quotable
quotient

R
rabies
raconteur
radiating
raising
ramification
rapidity

rarely
rarity
rationalize
readily
readmitted
reality
realize
really
reasonable
rebel
receive
receiving
receptacle
recipient
recognize
recollect
recommend
reconciling
recoup
recoverable
recreation
rectangular
rectified
recurrence
redoubling
reexamining
referring
refrigerate
regard
registrant
regretful
regulating
rehearsal
reimbursement
reissuing
reiterate
rejuvenate
relative
relevant
reliability
relieve
religion
remarkable
remember
reminisce
remotely
renaissance
repeatedly
repelled
repentance
repetition
replacement
reprehensible
represent
reprieve
reproachfully

reproducible
repudiating
repulsion
reputable
requisite
rescind
resembling
resignedly
resources
respectful
response
responsible
restaurant
resurrect
resuscitate
retaliating
retrieve
revealed
revenging
reverence
revering
reversible
revising
revocable
revolutionize
rhapsodies
rhinoceros
rhyming
rhythm
ricochet
ridicule
ridiculous
rigidity
risqué
ritualistic
rogue
rollicking
romantically
roommate
rottenness
rudely

S
sabbatical
sacrifice
sadistically
safety
salacious
salutary
sanatorium*
sanitarium*
sapphire
sarsaparilla
satellite
satiety
satisfied
satisfy

saturating
sauerkraut
saxophone
scandalous
scared
scarred
scene
schedule
schemer
scintillating
scissors
sclerosis
scoundrelly
scrupulous
scurrilous
scurrying
secretive
secureness
sedentary
seducible*
seemingly
seize
self-abasement
self-conscious
semantics
senatorial
sensitivity
sensuality
sentence
sentience*
sentimentality
separable
separate
separation
sergeant*
serviceable
seventieth
sexually
Shakespearean*
shamefacedly
shellacked*
shepherd
shining
short circuit
short-lived
shredded
shrinkage
shrubbery
shyly
sibilance
sickliness
sidesplitting
sideways
siege
significance
silhouette

similar
simile
sincerely
situating
skied
skyscraper
slatternly
sleepily
sleigh
sleight of hand
sliest
slipperiness
slurred
smoky*
smuggest
snobbery
snowcapped
sobriety
sociability
socialistic
sociology
solemnity
solicitude
solidity
solitaire
solvable
somnambulist
soothe
sophomore
soporific
sorcery
sorely
sorrier
source
souvenir
spaghetti
sparing
sparsely
speaking
spectrum
speech
speedometer
spirituality
spitefulness
sponsor
spontaneity
spurious
squalid
squarely
squaring
stabilization
starry
startling
stationary
stationery
statuary

stealthy
stepped
stiffen
stimulating
stodginess
stoically
stolidity
straight
strangely
strategy
strength
stretch
stretchable
stubborn
studying
stultify
stupefaction
stylistic
suavely
subjectivity
sublimity
submissiveness
submitted
subsidiary
subsistence
substantial
substituting
subterranean
subtle
succeed
succession
sufficient
suggestible
suitable
summary
summed
superannuate
superficially
superintendent
superlatively
supersede°
superstitious
suppress
supremacy
surcease
surfeited
surreptitious
surrounding
surveillance
susceptible
suspense

suspicious
sustenance
swimming
syllabication
syllable
symbol
sympathetic
symphonic
synonymous
synthesis
systematically

T
tableau
tabooed°
taciturn
tactically
talkativeness
tangible
tassel
tasteless
taught
taut
tawdriness
technique
tedious
telepathy
temperament
temporarily
tenacious
tendency
tentatively
tenuous
terminology
terrifically
terrifying
testicle
thankfully
thatched
themselves
theories
theory
therapeutic
therefore
thesaurus
theses
thesis
thieve
thinkable
thirstily
thirties

thorough
thought
thriving
through
ticklish
timidity
timing
tiresomely
titillate
to
tobaccos
together
tolerable
tomato
tomatoes
tomorrow
too
topography
tormentor
torpedoes
torrential
totally
tousled°
tragedy
tragically
tranquillity°
transcendental
transferred
translucence
transmitter
transparent
treachery
tremendous
trichinosis
tricycle
trivially
tropical
truculence
tubular
tumultuous
tuneful
turmeric°
turquoise
tying
typewriter
tyranny
U
ugliness
ukulele°
ultimately
umbrella

unaccountable
unanimous
unconcernedly
unctuous
undeniable
undoubtedly
unfortunately
uniformity
uniquely
unlikely
unnecessary
unoccupied
unprincipled
unruliness
unusually
urbanely
useful
useless
using
utterly

V
vacating
vacillate
vacuum
validity
valuable
vanquish
vaporous
variegated
varies
various
velocity
venerable
vengeance
ventriloquist
veracity
veritable
vernacular
versatility
vicarious
vicissitude
villain
vinegar
virtually
virulence
visibility
visitor
visualize
vitally
vivacity

vocalist
vociferous
voicing
voluminous
voluntarily
voluptuous
voracity
voucher
vulnerable

W
wakefully
wantonness
wariness
warrant
watery
weakened
wearisome
weather
weighty
weird
weren't
wheeze
where
whether
whistling
whole
wholly
whose
wieldy
wiliness
willfully°
winery
wintry
wireless
wishful
witticism
woeful
wonderfully
wondrous
workable
worrying
wrathfully
wrench
wretchedness
writhe
writhing
writing
wryly

Misuse of the Word

FAULTY DICTION

Aggravate, *to increase,* does not mean *to irritate.*

Ain't, a contraction of *am not,* should be avoided.

Alternative, *one of two things,* may not correctly be applied to more than two.

Among should be applied to more than two persons or things; *between* to two.

Any (every, no, some) place should not be used adverbially for *anywhere (everywhere, nowhere, somewhere).*

And which should be used only when preceded by *which.*

As should not take the place of *that* or *whether,* and preferably not of *because.*

As . . . as are correlatives to be used with positive; with negative use *so . . . as.*

As good as and **better than** are idioms. If they are used in the same sentence, neither *as* nor *than* may be omitted. The following sentence is, therefore, incorrect: *Brazil is as good, if not better, than Argentina in climate.*

As yet is redundant. Omit *as.*

Awful means *profoundly impressive.* It should not be used loosely to mean *very bad.*

Badly should not be used for *very much.*

Balance should not be used for *remainder* except in connection with a financial statement.

Barefoot is preferred to *barefooted.*

Because should not be used instead of *that* if preceded by *the reason why . . . is.* Nor should it be used instead of *the fact that.*

Blame it on him should not be used for *place the blame for it on him* or *blame him for it.*

Bring up or **rear** is preferable to *raise* in speaking of children.

Bursted, bust, and **busted** should not be used for *burst.*

But should not be used with a negative in expressions like *isn't but.*

But what is less desirable than *but that.*

Cannot but should not be confused with *can but.*

Certainly should not be overused.

Claim is a strong word. It should not be used for *maintain.*

Common, meaning *shared similarly,* should not be confused with *mutual,* meaning *reciprocal.* The expression *a friend in common* is naturally preferable to *a common friend.*

Comparison. Two standards should not be combined in one sentence. *Largest (tallest, best)* should be followed by a singular; if preceded by *one of,* by a plural. It is, therefore, incorrect to say, *The* Paul Revere *is New England's fastest, and one of America's best, planes.*

Considerable is overused. It may not be used as a noun.

Contact, used as a verb in business, should be avoided.

Could of is illiterate for *could have.*

Cute is used colloquially to mean *clever.* The word should be avoided.

Criticize, in literature, means *to judge.*

Date may not be used as a verb to mean *make an appointment,* or as a noun to mean *the one with whom an appointment has been made;* it is colloquial for *appointment.*

Different from is the preferred idiom.

Don't, a contraction of *do not,* may not be used in the third person singular.

Drownded is illiterate.

Each other should be used only with two persons or things; *one another* with more than two.

Either and **neither** should be used only with two persons or things. The elements of the correlatives *either . . . or* and *neither . . . nor* may not be interchanged.

Enthuse, a colloquialism, may not be used in formal writing.

Etc. is an overused and almost meaningless abbreviation. It should not be used, especially with *and.*

Every bit is colloquial.

Except, which is not a conjunction, should not be used for *unless.*

Expect should not be used for *think* or *suppose.*

Extra means *beyond that which is usual,* not *extraordinarily.*

Feel bad (not *badly*) is correct but confusing; *feel ill* is preferable. *Feel good* refers to a moral, not a physical, state.

Fellow is colloquial when it means *person* or *fiancé.*

Fewer is used with number; *less* with degree or quantity.

Fine means *finished, refined,* or *perfect.* It should not be used loosely.

Fix (up) is colloquial for *to arrange* or *to repair.*

Former may be used with only two persons or things; likewise *latter.*

Get to go is provincial for *to be able to go.*

Goings on is a vulgar expression.

Good may not be used as an adverb to mean *well*.

Got is an abused word: it is colloquial for *possess*, as is *have got* for *must*.

Gotten, except in a few crystallized expressions, has now been supplanted by *got*.

Grand means *magnificent* or *impressive*. It should be used with care.

Guess, when used to mean *believe* or *suppose*, although possessing a long history in that sense, should be used infrequently if at all.

Had ought is illiterate.

Hardly should not be used with a negative in expressions like *couldn't hardly*.

Have got is both colloquial and redundant. Omit *got*.

Heap(s) is colloquial when meaning *much* or *many*.

Hear to it is vulgar.

Honorable should be preceded by *the* and followed by the first name or *Mr.*

If is less desirable than *whether* after *ask, doubt*, and similar words.

Inside of for *within* is colloquial; in other cases, *of* should be omitted.

Kind and **sort** are singular: *this kind* or *these sorts*.

Kind of and **sort of** are colloquial when meaning *rather*. These phrases in sentences like *You plan to create a kind of game preserve?* should not be followed by the indefinite article, for the noun is used generically.

Lady is correctly applied to one of culture or social distinction; *woman* is, however, entirely correct and is preferred in compounds like *saleswoman*.

Learn means *to gain knowledge; teach* means *to give instruction*. These words must not be confused.

Let's, a contraction of *let us*, should not be followed by *we, don't*, or any other illogical words.

Like, never a conjunction, may not be followed by a clause, thus taking the place of *as* or *as if*.

Line is slang for *kind*, as in *line of work*.

Literally means *true to the fact*. It should not be used untruly for intensification.

Locate means *to place;* it is colloquial when it means *to take up residence*.

Lose out is redundant; omit *out*.

Lovely means *delicate* or *exquisite*. It should not be overused colloquially to mean *very pleasing*.

Mad means *insane* or *enraged*, not *angry*.

Mean, as an adjective, is a synonym for *humble* or *ignoble;* it is colloquial for *ill-tempered* or *selfish*.

Mighty means *powerful* or *wonderful*. *Mighty tired* is, therefore, incorrect.

Miss, Ms., Mr., Dr., Professor, and similar titles must be followed by the name.

More than means *in a greater number* or *amount;* it should not be confused with *over*, meaning *beyond*.

Mrs. should never be followed by the title or profession of the husband or a married woman: *Mrs. Judge Watson, Mrs. Lawyer Williams, Mrs. Major Wilkinson, Mrs. Director of Public Works Warren*.

Nice means *discriminating, pleasing, or scrupulous*. A more precise word is preferred.

No good is colloquial when used to modify a noun.

Notorious means *discreditably known; noted* means *celebrated*.

No use, except in informal speech, should be preceded by *of*.

Nowhere near is colloquial for *not nearly*.

Of is redundant when preceded by *outside (the house)* or *off;* it is illiterate when used for *have*, as in *could of*.

On account of is not a conjunction and may not be followed by a clause.

One repeated is stiff: *One may earn one's living if one tries*. The shift from *one* to *he* or *his* is sometimes awkward. *A person... his... he* is perhaps preferable to either.

One of, followed by a group into which it falls, does not govern the number of the verb which follows the group. Thus it is correct to say, *Black Beauty is one of the horses which run at Havre de Grace*.

Only should be placed properly in a sentence. Note the difference in meaning: *Only America won the war. American only won the war. America won the only war. America won the war only*.

Out loud, a colloquialism, should be replaced by *aloud*.

Outside of, meaning *besides* or *except for*, is objectionable.

Over with is redundant; omit *with*.

Overly is unknown to good usage.

Party means one person on one of two sides of a cause, or one entire group. It does not mean *any person*.

Per, coming from the Latin, should be used only with Latin words like *annum, capita, cent*, not with *acre, dozen*, and similar words.

Per cent should be used only after numbers; otherwise *percentage* should be used.

Perfectly is an abused and often unnecessary adjective, as in *perfectly darling* or *perfectly beautiful*.

Piano, voice, violin, vocal, and **instrumental** should not be used alone when speaking of instruction: *lessons* or *instruction* should follow.

Plan on is redundant; omit *on.*

Proven, except in the law, is archaic; *proved* is the modern past participle.

Quite means *completely;* when used to mean *to a great extent,* it is colloquial. It should not be used as by the English, excessively and often absurdly, as a meaningless ejaculation.

Quite a (bit, few, little, number) is colloquial.

Rarely ever and **seldom ever** should be avoided as confusions of *hardly ever* or *rarely (seldom) if ever.*

Real is an adjective or a noun; *really* is an adverb. *I was real happy* is, therefore, incorrect.

Render means *to give, to yield, to extract,* or *to inflict.* One may *render lard,* but one should not *render a vocal selection.*

Reverend should be preceded by *the* and followed by the first name or *Mr.*

Right, meaning *precisely (right here and now)* or *to a large degree (right nice girl)* is colloquial. *Right smart* is dialectal.

Right along (away, off) is colloquial.

Run, when meaning *to conduct* or *to manage,* is colloquial.

Said, when meaning *previously mentioned,* should be avoided except in the law. *Aforesaid* is permissible.

Same, except in the law, should not be used as a pronoun.

Says is the third person singular of *say;* it may not be used with *I. Says* should not be used when the past tense, *said,* is required.

See where is a misuse of *see that.*

Show is colloquial for *drama* or *concert.*

Show up is colloquial for *appear.*

So should not be used as a mere intensive in an incomplete construction: *I am so angry. Because* is preferable to the colloquial *so* in joining coordinate clauses: *He came; so we held a reception* should be rephrased: *Because he came, we held a reception. So* should not be used instead of *so that.* The correlative *as . . . as* are used positively; *so . . . as* are used negatively.

Some is colloquial for *somewhat.*

Stop means *to arrest progress.* A person *stays* at a hotel.

Such should not be used as a mere intensive in an incomplete construction: *I have heard such good things about you* is incomplete. A clause of result following *such* should be introduced by *that,* not

as: There was such a noise that I could not hear. A relative clause following *such* should be introduced by *as: He will follow such directions as the governor may give.*

Superlatives should not be used for intensification in an incomplete construction, as in *I had the best time.*

Sure is slang when it means *certainly. Surely* should be used.

Suspicion may never be used as a verb.

Take or **take it** should not be used to introduce an example.

The should not take the place of *a: Bittersweet candy is fifty cents the pound* is incorrect because a specific pound is not intended.

That is used colloquially to mean *to such a degree: I am not that tired that I must rest. So* should be used.

There as an expletive should be avoided.

This here *(these here, that there, those there)* is a vulgarism.

These should not be used loosely without any feeling of the demonstrative: *He is one of these modern cowboys who broadcast.*

Those should be followed by a relative clause: *He is one of those militarists* should be completed by adding a clause like *who would involve us in war;* or *He is a militarist.*

Through should not be used before a gerund: *I am through working* should be changed to *I have finished my work.*

Try and should be replaced by *try to.*

Ugly means *hideous* or *offensive morally.* It is used colloquially to mean *unpleasant.*

Up is redundant when preceded by a verb. It may not be used as a verb to mean *to increase,* as in *He upped the price ten dollars.*

Used to could is illiterate.

Verse, when used with the indefinite article, means *a line of poetry.* It should not be confused with *stanza,* a group of verses.

Very much is preferred to *very* when followed by a past participle not yet recognized as an adjective.

Way must be preceded by a preposition if used adverbially: *He works in that way.*

Who is this? when spoken over the telephone is both illogical and impolite.

Which as a relative pronoun should be used if the antecedent is inanimate or an animal; *who* if the antecedent is a person.

Without may not be used as a conjunction.

WORDS COMMONLY CONFUSED

accept, to receive
except, to exclude

access, approach
excess, superfluity

affect, to influence
effect, to execute

aisle, passage
isle, island

alley, lane
ally, associate

all ready, entirely prepared
already, at this time

all together, grouped
altogether, completely

allusion, indirect reference
illusion, deceptive appearance

altar, table
alter, vary

anachorism, violation of geography
anachronism, violation of time

angel, spiritual being
angle, corner

barbarous, almost savage
barbaric, showy, lacking restraint

berth, sleeping compartment
birth, beginning

beside, by the side of
besides, in addition to

boarder, one who takes meals
border, margin

Calvary, site of Christ's crucifixion
cavalry, horsemen

canvas, cloth
canvass, to solicit

capital, principal
capitol, statehouse

censor, examine
censure, condemn

centrifugal, proceeding from center
centripetal, proceeding toward center

chord, combination of tones
cord, small rope

cite, summon, quote
site, position

clothes, garments
cloths, fabrics

coarse, common, harsh
course, route

complement, addition, to add
compliment, to praise

congenial, kindred in taste
genial, cheerful

conscience, moral faculty
conscious, cognizant

consul, commercial representative
council, assembly
counsel, advice, attorney

contemptible, despicable
contemptuous, insolent

continual, in close succession
continuous, uninterrupted

corps, unit of organized establishment
corpse, dead body

credible, trustworthy
creditable, deserving of praise
credulous, inclined to believe

currant, raisin
current, motion

dairy, place for milk and its products
diary, daily record

desert, arid region; v. t., to leave, to abandon
dessert, course at end of meal

disinterested, uninfluenced by personal
    advantage
uninterested, apathetic

dual, twofold
duel, combat

elegy, lament
eulogy, commendatory oration

emigrant, one who leaves
immigrant, one who enters

enormity, wickedness
enormousness, immensity

euphemism, softened statement
euphony, pleasant sound
euphuism, artificial statement

exceptional, uncommon
exceptionable, objectionable

factious, dissentient
factitious, artificial
fictitious, feigned
fractious, unruly

faint, swoon
feint, pretense

farther, applied to distance, space
further, applied to extent, degree

forceful, possessing power
forcible, violent

feat, deed
feet, terminals of legs

formally, conventionally
formerly, heretofore

forth, onward
fourth, ordinal of *four*

hanged, executed
hung, suspended

healthful, wholesome
healthy, well, vigorous

ingenious, clever
ingenuous, candid

indict, to charge
indite, to write

inhumane, lacking in human kindness
inhuman (also *unhuman*), savage

later, afterward
latter, the second of two

lay (also past of *lie*), to place
lie, to recline

liable, obliged
likely, probably

lightening, relieving
lightning, flashing of light

loose, unattached
lose, to miss

luxuriant, profuse
luxurious, costly, ornate

mantel, shelf
mantle, cloak

misogamist, marriage hater
misogynist, woman hater

noted, renowned
notorious, disgraceful

O, used in invocation
oh, exclamation

observance, act of custom
observation, attentive consideration

passed, crossed
past, bygone

persecute, to afflict
prosecute, to carry on

personal, private
personnel, group collectively employed

plain, level land
plane, level surface

practical, useful, skillful
practicable, feasible

precedence, priority
precedents, antecedents

principal, chief
principle, doctrine

prodigy, wonder
progeny, offspring

propose, to offer
purpose, to resolve

prophecy, prediction
prophesy, to predict

quiet, undisturbed
quite, wholly

raise, to erect (in good use, not a noun)
rise, to ascend

recipe, formula
receipt, written acknowledgment

respectful, deferential
respective, individual

sciolist, pretender
scholiast, commentator

sensual, fleshly
sensuous, pertaining to the senses

sentiment, feeling
sentimentality, excessive feeling

stationary, fixed
stationery, paper

statue, image
stature, height
statute, law

stimulant, alcoholic beverage
stimulus, incentive

specie, coin
species, variety

suit, apparel
suite, set

their, possessive of *they*
there, in that place

therefor, for that
therefore, hence

to, toward
too, also
two, the number

troop, a collection
troupe, company of actors

venal, mercenary
venial, excusable

waive, to relinquish
wave, to swing

weather, condition of atmosphere
whether, if

who's, contraction of *who is* or *who has*
whose, possessive of *who*

your, possessive of you
you're, contraction of *you are*

USING THE TOOLS

Effective Sentences

To write effective sentences, you must learn not only to avoid certain basic errors, but also how to employ the tools of good writing. Often the "tool" to be used is simply on the other side of the coin from the error to be avoided. For example, to correct a *wordy* sentence, you take all unnecessary words out of the sentence; however, you should try to avoid wordiness by writing concisely, by writing no unnecessary words in the first place. Below you will find some constructive suggestions on how to write effective sentences.

Note the word *effective*. It carries the implication that, in writing, we wish to *do* something to our reader, to have an "effect" on him. If we don't take the time and make the necessary effort to determine what this effect is to be, our sentences will be ineffective. On the other hand, if we do assign a purpose to everything we write, something specific that we want to say—a "point of view"—we will have found one pathway toward errorless and effective writing.

MAKING SENTENCES EFFECTIVE

Use Concrete Language

A good writer uses concrete and definite words frequently, and avoids vague or abstract words. Concrete language gives the reader a specific picture rather than a general statement. It builds images that the reader can readily grasp.

General The lovely sounds of nature woke me.

Specific The wind in the trees and a bird's chirping woke me.

Be Positive

Good writing makes direct, positive statements; it avoids indirect, non-committal language. Use the word "not" only when the negative idea is emphatic; otherwise express what you want to say in the positive form.

Indirect He did not like Mr. Harvey's approach to grammar.

Direct He disliked Mr. Harvey's approach to grammar.

Indirect I did not think the trip would be very interesting.

Direct I thought the trip would be a bore.

Indirect Mr. Alexander was perhaps our best committee chairman. He was not long-winded, he was never biased, and he never failed to get the business before us covered.

Direct Mr. Alexander was the best committee chairman we ever had. He was direct, unbiased, and efficient.

Use the Active Voice

A careless writer uses the passive voice when there is no specific reason for doing so, and thereby weakens his effectiveness. Use the passive voice only when the subject is unknown or when the fact that something was *done to* the subject is of primary importance. Otherwise use the active voice. (See *Verbs: Voice*.)

Vary Your Sentences

A good stylist avoids monotonous writing by keeping his sentences varied, in both structure and length. To achieve a varied style one must keep one's ear open to the *sound* of his writing. (See *Basic Sentence Errors: Monotony*.)

Use a Climactic Order

Gain emphasis by placing important words or ideas at the important positions in the sentence—at the beginning or at the end, especially at the end. Sentences which state supporting ideas first and which withhold the important idea until the end are known as "climactic" or "periodic" sentences. Sentences which state the important idea first and then add supporting ideas are called "loose" sentences. Either kind of sentence is effective, but a preponderance of one or the other is decidedly ineffective and artificial. Whatever kind of sentence you select to express an idea, be sure to tuck away illustrative details and parenthetical expressions in the middle of the sentence. As a rule, loose sentences are preferred in informal writing; periodic sentences are more common in formal writing.

Periodic	The alternative we must avoid at all costs is armed conflict.
Loose	Armed conflict is the alternative we must avoid at all costs. (Important idea expressed first and followed by explanatory comment)
Periodic	Against the spangled backdrop of a dark night sky filled with unending stars shone the moon, white and fluorescent.
Loose	A white, fluorescent moon shone against the spangled backdrop of a dark night sky filled with unending stars.

Euphony and Rhythm

Euphony is the smooth, pleasant flow of agreeable sounds. An experienced writer chooses and arranges his words so that they form patterns of sound that are rhythmical and euphonious when read aloud. The more experienced and skillful the writer, the more pleasant are the sounds he produces. The ability to produce these sound effects comes only from experience.

Do not repeat words that have the same sound. Do not alliterate. Do not confuse rhythm with rhyme. An alliteration is the repetition of an initial sound in two or more words in the same phrase or clause. It is an eye-catching device used by advertising copy writers, but it has no place in formal prose writing. Rhyme, the repetition of end sounds, is a device of verse, not of prose. The first example below illustrates how euphony can be destroyed by alliteration; the second, by rhyme.

Alliteration	In a fury I flew into the fray.
Rhyme	I yearn to learn who she is.

Figures of Speech

A prevalent belief among students is that figures of speech are old-fashioned and should be confined to rhetoric and poetry. This is a false belief. We all use figurative language every day, and more often than not, without realizing it. *Hungry as a bear, quick as lightning, time flies, drive a bargain*—these are common figurative expressions. A figure of speech is any deviation from the literal meaning or ordinary use of words designed to make a thought clearer or more forceful. Suppose we express how a girl sings by comparing her with a nightingale. *May sings like a nightingale.* We do not say literally how May sings. We

suggest the image of the nightingale and leave it to the reader's imagination to know the quality of May's voice. This is communication in figurative language. The example of May's voice is a figure of speech known as a *simile*. The simile expresses a figurative resemblance or comparison between essentially different things. One thing is said to be like another, and the resemblance is usually introduced by *like* or *as*. *Hungry as a bear* and *quick as lightning* are also similes. Actually, the best similes compare things which are in most respects unlike, but which have at least one point of striking resemblance.

The "Intentional Fragment"

The grammatical structure of the sentence has been analyzed. We have already stated that a sentence need not necessarily contain a subject and a verb, although by far the majority of our written sentences do. Expressions such as "Why not?" or a conversational colloquialism such as "Me, too" are considered to be sentences. In writing, the sentence that intentionally lacks a subject or a verb is called an "intentional fragment." Professional writers use intentional fragments for stylistic effect. Beginning writers, however, are best advised not to use fragments of any kind.

Idioms

In every language, combinations of words have developed which appear completely proper to the natives of the country where the language is spoken, but which sound peculiar to a foreign visitor. Such expressions are known as *idioms*.

Sometimes idioms conform to grammatical rules, and at other times they may conflict with such rules, but idiomatic usage has established the expression as proper.

The prepositional idiom is a type of expression that gives even the native some difficulty. A seemingly well-written sentence will be ruined by a careless use of a prepositional idiom. The trouble arises in determining the correct preposition. For example: Is it *faced with* or *faced by*? Idiomatic usage has established *faced by* as the proper expression. To determine which preposition an idiom takes, see a good dictionary.

Synonyms

Synonyms are good words to become familiar with. They help give variety to sentences, and their proper use avoids repetitious phrases. A *synonym* actually is a word that means the same or nearly the same as another word. Practical students often resort to synonyms as a device to avoid using words they do not know how to spell. A student may want to use *lugubrious* on his essay examination but, unsure of the spelling, resorts to the word *dismal*. Careless substitution can change the subtle meaning of a sentence, even if it would appear that the two words are almost identical. To *plagiarize* and to *copy* often mean the same thing; there is, however, a distinct difference. To *plagiarize* definitely means to steal another person's literary effort and pass it off as one's own, whereas one may *copy* another person's work, with or without intent to steal it.

Antonyms

This is a word that means the opposite of another word. But even antonyms can be useful in giving sentences a greater variety if properly used. *Happy* and *sad* are antonyms. Seemingly, it would appear they are not interchangeable in a sentence, yet the writer may feel that the word *happy* is too strong, and he may decide, despite the admonition against the use of the negative, that *not sad* is just the right state he is trying to describe.

BASIC SENTENCE ERRORS

The Fragment

The *fragment* is a statement that fails to state a complete thought; it is an incomplete sentence. Generally, the error can be corrected by simply attaching the fragment to the sentence before or after it, as in each of the corrections below. Unintentional fragments used as complete sentences generally consist of phrases, appositives, or dependent clauses.

Fragment   The soldiers stood stoically in the rain. *Cursing quietly over their wretched luck.* (verbal phrase incorrectly used as a complete sentence)

Complete   The soldiers stood stoically in the rain, cursing quietly over their wretched luck.

Fragment   He was an unbelievable person. *A man as well read and as outspoken as any I've ever met.* (an appositive incorrectly used as a complete sentence)

Complete   He was an unbelievable person, a man as well read and as outspoken as any I've ever met.

Fragment   The settlers were careful to place twenty-four-hour guards around the encampment. *So that they would not be caught off guard by an Indian attack at any time.* (dependent clause used incorrectly as a complete sentence)

Complete   The settlers were careful to place twenty-four-hour guards around the encampment, so that they would not be caught off guard by an Indian attack at any time.

The Run-on Sentence

The *run-on sentence* occurs when the writer has failed to separate properly two sentences or independent clauses, with the result that the two "run into" each other. Two major types of run-on sentences occur. The first type contains no punctuation at all between the sentences. Such sentences are known as "fused sentences" or "stringiness." The second type of run-on sentence is one in which a comma has been improperly used. This is often called a "comma splice."

Run-on   Let us be wary but let us not fall prey to fear. (fused: failure to use punctuation between independent clauses)

Improved   Let us be wary, but let us not fall prey to fear.

Run-on   A soft answer turns away wrath, grievous words stir up anger. (comma splice: comma incorrectly used to separate independent clauses)

Improved   A soft answer turns away wrath; grievous words stir up anger.

To avoid writing run-on sentences, one must know the four possible ways of connecting independent clauses. (See also *Punctuation: The Comma.*) As a general rule, if the ideas are to receive equal emphasis, use the period and place the ideas in different sentences, or use the semicolon alone. If one idea is more important than the other, use the comma and a coordinating conjunction, or the semicolon and a conjunctive adverb.

Mixed Constructions

A *mixed construction* results when one part of a sentence does not agree grammatically with another part of the sentence. The two major types of mixed construction involve subject and verb disagreement, and pronoun and antecedent disagreement.

Wrong   A series of lectures were given by Mr. Olsen. (Plural verb *were* does not agree with singular subject *series*.)

Right   A series of lectures was given by Mr. Olsen. (Verb agrees with subject.)

Wrong   Sometimes circumstantial evidence will convict a person of a crime they did not commit. (Plural pronoun *they* does not agree with singular antecedent *person*.)

Right   Sometimes circumstantial evidence will convict a person of a crime he did not commit. (Pronoun agrees with antecedent.)

Dangling Modifiers

The *dangling modifier* is a verbal phrase that either has no word in the sentence to modify or is placed in such a way that it appears to modify unintended words in the same sentence.

Dangling   Making a flying tackle, Sam's shoe came off. (The participial phrase is *Making a flying tackle*, but the subject of the clause that follows is *shoe*. *Making a flying tackle* cannot possibly refer to a shoe.)

Improved   Making a flying tackle, Sam lost his shoe. (*Sam* is now the subject to which the participial phrase properly refers.)

Dangling   To be sure of a good seat, your tickets must be bought far in advance. (The understood subject of the infinitive phrase *To be sure* is not the same as the subject of the clause that follows.)

Improved   To be sure of a good seat, you must buy your tickets far in advance. (The infinitive phrase modifies *you*, the subject of the sentence.)

Dangling   After waiting an hour, the train finally came. (The train waited an hour? Obviously not. *After waiting an hour* has no word in this sentence to modify.)

Improved   After waiting an hour, we finally caught our train. (*After waiting an hour* refers to *we*, the subject of the sentence.)

Squinting Modifiers

A *squinting modifier* is one that is carelessly placed so that it appears to modify both the words preceding and the words following it. The reader has to stop reading to figure out what is being modified.

Squinting   The man who shoved his way to the platform angrily addressed the crowd. (What does *angrily* modifiy? The way the man made his way to the platform? Or the way he addressed the crowd?)

Improved   The man who angrily shoved his way to the platform addressed the crowd. *OR* The man who shoved his way to the platform addressed the crowd angrily.

There are two types of verbal phrase constructions that are independent of the rest of the sentence and that need not modify the subject of the clause that follows it. The first type is the *absolute phrase* consisting of a noun or pronoun followed by a participle.

The play having finished, the audience left.

The second type of verbal phrase that can be independent of the rest of the sentence is a phrase that states a general truth. A general truth does not refer to the action of a specific person or thing. Such expressions as *taking everything into consideration* and *to put it another way* are verbal phrases that can stand apart from the rest of the sentence.

Monotony

The most common form of this fault is the dull repetition of a subject-verb sentence pattern. Monotony also occurs when the writer fails to vary the length of his sentences. Monotony results, in fact, from any continued, dull repetition of sentence structure or length.

Not Varied   He opened the car door. He stepped out. He walked towards the store. He tried to remember all the things his wife had told him to buy. He hated shopping!

Varied   Opening the car door, he stepped out and walked towards the store, trying to remember all the things his wife had told him to buy. How he hated shopping!

Faulty Parallelism

A series of related ideas of equal importance can often be most effectively expressed by writing them in what is called "parallel form." Parallelism, which treats like ideas in like form, balances words, phrases, and clauses against one another. In a series, for example, words should be in the same class and in the same parts of speech. One may begin a series of parallel forms, then lose the parallelism, and thus commit the error known as "faulty parallelism."

Not Parallel   Although very good-looking, Ted was modest, shy, and didn't talk much. (The parallel adjectives *modest* and *shy* demand a third adjective rather than a clause to follow them, in order that the sentence should read smoothly and clearly.)

Parallel   Although very good-looking, Ted was modest, shy, and quiet.

Not Parallel   The man at the desk ordered me to be silent, to sit down, and that I should wait until I was spoken to. (The two infinitives and the phrase beginning *and that* constitute unparallel form.)

Parallel   The man at the desk ordered me to be silent, to sit down, and to wait until I was spoken to. (A third infinitive has been added to complete the parallelism begun by the first two.)

Correlative Conjunctions and Parallelism

The use of the correlative conjunctions can lead the writer to make mistakes in parallelism. These conjunctions–*either . . . or, neither . . . nor, not only . . . but also*–help tighten sentence structure and strength expression, but they must be used logically. That is, the same kinds of words and the same grammatical structure must appear on both sides of the correlatives, otherwise, parallelism and sense and effectiveness will be lost.

Not Parallel   Al is both a marvelous athlete and he dresses very well. (A modifying phrase on one side and an independent clause on the other)

Parallel   Al is both a marvelous athlete and a fine dresser. (Modifying phrase on either side)

Not Parallel   Your grandmother has not only a sharp mind but also her humor is lively.

Parallel   Your grandmother has not only a sharp mind but also a lively humor.

Mixed Metaphor

Combining two different comparisons or figures of speech that are inconsistent or incongruous with each other, produces the "mixed metaphor." The writer must be careful to maintain logic as he adds color with images and comparisons; he must make sure his comparisons "fit" one another. A "ship of state" cannot get "lost in the woods of diplomatic entanglements" (ships don't sail in the woods); "her eyes" could not be "glistening pebbles in the twilight sky" (pebbles do not glisten in the sky).

Mixed   With determination Ellen dug into the sea of work before her.

Logical   With determination Ellen dug into the pile of work before her. *OR* With determination Ellen plunged into the sea of work before her.

Mixed   Now, friend, chew upon this branch of my thoughts: all good looks are a snare that no man should let himself be drowned in.

Logical   Now, friend, chew upon this morsel of my thoughts: all good looks are a snare that no man should let himself be trapped in.

Inadequate Subordination

Immature minds seldom use subordination. It takes maturity to select one idea over another and to subordinate it to the important one. A child, for example, is likely to give new facts equal importance. Learning about Columbus, the child is likely to say: "Columbus was born in Portugal. He was given three ships by the Queen of Spain. He became famous as the discoverer of America. He died in poverty and neglect." A more mature version of these facts would be: "Columbus, who was born in Portugal, was given three ships by the Queen of Spain. He became famous as the discoverer of America; however, he died in poverty and neglect." Two simple words, the relative pronoun *who* and the conjunctive adverb *however*, place the facts about Columbus in truer perspective, by subordinating the less important facts to the more important ones.

Inadequate subordination is the sign not only of immaturity but of ineffective writing. It results in short, choppy sentences. The writer who combines ideas in sentences without proper subordination inevitably is guilty of an excessive number of *and* and *so* clauses. The rule to remember is: Put subordinate ideas in subordinate (dependent) clauses (or phrases), and main ideas in main (independent) clauses.

Inadequate Subordination	Tom was tired of listening to the lecture, and no one could see him, and so he slipped quietly out of the room. (Three ideas are placed in independent clauses, thereby giving each idea equal importance and resulting in no subordination at all.)
Improved	Tom was tired of listening to the lecture, and since no one could see him, he slipped quietly out of the room. (One idea has been made subordinate to the other two, by putting it in a dependent clause.) *OR* Since Tom was tired of listening to the lecture and as no one could see him, he slipped quietly out of the room. (two ideas made subordinate)

Faulty Subordination

When combining several ideas in one sentence, be sure not to make the mistake of subordinating the main idea. The less important of two ideas should always be in a dependent clause or phrase. Never introduce the main idea of a sentence with a conjunctive adverb.

Weak	Although he easily won the club tennis championship, he showed some signs of fatigue. (The main idea of the sentence is weakly introduced by the subordinating conjunction *Although*. The subordinate idea is in an independent clause.)
Improved	Although he showed some signs of fatigue, he easily won the club tennis championship. (The subordinate idea is properly placed in a subordinate clause, and the main idea is properly placed in the independent clause.)

"Fine" Writing

"Fine" writing is a ruse to cover up absence of knowledge. It is the use of big, pretentious words for simple, direct words. It is word exhibitionism at its worst. Students often resort to "fine" writing to impress, to make the reader think that they know what they are talking about. "Fine" writing is a puerile, sophomoric device, and it impresses nobody. Of course, writers often inject pretentious words into the speech of teenage delinquents, race track touts, and hoodlums of diverse sorts. This they do for comic irony, and the results can be hilarious. But it is pathetic to hear the same words uttered by high school and college students.

There is nothing wrong with big words, but they should normally be used only to express meanings and shades of meaning for which simpler words do not exist.

Split Infinitives

To split an infinitive is to insert an expression between the *to* and the verb. The inserted expression is usually an adverb (to *entirely* comprehend). The reason that split infinitives used to be condemned is that *to* is historically a preposition. Grammarians at one time insisted that a preposition should never be separated from its object by any other words. The rule now generally accepted sanctions the split infinitive when it results in a clearer meaning or a pleasanter sound. In the illustrations of acceptable split infinitives below, note how a transposition of the *to* would affect the meaning and the rhythm of the sentences.

Do you want us to really enjoy ourselves?

The judge refused to summarily dismiss the case.

He failed to entirely comprehend the charge.

The Double Negative

Avoid the double negative. Use a single negative to express a negative idea.

Wrong   I haven't no money left.

Right   I have no money left.

The following are troublesome words. They are all negative, or negative by implication, so should not be accompanied by a second negative word.

barely	no one
hardly	none
neither	not
never	nothing
nobody	only

Unneeded Words

Beware of repeating ideas already expressed.

Repetitious   Repeat what you said again.

Concise   Repeat what you said.

Repetitious   The reason I didn't do my homework was on account of the fact that I forgot the assignment.

Better   The reason I didn't do my homework was that I forgot the assignment.

Concise   I didn't do my homework because I forgot the assignment.

Let us go one step further. We don't simply say that May has a voice *like* a nightingale, but we say that her voice *is* the voice of a nightingale. *May has the voice of a nightingale.* The two voices are equated. This is a *metaphor*. It is simply an expanded simile. A simile states that one thing is *like* another; a metaphor, that one thing *is* another.

Simile   He mouths a sentence as curs mouth a bone.

Metaphor   All the world's a stage,
And all the men and women merely players.

Similes and metaphors are the most common figures of speech. Other common figures of speech are: *hyperbole* (extravagant but deliberate and fanciful exaggeration), *litotes* (deliberate understatement), *personification* (infusing life into inanimate things), and *metonymy* (naming one thing in terms of another which is part of it or associated with it).

Hyperbole   Thanks a million.

Litotes   Faulkner is not a bad writer (meaning he is a great writer).

Personification   Time flies.

Metonymy   She set a good table (meaning she prepared a good meal).

Weak Words

The weakest words in the English language are the intensives *very*, *little*, *rather*, and *pretty*. An *intensive* is a word that supposedly makes another word more forceful and emphatic. But the use of an adjective (as an adverb) to intensify another adjective often has the opposite effect. This is especially true of adjectives that have been used so often with so little regard for their true meanings that they have lost all the force they once had. Take the words *awful, dreadful, fearful,* and *horrible.* These are potent words when used to mean "to inspire awe" *(awful),* "to inspire dread" *(dreadful),* "to instill fear" *(fearful),* "to excite horror" *(horrible).* However, when these words are loosely used as intensives, they languish into impotence. They are especially absurd when they intensify words that contradict their own meanings. Expressions such as *awfully nice* and *horribly sorry* are not only feeble and placid but absurdly contradictory. The following is a list of words that should not be used as intensives. Unless you know the true meanings of these words, do not use them at all.

amazing	gorgeous	splendid
awful	grand	stunning
colossal	horrible	stupendous
devastating	huge	superb
dreadful	little	terrible
enormous	magnificent	terrific
fabulous	marvelous	tremendous
fearful	pretty	very
frightful	rather	wonderful

Slang

Slang is unacceptable in either ordinary conversation or formal writing. If it belongs anywhere, it is in light banter in an informal setting–but only if it is original and lively. Effective slang usually is a cleverly humorous or dramatically surprising play on words, achieved by taking words out of context, juxtaposing unexpected words, using very compressed metaphors, and the like. Unfortunately, slang ages quickly and becomes stale.

Why, then, is it so popular? Its chief attraction is that it makes a single word do so much. In an instant, a word of slang can communicate a reasonably exact meaning, suggest a humorous comparison, arouse emotion, and suggest personality. Think of how much more is said in the single word "Scram!" than in the sentence, "You may go now." In this very flexibility of slang lies one of its chief dangers: It may be used for so many things that it becomes a crutch for one's vocabulary. One may, for example, use the slang word "dig" in a variety of contexts: "I don't dig (understand) this equation"; "I dig (feel satisfied with) the mark I got in English"; "Baby, I dig (am attracted to) you." With so handy a word available the lazy or obtuse person will overuse it, quite failing to make distinct the various meanings he actually intends. Such dependence on slang prevents the development of a good vocabulary.

In sum, therefore, if you wish to inject slang into the dialogue of your fictional characters, by all means do so–with care and with a sparing hand. Incidentally, never enclose slang words within quotation marks, either single or double.

Solecisms

A *solecism* is the violation of correct grammatical structure. It is considered a blunder, not an illiteracy or a barbarism, and is usually the result of carelessness.

Colloquialisms

The chances are you have only a vague idea of what a colloquialism is. Most students confuse it with provincialisms or localisms and think it refers to sectional peculiarities of speech. Most students also attach some sort of stigma to the word and try to avoid using words or expressions that are labeled colloquial in the dictionary. A colloquialism really has nothing to do with sectional peculiarities, and there is nothing "bad" or improper about using it–under certain circumstances. The word simply labels expressions that are more acceptable in familiar or ordinary conversation than in formal speech and writing. For example, the president of a college, or the principal of a school, when talking with his colleagues, may quite properly use colloquialisms. However, when he dons cap and gown to deliver an address at the annual commencement exercises, he scrupulously avoids colloquialisms. The difference is in the setting.

It is perfectly all right to use colloquialisms when you are talking with members of your family, with friends, and when writing friendly letters and informal reports. An example of a colloquialism and its equivalent formal form is given below.

Colloquialism   What a close shave!

Formal   What a narrow escape!

Jargon

Dictionaries define *jargon* as language that is "unintelligible." This is an unfortunately broad definition. We usually associate the term with the "bureaucratic jargon" of officialdom, now widely referred to as *governmentese*. In this sense *jargon* has partly derisive, partly humorous connotations. In a stricter sense, *jargon* is the specialized vocabulary of persons who are engaged in the same trade or profession. The intelligibility of the specialized vocabulary naturally excludes the outsider, but for the insider it is loaded with meaning. A single expression can stand for a thought or idea that might otherwise take ten, twenty, or even a hundred words to express with a standard vocabulary. As long as the expression is kept within the specialized group, it is perfectly necessary and legitimate. It is only when the expression is employed outside the field in contexts where other vocabulary is available that it becomes jargon in the commonly accepted sense of the term. Thus, the expression "relate to" is a favorite in the vocabulary of psychologists. Employed by a psychologist outside his professional setting, or by the layman, this same expression loses its specialized meaning and becomes absurd jargon.

Trite Expressions and Clichés

A trite expression is an overused expression. It has been used so much that when the reader sees the first word or two, he can anticipate what follows. And when the reader can anticipate your words, you cannot hold his attention. "A good time was had by all" is a trite expression. A cliché is a figure of speech or turn of words that may have been original and clever once upon a time but that has become trite and stale through overuse. Like an oft-repeated joke, *it wears its welcome thin* (the expression in italics is a cliché). How do you tell when a cliché is a cliché? As happens with jokes, you hear one and you think it is original, or you think one up yourself. You hasten to tell it to your friends. But they have already heard it countless times. So it is with clichés. You must consciously be on the lookout for them in whatever you read or hear. Whenever you spot a cliché, make a mental note not to use it in your own writing.

Provincialisms and Localisms

A *provincialism* is a word, phrase, or idiom peculiar to a major geographical section or region. A *localism* is peculiar to a limited locality. When used in speech by persons who live in a particular section or locality, they are legitimate and proper. Since provincialisms and localisms are not in national usage, however, they do not appear in formal, expository writing. Obviously, both are essential to the speech of characters in fiction.

Barbarisms

Barbarism is the name grammarians give to the gross misuse of words. To use *eats* for *food,* as in "Pass me the eats," would be termed a barbarism. Another example of a barbarism is the use of *learn* for *teach,* as in "That will learn you a lesson."

Effective Paragaraphs

Any reader is aware that an indented sentence means a new paragraph. In dialogue, such indentation shows merely that a new speaker is being quoted. But the indentation at the beginning of the paragraph always indicates some change of subject or approach–in the description, the narration, the argument–whatever the type of the writing may be.

The new paragraph, however, does more for us than indicate a change in thought. For the paragraph is the real building block of any prose writing. The casual letter-writer, the student, the professional journalist, the novelist–all use paragraphing in their letters, essays, articles, or novels. In order to function correctly, that is, to fit neatly among the other blocks as well as help to hold them up, the paragraph must, itself, be a carefully completed and finely shaped unit. Perhaps the best definition of a *paragraph* might be: *the carefully rounded development of a single impression or idea.*

The reader should bear in mind that no absolute criteria exist for determining a good paragraph. There is agreement that a paragraph should contain the stylistic elements which effectively convey the writer's idea, or purpose. Such a paragraph is effective–it is good.

Paragraphs may be purely descriptive, or narrative, or expository, or they may include any mixture of these major types of writing. The principles of good paragraph-writing discussed below can be applied to all types of paragraphs.

PRINCIPLES

The Topic Idea

A good writer knows exactly why he is starting a new paragraph and why he is ending it. Within that one paragraph he is trying to say essentially *one thing* as clearly and as completely as he possibly can. That one thing we call the "topic idea" of a paragraph. Often this topic idea is expressed in a *topic sentence* that generally comes at or near the beginning of the paragraph. The topic sentence, however, need not come at the beginning, nor does the paragraph have to have a topic sentence, so long as the single idea is clear.

Adequate Development

The topic idea can be conveyed only if the writer makes sufficient effort to "show what he means" to his reader. The different methods of "showing" are enumerated below, but it is important to remember that no matter how you construct your paragraph, it must give enough details, facts, examples, or reasons to hold and convince the reader.

Inadequate   Everyone should play some sport from which he gets both enjoyment and physical toughening. Sports have always been considered important. They make you strong and you can have a lot of fun with them. Furthermore, friendships can be made through sports. Nobody can deny that for many reasons, sports are a "must."

In the above paragraph, note that most of the sentences are mere restatements of the topic sentence or of each other, and that they are extremely general. The way to construct your paragraphs well consists of your ability to give details, facts, specifics, in concise and *concrete* language.

Unity

The well-written paragraph sticks relentlessly to its topic idea and departs from that idea only to bring in closely related material. A careless writer, on the other hand, "wanders" from his topic, and thereby loses the concentrated focus, or "unity," that writing must have if it is to be effective. The best way to keep each paragraph unified is to make the subject of most of your sentences the same as the subject of your topic sentence; hold on to your subject, and you will hold on to your topic idea.

Transition

Transition is "going across" or–in writing–getting the reader smoothly from one thought to another, one image to another, one sentence to the next. You can achieve good transition by practicing these two important principles:

a) *Arrange the sentences of each paragraph in logical order so that each follows the one before it as naturally as possible.*

Failure to build the paragraph on such a pre-determined order can result in confusion and lack of transition. Presenting images or events simply in their *order of occurrence in time* or in their "narrative order" is one of the most common methods of developing a paragraph logically.

You could also arrange the ideas or arguments in a predetermined "order of importance."

b) *Wherever necessary, use words and phrases that tie your ideas together as closely as possible.*

These words and phrases, sometimes called "transitional devices," can be categorized under three headings: pronouns, key (or "echo") words, and connectives.

1) Pronouns

Using pronouns whose antecedents are the subject of the paragraph makes transition stronger. The most useful of these for transitional purposes are the demonstratives: *this, that, these, those.*

> Nothing in the way of equipment was overlooked. It was because of *this* preparation that the expedition was so successful.

2) Key words

These are words that relate to or "echo" the topic idea, and their inclusion holds the paragraph–and the reader–to the subject.

> The men fought the *fire* mightily for three days. However, the *blaze* was too much for them; the *flames* would not be extinguished. Such *holocausts* cost Americans millions of acres in valuable forest every year.

3) Connective words and phrases

This group of transitional devices is extensive, and we use many of them quite naturally in our everyday speech. The group includes all conjunctions–subordinate, correlative, and coordinate–plus a large number of "connective" adverbs and adverb phrases.

The following paragraph has employed transitional words and phrases. Note that the "flow" is smooth and its thought easy to follow.

> My black, furry poodle, Totor, is a real problem to me. *Ever since* I bought him from a pet shop, he has caused me nothing but trouble. *However,* I do like him, *because* he has such a charming, lively personality. *But* this liveliness is also the source of my problem, *for* it leads him to do the most dreadful things. *For instance,* he hops up on the kitchen table and eats a whole ham. *Then* he chews the caps off the milk bottles and drinks all the cream. *And* he is always stealing shoes and chewing them apart. *Nevertheless,* he is worth it, *mostly because* I have learned how to outfox him–most of the time.

Necessary Design

The good paragraph is organically dependent upon its topic sentence or topic idea for its overall construction. It has a logical design that arises out of the purpose of the paragraph. Thus, if your purpose is to describe a room by putting the reader into the scene, your details would be arranged in an order in which he might see them, were he standing in the room. If, in another paragraph, your purpose is to convince your reader of a certain fact, you would list your points in such a way that they would have maximum effect on him (perhaps in an ascending or "climactic" order of importance).

DEVELOPING A PARAGRAPH

The way the writer develops his topic idea in any single paragraph must always be determined by the topic idea and the purpose that the writer has in mind for the paragraph. The six major ways in which a writer can develop a topic idea within any paragraph are described below:

Enumerate Examples or Illustrations

Sometimes we may be saying something that we cannot explain clearly, and our listener may suggest, "Well, suppose you give me an example." Examples, or illustrations, provide us with a way of putting something abstract and perhaps difficult to comprehend into images or pictures that are easy to understand. Examples are almost exactly the same as details, except that they are used for the specific purpose of making a general point. You give an example of something; you make an illustration of a point. Hence, this method of developing a paragraph is especially useful in *expository* and *argumentative* writing.

Use a Single Illustration

Often the easiest way to "say what you mean" is to tell a simple story that says it for you. Such a method of developing a topic idea can help you define a word, make a point clear, or explain an idea. Hence, the "single-illustration paragraph" is used most frequently in *expository* and *argumentative* writing.

Explain by Definition

In *expository* writing, we can sometimes more clearly discuss an idea or concept by *defining* the word that embodies the idea. The definition should expand the basic idea by presenting other ideas with which the reader is already familiar.

Explain by Analogy

An *analogy* is a single illustration that describes or explains one thing by describing something quite different, but at the same time similar, so that there is a clear parallel between the two. George Orwell's much-discussed novel *Animal Farm* is an analogy in the form of a novel. In this book, Orwell presents his attitude toward the aftermath of the Russian Revolution by telling a story of a group of very human animals on a farm. The analogy is often more dramatic than a simple illustration because of its suggestive powers. Thus, for example, Orwell's use of animals immediately suggests that the historical figures whom they represent were somewhat less than human in their behavior.

Illustrate by Comparison and/or Contrast

This method of developing a paragraph can take one of three forms, depending on the topic idea and the purpose of the writer:

a) showing comparisons or similarities
b) showing contrasts or dissimilarities
c) showing both comparisons and contrasts

As you can see, the third is a combination of the first two methods. This approach is especially useful when describing abstract ideas.

Give Reasons

The paragraph that uses reasons to develop its topic idea will be more effective if the reasons are listed in some logical or dramatic order, not haphazardly. The reasons are listed in increasing order of importance. Since the end of the paragraph—like the end of a sentence, or of an essay, or of a speech—is a high point of emphasis, this order is commonly used and is very effective. A "clincher" sentence is used at the end of the paragraph to restate the topic sentence for greater emphasis.

The Total Composition

Every composition has a clearly defined introduction, body, and conclusion, but these are not labeled as such or set apart when the paper is written.

The introduction should (1) arouse the reader's interest; (2) state the main idea of the composition; and (3) possibly preview the main topics. It contains your thesis statement (see "The Research Paper") and a number of other sentences designed to introduce your topic and let the reader know what the paper is about. This is your road map, guiding you through the rest of your paper until you reach your destination.

The body of the composition must develop, support, and explain the main ideas stated in your introduction, or thesis paragraph. It should include appropriate, specific examples and details to back up your thesis. An outline is essential for a well-constructed paper.

The conclusion of the paper should clinch the main points made in the body of the composition. It pulls together the details of the paper into a final statement, giving a feeling of completeness. It should not contain any new evidence. Depending on your objective, the conclusion may simply summarize your position, emphasize a main point, draw a conclusion, or even spur the reader to action.

However, the best ideas and the most detailed research are all to no avail if the end product, the written paper, is not *well* written, if it does not communicate effectively to the reader. Therefore, the mechanics of composition are of paramount importance to you. The three key words to consider in writing are *unity, coherence,* and *emphasis.*

The principle of unity applies to all components of the paper, to the paragraphs which are the building blocks of the paper like bricks in a wall, and to the paper as a whole. Each paragraph should contain only one thought, with the topic sentence controlling the idea of the whole paragraph. By the same token, each paragraph should develop, explain, or expand on the main point of the composition. Do not wander off on tangents; eliminate anything that does not fulfill your thesis statement.

Following the principle of coherence makes the paper understandable. It has to do with arranging your ideas in a clear order according to a definite plan, with the ideas linked together clearly and expressed in vivid, interesting language. Paragraphs should flow naturally from one to another with ideas arranged in logical order. Smooth transitions from one paragraph to the next are essential for the reader to understand the relationship between the ideas expressed in the individual paragraphs. Therefore transitions could be likened to the mortar holding together the separate building blocks of a wall.

Here are some linking expressions to bridge gaps between paragraphs.

To go from one point to another: finally, moreover, besides, in addition to, another, in the next place, also, furthermore, to sum up.

To indicate another time: next, soon, meanwhile, then, later, finally.

To indicate results: therefore, thus, consequently, as a result.

To show contrast: nevertheless, however, on the other hand, instead, in spite of.

To show relationships: accordingly, similarly, likewise.

To introduce examples: for instance, for example.

Style, the way words are put together, is extremely important in getting ideas across from your mind to your reader's mind. We all use our language in different ways. In everyday conversation we use contractions, slang, colloquialisms, even dialect. This is fine. In addition to our spoken language, we have our written language. When we write letters to friends, or even informal papers, we write in a chatty, informal style. This is fine too. Then there is formal written language. For serious papers informality is totally out of place, so do not use contractions, slang, or colloquial expressions. While avoiding being stodgy or flowery, do be formal or objective in expression, and refrain from using second person (you) or first person (I).

A writer must also be very careful not to be guilty of plagiarism, which is using another person's ideas, words, or even sentence structure as one's own without giving proper credit to the original author.

The third principle of writing concerns emphasis, meaning devoting more space to the more important points and explaining what needs to be explained fully. Put yourself in the reader's place and try to see if another person would have any unanswered questions after reading the paper. Would they really understand what you are trying to say?

It has been said that there is no such thing as good writing, only rewriting. All really great authors polish their works many times. After you have gotten your thoughts down on paper the first time, read it aloud to yourself and listen to what it has to say. Get another person to read it to see if it is understandable to an outsider. After you have reworked the paper for sense and style of writing, go over it again checking your grammar and punctuation. Make a third check just for spelling. After you have copied your paper in its final form, always go over it again proofreading for any copying errors.

Typed papers are always double spaced. If you write by hand, use blue or black ink on one side only of standard notebook paper.

Put the title in the center of the first line. Do not underline it or put it in quotes. Skip a line and begin the paper proper, indenting paragraphs one-half inch. Leave a margin on the left side to coincide with the red line of the notebook paper (about one and one-half inches). Leave a margin on the right side half the width of the left-hand margin. Do not skip lines between paragraphs and do not write on the last blue line at the bottom of the page. On all pages except the first, begin writing on the first blue line. Do not number the first page of the paper but number all other pages of the paper proper in the upper right-hand corner. Outline, end notes, and bibliography pages are not numbered. Never turn in a paper containing crossed-out words. For an example of a title page, see the model at the end of "The Research Paper."

SPECIAL COMPOSITIONS

Written communication falls into four kinds of writing: exposition, argument, description, and narration. Expository writing is to inform or explain. Argument is used to persuade by reason and/or emotion. Description paints a picture appealing to the five senses. Narration gives an account of action or events.

Probably more than 95 percent of contemporary writing is expository for it includes most scientific and technical books, textbooks, philosophical and political tracts (when not contentious), much of biography and history, the bulk of magazine writing, recipes and formulas, essays and editorials, and reviews and criticism, whether of art, music, or literature. Patches of exposition may be found also in argumentation, narration, and description. When a debater pauses to explain or clarify a situation, the temporary digression may serve to strengthen his case. He is then no longer contending for a point but is engaging in exposition. If the author of a detective story pauses to discuss the layout of the apartment in which the crime occurs he is similarly engaged in exposition. In a book like Rachel Carson's *The Sea Around Us*, the text is about evenly divided among narration, description, and exposition.

Since expository writing is so important, we will go into detail about some specific kinds: the research paper, the book report (or review), the précis, and the science project report.

THE RESEARCH PAPER

A research (or library or term) paper is a documented prose work resulting from an organized analysis of a subject. It presents the results of careful investigation of some chosen topic in an interesting, orderly, and clear manner. It is an original paper by a student who has searched with intelligence through varied sources, selecting facts that he recognizes as essential to his stated subject. The student takes a relevant idea from one author, a telling quotation from another and, having gathered together a body of such information, will then, by using his imagination and knowledge, create something new. It is written in his own words unless a direct quotation is attributed to its original author.

STEPS TO FOLLOW

1. CHOOSE, THEN LIMIT YOUR SUBJECT. You will do best with a subject that interests you, that you can understand, that has sufficient information available about it, that is limited in its scope so that it can be covered adequately in a paper of the assigned length.

2. SURVEY YOUR RESOURCES. Check the card catalog of the library for books dealing with

your proposed topic. Determining the key word to look under is a basic problem in library research. No matter what library tool you use—card catalog, *Reader's Guide,* indexes to books—you must ask yourself this question: "What key word will lead me to the information I seek?" The same key word does not always apply to every reference tool. For instance, the *Reader's Guide* may use "Impeachment," while the card catalog may use "Presidents—U. S.—Impeachment." Remember the topic may encompass many subject headings. For instance, the broad subject of "Crime and Criminals" would include these subject headings and many more: Crime prevention; Criminal law; Administration of justice; Juvenile deliquency; Murder; Organized crime; Police; Prisons; Punishment; Racketeering; Social ethics, etc.

Write down the call numbers for books you think you could use, then go to the shelves to find them. Look at books with similar call numbers. Scan tables of contents to see what the books are about. In the card catalog also note references to pamphlets and clippings in the library's Vertical File and to nonbook materials such as filmstrips and multimedia kits. Consider knowledgeable people in the field to interview. Systematically look at the various issues of the *Reader's Guide,* checking off each volume as you finish it.

3. MAKE A PRELIMINARY STATEMENT OF OBJECTIVE (THESIS STATEMENT). At some point during your survey of resources, you may find there is not enough information on your topic. Change topics immediately. If you find much information, you will need to narrow it very soon, but surveying your resources helps you see the different facets of the topic, to help with your narrowing decision. But very soon you must hone in on your chosen objective in order to find all you need to know about it and not to waste time on information not essential to it. Making a preliminary thesis statement helps keep you on track.

Possible topics:

The Supreme Court—No! Impossibly broad!

Recent Supreme Court Decisions—No! Still impossible!

Supreme Court Decisions Pertaining to School Desegration—Still too big!

The Effect of Supreme Court Decisions on Nashville Schools—OK

Thesis Statement: Dramatic changes in the structure of Nashville's school system occurred in the 1950s, in 1971, and in 1983 as a result of Supreme Court decisions.

4. MAKE A WORKING BIBLIOGRAPHY. Once you have settled on what you are looking for, it is time to begin gathering material in earnest. Set up a Working Bibliography on a sheet of notebook paper listing everything that might possibly be of use to you. Here you copy all magazine articles exactly as the information is given you in the *Reader's Guide.* Make notations of those unavailable in your school library so you can check the public library. Scratch off those that prove useless. Enter all books, pamphlets, nonbook materials, people. The Working Bibliography is a good place to list all the varied subject headings you need to check to find available material. This is a valuable tool, so preserve it carefully until you have finished your paper.

5. SCAN YOUR MATERIAL. As you find information, glance through it quickly to see if it contains information you want. You must understand the material and then translate it into an intelligible presentation of your own. Ask yourself, "What is the author trying to say?" "What are the main points he is trying to make?" If the answers to these questions have a bearing on your thesis, prepare to go over the material more thoroughly.

6. MAKE A BIBLIOGRAPHY CARD, separate, complete, and accurate, for each source of information you consult. Do this before you take any notes from that source and keep your master bibliography cards separate from your note cards.

For a book, get your information from the title page and, if no date is listed there, the copyright date from the back of the title page. Book information includes author (full name, last name first), title, place of publication, publisher, and date.

For a magazine you must have the author of the article (if any); name of magazine; its volume number in arabic numerals; its date; and the pages the article is found on, such as pp. 37–41.

7. TAKE GOOD NOTES. If they are prepared properly, writing the paper is relatively easy, and you should not have to consult your sources again. Follow this procedure:

(a) write on 3 x 5 or 4 x 6 cards;

(b) write on one side of the card only;

(c) put only one idea from one source to a card;

(d) include on each card four things—(1) a slug, identification of the specific subject treated on the card; (2) the source, shortened title or author's name so you can tell where the information came from; (3) your notes; (4) the exact page where the material appears.

Do not write down obvious, easily remembered,

well known, or general information. As you read, stop to think what the main idea is. Close your eyes and say it in your own words. Write the notation on the notecard. Check back to see that you have understood the idea correctly. Be careful to avoid misrepresentation by lifting material out of context or by twisting the interpretation to suit your own conclusion. Put the information in your own words, never using words in the book. However, if you think you would like to quote the material from your source, copy it exactly and enclose it in quotation marks.

Here are samples of a bibliography card and a note card made from it.

> Muir, Frank
> Christmas Customs & Traditions
> New York, Taplinger Publishing Company
> 1975

> Preparations - Cookery   Muir
>   Stir Up Sunday - Sun. before Advent
>   last time to make Christmas
>   pudding to be ready in time.
> p.22 Gets name from Church Collect for
>   that day which begins "Stir up
>   we beseech thee, O Lord, the wills of
>   thy faithful people...."

8. During this reading process, MAKE A PRELIMINARY OUTLINE, so you can see exactly what information you need on various points and how much you will need. (See "Outlining.") Outline topics make good slugs for notecards.

9. CONTINUE READING AND NOTE TAKING. Remember the outline is like a skeleton which your paper will flesh out. The preliminary outline may show that your skeleton lacks an arm, or one arm is much smaller than the other. Your reading and note taking now can fill in what the outline revealed was needed.

10. MAKE UP AN INTERESTING TITLE.

11. WRITE YOUR THESIS STATEMENT IN ITS FINAL FORM. Remember the thesis tells exactly what your paper is about, what it is to cover; and the outline shows how you accomplish the objective of the thesis. In the preliminary stages you may need to adjust both the original thesis and the original outline. Now is the time to get your thesis in precise final form. Play with words, work to express your thesis so it will convey exactly the ideas you want it to in an interesting manner.

12. REVISE OUTLINE into its final form.

13. WRITE AN INTERESTING INTRODUCTION that (1) attracts the reader's attention; (2) states what the paper is about; and (3) previews the main topics. Incorporate your thesis in the introduction.

14. SORT YOUR NOTE CARDS to conform to your outline. Write the paper in your words using formal, objective style. Avoid the use of "you" and "I." The research paper is not an informal essay, although you need to make it interesting and may use imagination in making deductions and drawing conclusions.

Have your end note page beside you and make your end notes as you write. Be specific but do not worry about exact form at this time, as you can go back and set your end notes in precise form later. Just be sure your numbers coincide. End note' in your paper must refer to 'on your end note page.

Even though you are writing in your own words, you have used information supplied by others. You will also want to use direct quotations (but only sparingly, to emphasize an important point or as proof of your conclusions). These must be acknowledged. Use a footnote or an end note to give credit for a direct quotation; to give credit for an original or unusually interesting opinion or interpretation which you have put in your own words; to give credit for all statistics, figures, definitions, illustrations. The question always arises, "Since I knew nothing about this subject before researching it, do I have to footnote every piece of information used?" Obviously that would be impractical. If the ideas seem to be general knowledge of authorities in the field, do not footnote unless you are quoting exactly. (See "Endnoting/Footnoting" for exact details.)

Direct quotations are handled in two different ways. For a short quotation (one that would be four typed lines or less) enclose it in quotation marks and "work it in smoothly as part of your own sentence."[1]

A long quotation (one that is five lines or more of type) should be handled this way:

Double-space (or skip a line of notebook paper) above and below the quotation. Single-space the quotation if you are typing. Indent the quoted material an extra half-inch on each side. Do not use quotation marks around it. Remember always at the end of a quotation, whether it is short or long, that you must put a number slightly above the line to refer to the same number in your footnotes.[2]

15. WRITE A GOOD CONCLUSION that rounds out your paper, sums it up, gives a feeling of completeness.

16. REVISE YOUR PAPER.

17. COPY YOUR PAPER, then proofread for copying errors. Doublecheck footnotes for accuracy and for form.

18. MAKE YOUR BIBLIOGRAPHY. Arrange your bibliography cards alphabetically according to the author's last name. If there is no author, alphabetize by the first word of the title (skipping "A," "An," and "The." If the reference is published by an organization with no author, use the organization as author. Make your bibliography according to the prescribed forms. Often teachers want you to include in your bibliography only the sources you actually used in writing the paper, not a complete listing of sources you may have consulted. (See "Bibliography.")

19. MAKE THE TITLE PAGE. (See form.)

20. ASSEMBLE THE PAPER. The usual order is: (1) title page; (2) outline, which substitutes for a table of contents in a school paper; (3) the paper itself; (4) end notes; (5) bibliography.

ABBREVIATIONS

Common abbreviations found in doing research are:

ca., c.	about (circa)
ch., chs.	chapter, chapters
cf.	compare, confer
et al.	and others (**et alii or alibi**)
ed.	edited, edition, editor
e.g.	for example (**exempli gratia**)
f., ff.	and the following page, pages
illus.	illustrated
ibid.	in the same place (**ibidem**) (obsolete)
id.	the same (**idem**)
l., ll.	line, lines
i.e.	that is (**id est**)
loc. cit.	in the place cited (**loco citato**) (obsolete)
lit.	literally
MS, MSS	Manuscript, Manuscripts
N.B.	note well (**nota bene**)
n.d.	no date given
no., nos.	number, numbers
op. cit.	in the work cited (**opere citato**) (obsolete)
p., pp.	page, pages
trans.	translator/translation
viz.	namely
vol., vols.	volume, volumes

OUTLINING

An outline is to a paper what a road map is to a journey. The thesis statement states your destination, and the outline shows you how to get there. Thesis: I am going to Yazoo City, Mississippi, from Nashville, Tennessee. Outline: Take I-40 to Memphis; then I-55 toward Jackson; at Exit 181 go west on Highway 16. . . . The purpose of outlining is to prevent wandering off the subject; to give a quick overall view of the essay; to insure proportionate space to each part; to aid in organizing and giving order to the essay; to enable you to spot missing or irrelevant matter. Some ways to organize are: by time, by space, by likenesses and differences, in order of importance, by cause and effect.

An outline includes only main ideas and important details. Flesh in the outline when you write the paper.

There must always be under any topic more than one subtopic. Subtopics are divisions of the topic above them, and you cannot divide anything into fewer than two parts. If you find yourself wanting to use a single subtopic, rewrite the topic above it so that this "sub idea" is included in the main topic.

Wrong: C. Hostesses

    1. Those who nag

Right: C. Nagging Hostesses

A subtopic must belong under the main topic beneath which it is placed. It must be closely related to the topic above it.

Wrong: A. Dull games

    1. Bingo

    2. Not enough refreshments

Terms such as "Introduction," "Body," and "Conclusion" should not be included in the outline. Of course, you should have them as definite parts of your paper (though never so designated) but these are not topics that you intend to discuss.

There are two kinds of outlines, the topic and the sentence. The topic is composed of words or phrases throughout all divisions. It is used for conciseness and brevity, and no end punctuation is needed. A sentence outline uses sentences throughout its divisions, so end punctuation is needed. It is fuller, clearer, and more exact than a topic outline.

How to Prepare an Outline

To outline a chapter in a book is easy because the information was outlined before it was written. The difficult part of outlining is taking a large body of information and organizing it into a logical, coherent form. Here are some tips to help you do this for your research paper. Notice it is in sentence outline form.

I. Select the subject of your paper.
   A. Decide on a general topic.
      1. Survey available resources.
      2. Note the various aspects of the subject.
   B. Limit your topic to a narrow aspect that can be adequately covered in a paper of your designated length.
   C. Write a thesis statement that exactly pinpoints your objective.

II. Make a rough draft of your outline.
   A. Jot down at random all the points about your paper that come to mind.
   B. Group similar ones together.
   C. Decide what pattern would be best to follow.
      1. It could be chronological.
      2. It could be spatial (geographical).
      3. It could be a study of contrasts or comparisons.
      4. It could be cause-and-effect.
      5. It could be a study of influences.
   D. Write a simple topic outline.
      1. Choose two to four most important points for the major divisions.
      2. Place remaining ideas as subtopics under them.
   E. Assess the result.
      1. Consider if you are fulfilling your thesis statement.
      2. Consider if you have covered the subject adequately.
      3. Check to see that each subtopic falls logically under its larger topic.

   4. Eliminate any material that does not fit.
      (a) This means irrelevant matter.
      (b) This means unnecessary (too detailed) matter for an outline.
   5. Determine if you need to look for additional information.
      (a) Should this information be for an added topic?
      (b) Should it be to expand on an existing topic?

III. Write the outline in final sentence form.
   A. Word the main topics to make them concise, clear, and parallel.*
   B. Fill in the subtopics by the same criteria.
   C. See that the outline is in correct outline form.

* Parallelism means using similar wording for various divisions of equal rank. Here is a topic outline illustrating this.

Wrong
How to Do the Laundry
   I. Sorting by colors
   II. To start the machine
   III. Proper water temperature
   IV. How to handle delicate fabrics

Right
How to Do the Laundry
   I. Sorting by colors
   II. Starting the machine
   III. Choosing proper water temperature
   IV. Handling delicate fabrics

Picture of an Outline

Title of Paper

Thesis Statement: . . . .
   I. Major division
      A. Subdivision
         1. Sub-subdivision
            a.
               (1)
                  (a)
                  (b)
               (2)
            b.
         2.
      B.
   II.

FOOTNOTING/ENDNOTING

The distinction has been made that footnotes are properly used in dissertations and end notes are to be used in research papers. The difference is that footnotes appear at the bottom of the page containing the cited material, while end notes are arranged on one or two pages at the end of the paper. It is much easier to do end notes because in footnotes the writing has to be spaced very carefully to allow sufficient room at the bottom of the page. Teachers vary in which they require. People generally speak of footnotes to mean both those at the foot of the page and those at the end of the paper.

These instructions are for end notes.

* Number them consecutively throughout the paper.

* In the body of your paper put a number slightly above the line *at the end* of the material to be acknowledged. No period follows an end note number.

* On your end note page put the same number as its corresponding number in the paper (again above the line and without a period). Indent the first line of each end note and start the second line even with the left margin.

* The author's *given name* should be written *first.*

When the same source is repeated, it is not necessary to give the full information about that source a second time. Use a shortened form to identify the reference. Formerly Latin terms such as "ibid.," "op. cit.," and "loc. cit." were used. These are now considered obsolete. When the same source is used a second or subsequent time, simply write the end note number, then the author's last name, and then the page number on which the material can be found.

If you have made your bibliography cards properly, you will have there all the information you will need for your end notes, except for the exact page on which that bit of material was found, which will be on your note card. Never end note for several pages in a source; the only time you would indicate two pages is when the sentence on the source page runs over onto a second page.

Examples of End Notes

(First use of book by one author)

[1]Robert W. Kirk, *First Aid for Pets* (New York: E. P. Dutton, 1978), p. 40.

(Second and subsequent uses of preceding book)

[2]Kirk, p. 41.

(First use of book by two authors)

[3]Mary Bray Wheeler and Genon Hickerson Neblett, *Hidden Glory: The Life and Times of Hampton Plantation, Legend of the South Santee* (Nashville: Rutledge Hill Press, 1983), pp. 21-22.

(For a book with no author)

[4]*Webster's Geographical Dictionary* (Springfield: G. & C. Merriam Co., 1981), p. 535.

(For an organization as author)

[5]U.S. Department of Commerce, Bureau of the Census, *Statistical Abstract of the United States 1982–83* (Washington, D.C., Government Printing Office, 1982), p. 1065.

(For a book with an editor)

[6]Lois Decker O'Neill, ed., *The Women's Book of World Records and Achievements* (New York: Doubleday, 1979), p. 84.

(For a magazine article with an author; note the volume number before the date.)

[7]Michael M. Lombardo, "The Intolerable Boss," *Psychology Today,* 18(Jan., 1984), p. 45.

(For the same article, second and subsequent quotings)

[8]Lombardo, p. 46.

(For a magazine article with no author)

[9]"The Muffin-Mix Scare," *Time,* 123(Feb. 13, 1984), p. 20.

(For the same article, second and subsequent quotings)

[10]*Time,* p. 22*

* If you are quoting from several *different* issues of *Time,* include the date in parentheses: *Time,* (Feb. 13, 1984), p. 22. This will indicate which issue you refer to.

(For a newspaper article with a by-line)

[11]Patricia McCormack, "Special Diet Urged to Thwart Cancer," *Nashville Tennessean,* (Feb. 11, 1984), Sec. D, p. 2.

(For a newspaper article with no by-line)

[12]"Moslems Take West Beirut," *Nashville Banner,* (Feb. 8, 1984), Sec. A, p. 1.

(For an encyclopedia article)

[13]"Jet Propulsion," *World Book Encyclopedia,* (1979 ed.), vol. 11, p. 386.

(For an interview)

[14]Richard Fulton, Mayor of Nashville, interviewed by Mary Smith (Metropolitan Courthouse, Nashville, Tenn.), 10 A.M., Jan. 15, 1984.

(For a personal letter)

[15]Personal letter from Lamar Alexander, Governor of Tennessee, to Jason Jones, Feb. 16, 1984.

(For material from one source quoted in another)

[16]James Boswell, *The Life of Samuel Johnson,* quoted by Robert Byrne in *Cat Scan* (New York: Atheneum, 1983), p. 7.

If there are two or more works by the same author, or two or more authors with the same name, a shortened title of the cited work is used after the author's last name. Let us assume you are quoting from two books by Louise Davis, *Nashville Tales* and *Frontier Tales.*

(First citation)

[17]Louise Littleton Davis, *Nashville Tales* (Gretna, LA: Pelican Publishing Co., 1981), p. 35.

(Second citation)

[18]Davis, *Nashville,* p. 4.

Notice the differences between the pattern of end notes and of a bibliography. In end notes the arrangement is strictly numerical in the order the material is cited from the work; the author's first name comes first; the first line is indented and the second line is flush with the left-hand margin. In a bibliography the arrangement is alphabetical by the author's last name and the first line is flush with the left-hand margin with the second line being indented. Here is a bibliography of the works cited in the example of footnotes.

BIBLIOGRAPHY

Alexander, Lamar, Governor of Tennessee, to Jason Jones, Feb. 16, 1984.

Byrne, Robert. *Cat Scan.* New York: Atheneum, 1983.

Davis, Louise Littleton. *Frontier Tales.* Gretna, LA: Pelican Publishing Co., 1980.

———, *Nashville Tales.* Gretna, LA: Pelican Publishing Co., 1981.

Fulton, Richard, Mayor of Nashville, interviewed by Mary Smith, Metropolitan Courthouse, Nashville, Tenn., 10 A.M., Jan. 15, 1984.

"Jet Propulsion." *World Book Encyclopedia,* 1979 ed., vol. 11, p. 386.

Kirk, Robert W. *First Aid for Pets.* New York: E. P. Dutton, 1978.

Lombardo, Michael M. "The Intolerable Boss." *Psychology Today,* 18 (Jan., 1984), pp. 45–48.

McCormack, Patricia. "Special Diet Urged to Thwart Cancer." *Nashville Tennessean,* (Feb. 8, 1984), Sec. D, p. 2.

"Muffin-Mix Scare." *Time,* 123 (Feb. 13, 1984), pp. 20-21.

O'Neill, Lois Decker, ed. *The Women's Book of World Records and Achievements.* New York: Doubleday, 1979.

U. S. Department of Commerce, Bureau of the Census, *Statistical Abstract of the United States 1982#83.* Washington, D.C.: Government Printing Office, 1982.

Webster's Geographical Dictionary. Springfield: G. & C. Merriam Co., 1981.

Wheeler, Mary Bray, and Neblett, Genon Hickerson. *Hidden Glory: The Life and Times of Hampton Plantation, Legend of the South Santee.* Nashville: Rutledge Hill Press, 1983.

You will find slight variations, especially in punctuation, among the many handbooks available showing forms for footnotes and bibliographies. The important thing for you to do is to choose one source as your model and then be scrupulous in following it exactly so your paper is consistent throughout.

(Sample of Title Page)

RAIN OF DEATH: THE IMPACT OF ACID RAIN

ON NATURAL RESOURCES IN THE UNITED STATES

by

Nathan Elliott

American History, Fourth Period

February 21, 1984

Argumentative Writing

That category of writing which attempts to strengthen a view already held, to weaken or undermine such a view, or to persuade the reader to adopt another is called argumentation. The name, though well established, is unfortunate, for one immediately infers that it involves a contentious type of discussion. Persuasion would be a better name, for the aim is to incline another's will to one's own view rather than to controvert it or break it. The writer who conceives his task as persuasion must also assume (even though he may suspect the contrary to be true) that his reader has not taken a firm position, and, as a reasonable man, would be delighted to follow him into his stand. Therefore, from the very start, he tries to confine his attack, so far as he must attack, to issues rather than to persons. The attitude of the persuader must be understanding and generous. He writes, "It would appear . . . ," "It seems . . ." rather than "It is . . ." or "It must be. . . ."

Analysis of the Question

1. DEFINITION OF TERMS

Should a writer wish to contend that New York City is the true capital of America, he would have to define what he means by his terms. Does he mean "Greater New York," or does he mean the financial district? Does "true" have the same sense as "real"? Is "capital" used as "the governing political center" or the "dominant financial center"? By "America" does he mean the United States, North America, or the Western Hemisphere? It will be observed that until these terms are clarified the issue is confused. The process of clarification which must be undertaken by the writer at the outset is known as "defining the terms."

2. HISTORY OF THE QUESTION

Many issues are of long standing and have been discussed before. If the previous discussion has swayed public opinion in any discernible way, the writer may possibly profit by rehearsing previous discussions if their results favor him. Such a presentation is known as "giving the history of the question." If, on the other hand, he can show that his view has in the past received scant attention, has been rudely treated or suppressed, he may actually profit from rehearsing this history.

3. DETERMINING THE ISSUES

Whenever there is a difference of opinion, the holders of opposing views frequently find themselves separated on a multiplicity of issues, many of which may be extremely trivial. If one urges trivial issues, even successfully, when major issues are decisive, his power to persuade will fail. The best way to determine the major issues is to set up the chief issues for each side and to select the ones that collide most sharply; these are the major issues.

Planning Persuasive Measures

Once he has determined the issues, the writer plans the order in which he will present them. He will have to decide on one of two approaches, depending on whether he feels he can easily overcome opposition or will have to work hard to be persuasive. In the former situation he should choose and present his strongest point first, with the intent of putting his opposition to rout; in the latter, he should study the issues to see if there is not one that may be conceded to him without too great a struggle, and use that as an entering wedge. To persuade successfully one must consider every possible factor that can be turned to advantage, but yet must avoid seeming to do so. The tone of persuasion should be concessive, generous.

Briefing

If the issue involves grave consequences or the opposition is entrenched and well armed, it is wise to prepare a formal brief, covering the major issues and indicating the proof to be supplied. The practice of briefing, incidentally, provides an excellent discipline for the reasoning faculties. The form is well established and should be conscientiously adhered to:

The United States should support the U.N., *for*

I. It is the major instrument for world peace, *for*
    A. Balance of power is impossible, *for*
        1. Unilateral action can undermine the balance, *for*
            a. China does not accept Russian leadership in the East.
            b. France is uncooperative in the West.

B. Treaties are good only so long as the parties will honor them.

C. Neutral nations within the organization are a deterrent to immoral action.

II. It is a major instrument for social betterment, *for*

A. Its agencies combat disease and crime, etc.

Proof

1. TESTIMONIAL EVIDENCE

Once the writer has outlined his case, either in his own mind or in a formal brief, his next step is to muster the best proofs of his arguments that he can summon. Such proof is called evidence, and of evidence there are two kinds, testimonial and circumstantial. The first is the evidence of persons or witnesses; the second is that of the facts in the case.

Testimonial evidence is persuasive to the degree that the fairness and credibility of the witness may not be impugned. If the witness has something to gain from his testimony, its value is greatly reduced; in fact, it may be disproportionately reduced if the fact is discovered first by the opposition. The best witness is one who has no personal motivation in his testimony. In certain instances, in order to be judged reliable a witness should have no physical or mental handicaps. If a motorist has driven through a red light, and it can be shown that the only witness to his act is color blind, the case against him may be dismissed. Witnesses may be called upon to estimate the alleged speed of a traveling car, but if they cannot judge distances approximately in the courtroom their evidence may be impugned. The testimony of a witness may be impaired by showing that his morality is suspect because of some past dereliction, for while it is open to question whether a man who has stolen will lie, the world is all too ready to suspect that he will.

Whenever an issue involves special technical or scientific knowledge, it is customary to solicit the testimony of experts. In technical language, this is known as *the appeal to authority*. If responsibility in a boiler explosion is an issue, the testimony of an engineer is obviously worth more than that of a ribbon clerk, but if the quality of yardgoods is in question, the clerk, particularly if he is also a buyer for the store, is the better witness. The appeal to authority may also be invoked to summon the expert testimony of those dead and revered, as for example that of John Marshall (Chief Justice of the United States, 1801-1935) on constitutional questions. But so far as the expert testimony is concerned, it must be remembered that it is good only in the field of competency.

2. CIRCUMSTANTIAL EVIDENCE

Circumstantial evidence is evidence from the facts, but it is evidence from the facts as determined by human reasoning. One car, out of control, collides with another, catapulting its occupant into the street. An eyewitness may testify that the victim is a casualty of reckless driving, but it is disclosed that the victim, an elderly man and quite ill, was being driven to a hospital, and an autopsy reveals that he had been dead some time when the accident occurred. The facts of the autopsy, especially the blood clot closing the aorta, are interpreted as more convincing than the testimony of the eyewitness, though they are all circumstantial facts. (The illustration is a mixed one, for here the facts are presented by a physician and are reinforced by his authority; nevertheless, the court acts on his arrangement of them.) A man caught near the scene of a crime with a recently fired revolver of the same caliber as that of a bullet extracted from the body of the slain man has an impressive array of facts against him, despite a lack of any witness to the shooting. If we conclude he is guilty of the crime, our conclusion is based wholly on our reasoning from the facts. There may be others, however, that we have not taken into consideration. What if he was a friend of the victim who had picked up the murderer's gun and was searching for him? It must ever be kept in mind that in large areas of human experience circumstantical evidence at best produces only a "reasonable certainty."

3. TESTING CAUSAL RELATIONSHIPS

The initial presumptions that both the driver of the car out of control and the friend with the murderer's weapon in his hand were guilty are based upon one of the most fundamental tenets of all human thinking; namely, that nothing takes place without a cause. When the mind deals with an effect (natural death, in the first instance, and violent death, in the second) and searches for its cause, it is likely to commit certain well-known errors. The situation may be searched from the other direction, that is, from cause to effect. First, we may ask if the assumed cause was adequate to produce the effect. In both instances that we have hypothesized, it was; hence, the ready conclusion of guilt. Second, we may ask if the assumed cause is the only cause that could have operated. We have seen that, in each instance, it was not. When we are arguing that a certain cause will produce a "known" effect, we have these variants of the common errors to consider: Is the cause strong enough in this instance to produce the effect? May not some other cause intervene in the relationship?

The Argument from Analogy

Nothing is more enticing to a thinker bent on persuasion than the argument from analogy. It is based on the presumption that if two things have some elements in common, they have others also–a presumption which, of course, does not necessarily follow. Just as persons are always seeing family resemblances, they are quick to apprehend resemblances between things or situations.

There are two tests of real value with an analogy: (1) Are the resemblances really essential or vital resemblances? and (2) Despite the resemblances between the things compared, are there still more important differences between them? Dissenting from the relief measures that Franklin D. Roosevelt put into effect, William Allen White wrote, "If I was the underdog, I should bury my bones against the day of hunger." Mr. White believed that Roosevelt did not understand the "underdog" and, hence, would abandon him. Unfortunately for his analogy, many of the underdogs had no bones to bury, save those that Roosevelt's measures provided.

Generalizing Processes

1. INDUCTION

Every person who reasons inevitably generalizes. After discovering that a law operates in several examples of a kind, the mind finds it an enormous convenience to assume that it operates in all examples of that kind. When a scientist draws a conclusion from a reasonable number of cases, it is called an *induction*. We must remember, however, that there are few perfect inductions, that is, not *all* cases have been surveyed or could be surveyed.

There are four tests that an induction may be subjected to: Is the relative number of the instances observed, as compared with those unobserved, sufficiently large? Are the observed instances fair examples? Are there no invalidating exceptions? Is there an initial probability that the generalization is true?

2. DEDUCTION

It is a general assumption that all science is a product of the inductive method, but scientists fre-

quently imply that the discovery or law was a "hunch" or generalization for which the proof had later to be found by laborious investigation. Be that as it may, there is an almost equal tendency to assume generalizations and to find the assumed law operating in the instance under discussion. This process is called deduction. It is possible to state all deductions in this form, known as a *syllogism:*

All iron objects are subject to oxidation.
A steel rail is an iron object.
Therefore, a steel rail is subject to oxidation.

In the above syllogism, the statement "All iron objects are subject to oxidation" is called *the major premise;* "A steel rail is an iron object," *the minor premise;* and "Therefore, a steel rail is subject to oxidation," *the conclusion.* Mere ability to put a deduction in syllogistic form, however, does not guarantee its validity. Thus, for example:

All men are liars *(major premise).*
Green is a man *(minor premise).*
Therefore, Green is a liar *(conclusion).*

This syllogism is completely correct *if* we accept the major premise. But the major premise is the result of a previous faulty induction.

The ancients discovered that the syllogistic statement could be readily tested for its validity. It must conform to these rules:

a. Every syllogism has three, and only three, terms.

b. Every syllogism contains three, and only three, propositions or statements.

c. The middle term must be distributed (that is, universally applied), once at least, and must not be ambiguous.

d. No term must be distributed in the conclusion which was not distributed in one of the premises.

e. From negative premises nothing can be inferred.

f. If one premise is negative, the conclusion must be negative; and vice versa, to prove a negative conclusion one of the premises must be negative.

g. From two particular premises no conclusion can be drawn.

h. If one premise be particular, the conclusion must be particular.

A *term* denotes an individual or group of individuals or an attribute or a group of attributes. Thus in the syllogism attempting to show Green a liar, the terms are men (man), liars (liar), and Green. The *middle term* is the term which does not appear in the conclusion. With the help of a book on logic, or without it by trial and error, one may discover the complete validity of these rules.

The Common Fallacies

Thus far we have examined errors which occur in logical processes of reasoning, but a person engaged in the process of persuasion may adopt one of two illogical processes of reasoning and be quite unaware that they are illogical processes. Indeed, in practice they may each prove quite effective until an opponent exposes them. They are the common fallacies of *ignoring the question* and of *begging the question.*

1. IGNORING THE QUESTION

A writer ignores the question by substituting an issue which appears to be the same as the one under discussion. Because every writer becomes identified with the cause for which he stands, one of the commonest exhibitions of this fallacy occurs whenever an opponent attacks the writer, rather than his cause or the real issue under discussion.

2. BEGGING THE QUESTION

Whenever a reasoner assumes as true the thing which he is trying to establish, he is said to beg the question. Two forms of this fallacy are common: first, using question-begging epithets, and second, arguing in a circle. The first of these errors is regularly indulged in by impassioned or dishonest propagandists. When one writes, "In the *decadent* South a Negro can expect *no* justice from the *brutal* police," he is really begging the question; purged of these epithets, the proposition should read: In Chicago, Detroit, New York, or the South, the Negro can expect little justice from the police.

Refutation

In formal debate, replying to an opponent is usually left to the rebuttal speeches, though in presenting his case the debater may anticipate counterarguments. In a persuasive article there is no opportunity for rebuttal; hence the anticipation must be complete. Experienced writers know, as a rule, what may be offered in opposition to their views. Yielding an unimportant issue creates an impression of a judicious, a reasonable mind. It is in refutation that the reasoner probably should be most conscious, not of his ability to contend, but of his ability to persuade. Even if there is no chance of this with a dogmatic opponent, the persuasive attitude may win over more undecided listeners and readers than the dogmatism of the opponent. The successful reasoner treats his opponent with respect.

Narrative Writing

That form of writing which presents an event or a sequence of events involving animate beings is called narrative writing. While usually the actors in such a narrative are human beings, narrative writing is not restricted to their participation. The range of actors may be from insects and animals to trolls and fairies, to mechanical creatures and visitors from other planets. One thinks of the fat spider which disturbed little Miss Muffet, the boll weevil, Br'er Rabbit, Donald Duck, the Three Bears, the Rat-Wife, the Snow Princess, Superman, Tommy Tractor, Frankenstein, and the Man from Mars, whose antics may, or may not, bear some resemblance to human behavior. They do, however, have the capacity to carry the reader through an event or series of episodes, a characteristic which represents the primary function of characters in narrative writing.

Simple Narrative

The simplest event that can occur presents an actor in a role that is to some slight degree worth remarking. The commonest form of this narrative is the anecdote; the more familiar the actor, the less the writer has to supply by way of characterization. In repeating the legend of Newton's discovery of the law of gravitation from the falling apple which struck him on the head, the writer can count on persons' generally knowing who Newton was. Elaboration turns an anecdote into a narra-

tive allusion or after-dinner story. A narrative anecdote–it need not be true–that strikes at some foible in human behavior or belief is usually well received.

Fictional Narrative

Characters

To assure plausibility in a fictional narrative, start with the persons to be involved in the action. Ivan Turgenev, the Russian novelist, told the young Henry James that his fictions began *"always with the vision of some person or persons, who hovered before him, soliciting him, as the active or passive figure, interesting him and appealing to him just as they were and by what they were"* [italics ours]. That is, Turgenev started with a real person and transferred that person with his or her potentialities to his book. No procedure more surely guarantees plausibility than this one, for once the character is established he or she can do nothing "out of character"–both the artist and his reader would be instantly aware of the inconsistency. An axiomatic statement in fiction is, "Character governs action."

Plot

The persons in a work of fiction should determine the action; if they do not, it will not move. If three persons are placed together and two of them have traits that clash, the third is either bound to take sides or disintegrate, either through his effort to remain neutral or shift sides–and a "plot" is born. Imposing a plot on characters already assembled leads to distortion, unnaturalness, and eventually to implausibility. Increasing the number of characters usually multiplies the possibility of plot intricacy because of the alignment of loyalties. There are only two restrictions on the ramifications of plot: (1) The behavior of the characters must be wholly consistent with their natures, and (2) the high cost of typesetting limits the extent of any story. For the latter reason, three-volume novels and twenty-thousand-word short stories are not the fashion of the twentieth

century, though they were common enough in the nineteenth.

All conflicts in life move toward either stalemate or some sort of resolution, but in fiction they must move toward resolution. The ultimate clash of forces we term the *climax* of the tale; the results or consequences of this collision we call the *dénouement*. It is the highest art to make this as brief as possible.

Setting

The leisurely novel of the nineteenth century took much pains to set the stage fully for the action of its story. Frequently these novels began with a descriptive passage on which the author expended much conscious art.

But few writers could afford it today. Forced to economize, they have done so by eliminating extended descriptions of their stages. Instead they give the details of their settings as they proceed with their narratives. Scattering graphic bits of description through the narrative seems the best way to impress upon the reader with the greatest economy of means the setting for modern narrative. In order to impart a real sense of the scene, the writer should prepare a good many notes on his setting in order to select from among them.

Point of View

After a writer has chosen his characters, determined the nature of the conflict among them (even perhaps imagined the course of his plot), and determined where the events of his narrative will take place, he still must ask himself an important question: From what point of view shall I tell this story? He must follow this in his mind by other questions: Should the narrator be outside the tale? Should he know everything that takes place?

Should he be a participant in the action? Should he be a major figure or a minor figure? Should he be a limited or prejudiced observer?

If the narrator is to be outside the tale, he may definitely be identified with the author. Both Fielding and Thackeray do this and are frankly partisan in the conflicts which they imagine. The advantage of this point of view is that converts are more readily made to the author's views; but the limitations are those of partisanship–the intruding voice, the sense of manipulated characters. Because of these intrusions the narrative is always fiction–it loses a degree of verisimilitude; it becomes something less than life, whereas, if art is selective, it should be something more than life. Another choice from outside the action is to adopt what is known as the "omniscient" point of view. Still another choice remains–to plant a spectator on the periphery of the tale to report what goes on.

The recent tendency of writers of fiction seems to be to locate the point of view "in" one of the participants in action in the tale, either a major or a minor character. The author may identify with the hero of the tale and become this "I" narrator of his own adventure. The merit of this is its immediacy; it has, however, the grave limitation of closing to the reader the emotions and thoughts (save as they are overt) of other characters in the tale. And what is more boring than one who talks all the time?

Dialogue

Just as character determines the action in a narrative, so also character determines the dialogue. Relations between characters define what they will express and what they will repress. The talk must advance the story, and it does this either by revealing hidden motives or by suggesting aims and devices. The author has to remember also that a character can divine more than is said from what is unskillfully repressed. To expose the play of mind on mind is one of the most exciting challenges of a writer's career. No talk in good narrative should be pointless.

Description

That form of writing which depicts objects, living things, and the static elements in fantasies is called *description*. It is the vehicle through which we become acquainted with the world, its animals and machines, and the furnishings of its dreams and visions.

Independent Description

Required to write a description of a given thing, the writer should ask himself for whom he is describing it. If he is a professional writer preparing material for a wholesale hardware magazine distributed to retailers, he may assume some knowledge of his object or device, but if he is the same writer describing the same device for the general catalog of a mail order house, he can assume very little; he also has the limitation of space since so many objects are presented through his medium. The amount of description will be further reduced if the catalog uses illustrations and formulas, but his familiarity must include these to compensate for what is not depicted or formu-

larized. The householder without experience may write as good an advertisement of the home he wishes to sell as would the real estate agent (he should; he knows it better) but he does not know so well the purchaser or what will appeal to that purchaser.

Contributory Description

Skill in descriptive writing makes for interest in horticultural books, pleas for the preservation of wildlife, travel literature, and adventure stories, though these works may be chiefly narrative or persuasive. As with independent description, it is helpful to the reader to discover in an involved description a familiar image that will help him to see the scene with his mind's eye.

Long descriptive passages in fictional narrative are not so frequent today as they once were. The fiction writer manages to weave more of his descriptive detail into his narrative as it proceeds. The device is an old one; it is merely utilized more commonly now.

The Book Report/Review

Three conventional ways of writing about books are: (1) book reports, (2) book reviews, and (3) literary criticism. The book report is the traditional method whereby a teacher checks to see that an assignment has been completed and understood. It is the most elementary form. The third type, literary criticism, is an analysis, evaluation and judgment, presupposing critical knowledge on the part of the critic and the reader. You can work up to this.

The second type, the book review, is about halfway between the two, combining elements of both of the other types. Its purpose is (a) to inform the readership that a certain book is available; (b) to tell enough about the book to whet the appetite for someone to want to read it or to allow the reader to decide that he does not want to read it; (c) to make some judgment about its merit, although many reviewers are not acknowledged literary critics.

Students in elementary and middle schools need a lot of practice in doing book reports so when they reach high school they can move up into reviewing and make a good start toward real critiquing.

The way to approach writing a standard book report varies depending on the kind of book and the teacher's objective in making the assignment, so the teacher will often give specific guidelines to follow. However, there are many helpful hints the wise student will utilize which can make the difference between an "A" and a "C" report.

Keep in mind always that a book report is a hybrid, part fact and part fancy. It gives hard information about the book, yet it is your own creation, giving your opinion and judgment of it. Any report should tell at the beginning the author's full name, the title, the publisher, and the date of publication. It also makes very clear exactly what kind of book is being reviewed (fiction, or biography, or factual book about science, current events, history, etc.). Each type is judged by different standards which will be discussed later.

But no matter what kind of book is read, good book reporters and good book reviewers always read with the review constantly in the back of their minds. They mark in the book (if it belongs to them) or they make notes as they read to help them remember important things they want to say about the book and to help them find pertinent passages to quote in the review.

And they read imaginatively which is a skill that is necessary to complete the act of writing, for the greatest work ever written is only a piece of paper until a reader reacts to it. The reader actually helps create literature by responding to what the writer has to say. A thoughtful and imaginative reader considers both what the writer tries to say and how he says it. This gives him or her greater enjoyment in reading, and the critical skills develop with use, just as muscles do.

Usually when you finish a book you have a feeling. It may be of sorrow that the book has ended, or of satisfaction, or even of exhilaration. It may be a let-down feeling or plain indifference. Before you lose these emotions, before they fade away, jot down random notes capturing these reactions to the book. Then let your thoughts simmer on the back burner before actually writing the review.

REVIEWING FICTION

Most likely the majority of your class assignments for review will be in fiction, so you need to keep in mind these elements of literature as you read. First there is *characterization*. A writer may want to describe actions or ideas, but he must also describe the people who do the acting or have the ideas.

Then there is *motivation,* which means the reasons for the characters' actions. The writer should try to make his characters act like real people.

The *setting* is the place in which a character's story occurs. Literary characters, like the persons who read about them, do not exist in a vacuum. They act and react with one another, responding to the world in which they live.

The *plot* tells what happens to the characters in the story. It is built around a series of events that take place within a definite period of time. The leading character has a problem, he faces the problem, he overcomes it or is overcome by it.

Theme is what the author is trying to say, the basic idea behind writing the novel, the statement the author wants to make to the world. Seldom is it expressed in direct words; more often it is implied by the entire work. The mark of a sophisticated reader is being able to understand from the book what the author is trying to say above and beyond the simple story line of who did what to whom. The author may be saying that he thinks life is meaningless, that animals are superior to people, that love is the greatest power on earth, that all people need other people and cannot live alone, or whatever, *ad infinitum.*

Style is the way a writer uses words to create literature, to evoke emotions, to describe beauty or ugliness, to make characters come to life, to make events seem real.

As a mature reader you will understand these elements of literature and will assess them as you read, for they will color your evaluation.

You are now ready to plan your review. You have your notes made during the reading and your notes taken when you finished, and you have allowed your thoughts to take form. Ask yourself these questions:

* What was the author's real goal in writing the book? What was his theme? What was he trying to make me see, feel, or think? Did he accomplish his objective?

* Was the plot convincing? Did the incidents follow one another logically so I felt the story really could have happened?

* Did the characters seem human? Did I really care what happened to them? Did they act like real people or like puppets on a string? Did I learn anything about human nature after meeting these characters?

* Was the dialogue believable? Was it in keeping with the personalities of the characters? Did the dialogue move the story along or hinder it?

* Did the setting come to life? Could I actually see in my mind's eye the places described? Did the author fill in with vivid details?

* Was the style suitable to the plot and theme? Did it blend with the book or was I conscious of inept wording so it detracted from the story?

Make notes of your answers to these questions giving specific details to justify your reasons. Criticize where criticism is justified, but do not feel you must be critical to sound smart.

Summarize the plot briefly, never going into lengthy detail nor revealing an unexpected ending which would spoil the suspense if someone else were to read it. Never, never give a blow-by-blow account of the action; you are not rewriting the book but are judging the elements of the book and evaluating it as a whole. You may describe one particular scene in detail to try to capture the flavor of the book for your audience.

Take into consideration the exact nature of the book. If it is an historical novel, it is set in some specific place and period, so be sure to note the time, place, events, and historical persons involved. For instance, if you read the book *Tituba of Salem Village,* look up Tituba in an encyclopedia and point out that she was a real person and tell how the book followed (or did not follow) the actual events in her life. Read a little about the witchcraft trials in Salem, Massachusetts, so you can fix the book knowledgeably in its historical background.

Sometimes the title of the book needs explanation. If you read *The Magnificent Mutineers,* you should certainly include a paragraph about how mutineers, who are usually thought of as criminals, could be considered "magnificent."

Now ask yourself, What information do I want to get across to my readers about this book, what will *my* theme be? Take all your notes and form them into a logical outline that covers all that you want to say. Begin with the most factual parts and end with your own personal impressions.

Necessary for any good writing is a good introduction which entices the reader to read on and gives an overview of what is to come. Then the body of the work presents all the points the writer wishes to make. Equally critical is the conclusion that wraps up the writing, giving a feeling of completeness to the work.

The reviewer's own style of writing is important, with one word following another logically and interestingly, and with good paragraphs leading from one to the other smoothly. Use of transitional words or phrases between paragraphs helps the reader to follow the writer's meaning. All writing must be grammatically correct, with no misspelled words, and properly proofread.

Revise and polish your rough draft. Read the review over objectively. How do you think a reader of *your* work would evaluate it? Does it make a point? Does it give sufficient information for an outsider to form a valid opinion of the book? Is it dull? Is it a trustworthy evaluation? Be as thorough and critical of your own work as you were of the author's work!

REVIEWING A BIOGRAPHY

In reviewing a biography you must do much more than just tell the facts of the person's life which anyone can look up in an encyclopedia. Do summarize the person's life, telling when and where he lived and why he was worthy of having a book written about him.

A main factor to consider is what the author was trying to say about the person, what area of his life the author stressed. For instance, a biography about Thomas Jefferson might focus on Jefferson the president and what he did during his administration, such as enlarging the country through the Louisiana Purchase. Or the author might aim at showing how multitalented he was in the sciences and the arts. Or the concentration could be on his role in the Revolution as the author of the Declaration of Independence. Perhaps the main thrust was on the personality of Jefferson and his relationships with the people he loved.

Ask yourself these questions:

* Is the biographee presented as a real human being, with good traits and faults, or is he made into a stereotype, someone who is not quite real?

* Do the times and places come alive? Is the setting made real?

* Does the author explain what factors influenced the person? What conditions, or events, or people helped make the person what he became?

* Are the conversations as recorded believable?

* How does the author's style help or hinder the reading of the book?

* Would I have liked to have known the main character?

REVIEWING A SCIENCE BOOK

Here are some questions to ask yourself:

* Was the material easily understood? Did the author explain things clearly? Did I need more background to understand it or did the author write in too simple a manner?

* Were the facts accurate as far as I can tell?

* Were there enough illustrations, pictures, diagrams, and charts to help explain things?

* What are the author's qualifications? Is he a recognized authority in the field? How did he get his information, by actual experience or by research?

* What new sort of knowledge did I learn from reading the book? Is it just new to me or is it brand new scientific information? If it is new, does everyone agree with the author in his assessment of it? For instance, a book detailing how some scientists believe that birds are the direct descendants of dinosaurs would require relating this theory to older theories. Or a book about the discovery of "Lucy," a seven-million-year-old skeleton, would require fitting this information into opinions held by other scientists about how long man has been on this earth. But a book describing the life cycle of a butterfly might present nothing new or controversial although the information in it was new to you and helped enlarge your knowledge of the world about you.

REVIEWING HISTORY AND CURRENT EVENTS

* This type of book often deals with subjects from one point of view alone. What was the author's point of view? What was his purpose in writing it? Does he present only one side of a controversial question or did he look at it from many angles? For instance, a book about nuclear weapons can be slanted to the author's feeling or it can show different perspectives.

* Did my attitude change as I read the book?

* Was the book written in a clear manner so I could understand the various implications discussed?

* Did I feel the author distinguished fact from interpretation? Could I tell when hard facts were being given, those that can be checked elsewhere, and when the author was giving his assessment of the facts? Did he tell all the facts or did he distort or omit any? (This is a difficult thing to pinpoint, but reading a book with this possibility in mind helps open your eyes to the insidious nature of propaganda.)

* What are the author's qualifications for writing the book, his personal background?

A Précis

A précis is a concise summary of the essential points of a longer piece of writing in your own words, usually one-fourth to one-third as long as the original. Learning how to do this provides excellent training in reading for comprehension and in mastering the technique of clear, concise, and accurate writing. It is a useful skill, if mastered, and will be a valuable tool both for school work and later in the business world.

Fully recognize first of all that a précis is not a paraphrase, which is a restatement in different words of what the original said, often of the same length as or longer than the original. A précis, unlike a paraphrase, cuts wordage to the minimum, simplifying and getting to the essential meaning in very few words. It contains no details, examples, or illustrations, and it does not allow any comment or interpretation on your part. The French meaning of the word, "exact," "terse," describes it accurately.

Follow these steps:

* Read the selection quickly for a general overview.

* Reread it paragraph by paragraph several times very thoughtfully.

* In each paragraph look for the topic sentence and restate it, first to yourself, then write it down in your own words.

* Combine these ideas into a statement of the whole. Eliminate any that do not directly bear on the main idea of the paper.

* Revise your version checking to see that it is absolutely accurate in accordance with the author's version and that it follows the original in the same sequence of thoughts and facts.

* Go through your précis and cut it to one-fourth or one-third of the original length by tightening each sentence, cutting any extra words. Substitute a phrase for a clause or one word for a phrase.
Examples:

Wordy: If you do your studying right after school, you will be able to watch television at night.

Terse: Afternoon studying leaves night time free for TV watching.

Wordy: Miss Brown spoke to me in a pleasant manner.

Terse: Miss Brown spoke to me pleasantly.

Science Project Report

Writing a science project report involves a special format, although not all of the items listed below must be included for every project, as the nature of the investigation sometimes imposes limitations. However, knowing what can be required helps the student in planning and executing a successful project conducted according to approved scientific methods.

The writing must be clear and concise, using formal style, which means no colloquial expressions, no contractions, and in the third person (avoiding the words "you" and "I.") Define all terms that might need clarification.

1. *Title:* This should convey exactly what the report is about, being very specific and factual in wording. Cute or catchy titles are out of place. For example, "Sit, Lie Down, Play Dead" would not be a suitable title for a research report about how to train a dog. Instead, "Training a Dog to Follow Simple Commands," would be better.

2. *Abstract:* A one-paragraph summary of the report should introduce the paper telling the purpose of the project, general methods or procedures used, and the main results produced or conclusions reached. The reason for writing the abstract is to allow another busy scientist to decide if he/she wishes to study the entire report.

3. *Introduction:* This includes the importance of

the area under investigation, why you chose it, something of the historical background, and an overview of what other people have done in the field. This literary support requires using the *Readers' Guide* or other indexes to find references to what has already been done on the subject. You will need to document (give credit to) the sources you consulted. Either use conventional footnotes or put in parentheses after a statement a shortened version of the source (Jones, *Science Reports,* 1984) to refer to the work in a bibliography which you will include following the paper itself.

4. *The Problem:* Clearly state what it is you planned to do. Tell if you were testing several hypotheses, were looking for a hypothesis, were suggesting a theory, or were reporting some observations made under certain specific, controlled conditions. If possible, include how your problem relates to other theories. A hypothesis is a tentative assumption made in order to draw out and test its logical consequences.

5. *Hypotheses:* State all hypotheses that you were testing and, if possible, what the results of your experiments will mean as to the acceptance or rejection of these hypotheses.

6. *Procedures:* Describe in detail exactly how you did your experiments so other people can do the same thing with the same results. List all equipment you used, a step-by-step account of procedures followed, an exact description of the conditions influencing the results. Include all failures as well as successes so others will not waste time doing things that will not work. Diagrams and drawings can be used.

7. *Observations and Interpretations:* Record chronologically, perhaps in diary form, the facts you observed as you were conducting your experiments. Compile tables or graphs to present statistics, measurements, and other numerical data. Explain what your observations mean in connection with the hypothesis that was being tested.

8. *Conclusions:* Each hypothesis should be examined in light of your observations and interpretations so that the hypothesis may be rejected outright or accepted with reservations for more testing. Rarely does student work result in a fully accepted hypothesis.

9. *Generalizations:* Here you tell the implication or meaning of your research in relation to its larger field of science. Perhaps your study can suggest some new problems or further areas of study.

10. *Summary:* Write a brief summary of your investigation, listing the principal findings of the project.

Mechanical Details

TYPING TIPS

1. Use good quality bond paper, white, 8½ x 11 inches in size.
2. Use black ribbon and type on one side of the paper only.
3. Always make a carbon copy or photocopy your manuscript.
4. Double space the body of the manuscript, following the single spacing rules for long quotations, footnotes, endnotes, and bibliography entries.
5. The left margin should be 1½ inches wide; the right margin, as nearly as possible 1 inch wide; and the bottom margin, 1½ inches. This results in a page of 25 lines averaging about 10 words each, or a total of 250 words to a page.
6. On the first page, 12 spaces below the top of the paper, type the title, centered, in all capital letters.
7. Begin the paper proper three spaces below the title.
8. Indent each paragraph five spaces.
9. Do not number the first page, but do place a page number on each page of the paper beginning with page 2. Do not number outline, endnote, bibliography, or any appendix pages. The page number should be placed 1 inch from the top of the paper and 1 inch from the right margin. Do not use any punctuation with the number.

10. On all pages after the first continue the body of the text two spaces below the page number.
11. One reason for dividing words at the ends of lines is to keep the right margin as even as possible. However, correct syllabication must be observed. Consult the dictionary.
12. Leave one space after a comma or a semicolon. Leave two spaces after any punctuation mark that ends a sentence. Leave two spaces after a colon when the next word or sentence begins with a capital letter.
13. Center any columns. Figures are usually aligned so the right margin will be in block form.
14. Do not "x" out mistakes. Correct neatly with a whitening agent.
15. Always proofread for typographical errors.
16. Enclose your paper in a folder or stiff paper cover.

HANDWRITTEN MANUSCRIPTS

One of the most valuable skills a student can possess is to be able to type. If you have not had typing and must handwrite your paper, follow these rules.

1. Use standard notebook paper with wide-spaced lines, not paper torn from a spiral notebook.
2. Follow the typing rules as closely as possible.
3. Use the red line for the left margin space.
4. Write very legibly in blue-black or black ink.

Letters and Employment Resumes*

Whenever you write a letter–whether personal or business–those lines of writing become *you* in the mind of your reader. Your letters will, of course, vary in purpose and formality, as the occasion requires, yet each letter you write is, for your reader, like a face-to-face meeting with you. Let your letters be a credit to you in appearance, appropriateness, and good taste; make them also carry something of the naturalness and vitality your reader would experience in a person-to-person visit. Practically all letters can be included within three general classifications:

1. *The social "duty" letter,* a type of letter–formal or informal–demanded by good manners

2. *The personal letter,* a type of informal letter written to share the pleasures of life with friends and relatives

3. *The business letter,* a type of letter written in the conduct of commercial, professional, or administrative affairs

THE SOCIAL "DUTY" LETTER

Social "duty" letters are used as invitations, to acknowledge invitations, to thank friends for favors and gifts, to console relatives and friends in times of trouble. You will want to know how to write them.

Formal Social Letters

Very formal affairs–weddings, receptions, and formal dinners–still require a formal correspondence ritual. Guests are invited in a nonpersonal, formal manner, as is to be seen in the example below. The invitations are usually engraved or printed; they may be written in longhand. Guests responding to such invitations employ the same formal, nonpersonal language that they find in the invitation, but the responses are always handwritten.

---

*The acute accent over the final *e* in resumé has been omitted in the text of this chapter as this seems to be the rule in most United States business correspondence. In formal writing, the acute accent should be included even if the mark has to be inserted by hand. The Merriam–Webster *Third New International Dictionary* also carries the accent over the first *e*.

INVITATION

Mr. and Mrs. Eugene Parsons
request the honor of your presence
at the marriage of their daughter
Sue Ellen
to
Mr. Harvey Henderson
on Saturday, the first of June
at ten o'clock
Saint Mark's Church
New York

ACCEPTANCE

Thomas Olderbach
accepts with pleasure
the kind invitation of
Mr. and Mrs. Eugene Parsons
to the marriage of their daughter
Sue Ellen
to
Mr. Harvey Henderson
on Saturday, the first of June
at ten o'clock
Saint Mark's Church
New York

Informal Social Letters

Most social occasions that require letters are informal. When a hostess wants a few friends to attend a small dinner party, she does not send out engraved invitations. She writes a short personal note to each of them or she may even telephone. When a weekend guest returns home, he writes a so-called bread-and-butter thank-you note to his hostess.

Dear Mrs. Parsons,

That Saturday morning sunrise over the valley, those gay voices of the twins, and that stimulating table talk are still with me. Every moment of the weekend was perfect, but one—departure. How I hated to have it end!

I loved every moment at Oakridge Manor and I want to thank you very much for a wonderful time.

Sincerely,
Harvey Henderson

Gifts, favors, congratulations, and condolences—all are acknowledged in short notes which are set up like letters, rather than formal announcements. These social letters are written in natural, everyday language, with a friendliness of style appropriate to the relationship between writer and reader. Although a telephone call, greeting card, bouquet, or telegram may substitute for social letters on some occasions, letters are to be written:

Whenever you receive gifts, courtesies, favors, congratulations, or good wishes

Whenever you stay overnight as a guest in someone's home

Whenever you receive an invitation to a dinner or luncheon

Whenever you express or acknowledge condolence

In addition to such "duty" letters, there are innumerable kinds of social notes which it is always becoming to write. There are "cheer-up" notes which you send to the sick. There are "well-done," "best-wishes," "happy-journey," and "welcome-home" notes you can write on other occasions.

Stationery for the Social Letter

Formal social letters should be written on a good quality, white, side-folded letter sheet approximately 5½ inches x 7½ inches, in black or blue-black ink. Informal social letters may also be written on this type of stationery, on greeting cards, or on any of the personal stationery used in friendly correspondence. Less formal social letters may be typed, including the following, which at one time were handwritten only: letters of sympathy and replies to letters of sympathy, letters expressing and letters acknowledging good wishes, and letters acknowledging wedding gifts.

THE PERSONAL LETTER

Those letters which help us share with friends and relatives the joys of living are called *personal letters*. There is a single test for evaluating the personal letter: Does it provide the writer and the reader with shared satisfaction of friendship? The few principles of personal letterwriting that do exist are designed to help writer and reader enjoy to the full the pleasures of correspondence.

1. Note how Thackeray's daughter achieves the vividness of face-to-face contact in a letter:

I have been imagining you in my favorite corner of my favorite city. Have you opened your windows and looked out, does it smell—rumble—taste—Paris? I'm sure it does. Even the little tin water cans are unlike anything anywhere else.

2. Make your letters as cheerful and constructive as you can; nobody likes a complaining, gloomy, nagging letter.

3. Avoid any statement or hint that writing is a chore. It is impolite to tell a correspondent that you just could not get around to writing, that there is nothing to say, or that you are hastily dashing off a few lines.

4. Avoid putting into a letter any statement that could prove unbecoming if the letter were to fall into the hands of another. Remember, letters are permanent records.

Stationery for the Personal Letter

Close friends may correspond on any kind of stationery available, the only restrictions rising from personal choice and consideration for the reader. Untidy, blotted, scratched-out, or soiled letters are unbecoming to the writer and a discourtesy to the reader. Legibility is only common politeness. Writing in pencil, writing around the edges of the sheet, or writing on lined paper may also be resented, even among friends.

THE BUSINESS LETTER

The importance of the letter as a tool in business, government, the professions, and other administrative activities has developed the type known as *the business letter*.

For all practical purposes, the great variety of business letters may be classified under four basic headings:

1. *Letters that handle routine business*. Most business letters have a simple, routine mission; they carry needed details and short statements of information from businessman to businessman. Letters that order goods, acknowledge orders, and handle remittances make up the bulk of mail interchanged by business organizations. The main qualities these routine letters must possess are brevity and clearness. They must be complete in supplying all details as to style, color, price, conditions, procedures, and the like.

2. *Letters that grant requests*. Many business letters are written to grant requests; they supply information sought by other businessmen and the public; they send out samples and booklets; they open charge accounts; they make adjustments. When a request is granted, it should be done graciously and with good will, usually in the opening sentence of the letter:

We are pleased to send the samples of Kioba Fabric requested in your letter of January 23.

The middle of the letter can then supply the necessary detail. The ending is usually a further statement of good will.

3. *Letters that deny requests*. Many business letters have to deny requests. The best tactics for making a denial are (a) open with a statement that the reader will find agreeable–*we appreciate very much your detailed description of your recent experience with our Toast-Browner;* (b) give reasons for the denial; (c) make the denial; (d) seek the good will of the reader.

4. *Letters that persuade and sell*. Many business letters have a persuasive mission; they must move the minds and wills of their readers. Some of them must assist in selling goods and services; some of them must collect money; some of them must debate issues. All of them must employ techniques of persuasion.

The sales letter is usually constructed on a patterning of steps which lead to the sale–attention, desire, conviction, and action.

DEAR MR. JONES:

Attention Did you ever wish that your typewriter had an eraser key–one that could correct the original and all copies with a stroke of the finger? Well, here's your chance to get something even better–TYPERASO*–the magic insert and carbon pack that is self-erasing.

Desire With TYPERASO an error can be corrected with the flick of a key. All you have to do is slip the TYPERASO mounting over the error, pull up the TYPERASO carbon, and strike any key. In an instant, the error is gone. What a saving to you in time, money, and nerves.

Conviction TYPERASO has been approved by all leading banks, insurance companies, and typewriter manufacturers. We will give you double your money back if you are not delighted with your TYPERASO pack.

Action Pick up a TYPERASO pack at any office supply store. There's a pack waiting for you right now.

Sincerely,

*This is an imaginary product.

FORMATS OF THE LETTER

The general setup of a letter on a page is called its *format*. Formal invitations and replies, as already noted, are set up like announcements; their formats are different from the more usual letter formats.

Parts of the Letter

There are seven basic parts of a letter. Business and other "official" letters require all seven, and often several additional ones. Social and personal letters usually omit one or two of these parts, as explained below.

1. HEADING. The writer's address, engraved, printed, or written at the top of the sheet, constitutes the heading of the letter. As noted, personal stationery may have the writer's monogram, or name and address, or name alone, or address alone, imprinted upon the letter sheet. If the address does not appear on personal stationery, it must be written or typed at the top of the sheet. This same practice is followed in preparing a business letter when an individual (say, a job applicant) does not have printed letterhead stationery. Business firms and most other organizations have their names and addresses imprinted at the top of their letter sheets.

2. DATE LINE. All letters must be dated. The usual place for a letter date is to the top and right, on a lower line than the heading. Informal social letters, however, often carry their dates as a last element of the letter, at the left margin. The most usual form of date employed in letters is *January 23, 1965*, but social letters often omit the year; sometimes they are dated with a mere *Monday*, or *At home*. Never use such forms as January 23rd, 1965 or 1/23/65.

3. INSIDE ADDRESS. Business and other "official" letters always carry the name and address of the recipient of the letter. This *inside address* is generally placed four or five lines below the date line, beginning flush with the left margin.

4. SALUTATION. The greeting, *Dear Tom* or *Dear Sir*, so characteristic of the letter format, is called the *salutation*. In social and personal letters the salutation is followed by a comma and is generally informal–*Dear Tom, Tom dear*, etc. In business letters the salutation is followed by a colon and is generally formal, unless the writer and reader enjoy a close acquaintanceship–*Dear Mr. Smith:*,

Dear Sir:. The formality of the salutation must always match the formality of the complimentary close. See table on Forms of Address, pp. 73-74.

5. BODY. The part of the letter which carries the message is called the *body*.

6. COMPLIMENTARY CLOSE. The closing, *Sincerely yours* or *Very truly yours*, is called the *complimentary close*. In social and personal letters the complimentary close may take such forms as *Affectionately* or *With love*, but in business letters more formal complimentary closes are employed– *Cordially, Sincerely, Yours very truly,* or (to superiors) *Respectfully, Respectfully yours*.

7. SIGNATURE. All letters, typed and handwritten, must be signed by the writer. In social and personal letters the signature may be very informal, consisting of a first name or even a nickname. In business letters the written signature is often followed by a typed signature and an indication of the writer's position in the firm. Titles such as *Mr.* or *Dr.* are never written as part of a signature.

Additional letter parts, often found in business letters are (a) the subject line, (b) the attention line, (3) the identification initials. The subject line identifies the topic of the letter. The attention line (used only in letters addressed to a firm) directs the letter to a particular person within the firm, when the writer feels that the person has a special interest in the subject discussed. The identification initials indicate the person who dictated the letter and the secretary who typed it. The placement of these additional letter parts will be found in a letter model provided later.

Setup of the Letter

The informal social "duty" letter and the personal letter employ the same format with one exception: The date of the informal social "duty" letter may follow the signature, at the left margin.

Typed business letters are usually set up in a *block* format. Parts like the inside address are not staggered as they are in many handwritten letters.

Envelopes must always match letter pages in quality and color, and in style of addressing. In handwritten letters, the envelope address is usually indented. In business letters the envelope address is usually blocked, matching in detail the inside address. The return address is placed in the upper left corner of the envelope, following post office preference; but many writers of social and personal letters place the return address on the back flap of the envelope.

Forms of Address

PERSON	INSIDE ADDRESS	SALUTATION	COMPLIMENTARY CLOSE
President	The President The White House Washington, D.C.	Sir: *or* My dear Mr. President:	Most respectfully yours, *or* Respectfully yours,
Senator	The Honorable John Doe The United States Senate Washington, D.C.	Sir: *or* My dear Senator:	Very truly yours,
Congressman	The Honorable John Doe The House of Representatives Washington, D.C.	Sir: *or* My dear Mr. Doe:	Very truly yours,
Governor	The Honorable John Doe Governor of New York Albany, New York	Sir: *or* Dear Governor Doe:	Very truly yours,
Mayor	The Honorable John Doe Mayor of the City of Troy City Hall Troy, Colorado	Sir: *or* Dear Mayor Doe:	Very truly yours,
College Registrar	The Registrar Finn University Tobin City, N.J.	Dear Sir:	Very truly yours,
Rabbi	Rabbi John Doe	My dear Sir: *or* Dear Rabbi Doe:	Respectfully yours, *or* Very truly yours,
Protestant Clergyman	The Reverend John Doe	Reverend Sir: *or* My dear Mr. Doe:	Respectfully yours, *or* Very truly yours,
Priest	The Reverend John Doe	Reverend and dear Father: *or* Dear Father Doe:	Respectfully yours, *or* Very truly yours,
Nun	Sister Lioba, O.S.B.° . . . . (°Indicate order)	Reverend and dear Sister: *or* Dear Sister Lioba:	Respectfully yours, *or* Faithfully yours,
Woman Formally in a Business Letter	Miss Mary Doe *or* Mrs. John Smith	My dear Madam: *or* My dear Miss Doe:	Very truly yours,
Man Formally in a Business Letter	Mr. John Doe	My dear Sir: *or* My dear Mr. Doe:	Very truly yours,
Man or Woman in Less Formal Business Letters	Mr. John Doe *or* Miss Mary Doe	Dear Sir: *or* *more usually* Dear Mr. Doe: Dear Miss Doe:	Sincerely yours, *or* Sincerely,

PERSON	INSIDE ADDRESS	SALUTATION	COMPLIMENTARY CLOSE
Business Firm	Perfect Corporation	Gentlemen:	Very truly yours,
Man or Woman in a Social or Personal Letter	(No inside address needed, but be certain to use Mr., Mrs., Miss, Dr., or other title of courtesy before name on the envelope.)	Dear Mr. Jones, Dear Mrs. Doe, Dear Tom, Dear Jane, *or in friendly letters any familiar salutation in good taste*	Sincerely, *or any more intimate closing in good taste, such as* Affectionately yours, Lovingly,

SOLVING THE SEX QUESTION IN LETTER WRITING

With more and more women holding prominent career positions, the question constantly arises about the use of the traditional "Dear Sir" when the identity of the recipient of a business letter is unknown. Many sources suggest using "Dear Sir or Dear Madam," but this is cumbersome. The time-honored "Gentlemen" could be increased to "Gentlemen and Ladies" but this is stilted, and both retain the masculine precedence. A reversal of order might be employed.

However, a simpler solution is to use the title of the person addressed: "Dear Personnel Director"; "Dear Registrar"; "Dear Principal"; "Dear Public Service Commissioners." The same idea can be used in writing to a company: "Dear Jones Bookstore"; "Dear Executive Tax Service."

If it is known that the addressee is a woman, and her preference of titles is known, then address her as "Miss Mary Alston," or "Mrs. Joan Krantz," or "Ms. Sara Ledbetter." However, in many cases the correct choice is unknown and a wrong choice can sour a good relation before it has a chance to develop. If in doubt, simply write "Dear Eunice Reynolds." Or better still, incorporate her title in the salutation as "Dear Professor Caffey" or "Dear Director Smith."

With so many single parents these days, teachers have discarded the former "Dear Mother," in favor of "Dear Parent or Guardian."

COMMUNICATING IDEAS IN A LETTER

A successful letter is one that wins a favorable response. When you write a social "duty" letter, you seek a specific response—*I want Ann to realize how much I appreciate the silver tray she sent.* When you write a business letter, you also seek a specific response—*I want the bookkeeper at Greynolds, Inc., to understand that the 2% discount he took is not justified and that a check for $5.64 must be sent to me.* When you write a personal letter, you seek a much less tangible and much less specific response of friendship shared—*I want Tom to get pleasure and knowledge from the news I send and a deepened appreciation of our friendship.* In all of these types of letters, the success of the letter is judged by the response.

The Response Desired

So important is this response that the first principle of effective letter writing is: *Let the response you desire be your guide throughout the letter.*

A good practice is to pause a moment before beginning to write and answer the following questions:

Just why am I writing this letter?

Just how do I want my reader to feel when he finishes this letter?

In a particularly important letter, you may want to write out for yourself in a sentence or two the response you desire. But in most letters it will be enough if you get the response desired clearly in your own mind before you start writing.

The You-Attitude

When you have determined the desired response, you must next consider that goal from your reader's point of view. Imagine yourself the reader. Then select a plan for your letter, a set of ideas, a tone of approach, and a phrasing that would move *you* to the response desired.

This tactic of viewing a letter problem through the reader's eyes may be called the *you-attitude.* So important is the you-attitude that the second principle of effective letter writing is: *Let your reader's interests be your guide in the selection and phrasing of ideas.*

A letter which concentrates on the selfish interests of the writer is apt to be dull, and generally ineffective. Readers respond best when their own interests are being considered. In writing personal letters, you should stick to subjects that will give pleasure to your reader. Respond to the main points of his last letter to you. Involve him as much as possible in what you say. Instead of saying: "I found the view from the bridge over the rushing waters very impressive," say: "If only you could have shared that view from the dam with me. I know you would have thought, as I did, 'It's just like the Ausable River.'"

When you write business letters, you are always concerned with the advancement of some interest–getting a job, making a sale, collecting an account. Yet, these letters as well must be written with the you-attitude if they are to gain the response desired and win good will for the writer and his firm. A job applicant should tell how his training and experience will benefit the reader. The writer of a collection letter should stress the advantage his reader will gain through prompt payment–satisfaction in knowing his debts are paid or the protection of his credit standing.

Expression Skill

With the exception of formal correspondence, letters are best written in a natural conversational tone. After all, as already mentioned, the letter substitutes for a person-to-person meeting and should employ language appropriate to such meetings. Stilted language, artificiality, or phrases designed to impress have no place in a letter.

Writing skill, however, is very important to the letter writer. Actually, a letter is *not* a person-to-person meeting, and it requires skill to convey an idea and a set of feelings precisely and naturally through the written word.

The need to write well leads to a further principle of effective letter writing: *Let your ideas and feelings find expression in language that is clear, persuasive, natural, thoughtful, and interesting.*

The basic method of improving your ability to express yourself in writing is to read good writing and to practice as much writing as possible. As you read good writing notice how logical and constructive is the thought behind it. Notice how the writer phrases his ideas precisely. Notice how easily and

naturally the writer expresses himself. Such attention to the techniques of skillful writing will enhance your own writing skill.

When you practice writing, concentrate on the ideas and feelings you want your writing to convey, rather than on techniques and style. Think hard until you have an idea worthy of expression. Make yourself feel the mood you want to convey–cheeriness, sympathy, friendliness, or whatever that mood may be. Concentrate on that idea and feeling until the right phrasing comes to you. With an increase of experience, you will discover that you are acquiring skill, that the right words and phrasing come more and more readily.

When you concentrate on the ideas and feelings you want to convey, language will begin to flow; the trick is to keep it flowing. Your first attempt to express a business-letter idea may be, "Please do something about this." Obviously, this idea needs more definite thought and expression. If you concentrate upon it, you will gain not only a clearer thought but also more precise expression of that thought, and you will be writing, "Please pick up the damaged table on Saturday morning."

You can speed up this skill-building process further if you bear in mind the writing principles discussed in other chapters of this book.

WATCH THESE EXPRESSIONS

accept, except Do not confuse. *I shall accept* (receive) *the letter. I shall except* (exclude) *this sum from the list.*

affect, effect Do not confuse. *The news will affect* (influence) *his mood. The manager will effect* (bring about) *a new schedule. The effect* (the noun form) *of television is obvious.*

busy In personal letters never write *I would have answered sooner but I was too busy* or any similarly rude expression.

beside, besides Do not confuse. *The wastebasket is beside* (alongside of) *the desk. Who is going besides* (in addition to) *you?*

due to Do not use *due to* in place of *because of* or *owing to. Due* is an adjective and makes a questionable preposition.

favor Do not refer to a letter as a *favor* in such trite expressions as *Your favor of June 1 received.*

good, well Do not use *good* as an adverb. *This program works well* (not *good*).

hoping Avoid such letter endings as *hoping to hear from you.*

I am, I remain Avoid these old-fashioned phrases in your letter closings.

its, it's Do not confuse. *Every machine has its* (possessive) *own cover. It's* (it is) *going to be warm today.*

said Avoid such expressions as *the said program* or *the said matter.*

thanking you Avoid such expressions as *thanking you for your interest* followed by a complimentary close.

AVOID THESE EXPRESSIONS

anticipating
as per, as regards
at your earliest convenience
awaiting, we await
beg
duly noted
esteemed
recent date
trusting that this is satisfactory
valued
we are, we remain
we trust
we wish to
with due regard
with reference to the matter
yours

THE LETTER OF APPLICATION

A particularly important kind of sales letter is the *letter of application,* the letter a job seeker sends to a prospective employer requesting a job interview. The application letter is apt to get attention when it is written or typed neatly upon good, white, bond paper and opens with a statement that is distinctive. Far too many application letters begin with a trite, "I am writing this letter to apply for the job advertised in today's *Herald.*" Much better would be an opening like the following:

> My basic training in computer programing and my two years of part-time experience in data processing are the work advantages I can best offer in a letter. But if I could call upon

you, in response to your advertisement in today's *Herald,* I know that I could show you why I am the young man you need in your new automated division.

The application letter builds desire by outlining details of experience, education, and skill which will be useful in the job that is being sought. With desire built, the applicant can provide proof in the form of references and possibly samples of his work. Finally, the applicant moves his reader to action by requesting an interview, making himself available at any time convenient to the prospective employer.

Here are a few *do's* and *don'ts* on application letters:

DO'S

Write or type neatly on one side only of good quality, white paper.

Write large numbers of application letters. Write to firms that advertise, and write to firms that don't. Keep writing.

Learn as much as possible about your prospective employer and gear your letter to the way your education and experience will help him.

Exhibit confidence in your background and ability.

Request an interview at the end of the letter.

Write follow-up letters.

DON'TS

Don't write on letterheads of other business firms, hotel or club stationery.

Don't limit your job-seeking efforts to openings provided you by friends, relatives, and the local press. Don't wait for an answer from one firm before writing to another.

Don't make a vague offer to do anything.

Don't be timid and apologetic or conceited and boasting. Don't end vaguely at one extreme or attempt to pressure your reader into action at the other.

Don't neglect to thank the prospective employer for the courtesy of the interview he granted, even when you don't get the job.

How Businessmen Evaluate Applications

Today's business executive has very little time to read long letters. Most executives stress that they are more likely to reply to a short, well-written letter that makes the applicant's point quickly.

A vice president of a large chemical company submits the following letter as an example of a good application. It was received by his company in reply to a blind-box advertisement:

For your review I enclose a copy of my current resume which describes my qualifications for the position advertised in the March 25 issue of the New York Times.

My background and experience closely parallel the requirements outlined in your advertisement. I am, therefore, reasonably sure that I can make a valuable contribution to your company. Won't you call me at 586-3657 to arrange for an interview.

The vice president of a school-supply company received the following letter from a college student. He considers it to be an excellent letter of application:

In answer to my inquiry, the Atlanta Chamber of Commerce sent me your name as one of the firms in your city that hires college students for temporary summer work.

Although my home is San Francisco, and I attend Stanford University, I plan to take a one-day-a-week course at Georgia Tech this summer. This course will be given on Monday of each week and will run for six weeks.

It was a fortunate coincidence for me that your firm's name was submitted, because you are engaged in the type of business in which I hope to make my future.

At present, I am a sophomore at Stanford University, majoring in economics. Scholastically, I am in the top 10 per cent of my class, and I am a reporter on our college newspaper.

I realize that for the first six weeks of my twelve-week vacation, I will be able to work only four days a week. However, since I do not have to be back to school until the end of September, I will be able to work a full week for the last six weeks of my summer vacation.

I wish to learn every aspect of the writing-paper and school-supply business; therefore, I am willing to work in any phase of it—stockroom, manufacturing, sales, or office administration.

I will be in Atlanta on June 12. May I then call you and present myself for an interview?

Very truly yours,

The vice president of marketing of a business machine manufacturing company received the following letter, which accompanied a well-organized resume:

I am presently attending the University of Pennsylvania and will be graduated in June. I have decided that my educational background and experience in summertime and part-time employment is such that selling offers me the best opportunity for personal advancement and financial success. I have been impressed with your ads in recent issues of the Wall Street Journal *and I want to investigate the opportunities in your organization for a selling-trainee opening.*

Please write to me if I may phone for an interview.

Here's an example that the personnel manager of one of the largest merchandising corporations considers to be an effective letter-resume combination:

Your very fine company has impressed me for some time as the type of organization with which I would like to become associated. Your progressive merchandising policies and steady growth provide the type of opportunity I am seeking.

You will note from the attached resume that I am presently employed. I find working for my employer and my relationships with my associates most enjoyable. However, the firm is small and presents little in the way of opportunity for either personal growth or advancement.

I know I do not have much in the way of experience which could be utilized by a company such as Sears. However, I can assure you I would take an enthusiastic approach to learning. I would display mature judgment in viewing business problems after a limited amount of training. Above all, I have considerable ambition and am willing to sacrifice in order to obtain an opportunity.

My plans are such that I will be in Chicago the week of August 10, during which time I would like to have an interview at your convenience. May I call you for an appointment?

Very truly yours,

AN EMPLOYMENT RESUME

The employment resume is designed to introduce you to a prospective employer. You are looking for a job; he is looking for someone to fill the job; it goes without saying that you want the introduction to be a favorable one. So it is up to you to supply him, *briefly and clearly*, with the facts about yourself, your background, your education, and your work experience, in such a way that he will want to hire *you* instead of another applicant.

RULE NUMBER ONE: Be as brief as possible, yet include all pertinent facts.

RULE NUMBER TWO: Present yourself in the best possible light.

Some employment applicants have their employment resumes made up in quantity, either by mimeographing or multigraphing, and send them out with a covering letter to prospective employers. Some carry their resumes about with them when they go to answer advertisements that have appeared in newspapers or periodicals. Some resumes are supposed to be filled out on forms provided by the employment agency to which you have applied for help in finding a job. Whichever way your employment resume is used, it is obvious that it should present you most favorably. Use a typewriter and be sure the copy is letter perfect–no misspellings, no mistakes in grammar; also, no corrections, no strike-overs, no noticeable erasures. And see to it that your typewriter ribbon is dark and legible.

Most employment agencies will require you to fill out their form in ink while you are in their office. In such cases, before starting on the rounds of the agencies, take time and thought to prepare in advance, and to bring with you, a typed employment resume. Even if it is not possible for you to use this resume in its exact form, it is still likely that a great deal of what you have thought out can be used to good advantage.

In gathering material for this section, a number of employment agency directors were interviewed. Without exception they emphasized the point that the employment resume should be *brief, inclusive, and factual*. There is no place in an employment resume for attempts to be funny or clever.

Some employers will be interested in having, in addition, such personal information as:

Height
Weight
Marital Status
Number of Dependents
Military Experience
Present Military
    Status, etc.

A good resume has the following advantages over the overly comprehensive resumes so popular a number of years ago: It is brief, which assures that it will be read; it cites the essential information that the applicant wants the prospective employer to know at present; it shows, by its conciseness and organization, that the applicant is a methodical individual who knows how to bring out essential facts.

Below is an example of a resume described in the previous paragraph:

RESUME OF CHARLES DEERING, JR.

PERSONAL DATA: Married, One Child
                            Excellent Health

MILITARY SERVICE: U.S. Navy–Two years
                                Lt. Jr. Grade

EDUCATION: DePauw University, Indiana
                        B.A.–Economics (major)
                        Speech (minor)

PREVIOUS EXPERIENCE:

Trainee   One year
Merchandise and Operating
    Assistant Manager   One year

RETAIL EXPERIENCE:

Approximately two years experience in retail stores ranging in sales volume from $500,000 to $1,200,000. Responsibilities included department management, merchandising, advertising, personnel and operating assignments.

The Library: Indispensable Aid

A crucial skill for a literate person is the ability to use the library effectively. Not only is it essential for any organized research project, but it enhances the caliber of all other kinds of writing, and it provides a basis for the fullest enjoyment of pleasure reading.

Since the core of the library is the book collection, people need to know how to find and use books most effectively.

PARTS OF A BOOK: In addition to the main body of printed matter, each book contains some or all of the following parts. Every book has a *title page*, the right-hand page near the front on which are printed the title, the author, the publisher, and the place of publication. Sometimes there is a subtitle printed beneath the title which is added to give a better idea of the scope of the book.

The date on the title page may merely indicate when the book was printed, so the date on the reverse side of the title page is more important, as it tells the *copyright date,* near the time when the book was actually completed. The listing of more than one copyright date often means that additions or revisions were made to the original book. In a bibliography use the latest copyright date.

The *foreword* and *preface* are very similar. They tell something about the purpose of the book, how it can be used, or they acknowledge people who have helped prepare it. An *introduction,* written by the author or an authority on the subject, can summarize the book or introduce the subject.

The *Table of Contents* appears in the front and lists the chapters in order of their appearance, while the *index* is found on the last few pages and is an alphabetical arrangement listing specific persons, places, and topics with the exact page numbers where they are found.

Lists of maps, illustrations, charts are usually found immediately after the Table of Contents. Many books have an appendix near the back containing material that is not really part of the text but which is closely related to it. A United States history book, for example, may have in its appendix a copy of the Constitution.

Many books containing scientific, foreign, or other words that people may not understand have a *glossary* to define these terms.

TYPES OF BOOKS: To help people find books libraries classify, or arrange, books according to a clearly defined plan so that those which are similar in some way stand together on the shelves. They usually first divide the books into *fiction, biography,* and *non-fiction* categories. Fiction is a made-up story, although it can have much truth in it in the way of factual details, real-life characters, and actual settings. Novels such as *The Outsiders,* and short stories, are fiction.

A *biography* is the account of someone's life, and an *autobiography* is the account of one's own life. *Amos Fortune, Free Man* by Elizabeth Yates is a biography, while *The Story of My Life* by Helen Keller is an autobiography.

All other books in the library are usually designated non-fiction, or factual books, although this also includes such special types as folklore, mythology, poetry, drama, and essays.

DEWEY DECIMAL SYSTEM: In school and public libraries non-fiction is cataloged by the *Dewey Decimal System,* named for Melvil Dewey who in 1876 divided all knowledge into ten main classes and assigned numbers to each. Here is a listing of the Dewey class numbers:

CLASS NUMBER	MAIN CLASS
000—099	General Works
100—199	Conduct of Life (Philosophy)
200—299	Religion
300—399	Social Sciences
400—499	Language
500—599	Pure Sciences
600—699	Applied Science/Technology
700—799	Fine Arts and Recreation
800—899	Literature
900—999	History, Geography, Biography

Each of the main classes is subdivided into ten subdivisions. For instance, Pure Science is broken down this way:

510—Mathematics
520—Astronomy
530—Physics
540—Chemistry
550—Earth Sciences
560—Fossils
570—Biology
580—Botany
590—Zoology

Each subdivision is further broken down. For example, within the subclass 790—799 (Recreation), there is 796, outdoor sports; 797, water and air sports; 798, horse and other animal racing; 799, fishing. Further subdivision comes after the decimal. Thus 796.3 is for ball games, while 796.32 is for basketball; 796.33 is for football; 796.34 is for racquet games; and 796.35 is for baseball, etc.

CALL NUMBERS: In addition to the class number, each book also has an author designation which is placed under the class number. These two lines make up the call number which appears on the spine of the book and the catalog card. The call number for *The Many Faces of the Civil War* by Werstein:

> 973.7 = Dewey # for U. S. history, Civil War period
> W498m = W498 for Werstein, the "m" for first word of title.

READING SHELVES: You "read" shelves of books just as you read pages in a book, left to right, line by line (or row by row), with shelf dividers setting off the different "pages." Dewey numbers range from lower numbers on the left to higher on the right, with authors alphabetized within the same number. This is the correct placement of books on a shelf:

155	155.03	155.1	155.1	155.12	155.22
N36g	B42k	M32q	N19h	K14b	A12n

CLASSIFYING FICTION/BIOGRAPHY: Although fiction can fall within the 800s of the Dewey system, and biography in the 900s, most school and public libraries pull these books out and arrange them separately. Fiction is arranged alphabetically by the author's last name. If two authors have the same last name, then the first name is alphabetized, so books by Elizabeth Allen come before those by Merritt Allen. Novels by the same author are alphabetized by title, so Stevenson's *Kidnapped* comes before his *Treasure Island.*

Many libraries give fiction an "F" classification for the first line of the call number, with an author code below it for the second line. A library might have this call number for *Little Women* and *Little Men*, both by Louisa May Alcott:

> F = Fiction
> Alc = Alcott

Biographies are arranged alphabetically by *the person being written about,* so all the books about a person will stand together on the shelf. Often libraries give these books a "B" classification, or sometimes a 92 (part of the Dewey number for biographies.) Thus two biographies of Abraham Lincoln, one by Judson and one by Nolan, would have almost identical call numbers:

> B B (The only difference is the author designation
> L63j L63n at the end of the number representing Lincoln)

A collective biography, containing the lives of several people, is placed in the Dewey category for biography, 920—928, and has a regular author number.

SPECIAL COLLECTIONS: Sometimes there are other special collections that are housed separately. Short stories may be pulled out of their regular 800 number and put in a place designated S. C. (for story collection). Reference books are routinely shelved by themselves. Here is the call number for the reference book *Twentieth Century Authors* by Kunitz:

> R
> 928
> K96t

It is interesting how books from all these sections can be brought together for a special use. A teacher of American history preparing for a class unit on colonial life and the Revolution might go to the library and choose books from every single Dewey class number plus the other designations. Here are some books she might pick, with their broad class numbers: (Notice every class number is used.)

Subject	Class Number
Schools in colonial times	300
Signers of the Declaration (collected biography)	900
Development of constitutional government	300
Revolutionary war weapons	600
Sports and games in colonial days	700
A biography of George Washington	B
Johnny Tremain, a novel laid in Revolutionary days	F
The poem "Paul Revere's Ride"	800
How to embroider a sampler	700
A U. S. history book	900
Slavery	300
Tools used to build a log cabin	600
Foods and recipes	600
Story behind the song "Yankee Doodle"	700
Indian words adopted into our language	400
A description of Monticello, Jefferson's home	900
Colonial costumes	300
The founding of Pennsylvania by Quakers	200
Witchcraft in Salem village	100
Skits from American history	800
An encyclopedia article	000
Native birds painted by Audubon	500

LIBRARY OF CONGRESS CLASSIFICATION SYSTEM: A classification system especially suited to very large libraries or those with large collections of books on one subject find that the Library of Congress System suits their needs better because it can be divided into more precise categories than the Dewey Decimal System. Major classes are indicated by letters rather than by numbers, subdivided then by other letters and numbers. A book, *The Loch Ness Monster* by Cooke would have the L.C. number QL89.C65, while its Dewey call number would be: 001.94

> C772l

THE CARD CATALOG is the file for the library

containing alphabetized cards for every book in the library. For each book there is an author card, a title card, and as many subject cards as are necessary to cover the subjects dealt with in the book. Books of fiction have subject cards only if they contain authentic information about a location, a time period, specific events or people. Subject cards are distinguished because they are typed either in red or all capital letters. Here are examples of catalog cards.

USING THE CARD CATALOG: How do you look up a person in the card catalog? Do it as you do someone in the telephone book, last name first. This is true if the person is the author of a book or if the person is the subject of the book.

To find a title, look up the first word of the title unless the first word is "A," "An," or "The." If the first word is an article, go to the second word.

Numbers and abbreviations are filed as though they were spelled out.

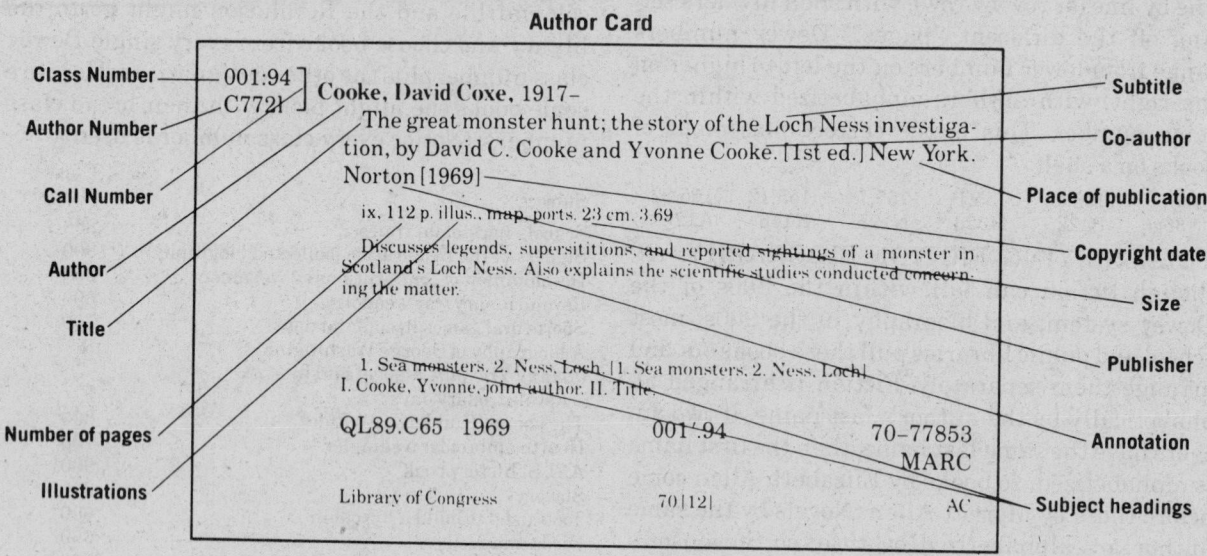

Author Card

Class Number — Author Number — Call Number — Author — Title — Number of pages — Illustrations

Subtitle — Co-author — Place of publication — Copyright date — Size — Publisher — Annotation — Subject headings

```
001:94
C772l      Cooke, David Coxe, 1917–
              The great monster hunt; the story of the Loch Ness investiga-
           tion, by David C. Cooke and Yvonne Cooke. [1st ed.] New York.
           Norton [1969]
              ix, 112 p. illus., map, ports. 23 cm. 3.69
              Discusses legends, superstitions, and reported sightings of a monster in
           Scotland's Loch Ness. Also explains the scientific studies conducted concern-
           ing the matter.

              1. Sea monsters. 2. Ness, Loch. [1. Sea monsters. 2. Ness, Loch]
           I. Cooke, Yvonne, joint author. II. Title.

           QL89.C65  1969          001'.94          70–77853
                                                     MARC
           Library of Congress        70[12]          AC
```

Title Card

The great monster hunt

```
001:94
C772l      Cooke, David Coxe, 1917–
              The great monster hunt; the story of the Loch Ness investiga-
           tion, by David C. Cooke and Yvonne Cooke. [1st ed.] New York.
           Norton [1969]
              ix, 112 p. illus., map, ports. 23 cm. 3.69
              Discusses legends, superstitions, and reported sightings of a monster in
           Scotland's Loch Ness. Also explains the scientific studies conducted concern-
           ing the matter.

              1. Sea monsters. 2. Ness, Loch. [1. Sea monsters. 2. Ness, Loch]
           I. Cooke, Yvonne, joint author. II. Title.

           QL89.C65  1969          001'.94          70–77853
                                                     MARC
           Library of Congress        70[12]          AC
```

Subject Card

Sea Monsters

```
001:94
C772l      Cooke, David Coxe, 1917–
              The great monster hunt; the story of the Loch Ness investiga-
           tion, by David C. Cooke and Yvonne Cooke. [1st ed.] New York.
           Norton [1969]
              ix, 112 p. illus., map, ports. 23 cm. 3.69
              Discusses legends, superstitions, and reported sightings of a monster in
           Scotland's Loch Ness. Also explains the scientific studies conducted concern-
           ing the matter.

              1. Sea monsters. 2. Ness, Loch. [1. Sea monsters. 2. Ness, Loch]
           I. Cooke, Yvonne, joint author. II. Title.

           QL89.C65  1969          001'.94          70–77853
                                                     MARC
           Library of Congress        70[12]          AC
```

All names beginning "Mc," "Mac," "M'" are filed as though they were spelled "Mac."

In parentheses are the first three letters of the word you would look behind for the following titles:

Mr. Roberts (Mis); *McGregor Strikes Back* (Mac); *1001 Questions about Birds* (One); *A Moveable Feast* (Mov); *Jane Eyre* (Jan); *The Count of Monte Cristo* (Cou); *And Now Tomorrow* (And because the first word is not "An").

Cards for books by a person come before cards for books about that person: Irving, Washington (author of "Rip Van Winkle") precedes IRVING, WASHINGTON (subject of a biography).

Periods in history are arranged chronologically, factual books first, then fiction.

> U. S.–History
> U. S.–History-Revolution
> U. S.–History-Revolution-Fiction
> U. S.–History-Civil War
> U. S.–History-Civil War-Fiction
> U. S.–History-20th Century

ALPHABETIZING: Most people think they know how to arrange in correct alphabetical order, yet they still have trouble finding things in the card catalog. One reason is that there is more than one system of alphabetical arrangement. The library uses the "word-by-word" system, meaning alphabetizing by letters to the end of each word, short words before long words. The other system, used by many encyclopedias and people who index books, is the letter-by-letter system, which is a strict alphabetical arrangement of all letters disregarding the ending of words.

LIBRARY SYSTEM	OTHER SYSTEM
New Amsterdam	New Amsterdam
New Delhi	Newark
New Zealand	New Delhi
Newark	New Zealand

SUBJECT HEADING: The most difficult part of library research seems to be establishing the key word or phrase that will lead you to the information you seek—finding the right subject heading. This is true not only for the card catalog but also for any other index, in books, encyclopedias, the *Reader's Guide*, etc.

One help is the existence of cross references, "See" and "See also" cards. A "See" card means there is nothing here, that you must look elsewhere. A "See also" card means there is something here but the information you seek may be listed under another heading. For instance, if you look up "Child abuse," you may be told to see the correct subject heading which is "Cruelty to children." Or if you look up "Energy," there may be a "See also" reference which tells you that "Energy" is a valid subject heading (for books about the physics of force and energy) but if you want something about energy as a fuel you should "See also" the alternative heading, "Power resources."

Here are some questions to ask yourself if you are having trouble with subject headings:

* Is there a larger subject that might include it? (U. S.—History—Civil War, rather than Gettysburg, Battle of).

* Is there a smaller subject? (American poetry, rather than Poetry).

* Does your subject overlap another? (Are you searching for the entertainment or the electronics aspect of television?)

* Is there another way to spell it or say it? (Cookery, French vs. French cookery; or Balzac, Honoré de vs. de Balzac, Honoré).

* Does it have a prefix? (U. S. Supreme Court instead of just Supreme Court).

* If your topic is a person, where and when did he live? What was he famous for? (For a report on Michelangelo you would probably do much better not reading a full-length biography but using information under Art—History; European history; Painting—History; Renaissance; Sculpture.

OTHER SOURCES: While today's libraries still find books the most useful sources of information, do not overlook the many non-book materials in its collection. Catalog cards will direct you to recordings, tapes, filmstrips, microfilm, microfiche, pictures, etc. The Vertical File contains pamphlets, clippings, maps, and other materials arranged alphabetically by subject matter in a filing cabinet or pamphlet boxes.

OTHER INFORMATION RETRIEVAL SOURCES: We have discussed at length using the card catalog, for it is a comprehensive index to materials in the library. However, there are additional useful indexes to help you out. Indexes are lists (or catalogs) of subjects, authors, or titles with information about where to find more material.

* Computers, besides storing information can tell where it is located, both within a library and in other places.

* Indexes to books and to encyclopedias are a useful aid to finding material in a book or encyclopedia. Too many people commonly ignore the index volume of an encyclopedia set (usually the last volume), but it is an invaluable tool, as it locates all the information in the entire set and often pinpoints where material is found that has no sepa-

rate article in the alphabetical listing. It can save time, also, as different encyclopedias head the same information differently, i.e. Man, Prehistoric; Prehistoric man; Fossil man; Evolution of Man.

Here is a typical index listing:

Newton, Sir Isaac (English physicist) N:306 with picture
    Aerodynamics A: 78-79
    Calculus (History) C:22
    Color Ci:666
    Dynamics D: 321
    Gravitation G:320
(Specific information about Newton's Theory of Gravity will be found in volume G on page 320).

* Reference books, such as *Play Index, Short Story Index, Poetry Index* tell in which books specific plays, stories, and poems are located.

* Some magazines and newspapers, such as *National Geographic* and the *New York Times* have indexes to back issues of their publications. Larger libraries index the local newspaper and put it on microfilm or microfiche.

* One of the most valuable indexing tools is the *Reader's Guide to Periodical Literature,* which indexes almost two hundred magazines of general interest. Paperback supplements are published twice a month, which are combined into three-month supplements. Then a full year's guide is bound in a single hardcover volume. There is also an *Abridged Readers' Guide* covering fewer magazines. This service is especially useful for finding recent, current information. Here is a typical entry, with explanation:

Under "Libraries" there are four sub-heads in one issue: Automation; Circulation; Federal aid; and Fines. Under "Fines" is found this entry:

A librarian throws the book at overdue borrowers. L. Giuliano. il por People Wkly 17:133 Ap 5 '82

This means L. Giuliano has written an article titled "A librarian throws the book at overdue borrowers" which is found in the magazine *People Weekly,* dated April 5, 1982, on page 133. The volume number for that issue is 17. The article also contains pictures (il) and a portrait (por).

A HOME REFERENCE LIBRARY: Reference books, which are usually expensive, are not in-tended for straight-through reading, but are designed to impart specific information quickly. The reference collection in a library is usually extensive and is not available to be checked out. Everyone should make a survey of what is available at their favorite library, but most people like to build a small home collection which can prove to be very useful at odd times of the day or night. Many of these books can be purchased in paperback so they fit into the average family's budget.

Indispensable in the home is a good *dictionary* which defines words, gives correct spelling and syllable division, and contains a great deal of additional front and back matter. An unabridged dictionary contains almost all the words in the language, while an abridged one is shortened.

Equally important for the home is a multi-volume general *encyclopedia* containing information about people, places, things, ideas, and events. Annual yearbooks keep it up-to-date. While a one-volume encyclopedia is ideal for quick reference, the more comprehensive multi-volume set is naturally better for detailed information such as school reports.

A handy tool is an *almanac,* such as the *World Almanac,* which is published yearly in paperback and is chock full of lists, tables, statistics, and all kinds of facts and figures.

For anyone who writes anything a *thesaurus* is most helpful. Also available in paperback, it is a dictionary of synonyms, to help the writer find the exact word needed.

Quotation books, again in paperback, allow the reader and writer to identify a quotation, to cite it in full, and to find an apt one on a particular theme.

Also useful in the home is an *atlas,* a book of maps, which is indispensable for planning trips as well as for obtaining information on political divisions, population, climate, resources, etc.

If a family has special hobbies or students pursuing special interests, there are innumerable handbooks covering single subjects and other reference books that could be purchased. It is always advisable to make friends with the local librarian, who can direct you to almost any information you seek.

Foreign Words and Phrases

In a language like English, whose vocabulary is at least 80 per cent borrowed from other language sources, it is not always easy to judge whether a word or expression should be considered as "foreign" or "naturalized." The choice is easier when it comes to full sentences and sayings. The chief sources of our foreign words and phrases are French and Latin. Other heavy contributors are Italian (particularly for musical terms), German, Greek, and Spanish. But English is a ready borrower and adapter, and we find in our list contributions from other European languages (Russian, Dutch, Scandinavian, Portuguese, etc.); from Semitic tongues, such as Hebrew and Arabic; from languages of Asia, such as Japanese, Chinese, Persian, and Turkish; from the tongues of the American Indians; and even from languages of the far Pacific, notably Hawaiian.

In each case, we have given the pronunciation of the word or expression with an approximation to the language of origin, even where usage has established a current English pronunciation; for instance, while there is a current English pronunciation of a Latin term like *bona fide,* our transcription approximates the sound of the original Latin because the current pronunciation is already commonly known.

The system of transcription is for the most part self-explanatory. Place the stress on the syllable that appears in capitals. Pronounce: AH like the *a* in *father;* EH like the *e* in *met;* EYE as in *eye;* OH like the *o* in *or;* OO as in *fool;* EE as in *seen;* OW as in *fowl;* ZH like the *s* in *pleasure;* AW as in *awe;* AY as in *lay.* In French words, ĀH, ĒH, ĀW, ŪH represent the four French nasal sounds of *an, vin, on, un,* respectively; shut off completely the passage between nose and mouth, so that your breath-stream is forced into the nose, and pronounce at the same time AH, EH, AW, UH. The transcription Ö represents a sound halfway between the *e* of *met* and the *o* of *or* (for which the French spelling is *eu* or *oeu*); the transcription Ü represents a sound intermediate between the *oo* of *fool* and the *ee* of *seen* (purse lips for *oo,* and try to say *ee*). In German words, KH represents the sound of *ch* in *ach,* Ç the sound of *ch* in *ich* (the nearest English approximation is the *h* of *huge*). Abbreviations for the names of the source language are as follows:

F	French	Jap	Japanese
L	Latin	Ch	Chinese
It	Italian	Du	Dutch
Sp	Spanish	Pers	Persian
G	German	Swed	Swedish
Pt	Portuguese	Yid	Yiddish
R	Russian	Arab	Arabic
Gk	Greek	Turk	Turkish
Sk	Sanskrit	Hind	Hindi
Heb	Hebrew	Norw	Norwegian

Other languages of rare occurrence (Hungarian, Irish, Welsh, Icelandic, Basque, Egyptian, Hawaiian, etc.) are left unabbreviated.

The translations given are sometimes literal, but more often aim at rendering the meaning of the foreign word or expression.

The italicized words and expressions are still considered "foreign." These words should be underlined in the original manuscript and italicized when printed. Not all authorities will agree with this list. When you "naturalize" a word or phrase, be prepared to defend your act. A quick rule to follow is: If the word or phrase does not appear in one of the major dictionaries, then it is still "foreign."

India—Hall of Special Audience in Red Fort, Delhi

A

ab initio (ahb ee-NEE-tee-oh), from the beginning (L)

à bon marché (a bāw mar-SHAY), cheap, a bargain (F)

ab ovo (ahb OH-woh), from the egg, from the very start (L)

absinthe (ap-SĒHT), wormwood, absinth (F)

a cappella (ah kahp-PEHL-lah), church style, without accompaniment (It)

accelerando (ah-chay-lay-RAHN-doh), with increasing speed (It)

Achtung (AKH-toong), attention (G)

adagio (ah-DAH-joh), slowly (It)

ad astra per aspera (ahd AH-strah pehr AH-speh-rah), to the stars through difficult places (L)

addendum (ahd-DEHN-doom) (pl. addenda, ahd-DEHN-dah), to be added (L)

Adeste Fideles (ah-DEHS-teh fee-DEH-lehs), Come, ye faithful (L)

ad hoc (ahd HOHK), for this, for this purpose (L)

adieu (a-DYÖ), farewell, good-bye (F)

ad infinitum (ahd een-fee-NEE-toom), to infinity, on and on (L)

adiós (ah-DYOHS), farewell, good-bye (Sp)

ad lib(itum) (ahd Lee-bee-toom), at pleasure (usually abbr. ad lib) (L)

ad nauseam (ahd NOW-seh-ahm), to the point of disgust (L)

ad valorem (ahd wah-LOH-rehm), in proportion to value or valuation (L)

affaire de coeur (a-FEHR duh KÖR), love affair (F)

affaire d'honneur (a-FEHR daw-NÖR), matter involving honor (F)

aficionado (ah-fee-thyoh-NAH-doh), fan, enthusiast (Sp)

a fortiori (ah fohr-tee-OH-ree), with greater reason, all the more (L)

agenda (ah-GHEHN-dah), things to be done (L)

agent provocateur (a-ZHĂH praw-vaw-ka-TÖR), one who provokes others into unlawful actions (F)

agio (AH-joh), ease; currency differential (It)

Agnus Dei (AHG-noos DEH-ee), Lamb of God (L)

agora (AH-goh-rah), marketplace (Gk)

aguardiente (ah-gwahr-DYEHN-teh), firewater, brandy (Sp)

aide-de-camp (EHD duh KĂH), field aide (F)

aigrette (eh-GREHT), egret, spray of feathers (F)

aiguillette (eh-ghee-YEHT), shoulder-knot (F)

à la (a la), in the–fashion (à la française, French style) (F)

à la carte (a la KART), according to the menu, picking out individual items (F)

alameda (ah-lah-MEH-dah), poplar grove (Sp)

à la mode (a la MAWD), in the fashion (F)

alcázar (ahl-KAH-thahr), fortress, fortified palace (Arab-Sp)

al fresco (ahl FRAYS-koh), in the open air (It)

alias (AH-lee-ahs), otherwise, at another time (L)

alibi (AH-lee-bee), elsewhere (L)

allegro (ahl-LAY-groh), quick, lively, merry (It)

alma mater (AHL-mah MAH-tehr), fostering mother, school or college (L)

aloha oe (ah-LOH-hah OH-eh), farewell to you (Hawaiian)

Alpenstock (AHL-pen-shtok), iron-tipped staff used in mountain climbing (G)

alpha-omega (AHL-fah OH-may-gah), beginning and end (Gk)

alter ego (AHL-tehr EH-goh), another I, close and inseparable friend (L)

alto (AHL-toh), low female voice (used for *contralto*, "counter high") (It)

alumnus, alumna (ah-LOOM-noos, ah-LOOM-nah), graduate of an institution (L)

amabile (ah-MAH-bee-lay), amiable, pleasing (It)

amanuensis (ah-mah-noo-EHN-sees), clerk, secretary (L)

amicus curiae (ah-MEE-koos KOO-ree-eye), friend of the court (L) *amour propre* (a-MOOR PRAW-pruh), self-love, pride (F)

ancien régime (äh-SYĒH ray-ZHEEM), old, prerevolutionary regime (F)

animato (ah-nee-MAH-toh), animated, with spirit (It)

anno Domini (AHN-noh DOH-mee-nee), in the year of our Lord (abbr. A.D.) (L)

Anschluss (AHN-shloos), annexation, union (G)

ante bellum (AHN-teh BEHL-loom), before the war (L)

ante meridiem (AHN-teh meh-REE-dee-ehm), before noon, morning (abbr. A.M.) (L)

antipasto (ahn-tee-PAH-stoh), appetizer, hors d'oeuvre (It)

apartheid (a-PART-hayt), South African policy of racial segregation (Du)

apéritif (a-pay-ree-TEEF), appetizer, before-meal drink (F)

aplomb (a-PLAW), self-possession, poise (F)

a posteriori (ah pohs-teh-ree-OH-ree), with hindsight, reasoning backwards from observed facts (L)

appassionato (ahp-pahs-syoh-NAH-toh), passionately (It)

Après moi le déluge! (a-PREH MWAH luh day-LÜZH), after me the deluge, I don't care what happens after I'm gone (F)

a priori (ah pree-OH-ree), reaching conclusions before gathering facts (L)

apropos (a-praw-POH), opportunely, by the way, with regard to (F)

aquavit (ah-kwah-VEET), brandy (Swedish, from Latin *aqua vitae*, water of life)

arbiter elegantiarum (AHR-bee-tehr eh-leh-gahn-tee-AH-room), arbiter of style or taste (L)

argot (ar-GOH), slang, thieves' cant (F)

argumentum ad hominem (ahr-goo-MEHN-toom ahd HOH-mee-nehm), diversion of a discussion to the personality of the opponent (L)

aria (AH-ryah), vocal solo passage in an opera (It)

arista (AH-rees-tah), the best, honors group in a high school (Gk)

arpeggio (ahr-PAY-joh), notes of chord played in harplike succession (It)

arrière-pensée (a-RYEHR päh-SAY), mental reservation, afterthought (F)

arroz con pollo (ahr-ROHTH kohn POH-lyoh), chicken with rice and condiments (Sp)

ars amandi (AHRS ah-MAHN-dee), the art of loving (L)

ars gratia artis (AHRS GRAH-tee-ah AHR-tees), art for art's sake (L)

ars longa, vita brevis (AHRS LOHN-gah, WEE-tah BREH-wees), art is long, but life is fleeting (L)

attaché (a-ta-SHAY), diplomatic official attached to an embassy (F)

au courant (oh koo-RÄH), posted, informed (F)

auf Wiedersehen (owf VEE-duhr-zayn), good-bye, till we meet again (G)

France—The Sacré Coeur, Paris

au gratin (oh gra-TĒH), baked with crumbs or cheese on top (F)

au jus (oh ZHÜ), in its natural juice or gravy (F)

aurea mediocritas (OW-ray-ah meh-dee-OH-kree-tahs), the golden mean (L)

au revoir (oh ruh-VWAHR), good-bye, till we meet again (F)

auri sacra fames (OW-ree SAH-krah FAH-mehs), sacred lust for gold (L)

aurora borealis (ow-ROH-rah boh-ray-AH-lees), the northern lights (L)

Aut Caesar aut nullus (owt KEYE-sahr owt NOOL-loos), either everything or nothing (L)

Autobahn (OW-toh-bahn), automobile highway (G)

auto da fé (OW-toh dah FEH), burning at the stake on a charge of heresy (Pt)

Aux armes! (oh-ZAHRM), to arms! (F)

avant-garde (a-VÄH-GAHRD), in the van or forefront (F)

Ave atque vale! (AH-weh AHT-kweh WAH-leh), hail and farewell (L)

Ave Caesar, morituri te salutamus (AH-weh KEYE-sahr, moh-ree-TOO-ree teh sah-loo-TAH-moos), Hail, Caesar, we who are about to die salute you (L)

Ave Maria (AH-weh mah-REE-ah), Hail, Mary (L)

à votre santé! (a VAW-truh SÄH-tay), to your health! (F)

B

baba (bah-BAH), light cake (F)

babu (BAH-boo), gentleman, Mr. (Hindi)

babushka (BAH-boosh-kuh), scarf over the head, tied under the chin "little grandmother" fashion (R) *baklava* (or *paklava*) (bah-KLAH-vah), Turkish pastry made with nuts and honey (Turkish)

bakshish (BAHK-sheesh), tip, money (Persian)

balalaika (buh-luh-LEYE-kuh), three-stringed triangular guitar (R)

bambino (bahm-BEE-noh), baby, child (It)

banderilla (bahn-deh-REE-lyah), dart with streamer used in bullfight (Sp)

banditti (bahn-DEE-tee), incorrect spelling for *banditi*, "bandits" (It)

banzai (BAHN-zeye), cheer or battle cry, "ten thousand years" (Jap)

bar mitzva (BAHR-MEETS-vah), confirmation ceremony (Heb)

baroque (ba-RAWK), irregular in shape, over-ornamental (F)

bas bleu (BAH BLÖ), blue-stocking, over-intellectual woman (F)

bas-relief (bah-ruh-LYEHF), sculpture with figures projecting from background (F)

basso profundo (BAHS-soh proh-FOON-doh), deep bass voice (It-L)

bathos (BAH-thos), false pathos; an anti-climax (Gk)

beau geste (BOH ZHEHST), fine gesture or deed (F)

beau monde (BOH MAWD), high society (F)

beaux arts (BOH-ZAHR), fine arts (F)

béchamel (bay-sha-MEHL), rich white sauce (F)

beige (BEHZH), undyed, grayish tan (F)

Beiheft (BEYE-heft), supplement, supplementary volume (G)

bel canto (behl KAHN-toh), fine singing (It)

belladonna (behl-lah-DAWN-nah), lovely lady, poisonous plant, eye-drug (It)

belles-lettres (behl-LEH-truh), literature, the humanities (F)

Bel Paese (behl pah-AY-say), beautiful country, a creamy cheese (It)

berceuse (behr-SÜZ), cradle-song, lullaby (F)

béret (bay-REH), flat, round cap (F)

béte noire (BEHT NWAHR), black beast, pet abomination (F)

bétise (beh-TEEZ), foolish act or word (F)

beurre noir (BÖR NWAHR), black butter sauce (F)

billet-doux (bee-YEH DOO), love note or letter (F)

bis (BEES), twice, encore (L)

bisque (BEESK), rich soup (F)

bistro (bee-STROH), cabaret, wine-shop (F)

blanc mange (BLAH MAHZH), white pudding (F)

blasé (bla-ZAY), jaded, satiated, bored (F)

blintzi (BLEEN-tsy), cheese or meat wrapped in pancake (R)

Blitzkreig (BLITZ-kreek), lightning war; swift, sudden attack (G)

Blut und Boden (BLOOT unt BOH-duhn), blood and soil (G)

Blut und Eisen (BLOOT unt EYE-zuhn), blood and iron (G)

B'nai B'rith (BNEYE BREETH), sons of the covenant, Jewish service organization (Heb)

bocce (BAW-chay), an Italian bowling game (It)

boeuf á la mode (BÖF a la MAWD), larded and pot-roasted beef (F)

Boer (BOOR), peasant or settler in South Africa (Du)

Bohême (boh-EHM), gypsy-like, unconventional living (F)

bolero (boh-LEH-roh), a Spanish dance (Sp)

Bolsheviki (buhl'-shuh-vee-KEE), Maximalists, Lenin-led Communists (R)

bombe glacée (BAWB gla-SAY), frozen dessert (F)

bona fide (BOH-nah FEE-day), in good faith (L)

bon ami (BAW-na-MEE), good friend (F)

bonanza (boh-NAHN-thah), windfall, run of luck (Sp)

bonbon (Baw-BAW), candy (F)

bon gré mal gré (baw-GRAY mal-GRAY), willy-nilly (F)

bon marché (baw mar-SHAY) (*see* à bon marché)

bon mot (baw MOH), witticism (F)

bonne (BAWN), maid, nursemaid (F)

bonus (BOH-noos), extra payment (L)

bon vivant (baw-vee-VAH), one who likes to live well (F)

bon voyage (baw-vwa-YAHZH), a happy trip (F)

borsch (BAWRSHCH), Russian beet soup, usually with sour cream (R)

boudoir (boo-DWAHR), lady's private sitting-room (F)

bouffant (boo-FAH), puffed out, full (F)

bouillabaisse (boo-ya-BEHS), seafood soup (F)

bouillon (boo-YAW), clear beef or chicken broth (F)

bourgeoisie (boor-zhwah-ZEE), middle class (F)

boutonnière (boo-taw-NYEHR), buttonhole, flower for a buttonhole (F)

bravo, brava (BRAH-voh, BRAH-vah), cry of approval; hired killer (It)

Brie (BREE), a creamy French cheese (F)

brio (BREE-oh), vivacity, liveliness (It)

brioche (bree-AWSH), bun, light roll (F)

Iran—Street Scene, Teheran

broccoli (BRAWK-koh-lee), green variety of cauliflower (It)

brochure (braw-SHÜR), pamphlet (F)

brut (BRÜ), raw, unadulterated (F)

Bund (BOONT), league; union, organization (G)

Bundesrepublik (BOON-duhs-reh-poo-bleek), West German Federal Republic (G)

burro (BOOR-roh), donkey (Sp)

bushido (BOO-shee-doh), code of honor of *samurai* class (Jap)

C

ca. See *circa*

cabala, kabala (kahb-ah-LAH), Hebrew occult religious philosophy (Heb)

cacciatora (kah-chah-TOH-rah), hunter style (It); more properly *alla cacciatora*

caciocavallo (kah-choh-kah-VAHL-loh), piquant Italian cheese (It)

cacique (kah-THEE-kay), American Indian chief, political leader (Carib-Sp)

caesura (keye-SOO-rah), break in line of poetry (L)

café (ka-FAY), coffee shop, saloon (F);—**au lait** (oh LEH), coffee with milk;—**noir** (NWAHR), black coffee

caffè espresso (kah-FEH ays-PREHS-soh), strong black coffee, machine-made (It)

Calvados (kal-va-DOHS), apple brandy from the French region of the same name (F)

camaraderie (ka-ma-rad-REE), loyalty, comradeship, good fellowship (F)

camarilla (kah-mah-REE-lyah), clique, group of special advisors (Sp)

Camembert (ka-mäh-BEHR), a soft French cheese (F)

camino real (kah-MEE-noh reh-AHL), royal or main highway (Sp)

camorra (kah-MAWR-rah), Neapolitan secret society (It)

campanile (kahm-pah-NEE-lay), bell tower (It)

campo santo (KAHM-poh SAHN-toh), graveyard, cemetery (It)

canaille (ka-NA-yuh), rabble (F)

canapé (ka-na-PAY), open sandwich served as appetizer (F)

canard (ka-NAHR), duck, hoax (F)

canasta (kah-NAHS-tah), basket, card game (Sp)

can can (käh-KÄH), kicking dance (F)

cannelloni (kahn-nayl-LOH-nee), large hollow macaroni stuffed with meat (It)

cantabile (kahn-TAH-bee-lay), singable, in singing style (It)

cantata (kahn-TAH-tah), musical composition for solos or choruses (It)

canton (käh-TÄW), political subdivision of Switzerland (F)

cap-à-pied (ka-pa-PYEH), head-to-foot armor (F)

capias (KAH-pee-ahs), "you may take"; arrest warrant (L)

capriccio (kah-PREE-choh), free musical composition, caprice (It)

carabiniere (kah-rah-bee-NYEH-ray), Italian military policeman (It)

carioca (kah-RYOH-kah), native of Rio; Brazilian dance (Pt)

carpe diem (KAHR-peh DEE-ehm), "seize the day"; make hay while the sun shines (L)

carte blanche (KART BLÄHSH), free hand; authorization to act as one will (F)

cartel (kar-TEHL), monopoly trust; organized group of business interests (F)

Carthago delenda est (kahr-TAH-goh deh-LEHN-dah EHST), Carthage must be destroyed (L)

cartouche (kar-TOOSH), cartridge; oval space for inscription of name of Egyptian Pharaoh (F)

casserole (kas-RAWL), clay saucepan for cooking and serving; contents thereof (F)

casus belli (KAH-soos BEHL-lee), occurrence giving rise to war (L)

caudillo (kow-DEE-lyoh), chief, leader (Sp)

cause célèbre (KOHZ say-LEH-bruh), famous or sensational trial (F)

causerie (kohz-REE), chat, informal talk (F)

cavatina (kah-vah-TEE-nah), short song (It)

caveat (KAH-weh-aht), let (him) beware (L);—**emptor** (EHMP-tohr), let the buyer beware

cave canem (KAH-weh KAH-nehm), beware of the dog (L)

cello (CHEHL-loh); abbr. of *violoncello*, musical instrument (It)

certiorari (kehr-tee-oh-RAH-ree), "to be ascertained"; writ to procure records (L)

c'est-à-dire (seh-ta-DEER), that is to say (F)

c'est la vie (seh-la-VEE), that's life (F)

ceteris paribus (KEH-teh-rees PAH-ree-boos), other things being equal (L)

chacun à son goût (sha-KÜH a-sâw-GOO), everyone to his taste (F)

chacun pour soi (sha-KÜH poor SWAH), every man for himself (F)

chaise longue (SHEHZ LÄWG), reclining chair or sofa (F)

champagne (shäh-PA-nyuh), French sparkling wine (F)

champignon (shäh-pee-NYÄW), mushroom (F)

chanteuse (shäh-TÖZ), female singer (F)

chargé d'affaires (shar-ZHAY da-FEHR), minor government official temporarily replacing a higher diplomat (F)

charivari (sha-ree-va-REE), mock serenade or raucous music (F)

chasseur (sha-SÖR), hunter; light-infantryman; footman (F)

château (sha-TOH), castle, palace (F)

chef (de cuisine) (SHEF duh kwee-ZEEN), head cook (F)

chef d'oeuvre (SHEH DÖ-vruh), masterpiece (F)

Cherchez la femme! (shehr-SHAY la FAM), look for the woman in the case (F)

chérie (shay-REE), dearie, sweetheart (F)

chetnik (CHET-neek), Yugoslav resistance fighter (Serbo-Croatian)

chevaux-de-frise (shuh-VÖH duh FREEZ), barrier of spikes in timber (F)

chez (SHAY), at the home of (F)

Chianti (KYAHN-tee), Italian wine (It)

chiaroscuro (kyah-roh-SKOO-roh), light and dark effect (It)

chic (SHEEK), elegant, elegance (F)

chiffon (shee-FÄW), rag; silk crepe, whipped ingredients in pie (F)

chile con carne (CHEE-leh kohn KAHR-neh), Mexican dish consisting of kidney beans, ground meat, and red peppers (Sp)

chop suey (TSAH SOO-ee), Chinese-American dish of meat and vegetables (Ch)

chow mein (CHOW MYEHN), Chinese dish of fried noodles, with meat or vegetables (Ch)

Cid (THEED), chieftain, leader (Sp, from Arab *sayyid*)

ci-gît (see-ZHEE), here lies (F)

cinquecento (cheen-kway-CHEHN-toh), 16th century (It)

circa (KEER-kah), about, approximately; abbr. ca. (L)

Civis Romanus sum (Kee-wees roh-MAH-noos SOOM), I am a Roman citizen (L)

Civitas Dei (KEE-wee-tahs DEH-ee), the City of God (L)

clair de lune (KLEHR duh LÜN), moonlight (F)

claret (kla-REH), light red wine (F)

clef (KLAY or KLEHF), key (F)

cliché (klee-SHAY), stereotype; hackneyed expression (F)

clientèle (klee-äh-TEHL), customers or patrons (F)

clique (KLEEK), set; group (F)

clôture (kloh-TÜR), closure of debate (F)

cocido (koh-THEE-doh), Spanish stew (Sp)

coda (KOH-dah), tail; concluding musical passage (It)

Code Napoléon (KAWD na-poh-lay-ÄW), code of civil law of France of 1804, applied with modifications in Louisiana (F)

codex (KOH-dehks), body of laws; manuscript on parchment (L)

Cogito, ergo sum (KOH-ghee-toh, EHR-goh SOOM), I think, therefore I exist (L)

cognac (kaw-NYAK), French brandy (F)

cognoscenti (erroneous for *conoscenti*, koh-noh-SHEHN-tee), experts (It)

coiffeur (kwa-FÖR), hairdresser (F)

coiffure (kwa-FÜR), hairstyle (F)

coloratura (koh-loh-rah-TOO-rah), embellishment in vocal music; soprano (It)

commando (koh-MAHN-doh), raiding troops (Du. from Pt)

comme ci, comme ça (kawm SEE, kawm SA), so-so (F)

comme il faut (kawm eel FOH), proper; properly; in the right fashion (F)

commedia dell'arte (kohm-MEH-dyah dayl-LAHR-tay), guild players' comedy, often improvised (It)

commissar (kuhm-mee-SAHR), government official (R, from F *commissaire*)

commune (kaw-MÜN), self-governing town; French revolutionary movement (F)

communiqué (kaw-mü-nee-KAY), official statement or dispatch (F)

compote (käw-PAWT), stewed fruit (F)

compte rendu (KÄWT räh-DÜ), book review; report (F)

con amore (kohn ah-MOH-ray), lovingly (It)

concerto (kohn-CHEHR-toh), musical composition for solo instrument(s) with orchestral accompaniment (It)

concierge (käw-SYEHRZH), janitor, superintendent (F)

concordat (käw-kawr-DAH), pact, agreement (F from Latin *concordatus*)

condottiere (kohn-doht-TYEH-ray), Italian Renaissance leader of mercenary troops (It)

confer (KOHN-fehr), compare; see; abbr. cf. (L)

confetti (kohn-FEHT-tee), candies; plaster or paper imitations used at feasts (It)

confrère (käw-FREHR), colleague; associate (F)

conga (KAWN-gah), Latin-American dance (Sp or Pt)

con moto (kohn MAW-toh), with movement; fast (It)

connoisseur (kaw-neh-SÖR), expert; one who knows (F)

conquistadores (kohn-kees-tah-DOH-rehs), conquerors (Sp)

console (käw-SAWL), ornamental bracket for supporting shelf; table with ledges (F)

consommé (käw-saw-MAY), concentrated meat broth (F)

consortium (kohn-SOHR-tee-oom), international finance control group (L)

contra (KOHN-trah), against (abbr. con; L)

contrabasso (kohn-trah-BAHS-soh), double-bass viol (It)

copula (KOH-poo-lah), connective; the verb "to be" or a similar verb (L)

coq au vin (KAWK oh VÉH), chicken braised in wine (F)

coquetterie (kaw-keht-REE), flirtatiousness (F)

coram populo (KOH-rahm POH-poo-loh), publicly (L)

cordillera (kohr-dee-LYEH-rah), mountain range (SP)

cornu copiae (KOHR-noo KOH-pee-eye), horn of plenty (L)

corona (koh-ROH-nah), crown (L)

corps de ballet (KAWR duh ba-LEH), ballet troupe (F)

corpus (KOHR-poos), body; collection (L)

corpus delicti (KOHR-poos deh-LEEK-tee), the body or tangible evidence of a crime (L)

corpus juris (KOHR-poos YOO-rees), the body of the law; collection of laws (L)

corrida (kohr-REE-dah), bullfight (Sp)

corrigenda (kohr-ree-GHEHN-dah), things to be corrected (L)

corsage (kawr-SAHZH), bodice; flowers worn on bodice (F)

cortège (kawr-TEHZH), procession (F)

corvée (kawr-VAY), forced labor (F)

cosi cosi (koh-SEE koh-SEE), so-so (It)

coterie (kawt-REE), small, intimate group or circle (F)

coup de grâce (KOO duh GRAHS), death-blow (F)

coup de main (KOO duh MÊH), sudden blow (F)

coup d'état (KOO day-TAH), seizure of government by sudden stroke (F)

couturier (koo-tü-RYAY), dressmaker (F)

crèche (KREHSH), crib, manger, public nursery (F)

credenza (kray-DEHN-tsah), small table or cupboard (It)

credo (KREH-doh), belief, article of faith, creed (L)

crème de menthe (KREHM duh MÂHT), peppermint liqueur (F)

crêpe (KREHP), thin cloth of silk, rayon, wool, etc. (F)

crêpe suzette (KREHP sü-ZEHT), thin pancake (F)

crescendo (kray-SHEHN-doh), gradual increase in loudness or intensity (It)

critique (kree-TEEK), criticism (F)

croissant (krwa-SÂH), crescent-shaped roll (F)

Croix de Guerre (KRWAH duh GHEHR), war cross, French military decoration (F)

croquette (kraw-KEHT), fried meat or fish, covered with bread crumbs (F)

croupier (kroo-PYAY), man who rakes in stakes at gambling table (F)

crux (KROOKS), cross; main point at issue (L)

cucaracha (koo-kah-RAH-chah), cockroach (Sp)

cui bono? (KOO-ee BOH-noh), to whose advantage? (L)

cuisine (kwee-ZEEN), cookery, cooking (F)

cul-de-sac (KÜL-duh-SAHK), blind alley, dead end (F)

cum grano salis (koom GRAH-noh SAH-lees), with a grain of salt (L)

cum laude (koom LOW-deh), with praise, with honor (L)

curé (kü-RAY), parish priest (F)

curriculum (koor-REE-koo-loom), year's course of studies (L);—**vitae** (WEE-teye), outline of one's life

czar (more precisely *tsar*, TSAHR), Russian emperor, autocrat (R)

czardas (more precisely *csárdás*, CHAHR- dahsh), Hungarian dance (Hungarian)

D

da capo (dah KAH-poh), from the start (It)

Dachshund (DAHKS-hoont), short-legged dog (G)

dal segno (dahl SAY-nyoh), from the sign (It)

data (DAH-tah) (sg. **datum**), information at one's disposal (L)

débâcle (day-BAH-kluh), disaster, collapse (F)

débris (day-BREE), wreckage, rubbish (F)

début (day-BÜ), coming out, first appearance (F)

débutante (day-bü-TÂHT), girl making first social appearance (F)

décolleté (day-kawl-TAY), low-necked (F)

décor (day-KAWR), stage setting, room setting (F)

de facto (deh FAHK-toh), in existence, in actuality (L)

deficit (DEH-fee-keet), amount less than what is needed (L)

de gustibus non est disputandum (deh GOOS-tee-boos nohn EHST dees-poo-TAHN-doom), there is no arguing about tastes (L)

Dei gratia (DEH-ee GRAH-tee-ah), by the grace of God (L)

déjeuner (day-zhö-NAY), lunch, breakfast (F)

de jure (deh YOO-reh), legally, legitimately (L)

dele (DEH-leh), erase, strike out, delete; abbreviation (L)

delenda est Carthago (deh-LEHN-dah EHST kahr-TAH-goh), Carthage must be destroyed (L)

delicatessen (day-LEE-kaht-EHS-suhn), prepared foods (G)

delirium tremens (deh-LEE-ree-oom TREH-mehns), alcoholic brain disease (L)

de luxe (duh LÜKS), luxurious, very fancy (F)

démarche (day-MAHRSH), diplomatic approach, step (F)

dementia praecox (deh-MEHN-tee-ah PREYE-kohks), adolescent mental illness (L)

demi-tasse (duh-MEE-TAHS), small cup of coffee (F)

demi-monde (duh-MEE-MAWD), fringe of society (F)

de mortuis nihil nisi bonum (deh MOHR-too-ees NEE-heel NEE-see BOH-noom), say nothing but good about the dead (L)

denarius (deh-NAH-ree-oos), Roman silver coin (L)

denier (duh-NYAY), small coin, unit of weight for hosiery (F)

dénouement (day-noo-MÂH), unraveling, solution of plot (F)

de novo (deh NOH-voh), anew, again from the start (L)

Deo volente (DEH-oh woh-LEHN-teh), God willing (L)

de profundis (deh proh-FOON-dees), out of the depths (L)

de rigueur (duh ree-GÖR), indispensable, required (F)

dernier cri (dehr-NYAY KREE), latest style, last word (F)

derrière (deh-RYEHR), back part, buttocks (F)

descamisado (dehs-kah-mee-SAH-doh), shirtless, follower of Evita Perón (Sp)

déshabillé (day-za-bee-YAY), in state of informal undress (F)

desideratum (deh-see-deh-RAH-toom; pl. **desiderata**, deh-see-deh-RAH-tah), what is desired (L) *détente* (day-TÃHT), release of strained relations (F)

de trop (duh TROH), in excess, superfluous, not wanted (F)

deus ex machina (DEH-oos ehks MAH-kee-nah), outside intervention to solve a crisis (L)

Deus vobiscum (DEH-oos woh-BEES-koom), God be with you (L)

diaspora (dee-AHS-poh-rah), dispersion, scattering (particularly of Jews after destruction of Jerusalem) (Gk)

dictum (DEEK-toom), saying, pronouncement (L)

diminuendo (dee-mee-noo-EHN-doh), diminishing in volume (It)

Dirndl (DEERNDL), peasant-girl dress (G)

diseur (fem. diseuse; dee-ZÖR, dee-ZÖZ), monologist (F)

diva (DEE-vah), female opera singer (It)

divertissement (dee-vehr-tees-MÃH), lively piece between acts (F)

divide et impera (dee-WEE-deh eht EEM-peh-rah), divide and conquer (L)

doge (DAW-jay), medieval ruler of Venice (It)

dogma (DOHG-mah), belief, article of faith (Gk)

dolce far niente (DOHL-chay FAHR NYEHN-tay), sweet idleness (It)

dolce stil nuovo (DOHL-chay STEEL NWAW-voh), sweet new literary style of 14th century (It)

Dominus vobiscum (DOH-mee-noos woh-BEES-koom), the Lord be with you (L)

don (DOHN), tutor at English universities; Spanish and Italian title of respect; Mafia leader (It, Sp)

donna (DAWN-nah), lady, woman (It)

Doppelgänger (DOH-pehl-gheng-uhr), ghostly double (G)

dossier (daw-SYAY), file (F)

double entendre (DOO-blāh-TÃH-druh), expression with double meaning (F)

dramatis personae (DRAH-mah-tees pehr-SOH-neye), cast of characters (L)

droshky (DRAWSH-kee), cab, carriage (R)

duce (DOO-chay), leader (It)

dueña (DWEH-nyah), chaperone (Sp)

duomo (DWAW-moh), cathedral (It)

dybbuk (DEE-book), bewitched person; evil spirit entering living body (Heb)

E

eau de vie (OH duh VEE), brandy (F)

ecce homo (EHK-keh HOH-moh), behold the man (L)

échelon (aysh-LÃW), steplike formation of troops, any hierarchical arrangement (F)

éclair (ay-KLEHR), pastry filled with cream (F)

éclat (ay-KLAH), success, prestige (F)

Edda (EHD-dah), old Scandinavian poetry (Icelandic)

Edelweiss (AY-duhl-veyes), white Alpine flower (G)

editio princeps (eh-DEE-tee-oh PREEN-kehps), original edition (L)

eisteddfod (ay-STETH-vohd), musical or poetic contest (Welsh)

élan (ay-LÃH), sparkle, liveliness (F)

el dorado (ehl doh-RAH-doh), fabulous South American land of gold (Sp)

Eli (EH-lee), my God (Heb)

élite (ay-LEET), select few (F)

Elohim (eh-loh-HEEM), God, Supreme Being (Heb)

embarras du choix (ãh-ba-RAH dü SHWAH), trouble making up one's mind (F)

embonpoint (ãh-baw-PWĒH), plumpness (F)

emeritus (eh-MEH-ree-toos), retired with honor (L)

émigré (ay-mee-GRAY), emigrated, exiled (F)

en bloc (ãh BLAWK), together; as a unit (F)

en brochette (ãh braw-SHEHT), on a skewer (F)

enceinte (ãh-SĒHT), pregnant, with child (F)

en coquille (ãh kaw-KEE-yuh), served in a shell (F)

encore (ãh-KAWR), again; repeat (F)

enfant gâté (terrible) (ãh-FAH gah-TAY, teh-REE-bluh), spoiled child, brat (F)

en masse (ãh MAHS), all together, in a mass (F)

ennui (ãh-NWEE), boredom (F)

en passant (ãh pa-SÃH), incidentally; by the way (F)

ensemble (ãh-SÃH-bluh), together, in a group (F)

entente (ãh-TÃHT), understanding; international agreement, alliance (F)

entourage (ãh-too-RAHZH), surrounding company (F)

entr'acte (ãh-TRAKT), between the acts (F)

entrée (ãh-TRAY), entrance; main dish (F)

entre nous (ãh-truh-NOO), between us (F)

entrepreneur (ãh-truh-pruh-NÖR), one who undertakes or manages (F)

envoi (ãh-VWAH), postscript (F)

épater le bourgeois (ay-pa-TAY luh boor-ZHWAH), to bedazzle and befuddle people (F)

epaulette (ay-poh-LEHT), shoulder piece (F)

e pluribus unum (eh PLOO-ree-boos OO-noom), one out of many (L)

ergo (EHR-goh), therefore, consequently (L)

Erin go bragh (EH-reen goh BRAH), Ireland forever (Ir)

errare humanum est (ehr-RAH-reh hoo-MAH-noom EHST), to err is human (L)

erratum (pl. errata; ehr-RAH-toom, ehr-RAH-tah), error, mistake (L)

ersatz (EHR-zatz), substitute, synthetic replacement (G)

escargots (ehs-kar-GOH), snails (F)

espada (ehs-PAH-dah), sword; the matador who kills the bull with a sword (Sp)

esprit de corps (ehs-PREE duh KAWR), spirit of loyalty to one's group (F)

et alii (eht AH-lee-ee); abbr. et al., and others (L)

Sweden—River front, Stockholm

et cetera (eht KEYE-teh-rah); abbr. etc., and others, and other things (L)

ethos (EH-thos), custom, national character (Gk)

et passim (eht PAHS-seem), abbr. et pass., and everywhere, scattered throughout a work (L)

et tu Brute? (eht TOO, BROO-teh), you, too, Brutus? (L)

étude (ay-TÜD), study; short musical composition (F)

et uxor (eht OOK-sohr); abbr. et ux., and wife (L)

eureka! (EH-OO-reh-kah), I have found it! (Gk)

ewig Weibliche (AY-vik VEYEB-li-çe), eternal feminine (G)

ex cathedra (ehks KAH-theh-drah), authoritatively, pontifically (L)

excelsior (ehks-KEHL-see-ohr), ever higher (L)

exempli gratia (ehk-SEHM-plee GRAH-tee-ah), abbr. e.g., for instance (L)

ex libris (ehks LEE-brees), from among the books of (L)

ex officio (ehks ohf-FEE-kee-oh), by virtue of his office (L)

exposé (ehks-paw-ZAY), statement, explanation, revelation (F)

ex post facto (ehks pohst FAHK-toh), after the fact (L)

extempore (ehks-TEHM-poh-reh), without previous preparation (L)

extra (EHKS-trah), beyond, in addition (L)

ex voto (ehks WOH-toh), as a vow; tablet or inscription recording an accomplished vow (L)

F

facsimile (fahk-SEE-mee-leh), exact reproduction (L)

fait accompli (FEH-ta-kolaw-PLEE), thing already done (F)

falsetto (fahl-SAYT-toh), excessively high tone (It)

fandango (fahn-DAHN-goh), Spanish dance (Sp)

farina (fah-REE-nah), flour or meal (L)

fatti maschi, parole femmine (FAHT-tee MAHS-kee, pah-RAW-lay FAYM-mee-nay), deeds are masculine, words feminine (It)

faute de mieux (FOHT duh MYÖ), for lack of anything better (F)

faux pas (FOH PAH), false step, blunder (F)

feis (FAYS), Irish song festival (Ir)

femme de chambre (FAM duh SHĀH-bruh), chambermaid (F)

femme fatale (FAM fa-TAL), enchantress, "vamp" (F)

festina lente (fehs-TEE-nah LEHN-teh), make haste slowly (L)

Festschrift (FEHST-shrift), memorial or commemorative volume (G)

fiacre (FYA-kruh), cab (F)

fiancé, fiancée (fyāh-SAY), betrothed (F)

fiasco (FYAHS-koh), failure (It)

fiat (FEE-aht), administrative order without legislative authorization (L)

fiesta (FYEHS-tah), festival (Sp)

filet mignon (fee-LEH mee-NYĀW), tenderloin steak (F)

financière (fee-näh-SYEHR), spicy stew (F)

fin de siècle (FĒH duh SYEH-kluh), end of the century; decadence (F)

fine champagne (FEEN shāh-PAH-nyuh), brandy (F)

fines herbes (FEEN ZEHRB), minced chives, parsley, etc. (F)

finis (FEE-nees), end (L)

finocchio (fee-NAWK-kyoh), fennel (It)

fleur de lis (FLÖR duh LEE), lily emblem of France (F)

foie gras (FWAH GRAH), goose liver (F)

fondue (fāw-DÜ), melted cheese (F)

force majeure (FAWRS ma-ZHÖR), superior force (F)

fortissimo (fohr-TEES-see-moh), very loud (It)

foulard (foo-LAHR), neckerchief of silk fabric (F)

franc-tireur (frāh-tee-RÖR), sniper, guerrilla fighter (F)

frappé (fra-PAY), whipped, semifrozen (F)

Frau (FROW), lady, madam, Mrs. (G)

Fräulein (FROY-leyen), Miss, young lady (G)

fresco (FRAYS-koh), mural painting (It)

fricassé (free-ka-SAY), diced meat in thick sauce (F)

frijoles (free-HOH-lehs), kidney beans (Sp)

friseur (free-ZÖR), hairdresser (F)

fritos (FREE-tohs), fried potatoes, etc. (Sp)

fromage (fraw-MAZH), cheese (F)

Führer (FÜ-ruhr), leader (G)

G

gabelle (ga-BEHL), salt tax (F)

gaffe (GAF), bad blunder (F)

gala (GAH-lah), festive (It)

garbanzos (gahr-BAHN-thohs), chick-peas (Sp)

garçon (gar-SÅW), boy, waiter (F)

garni (gar-NEE), garnished (F)

gâteau (gah-TOH), cake (F)

gaucherie (gohsh-REE), awkward or tactless action (F)

gaucho (GOW-choh), South American cowboy (Sp)

gaudeamus igitur (gow-deh-AH-moos EE-ghee-toor), let us therefore rejoice (L)

Gauleiter (GOW-leye-tuhr), Nazi district leader (G)

gazpacho (gath-PAH-choh), Spanish cold soup (Sp)

gefilte fish (guh-FEEL-tuh FISH), stuffed fish (Yiddish)

geheime Staatspolizei (guh-HEYE-muh SHTATS-poh-lee-tseye), abbr. Gestapo, secret state police (G)

geisha (GAY-shah), Japanese professional girl entertainer (Jap)

Gemütlichkeit (guh-MÜT-liç-keyet), congeniality, coziness (G)

gendarme (zhāh-DARM), policeman, constable, state trooper (F)

generalissimo (jay-nay-rah-LEES-see-moh), general in chief (It)

genre (ZHÅHR), kind, sort, species (F)

Gestalt (guh-SHTAHLT), shape, form, pattern (G)

Gestapo (guh-STAH-poh), see geheime Staatspolizei

Gesundheit (guh-ZOONT-heyet), (good) health (G)

ghetto (GAYT-toh), restricted section for Jews or others (It)

gigolo (zhee-goh-LOH), man paid to be dancing partner or companion (F)

glacé (gla-SAY), iced, sugared (F)

Gleichschaltung (GLEYEÇ-shahlt-ung), coordination, assimilation (G)

glissando (glees-SAHN-doh), gliding (F-It)

Glockenspiel (GLOK-uhn-shpeel), carillon (G)

gloria in excelsis Deo (GLOH-ree-ah een ehks-KEHL-sees DEH-oh), glory to God on high (L)

gnocchi (NYAWK-kee), flour or potato small dumplings (It)

golem (GOH-lehm), robot created for an evil purpose (Heb)

goniff (GOH-nif), thief (Yiddish)

gorgonzola (gohr-gohn-TSAW-lah), Italian green mold cheese (It)

Gott mit uns! (GAWT mit OONS), God is with us! (G)

Gott sei dank! (GAWT zeye DAHNK), thanks be to God (G)

goulash (more properly *gulyás*, GOO-LYAHSH), Hungarian meat stew (Hungarian)

gourmet (goor-MEH), epicure, lover of good food (F)

goy (GOY), Gentile, non-Jewish (Heb)

Graf (GRAHF), count (G)

graffiti (grahf-FEE-tee) scratched inscriptions (It)

grande dame (GRÅHD DAHM), great lady (F)

grand prix (GRÅH PREE), first prize (F)

granita (grah-NEE-tah), ice pudding (It)

gratin (gra-TÊH), dish prepared with cheese or bread crumbs (F)

gratis (GRAH-tees), free, without charge (L)

gringo (GREEN-goh), U.S. American (Sp)

gruyère (grü-YEHR), Swiss cheese (F)

guerrilla (ghehr-REE-lyah), warfare by irregulars (Sp)

guru (GOO-roo), teacher (Hindi)

gusto (GOOS-toh), taste, enjoyment (It)

H

habeas corpus (HAH-beh-ahs KOHR-poos), you may have the body; writ to bring someone into court (L)

hacienda (ah-THYEHN-dah), plantation (Sp)

Hadassah (hah-DAHS-sah), Jewish women's organization (Heb)

hallelujah (hah-lay-LOO-yah), praise the Lord (Heb)

hanukkah (HAH-nook-kah), dedication, feast of lights (Heb)

hapax legomenon (HAH-pahks leh-GOH-meh-non), something said only once (Gk)

hara-kiri (HAH-rah-kee-ree), belly-cutting, ceremonial suicide (Jap)

haricots verts (ah-ree-KOH VEHR), green beans (F)

Hasenpfeffer (HAH-zehn-pfef-fuhr), marinated hare (G)

Hasidim (khah-SEE-deem), Jewish religious sect (Heb)

haute couture (OHT koo-TÜR), group of high class dress designers (F)

Heft (HEHFT), volume (G)

hegira (more properly *hijra*, HEEJ-rah), Mohammed's flight; escape; moving day (Arab)

Heimweh (HEYEM-vay), homesickness (G)

Heimwehr (HEYEM-vehr), home guard, militia (G)

Herrenvolk (HEHR-ren-folk), master race (G)

hetaira, **hetaera** (HEH-teye-rah), courtesan (Gk)

hiatus (hee-AH-toos), split, break in line, pause between vowels (L)

hic jacet (HEEK YAH-keht), here lies (L)

hidalgo (ee-DAHL-goh), nobleman, man of gentle birth (Sp)

hierba maté (YEHR-bah mah-TEH), Paraguayan tea (Sp)

hodie mihi, cras tibi (HOH-dee-eh MEE-hee, KRAHS TEE-bee), today to me, tomorrow to you (L)

hoi polloi (hoy pohl-LOY), the many, rabble (Gk)

homard (aw-MAHR), lobster (F)

hombre (OHM-breh), man (Sp)

homo homini lupus (HOH-moh HOH-mee-nee LOO-poos), man is a wolf to his fellow-man (L)

homo sapiens (HOH-moh SAH-pee-ehns), man as a thinking animal or as a genus (L)

honni soit qui mal y pense (aw-NEE SWAH kee MAHL ee PÅHS), evil to him who evil thinks (F)

honoris causa (hoh-NOH-rees KOW-sah), bestowed in recognition of merit (L)

horribile dictu (hohr-REE-bee-leh DEEK-too), horrible to relate (L)

hors de combat (AWR duh kōh-BAH), disabled, out of the fight (F)

hors d'oeuvres (AWR DÖ-vruh), appetizers, relishes (F)

hôtel de ville (hoh-TEHL duh VEEL), town hall (F)

houri (HOO-ree), Mohammedan nymph of paradise (Persian)

hukilau (hoo-kee-LAH-OO), feast (Hawaiian)

hula-hula (HOO-lah-HOO-lah), Hawaiian dance (Hawaiian)

humanum est errare (hoo-MAH-noom EHST ehr-RAH-reh), to err is human (L)

hybris (HOO-brees), transgression of moral law; act of defiance (Gk)

hysteron proteron (HOOS-teh-rohn PROH-teh-rohn), putting the cart before the horse (Gk)

I

ibidem (ee-BEE-dehm), abbr. ibid., in the same place (L)

idée fixe (ee-DAY FEEKS), preconceived notion (F)

id est (EED EHST), abbr. i.e., that is (L)

Iesus Nazarenus Rex Iudaeorum (YEH-soos nah-zah-REH-noos REHKS yoo-deye-OH-room), abbr. I.N.R.I., Jesus of Nazareth King of the Jews (L)

ignis fatuus (EEG-nees FAH-too-oos), will-of-the-wisp (L)

illuminati (eel-loo-mee-NAH-tee), enlightened ones, deep thinkers (L)

imbroglio (eem-BRAW-lyoh), mix-up, mess (It)

impedimenta (eem-peh-dee-MEHN-tah), baggage, hindrances (L)

imprimatur (eem-pree-MAH-toor), license to print, sanction (L)

in absentia (een ahb-SEHN-tee-ah), in one's absence (L)

in articulo mortis (een ahr-TEE-koo-loh MOHR-tees), on the point of death (L)

in camera (een KAH-meh-rah), in chambers; in private (L)

incognito (een-KAW-nyee-toh), in disguise, not revealing one's identity (It)

Japan—Ginza by night, Tokyo

incomunicado (een-koh-moo-nee-KAH-doh), cut off from communication with the outside (Sp)

index expurgatorius (EEN-dehks ehks-poor-gah-TOH-ree-oos), list of forbidden books (L)

in esse (een EHS-seh), in being, existing (L)

in extenso (een ehks-TEHN-soh), in full (L)

in extremis (een ehks-TREH-mees), on the point of death (L)

influenza (een-floo-EHN-tsah), respiratory disease, flu (It)

in folio (een FOH-lee-oh), once folded sheet of printing (L)

infra (EEN-frah), below (L)

ingénue (ĕh-zhay-NÜ), innocent feminine character (F)

in hoc signo vinces (een hohk SEEG-noh WEEN-kehs), in this sign you will conquer (L)

in loco parentis (een LOH-koh pah-REHN-tees), in the place of a parent (L)

in medias res (een MEH-dee-ahs REHS), into the thick of things, without introduction (L)

in memoriam (een meh-MOH-ree-ahm), in memory of (L)

innamorato (een-nah-moh-RAH-toh), lover (It)

innuendo (een-noo-EHN-doh), hint, insinuation (L)

in primis (een PREE-mees), among the first (L)

in quarto (een KWAHR-toh), printing sheet folded twice (L)

in re (een REH), in the matter of (L)

in rem (een REHM), proceedings against a thing rather than a person (L)

in saecula saeculorum (een SEYE-koo-lah seye-koo-LOH-room), for ever and ever (L)

insignia (een-SEEG-nee-ah), distinguishing marks (L)

insouciance (ĕh-soo-SYĂHS), indifference, studied carelessness (F)

intaglio (een-TAH-lyoh), decoration cut into a stone (It)

integer vitae scelerisque purus (EEN-teh-ghehr WEE-teye skeh-leh-REES-kweh POO-roos), upright in life and free of guilt (L)

intelligentsia (een-tehl-lee-GHEHN-tsyah), informed intellectual people collectively (R)

inter alia (EEN-tehr AH-lee-ah), among other things (L)

inter alios (EEN-tehr AH-lee-ohs), among others (L)

interim (EEN-teh-reem), meanwhile (L)

intermezzo (een-tayr-MEH-dzoh), music played during intermission (It)

inter nos (EEN-tehr NOHS), between us (L)

in toto (een TOH-toh), completely, entirely (L)

intra muros (EEN-trah MOO-rohs), within the walls (L)

in vino veritas (een WEE-noh WEH-ree-tahs), in wine is the truth (L)

ipse dixit (EEP-seh DEEK-seet), he himself said it; the master has spoken (L)

ipso facto (EEP-soh FAHK-toh), by the very fact (L)

item (EE-tehm), likewise (L)

ite, missa est (EE-teh, MEES-sah EHST), go, the service is finished (L) *izvestiya* (eez-VYEHS-tee-yuh), news, information (R)

J

jai-alai (HAH-ee ah-LAH-ee), Basque ball game (Basque)

jardinière (zhar-dee-NYEHR), mixed vegetables; ornamental flower pot (F)

je ne sais quoi (zhuh nuh SEH KWAH), I don't know what (F)

jeu d'esprit (ZHÖ dehs-PREE), witticism (F)

jeunesse dorée (zhö-NEHS daw-RAY), gilded youth, elegant young people (F)

jihad (JEE-hahd), holy war (Arab)

jinni (JEEN-nee), supernatural being that can take human shape (Arab)

jinrickisha (JEEN-REEK-shah), mandrawn two-wheeled cab (Jap)

jodhpur (JOHD-poor), a kind of riding breeches (Hind)

joie de vivre (ZHWAH duh VEE-vruh), joy of being alive (F)

jongleur (zhaw-GLÖR), minstrel, juggler (F)

judo (JOO-doh), Japanese system of wrestling (Jap)

jujutsu (JOO JOO-tsoo), see judo (Jap)

junta (HOON-tah), administrative council or committee (Sp)

Jupiter Pluvius (YOO-pee-tehr PLOO-wee-oos), Jupiter of the rain (L)

jus gentium (YOOS GHEHN-tee-oom), law of nations, international law (L)

K

ka (KAH), the soul (Egypt)

kabuki (KAH-boo-kee), Japanese form of drama (Jap)

Kaddish (KAHD-deesh), prayer for the dead (Heb)

Kaffeeklatsch (kahf-FAY-klahtch), gathering for coffee and chatting (G)

kamikaze (KAH-mee-kah-zeh), divine wind; suicide dive bomber (Jap)

Kapellmeister (kah-PEHL-MEYE-stuhr), orchestra or chorus leader (G)

kaput (kah-POOT), finished, done for (G)

Katzenjammer (KAHT-suhn-yahm-muhr), hangover (G)

kibbutz (keeb-BOOTS), Israeli collective farm settlement (Heb)

kibitzer (KIB-its-uhr), onlooker at game, offering unwanted advice; meddler (Yid)

kimono (KEE-moh-noh), Japanese outer garment with sash and loose sleeves (Jap)

Kirschwasser (KEERSH-VAHS-suhr), cherry brandy (G)

Kismet (KEES-meht), fate, lot, will of Allah (Turk)

Knesset (KNEHS-seht), unicameral Israeli parliament (Heb)

koine (koy-NAY), language common to a large area (Gk)

koinos topos (koy-NOHS toh-POHS), commonplace (Gk)

kolkhoz (kuhl-KHAWS), collective farm (R)

Kol Nidre (KOHL NEE-dray), all vows; prayer of atonement; melody to which prayer is sung (Heb)

Kommandatura (kohm-mahn-dah-TOO-rah), command headquarters (G)

Komsomol (KOHM-suh-muhl), Communist youth organization (R)

Konzertmeister (kohn-TSEHRT-MEYE-stuhr), chief violinist of orchestra (G)

kopek (more properly *kopeika*, kuh-PYEY-kuh), small Russian coin (R)

kraal (KRAHL), South African village or enclosure (Du, from Pt *curral*)

Krasnaya Zvezda (KRAHS-nuh-yuh zviz-DAH), Red Star, Soviet Army organ (R)

Kremlin (more properly *kreml'*, KRYEHML'), citadel of Moscow, seat of government (R)

Kriegspiel (KREEK-shpeel), war game (G)

kulak (koo-LAHK), fist, tight-wad, well-to-do peasant (R)

Kultur (kool-TOOR), civilization, culture German style (G)

Kulturkampf (kool-TOOR-KAHMPF), Prussia's struggle to dominate Catholic Church (G)

kummerbund (KUM-muhr-buhnd), man's sash for waist (Pers)

Kuomintang (GWOH-meen-tahng), national people's party (Ch)

L

la belle dame sans merci (la BEHL DAM SÄH mehr-SEE), the beautiful lady without mercy (F)

labor omnia vincit (LAH-bohr OHM-nee-ah WEEN-keet), labor overcomes everything (L)

lagniappe (la-NYAP), small present to purchaser with purchase (F from Sp from Quechua)

laissez faire (leh-SAY FEHR), let things alone, noninterference (F)

Landwehr (LAHNT-vehr), home guard, militia (G)

lapsus calami (LAHP-soos KAH-lah-mee), slip of the pen (L)

lapsus linguae (LAHP-soos LEEN-gweye), slip of the tongue (L)

largo (LAHR-goh), broad, slow tempo (It)

lasagne (lah-SAH-nyay), broad, flat macaroni (It)

laudator temporis acti (low-DAH-tohr TEHM-poh-rees AHK-tee), one who praises the good old days (L)

lb. (abbr. for *libra*, LEE-brah), pound (L)

Leben Sie wohl (LAY-buhn ZEE VOHL), good-bye, be well (G)

Lebensraum (LAY-buhns-rowm), living space (G)

legato (lay-GAH-toh), bound, with no pause between notes (It)

Légion d'Honneur (lay-ZHÄW daw-NÖR), military and civil order (F)

lei (LAY), wreath of flowers worn around the neck (Hawaiian)

leitmotiv (LEYET-moh-teef), guiding theme (G)

lento (LEHN-toh), slow tempo (It)

lèse-majesté (LEHZ-ma-zhehs-TAY), treason, offense against ruler (F)

l'état, c'est moi! (lay-TAH seh MWAH), *I* am the state! (F)

liaison (lyeh-ZÅW), linking, connection (F)

libido (lee-BEE-doh), psychic drive associated with the sexual instinct (L)

Liederkranz (LEE-duhr-krahnts), singing society; type of cheese (G)

Limburger (LEEM-boor-guhr), type of cheese (G)

lingerie (lĕh-zhuh-REE), women's underwear (F)

lingua franca (LEEN-gwah FRAHN-kah), international or common language in multilingual area (L or It)

lira (LEE-rah), Italian unit of currency (It)

literati (lee-teh-RAH-tee), educated or cultured people, literary men (L)

loggia (LAWJ-jah), portico projecting from a building (It)

logos (LOH-gohs), word (Gk)

luau (loo-AH-oo), Hawaiian banquet (Hawaiian)

Luftwaffe (LOOFT-vahf-fuh), German air force (G)

lycée (lee-SAY), high school (F)

M

macabre (ma-KAH-bruh), gruesome (F)

macédoine (ma-say-DWAHN), mixture of fruits or vegetables (F)

mademoiselle (mad-mwah-ZEHL), young lady, Miss (F)

Madonna (mah-DAWN-nah), my Lady; the Virgin Mary (It)

maestoso (mah-ays-TOH-soh), majestic (It)

maestro (mah-AYS-troh), master, teacher (It)

Mafia (MAH-fyah), Sicilian secret organization (It)

Magna Charta (MAHG-nah KAHR-tah), Great Charter; English Bill of Rights (L)

magna cum laude (MAHG-nah koom LOW-deh), with great praise or distinction (L)

magnifico (mah-NYEE-fee-koh), magnificent; great man (It)

magnum bonum (MAHG-noom BOH-noom), great good; great benefit (L)

magnum opus (MAHG-noom OH-poos), great work, masterpiece (L)

maharajah (mah-hah-RAH-jah), great king (Hind)

maharani (mah-hah-RAH-nee), great queen (Hind)

Mahatma (mah-HAHT-mah), great soul, teacher (Sk)

mais où sont les neiges d'antan? (MEH-ZOO sãw lay NEHZH dãh-TÃH), but where are the snows of yesteryear? (F)

maître d'hôtel (MEH-truh doh-TEHL), head steward, head butler (F)

major domo (MAH-yohr DOH-moh), chief steward, head servant (L)

maladroit (ma-la-DRWAH), awkward, tactless (F)

malaria (mah-LAH-ryah), illness transmitted by mosquito bite (It)

mal de mer (MAL duh MEHR), seasickness (F)

malentendu (ma-lãh-tãh-DÜ), misunderstanding (F)

malgré lui (mal-GRAY LWEE), in spite of himself (F)

mañana (mah-NYAH-nah), tomorrow (Sp)

mandamus (mahn-DAH-moos), we order; legal writ (L)

manicotti (mah-nee-KAWT-tee), stuffed pasta rolls (It)

manifesto (mah-nee-FEHS-toh), declaration (It)

maquis (ma-KEE), French freedom fighters (F)

maraca (mah-RAH-kah), gourd used as musical instrument (Sp)

mardi gras (mar-DEE GRAH), Shrove Tuesday (F)

mare nostrum (MAH-reh NOHS-troom), our sea (L)

mariage de convenance (ma-RYAZH duh kãw-vuh-NÃHS), marriage of convenience (F)

marimba (mah-REEM-bah), wooden xylophone (Sp)

marina (mah-REE-nah), settled and landscaped seashore (It)

marrons glacés (ma-RÔH gla-SAY), candied chestnuts (F)

Marsala (mahr-SAH-lah), Sicilian sweet wine (It)

masseur, masseuse (ma-SÖR, ma-SÖZ), male, female massage expert (F)

matador (mah-tah-DOHR), bullfighter who kills bull with sword (Sp)

maté (mah-TEH), see hierba maté

materia medica (mah-TEH-ree-ah MEH-dee-kah), drugs, pharmacology (L)

matsoth (MAH-tsoth), Passover unleavened bread (Heb)

maxixe (mah-SHEE-shuh), Brazilian dance (Pt)

mazuma (mah-ZOO-mah), money (Yid)

mazurka (mah-ZOOR-kah), Polish dance (Pol)

mazzeltov (MAH-zuhl-tohv), good luck (Heb)

mea (maxima) culpa (MEH-ah MAHK-see-mah KOOL-pah), my (greatest) fault (L)

Meerschaum (MEHR-showm), mineral substance for making smoking pipes (G)

Mein Kampf (meyen KAHMPF), my battle, my struggle (G)

Meistersinger (MEYE-stuhr SING-uhr), master singer (G)

mélange (may-LÃHZH), mixture (F)

mêlée (meh-LAY), mix-up, fight, brawl (F)

memorabilia (meh-moh-rah-BEE-lee-ah), things worth remembering (L)

memorandum (meh-moh-RAHN-doom), something to be remembered, a note to that effect (L)

ménage (may-NAHZH), household (F)

Menorah (meh-NOH-rah), Jewish seven-candle candelabrum (Heb) *mens sana in corpore sano* (MEHNS SAH-nah een KOHR-poh-reh SAH-noh), a sound mind in a sound body (L)

menu (muh-NÜ), bill of fare (F)

meringue (muh-RĔHG), beaten and baked egg whites (F)

mesa (MEH-sah), tableland, plateau (Sp)

mésalliance (may-za-lee-ĂHS), marriage with a person of inferior social position (F)

mestizo (mehs-TEE-thŏh), half-breed (Sp)

métier (may-TYAY), trade, craft (F)

Métro (may-TROH), Paris subway (F)

mezzo (MEH-dzoh), half (It)

midi (mee-DEE), south (F)

migraine (mee-GREHN), headache (F)

miles gloriosus (MEE-lehs gloh-ree-OH-soos), braggart, swaggerer (L)

minestrone (mee-nehs-TROH-nay), vegetable soup (It)

mirabile dictu (mee-RAH-bee-leh DEEK-too), wonderful to relate (L)

mirabile visu (mee-RAH-bee-leh WEE-soo), wonderful to see (L)

mirabilia (mee-rah-BEE-lee-ah), wonderful things (L)

mise en scène (MEE-zăh-SEHN), stage setting (F)

miserere (mee-seh-REH-reh), have mercy (L)

modicum (MOH-dee-koom), proper or small measure (L)

modus operandi (MOH-doos oh-peh-RAHN-dee), way of working (L)

modus vivendi (MOH-doos wee-WEHN-dee), way of living (together) (L)

mores (MOH-rehs), customs, folkways, conventions (L)

mot juste (MOH ZHÜST), the right word for the occasion (F)

moue (MOO), pout, grimace (F)

mousse (MOOS), frozen whipped dessert (F)

Moyen Age (mwa-YĔH-NAHZH), Middle Ages (F)

mufti (MOOF-tee), civilian judge; civilian garb (Arab)

mutatis mutandis (moo-TAH-tees moo-TAHN-dees), with the appropriate changes (L)

muzhik (moo-ZHEEK), Russian peasant (R)

N

naive (na-EEV), innocent, guileless (F)

naiveté (na-eev-TAY), innocence, guilelessness (F)

née (NAY), born; having as a maiden name (F)

négligée (nay-glee-ZHAY), loose indoor robe for women (F)

ne plus ultra (neh PLOOS OOL-trah), no further (L)

nihil obstat (NEE-heel OHB-staht), there is no impediment (L)

nil admirari (NEEL ahd-mee-RAH-ree), be surprised at nothing (L)

nil desperandum (NEEL dehs-peh-RAHN-doom), never despair (L)

n'importe (nĕh-PAWRT), it doesn't matter (F)

Nirvana (neer-VAH-nah), extinction; oblivion; Buddhist paradise (Sk)

Nisei (NEE-say), second-generation Japanese-Americans (Jap)

nisi (NEE-see), unless (L)

noblesse oblige (naw-BLEHS aw-BLEEZH), high rank involves responsiblitity (F)

Noël (naw-EHL), Christmas (F)

nolle prosequi (NOHL-leh PRŎH-seh-kwee), I will prosecute no further (L)

nolo contendere (NOH-loh kohn-TEHN-deh-reh), no contest (L)

nom de guerre (NŎH duh GHEHR), pseudonym (F)

nom de plume (NŎH duh PLÜM), pen name (F)

non compos mentis (nohn KOHM-pohs MEHN-tees), insane, not sound in mind (L)

non sequitur (nohn SEH-kwee-toor), it does not follow; logical inconsistency (L)

nota bene (NOH-tah BEH-neh; abbr. n.b.), note well (L)

note verbale (NAWT vehr-BAHL), verbal communication on diplomatic matter (F)

novella (noh-VEHL-lah), short story (It)

nuance (nü-ĂHS), shade, delicate degree of difference (F)

nuncio (NOON-chyoh), Papal envoy (It)

O

obbligato (ohb-blee-GAH-toh), solo passage, not to be omitted (It)

obit (OH-beet), he died (L)

obiter dictum (OH-bee-tehr DEEK-toom), spoken incidentally (L)

objet d'art (awb-ZHEH DHAR), object of art (F)

odium (OH-dee-oom), hatred; blame (L)

olla podrida (OH-lyah poh-DREE-dah), stew, hodgepodge (Sp)

omnia mutantur, nos et mutamur in illis (OHM-nee-ah moo-TAHN-toor NOHS eht moo-TAH-moor een EEL-lees), all things change, and we change with them (L)

omnia vanitas (OHM-nee-ah WAH-nee-tahs), all is vanity (L)

omnia vincit amor (OHM-nee-ah WEEN-keet AH-mohr), love overcomes everything (L)

omnium gatherum (OHM-nee-oom-GA-ther-um), miscellaneous collection (L and mock L)

onus probandi (OH-noos proh-BAHN-dee), the burden of proof (L)

opera (OH-peh-rah), works (L); musical drama (It)

opéra bouffe (oh-pay-RAH BOOF), comic opera, musical comedy (F)

opera omnia (OH-peh-rah OHM-nee-ah), all the works (L)

operetta (oh-pay-RAYT-tah), light opera, musical comedy (It)

opus (OH-poos), work (L)

opus citatum (OH-poos kee-TAH-toom), abbr. op. cit.; the work previously cited (L)

ora et labora (OH-rah eht lah-BOH-rah), pray and work (L)

ora pro nobis (OH-rah proh NOH-bees), pray for us (L)

oratorio (Oh-rah-TAW-ryoh), musical drama on sacred topic (It)

osso buco (AWS-soh BOO-koh), marrow bone of veal (It)

o tempora! o mores! (OH TEHM-poh-rah OH MOH-rehs), O, times and customs! (L)

outré (oo-TRAY), extreme, excessive (F)

oyer and terminer (oh-YEHR tehr-mee-NEHR), higher criminal court (Old F)

oyez (oh-YEHTS), hear ye! (Old F)

P

paella (pah-EH-lyah), South Spanish dish of rice and meat or fish (Sp)

palette (pa-LEHT), artist's color-mixing board (F)

palio (PAH-lyoh), Siena horse-race (It)

pampa (PAHM-pah), grassy plain in Argentina (Sp, from Quechua)

panache (pa-NASH), plume (F)

panem et circenses (PAH-nehm eht keer-KEHN-sehs), bread and games (L)

Panzer (PAHN-tsuhr), armored car, tank (G)

papier-mâché (pa-PYAY-mah-SHAY), paper pulp, cardboard (F)

par excellence (pa-rehk-seh-LÄHS), to a superlative degree (F)

parfait (par-FEH), ice cream with syrup or fudge (F)

pariah (PAH-ree-ah), outcast, rejected (Tamil)

pari passu (PAH-ree PAHS-soo), side by side, evenly (L)

parmigiana (pahr-mee-JAH-nah), Parma style, with melted cheese and tomato (It)

parmigiano (pahr-mee-JAH-noh), Parma cheese, usually for grating (It)

parti pris (par-TEE PREE), preconceived idea (F)

paso doble (PAH-soh DOH-bleh), two-step; Spanish dance (Sp)

passacaglia (pahs-sah-KAH-lyah), slow Italian dance or music (It)

passim (PAHS-seem), abbr. pass.; scattered everywhere (L)

pasta (PAHS-tah), dough; any macaroni product (It)

pâté (pah-TAY), paste (F);—*de foie gras* (duh FWAH GRAH), goose-liver paste

pater familias (pah-tehr-fah-MEE-lee-ahs), head of family (L)

Pater Noster (PAH-tehr NOHS-tehr), Our Father, Lord's Prayer (L)

pater patriae (PAH-tehr PAH-tree-eye), father of his country (L)

patio (PAH-tyoh), courtyard, inner courtyard (Sp)

pâtisserie (pah-tees-REE), pastry (F)

patois (pa-TWAH), local dialect (F)

Italy—Amphitheatre, Pompeii

pax romana (PAHKS roh-MAH-nah), Roman peace, enforced peace (L)

pax vobiscum (PAHKS woh-BEES-koom), peace be with you (L)

peineta (pay-NEH-tah), tall comb (Sp)

penchant (päh-SHÄH), leaning, inclination (F)

per annum (pehr AHN-noom), by the year (L)

per capita (pehr KAH-pee-teh), by the head, apiece (L)

per diem (pehr DEE-ehm), by the day (L)

per se (pehr SEH), in itself, inherently (L)

persona non grata (pehr-SOH-nah nohn GRAH-tah), not acceptable diplomatic representative (L)

Pesach (PAY-sakh), Passover (Heb)

peseta (peh-SEH-tah), Spanish coin (Sp)

peso (PEH-soh), Latin American unit of currency (Sp)

petit bourgeois (puh-TEE boor-ZHWAH), lower middle class (F)

petite (puh-TEET), small, trim in figure (F)

petitio principii (peh-TEE-tee-oh preen-KEE-pee-ee), begging the question (L)

petits fours (puh-TEE FOOR), little sponge or pound cakes (F)

petits pois (puh-TEE PWAH), green peas (F)

phobia (FOH-bee-ah), fear, hatred (Gk)

pianissimo (pyah-NEES-see-moh), very softly (It)

piano (PYAH-noh), softly (It)

pibroch (PEE-brokh), bagpipe (Gaelic)

picador (pee-kah-DOHR), mounted bullfighter with lance (Sp)

piccolo (PEEK-koh-loh), small flute (It)

pièce de résistance (PYEHS duh ray-zees-TÄHS), main course (F)

pilaf (pee-LOW), Oriental rice dish (Persian)

piroshki (pee-RAWSH-kee), stuffed puffcakes (R)

pirouette (pee-roo-EHT), spin on one foot or in air (F)

più (PYOO), more (It)

pizza (PEE-tsah), pie, pancake (It)

pizzicato (pee-tsee-KAH-toh), plucking the strings of a musical instrument (It)

placebo (plah-KEH-boh), pacifier, medicine of no efficacy (L)

plaza de toros (PLAH-thah deh TOH-rohs), bullring (Sp)

plus ça change, plus c'est la même chose (PLÜ sa SHÄHZH PLÜ seh la mehm SHOHZ), the more it changes, the more it's the same thing (F)

pogrom (puh-GRAWM), devastation, massacre (R)

point d'appui (PWĚH da-PWEE), fulcrum, support point (F)

polenta (poh-LEHN-tah), thick gruel of corn, chestnuts, etc. (It)

polka (POHL-kah), fast Slavic dance (Czech)

pollice verso (POHL-lee-keh WEHR-soh), thumbs down (L)

Poltergeist (POHL-tuhr-geyest), racketing or prank-playing ghost (G)

pommes frites (PAWM FREET), fried potatoes (F)

poncho (POHN-choh), blanket with opening for head (Sp)

pons asinorum (POHNS ah-see-NOH-room), bridge of donkeys; hard problem for beginners (L)

portico (PAWR-tee-koh), covered gallery open on one side (It)

portmanteau (PAWRT-mäh-TOH), traveling bag (F)

posada (poh-SAH-dah), inn (Sp)

posse (comitatus) (POHS-seh koh-mee-TAH-toos), force of a county, sheriff and assistants (L)

post bellum (pohst BEHL-loom), after-war (L)

post hoc, ergo propter hoc (pohst HOHK EHR-goh PROHP-tehr HOHK), after, therefore in consequence of something else (L)

post meridiem (pohst meh-REE-dee-ehm), abbr. p.m., P.M.; after noon (L)

post-mortem (pohst MOHR-tehm), after death, autopsy (L)

post scriptum (pohst SKREEP-toom), abbr. P.S.; written after main letter (L)

potage (paw-TAHZH), soup (F)

potpourri (poh-poo-REE), mixture, medley (F)

pourparler (poor-par-LAY), talk, negotiations (F)

pravda (PRAHV-duh), truth (R)

préciosité (pray-syoh-zee-TAY), excessive refinement (F)

première (pruh-MYEHR), first showing (F)

première danseuse (pruh-MYEHR däh-SÖZ), first female dancer (F)

prestissimo (prays-TEES-see-moh), very fast (It)

prima donna (PREE-mah DAWN-nah), female opera star; anyone who wants to be first (It)

prima facie (PREE-mah FAH-kee-eh), at first glance, on the face of it (L)

primus inter pares (PREE-moos EEN-tehr PAH-rehs), first among equals (L)

prix fixe (PREE FEEKS), fixed price (F)

pro bono publico (proh BOH-noh POO-blee-koh), for the public good (L)

.**pro et con(tra)** (PROH eht KOHN-trah), for and against (L)

profanum vulgus (proh-FAH-noom WOOL-goos), the fickle crowd (L)

pro forma (proh FOHR-mah), as a matter of form (L)

propaganda (proh-pah-GAHN-dah), that which is to be spread (L)

pro rata (proh RAH-tah), in proportion, in accordance with fixed rate (L)

prosciutto (proh-SHOOT-toh), salted Italian-style ham (It)

prosit (PROH-seet), to your health or success (L)

protégé (praw-tay-ZHAY), one taken under another's sheltering wing (F)

pro tempore (proh TEHM-poh-reh), abbr. pro tem; temporarily (L)

provolone (proh-voh-LOH-nay), spicy Italian cheese (It)

puchero (poo-CHEH-roh), South American stew (Sp)

pudenda (poo-DEHN-dah), genital organs (L)

pueblo (PWEH-bloh), village, town (Sp)

puissance (pwee-SÄHS), power (F)

pulque (POOL-kah), alcoholic beverage of Mexico (Sp from Nahuatl)

pundit (PUN-deet), man of learning (Hind)

purdah (PUR-dah), veil, feminine seclusion (Hind)

purée (pü-RAY), thick cream soup (F)

Purim (POO-reem), Jewish feast of deliverance (Heb)

Putsch (POOCH), abortive revolutionary attempt (G)

Q

qua (KWAH), considered as, in the capacity of (L)

quantum (KWAHN-toom), how great, how much (L)

quasi (KWAH-see), as if, as though (L)

que será será (KEH seh-RAH seh-RAH), what will be will be (Sp)

quidnunc (KWEED-nunk), what now, gossip, newsmonger (L)

quid pro quo (KWEED proh KWOH), something in return for something else (L)

¿**quién sabe?** (KYEHN SAH-veh), who knows? (Sp)

qui s'excuse s'accuse (KEE sehks-KÜZ sa-KÜZ), he who excuses himself accuses himself (F)

qui vive (KEE VEEV), on the alert, watchful (F)

qui va là? (KEE va LA), who goes there? (F)

quod erat demonstrandum (KWOHD EH-raht deh-mohn-STRAHN-doom), which was to be proved (L)

quod vide (KWOHD WEE-deh); abbr. q.v.; which see (L)

quondam (KWOHN-dahm), former, formerly (L)

quorum (KWOH-room), majority of legislative body for voting purposes (L)

quot homines, tot sententiae (KWOHT HOH-mee-nehs TOHT sehn-TEHN-tee-eye), as many opinions as there are people (L)

quo vadis? (KWOH WAH-dees), where are you going? (L)

R

ragout (ra-GOO), spicy stew (F)

raison d'état (reh-ZÖH day-TAH), reason of state (F)

raison d'être (reh-ZÖH DEH-truh), reason for existing (F)

rajah (RAH-jah), king, ruler (Sk)

rallentando (rahl-layn-TAHN-doh), slowing up (It)

rani (RAH-nee), queen (Sk)

rapprochement (ra-prawsh-MÄH), reestablishing of friendly relations (F)

rara avis (RAH-rah AH-wees), rare bird (L)

Rathskeller (RAHTS-KEHL-luhr), basement restaurant and bar (G)

ravioli (rah-VYAW-lee), dumplings stuffed with meat or cheese (It)

re (REH), in the matter of (L)

realia (reh-AH-lee-ah), materials for teaching foreign cultures (L)

Reconquista (reh-kohn-KEES-tah), reconquest of Spain from the Moors (Sp)

recto (REKH-toh), on the right-hand page (L)

regata (ray-GAH-tah), Venetian gondola race (It)

Reich (REYEÇ), German state; empire (G)

Reichstag (REYEKS-tahk), German Parliament (G)

rendezvous (räh-day-VOO), appointment, assignation (F)

répondez s'il vous plait (ray-pöh-DAY seel voo PLEH), abbr. R.S.V.P.; please reply (F)

requiem (REH-kwee-ehm), rest; prayer for dead (L)

requiescat in pace (reh-kwee-EHS-kaht een PAH-keh), abbr. r.i.p.; may he rest in peace (L)

residuum (reh-SEE-doo-oom), remnant, residue (L)

résumé (ray-zü-MAY), summary (F)

ricksha (REEK-shaw), see jinrickisha

ricochet (ree-kaw-SHEH), bounce, rebound (F)

ricotta (ree-KAWT-tah), soft white Italian cheese (It)

rigor mortis (REE-gohr MOHR-tees), stiffness of death (L)

Rinascimento (ree-nah-shee-MAYN-toh), rebirth (It)

ris de veau (REE duh VOH), sweetbreads (F)

Risorgimento (ree-sohr-jee-MAYN-toh), Italian movement for unity (It)

risotto (ree-SAWT-toh), Italian rice dish (It)

rissolé (ree-saw-LAY), golden brown (F)

ritardando (ree-tahr-DAHN-doh), slowing up (It)

robot (ROH-boht), automaton trained to do man's work (Czech)

rodeo (roh-DEH-oh), roundup (Sp)

Roma caput mundi (ROH-mah KAH-poot MOON-dee), Rome, head of the world (L)

Rosh Hashanah (ROHSH hah-shah-NAH), head of year, New Year's Day (Heb)

rota (ROH-tah), wheel, Papal court (L)

rôti (roh-TEE), roast (F)

rôtisserie (roh-tees-REE), grill restaurant (F)

rotunda (roh-TOON-dah), circular building with dome (L)

roulette (roo-LEHT), gambling wheel (F)

rubaiyat (ROO-beye-yaht), quatrains, poems (Arab)

Rucksack (RUK-zahk), knapsack (G)

rupee (ROO-pee) Indian currency (Hind)

S

sabotage (sa-baw-TAHZH), intentional damage to arrest production (F)

sabra (SAH-brah), native Israeli (Heb)

sachet (sa-SHEH), small bag of perfume (F)

safari (sah-FAH-ree), hunting trip in Africa (Arab)

sahib (SAH-heeb), sir, master, title of respect (Arab)

salaam (sah-LAHM), peace, form of greeting (Arab)

salame (sah-LAH-meh), spiced sausage (It)

salmagundi (sal-ma-GOON-dee), spicy mixture (doubtful origin)

salon (sa-LAW), drawing room, exhibition room (F)

salus populi suprema lex (SAH-loos POH-poo-lee soo-PREH-mah LEHKS), the welfare of the people is the supreme law (L)

salve (SAHL-weh), hail (L)

samba (SAHM-bah), Brazilian dance (Pt. from Am. Indian)

samovar (suh-muh-VAHR), Russian tea urn (R)

samurai (SAH-moo-reye), Japanese feudal nobleman (Jap)

sanctum sanctorum (SAHNK-toom sahnk-TOH-room), holy of holies (L)

sangfroid (säh-FRWAH), coolness in the face of danger (F)

Yugoslavia—Dubrovnik

sans façon (sãh fa-SAW), unceremoniously (F)

sans gêne (sãh ZHEHN), without embarrassment, nervy (F)

sans souci (sãh soo-SEE)ꞏ carefree, free from worry (F)

sarape (sah-RAH-peh), Mexican blanket (Sp)

sari (SAH-ree), Hindu female costume (Hindi)

sartor resartus (SAHR-tohr reh-SAHR-toos), tailor retailored, tit for tat (L)

Saturnalia (sah-toor-NAH-lee-ah), Roman December festival (L)

Sauerbraten (ZOW-uhr-BRAH-tuhn), marinated roast (G)

Sauerkraut (ZOW-uhr-krowt), pickled cabbage (G)

sauté (soh-TAY), fried in small amount of fat (F)

sauve qui peut (SOHV kee PO), every man for himself (F)

savoir faire (sa-VWAHR FEHR), tact, ability to do the right thing (F)

savoir vivre (sa-VWAHR VEE-vruh), knowledge of how to behave and get along (F)

sayonara (SAH-yoh-nah-rah), good-bye (Jap)

scherzo (SKAYR-tsoh), lively, jesting musical composition (It)

schlemiel (shluh-MEEL), easy mark, dumbbell (Yid)

Schmalz (SHMAHLTS), fat; silly sentimentality (G)

Schnapps (SHNAHPS), brandy, whiskey (G)

Schnitzel (SHNIT-suhl), cutlet (G)

schnorrer (SHNOHR-ruhr), beggar (Yid)

Schrecklichkeit (SHREHK-liç-keyet), frightfulness, policy of deliberate atrocity (G)

scilicet (SKEE-lee-keht), that is to say, to wit (L)

séance (say-ÃHS), session, sitting (F)

sec (SEHK), dry (F)

Sehnsucht (ZEHN-zookht), longing, nostalgic feeling (G)

semper fidelis (SEHM-pehr fee-DEH-lees), forever faithful (L)

semper paratus (SEHM-pehr pah-RAH-toos), ever ready (L)

senatus populusque romanus (seh-NAH-toos poh-poo-LOOS-kweh roh-MAH-noos), abbr. S.P.Q.R., the Roman Senate and people (L)

se non è vero, è ben trovato (say nohn eh VAY-roh, eh behn troh-VAH-toh), if it isn't true, it's a good lie (It)

sforzando (sfohr-TSAHN-doh), with force or vigor (It)

shah (SHAH), king of Persia (Persian)

shalom (shah-LOHM), peace, form of Hebrew or Israeli greeting (Heb)

shashlik (SHAHSH-leek), meat on skewer (R)

sheikh (SHEYEKH), old man, religious leader (Arab)

shekel (SHEH-ķehl), unit of weight or money (Heb)

shillalagh (shil-LAY-lee), cudgel (Irish)

Shinto (SHEEN-toh), way of the gods; Japanese religion (Jap)

shish kebab (SHEESH keh-BAHB), lamb on skewer (Turk)

sic (SEEK), thus, precisely as it appears (L)

sic semper tyrannis (SEEK SEHM-pehr tee-RAHN-nees), may it always go thus with tyrants (L)

sic transit gloria mundi (SEEK TRAHN-seet GLOH-ree-ah MOON-dee), thus passes away the world's glory (L)

Siglo de Oro (SEE-gloh deh OH-roh), golden century (Sp)

s'il vous plait (seel voo PLEH), please (F)

similia similibus curantur (see-MEE-lee-ah see-MEE-lee-boos koo-RAHN-toor), like is cured with like (L)

sine die (SEE-neh DEE-eh), without assigning a day (L)

sine qua non (SEE-neh KWAH NOHN), indispensable requisite or condition (L)

Sinn Fein (SHIN FAYN), we ourselves; Irish revolutionary movement (Irish)

si vis pacem, para bellum (see wees PAH-khem, PAH-rah BEHL-loom), if you want peace, prepare for war (L)

skoal (SKOHL), to your health (Norw)

slalom (SLAH-lum), downhill skiing race (Norw)

smörgasbord (SMOR-gus-boord), table of appetizers and other foods (Swed)

soi-disant (swah-dee-ZÃH), self-styled (F)

soirée (swah-RAY), evening gathering (F)

solfeggio (sohl-FAY-joh), singing by notes (It)

solitaire (saw-lee-TEHR), alone, single (F)

solo (SOH-loh), alone, musical piece for one person (It)

sombrero (sohm-BREH-roh), hat (Sp)

sotto voce (SOHT-toh VOH-chay), in an undertone (It)

soubriquet (soo-bree-KEH), nickname (F)

soufflé (soo-FLAY), puffed up, baked custard (F)

soupçon (soop-SAW), suspicion, dash, trace (F)

soviet (suh-VYEHT), council of delegates (R)

spa (SPAH), watering place (Belgian place name)

spoor (SPOHR), track of animal (Du)

Sprachgefühl (SHPRAHKH-guh-FUL), feeling for language (G)

spumone (spoo-MOH-nay), Italian ice cream (It)

sputnik (SPOOT-neek), co-traveler, space satellite (R)

staccato (stahk-KAH-toh), having short notes (It)

Stakhanovite (stuh-KHAHN-uhv), champion speed worker in USSR (R)

stanza (STAHN-tsah) room; subdivision of poem (It)

status quo (STAH-toos KWOH), existing or previously existing state of affairs (L)

stet (STEHT), let it stand; disregard correction (L)

Strudel (SHTROO-duhl), type of cake (G)

stucco (STOOK-koh), mixture of lime and pulverized stone (It)

Stück (SHTUK), piece; selection (G)

studio (STOO-dyoh), study; place for studying or working (It)

Sturm und Drang (SHTOORM oont DRAHNG), storm and stress (G)

sub judice (soob YOO-dee-keh), not yet decided (L)

Ireland—Ashford Castle, County Mayo

subpoena (soob-POY-nah), under penalty; required appearance in court (L)

sub rosa (soob ROH-sah), under cover; in secret (L)

succès d'estime (sük-SEH dehs-TEEM), favored by critics and experts, but not by mass (F)

sui generis (SOO-ee GEH-neh-rees), in a class by itself; unique (L)

sukiyaki (SKEE-yah-kee), Japanese dish of meat and vegetables (Jap)

summa cum laude (SOOM-mah koom LOW-deh), with the highest praise (L)

summum bonum (SOOM-moom BOH-noom), the supreme good (L)

suo nomine (SOO-oh NOH-mee-neh), in his own name (L)

sûreté (sür-TAY), security; French security police (F)

suum cuique (SOO-oom kwoo-EE-kweh), to each his own (L)

svaraj (SVAH-rahj), self-rule, independence (Sk)

T

table d'hôte (TA-bluh DOHT), regular menu, no choice (F)

tabula rasa (TAH-boo-lah RAH-sah), clean slate (L)

tamale (tah-MAH-leh), Mexican dish of corn, meat, and red pepper (Sp)

tant mieux (pis) (TÄH MYÖ PEE), so much the better (worse) (F)

tarantella (tah-rahn-TEHL-lah), swift Italian dance (It)

Te Deum Laudamus (TEH DEH-oom low-DAH-moos), hymn of thanksgiving (L)

tempo (TEHM-poh), time, rate, rhythm, beat (It)

tempus fugit (TEHM-poos FOO-gheet), time is fleeting (L)

terminus (a quo, ad quem) (TEHR-mee-noos ah KWOH, ahd KWEHM), limit or boundary from which or to which (L)

terra cotta (TEHR-rah KAWT-tah), baked clay, earthenware (It)

terra firma (TEHR-rah FEER-mah), solid ground, mainland (L)

terra incognita (TEHR-rah een-KOHG-nee-tah), unknown land (L)

tertium quid (TEHR-tee-oom KWEED), a third factor (L)

tête-à-tête (TEH-ta-TEHT), face to face; intimate conversation (F)

thé dansant (TAY däh-SÄH), afternoon tea and dance (F)

thesaurus (teh-SOW-roos), treasure trove; idea dictionary (L)

timbale, timballo (teh-BAL, teem-BAHL-loh), baked in a mold (F, It)

timeo Danaos et dona ferentes (TEE-meh-oh dah-NAH-ohs eht DOH-nah feh-REHN-tehs), I fear the Greeks even when they bear gifts (L)

toga (TOH-gah), loose, flowing robe of Romans (L)

toreador, torero (toh-reh-ah-DOHR, toh-REH-roh), bullfighter (Sp)

torso (TOHR-soh), upper part of body without head (It)

Totentanz (TOH-tuhn-tahnts), dance of death (G)

touché (too-SHAY), touched; remark that strikes home (F)

toujours (too-ZHOOR), always, forever (F)

toupet (too-PEH), wig, false hair (F)

tour de force (TOOR duh FAWRS), special feat of dexterity (F)

tournure (toor-NUR), roundness, gracefulness of line (F)

tout de suite (TOO duh SWEET), at once (F)

tovarishch (tuh-VAH-reeshch), comrade (R)

traduttore, traditore (trah-doot-TOH-ray, trah-dee-TOH-ray), a translator is a traitor (It)

trauma (TROW-mah), blow, wound, injury (Gk)

tricolore (tree-kaw-LAWR), French Flag, red, white, and blue (F)

Trimurti (tree-MOOR-tee), Hindu trinity, Brahma, Vishnu, and Shiva (Sk)

trio (TREE-oh), group of three (It)

trivia (TREE-vee-ah), commonplace things (L)

troika (TROY-kuh), vehicle drawn by three horses (R)

troppo (TRAWP-poh), too much (It)

trouvère (troo-VEHR), minstrel (F)

tsar (see czar)

tu quoque (TOO KWOH-kweh), you, too (L)

tutti-frutti (TOOT-tee FROOT-tee), all fruits, mixed fruits (It)

U

ubique (oo-BEE-kweh), everywhere (L)

ukaze (oo-KAHS), imperial edict (R)

ukulele (oo-koo-LEH-leh), Hawaiian guitar (Hawaiian)

ultima Thule (OOL-tee-mah TOO-leh), faraway, mythical locality (L)

ultimo (OOL-tee-moh), last (month; abbr. ult.) (L)

ultra (OOL-trah), beyond, outside of (L)

ultra vires (OOL-trah WEE-rehs), beyond one's strength or capacity (L)

und so weiter (oont ZOH VEYE-tuhr), and so forth; etc. (G)

uno animo (OO-noh AH-nee-moh), with one mind (L)

Untergang des Abendlandes (OON-tuhr-gahng dehs AH-buhnt-LAHN-duhs), decline of the West (G)

urbi et orbi (OOR-bee eht OHR-bee), to the city and to the world (L)

ut supra (OOT SOO-prah), as above (L)

V

vade mecum (WAH-deh MEH-koom), a book carried as a constant companion, a handbook (L)

vae victis (WEYE WEEK-tees), woe to the vanquished (L)

vale (WAH-leh), good-bye, farewell (L)

valuta (vah-LOO-tah), currency, foreign exchange (It)

vaquero (bah-KEH-roh), cowboy (Sp)

Veda (VEH-dah), knowledge, book of knowledge (Sk)

veld (FEHLT), open grassy country (Du)

veni, vidi, vici (WEH-nee WEE-dee WEE-kee), I came, I saw, I conquered (L)

verbatim (wehr-BAH-teem), word for word (L)

verbum sat sapienti (WEHR-boom SAHT sah-pee-EHN-tee), a word to the wise is sufficient (L)

Verein (fehr-EYEN), union, club (G)

vermicelli (vayr-mee-CHEHL-lee), thin spaghetti (It)

versus (WEHR-soos), abbr. vs.; against (L)

veto (WEH-toh), I forbid; executive prohibition (L)

Via Crucis (WEE-ah KROO-kees), the Way of the Cross (L)

vibrato (vee-BRAH-toh), with vibration (It)

vice versa (WEE-keh WEHR-sah), the other way around (L)

vide (WEE-deh), see (L)

videlicet (wee-DEH-lee-keht), abbr. viz.; to wit, namely (L)

vignette (vee-NYEHT), illustration, short essay (F)

vinaigrette (vee-neh-GREHT), seasoned with vinegar (F)

vin ordinaire (VĒH nawr-dee-NEHR), common table wine (F)

viola da gamba (VYAW-lah dah GAHM-bah), large viol (It)

virtuoso (veer-too-AW-soh), master performer or singer (It)

vis-à-vis (vee-za-VEE), face to face (F)

vista (VEES-tah), view, panorama (It)

viva voce (WEE-wah WOH-keh), orally, by word of mouth (L)

vive (VEEV) long live (F)

vodka (VAWT-kuh), grain spirits (R)

volaille (vaw-LA-yuh), fowl (F)

vol-au-vent (VAW-loh-VĀH), large, light patty; baked pastry shell (F)

Volkswagen (FOHLKS-vah-guhn), people's car; German automobile (G)

volte-face (VAWLT-FAS), about face; reversal (F)

vomitorium (woh-mee-TOH-ree-oom), exit of large public building (L)

von (FUN), of, from, prefix to noble family name (G)

voortrekker (FOHR-TREHK-kuhr), early settler, pioneer (Du)

vox clamantis in deserto (WOHKS klah-MAHN-tees een deh-SEHR-toh), the voice of one shouting in the wilderness (L)

vox populi, vox Dei (WOHKS POH-poo-lee, WOHKS DEH-ee), the voice of the people is the voice of God (L)

vraisemblance (vreh-sāh-BLĀHS), likelihood, verisimilitude (F)

vulgo (WOOL-goh), commonly, popularly (L)

W

wagon-lit (va-GÔH-LEE), sleeping car (F)

wahini (wah-HEE-nee), woman (Hawaiian)

wanderlust (VAHN-duhr-loost), desire for travel (G)

Wehrmacht (VEHR-makht), armed forces (G)

Weinstube (VEYEN-SHTOO-buh), wine tavern (G)

Weltanschauung, Weltansicht (VEHLT-ahn-show-ung, VEHLT-ahn-zict), general outlook, conception of things (G)

Weltschmerz (VEHLT-shmehrts), sorrow for the world, pessimism (G)

wunderbar (VOON-duhr-bahr), wonderful (G)

Wurst (VOORST), sausage (G)

X

xenophobia (KSEH-noh-FOH-bohs), fear or hatred of the foreign (Gk roots)

Y

Yahweh (YAH-veh), Jehovah, God (Heb)

Yoga (YOH-gah), yoking; restraint; Indian philosophy (Sk)

Yogi (YOH-ghee), follower of Yoga (Sk)

Yom Kippur (YOHM keep-POOR), day of atonement, Hebrew holiday (Heb)

Z

zabaione (dzah-bah-YOH-nay), custard mixed with Marsala wine (It)

Zeitgeist (TSEYET-gheyest), spirit of the times (G)

zucchini (dzook-KEE-nee), green squash (It)

Zwieback (TSVEE-bahk), toasted biscuit (G)

Spain—Patio de la Acequia, Granada

READING SKILLS

It is important for student and nonstudent alike to be able to read well and quickly. Every student must be able to master without undue delay the contents of the textbooks or other materials that form a part of his course. The good student is an efficient reader. He reads rapidly with good comprehension, he is able to read critically, and he retains what he has read.

PREVIEWING

A good way for a reader to approach a new text is to devote a few minutes to *previewing* the material. This is a useful reading technique by which the reader familiarizes himself with the general contents of the text before he begins the actual reading. To preview a selection:

1. *Read the title and subtitles.* If the titles have been well prepared, they will indicate the main ideas of the material. The subtitles generally indicate the various points that go logically under the main idea. To read subtitles in order is apt to provide you with a good outline of the material.

2. *Examine the diagrams, charts, and other visual aids.* These visual aids are included to help explain difficult concepts or to repeat essential points.

3. *Pay attention to the length of paragraphs,* and let them determine the speed at which you will read the selection. Long paragraphs are apt to mean more detailed texts; short ones give fewer details and constitute easier texts. Read the long ones more slowly, the short ones more quickly.

Here is an example of the preview technique, making use of a feature story that appeared in a newspaper, with its headline, subheadline, and subtitles. Note that in textbooks, chapter titles and subtitles perform the same function.

Headline	KEY PROBLEMS IN FOREIGN POLICY
Subheadline	How can the President alert the nation to this many-angled crisis?
Subtitles	More "Fireside Chats" Reform of the Press Conference Continuation of the Forums Less Consideration of "World Opinion"

In its original form the story had additional subtitles, but it is apparent that the four subtitles listed are most pertinent. In a very short time the reader has learned the basic theme of the article and the various points the author suggests. The article goes into greater detail, but the preview has provided the reader, in a nutshell, with the essential points. Since the paragraphs in this particular selection are fairly long, the reader will do well to proceed with caution and allow sufficient time for the comprehension of the material.

It is a good idea to preview everything you read–textbooks, newspapers, magazines, technical journals, essays, and so on. This applies especially to material that has a title, subtitles, and visual aids. The few minutes it will take you will pay off in time saved and greater reading efficiency.

FINDING MAIN IDEAS

In presenting factual-type material, the author has set out to convey to you, the reader, in as logical and lucid a manner as possible, the ideas he wishes to impart. In a single paragraph he usually presents the one basic idea; this may be contained in a single sentence, or it may be implied in various sentences in the paragraph. Further, in any given paragraph, most sentences will contain details that explain, illustrate, amplify, or in some way develop the main idea.

You, as the reader, will want to command those skills that will help you to pick out as quickly as possible the central thought of a paragraph. This implies the ability to understand the relationship between the main idea and the supporting details.

Here are some guides to finding the main idea:

1. The main idea may be directly stated in the first sentence of the paragraph.

> *The President tells the visitor that he is giving three-fourths of his time to international affairs.* The White House staff works unclocked hours on problems ranging from Cambodia to the Common Market, from Mongolia to megatons. The foreign callers come to consult and to be feted in a seemingly endless procession–some, seventy-five times since the President took office.

Note the central thought in the first sentence; note also how the following sentences amplify the thought by providing examples of how the President devotes most of his time to the consideration of foreign affairs problems.

2. The main idea may be directly stated in the first sentence and repeated, for emphasis, in the last sentence of the paragraph.

> Many people think that whisky is a good cure for *rattlesnake bites, but scientists claim that whisky is the worst possible medicine.* It acts as a stimulant and therefore makes the heart beat faster. As a result, the heart pumps blood more rapidly all over the body. Rattlesnake poison is dangerous because it gets into the blood stream. If the blood is forced to travel rapidly over the body, then so does the rattlesnake poison that is in the blood. *"Send for the doctor–not for the whisky bottle" is good advice if you're bitten by a rattler.*

Note how the main idea is stated in the first sentence and repeated, for emphasis and as a summary, in the last. The remaining sentences *explain* the main idea.

The above-quoted paragraph illustrates another common technique for presenting the main thought of a paragraph. Often, as here, only a *part of a sentence* contains the main thought. Textbook writers, because paragraphs in textbooks are short, often employ this technique.

3. The main thought may be directly stated in a sentence located in the middle of a paragraph.

> In spite of the disapproval of a number of community organizations, New York State is considering undertaking vast fall-out shelter construction. State officials have been urging comparable projects for years. *However, opinion is divided over the necessity for fall-out shelters.* Local pacifist groups are condemning such projects. Many well-known scientists consider it futile. The federal government has condoned construction of shelters but has not taken positive steps to implement their construction.

Again, note how the main thought appears in a single sentence, and how the remaining sentences explain this main thought.

Of course, not all writers prepare their material in precisely this way. Individual styles of writing and the nature of the material often suggest other ways of presenting one's thoughts.

There may be paragraphs that contain sentences only *implying* the main thought; they do not specifically state it in any one sentence. Other paragraphs may be so short that it becomes difficult to determine the central thought. Or a paragraph may contain two equally important ideas.

Here is a suggestion for finding the main thought in a paragraph, regardless of the type of paragraph construction. Ask yourself two questions in regard to the paragraph; then put together the two answers to these questions into a single sentence. This sentence will provide the main idea. Thus:

a. Ask yourself who or what the paragraph is about.

b. Ask yourself what this paragraph says about the subject.

c. Combine the answers to these two questions into a single sentence, and you will have the main idea.

This technique can be applied whether the main idea is definitely stated, or whether it is implied. The same technique can be used in determining the basic theme of an essay, a chapter, or a short story.

Using this technique, see if you can find the main idea of the following paragraph:

The room was entirely carpeted with a thick, soft rug. Drapes, spun of gold thread, bedecked the large picture windows. Sterling silver candlesticks flanked a gold clock on the mantelpiece. Crimson velvet covered the large sofa. A Steinway grand piano stood in the center of the room.

What is the subject? *A room.*

What is distinctive about this room? *It is richly or expensively decorated.*

The main idea: The room was expensively decorated.

In stressing main ideas, you are not to infer that they alone are important, and that the details are useless. The sentences containing the details often furnish the "substance" of the story. Details can provide nuances of meaning; they can involve the reader's imagination.

CRITICAL READING

Reading quickly with adequate comprehension is not enough. The efficient reader must also be able to read critically, to evaluate what he reads. Such critical reading is a refinement of skill in reading. It requires that the reader be aware of the sources of the author's information; that he recognize the possible use of propaganda techniques; that he be able to differentiate between fact and opinion. Once you realize you are reading an opinion, accord it only the value you consider it to be worth. This does not mean that all opinion should be arbitrarily dismissed. Not at all. But not all opinion is worth accepting. Before you accept an opinion, evaluate it.

First, consider the author. Who is he? Is he or is he not an expert on the subject he is dealing with? You would not be very likely to accept the opinion of your neighbor, a carpenter, if he were to write an article on the causes of heart disease. But the chances are that you would believe implicitly the statements on heart disease made by Dr. Paul Dudley White, the eminent cardiologist. The critical reader does not blindly accept what he reads without knowing something about the author and his qualifications.

Guard against accepting overgeneralizations. Remember, things are not all white or all black. Don't let yourself be taken in by language that is emotionally tinged.

RATE OF READING

Most readers can improve their rate of reading without losing the essential ability to comprehend. (Obviously, there is no value or virtue in speed without comprehension.) Let your rate be determined by the purpose for which you read, and by the difficulty of the material.

For difficult factual reading, a reader's rate should be only two-thirds as fast as his most rapid reading. It is all very well to race through a popular magazine article or a book of light fiction; in reading *Moby Dick* or *Macbeth*, you will have to go more slowly if you wish to explore the deep meaning of these classics and to enjoy the beauty of the language. Nor should the student try to rush through a chapter of his physics or history text. What he wants to do is to absorb and digest, and make a part of his mental make-up, every fact and idea he comes upon in his reading.

Some of the more important rate-of-reading skills are skimming, skim-reading, and reading for key words.

Skimming

Skimming and reading are not one and the same. Skimming is a subskill in the reading process. Most readers who claim that they can "read" five or ten thousand words an hour are probably skimming, not reading at all.

In skimming you leave out whole sentences, whole paragraphs, even whole pages. When you glance at the headlines and subheadlines of your morning newspaper, you are skimming, not reading. The basic rule is to *skim for a definite purpose.* You will skim for a specific answer to a question, and you will skim when you want to get a general idea of the contents of some printed material.

1. SKIMMING FOR AN ANSWER TO A QUESTION. It may be a telephone number, or some general's middle initial, or the birth date of a President. Here is what you do:

a. *Preview the material* to find the answer you are looking for.

b. *Use guide words or phrases* to help direct you to the answer. For example, for George Washington's date of birth, turn to "Washington, George" in the encyclopedia, almanac, or other source book. Try to locate the words *birth, birthday, born,* or the like.

c. In skimming, *let your eyes move rapidly and*

efficiently over the text. You will not be moving your eyes from left to right from line to line as you do in ordinary reading; instead, there are two different ways you can let your eyes move. When the printed column is narrow (as in most newspapers, some textbook chapters, some magazine articles, etc.), your eyes can follow a vertical path down the center of the column. They will be able to see words to the left and to the right. As soon as you come upon the guide word or words, stop and read carefully. Another procedure is to let your eyes move in a left-to-right, then a right-to-left progression, taking in two or three lines of print as you go along, somewhat like an automobile going downhill, careening from side to side and so on down the hill. You can with this procedure observe words near the center of the zigzag path your eyes are taking.

In skimming, speed is essential. Go ahead as fast as you can.

2. SKIMMING IN ORDER TO GET A GENERAL IDEA OF THE CONTENTS. This can be a valuable procedure, for most of us just do not have the time to read thoroughly every bit of reading material that comes to our attention. The procedure is simple: First *preview* the article; then *read* the *first paragraph;* next *read* the *first sentence* of each following *paragraph;* last, *read* the *last paragraph* thoroughly.

Skim-Reading

This is a combination of reading and skimming. You read the important sections and skim the less important ones.

You can increase your rate of reading by reading the key words in sentences. Utilizing what may be called the "telegram style," perhaps 50 percent or more of a sentence is left out, without the reader's losing the meaning of the sentence. In the following paragraph, the key words have been italicized. By reading them, and them only, the reader will get the sense of the material.

> Our *forefathers fought* bloody *wars* and *suffered torture* and *death* for the *right to worship God according* to the varied *dictates* of *conscience.* Complete *religious liberty* has been *accepted* as an unquestioned personal *freedom* since our *Bill of Rights* was *adopted.* We have insisted only that *religious freedom* may *not* be pleaded as an *excuse for criminal* or clearly *antisocial conduct.*

A word of caution: Such words as *no, not, only,* and *less* are extremely important; so watch out!

Finally, your attitude when reading is important. Don't be afraid of the printed page! With material that is not especially difficult or technical, read on just as fast as you can without losing comprehension. Enter every reading situation with confidence and enthusiasm, and you will find this frame of mind will be a great help.

For further material on reading skills, refer to the books listed below:

1. Liddle, William, *Reading for Concepts* (New York: McGraw-Hill, 1977). Books "A" through "H" of this series are designed for readers in the seventh through twelfth grades.

2. Pauk, Walter, *How to Read Factual Literature* (Chicago: Science Research Associates, 1970). This book was written for readers in the seventh and eighth grades.

3. Pauk, Walter and Wilson, Josephine M., *How to Read Creative Literature* (Chicago: Science Research Associates, 1970). This book was written for readers in the ninth grade through adult level.

Where To Write for Vital Records

Introduction

This publication, *Where to Write for Vital Records: Births, Deaths, Marriages, and Divorces,* supersedes and incorporates three publications: *Where to Write for Birth and Death Records: United States and Outlying Areas* (DHEW Pub. No. (PHS) 80-1142, revised 1979), *Where to Write for Marriage Records: United States and Outlying Areas* (DHEW Pub. No. (PHS) 80-1144, revised 1979), and *Where to Write for Divorce Records: United States and Outlying Areas* (DHEW Pub. No. (PHS) 80-1145, revised 1979).

An official certificate of every birth, death, marriage, and divorce should be on file in the locality where the event occurred. The Federal Government does not maintain files or indexes of these records. These records are filed permanently either in a State vital statistics office or in a city, county, or other local office.

To obtain a certified copy of any of the certificates, write or go to the vital statistics office in the State or area where the event occurred. Addresses and fees are given for each event in the State or area concerned.

To ensure that you receive an accurate record for your request and that your request be filled with all due speed, please follow the steps outlined below for the event in which you are interested:

- Write to the appropriate office to have your request filled.

- For all certificates send a money order or certified check because the office cannot refund cash lost in transit. All fees are subject to change.

- Type or print all names and addresses in the letter.

- Give the following facts when writing for BIRTH OR DEATH RECORDS:

1. Full name of person whose record is being requested.
2. Sex and race.
3. Parents' names, including maiden name of mother.
4. Month, day, and year of birth or death.
5. Place of birth or death (city or town, county, and State; and name of hospital, if any).
6. Purpose for which copy is needed.
7. Relationship to person whose record is being requested.

- Give the following facts when writing for MARRIAGE RECORDS:

1. Full names of bride and groom (including nicknames).
2. Residence addresses at time of marriage.
3. Ages at time of marriage (or dates of birth).
4. Month, day, and year of marriage.
5. Place of marriage (city or town, county, and State).
6. Purpose for which copy is needed.
7. Relationship to persons whose record is being requested.

- Give the following facts when writing for DIVORCE RECORDS:

1. Full names of husband and wife (including nicknames).
2. Present residence address.
3. Former addresses (as in court records).
4. Ages at time of divorce (or dates of birth).
5. Date of divorce or annulment.
6. Place of divorce or annulment.
7. Type of final decree.
8. Purpose for which copy is needed.
9. Relationship to persons whose record is being requested.

Place of event	Cost of copy	Address	Remarks
ALABAMA			
Birth or Death	$5.00	Bureau of Vital Statistics State Department of Public Health Montgomery, AL 36130	State office has had records since January 1908. Additional copies at same time are $2.00 each. Fee for special searches is $5.00 per hour.
Marriage	$5.00	Same as Birth or Death	State office has had records since August 1936.
	Varies	See remarks	Probate Judge in county where license was issued.
Divorce	$5.00	Same as Birth or Death	State office has had records since January 1950.
	Varies	See remarks	Clerk or Register of Court of Equity in county where divorce was granted.

Place of event	Cost of copy	Address	Remarks
ALASKA			
Birth or Death	$5.00	Department of Health and Social Services Bureau of Vital Statistics Pouch H-02G Juneau, AK 99811	State office has had records since 1913.
Marriage	$5.00	Same as Birth or Death	Records since 1913.
Divorce	$5.00	Same as Birth or Death	Records since 1950.
	Varies	See remarks	Clerk of the Superior Court in judicial district where divorce was granted. Juneau and Ketchikan (First District), Nome (Second District), Anchorage (Third District), Fairbanks (Fourth District).
AMERICAN SAMOA			
Birth or Death	$2.00	Registrar of Vital Statistics Vital Statistics Section Government of American Samoa Pago Pago, AS 96799	Registrar has had records since 1900.
Marriage	$2.00	Same as Birth or Death	
Divorce	$1.00	Same as Birth or Death	
ARIZONA			
Birth (long form)	$5.00	Vital Records Section	State office has had records since July 1909 and abstracts of records filed in counties before then.
(short form)	$3.00	Arizona Department of Health Services	
Death	$3.00	P.O. Box 3887 Phoenix, AZ 85030	
Marriage	Varies	See remarks	Clerk of Superior Court in county where license was issued.
Divorce	Varies	See remarks	Clerk of Superior Court in county where divorce was granted.
ARKANSAS			
Birth	$5.00	Division of Vital Records	State office has had records since February 1914 and some original Little Rock and Fort Smith records from 1881.
Death	$4.00	Arkansas Department of Health 4815 West Markham Street Little Rock, AR 72201	
Marriage	$5.00	Same as Birth or Death	Records since 1917.
	$2.00	See remarks	Full certified copy may be obtained from County Clerk in county where license was issued.
Divorce	$5.00	Same as Birth or Death	Coupons since 1923.
	Varies	See remarks	Full certified copy may be obtained from Circuit or Chancery Clerk in county where divorce was granted.
CALIFORNIA			
Birth	$11.00	Vital Statistics Branch	State office has had records since July 1905. For earlier records, write to County Recorder in county where event occurred.
Death	$7.00	Department of Health Services 410 N Street Sacramento, CA 95814	
Marriage	$11.00	Same as Birth or Death	State office has had records since July 1905. For earlier records, write to County Recorder in county where event occurred.
Divorce	$11.00	Same as Birth or Death	Fee is for search and identification of county where certified copy can be obtained. Certified copies are not available from State Health Department.

Place of event	Cost of copy	Address	Remarks
	Varies	See remarks	Clerk of Superior Court in county where divorce was granted.
CANAL ZONE			
Birth or Death	$2.00	Panama Canal Commission Vital Statistics Clerk APO Miami 34011	Records available from May 1904 to September 1979.
Marriage	$1.00	Same as Birth or Death	Records available from May 1904 to September 1979.
Divorce	$0.50	Same as Birth or Death	Records available from May 1904 to September 1979.
COLORADO			
Birth or Death		Vital Records Section Colorado Department of Health 4210 East 11th Avenue Denver, CO 80220	State office has had death records since 1900 and birth records since 1910. State office also has birth records for some counties for years before 1910.
Regular Service	$6.00		
Priority Service	$10.00		
Marriage	See remarks	Same as Birth or Death	Statewide index of records for all years except 1940-75. Inquiries will be forwarded to appropriate office. Certified copies are not available from State Health Department.
	Varies	See remarks	County Clerk in county where license was issued.
Divorce	See remarks	Same as Birth or Death	Statewide index of records for all years except 1940-67. Inquiries will be forwarded to appropriate office. Certified copies are not available from State Health Department.
	Varies	See remarks	Clerk of District Court in county where divorce was granted.
CONNECTICUT			
Birth or Death	$3.00	Department of Health Services Vital Records Section Division of Health Statistics State Dept. of Health 150 Washington Street Hartford, CT 06106	State office has had records since July 1897. For earlier records, write to Registrar of Vital Statistics in town or city where event occurred.
Short form	$2.00		
Marriage	$3.00	Same as Birth or Death	Records since July 1897.
	$3.00	See remarks	Registrar of Vital Statistics in town where license was issued.
Divorce	See remarks	Same as Birth or Death	Index of records since 1947. Inquiries will be forwarded to appropriate office. Certified copies are not available from State office.
	Varies	See remarks	Clerk of Superior Court in county where divorce was granted.
DELAWARE			
Birth or Death	$5.00	Bureau of Vital Statistics Division of Public Health P.O. Box 637 Dover, DE 19903	State office has records for 1861 to 1863 and since 1881 but no records for 1864 to 1880.
Marriage	$5.00	Same as Birth or Death	Records since 1847.
Divorce	See remarks	Same as Birth or Death	Records since 1935. Inquiries will be forwarded to appropriate office. Fee for search and verification of essential facts of divorce, $2.50. Certified copies are not available from State office.
	$2.00	See remarks	Prothonotary in county where divorce was granted up to 1975. For divorces granted after 1975 the parties concerned should contact Family Court in the county where the divorce was granted.

Place of event	Cost of copy	Address	Remarks
DISTRICT OF COLUMBIA			
Birth or Death	$5.00	Vital Records Branch Room 3009 425 I Street, NW Washington, DC 20001	Office has had death records since 1855 and birth records since 1871, but no death records were filed during the Civil War.
Marriage	$5.00	Same as Birth or Death	Records since January 1, 1982.
	$5.00	Marriage Bureau 515 5th Street, NW Washington, D.C. 20001	Fee for proof of marriage, $2.50; proof of age, $2.50.
Divorce	$2.00	Same as Birth or Death	Records since January 1, 1982
	Varies	Clerk, Superior Court for the District of Columbia, Family Division 500 Indiana Avenue, NW Washington, D.C. 20001	Records since September 16, 1956.
	Varies	Clerk, U.S. District Court for the District of Columbia Washington, D.C. 20001	Records before September 16, 1956.
FLORIDA			
Birth	$6.50	Department of Health and Rehabilitative Services Office of Vital Statistics P.O. Box 210 Jacksonville, FL 32231	State office has had some birth records since April 1865 and some death records since August 1877. The majority of records date from January 1917. (If the exact date is unknown, the fee is $6.50 (for births) or $2.50 (for deaths) for the first year searched and $1.00 for each additional year up to a maximum of $25.00. Fee includes one copy of record if found.)
Death	$2.50		
Marriage	$2.50	Same as Birth or Death	Records since June 6, 1927. (If the exact date is unknown, the fee is $2.50 for the first year searched and $1.00 for each additional year up to a maximum of $25.00. Fee includes one copy of record if found.)
Divorce	$2.50	Same as Birth or Death	Records since June 6, 1927. (If the exact date is unknown, the fee is $2.50 for the first year searched and $1.00 for each additional year up to a maximum of $25.00. Fee includes one copy of record if found.)
GEORGIA			
Birth or Death	$3.00	Georgia Department of Human Resources Vital Records Unit Room 217-H 47 Trinity Avenue, SW Atlanta, GA 30334	State office has had records since January 1919. For earlier records in Atlanta or Savannah, write to County Health Department in county where event occurred. Additional copies of same record ordered at same time are $1.00 each.
Marriage	$3.00	Same as Birth or Death	Centralized State records since June 9, 1952. Certified copies are not issued at State office. Inquiries will be forwarded to appropriate office.
	$3.00	See remarks	Probate Judge in county where license was issued.
Divorce	Varies	Same as Birth or Death	Centralized State records since June 9, 1952. Certified copies are not issued at State office. Inquiries will be forwarded to appropriate office.
	$3.00	See remarks	Clerk of Superior Court in county where divorce was granted.

Place of event	Cost of copy	Address	Remarks
GUAM			
Birth or Death	$2.00	Office of Vital Statistics Department of Public Health and Social Services Government of Guam P.O. Box 2816 Agana, GU, M.I. 96910	Office has had records since October 26, 1901.
Marriage	$2.00	Same as Birth or Death	
Divorce	Varies	See remarks	Clerk, Superior Court of Guam, Agana, GU, M.I. 96910.
HAWAII			
Birth or Death	$2.00	Research and Statistics Office State Department of Health P.O. Box 3378 Honolulu, HI 96801	State office has had records since 1853.
Marriage	$2.00	Same as Birth or Death	
Divorce	$2.00	Same as Birth or Death	Records since July 1951.
	Varies	See remarks	Circuit Court in county where divorce was granted.
IDAHO			
Birth or Death	$6.00	Bureau of Vital Statistics, Standards, and Local Health Services State Department of Health and Welfare Statehouse Boise, ID 83720	State office has had records since 1911. For records from 1907 to 1911, write to County Recorder in county where event occurred.
Marriage	$6.00	Same as Birth or Death	Records since 1947.
	Varies	See remarks	County Recorder in county where license was issued.
Divorce	$6.00	Same as Birth or Death	Records since January 1947.
	Varies	See remarks	County Recorder in county where divorce was granted.
ILLINOIS			
Birth or Death		Division of Vital Records State Department of Public Health 605 West Jefferson Street Springfield, IL 62702	State office has had records since January 1916. For earlier records and for copies of State records since January 1916, write to County Clerk in county where event occurred. ($5.00 fee is for search of files and one copy of record if found. Additional copies of same record ordered at same time are $2.00 each.)
Certified copy	$15.00		
Certification	$10.00		
Marriage	See remarks	Same as Birth or Death	Records since January 1962. All items may be verified (fee $3.00). Inquiries will be forwarded to appropriate office. Certified copies are not available from State office.
	$3.00	See remarks	County Clerk in county where license was issued.
Divorce	See remarks	Same as Birth or Death	Records since January 1962. Some items may be verified (fee $5.00). Certified copies are not available from State office.
	Varies	See remarks	Clerk of Circuit Court in county where divorce was granted.
INDIANA			
Birth	$6.00	Division of Vital Records State Board of Health 1330 West Michigan Street P.O. Box 1964 Indianapolis, IN 46206	State office has had birth records since October 1907 and death records since 1900. Additional copies of same record ordered at same time are $1.00 each. For earlier records, write to Health Officer in city or county where event occurred.
Death	$4.00		

Place of event	Cost of copy	Address	Remarks
Marriage	See remarks	Same as Birth or Death	Marriage Index since 1958. Inquiries will be forwarded to appropriate office. Certified copies are not available from State Health Department.
	Varies	See remarks	Clerk of Circuit Court or Clerk of Superior Court in county where license was issued.
Divorce	Varies	See remarks	County Clerk in county where divorce was granted.
IOWA			
Birth or Death	$6.00	Iowa State Department of Health Vital Records Section Lucas State Office Building Des Moines, IA 50319	State office has had records since July 1880.
Marriage	$6.00	Same as Birth or Death	State Office has had records since July 1880.
Divorce	See remarks	Same as Birth or Death	Brief statistical record only since 1906. Inquiries will be forwarded to appropriate office. Certified copies are not available from State Health Department.
	$6.00	See remarks	Clerk of District Court in county where divorce was granted.
KANSAS			
Birth or Death	$6.00	Office of Vital Statistics Kansas State Department of Health and Environment 900 Jackson Street Topeka, KS 66612-1290	State office has had records since July 1911. For earlier records, write to County Clerk in county where event occurred. Additional copies of same record ordered at same time are $3.00 each.
Marriage	$6.00	Same as Birth or Death	Records since May 1913.
	Varies	See remarks	Probate Judge in county where license was issued.
Divorce	$6.00	Same as Birth or Death	Records since July 1951.
	Varies	See remarks	Clerk of District Court in county where divorce was granted.
KENTUCKY			
Birth	$5.00	Office of Vital Statistics Department for Human Resources 275 East Main Street Frankfort, KY 40621	State office has had records since January 1911 and some records for the cities of Louisville, Lexington, Covington, and Newport before then.
Death	$4.00		
Marriage	$4.00	Same as Birth or Death	Records since June 1958.
	Varies	See remarks	Clerk of County Court in county where license was issued.
Divorce	$4.00	Same as Birth or Death	Records since June 1958.
	Varies	See remarks	Clerk of Circuit Court in county where decree was issued.
LOUISIANA			
Birth (Long Form)	$8.00	Division of Vital Records Office of Health Services and Environmental Quality P.O. Box 60630 New Orleans, LA 70160	State office has had records since July 1914. Birth records for City of New Orleans are available from 1790, and death records from 1803.
Short Form	$3.00		
Death	$5.00		
Marriage	See remarks	Same as Birth or Death	Certified copies are not available from State Health Department. Inquiries will be forwarded to appropriate office.
Orleans Parish	$5.00	Same as Birth or Death	

Place of event	Cost of copy	Address	Remarks
Other Parishes	Varies	See remarks	Certified copies are issued by Clerk of Court in parish where license was issued.
Divorce	$3.00	Same as Birth	Clerk of Court in parish where divorce was granted. For Orleans Parish, copies may be obtained from State office for $3.00.

MAINE

Place of event	Cost of copy	Address	Remarks
Birth or Death	$5.00	Office of Vital Records Human Services Building Station 11 State House Augusta, ME 04333	State office has had records since 1892. For earlier records, write to the municipality where event occurred.
Marriage	$5.00	Same as Birth or Death	
	$2.00	See remarks	Town Clerk in town where license was issued.
Divorce	$2.00	Same as Birth or Death	Records since January 1892.
	$5.00	See remarks	Clerk of District Court in judicial division where divorce was granted.

MARYLAND

Place of event	Cost of copy	Address	Remarks
Birth or Death	$3.00	Division of Vital Records State Department of Health and Mental Hygiene State Office Building P.O. Box 13146 201 West Preston Street Baltimore, MD 21203	State office has had records since August 1898. Records for City of Baltimore are available from January 1875.
Marriage	$3.00	Same as Birth or Death	Records since June 1951.
	Varies	See remarks	Clerk of Circuit Court in county where license was issued or Clerk of Court of Common Pleas of Baltimore City (for licenses issued in City of Baltimore).
Divorce	$3.00	Same as Birth or Death	Records since January 1961. Certified copies are not available from State office. Some items may be verified. Inquiries will be forwarded to appropriate office.
	Varies	See remarks	Clerk of Circuit Court in county where divorce was granted.

MASSACHUSETTS

Place of event	Cost of copy	Address	Remarks
Birth or Death	$3.00	Registry of Vital Records and 150 Treemont St. Room B-3 Boston, MA 02111	State office has had records, except for Boston, since 1841. For earlier records, write to the City or Town Clerk in place where event occurred. Earliest records available in the Boston office are for 1848.
Marriage	$3.00	Same as Birth or Death	Records (except for Boston) since 1841. Earliest Boston records are for 1848.
Divorce	See remarks	Same as Birth or Death	Index only since 1952. Inquirer will be directed where to send request. Certified copies are not available from State office.
	$3.00	See remarks	Registrar of Probate Court in county where divorce was granted.

MICHIGAN

Place of event	Cost of copy	Address	Remarks
Birth or Death	$10.00	Office of Vital and Health Statistics Michigan Department of Public Health 3500 North Logan Street Lansing, MI 48914	State office has had records since 1867. Copies of records since 1867 may also be obtained from County Clerk in county where event occurred. Detroit records may be obtained from the City Health Department for births occurring since 1893 and for deaths since 1897.

Place of event	Cost of copy	Address	Remarks
Marriage	$10.00	Same as Birth or Death	Records since April 1867.
	Varies	See remarks	County Clerk in county where license was issued.
Divorce	$10.00	Same as Birth or Death	Records since 1897.
	Varies	See remarks	County Clerk in county where divorce was granted.
MINNESOTA			
Birth	$11.00	Minnesota Department of Health Section of Vital Statistics 717 Delaware Street SE P.O. Box 9441 Minneapolis, MN 55440	State office has had records since January 1908. Copies of earlier records may be obtained from Clerk of District Court in county where event occurred or from the Minneapolis or St. Paul City Health Department if the event occurred in either city.
Death	$8.00		
Marriage	See remarks	Same as Birth or Death	Statewide index since January 1958. Inquiries will be forwarded to appropriate office. Certified copies are not available from State Health Department.
	$8.00	See remarks	Clerk of District Court in county where license was issued.
Divorce	See remarks	Same as Birth or Death	Index since January 1970. Certified copies are not available from State office.
	$8.00	See remarks	Clerk of District Court in county where divorce was granted.
MISSISSIPPI			
Birth	$10.00	Vital Records State Board of Health P.O. Box 1700 Jackson, MS 39205	State office has had records since 1912. Full copies of birth certificates obtained within 1 year after the event are $5.00. Additional copies of same record ordered at same time are $1.00 each.
Short Form	$5.00		
Death	$5.00		
Marriage	$5.00	Same as Birth or Death	Statistical records only from January 1926 to July 1, 1938, and since January 1942.
	$3.00	See remarks	Circuit Clerk in county where license was issued.
Divorce	$.50 per page plus $1.00 for verification	Same as Birth or Death	Records since January 1926. Certified copies are not available from State office. Inquiries will be forwarded to appropriate office.
	$2.00	See remarks	Chancery Clerk in county where divorce was granted.
MISSOURI			
Birth or Death	$4.00	Division of Health Bureau of Vital Records P.O. Box 570 Jefferson City, MO 65102	State office has had records since January 1910. If event occurred in St. Louis (city), St. Louis County, or Kansas City before 1910, write to the City or County Health Department. Copies of these records are $3.00 each in St. Louis City and County. In Kansas City, $6.00 for first copy and $3.00 for each additional copy ordered at same time.
Marriage	No fee	Same as Birth or Death	Indexes since July 1948. Correspondent will be referred to appropriate Recorder of Deeds in county where license was issued.
	Varies	See remarks	Recorder of Deeds in county where license was issued.
Divorce	See remarks	Same as Birth or Death	Indexes since July 1948. Certified copies are not available from State Health Department. Inquiries will be forwarded to appropriate office.
	Varies	See remarks	Clerk of Circuit Court in county where divorce was granted.
MONTANA			
Birth or Death	$5.00	Bureau of Records and Statistics State Department of Health and Environmental Sciences Helena, MT 59620	State office has had records since late 1907.

Place of event	Cost of copy	Address	Remarks
Marriage	See remarks	Same as Birth or Death	Records since July 1943. Some items may be verified. Inquiries will be forwarded to appropriate office. Apply to county where license was issued if known. Certified copies are not available from State office.
	Varies	See remarks	Clerk of District Court in county where license was issued.
Divorce	See remarks	Same as Birth or Death	Records since July 1943. Some items may be verified. Inquiries will be forwarded to appropriate office. Apply to county where license was issued if known. Certified copies are not available from State office.
	Varies	See remarks	Clerk of District Court in county where divorce was granted.
NEBRASKA			
Birth	$6.00	Bureau of Vital Statistics State Department of Health 301 Centennial Mall South P.O. Box 95007 Lincoln, NE 68509-5007	State office has had records since late 1904. If birth occurred before then, write the State office for information.
Death	$5.00		
Marriage	$5.00	Same as Birth or Death	Records since January 1909.
	Varies	See remarks	County Court in county where license was issued.
Divorce	$5.00	Same as Birth or Death	Records since January 1909.
	Varies	See remarks	Clerk of District Court in county where divorce was granted.
NEVADA			
Birth or Death	$6.00	Division of Health - Vital Statistics Capitol Complex Carson City, NV 89710	State office has had records since July 1911. For earlier records, write to County Recorder in county where event occurred. Additional copies of Death Records ordered at the same time are $4.00 for second and third copies, $3.00 each for the next three copies, and $2.00 each for any additional copies.
Marriage	See remarks	Same as Birth or Death	Indexes since January 1968. Certified copies are not available from State Health Department. Inquiries will be forwarded to appropriate office.
	Varies	See remarks	County Recorder in county where license was issued.
Divorce	See remarks	Same as Birth or Death	Indexes since January 1968. Certified copies are not available from State Health Department. Inquiries will be forwarded to appropriate office.
	Varies	See remarks	County Clerk in county where divorce was granted.
NEW HAMPSHIRE			
Birth or Death	$3.00	Bureau of Vital Records Health and Welfare Building Hazen Drive Concord, NH 03301	State office has had some records since 1640. Copies of records may be obtained from State office or from City or Town Clerk in place where event occurred.
Marriage	$3.00	Same as Birth or Death	Records since 1640.
	Varies	See remarks	Town Clerk in town where license was issued.
Divorce	$3.00	Same as Birth or Death	Records since 1808. Fee includes search and one copy if found.
	Varies	See remarks	Clerk of Superior Court where divorce was granted.

Place of event	Cost of copy	Address	Remarks
NEW JERSEY			
Birth or Death	$4.00	State Department of Health Bureau of Vital Statistics CN 360 Trenton, NJ 08625	State office has had records since June 1878. Additional copies of same record ordered at same time are $2.00 each. If the exact date is unknown, the fee is an additional $1.00 per year searched.
		Archives and History Bureau State Library Division State Department of Education Trenton, NJ 08625	For records from May 1848 to May 1878.
Marriage	$4.00	Same as Birth or Death	If the exact date is unknown, the fee is an additional $0.50 per year searched.
	No fee	Archives and History Bureau State Library Division State Department of Education Trenton, NJ 08625	Records from May 1848 to May 1878.
Divorce	$2.00	Superior Court, Chancery Division State House Annex, Room 320 CN 971 Trenton, NJ 08625	The fee is for the first four pages. Additional pages cost $0.50 each.
NEW MEXICO			
Birth or Death	$10.00	Vital Statistics Bureau New Mexico Health Services Division P.O. Box 968 Santa Fe, NM 87504-0968	State office has had records since 1920 and delayed records since 1880.
Marriage	Varies	See remarks	County Clerk in county where license was issued.
Divorce	Varies	See remarks	Clerk of District Court in county where divorce was granted.
NEW YORK (Except New York City)			
Birth or Death	$5.00	Bureau of Vital Records State Department of Health Empire State Plaza Tower Building Albany, NY 12237	State office has had records since 1880. For records before 1914 in Albany, Buffalo, and Yonkers or before 1880 in any other city, write to Registrar of Vital Statistics in city where event occurred. For the rest of the State, except New York City, write to State office.
Marriage	$5.00	Same as Birth or Death	Records from January 1880 to December 1907 and since May 1915.
	Varies	See remarks	Records from January 1908 to April 1915. County Clerk in county where license was issued.
	$5.00	See remarks	Records from January 1880 to December 1907. Write to City Clerk in Albany or Buffalo or Registrar of Vital Statistics in Yonkers if marriage occurred in one of these cities.
Divorce	$5.00	Same as Birth or Death	Records since January 1963.
	Varies	See remarks	County Clerk in county where divorce was granted.
NEW YORK CITY			
Birth or Death	$5.00	Bureau of Vital Records Department of Health of New York City 125 Worth Street New York, NY 10013	Office has had birth records since 1898 and death records since 1920. For Old City of New York (Manhattan and part of the Bronx) birth records for 1865-1897 and death records for 1865-1919 write to Municipal Archives and Records Retention, 52 Chambers St., New York, NY 10038.

Place of event	Cost of copy	Address	Remarks
Marriage	$10.00	See remarks	Records from 1847 to 1865. Municipal Archives and Records Retention Center, New York Public Library, 23 Park Row, New York, NY 10038, except Brooklyn records for this period, which are filed with County Clerk's Office, Kings County, Supreme Court Building, Brooklyn, NY 11201. Additional copies of same record ordered at same time are $2.00 each.
	$10.00	See remarks	Records from 1866 to 1907. City Clerk's Office in borough where marriage was performed.
	$7.00	See remarks	Records from 1908 to May 12, 1943. New York City residents write to City Clerk's Office borough of bride's residence; nonresidents write to City Clerk's Office in borough where license was obtained.
	$10.00	See remarks	Records since May 13, 1943. City Clerk's Office in borough where license was issued.
Bronx Borough	$10.00	Marriage License Bureau 1780 Grand Concourse Bronx, NY 10457	
Brooklyn Borough	$10.00	Marriage License Bureau Municipal Building Brooklyn Borough Hall Brooklyn, NY 11201	
Manhattan Borough	$10.00	Marriage License Bureau No. 1 Center Street Municipal Building New York, NY 10007	
Queens Borough	$10.00	Marriage License Bureau Queens Borough Hall 120-55 Queens Boulevard Kew Gardens, NY 11424	
Staten Island Borough (no longer called Richmond)	$10.00	Marriage License Bureau Staten Island Borough Hall St. George Staten Island, NY 11201	
Divorce			See New York State
NORTH CAROLINA			
Birth or Death	$5.00	Department of Human Resources Division of Health Services Vital Records Branch P.O. Box 2091 Raleigh, NC 27602	State office has had birth records since October 1913 and death records since January 1, 1930. Death records from 1913 through 1929 are available from Archives and Records Section, State Records Center, 215 North Blount Street, Raleigh, NC 27602.
Marriage	$5.00	Same as Birth or Death	Records since January 1962.
	$3.00	See remarks	Registrar of Deeds in county where marriage was performed.
Divorce	$5.00	Same as Birth or Death	Records since January 1958.
	Varies	See remarks	Clerk of Superior Court where divorce was granted.
NORTH DAKOTA			
Birth	$7.00	Division of Vital Records State Department of Health Office of Statistical Services Bismarck, ND 58505	State office has had some records since July 1893. Years from 1894 to 1920 are incomplete.
Death	$5.00		
Marriage	$5.00	Same as Birth or Death	Records since July 1925. Requests for earlier records will be forwarded to appropriate office.
	Varies	See remarks	County Judge in county where license was issued.

Place of event	Cost of copy	Address	Remarks
Divorce	See remarks	Same as Birth or Death	Index of records since July 1949. Some items may be verified. Certified copies are not available from State Health Department. Inquiries will be forwarded to appropriate office.
	Varies	See remarks	Clerk of District Court in county where divorce was granted.
OHIO			
Birth or Death	$5.00	Division of Vital Statistics Ohio Department of Health G-20 Ohio Departments Building 65 South Front Street Columbus, OH 43266-0333	State office has had records since December 20, 1908. For earlier records, write to Probate Court in county where event occurred.
Marriage	See remarks	Same as Birth or Death	Records since September 1949. All items may be verified. Certified copies are not available from State Health Department. Inquiries will be referred to appropriate office.
	Varies	See remarks	Probate Judge in county where license was issued.
Divorce	See remarks	Same as Birth or Death	Records since September 1949. All items may be verified. Certified copies are not available from State Health Department. Inquiries will be referred to appropriate office.
	Varies	See remarks	Clerk of Court of Common Pleas in county where divorce was granted.
OKLAHOMA			
Birth or Death	$5.00	Vital Records Section State Department of Health Northeast 10th Street & Stonewall P.O. Box 53551 Oklahoma City, OK 73152	State office has had records since October 1908.
Marriage	Varies	See remarks	Clerk of Court in county where license was issued.
Divorce	Varies	See remarks	Clerk of Court in county where divorce was granted.
OREGON			
Birth or Death	$8.00	Oregon State Health Division Vital Statistics Section P.O. Box 116 Portland, OR 97207	State office has had records since January 1903. Some earlier records for the City of Portland since approximately 1880 are available from the Oregon State Archives, 1005 Broadway, N.E., Salem, OR 97310.
Heirloom Birth	$25.00	Same as Birth or Death Presentation style calligraphy suitable for framing.	
Marriage	$8.00	Same as Birth or Death	Records since January 1906.
	Varies	See remarks	County Clerk in county where license was issued. County Clerks also have some records before 1906.
Divorce	$8.00	Same as birth or Death	Records since 1925.
	Varies	See remarks	County Clerk in county where divorce was granted. County Clerks also have some records before 1925.
PENNSYLVANIA			
Birth	$4.00	Division of Vital Statistics State Department of Health Central Building 101 South Mercer Street P.O. Box 1528 New Castle, PA 16103	State office has had records since January 1906. For earlier records, write to Register of Wills, Orphans Court, in county seat where event occurred. Persons born in Pittsburgh from 1870 to 1905 or in Allegheny City, now part of Pittsburgh, from 1882 to 1905 should write to Office of Biostatistics, Pittsburgh Health Department, City-County Building, Pittsburgh, PA 15219. For events occurring in City of Philadelphia from 1860 to 1915, write to Vital Statistics, Philadelphia Department of Public Health, City Hall Annex, Philadelphia, PA 19107.
Short Form	$5.00		
Death	$3.00		

Place of event	Cost of copy	Address	Remarks
Marriage	See remarks	Same as Birth or Death	Records since January 1941. Certified copies are not available from State Health Department. Inquiries will be forwarded to appropriate office.
	Varies	See remarks	Marriage License Clerks, County Court House, in county seat where license was issued.
Divorce	Varies	Same as Birth or Death	Records since January 1946. Certified copies are not available from State Health Department. Inquiries will be forwarded to appropriate office.
	Varies	See remarks	Prothonotary, Court House, in county seat where divorce was granted.
PUERTO RICO			
Birth or Death	$2.00	Division of Demographic Registry and Vital Statistics Department of Health San Juan, PR 00908	Central office has had records since July 22, 1931. Copies of earlier records may be obtained by writing to local Registrar (Registrador Demografico) in municipality where event occurred or by writing to central office for information.
Marriage	$2.00	Same as Birth or Death	
Divorce	$2.00	See remarks	Superior Court where divorce was granted.
RHODE ISLAND			
Birth or Death	$4.00	Division of Vital Statistics State Department of Health Room 101, Cannon Building 75 Davis Street Providence, RI 02908	State office has had records since 1853. For earlier records, write to Town Clerk in town where event occurred. Additional copies of the same record ordered at the same time are $2.00 each.
Marriage	$5.00	Same as Birth or Death	Records since January 1853. Additional copies of the same record ordered at the same time are $2.00 each.
	$5.00	See remarks	City or Town Clerk in place where marriage was performed.
Divorce	$1.00	Clerk of Family Court 1 Dorrance Plaza Providence, RI 02903	
SOUTH CAROLINA			
Birth or Death	$5.00	Office of Vital Records and Public Health Statistics S.C. Department of Health and Environmental Control 2600 Bull Street Columbia, SC 29201	State office has had records since January 1915. City of Charleston births from 1877 and deaths from 1821 are on file at Charleston County Health Department. Ledger entries of Florence City births and deaths from 1895 to 1914 are on file at Florence County Health Department. Ledger entries of Newberry City births and deaths from late 1800's are on file at Newberry County Health Department. These are the only early records obtainable.
Marriage	$5.00	Same as Birth or Death	Records since July 1950.
	Varies	See remarks	Records since July 1911. Probate Judge in county where license was issued.
Divorce	$5.00	Same as Birth or Death	Records since July, 1962.
	Varies	See remarks	Records since April 1949. Clerk of county where petition was filed.
SOUTH DAKOTA			
Birth or Death	$5.00	Center for Health Policy and Statistics Vital Records 523 E. Capital Pierre, SD 57501	State office has had records since July 1905 and access to other records for some events that occcurred before then. Additional copies requested at the same time are $1.00 each.
Marriage	$5.00	Same as Birth or Death	Records since July 1905. Additional copies requested at the same time are $1.00 each.

Place of event	Cost of copy	Address	Remarks
	$5.00	See remarks	County Treasurer in county where license was issued.
Divorce	$5.00	Same as Birth or Death	Records since July 1905. Additional copies requested at the same time are $1.00 each.
	Varies	See remarks	Clerk of Court in county where divorce was granted.
TENNESSEE			
Birth (Long Form)	$6.00	Division of Vital Records State Department of Public Health Cordell Hull Building Nashville, TN, 37219	State office has had birth records for entire State since January 1914, for Nashville since June 1881, for Knoxville since July 1881, and for Chattanooga since January 1882. State office has had death records for entire State since January 1914, for Nashville since July 1874, for Knoxville since July 1887, and for Chattanooga since March 6, 1872. Birth and death enumeration records by school district are available for July 1908 through June 1912. For Memphis birth records from April 1874 through December 1887 and November 1898 to January 1, 1914, and for Memphis death records from May 1848 to January 1, 1914, write to Memphis-Shelby County Health Department, Division of Vital Records, Memphis, TN 38105.
Short Form	$4.00		
Death	$4.00		
Marriage	$4.00	Same as Birth or Death	Records since July 1945.
	Varies	See remarks	County Court Clerk in county where license was issued.
Divorce	$4.00	Same as Birth or Death	Records since July 1945.
	Varies	See remarks	Clerk of Court in county where divorce was granted.
TEXAS			
Birth or Death	$5.00	Bureau of Vital Statistics Texas Department of Health 1100 West 49th Street Austin, TX 78756	State office has had records since 1903. Additional copies of same *death* record ordered at same time are $2.00 each.
Marriage	See remarks	Same as Birth or Death	Records since January 1966. Certified copies are not available from State office. Fee for search and verification of essential facts of marriage is $1.00.
	Varies	See remarks	County Clerk in county where license was issued.
Divorce	See remarks	Same as Birth or Death	Records since January 1968. Certified copies are not available from State office. Fee for search and verification of essential facts of divorce is $1.00.
	Varies	See remarks	Clerk of District Court in county where divorce was granted.
TRUST TERRITORY OF THE PACIFIC ISLANDS			
Birth or Death	$2.50	Commonwealth Courts Commonwealth Governments Saipan, Mariana Islands 96950	Clerk of Court in district where event occurred. (If not sure of district in which event occurred, write to Director of Medical Services to have inquiry referred to the correct district.) Courts have had records since November 21, 1952. Beginning 1950, a few records have been filed with the Hawaii Bureau of Vital Statistics.
Marriage	Varies	See remarks	Clerk of Court in district where marriage was performed.
Divorce	Varies	See remarks	Clerk of Court in district where divorce was granted.
UTAH			
Birth	$10.00	Bureau of Health Statistics Utah Department of Health 288 North 1460 West P.O. Box 16700 Salt Lake City, UT 84116-0700	State office has had records since 1905. If event occurred from 1890 to 1904 in Salt Lake City or Ogden, write to City Board of Health. For records elsewhere in the State from 1898 to 1904, write to County Clerk in county where event occurred.
Death	$7.00		

Place of event	Cost of copy	Address	Remarks
Marriage	$7.00	Same as Birth or Death	State office has had records since 1978. Only short form certified copies are available.
	Varies	See remarks	County Clerk in county where license was issued.
Divorce	$7.00	Same as Birth or Death	State office has had records since 1978. Only short form certified copies are available.
	Varies	See remarks	County Clerk in county where divorce was granted.
VERMONT			
Birth or Death	$5.00	Vermont Department of Health Vital Records Section Box 70 60 Main St. Burlington, VT 05401	Town or City Clerk of town where birth or death occurred.
Marriage	$5.00	Same as Birth or Death	
	$5.00	See remarks	Town Clerk in town where license was issued.
Divorce	$5.00	Same as Birth or Death	
VIRGINIA			
Birth or Death	$5.00	Division of Vital Records and Health Statistics State Department of Health James Madison Building P.O. Box 1000 Richmond, VA 23208	State office has had records from January 1853 to December 1896 and since June 14, 1912. For records between those dates, write to the Health Department in the city where event occurred.
Marriage	$5.00	Same as Birth or Death	Records since January 1853.
	Varies	See remarks	Clerk of Court in county or city where license was issued.
Divorce	$5.00	Same as Birth or Death	Records since January 1918.
	Varies	See remarks	Clerk of Court in county or city where divorce was granted.
VIRGIN ISLANDS (U.S.)			
Birth or Death			
St. Croix	$5.00	Registrar of Vital Statistics Charles Harwood Memorial Hospital St. Croix, VI 00820	Registrar has had birth and death records on file since 1840.
St. Thomas and St. John	$5.00	Registrar of Vital Statistics Charlotte Amalie St. Thomas, VI 00802	Registrar has had birth records on file since July 1906 and death records since January 1906.
Marriage	See remarks	Bureau of Vital Records and Statistical Services Virgin Islands Department of Health Charlotte Amalie St. Thomas, VI 00801	Certified copies are not available. Inquiries will be forwarded to appropriate office.
St. Croix	$2.00	Chief Deputy Clerk Territorial Court of the Virgin Islands P.O. Box 929 Christiansted St. Croix, VI 00820	
St. Thomas and St. John	$2.00	Clerk of the Territorial Court of the Virgin Islands P.O. Box 70 Charlotte Amalie St. Thomas, VI 00801	
Divorce	See remarks	Same as Marriage	Certified copies are not available. Inquiries will be forwarded to appropriate office.

Place of event	Cost of copy	Address	Remarks
St. Croix	$5.00	Same as Marriage	
St. Thomas and St. John	$5.00	Same as Marriage	

WASHINGTON

Place of event	Cost of copy	Address	Remarks
Birth or Death	$6.00	Vital Records P.O. Box 9709, ET-11 Olympia, WA 98504-9709	State office has had records since July 1907. For King, Pierce, and Spokane counties copies may also be obtained from county health departments. County Auditor of county of birth has registered births prior to July 1907.
Marriage	$6.00	Same as Birth or Death	State office has had records since January 1968.
	$2.00	See remarks	County Auditor in county where license was issued.
Divorce	$6.00	Same as Birth or Death	State office has had records since January 1968.
	Varies	See remarks	County Clerk in county where divorce was granted.

WEST VIRGINIA

Place of event	Cost of copy	Address	Remarks
Birth or Death	$5.00	Division of Vital Statistics State Department of Health State Office Building No. 3 Charleston, WV 25305	State office has had records since January 1917. For earlier records, write to Clerk of County Court in county where event occurred.
Marriage	$5.00	Same as Birth or Death	Records since 1921. Certified copies have been available since 1964.
	Varies	See remarks	County Clerk in county where license was issued.
Divorce	See remarks	Same as Birth or Death	Index since 1968. Some items may be verified (fee $2.00). Certified copies are not available from State Office.
	Varies	See remarks	Clerk of Circuit Court, Chancery Side, in county where divorce was granted.

WISCONSIN

Place of event	Cost of copy	Address	Remarks
Birth	$7.00	Bureau of Health Statistics Wisconsin Division of Health P.O. Box 309 Madison, WI 53701	State office has scattered records earlier than 1857. Records before October 1, 1907, are very incomplete. Additional copies of the same record ordered at the same time are $2.00 each.
Death	$5.00		
Marriage	$5.00	Same as Birth or Death	Records since April 1836. Records before October 1, 1907, are incomplete. Additional copies of the same record ordered at the same time are $2.00 each.
Divorce	$5.00	Same as Birth or Death	Records since October 1907. Additional copies of the same record ordered at the same time are $2.00 each.

WYOMING

Place of event	Cost of copy	Address	Remarks
Birth	$5.00	Vital Records Services Division of Health and Medical Services	State office has had records since July 1909.
Death	$3.00	Hathaway Building Cheyenne, WY 82002	
Marriage	$5.00	Same as Birth or Death	Records since May 1941.
	Varies	See remarks	County Clerk in county where license was issued.
Divorce	$5.00	Same as Birth or Death	Records since May 1941.
	Varies	See remarks	Clerk of District Court where Divorce took place.

Where To Write for Birth and Death Records of U.S. Citizens Who Were Born or Died Outside of the United States and Birth Certifications for Alien Children Adopted by U.S. Citizens

Births Records of Persons Born in Foreign Countries Who Are U.S. Citizens at Birth

Births of U.S. citizens in foreign countries should be reported to the nearest American consular office as soon after the birth as possible on the Consular Report of Birth (Form FS-240). This report should be prepared and filed by one of the parents. However, the physician or midwife attending the birth or any other person having knowledge of the facts can prepare the report.

Documentary evidence is required to establish citizenship. Consular offices provide complete information on what evidence is needed. The Consular Report of Birth is a sworn statement of facts of birth. When approved, it establishes in documentary form the child's acquisition of U.S. citizenship. Filing a Consular Report of Birth is not authorized for children 5 years of age or older.

A $6.00 fee is charged for reporting the birth. The original document is filed in the Passport Services, Correspondence Branch, U.S. Department of State, Washington, D.C. 20524. The parents are given a certified copy of the Consular Report of Birth (Form FS-240) and a short form, Certification of Birth (Form DS-1350 or Form FS-545).

To obtain a copy of a report of the birth in a foreign country of a U.S. citizen, write to Passport Services, Correspondence Branch, U.S. Department of State, Washington, D.C. 20524. State the full name of the child at birth, date of birth, place of birth, and names of parents. Also include any information about the U.S. passport on which the child's name was first included. Sign the request and state the relationship to the person whose record is being requested and the reason for the request.

The fee for each copy is $4.00. Enclose a check or money order made payable to the U.S. Department of State.

The Department of State issues two types of copies from the Consular Report of Birth (Form FS-240):

- A full copy of Form FS-240 as it was filed.

- A short form, Certification of Birth (Form DS-1350), which shows only the name and sex of child and the date and place of birth.

The information in both forms is valid. The Certification of Birth may be obtained in a name subsequently acquired by adoption or legitimation after proof is submitted to establish that such an action legally took place.

Birth Records of Alien Children Adopted by U.S. Citizens

Birth certifications for alien children adopted by U.S. citizens and lawfully admitted to the United States may be obtained from the Immigration and Naturalization Service (INS), U.S. Department of Justice, Washington, D.C. 20536, if the birth information is on file.

Certification may be issued for children under 21 years of age who were born in a foreign country. Requests must be submitted on INS Form G-641, which can be obtained from any INS office. (Address can be found in a telephone directory.) For Certification of Birth Data (INS Form G-350), a $5.00 search fee, paid by check or money order, should accompany INS Form G-641.

Certification can be issued in the new name of an adopted or legitimated child after proof of an adoption or legitimation is submitted to INS. Because it may be issued for a child who has not yet become a U.S. citizen, this certification (Form G-350) is not proof of U.S. nationality.

Certificate of Citizenship

U.S. citizens who were born abroad and later naturalized or who were born in a foreign country to a U.S. citizen (parent or parents) may apply for a certificate of citizenship pursuant to the provisions of Section 341 of the Immigration and Nationality Act. Application can be made for this document in the United States at the nearest office of the Immigration and Naturalization Service (INS). The INS will issue a certificate of citizenship for the person if proof of citizenship is submitted and the person is within the United States. The decision whether to apply for a certificate of citizenship is optional; its possession is not mandatory.

Death Records of U.S. Citizens Who Die in Foreign Countries

Reports of deaths of U.S. citizens who die in foreign countries are made to the nearest U.S. consular office. The reports are permanently filed in the U.S. Department of State. (See exception given below.)

To obtain a copy of a report, write to Passport Services, Correspondence Branch, U.S. Department of State, Washington, D.C. 20524. The fee for a copy is $4.00.

Exception: Reports of deaths of members of the Armed Forces of the United States are made only to the branch of the service to which the person was attached at the time of death—Army, Navy, Air Force, or Coast Guard. In these cases, requests for copies of records should be directed as follows.

For members of the Army, Navy, or Air Force:

Secretary of Defense
Washington, D.C. 20301

For members of the Coast Guard:

Commandant, P.S.
U.S. Coast Guard
Washington, D.C. 20226

Records of Births and Deaths Occurring on Vessels or Aircraft on the High Seas

When a birth or death occurs on the high seas, whether in an aircraft or on a vessel, the determination of where the record is filed is decided by the direction in which the vessel or aircraft was headed at the time the event occurred.

a. If the vessel or aircraft was outbound or docked or landed at a foreign port, requests for copies of the record should be made to the U.S. Department of State, Washington, D.C. 20520.

b. If the vessel or aircraft was inbound and the first port of entry was in the United States, write to the registration authority in the city where the vessel or aircraft docked or landed in the United States.

c. If the vessel was of U.S. registry, contact the U.S. Coast Guard facility at the port of entry.

Records Maintained by Foreign Countries

Most, but not all, foreign countries record births and deaths. It is not feasible to list in this publication all foreign vital records offices, the charges they make for copies of records, or the information they may require to locate a record. However, most foreign countries will provide certifications of births and deaths occurring within their boundaries.

U.S. citizens who need a copy of a foreign birth or death record may obtain assistance by writing to the Office of Special Consular Services, U.S. Department of State, Washington, D.C. 20520.

Aliens residing in the United States who seek records of these events should contact their nearest consular office.

THE BUSINESS WORLD

Whether or not you work in a business office, you're involved in business dealings every day. When you cash a paycheck, buy groceries, repair your car, or do any number of things, you must handle your money or credit in a business-like way. But how well do you run your own business affairs? This chapter will give you some basic information that should help you handle your money more wisely.

We've included a section on the duties of a secretary to help business executives and secretaries plan their work. At the end of the chapter you'll find an explanation of several common business terms.

How to Make and Use a Family Budget

The most important rule for making a family budget is: *Keep it simple.* If you try to set up a complicated system, you'll waste time with unnecessary bookkeeping. A budget is supposed to help you plan how you will spend your money, and it should help you keep track of how your plan worked. If it's so complex that you can't understand it, why bother?

Design your budget to fit your own needs. Don't try to imitate someone else's budget, because your own income and expenses are unique.

First, notice where you're spending your money now. The easiest way to do that is to study the checks you wrote last month. (The bank sends them back to you after they've been processed.) Make a stack of these, along with any bills or receipts that show how you spent your cash last month.

In another stack, collect the stubs from last month's paychecks and any other checks you received. On a slip of paper, note any cash you received and put it in this stack, too. This can be very important if you get part of your income in cash every month—for example, if you're a waitress and your customers leave you tips.

Now go through each of these stacks, making a list of your income and expenses. Under expenses, you should note how much you spent last month for:

1. Rent or house payments
2. Education
3. Insurance
4. Loan Payments
5. Food
6. Clothing
7. Transportation
8. Medical Expenses
9. Savings
10. Recreation
11. Miscellaneous Expenses

Under the income, list the different sources of your income last month:

1. Fixed Income (your paycheck, Social Security checks, or other regular income)

2. Other Income (income that varies every month, like interest from a savings account or money you get from babysitting)

Now add up the money on each list. If the total of expenses is bigger than the total list of income, it means you're trying to spend more money than you earn. Doing that over a long period of time will drive you into bankruptcy.

How much money *should* you be spending for each item? That depends on your own needs and style of life. The federal government has found that the average family of four in the United States is dividing its money something like this:

HOUSING 33%
FOOD 25%
TAXES 20%
TRANSPORTATION
& CLOTHING 10%
MEDICAL EXPENSES 5%
OTHER PERSONAL
EXPENSES 7%

This is only an average. Your own budget will probably call for spending more money on certain items and less on others.

Before you make a plan for spending your money, find how much you're able to spend. Work only with your *take-home pay*—your wages or salary *after* your employer has subtracted taxes and Social Security payments.

You must pay a specific amount for some items every month, such as your house rent or mortgage payment, insurance, loan payments, and so on. List these on the budget sheet first. Then look at the expenses that vary each month, such as food, clothing, and transportation. You can control the amount that you spend for these items; so if you need to spend less money, cut the amount you spend for these "variables" first.

If you're planning to make a big purchase (such as a car or a house), decide how much money you can save each month toward this expense and put it in a savings account at your bank. You may also want to put some money in a savings account to build up an emergency fund for unexpected bills.

If you're like most people, you will want to budget some money for recreation, entertainment, and impulse buying. Reduce the money you spend for these things if your budget is pinched.

After you've budgeted a sensible amount of money for every item, you may find that you've exceeded your income. If so, you need to find ways to earn more money or reduce your total spending. You may need to reduce the amount you plan to spend for several items on your budget.

Most people are learning to do some jobs for themselves instead of hiring professionals to do them. You can take care of simple car repairs, home remodeling, and yardwork by yourself. Manufacturers are offering new products to help you do these jobs at a fraction of what you'd pay someone else.

Watch for "sales" on items you know you'll need in upcoming months. Often you can plan your buying to take advantage of seasonal close-outs. For example, you can buy lawn furniture cheaply at the end of the summer and store it to use next summer.

Always try to get the best value for the dollars you spend. When you're buying a new product, compare several brand names to see which one gives you the best quality at the price you can afford to pay.

After you've worked with your budget for a while, you may want to get the advice of a money expert. Ask for help at your local bank or savings-and-loan association. If you belong to a credit union, ask their staff for the advice you need. A stock broker can give you sound advice about investments.

Whatever you do, *stick with the budget you've planned*. You will need to change it from time to time as your personal situation changes. But remember: If you spend more than you planned in one area, you'll need to spend less in other areas. Otherwise, your budget won't balance at the end of the month.

Use good common sense when you plan your budget. Your success or failure depends on you alone. It's your money and you must decide how to spend it.

How to Buy a House

Whether it's large or small, a house is probably the most expensive purchase you'll ever make. It's an important step toward financial security.

But you need to remember several things when you think about buying a house. For one thing, it will require you to spend money on other items besides the house payment. Can you afford the insurance, utilities, property taxes, and maintenance costs that come with a house? You need to know that before you buy.

Take time to compare several houses and find the one that's best for you. You'll probably live there for several years, so get a house you'll enjoy.

Of course, there are all kinds of houses to choose from. So where do you start looking? Naturally, the first big factor is *price*. There's no need to waste time looking at houses you can't afford. Here's a good rule of thumb to use for deciding how much you can spend on a house: *Multiply your annual income by two-and-a-half.* For example, if you earn $20,000, you could probably afford to buy a house that costs $40,000 to $50,000, assuming that the other house money you spend each month doesn't wreck your budget. The basic monthly expenses for your house—the total of mortgage payment, taxes, and insurance—should not be more than one-sixtieth of your annual income. In other words, if you earned $20,000 each year, you'd divide that by 60 and find your basic housing expenses shouldn't be more than $333 each month. Remember, though, that you will be paying for some variable housing expenses, such as utilities and maintenance, on top of that.

The Federal Housing Administration uses another guideline that might help you. The FHA says the total of *all* housing expenses—mortgage payments, taxes, utilities, and maintenance—should be no more than 35 percent of your take-home pay. For example, if your take-home pay is $1,000 per month, you shouldn't spend more than $350 for all of your housing expenses.

Let us say you've decided how much you can afford to pay and you've found the house you want to buy. Now you need to decide how you'll buy it. Most people can't afford to pay cash for the total price of a house, but there are several other ways you might buy it:

1. Contract. The seller may let you pay him a small down payment and sign a contract to pay him the rest in monthly installments. He does not give you the title to the house until you've paid him all of the money that the contract requires.

2. Bank Loan. You can give the seller a down payment of your own and borrow the rest of the money from a bank. The bank will loan you the money only if the house is in good condition and you've made a large enough down payment. The bank requires you to make a smaller down payment for newer houses. Under this plan, the bank holds the title to your house until you pay off the loan. If you fail to make your monthly payments, the bank can sell your house to get the rest of the money you owe. Savings-and-loan associations loan money in the same way, and sometimes they charge less interest than local banks. Mortgage companies and private loan companies can do this, too, but they often charge more interest than the banks.

3. VA Loan. If you've ever served in the United States military, you can borrow money for your house and the Veterans Administration will agree to pay off the loan if you fail to pay. Usually you don't need to put down as much of your own cash, and you pay less interest on the loan. But if you fail to make your monthly payments, the VA can sell your house to get the money you owe.

4. FHA Loan. If at least two banks refuse to loan you the money to buy a house, and if you have a fairly low income, you may get the Farmer's Home Administration to agree to pay off the loan if you fail. If the FHA agrees to do this, you'll need very little money for the down payment and you'll pay less interest than with a regular bank loan. But the FHA will want to make sure that you can afford to make the monthly payments, and the agency will check the house to see that it is a sound investment. The FHA will also require the seller to pay extra fees for setting up this kind of loan. For this reason, some people may not sell their property to you if you plan to buy it with an FHA Loan. You can buy a new house with an FHA Loan; but the house must be modest and economical to maintain. If you have an unusually low income, the FHA may give you *interest credit*, which allows you to pay much less than the normal rate of interest.

When most people buy a house, they seek the

help of a real estate broker. Home sellers usually ask brokers to offer their houses for sale, so a broker can show you several different homes in your price range. The broker will probably ask you to make a small down payment when you offer to buy a house; this is called *earnest money,* because it shows the seller that you're really interested in buying the house. If the seller accepts your offer, the earnest money will go toward buying the house; if he rejects your offer, the broker will usually give your earnest money back to you.

After you've agreed to purchase a house and you've secured the financing, you may be asked to pay certain fees for the transaction. This varies with the different types of loans, and you should ask the broker to explain these *closing costs* before you offer to buy a house.

Be sure that a lawyer examines the title papers on the property. If anything is out of order, the seller should correct it before you close the deal. Otherwise, you may discover later that other debts were standing against the house, and you may have to pay them.

To put it simply, you should know whether you can really afford to buy a house—and if so, how much you can pay—before you begin shopping for one. And you should rely on professional lawyers and real estate brokers to help you make the transaction. If you don't, you could make some costly mistakes.

How to Make a Will

A person writes a *will* to distribute his property after he dies. The will is a legal document that names the persons or institutions who will receive his belongings, and often it tells who will divide this property among the ones who receive it. A husband and wife should each have a will; their wills should work together, so that the property will be handed out properly if *both* of them die at the same time.

You should review your will and update it periodically. As your personal situation changes, you'll probably want to change your will. If you prepare a new will, you should destroy the old ones; two wills would complicate matters after you died.

It is best to consult a lawyer when you're drawing up your will. He will want a list of your property, including any real estate, money, vehicles, insurance policies, or stocks and bonds. Usually you would give all of these things to your spouse, if you are married. But be sure the will explains who will receive these things if you and your spouse die at the same time. Also be sure that the will names someone to care for your children. If you want to give part of your estate to schools, churches, or other organizations, you must name these agencies in your will and tell exactly how much you want each one to receive.

Decide who will distribute your property and carry out the other duties you mentioned in your will; you must name this person in the document. This person is called the *executor* (if male) or an *executrix* (if female).

After you have written your will and gotten a witness to sign it, put it in a secure place. Usually this would be a safety deposit box that you can rent at your local bank. Ask your lawyer to keep another copy in case yours is stolen, lost, or destroyed.

The Business Secretary

Many people dream of being secretary to an important person. The work is varied and full of interest, responsible and challenging. The compensation will match the responsibilities involved. A good secretary is held in high esteem.

Just what must you do to prepare yourself for this valued niche in the world of action?

You should have the background of a good education; your interests should be broad; your reading should be comprehensive. In addition, you should master the tools of your trade. Your stenography and typing must be perfect; you must know how to write good letters and file important papers. A secretarial course at any good business school will see to that. All this, naturally, has to be coupled with your firm determination to emerge as an expert practitioner of the required skills.

But beyond this, there is a *plus* that makes the difference between being just a routine secretary (the kind that comes by the dozen) and that topnotch, "crackerjack" secretary that every busy executive is proud to have. Such a secretary makes life in the office so much smoother for him and the rest of the organization that he is glad to turn over to his secretary much of the work of the office. An executive who has a good secretary is relieved of many of his routine responsibilities and is left free to make the big decisions that can vastly improve the performance of the firm.

PERSONALITY

Understanding, tact, judgment, memory, dependability, initiative, patience, self-control—these might head the list of qualities of the ideal secretary you are aspiring to be.

An employer expects that his secretary will be understanding and well educated, have exemplary manners, know what constitutes good business customs, and be able to practice them. The secretary should also have poise. Who would want a secretary who is shy and afraid to meet people, or one who is brash, forward, obtrusive, and loud? When it comes to personal appearance, the secretary should be neat, but not gaudy. Dress, carriage, grooming, and hair should be attractive without being in any way extreme. The secretary

should have a pleasant voice; every caller is exposed to the secretary's voice. It must combine warmth and impersonality, friendliness and restraint. Surely, it is no easy task to be an excellent secretary.

ATTITUDE

Perhaps the word *loyalty* best describes the attitude the secretary should have toward job and employer. It is important to have a sincere interest, not only in the particular work being done, but in the overall welfare of the company. In every task undertaken, the good secretary puts forth the very best effort possible. Loyalty will make the job easy.

Sometimes in large organizations "the boss's secretary" gets into the habit of assuming or taking for granted privileges that others do not have. This is to be avoided. In the last analysis, you are there to do your part—and not an inconsiderable part—to guarantee this smooth functioning of the office.

DUTIES

As secretary, you keep the records; you attend to correspondence, both incoming and outgoing; you see or talk to visitors and telephone callers. In some cases you do the personal filing for your particular employer. You are ready to be called upon for what may be required in the way of business tasks.

Records

When Mr. Jones, president of the ABC Company, arrives at his office in the morning, he naturally wants to know what his day is going to bring, insofar as this is predictable. It is a good idea to let him see at a glance just what appointments and commitments he has for that day. So arrive at the office ahead of him and place on his desk, neatly typed up, a list of the day's activities. To do this, you should keep three calendars: your own, one for your employer, and a follow-up calendar (the so-called tickler file). This third file consists of a file box or drawer with 12 tab cards, one for each month of the year, and 31 tab cards, one for each day of the month. Behind the appropriate month and day (which is moved forward daily to the front of the box or file) you place notations on appointments, meetings, commitments, reminders, and so on. Each morning, you go through the material for the particular day, discarding what may have lost validity and typing up the day's schedule for Mr. Jones' desk.

Mr. Jones may also want to be reminded of significant family dates and anniversaries, holidays, pending trips, dates of payments and taxes due, and the like. If so, you should give him these reminders at the proper time. Thus, if he is planning to send a birthday check or other present to his daughter at college, remind him of this a week in advance, again three days before, and possibly on the very day (since he may want to call her long distance).

If Mr. Jones sets aside a few minutes at the start of the business day for a short conference, during which the two of you can go over the program for the day, it will make the day easier for you both. Of course, that is up to Mr. Jones. But such conferences have worked out splendidly in many offices.

Correspondence

Generally, mail addressed to a particular executive is placed unopened on his secretary's desk as soon as it arrives. It then becomes your duty to open this mail and arrange for its proper distribution. A good idea is to make a preliminary division into four categories:

1. Correspondence
2. Bills and statements
3. Newspapers and periodicals
4. Advertisements and circulars

Each of these initial piles is then further subdivided into: (a) for the employer's attention; (b) for the attention of others in the organization; (c) for the secretary's own attention; (d) possible discards. This last applies only to the fourth category above, and must depend on the very careful discretion of the secretary.

The procedure for mail marked "Personal" varies with the particular organization and the wishes of your employer. Mr. Jones may or may not want you to leave this mail unopened for him to handle himself. Perhaps he prefers to have you open *all* his mail, regardless of the notation on the envelope. He may wish to have such letters placed in a separate folder. You carry out his wishes, of course.

You may prepare letters regarding company business, personal letters, and miscellaneous courtesy letters. When you are expected to write such letters, bear in mind the newspaper reporter's essential five: Who, What, When, Where, and Why. "Short and to the point" is the rule.

For spellings, word divisions, and distinctions among synonyms, *never guess;* consult a standard dictionary. For punctuation, capitalization, and abbreviations, consult the dictionary or a good style book. As for vocabulary and grammar, follow correct usage. Much of what you will need to know will be found in the early sections of this book.

You may need to compose replies to all but the most personal letters. Or it may be Mr. Jones' custom to spend a session with you daily, going over that day's incoming mail. He may dictate all or most of his letters to you, but there are no hard and fast rules. Your employer's wishes are law; carry them out according to the letter and spirit of these wishes.

In general, toward the end of the business day, you bring all outgoing mail to Mr. Jones for his signature. Then you must check every letter to be sure that it is signed, that any enclosures are included, and that the addresses inside the letter and on the envelope conform. Only then is the outgoing mail ready for mailing. You keep copies of any of the letters that your employer wants you to file.

Callers

In seeing your employer's visitors and greeting his telephone callers, you must combine the functions of a receptionist, a diplomat, a welcoming committee, a watchdog, and even a "bouncer." When you greet the caller, you must find out the purpose of his visit and make him comfortable. On some occasions you must be able to get rid of him as quickly and expeditiously as possible. But no matter what your purpose, you must remain polite. You must not convey an air of impatience or hostility. You must not antagonize the visitor or caller; you can be firm, but you must remain friendly. A good secretary soon learns whom an employer wants to see and whom he doesn't, whether to refer the caller to someone else in the organization, or whether to deal with the caller's problem yourself. This aspect of your job calls for excellent judgment and quick decisions. It demands poise, tact, good manners, and adaptability. In making these first contacts with visitors and telephone callers, remember you are serving both your employer and the caller.

Filing

Less than twenty-four hours after the tragic death of President Kennedy, the television screen showed his private files being removed from the Presidential office. In some offices, there is a central filing system that includes all but the most personal correspondence. But in some offices the filing of an executive's private and business correspondence is his secretary's responsibility. It has been said that if you file something correctly, there is only one place where it can be found. But if you file something incorrectly, you may have to look in a thousand places and then not find it. See to it that everything you file is filed in the most logical place it belongs.

CONDENSED WORLD GAZETTEER

Keyed to the Quick Reference World Map (next two pages)

Latest Estimated Population Figures

AFGHANISTAN (E-23) People's Republic. Area 252,000 sq. mi. Pop. 15,056,000. Capital Kabul.

ALBANIA (D-20) Communist. Area 11,000 sq. mi. Pop. 3,046,000. Capital Tirane.

ALGERIA (E-19) Republic. Area 896,593 sq. mi. Pop. 22,107,000. Capital Alger (Algiers).

ANDORRA (D-19) Co-Principality. Area 179 sq. mi. Pop. 43,000. Capital Andorra la Vella.

ANGOLA (J-20) People's Republic. Area 481,350 sq. mi. Pop. 7,948,000. Capital Luanda.

ARGENTINA (L-14) Republic. Area 1,072,163 sq. mi. Pop. 30,708,000. Capital Buenos Aires.

AUSTRALIA* (K-3) Federal Parliamentary State. Area 2,967,900. sq. mi. Pop. 15,345,000. Capital Canberra.

AUSTRIA (D-19) Area 32,375 sq. mi. Pop. 7,451,000. Capital Wien (Vienna).

BAHAMAS* (F-14) Independent Commonwealth. Area 5,382 sq. mi. Pop. 230,000. Capital Nassau.

BAHRAIN (F-22) Independent Monarchy (Emirate). Area 256 sq. mi. Pop. 431,000. Capital Al Manama.

BANGLADESH* (F-1) Area 55,126 sq. mi. Pop. 101,408,000. Capital Dacca.

BARBADOS* (G-15) Parliamentary State. Area 166 sq. mi. Pop. 252,000. Capital Bridgetown.

BELGIUM (C-19) Constitutional Monarchy. Area 11,782 sq. mi. Pop. 9,858,000. Capital Bruxelles (Brussels).

BELIZE* (G-13) Parliamentary. Area 8,866 sq. mi. Pop. 166,400. Capital Belmopan.

BENIN (DAHOMEY) (H-19) Marxist-Leninist. Area 43,475 sq. mi. Pop. 4,005,000. Capital Porto Novo.

BHUTAN (F-1) Monarchy. Area 18,000 sq. mi. Pop. 1,417,000. Capital Thimphu.

BOLIVIA (J-14) Republic. Area 424,165 sq. mi. Pop. 6,195,000. Capital La Paz and Sucre.

BOTSWANA* (K-20) Republic. Area 222,000 sq. mi. Pop. 1,068,000. Capital Gaborone.

BRAZIL (J-15) Federal Republic. Area. 3,286,488 sq. mi. Pop. 135,000,000. Capital Brasília.

BRUNEI* (H-2) Sultanate. (United Kingdom Prot.) Area 2,226 sq. mi. Pop. 232,000. Capital Bandar Seri Begawan.

BULGARIA (D-20) Communist. Area 42,823 sq. mi. Pop. 8,974,000. Capital Sofiya (Sofia).

BURMA (F-1) Socialist Republic. Area 261,789 sq. mi. Pop. 36,919,000. Capital Rangoon.

BURUNDI (I-20) Republic. Area 10,747 sq. mi. Pop. 4,673,000. Capital Bujumbura.

CAMBODIA (G-2) People's Republic. Area 69,898 sq. mi. Pop. 6,249,000. Capital Phnom Penh.

CAMEROON (H-19) Republic. Area 179,558 sq. mi. Pop. 9,737,000. Capital Yaoundé.

CANADA* (B-12) Federal Parliamentary State. Area 3,851,809 sq. mi. Pop. 25,399,000. Capital Ottawa.

CANAL ZONE (H-13) U.S. Terr. Area 647 sq. mi. Pop. 45,200. Capital Balboa Heights.

CAPE VERDE (G-16) Independent Republic. Area 1,557 sq. mi. Pop. 312,000. Capital Praia.

CENTRAL AFRICAN REPUBLIC (H-20) Republic. Area 241,305 sq. mi. Pop. 2,664,000. Capital Bangui.

CHAD (G-20) Republic. Area 495,750 sq. mi. Pop. 5,036,000. Capital N'Djamena.

CHILE (L-14) Military Dictatorship. Area 292,258 sq. mi. Pop. 12,042,000. Capital Santiago.

CHINA (E-2) People's Republic. Area 3,691,500 sq. mi. Pop. 1,037,588,000. Capital Peiping (Peking).

COLOMBIA (H-14) Republic. Area 439,737 sq. mi. Pop. 29,347,000. Capital Bogotá.

COMOROS (J-21) Republic. Area 863 sq. mi. Pop. 469,000. Capital Moroni.

CONGO (I-19) People's Republic. Area 132,046 sq. mi. Pop. 1,798,000. Capital Brazzaville.

COSTA RICA (H-13) Democratic Republic. Area 19,652 sq. mi. Pop. 2,644,000. Capital San José.

CUBA (F-13) Communist Dictatorship. Area 42,827 sq. mi. Pop. 10,105,000. Capital Habana (Havana).

CYPRUS* (E-21) Republic. Area 3,572 sq. mi. Pop. 665,000. Capital Nicosia.

CZECHOSLOVAKIA (D-20) Communist. Area 49,374 sq. mi. Pop. 15,502,000. Capital Praha (Prague).

DENMARK (C-19) Constitutional Monarchy. Area 16,630 sq. mi. Pop. 5,105,000. Capital København (Copenhagen).

DJIBOUTI (G-21) Republic. Area 8,900 sq. mi. Pop. 297,000. Capital Djibouti.

DOMINICAN REPUBLIC (G-14) Representative Democracy. Area 18,658 sq. mi. Pop. 6,614,000. Capital Santo Domingo.

ECUADOR (I-13) Republic. Area 109,484 sq. mi. Pop. 9,378,000. Capital Quito.

EGYPT (F-20) Republic. Area 386,900 sq. mi. Pop. 49,000,000. Capital Cairo.

EL SALVADOR (G-13) Republic. Area 8,124 sq. mi. Pop. 4,961,000. Capital San Salvador.

EQUATORIAL GUINEA (H-19) Unitary Republic. Area 10,830 sq. mi. Pop. 350,000. Capital Malabo.

ETHIOPIA (H-21) Military Dictatorship. Area 471,800 sq. mi. Pop. 42,266,000. Capital Addis Ababa.

FIJI* (J-6) Independent Parliamentary State. Area 7,055 sq. mi. Pop. 700,000. Capital Suva.

FINLAND (B-20) Republic. Area 130,129 sq. mi. Pop. 4,908,000. Capital Helsinki.

FRANCE (D-19) Republic. Area 210,039 sq. mi. Pop. 55,041,000. Capital Paris.

FRENCH GUIANA (H-15) Overseas Department. Area 34,750 sq. mi. Pop. 82,700. Capital Cayenne.

GABON (I-19) Republic. Area 103,347 sq. mi. Pop. 988,000. Capital Libreville.

GAMBIA, THE* (G-17) Republic. Area 4,467 sq. mi. Pop. 751,000. Capital Banjul.

GERMANY, EAST (C-19) Communist. Area 41,650 sq. mi. Pop. 16,686,000. Capital East Berlin.

GERMANY, WEST (C-19) Federal Republic. Area 95,985 sq. mi. Pop. 60,950,000. Capital Bonn.

GHANA* (H-18) Authoritarian. Area 92,100 sq. mi. Pop. 13,004,000. Capital Accra.

GIBRALTAR* (E-18) United Kingdom Colony. Area 2.25 sq. mi. Pop. 30,000. Capital Gibraltar.

GREECE (E-20) Republic. Area 50,960 sq. mi. Pop. 9,921,000. Capital Athínai (Athens).

GREENLAND (A-16) Danish Colony. Area 840,000 sq. mi. Pop. 53,000. Capital Godthaab.

GRENADA* (G-15) Parliamentary State. Area 133 sq. mi. Pop. 113,000. Capital Saint George's.

GUAM (G-4) U.S. Terr. Area 209 sq. mi. Pop. 119,540. Capital Agana.

GUATEMALA (G-12) Military. Area 42,042 sq. mi. Pop. 8,346,000. Capital Guatemala.

GUINEA (G-18) Republic. Area 94,926 sq. mi. Pop. 5,597,000. Capital Conakry.

GUINEA-BISSAU (G-17) Republic. Area 13,948 sq. mi. Pop. 858,000. Capital Bissau.

GUYANA* (H-15) Republic. Area 83,000 sq. mi. Pop. 768,000. Capital Georgetown.

HAITI (G-14) Dictatorship. Area 10,714 sq. mi. Pop. 5,762,000. Capital Port-au-Prince.

HONDURAS (G-13) Democratic Constitutional Republic. Area 43,277 sq. mi. Pop. 4,499,000. Capital Tegucigalpa.

HONG KONG* (F-2) United Kingdom Colony. Area 403 sq. mi. Pop. 5,287,600. Capital Victoria.

HUNGARY (D-20) Communist Unitary State. Area 35,920 sq. mi. Pop. 10,644,000. Capital Budapest.

ICELAND (B-17) Republic. Area 39,769 sq. mi. Pop. 241,000. Capital Reykjavik.

INDIA* (F-24) Federal Republic. Area 1,269,420 sq. mi. Pop. 767,681,000. Capital New Delhi.

INDONESIA (I-2) Republic. Area 782,663 sq. mi. Pop. 173,103,000. Capital Jakarta.

IRAN (PERSIA) (E-22) Islamic Republic. Area 636,000 sq. mi. Pop. 45,191,000. Capital Tehran.

IRAQ (E-21) Ruling Council. Area 168,928 sq. mi. Pop. 15,507,000. Capital Baghdad.

IRELAND (EIRE) (C-18) Republic. Area 27,136 sq. mi. Pop. 3,588,000. Capital Baile Atha Cliath (Dublin).

ISRAEL (E-21) Parliamentary Democracy. Area 7,992 sq. mi. Pop. 4,128,000. Capital Jerusalem.

ITALY (D-19) Republic. Area 116,313 sq. mi. Pop. 57,116,000. Capital Roma (Rome).

IVORY COAST (H-18) Republic. Area 123,484 sq. mi. Pop. 10,090,000. Capital Abidjan.

JAMAICA* (G-13) Constitutional Monarchy. Area 4,244 sq. mi. Pop. 2,366,000. Capital Kingston.

JAPAN (E-4) Parliamentary Democracy. Area 145,747 sq. mi. Pop. 120,731,000. Capital Tokyo.

JORDAN (F-21) Constitutional Monarchy. Area 36,832 sq. mi. Pop. 2,668,000. Capital Amman.

KENYA* (H-21) Republic. Area 224,961 sq. mi. Pop. 20,194,000. Capital Nairobi.

KOREA, NORTH (D-3) Communist State. Area 46,800 sq. mi. Pop. 20,082,000. Capital Pyongyang.

KOREA, SOUTH (E-3) Republic. Area 38,130 sq. mi. Pop. 42,643,000. Capital Seoul.

KUWAIT (F-22) Constitutional Monarchy. Area 6,880 sq. mi. Pop. 1,710,000. Capital Al Kuwait.

LAOS (G-2) Communist. Area 91,400 sq. mi. Pop. 3,605,000. Capital Vientiane.

LEBANON (E-21) Republic. Area 3,950 sq. mi. Pop. 2,619,000. Capital Bayrut (Beirut).

LESOTHO* (K-20) Constitutional Monarchy. Area 11,720 sq. mi. Pop. 1,512,000. Capital Maseru.

LIBERIA (H-18) Military. Area 43,000 sq. mi. Pop. 2,232,000. Capital Monrovia.

LIBYA (F-20) Socialist Republic. Area 675,000 sq. mi. Pop. 3,752,000. Capital Tripoli.

LIECHTENSTEIN (D-19) Hereditary Constitutional Monarchy. Area 62 sq. mi. Pop. 27,000. Capital Vaduz.

LUXEMBOURG (D-19) Constitutional Monarchy. Area 999 sq. mi. Pop. 366,000. Capital Luxembourg.

MACAO (F-2) Port. Overseas Province. Area 6 sq. mi. Pop. 340,000. Capital Macao.

MADAGASCAR (J-22) Republic. Area 226,658 sq. mi. Pop. 9,941,000. Capital Antananarivo.

MALAWI* (J-21) Republic. Area 45,747 sq. mi. Pop. 7,056,000. Capital Lilongwe.

MALAYSIA* (H-2) Federal Constitutional Monarchy. Comprises West Malaysia and East Malaysia (Sarawak and Sabah). Area 127,316 sq. mi. Pop. 15,467,000. Capital Kuala Lumpur.

MALDIVES (H-23) Republic. Area 115 sq. mi. Pop. 182,000. Capital Male.

MALI (G-18) Republic. Area 478,822 sq. mi. Pop. 7,721,000. Capital Bamako.

MALTA* (E-19) Republic. Area 122 sq. mi. Pop. 355,000. Capital Valetta.

MAURITANIA (G-18) Military Republic. Area 398,000 sq. mi. Pop. 1,656,000. Capital Nouakchott.

MAURITIUS* (K-22) Parliamentary State. Area 787.5 sq. mi. Pop. 1,024,900. Capital Port Louis.

MEXICO (F-12) Federal Republic. Area 761,604 sq. mi. Pop. 79,662,000. Capital Mexico City.

MONACO (D-19) Constitutional Monarchy. Area 0.73 sq. mi. Pop. 28,000. Capital Monaco-Ville.

MONGOLIA (D-1) People's Republic. Area 604,000 sq. mi. Pop. 1,893,000. Capital Ulaanbaatar (Ulan Bator).

MOROCCO (E-18) Constitutional Monarchy. Area 177,117 sq. mi. Pop. 23,117,000. Capital Rabat.

MOZAMBIQUE (J-21) People's Republic. Area 308,642 sq. mi. Pop. 13,638,000. Capital Maputo.

NAMIBIA (SOUTH-WEST AFRICA) (K-20) South Africa Terr. Area 318,261 sq. mi. Pop. 1,090,000. Capital Windhoek.

NAURU* (I-6) Republic. Area 8.2 sq. mi. Pop. 8,000. Capital Yaren.

NEPAL (F-24) Constitutional Monarchy. Area 54,362 sq. mi. Pop. 16,966,000. Capital Kathmandu.

NETHERLANDS (C-19) Constitutional Monarchy. Area 15,892 sq. mi. Pop. 14,481,000. Capital Amsterdam.

NEW ZEALAND* (M-6) Parliamentary State. Area 103,747 sq. mi. Pop. 3,271,000. Capital Wellington.

NICARAGUA (G-13) Republic. Area 50,000 sq. mi. Pop. 2,232,000. Capital Managua.

NIGER (F-19) Republic. Area 489,000 sq. mi. Pop. 6,491,000. Capital Niamey.

NIGERIA* (H-19) Military Dictatorship. Area 356,699 sq. mi. Pop. 102,783,000. Capital Lagos.

NORWAY (B-19) Hereditary Constitutional Monarchy. Area 125,053 sq. mi. Pop. 4,152,000. Capital Oslo.

OMAN (F-22) Absolute Monarchy. Area 82,000 sq. mi. Pop. 1,228,000. Capital Masqat (Muscat).

PAKISTAN (F-23) Martial Law Regime. Area 307,374 sq. mi. Pop. 99,199,000. Capital Islamabad.

PANAMA (H-13) Constitutional Democracy Centralized Republic. Area 29,209 sq. mi. Pop. 2,180,000. Capital Panama.

PAPUA NEW GUINEA (I-4) Parliamentary Democracy. Area 178,260 sq. mi. Pop. 3,326,000. Capital Port Moresby.

PARAGUAY (K-15) Republic. Area 157,048 sq. mi. Pop. 3,989,000. Capital Asuncion.

PERU (I-13) Constitutional Republic. Area 496,224 sq. mi. Pop. 19,696,000. Capital Lima.

PHILIPPINES (G-3) Republic. Area 115,800 sq. mi. Pop. 56,808,000. Capital Manila.

POLAND (C-20) Communist. Area 120,725 sq. mi. Pop. 37,160,000. Capital Warszawa (Warsaw).

PORTUGAL (E-18) Parliamentary Democracy. Area 35,383 sq. mi. Pop. 10,046,000. Capital Lisboa (Lisbon).

PUERTO RICO (G-14) U.S. Commonwealth. Area 3,421 sq. mi. Pop. 3,279,231. Capital San Juan.

QATAR (F-22) Independent Emirate. Area 4,400 sq. mi. Pop. 301,000. Capital Doha.

RHODESIA (J-20) Republic. Area 150,875 sq. mi. Pop. 6,530,000. Capital Salisbury.

ROMANIA (D-20) Communist. Area 91,700 sq. mi. Pop. 22,734,000. Capital Bucuresti (Bucharest).

RWANDA (I-20) Republic. Area 10,169 sq. mi. Pop. 6,115,000. Capital Kigali.

SAN MARINO (D-19) Independent Republic. Area 24 sq. mi. Pop. 22,300. Capital San Marino.

SÃO TOMÉ AND PRÍNCIPE (H-19) Democratic Republic. Area 372 sq. mi. Pop. 105,000. Capital São Tomé.

SAUDI ARABIA (F-21) Monarchy. Area 865,000 sq. mi. Pop. 11,152,000. Capital Riyadh.

SENEGAL (G-18) Republic. Area 78,685 sq. mi. Pop. 6,755,000. Capital Dakar.

SEYCHELLES* (I-22) Single Party Republic. Area 107 sq. mi. Pop. 66,000. Capital Victoria. Mahé.

SIERRA LEONE* (H-18) Republic. Area 27,925 sq. mi. Pop. 3,883,000. Capital Freetown.

SINGAPORE* (H-2) Parliamentary Democracy. Area 227 sq. mi. Pop. 2,556,000. Capital Singapore.

SOMALIA (H-22) Independent Republic. Area 246,300 sq. mi. Pop. 7,595,000. Capital Mogadishu.

SOUTH AFRICA (K-20) Tricarmel Parliamentary. Area 471,445 sq. mi. Pop 32,465,000. Capitals Pretoria and Cape Town.

SPAIN (D-18) Constitutional Monarchy. Area 194,885 sq. mi. Pop. 38,829,000. Capital Madrid.

SRI LANKA (CEYLON)* (H-24) Republic. Area 25,332 sq. mi. Pop. 16,344,000. Capital Colombo.

SUDAN (G-20) Republic. Area 967,500 sq. mi. Pop. 22,972,000. Capital Khartoum.

SURINAME (H-15) Military-Civilian Executive. Area 70,060 sq. mi. Pop. 395,000. Capital Paramaribo.

SWAZILAND* (K-21) Parliamentary Monarchy. Area 6,704 sq. mi. Pop. 636,000. Capital Mbabane.

SWEDEN (B-20) Constitutional Monarchy. Area 173,732 sq. mi. Pop. 8,348,000. Capital Stockholm.

SWITZERLAND (D-19) Federal State. Area 15,943 sq. mi. Pop. 6,457,000. Capital Bern.

SYRIA (E-21) Socialist. Area 71,498 sq. mi. Pop. 10,535,000. Capital Dimashq (Damascus).

TAIWAN (FORMOSA) (F-3) One-Party System. Area 13,893 sq. mi. Pop. 19,338,000. Capital Taipei.

TANZANIA* (I-21) Republic. Area 364,943 sq. mi. Pop. 21,701,000. Capital Dar es Salaam.

THAILAND (SIAM) (G-1) Constitutional Monarchy. Area 198,500 sq. mi. Pop. 51,546,000. Capital Krung Thep (Bangkok).

TOGO (H-19) Republic. Area 21,925 sq. mi. Pop. 3,023,000. Capital Lomé.

TONGA* (K-7) Constitutional Monarchy. Area 225 sq. mi. Pop. 103,000. Capital Nuku'alofa.

TRINIDAD-TOBAGO* (H-14) Parliamentary Democracy. Area 1,980 sq. mi. Pop. 1,186,000. Capital Port of Spain.

TUNISIA (E-19) Republic. Area 63,379 sq. mi. Pop. 7,259,000. Capital Tunis.

TURKEY (E-21) Republic. Area 300,948 sq. mi. Pop. 50,661,000. Capital Ankara.

UGANDA* (H-21) Military Dictatorship. Area 93,104 sq. mi. Pop. 14,689,000. Capital Kampala.

UNION OF SOVIET SOCIALIST REPUBLICS (C-22) Federal Socialist Republic. Area 8,600,340 sq. mi. Pop. 277,504,000. Capital Moskva (Moscow).

UNITED ARAB EMIRATES (F-22) Federation. Area 32,300 sq. mi. Pop. 1,283,000. Capital Abu Dhabi.

UNITED KINGDOM (GREAT BRITAIN and NORTHERN IRELAND)* (C-18) Constitutional Monarchy. Area 94,217 sq. mi. Pop. 56,423,000. Capital London.

UNITED STATES (E-12) Federal Republic. Area 3,615,122 sq. mi. Pop. 238,631,000. Capital Washington, D.C.

BURKINA FASO (G-18) Republic. Area 105,869 sq. mi. Pop. 6,907,000. Capital Ouagadougou.

URUGUAY (L-15) Republic. Area 68,536 sq. mi. Pop. 2,936,000. Capital Montevideo.

VATICAN CITY (D-19) Independent Sovereignty. Area 108.7 acres. Pop. 1,000.

VENEZUELA (H-14) Federal Republic. Area 352,144 sq. mi. Pop. 17,317,000. Capital Caracas.

VIETNAM (G-2) Communist People's Republic. Area 130,653 sq. mi. Pop. 60,492,000. Capital Hanoi.

WESTERN SAMOA* (J-7) Parliamentary Democracy. Area 1,133 sq. mi. Pop. 160,000. Capital Apia.

YEMEN (G-21) Republic. Area 77,200 sq. mi. Pop. 6,159,000. Capital San'a.

YEMEN, PEOPLE'S DEMOCRATIC REPUBLIC OF (G-22) Republic. Area 111,074 sq. mi. Pop. 2,209,000. Capital Aden.

YUGOSLAVIA (D-20) Federal Socialist Republic. Area 98,766 sq. mi. Pop. 23,124,000. Capital Beograd (Belgrade).

ZAIRE (I-20) Republic. Area 905,365 sq. mi. Pop. 30,505,000. Capital Kinshasa.

ZAMBIA* (J-20) Republic. Area 290,586 sq. mi. Pop. 6,832,000. Capital Lusaka.

**Member British Commonwealth of Nations.*

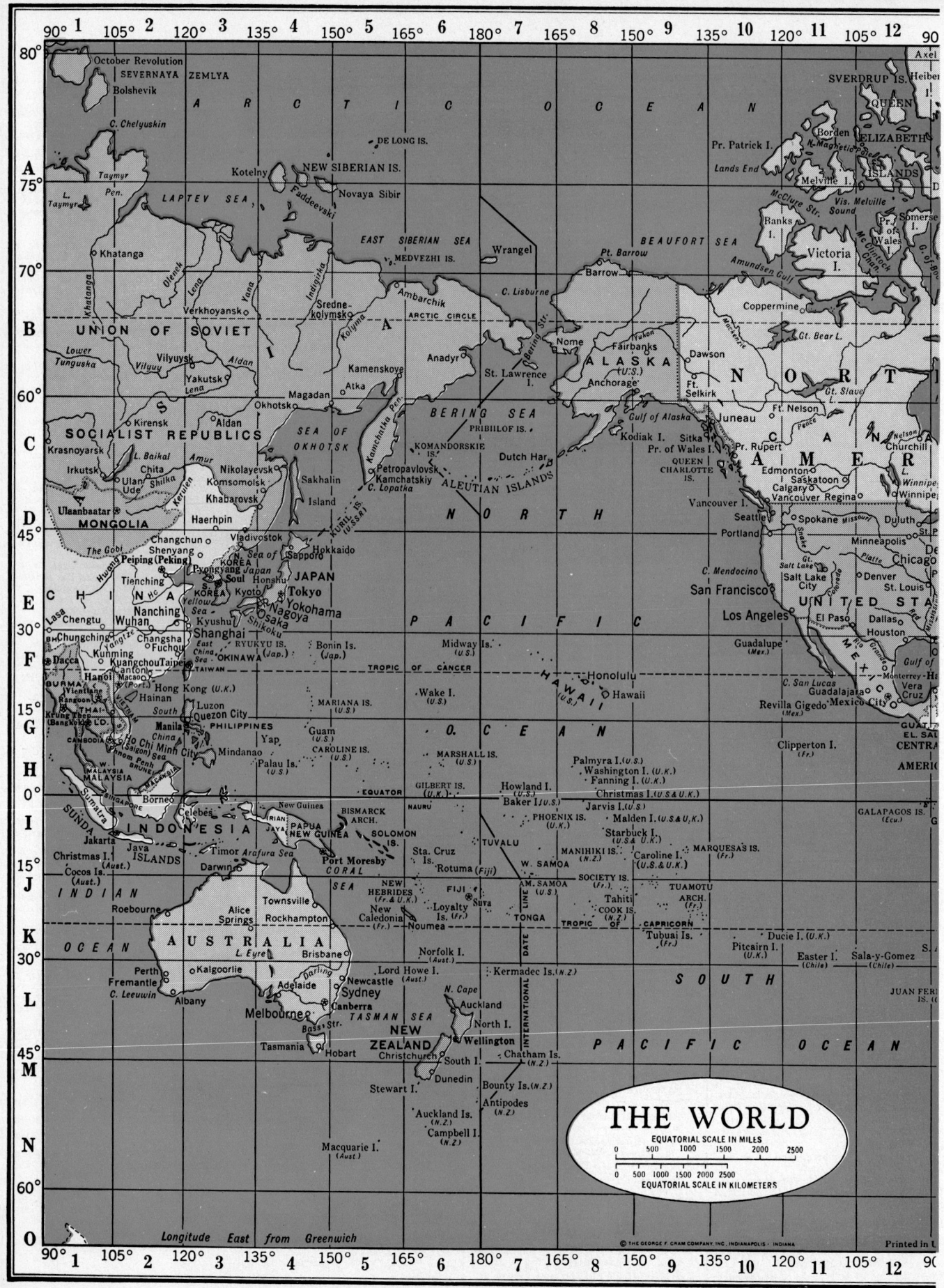

THE WORLD

EQUATORIAL SCALE IN MILES
0 500 1000 1500 2000 2500

0 500 1000 1500 2000 2500
EQUATORIAL SCALE IN KILOMETERS

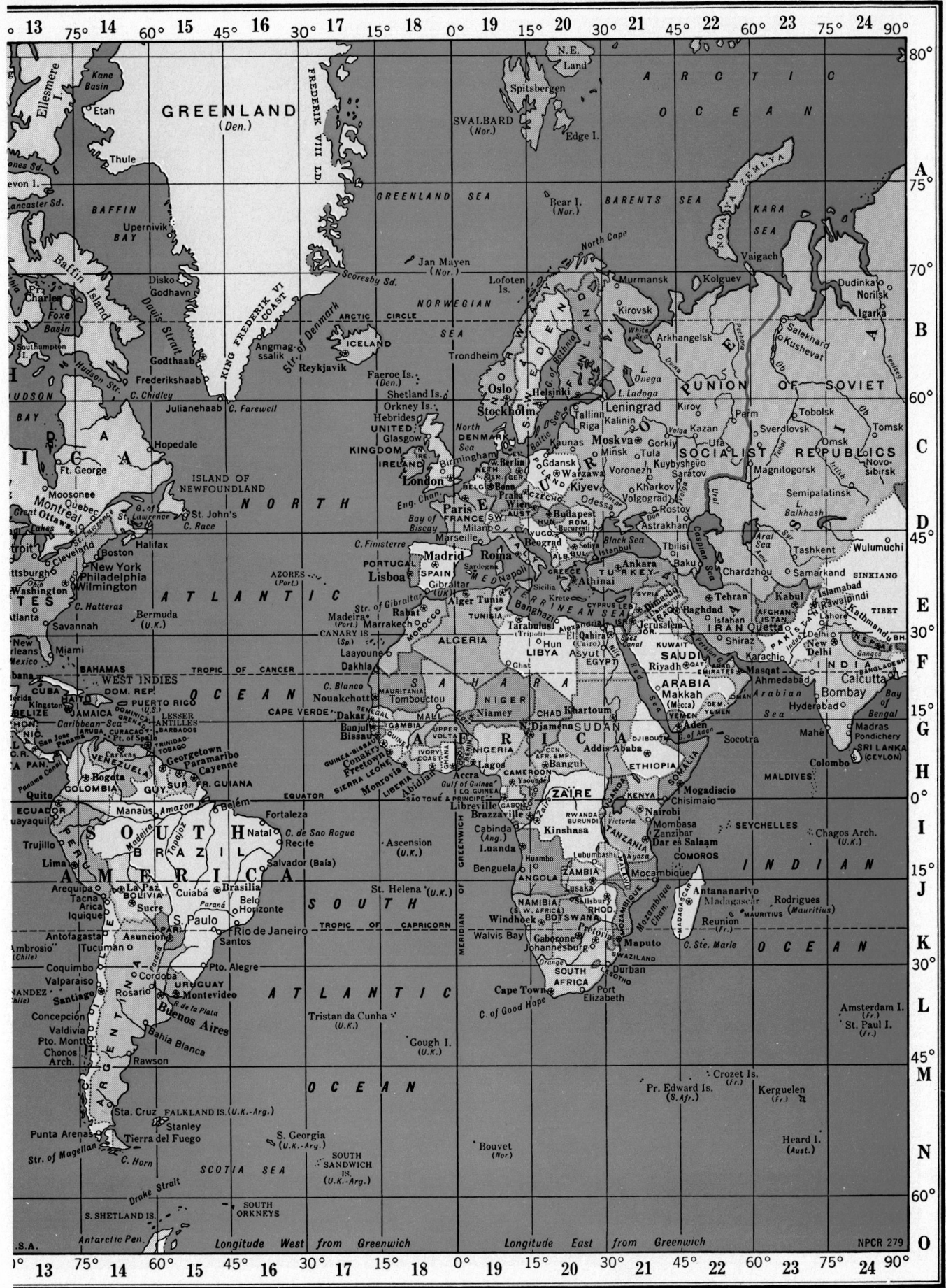

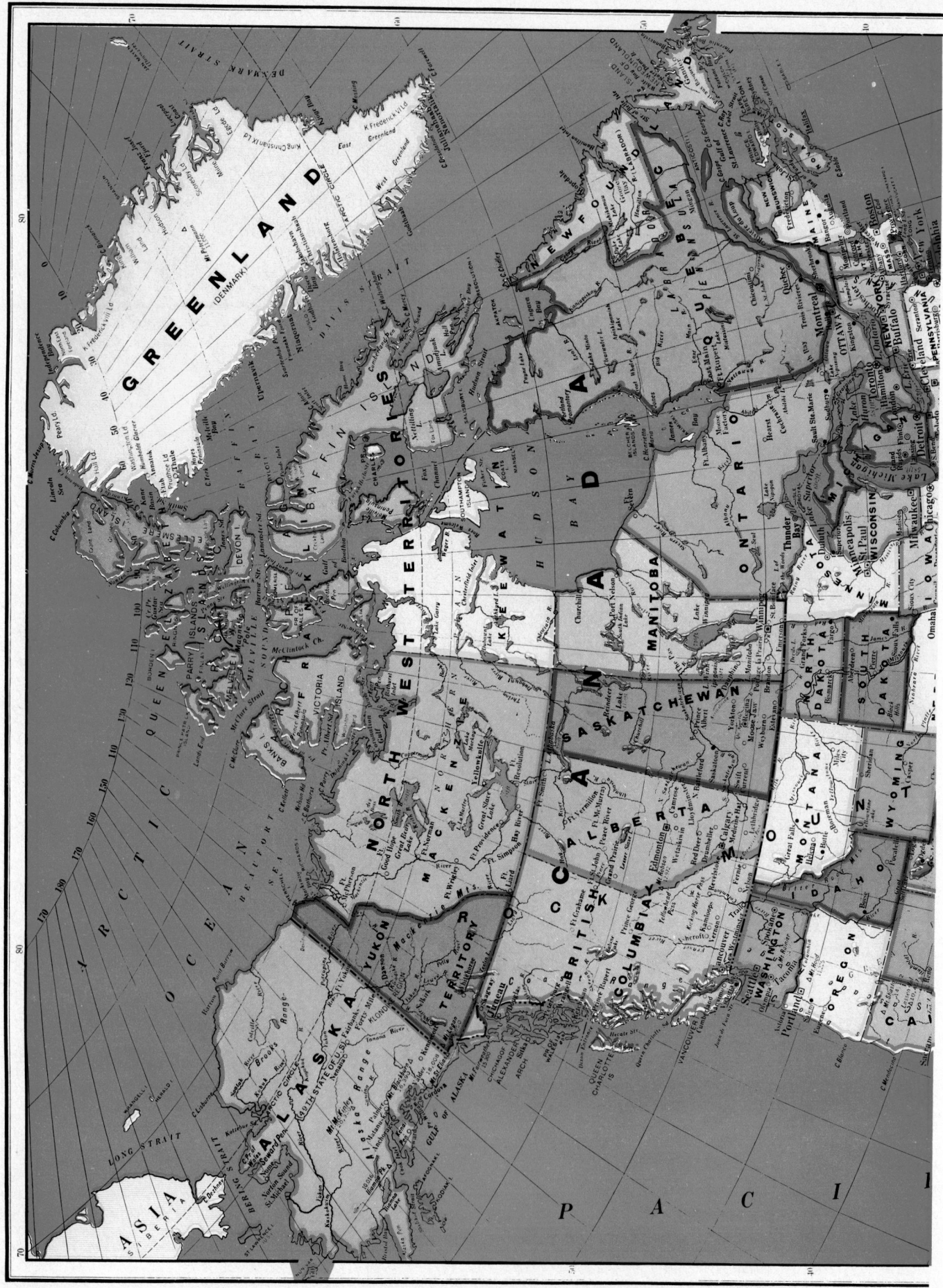

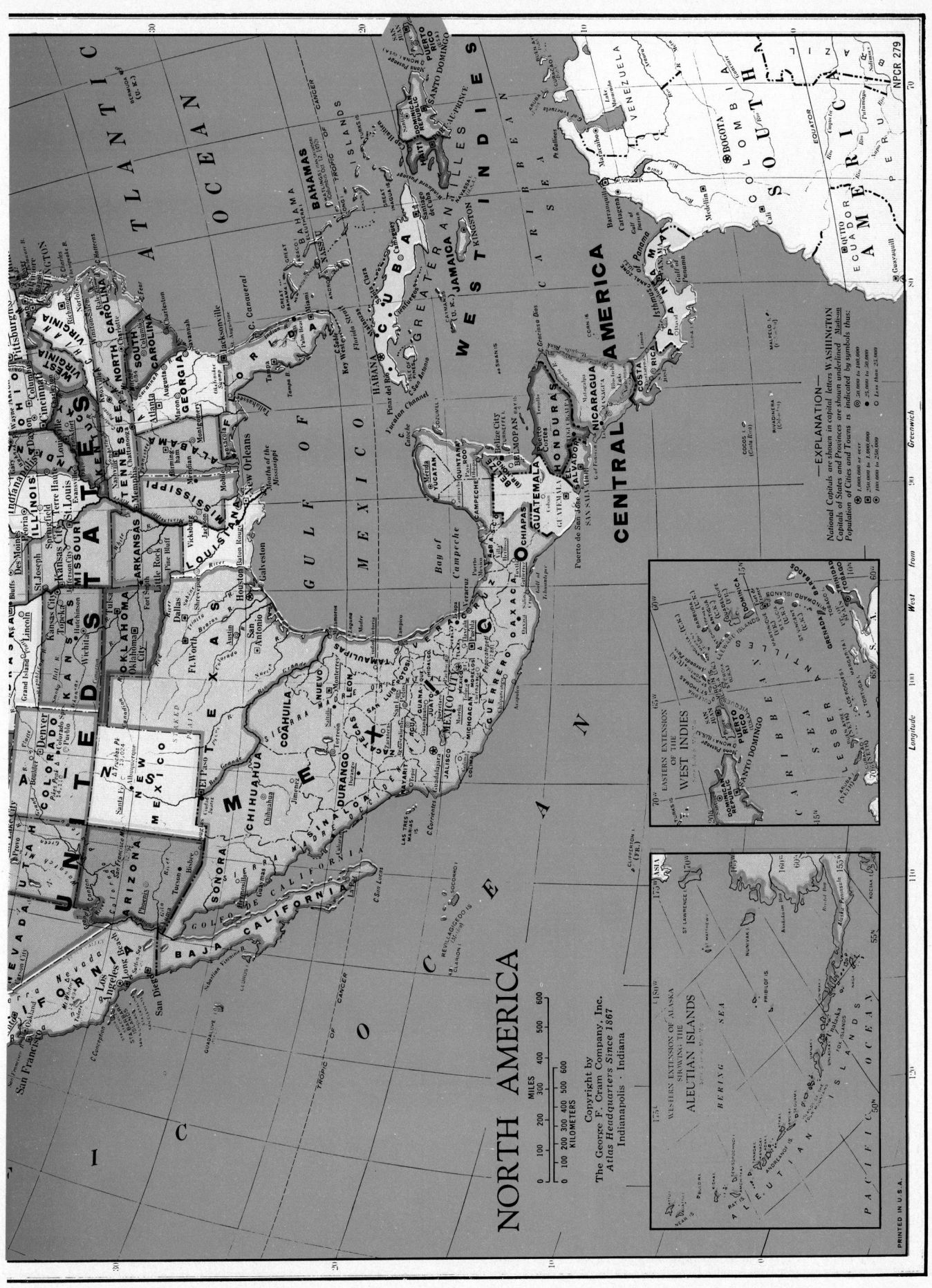

NORTH AMERICA

MILES
0   100   200   300   400   500   600

0 100 200 300 400 500 600
KILOMETERS

Copyright by
The George F. Cram Company, Inc.
Atlas Headquarters Since 1867
Indianapolis · Indiana

—EXPLANATION—

National Capitals are shown in capital letters WASHINGTON
Capitals of States and Provinces are shown underlined Madison
Population of Cities and Towns is indicated by symbols thus:

◎ 1,000,000 or over   ● 50,000 to 100,000
◉ 250,000 to 500,000   ● 25,000 to 50,000
◉ 100,000 to 250,000   ● Less than 25,000

EASTERN EXTENSION
OF THE
WEST INDIES

WESTERN EXTENSION OF ALASKA
SHOWING THE
ALEUTIAN ISLANDS

PRINTED IN U.S.A.

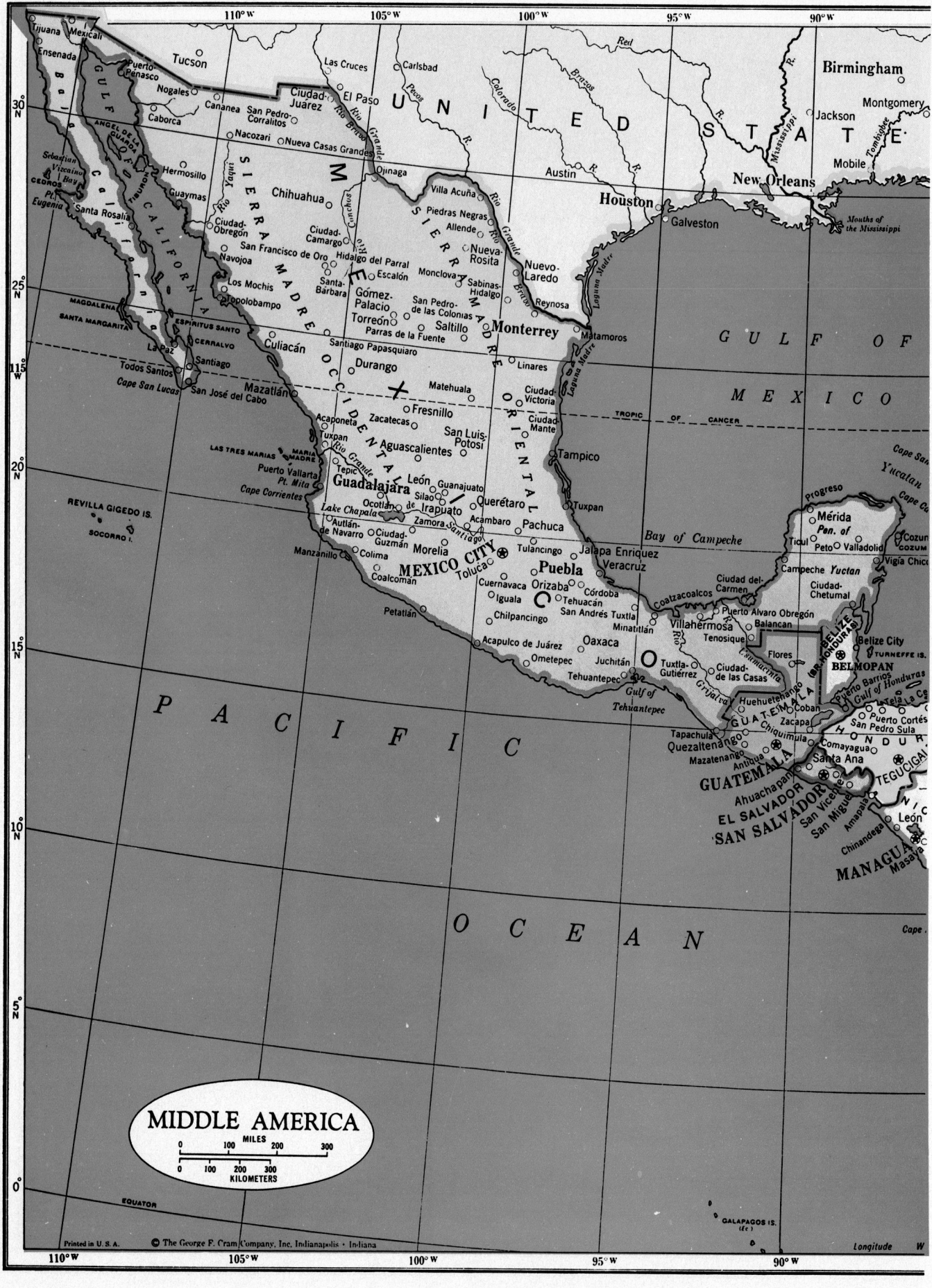

MIDDLE AMERICA

MILES
0   100   200   300

0 100 200 300
KILOMETERS

Printed in U.S.A.   © The George F. Cram Company, Inc, Indianapolis • Indiana

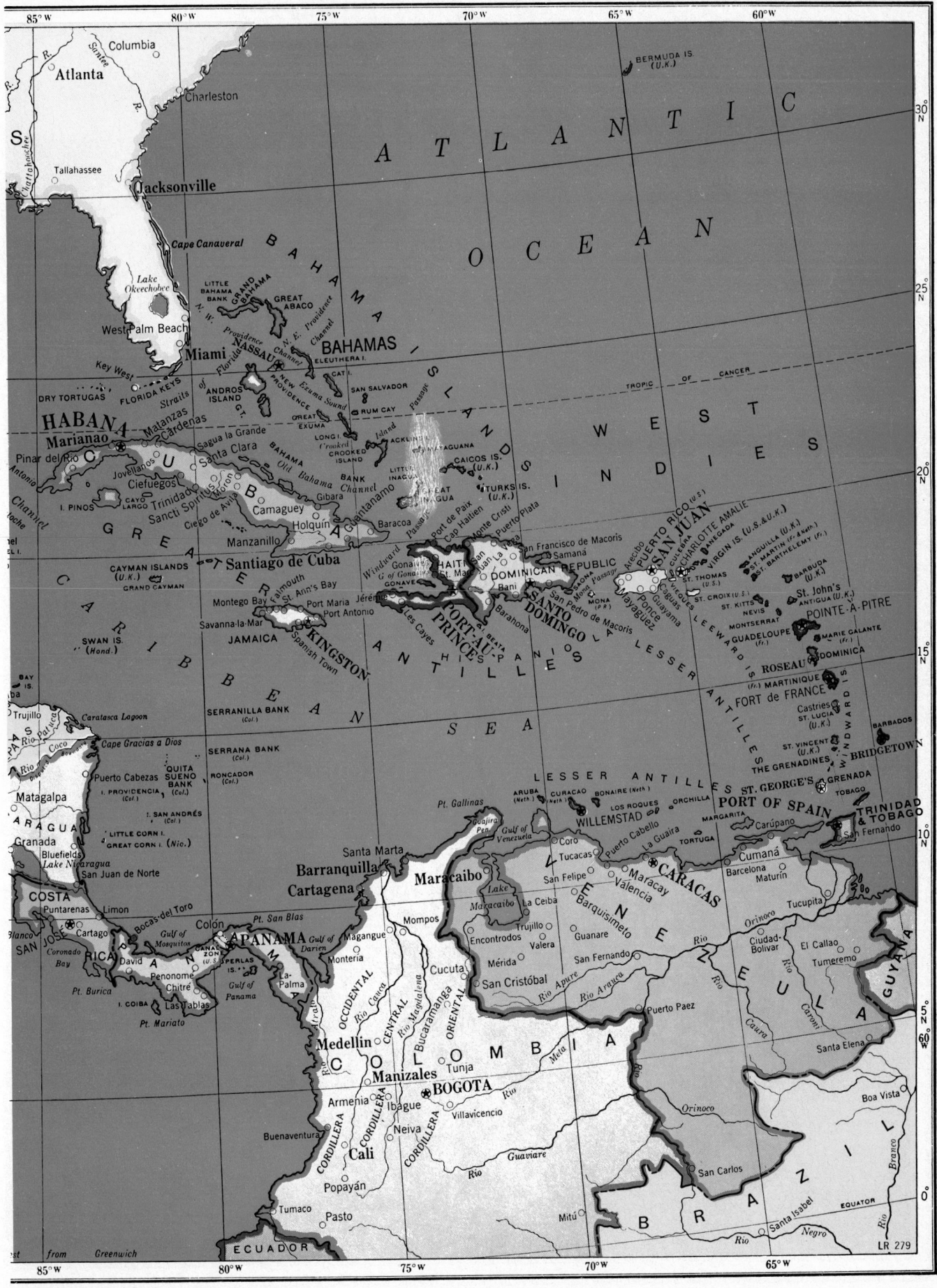

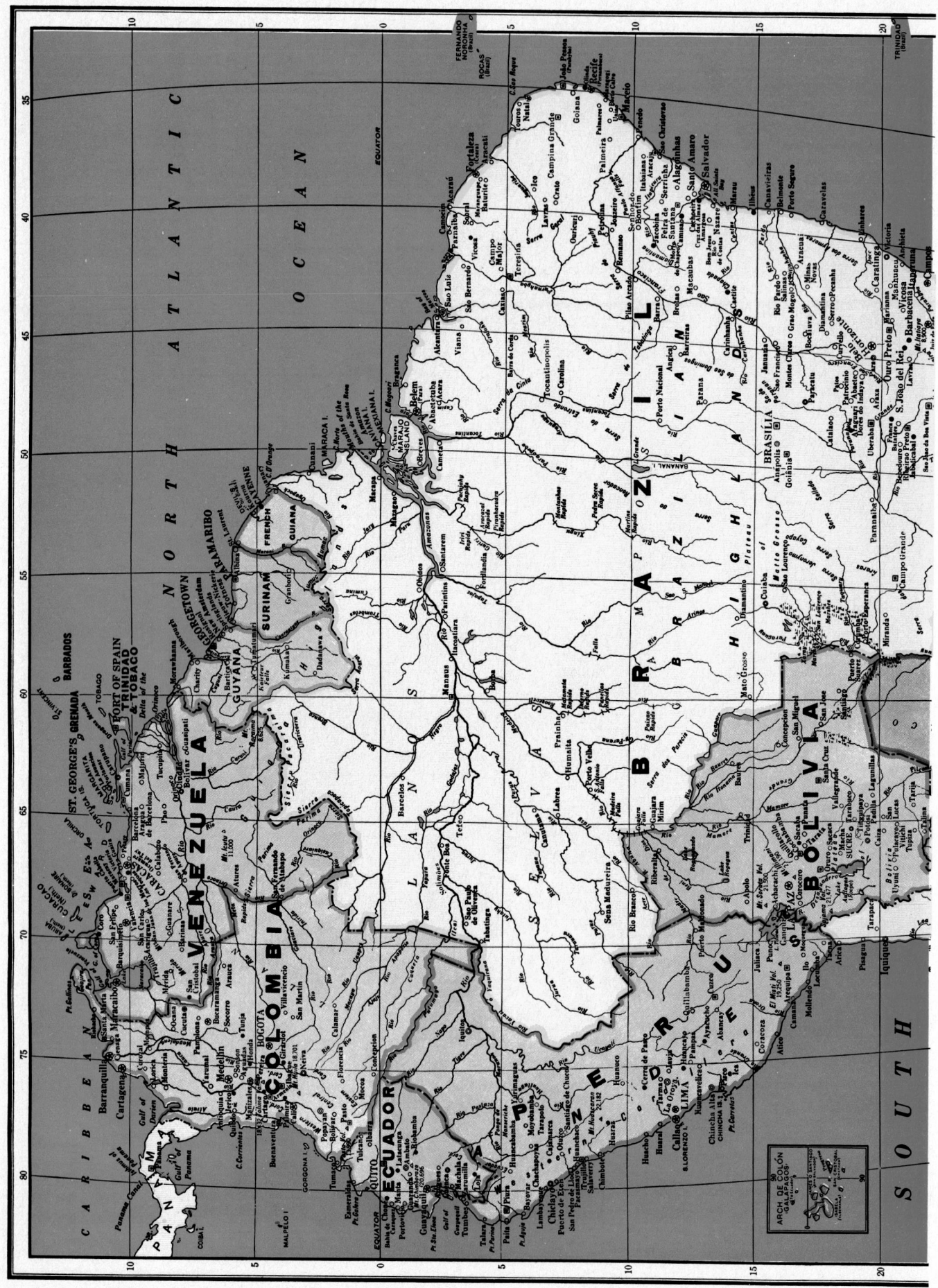

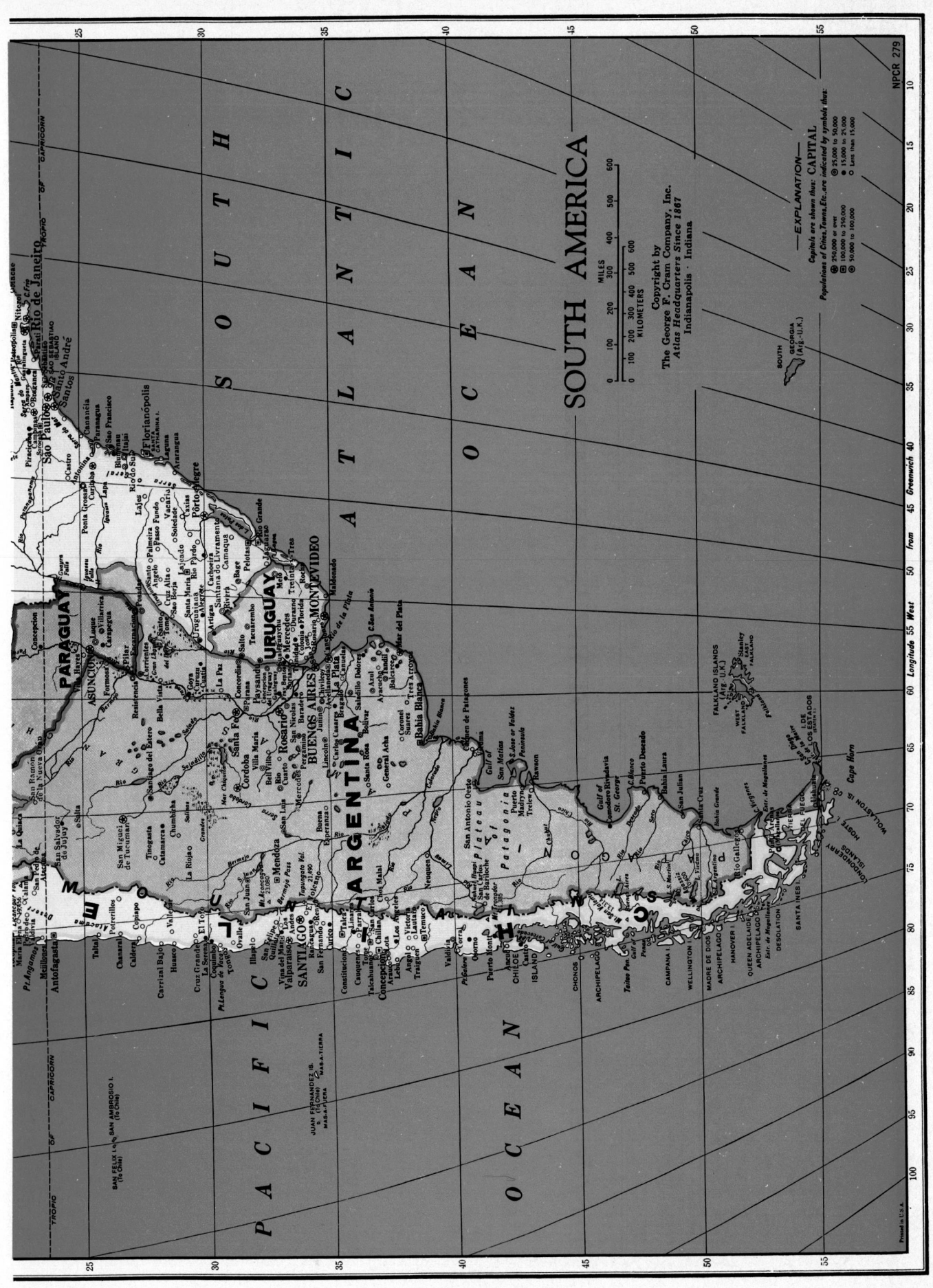

SOUTH AMERICA

Copyright by
The George F. Cram Company, Inc.
Atlas Headquarters Since 1867
Indianapolis · Indiana

MILES
0 100 200 300 400 500 600
0 100 200 300 400 500 600
KILOMETERS

—EXPLANATION—
CAPITAL
Capitals are shown thus: CAPITAL
Capitals of Cities, Towns, Etc., are indicated by symbols thus:
⊛ 250,000 or over
⊕ 100,000 to 250,000
⊙ 50,000 to 100,000
Populations of Cities, Towns, Etc.
◉ 25,000 to 50,000
◎ 15,000 to 25,000
○ Less than 15,000

S O U T H   A T L A N T I C   O C E A N

P A C I F I C   O C E A N

PARAGUAY

ASUNCIÓN

URUGUAY

MONTEVIDEO

ARGENTINA

BUENOS AIRES

SANTIAGO

C H I L E

São Paulo

Rio de Janeiro

SOUTH
GEORGIA
(Arg.-U.K.)

FALKLAND ISLANDS
(Arg.-U.K.)

WEST
FALKLAND

EAST
FALKLAND

Stanley

Cape Horn

TIERRA DEL FUEGO

WOLLASTON IS.

Patagonia

NPCR 279
10
15
20
25
30
35

Printed in U.S.A.

EUROPE

MILES

Copyright by
The George F. Cram Company, Inc.
Atlas Headquarters Since 1867
Indianapolis · Indiana

EXPLANATION

Capitals are shown in capital letters thus: **PARIS**
Population of Cities and Towns is indicated thus:

⊕ 1,000,000 or over	**Glasgow**	● 50,000 to 100,000	Koblenz
⊡ 250,000 to 1,000,000	Lyon	● 25,000 to 50,000	Cherbourg
⊚ 100,000 to 250,000	Zürich	○ Less than 25,000	Gaeta

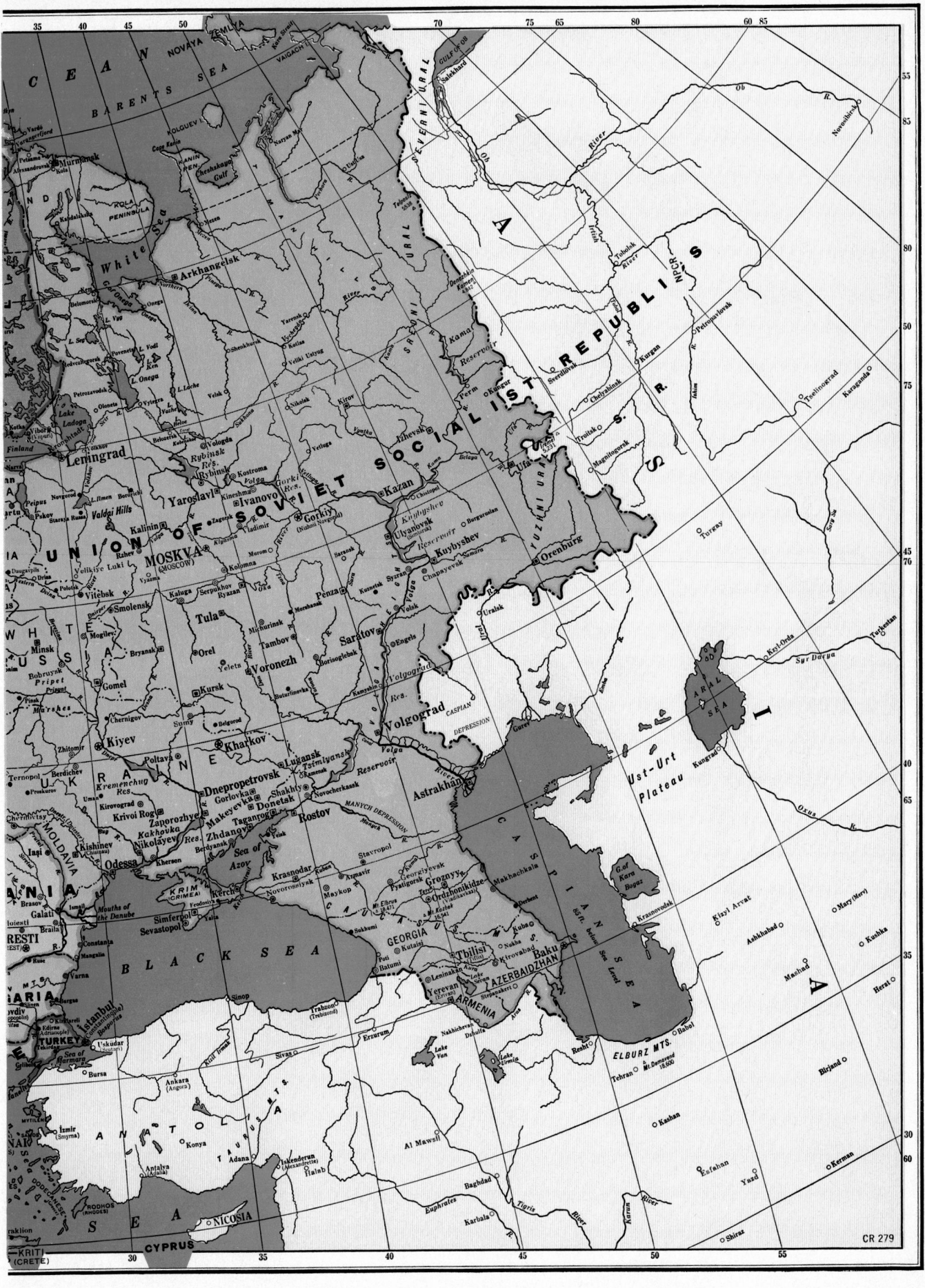

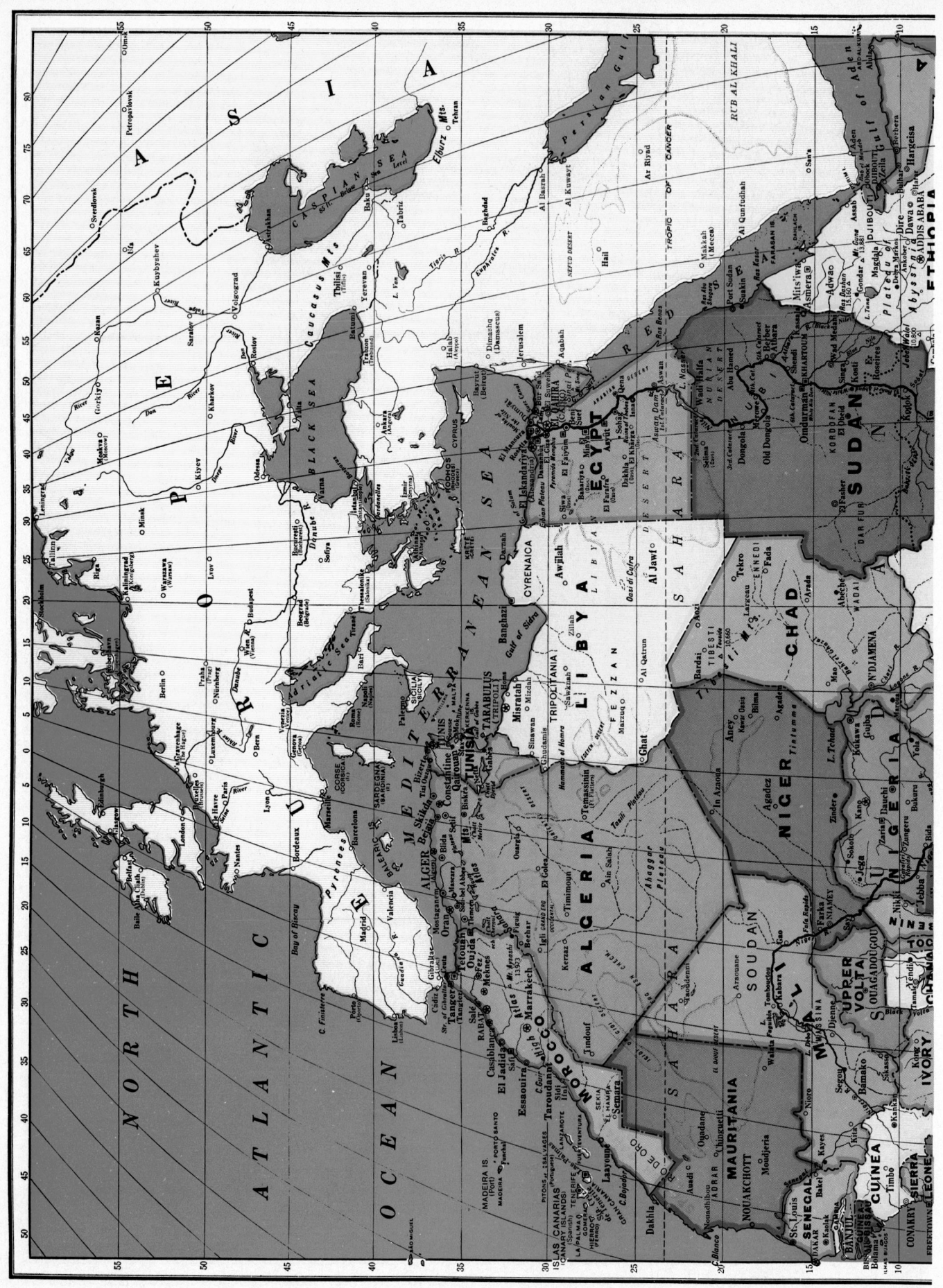

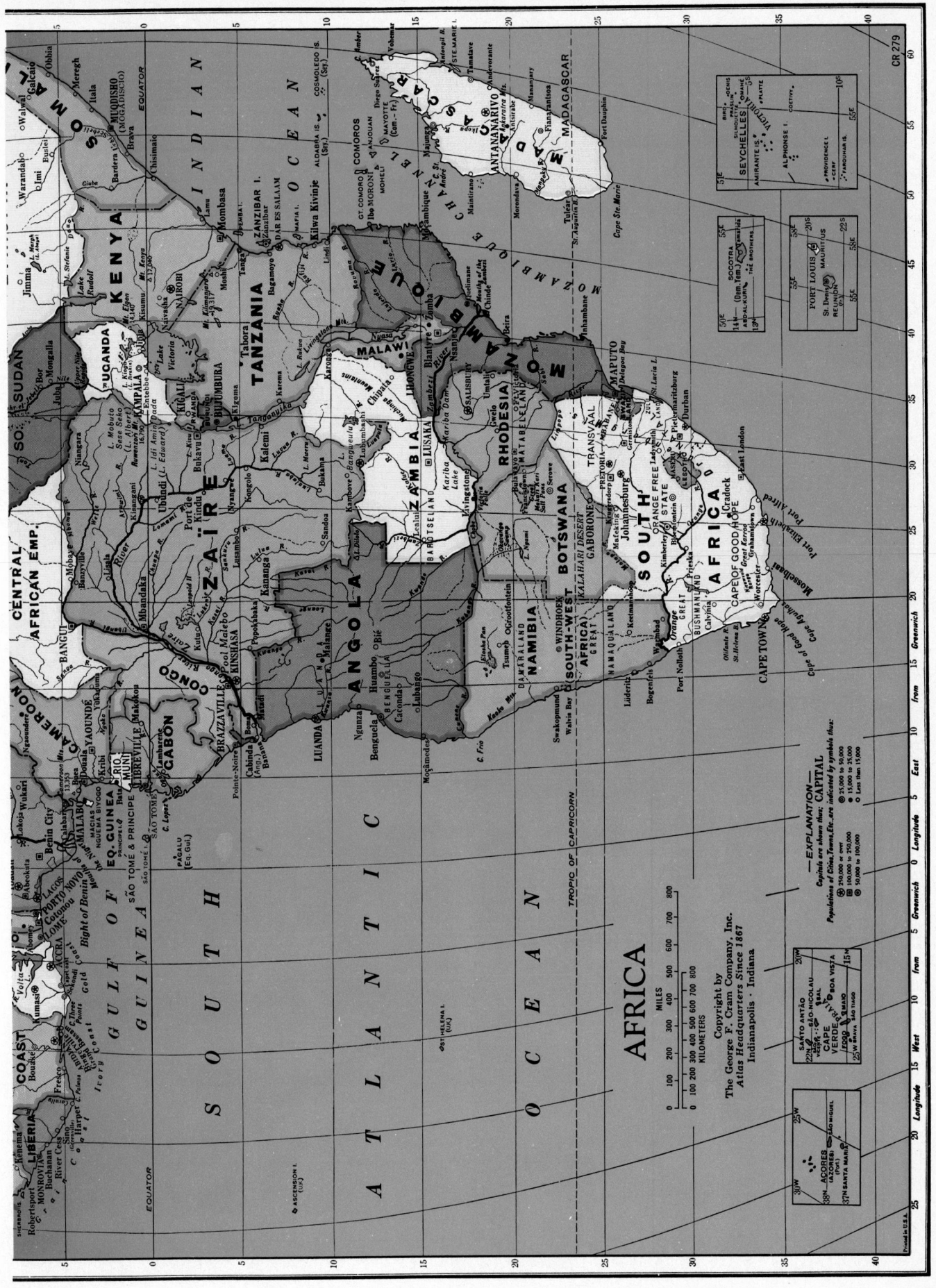

AFRICA

MILES
0 100 200 300 400 500 600 700 800

KILOMETERS
0 100 200 300 400 500 600 700 800

Copyright by
The George F. Cram Company, Inc.
Atlas Headquarters Since 1867
Indianapolis · Indiana

— EXPLANATION —
Capitals are shown thus: CAPITAL
Populations of Cities, Towns, Etc., are indicated by symbols thus:
⊛ 250,000 or over   ⊕ 25,000 to 50,000
⊛ 100,000 to 250,000   ⊙ 15,000 to 25,000
⊛ 50,000 to 100,000   ○ Less than 15,000

CR 279

Printed in U.S.A.

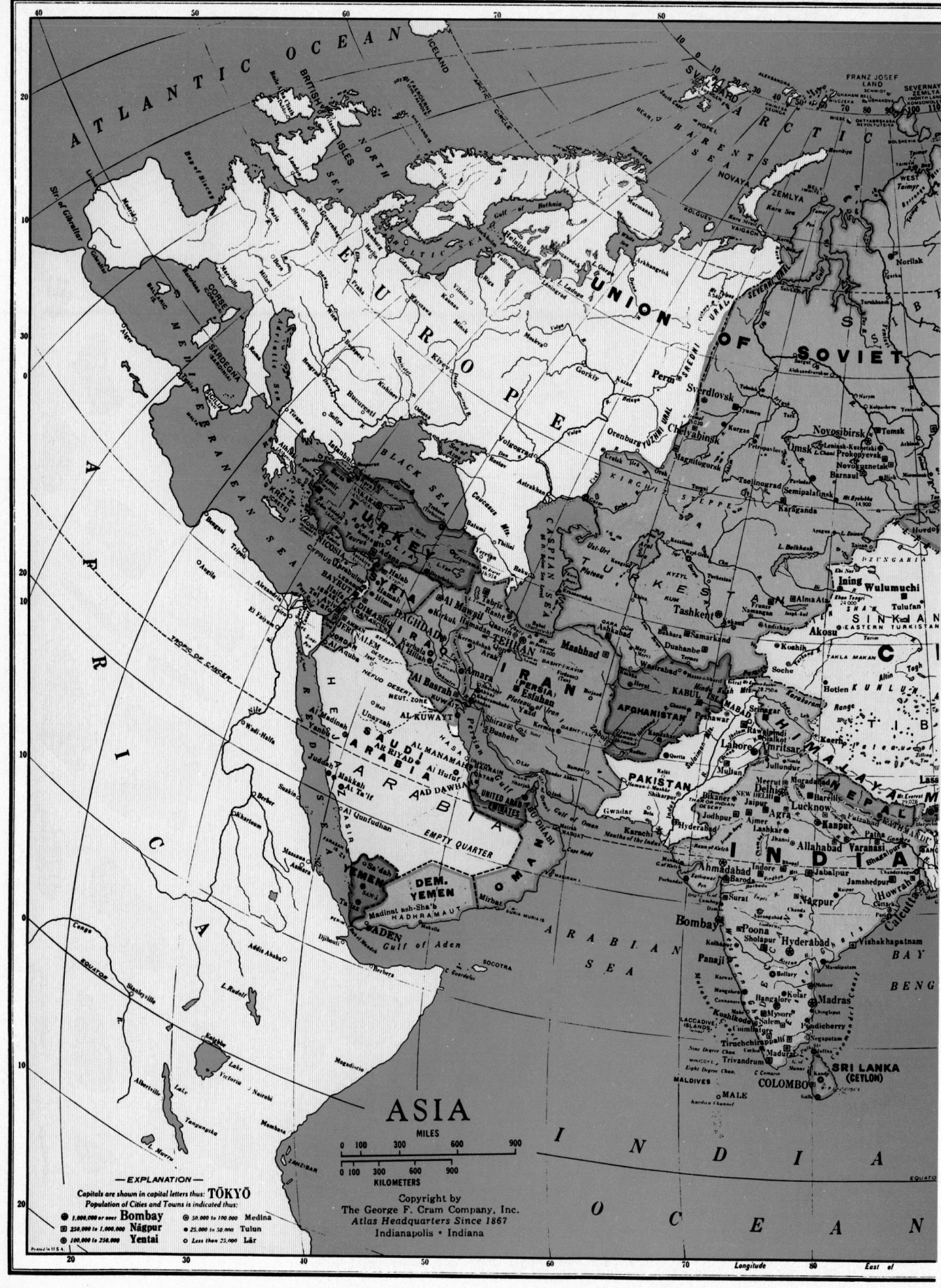

ASIA

MILES

0 100   300   600   900

0 100   300   600   900

KILOMETERS

Copyright by
The George F. Cram Company, Inc.
Atlas Headquarters Since 1867
Indianapolis • Indiana

— EXPLANATION —

Capitals are shown in capital letters thus: **TŌKYŌ**
Population of Cities and Towns is indicated thus:

● 1,000,000 or over   **Bombay**   ⊕ 50,000 to 100,000   Medina
■ 250,000 to 1,000,000 **Nāgpur**   ◉ 25,000 to 50,000   Tulun
◎ 100,000 to 250,000 **Yentai**   ○ Less than 25,000   Lār

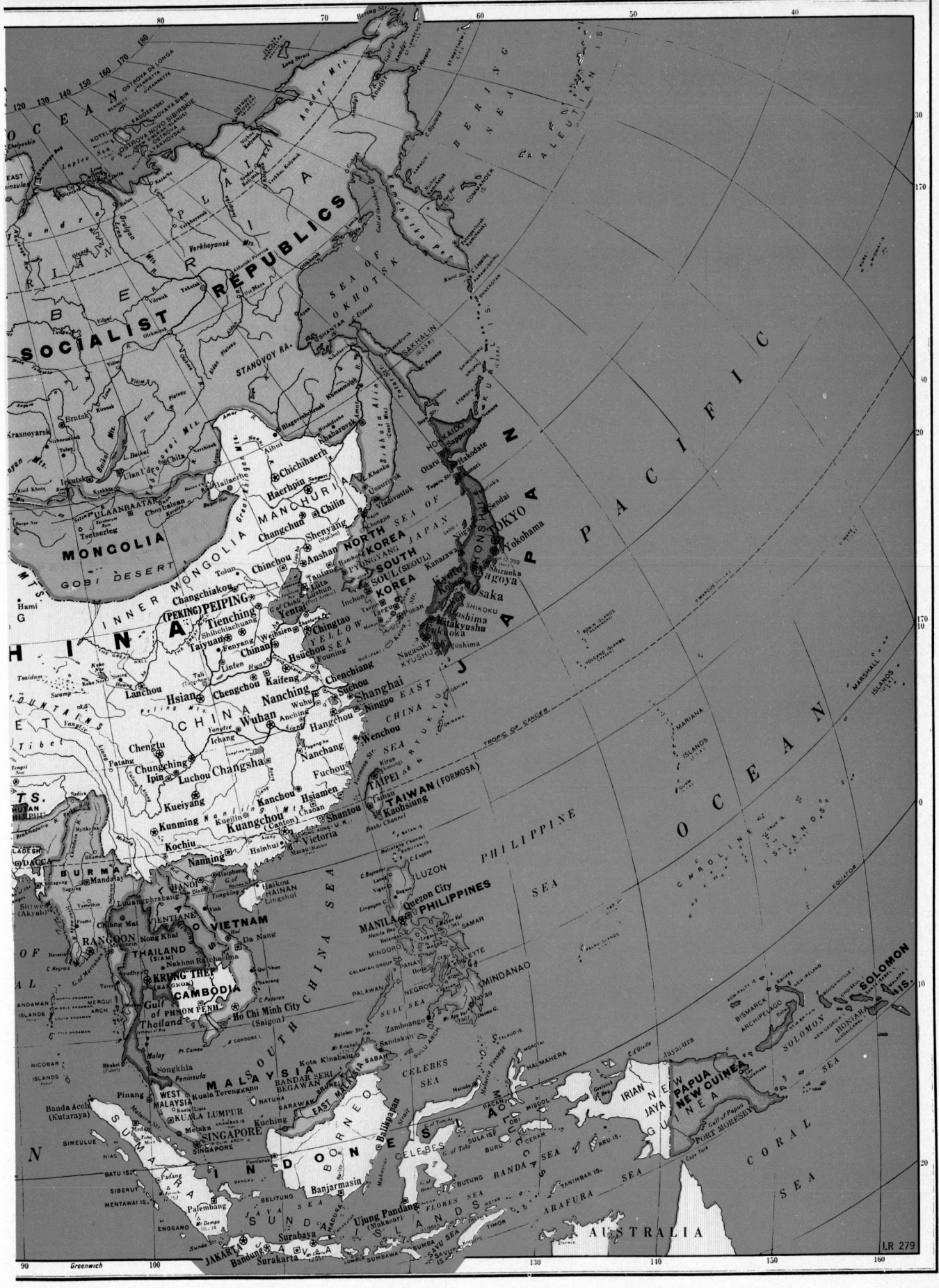

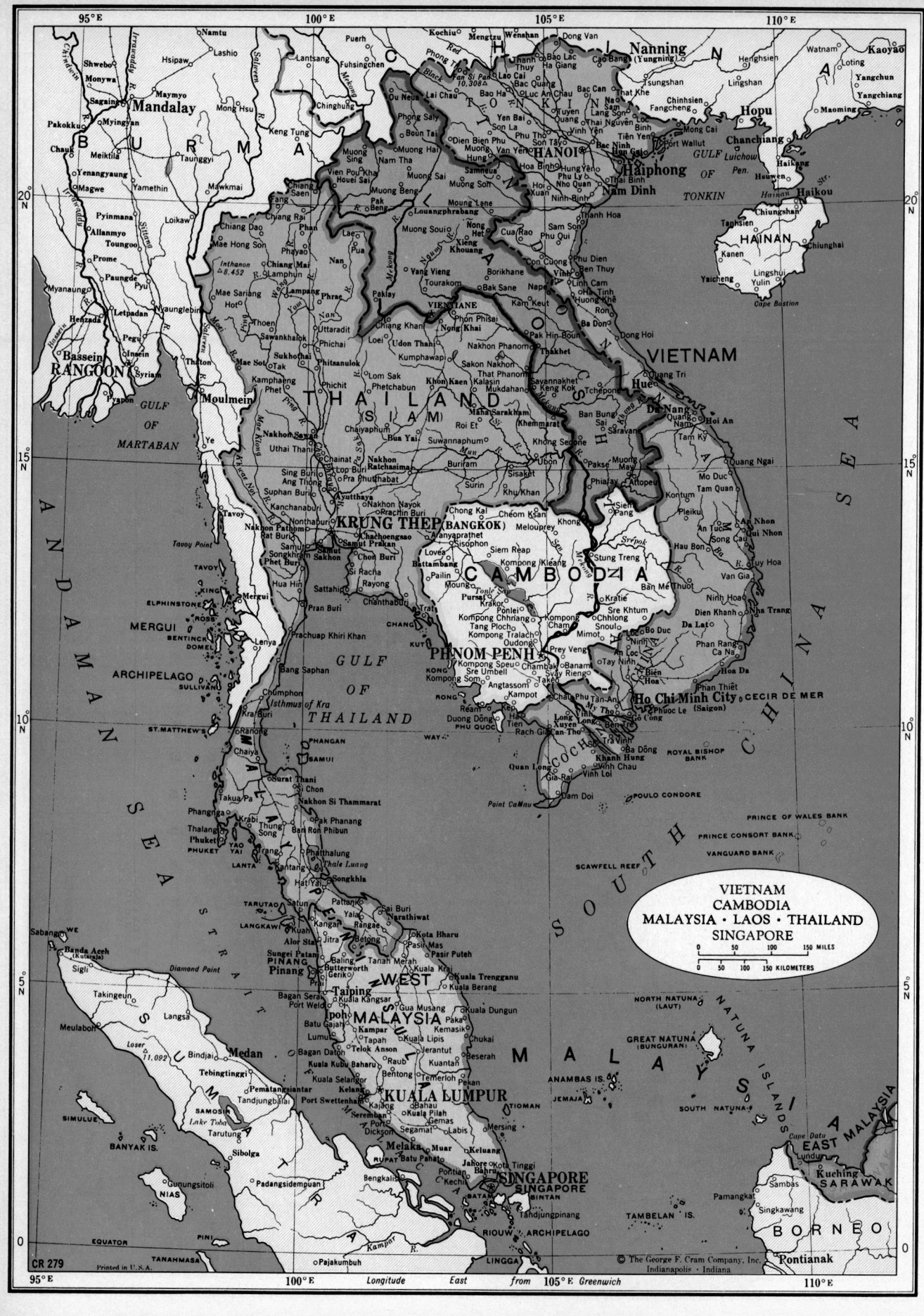

WORLD HISTORY

CULTURE AND CIVILIZATION

Only man is capable of producing a culture and his history is inseparable from it. **Culture (in the broadest sense of the term) is the whole of social experience—the knowledges, technics, moral codes, customs and traditions that are transmitted by human groups from generation to generation. Each social group has a unique culture, but cultural anthropologists do distinguish these common elements in culture: the basic patterns are stable but with the years change in details; culture is conservative in its ends, but flexible in its means; it is greater and more enduring than any individual within it, but is realized only through individuals; and it is transmitted by symbols in the form of language, myth, art, religion, etc.** When does a "culture" become a "civilization"? The answer to this question is quantitative. **Culture becomes civilization when it produces an economic surplus, develops mastery over the environment, and has a relatively complex economic organization, a classsystem, urban communities, recognized government, systematized law, a form of writing and elevated thought and esthetic patterns.**

Tool Culture. Cultural anthropologists have learned to make a virtue of necessity. The most numerous material remains of prehistoric cultures are the tools and weapons that prevailed. Considerable information about a culture can be derived from a tool. Nor can the importance of the tool in man's development be underestimated. It sharpened his cortico-motor reflexes, developed his sense of spatial relationships, increased his creative powers, extended his muscle power, introduced his first concepts of the possible mechanization of work, expanded his speech powers in

order to transmit the tool-heritage and began the important process of division of labor and specialization of work. That this is no exaggeration can be judged by examining the importance of the tool or machine in our own civilization.

THE AGES OF MAN

Tools provide us with the basis for periodizing the cultural history of mankind.

The Eolithic or Dawn Stone Age. The **Eolithic** or Dawn Stone Age covered the first half million years of proto-human history. It was the time of Java or Peking Man. Its primary tool and weapon was a multiple-purpose ealith (a stone shaped by nature and unaltered by man) which fitted the hand and could be used to stab, cut or hack. In these first days the economy was **collectional**—the gathering of berries, roots, small animals and larvae for food. There is some evidence that spoken language and control of fire appeared at the end of Eolithic—but this is not certain. Nor is there any certainty about the grouping of men. It is assumed that the family was the basic unit of social organization and that kinship groups roamed as hunting packs or herds under the leadership of the strongest and craftiest. Nothing at all is known of the clothing or type of habitation used for shelter.

The Paleolithic or Old Stone Age. Since the **Paleolithic** or the Old Stone Age extended from ca. 500,000 B.C. to 10,000 B.C., and since material remains increase abundantly as times become more recent, it has been necessary to divide Paleolithic into **Upper** which ends about 130,000 B.C.,

Middle which ends about 70,000 B.C. and **Lower** which brought the age to an end about 10,000 B.C. While Java and Peking men may have continued on from Eolithic into Paleolithic, the epoch is predominantly that of Heidelberg and Neanderthal and Cro-Magnon men. Spurred by economic and defense needs, Paleolithic men invented the **manufactured tool.** Two types of stone-tool "industries" flourished during Lower and Middle Paleolithic—the "core" and the "flake." Core tools were produced by knocking chips off a large lump of flint or volcanic glass until it was reduced to a standard form, the *coup de poing* or "fist-hatchet." Flakes were produced by the Levalloisian technique: the shape of the tool desired was etched on the core; then, by either percussion or spatula-pressure, a flake was detached; the detached pieces were then shaped to desired sharpness by chipping. Earliest Paleolithic tools were undifferentiated. Over the years, however, the core tool became a primary one, that is, designed to produce secondary or specialized tools for perforating, chopping, cutting, scraping or sawing. By the time of Upper Paleolithic, highly specialized tools appeared and took the forms of bone needles, harpoons, pronged fish-hooks, dart-throwers and bows and arrows.

Advances. Tooling revolutionized the food industry of primitive men. The mode of economy now became that of fishing and hunting. The fist-hatchet made the stalking and capture of animals safer and more certain. With the invention of the sling, the dart and the bow and arrow, man could capture animals at a distance; he was now provided with a relatively permanent food supply. With the further invention of the harpoon and fishhook, an increase in the food supply took place. Mastery of fire, moreover, gave Paleolithic men a varied food diet—as well as defense, heat and light. Now began an increase in creature comforts. Paleolithic men donned sewn clothing made from animal skins; they initiated the permanent residence, first in caves and then in crudely constructed shelters; and their men and women began to ornament themselves with beads, necklaces and pendants.

Cultural Advances. During Paleolithic, the family grouping of men expanded into larger kinship groups tracing their origin, either matri- or patri-linearly, from a common ancestor. Out of this kinship grouping came the first cultural institutions —economic, political, educational and religious. Men assumed all the duties of the hunt; women concerned themselves with the collectional and household manufacturing activities. Government was probably concerned with the maintenance of internal peace; and the mightiest hunters and the older men probably arbitrated conflicts, enforced taboos and distributed food equitably. Protection of the hunting lands turned the hunters, on occasion, into warriors. All strangers were, therefore, suspect. But good relations existed among neighboring groups of necessity. Often flint supplies gave out and had to be secured outside the locality by trade; or animals were forced by sudden climatic change to new grazing lands; or population decline caused by an imbalance of males and females may have threatened the survival of the group.

Education was for individual survival. Until puberty the child's education was in the hands of the women of the family. Thereafter, men took over the boy's training. He now underwent a severe initiation which included fasting, keeping long vigils and even mutilation; he was instructed in proper behavior to people and to things in the world about him; finally, he was taught to hunt safely and efficiently. Religious guidance was fundamental to the education of both girls and boys for there were many prescriptions and proscriptions to be heeded. Remains of burial and funerary practices make clear that late in Paleolithic men began to experience religious thought and feeling. It would seem that their religious outlook included concepts of a soul or spirit belonging to each individual, and of its persistence after death. Natural forces were regarded as being motivated by a mysterious, supernatural power or "mana." Later this undifferentiated supernatural force took the shape of spirits or ghosts present unseen, everywhere, and in all things in the universe (**animism**). These spirits or ghosts were capable, as was perfectly obvious from the great insecurity in which men lived, of inflicting great harm unless propitiated. To placate these unseen powers, paleolithic men introduced religious rites. They carved female figurines as symbols of fertility with exaggerated sexual organs and worshipped them. They invented sympathetic magic or the practice of destroying an enemy by first mutilating his spirit resident in some effigy of him. They warded off evil by wearing amulets and talismans of beads or pendants. Finally, they created a class of professional religious practitioners called **shamans** who were possessed of powers of healing, divining and casting magical spells.

Though he accepted fully a supernatural explanation of the world of nature, paleolithic man was a close observer of things that mattered most to him. This was evident in his art work. For example, on the walls of caves he carved and painted reproductions of the animals which his band hunted—bison, mammoth, stags, reindeer, wolves. The realism, the naturalistic modeling, the use of light and dark masses, the employment of harmonious or agitated rhythms, the rigorous attention to detail, the ability to suppress detail to create a center of interest, the accuracy and sureness of drawing, the arresting of movement and action, the use of polychromatic effects—any or all of these characteristics of Cro-Magnon art establish the paleolithic artist as a very accomplished one. Nor was his skill limited to murals. He decorated his tools with small sculptures that never interfered with the function of the tool and made etchings that again illustrate his sense of realistic design. Paleolithic art was unquestionably functional in that it served the purposes of sympathetic magic; it was a form of religious ritual. But its esthetic values are timeless and universal.

The Neolithic or New Stone Age. Neolithic men exhausted the possibilities of stone technology. Since surface flint deposits were nearly depleted by 10,000 B.C., a mining industry was begun. Shafts were sunk and chalk veins were tapped with deerhorn picks for the flint they might yield. When required, Neolithic men burrowed long transverse tunnels in their mine pits. All tools were highly specialized now. In addition they were smoothed down to fine cutting edges on whetstones. Handles were attached to all chopping tools and they assumed distinctively modern appearances.

Toolmaking did not account for the profound revolution which occurred during the Neolithic Age. Discovery of agriculture and the domestication of animals did. When or how these two epoch-making discoveries took place is not known. There is some evidence for the prevailing belief that women first hit upon the art of cultivation; for many years it was they who farmed the land with picks, digging sticks and hoes while the men continued to hunt and fish. Domestication of animals lessened the need to hunt and fish and permitted the man to settle down as a cultivator.

What were the effects of this agricultural revolution? Permanent settlements along river valleys made their appearance; men experienced with new forms of durable housing—mud and thatch affairs or lake dwellings on high piles. Diets were enriched with large varieties of grains, fruits and vegetables; where rivers overflowed, large scale drainage and irrigation projects were begun; grain surpluses led to increased trade and this, in turn, effected a revolution in transportation on land and water—the wheeled vehicle and the sail were invented. Mankind developed new, civilized habits—a sense of property ownership, patience, industry and planning; soil-rootedness made him conscious of the seasons and the stars; new scientific curiosities led him to inventions such as pottery (for storage and cooking purposes) from baked clay, stone mills to grind grain, etc.

Animals continued, of course, to serve as sources of food, but they also provided man with a new source of motive power, new supplies of raw materials for textiles and a new means of transportation. Because of the availability of animals, plows and wheeled carts were invented; the textile industries of spinning and weaving took root. Civilization, clearly, was beginning to take shape.

Social reorganization followed upon economic revolution. Population increased rapidly and lived longer as the result of more abundant and more reliable food supplies. Though kinship grouping persisted in Neolithic times, it had become a fiction; the reality was the large tribe centered in a fixed locality. Tribal organization took on concrete form. Members of the tribe delegated to either strong men or elders authority to adjudicate an increasing number of disputes over property rights, to interpret tradition in changing circumstances, to defend the village against raids by hungry nomads, etc. This delegation of authority was the rudiment of formal government. Near the end of Neolithic times, representative governments gave way to absolute monarchies, out of necessity. An increase in the number, intensity and dire consequences of war was directly responsible. A lost war resulted in either annihilation, dispersal, subjugation or slavery. To prevent this, Neolithic groups submitted themselves to the authoritative leadership of war-chiefs.

Neolithic men carried religious belief forward from its state of a generalized animism to that of **polytheism.** The vague spirits of Paleolithic belief now became numerous specific gods possessing immortal but human or anthropomorphic personalities. These gods resided in stones, animals, springs, trees, caves and mountains. Methods for appeasing angry gods proliferated and took the forms of human sacrifice, animal slaughter, self-mutilation or torture, sacramental sexual relations or ritual cannibalism. Belief in an after-life also grew more concrete. Burials as a result became more elaborate: chambered tombs were constructed above the graves; into the tombs were piled furniture, weapons, clothing and food for the spirit of the departed. The first form of temple worship was that of worship at monumental stone structures—dolmens or trilithons (two upright stones with a covering slab, post-and-lintel style); or just megaliths, tremendous stones set individually in long rows (some were 70 feet high!); or cromlechs, like the famous one at Stonehenge, England, combining dolmens and megaliths in a circle.

Art declined during the Neolithic Age. Naturalism disappeared and was replaced by abstract representations of concentric lines, zigzags, spirals, dots and chevrons which were scratched or painted as decorative motifs on pottery.

ANCIENT EGYPT

The Land. As history recedes into the remoter past, geography emerges as a dominating, if not quite the dominant, factor. Ancient Egypt was, to a considerable extent, the product of a river, cataracts, delta and desert. "Egypt," said the Greek historian, HERODOTUS, "is the gift of a river." It lay along the Nile and annually that river overflowed to provide Egypt with the only moisture it had and with rich deposits of alluvial soil. Egypt proved equal to the challenge and evolved political, economic and social institutions that enabled her to capture, store and distribute the floodwaters. Canals, dikes and reservoirs appeared early in the history of civilization. The cataracts were in the southern Nilotic waters and created a natural boundary there which acted as a barrier both to expansion and invasion. The desert, too, was a formidable barrier. Geography kept Egypt at peace for centuries. The mouth of the Nile spread into a fertile delta; this region made Egypt the granary of the ancient world and gave her a valuable trading link to the Mediterranean world when she finally emerged from her isolation.

Predynastic Egypt. No written records exist from the period prior to the first families of **pharaohs** (called **dynasties**). Excavations reveal, however, that predynastic Egyptians had made important strides toward civilization. Stone was being abandoned for copper, and Egyptians had already mastered the art of smelting and casting this metal. As a people, the Egyptians were racially mixed, lived in villages as farmers and animal herders, fashioned stone, wood and copper tools, decorated pottery and wove linen goods. They had reclaimed swamplands and had begun local irrigation projects. Political units called **nomes** existed and were ruled by local nomarchs. Powerful nomarchs had effected early union of Upper and Lower Egypt. Some form of preternatural belief existed, for the dead were buried in graves along with their implements and with symbolic figurines.

THE PERSIANS

Persia lay on the Iranian plateau stretching eastward from the Tigris River to the Indus River. About 1800 B.C. an Aryan-speaking people occupied the northeastern edge of this plateau. For centuries they were subject to the rule of the Elamites; but Ashurbanipal, the Assyrian, devastated Elam and its capital at Susa (ca. 640 B.C.). When the Assyrians were destroyed in turn, the Medes under Cyaxeres (625–593 B.C.) took over the former Elamite Kingdom. But the Persians now made their bid for power. In 550 B.C. CYRUS THE GREAT took over the Median Kingdom and then continued westward to conquer Lydia and Chaldea. Cyrus's son, Cambyses (530–521 B.C.) added the Egyptian Empire to the Persian. At this point, the empire of the Persians was the largest of all those of the ancient world.

Darius I (521–485 B.C.) added little new territory to this vast empire but devoted his high intelligence to organizing it for efficient administration. His basic principle of organization was centralization through the monarch. Thus he built for himself four capitals with royal residences at Susa, Persepolis, Ecbatana and Babylon. These were interconnected with modernized highways over which flowed normal trade, postal communication and military patrols. The King made a regular circuit of his capitals and while in each he disposed of accumulated local problems. Reporting to him regularly were twenty *satraps* or governors appointed by and responsible solely to himself. (The empire had been divided into twenty *satrapies* or administrative divisions.) Each governor was responsible for the imperial tax and the army levies. In all other matters local autonomy was permitted and everywhere native cultures were tolerated. (Under the Persians, for example, the Hebrews were permitted to return from Babylon to Palestine.) But, to guarantee efficiency and to ward off the evils of bureaucratic corruption, the King appointed official spies known as "The King's eyes and the King's ears" who traveled about the empire incognito and reported back to the King the evils they observed or heard about. The Persian government itself was an absolute hereditary monarchy "by the grace of Ahura-Mazda." There were important limitations on the King's absolutism: he was expected to consult with the nobility, to base his law-making upon the Law of the Medes and the Persians and to be guided by precedents in the law. This was the empire that persisted in the Middle East until 333 B.C. It received its first important setback at the hands of the Greeks at the Battle of Marathon in 490 B.C.; and it was destroyed by Alexander the Great. Its influence, however, continued long after its demise.

CRETE

Between Persia and Ancient Greece lay the Aegean Sea and around that sea there flourished a number of civilizations which became transitional to the Greek. Earliest of these was the **Minoan** civilization which flourished on the island of Crete and which was revealed to the modern world by the brilliant excavations about 1900 (A.D.) of SIR ARTHUR EVANS. Knowledge of the Minoan civilization is still limited because its language is still undeciphered; what is known is due to archaeological discoveries. From these it is known that Minoan civilization flourished between 3000 and 1200 B.C. In this period, they dominated the Mediterranean sea with their trade and military power.

Their power was manifest in the mighty cities which they built at Cnossus and Phaestus on the island itself. Cnossus, for example, was dominated by the king's palace which was at least two stories high, contained a maze of living rooms, store rooms, workshops, offices, etc., was equipped with plumbing that provided running water and efficient sewage. Attached to the palace were factories which turned out articles for export—pottery, textiles and metal goods.

Unearthed figurines indicate that Minoan worship centered about a snake goddess, a symbol of fertility and of destruction. The dead were buried with their implements of war and livelihood; gods were appeased by sacrifice. There were, however, no temples. Minoan murals are exceptionally revealing: they show the people as unusually sports-loving and engaging in bull fights, boxing, races, etc. Women held an exceptionally high position; they play and work side by side with the men. All this is shown by the archaeological record. This record also reveals that about 1400 B.C. Minoan civilization took root in northwestern Asia Minor about the site of Troy and in a group of Greek islands centered about Mycenae on the mainland. Similar pottery, artistic design and "beehive" tombs prove this. Esthetic analysis of Mycenaean remains, however, shows that the creative flame was gone by 1400 B.C. Minoan art, at its height, is a rare combination of naturalism and spontaneity combined with exquisite delicacy; Mycenaean art is derivative and dull by comparison. The Minoan artist was master of the miniature: the figurine, the painted dagger, jewelry, inlay; Mycenaean is large and crude by comparison. The real influence of the Minoan Cretans was not upon the rough Trojans and Mycenaeans but upon those that conquered them, the ancient Greeks of Dorian and Ionian stock.

Greece

ORIGINS

Greek civilization did not spring full-blown from the soil of Greece. It took a millenium before the Greeks cast off their original barbarism. The earliest Greeks lived in the valley of the Danube; they spoke a common Indo-European tongue. By 2000 B.C., however, their language had become differentiated enough to enable us to divide them into Achaeans, Aeolians, Ionians, Illyrians, Boetians, Dorians, etc. About that time, too, they were uprooted from their homeland and began a folk-wandering southward into the Balkan peninsula; they came, that is, as conquerors.

The first to enter may have been the Achaean Hellenes (ca. 2000 B.C.). Over a period of 700 years these people filtered into central and southern Greece and then into the Aegean islands. They seem to have assimilated with the indigenous Greeks, and absorbed their superior culture; but they imposed upon them the Achaean language and rule. Ionians are found in western Greece as early as 1500 B.C. They, too, settled down, absorbed and assimilated with the natives. But about 1300 B.C. a barbarous tribe of Illyrians swept down into Thessaly and uprooted the Achaeans and the Ionians and forced them to scatter into the remoter regions of the peninsula and overseas to Asia Minor. It is quite likely that this upheaval, rather than the legendary kidnapping of Helen, brought the Achaeans under Agamemnon into collision with the Trojans in Asia Minor. This Illyrian conquest was followed by an even more devastating **Dorian invasion** which re-scattered the Achaeans and Ionians. After 1000 B.C. the invasions ended and Greece entered a period of incubation.

Invasion and dispersion were not without positive results. The decadent remnants of Minoan-Mycenean culture were destroyed, paving way for a new culture; the Greek nation differentiated into varied and conflicting types each occupying a fixed territory, and this spurred the growth of individualism; Greek culture became Mediterranean rather than Balkan; overseas, the Greeks came into contact with the civilizing ways of the Near East; and passage over the seas required that the Greeks become "maritime-minded" and oriented to a life of trade and commerce.

The Land. Trade and commerce were vital preconditions for the development of Greek civilization for the Balkan peninsula was a singularly barren land. Criss-crossing mountain ranges covered two-thirds of the land surface; arable plains made up a bare one-sixth. The rivers were nonnavigable and varied between winter flood and summer dry-bed. Lakes were rare and inclined, because of poor drainage, to become malarial swampland. Scrubby pasture supported meager flocks of sheep and goats. Deforestation was acute; and there were only thin veins of metals basic to the ancient civilizations—gold, silver, lead, iron and copper. The historian HERODOTUS defined it accurately when he said that poverty was foster-sister to the Greeks. But while geography was, in the main, a barrier to civilization, it did open some opportunities. For example, there were rich deposits of stone and marble and potter's clay; natural harbors abounded along the eastern shore; the Aegean islands were natural stepping-stones to the Asiatic mainland and by occupying them, the Greeks made the Aegean Sea into a Grecian Lake.

The "Homeric" Greeks. Homer's *Iliad* and *Odyssey* are timeless masterpieces of epic poetry; they qualify as such by every standard of literary criticism—by clear, vivid and natural diction; by **epithets** that serve as haunting refrains and impress the *dramatis personae* upon the memory; by an **"heroic" meter, the hexameter;** by suspenseful beginnings *in media res* (in the middle of things) to avoid tedious or interruptive background material; by the music of their language; and by their wide range of human emotions, their varieties of style to fit the scenes, their plenitude of imagery and matchless rhetoric. They are "things of beauty," of "Attic shapes" in motion and as such their influence has not waned in the 2800 years of their lives. In a study of Greek and Roman influences on western civilization (*The Classical Tradition*), Gilbert Highet was compelled to make more than 250 references to Homer's epics. Here we can do no more than note Homer's literary impact. Our interest must be in what he revealed about the "dark age" in the preliterary history of Greece.

Homer's interest was in his own past; but he

was unable to escape his present. So, from between his lines, we are able to piece out that part of Greek history which is called the **"Homeric Age."**

Primitive Society. Homer's Greeks lived in a relatively primitive society. Their methods of wealth-gathering centered upon crude agriculture, herding and plundering on land and sea. Technologically they had passed from the Bronze to the threshold of the Iron Age. Some specialization of craft had begun for the epics speak of **freemen** who were smiths, potters, saddlers, masons, carpenters and cabinetmakers. Costlier goods, however—objects of art, weapons, fancy raiment and gold beakers—seen to have been imported. Trading was very limited and conducted by means of primitive barter. There was no coinage and wealth was estimated in flocks. The ox served as a medium of exchange. Most manufactured goods were produced in the home by slaves with the assistance of their masters and mistresses.

Private ownership, as an institution, had not yet appeared; landed property was owned by the family with the father as chief administrator. While the father could determine the use of the land, he could not sell it. He had to transmit it, by the common law of **primogeniture,** to his eldest son who became head of the household upon his father's death. The family unit was patriarchal; it was, in fact, a patriarchal despotism for the father could, if he wished, take concubines for himself or offer them to his guests, or commit infanticide, or slaughter his children as sacrifices to the gods. Fathers, however, rarely employed such practices. Homeric families are, for the most part, monogamous; intimacy and affection exist between husband and wife and between father and children; the position of the woman in the household is high and free even though marriage was by purchase. (Women were to lose this high status as Greek society developed.)

Homeric men could and did commit unspeakable barbarities upon one another; but concepts of a common humanity tempered their crudities. They are never far from tenderness, sentiment and tears; deep friendships are common; they show rare hospitality to strangers for they bathe them, clothe them, wine-dine-and lodge them, and then send them off with gifts; slaves have a rare position of equality in the household. On the other hand, they are never far from what we would consider immoralities either. Women are offered as prizes in athletic contests; wanton, cruel sacrifices are made upon funeral pyres; slavery and concubinage follow upon conquest; piracy is an honorable profession and pillage a necessary one; they admire unabashed lying, deceit and treachery. This was their response to an insecure world in which human life was cheap; to survive, a man must have the qualities of Ares, the God of War— strength, guile and deception. Fair was foul, and foul was fair. (These, in fact, are among Odysseus' most conspicuous traits.)

Politics. Political institutions were equally primitive though considerably advanced over Oriental forms as no divine-right absolute monarch existed in Homeric Greece. There was a **basileus or dynastic king** who served as commander in chief, high priest and chief justice. He was, however, a chief among equals. His equals were a landed aristocracy who claimed, as did the basileus, divine descent. They met on important occasions as a council and through this agency they checked any exercise of arbitrary power by the basileus. Within the council the nobility enjoyed complete freedom of speech. As a further check on absolutism there existed an assembly of all freemen who could, in a crisis of war or peace, approve or reject proposals made by the king or nobles. Government was completely decentralized; the power of the king extended, on a "feudal" basis, only as far as his noble retainers obeyed him. For example, while his anger was upon him and he did not choose to fight, Achilles ignored every demand and plea to do so made by King Agamemnon. There was no fixed law but custom; justice was administered by the family-feud—though there is some evidence that justice by trial was beginning to take root.

Religion. Homeric Greeks conceived the ideas that they lived on an earth that was a flat disk floating on Oceanus. Above them was the solid dome of heaven kept aloft by Atlas. Around them the seas abounded with marvels and foreign lands with freaks. Natural forces resulted from the actions of unseen gods who dwelt on Mt. Olympus. Gods were distinguished from men only by their immortality and their extraordinary powers; otherwise they had the shape of humans and all of the virtues and vices of mankind. They fought, feasted, made love, played tricks, lied, deceived, made music, roared with laughter, fell in love with mortals and produced thereby generations of illegitimate progeny. They were, indeed, a capricious lot and therefore had to be cajoled, persuaded or "bought off" by prayers, votive offerings and sacrifices. The head of each Greek family was qualified to conduct these religious rites and therefore there were, among the Homerics, no temples, no organized priesthood. Relations between these Greeks and their gods were earthbound for the Greeks seemed not to believe in underworld ghosts, or spirits, or, in fact, in any last judgment and afterlife punishment. Hence they had only the most rudimentary sense of sin. Life was to be lived on earth and religious devotion was centered upon extending it as long as possible with the aid of favoring gods or by outwitting unfavoring ones through developing the gift of prophecy or omen-reading.

THE WARS OF ANCIENT GREECE

The Greek nations were forced to fight their way to freedom because they were caught between the Persian Empire expanding westward from Asia Minor and Carthage expanding eastward from North Africa. The Persian menace first struck the Ionian Greeks who were resident in Asia Minor; by 546 B.C. Cyrus had subdued all the Greek cities there. Mainland Greece was now faced with the possibility that the Persians would cross over the Hellespont into Europe. Already the Persians were seeking to dominate the sea trade on the Mediterranean. When, therefore, Aristagoras in 499 B.C. led the Ionian cities in revolt against DARIUS, Athens risked the fury of the Persians by sending them naval assistance; Sparta refused to send aid. Darius gathered tremendous land and naval forces for an assault on Greece itself.

The Persians first landed at **Marathon** (490 B.C.). This direct threat to the independence of all the Greeks failed to unify them; the Athenian army was left to face the Persians alone. Under the military leadership of Miltiades and Callimachus the Persians were routed and driven into the sea. The results of this victory were immense: it showed that the Persians were not invincible; it delayed a second Persian attack for ten years; it began the Athenian leadership of Greece; it spelled the end of the tyranny as a form of government (for the Persians were fostering this form on the Ionian shore); it inspired the great classics of Aeschylus and Herodotus; it ensured that "western civilization" as opposed to "oriental civilization" would prevail in Europe. Of more immediate

value, it forced the Greek cities to unite against the certainty of the second attack.

This attack came in 480 B.C. XERXES, the son of Darius, had gathered a force of 200,000 men for the attack and had selected **Thermopylae** as the battleground. LEONIDAS made his immortal stand against the Persians here and delayed them long enough to permit the evacuation of Athens. The Greeks were unable to prevent the destruction of Athens; nor did they make strenuous efforts to defeat the Persians on land. Greek strategy was to achieve a decisive victory on the sea. They met the Persians, as planned, at Salamis and wiped out the Persian fleet and army there. On the same day Persia's Carthaginian allies were routed. One year later, at Platea, the Persians were defeated on land and driven out of Europe.

The Peloponnesian Wars (431–404 B.C.) The unity finally achieved in the war against the Persians did not last. Capitalizing upon her leadership, Athens, in 478 B.C., organized the **Delian League,** a confederacy of about 200 city-states; then, led by Themistocles and Aristides, Athens converted this League into an imperialist grab-bag for herself. She intervened by occupation and threat of occupation in the internal affairs of the League members; she forced them to pay a tribute to Athens for "protection"; she dominated all their commercial activities. Athenian imperialism forced Sparta, in alliance with Corinth, to take steps against the possible loss of their own independence by strengthening the Peloponnesian League.

Thus matters stood when Pericles came to power in Athens. Democratic at home, Pericles pursued an aggressive imperialist policy abroad; he broke a long-standing alliance with Sparta; he allied with the enemies of Sparta and Corinth (Argos, the landed nobility of Thessaly, Megara, etc.); he helped a group of rebellious helots to colonize in Athenian territory; he began a policy to drive Corinthian trade out of the Aegean. Anticipating the reaction of the Spartans, Pericles completed the fortification of Athens by building the Long Walls connecting Athens with the port of Peiraeus, a distance of four and a half miles.

These preparations were made none too soon for in 431 B.C. Sparta and her allies declared war on Athens. The war lasted 27 years. It was featured, as Thucydides pointed out, by "calamities such as Hellas had never known."

After years of stalemate, the Athenians were

defeated at **Syracuse** in the west (413 B.C.) and ultimately at Athens in 404 B.C. The results of the Peloponnesian wars were calamitous in the extreme: the great age of Athens ended; Spartan hegemony was destroyed by the city-state of Thebes under the leadership of Epaminondas; war and confusion prepared the way for a new power rising in the north and readying itself to spring southward.

THE RISE OF MACEDONIA

Philip. At the beginning of the fourth century B.C. Macedonia was a semi-barbarian state on the northern fringe of Greece. PHILIP came to the Macedonian throne in 359 B.C. As a youth he had been taken as a hostage to Grecian Thebes; there he learned to hold Greek culture in great reverence and to disdain Greek politics, which had deteriorated.

Philip, it seems, determined to save Greece from itself by a liberating Macedonian conquest. He would unite her under his single rule and spread her culture abroad. His policy of conquest was to be by devious political fracturing of whatever Greek unity existed and then by direct military assault. With this goal before him, he developed a powerful army and seized the gold mines of Grecian Amphipolis. When the opportunity presented itself he entered a "sacred war" against Phocis on the side of ruling Thebes and this netted him Greek citizenship and a place on the Amhyctyonic Council.

At this time, only one Greek saw through Philip's maneuvering—DEMOSTHENES, and in his **"Philippics"** he warned of conquest to come and urged unity—military and political—upon the Greek city-states. His passionate and eloquent words went unheeded, even laughed at—Philip was such a cultured gentleman who lived so far away! With this advantage Philip defeated Olynthus and neutralized Athens herself. Against the advice of Demosthenes Athens permitted Macedonia to cooperate with her in a second "sacred war" against Amphissa. In the course of this campaign Philip took over all of central Greece. Thoroughly alarmed, Athens and Thebes permitted Demosthenes to organize a counter-Macedonian **Pan-Hellenic League**—which Philip crushed. He was now sole ruler in Greece. His policy toward the conquered Greeks was one of firm kindness; he even offered them an honored place in an expedition against the Persians that he was now planning. But in 336 B.C. he was murdered. His son Alexander succeeded.

Alexander. ALEXANDER THE GREAT was tutored by the great Greek philosopher Aristotle; and no more thoughtful world conqueror ever existed. Better than most, Alexander knew and appreciated the glory of Greek culture. But he knew that no Greek was safe from barbarian conquest until Greece had conquered all the world. He brought all his genius for military tactics, propaganda and political strategy to bear upon the realization of this goal.

First, Alexander crushed an uprising of Spartans in Greece itself; then, with half his army he went to meet the Persians in Asia Minor. He met them at Granicus in 334 B.C. and at Issus in 333 B.C. and routed them each time. Choosing not to pursue Darius, Alexander turned south and subdued the Phoenican coast; he then descended deeper into Egypt. Here his purpose was revealed fully for he launched a huge public works program to restore all things Egyptian and then recruited thousands of Greek intellectuals and workingmen to build for him a huge Greek city in Egypt itself; this city became **Alexandria,** the first cosmopolitan city in the world, a meeting-place for people from all over the world.

This done, Alexander now returned to meet Darius who had regrouped and enlarged his armed forces until they far outnumbered Alexander's; at Arbela, in 331 B.C., Darius was defeated again. Though Darius escaped, he was murdered by his own men; Alexander then assumed for himself the Persian title of the "Great King." He took over Persia's capitals and its treasuries; he assumed Oriental mannerisms and even his Macedonians had to now prostrate themselves before him. In pursuit of the murders of Darius Alexander now pushed on to conquer Bactria and India; but exhaustion had set in.

Alexander moved on to Babylon, where he contracted the swamp fever and died. He was thirty-three years old; but in his brief lifetime he had changed the face of the world. Alexander's empire died with him. PTOLEMY, a follower, seized Egypt and instituted a pharaonic rule; Seleucus took Syria and the lands of the Persian Empire; Greece degenerated into an internecine war between an Aetolian League and an Achaean League and Macedonia. The world awaited a new unifier and a new peace. In Italy one such was coming slowly to life and power.

Though chaos succeeded Alexander's efforts, what his conquest accomplished was incalculable. He broke down the barriers which had persisted for three millenia between Oriental and Occidental; out of the intermixture of cultures came a new, brilliant Hellenistic civilization; hieroglyphic and cuneiform fell to superiority of the Greek tongue; release of the Persian treasures stimulated trade and commerce to new heights; trade lanes now began to extend from the Pacific Ocean to the Atlantic; new cities grew up and old ones were revitalized all along the trade lanes. He had decisively altered his world.

Rome

THE BASES OF ROMAN CIVILIZATION

Geography. The mountains of Italy were not obstacles to political unification as were those of Greece; while precipitous, they terminated in the broad plains of Latium—large and fertile areas capable of intensive cultivation. The Appenines, however, forced the Romans to face westward, away from the civilizations of the eastern Mediterranean; and this gave the Romans the isolation they needed for independent development. Italy's peninsular form made it inevitable that, when able, the Romans would concentrate upon domination of the Mediterranean Sea. The open land areas, the easy invasion of Italy from northern lands and surrounding seas, forced the Romans on the defensive from their earliest days; militarism became synonymous with survival. Finally, the situation of Rome itself atop seven hills commanding the Tiber River gave her a powerful position on the peninsula.

People. The original Italian peoples are lost in the mists of the past. When the Romans emerged they were a linguistic, cultural and racial mixture of Samnites, Umbrians, Latins, Gauls, Greeks and Etruscans. Greek influence was particularly strong; but most profound was that of the **Etruscans,** an Oriental people whose high civilization was absorbed by the Romans. The earliest Romans were subject for many years to the overlordship of these Etruscans. Etruscan practices of many kinds seeped into Roman life and remained long after the Etruscans themselves had vanished.

Political Institutions. Because they began as a conquered people under absolute monarchy, the Romans created political institutions to defend themselves from the exercise of arbitrary power. When they became a free people, they placed supreme power in the hands of two political bodies —the **Assembly** and the **Senate.** The Assembly included all male citizens of military age. It was basically a ratifying body and as such had an absolute veto on executive decrees in matters of war, peace and justice. The Senate was a council of elders whose membership derived from traditional clans. Senators comprised, for the most part, a conservative, landowning aristocracy; they were charged with choosing successors to the monarchy and with safeguarding the **law of custom** from invasion by either the King or the Assembly. Such were the **checks and balances** that characterized the Roman government when it began its independent existence in 509 B.C.—the year the Etruscan kings were finally expelled.

Socio-Economic Institutions. The family was the basic unit in primitive Roman society. Its sole legal personality was the *pater* (father) who had the power of life and death within the family. Custom and the position of the Roman matron acted as restraints on the absolutism of this *paterfamilias.* The social group was separated by rigid class divisions: there were **patricians** or large landowners of noble birth, a privileged class who served in the Senate, monopolized army offices, and conducted public religious ceremonials. Then there were the **plebeians,** a free citizenry drawn from the the small farming and artisan classes. They served in the Assembly and enjoyed the right of trading, property holding, and judicial self-defense. But they were barred from entry into the Senate, they could not intermarry with the patricians, and had no recorded bill of rights. **Clients** or tenant farmers and slaves completed the class structure; they were without freedom or rights.

Religion. Religion cemented Romans of all classes. There were no priestly castes; religion was related to civic activities. However, specialists in religious knowledge did exist: *haruspices* who inspected the vital organs of sacrificed animals; *augurs* who interpreted omens.

Household and farm deities predominated: Janus, the Spirit of the Doorway; Vesta, The Spirit of the Hearth; the Penates, the Guardians of Household Stores; the Lares, The Guardians of Family Property; and the Genius or Guardian Spirit.

Religious devotion was quite materialistic: it was based on bargaining and contracting with the gods and such bargains and contracts were enforced by law, duty and taboo. Late in the monarchical period national gods made their appearance: **Jupiter,** the sky-god and chief over all; **Juno,** Jupiter's spouse and protector of matrons; **Minerva,** the artisan's divinity; and **Mars,** god of war. With national deities asserting themselves, the gods left the Roman household and entered into temples; worship became cultish.

The Roman Ideal. Where the Greeks found their ideal within themselves, the Romans looked back to their founding ancestors for theirs. For it seemed to Romans that these founders were worthy of worship. They had set the ideal of "sterling integrity, stern dignity, stoic endurance, rugged simplicity, hard economy and sturdy industry" for all posterity. They were unselfish patriots, austere puritans, practical utilitarians—without philosophy, imagination or culture.

FROM CITY-STATE TO NATION-STATE

From 509 to 265 B.C. the small city-state of Rome expanded its dominion until it was master of the whole Italian peninsula. This 250 year expansion was piecemeal and resulted from the efforts of the Romans to make themselves defensively secure against hostile neighbors and to solve their problem of a landless population at the expense of their neighbors.

The Fifth Century B.C. Etruscan power declined steadily during the fifth century B.C. and released a large number of Italian tribes for war and expansion. Rome was threatened by engulfment by any one or all of them. Cities in Latium had formed a **Latin League** and were pressing upon Rome. After many years of defensive battling, Rome brought the Latin League to terms by a tremendous victory at **Lake Regillus** (486 B.C.). Members of the Latin League were forced into an offensive-defensive alliance with Rome, an alliance that held for 150 years in wars against the Etruscans, the Aequi, and the Volsci. Aggressive advances by the northern Sabellians had set the Aequi and Volsci in motion against Rome. Under the leadership of CORIOLANUS the Aequi were vanquished; and under that of CINCINNATUS, the Volsci. Momentarily secure on her farther borders, Rome attacked and eliminated an Etruscan stronghold at Veli—twelve miles to her North across the Tiber. This latter victory enabled Rome to double her territory and to emerge as the leader of the Latin League.

The Fourth Century B.C. The fourth century B.C. opened with a disastrous invasion by barbarous **Gauls** which ended in the sack of Rome and the impoverishment of its people. Under Camillius the Romans painfully rebuilt their razed city, built strong walls around it, reorganized their army into more flexible units, introduced iron weapons, and revised their requirements for Roman citizenship.

Chastened and strengthened, the Romans were occupied for most of the rest of the century with eliminating the strong threat of the Samnites, war-like mountaineers who were threatening Rome's fertile lands in Campania. A victory over the Samnites had the effect of stirring Rome's allies in the Latin League to attack her; she was becoming too big and powerful for the security of other Italian states on the peninsula. But Rome defeated their combined effort. The Latin League was dissolved; its cities were isolated by separate treaties; some were made colonies; others were given a suffrageless Roman citizenship.

Rome became the capital of all Latium and the protector of all under her dominion. Colonies of Roman citizens were settled within the conquered territories to relieve the pressure of the landless upon Rome's land. The Samnites, defeated but not conquered, now (327 B.C.) attempted to organize all of the conquered people into a federation for independence. To meet this new threat, Appius

Claudius made further reforms in the army, built a navy, broadened the base for both military and tax levies, and constructed the first of the great Roman military highways (**The Appian Way**). The result was the complete defeat of the Samnites and their allies at the Battle of **Sentium** (296 B.C.). All Italy was within the grasp of the Romans.

The Conquest of Italy. The remainder of Italy was taken in the third century B.C. This was southern Italy where Greek cities predominated. When war between the Greek cities and Rome threatened, the city of Tarentum called upon King Pyrrhus of Epirus (in Greece) for aid. Pyrrhus responded and at Heraclea (280 B.C.) won a bitter and costly victory—hence the phrase "Pyrrhic victory." Pyrrhus's advantage came from the use of terror-spreading elephant cavalry. Rome now allied with her powerful North African neighbor, Carthage, in a defensive alliance against Pyrrhus. By 275 B.C. Pyrrhus was forced to leave Italy, and Tarentum fell; all of southern Italy now succumbed. Rome occupied Italy from the toe to the Po River.

Why Rome Conquered. Many reasons are given for Rome's success. Her enemies were disunited and Rome's policy of divide and rule was effective; Rome's allies were weakened by continual wars with *Rome's* enemies; Roman statesmen kept internal strife at a minimum by generous land grants, liberal division of the spoils of war and extension of democratic rights. Rome's victims were forced to place their armies at her disposal. Highway trunklines were built with each new conquest, colonies and garrisons were placed at all strategic outposts, bilateral treaties militated against new combinations against Rome.

Most important, however, was the use made of Roman citizenship.

Conquered peoples fell into four classes: **citizens, municipia, Latin Allies** and **Italian Allies.**

Roman citizens had full rights and privileges of citizenship.

Municipia had Roman citizenship *without* suffrage rights; they enjoyed local autonomy and the rights of trade; they served in the army and paid taxes.

The Latin Allies had no citizenship but still enjoyed the rights of trade; they furnished Rome with foreign legions and had some local autonomy.

The Italian Allies were Roman protectorates; they sent troop levies to Rome, levies that were supported at Roman expense and shared in the war booty.

Though the bulk of the Italians thus lost their independence, were bound to do Roman military service and had to pay numerous special taxes to their Roman rulers, Roman rule brought them many advantages: a *pax Romana* (Roman peace), an end to inter-tribal warfare, defense against external aggression, partial freedom and the possibility of full citizenship, economic unity, the use of Roman public works (aqueducts, roads, bridges, etc.) and a share in the new prestige that Rome had won for Italy.

Effects on Rome—Military, Economic, Cultural. The Roman army took on permanent form. It was a paid, national militia based on universal conscription of all property holders for service at home or abroad. The military unit was the phalanx of heavy and light infantry; the sub-unit was the centuriate (100 men). During the fourth century a more flexible form of legion (4000 infantry) was adopted. It was divided into 120 maniples for maneuverability. Larger units of cavalry were added and by the middle of the fourth century the Romans had a navy as well.

The Italian conquest extended the importance of agriculture in Rome's economy, since large tracts of arable soil were added to her holdings. Labor power for these expanded estates was provided by the slaves who were taken as war-prisoners. From the conquered people new techniques of farming were borrowed and applied (particularly in wine and olive production). War profits increased the demand for foreign luxury goods; trade expanded and with trade there came a money economy. Trade brought the trader—a new class of rich men that began to press for a larger share in government.

Latin translations of Greek works began to spread through Italy. Greek gods were adopted and given Roman "citizenship." Hellenistic philosophies began to capture the imagination of the intellectuals and to undermine the traditional beliefs.

THE ROMAN EMPIRE

Rise. Caesar had willed his rule to his nephew OCTAVIUS. Octavius had to fight for his bequest against MARC ANTONY and LEPIDUS—both Caesar's friends and both commanding effective military power. All three, however, had a common enemy in the republican forces led by Cassius and Brutus. **A Second Triumvirate** was therefore formed which consisted of Octavius, Antony and Lepidus. At **Philippi** the republicans were overwhelmed. Antony moved on to Egypt and to Cleopatra while Octavian (Octavius) returned to Rome to consolidate his position. When Antony divorced Octavia (Octavian's sister) to marry Cleopatra, Octavian declared war. At the **Battle of Actium, 39 B.C.**, his fleet won a decisive victory over Antony and Cleopatra. Octavian was now without opposition.

The Principate. Julius Caesar had sought to transform Roman society; Octavian sought to reestablish it — within a new order. Octavian, for example, forced Caesar's appointees from the Senate if they were not descended from the highest Roman nobility. He decreed that no Roman citizen could marry a freeman, or outside his rank. Old Temples were restored—in marble. Republican forms were scrupulously observed. When Octavian acted it was *through* the Senate and Assembly. In 27 B.C. Octavian laid down all his extraordinary powers and it was the Senate that granted them to him anew by popular acclaim. Thus by senatorial proclamation Octavian became

> *Princeps*—the head of the Senate and first citizen of the State
>
> *Imperator Caesar Divi filius*—commander-in-chief of the armed forces and son of the Divine Julius (hence he could become the object of religious worship)
>
> *Augustus*—restorer and augmenter of the state (a title formerly bestowed on certain gods).

In these bestowals the Senate recognized that the old order was gone; new times, new governmental forms. After a century of civil war the great desire of all Romans was peace and order. And Augustus Caesar was the one to give it to them.

Reforms. Augustus brought the *Pax Romana* to the Romans and to the world. The Roman army, recruited from the ranks of Roman citizens and officered by men from the aristocratic classes, stood guard at all the frontiers and within all troubled areas in the Empire. In Rome Augustus kept for himself a small praetorian guard. A standing navy was added to the armed forces. Military affairs were made the exclusive perogative of Augustus himself. Competence over the provinces was divided: those pacified and near at home were granted to the Senate; others were administered by the Imperator.

Within all provinces Augustus decided upon all military matters. To meet the rise in state expenditures for the military, for public works, for grain distribution and the like, Augustus made tax collection a state function; taxes were now collected efficiently and new import taxes were introduced. To keep expenses down, no new foreign conquests were undertaken—particularly after the resounding defeat suffered by the Romans under Varus at the hands of Arminius, a Germanic barbarian.

Height. Augustus died in 14 A.D. and his stepson TIBERIUS was nominated by the Senate as his successor. Tiberius abolished the *comitia tributa*, transferred certain provinces from the Senate to himself in order to reform them, suppressed two great mutinies in the ranks of the legionnaires and many personal plots against himself. He died unpopular in 37 A.D.

CALIGULA (37–41 A.D.) who succeeded him was insane and managed to dissipate the treasury in drunken revels and bizarre celebrations. The Praetorian Guard disposed of him. It was they who named Claudius as successor.

CLAUDIUS (41-54 A.D.) ruled well. He reoccupied Britain; reformed the bureaucracy by instituting special divisions; he completed the construction of two aqueducts and improved the great harbor at Ostia. Because she plotted against him, Claudius had his wife, Messalina, executed. He then married his niece, Agrippina, who bore him a son Nero. Agrippina then disposed of Claudius by poisoning him.

NERO (54-70 A.D.) was probably insane. His administration was filled with plot and counterplot, with assassination and execution, with persecution of the Christians who were made the scapegoat for a fire that swept Rome in 64 A.D., and with border revolts extending from Britain to Judea. When the Senate finally condemned Nero, he committed suicide.

VESPASIAN (70-79 A.D) proved a wise choice: he reformed the tax structure, recovered large tracts of public lands from extortionists, introduced rigid governmental economy, increased the income of the state, restored discipline in the ranks of the army and kept the peace. His successor, TITUS, ruled for two years only (79-81 A.D.) and was followed by Domitian.

DOMITIAN (81-96 A.D.) built the lines of forts between the Germanic and Roman lands where no natural boundaries existed. This established peace in the northeast. Murder and assassination, including his own, featured Domitian's rule.

NERVA'S (96-98 A.D.) brief rule produced an interesting agricultural scheme: to encourage agriculture in Italy a revolving fund was set up by the state; farmers could borrow from the fund at low interest rates; upon repayment, the principal was returned to the fund, and the interest was used for relief for indigent widows and orphans. Nerva began the adoptive system of imperial succession when he adopted Trajan as his son and successor.

TRAJAN (98-117 A.D.) was the first provincial to become an emperor. He was a brilliant military commander and during his rule he brought the Roman Empire to the Tigris and Euphrates Rivers—its widest extent. He also made important reforms in the imperial administration. He adopted Hadrian as his son.

HADRIAN (117-138 A.D.) was a most unmilitary ruler. His interests were in languages, literature, philosophy and art. To avoid the bother of empire, he ceded Mesopotamia and Assyria to the Parthians; granted independence to Dacia; completed the northern forts; built a wall in Britain between Roman and Celtic lines; destroyed Jerusalem and scattered the Jews far and wide through the Empire. Internal administration was reformed and the praetorian edicts were codified. Hadrian's Tomb (The Castle of Saint Angelo) on the banks of the Tiber is a most fitting memorial of this most esthetic of the Roman emperors.

ANTONINUS PIUS (139-161) ruled long and peacefully; his successor MARCUS AURELIUS (161-180) ruled long, was a man of peace, but lived through troubled times. There were local wars against the Parthians, Germanic tribes and others; there were severe persecutions of the Christians. These external exertions were in direct contradiction to the inner life of Marcus who, in his famous *Meditations*, a treatise on Stoicism, revealed himself as simple, conscientious, retiring, philosophical and ascetic.

COMMODUS (180-192) was a true son of Marcus Aurelius, at least in the flesh. The spirit of Commodus—cruel, sensuous and cowardly—was far removed from that of his father. With Commodus begins the decline of Rome.

THE DECLINE OF ROME

Rome's decline extended over centuries; it had no sudden fall. Many factors contributed to the decline. Science and technology did not keep pace with Roman expansion and Romans found that they were unable to handle efficiently the food, tools and transport problems that arose. The immense size of the empire was also a factor. It was impossible for the best-intentioned emperor to cope with the ceaseless problems of rising nationalisms, border attacks, graft and corruption in the provinces, inefficient bureacracy, gross waste of limited resources. The drain on the public treasury was continuous. The wider the empire became, the less intense became the degree of patriotism; loss of patriotism engendered corrupt political behavior. The army was sensitive to the decline particularly as it lost its Roman character and became increasingly provincial. With decline in emperor character, the army became a prime political force. It began to make and unmake emperors so frequently that one can say accurately that between the rule of Commodus (d. 192 A.D.) and the rise of DIOCLETIAN (284 A.D.) military anarchy prevailed in the Empire.

Political decline hastened the factors making for economic decline. Small farmers, the backbone of the Roman Republic, virtually disappeared or rather were absorbed into the immense estates as semi-slaves. The purchasing power represented by these small farmers disappeared and helped to ruin the city artisans who had produced manufactured goods for sale to the small farmers; besides, an important source of tax revenue also disappeared. With the ruin of the small farming and artisan classes, the state became the primary producer of goods, a factor which destroyed the initiative of the Romans. Resulting shortages of goods produced a steady inflation. Coinage began to disappear; what remained was debased and became worthless. The result was a reversion to barter. This had a tremendous impact upon the trading or middle classes who had become the backbone of the Empire. Foolish imperial decrees hastened the decline of this group. They were made responsible for the collection of taxes in the municipalities. Whatever they did not raise of the quota assigned them, they had to pay out of their own pockets. They could not meet their quotas because the artisans had been ruined with the decline of the small farmers. Soon the middle class followed the artisans into ruin.

Some social factors entered the picture too. Population declined all during the imperial period. War, epidemic and plague were chiefly responsible; and, as times grew harder, natural birth rates declined among the poor as well as the rich. Of equal importance was the failure of nerve which accompanied physical decline. This was revealed in the search for security above enterprise, in the widespread superstitions that developed, in the rush to join mystical cults that guaranteed, at least, some reward in the hereafter, in the loss of patriotism, in the wild and bestial indulgences of the rich, etc.

The Fall. Several strenuous efforts were made to halt the decline of the empire. Most notable was that of DIOCLETIAN (284-305 A.D.). Diocletian tried to augment the powers of the Emperor by introducing Oriental features of absolutism into his rule. He reformed the army; tried to halt inflation by instituting both price and wage controls; and made significant changes in imperial administration. This latter was most important for the future of European history. The Empire was divided in two, a western and eastern half and Diocletian ruled from the east. This division became permanent when CONSTANTINE (306-337) made Constantinople into a second Rome. When the fall came, it was the western half that collapsed; **the eastern half continued for more than a thousand years to preserve and disseminate the culture of the Roman Empire.**

The Foundations of Medieval Civilization

The **Medieval** or **Middle Ages** of European History are those that lie between the Greco-Roman Age and the Age of the Renaissance—approximately from 476 A.D. to about 1350. These Middle Ages reached their height between the 11th and 13th centuries. Our concern in this chapter is with Medievalism at its height and with only the broadest aspects of its civilization and culture.

FEUDALISM

A distinguishing feature of the Middle Ages was the **Feudal System,** a system that pivoted upon a **personal, contractual relationship** between two nobles—**a lord and a vassal.** A nobleman became a **lord** when he made a grant of a **fief** (a section of land with its peasant inhabitants) to another nobleman in exchange for the latter's services, chiefly military. A nobleman became a **vassal** when he accepted the fief and swore homage and fealty to his lord. It is important to remember that both the lord and the vassal were noblemen and freemen.

Origins of the Feudal System. Both Roman and German influences contributed to the creation of the Feudal System. It was not unusual in Roman times for a freeman to attach himself to a wealthy or influential man as a "client." In exchange for services, the client received protection. In more troubled times the practice of **commendation** arose. A client would "commend" both himself and his land to a patron in exchange for protection. In reverse, it was also a common practice for a wealthy landed patron to grant a client a *precarium* (land with precarious or uncertain tenure) ; in time this became a *beneficium* or a grant of land for a fixed period of time, say, a lifetime or two generations, in exchange for services. This land-services practice became merged with the Germanic practice of establishing a personal military relationship between a chief and his freeman-warriors. The Germans also introduced a practice of "immunity-grants" whereby powerful noblemen were granted free, unsupervised sovereignty over fixed territorial areas.

The Fief. In the tenth century the practice became fixed to **invest** a warrior-vassal with a fief. The fief might be a single, small holding or an entire duchy of many holdings. It was an *hereditary* holding and was transmitted by succession through the eldest son. Within the boundaries of the fief the vassal exercised sovereign rights: he collected taxes, coined money, exploited the resources, raised armies, provided for the public defense, administered justice, established and regulated markets and the like. The investiture of a fief was often recorded in a written contract. In the written contract was also included a listing of the services which the vassal would render to his lord. A fief could be *sub-infeudated* or divided among sub-vassals.

The Services of the Vassal. The basic obligation of the vassal to his lord was military service; in time this came to be limited to about forty days of military action. The number of fully equipped men that each vassal contributed depended upon the number of sub-vassals that he controlled. Vassals were also expected to help garrison the lord's fortress or castle and to engage in administrative activities. A vassal, then, might be chief administrative agent of fief and household; a constable or commander of the castle; a marshal or supervisor of the horses; a butler or supervisor of the wine supplies. Vassals were expected to attend the lord's court and to serve as judges in inter-vassal disputes, thus giving rise to a "trial by one's peers."

Feudal aids or monetary payments accompanied the personal services of the vassal; occasions for such payments were numerous. If the lord was captured in battle, the vassal had to contribute to ransom him back; if the lord planned an expensive undertaking in the nature of a pilgrimage or crusade, the vassal had to provide monetary assistance; if a vassal died, the inheriting son had to pay an inheritance tax. To protect himself against the possibility that an enemy would take legal possession of a fief, the lord secured the right to himself to veto a marriage proposal made to the vassal's daughter or widow; to assign custody over minors, who had inherited a fief, to a male regent. If a vassal failed to deliver his services, he could be forced to forfeit his fief and if he died without an heir, the fief would revert to the lord.

Feudal Hierarchy. Medievalism was patterned on the needs of these broad social groups: the peasants, the military nobility, and the clergy. These three groups formed **estates** and the first was the clergy, the second, the nobility, and the third, the peasantry and other producers (the townsmen did not fit easily into this medieval pattern—as we shall see).

In theory, the feudal hierarchy was carefully pyramided. At the top, as lord of all vassals, was the king; counts, dukes, and viscounts followed; beneath them were the barons or seignors; and knights or chevaliers made up the lowest rank. The Church held a special position in the hierarchy. In the 9th and 10th centuries many churchmen gave military service for feudal allotments and when this was prohibited on moral grounds, church fiefs were usually sub-infeudated among lay knights who could fulfil by proxy the Church's military duties.

Within the hierarchy, the king was potentially powerful but actually limited in his power to his own estate. Theoretically he owned all the land; in reality it was in the inalienable possession of the powerful nobility. Theoretically—as in Germany—the king ruled by divine right (The Holy Roman Emperor); in reality, he was an *elective* monarch chosen by the nobility and the clergy. Theoretically, the king commanded the allegiance of all his subjects; in reality, they obeyed him to the extent of their oath of allegiance and feudal contract. The point of this comparison is that the seeds of royal absolutism were buried in the medieval order and could be released the moment the power of the feudality weakened. This is precisely what happened by the 15th century.

Feudal Life. While feudalism prevailed, violence and turbulence characterized the life of the nobility as they contended over matters of inheritance and succession, of lay and ecclesiastical supremacy, of infractions of the feudal contract and the like. With war as an almost constant condition, feudal lords were forced to convert their homes into fortresses. The castle was a fortress. Its thick walls, crenelated towers, deep donjons, inner and outer battlements, surrounding moat, iron-toothed portcullis and drawbridge made it virtually unassailable by feudal armies except by seige and starvation.

The state of permanent war conditioned the education of youth. Feudal youth were trained to become knights or warriors. Like his Spartan prototypes, the feudal youth was removed from parental care at the age of seven or eight and sent to another feudal household for upbringing. He served as a page until he was sixteen and as a squire until he was twenty-one. Throughout these early years, he was made to live a hard life in the course of which he was taught the use and care of arms and horses. When he was battle-ready, he became a knight. This occasion was an impressive religio-feudal ceremony during which the knight-to-be knelt before another knight and received an *accolade* which was originally a sharp blow with the flat of a sword intended to knock the initiate out but was later modified to a slight tap on the head or shoulder. Once knighted, the warrior spent his time in war or warlike games which took the forms of hunting and tournaments or jousts.

ENGLAND

England was brought into the compass of European civilization by the Romans. In the fifth century A.D., however, the Romans had to retire before the onslaughts of the barbarian Angles, Saxons, Jutes and Frisians. The chaos which resulted was brought into some kind of order as a result of the missionary work of the Irish and Roman clergy. In 664, at the Synod of Whitby, Roman Catholic Christianity was officially adopted by the ruling tribes.

These tribes were divided into seven kingdoms, the so-called **Heptarchy.** By the ninth century, the kingdom of Wessex rose to power and produced one of England's great leaders, ALFRED THE GREAT (871-901). Alfred was able to establish a working relationship with the Danes who were threatening Anglo-Saxon England with extinction and then to initiate in England something of a "renaissance" of learning. He established schools and fostered the translation of Latin classics (e.g., Boethius' *Consolation of Philosophy*, Venerable Bede's *Ecclesiastical History of the English Nation*). He himself helped produce the *Anglo-Saxon Chronicle* and inspired the work of CAEDMON and CYNEWULF, founders of English literature. By codifying the laws and by remarkable defense of his realm, Alfred gave the English a tradition of strong kingship that soon became legendary. His work was undone by weak successors and by the conquest of England by KING CANUTE, the Dane (1016-1035). Canute's invasion forced many of the Anglo-Saxon nobility to flee to Normandy in France.

William the Conqueror. One such who fled was EDWARD THE CONFESSOR who in 1042 returned from Normandy to the throne of England. Edward brought with him many Norman advisers. Great rivalry developed between the Anglo-Saxon earls and these Norman nobles. When Edward died, the Witan (Council) selected Harold the Saxon (of Wessex) as king. WILLIAM, DUKE OF NORMANDY opposed this selection saying that Edward had promised the kingdom to him. In 1066 William invaded England and at the **Battle of Hastings** defeated Harold and his Anglo-Saxon forces. All of England fell as a feudal fief to the Conqueror.

Showing rare wisdom, William kept the government institutions he found in England and infused them with a new life. William destroyed the Anglo-Saxon earldoms, dividing them into smaller administrative units; over them he placed officials directly responsible to himself. Thus he merged Anglo-Saxon institutions with Norman institutions.

William's intention was to build a strong, centralized monarchy in England. His position was unique for he held all of England as a fief and could therefore make every landholder his vassal; every landholder had to serve in William's army. To further strengthen his position William kept a private standing militia for his use and prohibited private warfare. He issued a uniform royal currency. Even more remarkable for his time, William based his taxation upon the Domesday Survey (1085-1086), a national census of property holders and property! To defend his realm, William built castles everywhere and armed them with his own retainers.

Henry I (1100-1135). When William died the nobles tried to disrupt his plans for centralization. HENRY I consolidated his position by creating a permanent council of advisers—a bureaucracy of professional civil servants—and a group of "circuit" judges who traveled about the kingdom bringing the king's justice to all parts.

Henry II (1154-1189). Following Henry I's death, feudal and civil wars reduced England to a state of anarchy. Order was eventually restored by HENRY II, one of the greatest of all English kings. Henry was founder of the **Plantagenet dynasty** and ruled a land that extended from Scotland to the Pyrenees; his wife was the brilliant Eleanor of Aquitaine.

During the course of his reign, the English monarchy was considerably strengthened, particularly in the arena of judicial control. Henry's judicial reforms entered not only into the blood stream of the English nation, but into that of the United States as well. In the Assize of Clarendon of 1166 Henry did more than strengthen the king's justice. He initiated the participation of the people in the law-making process. The Clarendon Assize established the circuit judge as a permanent part of the English judicial system. When the circuit came to town, it was the duty of the sheriff to call up witnesses to give the judges information of existing wrongs. This practice created the **grand jury** which made "presentments" to the judges. In time these presentments were turned over to a **petit jury** ("twelve good men and true") to hear the presentments and pass judgment. He enlarged the jurisdiction of the King's Bench by permitting—contrary to feudal practice—civil as well as criminal cases to come before the circuit judges. This reduced considerably the power of the local, feudal baronial court.

Henry also resolved to reduce the power of the church courts by limiting the claim of "benefit of clergy" to major officials of the church. In this he was opposed by THOMAS A BECKET, the Archbishop of Canterbury. When Henry promulgated in 1164 the **Constitutions of Clarendon** which ordered that church officials accused of a crime should be taken before a royal court, Becket ordered churchmen to ignore the decree. After six years of dispute, at Henry's instigation a group of his followers murdered Becket.

The church and baronial courts having been curbed, the king's justices were free to consolidate English law and practice and out of their procedures there grew up the great system of **English Common Law.** Unlike Roman Law, the Common Law was never codified; it consisted of **customs and precedents.** In spite of this, it is wholly proper to call Henry II the "English Justinian."

Magna Carta (1215). Centralization of monarchical power suffered greatly under the rules of RICHARD THE LIONHEARTED and KING JOHN. Richard spent his father's bequest fighting as a knight errant in the Holy Land. John, whose goals of a centralized monarchy were consistent with Henry's but whose abilities and character were far inferior, became involved in a war with the feudal nobility and in a terrible quarrel with Pope Innocent III. As a result of his quarrel with Innocent, he lost all of his kingdom to the pope as a fief; and as a result of his war with the nobility, having been defeated in the **Battle of Runnymede,** he was compelled to sign the **Magna Carta** which placed severe restrictions on the power of the king in matters of taxation and judicial trial. At the time it was signed, Magna Carta served the interests of the feudal system. Only later did it become the **"charter of English liberties."** To cap

this sad climax to the efforts of Henry II to establish the royalty in England, John proceeded to lose all of England's French possessions.

Edward I (1272–1307). When he came to the throne, EDWARD I resumed the reforms that were begun by the two Henrys. He further weakened the baronial and church courts; he strengthened the civil service; he gave strong impetus to a new institution, the English Parliament; he began the union of all the British Isles under one crown by conquering Wales (and creating a post of Prince of Wales as successor to the Crown) and Ireland. His work with Parliament deserves special mention since herein was the "wave of the future."

The Development of Parliament. Parliament is traced to the Anglo-Saxon Witan, a council of prominent nobles. William the Conqueror converted this into a Grand Council of nobles which served him in a judicial and advisory capacity.

Parliaments became popular in Europe during the second half of the thirteenth century as kings sought for revenues outside feudal dues to carry out their programs of national aggrandizement. It became customary to convene an assembly of three "estates," the lords, the clergy and townsmen (bourgeoisie) as a means of raising money. Spain had its **cortes,** France its **Estates General,** Germany its **diet** and England its **Parliament.** In 1265 SIMON DE MONTFORT had convened, on behalf of the feudal lords, the first British Parliament. But it was Edward I who convened the "Model Parliament."

Edward's purpose was to reduce his dependence upon the nobility for moneys and he therefore agreed, in 1297, that certain taxes would be levied only with the consent of Parliament. By the 14th century, this Parliamentary "power of the purse" was ingrained in English practice—to the considerable regret of the monarchs who followed Edward. Not only had this custom begun to prevail, but it also became a custom for the lords temporal and lords spiritual to sit together as the House of Lords, while the others sat separately as the House of Commons.

Furthermore, when Parliament met, it became the practice of the House of Commons to submit to the king a "list of grievances" which had to be taken care of before any money was voted. When England became involved in the Hundred Years War, and the financial drain became severe, the House of Commons began to insist on directing how the funds should be spent. For this to be legal, it became further necessary for the Commons to draw up a law which stipulated the way the money should be spent. Thus, in the Middle Ages, grew up one of the primary forms of modern democracy.

The Hundred Years War (1337-1450). The wars between England and France in the years between 1337 and 1450 were largely inspired by the desire of the kings of England who followed Edward to repossess their French holdings. As a result of these wars, England was driven permanently off the continent and forced to concentrate upon the British Isles. British kings became more and more independent in such matters as freedom of Parliamentary debate, extension of suffrage for Parliamentary members, the right of all money bills to originate in the House of Commons and not the House of Lords. The kings' power having been weakened by war and parliament, the power of the nobility rose.

The Wars of the Roses (1453-1485). The English baronial class split into two factions, **Lancaster** and **York**—Lancaster of the "Red Rose," and York of the "White Rose." (their emblems). Both factions struggled for control of the monarchy and of Parliament. The result was a lengthy civil war known as the **Wars of the Roses** (celebrated in Shakespeare's History Plays). As a result of this civil war, the feudal nobility virtually exterminated one another and permitted Henry VII of the **House of Tudor** to gain power. With Henry VII, England moves from the Middle Ages to modern history.

THE HOLY ROMAN EMPIRE

While other European nations took the path of national unity, Germany and Italy did not become united nations until the nineteenth century. The reasons for this failure were numerous. German emperors dissipated their energies in an effort to unite Germany and Italy, a policy that was opposed, as we have seen, by the papacy and the powerful Italian towns. The popes were particularly effective in preventing this union. They openly interfered in imperial elections within Germany and kept that nation split in perpetual war between Guelph and Ghibelline, they used their extensive powers of excommunication and

interdict against such strong rulers as Barbarossa, Henry VI and Frederick II, and, when these failed, they invited foreigners like Charles of Anjou (1265) to make war on the Germans.

The Germans themselves made a unified nation nearly impossible by measures continually adopted to weaken the Emperor. For five hundred years thereafter there was no Germany—just a series of archduchies, margravates, counties, duchies and free cities known as the Germanies.

Italy suffered the same fate. The lead in preventing the unification of the Italian states was taken once more by the popes who feared for their vast possessions in Italy and by the short-sighted Italian cities. Constant invasion plagued the Italians as well. Following the decline of the Carolingian power Italy was invaded by the Normans who settled in Sicily. The Normans provided Italy with models of intelligent rule: laws were codified; a parliament was created (1225); trade and commerce were fostered. Because it threatened their power, the popes invited the French Angevins into Italy as conquerors. So bitter was the Italian resentment against the French that in 1282 at Palermo they rose up, at the house of vespers, and murdered every Frenchman they could find. (This massacre is known in history as the "Sicilian Vespers.") When the French left it became the turn of the Spaniard Alfonso of Aragon to conquer Sicily and Naples (1443). In 1494 Charles the VIII of France invaded Italy . . . but by this time Italy's will to exist as a nation was destroyed.

Out of this failure in government a new state was born—Switzerland. While Frederick II was King he permitted two Swiss cantons to become self-governing—subject to his overlordship. A habit of independence was born. When in 1291 Rudolph of Hapsburg, the German ruler decided to remove their independent rights, the Swiss cantons formed a Perpetual Compact or alliance directed against Rudolph. Their resistance was successful. In 1315 the frustrated Hapsburgs moved an army against the Swiss and were soundly beaten by boulders rolled down the declivities of the cantons. Their success encouraged the Swiss to organize a confederation. In 1394 the Hapsburgs compromised with necessity and recognized Swiss independence. Out of this struggle came the legend of **William Tell.**

The Economic Transition to Modern Times

THE COMMERCIAL REVOLUTION

Statistics of the growth of European commerce between 1350 and 1650 are not available; but some indication of the growth is reflected in the fact that by the latter date there were an estimated 2,000,000 tons of shipping afloat. We are concerned with this fact because with each increase in Europe's trade **the power and position of the middle class grew.** Fixed capital such as landed property began to take second place to fluid capital in the form of money. Manufacturing was becoming a competitor of agriculture for available investment capital. There still were many medieval shackles upon the free flow of trade—feudal tolls and tariffs, religious prohibitions, guild restrictions, and the like. But these were being shaken loose by the rise of **national states** under *national* monarchies, by the wave of humanism and new learning sweeping Europe, and by the religious reformation. Taking advantage of these dissolvents of the medieval order, the middle class began to develop forms of manufacturing that evaded the boundaries set down by the guilds. In the mainstream of all these charges, however, was the revolution in commerce that made itself felt by the fifteenth century.

Trade and Commerce. By 1400 European markets were no longer restricted to the luxury trade from the Near East. These still commanded an imposing position in the trade picture, but trading was as much concerned now with new European foodstuffs, textiles, shipbuilding materials and tools. Markets were no longer restricted to a few favored areas since goods could now travel along the king's roads protected by the king's police and the king's courts. The supply of money had increased; European deposits of gold and silver were dug with intensified fervor and North African mineral sources were tapped. When the Americas were discovered—just as European deposits were almost exhausted—a flood of gold and silver bullion re-entered the trade stream.

Manufacturing. Traders clamored for manufactured products to be sold abroad in exchange for luxury goods and for foodstuffs. Throughout these early years, in fact, the drain of gold and silver out of Europe was very heavy. Europe suffered from an almost continual unfavorable balance of trade which kept her prices low (deflation) and her debts high. When the political power of the guilds declined, entrepreneurs (early capitalists) appeared who discovered and invested in a new mode of production of manufactured goods, the **domestic** or "putting out" system.

Under this system the entrepreneur contracted with many craftsmen to supply them with raw materials and to pay them for the goods they manufactured out of the raw materials. The entrepreneur then disposed of the manufactured goods in the local or international market. This was a very attractive offer to the craftsman. He already owned his own tools, he could do the work at home (hence domestic), he did not have to worry about purchasing raw materials' and selling his products, he could keep a garden patch and do some farming to supplement his income from manufacture.

To the entrepreneur this system was still not ideal: the cost was high since the craftsman made the whole product and insisted in producing quality goods, the entrepreneur depended upon the craftsman who owned the tools, the small number of craftsmen kept wages high, production was limited, invention of new tools was discouraged since craftsmen could not afford to finance them, etc. Over the years, the attractiveness of the craftsman's position brought many new workers into the field. Entrepreneurs took advantage of this situation by lowering wages considerably. The lowering of wages had the effect of increasing the dependence of the craftsman upon the entrepreneur. To get more money, the craftsman had to give up his farming and put his wife and children to work. Under pressure to make more, the craftsman became less concerned with the quality of the product. The entrepreneur, in turn, got poorer goods and found it increasingly difficult to supervise many workers in their homes. The time soon came when a more radical innovation in manufacturing processes would have to be made. For this period, however, the domestic system served admirably to build up the quantity of trade, the wealth of the entrepreneurs and to destroy effectively the power of the guilds.

Finance. Financing by means of money grew side by side with commerce and manufacturing.

Professional money lending was an old practice by 1400. As early as the 10th century monasteries began to engage in extensive money lending, generally to local peasants and landlords. Political loans were on occasion made to Emperors, Popes and high feudal lords. Later, the knightly orders (Templars, Hospitalers, etc.) played the part of kings of finance and supplied credit needs.

In the medieval cities the role of professional lenders fell to the Lombards, Jews and money changers. Medieval Jews, prohibited from becoming farmers or artisans, had been among the first to engage in commerce. The rise of Christian merchants forced them out of this business and into the business of money-lending since they were not subject to church prohibitions and money-lending was a necessary function in an expanding economy. Christians permitted them to settle in specified areas *only if they would make loans;* Jews paid with their lives *if they refused to make a loan when security was offered.* Jews, then, won "toleration" so that Christians might evade the church's prohibition of "usury"—though the latter of course reaped the rewards of usury.

Soon, however, the Italian Lombards became active competitors of the Jews. Their loans went out to the urban merchants, feudal lords and handicraftsmen. The Lombards discovered that they might lend out more money than they had (since some was always being paid back)—but not safely. Therefore, they began to solicit interest-bearing deposits (a practice forbidden to the Jews). This was the origin of commercial banking. Other methods—such as bills of exchange, bank drafts and bank acceptances—were soon instituted.

Business Organization. Forms of **partnership,** family and non-family, had developed in the Middle Ages and were continued into the modern period. So too was the **regulated company**—an association of merchants created to monopolize and exploit some branch of trade. It received its charter from the government. Each associated merchant worked as an individual entrepreneur but contributed to a common treasury to finance a central body which maintained foreign trade centers, gave protection to the membership and laid down the rules for the proper conduct of business.

But the most modern of the forms developed in this period was the **joint stock company.** The others were a union of persons; this was a union of capital. A number of investors put their money into a venture and then chose a board of directors to conduct the venture; they then shared the profits and the risks.

When joint stock companies came to be linked to regulated companies, they were called **chartered commercial companies.** A good example of one such was the famous English **East India Company.** Its capital was derived from shareholders but it did more than engage in commercial ventures. Its charter granted it monopoly rights to trade anywhere in the Pacific and Indian Oceans; to buy land in unlimited quantity; to deal with foreign potentates; to wage war and to make peace treaties. With these freedoms permitted to it, chartered companies began to colonize the world on behalf of the mother country.

DISCOVERY AND COLONIZATION

Colonization was first attempted, unsuccessfully, by the Crusaders. The germ of the colonial concept was also present in the trading posts which were set up in Europe and the Near East by the Venetians and the Hanseatic League in the 13th and 14th centuries. But these ventures were in relatively settled and civilized areas. Modern colonization began when a vast new world of either sparsely settled or barbarous regions were suddenly discovered, explored and found more than useful. The first burst of such exploration and discovery came in the half century between 1450 and 1500. Why at that time?

Causes. Many factors combined to produce the burst of overseas exploration in 1450–1500. Nations along the Atlantic coast were growing desperate for gold and silver with which to offset the unfavorable balance of trade with the Near East. They resented more and more bitterly the stranglehold which the free cities of Italy had upon that area and upon the Mediterranean Sea. Momentarily the Italian monopoly had been threatened when the Ottoman Turks in 1453 had captured Constantinople and overthrown the Byzantine Empire. (Indeed, they had advanced deep into Europe itself and had overrun Serbia, Wallachia, Bosnia and Greece.) The Turks, however, anxious to keep the favorable balance of trade with Western Europe, had renewed Venice's privileges in the Near East. Even had there not been this political domination of the Near East, the price of Far

Eastern commodities was extremely high since the price reflected the great distances by sea and overland that the goods had to come, the tariff that had to be paid en route, the brigandage that lined the whole trade route, etc. It was clear to thoughtful merchants that there was but one answer to this distressing problem: some all-water route to the Far East—either around Africa or by a westward sailing.

Successes. MARCO POLO and other travelers had returned to Europe with the news that Far Eastern lands were washed by some mighty water. Why could it not be the same mighty water that washed the Atlantic shores of Europe? Europeans became convinced that it was and began the systematic conquest of this water—which held so many terrors for the uninformed.

By 1450 improvements in seafaring were far advanced. The magnetic compass was in general use; the astrolabe to measure latitude out at sea was perfected; new scientific maps were in circulation; shipbuilding had advanced toward larger and more powerful vessels. With the invention by JOHANN GUTENBERG of the printing press, geographical, maritime and astronomical information was diffused over wide areas. In particular it became better and better known that the earth was a sphere and that one could reach east by sailing west.

Southward and westward sailing were in the minds of many men by 1450. National states were well advanced by that time and the monarchs hungered for more revenue with which to counter the feudal nobility; dispossessed nobles hungered for a new chance to recoup their fortunes. Individuals stirred by the Renaissance stress on man sought new adventures and new glories. Men looked to Africa and to the Far East as vast potential fields of conquest.

Now Europe needed bold and fearless navigators to try the dangers of the unknown sea. One who did not fear the sea was Prince HENRY THE NAVIGATOR, son of King John I of Portugal. Motivated by a zealot's hatred for the Moslems and a desire to conquer them by outflanking them in the south of Africa, Henry organized a navigational center on the southern tip of Portugal facing the Atlantic. Here captains were trained in the making of maps, the reading of them, the use of navigational instruments, etc.

Their training completed, Portuguese navigators began to edge cautiously down the western coast of Africa. In 1488 (twenty years after Henry's death) BARTHOLOMEW DÍAZ reached the Cape of Good Hope. Ten years later VASCO DA GAMA sailed around Africa to India. The southward route had been breached. Six years before da Gama's feat, however, the Western route was opened by the world-shaking voyage of CHRISTOPHER COLUMBUS (1492). Some years had to pass before Europeans came to realize that Columbus had discovered a huge continent that blocked the way to the Far East. The first to see the ocean on the other side of the New World was VASCO NUNEZ DE BALBOA; and the first to circumnavigate the globe by sailing westward was FERDINAND MAGELLAN and his crew (Magellan having been killed in the Philippines). By 1522 the Mediterranean Sea route to the luxury items of the Far East had been circumvented in two directions. Hegemony over Far Eastern Trade now passed to the nations on the Atlantic shores. The Commercial Revolution was complete.

The Renaissance

For many years historians took their understanding of the historical period known as the **Renaissance** from a book written by the great Swiss historian, JAKOB BURCKHARDT—*The Civilization of the Renaissance in Italy*. According to Burckhardt, the Renaissance was a spontaneous creation of the Italian people in the fifteenth century (the quattrocento); it was something new that had no roots in the past. From nowhere came a new birth of individuality; from nowhere, an outburst of genius that took the forms of great art and literature. Several concepts distorted Burckhardt's view of the Renaissance: he was primarily concerned with culture and ideas; he, therefore, paid insufficient attention to other factors—religious, political, social or economic; he believed in the "great man theory of history" which blinded him to large movements involving lesser people. In spite of these weaknesses, Burckhardt's study remains a major classic of historical research.

Historians still do not agree on all that the Renaissance was, but most will accept the statement that it was not a "rebirth" so much as a **transitional period between medieval and modern times.** As a transitional period the roots of the Renaissance derive from the medieval outlook; its tentacles stretch toward the dawning era of modern science; in itself it was neither medieval nor modern. Because it was an in-between period it was characterized by criticism of the *status quo*, by restless curiosity about all things, by the raising of questions rather than the answering of them. Such intellectual attitudes inevitably led the men of the Renaissance to place man himself under more intensive examination and it was out of this emphasis upon *man* that the distinctive features of the Renaissance emerged. In this matter, Burckhardt cannot be denied; the Renaissance did burst with creativity and the artists of that period were great men even if they were not the *sole* determinants of the course of history during the Renaissance.

Renaissance Versus Medievalism. There was much in medieval life that Renaissance men openly rejected or disagreed with. While medieval men revered some of the Greco-Roman classics, Renaissance men hailed them all, no matter how pagan, how un-Christian. They made war against medieval Latin and 14th century vernacular and sought to return to the "pure Latin" of Cicero— a virtually unknown tongue. They were optimistic, worldly, and individualistic. They rejected "Gothic" architecture as "barbaric"; they no longer gave unthinking credence to Ptolemaic astronomy which placed man at the center of the universe; they pursued knowledge for knowledge's sake without fearing for their faith; they mocked at chivalry, scholastic philosophy, medieval economics; in short, they affirmed life with enthusiasm and joy.

Causes of the Renaissance. What forces accelerated this drive toward a "new birth?" Many of them lay in earlier developments: contact with Moslem and Byzantine civilizations; the Commercial Revolution with its interchange of goods and ideas; the new learning of the thirteenth century that flowered in scholasticism; the rise of national monarchies bolstered by the Bolognese revival of Roman law; the spread of universities; the near-scientific emphasis of the Nominalist movement within scholasticism; the growth of a wealthy, leisured middle-class seeking prestige as patrons of the arts. These might very well be designated **fundamental causes.** (It is worth re-emphasizing that most of these causes lay, chronologically, *within* the medieval period.) For the more immediate causes, we must turn to the history of Italy in the fourteenth and fifteenth centuries.

IDEAS OF THE RENAISSANCE

The rise of the Renaissance dictators was accompanied by a rationalization of their activities and behavior. One such rationalization was the ideal of *virtù*. A man was to be judged by the bravery and skill with which he achieved his personal goals and by the subtlety and finesse of the means he employed. In pursuit of virtù, conscience was irrelevant. So wrote MACHIAVELLI in *The Prince*.

Machiavellanism. Machiavelli wrote *The Prince* out of a deep sense of frustration with the political condition of Italy—its helplessness before the might of Spanish and French invaders, its lack of patriotism, its dependence upon mercenary soldiers, its state of warring disunity. His dream was of a unified Italy, completely sovereign, untrammeled by church, religion or morals, free to undertake whatever was necessary to bolster its unlimited sovereignty over the lives of its subjects. The end of unity could only be achieved by a patriotic and ruthless prince, possessed of virtù, who by craft and force would reduce the peninsula of Italy to a single sway.

Such a prince, thought Machiavelli, was CESARE BORGIA. Why was Cesare qualified? He took the world as it was and men for what they were—as motivated primarily by evil purposes. He therefore planned to make evil his ally. He did not scruple to break his word when his promise no longer served his purpose; he strove to make himself both loved and feared by giving the appearance of being virtuous but doing all the evil required to maintain himself in power. All means are justified, argued Machiavelli, that serve the end of attaining and retaining political power. Ruse, cunning, artifice, conspiracy—these were the methods of the prince with grandeur of soul, strength of body and mind. Poison to the prince were such Christian ideals as humility, lowliness and contempt of worldly objects.

Such goals were not confined during the Renaissance to princes alone. They can be seen operating in the interesting lives of such Renaissance figures as Pope Alexander VI, Machiavelli, himself, the utterly unscrupulous critic Pietro Aretino, the adventurer Castagno, the braggart Benvenuto Cellini and even in the youth of Leonardo da Vinci.

The Perfect Courtier. The ideal of the "very perfect knight" of chivalry had decomposed by the time of the Renaissance; in its place appeared the ideal of the "very perfect gentleman." BALDASSARE CASTIGLIONE (1478–1529) established this ideal in his book *Il Cortigiano* (*The Courtier*). Who was the gentleman? He was born to a family of good manners or gentility, aristocrats in mind and body, standards and taste. In such an environment he would grow up skilled in sport and the use of arms, a graceful dancer and skilled musician, a master of several languages including Latin, familiar with great works of literature and art, and completely at ease in the company of accomplished women.

Women, said Castiglione, are a necessary part of the environment that makes the gentleman for they refine whatever brute instincts are the natural endowment of man. But women have to be trained in their role of complement to the gentleman and the first requirement was to be feminine in carriage, manners, speech and dress. To be the conversational equals of men, women, too, must undergo the studies that would provide them with ideas on literature, art and statecraft, with facility in many languages. Compared, then, with the medieval ideal of womankind, Renaissance woman was a real woman—rather than an ethereal ideal

—and was celebrated as such in paintings of artists like Raphael and Andrea del Sarto both of whom used *live* models for their Madonnas. Gentlemen and gentlewomen, pursuing the ideal of *cortesia* (gentility) inevitably became patrons of the arts.

Art Patronage. Responding to the heightened interest in the remains of classical antiquity, the nobility and wealthy merchants began to collect antiques, to finance projects designed to spread classical, learning, and to give support to local, native artists who possessed unusual talent. The Medici, for example, built a museum for the study of antique art, financed diggings among Etruscan and Roman ruins, invited and supported artists like Bertoldo, Michelangelo, Leonardo and Verrochio to work in the museum on original projects. Lorenzo de Medici was himself exceptionally gifted as a poet and composer.

Artistic Individualism. While the artists appreciated these endowments and made much use of them, they resisted all efforts to form them into guilds or corporations so characteristic of the medieval outlook. The earliest of the great artists worked in guild workshops under the usual guild regulations and restrictions. Gradually the cult of individualism developed; artists of genius established themselves in individual studios and assumed an independent role. They still depended on commissions from the aristocracy and the church, but the subject matter and form of the artwork was to be exclusively their own. The result was that fine art was separated from the crafts; painting, sculpture and architecture became individual liberal arts, each with its own esthetic, or canons of taste and judgment.

As individual artists became recognized, there flocked about them groups of worshipping and imitating students. To bring some kind of order into art instruction, some of the masters began to organize art academies. From the art academies sprang the various schools of art which characterized the Renaissance.

The Protestant Reformation

FUNDAMENTAL CAUSES

Between 1517 and 1648 the "universality" of the Roman Catholic Church was shattered beyond repair. Roman Catholicism now had to share its leadership of Christians with a large number of national churches and private sects, each with its dogma, doctrine, ritual and sacramental acts. This momentous schism began as a reformation within the Roman Church but ended as a series of transformations outside it. The political, economic, social and cultural consequences of this schism in Christian thought and practice were explosive in the days of its origin and remain so in our own day, 300 years later. Reform movements within the Catholic fold had occurred previously, as we have seen; they were part of the evolution of the church's structure to meet changing social conditions. Why, then, should the reform inaugurated by MARTIN LUTHER have had such drastic consequences?

Church abuses. The number of church abuses had multiplied, but not significantly, over those that existed at the time of the Cluniac Reform. Many clergymen were ignorant and ineffective as priests; many led scandalous lives and in so doing broke their vows of poverty and chastity. The papal office was held by a number of Renaissance popes notorious for their loose and indulgent living and who were incredibly corrupt. They made a business out of the sale of religious offices and benefices; church offices and dispensations were placed on the auction block and those who won the bids and became church officers got their money back by charging outrageous fees for priestly services.

Still other venerated church practices were converted into profit-making enterprises. Two that figured largely in Luther's protest were the sale of relics and the sale of indulgences. Relics were objects believed to have been used by Christ, the Virgin and the saints and therefore possessed of miraculous power to cure the afflicted and to protect the threatened. Unrestrained and unreproved, relic-hawkers traveled through Europe selling unlimited quantities of holy splinters from the "true" cross or from the "bones" of saints. When the fantastic proportions reached by this traffic were exposed by the Humanists, a great revulsion followed. Even more controversy centered about the sale of indulgences.

An indulgence was a remission of all or part of the punishment for sinning in this life; it was effective in purgatory but not in hell. The practice was an ancient one and in the beginning granted after works of charity, fasting and the like. Church teaching held that Christ and the saints had accumulated a large "treasury of merit" while they were on earth; this treasury was deposited in heaven and the Pope, possessed of "the power of the keys and the authority to bind and loose," could draw upon the treasury to remit punishment both on earth and in purgatory. No indulgence was valid unless the recipient was truly contrite, confessed his sins and was absolved. Since canonical penalties often inflicted hardships and inequities upon helpless people, the church began the practice of commuting penalties into almsgiving. From almsgiving to the sale of indulgences was a natural step for the Renaissance popes who cared little for the spiritual significance of the indulgence and much for its possibilities for fundraising. In fact, one of the popes turned over the traffic in indulgences to a banking firm which collected one-third of the "take" as their share of the "profits." When exposed, this, too, caused great indignation among the faithful.

All these things had been before and had brought on reform movements; why should these series of abuses have brought on a schism? The reason must lie deeper. Old abuses gather new force when they occur in a changed environment.

Waves of Doctrine. Disgust with the Pope's exercise of temporal power had stirred JOHN WYCLIFFE (1324?–1384) to denounce it, and to follow this denunciation with demands that the Scriptures be elevated above papal power, and that the clergy be permitted to live secular lives (marriage, etc.) to reduce the amount of corruption that prevailed among them. He thought, too, that the Bible ought to be translated into the vernacular so that all who could would read it.

The fall of the papacy into the "Babylonian Exile" revived Wyclifism after it had been suppressed and found an eloquent spokesman and martyr in the person of JOHN HUS (1369-burned 1415). Humanism added to the amount, not the depth, of anti-clericalism for it did so from within the church. Valla, Mirandola, Le Fevre, Colet, Reuchlin, von Hutten and Erasmus were merciless in their exposure of hair-splitting scholasticism, monkish practices of celibacy, poverty and obedience, church practices like worship of saints and relics, confession and absolution (on the ground that research did not reveal these practices among the first Christians). Humanists generally favored a return to a simpler form of Christian practice.

What the Humanists favored the Mystics in the Church (Thomas à Kempis, Meister Eckhart, Heinrich Suso, Johann Tauler, and others) practiced. In "imitation of Christ" they rejected mechanical schemes of salvation for more direct and personal ones. By contemplation, prayer and fasting they tried to come into direct communion with God without any intermediary—that is, without the church. These men were placing considerable reliance upon justification by faith alone and not upon St. James's, doctrine of "good works." Emphasis upon man's corruptibility and his need of faith caused a revival of interest in the epistles of St. Paul; Jacques Le Fevre made a translation of them into Latin and John Colet delivered a popular series of lectures upon them. The very bases of church practice were being challenged.

Religion and Nationality. While the Church's power prevailed, criticism had, perforce, to be cautious; why did it suddenly become bold and clamorous? When church critics found secular powers to support them by force of arms, they ceased to be fearful and did not hesitate to draw the conclusions from their criticisms.

Everywhere in Europe, save Germany and Italy, new national states had arisen and were making a strong assertion of secular sovereignty. In France, by the Pragmatic Sanction of Bourges (1438) and the Concordat of Bologna (1516), the kings succeeded in winning for themselves the right to dictate ecclesiastical appointments, jurisdiction and tax levies; by the Statute of Provisors (1351, 1390) and the Statute of Praemunire (1353, 1390), the English kings had made a similar assertion; nor were the Spanish kings far behind the French and English in their demands. These gains against the church stimulated rather than appeased royal appetites. They eyed enviously the vast domains of the church; and they resented the flow out of their countries of vast sums collected by the church in the form of annates, "Peter's Pence," indulgence fees, church court fines, income from vacant benefices, fees for bestowing the pallium upon bishops, etc. They felt that every effort of the church to excommunicate or to interdict was a violation of their sovereignty; they even turned hostile eyes upon the presence in their lands of church courts sharing judicial power with royal courts.

The bourgeoisie (middle class) fully supported the kings, for different reasons. They viewed the vast church holdings as immobilized capital that, if freed, could be used as a base for a great credit expansion; and they bitterly resented being deprived of the fluid capital they had in the form of countless payments to the church. And, since the chief burden of payment fell upon the lowly backs of the peasantry, they, too, echoed the bitter resentment of the kings and the bourgeoisie.

In such an atomosphere, church abuses became the sparks of a revolutionary movement to transform the church. This movement found its voice in Martin Luther whose career is a clear illustration of the causes at work in the Protestant Reformation.

The French Revolution

Revolution is a product of national paralysis. Between 1788 and 1789 the French monarchy entered into a period of crisis, chiefly financial. War, royal extravagance, reckless borrowing, inefficient taxation and the short-sighted inflexibility of the ruling groups had emptied the royal treasury; existing revenues were inadequate to meet obligations of the national debt; existing taxes on the peasantry and bourgeoisie were already crushing.

Potentially prosperous, the French nation was experiencing widespread poverty. Prices had risen because of crop failures; wages lagged far behind prices; business failures were increasing as a result of a British invasion of the French markets; large numbers of wage earners (which included part-time peasant workers) were unemployed. Economists like Turgot, Necker and Calonne, called in to solve the financial crisis did their best to delay collapse by minor economies and major loans. Each realized that France's salvation lay in opening the untaxed wealth of the privileged classes to taxation as the only solution; and for recommending this as national policy, each was dismissed.

At Calonne's suggestion, Louis XVI convened in 1787 an Assembly of Notables. These privileged groups were asked to tax themselves. They refused but did suggest that an Estates General or parliament of the three estates (clergy, nobility and the Third Estate) be called to consider the matter of taxation. The current finance minister, Archbishop de Brienne, coldly dismissed the suggestion of the Notables and undertook to float a new loan.

Popular Reaction. Encouraged by vocal popular support, the *parlement* (court) of Paris (on whose bench sat spokesmen for the bourgeoisie) refused to register de Brienne's new loan, or any loan or tax, unless it was approved by an Estates General. This was subversion and the king moved against the court with troops. But the soldiers refused to arrest the judges and in this act they were supported by menacing mobs in Paris. Uncomprehending and bewildered, Louis was compelled to summon the Estates General. Neither he, nor any Frenchman, foresaw the consequences of this act.

The Estates General. In 1789 the Estates General was only an historical memory since it had not met since 1614. At that time it consisted of three estates—the clergy, the nobility and the Third Estate, each meeting and voting as separate bodies. The least of the three had been the Third Estate. That this was no longer possible was clearly stated in an influential pamphlet written by the Abbé Sieyès. "What is the Third Estate?" asked the Abbé. And he answered: "It is everything. What has it been hitherto in the political order? Nothing! What does it desire? To be something!" Advisers of Louis accepted the truth of the Abbé's formulation and in assigning delegates, the Third Estate was permitted to choose 600 out of a total of 1200.

Elections were held in the early months of 1789 on the basis of almost universal male suffrage. In the course of electoral gathering local communities drew up *cahiers*—lists of grievances which the delegates were instructed to correct. It is interesting to note how un-revolutionary national sentiment was on the eve of the Revolution. The cahiers almost universally proclaimed the delegates loyal to the king and to the idea of hereditary succession. But they did propose hundreds of reforms. In general these reforms centered upon limiting by constitution the powers of the king and the bureaucracy; upon no taxation without representation; upon increased elective local autonomy; upon *universal* taxation; upon humane reformation of the criminal law and its procedures; upon immediate relief of the economic crisis.

Paralysis and Revolution. On May 5th the delegates gathered into a temporary structure called (ironically) the Hall of the (King's) Lesser Pleasures. The first important dispute was on a procedural question: How should the delegates vote? The first two estates insisted on each estate casting a single vote, as in the traditional manner. Realizing that this would place them at the mercy of the privileged groups, the Third Estate insisted on voting by head (one delegate—one vote) in a single body. Third Estate strategy rested on the knowledge that some nobility and many parish priests would vote with the Third Estate to give it a majority.

The result was a temporary paralysis; the first two estates met as separate orders and organized for action; the Third Estate refused to organize until its demands for meeting as a single body were met. The impasse lasted for five weeks. Then, on June 12, the Third Estate organized itself and invited the others to join it. To distinguish itself from the others, the Third Estate, on June 17, assumed the title of **National Assembly** and declared that it had sovereign power to act for the nation. The king's government was set aside. The Revolution had begun.

The National Assembly. On the same day (June 17) the National Assembly began quietly but ominously to reform the state of France. All of the royal taxes were abolished; committees were created to draw up a reformed financial structure and to take steps to relieve the distress among the poor. Louis had not yet acted. On the 20th of June Louis suspended the sessions of the Estates General. The Third Estate, in the form of the National Assembly, withdrew to a neighboring tennis court and there took an oath (The "Tennis Court Oath") not to disband until France had a constitution. This was done with great confidence because by this time many of the parish priests and nobility had joined the National Assembly.

On the 27th of June, Louis seemed to capitulate to the National Assembly by ordering the first two estates to sit with it; he began, however, to gather mercenary troops and to station them in Paris for a showdown. With each new detachment of troops, popular indignation and violence grew. It came to a head when, on July 14, the populace stormed and took the Bastille. Violence now rolled out of Paris into the countryside as enraged peasantry attacked the chateaux of the landed nobility. By the late summer of 1789, France was in the hands of the people; the authority of the crown had vanished. All eyes were turned to the National Assembly which in August had begun to reform France.

The Reforms of the National Assembly. Abolition of feudal privileges. In abolishing the survivals of the feudal past, the nobility in the National Assembly itself took the leadership. One after another the nobles rose to propose destruction of such privileges as exemption from taxation, collection of feudal taxes, monopoly rights, distinctions of rank, vested interests, hunting and fishing rights and the like.

The Declaration of the Rights of Man. Taking its lead from the example of the American Revolution, the French Revolutionists turned to a statement of general principles as a guide to further and more permanent reform. They drew up a **Declaration of the Rights of Man and of the Citizen.**

Three pillars of freedom were erected in the ideological structure. One was **property rights**: men were to be protected in their right to private ownership of property; no one could be deprived of property except in case of public necessity; anyone deprived of property had a basic right to compensation. A second was **personal rights**: these included the basic freedoms; religious toleration; equality before the law; due process of law . . . and the like. A third was **democracy**: sovereignty resided with the people; only the people could delegate sovereignty to government; and the people reserved the right of revolution against tyranny.

Secularization of the church. Church lands were confiscated and were sold in parcels to impoverished peasantry and were also used as backing for a new currency issued to meet the financial crisis. A Civil Constitution of the Clergy was then drawn up which made the priesthood elective civil serv-

ants of the state. All clergy were forced to take an oath of allegiance to the state to qualify for the priesthood. The Pope, of course, condemned this feature and prohibited oath-taking. The result was that the French clergy were divided into those who did (juring) and those who did not (nonjuring) take the oath.

The Constitution of 1791. To complete their essentially conservative revolution, the French Revolutionists drew up a constitution for France which established a limited monarchy on the principle of the separation of powers. A Legislative Assembly was created with full power to make the law; it was to be indirectly elected by electoral colleges. The executive power was given to the king. As a check upon absolutism the king was shorn of control of the army, church and local government and was removed from the legislative process by being given a veto that could be overridden by the Legislative Assembly.

The Radical Phase. By 1791 the conservative phase of the Revolution was complete. Events soon propelled the Revolution into a more radical phase. To begin with, the economic demands of the impoverished wage-earners were not met; if anything, the situation grew worse due to a currency inflation. Restless, hungry workers had become organized mobs directed by leaders of radical clubs which had begun to flourish in Paris. These clubs reflected the political spectrum which early made its appearance in the National Assembly. Conservatives, those who favored a status quo, concentrated in the **Girondist Party**; Radicals, those who favored complete abolition of the monarchy and a sharp limitation on the rights of the bourgeoisie as well as the clergy and nobility, gravitated to the **Jacobin Party.**

Emigres—those who managed to flee from France to the more hospitable lands of Prussia and Austria and England—had created enough anxiety there to cause the monarchs of these countries to issue an ultimatum to the French Revolutionists to desist in their persecution of church and nobility. National irritation with this unwarranted interference resulted in a declaration of war by the Legislative Assembly on Prussia and Austria. Invasion of France by these two nations created a national emergency. National mobilization of a citizen army to meet the threat of foreign invasion followed. The king and queen actively cooperated with the emigres abroad and, on one occasion, even attempted escape. To the Radicals in France, it seemed that the very Revolution was at stake. In 1792 they moved to take over the government.

THE RADICAL PHASE OF THE FRENCH REVOLUTION

Terror. The radical phase of the French Revolution was distinguished by increased use of terrorization as political policy. "Madame Guillotine" became the symbol of this period. Under the loose designation of "enemies of the people" thousands of people were slaughtered. Some were, of course, guilty of treasonable activity, of conspiracy with the emigres abroad and the instigators of civil war at home; some were guilty of no more than association by birth with suspected elements in the population; others were victims of spite, revenge, rivalry and the like. Terror, like power, corrupts; and corruption was no more evident than in the popular jubilation which attended the ceremonies of execution.

Those who used terror were themselves victimized by it. In January 1793 Louis XVI and Marie Antoinette were executed. Only the Girondists opposed this decision. DANTON and ST. JUST, by brilliant oratory, turned the National Convention to this decision. It was not long before the Girondists were made the victims of the terror by the Jacobins led by Danton, ROBESPIERRE and others. This done, it was Danton's turn and he was executed because he felt that it was time to call halt to the terror. Under Robespierre, the guillotine was employed with increasing frequency. But in 1794 he too lost his head though he was almost dead of bullet wounds.

Dictatorship. In September 1792 the monarchy was deposed and the First French Republic declared. An election was then held for a National Convention to frame a new constitution. In 1793 the constitution was published. It was democratic to the core and provided for universal male suffrage, an elected legislature, an executive elected by the legislature, annual elections and the like. But it was not put into effect.

Arguing that the national situation of civil war, foreign war and economic depression was too dire to permit the processes of democracy, the Jacobins set aside the constitution and created instead a dictatorial Committee of Public Safety composed of nine members. This Committee assumed all the powers of government; it sent its agents abroad to check on the loyalty of Frenchmen and to negotiate with foreign governments; it created revolutionary tribunals with virtually unlimited power to try and execute "enemies of the people"; it raised armies and fought the foreign enemies; it nationalized economic enterprise much more effectively than the absolute monarchs of France. For two years there was little but the outer trappings to distinguish Robespierre from Louis XVI.

The fall of Robespierre brought a reaction to terror and dictatorship (the **Thermidorean Reaction**). A new constitution was written in 1795 which returned France to a moderate course. Power was divided between a bicameral legislature and a Directory or executive of five members. Voting was restricted to property owners; age-limits for holding office were raised; two-thirds of the membership of a new legislature had to be chosen from the old. Terror had made men suspicious of democracy.

Reforms. Under the dictatorship some permanent reforms were effected. Price controls stopped the inflation; the metric system was adopted; a commission to revise the law code of France began its work by providing for prison reforms, abolition of imprisonment for debts, abolition of slavery in the colonies; public education was expanded with the creation of Normal schools and Polytechnical institutes; a national library was set up; confiscated land was sold to peasants and made France into a nation of small farmers. Above all, the civil war was suppressed and foreign enemies were forced into signing the peace treaties of 1795 which declared an end to foreign efforts to suppress the French Revolution and French efforts to spread it abroad. These accomplishments left permanent effects.

Not so were the efforts of the radical Jacobins to abolish *Monsieur* and *Madame* in favor of *Citizen;* to introduce a new calendar with 1792 as the Year I and with the months renamed to celebrate nature and her wonders; to institute and enforce the worship of the goddess Reason; to inaugurate an official Reign of Virtue and the like.

NAPOLEON BONAPARTE

The Directory ruled France for four years (1795–1799) and then succumbed to a bloodless *coup d'état* unleashed by NAPOLEON BONAPARTE who then ruled France until 1815.

In those five years the Directory so alienated the affections of the French people that they accepted Napoleon as their savior. The Directory was unable to cope with renewed inflation; when it issued a new currency, it could not force popular acceptance of it. Nor could it cope with increasing pressure by the clergy, widely supported by the people, for some restoration of their property and rights. Unbelievable corruption characterized the Directors, each of whom ruled for a price. Peace had been concluded with Prussia, Holland and Spain; but negotiations with England and Austria had fallen through because the Directory insisted upon an extension of France's boundaries to the Rhine.

On October 5, 1795 a Paris mob attacked the Directory and only the quick and ruthless wit of an artillery officer named Napoleon Bonaparte, a Corsican, saved it. On this "whiff of grapeshot" Napoleon marched into history as the prototype of the modern dictator.

What Makes A Dictator? No man in history has been more analyzed than Napoleon, who rose from complete obscurity to become European conqueror. A boundless ambition seems a first requirement. Napoleon had this in abundance.

Recognition of opportunity or rank opportunism coupled with unscrupulous and amoral actions speeded him. He did not hesitate to use artillery against an unarmed crowd, or to enter into a loveless marriage for advancement or to cajole the support of any group that could be useful to him. He permitted himself loyalty to no man; he was his own cause; and this limitless egotism seems a requisite for the temperament of a dictator. Ability, too, is needed; genius is preferable. Napoleon had both military and administrative genius.

The Rise To Power. Having saved the Republic and won the hand of Josephine Beauharnais who had great influence in the Directory, Napoleon in 1796 secured command of the Army of Italy; his instructions were to use his ragged force of 30,000 men to divert the Austrians from the south while the main thrust was made in the North. Napoleon turned this diversionary movement into a major thrust and virtually marched north on Vienna. The Austrians were forced to sue for peace. Acting on the principle that what is done can often not be undone, Napoleon, *without consent of the Directory*, negotiated the Treaty of Campo Formio

which forced Austria to recognize French claims to the Rhine, to release her Italian possessions and to surrender Lombardy and Belgium to the French.

This done, Napoleon proceeded with political reorganization of the Italian states into the Cisalpine and Ligurian Republics. He announced himself as the liberator of Italy, the son of the French Revolution and imposed "liberty and equality" on the occupied lands. Beneath this role of liberator lay the more obvious role of terrorist; opposition to French booty-taking was punished with shocking brutality. Napoleon returned to Paris as a conquering hero. What could the Directory do? The army worshipped their commander.

The Egyptian Maneuver. It was clear to Napoleon that the Directory could not long survive. He, Napoleon, must not lend his strength to support their weakness. With keen political astuteness Napoleon therefore proposed that he undertake an Egyptian Campaign as a first step to deprive England of her life-line to Italy. Anxious to get rid of this rising menace, the Directory gave its ungrudging consent to the campaign. In July of 1798 Napoleon evaded the watchful British navy led by Admiral Nelson and landed in Egypt. In the Battle of the Nile, Nelson destroyed Napoleon's fleet and trapped him inside Egypt. Though Egypt fell an easy prey, Napoleon was unable to remove his army from Egypt. He therefore deserted it when news came that France was his for the taking.

A new coalition of powers (England, Russia, Austria, Portugal, Turkey and Naples) had been formed for an attack on France; along the Rhine and in the Italies the French armies were steadily being pushed back. Leaving his scruples in Egypt to follow his star, Napoleon barely evaded Nelson's fleet and returned to Paris as the conqueror of Egypt, as another Caesar. A conspiracy to overthrow the Directory was effected with the aid of three directors and the upper house of the legislature. On November 9, 1799 Napoleon's armed force took possession of the state.

Dictators prefer to act constitutionally. Having seized power, Napoleon wrote a new constitution establishing an elected **Consulate** with himself as First Consul. He created a legislative apparatus but made it impotent. By 1802, Napoleon was ready to throw off the disguise of democracy. He was elected consul for life. Two years later he became Emperor of the French with rights to hereditary succession.

Wherever possible he remained close to popular acceptance. After each coup he submitted the accomplished fact to a popular vote. Since these votes were conducted without free discussion, with no possible alternatives and under army rule, they were overwhelmingly for each of Napoleon's acts. (There is little doubt, on the other hand, that as long as he was successful, Napoleon did command the loyalty of the French people.)

Conqueror. In 1810 Napoleon ruled France, the eastern half of Italy, Belgium, Holland, the Rhineland—directly; indirectly he controlled the vast Confederation of the Rhine (the Germanies), the Grand Duchy of Warsaw (Poland), the Kingdom of Italy, the Kingdom of Naples, Switzerland and the Kingdom of Spain. Within the French orbits lay Denmark and Norway, Prussia and Austria. This overlordship was achieved by conquest in war.

Napoleon's victories at Ulm, Austerlitz, Jena, Friedland are classics of military strategy and are still studied in military academies. His military principles included: simplicity, rapidity, superiority of forces in localized areas, concentration, quick decision on the spot, meticulous study of positions and alternatives, keen perception of the psychology of the opponent, judicious use of all information, material and moral, attention to the most insignificant of details, obedient officers who took no initiative, rigid discipline and self-confidence. Yet, within five years of his position in 1810, his armies were defeated and his kingdom gone. What brought this conqueror so low?

Decline and Fall. Many factors served to bring about the collapse of Napoleon. None was more important than England's dogged resistance and her command of the seas and her ability to inspire and to supply opposition to Napoleon. England's chief weapon was her shops and her chief warrior shopkeepers who produced manufactured goods that were far more durable and cheap than any produced on the continent.

Napoleon hoped to choke off all British trade with the continent. By a series of decrees he placed a paper blockade around Europe and around England; no English ship could deliver goods to Europe; and no non-English ship could deliver goods to England. England retorted with her own blockade on French ships and on foreign ships trading with the French. Europeans felt severely the prohibition on entry into Europe of British goods and evaded Napoleon's **Continental System** by widespread smuggling.

It was the Continental System that led to Napoleon's disastrous Spanish campaign and march into Russia. In Spain Napoleon had to fight a species of guerilla warfare that drained men and supplies and could not be brought to a decision. In Russia he encountered similar warfare accompanied by a "scorched earth" policy and then by bitter winter fighting for which the French were unprepared. Half-a-million men were lost in the **Russian Campaign of 1812.** Moreover, willingness to fight the French resulted from the insurgence of nationalism that arose out of disillusionment with Napoleon's promises of liberation and out of national humiliation resulting from constant defeat at Napoleon's hands. Freedom proved a double-edged sword for the conqueror.

So, too, did Napoleon's efforts to unify such countries as Italy, Germany and Poland. Napoleon's aim was efficiency in French domination. But having tasted the sweets of unification, these countries now demanded the fruits—independence from French domination.

Finally, continual war exhausted the French materially and spiritually. Only a few Frenchmen reaped the benefits of war profits; on most fell the burdens of French taxation and the loss and mutilation of their loved ones. All of these factors collected at Leipzig in 1814 and in the **Battle of Nations** Napoleon suffered total defeat. He was sent to **Elbe** in exile but escaped and for "100 Days" gave Europe a fright until in 1815 he was finally destroyed at **Waterloo.** Once more he was sent into exile on the island of **St. Helena** in the mid-Atlantic. There he "ruled" until he died on May 5, 1821.

The Industrial Revolution

The Industrial Revolution spread out of England slowly; in 1850 the primary productive pattern in the western world was still agriculture and it was not until 1870 that manufacturing began to overtake agriculture.

There are many explanations for this slow progress. Europe, for example, spent the first quarter of the 19th century recovering from the Napoleonic Wars. Many of the countries lacked some one or more of the basic factors required for industrial progress. Social or cultural lag existed in mental outlook and educational system. In the United States wide stretches of free or almost free land acted as a deterrent and prevented large capital accumulation. England's initial superiority gave her a competitive advantage that handicapped other nations. In spite of these many handicaps, however, the Industrial Revolution spread into Europe, particularly into France, Belgium and Germany; Italy and Russia lagged until the very end of the 19th century.

Stages In The Industrial Revolution. Primary concentration in the first stage (ca. 1750–1850) was upon elaboration of the productive process: discovery of required raw materials, refinement of processes in the extraction of raw materials, extensions of the uses of the steam engine, construction of factories and the development in workers of factory discipline, laying the groundwork for an improved system of transportation and solving the problem of maximizing profits (capital accumulation).

In the second stage of the Industrial Revolution (1850–1900) productive inventiveness continued at a rapid pace; but the other factors of labor, distribution and exchange became the center of concentration. To reduce labor costs and the growing "threat" of labor organization, manufacturers began to invest in machines that would break down production into minute processes and destroy the basis of skilled labor. Symbolic of this trend was the work of the American, FREDERICK WINSLOW TAYLOR (1856–1915), in the field of scientific management. Taylor began experimental studies ("time-and-motion" studies) to set standards of efficient working performance. During this period the corporative form of business organization was elaborated as was the relation of business to banking.

In the field of invention a revolution was effected in transportation and communication. By 1850 the railroad had proved its effectiveness and a rush was begun in all countries to lay track. Problems involved in railroad transport were soon overcome by invention of high powered locomotives, air brakes, standard gauges, signal systems, refrigeration cars, sleepers and the like. Steamboating kept pace with railroading.

More and more industrialism, in this period, began to rely upon pure science. This was nowhere more true than in the field of communications. Out of the work of such men as Franklin, Galvani, Volta, Ampere, Ohm, Maxwell and Faraday came the possibility of communication by electrical impulses. An electric telegraph was invented independently by Carl Steinheil, a German, Charles Wheatstone, an Englishman, and Samuel Morse an American. The telegraph, however, was landbound until Cyrus W. Field solved the oceanographic problems required to lay a trans-Atlantic cable; this was accomplished in 1866.

Important advances were registered, too, in the field of lighting. The kerosene lamp was perfected in 1784. More useful, however, was the gaslighting device perfected by Murdock, Bunsen and Welsbach in the mid-nineteenth century. Toward the end of this period, electric lighting made its appearance as a result of the researches of Davy, Marks, Edison and many others.

The third stage of the Industrial Revolution had little unity—expansion occurred in every imaginable direction. Invention itself was systematized and accelerated through creation of subsidized laboratories. Of special note was the rise of the chemist as an adjunct to industry. Upon him fell the responsibility of discovering new uses for old resources and the manufacture of synthetic resources as substitutes for natural products.

Out of the invention of the internal combustion engine and the electric motor whole new worlds appeared: the automobile industry, the industries of radio and television, great hydroelectric plants, the airplane industry and the like. Of equal importance was the development of the precision instrument—a development that gave to the physicist the same status as the chemist in the industrial world. The engineer, of course, became a key figure as the demand for roads, bridges, communications, building structures, electrical appliances and the like rose.

Mass production became a startling reality when the factory was rationalized through use of assembly lines and standardized parts. Of primary importance was the distribution of this mass production. Problems of transport were solved through further developments of railroad and steamship and the introduction of trucks and airplanes. But the sale of goods required the transformation of advertising into a national industry. This in turn put pressure on the creation of mass media of communication. The linotype machine, typewriter, and rotary press accommodated this need; radio and television enhanced it. Along with the revolution in advertisement of products, came a revolution in the financing of the purchase of goods—installment buying. With exhaustion of resources at home began a worldwide search for raw materials such as rubber, tin, nitrates, manganese, magnesium, chromium, nickel, lead, copper, hardwoods, etc.

With the discovery of thermonuclear power a new and fourth stage in the Industrial Revolution loomed. This stage brought the physicist to the fore. It is too early to project the transformations that will be made as a result of this discovery of a new power-source. The peaceful uses of atomic energy have been probed—chiefly in the areas of medical research, agricultural production, new sources of power and the like. The world is waiting for a new dawn.

RESULTS OF THE INDUSTRIAL REVOLUTION

General. In essence, the Industrial Revolution was a transfer from hand tool to machine process; from muscle-wind-and-water power to steam-gas-electricity-and-atomic power. Manufacturing became a way of life emphasizing compulsory centralization of the labor force around the machine, complete dependence of the labor force upon the machine for a livelihood, impersonalization of the relations between worker and employer and regimentation of the life of the worker to the demands of production. From the factory flowed ever-increasing production and this was reflected in expanding commerce, accumulated capital, national and international corporations, business combinations in the forms of merger, trust, holding company, interlocking directorates, cartels and the like. Increased standards of living resulted and this

was followed by rapid increases of population for the most part gathered into urban areas where cultural life blossomed on the nurture provided by increased educational facilities. But culture, too, followed the pattern of standardization; mass media threatened to produce mass minds, mass behavior.

Machine Culture. Mankind came to depend upon invention for innovation; progress was equated with multiplication of gadgets. There was no limit to inventiveness. In the wake of the mechanization of society came many problems affecting human welfare: overcrowded cities, indebtedness, increasing destructiveness of wars, labor-management conflict, and the like.

The Workingman. The brunt of the inhumanity in the machine civilization fell upon the workingman. Skilled workers of the late 18th and early 19th centuries resented and resisted the introduction of the factory system; they became, in fact, "machine-wreckers." Factory processes reduced the workingman to a mechanical unit engaged in some small specialized task that produced fatigue and boredom.

Moreover, in the early period of capital accumulation working conditions were abominable. Factories were hastily and cheaply built; no provisions were made for the health or safety of the employees in matters of ventilation, lighting or provisions for creature comforts. Child labor was brutally exploited in the form of pauper apprentices. Hours of work ranged between 14 and 16 a day. Wages were miserably low.

From impoverished conditions in the factory, workers moved to even worse conditions at home. Slums made up the bulk of dwelling quarters in factory towns. Crime and epidemic disease were the consequences of these miserable hovels in which workers dwelt. Added to these inadequate conditions of work was the continuous insecurity that hung over the heads of the working people. They were completely unprotected in the face of unemployment produced by technological change or depressions, of illness and accident for which there was no compensation, and of old age—a variable figure depending on the supply of workers available. This, then, was the social lag behind industrial progress.

Overcoming The Social Lag. To overcome the social lag to industrial progress, a humanitarian revolution in the minds of the rulers of mankind had to be effected. Horrible conditions had first to be seen as horrible, and felt as such. This required intensive education through propaganda and agitation, a campaign that was launched by workers' organizations, philosophers like Jeremy Bentham and William Godwin, poets like Shelley and Thomas Hood, novelists like Charles Dickens and George Eliot and politicians like Benjamin Disraeli, William Gladstone, Otto von Bismarck, Andrew Jackson. These men helped to transform the problem of working conditions into a *moral* question.

The result of all this agitation and propaganda was a series of social laws passed by interested governments which set out to reform the conditions under which men labored in factories and mines. In England, for example, between 1802 and 1860, a large number of factory acts were passed. These had the effect of reducing by law the number of hours of work, of discouraging the employment of child labor, of limiting the employment of women, of compelling the introduction of health, sanitation and safety devices in factories. Later legislation in England (1870–1920) freed workers to organize into labor unions and to strike for increased wages and improved working conditions.

Germany, under OTTO VON BISMARCK, took the leadership in framing the first social security laws, laws providing for workman's compensation in the event of accident on the job, for old age pensions, for sickness and unemployment insurance. These laws were eventually introduced into all the industrialized nations of the world.

The Capitalist System. Capitalism came to full growth under the impetus of the Industrial Revolution. It was the primary agency in the transformation of society from a low-producing to a high-producing level. In the course of its development, capitalism moved through several stages. The earliest was the stage of industrial capitalism—where individual capitalists owned the factories as single proprietorships or as partnerships. To a great extent these capitalists relied upon their own resources for expansion. As business grew, however, the single proprietorship and partnership proved to be inadequate as financial vehicles. The result was that capitalists began to depend more and more on the corporation—and the sale of stocks and bonds—as a means for gathering in wealth. Increasingly, in this second stage of capitalist development, industrialists began to turn to the banks for loans for expansion.

This led to the third stage, that of finance capitalism. In this stage industrial and banking elements in the economic process merged to provide industry with a virtually unlimited capital expansion base. In this area, as in the area of mechanization, a social lag appeared.

Ownership and management were divorced, a divorce that produced the possibilities of mismanagement. Mismanagement resulted in practices which strangled free competition by monopolization; which defrauded stockholders through issuance of "watered" stock, or failure to declare dividends; which practiced fraud on consumers through price fixing, adulteration of product and the like; which encouraged corrupt political practices like bribery of legislators. The social lag was somewhat remedied in most countries by government intervention that resulted in anti-trust laws, laws regulating the issuance of corporate securities, pure food and drug laws, income and corporate tax laws and the like.

Abandonment of Laissez Faire. Government intervention in the economic process is the antithesis of laissez faire, the system of ideas under which capitalism grew to maturity. As taught by Adam Smith in his *Wealth of Nations,* the doctrine of laissez faire assumed that there were rational, natural laws that governed economic behavior. Men left alone to pursue selfish ends in the use of their capital and labor would ultimately produce social good. The laws of free trade and of competition, of supply and demand, would determine success and failure in the economic struggle for existence; but the end result would be an increase in the total national wealth.

Smith founded the school of liberal or **classical economists,** members of which searched for "natural laws" in the economy of capitalism. Thus THOMAS MALTHUS proposed an "iron law" of population and demonstrated that famine, war, disease and population control are advantageous since population increases geometrically while food supply increases arithmetically. DAVID RICARDO "proved" that wages sink to the mere level of subsistence. Nassau Senior "demonstrated" that hours of work could not be lowered without disastrous consequences to profits. McCulloch "proved" on the basis of and existing "wages-fund" that wage increase to one group had to result in wage decrease for another.

All of this theorizing resulted in a pattern of beliefs that called for abolition of tariffs and subsidies, free contracting, treatment of labor organization as conspiracy, free competition, and no government restraint upon economic free choice. Between 1800 and 1860 the English government, for example, followed this doctrine to the letter. The "corn laws (tariffs)" were repealed, mercantilist regulations concerning the granting of monopolies were removed from the legislative books, laws protecting apprentices were abrogated. We have seen the abuses that followed upon this adoption of the complete policy of laissez faire. (There is little doubt that if we ignore humanitarian considerations, laissez faire did accomplish miracles in production at a time when the resources for such productive effort were limited.)

No country followed England in its application of the policy of laissez faire. From their inception, the classical economists were challenged on theoretical lines. From America and Germany came economic doctrines defending protectionism as a means for hastening industrial advance. Population theorists challenged Malthus when it became obvious that the industrial revolution would extend to the farm and result in fabulous increases in food production. The most serious challenge, however, came from the "socialists" who took the abuses of the capitalist as their starting point and ignored the many efforts being made by governments to correct these abuses.

Socialism. Socialism was as much an *ethical* as an economic discipline; its theories were in part formed out of a preconceived utopian dream in which all men were economically equal and lived in the midst of abundance.

Early socialists like SAINT-SIMON (1760–1825), FOURIER (1772–1837) and ROBERT OWEN (1772–1858) were labelled "Utopians" by later socialists like KARL MARX (1818–1883). This derogatory label was not directed against the ultimate plans of the Utopians, for these plans envisaged the abolition of the capitalist class and the substitution of some form of workingclass ownership and control of the means of production (as socialism is defined). Derogation was directed against the means by which these theoreticians proposed to eliminate the capitalist class.

Saint-Simon hoped to bring socialism by the arts of persuasion and appeal to Christian doctrine; Fourier proposed that workers and others form voluntary socialist societies which he called "phalanxes" where all would work for all; Owen hoped to convince capitalists by his own example to build model socialist communities with their capital. (Fourierism caught on somewhat in the United States in the 1830's and '40's where experiments like Brook Farm and Oneida were tried and failed. Owen went bankrupt after his ventures in capitalist socialism at New Harmony, Indiana.) LOUIS BLANC (1813–1882)—an influential figure in the Revolution of 1848 in France—advanced the concept of government financed socialist communities, a scheme for turning over factories to workers and financing them until they were able to stand on their own feet. In practice this system turned out to be a huge financial dole that almost bankrupted the government.

Karl Marx (author of *Capital* and co-author with Frederick Engels of *Communist Manifesto*) condemned all of these efforts and proposed instead his own brand of "scientific" socialism. He advocated both peaceful and violent waging of a "class war" to overthrow capitalism. His followers, who believed in peaceful "class war" became latter-day socialists; those who favored force and violence to establish a "dictatorship of the proletariat" became communists. Marxism, then, was both a theory about capitalist society and a blueprint for its replacement.

Imperialism and World War I

IMPERIALISM

About 1875 territorial aggrandizement became the dominant drive of the large European powers, and of the United States of America. No one cause can account for this phenomenon. The Industrial Revolution was certainly a most important factor.

As industry expanded so did the need for raw materials, many of them unavailable in the industrialized lands. This caused a search for basic materials, particularly for such materials as rubber, tin, petroleum, tungsten, etc.

As mass production mounted, nations began to seek potential "outlets" for surplus goods; colonies could be excellent dumping grounds for these goods and in many cases imperialized markets were the "margin of profit" for manufacturers. Similarly with surplus capital that now began to accumulate. Investments at home rarely brought the rate of return that could be gained by investment in colonial areas where labor was cheap and monopoly assured by government fiat.

Accompanying these economic motives for imperialism were equally strong political, social, psychological and religious ones. Nationalism virtually dictated that each nation should seek some "place in the sun"; national pride was fostered by each new splatter of color on the map that showed national expansion; national propaganda led to widespread belief that each nation was engaged in a civilizing mission. Very popular, though little founded in fact, was the prevailing argument that all nations, riding the crest of tremendous population increases, needed outlets for "surplus" population. Enough people did emigrate to the colonies to make this fiction seem a fact. Also there was the revival in this period of missionary activities that opened wide new worlds to the West.

Finally, imperialist expansion was strongly advocated by military leaders in all nations as the best means for securing naval bases and an adequate supply of strategic raw materials. To the support of these military men came the geographers who developed anew the doctrines of geopolitics, the science of national security that determined what heartland and fringelands were vital to "defense"—even though they were inhabited by other peoples. Geopolitics became power-politics, politics supported by military force. In reality, it was a "scientific" rationale for world conquest or domination.

Methods and Forms of Imperialism. International trade, investments and loans are not imperialistic but are part of a normal process of international intercourse. They become imperialistic when they are used as excuses for territorial conquest or for establishing exclusive economic control. During the late nineteenth century it often happened that rulers of undeveloped areas borrowed heavily from the investment bankers of the west. In exchange for such loans favored concessions were made to European investors. If such rulers defaulted on their debts or were unable to protect the investments in railroads, mines, etc., it often happened that the rulers of the powerful

investor nations sent troops into that area to "protect" the lives and property of their nationals. It was at this point that imperialism began. Under foreign control these areas lost their political freedom and the right to exploit their own national wealth.

Out of this pattern emerged four forms of imperialist control: the **colony** or direct political control where the powerful nation openly ruled the undeveloped area as a possession; the **protectorate** or indirect political control where the powerful nation ruled the undeveloped area through a native puppet; the **concession** or exclusive direct control over some particular resource; and the **sphere of influence** or indirect economic control over the whole of the undeveloped area. These basic forms intermingled freely. The imperialist test for any of them was the degree of freedom retained by the undeveloped area.

THE FIRST WORLD WAR

The basic causes of the first World War were the rival imperialist ambitions among the western powers, their excessive nationalistic pride, the armaments race that developed in the face of political and economic rivalry, the struggle of suppressed peoples for independence, the geopolitical drive to reach "natural boundaries" and the absence in the world of any effective world organization that might have prevented war through peaceful settlement of disputes. These fundamental causes worked themselves out in a series of international events the primary effect of which was to create two great systems of alliances that opposed each other in a menacing **balance of power.**

The Triple Alliance vs. The Triple Entente. The **Triple Alliance** of Germany, Austria-Hungary and Italy (and allied satellites) was born from Bismarck's desire to isolate France so that she could never wage a war of revenge against Germany after her ignominious defeat in the Franco-Prussian War. By promise and perfidy Bismarck secured a secret defensive alliance with Austria-Hungary, a "gentleman's agreement" with Russia, an alliance with Italy directed against France, English neutrality, Serbian and Rumanian allegiance, and Turkish friendship.

To each of these nations Germany promised diplomatic support for nationalist aspiration—no matter how contradictory these promises were. Thus Russia and Austria-Hungary were bitter rivals in the Balkans as were Serbia and Austria-Hungary; Italy had many grievances against Austria-Hungary with respect to *Italia Irridenta;* Rumania and Turkey could not be friends. Yet Bismarck accomplished the impossible as long as Germany pursued a non-imperialist policy of its own. When William II overrode Bismarck and began an aggressive policy of imperialism, economic rivalry and arms supremacy, the grand alliance fell apart. Out of its pieces was born the **Triple Entente.**

Russia was the first to leave and to join France in a Dual Alliance in 1894. When Germany rejected Russia's request for large modernization loans, France granted them in exchange for a military convention that amounted to a defensive alliance. (This agreement, incidentally, was as much directed against England as against Germany, for England was threatening France in the Sudan and Russia in Persia and the Far East.)

By 1900 a number of factors compelled England to reconsider her policy of "splendid isolation" from continental affairs. Germany had begun to construct a formidable navy and to challenge England's markets in all parts of the world. She was the chief obstacle to the union of British territories in east Africa. Now she proposed to construct a Berlin to Baghdad Railroad through Turkey which would possibly destroy England's trade advantage in the Near East and India. The result was the **Entente Cordiale** with France (1904), a settlement of all territorial differences and an implied defensive alliance. Russian-English differences over Persia and the Far East were finally settled in an entente that settled differences in Persia and Afghanistan by division of those territories. By 1907 the Triple Entente was complete and faced the Triple Alliance in a delicate balance of power.

International Crises. War approached by a series of international crises in North Africa and the Balkans. In 1905 France began a series of familiar maneuvers westward from Algeria into Morocco, an area that Germany had selected as her own hunting grounds. The Kaiser promised the Moroccan ruler support if he resisted French overtures and then went on to demand that the "Moroccan Question" be submitted to an international conference. Such a conference was held in 1906 at Algeciras and Germany forced through a policy of the "open door" in Morocco to France's chagrin.

In 1911 an uprising in Morocco gave the French an excuse to move in with troops. The Germans sent the "Panther," a gunboat, to challenge French occupation. War hung in the balance. At that moment English warships began to maneuver around the "Panther," and Germany decided that the time was not ripe for a challenge. In exchange for a part of the French Congo Germany gave France a "free hand" in Morocco.

Attention was now focused on the Balkans. In 1908 a group of humiliated **Young Turks,** resentful of the slow disintegration of the Turkish Empire, undertook a revolution. Austria-Hungary took advantage of this situation to annex Balkan territory. Russia, fearful of Austro-Hungarian moves, had secured a promise from her that she would support Russian moves in the Dardenelles area in exchange for Russian support for Balkan seizures by Austria-Hungary. This was the infamous "Buchlau Bargain."

Austria-Hungary violated the bargain by annexing Bosnia and Herzegovina without support for Russia's territorial ambitions. Russia was infuriated and resolved to make war on the first occasion that presented itself. She began to provoke Serbia into anti-Austrian activities. At the same time Russia continued maneuvering against Turkey by organizing a Balkan League (Montenegro, Serbia, Bulgaria and Greece) for an assault on Turkey. This assault came in 1912 and 1913 in two Balkan Wars. Once again Austria frustrated Russian ambitions by creating the buffer state of Albania. Europe became a "powder magazine."

The spark that blew it up occurred in Sarajevo, Bosnia when the Austrian Archduke Ferdinand was assassinated by a member of a secret society for the creation of a greater Serbia. Austria delivered an ultimatum to Serbia to stop all anti-Austrian propaganda, to suppress all anti-Austrian publications, to dismiss Serbian officials implicated in the assassination plot, to permit Austrian police forces to enforce the ultimatum. Serbia temporized and on July 28, 1914 Austria declared war on Serbia. On July 30 Russia mobilized. On July 31 Germany warned Russia to cease mobilizing; Russia refused. On August 1 Germany declared war on Russia and sent an ultimatum to France to remain neutral. France temporized. On August 3 Germany declared war on France and began to pass through Belgium whose neutrality had been guaranteed by all the European powers. On August 4, when Germany refused to respect Belgian neutrality, England declared war. The holocaust was on. Who was responsible?

The Military Phase. From 1914 to 1918 the greatest war in history to that date was fought. Before it was over, thirty nations had become participants, 65,000,000 men bore arms, 8,500,000 soldiers were killed, 29,000,000 were wounded, an inestimable number of civilians were destroyed and some $200,000,000,000 had been expended.

After initial German successes, the war settled down to a stalemate fought in "no-man's lands" from fixed trenches along the western front. Following an initial push to Paris, the Germans were stopped at the Marne; thereafter they were held in spite of such mighty pushes as the one at Verdun.

Allied counter-attacks came similarly to grief. Efforts of the Allies to take Turkey in the Gallipoli campaign were repulsed. The Austrians were checked in the Balkans. Italy deserted the Triple Alliance for the Allied cause but proved more of a handicap than an aid particularly following her defeat at Caporetto. In only one direction did the war move to a completion, that of Germany's assault on Russia. Then came the Russian revolution, and the Bolsheviks, who seized power from the democratic liberals in November of 1917, decided to seek peace. In 1918 they signed the **Treaty of Brest-Litovsk** which ceded Poland, Lithuania, Courland, Bessarabia, the Caucasus, Finland, Estonia, Latvia and the Ukraine to the Central Powers.

Germany did not win the war chiefly as a result of the entry of the United States in 1917. Provoked by unrestricted submarine warfare, sabotage, plots with Mexico and German sabre rattling, and led by economic stakes in the Allied cause and effective Allied propaganda in the United States, America declared war on April 6, 1917, resolved to make the world safe for democracy and to fight a war to end all wars. So did Woodrow Wilson frame the goals of the Allied cause. Entry of men and material from America in 1918 gave the Allied powers the strength to mount a final offensive in 1918, one that broke through German lines and forced the Germans to sue for peace on November 11, 1918.

The Versailles Treaty. Vision and reality met in battle on January 18, 1919 when the victorious powers met to determine the fate of their conquered enemies. The vision was in the person of Woodrow Wilson, President of the United States, who had boldly announced in January 1918 his **Fourteen Points** for an enduring peace. Wilson foresaw a post-war world where secret diplomacy would be outlawed; where the seas would be free; where all economic barriers to international trade would be removed; where armaments races would end; where imperialism would be eliminated on moral grounds; where national aspirations would be respected; where closed waters, such as the Dardenelles, would be forever open; and where a league of nations would be established to settle once for all all international disputes by conciliation, arbitration and judicial settlement. It was a splendid vision, one that captured the imagination of people all over the world.

The reality was in the persons of LLOYD GEORGE of England, CLEMENCEAU of France and ORLANDO of Italy who comprised a "Big Three" determined to make the Peace of Versailles a vengeful and profitable one at the expense of the conquered nations. What emerged was in the nature of a compromise between the vision and the reality.

Germany, Austria-Hungary, Turkey and Bulgaria were punished. Germany ceded Alsace-Lorraine back to France, Eurpen and Malmedy to Belgium and a corridor through West Prussia for Poland to reach the sea. Schleswig was returned to Denmark; Lithuania secured Memel; Danzig became an internationalized "free city"; the Saar was placed under the political control of the League of Nations and the economic control of France for fifteen years after which there was to be a plebiscite held in which the Saarlanders could vote for a permanent political settlement of their fate. Germany lost all of her Pacific holdings to the League of Nations which received them as "mandates" and which distributed them to the victorious powers for education and eventual release as independent states. (Such was Wilson's plan for the eventual elimination of imperialism.)

Germany was then stripped of all military power—armed forces, navy, fortifications—and had to submit to occupation of her territory to ensure enforcement of the terms of the treaty. At the same time, Germany was declared to be guilty of having provoked the war and was therefore made to bear the expense of repairing the damage. Reparations costs ran to some sixty billion dollars. As immediate payments on this reparations bill, Germany was stripped of railroads, capital equipment, livestock and coal. Out of the treaties of St.

Germain, Neuilly and Serves with Austria, Hungary and Turkey respectively came the birth of many new nations and additional mandated territories to be granted to the victorious powers.

The League of Nations. In exchange for many concessions to the nationalist and imperialist aims of the victorious allied powers, Wilson demanded that as Article I of the Versailles Treaty appear a covenant for a League of Nations to which all the victorious powers would belong and which would be given sufficient power to end all future wars.

To some degree this was accomplished. An international organization was framed which would include an Assembly of all the member nations, each with a single vote; an executive Council of permanent big-power members and non-permanent elected members to enforce decrees of the Assembly; a World Court for the judicial settlement of disputes; a Secretariat for arranging meetings and recording results. The covenant also provided for a mandate system to eliminate imperialism. It was projected, too, that the League would form committees to alleviate some of the basic economic, health, education and communication problems of the world.

That there would be an end to war seemed a realizable hope in the year 1919. Countries were already projecting a series of disarmament conferences that would reduce the burden of maintaining powerful armed forces. Nationalism had been satisfied in the creation of the "succession states" of Poland, Czechoslovakia, Austria, Hungary, Yugoslavia and others. Imperialism would end as mandatory nations fulfilled their obligations to their territories and prepared them for the status of independent nations who would then join the League. International anarchy was to end with the establishment and growth in the power of the League of Nations and the World Court. International cooperation was to replace economic rivalry. What causes for any future war were possible?

But twenty years later came a second, and even more terrible, war. What went wrong with the vision?

The Shaping of the Modern World

SOVIET RUSSIA

In March 1917 the Tsar was overthrown and a liberal democratic state set up under the leadership of Prince Lvov and Professor Miliukov. Instrumental in this overthrow were the numerous "soviets" or local government that had made their appearance during the stages of the first revolution. In the elected Soviets the Bolsheviks (communists) led by Lenin had no control.

In the first All-Russian Congress of Soviets held in June of 1917 Kerensky Social Revolutionaries and Menshevik socialists-groups favoring democratic processes of government—were voted control of the government. Even after the Bolsheviks had seized control of the government of Petrograd in November 7th they could not secure approval from a constitutional assembly called in January 1918 to confirm the seizure. This constitutional assembly was freely and democratically elected. However, when it voted down Bolshevik proposals with respect to making peace, distributing land and disarming all of the Russians but the workers, it was abruptly dismissed and in its place was created a dictatorship under the leadership of Nicolai Lenin, Leon Trotsky and Joseph Stalin.

Many circumstances played into the hands of the Bolsheviks to enable them to maintain and to consolidate their power. They voluntarily signed the Treaty of Brest-Litovsk with Germany in which they surrendered a considerable portion of European Russia. Moreover, they published secret treaties that revealed many of the imperialist aims of the warring allied powers.

Frightened by the success of the Bolsheviks, the Allied powers dispatched an international force to aid the "White Russians" in their effort at a counter-revolution. Since these "White Russians" contained many of the elements of the hated Old Regime the Allied intervention was strongly opposed.

Meanwhile, the Bolsheviks set up the Cheka—

secret police and revolutionary tribunals—which destroyed not only elements of the old regime but *all* opposition to Bolshevism. At the same time, to give meaning to their "socialist" revolution, the Bolsheviks temporarily turned factories over to workers' committees, distributed land to the peasants, as much as each could work, nationalized all industry without compensation, confiscated all Tsarist obligations to domestic and foreign lenders and removed money as a means of exchange.

Consolidation. In 1919 a Supreme Economic Council was created to make plans for the eventual creation of complete state ownership and operation of the means of production. The productive system collapsed and in 1921 there was desperate poverty.

In 1921, therefore, Lenin ordered a "new economic policy" to be instituted. The base of the new economic policy was state ownership of about 85 per cent of the means of production. In the remaining 15 per cent the Communists permitted foreign investors to invest funds at high rates of interest. Opposition abroad was considerably disarmed by this maneuver; Western nations were led to believe that Russia would some day return to the family of capitalist nations. In 1924 Communist Russia was officially recognized by Great Britain, France and Italy. Not until 1934 did the United States follow suit.

The "Plan" was fulfilled in a series of "five-year plans" launched by JOSEPH STALIN in 1928. All foreign influence in Russian industry was abolished. A state planning commission drew up goals for a five-year increase in industrialization, mechanization and electrification of state owned industries. Every type of incentive was used to increase worker productivity; this was needed, for productivity increase was linked to a decrease in consumption—the surplus being used to purchase basic machinery abroad. Meanwhile, the process of forcible collectivization of farms was begun.

Thus straitjacketed the Russian economy did move into the high gear of production. Opposition to collectivization was so strong, however, that Russia suffered another severe food famine in 1934. A second five-year plan eased the consumption picture somewhat; a third was just begun when Russia was attacked by the Nazi forces. Her industrialization, considerably aided by American "lend-lease," stood her in good stead and enabled her to make a rapid recovery after the war.

Dictatorship. Protest in Russia could find no effective means of expression once the Bolsheviks had imposed their dictatorship. All political opposition was suppressed. The "purge" and staged trials became an institution by which Joseph Stalin periodically eliminated potential rivals.

Yet the Communists could not forever ignore the need for some form of national consent. In 1936 they granted a constitution which constructed a tremendous facade of republican institutions that were designed to conceal the dictatorship. A bicameral legislature representing all the people and their nationalist divisions was created; an elective ministry headed by a premier was set up as executive. An extensive "bill of rights" was added. But the realities in these political forms are evident in the facts that in Soviet elections only one party is permitted, that only members of the Communist Party may hold high office, in the control which the state holds over all means of communication, in the secret police, in the use of secret trials and summary executions, in the absence of all debate at the meetings, when called, of the legislature, in the rigid control of ingress and egress from Russia itself, in antireligious official attitudes and propaganda, in the strict control of education.

FASCIST ITALY

BENITO MUSSOLINI, founder of Italian Fascism, came to power by a coup d'etat on October 28, 1922. He and his "Black Shirts"—a private army —"marched on Rome" and took possession of the state apparatus. Only the complete breakdown of the democratic apparatus of the Italian government could have permitted this to take place. This breakdown was due to Italy's multi-party system that, at the crucial moment, was unable or unwilling to form a government to counteract this coup. A breakdown in government was the result of accumulating difficulties resulting from widespread postwar depression, unemployment, radical efforts to seize factories, peasant revolts, etc.

Once in power, Mussolini destroyed all opposition and civil liberty, ruled by terror and secret police, resorted to political assassination and prepared Italy for a series of wars that would make the Mediterranean an Italian lake. Both industry and labor were harnessed to state purposes. Industrialists had no choice but to produce what the state required; labor was denied every form of free action on its own behalf. Both were organized into "corporations" (hence the "corporate state") and these were directed by state-appointed bureaucrats. Propaganda and militarization took the place of education. From earliest age, the youth were organized as military cadres and taught implicit obedience to the dictates of *Il Duce* ("The Leader").

The economy felt the artificial stimulation of increased war production and Mussolini was able to secure a surplus which enabled him to make Italy somewhat more self-sufficient by the draining of marshes, improvement of railroads, large hydroelectric and reclamation projects, subsidies for overseas trade, construction of a merchant marine, etc. But the intent of this program of reform was war and renewed imperialistic attacks on those powers which held territories overseas particularly England and France.

NAZI GERMANY

ADOLPH HITLER'S coup came in January 1933. As in Italy, the normal process of democratic government had broken down when the major parties in the Reichstag were unable to agree on a government bloc. Few governments were more democratically oriented than Germany under the Weimar Republic, a government created to replace that of the German Kaiser. When faced with large scale unemployment and dissatisfaction resulting from the world depression in 1933, the radical and liberal parties were unable and unwilling to combine to suppress the threat of the author of *Mein Kampf* and his private army of Brown Shirts.

Adolph Hitler was a master of vicious propaganda; he exploited every grievance of the Germans by centering them upon a few scapegoats —the Treaty of Versailles, the Jews, the German need for *lebensraum* (living space). To justify the use of these scapegoats, he constructed out of a long history of racist theorizing (DE GOBINEAU, HOUSTON STEWART CHAMBERLAIN) the doctrine of the racial superiority of the German Nordic. He convinced the German people by ceaseless dinning through every means of communication that they were the only source of civilization, that they stood in dread danger of corruption and bestialization through intermingling with inferior race, that they must save the world by conquering it for humanity and civilization, etc.

At best one might say that the German people had little inkling—though the unspeakable brutality of the Nazi Storm Troopers must have been evident to them from the day Hitler took power— that these false and vicious doctrines were soon to be translated into furnaces that would burn up more than 6,000,000 people whose only crime was that they were of different religions and nationalities from the ruling German cliques.

After 1934 Hitler became *Der Führer* ("the Leader"). The German state was completely totalitarianized. Industry and labor were organized in similar fashion to that of Mussolini. Capitalism was retained but placed at the beck and call of state needs. War production was immediately begun in preparation for a series of adventures to test the democracies' will to resist and eventually for a bid for world conquest. German freedom disappeared and the Gestapo and the Storm Troopers combined to produce absolute terror.

THE WEAKENING OF THE DEMOCRACIES

World War I proved to be empty victories for the democracies. In 1921 and again in 1931 they suffered depressions of unparalleled dimensions. England, in particular, found that economically she was slipping into the place of a second rate power in the face of American and Japanese competition. Unemployment, exhaustion of native resources, mounting taxes which destroyed considerable investment capital, the failure of Germany to produce any sizeable reparations, widespread strikes among the transport workers and coal miners—all of these factors helped keep successive British governments reeling. In 1923 the first Labor government, under Ramsey Macdonald, was elected; but it was no more able to manage the various crises than the Conservatives.

With the onset of the Great Depression England experimented with a coalition government of Conservative and Laborites. The great achievement of this government was the final abandonment of England's free trade policy for a policy of imperial preference and the Statute of Westminster. The latter was virtually a declaration of independence for all British dominions. It created the British Commonwealth of Nations for the dominions, a system which permitted any dominion to leave the Empire when it wished and if it stayed within the Empire to enjoy absolute local autonomy. (No dominion has left the Commonwealth except Ireland, which in 1922 became Eire, a free state without any political ties to England.)

As the Fascist menace rose to challenge England's position, England began a rearmament program that stimulated the economy to slow revival. Out of the general feeling of helplessness that England felt, however, was generated her policy of "appeasement"—a policy associated particularly with Prime Minister Neville Chamberlain. This policy had as its central aim the strengthening of Fascism to a point where it could successfully attack Communism. In the struggle which ensued, England hoped, both would destroy each other.

French difficulties were similar to those of England with this addition—under the impact of economic crisis the normally unstable French Governments became even more so. France felt keenly Germany's inability to meet her reparations payments since France had been the chief sufferer among the western powers of the first World War. High taxes and shortages of goods produced an astronomical inflation in France in 1926. Unemployment, loss of foreign markets, colonial difficulties and the threat of both Germany and Italy to her security kept France off balance throughout the two decades and made her a leading exponent of appeasement. She, more than any, sought to direct Hitler's power eastward toward Russia.

Finally, the United States withdrew completely from the arena of international responsibility. She rejected the League of Nations, refused to enter the World Court and adopted a series of neutrality laws that were designed to remove her physically from direct or indirect participation in any future European conflict. The world depression of 1931 struck the United States with especial force. Unemployment mounted to 16,000,000, factory production fell by fifty per cent, emergency relief drained the treasury and forced the policy of government borrowing that was to become the greatest government debt in history following the second world war. These difficulties intensified America's desire to remove itself from the arena of world affairs and to concentrate upon her own revival.

Finally, the hope of the democracies resided in the League of Nations; but it proved to be a weak vessel. Weakened by the requirement of unanimity for any decisive action, by the provision in the covenant permitting an aggressor to leave the League after two years' notice, by the absence

from the membership rolls of both the United States and the Soviet Union—the League had proved itself incapable of coping with any threat to the peace involving a major power. Its successes were on the fringes of international politics.

Lack of confidence in the League was reflected in the successive disarmament conferences that were held outside League auspices. Though none of these conferences was an unqualified success, the earliest ones—particularly the Washington Arms Conference of 1921–1922—did manage to provide for a cessation in the armaments race for a ten-year period. Japanese ambitions in the Far East were effectively curbed by a Nine-Power Treaty and a Four-Power Treaty which made her sign support for the open door policy, for preservation of China's territorial integrity and for the integrity of the Pacific island possessions of the western powers. (Japan freely violated all these commitments since no effective check was provided for to ensure that she fulfilled them.) Even the idealist Kellogg-Briand Peace Pact which "outlawed war" was negotiated by America and France outside the League. Moreover, both France and England placed their reliance on the construction of a wide system of security alliances (the Little Entente, the Locarno Pacts, etc.) rather than on the force of the League. International anarchy was as prevalent with the League as in the days before the League. With this state of affairs in the world there was no reason for the aggressive fascist nations to hesitate in their new imperialist policy . . . the second factor leading to World War II.

THE NEW IMPERIALISM

The old imperialism was, for the most part, directed against helpless, undeveloped areas; the new imperialism unleashed by the powers of the Rome-Berlin-Tokyo Axis was directed against strong, advanced nations. In 1931 Japan began what she called a punitive expedition against Chinese bandits, an expedition that ended with the conquest of all of Manchuria. When the League investigated this aggression through the Lytton Commission and condemned the actions of Japan, Japan left the League, and converted Manchuria into the puppet state of Manchukuo. From this as a base, Japan in 1933 spilled over into the province of Jehol.

It was now Hitler's turn. In 1935, Hitler ordered general conscription and then marched his troops into the Rhineland. Both these actions had been forbidden in the Treaty of Versailles. The French met this threat with the construction of an "impassable" Maginot Line; Hitler built the "Siegfried Wall" opposite it.

In 1936, Generalissimo Francisco Franco, aided and equipped by both Mussolini and Hitler, began an assault on the Spanish Republic with the avowed purpose of setting up a fascist regime in Spain. Spain became an experimental laboratory for the use of Axis weapons and troops; pursuing the policy of "non-intervention" the democratic nations stood aside while these tactics were being employed. After a gallant but hopeless defense, the Spanish Republic collapsed in 1939. Once again the democracies gave evidence that they would not resist fascist aggression until it was directed against themselves.

In 1936, Mussolini began his assault on Ethiopia to revenge the defeat at Adowa and to outflank England on the east coast of Africa. Worried now, England attempted to force the League to adopt sanctions against Italy, particularly sanctions on the sale of oil. But United States oil companies took this as an opportunity to capture the Italian market. As a result, Italy proceeded unchecked until Ethiopia was hers.

Meanwhile, Hitler's "Fifth Column" of Nazi Austrians had begun to agitate for *anschluss* (union) of Germany and Austria. The Austrian Chancellor Schussnigg resisted Hitler's demands. As European eyes focussed on this crisis, the Japanese, in 1937, began their plunge into the deep south of China, a plunge that Chiang Kai shek—China's President and Generalissimo—could do no more than delay. With attention shifted to the Far East, Hitler on March 11, 1938, simply walked in and took over Austria without a struggle. Within weeks Austria was nazified by the well-organized fifth column which had been in secret preparation for many years.

A few months later Hitler, at a Nuremberg Conference, began agitating for the Sudetenland of Czechoslovakia—a section of Czechoslovakia that contained many German-speaking people. This demand led to a remarkable series of meetings in which England's Chamberlain and France's Daladier granted to Hitler his demands upon Czechoslovakia because this was the only way to achieve "peace in our time" and because this was to be Hitler's "last request!" In the face of this complete acquiescence, Hitler took over all of Czechoslovakia and permitted Poland and Hungary small slices bordering their lands.

Italy, early in 1939, took over Albania. This was no sooner done, than Hitler began to agitate for a return of the Polish Corridor to Germany. This was absolutely his last demand. But in August of 1939 came a "diplomatic revolution" that changed the international situation overnight.

THE SECOND WORLD WAR

Poland was crushed by Hitler in five weeks; the Nazis unleashed the *Blitzkreig* tactic, a combined bombing and armored vehicle attack that was both mobile and paralyzing. Poland's allies lent her no assistance. Russia now moved to collect its dividends on the Nazi-Soviet pact. Lithuania, Latvia, Estonia, the Rumanian provinces of Bessarabia and Bukowina, and (1940) Finland were conquered by the Red Army.

In April 1940 the Nazis overran Denmark and Norway. British failure forced Chamberlain out of office and Winston Churchill became Prime Minister on May 10, 1940. On that very day came the Nazi attack on the Low Countries and France. France fell in one of the most ignominious defeats in military history on June 21, 1940. Collaborationists like Laval set up a new French government at Vichy; Italy formally entered the war by an assault on British positions in North Africa; England was without allies; the United States began to drop its aloofness as Roosevelt began his campaign to win Americans to the support of England. Such were the consequences of the fall of France.

Germany now began its air assault on England and against meager opposition. Hitler's air blitz on England failed. The small Royal Air Force proved marvelously effective and destroyed 3,000 German planes; British morale grew sturdier with each attack; supplies, protected by the British navy, began to pour in; American aid grew mountainously especially after the passage of the Lend-Lease Act; Hitler was forced to pull his Italian ally out of difficulties in North Africa and the Balkans and this diverted his energies eastward.

In June 1941 Hitler attacked Russia without warning in a hope to break through the Caucusus into India and to join there with the Japanese who had already advanced far into Southeast Asia in the direction of eastern India. Initial successes brought the Nazis to the gates of Moscow and far south to the city of Stalingrad. On December 7, 1941, Japan attacked the U.S. naval base at Pearl Harbor. America now entered the conflict.

In 1942 the counteroffensive against the Axis powers began. Russia destroyed the Nazi army at Stalingrad and began an offensive that carried her to Berlin in 1945. England defeated the Nazi-Fascist forces deep in Egypt at El Alemain and took the offensive that ended only when the British met the American forces who had landed in western North Africa to spring a trap on the Nazis. The U.S. began its island-hopping campaign that brought her to the perimeter of the Japanese Islands. No assault had to be made on these islands for the dropping of atom bombs on Hiroshima and Nagasaki convinced the Japanese military that further resistance was useless. Russia completed the demolition of the Japanese by destroying its Manchurian armies.

From North Africa Anglo-American forces crossed over to Italy and began a northward assault on German-held positions. But the greatest water-borne assault in history came on D-day— June 6, 1944—when Anglo-American forces invaded Normandy and continued rolling until all of western Germany had fallen. Victory in Europe came on May 7, 1945; Victory in Japan came on August 14, 1945. The most devastating war in the history of mankind was over. Its total cost in money, lives, disease, broken bodies, broken minds will probably never be fully calculated; its effects upon the political, social, economic, psychological and cultural institutions of the civilized world are as yet incalculable. Yet it, more than any other phenomenon, shaped the frame and features of the world today. We can do no more than indicate some of the vectors that have revealed themselves since 1945 and wait for their unraveling in the future.

THE POST-WAR WORLD

"One World." World War II was fought on a high ideological level. In August 1941 Churchill and Roosevelt met to frame the "Atlantic Charter." The nobility of the cause of the united nations was framed in the words of this document, words that bear repetition especially today. The allied nations agreed that

they will seek no aggrandizement, territorial or otherwise;

territorial changes will be made in accord with the freely expressed wishes of the people concerned;

people will choose the form of government under which they will live;

they will see to it that people who have forcibly lost their self-government will get it back;

with due respect for existing obligations, they will see to it that all States have access, on equal terms, to the trade and raw materials of the world;

they will get all nations to collaborate to improve labor standards, economic advancement, and social security;

they will establish a peace in which men may live out their lives free from fear and want;

they will assure freedom of the seas; and

they will disarm aggressors and will remain armed themselves until permanent security is established.

Out of this drive for world peace came the United Nations organization.

THE UNITED NATIONS

A United Nations Organization had been projected simultaneously with the issuance of the Atlantic Charter. At the Moscow Conference—and other military meetings during the war—the need for such an organization was officially proclaimed and the basic principle of the equality of states was announced (1943).

At Teheran (1943) a planning committee was projected. It met at Dumbarton Oaks (1944) and consisted of the Big Four—the United States, the United Kingdom, the Soviet Union and China. Ninety percent of the Charter of the United Nations was hammered out at Dumbarton Oaks. The remainder was completed at Bretton Woods (N.H.) where an International Bank for Reconstruction and Development and an International Monetary Fund to stabilize world currencies were set up; at Yalta where the formula on the voting procedures in the Security Council was agreed upon and each of the great powers was granted an absolute veto on all matters except procedure; and at San Francisco (April-June 1945) where the addition of the important Article 51 was made, the article that provided for regional pacts for individual or collective self-defense pending action by the Security Council.

Purposes. Article I of the Charter of the UN sets forth its major goals: "To maintain international peace and security, and to that end: to take effective collective measures for the prevention and removal of threats to the peace . . ."; and "To achieve international cooperation in solving international problems of an economic, social, cultural or humanitarian character . . ."

Membership. All independent, peace-loving nations are eligible if they accept the obligations of the UN and are willing and able to carry them out. On January 1, 1957 there were over eighty member nations.

Structure. There are six main organs of the UN: **The General Assembly** composed of all member states. Each state may send five delegates but each state is entitled to only one vote. On most matters a two-thirds vote prevails. The Assembly must meet at least once a year but may meet in special session. After the creation in 1947 of an interim committee called the "Little Assembly" one may now say that the General Assembly is in continuous session.

The Security Council. This was to have been the leading organ of the UN. It consists of eleven members, five (U.S., U.K., USSR, France and China) with permanent seats and six elected by the General Assembly for two-year terms. It is in continuous session and has the primary responsibility for maintaining peace and security; all other members of the UN are bound to carry out its decisions. But its decisions have been few since each of the permanent members has an absolute veto on all substantive matters. Its *potential* power remains virtually limitless.

The Economic and Social Council (ECOSOC). ECOSOC's 18 member council is chosen for staggered three-year terms by the General Assembly. It is charged with carrying out programs of international and social improvement. The most spectacular accomplishments of the UN have been in the work of this organ through its many specialized agencies whose titles clearly indicate their functions: The International Labor Organization (ILO), the Food and Agricultural Organization (FAO), the United Nations Educational Scientific and Cultural Organization (UNESCO), the International Civil Aviation Organization (ICAO), The International Bank for Reconstruction and Development (IBRD), the International Monetary Fund (IMF), the International Telecommunications Union (ITU), the World Health Organization (WHO), the International Trade Organization (ITO). Through these organizations particularly does the light of "one world" shine through.

The Trusteeship Council. This organ supervises territories previously administered by the League of Nations as mandates as well as such territories that nations have voluntarily placed under trusteeship with the UN. Six UN members are at present charged with advancing the political and economic development of 20,500,000 people in eleven African and Pacific areas. The Council sends out questionnaires, hears reports, listens to complaints from natives and sends out on-the-spot investigating committees—unless the trust-holding power designates its trust territory as "strategic."

U.N. Successes and Limitations. Since 1945, the United Nations has scored many successes. It caused Russian withdrawal of troops from Iran (1946); it halted Civil War in Greece and set up the U.N. Balkan Commission; it created the independent states of Israel, Indonesia and Libya; it fought the Korean War to a truce; it halted intense religious battles between India and Pakistan over the disputed territory of Kashmir; it halted similar strife in the Israeli-Arab War of 1948–9; it stopped a tripartite invasion of Egypt by England, France and Israel in 1956 (caused these nations to withdraw from Egyptian territory). In 1948, the General Assembly adopted the Declaration of Human Rights, a world charter of human civil liberty; and in the same year approved the Genocide Convention to protect any ethnic group from extinction. The U.N. sponsored GATT., a general agreement on tariffs and trade to limit world economic nationalism.

U.N. limitations, however, were evident in the rapid increase of regional agreements for collective security (NATO and the WARSAW PACT); the constant use of the veto power by the Soviet Union in the Security Council; inability of the U.N. to establish a permanent international armed force; existence within the U.N. of political blocs (American, Soviet, Afro-Asian), inability to act on such matters as suppression of the Hungarian revolt, etc.

THE COLD WAR

Communist Imperialism. By 1947, the "One World" built during the war was replaced by a so-called Cold War between two power blocs: a Western bloc headed by the United States and an Eastern bloc headed by the Soviet Union. Conflicting military and economic goals were the basic causes of the Cold War. Russian satellite states were created in Albania, Bulgaria, Hungary, Rumania, Czechoslovakia, Poland and East Germany. Yugoslavia, under Marshall Tito, broke from her satellite status but retained a Communist form of government. Estonia, Latvia, Lithuania, the Karelian Isthmus of Finland, Finnish Petsamo, Bessarabia and the eastern provinces of Poland were absorbed into the U.S.S.R. itself. The Chinese Communists drove Chiang Kai shek off the mainland on to Taiwan (Formosa) and assumed control of China; later, the Chinese Communists conquered Tibet. Chinese Communists aided in the formation of Communist North Korea. In each of these conquered or absorbed territories, the Communists instituted political dictatorship and economic totalitarianism modeled after the Soviet state. Efforts at protest or revolt in Czechoslovakia, Poland, East Germany, Hungary and Tibet were crushed. The Communists inspired hostilities in Greece, the Philippines and Malaya; and major wars in Korea and Indo-China. They were constantly active in the Middle East and Latin America, and important inroads were made in Indonesia and Africa. Meanwhile Russia's military power was enhanced by the successful firing of a thermonuclear bomb and by the launching of a 3000-pound space missile. Soviet diplomats combined the diplomacy of threat with an increased program of foreign aid to backwood nations. Through shipments of military equipment, Communist prestige increased in the Middle East and in Africa.

Counterattack. The Western counterattack to Soviet-bloc expansion evolved with events and took three forms.

Containment. In 1947, President Truman called for an end to Communist expansion and in the **Truman Doctrine** offered American military, economic and financial aid to any nation under attack or threat of attack by Communist-bloc nations. Subsequently, the United States intervened directly and unilaterally to counter Communist attacks or threats in Greece, Turkey, Korea, Indo-

China, the Philippines and Malaya. This was followed by the formation of a series of defensive military alliances designed to "contain" Communist expansion.

On April 4, 1949, the North Atlantic Treaty Organization (NATO) was formed. Original members included Belgium, Canada, Denmark, France, Greenland, Iceland, Italy, Luxemburg, the Netherlands, Norway, the United Kingdom and the United States; subsequently Greece, Turkey and West Germany were added to the alliance to form a community embracing more than 400,000,000 people. NATO, located in Paris, is composed of a ruling Civilian Council and a Military Council, with a Supreme Commander who controls motorized infantry divisions, air and naval fleets, complex and instantaneous communication systems, suppliers and, of course, conventional and atomic weapons. In its first decade NATO was able to overcome difficulties created by the failure of member nations to meet personnel quotas, forces withdrawn from non-NATO operations (French withdrawal of troops for use in Indo-China and Algeria), competition among members for favored posts and commands and non-NATO rivalries among members (England vs. Greece vs. Turkey over Cyprus; England vs. Iceland over North Atlantic fisheries). The most serious threat to NATO, however, was the demand by President De Gaulle of France for complete parity with the United States and England in Mediterranean commands and over control of atomic weapons (the latter forbidden by the United States without the consent of Congress). As a result, the United States was forced to move all its French-based atomic equipment to other sites.

Less effective than NATO was the alliance formed in Southeast Asia (SEATO) among Australia, New Zealand, Pakistan, the Philippines, Thailand, France, England and the United States. This alliance is purely consultative and it suffers considerably from the absence of India, Burma, Indonesia, Taiwan (the Republic of China) and Japan.

Least effective is the Middle East Treaty Organization (METO) organized by England but financed by the United States. It includes only Turkey, Iran, Pakistan and England (Iraq having dropped out in 1959) and is merely consultative; moreover, Egypt and the Arab League are violently opposed to it. Because these multilateral alliances have been strengthened by bilateral agreements between the United States and countries across the world, American troops are provided with military bases along the fringe of the Communist world. That the United States has not abandoned unilateral action is evident in the 1957 adoption of the **Eisenhower Doctrine** which provides for armed assistance to repel Communist aggression in the Middle East, if requested by a Middle Eastern nation.

Strengthening Europe's Economic Defenses. The United States launched its Marshall Plan (1948–1952) to remove the ruins of war, to rebuild Europe's economy and to reduce the effectiveness of the Communists throughout Europe. This economic and financial aid was distributed in Europe by the **Organization of European Economic Cooperation** (OEEC). European cooperation within the OEEC was the first step in a move toward European integration. In 1946 Belgium, the Netherlands and Luxemburg organized a tariff union (Benelux) within the OEEC. In 1949 a Council of Europe was formed to examine the possibilities of political unity of the OEEC powers. Then in 1952, France, Italy, West Germany and the Benelux nations adopted the Schuman Plan which integrated the economies of these six countries into a coal and steel community under a unified high authority which planned the production, the distribution and the labor forces available for the making of steel. In 1957, Euratom was created to promote common production of nuclear energy; and in 1959, the Schuman Plan nations began Euromarket designed to eliminate all tariffs within the community and to adopt a common tariff against all nations outside the community. England proposed a wider free-trade area to embrace all Western Europe. Finding no approval for this plan by Euromarket, England began to organize its own free-trade area to include itself, Sweden, Norway, Denmark, Austria, Switzerland and Portugal.

Strengthening Non-European Economic Defenses. To offset Communist inroads into the more backward areas of the world, the United States and its allies have begun large-scale programs of economic aid to these areas. Technical assistance to improve control over natural resources was made available under President Truman's Point Four program and a similar United Nation's project. Loans and grants-in-aid were provided for Southeast Asia in the British-sponsored and American-financed Colombo Plan; and to all the rest of the world in the United States' **Development Loan Fund** and **Agricultural Trade and Development Loan Funds** (which distributes America's farm surpluses to needy nations). Other sources of loans for approved projects were the **American Export-Import Bank** and the **International Bank for Reconstruction and Development.** Billions of dollars and pounds poured into these backward areas have successfully halted important Communist gains, and have kept the governments of these nations, generally inclined to Communism, on a neutral path.

Support for Former Enemies. Since enemies of Communism are not necessarily friends of democracy, the Western powers have taken active steps to obtain necessary allies. Thus, Marshall Tito, heading a Communist state in Yugoslavia, was aided by loans and military support to defy the Soviet bloc and retain his independence; Generalissimo Franco, heading a Fascist state in Spain, was encouraged to be friendly to the Western powers by a defense agreement with the United States in which air bases were exchanged for military and economic aid. Similarly, Japan, having been effectively democratized, was permitted to rearm, admitted to the United Nations, granted large sums of rehabilitory aid, and made a defense bastion in the Far East. Most significant, however, was the treatment accorded to Germany.

The Yalta and Potsdam agreements of 1945 provided that both Germany and its historic capital, Berlin, were to be partitioned until the country was completely demilitarized, denazified and democratized. When this was accomplished Germany was to be reunited as a minor power. Unilateral Russian action, however, in changing Germany's boundaries within the eastern zone, in blockading Berlin, and in converting the Russian zone into the satellite nation of East Germany, caused the Western powers to take positive steps. West Germany became an independent state; the German General Staff was recreated; West Germany was militarized and admitted to NATO. The Western powers maintained their position in West Berlin despite the efforts of Russian Premier Khrushchev who threatened to turn West Berlin, located well within the territory of the East German state, over to East Germany, and conclude a separate peace treaty with East Germany.

East and West met at the conference table at Geneva in 1959 in an attempt to solve the problem of a united Berlin and a united Germany.

Decade of Turmoil. The 1960s brought internal strife to many countries of the world as new political groups fought to gain more personal freedoms.

Civil war gave birth to several new nations in Africa, while others claimed their independence from the rule of Great Britain and France. Military leaders vied for control of Greece, Portugal, and a number of countries in Latin America.

The National Association for the Advancement of Colored People (NAACP) led by Roy Wilkins and the Southern Christian Leadership Conference (SCLC) led by Martin Luther King, Jr., championed the cause of racial equality in the United States. Their protest marches and boycotts in the early 1960s won some changes in the law. Later more radical groups stirred up violent riots in the large urban areas, reacting against the bitter plight of blacks and similar minorities.

In Northern Ireland the age-old conflict between (middle-class) Protestants and (lower-class) Catholics erupted again when Catholics called for total independence from Great Britain. Tempers flared and terrorist groups roamed the streets, frightening and murdering their opponents in the cause. The conflict worsened as the decade rolled on.

In Czechoslovakia the democratic policies of President Alexander Dubcek earned the scorn of nearby Russia. To make sure the reforms didn't spread to other Communist satellites, the Soviet government sent its army into Czechoslovakia in August 1968 to sweep Dubcek from power.

Military Challenges. During the 1960s the powers of East and West tested their strength in several crucial showdowns.

When Cuban Premier Fidel Castro brought Russian missiles onto his island fortress in 1962, President John F. Kennedy placed a naval blockage against the shipments. He said Castro and his Russian partners had violated the Monroe Doctrine–the policy which President James Monroe laid down over a hundred years earlier, when he declared that the United States would not allow foreign powers to stake new claims in the Western Hemisphere.

In Southeast Asia, Communist super-powers supported the government of North Vietnam as it tried to take South Vietnam. The United Nations sent military advisors to South Vietnam, then troops. The conflict spread to the neighboring countries of Cambodia, Laos, and Thailand. The United States pledged to defend South Vietnam if the conflict became a full-scale war; Russia and China did the same for North Vietnam. But both

sides wanted to keep the conflict from growing into another world war. The United States committed over 500,000 soldiers to the contest, but by the end of the sixties most American leaders knew the effort would fail. At home, college students demonstrated against America's role in Asia and many young men burned their draft cards to show their contempt for what they called an "immoral war."

DÉTENTE

Richard M. Nixon took office as President of the United States in 1969 with two goals for his administration: (1) to settle the unrest in America's streets, and (2) to establish a more peaceful climate on the world scene. He knew the first goal depended on reaching the second. He also realized that if America was to find world peace, it had to melt the ice of its "cold war" with the Communist powers. Mr. Nixon called this process *détente*, using a French term that means "to relax tension."

The United States began a round of Strategic Arms Limitation Talks (SALT) with the Soviet Union. At these conferences the diplomats from both nations agreed to limit the number of new weapons they made–especially atomic weapons. At the same time the United States invited Chinese athletes to visit North America for what newspaper columnists jokingly called "ping-pong diplomacy." Relations grew more friendly between the two nations and climaxed with President Nixon's courtesy trip to China in early 1972. A treaty between the United States and North Vietnam ended the long stand-off in Southeast Asia with American troops leaving the area at the end of 1972. In April 1973, North Vietnamese troops took the last major cities in South Vietnam and united the country with their own.

Economic Problems. Israel and its Arab rivals called for military aid in their long-time dispute, but the spirit of *détente* led major world powers to keep "hands off." Arab nations banded together to resist this policy, and in the fall of 1973 they refused to ship oil to the United States. They ended the boycott several months later, but the Arab-controlled group of Oil Producing and Exporting Countries (OPEC) doubled the price of crude oil. This triggered a new surge of inflation in the United States and other Western countries. China, Russia, and most Communist countries in Eastern

Europe produced enough oil for their own needs, so the price hike did little to harm their economies.

By the time James Earl (Jimmy) Carter became President in 1977, the cost of living in the United States was rising by about eight percent each year. The United States imported much more than it sold to other nations, and had to borrow billions of dollars' worth of credit to cover the difference. This **balance of payments deficit** loomed as a primary concern of the Western world. It meant that the American dollar was worth less than it was a year earlier–or even a month earlier. Because the United States was so active in the business of the Western world, its growing debt threatened to disrupt international economy. President Carter proposed new programs to make the United States able to produce more of its own energy. In early 1978 he met in Munich, West Germany with other Western leaders to seek ways of strengthening the international system of trade. Ironically, by this time the European continent and Japan had bounced back from World War II even better than the United States and Great Britain.

Détente seemed threatened by President Carter's demand for human rights in Communist countries. He cited the Helsinki pact of 1973, in which the Soviet Union pledged to give its citizens freedom of speech, freedom of worship, and other concessions. Carter and his aides criticized the Soviet Union for putting political and religious dissenters on trial: the Soviet government warned the United States to stop meddling in Russia's domestic affairs.

Yet the period of *détente* had real benefits. Because of easing tensions in the Middle East, President Carter could invite President Anwar Sadat of Egypt and Prime Minister Menachem Begin of Israel to a summit conference at Camp David, in the Maryland hills near Washington, D.C. On September 17, 1978, the three men signed a "Framework for Peace in the Middle East," which outlined steps for ending the 30-year dispute between Israel and its Arab neighbors.

AMERICAN HISTORY

Origins

The origins of American history may be found in developments in Europe. The fourteenth and fifteenth centuries saw extraordinary developments taking place in Europe. These included the rise of a middle class, the appearance of independent nations, the growth of industry and commerce, the invention of printing, a new interest in science, the development of religious conflict. These changes led Europeans to explore the world. Columbus' discovery of America in 1492 was but one of many attempts on the part of Europeans to find an all-water route to the Far East.

A year after Columbus' first voyage on behalf of Spain, the Pope gave Spain title to all of the New World, with the exception of the eastern part of South America, known today as Brazil, which was awarded to Portugal. Spain ruled her vast empire despotically. There was no religious freedom, Indians were treated harshly, and self-government was denied to the colonists.

In 1608, the French founded Quebec. For a century afterward, they continued to explore North America, following the great waterways of the continent–the St. Lawrence River, the Great Lakes, and the Mississippi River. However, by 1750 only about 80,000 settlers had come to New France. Like Spain, France denied her colonies the right of self-government. Furthermore, since France was interested mainly in the fur trade, settlers who wished to farm the land were discouraged from migrating to the colonies.

In 1607, the English founded Jamestown in Virginia, and in 1620, what was to become Plymouth in Massachusetts. In 1664, they forced the Dutch to surrender their colony of New Netherlands, which included what is now New York, New Jersey, Pennsylvania, and Delaware. The English flag now floated from Maine to the border of Florida. The English colonies, unlike those of Spain and France, attracted large numbers of settlers. By 1750 there were nearly 1,500,000 people living in the thirteen colonies strung along the Atlantic coast.

These settlers had come for many reasons. Some hoped to find religious freedom; some sought political liberty; others hoped to improve their economic lot. The prospect for the small farmer was far brighter in the English colonies because land ownership was widespread, especially in New England and in the middle colonies. England granted more political, religious, and economic freedom than either Spain or France.

English colonists came to believe that all men were equal and should have equal opportunities. They insisted that the political rights won by their fellow countrymen in England over the centuries were also rightfully theirs. Building upon their heritage of the Magna Charta (1215), the Petition of Rights (1628), and the Bill of Rights (1689), the English colonists developed their own democratic institutions. In Virginia the House of Burgesses, established in 1619, was the first elected legislature in the New World. In 1639, Connecticut drew up the Fundamental Orders, the first written constitution in America. New England town meetings involved the participation of qualified citizens in making local decisions and choosing their officials. By 1750 most of the colonial legislatures had some measure of control over the royal governors by virtue of "the power of the purse," that is, the right to grant or withhold taxes.

Religious freedom also developed in the English colonies. Roger Williams founded Rhode Island as a colony affording complete religious freedom for all, with separation of church and state. Maryland's Act of Toleration granted freedom of worship to all Christians. William Penn, in 1682, granted religious freedom in Pennsylvania.

Beginning in 1689, England and France were engaged in a worldwide struggle for colonies and commerce. In 1754, the fourth and most decisive of these wars broke out. In the New World it was known as the French and Indian War. Its outcome was a complete defeat for the French. The Treaty of Paris (1763) gave to England Canada and all of the French territory east of the Mississippi, with the exception of New Orleans.

The victory proved to be a mixed blessing for England. Before 1763, she had paid little attention to the colonies which had had virtual self-government. The Navigation Acts, which had been designed to compel the colonies to trade almost entirely with the mother country, in accordance with the mercantilist theory, had not been enforced. After the French and Indian War, England's attitude changed. To protect the colonists from Indians, England needed an army of 10,000 in the colonies, at a cost of one million dollars a year. Added to this sum was the huge debt with which the English were saddled as a consequence of the war. She determined to make the colonies pay part of the cost of maintaining the army as well as the interest on the war debt. Furthermore, British officials began to collect customs duties, which had long been evaded by colonial smugglers.

There followed a series of British enactments which became increasingly objectionable to the colonists. The lands west of the Appalachians were closed to colonial settlers. The Sugar Act, the Stamp Act, and the Townshend Acts, all designed to increase revenue for Britain, aroused anger among the colonists. Committees of Correspondence succeeded in organizing opposition to Britain, coordinating the efforts of patriots in the various colonies.

On April 19, 1775, fighting broke out at Lexington, Massachusetts. The news spread quickly. Harsh measures by the British convinced many colonists that independence was the next logical step. On July 4, 1776, the Second Continental Congress adopted the Declaration of Independence, written chiefly by Thomas Jefferson, which expressed the democratic ideals of the American Revolution.

The war between England and her American colonies was a long and a bitter one. Under the inspiring leadership of George Washington, the colonists, with the help of France, scored a series of remarkable victories. The Treaty of Paris (1783) ended the war, granting full independence to the colonies.

Once free, the colonies became thirteen independent states, loosely bound together under the Articles of Confederation. The period from 1781 to 1789 has been called the Critical Period, because it seemed that the weak central government would fail to solve its economic and political problems. In 1787, the representatives of twelve of the thirteen states met in Philadelphia to strengthen the powers of the central government. Instead of merely revising the Articles of Confederation, however, they drew up an entirely new plan of government for the nation and wrote a new constitution. This document, the Constitution of the United States, has remained the basis of our federal system of government.

A task which was uppermost in the minds of the representatives was the prevention of tyranny. They agreed with the famous French philosopher Montesquieu that there could be no liberty when the powers to make the laws and to enforce the laws were given to the same person or group or when the power of judging was not separated from legislative and executive powers. Accordingly, they decided to set up a system in which no one person or agency could make a law, arrest a violator, find him guilty, and punish him.

In the section "American Government," we shall examine the three main branches of our Federal Government in order to understand the responsibilities of each, as well as the relationships among the branches.

Development

During the quarter century between the inauguration of President Washington and the end of the War of 1812, the new nation achieved maturity and general recognition from the international community.

It was first necessary to learn whether the Constitution could adequately provide guidance in transforming the sovereign states into a federal nation. Some leaders were at least as strongly devoted to their state–Jefferson always called Virginia his "country"–as to the Union. Others considered that the United States relegated the states to subdivisions. This division appeared to some extent in the platforms of political leaders and, as they developed, of political parties. As the nation evolved, the aggregation of states, the region–New England, the South, the West–tended to replace the state in its capacity to attract primary loyalties, especially when the region could be identified with a minority position. Nevertheless, political regionalism invariably was disguised as the doctrine of states' rights, because under the Constitution the state was a political entity that had specific rights, whereas the region had no standing of any kind.

POLITICAL PARTIES

Nor did the Constitution recognize the existence of political parties, or factions (the term in vogue in the eighteenth century), and all the Constitution-builders professed an aversion to factionalism. At first only one's opponents were described as forming a faction. Those who favored the strengthening of the new central government described themselves as Federalists. Their opponents, who preferred minimal government administered locally, were therefore dubbed Antifederalists, or simply Antis. But the latter, choosing to emphasize positive concepts, such as liberty, professed to see a trend toward monarchism among the Federalists, and so called themselves Democratic-Republicans, soon shortened to Republicans. With polarization, the factional names acquired symbolic value, and by the time John Adams became President a two-party system was operative.

It then became necessary for that system to de-velop effective mechanisms. The election in 1796 of an Executive team of antithetical politicians, the Federalist President John Adams and the Republican Vice President Thomas Jefferson, disclosed the absurdity and the need for reform. When the electoral process in the election of 1800 returned a tie vote for two Republican candidates, Jefferson and Aaron Burr, that was resolved under Constitutional procedures only after 36 ballots in Congress just a week before inauguration day, reform became imperative. The result was the Twelfth Amendment, ratified in 1803 and operative in 1804, which required a separate ballot for the President and Vice President.

Once the legitimacy of party organization was accepted, the Congressional members of the several parties (known as *caucuses*) assumed the prerogative of selecting candidates. Federal caucuses nominated John Adams, Charles Pinckney, DeWitt Clinton, and Rufus King in the elections from 1800 through 1816, while Republican caucuses named Thomas Jefferson, James Madison, and James Monroe. After three successive two-term Republican administrations, the Federalist Party ceased to exist nationally in 1820. Four years later the Republican Party, lacking external opposition, was internally in turmoil. Only one-third of the Republicans in Congress attended the caucus that named William Crawford to run for the Presidency. Three competitors found it expedient to announce their candidacies through the sponsorship of state legislatures: Andrew Jackson, John Quincy Adams, and Henry Clay. When the two-party system began to function once more in the 1830s, the caucus had lost its nominative function. It was replaced by the party convention, which had nominated candidates for state office since the 1790s. The first Democratic national convention met in 1832, but two minor parties, the Anti-Masonic and National Republican parties, nominated Presidential candidates in 1831.

FOREIGN RELATIONS

The confrontation between Federalists and Republicans had been well defined during President Washington's Administration, from 1789 to 1797, when Alexander Hamilton and Thomas Jefferson

POLITICAL RACE COURSE - UNION TRACK - FALL RACES 1836

A cartoon satirizes the 1836 presidential election campaign.

Another cartoon looks at the presidential campaign of 1856.

The Resignation of George Washington (detail).

were their recognized spokesmen. Both foreign and domestic policy were matters of partisan controversy. The French Revolution and the Napoleonic Wars had an impact because interested parties abroad sought support within the United States.

The Republicans considered the early phases of the French Revolution a continuation of the American Revolution. Thomas Paine, Thomas Jefferson, and James Monroe were ardent advocates of the French republic, whereas such Federalists as Alexander Hamilton, John Adams, and John Jay supported a counterrevolutionary backlash. Washington was initially neutral, but gradually turned toward the Federalist position. As the Terror of 1793 was succeeded by the general warfare of the Napoleonic period, even the Republicans were disillusioned.

The break in the alliance between France and the United States was a direct result of the "XYZ Affair" of 1797, a demeaning and unsuccessful attempt by the French Directory to browbeat President Adams' administration by insulting American negotiators. A state of undeclared war in 1798 was accompanied by the establishment of an American navy, while France under Napoleon embarked on full-scale war against Great Britain and neighboring European countries. As the tempo of the European war accelerated, the two major belligerents alternately wooed and abused the United States. Under such conditions, Napoleon unexpectedly sold Louisiana to the United States in 1803. American merchant shipping throve on risky but profitable wartime ventures. After 1805 the attempts of three American Presidents to enforce neutrality through "nonintercourse" and embargoes aroused resentment on the part of American commercial interests and retaliation at the hands of the belligerents. The practice that most outraged Americans was that of "impressment"–removing sailors from United States ships under the pretext that they were British deserters, as was often the case.

THE WAR OF 1812

The years of frustration ultimately played into the hands of a new generation of political leaders from the West, who welcomed an excuse to advocate an offensive foreign policy. Known as the War Hawks, they proposed to smite the Spanish in the Floridas and the British in Canada, to secure the southern and northern borders of the United States. The ensuing War of 1812 proved militarily indecisive, despite moments of naval glory and the spectacular victory for the United States at New Orleans. The political significance of the war makes the Treaty of Ghent, signed in 1814, a landmark in United States history. The world was impressed that a hitherto untried nation could hold to a standstill Europe's foremost naval power, the conqueror of Napoleon.

The development of American internal politics was no less dramatic. The Republicans in 1798 and 1799 had sponsored the Kentucky and Virginia Resolutions, proclaiming the concept that the Union was a revocable compact among sovereign states. Now they had become a nationalist party of militant expansionists. The Federalists, on the other hand were virtually insulated in New England. They compromised their original position by considering, at the Hartford Convention of 1814, whether their region might not be more prosperous outside than within the Union. The Treaty of Ghent made such notions irrelevant, and enabled the country to devote its full energies to the consolidation of the vast territories it now controlled.

ORGANIZING AN EMPIRE

The United States had undergone a remarkable physical change between the treaties of 1783 and 1814. At the end of the Revolutionary War, the thirteen original states claimed a hinterland extending to the Mississippi, with undefined and insecure borders south and north. Spain claimed the entire Gulf coast. British troops continued to occupy strategic points that admittedly belonged to the United States, pending France's fulfillment of all the terms of the Treaty of Paris. Jay's Treaty of 1794 with Great Britain settled some of the disputes with Britain, and Thomas Pinckney's Treaty of San Lorenzo with Spain in 1795 gave Georgia a disputed strip in the hinterland of Florida. These were holding operations, maintaining instability.

Meanwhile, Congress under the Articles of Confederation and later under the Constitution established a pattern of organization for the trans-Appalachian territories. Georgia west of the Chattahoochee was ceded to the Federal Government in 1802 and became Mississippi Territory. The Territory Southwest of the River Ohio, originally the western sections of Virginia and North Carolina, became the states of Kentucky and Tennessee in 1792 and 1796 respectively. The Territory North of the River Ohio (Northwest Territory for short) was organized in 1787 with the provision that it would be formed into states, each of which would be admitted to the Union upon attaining a population of 60,000. A further provision prohibited the institution of slavery throughout the entire area. The authority of the Federal Government to organize and legislate for territories that would be guaranteed statehood was thus established even before the Constitution was ratified.

THE NEW WEST

In 1803, Ohio–the first state carved out of the Northwest Territory–was admitted to the Union. That same year, the total area of the United States was doubled by the acquisition of Louisiana. This vast tract extended the sovereignty of the United States west to the Rocky Mountains. Some questioned the authority of the Federal Government to acquire territory by purchase (as in this instance) or by conquest; but Jefferson set a precedent that met with general approval. The Louisiana Purchase–soon renamed Missouri Territory–was expected to evolve into states and be added to the Union. However, it was not so generally conceded that the Federal Government could legislate concerning the extension of the institution of slavery into the Missouri Territory.

It was anticipated that this territory would be settled mostly by small farmers, who would adhere to the Republican ideals of Jefferson. Within the agrarian South itself, however, planters already prevailed over yeomen, and cotton plantations were taking the place of tobacco plantations to such an extent that the region had virtually developed a one-crop economy: cotton was "king." This resulted in the rejuvenation of the institution of slavery, the narrowing of trade relations to the

The Aaron Burr—Alexander Hamilton Duel (detail)

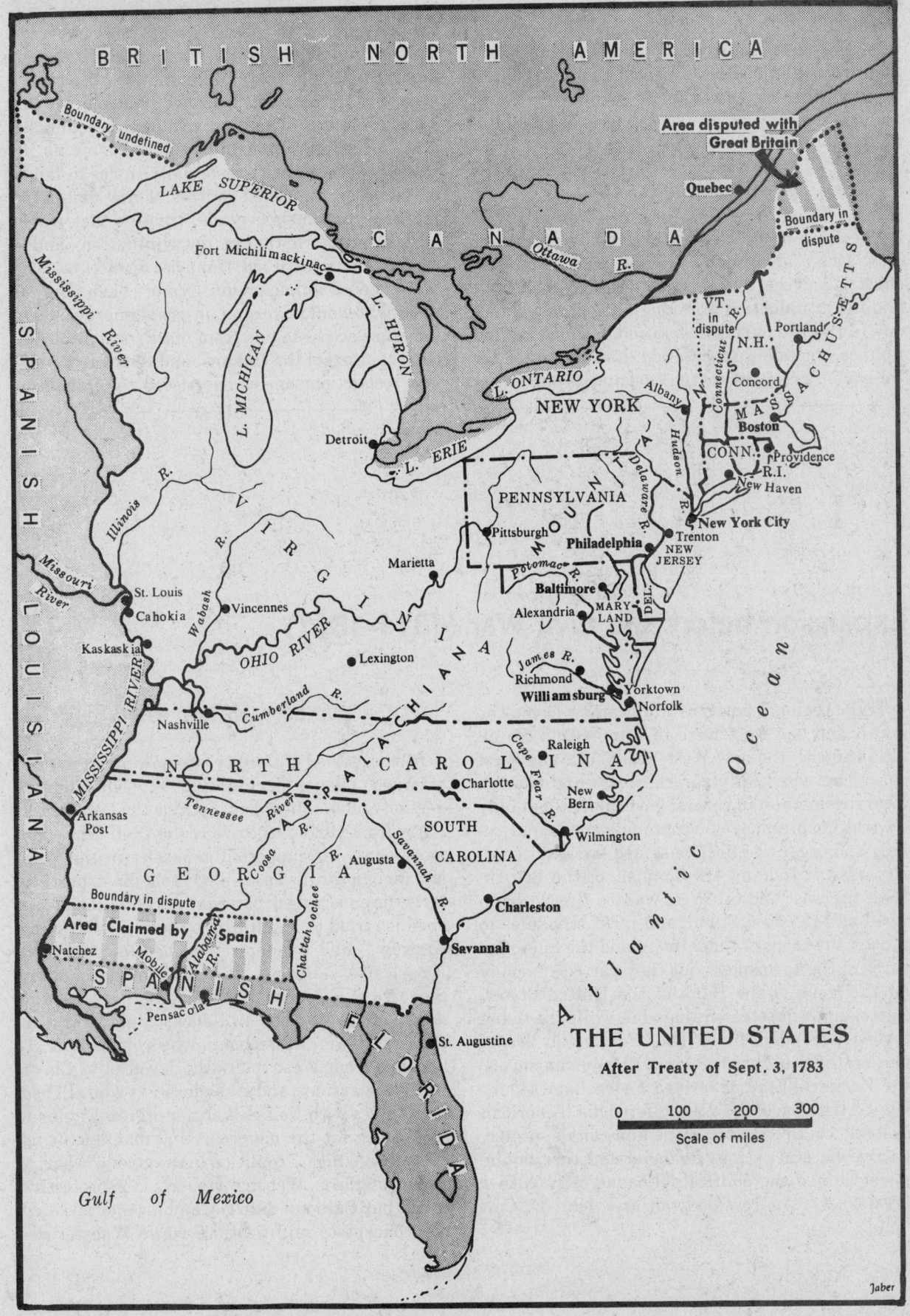

BRITISH NORTH AMERICA

Boundary undefined

LAKE SUPERIOR

CANADA

Ottawa R.

Area disputed with Great Britain

Quebec

Boundary in dispute

Fort Michilimackinac

L. HURON

L. MICHIGAN

L. ONTARIO

Albany

VT. in dispute

N.H.

Portland

Concord

Connecticut R.

M A S S A C H U S E T T S

Detroit

L. ERIE

NEW YORK

Boston

CONN.

Providence

R.I.

New Haven

Mississippi River

Illinois R.

SPANISH LOUISIANA

Missouri River

St. Louis

Cahokia

VIRGINIA

Wabash R.

Vincennes

Marietta

PENNSYLVANIA

Pittsburgh

Hudson R.

Trenton

New York City

Philadelphia

NEW JERSEY

Delaware R.

Potomac R.

Baltimore

DEL.

Alexandria

MARYLAND

Kaskaskia

OHIO RIVER

Lexington

James R.

Richmond

Williamsburg

Yorktown

Norfolk

MISSISSIPPI RIVER

Cumberland R.

Nashville

NORTH CAROLINA

A P P A L A C H I A N

Raleigh

Cape Fear R.

New Bern

Arkansas Post

Tennessee River

Charlotte

SOUTH CAROLINA

Wilmington

Coosa R.

Augusta

Savannah R.

GEORGIA

Boundary in dispute

Area Claimed by Spain

Chattahoochee R.

Alabama R.

Natchez

Mobile

SPANISH FLORIDA

Pensacola

St. Augustine

Charleston

Savannah

Atlantic Ocean

THE UNITED STATES

After Treaty of Sept. 3, 1783

0   100   200   300

Scale of miles

Gulf of Mexico

Jaber

export of cotton, and the substitution of South Carolina for Virginia as the regional headquarters. Nor were the interests of the cotton South identical with those of the new West on such questions as the protective tariff (which the South abhorred) or the need to build roads or canals.

THE CHANGING EAST

The East–or the North, by which was meant New England and the Middle states–was also changing, largely as a result of the War of 1812 and the introduction from England of the technology of the Industrial Revolution. Commerce and finance, including speculation, had accounted for the earlier prosperity of the East and its prevailing political pattern of Federalism. But now the country had abandoned colonial habits and discovered the function of new devices behind which a manufacturing industry could flourish. While traders needed a strong navy and merchant marine, favored commercial treaties with foreign countries, and valued an expanding hinterland for its investment possibilities (especially in cheap land), manufacturers needed sources of raw materials, markets for finished goods, treaties that would permit selective import discrimination, and a strong and controlled financial structure. The West needed ample credit, free or cheap land for those who would live on it, internal improvements to assure access to and from markets, a militia to control or expel the Indians, and removal of property restrictions on the exercise of the franchise.

Expansion before the Civil War (1814-1861)

Three regional patterns were taking form. The South and the East were in competition for an alliance with the new West. The South and West shared an essentially agrarian base and trust in local rather than in central government; but only central government could provide roads and canals and organize effective armed forces for security against Indians, the Spanish, or the British. Both the East and the West wanted the National Road and the Erie Canal, and tariff schedules to protect the crops of the farmers and the manufactures of the townsmen; but they parted company on the issue of the Bank of the United States. Borrowing homesteaders hated it, while the rising tycoon depended on it. The West could accept neither the Southern version of Republicanism nor the Eastern brand of revived Federalism. Henry Clay, a true son of the West, offered his "American system" that combined roads and canals, protective tariffs, and a strong financial structure, but he never gained the political following of two other Westerners, Andrew Jackson and John C. Calhoun.

JACKSONIANS AND WHIGS

After a period of fluidity two new major parties emerged. One, a Jacksonian (not Jeffersonian) version of Republicanism, became the Democratic Party from 1828 to the eve of the Civil War. This movement was supported generally in the West and among the disfranchised in the East, particularly the emerging urban working class. Jackson's enemies tried to insult him by calling him "King Andrew," and by depicting the Democrats as American-style Tories. In the current jargon, the converse of a Tory was a Whig, and this was the name adopted by the anti-Jacksonians. They included followers of Calhoun, who switched his allegiance from West to South; devotees to Clay's American system; and ex-Federalists who aligned themselves with Daniel Webster of New England, spokesmen for the merchant and manufacturing class. The Whigs, a coalition in the guise of a party, had no platform. Webster supported the protective tariff, but Calhoun didn't. Calhoun reformulated the concept of nullification, while Webster demanded loyalty to the Union. The Whigs finally elected a President after the issueless campaign of 1840. He was the picturesque but nonpolitical William Henry Harrison, who died within a month and was succeeded by an anti-Jacksonian Democrat, John Tyler.

THE ISSUE OF SLAVERY

One issue that did not appear crucial to the major political figures in the decades after the War of 1812 was that of slavery, although such discerning experts as Jefferson and John Quincy Adams suspected its potential gravity early on. The point became controversial in national politics rather indirectly, in connection with the procedure for admitting new states. Eight of the 16 states that comprised the Union in 1803 were "slave" states; that is, their economy significantly depended on the use of slave labor. They shared power in the Senate with an equal number of "free" states, while in the House of Representatives the ratio of delegates was 49 "slave" to 57 "free." However, some of the slave-state Congressmen held office only because the Constitution gave every five blacks as much representation in the House of Representatives as every three whites (although the blacks had no other political existence). Whatever resentment the North felt against this advantage exercised by the slave interests was mitigated by the fact that only three more territories open to slavery remained east of the Mississippi, whereas at least four territories would be formed out of the Northwest Territory, where slavery was prohibited under the Ordinance of 1787. In spite of an initial proslavery handicap, the slave power would soon inevitably be a minority in both Houses.

The trans-Mississippi acquisition postponed the doom of the slave power. In 1820 the 22 states then in the Union were evenly divided, and the "slave" minority in the House had slipped only from 44 percent to 42 percent. The pending admission of Missouri as a slave state would tip the balance against the free-soil power. Henry Clay, known as a compromiser, proposed that the District of Maine in Massachusetts, having long sought statehood, should be matched with Missouri to maintain equilibrium. He also proposed that henceforth a line be extended westward along Missouri's southern border, north of which slavery would be banned just as it had previously been banned in the Northwest Territory. This Missouri Compromise of 1820 was forthwith adopted, and a crisis was averted for a decade or so. But the South did not fail to observe the shape of the remaining territory, of which only a relative sliver remained potential slave territory. The only solution for the slave power was to annex additional land south of the slave-free border: the Spanish Southwest.

ANNEXATION, SOUTH AND NORTH

The notion of annexing contiguous territory was neither novel nor unexplored. As soon as it had become clear that the Louisiana deal did not include any part of Spanish Florida, frontiersmen began to infiltrate their neighbor's domain. West Florida between the Mississippi and Pearl rivers was occupied in 1810 and two years later was annexed to the new state of Louisiana. The process–settlement of Americans on foreign territory, liberation of the area, annexation–was to be repeated on almost every occasion, from Texas to Hawaii. In Florida, the next step was the invasion of Mobile and the extension of American claims eastward to the Perdido in 1813. The rest of Florida was bought in 1819 for a minimal price from Spain, which was in no position to defend its holdings; for much of Spanish America was authentically in a state of revolution. The Adams-Onís Treaty of 1819 not only added Florida to the United States; it also defined for the first time the southern border of the Louisiana Purchase.

Meanwhile, the northern border was also subject to negotiation. There was no question that the United States had hoped to annex part of Canada during the War of 1812. The Treaty of Ghent with Great Britain ended this prospect, and a series of agreements culminated in the Convention of 1818, which made the forty-ninth parallel the permanent boundary between the United States and British North America from the Lake of the Woods to the Rocky Mountains. Between the Rockies and the Pacific Ocean, north of the present northern border of California and south of the still undefined Russian border, was a vast tract known as the Oregon country, still the preserve of fur traders and mountain men. British and American claims to Oregon remained unresolved by mutual agreement, and the region was in effect open to all.

THE MONROE DOCTRINE

These border problems having been settled, the United States asserted a sphere of influence. As the Spanish possessions in South America became independent during the years 1810 to 1825, they sought approval and recognition from the United States. Until pending disputes between the United States and Spain were resolved, these appeals from South America were ignored, but with the ratification of the Adams-Onís Treaty in 1821, the United States took steps to enter into relations with the ex-colonies. When it appeared that a league of European powers (the Holy Alliance) proposed to help Spain recover these colonies, President James Monroe proclaimed his doctrine: "The American continents . . . are henceforth not to be considered as subjects for future colonization by any European powers."

THE MEXICAN WAR

This proclamation, which in fact required the British navy for its enforcement, was not a self-denying ordinance. For an American colony had already infiltrated Spanish Mexico in 1821, and continued to enlarge after Mexico had achieved its independence. The initial step toward acquiring the Mexican state of Texas was undertaken by President Jackson in 1829. Thereafter it was only a matter of time until the sequence of revolution, liberation, and annexation was pursued. This time it required a full-scale war between the United States and Mexico to confirm the objective, but in 1848, under the terms of the Treaty of Guadalupe Hidalgo, the Mexican territories became the American Southwest, adding New Mexico and

California to the already admitted state of Texas. In 1846 an agreement had been concluded with Great Britain that extended the forty-ninth parallel westward from the Rocky Mountains through the Oregon country. The ultimate shape of the United States was virtually attained, fulfilling the dogma of Manifest Destiny "to overspread the continent allotted by Providence for the free development of our yearly multiplying millions"–which by 1848 exceeded 20 million.

COMPROMISE OF 1850

The organization of all this territory again raised the problem that had vexed the country in 1820 and had brought about the Missouri Compromise. The Presidential election of 1848 was the first in which the question of slavery, or at least its extension into the territories, was the principal issue. During the Mexican War, the House of Representatives had passed the Wilmot Proviso that would have excluded slavery from any ceded territory, but the South mustered enough support in the Senate to beat back this offensive. In 1848 both parties were split on the question of slavery extension. In the very week during which Wisconsin's admission restored a balance of 15 states on each side, the Democrats picked Lewis Cass for their Presidential candidate. Cass had developed the concept of "popular sovereignty." He wanted to discard the old principle of a demarcation between free and slave territories; he believed that the settlers should vote their preferences on the issue. Inasmuch as hardly any of the remaining unorganized territory would support the use of slave labor, the North could accept popular sovereignty in principle. The South might well endorse a pro-

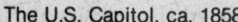
The U.S. Capitol, ca. 1858

gram _____ ___ remove the thorny issue from
Congr _____ _at ___ where they could no longer hope to
break ss, where they could no longer hope to

The W___ higs again nominated a nonpolitical general, Za___ hary Taylor, taking no stand on the crucial que___ tions—and won. Their victory was made
possible, however, by the swing vote of the Free-
Soil Party, composed of antislavery Democrats and
Whigs, who won enough votes in New York to
deprive Cass of the Presidency.

The gold rush that swelled the population of
California indirectly canceled the truce, for it was
imperative to provide law and order on the West
Coast. California applied for immediate statehood
in 1849 under a free-soil constitution, although
most of the proposed state was on the "slave" side
of the Missouri Compromise line. Congress delayed the admission of California despite President Taylor's plea for prompt action, and the
Californians set up "vigilantes" to assume the
police role. In 1850 Clay again came to the rescue
with a compromise. Its basic elements were (for the
North) the admission of a free-soil California and
(for the South) a strict law enforcing the return of
fugitive slaves to their masters. Moreover, two
other proposed territories (Utah and New Mexico)
north and south of the line of demarcation would
be organized under the concept of popular sovereignty. The Compromise of 1850 was unenthusias-
tically adopted.

THE FAILURE OF COMPROMISE

The nation now attempted to consolidate its acquisitions. During the next decade there was a
great leap forward of immigration, homesteading,
railroad building. The peopling of the Great Plains
inevitably hastened the development of territories
into states, and again the slavery issue appeared.
In 1854 the Kansas-Nebraska Bill proposed to
apply the principle of popular sovereignty to the
next tier west of Iowa and Missouri, extending
from British North America south to the territory
reserved for the Indians, and west to Utah and
New Mexico. Under the Missouri Compromise,
these territories were both destined for free soil;
the new dispensation would give the slave power a
chance. Once the bill was signed, partisans with
strong convictions and guns were sent into the
territories to frame constitutions.

The pro-slavery forces showed special capacity
for organization in Kansas Territory (where rival
constitutions appeared), accompanied by terrorist
campaigns that gave rise to the popular allusion to
"bleeding Kansas." By the time of the election of
1856, a national Republican Party had succeeded
the transitory Free-Soilers. It held its first convention and nominated John C. Frémont for President. Frémont, with 33 percent of the popular
vote, brought the Republicans to the rank of a
major party. The Whigs joined the Federalists in
the archives of history.

The stroke that ended all possibility of compromise on slavery was applied by the U.S. Supreme Court. The judiciary, under the brilliant
and durable guidance of Federalist John Marshall,
had established beyond question its role as stabilizer and sustainer of balance between the Executive and Legislative branches. Often upholding
the Federal government against the states, sometimes protecting states' rights, only once had the
Supreme Court (in *Marbury v. Madison* in 1803)
declared an act of Congress unconstitutional. Now,
more than half a century later (in *Dred Scott v.
Sandford* in 1857), the Court declared that no
legislature—national, state, or territorial—could
prohibit the institution of slavery. Where the
Kansas-Nebraska Act had removed the thorny
controversy from Congress to territorial conventions, the Court now forced it to the battlefield. The
moderates who had hoped to contain the institution or to control its spread, were driven from
contention, leaving as contestants only
those who refused to limit slavery or those who
would abolish it.

As so many grave issues had taken on the aspect
of a clash between Federal and states' rights, so the
issue of slavery was transformed into a contest
between (1) those who would secede rather than
compromise on slavery and (2) those who identified hostility toward slavery with loyalty to the
Union. Their predicament was personalized by the
Republican candidate for the Presidency in 1860,
Abraham Lincoln. Within a few years, on taking
office and under the stress of Civil War, Lincoln
passed from a free-soil to an abolitionist position.
The war was essentially a defense of the Union, as
Lincoln and most in the North understood it. But
in Southern eyes it was a defense not only of the
right of states to leave the Union, but a defense of
an institution vital to the economy of the South.

Thomas J. ("Stonewall") Jackson

Jefferson Davis

The Civil War—Black Union soldiers

THE CIVIL WAR

The population of the United States at the outbreak of the Civil War was about thirty-one million, of whom more than 60 percent lived in the North. One-third of the Southern minority were slaves. The economy of the South had long since ceased to compete with that of the North. The South was in effect a colonial supplier of cotton to British and Northern factories. The North, on the other hand, had embraced industrialization and was capable of supplying the potential market of the West and drawing upon its untapped resources. The West had already received more free immigrants than the entire servile labor force of the South. An economic alliance between the West and the North awaited only the building of railroads to link the two regions.

Under these circumstances, few people could expect the South to stave off the Northern military offensive for more than four years. Even during the Civil War, the Union lacked actual unity. The exigencies of war brought a boom to Western farmers, fortunes to profiteers, and a decline in the real income of workers and artisans. It irreversibly altered the economy of the nation.

Readjustment and Reconstruction (1864–1876)

The first postwar decade was devoted to Reconstruction. The Federal Government had to restructure the relationships between the states of the defeated Confederacy and the triumphant Union. President Lincoln and (after his assassination) President Andrew Johnson proposed to bind the nation's wounds by restoring autonomy to the South consistent with the termination of slavery, as formulated in the Thirteenth Amendment ratified in December 1865. This charitable policy would have to be achieved at the expense of the ex-slaves.

THE SOUTH IS READMITTED

A spate of "black codes" enacted by the first popular legislatures throughout the South angered the Republicans who controlled Congress. A Freedmen's Bureau, with the function of protecting the interests of the blacks, had been set up temporarily in March 1865, and was given permanent status over Johnson's veto in July 1866. Inasmuch as the Southern representation in the House of Representatives would increase when the blacks achieved full (rather than three-fifths) representation, Congress refused to readmit the former states until they accepted the Fourteenth Amendment, which spelled out the civil rights of blacks. When all of the "sinful ten" states had "flung back into our teeth the magnanimous offer of a generous nation" (in the words of Congressman James A. Garfield), Congress passed in March 1867 a Reconstruction Act that instituted martial law throughout the South.

By the end of 1869 most of the Southern states were in the fold and the Fifteenth Amendment ratified in March 1870 gave voting privileges to all male blacks, North and South. For the next five or six years the Republican Party closely supervised the legislatures of the Southern states, imposing civil rights through a series of so-called Force Acts. Under this umbrella a combination of freedmen, white Republicans of Northern origin (derisively called "carpetbaggers"), and white Southern Republicans (who were ridiculed as "scalawags") enacted social legislation that was unacceptable to the white supremacists. When the Northern Republicans chose to relax their supervision, the unreconstructed Southern whites resumed their opposition to blacks, both through the underground Ku Klux Klan and an official Democratic Party. Around this party a political structure known as the "solid South" was firmly established.

THE NEW NORTH

The same administration that presided over Reconstruction in the South was responsible for the transformation of the North. There the main drive of the Republican Party was to serve the industrialists and financiers who were building railroads, operating steel mills, mining coal, iron, and the recently discovered petroleum, and in general developing an industrial plant suitable for a powerful modern nation. The legislation to encourage these activities, forming the essential Republican platform, included high tariffs and sound currency. Other ingredients that did not appear in party manifestoes included subsidies for the railroads, relaxation of free enterprise in favor of various patterns of monopoly, and tolerance of corruption. In this era politicians such as William Tweed were able to plunder cities of millions of dollars, slums appeared in large urban centers, and scandals on a large scale demeaned the Presidency.

The first railway from New York to Chicago had been completed in 1865, and four years later the Union Pacific and Central Pacific met in Utah Territory. Railroads had given the Union the edge in the Civil War, and they determined which communities in the West would survive to become cities. In earlier times, commerce and enterprise exemplified in the career of John Jacob Astor had built the great fortunes, but the capital accumulation that followed the Civil War was in the hands of such pioneers as the railroad builder, Cornelius Vanderbilt. Railroads also introduced coolie labor to the United States, and the first serious confrontation between capital and labor alarmed the nation when the railroad workers of the Baltimore and Ohio struck in 1877. Finally, in reaction against the ruthless power exercised in rural areas by the railroads, the Grange (a farmers' social and welfare society) turned toward lobbying for anti-railroad legislation on a state level.

The Urbanization of America (1876–1917)

The Reconstruction program formally ended as a result of the Presidential election of 1876. A depression in 1873 and 1874, revulsion against the spread of corruption, firm resistance to civil rights in the South, and even the humiliating defeat of General George Custer by the Sioux in Montana Territory combined to bring about a state of general discontent. The time had come for an understanding between the Democrats (who wished to assume political jurisdiction in the South) and the Republicans (who were frightened when the Democrats gained control of the House of Representatives in 1874, for the first time since the Civil War). In 1876 the Democratic Presidential candidate, Samuel J. Tilden, won a popular majority but was one vote short in the electoral college. A deal was made whereby the Democrats would deprive Tilden of the Presidency in favor of the Republican candidate, Rutherford B. Hayes, if Hayes would withdraw Federal troops from the South. Immediately after the withdrawal the Democrats took over the state governments in the former Confederacy, and within a few years the blacks were

tenant farmers, or sharecroppers. They were excluded by economic pressure and by force from exercising civil and political rights they had briefly acquired. The economy of the South continued to produce mainly cotton, recovering from wartime collapse but remaining outside the mainstream of postwar prosperity.

END OF THE FRONTIER

In the North and in the West that prosperity was neither under control nor equitably distributed. At the beginning of this period, which comprised the last quarter of the nineteenth century, about one-fourth of the population lived in communities exceeding twenty-five hundred inhabitants. The total population rose, with the help of some nine million immigrants, from about fifty million in 1880 to about seventy-five million in 1900. Most of the newcomers settled in rural areas and the West was settled so thoroughly that no discernible frontier existed after 1890. The plains proved as fertile as anticipated, once the range was largely enclosed and made arable; and crops were so abundant that their prices fell steadily and farmers could not live on what they produced.

PROBLEMS OF RISING REVENUES

At the same time huge fortunes were accumulated, private enterprise was short-circuited to permit the reckless manipulation of public resources. Financial crises (called "panics") recurred and credit was kept tight. Small entrepreneurs found it difficult to finance a grubstake, but magnates such as John D. Rockefeller and Andrew Carnegie organized industrial empires. The accumulation of private capital was exceeded only by that in the United States Treasury. With revenues constantly exceeding expenditures, the Federal Government no longer needed high tariffs to provide income. Tariffs favored manufacturers and made manufactured goods expensive for farmers and workers, so tariff reduction became a perennial slogan of reformers. Another catchphrase was "cheap money," which usually meant the coinage of silver, a metal increasingly produced in the West and therefore a significant commodity. Groups in every part of the country were for or against high tariffs or free coinage, and geographical sectionalism was giving way to confrontations between the Establishment–big business and big politics–and its victims.

THE 1880s AND 1890s

In three consecutive Presidential elections, 1880 through 1888, the Democratic and Republican candidates evenly shared the electorate, with less than one percentage point separating their popular votes. The Democrat, Grover Cleveland, won the Presidency in 1884. The prize went to Republicans James A. Garfield and Benjamin Harrison respectively in the preceding and following campaigns. But issues played a negligible role in each instance. During the 1890s, however, the monetary system and tariffs began to arouse interest and as tariffs rose, so did passion concerning the imposition of the "cross of gold." After the McKinley Tariff of 1890 and the Panic of 1893, the fervor

of the cheap-money partisans was expressed when an eloquent Democratic politician, William Jennings Bryan, reminded the urban gold advocates "that the great cities rest upon our broad and fertile prairies."

LABOR UNIONS

Both workers and farmers attempted to organize in the late nineteenth century. The unions, speaking for an abused minority, were suppressed or controlled by the most powerful segments of society. The mushroom growth of the Knights of Labor in the 1880s was stifled by the thrust of the American Federation of Labor as organization by craft, a narrow but more intensive base, proved more successful than organization by class. After several violent confrontations between labor and management in this period, notably at Haymarket Square in Chicago in 1886 and at the Homestead, Pennsylvania, plant of the Carnegie corporation in 1892, unionism made little progress before the turn of the century.

FARM ORGANIZATIONS

The farmers who were an abused majority, made impressive political progress. Within the Democratic Party, the Farmers' Alliances that developed from the Grange elected nine Congressmen and two Senators in 1890 and began to consider forming an independent party. The convention of the People's Party in 1892 picked a Presidential candidate who won 8.5 per cent of the popular vote and the ballots of 22 electors from four states. Their platform was based on the free coinage of silver, national ownership of rail, telegraph, and telephone facilities, a graduated income tax, an eight-hour day, and the popular election of Senators–several of which proposals were eventually adopted by the traditional parties and enacted into law. The Populists increased their strength in 1894, but in 1896 they were persuaded to endorse the Democratic candidate, Bryan. His defeat terminated third-party efforts for many decades and prolonged the ascendancy of the Republican alliance with big business.

The Spanish-American War—The Battle of Manila Bay, Philippine Islands, May 1898

THE NATION REACHES FULL GROWTH

Through a combination of aggressive enterprise, indulgent government, enormous resources, and geographical isolation, the United States emerged into the twentieth century as a major power. The gold standard and a record tariff were on the books. Farm production began to satisfy an expanding domestic market. The United States produced more steel than any country in the world. For a quarter-century the trade balance was increasingly favorable, and soon after the turn of the century the United States became a creditor rather than a debtor in the international market. The circumstances favored a new manifestation of expansionism, which had been almost dormant in the second half of the nineteenth century; only the purchase of Alaska from the Russians in 1867 significantly added to the national domain. Just before the end of the century the contagion of European imperialism spread to the Western Hemisphere. The vigorous economy would soon require new markets, new sources of raw material, new fields for the investment of capital.

THE SPANISH-AMERICAN WAR

In such an environment, the plight of the off-shore island of Cuba proved to be a catalyst. The drive to annex Cuba to the United States had diminished once the island was no longer potential slave territory. But Spain's poor administration of Cuba, in which American capital was heavily invested after the Civil War, provided a reason for intervention. More dramatic justification developed—according to some sources, was provided—when the U.S. battleship *Maine* was blown up in Havana harbor in February 1898. The Spanish-American War began in April; by August, Spain sought peace; and the treaty signed in Paris in December transferred to the United States possession of the Philippine Islands, Puerto Rico, and Guam, as well as the mandate of Cuba. In that year the annexation of the Hawaiian Islands, governed as a "republic" by Americans since 1893, was also consummated. Thus the United States found itself responsible for the administration of widely scattered dependencies inhabited by large populations whose integration into the existing American system was not contemplated.

The Spanish-American War—Wreck of the *Maine*

Emergence as a World Power (1896–1917)

The United States adopted its colonial role vigorously. The attempt by the Filipinos to assert their independence from foreign dominion was suppressed over a period of two years. Cuba was recognized as sovereign only after accepting a constitution that permitted arbitrary American intervention and after ceding Guantánamo for use as a United States military base. In the Insular Cases of 1901, the U.S. Supreme Court ruled that the acquisitions from Spain were not part of the United States, but were to be administered without representation. Hawaii, on the other hand, became a territory and received as its first governor Sanford B. Dole, its erstwhile president. The interests of the United States in China were safeguarded by the unilateral declaration of the Open Door Policy, which won international acceptance in 1900. The United States, in turn, participated in the joint effort by Western powers to suppress the Boxer Rebellion against the Chinese government.

THE BIG STICK

Assured of its status as a Caribbean and Pacific power, the United States planned to protect its interests by building a canal across Central America between the Caribbean Sea and the Pacific Ocean. This was made possible in 1903 when the province of Panama withdrew from Columbia, under the protection of the U.S. Navy. The new republic of Panama then leased a canal zone to United States in perpetuity. United States armed forces were used to protect the interests of businessmen and investors in Santo Domingo in 1905, in Cuba from 1906 through 1909, in Nicaragua in 1909, and in Haiti in 1915.

Perhaps more significant than the establishment of Caribbean protectorates was the extension of the Monroe Doctrine by the so-called Roosevelt Corollary of 1904, which proclaimed the intention of the United States to intervene anywhere in Latin America when local authorities appeared incapable of maintaining law and order. Mexico was a target of this policy during its revolution that began in 1911. President Wilson announced that he would recognize only a chief executive who

had been legally elected. In 1914 he dispatched a force to seize Veracruz on a pretext. When Francisco Villa, one of the generals contending for the Mexican presidency, led raids across the border in 1916 to retaliate against the incursion into his country, Wilson sent an American contingent on a counterraid that provoked the indignation of Villa's opponent, President Venustiano Carranza.

PROGRESSIVE POLITICS

The display of energy in foreign policy during the first decade of the twentieth century was matched by a zeal to loosen the ties between big business and the government. The change in policy was a reaction to abuses by such tycoons as J. P. Morgan, John D. Rockefeller, and the railroad magnates James J. Hill and E. H. Harriman, all of whom combined to create a massive trust known as Northern .Securities. The Progressive movement led by Congressman Robert M. La Follette weakened monopolies on the state level, and national leaders presented themselves as enemies of corporate arrogance. In 1902 President Theodore Roosevelt used the Sherman Antitrust Act to break up Northern Securities, which gave him the reputation of a "trust-buster." Other accomplishments of his Administration included regulative agencies and legislation, such as the Interstate Commerce Commission and the Pure Food and Drug Act, both in 1906. The succeeding Administration of William Howard Taft attempted to stem the Progressive trend in the Republican Party, driving Roosevelt into opposition.

The political feud within the Republican camp gave the Presidency in 1912 to Woodrow Wilson, the first Democrat other than Cleveland to achieve that office since the Civil War. Wilson rode the Progressive tide under the slogan of the New Freedom. The major domestic achievement during his first term was the ratification in 1912 of the Sixteenth Amendment, which imposed an income tax and thus met a major objective of the Populist movement. Wilson convinced Congress to strengthen the drive against monopoly in 1914 by passing the Clayton Antitrust Act, which specifically exempted trade unions from classification as a "trust," and by creating the Federal Trade Commission. Other reforms and changes in direction under Wilson's purposeful leadership included reorganization of the banking system under the Federal Reserve Act of 1913. Wilson provided Federal aid in the building of highways in 1916 as it became evident that the automobile was here to stay.

DRIFT TOWARD WAR

The course of developing the New Freedom was interrupted by events in Europe, where rival blocs were competing for control of the world's markets. In the approaching showdown between the long-established colonial powers–Great Britain, France, and Russia (the Allies) and the less stable empires of Germany and Austria-Hungary (the Central Powers)–the United States had little interest. But as in the nineteenth-century contest between Great Britain and Napoleonic France, neutrality was difficult to maintain. British conduct toward neutral shipping was often as high-handed as that of the Germans, yet the German embargo of the British Isles threatened the

flourishing commerce between Great Britain and the United States. Britain's status as a major customer made it possible for the United States to overlook minor breaches. On the other hand, the Germans had no weapons other than submarines to enforce its blockade, so it inevitably brought about innocent American deaths on the high seas. This swept the United States into the camp of the Allies. Wilson, who was reelected in 1916 because "he kept us out of war," asked Congress for a declaration of war in April 1917; and the United States entered the First World War–not as an "ally," but as an "associated power."

FIRST WORLD WAR

The nation met its responsibilities as a belligerent with efficiency; it accepted unprecedented restrictions on its economy and liberty. The War Industries Board concentrated the forces of industry, agriculture, and manpower. Civilians were conscripted into the armed forces, and the Committee on Public Information mobilized public opinion. Once the war was over, the American people found them so uncomfortable that they rallied around the slogan of a "return to normalcy."

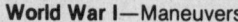

World War I—Maneuvers

World War I—Capt. Eddie Rickenbacker and his Spad Airplane

Between World Wars (1918–1945)

Nevertheless the First World War transformed the United States into a world power, and President Wilson became for a season the hero of the victorious Allies. The Fourteen Points proposed by Wilson to Congress in January 1918 as a peace platform became the framework for peace negotiations in which he participated personally at Versailles in 1919, winning the Nobel Prize for peace en route. He was responsible for formulating a Covenant for a League of Nations that was incorporated into the proposed peace treaty. Its purpose was to set up a forum where a stabilized world could conduct international business without recourse to arms. When the treaty, with its Covenant, was brought to the Senate for ratification in March 1920, it was passed by a majority short of the required two-thirds. Wilson was unable to convert either the Senate or the electorate to his vi-

sion. The United States recoiled from the possibility of compromising a particle of its sovereignty. In 1921 a relatively unknown Republican Senator, Warren G. Harding, became the first "dark horse" of the century to achieve the Presidency in the first election in which women were eligible to vote. The country turned back to business as usual.

DECADE OF PROSPERITY

The relaxation of discipline was sudden. The armed forces were demobilized, the railroads were returned to private control, tariffs were raised to peak levels and extended to protect industries that had not existed in prewar days and crops never before shielded. Taxes that confiscated fortunes

The *Question Mark*, a Fokker C-2, with the help of a refueling plane
sets an endurance record of almost 151 hours in 1929.

were repealed and monopolistic practices were revived. These changes brought a decade of unprecedented prosperity. Among the contributing factors were a population of well over one hundred million, more than half of whom were urban; advances in technology, particularly in chemistry and the use of electric power; above all the development of the automobile, which paralleled in its economic and social influence the development of the railroad in the mid-nineteenth century. Just as the automobile increased the mobility of persons and goods, so the new medium of radio increased the spread of information. The broadcasting network exemplified the complex modern enterprise, just as the marketplaces of the land were being forged into linked chains. Transportation, communications, and merchandising assumed their modern characteristics, and in turn stimulated such industries as steel, glass, rubber, oil, and advertising. Only the liquor industry was depressed, for during the war the temperance movement convinced the American people of the evils of alcohol. Prohibition became effective one year after the ratification of the Eighteenth Amendment in January 1919.

DRIFT TOWARD DEPRESSION

The United States did not cut itself off entirely from the world. The nation's role on the world stage required its involvement in international trade. Although production and credit were expanding rapidly within the United States after the war, these activities were disrupted on the world scene by maneuvers around the war debt and reparations. Perhaps the inequitable distribution of wealth aggravated the difficulties. In any case, the world's consuming market could no longer profitably absorb the abundance produced. A panic in the stock exchange in September and October 1929, preceded a rapid decline in business activity and employment. The ensuing depression spread from the United States throughout the world. Its effects were profound. It altered the course of American economy and internationally contributed to the political circumstances that led directly to the Second World War.

The Wall Street "crash" occurred seven months after President Herbert Hoover's inauguration, at which he predicted the final victory over poverty. The remainder of Hoover's Administration was engaged in an effort to achieve recovery in a manner consistent with Republican policies. Government could intervene in the private economy sector only if it benefited business, for prosperous industry was considered the prerequisite to general prosperity. Accordingly, the Reconstruction Finance Corporation (RFC) was created in January 1932, with the mission of distributing Federal funds where they would presumably do the most good. Banks and big business received help. Direct relief to victims of the economic disaster was not within the jurisdiction of the RFC.

THE NEW DEAL

This program did not appeal to the stricken electorate. They returned the Democratic Party to power by voting for Franklin D. Roosevelt as Pres-

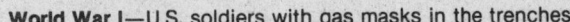

World War I—U.S. soldiers going over the top

World War I—U.S. soldiers with gas masks in the trenches

ident. The crisis of bank failures in 1933 coincided with his inauguration, but Roosevelt told his countrymen that they had "nothing to fear but fear itself." In this spirit of indomitable optimism, a series of bold, innovative measures were directly addressed to the catastrophe. Roosevelt's program, known as the New Deal, included relief for the farmer in the Agricultural Adjustment Act (AAA), for small as well as big business in the National Industrial Recovery Act (NIRA), for the youthful unemployed in the Civilian Conservation Corps (CCC) and the National Youth Administration (NYA), and for jobless adults in the Public Works Administration and successively in the Civil Works, Works Progress, and Work Projects administrations (CWA, WPA). Insurance against bank failures was guaranteed by the Federal Deposit Insurance Corporation (FDIC); and insurance against the effects of severed income was provided in the Social Security system, which also fostered the passage of state unemployment insurance laws. Collective bargaining between management and labor was encouraged by the National Labor Relations Act. The proliferation of what became known as "alphabet agencies" continued. Most of them survived the constitutional test, although the Supreme Court struck down NIRA and AAA. This led to a logistic attack against the Court by Roosevelt, usually referred to as "packing" the Court. Although neither the Constitution nor tradition limited the number of Justices, Roosevelt's lunge proved unpopular. After a series of Court rulings more favorable to the New Deal, the "packing" attempt was abandoned.

At first the business community supported the New Deal. But when the safety of the capitalist system was assured, Roosevelt began to lose business approval. On the other hand, a powerful new labor organization, the Committee for (later Congress of) Industrial Organization (CIO), arose within the established American Federation of Labor (AFL). The CIO organized workers by industry rather than according to craft in the AFL tradition. Spurred by favorable legislation and a friendly government, the unions almost tripled their membership in the eight years after 1933, and could be numbered safely in the Democratic fold. Most of the voting blacks were in Northern working-class precincts and were likely to find more in common with the party of Roosevelt than with the Republicans, whose ties with Lincoln appeared tenuous. Additional support for Roosevelt was gained when, in 1933, the Twenty-First Amendment repealed Prohibition; this reform had been in the Democratic platform. The Depression lingered on despite the best efforts of the first two Administrations of Franklin Roosevelt; yet the New Deal remained popular and even the Republican candidate in 1940, Wendell Willkie, did not attack it in principle. Roosevelt easily won an unprecedented third term. To a great degree, however, his foreign policy accounted for his victory in 1940. The Second World War was already under way, sending shock waves across both oceans. The American people felt it was no time to change leadership.

WAR CLOUDS AGAIN

During the first two Roosevelt Administrations, Adolf Hitler had risen to power over Europe and made a partnership in an anticommunist axis with

World War II—A montage of photographs depicting the attack of Pearl Harbor

SECOND WORLD WAR

imperial Japan and fascist Italy. This aroused mixed reactions among Americans. Antipathy toward communism prevailed in the United States, which waited 16 years to recognize the obviously stable government of the Soviet Union. However, few Americans considered the dictators of Italy and Germany and the martial emperor of Japan champions of enlightened capitalism. They observed with distaste the ruthless treatment of Jews and dissidents in Germany, Italy's conquest of Ethiopia, the cynical participation of Italian and German troops in Spain's civil war, and the even more cynical absorption of Austria and Czechoslovakia by Hitler. On the other hand, sentiments of neutralism were strong. This caused the United States to play an ambiguous role toward Spain, to abstain from participation in the League of Nations, and to observe with aloofness the Japanese aggression against China. The Soviet Union, perhaps aware that anticommunist Europe was willing to support Hitler in an eastward drive, formed an alliance with Hitler in 1939. Most of Western Europe was overrun by the Nazis in 1940, and the United States prepared to face the imminent danger, adopting peacetime conscription for the first time in September 1940. Modest aid was tendered to Great Britain. The neutrality laws were revised. And in anticipation of the approaching Presidential campaign, Roosevelt named Republicans to the sensitive Navy and War posts in his cabinet.

Only after the Hawaiian Islands were directly attacked by the Japanese on December 7, 1941, did the United States enter the Second World War. The nation immediately became the "arsenal of democracy," and its contribution of goods and personnel undoubtedly assured the reversal of Axis aggression. Once more the entire economy was geared to a single task, this time under the Office of War Mobilization. The vast production capacity was now fully utilized, bringing an end to the Depression and even restoring prosperity to the farmers, who had languished since the end of the First World War in near-poverty. Organized labor, committed to abstain from striking for the duration, enrolled members at an accelerating pace. Among these were large numbers of women and black ex-sharecroppers who had found factory jobs in Northern cities. The prosecution of the war was conducted with enthusiasm. President Roosevelt, elected to a fourth term in 1944, maintained active leadership, attending countless conferences. These began in August 1941, with a secret meeting between Roosevelt and British Prime Minister Winston Churchill on the high seas to formulate the Atlantic Charter. This document became the basis of the United Nations Declaration of January 1942. Summit meetings of the allied leaders continued in 1943 at Casablanca, Cairo, and Teheran. The meeting at Yalta in February 1945, was

World War II—"D" Day, U.S. troops land on a beachhead in Northern France.

World War II—U.S. 3rd Infantry Division passes the shattered remains of a German convoy.

World War II—Nagasaki, Japan, following the explosion of the second U.S. atomic bomb.

World War II—Japanese Foreign Minister Mamoru Shigemitsu signs surrender terms on board the U.S.S. *Missouri*.

World War II—U.S. military personnel gather in Paris to celebrate the end of the war.

the last attended by Roosevelt, whose death in April placed his Vice-President, Harry S. Truman, in charge of the peacemaking activities.

THE BOMB AND THE UNITED NATIONS

Before the war was concluded, President Truman made the fateful decision to drop the first atomic bombs in history, over the Japanese cities of Hiroshima and Nagasaki, on August 6 and 9, 1945. This event occurred three months after the Germans had surrendered and a few days after the conclusion of the Potsdam Conference, at which the organization of the postwar world was discussed by those who would be in charge.

Meanwhile, from April to June 1945, the United States hosted a meeting in San Francisco of the nations which had signed the 1942 declaration concerning war aims. These nations now signed a charter establishing a new international organization to "maintain international peace and security," to "develop friendly relations among nations," and in general to reincarnate the League of Nations in the coming era. The United States was a charter member of this organization, the United Nations. The prospects for the international community after the Second World War seemed more promising than those for the peoples of the world after the First World War.

The Cold War (1946–1972)

Before the surrender of Japan on September 2, 1945, the friendship among the allies began to fray, revealing a schism between its communist and anticommunist members. It soon became apparent that the powers would divide into two blocs, led by the surviving superpowers, the United States and the Soviet Union. All the nations were weary of war and no power on earth would dare provoke the United States to demonstrate once more that its nuclear monopoly could bring intolerable destruction. The Soviet Union, however, chose not to relinquish this unique opportunity to establish a tier of buffer states around its heartland. Therefore, there ensued a condition between belligerency and amity between the two major powers that came to be known as "cold war."

TRUMAN DOCTRINE AND MARSHALL PLAN

Each bloc attempted to blame the other for the onset of this unwelcome atmosphere. In one version, the declaration of this "war" was attributed to Churchill, who made a speech at Fulton, Missouri, on March 5, 1946. There he described an "iron curtain" stretching across Europe from the Baltic to the Adriatic, dividing the contending camps. A year later the United States opened what may be viewed as an offensive in the contest–the proclamation of the Truman Doctrine, in the tradition of the Monroe Doctrine and the Roosevelt Corollary. President Truman declared in March 1947 (on the occasion of providing aid to the Greek government against communist insurgents) that it would be "the policy of the United States to support free peoples who are resisting attempted subjugation by armed minorities or by outside pressures." This formula was soon abbreviated to the concept of "containment" of communism. In June 1947, Secretary of State George Marshall proposed a plan to provide economic aid to the devastated countries of Europe, without discrimination. The Soviet government refused aid on behalf of its client states. Certain beneficiaries of the Marshall Plan banded together in 1949 as the North Atlantic Treaty Organization (NATO), which functioned as the military arm of the anticommunist bloc in Europe.

The first overt clash between the blocs in Europe occurred over Berlin, a disputed enclave geographically within the communist-occupied sector of

Germany. The United States supported the besieged city with an impressive airlift in 1948 and 1949. As a result, each bloc took control of a part of the former capital, and before the end of 1949 two Germanies were established as independent countries.

KOREA AND INDOCHINA

The decisive military superiority of the anticommunist camp ended when the Soviet Union demonstrated its own atomic capacity in 1949. In the same year communist power expanded with the military victory of the forces of Mao Tse-tung in China. In 1950 the communist North Koreans attacked the anticommunist South Koreans. Although the military defense of the anticommunist cause was undertaken by the United Nations (during a brief boycott of the organization by the Soviet Union), the actual conduct of the ensuing Korean War was led by the United States. China became involved and the fighting ended in a truce in 1953 that restored the lines breached in 1950.

General Dwight D. Eisenhower, supreme Allied commander in Europe during the Second World War and more recently supreme commander of the NATO forces in Europe, was elected President in 1953 to succeed Truman. One of his preelection promises was to end the war in Korea. He kept this promise. He also restrained his Secretary of State, John Foster Dulles, from providing the French in Indochina with more than economic aid in their effort to regain their colony in that area. When the French were expelled in 1954, however, Eisenhower was convinced that the Indochinese independence movement with headquarters in Hanoi was completely under communist control. During his Administration an anticommunist regime was established in Saigon with United States help. This regime proved unstable, but its maintenance as an anticommunist nucleus was considered essential. It received ever-increasing military and economic aid and finally the reinforcement of manpower. The Southeast Asia Treaty Organization was set up in 1954 in the NATO pattern. Its futility was matched only by the so-called Eisenhower Doctrine in support of any nation in the Middle East that should request aid "against armed aggression from any country controlled by international communism." In 1961 President John F. Kennedy inherited not only a bellicose policy against the communist bastion in Cuba, but also the execution of an ill-conceived military expedition against Cuba. In 1962 Kennedy compelled the Soviet Union to desist from its projected buildup of missiles in Cuba.

The Korean War—U.S. paratroopers descend on a designated location.

The Korean War—A railroad depot in North Korea minutes after being bombed by U.S. planes

BALANCE OF POWER

As the scope of the cold war widened and confrontations increased, both camps became aware of their roles. The communists, in a mirror image of the Truman Doctrine, declared that they would aid any war of "national liberation." Although nuclear war was intolerable, conventional (or "brushfire") wars could be waged. Meanwhile, both camps were subject to internal stress. Two of the anticommunist powers, France and Great Britain, joined Israel in attempting to seize the Suez Canal in 1956. The United States and the Soviet Union joined to support the United Nations' condemnation of the aggression against Egypt. On the other hand, a rift developed and widened between the Soviet and Chinese communists. Each of these major sections of the communist camp competed for goodwill within the Third World, as the uncommitted or unaligned nations–many of them liberated ex-colonies–came to be called. Finally, in the 1960s, the growing stability of China and its potential capacity to wield atomic warfare began to alter the polarity of the contest, and a triangular balance of power began to emerge. This fluid situation was of little advantage to the United States. After decades of costly effort in Indochina, the United States was left with only the certainty of defeat and diminished status.

The United Nations constantly admitted members of the Third World who tended to drift toward one of the communist groupings and almost never were attracted to the anticommunist camp. The United States found itself in the unaccustomed role of spokesman for a minority. The Nixon and Ford Administrations looked to Secretary of State Henry Kissinger as the architect of their foreign policy. They sought to adjust to the situation by establishing a détente with the Soviet Union and initiating modified diplomatic relations with China. This reversal of policy was exemplified by the admission of the People's Republic of China to the United Nations in 1971 and by an agreement with the Soviet Union in 1972 to limit the use of strategic missiles.

The Korean War—U.S. troops in action

SPACE RACE

The competition between the Soviet Union and the United States for political power on earth was paralleled by a race for the exploitation of space. The development of missiles led directly to the production of artificial satellites. The Soviet Union sent the first satellite into orbit on October 4, 1957, and less than four months later the United States sent its first satellite around the earth. The Soviet Union first made physical impact on the moon in 1959 and first sent a man into orbit in 1961, but the United States was the first to land a man on the moon's surface in 1969. The rivalry was officially terminated by a joint manned space mission in July 1975. But the competitors still covet the military and intelligence by-products that continue to accrue.

THE HOME FRONT HEATS UP

The cold war had a pronounced effect on the domestic affairs of the United States, from the Truman through the Nixon Administrations. So Under the cloak of anticommunism, dissidence of every sort was repressed. Landmark events were the "loyalty" check of government employes instituted in 1947 by Truman, the indictment of communists under the Smith Act in 1949, the enactment of the Subversive Activities Control Act and the Internal Security Act in 1950, and the series of investigations conducted or inspired by Senator Joseph McCarthy from 1950 to 1954.

Several minority groups–particularly blacks –crusaded for more civil rights in the 1950s and 1960s. The Supreme Court decision of 1954, *Brown v. Board of Education of Topeka,* reversed the 1896 ruling of *Plessy v. Ferguson* by declaring unconstitutional the segregation of blacks in public schools. This was followed by a vigorous movement to enforce and amplify the full exercise of black citizenship. The Montgomery, Alabama bus boycott began in 1955 to assert the right of blacks to equal public accommodations. It was the opening skirmish on behalf of civil rights led by the Reverend Martin Luther King, Jr., and his Southern Christian Leadership Conference. The struggle against segregation continued in its nonviolent phase as Freedom Riders tested the manner in which legal victories were translated into practice. This phase reached its climax in a mass march on Washington in 1963. A more militant phase of the movement attempted to enforce the political rights of blacks, culminating in a spectacular march from Selma to Montgomery, Alabama in 1965.

Simultaneously resistance to the war in Indochina began to peak. The antiwar and civil rights movements merged, resulting in the so-called "revolt on the campus" and the street tumult coinciding with the 1968 Democratic national convention in Chicago. Both President Lyndon Johnson and President Richard Nixon were disturbed by the rising discontent.

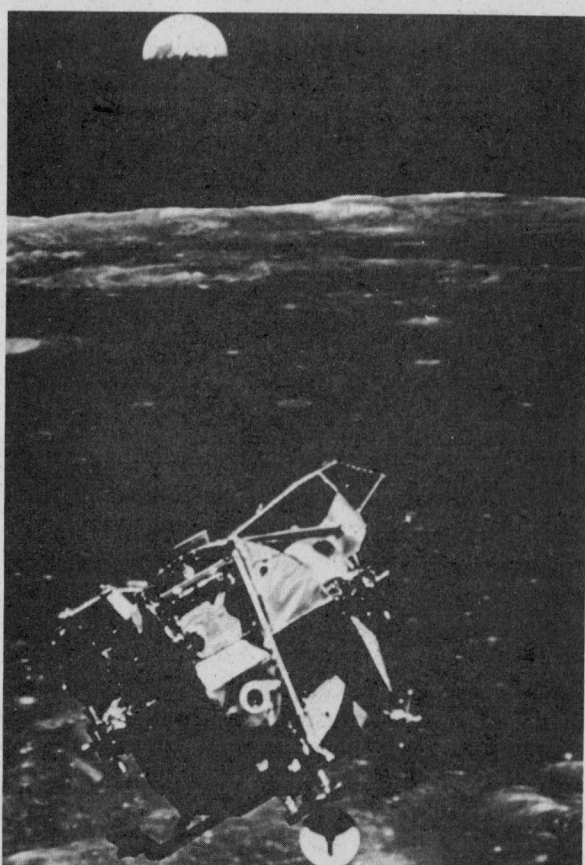

Astronaut Edwin E. Aldrin, Jr. stands alongside the U.S. flag deployed by him and Astronaut Neil A. Armstrong after they landed on the moon in *Apollo 11*.

The *Apollo 11* Lunar Module ascent stage on its way to a docking rendezvous prior to returning to earth.

An *Apollo 12* astronaut examines the TV camera on the surface of the moon. The Lunar Module is in the background.

Apollo 15 Astronaut James B. Irwin rides on the surface of the moon in the Lunar Rover.

The Skylab II Space Station, photographed from the Command Module.

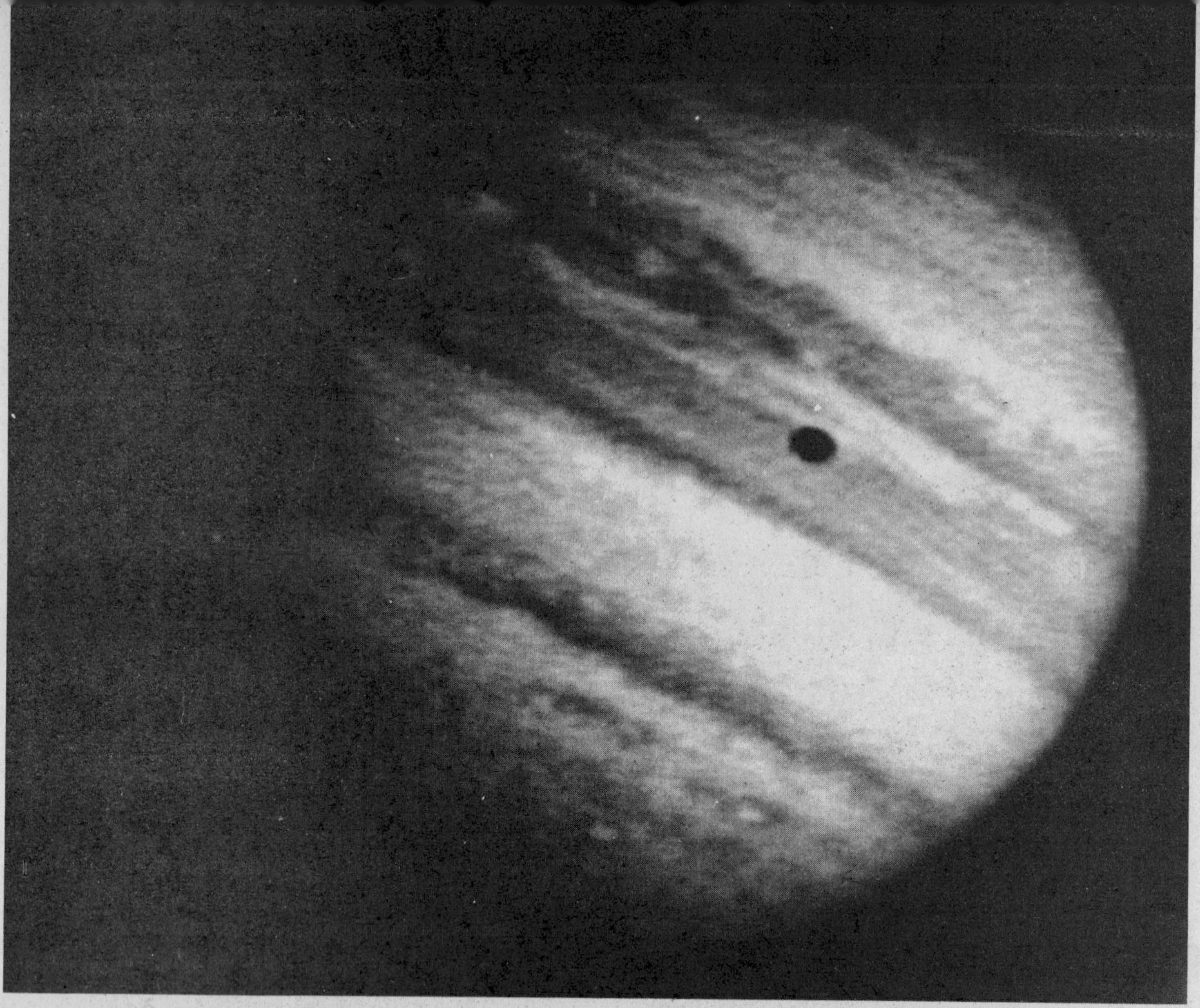

Jupiter's red spot and a shadow of the moon as photographed by *Pioneer 10*

Civil Rights Demonstration
Montgomery, Alabama, March 17, 1965

Dr. Martin Luther King, Jr.

Profile of a Superpower Since 1955

After the Second World War, the United States recovered economically far more robustly than in the period after the First World War. Following an interval of mild recession and readjustment, an upswing began during the first Eisenhower Administration with the end of the Korean War. The real gross national product in 1955 was more than twice that of 1929, and the Federal balance for fiscal 1955 and 1956 showed a surplus. Eisenhower warned of the rise of a "military-industrial complex." He was succeeded in 1961 by John F. Kennedy, whose ambitious domestic program included considerable social legislation, conservation, and accelerated space exploration. Alhough the Mercury, Gemini, and Apollo projects were virtually completed in the Kennedy and Johnson Administrations, the struggle in Indochina depleted the resources of the country at the expense of the social reforms. It so undermined the "war on poverty" declared in 1964 by President Johnson that the "great society" had to be aborted.

In November 1967, the population of the United States reached 200 million. This was double the population during the First World War, when the country first became predominantly urban. By 1967 about three-fourths of the population lived in cities. An unusually large proportion of the population were immigrants or offspring of recent immigrants, who tended to settle in urban areas. Of the 32 million immigrants who arrived in the United States by 1920, those who came before 1900 were mostly from the countries of northern Europe, but thereafter an increasing proportion came from southern and eastern Europe and were considered less capable of being assimilated. A similar attitude toward the influx of Chinese and Japanese unskilled labor in the second half of the nineteenth century resulted in discriminatory immigration laws and even total exclusion. An immigration act of 1924 restricted the proportion of south and east Europeans who could acquire permanent residence. This policy was reversed in 1965, essentially by altering the primary basis of admission from country of origin to the skill of the immigrant.

TECHNOLOGICAL INFLUENCES

At the turn of the century the highway began to take the place of the railroad as the principal mode of transport. After the Second World War, passengers and freight began to take to the air. In the aerospace age, automation was augmented by computer technology. Mobility increased and the population dispersed geographically. As manufacturing had previously gained at the expense of agriculture, now the service industries and the government bureaucracies began to draw workers away from the farms, mines, and factories. The surplus of products required new markets, either at home or abroad, while personal income failed to keep pace. Government intervention attempted to cushion the effects of inflation and a rising rate of unemployment.

POLITICAL CHANGES

The increasing role of the Federal government and tension between the executive and legislative branches of government became controversial during the third quarter of the twentieth century. The spectrum in both political parties ran from liberal to conservative; each party had a contingent favoring the reduction of government power, whether in central or local sphere. Services were expected from government, but they were costly and offered excessive opportunity for corruption. Conservatives generally proposed that the Federal Government shed its bureaucracies and allow local communities to monitor their own affairs. Liberals preferred to make sure that hard-won benefits would not be lost. Many sought a balance between laissez faire and the welfare state, and debated whether to entrust significant areas of administration to city hall, the state house, or the District of Columbia. "Strong" Presidents were somewhat out of favor, largely because of the abuse of power revealed in the aftermath of the Watergate scandal of Nixon's Administration. However, few believed that Congress could pro-

A caisson bearing the body of the assassinated black leader, Martin Luther King, Jr.

vide the world's most powerful and richest country with the leadership demanded by the contemporary situation.

CONSTITUTIONAL CHANGES

During the twentieth century, flaws in the political process were corrected several times by amendments to the Constitution, a procedure that had already rationalized the mode of Presidential elections with the Twelfth Amendment. The Seventeenth Amendment, ratified in 1913, required direct popular election of Senators instead of their selection by state legislatures. This reform was adopted after 29 of the 48 states had already passed laws compelling their legislatures to do this. In 1967 new procedures for Presidential succession in an emergency were incorporated in the Twenty-fifth Amendment. The heart attacks of President Eisenhower (during which Vice-President Nixon had tentatively assumed Executive authority) and the lingering disability of Presidents Garfield and Wilson stimulated the reform. The amendment defined the circumstances under which Presidential duties may be assumed by the Vice-President, and also prescribed the filling of a Vice-Presidential vacancy. An occasion for utilizing the Twenty-fifth Amendment occurred in 1973, when a criminal indictment forced Vice-President Spiro Agnew to resign. Nixon then appointed Congressman Gerald Ford to replace Ag-

new. In 1974, President Nixon also resigned and Ford succeeded to the Presidency; he in turn appointed Nelson Rockefeller to the Vice-Presidency. Thus from 1974 through 1976 the executive branch was headed by unelected but duly constituted chiefs.

TEST OF MATURITY

In general, the Constitutional procedures served well. The black population gained appropriate political power largely in the courts and by using the rights to petition, assemble, and speak freely. It took the Twenty-fourth Amendment in 1964 to eliminate the poll tax, long an instrument for denying the franchise. The threat of impeachment forced President Nixon to resign when his role in obstructing justice was established. Convictions were handed down against some of Nixon's most powerful associates in the Watergate affair. This proved to many Americans that the Constitutional process works creditably. Others, however, were so disgusted by the deeds of recent Administrations that they shunned politics altogether.

The United States entered its bicentennial year soberly, knowing that the fate of the Western world depended on the kind of example it could provide. Its economy was faltering but did not appear likely to disintegrate. Its enemies were divided; its friends were critical but could be rallied; its own population was frustrated but capable. At

Vietnam War—U.S. troops guard captured Vietcong soldiers.

Vietnam War—U.S. troops move into action.

the nation's two-hundredth birthday the United States faced inexorable tests of its maturity.

Thus it seemed quite appropriate that 1976 should be an election year. After a hotly contested round of primaries, Georgia's Governor James Earl ("Jimmy") Carter emerged as the Democratic presidential choice. The Republicans rallied around Gerald Ford, hoping that his experience in the White House would earn official sanction at the ballot box. Carter promised to reduce unemployment and turn back the tide of inflation. He pledged to bring Washington a government that was "as good, decent, and honest as the American people themselves"—an appeal to the voters disgruntled by Watergate. On the other hand, Ford proposed to continue the policy of détente with the Soviet Union, and he predicted that the economic problems at home would take care of themselves as America developed more of its own energy resources.

Carter won the election, but soon discovered how hard it was to deliver what he'd promised. The high cost of oil, a long miners' strike in the coal industry and a series of harsh winters pushed inflation ahead. The Carter Administration created thousands of new public-service jobs, but not enough to absorb the growing number of unemployed people. Congress balked at the President's proposal to streamline the Federal government. Labor unions rejected his pleas to soften their wage demands. The public reacted skeptically to the Administration's treaty with Panamanian President Omar Trujilos, which would give the Canal Zone back to Panama by the year 2000. (The treaty passed Congress by a slim margin.) All in all, Carter fared poorly during his first year in the White House.

As time went on, Carter made better progress in foreign affairs. In a surprise move, he invited Egyptian President Anwar Sadat and Israeli Prime Minister Menachem Begin to a summit conference at Camp David in September 1978. There they drafted a "Framework for Peace in the Middle East" and vowed to sign a formal peace treaty within three months. American envoys met Soviet negotiators for a second series of Strategic Arms Limitation Talks (SALT), to hammer out an agreement on sophisticated new weapon systems.

Meanwhile, President Carter bargained with Japanese and Arab leaders in an effort to right America's balance of trade. Economic problems became a major concern of the Carter administration, in both the domestic and foreign arenas.

A group of Iranian students seized the United States embassy in Tehran on November 4, 1979, beginning one of the most tense confrontations of Carter's Administration. The students held 50 hostages for several months, ignoring the pleas of the United Nations and the new Islamic government of Iran.

Five divisions of Soviet troops invaded Afghanistan on January 3, 1980 to replace the socialist government of President Hafi-zulla Amin with leaders who would be more responsive to Russia's directives. The United States protested the invasion.

AMERICAN GOVERNMENT

The U.S. Constitution separates the powers of government as a safeguard against dictatorship. You will note that Article I of the Constitution begins with the phrase: "All legislative powers herein granted shall be vested in a Congress . . . ." Article II begins with a parallel phrase: "The executive power shall be vested in a President . . . ," while Article III states: "The judicial power of the United States shall be vested in one Supreme Court, and in . . . inferior courts. . . ." Each of these branches is independent of the others.

THE EXECUTIVE BRANCH

The office of the President has developed over the years. Many changes have taken place in the method of electing the President. The authors of the Constitution wanted to avoid having the President chosen directly by the people; they feared the public would not know the qualifications of the candidate and might choose unwisely. Consequently, they provided that every four years each state should select "electors" equal in number to the total number of the state's representatives and senators in Congress. These presidential electors would use their own judgment in electing a President and Vice-President, voting as they saw fit. Groups of electors (known as "electoral colleges") would meet in the capitals of their respective states and cast their ballots for President and Vice-President, writing two names on each ballot. The votes of the electoral colleges would then be sent to the president of the Senate, who would open and count the votes. The candidate who received a majority of all of the electoral votes cast would be declared the President-elect; the candidate with the next highest number would be the Vice-President-elect.

This system was soon changed. By 1800 two political parties had grown up, each putting forth its own candidates for office. Electors were pledged to one of these parties. They became "rubber stamps" who cast the state's electoral vote for the candidate of the party they represented. Today each party chooses a slate of electors; most voters in the state don't know them. On Election Day, voters continue to choose electors, convinced that the elector will vote for the candidate whom the voter wants. However, in the elections of 1948, 1956, 1960, 1968, and 1972 a few electors exercised their constitutional rights and voted for candidates of their own choice rather than that of the voters.

Political parties brought another important change in the method of electing the President. In 1796, John Adams became our second President because he had received the largest number of electoral college votes. Thomas Jefferson became the Vice-President, even though he and Adams were of different political parties. Furthermore, if each elector wrote on his ballot the names of the two candidates of his political party, a tie for first place might easily result. (This actually happened in 1800. The election went to the House of Representatives, where Thomas Jefferson was chosen on the thirty-sixth ballot.)

To remedy these defects, Amendment XII was added to the Constitution in 1804. It provided that the President and Vice-President be chosen on separate ballots.

Many voters dislike the electoral college system because it can elect a "minority President" who has not received even 50 percent of the popular vote. Each state's entire electoral vote goes to the candidate who polls the most votes in the state, no matter how narrow the margin of victory over his opponent. Consequently, a candidate can receive a majority of the popular vote and yet fail to win the election. This happened in 1888, when Grover Cleveland had clear majority over Benjamin Harrison, yet Harrison became President because he had more of the electoral college votes. Harrison carried the states with a large electoral vote, while Cleveland carried the states with a small electoral vote.

Reformers have often tried to make the method of electing a President more democratic. One proposal is to elect the President directly by popular vote, abolishing the electoral college. Another has been to divide each state's electoral vote among the candidates according to the popular vote.

Powers of the President

On the White House desk of President Harry S. Truman was a small sign that read, "The buck stops here." This meant that the President had to make the final decisions about a tremendous number of problems which arose each day. The Presidency has been called "the world's biggest job." As a matter of fact, it is really six different jobs:

1. The President as Chief Administrator. The Constitution states: "The executive power shall be vested in a President of the United States of America." This includes primarily the job of enforcing the laws. However, this duty is so great that the President must delegate some of this power. The President is the head of nearly two and a half million federal employees who run the approximately 2,200 government departments, bureaus, boards, and other administrative agencies.

Directly under his command is the executive office of the President. Included in this office are several staff agencies. The White House office itself includes the President's press secretary, a legal counsel, a correspondence secretary, an appointments secretary, and a number of political, legislative, and administrative aides.

The President's chief lieutenants are the eleven members of his cabinet, who head the Departments of State; Treasury; Defense; Justice; Interior; Agriculture; Commerce; Labor; Health, Education and Welfare; Housing and Urban Development; Transportation.

Four presidential staff agencies work closely with the President:

A. *Office of Management and Budget.* The director of the budget advises the President on the fiscal requirements of the many government agencies. The Bureau advises him about legislation that concerns the costs of operating these agencies. The Office of Management and Budget has been called "Chief Housekeeper," since it tries to improve the efficiency of the Administration.

B. *Council of Economic Advisors.* This board is made up of three members who advise the President concerning economic trends. It also suggests new laws regarding the economy of the nation and helps the President prepare reports on the economic state of the nation.

C. *National Security Council.* This is an important agency concerned with national defense. It includes the Secretary of State, Secretary of Defense, director of the Central Intelligence Agency, and the director of the Office of Emergency Preparedness. It is the nation's top strategy planning body, meeting weekly with the President and Vice-President.

D. *Office of Emergency Preparedness.* This staff agency advises the President on the status of our country's raw materials, manpower, industry, military and civilian defense. It also coordinates, directs, and plans all civil and defense mobilization.

In addition to these agencies and departments, a number of others work closely with the President. These include the United States Information Agency, the Veterans' Administration, the Small Business Administration, and others.

Lastly, there are the many so-called independent agencies created by Congress. These include the Civil Aeronautics Board, the Atomic Energy Commission, the Interstate Commerce Commission, and the Federal Power Commission. These are formally part of the executive branch. (In theory, the constitution was designed to prevent executive, legislative, and judical power from being concentrated within any one of our three branches. However, these agencies do function in all three areas. They make rules, judge offenders, and execute their own laws.)

2. The President as Legislator. In spite of the separation of powers, our Chief Executive has important law-making powers. The Constitution states that the President "shall from time to time give to the Congress information on the State of the Union, and recommend to their consideration such measures as he shall judge necessary and expedient." This is how the President plays a major note in shaping national legislation. The President appears before Congress and urges legislation he considers important. The Constitution gives him the power to veto bills of which he does not approve. Congress usually cannot muster the two-thirds vote necessary to pass a bill over the President's veto. So Congress usually writes a bill to be in line with what the White House will accept.

3. The President as Chief Diplomat. In today's troubled world, the conduct of foreign relations may well be the President's most vital role. He appoints United States diplomats to their overseas posts, with the advice and consent of the Senate. The Constitution gives him also the responsibility of receiving foreign ambassadors. This involves the important power to recognize foreign governments. After the Communist revolution in 1917, Presidents Coolidge and Hoover refused to receive a Russian ambassador, thus refusing to recognize the Soviet government. Furthermore, the President has the power to make treaties, which must be approved by two-thirds of the Senate. However, he can also make executive agreements which do not require Senate approval. In 1939, for instance, President Roosevelt traded fifty United States destroyers to Great Britain for island bases without the Senate's approval.

4. The President as Chief of State. Unlike members of Congress, the President represents all Americans rather than those of a particular section. He appears at important public ceremonies. He is in a unique position to help mold public thinking, through press conferences, radio, and television. Presidents Franklin D. Roosevelt and Jimmy Carter, for example, used "fireside chats" to help gain the nation's support for their programs.

5. The President as Commander in Chief. The Constitution places the President at the head of all of the armed forces of the United States. He must approve all military promotions and is responsible for the nation's defense and military preparedness. Although the Constitution gives Congress the power to declare war, the President may determine whether or not a state of war exists. President Truman, for example, ordered United States troops into Korea in 1950, although Congress had not formally declared war. Once war comes, the President decides when, where, and how our military power will be used.

6. The President as Party Chief. Although political parties are not mentioned in the Constitution, the President is the head of his political party. He is responsible for choosing the party's national chairman. As chief executive he can award hundreds of government jobs in Washington and throughout the country, a power known as "patronage." Often, he uses these positions to reward loyal members of the party. The President often uses his prestige to support some of his party's candidates in Congressional or state elections.

Presidential Succession

John Adams, the first Vice-President of the United States, once remarked that an appropriate title for the Vice-President would be "Your Superfluous Excellency." He referred to the fact that the main responsibility of the office was to preside over the Senate. In that position, the Vice-President does not even have the privilege of voting, except in case of a tie.

Yet the constitutional qualifications for the Vice-President are the same as for the Presidency. The history of our nation has given ample evidence that this was a wise precaution. Eight of our presidents have died in office, four of them by assassination. If the President dies, the Vice-President takes office. The Constitution did not say he would necessarily become President in name. It provided that the *duties* of the chief executive would be performed by the Vice-President in case of the President's "death, resignation, or inability to discharge the duties" of his office.

While Dwight D. Eisenhower was President, he suffered two serious illnesses. The public became aware of the fact that the Constitution, in the phrase quoted above, left unanswered two important questions: (1) Who determines whether the President is incapable of serving as chief executive? (2) What happens if a President is declared unable to serve, and then recovers his health and capacities?

In 1965, Congress proposed the Twenty-fifth Amendment to the Constitution. Ratified on February 10, 1967, this amendment provides that in the event of death, resignation, or impeachment of the President, the Vice-President actually becomes the President; he does not simply perform the duties of the Chief Executive. He appoints a new Vice-President, who must be confirmed by a majority vote of Congress. Further, the amendment details the procedures to be followed if the President becomes temporarily or permanently incapacitated and unable to serve.

Presidential Tenure

How long can a President serve in office? The Constitution did not limit the number of terms of office a President might serve. Both Washington and Jefferson, however, decided that two terms were sufficient. This remained an "unwritten precedent" until 1940. In that year Franklin D. Roosevelt ran for reelection to a third term. Because he was so popular, and because World War II had broken out in Europe, the voters gave him an easy victory. In 1944, he was chosen again for a fourth term.

Many people felt that no man should be permitted to serve for so long a period. They led a movement which resulted in the adoption of the Twenty-second Amendment, which went into effect in 1951. This Amendment forbids any person from serving as President for more than two full terms. A person who has come to the Presidency from the Vice-Presidency as the result of the death of the President is considered to have had a "full term" if he holds office for over two years.

THE LEGISLATIVE BRANCH

Of the three branches of the Federal Government, the legislative branch is the only one elected *directly* by the people. The Constitution granted the power of making all federal laws to Congress, composed of the Senate and the House of Representatives.

The House of Representatives

Representation in the House is based upon population, each state being guaranteed at least one representative. There are 435 members. Most representatives are elected from a congressional district, whose area is determined by the state legislature. Some states also have Congressmen-at-large, elected by the voters of the entire state. Members of the House of Representatives serve for two years.

In addition to the law-making powers which it shares with the Senate, the House of Representatives has three special powers. It has the sole power to initiate revenue bills. It alone has the power to impeach the President or any other civil officer of the United States for "Treason, Bribery, or other high Crimes and Misdemeanors." Lastly, the House of Representatives elects the President if the electoral college fails to do so. This happened in 1800 and 1824.

The Senate

The Constitution provided that the Senate be made up of two senators from each state. Hence all states, regardless of their size or population, have an equal voice in the Senate. All senators are elected for six years. Since one-third of the Senate comes up for election every two years, the Senate never changes more than one-third of its membership at any time, as the House of Representatives may.

The Senate has three special powers, which permit it to check the power of the President. Its approval is needed for Presidential appointments to cabinet posts, ambassadorships, and other high offices. The two-thirds vote of the Senate required for ratification of treaties has given it a significant role in foreign relations. Finally, the Senate sits as a court of trial in impeachment cases, a two-thirds

vote being necessary for conviction. (The Senate also has the power to elect the Vice-President when the electoral college fails to do so. However, this power has been used only once, in the election of 1836.)

The Powers of Congress

Most of the legislative powers granted to Congress are found in Article I, Section 8. In addition to granting 17 specific powers to Congress, this section also contains the so-called *elastic* clause. This provides that Congress shall have the power "to make all laws which shall be necessary and proper for carrying into execution the foregoing powers. . . ." This clause has made possible a tremendous growth of the Federal Government.

Although Congress's powers are vast, it does not have the power to legislate as it sees fit. Article I, Section 9, and the first ten Amendments (The Bill of Rights) limit the right of Congress in many ways. For example, Congress may not tax exports, appropriate money for the Army for a period of over two years, suspend the privilege of the writ of *habeas corpus*, or grant a title of nobility.

How a Bill Becomes a Law

A bill must be introduced by a member of Congress, in either one of the two houses (except for bills for the raising of revenue, which must originate in the House of Representatives). Thousands of bills are introduced in each session of Congress. Out of this number, fewer than one thousand become laws. The process by which a bill becomes a law is often long and complicated.

1. *The bill is introduced.* In the Senate, a sponsor introduces the bill from the floor, usually without discussion. In the House of Representatives, a sponsor of the bill drops it into a box known as the "hopper" at the desk of the Speaker of the House. (The Speaker is chosen at the start of each new Congress from the majority party. He ordinarily votes on issues only in case of a tie.)

2. *A committee studies the bill.* Because of the thousands of bills which are introduced during a session of Congress, the committee system was set up. In the House of Representatives there are 19 "standing" or regular committees; in the Senate there are 15. Large committees are generally broken down into subcommittees, each responsible for part of the parent committee's work. Each committee is made up of members from both political parties. Generally, the committee reflects the relative party strengths in the particular house of

Congress, so that the majority party controls each committee.

Seniority determines who will be chairman of the committee. That is, the position is usually held by a member of the majority party who has had the longest period of service on the committee.

In the House of Representatives, the Speaker assigns the bill to the appropriate committee. Senators state their choice of committee on all bills they introduce.

The committee may announce public hearings, at which supporters and opponents of the bill may appear and state their positions. At the close of the hearings, the committee decides whether to report the bill favorably or to pigeonhole it–that is, not report it at all. Over 90 percent of all bills introduced in Congress are killed in committee.

Most committee hearings are for the purpose of examining bills introduced. However, Congress also has the power to use committee hearings to "investigate," in order to see how well the laws of Congress are being executed and to find out whether new legislation is needed. In recent years, investigatory hearings into crime, Communism, and corruption have attracted widespread public attention.

3. *Bills reach the floor.* After the committee has reported a bill favorably, the bill goes on the calendar of the house to which the committee belongs. Some bills are considered more important than others. In the House of Representatives the Rules Committee may decide when a bill shall be called up. Some bills may never be reached at all if this committee places them at the bottom of the list. In the Senate, the policy committee of the majority party determines priorities.

The members debate the bill on the floor. In the House, the large membership has made it necessary to limit the time each member is allowed to speak. But in the Senate there is unlimited debate. A Senator or group of Senators can try to "talk a bill to death" to prevent its being brought to a vote. This strategy is called a "filibuster."

Each house may revise or amend the bill in the course of debate. The vote is finally taken. If a majority approves, the bill is sent to the other house for consideration. There the entire process starts all over again. The bill may be pigeonholed in committee, defeated on the floor, or approved. (Sometimes the procedure is speeded up by having similar bills start at the same time in both houses.)

4. *A conference committee may consider the bill.* In the course of its travel through both houses, the bill may have been changed considerably, so that the House version and the Senate version differ in details. In such a case, a conference committee, made up of members of both houses, meets to adjust these differences. The bill is then sent back to both houses for final approval.

5. *The bill goes to the President.* The bill becomes law after receiving the President's signature. If he holds it for a period of ten days (Sundays excepted) while Congress is in session, it also becomes law. (If Congress is not in session and the President holds the bill for ten days, it is automatically killed. This is called a "pocket veto.") If the President disapproves of the bill, he returns it to the house in which it started, with a statement of his objections, called a "veto message." If two-thirds of each house again vote for it, it becomes a law in spite of his veto.

THE JUDICIAL BRANCH

The judicial branch can be understood better if we contrast it with the legislative and executive branches. The primary function of Congress is to make laws. The primary function of the executive branch is to carry these laws into effect. The courts settle legal disputes in terms of existing law.

In the United States the courts have a particularly important role to play. Our Constitution is based upon the idea of limited government. The judicial branch has been given a major responsibility for seeing that government does not exceed the powers the people have given it.

How Federal Courts Are Organized

In Article III, Section 1, the Constitution provides for a Supreme Court and ". . . such inferior [lower] courts as the Congress may from time to time ordain and establish." In accordance with this, Congress created the Federal court system, consisting of three types of courts (and one special court, the Court of Claims).

1. *Federal District Courts.* At the base of the Federal court system are the 84 District Courts. Since these are the first to hear most cases, they are said to have *original* jurisdiction. Only one judge ordinarily sits on a case, although three may sit as a court in special circumstances. Like all other federal judges, District Court judges are appointed for life by the President, subject to the advice and consent of the Senate. In the District

Courts are tried most cases of crime against the United States and suits between individual citizens of different states.

2. *The United States Courts of Appeals.* Immediately above the District Courts are the eleven Courts of Appeals. These are ordinarily three-judge courts. Since they hear cases on appeal from the District Courts, they are said to have appellate jurisdiction. They are concerned primarily with questions of law rather than with findings of fact. Thus they relieve the Supreme Court of some of the tremendous burden of appellate work.

Usually, the decision of a Court of Appeals is final. Unless a case involves an extremely complex and important point of law, the Supreme Court would not have time to review it. Only a small fraction of cases go from the Courts of Appeals to the United States Supreme Court.

3. *The Court of Claims.* The Court of Claims was created in order to handle debt claims against the United States Government. Most of these claims arise out of government contracts. The Court of Claims has five judges.

4. *The Supreme Court of the United States.* The nation's highest tribunal consists of nine judges. Since the Constitution does not specify the number of judges, Congress decides this by law. (At first the Supreme Court had six judges. Congress has set the number at as many as ten and as few as five.)

One of the judges is designated as the chief justice. His decisions, however, have no more legal weight than those of his fellow justices. The Court ordinarily hears arguments for two weeks and then recesses for two weeks to reach decisions and write opinions. Cases are decided by a majority vote of the justices. (Many important cases have been decided by a five-to-four vote.) In addition to the majority decision, there may be a *dissenting,* or minority, opinion. In case a justice agrees with the majority decision but differs with the reasoning behind it, he may write a *concurring* opinion.

The Supreme Court has wide discretion to decide which cases it will hear on appeal from lower courts and which it will refuse to hear. In general, the Court will hear cases that have been decided differently in two or more lower courts. You will recall that unless there is a real constitutional issue or an important point of federal law involved, the Court will usually decline to hear an appeal. Thus, out of about 1,500 cases, the Court will hear only about 200.

In addition to the cases brought to the Supreme Court on appeal, the Court has original jurisdiction in certain cases. These cases are prescribed by the Constitution and are relatively rare. They include cases involving foreign diplomats and suits brought by one state against another.

Our Dual Court System

It should be noted that each of the states has its own court system. Since the United States Consitution is the supreme law of the land, any case involving federal law or the federal Constitution is heard in a United States court rather than in a state court. The Supreme Court of the United States exercises the power to void laws passed by state legislatures and to overrule decisions of state courts, when it deems these laws or decisions to be in conflict with federal law or the United States Constitution.

CHECKS AND BALANCES

We have examined the responsibilities of each of the three main branches of our government. The Constitution provided a system of checks and balances to prevent any branch from invading the rights of the others. There have been occasions in our history, however, when conflict arose because one of the branches considered that its independence was being threatened. Let us review the important checks and balances and note some of the notable instances of conflict among the three branches.

Congress and the President

As noted above, the President may check Congress by using his veto power over legislation. He may also call Congress into special session and recommend legislation to Congress. Through the prestige of his office, he can exert great influence on public opinion and on Congress.

Meanwhile, Congress can check the President by the use of its constitutional powers. The administration must depend upon Congress for money. If Congress refuses to appropriate funds the President needs to enforce a law, it can tie his hands. Furthermore, although the President is commander in chief of the armed forces, Congress determines the size and equipment of those forces. Both houses may override the President's veto by two-thirds vote. In addition, the Senate may check the President by refusing to approve his appointments or by refusing to ratify treaties. The Constitution provides that the House of Representatives may bring impeachment charges against the President, and the Senate has the power to try him on these charges.

Conflict between the executive and legislative branches has been a part of our history since the days of George Washington. In 1789, President Washington tried to hasten the Senate's ratification of an Indian treaty by going to the Senate with his advisors to answer any questions the Senators had. The Senators sat in silence, resenting what they considered to be an intrusion on their powers. Washington walked out, vowing never to set foot in the Senate chamber again. No President did, in fact, until President Wilson appeared before the Senate 130 years later. Washington's successor, John Adams, remarked that Congress and the President were "natural enemies."

During the Civil War, Abraham Lincoln not only used the constitutional powers of the President but also some that belonged to Congress. According to the Constitution, only Congress may "raise and support armies," yet Lincoln issued a call for volunteers, declared martial law, and ordered the Treasury to pay funds for military purposes. He waited until Congress had adjourned to issue his Emancipation Proclamation. He said, "I felt that measures, otherwise unconstitutional, might become lawful by becoming indispensable to the preservation of the Constitution . . ." After Lincoln's assassination, Andrew Johnson continued to insist upon the powers of the President. His conflict with Congress was climaxed by his impeachment trial, which failed of conviction by just one vote.

Woodrow Wilson believed strongly that the President must give legislative leadership to Congress. He insisted upon appearing in person before Congress on major proposals for legislation. When the Senate refused to allow the United States to join the League of Nations after World War I, he "went to the people." On a cross-country tour he urged the voters to make Congress vote for his measure.

In 1933, Franklin D. Roosevelt continued the Wilson pattern of Presidential leadership in legislation. He spoke to Congress of "building a strong and permanent tie between the legislative and executive branches of the government." When he felt that an individual Senator failed to support his program, he did not hesitate to go into the Senator's home state to campaign against his reelection.

Conflcts between the legislative and executive branches have also arisen out of the activities of congressional committees. Congressional investigations have often served useful purposes, such as the uncovering of the Teapot Dome scandal during the administration of President Harding and the revelation of corruption in the Internal Revenue Department during the 1950s. However, important questions concerning the independence of each branch arise out of these hearings. How far may a committee go in requiring officials of the executive branch to appear before it and testify? The President clearly may not be so forced, but what of cabinet officers? May the President order his subordinates not to give information to a congressional committee? These and other questions arose during the hearings on the role of communism in the government and the army conducted by Senator Joseph McCarthy in 1953–1954, and the Senate investigation into campaign wrongdoings in 1973.

The Supreme Court and the Other Branches

The Constitution provides for checks by the President on the judicial branch. He has the power to appoint new Supreme Court judges and other federal judges to fill vacancies. Furthermore, he may grant pardons and reprieves, except in cases of impeachment. The Senate checks on the courts by its power to refuse to ratify Presidential appointments. Impeachment charges against federal judges are brought by the House of Representatives and tried by the Senate.

The Supreme Court, on the other hand, exercises a tremendously important check upon the other two branches. It may set aside any law passed by Congress and approved by the President if a majority of the Court's members find that the law violates any part of the Constitution. Furthermore, it may also declare any actions of the executive branch unconstitutional.

This power, known as *judicial review,* is not expressly granted to the Supreme Court by the Constitution. In 1803 Chief Justice John Marshall first declared an act of Congress unconstitutional, in the celebrated case of *Marbury* v. *Madison.* In his decision, Marshall declared: "It is emphatically the province and duty of the judicial department to say what the law is. . . . A law repugnant to the Constitution is void. . . ."

This power of judicial review has been a major

source of conflict. Thomas Jefferson strongly criticized the doctrine as making the Constitution "a mere thing of wax in the hands of the judiciary, which they might twist, and shape into any form they please." He insisted that each branch should have the authority to interpret its own powers. Andrew Jackson is reported to have said about a decision with which he disagreed: "John Marshall has made his decision, now let him enforce it!" Few decisions in our nation's history have been as unpopular as the Court's ruling in the Dred Scott case, in 1857, that Congress lacked the power to exclude slavery from the territories.

The argument over the power of judicial review reached a climax in the 1930s, when the Supreme Court held so many New Deal laws unconstitutional that President Franklin D. Roosevelt proposed to Congress that he be allowed to "pack" the Court by making as many as six new appointments to the Court. In this way, he hoped to get more favorable decisions. Congress refused to support him in his effort, however.

In 1952, President Harry S. Truman, in order to forestall a steel strike which he felt would imperil national defense at a time when the country was engaged in the war in Korea, ordered his Secretary of Commerce to seize and operate the steel mills. The Supreme Court held his action to be unconstitutional. It argued that the President normally has only those powers specifically granted to him by the Constitution and the laws. In grave emergencies, however, he may exercise powers beyond these *if Congress agrees*. Here we see a basic role of the Court: to act as the "guardian of the Constitution" by curbing the power of the other branches.

The Constitution of the United States

WE THE PEOPLE of the United States, in Order to form a more perfect Union, establish Justice, insure domestic Tranquility, provide for the common defence, promote the general Welfare, and secure the Blessings of Liberty to ourselves and our Posterity, do ordain and establish this CONSTITUTION for the United States of America.

ARTICLE I.

SECTION 1. All legislative Powers herein granted shall be vested in a Congress of the United States, which shall consist of a Senate and House of Representatives.

SECTION 2. [1] The House of Representatives shall be composed of Members chosen every second Year by the People of the several States, and the Electors in each State shall have the Qualifications requisite for Electors of the most numerous Branch of the State Legislature.

[2] No person shall be a Representative who shall not have attained to the Age of twenty five Years, and been seven Years a Citizen of the United States, and who shall not, when elected, be an Inhabitant of that State in which he shall be chosen.

[3] *[Representatives and direct Taxes shall be apportioned among the several States which may be included within this Union, according to their respective Numbers, which shall be determined by adding to the whole Number of free Persons, including those bound to Service for a Term of Years, and excluding Indians not taxed, three fifths of all other Persons.]** The actual Enumeration shall be made within three Years after the first Meeting of the Congress of the United States, and within

NOTE.–This text of the Constitution follows the engrossed copy signed by Gen. Washington and the deputies from 12 States. The superior number preceding the paragraphs designates the number of the clause; it was not in the original. Spelling and punctuation in the Constitution are set according to copy supplied by the United States Government Printing Office; 88th Congress, 1st Session; House Document No. 112.

* The part included in heavy brackets was changed by section 2 of the fourteenth amendment.

every subsequent Term of ten Years, in such Manner as they shall by Law direct. The Number of Representatives shall not exceed one for every thirty Thousand, but each State shall have at Least one Representative; and until such enumeration shall be made, the State of New Hampshire shall be entitled to chuse three, Massachusetts eight, Rhode-Island and Providence Plantations one, Connecticut five, New-York six, New Jersey four, Pennsylvania eight, Delaware one, Maryland six, Virginia ten, North Carolina five, South Carolina five, and Georgia three.

4 When vacancies happen in the Representation from any State, the Executive Authority thereof shall issue Writs of Election to fill such Vacancies.

5 The House of Representatives shall chuse their Speaker and other Officers; and shall have the sole Power of Impeachment.

SECTION 3. 1 The Senate of the United States shall be composed of two Senators from each State, [chosen by the Legislature thereof,]* for six Years; and each Senator shall have one Vote.

2 Immediately after they shall be assembled in Consequence of the first Election, they shall be divided as equally as may be into three Classes. The Seats of the Senators of the first Class shall be vacated at the Expiration of the second Year, of the second Class at the Expiration of the fourth Year, and of the third Class at the Expiration of the sixth Year, so that one third may be chosen every second Year; [and if Vacancies happen by Resignation, or otherwise, during the Recess of the Legislature of any State, the Executive thereof may make temporary Appointments until the next Meeting of the Legislature, which shall then fill such Vacancies]. **

3 No Person shall be a Senator who shall not have attained to the Age of thirty Years, and been nine Years a Citizen of the United States, and who shall not, when elected, be an Inhabitant of that State for which he shall be chosen.

4 The Vice President of the United States shall be President of the Senate, but shall have no Vote, unless they be equally divided.

5 The Senate shall chuse their other Officers, and also a President pro tempore, in the Absence of

the Vice President, or when he shall exercise the Office of President of the United States.

6 The Senate shall have the sole Power to try all Impeachments. When sitting for that Purpose, they shall be on Oath or Affirmation. When the President of the United States is tried, the Chief Justice shall preside: And no Person shall be convicted without the Concurrence of two thirds of the Members present.

7 Judgment in Cases of Impeachment shall not extend further than to removal from Office, and disqualification to hold and enjoy any Office of honor, Trust or Profit under the United States: but the Party convicted shall nevertheless be liable and subject to Indictment, Trial, Judgment and Punishment, according to Law.

SECTION 4. 1 The Times, Places and Manner of holding Elections for Senators and Representatives, shall be prescribed in each State by the Legislature thereof; but the Congress may at any time by Law make or alter such Regulations, except as to the Places of chusing Senators.

2 The Congress shall assemble at least once in every Year, and such Meeting shall [be on the the first Monday in December,]*** unless they shall by Law appoint a different Day.

SECTION 5. 1 Each House shall be the Judge of the Elections, Returns and Qualifications of its own Members, and a Majority of each shall constitute a Quorum to do Business; but a smaller Number may adjourn from day to day, and may be authorized to compel the Attendance of absent Members, in such Manner, and under such Penalties as each House may provide.

2 Each House may determine the Rules of its Proceedings, punish its Members for disorderly Behavior, and, with the Concurrence of two thirds, expel a Member.

3 Each House shall keep a Journal of its Proceedings, and from time to time publish the same, excepting such Parts as may in their Judgment require Secrecy; and the Yeas and Nays of the Members of either House on any question shall, at the Desire of one fifth of those Present, be entered on the Journal.

4 Neither House, during the Session of Congress, shall, without the Consent of the other, adjourn for more than three days, nor to any other Place than that in which the two Houses shall be sitting.

---

* The part included in heavy brackets was changed by section 1 of the seventeenth amendment.

** The part included in heavy brackets was changed by clause 2 of the seventeenth amendment.

*** The part included in heavy brackets was changed by section 2 of the twentieth amendment.

SECTION 6. [1] The Senators and Representatives shall receive a Compensation for their Services, to be ascertained by Law, and paid out of the Treasury of the United States. They shall in all Cases, except Treason, Felony and Breach of the Peace, be privileged from Arrest during their Attendance at the Session of their respective Houses, and in going to and returning from the same; and for any Speech or Debate in either House, they shall not be questioned in any other Place.

[2] No Senator or Representative shall, during the Time for which he was elected, be appointed to any civil Office under the Authority of the United States, which shall have been created, or the Emoluments whereof shall have been encreased during such time; and no Person holding any Office under the United States, shall be a Member of either House during his Continuance in Office.

SECTION 7. [1] All Bills for raising Revenue shall originate in the House of Representatives; but the Senate may propose or concur with Amendments as on other Bills.

[2] Every Bill which shall have passed the House of Representatives and the Senate, shall, before it become a Law, be presented to the President of the United States; If he approve he shall sign it, but if not he shall return it, with his Objections to that House in which it shall have originated, who shall enter the Objections at large on their Journal, and proceed to reconsider it. If after such Reconsideration two thirds of that House shall agree to pass the Bill, it shall be sent, together with the Objections, to the other House, by which it shall likewise be reconsidered, and if approved by two thirds of that House, it shall become a Law. But in all such Cases the Votes of both Houses shall be determined by Yeas and Nays, and the Names of the Persons voting for and against the Bill shall be entered on the Journal of each House respectively. If any Bill shall not be returned by the President within ten days (Sundays excepted) after it shall have been presented to him, the Same shall be a Law, in like Manner as if he had signed it, unless the Congress by their Adjournment prevent its Return, in which Case it shall not be a Law.

[3] Every Order, Resolution, or Vote to which the Concurrence of the Senate and House of Representatives may be necessary (except on a question of Adjournment) shall be presented to the President of the United States; and before the Same shall take Effect, shall be approved by him, or being disapproved by him, shall be repassed by two thirds of the Senate and House of Representatives, according to the Rules and Limitations prescribed in the Case of a Bill.

SECTION 8. [1] The Congress shall have Power To lay and collect Taxes, Duties, Imposts and Excises, to pay the Debts and provide for the common Defence and general Welfare of the United States; but all Duties, Imposts and Excises shall be uniform throughout the United States;

[2] To borrow Money on the credit of the United States;

[3] To regulate Commerce with foreign Nations, and among the several States, and with the Indian Tribes;

[4] To establish an uniform Rule of Naturalization, and uniform Laws on the subject of Bankruptcies throughout the United States;

[5] To coin Money, regulate the Value thereof, and of foreign Coin, and fix the Standard of Weights and Measures;

[6] To provide for the Punishment of counterfeiting the Securities and current Coin of the United States;

[7] To establish Post Offices and post Roads;

[8] To promote the Progress of Science and useful Arts, by securing for limited Times to Authors and Inventors the exclusive Right to their respective Writings and Discoveries;

[9] To constitute Tribunals inferior to the supreme Court;

[10] To define and punish Piracies and Felonies committed on the high Seas, and Offenses against the Law of Nations;

[11] To declare War, grant Letters of Marque and Reprisal, and make Rules concerning Captures on Land and Water;

[12] To raise and support Armies, but no Appropriation of Money to that Use shall be for a longer Term than two Years;

[13] To provide and maintain a Navy;

[14] To make Rules for the Government and Regulation of the land and naval Forces;

[15] To provide for calling forth the Militia to execute the Laws of the Union, suppress Insurrections and repel Invasions;

[16] To provide for organizing, arming, and disciplining the Militia, and for governing such Part of them as may be employed in the Service of the United States, reserving to the States respectively, the Appointment of the Officers, and the Authority of training the Militia according to the discipline prescribed by Congress;

[17] To exercise exclusive Legislation in all Cases whatsoever, over such District (not exceeding ten Miles square) as may, by Cession of particular States, and the Acceptance of Congress, become the Seat of the Government of the United States, and to exercise like Authority over all Places purchased by the Consent of the Legislature of the State in which the Same shall be, for the Erection of Forts, Magazines, Arsenals, dock-Yards, and other needful Buildings;–And

[18] To make all Laws which shall be necessary and proper for carrying into Execution the foregoing Powers, and all other Powers vested by this Constitution in the Government of the United States, or in any Department or Officer thereof.

SECTION 9. [1] The Migration or Importation of such Persons as any of the States now existing shall think proper to admit, shall not be prohibited by the Congress prior to the Year one thousand eight hundred and eight, but a Tax or duty may be imposed on such Importation, not exceeding ten dollars for each Person.

[2] The Privilege of the Writ of Habeas Corpus shall not be suspended, unless when in Cases of Rebellion or Invasion the public Safety may require it.

[3] No Bill of Attainder or ex post facto Law shall be passed.

*[4] No Capitation, or other direct, Tax shall be laid, unless in Proportion to the Census or Enumeration herein before directed to be taken.

[5] No Tax or Duty shall be laid on Articles exported from any State.

[6] No Preference shall be given by any Regulation of Commerce or Revenue to the Ports of one State over those of another: nor shall Vessels bound to, or from, one State be obliged to enter, clear, or pay Duties in another.

[7] No Money shall be drawn from the Treasury, but in Consequence of Appropriations made by Law; and a regular Statement and Account of the Receipts and Expenditures of all public Money shall be published from time to time.

[8] No Title of Nobility shall be granted by the United States: And no Person holding any Office of Profit or Trust under them, shall, without the Consent of the Congress, accept of any present, Emolument, Office, or Title, of any kind whatever, from any King, Prince, or foreign State.

---

*See also the sixteenth amendment.

SECTION 10. [1] No state shall enter into any Treaty, Alliance, or Confederation; grant Letters of Marque and Reprisal: coin Money; emit Bills of Credit; make any Thing but gold and silver Coin a Tender in Payment of Debts; pass any Bill of Attainder, ex post facto Law, or Law impairing the Obligation of Contracts, or grant any Title of Nobility.

[2] No State shall, without the Consent of the Congress, lay any Imposts or Duties on Imports or Exports, except what may be absolutely necessary for executing it's inspection Laws: and the net Produce of all Duties and Imposts, laid by any State on Imports or Exports, shall be for the Use of the Treasury of the United States; and all such Laws shall be subject to the Revision and Controul of the Congress.

[3] No State shall, without the Consent of Congress, lay any Duty of Tonnage, keep Troops, or Ships of War in time of Peace, enter into any Agreement or Compact with another State, or with a foreign Power, or engage in War, unless actually invaded, or in such imminent Danger as will not admit of delay.

ARTICLE II.

SECTION. 1. [1] The executive Power shall be vested in a President of the United States of America. He shall hold his Office during the Term of four Years, and, together with the Vice President, chosen for the same Term, be elected as follows

[2] Each State shall appoint, in such Manner as the Legislature thereof may direct, a Number of Electors, equal to the whole Number of Senators and Representatives to which the State may be entitled in the Congress: but no Senator or Representative, or Person holding an Office of Trust or Profit under the United States, shall be appointed an Elector.

[*The Electors shall meet in their respective States, and vote by Ballot for two Persons, of whom one at least shall not be an Inhabitant of the same State with themselves. And they shall make a List of all the Persons voted for, and of the Number of Votes for each; which List they shall sign and certify, and transmit sealed to the Seat of the Government of the United States, directed to the President of the Senate. The President of the Senate shall, in the Presence of the Senate and House of Representatives, open all the Certificates, and the Votes shall then be counted. The Person having the greatest*

Number of Votes shall be the President, if such Number be a Majority of the whole Number of Electors appointed; and if there be more than one who have such Majority, and have an equal Number of Votes, then the House of Representatives shall immediately chuse by Ballot one of them for President; and if no Person have a Majority, then from the five highest on the List the said House shall in like Manner chuse the President. But in chusing the President, the Votes shall be taken by States, the Representation from each State having one Vote; A quorum for this Purpose shall consist of a Member or Members from two thirds of the States, and a Majority of all the States shall be necessary to a Choice. In every Case, after the Choice of the President, the Person having the greatest Number of Votes of the Electors shall be the Vice President. But if there should remain two or more who have equal Votes, the Senate shall chuse from them by Ballot the Vice President.] *

³ The Congress may determine the Time of chusing the Electors, and the Day on which they shall give their Votes; which Day shall be the same throughout the United States.

⁴ No Person except a natural born Citizen, or a Citizen of the United States, at the time of the Adoption of this Constitution, shall be eligible to the Office of President; neither shall any Person be eligible to that Office who shall not have attained to the Age of thirty five Years, and been fourteen Years a Resident within the United States.

⁵ In Case of the Removal of the President from Office, or of his Death, Resignation, or Inability to discharge the Powers and Duties of the said Office, the Same shall devolve on the Vice President, and the Congress may by Law provide for the Case of Removal, Death, Resignation or Inability, both of the President and Vice President, declaring what Officer shall then act as President, and such Officer shall act accordingly, until the Disability be removed, or a President shall be elected.

⁶ The President shall, at stated Times, receive for his Services, a Compensation, which shall neither be encreased nor diminished during the Period for which he shall have been elected, and he shall not receive within that Period any other Emolument from the United States, or any of them.

Before he enter on the Execution of his Office, he shall take the following Oath or Affirmation:–"I do solemnly swear (or affirm) that I will faithfully execute the Office of President of the United States, and will to the best of my Ability, preserve,

protect and defend the Constitution of the United States."

SECTION 2. ¹ The President shall be Commander in Chief of the Army and Navy of the United States, and of the Militia of the several States, when called into the actual Service of the United States; he may require the Opinion, in writing, of the principal Officer in each of the executive Departments, upon any Subject relating to the Duties of their respective Offices, and he shall have Power to grant Reprieves and Pardons for Offences against the United States, except in Cases of Impeachment.

² He shall have Power, by and with the Advice and Consent of the Senate, to make Treaties, provided two thirds of the Senators present concur; and he shall nominate, and by and with the Advice and Consent of the Senate, shall appoint Ambassadors, other public Ministers and Consuls, Judges of the supreme Court, and all other Officers of the United States, whose Appointments are not herein otherwise provided for, and which shall be established by Law: but the Congress may by Law vest the Appointment of such inferior Officers, as they think proper, in the President alone, in the Courts of Law, or in the Heads of Departments.

³ The President shall have Power to fill up all Vacancies that may happen during the Recess of the Senate, by granting Commissions which shall expire at the End of their next Session.

SECTION 3. He shall from time to time give to the Congress Information of the State of the Union, and recommend to their Consideration such Measures as he shall judge necessary and expedient; he may, on extraordinary Occasions, convene both Houses, or either of them, and in Case of Disagreement between them, with Respect to the Time of Adjournment, he may adjourn them to such Time as he shall think proper; he shall receive Ambassadors and other public Ministers; he shall take Care that the Laws be faithfully executed, and shall Commission all the Officers of the United States.

SECTION 4. The President, Vice President and all civil Officers of the United States, shall be removed from Office on Impeachment for, and Conviction of, Treason, Bribery, or other high Crimes and Misdemeanors.

*This paragraph has been superseded by the twelfth amendment.

ARTICLE III.

SECTION 1. The judicial Power of the United States, shall be vested in one supreme Court, and in such inferior Courts as the Congress may from time to time ordain and establish. The Judges, both of the supreme and inferior Courts, shall hold their Offices during good Behaviour, and shall, at stated Times, receive for their Services a Compensation, which shall not be diminished during their Continuance in Office.

SECTION 2. [1] The judicial Power shall extend to all Cases, in Law and Equity, arising under this Constitution, the Laws of the United States, and Treaties made, or which shall be made, under their Authority;–to all Cases affecting Ambassadors, other public Ministers and Consuls;–to all Cases of admiralty and maritime Jurisdiction;–to Controversies to which the United States shall be a Party;–to Controversies between two or more States;–between a State and Citizens of another State;*–between Citizens of different States;–between Citizens of the same State claiming Lands under Grants of different States; and between a State, or the Citizens thereof, and foreign States, Citizens or Subjects.

[2] In all Cases affecting Ambassadors, other public Ministers and Consuls, and those in which a State shall be Party, the supreme Court shall have original Jurisdiction. In all the other Cases before mentioned, the supreme Court shall have appellate Jurisdiction, both as to Law and Fact, with such Exceptions, and under such Regulations as the Congress shall make.

[3] The Trial of all Crimes, except in Cases of Impeachment shall be by Jury; and such Trial shall be held in the State where the said Crimes shall have been committed; but when not committed within any State, the Trial shall be at such Place or Places as the Congress may by Law have directed.

SECTION 3. [1] Treason against the United States, shall consist only in levying War against them, or in adhering to their Enemies, giving them Aid and Comfort. No Person shall be convicted of Treason unless on the Testimony of two Witnesses to the same overt Act, or on Confession in open Court.

[2] The Congress shall have Power to declare the Punishment of Treason, but no Attainder of Treason shall work Corruption of Blood, or Forfeiture except during the Life of the Person attainted.

ARTICLE IV.

SECTION 1. Full Faith and Credit shall be given in each State to the public Acts, Records, and judicial Proceedings of every other State. And the Congress may by general Laws prescribe the Manner in which such Acts, Records and Proceedings shall be proved, and the Effect thereof.

SECTION 2. [1] The Citizens of each State shall be entitled to all Privileges and Immunities of Citizens in the several States.

[2] A Person charged in any State with Treason, Felony, or other Crime, who shall flee from Justice, and be found in another State, shall on Demand of the executive Authority of the State from which he fled, be delivered up, to be removed to the State having Jurisdiction of the Crime.

[3] [*No Person held to Service or Labour in one State, under the Laws thereof, escaping into another, shall, in Consequence of any Law or Regulation therein, be discharged from such Service or Labour, but shall be delivered up on Claim of the Party to whom such Service or Labour may be due.*]**

SECTION 3. [1] New States may be admitted by the Congress into this Union; but no new State shall be formed or erected within the Jurisdiction of any other State; nor any State be formed by the Junction of two or more States, or Parts of States, without the Consent of the Legislatures of the States concerned as well as of the Congress.

[2] The Congress shall have Power to dispose of and make all needful Rules and Regulations respecting the Territory or other Property belonging to the United States; and nothing in this Constitution shall be so construed as to Prejudice any Claims of the United States, or of any particular State.

SECTION. 4. The United States shall guarantee to every State in this Union a Republican Form of Government, and shall protect each of them against Invasion; and on Application of the Legislature, or of the Executive (when the Legislature cannot be convened) against domestic Violence.

---

* This clause has been affected by the eleventh amendment.
** This paragraph has been superseded by the thirteenth amendment.

ARTICLE V.

The Congress, whenever two thirds of both Houses shall deem it necessary, shall propose Amendments to this Constitution, or, on the Application of the Legislatures of two thirds of the several States, shall call a Convention for proposing Amendments, which, in either Case, shall be valid to all Intents and Purposes, as Part of this Constitution, when ratified by the Legislatures of three fourths of the several States, or by Conventions in three fourths thereof, as the one or the other Mode of Ratification may be proposed by the Congress: Provided, [*that no Amendment which may be made prior to the Year One thousand eight hundred and eight shall in any Manner affect the first and fourth Clauses in the Ninth Section of the first Article; and*]* that no State, without its Consent, shall be deprived of its equal Suffrage in the Senate.

ARTICLE VI.

¹ All Debts contracted and Engagements entered into, before the Adoption of this Constitution shall be as valid against the United States under this Constitution, as under the Confederation.

² This Constitution, and the Laws of the United States which shall be made in Pursuance thereof; and all Treaties made, or which shall be made, under the Authority of the United States, shall be the supreme Law of the Land; and the Judges in every State shall be bound thereby, any Thing in the Constitution or Laws of any State to the Contrary notwithstanding.

³ The Senators and Representatives before mentioned, and the Members of the several State Legislatures, and all executive and judicial Officers, both of the United States and of the several States, shall be bound by Oath or Affirmation, to support this Constitution; but no religious Test shall ever be required as a Qualification to any Office or public Trust under the United States.

ARTICLE VII.

The Ratification of the Conventions of nine States, shall be sufficient for the Establishment of this Constitution between the States so ratifying the Same.

DONE in Convention by the Unanimous Consent of the States present the Seventeenth Day of September in the Year of our Lord one thousand seven hundred and Eighty seven and of the Independence of the United States of America the Twelfth IN WITNESS whereof We have hereto subscribed our Names,

G⁰ WASHINGTON—
Presidᵗ. and deputy from Virginia.

[Signed also by the deputies of twelve States.]

New Hampshire.
JOHN LANGDON,
NICHOLAS GILMAN.

Massachusetts.
NATHANIEL GORHAM,
RUFUS KING.

Connecticut.
WM. SAML. JOHNSON,
ROGER SHERMAN.

New York.
ALEXANDER HAMILTON.

New Jersey.
WIL: LIVINGSTON,
DAVID BREARLEY,
WM. PATERSON,
JONA: DAYTON.

Pennsylvania.
B FRANKLIN,
ROBᵀ MORRIS,
THOS. FITZSIMONS,
JAMES WILSON,
THOMAS MIFFLIN,
GEO. CLYMER,
JARED INGERSOLL,
GOUV MORRIS.

Delaware.
GEO: READ,
JOHN DICKINSON,
JACO: BROOM,
GUNNING BEDFORD, jun,
RICHARD BASSETT.

Maryland.
JAMES MCHENRY,
DANᴸ CARROLL,
DAN OF Sᵀ THOS. JENIFER.

Virginia.
JOHN BLAIR—
JAMES MADISON Jr.

---

* Obsolete.

North Carolina.
   WM. BLOUNT,
   HU WILLIAMSON,
   RICH'D DOBBS SPAIGHT.

South Carolina.
   J. RUTLEDGE,
   CHARLES PINCKNEY,
   CHARLES COTESWORTH PINCKNEY,
   PIERCE BUTLER.

Georgia.
   WILLIAM FEW,
   ABR BALDWIN,
   Attest: WILLIAM JACKSON, *Secretary.*

ARTICLES IN ADDITION TO, AND AMENDMENT OF, THE CONSTITUTION OF THE UNITED STATES OF AMERICA, PROPOSED BY CONGRESS, AND RATIFIED BY THE LEGISLATURES OF THE SEVERAL STATES PURSUANT TO THE FIFTH ARTICLE OF THE ORIGINAL CONSTITUTION

ARTICLE [I] *

Congress shall make no law respecting an establishment of religion, or prohibiting the free exercise thereof; or abridging the freedom of speech, or of the press, or the right of the people peaceably to assemble, and to petition the Government for a redress of grievances.

ARTICLE [II]

A well regulated Militia, being necessary to the security of a free State, the right of the people to keep and bear Arms, shall not be infringed.

ARTICLE [III]

No Soldier shall, in time of peace be quartered in any house, without the consent of the Owner, nor in time of war, but in a manner to be prescribed by law.

* Only the 13th, 14th, 15th, and 16th articles of amendment had numbers assigned to them at the time of ratification. Articles of amendment that did not have numbers assigned to them at ratification are shown here in proper order with the corresponding number placed in light brackets.

ARTICLE [IV]

The right of the people to be secure in their persons, houses, papers, and effects, against unreasonable searches and seizures, shall not be violated, and no Warrants shall issue, but upon probable cause, supported by Oath or affirmation, and particularly describing the place to be searched, and the persons or things to be seized.

ARTICLE [V]

No person shall be held to answer for a capital, or otherwise infamous crime, unless on a presentment or indictment of a Grand Jury, except in cases arising in the land or naval forces, or in the Militia, when in actual service in time of War or public danger; nor shall any person be subject for the same offence to be twice put in jeopardy of life or limb, nor shall be compelled in any criminal case to be a witness against himself, nor be deprived of life, liberty, or property, without due process of law; nor shall private property be taken for public use without just compensation.

ARTICLE [VI]

In all criminal prosecutions, the accused shall enjoy the right to a speedy and public trial, by an impartial jury of the State and district wherein the crime shall have been committed; which district shall have been previously ascertained by law, and to be informed of the nature and cause of the accusation; to be confronted with the witnesses against him; to have compulsory process for obtaining Witnesses in his favor, and to have the Assistance of Counsel for his defence.

ARTICLE [VII]

In Suits at common law, where the value in controversy shall exceed twenty dollars, the right of trial by jury shall be preserved, and no fact tried by a jury shall be otherwise reexamined in any Court of the United States, than according to the rules of the common law.

ARTICLE [VIII]

Excessive bail shall not be required, nor excessive fines imposed, nor cruel and unusual punishments inflicted.

ARTICLE [IX]

The enumeration in the Constitution, of certain rights, shall not be construed to deny or disparage others retained by the people.

ARTICLE [X]

The powers not delegated to the United States by the Constitution, nor prohibited by it to the States, are reserved to the States respectively, or to the people.

ARTICLE [XI]

The Judicial power of the United States shall not be construed to extend to any suit in law or equity, commenced or prosecuted against one of the United States by Citizens of another State, or by Citizens or Subjects of any Foreign State.

ARTICLE [XII]

The electors shall meet in their respective states and vote by ballot for President and Vice-President, one of whom, at least, shall not be an inhabitant of the same state with themselves; they shall name in their ballots the person voted for as President, and in distinct ballots the person voted for as Vice-President, and they shall make distinct lists of all persons voted for as President, and of all persons voted for as Vice-President, and of the number of votes for each, which lists they shall sign and certify, and transmit sealed to the seat of the government of the United States, directed to the President of the Senate;–The President of the Senate shall, in presence of the Senate and House of Representatives, open all the certificates and the votes shall then be counted;–The person hav-ing the greatest number of votes for President, shall be the President, if such number be a majority of the whole number of Electors appointed; and if no person have such majority, then from the persons having the highest numbers not exceeding three on the list of those voted for as President, the House of Representatives shall choose immediately, by ballot, the President. But in choosing the President, the votes shall be taken by states, the representation from each state having one vote; a quorum for this purpose shall consist of a member or members from two-thirds of the states, and a majority of all the states shall be necessary to a choice. [*And if the House of Representatives shall not choose a President whenever the right of choice shall devolve upon them, before the fourth day of March next following, then the Vice-President shall act as President, as in the case of the death or other constitutional disability of the President.*] * The person having the greatest number of votes as Vice-President, shall be the Vice-President, if such number be a majority of the whole number of Electors appointed, and if no person have a majority, then from the two highest numbers on the list, the Senate shall choose the Vice-President; a quorum for the purpose shall consist of two-thirds of the whole number of Senators, and a majority of the whole number shall be necessary to a choice. But no person constitutionally ineligible to the office of President shall be eligible to that of Vice-President of the United States.

ARTICLE XIII

SECTION 1. Neither slavery nor involuntary servitude, except as a punishment for crime whereof the party shall have been duly convicted, shall exist within the United States, or any place subject to their jurisdiction.

SECTION 2. Congress shall have power to enforce this article by appropriate legislation.

ARTICLE XIV

SECTION 1. All persons born or naturalized in the United States, and subject to the jurisdiction thereof, are citizens of the United States and of the

* The part included in heavy brackets has been superseded by section 3 of the twentieth amendment.

State wherein they reside. No State shall make or enforce any law which shall abridge the privileges or immunities of citizens of the United States; nor shall any State deprive any person of life, liberty, or property, without due process of law; nor deny to any person within its jurisdiction the equal protection of the laws.

SECTION 2. Representatives shall be apportioned among the several States according to their respective numbers, counting the whole number of persons in each State, excluding Indians not taxed. But when the right to vote at any election for the choice of electors for President and Vice-President of the United States, Representatives in Congress, the Executive and Judicial officers of a State, or the members of the Legislature thereof, is denied to any of the male inhabitants of such State, being twenty-one years of age, and citizens of the United States, or in any way abridged, except for participation in rebellion, or other crime, the basis of representation therein shall be reduced in the proportion which the number of such male citizens shall bear to the whole number of male citizens twenty-one years of age in such State.

SECTION 3. No person shall be a Senator or Representative in Congress, or elector of President and Vice-President, or hold any office, civil or military, under the United States, or under any State, who, having previously taken an oath, as a member of Congress, or as an officer of the United States, or as a member of any State legislature, or as an executive or judicial officer of any State, to support the Constitution of the United States, shall have engaged in insurrection or rebellion against the same, or given aid or comfort to the enemies thereof. But Congress may by a vote of two-thirds of each House, remove such disability.

SECTION 4. The validity of the public debt of the United States, authorized by law, including debts incurred for payment of pensions and bounties for services in suppressing insurrection or rebellion, shall not be questioned. But neither the United States nor any State shall assume or pay any debt or obligation incurred in aid of insurrection or rebellion against the United States, or any claim for the loss or emancipation of any slave; but all such debts, obligations and claims shall be held illegal and void.

SECTION 5. The Congress shall have power to enforce, by appropriate legislation, the provisions of this article.

ARTICLE XV

SECTION 1. The right of citizens of the United States to vote shall not be denied or abridged by the United States or by any State on account of race, color, or previous condition of servitude.

SECTION 2. The Congress shall have power to enforce this article by appropriate legislation.

ARTICLE XVI

The Congress shall have power to lay and collect taxes on incomes, from whatever source derived, without apportionment among the several States, and without regard to any census or enumeration.

ARTICLE [XVII]

The Senate of the United States shall be composed of two Senators from each state, elected by the people thereof, for six years; and each Senator shall have one vote. The electors in each State shall have the qualifications requisite for electors of the most numerous branch of the State legislatures.

When vacancies happen in the representation of any State in the Senate, the executive authority of such State shall issue writs of election to fill such vacancies: *Provided,* That the legislature of any State may empower the executive thereof to make temporary appointments until the people fill the vacancies by election as the legislature may direct.

This amendment shall not be so construed as to affect the election or term of any Senator chosen before it becomes valid as part of the Constitution.

ARTICLE [XVIII]

[*SECTION 1. After one year from the ratification of this article the manufacture, sale, or transportation of intoxicating liquors within, the importation thereof into, or the exportation thereof from the*

United States and all territory subject to the jurisdiction thereof for beverage purposes is hereby prohibited.

[*Section 2. The Congress and the several States shall have concurrent power to enforce this article by appropriate legislation.*

[*Section 3. This article shall be inoperative unless it shall have been ratified as an amendment to the Constitution by the legislatures of the several States, as provided in the Constitution, within seven years from the date of the submission hereof to the States by the Congress.*]*

ARTICLE [XIX]

The right of citizens of the United States to vote shall not be denied or abridged by the United States or by any State on account of sex.

Congress shall have power to enforce this article by appropriate legislation.

ARTICLE [XX]

Section 1. The terms of the President and Vice-President shall end at noon on the 20th day of January, and the terms of Senators and Representatives at noon on the 3d day of January, of the years in which such terms would have ended if this article had not been ratified; and the terms of their successors shall then begin.

Section 2. The Congress shall assemble at least once in every year, and such meeting shall begin at noon on the 3d day of January, unless they shall by law appoint a different day.

Section 3. If, at the time fixed for the beginning of the term of the President, the President elect shall have died, the Vice-President elect shall become President. If a President shall not have been chosen before the time fixed for the beginning of his term, or if the President elect shall have failed to qualify, then the Vice-President elect shall act as President until a President shall have qualified; and the Congress may by law provide for the case wherein neither a President elect nor a Vice-President elect shall have qualified, declaring who shall then act as President, or the manner in which one who is to act shall be selected, and such person

shall act accordingly until a President or Vice-President shall have qualified.

Section 4. The Congress may by law provide for the case of the death of any of the persons from whom the House of Representatives may choose a President whenever the right of choice shall have devolved upon them, and for the case of the death of any of the persons from whom the Senate may choose a Vice-President whenever the right of choice shall have devolved upon them.

Section 5. Sections 1 and 2 shall take effect on the 15th day of October following the ratification of this article.

Section 6. This article shall be inoperative unless it shall have been ratified as an amendment to the Constitution by the legislatures of three-fourths of the several States within seven years from the date of its submission.

ARTICLE [XXI]

Section 1. The eighteenth article of amendment to the Constitution of the United States is hereby repealed.

Section 2. The transportation or importation into any State, Territory, or possession of the United States for delivery or use therein of intoxicating liquors, in violation of the laws thereof, is hereby prohibited.

Section 3. This article shall be inoperative unless it shall have been ratified as an amendment to the Constitution by conventions in the several States, as provided in the Constitution, within seven years from the date of the submission hereof to the States by the Congress.

ARTICLE [XXII]

Section 1. No person shall be elected to the office of the President more than twice, and no person who has held the office of President, or acted as President, for more than two years of a term to which some other person was elected President

---

*Repealed by section 1 of the twenty-first amendment.

shall be elected to the office of the President more than once. But this article shall not apply to any person holding the office of President when this Article was proposed by the Congress, and shall not prevent any person who may be holding the office of President, or acting as President, during the term within which this Article becomes operative from holding the office of President or acting as President during the remainder of such term.

SECTION 2. This article shall be inoperative unless it shall have been ratified as an amendment to the Constitution by the legislatures of three-fourths of the several States within seven years from the date of its submission to the States by the Congress.

ARTICLE [XXIII]

SECTION 1. The District constituting the seat of Government of the United States shall appoint in such manner as the Congress may direct:

A number of electors of President and Vice-President equal to the whole number of Senators and Representatives in Congress to which the District would be entitled if it were a State, but in no event more than the least populous State; they shall be in addition to those appointed by the States, but they shall be considered, for the purposes of the election of President and Vice-President, to be electors appointed by a State; and they shall meet in the District and perform such duties as provided by the twelfth article of amendment.

SECTION 2. The Congress shall have power to enforce this article by appropriate legislation.

ARTICLE [XXIV]

SECTION 1. The right of citizens of the United States to vote in any primary or other election for President or Vice-President, for electors for President or Vice-President, or for Senator or Representative in Congress, shall not be denied or abridged by the United States or any State by reason of failure to pay any poll tax or other tax.

SECTION 2. The Congress shall have the power to enforce this article by appropriate legislation.

ARTICLE XXV

SECTION 1. In case of removal of the President from office or of his death or resignation, the Vice-President shall become President.

SECTION 2. Whenever there is a vacancy in the office of the Vice-President, the President shall nominate a Vice-President who shall take office upon confirmation by a majority vote of both Houses of Congress.

SECTION 3. Whenever the President transmits to the President pro tempore of the Senate and the Speaker of the House of Representatives his written declaration that he is unable to discharge the powers and duties of his office, and until he transmits to them a written declaration to the contrary, such powers and duties shall be discharged by the Vice-President as Acting President.

SECTION 4. Whenever the Vice-President and a majority of either the principal officers of the executive departments or of such other body as Congress may by law provide, transmit to the President pro tempore of the Senate and the Speaker of the House of Representatives their written declaration that the President is unable to discharge the powers and duties of his office, the Vice-President shall immediately assume the powers and duties of the office as Acting President.

Thereafter, when the President transmits to the President pro tempore of the Senate and the Speaker of the House of Representatives his written declaration that no inability exists, he shall resume the powers and duties of his office unless the Vice-President and a majority of either the principal officers of the executive department or of such other body as Congress may by law provide, transmit within four days to the President pro tempore of the Senate and the Speaker of the House of Representatives their written declaration that the President is unable to discharge the powers and duties of his office. Thereupon Congress shall decide the issue, assembling within forty-eight hours for that purpose if not in session. If the Congress, within twenty-one days after receipt of the latter written declaration, or, if Congress is not in session, within twenty-one days after Congress is required to assemble, determines by two-thirds vote of both Houses that the President is unable to discharge the powers and duties of his office, the Vice-President shall continue to discharge the same as Acting President; otherwise, the President shall resume the powers and duties of his office.

ARTICLE XXVI

SECTION 1. The right of citizens of the United States, who are eighteen years of age or older, to vote shall not be denied or abridged by the United States or by any State on account of age.

SECTION 2. The Congress shall have power to enforce this article by appropriate legislation.

ARTICLE XXVII

This Article had not completed ratification by the end of 1979, and Congress extended the term for ratification to 1982.

1. Equality of rights under the law shall not be denied or abridged by the United States or by any State on account of sex.

2. The Congress shall have the power to enforce, by appropriate legislation, the provisions of this article.

3. This amendment shall take effect two years after the date of ratification.

WEBSTER'S NEW REFERENCE LIBRARY

AUTHORS AND THEIR WORKS

A knowledge of literature is the greatest humanizing force available to man. It teaches him respect for segments of mankind with whom he can have no direct acquaintance. It obligates him to compare his standards with the aims and codes of others. It provides him with illustrations of exemplary conduct, as well as of behavior to be reprobated. And it assures him of the immortality of the works of man, if not of man himself. The following brief biographical and critical accounts of some of the world's most famous writers is provided for reference.

Aeschylus (525?–456 B.C.), the Greek poet, is thought to have written about sixty plays. Only seven of his plays, dealing with the relationships of man with the gods and filled with accounts of murder, torture, revenge, and punishment, survive in their entirety. They are: the *Persae, Seven Against Thebes,* the *Agamemnon,* the *Choephori,* the *Eumenides, Prometheus Bound,* and the *Suppliant Women.*

Aesop (fl. ca. 570 B.C.), throughout classical antiquity was looked upon as the master of fables. However, it is unlikely that he left any written works. The short animal fables for which he is famous were used by him to make his point in debating.

Greek authors who were the creators of fables before the time of Aesop and other examples of fables have been found in the wisdom literature of the Sumerians, Babylonians, and Assyrians. About two hundred and thirty fables credited to Aesop, but probably spurious, are in the *Augustana,* which was printed in 1812.

Alcott, Louisa May (1832–1888), United States author, best known for her autobiographical *Little Women* (1868–1869), one of the most popular books ever written for girls.

Other books, drawn from her early experiences, were: *An Old-Fashioned Girl; Aunt Jo's Scrap Bag,* 6 vols.; *Little Men; Jo's Boys.* Her *Hospital Sketches* (1863) is valued for its vivid account of a nursing experience in the Civil War.

Andersen, Hans Christian (1805–1875), Danish author of some of the world's best-known stories. In 1822, when Andersen was seventeen, his first book, *Ungdoms-Forsog* (*Youthful Attempts*), was published under the pen name William Christian Walter. His first poem, "Det doende Barn" ("The Dying Child"), appeared in 1827; he became better known with the publication of *Fodreise fra Holmens Kanal til Østpynten af Amager* in 1829, the same year his first play was performed. *Improvisatoren* (1835), an autobiographical novel with an Italian setting, was his first and most successful novel. While this book was being printed, Andersen began to write the children's stories that were to bring him lasting fame. Such fairy tales as "The Tinderbox," "Little Claus and Big Claus," "The Princess and the Pea," "Little Ida's Flowers," "The Tin Soldier," and "The Emperor's New Clothes" have been translated into eighty languages and are known and loved the world over.

Anderson, Maxwell (1888–1959), United States playwright who contributed to the development of modern American drama. His plays, some of which are written in a form of blank verse, include comedy, historical drama, and political satire. The World War I comedy *What Price Glory?* (1924) was written in collaboration with Laurence Stallings. He turned to history for *Elizabeth the Queen, Mary of Scotland,* and *Anne of the*

Thousand Days (1947). The very successful *Both Your Houses* was awarded the Pulitzer Prize. With two poetic plays, *Winterset*, inspired by the Sacco-Vanzetti case, and *High Tor*, he expressed his displeasure with the materialism of the modern world. In 1955 he wrote *The Bad Seed*.

Anderson, Sherwood (1876–1941), United States author whose stories presented sympathetically the lives of Middle Western townspeople. His first novel was *Windy McPherson's Son;* his reputation was made by *Winesburg, Ohio* (1919), which he called "A Book of the Grotesque"; it is a fictional study of repressed characters in a country village. This and the short stories in *The Triumph of the Egg, Horses and Men,* and *Death in the Woods* are considered his best work. In *Poor White* he studied the effects of the change to industry on a small town and its inhabitants. *Dark Laughter* and *Kit Brandon* are others of his works.

Aquinas, Saint Thomas (1225?–1274), medieval Italian philosopher, theologian, and the greatest organizer of Roman Catholic thought. His writings include theological and philosophical commentaries, discussions of doctrine, several short treatises, and two famous summaries of doctrine. The *Summa Contra Gentiles,* a manual of Catholic doctrine, was intended for use by missionaries in Spain. The *Summa Theologiae,* a large theological synthesis, was left unfinished.

Aquinas had immense influence on later theological thought and his doctrine has been officially endorsed by two encyclicals–Leo XIII's *Aeterni Patris* (1879) and Pius XI's *Studiorem Ducem* (1923). His eucharistic hymns, especially the "Lauda Sion" and the "Pange Lingua," are classed with the great medieval Latin lyrics.

Archimedes (ca. 287?–212 B.C.), Greek mathematician and inventor, was  the only one of his age to make any real contribution to the theory of mechanics and to hydrostatics. His *On the Equilibrium and the Center of Gravity of Planes* may be considered the foundation of theoretical mechanics. The endless screw and the Archimedes screw are among the inventions ascribed to him. His other works include *On the Sphere and Cylinder, The Measurement of the Circle, On Conoids and Spheroids, On Spirals, The Quadrature of the Parabola, On Floating Bodies, The Sand Reckoner, The Method,* and *A Collection of Lemmas.*

Aristophanes (ca. 450–ca. 388 B.C.), most fa-  mous of all Greek writers of comedy, is credited with having written fifty-four plays, of which only eleven are extant. Those belonging to his first writing period are *Acharnians, Knights, Clouds, Peace,* and *Wasps.* The *Clouds* (423 B.C.) attacks "modern" education and morals, as they were taught by the Sophists. In the play, which ridicules Socrates and his pupils, their school known as the *Phrontisterion* or "Thinking Shop" is burned to the ground. *Wasps* (422 B.C.) satirizes the Athenians' penchant for lawsuits. To the second period belong *Birds, Lysistrata, Thesmophoriazusae,* and *Frogs.* In these the political satire is milder; *Frogs* is a literary rather than a "social" comedy. *Ecclesiazusae* and *Plutus* are the last of Aristophanes' plays. In the former, the women of Athens, instead of the men, are in power and the communism of wealth, property, and sex which is introduced is strongly reminiscent of that in the fifth book of Plato's *Republic.*

Aristotle (384–322 B.C.), a Greek famous in the fields of philosophy, logic, morals, politics, psychology, biology, and literary criticism. His theory of reasoning was the first, with modern additions, to survive to the present day as deductive logic. His treatises are concerned chiefly with logic (analytics), rhetoric, poetics, physics, psychology, and biology. In the *Poetics* is stated his theory of catharsis: tragedy "by raising pity and fear, purges the mind of these passions." Among his well known works are the *Organon,* concerning science or scientific reasoning; *Physics,* on inorganic nature; *Parva naturalia,* on such subjects as sensation, memory, sleep, and dreams; *Historia animalium,* a record of natural history data. Other important works include the *Eudemian Ethics* and the *Nicomachean Ethics.*

Arnold, Matthew (1822–1888), English poet and critic. The undercurrent of sadness found in much of his poetry, as in "Dover Beach," reflects his feelings about the conflict between longcherished beliefs and science. Other noted poems are the long narrative "Sohrab and Rustum" and "The Scholar Gypsy." Arnold's outstanding critical essays are *Essays in Criticism* (1865, 1888), a discussion of the scope and importance of criticism; *Culture and Anarchy* (1869), an attack on the smugness and money-worship of Victorian England; and *The Study of Poetry,* which presents the thesis that poetry will have to replace religion.

Arouet, François Marie (1694–1778), who wrote under the pen name of Voltaire, French philosopher and author. *Zaire* is possibly the best of his tragedies that follows along classical lines. It probably is one of the ten or twelve best plays of the French classical school. His *Letters Concerning the English Nation* profoundly influenced other writers.

His two great historical works were *Siècle de Louis XIV* and *Essai sur l'histoire générale et sur les moeurs et l'espirit des nations* (7 volumes) with special attention given to cultural and economic developments. His short "philosophical novels" are popular today, particularly *Candide* (1759), a masterpiece of saucy satire. Voltaire was a prolific writer, and his voluminous correspondence is very revealing about himself.

Austen, Jane (1775–1817), English novelist.

The writings that established Jane Austen's literary reputation were *Pride and Prejudice,* a gently humorous novel of conflict between the heroine and hero; *Emma,* whose heroine is an engaging personality in spite of her meddling with the lives of others; *Sense and Sensibility,* which presents two heroines, one practical, the other inclined toward the romantic. *Mansfield Park, Northanger Abbey,* and *Persuasion* are other popular novels. Most of her fame and popularity came after her death.

Bacon, Francis (1561–1626), English phi-

losopher, statesman, and man of letters. Among his greatest professional, philosophical, and literary works are *The History of Henry VII;* the *Essays* (1597), an indication of his complete thoughts; and *New Atlantis,* a philosophic romance. He is also noted for his plan to develop a system of inductive logic. Of his plans to reorganize

knowledge, in a philosophical work, *Instauratio Magna,* he completed, *The Advancement of Learning* and *Novum Organum.*

Balzac, Honoré de (1799–1850), French novelist, one of the greatest and most productive writers of fiction of all time. His first success came with the publication of *Les Derniers Chouans* in 1829. He conceived the idea of presenting an all-inclusive picture of modern civilization in *La Comédie Humaine.* It includes partly interconnected novels which recreate French society and picture in exact detail individuals of all classes and professions. Among the best known of his 85 novels are *Eugénie Grandet, Le Père Goriot, La Cousine Bette, Le Cousin Pons, The Magic Skin,* and the Sweden-borgian *Seraphita.*

Baudelaire, Charles Pierre (1821–1867), French poet and critic. He is noted mainly for *Les Fleurs du mal (Flowers of Evil),* a volume of verse condemned as obscene. He excelled in writing of the macabre and the morbid, and exhibited this talent in his sympathetic translations of Poe's works. His only novel was the autobiographical *La Fanfarlo.*

Bellamy, Edward (1850–1898), United States writer, best known for his idealistic romance, *Looking Backward* (1888). This described a coming Utopian society that stressed cooperation, brotherhood, and especially technological adjustment to the needs of humans in A.D. 2000. Several tales combined in *The Blindman's World and Other Stories* subtly criticized conventional America.

Benét, Stephen Vincent (1898–1943), United States poet, novelist, and short story writer, best known for *John Brown's Body,* a long narrative poem of the Civil War which was awarded the Pulitzer Prize in 1929. His work is notable for a sense of drama and patriotism. Other well-known poems are "The Portrait of a Southern Lady" and "Ballad of William Sycamore." "The Devil and Daniel Webster" is one of his most imaginative short stories.

Beyle, Marie Henri (1783–1842), French writer who used the pseudonym of Stendhal, was one of the most creative and distinguished of French essayists and novelists. Although almost unknown during his lifetime, Stendhal wrote masterpieces which, for their psychological analysis, are among the greatest novels of all times. *The Red and the Black* is a brilliant picture of an ambitious young Frenchman to whom his own country seems foreign. *The Charterhouse of Parma* is a colorful, delightful novel of amour and politics. *Lucien Leuwen* is an unusually realistic and revealing political novel which was published in the United States as two novels: *The Green Huntsman* and *The Telegraph.*

Boccaccio, Giovanni (1313–1375), Italian writer and humanist, one of the principal figures of the Italian renaissance. *The Decameron,* his most famous work, was probably written during the years 1348–1358. It is composed of 100 stories told during a ten-day period by seven ladies and three gentlemen who, in 1348, flee to the country from plague-stricken Florence. The plots of the stories are based on popular tales of that period, especially the fabliaux, which had come to Italy from France. The word *Decameron* means "ten days' work." Boccaccio's other works include *Filicolo, Filostrato,* and *Teseida.*

Boswell, James (1740–1795), Scotsman, friend and biographer of Samuel Johnson, and one of the world's greatest diarists. His first literary fame came from *An Account of Corsica, the Journal of a Tour to That Island* and from his *Memoirs of Pascal Paoli.* However, it is for the *Life of Johnson* (1791) that Boswell continues to retain his place in English letters.

Brecht, Bertolt (1898–1956), German poet and playwright. His early plays, *Baal* and *Trommeln in der Nacht* (1922), won the contemporary critics' acclaim. Both these and *Im Dickicht der Städte* were expressionist. Brecht used stark realism and simplicity of style, as he had also used them in his early lyrics and ballads, collected under the satirical title *Die Hauspostille (Book of Family Devotions).* Brecht's greatest theatrical success was his *Die Dreigroschenoper (The Threepenny Opera),* with music by Kurt Weill. It is an adaptation of Gay's *Beggars' Opera* and portrays human greed, indolence, and bewilderment.

Brecht's claim to fame is based on plays that deal with human issues from a Marxist point of view: *Mutter Courage und ihre Kinder,* a chronicle of the Thirty Years' War; *Leben des Galilei; Herr Puntila und sein Knecht;* and the dramatic parables, *Der gute Mensch von Sezuan* and *Der kaukasische Kreidekreis.*

Brontë, Charlotte (1816–1855), English novelist. Charlotte Brontë recorded her memories of the school she attended in *Jane Eyre* (1847), her most famous novel. It is a fascinating tale of wild melodrama. Her book *Shirley* is the first English regional novel. The three Brontë sisters–Charlotte, Emily, and Anne–collaborated on *Poems* in 1846.

Brontë, Emily (1818–1848), English novelist and poet. Her *Wuthering Heights* (1847) is an intensely dramatic, creative work of fiction, a tale of psychological horror, technically interesting for its narrative point of view.

Browning, Elizabeth Barrett (1806–1861),

English poet, wife of the poet Robert Browning. She was born Elizabeth Barrett, under which name she wrote and published *Sonnets from the Portuguese* (1850). This is considered her best work–gentle, yet deeply sincere–and assures her of a permanent place among English poets. Other works include *Casa Guidi Windows* and a novel in verse, *Aurora Leigh.*

Browning, Robert (1812–1889), English poet. For some years Browning wrote verse-drama, including his popular *Pippa Passes.* He then turned to shorter poems, such as "Home Thoughts from Abroad," "The Pied Piper of Hamelin," and "Waring," but won his greatest fame with such dramatic monologues as "My Last Duchess," "Andrea del Sarto," and "The Bishop Orders His Tomb at Saint Praxed's Church." The most outstanding works of his last years included *The Ring and The Book,* his greatest poem (1868), and his long dramatic or narrative poems, *Fifine at the Fair, The Inn Album, Dramatic Idyls,* in two series, *Pauline,* and *Sordello.*

Buck, Pearl S. (1892–1973), United States novelist who won the 1938 Nobel Prize in Literature. Until 1934 she spent most of her life in China, where her parents and her first husband were missionaries. Her first novel, *East Wind: West Wind* (1930), was followed by *The Good Earth* (1931), which won the Pulitzer Prize. Her later books include *The Patriot, Dragon Seed,* and *Peony.* Her works are notable for the vivid descriptions of Oriental life and problems, and for their understanding of humanity.

Burke, Edmund (1729–1797), was born in Ireland but became a British political thinker, statesman, and parliamentary orator. He was outstanding in protests against the Crown in favor of the American colonies. Two speeches, *On American Taxation* and *On Moving His Resolutions for Conciliation with the Colonies,* expressed Burke's pro-American sentiments. Two others of Burke's well-known speeches were on affairs in India–*On Mr. Fox's East India Bill* and *On the Nabob of Arcot's Debts.* He was hostile to the French Revolution and wrote his *Reflections on the French Revolution* as a protest.

Burns, Robert (1759–1796), one of the greatest Scottish poets. His *Poems, Chiefly in the Scottish Dialect* won him immediate acclaim. Among his better known poems are "Holy Willie's Prayer," a satiric poem; "The Cotter's Saturday Night," and "Tam O'Shanter." His songs "O Wert Thou in the Cauld Blast," "Flow Gently, Sweet Afton," "Ae Fond Kiss," "Auld Lang Syne," and "Coming thro' the Rye" are well loved in all English-speaking parts of the world.

Byron, George Gordon, 6th Baron (1788–1824), English poet and satirist. *Childe Harold* (1812–1818) and *Don Juan,* long romances in verse, are autobiographical, as was his poetic drama *Sardanapalus.* Byron's *The Vision of Judgment* is a satire on Southey. His letters were conversational and witty. Many of them, first published in the twentieth century, have enhanced his literary reputation. Other long poems include *The Bride of Abydos, Manfred,* and *Mazeppa.* A shorter piece, *The Prisoner of Chillon* (set in the Fortress of Chillon in Montreux, Switzerland) is today one of his most familiar works.

Carlyle, Thomas (1795–1881), Scots essayist and historian. His translation in 1824 of Goethe's *Wilhelm Meister's Apprenticeship* is a masterpiece. His book *The French Revolution* (1837) is his greatest work. He saw the French Revolution as a judgment of monarchy. He expressed his preference for the Middle Ages over the present in *Past and Present.* Another important work is *Latter-Day Pamphlets. Sartor Resartus* expressed his views on British society.

Cather, Willa (1873–1947), United States novelist of the frontier. In her pioneer novels, adventure was replaced by ordinary daily living. *O Pioneers!* (1913) was her first great success and *One of Ours* (1922) won the Pulitzer Prize. Other outstanding novels of Willa Cather's were *My Antonia,* about the Nebraska girlhood of a Bohemian immigrant; *A Lost Lady,* which mourned the passing of the pioneer spirit of the Middle West; and *Death Comes for the Archbishop,* an account of the establishment of the Catholic Church in the Southwest.

Cato, Marcus Porcius [called **The Censor**] (234–149 B.C.), Roman statesman, orator, and first Latin prose writer of importance. He wrote the first history of Rome in Latin, the *Origines,* but it is now lost. His only surviving work is *De Re Rustica,* written about 160 B.C., which dealt with the production of wine, oil, and fruit, and with grazing. He compiled an encyclopedia and maxims, and works on medicine, military science, and law.

Catullus, Gainus Valerius (84?–54 B.C.), Roman lyric poet. His many poems, of which about one hundred or so survive, include satires, epigrams, and especially passionate lyric poems addressed to the lady Lesbia.

Cervantes Saavedra, Miguel de (1547–1616), Spanish novelist, playwright, poet, and creator of Don Quixote. In January, 1605, his immortal work, *El Ingenioso Hidalgo Don Quixote de la Mancha,* appeared in Madrid. It was a mad, kindly satire on the pretensions inspired by chivalry and romance. The second part of *Don Quixote* was not completed until 1615. Of the twenty to thirty plays he wrote, only two, *El Trato de Argel* and *La Numancia,* have survived. A pastoral novel, *La Galatea,* appeared in 1584; his twelve excellent short novels, *Novelas ejemplares,* in 1613. The following year *Viaje del Parnaso,* a burlesque poem, and the *Adjunta al Parnaso,* in prose, appeared. Shortly before his death, Cervantes returned to his first enthusiasm, drama, with the *Ocho comedias y ocho entremeses nuevos.* By virtue of *Don Quixote,* Cervantes ranks as one of the world's great writers.

Chaucer, Geoffrey (ca. 1340–1400), probably the greatest English poet before Shakespeare. *The Canterbury Tales* has always been the most popular of Chaucer's works. In it some 30 pilgrims are described on their travels from a suburb in London to Canterbury. The pilgrims, drawn from different classes and occupations, are treated with gentle irony and humor as they tell their tales. Others of Chaucer's outstanding works are *Troilus and Criseyde* and *The Legend of Good Women*. He also wrote short poems and addresses.

Chekhov, Anton Pavlovich (1860–1904), Russian playwright and short story writer. His works present a graphic picture of middle-class Russia at the turn of the century. There is also a quality of timelessness created by his heroes who struggle against static forces of almost overwhelming inertia. His first full-length play, *Ivanov* (1887), was followed by *The Wood Demon* and *The Seagull* (1896). The plays usually considered his masterpieces are *Uncle Vanya; The Three Sisters* (1901), which is his most profound dramatic work; and *The Cherry Orchard*.

The best and best known of his many short stories are "The Lady with the Dog," "In the Ravine," "The Chorus Girl," "A Woman's Kingdom," "Peasants," and "Three Years," a story of Moscow life which includes much autobiographical material.

Cicero, Marcus Tullius (106–43 B.C.), Roman statesman, orator, scholar, and writer. His correspondence reveals the political, social, literary, and economic life of Rome. His best-known poems (they survive only in fragments) were the epics *On His Consulship* and *On His Life and Times*.

Four collections of Cicero's letters–to Atticus, to his friends, to Brutus, and to his brother–form a revealing historical source of the ancient world of his time.

Clemens, Samuel Langhorne (1835–1910), who wrote under the pen name of Mark Twain, United States' most famous humorist and the author of popular and outstanding autobiographical works, travel books, and novels. One of Twain's best books, *The Adventures of Tom Sawyer* (1876), is certainly his best for young people. It takes place in the river town of Hannibal, Missouri, and is a contrast of boys' "orneriness" with their natural decency. By general agreement, *Huckleberry Finn* (1884) is Twain's finest book and an outstanding American novel. Huck wants to be "free and satisfied." The book runs the gamut from humor to drama. *The Prince and the Pauper* is a historical novel making use of the ancient artifice of exchanged identities. Another historical fiction is *A Connecticut Yankee in King Arthur's Court*. Other works include: *Life on the Mississippi, Innocents Abroad* (1869), *Roughing It, The Gilded Age, Pudd'nhead Wilson* (1894), and many short stories.

Coleridge, Samuel Taylor (1772–1834), English poet, lecturer, journalist, and critic of literature, theology, philosophy, and society. His best known poems are: "The Rime of the Ancient Mariner" (1798), a narrative tale showing the poet's insight into the sense of the Infinite, "Christabel," and "Kubla Khan." The "Ancient Mariner" remains outstanding among narrative poems in English. He and William Wordsworth

published *Lyrical Ballads* in 1798. Later poems include *Sybilline Leaves* and the critique *Biographia Literaria*.

Congreve, William (1670–1729), English dramatist. In 1692 he published the delightful *Incognito*, or *Love and Duty Reconcil'd*. In 1693 he achieved fame with the staging of *The Old Bachelor*. *Love for Love* is best suited for the stage. A tragedy, *The Mourning Bride*, is now remembered for its lyrics "Music Hath Charms" and "Hell Hath No Fury." *The Way of the World*, which appeared in 1700, is considered to be Congreve's masterpiece.

Conrad, Joseph (1857–1924), British seaman and novelist, born in Poland and named Teodor

Jósef Konrad Korzeniowski. He became one of the greatest novelists and short story writers in the English language. Conrad's first novels, *Almayer's Folly* (1895) and *An Outcast of the Islands* (1896), were set in the East Indies. They were followed by *The Nigger of the "Narcissus," Lord Jim* (1900), and *Chance* (1914). When *Chance* became famous, readers rediscovered *Lord Jim. Nostromo* (1904), his most elaborate novel, is a story of revolution, politics, and graft in a South American republic and is considered Conrad's masterpiece.

Cowper, William (1731–1800), once one of the most widely read of English poets. In 1784 he wrote the ballad *The Diverting History of John Gilpin*, which was soon sung throughout London. In 1779 the *Olney Hymns*, a book of religious verse, appeared. *The Castaway* was one of his longer tragic poems.

Crane, Stephen (1871–1900), United States novelist, poet, and short story writer. His novel, *Maggie: a Girl of the Streets*, is a naturalistic study of life in a New York slum. *The Red Badge of Courage* (1895), his most famous work, is a Civil War novel exploring the fear, shame, disgust, and courage of a Union soldier. Its realistic descriptions of battle scenes have great verisimilitude. Crane was the author of two books of poems, *The Black Riders* and *War Is Kind*.

Cummings, e. e. (1894–1962), United States poet and artist, whose volume of *Collected Poems* is probably his best known; his work shows deep poetic insight, strongly expressed in unusual ways–he was most unorthodox in punctuation, including the use of small letters for capital letters. *Viva, No Thanks, One Times One*, and *95 Poems* are among his volumes of verse. One of the better World War I novels was Cummings' *The Enormous Room*.

Dana, Richard Henry (1815–1882), United States lawyer and author, whose literary fame rests on a single book, *Two Years Before the Mast* (1840). It describes a voyage he himself made around Cape Horn to California and back and presents "the life of a common sailor at sea as it really is."

Dante [full name **Dante Alighieri**] (1265–1321), the greatest poet of Italy, author of the allegorical Christian poem, the sublime *Divina Commedia* or *Divine Comedy*. His other works include the *Vita Nuova* and *Monarchia*, on world government. Among his unfinished works are *Convivio* and *De vulgari eloquentia*.

Darwin, Charles Robert (1809–1882), English naturalist. In 1859, Darwin published his great work *On the Origin of Species by Means of Natural Selection, or the Preservation of Favoured Races in the Struggle for Life*. As an explanation for evolution he gave first place to the "survival of the fittest."

Defoe, Daniel (1659?–1731), English novelist and political pamphleteer. His pamphlet, *The Shortest Way with the Dissenters* (1702), resulted in a fine and imprisonment at Newgate. On his release, he started the periodical *The Review*, incorporating commercial interests and domestic and political articles. Defoe's political and domestic writings are now all but forgotten. His fame rests largely on *The Review*, which is important in the history of journalism, and on two novels, *Robinson Crusoe* (1719), one of the most famous books ever written, and *Moll Flanders* (1722).

Demosthenes (384/383–322 B.C.), Greek statesman and orator. The contents of his speeches illuminate the political, social, and economic life of Athens in the fourth century B.C. Among the most famous of his orations are the *Olynthiacs*, occasioned by Philip of Macedon's attack on the state of Olynthus, and the *Philippics*, directed against Philip. Demosthenes' famous speech, *On the Crown*, was used to vindicate himself at a trial held in 330 B.C.

De Quincey, Thomas (1785–1859), English writer, author of *Confessions of an English Opium-Eater* (1822). Of De Quincey's works, the most important are his autobiographical writings, his literary criticism, and the unfinished *Suspiria de Profundis*, with its theme that grief and pain are essential to the development of the soul. In the *Autobiographic Sketches*, his objective is to trace the growth and development of his own mind. The "Daughter of Lebanon," found at the end of the *Confessions*, even though only a fragment, is a splendid example of De Quincey's prose.

Descartes, René (1596–1650), French philosopher and mathematician, who extended mathematical ideas and proofs to all facets of knowledge and to knowledge itself. Descartes' outstanding work is the *Discourse on the Method of Properly Guiding the Reason in the Search for Truth in the Sciences*. This book established as the basis for modern

rationalism, scientific doubt and mathematical logic. Part is titled *Also the Dioptric, the Meteors and the Geometry, which are Essays in this Method* (Leyden, 1637). Descartes thus, in addition to his theoretical studies, also presents fully worked-out examples of his method's application. Other philosophical works are *Meditationes de Prima Philosophia* (1641) and *Principia Philosophiae* (1644). The *Geometry* (1637) embodies his discovery and formulation of coordinate geometry; much of this work has now been adopted by modern textbooks.

Dickens, Charles (1812–1870), one of the greatest English novelists. Dickens' humanitarian novels describe vividly the scenes of the poor of his time, including the poorhouse and the debtors' prison. In *David Copperfield* (1849–1850) he uses incidents from his own bitter childhood. The *Pickwick Papers* charmingly recreates the life of stagecoach and country inn. *Hard Times* may be considered historically important as Dickens' most radical book. As in all the novels that follow, Dickens demands social reform and the regeneration of men. Other Dickens novels include *Little Dorrit; A Tale of Two Cities*, a historical romance of the French Revolution; *Great Expectations; Oliver Twist* (1837–1839); and *Martin Chuzzlewit.*

Dickinson, Emily (1830–1886), United States poet, considered one of the great women poets of the nineteenth century, only six of whose poems were published in her lifetime. Thomas Wentworth Higginson published 116 poems in 1890–1891, and other collections appeared at intervals. In 1945 over 600 new poems were presented in *Bolts of Melody.*

Donne, John (1573–1631), English cleric, poet, and prose writer. Donne's life reflected the device he used in his writing the *Paradox.* His sensual, witty *Elegies* and the caustic *Satires* are examples of his early poetry. In later life, when he had left Roman Catholicism and embraced the Church of England, becoming Dean of St. Paul's, his writings became devotional. His works include, among others, the lyric *The Songs and Sonnets* and the prose *Paradoxes and Problems.*

Dos Passos, John (1896–1970), United States novelist. Dos Passos won fame with his novel about World War I, *Three Soldiers* (1921). In 1925 *Manhattan Transfer* appeared. The book presented a view of New York life, using an experimental technique. This same "collage" technique was carried forward in the trilogy *U.S.A.,* an important record of the United States from 1900 to the 1930s. The trilogy contains his best-known novels–*The 42nd Parallel; 1919,* a story of the World War I years; and *The Big Money,* which dealt with the frantic money-making of the post-World War I period. Dos Passos' later works include such novels as *The Grand Design, The Great Days,* and *Mid-century* (1961), as well as travel books, historical studies, and documentaries.

Dostoevski, Fëdor Mikhailovich (1821–1881), Russian novelist whose first novel, *Poor Folk,* brought him quick recognition. Between 1861 and 1881, he wrote several long novels, the best known of which are *Crime and Punishment* and *The Brothers Karamazov. Crime and Punishment* is the story of the murder of an old woman by a half-starved student; *The Brothers Karamazov* relates the love of a father and son for the same girl, with the son murdering the father. Other novels are *The House of the Dead, The Idiot,* and *The Possessed.* Of his short novels, *Notes from the Underground* is considered the best.

A giant of literature, Dostoevski continues to be one of the most widely read novelists of all times as new editions of his greatest works keep appearing.

Doyle, Sir Arthur Conan (1859–1930), English novelist and historian. It was through his cycle of Sherlock Holmes stories that Conan Doyle gained fame. The ingenious methods he suggested in these stories for the detection of crime are said to have influenced law enforcement agencies in developing scientific methods of crime detection. Doyle's Sherlock Holmes stories have been made into movies, plays, radio, and television shows. The best-known Holmes stories are *The Hound of the Baskervilles, The Sign of the Four,* and *The Memoirs of Sherlock Holmes.*

Dreiser, Theodore (1871–1945), United States author, distinguished for his naturalistic novels. His first novel, *Sister Carrie* (1900), was a starkly realistic picture of the poor conditions under which factory girls worked. Practically suppressed by its publisher, it attracted little attention. *Jennie Gerhardt* (1911) was also controversial, but it won success. Only then was a new edition of *Sister Carrie* accepted on its merits. The next year Dreiser brought out *The Financier,* first of a trilogy about a businessman whose career in many respects resembled that of an actual financial magnate. The others in the series were *The Titan* and *The Stoic*. The best of his novels, *An American Tragedy* (1925), was based on an actual murder case and brought Dreiser worldwide recognition as a major novelist.

Dudevant, Amandine Lucile Aurore (1804–1876), née Dupin [also **Baronne Dudevant**], French novelist, who used the pseudonym George Sand. Among her best-known novels are *Indiana, La Mare au Diable (The Haunted Pool)*, and *La Petite Fadette (Fanchon the Cricket). Elle et Lui* is her version of her affair with Musset; *Un Hiver à Majorque (A Winter in Majorca)* tells of her life on the island with Chopin. The dramatization of several of her plays met with some success—*Le Marquis de Villemer* was a triumph.

Dumas, Alexandre, the Elder, (1802–1870), French novelist and dramatist. He is known for his famous romances: *The Count of Monte Cristo*, an exciting story of melodramatic revenge, romance, and adventure, *The Three Musketeers, Twenty Years After*, and *The Vicomte de Bragelonne*, which depict French life under Louis XIII. His *Louis XIV et Son Siecle* is the most important of his historical works, and his best-known play is *La Taur de Nesle*.

Dumas, Alexandre, the Younger (1824–1895), French playwright and novelist, son of Alexandre Dumas, the Elder. His novel *La Dame aux Camelias (Camille)* won him immediate acclaim. He wrote many plays and novels about contemporary trends in politics, business, and romance which became the bases for successful stage plays. Verdi's *La Traviata* is based on Dumas' *Camille*.

Eliot, T. S. (1888–1965), American-born British poet, playwright, and critic. His first book of poems, *Prufrock and Other Observations,* appeared in 1917; the next volumes were *Poems* (1920), *The Waste Land*, and *Ash Wednesday*. In 1944, he published *Four Quartets,* a modern metaphysical poem. He received the Nobel Prize for Literature in 1948. He wrote two religious verse plays, *The Rock* and *Murder in the Cathedral*, and returned to the theater with *The Family Reunion, The Cocktail Party, The Confidential Clerk,* and *The Elder Statesman.*

Emerson, Ralph Waldo (1803–1882), United States essayist, poet, lecturer, and one of the most stimulating thinkers of the nineteenth century. His Phi Beta Kappa oration at Harvard in 1837, later known as *The American Scholar*, was called by Oliver Wendell Holmes our intellectual Declaration of Independence. Emerson's views on democracy, conformity, individual liberty, American customs of the time, and a host of other subjects, were delivered as lectures and subsequently were published under a variety of titles. Among them were *Essays: First and Second Series, Representative Men, Society and Solitude,* and *English Traits.* His best-known poems include "Brahma," "The Concord Hymn," "The Problem," "Ode to Beauty," and "The Rhodora." Emerson, a Protestant minister, gave up the pulpit because of his nonconformist views.

Epicurus (341–270 B.C.), Greek philosopher. Most of our information on Epicurus comes from other sources. His own observations are expressed in forty short, pithy statements in *Principal Doctrines* and in three letters: *To Herodotus, To Pythocles,* and *To Menoeccus.* Epicurus' great work *On Nature* (originally in 37 books) was found in the papyrus rolls discovered at Herculaneum in the years 1752–1754. The doctrines of Epicurus offer the human soul outlets for its anxieties and show how the simple fact of being can be the foundation for real happiness.

Euripides (ca. 485–407 B.C.), youngest of the three great Greek tragedians, following Aeschylus and Sophocles. Of his 19 surviving plays the best known are *Medea, Electra, The Trojan Women, Orestes,* and *Alcestis*. The struggle of the human will to overcome human passions is a central theme in many of Euripedes' plays, as in *Medea*. Medea was wronged by Jason, who owed his achievements and his life to her. When he cast her off to marry a Greek princess, she punished him by killing his wife and her own children by him, leaving him to grow old alone.

Evans, Mary Ann (1819–1880), who used the pen name of George Eliot, was one of the great English novelists of the Victorian age. Her early novels were based on her memories of life in the English countryside of Warwickshire; they are considered somewhat autobiographical. Her first was *Scenes of Clerical Life*. Then came *Adam Bede*, her first long novel, which she described as a "country story–full of the breath of cows and the scent of hay." In *The Mill on the Floss* she again turned to the scenes of her early life and her relations with her brother Isaac. *Middlemarch* is her most substantial work. In the classroom she is well known for her *Silas Marner*, the story of a weaver whose lost gold is replaced by a strayed child.

Faulkner, William (1897–1962), United States author. With his first novels about mythical Yoknapatawpha County, Mississippi, *Sartoris* and *The Sound and the Fury* (both 1928–1929), Faulkner began a series of books about social and racial problems in the South. Others in the series are *As I Lay Dying; Light in August; Absalom, Absalom!;* "The Bear" [in *Go Down, Moses and Other Stories*]; and *Intruder in the Dust* (1948). He was awarded the 1949 Nobel Prize in Literature.

Aside from the Yoknapatawpha series, a trilogy on the Snopes family, *The Hamlet, The Town*, and *The Mansion*, began brilliantly but slackened as it progressed. Faulkner's most ambitious work was the novel *A Fable*, which won the Pulitzer Prize in 1955.

Fielding, Henry (1707–1754), English jurist, novelist, and playwright, is best known for one of the  greatest of realistic novels, which he wrote toward the end of his career. This novel is *Tom Jones, or the History of a Foundling*, the long and zestful story of a lively hero, richly filled with adventures and characters.

Fielding's numerous plays include *Love in Several Masques, The Author's Farce, Tom Thumb*, and *The Coffee House Politican*. Prior to *Tom Jones* he had written the novels *Joseph Andrews* and *Jonathan Wild*. His prolific pen also produced poetry, essays, and treatises. In addition to his literary writings, he produced two newspapers and was called to the bar. Fielding was influential on such writers as Dickens and Thackeray.

FitzGerald, Edward (1809–1883), English translator. In 1859 an anonymous translation from the Persian was published as *The Rubaiyat of Omar Khayyám*. The translation was by FitzGerald. Regardless of the merit of the *Rubaiyat*, the translation was recognized immediately as a literary work of consequence. FitzGerald produced translations of *Agamemnon* of Aeschylus, Oedipus tragedies of Sophocles, and some plays of Calderón.

Fitzgerald, F. Scott (1896–1940), United States novelist who captured the spirit of the 1920s. The first of his best works, *This Side of Paradise* (1920), largely autobiographical, was about the rebellious youth of the twenties. It was followed by two volumes of short stories, *Flappers and Philosophers* and *Tales of the Jazz Age*, and a second novel, *The Beautiful and the Damned*, which revolved around the revolt of sophisticated youth and the meaninglessness of life. *The Great Gatsby*, Fitzgerald's best-known book, satirized wealthy Long Island society in the 1920s and revealed his literary merit. Some of his finest short stories were included in *All the Sad Young Men*, and another novel, *Tender Is the Night*, exploits his own sadly tortured domestic situation. He died before completing *The Last Tycoon* (published posthumously in 1941).

Flaubert, Gustave (1821–1880), French novelist. Many French critics call *Sentimental Education* Flaubert's best work. It is about the disillusionment of a young Parisian through love. His *Salammbô* is a barbaric, colorful story of love and war in ancient Carthage. In *Madame Bovary*, sometimes called "the perfect novel," Flaubert took a run-of-the-mill story of adultery in a small French village and turned it into a work of enduring literary merit.

Freud, Sigmund (1856–1939), Austrian physician and author, was the  founder of psychoanalysis, which began as a technique for the analysis and cure of mental illness. His psychoanalytic principles have influenced medicine, psychology, the arts, religion, education, and the social sciences. He is considered one of the outstanding thinkers of the twentieth century. Through his early work on the treatment of hysteria by hypnosis he became aware of the importance of the unconscious in men's minds. Later he gave up the use of hypnosis, substituting for it the technique of "free association of ideas" for bringing unconscious memories and emotions into consciousness. Among his leading works are *Studies in Hysteria* (with Josef Breuer) (1895); *The Interpretation of Dreams* (1899); *Introductory Lectures on Psychoanalysis* (1916); *Beyond the Pleasure Principle* (1920); *The Future of an Illusion* (1927); *Civilization and Its Discontents* (1930); and *Moses and Monotheism* (1939).

Frost, Robert Lee (1874–1963), four times winner of the Pulitzer Prize in Poetry, United States poet of the people, of New Englanders, of New England itself, its hills, its hardships, its humor, and inverse tenderness. While his poetry has a regional quality, its real subject is human life and destiny. His works include *A Boy's Will, North of Boston, New Hampshire, West-Running Brook, A Witness Tree, A Masque of Mercy,* and *Complete Poems.* Among his latest poems are "The Gift Outright," the poem delivered at the inaugural of President John F. Kennedy, which was included in a volume of poetry published in 1962, entitled *In the Clearing.* As a distinguished man of letters he received many awards and honorary degrees.

Galsworthy, John (1867–1933), British playwright and novelist, winner of the Nobel Prize in Literature in 1932. Galsworthy attracted wide attention with his novels, *The Man of Property* in 1906 and *The Island Pharisees* in 1908. The former was the first of *The Forsyte Saga* series. *The Indian Summer of a Forsyte, In Chancery, Awakening,* and *To Let* were others in the series. In 1942 Galsworthy published *The White Monkey,* the first of a trilogy about London after World War I, of which *The Silver Spoon* and *Swan Song* were the other two. *The Silver Spoon* shows Galsworthy's rapport with youth and beauty. Among his plays are *Strife, The Silver Box, Justice,* and *The Forest.*

Germaine, Anne Louise (1766–1817), who used the pen name Madame de Staël, French novelist and writer, wrote two very successful novels, *Delphine* and *Corinne.* Her chief work was *De l'Allemagne,* which through its enthusiasm for German romanticism, strongly influenced French literature.

Gibbon, Edward (1737–1794), English historian. Gibbon's monumental six-volume *Decline and Fall of the Roman Empire* (1788) remains one of the outstanding achievements in all historical writing. It displays a mastery of the architectonics of English prose. The *Decline* covers the period A.D. 180–641 exhaustively; and the period A.D. 641–1453 in summary form. Gibbon also wrote his autobiography, *Memoirs of My Life and Writings.*

Goethe, Johann Wolfgang von (1749–1832), dramatist, novelist, the greatest of German poets. His *Kleine Blumen* and *Kleine Blätter* ushered in a new epoch in German lyric poetry. One of the most beautiful love stories in world literature is the idyll of Sessenheim in *Dichtung und Wahrheit.* The influence of Greek tragedy is found in the quiet beauty of his new iambic version of *Iphigenie auf Tauris;* Renaissance classicism runs throughout the drama of *Torquato Tasso. Wilhelm Meisters Lehrjahre* tells the history of a young man's apprenticeship in the theater. This novel proved to be an instant and enduring influence on German literature. In *The Sorrows of Young Werther* the hero commits suicide because his love is unrequited.

The crowning achievement of Goethe's career was *Faust,* a philosophical drama that is at once profound and exciting.

Gogol, Nikolai Vasilievich (1809–1852), Russian novelist and dramatist. His first success came with *Evenings on a Farm* and "Taras Bulba," the best known of the *Cossack Tales.* He also published *Arabesques,* a collection of essays and stories, and a number of other short stories, including *Old World Gentlefolks.* He is best known in the English-speaking world for the *Inspector-General* [in Russian the *Revizor*] and *Dead Souls.* The *Inspector-General* is about a simple Russian who is mistaken for a high Russian official. *Dead Souls* is the story of a Russian scoundrel who goes about the countryside buying up "dead souls" or dead serfs.

Goldsmith, Oliver (1728–1774), English poet, playwright, and novelist. Until the publication of his poem "The Traveler" Goldsmith had written considerable popular material, mostly unsigned or under a pseudonym. Most of this early work which would now be labeled "commercial" was written to sustain himself. "The Traveler" was the first to appear under his own name and at once became a success. Then followed the great *Vicar of Wakefield*, which still is required reading in many English literature courses. In 1773 Goldsmith's play *She Stoops to Conquer* was staged. This incomparable farce is a great stage success to this day. Other works include a poem, "The Deserted Village," and a children's classic, *Little Goody Two-Shoes*.

Gorky, Maxim (1868–1936), Russian author. Gorky's famous play is *The Lower Depths* (1902). "My Fellow Traveler" and "Twenty-six Men and a Girl" are the best of his early stories. An autobiographical trilogy was composed of *Childhood, In the World* (V. Lyndyakh), and *My Universities*. The trilogy, a volume of *Recollections,* and *Fragments from My Diary* constitute Gorky's best works.

Gray, Thomas (1716–1771), English poet, whose "Elegy Written in a Country Churchyard," one of his most familiar poems, expresses feelings that are common to most people. He was not a prolific writer, yet he published enough to be considered one of England's great poets. His love for the beautiful local countryside inspired his "Ode on the Spring."

Grimm, Jacob Ludwig Carl (1785–1863), and  **Wilhelm (Carl)** (1786–1859), German folklorists and philologists. Together they were the collectors and editors of Grimms' *Fairy Tales* and were generally known as The Brothers Grimm; Jacob was the grammarian, and Wilhelm the literary scholar.

Jacob Grimm's *Deutsche Grammatik* (1819–1822) was the result of both brothers' previous philological work. In 1811 Jacob published a purely literary work, *Über den altdeutschen Meistergesang* and Wilhelm brought out his volume of translations *Altdänische Heldenlieder, Balladen und Märchen übersetzt*. In 1812 the brothers published the two ancient fragments of the *Hildebrandslied* and the *Weissenbrunner Gebet;* in 1812–1815 they jointly edited the first edition of the *Kinder-und Hausmärchen*, the *Fairy Tales*, which have penetrated practically every household of the civilized world, and became a basis for the scientific study of comparative folklore.

Hamsun, Knut (1859–1952), Norwegian author, winner of the Nobel Prize in Literature in 1920, is best known throughout the English-speaking world for three novels, *Hunger, Growth of the Soil,* and *The Woman at the Well*. His interests were centered around the psychological analysis of people with real and simple problems such as hunger.

Hardy, Thomas (1840–1928), English novelist and poet, whose first popular success was *Far from the Madding Crowd*. Then came, among others, *The Hand of Ethelberta*, subtitled a "Comedy in Chapters"; *The Return of the Native*, the most melancholy and perhaps the most powerful; *Two on a Tower*, a long ironic story; and Hardy's most famous novel, *Tess of the D'Urbervilles*, which was, like his other novels, a gloomy, naturalistic study of character and environment. Adverse criticism turned him to poetry in which he expressed his pessimism in such books as *Wessex Poems, The Dynasts*, and *Moments of Vision*.

Harris, Joel Chandler (1848–1908), United States author, whose "Tar Baby Story" (1879) started the vogue for a new and different kind of dialect literature. Harris wrote just as the plantation Negro talked, adding humor and descriptive narrative. *Uncle Remus, Nights with Uncle Remus, The Tar Baby* and *Brer Rabbit* are good examples of his style. He also wrote a series of children's books: *The Story of Aaron* and *Gabriel Tolliver. On the Plantation* was autobiographical.

Harte, Francis Brett (1836–1902), United  States author who wrote under the name of Bret Harte. He created a new type of short story and a new movement in American literature–the "local color" school. His first story, "The Luck of Roaring Camp," a tale of life in a western mining town, appeared in the *Overland Monthly* in 1868 and made his reputation. It was followed by "The Outcasts of Poker Flat" and "Tennessee's Partner." Harte's reputation was further strengthened by "Plain Language from Truthful James" (better known as "The Heathen Chinee"), a poem that attracted national attention. His "An Ingenue of the Sierras" and "A Protégée of Jack Hamlin's" were written in 1893.

Harte's most successful books were *The Luck of Roaring Camp and Other Sketches* (1870) and *Tales of the Argonauts*. His best play was *Ah Sin,* written in collaboration with Mark Twain and based on Harte's famous poem, "Plain Language from Truthful James."

Hawthorne, Nathaniel (1804–1864), one of the greatest fiction writers in United States literature. *Twice-Told Tales,* his first collection of short stories, was published in 1837. *The Scarlet Letter* (1850) ranks among his finest works and is one of the great works of fiction in the English language. The theme of the book is the revelation of sin, but Hawthorne was not so much interested in this as in its psychological consequences. Some of his other major novels are *The House of the Seven Gables,* about sinister influences within an old New England family; *The Marble Faun,* concerning several characters in Italy; and a partly autobiographical novel, *The Blithedale Romance,* growing out of Hawthorne's participation in the Brook Farm experiment in socialism.

Hegel, Georg Wilhelm Friedrich (1770–1831), German philosopher. Although his essay on *The Spirit of Christianity* is one of Hegel's most remarkable works, it was unpublished until 1907. His first great work, the *Phenomenology of Mind* was finished and published in 1807.

After the publication of his *Philosophy of Right* he appears to have devoted himself to his lectures. These were published as *Aesthetics,* the *Philosophy of Religion,* the *Philosophy of History,* and the *History of Philosophy.* The *Philosophy of History* sees civilizations as a struggle toward rational freedom.

Heine, Heinrich (1797–1856), an outstanding satirist and publicist, and one of the greatest German lyric poets. His *Buch der Lieder* placed him among the world's great poets. His poems such as "Lorelei" are musical and have a folk-like quality; often they are sharpened by subtle irony or dissonant endings. He wrote the famous verse satires *Atta Troll, Deutschland,* and *Gedichte.* His *Harzreise,* one of his prose travel sketches, shows his lyric emotion and wit.

Hemingway, Ernest (1899–1961), United States novelist and short story writer, noted for his gift for dialogue and understatement. *The Sun Also Rises* (1926), a touching fictional reminiscence of the "lost generation" of expatriates after World War I, brought Hemingway his first notable success. His stature as a novelist was increased with the publication of *A Farewell to Arms* (1929), a deep love story of World War I, and *For Whom the Bell Tolls* (1940), a story of love and bravery in the Spanish Civil War. His short novel, *The Old Man and the Sea* (1952), is the heroin story of an old Cuban fisherman's expedition in search of and struggle for a great fish in the Gulf Stream north of the island. For it Hemingway was awarded the Pulitzer Prize in 1953, and in 1954 he received the Nobel Prize in Literature.

Herodotus (fifth century B.C.), Greek author of  a single work, a history of the Persian Wars; probably the first real historian. In the *History,* his theme is the war between democratic Greece and totalitarian Persia. Not only is it, for all its mistakes and fantasies, an artistic masterpiece, but also a leading source book for Greek history of the particular period and for much of that of western Asia and Egypt. Divided into nine books, it is sometimes referred to as the "Histories."

Holmes, Oliver Wendell (1809–1894), United  States poet and humorist, famous for poems such as "Old Ironsides," "The Chambered Nautilus," and "The Deacon's Masterpiece." Collections of his famous and popular sketches contain *The Autocrat of the Breakfast Table* and *The Poet at the Breakfast Table.* He also wrote *Elsie Venner,* which has been called the first American psychological novel.

Homer (seventh or eighth century B.C.), early Greek poet, credited with being the author of two masterpieces of world literature, the epic poems *The Iliad* and *The Odyssey. The Iliad* masterfully tells the story of the long siege of Troy by the Greeks; *The Odyssey* relates the ten-year struggle of Odysseus to return to Greece from Troy.

Horace [Quintus Horatius Flaccus] 65–8 B.C.), celebrated Roman poet, was a contemporary and friend of Virgil. His works are made up of short, thoughtful, personal poems, and longer verse-essays dealing in a worldly-wise way with everyday manners and moral philosophy and literary criticism.

Of Horace's works there are extant only 121 lyric poems, *Odes, Epodes,* and *Carmen saeculare,* and 41 verse essays, *Satires,* sometimes called *Sermones, Epistles,* and *Ars poetica.* The descriptive power of Horace's verse greatly influenced English poetry.

Howells, William Dean (1837–1920), United States novelist and critic, was the spokesman of realism in American fiction. Howells' strongest novel was *A Modern Instance,* a realistic study of an average couple and their marital difficulties. His best-known novel, *The Rise of Silas Lapham,* depicts the newly rich Lapham trying to rise into Boston society.

Hughes, Langston (1902–1967), black United States poet and novelist. Langston Hughes is best known for his poetry, much of which has been translated into many languages. His books of verse include *The Weary Blues, Shakespeare in Harlem,* and *Freedom Blows.*

Hugo, Victor Marie (1802–1885), French poet, novelist, and dramatist. His plays include *Cromwell, Le Roi s'amuse* (the basis of Verdi's *Rigoletto*), and *Ruy Blas. Les Orientales,* a series of poems about the Levant, was published in 1829. In 1831 he published his first novel, *The Hunchback of Notre Dame (Notre Dame de Paris),* a great historical novel laid in the fifteenth century. In 1862 he published the novel *Les Misérables,* in which the poor of post-Napoleonic France are portrayed with great pathos. *The Toilers of the Sea* is another of his great novels upon which his popularity in the English-speaking world is founded.

Hume, David (1711–1776), British (Scottish) philosopher, historian, economist, and essayist. His *History of England,* extending from Caesar's invasion to 1688, in six volumes, and his *Political Discourses* brought him fame in England and abroad. In *A Treatise of Human Nature,* commonly referred to as the *Treatise,* and in the *Enquiry concerning Human Understanding,* Hume stated his philosophical theories.

Huxley, Thomas (1825–1895), English biologist, whose researches and studies in philosophy and religion made him a strong supporter of agnosticism. His scientific writings, such as *Man's Place in Nature,* backing Darwin's theory of evolution, and *The Theory of the Vertebrate Skull,* are among his most famous works. His *Collected Essays* (in nine volumes) and *Life and Letters of Thomas Huxley* (in two volumes) report his scientific lectures and his reasons for supporting agnosticism.

Ibsen, Henrik Johan (1828–1906), Norwegian poet and dramatist. His most famous plays are *A Doll's House, The Wild Duck, Hedda Gabler, Ghosts,* and *The Master Builder.*

Two of Ibsen's most outstanding literary works, *Brand* and *Peer Gynt,* awakened the moral sense of all Scandinavia with their ethical lessons. Ibsen wrote many other plays, including *St. John's Night, The Vikings of Helgeland, The Pretenders, Little Eyolf,* and *John Gabriel Borkman.*

Irving, Washington [known also by a number of pseudonyms, including **Geoffrey Crayon** and **Diedrich Knickerbocker**] (1783–1859), has been called "first American man of letters," "dean," or "father of American literature," "inventor of the short story."

Irving won his greatest literary success with *The Sketch Book* (1819–1820) in which "Rip Van Winkle" and "Legend of Sleepy Hollow" are the best-known stories. *Diedrich Knickerbocker's History of New York* is a humorous history of Dutch rule, prefaced by a mock-learned account of the world from the beginning. Irving wrote three biographies: *Oliver Goldsmith, Mahomet and His Successors,* and *George Washington.* Other works include: *Bracebridge Hall* (1822), *Tales of a Traveller* (1825), and *The Alhambra* (1832).

James, Henry (1843–1916), prolific writer, and one of the most celebrated of United States novelists. Beginning in 1865, he produced brilliant literary reviews and short stories. Most famous for his novels–he was the recognized master of the psychological novel–James also wrote dramas, travel books, literary criticism, and autobiographical works which include *A Small Boy and*

Others. Such novels as *The American, The Portrait of a Lady* (1881), *The Wings of the Dove,* and *The Ambassadors* won him acclaim, but *Daisy Miller,* a novelette, surpassed all in popularity. His most famous short fiction, *The Turn of the Screw* (1898), a psychological ghost story, added further laurels.

Other works include *The Spoils of Poynton, What Maisie Knew, The Golden Bowl,* and *The American Scene,* the last-named remarkable for its prose picture of, and brooding concern with, the materialistic drift of American life.

Jonson, Ben (1573?–1637), English dramatist. In 1598 Ben Jonson produced one of the most famous English comedies, *Every Man in His Humour,* a play in which Shakespeare is said to have played. Two of his better plays are the comedies *Volpone,* whose theme is greed, and *The Alchemist,* which deals with quackery. *The Silent Woman* (1609) and *Bartholomew Fair* (1614) are considered his masterpieces. In his later years, he wrote two comedies, *The Magnetic Lady* and *The Tale of a Tub,* and some masques. His beautifully written pastoral drama, *The Sad Shepherd,* was left unfinished; it was published four years after his death.

Joyce, James (1882–1941), Irish writer, whose first publication, *Chamber Music,* a volume of poems, appeared in 1907. He is best known for the short stories in the *Dubliners,* and the novels, *Portrait of the Artist as a Young Man* (1917), *Ulysses* (1922), and *Finnegans Wake* (1939). Joyce rejected the accepted conventions of novel-writing. He developed the "stream-of-consciousness" technique, which reveals his characters' thoughts, experiences, and impressions and shows how these affect their lives and behavior. He also used language like music to convey thoughts and impressions which he felt could not be captured in conventional statement.

Jung, Carl Gustav (1875–1961), Swiss psychologist and psychiatrist, founder of analytic psychology (a name he preferred to *psychoanalysis*), was second only to Freud in the psychoanalytic field. Jung's works in English translation include: *Psychology of Dementia Praecox, The Theory of Psychoanalysis, Psychology of the Unconscious, Studies in Word Association, Psychological Types,*

Contributions to Analytical Psychology, The Secret of the Golden Flower, with Richard Wilhelm, *Modern Man in Search of a Soul, Psychology and Religion, Integration of the Personality, Essays on Contemporary Events,* and *Essays on a Science of Mythology,* with C. Kerenyi. Jung first introduced the terms *extroversion* and *introversion.*

Kant, Immanuel (1724–1804), German philosopher, greatest of the idealists, and one of the most important thinkers of modern times. His classic, *The Critique of Pure Reason,* shows that human sensations and perceptual apparatus produce the immediate objects of perception. The three chief ideas of reason–God, freedom, and immortality–are developed in *Prolegomena, Groundwork to a Metaphysics of Morals,* and *Critique of Practical Reason.* In *Critique of Judgment,* Kant discusses the philosophical problems of aesthetics.

Keats, John (1795–1821), English lyric poet, whose great work *Endymion* tells the story of Endymion and the moon goddess. *Hyperion* is a blank verse epic. In "Lamia," the meter is rhymed heroics. It is in the great odes, new in form and spirit, that Keats pioneered. Of these, "Ode on a Grecian Urn" and "Ode to a Nightingale" are the best known, as is also the unfinished narrative *Hyperion.* Romantic medievalism is shown at its best in "The Eve of St. Agnes" and "La Belle Dame sans Merci."

Kipling, Rudyard (1865–1936), British author, whose collections of short stories, *Plain Tales from the Hills* (1888) and *Soldiers Three,* made his reputation in England. Two successful collections of poems, *Barrack Room Ballads* (1892) and *The Seven Seas,* followed. Kipling's two *Jungle Books* became generally familiar animals stories; he published *Kim* in 1901 and the classic children's book, *Just So Stories,* in 1902. His later works were *Puck of Pook's Hill, Rewards and Fairies,* and *Something of Myself* (1937), which was largely autobiographical. His patriotism is apparent in his writings; he also criticized some of the worst aspects of British colonialism. He received the Nobel Prize in Literature in 1907.

La Fontaine, Jean de (1621–1695), French poet. His most famous works are the *Contes* and the *Fables*. In the *Fables* he has adapted, to the not-too-nice world of Louis XIV, stories of all-too-human animals from Aesop and other sources. The child, the student, the man of the world–all find delight in these stories. The *Contes*, imitations in verse of Boccaccio and Ariosto, the *Cent Nouvelles, Nouvelles*, and others, illustrate La Fontaine's marvelous knack of saying shocking things in the most courteous and gentlemanly manner.

Lamb, Charles (1775–1834), English essayist and critic. In 1807 appeared *Tales from Shakespeare,* by Charles and Mary Lamb, in which Charles wrote about the tragedies and his sister Mary about the comedies. The following year, *Specimens of English Dramatic Poets who Lived about the Time of Shakespeare,* with short but suitable critical notes, established Lamb as a literary critic. His essays, despite their informal, familiar tone, placed him on a par with Montaigne, Steele, and Addison.

Lewis, Sinclair (1885–1951), United States

novelist and social critic, who wrote several minor works before he won recognition with his *Main Street* (1920). This novel was the first in a series in which Lewis satirized the intolerance and materialism of American life. He also criticized the emptiness of the superficial intellectual who despised this kind of life but had nothing better to offer. *Babbitt* (1922), which added a new word to the English language, dealt with the complacent American, sucked dry of his individuality by the general pressure for conformity. *Arrowsmith,* for which Lewis refused a Pulitzer Prize, satirized the medical profession and emphasized the crushing of high scientific ideals. *Elmer Gantry* attacked ignorant, predatory religious leaders, and *Dodsworth* dealt with the European tour of a retired Midwestern manufacturer and his wife. Lewis was awarded the Nobel Prize in Literature in 1930, the first United States author to be so honored. His later works include *It Can't Happen Here, Cass Timberlane,* and *Kingsblood Royal.*

Lindsay, Vachel (1879–1931), United States poet, whose fame began with the publishing of his *General William Booth Enters into Heaven*. This type of poetry, based on the very heartthrob of American crowds and on camp-meeting rhythms, was widely acclaimed. The poems he recited and which his audiences continued to call for were "General William Booth," "The Congo," "Bryan, Bryan, Bryan," "Johnny Appleseed," and "The Santa Fe Trail." They have become a part of America's heritage. By 1920 Lindsay's best work was done. Lindsay's principal works include *General William Booth Enters into Heaven and Other Poems, Adventures While Preaching the Gospel of Beauty* (prose), *The Congo and Other Poems,* and *The Golden Whales of California, and Other Rhymes in the American Language.*

Livy [Titus Livius] (59 B.C.–A.D. 17), most famous of Roman historians. His *History of Rome* was originally in over 140 books and covered Roman history from the arrival of Aeneas in Italy to the death of Orusus, brother of the emperor Tiberius, in 9 B.C. Of this immense work only 35 books survive. Livy's history portrays Rome in the light of men and events, which he describes and interprets in universal terms.

Locke, John (1631–1704), English philosopher, one inspirer of the Age of Enlightenment and of Reason in England and in France. In 1690 Locke gave to the world *An Essay concerning Human Understanding,* which advanced an empirical theory of knowledge. Among Locke's posthumously published writings was *The Conduct of the Understanding,* which was very characteristic of his work. In *Two Treatises on Government,* he wrote in justification of constitutional monarchy, in essence a plea for the kind of democracy found in the United States Constitution. His last days were occupied in composing a *Fourth Letter on Toleration* which was never finished.

London, Jack (1876–1916), United States

novelist, famous for his romantic tales of rugged adventure. Before turning to writing, he had worked as a sailor, trapper, and miner and found in these occupations material for his fiction. His first book, *The Son of the Wolf,* gained him a wide audience. *Martin Eden* (1909) is a partly autobiographical account of a struggle against

adverse economic and social conditions. *The People of the Abyss* is based on the time he spent in the London slums, and *The Cruise of the Snark* tells of his adventures sailing the South Pacific. Some of London's other outstanding works are *The Call of the Wild, White Fang, Burning Daylight, The Sea-Wolf, The Iron Heel,* and *The Valley of the Moon.*

Longfellow, Henry Wadsworth (1807–1882), the most popular United States poet of the nineteenth century. His book of poetry, *Ballads and Other Poems,* appeared in 1841 and was immensely popular. It included such well-known poems as "The Skeleton in Armor," "The Wreck of the Hesperus," "Excelsior," and "The Village Blacksmith." *Evangeline* (1847), a tale of the French exiles of Acadia, is one of his most popular poems. Others are *The Song of Hiawatha* (1855), *The Courtship of Miles Standish,* and *Tales of a Wayside Inn* which includes the national favorite, "Paul Revere's Ride." Longfellow translated Dante's *Divine Comedy.*

Lowell, Amy (1874–1925), United States poet, critic, and lecturer who was a major force in the Imagist movement. The characteristic qualities of her work include her mastery of the free verse technique, her brilliant use of sensuous impressions in describing the external world, and the restrained beauty of many of her shorter poems.

With her first volume, *A Dome of Many-Coloured Glass,* Amy Lowell was well on her way to fame. *Sword Blades and Poppy Seed* included her first poems in *vers libre* and "polyphonic prose." Other famous works include *Six French Poets; Men, Women and Ghosts; Tendencies in Modern American Poetry; Pictures of the Floating World,* which reflected her new interest in Oriental poetry; *Fir-Flower Tablets* (1921), with Florence Ayscough; A *Critical Fable;* a biography of John Keats; *East Wind;* and *Ballads for Sale.*

Lowell, James Russell (1819–1891), United States poet and critic, who became well known through his satiric *Bigelow Papers* (serialization begun in 1846), written in New England dialect. These charged that the Mexican War was an attempt to extend the area of slavery. "The Vision of Sir Launfal," with its theme that "the gift without the giver is bare," and the jolly and witty *Fable for Critics,* which measured very acutely some of his contemporaries, also brought fame to Lowell.

Partly through his co-editorship of the *North American Review* (1864–1872), Lowell published his critical essays on the great masters including Dante, Chaucer, Shakespeare, Cervantes, Milton, Fielding, Lessing, Wordsworth, Carlyle, Emerson, and many others. He was also the first editor of *The Atlantic Monthly.*

Lucretius [Titus Lucretius Carus] (earlier half of the last century B.C.), Latin poet and philosopher. His one celebrated poem of six volumes, *De rerum natura (On the Nature of Things)* presents in hexameter verse his appeals to man to be his own master, not to fear gods or death. Lucretius used Epicurus' atomic theory to convince man that the universe developed through the workings of natural laws in the combining of atoms.

Macaulay, Thomas Babington (1800–1859), English historian, poet, and essayist. Published in 1842, Macaulay's poetry, *Lays of Ancient Rome,* was very popular. In the following year he published his comprehensive collection of *Essays.* His *History of England from the Accession of James the Second,* in five volumes, was his major work, although he died before he could perfect the fifth volume.

Machiavelli, Niccolò (1469–1527), Italian statesman and writer. His most famous works, *The Prince* and *The Discourses,* use the life of Cesare Borgia to express his belief that such methods of conquest, the cementing of a new state out of scattered elements, and the dealing with false friends or doubtful allies, were worthy of commendation and imitation. *The Prince* is an analysis of the methods by which an ambitious man may rise to power. Machiavelli's other works include the *Mandragola,* a powerful play; lesser plays such as the *Clizia;* the *History of Florence;* and a novel, *Belfagor.*

Mann, Thomas (1875–1955), the greatest modern German novelist. His masterpiece, *Buddenbrooks* (1901), tells the story of a family much like his own, and follows its decline through four generations. A number of short novels next appeared, *Tonio Kröger, Tristan,* and *Death in Venice. The Magic Mountain* (1924), a study in microcosm of the forces which adversely influenced European society, won Mann the Nobel Prize in Literature in 1929.

The novels of Mann's exile included the biblical tetralogy, *Joseph und seine Brüder,* dealing with ancient Egypt and the biblical saga of Joseph; *Lotte in Weimar; Dr. Faustus* (1948); *Die Betrogene;* and the unfinished *Bekenntnisse des Hochstaplers Felix Krull,* a comic novel expanded from an early short story.

Maupassant, Guy de (1850–1893), French writer of short stories and novels. Of his almost 300 short stories, many are unsurpassed in style, craftsmanship, and psychological realism. Among these are "Boule de Suif" ("Tallow Ball"), "La Ficelle" ("The Piece of String"), and "Miss Harriet." Probably his most popular story is "The Necklace." His famous novels are *Bel-Ami,* in which a scoundrel succeeds because of his good looks, and *Une Vie (A Woman's Life),* which gives an analysis of a French woman's life and her frustration. Maupassant has had great influence on short story writing.

Melville, Herman (1819–1891), United States author whose first book, *Typee,* was based on his involuntary stay with a savage tribe in the South Seas. The adventures of the short voyage which followed furnished Melville with the ideas for his second and most humorous book, *Omoo.*

Melville began work on *Moby Dick,* his masterpiece, as a simple tale, a gusty account of a whaling voyage. Before he ended it, it had developed into an allegory, probing into the spiritual torments of a man who set himself the task of implacable vengeance. *Billy Budd, Foretopman,* a superb short novel, is Melville's most haunting sea story, published posthumously in 1924.

Menander (ca. 343/342–291/290 B.C.), Greek poet and outstanding representative of the comedy of his period. Only some fragments, and some of those of uncertain authorship, remain of Menander's work. The most important is the Cairo papyrus, discovered in 1905, containing 659 lines from *Epitrepontes,* 83 from *Heros,* 341 from *Samia,* 324 from *Perikeiromene,* and 61 from an uncertain play. In Menander's plays, as contrasted to Aristophanes', the chorus was not used, the debate type of speaking between two antagonists disappeared, and the theme changed from political or social philosophy to an everyday plot in Athenian life. *The Flatterer, The Superstitious Man,* and *The Lady from Andros* are good examples of Menander's new type of comedy.

Mencken, Henry Louis (1880–1956), United States editor, writer, and controversialist. For two decades the most ironic critic of American life and letters, Mencken often used literary criticism as a starting point for his ideas. He wrote enough reviews and miscellaneous essays to fill six volumes, aptly titled *Prejudices.* Many readers found it refreshing, after hearing others endlessly praise their nation, to find Mencken's description of the American people as "the most timorous, sniveling, poltroonish, ignominious mob of serfs and goosesteppers ever gathered under one flag in Christendom since the end of the Middle Ages." The famous platform for his ideas was the magazine *American Mercury,* which he helped found in 1924, after leaving the *Smart Set.*

His great work, *The American Language* (1918), brought together examples of American, not English, expressions and idioms. His autobiographical trilogy, *Happy Days* (1940), *Newspaper Days,* and *Heathen Days* (1943), deals largely with his experience in journalism.

Mill, John Stuart (1806–1873), British philosopher, economist, and reformer. Some of his essays written for journals were collected in the first two volumes (1859) of his *Dissertations and Discussions* and show wide interests. The twin essays on Bentham and Coleridge are perhaps his finest writings and show the new spirit he tried to inject into English radicalism. Among his important works are *System of Logic,* with its four canons of inductive method, published in 1843; *Principles of Political Economy;* and the brilliant essay "On Liberty" (1859).

Millay, Edna St. Vincent (1892–1950), United States poet. She first attracted attention with a long poem, "Renascence," written when she was only nineteen. This was later incorporated into a poetry volume, *Renascence and Other Poems*. She attracted a still larger audience with *A Few Figs from Thistles* and *Second April*. In 1921 she published three plays: *Two Slatterns and a King, The Lamp and the Bell*, and *Aria Da Capo. The Harp-Weaver and Other Poems* showed a new maturity; the title poem was awarded a Pulitzer Prize in 1922.

Milton, John (1608–1674), English poet. Milton's first great poem in English was "On the Morning of Christ's Nativity." Some of his other famous early works include *L'Allegro, Il Penseroso,* the masque *Comus,* and the elegy *Lycidas*. His *Areopagitica* was written in defense of the press; his *Of Reformation in England* had to do with church government. After Milton became completely blind, he dictated his famous and timeless epics, *Paradise Lost,* in which he tells of Satan's rebellion against God and the fall of man, and *Paradise Regained,* where Christ (the second Adam) gains back for mankind that which Adam and Eve lost. His *Samson Agonistes* is modeled after Greek drama.

Montesquieu, Charles Louis de Secondat (1689–1755), French political philosopher and man of letters, whose *Lettres Persanes* ("Persian Letters"), a satirical picture of European society, is a masterpiece of irony. His *Considérations sur les causes de la grandeur des Romains et de leur decadence.* ("Reflections on the Causes of Grandeur and Declension of the Romans") presents an interesting philosophy of history. His famous work, *The Spirit of the Laws,* is a study of comparative governments. Its checks and balances theory was incorporated into the Constitution of the United States. *Defense of the Spirit of the Laws* is the most brilliantly written of all his works.

Moore, Thomas (1779–1852), Irish poet whose *Irish Melodies* appeared in 1808, containing some of his best and most popular work, such as, "Believe Me If All Those Endearing Young Charms," and "Oft in the Stilly Night." *Lalla Rookh,* a poetic romance, was published in 1817 and became an immediate success. In 1831 Moore completed his *Life and Death of Lord Edward Fitzgerald,* probably his best piece of prose.

Nietzsche, Friedrich (1844–1900), German philosopher, one of the most influential thinkers of modern times. *Die Geburt der Tragödie* ("The Birth of Tragedy") was his first well-known work. His most perplexing work, and the most difficult to understand, *Also sprach Zarathustra* ("Thus Spake Zarathustra"), censures conventional Christian morality as something which the masses follow blindly; it preaches that superior to it is the morality of the natural aristocrats. According to Nietzsche, the will of man must create the superior man, the superman, who would rise above good and evil and be able to destroy deteriorating democracy. *Zarathustra* was Nietzsche's first attempt to systematize his thought. Then came *Jenseits von Gut und Böse* ("Beyond Good and Evil") and *Zur Genealogie der Moral* ("The Geneaology of Morals") which further presented his ideas. His last work was *Nietzsche contra Wagner,* slightly revised, a compilation of some parts of his earlier books. This is his briefest and probably his most beautiful book.

O'Neill, Eugene Gladstone (1888–1953), United States dramatist, the country's greatest playwright, and an artist of international renown.

O'Neill loved the sea and some of the best of his 47 plays *(The Moon of the Caribbees, The Long Voyage Home)* are salty as the sea. In 1920 O'Neill won a Pulitzer Prize with his first full-length play, *Beyond the Horizon,* a bitter domestic tragedy, written for the Provincetown Players. He won two more Pulitzer Prizes with *Anna Christie* and *Strange Interlude,* and in 1936 became the second American (after Sinclair Lewis) to win the Nobel Prize in Literature. He thrilled theatergoers with tom-toms (*Emperor Jones*), masks (*The Great God Brown*), verbalized subconscious ideas (*Strange Interlude*), and choral chants (*Lazarus Laughed*). His great tragedy was *Mourning Becomes Electra. Ah, Wilderness* was the only comedy he wrote.

When O'Neill died he left at least three plays in manuscript, including the autobiographical *Long Day's Journey Into Night.* A fourth Pulitzer Prize, for *Long Day's Journey Into Night,* was awarded him posthumously in 1957.

Ovid [Publius Ovidius Naso] (43 B.C.–A.D. 18), Roman poet, famous for his love poems. Ovid's poems fall into three groups: erotic poems, such as *Art of Love;* mythological poems, particularly his greatest work in hexameters, *Metamorphoses* ("Transfigurations"); and poems of exile, of which *Tristia,* an autobiographical poem written during his years of exile, is a good example. This poem depicts the wretched life of his exile (for having written *Art of Love*) and pleads with Emperor Augustus for forgiveness.

Pascal, Blaise (1623–1662), French scientist and writer on religious subjects. The eighteen *Lettres écrites par Louis de Montalta à un provincial* (1656–1657), better known as *Les Provinciales,* help us to follow Pascal in his spiritual and theological beliefs and practices. Pascal's religious writings, which are mystical and in a pure literary style, are named *Pensées.* As a scientist, he is most famous for Pascal's law.

Pepys, Samuel (1633–1703), English diarist.

Pepys was revealed as author and man about town in 1825 when his secret diary was published in part. The first entry was dated January 1, 1660, the last, May 31, 1669. The *Diary* (in six volumes) furnishes an invaluable picture of the Restoration period. During his lifetime Pepys' only known publication was the *Memoirs of the Royal Navy.*

Petrarch [Francesco Petrarca] (1304–1374), Italian poet, the first humanist and the first modern lyric poet, surpassed in Italian literature only by Dante. He adapted, among other things, the Ciceronian oration *Pro Archia,* that great declaration of the nature of poetry. Two of his ambitious and significant Latin works are *De viris* and the *Africa* (begun 1338 or 1339). He is honored for his Latin *Trionfi.* He also wrote *Bucolicum carmen, De vita solitairia,* and *De otio religioso.* His famous work *Canzoniere* contains songs and sonnets.

Pindar (ca. 522–443 B.C.), great lyric poet of ancient Greece. Forty-four complete odes and numerous fragments of his work still exist. Pindar's works are chiefly choral lyrics. He also developed the triumphal ode celebrating athletic victories, but generally having to do with myths. The Pindaric Ode influenced English verse form in the seventeenth and eighteenth centuries. *Epinicia* in ode form commemorates successes in the great athletic games.

Plato (428/427–348/347 B.C.), Greek philosopher who has deeply influenced Western thought for more than 2,400 years. His dialogues express his philosophy and are outstanding masterpieces of world literature through their beauty of style, depth, and range of thought. Among the dialogues are the early defense of Socrates in *Apology, Charmides, Phaedras,* with *Republic* perhaps the most noted. The world of Platonism is order, and all disorder is evil.

Plautus (254?–184 B.C.), comic dramatist of ancient Rome. His 21 surviving plays are vigorous portrayals of middle- and lower-class life. Plautus' plays are essentially translations of the Greek new comedy school of plays, but he was more than a translator; his command of Latin was such that his plays become originals. Among his extant plays are *Amphitruo, Asinaria, Captivi, Mercator, Miles Gloriosus, Pseudolus,* and *Stichus.*

Pliny, the Elder **[Gaius Plinius Secundus]** (A.D. 23 or 24–79), Roman savant and author. Pliny's *Natural History* is often inaccurate and most of the information in it is second-hand; but there are accounts of ancient arts and culture, such as sculpture and painting, which cannot be found in any other sources.

Pliny, the Younger **[Gaius Plinius Caecilius Secundus]** (61 or 62–ca. A.D. 113), Roman author and administrator, nephew of the elder Pliny. His official correspondence was an unusual collection, well written, portraying public and private life at the height of the Roman Empire. *The Letters* (in nine books) suggest a highly sophisticated poseur.

Plutarch (ca. A.D. 46–120), Greek biographer and writer. *Forty-six Parallel Lives* brought him fame and popularity. This series reflects Plutarch's learning and research in preparing the long lists of authorities to which he refers, and the comprehensive information on each person about whom he writes. Plutarch wrote a great deal, covering many topics. Some of his works, published under the title *Opera moralis,* include dialogues and essays on ethical, literary, and historical subjects.

Pope, Alexander (1688–1744), English poet, whose first publication was *Pastorals,* in 1709. His next publication, the *Essay on Criticism* (1711), was a poem outlining contemporary critical tastes and standards. His best-known work is *The Rape of the Lock.* For 12 years Pope worked on his translation of Homer. He also wrote *Elegy to the Memory of an Unfortunate Lady* and *Eloisa to Abelard.*

Poe, Edgar Allan (1809–1849), United States poet, critic, and short-story writer. In 1831 he brought out a first volume of *Poems.* His story, "A MS. Found in a Bottle," won a contemporary literary award. He also wrote "William Wilson" and "The Fall of the House of Usher," stories of supernatural horror, and published the first detective story, "The Murders in the Rue Morgue." In 1843 his "Gold Bug" also won a prize. His most famous poem, "The Raven" (1845), brought him national fame. Other well-known poems are "To Helen," "Israfel," and "The City in the Sea." *Tales of the Grotesque and Arabesque* comprise a collection of his short stories.

Porter, William Sidney (1862–1910), wrote under the pen name of O. Henry. This United States short-story writer saw and wrote about love, pathos, and small acts of heroism in the lives of ordinary people. Despite occasional clowning, his stories are artistically told and have social implications. His fame rests on his short stories *Bagdad on the Subway.* His first book, *Cabbages and Kings* (1904), portrayed unreal characters against strangely beautiful Honduran backgrounds. *The Four Million* revealed the lives of the people of New York City. *The Trimmed Lamp* and *Heart of the West* presented true and fascinating pictures of the Texas range.

Pound, Ezra Loomis (1885–1972), United States poet, translator, and critic. His major poems are *Homage to Sextus Propertius, Hugh Selwyn Mauberley,* and *The Cantos.* Some of his translations include the Anglo-Saxon *Seafarer,* the Chinese *Cathay,* and *Classic Anthology.* His *Letters* were published in 1950 and a selection of his *Literary Essays* in 1954.

Proust, Marcel (1871–1922), French novelist. *A la recherche du temps perdu (Remembrance of Things Past),* comprising seven novels, is Proust's outstanding work. In it he shows the many-sidedness of French society. The author takes the leading part, with musings and reverie as his method. The first part, *Du coté de chez Swann (Swann's Way),* shows the freshness and minuteness of recollections of childhood and is the best-known volume of the set.

Pushkin, Alexander (1799–1837), Russian poet. In 1825 Pushkin wrote his most outstanding work, the tragedy *Boris Godunov.* In 1829 *Poltava* appeared. The lyrics of his *A Voyage to Arzrum* are delightful. The *History of the Revolt of Pugachev* is a fine piece of historical writing. *The Captain's Daughter,* the one long novel he completed, is a good example of his prose. *Boris Godunov* and *Eugene Onegin* were used for operas by Mussorgsky and Tschaikovsky. Of Pushkin's short stories, "The Queen of Spades" is the most famous.

Rabelais, François (ca. 1495–1553), French author. The works that made Rabelais immortal were his history of the giant *Gargantua* and his history of the son of Gargantua, *Pantagruel.* These fabulous giant-heroes fight, eat, drink, and jest; besides, the story in each case reveals the education, politics, and philosophy of Renaissance France. The stories really are satires against the vulgarity and abuses of French society.

Racine, Jean (1639–1699), French tragic dramatist. *Andromaque,* a tragedy, was the first of many of his dramatic successes. Two of his masterpieces are *Phédre* and *Athalie. Athalie* was the means of introducing new ideas for plays, such as choruses. *Les Plaideurs* is a successful charming comedy. His tragedies were, *Britannicus, Mithridate, Iphigenie, Phédre,* and *Esther,* a masterpiece based on a biblical theme.

Robinson, Edwin Arlington (1869–1935), United States poet. Robinson's first success was *Captain Craig* (1902). He won three Pulitzer prizes in Poetry–*Collected Poems* (1921); *The Man Who Died Twice* (1924); and *Tristram* (1927). His forte was the short narrative poem, such as "Richard Cory" and "Miniver Cheevy." Three of his long poems, *Merlin, Lancelot,* and *Tristram* were taken from the King Arthur stories. His psychological studies found expression in *Avon's Harvest, Matthias at the Door,* and *Amaranth.*

Rolland, Romain (1866–1944), French novelist and biographer. The biographies include *Mahatma Gandhi,* an impassioned defense of the Indian leader; *Beethoven the Creator;* and books on Tolstoy and Michelangelo. His ten-volume novel, *Jean Christophe,* is the work upon which rests his fame. In this novel a musical genius battles poverty, attains success, and finally wins peace in death. Rolland's best-known play is *Les Loups (The Wolves).* He received the Nobel Prize in Literature in 1915.

Rossetti, Dante Gabriel (1828–1882), English painter and poet. In December, 1850, some of his most famous poems appeared, including "The Blessed Damozel." His *Ballads and Sonnets* contained much of his best work, including the completed *House of Life,* the great sonnet sequence, and the ballads, "Rose Mary," "The White Ship," "The King's Tragedy," and "Sister Helen."

Rostand, Edmond (1869–1918), French dramatist, the repeated production of whose comedy *Cyrano de Bergerac* continues to delight theatergoers to this day. In *L'Aiglon,* another famous play, Rostand's theme is the unhappy life of Napoleon II. *Chantecler,* the barnyard fable, was extremely successful. Besides plays Rostand also wrote patriotic verse.

Rousseau, Jean Jacques (1712–1778), French-Swiss moralist. Fame came to Rousseau through his essay, *Discours sur les sciences et les arts.* His *La Nouvelle Héloise,* a novel, was immediately and enormously popular. *Du Contract Social (The Social Contract)* was a French document of great influence for the French Revolution. The novel *Emile* expressed Rousseau's ideas on progressive education. Rousseau's autobiography, *Confessions,* is an uninhibited self-revelation anticipating the vogue for stark realistic descriptions in current literature. One of his last works was *Reveries d'un Promeneur Solitaire.*

Ruskin, John (1819–1900), English writer and critic. *Modern Painters* in five volumes and *The Seven Lamps of Architecture,* the latter appearing with Ruskin's own etchings, made a great reputation for him. Other works included *Ethics of the Dust,* and *The Crown of Wild Olive.* A more serious work was *Time and Tide,* a collection of "Thoughts" which gives a good picture of Ruskin's social and economic program. In 1871 Ruskin began *Fors Clavigera,* written for the English working man.

Sandburg, Carl (1878–1967), United States poet, historian, novelist, and folklorist. Sandburg was one of the group of writers who, in the days before World War I, brought about the "Chicago Renaissance" in letters. He later described his early years in his autobiography, *Always the Young Strangers.* His poems reflect industrial America. In 1914 a group of his *Chicago Poems* appeared in *Poetry;* later they were issued in book form. The favorable impression he made was strengthened with succeeding volumes–*Cornhuskers, Smoke and Steel,* and *Slabs of the Sunburnt West. The American Songbag* and *Carl Sandburg's New American Songbag* were collections of folk songs. Sandburg wrote one of the finest Lincoln biographies, *Abraham Lincoln: The Prairie Years* (2 volumes) and *Abraham Lincoln: The War Years* (4 volumes, which won the Pulitzer Prize for History, 1940). In 1948 he published a long novel, *Remembrance Rock,* dealing with the American experience from Plymouth Rock to

World War II. *Complete Poems* won him the Pulitzer Prize for Poetry in 1951.

Sappho (early sixth century B.C.), the greatest woman poet of Greece. Only eight books of her lyrical poems are known. The only complete collection of the known material is in *Sapphous Mele.* Her verse is a fine example of the "pure" love lyric, characterized by very strong expressions of passion and excellent control of meter. Simple language and deep feeling as well as perfect form are everywhere evident in her work.

Schopenhauer, Arthur (1788–1860), German philosopher, outstanding as a promoter of a metaphysical doctrine of the will as opposed to Hegelian idealism. His principal work is *Die Welt als Wille und Vorstellung (The World as Will and Idea).* His pessimism was clearly stated in both *Über den Willen in der Natur (On the Will in Nature)* and in *Two Essays.*

Scott, Sir Walter (1771–1832), Scottish poet and novelist. Scott is known for his narrative poems–*Lay of the Last Minstrel, Marmion,* and *The Lady of the Lake.* Of his novels, *Guy Mannering, The Heart of Midlothian,* and *The Bride of Lammermoor* are among the finest. *Ivanhoe* was the first of a long series of romances of British history, which included *Kenilworth, Quentin Durward,* and *The Talisman.* The splendid, heroic spirit of Scotland is found in his poems "Lochinvar" and "Proud Maisie."

Seneca, Lucius Annaeus (ca. 4 B.C.–A.D. 65), Roman philosopher, dramatist, and statesman. The most important of Seneca's works are his philosophical writings. These consist of a series of essays on practical ethics that preach Stoicism in a modified form, such as *De vita beata.* His nine tragedies, which include *Medea, Phaedra, Agamemnon, Oedipus,* and *Thyestes,* were most influential in Europe during and after the Renaissance.

Shakespeare, William (1564–1616), English poet and playwright. No one man in English literature–or for that matter in the literature of any language–has had his genius so universally acknowledged.

Today, more than 400 years after his birth, there is no country with even a single theatrical stage where his works are not produced at one time or another. There is no library where a copy or a translation of one of his books is not available. Every actor's ambition is to play Hamlet, and every actress hopes to play Juliet.

Of Shakespeare's poems the best-known are "Venus and Adonis", "The Rape of Lucrece," and "The Phoenix and the Turtle." Shakespeare's comedies and tragedies, written between 1589 and 1613, are given chronologically:

Henry VI (Parts 2 and 3), *Henry VI* (Part 1), *Comedy of Errors, Titus Andronicus, Richard III, Taming of the Shrew, Two Gentlemen of Verona, Love's Labour's Lost, Romeo and Juliet, Richard II, A Midsummer Night's Dream, King John, Merchant of Venice, Henry IV* (Parts 1 and 2), *Much Ado About Nothing, Henry V, Julius Caesar, As You Like It, Twelfth Night, Merry Wives of Windsor, Troilus and Cressida, All's Well that Ends Well, Hamlet, Measure for Measure, Othello, King Lear, Macbeth, Antony and Cleopatra, Coriolanus, Timon of Athens, Pericles, Cymbeline, Winter's Tale, Tempest, Henry VIII,* and *Two Noble Kinsmen.*

Shaw, George Bernard (1856–1950), Irish critic, pamphleteer, and playwright. His important plays include *Heartbreak House* (on World War I), *Back to Methuselah, Androcles and the Lion,* and *Saint Joan,* the latter about heroism and saintliness. Among his other plays are *Pygmalion, Candida* (on love as pity), *Arms and the Man* (a satire on the military profession), *The Doctor's Dilemma, You Never Can Tell, Man and Superman* (on eugenics), and *Fanny's First Play.* For a time he was a music critic and a dramatic critic and also wrote essays on a variety of subjects. He was awarded the Nobel Prize in Literature in 1925.

Shelley, Percy Bysshe (1792–1822), English poet. Shelley's chief works include the drama of *Hellas,* hoping for better things to come for mankind; *Alastor,* followed by *The Revolt of Islam* and *Julian and Maddalo;* the grand tragedy of *The Cenci;* and the sublime drama, *Prometheus Unbound.* The latter is his masterpiece and depicts the world moving from slavery

ever onward. *The Witch of Atlas*, the most perfect of Shelley's longer poems, is sheer imagination. *Adonais*, the elegy on Keats, followed in 1821. Shelley's letters to Thomas Love Peacock and others, and his incomplete *A Defence of Poetry*, are excellent prose. Of Shelley's lyrics some of the best loved are "Ode to the West Wind," "To a Skylark," and "The Indian Serenade."

Sinclair, Upton (1878–1968), United States author of the "muckraking" school, is noted for social protests. Sinclair's first recognition was won with *The Jungle* (1906), a realistic study of conditions among immigrants and in the Chicago packing houses where they worked. Sinclair continued to be a propaganda novelist with such works as *King Coal*, which took up the Colorado coal strike in 1913; *100%*, based on the Tom Mooney Preparedness Day bombing case; *Oil!*, an investigation of the Teapot Dome scandal, the film industry, and popular evangelism; and *Boston*, dealing with the Sacco-Vanzetti case. He also wrote nonfiction studies of such aspects of United States life as religion, journalism, and education.

In 1940 Sinclair began his popular series of contemporary historical novels, covering the period before and during World War II. The hero of the series, Lanny Budd, sees the rise of Nazism in Germany and later becomes a personal representative of President Franklin D. Roosevelt. Among the books included in the series are *World's End; Between Two Worlds; Dragon's Teeth* (1942 Pulitzer Prize for Fiction); *Presidential Agent; A World to Win; Presidential Mission;* and *O Shepherd, Speak!* In 1953 Sinclair published *The Return of Lanny Budd*.

Socrates (ca. 470 B.C.–399 B.C.), Athenian philosopher. There is no evidence that Socrates wrote anything. Information about his personality and doctrine is to be sought chiefly in the dialogues of Plato and the *Memorabilia* of Xenophon. Socrates dedicated himself to combating skepticism and arousing the love of truth and virtue. The Socratic method was to ask a question, then to show the inadequacy of the answer by further skillful questioning–all directed toward finding a sounder answer.

Sophocles (497–406 B.C.), one of the three great Greek tragic poets. His most famous play was *Oedipus Tyrannus (Oedipus Rex)*. Other plays of Sophocles include *Antigone,* the *Trachiniae, Electra, Philoctetes, Oedipus at Colonus,* and *Ajax*. Besides these seven complete tragedies, there remain about four hundred lines of a satyr play, *The Ichneutai,* and several hundred fragments of plays.

Spenser, Edmund (1552–1599), English poet. Among his outstanding contributions were *The Shepheardes Calender,* consisting of 12 pastoral eclogues. Other works include *Astrophel, Amoretti,* which expresses wooing; and *Epithalmion,* which tells about Spenser's wedding. *The Faerie Queene,* Spenser's unfinished masterpiece (Books I–VI), is an allegory and expresses Spenser's beliefs in the areas of morals, religion, and politics.

Stein, Gertrude (1874–1946), United States author. A literary "cubist" who utilized her theories of abstract art in her writing, Gertrude Stein seemed to carry to extremes her unconventional, repetitious manipulation of words. One of her celebrated phrases is "a rose is a rose is a rose." In the very well done *The Autobiography of Alice B. Toklas,* Miss Stein, while seeming to write the life of her secretary and companion, actually wrote her own life. Among Miss Stein's better-known works is *Three Lives* (1908), a story of three women told in a unique style. Other works are a book of verse, *Tender Buttons;* a play, *Four Saints in Three Acts;* and *Everybody's Autobiography.*

Steinbeck, John Ernst (1902–1968), United States novelist and Nobel Prize winner in Literature. He is best known for his social novel, *The Grapes of Wrath,* which won the 1940 Pulitzer Prize. *The Grapes of Wrath* has remained an all-time best-seller and has been translated into many foreign languages.

Among other Steinbeck works are *Tortilla Flat* (1935), *In Dubious Battle, Of Mice and Men, The*

Moon Is Down, Cannery Row, The Winter of Our Discontent, and *Travels with Charlie in Search of America* (1962).

Sterne, Laurence (1713–1768), English humorist, who is mainly noted for *The Life and Opinions of Tristram Shandy, Gentleman (1860–1867),* and *The Sentimental Journey through France and Italy.* Sterne started the trend toward the sentimental novel.

Stevenson, Robert Louis Balfour (1850–1894), Scottish novelist, essayist, and poet. *Virginibus Puerisque* (1881) contains his best essays. Short stories and travel appear in books such as *Travels with a Donkey* and *Inland Voyage.* His popular books include *Treasure Island* (1883), a story of pirates and a cabin boy and their adventures with mutiny and buried gold; *Kidnapped,* a young Scot's romantic adventures on sea and land; and *A Child's Garden of Verses* (1885), an adult remembering his childhood. *The Strange Case of Dr. Jekyll and Mr. Hyde* (1886) is a psychological study of the struggle between right and wrong within man's soul.

Stowe, Harriet Beecher (1811–1896), United States writer, best known as the author of *Uncle Tom's Cabin; or Life Among the Lowly* (1852). Its publication in book form was an important factor in bringing to a head the antislavery sentiment in the North. She wrote a second antislavery novel, *Dred* (1856), and several books dealing with New England, such as *The Minister's Wooing* and *Oldtown Folks.*

Strindberg, August (1849–1912), Swedish playwright, novelist, short story writer, and poet. He is noted for his conception of "the war of the sexes." His first important work and the first living piece of modern Swedish drama was *Master Olaf,* completed in 1880. His first novel, *The Red Room,* an ironical account of the vagaries of Stockholm society, made him famous. His other plays include *Lucky Peter's Travels, The Dance of Death,* and *The Bridal Crown.* The best of his historical plays is *Gustav Vasa.* His short stories include the collection called *Married,* that led to a prosecution for blasphemy of which he was acquitted. In later life he acquired a new faith, with overtones of Swedenborgianism, which produced a drama in three parts, *The Road to Damascus.*

Swift, Jonathan (1667–1745), British satirist, a good example of whose satire was the *Argument to prove that the abolishing of Christianity in England, may, as things now stand, be attended with some inconveniences.* His best narrative poem was *Baucis and Philemon.* His most famous work was *Travels Into Several Remote Nations of the World,* in four parts, commonly known as *Gulliver's Travels* (1726). This story which delights children is actually a bitter attack on mankind.

Swinburne, Algernon Charles (1837–1909), English poet and critic. Probably his two most famous dramas are *The Queen Mother* and *Rosamond.* He is more famous for *Poems and Ballads,* a revolt against moral conventions. *Song of Italy* and *Songs before Sunrise* show Swinburne's enthusiasm for Mazzini's revolt in Italy. *Tristram of Lyonese,* a poetic drama, retells a medieval legend. *Atlanta in Calydon* is a poetic drama; "When the hounds of spring" is his best known chorus; and "The Garden of Proserpine," one of his shorter poems, is a fine example of his masterly writing.

Tacitus, Cornelius (ca. 55–120), Roman historian. His works consist of the *Dialogue on Orators;* the *Life of Agricola; Germania (Germany),* an authentic account of the Germanic tribes; *Historiae (the Histories),* of which four books and a fragment survive, covering Galba's reign and the beginning of Vespasian's; and the *Annals,* of which twelve books survive, dealing with the reign of Tiberius and parts of the reigns of Claudius and Nero.

Tarkington, Booth (1869–1946), United States novelist and dramatist who wrote of Midwesterners in a satirical vein. The author of many kinds of writings, Tarkington won early recognition with his novel about political corruption, *The Gentleman from Indiana.* This was followed by the very popular romance *Monsieur Beaucaire,* which Tarkington later adapted for the stage. *The Conquest of Canaan,* a "problem" novel, was probably his most mature early work. His witty pictures of boyhood and adolescence, *Penrod* and *Seventeen,* enjoyed a considerable vogue. He was equally successful when he wrote about Midwestern life and character as shown by *The Turmoil* and *The Magnificent Ambersons* (Pulitzer Prize for Fiction, 1919). *Alice Adams* (Pulitzer Prize for Fiction, 1922), a deep character analysis of 22-year-old Alice and her problems, is perhaps his most polished novel.

Tennyson, Alfred, First Baron (1809–1892), English poet. The following won him wide acclaim: the volume of *Poems* which included "The Lady of Shalott," "The Dream of Fair Woman," "The Lotus Eaters," and "The Miller's Daughter," together with a score of other lyrics.

In Memoriam was published, in its original anonymous form, in 1850. Other famous works include "Ulysses"; *Tiresias and Other Poems; Jocksley Hall Sixty Years After;* "The Charge of the Light Brigade," a story of the Crimean War; *The Idylls of the King* (King Arthur), seven in number; *Enoch Arden;* and *Ballads and Other Poems,* which contains the gloomy and magnificent "Rizpah."

Thackeray, William Makepeace (1811–1863), English novelist. Thackeray's masterpieces are *Henry Esmond* (1852), a realistic story of Queen Anne's reign; *Pendennis,* a story of a selfish man; and *Vanity Fair* (1847), a comparison of a sweet, simple girl with a conniving, fascinating one. Some of his best essays are found in the *Roundabout Papers.*

Thibault, Jacques Anatole (1844–1924), French author and man of letters, who wrote under the pen name Anatole France, was awarded the Nobel Prize in Literature in 1921. His first novel, *Le Crime de Sylvestre Bonnard,* quickly won him literary acclaim. In forty years of writing France produced thoughtful, deep, lively, and beautifully written works. "Balthazar" and "L'Etui de Nacre" are fine examples of his keenly clever short stories. Among other works are *Le Puits de Sainte-Claire;* the thoughtful and critical books, *Les Opinions de Jérome Coignard* and *La Vie littéraire* (4 volumes); *La Rôtisserie de la Reine Pédauque,* a philosophical novel; and, a historical and philosophical work, *Thaïs,* set in Alexandria in the first century, in which a courtesan becomes a Christian through the efforts of a monk, but all for naught.

Thoreau, Henry David (1817–1862), United States writer, poet, and naturalist, whose greatest book is *Walden* (1854). In this, Thoreau, an individualist, wrote of his experiences while living alone with nature. Another well-known book is *A Week on the Concord and Merrimack Rivers.* His finest essays, *The Maine Woods, A Yankee in Canada,* and *Cape Cod,* contain his discoveries of what early America was like before civilization changed it. His essay *Civil Disobedience* inspired men such as Gandhi to try civil disobedience as a political tactic.

Thucydides (471?–400 B.C.), Greek historian. His great *History,* a recounting of the Peloponnesian War of 411 B.C., has been divided into eight books. It has no social and political references except as relating to the war and is noted for famous speeches, such as Pericles' funeral oration.

Thurber, James (1894–1961), United States writer and artist, considered by many the country's best humorist since Mark Twain. A serious writer as well as a comic artist, Thurber produced writings and drawings showing odd characters in surprising situations, humorous aspects of the war between men and women, and startling studies into the subconscious of unusual dogs and other animals, both real and imaginary. *My Life and Hard Times* is a hilarious autobiography. "The Secret Life of Walter Mitty" is his best-known short story. A successful stage play, *The Male Animal,* was written together with Elliott Nugent. While there is a satirical sense in many essays, parodies, and burlesques, a gentle humor is found in such fairy tales as *The Thirteen Clocks. The Years with Ross* is a witty record of associates on the *New Yorker* magazine.

Tolstoy, Leo Nikolayevich, Count (1828–1910), Russian novelist, playwright, and moral philosopher. His first story, *Childhood,* part of an autobiographical trilogy, was enthusiastically received. The ineffectualness, meanness, and crudeness of civilized man are revealed again and again in *Two Hussars, Lucerne, Three Deaths,* and *Kholstomer.* Tolstoy's philosophy found its full expression in the first of his great works, *War and Peace* (1863–1869). Considered one of the world's greatest novels, it traces the fortunes of two noble families and Russia's battles, defeat, and final victory over Napoleon. In 1873 he began *Anna Karenina*, a story of an adultery among the Russian nobility. *Resurrection* (1899–1900), a novel, tells of a Russian prince's seduction of a peasant girl and his repentance.

Tolstoy's plays include *The Power of Darkness*, a powerful drama of peasant life; *The Fruits of Enlightenment*, a light comedy satirizing the "fads" of society; and *The Living Corpse*.

Turgenev, Ivan Sergeyevich (1818–1883), Russian novelist generally contrasted with Flaubert, the naturalist, as the champion of realism. His first great success was *A Sportsman's Sketches*. Turgenev's masterpieces include short stories like "The Backwater," "Asya," "First Love," and the more complicated novels, *Rudin, A Nest of Gentlefolk, On the Eve,* and *Fathers and Sons* (1861). His best-known work in the United States is probably *Fathers and Sons*. Turgenev's last long works were *Smoke* and *Virgin Soil*.

Undset, Sigrid (1882–1949), Norwegian writer and Nobel Prize winner in Literature in 1928. Her most famous work, *Kristin Lavransdatter* (1920–1922) is a trilogy of Scandinavia. Mme. Undset's work demonstrates her ability to think in psychological terms and to judge the thinking and feelings of years gone by. Her work *Olav Amundsen* is a novel of the thirteenth century. Other books are *Jenny, Tree Marta Oulie, In the Wilderness, The Burning Bush, The Faithful Wife,* and *Men, Women, and Places,* an autobiography.

Villon, Francois (1431–ca. 1463), French poet, whose chief works took the form of mocking bequests to his family, friends, and particularly to his enemies. They were the *Petit Testament* and the *Grand Testament*. Throughout the *Grand Testament* are ballads and lyrics. The vainness of human life is the theme of all his poetry and is the very essence of his most famous and beautiful piece, the "Ballade des dames du temps jadis." His later poems include "The Ballad of the Hanged."

Virgil or **Vergil [Publius Vergilius Maro]** (70–19 B.C.), Roman poet. The *Eclogues*, the first of his certain works, is made up of ten pastoral poems that combine the beauty of nature with political life. This brought him recognition as one of Rome's leading poets. Then came the *Georgics*, four books on "tillage, trees, cattle, bees" showing that he was an expert on farming. Last came the *Aeneid*, a great national epic, which glorifies Rome, historically and culturally.

Wells, Herbert George (1866–1946), English novelist, journalist, and popular historian. His most popular work was *The Outline of History* (1920), a brief, clear history of mankind. The novels, *Kipps* and *Tono-Bungay*, exhibit his humor and social satire, both with a Dickensian touch. Wells also wrote a kind of science fiction to call attention to needed social reform. These works include *Men Like Gods, The Time Machine, The War of the Worlds,* and *The World Set Free*.

Whitman, Walt (1819–1892), United States poet. His *Leaves of Grass* (1855) demonstrated the inherent power of the free verse line, which he was the first to bring to perfection. His work revealed him as a mystic and a believer in pantheism, with high regard for all humanity. All of his works reflected his thinking and beliefs. Some of his poems, such as "Song of Myself" and "Out of the Cradle Endlessly Rocking," contain a spiritualized view of sex. Among his best poems are *Drum-Taps* and *Sequel to Drum-Taps*, containing the popular "When Lilacs Last in the Dooryard Bloom'd" and "O Captain! My Captain!" *Specimen Days* and *Democratic Vistas* are Whitman's chief prose works.

Whittier, John Greenleaf (1807–1892), United States poet and abolitionist. His best-known work is "Snowbound" (1866), an idyll of New England farm life. *Legends of New England,* a collection of short stories and poems, was his first book. He wrote in both prose and poetry—*Old Portraits and Modern Sketches, Literary Recreations and Miscellanies, Songs of Labor, The Chapel of the Hermits* and *Panorama,* the latter containing such favorites as "The Barefoot Boy" and "Maud Muller." *Home Ballads and Poems* contains "Telling the Bees," "My Playmate," and "Skipper Ireson's Ride." His best-known war poem, "Barbara Frietchie" is found in *In War Time*.

Wilde, Oscar (1854–1900), English author. The outstanding works of Wilde are the novel, *The Picture of Dorian Gray*, and the clever, facetious plays, *The Importance of Being Earnest* and *Lady Windermere's Fan*. His powerful *Ballad of Reading Gaol* was published in 1898. His *Collected Poems* show that he might have made a considerable reputation as a poet had he not neglected this talent.

Wilder, Thornton (1897–1975), United States novelist and playwright. Wilder's novels, almost all historical, include *The Cabala, The Woman of Andros,* and *Heaven's My Destination. The Ides of March* is about the assassination of Julius Caesar. *The Bridge of San Luis Rey* is a novel showing that life may contain more design than is apparent. It won the Pulitzer Prize in 1928. His plays *Our Town, The Matchmaker,* and *The Skin of Our Teeth* (Pulitzer Prize, 1943) won both popular and critical acclaim.

Williams, Tennessee (1914–1983), United States author dramatist and the pen name of Thomas Lanier.

Williams' first public recognition came with the successful Broadway production of *The Glass Menagerie*. He won the New York Drama Critics' Circle Award three times–for *The Glass Menagerie, A Streetcar Named Desire,* and *Cat on a Hot Tin Roof*–and Pulitzer prizes for the latter two. Williams' characters all appear mentally sick. For such characters, no hope can be offered; but with his poetic language, Williams grants them sympathy. Other plays include *Summer and Smoke, The Rose Tattoo, Orpheus Descending, Suddenly Last Summer,* and *Night of the Iguana*.

Wolfe, Thomas Clayton (1900–1938), United States author. His novel *Look Homeward, Angel* (1929) has become an American classic. It is at the same time realistic and lyrical. It was followed by *Of Time and the River. The Web and the Rock* and *You Can't Go Home Again* were published after Wolfe's death. *You Can't Go Home Again* is considered the most mature of his autobiographical narratives. *The Hills Beyond* contains semibiographical stories somewhat like his novels.

Wordsworth, William (1770–1850), English poet. His collection of poetry in *Poems in Two Volumes* shows his extensive poetical power. His use of the sonnet and the ode give these poetic forms new vigor. *The Prelude,* the *Recluse,* and *Margaret, or the Ruined Cottage* place Wordsworth with the greatest poets.

Wright, Richard (1908–1960), black United States novelist. His most famous work, *Native Son* (1939), won the Springarm medal. Wright dealt with social problems in his novels, particularly those relating to black Americans. Other well known works include *Uncle Tom's Children, Black Boy,* and *White Man, Listen*.

Xenophon (ca. 430 B.C.–after 355 B.C.), Greek historian and man of letters. *Anabasis* is the most popular of Xenophon's writings. It tells about the military campaigns of Cyrus, the Persian king, and the withdrawal of the Greek hired soldiers to the Black Sea. The first two-thirds is a running narrative not too deep in thought, but vigorous, detailed, and exact. The *Hellenica* is the only history of this period (411–362 B.C.) written by a contemporary. The *Memorabilia* tells of the life and opinions of Socrates, with many of Xenophon's opinions included.

Yeats, William Butler (1865–1939), Irish twentieth-century poet, dramatist, and critic. First among Yeats' many poetic successes was *The Wanderings of Oisin. Purgatory* is a brief but important verse-drama. Other notable poetic dramas are *The Countess Cathleen, Cathleen Ni Houlihan, The Land of Heart's Desire,* and *Deirdre*. These plays established him as a stalwart of the Abbey Theatre in Dublin.

Yeats edited *The Oxford Book of Verse* and prefaced it with a long essay. He received the Nobel Prize in Literature in 1923.

Zola, Émile (1840–1902), French novelist. Zola wrote "scientific" novels in which the characters are governed by environment and heredity; of these his 20-volume series, *Les Rougon Macquart,* is an example. The series includes *Germinal* (1885), a clear, forceful account of an unsuccessful coal miners' strike and the misery of the children and adults who work in the mines; *L'Assommoir (The Dram-Shop),* a warning of the evils of alcohol; and *Nana,* an account of the crudeness of the demimonde of the Second Empire. *La Terre* is a powerful novel dealing with selfishness and brutality in peasant life. His *J'accuse* (1898) reflects his strong stand in the Dreyfus Affair. *Le Roman expérimental* states his theory of fiction and is the most widely known statement of naturalistic aims.

STATES AND COUNTRIES

The Fifty States of the United States

From the original 13 colonies, the United States has grown to the present 50 states. It is not unreasonable to assume that the number may still grow, now that the non-contiguous territories of Alaska and Hawaii have become states. Of course, this growth cannot be at the nineteenth-century rate because the possessions are now limited.

This section gives a brief history of each state including government and economy, and at the end of the next section there is a table with statistics related to the states.

ALABAMA

Alabama advertises itself as "The Heart of Dixie." It is, indeed, one of the original "Cotton Belt" states of the Old South. The first settlement in what is now Alabama was made by the French on Mobile Bay, in 1702. The French lost control of the area to the British in 1763. At the end of the War for Independence, all of the present state except the Mobile area was ceded to the United States. Mobile was then ceded to Spanish Florida, but regained by the United States in 1813.

Alabama was set up as a territory in 1817. It was then reorganized and admitted into the Union on December 14, 1819, as the twenty-second state. Alabama seceded from the Union on January 11, 1861, and joined the Confederate States of America. The first Confederate capital was located at Montgomery, Alabama. With the surrender of Mobile after the Battle of Mobile Bay in 1865, the defeat of Alabama was completed. Devastation due to the war was less severe than in other states of the South, but the economy of the state was wrecked and industry almost ceased. The state was readmitted in 1868, but federal troops were not withdrawn until four years later.

With the antebellum pattern of life destroyed, years of confusion and slow rebuilding followed. The economy revived somewhat in the eighties when steel production began in the Birmingham area. Other industries began to expand rapidly. A great industrial boom has taken place in Alabama during the twentieth century. This rapid industrial growth, combined with a revitalized agriculture that is no longer dependent solely upon cotton, has brought about vigorous change and revolutionary progress in "The Heart of Dixie."

Government. The state constitution dates from 1901. The state sends two senators and seven representatives to the U.S. Congress. The legislature consists of a senate of 35 members and a house of representatives of 106 members. The state is divided into 67 counties; in 1970 there were 35 cities with a population of more than ten thousand.

Economy. Major resources include iron, coal, limestone, and the "black soils" for agriculture. The great TVA projects that have arisen along the Tennessee River have brought extensive industrial expansion to northern Alabama. The presence of iron, coal, and limestone (all of which are major components of steel-making) in the same area of north-central Alabama has made Bir-

Alabama—Bellingrath Gardens near Mobile

mingham the leading iron and steel center of the South.

Alabama is also one of the leading lumber-producing states. Over 634,000 acres of national forests existed in Alabama in 1970. The chief crops grown in Alabama are cotton, corn, peanuts, and oats. Special crops include tung oil and pecans, both derived from nut trees. The raising of cattle and hogs is becoming significant in the state's economy.

ALASKA

Alaska was discovered in 1741 by Vitus Bering, a Danish explorer in the service of Russia. Russian fur traders and trappers followed the explorers. In 1784 they founded the Kodiak settlement and Sitka, the capital of Russian America, in 1799. On March 30, 1867, Alaska was sold to the United States by Czar Alexander II to prevent its capture by the British, with whom Russia was then at war. The United States paid $7,200,000, or less than two cents per acre!

President Andrew Johnson and Secretary William H. Seward were derided for making what was thought to be a useless purchase. The area of the present state was set up as a district and governed under the general laws of Oregon, although it was not governed by that state itself. After a series of gold discoveries in the district, Alaska was organized into a territory on August 24, 1912. The development of salmon fisheries, copper mining, and the growth of a tourist industry during the twenties and thirties strengthened the economy of the territory and generated a strong campaign for statehood. During World War II the statehood issue was set aside. The territory's strategic location and its natural wealth attracted the Japanese. They attempted an invasion in 1942 and managed to occupy Attu and Kiska islands in the Aleutian Archipelago of Alaska. The United States poured millions of dollars into Alaskan defenses, and in 1943 the Japanese were expelled.

The postwar economy was strengthened by further heavy defense spending, with the consequent expansion of industry and population. A renewed campaign for statehood resulted in victory on January 3, 1959, when Alaska entered the Union as the forty-ninth state.

Government. Alaska's executive branch consists of 20 departments under the governor's office. The legislature consists of a senate of 20 members and a house of representatives of 40 members. The state sends two senators and one representative to Congress. There are no counties in Alaska, but a system of boroughs performs the same functions. There were five cities in 1970 with a population of over 10,000.

Economy. Much economic activity centers around fishing, forestry, and the tourist industry. It is now fairly certain that Alaska's Kenai Peninsula and the Arctic Slope form two of the world's major petroleum areas, and someday may rival or even surpass production in the Middle East. An 800-mile trans-Alaska pipeline was completed in 1977 to carry oil from the North Slope to the Gulf of Alaska in the south.

Agriculture is well developed in the Matanuska Valley of southern Alaska and in the interior around Fairbanks. Hay, potatoes, wheat, and rye are the major crops. Some dairying and ranching is carried on near Anchorage, the state's largest city. Sawmills and canneries are concentrated in the panhandle.

The state's transportation system includes one railroad, 470 miles long, serving the interior between Fairbanks and Anchorage. Travel to Alaska is possible by automobile on the Alaska Highway,

Alaska—Mt. McKinley

1,523 miles long. This road lies mostly in Canada, and extends from Dawson Creek in British Columbia, to Fairbanks, Alaska, with several spur routes in both Alaska and Canada.

ARIZONA

Many of the Indians that live in Arizona today are the descendants of two highly advanced cultures that developed there in prehistoric times. Abandoned cliff-cities and other ruins scattered over Arizona belonged to the famous Basket-Maker people and their successors, the Pueblo people. A great 30-year drought during the thirteenth century is thought to be the chief cause of the abandonment of most of the cliff-cities. The descendants of the cliff-dwellers were found living in fortified towns and mesas, or near watercourses when Coronado's Spanish expedition entered the region in 1540.

Spanish settlement began in 1752, although Spanish missionaries had been active in Arizona since the end of the sixteenth century. Arizona became a part of independent Mexico in 1821. Most of the present state was ceded to the United States in 1848 by the Treaty of Guadalupe Hidalgo. That part lying south of the Gila River formed part of the Gadsden Purchase that was added in 1854 (*see also* New Mexico). Arizona was organized as a territory in 1863 and entered the Union as the forty-eighth state on February 14, 1912.

Government. The state constitution dates from 1910. The legislature consists of a senate of 30 members and a house of representatives of 60 members. The state sends to the national Congress two senators and four representatives. Arizona is divided into fourteen counties, and in 1970 there were 13 cities with a population of more than ten thousand.

Economy. The state's greatest resource is copper, and 40 to 50 percent of the entire United States production is mined in Arizona. Silver, uranium, zinc, molybdenum, gold, and other minerals are mined. Tourists, attracted by the healthful dry climate and many great natural wonders, provide a major source of revenue.

Water is always a precious mineral, and particularly so in Arizona, where it is in short supply. Four major dams on the Colorado and two on the Salt and Gila rivers provide water for irrigation and other uses. Through irrigation, deserts give way to fields of lettuce, cantaloupe, cotton, and citrus trees. Hoover Dam (formerly Boulder Dam), on the Colorado River in the northwest, is the

Arizona—Petrified Forest and Teepee Formations

highest in the U.S. and one of the highest in the world. It forms Lake Mead, which is shared with Nevada. Generators at the dam supply a large percentage of the electric power that is used in Arizona. Over one million acres of land are under irrigation in the state.

The most important crops are cotton, grain sorghums, and barley. Pasturing of sheep is heavy but diminished from earlier years.

ARKANSAS

The area of the present state of Arkansas was visited by Hernando de Soto in 1541–1542. It was

Arkansas—Observation Tower, Hot Springs Mountain

claimed for France in 1682 by Sieur de La Salle as a part of the Mississippi drainage area. The French yielded the region to Spain in 1762 but it was given back to France in 1800. (French trappers established the first permanent settlement within the present state in 1686 and called it Arkansas Post. It was located at the confluence of the Arkansas River with the Mississippi River.) The region became a part of the Louisiana Purchase in 1803 and came under the American flag. Arkansas Territory was organized in 1819 from a part of Missouri Territory. It assumed its present boundaries (by excluding what is now Oklahoma) and was admitted to the Union as the twenty-fifth state on June 15, 1836.

The people of Arkansas were seriously divided on the issue of slavery and secession, but on May 6, 1861, the state voted to secede and join the Confederate States of America. Union forces won a costly battle at Pea Ridge in northwestern Arkansas in 1862, and captured Little Rock the following year. In 1868 Arkansas was readmitted to the Union.

Government. The legislature of Arkansas is called the General Assembly (*see* Colorado) and is composed of a senate of 35 members and a house of representatives of 100 members. The governor and lieutenant governor are elected for two years. Arkansas is represented in Congress by two senators and four representatives. The state is divided into 75 counties, and in 1970 there were 25 cities and towns with a population of more than ten thousand.

Economy. Arkansas is an agricultural state. Cotton is the chief crop; and rice, soybeans, wheat, fruit, and sweet potatoes are grown in significant amounts. The state ranks fifth in the production of cotton. Erosion is a serious problem in the state.

Large portions of the state's land is thought to require drastic corrective measures. Forests cover three-fifths of the state and hardwood timber forms the basis for most of the state's manufacturing.

Mineral production centers around bauxite, an ore of aluminum. Most of this (97 percent of the U.S. domestic supplies) is taken from mines just southwest of Little Rock. Titanium, lead, oil, natural gas, and coal are also mined. The tourist industry has developed greatly in recent decades. Numerous springs, caves, cool highlands, and scenic spots, along with the great many lakes, have attracted vacationers and sightseers in large numbers.

CALIFORNIA

The name *California* was first used in a book published in 1510 by Garcia Ordoñez de Montalvo. The first European known to have seen California was Juan Rodriguez Cabrillo, who passed up the coast of the present state in 1542. San Diego and Monterey were settled in 1769 and 1770, respectively, as fortified outposts and missions. It was in 1823 that Mexico achieved independence and came into possession of California. There were 21 missions in the state, strung along the coast about a day's journey apart.

San Francisco was founded in 1776 and was called Yerba Buena until 1847. Los Angeles was founded in 1781 as Neustra Señora la Reina de Los Angeles, (city of Our Lady, Queen of the Angels). By 1844 all the missions were broken up or sold by the Mexican government to private interests.

Relations with Mexico were altered in 1838 when that government recognized the separate existence of California within the Mexican Union. A final attempt to install a Mexican governor was thwarted in 1845. About this time, Americans began settling in the state, especially in the Great Central Valley, around Sacramento. In June 1846, John C. Fremont challenged Mexican authority by capturing Sonoma and setting up the famous "Bear Flag Republic." This movement was at first disavowed by the United States Government, but the onset of war between Mexico and the United States led to the recognition of Fremont's Bear Flag revolt. Fremont was persuaded to place his troops under the command of Commodore John D. Sloat, and the United States then proceeded to

occupy California. In 1848 Mexico surrendered all claims to California and on September 9, 1850, California was admitted to the Union as the thirty-first state. Two years earlier, James Marshall, a lumberjack, found gold nuggets while building a sawmill for John Sutter on the American River. This started the famous "Forty-niner" gold rush and the rapid development of the state's natural resources.

Government. The legislature consists of a senate of forty members and an assembly of eighty members. The governor and lieutenant governor are elected for four years. The state sends two senators and 43 representatives to the U.S. Congress. The state is divided into 58 counties. San Bernardino County, covering 20,131 square miles, is the largest county in the United States. In 1970, there were 288 cities and towns in California with a population of more than ten thousand.

Economy. California's economic activities are as

California—San Francisco

varied as are the climate and landforms. The state leads in the total value of farm products. In the agricultural picture, specialty crops and fruits are especially important. In addition, cotton, wheat, barley, rice, poultry, and vegetables are grown in large quantities. The chief specialty crops are raisin and wine grapes, plums, prunes, apricots, citrus fruits, including oranges, lemons, and grapefruit, nuts, and dates. California produces 85 percent of the nation's wine.

California ranks second in the nation in cotton production and leads all states in sugar beets, fishery products, persimmons, seed crops, lemons, walnuts, almonds, apricots, avocados, figs, grapes, olives, peaches, pears, plums, prunes, artichokes, cantaloupes, carrots, strawberries, dates, asparagus, green limas, broccoli, cauliflower, and celery. The specialty crops and fruit are grown mainly in the Great Central and the Imperial valleys, largely on irrigated lands.

The principal mineral is petroleum, in the production of which California regularly ranks third, after Louisiana and Texas. Other major minerals mined are gypsum, mercury, natural gas, tungsten, lead, zinc, copper, and iron ore. The state was fifth in the production of gold in 1960. Only Texas outranks California in total mineral production. In lumber production, California ranks second to Oregon.

However large other industries of the state are, most of California's income is derived from manufacturing. The state ranks first in slaughtering of cattle, in value of processed foods, and in the production of wine and olive oil. Iron and steel production is centered in the Los Angeles area, while shipbuilding is concentrated in San Francisco and San Diego. Palo Alto is the center of the electronics industry and of aircraft building.

Outstanding natural features such as wa-terfalls, canyons, and desert scenery, have been enclosed or preserved within both state and federal parks and monuments, providing the basis for a large tourist industry. In addition, sport centers, winter and summer resorts are located all over the state. Several million persons visit California every year as tourists or vacationers.

COLORADO

Spanish explorers had visited Colorado during the sixteenth and seventeenth centuries. However, it was not until 1706 that Juan de Uribarri took formal possession of the region for Spain, despite a claim by France originating with Sieur de La Salle in 1682. The eastern part of the present state eventually was included in the Louisiana Purchase and came under the American flag in 1803. The remainder of Colorado passed into United States possession in 1848 as a part of the Mexican cession.

Zebulon M. Pike explored Colorado in 1806, discovering the peak now named for him. Between 1820 and 1850 Major Stephen Long and John C. Fremont explored parts of the present state. The discovery of gold at Cherry Creek in 1858 attracted settlers; the first settlement was made at Auraria (now part of Denver). Colorado was organized as a territory in 1861. Movements for statehood failed on several occasions, but were successful in 1876 when Colorado was admitted to the Union as the thirty-eighth state. In 1906, the United States mint opened at Denver, and Mesa Verde National Park was established to preserve abandoned cliff-cities of a former Indian civilization (*see* Arizona).

Government. The state's legislative body is called the General Assembly (in other states this

Colorado—Mesa Verde National Park

name is often applied to the lower legislative chamber). It consists of a senate of 35 members and a house of representatives of 65 members. The governor and lieutenant-governor are elected for four years. The state sends two senators and five representatives to Congress. Colorado is divided into 63 counties, and in 1970 there were 26 cities and towns having a population of more than ten thousand.

Economy. More than 250 different minerals are mined in Colorado, the major ones being coal, oil, molybdenum, zinc, lead, vanadium, and uranium. Colorado has huge reserves of oil in the form of oil shales, but their mining awaits fuller development of methods to extract the oil from the shale.

Colorado is a leading sheep-raising state, and Denver is said to be the world's largest sheep-marketing center. The state's agriculture relies heavily upon irrigation and more than 20 percent of the crop lands are seriously eroded. Nevertheless, the state ranks first in the production of broomcorn, second in sugar beets, second in onions, fourth in beans, and eighth in barley. In addition, Colorado is a leading producer of celery, potatoes, wheat, peaches, cherries, and cattle feed. National forests cover nearly fourteen million acres. Tourism is a large industry, based chiefly on the big game for hunters and the Rocky Mountain scenic and ski areas.

CONNECTICUT

Connecticut is one of the 13 original states. A Dutch navigator named Adraen Block discovered and explored the Connecticut River in 1614. A Dutch trading post, established at Hartford in 1633, was replaced by an English settlement in 1635. Windsor and Wethersfield were founded in 1634. The Dutch attempted to expel the English but failed. In 1639 the three towns drew up a constitution which governed them until Charles II granted a charter in 1662. This famous charter served the colony and then the state of Connecticut until 1818. In 1687 King James II of England called upon Connecticut to surrender the charter. The colonists refused and hid it in an oak tree. However, the existing government was dissolved and the colony was despotically ruled until the overthrow of King James II in 1689. The famous Charter Oak is shown on a United States postage

stamp, issued in 1935 to commemorate the three-hundreth anniversary of the state.

The charter struggle and other events in Connecticut were closely observed by other colonies and had a strong influence in arousing public opinion against England. Connecticut contributed large amounts of supplies to the Continental Army. It was the only colony in which the British governor supported the Colonists and continued in office during the Revolution. Fifteen percent of the population participated in the war. Nathan Hale, a Connecticut schoolteacher, was hanged as a spy by the British in 1776. Connecticut joined the Union as the fifth state on January 9, 1788.

Government. Our present system of representation in Congress was proposed by the Connecticut delegation to the Constitutional Convention in 1787. It was adopted and is called the Connecticut Compromise. Connecticut's legislative body is called the General Assembly (*see* Colorado); it consists of a senate of 36 members, and a house of representatives of 177 members. The governor and lieutenant-governor are elected for four years. The state sends two senators and six representatives to the U.S. Congress. County government, established in 1666, was formally abolished by the General Assembly in 1960. The eight former counties remain only as geographical subdivisions. In 1970,

Connecticut—Nathan Hale Schoolhouse, East Haddam

there were 78 cities and towns in Connecticut with a population of more than ten thousand. (For a note on New England towns, *see* Massachusetts.)

Economy. Only three minerals (mica, beryl, and feldspar) are of economic importance. The chief industry of Connecticut is manufacturing. In 1970 the state ranked thirteenth in the nation in value added by manufacturing. It was a leader in the production of hats, firearms, clocks, watches, aircraft engines, needles, pins, nails, and hardware.

A high-quality leaf tobacco is grown in Connecticut, and the Connecticut Valley is a major fruit-growing region.

DELAWARE

Delaware is one of the 13 original states. The first attempted settlement, made near Lewes by the Dutch in 1631, was destroyed by the Indians. In 1638 the Swedes established a successful colony at Fort Christina, now Wilmington. This colony, called New Sweden, prospered until it was overwhelmed by a Dutch invasion in 1655. Nine years later (1664), the Dutch were conquered by the British.

The colony was deeded to William Penn in 1682. However, the area remained a distinct unit within Penn's territory and was called the "Three Lower Counties." A long dispute between William Penn and the Baltimores (proprietors of the Maryland

Delaware—Caesar Rodney Statue, Rodney Square, Wilmington

colony) was settled when Mason and Dixon surveyed the region in 1763.

The same governor and General Assembly served both colonies until 1704 when a dispute over defense caused the Three Lower Counties to form their own General Assembly. The two colonies continued to share the same governor until the War for Independence.

In 1776 the Three Lower Counties became "Delaware State," and joined with 12 other colonies to prosecute the war with the British. The first star in the American flag represents Delaware State, because it was the first to ratify the new federal constitution creating the United States, on December 7, 1787. In 1792 a new state constitution changed the name "Delaware State" to "State of Delaware." Delaware remained in the Union throughout the Civil War (1861–1865).

Government. The legislature of Delaware is called the General Assembly and consists of a senate of 19 members and a house of representatives of 39 members. The state has one representative-at-large and two senators in the U.S. Congress. The state is divided into three counties. Delaware is the only state today that subdivides the counties into "hundreds." The hundred is an ancient unit, meaning originally a piece of land that could provide 100 men for use in time of war. It was once used in Delaware as the basis for representation in the General Assembly, but today is used only for tax and other minor purposes.

Economy. Delaware is mainly an industrial state. Wilmington is one of the chief chemical manufacturing centers of the world. Textiles rank next to chemicals, followed by leather-making. Shipbuilding is also important. Wilmington is the chief industrial and urban complex. Commercial fishing centers around Lewes, a port on the Atlantic Ocean. Wilmington and New Castle are major seaports. The Chesapeake and Delaware Canal, completed in 1829 and widened in 1919, provides a shortcut between Delaware Bay and Chesapeake Bay through the Delmarva Peninsula.

Excellent highways cross Delaware in all directions. Surf bathing and harness racing attract many visitors and vacationers to the state.

FLORIDA

Florida was visited twice from 1513 to 1521 by Ponce de Leon, a Spanish adventurer. He named the country Florida. Hernando de Soto marched through the interior of the Florida Peninsula in 1539.

A settlement of French Huguenots, established in 1564 at Fort Carolina on the St. John's River, was wiped out by the Spanish in 1565. In the same year the first permanent white settlement in what is now the United States was founded at St. Augustine by Spanish colonists.

Spain ceded Florida to the English in 1763, but a fierce three-way war broke out among the English, the Indians, and the Spanish colonists. This war merged into the American Revolution. Florida was used as a base for raids on Carolina and Georgia towns. In 1783 the British gave Florida back to Spain, and in 1795 Spain sold a part of Florida on the gulf coast to France. The United States occupied that part in 1812, claiming that France had included it in the sale of Louisiana to the United States in 1803.

In the War of 1812, the British captured Pensacola but were driven out by Andrew Jackson. He abandoned it and had to recapture it in 1818. In the following year Spain sold all of Florida to the United States for five million dollars.

In 1835, war broke out between the United States and the Seminole Indians. The Seminole War was merely a more serious phase of a war that had been going on since Andrew Jackson invaded Florida in 1818.

After more than a thousand Seminoles and their allies had been rounded up and sent west of the Mississippi (*see* Oklahoma), a treaty of peace was concluded in 1839. But sporadic fighting continued until 1842. On March 3, 1845, Florida was admitted to the Union as the twenty-seventh state. Florida seceded from the Union on January 10, 1861, and was readmitted on February 6, 1868.

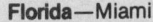

Florida—Miami

Government. The legislature of Florida consists of a senate of 48 members and a house of representatives of 119 members. The state has no lieutenant-governor. Florida sends two senators and 15 representatives to the U.S. Congress. There are 67 counties, and in 1970 there were 87 cities and towns with a population of more than ten thousand.

Economy. The great citrus fruit belt for which Florida is so famous lies in the highland section of the peninsula, among the lakes. Grapefruit and oranges are the leading citrus crops. Florida is the leading state in the production of oranges, grapefruit, and limes. Tobacco, cotton, peanuts, and sugar cane are other major crops in the state.

The state has rich mineral deposits. Three-fourths of phosphate mined in the United States comes from Florida. Fuller's earth, uranium (recovered from phosphate deposits), ilmenite and rutile (ores of titanium) are also mined in Florida.

Industrial growth has been rapid in recent years, chiefly in processed foods. The greatest industry of Florida is tourism. The long beaches, pleasant climate, and the tropical Everglades are contributing factors in the fame of Florida as a vacation land.

GEORGIA

Georgia is one of the original 13 states, and it was the last English colony to be established in what is now the United States. Before the white settlers came, Creek Indians lived on the southern plains and lowlands while the Cherokees inhabited the highlands.

Hernando de Soto visited the region in 1540 and French explorers followed a few years later. The English claimed the region in 1629 as part of the Carolina grant made by King Charles I, but did not attempt to plant a colony there until 1732. In that year, George II deeded the region to a group led by General James Oglethorpe, and Oglethorpe landed the first settlers the following year. Georgia ratified the U.S. Constitution on January 2, 1788, and in 1802 the state sold all of its claims west of the Chattahoochee River. In 1832, the Creek Indians in the state were deported westward, followed by the Cherokees in 1838. Georgia seceded from the Union on January 19, 1861.

Georgia suffered heavily in the Civil War. Several of the engagements in the state were bitterly

Georgia—Fort Pulaski Moat

fought and costly in terms of men and material. Toward the end of the war, General Sherman's troops burned Atlanta and marched toward the sea, causing such great destruction through fire and looting that the line of march is still discernible from the air. Georgia was readmitted to the Union in 1868, but expelled in 1869 and again readmitted in 1870.

Government. The constitution of 1945 is the eighth one adopted in Georgia. The Georgia legislature consists of a senate of 24 members and a house of representatives of 195 members. The minimum voting age is 18. Georgia has two senators and ten representatives in the U.S. Congress. The state is divided into 159 counties, the largest number of counties in any state except Texas. In 1970, there were 39 cities and towns with a population of more than ten thousand.

Economy. Georgia furnishes 78 percent of the nation's kaolin, or china clay. Gold was discovered in 1828 and until 1849 most of the gold in the United States came from Georgia. The quarrying of granite and marble is an important industry. Iron and coal are mined in the Appalachians. Forests cover about two-thirds of the state, and Georgia leads in the production of turpentine and resin, both derived from the sap of trees. The principal agricultural crops are cotton, peanuts, hogs, tobacco, and poultry. The state is the largest producer of sea island cotton. Georgia leads the nation in pecan and peanut production.

HAWAII

The Hawaiian Islands, formerly called the Sandwich Islands, were discovered in 1778 by Captain James Cook. Cook returned to the islands the following year after exploring the coast of North America (*see* Oregon). He was killed on the main island of Hawaii as he tried to retrieve a stolen boat.

Between 1795 and 1819, the island archipelago was united into a kingdom by Kamehameha I. Christian missionaries began working there in 1820. The kingdom adopted its first constitution in 1840. Immigration from Asia and Europe in large numbers began with Chinese in 1852, followed by Polynesians from other Pacific islands in 1859, Portuguese in 1878, Japanese in 1886, and Filipinos in 1906.

The pineapple industry was established by Captain John Kidwell in 1882, using plants imported from Jamaica. By 1893, American owners of the sugar cane and pineapple industries formed the strongest groups in the islands. The instability of the kingdom and the desire of the growers to export under more favorable conditions led to a revolt in 1893, and the establishment of a Hawaiian Republic under Sanford B. Dole.

American businessmen managed to get the islands annexed to the United States in 1898. The Territory of Hawaii was organized on June 14, 1900. A plebiscite for statehood was not held until 1940. Japanese forces attacked Pearl Harbor on December 7, 1941, forcing the United States into World War II. A constitution was adopted in 1950

Hawaii—Mauna Loa

and statehood was achieved on August 21, 1959. Thereby, Hawaii became the fiftieth state.

Government. The legislature consists of a senate of 25 members and a house of representatives of 51 members. The governor and lieutenant-governor are elected for four years. The state sends two senators and two representatives to the U.S. Congress. Hawaii is divided into five counties. There are 34 municipalities having more than 2,500 inhabitants (1970). Nine of these had a population of more than ten thousand in 1970.

Economy. The mainstays of the state's economy are military expenditures, agriculture, and tourism. Plantation agriculture is highly developed with sugar cane the most important crop. Crops vary with altitude zones. Sugar grows in the lowlands. Pineapples, the second largest crop, grow on the terraced uplands. The plantations of Hawaii are outstandingly efficient and some are highly mechanized. The people enjoy a high standard of living. Some diversified agriculture is beginning to be practiced.

IDAHO

The early history of Idaho is that of the Oregon country, especially with regard to the Oregon boundary dispute, the explorations of Lewis and Clark, and other explorations (*see* Oregon). After 1853, however, what is now Idaho became a part of the new Washington Territory. The region of Idaho became known to white men after the discovery of gold in 1859 near the present Lewiston. By 1862 there were thirty thousand white people in the region. In March 1863, Idaho was organized into a territory, with the capital at Lewiston. It included Montana until 1864, and Wyoming until 1868. These separations reduced the territorial limits to about what they are today. However, errors in earlier surveys of boundaries necessitated changes at various times.

Serious Indian troubles developed between 1877 and 1879, in which many settlers and soldiers were killed. The Snake River Valley was opened by the laying of tracks for the Oregon Short Line Railroad in 1880. Idaho was admitted to the Union on July 3, 1890 (forty-third state). Labor trouble in the Coeur d'Alene area led to rioting and the blowing up of a mill. In 1905 Governor Steunenburg was assassinated. This resulted in the famous trial of a member of the western Federation of Miners, who was sentenced to life imprisonment.

Government. Idaho is governed under its original constitution of 1889. The legislature consists of a senate of 35 members and a house of representatives of 70 members. The governor and lieutenant-governor are elected for four years. The state is represented in the U.S. Congress by two senators and two representatives. Idaho is divided into 44 counties, and in 1970 there were nine cities and towns with a population of more than ten thousand.

Economy. Silver, lead, zinc, and antimony are the chief minerals mined in Idaho. The state ranks high in the mining of antimony, lead and cobalt, and it produces 44 percent of the domestic silver. Other major minerals produced are phosphate rock, garnet, nickel, columbium, tantalum, copper, gold, and mercury. Beryllium has been recently discovered, and other minor minerals are produced.

Although large areas are arid, agriculture is a leading industry in Idaho. Irrigation is widely practiced and there are over three million acres under irrigation in the state. The most important cash crops are cereals, over 50 percent of which is wheat. The growing of hops, a new industry, is spreading. Other crops include sugar beets, potatoes, oats, barley, beans, apples, and prunes.

Idaho—Craters of the Moon National Monument

Illinois—Chicago

ILLINOIS

Illinois was discovered in 1673 by the French explorers Father Jacques Marquette and Louis Joliet.

The early history of the state is that of French exploration and settlement. Sieur de LaSalle several times crossed Illinois between Lake Michigan and the Mississippi River by using the historic portage route to the Illinois River, and thence down that river to the Mississippi. La Salle built Fort Crevecoeur near the present Peoria. In about 1700 two settlements were established near the mouth of the Illinois River. They were Kaskaskia and Kahokia. Both were settled by missionaries, traders, and Indians.

In 1717 these settlements were called the Illinois District and were annexed to the French province of Louisiana. By 1720 there were three additional villages in the district. In 1763 France ceded the district to the British, who annexed it to Quebec in 1774.

George Rogers Clark led a military expedition of Virginians into the Illinois country (1778–1779). Largely because of this expedition, the entire region was ceded to the United States in 1783. When Indiana Territory was set up in 1800 (*see* Indiana), Illinois was a part of it. In 1809 Illinois Territory was organized with the seat of government at Kaskaskia. Illinois was admitted to the Union as the twenty-first state on December 3, 1818.

Government. The Illinois legislature consists of a senate of 58 members and a house of representatives of 177 members. The governor and lieutenant-governor are elected for four years. The state sends two senators and 24 representatives to the United States Congress. The state is divided into 102 counties. In 1970 there were 147 cities and towns in Illinois with a population of more than ten thousand. Chicago is the second largest city in the United States and the thirteenth largest in the world.

Economy. Illinois is mainly an agricultural state despite the fact that it ranks fourth in value added by manufacturing. The state ranks fourth in the nation in cash receipts from farming. Nineteen percent of the total value of all farm commodities is from corn, and 16 percent of the remainder is from soybeans. Other major crops include wheat and oats. Over seven million hogs are raised every year in Illinois.

Illinois ranks eleventh among the states in mineral production; it is a leading producer of fluorspar and tripoli; and it ranks high in building stone and coal.

Chicago is the key city of the second largest manufacturing region in the United States. The Chicago area is the machinery-making center of the nation, and northern Illinois is one of the fastest growing industrial districts.

Chicago's leadership in meat-packing has been lost to such cities as Omaha and Kansas City. Some of the world's largest printing establishments and food processing plants are located in Chicago. Heavy industry, including great steel mills and oil refineries extend southeastward from Chicago and into Indiana along Lake Michigan. The great inland seaport of Indiana Harbor also serves Chicago and parts of Illinois.

INDIANA

Indiana is one of the states that formerly comprised the old Northwest Territory. The region was inhabited mainly by the Potawatomi and Miami Indians when French explorers visited there in 1679. After several unsuccessful trips, the French were able to establish a permanent settlement in 1732, at the present city of Vincennes. However, only 31 years later the entire area of the present Indiana was lost to the British. The British were driven out by Americans under George Rogers

Clark in 1779. The territory northwest of the Ohio River was organized into the Northwest Territory in 1787. Indiana Territory—an area comprising all of the present Indiana, Illinois, Wisconsin, and parts of other states—was carved out of the Northwest Territory in 1800. William Henry Harrison, later the ninth President of the United States, became the territorial governor, with his capital at Vincennes. Harrison was forced into a showdown fight with the Prophet, a famous Indian leader. At the Battle of Tippecanoe on November 7, 1811, Indian power in the Territory was broken. Congress formally admitted Indiana into the Union on December 11, 1816, as the nineteenth state. However, its area was greatly reduced from the original extent of Indiana Territory.

Government. The state's legislative body is called the General Assembly. It consists of a senate of 50 members and a house of representatives of 100 members. The state is represented in Congress by two senators and eleven representatives. Indiana is divided into 92 counties. In 1970 there were 53 cities and towns that had a population of more than ten thousand.

Economy. This is a major manufacturing state, ranking eighth in the nation; but it is also a "Corn Belt" prairie state, ranking tenth in cash income from sale of agricultural crops.

The metal industries employ six of every ten persons engaged in manufacturing. The state

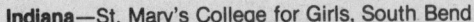
Indiana—St. Mary's College for Girls, South Bend

ranks third in steel production, provides 80 percent of all limestone used in the nation, and makes 12 percent of all household furniture. Other large industries include brick and tile making, rubber processing, the manufacture of prefabricated houses, and automotive parts.

Corn is the major farm crop, but most of it is marketed as livestock feed, mainly for hogs. Indiana is third in the nation in production of soybeans, third in corn, and third in hogs.

IOWA

Iowa was a part of the original Louisiana Purchase territory. Father Marquette and Louis Joliet visited the area of the present state in 1673, stopping at the mouth of the Des Moines River. The first settlement was made in 1785 by Julien Dubuque near the city that now bears his name. He was attracted by the lead deposits nearby.

In 1763, the entire region of Louisiana was ceded to Spain, and returned to France in 1800. In 1803, the United States purchased Louisiana. After the state of Louisiana took this name and entered the Union in 1812, the name of the entire region north of the new state of Louisiana was changed to Missouri. In 1821, the state of Missouri came into existence, leaving Iowa without a name or a government. In 1834, it became a part of Michigan Territory and then a part of Wisconsin Territory. Iowa was established as a territory in 1838 and separated from Wisconsin Territory. At that time it embraced the greater part of Minnesota and all of the two Dakotas. On December 28, 1846, Iowa was admitted to the Union as the twenty-ninth state. During the Civil War Iowa remained loyal to the Union and furnished nearly eighty thousand men to the federal armies.

Government. The legislature is called the General Assembly and consists of a senate of 50 members and a house of representatives of 100 members. The governor and lieutenant-governor are elected for two years. The state is represented in the U.S. Congress by two senators and six representatives.

Iowa is divided into 99 counties. Most of the county lines meet at right angles, forming tiers and rows of squares, with county seat towns nearly in the center of the square counties. These counties also contain neat rows and tiers of townships, at least twelve to a county. Nearly every community

Kansas—State House, Topeka

in Iowa is an incorporated place, but in 1970 only 27 of them had a population of more than ten thousand.

Economy. Iowa is the richest state in agriculture, with nearly 96 percent of the state under cultivation. Iowa leads all states except California in cash receipts from farming. Although it is only one-third the size of California, Iowa has almost the same amount of land as California under cultivation (36 million acres).

Corn grows on about one-third of the farm acreage of the state, and Iowa leads all other states except Illinois in corn growing. In oats Iowa leads all states. Other major crops are sugar beets, wheat, barley, buckwheat, flax, rye, alfalfa, soybeans, and red clover.

Iowa ranks thirty-first in mining, but is third in the mining of gypsum. Coal underlies large areas of the state. Meat packing leads all other manufacturing industries. Cedar Rapids has the largest cereal mill in the world.

KANSAS

The first white men to gaze upon the wide prairies of Kansas were the Spanish explorers led by Coronado in 1541. All but the southwestern section was included in the Louisiana Purchase of 1803. The southwestern area was a part of Texas until 1850 when it was turned over to the United States and became a part of the Missouri Territory. The name *Missouri* had been adopted in 1812 as the name of the remaining part of the Louisiana Purchase after the state of Louisiana had entered the Union (*see* Louisiana).

Kansas was separated from Missouri Territory and organized into a territory under provisions of the Kansas-Nebraska Bill of 1854. Immigrants from both slave and free areas further east began to pour into Kansas. Serious political conflict soon arose between pro-slavery and anti-slavery groups.

A pro-slavery government, set up in 1855, expelled anti-slavery supporters from the legislature. Free-state factions organized a new government, declaring the existing government to be illegal. Violence attended these actions. The town of Lawrence was destroyed twice, and other towns were burned in attacks and reprisals. The pro-slavery faction drew up another constitution at Lecompton and presented it to the voters, who defeated it in 1858. Thereupon the "Wyandotte" constitution, drawn up by free-state groups, was passed and adopted by large majorities. On January 29, 1861, Kansas was admitted to the Union as the thirty-fourth state. However, guerilla warfare broke out and the conflict merged with the greater war being fought in the east. Quantrill's raiders and other groups devastated large areas of Kansas before the Confederacy was defeated in 1865.

Government. The legislature consists of a senate of 40 members and a house of representatives of 125 members. The governor and lieutenant-governor are elected for two years. Kansas sends two senators and five representatives to the United States Congress. The state is divided into 105 counties, and in 1970 there were 34 cities and

Iowa—The Capitol Building, Des Moines

towns with a population of more than ten thousand.

Economy. Kansas is the nation's number one wheat producer, and the state is primarily agricultural. Kansas is second in sorghums, and ranks fourth in the number of cattle. Corn, hay, soybeans, barley, oats, and sugar beets are also major crops. In industry, the manufacture of transportation equipment (including aircraft) has become important in recent years. This industry group is especially prominent in Wichita and Kansas City. Kansas ranks fifteenth in mining. Petroleum, natural gas, and zinc are the principal minerals.

KENTUCKY

Kentucky's recorded history began, as did that of many other states, with the journeys of great French explorers. Robert Cavelier, Sieur de La Salle (1648–1687), considered the greatest of them, passed down the Ohio River (Kentucky's northern boundary) in 1669. The French claimed the region until they released it to Spain in 1762, despite a standing British claim. France dispatched at least one expedition to the present Kentucky to police Indian attempts to reclaim the

Kentucky—Mammoth Cave National Park

area. The English entered Kentucky as early as 1750, when it formed a part of Virginia, but were driven out by the Indians.

A group of settlers from Pennsylvania managed to establish Harrodsburg on the Kentucky River in 1775. In the following year, Daniel Boone led colonists through historic Cumberland Gap and founded Boonesboro as a fort and settlement. Violence began immediately, for even chance encounters between Indians and white people generally resulted in bloodshed. Boonesboro was attacked several times, but withstood the sieges.

Through the efforts of George Rogers Clark, hero of the Revolutionary War in the west, Kentucky was established as a county of Virginia in 1776. It had been divided into three counties by 1780 and a statehood movement was growing. Virginia refused to consent to statehood until after 1789. On June 1, 1792, Kentucky was admitted to the Union as the fifteenth state.

During the War of 1812, the threat to New Orleans (the chief port for Kentucky goods) aroused Kentuckians to take a leading part in Andrew Jackson's campaign to defend New Orleans against the British. Kentuckians helped explore and settle the newly acquired Louisiana region. Even the restless Daniel Boone moved westward (he died in Missouri in 1820 at the age of 86, less than a year before that state entered the Union).

Government. The legislative body of Kentucky is called the General Assembly and consists of a senate of 38 members and a house of representatives of 100 members. The governor and lieutenant-governor are elected for four years. The state sends two senators and seven representatives to the U.S. Congress. Kentucky is divided into 120 counties. In 1970 there were 37 cities and towns having a population of more than ten thousand.

Economy. Kentucky is an agricultural state. The chief crop is tobacco (the state ranks second to North Carolina). Corn, apples, strawberries, popcorn, fescue seed, bluegrass seed, hay, and soybeans are also major crops. The state is acclaimed as the home of the world's finest race horses, most of which are raised in the Bluegrass region around Lexington.

Coal is the principal mineral of Kentucky, and chiefly because of it, the state ranks ninth as a mineral producer.

LOUISIANA

Hernando De Soto entered what is now Louisiana in 1541, claiming it as a part of Spanish Florida. In 1682 the entire Mississippi and Missouri valley region was claimed for France by La Salle, and named Louisiana. In order to strengthen her claim, France sent Iberville to found the first settlement at Mobile (see Alabama). The first settlement in the present Louisiana was made at Natchitoches, on the Red River, in 1714. Bienville founded New Orleans in 1718 and in 1722 it became Louisiana's capital.

The entire region was ceded to Spain in 1762, but by the Treaty of San Iledefonso in 1800, it was returned to France. On April 30, 1803, Napoleon sold all of Louisiana to the United States for 15 million dollars, at a rate of about four cents per acre. That part lying west of the Mississippi was organized into the Territory of Orleans in 1804. Shortly afterwards the area east of the Mississippi was added and the combined areas were admitted to the Union under the name of Louisiana on April 30, 1812. The state seceded January 26, 1861. In 1862 New Orleans was captured by federal forces and occupied until the end of the war. The state was readmitted to the Union in 1868 and federal troops were withdrawn in 1877.

Government. The legislature consists of a senate of 39 members and a house of representatives of 105 members. Both governor and lieutenant-governor are elected for four years. The state sends two senators and eight representatives to the U.S.

Louisiana—Mississippi River loading dock, Baton Rouge

Congress. Louisiana is divided into 64 parishes that correspond to counties in other states. In 1970 there were 37 cities and towns with a population of more than ten thousand.

Economy. About one-third of the state is composed of rich delta land. Louisiana produces most of the cane sugar and rice grown in the United States. Forests cover about 56 percent of the state and lumbering is an important industry. Louisiana is second only to Texas in petroleum output. The largest oil refinery in the United States is at Baton Rouge. The state is the second largest producer of sulphur. The port of New Orleans is second only to New York in tonnage handled. It is the chief port of entry for Latin American products. Baton Rouge and Lake Charles are also major ports. Aside from New Orleans, Shreveport in the northwest is the chief industrial and trade center.

MAINE

Giovanni da Verrazano is credited with having discovered the coast of Maine in 1524. However, it was not until a century later that systematic exploration of Maine began. One of the first explorations was that of John Smith in 1614. Temporary settlements were made in 1604 (Neutral Island), 1607 (Sabino Point), 1608 (Mount Desert Island), and 1623 (Monhegan Island). The first permanent settlement was made at Pemaquid in 1625.

Various grants of land in the region were confusing and led to disputes that lasted for two centuries. Massachusetts disputed all claims and completed the possession of Maine by 1691.

Maine's association with Canada has often been bitter. New Brunswick and Maine fought a war over their boundaries until settlement was made in 1842 by the terms of the Ashburton Treaty.

For a long time Maine was restless under the government of Massachusetts. Opportunity for separation came from the growing slavery question. Missouri had applied for admission to the Union as a slave state. This led to the famous Missouri Compromise in which a free state (in this case, Maine) was to be admitted along with Missouri, a slave state. Maine was separated from Massachusetts and entered the Union on March 15, 1820, as the twenty-third state.

Maine—Coastline at Schoodic

Government. The legislature consists of a senate of 32 members and a house of representatives of 151 members. The constitution of statehood (1820) is still in force. The governor is elected for four years. There is no office of lieutenant-governor. Maine has an Executive Council of seven members to advise the governor. Massachusetts and New Hampshire are the only other states that have executive councils. Maine sends two senators and two representatives to the U.S. Congress. The state is divided into 16 counties.

Many of the functions that are performed by counties in other states are performed by "towns" in Maine (*see* Massachusetts; Connecticut). The "town" of New England is roughly equivalent to "township" in other states except Wisconsin. The New England word "town" should *never* be confused with "town" as popularly used for any small community (as it is used in the next sentence.) In 1970, there were 18 cities and towns with a population of more than ten thousand.

Economy. Maine is a leading state in the manufacture of paper and other wood products. The chief types of trees used commercially are spruce, fir, beech, cedar, hemlock, white pine, birch, maple, and aspen. Nearly half the communities are engaged in wood products industries of one kind or

another. There are numerous plants making paper, some of which are among the largest in the world. Maine is the second leading producer of potatoes in the United States. Granite is another major product of the state. Fishing is a major industry. Clams (soft-shell), lobsters, scallops, sardines, cod, haddock, and mackerel are the chief kinds of fish caught. Portland and Rockland are the chief fishing ports.

MARYLAND

Maryland is one of the 13 original states. The grant of the present state was made in 1632 by Charles I to George Calvert, first Lord Baltimore. Lord Baltimore's purpose in acquiring the grant was to establish a refuge for persons of the Catholic faith who were at that time being persecuted.

About two hundred colonists landed in Maryland in 1634, and founded the settlement of St. Mary's. The young colony experienced setbacks from several quarters and for a time (1645–1646) St. Mary's was occupied by dissident groups. In 1649 the famous Toleration Act was passed. This document guaranteed the freedom of worship to all Christians. However, several Puritan (Protestant) groups continued to be hostile, and took up separate settlements in Maryland. The Puritans revolted and held the province from 1654 to 1657. In 1657, Lord Baltimore was restored to control of Maryland. In 1692 Maryland was converted to a royal colony directly under the King of England. In 1715 the Baltimores regained possession of the

Maryland—Hampton House "Ghost Room"

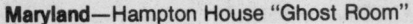

colony and retained it until the Revolutionary War. A 50-year dispute with Pennsylvania was finally settled by the surveys of Mason and Dixon (the Mason-Dixon Line) from 1763 to 1767. The city of Baltimore was founded in 1730. Maryland took an active part in the struggle for independence. Congress met at Annapolis in 1783. Maryland ratified the Constitution on April 28, 1788 (seventh state).

During the War of 1812, rioting occurred in Baltimore and the city was under siege by British ships. Fort McHenry withstood the siege, an event commemorated by Francis Scott Key in our national anthem. Maryland was divided in sympathy during the Civil War, but remained loyal to the Union. In September 1862, the fierce battle of Antietam (Sharpsburg) was fought in Maryland.

Government. The legislative body is called the General Assembly and consists of a senate of 43 members and a house of delegates of 142 members. The governor is elected for four years. There is no office of lieutenant-governor. The state sends two senators and eight representatives to the U.S. Congress. The United States capital is located in the District of Columbia, which forms an enclave in Maryland and has no connection whatever with the state. Maryland is divided into 23 counties, and in 1970 there were 57 cities and towns with a population of more than ten thousand. Baltimore, the state's largest city, has the status of a county and is an enclave in Baltimore County but not a part of the county. Baltimore is the seventh largest city in the United States.

Economy. Manufacturing industries form the major part of the economy. Aluminum, chemicals, ships, missiles, clothing, rubber, and machinery are manufactured. Baltimore is a leading port, commercial and trade center. It is also a major steel center. The seafood industry is of major importance; and Maryland is a leader in its catch of striped bass, soft-shell clams, and oysters.

MASSACHUSETTS

Massachusetts is one of the 13 original states. A Protestant group in England, at first called "Separatists," and later "Pilgrims," sought refuge from religious intolerance in Holland (The Netherlands), and then set sail for North America in 1620. They established the first permanent white settlement within the present Massachusetts, at Plymouth in December 1620. They also instituted a form of democratic government in accordance with terms they had drawn up among themselves before landing—the historic Mayflower Compact. Others, seeking religious freedom, began to found settlements all along the coast, and in 1630 the Massachusetts Bay Colony was chartered to unify the settlements. Boston was settled in 1630, and Massachusetts was made a royal colony in 1691.

The people of Massachusetts were foremost in the movement that brought about a break with England and the independence of the United States. The movement began with rioting and boycotts that eventually led to the Boston Massacre of March 5, 1770, when British soldiers fired into a crowd of colonists. In 1773, cargoes of tea were dumped into Boston Harbor by a group disguised as Indians and led by Samuel Adams. In retaliation, Boston was occupied and the port closed. Patriots then called the First Continental Congress, which ordered a general boycott of all English goods. The siege of Boston followed the first engagements of the War for Independence at Lexington and at Concord Bridge. George Washington took command of the Continental Army at Cambridge on July 3, 1775. The Battle of Bunker Hill, March 17, 1776, led to the British evacuation of Boston, to which the British were never able to return. Following the end of the war, a period of economic depression set in, which lasted until Massachusetts adopted the federal Constitution on February 6, 1788.

Massachusetts—Paul Revere Statue, Boston

Government. The legislative body of the state is called the General Court of the Commonwealth and consists of a senate of 40 members and a house of representatives of 240 members. Both governor and lieutenant-governor are elected for four years. The state sends two senators and twelve representatives to the U.S. Congress in Massachusetts. As in other New England states, the "town" (roughly similar to the "township" in other states) is of greater significance in local government than is the county. There are over 300 towns within the state. In addition, there are 152 cities with a population of more than ten thousand.

Economy. Massachusetts is overwhelmingly a manufacturing state, and is the nation's oldest manufacturing region. Textiles have usually been prominent, but the state is known for the great variety of its manufactured products. Few minerals or other raw materials for industry originate within the state.

More than half of the state's population lives in the metropolitan area of Boston. The city is a major world seaport, the largest fishing port in the nation, as well as one of the leading manufacturing centers. Research is a major industry in Massachusetts. Some 338 research laboratories employing numerous scientists, engineers, and technicians are located in the state.

MICHIGAN

The French explorer Étienne Brulé (who met a tragic death as a sacrificial victim among his former friends, the Huron Indians) may have been the first white man to see what is now the state of Michigan in 1610. Jesuit missionaries and French explorers gradually opened up the region, and Father Marquette founded the first settlement at Sault Sainte Marie in 1668. Detroit was founded in 1701. After the French and Indian War, the British came into control of Michigan, annexing it to Canada in 1774. By the Treaty of Paris (1783) it was ceded to the United States. In the following years British agents stirred up Indian trouble for the settlers. Organized Indian forces defeated General Saint Clair but met disastrous defeat at the hands of General "Mad" Anthony Wayne at Fallen Timbers in 1794 (*see* Ohio).

In 1805 Michigan Territory was organized, embracing the lower peninsula and with a southern boundary farther south than at present. In 1834, the territory was expanded to include the entire region between Lake Erie and the Missouri River. The opening of the Erie Canal brought commerce and a rapid increase in population. A serious boundary dispute known as the "Toledo War" (*see* Ohio) was settled, resulting in the moving of the southern boundary northward. As compensation, Michigan was given the entire upper peninsula. The peninsula turned out to be a hidden treasure of copper, iron, and other valuable resources. Michigan was reduced to its present size by 1837 and admitted to the Union on January 26 of that year as the twenty-sixth state.

Government. The legislature consists of a senate of 38 members and a house of representatives of 109 members. The governor and lieutenant-governor are elected for four years. The state sends two senators and 19 representatives to the U.S. Congress. Michigan is divided into 83 counties. In 1970 there were 78 cities with a population of more than ten thousand. Detroit is the fifth largest city in the United States, behind Philadelphia and ahead of Houston (1970).

Economy. The state has well-diversified and highly-developed agricultural industries, including dairying. The principal crops are plums, peaches, cherries, honey (a by-product of the fruit-growing industry), apples, corn, hay, oats, winter wheat, and sugar beets.

Michigan—Isle Royale National Park

Despite its agricultural wealth, Michigan is predominantly an industrial state. The manufacture of automobiles is by far the leading industry, employing more than half the industrial workers of the state. Iron ore is the chief mineral mined in Michigan, most of it coming from the upper peninsula. Copper, petroleum, natural gas, salt, and limestone (some of the largest quarries in the world) are also mined in the state. The Great Lakes are ice-free from April to November, and they form the busiest waterway in the world. The famous Soo Canal between Lake Superior and Lake Huron handles twice as much tonnage annually as does the Panama Canal, even though the latter is open all year.

MINNESOTA

French fur traders came to Minnesota by way of the Great Lakes in about 1658. Little was known of the region until Jesuit missionaries penetrated Minnesota in 1680. Father Hennepin traveled up the Mississippi River in that year and discovered the Falls of St. Anthony, which he named (located in present-day Minneapolis). The French claimed the region east of the Mississippi River but ceded it to England in 1763. In 1783 the United States acquired this part, and the remainder of the future state was acquired as a part of the Louisiana Purchase of 1803. Zebulon Pike (*see* Colorado) traced the Mississippi's upper course to Cass Lake in 1806. Henry R. Schoolcraft traced the great river to its source in 1832, and found it to be in Lake Itasca in northcentral Minnesota.

The first settlement was made in 1819 at Fort St. Anthony (name changed to Fort Snelling in 1824). Eastern Minnesota became a part of the Northwest Territory, set up by Congress in 1787. Minnesota then became successively a part of Indiana, Illinois, Michigan, and finally Wisconsin Territories. Western Minnesota, acquired in 1803, was at first a part of Louisiana, then of Missouri, Michigan, Wisconsin, and Iowa Territories. In 1849 the two sections were at last put together to form Minnesota Territory. Minnesota became the thirty-second state on May 11, 1858.

While the Civil War was on, the Sioux Indians started a war of their own, nearly succeeding in driving white people out of southern Minnesota. Five hundred white settlers died in the Sioux War, and damage ran into millions of dollars. The war ended with the defeat of the Indians at Wood Lake (1862).

Minnesota—Minneapolis

Government. The legislature consists of a senate of 67 members and a house of representatives of 133 members. The governor and lieutenant-governor are elected for four years. The state sends two senators and eight representatives to the U.S. Congress. Minnesota is divided into 87 counties, and in 1970 there were 54 cities and towns with a population of more than ten thousand. The city of Minneapolis ranks thirty-second in the nation, while St. Paul ranks forty-sixth.

Economy. Agriculture, mining, and manufacturing are all chief industries in the state. Manufacturing is chiefly in the south and in the Duluth area around Lake Superior. The state consistently ranks first in creamery butter, oats, turkeys, and sweet corn. Other major crops are corn, soybeans, and green peas. Minnesota's principal mineral is iron ore, most of it coming from three major mining districts in the northeast. The iron is taken mainly by rail to the Lake Superior ports of Duluth and Two Harbors, where it is loaded on ore boats and sent to the great steel mills and furnaces in the lower Great Lakes region (Cleveland, Lorain, Gary, Pittsburgh, and Buffalo). The city of Duluth itself is also a steel-making center. The state supplies more than half of the nation's iron ore. The great new ore deposits of Quebec and Venezuela now pose serious competition to Minnesota iron ore.

MISSISSIPPI

Spanish explorers led by Hernando de Soto were the first white men to enter what is now Mississippi. De Soto discovered the Mississippi River in 1541. The first permanent settlement in the state was made by the French on the Gulf Coast of the future state in 1699. Natchez was settled in 1716 in an attempt by the French to secure a more firm control of the Mississippi Valley. But they lost the region to the British in 1763. After the independence of the United States, Mississippi was ceded to the United States by England. However, it was still claimed by Spain. The treaty of San Lorenzo in 1795 secured the area to legal United States control. Mississippi Territory was organized in 1798. The boundaries were extended in 1804 and in 1812 by the addition of parts of the Louisiana Purchase. On December 10, 1817, Mississippi was admitted to the Union as the twentieth state.

Mississippi seceded from the Union on January 8, 1861, the second state to do so. The chief struggle during the war that followed was for control of the Mississippi River. The siege of Vicksburg, a vital port on the river, became one of the most critical battles of the war. When Vicksburg fell on July 4, 1863, the fate of the Confederacy was sealed, although other engagements were fought in the state before the end came. Mississippi was readmitted to the Union in 1870.

Government. The legislature consists of a senate of 52 members and a house of representatives of 140 members. The governor and lieutenant-governor are elected for four years. The state is represented in the U.S. Congress by two senators and five representatives. Mississippi is divided into 82 counties. In 1970, there were 24 cities having a population of more than ten thousand.

Economy. Mississippi's greatest resources are her soils and forests. Cotton is the major crop; the state ranks third in the production of that commodity. The state leads in the output of tung-oil nuts. Other major crops include pecans, sweet potatoes, corn, rice, wheat, oats, sugar cane, and sorghum. The state ranks eighth in broiler-chicken production. It is also the tenth ranking oil producer in the nation. Mississippi is one of the major lumbering states, and about 58 percent of its area is covered by forests, including over a million acres in national forests. Shrimp fishing is important on the Gulf Coast at Biloxi and Gulfport.

Mississippi—D'Evereux Home

MISSOURI

The Southern part of what is now the state of Missouri was visited by De Soto in 1541 when he crossed the Mississippi River near Memphis. On the basis of the explorations of Marquette, Joliet, and La Salle, the region was claimed by France. In 1705, a party of French explorers ascended the Missouri River to the present site of Kansas City. The territory, then called Louisiana, was ceded to Spain in 1763 and given back to France in 1800 (*see* Louisiana). The United States came into possession of the area in 1803 as a part of the Louisiana Purchase. When the state of Louisiana entered the Union in 1812, the name Missouri became applied to the remainder of the Purchase, which included the entire Missouri River Valley. Daniel Boone (*see* Kentucky) moved into Missouri in 1795 and was an active agent in the state's development. Under terms of the Missouri Compromise, the state of Missouri entered the Union on August 10, 1821 (*see* Maine). The boundary was much the same as today except for a small area that was added in the northwest in 1837. The remainder that was once called Missouri Territory gradually became organized into smaller units, taking on names that had already been growing in popularity or had already existed, such as Dakota, Nebraska, and Kansas.

Missouri—The climatron, Missouri Botanical Garden, St. Louis

Government. The legislative body is called the General Assembly and consists of a senate of 34 members and a house of representatives of 163 members. The governor and lieutenant-governor are elected for four years. The state sends two senators and ten representatives to the U.S. Congress. Missouri is divided into 114 counties. In 1970 there were 54 cities and towns with a population of more than ten thousand. St. Louis has the status of a county and is separate from St. Louis County (*see* Maryland for a similar condition). In 1970 St. Louis was the eighteenth largest city in the United States and Kansas City was the twenty-sixth.

Economy. Missouri is a leading livestock-raising state, ranking fourth in number of hogs and sixth in cattle. The chief crops are soybeans, wheat, corn, and clover. Missouri mines about 45 percent of the United States' lead. Other major minerals mined are barite, lime, iron, copper, and coal. Missouri's largest manufacturing industries are in transportation equipment and food processing. A unique industry in the state is the making of corncob pipes (mainly at the town of Washington). Kansas City (not to be confused with Kansas City, Kansas) and St. Louis have two-thirds of the state's total number of factories. The making of shoes and leather products are also important industries in Missouri.

MONTANA

About a third of the present Montana was included in the original Oregon country, while the remainder formed part of the Louisiana Purchase. The region was explored in 1742–1743 by Sieur de la Verendrye, a French explorer. In 1805 the Lewis and Clark expedition crossed the region. A fort was built at the mouth of the Big Horn River in 1807. The first settlements were made between 1809 and 1829. Jesuit missionaries established missions among the Flathead Indians in 1841.

The discovery of gold on Hell Gate River in 1852 and 1857 was the real beginning of Montana's modern history. Mining settlements sprang up, attracting trade, exploration, and industry.

Conflict with the Indians culminated in the disastrous battle of the Little Big Horn River on June 25, 1876, in which General George Armstrong Custer and his entire force were wiped out by Sioux Indians under Sitting Bull.

Copper and silver mining in the 1880s resulted in rapid development of the region. Montana became a state on November 8, 1889, the forty-first (six days after the two Dakotas).

Government. The Montana legislature consists of a senate of 50 members and a house of representatives of 100 members. The governor and lieutenant-governor are elected for four years. The state is

Montana—Custer's Last Stand (Marker)

represented in the U.S. Congress by two senators and two representatives. Montana is divided into 56 counties, and in 1970 there were eight cities and towns with a population of more than ten thousand.

Economy. Irrigation plays a significant part in agriculture. Montana is a major producer of wheat, barley, sugar beets, and potatoes. Cattle and sheep are also important. Forests cover nearly twenty million acres, or about one-fourth of the state.

Montana is the third-ranking copper producer, and is the number one producer of vermiculite and chromite. (Vermiculite is a form of mica and is used for heat insulation. Chromite is the ore of the metal chromium.) The state also ranks second in the mining of zinc, silver, and fluorspar. Montana is also a large producer of crude petroleum.

NEBRASKA

Nebraska's wide prairies were first seen by Europeans when Coronado reached the region in 1541. As a part of the Louisiana region, it was ceded by France to Spain in 1763. Spain returned it to France in 1800, and the area was sold by Napoleon to the United States in 1803. The explorers Lewis and Clark crossed the future state in 1804. The first settlement was made at Bellevue in 1823, although trading posts had been set up by fur traders as early as 1810. It is estimated that between 1840 and 1866 over two and one-half million people crossed Nebraska on the Overland Trail to California. Settlers began squatting on Indian lands during those years, until in 1854 the entire region (known as Missouri Territory) was opened to settlement. The Kansas-Nebraska Bill of 1854 divided Missouri Territory into Nebraska Territory and Kansas Territory.

With the breaking of ground for the Union Pacific Railroad in 1863, a period of Indian warfare ensued that lasted until the 1870s. Nebraska became a state on March 1, 1867, the thirty-seventh state. In 1882 it annexed part of Dakota Territory and in 1908 received another piece of territory from South Dakota.

Government. By an amendment to the 1875 constitution, Nebraska adopted a single-house legislature, the only state with such a body. This

Nebraska—Chimney Rock located on U.S. Highway 26

legislature consists of 49 members, elected for two years. The governor and lieutenant-governor are elected for two years. Nebraska is represented in the U.S. Congress by two senators and three representatives. Although there are a total of 536 incorporated villages and cities in the state, only 12 of them had a population of more than ten thousand in 1970.

Economy. Three-fourths of the population live in the eastern third of the state. Agriculture is the chief industry, although the processing of meats and other farm products are large industries that are dependent upon the rich farm lands. Farming provides 80 percent of the state's income. The state is third in number of cattle.

Oil and natural gas have been discovered in the western part of Nebraska. Other minerals mined include potash, pumice, gypsum, salt, shale, and clay. Omaha, on the Missouri River, is one of the largest livestock markets in the world and the largest meat-packing center in the United States. The city ranks second in frozen-food production.

Nevada—Hoover Dam

NEVADA

Nevada was first visited by Europeans in 1738 when Franciscan friars crossed the state. Peter Ogden of the Hudson's Bay Company discovered the Humboldt River in 1825. John C. Fremont led an exploring party through the region (1843–1844). The first settlement was made by Mormons in 1849 in the valley of the Carson River. The area had become a part of the United States one year earlier, with the Mexican Cession. Nevada became a part of Utah Territory in 1850, but a separate government was soon established and requested annexation to California. The request was turned down, and the area was then organized into Nevada Territory (1861). The state was admitted to the Union on October 31, 1864. In 1866, a section of land was added to the state from Arizona.

The discovery of silver in the Comstock Lode region in 1859 initiated the rapid development of the state. A decline set in when the Comstock worked out, but a revival was made with the discovery of gold southeast of the Comstock region, early in the twentieth century.

Government. The legislature consists of a senate of 20 members and an assembly of 40 members. The governor and lieutenant-governor are elected for four years. Carson City, the capital, is the smallest capital city in the United States. Nevada sends two senators and one representative to the U.S. Congress. The state is divided into 17 counties. Nye County (18,064 square miles) is the third largest county in the nation. Elko (17,126 square miles) is fourth. In 1970 there were nine cities and towns with a population of more than ten thousand. (Compare this with 288 such cities and towns in California.)

Economy. Despite its dry climate, Nevada is covered with 20 million acres of forests. However, only a small amount of this is commercial timber. Ranching is the main agricultural concern. Alfalfa is raised. Some irrigation is practiced. Other crops include wheat, barley, oats, and potatoes.

Nevada has rich mineral resources, and these form the mainstay of the state's economy. Mercury, manganese, copper, tungsten, gold, uranium, and barite are the chief minerals mined. The state currently ranks fourth in copper production. Gambling and tourism also bring dollars to the state.

NEW HAMPSHIRE

New Hampshire is one of the 13 original states. The area of the present state was first explored in 1603 by Sir Martin Pring. John Smith explored the coastline in 1604. The region was originally a part of the First Charter of Virginia of 1606, but was given to the Plymouth Company in 1620. In 1629, Captain John Mason secured a claim to all the

New Hampshire—Dartmouth College

land between the Piscataqua and the Merrimack rivers, extending northward to Lake Champlain. This he called New Hampshire, for his native district of Hampshire, England. The first permanent settlement was made at Little Harbor in 1623 by David Thompson.

Upon the death of Mason the colony was placed under the protection of Massachusetts (1641). New Hampshire was made a royal colony in 1679. Boundaries were disputed by the Mason family, and they remained to plague the colony and later the state of New Hampshire. Controversy between New Hampshire and New York developed over the land between the Connecticut River and Lake Champlain, north of Massachusetts. Eventually New York won, but the citizens of the disputed area revolted and declared themselves to be the independent state of "New Connecticut" (*see* Vermont).

Early in 1775, New Hampshire declared for independence and was the first to draw up a new constitution. In the war, a notable victory was achieved by New Hampshire and Vermont troops at Bennington (August 16, 1777). New Hampshire ratified the federal Constitution (the ninth state) in 1788.

Government. The legislature consists of a senate of 24 members and a house of representatives whose membership is restricted to from 375 to 400 members. The governor and five administrative officers (called councilors) are elected for two years. There is no office of lieutenant-governor. The state sends two senators and two representatives to the U.S. Congress. The state is divided into ten counties, but they are not as important governmentally as are the cities and towns located in

them (*see* Massachusetts.) In 1970, there were 13 cities having a population of more than ten thousand.

Economy. Location, resources, and the traditions of the people have combined to make the state a land of small farms and small towns. The chief field crops are hay, potatoes, and vegetables. Granite is quarried in several places and is the chief mineral of the state. Manufacturing is concentrated in the larger cities and towns of the south and east.

NEW JERSEY

New Jersey is one of the original 13 states. It was first settled by the Dutch, who built a trading post at Bergen on the Hudson River in 1618. In 1664, the area of the present state was taken from the Dutch by the English. The Duke of York, brother of Charles II, King of England, gave the state its identity in 1664, when he granted the land between the Hudson and Delaware rivers to Lord John Berkeley and Sir George Carteret. Today, the boundaries of New Jersey are exactly those set by the Duke of York in his original deeds of lease. However, from 1674 to 1702 the state was divided into the two colonies of East New Jersey and West New Jersey. On April 17, 1702, Queen Anne reunited the two Jerseys into one royal colony.

The people were divided in feelings during the War for Independence. Those favoring independence won out when a new constitution was adopted in 1776. Because of its strategic location between New York City and Philadelphia, New Jersey became a major battleground. Washing-

New Jersey—Morven, The Executive Mansion of New Jersey at Princeton

ton's Continental Army spent a large part of its time in the state, including three winters at encampments. Nearly one hundred battles were fought by the forces of the Continental Army on New Jersey soil. New Jersey became the third state to ratify the Constitution of the United States, on December 17, 1787.

Government. The legislative body is called the Legislature and is composed of a senate of 40 members and a General Assembly of 79 members. New Jersey is represented in Congress by two senators and 15 representatives. The governor is elected for a four-year term. There is no lieutenant-governor. New Jersey is divided into 21 counties. In 1970, there were 177 cities having a population over ten thousand.

Economy. After tourism, manufacturing is the largest industry. The state ranks seventh in manufacturing in the nation. Manufacturing in the state is concentrated in a 15-mile-wide corridor between Philadelphia and New York. The state is the "core" area of research and science laboratory work in the United States, with more than four hundred research laboratories in the area. Heavy industry in the corridor is concentrated along the Delaware River and in the northeastern counties, opposite New York City.

A favorable climate and almost an unlimited market have given rise to large gardening and dairying industries. The principal farm crops are corn, wheat, potatoes, cranberries, and apples. The chief minerals of New Jersey are stone, glass sand, gravel, iron ore, and clay.

NEW MEXICO

Because of the high level of culture reached by the ancient cliff-dwellers and their descendants, the Pueblo Indians, the pre-Columbian history of New Mexico becomes a significant part of the state's heritage. Most of the larger ruined cities are enclosed within state and national parks and monuments. Many of these sites have museums and collections that portray the everyday life and cultural contributions of the past civilization in what is now New Mexico.

The earliest white explorers were Spaniards who governed the region. Cabeza de Vaca, Coronado, and Nuño de Guzman were the principal explorers. Juan de Oñate conquered the region (1588–1599) and founded the first settlement at San Gabriel. By 1630, Franciscan friars had established about fifty missions throughout New Mexico. Santa Fe was founded in 1605 or 1606 . In 1680 a great Indian revolt expelled all the Spanish from the region and it was not reconquered until 1692.

In 1821, the area became a province of the Republic of Mexico under the name of New Mexico. This entire province was ceded to the United States under terms of the Treaty of Guadalupe Hidalgo, after Mexico's defeat in the Mexican War of 1846–1848.

New Mexico—Acoma Mission

In 1850, all of the land west of Texas and east of California was organized into New Mexico Territory. These limits were changed by the addition of the Gadsden Purchase (*see* Arizona) in 1854, by the transfer of the northeastern corner to Colorado in 1861, by the transfer of the northwestern corner to Nevada in 1866, and by the organization of the western half into Arizona Territory in 1863.

Statehood was hotly debated for more than sixty years, but on January 6, 1912, New Mexico became the forty-seventh state. (Arizona followed about a month later.)

Government. The legislature consists of a senate of 42 members and a house of representatives of 70 members. The governor and lieutenant-governor are elected for four years. The state is represented in the U.S. Congress by two senators and two representatives. New Mexico is divided into 32 counties. In 1970, there were 15 cities and towns with a population of more than ten thousand.

Economy. Agriculture is a major industry in New Mexico. Irrigation is extensively practiced. The chief crops are lint cotton, cottonseed, sorghums, hay, and vegetables.

New Mexico is at present the largest domestic source of uranium, with about 66 percent of the total reserves of that metal. Petroleum, natural gas, copper, zinc, and perlite are other major minerals produced in the state. Lumbering is also important in the state's economy.

NEW YORK

New York is one of the original 13 states. Giovanni da Verazzano, sailing for France, discovered New York harbor and the lower Hudson River in 1524. In 1609, Henry Hudson explored the river that is named for him, and his voyage was the basis for the Dutch claim to all the region drained by the river. Permanent settlements were made near the present Albany in 1624, and on Manhattan Island (now a part of New York City) in the same year. The entire Dutch-settled region was called New Netherland. The chief towns were Fort Orange, now Albany, and New Amsterdam, now New York City.

Dutch rule, lasting fifty years, was notable for the famous "Patroonship" system, designed to encourage further settlement. This was the giving of feudal rights, including perpetual land tenure, to the "Patroons" who purchased land from the Indians.

In 1664, the English seized the colony. They renamed Fort Orange, Albany and changed New Amsterdam to New York, both in honor of the Duke of York and Albany.

During 110 years of British rule, many events occurred that contributed to the founding of the United States. The trial of John Peter Zenger in 1735 led to an early victory for freedom of the press in the colonies. A plan proposed in 1754 by Benjamin Franklin for the federal union of the colonies was the forerunner of the Declaration of Independence. The Stamp Act Congress, organized to protest British taxes, met in New York City in 1765.

New York's strategic location as a middle colony with a major trade route (the Hudson-Mohawk route) made it one of the most important battlegrounds during the War for Independence. In 1776 the British fleet took possession of New York City and retained it throughout the war, despite American efforts to capture the city. Washington was able, however, to draw large quantities of supplies from the free area of the colony. In 1777, a British campaign to split the 13 colonies by a three-way drive on Albany was defeated at Saratoga, in one of the world's most decisive battles. Contributing to this victory was the heroic stand made by General Herkimer at Oriskany, preventing the British from uniting their invading forces.

Washington fortified the lower Hudson in 1778, and the Iroquois Indians' alliance with the British was broken in western New York in the following year. General Washington established the Continental Army headquarters in April 1782, at Newburgh on the Hudson River, and it remained there until the end of the war. The last battle of the war was fought at Johnstown, N.Y., on October 25, 1781. After the reoccupation of New York City by the American Army in 1783, Washington bade farewell to his officers at Fraunces Tavern. Six years later he returned to the city (the first capital of the United States under the Constitution) for his inauguration as the first president of the nation. New York had entered the Union on July 26, 1788, as the eleventh state.

New York—The United Nations Building

Government. The legislative power of the state is vested in a two-house legislature. It consists of a senate of 58 members and an assembly of 150 members. Both the governor and the lieutenant-governor are elected for four years. The state sends two senators and 39 representatives to the U.S. Congress. New York is divided into 62 counties, five of which are within the city of New York. In 1970 there were 158 cities and towns with a population of more than ten thousand. New York City is the largest in the United States and third largest in the world (after Tokyo and London). Buffalo, the state's second largest city, ranks twenty-eighth in the nation.

Economy. New York has been the nation's leading state in the value of manufactured products since 1830. It also outranks all other states in the variety and extent of manufacturing.

Apparel is the largest single industry in the state. About 36 percent of all apparel produced in the nation comes from New York State. Ranking next in terms of employment are machinery, printing, and publishing. One-fourth of the printing in the United States is done in the state. The manufacture of paper, pulp, and paperboard is concentrated in the north and northwest. Instrument industries in New York employ 29 percent of the nation's workers in this field, and the photographic industry employs two-thirds of all the nation's workers in that field.

New York is not often thought of as a mineral-rich state, yet it leads the nation in the mining of industrial talc, garnet, wollastonite, emery, and titanium. It is a major producer of zinc, gypsum, salt, sand and gravel, and mines about 5 percent of the iron ore in the United States. New York leads all states in the utilization of radioactive materials in medical research, diagnosis, and treatment.

It is well to note that fully 25 percent of all the people in the United States live within a 250-mile radius of New York City, so New York State ranks unusually high as a wholesale market region. The state leads all others in both retail and wholesale activities. In banking and finance, New York is also the leader, having 518 banks with resources amounting to 78 billion dollars. This makes the state, and in particular, the city of New York, the financial center of the world (New York City is also the largest insurance center in the nation).

The Port of New York has about 600 miles of piers and handles about 24 percent of the waterborne foreign trade in the country. The Port of New

York Authority is a bi-state agency of New York and New Jersey, set up to develop and promote this port district.

The Port of Buffalo is the largest state port on the Greak Lakes, in terms of value and in tonnage. The city has 37 miles of waterfront on Lake Erie. The opening of the St. Lawrence Seaway in 1959 provided a new seacoast for ocean commerce along the river and the Great Lakes. This project stimulated plans for deep-water ports by Massena, Ogdensburg, Oswego, Rochester, and other cities in the state.

Dairying is the largest agricultural industry, and the state is second in the nation in the number of dairy cows and in the production of milk. Other major agricultural crops include grapes, apples, peaches, potatoes, maple syrup, and buckwheat. The state ranks fourth in total vegetable production and second in the production of cheese and ice cream.

North Carolina—Wright Monument in Wright Brothers National Memorial near Kitty Hawk

NORTH CAROLINA

North Carolina is one of the 13 original states. The first English attempts to establish settlements in what is now the United States were made in North Carolina in 1584, 1585, and 1587. In the year 1587, Roanoke Island became the site of a colony, established by Sir Walter Raleigh, in which the first white child was born in America. Her name was Virginia Dare. This was the famous "Lost Colony." Its disappearance was so complete that the only clues ever found were the word *Croatoan* (the name of another island) and a few pieces of armor. The state was not permanently settled until 1663.

In 1629, King Charles I of England granted what is now North and South Carolina to Sir Robert Heath. In 1663 King Charles II gave the area to a group of "proprietors." In 1710 North and South Carolina were separated. Beginning in 1712, each had a separate capital and governor. In 1729, North Carolina became a royal colony (the King having bought out the proprietors). North Carolina entered the Union on November 21, 1789, the twelfth state to ratify the new federal Constitution.

North Carolina was the last state to secede from the Union. It did so on May 20, 1861, and was readmitted in July 1868.

Government. The state legislature consists of a senate of 50 members and a house of representatives of 120 members. The governor may not succeed himself, and has no veto power. The state sends two senators and 11 representatives to the U.S. Congress. North Carolina is divided into 100 counties. In 1970 there were 41 cities and towns having a population of more than ten thousand.

Economy. The state is rich in natural resources. Its climate and soil permit a wide range of economic activities.

North Carolina's Piedmont region is dotted with the world's largest concentration of textile, tobacco, and furniture factories. The state leads the nation in all three. Value added by manufacturing is the largest in the South and fourteenth in the nation.

In agriculture, North Carolina is the number one producer of tobacco in the United States. Other major cash crops are corn, soybeans, cotton, and peanuts. Also grown extensively are wheat, oats, barley, sweet potatoes, hay, peaches, and apples. North Carolina is first in the country in farm population and eleventh in farm production. Its timber covers 20 million acres, and furnishes about 7 percent of the total value of the state's farm products.

An astounding variety of minerals are found in North Carolina. There are 300 types, leading all states in variety. The state produces 74 percent of all the sheet mica in the United States. The state is also a leading producer of feldspar, kaolin clays, talc, and stone (chiefly granite).

NORTH DAKOTA

Most of North Dakota lies in the drainage basin of the Missouri-Mississippi system which was claimed by Sieur de La Salle for France in 1682. This claim was transferred to Spain in 1762. The British obtained title to part of the state in the north and east in 1763. The United States received all but the British-claimed area in 1803, as a part of the Louisiana Purchase. In 1818, the British-claimed area was formally ceded to the United States, although French and English fur traders continued to explore the region.

Lewis and Clark crossed North Dakota on their famed journey of exploration (1804–1806). David Thompson, the great English geographer, had explored and mapped the Souris and Missouri river basins in 1797.

Attempts at settlement occurred in the early nineteenth century at Pembina in the northeast, but the present state remained virtually unoccupied except for Indians and trading posts until the 1850s. In 1829, the American Fur Company built Fort Union at the mouth of the Yellowstone River. In 1857 the first military outpost was established at Fort Abercrombie on the Red River of the North. By 1860 regular steamboat service was available on both the Missouri and Red River of

North Dakota—Theodore Roosevelt National Memorial Park

the North. Dakota Territory was organized in 1861 and included both North and South Dakota, plus parts of Wyoming and Montana.

Dakota Territory was opened for homesteading in 1863. Railroads began to cross the territory in 1871. In 1889 the Dakota Territory was divided into two territories. The division was made along the seventh standard parallel. North Dakota and South Dakota were admitted to the Union on November 2, 1889. President Benjamin Harrison apparently never revealed which statehood bill he signed first, so that it will never be known which of the two sister states was the first to be admitted to the Union. North Dakota is generally given as the thirty-ninth state only because of its alphabetical position, but either state could be placed thirty-ninth or fortieth.

Government. The present constitution dates from statehood. The law-making body is called the Legislative Assembly and consists of a senate of 50 members and a house of representatives of 108 members. The governor and lieutenant-governor are elected for four years. The state is represented in the U.S. Congress by two senators and one representative. North Dakota is divided into 53 counties. There are 356 municipalities, of which 10 had a population of more than ten thousand in 1970.

Economy. Agriculture is the chief industry. Large-scale mechanized farms are common. The state leads in the production of barley, ranks second in rye, and second in wheat. Other important crops include flax seed, potatoes, hay, oats, and corn.

North Dakota is the newest oil-boom state, and petroleum is the most valuable mineral found there. The state ranks ninth in reserves. The major fields are located around Williston. Refineries are located at Dickinson, Williston, and Mandan.

OHIO

The first recorded inhabitants of Ohio were the Mound Builders, prehistoric Indians. Those living in Ohio left more than ten thousand burial and ceremonial mounds. Most of the Mound Builders of Ohio belonged to the Hopewell culture. Artifacts found in the mounds indicate advanced cultural progress and social life.

Early in the seventeenth century Jesuit priests and French explorers began entering the region.

Moravian missionaries founded a settlement which they called Schoenbrunn in eastern Ohio in 1772. This settlement was destroyed in 1776. Marietta on the Ohio River was founded in 1788, becoming the first permanent town in the future state.

After the Revolutionary War the British continued to encourage the Indians to violence in the region north of the Ohio River. The new federal Government was determined to put an end to the Indian troubles and sent General "Mad" Anthony Wayne to deal with the situation. In 1794, Wayne brought a disastrous defeat upon the Indians at Fallen Timbers, near present Toledo. In 1795, Wayne secured the Greenville Treaty, bringing about peace in Ohio.

New towns began to spring up soon after the treaty was signed. In 1796, the famous Western Reserve surveys began. Ohio became the first state to be carved out of the old Northwest Territory. It unofficially entered the Union as the seventeenth state on February 19, 1803. The entrance was made official on August 8, 1853, retroactive to the original 1803 date. A serious border dispute between Ohio and Michigan in 1835 resulted in the "Toledo War." Ohio was awarded the disputed area and Michigan was given what proved to be a tremendous bargain–the copper-rich Upper Peninsula.

Government. The legislative body of Ohio is called the General Assembly. It consists of a senate of 33 members and a house of representatives of 99 members. The governor and lieutenant-governor are elected for four years. Ohio sends two senators and 23 representatives to the U.S. Congress. The state is divided into 88 counties, and in 1970 there were 153 cities and towns with a population of more than ten thousand. Cleveland ranks tenth in the nation, and Columbus ranks twenty-first.

Economy. Although Ohio ranks third among the states in manufacturing, it is also a major farming state, ranking eighth in gross value of farm production. Agriculture in the state is varied, including even greenhouse farming, the largest such industry in the nation. Along Lake Erie is a major fruit-growing region, aided by the lake's influence on the climate. In addition, the state ranks fifth in corn, first in timothy seed, fifth in oats, third in popcorn, and sixth in hogs.

Iron and steel products are the largest group of manufactured products. Steel mills and blast furnaces are concentrated along Lake Erie, especially at Cleveland and Lorain. Ohio ranks first in business machines, clay products, electrical machinery, tires and tubes, and machine tools.

Cleveland, Toledo, Lorain, Ashtabula, and Sandusky now rank as seaports since the completion of the Great Lakes-Saint Lawrence Seaway (*see* New York). In fact, Toledo has a substantial foreign trade zone, and is the world's greatest coal-shipping port. The chief minerals mined in Ohio are coal, clay, lime, and salt.

Ohio—University of Cincinnati campus

OKLAHOMA

The recorded history of Oklahoma began in 1541 when De Soto visited the eastern part of the region and the Spanish Coronado expedition crossed central Oklahoma. The section was not known as Oklahoma until 1866, and then not officially until 1890. Little was known of the area until it became a part of the Louisiana Purchase in 1803. American explorers then made maps of the region.

Oklahoma early became a refuge for Indians who were driven from east of the Mississippi, and this role shaped the destiny of the future state. Between 1820 and 1840, Indian treaties were signed with Cherokee, Choctaw, Chickasaw, Seminole, and Creek tribes. These five tribes were allotted areas for settlement and were given land by the Government. They eventually set up their

Oklahoma—Travertine Creek, Platt National Park

Economy. Agriculture is the major industry of Oklahoma. However, soil erosion is a serious problem because the state lies in a region of erratic rainfall, some years being rainy and others being too dry. Farmers in the state are often faced with the problem of protecting topsoils either from severe drought or severe flooding. The most important crop is wheat and production is the second-highest in the United States. Other crops include cotton, grain, sorghums, and broomcorn.

Oklahoma ranks fourth in the production of petroleum. Natural gas, coal, gypsum, zinc, and salt are also produced. Petroleum refining is the chief nonagricultural industry.

own governments and became autonomous areas with their own capital cities. The Five Nations were divided on the issues of the Civil War, and considerable internal strife resulted.

Cattle drives northward through the Indian country required many grazing leases on Indian lands. The railroads brought an influx of white people to the country. After the Civil War, Creek and Seminole peoples ceded large areas in the central part of the future state to the United States. These lands were opened for white settlement on April 22, 1889. On opening day, fifty thousand people were on hand. By nightfall, tent cities had sprung up and six counties had been created. The following year Oklahoma was designated a territory. By 1895 all of southwestern Oklahoma had been opened to white settlement.

The Indians struggled to remain independent of Oklahoma Territory. They attempted to become a separate state in 1905, but were defeated. In 1906 President Theodore Roosevelt joined the white and Indian territories into a single state. Oklahoma was declared the forty-sixth state on November 16, 1907.

Government. The state has a senate of 48 members and a house of representatives of from 120 to 123 members. The governor and lieutenant-governor are elected for four years. The state is represented in Congress by two senators and six representatives. Oklahoma is divided into 67 counties. In 1970, 30 cities and towns had a population of more than ten thousand.

OREGON

The name *Oregon* was originally applied to the whole region of what is now the Pacific Northwest and includes Oregon, Washington, parts of Idaho, Montana, and Canada's British Columbia. Discovery and exploration were first carried out by sea voyages along the coast. Spanish sailors from Mexico, in 1543, were the first white men to see the Oregon country. Spanish claims were challenged by the British after the visits of Sir Francis Drake in 1579, and especially after the voyages of exploration of Captain James Cook (1778), and George Vancouver (1792). The Russians, too, claimed the region as a result of their fur-trading expeditions in the latter part of the eighteenth century. American interest was stimulated by the overland expedition of Lewis and Clark in 1804–1806, and by the sea voyage to the coasts by Captain Robert Gray in 1791 and 1792.

Russian and Spanish claims lapsed by agreement, but British and American rivalry in the fur trade and between settlements brought about serious conflicts. An agreement made in 1818 for joint occupancy was finally terminated by treaty in 1846, after the so-called Oregon Question threatened to involve the United States in war with Great Britain. The original American demand was "Fifty-Four Forty or Fight," but the forty-ninth parallel of latitude was finally accepted as the boundary between the United States and British-controlled Canada.

Settlement began when the Pacific Fur Company established Astoria in 1811. In 1813 Astoria was sold to the Northwest Company. That company was then absorbed by the Hudson's Bay

Oregon—Ice Lake, Wallowa Mountain

Company, which actually governed the region of present Oregon until the treaty in 1846. Settlements were established in 1829 in the Willamette River valley. American settlers formed a provisional government in 1843 and Oregon Territory was organized in 1848. Oregon was admitted to the Union on February 14, 1859, as the thirty-third state.

Government. The present constitution of Oregon dates from statehood. The legislative body is called the Legislative Assembly and consists of a senate of 30 members and a house of representatives of 60 members. The governor is elected to a four-year term. There is no lieutenant-governor. The state is divided into 36 counties. Harney County (10,131 square miles) is the eighth largest of the more than three thousand counties in the United States. In 1970 there were 24 cities and towns with a population of more than ten thousand.

Economy. Nearly 30 million acres of standing forests blanket the state, and Oregon leads the nation in lumbering. Oregon produces annually nearly eight million board feet of lumber, or about 25 percent of the total United States' production. Agriculture is another major industry. The state is a leading producer of peppermint, filberts, black raspberries, beans, beets, lily bulbs, holly, and seedling root stocks. The most productive farm land lies in the Willamette Valley between Portland and Eugene.

Manufacturing ranges from lumber products through aluminum, textiles, and fertilizers. Mining includes gold, silver, mercury, copper, and nickel. Oregon is one of the few states with commercial deposits of quicksilver and chromite ores, and one of two states producing nickel.

Fishing is important along the coast and on the Columbia River; salmon, trawl fish, clams, crabs, and tuna are the chief kinds taken.

PENNSYLVANIA

Pennsylvania is one of the 13 original states. William Penn (1644–1718), an English Quaker, received the grant of Pennsylvania from Charles II in 1681. It has been said that the immediate purpose of Charles' act was to get rid of "the troublesome Quakers." If so, he must have been roundly satisfied, because the Quakers flocked to Pennsylvania in the first few years. Penn himself came in 1682, and Philadelphia was laid out in the same year.

Penn set about concluding a number of treaties with the Lenni-Lenape and other tribes of Indians. His work saved years of bloodshed during the opening up of the land for settlement. Penn's domain was enlarged in 1682 by the grant of the "Three Lower Counties," which were retained as a nominal part of Pennsylvania until 1776 (*see* Delaware). The constitution devised in 1701 lasted until the Revolution.

Pennsylvania was often involved in long disputes over the colony's boundaries, and later over state lines. Some of these led to violence, as in the "Pennamite" and "Yankee" wars. The last change in the boundary was the adding of a triangle in 1792 to give the state an outlet on Lake Erie in the west.

Pennsylvania took a leading part in the Revolution. The Declaration of Independence was signed at Philadelphia in 1776. During a large part of the war, Pennsylvania served as Washington's base of operations. Except for a brief period when Philadelphia was occupied by the British, the city was the seat of the Continental Congress. Winter quarters were established at Valley Forge by the Continental Army during the winter of 1777–1778. The state ratified the federal Constitution on December 12, 1787, the second state to do so (following Delaware).

Government. Pennsylvania's legislative body is called the General Assembly and consists of a senate of 46 members and a house of representatives of 202 members. The governor and lieutenant-governor are elected for four years. The state sends two senators and 25 representatives to the U.S. Congress. Pennsylvania is divided into 67 counties (including the city of Philadelphia, whose boundary includes all of Philadelphia County). Philadelphia is the fourth largest city in the United States. Pittsburgh ranks twenty-fourth in the nation. In 1970 there were 101 cities and towns with a population of more than ten thousand.

Economy. Despite a varied agriculture and some of the richest soils in the nation, Pennsylvania is predominantly an industrial state. However, the state ranks second in the nation in egg production and fifth in dairying. The chief farm crops are corn, wheat, tobacco, and potatoes. Pennsylvania ranks second (to West Virginia) in coal mining. The principal coal seams are those of hard coal (anthracite) in the northeastern counties, and soft coal (bituminous) in the southwest. Half of the world's supply of anthracite coal comes from Pennsylvania. The state also ranks fourth in kaolin and second in limestone. Petroleum and natural gas are produced in large quantities. The state leads the nation in the production of iron and steel. Heavy industry is concentrated in the Pittsburgh and Philadelphia areas. Seventeen million tons of iron and steel come from the blast furnaces of Johnstown, Pittsburgh, Morrisville, Bethlehem, Steelton, and Coatesville each year. Most of the iron ore used comes from Minnesota over the Great Lakes route. Textile manufacturing is also a large industry, concentrated mainly in Philadelphia, Allentown, and Reading. The world's largest knitting mill is located at Reading (pronounced "Redding").

Pennsylvania—Memorial Chapel, Valley Forge

RHODE ISLAND

Rhode Island is one of the 13 original states. Rhode Island and Providence Plantations (still the official name of the state) was founded by Roger Williams in 1636. Williams had been exiled from Massachusetts for his religious beliefs. He persuaded several settlers to go with him into exile, and obtained land near the present Providence by purchase from the Indians of the Narragansett Bay region. The town of Newport was founded in 1639.

The New England Confederation, which had been formed for defensive purposes in 1643, threatened the little colony along Narragansett Bay. This prompted Roger Williams to hurry off to England where he got a charter for his colony (1652). This charter remained the governing law of Rhode Island until 1842. During the colonial period Rhode Island became a principal refuge for those who were persecuted because of their political beliefs. It was one of the first colonies to resist British oppression by burning the British cruiser *Gaspée.* Nathaniel Greene, a leading hero of the war, led a thousand Rhode Island men to Boston upon the outbreak of war.

Rhode Island was suspicious of the larger states throughout the early years of independence, and was at first fearful of joining a stronger union in which the small states could be trampled upon. Threats of annexation and of cutting off trade forced Rhode Island into ratifying the federal Constitution as the thirteenth state on May 29, 1790.

Government. The legislative body is called the General Assembly and consists of a senate of 50 members and a house of representatives of 100 members. The governor and lieutenant-governor are elected for two years. Rhode Island is represented in the U.S. Congress by two senators and two representatives. The state has five counties, but they have no political functions whatever. The town and city are the major units of local government. Of the 43 towns and cities in 1970, 27 had a population of more than ten thousand.

Economy. Rhode Island's larger cities are still the stronghold of the textile industries which have been on the decline elsewhere in New England. Woolens and worsteds are the leading textiles manufactured. Machinery, fabricated metal products, and jewelry are other leading industries. Agriculture and mining in Rhode Island are not important on a national level.

Rhode Island—Kitchen of James Mitchell
Varnum House, East Greenwich

South Carolina—Fort Sumter, Charleston

SOUTH CAROLINA

South Carolina is one of the original 13 states. Spanish explorers visited the area as early as 1520. However, England claimed the future South Carolina along with the entire North American coast on the basis of the voyages of discovery of John and Sebastian Cabot. In 1629, Charles I granted the region to Sir Robert Heath, who made no attempt to establish settlements. In 1663, Charles II made a second grant of the same area (which included the present North Carolina) to eight "proprietors." This colony was called Carolina. The first settlement was made in 1670 at Charlestown. This settlement was later moved and renamed Charles Town (changed to Charleston in 1783). In 1729, Carolina was divided into North Carolina and South Carolina (although actually there always had been two separate governments).

During the Revolutionary War, South Carolina contributed more money to the cause than any other state except Massachusetts. The colony had been prosperous from the very beginning, and for a time Charleston was a leading center of wealth and culture in North America. However, the state of South Carolina suffered heavily in the war. Charleston was besieged and forced to surrender. Much of the war was waged in guerrilla fashion by such leaders as Francis Marion ("Swamp Fox"), Sumter, and Pickens. South Carolina ratified the federal Constitution on May 23, 1788, the eighth state to sign.

The Civil War began in South Carolina after that state seceded from the Union on December 20, 1860. The bombardment of Fort Sumter in Charleston Harbor were the opening shots of the war (April 12–13, 1861). Tremendous damage was inflicted on the state, especially along the route of General Sherman's army in the famous march to the sea (*see* Georgia). At the close of the war a military government was imposed upon the state for twelve years. On June 25, 1868, the state was readmitted to the Union but was one of the worst sufferers during the period of Reconstruction.

Government. The legislative body is called the General Assembly. It consists of a senate of 46 members and a house of representatives of 124 members. The governor and lieutenant-governor are elected for four years. The state sends two senators and six representatives to the United States Congress. South Carolina is divided into 46 counties, and in 1970 there were 20 cities with a population of more than ten thousand.

Economy. South Carolina is an agricultural state. The principal crops are tobacco, corn, lint cotton, soybeans, and peaches. Of the minerals, large reserves of rare-earth minerals exist, although the state now ranks only forty-first in the value of minerals produced. The state ranks second in kaolin and kyanite clays. The state has a trend toward metals manufacturing, but textiles are by far the leading manufacture.

SOUTH DAKOTA

South Dakota was a part of the Louisiana Purchase of 1803. The state was first explored in 1743, mainly by the Verendrye brothers, who were French explorers from Canada. They buried a lead plate to serve as proof of their visit and of the claim of France to the region. The plate was found in 1913. The Lewis and Clark Expedition passed through the state in 1804 and 1806. Fort Teton (Fort Pierre) was established as a trading post in 1831. Steamboat service on the Missouri started the following year. Fort Pierre became a United States military post in 1855, and Sioux Falls was founded in 1857. South Dakota was successively placed under the governments of Missouri Territory (1812), Michigan Territory (1834), Wisconsin Territory (1836), Iowa Territory (1838), Minnesota Territory (1849), and then a part became part of Nebraska Territory in 1854. Dakota Territory was organized in 1861 and until 1863 included parts of Montana and Wyoming. Railroad construction initiated rapid settlement and development of the state. On November 2, 1889, South Dakota became either the thirty-ninth or the fortieth state (*see* North Dakota). A great land rush ensued when nine million acres of former Sioux Indian lands were sold in 1892.

Government. The legislature consists of a senate of 35 members and a house of representatives of 75 members. The governor and lieutenant-governor are elected for two years. South Dakota is divided into 67 counties (Armstrong County was abolished in 1959). The state sends two representatives and, of course, two senators to the Congress. Three counties remain unorganized and without government functions. In 1970 there were eight cities and towns with a population of more than ten thousand.

Economy. South Dakota is a farming state, and the farms are generally large (averaging over 800 acres) and highly mechanized. The state is a major producer of wheat, barley, oats, corn, rye, and flaxseed.

The state leads in the mining of gold (the Homestake Mine), although South Dakota ranks only forty-second in the value of minerals produced. Beryllium and mica are also mined in large quantities.

South Dakota—Mount Rushmore

TENNESSEE

In April 1541, De Soto reached the present Memphis, Tennessee area and crossed the Mississippi there into what is now Arkansas. Early in 1682 Sieur de La Salle built Fort Prud'homme. A French trading post was established near Nashville in 1714 and French settlers founded Fort Assumption. The English settled at Fort Loudoun near Knoxville in 1756. This fort was captured by the Cherokees in 1760 and the garrison was massacred. A series of permanent settlements were established in the valleys of the Holston and Watauga rivers in 1769 by colonists from Virginia and North Carolina.

A number of pioneers, including Daniel Boone, founded the state of Transylvania. They drew up a form of government in 1780 and founded a settlement at Nashville. However, Virginia refused to sanction the new state. John Sevier founded another state that was called Franklin. This time North Carolina refused to sanction the state and regained control over the territory in 1788.

After North Carolina and Virginia had given up their claims to Tennessee, the region was organized as "Territory South of the Ohio," but this did not include Kentucky (which was a Virginia County at that time). Statehood came on June 1, 1796, when Tennessee became the sixteenth state (four years after Kentucky had entered the Union).

The Tennessee people took a leading part in exploring and settling the American Southwest. In the war with Mexico, Tennessee became known as the "Volunteer State" because 30,000 soldiers volunteered for the war when only 2,800 had been called for.

Next to Virginia, Tennessee was the main battleground in the Civil War. Shiloh and the engagements around Chattanooga were bloody and crucial battles in the war. Tennessee had withdrawn from the Union on June 24, 1861, and was readmitted on July 24, 1866.

Government. The legislative body is called the General Assembly and consists of a senate of 63 members and a house of representatives of 99 members. The governor is elected for a four-year term. There is no office of lieutenant-governor. Tennessee sends two senators and eight representatives to the U.S. Congress. The state is divided into 95 counties, and in 1970 there were 32 cities and towns with a population of more than ten

Tennessee—Confederate Monument, Fort Donelson

thousand. The largest city is Memphis, which ranks seventeenth among the United States cities in population.

Economy. The chief crops of Tennessee are cotton, tobacco, soybeans, and corn. Coal fields cover over 5,000 square miles of the state, and Tennessee is a leading producer of coal. Tennessee leads in the mining of zinc and is second in phosphate rock. The state ranks twenty-eighth in mineral production; about 30 different minerals are mined commercially. Chemicals, iron, and steel products are the chief manufactures. Memphis is Tennessee's major port. Oak Ridge was founded by the U.S. Government in 1942 for atomic energy development and research in nuclear physics.

TEXAS

The Spanish initiated the exploration of Texas in 1519, when Alonso Álvarez de Peñeda was sent out to explore and map the coast along the Gulf of Mexico. Cabeza de Vaca added to European knowledge of the region by spending six years with the Indians there. In 1685, the French began exploring Texas. Thus, the claims of France and Spain overlapped until the defeat of France in 1763 by the British. Texas was then Spanish until it passed to an independent Mexico in 1821. During the Spanish period, missions and forts were established throughout the region. The first settlement in Texas dates from 1686.

American settlers, led by Moses Austin and later by his son, Stephen F. Austin, established homes in Texas while it was governed by Mexico. A flood of American settlers soon ran into conflict with Mexican sovereignty. In 1835, the colonists revolted against Mexico and set up a provisional government. Santa Anna, the Mexican general who had already overthrown his own government, set out to crush the revolt. Texans captured San Antonio in December 1835, but were crushed when Santa Anna's superior forces overwhelmed the small garrison in the Alamo, the chapel of an old Spanish mission, on March 6, 1836. There were no survivors; all died fighting, including Davy Crockett, Jim Bowie, and William Travis.

After the fall of the Alamo, Santa Anna was caught by surprise at San Jacinto. Forces under Sam Houston annihilated the Mexican Army and captured Santa Anna. This ended Mexican sovereignty over Texas. The Texas Republic came into existence on March 2, 1836 and lasted until the state entered the Union voluntarily on December 29, 1845, as the twenty-eighth state. Texas seceded from the Union in 1861 and was readmitted March 30, 1870.

Government. The present constitution dates from 1876. The Texas legislature consists of a senate of 31 members and a house of representatives of 150 members. The governor and lieutenant-governor are elected for two years. Texas sends 24 representatives besides the two senators to the Congress. Texas is divided into 254 counties, the largest number of counties in any state. In 1970 there were 125 cities and towns with a population of more than ten thousand.

Economy. Texas leads all states by a wide margin in the production of petroleum and helium. The total value of minerals is 22 percent of the United States total. More than three-fifths of all natural gas used in the country comes from Texas. Other minerals include sulphur, salt, gypsum, asphalt, and magnesium (from seawater).

Great chemical industries have grown up in the Houston area. The Port of Houston is connected to the Gulf of Mexico by the Houston Ship Canal (57.3 miles long). Houston itself is the largest inland cotton market in the world.

Texas ranks as one of the leading agricultural states. Large farms dominate the state's agriculture. Texas leads in the production of cotton and grain sorghum. Other important crops include pecans, corn, winter wheat, oats, rice, castor beans, potatoes, sweet potatoes, peanuts, and grapefruit.

Texas—The Alamo

The state also leads in the livestock industry. It has more cattle and sheep than any other state. Tourism is an important industry in southern and western Texas.

UTAH

The first white men to see Utah were Spanish explorers and the Franciscan friars. Captain James Bridger discovered Great Salt Lake in 1825. The first settlement was made at Salt Lake City in July 1847, by a group of about 150 Mormon settlers.

The Mormon Church (properly called the Church of Jesus Christ of Latter-Day Saints) was founded at Fayette, New York, in 1830 by Joseph Smith. Persecution and opposition forced the Mormons to move westward. Brigham Young joined the group after it had reached Kirtland, Ohio (near Cleveland) in 1832. They were driven from Ohio and then from Missouri. In 1840, they were at Nauvoo, Illinois; by 1844 Nauvoo had become the largest town in Illinois because of the influx of converts and settlers. Joseph Smith and his brother Hyram were jailed and then shot by a mob on June 27, 1844. The charter of Nauvoo was revoked and the Mormons were again forced to flee westward. They reached the Great Salt Lake and founded Salt Lake City in 1847. Mormons attempted to enter the Union as the State of Deseret; they were finally admitted as the Territory of Utah in 1850.

Utah early came into conflict with federal authorities over the practice of polygamy, which had been outlawed by the United States in 1862. The Edmunds Bill took citizenship away from polygamists, and in 1890 the court declared their church property forfeited. This forced the Mormons into accepting monogamist laws. Thereupon Utah was admitted to the Union as the forty-fifth state, on January 4, 1896.

Government. The Utah legislature consists of a senate of 28 members and a house of representatives of 69 members. The governor is elected for four years. There is no office of lieutenant-governor. Utah is represented in the U.S. Congress by two senators and two representatives. The state is divided into 29 counties, and in 1970 there were 15 cities and towns with a population of more than ten thousand.

Utah—Temple Square in Salt Lake City

Economy. The raising of sheep and the production of wool are a leading agricultural industry. Most farming in Utah is done by irrigation, although some dry farming is practiced. Utah is primarily a mining state, ranking sixteenth in the nation. The state is second in asphalt production, and also in copper, gold, silver, molybdenum, and vanadium; third in uranium, lead, and potassium salts; fourth in iron ore.

VERMONT

Samuel de Champlain was the first European to see Vermont. He discovered Lake Champlain in 1609. The first settlement was made by the French on La Motte Island in Lake Champlain in 1666. Fort Dummer (now Brattleboro) was the site of the first English settlement, established in 1724 by colonists from Massachusetts.

The early history of Vermont centers on the disputes over the Mason Land Grants and the earlier charter grants by both England and France. Later, the charters of both New Hampshire and Massachusetts included parts of the present Vermont. This conflict was settled in favor of New Hampshire in 1740. But the New Hampshire colony inherited a dispute with New York that had been in progress over the eastern boundary of New York. The king was asked to decide and did so—in favor of New York. The latter colony ignored the claims and rights of settlers who had purchased their lands from New Hampshire. Armed conflict resulted, especially at Bennington (now in Vermont).

In 1775, a convention met at Westminster and declared for independence, and a second convention declared for an independent state to be called New Connecticut. A third convention in 1777 changed the name of the region to Vermont. Be-

Vermont—The State House, Montpelier

cause of bitter opposition from New York and New Hampshire, Vermont was denied statehood for 14 years. The Vermonters were finally able to settle claims of both the other states and on March 4, 1791, Vermont became the first state to be admitted to the Union after the original 13 states had ratified the federal Constitution. During the War for Independence, Vermont fought independently and was for a time seeking an independent peace. But eventually it joined the other former colonies in the peace negotiations. The capture of Fort Ticonderoga (in New York) by Vermont hero Ethan Allen and his Green Mountain Boys was one of the major events of the war.

Government. The state legislature consists of a senate of 30 members and a house of representatives of 150 members. Vermont sends two senators and one representative to the U.S. Congress. The state is divided into 14 counties and 246 towns and cities (*see* Maine for a note on "town" and on New England counties). In 1970 there were eight cities with a population of more than ten thousand, and 47 cities and towns with a population of more than twenty-five hundred.

Economy. Manufacturing is the principal industry, although tourism and recreation have become much more important in recent years. Vermont leads in maple syrup production. Other crops grown are potatoes, oats, apples, and hay. Granite is the principal mineral produced, although the state is the number one producer of asbestos.

VIRGINIA

Virginia is one of the 13 original states. It was settled under a charter issued in 1606 by King James I. The first permanent settlement (at Jamestown in 1607) was established only after several unsuccessful attempts (*see* North Carolina).

The first legislative assembly in the Western Hemisphere, the House of Burgesses, convened in Jamestown in 1619. In 1622, Indians massacred nearly one-third of the settlement's inhabitants. In 1624, Virginia was made a crown colony.

After a revolution in England had overthrown the king and Cromwell had assumed the powers of government, Virginia obtained a new charter of self-government. However, the colony reverted to the crown when Charles II came to power. An era

Virginia—Houdon Statue of George Washington, in the State Capitol, Richmond

of prosperity in Virginia ensued, based mainly on the growing of tobacco on the Tidewater plantations, using slave labor.

The Navigation Acts of 1660 and 1663 ushered in a period of remonstrance and protest that foreshadowed the Revolution which came a century later. The Navigation Acts imposed unwanted restrictions upon Virginia's trade. Soon after, Governor Sir William Berkeley placed drastic limitations upon democratic government and the House of Burgesses. This led to Bacon's Rebellion of 1676. Savage reprisals and brutal hangings by Berkeley ended the rebellion. In 1699, during the reign of William and Mary in England, the Virginia capital was removed to Middle Plantation, and that town's name was changed to Williamsburg. Williamsburg became one of the great social, cultural, and political centers of American life. The city declined after removal of the capital to Richmond in 1780. In 1927 the restoration of Williamsburg to its original condition was begun and has been nearly completed at a cost, so far, of more than sixty-eight million dollars.

By 1763, Virginia was moving toward revolution and independence. Virginians disputed the Hillsborough Proclamation of 1763, prohibiting settlement of Virginians beyond the crest of the Allegheny Mountains in the west. England asserted Parliament's right to legislate for the colonies. This brought a series of events that led to war.

Virginia took the lead among the colonies and provided most of the leaders in the war that resulted. The rise of Virginia politicians and farmers to the status of great American statesmen was exemplified in the careers of Jefferson, Richard Henry Lee, Patrick Henry, Madison, Pendleton, Randolph, Mason, Washington, and others. The Colonial Assembly adjourned on June 20, 1775, and never met again.

The Second Continental Congress elected George Washington commander in chief on June 14, 1775. He proceeded to Cambridge, Massachusetts, to take control of the army (*see* Massachusetts).

Virginia's second governor, Thomas Jefferson, wrote the Declaration of Independence for the colonies. George Mason drafted the Declaration of Rights—the model for the Bill of Rights that was later added to the United States Constitution. "Light Horse Harry" Lee, Daniel Morgan, John Paul Jones, George Rogers Clark, and George Washington all took leading parts in fierce battles that led to victory. Virginia became the tenth state on June 25, 1788. The state gave up its claims to the vast region west of the mountains and north of the Ohio River.

Upon the outbreak of the Civil War in 1861, Virginia decided upon secession. Again the state provided great leaders in such men as Robert E. Lee, "Stonewall" Jackson, J. E. B. Stuart, and Joseph E. Johnston. The critical battles of the war were fought in Virginia, and the capture of Richmond (the Confederate capital from April 1861) was the primary object of the boldest strikes made during the war by Union commanders. Virginia was the battlefield upon which the South's greatest victories were won. But it was also at Appomattox, Virginia that General Lee was forced to surrender, ending one of the bloodiest wars in the history of the world up to that time.

Government. In 1776, the House of Burgesses was converted into the General Assembly of two houses, the senate, presently made up of 40 members, and the house of delegates, now having 100 members. The governor and lieutenant-governor are elected for four years. The state sends two senators and 10 representatives to the U.S. Congress. As of 1963, the state was divided into 96 counties and 35 independent cities which have the status of counties. In 1970 there were 29 cities and towns having a population of more than ten thousand.

Economy. Coal is the most important mineral, including high-grade coking coal. Lead, stone, gypsum, manganese, lime, and titanium are also produced. The state has diversified agriculture, but livestock-raising and tobacco-growing are leading activities. Tobacco is the leading cash crop today, just as it was in colonial times.

WASHINGTON

The early history of Washington is that of the Oregon country (*see* Oregon). American interests grew strong and came in conflict with those of the British after the overland expedition of Lewis and Clark (1804–1806). An agreement between England and the United States in 1818 allowed both nations to occupy the region. The United States advanced its claim to the Columbia River basin during the presidential campaign of James K. Polk in 1844. The dispute was arbitrated in 1846 and a treaty was signed, establishing the boundary of Oregon on the forty-ninth parallel of latitude, which is the present international boundary. Later, a dispute over the San Juan Islands was also arbitrated and settled.

In 1848, Oregon Territory was formed, and it included the present state of Washington. In 1853, Washington Territory was separated and organized. Agitation for statehood began in 1876 and ended when Washington was admitted to the Union as the forty-second state on November 11, 1889.

Washington—Olympic National Park

Government. The legislature consists of a senate of 49 members and a house of representatives of 99 members. The governor and lieutenant-governor are elected for four-year terms. Washington sends two senators and seven representatives to the U.S. Congress. The state is divided into 39 counties, and in 1970, there were 39 cities and towns with a population of more than ten thousand. The city of Seattle, largest in the state, ranks twenty-second in the nation.

Economy. Because the state has the greatest potential power supplies, the aluminum industry was attracted there. Vast forests of principally hemlock, fir, and pine make the forestry industries among the largest in the nation. The manufacture of wood products, including paper and pulp, is the largest single industry in Washington, and the state ranks third in this field. Agriculture is also a major industry, with much of it practiced on irrigated lands. Western Washington has large dairy farms and berry fields, while in the east the growing of wheat and ranching are the chief agricultural industries. Washington leads all states in the production of apples, hops, mint; ranks second in Bartlett pears, filberts, apricots; fourth in winter wheat.

WEST VIRGINIA

West Virginia is the youngest state east of the Mississippi River. It was originally a part of Virginia. But when that state seceded from the Union in 1861, the western counties (most of the present state of West Virginia) seceded from Virginia. By a proclamation of President Lincoln on June 20, 1863, these counties were admitted to the Union as the thirty-fifth state.

Government. West Virginia is governed by a senate with 34 members and a house of delegates with 100 members. The state sends two senators and four representatives to the U.S. Congress and has six electoral votes in federal elections. There is no lieutenant-governor. The major unit of local government is the county. West Virginia is divided into 55 counties.

Economy. Coal underlies nearly two-thirds of the state. West Virginia has led the nation in the mining of coal since 1936. Over a hundred million tons are mined every year, accounting for 80 percent of the state's total mineral production. Other minerals produced include petroleum, natural gas, salt, and limestone.

Although there are about seven million acres of farm land, only about one million acres are in crops. Sixty-five percent of the state is in woodlands, including nearly a million acres of national forests. The chief crops grown in West Virginia include tobacco, fruit, wheat, corn, oats, and potatoes. The eastern panhandle is a noted apple-growing region.

Manufacturing in West Virginia is centered in the valley of the Kanawha River and along the Ohio River. The Kanawha Valley is one of the major chemical-producing areas of the United States.

West Virginia—Capitol Building, Charleston

WISCONSIN

Wisconsin was explored by the French from bases in Canada. Jean Nicolet visited eastern Wisconsin in 1534. A fuller exploration was conducted by the traders Radisson and Groseilliers (1658–1659). Father Allouez established a mission near the present Green Bay in 1665. The first permanent settlement was made near the same place in 1670. The entire state was a part of New France until the French defeat in 1763. The sympathies of the early settlers were generally with the English, and they retained this allegiance during the Revolutionary War.

The United States acquired Wisconsin as a result of the Treaty of Paris in 1783, ending the war and establishing American independence. The region was included in the Ordinance of 1787, establishing the Northwest Territory. When Indiana

Territory was separated from this in 1800, Wisconsin was included in Indiana. In 1805, it became a part of Michigan Territory, and from 1808 until 1818 it was a part of Illinois Territory. Wisconsin was again transferred to Michigan Territory after Illinois became a state in 1818, and there it remained until 1836. In that year Wisconsin Territory was organized, thus ending a complicated series of changes in government. At that time Wisconsin Territory included parts of Minnesota, Iowa, and the Dakotas. Iowa was separated in 1838. On May 29, 1848, Wisconsin became the thirtieth state and was reduced to its present boundaries.

Government. The law-making body is called the Legislature, as in most states, and consists of a senate of 32 members and an assembly of 100 members. The governor and lieutenant-governor are elected for four years. The state sends two senators and nine representatives to the U.S. Congress. Wisconsin is divided into 72 counties (Menominee became the seventy-second county in 1961). In 1970 there were 52 cities and towns with a population of more than ten thousand. Milwaukee, the state's largest city, ranks twelfth in the nation.

Economy. Wisconsin is famous for its dairy products, but agriculture has recently been surpassed in importance by the rising industrial complexes centering around Milwaukee and the southeast. Although the state has little coal, about 85 percent of the nation's iron ore is within easy reach in the Greak Lakes area and the lakes themselves form a major transportation route for incoming raw materials and outgoing finished products. The fabrication of iron and steel products is the largest industry. Textiles, footwear, furniture, chemicals, and shipbuilding are other major manufactures. In agriculture, the dairying industry is concentrated in the southern counties. In 1970 the state ranked first in milk and cheese and second in creamery butter. The principal crops are those used in feeding cattle, such as corn, oats, and hay. The best cash crop is potatoes, grown mainly in northern Wisconsin.

WYOMING

Chevalier de la Verendrye, a member of a remarkable family of Canadian explorers passed through the Wyoming Wind River region in 1743–1744. Wilson Hunt explored the Powder River on his way to Oregon in 1811. John Colter spent the winter of 1806–1807 in Wyoming, and discovered the Yellowstone region. In 1842 John C. Fremont ascended Fremont Peak in Wind River Range, accompanied by Kit Carson. The first white settlement in Wyoming was made in 1834 at Fort William (later changed to Fort Laramie) by William Sublette and Robert Campbell. This post was sold to the United States government in 1849. Part of the Mormon migration to Utah (*see* Utah) stopped in Wyoming and settled at Fort Bridger in 1853.

Wyoming came to the United States in three sections. The greater part was included in the Louisiana Purchase of 1803. More was added by the settlement of the Oregon dispute in 1846, and Mexico ceded the remainder in 1848 as a result of the Treaty of Guadalupe Hidalgo.

The discovery of gold in 1867 and the completion of the Union Pacific Railroad in Wyoming in 1868 caused a wave of settlement. The Territory of Wyoming was organized in 1868 from parts of Utah, the Dakota Territory, and Idaho Territory. The great natural wonders of the Yellowstone region were set aside as a national park in 1872 (the oldest national nature park). Wyoming became the forty-fourth state on July 10, 1890.

Government. The legislature consists of a senate of 30 members and a house of representatives of 61 members. The governor is elected for a four-year term. There is no office of lieutenant-governor in Wyoming. The Territory of Wyoming was the first government under the American flag to guarantee equal suffrage to women (in 1869). The state sends

Wisconsin—Ancient quartzite cliffs overlooking Devils Lake, Baraboo

two senators and one representative to the U.S. Congress. Wyoming is divided into 23 counties, and in 1970 there were five cities with a population of more than ten thousand.

Economy. Many of the soils of the state are very fertile and produce well when water is provided.

About two million acres of land are already under irrigation, and more is planned to be placed under irrigation. Wyoming's agriculture revolves around the cattle industry and sheep-raising. The chief mineral produced is oil. Natural gas is also found in large quantities and uranium has recently become a major mineral product.

Wyoming—Thousands of Oregon Trail travelers carved their names on Register Cliff near Guernsey (Inset shows actual names)

Districts, Commonwealths, Possessions, and Trust Areas Of the United States

Besides the District of Columbia and the Commonwealth of Puerto Rico, this section includes lands and peoples associated with the United States in the form of possessions, territories, or trust areas. At some time in the future these areas may become one of the United States.

DISTRICT OF COLUMBIA

The District of Columbia is the seat of government and the location of the federal capital of the United States. It is limited to the city of Washington.

Rivalry developed between northern and southern congressmen over the location of the nation's capital. The institution of slavery was one issue in the arguments. Finally, in 1790, Alexander Hamilton and Thomas Jefferson worked out a compromise.

The District of Columbia was organized from lands ceded by Maryland and Virginia. The District then was a perfect square, measuring ten miles along each of the four sides. However, in 1846 the part ceded originally by Virginia and lying across the south bank of the Potomac River was returned to Virginia, and now forms Arlington County of that State.

In 1791, President Washington chose the exact site for the Capitol Building and the city of Washington. He then commissioned Pierre L'Enfant, a French engineer, to design a layout for the city of Washington. L'Enfant's ideas for wide avenues and streets were considered wasteful by many, but Washington approved the plans himself and laid the cornerstone of the Capitol Building on September 18, 1793. President John Adams, Washington's successor, was the first President to serve the nation from the new capital. He moved from Philadelphia to Washington on June 3, 1800. The city of Washington was incorporated in 1802.

The original Capitol Building was burned (along with the White House) by the British during the War of 1812. Both the present White House and Capitol Building date from 1818. The Capitol was not actually completed until 1863.

The White House is the official residence of the President. The cornerstone of the original building was laid by Washington on October 13, 1792. Extensive alterations have been made, in 1902–1903 under President Theodore Roosevelt and in 1948–1952 under President Truman. A major redecorating project was carried out under Jacqueline Kennedy in 1963.

The Capitol is one of the chief attractions of the District of Columbia. It crowns the summit of Capitol Hill, 88 feet above the level of the Potomac River. It covers four acres and its height is 287 feet, 5.5 inches. The original plan was drawn by Dr. William Thornton of the Virgin Islands. Benjamin Latrobe and Charles Bulfinch had charge of repair and reconstruction after the British burning of the building in 1814. The present Senate and House wings were added in 1851. The bronze statue of Freedom on top of the great dome is 19.5 feet tall, and weighs 15,000 pounds. The rotunda is 180 feet high and has a diameter of 97 feet.

Government. The city of Washington (District of Columbia) is governed by a mayor, an assistant, and a 13-member city council elected by the district's voters. The district has one Delegate to the House who may vote in committees but not on the floor. Amendment Twenty-three to the Constitution of the United States gave the citizens of the District the right to vote in national elections. This amendment was ratified by the requisite number of states and became law in 1961.

Buildings and Monuments. The Lincoln Memorial in West Potomac Park was dedicated in 1922. Its famous statue of President Lincoln was the work of Daniel Chester French. The memorial is of Colorado-Yule marble. The wells are enclosed by a colonnade of 38 Doric columns. Inside are three memorials—a seated figure of Lincoln, a passage from Lincoln's Second Inaugural Address, and his Gettysburg Address.

The Thomas Jefferson Memorial was dedicated in 1943. Its central circular chamber is occupied by a huge statue of Jefferson. The building incorporates pantheonic design of Vermont and Georgia marble.

The Washington National Monument is an obelisk of white marble 555.5 feet tall. It was

District of Columbia—Capitol Building, Washington, D.C.

begún in 1848 and completed in 1885. An elevator takes visitors to the 500-foot level.

Other famous buildings and monuments in the District include the National Archives, Smithsonian Institution, the National Geographic Society, the Folger Shakespeare Library, and the National Gallery of Art. In nearby Arlington are the Pentagon, the Iwo Jima Memorial, the Tomb of the Unknown Soldier, and the Custis-Lee Mansion (the last two are in Arlington National Cemetery).

Economy. Most of the people either work for the federal Government or are in wholesale and retail businesses. There are six hundred manufacturing firms in the District. Printing and publishing is the largest single industry.

Outlying U.S. Areas

AMERICAN SAMOA

These comprise the seven eastern islands of the Samoa group in the South Pacific, 2,300 miles southwest of Hawaii. They became a United States territory in 1900. The larger islands of the Samoan group (Western Samoa) form an independent nation. Administered by the Interior Department, American Samoa elects its own governor, bicameral legislature and a non-voting delegate to Congress. Chief port is Pago Pago (pronounced "Pango Pango") but the seat of government is the nearby town of Fagatogo on the Island of Tutuila.

The islands are of volcanic origin; they have a mild climate with a distinct dry season, and are heavily forested. The people are Polynesians. The chief exports are canned fish, *copra* (dried coconut), cocoa, and handicrafts.

COMMONWEALTH OF PUERTO RICO

(Estado Libre Asociado de Puerto Rico)

The spelling *Porto Rico* is today unacceptable, having been replaced by *Puerto Rico* by an Act of

Congress in 1932. Columbus discovered Puerto Rico in 1493. The famous Ponce de León (*see* Florida) founded San Juan in either 1506 or 1508. The chief purpose was to protect Mona Passage, which at that time was the principal gateway to the Spanish possessions that lay in and along the Caribbean Sea.

San Juan was fortified early because of raids and sieges by English buccaneers. Dutch warships also attacked the town and destroyed a large part of it in 1625. La Fortaleza, El Morro, and San Cristóbal are three fortresses that were built at various times as a means of defense. Puerto Rico remained a Spanish possession until 1898.

The Treaty of Paris in 1898 ended the Spanish-American War and ceded Puerto Rico (along with Guam and the Philippines) to the United States. The troops led by General Nelson Miles had captured the island without serious fighting on July 25, 1898.

The territorial status of Puerto Rico was determined by the Jones Act of 1917; this status was retained until July 25, 1952, when the Commonwealth of Puerto Rico was proclaimed.

Government. The Commonwealth form of government is defined as a "compact," establishing an association between the United States and Puerto Rico. The electorate chooses a delegate (resident commissioner) who sits in the U.S. House of Representatives, but has no vote. The citizens of Puerto Rico are citizens of the United States and subject to most of the same national laws, except the internal revenue statutes. Puerto Rico is not subject to United States taxes, including income tax.

The commonwealth is autonomous in local government. The executive power is vested in a governor, elected for four years. The Council of Secretaries (10 members) advises the governor. The legislature consists of a senate of 27 members and a house of representatives of 51 members. Spanish is the mother language, but English is widely spoken and its use is growing. All instruction below high-school level is given in Spanish.

Economy. Manufacturing is the leading industry. Textiles and apparel, plastics and chemicals, and electronic equipment are among the leading products. The processing of sugar cane is still an important industry but the income from dairy and livestock products is now greater. Tourism is also a large revenue producer.

San Juan is the chief port of entry by both air and water. The city is the governmental, cultural, and industrial heart of Puerto Rico. The chief agricultural crop is sugar cane; coffee, tobacco, and pineapples are next in importance, in that order. Eighty-seven percent of all trade is with the United States mainland.

GUAM

This is the largest and southernmost island of the Marianas group, located south of Japan and east of the Philippines. The island is not a part of the United States Trust Territory of the Pacific Islands, but serves as headquarters for the administration of that territory. One of the largest United States military installations in the Pacific is located on Guam. Under the administration of the Interior Department, Guam elects its own governor, legislature, and one delegate to the United States House of Representatives who can vote in committee but not on the floor. Residents who are American citizens cannot vote in presidential elections. It was discovered by Magellan in 1521 and acquired by the United States in 1898 as a result of the Spanish-American War. It was captured by the Japanese in 1941 but was regained after bitter

fighting in 1944. It was then used as a base for the B-29 bomber raids against Japan.

NORTHERN MARIANAS

Extending in a 500-mile arc east of the Philippines and southeast of Japan, the Mariana islands (with the exception of Guam, which is separate) are in process of becoming a United States commonwealth like Puerto Rico. They were formerly part of the United States Trust Territory of the Pacific Islands but they have already elected their own governor and legislature. Military bases on the islands are important for United States defense.

TRUST TERRITORY
OF THE PACIFIC ISLANDS

Assigned to United States administration by the United Nations, this group of almost 2,000 islands, 98 of them inhabited, is scattered over three million square miles in the western Pacific Ocean. Often called Micronesia, they consist of the Caroline and Marshall islands, including some noted for World War II battles (Truk, Enewetak, and Kwajalein) and as nuclear testing sites (Bikini). Negotiations are underway for full self-government, with the United States retaining responsibility for defense. When this happens the UN will end the trusteeship of the United States.

UNINCORPORATED TERRITORIES

Howland, Jarvis, and Baker Islands are south of Hawaii, uninhabited since World War II, and are under the Interior Department.

Johnston Atoll, southwest of Hawaii, is operated by the Nuclear Defense Agency. It has a population of 300 on one square mile. An atoll is an island formed by coral deposits.

The Midway islands consist of two coral atolls at the northwestern end of the Hawaiian chain of islands. They served as a "China Clipper" transoceanic flight base before World War II. During the war the Japanese were defeated in the great Battle of Midway in June 1942. Consisting of two square miles, with a population of 2,256, they are administered by the United States Navy.

Wake Island, the scene of a great World War II

battle in 1945, is on a direct route from Hawaii to Hong Kong. With its sister islands of Wilkes and Peale, it is administered by the United States Air Force.

VIRGIN ISLANDS

The United States' group comprise about 50 islands in the West Indies just east of Puerto Rico. They were discovered by Columbus in 1493, and acquired by the United States from Denmark in 1917. The people, mainly of African origin, have been United States citizens since 1927. St. Croix, the largest island, has a jet airport. St. Thomas Island is the site of the capital. Tourism is the most important industry. The making of rum, raising of cattle, and growing of sugar cane are also important. The chief export is rum. A 1972 law allows the people to elect one delegate to the United States House of Representatives who can vote in committee but not on the floor.

CANAL ZONE

The Canal Zone is no longer an outlying territory of the United States. Two treaties signed by the United States and the Republic of Panama in 1978 dealt with the operation and defense of the Canal Zone until 1999 and with the guarantee of its permanent neutrality. At that time Panama assumed general territorial jurisdiction over the former Canal Zone. The United States maintains control over the land, water and installations of the canal itself, including military bases necessary to operate and defend the zone, until December 31, 1999. Until 1990 the canal administrator is a United States citizen with a Panamanian deputy.

After that, until 1999, the administrator will be a Panamanian with the deputy being a United States citizen.

The building of the Panama Canal was one of the greatest engineering projects in all history. Plans for a canal across the Isthmus of Panama had been put forward even before Columbus died. Plans were made on several occasions, down to the nineteenth century.

It remained for the French to actually begin the work. Ferdinand de Lesseps headed the construction of the Suez Canal, which opened in 1869. He was a national hero in France because of his success, and when he proposed the Panama project he received enthusiastic support.

The problems in Panama were vastly more difficult to overcome than in the Suez project. The French effort ended after an expenditure of 300 million dollars. The De Lesseps project began on New Year's Day, 1880, and ended in bankruptcy in 1888.

In 1903, the United States signed a treaty with Colombia to acquire land and construction rights in the Isthmus of Panama, which was a part of Colombia to acquire land and construction rights in the Isthmus of Panama, which was a part of Colombia at that time. However, Colombia balked at the terms of the treaty, which led to a local revolution against Colombia. A treaty with an independent Panama was then signed, granting the United States sovereignty over a Canal Zone. In 1921, Colombia accepted 25 million dollars as compensation for the loss of Panama, and established relations with the new republic in 1924 (*see* Panama).

The United States began construction in 1904, using some of the partially excavated route of the French project. However, the cost ran to almost 400 million dollars. The canal was opened to traffic on August 15, 1914.

Statistics for the United States

NAME OF STATE (ZIP CODE ABBREVIATION) NICKNAME	POPULATION RANK IN POP. AREA (SQ. MI.) RANK IN AREA	CAPITAL* LARGEST CITY	BIRD FLOWER	DESCRIPTION OF FLAG
Alabama (AL) Heart of Dixie Cotton State	3,943,000 22 51,609 29	Montgomery* 178,157 Birmingham 284,413	Yellowhammer Camellia	A crimson St. Andrew's cross on a square white field
Alaska (AK) No official nickname	438,000 50 586,412 1	Juneau* 19,528 Anchorage 173,017	Willow ptarmigan Forget-me-not	A deep blue field with seven gold stars in the shape of the Big Dipper constellation at the left and a single gold star representing Polaris in the upper right-hand corner.
Arizona (AZ) Grand Canyon State	2,860,000 29 113,909 6	Phoenix* 764,911	Cactus wren The blossom of the saguaro cactus	The lower half is a blue field; the upper half is composed of red and yellow rays, emanating from a large, copper-colored five-pointed star superimposed on the center of the flag.
Arkansas (AR) Land of Opportunity	2,291,000 33 53,104 27	Little Rock* 158,461	Mockingbird Apple blossom	A white diamond outlined in blue centered on a red field; twenty-five white stars arranged around the blue border of the diamond indicate Arkansas' position as the twenty-fifth state to enter the Union; within the white diamond are four large blue stars and the word "Arkansas"; three of these stars, placed below "Arkansas," signify the three nations of Spain, France, and the United States, to which Arkansas successively belonged; the star above "Arkansas" commemorates the Confederacy, and the diamond itself signifies that Arkansas is the only diamond-producing state in the Union.
California (CA) Golden State	24,724,000 1 158,693 3	Sacramento* 275,741 Los Angeles 2,966,763	California valley quail Golden poppy	A California grizzly bear set in the center of a white field; at the top left is a red star; below the bear the words "California Republic" appear above a broad red stripe. Known as the Bear Flag.
Colorado (CO) Centennial State	3,045,000 27 104,247 8	Denver* 491,396	Lark bunting White and lavender Rocky Mountain columbine	Three equal stripes, two of which are blue, representing the sky, and one white, representing snow-capped mountains; on the left is a red "C" encircling a disk of yellow.
Connecticut (CT) Constitution State Nutmeg State	3,153,000 26 5,009 48	Hartford* 136,392 Bridgeport 142,546	Robin Mountain laurel	A blue background with a white shield bearing the state seal in the center; beneath the shield is the state motto; the flag is bordered with a gold fringe.
Delaware (DE) First State Diamond State	602,000 47 2,057 49	Dover* 23,512 Wilmington 70,195	Blue hen chicken Peach blossom	A buff-colored diamond bearing the state seal is placed in the center of a blue field; below the diamond are the words "December 7, 1787," the date when Delaware ratified the Constitution of the United States.
Florida (FL) Sunshine State	10,416,000 7 58,560 22	Tallahassee* 81,548 Jacksonville 540,898	Mockingbird Orange blossom	The state seal lies in the center of a white field, crossed by diagonal red bars, which stand for the bars of the Confederate flag.
Georgia (GA) Empire State of the South Peach State	5,639,000 12 58,876 21	Atlanta* 425,022	Brown thrasher Cherokee rose	A combination of an earlier flag with a field of blue containing the state seal, and the battle flag of the Confederacy with its field of red containing crossed blue bars and thirteen white stars.
Hawaii (HI) The Aloha State	994,000 39 6,450 47	Honolulu* 365,048	Nene (Hawaiian goose) Hibiscus	Eight horizontal stripes which, from the top, are alternately white, red, and blue; in the upper left-hand corner is the British Union Jack.
Idaho (ID) Gem State	965,000 40 83,557 13	Boise* 102,451	Mountain bluebird Syringa	A dark-blue field bordered by a gold fringe; in the center is the state seal; below this a red band contains the words "State of Idaho" in gold.
Illinois (IL) The Inland Empire	11,448,000 5 56,400 24	Springfield* 99,637 Chicago 3,005,072	Cardinal Violet	In the center of a white field fringed in gold is a symbol based on the state seal.
Indiana (IN) Hoosier State	5,471,000 14 36,291 38	Indianapolis* 700,807	Cardinal Peony	A flaming torch in gold against a blue field surrounded by a circle of thirteen stars; below is a semicircle of five stars; above the torch is a larger star and the word "Indiana."

NAME OF STATE (ZIP CODE ABBREVIATION) NICKNAME	POPULATION RANK IN POP. AREA (SQ. MI.) RANK IN AREA	CAPITAL* LARGEST CITY	BIRD FLOWER	DESCRIPTION OF FLAG
Iowa (IA) Hawkeye State	2,905,000 28 56,290 25	Des Moines* 191,003	Eastern goldfinch Wild rose	A white field bordered on the staff end by a blue band and on the opposite end by a red band; centered in the white field is an eagle bearing the state motto.
Kansas (KS) Sunflower State	2,408,000 32 82,264 14	Topeka* 115,266 Wichita 279,272	Western meadowlark Sunflower	The flag has a wreath above the seal to represent the Louisiana Purchase. The yellow sunflower stands for the state's prairies and for the golden future.
Kentucky (KY) Bluegrass State	3,667,000 23 40,395 37	Frankfort* 25,973 Louisville 298,451	Cardinal Goldenrod	The center of the state seal on a field of blue; the words "Commonwealth of Kentucky" appear in gold around the top half of the seal, and a garland of goldenrod is below the seal; the flag is fringed in gold.
Louisiana (LA) Pelican State	4,362,000 18 48,523 31	Baton Rouge* 219,486 New Orleans 557,482	Brown pelican Magnolia	In the center of a blue field is a white pelican feeding its young; beneath the pelican is a white ribbon inscribed in blue with the state motto.
Maine (ME) Pine Tree State	1,133,000 38 32,215 39	Augusta* 21,819 Portland 61,572	Chick-a-dee Pine cone and tassel	The state seal lies in the center of a blue field.
Maryland (MD) Old Line State Free State	4,265,000 19 10,577 42	Annapolis* 31,740 Baltimore 786,775	Baltimore oriole Black-eyed Susan	Bears the coat of arms of the Calvert and Crossland families, Crossland being the maiden name of the wife of the first Lord Baltimore. The Maryland flag is the only state flag embodying recognized armorial bearings.
Massachusetts (MA) Bay State Old Colony	5,781,000 11 8,257 45	Boston* 562,994	Chick-a-dee Mayflower (ground laurel or trailing arbutus)	One side bears the state coat of arms on a white field; the reverse has a white field in the center of which is a blue shield bearing a green pine tree.
Michigan (MI) Great Lake State Wolverine State	9,109,000 8 58,216 23	Lansing* 130,414 Detroit 1,203,339	Robin Apple blossom	The symbols of the state seal appear on a dark-blue field.
Minnesota (MN) North Star State Gopher State	4,133,000 21 84,068 12	St. Paul* 270,230 Minneapolis 370,951	Loon Pink and white lady's-slipper	The state seal is placed in the center of a blue field.
Mississippi (MS) Magnolia State	2,551,000 31 47,716 32	Jackson* 202,895	Mockingbird Magnolia	In the upper left-hand corner is a Union Jack with a ground of red and saltier of blue bearing thirteen white stars; the remainder of the flag is divided into three horizontal bars of equal width, the upper blue, the center white, and the lower red.
Missouri (MO) Show Me State	4,951,000 15 69,686 19	Jefferson City* 33,619 St. Louis 453,085	Bluebird Hawthorn	Three horizontal bands of equal width, the top one of red, the center one of white, and the bottom one of blue; in the middle is the state seal surrounded by a band of blue bearing twenty-four white stars.
Montana (MT) Treasure State	801,000 44 147,138 4	Helena* 23,938 Billings 66,798	Western meadowlark Bitterroot	The state seal is centered on a bright blue field; gold fringe borders two upper and lower edges.
Nebraska (NE) Cornhusker State	1,586,000 35 77,227 15	Lincoln* 171,932 Omaha 311,681	Western meadowlark Goldenrod	The state seal is gold and silver against a blue field.
Nevada (NV) Sagebrush State Battle Born State	881,000 43 110,540 7	Carson City* 32,022 Las Vegas 164,674	No official state bird; however, the mountain bluebird is used. No official flower; however, the sagebrush is sometimes used.	Two sprays of green sagebrush with stems crossed at the bottom to form a half-wreath in the upper left-hand corner of a field of cobalt blue; above, and completing the circle, is a yellow scroll bearing the words "Battle Born"; centered in the circle is a five-pointed star surrounded by the word "Nevada."

NAME OF STATE (ZIP CODE ABBREVIATION) NICKNAME	POPULATION RANK IN POP. AREA (SQ. MI.) RANK IN AREA	CAPITAL* LARGEST CITY	BIRD FLOWER	DESCRIPTION OF FLAG
New Hampshire (NH) Granite State	951,000 42 9,304 44	Concord* 30,400 Manchester 90,936	Purple finch Purple lilac	A blue field on which is centered the state seal surrounded by laurel leaves interspersed with nine stars.
New Jersey (NJ) Garden State	7,438,000 9 7,836 46	Trenton* 92,124 Newark 329,248	Eastern goldfinch Purple violet	The state seal is centered on a buff-colored field.
New Mexico (NM) Land of Enchantment	1,359,000 37 121,666 5	Santa Fe* 48,899 Albuquerque 331,767	Roadrunner Yucca flower	A field of gold with the ancient Zia Sun symbol in red in the center.
New York (NY) Empire State	17,659,000 2 49,576 30	Albany* 101,727 New York 7,071,030	Bluebird (unofficial) Rose	The state seal lies in the center of a dark-blue field.
North Carolina (NC) Tar Heel State Old North State	6,019,000 10 52,586 28	Raleigh* 149,771 Charlotte 314,447	Cardinal Dogwood	At the right are two horizontal stripes, one red and one white; on the left is a vertical blue stripe; at the top of the vertical stripe is a gold scroll inscribed with the date "May 20 1775" commemorating the Mecklenburg Declaration of Independence; at the bottom, in another golden scroll is the date "April 12th 1776," commemorating the Halifax Resolves, which instructed North Carolina's delegates to the Continental Congress to vote for independence; in the center, between these two scrolls, are the initials "N" and "C" separated by a white star.
North Dakota (ND) Sioux State Flickertail State	670,000 46 70,665 17	Bismarck* 44,485 Fargo 61,308	Western meadowlark Wild prairie rose	On a field of blue a bald eagle with widespread wings holds a group of arrows in its left claw and an olive branch in its right claw; in its beak is a scroll that reads "E Pluribus Unum"; beneath the eagle on a red scroll are the words, "North Dakota"; above the eagle is a double semicircle of stars representing the original thirteen states.
Ohio (OH) Buckeye State	10,791,000 6 41,222 35	Columbus* 564,871 Cleveland 573,822	Cardinal Scarlet carnation	A swallow-tailed pennant bearing three red and two white horizontal stripes; on the left is a blue union, on which seventeen stars are disposed about a white "O" centered on red.
Oklahoma (OK) Sooner State	3,177,000 25 69,919 18	Oklahoma City* 403,213	Scissor-tailed flycatcher Mistletoe	In the center of a blue field is the buckskin shield of an Osage Indiana warrior; the shield is decorated with six painted crosses; seven eagle feathers form a fringe at the bottom; a peace pipe crossed by an olive branch appears on the face of the shield.
Oregon (OR) Beaver State	2,649,000 30 96,981 10	Salem* 89,233 Portland 366,383	Western meadowlark Oregon grape	A navy blue field bearing the shield of the state seal in gold, supported by thirty-three gold stars and topped by the words "State of Oregon"; the reverse shows a gold beaver.
Pennsylvania (PA) Keystone State	11,865,000 4 45,333 33	Harrisburg* 53,264 Philadelphia 1,688,210	Ruffed grouse Mountain laurel	The state shield, with eagle and wreath, supported by two harnessed draft horses; streamers below the state motto; the field is dark blue.
Rhode Island (RI) Little Rhody Ocean State	958,000 41 1,214 50	Providence* 156,804	Rhode Island Red Violet (unofficial)	In the center of a white field is a gold anchor; beneath the anchor on a blue ribbon is the motto "Hope"; all this is surrounded by a circle of thirteen gold stars; the flag is edged with a yellow fringe.
South Carolina (SC) Palmetto State	3,203,000 24 31,055 40	Columbia* 99,296	Carolina wren Carolina jessamine	A field of blue with a white palmetto tree in the center and a white crescent in the upper corner near the staff.
South Dakota (SD) Coyote State Sunshine State	691,000 45 77,047 16	Pierre* 11,973 Sioux Falls 81,343	Ring-necked pheasant Pasqueflower	On a field of blue is a blazing sun surrounded by the words "South Dakota, The Sunshine State"; on the reverse is the state seal.
Tennessee (TN) Volunteer State	4,651,000 17 42,244 34	Nashville* 455,651 Memphis 646,356	Mockingbird Iris	In the center of a crimson field is a circle of blue with a rim of white; in the center of the circle are three white stars; on the edge are two vertical bars—one blue and one white.

NAME OF STATE (ZIP CODE ABBREVIATION) NICKNAME	POPULATION RANK IN POP. AREA (SQ. MI.) RANK IN AREA	CAPITAL* LARGEST CITY	BIRD FLOWER	DESCRIPTION OF FLAG
Texas (TX) Lone Star State	15,280,000 3 267,338 2	Austin* 345,496 Houston 1,594,086	Mockingbird Bluebonnet	A blue vertical stripe next to the staff and two horizontal stripes, the upper white and the lower red; a white star is in the center of the blue stripe.
Utah (UT) Beehive State	1,554,000 36 84,916 11	Salt Lake City* 163,033	Sea gull Sego lily	Within a gold circle in the center of a blue field is the state seal; the flag is fringed in gold.
Vermont (VT) Green Mountain State	516,000 48 9,609 43	Montpelier* 8,241 Burlington 37,712	Hermit thrush Red clover	The state coat of arms against a field of blue; the coat of arms contains a shield bearing a landscape scene with pine tree, cow, and sheaves of grain; a buck's head as the crest; a badge of crossed pine branches; and a red scroll bearing the state motto and the word "Vermont."
Virginia (VA) Old Dominion	5,491,000 13 40,817 36	Richmond* 219,214 Norfolk 266,979	Cardinal American dogwood	The state seal in the center of a deep blue field; a white fringe borders the edge farthest from the flagstaff.
Washington (WA) Evergreen State	4,245,000 20 68,192 20	Olympia* 27,447 Seattle 493,846	Willow goldfinch Rhododendron	A dark green field with the state seal in the center.
West Virginia (WV) Mountain State	1,948,000 34 24,181 41	Charleston* 63,963	Cardinal Rhododendron maximum (big laurel)	The state coat of arms (the central scene from the state seal) in a field of white bordered by a strip of blue; above the coat of arms is a ribbon bearing the words "State of West Virginia" and below is a wreath of rhododendron maximum.
Wisconsin (WI) Badger State	4,765,000 16 56,154 26	Madison* 170,616 Milwaukee 636,212	Robin Wood violet	The Wisconsin coat of arms is centered on a field of dark blue, the edges of which are trimmed with a knotted fringe of yellow silk.
Wyoming (WY) Equality State	502,000 49 97,914 9	Cheyenne* 47,283 Casper 51,016	Meadowlark Indian paintbrush	A white silhouetted buffalo in the center of the blue field with a border of white and an outer border of red; the state seal appears on the buffalo's side.
District of Columbia (DC)	631,000 67			

Statistics for Outlying United States' Areas

NAME OF OUTLYING AREA ZIP CODE ABBREVIATION	POPULATION	CAPITAL* LARGEST CITY	AREA (SQ. MI.)
American Samoa (AS)	32,297	Fagatogo* Island of Tutuila	76
Commonwealth of Puerto Rico (PR) (Estado Libre Asociado de Puerto Rico)	3,196,520	San Juan* 434,849	3,435
Guam (GU)	106,000	Agana* 4,180 Dededo 23,644	209
Johnston Atoll	300	None	1
Midway Islands	2,256	None	2
Northern Mariana Islands (CM)	16,758	None	181.9
Trust Territory of Pacific Islands (TT)	116,149	None	533
Virgin Islands (VI) (St John, St. Croix, St. Thomas)	96,569	Charlotte Amalie* on St. Thomas 11,671	133
Wake Island	300	None	3

Countries of the World

This section contains a brief history of each country of the world. Statistics will be found in the tables at the end of the section.

AFGHANISTAN

The history of Afghanistan is that of a succession of foreign conquests, by the Persians under Cyrus the Great in 516 B.C., and by Alexander the Great around 334 B.C. In the tenth century, the Turks, who brought Islamic culture with them, gained control. The Mongol hordes of Genghis Khan invaded and remained in power for two centuries. Later, another Mongol, Tamerlane, seized control.

In the seventeenth century, Afghans began a series of uprisings against foreign domination, and for centuries there was unrest in the country. An Anglo-Indian army invaded Afghanistan, precipitating the First Afghan War, lasting from 1838 to 1842, in which the Afghans were defeated. The British re-invaded the country in the Second Afghan War, in which the Afghans were again defeated. A new ruler stabilized the country, concluded treaties of demarcation with India and Russia, and curbed the power of tribal chiefs.

In 1919, while Britain was having difficulties with the liberation movement in India, Afghanistan seized the opportunity to declare war on England. Britain soon recognized Afghan independence. The country remained neutral in both world wars, and was admitted to the United Nations on November 19, 1946.

In December 1979 the U.S.S.R. invaded the country but found much guerrilla resistance. Fighting continued in 1984.

ALBANIA

Albania occupies the region that the classical Greeks called Illyria. The Greeks were never able to conquer all of Illyria, but the Romans succeeded in doing so in the second century A.D. In later centuries, their control was never firmly established. The region of present Albania fell under the control of successive invaders, including Byzantines, Bulgars, Normans, Venetians, Neapolitans, and finally the Turks. Turkish control lasted from 1479 until 1912.

Independence movements began in 1878 and ended in 1912 when, after the First Balkan War, Albania was established as a nation. After World War I, the country gradually became an Italian protectorate. A threat to partition Albania resulted in the establishment of a republic under Ahmed Zog, who proclaimed himself king in 1928. In 1939 Italy annexed Albania.

During World War II, Albania became the base for an Italian invasion of Greece. Communist-led guerrillas under Enver Hoxha freed Albania with Allied assistance. In 1946 the country was declared a People's Republic. Relations with Yugoslavia became strained and were broken in 1948.

Albania's relations with the Soviet Union deteriorated until they were broken completely in 1961. Albania was admitted to the United Nations on December 14, 1955. In 1971, the country renewed diplomatic ties with Greece and Yugoslavia.

ALGERIA

The coast of North Africa was first colonized in historic times by Phoenicians from the Mediterranean coast of Asia. Carthage, one of the Phoenician cities, controlled the entire coast until the city's destruction by Rome in 146 B.C. Romans called the region Numidia. Roman culture and economic activity progressed in Numidia until it became a wealthy cultural center of the Roman world. Invasions by Vandals and revolts by the native inhabitants (Berbers) brought an end to Roman rule in the fifth century.

The Arab conquest took place in A.D. 637, and successive waves of Arabs swept over Algeria until after the eleventh century. The Berbers gradually accepted Islam but retained their own customs and language. Spain occupied parts of the coast in the sixteenth century but a Turkish pirate named Horuk Barbarossa expelled the Spaniards. Thereafter, piracy developed along the "Barbary Coast," as the region was called after the sixteenth century. Turkish control of the region was carried out

Algeria—The Harbor, Algiers

by a series of officials known according to their rank as beylerbeys, pashas, aghas, and deys. In the seventeenth century, the city of Algiers became the chief center of piracy and the strongest state of the Barbary Coast.

Algiers began to defy even the Turkish (Ottoman) emperors in the eighteenth century and piracy thrived as never before. Early in the nineteenth century a United States fleet, and later a combined Dutch and British fleet, smashed the major strongholds along the Barbary Coast. In 1830 France invaded Algeria and took over complete control. The name Al-Jazair, the Arabic name, was changed to Algérie in French and after 1838 this became the general name for the region.

Throughout the nineteenth century movements for either independence or greater autonomy resulted in several revolts against the French. It was not until after World War II that a strong movement for independence or assimilation developed. Guerrilla warfare, initiated by an organization known as Front de Libération Nationale (FLN), eventually caused the fall of the Fourth French Republic. General Charles de Gaulle was called in to lead the Fifth Republic and to solve the Algerian crisis. He offered Algeria self-determination and a cease-fire agreement was signed in 1962.

In the meantime, many French settlers in Algeria revolted against France. The French Army in Algeria waged a heavy campaign against the rightist group among the settlers. On April 8, 1962, Algeria gained its independence, thus ending 132 years of French rule. It was admitted to the United Nations in October of the same year. Algeria's socialist government is trying to relieve the nation's deep poverty, but with only partial success.

ANDORRA

Andorra is a co-principality, and the official long form of the name is *Valls d'Andorra* ("Valleys of Andorra" in the Catalan language). The country dates from the time of Charlemagne. The counts of Foix of France and the Spanish Bishop of Urgel were the original inheritors of the principality. When Henry II of Navarre ascended the French throne, he was established along with the Bishop of Urgel as co-prince of Andorra. It has remained a co-principality to this day, except for a brief interlude of occupation by the French (1793–1806). The president of France is now co-prince with the Bishop of Urgel.

The people are mainly pastoral, but iron and lead are mined. Smuggling activities have long been associated with Andorra.

ANGOLA

The Portuguese colonized Angola in 1574. Luanda, the present capital, was founded in 1575. The Portuguese kept full possession of the huge region except for a brief occupation by the Dutch from 1641 to 1648.

Pro-independence forces have been active in Angola since World War II. In 1962 the United Nations General Assembly voted to condemn Portugal's "colonial war" against the people of Angola. In 1974 a revolution in Portugal resulted in that country's withdrawal from its African colonies. Angola was declared independent on November 11, 1975. The three main Angolan groups which had fought against the Portuguese could not agree to form a coalition government, and civil war broke out. Financial aid from Russia and about fifteen thousand Cuban troops helped the Popular Movement win most of the country in May 1977. Russian influence continued strong in 1984.

ARGENTINA

The name *Argentina* is derived from the Latin word for silver. The Spanish explorers referred to the region as *Plata*, or "silver," because they saw Indians using silver and assumed that there were rich mines in the region.

Juan Diaz de Solis was the first European to visit what is now Argentina. The first permanent settlement was made in 1553 at Santiago del Estero by colonists from Chile. Buenos Aires was founded in 1536, but was wiped out by the Indians and was reestablished in 1580.

The early settlements were ruled from Bolivia and Peru. It was not until 1776 that the huge region achieved the status of a viceroyalty in the Spanish Empire. In 1810, revolution broke out against Spanish authority. José de San Martín led the revolt that ended in independence in 1817. Soon after, San Martín collected an army and crossed the Andes to liberate Chile and Peru from Spanish rule.

The country got off to a bad start as a nation. Internal strife, combined with a series of dictatorial regimes, characterized Argentina until 1853. The War of the Triple Alliance occurred between 1856 and 1870. In this war Argentina, Brazil, and Uruguay joined to fight Paraguay.

In 1943, a pro-Axis government installed itself to prevent Argentina from joining the Allies in World War II. Colonel Juan D. Perón became president in 1946 and large-scale reforms were enacted. In 1955 Perón was overthrown by a military junta. He returned in 1973 to be elected president once again, but died 10 months later. His wife Isabel then became president. After several years of terrorism and kidnappings, the country came under the control of another military junta in 1976, when Mrs. Perón was ousted. The 1983 elections brought civilian control.

AUSTRALIA

Many Europeans believed in the existence of a great southern continent long before it was discovered. On old maps this supposed continent was named *Terra Australis Incognita* ("Unknown Southern Land").

In 1606, a Dutch navigator named Jansz sighted what is now Cape York Peninsula. Another Dutch navigator, Dirck Hartog, landed on the west coast in 1616. Dirck Hartog Island is named in his memory. In 1642 the explorer Abel Tasman discovered Tasmania (the Tasman Sea is also named for him) and New Zealand. None of the early explorers and navigators made any attempt to claim the land or even to ascertain how large it was. That was left for the greatest navigator in English history—Captain James Cook (1728–1779).

Captain Cook's first voyage (he made three to the South Pacific region) was made to observe the transit of the planet Venus from below the equator. From Tahiti (where he made the observation) he traveled westward, circled New Zealand,

Australia—Aerial view of Sydney

and then passed up the eastern coast of Australia, mapping it with remarkable precision. Cook took possession of the land for Britain. The first settlement was made in 1788 by Captain Arthur Phillip, at what is now Sydney. He landed a total of 1,030 men, of whom 736 were convicts. (Many were political prisoners with education and talent, whose offenses would today be considered misdemeanors only. All penal settlements were abolished by 1868.)

The interior grasslands beyond the great eastern mountain barrier were discovered in 1813. Settlements increased along the coasts and developed into colonies, some of which became states. The discovery of gold in 1851 made Australia famous in a short time. The population grew quickly and railroads began to open up the interior to farming. Wool and wheat were two of the commodities that helped to develop Australia. A flock of only 105 sheep in 1792 has grown to 150,000,000

The present Australian states were originally British colonies. New South Wales was founded in 1786; Tasmania in 1825; Western Australia in 1829; South Australia in 1834; Victoria in 1851; and Queensland in 1859.

On January 1, 1901, the above colonies were federated under the name Commonwealth of Australia, and the term *colony* was replaced by *state*. Northern Territory was established in 1911, the same year that the Australian Capital Territory was acquired from New South Wales. The capital was moved there in 1927. In recent times a number of dependencies were acquired. The most important of these is the Trust Territory of New Guinea which Australia first occupied in 1914. Australia was confirmed as trustee by the League of Nations in 1921 and by the United Nations in 1946. Australia became a member of the United Nations on November 1, 1945.

During World War II, Australia was threatened with invasion by the Japanese. However, the Japanese were turned back in the Solomon Islands engagements and in the famous naval battles of the Coral Sea. Japan is now Australia's most important trade partner.

AUSTRIA

The Austro-Hungarian monarchy had its origins in the eighth century under Charlemagne. After the Napoleonic Wars, the Congress of Vienna in 1815 left Austria as the dominant power on the continent. In 1919 after World War I, the monarchy was dissolved. There followed years of chaos. The Social Democrats introduced important economic reforms, which were checked by an army-supported dictatorship. After Adolf Hitler came to power in Germany, Austria was occupied by the Nazis and forcibly annexed to Germany in March 1938.

After World War II, the United States and Great Britain declared the Austrians a "liberated" people, although the country was occupied by foreign troops until 1955. Austria was admitted to the United Nations on December 14, 1955. The Socialist Party dominates Austria's government.

BAHAMA ISLANDS

The Bahama Islands, or Bahamas, are the site of Columbus' first landfall in the New World on October 12, 1492. The British have controlled the islands since the seventeenth century. At first they were merely the base for pirates; but under royal governors, appointed after 1717, the pirates were driven out. The islands became a crown colony in 1767, after many Loyalists from the Thirteen Colonies settled there. The slaves were emancipated in 1838.

In 1964, the Bahamas were granted autonomy. The population (mostly black) achieved independence on July 10, 1973, and the Commonwealth of the Bahamas was admitted to the United Nations on September 18, 1973. Banking and tourism are the major business activities.

BAHRAIN

Bahrain is one of the Persian Gulf states. It comprises several islands close to the mainland of Saudi Arabia. It is governed by an amir, whose ancestors concluded a treaty in 1882 giving the United Kingdom control over the nation's foreign affairs. On August 15, 1971, Bahrain declared its independence. On September 21, 1971, it became a member of the United Nations. Its first parliament convened in 1973.

Bahrain is one of the countries that declared an oil embargo against the United States and other nations in 1973–1974.

Austria—Ringstrasse with the Parliament, City Hall, and Votive Church, Vienna

BANGLADESH

Originally a part of British India, the territory of the present republic of Bangladesh became the eastern part of Pakistan in 1947, when the British withdrew from the subcontinent. East Pakistan was separated from West Pakistan by a thousand miles of Indian territory. Although both parts of Pakistan shared a common religion, Islam, East Pakistan, with the larger population and more advanced industry, resented the political control maintained by West Pakistan.

An independence movement, led by Sheikh Mujibur (Mujib) Rahman, culminated in a bloody revolution in December 1971. With the help of the Indian army, East Pakistan defeated the troops of West Pakistan.

The country declared its independence and adopted a parliamentary democracy on December 16, 1972, remaining part of the British Commonwealth, under the name of Bangladesh. It was admitted to the United Nations on September 17, 1974. In January 1975, Mujibur Rahman was made president of a one-party republic. He was executed during a coup on August 15, 1975. A new government came to power in 1977.

Other coups ensued, and in 1982 the Army took over and placed the country under martial law.

BARBADOS

The island of Barbados in the Caribbean Sea was occupied by the British in 1627. It remained a British crown colony for almost 340 years. In 1652, it elected its own assembly. In 1834, the slaves on Barbados were freed.

Barbados achieved autonomy in 1961, and its prime minister, Sir Grantley Adams, a black Barbadian, became prime minister of the short-lived West Indies Federation. On November 30, 1966, Barbados was made independent, and remained within the Commonwealth. The island was admitted to the United Nations on December 9, 1966.

In 1982, President Reagan became the first United States president to visit the island.

BELGIUM

The name of the country is derived from the Belgae, an ancient people who were conquered by the Romans under Julius Caesar in about 50 B.C. The present area of Belgium was a Roman province until overrun by the Germanic Franks in the fifth century A.D.

After the decline of Frankish rule under Charlemagne and his successors, the region became broken up into a series of duchies. Flanders arose as a power in the fourteenth century, united with Burgundy, and as a result of a series of princely marriages became part of the possessions of the House of Hapsburg. Charles of Hapsburg, a native of Ghent, inherited this entire region, known as the Netherlands (or Low Countries), as well as Spain and the Spanish possessions in America. In 1519 he also became Holy Roman Emperor. The

Bahamas—The Sheraton British Colonial Hotel, Nassau

present Belgium, then the southern Netherlands, was then the most prosperous part of Europe. His son, Philip II of Spain, ruled the Netherlands as a Spanish dependency. In 1568, the Netherlands revolted and in 1579 the northern provinces became the Dutch Republic.

The southern provinces remained in Hapsburg control, first ruled by Spain, after 1713 by the Austrian branch of the family. In the French revolutionary and Napoleonic periods, the Austrian Netherlands were annexed by France. From 1815 to 1830 this region was reunited with the provinces to the north as the Kingdom of the Netherlands. The southern provinces, which differed in language, religion, and culture from those in the north, revolted in 1830 and declared their independence. Prince Leopold of Saxe-Coburg became the king of the new Kingdom of Belgium.

Belgium's neutrality was guaranteed by neighboring powers. Despite this, the German armies overran Belgium during World War I. Again, during World War II, Belgium fell under German occupation.

After the war, Belgium became part of an economic union with the Netherlands and Luxembourg called Benelux. Two languages, Flemish and French, are spoken in Belgium, and the country is divided into two linguistic zones.

BELIZE

Formerly known as British Honduras, this British colony in Central America was settled by Jamaicans in the seventeenth century and was made a dependency of Jamaica in 1862. By 1884 it had become a separate colony.

British Honduras was given self-government in 1964. As an indication of its intention to seek independence, the local government changed the name of the colony to Belize, which is also the name of its largest city and former capital. Belmopan is now the capital.

Guatemala, which borders Belize to the west, has long claimed the region. The claim is based on the fact that the region was part of the Spanish captaincy-general of Guatemala when the Central American nations became independent. The inhabitants of British Honduras rejected a proposal made in 1968 by a mediator that they enter into a close relationship with Guatemala. Great Britain sent troops to Belize in 1977 to help keep peace with Guatemala.

The country achieved independence September 21, 1981.

BENIN

Formerly called Dahomey, this West African country is made up of several small native kingdoms, and its boundaries were formed through the political conflicts attending French and English territorial rivalry. However, the Portuguese were the first Europeans to explore and establish trading posts in what is now Benin. They founded Porto-Novo, the present capital. The French gradually pushed the English aside in the region, and the present boundaries took shape at the end of the nineteenth century. The area became a colony and part of the loose federation of French West Africa in 1904. In 1946 it became an overseas territory of France.

On December 4, 1958, Dahomey established its National Constituent Assembly and proclaimed the Republic of Dahomey as a member of the French Community. It became independent on August 1, 1960. It was admitted to the United Nations on September 20, 1960. The country withdrew from the French Community by agreement with France on April 24, 1961. On December 1, 1975, Dahomey changed its name to Benin.

BERMUDA

Bermuda was named for Juan de Bermúdez, who discovered the islands in 1500. Colonization began with the shipwrecked survivors of the *Sea Venture* in 1609. Until 1684 Bermuda was a part of the Virginia Company's grants. Hamilton became the capital in 1815. The United States built air and naval bases there during World War II.

Bermuda is a British dependency with semirepresentative government. Its parliament, established in 1620, is the oldest British parliament outside Britain.

BHUTAN

Little is known of Bhutan before the conquest of the region by a Tibetan warlord in the sixteenth century. With Tibet, Bhutan fell under Chinese control in the eighteenth century. The British sought trade privileges in Bhutan, and by 1910 they were able to win control over Bhutan's foreign policy in return for a subsidy. India succeeded Britain in 1947 as protector of Bhutan.

Bhutan became a hereditary monarchy in 1907. The present constitutional monarchy was instituted in 1967. Bhutan was admitted to the United Nations on September 21, 1971.

BOLIVIA

Bolivia was the site of two Indian civilizations of a high level in pre-Columbian times. The first was that of the Tiahuanaco people that arose on the shores of Lake Titicaca in about A.D. 600 and lasted until A.D. 900. These people were noted for their great stone buildings, statues, and elaborate art work in pottery. The second civilization was that of the Quechua Inca Empire that spread down into Bolivia from the north. The empire developed in about A.D. 1200. Under the leaders Pachacuti and his son Topa (1471–1493) the empire expanded to include the present Ecuador, Peru, Bolivia, and part of Chile, plus other areas.

The Incas were noted for great works in stone set without mortar, and so precisely set that the blade of a knife cannot be inserted between stones. They also farmed by irrigation, built great highways with retaining walls, fabricated colorful costumes and had an elaborate government, religion, and social life. The Inca Empire was split and weakened before the coming of the Spanish. It is possible that Pizarro, the Spanish conquistador, would not have been able to conquer the empire, had not a civil war been in progress when he came in 1532.

In 1539, the town of La Plata (later changed to Sucre) was founded and became the capital of Alto Peru, the early name of the region that is now Bolivia. In 1559, it became a vice-royalty of Spanish Peru. The Indians rebelled several times in later centuries but were crushed. Spain held on to Alto Peru until 1824, when Antonio Jose de Sucre, one of Simón Bolivar's generals, marched in and captured the region. In 1825 Bolivia declared its independence and took its name from the great South American liberator, Simón Bolivar.

A war with Chile, called the War of the Pacific, broke out over nitrate deposits, and because Bolivia was seeking an outlet to the Pacific Ocean. Bolivia was aided by Peru, but Chile defeated both and seized the province of Atatcama and part of southern Peru. Ever since, Bolivia has remained a landlocked nation. In a war with Paraguay (1932–1938), Bolivia lost additional territory.

Bolivia became a member of the United Nations on November 14, 1945. In 1967 Bolivian soldiers captured and executed Che Guevara, a naturalized Cuban Communist and guerrilla leader.

After a series of coups and revolts, a military regime took control of Bolivia in 1974 and banned all civilians from public office. The military officers resigned in October 1982, allowing a congress elected by the people to take over and elect a president.

BOTSWANA

Formerly known as Bechuanaland, this country wedged between Rhodesia and South Africa was made a British protectorate in 1885 at the request of its Bantu inhabitants, who feared the advance of the Boers from the Transvaal. In 1895, its southern part was annexed to Cape Colony (now part of South Africa), but the larger northern part of Bechuanaland remained a protectorate.

On September 30, 1966, the protectorate became the independent republic of Botswana, part of the Commonwealth. It remained economically dependent, however, on South Africa. Botswana has a one-chamber assembly, which is also advised by a council of chiefs of the principal tribes.

BRAZIL

The first European to visit Brazil was the Spanish navigator Vincent Yañez Pinzón, who landed near Recife in January 1500. By the terms of the Treaty of Tordesillas, Brazil was granted to Portugal, and Pedro Alvarez Cabral formally claimed the land for Portugal on Easter Sunday, 1500. Cargoes of dyewood called *pau brasil* had been obtained along the coast by early navigators. The name Brazil was derived from the name of this wood, although Cabral had named the region Terra de Vera Cruz.

The first settlement was made in 1532 at São Vicente. A French colony was established at Rio de Janeiro in 1555. It was abolished in 1567 with the founding of the present city of Rio de Janeiro by the Portuguese on the same spot. From 1578 to 1640, Brazil was under Spanish rule. Dutch settlements were expelled in 1654. The discovery of gold in 1693, and of diamonds in 1729, brought fresh waves of immigrants.

In 1808, the royal family of Portugal was driven out by Napoleon; they took refuge in Brazil. Dor

João VI opened Brazil to foreign commerce and removed other restrictions, which helped bring about greater prosperity and economic activity. Dom João returned to Portugal in 1821, but left his son to rule. The prince opposed his father and declared himself Dom Pedro I, Emperor of Brazil. Thereafter, Brazil's history is separate from that of Portugal.

The new empire plunged deep into internal troubles soon after independence. In 1831 Dom Pedro abdicated in favor of his son Dom Pedro II, who was not crowned until 1840 because of his youth. His reign lasted until he was desposed in 1889. The nation was then organized into the United States of Brazil with a constitution modeled after that of the United States of America.

The early years of the republic were marked by repeated revolts. However the nation adjusted nearly all its boundaries with neighboring states between 1900 and 1928. The disputed boundaries had resulted in major wars with Argentina in 1852, and with Paraguay in 1856–1870.

Brazil joined the Allies in World War I and again in World War II. In the latter war, Brazilian troops fought in Europe. The long regime of Getulio Vargas (1937–1945) improved Brazil's economic situation somewhat, but the loss of her rubber monopoly and the overproduction of coffee after World War II left Brazil with serious internal weaknesses.

Two ambitious projects were undertaken after the war. One was the building of the new capital city, Brasília, which was begun in 1957. Three years later it was officially designated the capital, and by 1975 it had a population of more than half a million. The other project was the construction of the Trans-Amazon Highway from the Atlantic Ocean to the border of Peru, a distance of more than 3,000 miles. It was complete in 1974. Meanwhile, the phenomenal growth of the city of São Paulo occurred without plan. It is now the largest city in South America.

Brazil became a member of the United Nations on October 24, 1945.

In recent years, the country has been beset by economic troubles. In the early '80s it had huge oil debts and 95 percent inflation.

BRITISH ANTARCTIC TERRITORY

The British Antarctic Territory is a crown colony, formed in 1962 from parts of the Falkland Islands and dependencies. It comprises all British-administered, claimed, or held territories south of latitude 60° South. The chief units of the colony are South Shetland Islands (1,800 square miles) and Antarctic Peninsula.

The Falklands remain a British dependency, although Argentina, which calls them *Islas Malvinas,* claims them also. When Argentina invaded them April 2, 1982, Britain sent a task force to the area and forced an Argentine surrender.

BRITISH INDIAN OCEAN TERRITORY

A group of islands in the Indian Ocean that were formerly dependencies of Seychelles Or Mauritius were formed in 1965 into a separate British colony. They included the Chagos Archipelago and the islands of Aldabra, Farquhar, and Desroches.

Brazil—Palácio da Alvorada, Brasília

In 1973, one of the Chagos group, Diego Garcia was turned over to the United States, which two years later began building a naval base there.

BRUNEI

Brunei was once (sixteenth century) a powerful state that controlled all of the large islands of Borneo, plus parts of the Sulu and Philippine islands. But today, Brunei consists of two small enclaves on the north coast of Borneo in southeast Asia. Brunei is surrounded by the Sarawak section of the Federation of Malaysia.

The government is supported mainly by revenues from oil wells in the state. Oil production, though very large, has passed its peak. The island of Labuan lies just off the coast of Brunei but is not now a part of it. Brunei became self governing in 1971 and achieved independence January 1, 1984, becoming the world's newest nation.

BULGARIA

The Bulgars were a tribe who migrated from central Asia in A.D. 679. They mixed with the Slavic peoples already there to form the modern Bulgarians. The Bulgars founded an empire in the seventh century, but declined under pressure from the Byzantine Empire. A second empire grew up under Semeon II (893–927), but was conquered again by the Byzantines.

Bulgaria was conquered by the Turks in 1396. In 1876 the Bulgarians revolted, and with the aid of Russia, gained their independence. The Kingdom of Bulgaria that was established included all of the present Bulgaria plus Macedonia and most of what is now European Turkey. In 1885, the region of Rumelia was added.

The Bulgarian struggle to get or to keep a coastline on the Aegean Sea (and hence on the Mediterranean Sea) involved the country in the Balkan Wars, World War I, and World War II. The nation allied itself with Nazi Germany in World War II and withdrew too late to prevent a Russian invasion and an eventual Communist-backed revolution that destroyed the monarchy (1944–1946).

The country is now known as the People's Republic of Bulgaria. It was admitted to the United Nations on December 14, 1955. It is a close ally of the Soviet Union.

BURMA

Burma first became a united country in 1044 when Anawrahta founded a kingdom that was to last for two hundred years. Five hundred years of disunity followed, ending in 1754, when Alaungpaya established another kingdom over nearly all of the present Burma. British conquest began in 1824 and was completed with the annexation of Burma to the empire in 1886.

Burma gradually regained self-government, starting with a legislative council in 1897. Further steps toward political independence were taken in 1937. The long fight for independence ended in 1948 when the Union of Burma became a reality under the leadership of U Nu. In 1962, a socialist revolution deposed U Nu and General Ne Win became the head of a new government, proclaimed as the Socialist Republic of the Union of Burma in 1974. At that time Burma left the Commonwealth.

Burma was the scene of heavy fighting during World War II. The famous Burma Road led across great mountains from Lashio in Burma to southern China, and was used by the Allied armies to supply Chinese resistance forces in the war with Japan. Burma was admitted to the United Nations on April 19, 1948.

BURUNDI

The Watutsi, or Tutsi, people came to the area of the present Burundi in the fifteenth century. They gradually subjugated the Bahutu, or Hutu peoples. This was the situation when Germany, during the nineteenth century, established a zone of influence in the region.

After World War I, the League of Nations mandated the portion of German East Africa known as Ruanda-Urundi to Belgium. It was attached, for administrative purposes, to the Belgian Congo (now Zaire), but the ancient indigenous monarchies of Ruanda and Urundi were maintained.

Ruanda-Urundi became a Belgian trust territory under United Nations auspices after World War II. In 1960 separate elections were held in each of the kingdoms, and two years later they became independent as the republic of Rwanda and the kingdom of Burundi, refusing to reunite.

Both were admitted to the United Nations on September 18, 1962. In 1966 the premier of Burundi declared that country a republic and he became its president. Burundi has no constitution.

CAMBODIA

For almost a thousand years, from the sixth to the fifteenth century, the strongest power in southeastern Asia was the Khmer Empire. The magnificent ruins of Angkor are the remains of monuments that were constructed between the ninth and thirteenth centuries, at the height of that empire. It succumbed to attacks from the Thais, one of its vassal peoples, from the Annamese, and from the Mongols. After several centuries, the remnants of the Khmer Empire, the present Cambodia, became a French protectorate in 1863.

France ruled Cambodia, while maintaining its royal house in nominal authority, until after World War II. The nationalist movement that emerged under the Japanese occupation rode on the coattails of the more aggressive movement in adjoining Vietnam (Annam and Tonkin), and Cambodia was given its independence in 1949 as an "associated state of the French Union."

The Vietnamese nationalists, under the leadership of Ho Chi Minh, attempted to involve Cambodia in total repudiation of French rule, especially after the Vietnamese defeat of the French at Dien Bien Phu in 1954. The anticommunist Southeast Asia Treaty Organization, on the other hand, unilaterally guaranteed Cambodian independence.

King Norodom Sihanouk abdicated his throne in March, 1955, was elected premier in September, and withdrew Cambodia from the French Union. On December 14, 1955, Cambodia was admitted to the United Nations.

As head of state, Prince Norodom Sihanouk steered his country on a neutralist course to avoid being involved in the armed struggle under way in Vietnam.

In 1970, a pro-Western coup by Lon Nol deposed the prince, and the United States and South Vietnamese forces bombed and sent troops into Cambodia to drive out the North Vietnamese forces that were based there.

A civil war developed between the Lon Nol Government and insurgents known as the Khmer Rouge. In April 1975, Lon Nol fled from Cambodia and the Khmer Rouge forces took over the country and immediately named Norodom Sihanouk chief of state for life, although his authority was entirely honorary. He resigned in 1976.

The Khmer Rouge government kept the nation's activities a secret, but refugees said that hundreds of thousands were killed in a post-war purge. The communist regime renamed the nation "Democratic Kampuchea," but the traditional name of Cambodia is still commonly used.

In January 1979, communist troops from Vietnam seized control of the country. China protested this action, because the Soviet Union had supported the new take-over, and the Chinese feared that the Soviets would use Cambodia as a base of operations against them.

Clashes between Vietnamese and anti-Communist forces continued in 1983.

CAMEROON

The Cameroon region was visited late in the fifteenth century by the Portuguese. Trading posts were established there in the seventeenth century. From 1888 to 1914, Germany occupied Cameroons. The territory was invaded by French and British troops during World War I.

After the defeat of Germany, the region was divided into a western Cameroons under British control and a larger eastern Cameroons under French control.

The portion assigned to France obtained internal autonomy in 1959 and complete independence in 1960. The part under British control consisted of two parts. The northern part decided by plebiscite in February 1961 to join the Federation of Nigeria. At the same time a plebiscite was held in the southern part and as a result that section united with the former French area, all of which became the Federal Republic of Cameroon in 1961. In 1972 a unitary state was instituted. The republic was admitted to the United Nations on September 20, 1960.

CANADA

Both France and Great Britain based their claims to Canadian territory on the landings of explorers: that of John Cabot on Cape Breton Island for England in 1497; and that of Jacques Cartier on the Gaspé coast of Quebec for France in 1534. But neither the British nor the French tried to take permanent physical possession of any part of the territory before the seventeenth century.

The French explorer Samuel de Champlain tried unsuccessfully to establish a station in the vicinity of the Bay of Fundy in 1604 and 1605. In 1608 he was able to locate the first permanent post at

Canada—Parliament Buildings, Ottawa

Quebec. In 1610, Henry Hudson sailed into the bay named after him, still seeking a water route to Asia. On the basis of Hudson's voyage, Charles II of England granted the entire northeastern wilderness to a private trading corporation, the Hudson's Bay Company.

The French government chartered private trading companies to exploit New France for more than a half-century. Their settlements were persistently harassed by the English. A post set up by Champlain at Port Royal was destroyed by a Virginia raiding party in 1613 and twice thereafter; eventually it became British in 1713 as Annapolis Royal in Nova Scotia. Quebec was subject to a series of similar raids.

Louis XIV declared New France—the combined settlements of Acadia in the Bay of Fundy area and Canada in the St. Lawrence valley—to be a Crown colony in 1663. He appointed a governor to act as chief of state. For a century New France developed under this regime, although in the early stages of the French and Indian Wars much of Acadia was lost to the British.

The colonial wars in North America ended in 1763 with the total cession of New France to Great Britain.

But in 1774, the former New France was reorganized as an extended province called Quebec. Parliament hoped that the Quebec Act would preserve the overwhelmingly French character of the recently conquered territory, lest the French colonists find common cause with disaffected settlers

William Lyon Mackenzie.

to the south. The statute only further outraged the English-speaking colonists.

The decade following the Quebec Act was critical. English-speaking refugees from the rebellious lower colonies began to populate widely separated areas of Nova Scotia and Quebec, laying the foundation for the emerging provinces of New Brunswick, Prince Edward Island, and Upper Canada (Ontario).

In the next generation some of the ideas associated with Jacksonian democracy in the United States began to penetrate the Canadian border. Such influences inspired the uprisings of 1837, led by Louis Papineau in Lower Canada and by William Lyon Mackenzie in Upper Canada.

The Earl of Durham was sent to British North America to study the situation. He recommended the adoption of representative government for the two Canadas. Since many of the colonists were moving West, he also urged that the two provinces be reunited to guarantee a minimum French im-

pact once the democratic regime was instituted. In 1840 Parliament created the province of Canada (in which two districts, Canada West and Canada East, were recognized). But only after Nova Scotia was granted representative government in 1848 was the same privilege extended to Canada.

The British Parliament was apprehensive of the increasing power of the United States in the second half of the nineteenth century. The British government was able to resolve several border disputes: In 1818 the forty-ninth parallel became the line of demarcation from the Lake of the Woods to the Rocky Mountains; a controversial border between Maine and New Brunswick was peaceably settled in 1842; and in 1846 the dangerous Oregon question was resolved when the forty-ninth parallel was extended almost to the Pacific Ocean. But some leaders in the United States pressed for more acquisition of British American territory. Parliament feared that British recognition of the Southern Confederacy during the American Civil War

Louis Joseph Papineau.

might serve as a pretext, following Union victory, for hostile movements across the border, and so Parliament encouraged the provinces to consolidate their powers. This was the reasoning behind Parliament's British North America Act of 1867. The Dominion of Canada was created by this act. It was a confederation of British colonies under the authority of the British Parliament. Its original members were two of the Atlantic provinces, Nova Scotia and New Brunswick, and the two sections of the province of Canada—Ontario and Quebec. The act provided for the eventual admission of all British North America.

The Hudson's Bay Company returned its holdings to Great Britain, which immediately ceded them to the Dominion of Canada. They became the Northwest Territories in 1870. The only settled district within the Territories was organized within the year as the fifth province of Canada, under the name of Manitoba. In 1871 the colony of British Columbia agreed to join the Dominion as a sixth province if a railway would be constructed to link it with the eastern provinces. Prince Edward Island became the seventh province in 1873.

The last years of the nineteenth century brought a spectacular westward shift in Canada's population. In 1898, Yukon Territory was detached from the Northwest Territories adjoining Alaska. By 1905 settled sections of the Territories between Manitoba and British Columbia were organized into the new provinces of Saskatchewan and Alberta. Except for Newfoundland (which became part of Canada in 1949), the Dominion attained its ultimate territorial extent and virtually its final political organization by 1905.

Government. The trend in Great Britain was to relax its tight control over its possessions and to encourage them to run their own affairs. The power of the Crown was vested in an appointed governor-general and in appointed lieutenant-governors of each province. Most law-making powers were assigned to a Senate, whose members were appointed for life. (Those appointed after 1965 must retire at the age of 75.) The Canadian House of Commons was, like that of the United Kingdom, elective and based on population. While the provinces have their own constitutions, which they alone may amend, they have authority only over their internal affairs to the degree authorized under the constitution. This document, the British North America Act, specifies the powers granted to the provinces. Powers not so enumerated are to be exercised by the federal government. (This is the reverse of the system in the United States, where the specified authority of the federal government is defined and residual powers are granted to the states.)

Although not quite a nation, the Dominion was admitted to the League of Nations and independently participated in foreign affairs. Great Britain called an imperial conference in 1926, at which it declared that the dominions were autonomous and equal members of a Commonwealth of Nations, headed by a single sovereign. This concept was formalized by the British Parliament in 1931 as the Statute of Westminster. Under this statute Canada formally attained sovereignty and nationhood.

Perhaps the most significant subsequent constitutional development was the ruling in 1949 that Canadian citizens could no longer appeal the decisions of the Supreme Court of Canada to the British Privy Council. In the same year the British Parliament passed the second British North America Act, which made it clear that amendments to the first British North America Act could not be made without the participation of the Canadian Parliament.

Canada's international role has been distinctive. Its national policy is independent of the United States, despite strong economic pressures. In its internal policies, however, Canada suffers from chronic controversy concerning the balance between federal and provincial authority. A cohesive and articulate French minority comprises a majority within the province of Quebec. The French nationalist movement is itself divided into factions, one of which agitates for separation and sovereignty. The use of the French language has parity throughout Canada and supersedes the English language within the province of Quebec.

Economy. Canada proved to be a late bloomer. The first years of the twentieth century saw the anticipated development of agriculture, mining, and industry. The United States had already peopled its West, and the Canadian prairies received the overflow—not only from the states, but from every part of Europe and even from the Orient. At first Canadians feared direct economic encroachment from the United States, and a policy of trade protectionism was adopted. But capital investment from the United States has become sufficiently dominant to appear as a possible menace to many Canadians.

Cape Verde Islands—Cape Verdeans display portraits of two leaders of their country.

CAPE VERDE ISLANDS

An archipelago about 375 to 525 miles west of Senegal in Africa was discovered by the Portuguese sailor Diogo Gomes in 1460. Two years later Portuguese settlers and their African slaves populated the uninhabited islands. They were transferred to the Portuguese crown in 1495 and a century later the first governor was appointed.

In modern times the Cape Verde Islands were made an overseas province of Portugal. The leaders of the independence movement in Portuguese Guinea (now Guinea-Bissau) were mostly from Cape Verde. When the Portuguese withdrew from their African colonies, both the mainland and the islands became independent. Cape Verde became a republic on July 5, 1975. On September 16, 1975, the country was admitted to the United Nations.

CAYMAN ISLANDS

These coral islands in the Caribbean Sea south of Cuba were discovered by Columbus in 1503 and were colonized from nearby Jamaica.

Until 1959, the Caymans were administered as a dependency of Jamaica. In 1962, they were given self-government as a separate colony with a partly elected legislature. The free port of Georgetown is used as a tax haven for foreign corporations and individuals.

CENTRAL AFRICAN EMPIRE

During the last decade of the nineteenth century, the French explored what is now the Central African Empire. In 1894, the Territory of Ubangi-Shari was established, and was merged in 1905 with Chad to form Ubangi-Shari-Chad. In 1910, Gabon and Middle Congo were added to this group to form French Equatorial Africa.

That loose federation came to an end when the constituent states chose to become autonomous states within the French Community of Nations in 1958. On December 1, 1958, the Ubangi-Shari section became the Central African Republic and was proclaimed an independent nation two years later. It was admitted to the United Nations on September 20, 1960. In 1976 President Jean-Bedel Bokassa changed the country's name to Central African Empire and declared himself its first emperor.

The Central African Empire exports diamonds, uranium, textiles, and other goods. It has not been able to develop many of its natural resources because it is cut off from the major trade routes.

CHAD

Arabs visited this general area in Africa many centuries ago, but it was not explored until late in the nineteenth century. Various African tribes inhabited the region, alternately warring and living in some sort of peace. Slave traders scoured the territory for their exports of human beings to Egypt and the Near East, while other traders sought ostrich feathers and ivory.

The French helped put an end to the slave trade in the Chad area, and by 1910 it had become part of French Equatorial Africa. In 1920 it was given separate administration and it became an autonomous member of the French Community in 1958. It declared its independence on August 11, 1960, and was admitted to the United Nations on September 20, 1960.

Chad suffered from conflicts between the Moslem, pro-Arab, and conservative population of the north and the black, more progressive population of the south. Years of scanty rainfall have also been destructive.

Chad has consistently tried to africanize its proper names. President François Tombalbaye change his first name to Ngarta. The capital, Fort Lamy, was renamed N'Djamema. After fifteen years in the presidency Tombalbaye was killed in a military coup in 1975.

Libya took advantage of the confusion in Chad's government to annex 37,000 square miles of territory in northern Chad in 1976. Libyan troops were withdrawn in November 1981.

CHANNEL ISLANDS

William the Conqueror, of Normandy, who invaded England in A.D. 1066 and became king of England, was already ruler of the Channel Islands. They have remained a territory of the English Crown ever since.

CHILE

In 1520, during his epic voyage around the earth, Ferdinand Magellan landed on an island near a region of South America called "Tchili" by the natives of the area. This was the first visit by Europeans to what is now called Chile. In 1535, Diego de Almagro was sent to explore the land to the south of Peru. He was not successful in the venture, but five years later Pedro Valdivia annexed the present-day Chile down to the Maipú River, near where Santiago, the capital of Chile, now stands. The chief obstacles to Spanish conquest were the fierce Araucanian Indians, who continued to resist long after Chile had become an independent nation.

In 1810, Chile declared its independence, and the war that followed with Spain was fought by Chileans under the leadership of Bernard O'Higgins and José de San Martin. The Spanish were finally driven from the country in 1818.

Chile passed through a turbulent and unstable period after independence. By 1837 the nation fought a bitter war that destroyed a Peruvian-Bolivian confederation against her. Again in 1879–1883, Chile fought the War of the Pacific against the combined armies of Peru and Bolivia, and won. In that war Bolivia lost its outlet to the sea to Chile (the Atacama region). Chile was admitted to the United Nations on October 24, 1945.

Among South American nations, Chile has a reputation for political stability. The accession by normal political processes of a Marxist president, Salvador Allende Gossens, in 1970 was unprecedented. However, the country was disunited. Foreign influence, including that of the United States, was brought to bear. In 1973, Allende was deposed by a military junta and murdered. The succeeding administration reversed Allende's policies.

The military continued control in 1983.

Chile—University of Concepcion

CHINA
(People's Republic of China)

The Chinese state has existed without interruption for over four thousand years. The Chinese were experiencing one of their periods of cultural and intellectual Golden Ages when Europe was still in the Stone Age. The original home of the Chinese people appears to have been in the valley of the Wei River in the present Shensi Province area. In about the twenty-eighth century B.C. a loose empire appeared under the Hsia dynasty. This was the first recorded state. Its successor, the Shang dynasty, left written records about the first important cultural development (1750–1122 B.C.).

The period of the Chou dynasty (1122–221 B.C.) was a great feudal period. About 770 B.C., the capital was moved from Sian to Loyang on the Yellow River. The period of the new state, called the Eastern Chou dynasty, was the time when the great philosophers Confucius and Lao-tzu lived. It was a classical age in literature and art.

From 221 to 206 B.C. one of the notable men in world history was the ruler of China. His name was Shih Huang-ti and his dynasty was known as Ch'in or Chin, from which the word *China* was derived. He was the Charlemagne of China. Although he was a "book-burner," he left the Great Wall as one of his legacies, and is the founder of modern China. The wall extends from Mongolia to the Yellow Sea, and remains as a colossal monument to Chinese ingenuity and imagination.

The Han dynasty (206 B.C.–A.D. 220) followed. The classics were restored, Buddhism was introduced, sculpturing as a fine art began, and paper was invented. The Han rulers expanded the Chinese Empire westward into the heart of Asia. They established contact with the Roman Empire in the west. The Han rulers began the system of civil service examinations that lasted to 1911.

The Grand Canal, another spectacular feat of Chinese workmanship, was begun under the Sui (A.D. 581–618) and T'ang (618–907) dynasties. The T'ang dynasty is usually considered the most splendid in Chinese history. Under Emperor Tai Tsung (627–649) China became powerful. A great system of roads was built from Sian, the capital. Handicrafts and arts flourished as never before. China reached its greatest area in 650. At that time it included all of today's China, plus southeast Asia and other areas. Printing was invented, the use of silk developed, and poetry and painting advanced. The invention of movable type, gunpowder, and the magnetic compass followed.

The Mongols crashed through the Great Wall in the thirteenth century, at the same time that they were invading western Europe. Genghis Khan established the Mongol dynasty and extended his rule as far south as the present Fukien province. Chinese civilization persisted, as was witnessed by Marco Polo who visited China during the short period of Mongol domination. During the reign of the Manchu emperors (1644–1911), the last dynasty, China declined rapidly. In the nineteenth century, rebellion weakened the ruling Manchus (Ming dynasty) and foreign interference developed. The Portuguese had reached China in 1516, the Spanish in 1557, the Dutch in 1606, and the English in 1637. Western governments supported the Manchus in the Taipeng Rebellion (1850–1864) in order to get access to Chinese commerce and trade privileges. The Boxer Rebellion (1900) was put down by foreign troops, including those of the United States. China suffered heavy losses and was further weakened in a war with Japan (1894–1895). The imperial government was finally overthrown in 1911.

Sun Yat-sen, the founder of the Republic of China (1912), lost control to a group of military chiefs or warlords. Chiang Kai-shek gained control and was for a time allied with the Communists. A split developed in 1927 between Chiang Kai-shek and the Communists. Japan, taking advantage of disunity, occupied Manchuria in 1931. The Sino-Japanese War began in 1937 and merged into World War II. During the war, American aid reached China mainly over the Burma Road and by air. By 1945 the Japanese were completely expelled. The Communist forces had been attacked by Chiang Kai-shek in 1936, and had transferred their center of power to Shensi in northern China, by means of a great land journey known as the "Long March." Their strength had been greatly reduced, but by the end of World War II, the Communist movement was again threatening Chiang Kai-shek.

Although supported by the United States, Chiang Kai-shek steadily lost ground in the civil war that erupted after World War II. By 1949 the Nationalist forces had been expelled from the mainland, and took refuge on Taiwan (Formosa).

The People's Republic of China was proclaimed in 1949 by the Communists under Mao Tse-tung. In 1950 China retrieved Tibet, which had broken away in the fall of the Manchu dynasty. For many years the Peking regime was denied membership in the United Nations, where China's seat was held by representatives of the government on Taiwan that called itself the Republic of China. In 1971 the United Nations voted to expel the dele-

U.S. President Richard M. Nixon is greeted on Feb. 21, 1972 by Chairman Mao Tse-tung of the Peoples Republic of China.

gates from Taiwan and to seat those of the People's Republic. The United States had long opposed this move, and continued to withhold full diplomatic recognition of the Peking regime. But the animosity was dissipated after President Richard Nixon visited Peking in 1972 and met with Chinese leaders Mao Tse-tung and Chou En-lai. In December 1978, President Jimmy Carter's administration announced plans to establish formal diplomatic ties with the People's Republic of China.

The Reagan administration has continued the good will policy toward both China and the Republic of China on Taiwan.

CHINA
(Republic of China)
See Taiwan

COLOMBIA

Columbus explored the northern coast of what is now Colombia in 1502 on his last voyage to the New World. The city of Bogotá, deep in the interior, was founded in 1538. Shortly after this, the region began to be called New Granada. It included the present Colombia, Panama, Ecuador, and Venezuela. The state was ranked as a viceroyalty within the Spanish American empire.

A war for independence was begun in 1810 and continued until 1819, when Bolivar and Santander won the Battle of Boyaca. From 1819 to 1830 Colombia was a part of Bolivar's Gran Colombia that included nearly the same area as did the old Spanish viceroyalty. By 1832, Ecuador and Venezuela had seceded from Gran Colombia. The remainder changed its name to Colombia and became a republic. During the turbulent nineteenth century in Colombia no less than ten different constitutions were promulgated.

In 1903, the country lost Panama to a United States-instigated revolt which established the Republic of Panama. The first seven decades of Colombia's twentieth-century history have been relatively more peaceful and accompanied by considerable economic and social progress. The nation has been experiencing severe economic and political difficulties in the past few years. Colombia became a member of the United Nations on November 5, 1945.

COMORO ISLANDS

The Comoro archipelago was acquired by France in 1886, although the island of Mayotte had been occupied since 1843. In 1912, the archipelago was declared a colony and attached to Madagascar (now the Malagasy Republic) for administration. Upon the latter's independence, the Comoro group became an overseas territory of France.

When the inhabitants voted for independence in 1974, France did nothing to impede their desire, although Mayotte had voted against independence. On July 6, 1975, the Comoro legislature declared their independence. On November 12, 1975, the country was admitted to the United Nations.

CONGO

A Portuguese navigator, Diego Cam, discovered the mouth of the Congo (Zaire) River in 1484. Thereafter, exploration was mainly done by French missionaries and slave-traders. In the nineteenth century Henry M. Stanley (in the service of Belgium) and Pierre Savorgnan de Brazza (in the service of France) opened up the country to European penetration and established claims to the region. The French claims to what is now the Republic of Congo were recognized at the Congress of Berlin in 1855. In 1903, the territory was organized into Moyen (Middle) Congo, and it became a part of French Equatorial Africa (a loose federation) in 1908. On September 28, 1958, Middle Congo became the Republic of Congo, an autonomous member of the French Community. It remained in the Community when it became an independent nation on August 15, 1960, as the Republic of Congo. It was admitted to the United Nations on September 20, 1960. In 1970, it changed its name to the People's Republic of the Congo.

This country should not be confused with Zaire, known from 1960 to 1971 as the Democratic Republic of Congo. During those years Zaire was called "Congo (Kinshasa)" to distinguish it from the country by the same name north of the Congo River, known as "Congo (Brazzaville)."

Communistic influence has been strong since 1963, and in 1981 a treaty of "friendship" was signed with the Soviets.

COSTA RICA

Costa Rica was discovered in 1502 by Christopher Columbus. It was conquered by the Spanish and made a royal province before the middle of the sixteenth century.

In 1821, Costa Rica declared its independence, but was annexed by Mexico. From 1823, when the Mexican Empire broke up, until 1839, Costa Rica was a member of a loose federation called the United Provinces of Central America.

The country became wholly independent in 1840, and proclaimed itself a republic in 1848. Many boundary disputes were settled, including one with Nicaragua and another with Panama.

Up to 1948, Costa Rica had enjoyed internal peace. In that year, a disputed presidential election resulted in new elections and a new constitution in 1949. Unrest continued to plague the country, and terrorist activity went on for several years. In 1954 Costa Rica charged Nicaragua with meddling in its internal affairs. The dispute ended in an agreement by both countries to curb terrorist activity. Costa Rica was admitted to the United Nations on November 2, 1945.

CUBA

The island of Cuba was discovered by Christopher Columbus on his first voyage in 1492. Santiago de Cuba was founded in 1514 by Diego Velásquez and was the capital until 1589. Cuba was the base for the historic expeditions of Cortés to Mexico and of De Soto to Florida. Havana was founded in 1519, captured by the British in 1762, and returned to Spanish control the following year.

Unsuccessful revolts occurred in 1868, in 1875, and in 1895. In the latter part of the nineteenth century the brilliant leader, José Marti, was mainly responsible for the development of national consciousness in Cuba.

The United States declared war against Spain after the sinking of the American battleship *Maine* in Havana harbor on February 15, 1898. The slogan, "Remember the Maine," aroused a patriotic sentiment in the United States for war against Spain. The land battles of ElCaney and San Juan Hill and the naval battle at Santiago resulted in Spain's loss of Cuba. By the terms of the Platt Amendment to the new Cuban constitution of 1901, Cuba became virtually a protectorate of the United States and was occupied by the United States Marines on three occasions. In 1934 the Platt Amendment was repealed but the United States kept its Guantanamo naval base.

A military dictatorship was inaugurated in Cuba in 1952 by Fulgencio Batista. In 1953, opposition to the Batista regime developed into a large-scale revolt. The leader of the rebel group was Fidel Castro, who operated mainly from fortified positions in the Sierra Maestra (mountains) in eastern Cuba. Several unsuccessful revolts were staged before 1958, when full civil war developed. Batista fled to exile in the Dominican Republic and Castro's rebels took over the government. At first Castro was on friendly terms with the United States, but in 1960 his government began seizing the properties of United States companies.

The United States severed diplomatic relations in 1960, and Cuba increasingly turned toward the Soviet Union for support and aid. In April 1961, a United States-sponsored invasion force landed on the Bay of Pigs at the south coast of Cuba, but was defeated in 72 hours with a loss of 1,200 prisoners. In October 1962, United States high-altitude photographs showed Soviet missiles in Cuba. The discovery nearly precipitated a war between the United States and the Soviet Union. After the United States threw up a naval blockade of Cuba, the Soviet Union withdrew the missiles and most of the troops.

Tension between the United States and the Soviet Union eased considerably, but Cuba-United States relations continued strained. Cuba has been a member of the United Nations since October 24, 1974.

Since 1975, Cuba, with considerable encouragement from the Soviets, has continually expanded its revolutionary operations in Africa and more recently in Latin America.

CYPRUS

Cyprus was famous in the ancient world for its rich copper deposits. The word *copper* is derived from the name *Cyprus*. The Egyptians occupied the island until 1450 B.C., and the Greeks came in 1400 B.C. Between 500 B.C. and A.D. 1562, Phoenicia, Egypt, Persia, Greece, Rome, the Byzantine Empire, Venice, and finally the Ottoman Empire (Turks) all held Cyprus.

The United Kingdom administered Cyprus after 1878, and in 1914 the British annexed the island. In modern times Greek Cypriots have often attempted to unite Cyprus with Greece. Although the Greeks form a majority of the population, a large Turkish minority always opposed such a move. Violence broke out in 1955 between the two groups. Civil war developed and ended only after an unexpected proposal for an independent Cyprus was suddenly accepted by the Greek Cypriots. On August 16, 1960, Cyprus became an independent republic. The country was admitted to the United Nations on September 20, 1960.

Tension between the Greek and Turkish populations of Cyprus continued to flare into open clashes, particularly in 1964. In 1974 an advocate of *enosis* (union with Greece) tried to seize control of the island. This was followed by a Turkish invasion. Finally the two groups reached a truce. The Turks maintained an enlarged sector in the northeast and refused to accept any alternative to a federal state. United Nations peace-keeping forces were sent to prevent further violence until an agreement among the Cypriots could be reached. However, the peace talks failed and fighting broke out again. The Turks enlarged the territory under their control, and on June 8, 1975, they voted to form a separate Turkish state.

Under Turkish control some 200,000 Greeks have been expelled and thousands of Turks have moved in from the Turkish mainland.

CZECHOSLOVAKIA

Czechs and Slovaks settled in the present region before the sixth century ended. The Slovaks were conquered by the Magyar people and for a thousand years had no independent existence. The Czechs, however, formed the Kingdom of Bohemia in the tenth century.

Bohemia had a golden age of cultural growth in the fourteenth century that lasted until 1620. Prague, its capital, became a great center of Latin learning. In 1526, Bohemia came under Hapsburg rule and the Czech population was subjected to German and Austrian influences. The revolt of 1618 ended disastrously at the Battle of White Hill (White Mountain) in 1620, which crushed Czech national aspirations until the mid-nineteenth century.

The breakup of the Austro-Hungarian Empire presaged a serious move for independence during World War I. A Czech state came into existence on October 28, 1918. Two days later the Slovak National Council indicated its desire to unite with the Czechs in a single state. The Republic of Czechoslovakia was declared on November 14, 1918.

Czechoslovakia became a victim of Nazi expansionist aims in 1938. The republic was dismembered and abolished in 1939. A German-sponsored Slovak state was not recognized by the Allies, who supported a government-in-exile led by Dr. Eduard Beneš in London. Czechoslovakia regained its territory in 1944, and all severed sections were eventually reunited, except for part of Ruthenia.

Czechoslovakia moved in two stages into a Communist form of government. In February 1948, Beneš had to accept Clement Gottwald, a Communist, as Prime Minister, after the Communists had taken over control of much of the machinery of government. In June 1948, President Beneš was forced to resign after an election in which the people were permitted to vote only for candidates on a slate approved by the Communists. Czechoslovakia became a member of the United Nations on October 24, 1945.

Alexander Dubček became the leader of Czechoslovakia's Party in early 1968 and announced new liberal policies for the nation. Russia and other Warsaw Pact nations invaded the country on August 20, 1968 to halt Dubček's reforms.

Despite the activity of intellectuals and liberals, Russia has continued to keep a tight rein on the country.

DENMARK

Recent excavations from Danish peat bogs have provided proof that man lived in the Jutland region of Denmark at least eleven thousand years ago.

In ancient times Jutland was colonized by Norway, which lies to the north across the Skagerrak (strait). People from Denmark invaded England in the ninth century after Christ, Harald "Bluetooth" united Denmark for the first time in the tenth century and his son Sweyn conquered England.

During these centuries the Danish Vikings took part in raids along the shores of Western Europe. During the reign of Canute the Great (1014–1035), England, Denmark, and Norway were united. During the next three centuries, Denmark continued to expand, and under the reign of Valdemar II (1202–1241) it became the leading power of northern Europe. In the reign of Margarethe (1387–1412), Denmark, Sweden, and Norway were united. This union was dissolved in 1532, but Norway remained a part of the Crown of Denmark until 1814.

Danes settled Greenland in 1721. Serfdom was abolished in 1788. In the mid-nineteenth century, Denmark lost territory on the south of the Jutland

Peninsula to Prussia. In 1918, the independence of Iceland was recognized. Germany attacked the kingdom on April 9, 1940, conquering it in a few hours. However, the conquest was costly to maintain because the Danes became expert saboteurs and the Danish fleet was scuttled by its own officers in the harbor of Copenhagen. The nation was liberated on May 5, 1945. Denmark became a member of the United Nations on October 24, 1945.

DJIBOUTI

This nation on the northeast coast of Africa was formerly French Somaliland. It was taken by France in the late nineteenth century. The country held a strategic location at the strait leading to the Suez Canal, and for many years it was Ethiopia's only link with the sea.

In 1967, the people voted to remain under French control, and the region became known as the Terri-

Denmark—Tivoli Gardens, Copenhagen

tory of the Afars (related to the Ethiopians) and the Issas (related to the Somalis). Immigrants from both countries kept pouring into the area and bitter fighting flared up between them. On June 27, 1977, the territory proclaimed its independence from France and adopted the name of Djibouti, the capital city. Both Ethiopia and Somalia still claim the area as their own.

DOMINICAN REPUBLIC

The island of Hispaniola, on which the present Dominican Republic is located, was discovered and named by Christopher Columbus during his first voyage in 1492. The city of Santo Domingo was founded by his brother, Bartholomew Columbus, in 1496. The island became a base for Spain's discovery and exploration of the New World. The Spanish lost Hispaniola to the French in 1697, but regained the eastern two-thirds of the island in 1809. The remainder of the island became the independent Haiti, now the Republic of Haiti.

A revolt by Dominicans in 1821 freed the country from the Spanish, but in 1822 Haiti occupied Santo Domingo (the name of the former Spanish-held area at that time). Haitians remained until expelled by another revolt in 1844, and the name was changed to the Dominican Republic. Independence was short-lived, however, because Spain regained the country in 1861. The Spanish withdrew in 1865.

The next half-century was one of corrupt rule, confusion, and dictatorship for Santo Domingo. In 1907, the United States undertook control of the country's finances; and in 1915, the U.S. Marines occupied the country. They remained until 1924. In 1930, Rafael Leonidas Trujillo Molina assumed power. He and members of his family maintained a tight control until he was assassinated in 1961. The Dominican Republic was admitted to the United Nations on October 24, 1945.

After Trujillo's assassination, Joaquin Balaguer resigned as president; and in 1962, the first real election in almost forty years returned Juan Bosch to the presidency. Bosch was deposed in a coup the next year, and civil turmoil continued. In 1965 the United States sent in Marines to protect American lives and property, and to prevent the possibility of a government of the Castro type. In the first election after the troops were withdrawn, Balaguer defeated Bosch, and was reelected in 1970 and 1974.

EAST GERMANY

For the history of Germany prior to the provisional partition in 1945, see West Germany (Federal Republic of Germany). The failure of the Allies to agree upon the future disposition of defeated Germany after World War II resulted in the formal division of Germany into an eastern and a western section. In June 1948, the Russians instituted a series of unilateral changes, including the use of a new currency in the eastern zone. They also blockaded Allied traffic into the western section of Berlin. That city was forced to rely upon airlifted supplies until the blockade was broken. Five months after the Federal Republic of Germany had been established in the western zone, the German Democratic Republic was organized by the Russians in the eastern zone on October 7, 1949.

The Democratic Republic was maintained largely under Soviet protection. It seemed that the unification of Germany was not imminent, and the two Germanies began to deal with one another. They finally signed their first treaty in May 1972. Both were admitted to the United Nations on the same day, September 18, 1973.

ECUADOR

The area of what is now Ecuador became a part of the great South American empire of the Inca Indians a few years before the voyages of Columbus to the New World.

The Spanish Conquistador Francisco Pizarro began the conquest of the Inca Empire in 1530. One of Pizarro's men founded Quito (the present capital of Ecuador) in 1534. Spanish colonial domination lasted until 1822. In that year the revolutionary generals Simón Bolívar and José San Martín met at Guayaquil, Ecuador, to decide on the future of the liberated regions of northern South America. The result of this meeting was the formation of Gran Colombia, which included the present states of Venezuela, Colombia, Panama, and Ecuador. This union collapsed in 1830 and Ecuador became an independent republic. Since 1830, the country has rarely been administered by a stable government. It was admitted to the United Nations on December 21, 1945.

EGYPT

The civilization of ancient Egypt arose in the lower valley of the Nile River over five thousand years ago. By 3200 B.C. the land of Egypt was unified by King Menes, who ruled as "King of Upper and Lower Egypt." The use of writing developed in Egypt at this time. From small beginnings a mighty empire and a high civilization arose, led mainly by priest-kings and kings who called themselves gods. Their civilization

Egypt—Sphinx and Pyramids

flourished for 2,500 years. The Egyptians built great cities, temples, pyramids, and statues; they opened sea and land routes of trade, and their armies commanded respect throughout the world.

In 1150 B.C., civilized peoples elsewhere discovered iron and how to use it. Egypt had no iron resources, and this contributed to the decline of its power. The history of ancient Egypt came to an end with the conquest by Alexander the Great in 332 B.C.

In 30 B.C., Roman legions entered Egypt. It became the chief source of grain in the Roman world. Byzantine (Eastern Roman Empire) rule began in A.D. 395 and lasted until the Arab conquest in A.D. 600. Egypt gradually developed into a Moslem nation with a strong Arabic culture. Arabic rule lasted to the sixteenth century and then gave way to a long period of Turkish (Ottoman Empire) rule.

In 1881, a revolution against the Turkish authorities resulted in French and British intercession. Egypt became a British protectorate in 1882. The protectorate ended in 1922, and Egypt became a self-governing kingdom in 1936. In 1951, an army junta overthrew the monarchy; and in 1956 Egypt nationalized the famous Suez Canal, over the objections of many foreign powers.

A short war between Egypt and Israel broke out in October 1956, in which the United Kingdom and France joined in attacking Egypt. It was ended when the United Nations interceded. In 1958, Egypt and Syria united to proclaim a United Arab Republic. In 1961, Syria withdrew from the union, but the name United Arab Republic was retained by Egypt as the nation's official title until 1971. Then the official designation of the country became Arab Republic of Egypt. Under one name or another, Egypt has been a member of the United Nations since it was first admitted on February 1, 1958.

Egypt sought with varying degrees of zeal to act as the spokesman of the Arab world, particularly in its relations with Israel. Hostility between Israel and Egypt developed into active warfare in June 1967. Israel emerged after six days of combat with total victory. Israel occupied Egypt's Sinai Peninsula and a truce continued until 1973. In October of that year, Egypt took the offensive, and forces of each country were able to cross the Suez Canal to establish beachheads on the other's territory. In the ensuing negotiations, Israel withdrew from the west bank of the canal and from a strip along its east bank, and Egypt reopened the canal for the first time in eight years.

El Salvador—The National Palace in the city of San Salvador

In the late '70s, Egypt's president, Anwar Sadat, emerged as a leading figure for world peace, with special attention to the Middle East. His efforts ended with his assassination October 6, 1981.

EL SALVADOR

The history of El Salvador began in 1524 with its conquest by the Spanish conquistador Pedro de Alvarado. San Salvador was founded in 1528 at its present location. Throughout the Spanish colonial period the area of the present republic formed two provinces of the captaincy-general of Guatemala.

Independence from Spain was achieved as a part of Guatemala in 1821. In 1824, the area became a part of the United Provinces of Central America, a federation of Central America that lasted until 1839. El Salvador became a separate nation on January 1, 1841. The Organization of Central American States (ODECA), formed in 1951, includes El Salvador. The capital of this loose association of states is at San Salvador. The political history of El Salvador during the past century has been marked by violence and rapid changes in government. El Salvador became a member of the United Nations on October 24, 1945.

During the early '80s, El Salvador became a battleground for competing ideologies, with the United States supporting the government (to the tune of $20 million in 1983) and Russia and Cuba backing the leftist guerrillas seeking its overthrow.

EQUATORIAL GUINEA

Equatorial Guinea is the former Spanish

Guinea. It consists of Rio Muni (an enclave on the equatorial coast of West Africa) and two islands in the Gulf of Guinea. One of these islands, formerly called Fernando Póo and renamed Macias Nguema (after the first president of the country), is about 20 miles offshore. The other, formerly named Annobón and renamed Pigalu, is about four hundred miles to the southwest. All were acquired by Spain in 1778. The islands were used as stations in the slave trade. No attempt to occupy Río Muni was made until the last quarter of the nineteenth century.

In 1959, the territories were designated as two provinces of Spain. In 1963, they were granted a degree of autonomy and called Equatorial Guinea. A referendum concerning independence was held in 1968, and on October 12, 1968, full independence was granted. The country was admitted to the United Nations on November 12, 1968.

ETHIOPIA

In ancient times the power of Egypt's pharaohs extended southward into what is now Ethiopia and along the headwaters of the Nile River. By the eleventh century before Christ, Ethiopian rulers had turned the tables and ruled mighty Egypt for a few centuries. During this period of expansion the Ethiopians absorbed much Egyptian culture. Christianity was introduced in about A.D. 330.

In the following centuries Ethiopia continued as a powerful state, although it ceased to rule Egypt. Through contacts with foreign regions, trade and immigration expanded. By the fifteenth century, however, Ethiopia had become divided into many small kingdoms.

Modern Ethiopia dates from the time of Menelik I (1844–1913) who pieced the country back together again. It grew into an empire, but the former kingdoms that made up the empire now form mere provinces in modern Ethiopia.

The Italian occupation and colonization of parts of Ethiopia began in the late nineteenth century. Italian expansion culminated in a full-scale invasion and conquest of the empire in 1935.

In 1941, during World War II, British and Ethiopian troops reconquered the country. Ethiopia became a member of the United Nations on November 13, 1945. In 1952, the former Italian colony of Eritrea was made an autonomous part of Ethiopia; but in 1962, it was reduced to the status of a province. A movement for the secession of Eritrea erupted into armed clashes by 1970.

After his appearance in defense of Ethiopia before the League of Nations in 1936, the Emperor Haile Selassie became an international figure. He was deposed by a military junta in 1974, after a reign of 44 years, and the monarchy was abolished in 1975. The capital of Ethiopia, Addis Ababa, is the headquarters of the Organization of African Unity, established there in 1963. The new government signed a pact with Russia in 1977.

The following year, Cuba sent 20,000 troops in to help repulse an attack by Somali forces.

FAROE ISLANDS

About A.D. 1000, the Vikings came to the Faroe Islands from Norway. At first a Norwegian dependency, they were attached to the Danish Crown, along with Norway, in 1380. In 1709, they became a part of the Danish kingdom. In 1814, when Norway was ceded to Sweden, the Faroes remained with Denmark, along with Iceland and Greenland.

In 1940, when the Nazis invaded Denmark and the Low Countries, the British sent forces to secure the islands from German occupation; at the end of the war they withdrew. A plebiscite for self-determination resulted in such a close vote (5,660 for independence, 5,499 against) that the Danish government declared the voting indecisive. Renewed negotiations led to a degree of autonomy, especially in economic matters. The islands acquired their own currency, which had to be covered by the Danish kroner, and the right to fly their own flag at sea.

FIJI

The Fiji Islands were discovered by Abel Tasman in 1643 and were visited by Captain James Cook in 1774. Captain William Bligh was the first to describe Fiji to any extent. Missionaries came to the islands in 1835 and helped to eradicate cannibalism.

The islands were annexed by Great Britain in 1874 and were administered by the colonial office until 1970, when a parliamentary system was set up and Fiji became an independent nation. It was admitted to the United Nations on October 13, 1970.

Finland—Helsinki

FINLAND

The Finnish people came originally from the Volga region of what is now the Soviet Union. They arrived in the present area of Finland sometime during the seventh century A.D. The Swedes began to penetrate Finland in the twelfth century. Swedish invasions took the form of religious crusades to convert the people to Christianity. This struggle against pagan Finns lasted two hundred years, ending with the complete conquest of Finland by the Swedes in 1293.

Russia annexed parts of Swedish-held areas in 1721, and the remainder of Finland in 1809. Finland was a grand duchy of the Russian Empire until 1917. The revolution in Russia gave the Finns a chance to proclaim independence.

In the great civil war that followed the Bolshevik victory in November 1917, Germany intervened on behalf of Finland and secured the *de facto* separation from Russia, but intended to establish a German-controlled government. However, after Germany's defeat, Finland emerged in 1919 as a parliamentary republic.

The Aland Islands were secured from Sweden in 1921. In 1939, the Soviet Union and Finland broke relations and two short wars followed that merged with World War II. Finland was defeated and had to pay, both in money and in the loss of some territory. Finland paid her reparations by 1952 and the Soviet Union abandoned the Porkkala naval base, returning it to Finland. However, parts of Karelia and the Petsamo region are ap-

parently permanently lost. Finland was admitted to the United Nations on December 14, 1955.

FRANCE

Classical Greek colonies were founded on the Mediterranean coast of what is now France as early as 600 B.C. However, very little was known of the region until Julius Caesar began his conquests in 58 B.C. The Celtic tribes who lived in the present France were called "Gauls" by the Romans. Gallic legends, traditions, and influence have remained an integral part of French culture. Gallic France achieved a high order of civilization. The region was richly endowed with prosperous cities, a thriving trade, and with great works of both Roman and Gallic engineering and architecture.

After A.D. 180, Gaul experienced violent invasion and wholesale destruction. Visigoths, Ostrogoths, Vandals, Lombardi, Alemanni, Burgundians, and many other invaders passed through Gaul, or conquered parts of it.

In A.D. 476 the Western Roman Empire came to an end and Gaul was left to fend for itself. The Franks, a Germanic tribe, entered Gaul and by A.D. 486 had united under Clovis, who became a convert to Christianity in 496. The Franks gradually conquered most of Gaul, but their Merovingian dynasty was unable to maintain control over large areas.

Under the later Merovingians, power passed to the mayors of the palace. Eventually these mayors took over the kingship titles, and in this way the

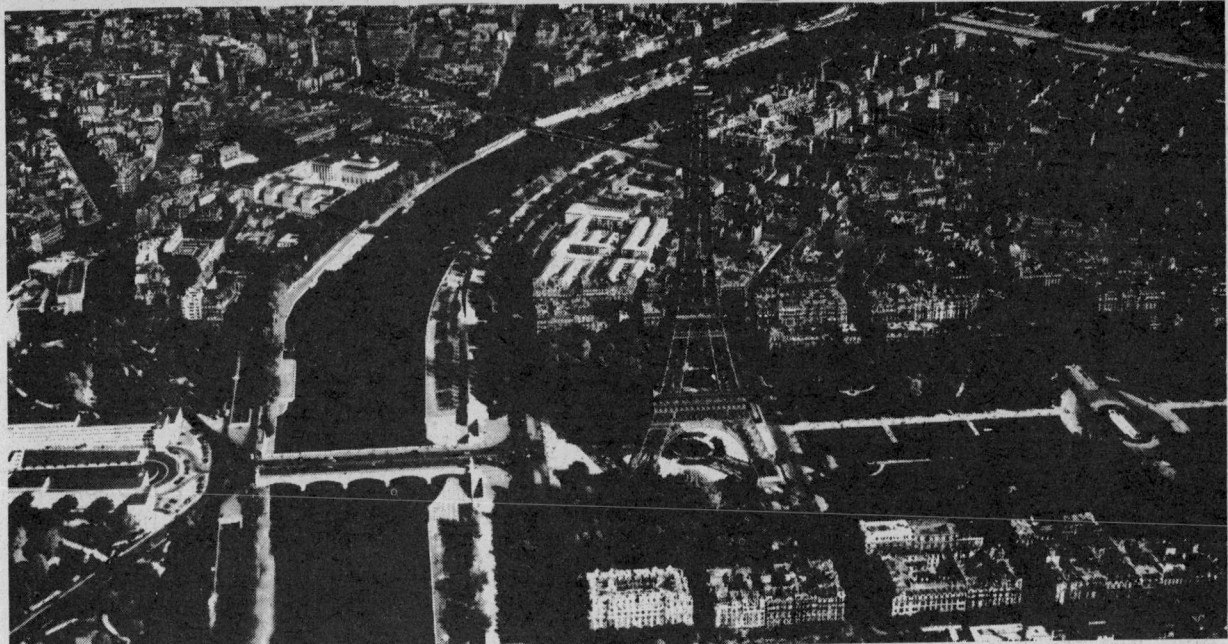

France—Paris

Carlovingians became the ruling dynasty of the region that was beginning to be called "France."

Charlemagne (768–814), also called Charles the Great, raised the Frankish people to the height of power in western Europe. Charlemagne ruled not only what is now France, but most of Germany and Italy as well. He had a difficult task in defending his realm from the Vikings and hundreds of other great and small groups. France became one great battlefield.

Huge castles rose over the ashes of formerly beautiful Roman cities. People locked themselves into these bastions for defense against the rising violence and lawlessness that gradually pervaded all western Europe. The population sold its freedom for protection, and serfdom became an established institution—the Age of Feudalism had come to France.

After his death the empire of Charlemagne fell apart. What was left of the once-great empire—a small area centered around Paris—went to Hugh Capet, who founded the third dynasty of French kings. His family was to rule France for 800 years.

The Capetian kings gradually expanded their authority and began to establish order in the lands they controlled. The fashioning of a new France by the Capetian kings was done at the expense of feudal elements and with the aid of a rising new middle class of merchants and nonfeudal groups.

Louis IX (1226–1270) overcame the feudal nobility by making the kingship popular to all groups—even to the peasantry. He outlawed a number of feudal practices and his capital became the intellectual center of Europe. Louis IX died while on a Crusade to the Holy Lands.

The Crusades began in 1096 and lasted until the fourteenth century. Most of the leaders in the first four Crusades were of the French nobility. France learned many lessons in warfare, and received from the Crusades the benefits of greater commerce and quickened industrial activity. These things stimulated a Renaissance in France and helped to lift Europe out of the "Dark Ages."

French power and the Capetian dynasty itself were challenged from England, first by Henry II (1154), and then by Henry's sons, Richard and John. The French kings were able to hold most of their territory in this first great encounter with English power.

In 1328, Edward III again challenged the right of the Capetian house to the French throne. The fighting began in 1337 and lasted for over one hundred years. It was during this "One Hundred Years' War" that Joan of Arc inspired French arms and helped to crown Charles VII king of France. Joan was captured and burned at the stake as a witch, but French armies advanced and by 1461 had driven the English out of France.

It should be noted that French-speaking nobility fought on both sides in this war. Yet France came out of the war more united than ever before. The next two centuries saw discord once more, but this time the conflict was a religious one.

The Protestant Reformation did not have as strong an effect on France as it did on other countries. But large areas of the population that did become Protestant were persecuted by the Catholics.

Under Louis XIV (1643–1715) kingship reached its greatest heights. The Sun King built a magnificent court and did much to make France the center of Western civilization.

The splendor of monarchial France did not last. The end came during the reign of Louis XVI, when a revolution overturned the throne in 1789. The

French Revolution abolished the divine right principle, replacing it with political authority. The bloody civil war that ensued ended only when Napoleon Bonaparte took control. Napoleon led the French nation in conquests and empire-building that ended in his defeat at Waterloo (a town in present Belgium).

The First Empire was succeeded by a monarchy (1814–1848) and the Second Republic (1848–1852). Memories of Napoleon were revived during the short Second Empire that lasted from 1852 to 1870, led by Napoleon III. After 1870, France blundered into a conflict with a newly united Germany. She was beaten, and then revolution overthrew the Empire, creating the Third Republic (1875).

A chance for revenge against German came in 1914. In that year World War I began and France became the main battlefield. Although victorious, France was greatly weakened.

World War II began in 1939 and again German armies crossed the frontiers of France. This time the nation's resistance against a large German army lasted only six weeks. A government was established to administer the German occupation. An "unoccupied" zone was governed from Vichy. Meanwhile, a government-in-exile functioned from London under the leadership of General Charles de Gaulle. French guerrilla fighters (the Resistance) worked closely with the De Gaulle headquarters and the Allies. Following the invasion by the Allies, France was liberated by October 1944.

De Gaulle retired in 1946. The Fourth Republic that governed from 1946 to 1958 lost major French colonies, including those in the Middle East, Indochina, Tunisia, and Morocco. But it made a bitter and vain effort to retain Algeria. Recalled to take the leadership of the Fifth Republic, De Gaulle granted independence to this colony in 1962. Although he resigned once more in 1969, many of his policies were continued by his successor, Georges Pompidou.

France was a charter member of the United Nations on October 24, 1945. The country also joined the North Atlantic Treaty Organization; but in that alliance French policy was independent and unpredictable.

While France has resisted communism, it has drifted toward socialism, culminating with the election May 10, 1981, of Francois Mitterrand, a socialist candidate, over Giscard D'Estaing. Mitterrand proceeded to nationalize five major industries and most banks.

FRENCH GUIANA

French Guiana was settled in 1604 and has been a French possession since 1667. It was long the site of a penal colony named Devil's Island, but the last prisoners were removed in 1945. In 1946, French Guiana became an overseas department of France. It is the last European dependency on the mainland of South America.

FRENCH POLYNESIA

The Overseas Territory of French Polynesia was formerly called French Settlements in Oceania. The major island groups that comprise the territory were made protectorates of France in 1844 and colonies in 1880. The Marquesas and Gambier groups were annexed in 1881. The entire region became a member of the French Community in 1958.

FRENCH SOUTHERN TERRITORIES

This Overseas Territory of France includes: (1) the Kerguelen Archipelago of three hundred islands, discovered in 1772 by Yves de Kerguelen. With an area of 2,700 square miles, they are located in the Indian Ocean southeast of Madagascar and used mainly in scientific research; (2) the Crozet Archipelago, discovered in 1772 by Marion-Dufressne. These 15 islands in the Indian Ocean, with an area of 193 square miles, are uninhabited; (3) St. Paul, an uninhabited island of 3 square miles south of Madagascar in the Indian Ocean; (4) New Amsterdam, an island of 19 square miles, discovered in 1522 by Magellan's ships. It is located in the south Indian Ocean and used as an administrative center; and (5) the Adelie Coast (Terre Adèlie) of the Antarctic continent, an estimated 150,000-square-mile area, discovered in 1840 by Dumont d'Urville.

In 1960, other islands were added to the territory. These include Europa, Juan de Nova (Saint-Christophe), Bassas-de-India, and the Glorioso Islands, all located in Mozambique Channel and having a total area of 23 square miles.

GABON

In the mid-nineteenth century, the region of

Gabon and the city of Libreville, together with other African republics of today, were established under French control and lumped together under the name of "French Equatorial Africa." In 1910, the colony of Gabon was officially organized as part of that region.

In 1946, the French Union was established and Gabon became an overseas territory. In 1960, it became completely independent within the French Community. Gabon was admitted to the United Nations on September 20, 1960.

GAMBIA

An enclave within Sierra Leone on the coast of West Africa is the tiny nation of Gambia, the smallest on the African mainland. It was formed out of the colony and protectorate of the same name. Great Britain acquired both in the seventeenth century and usually administered them from Sierra Leone.

In 1963, Gambia was given autonomy, and on February 18, 1965, it was made a member of the Commonwealth. On September 21, 1965, Gambia became a member of the United Nations. In 1970 the Gambians voted to become a republic, but to retain Commonwealth membership.

GHANA

The first authenticated landing of Europeans in this region of Africa was that of some Portuguese in 1470. The first British trading expedition came in 1553. Over the centuries Danes, Dutch, Germans, Portuguese, and British controlled parts of what was then called the Gold Coast.

During the eighteenth century slave trade developed, and by 1821 the British won increasing control of the region. The Crown took over the private trading-post settlements. In time the Danish forts were purchased by Britain. The Fanti chiefs approved a pact that allowed British agents to participate in administering justice.

Ghana was granted autonomy in 1951 and independence on December 12, 1956. It remained within the Commonwealth, became a member of the United Nations on March 8, 1957, and became a republic within the Commonwealth on July 1, 1960. The presidency was abolished in 1972.

GIBRALTAR

Located on a peninsula jutting out from Spain's southern coast, and guarding the Mediterranean Sea, the rock of Gibraltar was captured by England from Spain in 1704. It has been a British colony ever since, despite frequent Spanish protests. It was granted local autonomy in 1969.

GILBERT AND ELLICE ISLANDS

A group of archipelagoes in the Pacific Ocean comprise the British colony of the Gilbert and Ellice Islands, formed in 1915. It includes the Gilbert Islands on each side of the Equator, whose inhabitants are Micronesians; the Ellice Islands, south of the Equator, whose inhabitants are Melanesians; and several other islands. The colony was granted self-government in 1971. At the end of 1975, the Ellice Islands separated from the others and renamed itself the territory of Tuvalu.

GREECE

Historians regard the ancient Greeks as the founders of Western civilization. The Greeks were the first to develop the concept of democracy. They became Western civilization's first great dramatists, philosophers, scientists, doctors, geographers, orators, and poets. After two thousand years, the Greek world passed its vast heritage on to Rome. In a real sense, Greek civilization did not die; it merely moved to Rome, changed its form, and then brought forth a new civilization—that of modern times.

The recorded story of Ancient Greece began on the island of Crete, which lies on the southern limits of the Aegean Sea south of the mainland of the Greek peninsula. The Cretan civilization, also known as the Minoan, developed about 3000 B.C. It flourished until about 1600 B.C., when it was overpowered by an invasion from the mainland.

The mainland Greeks then developed the Mycenaean civilization on the mainland. By this time Greeks had entered the Bronze Age. They built fortified cities and ships that crossed the Mediterranean Sea to carry on trade with other peoples. Finally they developed a written language (deciphered in 1953). Mycenae in southern

Greece—The Acropolis, Athens

Greece was the central city of this civilization. Mycenaean civilization produced the events described in the *Iliad* and the *Odyssey*.

The Mycenaeans were eventually overwhelmed by invaders from the north. The invaders came in three separate waves, each wave displacing earlier ones. The invasions ended about 1000 B.C. All four groups (including the original Mycenaeans) settled down, intermingled, and finally created the Greek Golden Age.

About 750 B.C., Greeks began to establish colonies along the Mediterranean coast. Some of the more famous colonies were Lisbon, Marseille, Odessa, Naples, Pompeii, and Syracuse. During the Golden Age (480–399 B.C.) there were more than 150 Greek states and colonies strung along the Mediterranean and Black Seas from Spain in the West to the Caucasus, on the edge of Asia in the East.

The first coinage in the Western world appeared in Asia Minor (Kingdom of Lydia) as a result of the rise of Greek trade and commerce there. The coins of Athens became world famous for their reliability, and those of Syracuse were of unsurpassed workmanship and design.

Invasions by Persians from the east (Asia Minor) stirred the Greek world into a movement to unify the scattered states for defensive purposes. The Persian invasions were halted in a series of great battles by the Greeks. A united Greek army crushed the Persians at Platea in 479 B.C. It was at the end of the Persian Wars that the Golden Age flourished.

Athens was the center of Greek intellectual and artistic ferment during this period. The greatest works of sculpture, architecture, drama, and history were produced at Athens at that time. However, nearly all the Greek states shared in the Golden Age. As the power of Athens grew, so did the jealousies of her neighbors. In particular, Sparta became the bitter enemy of Athens. Sparta was a militaristic, highly disciplined, and regimented state. The wars that followed between Athens and her enemies were won by Sparta and the Golden Age came to an end.

Sparta was herself defeated soon after, and all Greece lay weakened by warfare—the ripe fruit for any determined conqueror. Alexander the Great seized the opportunity and in 338 B.C. conquered all of Greece.

Alexander the Great spread Greek culture and ideas throughout the known world. However, his great empire crumbled after his death in 323 B.C.

The Roman army easily conquered a divided Greece in 197 B.C. and again in 167 B.C. Greece became a mere province in the Roman Empire. It was called Achaea. The name *Greek* was first used by the Romans. The classical Greeks called themselves "Hellenes" and their land "Hellas."

After the fall of Rome, Greece became part of the Byzantine, or Eastern Empire. After A.D. 1261, a group of independent states arose and flourished until all were conquered by the Turks in 1460. Some of the islands remained in the possession of Venice until the eighteenth century.

In the nineteenth century the spirit of national independence was reawakened. Following an unsuccessful attempt in 1770, the Greeks proclaimed an independent state in 1821. Their independence was supported by Britain, France, and Russia, and was defended by those powers in 1827. The London Protocol of 1830 secured international recognition of the Greek state.

Greece became a monarchy—first under a Bavarian royal house, then under a Danish prince, who took the throne as George I in 1863. As the result of several wars, Greece acquired Crete, parts of Macedonia and Thrace, and parts of European Turkey. This led to a disastrous war with Turkey, after which some two million Greeks were exchanged for more than a million Turks living in Greece.

During World War II, Greece was under German occupation. The monarchy found exile in Cairo, while the resistance forces fought on in Greece. After the war, the resistance (which included communists) tried to seize power. But a plebiscite in 1946 accepted the monarchy.

A military junta took power in 1967 and forced Constantine, the last king, to flee. The dictatorship was overthrown in 1973, and a parliamentary republic was restored by referendum in 1974.

In 1981, Andres Papandreou of the Panhellenic Socialist Movement was elected prime minister. Greece is a member of the NATO military alliance.

GREENLAND

The huge island of Greenland was discovered and colonized at the end of the tenth century by Eric the Red. Two centuries later it was claimed by Norway, but thereafter the colony was neglected. Although many explorers passed the west coast of Greenland, only traces of the old colony remained when the island was revisited in 1721 by Danish missionaries.

Greenland was again colonized, receiving only enough aid to support the missions and provide a base for explorations.

After the Napoleonic Wars, Denmark and Norway were separated, and Greenland remained with Denmark. In 1979 it was granted home rule, electing a socialist-dominated legislature. It also translated its official name into the Greenlandic language, Kalaallit Nunaat.

GRENADA

The most southerly of the British Windward Is-

lands, Grenada was discovered by Columbus in 1498. It was held alternately by the French and British until 1784. The Windward Islands were given autonomy in 1967, with the status of associated states in the British Commonwealth, and it declared its independence in 1974.

In 1983, acting on intelligence reports of a buildup by Soviet and Cuban operatives, the United States sent in a military detachment to secure the island. American troops were later withdrawn.

GUADELOUPE

Guadeloupe was discovered by Columbus in 1493. It was colonized in 1635 and became a French possession in 1674. It was made an overseas department of France in 1946. Its dependencies include Marie Galante, Les Saintes, Désirade, St. Barthélemy, and part of St. Martin.

GUATEMALA

The ancestors of modern-day Guatemalans were the Mayan peoples who developed a remarkable civilization between A.D. 300 and 900. The Maya were a short, stocky people who lived originally in what is now Mexico, Guatemala, Honduras, British Honduras, and El Salvador. The classic civilization (ca. A.D. 350 to 600) may have included two million people. The Maya developed mathematics, a 365-day calendar, ideographic writing, sculpture, music, and literature. Their great cities now lie abandoned, deep in the jungles of Central America. Their decline is partly a mystery. By the time the Spanish came, the cities had already been abandoned; the people had become food-gatherers and sedentary agriculturalists.

The Spanish conquest began in 1524 and was completed by 1550. The capital was established at Guatemala City in 1776. In 1821, all the Central American colonies declared their independence of Spain and joined the Mexican Empire. Soon they withdrew to form the United Provinces of Central America. This union was weak and collapsed in 1939, and Guatemala the same year became a republic. Its government has been among the least stable in Central America. Guatemala was admitted to the United Nations on November 21, 1945.

GUINEA

European penetration and exploration of what is now Guinea began in the fifteenth century under the Portuguese. France began to trade and acquire territory there early in the seventeenth century. France administered all her Guinea region as a part of Senegal until 1845. Resistance to French rule was bitterly carried out by Samory Touré, who fought the French from 1882 until he was captured in 1898. The boundaries of Guinea were established in 1882.

In 1946, Africans in Guinea became French citizens and a territorial legislature was organized. At that time it became a part of the loose federation of French West Africa. In 1958, Guinea was given the choice of becoming an independent nation, either in the French Community or outside it. Guinea chose independence without association with the Community. It was admitted to the United Nations on December 12, 1958.

GUINEA-BISSAU

Located on the West African coast between the former French colonies of Senegal and Guinea, this region belonged to Portugal since Bissau was set up as a Portuguese post in 1687. Before that, since its discovery by Nuno Tristão in 1446, this part of Guinea was active in the slave trade. Its status as a Portuguese colony was settled by an agreement with France in 1886. Initially administered from Cape Verde, Portuguese Guinea became a separate colony in 1879. In 1951, it was designated an overseas territory. Its independence was recognized by Portugal on September 7, 1974, and ten days later Guinea-Bissau was admitted to the United Nations.

GUYANA

The westernmost of the three European colonies known as the Guianas, this area was first colonized by the Dutch. It was traded to the British after the Napoleonic era.

The three settlements of Berbice, Essequibo, and Demerara were combined in 1831 to form British Guiana, and became a crown colony in 1928. Local autonomy was introduced in 1953, and a contest developed between the black and East Indian inhabitants for control. The black faction prevailed, and on May 22, 1966, the independence of the country was recognized. On September 20, 1966, Guyana was admitted to the United Nations.

HAITI

That portion of the island of Hispaniola that is now the Republic of Haiti was ceded to France in 1697. It became known as St. Domingue, while the Spanish portion of Hispaniola was called Santo Domingo.

French control was swept away by a revolution in 1803. Jean Jacques Dessalines named the country Haiti, and was proclaimed emperor. He was assassinated in 1806. From that date until 1820, Haiti was divided into a kingdom and a republic. Haiti was reunited in 1822 by Jean Pierre Boyer, who also seized Santo Domingo. He ruled the entire island of Hispaniola until 1844. The future Dominican Republic withdrew in that year.

From 1915 to 1934, Haiti was occupied by the United States. It became a member of the United Nations on October 24, 1945.

HONDURAS

In 1502, Christopher Columbus discovered the region that is now Honduras. The Spanish explorer Hernan Cortés made the first settlement there in 1524 and claimed the land for Spain.

Honduras remained under the rule of Spain until 1821, when the country revolted and was annexed to Mexico. From then on, Honduras' history includes a series of alliances and wars with neighboring countries. Starting in 1883 and continuing for twenty years, Honduras was in continuous revolt and civil disorder. In 1911 the United States intervened in the strife between Honduras and Guatemala. Civil war followed World War I. The United States intervened again in 1915, and the 1930s were turbulent.

Honduras was admitted to the United Nations on December 17, 1945.

HONG KONG

Hong Kong was occupied in 1841 by the British. In 1860, the Kowloon peninsula was added. Additional territory was added by a lease agreement in 1898. Hong Kong is a crown colony, administered by a governor assisted by an executive council. Most of the people are Chinese.

HUNGARY

Within historic times the area of the present Hungary was a part of the Roman provinces of Pannonia and Dacia. Germanic tribes displaced the Romans in the second century A.D., and were, in turn, conquered by Attila the Hun in the fifth century.

The Magyars (Hungarians) were originally located in what is now central Russia. They invaded and occupied the lands between the Tisza and Danube rivers in A.D. 895. Christianity was introduced during the reign of the first great Hungarian king, Stephen I (canonized in 1083).

The Magyars fought wars on all sides. Their greatest period of expansion was during the reign of Louis the Great (1342–1382) which was after the country had been overrun by the Mongols (1235–1270) from Asia. Hungarian power was broken by the Turks in 1526. Thereafter, the nation was split into several petty baronies and duchies.

The Hapsburg kings of Austria defeated the Turks and gradually united the Magyar people under Austrian control. Hungary was finally driven to revolt by the repressive policies of Prince Metternich in 1848. The revolt was crushed in 1849. Austria was gradually weakened by war with Prussia, and was forced to give in to Hungarian national aspirations in 1867. In that year a dual monarchy was established, called Austria-Hungary.

Austria-Hungary expanded into the Balkans in the twentieth century. By this time it was also known as the Austro-Hungarian Empire. Political annexations aimed at Turkey precipitated the Balkan Wars, and Austria-Hungary became deeply implicated in Balkan affairs. The assassination of the heir to the throne of Austria-Hungary in 1914 precipitated World War I, in

Hong Kong—General view of Victoria Island

which the dual monarchy entered on the side of Germany. After the war, the dual monarchy collapsed.

Hungary was separated from Austria and stripped of nearly two-thirds of its territory. In 1920, it became a kingdom, but without a king. In the hope of retrieving lost territory, Hungary in World War II joined the Axis powers and was again defeated along with Germany. She again lost territory, this time what had been acquired after 1937.

In 1948, the Hungarian Workers party (Communist) seized control and established the one-party (Communist) People's Republic of Hungary. A revolt occurred in 1956 which was directed against the Communist regime. After temporary success, the revolt was crushed with the aid of military forces from the U.S.S.R. Hungary was admitted to the United Nations on December 14, 1955.

By the late 1970s, Hungarian laws had relaxed to allow more personal freedoms than most other communist nations. Many Hungarians who fled the country in 1956 have returned to their homeland.

ICELAND

Iceland was settled shortly before A.D. 900, mainly by Norsemen. Christianity appeared at the beginning of the twelfth century, and with it certain reforms which helped to stablize the various fighting clans. In the mid-thirteenth century, both sides in a civil war appealed to Norway for intervention; the result was unification with that country in 1262–1264.

Then followed a succession of events which nearly wiped out the island: harsh Norwegian rule, volcanic eruptions, and bubonic plague. Iceland passed into Danish hands in 1483 when the king of Denmark came to the Norwegian throne.

With the decline of the monarchs, Iceland began its struggle for freedom, and in 1874 won limited home rule. By 1918, it had become a sovereign nation under Denmark's crown. On June 17, 1944, Iceland became a completely independent republic.

During World War II, Iceland served as an important naval station for United States warships. Iceland was admitted to the United Nations on November 19, 1946. In 1972, Iceland banned foreign fishing fleets from within 200 miles of its shores.

INDIA

The earliest civilization known to have existed on the subcontinent of India developed in the Indus River valley of what is now Pakistan about five thousand years ago. The ruins at Mohenjodaro indicate a very high degree of civilization.

Mystery surrounds the fate of that civilization. The Aryan invasions began about four thousand years ago, and their influence gradually spread throughout India. They established Hinduism, the family pattern of India, and the caste system. Alexander the Great came to India by way of the Khyber Pass in 326 B.C., but Greek influence was not felt east of the Indus valley. The Maurya Empire arose after Alexander's visit. Under Asoka (273–232 B.C.), India was finally united into one state. It included nearly all of the present India, Pakistan, and other parts of southern Asia. After Asoka, India was subdivided into many competing states. The Gupta rulers became the first Hindu kings and brought about a "golden age" of Sanskrit learning. Rich cities and great universities were founded. By about A.D. 1000, the Hindu period had reached its peak. Many of the great works of art and architecture in India that still survive date from this period.

The next age of flourishing civilization was initiated by the Moslem invaders who had gradually spread their power and influence throughout northern India from the eighth to the sixteenth century. The unification of India began again in 1526. Babar, Akbar, Shah Jahan, and Aurangzeb established the Mogul Empire and caused the rise of a new and even richer civilization in India. Aurangzeb, the last of the great emperors, tried to convert the people to Islam by force. This, together with the extravagance of the Mogul rulers, led to the downfall of Mogul power. Their demise made it easier for the Europeans to obtain a foothold on the subcontinent.

Vasco da Gama (Portuguese) reached Calicut (on the west coast of India) in 1498. Thereafter the Portuguese, English, and French began a mad scramble for spheres of trade and colonies. The British eventually won. By the middle of the nineteenth century they controlled most of India in one form or another. British withdrawal was sudden and decisive in 1947. India was then a single independent nation, but was still divided in many other ways.

The most serious division was between Hindu and Moslem. Bloodshed and civil war resulted

India—Golden Temple of Amritsar

when the Moslem state of Pakistan was proclaimed upon the date of Indian independence. Other serious problems that still plague the Indian nation are the many language and ethnic barriers; the system of caste and other religious issues; the poverty of the masses of Indians; and the lack of a genuine national tradition and spirit for the nation as a whole.

India has attempted to remain neutral between communist and capitalist nations. She tried to defend her borders against Chinese claims and invasions. India also was engaged in a serious dispute over Kashmir. Kashmir is divided between India and Pakistan, and only an armed truce prevents warfare along that frontier. India has been trying to lessen the linguistic differences and problems by establishing states on the basis of language or of national ethnic minorities. India became a member of the United Nations on October 30, 1945.

INDONESIA

According to Indonesian history, the people of the original archipelago were overwhelmed by countless migrations from the Asian mainland. Some two thousand years ago, Hindu traders introduced their religion and culture. Then followed

Indian Buddhists who also greatly influenced the natives. The Islamic religion entered at the end of the fifteenth century and gained a firm foothold.

Portuguese traders came next. They were soon pushed out by the Dutch, under whom the islands became a highly important colony until World War II. From the beginning of the nineteenth century on, the Dutch rulers put down several attempts at revolution. World War II ended the Japanese occupation, and the Dutch attempted to return to power. A self-proclaimed independence followed, with both open and guerrilla warfare. At the end of 1949, the Dutch officially relinquished sovereignty. On September 28, 1950, Indonesia became a member of the United Nations.

A dispute with the Netherlands arose over the disposition of Dutch New Guinea, which Indonesia claimed as her province of West Irian. In 1963, West Irian was turned over to Indonesia by the United Nations. Meanwhile, the parliamentary system was changed to an authoritarian regime, based on the slogan of "guided democracy." A military coup in 1965 suppressed the strong communist faction of Indonesia. In 1967, it deposed President Sukarno. The leader of the junta, Suharto, became president and prime minister. Indonesia, which had been a charter member of the United Nations, withdrew from the organization in January 1965. But she resumed membership on September 28, 1966.

IRAN

Iran was called Persia until 1935. The history of Persia dates back to the time of the Medes, a people who settled in what is now Iran in 1500 B.C. The Medes dominated the Persians until the time of Cyrus the Great. In about 549, Cyrus conquered the Medes and extended his Persian kingdom. Persia conquered Babylonia, restoring Jerusalem to the Jews in 538 B.C. Persia failed to capture the Greek city-states in 490 and 480 B.C., and was itself defeated by Alexander the Great in 331 B.C.

The Parthians prevented the Romans from conquering Persia. They controlled the area until the third century A.D., and were followed by the Sassanians, who ruled for another four centuries.

The Arabs brought Islam to Persia in the seventh century A.D., and for centuries afterward religious caliphates ruled in Persia. The Mongols invaded in A.D. 1250. After the defeat of the caliphate in 1502, Persia was ruled by a shah (king). A constitution was granted in 1906. The period following was marked by attempts of foreign powers to gain spheres of influence in Persia. During World War II, Iran was occupied by the Allies to prevent German access to the rich Iranian oil fields. The sovereignty of Iran was reaffirmed by the Allies at the Tehran Conference in 1943. Iran joined the United Nations on October 24, 1945.

Iran is now one of the largest exporters of oil in the world. Its income allows the nation to invest in a wide variety of foreign enterprises. Iran is purchasing nuclear power plants from France and the United States; and in 1974, it loaned money to Great Britain to shore up the sagging British economy.

Popular protests forced the shah of Iran to leave the country in January 1979. Religious leader Ayatollah Khomeini seized control and shortly thereafter the American Embassy was stormed with 90 persons captured. Among them were 52 Americans who were held for 444 days before being released unharmed January 20, 1981.

IRAQ

Modern Iraq occupies the area the ancient Greeks called Mesopotamia, one of the cradles of modern civilization. As such, the history of Iraq extends back to the very beginning of writing, about 4000 B.C., and archaeologically even farther.

Eridu, Ur, Nineveh, and Babylon were among the earliest cities in human civilization. The Sumerian culture developed in about 3000 B.C. and later influenced the culture of Egypt, and the rising new civilizations of Greece and Crete.

The Sumerians were succeeded by Akkadians, Assyrians, Scythians, Persians, and finally Romans. The Arabs conquered Iraq in A.D. 637. Baghdad became a brilliant center of cultural and intellectual life.

The Mongol invasions of the thirteenth century ended the prosperity, destroyed the remarkable irrigation system, and turned the land of former greatness into a desert. The Ottoman Turks swept into Iraq in 1638 and maintained their control until, during World War I, British troops wrested it from them. The League of Nations established a British mandate over Iraq, and a monarchy was established in 1921. The mandate was terminated in 1932. The monarchy was overthrown in 1958, shortly after Iraq and Jordan had joined in a feder-

ation. The federation was terminated and Iraq was declared a republic.

Hostilities between Iraq and Iran flared into open warfare in September 1980. Two years later, Iraq had counted 40,000 dead and 100,000 wounded or captured.

IRELAND

Recorded Irish history begins with the arrival of St. Patrick on the Emerald Isle in the fifth century. Christianity spread rapidly thereafter and Ireland became dotted with great monasteries that were centers of learning and of Gaelic and Latin culture. The Viking invasions of the eighth century nearly put an end to Irish learning, but Viking power was finally broken at the Battle of Clontarf in 1014.

Anglo-Norman invasions began soon after. For 800 years, Ireland grappled with neighboring Britain for a separate and independent existence. Successive British monarchs attempted to control, cajole, or colonize Ireland, but usually ended up persecuting the inhabitants, either for religious or political reasons. Rebellions during the nineteenth century were fair warning that Irish nationalism was growing strong and ever more resentful of English control.

A civil war and political turmoil marked the period of 1916–1921 that ended with the establishment of the Irish Free State with dominion status in the British Commonwealth of Nations. In 1937, a further change came about when the

Ireland—Glendalough

British governor-general was replaced by a president. The name was then changed to Ireland (in Gaelic, *Eire*). In 1948, Ireland withdrew from the Commonwealth and on April 15, 1959 became a republic. The republic became a member of the United Nations on December 14, 1955.

Protestant and Catholic groups still wage a sporadic war of terrorism against one another.

ISLE OF MAN

The Isle of Man has been attached to the Crown of England since 1346. It is administered under its own laws and form of government consisting of legislative council, governor, and the Court of Tynwald. The people are Celtic in origin, and are called Manx, or Manxmen. Manx and English are spoken.

ISRAEL

Israel is the collective name that was applied to the descendants of Jacob, those Hebrew peoples who migrated under Abraham from Mesopotamia to Canaan sometime during the twentieth century before Christ.

The Israelites conquered most of the Canaanites, adopted their language and some of their culture. Later, some of the remaining Canaanites became known as Phoenicians. The land of Canaan is now called Palestine, part of which forms modern Israel.

In about 1100 B.C., the Israelites formed a loose organization of tribes. A united kingdom was established by Saul (1010 B.C.–970 B.C.). It became the heart of a great Hebrew civilization that flourished under David and his son, Solomon. After the death of Solomon, the kingdom split into two parts. In 722 B.C., northern Israel was conquered by the Assyrians. The southern part, Judea, held out until 586 B.C., when the Babylonians captured Jerusalem and exiled the Jews. Judea arose again after 538 B.C. and continued to flourish until A.D. 70, when Roman legions captured Jerusalem, bringing an end to ancient Israel.

The Arabs seized Palestine (the Roman name for Canaan) in A.D. 636. Four hundred years of Moslem rule followed, in which Christians and Jews were tolerated. The Turks seized the region in 1065, and the Crusades were begun in order to free the Holy Land of Christendom. Successive waves of invasions continued after the Crusades, and the Turks managed to recapture or retain most of Palestine until 1917. Jews began to return to Palestine in 1878. Britain occupied it from 1917 until 1948.

Zionism is the name of the national movement for the restoration of Palestine to the world's Jews. The Balfour Declaration of Britain (1917) supported the idea behind Zionism. Under the United Kingdom's mandate, Jewish immigrants arrived in large numbers, particularly under Nazi persecution of the European Jews and during World War II. Jews attempted to find refuge in Palestine, which they considered their historic homeland (Zion); their hopes collided with the aspirations of some Arabs, who wanted to establish independent Arab states in the area. Britain, caught between conflicting pressures, restricted Jewish immigration to Palestine. Eventually, Britain therefore precipitously abandoned the mandate, leaving the United Nations to provide a solution.

The solution proposed was the creation of a Jewish state and an Arab state in Palestine. On May 14, 1948, the Jews proclaimed their state, which they called Israel. The states of the Arab League immediately attacked Israel, were beaten off, and signed an armistice in 1949. However, no peace was established.

The Israeli government was forced to protect its population from constant sporadic attacks from all sides. The Palestinian Arabs either fled or accepted minority status within Israel. The issue of the displaced Palestinians became a critical factor in the Middle East question, along with the issue of Arab recognition of the state of Israel.

Warfare broke out in 1956, when Israel invaded Egypt and defeated the Egyptian army. The intervention of French and British forces on their behalf brought about a settlement by the United Nations. In 1967, Egypt took the offensive and was decisively defeated within six days. In 1973, Egypt forcibly recovered part of the territory occupied since 1967 by Israel. In all these conflicts Syria and other Arab states participated against Israel. On numerous occasions the issue was brought before the United Nations (to which Israel was admitted on May 11, 1949). After the acquisition of Arab territory in the 1967 war, most United Nations resolutions were unfavorable to Israel. The forging of peaceful relations between Israel and her Arab neighbors remained a major international problem.

ITALY

The roots of Italian history lie in the Roman period, and the history of Rome rested upon Greek and Etruscan civilizations.

Roman civilization began as an offshoot of that of the Etruscans whom the early Romans conquered about 200 B.C. Etruria (modern Tuscany) lay in the north-central part of the Italian peninsula. The Etruscan civilization spread into the Po River valley and reached its greatest development about 600 B.C. Etruscan control over Latium (Rome) lasted to about 500 B.C., and over southern Italy for another hundred years. Their influence upon Roman civilization is seen through the development of urban centers, large public works, maritime commerce, and in art forms. The Etruscans borrowed from Greece, and probably also from Lydia in Asia Minor.

When Rome conquered the Etrurian states in Southern Etruria in about 400 B.C., the Greek states and colonies in that area collapsed. By 272 B.C., the entire Italian peninsula had come under Roman rule.

The period of unification was followed by overseas expansion. Three wars were fought for control of the Mediterranean Sea with the Phoenician city of Carthage (near present-day Tunis in Africa). After one hundred years of war, Carthage was overwhelmed in 146 B.C.

Rome had been a republic since its founding, but because of the wars of conquest and expansion, an imperial form of government was established in 27 B.C. The first 200 years of the empire were marked by a golden age of peaceful development, prosperity, and progress in literature, the arts, engineering, architecture, and government. Despite the personal rule of some incompetent emperors, the Roman Empire flourished primarily through efficient administrative machinery, and through the occasional genius of such emperors as Augustus (27 B.C.–A.D. 14), Trajan (98–117), Hadrian (117–138), and Marcus Aurelius (161–180).

The empire eventually became too large and troublesome for the personal rule of one emperor. It was split in A.D. 395 into the Eastern Roman Empire with the seat of government at Constantinople (the present Istanbul) and a Western Roman Empire whose capital remained at Rome. Following the death in 337 of Emperor Constantine, who ruled both empires, open rebellions broke out. Spain, Gaul (France), and all the African territories had already been lost when

Italy—Milan Cathedral

Odoacer, a German prince, established a kingdom in the Italian peninsula in A.D. 476. The Western Roman Empire had ended. The Eastern Roman Empire survived and flourished until 1453, when the Turks overran it and captured Constantinople.

From the sixth century down to the thirteenth, Italy suffered from invasions—including those of the Lombards, Franks, Saracens, and Germans. From the tenth to the fourteenth century the Holy Roman Empire of German kings and the Christian Church, centered in Rome, became the leading contenders for power in the Italian peninsula. However, the rise of small city-states with powerful maritime interests upset the balance between papal and German rule. The south became united in the Kingdom of Naples, and the Papal States were established in central Italy; and most of the city-states were located in the north and along the coasts of both the Adriatic and Tyrrhenian seas.

Beginning in the thirteenth century, a revival of trade, commerce, and learning spread out from the main centers of both the Byzantine and the Western Christian world. This was stimulated, to a large degree, by the Crusades of Europeans against Moslem control of the Holy Lands of Christendom.

Modern Italian history dates from the rise of the new commerce, trade, and industrial centers of the Italian peninsula during and after the great Crusades. The Italian peninsula emerged as the heart of an unparalleled surge in art, music, literature, science, and philosophical movements. Industry, trade, commerce, farming, and orderly government revived. Milan, Florence, Genoa, Pisa, Lucca, Venice, and Bologna vied with one another for leadership in the Renaissance of the Western world.

In later centuries the Italian city-states were overwhelmed by other European powers. Venice, Milan, and the Kingdom of Piedmont (in the northwest) managed to keep alive ideas of national unity and their own independence.

Modern Italian national consciousness was greatly influenced and strengthened by the "Resorgimento" movement, led by Giuseppe Mazzini and Count Camillo Cavour, in the nineteenth century. The Kingdom of Piedmont and its ruling House of Savoy served as the rallying point for Italian unification. Giuseppe Garibaldi initiated a series of military adventures that helped lead to a united Italy in 1870. Rome became the capital of the kingdom in that year, but the Roman Catholic Church continued in bitter opposition to unification for another 60 years.

Italy suffered heavy losses during World War I. This setback, combined with a severe economic depression, ushered in a Fascist dictatorship led by Benito Mussolini in 1922. During World War II, Italy joined Hitler's Nazi regime in Germany. The nation became a major battlefield of the war and was devastated by land invasion and air attack. Mussolini's Fascist empire collapsed near the end of the war; and in 1945, the Italian Social Republic was set up. In 1946, this was transformed into a constitutional republic. The reign of the House of Savoy came to an end. Italy became a member of the NATO alliance in 1949 and a member of the United Nations on December 14, 1955.

The Italian constitution does not allow the reorganization of the Fascist Party, but it does allow the Communist Party to take an active role in government. Inflation and uneasy labor relations have brought down a number of Italian premiers in recent times.

IVORY COAST REPUBLIC

Portuguese navigators first landed in the late fifteenth century in what is now the Ivory Coast Republic. For the next 200 years, European traders dealt extensively in ivory and slaves taken from the region. French missionaries established themselves there in 1687, and at the beginning of the eighteenth century a trading post was set up by the French near Abidjan. Additional settlements by the French were established in the nineteenth century.

On March 10, 1893, the Ivory Coast became a French colony and later was consolidated with other French-controlled regions to form French West Africa. The colony was designated a territory within the French Union in 1946. On August 7, 1960, the Ivory Coast became an independent republic associated with the French Community. It was admitted to the United Nations on September 20, 1960.

JAMAICA

Columbus discovered Jamaica in 1494 on his second voyage. The island was colonized by the Spanish in 1523. The British captured it in 1655, and it was formally ceded by Spain in 1670. Jamaica acquired internal self-government in 1944 and cabinet government was introduced in 1953.

Jamaica joined a British-sponsored Federation of West Indies in 1958. However, the island withdrew in 1961 and became an independent nation on August 6, 1962. Jamaica was admitted to the United Nations on September 18, 1962.

In 1974, the Jamaican government took half ownership in American companies that have Jamaican mines for bauxite (aluminum ore).

In recent years, Jamaica's relations with the United States under the leadership of Prime Minister Seaga have improved. The country severed relations with Cuba in 1981 and President Reagan visited Jamaica in 1982.

JAPAN

According to legend, the Japanese Empire was founded in 660 B.C. The first capital was at Nara and was removed to Kyoto in A.D. 784. Buddhism and Chinese culture entered Japan during the Nara period. The Chinese influences were molded and changed to suit native forms. The shogunate form of government (in which real power lay not with the emperor but with military leaders called "shoguns") began in 1192 and continued until 1867.

The first contacts with the West occurred when Portuguese traders arrived in southern Japan in 1543. However, Japan remained generally sealed off to Westerners except for a few Dutch and Chinese merchants until the coming of Commodore Matthew C. Perry from the United States in 1853. The signing of a treaty of peace and friendship with the United States caused turmoil among the ruling forces and eventually led to the destruction of feudalism in Japan. In 1867, the emperor won back full control of the throne from the feudal shoguns.

The opening up of Japan to Western influence also ushered in a period of Japanese expansion. Japan defeated China in 1895, Russia in 1905, and Korea in 1910. By 1922, Japan was the third naval power of the world and one of the five "great powers." Military factions dominated Japan after 1926, and events that led up to World War II began with an invasion of China in 1931. By 1936, the military were in full control. Manchuria (a region of China) had been conquered and organized into a puppet state called Manchukuo. In 1936, Japan withdrew from the League of Nations and set up close relations with the Axis Powers (Germany and Italy).

Japan launched a full-scale invasion of China in 1937. The United States was sympathetic to China and extended her credit, placing embargoes on the shipping of aircraft and other war materials to Japan. Japan retaliated with a sneak attack on the United States Pacific naval base at Pearl Harbor,

Hawaii, on December 7, 1941. This was the beginning of World War II in the Pacific area. (The war had been under way in Europe since 1939, when Germany invaded Poland.)

The Pacific war was marked by a series of great naval battles. On land it was a bitter jungle war and a series of beachhead landings from island to island. The Japanese reached the Coral Sea off Australia in May 1942, where they were stopped in the great Battle of the Coral Sea. Their eastward move was halted at Midway Island in June 1942, and in Alaska at the same time. Thereafter, the war went against Japan, as Allied strength began to build up. The most decisive battle was probably Leyte Gulf (October 23, 1944), the biggest naval battle in history. The Japanese fleet was crushed and Japanese aircraft resorted to suicide "Kamikaze" dives on American ships. By October 26, the Japanese fleet no longer existed as a force.

The final blow was an atomic bomb attack launched by the United States against Hiroshima on August 6, 1945, and against Nagasaki on August 9, 1945. Japan surrendered, signing the terms on August 14 aboard the battleship *Missouri* in Tokyo Bay. The Japanese people participated enthusiastically in the great changes that transformed Japan from a feudal militaristic empire into a progressive and democratic nation.

Japanese economic recovery was phenomenal,

Japan—Nijubashi Bridge, main entrance to Imperial Palace

but also important were the basic changes made in the life and culture of Japan. The new Japan has become a Westernized nation in many of its social patterns. Japan became a member of the United Nations on December 18, 1956.

In September 1972, Japan broke its diplomatic ties with the Chinese government-in-exile on Taiwan and restored friendly relationships with mainland China. The United States has withdrawn most of its military forces from Japan and has given virtually all of its bases there to the Japanese government.

In its rise to leadership among industrial nations of the world, Japan has become a fierce competitor to the United States in the manufacture of automobiles, electronics, computers and many other products. The rivalry has resulted in some modifications of Japan's trade policies and the imposition of some sanctions by the United States.

JORDAN

The nation is named for the famous river of Jordan whose valley forms one of the earliest sites of human civilization. Excavations at Jericho, near the Dead Sea, reveal a Neolithic culture eight thousand years old. The history of western Jordan is much the same as that of Palestine (*see* Israel). However, Jordan's history has one other chapter not included in that of Palestine. This is the era of the Nabataeans, a mysterious Arabic people who built one of the finest of all ancient cities in the desert of what is now southern Jordan. The ruins of Petra, the capital city, were discovered in A.D. 1812. The Nabataeans controlled the trade routes between the Dead Sea and Red Sea. Their empire developed an alliance with Rome that could have changed the history of the world, had it lasted. Petra developed a unique Arabic-Greco-Roman culture. The kingdom was annexed by the Romans in the second century after Christ.

The great northward invasion of the Arabs in A.D. 633 brought Islam to the region. From the twelfth century until the Ottoman conquest in 1517, the area was controlled by Christian Crusaders from Europe. The Ottoman Turks ruled this entire part of southwestern Asia until 1917, when T. E. Lawrence (known as Lawrence of Arabia) led Arab troops against the Turks to a decisive victory. As a result, an Arab state was set up in the eastern part of Britain's Palestinian mandate.

In 1921, Abdullah ibn Hussein (head of the Hashemite family of Arabia) was installed by the British as king of the new state, which was known as Transjordan because it was on the far side of the river. In 1927, it was recognized as a state under British protection. The mandatory power signed a treaty with Abdullah in 1946 recognizing him as ruler of the Hashemite Kingdom of Transjordan. Two years later the Palestinian mandate ended, Israel was formed under United Nations auspices in western Palestine, and Transjordan joined with other Arab states in a military attack on Israel. Much Palestinian territory west of the Jordan was annexed to Abdullah's kingdom, which then changed its name to Jordan. Part of the city of Jerusalem thus fell to Jordan. The state was admitted to the United Nations on December 14, 1955.

Under Abdullah's grandson, Hussein, Jordan continued to oppose Israel along with Egypt and other Arab states. During the Arab-Israeli War of 1967, Israel captured Jordan's west-bank territory. The continued occupation of the west bank became a major obstacle to peace in the Middle East. Jordan became more moderate in her relations with Israel than the Palestinians did. In fact, the Palestinians almost seized control of Jordan's kingdom, and were forced to transfer their bases to Syria in 1970. Hussein joined the other Arab states in the attack on Israel in 1973.

KENYA

Settlements of Arabs from nearby Zanzibar were established in what is now Kenya as early as the seventh century A.D. After the fifteenth century, the Portuguese competed with the Arabs for control of the coast. After 1740, the sultanate on Zanzibar Island became the ruler of most of eastern Kenya until 1887. Zanzibar then came under British influence and other opportunities, and the British East Africa Protectorate was created in 1895. Britain then induced Europeans to settle in the region, which was valued as a gateway to Uganda. Most of the usable land was occupied by Europeans, and the local tribesmen were driven to the least desirable locations. In 1920, Kenya became a colony.

A movement for African control and for independence began within the decade. The tribes organized in a guerrilla strike force known as the Mau Mau, and eventually brought self-government by stages. Jomo Kenyatta became a member of the colonial cabinet in 1962 and was prime minister when Kenya became independent on December 12, 1963. Four days later the country was admitted to the United Nations.

KUWAIT

In 1716, settlements were established in Kuwait by migrants from the neighboring Arabian Desert. The present ruling dynasty dates from 1756. British protection was extended upon the invitation of the Sheikh Mubarak al-Sabah (1896–1915), to prevent occupation by the Turks. After World War I Kuwait became independent, but remained under the protection of the British Crown. On June 19, 1961, that protection was terminated by mutual consent.

On May 14, 1963, the United Nations admitted Kuwait to membership. Kuwait exercises a great influence on Middle East and world affairs because of her enormous oil resources, which were largely developed by American companies since World War II. The country consistently supports the Arab anti-Israeli position.

LAOS

In the thirteenth century the Thai (Siamese) people migrated southward from China into Indochina, where they organized Lao tribes into a powerful kingdom that reached its peak in the seventeenth century, with its capital at Vientiane. The decline of this kingdom was complete with the fall of Vientiane to the Thais in 1827. The French, who had acquired a foothold on the Indochinese coast (in Annam and Tonkin, now North Vietnam), attached Laos to their Union of Indochina in 1893. In 1899 Laos became a French protectorate.

Japan occupied Indochina in World War II. Upon their withdrawal, resistance movements arose in all the Indochinese states. The most influential movement was that of the Vietminh, led by Ho Chi Minh in Vietnam. In 1949, a Laotian monarchy was reinstated and its government was recognized as independent within the French Union; but a dissident faction, the Pathet Lao, arose in 1953. Generally sympathetic with the Vietminh, the Pathet Lao participated at times in government with the monarchy. The kingdom of Laos became a member of the United Nations on December 14, 1955, and was assured of the protection of the anticommunist Southeast Asia Treaty Organization.

As the Pathet Lao accepted more and more aid from North Vietnam, it was inevitable that the Indochina War would involve Laos. One of the main routes used by North Vietnamese forces to reach their targets in South Vietnam passed through eastern Laos. In 1970, United States and South Vietnamese forces made a brief and unsuccessful incursion into southern Laos. With the victory of the communist forces in Indochina in 1975, the coalition and the monarchy yielded to Pathet Lao control.

LEBANON

The name *Lebanon* is derived from a great mountain range that extends through the country. The history of Lebanon has been associated with that of Syria since Phoenician times. Tyre, Sidon, and Byblos were famous Phoenician trade centers which sent colonists to found Carthage, Marsailles, Cádiz, and other cities along the Mediterranean Sea. Syria and Lebanon were united under Alexander the Great, under Rome, and later under the Arabs and Turks. Christians from Syria sought refuge in Lebanon, and the Druze sect of Islam also escaped to the Lebanese mountains and forests for protection. The Crusaders controlled parts of Lebanon in the thirteenth century, and left descendants there.

Modern Lebanon dates only from the 1860s, when France intervened in the Turkish rule of Lebanon in order to protect Maronite Christians who had revolted against the Druzes. From 1864 until World War I, the Turks ruled Lebanon under an agreement that permitted Christian freedom. During the war, France and Britain came to an agreement concerning the postwar division of the Middle East. Syria and Lebanon were allotted to France, and this change was approved by the League of Nations in 1923. At this time the state of Greater Lebanon was created, with a population about evenly divided between Moslems and Christians. The constitution of 1926 provided that the division would be reflected in the political institutions. This originated the tradition that the president should be a Christian and that he appoint a Moslem prime minister. As the Moslem population began to outnumber the Christians, this failed to be reflected in the legislature.

Plans for Lebanese independence were suspended by the conditions of World War II, when the Vichy French who controlled Lebanon were displaced in 1941 by the Free French. In 1945, the independence of Lebanon was recognized, and the country was admitted to the United Nations on October 24, 1945.

The government was fairly stable and the country was the most prosperous in the Arab world. In the conflict between the Arab states and Israel, Lebanon sided with the Arabs. The possibility of Communist influence in 1958 led President Dwight D. Eisenhower to send a large contingent of American troops to Lebanon, but they were not used in combat.

In the 1970s, the Palestinian Arabs used Lebanese soil to establish bases for raids on Israel, and this resulted in Israeli raids on Lebanon. A civil war broke out in 1975, with the Christian minority arrayed against a combination of Palestinians and Lebanese Moslems. The principal issue appeared to be the inequity of Moslem representation in Lebanese government.

The problem has been seriously exacerbated by the action of neighboring Mideast nations to protect their own interests, among them Israel and Syria. In 1982, the United States, France and Italy sent in a "peacekeeping force" that failed in its objective. In early 1984, all three nations were preparing to withdraw their forces.

LEEWARD ISLANDS

The most northerly group of islands in the Lesser Antilles of the British West Indies is called the Leeward Islands. They were discovered by Columbus in 1493, and they all have had a great degree of autonomy under British administration.

The British Virgin Islands may be considered part of this group. They were acquired in 1666 and never formed part of the West Indies Federation that existed from 1958 to 1962. All the other Leeward Islands did belong to this federation.

Antigua and Barbuda, St. Kitts-Nevis, and Anguilla are now independent nations.

LESOTHO

A small enclave within South Africa, the kingdom of Lesotho is administered under its own constitution by a hereditary monarchy. Its people, however, depend for their livelihood on the economy of the surrounding republic. The Basutos, a

Lebanon—Temple of Bacchus (or Venus), Baalbek

Lesotho—Women building a road

Bantu people, sought British aid against the threatened encroachments of the Boers in 1867. In 1868, the area was acquired by Britain, and three years later it was annexed to Cape Colony (now Cape Province of South Africa). After a revolt of the Basutos, their territory became the crown colony of Basutoland in 1884. It was excluded from South Africa when the Union was formed in 1909.

When the Union became the Republic of South Africa in 1961, the continued separation of Basutoland was reconsidered. The British had permitted the Basuto monarchy to function, and the republic chose not to challenge the tradition. On October 4, 1966, Basutoland became the independent country of Lesotho. It was admitted to the United Nations on October 17, 1966. It chose to remain within the British Commonwealth.

After the government of Prime Minister Chief Leabua Jonathan lost an election in 1970, Jonathan suspended the constitution and parliament and the king was forced to flee from Lesotho. In 1973, Jonathan promised that a constitutional system would be reinstated.

LIBERIA

Liberia was founded in 1822 by the American Colonization Society. It was designed to promote the establishment of a country for free American blacks. The first settlement was made near the present city of Monrovia (named for James Monroe, fourth President of the United States). Immigration by blacks continued even after the American Civil War.

In 1847, the Republic of Liberia was established. Before it became well established, it lost a considerable amount of territory to French and British colonies. The United States aided in the country's finances, military organization, and in settling boundary disputes.

Liberia joined the United Nations on November 2, 1945.

LIBYA

Phoenician and Greek states competed for the control of the fertile Mediterranean coast of what is now Libya from 500 B.C. to 250 B.C. Romans replaced the Greeks in the third century before Christ. During the Phoenician, Greek, and Roman periods, some of the most prosperous and beautiful cities in the ancient world flourished along the coast.

Beginning with Vandal invasions in the fourth century A.D., Libya (the Greek name for the region) was looted and the cities were ruined. The region was then ruled in succession by the Byzantines, Arabs, and Turks (Ottoman Empire) down to the nineteenth century. It became part of the Barbary Coast of pirate strongholds, ruled by feudal deys. Between 1802 and 1805, the United States fought the pirates of Tripoli. United States Marines stormed the city in 1805. (Tripoli in Libya should not be confused with the ancient Tripoli in Lebanon).

Italy occupied Libya in 1911, but was unable to secure full control until the defeat of the Sanusi movement in 1931. In World War II, Libya became a major battlefield between the British Eighth Army and Field Marshal Rommel's German Africa Corps. Fierce tank battles developed as Rommel advanced along the coast to threaten Egypt. The battle of El Alamein in Egypt, in June 1942, was one of the critical engagements of World War II. It resulted in the defeat of Rommel, his long retreat westward back through Libya, and his final expulsion from Africa (*see* Tunisia).

Libya was not returned to Italy, which had sided with the Axis powers in the war. After a brief period of British and French control, the United Nations recognized the independence of the country under a monarchy.

With the discovery of oil in Libya and the rising resentment against remnants of British and American control, an insurrection occurred in 1969, led by a military junta. Its principal leader, Muammar al-Qadaffi, became dictator of the country.

Libya began buying jet fighters and other advanced weapons from France and the Soviet Union. In 1977, the Libyan army fought several border battles with Egypt, and Chad accused Libya of invading its northern uranium fields.

Deterioration of relations between the United States and Libya led to the closing on May 6, 1981, by the United States of the Libyan mission in Washington.

LIECHTENSTEIN

The history of Liechtenstein dates back to 1342. Its present boundaries were fixed in 1434. Liechtenstein is a sovereign European state, described as a constitutional monarchy and ranked as a principality. It consists of two counties (Vaduz and Schellenberg); it is bordered on the east by Austria, on the west by Switzerland.

LUXEMBOURG

The present Duchy of Luxembourg was originally a part of Roman-held territories called Belgica, from which the name Belgium was derived. It became a part of Charlemagne's empire from A.D. 800 until A.D. 963.

Luxembourg was founded in 963 by Count Sigefroid, a son of Charlemagne. The territory was greatly enlarged under Countess Ermesinde (1196–1247). Charles IV (1346–1378) became also emperor of the Holy Roman Empire, and it was he who made Luxembourg a duchy. After 1443, the duchy remained under foreign control for four hundred years.

The duchy was awarded to the Netherlands' king as a grand duchy in 1815; and in 1839, it lost more than half of its territory to the new Kingdom of Belgium. By the Treaty of London in 1867 Luxembourg was declared an independent state under the protection of the Great Powers.

The duchy was overrun in World Wars I and II, but in each case its territory was restored after the war. Luxembourg was admitted to the United Nations on October 24, 1945.

MACAO

Located on the coast of China southwest of Hong Kong, Macao was acquired by the Portuguese in 1557 and remained in their hands by an agree-

Libya—Theatre Sabratha near Tripoli

ment with the Chinese Empire in 1887. The Communist Chinese made no attempt to recover the peninsula and two small islands.

Macao, previously an overseas province of Portugal, was given increased autonomy in 1976 when it was redesignated a territory. Statutes passed by its assembly became as binding as laws, rather than as provisional decrees subject to Portuguese approval, and the territory was made responsible for its own defense and security.

MALAGASY REPUBLIC

The name *Madagascar* is applied generally to the large island off Africa's east coast, but it is often also used as an alternate name of the Malagasy Republic. The culture and language of the Malagasy people reveal a clear relationship with Indonesian peoples, and it has been established that the island was first colonized by Indonesians before the Christian era. Arabs, Phoenicians, and Chinese have also visited Madagascar in historic times. The Portuguese were the first Europeans to sight the island (1500). French, Dutch, and British competed in the seventeenth century for trading rights on the island.

The French gradually won out but had to deal with strong native kingdoms and were expelled for a time (1672) in an uprising of the native peoples. The French maintained a tenuous control until the twentieth century. In 1896, they made Madagascar a colony, and achieved military supremacy over the natives. National feelings continued to run high after the conquest.

France gradually permitted internal self-government. In 1947, rebellion broke out and thousands died in the year of fighting that followed. In 1958, Madagascar voted to join the new French Community of Nations. The Malagasy Republic was established in 1959 and became a sovereign state on June 26, 1960. It was admitted to the United Nations on September 20, 1960.

A coup in 1972 threw out the French-supported government in favor of a new socialist regime. The Malagasy leaders closed down French businesses and a United States satellite-tracking station. They turned to Communist China for financial aid. Several Arab business concerns have opened offices on the island.

MALAWI

Formerly known as Nyasaland, the area west and south of Lake Nyasa was crossed by David Livingstone in 1859. It became a British protectorate (British Central Africa) in 1891, and was renamed Nyasaland in 1907. In 1953, the protectorate was joined with Northern and Southern Rhodesia to form the Central African Federation, but nine years later Nyasaland withdrew from the federation, which was dissolved in 1963. On July 6, 1964, Nyasaland became the independent state of Malawi, and on December 1, 1964, it became a member of the United Nations. In 1966, Malawi decided to become a republic, although it remained within the British Commonwealth.

MALAYSIA

The Peninsula of Malaya lies across the Strait of Malacca from the island of Sumatra. For centuries it has been a land bridge between the Asian continent and the South Pacific islands. By the thirteenth century, Indian, Chinese, and Islamic cultures had reached and mingled here. Europeans entered Malaya during the fifteenth and sixteenth centuries (first the Portuguese, then the Dutch). British influences appeared in the eighteenth century, when Britain took Malacca from the Dutch. They also leased Penang Island; and in 1819, they acquired Singapore at the tip of Malaya.

The opening of the Suez Canal and the introduction of rubber trees from South America changed the economy of Malaya. By the end of the first decade of the twentieth century, Britain had treaty relationships with rulers of all the Malay states. Japan occupied the area during World War II. In 1946, these protectorates were formed into a Union and two years later into the Federation of Malaya, which also absorbed from the former crown colony of the Straits Settlements both Penang and Malacca (Singapore having been made a separate colony). The Federation of Malaya was granted independence within the British Commonwealth on August 31, 1957. And on September 17, 1957, it joined the United Nations. On September 16, 1963, two British Colonies in Borneo—Sarawak and North Borneo (renamed Sabah—and the independent state of Singapore joined the Federation, which changed its name to Malaysia. In 1965, Singapore withdrew to become an independent country once more.

Malaysia—Town of Lota Kinabalu, capital of Sabah

MALDIVE ISLANDS

This group of coral islands lies some four hundred miles south of Sri Lanka (formerly Ceylon). They were a protectorate of Ceylon after the seventeenth century; when the British acquired Ceylon, they also took over the protectorate. The islands served as a British military base until 1976.

With the independence of Ceylon in 1948, British protection was maintained. On July 26, 1965, the Maldives became independent. The country was admitted to the United Nations on September 21, 1965, and became a republic in 1968.

MALI

A great Moslem empire named Mali flourished in the western Sudan during the early part of the fourteenth century. Its ruler, Mansa Musa, conquered Timbuktu (now Tombouctou) and became legendary in African history. The empire disintegrated long before the French reached the region in the late nineteenth century. They established French West Africa in 1904, and within it the territory called French Sudan, east of Senegal.

After World War II, the French Sudan became an overseas territory; and in 1957, it was granted the right to rule itself. In 1958, the Sudanese Republic was formed within the French Union. In 1959, this republic joined with its neighbor, Senegal, as the Federation of Mali.

Senegal withdrew from the federation the next year, and the independent Republic of Mali emerged on September 22, 1960. Six days later Mali became a member of the United Nations.

The constitutional regime endured until 1968, to be replaced by a military dictatorship.

MALTA

Malta has been under the rule of Phoenicians, Greeks, Carthaginians, Romans, and Arabs. In A.D. 1090, it became a part of Sicily; and in 1530, it was taken by the Knights of St. John. It was ruled by them until Napoleon captured it in 1798. After the defeat of Napoleon in 1814, the island was annexed to the British Crown.

Because of its strategic location between Sicily and North Africa, Malta has always been of great military importance. It was so useful to the British during World War II that its people were given a unique unit citation, the George Cross, for their contribution. The Maltese were accustomed to considerable local self-government, but British international policy slowed down the drive toward genuine autonomy. When the State of Malta was officially created in 1961, defense and external affairs were kept in British hands.

Following a referendum on the island, Malta acquired its independence on September 21, 1964. It remained within the Commonwealth, but chose to become a republic in 1974. It became a member of the United Nations on December 1, 1964.

MARTINIQUE

Martinique was discovered by Columbus in 1502 and colonized by the French in 1635. It has remained a French possession since 1815, first as a colony and since 1946 as an overseas department.

MAURITANIA

Like other North African countries, the territory of Mauritania derives its name from its Moorish population. However, the modern Mauritania has no other relationship to ancient Mauretania.

European traders were attracted to this barren region of northwest Africa as early as the fifteenth century, because it produced the valuable commodity called "gum arabic." The Berbers brought Islam to the region in the eleventh century, and they were in turn supplanted by Arabs. But enduring European control was imposed by the French, who set up French West Africa in 1904, including the protectorate established the preceding year over Mauritania. The colony of this name was organized in 1920, and it became an overseas territory in 1946.

On November 28, 1960, independence was granted to the Islamic Republic of Mauritania. On October 27, 1961, the country was admitted to the United Nations. In 1975, Mauritania annexed the southern part of the former Spanish Sahara, but Saharan guerrillas resisted the change.

MAURITIUS

An uninhabited island in the Indian Ocean east of Madagascar attracted Dutch colonists early in the seventeenth century. They named the island for Prince Maurice, son of William of Orange. African slaves were imported by the next owners of the land, the French; and after the British seized it in 1810, they brought in laborers from India, who became a majority of the island's dense population.

On March 12, 1968, Mauritius became an independent state within the British Commonwealth. She joined the United Nations on April 24, 1968.

MEXICO

The pre-Columbian history of Mexico is that of three related civilizations that grew up in the Valley of Mexico and the Yucatan region. Two of these civilizations were the most advanced cultures in pre-Columbia America. The first was the Mayan, described elsewhere (*see* Guatemala). The great cities of Chichen Itza, Mayapan, and Uxmil were located in present-day Mexico, in the Yucatan re-

Mexico—Metropolitan Cathedral, Mexico City

gion. The Mayan civilization flourished from the third century B.C. until about the thirteenth century A.D. The Nahua group of people, which includes the Toltecs and the later Aztecs, developed a high culture in the Great Valley of Mexico about the tenth century A.D. The Aztecs, who conquered the Toltecs, built the brilliant culture that Cortés found and destroyed in A.D. 1519. The Spanish brought their Catholic religion, legal and economic systems, and imposed them upon the Aztecs, enslaving part of the population.

The Spanish gradually extended their control outward from the Valley of Mexico until their possessions extended as far north as northern California and as far south as Guatemala. A movement for independence developed after the Napoleonic occupation of Spain had weakened the Spanish monarchy and imperial control over outlying areas. In 1810, a revolt broke out, led by a priest, Miguel Hidalgo, and later by another priest, José Maria Morelos. Finally, in 1821, Mexican independence was achieved under Vicente Guerrero and Agustin de Iturbide.

Mexico became a republic in 1823. But between 1834 and 1849 the government was controlled by dictators. Texas seceded in 1835 and joined the United States. The subsequent war between the United States and Mexico ended in defeat for Mexico and the loss of its northwestern region.

A reform government was inaugurated in 1855, but France invaded Mexico in 1861. Archduke Maximilian of Austria was placed on the throne of a French puppet state. The Mexicans revolted, executed Maximilian, and restored the republic in 1867.

In the twentieth century, Mexico has become a powerful nation, playing a leading role in Latin American affairs. Its abundant oil supply gave its economy a boost during the height of the oil shortage of the '70s but inflation and the drop in oil prices caused an economic crisis. The peso was devalued and private banks were nationalized. The U.S. maintains friendly ties with the "south of the border" country.

MONACO

Monaco dates from A.D. 1338 when the principality was established. In 1815 it was placed under the protection of the Kingdom of Sardinia (now part of Italy). It was at that time larger than it is today. It lost territory to Sardinia and France in 1848 and 1861.

In 1861, Monaco became a protectorate of France but remained otherwise independent. It is a favorite resort area.

MONGOLIA

Mongolia is an ancient land, the original center of a powerful empire that extended from the Pacific Ocean to the Danube. The most famous Mongol khan was Genghis, who led the invasion of India and Russia in the thirteenth century. More enduring empires were formed by the Golden Horde in Russia, by the Tartars in southern Asia, and by Kublai, who founded a Chinese dynasty that lasted nearly a century (1279–1368). Later, India was ruled by Mongols (known as Moguls), and Tamerland threatened Europe with a Mongol invasion.

In modern times Mongolia refers to a region north of China. The Manchus brought some of the Mongols under their control in the seventeenth century. The rest of the Mongols were not subjugated until the eighteenth century.

In 1911, the Manchu dynasty of China was overthrown, and the area known as Outer Mongolia declared its independence, while Inner Mongolia was incorporated into China. Outer Mongolia was ruled by the so-called "Living Buddha," who died in 1924. During the Russian Revolution, anticommunist ("white") Russians seized control of the region until communist forces defeated them in 1921. The communists allowed the monarchy to remain until 1924, when the Mongolian People's Republic was established in the Soviet image. This republic was not recognized by China until 1946. It was admitted to the United Nations on October 28, 1961. Treaties between Mongolia and the Soviet Union in 1966 and 1976 have brought large numbers of Russian troops to the country.

MOROCCO

The Phoenicians discovered and colonized the coast of what is now Morocco in about 1200 B.C. The Carthaginians later established control and expanded their area. Roman legions took over after the fall of Carthage in 146 B.C. The region was called Mauretania by the Romans (not to be confused with the modern republic of Mauritania).

As the Roman Empire disintegrated, northern Africa was subjected to invasions. The Vandals crossed from Spain to conquer the region early in the fifth century and were not expelled until the middle of the sixth century by the Byzantine general Belisarius. Arabs brought the religion of Islam as they swept westward across Africa in the seventh century. They united with the native Berbers in a dynasty that consolidated a great empire in what is now Morocco, Spain, Portugal, Algeria, Tunisia, and Libya. This empire flourished under the Almorovids, Almohades, Marinids, and finally the Sa'adi dynasties. The last dynasty brought about the great golden age of Moroccan history. Vast treasures in gold and ivory were amassed in the magnificent capital of Marrakech. This dynasty fought fierce wars with the Great Mali Empire and captured Timbuktu (Tombouctou) in 1591 (*see* Mali). The present dynasty of Morocco was established in 1649, and still occupies the throne.

Morocco was drawn into European conflicts chiefly because of its strategic location in Africa. France had conquered neighboring Algeria in 1832 and also became interested in Morocco. The French defeated a combined Algerian and Moroccan army in 1844. Thereafter French influence began to grow in the country.

Spain invaded northern Morocco in 1860. The next 50 years were marked by rivalry between France and Spain for control of Morocco. This rivalry almost caused a world war until the Treaty of Algeciras settled the rivalry in favor of France. Spain retained the "Rif" region of northern Morocco until expelled in the Rif War of the 1930s that helped bring on the Spanish Civil War (*see* Spain). In 1912, Morocco became officially a protectorate of France. In 1923, Tangier was separated and established as an international trading and financial zone.

In 1953, the French tried to overcome the movement toward independence by deposing the Sultan Mohammed V. On March 2, 1956, France acknowledged the independence of Morocco. On April 7, 1956, Spain followed suit. Tangiers was turned over to Morocco on October 29, 1956, and the country was admitted to the United Nations on November 12, 1956. Only the so-called Spanish presidios within Morocco remained under Spanish rule. In 1975, Spain allowed Morocco to acquire the northern part of its former colony of Spanish Sahara.

MOZAMBIQUE

Mozambique was discovered by Vasco da Gama for Portugal in 1498 and was colonized by the Portuguese in 1505. The boundaries became fixed at the end of the nineteenth century. It generally became known as Portuguese East Africa. In 1951, Mozambique was designated an overseas province of Portugal. In 1962, some inhabitants of the province formed the Mozambique Liberation Front, or *Frelimo,* to win independence. The Portuguese revolution of 1974 resulted in the victory of Frelimo in Mozambique, for independence was granted on June 25, 1975. The country became a member of the United Nations on September 16, 1975.

NAMIBIA

In 1884, Germany was given control of the region known as South-West Africa. The Germans turned the area over to South Africa in 1915, and it was governed under supervision of the League of Nations. The United Nations tried to assume this advisory role, but South Africa rejected its instructions.

In May 1968, the United Nations formed a council to plan the liberation of South-West Africa. The UN renamed the area "Namibia" and criticized South Africa for claiming the land. Marxist groups have begun raids on South African strongholds in Namibia, in an effort to force the country's independence.

NAURU

A tiny island in the Pacific Ocean, northeast of the Solomons, Nauru was annexed by Germany in 1888. After World War I, it was mandated to Australia. After World War II, Australia continued to administer Nauru under United Nations auspices. On January 31, 1968, Nauru became an independent republic with a special relationship with the British Commonwealth.

NEPAL

Little was known about the land until the fourteenth century A.D., when a Rajput ruler established a dynasty which lasted into the eighteenth. Later, Gurkhas and Chinese invaded and occupied the land.

The nineteenth century brought more conflict. As a result of border disputes, British-Nepalese relations deteriorated and the war of 1814 followed, with Britain victorious. During World War I, Nepal aided British forces and was granted independence in 1923. In World War II, Nepal was again on the Allied side.

An attempt to institute parliamentary government failed in 1959. Nepal was admitted to the United Nations on December 14, 1965. The nation has forged closer links with India and Communist China in recent years.

NETHERLANDS

Recorded history in the Netherlands began with the conquest by Julius Caesar in 55 B.C. The end of Roman rule triggered clashes between Saxon and Frankish forces over control of the region. (Christianity was introduced about A.D. 800.) Charlemagne and the Franks won control, but after his death the area of the present Netherlands became a part of the Holy Roman Empire.

The seeds of capitalism and individual enterprise were being sown at the same time. This was evident in the towns where a craftsman and merchant group began to challenge the ruling nobility, even during the Middle Ages. The country had several small, competing duchies and other feudal units.

Netherlands—Harbor of Rotterdam

first settled in the seventeenth century by Europeans. It is much smaller and is represented by a single legislator. The islands in this group are Saba, St. Eustachius, and Sint Maarten (the southern half of an island shared with France).

NEW CALDEDONIA

New Caledonia was discovered in 1768 by Louis Antoine de Bougainville. Captain James Cook named the island when he landed there in 1774.

New Caledonia became a French possession in 1853. It was long used as a penal colony. It became an overseas territory of France in 1946.

In 1477, the Spanish branch of the Hapsburg family acquired control of the Netherlands. By 1549, the Netherlands, Spain, and Austria were united under Hapsburg rule.

Soon thereafter the Dutch people began to revolt. By 1581, they had established a new republic, called United Provinces. In the seventeenth century, the United Provinces became one of the world's leading maritime and commercial powers. Rivalry with Britain wore down the republic's strength, however, and it succumbed to Napoleon's great invasion of 1795. The Netherlands were reestablished by the Congress of Vienna (1815), and remained independent until they were overwhelmed by the German blitzkrieg ("lightning war") invasion of 1940. After World War II, the rich Dutch East Indies were lost in a revolt which led to the creation of the Republic of Indonesia. The Netherlands joined the United Nations on December 10, 1945.

NEW HEBRIDES

These islands were discovered in 1606 and have been administered jointly by the United Kingdom and France. The people of the islands are mainly Melanesians.

The New Hebrides consist of 12 large islands and about 60 smaller islands. The group is located roughly 500 miles west of Fiji and 250 miles northeast of New Caledonia, in the South Pacific Ocean.

NEW ZEALAND

The Polynesian Maori people in the fourteenth century invaded the islands that now comprise modern New Zealand. The Dutch navigator Abel Tasman discovered New Zealand for Europeans in 1642. In 1769, Captain James Cook sailed around the island to determine its size. New Zealand was largely ignored thereafter until the nineteenth century when Britain took formal possession (1840).

NETHERLANDS ANTILLES

Two groups of islands in the Caribbean Sea constitute the Dutch dependency of the Netherlands Antilles.

The Leeward group, off the coast of Venezuela, comprises the islands of Curaçao, Aruba, and Bonaire, each of which is represented in the legislature. Discovered in 1499, they have been under Dutch control since 1634.

The Windward group, east of Puerto Rico, was

New Zealand—Wellington City and Harbor from Tinakori Hills

Colonization resulted in conflict with the native Maoris, and war with them continued until 1864. In 1867, Maoris were granted their own representatives in government. With the introduction of refrigeration, in 1882, New Zealand became a leading world exporter of dairy produce and meat. From then on economic development became rapid.

New Zealand became a colony in 1852, a dominion in 1907, and a sovereign state within the British Commonwealth in 1947. It was admitted to the United Nations on October 24, 1945.

NICARAGUA

Columbus discovered the coast of Nicaragua and landed there in 1502. The Spanish founded Granada and León in 1524. Throughout most of the colonial period the entire region was ruled by the Spanish from bases in Guatemala. The Central American areas of the Spanish Empire declared their independence on September 15, 1821. The United Provinces of Central America, a federation, was established in 1823, and Nicaragua was a part of it. Nicaragua withdrew from the federation in 1838 and became a republic.

During the nineteenth century Nicaragua was often considered as a possible site for a transcontinental canal. In the end, the canal was built across the Isthmus of Panama. Conditions in Nicaragua became unstable, and the United States occupied the country from 1912 to 1925, and from 1926 to 1933.

Marxist rebels began a round of terrorist murders and kidnappings in the early 1970s, and President Anastasio Somoza imposed martial law. The guerrillas, led by the Marxist Sandinista, invaded Nicaragua May 29, 1979, and the Somoza government toppled seven weeks later. The United States has since actively supported the anti-Sandinista rebels and imposed trade restrictions on Nicaragua's sugar exports.

NIGER

The first European explorers to enter the region that is now the Republic of Niger arrived in the mid-nineteenth century. In 1890, the French began to settle in the area, and its status progressed from military territory in 1900, to autonomous territory in 1922, to overseas territory in 1946. On August 3, 1960, Niger became an independent country. It was admitted to the United Nations on September 20, 1960.

NIGERIA

The eastern Guinea coast of Africa was first visited by the Portuguese in 1472. All of the maritime nations of Europe participated thereafter in its lucrative slave trade.

Britain abolished this trade and began to promote trade in palm oil in its place. To protect this interest, the British seized the town of Lagos in 1851. In 1861, the surrounding area was annexed as a colony. In 1888, the Yoruba country in the interior was also brought under British protection, a claim that won international recognition.

In 1900, the protectorate of Southern Nigeria was formed; and in 1906, it became the Colony and Protectorate of Southern Nigeria. Simultaneously, Britain increased her control of the hinterland. Northern Nigeria became a protectorate and was combined with Southern Nigeria in 1914. A threefold division was made: the Lagos region became the Colony of Nigeria, while the remainder became the Eastern and Western provinces of the protectorate. In 1954, the Federation of Nigeria was formed under a single administration. The Eastern and Western regions were granted autonomy in 1957, the Northern in 1959. On October 1, 1960, the Federation of Nigeria became an independent state. It joined the United Nations six days later. In 1963, it became a republic.

The geographical divisions concealed a significant disunity within Nigeria, based on tribal allegiances—particularly involving the Hausa and Fulani in the north, the Yoruba in the west, and the Ibo in the east. This caused a savage civil war from 1967 through 1970, during which the Ibo attempted to form a separate state of Biafra. This disaster cost over a million casualties.

Calm settled over the nation with the restoration of civilian government in 1979 following 13 years of military government.

NORTH KOREA

Korea was recovered from Japanese occupation at the end of World War II. An administrative dividing line was established at the thirty-eighth parallel, pending an agreement between the Soviet Union and the United States liberation forces. Negotiations failed, but the division between the northern and southern parts of the country remained. North Korea was organized on May 1, 1948 on the Soviet model.

In 1950, North Korean forces invaded South Korea. The border war lasted three years and ended in a truce, with no territorial change. (For the history of Korea, *see* South Korea.)

NORWAY

The recorded history of Norway began during the eighth century, when a series of small kingdoms were established along the rocky coasts and deep inlets (called *fjords*) of Norway. The people who established these kingdoms were called Vikings.

The Viking period of Norwegian history lasted from about A.D. 800 to about A.D. 1050. In these years, the Vikings sailed sturdy longboats over the North Atlantic, reaching Ireland, the Hebrides, and southern Europe. They also sailed westward to Iceland, Greenland, and North America. Recent evidence has been found in Canada that proves Vikings spent some time there in about A.D. 1024. The Vikings also colonized Iceland, Greenland, and parts of western Europe. One of their most famous colonies was on the coast of northwestern France; this colony became Normandy, and the Vikings there became known as Normans. Their descendants conquered England and Ireland.

Norway was united for the first time in A.D. 860 by Harold the Fairhaired. King Olaf I introduced Christianity. After the close of the Viking period, Norway was weakened by the loss of trade to Hanseatic League cities and by internal dissension.

Norway lost its independence in 1380 when King Haakon of Denmark inherited the Norwegian kingdom. Denmark and Norway were united for more than four hundred years, and Norway was little more than a province in the Danish kingdom. Sweden was a part of this union from 1397 to 1523.

Denmark sided with Napoleon in the early years of the nineteenth century. As a result of Napoleon's defeat, Denmark was forced to give up Norway, which was then united with the Crown of Sweden. Denmark retained the former island colonies of Norway (Greenland, Iceland, and the Faroe Islands) that had come to be administered by Denmark during the union of the two countries.

Sweden and Norway remained united until 1905. Norway became a major maritime nation and selected King Haakon VII to be its king, despite Swedish opposition. The Swedes later recognized Norwegian independence.

Norway was neutral during World War I but was overrun by the Nazis during World War II. King Haakon and the government escaped to England. After the war, Norway joined NATO and abandoned her former neutral position. The kingdom was admitted to the United Nations on November 27, 1945.

OMAN

Oman is the southeastern part of the Arabian Peninsula, extending along the Arabian Sea. It is under the control of an Arab sultan whose forebears came from Yemen in 1744 and expelled the Persians. In 1798, the descendants of this Yemenite conqueror obtained protection from the British and succeeded in building an empire (called Muscat and Oman) that included Zanzibar and part of the East African coast, as well as a coastal section of Baluchistan. Only in 1958 did the small empire give its last enclave in Baluchistan back to Pakistan. In 1965, the United Nations recommended that Britain end its protectorate, but no formal action was taken. The sultan who seized the throne from his father in 1970 changed the country's name to Oman. On October 7, 1971, Oman was admitted to the United Nations.

PAKISTAN

The religion of Islam spread rapidly over southern Asia after the eighth century. In the tenth century a Moslem warrior group swept into India by way of the Khyber Pass in the west. Moslem power and influence moved eastward along the Ganges Plain and southward in the valley of the Indus River. By the sixteenth century it had reached Bengal on the far eastern edge of the Indian subcontinent and included most of the lower Ganges and Bengal regions.

Under British influence during the eighteenth and nineteenth centuries, the Moslem position was threatened by the rise of Hindu patriotism. In

1906, the All-India Moslem League was founded to help create a Moslem state.

The Moslem leader Mohammed Ali Jinnah invented the name *Pakistan* (from the first letters of "Punjab," "Afghan," and "Kashmir," and the remainder from "Baluchistan"). The Dominion of Pakistan came into existence amid riots and bloodshed in 1947. On March 3, 1956, Pakistan was proclaimed the Islamic Republic of Pakistan, but retained full membership in the British Commonwealth of Nations. The constitution proved unsatisfactory and was abolished within two years. A new constitution in 1962 provided for two provinces—West Pakistan and East Pakistan— each with its own legislature. This arrangement also proved unworkable, for the Bengalis of East Pakistan felt they were at a disadvantage. Again the constitution was abolished in 1969, and in the elections of 1971 the East Pakistan voters exerted their full powers.

When the president of Pakistan delayed convening of the legislature, East Pakistan declared itself independent. A rebellion broke out, and it was only with the aid of India that East Pakistan was able to defeat West Pakistan late in 1971. As a result, East Pakistan became the independent state of Bangladesh, and only West Pakistan remained to bear the name of the country. Once more a constitution was framed, and the country adopted the name of the Islamic Republic of Pakistan. But this time it withdrew from the Commonwealth, in which Bangladesh chose to remain.

Pakistan—Badshahi Mosque at Lahore

Pakistan's proximity to Afghanistan has made it a refuge for Afghans fleeing the Russian invasion of their country. The United States began sending economic and military aid to Pakistan in 1981.

PANAMA

The Isthmus of Panama was first seen by white men in 1501 when the Spaniard Rodrigo de Bastides landed near the present Portobelo. Columbus saw the isthmus the following year and claimed it for Spain. Balboa crossed the isthmus in 1513 and discovered the Pacific Ocean (which he named). Balboa also became the first governor of the region.

When the Spanish conquistadores began their conquest of the fabulous Inca Empire in South America, they used the Isthmus of Panama to carry supplies, soldiers, and captured treasures. British buccaneers made daring raids against strong points in Panama and against Spanish galleons that sailed to and from Panama, laden with gold and other loot from the Inca Empire.

In 1739, Panama was attached to the viceroyalty of New Granada that included the present Colombia, Panama, and Venezuela. In 1821, Panama became a part of the independent Gran Colombia, a new state that comprised the present Colombia, Venezuela, Ecuador, and Panama. Upon dissolution of Gran Colombia in 1830, Panama remained a part of Colombia. With the help of the United States, it was separated from Colombia in 1903 to facilitate the building of a projected canal across the isthmus. From time to time, Panama demanded that the zone (leased in perpetuity to the United States) be restored to Panamanian sovereignty. The United States signed a treaty to that effect in 1978.

For up-dated information on the Canal Zone, see "Outlying U.S. Areas."

PAPUA NEW GUINEA

New Guinea is an island north of Australia, also known as Papua or Irian. Its western half was once Netherlands New Guinea and was annexed in 1963 by Indonesia. The eastern half of New Guinea is itself divided into two portions, the most northerly of which was known as German New Guinea from 1884 to 1914. It was captured during World War I by Australia and became an Australian mandate, the Territory of New Guinea, in 1920. The southeastern quarter of the island was seized in 1883 by the British colony of Queensland (Australia). It was annexed by Great Britain as the colony of British New Guinea in 1888, and handed over to Australia in 1906 to become the Territory of Papua.

None of these incursions by Europeans profoundly involved the native population, which is largely Melanesian or black. The Territory of New Guinea has been administered by Australia since 1949. With the gradual increase of self-government, Papua New Guinea became capable of achieving independence, which was granted on September 16, 1975. Papua New Guinea was admitted to the United Nations on October 10, 1975.

PARAGUAY

The region of present Paraguay was first visited by Europeans in the expedition of Juan de Salazar that founded Asunción in 1537. The Jesuits came later and gathered together the Guaraní Indians to build a remarkable series of prosperous Guaraní communities in the region. Spanish colonists initiated a campaign of slander against the Jesuits that led to the destruction of the mission communities. The Guarani were eventually destroyed as a people.

The Spanish ruled Paraguay as a part of the viceroyalty of Peru and then as part of La Plata. La Plata declared independence from Spain in 1810. After the expulsion of the Spanish, Uruguay and Paraguay then fought Argentina, which was attempting to annex them.

Nearly all of Paraguay's history since that time has been concerned with wars and dictatorial rule. The War of the Triple Alliance (1865–1870) was the bloodiest in the history of Latin America. It was fought by Brazil, Uruguay, and Argentina against Paraguay. Paraguay was crushed, her economy completely ruined; she has never recovered from this disaster. In 1932, a long dispute between Paraguay and Bolivia erupted into another war that lasted until 1938. Economic difficulties and dictatorial rule have continued in the post-World War II period. Paraguay became a member of the United Nations on October 24, 1945.

Paraguay has joined its modernized neighbor, Brazil, in a series of projects to aid the economies of both. They have built a highway linking the two countries; and in 1974, they signed a pact to build the world's largest electric generator on the Paraná River.

PERU

The Inca civilization that developed in pre-Columbian Peru arose slowly from a nucleus in the Cusco Valley about A.D. 1200. In 1438 the empire began to expand under Pachacuti and his son Topa Inca. At its height, the empire had about twelve million people and included most of what is today Peru, Bolivia, Chile, Ecuador. The Incas built great palaces, irrigation works, highways, and cities. Arts, handicrafts, and agriculture were developed to a degree equalled only by the Mayan people of Mexico and Guatemala.

Francisco Pizarro brought down the empire in 1532 and 1533. In 1535, the city of Lima was founded. It became the capital of a wealthy Spanish empire in America. Treasures of gold and silver poured a veritable flood into the Spanish treasury. Indians were enslaved to work the gold mines. The Spanish treasure galleons bound from Peru became the favorite target of English "sea dogs."

Simón Bolívar and José de San Martín landed in Peru in 1820 and by 1824 (Battle of Ayacucho) had destroyed the Spanish Empire in America. Peru thereafter was a republic, but experienced harsh rule under a rigid militarist group until the twentieth century. Peru lost a nitrate-rich region to Chile, in the War of the Pacific (1879–1884). Then Peru became a relatively stable country, with a constitution. It became a member of the United Nations on October 31, 1945.

Peru—San Martín Square, Lima

PHILIPPINES

The Philippines were discovered by Ferdinand Magellan while on his epic voyage around the world in 1521. Magellan was killed in the islands by native Filipinos. Despite revolts by Filipinos, the Spanish were able to retain control over the Philippines until the end of the nineteenth century. The islands were named for Philip II, King of Spain.

Revolutions in Central and South America stimulated an independence movement in the Philippines. A Filipino doctor named Emilio Aguinaldo stirred up a revolt in 1896 which merged with the Spanish-American War.

After the war had ended, Aguinaldo demanded independence. The Americans refused, and Aguinaldo revolted against them as well. He was captured in 1901. It was not until after World War II that the Philippines finally achieved independence.

In 1941, the Japanese invaded the Philippines. The fall of the Corregidor fortress in the harbor of Manila was a major event of World War II. Americans under Douglas MacArthur returned to the Philippines with a massive invasion force on October 20, 1944. Fighting had to be waged from island to island throughout the huge archipelago.

On July 4, 1946, the Philippines were granted independence. Aguinaldo, who was nearly one hundred years old, saw his dream realized. The Philippines were admitted to the United Nations on October 24, 1946.

At first the Philippines was a republic; but in 1973, President Ferdinand Marcos instituted a parliamentary dictatorship.

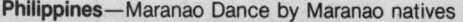

Philippines—Maranao Dance by Maranao natives

PITCAIRN

Pitcairn was discovered by Philip Carteret in 1767. In 1790, the island was occupied by nine mutineers from the British ship the *Bounty*, who brought with them 12 Tahitian women. Nothing more was heard of the island until the visit of an American ship in 1808. It was learned then that all the men had killed each other, except John Adams, who ruled the colony. In 1838, Britain took formal possession of the island. In 1856, all of the colonists were removed. Forty of them later returned, but the population never exceeded one hundred. The colony is administered from New Zealand.

POLAND

Poland dates from the unification of several small Slavic states in the tenth century. In A.D. 966, Christianity was introduced. Boleslaus the Brave (992–1025) made Poland an independent kingdom.

In 1241, the Mongols invaded Poland. The Teutonic knights helped to expel the Mongols, but remained to threaten Poland's independence. For centuries Poland has contended with German pressure from the west. Poland reached the height of her power from the fourteenth to sixteenth centuries under the Jagellon dynasty of rulers. She defeated the German Tannenberg order in 1410 and annexed Lithuania in 1569.

Polish power declined under German (Prussian), Swedish, and Russian invasions. The country eventually was divided among neighboring powers.

Napoleon's Grand Duchy of Warsaw partially revived Poland, but the revival ended in 1815 when Napoleon was defeated. Revolts in 1830, 1831, and 1863 were crushed. After the Allied victory in World War I, Poland became a republic in 1918. It was divided between Germany and the Soviet Union in 1939. The Nazi invasion of Poland was the opening phase of World War II. The Poles fought fiercely, especially around Warsaw, which was nearly destroyed. After Germany's invasion of the Soviet Union, Poland's forces fought their way back into German-occupied Poland.

After World War II, Poland was reconstituted with new borders. She gained territory from Germany and yielded territory to the Soviet Union; thus the entire country shifted toward the west. As the result of an election in 1947, a procommunist government was formed, which framed a constitution of the Soviet type in 1952.

Militant labor activists led a movement that culminated in 1980 with the government's granting workers the right to form independent trade unions and to strike. Further demands by the principal trade union, Solidarity, led the government to declare martial law. The United States imposed economic sanctions, and martial law was lifted in December 1982. Meanwhile, the government arrested Lech Walesa and other Solidarity leaders, who had called for a nationwide strike that did not materialize, but they were later released.

PORTUGAL

The Iberian Peninsula was wrested from Carthage by Roman armies in about 138 B.C. The section now known as Portugal was then called Lusitania. Starting in the fifth century A.D. and continuing until 711, Portugal was overrun by a succession of invaders, including Alans, Suevi, Visigoths, and Celtic peoples. In 711, the Arabs conquered the region, but Ferdinand of Castile regained it in 1139. By the thirteenth century, the boundaries of the nation were established and Lisbon was the capital.

During the reign of John (João) I (1385–1433), the Portuguese defeated the Spanish and began a period of growth and progress. Portuguese explorations of unknown regions began under John, who founded a school for navigation. A series of brilliant navigational exploits resulted in the establishment of a Portuguese Empire by the six-

teenth century. Bartholomew Diaz rounded the Cape of Good Hope in Africa (1486), discovering a new route to India. Vasco da Gama made the voyage to India in 1497, and Portuguese navigators discovered Brazil in 1500.

In 1580, Spain took over Portugal and its empire, but sovereignty was restored by a rebellion in 1640. A long war ensued. In 1668, Spain recognized Portugal's independence. Brazil was lost by Portugal in 1822, and the Bragança royal house was overthrown by a revolution in 1910. But instability plagued the nation until the rise of António de Oliveira Salazar, who became prime minister in 1932. He established a conservative dictatorship. In 1974, his successor, Marcello Caetano, was overthrown by a military junta. The administration wavered in its domestic policies, but abandoned the colonial empire that it was incapable of preserving. All the overseas territories of Africa became independent in 1974 and 1975, and Macao became an autonomous territory.

QATAR

On a peninsula jutting into the Persian Gulf, west of the United Arab Emirate is Qatar, formerly a British protectorate. It ended this relationship when it declared its independence on September 1, 1971. Admission to the United Nations followed in twenty days.

Qatar exports about one hundred seventy-eight million barrels of crude oil each year. The income from oil gives Qatar the second highest income per capita of any nation in the world.

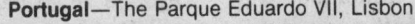
Portugal—The Parque Eduardo VII, Lisbon

RÉUNION

The largest island of the Mascarene group in the Indian Ocean was discovered by a Portuguese navigator in 1528, claimed by the French in 1638, and colonized by them in 1662. It was named Ile de Bourbon until after the French Revolution, when it was renamed La Réunion. In 1946, it became an overseas territory of France.

RHODESIA (Zimbabwe)

Cecil Rhodes, who organized the British South Africa Company in 1889, was responsible for the northward expansion of British holdings from Cape Colony at the tip of South Africa. By 1895, the Zambesi region was named Rhodesia, after Rhodes. The company administered the area under a British charter until the European settlers voted in 1923 to accept self-government, rather than join the Union of South Africa.

Meanwhile, the company had expanded its operations further north. These holdings were designated Northern Rhodesia in 1911, so the autonomous portion became known as the colony of Southern Rhodesia.

Government leaders were unable to bring the two regions together because Southern Rhodesia was controlled by its minority of white settlers, a prospect inacceptable to the black population of Northern Rhodesia. Nevertheless, the British government decided in 1953 to form a federation to include the two Rhodesias and adjoining Nyasaland. The federation was dissolved in 1963.

By this time, Southern Rhodesia had adopted a new constitution and committed itself against extending powers of government to its black majority. Great Britain disapproved this policy. So the government of Southern Rhodesia (which was renamed Rhodesia in 1964) declared its independence on November 11, 1965.

The United Nations asked all its members to impose economic sanctions against Rhodesia. Only Portugal and South Africa ignored the resolution. Rhodesia prospered as an independent nation and declared itself a republic in 1970.

Guerrilla forces began raiding government outposts to try to press the white leaders into a compromise. But peace talks failed, and the bush war spread into Mozambique. In 1977, the United States stopped buying chrome from Rhodesia to protest that government's hard line against black rule. Early in 1979, the white Rhodesians voted to relinquish their control of the government in coming years.

Elections were held and the country achieved independence on April 18, 1980.

ROMANIA

Most of the present Romania became a part of the Roman province of Dacia after Emperor Trajan conquered the Dacians in the fierce campaign of A.D. 101–106. Roman influence remained even after numerous invasions by other peoples in later centuries. The Dacians gradually emerged as the Vlachs or Wallachians who were converted to Christianity during the eleventh century.

Wallachia and another state called Moldavia developed in the region late in the thirteenth century. Wallachia was seized by the Turks in 1476 and Moldavia was taken over in 1513.

The Ottoman Empire's control over both areas was challenged from time to time by Russia. The latter took Bessarabia from Moldavia in 1812, and Austria seized Bucovina from Wallachia in 1775. The Russians invaded both areas in 1828, but released them in 1834.

The Congress of Paris established Wallachia and Moldavia as separate states, and they were united under Alexander Cuza in 1859. The resulting new nation was called Romania or Rumania.

During World War I, Romania joined the Allies, but was defeated by Germany early in 1918. Later that year Romania came back into the war on the Allied side. After the war Romania received the regions of Bucovina, Bessarabia, Transylvania, and Banat.

King Carol II, who had renounced the throne in 1925, was returned in 1930. Romania was caught in a series of threats and power moves by Russia, Germany, and Italy. King Carol abdicated and the country entered an alliance with the Axis powers on the side of Germany.

King Michael (son of Carol II) engineered a coup d'état in 1944. Romania then entered the war on the Allied side.

The communists gained election victories in 1947, and King Michael was forced to resign. Romania was then proclaimed a people's republic (in 1952 changed to "socialist republic"). It became a member of the United Nations on December 14, 1955.

RWANDA

The history of Rwanda is closely associated with the Tutsi (Watutsi) and Hutu Bahutu peoples. (The latter are a Bantu group.) The Tutsi early managed to become the ruling tribe and the Hutu became the feudal lower "caste." These conditions failed to change even when the white men came. Germany was awarded the country along with Urundi (the future Burundi) in 1884, and relations were peaceful with the native ruling Tutsi people. During World War I, Belgium occupied both Ruanda (the future Rwanda) and Urundi. The League of Nations attached both countries to the Belgian Congo in 1920. After World War II, Ruanda and Urundi (then called Ruanda-Urundi) became a single trust territory of the UN.

In 1959, clashes erupted between the Tutsi and the Hutu, the latter demanding basic freedoms. Tensions mounted until the United Nations called for popular elections, which abolished the monarchy in Ruanda. The UN hoped that the two sections would become a single independent state. However, internal differences prevented their unification. On July 1, 1962, Rwanda (with a slight change in spelling) became an independent nation. It was admitted to the United Nations on September 18, 1962.

ST. HELENA

The Portuguese discovered St. Helena in 1502. It has belonged to the United Kingdom since 1673.

St. Helena is a crown colony with several dependencies: Ascension Island, 700 miles to the northwest (administered with St. Helena since 1922), and the Tristan da Cunha archipelago, far to the south (so administered since 1938).

ST. PIERRE AND MIQUELON

These small islands lying ten miles south of Newfoundland are all that remain of the once-great French empire in North America. First settled by the French in 1604, they have been permanently French since 1816. The colony was given autonomy in 1935 and made an overseas territory in 1946.

SAMOA

This group of islands is located in the South Pacific, just east of Fiji and north of Tonga. It was a German colony from 1899 to 1914, when New Zealand landed troops on the main island and seized control. The League of Nations allowed New Zealand to administer the government of Samoa; and in 1945, the United Nations affirmed New Zealand's responsibility for the area.

The Samoans elected their own government in October 1959. The country became an independent monarchy on January 1, 1962, although New Zealand continues to give financial aid.

SAN MARINO

San Marino is the oldest republic in the world. According to tradition, it was founded in the fourth century by a Christian refugee from persecution. Its monastery has been occupied since A.D. 885. A tiny district in the midst of Italy's Apennine Mountains, San Marino preserved its independence throughout the Middle Ages and modern wars. A republic, it has a trade treaty with Italy.

SÃO TOMÉ AND PRÍNCIPE

São Tomé and Príncipe were discovered in 1471 and have been Portuguese territory since 1522. The islands became an overseas province in 1951 and were granted independence on July 12, 1975. Admission to the United Nations followed on September 16, 1975.

The country's first president, Manuel Pinto da Casta, was trained in East Germany.

SAUDI ARABIA

Saudi Arabia was founded by Abdu-l-Aziz ibn Sa'ud (1880–1953). However, the history of Saudi Arabia is closely associated with that of the Arabian peninsula, of which it occupies the greater part. (*See also* Kuwait and Yemen).

The Arabian peninsula has been inhabited throughout historic times by Semitic peoples, but unified states were not formed until the arrival of

Mohammed (A.D. 570–632), who founded Islam. Through Islam, the land of Arabia became famous throughout the world. Mohammed and his successors led the Arabians out of Arabia and spread their religion from the Atlantic Ocean to the borders of China and the Pacific Ocean. The Arabian language and culture became nearly as widespread as the religion of Islam, and remains so today.

Arabia declined soon after the Arab civilization reached other parts of the world. Little was known of life within Arabia for a thousand years thereafter.

The puritanical Islamic sect of Wahhabism was fused with the Sa'udi family in the eighteenth century, thus leading to the beginnings of the present kingdom of Saudi Arabia. By 1830, the Sa'udi family controlled Nejd, Hasa, and Oman. Setbacks occurred in the following years; but in 1901, Abdu-l-Aziz resumed his conquest of all Arabia. In 1906, he broke the power of the leading competing tribes. He captured Mecca in 1924, the Kingdom of Hejaz in 1926, and the Kingdom of Nejd in 1927. British recognition was accorded in 1927.

When Abdu-l-Aziz ibn Sa'ud died in 1953, he left a state that was largely his own creation. Arabia became a member of the United Nations on October 24, 1945.

King Faisal led the development of Saudi Arabia's crude oil reserves. The nation took control of the Arabian American Oil Company between 1973 and 1976, then launched a massive economic development program. Saudi Arabia gave financial aid to Egypt and other Arab countries in their conflict with Israel. Then King Faisal stopped oil shipments to the United States and other nations in 1973–1974 to protest American military aid to Israel.

Faisal was assassinated in March 1975, and Crown Prince Khalid became the new king.

Following Khalid's death, Fahd became king in June 1982. The United States had maintained friendly relations with the Saudis, who have exercised a moderate position in meetings of OPEC.

SÉNÉGAL

Prior to the coming of white men, Sénégal was at various times a part of the famous ancient empires of Ghana and of Mali. The Portuguese visited the present Sénégal in the fifteenth century. The French established Saint-Louis as a trading post at the mouth of the Sénégal River in 1659. From about 1870 to the end of the century, France secured Sénégal and consolidated its control.

The colony was transformed into a territory in 1946 and became autonomous in 1958. In January 1959, Sénégal and Sudan (the future Mali) joined in the Federation of Mali, but the federation broke up shortly after it became independent. Sénégal proclaimed its independence on August 20, 1960, and remained within the French Community of Nations. The country was admitted to the United Nations on September 28, 1960.

SEYCHELLES

The Seychelles archipelago was colonized by the French in the eighteenth century. The islands were captured by the British in 1794, included as a part of Mauritius in 1814, and organized as a colony in 1888. They became a crown colony in 1903, and were granted independence as of June 29, 1976.

SIERRA LEONE

Little is known of the history of Sierra Leone before its discovery by Europeans. About 1460, a Portuguese adventurer named Pedro da Cintra visited the region and gave it the present name. Some hundred years later an Englishman, Sir John Hawkins, landed an expedition to obtain slaves. Other slave traders followed.

During the seventeenth and eighteenth centuries, Sierra Leone was a pirate haunt. Around 1787, English abolitionists succeeded in having the government declare Sierra Leone to be the home for England's freed slaves.

By 1808, Sierra Leone was made a British colony with a Crown-appointed governor and advisory council. Schools were founded, frontiers with Liberia were agreed upon, and Africans were appointed to the executive council in an unofficial capacity. It was a long and slow, but orderly process.

In April 1961, Sierra Leone became independent and a member of the British Commonwealth of Nations. It maintains close ties with Great Britain. Sierra Leone was admitted to the United Nations on September 27, 1961.

SINGAPORE

A small island at the tip of the Malay Peninsula, Singapore, was founded by Sir Stamford Raffles in 1819. It was a trading post controlled by the British East India Company. Along with Penang and Malacca, it was designated as the colony of the Straits Settlements in 1867.

In 1946, Singapore became a separate crown colony and was given autonomy in 1959. Singapore joined the Federation of Malaysia in 1963, but chose to secede and become an independent republic on August 9, 1965. Shortly thereafter it joined the British Commonwealth, having already become a member of the United Nations on September 21, 1965.

SOLOMON ISLANDS

East of New Guinea is an archipelago, the Solomon Islands, that came under British protection in the last decade of the nineteenth century. They were the scene of heavy naval fighting during World War II. In the 1970s, they attained considerable self-government.

Not to be confused with this British protectorate (which includes such large islands as Guadalcanal and New Georgia) are a smaller chain of Solomon Islands to the west. This chain, including Bougainville, is part of the state of Papua New Guinea.

SOMALIA

The name *Somalia* is used here as the short form for the Somali Republic and should not be confused with the region of Somalia or Somaliland, of which it is only a part. The region includes parts of what are now Ethiopia, Kenya, and the Territory of Afars and Issas (former French Somaland).

The former Somaliland protectorate was under Egyptian control until it was acquired by Britain in 1884. It was administered as a dependency of India from Aden, until the Italians occupied it during World War II.

The colony of Italian Somaliland was established in 1889 south of the British protectorate, on a coast previously belonging to Zanzibar and to Kenya. During the war with Ethiopia in 1934, Italy added the Ethiopian province of Ogaden to its Somali colony. This colony became known as Italian East Africa; it was taken over by Britain during World War II. In 1950, the United Nations returned the former Italian Somaliland to Italy under mandate.

In June 1960, the British and Italian lands became independent and merged to form the Somali Republic on July 1. The country joined the United Nations on September 20, 1960. In 1970, a military coup changed the name to the Democratic Republic of Somalia. The new government permitted Soviet military bases to be built on Somali territory.

SOUTH AFRICA

Portuguese sailors rounded the Cape of Good Hope in 1488. One of them, Vasco da Gama, discovered the Natal coast in 1497. The first European settlement in the region was made by the Dutch at the Cape of Good Hope in 1652. Primitive Bushmen and Hottentots were the principal peoples that the white settlers found in southern Africa. They soon, however, came into contact with migrating Bantu peoples from the north. As settlement increased, conflict with Bantus arose in four separate wars, that occurred between 1779 and 1812.

The British occupied the Cape in 1795. As a result of the Napoleonic Wars, the entire colony was ceded to Great Britian in 1815. British settlers came in 1820 and slavery was abolished in 1834. The descendants of the Dutch became known as Afrikaners. Disputes with British policies led to the "Great Trek," a migration by the Afrikaners in 1836. They settled in Natal and north of the Vaal River (Transvaal). The British extended their control into those regions by the middle of the century, beginning with the annexation of Natal in 1843. By 1897, all of southern Africa, except the Orange Free State and the Transvaal, was under British rule of one form or another.

Meanwhile conflict with Africans resulted in the establishment of various *apartheid* projects, in which separate white and nonwhite settlements were developed. Nonwhite labor was essential to the economy, so *apartheid* could go only so far. The discovery of gold and diamonds brought an influx of immigrants and, with them, rising conflict between Afrikaners and the British government.

The conflict centered on the Afrikaner-controlled regions of Transvaal and the Orange

Free State. The latter had been independent since 1854, and the former since 1877.

The unsuccessful Jameson Raid of 1895 was followed by the Boer War of 1899–1902. (The descendants of the first Dutch settlers were also called Boers.) This war was between the British and an alliance of the Orange Free State and Transvaal. The two Boer republics lost their independence. In 1909 four states in southern Africa were combined to form the Union of South Africa, which was accepted as a member of the British Commonwealth of Nations (1926).

After World War II the Afrikaner segment of the population gained political control and legislated the separation of races. South Africa withdrew from the Commonwealth in 1960 and became a republic the following year.

South Africa became a member of the United Nations on November 7, 1945. Within the organization, she has been criticized by an increasing number of member states, partly because of her policy of *apartheid*.

In 1963, South Africa began setting up separate units for its black population known as *Bantustans*. Within a decade or so, most of the projected "homelands" were well under way. This did not improve the nation's image in black Africa.

SOUTH KOREA

The recorded history of Korea began with the migration of Tungusic people into northern Korea from Manchuria about four thousand years ago. At the beginning of the Christian era there were three kingdoms in Korea. One of these (the Silla dynasty) united all Korea in A.D. 669.

For many centuries thereafter, Chinese, Japanese, and Mongolians fought for possession of Korea. After the empire of Mongols fell in the thirteenth century, their power in the peninsula of Korea disappeared. In 1392, the strong Yi dynasty assumed the reins of government. A brilliant age of cultural development followed, in which the Korean alphabet was introduced and arts flourished.

A great war of survival against Japan broke out in 1592. Korea won the war but the country was left in a weakened condition.

The United States opened relations with Korea in 1882. Japan invaded Korea in 1904 and annexed the country in 1910, naming it Chosen. After the defeat of Japan in World War II, Korea was divided

temporarily at the thirty-eighth parallel between Soviet and United States jurisdictions, according to agreements made at Potsdam. When the two liberating nations failed to agree, separate regimes were set up at Pyongyang and at Seoul. The former organized a procommunist government (*see* North Korea) and the latter formed the Republic of Korea, usually known as South Korea, on August 15, 1948.

On June 25, 1950, a North Korean army struck across the border without warning. Within two days, and with United Nations authorization, the United States ordered its armed forces to protect South Korea against the aggressors. Several other countries supplied small contingents to fight under the United Nations command. Seoul, the capital of South Korea, fell to the North Koreans, who advanced almost to the southern tip of the peninsula. After United States forces landed at Inchon, the North Koreans were driven back almost to their border with China. This brought the Chinese Communists into the war, and the United Nations forces retreated to the thirty-eighth parallel. In July 1953, an armistice was signed. No significant territorial change occurred.

During the intervening 30-plus years, an uneasy peace has existed between the North and South Koreans separated by a demilitarized zone (DMZ), and numerous incidents have occurred between the forces (that include American troops) on the south and those on the north.

SOUTH YEMEN

This name is generally used for an independent state that is officially called the People's Republic of Yemen. Although its population is largely Arab, it must not be confused with its neighbor to the north, the Yemen Arab Republic, generally known as Yemen.

The ancient port of Aden at the southwest corner of Arabia was acquired by Britain in 1839. Its strategic importance was increased with the opening of the Suez Canal. Long a dependency of British India, it became a crown colony in 1937. Surrounding the colony were a number of Arab sultanates that Britain loosely organized in 1937 under a protectorate. Between 1959 and 1962 the protectorate was transformed into a Federation of South Arabia, to which the colony of Aden was attached in 1963. A period of civil warfare ended when South Arabia declared its independence as the Southern Yemen People's Republic on November 30, 1967. Under that name, Southern Yemen joined the United Nations on December 14, 1967. On November 30, 1970, it assumed its present name.

SPAIN

The recorded history of Spain began about 1100 B.C. with the Phoenician colonies. The present city of Cádiz, on the southwest coast, founded by Phoenicians in 1130 B.C., may be the oldest city in Europe. Carthage also planted colonies along the coast of Spain, beginning about 500 B.C. The present city of Barcelona began as a Carthaginian colony.

Rome sought the Iberian peninsula mainly for its rich gold and silver mines. Spain was called Hispania by the Romans, who conquered it from Carthage during the Second Punic War (218–200 B.C.). Roman Hispania became a rich and prosperous center of Roman culture. Several great Roman writers (such as Seneca and Quintilian) and even some of the emperors (including Trajan and Hadrian) came from Roman Spain. Large cities, highways, aqueducts, and other great engineering works dotted the land.

In the fifth century a series of invasions ended the prosperity of Spain. The Moorish invasions from Africa, beginning in A.D. 711, had a lasting effect upon the future of the Iberian Peninsula. Moorish domination throughout most of what is now Spain continued from 711 until 1492.

Moorish Spain left a rich heritage, including prosperous cities, great philosophers, a distinctive architecture, fine craftsmanship in design and art work, and brilliant writers and physicians. The Moors introduced an efficient irrigation system that still serves Spanish farmers in some areas. The Moorish occupation left Spain with a higher civilization than that of most of Europe at the time.

In 1479, the kingdoms of Aragon and Castile were united. Granada, the last of the Moorish states, fell before the armies of King Ferdinand and Queen Isabella in 1492. This period of Spanish history was noted for the cruelty of the Inquisition, which tortured any group standing in the way of royal power. It was also the period during which Spain began her rise to world power through voyages of exploration and discovery.

The Spanish golden age came during the sixteenth century, when the treasures from her colonial empire began pouring into the country. The armies of Spain were the strongest of Europe, and on the high seas only the English pirates and buccaneers presented serious difficulties.

The beginning of decline in Spanish power dates from the defeat of the Armada that King Philip II sent in 1588 to punish England's Queen Elizabeth I. The great fleet of over one hundred thirty warships was wiped out by a combination of storm and the smaller, more maneuverable English ships. Wars sapped the strength of the empire. By the time Napoleon had come to power in France, Spain was on the verge of internal collapse. Joseph Bonaparte, brother of the Emperor, was proclaimed King of Spain. However, a Spanish revolt restored the Bourbon's throne (1816).

Spain grew still weaker, losing nearly all her American colonies to independence movements early in the nineteenth century. In 1898, the United States crushed the Spanish Empire by capturing the Philippines, Puerto Rico, and Guam, and by freeing Cuba in a short war.

Spain chose to remain neutral during World War I. The African colony of Morocco revolted in 1921 and the Spanish army was overwhelmed by Moroccan soldiers. This was the signal for a reform movement in Spain.

General Miguel Primo de Rivera made himself dictator in 1923. However, in 1930, he was overthrown and the monarchy was reestablished. In 1931, a republic was proclaimed.

In 1936, an election gave the leftist parties a strong majority. Army officers revolted later that year, setting off a violent civil war that lasted until the victory of General Francisco Franco in 1939. In the civil war, the Republican group was opposed by a rightist Nationalist group that included Fascist elements. Germany tested many of her World War II weapons by turning them over to the Nationalists while the Soviet Union contributed weapons to the Republican group.

Franco's victory resulted in the formation of a "corporative republic." Spain then proceeded to aid the Nazis during World War II, though refraining from active participation in the war. As a result of her stand, Spain was isolated diplomatically after the War. Spain was admitted to the United Nations in 1955.

The dictatorship established after the civil war endured through Franco's lifetime. He named as his successor the son of the Bourbon pretender to the throne. In November 1975, Juan Carlos de Bourbón was restored to a kingdom unlike that of his grandfather, 44 years earlier.

SRI LANKA

For nearly two thousand years, Sinhalese kings ruled Ceylon with only occasional interruptions. Many wars were fought against invaders from southern India and China. Early in the sixteenth century the Portuguese established relations with Ceylon and began a conquest of the island. By the end of the century they had gained control. The Dutch supplanted them in the middle of the seventeenth century. In 1796, the British expelled the Dutch and annexed their settlements to one of their administrations in India. In 1802, Ceylon was constituted a crown colony.

The British firmly suppressed attempted native rebellions; they introduced tea and rubber plantations, importing Tamils as coolie laborers. Internal struggles broke out between Buddhists and Moslem traders. In addition, the inhabitants strove constantly for a voice in their own government.

On February 4, 1949, Ceylon became a Dominion within the British Commonwealth. On December 14, 1955, the country became a member of the United Nations. It changed from a monarchy to a republic on May 22, 1972, and at that time also chose to use its Sinhalese name, Sri Lanka.

SUDAN

The region known as Nubia was invaded by Egyptians around 3000 B.C.; and Egypt ruled it continuously until the eighth century B.C., when the Sudanese defeated and subjugated the Egyptians.

Gradually the country became Christianized. It was invaded in the sixteenth century by Arabs from the north and Moslem blacks from the Blue Nile Valley.

In the nineteenth century, Egypt, then a Turkish province, launched a successful invasion that made Sudan an Egyptian province. The region remained under Egyptian-Turkish rule for 60 years, a period marked by native unrest. A series of revolts beginning in 1880 smashed Egyptian rule

but brought little improvement in conditions. Constant wars of expansion were waged against neighboring tribes, and an attempted conquest of Egypt in 1889 ended in disaster.

Following this debacle, French influence began to spread in the Sudan. Alarmed at growing French power, Britain sent a joint British-Egyptian force into the region and won a complete victory. In 1899, Britain and Egypt assumed joint control in Sudan.

Following World War II, Egypt became dissatisfied with the joint arrangement and demanded British withdrawal. An agreement was finally reached that provided for Sudanese independence. After an election, Sudanese officials took office in 1954 and began the process of replacing all foreigners in government and military positions. On January 1, 1956, the Republic of Sudan was established, and on November 12, 1956, it was admitted to the United Nations.

Sudan has found itself in the midst of recent terrorist revolts in the Arab world. In March 1973, eight Palestinian rebels murdered the American ambassador, a Belgian diplomat, and the French *chargé d'affaires* in Khartoum. The Sudanese government released the terrorists to another revolutionary group in Egypt. Sudan also supports the Eritrean guerrillas in Ethiopia.

SURINAM

In 1667, the Dutch acquired Surinam from the British in exchange for New Netherland (an area that now includes New York) in North America. It remained a colony called Netherlands Guiana (or Dutch Guiana) until 1954, when it was given the status of a dependency of the Dutch crown. The home government was more than willing to grant this country its freedom. Most of the population of Surinam are East Indians or descendants of slaves brought over from Africa. The republic of Surinam was proclaimed on November 25, 1975, and it was admitted to the United Nations on December 4, 1975.

SWAZILAND

The Swazis, a Bantu people in southern Africa, gradually bargained away their resources to the

British and Boer colonists who were their neighbors at the end of the nineteenth century.

Sobhuza II became king of Swaziland in 1921. He remained king after Swaziland became an independent state within the British Commonwealth on September 6, 1968. Swaziland was admitted to the United Nations on September 24, 1968. A parliamentary system installed in 1967 was discarded by King Sobhuza in 1973.

SWEDEN

The first mention of the Swedes by Europeans was made by the Roman historian Tacitus in about A.D. 100. He described them as having "mighty ships and arms." Uppsala was founded about A.D. 500.

Swedes explored interior Russia. Rurik (probably a Viking from Sweden) founded the Russian State (see U.S.S.R.).

A long series of wars against Finland began in 1157, ending with the conquest and Christianization of Finland in 1293. In 1319, Norway and Sweden were united; and in 1397, all of Scandinavia was united under Queen Margarethe of Denmark.

Sweden broke away in 1523 and elected Gustavus Vasa (Gustaf I) as king. Gustavus freed the country from the rule of Danish nobles and the Hanseatic League cities. By 1560, Sweden was the strongest power in northern Europe. Between 1611 and 1718 Sweden expanded to be the foremost Protestant power.

Sweden declined through internal dissension and the combined efforts of Prussia, Russia, and Hanover. The last war ever fought by Sweden was against Napoleon in 1814. Norway was united to Sweden (taken from Denmark) between 1814 and 1905. Sweden gradually became a democratic nation as the king handed over more and more power to the Riksdag (Parliament). Sweden has mantained strict neutrality since 1814, but joined the United Nations on November 19, 1946.

SWITZERLAND

When Julius Caesar set about his conquest of Gaul, one of the peoples he conquered on the way were the Helvetii. Even now Switzerland calls itself by the Latin name of *Helvetia* on postage stamps. The area came under the control of various Germanic peoples in the fifth century A.D. It was part of Charlemagne's Frankish domain in the eighth century and part of the Holy Roman Empire by the eleventh century. In the thirteenth century it came under Hapsburg rule.

Oppressive rule by the Hapsburgs led to an "eternal alliance" between the cantons of Schwyz (the name from which "Switzerland" is derived), Uri, and Unterwalden in 1291. This was the first step toward a Swiss nation. In 1315, the Swiss defeated the Hapsburgs at Morgarten Pass. Thereafter the Swiss became renowned throughout Europe as great fighters and tough soldiers. Other countries hired Swiss mercenaries to do their fighting. The Swiss defeated Charles of Burgundy in 1477. The number of cantons in the alliance had grown to eight by then. Four more victories over Austria followed within a century. The country secured complete independence from the Holy Roman Empire at Basel in 1499.

The confederation had grown to 13 (plus some allied cantons) by 1513. Then the Reformation troubles began. The conflict between Catholic and Protestant in Switzerland plagued the federation until 1847. A number of rebellions occurred, but were unsuccessful. Switzerland was occupied by Napoleon's forces for a time; but it was restored with its 22 cantons in 1815 by the Congress of Vienna.

Since 1874 Switzerland has operated under an enlarged federal authority, with a constitution similar to that of the United States. The nation has managed to remain neutral in all wars since 1815. At the same time, it has been a refuge for exiles and has offered Swiss services to international organizations. Switzerland was the headquarters of the League of Nations, and the Swiss also offered the city of Geneva as the site of the United Nations. However, Switzerland is not a member of the United Nations.

SYRIA

Syria is the name of an ancient region that included the present Syria, Lebanon, Israel, and Jordan. In 1471 B.C., Egypt conquered ancient Syria. Successive invasions by Babylonia, Assyria, Persia, and Macedonia eventually destroyed the outline of Syria.

The region of the present-day Syria, centered around the city of Damascus (reputedly the oldest inhabited city in the world), became a notable trading area. Famous caravan routes between the Persian Gulf and the Mediterranean Sea passed through Palmyra and Damascus. In A.D. 105, the entire region came under Roman rule. Palmyra rose to great fame under Queen Zenobia, but was destroyed by the Roman Emperor Aurelian in A.D. 273. In A.D. 637, Damascus became the capital of a large Arab empire called the Caliphate of Omayyad, which extended all the way to India. The Christian Crusaders invaded Syria in the twelfth century. A series of small Crusaders' states grew up in Syria that lasted until the coming of the Ottoman Empire in the sixteenth century. Ottoman rule continued until after World War I. After the war, the League of Nations gave Syria the control of France. The Syrians were dissatisfied with the mandate and demanded home rule. Rebellions were crushed by the French in 1925 and 1927.

In 1941, Syria was proclaimed an independent republic. The Arab League was formed in 1945 with Syria as a member. The French withdrew in 1946, and Syria joined the Arab League to resist the formation of Israel. Syria was defeated, along with the Arab League, and an internal struggle developed. In 1958, Syria joined with Egypt to form the United Arab Republic, which was dissolved in 1961. When Syria entered the war against Israel in 1967, she lost her southwestern corner (the Golan Heights) to Israel. Syria continued to allow guerrilla units to stage raids on Israel from her territory. She refused to negotiate peace with Israel until the Golan Heights were restored and the issue of the Palestinian refugees was settled.

Syria has been the most militant of the Arab countries and has engaged in every conflict that has occurred in the Middle East over the past 30 years. In 1984, Syrian forces were in the thick of the fighting in Lebanon.

TAIWAN

This large island 110 miles east of the Chinese mainland probably received Chinese immigrants during the Tang Dynasty (A.D. 618–907), but it was not part of the Chinese Empire until the end of the seventeenth century. The Portuguese first saw the island in 1544 and named it *Formosa* ("beauti-

ful"). By 1624, there were Dutch forts on the island; but Chinese refugees drove out the Dutch, even before others came from the mainland to conquer the island in 1662.

After the Japanese victory in her war with China in 1895, Taiwan was ceded to Japan. It remained Japanese for half a century, during which its economy was improved but its culture was blighted. It was restored to Chinese control after World War II. Within a few years, the Taiwanese began to revolt against the Chinese government. At this time, the Chinese government was being driven out of the mainland by the Chinese Communists; so the anticommunist or Nationalist governments took refuge on Taiwan, which became the official seat of administration for Nationalist China.

The Nationalist administration tried to bring peace and order to its new home, from which it expected to launch a reconquest of the mainland. It improved the economy of the island and represented China in many world capitals. It was a member of the United Nations from October 24, 1945 until 1971, when the organization voted to transfer the Chinese seat to the representatives of the People's Republic of China.

The main support of the Nationalist government was the United States. Even after 1971 the United States continued to recognize the Nationalists while negotiating with the People's Republic. Both Chinese governments agreed in principle that Taiwan is part of China.

TANZANIA

The name of this republic was coined from that of its two component units, Tanganyika and Zanzibar, which had separate histories before their merger in 1964.

Vasco da Gama was the first modern European to visit the east coast of Africa in 1498. He found the Arabs entrenched there, and they remained in control as slave traders, despite Portuguese efforts to gain a foothold. In the early eighteenth century, the dominant power was that of the sultan of Muscat and Oman, whose headquarters were on the offshore island of Zanzibar (*see* Oman).

In 1884, the coast became part of German East Africa. This colony was split after World War I, and the bulk of it was mandated in 1922 to Britain under the name of the large lake on its west border, Tanganyika. It became a United Nations trust territory in 1946. After achieving local autonomy in 1960, Tanganyika became independent on December 9, 1961. Five days later it became a member of the United Nations. On its first anniversary, Tanganyika became a republic within the British Commonwealth.

Meanwhile, Zanzibar and the nearby island of Pemba acquired a population from southern Asia, and its Arab masters were supplanted by Portuguese, who dominated during the sixteenth and seventeenth centuries. In 1699, the Portuguese were driven out by Arabs from Oman. Zanzibar became one of the leading slave trading centers in eastern Africa.

British interest required the ban of this commerce with her colonies; and in 1822, the Imam of Oman signed a treaty with Britain containing this provision. Thus began an era of British protection that continued when Zanzibar was separated from Oman in 1856. The region became a colony of Great Britain during World War I. Autonomy was granted in 1963; and on June 24 of that year, the sultanate became independent. On January 12, 1964, the sultan was deposed and the People's Republic of Zanzibar was proclaimed.

Zanzibar had been admitted to the United Nations on December 16, 1963. But on April 26, 1964, Zanzibar and Tanganyika united to form a single republic. Thereafter only one membership was retained in the United Nations. The name was changed on October 29, 1964 to United Republic of Tanzania.

THAILAND

Tribes of Indochina began a migration during the sixth century B.C. into the area now called Thailand. In the middle of the fourteenth century, a unified Thai kingdom was established. It expanded over the centuries by wars of conquest against neighboring small states. It continued for 400 years. By the sixteenth century, contact with Europeans had been established, and Thailand enjoyed a flourishing trade with various Asian and European countries.

There were intermittent wars with Burma until 1764. Then Thailand was invaded by the Burmese and the Thai capital was destroyed. Shortly after-

ward, the Thais succeeded in driving out the Burmese and established a new capital at Bangkok.

Late in the nineteenth century, Thailand engaged in a boundary dispute with the French, who at that time controlled Indochina. France sent troops and warships that forced Thailand to give up territorial rights in Cambodia. Later, the Thais gave up additional territory to France and Great Britain.

Thailand was an absolute monarchy until 1932, when a revolt set up a representative government with universal suffrage. In 1939, the country (which had until then been known as Siam) officially changed its name to Thailand.

While France was embroiled in World War II, Thailand demanded that territory taken from it be returned. Japan mediated the dispute; this strengthened relations between Thailand and Japan. Immediately after the attack on Pearl Harbor, Japan was granted the right to move troops across Thai territory to the Malay area. In January 1942, Thailand declared war against the Allies. The pro-Japanese government was overthrown in 1944, and the new leaders expressed sympathy for the Allied cause. However, Japan remained in control of Thailand until the war ended. Thailand was admitted to the United Nations on December 16, 1946.

After World War II, the country generally sided with the anticommunist powers in the Cold War. During the war in Indochina, Thailand became a staging area for United States air forces that raided Indochina. Thailand was one of the few Asian members of the Southeast Asia Treaty Organization. Its government was overthrown by a military junta in 1971, which was in turn succeeded by a constitutional government in 1973. In 1975, the first elections ever held in Thailand returned a coalition government, but the military regained power in a coup in 1976.

TOGO

Togo should not be confused with Togoland, a term formerly used for a political unit which no longer exists. Togo was originally colonized by the Ewe people, who now form part of the population in Togo and in neighboring Ghana. The Portuguese began taking slaves from the Togo region in the fifteenth and sixteenth centuries. After competing with both France and Britain for control, Germany established a formal protectorate over the area in 1894.

The original region of which Togo now forms a part was called Togoland. It was held by the Germans until after World War I. In 1919, Togoland was divided into British-administered Togoland and French-administered Togoland, both under trusteeship. Trusteeship was continued under the United Nations after World War II. In 1956, the people of British-held Togoland voted to join the Gold Coast Colony, which became Ghana. British Togoland then ceased to exist.

In 1956, the French-held area voted to terminate trust status, but the vote was not accepted by the United Nations. In April 1958, elections were held under United Nations supervision; this time Togo was given permission to negotiate with France for independence. Full independence was granted on April 27, 1960, and the country was admitted to the United Nations on September 20, 1960.

TONGA

The archipelago of Tonga in the Pacific Ocean has been ruled by a monarchy that is at least 900 years old. The Dutch were the first Europeans to visit the islands, but it was Britain that signed a treaty establishing her protectorate in 1900. By a similar agreement, the islands regained their independence on June 4, 1970, and became a member of the British Commonwealth.

TRINIDAD AND TOBAGO

The islands of Trinidad and Tobago were discovered by Christopher Columbus in 1498, on his third voyage to the New World. The original inhabitants (Carib and Arawak Indians) were killed off or enslaved by the Spanish. The Spanish at first used both islands as centers for the expeditions of discovery and conquest in what is now Latin America.

Colonization of both islands began in the sixteenth century. Tobago was colonized by English settlers from nearby Barbados, and eventually changed hands between the Spanish and English many times before finally becoming a British colony in 1814.

Trinidad is much larger and richer in resources than Tobago. It was colonized by Spanish immigrants, who were later augmented by colonists from other lands. Slaves were introduced early to work sugar cane plantations. During the last half of the nineteenth century many people from South Asia came as laborers in the fields and forests of Trinidad. Trinidad was captured by the British in 1797.

Both islands were at first ruled as separate colonies. Trinidad became a crown colony in 1802, and Tobago was administered as a part of the Windward Islands until 1877, when it also became a crown colony. However, Trinidad and Tobago were united in 1888.

The Federation of West Indies was created in 1958 and included as one of its members a combined Trinidad and Tobago. On February 6, 1962, the British government dissolved the federation. Trinidad and Tobago were then united into an independent nation on August 31, 1962. The new nation became a member of the United Nations on September 18, 1962.

TUNISIA

The ancient city of Carthage was founded in 850 B.C., not far from the present city of Tunis. Following the destruction of Carthage in the Punic Wars, the region came under the domination of various peoples (including the Romans, Byzantines, Vandals, Arabs, Spanish, Turkish, and French). Relics of all these civilizations are still to be found throughout the country; the strongest imprint was left by the Arab-Moslem culture.

Under the Husseinite dynasty, which began early in the eighteenth century, a major source of revenue was piracy. In the nineteenth century, United States naval forces destroyed pirate bases along the so-called Barbary Coast and made the high seas safe for shipping.

In 1881, the French entered Tunisia from Algeria and forced it to become a protectorate, a status which lasted well into the twentieth century. Important World War II battles were fought in Tunisia.

After achieving autonomy, the Tunisians declared their independence on March 20, 1956. Ignoring the monarchy, they instituted a republic on July 25, 1957. Tunisia became a member of the United Nations on November 12, 1956.

TURKEY

About 1900 B.C., the Hittite people invaded Asia Minor from either Europe or Central Asia. Their language and customs persisted for 700 years in Asia Minor. Greeks from the west and Assyrians from the east eventually destroyed their empire, and they gradually disappeared from history.

From about 1000 B.C., the Greeks, Lydians, and others dominated Asia Minor. The Kingdom of Lydia is best known for minting the first coins in the Western world. The Greeks became the most influential people and established great centers of classical Greek culture at such cities as Ephesus, Pergamum, Miletus, and Halicarnassus.

The Persians overran most of Greek-controlled Asia Minor, but all of it was recaptured by Alexander the Great in 333 B.C. The Romans conquered Asia Minor in 63 B.C.

The Byzantine or Eastern Roman Empire continued Roman rule until the Seljuk Turks (a Moslem people from central Asia) invaded and conquered the area in the eleventh century. These Seljuks were the ancestors of the present-day Turks. The Crusades by Western Europeans were directed at the Seljuks. But they were conquered instead by the Mongolians of Central Asia. Turkish power revived under the Ottoman Turks after the Mongol invasions receded. The Ottoman Empire expanded at the expense of Christian and other Moslem states. Constantinople, the last Christian imperial capital in eastern Europe, fell in 1453. The city was made the Ottoman capital under the name *Istanbul.*

The history of modern Turkey begins with the decline of the Ottoman power that started in 1529, when the Ottomans failed to take Venice in a bloody siege. Throughout the later centuries, the Ottoman Empire fought defensive wars and continued to lose them. It became derisively known as the "Sick Man of Europe." The Greeks regained their independence in the 1820s. The North African territories—Egypt, Algeria—were detached. Serbia was removed from Turkish control, even after a Turkish victory in the Crimean War. The Balkans became the target of European power grabs, while Turkey was left with only a small enclave around Istanbul as a souvenir of her European holdings.

These territorial losses and the despotic domestic policy aroused patriots within the country (known as Young Turks) to force the sultan to establish a constitutional monarchy in 1909. Italy took Libya from the Turks in 1911. In a gamble to recover some power in Europe, Turkey allied herself with Germany in World War I, and lost her Middle East possessions. Out of the ruins came a revolution headed by Kemal Ataturk, who drove the Greeks out of Asia Minor and proclaimed a republic on October 29, 1923.

Turkey remained neutral throughout World War II, joining the victorious Allies only in February 1945, in time to participate as a belligerent in the peace negotiations. Turkey joined the United Nations on October 24, 1945. In 1950, Turkey sent a token contingent to fight in Korea; and in 1952, she became a signatory of the North Atlantic Treaty Organization. Relations with Greece were strained in 1974 because of the dispute over Cyprus. The Turkish invasion of Cyprus resulted in an arms embargo by the United States, and this in turn endangered Turkish membership in the North Atlantic Treaty Organization. Turkey ordered the United States to leave its Turkish military bases; but in 1976, they signed a new treaty that allowed the Americans to stay.

Turkey signed a non-aggression pact with Russia in 1978.

TURKS AND CAICOS ISLANDS

The Turks and Caicos, discovered by Ponce de León in 1512, are geographically a part of the Bahama Islands group in the West Indies. They were administered as part of Jamaica from 1848 until Jamaica became independent in 1962. After that, the Turks and Caicos became a British dependency.

UGANDA

Arab and English immigration into this region of Africa began about the middle of the nineteenth century. The British established a protectorate in 1894. Progress toward self-government was begun in 1920.

On October 9, 1962, Uganda became an independent nation within the British Commonwealth. Sixteen days later, Uganda became a member of the United Nations; and in 1967, the nation became a republic. Its government lacked stability until Idi Amin seized the presidency in 1971 and established a dictatorship. He aroused ill will in Europe and the United States by expelling the large Asian population of Uganda in 1972. The United States cut off economic aid in 1973, and Amin called for Soviet help. He was driven into exile in 1979.

UNION OF SOVIET SOCIALIST REPUBLICS

The region that now comprises the heart of the U.S.S.R. (also called the Soviet Union) was known as Scythia to the ancient Greeks. The people were called Scythians. Greek colonies were established along the northern shores of the Black Sea in Scythia about 1000 B.C.

The modern history of the Soviet Union is largely that of the Russians (also called Great Russians to distinguish them from Ukrainians, or Little Russians, and Byelorussians, or White Russians).

The first state in the region of the present European Soviet Union was founded by three Scandinavian brothers named Rurik, Sineus, and Truvor. Their seat of government became the Slavic city of Novgorod (New Town) in A.D. 862. Novgorod (also called Novgorod the Great) seems to have had a long previous association with bands of Vikings, and it is possible that the three brothers were Vikings. Rurik (from whose name the word *Russia* may have been derived) eventually became the sole ruler of Novgorod. After Rurik's death in A.D. 879, the center of political power gradually shifted southward to Kiev on the Dnieper River in the present Ukraine.

Novgorod and Kiev were growing political centers in the ninth century. They were trading posts and commercial centers on the famous trade route across Europe that has since become known as the

Russia—Nevsky Prospect, Leningrad

"Water Road." The Water Road was a wilderness system of river, lake, and portage routes that connected the Baltic and Black seas through what is now the western part of European Russia.

Several princely states gradually grew up along the Water Road, but Novgorod and Kiev remained the leading centers until the coming of the Mongol invaders during the thirteenth century. Between 879 and 1242, Kiev expanded and grew to become the "mother" of Slavic culture and chief seat of learning.

The death blow to Kiev as a national center came early in the thirteenth century when the Mongol invasions began. The Mongols (called Tatars by Russians) swept over southern Russia, toppling one princely state after another. Many of the leaders, including those from Kiev, fled to the great forest where they established new cities and prepared for defense against the oncoming Mongolian armies. Kiev was overpowered and ruined by the Mongols in 1240.

Soon all the Russian states were paying tribute to the Mongols—all but Novgorod, which withstood the attacks. Alexander Nevsky, the first great Russian national hero, became the ruler of free Novgorod in 1240 and of Vladimir in 1252. In 1240, he defeated an invasion by Swedes and then crushed the Teutonic Knights on frozen Lake Peipus (Chudskoye) in 1242. However, he was no match for the "Golden Horde," and soon even Novgorod was paying taxes to the Mongol princes.

It should be noted that the Mongols did not destroy the Orthodox Church, nor did they disrupt the system of government by "Grand Princes" that had prevailed in Russia before the invasion. They simply exacted taxes from the ruling princes.

A century after the invasions, Moscow began to rise as a religious and political center. Ivan (Russian for John) Kalita, "The Purse," ruler of Moscow from 1328–1340, persuaded the head of the Christian Church to move from Vladimir to Moscow. Ivan then had himself crowned "Grand Prince of Vladimir and all Rus." This was the beginning of Muscovite expansion.

Mongol power was broken under the steady fighting of Muscovite princes. Ivan III (1462–1505) finally freed Russia from Mongol domination. Ivan also put an end to the independence of Novgorod the Great, although that city is still a prosperous industrial center of the Soviet Union.

A series of powerful rulers, including Ivan IV ("the Terrible"), continued to expand the Muscovite state. They crushed all opposition to autocratic rule and established serfdom. Peter the Great (1682–1725) founded St. Petersburg (now Leningrad) in 1703 as a glittering European capital city. After Peter, Russia began to accept Western Europe's culture, fashions, and science. The rules of Peter, Elizabeth, and Catherine the Great added Ukraine, Byelorussia (White Russia), Bessarabia, Crimea, and other areas to the growing empire. Siberia, Central Asia, and Alaska were added by Catherine the Great and Tsars Alexander I and Nicholas I.

Petty wars, heavy taxation, and repression gradually brought on a crisis in the empire. The crisis began with the Pugachev Revolt in 1773 and continued until the overthrow in 1917. Serfs had been freed in 1861 by Tsar Alexander II, who tried to stem the tide of demands by granting several reforms. (It was this Alexander who sold Alaska to the United States in 1867.) Alexander was assassinated in 1881.

World War I found Russia on the Allied side. But the war brought only defeats and privations for the Russian army. The army was finally unable to get supplies or to get clear decisions from the head of government. In March 1917, a moderate government took over upon the abdication of Tsar Nicholas II, who was no longer able to control the government. In November 1917, the moderate government was overthrown by a revolutionary Marxist group called the Bolsheviks. All authority for government was then handed over to councils of workers and peasants (the word for council in Russian is *soviet*). All major industrial and commercial activities were nationalized. A great civil war followed. Despite foreign intervention, the Bolsheviks were victorious by 1921.

The creation of the Soviet Union was the greatest act in the long career of V. I. Lenin, revolutionary leader and Marxist philosopher. After the death of Lenin in 1924, factional disputes arose. These took the form of purges and finally the redirection of state power toward the building of heavy industry. Communist leaders abandoned the idea of the world Marxist movement for immediate revolution and internal growth. Joseph Stalin ushered in a period when the Soviet Union consolidated its power internally. Heavy industry was planned and activated at the expense of consumer products and agriculture. The Stalin group laid heavy hands upon the freedom of the Russian people.

The Soviet Union was invaded by German forces in June 1941. The resulting battles on Russian soil were among the bloodiest ever fought. German armored divisions succeeded in reaching the Volga River at Stalingrad (now Volgograd), where they besieged the city for two months. This action marked the turning point in the war. United States military assistance reached the Soviet Union chiefly through the northern sea route and over the southern land route.

After the war and the death of Stalin (1953), the Soviet Union changed directions in political, social, and economic matters. A more relaxed attitude toward other nations began to appear. When Nikita Khrushchev assumed power in 1956, he denounced Stalinist excesses and tensions began to ease. The so-called Cold War between Western democracies and the Soviet Union tapered off.

The Soviets never let up, however, in their relentless effort toward world conquest. Massive military and economic help in Indo-China and aid to African and Latin American countries helped in the ideological war against the free world; and the success of their efforts is beyond question.

Khrushchev was deposed in 1964. His successor was Leonid Brezhnev who died in 1982 to be succeeded by Yuri Andropov, who died in 1984. Konstantin Chernenko was chosen his successor.

UNITED ARAB EMIRATES

Along the south coast of the Persian Gulf between Qatar and Oman are seven Arab sheikhdoms, whose main resource is oil.

In earlier times their principal activity was piracy. In the nineteenth century, they came under British influence and signed a truce to abstain from such violations of international law. This gave them the name of the Trucial States, and they became a collective British protectorate while their sheikhs maintained their local power. On December 2, 1971, the states became the United Arab Emirates and signed a treaty with Britain as an independent country. A week later the United Arab Emirates became a member of the United Nations.

UNITED KINGDOM

The full form of the name is the United Kingdom of Great Britain and Northern Ireland. This name evolved slowly, beginning in 1707. At that time the Crowns of England and Scotland were united to form the Kingdom of Great Britain. The name was correctly used for both the island and the kingdom. In 1801, the name *Ireland* was added as a result of the union of Ireland with the Crown. The last change occurred in 1927, when Ireland withdrew from the union of kingdoms, leaving behind the six counties of Ulster. These became Northern Ireland, which replaced "Ireland" in the full name of the United Kingdom.

The island of Great Britain was inhabited in pre-Roman times by Celtic peoples who lived mainly in the southern part. The chief tribe was the Briton, from which the name *Britain* is derived.

Julius Caesar was unable to conquer the island during his expedition of 54 B.C. However, the island was conquered by the Roman Emperor Claudius in A.D. 43, and Roman rule was gradually extended northward. The Romans built a great wall (part of which still stands) to mark the northern limits of their government and to keep out the warlike Picts of present-day Scotland. Roads were built. Christianity was introduced; many cities and towns were founded during the Roman period. The Romans withdrew gradually as pressure mounted from invading forces of Nordic peoples. By A.D. 410, they had left the island to the invaders.

A period of confusion and invasion followed. After the Roman departure, Danes, Saxons, Angles, and Jutes gained territory in Britain. The Celtic peoples gradually withdrew deeper into the secluded forests and uplands of what is now Wales and Scotland. The Welsh people are largely the descendants of the ancient Celts who first inhabited Britain.

England—Westminster, Big Ben, and the Houses of Parliament, also showing Westminster Abbey

Many small kingdoms developed, especially in the southern part of Britain. Some of them were united to form larger kingdoms; by the eighth century, Wessex had become the strongest. Its greatest leader was Alfred the Great (849–899), who defeated the Danes. However, Danish rule was reinstituted in 954. From 1017 to 1035, most of what is now England was united to the Crown of Denmark under King Canute.

The modern history of Britain began in 1066 when William the Conqueror, himself the descendant of Norse (Norman) invaders of France, invaded and defeated the last Saxon king at Hastings. William built a strong government. French was introduced as the language of the nobility. Under William and his descendants, the English language began to take form. This is called the Norman period (William was also king of Normandy, a region in France). In 1154, the Plantagenet family of kings introduced further refinements in government, including the jury system. Repressive taxes caused the nobility to revolt. In 1215, King John was forced to sign the Magna Charta, or Great Charter, that established several basic limits in government. The beginnings of a parliamentary system were made under Edward I (1272–1307). The "model parliament" of 1295 included clergymen and townspeople, as well as lesser nobility. It established a trend toward democracy in government.

The Hundred Years' War represented for Britain and France the final flowering of feudalism and the end of the Middle Ages. The use of gunpowder signaled the end of the armored knight on horse, as well as the great castle bastions of feudal times. A trend toward strong central government began in Britain. Trade and commerce revived, along with the beginnings of competition for markets and colonies outside Britain. As an island kingdom with a long seafaring tradition, Britain was well prepared to compete with the Dutch, Spanish, French, and others for the control of newly discovered lands.

The reign of Elizabeth I (1558–1603) initiated the golden age of British culture and history. The flowering of art, drama, and literature went hand-in-hand with expansion overseas. British power eventually gained an empire that spread over the known world and was the largest empire in history. Britain achieved supremacy in commerce and trade, as well as in naval and military power.

A period of absolute monarchy after Elizabeth I was followed by the outbreak of civil war in 1642.

When monarchy was restored in 1688, it was no longer under the "divine right" concept. Parliament passed a "Bill of Rights" in 1689, which has served as a model for many other nations of the world.

After the wars with France in the seventeenth and eighteenth centuries, the British Empire had reached its greatest extent. The Industrial Revolution reached Britain and an era of political and social reform followed. The Victorian period under Queen Victoria (1837–1901) saw the rise of great parliamentarians and the beginning of the colonial movement for self-government or independence. The empire began to break up, often with violence. But in some cases, the colonies made a peaceful transition from empire to the new "commonwealth" concept. The American colonies were lost in 1783; Canada became a dominion (an associated state) in 1867; New Zealand, Australia, and South Africa, at the beginning of the twentieth century; Ireland withdrew in 1922, and Egypt in 1936. India gained her independence in 1947.

The Commonwealth of Nations, formerly called the British Commonwealth, is a loose association of Great Britain and about 35 countries which were her former colonies, although not all chose to be included. Heads of these nations meet at intervals to discuss mutual goals and problems.

The United Kingdom in the twentieth century has engaged in two world wars. The most critical of these was World War II, in which Britain was severely bombed and 360,000 British service men lost their lives.

The British of recent years have been preoccupied with problems such as the struggle in Northern Ireland, which has on occasion reached the streets of London; inflation and high unemployment; and the pesky invasion in 1982 by Argentina in the Falkland Islands. Prime Minister Margaret Thatcher's handling of that situation and her austere program to get the country back on a sound financial footing helped her win reelection in 1983. Britain has profited from huge oil discoveries in the North Sea. The United Kingdom continues as one of the United States' staunchest allies.

UNITED STATES OF AMERICA
(See Pages 1079–1134)

UPPER VOLTA

The history of Upper Volta until the end of the nineteenth century A.D. was that of the empire-building Mossi people. Their origin is somewhat obscure, but they probably came from eastern Africa sometime in the eleventh century A.D. They first established small kingdoms in the region of the present Ghana and then spread out northward along the Black, Red, and White Volta rivers.

The original empire was centered on the present city of Ouagadougou. It persisted down to modern times. The Mossi people sacked the city of Timbuktu (Tombouctou) in 1333. They also fought the Mali and Songhai peoples that were near neighbors. Mossi power declined after the eighteenth century.

By 1896, the empires of the region were weak and the French were able to establish a protectorate. In 1919, the former kingdoms were united into a territory called Upper Volta, and were added to the French West African group of colonies. In 1932, Upper Volta was dismembered and abolished. However, on September 4, 1947, the Territory of Upper Volta was reestablished with the 1932 boundaries. This was done to avoid political conflict. On December 11, 1958, Upper Volta became the autonomous Voltaic Republic. In 1959, the name was changed back to Upper Volta. Upper Volta became an independent nation on August 5, 1960. It was admitted to the United Nations on September 20, 1960.

URUGUAY

Juan de Solis discovered the Uruguay region in 1516. Colonia del Sacramento was founded by the

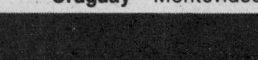

Uruguay—Montevideo

Portuguese as a rival to Spanish Buenos Aires, located just a few miles away (across the Río de la Plata estuary). Rivalry between the Portuguese in Uruguay and the Spanish in Argentina continued until the Uruguay region was annexed to the vice-royalty of Buenos Aires. Uruguay revolted against Spain in 1810. It had to fight not only the Spanish, but also Brazil and Argentina, both of which tried to annex the country. Independence was achieved in 1825 from Argentina and in 1828 from Brazil. Uruguay became a republic.

During the rest of the nineteenth century, Uruguay had mostly unstable governments; but in 1903, President José Batlle y Ordónez initiated a series of reforms that made Uruguay one of South America's most progressive democracies. It became a member of the United Nations on December 18, 1945.

In 1952, the presidential system was abandoned and the executive power was shared by a board of nine members—six from the majority and three from the minority party. The presidential system was restored in 1957, then again abrogated in 1973 for a military dictatorship.

VATICAN CITY

The Vatican City is an independent state located in Italy, within the city of Rome.

The state's modern history dates from February 11, 1929, when the Lateran Treaty was signed be-

tween Italy and His Holiness, the Supreme Pontiff (pope) of the Roman Catholic Church. The treaty established the boundaries and guaranteed the independence of the state. Vatican City issues its own coins and stamps and maintains diplomatic relations with about 70 nations, the United States becoming one in 1983.

VENEZUELA

Venezuela was discovered by Columbus in 1498, but until Caracas was founded in 1567 there were no important settlements. As part of New Granada (*see* Colombia) it participated in the revolt led by Simón Bolívar and Francisco de Miranda in 1810 and 1811, and after independence was won in 1821 remained part of the new state of Gran Colombia. But this state disintegrated; and in 1830, Venezuela became independent. Throughout the nineteenth century, and until the presidency of Romulo Betancourt in 1958, a succession of dictators ruled Venezuela. The constitution of 1961, and reforms of succeeding presidents, apparently made democracy work in Venezuela. The country became a member of the United Nations on December 18, 1945.

VIETNAM

The history of Vietnam can be traced back to the fourth century B.C., when a group of people called

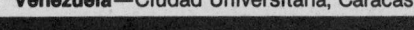

Venezuela—Ciudad Universitaria, Caracas

the Viets entered the Tonkin Gulf area of Southeast Asia. They conquered and intermarried with the local people. About 200 B.C., they set up the kingdom of Nam-Viet, which was later conquered by Chinese armies.

The Chinese ruled Nam-Viet until A.D. 938, when Viet leaders expelled them and planted the new kingdom of Vietnam. France captured Vietnam in the eighteenth century and set up a protectorate there in 1884.

Japan took control of the country in World War II and established the puppet state of Bao Dai. In 1946, Communist forces known as the Vietminh overthrew the Bao Dai. They refused to accept French rule, and France launched a full-scale attack on the country. The French forces were defeated at Dien Bien Phu in 1954.

A peace conference in Geneva divided the country into North and South Vietnam to separate the pro-communist and and anticommunists forces until elections could be held in 1956. But the elections were never held, and the two nations remained hostile toward one another.

In 1963, a guerrilla movement emerged in South Vietnam to overthrow the South Vietnamese government. A series of military chiefs held the presidency of South Vietnam, but each failed to quash the Vietcong guerrillas. The United States poured money and troops into the conflict, to no avail. South Vietnam fell to the communist forces in the spring of 1975, after more than a million Vietnamese civilians and over 200,000 Vietnamese soldiers had been killed. More than 47,000 American soldiers also died in the war.

The country was officially reunited on July 2, 1976. It adopted the flag, capital, and government of the former North Vietnam. In 1977, the United States agreed to allow Vietnam to join the United Nations. Since then, Vietnam troops have engaged troops in neighboring Cambodia and Thailand.

WALLIS AND FUTUNA

The islands were ruled by kings and as a protectorate of France from 1842 until 1961, when they became an overseas territory of France. The territory is located in the South Pacific Ocean.

WESTERN SAMOA

Western Samoa was made a German protecto-rate in 1900. It became a League of Nations mandated territory of New Zealand in 1920. Partial self-government was achieved in 1947. By 1961, the islands were ready for full independence, which had been pledged to them by New Zealand in 1946. Independence was granted on January 1, 1962.

WEST GERMANY

The Romans used the name *Germania* to designate an area that was almost the same as that of modern Germany. The inhabitants of Germania were described as being divided into classes of noblemen, freemen, vassals, and slaves. The Romans waged war against various tribes that came from this region, beginning with Cimbri and Teuton peoples in the second century A.D. In later centuries German peoples came over to the Roman areas peacefully and often joined up with the legions of Imperial Rome. Still later, they began to invade Roman provinces, and finally aided in the destruction of the Roman world.

The rise of Frankish power and the establishment of a Frankish empire under Merovingians marked the beginning of a long series of unification attempts in what is now Germany. Charlemagne inherited the region from the Merovingians. His Frankish empire included what is now France, Germany, and part of Italy. Upon his death the empire dissolved. Germany was again united in the Holy Roman Empire that was set up in 962. The Holy Roman Empire dominated Central Europe until the Reformation. The empire crumbled from lack of a steady central authority and from internal dissension. The rise of national kingdoms and prosperous trading cities also helped destroy the effective authority of the empire. The Thirty Years' War of 1618–1648 split Germany and the Holy Roman Empire into a maze of fragments, including over three hundred separate states and independent cities.

The rise of Prussia under Frederick II (1740–1786) once again presented an opportunity for the establishment of a German nation. German nationalism asserted itself during the French Revolution and the Napoleonic era. A successful movement for unification came into being under the leadership of Otto von Bismarck, Chancellor of Prussia. Rivalry between Prussia and Austria for the control of Germany developed into a series of wars (1864–1871) which Prussia won, assuming the position of the leading economic and military power on the Continent. An intricate system of alliances established a delicate balance of political power in Europe. This balance was finally upset in the Balkans by the 1914 murder of the heir to the throne of the Austro-Hungarian Empire, which led to World War I.

World War I ended in the defeat of Germany and the destruction of the German Empire. In the social disorder that followed, National Socialism, or Nazism, gained a powerful following under the leadership of Adolf Hitler. In 1933, Hitler converted the Weimar Republic of Germany into the German Third Reich, a Nazi dictatorship.

Expansionist policies, the persecution of political minorities, and the execution of plans to exterminate the Jewish population of Germany marked the Nazi regime. In 1938, Hitler annexed Austria and then Czechoslovakia. World War II was precipitated by the sudden German invasion of Poland on September 1, 1939. The Soviet Union had signed a nonaggression pact with Hitler and had helped in the partition of Poland. Yet German forces invaded Russia in a lightning-like stroke on June 22, 1941. On December 7, 1941, Japan, which had become allied with Germany, without warning attacked Pearl Harbor. While the Americans adopted a holding action in the Pacific, they planned, along with the Allies, an invasion of Europe. The German armies, in the meantime, pushed further into Russia and were finally halted at Stalingrad (*see* U.S.S.R.). The allied invasion began in Africa in November 1942, and continued in Sicily and Italy, gradually splitting the Axis forces and sapping German military strength. On June 1, 1944, a great Allied invasion force landed on the coast of Normandy in France. The Nazi military machine was crushed. On May 8, 1945, Germany surrendered.

On June 5, 1945, Germany was divided into four zones of occupation. The four occupation powers (the United Kingdom, France, the Soviet Union, and the United States) set up an Allied Control Council for the government of the German capital city of Berlin, which became an island in the Soviet Union's zone of occupation.

The failure of the Allies to agree upon procedures and upon the future disposition of defeated Germany ended the policy of cooperation and brought about the demise of the Allied Control Council for Berlin. In 1949, Germany was formally divided into western and eastern sections. The western part became the Federal Republic of Germany with a provisional capital at Bonn, on the Rhine River in Westphalia. Territories in the east that included East Prussia were partitioned by Poland and the Soviet Union. Berlin, originally di-

West Germany—The Lukaskirche, Protestant Church, Munich

vided into four zones of occupation, eventually consisted of only two zones—West Berlin, which was associated with the Federal Republic, and East Berlin, which was under the administration of the German Democratic Republic (the Soviet zone). The Saar region was formally united to the Federal Republic after agreement between France and the Federal Republic, after free elections had been held.

Since World War II, West Germany has become one of the leading industrial nations of the world and, like Japan, a keen competitor with U.S. auto makers. Its agreement to allow the deployment of nuclear missiles within its borders sparked huge demonstrations in 1983 but government leaders reaffirmed their determination to stick to their decision.

WINDWARD ISLANDS

The more southerly group of islands in the Lesser Antilles of the British West Indies is called the Windward Islands. They comprise, from north to south, Dominica, St. Lucia, St. Vincent, and Grenada. They were members of the West Indies Federation that existed from 1958 to 1962. Discovered by Columbus and often in dispute between the French and English, while the indigenous Carib Indians fiercely resisted conquest by Europeans, these islands were before 1958 organized as the colony of Windward Islands and in 1967 were made associated states. As such, they had maximum self-government short of independence. In 1974, Grenada declared its independence (*see* Grenada), but the others remained associated states.

Yemen—View of Sana'a, the capital

YEMEN

Yemen is the heart of the famous "Arabia Felix" of ancient times. It was the site of the Kingdom of Saba (950–115 B.C.), supposedly ruled for a time by the great Queen of Sheba.

The Yemen region was conquered by the Ottoman Turks in 1517 and remained under their loose control until they were expelled by the British in World War I (1918). Turkish control had been only nominal after 1913. Yemen became a member of the United Nations on September 30, 1947.

The ruler of Yemen was the hereditary imam until military forces proclaimed the Yemen Arab Republic on September 18, 1962.

Today two countries are recognized, North Yemen or the Yemen Arab Republic, and South Yemen or the People's Democratic Republic of Yemen.

The People's Republic of Yemen went to war with Yemen in 1979. The war was short-lived and a mutual withdrawal of forces was agreed to.

YUGOSLAVIA

The South Slavs migrated to the Balkans from the east and north during the sixth century A.D. and later. Most of them were converted to Christianity during the eighth and ninth centuries, but under later Turkish rule many became Moslems. Of the many attempts to form lasting states, only the Serbians were partially successful.

In the second half of the nineteenth century, just prior to the national liberation movements centering around Serbia, the South Slavs consisted of Serbians, Slovenes, Croatians, Bosnians, Macedonians, and Montenegrins. In 1878, Serbia achieved independence. The Balkan Wars of 1911–1913 led to a series of events that eventually became the immediate cause of World War I. After the war a unified Slavic state emerged, comprising Serbia, Croatia, Bosnia and Herzegovina, Slavonia, and Dalmatia. This new state was called the Kingdom of the Serbs, Croats, and Slovenes. The state

U.S. Secretary of State, Henry Kissinger (left) with President Josip Broz Tito of Yugoslavia (right) during the former's visit to Yugoslavia in November 1974. (With them is an interpreter.)

proved unstable, and the king declared himself dictator in 1929 and renamed the country Yugoslavia.

During World War II pressure was used by both the Axis and Allied powers to secure Yugoslav support. The Germans invaded the country in April 1941, and the king thereafter ruled from exile in London. Several resistance groups emerged within Yugoslavia, the most enduring of which was led by Tito, a communist, who was eventually supported by the Soviet Union, the British, and the Americans. Yugoslavia was a charter member of the United Nations on October 24, 1945.

On November 29, 1945, Yugoslavia was proclaimed a republic, and the constitution of 1946 made it a federal republic. The leader in the Soviet-type government was Tito, although he did not become president until 1953, when a new constitution provided for that office. By this time, relations between the Soviet Union and Yugoslavia had deteriorated. The differences between two communist countries revealed for the first time that nations could belong to the communist camp and yet not be "satellites" of the Soviet Union. Yugoslavia became a leader of the so-called unaligned bloc.

Under the constitution of 1963, the official name was changed to the Socialist Federal Republic of Yugoslavia.

Following Tito's death in 1980, a rotating system of succession was established among members representing each republic and autonomous province.

ZAIRE

This name is an African equivalent of Congo, and was adopted by the government formerly known as Republic of the Congo, with its capital at Kinshasa, both for itself and for the river. An even earlier name of this state was Belgian Congo, before independence was achieved.

The mouth of the Congo River was discovered by the Portuguese explorer Diego Cam. Exploration into the interior began when David Livingstone and Henry Stanley, in the nineteenth century, followed the Congo through the great rain forest. Stanley was in the service of Belgian King Leopold II who subsidized several of Stanley's expeditions. Conflicts between European nations over the Congo area were prevented by the Berlin Conference of 1884, which established the Belgian king's claims to the main basin of the Congo River.

The personal rule of the king ended in 1908 when the Congo region was organized into the colony of Belgian Congo. Serious movements toward independence did not occur until 1959. Belgium agreed to grant independence on June 30, 1960.

No sooner had the nation become independent than its army mutinied. The national army then became an uncertain and undisciplined force that supported various leaders at different times. Katanga province, rich in minerals, seceded from the republic. A special United Nations force tried to maintain some semblance of order but failed. The nation's first prime minister was murdered under

President Joseph Mobutu of Zaire (right) with U.S. heavyweight challenger Muhammad Ali. The latter was in Zaire for a title bout with George Foreman.

mysterious circumstances; and in 1961, the Congolese Parliament convened under United Nations auspices and protection. The central government tried to negotiate with the secessionist Katanga Province, but its leader, Moise Tshombe, refused to carry out agreements. UN Secretary-General Dag Hammarskjöld was killed in a plane crash while flying into Katanga Province in order to secure an agreement. A new constitution was drafted in 1962 but led to still another secessionist movement, in Kasai Province. By the latter part of 1963, both secessions had ended, and United Nations supervisory forces were able to leave the country by the end of June 1964.

The constitution in effect was superseded by another imposed in 1966 by President Joseph Mobutu. He remained in that office under a new constitution adopted by referendum in June 1967. As part of the africanization program, he changed his name to Mobutu Sese Seko, and that of the country to Zaire, in 1971.

Most foreign business owners sold their interests to native operators in 1974, but the government of Zaire asked them to return. Low copper prices hurt the economy of the country; and in 1977, a force of Cuban-trained guerrillas invaded Zaire from Angola. Troops and planes from Morocco, Egypt, and France helped President Mobutu repel the attack. Another invasion was attempted in 1978 but without success.

ZAMBIA

After the federation of Rhodesia and Nyasaland was dissolved on the last day of 1963, the British protectorate of Northern Rhodesia was given autonomy. (For the history of Northern Rhodesia, see Rhodesia.) On October 24, 1964, the protectorate was given its independence within the Commonwealth, as the republic of Zambia. On December 1, 1964, it joined the United Nations. Relations between black-ruled Zambia and her white-ruled neighbor, Rhodesia, continued to be unfriendly; and for a time in 1973, their borders were closed. An alternate link to the coast was provided by the building of a highway and railroad through Tasmania to the port of Dar es Salaam.

The main street of Lusaka, Zambia.

Statistics for Countries of the World

NAME OF COUNTRY	POPULATION	CAPITAL* LARGEST CITY	AREA (SQUARE MILES)	GOVERNMENT	MAJOR LANGUAGES
Afghanistan Democratic Republic of Afghanistan	15,056,000	Kabul* 891,750	252,000	Military government, U.S.S.R. control	Pushtu, Persian
Albania People's Socialist Republic of Albania	3,046,000	Tirana* 198,000	11,000	1 party, Communist state	Albanian
Algeria Democratic and Popular Republic of Algeria	22,107,000	Algiers* 2,200,000	896,593	Presidential regime	Arabic, French
Andorra Principality of Andorra	43,000 (scattered through 7 small villages)	Andorra la Vella* No population figure available	179	Co-principality, France and Spain, Council of 24 members	Catalan
Angola People's Republic of Angola	7,948,000	Luanda* 475,300	481,350	1 party, committee rule	Portuguese, Bantu
†Antigua and Barbuda	77,000	St. John's* 25,000	171	2 party, parliamentary government	English
Argentina Argentine Republic	30,708,000	Buenos Aires* 2,922,800	1,072,163	Federal republic. Long under military control, but Oct., 1983, defeat of Peronists gave civilian control.	Spanish
†Australia Commonwealth of Australia	15,345,000	Canberra* 246,100 Sydney 3,231,700	2,967,500	Multi-party, democratic federal state system, parliamentary government	English
Australian External Territories: Norfolk Island Coral Sea Island Territory of Ashmore and Carter Island Cocos (Keeling) Island Christmas Island Australian Antarctic Territory	1,800 3,184 3,184		13½ 1 2 5½ 52 2,472,000		
Austria Republic of Austria	7,451,000	Vienna* 1,504,200	32,375	Multi-party, federal republic	German
†The Bahamas Commonwealth of the Bahamas	230,000	Nassau* 138,000	5,382	Independent within British Commonwealth, multi-party, parliamentary government	English
Bahrain State of Bahrain	431,000	Manama* 300,000	256	No parties, traditional Emirate	Arabic
†Bangladesh People's Republic of Bangladesh	101,408,000	Dacca* 3.4 million (metropolitan area)	55,126	Military rule	Bengali, English
†Barbados	252,000	Bridgetown* 7,600	166	Independent sovereign state within British Commonwealth; multi-party, parliamentary government	English
Belgium Kingdom of Belgium	9,858,000	Brussels* 1,000,221 (metropolitan area)	11,782	Multi-party, parliamentary democracy under constitutional monarch	Flemish French
†Belize	166,400	Belmopan* 2,932 Belize City 39,887	8,866	2 party, parliamentary government	English, Spanish, Indian languages
Benin People's Republic of Benin	4,005,000	Porto-Novo* 123,000 Cotonou 215,000	43,475	No political parties, Marxist-Lenist military government	French, Fons, and Adjas

NAME OF COUNTRY	POPULATION	CAPITAL* LARGEST CITY	AREA (SQUARE MILES)	GOVERNMENT	MAJOR LANGUAGES
Bhutan Kingdom of Bhutan	1,417,000	Thimphu* 10,000	18,000	No political parties, absolute monarch	Dzong Ka, Nepali, others
Bolivia Republic of Bolivia	6,195,000	Sucre (legal)* 63,259 LaPaz (de facto)* 881,400	424,165	Multi-party, centralized republic	Spanish, Aymara Quechua
†Botswana Republic of Botswana	1,068,000	Gaborone* 59,000	222,000	Multi-party, parliamentary democracy	English, Tswana, and other Bantu languages
Brazil Federative Republic of Brazil	135,000	Brasilia* 411,305 Sao Paulo 7 million	3,286,488	2 party federal government	Portuguese
Brunei	232,000	Bandar Seri Begawan*	2,226	Sultanate	English, Malay
Bulgaria People's Republic of Bulgaria	8,974,000	Sofia* 1,056,900	42,823	Communist state	Bulgarian
Burma Socialist Republic of the Union of Burma	36,919,000	Rangoon* 2,186,000	261,789	1 party, socialist republic	Burmese, Shan, others
Burundi Republic of Burundi	4,673,000	Bujumbura* 200,000	10,747	1 party, presidential regime	Kirundi, French, others
**Cambodia (Kampuchea) Cambodian People's Republic	6,249,000	Phnom Penh* 500,000	69,898	1 party, communist state	Khmer, French Annamese
Cameroon United Republic of Cameroon	9,737,000	Yaounde* 400,000 Douala 500,000	179,558	1 party, presidential regime	French, English, others
†Canada	25,399,000	Ottawa* 695,000 Montreal 2,800,000	3,851,809	Multi-party, confederation with parliamentary democracy.	English, French
**Cape Verde Republic of Cape Verde	312,000	Praia* 36,600 Mindelo 40,000	1,557	1 party, constitutional assembly	Portuguese, Bantu
Central African Republic	2,664,000	Bangui* 367,100 (metropolitan area)	241,305	Republic	French, Sangho, others
Chad Republic of Chad	5,036,000	N'Djamena* 303,000 (metropolitan area)	495,750	1 party, military government	French, Arabic, Sara, others
Chile Republic of Chile	12,042,000	Santiago* 3,448,700	292,258	Political activity suspended, military government	Spanish
**China People's Republic of China	1,037,588,000	Peking* 8,500,000 Shanghai 12,000,000	3,691,500	1 party, communist state	Chinese
China (Taiwan) Republic of China	19,388,000	Taipei* 2,298,000 (metropolitan area)	13,893	Multi-party, presidential regime	Chinese
Colombia Republic of Colombia	29,347,000	Bogota* 4,486,200	439,737	Multi-party, parliamentary government	Spanish
Comoros Federal Islamic Republic of the Comoros	469,000	Moroni* 22,000 (metropolitan area)	863	Republic	Malagasy, French
Congo People's Republic of the Congo	1,798,000	Brazzaville* 200,000 (metropolitan area)	132,046	1 party, military government	French, Kongo, Batéké, M'Bochi

NAME OF COUNTRY	POPULATION	CAPITAL* LARGEST CITY	AREA (SQUARE MILES)	GOVERNMENT	MAJOR LANGUAGES
Costa Rica Republic of Costa Rica	2,644,000	San Jose* 867,800	19,652	Multi-party, federal republic	Spanish
Cuba Republic of Cuba	10,105,000	Havana* 1,008,500	42,827	1 party, communist state	Spanish
***†Cyprus Republic of Cyprus	665,000	Nicosia* 121,500	3,572	Multi-party, parliamentary government	Greek, Turkish
Czechoslovakia Czechoslovak Socialist Republic	15,502,000	Prague* 1.1 million	49,374	1 party, communist state	Czech, Slovak
Denmark Kingdom of Denmark	5,105,000	Copenhagen* 654,437	16,630	Multi-party, parliamentary constitutional monarchy	Danish
Greenland (Kalaallit Nunaat*) *official name now	53,000	Nuuk* 9,717	840,000	Formerly an integral part of Denmark, it was granted home rule in 1979; has socialist-dominated legislature	Greenlandic, Danish
Djibouti Republic of Djibouti	297,000	Djibouti* 200,000 (metropolitan area)	8,900	Multi-party, parliamentary government	French, Somali
†Dominica Commonwealth of Dominica	100,000	Roseau* 20,000	290	Parliamentary	English
Dominican Republic	6,614,000	Santo Domingo* 1.3 million	18,658	Multi-party, centralized republic	Spanish
Ecuador Republic of Ecuador	9,378,000	Quito* 918,900 Guayaquil 1,278,900	109,484	Multi-party, republic	Quechau, Spanish, Jivaroan
Egypt Arab Republic of Egypt	49,000,000	Cairo* 5,084,463	386,900	Presidential regime	Arabic
El Salvador Republic of El Salvador	4,961,000	San Salvador* 400,000	8,124	Military-dominated	Spanish
Equatorial Guinea Republic of Equatorial Guinea	350,000	Malabo* 25,000	10,830	Military regime	Spanish, English, Fang
Ethiopia Socialist Ethiopia	42,266,000	Addis Ababa* 1,200,000	471,800	Military regime	Amharic, others
†Fiji Dominion of Fiji	700,000	Suva* 64,000	7,055	Parliamentary democracy	English, Fijan, Hindustani
Finland Republic of Finland	4,908,000	Helsinki* 490,204	130,129	Multi-party, parliamentary government	Finnish, Swedish
France French Republic	55,041,000	Paris* 2,296,945	210,039	Multi-party, Republic	French
French Overseas Departments: French Guiana Guadeloupe Martinique Mayotte Reunion St. Pierre and Miquelon	 82,700 300,000 300,000 41,000 500,000 6,000		 34,750 687 431 146 970 93		
French Overseas Territories: French Polynesia comprises 130 islands administered from Tahiti, including Society Islands, Windward and Leeward islands, Marquesas Islands, the Tuamotu Archipelago including the Gambler Islands, and the Austral Islands.	200,000		1,544		

NAME OF COUNTRY	POPULATION	CAPITAL* LARGEST CITY	AREA (SQUARE MILES)	GOVERNMENT	MAJOR LANGUAGES
France–continued					
French Southern and Antarctic Lands comprises Adelie Land and island groups in Indian Ocean, Kerguelen Archipelago, and Crozet Archipelago.					
New Caledonia	139,600		8,548		
Wallis and Futana Islands	11,000		106		
Gabon Gabonese Republic	988,000	Libreville* 225,200	103,347	1 party, presidential regime	French, Fange, Omyere
†The Gambia Republic of The Gambia	751,000	Banjul* 40,000	4,467	Republic	English, Mandinka, Wolof
Germany, East German Democratic Republic	16,686,000	East Berlin* 1,145,743	41,650	1 party, communist state	German
Germany, West Federal Republic of Germany	60,950,000	Bonn* 289,400 Berlin 2 million	95,985	Multi-party, federal republic	German
†Ghana Republic of Ghana	13,004,000	Accra* 998,800	92,100	Military government	English, Twi, Fanti, Ga
Greece Hellenic Republic	9,921,000	Athens* 3,300,000 (metropolitan area)	50,960	Multi-party, parliamentary government	Greek
†Grenada State of Grenada	113,000	St. George's* 30,813	133	After the U.S. invasion, Oct., 1983, government administered by a British Governor and a 9-man council until new elections could be held, presumably under a democratic constitution	English, French-African patois
**Guatemala Republic of Guatemala	8,346,000	Guatemala City* 1,307,300	42,042	Military government	Spanish, Indian languages
Guinea People's Revolutionary Republic of Guinea	5,597,000	Conakry* 575,000	94,926	1 party, presidential regime	French, Fulani
Guinea-Bissau Republic of Guinea-Bissau	858,000	Bissau* 109,500	13,948	Revolutionary council	Portuguese, Criouio
†Guyana Cooperative Republic of Guyana	768,000	Georgetown* 170,000	83,000	Multi-party, presidential regime	English, Hindi, Portuguese, Negro patois
Haiti Republic of Haiti	5,762,000	Port-au-Prince* 745,700	10,714	1 party, presidential regime	French, French-Creole
Honduras Republic of Honduras	4,499,000	Tegucigalpa* 472,700	43,277	Strong military influence	Spanish, Indian languages
Hungary Hungarian People's Republic	10,644,000	Budapest* 2,085,615	35,920	1 party, communist state	Hungarian
Iceland Republic of Iceland	241,000	Reykjavik* 84,600	39,769	Multi-party, parliamentary government	Icelandic, Danish
**India Republic of India	767,681,000	New Delhi* 5.2 million Calcutta 9.1 million	1,269,420	Multi-party, parliamentary government	Hindi, Urdu, English, and others
Indonesia Republic of Indonesia	173,103,000	Jakarta* 5,500,000	782,663	No parties, military government	Bahasa Indonesian (Malay), Javanese
Iran Islamic Republic of Iran	45,191,000	Teheran* 4,496,159	636,000	Islamic republic	Farsi Persian Kurdish
Iraq Republic of Iraq	15,507,000	Baghdad* 3,205,645	168,928	1 party, military government	Arabic, Kurdish
Ireland Irish Republic	3,588,000	Dublin* 525,360	27,136	Multi-party, parliamentary government	English, Gaelic

NAME OF COUNTRY	POPULATION	CAPITAL* LARGEST CITY	AREA (SQUARE MILES)	GOVERNMENT	MAJOR LANGUAGES
Israel State of Israel	4,128,000	Jerusalem* 398,000	7,992	Multi-party, parliamentary government	Hebrew, Arabic
Italy Italian Republic	57,116,000	Rome* 2.9 million	116,313	Multi-party, parliamentary government	Italian
Ivory Coast Republic of Ivory Coast	10,090,000	Abidjan* 1,686,100 (metropolitan area)	123,484	1 party, presidential regime	French, Mande languages
†Jamaica	2,366,000	Kingston* 671,000	4,244	2 party, parliamentary government	English
Japan	120,731,000	Tokyo* 8.2 million	145,747	2 party, parliamentary constitutional monarchy	Japanese
Jordan Hashemite Kingdom of Jordan	2,668,000	Amman* 684,600	36,832	1 party, constitutional monarchy	Arabic
Kenya Republic of Kenya	20,194,000	Nairobi* 959,000 (metropolitan area)	224,961	1 party, presidential regime	Swahili, Kikuyu, English, others
Kiribati Republic of Kiribati	62,000	Tarawa* 22,148	264	Parliamentary	English, Gilbertese, Ellice
Korea, North Democratic People's Republic of Korea	20,082,000	Pyongyang* 1,283,000	46,800	1 party, communist state	Korean
Korea, South Republic of Korea	42,643,000	Seoul* 8,000,000	38,130	Military rule	Korean
Kuwait State of Kuwait	1,710,000	Kuwait* 60,400 Hawalli 152,300	6,880	No political parties, constitutional monarchy	Arabic
Laos Lao People's Democratic Republic	3,605,000	Vientiane* 200,000	91,400	1 party, communist state	Lao, French, others
Lebanon Republic of Lebanon	2,619,000	Beirut* 1,100,000	3,950	Multi-party, parliamentary government	Arabic, French
Lesotho Kingdom of Lesotho	1,312,000	Maseru* 75,000	11,720	Multi-party, constitutional monarchy	English, Sesotho
Liberia Republic of Liberia	2,232,000	Monrovia* 306,000	43,000	Political activity suspended, military rule	English, African languages
Libya Socialist People's Libyan Arab Jamahiriya	3,752,000	Tripoli* 858,500	675,000	1 party, military government	Arabic
Liechtenstein Principality of Liechtenstein	27,000	Vaduz* 5,000	62	2 party, hereditary constitutional monarchy	German
Luxembourg Grand Duchy of Luxembourg	366,000	Luxembourg* 80,000	999	Multi-party, constitutional monarchy	French, German, Luxembourgian
Madagascar Democratic Republic of Madagascar	9,941,000	Antananarivo* 600,000	226,658	Political activity suspended, military government	French, Malagsy
Malawi Republic of Malawi	7,056,000	Lilongwe* 75,000 (metropolitan area)	45,747	1 party, presidential regime	English, Nyanja
Malaysia	15,467,000	Kuala Lumpur* 1,081,000 (metropolitan area)	127,316	Parliamentary democracy under a constitutional monarchy	Malay, English, Chinese, Dayak
†Maldives Republic of Maldives	182,000	Male* 32,000	115	Parliamentary government, limited democracy	Divehi
Mali Republic of Mali	7,721,000	Bamako* 620,000 (metropolitan area)	478,822	1 party, military government	French, Mande languages

NAME OF COUNTRY	POPULATION	CAPITAL* LARGEST CITY	AREA (SQUARE MILES)	GOVERNMENT	MAJOR LANGUAGES
†Malta	355,000	Valletta* 14,000	122	Multi-party, parliamentary government	Maltese, English, Italian
Mauritania Islamic Republic of Mauritania	1,656,000	Nouakchott* 250,000	398,000	Military government	Arabic, French
Mauritius	1,024,900	Port Louis* 146,884	787	Multi-party, parliamentary democracy under a constitutional monarchy (Queen Elizabeth)	English, French, Creole
**Mexico United Mexican States	79,662,000	Mexico City* 15 million	761,604	1 party, federal republic	Spanish, Indian languages
Monaco Principality of Monaco	28,000	Monaco-Ville* 1,700	0.73	1 party, constitutional monarchy	French
Mongolia Mongolian People's Republic	1,893,000	Ulaanbaatar* 435,400	604,000	1 party, communist state	Khalkha, Mongolian
Morocco Kingdom of Morocco	23,117,000	Rabat* 435,510 (Rabat-Sale) Casablanca 1,371,330	171,117	Multi-party, constitutional monarchy	Arabic, French, Spanish, Berber
Mozambique People's Republic of Mozambique	13,638,000	Maputo* 755,300	308,642	Marxist one-party state, committee rule	Portuguese, Bantu
†Nauru Republic of Nauru	8,000	Yaren* (no population figure available)	8.2	2 party, parliamentary government	Nauruan, English
Nepal Kingdom of Nepal	16,966,000	Kathmandu* 125,000	54,362	No political parties, monarchy	Nepali, others
Netherlands Kingdom of the Netherlands	14,481,000	Amsterdam* 712,294	15,892	Multi-party, parliamentary democracy under a constitutional monarchy	Dutch
Netherlands Antilles	200,000	Willemstad* On Curacao 50,000	383	Constitutionally on level of equality with the Netherlands within the Kingdom	
Curacao, Aruba, Bonaire, St. Eustatius, Saba, St. Maarten					
†New Zealand	3,271,000	Wellington* 342,000 Auckland 818,000	103,747	2 party, parliamentary government	English, Maori
**Nicaragua Republic of Nicaragua	2,232,000	Managua* 552,900	50,000	Republic	Spanish
Niger Republic of Niger	6,491,000	Niamey* 300,000	489,000	Political activity banned, military government	French, Hausa
†Nigeria Federal Republic of Nigeria	102,783,000	Lagos* 1,404,000	356,699	Multi-party, federal republic	English, Housa, Ibo, Yoruba
Norway Kingdom of Norway	4,152,000	Oslo* 452,023	125,053	Multi-party, parliamentary constitutional monarchy	Norwegian
Oman Sultanate of Oman	1,228,000	Muscat* 50,000	82,000	No political parties, absolute monarchy	Arabic
Pakistan Islamic Republic of Pakistan	99,199,000	Islamabad* 201,000 Karachi 3,498,634	307,374	Military rule	Urdu, English, others
Panama Republic of Panama	2,180,000	Panama* 655,000	29,029	Republic	Spanish, English
†Papua-New Guinea	3,326,000	Port Moresby* 116,900	178,260	Parliamentary government	English, Papuan

NAME OF COUNTRY	POPULATION	CAPITAL* LARGEST CITY	AREA (SQUARE MILES)	GOVERNMENT	MAJOR LANGUAGES
Paraguay Republic of Paraguay	3,300,000	Asunción 481,706	157,018	Presidential dictatorship	Spanish, Guarani
Peru Republic of Peru	18,600,000	Lima* 3.1 million	496,224	Multi-party, republic	Spanish, Quechua, Aymara
Philippines Republic of the Philippines	51,600,000	Quezon City* 1.1 million Manila is defacto capital 1.6 million	115,800	Multi-party, presidential regime	Tagalog, English, Spanish, others
Poland Polish People's Republic	36,300,000	Warsaw* 1.5 million	120,725	1 party, communist state	Polish
Portugal Republic of Portugal	9,930,000	Lisbon* 812,400	35,383	Multi-party, parliamentary government	Portuguese
Qatar State of Qatar	250,000	Doha* 190,000	4,400	No political parties, Traditional Emirate	Arabic
Romania Socialist Republic of Romania	22,600,000	Bucharest* 1,861,007	91,700	1 party, communist state	Romanian
Rwanda Republic of Rwanda	5,400,000	Kigali* 156,650	10,169	No political parties, military government	Kinyawanda, French
St. Kitts-Nevis	52,000	Basseterre* 14,725	101	Multi-party, parliamentary government	English
†Saint Lucia	124,000	Castries* 45,000	238	Parliamentary government	English
†Saint Vincent and the Grenadines	120,000	Kingstown* 23,200	150	Multi-party, parliamentary government	English
San Marino Most Serene Republic of San Marino	21,537	San Marino* 3,000	24	Multi-party, parliamentary government	Italian
Sao Tomé and Principe Democratic Republic of Sao Tome-Principe	100,000	Sao Tome 25,000	372	1 party, republic	Portuguese, Bantu
Saudi Arabia Kingdom of Saudi Arabia	11,100,000	Riyadh* 1,793,000	865,000	No political parties, absolute monarchy	Arabic
Senegambia	6,700,000	Dakar* 978,553	78,685	Multi-party, parliamentary government created in 1982 from union of Senegal and Gambia; cabinets function separately.	French, English, Wolof, Mande
†Seychelles Republic of Seychelles	67,000	Victoria* 23,000	107	Single party, republic	Creole, English, French
†Sierra Leone Republic of Sierra Leone	3,700,000	Freetown* 500,000	27,925	1 party, presidential regime	English, African languages, Creole
†Singapore* Republic of Singapore	2,500,000	Singapore* 2,334,400	227	Multi-party, parliamentary government	English, Malay, Chinese, Tamil
†Solomon Islands	240,000	Honiara* 19,200	11,500	Multi-party, parliamentary government. Within the Commonwealth of Nations	Pidgin English, English
Somalia Somali Democratic Republic	4,600,000	Mogadishu* 400,000	246,300	No political parties, military government	Somali, Italian, Arabic
South Africa Republic of South Africa	30,000,000	Cape Town* (legislative) 213,830 Pretoria* (administrative) 528,407 Bloemfontein* (judicial) 230,688	471,445	2 party, parliamentary government (limited to white adults)	English, Africaans, Shosa, Zulu, Sotho

NAME OF COUNTRY	POPULATION	CAPITAL* LARGEST CITY	AREA (SQUARE MILES)	GOVERNMENT	MAJOR LANGUAGES
Namibia (South-West Africa)	1,038,000	Windhoek* 64,095	318,827	On Jan. 18, 1983, South Africa dissolved the Namibian General Assembly and assumed direct control of the territory	
**Spain Spanish State	37,900,000	Madrid* 3,520,320	194,885	Multi-party, parliamentary monarchy	Spanish
The Balearic and the Canary Islands are provinces of Spain					
†Sri Lanka Democratic Socialist Republic of Sri Lanka	15,200,000	Colombo* 585,776	25,332	Multi-party, parliamentary government	Sinhalese, Tamil, English
Sudan Democratic Republic of the Sudan	19,900,000	Khatoum* 333,921	966,757	1 party, presidential regime	Arabic, English, African languages
Suriname	420,000	Paramaribo* 67,700	63,037	Military government	Taki-Taki, Dutch, Spanish, others
†Swaziland Kingdom of Swaziland	600,000	Mbabane* 33,000	6,704	No political parties, constitutional monarchy	English, siSwati
Sweden Kingdom of Sweden	8,310,000	Stockholm* 1,386,980	179,896	Multi-party, parliamentary constitutional monarchy	Swedish
Switzerland Swiss Confederation	6,343,000	Bern* 145,000 Zurich 375,000	15,941	Multi-party, parliamentary government	German, French, Italian, Romansch
Syria Syrian Arab Republic	9,700,000	Damascus* 1,142,000	71,498	Multi-party, presidential regime	Arabic, Kurdish, Armenian
†Tanzania United Republic of Tanzania	19,900,000	Dar-es-Salaam* 700,000	364,886	1 party, presidential regime	Swahili, English
Thailand Kingdom of Thailand	49,800,000	Bangkok* 4.7 million	198,500	Political activity suspended, military government	Thai, Chinese, English, others
Togo Republic of Togo	2,800,000	Lomé* 283,000	21,853	1 party, presidential regime	French, African languages
†Tonga Kingdom of Tonga	100,000	Nuku'alofa* 19,900	270	No political parties, constitutional monarchy	Tongan, English
†Trinidad and Tobago Republic of Trinidad and Tobago	1,100,000	Port-of-Spain* 250,000 (metropolitan area)	1,970	2 party, parliamentary government	English, Creole
Tunisia Republic of Tunisia	6,700,000	Tunis* 1,000,000	63,378	1 party, presidential regime	Arabic, French
Turkey Republic of Turkey	47,700,000	Ankara* 1,877,755 Istanbul 2,772,708	300,948	Military rule	Turkish, Kurdish, Arabic
†Tuvalu	9,000	Funafuti* 2,200	10	Parliamentary government	English, Samoan, Gilbertese
†Uganda Republic of Uganda	13,700,000	Kampala* 458,000	91,104	Presidential regime	English, African languages
Union of Soviet Socialist Republics	268,800,000	Moscow* 8.2 million	8,649,490	1 party, communist state	Russian, and other languages
United Arab Emirates	1,200,000	Abu Dhabi* 449,000	32,000	Federal system, monarchs rule member states	Arabic
United Kingdom of Great Britain and Northern Ireland	56,100,000	London* 6,696,008	94,222	Multi-party, parliamentary constitutional monarchy	English, Welsh, Gaelic
British possessions: Channel Islands	130,000		75	Separate legal existence, lieut. gov. named by Crown	
Isle of Man	61,000		227	Lieut. gov. named by Crown	

NAME OF COUNTRY	POPULATION	CAPITAL* LARGEST CITY	AREA (SQUARE MILES)	GOVERNMENT	MAJOR LANGUAGES
Gibraltar	29,000		2.25	A dependency	
British West Indies:					
Montserrat	12,000		40	Possession	
Anguilla	7,000		35	Autonomous elected government	
Cayman Islands	23,000		100	Dependency	
Turks and Caicos					
Islands	7,000		193	Separate possessions	
Bermuda	58,000		20 (360 small islands)	A dependency	
South Atlantic Dependencies:					
Falkland Islands	2,000		4,700		
St. Helena	9,000		47		
Tristan da Cunha	262		40		
Ascension	1,179		34		
Asia and Indian Ocean Colony					
Hong Kong	5,287,000		403	A Crown colony	
Pacific Ocean Colony					
Pitcairn Island	55		1.75	A colony	
**United States of America (For information on U.S. Possessions see pp. 341-344)	238,631,000	Washington, DC* 3,060,922 (metropolitan area) New York 9,120,346 (metropolitan area)	3,165,122	2 party, federal republic	English
Upper Volta Republic of Upper Volta	6,907,000	Ouagadougou* 200,000	105,869	Military junta	French, Mande, Voltaic languages
Uruguay Oriental Republic of Uruguay	2,936,000	Montevideo* 1,260,600	68,536	Political activity banned, military government	Spanish
†Vanuatu Republic of Vanuatu	125,600	Vila* 15,100	4,707	Multi-party, parliamentary government	English, French
Vatican State of Vatican City	1,000	Vatican City	0.17	No parties, papal state	Latin, Italian
Venezuela Republic of Venezuela	17,317,000	Caracas* 2,700,000	352,144	Multi-party, federal republic	Spanish
Vietnam Socialist Republic of Vietnam	60,492,000	Hanoi* 2 million Ho Chi Minh City 3.5 million	130,653	1 party, communist state	Annamese, Chinese, French
Western Samoa	160,000	Apia* 33,400	1,133	2 party, parliamentary constitutional monarchy	Samoan, English
Yemen, North Yemen Arab Republic	6,159,000	Sanaa* 277,800	77,200	No parties, military government	Arabic
Yemen, South People's Democratic Republic of Yemen	2,209,000	Aden* 264,326	111,074	1 party, presidential council	Arabic
Yugoslavia Socialist Federal Republic of Yugoslavia	23,124,000	Belgrade* 1,300,000	98,766	1 party, communist state	Slovene, Macedonian, Serbo-Croat
Zaire	30,505,000	Kinshasa* 3,000,000	905,365	1 party, presidential regime	French, Swahili, Lingala
†Zambia Republic of Zambia	6,832,000	Lusaka* 538,000	290,586	1 party, presidential regime	English, Bantu
†Zimbabwe	8,678,000	Harare* 657,000 (metropolitan area)	150,875	Multi-party, parliamentary government	English, Shona, Sindebele

† (Before name of country) means it belongs in the Commonwealth of Nations formerly called the British Commonwealth. Some have monarchs other than Queen Elizabeth II, some are dictatorships, etc. The Commonwealth is simply a loose association of self-governing nations plus some colonies and protectorates.

** Some countries described as one-party or two-party systems may actually have more legal political parties, but they are not viable politically, i.e. Mexico has five, but only one has governed since 1929. Also, in the U.S. other parties come and go, but there are only two major parties.

Population figures in most cases are 1982 estimates.

The United Nations

The United Nations does not represent the first attempt at world cooperation. After World War I, President Wilson and others conceived the idea of a League of Nations, an organization devoted to the settlement of disputes and the prevention of war. The main defect of the League was that it had no independent strength with which to punish aggressor nations or to enforce the peace. The League's failure during the 1930s to stop Japan from attacking Manchuria and Italy from attacking Ethiopia and its inability to stop World War II marked the demise of this well-intentioned organization.

Throughout World War II, a realization was growing that a more effective international body would have to be created. The Atlantic Charter, signed in 1941 by President Roosevelt and British Prime Minister Churchill, stressed the concept of full cooperation between nations. Later twenty-six countries signed the Declaration of the United Nations which reasserted this concept. Conferences held in 1943 at Moscow and Tehran paved the way for an organization ". . . for the maintenance of international peace and security." Still later, representatives of the United States, the United Kingdom, China, and the Soviet Union met at Dumbarton Oaks, near Washington, D.C., to work out a more detailed blueprint for the new world organization, which they agreed to call the United Nations.

On April 12, 1945, one of the chief architects of the United Nations, Franklin D. Roosevelt, died. Two weeks after his death the San Francisco Conference met at the Opera House in that city. After eight weeks of hard work, delegates from fifty countries approved the Charter of the United Nations. The solemn signing took eight hours.

THE BASIC STRUCTURE OF THE UNITED NATIONS

"We the peoples of the United Nations determined to save succeeding generations from the scourge of war, which twice in our lifetime has brought untold sorrow to mankind . . . do hereby establish an international organization to be known as the United Nations."

These are the words of the Preamble of the Charter of the United Nations. The Charter goes on to state the purposes of the organization and to describe its organization.

Purposes. The Charter sets forth three basic purposes:

1. To maintain international peace and security by preventing aggression and settling disputes peacefully.
2. To develop friendly relations among nations based on respect for equal rights and self-determination of peoples.
3. To achieve international cooperation in solving economic, social, cultural, and humanitarian problems and in promoting respect for human rights and fundamental freedoms for all.

In accordance with these purposes, all members agree to (1) settle disputes peacefully, (2) to refrain from threat or use of force against another state, and (3) to assist the United Nations in its undertakings and not to aid any state against which the United Nations is acting.

Bearing in mind the arguments which helped keep the United States out of the League of Nations, the Charter specifically states that there is to be no intervention in matters essentially within the domestic jurisdiction of any state.

Any amendment to the Charter must be approved by a two-thirds vote of the General Assembly and ratified by two-thirds of the members of the United Nations. The first amendments were ratified in 1965 and became effective on January 1, 1966. They increased the number of members of the Security Council and the Economic and Social Council.

Membership. The Charter provides that membership shall be "open to all . . . peace-loving states which accept the obligations contained in the present Charter and which, in the judgment of the organization, are able and willing to carry out these obligations." Members are admitted by vote of the General Assembly upon recommendation of the Security Council.

As will be explained later, the permanent members of the Security Council have a veto. During the first ten years, the Soviet Union vetoed for membership every country it considered too favorable to the West, including Italy, South Korea, and Japan. At the same time, when the Soviet Union

United Nations—The San Francisco Conference, June 26, 1945

THE GENERAL ASSEMBLY

The central body of the United Nations is the General Assembly. All member states are members of the Assembly, each having one vote, although each nation may send up to five representatives. Often called "the Town Meeting of the World," the General Assembly meets in annual, regular sessions, although special sessions can be called by the Secretary-General at the request of the Security Council or of a majority of the members of the United Nations.

The General Assembly can discuss and make recommendations on all matters within the scope of the Charter, except that it may not discuss issues which are at that time on the agenda of the Security Council. However, at the time of the Korean conflict in November 1950, the General Assembly adopted the "Uniting for Peace" resolution. This greatly increased the power of the General Assembly. It provided that if the Security Council should, because of the use of the veto by one of its permanent members, fail to act in a situation threatening international peace, then the General Assembly might hold an emergency session within twenty-four hours and recommend collective action, including the use of armed force. You may recall that it was the failure of the Council of the League of Nations to take action to halt aggression which weakened that organization's efforts. The

put up Hungary, Romania, and Bulgaria for membership, the majority on the Security Council voted them down as being "satellite states" under Soviet domination. In 1955, however, a "package deal" was arranged, and sixteen nations came in together. Since then a number of other nations, including the new nations of Africa, have been admitted, making a total membership of well over 140 nations.

United Nations—Eighteenth Regular Session of the General Assembly

"Uniting for Peace" resolution was designed to prevent a repetition of that failure.

Decisions of the General Assembly on important matters, such as those involving the maintenance of peace, the admission of members, and the election of the nonpermanent members of the Security Council, are decided by a two-thirds majority. Other less important matters are decided by a simple majority.

THE SECURITY COUNCIL

The Charter places "the primary responsibility for the maintenance of peace and security" on the Security Council. It has fifteen members including five permanent members—China, France, the Union of Soviet Socialist Republics, the United Kingdom, and the United States—and ten nonpermanent members. Each year, the General Assembly elects five nonpermanent members for a two-year term. These nonpermanent members are not eligible for immediate reelection to the Security Council.

Although the Security Council meets periodically, it is set up so as to be able to function at any time. It is said to be "in continuous session," because each member is always represented at UN Headquarters.

Each member of the Security Council has one vote. Routine, or "procedural" matters, as the Charter says, are decided by an affirmative vote of any nine of the fifteen members. However, in all other cases, the five permanent members must either cast affirmative votes or abstain. The Security Council may not take action if any permanent member casts a negative vote on a substantive matter.

The power of veto in the Security Council means that no enforcement action will be taken against any permanent member, for no nation is likely to vote against itself. The veto was written into the Charter at the insistence not only of the Soviet Union, but of the United States as well, because of the fear that otherwise the United States Senate might not ratify the Charter.

The argument against the veto power is that its abuse by the Soviet Union has weakened the ability of the United Nations to act effectively. However, the "Uniting for Peace" resolution, as we have seen, provides a method by which the General Assembly can undertake to solve a problem when a veto in the Security Council blocks action.

It is important to remember that the main aim of the United Nations is not to fight any of its members but rather to provide machinery for peaceful settlement of disputes. Hence, the Security Council may call upon disputing nations to settle their dispute by such means as negotiation or by settlement by the International Court of Justice (see below). If the dispute is not settled, the Security Council may itself recommend a settlement.

The Council is given the authority, if all attempts at a peaceful settlement fail, to call upon the members of the United Nations, who are pledged to make armed forces available to the Security Council for land, sea, and air forces to use in blockades or "other operations" against the nation whose action is threatening the peace.

THE ECONOMIC AND SOCIAL COUNCIL

The founders of the United Nations were convinced that part of the job to be done by the international organization was the improvement of living conditions all over the world. Chapter IX of the Charter states that "the United Nations shall promote higher standards of living, full employment, conditions of economic and social progress . . . international, cultural, and educational cooperation . . . universal respect for . . . human rights and fundamental freedoms for all without distinction as to sex, race, language, or religion."

In accordance with these objectives, the Economic and Social Council (ECOSOC) was provided for. ECOSOC has members, elected annually for three-year terms in groups of eighteen by the General Assembly. The Council meets as often as necessary to perform its duties, usually for two sessions a year.

The functions of the Economic and Social Council are to make studies on international health, social, economic, cultural, and educational problems, and to make recommendations to the General Assembly on the basis of these studies. It may call international conferences on matters related to these fields. In connection with these very broad areas of interest, the Council often calls upon the cooperation of private organizations and experts to help in its work. The Specialized Agencies, which will be discussed in detail later, are brought into relationship with the United Nations through the Economic and Social Council.

United Nations—Trusteeship Council concludes examination of conditions in Tanganyika, July 13, 1961.

THE TRUSTEESHIP COUNCIL

When World War I ended, Germany's colonies were taken from her and handed over to various other nations for administration as "mandates." This meant that they were no longer to be considered colonies. Instead, the administering countries promised to rule them fairly and to report regularly to the League of Nations. After World War II, most of the mandates were transferred to the United Nations, whose Charter established a Trusteeship Council to supervise the governing of trust territories. The goal is to advance these territories to the point where they will be able to govern themselves or achieve complete independence.

Trust territories include, in addition to those formerly held as mandates under the League of Nations, territories taken from Axis powers after World War II and dependent territories voluntarily turned over to trusteeship by the nations controlling them.

The Trusteeship Council is made up of those United Nations members which administer trust territories and an equal number of those which do not. Included in the number, however, must be the five permanent members of the Security Council. The Trusteeship Council holds two regular sessions a year, as well as special sessions which may be required. Decisions are made by a simple majority vote.

As the number of trust territories gaining their independence has increased, the work of the Trusteeship Council has lessened. The members are charged with taking an active part in the governing of the remaining trust territories. Each year, the administering government has to report to the Council about economic, political, and educational progress made in the trust territory during the year. Thousands of petitions and complaints are received by the Council from people in trust territories all over the world. Special missions are sent out to territories to investigate conditions. The Council reports to the General Assembly on developments in the trust territories.

THE INTERNATIONAL COURT OF JUSTICE

The principal judicial organ of the United Nations is the International Court of Justice. It is the successor of the Permanent Court of International Justice, often called the World Court. Located at The Hague, Netherlands, it has fifteen judges, no two from any one nation. They are chosen by the Security Council and the General Assembly for nine-year terms. All members of the United Nations are automatically associated with the Court. Other nations may join upon the consent of the General Assembly and the Security Council.

The function of the Court is to decide points of international law over which a dispute may arise between nations. Only nations, not individuals, may bring a case before the Court. All United Nations members undertake to obey the Court's decisions. If a nation should fail to do so, an appeal may be made to the Security Council, which may take any action it sees fit. A nation may, if it wishes, promise in advance that it will always be ready to submit to the Court's decision in certain types of cases, provided the opposing nation does the same. The United States reserved the right to decide in each specific case whether it would allow

United Nations—Security Council meets on the Cypress Question, March 3, 1964.

the matter to come before the Court. The International Court of Justice may also give advisory opinions on legal questions which the other organs of the United Nations may submit to it.

The services of the Court have been extensively used by the members of the United Nations. Cases have involved disputes between Albania and the United Kingdom over damage to British warships by mine explosions in the Corfu Channel, between the United States and France over the rights of Americans in Morocco, between Cambodia and Thailand over ownership of a holy temple, and many others.

THE SECRETARIAT

The day-to-day work of the United Nations is entrusted to a staff known as the Secretariat. About four thousand people from all over the world make up the Secretariat. They do not represent their own nations but are bound by the Charter to serve as international public servants.

Members of the Secretariat make the arrangements for conference, draft reports, and collect information for use by the delegates. Skilled interpreters sit in soundproof boxes overlooking meetings of various UN bodies and provide simulta-

neous translations for transmission by the language earphones that are provided at every seat on the floor. No matter what language is being spoken, a delegate can hear a translation in English, French, Spanish, Russian, or Chinese.

At the head of the Secretariat is the Secretary-General. He is elected by the General Assembly on the recommendation of the Security Council for a five-year term. As the chief administrative officer of the United Nations, he serves all the main organs of the world organization except the Court. He reports annually to the General Assembly. He supervises the staff of the Secretariat, assisted by under-secretaries and other officials.

One of the most important roles of the Secretary-General arises out of his right to go before the Security Council at any time and call its attention to a situation which he regards as a threat to world peace. This places the Secretary-General at the center of most international disputes, in a position to exercise tremendous influence in world affairs. In 1960, for example, the Security Council passed a resolution giving Secretary-General Dag Hammarskjöld, who had succeeded Trygve Lie in the post, full authority for organizing a force to secure peaceful conditions in the newly independent Congo. On September 18, 1961, while he was en route to a meeting in Africa to strengthen peace efforts, Hammarskjöld was killed when his plane crashed in flames. His successors, U Thant of Burma and Kurt Waldheim of Austria, have continued to stress the fact that the Secretary-General must take the initiative in attempting to bring about permanent peace.

SPECIALIZED AGENCIES

Associated in a close relationship with the United Nations are agencies of various kinds that are not actually part of the world organization but are related to it by special agreements through the Economic and Social Council. These agencies are called the "Specialized Agencies" because each one has a special field of work, such as education, health, or finance. Although these agencies report regularly to the United Nations through ECOSOC, they are largely independent, each having its own membership, officers, treasury, and budget. Membership in the Specialized Agencies is not dependent upon United Nations membership. Consequently, the number of nations participating is not necessarily the same as the number of nations belonging to the United Nations.

About four billion people are in the world. It has been estimated that more than half of them are ill-fed or underfed or both. These are, in the main, the people of Asia, the Middle East, much of Africa,

Nepal—Workers at Government Forest Nursery at Thankot

and large areas of Latin America. Much of the problem is due to primitive and unscientific methods of farming.

The problem of food shortages is not a new one. However, it has been complicated by the so-called "population explosion." The number of people in the world is increasing faster than ever before. In 1900, the population of the world was about one and a half billion people. Today, as we have seen, it is four billion. It is estimated that by the year 2000 there will be more than six billion people in the world.

The Food and Agriculture Organization is an agency concerned with improving the production, distribution, and consumption of food from agriculture and fisheries. Its work falls into three main classes: (1) collecting and distributing information from all over the world, (2) meetings and conferences of experts to discuss ways of solving the problem of food shortages, (3) sending experts to countries whose governments ask for help in developing food resources.

FAO's varied activities have been worldwide in scope. Fishermen in Chile have been helped to discover better fishing grounds. Farmers in Ethiopia have learned to fight animal diseases and those in the Middle East, to fight desert locusts. Sri Lanka was aided in the setting-up of timber mills. Tough grasses and hardy trees have been planted in the deserts of North Africa. Israeli farmers have been taught new methods of dairy farming.

It has been estimated that fully half of the people in the world are suffering from diseases that are preventable by knowedge, skills, and techniques already at hand. The problem is to find a way of bringing the knowledge to the place where it is needed. The World Health Organization was created to direct and coordinate health work in order to raise the health standards of people all over the world.

WHO sends public health experts and demonstration teams for disease control to countries requesting this service. It helps to train health workers of all kinds and provides hundreds of fellowships for doctors and nurses to study abroad.

The results of its efforts have been very impressive. In 1950, Indonesia asked for help against yaws, a crippling disease of which there were ten million victims in Indonesia. In four years, medical teams trained by WHO had cured 1,300,000 cases. Egypt has been helped in the fight against bilharziasis, a disease which used to cause one out of every five deaths in that country. Malaria-

Peru—A census-taker in the village of Chinchera

control teams have worked in all corners of the globe and millions of people have been vaccinated against a variety of dread diseases including polio, diphtheria, and yellow fever. WHO has also worked to encourage medical research into such areas as cancer and heart disease.

World War II resulted in the destruction of schools and colleges all over Europe. Even before the war ended, representatives of various nations met to make plans for rebuilding their educational systems after the war. An agency to coordinate this effort was to be set up. However, the idea of an agency devoted only to rehabilitation gradually changed to the notion that a permanent educational and cultural organization should be set up under the United Nations.

The preamble to UNESCO's constitution expresses the basic aim of the agency: "Wars begin in the minds of men, and it is therefore in the minds of men that the defenses of peace must be constructed." The idea has been put in another way: "One idea is worth more than a hundred thousand bayonets."

At present, there are six main items in UNESCO's program: (1) compulsory primary education, (2) scientific research for the improvement of living conditions, (3) the elimination of racial and social tensions, (4) the development of mutual appreciation by peoples all over the world of the cul-

ture of other peoples, (5) the growth in freedom of information, and (6) "fundamental education," meaning learning to live properly as regards diet and health, as well as to read and write.

In recent years UNESCO has engaged in several major projects. Latin American governments have been helped to increase primary education for the children of their countries. Scientific research for the development of natural resources in the arid zone from Morocco to India has been encouraged. Appreciation of Asian and Western cultural values, primarily through international visits and exchange of ideas, literature, and art, has been promoted. Teams of experts have gone out to India, Mexico, and Egypt to set up teacher-training institutes. An extensive fellowship program has been organized to promote the exchange of students and teachers. The first committee of the International Geophysical Year was organized with the help of UNESCO. An extensive survey of the Indian Ocean has been made in an effort to provide new sources of food for much of the world's population.

The International Labor Organization was founded in 1919 as part of the League of Nations. Its aim is ". . . universal and lasting peace . . . based upon social justice." It strives to persuade nations to improve labor conditions and living standards. It is made up of representatives of employers, labor, and the governments of the member nations. Its headquarters are in Geneva, with branch offices around the world.

A major part of ILO's work is the development of "Conventions" (or treaties) dealing with such matters as safety and health for workers, minimum age for employment, collective bargaining, and equal pay for equal work. These conventions are the product of long study and debate. They are submitted to the member governments for ratification. A country that ratifies binds itself to report each year on what progress it has made toward putting into effect the laws recommended by the Convention.

ILO also conducts training courses, does research, and publishes many economic and statistical reports. It cooperates with other Specialized Agencies in the task of raising living standards through advice on how to produce more and better goods. Recent studies by ILO have dealt with automation and its effects, protection of workers against radiation, and discrimination in employment.

In 1946, a new kind of bank was ready for business. Its aim was to help nations to finance the rebuilding of areas devastated by war and to aid underdeveloped nations. It was named the International Bank for Reconstruction and Development, with headquarters in Washington, D.C. Member nations bought stock in the Bank. Each has a representative on the Board of Directors, which meets once a year, and passes on all loans. The Bank lends money to member governments or to private enterprises where payment is guaranteed by the government. It will provide funds, however, only where it is reasonably sure that the loan can be paid back with interest and where private banks will not handle the loan. The Bank obtains funds not only from the sale of its stock but also by issuing bonds, which are bought by private investors in various countries.

The effects of the Bank's activities have been felt all over the world. The Pacific Railroad of Mexico was modernized with a very large loan. Through the Bank, Colombia added 190 miles of railway and Sri Lanka was able to build hydroelectric installations. India built a power plant near Bombay. Peru was helped to irrigate 125,000 acres of land. A loan helped Israel develop the Dead Sea Potash Works.

In 1960, a new agency, affiliated with the International Bank for Reconstruction and Development, was established. It was the International Development Association, set up to help finance economic growth to the less-developed countries. Its loans are made on very flexible terms, with long periods of repayment, low rates of interest, or no interest at all.

Another agency affiliated with the Bank is the International Finance Corporation. Like IDA, it is concerned with helping less-developed countries build dams, schools, hospitals, and roads. IFC aids economic development by encouraging productive private enterprise, in association with private investors, without requiring government guarantee of repayment. It has assisted in the development of private enterprises in Brazil, Chile, Pakistan, and Australia.

The International Monetary Fund works in close association with the Bank. In fact, a government must be a member of IMF in order to join the Bank. The Fund's purpose is to help a nation which is temporarily short of gold or foreign currency because its exports are not earning enough to pay for its imports. In such a case, the nation may buy the necessary foreign money from IMF, which has available the currency of all member nations. The Fund also provides technical assistance by sending experts who advise governments on monetary questions.

The basic aim of the International Civil Aviation Organization is to make flying from one country to another safer and easier. Its headquarters are in Montreal, but it holds regional meetings all over the world.

ICAO has drafted a set of rules and regulations to standardize international air operations, and immigration, customs, and health procedures at international airports. ICAO experts make recommendations to member governments regarding suitable airport sites and the improvement of weather information and of search and rescue operations. Much of its work is directed toward meeting new requirements for jet operations. Nations with inadequate roads or railways are helped to improve air service for quick and easy transportation.

The Universal Postal Union was set up in 1874 in Berne. It is now part of the United Nations. As a result of its work, several billion pieces of mail are carried safely from one country to another. The Union guarantees the delivery of mail under the established rates throughout the world and its return to place of origin, if it cannot be delivered.

Similar to the UPU is the International Telecommunication Union, which dates back to 1865. Although in its early days it was concerned largely with improving international telegraph service, today much of its work involves radio broadcasting. If stations in different countries were to broadcast on any wave length they wished to, radio communications among nations would be extremely difficult, since there would be a great deal of interference. To prevent this, ITU records the frequency assignments made by individual nations and tries to persuade them to agree on an orderly sharing of radio frequency bands.

The scientific study of weather conditions has become increasingly important in the age of the airplane, television, and radio. The World Meteorological Organization, with headquarters in Geneva, aims to collect and exchange, among weather stations all over the world, accurate meteorological information. It also provides technical assistance to member nations to improve

Bangladesh—Dacca, Bengali women learning to cut cloth and sew

weather forecasting services. It has recently added to its work the spreading of information based upon the observations of weather satellites.

In 1957, the International Atomic Energy Agency was established in order to help put the power of the atom to work for peaceful uses. Its headquarters are in Vienna. Unlike the other Specialized Agencies, IAEA is an intergovernmental agency which makes an annual report directly to the General Assembly.

IAEA supplies advice to nations wishing help in establishing atomic installations for peaceful purposes, and arranges for the exchange of atomic materials.

The Intergovernmental Maritime Consultative Organization (IMCO) began operations in 1958 with headquarters in London. It seeks to promote cooperation in regard to the regulation of ocean shipping and the improvement of safety at sea.

In force since 1948, the General Agreement on Tariffs and Trade seeks to reduce barriers to international trade. To aid developing countries, GATT set up the International Trade Center in 1964.

THE UNITED NATIONS IN ACTION

One evaluation of the work of the United Nations ended with this comment: "To measure the UN's contribution, one need only ask how much meaner and poorer, how much less touched by hope or reason, would be the world scene if it suddenly ceased to exist."

Since its establishment, the United Nations has done much to provide hope for people all over the world. In 1953, the United Nations Children's Fund, known as UNICEF, was set up as a permanent agency. It works with WHO and other Specialized Agencies to help children grow strong and healthy. UNICEF is supported by contributions from governments and from private persons and organizations.

Another program which coordinates the work of various Specialized Agencies is the Expanded Program of Technical Assistance (EPTA). A Technical Assistance Board, composed of the Secretary-General of the United Nations or his representative and the heads of the cooperating agencies, administers a special fund, which it distributes to be used for work that no agency by itself is equipped to undertake. By coordinating the work of WHO, WMO, ILO, FAO, and other agencies, TAB has provided training for doctors, nurses, and nutritionists, with the host government providing the hospitals and Specialized Agencies of the UN providing expensive equipment. Other projects have included providing engineers and other experts to help in town planning, in building dams and hydroelectric projects, and in setting up fisheries. In 1959, a new program called the Special Fund was established. It concentrates on a few large projects which are considered to be especially urgent. It is hoped that the success of these projects will open the way for investment of much larger sums by private business in countries that badly need new enterprises.

At its first meeting in 1946, the Economic and Social Council elected a Commission on Human Rights to draw up an international bill of rights for all people. On December 10, 1948, the Universal Declaration of Human Rights was unanimously adopted by the General Assembly. It proclaims that all people are born free and equal and are entitled to life, liberty, and security of person, the right to travel freely and live where they please, and freedom of speech, press, assembly, and worship.

ECOSOC has also worked for human welfare in other ways. Its Commission on the Status of Women has made a number of studies and recommendations to insure equality of rights and duties between men and women. Another commission of the Council is the Commission on Narcotic Drugs which works to strengthen control over international traffic in drugs.

A special committee of ECOSOC drafted the Genocide Convention, which the General Assembly adopted in 1958. This Convention is designed to outlaw the crime of *genocide,* defined as an attempt to destroy "a national, ethnical, racial, or religious group as such." A year later the Assembly unanimously adopted a Declaration of the Rights of the Child, which asserts the right of every child to be given proper food, shelter, medical care, and education, the right to play, and to be taught the spirit of universal brotherhood.

Another problem with which the United Nations has concerned itself has been aid to refugees. The UN Office of the High Commissioner for Refugees gives international protection to people driven out of their homelands. Refugees from Communist China, Morocco, Tunisia, Hungary, Israel, and East Germany have been given emergency relief and have been aided in finding homes and employment.

THE U.N. MEETS MANY CRISES

The United Nations has faced many serious crises, several of which could have resulted in a major war and in the destruction of the UN itself. The UN did not succeed in reaching a settlement in every one of these crises. It is important to remember, however, that a successful settlement depends upon the willingness of governments to cooperate in order to avoid war.

Math Formulas/Equivalent Measures

CIRCUMFERENCE

Circle .... $C = d\pi$, in which π is 3.1416 and d the diameter.

AREA

Circle .... $A = r^2\pi$, in which π is 3.1416 and r the radius.

Rectangle .... $A = ab$, in which a is the base and b the height.

Sphere .... $A = 4r^2\pi$, in which r is the radius.

Trapezoid .... $A = \dfrac{h(a+b)}{2}$, in which h is the height, a the longer parallel side, and b the shorter.

Triangle .... $A = \dfrac{ab}{2}$, in which a is the base and b the height.

VOLUME

Cone .... $V = \dfrac{r^2\pi h}{3}$, in which π is 3.1416, r the radius of the base, and h the height.

Cube .... $V = a^3$, in which a is one of the edges.

Cylinder .... $V = r^2\pi h$, in which π is 3.1614, r the radius of the base, and h the height.

Pyramid .... $V = \dfrac{Ah}{3}$, in which A is the area of the base and h the height.

Rectangular Prism .... $V = abc$, in which a is the length, b the width, and c the depth.

Sphere .... $V = \dfrac{4\pi r^3}{3}$, in which π is 3.1416 and r the radius.

FALLING BODIES

Speed per second acquired by falling body: $S = 32t$, in which t is the time in seconds.

Distance in feet traveled by falling body: $D = 16t$, in which t is the time in seconds.

SPEED OF SOUND

Speed of sound in feet per second through any given temperature of air: $S = \dfrac{1087\sqrt{273+t}}{16.52}$, in which t is the temperature in Centigrade.

ENERGY AND MATTER

Conversion of matter into energy (Einstein's theorem): $E = mc^2$, in which E is the energy in ergs, m the mass of the matter in grams, and c the speed of light in centimeters per second. ($c^2 = 9.10^{20}$).

FORMULAS USED IN SOLID GEOMETRY

LATERAL AREA

Cone of revolution .... $L = \pi rs$
Cylinder of revolution .... $L = 2\pi rh$
Frustum of cone of revolution .... $L = \frac{1}{2}s(c + c')$
Frustum of regular pyramid .... $L = \frac{1}{2}s(p + p')$
Prism .... $L = ep$
Regular pyramid .... $L = \frac{1}{2}sp$

TOTAL AREA

Cone of revolution .... $T = \pi r(r + s)$
Cylinder of revolution .... $T = 2\pi r(r + h)$
Sphere .... $S = 4\pi r^2$
Zone .... $S = 2\pi rh$

VOLUME

Circular cone .... $V = \frac{1}{3}\pi r^2 h$
Circular cylinder .... $V = Bh$
Cube .... $V = e^3$
Cylinder of revolution .... $V = \pi r^2 h$
Frustum of circular cone .... $V = \frac{1}{3}\pi h(r^2 + r'^2 + rr')$
Frustum of pyramid .... $V = \frac{1}{3}h(B + B' + \sqrt{BB'})$
Prism .... $V = Bh$
Prismatoid .... $V = \frac{1}{6}h(B_1 + B_2 + 4M)$
Pyramid .... $V = \frac{1}{3}Bh$
Rectangular solid .... $V = lwh$
Sphere .... $V = \frac{4}{3}\pi r^3$
Spherical sector .... $V = \frac{2}{3}rS$

PHYSICAL CONSTANTS

QUANTITY	SYMBOL	VALUE
Gravitational constant	G	$6.67 \times 10^{-11}\ n \cdot m^2/kg^2$
Acceleration of gravity at earth's surface	g	$9.81\ m/sec^2 = 32.2 ft/sec^2$
Atmospheric pressure at sea level	(none)	$14.7\ lb/in^2 = 1.01 \times 10^5\ n/m^2$
Absolute zero	$0°K$	$-273°C$
Boltzmann's constant	k	$1.38 \times 10^{-23}\ j/°K$
Electrostatic constant	C	$9.00 \times 10^9\ n \cdot m^2/coul^2$
Electromagnetic constant	μ	$1.26 \times 10^{-6} \cdot weber/amp \cdot m$
Charge of electron	e	$1.60 \times 10^{-19}\ coul$
Electron rest mass	m_e	$9.11 \times 10^{-31}\ kg$
Proton rest mass	m_p	$1.67 \times 10^{-27}\ kg$
Neutron rest mass	m_n	$1.67 \times 10^{-27}\ kg$
Speed of light	c	$3.00 \times 10^8\ m/sec$
Planck's constant	h	$6.63 \times 10^{-34}\ j \cdot sec$

TABLES OF INTERRELATION OF UNITS OF MEASUREMENT
UNITS OF LENGTH

Units	Inches	Links	Feet
1 inch =	1	0.126 262 6	0.083 333 33
1 link =	7.92	1	0.66
1 foot =	12	1.515 152	1
1 yard =	36	4 545 45	3
1 rod =	198	25	16.5
1 chain =	792	100	66
1 mile =	63 360	8000	5280
1 centimeter =	0.393 700 8	0.049 709 70	0.032 808 40
1 meter =	39.370 08	4.970 970	3.280 840

Units	Yards	Rods	Chains
1 inch =	0.027 777 78	0.005 050 505	0.001 262 626
1 link =	0.22	0.04	0.01
1 foot =	0.333 333 3	0.060 606 06	0.015 151 52
1 yard =	1	0.181 818 2	0.045 454 55
1 rod =	5.5	1	0.25
1 chain =	22	4	1
1 mile =	1760	320	80
1 centimeter =	0.010 936 13	0.001 988 388	0.000 497 097 0
1 meter =	1.093 613	0.198 838 8	0.049 709 70

Units	Miles	Centimeters	Meters
1 inch =	0.000 015 782 83	2.54	0.025 4
1 link =	0.000 125	20.116 8	0.201 168
1 foot =	0.000 189 393 9	30.48	0.304 8
1 yard =	0.000 568 181 8	91.44	0.914 4
1 rod =	0.003 125	502.92	5.029 2
1 chain =	0.012 5	2011.68	20.116 8
1 mile =	1	160 934.4	1609.344
1 centimeter =	0.000 006 213 712	1	0.01
1 meter =	0.000 621 371 2	100	1

UNITS OF VOLUME

Units	Cubic inches	Cubic feet	Cubic yards
1 cubic inch =	1	0.000 578 703 7	0.000 021 433 47
1 cubic foot =	1728	1	0.037 037 04
1 cubic yard =	46 656	27	1
1 cubic centimeter =	0.061 023 74	0.000 035 314 67	0.000 001 307 951
1 cubic decimeter =	61.023 74	0.035 314 67	0.001 307 951
1 cubic meter =	61 023.74	35.314 67	1.307 951

Units	Cubic Centimeters	Cubic decimeters	Cubic meters
1 cubic inch =	16.387 064	0.016 387 064	0.000 016 387 064
1 cubic foot =	28 316.846 592	28.316 846 592	0.028 316 846 592
1 cubic yard =	764 554.857 984	764.554 857 984	0.764 554 857 984
1 cubic centimeter =	1	0.001	0.000 001
1 cubic decimeter =	1 000	1	0.001
1 cubic meter =	1 000 000	1000	1

UNITS OF AREA

Units		Square inches	Square links	Square feet	Square yards
1 square inch	=	1	0.015 942 25	0.006 944 444	0.000 771 604 9
1 square link	=	62.726 4	1	0.435 6	0.048 4
1 square foot	=	144	2.295 684	1	0.111 111 1
1 square yard	=	1296	20.661 16	9	1
1 square rod	=	39 204	625	272.25	30.25
1 square chain	=	627 264	10 000	4356	484
1 acre	=	6 272 640	100 000	43 560	4840
1 square mile	=	4 014 489 600	64 000 000	27 878 400	3 097 600
1 square centimeter	=	0.155 000 3	0.002 471 054	0.001 076 391	0.000 119 599 0
1 square meter	=	1550.003	24.710 54	10.763 91	1.195 990
1 hectare	=	15 500 031	247 105.4	107 639.1	11 959.90

Units		Square rods	Square chains	Acres	Square miles
1 square inch	=	0.000 025 507 60	0.000 001 594 225	0.000 000 159 422 5	0.000 000 000 249 097 7
1 square link	=	0.001 6	0.000 1	0.000 01	0.000 000 015 625
1 square foot	=	0.003 673 095	0.000 229 568 4	0.000 022 956 84	0.000 000 035 870 06
1 square yard	=	0.033 057 85	0.002 066 116	0.000 206 611 6	0.000 000 322 830 6
1 square rod	=	1	0.062 5	0.006 25	0.000 009 765 625
1 square chain	=	16	1	0.1	0.000 156 25
1 acre	=	160	10	1	0.001 562 5
1 square mile	=	102 400	6400	640	1
1 square centimeter	=	0.000 003 953 686	0.000 000 247 105 4	0.000 000 024 710 54	0.000 000 000 038 610 22
1 square meter	=	0.039 536 86	0.002 471 054	0.000 247 105 4	0.000 000 386 102 2
1 hectare	=	395.368 6	24.710 54	2.471 054	0.003 861 022

Units		Square centimeters	Square meters	Hectares
1 square inch	=	6.451 6	0.000 645 16	0.000 000 064 516
1 square link	=	404.685 642 24	0.040 468 564 224	0.000 004 046 856 422 4
1 square foot	=	929.030 4	0.092 903 04	0.000 009 290 304
1 square yard	=	8 361.273 6	0.836 127 36	0.000 083 612 736
1 square rod	=	252 928.526 4	25.292 852 64	0.002 529 285 264
1 square chain	=	4 046 856.422 4	404.685 642 24	0.040 468 564 224
1 acre	=	40 468 564.224	4046.856 422 4	0.404 685 642 24
1 square mile	=	25 899 881 103.36	2 589 988.110 336	258.998 811 033 6
1 square centimeter	=	1	0.000 1	0.000 000 01
1 square meter	=	10 000	1	0.000 1
1 hectare	=	100 000 000	10 000	1

STANDARD CONVERSION FACTORS

1 m/sec = 3.28 ft/sec = 2.24 mi/hr = 3.60 km/hr

1 ft/sec = 0.305 m/sec = 0.682 mi/hr = 1.10 km/hr

1 mi/hr = 1.47 ft/sec = 0.447 m/sec = 1.61 km/hr

1 radian (rad) = 57.30° = 57°18′

1° = 0.01745 rad

1 revolution/minute (rev/min) = 0.1047 rad/sec

1 atomic mass unit (amu) = 1.66 X 10⁻²⁷ kg = 1.49 X 10⁻¹⁰ j = 931 Mev

1 newton (n) = 0.225 lb

1 pound (lb) = 4.45 n

1 joule (j) = 0.738 ft.lb = 2.39 X 10⁻⁴ kcal = 6.24 X 10⁻¹⁸ ev

1 kilocalorie (kcal) = 4.186 j

1 foot-pound (ft.lb) = 1.36 j

1 electron volt (ev) = 10⁻⁶ Mev = 1.60 X 10⁻¹⁹ j = 1.18 X 10⁻¹⁹ ft.lb = 3.83 X 10⁻²³ kcal

1 watt = 1 j/sec = 0.738 ft.lb/sec

UNITS OF CAPACITY LIQUID MEASURE

Units	Minims	Fluid drams	Fluid ounces
1 minim =	1	0.016 666 67	0.002 083 333
1 fluid dram =	60	1	0.125
1 fluid ounce =	480	8	1
1 gill =	1920	32	4
1 liquid pint =	7680	128	16
1 liquid quart =	15 360	256	32
1 gallon =	61 440	1024	128
1 cubic inch =	265.974 0	4.432 900	0.554 112 6
1 cubic foot =	459 603.1	7660.052	957.506 5
1 milliliter =	16.231 19	0.270 519 8	0.033 814 97
1 liter =	16 231.19	270.519 8	33.814 97

Units	Gills	Liquid pints	Liquid quarts
1 minim =	0.000 520 833 3	0.000 130 208 3	0.000 065 104 17
1 fluid dram =	0.031 25	0.007 812 5	0.003 906 25
1 fluid ounce =	0.25	0.062 5	0.031 25
1 gill =	1	0.25	0.125
1 liquid pint =	4	1	0.5
1 liquid quart =	8	2	1
1 gallon =	32	8	4
1 cubic inch =	0.138 528 1	0.034 632 03	0.017 316 02
1 cubic foot =	239.376 6	59.844 16	29.922 08
1 milliliter =	0.008 453 742	0.002 113 436	0.001 056 718
1 liter =	8.453 742	2.113 436	1.056 718

Units	Gallons	Cubic inches	Cubic feet
1 minim =	0.000 016 276 04	0.003 759 766	0.000 002 175 790
1 fluid dram =	0.000 976 562 5	0.225 585 9	0.000 130 547 4
1 fluid ounce =	0.007 812 5	1.804 687 5	0.001 044 379
1 gill =	0.031 25	7.218 75	0.004 177 517
1 liquid pint =	0.125	28.875	0.016 710 07
1 liquid quart =	0.25	57.75	0.033 420 14
1 gallon =	1	231	0.133 680 6
1 cubic inch =	0.004 329 004	1	0.000 578 703 7
1 cubic foot =	7.480 519	1728	1
1 milliliter =	0.000 264 179 4	0.061 025 45	0.000 035 315 66
1 liter =	0.264 179 4	61.025 45	0.035 315 66

Units	Milliliters	Liters
1 minim =	0.061 609 79	0.000 061 609 79
1 fluid dram =	3.696 588	0.003 696 588
1 fluid ounce =	29.572 70	0.029 572 70
1 gill =	118.290 8	0.118 290 8
1 liquid pint =	473.163 2	0.473 163 2
1 liquid quart =	946.326 4	0.946 326 4
1 gallon =	3 785.306	3.785 306
1 cubic inch =	16.386 61	0.016 386 61
1 cubic foot =	28 316.05	28.316 05
1 milliliter =	1	0.001
1 liter =	1000	1

UNITS OF CAPACITY DRY MEASURE

Units	Dry pints	Dry quarts	Pecks
1 dry pint =	1	0.5	0.062 5
1 dry quart =	2	1	0.125
1 peck =	16	8	1
1 bushel =	64	32	4
1 cubic inch =	0.029 761 6	0.014 880 8	0.001 860 10
1 cubic foot =	51.428 09	25.714 05	3.214 256
1 liter =	1.816 217	0.908 108 4	0.113 513 6
1 dekaliter =	18.162 17	9.081 084	1.135 136

Units	Bushels	Cubic inches	Cubic feet
1 dry pint =	0.015 625	33.600 312 5	0.019 444 63
1 dry quart =	0.031 25	67.200 625	0.038 889 25
1 peck =	0.25	537.605	0.311 114
1 bushel =	1	2150.42	1.244 456
1 cubic inch =	0.000 465 025	1	0.000 578 703 7
1 cubic foot =	0.803 563 95	1728	1
1 liter =	0.028 378 39	61.025 45	0.035 315 66
1 dekaliter =	0.283 783 9	610.254 5	0.353 156 6

Units	Liters	Dekaliters
1 dry pint =	0.550 595 1	0.055 059 51
1 dry quart =	1.101 190	0.110 119 0
1 peck =	8.809 521	0.880 952 1
1 bushel =	35.238 08	3.523 808
1 cubic inch =	0.016 386 61	0.001 638 661
1 cubic foot =	28.316 05	2.831 605
1 liter =	1	0.1
1 dekaliter =	10	1

UNITS OF MASS NOT LESS THAN AVOIRDUPOIS OUNCES

Units	Avoirdupois ounces	Avoirdupois pounds	Short hundred weights
1 avoirdupois ounce =	1	0.0625	0.000 625
1 avoirdupois pound =	16	1	0.01
1 short hundredweight =	1 600	100	1
1 short ton =	32 000	2 000	20
1 long ton =	35 840	2 240	22.4
1 kilogram =	35.273 96	2.204 623	0.022 046 23
1 metric ton =	35 273.96	2204.623	22.046 23

Units	Short tons	Long tons	Kilograms	Metric tons
1 avoirdupois ounce =	0.000 031 25	0.000 027 901 79	0.028 349 523 125	0.000 028 349 523 125
1 avoirdupois pound =	0.000 5	0.000 446 428 6	0.453 592 37	0.000 453 592 37
1 short hundredweight =	0.05	0.044 642 86	45.359 237	0.045 359 237
1 short ton =	1	0.892 857 1	907.184 74	0.907 184 74
1 long ton =	1.12	1	1016.046 908 8	1.016 046 908 8
1 kilogram =	0.001 102 311	0.000 984 206 5	1	0.001
1 metric ton =	1.102 311	0.984 206 5	1 000	1

SQUARE, SQUARE ROOTS, CUBES AND
CUBE ROOTS OF NOS. 1 TO 100

No.	Sq.	Cube	Sq. Root	Cube Root	No.	Sq.	Cube	Sq. Root	Cube Root
1	1	1	1.000	1.000	51	2601	132651	7.141	3.708
2	4	8	1.414	1.260	52	2704	140608	7.211	3.732
3	9	27	1.732	1.442	53	2809	148877	7.280	3.756
4	16	64	2.000	1.587	54	2916	157464	7.348	3.779
5	25	125	2.236	1.710	55	3025	166375	7.416	3.803
6	36	216	2.449	1.817	56	3136	175616	7.483	3.825
7	49	343	2.646	1.913	57	3249	185193	7.550	3.848
8	64	512	2.828	2.000	58	3364	195112	7.616	3.870
9	81	729	3.000	2.080	59	3481	205379	7.681	3.893
10	100	1000	3.162	2.154	60	3600	216000	7.746	3.915
11	121	1331	3.317	2.224	61	3721	226981	7.810	3.936
12	144	1728	3.464	2.289	62	3844	238328	7.874	3.958
13	169	2197	3.605	2.351	63	3969	250047	7.937	3.979
14	196	2744	3.742	2.410	64	4096	262144	8 000	4.000
15	225	3375	3.873	2.466	65	4225	274625	8.062	4.020
16	256	4096	4.000	2.511	66	4356	287496	8.124	4.041
17	289	4913	4.123	2.571	67	4489	300763	8.185	4.062
18	324	5832	4.243	2.621	68	4624	314432	8.246	4.082
19	361	6859	4.359	2.668	69	4761	328509	8.307	4.102
20	400	8000	4.472	2.714	70	4900	343000	8.367	4.121
21	441	9261	4.583	2.759	71	5041	357911	8.426	4.140
22	484	10648	4.690	2.802	72	5184	373248	8.485	4.160
23	529	12167	4.796	2.844	73	5329	389017	8.544	4.179
24	576	13824	4.899	2.884	74	5476	405224	8.602	4.198
25	625	15625	5.000	2.924	75	5625	421875	8.660	4.217
26	676	17576	5.099	2.962	76	5776	438976	8.718	4.236
27	729	19683	5.196	3 000	77	5929	456533	8.775	4.254
28	784	21952	5.292	3.037	78	6084	474552	8.832	4.273
29	841	24389	5.385	3.072	79	6241	493039	8.888	4.291
30	900	27000	5.477	3.107	80	6400	512000	8.944	4.309
31	961	29791	5.568	3.141	81	6561	531441	9.000	4.327
32	1024	32768	5.657	3.175	82	6724	551368	9.055	4.344
33	1089	35937	5.745	3.208	83	6889	571787	9.110	4.362
34	1156	39304	5.831	3.240	84	7056	592704	9.165	4.371
35	1225	42875	5.916	3.271	85	7225	614125	9.220	4.397
36	1296	46656	6.000	3.302	86	7396	636056	9.274	4.414
37	1369	50653	6.083	3.332	87	7569	658503	9.327	4.431
38	1444	54872	6.164	3.362	88	7744	681472	9.381	4.448
39	1521	59319	6.245	3.391	89	7921	704969	9.434	4.465
40	1600	64000	6.325	3.420	90	8100	729000	9.487	4.481
41	1681	68921	6.403	3.448	91	8281	753571	9 539	4.498
42	1764	74088	6.481	3.476	92	8464	778688	9.592	4.514
43	1849	79507	6.557	3.503	93	8649	804357	9.644	4.531
44	1936	85184	6.633	3.530	94	8836	830584	9.695	4.547
45	2025	91125	6.708	3.557	95	9025	857375	9.747	4.563
46	2116	97336	6.782	3.583	96	9216	884736	9.798	4.579
47	2209	103823	6.856	3.609	97	9409	912673	9.849	4.595
48	2304	110592	6.928	3.634	98	9604	941192	9.899	4.610
49	2401	117649	7.000	3.659	99	9801	970299	9.950	4.626
50	2500	125000	7.071	3.684	100	10000	1000000	10.000	4.641

CHEMICAL ELEMENTS, ATOMIC WEIGHTS

Element	Symbol	Atomic number	Atomic weight	Element	Symbol	Atomic number	Atomic weight
Actinium	Ac	89	(1)	Mercury	Hg	80	200.61
Aluminum	Al	13	26.98	Molybdenum	Mo	42	95.95
Americium	Am	95	(1)	Neodymium	Nd	60	144.27
Antimony	Sb	51	121.76	Neon	Ne	10	20.183
Argon	Ar	18	39.944	Neptunium	Np	93	(1)
Arsenic	As	33	74.91	Nickel	Ni	28	58.71
Astatine	At	85	(1)	Niobium	Nb	41	92.91
Barium	Ba	56	137.36	Nitrogen	N	7	14.008
Berkelium	Bk	97	(1)	Nobelium	No	102	(1)
Beryllium	Be	4	9.013	Osmium	Os	76	190.2
Bismuth	Bi	83	209.00	Oxygen	O	8	[2]16
Boron	B	5	10.82	Palladium	Pd	46	106.4
Bromine	Br	35	79.916	Phosphorus	P	15	30.975
Cadmium	Cd	48	112.41	Platinum	Pt	78	195.09
Calcium	Ca	20	40.08	Plutonium	Pu	94	(1)
Californium	Cf	98	(1)	Polonium	Po	84	(1)
Carbon	C	6	12.010	Potassium	K	19	39.100
Cerium	Ce	58	140.13	Praseodymium	Pr	59	140.92
Cesium	Cs	55	132.91	Promethium	Pm	61	(1)
Chlorine	Cl	17	35.457	Protactinium	Pa	91	(1)
Chromium	Cr	24	52.01	Radium	Ra	88	(1)
Cobalt	Co	27	58.94	Radon	Rn	86	(1)
Copper	Cu	29	63.54	Rhenium	Re	75	186.22
Curium	Cm	96	(1)	Rhodium	Rh	45	102.91
Dysprosium	Dy	66	162.51	Rubidium	Rb	37	85.48
Einsteinium	Es	99	(1)	Ruthenium	Ru	44	101.1
Erbium	Er	68	167.27	Samarium	Sm	62	150.35
Europium	Eu	63	152.0	Scandium	Sc	21	44.96
Fermium	Fm	100	(1)	Selenium	Se	34	78.96
Fluorine	F	9	19.00	Silicon	Si	14	28.09
Francium	Fr	87	(1)	Silver	Ag	47	107.880
Gadolinium	Gd	64	157.26	Sodium	Na	11	22.991
Gallium	Ga	31	69.72	Strontium	Sr	38	87.63
Germanium	Ge	32	72.60	Sulfur	S	16	[3]32.066
Gold	Au	79	197.0	Tantalum	Ta	73	180.95
Hafnium	Hf	72	178.50	Technetium	Tc	43	(1)
Helium	He	2	4.003	Tellurium	Te	52	127.61
Holmium	Ho	67	164.94	Terbium	Tb	65	158.93
Hydrogen	H	1	1.0080	Thallium	Tl	81	204.39
Indium	In	49	114.82	Thorium	Th	90	232.05
Iodine	I	53	126.91	Thulium	Tm	69	168.94
Iridium	Ir	77	192.2	Tin	Sn	50	118.70
Iron	Fe	26	55.85	Titanium	Ti	22	47.90
Krypton	Kr	36	83.80	Tungsten	W	74	183.86
Lanthanum	La	57	138.92	Uranium	U	92	238.07
Lawrencium	Lw	103	(1)	Vanadium	V	23	50.95
Lead	Pb	82	207.21	Xenon	Xe	54	131.30
Lithium	Li	3	6.940	Ytterbium	Yb	70	173.04
Lutetium	Lu	71	174.99	Yttrium	Y	39	88.92
Magnesium	Mg	12	24.32	Zinc	Zn	30	65.38
Manganese	Mn	25	54.94	Zirconium	Zr	40	91.22
Mendelevium	Md	101	(1)				

[1] These values are omitted because the elements do not occur in nature, and their atomic weight depends on which isotope is made.

[2] This is a defined value rather than an indicated one.

[3] Because of natural variations in the abundance ratio of the isotopes of sulfur, the atomic weight of this element has a range of ±0.003.

FOUR-PLACE LOGARITHMS

No.	0	1	2	3	4	5	6	7	8	9
10	0000	0043	0086	0128	0170	0212	0253	0294	0334	0374
11	0414	0453	0492	0531	0569	0607	0645	0682	0719	0755
12	0792	0828	0864	0899	0934	0969	1004	1038	1072	1106
13	1139	1173	1206	1239	1271	1303	1335	1367	1399	1430
14	1461	1492	1523	1553	1584	1614	1644	1673	1703	1732
15	1761	1790	1818	1847	1875	1903	1931	1959	1987	2014
16	2041	2068	2095	2122	2148	2175	2201	2227	2253	2279
17	2304	2330	2355	2380	2405	2430	2455	2480	2504	2529
18	2553	2577	2601	2625	2648	2672	2695	2718	2742	2765
19	2788	2810	2833	2856	2878	2900	2923	2945	2967	2989
20	3010	3032	3054	3075	3096	3118	3139	3160	3181	3201
21	3222	3243	3263	3284	3304	3324	3345	3365	3385	3404
22	3424	3444	3464	3483	3502	3522	3541	3560	3579	3598
23	3617	3636	3655	3674	3692	3711	3729	3747	3766	3784
24	3802	3820	3838	3856	3874	3892	3909	3927	3945	3962
25	3979	3997	4014	4031	4048	4065	4082	4099	4116	4133
26	4150	4166	4183	4200	4216	4232	4249	4265	4281	4298
27	4314	4330	4346	4362	4378	4393	4409	4425	4440	4456
28	4472	4487	4502	4518	4533	4548	4564	4579	4594	4609
29	4624	4639	4654	4669	4683	4698	4713	4728	4742	4757
30	4771	4786	4800	4814	4829	4843	4857	4871	4886	4900
31	4914	4928	4942	4955	4969	4983	4997	5011	5024	5038
32	5051	5065	5079	5092	5105	5119	5132	5145	5159	5172
33	5185	5198	5211	5224	5237	5250	5263	5276	5289	5302
34	5315	5328	5340	5353	5366	5378	5391	5403	5416	5428
35	5441	5453	5465	5478	5490	5502	5514	5527	5539	5551
36	5563	5575	5587	5599	5611	5623	5635	5647	5658	5670
37	5682	5694	5705	5717	5729	5740	5752	5763	5775	5786
38	5798	5809	5821	5832	5843	5855	5866	5877	5888	5899
39	5911	5922	5933	5944	5955	5966	5977	5988	5999	6010
40	6021	6031	6042	6053	6064	6075	6085	6096	6107	6117
41	6128	6138	6149	6160	6170	6180	6191	6201	6212	6222
42	6232	6243	6253	6263	6274	6284	6294	6304	6314	6325
43	6335	6345	6355	6365	6375	6385	6395	6405	6415	6425
44	6435	6444	6454	6464	6474	6484	6493	6503	6513	6522
45	6532	6542	6551	6561	6571	6580	6590	6599	6609	6618
46	6628	6637	6646	6656	6665	6675	6684	6693	6702	6712
47	6721	6730	6739	6749	6758	6767	6776	6785	6794	6803
48	6812	6821	6830	6839	6848	6857	6866	6875	6884	6893
49	6902	6911	6920	6928	6937	6946	6955	6964	6972	6981
50	6990	6998	7007	7016	7024	7033	7042	7050	7059	7067
51	7076	7084	7093	7101	7110	7118	7126	7135	7143	7152
52	7160	7168	7177	7185	7193	7202	7210	7218	7226	7235
53	7243	7251	7259	7267	7275	7284	7292	7300	7308	7316
54	7324	7332	7340	7348	7356	7364	7372	7380	7388	7396
55	7404	7412	7419	7427	7435	7443	7451	7459	7466	7474
56	7482	7490	7497	7505	7513	7520	7528	7536	7543	7551
57	7559	7566	7574	7582	7589	7597	7604	7612	7619	7627
58	7634	7642	7649	7657	7664	7672	7679	7686	7694	7701
59	7709	7716	7723	7731	7738	7745	7752	7760	7767	7774
60	7782	7789	7796	7803	7810	7818	7825	7832	7839	7846
61	7853	7860	7868	7875	7882	7889	7896	7903	7910	7917
62	7924	7931	7938	7945	7952	7959	7966	7973	7980	7987
63	7993	8000	8007	8014	8021	8028	8035	8041	8048	8055
64	8062	8069	8075	8082	8089	8096	8102	8109	8116	8122
65	8129	8136	8142	8149	8156	8162	8169	8176	8182	8189
66	8195	8202	8209	8215	8222	8228	8235	8241	8248	8254
67	8261	8267	8274	8280	8287	8293	8299	8306	8312	8319
68	8325	8331	8338	8344	8351	8357	8363	8370	8376	8382
69	8388	8395	8401	8407	8414	8420	8426	8432	8439	8445
70	8451	8457	8463	8470	8476	8482	8488	8494	8500	8506
71	8513	8519	8525	8531	8537	8543	8549	8555	8561	8567
72	8573	8579	8585	8591	8597	8603	8609	8615	8621	8627
73	8633	8639	8645	8651	8657	8663	8669	8675	8681	8686
74	8692	8698	8704	8710	8716	8722	8727	8733	8739	8745
75	8751	8756	8762	8768	8774	8779	8785	8791	8797	8802
76	8808	8814	8820	8825	8831	8837	8842	8848	8854	8859
77	8865	8871	8876	8882	8887	8893	8899	8904	8910	8915
78	8921	8927	8932	8938	8943	8949	8954	8960	8965	8971
79	8976	8982	8987	8993	8998	9004	9009	9015	9020	9025
80	9031	9036	9042	9047	9053	9058	9063	9069	9074	9079
81	9085	9090	9096	9101	9106	9112	9117	9122	9128	9133
82	9138	9143	9149	9154	9159	9165	9170	9175	9180	9186
83	9191	9196	9201	9206	9212	9217	9222	9227	9232	9238
84	9243	9248	9253	9258	9263	9269	9274	9279	9284	9289
85	9294	9299	9304	9309	9315	9320	9325	9330	9335	9340
86	9345	9350	9355	9360	9365	9370	9375	9380	9385	9390
87	9395	9400	9405	9410	9415	9420	9425	9430	9435	9440
88	9445	9450	9455	9460	9465	9469	9474	9479	9484	9489
89	9494	9499	9504	9509	9513	9518	9523	9528	9533	9538
90	9542	9547	9552	9557	9562	9566	9571	9576	9581	9586
91	9590	9595	9600	9605	9609	9614	9619	9624	9628	9633
92	9638	9643	9647	9652	9657	9661	9666	9671	9675	9680
93	9685	9689	9694	9699	9703	9708	9713	9717	9722	9727
94	9731	9736	9741	9745	9750	9754	9759	9763	9768	9773
95	9777	9782	9786	9791	9795	9800	9805	9809	9814	9818
96	9823	9827	9832	9836	9841	9845	9850	9854	9859	9863
97	9868	9872	9877	9881	9886	9890	9894	9899	9903	9908
98	9912	9917	9921	9926	9930	9934	9939	9943	9948	9952
99	9956	9961	9965	9969	9974	9978	9983	9987	9991	9996

Metric Conversions

TEMPERATURE

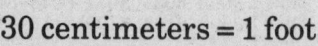

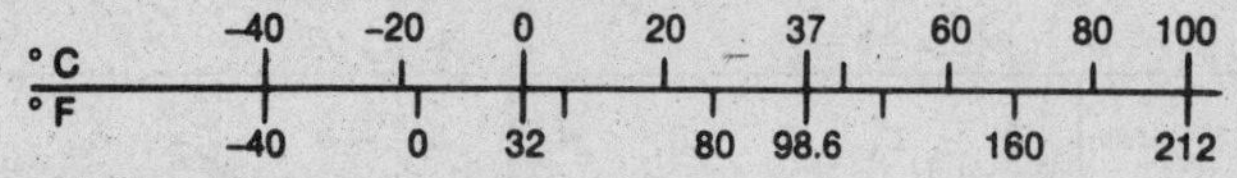

°C	-40	-20	0	20	37	60	80	100
°F	-40	0	32	80	98.6	160		212

To Convert Celsius to Fahrenheit:
Multiply the Celsius temperature by 2, subtract 10%, and add 32.
Example: 25″ C x 2 = 50 − 5 = 45 + 32 = 77″ F

To Convert Fahrenheit to Celsius, Reverse the Procedure.
Example: 72″ F − 32 = 40 + 4 = 44 ÷ 2 = 22″ C

Temperatures in degrees Celsius, as in the familiar Fahrenheit system, can only be learned through experience. The following may help to orient you with regard to temperatures you normally encounter.

0″ C	Freezing point of water (32″ F)
10″ C	A warm winter day (50″ F)
20″ C	A mild spring day (68″ F)
30″ C	Quite warm — almost hot (86″ F)
37″ C	Normal body temperature (98.6″ F)
40″ C	Heat wave conditions (104″ F)
100″ C	Boiling point of water (212″ F)

30 centimeters = 1 foot

KILOMETERS
MILES PER HOUR

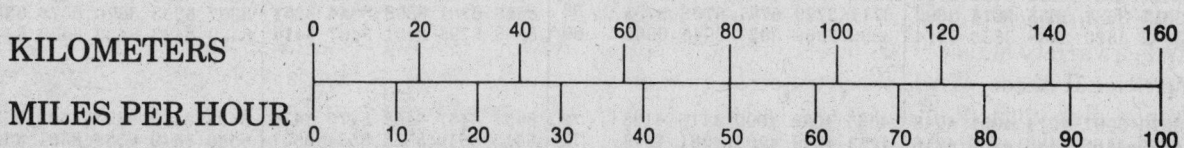

Inches = Millimeters		Feet = Meters		Pounds = Kilograms		Ounces = Grams		Pints = Liters		Gallons = Liters	
¹/₃₂	.79	1	0.3	1	0.5	¼	7.1	½	.236	1	3.8
¹/₁₆	1.59	2	0.6	2	0.9	½	14.2	1.0	.473	2	7.6
⅛	3.175	3	0.9	3	1.4	³/₂	21.3	1½	.709	3	11.4
¼	6.35	4	1.2	4	1.8	1	28.4	2.0	.946	4	15.1
⅜	9.53	5	1.5	5	2.3	2	56.7	2½	1.183	5	18.9
½	12.7	6	1.8	6	2.7	3	85.0	3.0	1.419	6	22.7
⅝	15.88	7	2.1	7	3.2	4	113.4	3½	1.656	7	26.5
¾	19.05	8	2.4	8	3.6	5	141.7	4.0	1.893	8	30.3
⅞	22.3	9	2.7	9	4.1	6	170.1	4½	2.129	9	34.1
1.0	25.4	10	3.0	10	4.5	7	198.4	5.0	2.366	10	37.9
1½	38.1	15	4.6	11	5.0	8	226.8	5½	2.602	11	41.6
2.0	50.8	20	6.1	12	5.4	9	255.1	6.0	2.839	12	45.4
2½	63.5	25	7.6	13	5.9	10	283.5	6½	3.075	13	49.2
3.0	76.2	30	9.1	14	6.4	11	311.8	7.0	3.312	14	53.0
3½	88.9	35	10.7	15	6.8	12	340.2	7½	3.549	15	56.8
4.0	101.6	40	12.2	16	7.3	13	368.5	8.0	3.786	16	60.6
4½	114.3	45	13.7	17	7.7	14	396.9			17	64.3
5.0	127.0	50	15.2	18	8.2	15	425.2			18	68.1
5½	139.7	55	16.8	19	8.6	16	453.6			19	71.9
6.0	152.4	60	18.3	20	9.1					20	75.7
6½	165.1	65	19.8	25	11.34					30	113.6
7.0	177.8	70	21.3	30	13.61					40	151.4
7½	190.5	75	22.9	40	18.14					50	189.3
8.0	203.2	80	24.4	50	22.68					60	227.1
8½	215.9	85	25.9	60	27.22					70	264.9
9.0	228.6	90	27.4	70	31.75					80	302.8
9½	241.3	95	29.0	80	36.29					90	340.7
10.0	254.0	100	30.5	90	40.82					100	378.5
10½	266.7			100	45.36						
11.0	279.4										
11½	292.1										
12.0	304.8										

Cookery and Nutrition

Every penny you spend on food should be an investment in good health. This doesn't mean that you have to devote hours every day to working with charts and slide rules. But to make the most of your food dollars, you do have to understand what kinds of food you need and what and how each contributes to basic nutritional requirements.

Quite simply, good nutrition means meeting the body's needs for growth, maintenance, energy, and tissue repair. Good nutrition also means family meals that are satisfying and enjoyable.

PLANNING YOUR MENUS

Well-balanced meals are easy to plan if you include a variety of foods that meet everyone's daily nutritional needs. While it's possible to provide a proper diet without following a daily plan, it's easier to stay within your budget while meeting your family's nutritional needs if you build your menus around the Basic Four Food Groups. All of us need something from each section every day, and since the foods within each group are similar in value, they can be used interchangeably for variety and interest. (The sample menu chart that follows shows you how to turn basic foods into excitingly different meals.) To review briefly, groups are:

1. Dairy. Included are milk, cheese, ice cream or ice milk—all of which supply calcium, riboflavin, protein, and Vitamin A, along with other essentials. *Daily need:* Three to four cups of milk for children and teenagers; two or more cups for adults; three or more cups for pregnant women; four cups for nursing mothers.

2. Meats. Other sources are poultry, fish, and eggs which we must have for animal protein, thiamine, riboflavin, niacin, and iron. *Daily need:* Two servings.

3. Fruits and vegetables. A daily must for nearly all of our Vitamin C and much of our Vitamin A, they also contribute minerals, calcium, iron, and some riboflavin. *Daily need:* Four or more servings, including one rich in Vitamin C and one of a dark green or yellow variety.

4. Breads and cereals. Alternates are spaghetti, macaroni, noodles, hominy, grits, rice, and crackers or other baked foods which provide essential B vitamins and iron. *Daily need:* Four or more servings.

Fortunately, all of the foods containing these nutrients are readily found in supermarkets. While each nutrient contributes to building, regulating, and repairing the body, it's important to remember that they work together as a team. An extra supply of one can't take the place of another.

Only the amounts of food should vary to meet individual needs based on age and activity—for example, smaller servings for children and dieters, larger servings for very active adults and teenagers. Following these pages you'll find a chart that lists the major nutrients, the reasons why they are needed, and their principal sources. Use it for quick reference; with a little practice, you'll notice that you soon think of each food in terms of what it provides.

Fiber While it is not a nutrient, fiber is essential to health. It consists of the indigestible elements of foods which pass through our bodies primarily unchanged. To keep our digestive systems functioning properly, we all need a certain amount every day. Whole-grain cereals and breads—especially bran—fruits, vegetables, and nuts are top contributors.

NUTRITIONAL LABELING— WHAT'S ITS USE?

Labels that spell out what's inside are now found on any canned, frozen, processed, or packaged foods for which a manufacturer makes a nutritional claim, or on foods to which nutrients have been added (fortified cereals or enriched breads). Read these labels carefully, for they can help you:

1. learn more about nutrition;
2. plan better balanced meals;
3. meet the nutritional needs of every member of your family;
4. count calories;
5. know how much of a specific nutrient a food contains.

At the same time, keep in mind that meats and fresh fruits and vegetables do not yet carry nutritional labels. Therefore, you can't use this information as your *only* guide to selecting foods.

Conveniently, all listings stated on the labels are given in single servings (2 slices, 1 cup, 1 ounce), along with the total servings in the container. This enables you to compare the nutritive values of different products, and as a result, find your best buys.

On the label, you'll also notice the term U.S.

RDA. This means Recommended Daily Allowances, the nutritional standards based on the amounts of nutrients the National Research Council believes are adequate for most healthy people. Since RDA's are given in percentage of the day's total, they can help you keep tabs on how your menus stack up nutritionally.

A GOOD BREAKFAST

For good health and energy, everyone should start the day with at least a quarter of his daily needs for protein, vitamins, minerals, and calories. Children and adults who skip or skimp on the day's first meal slow down in mid- or late morning because of fatigue. With no breakfast, weight control is harder since noontime hunger is greater, and the dieter is more likely to overeat.

A sound, basic breakfast pattern can be as simple as fruit or juice, cereal and milk, toast with butter or margarine, and extra milk as a beverage for youngsters or coffee for adults. Even though a family eats in shifts, this menu is easy enough for most children of school age to fix for themselves.

HOW IMPORTANT ARE SNACKS?

For good health, at any age, it isn't necessary to eliminate them—just plan them so that they carry their weight in food value.

Children's energy needs are great, so most need something to keep them going between meals. Cereal and milk, pudding, ice cream, fruit, crackers, raw vegetables, cheese, and peanut butter are top nutritional choices. It's best not to allow snacking too close to mealtime, however, or appetites won't be up to par for the next meal.

For teenagers, snacks are a part of their social life, and for boys, particularly, a source of the extra calories they need. But whatever they eat should provide more than just calories. Wise choices are hamburgers or cheeseburgers, pizza, milk, milk shakes, and high-protein chocolate-flavored beverages that come in the soft drink section of the supermarket.

Girls benefit from meat and cheese sandwiches, ice cream, fruit and fruit juices, and dry cereals to eat out of hand. All of these supply particular nutrients that are often lacking—or low—in their diets.

Adults and waistline-watchers can also enjoy snacks if they select them wisely and count their calories as part of their day's permitted total. Fruit and vegetable juices, bouillon, skimmed milk or buttermilk, and raw vegetable relishes take the edge off hunger, yet contain few calories.

COOK TO SAVE NUTRIENTS

How you cook is equally as important as what you cook, since sloppy methods or overcooking can destroy food value. This is particularly true of vegetables that lose their bright color and fresh flavor when drowned in water or left on the heat too long.

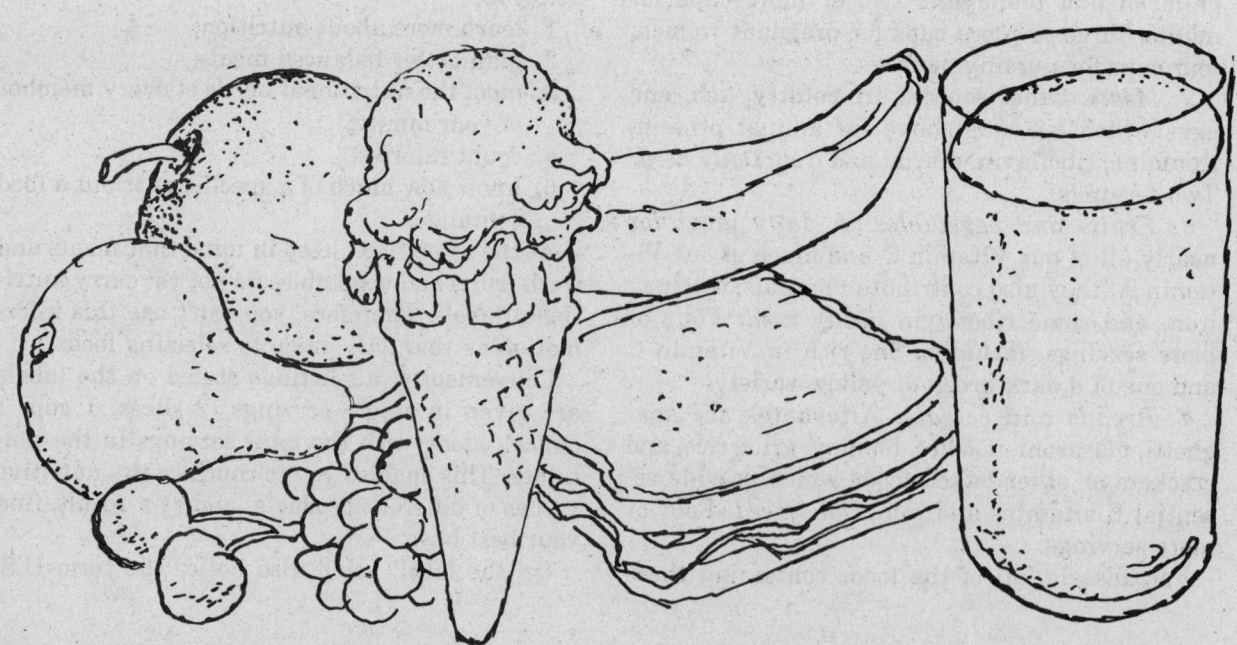

SAMPLE SEVEN-DAY MENU GUIDE
TO KEEP YOUR FAMILY FIT

BREAKFAST	LUNCH	DINNER
Chilled Grapefruit Juice 40% Bran Flakes Broiled Corned-beef Hash on Toasted Hamburger Buns Milk, Tea or Coffee	Chicken-vegetable Soup Tuna Casserole Raw Carrot Sticks Fresh Fruit Compote Milk, Tea	Beef Patties Parslied Noodles Green Beans Waldorf Salad Strawberry Sundaes Pineapple Drop Cookies Milk, Tea or Coffee
Sliced Oranges Toasted Frozen Waffles with Hot Blueberry Sauce Milk, Tea or Coffee	Lentil Soup Toasted Italian Bread Shredded Cabbage Salad with Cranberry-mayonnaise Dressing Canned Apricot Halves Milk, Tea	Salmon Soufflé Baked Potatoes Pimiento Peas and Limas Marinated Yellow Squash Sticks on Lettuce Butterscotch Pudding Milk, Tea or Coffee
Sliced Bananas with Granola-type Cereal Raisin French Toast Maple-blended Syrup Milk, Tea or Coffee	Spanish Rice with Shrimp Tossed Green Salad with Oil-and-vinegar Dressing Raspberry Gelatin Cubes with Custard Sauce Milk, Tea	Lamb Stew Pear, Orange, and Avocado Salad with French Dressing Chocolate Layer Cake Milk, Tea or Coffee
Tangerine Sections Scrambled Eggs with Diced Ham Toasted English Muffins Milk, Tea or Coffee	Broiled Hamburger Patties Hamburger Buns with Mustard Butter Mixed Raw Relishes and Pickles Caramel Cup Custards Milk, Tea	Baked Chicken and Rice Green Salad with Shredded Carrot and Sliced Cauliflowerets Corn Sticks Lemon Pie Milk, Tea or Coffee
Chilled Mixed Vegetable Juice Hot Oatmeal Cinnamon Toast Milk, Tea or Coffee	Bologna Sandwiches Lettuce Wedges with Russian Dressing Chocolate Ice Cream Bars Milk, Tea	Consommé Baked Haddock Potatoes au Gratin Steamed Spinach Mixed Green Salad with Cherry Tomatoes Peach Betty with Cream Milk, Tea or Coffee
Grapefruit Halves Open-face Toasted Cheese Sandwich Milk, Tea or Coffee	Spaghetti with Meat Balls Hot Garlic French Bread Celery Spears Fresh Apples and Grapes Milk, Tea	Sautéed Liver and Onions Whipped Potatoes Steamed Broccoli Raw Relish Tray Baking Powder Biscuits Gingerbread with Lemon Sauce Milk, Tea or Coffee
Chilled Orange Juice Small Whole-wheat Pancakes Brown-and-serve Link Sausages Strawberry Preserves Milk, Tea or Coffee	Mushroom Omelets with Cheese Sauce Marinated Mixed Vegetables on Lettuce Italian Bread Sticks Lemon Pudding Milk, Tea	Beef Pot Roast Romaine-radish Salad with Italian Dressing Hot Butterflake Rolls Dill Pickles Apple Pie Milk, Tea or Coffee

MAJOR NUTRIENTS: THEIR ROLES AND SOURCES

NUTRIENT	WHY NEEDED	WHERE FOUND
Protein	Promotes growth and repair of body tissues; supplies energy; helps to fight infections; forms an important part of blood, enzymes, and hormones to regulate body functions.	Lean meats; poultry; fish; shellfish; eggs; milk; cheese. Next best are the vegetable proteins such as dry beans and peas; nuts; peanut butter; bread; cereals; wheat germ. If served with a complementary animal protein food such as cheese, the combined protein value is high.
Carbohydrates (Starches and sugars)	Supply energy; spare protein for body building and repair; also necessary for bulk and proper elimination.	Breads; cereals; grits; corn; rice; potatoes; the macaroni and noodle families; bananas; sugar; honey; syrup; jam; jelly; molasses.
Fats	Supply concentrated energy; improve taste of food; help body use other nutrients; help maintain temperature; lubricate intestinal tract.	Butter; margarine; whole milk; ice cream; cheese; egg yolk; shortening; lard; chocolate; chocolate candy; pies; puddings; salad oils.
Calcium	Builds sturdy bones and teeth; helps blood clot; helps to keep nerves, muscles, and heart healthy; aids in healing wounds; helps fight infections.	Milk; ice cream; cheese; cottage cheese; kale; collards; mustard and turnip greens; salmon; sardines.
Iodine	Helps thyroid gland work properly in regulating energy.	Iodized salt; salt-water fish and shellfish.
Iron	Necessary to form hemoglobin (red substance in blood) which carries oxygen from lungs to body cells.	Liver; heart; kidneys; oysters; lean meats; egg yolk; clams; whole-grain and enriched cereals; dry beans; molasses; raisins and other dried fruits; dark green leafy vegetables.
Sodium	Preserves water balance in body.	Salt; meat; fish; poultry; eggs; olives.
Potassium	Keeps nerves and muscles healthy; helps to maintain fluid balance.	Meat; fish; fruits; cereals.
Phosphorus	Essential (with calcium) for bones and teeth; helps fat do its job in the body; aids enzymes used in energy metabolism.	Milk; ice cream; cheese; meat; poultry; whole-grain cereals; dry beans and peas; fish; nuts.
Magnesium	A must for strong bones and teeth; helps muscle contraction; aids in transmitting nerve impulses.	Cereals; dry beans; meats; milk; nuts.
Vitamin A	Helps maintain eyesight, especially in dim light; aids growth of healthy skin, bones, and teeth; promotes growth; helps resist infection.	Liver; broccoli; turnips; carrots; pumpkin; sweet potatoes; winter squash; apricots; butter; fortified margarine; egg yolk; fish-liver oils; cantaloupe.
Thiamine (Vitamin B_1)	Helps body cells obtain energy from food; aids in keeping nerves healthy; promotes good appetite and digestion.	Pork; lean meats; poultry; fish; liver; dry beans and peas; egg yolk; whole-grain and enriched cereals and breads; soybeans.
Riboflavin (Vitamin B_2)	Helps body use protein, fats, and carbohydrates for energy and for building tissues; aids in maintaining eyesight; promotes radiant skin.	Milk; cheese; liver; kidneys; heart; eggs; green leafy vegetables; enriched cereals and breads; yeast.
Niacin	Required for healthy nervous system, skin, and digestive tract; aids energy production in cells.	Lean meats; poultry; fish; variety meats; dark green leafy vegetables; whole-grain and enriched cereals and breads; peanuts; peanut butter.
Vitamin C (Ascorbic acid)	Aids in building the materials that hold cells together; helps in healing wounds and resisting infection; needed for healthy teeth, gums, and blood vessels.	Citrus fruits; strawberries; cantaloupe; tomatoes; potatoes; Brussels sprouts; raw cabbage; broccoli; green and sweet red peppers.
Vitamin D	Helps body use calcium and phosphorus to build bones and teeth.	Fortified milk; fish-liver oils; egg yolks; liver; salmon; tuna. Direct sunlight also produces Vitamin D.
Vitamin B_6	Aids body to use protein and maintain normal hemoglobin in blood.	Meats; wheat germ; liver; kidneys; whole-grain cereals; soybeans; peanuts.
Vitamin B_{12}	A necessity for producing red blood cells and for building new proteins in the body.	Meats; liver; kidneys; fish; eggs; milk; cheese.
Vitamin E	Function is not clearly understood, although it is thought to help form red blood cells, muscle, and other tissue.	Wheat-germ oil; salad oils; green leafy vegetables; nuts; dry beans and peas; margarine.
Vitamin K	Promotes normal blood clotting.	Green leafy vegetables; cauliflower; egg yolk; liver; soybean oil.
Water	Forms a vital part of all cells; carries nutrients to cells and waste from body; necessary for digestion; regulates body temperature.	Water; beverages; soups; fruit juices; milk; fruits and vegetables.

EVERYDAY HELPS

With all of our modern kitchen appliances, minute minders, and space savers, cooking is a joy, yet push buttons just can't do everything. Recipes still call for a human touch, and here's where it pays to know the techniques and shortcuts that will make the job easier and the results surer.

The following helps will give you quick answers to many of your daily cooking questions. How-to's on measuring ingredients and utensils help guarantee success and become second nature once you learn the right way. If you want to know how many whole onions it takes to make a cupful after they've been chopped, look here for a handy chart listing a number of foods.

For easy at-home reference—perhaps when you're planning meals or making up your shopping list—another table tells you what size cans certain foods come in so you can pick the pack that best fits your needs. Still another will guide you through emergency situations when you've started a recipe and find you've run out of a particular item you thought you had on hand. Sometimes there's an equally good counterpart you can use in its place, and this chart includes a few that have been worked out scientifically to eliminate mistakes and failures.

Finally, for these days when everyone's trying to save energy, there are tips to help you conserve it as well as get the most from what you do use.

BASIC COOKING TERMS AND WHAT THEY MEAN

BAKE: To cook food by dry heat in an oven or oven-type appliance.

BARBECUE: To roast or broil food on a rack or spit over or under a heating unit. Usually a special sauce is brushed over the food as it cooks.

BASTE: To moisten food as it cooks to prevent drying and add flavor. Pan drippings, fruit juices, salad oil, or special sauces are most often used.

BEAT: To make a mixture smooth with a quick even motion, using a spoon, wire whisk, or hand or electric beater.

BLANCH: To dip into boiling water to loosen skin from some foods or to scald as a step in preparing vegetables for freezing.

BLEND: To thoroughly mix two or more ingredients. Or to prepare food in an electric blender.

BOIL: To cook in liquid in which bubbles constantly rise to the surface and break.

BRAISE: To cook food slowly in a small amount of liquid in a tightly covered pan.

BROIL: To cook by direct heat on a rack or spit.

CARAMELIZE: To heat sugar slowly in a skillet until it melts and turns golden-brown.

CHILL: To refrigerate food or let it stand in a pan of ice and water until cold.

CHOP: To cut into small pieces with a knife or electric blender.

COAT: To cover all sides of food with another ingredient such as flour or bread crumbs.

CREAM: To make a mixture soft and smooth by beating with a spoon or electric mixer. Usually refers to blending fat and sugar together. Another meaning is to cook food in, or serve it with, a white or creamy sauce.

CRISP: To make a food firm and brittle by letting it stand in ice water or heating it in the oven.

CUBE: To cut food into cubes.

CUT: To combine shortening or solid fat with flour or other dry ingredients by using a pastry blender to distribute the shortening evenly.

DEEP-FRY: To cook in hot fat that's deep enough so the food floats on top.

DEVIL: To combine foods with one or more spicy-hot seasonings.

DICE: To cut foods into very small cubes, usually about ¼ inch.

DOT: To scatter bits of an ingredient such as butter or margarine over the surface of another food.

DREDGE: To coat or cover food with some dry ingredient such as flour, cornmeal, or sugar.

DUST: To sprinkle food with a dry ingredient such as flour or confectioners' powdered sugar.

FOLD: To combine delicate ingredients with other foods by cutting vertically down through the mixture with a spoon or spatula, sliding it across the bottom of the bowl, and bringing some of the mixture up and over the surface.

FRY: To cook in hot fat.

GRATE: To cut food into fine particles by rubbing it against a grater.

GREASE: To rub the surface of dish or pan

with shortening or other fat to keep food from sticking.

GRILL: To cook by direct heat.

GRIND: To cut food into tiny particles by putting it through a grinder.

JULIENNE: To cut food into long, slender strips.

KNEAD: To work a food mixture with hands by folding it toward you, then pressing down and pushing it away.

LARD: To cover meat with strips of fat or to insert them into meat to add flavor and prevent drying.

MARINATE: To let food stand in liquid for a period of time to enhance flavor or produce tenderness.

MELT: To use heat to turn a solid food into liquid.

MINCE: To cut into very fine pieces.

MIX: To combine ingredients until evenly blended.

PANBROIL: To cook, uncovered, in a skillet without fat.

PANFRY: To cook in a skillet in a small amount of fat.

PARBOIL: To boil food until partly cooked.

PARE: To trim skin, peeling, or outer covering from food with a knife or vegetable parer.

PEEL: To pull outer covering from food with hands.

PIT: To remove seed.

POACH: To cook gently in simmering liquid.

PUREE: To press food through a fine sieve or food mill, or twirl in a blender, until it becomes smooth.

RECONSTITUTE: To add water to concentrated food to return it to its natural form.

ROAST: To cook, uncovered, by hot air.

SAUTÉ: To cook in a small amount of hot fat.

SCALD: To heat a liquid to a point just below boiling.

SCORE: To make shallow cuts or slits in the surface of food to prevent fat from curling, to decorate, or to increase tenderness.

SEAR: To brown the surface of meat quickly by intense heat.

SHRED: To cut food into thin strips or slivers with a knife or shredder.

SIFT: To put through a sieve or sifter.

SIMMER: To cook slowly in liquid with the surface of the liquid barely rippling.

SKEWER: To fasten with wooden or metal pins.

STEAM: To cook directly over boiling water in a tightly covered container.

STEEP: To extract color and flavor by letting food stand in hot liquid.

STEW: To simmer in liquid.

STIR: To mix food with a circular motion for uniform consistency.

TOAST: To brown by dry heat.

TOSS: To mix foods lightly by lifting them with two forks or spoons.

WHIP: To beat rapidly to incorporate air and expand volume.

THE RIGHT WAY TO MEASURE

Start with proper equipment. Every cook should have these basics: a set of four nested measuring cups for dry ingredients, a 1-cup measure for liquids, and a set of four measuring spoons.

Nested—or graduated—cups in metal or plastic include ¼-, ⅓-, ½-, and 1-cup sizes. Liquid measures, available in glass or plastic, are designed with a rim above the cup level to prevent spilling, as well as lines that mark less than 1-cup amounts. For measuring larger quantities or bulky foods such as bread cubes or apple slices, pint and quart sizes are also handy. Standard measuring-spoon sets include a quarter and half teaspoon, one teaspoon, and one tablespoon.

To measure dry ingredients. Lightly spoon flour, granulated sugar, or confectioners' powdered sugar into cup or spoon until it overflows, then level it off with the edge of a spatula. Two other reminders in measuring flour: Be careful not to pack it down and never shake or tap the cup.

On the other hand, pack brown sugar into the cup with the back of a spoon, then level off. If properly measured, the sugar should hold the shape of the cup when it's turned out.

Solid shortening also calls for nested cups. Spoon the shortening directly from can to cup, packing it down lightly; level off; scrape the cup out cleanly with a rubber spatula.

Most stick butter and margarine comes in wrappers that are designed with tablespoon measurements, so it's easy to cut off what you need with a knife. If your particular brand isn't marked, remember that one-quarter pound or one stick makes ½ cup. For smaller amounts, follow the rule for solid shortening.

For all other solid ingredients—fruits, nuts, cereals, grated cheese, coconut, bread crumbs, biscuit mixes, and rice—use your nested cups.

Many times a recipe calls for ⅛ teaspoon of some ingredient such as salt, an herb, or a spice. In this case, measure ¼ teaspoon and level off, then divide the amount in half by drawing a knife lengthwise through the center. Push half back into the bottle or jar and use the other half.

To measure liquids. Place cup on a level surface and fill it to the line marked on the side, then bend down so you can read the amount at eye level. For spoon measurements, pour the liquid right to the rim but don't let it spill over. Never measure, even small amounts, directly over the food to which the liquid is being added. Your hand may tremble or slip and pour out more than you need.

Measure liquid shortening, salad oils, and melted butter or margarine the same as milk, water, fruit juices, wine, or other liquids.

HOW TO MEASURE PANS AND MOLDS

For best results, it pays to use the exact size pan, casserole, or mold called for in your recipe. This ensures attractive foods and even cooking, and avoids spillovers.

Many manufacturers stamp the size or capacity on the bottom of baking pans and dishes, pie plates, custard cups, and molds. But if you should have some that aren't marked, here's how to determine their size:

Casseroles and molds: Pour measured amounts of water into the utensil up to the rim. The total amount tells you how many cups or quarts the utensil holds.

Round cake pans and pie plates: For diameter, use a ruler and measure across the top from inside edge to inside edge. If it's depth you need, stand the ruler straight up along side.

Rectangular or square pans: Use your ruler again to measure length and width.

FAMILIAR CAN SIZES

NET WEIGHT OR FLUID MEASURE	CUPS	SERVINGS	PRODUCT PACKED
8 ounces	1	1 to 2	Fruits and vegetables; *specialties.
10½ to 12 ounces	1¼	2 to 3	Condensed soups; some fruits, vegetables, meats, and fish; *specialties.
12 ounces	1½	3 to 4	Mostly vacuum-pack corn.
14 to 16 ounces	1¾	3 to 4	Pork and beans; baked beans; meat products; cranberry sauce; blueberries; *specialties.
16 to 17 ounces	2	4	Fruits and vegetables; some meat items; ready-to-serve soups; *specialties.
20 ounces or 18 fluid ounces	2½	5	Juices; ready-to-serve soups; pineapple; apple slices; pie fillings; *specialties.
27 to 29 ounces	3½	5 to 7	Fruits; some vegetables such as pumpkin, sauerkraut, spinach, and tomatoes.
51 ounces or 46 fluid ounces	5¾	10 to 12	Fruit and vegetable juices; juice drinks; pork-and-beans.

*Specialties include such items as macaroni-and-cheese, Spanish rice, Mexican foods, and Chinese foods.

Juices now come canned or bottled in several sizes besides 18 or 46 fluid ounces.

Infant and junior foods are available in small cans and jars suitable for small servings. Check labels for content.

Cooking Measures

Dash (liquid) = Few drops
Dash, pinch, or
  few grains (dry) = Less than 1/8
                      teaspoon

3 teasp.	1 tablesp.
1/3 of 1 tablesp.	1 teasp.
1/3 of 2 tablesp.	2 teasp.
1/3 of 5 tablesp.	1 tablesp. + 2 teasp.
1/3 of 7 tablesp.	2 tablesp. + 1 teasp.
1/2 of 1 tablesp.	1 1/2 teasp.
1/2 of 3 tablesp.	1 tablesp. + 1 1/2 teasp.
1/2 of 5 tablesp.	2 tablesp. + 1 1/2 teasp.
1/2 of 7 tablesp.	3 tablesp. + 1 1/2 teasp.
2 tablesp.	1/8 cup
4 tablesp.	1/4 cup
5 tablesp. + 1 teasp.	1/3 cup
8 tablesp.	1/2 cup
10 tablesp. + 2 teasp.	2/3 cup
12 tablesp.	3/4 cup
16 tablesp.	1 cup
1/3 of 1/4 cup	1 tablesp. + 1 teasp.
1/3 of 1/3 cup	1 tablesp. + 2 1/3 teasp.
1/3 of 1/2 cup	2 tablesp. + 2 teasp.
1/3 of 2/3 cup	3 tablesp. + 1 2/3 teasp.
1/3 of 3/4 cup	1/4 cup
1/2 of 1/4 cup	2 tablesp.
1/2 of 1/3 cup	2 tablesp. + 2 teasp.
1/2 of 1/2 cup	1/4 cup
1/2 of 2/3 cup	1/3 cup
1/2 of 3/4 cup	6 tablesp.
2 cups	1 pt.
2 pt.	1 qt.
1 qt.	4 cups
4 qt.	1 gal.
8 qt.	1 peck
4 pecks	1 bushel
16 oz. (dry measure)	1 lb.

Oven Temperatures

	Fahrenheit
Very Slow	250°–275°
Slow	300°–325°
Moderate	350°–375°
Hot	400°–425°
Very Hot	450°–475°
Extremely Hot	500°–525°

Cooking Substitutes

■ 1 teaspoon baking powder = 1/3 teaspoon baking soda plus 1/2 teaspoon cream of tartar.

■ 1 cup bread crumbs = 3/4 cup cracker crumbs.

■ 1 cup butter = 1 cup margarine or 7/8 cup vegetable oil.

■ 1-ounce square unsweetened chocolate = 3 tablespoons cocoa plus 1 tablespoon margarine.

■ 1 tablespoon cornstarch, as thickener = 2 tablespoons flour.

■ 1 cup heavy cream = 3/4 cup milk plus 1/3 cup butter.

■ 1 cup light cream = 3/4 cup milk plus 3 tablespoons butter.

■ 2 egg yolks = 1 whole egg.

■ 1 cup all-purpose flour = 1 cup whole wheat flour.

■ 1 cup cake flour = 1 cup less 1 tablespoon all-purpose flour.

■ 1 teaspoon lemon juice = 1/2 teaspoon vinegar.

■ 1 cup whole milk = 1/2 cup evaporated milk plus 1/2 cup water.

■ 1 cup sour milk = 1 cup yogurt or buttermilk.

■ 1 cup sour cream, in baking = 7/8 cup buttermilk or sour milk plus 3 tablespoons margarine.

■ 1 cup sour cream = 1 cup yogurt.

■ 1 cup sugar, in baking bread = 1 cup honey plus a pinch of baking soda.

■ 1 cup sugar, main dishes = 3/4 cup honey.

■ 1 cup sugar, in baking = 7/8 cup honey plus a pinch of baking soda.

■ 1 cup brown sugar = 1 cup white sugar plus 2 tablespoons molasses.

■ 1/2 cup dry red or white wine = 2 tablespoons sherry or port.

■ 1 cup molasses, in baking = 1 cup sugar, omit baking soda, use baking powder.

■ 3/4 cup maple syrup, in baking = 1 cup sugar, increase liquid in recipe by 3 tablespoons.

■ 1 cup grated coconut = 1 1/3 cup flaked coconut.

■ 2 teaspoons tapioca, as thickener = 1 tablespoon flour.

■ 1 cup yogurt = 1 cup buttermilk.

■ 1 cup zucchini = 1 cup summer squash.

■ 1 pound almonds, in shell = approximately 3/4-1 cup shelled.

■ 1 pound apples = approximately 3 cups pared and sliced.

■ 1 pound dried apricots = approximately 3 cups.

Four-Year Colleges and Universities

Four-Year Public Colleges and Universities

ALABAMA

Alabama A and M University
Normal, AL 35762

Alabama State University
Montgomery, AL 36195

Athens State College
Athens, AL 35611

Auburn University
Auburn University, AL 36849

Auburn University—Montgomery
Montgomery, AL 36117

Jacksonville State University
Jacksonville, AL 36265

Livingston University
Livingston, AL 35470

Troy State University
Troy, AL 36082

Troy State University—Dothan/Ft. Rucker
Dothan, AL 36301

Troy State University—Montgomery
Montgomery, AL 36104

University of Alabama
University, AL 35486

University of Alabama—Birmingham
Birmingham, AL 35294

University of Alabama—Huntsville
Huntsville, AL 35807

University of Montevallo
Montevallo, AL 35115

University of North Alabama
Florence, AL 35632

University of South Alabama
Mobile, AL 36688

ALASKA

University of Alaska—Anchorage
Anchorage, AK 99504

University of Alaska—Fairbanks
Fairbanks, AK 99701

University of Alaska—Juneau
Juneau, AK 99803

ARIZONA

Arizona State University
Tempe, AZ 85281

Northern Arizona University
Flagstaff, AZ 86011

University of Arizona
Tucson, AZ 85721

ARKANSAS

Arkansas State University
State University, AR 72467

Arkansas Tech University
Russellville, AR 72801

Henderson State University
Arkadelphia, AR 71923

Southern Arkansas University
Magnolia, AR 71753

University of Arkansas
Fayetteville, AR 72701

University of Arkansas—Little Rock
Little Rock, AR 72204

University of Arkansas—Monticello
Monticello, AR 71655

University of Arkansas—Pine Bluff
Pine Bluff, AR 71601

University of Central Arkansas
Conway, AR 72032

CALIFORNIA

California State College—Bakersfield
Bakersfield, CA 93309

California State College—San Bernadino
San Bernadino, CA 92407

California State College—Stanislaus
Turlock, CA 95380

California State Polytechnic University—Pomona
Pomona, CA 91768

California State Polytechnic University—San Luis Obispo
San Luis Obispo, CA 93407

California State University—Chico
Chico, CA 95929

California State University—Dominquez Hills
Carson, CA 90747

California State University—Fresno
Fresno, CA 93740

California State University—Fullerton
Fullerton, CA 92634

California State University—Hayward
Hayward, CA 94542

California State University—Long Beach
Long Beach, CA 90840

California State University—Los Angeles
Los Angeles, CA 90032

California State University—Northridge
Northridge, CA 91330

California State University—Sacramento
Sacramento, CA 95819

Claremont Men's College
Claremont, CA 91711

Humboldt State University
Arcata, CA 95521

National University
San Diego, CA 92108

San Diego State University
Calexico, CA 92231

San Diego State University
San Diego, CA 92182

San Francisco State University
San Francisco, CA 94132

San Jose State University
San Jose, CA 95192

Sonoma State University
Rohnert Park, CA 94928

University of California—Berkeley
Berkeley, CA 94720

University of California—Davis
Davis, CA 95616

University of California—Irvine
Irvine, CA 92717

University of California—Los Angeles
Los Angeles, CA 90024

University of California—Riverside
Riverside, CA 92521

University of California—San Diego
La Jolla, CA 92093

University of California—Santa Barbara
Santa Barbara, CA 93106

University of California—Santa Cruz
Santa Cruz, CA 95064

COLORADO

Adams State College
Alamosa, CO 81102

Colorado School of Mines
Golden, CO 80401

Colorado State University
Fort Collins, CO 80523

Fort Lewis College
Durango, CO 81301

Mesa College
Grand Junction, CO 81501

Metropolitan State College
Denver, CO 80204

United States Air Force Academy
USAF Academy, CO 80840

University of Colorado
Boulder, CO 80309

University of Colorado Springs—Colorado Springs
Colorado Springs, CO 80907

University of Colorado—Denver
Denver, CO 80202

University of Northern Colorado
Greeley, CO 80639

University of Southern Colorado
Pueblo, CO 81001

Western State College of Colorado
Gunnison, CO 81230

CONNECTICUT

Central Connecticut State College
New Britain, CT 06050

East Connecticut State College
Willimantic, CT 06226

Southern Connecticut State College
New Haven, CT 06515

United States Coast Guard Academy
New London, CT 06320

University of Connecticut
Storrs, CT 06268

Western Connecticut State College
Danbury, CT 06810

DELAWARE

Delaware State College
Dover, DE 19901

DISTRICT OF COLUMBIA

University of the District of Columbia
Washington, DC 20004

FLORIDA

Florida A and M University
Tallahassee, FL 32307

Florida Atlantic University
Boca Raton, FL 33431

Florida International University
Miami, FL 33199

Florida State University
Tallahassee, FL 32306

Fort Lauderdale College
Fort Lauderdale, FL 33301

New College of the University of
South Florida
Sarasota, FL 33580

Panama Canal College
APO Miami, FL 34002

University of Florida
Gainesville, FL 32611

University of North Florida
Jacksonville, FL 32216

University of South Florida
Tampa, FL 33620

University of West Florida
Pensacola, FL 32504

GEORGIA

Albany State College
Albany, GA 31705

Armstrong State College
Savannah, GA 31406

Augusta College
Augusta, GA 30910

Columbus College
Columbus, GA 31993

Fort Valley State College
Fort Valley, GA 31030

Georgia College
Milledgeville, GA 31601

Georgia Institute of Technology
Atlanta, GA 30332

Georgia Southern College
Statesboro, GA 30458

Georgia Southwestern College
Americus, GA 31709

Georgia State University
Athens, GA 30303

Kennesaw College
Marietta, GA 30061

Medical College of Georgia
Augusta, GA 30912

North Georgia College
Dahlonega, GA 30533

Savannah State College
Savannah, GA 31404

Southern Technical Institute
Marietta, GA 30060

University of Georgia
Athens, GA 30602

Valdosta State College
Valdosta, GA 31601

West Georgia College
Carrollton, GA 30118

HAWAII

University of Hawaii—College of Arts
and Sciences
Hilo, HI 96720

University of Hawaii—Manoa
Honolulu, HI 96822

University of Hawaii—West Oahu
College
Aiea, HI 96701

IDAHO

Boise State University
Boise, ID 83725

Idaho State University
Pocatello, ID 83209

Lewis-Clark State College
Lewiston, ID 83501

University of Idaho
Moscow, ID 83843

ILLINOIS

Chicago State University
Chicago, IL 60628

Eastern Illinois University
Charleston, IL 61920

Governors State University
Park Forest South, IL 60466

Illinois State University
Normal, IL 61761

National American Educational
Service (s)
Chicago, IL 60640

Northeastern Illinois University
Chicago, IL 60625

Northern Illinois University
DeKalb, IL 60115

Sangamon State University
Springfield, IL 62708

Southern Illinois University
Edwardsville, IL 62026

Southern Illinois University—
Carbondale
Carbondale, IL 62901

University of Illinois—Chicago Circle
Chicago, IL 60680

University of Illinois—Medical
Center
Chicago, IL 60612

University of Illinois—
Urbana/Champaign
Urbana, IL 61801

Western Illinois University
Macomb, IL 61455

INDIANA

Ball State University
Muncie, IN 47306

Indiana State University—Evansville
Evansville, IN 47712

Indiana State University—Terre
Haute
Terre Haute, IN 47809

Indiana University—Bloomington
Bloomington, IN 47405

Indiana University—Kokomo
Kokomo, IN 46901

Indiana University—Purdue
University at Fort Wayne
Fort Wayne, IN 46805

Indiana University—Purdue
University at Indianapolis
Indianapolis, IN 46202

Indiana University—South Bend
South Bend, IN 46615

Indiana University—Southeast
New Albany, IN 47150

Purdue University
West Lafayette, IN 47907

Purdue University—Calumet
Hammond, IN 46323

Purdue University—North Central
Westville, IN 46391

IOWA

Iowa State University
Ames, IA 50011

University of Iowa
Iowa City, IA 52242

University of Northern Iowa
Cedar Falls, IA 50613

KANSAS

Emporia State University
Emporia, KS 66801

Fort Hays State University
Hays, KS 67601

Kansas State University
Manhattan, KS 66506

Pittsburg State University
Pittsburg, KS 66762

United States Army Command and
General Staff College
Fort Leavenworth, KS 66027

University of Kansas
Lawrence, KS 66045

University of Kansas—College of
Health Sciences and Hospital
Kansas City, KS 66103

Wichita State University
Wichita, KS 67204

KENTUCKY

Eastern Kentucky University
Richmond, KY 40475

Kentucky State University
Frankfort, KY 40601

Murray State University
Murray, KY 42071

Northern Kentucky University
Highland Heights, KY 41076

University of Kentucky
Lexington, KY 40506

University of Louisville
Louisville, KY 40208

Western Kentucky University
Bowling Green, KY 42101

LOUISIANA

Grambling State University
Grambling, LA 71245

Louisiana State University—A and M
College
Baton Rouge, LA 70803

Louisiana State University—
Shreveport
Shreveport, LA 71115

Louisiana Tech University
Ruston, LA 71272

McNeese State University
Lake Charles, LA 70609

Nicholls State University
Thibodaux, LA 70310

Northeast Louisiana University
Monroe, LA 71209

Northwestern State University
Natchitoches, LA 71457

Southeastern Louisiana University
Hammond, LA 70402

Southern University—Baton Rouge
Baton Rouge, LA 70813

Southern University—New Orleans
New Orleans, LA 70126

University of New Orleans
New Orleans, LA 70122

University of Southwestern
Louisiana
Lafayette, LA 70504

MAINE

Maine Maritime Academy
Castine, ME 04421

University of Maine—Augusta
Augusta, ME 04330

University of Maine—Farmington
Farmington, ME 04938

University of Maine—Fort Kent
Fort Kent, ME 04743

University of Maine—Machias
Machias, ME 04654

University of Maine—Orono
Orono, ME 04473
University of Maine—Presque Isle
Presque Isle, ME 04769
University of Southern Maine
Gorham, ME 04038

MARYLAND

Bowie State College
Bowie, MD 20715
Coppin State College
Baltimore, MD 21216
Frostburg State College
Frostburg, MD 21532
Morgan State University
Baltimore, MD 21239
Salisbury State College
Salisbury, MD 21801
St. Mary's College of Maryland
St. Mary's City, MD 20686
Towson State University
Towson, MD 21204
United States Naval Academy
Annapolis, MD 21402
University of Baltimore
Baltimore, MD 21201
University of Maryland—Baltimore County
Baltimore, MD 21228
University of Maryland—College Park
College Park, MD 20742
University of Maryland—Eastern Shore
Princess Anne, MD 28153
University of Maryland—University College
College Park, MD 20742

MASSACHUSETTS

Boston State College
Boston, MA 02115
Bridgewater State College
Bridgewater, MA 02324
Fitchburg State College
Fitchburg, MA 01420
Framingham State College
Framingham, MA 01701
Massachusetts College of Art
Boston, MA 02215
Massachusetts Maritime Academy
Buzzards Bay, MA 02532
North Adams State College
North Adams, MA 01247
Salem State College
Salem, MA 01970
Southeastern Massachusetts University
North Dartmouth, MA 02747
University of Lowell
Lowell, MA 01854
University of Massachusetts—Amherst
Amherst, MA 01003
University of Massachusetts—Boston
Boston, MA 02125
Westfield State College
Westfield, MA 01085
Worcester State College
Worcester, MA 01602

MICHIGAN

Central Michigan University
Mount Pleasant, MI 48858
Eastern Michigan University
Ypsilanti, MI 48197

Ferris State College
Big Rapids, MI 49307
Grand Valley State Colleges
Allendale, MI 49401
Lake Superior State College
Sault Ste. Marie, MI 49783
Michigan State University
East Lansing, MI 48824
Michigan Technological University
Houghton, MI 49931
Northern Michigan University
Marquette, MI 49855
Oakland University
Rochester, MI 48063
Saginaw Valley State College
University Center, MI 48710
University of Michigan—Ann Arbor
Ann Arbor, MI 48109
University of Michigan—Dearborn
Dearborn, MI 48128
University of Michigan—Flint
Flint, MI 48503
Wayne State University
Detroit, MI 48202
Western Michigan University
Kalamazoo, MI 49008

MINNESOTA

Bemidji State University
Bemidji, MN 56601
Mankato State University
Mankato, MN 56001
Metropolitan State University
St. Paul, MN 55101
Moorhead State University
Moorhead, MN 56560
Southwest State University
Marshall, MN 56258
St. Cloud State University
St. Cloud, MN 56301
University of Minnesota—Duluth
Duluth, MN 55182
University of Minnesota—Morris
Morris, MN 56267
University of Minnesota—Twin Cities
Minneapolis, MN 55455
Winona State University
Winona, MN 55987

MISSISSIPPI

Alcorn State University
Lorman, MS 39096
Delta State University
Cleveland, MS 38733
Jackson State University
Jackson, MS 39217
Mississippi State University
Mississippi State, MS 39762
Mississippi University for Women
Columbus, MS 39701
Mississippi Valley State University
Itta Bena, MS 38941
University of Mississippi
University, MS 38677
University of Mississippi Medical Center
Jackson, MS 39216
University of Southern Mississippi
Hattiesburg, MS 39401

MISSOURI

Central Missouri State University
Warren, MO 64093
Missouri Southern State College
Joplin, MO 64801

Missouri Western State College
St. Joseph, MO 64507
Northeast Missouri State University
Kirksville, MO 63501
Northwest Missouri State University
Maryville, MO 64468
Southeast Missouri State University
Cape Girardeau, MO 63701
Southwest Missouri State University
Springfield, MO 65802
University of Missouri—Columbia
Columbia, MO 65201
University of Missouri—Kansas City
Kansas City, MO 64110
University of Missouri—Rolla
Rolla, MO 65401
University of Missouri—St. Louis
St. Louis, MO 63121

MONTANA

Eastern Montana College
Billings, MT 59101
Montana College of Mineral Science and Technology
Butte, MT 59701
Montana State University
Bozeman, MT 59717
Northern Montana College
Havre, MT 59501
University of Montana
Missoula, MT 59812
Western Montana College
Dillon, MT 59725

NEBRASKA

Chadron State College
Chadron, NE 69357
Kearney State College
Kearney, NE 68847
Peru State College
Peru, NE 68421
University of Nebraska—Lincoln
Lincoln, NE 68508
University of Nebraska—Omaha
Omaha, NE 68182
Wayne State College
Wayne, NE 68787

NEVADA

University of Nevada—Las Vegas
Las Vegas, NV 89150
University of Nevada—Reno
Reno, NV 89557

NEW HAMPSHIRE

Keene State College
Keene, NH 03431
Plymouth State College
Plymouth, NH 03264
University of New Hampshire
Durham, NH 03824

NEW JERSEY

Glassboro State College
Glassboro, NJ 08028
Jersey City State College
Jersey City, NJ 07305
Montclair State College
Upper Montclair, NJ 07043
New Jersey Institute of Technology
Newark, NJ 07102
Rutgers University—Camden College of Arts and Sciences
Camden, NJ 08102

Rutgers University—College of Engineering
New Brunswick, NJ 08903
Rutgers University—College of Nursing—Newark
Newark, NJ 07102
Rutgers University—College of Pharmacy
New Brunswick, NJ 08903
Rutgers University—Cook College
New Brunswick, NJ 08903
Rutgers University—Douglass College
New Brunswick, NJ 08903
Rutgers University—Livingston College
New Brunswick, NJ 08903
Rutgers University—Mason Gross School of the Arts
New Brunswick, NJ 08903
Rutgers University—Newark College of Arts and Sciences
Newark, NJ 07102
Rutgers University—Rutgers College
New Brunswick, NJ 08903
Rutgers University—University College
New Brunswick, NJ 08903
Trenton State College
Trenton, NJ 08625
William Paterson College
Wayne, NJ 07470

NEW MEXICO

Eastern New Mexico University
Portales, NM 88130
New Mexico Highlands University
Las Vegas, NM 87701
New Mexico Institute of Mining and Technology
Socorro, NM 87801
New Mexico State University
Las Cruces, NM 88003
University of New Mexico
Albuquerque, NM 87131
Western New Mexico University
Silver City, NM 88061

NEW YORK

CUNY—Bernard Baruch College
New York, NY 10010
CUNY—Brooklyn College
Brooklyn, NY 11210
CUNY—City College
New York, NY 10031
CUNY—College of Staten Island
Staten Island, NY 10301
CUNY—Hunter College
New York, NY 10021
CUNY—John Jay College of Criminal Justice
New York, NY 10019
CUNY—Lehman College
Bronx, NY 10468
CUNY—Medgar Evers College
Brooklyn, NY 11225
CUNY—Queens College
Flushing, NY 11367
CUNY—York College
Jamaica, NY 11432
SUNY—Albany
Albany, NY 12222
SUNY—Binghamton
Binghamton, NY 13901
SUNY—Buffalo
Buffalo, NY 14214

SUNY—College at Brockport
Brockport, NY 14420
SUNY—College at Buffalo
Buffalo, NY 14222
SUNY—College at Cortland
Cortland, NY 13045
SUNY—College at Fredonia
Fredonia, NY 14063
SUNY—College at Genesco
Genesco, NY 14454
SUNY—College at New Paltz
New Paltz, NY 12561
SUNY—College at Old Westbury
Old Westbury, NY 11568
SUNY—College at Oneonta
Oneonta, NY 13820
SUNY—College at Oswego
Oswego, NY 13126
SUNY—College at Plattsburgh
Plattsburgh, NY 12901
SUNY—College at Potsdam
Potsdam, NY 13676
SUNY—College at Purchase
Purchase, NY 10577
SUNY—College of Agriculture and Life Science at Cornell
Ithaca, NY 14853
SUNY—College of Ceramics at Alfred
Alfred, NY 14802
SUNY—College of Environmental Science and Forestry
Syracuse, NY 13210
SUNY—College of Human Ecology at Cornell
Ithaca, NY 14853
SUNY—College of Technology
Utica, NY 13502
SUNY—Empire State College
Saratoga Springs, NY 12866
SUNY—Fashion Institute of Technology
New York, NY 10001
SUNY—Maritime College
Bronx, NY 10465
SUNY—School of Industrial and Labor Relations at Cornell
Ithaca, NY 14853
SUNY—Stony Brook
Stony Brook, NY 11794
SUNY—Upstate Medical Center
Syracuse, NY 13210
United States Merchant Marine Academy
Kings Point, NY 11024
United States Military Academy
West Point, NY 10996

NORTH CAROLINA

Appalachian State University
Boone, NC 28608
Davidson College
Davidson, NC 28036
East Carolina University
Greenville, NC 27834
Elizabeth City State University
Elizabeth City, NC 27909
Fayetteville State University
Fayetteville, NC 28303
North Carolina Agricultural and Technical State University
Greensboro, NC 27411
North Carolina Central University
Durham, NC 27707
North Carolina School of the Arts
Winston-Salem, NC 27107

North Carolina State University—Raleigh
Raleigh, NC 27650
Pembroke State University
Pembroke, NC 28372
Salem College
Winston-Salem, NC 27108
University of North Carolina
Ashville, NC 28814
University of North Carolina—Chapel Hill
Chapel Hill, NC 27514
University of North Carolina—Charlotte
Charlotte, NC 28223
University of North Carolina—Greensboro
Greensboro, NC 27412
University of North Carolina—Wilmington
Wilmington, NC 28403
Western Carolina University
Cullowhee, NC 28723
Winston-Salem State University
Winston-Salem, NC 27102

NORTH DAKOTA

Dickinson State College
Dickinson, ND 58601
Mayville State College
Mayville, ND 58257
Minot State College
Minot, ND 58701
North Dakota State University
Fargo, ND 58105
University of North Dakota
Grand Forks, ND 58202
Valley City State College
Valley City, ND 58072

OHIO

Bowling Green State University
Bowling Green, OH 43403
Central State University
Wilberforce, OH 45384
Cleveland State University
Cleveland, OH 44115
Kent State University
Kent, OH 44242
Miami University
Oxford, OH 45056
Ohio State University
Columbus, OH 43210
Ohio State University—Lima
Lima, OH 45804
Ohio State University—Mansfield
Mansfield, OH 44906
Ohio University
Athens, OH 45701
Ohio University—Lancaster
Lancaster, OH 43130
University of Akron
Akron, OH 44325
University of Cincinnati
Cincinnati, OH 45221
Write State University
Dayton, OH 45435
Youngstown State University
Youngstown, OH 44555

OKLAHOMA

Central State University
Edmond, OK 73034
East Central Oklahoma State University
Ada, OK 74820

Northeastern Oklahoma State University
Tahleguah, OK 74464
Northwestern Oklahoma State University
Alva, OK 73717
Oklahoma State University
Stillwater, OK 74078
Panhandle State University
Goodwell, OK 73939
Southeastern Oklahoma State University
Durant, OK 74701
Southwestern Oklahoma State University
Weatherford, OK 73096
University of Oklahoma—Health
Oklahoma City, OK 73190
University of Oklahoma—Norman
Norman, OK 73019
University of Science and Arts of Oklahoma
Chickasha, OK 73018

OREGON

Eastern Oregon State College
La Grande, OR 97850
Oregon College of Education
Monmouth, OR 97361
Oregon Institute of Technology
Klamath Falls, OR 97601
Oregon State University
Corvallis, OR 97331
Portland State University
Portland, OR 97207
Southern Oregon State College
Ashland, OR 97520
University of Oregon
Eugene, OR 97403
University of Oregon—Health
Portland, OR 97201

PENNSYLVANIA

Bloomsburg State College
Bloomsburg, PA 17815
California State College
California, PA 15419
Cheyney State College
Cheyney, PA 19319
Clarion State College
Clarion, PA 16214
East Stroudsbury State College
East Stroudsbury, PA 18301
Edinboro State College
Edinboro, PA 16412
Grove City College
Grove City, PA 16127
Indiana University of Pennsylvania
Indiana, PA 15705
Kutztown State College
Kutztown, PA 19530
Lock Haven State College
Lock Haven, PA 17745
Mansfield State College
Mansfield, PA 16933
Millersville State College
Millersville, PA 17551
Pennsylvania State University
University Park, PA 16802
Pennsylvania State University—Behrend
Erie, PA 16563
Pennsylvania State University—Capitol
Middletown, PA 17057

Shippensburg State College
Shippensburg, PA 17257
Slippery Rock State College
Slippery Rock, PA 16057
Temple University
Philadelphia, PA 19122
West Chester State College
West Chester, PA 19380

RHODE ISLAND

Rhode Island College
Providence, RI 02908
University of Rhode Island
Kingston, RI 02881

SOUTH CAROLINA

Clemson University
Clemson, SC 29631
College of Charleston
Charleston, SC 29401
Francis Marion College
Florence, SC 29501
South Carolina State College
Orangeburg, SC 29117
The Citadel
Charleston, SC 29409
University of South Carolina
Columbia, SC 29208
University of South Carolina—Aiken
Aiken, SC 29801
University of South Carolina—Coastal Carolina
Conway, SC 29526
University of South Carolina—Spartanburg
Spartanburg, SC 29303
Winthrop College
Rock Hill, SC 29733
Wofford College
Spartanburg, SC 29301

SOUTH DAKOTA

Black Hills State College
Spearfish, SD 57783
Dakota State College
Madison, SD 57042
Northern State College
Aberdeen, SD 57401
South Dakota School of Mines and Technology
Rapid City, SD 57701
South Dakota State University
Brookings, SD 57006
University of South Dakota
Vermillion, SD 57069
University of South Dakota of Springfield
Springfield, SD 57062

TENNESSEE

Austin Peay State University
Clarksville, TN 37040
East Tennessee State University
Johnson City, TN 37614
Memphis State University
Memphis, TN 38152
Middle Tennessee State University
Murfreesboro, TN 37132
Tennessee State University
Nashville, TN 37203
Tennessee Technological University
Cookeville, TN 38501
University of Tennessee—Center for the Health Sciences
Memphis, TN 38163

University of Tennessee—Chattanooga
Chattanooga, TN 37401
University of Tennessee—Knoxville
Knoxville, TN 37916
University of Tennessee—Martin
Martin, TN 38238

TEXAS

Angelo State University
San Angelo, TX 76909
Corpus Christi State University
Corpus Christi, TX 78412
East Texas State University
Commerce, TX 75428
Lamar University
Beaumont, TX 77710
Laredo State University
Laredo, TX 78040
Midwestern State University
Wichita Falls, TX 76308
North Texas State University
Denton, TX 76203
Pan American University
Edinburg, TX 78539
Prairie View A and M University
Prairie View, TX 77445
Sam Houston State University
Huntsville, TX 77340
Southwest Texas State University
San Marcos, TX 78666
Stephen F. Austin State University
Nacogdoches, TX 75962
Sul Ross State University
Alpine, TX 79830
Sul Ross State University—Uvalde Study Center
Uvalde, TX 78801
Tarleton State University
Stephenville, TX 76402
Texas A and I University—Kingsville
Kingsville, TX 78363
Texas A and M University
College Station, TX 77843
Texas A and M University at Galveston
Galveston, TX 77553
Texas Southern University
Houston, TX 77004
Texas Tech University
Lubbock, TX 79409
Texas Woman's University
Denton, TX 76204
University of Houston
Houston, TX 77004
University of Houston—Clear Lake City
Houston, TX 77058
University of Houston—Downtown
Houston, TX 77002
University of Houston—Victoria
Victoria, TX 77901
University of St. Thomas
Houston, TX 77006
University of Texas—Arlington
Arlington, TX 76019
University of Texas—Austin
Austin, TX 78712
University of Texas—Dallas
Richardson, TX 75080
University of Texas—El Paso
El Paso, TX 79968
University of Texas—Health Science Center—San Antonio
San Antonio, TX 78284

University of Texas Medical Branch—
Galveston
Galveston, TX 77550

University of Texas—Permian Basin
Odessa, TX 79762

University of Texas—San Antonio
San Antonio, TX 78285

University of Texas—Tyler
Tyler, TX 75701

West Texas State University
Canyon, TX 79016

UTAH

Southern Utah State College
Cedar City, UT 84720

Utah State University
Logan, UT 84322

Weber State College
Ogden, UT 84408

VERMONT

Castleton State College
Castleton, VT 05735

Johnson State College
Johnson, VT 05656

Southern Vermont College
Bennington, VT 05201

University of Vermont
Burlington, VT 05405

VIRGINIA

Christopher Newport College
Newport News, VA 23606

College of William and Mary
Williamsburg, VA 23185

George Mason University
Fairfax, VA 22030

James Madison University
Harrisonburg, VA 22801

Norfolk State University
Norfolk, VA 23504

Old Dominion University
Norfolk, VA 23508

University of Virginia—Clinch
Wise, VA 24293

Virginia Military Institute
Lexington, VA 24450

Virginia Polytechnic Institute and
State University
Blacksburg, VA 24061

Virginia State University
Petersburg, VA 23803

WASHINGTON

Central Washington University
Ellensburg, WA 98926

City College
Seattle, WA 98104

Eastern Washington University
Cheney, WA 99004

Evergreen State College
Olympia, WA 98505

University of Washington
Seattle, WA 98105

Washington State University
Pullman, WA 99164

Western Washington University
Bellingham, WA 98225

WEST VIRGINIA

Bluefield State College
Bluefield, WV 24701

Concord College
Athens, WV 24712

Fairmont State College
Fairmont, WV 26554

Glenville State College
Glenville, WV 26531

Marshall University
Huntington, WV 25705

Shepherd College
Shepherdstown, WV 25443

West Liberty State College
West Liberty, WV 26074

West Virginia Institute of Technology
Montgomery, WV 25136

West Virginia State College
Charleston, WV 25312

West Virginia University
Morgantown, WV 26506

WISCONSIN

University of Wisconsin—Eau Claire
Eau Claire, WI 54701

University of Wisconsin—Green Bay
Green Bay, WI 54302

University of Wisconsin—La Crosse
La Crosse, WI 54601

University of Wisconsin—Madison
Madison, WI 53706

University of Wisconsin—Milwaukee
Milwaukee, WI 53201

University of Wisconsin—Oshkosh
Oshkosh, WI 54901

University of Wisconsin—Parkside
Kenosha, WI 53141

University of Wisconsin—Platteville
Platteville, WI 53818

University of Wisconsin—River Falls
River Falls, WI 54022

University of Wisconsin—Stevens
Point
Stevens Point, WI 54481

University of Wisconsin—Stout
Menomonie, WI 54751

University of Wisconsin—Superior
Superior, WI 54880

University of Wisconsin—Whitewater
Whitewater, WI 53190

WYOMING

University of Wyoming
Laramie, WY 82071

GUAM

University of Guam
Mangilao, Guam 96913

PUERTO RICO

Bayamon Central University
Bayamon, PR 00619

VIRGIN ISLANDS

College of the Virgin Islands
St. Thomas, VI 00801

Four-Year Private
Colleges and Universities

ALABAMA

Birmingham-Southern College
Birmingham, AL 35204

Gately Christian University
Guntersville, AL 35976

Huntingdon College
Montgomery, AL 36106

International Bible College
Florence, AL 35630

Judson College
Marion, AL 36756

Miles College
Birmingham, AL 35208

Mobile College
Mobile, AL 36613

Oakwood College
Huntsville, AL 35806

Samford University
Birmingham, AL 35229

Selma University
Selma, AL 36701

Southeastern Bible College
Birmingham, AL 35256

Spring Hill College
Mobile, AL 36608

Stillman College
Tuscaloosa, AL 35401

Talladega College
Talladega, AL 35160

Tuskegee Institute
Tuskegee, AL 36088

ALASKA

Alaska Bible College
Glennallen, AK 99588

Alaska Pacific University
Anchorage, AK 99504

Sheldon Jackson College
Sitka, AK 99835

ARIZONA

Arizona College of the Bible
Phoenix, AZ 85021

Devry Institute of Technology
Phoenix, AZ 85016

Embry-Riddle Aeronautical
University
Prescott, AZ 86301

Grand Canyon College
Phoenix, AZ 85017

Southwestern Baptist College
Phoenix, AZ 85032

University of Phoenix
Phoenix, AZ 85004
Western International University
Phoenix, AZ 85021

ARKANSAS

Arkansas Baptist College
Little Rock, AR 72202
Arkansas College
Batesville, AR 72501
Central Baptist College
Conway, AR 72032
College of the Ozarks
Clarksville, AR 72830
Harding University
Searcy, AR 72143
Hendrix College
Conway, AR 72023
John Brown University
Siloam Springs, AR 72761
Ouachita Baptist University
Arkadelphia, AR 71923
Philander Smith College
Little Rock, AR 72203

CALIFORNIA

Ambassador College
Pasadena, CA 91123
Antioch University—West
San Francisco, CA 94108
Armstrong College
Berkeley, CA 94704
Art Center College of Design
Pasadena, CA 91103
Azusa Pacific College
Azusa, CA 91702
Bethany Bible College
Santa Cruz, CA 95066
Biola College
La Mirada, CA 90639
Brooks Institute
Santa Barbara, CA 93108
California Baptist College
Riverside, CA 92504
California Christian College
Fresno, CA 93703
California College of Arts and Crafts
Oakland, CA 94618
California College of Commerce
Long Beach, CA 90813
California Institute of Technology
Pasadena, CA 91125
California Institute of the Arts
Valencia, CA 91355
California Lutheran College
Thousand Oaks, CA 91360
California Maritime Academy
Vallejo, CA 94590
Center for Early Education
Los Angeles, CA 90048
Chapman College
Orange, CA 92666
Christ College Irvine
Irvine, CA 92715
Christian Heritage College
El Cajon, CA 92021
Cogswell College
San Francisco, CA 94108
Coleman College
La Mesa, CA 92041
College of Notre Dame
Belmont, CA 94002
Columbia College
Los Angeles, CA 90038
Dominican College of San Rafael
San Rafael, CA 94901

Dominican School of Philosophy and Theology
Berkeley, CA 95709
Fresno Pacific College
Fresno, CA 93702
Golden Gate University
San Francisco, CA 94105
Harvey Mudd College
Claremont, CA 91711
Heald Engineering College
San Francisco, CA 94109
Hebrew Union College
Los Angeles, CA 90007
Holy Family College
Fermont, CA 94538
Holy Names College
Oakland, CA 94619
John F. Kennedy University— Evenings
Orinda, CA 94563
L.I.F.E. Bible College
Los Angeles, CA 90026
Lincoln University
San Francisco, CA 94118
Loma Linda University
Loma, CA 92350
Loma Linda University—La Sierra
Riverside, CA 92515
Los Angeles Baptist College
Newhall, CA 91322
Loyola Marymount University
Los Angeles, CA 90045
Menlo College
Menlo Park, CA 94025
Mills College
Oakland, CA 94613
Monterey Institute of International Studies
Monterey, CA 93940
Mount St. Mary's College
Los Angeles, CA 90049
Music and Arts Institute of San Francisco
San Francisco, CA 94115
New College of California
San Francisco, CA 94110
Northrop University
Inglewood, CA 90306
Occidental College
Los Angeles, CA 90041
Otis Art Institute of Parsons School of Design
Los Angeles, CA 90057
Pacific Christian College
Fullerton, CA 92631
Pacific Oaks College
Pasadena, CA 91103
Pacific States University
Los Angeles, CA 90006
Pacific Union College
Angwin, CA 94508
Patten Bible College
Oakland, CA 94601
Pepperdine University
Los Angeles, CA 90044
Pepperdine University—Seaver College
Malibu, CA 90265
Pitzer College
Claremont, CA 91711
Point Loma College
San Diego, CA 92106
Pomona College
Claremont, CA 91711
San Francisco Art Institute
San Francisco, CA 94133

San Francisco Conservatory of Music
San Francisco, CA 94122
San Jose Bible College
San Jose, CA 95108
Scripps College
Claremont, CA 91711
Simpson College
San Francisco, CA 94134
Southern California College
Costa Mesa, CA 92626
Southern California Institute of Architecture
Santa Monica, CA 90404
Stanford University
Stanford, CA 94305
St. Mary's College of California
Moraga, CA 94575
St. Patrick's College
Mountain View, CA 94042
Thomas Aquinas College
Santa Paula, CA 93060
United States International University
San Diego, CA 92131
University of Judaism
Los Angeles, CA 90024
University of La Verne
La Verne, CA 91750
University of Redlands
Redlands, CA 92373
University of San Diego
San Diego, CA 92110
University of San Francisco
San Francisco, CA 94117
University of Santa Clara
Santa Clara, CA 95053
University of Southern California
Los Angeles, CA 90007
University of the Pacific
Stockton, CA 95211
University of West Los Angeles
Culver City, CA 90230
West Coast Bible College
Fresno, CA 93710
West Coast University—Evenings
Los Angeles, CA 90020
West Coast University—Orange County—Evenings
Orange, CA 92668
Western Apostolic Bible College
Stockton, CA 95205
Western States College of Engineering
Inglewood, CA 90301
Westmont College
Santa Barbara, CA 93108
Whittier College
Whittier, CA 90608
Woodbury University
Los Angeles, CA 90017
World College West
San Anselmo, CA 94960
Yeshiva University of Los Angeles
Los Angeles, CA 90035

COLORADO

Baptist Bible College of Denver
Broomfield, CO 80020
Belleview College
Westminster, CO 80030
Colorado College
Colorado Springs, CO 80903
Colorado Technical College
Colorado Springs, CO 80907
Colorado Women's College
Denver, CO 80220

Intermountain Bible College
Grand Junction, CO 81501
Loretto Heights College
Denver, CO 80236
Naropa Institute
Boulder, CO 80302
Regis College
Denver, CO 80221
Rockmont College
Denver, CO 80226
University of Denver
Denver, CO 80210
Western Bible College
Morrison, CO 80465

CONNECTICUT

Albertus Magnus College
New Haven, CT 06511
Bridgeport Engineering Institute
Bridgeport, CT 06606
Connecticut College
New London, CT 06320
Fairfield University
Fairfield, CT 06430
Holy Apostles College
Cromwell, CT 06416
Post College
Waterbury, CT 06708
Quinniplac College
Hamden, CT 06518
Sacred Heart University
Bridgeport, CT 06606
St. Alphonsus College
Suffield, CT 06078
St. Basil's College
Stamford, CT 06902
St. Joseph College
West Hartford, CT 06117
Trinity College
Hartford, CT 06106
University of Bridgeport
Bridgeport, CT 06602
University of Hartford
West Hartford, CT 06117
University of New Haven
West Haven, CT 06516
Wesleyan University
Middletown, CT 06457
Yale University
New Haven, CT 06520

DELAWARE

Goldey Beacom College
Wilmington, DE 19808
University of Delaware
Newark, DE 19711
Wesley College
Dover, DE 19901
Wilmington College
New Castle, DE 19720

DISTRICT OF COLUMBIA

Beacon College
Washington, DC 20009
Benjamin Franklin University
Washington, DC 20036
Catholic University of America
Washington, DC 20064
Corcoran School of Art
Washington, DC 20006
Georgetown University
Washington, DC 20057
George Washington University
Washington, DC 20052
Howard University
Washington, DC 20059

Mount Vernon College
Washington, DC 20007
Oblate College
Washington, DC 20017
Southeastern University
Washington, DC 20024
Strayer College
Washington, DC 20005
The American University
Washington, DC 20016
Trinity College
Washington, DC 20017
Washington International College
Washington, DC 20006

FLORIDA

Barry College
Miami Shores, FL 33161
Bethune-Cookman College
Daytona Beach, FL 32015
Biscayne College
Miami, FL 33054
Clearwater Christian College
Clearwater, FL 33519
College of the Palm Beaches
West Palm Beach, FL 33402
Eckerd College
St. Petersburg, FL 33733
Edward Waters College
Jacksonville, FL 32209
Flagler College
St. Augustine, FL 32084
Florida Beacon College
Largo, FL 33541
Florida Institute of Technology
Melbourne, FL 32901
**Florida Institute of Technology—
School of Applied Technology**
Jensen Beach, FL 33457
Florida Memorial College
Miami, FL 33054
Florida Southern College
Lakeland, FL 33802
Fort Lauderdale College
Fort Lauderdale, FL 33301
Jacksonville University
Jacksonville, FL 32211
Jones College
Orlando, FL 32803
Jones College—Jacksonville
Jacksonville, FL 32211
Miami Christian College
Miami, FL 33167
Nova University
Fort Lauderdale, FL 33314
Palm Beach Atlantic College
West Palm Beach, FL 33401
Ringling School of Art
Sarasota, FL 33580
Rollins College
Winter Park, FL 32789
Southeastern College
Lakeland, FL 33801
Stetson University
Deland, FL 32720
St. John Vianney College Seminary
Miami, FL 33165
St. Leo College
St. Leo, FL 33574
**Tampa College Medical Education
Center**
Tampa, FL 33609
Trinity College
Dunedin, FL 33528
University of Central Florida
Orlando, FL 32816

University of Miami
Coral Gables, FL 33124
University of Sarasota
Sarasota, FL 33577
University of Tampa
Tampa, FL 33606
Warner Southern College
Lake Wales, FL 33853
Webber College
Babson Park, FL 33827

GEORGIA

Agnes Scott College
Decatur, GA 30030
Atlanta Christian College
East Point, GA 30344
Atlanta College of Art
Atlanta, GA 30309
Berry College
Mount Berry, GA 30149
Beulah Heights Bible College
Atlanta, GA 30316
Brenau College
Gainesville, GA 30501
Carver Bible Institute and College
Atlanta, GA 30313
Clark College
Atlanta, GA 30314
**Emmanuel College School of
Christian Ministries**
Franklin Springs, GA 30639
Emory University
Atlanta, GA 30322
Georgia College
Milledgeville, GA 31601
La Grange College
La Grange, GA 30240
Mercer University—Atlanta
Atlanta, GA 30341
**Mercer University School of
Pharmacy**
Atlanta, GA 30312
Morehouse College
Atlanta, GA 30314
Morris Brown College
Atlanta, GA 30314
Oglethorpe University
Atlanta, GA 30319
Paine College
Augusta, GA 30910
Piedmont College
Demorest, GA 30535
Shorter College
Rome, GA 30161
Spelman College
Atlanta, GA 30314
Tift College
Forsyth, GA 31029
Toccoa Falls College
Toccoa Falls, GA 30598
Wesleyan College
Macon, GA 31297

HAWAII

Brigham Young University—Hawaii
Laie Oahu, HI 96762
Chaminade University of Honolulu
Honolulu, HI 96816
Hawaii Loa College
Kaneohe, HI 96744
Hawaii Pacific College
Honolulu, HI 96744
International College
Honolulu, HI 96809

IDAHO

College of Idaho
Caldwell, ID 83605
Northwest Nazarene College
Nampa, ID 83651

ILLINOIS

Aero-Space Institute
Chicago, IL 60610
**Antioch—Native American
Educational Services**
Chicago, IL 60640
Augustana College
Rock Island, IL 61201
Aurora College
Aurora, IL 60507
Barat College
Lake Forest, IL 60045
Blackburn College
Carlinville, IL 62626
Bradley University
Peoria, IL 61625
College of St. Francis
Joliet, IL 60435
Columbia College
Chicago, IL 60605
Concordia College
River Fores, IL 60305
De Lourdes College
Des Plaines, IL 60016
DePaul University
Chicago, IL 60604
DeVry Institute of Technology
Chicago, IL 60618
Elmhurst College
Elmhurst, IL 60126
Eureka College
Eureka, IL 61530
George Williams College
Downers Grove, IL 60515
Greenville College
Greenville, IL 62246
Hebrew Theological College
Skokie, IL 60076
Illinois Benedictine College
Lisle, IL 60532
Illinois College
Jacksonville, IL 62650
Illinois Institute of Technology
Chicago, IL 60616
Illinois Wesleyan University
Bloomington, IL 61701
Judson College
Elgin, IL 60120
Kendall College
Evanston, IL 60201
Knox College
Galesburg, IL 61401
Lake Forest College
Lake Forest, IL 60045
Lewis University
Romeoville, IL 60441
Lincoln Christian College
Lincoln, IL 62656
Loyola University of Chicago
Chicago, IL 60611
MacMurray College
Jacksonville, IL 62650
McKendree College
Lebanon, IL 62258
Midwest College of Engineering
Lombard, IL 60148
Millikin University
Decatur, IL 62522
Monmouth College
Monmouth, IL 61462

Moody Bible Institute
Chicago, IL 60610
Morrison Institute of Technology
Morrison, IL 61270
Mundelein College
Chicago, IL 60660
**National American Educational
Service(s)**
Chicago, IL 60640
National College of Chiropractic
Lombard, IL 60148
National College of Education
Evanston, IL 60201
**National College of Education—
Urbana**
Chicago, IL 60601
North Central College
Naperville, IL 60566
North Park College
Chicago, IL 60625
Northwestern University
Evanston, IL 60201
Olivet Nazarene College
Kankakee, IL 60901
**Parks College of Aeronautical
Technology of St. Louis
University**
Cahokia, IL 62206
Principia College
Elsah, IL 62028
Quincy College
Quincy, IL 62301
Rockford College
Rockford, IL 61101
Roosevelt University
Chicago, IL 60605
Rosary College
River Forest, IL 60305
**Rush University—Colleges of Nursing
and Health Sciences**
Chicago, IL 60612
Sangamon State University
Springfield, IL 62708
School of the Art Institute of Chicago
Chicago, IL 60603
Sherwood Music School
Chicago, IL 60605
Shimer College
Waukegan, IL 60085
Spertus College of Judaica
Chicago, IL 60605
St. Xavier College
Chicago, IL 60655
Trinity Christian College
Palos Heights, IL 60463
Trinity College
Deerfield, IL 60015
University of Chicago—The College
Chicago, IL 60637
**University of Health Sciences—
Chicago Medical School**
North Chicago, IL 60062
Vandercook College of Music
Chicago, IL 60616
Wheaton College
Wheaton, IL 60187

INDIANA

Anderson College
Anderson, IN 46011
Bethel College
Mishawaka, IN 46544
Butler University
Indianapolis, IN 46208
Calumet College
Whiting, IN 46394

DePauw University
Greencastle, IN 46135
Earlham College
Richmond, IN 47374
Fort Wayne Bible College
Fort Wayne, IN 46807
Franklin College
Franklin, IN 46131
Goshen College
Goshen, IN 46526
Grace College
Winona Lake, IN 46590
Hanover College
Hanover, IN 47243
Huntington College
Huntington, IN 46750
Indiana Central University
Indianapolis, IN 46227
Indiana Institute of Technology
Fort Wayne, IN 46803
Indiana University—Northwest
Gary, IN 46408
Manchester College
North Manchester, IN 46962
Marian College
Indianapolis, IN 46222
Marion College
Marion, IN 46952
Oakland City College
Oakland City, IN 47660
Rose-Hulman Institute of Technology
Terre Haute, IN 47803
St. Francis College
Fort Wayne, IN 46808
St. Joseph's College
Rensselaer, IN 47978
St. Mary-of-the-Woods College
St. Mary-of-the-Woods, IN 47876
St. Mary's College
Notre Dame, IN 46556
St. Meinrad College
St. Meinrad, IN 47577
Taylor University
Upland, IN 46989
Tri-State University
Angola, IN 46703
University of Evansville
Evansville, IN 47702
University of Notre Dame
Notre Dame, IN 46556
Valparaiso Technical Institute
Valparaiso, IN 46383
Valparaiso University
Valparaiso, IN 46383
Wabash College
Crawfordsville, IN 47933

IOWA

Briar Cliff College
Sioux City, IA 51104
Buena Vista College
Storm Lake, IA 50588
Central College
Pella, IA 50219
Clarke College
Dubuque, IA 52001
Coe College
Cedar Rapids, IA 51402
Cornell College
Mount Vernon, IA 52314
Divine Word College
Epworth, IA 52045
Dordt College
Sioux Center, IA 51250
Drake University
Des Moines, IA 50311

Faith Baptist Bible College
Ankeny, IA 50021

Graceland College
Lamoni, IA 50140

Grand View College
Des Moines, IA 50316

Grinnell College
Grinnell, IA 50112

Iowa Wesleyan College
Mt. Pleasant, IA 52641

Loras College
Dubuque, IA 52001

Luther College
Decorah, IA 52101

Meharishi International University
Fairfield, IA 52556

Marycrest College
Davenport, IA 52804

Morningside College
Sioux City, IA 51106

Mount Mercy College
Cedar Rapids, IA 52402

Mount St. Clare College
Clinton, IA 52732

Northwestern College
Orange City, IA 51041

Open Bible College
Des Moines, IA 50321

Simpson College
Indianola, IA 50125

St. Ambrose College
Davenport, IA 52803

St. Joseph Seminary College
St. Benedict, IA 70457

University of Dubuque
Dubuque, IA 52001

Upper Iowa University
Fayette, IA 52142

Vennard College
University Park, IA 52595

Wartburg College
Waverly, IA 50677

Westmar College
Le Mars, IA 51031

William Penn College
Oskaloosa, IA 52577

KANSAS

Baker University
Baldwin City, KS 66006

Benedictine College
Atchison, KS 66002

Bethany College
Lindsborg, KS 67456

Bethel College
North Newton, KS 67114

Friends Bible College
Haviland, KS 67059

Friends University
Wichita, KS 67213

Kansas City College and Bible School
Overland Park, KS 66204

Kansas Newman College
Wichita, KS 67213

Kansas Weselyan
Salina, KS 67401

Manhattan Christian College
Manhattan, KS 66502

Marymount College of Kansas
Salina, KS 67401

McPherson College
McPherson, KS 67460

Mid-America Nazarene College
Olathe, KS 66061

St. Mary College
Leavenworth, KS 66048

Ottawa University
Ottawa, KS 66067

Southwestern College
Winfield, KS 67156

Sterling College
Sterling, KS 67579

St. Mary of the Plains College
Dodge City, KS 67801

Tabor College
Hillsboro, KS 67063

Washburn University of Topeka
Topeka, KS 66621

KENTUCKY

Ashbury College
Wilmore, KY 40390

Bellarmine College
Louisville, KY 40205

Berea College
Berea, KY 40404

Brescia College
Owensboro, KY 42301

Campbellsville College
Campbellsville, KY 42718

Centre College of Kentucky
Danville, KY 40422

Cumberland College
Williamsburg, KY 40769

Georgetown College
Georgetown, KY 40324

Kentucky Christian College
Grayson, KY 41143

Kentucky Wesleyan College
Owensboro, KY 42301

Lexington Baptist College
Lexington, KY 40502

Louisville School of Art
Louisville, KY 40204

Morehead State University
Morehead, KY 40351

Pikeville College
Pikeville, KY 41501

Seminary of St. Pius X
Erlanger, KY 41018

Simmons University Bible College
Louisville, KY 40210

Spalding College
Louisville, KY 40203

Thomas More College
Fort Mitchell, KY 41017

Transylvania University
Lexington, KY 40508

Union College
Barbourville, KY 40906

LOUISIANA

Baptist Christian College
Shreveport, LA 71108

Centenary College of Louisiana
Shreveport, LA 71104

Dillard College
New Orleans, LA 70122

Louisiana College
Pineville, LA 71360

Loyola University
New Orleans, LA 70118

Our Lady of Holy Cross College
New Orleans, LA 70114

St. Mary's Dominican College
New Orleans, LA 70114

Tulane University
New Orleans, LA 70118

Xavier University of Louisiana
New Orleans, LA 70125

MAINE

Bates College
Lewiston, ME 04240

Bowdoin College
Brunswick, ME 04011

Colby College
Waterville, ME 04901

College of the Atlantic
Bar Harbor, ME 04609

Husson College
Bangor, ME 04401

Nasson College
Springvale, ME 04083

New England Baptist Bible College
Portland, ME 04101

Portland School of Art
Portland, ME 04101

St. Joseph's College
North Windham, ME 04062

Thomas College
Waterville, ME 04901

Unity College
Unity, ME 04988

**University of New England—
St. Francis College**
Biddleford, ME 04005

Westbrook College
Portland, ME 04103

MARYLAND

Baltimore Hebrew College
Baltimore, MD 21215

Capitol Institute of Technology
Kensington, MD 20795

College of Notre Dame of Maryland
Baltimore, MD 21210

Columbia Union College
Takoma Park, MD 20012

Goucher College
Towson, MD 21204

Hood College
Frederick, MD 21701

Johns Hopkins University
Baltimore, MD 21218

Loyola College
Baltimore, MD 21210

Maryland Institute of College of Art
Baltimore, MD 21217

Mount Saint Mary's College
Emmitsburg, MD 21727

Peabody Conservatory of Music
Baltimore, MD 21202

St. John's College
Annapolis, MD 21404

St. Mary's Seminary and College
Baltimore, MD 21210

Washington Bible College
Lanham, MD 20801

Washington College
Chestertown, MD 21620

Western Maryland College
Westminster, MD 21157

MASSACHUSETTS

American International College
Springfield, MA 01109

Amherst College
Amherst, MA 01102

Anna Maria College
Paxton, MA 01612

Assumption College
Worcester, MA 01609

Atlantic Union College
South Lancaster, MA 01561

Babson College
Wellesley, MA 02157
Bentley College
Waltham, MA 02154
Berklee College of Music
Boston, MA 02215
Berkshire Christian College
Lenox, MA 01240
Boston College
Chestnut Hill, MA 02167
Boston Conservatory of Music
Boston, MA 02115
Boston University
Boston, MA 02215
Bradford College
Bradford, MA 01830
Brandeis University
Waltham, MA 02254
Central New England College of Technology
Worcester, MA 01610
Clark University
Worcester, MA 01610
College of Our Lady of the Elms
Chicopee, MA 01013
College of the Holy Cross
Worcester, MA 01610
Curry College
Milton, MA 02186
Eastern Nazarene College
Quincy, MA 02170
Emerson College
Boston, MA 02116
Emmanuel College
Boston, MA 02115
Gordon College
Wenham, MA 01984
Hampshire College
Amherst, MA 01002
Harvard and Radcliffe Colleges
Cambridge, MA 02138
Hebrew College
Brookline, MA 02146
Hellenic College
Brookline, MA 02146
Lesley College
Cambridge, MA 02238
Massachusetts College of Pharmacy and Allied Health Sciences— Hampden
Springfield, MA 01119
Massachusetts Institute of Technology
Cambridge, MA 02139
Merrimack College
North Andover, MA 01845
Mount Holyoke College
South Hadley, MA 01075
New England Conservatory of Music
Boston, MA 02115
Nichols College
Dudley, MA 01570
Northeastern University
Boston, MA 02115
Pine Manor College
Chestnut Hill, MA 02167
Regis College
Weston, MA 02193
School of the Museum of Fine Arts/ Affiliated with Tufts University
Boston, MA 02115
Simmons College
Boston, MA 02115
Simon's Rock Early College of Bard College
Great Barrington, MA 01230

Smith College
Northampton, MA 01063
Springfield College
Springfield, MA 01109
St. Hyacinth College and Seminary
Granby, MA 01033
St. John's Seminary College of Liberal Arts
Brighton, MA 02135
Stonehill College
North Easton, MA 02356
Suffolk University
Boston, MA 02114
Swain School of Design
New Bedford, MA 02740
Tufts University
Medford, MA 02155
Wellesley College
Wellesley, MA 02181
Wentworth Institute of Technology
Boston, MA 02115
Western New England College
Springfield, MA 01119
Wheaton College
Norton, MA 02766
Wheelock College
Boston, MA 02215
Williams College
Williamstown, MA 01267
Worcester Polytechnic Institute
Worcester, MA 01503

MICHIGAN

Adrian College
Adrian, MI 49221
Albion College
Albion, MI 49224
Alma College
Alma, MI 48801
Andrews University
Berrien Springs, MI 49104
Aquinas College
Grand Rapids, MI 49506
Calvin College
Grand Rapids, MI 49506
Center for Creative Studies—College of Art and Design
Detroit, MI 48202
Cleary College
Ypsilanti, MI 48197
Condordia College
Ann Arbor, MI 48105
Detroit College of Business
Dearborn, MI 48126
General Motors Institute
Flint, MI 48502
Grace Bible College
Grand Rapids, MI 49509
Grand Rapids Baptist College
Grand Rapids, MI 49505
Great Lakes Bible College
Lansing, MI 48901
Hillsdale College
Hillsdale, MI 49242
Hope College
Holland, MI 49423
Jordan College
Cedar Springs, MI 49319
Kalamazoo College
Kalamazoo, MI 49007
Kendall School of Design
Grand Rapids, MI 49503
Lawrence Institute of Technology
Southfield, MI 48075
Madonna College
Livonia, MI 48150

Marygrove College
Detroit, MI 48221
Mercy College of Detroit
Detroit, MI 48219
Nazareth College
Nazareth, MI 49074
Northwood Institute
Midland, MI 48640
Olivet College
Olivet, MI 49076
Reformed Bible College
Grand Rapids, MI 49506
Shaw College of Detroit
Detroit, MI 48202
Sacred Heart Seminary
Detroit, MI 48206
Siena Heights College
Adrian, MI 49221
Spring Arbor College
Spring Arbor, MI 49283
St. Mary's College
Orchard Lake, MI 48033
University of Detroit
Detroit, MI 48221
Walsh College of Accountancy and Business Administration
Troy, MI 48084
William Tyndale College
Farmington Hills, MI 48018

MINNESOTA

Augsburg College
Minneapolis, MN 55454
Bethel College
St. Paul, MN 55112
Carleton College
Northfield, MN 55057
College of St. Benedict
St. Joseph, MN 56374
College of St. Catherine
St. Paul, MN 55105
College of St. Scholastica
Duluth, MN 55811
College of St. Teresa
Winona, MN 55897
College of St. Thomas
St. Paul, MN 55105
Condordia College
Moorhead, MN 56560
Concordia College
St. Paul, MN 55104
Dr. Martin Luther College
New Ulm, MN 56073
Gustavus Adolphus College
St. Peter, MN 56082
Hamline University
St. Paul, MN 55104
Macalester College
St. Paul, MN 55105
Minneapolis College of Art and Design
Minneapolis, MN 55404
Minneapolis Bible College
Rochester, MN 55901
North Central Bible College
Minneapolis, MN 55404
Northwestern College
Roseville, MN 55113
Pillsbury Baptist College
Owatonna, MN 55060
St. John's University
Collegeville, MN 56321
St. Mary's College
Winona, MN 55987
St. Olaf College
Northfield, MN 55057

St. Paul Bible College
Bible College, MN 55375

MISSISSIPPI

Belhaven College
Jackson, MS 39202
Blue Mountain College
Blue Mountain, MS 38610
Millsap College
Jackson, MS 39210
Mississippi College
Clinton, MS 39058
Mississippi Industrial College
Holly Springs, MS 38635
Rust College
Holly Springs, MS 38635
Southeastern Baptist College
Laurel, MS 39440
Tougaloo College
Tougaloo, MS 39174
Wesley College
Florence, MS 39073
Whitworth Bible College
Brookhaven, MS 39601
William Carey College
Hattiesburg, MS 39401

MISSOURI

Avila College
Kansas City, MO 64145
Baptist Bible College
Springfield, MO 65803
Calvary Bible College
Kansas City, MO 64147
Cardinal Glennon College
St. Louis, MO 63119
Central Bible College
Springfield, MO 65807
Central Christian College of the Bible
Moberly, MO 65270
Central Methodist College
Fayette, MO 65248
Columbia College
Columbia, MO 65216
Conception Seminary College
Conception, MO 64433
Culver-Stockton College
Canton, MO 63435
Drury College
Springfield, MO 65802
Evangel College
Springfield, MO 65802
Finlay Engineering College
Kansas City, MO 64114
Fontbonne College
St. Louis, MO 63105
Hannibal-Le Grange College
Hannibal, MO 63401
Harris Stowe State College
St. Louis, MO 63103
Kansas City Art Institute
Kansas City, MO 64111
Lincoln University
Jefferson City, MO 65101
Lindenwood Colleges
St. Charles, MO 63301
Maryville College—St. Louis
St. Louis, MO 63141
Missouri Baptist College
St. Louis, MO 63141
Missouri Institute of Technology
Kansas City, MO 64114
Missouri Valley College
Marshall, MO 65340
Ozark Bible College
Joplin, MO 64801

Park College
Kansas City, MO 64152
Rockhurst College
Kansas City, MO 64110
School of the Ozarks
Point Lookout, MO 65726
Southwest Baptist College
Bolivar, MO 65613
Stephens College
Columbia, MO 65215
St. Louis Christian College
Florissant, MO 63033
St. Louis College of Pharmacy
St. Louis, MO 63110
St. Louis Conservatory of Music
St. Louis, MO 63130
St. Louis University
St. Louis, MO 63103
Tarkio College
Tarkio, MO 64491
Washington University
St. Louis, MO 63130
Webster College
St. Louis, MO 63119
Westminster College
Fulton, MO 65251
William Jewell College
Liberty, MO 64068
William Woods College
Fulton, MO 65251

MONTANA

Big Sky Bible College
Lewiston, MT 59457
Carroll College
Helena, MT 59601
College of Great Falls
Great Falls, MT 59405
Rocky Mountain College
Billings, MT 59102

NEBRASKA

Bellevue College
Bellevue, NE 68005
College of St. Mary
Omaha, NE 68124
Concordia Teachers College
Seward, NE 68434
Creighton University
Omaha, NE 68178
Dana College
Blair, NE 68008
Doane College
Crete, NE 68333
Grace College of the Bible
Omaha, NE 68108
Hastings College
Hastings, NE 68901
Midland Lutheran College
Fremont, NE 68025
Nebraska Christian College
Norfolk, NE 68701
Nebraska Wesleyan University
Lincoln, NE 68504
Platte Valley Bible College
Scotts Bluff, NE 69361
Union College
Lincoln, NE 68506

NEVADA

Sierra Nevada College
Incline Valley, NV 89450

NEW HAMPSHIRE

Colby-Sawyer College
New London, NH 03257

Daniel Webster College
Nashua, NH 03063
Dartmouth College
Hanover, NH 03755
Franklin Pierce College
Rindge, NH 03461
Nathaniel Hawthorne College
Antrim, NH 03440
New England College
Henniker, NH 03242
New Hampshire College
Manchester, NH 03104
Notre Dame College
Manchester, NH 03104
River College
Mashua, NH 03060
St. Anselm College
Manchester, NH 03102

NEW JERSEY

Bloomfield College
Bloomfield, NJ 07003
Centenary College
Hackettstown, NJ 07840
College of St. Elizabeth
Convent Station, NJ 07961
Don Bosco College
Newton, NJ 07860
Drew University—College of Liberal Arts
Madison, NJ 07940
Fairleigh Dickinson University—Madison
Madison, NJ 07940
Fairleigh Dickinson University—Rutherford
Rutherford, NJ 07666
Fairleigh Dickinson University—Teaneck
Teaneck, NJ 07666
Felician College
Lodi, NJ 07644
Georgian Court College
Lakewood, NJ 08701
Kean College of New Jersey
Union, NJ 07083
Monmouth College
West Long Branch, NJ 07764
Northeastern Bible College
Essex Fells, NJ 07012
Princeton University
Princeton, NJ 08544
Rabbinical College of America
Morristown, NJ 07960
Ramapo College of New Jersey
Rahway, NJ 07430
Rider College
Lawrenceville, NJ 08648
Seton Hall University
South Orange, NJ 07079
Stevens Institute of Technology
Hoboken, NJ 07030
St. Peter's College
Jersey City, NJ 07306
Thomas A. Edison College
Trenton, NJ 08625
Upsala College
East Orange, NJ 07019
Westminster Choir College
Princeton, NJ 08540

NEW MEXICO

College of Santa Fe
Santa Fe, NM 87501
College of the Southwest
Hobbs, NM 88240

National College of Business—
 Albuquerque
 Albuquerque, NM 87108
St. John's College
 Santa Fe, NM 87501
University of Albuquerque
 Albuquerque, NM 87140

NEW YORK

Adelphi University
 Garden City, NY 11530
Albany College of Pharmacy
 Albany, NY 12208
Alfred University
 Alfred, NY 14802
American University in Cairo
 New York, NY 10017
Bard College
 Annandale-on-Hudson, NY 12504
Barnard College of Columbia
 University
 New York, NY 10027
Boricus College
 New York, NY 10025
Canisius College
 Buffalo, NY 14208
Cathedral College of the Immaculate
 Conception
 Douglaston, NY 11362
Clarkson College
 Potsdam, NY 13676
Colgate University
 Hamilton, NY 13346
College of Human Services
 New York, NY 10016
College of Insurance
 New York, NY 10038
College of Mount St. Vincent
 New York, NY 10471
College of New Rochelle—School of
 Arts and Sciences
 New Rochelle, NY 10801
College of St. Rose
 Albany, NY 12203
Columbia University—Columbia
 College
 New York, NY 10027
Concordia College
 Bronxville, NY 10708
Cooper Union
 New York, NY 10003
Cornell University
 Ithaca, NY 14850
Daemen College
 Amherst, NY 14226
Dominican College of Blauvelt
 Orangeburg, NY 10962
Dowling College
 Oakdale, NY 11769
D'Youville College
 Buffalo, NY 14201
Eisenhower College of Rochester
 Institute of Technology
 Seneca Falls, NY 13148
Elmira College
 Elmira, NY 14901
Fordham University—Lincoln Center
 New York, NY 10023
Fordham University—Rose Hill
 Bronx, NY 10458
Friends World College
 Huntington, NY 11743
Hamilton College
 Clinton, NY 13323
Hartwick College
 Oneonta, NY 13820

Hebrew Union College
 New York, NY 10023
Hobart College
 Geneva, NY 14456
Hofstra University
 Hempstead, NY 11550
Holy Trinity Orthodox Seminary
 Jordanville, NY 13361
Houghton College
 Houghton, NY 14744
Iona College
 New Rochelle, NY 10801
Ithaca College
 Ithaca, NY 14850
Jewish Theological Seminary of
 America
 New York, NY 10027
Julliard School
 New York, NY 10023
Keuka College
 Keuka Park, NY 14478
Le Moyne College
 Syracuse, NY 13224
Long Island University—Brooklyn
 Brooklyn, NY 11201
Long Island University—College of
 Pharmacy/Health Sciences
 Brooklyn, NY 11201
Long Island University—C.W. Post
 College
 Greenvale, NY 11548
Long Island University—
 Southhampton College
 Southhampton, NY 11968
Manhattan College
 Riverdale, NY 10471
Manhattanville College
 Purchase, NY 10577
Mannes College of Music
 New York, NY 10021
Marist College
 Poughkeepsie, NY 12601
Marymount College
 Tarrytown, NY 10591
Marymount Manhattan College
 New York, NY 10021
Medaille College
 Buffalo, NY 14214
Mercy College
 Dobbs Ferry, NY 10522
Molloy College
 Rockville Centre, NY 11570
Mount Saint Mary College
 Newburgh, NY 12550
Nazareth College of Rochester
 Rochester, NY 14610
New School of Social Research
 New York, NY 10011
New York Institute of Technology
 Old Westbury, NY 11568
New York Institute of Technology—
 Metropolitan Center
 New York, NY 10023
New York School of Interior Design
 New York, NY 10022
New York University
 New York, NY 10012
Niagara University
 Niagara University, NY 14109
Nyack College
 Nyack, NY 10960
Pace University
 New York, NY 10038
Pace University—College of White
 Plains
 White Plains, NY 10603

Pace University—Pleasant/Briarcliff
 Pleasantville, NY 10570
Parsons School of Design
 New York, NY 10011
Polytechnic Institute of New York
 Brooklyn, NY 11201
Pratt Institute
 Brooklyn, NY 11205
Rensselaer Polytechnic Institute
 Troy, NY 12181
Roberts Wesleyan College
 Rochester, NY 14624
Rochester Institute of Technology
 Rochester, NY 14623
Russell Sage College
 Troy, NY 12180
Sarah Lawrence College
 Bronxville, NY 10708
School of Visual Arts
 New York, NY 10010
Siena College
 Loudonville, NY 12211
Skidmore College
 Saratoga Springs, NY 12866
St. Bonaventure University
 St. Bonaventure, NY 14778
St. Francis College
 Brooklyn, NY 11201
St. John Fisher College
 Rochester, NY 14618
St. John's University Jamaica/
 Queens/Staten Island
 Jamaica, NY 11439
St. Joseph's College
 Brooklyn, NY 11205
St. Joseph's College—Suffolk
 Patchogue, NY 11772
St. Lawrence University
 Canton, NY 13617
St. Thomas Aquinas College
 Sparkill, NY 10968
Syracuse University
 Syracuse, NY 13210
The King's College
 Briarcliff Manor, NY 10510
Touro College
 New York, NY 10036
University of Rochester
 Rochester, NY 14627
Utica College of Syracuse University
 Utica, NY 13421
Vassar College
 Poughkeepsie, NY 12601
Wadhams Hall Seminary College
 Ogdensburg, NY 13669
Wagner College
 Staten Island, NY 10301
Webb Institute of Naval Architecture
 Glen Cove, NY 11542
Wells College
 Aurora, NY 13026
William Smith College
 Geneva, NY 14456
Yeshiva College—Main Center
 New York, NY 10033

NORTH CAROLINA

Atlantic Christian College
 Wilson, NC 27893
Barber-Scotia College
 Concord, NC 28025
Belmont Abbey College
 Belmont, NC 28012
Bennett College
 Greensboro, NC 27420

Campbell University
Buies Creek, NC 27506

Catawba College
Salisbury, NC 28144

Duke University
Durham, NC 27706

Elon College
Elon College, NC 27244

Gardner-Webb College
Boiling Springs, NC 28017

Greensboro College
Greensboro, NC 27420

Guilford College
Greensboro, NC 27410

High Point College
High Point, NC 27262

Johnson C. Smith University
Charlotte, NC 28216

Lenoir-Rhyne College
Hickory, NC 28601

Livingstone College
Salisbury, NC 28144

Mars Hill College
Mars Hill, NC 28754

Meredith College
Raleigh, NC 27611

Methodist College
Fayetteville, NC 28301

North Carolina Wesleyan College
Rocky Mount, NC 27801

Pfeiffer College
Misenheimer, NC 28109

Piedmont Bible College
Winston-Salem, NC 27101

Queens College
Charlotte, NC 28274

Roanoke Bible College
Elizabeth City, NC 27909

Sacred Heart College
Belmont, NC 28012

Shaw University
Raleigh, NC 27611

St. Andrew's Presbyterian College
Laurinburg, NC 28352

St. Augustine's College
Raleigh, NC 27611

Wake Forest University
Winston-Salem, NC 27109

Warren Wilson College
Swannanoa, NC 28778

Winston-Salem Bible College
Winston-Salem, NC 27102

NORTH DAKOTA

Jamestown College
Jamestown, ND 58401

Mary College
Bismark, ND 58501

Northwest Bible College
Minot, ND 58701

Trinity Bible Institute
Ellendale, ND 58436

OHIO

Allegheny Wesleyan College
Salem, OH 44460

Antioch College—Yellow Springs
Yellow Springs, OH 45387

Ashland College
Ashland, OH 44805

Baldwin-Wallace College
Berea, OH 44017

Bluffton College
Bluffton, OH 45817

Borromeo College of Ohio
Wickliffe, OH 44092

Capital University
Columbus, OH 43209

Case Western Reserve University
Cleveland, OH 44106

Cedarville College
Cedarville, OH 45314

Cincinnati Bible College
Cincinnati, OH 45204

Circleville Bible College
Circleville, OH 43113

Cleveland College of Jewish Studies
Beachwood, OH 44122

Cleveland Institute of Art
Cleveland, OH 44106

Cleveland Institute of Music
Cleveland, OH 44106

College of Mount St. Joseph on the Ohio
Mount St. Joseph, OH 45051

College of Wooster
Wooster, OH 44691

Columbus College of Art and Design
Columbus, OH 43215

Defiance College
Defiance, OH 43512

Denison University
Granville, OH 43023

Dyke College
Cleveland, OH 44114

Edgecliff College
Cincinnati, OH 45206

Findlay College
Findlay, OH 45840

Franklin University
Columbus, OH 43215

God's Bible School and College
Cincinnati, OH 45210

Heidelberg College
Tiffin, OH 44883

Hiram College
Hiram, OH 44234

John Carroll University
University Heights, OH 44118

Kenyon College
Gambler, OH 43022

Lake Erie College
Painesville, OH 44077

Malone College
Canton, OH 44709

Marietta College
Marietta, OH 45750

Mount Union College
Alliance, OH 44601

Mount Vernon Bible College
Mount Vernon, OH 43050

Mount Vernon Nazarene College
Mount Vernon, OH 43050

Muskingum College
New Concord, OH 43762

Notre Dame College
Cleveland, OH 44121

Oberlin College
Oberlin, OH 44074

Ohio Dominican College
Columbus, OH 43219

Ohio Institute of Technology
Columbus, OH 43209

Ohio Northern University
Ada, OH 45810

Ohio Wesleyan University
Delaware, OH 43015

Otterbein College
Westerville, OH 43081

Pontifical College Josephinum
Columbus, OH 43085

Rio Grande College/Community College
Rio Grande, OH 45674

Tiffin University
Tiffin, OH 44883

Union for Experimenting Colleges and University
Cincinnati, OH 45202

University of Dayton
Dayton, OH 45469

University of Steubenville
Steubenville, OH 43952

Urbana College
Urbana, OH 43078

Ursuline College
Pepper Pike, OH 44124

Walsh College
Canton, OH 44720

Wilberforce University
Wilberforce, OH 45384

Wilmington College of Ohio
Wilmington, OH 45177

Wittenberg University
Springfield, OH 45501

Xavier University
Cincinnati, OH 45207

OKLAHOMA

Bartlesville Wesleyan College
Bartlesville, OK 74003

Bethany Nazarene College
Bethany, OK 73008

Cameron University
Lawton, OK 73505

Flaming Rainbow University
Stillwell, OK 74960

Hillsdale Free Will Baptist College
Moore, OK 73153

Langston University
Langston, OK 73050

Midwest Christian College
Oklahoma City, OK 73111

Oklahoma Baptist University
Shawnee, OK 74801

Oklahoma Christian College
Oklahoma City, OK 73111

Oklahoma City University
Oklahoma City, OK 73106

Oklahoma Southwestern College
Oklahoma City, OK 73127

Oral Roberts University
Tulsa, OK 74171

Phillipe University
Enid, OK 73701

University of Tulsa
Tulsa, OK 74104

OREGON

Colegio Cesar Chavez
Mount Angel, OR 97362

Columbia Christian College
Portland, OR 97200

Concordia College
Portland, OR 97211

Eugene Bible College
Eugene, OR 97405

George Fox College
Newberg, OR 97132

Lewis and Clark College
Portland, OR 97219

Linfield College
McMinnville, OR 97128

Marylhurst College for Lifelong Learning
Marylhurst, OR 97036

Mount Angel Seminary
St. Benedict, OR 97373
Multnomah School of the Bible
Portland, OR 97220
Museum Art School
Portland, OR 97205
Northwest Christian College
Eugene, OR 97401
Pacific University
Forest Grove, OR 97116
Reed College
Portland, OR 97202
University of Portland
Portland, OR 97203
Warner Pacific College
Portland, OR 97215
Western Baptist College
Salem, OR 97302
Willamette University
Salem, OR 97301

PENNSYLVANIA

Albright College
Reading, PA 19603
Allegheny College
Meadville, PA 16335
Allentown College of St. Francis De Sales
Center Valley, PA 18034
Alliance College
Cambridge Springs, PA 16403
Alvernia College
Reading, PA 19607
Antioch University—Philadelphia
Philadelphia, PA 19108
Baptist College of Pennsylvania
Clarks Summit, PA 18411
Beaver College
Glenside, PA 19038
Bryn Mawr College
Bryn Mawr, PA 19010
Bucknell University
Lewisburg, PA 17837
Carlow College
Pittsburgh, PA 15213
Carnegie-Mellon University
Pittsburgh, PA 15213
Cedar Crest College
Allentown, PA 18104
Chatham College
Pittsburgh, PA 15232
Chestnut Hill College
Philadelphia, PA 19118
College Misericordia
Dallas, PA 18612
College of the Academy New Church
Bryn Athyn, PA 19009
Combs College of Music
Philadelphia, PA 19119
Curtis Institute of Music
Philadelphia, PA 19103
Delaware Valley College of Science and Agriculture
Doylestown, PA 18901
Dickinson College
Carlisle, PA 17013
Drexel University
Philadelphia, PA 19104
Duquesne University
Pittsburgh, PA 15219
Eastern College
St. Davids, PA 19087
Elizabethtown College
Elizabethtown, PA 17022
Franklin and Marshall College
Lancaster, PA 17604

Gannon University
Erie, PA 16541
Geneva College
Beaver Falls, PA 15010
Gettysburg College
Gettysburg, PA 17325
Gratz College
Philadelphia, PA 19141
Gwynedd-Mercy College
Gwynedd Valley, PA 19437
Hahnemann College of Allied Health Professions
Philadelphia, PA 19102
Haverford College
Haverford, PA 19041
Holy Family College
Philadelphia, PA 19114
Immaculate College
Immaculate, PA 19345
Juniata College
Huntingdon, PA 16652
King's College
Wilkes Barre, PA 18711
Lafayette College
Easton, PA 18042
Lancaster Bible College
Lancaster, PA 17601
La Roche College
Pittsburgh, PA 15237
La Salle College
Philadelphia, PA 19141
Lebanon Valley College
Annville, PA 17003
Lehigh University
Bethlehem, PA 18015
Lincoln University
Lincoln University, PA 19352
Lycoming College
Williamsport, PA 17701
Marywood College
Scranton, PA 18509
Mercyhurst College
Erie, PA 16546
Messiah College
Grantham, PA 17027
Moore College of Art
Philadelphia, PA 19103
Moravian College
Bethlehem, PA 18018
Muhlenberg College
Allentown, PA 18104
Neumann College
Aston, PA 19014
New School of Music
Philadelphia, PA 19103
Philadelphia College of Art
Philadelphia, PA 19102
Philadelphia College of Bible
Langhorne, PA 19047
Philadelphia College of Pharmacy and Science
Philadelphia, PA 19104
Philadelphia College of Textiles and Science
Philadelphia, PA 19144
Point Park College
Pittsburgh, PA 15222
Robert Morris College
Coraopolis, PA 15108
Rosemont College
Rosemont, PA 19010
Seton Hill College
Greensburg, PA 15601
Spring Garden College
Chestnut Hill, PA 19118

St. Francis College
Loretto, PA 15940
St. Joseph's University
Philadelphia, PA 19131
St. Vincent College
Latrobe, PA 15650
Susquehanna University
Selinsgrove, PA 17870
Swarthmore College
Swarthmore, PA 19081
Thiel College
Greenville, PA 16125
Thomas Jefferson University College of Allied Health Sciences
Philadelphia, PA 19107
United Wesleyan College
Allentown, PA 18103
University of Pennsylvania
Philadelphia, PA 19104
University of Pittsburgh
Pittsburgh, PA 15620
University of Pittsburgh—Bradford
Bradford, PA 16701
University of Pittsburgh—Greensburg
Greensburg, PA 15601
University of Pittsburgh—Johnstown
Johnstown, PA 15904
University of Scranton
Scranton, PA 18510
Ursinus College
Collegeville, PA 19426
Valley Forge Christian College
Phoenixville, PA 19460
Villa Maria College
Erie, PA 16505
Villanova University
Villanova, PA 16505
Washington and Jefferson College
Washington, PA 15301
Waynesburg College
Waynesburg, PA 15370
Westminster College
New Wilmington, PA 16142
Widener College
Chester, PA 10913
Wilkes College
Wilkes-Barre, PA 18766
Wilson College
Chambersburg, PA 17201
York College of Pennsylvania
York, PA 17405

RHODE ISLAND

Barrington College
Barrington, RI 02806
Brown University
Providence, RI 02912
Bryant College
Smithfield, RI 02917
Johnson and Wales College
Providence, RI 02903
Newport College—Salve Regina
Newport, RI 02840
Providence College
Providence, RI 02918
Rhode Island School of Design
Providence, RI 02903
Roger Williams College
Bristol, RI 02809
Roger Williams College—Providence
Providence, RI 02809

SOUTH CAROLINA

Allen University
Columbia, SC 29204

Baptist College at Charleston
Charleston, SC 29411

Benedict College
Columbia, SC 29204

Bob Jones University
Greenville, SC 29614

Central Wesleyan College
Central, SC 29630

Claflin College
Orangeburg, SC 29115

Coker College
Hartsville, SC 29550

Columbia Bible College
Columbia, SC 29230

Columbia College
Columbia, SC 29203

Converse College
Spartanburg, SC 29301

Erskine College
Due West, SC 29639

Friendship College
Rock Hill, SC 29730

Furman University
Greenville, SC 29163

Lander College
Greenwood, SC 29646

Limestone College
Gaffney, SC 29340

Morris College
Sumter, SC 29150

Newberry College
Newberry, SC 29108

Presbyterian College
Clinton, SC 29325

Southern Methodist College
Orangeburg, SC 29115

Voorhees College
Denmark, SC 29042

Wofford College
Spartanburg, SC 29301

SOUTH DAKOTA

Augustana College
Sioux Falls, SD 57197

Dakota Wesleyan University
Mitchell, SD 57301

Huron College
Huron, SD 57350

Mount Marty College
Yankton, SD 57078

National College of Business
Rapid City, SD 57709

Sinte Gleska College
Rosebud, SD 57570

Sioux Falls College
Sioux Falls, SD 57101

Yankton College
Yankton, SD 57078

TENNESSEE

American Baptist College
Nashville, TN 37207

Belmont College
Nashville, TN 37203

Bethel College
McKenzie, TN 38201

Bristol College
Bristol, TN 37620

Bryan College
Dayton, TN 37321

Carson-Newman College
Jefferson City, TN 37760

Christian Brothers College
Memphis, TN 38104

Covenant College
Lookout Mountain, TN 37350

David Lipscomb College
Nashville, TN 37203

Fisk University
Nashville, TN 37203

Freed-Hardeman College
Henderson, TN 38340

Free Will Baptist Bible College
Nashville, TN 37205

Johnson Bible College
Knoxville, TN 37920

Lee College
Cleveland, TN 37311

King College
Bristol, TN 37620

Knoxville College
Knoxville, TN 37921

Lambuth College
Jackson, TN 38301

Lane College
Jackson, TN 38301

Le Moyne-Owen College
Memphis, TN 38126

Lincoln Memorial University
Harrogate, TN 37752

Maryville College
Maryville, TN 37801

Memphis Academy of Arts
Memphis, TN 38112

Mid-South Bible College
Memphis, TN 38112

Milligan College
Milligan College, TN 37682

O'More College of Design
Franklin, TN 37604

Southern Missionary College
Collegedale, TN 37315

Southwestern—Memphis
Memphis, TN 38112

Steed College
Johnson City, TN 37601

Tennessee Temple University
Chattanooga, TN 37404

Tennessee Wesleyan College
Athens, TN 37303

Trevecca Nazarene College
Nashville, TN 37210

Tusculum College
Greeneville, TN 37743

Union University
Jackson, TN 38301

University of the South
Sewanee, TN 37375

Vanderbilt University
Nashville, TN 37212

TEXAS

Abilene Christian University
Abilene, TX 79601

Abilene Christian University—Dallas
Garland, TX 75041

American Technological University
Killeen, TX 76541

Arlington Baptist College
Arlington, TX 76012

Austin College
Sherman, TX 75090

Baylor College of Medicine
Houston, TX 77025

Baylor University
Waco, TX 76706

Bishop College
Dallas, TX 75241

Dallas Baptist College
Dallas, TX 75211

Dallas Bible College
Dallas, TX 75228

Dallas Christian College
Dallas, TX 75234

East Texas Baptist College
Marshall, TX 75670

Gulf Coast Bible College
Houston, TX 77008

Hardin-Simmons University
Abilene, TX 79601

Houston Baptist University
Houston, TX 77074

Howard Payne University
Brownwood, TX 76801

Huston-Tillotson College
Austin, TX 78702

Incarnate Word College
San Antonio, TX 78209

Jarvis Christian College
Hawkins, TX 75765

LeTourneau College (Le Tourneau Christian College)
Longview, TX 75602

Lubbock Christian College
Lubbock, TX 79407

McMurry College
Abilene, TX 79697

Our Lady of the Lake—University of San Antonio
San Antonio, TX 78285

Paul Quinn College
Waco, TX 76704

Rice University
Houston, TX 77001

Southern Bible College
Houston, TX 77015

Southern Methodist University
Dallas, TX 75275

Southwestern Adventist College
Keene, TX 76059

Southwestern Assemblies of God College
Waxahachie, TX 75165

Southwestern University
Georgetown, TX 78626

St. Edward's University
Austin, TX 78704

St. Mary's University of San Antonio
San Antonio, TX 78284

Texas Christian University
Fort Worth, TX 76129

Texas College
Tyler, TX 78155

Texas Lutheran College
Sequin, TX 78155

Texas Wesleyan College
Fort Worth, TX 76105

Trinity University
San Antonio, TX 78284

University of Dallas
Irving, TX 75061

University of Mary Hardin—Baylor
Belton, TX 76513

University of St. Thomas
Houston, TX 77006

Wayland Baptist College
Plainview, TX 79072

Wiley College
Marshall, TX 75670

UTAH

Brigham Young University
Provo, UT 84602

Westminster College
Salt Lake City, UT 84105

VERMONT

Bennington College
Bennington, VT 05201
Burlington College
Burlington, VT 05401
College of St. Joseph the Provider
Rutland, VT 05701
Goddard College
Plainfield, VT 05667
Green Mountain College
Poultney, VT 05764
Lyndon State College
Lyndonville, VT 05851
Marlboro College
Marlboro, VT 05344
Middlebury College
Middlebury, VT 05753
Norwick University
Northfield, VT 05663
School for International Training
Battleboro, VT 05301
St. Michael's College
Winooski, VT 05405
Trinity College
Burlington, VT 05401
Vermont College of Norwick University
Montpelier, VT 05602

VIRGINIA

Averett College
Danville, VA 24541
Bluefield College
Bluefield, VA 24605
Bridgewater College
Bridgewater, VA 22812
Eastern Mennonite College
Harrisonburg, VA 22801
Emory and Henry College
Emory, VA 24327
Ferrum College
Ferrum, VA 24088
Hampden-Sydney College
Hampden-Sydney, VA 23943
Hampton Institute
Hampton, VA 23668
Hollins College
Hollins College, VA 24020
Liberty Baptist College
Lynchburg, VA 24506
Longwood College
Farmsville, VA 23901
Lynchburg College
Lynchburg, VA 24501
Mary Baldwin College
Staunton, VA 24401
Marymount College of Virginia
Arlington, VA 22207
Mary Washington College
Fredericksburg, VA 22401
Radford University
Radford, VA 24142
Randolph-Macon College
Ashland, VA 23005
Randolph-Macon Women's College
Lynchburg, VA 24503
Roanoke College
Salem, VA 24153
Shenandoah College and Conservatory of Music
Winchester, VA 22601
St. Paul's College
Lawrenceville, VA 23868
Sweet Briar College
Sweet Briar, VA 24595

University of Richmond
Richmond, VA 23173
Virginia Commonwealth University
Richmond, VA 23284
Virginia Intermont College
Bristol, VA 24201
Virginia Union University
Richmond, VA 23222
Virginia Wesleyan College
Norfolk, VA 23502
Washington and Lee University
Lexington, VA 24450

WASHINGTON

Cornish Institute of Allied Arts
Seattle, WA 98102
Fort Wright College
Spokane, WA 99204
Gonzaga University
Spokane, WA 99258
Lutheran Bible Institute
Issaquah, WA 98027
Northwest College
Kirkland, WA 98033
Pacific Lutheran University
Tacoma, WA 98447
Puget Sound College of the Bible
Edmonds, WA 98020
Seattle Pacific University
Seattle, WA 98119
Seattle University
Seattle, WA 98122
St. Martin's College
Lacey, WA 98503
University of Puget Sound
Tacoma, WA 98416
Walla Walla College
College Place, WA 99324
Whitman College
Walla Walla, WA 99362
Whitworth College
Spokane, WA 99251

WEST VIRGINIA

Alderson Broaddus College
Philippi, WV 26416
Appalachian Bible College
Bradley, WV 25818
Bethany College
Bethany, WV 26032
Davis and Elkins College
Elkins, WV 26241
Salem College
Salem, WV 26426
University of Charleston
Charleston, WV 25304
West Virginia Wesleyan College
Buckhannon, WV 26201
Wheeling College
Wheeling, WV 26003

WISCONSIN

Alverno College
Milwaukee, WI 53215
Beloit College
Beloit, WI 53511
Cardinal Stritch College
Milwaukee, WI 53217
Carroll College
Waukesha, WI 53186
Carthage College
Kenosha, WI 53140
Concordia College
Milwaukee, WI 53208
Edgewood College
Madison, WI 53711

Holy Redeemer College
Waterford, WI 53185
Immanuel Lutheran College
Eau Clair, WI 54701
Lakeland College
Sheboygan, WI 53081
Lawrence University
Appleton, WI 54911
Marian College
Fon Du Lac, WI 54935
Marquette University
Milwaukee, WI 53233
Milton College
Milton, WI 53563
Milwaukee Institute of Art and Design
Milwaukee, WI 53211
Milwaukee School of Engineering
Milwaukee, WI 53201
Mount Mary College
Milwaukee, WI 53222
Mount Senario College
Ladysmith, WI 54848
Northland College
Ashland, WI 54806
Ripon College
Ripon, WI 54971
Silver Lake College
Manitowoc, WI 54220
St. Norbert College
De Pere, WI 54115
Viterbo College
La Crosse, WI 54601
Wisconsin Conservatory of Music
Milwaukee, WI 53202

FRANCE

American College in Paris 75007
Paris, France

ENGLAND

New England College
Arundel, Sussex BN18 ODA, England
Richmond College
London W8 5PN, England
University of Warwick
Coventry CVA 7AL, England

WEST GERMANY

Schiller International University 6900
Heidelberg, West Germany

GREECE

Deree College
Athens, Greece

HONG KONG

Hong Kong Baptist College
Kowloon, Hong Kong

LEBANON

American University of Beirut
Beirut, Lebanon

MEXICO

University of the Americas
Puebla, Mexico

PUERTO RICO

American College of Puerto Rico
Bayamon, PR 00619
Antillian College
Mayaguez, PR 00708

Computer Science

THE AGE OF COMPUTERS

The rise of the computer has been swift and remarkable. Businesses began using large computers as soon as they were made commercially available in the 1950s. Computer use grew rapidly throughout business, industry, and government. By the middle 1970s, these machines affected the lives of all Americans, yet few individuals had actually seen a computer. This changed with the introduction of the microcomputer, the personal computer. All across this country, on farms, in small towns, in large cities, families are buying computers, wishing they could buy one, or wondering if they should. Advertisements have appeared which imply that students will not do well in school without a computer at home. While this is questionable, it is true that a basic knowledge of computers—how they were developed and how they work—is fast becoming a necessity in today's society.

During the last half of the 20th century, history entered a new age, the Information Age. A major shift is being made from a focus on manufacturing to a focus on managing information. It is computers which have made this new age possible. Every year they become smaller, more efficient and able to do more complex tasks. As computers become increasingly woven into our day-to-day lives, it is important to remember that it is people who control computers. Computers are only tools to be used, and although they are very complex tools, they are becoming easier to use even as they become more powerful. Learning about computers, and how to use then, makes it possible to be more comfortable in this world of technology.

HISTORICAL BACKGROUND

The earliest important computing device is the abacus, which has been used for over two thousand years. There are different variations of the abacus, the most common being a series of beads that can be manually positioned along a set of wires. Each wire is given to represent one position in a numerical system of notation, such as ones, tens, hundreds, thousands, etc. The abacus is really a tool to assist the memory. The positions of the beads allow the user to remember steps in calculations. By manipulating the beads on the wires, complicated calculations can be performed. The abacus is still used both in business and in schools in China and Japan.

Pascal. The French philosopher, physicist, and mathematician, Blaise Pascal (1623-1662), designed and built one of the first adding and subtracting machines. One of the first of a series of computer whiz kids, Pascal was only nineteen years old when he designed the *Pascaline* to assist his father, a tax collector. This device, built in 1642, consisted of a complex assortment of gears, rods, and dials. Pascal gave a copy of it to Louis XIV, King of France. The use of Pascal's device, however, was not very widespread. Many clerks

Abacus

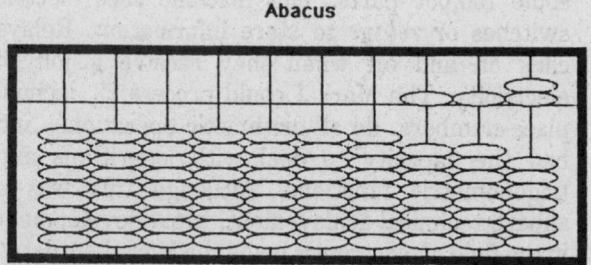

In an abacus, the position of a bead determines a numerical value.

and accountants refused to accept the machine because they feared that it might someday eliminate their own jobs.

The first commercially practical adding machines did not appear until about 1820. By the end of the nineteenth century, a variety of manually operated machines was available for business applications. Building calculating machines capable of solving mathematical problems posed by scientists, engineers, and mathematicians developed more slowly.

Charles Babbage. In 1822 the British mathematician Charles Babbage (1792–1871) built a prototype of his "difference engine." This device was an effort to make a machine capable of solving the repetitive computations required to compile mathematical tables. In 1833 Babbage radically changed his theoretical approach to the problem of constructing a computing machine. As a result, he devised plans for a device he termed the *Analytical Engine*. Although Babbage never completed his machine—he had envisioned an enormous array of cogged cylinders powered by a steam engine—his ideas were precursors of what would follow decades after his death.

Babbage had planned that his Analytical Engine would use punched cards similar to those invented by Joseph Jacquard for use on looms to control the weaving of complex patterns. These punched cards would provide the machine with the data and the instructions needed for operation. The machine would also have a primitive memory amounting to the storing of one thousand numbers of up to fifty digits each.

Lord Byron's daughter, Ada, the Countess of Lovelace, an accomplished mathematician herself, remarked that Babbage's Analytical Engine would weave "algebraical patterns just as the Jacquard loom weaves flowers and leaves." She was impressed by the work of the contemporary mathematician, George Boole, who devised a system of logic called *Boolean algebra*. Boole's work utilized the binary number system, and Ada used this system to write what could be considered the first computer programs—instruction for use with Babbage's theoretical machine.

Herman Hollerith. The next important development came in 1890 with the work of Herman Hollerith (1860–1929) for the United States Census Bureau. It had taken nearly eight years to tabulate the census of 1880. The United States population

punched card - once the most common computer input medium

was growing rapidly, and statisticians realized that the census of 1890 could not be completed before time to send the census takers out again in 1900. Hollerith developed the first electric machines that could "read" census information which had been punched onto cards. Thus the statistical work of the Bureau was more easily and quickly prepared, and the census of 1890 was counted in less than three years. Hollerith's machines were also used for census work in other countries, including Canada and Czarist Russia. In 1896 Hollerith founded the Tabulating Machine Company, which was one of the companies that would become International Business Machine (IBM) in 1924.

In the 1920s and 1930s companies marketed computing machines that handled between 50 and 250 punched cards per minute. This is very slow when compared to today's computers and calculators, but it was an important advance over previous technology. In 1928 the astronomers Wallace J. Eckert in America and John Cromie in England devised punched card machines capable of preparing calculations for astronomical and nautical tables.

Mark I. In 1944 the Harvard Mark I was unveiled. This electromechanical machine was developed by Howard Aiken and his associates and could perform the functions Charles Babbage had planned for his Analytical Engine. The Mark I was eight feet tall and fifty-five feet long and contained some 750,000 parts. This machine used electric switches or *relays* to store information. Relays click on and off when they receive a jolt of electricity. The Mark I could process 23 decimal place numbers, do all arithmetic operations, and had the capacity to deal with logarithms and trigonometric functions. Although this was a superb technical achievement, rapid development in the field of electronics made the Mark I outdated even as it became operational.

ELECTRONIC COMPUTERS

Modern computer history is often measured by generations of the electronic computer. *First generation computers* are based around the vacuum tube, which was used to transmit electricity within the machines. Vacuum tubes were both faster and more reliable than were the relays used in the Mark I. Credit for developing the first electronic computer goes to John Vincent Atanasoff, a physics professor at Iowa State College, and his teaching assistant, Clifford Berry. In 1939 Atanasoff developed a vacuum tube-based computer to carry out computations related to physics problems. Unfortunately, for many years Atanasoff's contributions were not generally recognized. In the early 1970s a court decision acknowledged this contribution to the field of computer science.

The 1940s were a time of rapid growth in many fields as scientists responded to the military needs of World War II. More advanced computers were needed to accurately calculate tables of trajectories for artillery fire. Researchers responded to this challenge.

ENIAC. In 1943 J. Presper Eckert and John W. Maunchly, with their associates at the University of Pennsylvania, planned a machine called an "electrical numerical integrator and calculator," or ENIAC. Finally completed in 1944, this all-electric machine was an advancement that incorporated some 18,000 vacuum tubes, expended 180,000 watts of power, and took up the floor area of a two bedroom house. ENIAC would be able to solve ballistics problems in fifteen seconds that formerly would have taken twenty hours if done by a person with a desk-top manual tabulator. ENIAC was also used to perform calculations for the atomic bomb project at Los Alamos, New Mexico.

A major advance in the field of computer science occured in 1945 when the mathematician John von Neumann proposed the idea of a stored memory capacity. This permitted the computer to store its instructions within itself. Neumann incorporated this concept into his design for the **EDVAC** machine (Electronic Discrete Variable Automatic Computer), which was completed in 1952.

In 1951 Eckert and Maunchly completed work on **UNIVAC** (Universal Automatic Computer), which the United States Census Bureau had ordered in 1945. UNIVAC, and other computers similarly designed, had delay-line memories and performed multiplication by repetitious addition. UNIVAC was the first commercial computer, and businesses found many uses for it. These giant computers received their instructions from stacks of punched cards, and as they became more widespread during the 1950s, the instructions not to "fold, spindle, or multilate" became a joke.

Grace Hopper. Few women are mentioned in the history of computers. A major exception is Grace Murray Hopper (1906–   ). At the beginning of World War II, Hopper was teaching college mathematics. When she joined the Navy to add her considerable skills to the war effort, she could not have imagined that she would not retire until August of 1986 as a Rear Admiral and the Navy's oldest active duty officer. Her contributions to the field of computer science are remarkable. In 1944 she was sent to Harvard to join the team which was working with the Mark I. Following in the tradition of Ada, Countess of Lovelace, her assignment was to program the computer. While working with the Mark I, she was responsible for originating a popular computer expression. One day the computer would not work. After much searching, the team found a dead moth caught in a relay. Hopper taped the moth into her log book and labeled it the first computer bug. From that time computer problems have been referred to as "bugs," and fixing those problems as "debugging."

Grace Hopper developed a compiler code for UNIVAC, which allowed her to write a program in five minutes rather than three weeks. This code was accepted in 1955 and was a major step forward in the programming field. She then directed a team of programmers at Remington Rand and developed the COBOL programming language which is still in use today.

In the late 1950s the standard for computer memories became ferrite cores, and the transistor, which had been developed in 1948, replaced the cumbersome vacuum tube. The transistor has been called the greatest invention of the 20th century. In 1956 John Bardeen, Walter Brattain, and William Shockley were awarded the Nobel Prize in physics for their work in its development. In the late 1950s the transistor made possible *second generation computers*. These transistor-based machines were smaller and more efficient than their predecessors. While the transistor serves to control the flow of electricity as does the vacuum tube, it is an incredible technological advance. Vacuum tubes generated so much heat that they could not be placed too close to one another. Special air-conditioning units were required to cool the giant tube based computers, but tubes frequently burned out and had to be replaced. An electrical storm, with loss of power, struck terror into computer room workers, and special generators were installed for emergencies. Transistors were much smaller than vacuum tubes, were cooler, did not burn out, and could combine several functions, reducing the number of devices needed.

Innovations in the programming of computers were just as important as were the technological advances. The concept of an "assembly language," which translated a computer's binary code into a more easily used set of instructions, came about in the 1950s. Higher-level languages, such as FORTRAN, ALGOL, and COBOL, more closely resembled human language or the logic of mathematics. These computer languages were developed in the late 1950s and early 1960s.

In the 1960s research focused upon building computers with expanded memories and functional capabilities. The two computers that stand out during this period were the "LARC" machine, built by the Sperry-Rand Corporation for the University of California, and "Stretch" built by IBM. Early attempts to photoprint electrical circuitry, thereby making computers smaller and faster, began about 1960.

Integrated circuits, or ICs, were a development of the early 1960s. These devices combined several transistorized components into one. Jack Kilby at Texas Instruments built the first IC in 1958, but it was the growing space program of the 1960s which accelerated their development and use. These circuits were placed onto tiny chips of silicon and soon came to be called chips. The *third generation computers* incorporated these integrated circuits.

1st Generation	2nd Generation	3rd Generation	4th Generation
vacuum tubes	transistors	integrated circuits (IC's)	large-scale integration (LSI)
1,000 calculations per second	10,000 calculations per second	1,000,000 calculations per second	10,000,000 calculations per second
1940s & 50s	early 1960s	late 1960s	1970-

FOUR GENERATIONS OF COMPUTERS

As computers became smaller, faster, and more efficient, their use in the business world was increasing. In 1963 the *Daily Oklahoman/Oklahoma City Times* was the first newspaper to set all classified and editorial text by means of computer. In 1964 American Airlines and IBM created the airlines reservation system called SABRE. The use of computers in science and engineering during the 1960s can best be illustrated by the successful Apollo lunar landing project. Without computers to calculate orbit configurations and rocket specifications, putting men on the moon would probably not have been possible.

Yet another technological advance made possible the development of *fourth generation computers*. In 1969 engineers at Intel Development Corporation in California developed a technique for large scale integration (LSI). This allowed the manufacture of chips which contained hundreds of components on a single chip. The first **microprocessor,** the Intel 4004, was released in 1971. This chip contained everything needed to process basic arithmetic and was used in electronic calculators. Within the next few years, chips were being produced which contained all the necessary circuits for a computer's "brain." These chips dramatically reduced the size of computers, and made possible

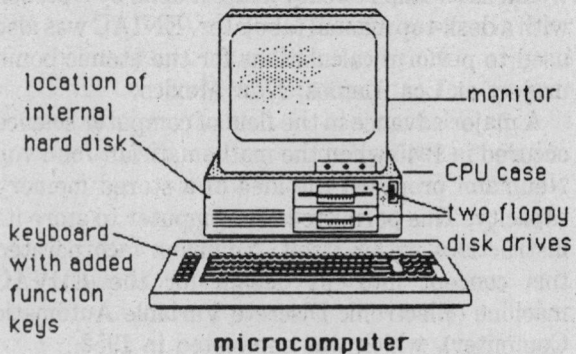

location of internal hard disk

monitor

CPU case

two floppy disk drives

keyboard with added function keys

microcomputer

"personal computers." In addition to development of small computers, the 1970s also witnessed the manufacture of huge, multimillion dollar "supercomputers" used for weather forecasting, oceanographic research, astrophysics, and nuclear engineering.

The 1980s can be called the decade of the personal computer. Companies such as IBM, Apple, Commodore Business Machines, and the Tandy Corporation have produced microcomputers designed for use in the home or small business. The companies that profited from the home video game craze also offered hardware that would convert their video games into modest home computers. In education, "computer literacy" became a growing concern for elementary and secondary schools and watchword in business, science, and government.

HOW A COMPUTER WORKS

The modern computer has two basic components: hardware and software. Hardware refers to the physical equipment of a computer system. It may include a keyboard, disk drives, a video monitor, and a printer. Increasingly it may also include a mouse, a hard or fixed disk drive, or extra floppy disk drives. Hardware items which are used to put information into the computer are called *input devices*. Information coming from the computer is sent to an *output device*. Software refers to the programming instructions that tell the computer how to perform any given task. Software programs now come in brightly colored packages which promise much and sometimes deliver. These are available in computer stores, software specialty stores, by mail order, and frequently in local bookstores and discount stores. Underneath the visible operation of a computer are the remarkable technical achievements which allow hardware and software to come together to accomplish particular goals.

The most important part of a computer is the central processing unit, or CPU. The CPU has two sections. One of these is an arithmetic and logic section that can perform mathematical functions such as addition and multiplication, and logical functions such as comparing two distinct quantities. The CPU also contains a control section that communicates with other parts of the computer system, such as output devices or a data storage disk drive. Although this vital part of the computer is called a *central* processing unit, the actual electrical circuitry that comprises the CPU may not be limited to one location within the computer.

Computers, thanks to semiconducting chips of silicon, can be built with two types of memory. RAM, or random-access memory, is a temporary memory capacity that can be altered by the CPU upon command of the user. RAM can be thought of as a kind of "scratch pad" upon which the user may write, erase, and write again.

ROM, or read-only memory, is the computer's permanent memory. The user, through the CPU, can read the ROM, but cannot alter it. Programs that are frequently used can be entered into a computer's memory during the manufacturing process. Many personal computers are sold with a common language, such as BASIC, already a part of the computer's ROM.

When a computer is turned on, the CPU will automatically read the instructions for it in the "boot ROM," which contains the initial directions a computer needs in order to function. These instructions will direct the CPU to the operating system which has been entered into a section of RAM so that the computer can follow it.

But how does a computer process data? The computer must translate all data into a binary code that can be represented as a series of O's and 1's. A bit (either 0 or 1) is the smallest instruction which can be given to a computer. Each group of eight bits is call a **byte**. Within the computer a continuous translation procedure occurs that changes input data into the machine's binary code, and after the data has been processed, back into a form the user can readily understand.

5 1/4 inch floppy disk (diskette)

hub of disk surrounds the hole in center of disk jacket

disk label goes here

write-protect notch (when this is covered, information can not be placed on the disk)

tough plastic jacket protects disk inside

magnetic media--touching this can cause data to be lost from disk

hard plastic cover

label

metal door slides back inside drive

3 1/2 inch floppy disk

Computer programs are usually stored on *floppy disks* or *diskettes*. Inside their protective cover, disks look like 45 rpm records made of recording tape. Information is stored on them magnetically, just as it is on tape. Indeed early personal computers used tape to store programs, as did larger computers. Disks are more efficient and less likely to fail than tapes. Disks for personal computers come in two sizes, 5¼ inches and 3½ inches. The newer small disks come in a hard plastic cover and can store much more information than the larger 5¼ inch ones. Computer owners have the option of buying a *hard* or *fixed disk*. This storage device can hold hundreds of programs. Hard disks may only be removed by a technician and are often built into the machine, though they can be added as an external device. Heavy computer users as well as businesses benefit from the use of a hard disk.

When a computer user *loads* a program into the CPU, the original program remains on the disk. Only a copy of the program is placed in the temporary memory (RAM) of the computer. Newer programs occupy so much memory that only a portion of their instructions may be copied in at once. The computer must go back to the disk from time to time as a program is being used. Newer computers with increased amounts of RAM are able to load more instructions at one time.

The keyboard is still the most common device a user has with which to enter data. When keys are hit, a keyboard processor within the computer interprets the sequence and location of the keys and translates into machine language. When the translation is completed and the desired task performed, processed data is sent to an output device, such as a video monitor or a printer. The user may then proceed either to continue data input or to make a transfer of the data to tape or disk for storage.

COMPUTER PROGRAMS

Computers need instructions in order to operate. The central processing unit of a computer understands instructions only if translated into a machine "language" it can read. For this reason different computer languages have been developed to perform the translation process. Still other computer languages have been developed for specific functional tasks.

The native language of a computer is *binary code*. Our number system is decimal, or base 10. It has ten digits, zero through nine, and has a ones'

place, a tens' place, hundreds' place, etc. The binary number system, or base two, has only two digits, 0 and 1. All numbers are written by using combinations of these two digits. Binary has a ones' place, a twos' place, fours' place, eights' place, etc. Each place has the value of the last place multiplied by two. A place is either empty or full, either 0 or 1. As an example, the decimal number 22 would be written as 10110 in binary.

Boolean algebra is a system of logic which conceives of all bits of information as either true or false. By combining the concept of Boolean algebra with the binary number system, computers can be given series of instructions in which each **bit** (**binary digit**) is either false or true, 0 or 1. Electricity flows along a path in the computer, meeting thousands of switches. Electronic switches are either set (closed) or unset (open). A bit with the value 0 unsets a switch, leaving it open. A bit with the value 1 sets a switch, closing it. Each switch can be thought of as a decision point at which electricity is forced to choose the only open path. Originally all instructions were given to a computer as strings of binary numbers. This changed with the development of computer languages.

Languages for computers are divided into two classes: low and high. A computer language which closely resembles a human language is considered a high-level language. Low-level languages are more similar in form to the machine's binary code.

Assembly language is a step higher than binary code. It lets programmers use *mnemonics* when they are writing instructions for the computer. A mnemonic is an aid to memory. For example, the mnemonic which tells the CPU to load data into a particular memory location is LD, followed by the location. The mnemonic LDA means to load data into the *accumulator*, which is located at a specific place in the computer's memory. The CPU interprets the direction LDA using a translation program called an *assembler*. The direction is translated into binary code and the CPU carries it out.

Example: LDA $C8
       STA $400   This assembly language
       LDA $C9   program will print
       STA $401   the word HI on the
                    monitor screen.

ST stands for store, and the $ symbol means that the code the programmer is using represents numbers in *hexadecimal* code (base 16), rather than binary. Hexadecimal numbers are often used by programmers, as they are easier to work with than binary numbers.

The development of high-level languages made computer programming much easier. Such languages use instructions which are very close to English, for example: LOAD or PRINT. In addition, high-level languages combine several machine code instructions into one.

Example: PRINT "HI"   This line of BASIC produces the same result as the series of assembly language commands above.

The first high-level language to become widely used was **FORTRAN**. FORTRAN (for **For**mula **tran**slation) is a language geared for mathematical applications. It was written by John Backus of IBM in 1954. FORTRAN was the first computer language learned by many of today's programmers, but use of the language has been decreasing as it is replaced by more recently developed ones.

BASIC (**B**eginner's **A**ll-purpose **S**ymbolic **I**nstruction **C**ode) is a language developed by John G. Kennedy and Thomas E. Kurtz of Dartmouth College. It was especially designed for students, particularly for those working in areas other than mathematics. BASIC has been a very popular computer language for beginners, and a version of it is provided with most personal computers. Despite its popularity, BASIC has been criticized as a language that encouraged sloppy programming, and many college computer science departments have stopped teaching it. Students are being encouraged to use more structured programming languages such as Pascal. Proponents of BASIC have responded to this criticism by writing new versions of the language.

Pascal was developed in 1968 by the Swiss computer scientist Niklaus Wirth and revised in 1972. The language is named in honor of Blaise Pascal, inventor of the Pascaline. Pascal has become a very popular programming language, as it is relatively simple to learn, but powerful. The structure of the language encourages its users to write clear programs which can be understood by other programmers. The high school advanced placement examination in computer science requires a knowledge of Pascal.

Another popular programming language is **Logo.** This language was developed at the Massachusetts Institute of Technology in the 1960s by Seymour Papert and his co-workers. Logo is usually associated with "turtle graphics" and is often used in elementary schools as a first programming language. Logo is especially suited to introducing the concepts of geometry. Drawing with Logo is done by moving a small triangle, called a turtle, about the screen. Logo is a complete programming language and may be taught on an advanced level.

The language **Ada** was developed by the U.S. Department of Defense for specialized applications. Professional programmers often use **C**, a very fast and powerful programming language which is related to Pascal. The growing field of Artificial Intelligence research uses such languages as **LISP** (List Processing) and **Prolog.** Computer languages vary widely in their approaches, and programs in recently developed languages look quite different from earlier ones.

Example: main 0   This is
{   the tradi-
    printf("Hello, world\n");   t i o n a l
}   first pro-
                                   g r a m

written in the C language. It causes *Hello, world* to appear on t h e screen.

The development of high-level programming languages has extended programming to those who are not mathematicians. While it is no longer necessary to use higher level mathematics in programming, it is important that a potential programmer be a good logical thinker. Computer programming is often taught at a beginning level in elementary and secondary schools to help develop thinking skills.

THE PERSONAL COMPUTER

Personal computers, also known as microcomputers, are quickly invading the home and affecting our traditional way of life. The individual who was only vaguely aware of computers is now presented with television computer ads during popular sports events and computer disks for sale at local discount stores. Used for everything from playing video games to tax preparation and word processing, the personal computer has yet to realize its full potential as a household information processor. Many analysts expect that soon the microcomputer will be a major factor in the way the American family shops, banks, communicates long-distance, and gains access to news and reference information.

The history of the personal computer has been one of "whiz kids," rapidly made fortunes, and, unfortunately, rapidly lost fortunes. A good beginning point is the story of Bill Gates and Paul Allen. These two young computer geniuses were working in the computer field while still in high school in Seattle, Washington. In December of

1974, Gates was a freshman at Harvard and Allen was working for Honeywell in Boston. This was the month that a soon-to-become legendary issue of *Popular Electronics* hit the newstands. It featured a cover story on the Altair computer, a personal computer kit which sold for $397. Allen and Gates realized that there were no programming languages or software available for purchasers of the Altair. Buyers had to write their own programs in machine code. The two young men called Ed Roberts, of MITS in Albuquerque, who was making the Altair, and offered him a version of BASIC for the computer. He told them he would be glad to buy it when he saw it actually running on the Altair. For the next six weeks, Gates and Allen frantically wrote day and night, using a mainframe which had been programmed to imitate the operation of the Altair's microprocessor. The BASIC was finished hours before Allen (at nineteen, the older of the two) caught a plane to Albuquerque where he successfully demonstrated the results of those hours of programming. This sale represented the beginning of the giant Microsoft Corporation, of which Bill Gates is now chairman of the board. At peaks in the stock market, Gates' Microsoft stock has made him a billionaire.

In California, another pair of computer enthusiasts, Steve Wozniak and Steven Jobs, were also creating a legend. The area around Cupertino, California, has been called the Silicon Valley because of the number of computer related businesses which have located there. It was natural that boys in this area would become interested in electronics and fortunate that these two boys developed this particular interest. Both had been interested in the computer field for years before they met in the early 1970s. Wozniak, known as "Woz," was five years older than Jobs. He had dropped out of college and was working for a small computer company when they were introduced. Eventually Jobs went to work for Atari, and Wozniak for Hewlett-Packard. In his spare time, Woz attended meetings of the Homebrew Computer Club, whose meetings in a garage drew many serious computer pioneers. In July of 1976 Woz designed a computer around the new 6502 microprocessor chip and demonstrated this computer, the Apple I, at a meeting of the Homebrew Computer Club. Working with 30 days credit, Jobs and Wozniak built and delivered 50 Apple I's. In the fall of the year Woz developed the Apple II, and the infant company was on its way. Steven Jobs was twenty-two, had long hair, and was often seen in jeans and bare feet. Today Jobs has left Apple to form another company, and Wozniak still maintains connections to the company. Both are multi-millionaires.

The giant IBM company initially saw no reason to enter the personal computer field. Their IBM PC was finally announced in August of 1981, and

Apple's Macintosh microcomputer

two floppy disk drives

IBM-PC case containing CPU

IBM predicted that total sales for the computer might reach 100,000 units. They underestimated. The reputation which the company had gained in the field of large computers followed it into this new area, and many businesses found themselves buying computers which they had previously thought of as "home computers." IBM became the industry leader in sales.

The late 1980s saw dramatic changes in personal computers. IBM introduced a new series of computers in the spring of 1987. This line completely replaced the traditional IBM, which had been imitated successfully by makers of IBM "clones." Many new IBM features reflected developments first seen in Apple's popular Macintosh line of computers. These included use of a mouse, small 3½ inch disks, and software which used "windows" and "pull-down menus." Apple in turn introduced their powerful Macintosh II, which some industry analysts saw as true competition for IBM. The amount of memory supplied with personal computers multiplied by leaps and bounds, and it was not uncommon for a computer to come with 512K or even a megabyte of memory built in. Large amounts of memory were needed for new graphics and sound capabilities. Laser printers gave the personal computer user the capability of publishing work on their own system. **Desktop publishing** became a common expression.

Today there is a wide variety of personal computers on the market. The person who wishes to buy a personal computer faces many choices. Which computer system and manufacturer is the best? Why does one system cost so much more than another? Whether to buy a dot-matrix, daisy wheel, or laser printer; whether a mouse, joystick, or modem is an essential; there are questions which must be answered. Unfortunately, there are no simple answers, and the solutions are as different as individuals.

Before purchasing a computer system, it is wise to consider who will be using the computer and what some of the uses will be. The world of computers is changing so rapidly that a buyer cannot forecast all potential uses. Often machines which have been bought for a teenager to practice computer programming are used for word processing, balancing the family budget, and even for managing a small business. A factor to consider is if the computer is easily expanded to allow for changing needs. New computer owners are sometimes dismayed when their purchase seems outdated by the latest breakthrough. They should remember that a good, expandable computer will give them good service for years, no matter what new products come on the market.

It may be possible to find a computer retailer who is willing to let customers try out programs and equipment before purchasing the expensive hardware. For example, some keyboards may not be responsive enough for speed typing, others may be too sensitive. Some software may be too complicated for the beginner to use. One way to be sure to get the hardware and software you can use is to try it out at the store.

The computer beginner should be especially careful with small order companies. There are many excellent ones, and the history of the personal computer begins with a mail-order computer, the Altair. There is one particular problem, however, with mail orders in the computer industry. The computer industry has a word, *vaporware*, for products that are announced but are not actually available. Advertisements may offer these products for sale for months, yet the product is either still under development or has proved unworkable. It is important to know whether the product being ordered actually exists.

The potential buyer should do research before making a decision. Computers are changing so rapidly that books quickly become outdated, but there are dozens of computer magazines on the market. Many of these magazines are specific to one brand of computer, some are general, and a few are aimed at families or businesses which are beginning in computing. These may be purchased or found at local libraries, and the information they contain should assist in the selection of a new computer.

WHAT IS WORD PROCESSING?

People have been processing words for thousands of years, but the term word processor has emerged in connection with the use of computers. The earliest word processors were *dedicated* computers, ones which could only be used for word processing. These word processors quickly spread through offices as their advantages became apparent. Mistakes could be easily corrected while the typed words showed on a screen. There was no need to print the completed copy until the material was edited. Another option was to print out a copy, note corrections and changes, and then enter those changes into the word processor and print the final copy. There was never a need to retype the material. These machines have saved thousands of hours of secretarial time. Writers discovered that the quality of their writing actually improved as they used a word processor. The easy use of the machine encouraged rewriting, which in turn produced a superior finished product.

In the home, word processing might be used to produce personal correspondence, school term papers, and diary entries. In business the word processor is used to produce "personalized" advertising, form letters, memoranda, project proposals, reports, and customer correspondence. The word processor also has the ability to store on disk anything it has created. All documents created can be filed, retrieved, printed again, or revised without being retyped.

Any personal computer can now be used as a word processor. Some companies provide word processing software with new computers, but most personal computer owners must purchase this software separately. Software developers produce a variety of word processing packages for personal computers. There are programs available for all brands, but the greatest variety is offered for the most popular ones. The computer owner is faced with choosing the program which will best meet his or her needs. The newest word processing programs often include spelling checkers, and some computers can use programs which allow

pictures or graphs to be included in the document. Word processing software gives the writer control of margins, permits word, line, and paragraph deletions or insertions; and some software will automatically construct footnotes or bibliographic citations. With such flexibility it is easy to understand why most newspapers and book publishers, as well as professional writers, have incorporated the word processor into their business procedures.

DESKTOP PUBLISHING

Desktop publishing refers to the use of microcomputers and printers to produce a variety of printed materials. While some privately published books have been created this way, it is more common to find newsletters, flyers, brochures, and business presentations emerging from the desktop. Personal computers have been used to produce greeting cards, banners, awards, and letterheads. New computer programs make it possible to create a professional looking newsletter while working on a computer at the kitchen table. This potential has given rise to many new home-based businesses. Laser printers are often used in desktop publishing. These machines can produce type with quality that is very close to that of printing presses. Laser printers are very expensive, though some newer models are dropping dramatically in price. Work done in the home or small business can often be printed on less expensive dot-matrix printers with excellent results, or taken on a disk to a quick printing shop which provides laser prints. Even traditional cut-and-space methods, when used on computer-

This is a sample of laser printer output.

This is a sample of laser printer output.

produced test and graphics, can result in a quality finished product.

New, more powerful computers, linked with better printers and devices such as scanners, open the door to even wider use of desktop publishing. It is possible to purchase a small scanner which will make a computer graphic from a photograph. Any picture can then be incorporated into a computer-generated text. There are a growing number of books available on this subject, and several magazines designed to assist the desktop publisher have come onto the market.

COMPUTER CAREERS

The computer industry is no longer an infant, and as it has grown up, it has lost some of its flexibility. As an industry matures, job definitions become distinct and job requirements more defined. This is particularly true as computer exposure becomes so widespread. Originally there was one person in a business or a school who was fascinated by a new computer system. This person soon became the local expert, and carved out a new job which was often called computer consultant or manager. Today people are entering the job market with computer experience acquired in school. In addition, computers have become so common in business and industry that there are few workers who have no computer familiarity. No longer is it true that there is one computer "guru" in an office to whom everyone must come with their computer related questions. The increased use of computers and the new functions which they are performing require a new variety of job descriptions and job opportunities. These jobs will continue to increase, but because there are many individuals getting computer training, the job market has become more competitive.

Many jobs require some computer expertise, but there are particular jobs which are more directly related to computers. There are three major divisions among computer careers. The first is **systems analysis.** People who work in this area are called systems analysts, and they design or improve the computer systems which a company uses. They also evaluate both current systems and new components to see how these might fit into the overall computer needs of the company. When a company plans to purchase a computer system, they first consult a systems analyst. A very large company will have systems analysts on their staff, but most companies will hire an outside consulting firm. Some of these firms only exist as computer consultants, but some companies, such as accounting firms, have added divisions which provide these services. Outside consultants come to a company and survey the people who will be using computer services to discover their specific needs.

After preparing a detailed description of the jobs which a computer system must do, they then examine currently available alternatives and recommend the selection of a system. Systems analysts usually have at least an undergraduate college degree and have often been computer programmers.

The second division is **computer programming.** Programmers write the instructions which allow computers to carry out functions needed by those who will use the completed program. Some programmers work for large software development companies. Generally, teams of programmers work together for months or even years to produce a piece of commercial software. These companies produce software which can be used by a wide range of individuals to do related jobs. For example, a company might produce a new word processing program which is particularly easy to use and contains many desirable up-to-date features. This program might be purchased and used by people in many different job categories, and could be used both at work and at home. Other programmers might write a new adventure game for home or school use. A major concern of software developers is that there is little awareness of the hundreds or thousands of hours necessary to produce these modern programs. As a result, programs may be copied illegally with very little thought.

Most working programmers are not employed by software developers. These programmers may work directly for the company which will use their work. Large companies have needs which are so specific that generic software will not be best for them. They hire programmers to design programs to meet those specific needs. Programmers review system requirements and then prepare the necessary programs. A large company will have many levels of programming jobs, ranging from an entry level trainee to a programming division manager. An undergraduate college degree in computer science, accounting, or math is almost always required for someone entering this field.

The third major division of computer careers is **computer operations.** Workers in this field physically operate the computer, entering data which must be processed and retrieving the results of the processed information. The lowest paying computer occupation is the data entry clerk, who may be required to enter information so rapidly that there is little awareness of the meaning of the data. Good data entry or keypunch clerks are in demand, but the work is very repetitive and opportunities for advancement are few. The importance of this job becomes apparent when we consider how data entry affects our lives. It is through data entry that deposits are entered into checking or savings accounts, social security contributions are credited, high school or college grades recorded, military records updated, and bill payments posted. In this computer age, it should be remembered that it is not the computer who makes mistakes, but the human who put information into the machine. Occasionally it is not the data entry clerk, but a flaw in the program being used that causes problems. Remember that the program was written by a person, and any point in a computer system requiring human input offers an opportunity for a human mistake.

More highly trained data processing professionals, often with an associate degree from a technical school or junior college or even with a college degree, have jobs which offer more responsibilities. A data base manager, for example, would decide under which categories to store information and would supervise those who enter the data. This job would require someone who could create data base files and be able to give instructions for easy retrieval of information. As in many other computer jobs, a data base manager must be able to encounter a totally new problem and solve it.

There are computer careers for technical writers, in computer sales, and in the growing field of robotics. A demand exists for computer service technicians and for computer trainers who can effectively teach others to work with computer systems. The use of computers has dramatically changed some traditional job descriptions. Librarians are changing into information managers, and their training now includes extensive computer work. The modern librarian may be expected to know how to get information electronically from a variety of on-line data bases. Musicians are using computers to create sounds which the human ear has never heard. All the instruments of the orchestra may now be generated artificially. A composer can sit down at a keyboard and create whatever music he can imagine. Industrial engineers can model their creations on a computer screen and evaluate performance. Reporters now enter their stories into computers, and may submit stories to their newspaper over telephone lines, with the use of a modem. The potential for future job opportunities is great and only limited by human imagination.

FUTURE POSSIBILITIES

If the next twenty years bring as many innovations in computer science and technology as have the last twenty years, it is very difficult indeed to foretell the extent to which computers will change our lives. However some general observation based on current research into new computer technology and applications can give us a glimpse of what the future might bring.

In the factory, computers will control robots designed to do the repetitive tasks of assembly line manufacturing. Already there exist automobile assembly lines in Japan, the United States, and Europe that rely almost exclusively upon the work of robots and the computers that control them. There are real problems to deal with in the areas of retraining workers and in finding appropriate job slots in our economy for those whose jobs have been lost to computer technology.

Computers will undoubtedly play an increased role in the advancement of medical science and health care services. Research into "bionics" offers the possibility of replacing diseased or damaged body parts with computer controlled limbs or organs. One application already in operation is a computer accessed data bank of symptoms, which doctors throughout the country can use to help them diagnose disease and illness. Experimenters are using computer technology to send impulses to paralyzed nerves, and in the future this may allow patients in wheelchairs to walk again. Other experimenters are training handicapped individuals to work with robots and with voice-activated computer systems. Computer technology may allow handicapped individuals to regain lost abilities.

Computers will also change our lifestyle. Some futurists foresee the time when almost all an American family's shopping, banking, communications, and access to information services will be by means of a home computer system. Sooner to come will be the wider use of magnetized plastic cards that will automatically debit the customer's bank account when presented at a grocery checkout, gasoline station, or department store. Such a situation would indeed take America closer to becoming a "cashless" society. In a scenario writer Alvin Toffler termed an "electronic cottage," more and more people will have jobs at home working at a computer, rather than in an office.

Technologically, computers will incorporate synthesized voices and be able to add complex speech patterns in a variety of languages to the output capacities now available. Computers will

also be able to recognize human language commands, thus being able to "listen" to the user, rather than being limited to a keyboard or keypad for data and command input. The technology for these capabilities exists today. Further research and testing will make them commonplace in the future. Computers may eventually be able to project three-dimensional holograph images. Such a capacity might be used in communications, theater, and art.

Perhaps the most interesting aspect of computer research is in the field of artificial intelligence. Several computer programming languages are particularly suited to this field, most notably LISP and Prolog. A number of computer scientists, Pulitzer Prize winner Douglas R. Hofstadter among them, are searching for computer programming that would create a "machine consciousness." Hofstadter believes this can be achieved only when a computer has an awareness of itself and of the method of its own problem-solving routines.

With whatever the future brings, fear of computers is unjustified. Rather, one should fear being ignorant of computers and their potential. This century has brought many changes, most of which were initially feared. As changes are incorporated into our lives, we adjust to them and find ways to effectively use them. Computers are merely the latest of these developments.

Computer Glossary

A COMPUTER GLOSSARY

ADA—A high-level language developed by the U.S. Department of Defense. The language is named for Ada, Countess of Lovelace, by tradition history's first computer programmer.

abacus—the first real calculating tool; consists of ten wires with beads inside a frame.

acoustic coupler—a device that permits the transmitting of data to or from a computer by way of telephone lines. A modem is an example of such a device.

Adding and Listing Machine—a popular ad-

ding and subtracting machine invented by Burroughs in 1886.

address—also called memory address; a number that refers to a specific memory location within a computer—that is, a location at which a unit of data can be stored. Addresses are given in the *hexadecimal* (base 16) number system.

adventure games—interactive computer games, the first of which, *Adventure,* was developed on a mainframe at Stanford and is still on most college mainframes in the United States.

algorithm—a sequence of steps for solving a problem

ALGOL—Algorithmic Oriented Language, a computer language developed in the 1960s which is more popular in Europe than in the United States.

American National Standards Institute Standard (ANSI standard)—the standard version of the BASIC programing language.

Analytical Engine—a gear-driven machine designed by Charles Babbage to add, subtract, multiply, and divide large numbers.

application software—software that tells hardware how to perform special tasks such as word processing or data processing.

architecture—the arrangement of circuits in computers.

argument—in a BASIC function, the term inside the parentheses.

artificial intelligence—the area of computer science which attempts to develop computers which can operate more like the human mind. Often abbreviated as AI.

ASCII—(pronounced "askey")—the American Standard Code for Information Interchange assigns numbers from 0 to 127 to a wide variety of symbols, including the twenty-six uppercase letters of the alphabet, the twenty-six lowercase letters, the ten numerals, and punctuation symbols such as the period, comma, and exclamation point.

assembler—a program that translates an instruction given in assembly language into machine language.

assembly language—a symbolic computer language in which each instruction, or *mnemonic*, represents a single machine language instruction, or *op-code*. Before it may be executed by a computer, an assembly language must first be translated into machine language by an assembler.

authoring language—a user language to design computer-based programs, often used to produce educational programs. An authoring language allows a user with no technical computer programming skills to produce software.

backup—an extra copy of computer information or instructions.

bar-code reader—an input device that enters the Universal Product Codes of supermarket purchases into the computer.

BASIC—Beginners All-purpose Symbolic Instruction Code; a computer language derived from and interactive with FORTRAN. Developed by John Kemeny and Thomas Furtz in the mid-1960s, it is called an instruction code because the programmer is writing instructions for the computer.

baud rate—the rate at which data may be transmitted over telephone lines, expressed in bits per second.

binary—also know as base 2, this is a number system which uses only the digits 0 and 1. Place values are multiples of 2, and each place is either full (1) or empty (0).

bit—short for binary digit. The smallest unit of information that can be stored in a computer, one bit is a 1 or 0 representing a set or unset switch in machine code.

Boolean algebra—mathematical system of logic, proposed in 1847 by the English mathematician George Boole, in which logical concepts "true" and "false" are made equal to the numbers 1 and 0.

booting—loading the disk operating system (DOS) into the computer.

branch—a decision point; one way that steps in a program can be written.

bug—a programming error, or an error caused by hardware malfunction.

bulletin board—See *electronic bulletin board*.

bus—a data path or communication channel within a computer utilizing a special set of circuit wires to pass data from one part to another.

byte—a group of eight bits. A byte may represent a single letter, number, or symbol.

C—a very fast high level computer language which resembles Pascal in structure.

CAD-CAM—computer-aided design and computer-aided manufacturing—software or dedicated computers that allow the design and manufacture of products.

CD ROM—mass storage device which utilizes a compact disc. (When discussing CD ROM, "disc" rather than "disk" is used.) An entire encyclopedia can be stored on one disc. CD ROM readers are attached to computers, and special software allows the users to look at information from the disc. Lasers are used to put the information on the disc. Currently computer users cannot use this technology to store their own information; they may only use commercially made discs.

cell—the location in a spreadsheet where a row and a column intersect.

Central Processing Unit (CPU)—the part of a computer where program instructions are processed and their execution coordinated. On a microcomputer, the CPU consists of a microcomputer plus several related circuits.

chip—a silicon wafer on which has been placed, through photoetching processes, an integrated circuit.

clone—a computer which has been designed to be compatible with another computer. For example, a good clone of an IBM PC might be able to use as much as 95% of the software written for the IBM machine.

COBOL—Common Business Oriented Language, a high-level computer language geared for business applications.

column—a vertical line of space in a computer's screen display, also a vertical line of space in a spreadsheet.

command—a direct order to a computer. It usually refers to instructions that are typed directly on the keyboard of the computer and executed immediately.

compiler—a program that changes high-level language into the computer's binary machine language before the programmer's work is stored and executed.

computer—a mechanical or electronic device for processing information. Usually this information is processed as a string of binary digits, resulting in the term "digital computer."

computer assisted instruction (CAI)—the use of computers to aid classroom instruction. Three types of programs common to CAI are drill and practice, simulation, and tutorial.

control unit—the part of the Central Processing Unit that manages the flow of data.

copy programs—computer software designed to allow legitimate copying of programs for backup disks.

copy protection schemes—ways to prevent or limit the illegal copying of software.

crash—a breakdown in a computer program.

cursor—the movable indicator displayed on a computer's monitor. It shows where information the computer user is inputting will appear on the display or marks the current position of some type of electronic pointer.

daisy-wheel—a mechanism in a printer that holds character symbols arrayed on spokes that originate from a common wheel. Printers using this technology produce "letter quality" work, but they are slower than other types of printers.

data base—a reservoir of data contained in an organized format for easy entry, retrieval, and revision. Data may be accessed according to a number of different criteria, or by key words or phrases.

data base management—the creating, updating, organizing, and accessing of data base files.

data disk—a disk on which is stored data for use with a specific applications program. This disk is used in conjunction with a program disk which contains the application (word processor or data base, for example).

data processing—the process of gathering, recording, organizing, storing, and retrieving data by using data base application software.

debugging—the process of finding and removing errors in a computer program.

decimal—the number system most commonly used in counting, which utilizes the ten digits from 0 through 9.

dedicated computers—computers which are designed to perform only certain limited tasks.

desktop publishing—term used to refer to the production of printed material using the latest in laser printing technology.

Difference Engine—a gear-driven machine designed by Charles Babbage to add and subtract large numbers.

digitalize—the process of transferring other media into a form which the computer can recognize. For example, scanning a photograph to produce a computer image, or interpreting musical notes into computer generated music.

disk—a magnetic plate for storage of data. See *floppy disk* or *hard disk*.

disk drive—a device which records or plays back the information stored on magnetic disks.

documentation—written instructions to the computer user on the operations of hardware or software.

DOS (disk operating system)—a program that tells the CPU how to communicate with devices connected to the computer. Common DOS programs include CP/M, MS-DOS, UNIX, ProDOS, and OS/2.

dot-matrix printer—a computer printer that prints letters, numbers, or symbols by printing selected dots from a rectangular matrix of dots. It is faster than letter-quality printers, can reproduce graphics (drawings), and recent models are capable of producing near letter-quality work.

downloading—taking information received via telecommunications and transferring it into a computer.

electronic bulletin board—a computerized telephone answering system which allows callers or user group members equipped with computers and modems to leave written messages, read messages left by earlier callers, and take advantage of other electronic services.

electronic funds transfer (EFT)—the process of moving money electronically to and from banks and individuals.

electronic mail (E-mail)—a mail system that uses telecommunications or a computer network to send messages.

field—a location in a data record in which the user enters information.

file—a block of data considered by the user as a logical grouping of information and which may be handled by the computer as a single unit. In word processing, a single document is called a file.

first generation computers—computers which were dependent on vacuum tubes.

fixed disk—term used by IBM for a hard disk. See *hard disk.*

floppy disk—a plastic plate with a magnetic surface which is sealed inside a plastic outer covering and on which information is stored by a computer. Floppy disks may be 3½, 5¼, or 8 inches in diameter. The trend is toward smaller disks which store more information.

flowchart—a diagram which shows the steps involved in solving a problem. Programmers have used flowcharts to assist them in planning programs. Flowcharting is not used as extensively today.

forecasting—term used in business to mean predicting with the use of an electronic spreadsheet.

formatting a disk—preparing a new disk for use with a specific disk operating system or for use with a particular program.

FORTRAN—Formular Translator, the first major high-level programming language developed in the mid–1950s under the sponsorship of IBM. It has been particularly used for mathematical operations important to engineers and scientists.

fourth generation computers—computers which are dependent on large-scale integration (LSI).

graphics—display of pictorial images on the monitor screen, which may be printed out on a printer with graphics capabilities. The techniques for producing graphics vary widely from computer to computer.

hacker—1. Someone who programs computers for pleasure. 2. A computer user who uses a computer with a modem and telephone to gain or attempt to gain unauthorized access to other computer systems. The term originated at the Massachusetts Institute of Technology in the late 1950s for people who were "hacking around" in the computer lab.

hard copy—computer output which has been printed out on paper.

hard disk—a computer information storage device that is most commonly hermetically sealed. A hard disk can store much more data than a floppy disk and is increasingly being used by serious computer users. Hard disks installed at the factory are located inside a computer, but can often be added to a computer system later and connected with a cable.

hardware—includes any of the mechanical or electrical devices of a computer system; excludes software.

hexadecimal—base 16, a number system using 16 digits: the numerals from 0 through 9 and the letters of the alphabet from A through F. This system is often used in machine and assembly language.

high-level language—computer programming language which usually uses English-like words. They are called "high level" because they are so far away from the machine language which is the computer's native tongue. They must, therefore, be translated into machine code before they can be understood by the CPU.

high-resolution graphics—computer graphic images containing a high degree of detail.

icon—a picture used to represent a menu option in a computer program. The use of icons is a popular trend in computer software.

immediate mode—an operating mode used in some computer languages, particularly BASIC, in which instructions, or commands, may be entered directly at the keyboard and executed immediately by the computer.

initializing a disk—See *formatting a disk.*

ink jet printer—a printer which creates characters by spraying ink with a very fine nozzle; used for commercial applications because of its speed and quality.

input—the entry of information into a computer.

input device—any device which accepts information from outside the computer, input, and then transfers it to the central processing unit or main memory of the computer.

input/output (I/O)—refers to the possible ways information may be entered and retrieved from a computer. Common input mechanisms are keyboards, mouse, joystick, and touch-sensitive screens. Output devices include video displays, printers, and voice synthesizers.

integrated circuit (IC)—electronic circuit containing a large number of smaller circuits "integrated" together on a silicon chip. These were used to build the smaller, faster, more powerful third generation computers.

integrated software—package or group or programs contained in a single software package which are intended to work together. Commonly an integrated software package includes a word processing program, a spreadsheet, and a data base program. Newer packages are adding graphics and telecommunications components.

interface card—small circuit board which can be inserted inside a computer to allow it to communicate with a specific peripheral device such as a printer.

joystick—input device consisting of a control rod with a ball joint mounted on a base, with one or two firing buttons included either on the base or on the tip of the stick. The term comes from aviation where a device of the same name and similar construction is used to guide airplanes.

K—or kilobyte; the symbol used to represent 1024 bytes. Computer memory size is expressed in kilobytes.

keyboard—an input device similar to a set of typewriter keys. Some computer keyboards come with a numerical keypad which is a separate arrangement of numbered keys useful for inputting digital data.

laptop computer—a portable computer with a small screen using a liquid crystal display similar to that of hand-held calculators. Laptops are widely used by employees, especially those who must make frequent business trips. Their use is growing, and soon laptop computers will be a common sight. They often come with business software included and frequently have built-in modems to

laptop (portable)

send files back to the office or to a home computer.

large scale integration (LSI)—mass production of chips containing hundreds of components which made possible the fourth generation of computers.

laser printer—computer printer which prints using technology similar to that used in photocopying machines.

letter quality—a designation given to a printer that produces fine quality characters suitable for formal letter or manuscript applications.

light pen—input device which allows the user to draw directly on the monitor screen.

LISP—high-level programming language used primarily by artificial intelligence (AI) researchers; short for list processor. Developed at MIT about 1960 by AI researcher John McCarthy.

load—the action of transferring data from a tape or disk into a computer.

local area network (LAN)—a number of microcomputers which are linked together, usually by cabling. Users are able to share information and applications which have been made available on the network.

Logo—high-level programming language which is related to LISP; developed at MIT in the early 1970s by a team of educators headed by Seymour Papert. Logo is often used in elementary schools.

log on—the process of a user gaining access to a computer system, usually of a network or bulletin board.

low-resolution graphics—graphic images containing much less detail than high-resolution graphics. "Low-res" graphics are often jagged and blocky looking.

low-level language—a programming language which is very close to the computer's native machine code.

machine language—only language understood by a computer's central processing unit; code made up of electronic signals formed by setting and unsetting switches.

mainframe—the term used to designate a large computer that may be accessed by many terminals.

management information systems (MIS)—system used in businesses to keep track of and control data.

mass storage device—any device other than ROM and RAM which stores large amounts of computer data.

memory—there are two types of computer memory: internal and external. There are two types of internal memory: RAM (random: access memory), which can store information temporarily, and ROM (read-only memory), which is the computer's permanent memory, containing, for example, its memory of the machine language. External memory is contained on media such as floppy disks.

menu—list of options offered by a computer program, just as a restaurant menu offers choices. The user of the program can choose the desired option. A program organized around a central menu is called *menu-driven.*

microcomputer—computer whose central processing unit is a microprocessor.

microprocessor—computer central processing unit on a silicon chip. This is the integrated circuit that is the brains of a microcomputer.

minicomputer—a computer that is smaller and less powerful than a mainframe computer. This is not a microcomputer.

model—to simulate or try out a design or a situation that cannot be easily observed. For example, a scientist might model the behavior of subatomic particles on a computer. A design engineer might model the functioning of a new car design.

modem—modulator demodulator; a device allowing a computer to be connected to a telephone line or a direct line, thereby permitting the transmitting or receiving of data. This converts computer data into audio tones, and vice versa.

monitor—the video screen on which computer data is displayed.

motherboard—the main circuit board inside a microcomputer.

mouse—an input device that manipulates a cursor, commonly an arrow, which the user points

mouse

at a chosen option on the screen. It looks like a small box, has a rolling ball on the bottom, and the connecting wire emerging from one end looks like a tail. The user rolls the mouse on a smooth surface. The motion is translated by the computer, which uses the information to move the cursor to a new location. The user commonly "clicks" a button on the mouse when the cursor points to the desired option.

nanosecond—a billionth of a second.

Napier's Bones—calculating device made of pieces of bone with digits marked on them.

network—See *local area network.*

octal—base 8.

on-line service—a service which can be accessed over telephone lines. The expression "going on-line" is used when a computer user connects to an electronic bulletin board via a modem.

optical mark reader—input device used to score tests when the answers have been marked on a special forum.

output—the sending of data from the internal memory of the computer to a peripheral device such as a screen, printer, disk drive, etc.

Pascal—structured high-level computer language developed by a team headed by Niklaus Wirth in the late 1960s and early 1970s. The language was named for the French mathematician Blaise Pascal. The high school advanced placement exam in computer science assumes knowledge of Pascal.

password—a code word which must be entered by a computer user before being allowed access to a system. Passwords are used to restrict computers to authorized users.

personal computer—see *microcomputer.*

peripheral—a piece of hardware connected to and controlled by a computer, such as a printer, modem, etc.

pixel—picture element; the smallest area of a video screen that can be affected by computer commands.

plotter—a computer printer which produces graphics output with a moving pen.

presentation graphics—graphics that present data in easy-to-understand ways such as charts and graphs. Some presentations are now being produced as computer-generated video displays.

printer—output device which will produce a printed copy of computer generated data.

program—a list of instructions that tells a computer to perform specified tasks.

pull-down menu—option menus which can be examined from within a program and which allow selections to be made without exiting that program.

Prolog—a high-level computer language often used in artificial intelligence research.

RAM—random-access memory; a temporary data storage capacity that must be transferred to tape, disk, or print-out before power is off, or it will be lost. Software programs which a user loads into a computer from a disk are stored in RAM.

real-time processing—handling data quickly enough to influence the environment from which the data came.

record—the part of a data base file that contains all the information about one item. For example, in a file of names and addresses, the information about one person would be a record.

recursion—a powerful feature of some programming language which allows a procedure to call itself.

robotics—the science of designing, building, and programming robots.

ROM—read-only memory; a memory storage capacity the user can read only and not alter. The information in ROM is built in at the factory.

run—to carry out a program. This is a commonly used expression and should be distinguished from the BASIC command RUN, a technical term in that language which is used to start BASIC programs.

scrolling—the feature in a word processor or spreadsheet which allows the computer to scroll some of the text off the screen to provide more blank lines or space.

searching—way to retrieve information from a program such as a data base by telling it to find all records containing specified information. For example, the user could tell the computer to find all records in an address file that are in Atlanta.

second generation computers—computers which were built using transistors.

silicon chip—See *chip*.

software—the instructions, programs, rules, etc., that make a computer work.

speech digitizer—computer output device which allows computers to use human sounding voices to respond to users.

spelling checker—special program for use with a word processor which checks the spelling of all words in a document.

spreadsheet—program which allows the user to create on the screen a chart which shows the relationships between numbers. Accountants keep books on spreadsheets, and the spreadsheet can be thought of as a page from a ledger. This electronic ledger will automatically do all calculations.

structured programming—use of a programming language which encourages planning from the top down, modular design, and structured coding.

supercomputer—fastest, most powerful type of computer. These are used for forecasting the weather.

system software—operating systems and utility programs which come with a computer system and manage computer functions.

telecommunications—refers to the transmitting of computer data over telephone lines.

template—a chart which shows the commands needed to operate a particular program. These often are available to fit around a computer keyboard, so that the user may find at a glance how to perform a particular function.

terminal—an input/output device with a keyboard for input and either a screen or a printer for output. It is connected to a mainframe or minicomputer, and does not contain its own CPU.

thermal printer—type or dot-matrix printer which forms printed characters by applying heat to chemically treated paper. While they are generally inexpensive, the paper they must use is not!

third generation computers—computers based upon integrated circuits.

time-sharing—a concept of handling many computer terminals so that each terminal has a satisfactory response time.

top down programming—a programming technique which starts with the whole problem and breaks it down into sets of smaller problems.

touch-sensitive screen—input device which allows the user to draw electronically directly onto the screen. Sometimes these are used to allow a person to touch the screen in order to choose a particular menu item in a program.

transistor—device used to transmit electricity.

user friendly—any computer equipment or software that is easy to understand and operate.

user's group—group of computer users who meet to discuss software, hardware, programs, etc. Most user's groups consist of people who use one particular brand of computer or are interested in one particular area of computer use.

utilities—system software which provides functions which the user may need. An example is a copy function for making backup disks.

vacuum tube—device used to transmit electricity in the first generation of computers.

vaporware—computer products which are advertised or reviewed, but are not actually on the market.

voice recognition system—an input device which allows the user to speak instructions to the computer. The computer can be taught to recognize and respond to one person's voice.

windowing—the capacity of a computer to allow portions of different displays to overlap on the screen at the same time.

word—a grouping of bits treated as a single unit by the CPU.

word processor—a computer program or system that is geared for the writing, editing, or correcting of written text.

WYSIWYG—(pronounced "wissywig") stands for "what you see is what you get." This common expression is used to describe a word processing program which shows on the screen *exactly* what will print on the printer.

Music Glossary

absolute music—"abstract" or "pure" music; instrumental music requiring for its appreciation neither words nor story nor any association beyond its basic statement.

absolute pitch—the capacity of identifying or singing any tone at proper pitch without the aid of an instrument.

a cappella—choral music sung without accompaniment.

accent—stress or pulse which emphasizes one note over others in a measure.

accidental—a natural, sharp, or flat not indicated by key-signature.

accompaniment—instrumental or choral support for soloists.

adagio—slow tempo; the name often given to a particular section of a musical work so characterized.

allegro—fast tempo; the name often given to a particular section of a musical work so characterized.

alto—a vocal range for a female voice which lies between soprano and contralto; sometimes mistakenly used for contralto; used to describe certain instruments like the viola.

andante—moderately slow tempo; the name often given to a particular section of a musical work so characterized.

antiphonal—the answering or alternation of two groups, choral or instrumental.

aria—a solo song or air in opera, oratorio, or cantata which often lends itself to a display of skill.

arpeggio—a chord, the notes of which are played successively in ascending or descending order.

art song—short song of high dramatic and formal value.

atonality—designating music in which there is no key center; a twentieth-century compositional style sometimes employing a twelve-tone scale.

augmentation—the repetition of a melody with changes provided by the use of proportionately longer notes.

ballet—an elaborate dance usually telling a story, with instrumental or full orchestral accompaniment for theatrical performance.

bar—a measure in musical notation.

baritone—male vocal register between tenor and bass.

baroque—musical style characteristic of composers from 1600 to 1750; includes works of Bach.

bass—deepest male voice.

beat—the rhythmic pulse of music marking time into relatively equal divisions in the measure.

bel canto—operatic singing technique used to produce a lyrical effect.

binary form—notable in music which uses two contrasting themes in a section.

bravura—great skill and expansiveness of style.

buffo—the character-comic in opera.

cadence—chords at the end of a tune, phrase, section, or movement, which have the effect of bringing the statement to a rest.

cadenza—an elaboration of the cadence, displaying the skill of a soloist.

canon—music, such as a round, in which two or more sections repeat the same melody, starting at different times but overlapping.

cantabile—emphasis upon a "singing" quality in the music.

cantata—an elaborate vocal and instrumental form with arias, recitatives, duets, and chorus, but not requiring dramatic or scenic implementation.

castrato—a eunuch with an adult male voice in the female range.

chamber music—music specifically intended for performance in a small hall, each part usually being taken by one instrument as contrasted with groups or sections of instruments in large orchestras.

chord—three or more tones sounded together.

chromatic—music with many half step intervals not in the diatonic scale.

classical music—the musical style of composers between 1750 and 1825, including the works of Mozart and Beethoven.

clef—sign on the left of each staff indicating sound or exact pitch.

coda—passage which rounds out a section or end of a composition.

coloratura—elaborate vocal passage demonstrating skill of both composer and soloist.

concert master—first violinist in orchestra, frequently also an assistant conductor.

concerto—composition for one or more instruments with orchestral accompaniment.

conductor—orchestra leader, chiefly responsible for musical interpretation.

contralto—lowest pitched female voice.

counterpoint—simultaneous use of two or more melodies.

crescendo—becoming gradually louder.

development—compositional exploration and restatement of thematic idea.

diatonic—opposite of chromatic; music confined to the use of notes in a given major or minor key.

discord—See dissonance.

dissonance—a combination of clashing tones requiring the addition of other tones for resolution.

divertimento—a light instrumental composition in several short movements.

dominant—fifth tone in the minor or major scale.

downbeat—first strong accent in each measure.

encore—repetition of a piece or performance of an additional one in response to applause.

enharmonic—a tone having several different forms of notation.

ensemble—combination of performers; also, overall quality of musical expression.

equal temperament—division of octave into twelve equal halftones; also characteristic method of tuning instruments.

étude—"study music" composed for practice purposes but often included in concert repertoires.

exposition—in sonata form, among others, a first section containing statement of themes to be developed.

expression—immediate personal and emotional interpretation of music by a performer.

falsetto—adult male voice used in an unnaturally high pitch.

fermata—a long pause.

finale—last section of a composition.

flat—notation indicating the lowering of a tone by a half step.

forte—loud.

fugue—a musical form similar to the canon but one in which various imitations of the melody occur in shorter phrases.

fundamental—primary note of a chord or harmonic series.

glissando—tonal effect produced by sliding finger over the strings or keys of an instrument.

grace note—an embellishing note, printed in smaller type.

Gregorian chant—early church music named for Pope Gregory I; used in Roman Catholic church services.

harmony—the simultaneous combination of tones into chords; also the study of chord functions and structure.

homophony—music composed of a melody supported by harmonic chordal accompaniment.

hymn—originally a religious song in praise of God; also used of songs with a patriotic theme.

imitation—technique of composition

which repeats theme or melody, making use of several instruments or voices as in canon, fugue, or round.

impressionism—the musical style of late nineteenth- and early twentieth-century composers, including Debussy and Ravel.

interval—the difference in pitch between two notes.

intonation—fidelity of pitch.

inversion—reversing or inverting the position of notes in chords or intervals.

-issimo—suffix meaning "very," added to many musical terms.

jazz—music of black American origin, initially called "ragtime," and characterized by syncopated rhythm.

key—scale; relating to a system of tonal relationships developed from a tonic keynote.

keynote—base or principal note from which a scale is derived.

largo—a very slow and deliberate tempo; the name often given to a particular section of a musical work so characterized.

legato—smooth transitions from note to note without breaks.

leitmotiv—thematic melody used recurrently to identify specific characters, events, places, ideas, or emotions; characteristically used by Wagner.

lento—slow tempo between andante and largo.

libretto—the entire literary text of a musical work utilizing singing and speaking.

lyrics—words set to music.

measure—a horizontally lined space between two vertical bar lines which mark off a section of a staff.

medieval music—styles of music developed during the thousand-year period beginning A.D. 500, primarily vocal; greatly influenced by church liturgy, by court and peasant life.

melodrama—scene or play in which a musical background accompanies action and dialogue.

melody—a succession of notes of varying pitch and duration having a distinct pattern.

meter—strong and weak accents in rhythmical pattern.

metronome—a clockwork pendulum invented to insure standard tempi.

mezzo—prefix meaning "half."

mezzo-soprano—female voice between soprano and alto ranges.

M.M.—letters indicating metronomic setting.

mode—general term for system(s) of arranging intervals of a scale.

moderato—moderate tempo.

modern music—styles of music de-

veloped from the beginning of the twentieth century, as distinguished from earlier styles still flourishing; among the former, works of Schoenberg and Bartok.

modulation—change of key or tonality through a succession of chords.

molto—very or much more, as in molto adagio (very slowly).

monophony—unaccompanied music composed only of a melodic line.

mordent—a grace note.

motive—a musical phrase which reappears irregularly.

movement—major division of a musical composition.

natural—symbol indicating the return of a tone to its natural pitch from a previous sharping or flatting.

notation—entire system employed for writing Western music.

obbligato—an accompaniment which is an indispensable and intrinsic part of the musical statement; by misuse, in some nineteenth-century music used in the opposite sense to refer to a part which is optional.

octave—the interval covering eight successive notes in the diatonic scale, e.g., middle C to the C above it.

opera—a form of drama set to orchestral music in which most of the dialogue is sung; generally presented in an elaborate production.

opus—a composition or set of compositions; customarily accompanied by a number to indicate its place in the chronological order of a composer's work.

oratorio—a form of drama set to orchestral music and voice; differing from opera in the absence of staging, costumes, and scenery; usually on a religious subject.

overture—introductory instrumental music to an opera or play; also now an independent form.

partita—originally, variations or a set of dances; by extension, used to mean "suite."

phrase—a short distinguishable part of a melody.

piano—softly.

pitch—degree of highness or lowness of a sound.

più—more; as in più lento (more slowly).

poco—a little.

polyphony—music composed of at least two melodies played simultaneously.

polytonality—simultaneous use of two different keys.

prelude—a short composition which can be a piece of a single movement, the beginning of a longer work, or an overture.

presto—very fast tempo; the name often given to a particular section of a musicat work so characterized.

program music—descriptive music which tells a story or describes a place; frequently employs explanatory or supportive program literature; the opposite of "absolute music."

progression—advance from one tone to another or from one chord to another.

quartet—an intimate musical form for four instruments or voices.

quintet—similar to quartet but refers to five instruments or voices.

recapitulation—repetition of a thematic statement after an intervening development and contrast.

reprise—repeat of a segment of music.

rest—musical notation indicating silence.

rhapsody—a very free musical form developed during the nineteenth century.

rhythm—recurrent pattern created by the accent and duration of notes.

rondo—a musical form in which the main theme is consistently repeated throughout.

scale—a series of consecutive tones forming an octave.

scherzo—usually the third movement of a larger composition; humorous and lively.

score—written or printed piece of music in which the different instruments or voices are entered on a separate staff, one above the other.

sharp—notation raising a tone by a half step.

signature—symbol placed at the beginning of a composition specifying key and tempo.

sonata—a composition for one or more instruments.

soprano—the highest female singing voice.

staff—the five horizontal lines and intervening spaces upon which musical notation is made.

symphonic poem—a tone poem; a form of program music.

symphony—major form of orchestral work, divided into movements.

syncopation—kind of rhythm created by altering the natural accent into a weak beat.

tempo (pl: tempi)—the rate of speed at which a piece or passage of music moves.

tenor—highest normal adult male voice; also the range of some instruments.

theme—melody used as the main musical line for development and variation.

tonality—the adherence to the keynote (tonic) as the referent of all chords and harmonies used in a composition or part of a composition.

tone—a note; sound with a fixed pitch.

tone poem—*See* symphonic poem.

transpose—changing key or pitch, leaving all other musical relationships intact.

treble—the highest register of musical sound.

upbeat—weak beat preceding a heavy accent.

variation—alteration of a melody that still retains its essential qualities.

GEOLOGY

Introduction

Derived from the Greek *geo*, "earth," plus *logos*, "discourse," geology is the science which deals with the origin, structure, and history of the earth and its inhabitants as recorded in the rocks.

To the geologist, the earth is not simply the globe upon which we live—it is an ever present challenge to learn more about such things as earthquakes, volcanoes, glaciers, and the meaning of fossils. How old is the earth? Where did it come from? Of what is it made? To answer these questions, the earth scientist must study the evidence of events that occurred millions of years ago. He must then relate his findings to the results of similar events that are happening today. He attempts, for example, to determine the location and extent of ancient oceans and mountain ranges, and to trace the evolution of life as recorded in rocks of different ages. He studies the composition of the rocks and minerals forming the earth's crust in an attempt to locate and exploit the valuable economic products that are to be found there.

In pursuing his study of the earth the geologist relies heavily upon other basic sciences. For example, **astronomy** (the study of the nature and movements of planets, stars, and other heavenly bodies) tells us where the earth fits into the universe and has also developed several theories as to the origin of our planet. **Chemistry** (the study of the composition of substances and the changes which they undergo) is used to analyze and study the rocks and minerals of the earth's crust. The science of **physics** (the study of matter and motion) helps explain the various physical forces affecting our earth, and the reaction of earth materials to these forces.

To understand the nature of prehistoric plants and animals we must turn to **biology**, the study of all living forms. **Zoology** provides us with information about the animals, and **botany** gives us some insight into the nature of ancient plants. By using these sciences, as well as others, the geologist is better able to cope with the many complex problems that are inherent in the study of the earth and its history.

The scope of geology is so broad that it has been divided into two major divisions: **physical geology** and **historical geology.** For convenience in study, each of these divisions has been subdivided into a number of more specialized branches of subsciences.

PHYSICAL GEOLOGY

Physical geology deals with the earth's composition, its structure, the movements within and upon the earth's crust, and the geologic processes by which the earth's surface is, or has been changed.

The broad division of geology includes such basic geologic subsciences as **mineralogy,** the study of minerals, and **petrology,** the study of rocks. These two branches of geology provide us with much-needed information about the composition of the earth. In addition, there is **structural geology** to explain the arrangement of the rocks within the earth, and **geomorphology** to explain the origin of its surface features.

These branches of physical geology enable the

geologist to make detailed studies of all phases of earth science. The knowledge gained from such research brings about a better understanding of the physical nature of the earth.

CASUAL OBSERVATION

How can we learn more about this fascinating earth and the stories to be read from its rocks? Actually it is very simple, for geology is all around us. The geologist's laboratory is the great outdoors, and each walk through the fields or drive down the highway brings us in contact with the processes and materials of geology.

For example, pick up a piece of common limestone. There are probably fossils in it. And these fossils may well represent the remains of animals that lived in some prehistoric sea which once covered the area.

Or maybe you are walking along a river bank. Notice the silt on the bank after the last high water stage. This reminds us of the ability of running water to deposit **sediments**—sediments that may later be transformed into rocks. Notice, too, how swift currents have scoured the river banks. The soil has been removed by **erosion**, the geologic process which is so important in the shaping of the earth's surface features.

Perhaps you see a field of black fertile soil supporting a fine crop of cotton or corn. It may surprise you to learn that this dark rich soil may have been derived from an underlying chalky white limestone—still another reminder of the importance of earth materials in our everyday life.

EARTH AS A PLANET

The earth is one of nine planets comprising the solar system. It is the largest of the four planets of the inner group (Mercury, Venus, Earth, and Mars) and is third closest to the sun (Fig. 1).

Shape of the Earth. The earth has the form of **an oblate spheroid.** That is, it is almost ball-shaped, or spherical, except for a slight flattening at the poles. This flattening, and an accompanying bulge at the equator, are produced by the centrifugal force of rotation.

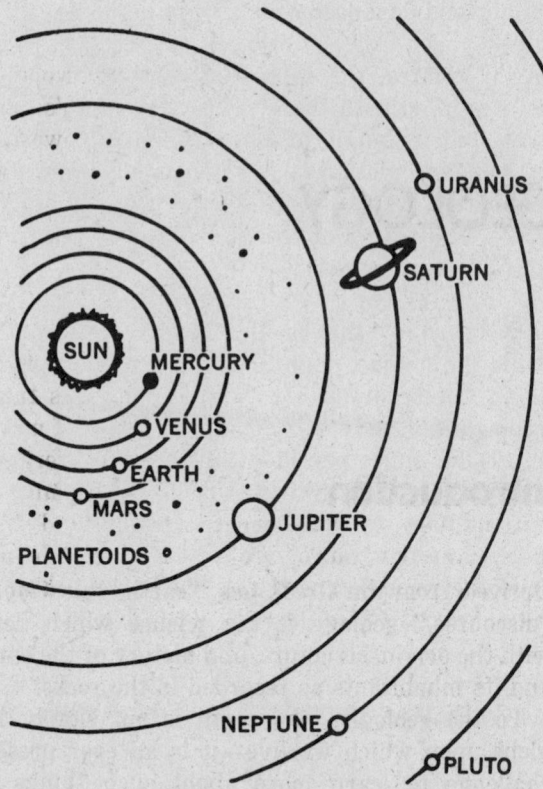

FIGURE 1. Planets of the solar system and their relation to the sun.

Size of the Earth. Although the earth is of great size, Jupiter, Saturn, Uranus, and Neptune all have greater equatorial diameters. Earth has a polar diameter of about 7900 miles (the equatorial diameter is approximately 27 miles greater because of the bulge described above). The circumference of the earth is about 24,874 miles, and the surface area comprises roughly 197 million square miles, of which only about 51 million square miles (29 per cent) are surface lands. The remaining 71 per cent of the earth's surface is covered by water.

Earth Motions. We have already learned that each of the planets revolves around the sun within its own orbit and period of revolution. In addition to its trip around the sun, the earth also rotates.

Rotation of the Earth. The earth turns on its axis (the shortest diameter connecting the poles), and this turning motion is called *rotation*. The earth rotates from west to east and makes one complete rotation each day. It is this rotating motion that gives us the alternating periods of daylight and darkness which we know as day and night.

As it rotates, the earth has a single wobble. This has to do with the fact that the earth's axis is tilted at an angle of 23½ degrees. However, this wobbling motion is so slow that it takes approximately 26,000 years to complete a single wobble. The tilting of the earth's axis is also responsible fcr the seasons.

Revolution of the Earth. The earth revolves around the sun in a slightly elliptical **orbit** approximately once every 365¼ days. During this time (a solar year), the earth travels at a speed of more than 60,000 miles per hour, and on the average, it remains about 93 million miles from the sun.

In addition to rotation, revolution, and the wobbling motion, our entire solar system is heading in the general direction of the star Vega at a speed of about 400 million miles per year.

PRINCIPAL DIVISIONS OF THE EARTH

The earth consists of air, water, and land. We recognize these more technically as the **atmosphere,** a gaseous envelope surrounding the earth; the **hydrosphere,** the waters filling the depressions and covering almost three-fourths of the land; and the **lithosphere,** the solid part of the earth which underlies the atmosphere and hydrosphere.

The Atmosphere. The atmosphere, or gaseous portion of the earth, extends upward for hundreds of miles above sea level. It is a mixture of nitrogen, oxygen, carbon dioxide, water vapor, and other gases (see Table 1).

GAS	PER CENT BY VOLUME
Nitrogen	78.084
Oxygen	20.946
Argon	.934
Carbon dioxide	.033
Neon	.001818
Helium	.000524
Methane	.0002
Krypton	.000114
Hydrogen	.00005
Nitrous oxide	.00005
Xenon	.0000087

TABLE 1. Analysis of gases present in pure dry air. Notice that nitrogen and oxygen comprise 99 per cent of the total volume of atmospheric gases.

Of great importance to man, the elements of the atmosphere make life possible on our planet. Moreover, the atmosphere acts as an insulating agent to protect us from the heat of the sun and to shield us from the bombardment of meteorites, and it makes possible the evaporation and precipitation of moisture. The atmosphere is an important geologic agent (see Chapter 9) and is responsible for the processes of weathering which are continually at work on the earth's surface.

The Hydrosphere. The hydrosphere includes all the waters of the oceans, lakes, and rivers, as well as **ground water**—which exists within the lithosphere. As noted earlier, most of this water is contained in the oceans, which cover roughly 71 per cent of the earth's surface to an average depth of about two and a half miles.

The waters of the earth are essential to man's existence and they are also of considerable geologic importance. Running streams and oceans are actively engaged in eroding, transporting, and depositing sediments; and water, working in conjunction with atmospheric agents, has been the major force in forming the earth's surface features throughout geologic time. The geologic work of the hydrosphere will be discussed in some detail in later chapters of this book.

The Lithosphere. Of prime importance to the geologist is the lithosphere. This, the solid portion of the earth, is composed of rocks and minerals which, in turn, comprise the continental masses and ocean basins. The rocks of the lithosphere are of three basic types, **igneous, sedimentary,** and **metamorphic.** Igneous rocks were originally in a molten state but have since cooled and solidified to form rocks such as granite and basalt. Sedimentary rocks are formed from sediments (fragments of pre-existing rocks) deposited by wind, water, or ice. Limestone, sandstone, and clay are typical of this group. The metamorphic rocks have been formed from rocks that were originally sedimentary or igneous in origin. This transformation takes place as the rock is subjected to great physical and chemical change. Marble, which in its original form was limestone, is an example of a metamorphic rock.

Most of what we know about the lithosphere has been learned through the study of the surface materials of the earth. However, by means of deep bore holes and seismological studies, geologists have gathered much valuable information about the interior of the earth. Additional geologic data are derived from rocks which were originally buried many miles beneath the ground but have been brought to or near the surface by violent earth movements and later exposed by erosion.

MAJOR PHYSICAL FEATURES OF THE EARTH

The major relief features of the earth are the **continental masses** and the **ocean basins.** These are the portions of the earth which apparently remained stable throughout all of known geologic time.

The Continental Masses. The continents are rocky platforms which cover approximately 29 per cent of the earth's surface. Composed largely of granite, they have an average elevation of about three miles above the floors of the surrounding ocean basins and rise an average of one-half mile above sea level (Fig. 2). The seaward edges of the continental masses are submerged and these are called the **continental shelves.**

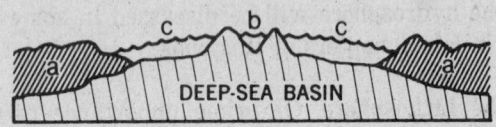

FIGURE 2. Relation between continents and ocean basins.
a—Continents.
b—Volcanic islands.
c—Sea level.

Although the continental surfaces appear to be very irregular to man, the difference in elevation between the highest mountain (Mount Everest—more than 29,000 feet above sea level) and the deepest part of the ocean (more than 35,000 feet deep, south of the Mariana Islands in the Pacific) is inconsequential when considered in relation to the size of the earth.

The Ocean Basins. The ocean basins contain the greatest part of the hydrosphere and cover more than 70 per cent of the earth's surface. The floors of the ocean were originally believed to be quite flat and featureless, but recent oceanographic studies indicate that this is not so. The surface of the ocean floor possesses as many irregularities

as the land and includes deep trenches, canyons, and submarine mountain ranges.

Of the five oceans, Arctic, Antarctic, Atlantic, Indian, and Pacific, the latter is deepest (about 35,000 feet) and largest, covering almost half of the earth. The bottoms of the deepest parts of the oceans are composed of basalt, a rather dense, dark, igneous rock. In many places the basaltic bottom is covered by layers of marine sediments.

The origin of the continents and ocean basins and their relationship to each other are discussed in later sections.

GEOLOGIC FORCES

Geologic investigation of almost any part of the earth's surface will reveal some indication of great changes which the earth has undergone. These changes are of many kinds and most have taken place over millions of years. They are, in general, brought about by the processes of **gradation, tectonism,** and **volcanism.**

Gradation. The surface rocks of the earth are constantly being affected by gradational forces. For example, the atmosphere attacks the rocks, weathering them both physically and chemically. In addition, the rivers and oceans of the hydrosphere are continually wearing away rock fragments and transporting them to other areas where they are deposited. Gradation, then, includes two separate types of processes: **degradation,** which is a wearing down or destructive process, and **aggradation,** a holding up or constructive process.

Degradation, commonly referred to as erosion, results from the wearing down of the rocks by water, air, and ice. Here are included the work of atmospheric weathering, glacial abrasion, stream erosion, wind abrasion, etc.

Aggradation, known also as deposition, results in the accumulation of sediments and the ultimate building up of rock strata. The principal agents depositing these sediments are wind, ice, and water. The work of each of these geologic agents is discussed elsewhere in this book.

Tectonism. This term encompasses all the movements of the solid parts of the earth with respect to each other. Tectonic movements, which are indicative of crustal instability, produce **faulting** (fracture and displacement), **folding, subsidence,** and **uplift** of rock formations. Known also as **diastrophism,** tectonism is responsible for the formation of many of our great mountain ranges and for most of the structural deformation that has occurred in the earth's crust. However, these tectonic features (such as folds and faults) are not usually seen until they have been exposed by the process of degradation, or erosion.

In addition, widespread tectonic movements are responsible for certain types of metamorphism.

The intrusion of **magma,** more closely associated with volcanism, may also bring about rock deformation by folding.

Volcanism. This term, known also as vulcanism, refers to the movement of molten rock materials within the earth or upon the surface of the earth. Volcanic processes produce the lavas, ashes, and cinders which are ejected from volcanoes. Volcanism is also responsible for the rocks, once molten, which solidified at great depth within the earth.

Minerals

We now know that the geologist is primarily interested in the earth's rocky crust, but before he can study rocks it is necessary to know something about minerals, for these are the building blocks of the earth's crust. Although geologists differ when defining the term mineral, the following definition is generally accepted: **Minerals are chemical elements or compounds which occur naturally within the crust of the earth.** They are **inorganic** (not derived from living things), have a definite chemical composition or range of composition, an orderly internal arrangement of atoms (crystalline structure), and certain other distinct physical properties. It should be noted, however, that the chemical and physical properties of some minerals may vary within definite limits.

Rocks are aggregates or mixtures of minerals, the composition of which may vary greatly. Limestone, for example, is composed primarily of one mineral—calcite. Granite, on the other hand, typically contains three minerals—feldspar, mica, and quartz.

Certain minerals, such as calcite, quartz, and feldspar, are so commonly found in rocks that they are called the **rock-forming** minerals. Other minerals, like gold, diamond, uranium minerals, and silver are found in relatively few rocks.

Minerals vary greatly in their chemical composition and physical properties. Let us now become acquainted with the more important physical and chemical characteristics that enable us to distinguish one mineral from the other.

CHEMICAL COMPOSITION OF MINERALS

Although a detailed discussion of chemistry is not within the scope of this book, an introduction to chemical terminology is necessary if we are to understand the chemical composition of minerals.

All matter, including minerals, is composed of one or more **elements.** An element is a substance that cannot be broken down into simpler substances by ordinary chemical means. Theoretically, if you were to take a quantity of any element and cut it into smaller and smaller pieces, eventually you would obtain the smallest pieces that still retained the characteristics of the element. These minute particles are **atoms.** Although atoms are so small that they cannot be seen with the most powerful microscope (it would take 100 million of them to make a line one inch long) we know a great deal about them. We know, for instance, that the nucleus of an atom is composed of **protons,** positively charged particles, and **neutrons,** or uncharged particles. Outside the nucleus and revolving rapidly around it are negatively charged particles called **electrons.** It is now known, of course, that certain elements have been broken down by atomic fission or "atom-smashing," but these are not considered to be "ordinary chemical means." Although there are only ninety-two elements occurring in nature, several more have been created artificially.

Some minerals, such as gold or silver, are composed of only one element. More often, however, minerals consist of two or more elements united to form a **compound.** For example, calcite is a chemical compound known as calcium carbonate. The chemical composition of a compound may be expressed by means of a chemical formula ($CaCO_3$ in the case of calcite) in which each element is represented by a symbol. The symbol is derived from an abbreviation of the Latin or English name of the element it represents. For many elements, the first letter of the element's name is used as its symbol—thus H for an atom of hydrogen, and C for an atom of carbon. If the names of two elements start with the same letter, two letters may be used for one of them to distinguish between their symbols. For example, an atom of helium may be represented as He, an atom of calcium as Ca. Some symbols have been derived from an abbreviation of the Latin name of the elements: Cu (from *cuprum*) represents an atom of copper, and Fe (from *ferrum*) an atom of iron. The small numerals used in a chemical formula represent the proportion in which each element is present. Hence, the formula for water, H_2O, indicates that there are two atoms of hydrogen for each atom of oxygen present in water.

As mentioned above, ninety-two elements have been found to be present in minerals; however, eight of these elements are so abundant that they constitute more than 98 per cent, by weight, of the earth's crust. These elements, their symbols, and the per cent by weight present in the earth's solid crust are as follows:

Oxygen (O)	46.60
Silicon (Si)	27.72
Aluminum (Al)	8.13
Iron (Fe)	5.00
Calcium (Ca)	3.63
Sodium (Na)	2.83
Potassium (K)	2.59
Magnesium (Mg)	2.09
Total	98.59

As indicated in the above table, two elements, oxygen and silicon, make up approximately three-fourths of the weight of the rocks. Both these elements are **nonmetals,** but the remaining six are **metals.** Metals are characterized by their capacity for conducting heat and electricity, their ability to be hammered into thin sheets (malleability) or to be drawn into wire (ductility), and their luster (the way light is reflected from the mineral's sur-

face). Such minerals as gold, silver, copper, and iron are included in the metals. The nonmetallic, or industrial minerals do not have the properties mentioned above. Some typical nonmetallic minerals are sulfur, diamond, and calcite.

CRYSTALS

When crystalline minerals solidify and grow without interference, they will normally adopt smooth angular shapes known as crystals. The planes that form the outside of the crystals are known as **faces.** These are related directly to the internal atomic structure of the mineral, and the size of the faces is dependent upon the frequency of the atoms in the different planes. The shape of the crystals and the angles between related sets of crystal faces are important in mineral identification.

PHYSICAL PROPERTIES OF MINERALS

Each mineral possesses certain physical properties or characteristics by which it may be recognized or identified. Although some may be identified by visual examination, others must be subjected to certain simple tests.

Physical properties especially useful in mineral identification are (1) hardness, (2) color, (3) streak, (4) luster, (5) specific gravity, (6) cleavage, (7) fracture, (8) shape or form, (9) tenacity or elasticity, and (10) certain other miscellaneous properties. The geologist must know how to test a mineral specimen for the above properties if he is to identify it correctly. Many of these tests do not require expensive laboratory equipment and may be done in the field. Some of them may be made by using such commonplace articles as a knife or a hardened steel file, a copper penny, a small magnet, an inexpensive pocket lens with a magnification of six to ten times, a piece of glass, a piece of unglazed porcelain tile, and a fingernail.

Hardness. One of the easiest ways to distinguish one mineral from another is by testing for hardness. The hardness of a mineral is determined by what materials it will scratch, and what materials will scratch it. The hardness or scratch test may be done with simple testing materials carried in the field. For greater accuracy, one may use the scale of hardness called **Mohs' scale.** This scale, named for the German mineralogist Friedrich Mohs, was devised more than one hundred years ago. In studying his mineral collection, Mohs noticed that certain minerals were much harder than others. He believed that this variation could be of some value in mineral identification, so he selected ten common minerals to be used as standards in testing other minerals for hardness. In establishing this scale, Mohs assigned each of the reference minerals a number. He designated talc, the softest in the series, as having a hardness of 1. The hardest mineral, diamond, was assigned a hardness of 10.

Mohs' scale, composed of the ten reference minerals arranged in order of increasing hardness, is as follows:

> No. 1—Talc (softest)
> No. 2—Gypsum
> No. 3—Calcite
> No. 4—Fluorite
> No. 5—Apatite
> No. 6—Feldspar
> No. 7—Quartz
> No. 8—Topaz
> No. 9—Corundum
> No. 10—Diamond (hardest)

Most of the minerals in Mohs' scale are common ones, which can be obtained in inexpensive collections. Diamond chips are more expensive, but not beyond reason. Note that Mohs' scale is so arranged that each mineral will be scratched by those having higher numbers, and will scratch those having lower numbers.

It is also possible to test for hardness by using the following common objects:

ITEM	HARDNESS
Fingernail	About 2½
Copper penny	About 3
Glass	5–5½
Knife blade	5½–6
Steel file	6½–7

Each of the above items will scratch a mineral of the indicated hardness. For example: the fingernail will scratch talc (hardness of 1) and gypsum (hardness of 2), but would not scratch calcite which has a hardness of 3.

In testing for hardness, first use the more common materials. Start with the fingernail; if that will not scratch the specimen, use the knife blade. If the knife blade produces a scratch, this indicates that the specimen has a hardness of between 2½ and 6 (see scale above). Referring to Mohs' scale, it is found that there are three minerals of known hardness within this range. These are: apatite (5); fluorite (4); and calcite (3). If the calcite will not scratch the specimen but the fluorite will, its hardness is further limited as between 3 and 4. Next, try to scratch the fluorite with the specimen. If this can be done, even with difficulty, the hardness is established as 4; if not, then it is between 3 and 4.

Color. Probably one of the first things that is noticed about a mineral is its color. However, the same mineral may vary greatly in color from one specimen to another, and with certain exceptions, color is of limited use in mineral identification. Certain minerals, for example, azurite, which is always blue, malachite, which is green, and pyrite, which is yellow, have relatively constant colors. Others, such as quartz or tourmaline, occur in a wide variety of colors; hence, color may be of little use in identifying these two minerals. Color variations of this sort are primarily due to minor chemical impurities within the mineral.

When using color in mineral identification, it is necessary to take into consideration such factors as (1) whether the specimen is being examined in natural or artificial light, (2) whether the surface being examined is fresh or weathered, and (3) whether the mineral is wet or dry. Each of these may cause color variations in a mineral. In addition, certain of the metallic minerals will tarnish and the true color will not be revealed except on a fresh surface.

Streak. When a mineral is rubbed across a piece of unglazed tile, it may leave a line similar to a pencil or crayon mark. This line is composed of the powdered minerals. The color of this powdered material is known as the streak of the mineral, and the unglazed tile used in such a test is called a **streak plate** (Fig. 3).

The streak in some minerals will not be the same as the color of the specimen. For example, a piece of black hematite will leave a reddish brown streak, and an extremely hard mineral such as topaz or corundum will leave no streak. This is because the streak plate has a hardness of about 7,

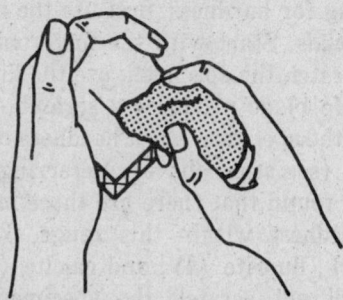

FIGURE 3. Testing for streak by means of streak plate.

and both topaz (8) and corundum (9) are harder than the streak plate, hence the mineral will not be powdered.

Luster. The appearance of the surface of a mineral as seen in reflected light is called luster. Some minerals shine like metals, for example, silver or gold. These are said to have metallic luster. Other lusters are called nonmetallic. The more important nonmetallic lusters and some common examples are shown below:

Admantine—brilliant glossy luster: typical of diamond
Vitreous—glassy, looks like glass: quartz or topaz
Resinous—the luster of resin: sphalerite
Greasy—like an oily surface: nepheline
Pearly—like mother-of-pearl: talc
Silky—the luster of silk or rayon: asbestos or satin-spar gypsum
Dull—as the name implies: chalk or clay

Submetallic luster is intermediate between metallic and nonmetallic luster. The mineral wolframite displays typical submetallic luster.

Terms such as **shining** (bright by reflected light), **glistening** (a sparkling brightness), **splendent** (glossy brilliance), and **dull** (lacking brilliance or luster) are commonly used to indicate the degree of luster present. Here too, one must take into consideration such factors as tarnish, type of lighting, and general condition of the mineral specimen being examined.

Specific Gravity. The relative weights of minerals are also useful in identification, for some minerals, such as galena (an ore of lead), are much heavier than others. The relative weight of a mineral is called its specific gravity. Specific gravity is determined by comparing the weight of the mineral specimen with the weight of an equal

volume of fresh water. Thus, a specimen of galena (specific gravity about 7.5) would be about 7½ times as heavy as the same volume of water.

In order to determine the specific gravity of a given specimen, the specimen is weighed in air on a spring scale (sometimes called a Jolly-Kraus balance) ; then lowered into a container of fresh water and weighed in the water. The specific gravity (Sp. Gr.) equals the weight in air divided by the loss of weight in water. When the specific gravity has been determined, it may then be compared with the known weight of other minerals in order to identify the specimen.

Cleavage and Fracture. Mineral crystals will break if they are strained beyond their plastic and elastic limits. If the crystal breaks irregularly it is said to exhibit **fracture**, but if it should break along surfaces related to the crystal structure it is said to show **cleavage.** Each break or **cleavage plane** is closely related to the atomic structure of the mineral and designates planes of weakness within the crystal. Because the number of cleavage planes

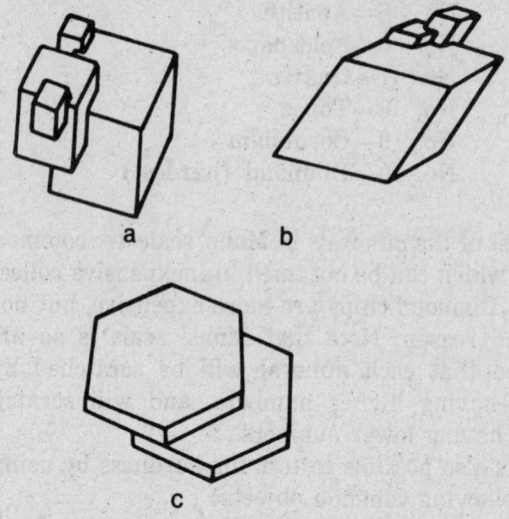

FIGURE 4. Three types of cleavage.
a—Cubic.   *b*—Rhombic.   *c*—Perfect basal.

present and the angles between them are constant for any given mineral, cleavage is a very useful aid in mineral identification.

Minerals may have one, two, three, four, or six directions of cleavage. The mineral galena, for example, cleaves in three planes (directions) at right angles to one another. Thus, if galena is struck a quick, sharp blow with a hammer, the specimen will break up into a number of small cubes. Calcite, on the other hand, has three cleavage planes that are not at right angles to one another. Therefore it will always produce a number of rhombohedral cleavage fragments. Hence, galena is said to have **cubic** cleavage, calcite **rhombohedral** cleavage.

Many minerals break or fracture in a distinctive way, and for this reason their broken surfaces (Fig. 5) may be of value in identifying minerals.

There are several types of fractures; some of the more common types (with example) are:

> Conchoidal—the broken surface of the specimen shows a fracture resembling the smooth curved surface of a shell. This type of fracture is typical of chipped glass: quartz and obsidian.
>
> Splintery or Fibrous—fibers or splinters are revealed along the fracture surface: pectolite.
>
> Hackly—fracture surface marked by rough jagged edges: copper, silver, and certain other metals.
>
> Uneven—rough irregular fracture of surface. This type of fracture is common in many minerals and is, therefore, of limited use in identification: jasper, a variety of quartz.
>
> Even—as the name implies: magnesite.
>
> Earthy—as the name implies: kaolinite.

Tenacity. The tenacity of a mineral may be defined as the resistance that it offers to tearing, crushing, bending, or breaking. Some terms used to describe the different kinds of tenacity are:

> Brittle—the mineral can be broken or powdered easily. The degree of brittleness may be qualified by such terms as tough, fragile, etc.: galena or sulfur.
>
> Elastic—the mineral, after being bent, will return to its original form or position: mica.
>
> Flexible—the mineral will bend but will not return to its original shape upon release of pressure: talc.

Other Physical Properties. In addition to those properties discussed above, the mineral characteristics below may also aid greatly in identification. Examples of minerals exhibiting these properties are given.

Play of Colors. Some minerals show variations in color when viewed from different angles: labradorite.

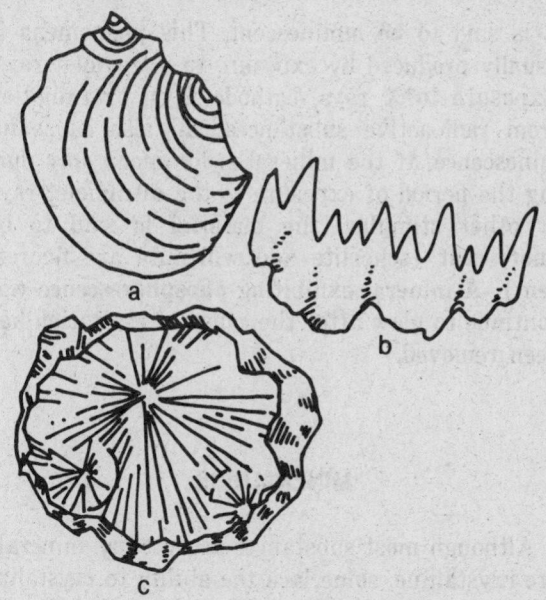

FIGURE 5. Some types of fracture.
a—Conchoidal. *b*—Hackly. *c*—Splintery.

> Sectile—the mineral can be cut with a knife to produce shavings: selenite gypsum and talc.
>
> Malleable—the mineral can be hammered into thin sheets: gold and copper.
>
> Ductile—the mineral can be drawn out into wire: gold, silver, and copper.

Asterism. This may be observed if the mineral exhibits a starlike effect when viewed either by reflected or transmitted light: certain specimens of phlogopite or the star-sapphire.

Diaphaneity or Transparency. This property refers to the ability of a mineral to transmit light. The varying degrees of diaphaneity are:

> Opaque—no light passes through the mineral: galena, pyrite, and magnetite.
>
> Translucent—light passes through the mineral but an object cannot be seen through it: chalcedony and certain other varieties of quartz.
>
> Transparent—light passes through the mineral and the outline of objects can be clearly seen through it: halite, calcite, clear crystalline quartz.

Magnetism. A mineral is said to be magnetic if, in its natural state, it will be attracted to an iron magnet: magnetite, or lodestone, and pyrrhotite.

Luminescence. When a mineral glows or emits light that is not the direct result of incandescence, it is said to be luminescent. This phenomena is usually produced by exposure to ultraviolet rays. Exposure to X rays, cathode rays, or radiation from radioactive substances can also cause luminescence. If the mineral is luminous only during the period of exposure to the ultraviolet rays or other stimulus, the material is said to be **fluorescent** (scheelite and willemite are fluorescent). A mineral exhibiting **phosphorescence** will continue to glow after the cause of excitation has been removed.

MINERALOIDS

Although most substances accepted as minerals are crystalline, some lack the ability to crystalize and occur instead as a hardened gel. Substances of this type are commonly referred to as mineraloids. They are also said to be amorphous—that is, without form, for example, opals.

ROCK FORMING MINERALS

Of some two thousand different minerals that are known to be present in the earth's crust, relatively few are major constituents of the more common rocks. Those minerals that do make up a large part of the more common types of rocks are called the rock-forming minerals. Most of the rock-forming minerals are silicates, that is, they consist of a metal combined with silicon and oxygen. Rock-forming minerals are such as feldspars, mica, and quartz.

RADIOACTIVE MINERALS

In this so called "atomic age," radioactive minerals have come to play an ever increasing part in modern technology. A radioactive mineral is distinguished because it emits radioactive isotopes which are detected usually with a geiger counter. Although there are a number of radioactive minerals, the two most widely known are uraninite and carnotite.

METALLIC OR ORE MINERALS

Metals are among the most valuable products known to man, and for this reason the metallic or ore minerals are of great interest to the geologist. These minerals are found in ore deposits —rock masses from which metals may be obtained commercially. Usually occurring with the valuable ore minerals are certain worthless minerals called gangue minerals. These, of course, must be separated from the more valuable ore minerals. Included here are aluminum, gold, copper, lead, and silver.

NONMETALLIC OR INDUSTRIAL MINERALS

Minerals that do not contain metals or that are not used as metals make up this group. It is in this vast category that such varied materials as coal, petroleum, sulfur, fertilizer, building stones, and gem stones are placed.

Metamorphism and Crustal Deformation

Metamorphic rocks are rocks (originally either igneous or sedimentary) that have been buried deep within the earth and subjected to high temperatures and pressures. These new physical conditions usually produce great changes in the solid rock and these changes are included under the term metamorphism (Greek *meta*, "change," and *morphe*, "form" or "shape").

During the process of metamorphism the original rock undergoes physical and chemical alterations which may greatly modify its texture, mineral composition, and chemical composition.

Thus, limestone may be metamorphosed into marble, and sandstone into quartzite. Let us now consider the types of forces that might bring about metamorphic changes.

TYPES OF METAMORPHISM

Although more technical classifications recognize several different kinds of metamorphism, only contact metamorphism, and dynamic, or kinetic, metamorphism will be considered here.

Contact Metamorphism. When country rock (the rock intruded by or surrounding an igneous intrusion) is invaded by an igneous body it generally undergoes profound change. Hence, limestone intruded by a hot magma may be altered for a distance of a few inches to as much as several miles from the igneous sedimentary contact. Some of the more simple metamorphic rocks have been formed in this so-called **baked zone** of the altered country rock (Fig. 6).

Physical change may be produced by contact metamorphism when the original minerals in the country rock are permeated by magmatic fluids which often bring about recrystallization. This process, which typically produces either new or larger mineral crystals, may greatly alter the texture of the rock. In addition, the magmatic fluids commonly introduce new elements and compounds

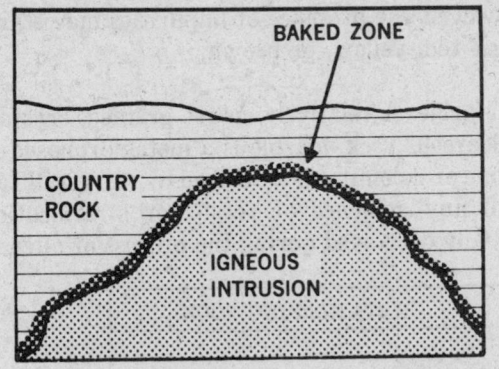

FIGURE 6. Baked zone in country rock surrounding an igneous intrusion.

which will modify the chemical composition of the original rock and result in the formation of new minerals.

Dynamic, or Kinetic, Metamorphism. Dynamic metamorphism occurs when rock layers undergo strong structural deformation during the formation of mountain ranges. The great pressures exerted as the rock layers are folded, fractured, and crumpled generally produce widespread and complex metamorphic change. Such pressures may result in tearing or crushing of the minerals, obliteration of any indication of fossils or stratification, realignment of mineral grains, and increased hardness. Because this type of metamorphism takes place on a relatively large scale it is also called **regional metamorphism.**

EFFECTS AND PRODUCTS OF METAMORPHISM

The effects of metamorphism are controlled to a large extent by the chemical and physical characteristics of the original rock and by the agent and degree of metamorphism involved. The more basic changes are in the texture and chemical composition of the rock.

TEXTURE

The rearrangement of mineral crystals during metamorphism results in two basic types of rock texture: foliated and nonfoliated.

Foliated Metamorphic Rocks. Foliated rocks are metamorphic rocks in which the minerals have been flattened, drawn out, and arranged in parallel layers or bands (Fig. 7). There are three basic types of foliation: slaty, schistose, and gneissic. Each of these, and some common rocks which exhibit them, is discussed below.

Slate. A metamorphosed shale, slate is characterized by a very fine texture in which mineral crystals cannot be detected with the naked eye. It does not show banding (see Fig. 7) and splits readily into thin even slabs. Slate occurs in a variety of colors, but is usually gray, black, green, and red. Its characteristic slaty cleavage (not to be confused with mineral cleavage) makes it especially useful for roofing, blackboards, and sidewalks.

Schist. Schist is a medium- to coarse-grained foliated metamorphic rock formed under greater pressures than those which form slate. It consists principally of micaceous minerals in a nearly parallel arrangement called **schistosity**. Schists usually split readily along these schistose laminations or folia, which are usually bent and crumpled. Commonly derived from slate, schists may also be formed from fine-grained igneous rocks. They are named according to the predominant mineral, such as mica schists, chlorite schists, etc.

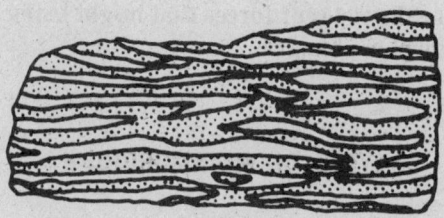

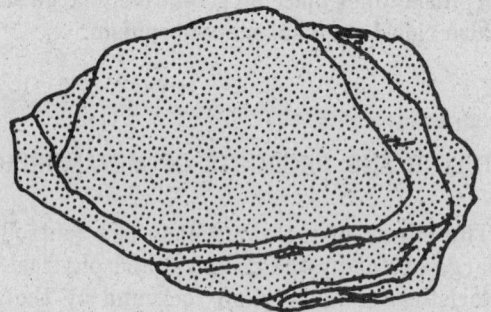

FIGURE 7. Schist, a foliated metamorphic rock.

Phyllite. Derived from the Greek word *phyllon* (a leaf), phyllites are more fine-grained than schists but coarser than slate. On freshly broken surfaces they have a characteristic silky luster or sheen due to the presence of fine grains of mica. Most have been formed from shales which have been subjected to pressures greater than those required to produce slate, but not of sufficient intensity to produce schists.

Gneiss. Gneiss (pronounced "nice") is a very highly metamorphosed coarse-grained banded rock. This rock is characterized by alternating bands of darker minerals such as chlorite, biotite mica, or graphite (Fig. 8). The bands are typically folded and contorted, and although some gneisses resemble schists, they do not split nearly as easily. Banding may be an indication of stratification in

FIGURE 8. Gneiss, a banded metamorphic rock.

the original bedded sedimentary rock, or caused by the alteration of coarse-grained igneous rocks containing light- and dark-colored minerals.

In general, gneisses have undergone a greater degree of metamorphism than have schistose rocks and are commonly formed as a result of intense regional metamorphism.

Nonfoliated Metamorphic Rocks. These are metamorphic rocks which are typically massive or granular in texture and do not exhibit foliation. Although some nonfoliated rocks resemble certain igneous rocks, they can be differentiated from them on the basis of mineral composition.

Quartzite. Quartzite is formed from metamorphosed quartz sandstone. One of the most resistant of all rocks, quartzite is composed of a crystalline mass of tightly cemented sand grains. When formed from pure quartz sand, quartzite is white; however, the presence of impurities may stain the rock red, yellow, or brown.

Marble. A relatively coarse-grained, crystalline, calcareous rock, marble is a metamorphosed limestone or dolomite. It is formed by recrystallization, and any evidence of fossils or stratification is usually destroyed during the process of alteration.

ORIGINAL ROCK	METAMORPHIC ROCK
Sedimentary	
Sandstone	Quartzite
Shale	Slate, phyllite, schist
Limestone	Marble
Bituminous coal	Anthracite coal, graphite
Igneous	
Granitic textured igneous rocks	Gneiss
Compact textured igneous rocks	Schist

TABLE 2. Some common igneous and sedimentary rocks and their metamorphic equivalents.

White when pure, the presence of impurities may impart a wide range of colors to marble.

Anthracite. When bituminous, or soft, coal is strongly compacted, folded, and heated, it is transformed into anthracite, or hard, coal. Because it has undergone an extreme degree of carbonization, anthracite coal has a high fixed carbon content and almost all of the volatile materials have been driven off.

CRUSTAL MOVEMENTS

The crust of the earth has undergone great structural change during past periods of earth history. Even today the earth's crust is continually being altered by three major forces—gradation, volcanism, and tectonism. Gradation and volcanism have been discussed in earlier sections of this book; let us now see how tectonic forces have affected our earth.

TECTONISM

As usually considered, tectonism includes those processes which have resulted in deformation of the earth's crust. Tectonic movements normally occur slowly and imperceptibly over long periods of time. But some—for example, an earthquake—may take place suddenly and violently. In some instances the rocks will move vertically, resulting in uplift or subsidence of the land. They may also move horizontally, or laterally (sidewise), as a result of compression or tension. The two major types of tectonic movements, **epeirogeny** (vertical movements) and **orogeny** (essentially lateral movements) are discussed below.

Epeirogenic Movements. Relatively slow movements accompanied by broad uplift or submergence of the continents are termed epeirogenic movements. Such movements affect relatively large areas, and typically result in tilting or warping of the land. An uplift of this type may raise wavecut benches and sea cliffs well above sea level; features of this sort are common along certain parts of the Pacific Coast. In a like manner, parts of the Scandinavian coast are rising as much as three feet per century. Subsidence of the continents may also take place. Thus, continental areas sink slowly beneath the ocean and become submerged by shallow seas. Similar movements

have caused the British Isles to become isolated from continental Europe and bays to be formed in drowned valleys along the New England coast. (Submergence may, of course, also be caused by a rise in sea level.)

Rock strata involved in epeirogenic movements are not usually greatly folded or faulted (fractured). As noted above, however, such strata may undergo large-scale tilting or warping.

Orogenic Movements. These are more intense than epeirogenic movements, and the rocks involved are subjected to great stress. These movements, known also as orogenies or mountain-making movements, normally affect long narrow areas and are accompanied by much folding and faulting. Igneous activity and earthquakes also commonly occur with this type of crustal disturbance. Although orogenic movements are slow, they do occur somewhat more rapidly than epeirogenic movements.

ROCK STRUCTURES PRODUCED BY TECTONISM

Tectonic movements, whether epeirogenic or orogenic, will result in rock deformation. Under surface conditions, ordinary rocks are relatively brittle and will fracture or break when placed under great stress. Deeply buried rocks, however, are subject to such high temperatures and pressures that they become somewhat plastic. When subjected to prolonged stress these rocks are likely to warp or fold.

Warping. As noted above, warping is usually caused by raising or lowering broad areas of the earth's crust. The rock strata in such areas appear to be essentially horizontal; close study, however, indicates that the strata are gently **dipping** (inclined). Warping movements are typically epeirogenic and are accompanied by little or no local folding and faulting.

Folding. Not only may rocks be tilted and warped, they may also be folded (Fig. 9). Folds, which vary greatly in complexity and size, are formed when rock strata are crumpled and buckled up into a series of wavelike structures. This type of structural development is usually produced by great horizontal compressive forces and may result in a variety of different structures.

Anticlines (Fig. 9a) are upfolds of rock formed when strata are folded upward. **Synclines** (Fig. 9b) may be created when rock layers are folded downward. Broad uparched folds covering large areas are called **geanticlines**; large down-warped troughs are known as **geosynclines**. Great thicknesses of sediments have accumulated in certain geosynclines of the geologic past, and some of these have been elevated to form folded mountain ranges. For example, the Appalachian Geosyncline received sediments throughout much of early Paleozoic time. Then about 225 million years ago

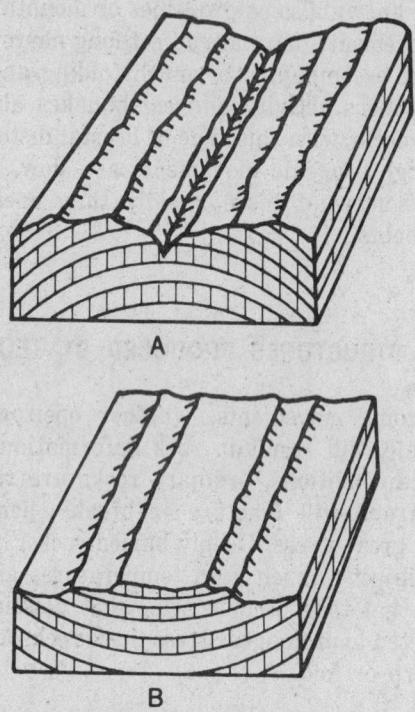

A

B

FIGURE 9. Types of folds.
a—Anticline.   *b*—Syncline.

these sediments (which had since become sedimentary rocks) were uplifted to form the Appalachian Highlands, of which the Appalachian Mountains are a part.

In studying folds we must be able to determine the **attitude** of the rock strata. Attitude—a term used to denote the position of a rock with respect to compass direction and a horizontal plane—is defined by **strike** and **dip** (Fig. 10). The strike of a formation is the compass direction of the line formed by the intersection of a bedding plane with a horizontal plane. Dip is the angle of inclination between the bedding plane and a horizontal plane. The direction of dip is always at

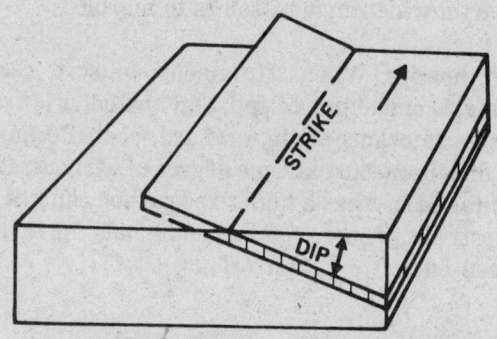

FIGURE 10. Strike and dip. The beds strike north-south and dip to the east.

right angles to the strike; thus, a rock stratum which dips due north would strike east-west.

Other types of folds include **monoclines**, simple steplike folds which dip in only one direction (Fig. 11); **domes**, a fold in which strata dip away from a common center; and **basins**, a fold in which the strata dip toward a common center.

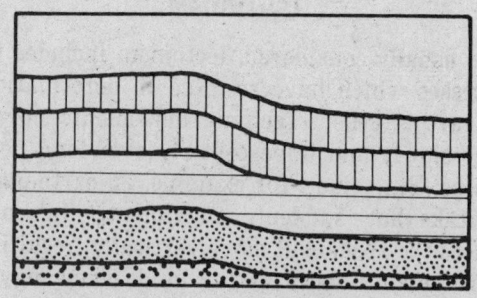

FIGURE 11. A monocline.

Fracturing. Rocks subjected to great stress near the surface are apt to fracture, thus producing joints and faults. A fracture along which there has been little or no movement is called a **joint** (Fig. 12). Joints occur in sets and are usually parallel to one another. Fractures of this sort have formed in igneous rocks as a result of contraction due to cooling and are common in certain dikes and sills. Joints are also created by tension and compression when rocks undergo stress due to warping, folding, and faulting.

Joint systems are developed when two or more sets of joints intersect. These intersecting joint patterns may be helpful in certain quarrying operations and in developing porosity in otherwise impervious rocks. Jointing will also hasten weathering and erosion, for they render the rocks more susceptible to attack from rain, frost, and streams.

Faults are fractures in the earth's crust along which movements have taken place (Fig. 13). The rocks affected by faulting are displaced along the **fault plane.** If the crust is displaced vertically, the rocks on one side of the fault may stand higher than those on the other. This may result in a cliff called a **fault scarp.** Large-scale faulting of this type may produce **fault block mountains,** such as the Sierra Nevada in California and the Lewis Range in Montana.

Some knowledge of fault terminology is prerequisite to an understanding of the different types of faults. (The parts of faults are illustrated in Fig. 13.) The rock surface bounding the lower side of an inclined fault plane is known as the **footwall** and that above as the **hanging wall.** The **strike** of a fault is the horizontal direction of the fault plane; **dip** is determined by measuring the inclination of the fault plane at right angles to the strike. **Displacement** refers to the amount of movement that has taken place along the fault plane.

The various types of faults are classified largely by the direction and relative movement of the rocks along the fault plane. A **normal or gravity fault** is one in which the hanging wall has moved downward with respect to the footwall (Fig. 14).

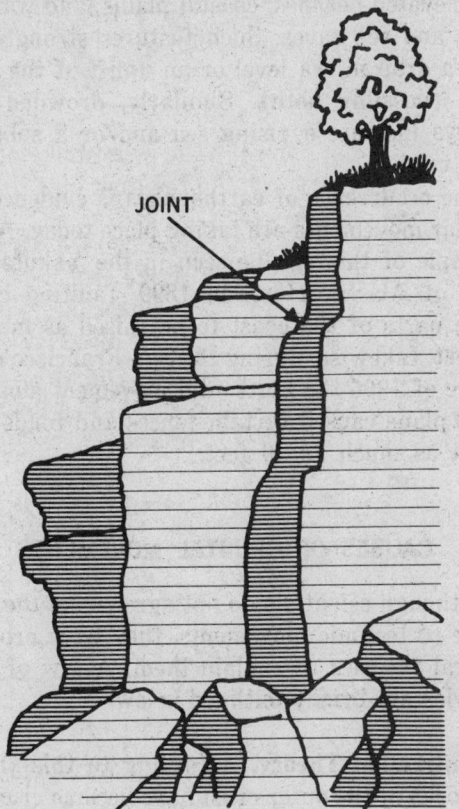

FIGURE 12. Vertical joints in limestone cliff.

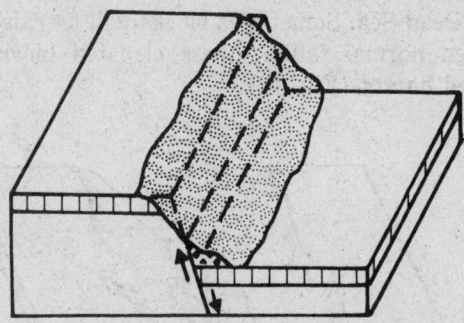

FIGURE 14. Normal or gravity fault.

If the hanging wall has moved upward with respect to the footwall, a **reverse fault** or **thrust fault** is produced (Fig. 15). A **strike-slip fault** will be

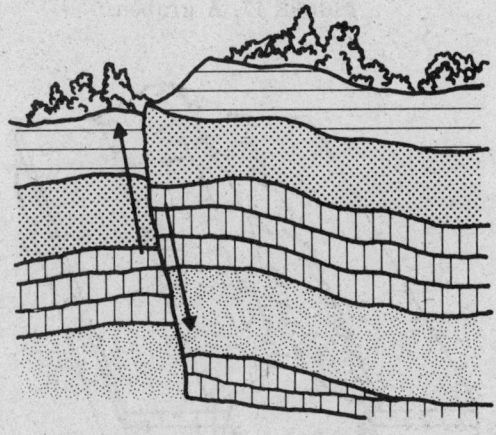

FIGURE 15. Reverse fault.

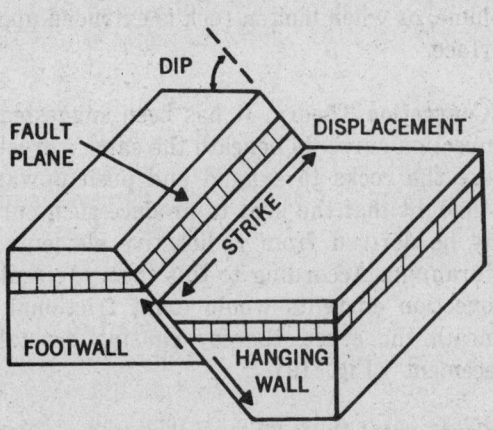

FIGURE 13. A normal fault, showing principal parts and terms used in describing faults.

produced if the movement is predominantly horizontal parallel to the fault plane (Fig. 16).

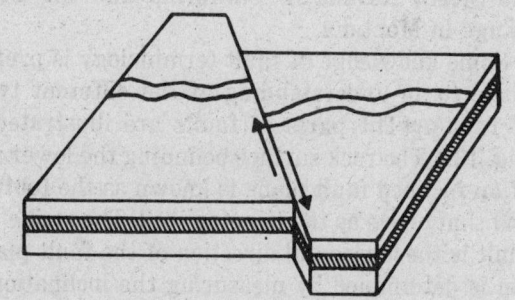

FIGURE 16. Strike-slip fault. (Note the road offset in center of block.)

In some areas a long narrow block has dropped down between normal faults, thereby producing a **graben** (Fig. 17). Large-scale grabens are called **rift valleys.** Two examples of grabens are the upper Rhine Valley and the depression containing the Dead Sea. Sometimes blocks will be raised between normal faults; these elevated blocks are called **horsts** (Fig. 18).

FIGURE 17. A graben.

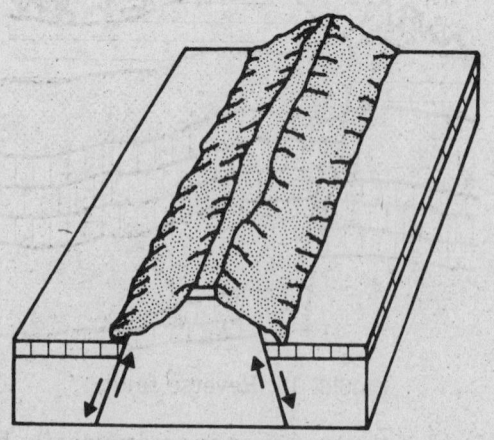

FIGURE 18. A horst.

EVIDENCE OF CRUSTAL MOVEMENTS

The rocks of the earth's crust present much evidence to show that many tectonic movements have taken place in the geologic past. We have already learned, for example, that the fossilized remains of sea plants and animals may be found thousands of feet above sea level. Common also are elevated beaches, coastal plains, and wave-cut cliffs and sea caves. Such features strongly suggest a drop in sea level or an uplift of the continent (possibly both). Similarly, drowned river valleys indicate a rising sea and/or a subsiding land mass.

The occurrence of earthquakes is evidence that similar movements are taking place today. A good example of this can be seen in the Yakutat Bay area of Alaska. Here, in 1899, faulting caused some parts of the coast to be raised as much as 47 feet. Likewise, during the San Francisco earthquake of 1906 the horizontal movement along the fault plane caused certain fences and roads to be offset as much as 20 feet.

CAUSES OF CRUSTAL MOVEMENTS

Although scientists do not agree upon the exact cause of tectonic movements, they have proposed several theories to explain them. A few of these theories are briefly outlined below.

Contraction Theory. According to this theory, the rocks of the outer crust have become crumpled and wrinkled as the interior of the earth cooled and contracted. Shrinkage may also come about as great pressures squeeze the earth into a smaller volume, or when molten rock is extruded upon the surface.

Convection Theory. It has been suggested that convection currents beneath the earth's crust may cause the rocks to expand and push upward. It is thought that the heat to produce such currents may be derived from radioactive elements such as uranium. According to this theory, circulating convection currents would exert frictional drag beneath the crust, thereby causing crustal displacement (Fig. 19).

Continental Drift Theory. This theory suggests that there was originally only one huge continent. At some time in the geologic past this continent

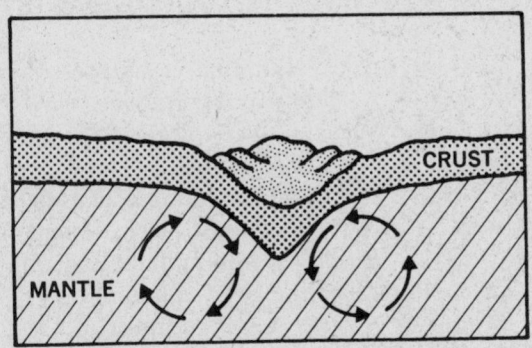

FIGURE 19. Convection currents in the mantle (circling arrows) and their relation to the overlying crust.

broke into several segments and drifted apart. This "drifting" or "floating" was possible because the continents, composed largely of granite, are lighter than the more plastic basaltic material beneath the crust. As the front of the drifting land mass moved forward, frictional drag with subcrustal material caused the continental margins to crumple up, thus forming the folded coastal mountain ranges of Europe and North and South America. Look at a globe and you will see how this idea originated. You will notice that the shorelines along both sides of the Atlantic Ocean match surprisingly well. Moreover, some of the older mountain belts in America appear to be continu-

ations of similar mountain belts in the eastern continents.

Isostasy. The theory of isostasy states that at considerable depth within the earth, different segments of the crust will be in balance with other segments of unequal thickness. The differences in height of these crustal segments is explained as the result of variations in density. Consequently, the continents and mountainous areas are higher because they are composed of lighter rocks; the ocean basins are lower because they are composed of denser (heavier) rocks (Fig. 20). As the continents are eroded and sediments deposited in the ocean, the ocean basin is depressed because of the added weight of the accumulating sediments. This causes displacement of the plastic subcrustal rocks which push the continents up. The upward displacement of the continent is aided by erosion which removes rock materials, thus making the continents lighter and more susceptible to uplift.

Because the movements of isostatic adjustment are essentially vertical in nature, this theory cannot account for forces of horizontal compression. Isostasy does, however, offer some explanation as to why the erosion of the continents and subsequent deposition in the ocean basins have not resulted in a continuous level surface on the face of the earth.

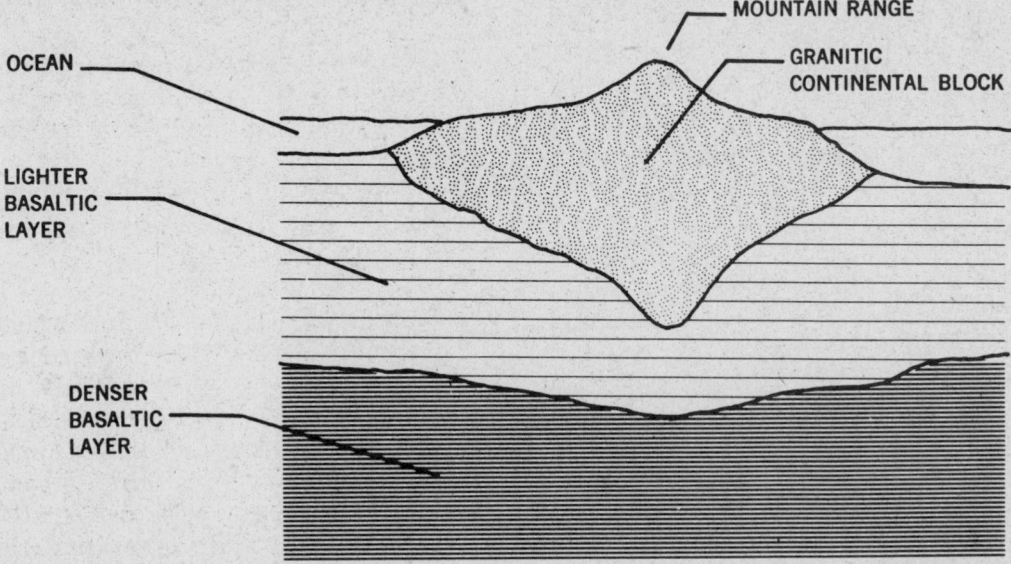

FIGURE 20. Relatively light granitic rocks of continent resting on denser basaltic substratum.

ASTRONOMY

A Brief History

The history of astronomy may be conveniently divided into three periods: the geocentric, the galactic, and the universal. The first had its beginnings in ancient history, and came to a close in the sixteenth century. The second extends from the seventeenth through the nineteenth centuries. And the third began and continues in the present century.

THE GEOCENTRIC PERIOD

Early astronomers believed the earth to be in the center of the universe; and assumed that the sun, moon, and stars revolved about that stationary earth. Their interest, hardly scientific in our sense of the term, was mainly in practical matters, in the real and supposed relation of celestial events to those on the earth; in searching the skies for clues to good and evil omens.

Even so, remarkable discoveries were made then. The calendar was developed with great accuracy. The apparent path of the sun among the stars—the ecliptic—was carefully defined. The complete cycle of solar and lunar eclipses was determined. And as early as the second century B.C., the motion of the earth's axis was well understood.

The great figure of Nicolaus Copernicus (1473–1543) is closely associated with the end of the primitive geocentric period in the sixteenth century.

THE GALACTIC PERIOD

Modern astronomy can be said to have begun in this period. Copernicus demonstrated that the earth, far from being the center of the universe, was merely one of the planets revolving about the central sun. Hardly unique, the earth was found to be a quite ordinary planet, going through ordinary motions in an ordinary way.

Indeed the central sun itself was realized to be merely one star among the multitudes in the heavens, one among billions of similar stars in every direction about us—some larger, some smaller, some heavier, some lighter than our sun.

In this period the approach became increasingly scientific, motivated largely by the desire to know, to understand the basic laws governing the motion of heavenly bodies, to explain what the eye saw.

Progress from the sixteenth through the nineteenth centuries resulted from the effective combination of extended observation, improved instruments, and the work of scientific genius.

Observation. Great quantities of data of fundamental importance were painstakingly gathered by careful observers, chief among whom is the great name of Tycho Brahe (1546–1601).

Instruments. The introduction of the telescope in 1610 by Galileo Galilei (1564–1642) was, of course, a milestone in the development of the science of astronomy; as was the later invention and introduction of the spectroscope. The two instruments complement one another: the telescope permits us to see the stars more clearly; the spectroscope analyzes stellar light, furnishing us with much information about the stars.

Genius. Like every science, astronomy requires for its advancement the labors of great minds that are able to apply to the observed data insight, imagination, intuition, as well as great learning.

Such minds were Johannes Kepler (1571–1630) and Sir Isaac Newton (1642–1727): Kepler by the discovery of the laws of planetary motion and Newton by the discovery of the Universal Law of Gravitation.

THE UNIVERSAL PERIOD

Now it became apparent that the galaxy of stars to which our sun belongs is merely one of many galaxies—some larger, some smaller than ours. To these much of the astronomical research of the last half century has been devoted, in an effort to achieve a "complete" picture of the universe. To aid this research ever greater optical telescopes, as well as gigantic radio telescopes, have been constructed.

The great theoretical genius associated most closely with this period in the public mind (although he was primarily a physicist and mathematician) is the late Dr. Albert Einstein (1879–1955). Cosmology and astrophysics depend more and more on his theory of relativity.

This is the astronomic period in which we live. And it is far from concluded.

The Universe

INTRODUCTION AND DEFINITIONS

For as long as man has been conscious of himself and the universe he inhabits, he has regarded the sky with awe and wonder—a source of constant and compelling fascination. Awe and wonder generate study and science; man seeking ceaselessly to conquer ignorance and solve mysteries, thus developing finally into the science of astronomy.

Astronomy is the science of the positions, motions, constitutions, histories, and destinies of celestial bodies. In the course of its development as a science, it has already discovered many of the basic laws governing those bodies. But it is the nature of scientific investigation that its work is never done—and here, as elsewhere, immense labors remain to be performed.

THE STUDY OF ASTRONOMY?

We study astronomy because the intelligent, inquiring mind must ask questions and seek answers; must know "Why?" and discover "How?" And from the beginning, whenever man has looked up, there was the sky—always confronting him with seemingly imponderable problems, always challenging him to solve its mysteries.

On one level, man has stated his reaction in magic and mythology, and this has been expressed in the world's art, literature, and religions. On another level, he has attempted to explain the celestial phenomena perceived by his senses in scientific terms—and these explanations are the subject matter of the science of astronomy.

THE COMPONENTS

The earth we live on is a planet—one of a number of planets that revolve about the sun. The unassisted eye is capable of detecting the sun, several planets, one satellite (our moon), several thousands of stars, shooting stars (meteors), and once in a great while a comet.

These celestial bodies are the components that constitute the universe, in much the same way that homes, churches, hospitals, and parks are components of a community.

To the best of our knowledge, the **universe consists of stars** (billions and billions of these), nebulae, planets, planetoids, satellites, comets, etc.

STARS

Stars are large globes of intensely heated gas, shining by their own light. At their surface, they reach temperatures of thousands of degrees; in their interior, temperatures are much higher.

At these temperatures, matter cannot exist either in solid or in liquid form. The gases constituting the stars are much thicker than those on the earth usually are. The extremely high values of their density are due to enormous pressures which prevail in their interior.

Stars move above in space, although their motion is not immediately perceptible. No change in their relative position can be detected in a year. Even in a thousand years, the stars will seem not to have moved substantially. Their pattern now is almost exactly that of a thousand years ago. This seeming fixedness is due to the vast distance separating us from them. At these distances it will take many thousands of years for the stellar pattern to undergo a noticeable change: This **apparent** constancy of position accounts for the popular name "fixed stars."

NEBULAE

A nebula is a vast cloud composed of dust and gas. The gases which compose it are extremely thin and of low temperature. Nebulae do not shine by their own light, but are made visible by the light of neighboring stars. When they are so visible, they appear to the unaided eye not unlike a fuzzy star. Their actual size and structure, however, can be determined only with the aid of a telescope. Other nebulae are dark and obscure the stars beyond them.

PLANETS

The planets that revolve around our sun are large, solid, nearly spherical masses. The best

known to us is, of course, our own earth. All of them are relatively cool and are made visible by reflected sunlight; several can be seen at one time or another by the unaided eye. Three planets, however, can be seen only with the aid of a telescope. At first glance, planets look very much like the multitude of stars that glitter in the sky; but an observer can identify a planet by one or more of the following characteristics:

A. Planets shine with a **steady** light, while stars do not. The light reaching our eyes from stars seems to change rapidly in both color and brightness. These changes in color and brightness cause the **twinkling** of the stars.

B. Planets **wander** in the heavens: A planet which at one time was close to one star may later be observed close to another star. Stars, on the other hand, seem to keep the same positions relative to one another. See Fig. 1. The very word "planet" is derived from a Greek word meaning "wanderer."

C. Planets, when observed through telescopes, appear as **small disks** of light. The greater the magnification, the larger will be the diameter of the disk. Stars, even with the largest telescope, appear only as points of light. Even in the 200-inch telescope, they appear as mere points, having no measurable diameter.

D. Planets may be found **only in a narrow strip** in the sky. Their motions are limited to the boundaries of this strip. Stars, of course, may be found in any part of the sky.

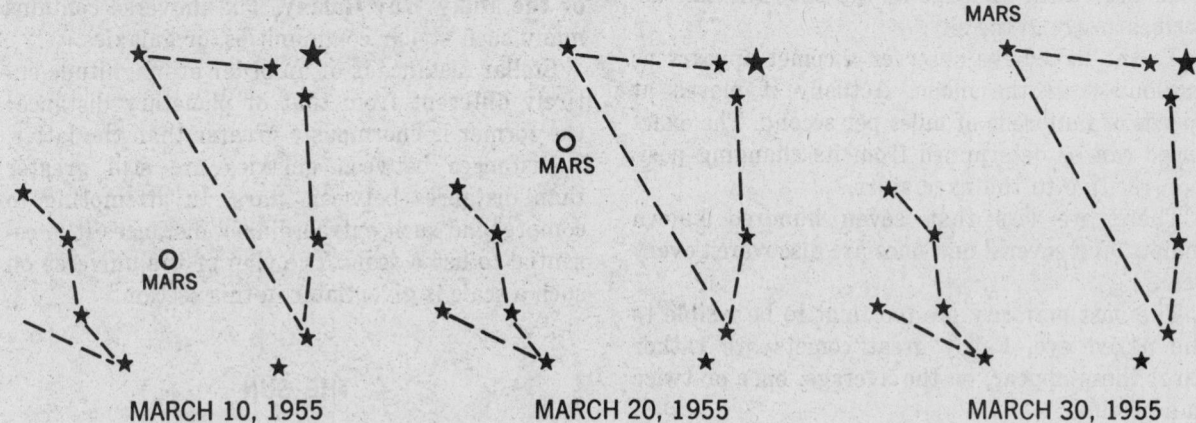

MARCH 10, 1955   MARCH 20, 1955   MARCH 30, 1955

FIGURE 1. Views of the same part of the sky on three different dates, March 10, March 20, and March 30, 1955. Note that the stars maintain the same relative position. The planet (Mars) has wandered considerably in that time.

PLANETOIDS

Planets are small, irregularly shaped solid bodies revolving, like the major planets, about the sun, and differing from planets primarily in size. They are also known either as asteroids or as minor planets. The largest planetoid, Ceres, has a diameter of 480 miles; but many of them have a diameter of only two miles. The first planetoid was discovered on January 1, 1801; many more have since been discovered. It is estimated that more than 100,000 planetoids can be photographed with one of the large telescopes.

They, too, shine by reflected sunlight; however, because of their small surface, the amount of reflected light is very small. They cannot be seen without the aid of a telescope.

SATELLITES

Six of the nine major planets have one or more moons revolving round them. These are called satellites. The earth has only one moon (satellite), while the planet Jupiter, for example, has fourteen. To date, thirty-four satellites have been discovered, the last as recently as 1975.

COMETS

Comets are celestial bodies of unique form and large size which appear from time to time. A typical comet consists of a luminous sphere, or head, connected to a long, tenuous cylinder, or tail. The head may seem as large as the sun; the tail describes an arc in the sky.

To the naked-eye observer a comet appears as motionless as the moon. Actually it moves at speeds of hundreds of miles per second. The exact speed can be determined from its changing position relative to the fixed stars.

There are less than seven hundred known comets, and several new ones are discovered every year.

The vast majority are too faint to be visible to the naked eye. Fairly great comets are rather rare; these appear, on the average, once or twice in a lifetime.

Of the 625 or so known comets, more than 259 are known to move in "closed orbits"—that is, in more or less elongated, cigar-shaped paths. The fact that the orbit is "closed," has no beginning or end, is of great importance. Comets moving in

them go round the same path continuously; many of them have been observed several times during their returns to the vicinity of the earth.

The orbits of the other 368 comets are either parabolic or hyperbolic. They very likely made only one appearance in the vicinity of the earth, coming, probably, from outer space, making a U-turn, and then left, never to be seen again.

METEOROIDS

Meteoroids are usually tiny (about the size of the head of a pin), solid objects traversing through space. Occasionally a group of meteoroids is attracted to the earth and becomes entangled in its atmosphere. The heat resulting from this encounter consumes the object; the dust resulting from this cremation falls to the earth. Hundreds of tons of meteoric dust descend each year. On rare occasions large meteoroids manage to reach the earth before they are consumed. The light phenomenon which results from the entry of the meteoroid into the earth's atmosphere is called meteor, or "shooting star," the glow of which may persist several seconds.

The universe is composed of stars, nebulae, planets, comets, and other celestial bodies. Here, the components are assembled to form the design of the universe.

The planets, planetoids, satellites, comets, and meteorites revolve about a single star: the star we call the sun. Together they form the Solar System. The sun, and billions of other stars, form the community of stars known either as Our Galaxy, or the Milky Way Galaxy. The universe contains many such stellar communities, or galaxies.

Stellar distance is of an order of magnitude entirely different from that of planetary distance: the former is enormously greater than the latter.

Distances between galaxies are still greater than distances between stars. In attempting to comprehend such extraordinary distances it is essential to use a scale. The plan of the universe on such a scale is given later in this section.

THE SUN

Although it may not seem so, the sun is just an ordinary star, similar to numerous other stars that we see in the sky.

The sun appears large to us because it is, relatively speaking, near to us. All other stars appear as small points of light in the sky because they are far away. See Figs. 2a and 2b. Our interest in this star (the sun) derives from the fact that the earth receives from it both heat and light—energy of

FIGURE 2a. The sun is just an ordinary star. All the other stars look tiny, as they are so remote that we see them only as mere points of light.

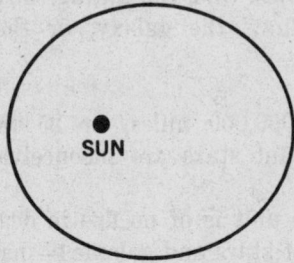

FIGURE 2b. Other objects, too, appear smaller with increasing distance. Note the apparent size of the distant tree.

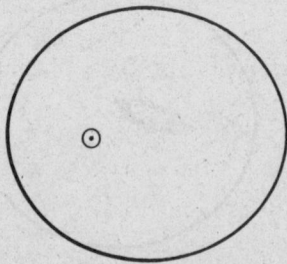

FIGURE 2c. The oval curve suggests the circumference of the whole universe. The dot represents the location of the sun.

fundamental importance in maintaining life. The oval curve in Figure 2c represents the universe and the dot the position of the sun within the universe. (Note that Fig. 2c, as well as Figs. 3, 4, and 5, are symbolic representations and not figures drawn to scale.)

PLANETS

There are nine planets revolving about the sun: Mercury, Venus, Earth, Mars, Jupiter, Saturn,

Uranus, Neptune, and Pluto. Mercury is closest to the sun, and at a somewhat greater distance is Venus; then, the earth; and the farthest known planet from the sun is Pluto.

The earth is 93 million miles from the sun. **This distance is often referred to as an Astronomical Unit.** Mercury is only four tenths the earth's distance from the sun. Pluto, the most distant planet, is forty times the earth's distance. The distance of Pluto can be stated as forty times 93 million miles, or simply as forty astronomical units.

A reducing scale may help to visualize these distances. The scale that is commonly used represents the sun-earth distance as one foot long:

93 million miles equal 1 foot; or,
1 astronomical unit equals 1 foot.

On this scale, Mercury is fourth tenths of a foot; Venus is seven tenths; and the earth is one foot away from the sun. The farthest planet is forty feet from the sun. A circular box of forty-foot radius could accommodate all the planets. The box could be quite shallow, as all the planets move approximately in the same plane.

THE SOLAR SYSTEM

The sun and the planets are the major components of the solar system. Other members of this system are:

1. the host of smaller planets known as planetoids or asteroids
2. the several moons, known as satellites, that revolve about six of these planets;
3. comets that appear from time to time;
4. the vast number of meteoroids.

The circle around the dot in Figure 3 represents the entire solar system.

FIGURE 3. The oval curve suggests the circumference of the whole universe. The dot and the small circle represent the sun and the solar system, respectively.

THE STARS

Distances to stars are immensely greater than distances to planets. Even the star nearest our own sun is at a distance of 270,000 astronomical units. Using the scale (one foot equals one astronomical unit, or 93 million miles), the star closest to our sun would be at a distance of fifty miles.

The two units should be carefully noted. Distances between planets are stated in **feet,** while those between stars are stated in **miles.** A mental picture might help to visualize this distinction. The sun, and all the planets, could be accommodated in a circular house of forty foot radius. The closest star, by our scale, would be in a house fifty miles away. Other stars, by our scale, are at scale distances of thousands and hundreds of thousands of miles from the sun.

OUR GALAXY

These stars form a large community called Our Galaxy or the Milky Way Galaxy. It is estimated that the number of stars in our galaxy is close to a hundred billion—otherwise stated as 100×10^9, or a hundred thousand million.

The outer surface of the galaxy is often compared either to a grindstone or to a lens.

A top view of the galaxy would reveal its circular shape as well as the spiral design formed by the stars. A side view would suggest its similarity to a lens, namely, that it is thick in the center, and thins out toward the edges.

Again using the one foot scale, the diameter of the circle would be close to a million miles, while the maximum thickness is only about one sixth of the diameter.

Our galaxy is represented in Figure 4.

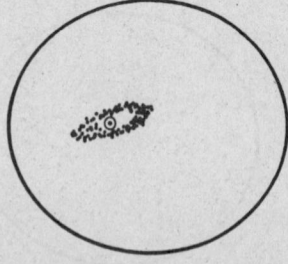

FIGURE 4. The oval curve represents the circumference of the universe. Our galaxy is indicated inside the oval. The dot and the circle represent the sun and the solar system, respectively.

OTHER GALAXIES

Ours is not the only galaxy in the universe: many have been discovered in recent years, strikingly similar to our own. The scale distances between them are from ten to twenty million miles. A highly simplified picture of the universe is shown in Figure 5.

OUTLINE OF THE UNIVERSE IN TERMS OF ACTUAL DISTANCES

The distance to the sun is 93 million miles; the distance to our nearest star, Alpha-Centauri, is

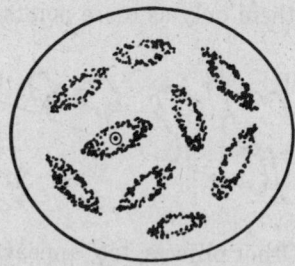

FIGURE 5. The "complete" universe consists of many galaxies. One, containing the sun, is known as our galaxy, the galaxy, or the Milky Way galaxy.

25,000,000,000,000 miles, or 25 million million miles. Distant stars are inconceivably more remote.

The mile unit is of no use in dealing with the distances of stars and galaxies—instead, astronomers use the unit "light-year": one light-year is the distance that a beam of light travels in one year. The distance covered by a beam of light in one second is 186,000 miles; hence:

One light-year =

$$186{,}000 \times 60 \left(\frac{\text{seconds}}{\text{minute}}\right) \times 60 \left(\frac{\text{minutes}}{\text{hour}}\right)$$

$$\times 24 \left(\frac{\text{hours}}{\text{day}}\right) \times 365\tfrac{1}{4} = 5{,}880{,}000{,}000{,}000 \text{ miles}$$

or 6 million million miles, approximately.

The star nearest the solar system is 4.3 light-years away. The diameter of our galaxy is about 100,000 light-years; its maximum thickness is 15,000 light-years. An average distance between galaxies would be approximately a million light-years.

The sun is only a minute fraction of a light-year from the earth. The distance to the sun may be stated as 8 light minutes.

Distances to heavenly bodies, when stated in terms of light, have an added meaning—for the sun, it implies that it takes a beam of sunlight 8 minutes to reach the earth.

So for the stars. A ray of light from Alpha-Centauri reaches the earth 4⅓ years after leaving the star.

The most distant object seen by the unaided eye is the Andromeda galaxy—2 million light-years away. The light entering the observer's eye has been en route for that time.

A BRIEF HISTORY OF THE UNIVERSE

The most tenable theory to date for the history of the universe is the one known as the "big bang theory." According to that theory, all the matter and all energy that is present in the universe was once concentrated in a small, enormously hot, preposterously dense ball.

Then 10, or more, thousand million years ago the ball exploded (big bang!), sending into space torrents of gas (primarily protons, neutrons, electrons, and some alpha particles), immersed in a vast ocean of radiation.

As time went on, concentration of matter formed in that turbulent gas—each concentration contracting in response to its own gravitational field, while moving outward in the ever-expanding universe.

These concentrations of gas (also known as nebulae) became galaxies when they fragmented into massive blobs to form protostars (masses of gas that in due course of time are destined to become stars).

Many of these protostars, while shrinking and flattening under influence of their own gravitational and centrifugal forces, became unstable, causing smaller masses of gas to break away and form protoplanets; and the protoplanets similarly produced protosatellites.

The protostars eventually became stars; the protoplanets and protosatellites, after proper cooling, condensing, and contracting, became planets and satellites.

To the best of our knowledge, the transition of our sun from a protostar to a star took place some 5 billion years ago. The planets and the satellites of the solar system were formed shortly thereafter.

UNAIDED OBSERVATION

On a clear night far away from city lights, the naked eye can see

A. Some 2,000 to 3,000 stars in each hemisphere of the sky. Some of these are only a few light-years away, others at distances of many hundreds of light-years.

NOTE: To the human eye, all of these stars appear equally distant and it is helpful to imagine that all these stars are attached to the inside of an imaginary large sphere called the celestial sphere. See Fig. 6.

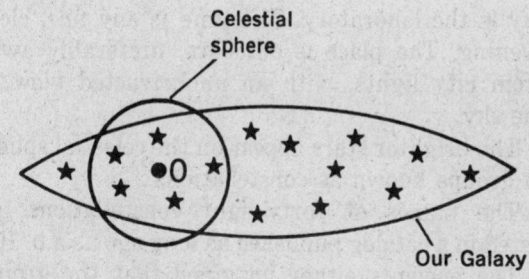

FIGURE 6. The celestial sphere is an imaginary spherical projection screen, upon which the observer, situated at the center, "sees" the stars and other celestial bodies.

B. Several planets traveling among the stars, each planet at its own characteristic velocity.

C. Meteors, five or ten every hour, each streaking across the sky and leaving a flash of light in its wake.

D. Comets, really bright ones—once or twice in a lifetime.

E. Nebulae—e.g., the great emission nebula in Orion or the dark Horsehead Nebula (also in Orion).

F. The Milky Way. An irregular belt describing a complete circuit of light on the surface of the celestial sphere. The belt varies from 5° to 50° in width. The light is due to the combined radiation emitted by the billions of stars along the long dimension of our flattened galaxy (lines AB in Figure 7). This band contrasts with the relative darkness (due to the paucity of stars) along the narrow dimension (lines AC) of the galaxy.

G. Other galaxies—e.g., the galaxy in Andromeda, that can be seen in northern latitudes and the two galaxies known as Magellanic Clouds in southern latitudes.

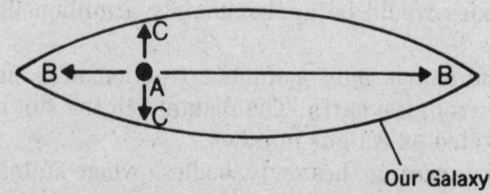

Our Galaxy

FIGURE 7. An observer at point A sees the merging light from billions of stars along lines AB. This forms the Milky Way. There are much fewer stars along lines AC, hence comparative darkness.

Identifying and Locating Stars Without a Telescope

Astronomy is one of the several sciences engaged in the study of nature. Much remains to be learned, and many important discoveries can still be made without the use of any equipment. The sky is the laboratory. The time is any fine, clear evening. The place is outdoors, preferably away from city lights, with an unobstructed view of the sky.

The brighter stars appear on the celestial sphere in groups known as constellations.

The names of forty-eight constellations are listed in a catalog published as long ago as A.D. 150.

The ancients either imagined that the groups formed pictures of gods, heroes, animals, etc., or they wanted to honor their gods, heroes, animals, etc., and named the constellations accordingly.

Modern astronomy recognizes eighty-eight constellations, each with its own clearly defined boundaries and each bearing the name originally given to it. The eighty-eight areas completely cover the celestial sphere.

NOTE: Celestial objects outside our own galaxy are also identified with the constellation in which they are seen. Hence the names "galaxy in Andromeda" or "galaxy in Ursa Major."

In this chapter, we shall pay particular attention to some thirty well-known constellations, such as Orion, the Big and Small Dippers, Cassiopeia, and so on, and we shall begin with the group that is probably easiest to identify—the Big Dipper. As its name implies, the stars form the outline of a dipper. It is important to become familiar with

that group of stars as it is with reference to it that the locations of other constellations are most often determined. The Big Dipper can be seen every clear evening in most of the northern hemisphere. This section deals primarily with the stars of that constellation.

THE STARS OF THE BIG DIPPER

Seven bright stars form the pattern of the Dipper. The four forming the "bowl" are known as Dubhe, Merak, Phecda, and Megrez, all Arabic names: Dubhe means "bear," Merak "loin," Phecda and Megrez, "thigh" and "the root of the bear's tail," respectively.

The stars forming the "handle" of the Dipper are known as Alkaid, Mizar, and Alioth, also Arabic names, meaning "the chief," and "the apron"; the precise meaning of the name "Alioth" is still disputed.

Close to Mizar is the small star Alcor. The Arabs called these two stars "the Horse and the Rider." The star Alcor was used by them in a test for good eyesight. See Fig. 8.

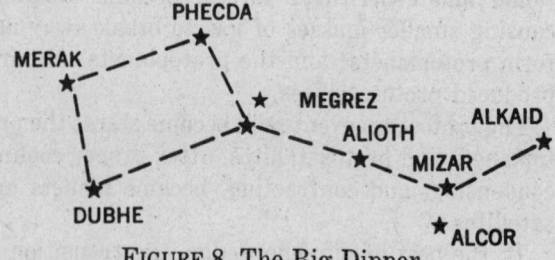

FIGURE 8. The Big Dipper.

SCALE OF ANGULAR DISTANCES

Locations of stars are stated in terms of angles or arcs. The angular distance, measured in degrees, is the angle or arc, subtended by these stars at the vantage point of the observer.

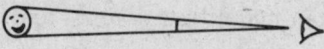

FIGURE 9. The angular distance of the full moon is about half a degree.

It is of importance to be able to gauge small angles in the sky. The diameter of the full moon is about half a degree, otherwise stated more formally as: The angle, or arc, subtended at our eye by the diameter of the full moon is .5°. See Fig. 9.

Another angular distance often used is the one between Dubhe and Merak—close to five degrees.

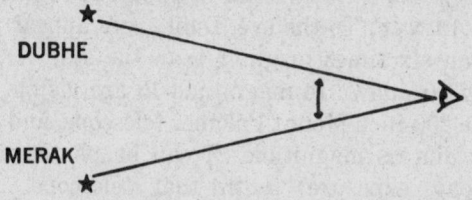

FIGURE 10. The angle subtended by Dubhe and Merak at the eye of a terrestial observer is close to 5°.

Ten moons could be placed side by side in the distance between these two stars. See Fig. 10.

PROBLEM 1:

Estimate the angular distance between Dubhe and Megrez.

Answer: 10°, approximately.

LEGENDS

One of the early names given to this constellation was the "Great Bear" and the Arabic names meaning "thigh," "loin," etc., describe parts of the bear. See Fig. 11.

FIGURE 11. The Great Bear. Note the position of the Big Dipper.

The reason for this is not known, as an observer can scarcely imagine the outline of a bear or any other animal in that constellation.

An ancient legend held that the Bear represented Callisto, a daughter of the King of Arcadia, beloved of Jupiter, who, in order to protect her, changed her into a Bear and transferred her to the skies.

Another legend held that the Great Spirit purposely put the Great Bear in the sky to act as a "calendar" for earthly bears. During the half year when the Great Bear is low in the sky, all earthly bears stay in their dens and keep warm. When the Bear is high in the sky, bears leave their dens, for summer has begun.

OTHER NAMES

The names Great Bear and Big Dipper are still in common use. The scientific name for the constellation is the Latin translation of Great Bear—Ursa Major. In England, the constellation is known as the Plough, or the Wain (for wagon).

NOTE: To be accurate, the term Big Dipper should be used to refer to the seven bright stars and the term Great Bear or Ursa Major to refer to all the stars in the constellation. Often, however, these terms are used interchangeably.

APPARENT BRIGHTNESS OF STARS

The seven stars of the Big Dipper differ materially in apparent brightness. The brightest star is Alioth; the faintest, Megrez.

Technically this is stated in terms of apparent magnitude. Alioth has the smallest apparent magnitude (1.7); Megrez, the largest (3.4).

HIPPARCHUS' CLASSIFICATION OF STARS ACCORDING TO BRIGHTNESS

The ancient Greek astronomers classified the visible stars according to their apparent brightness, into six classes. This basic classification, in the main, is still valid. To Hipparchus, who lived on the island of Rhodes in the second century B.C., goes the credit for this classification. The twenty brightest stars known to him were arbitrarily designated as stars of the **first magnitude**; and the next fifty in order of apparent brightness were designated as stars of the **second magnitude**; and so on. The designation of **sixth magnitude** was given to several hundred stars barely visible to the normal human eye. See Fig. 12. Thus a completely

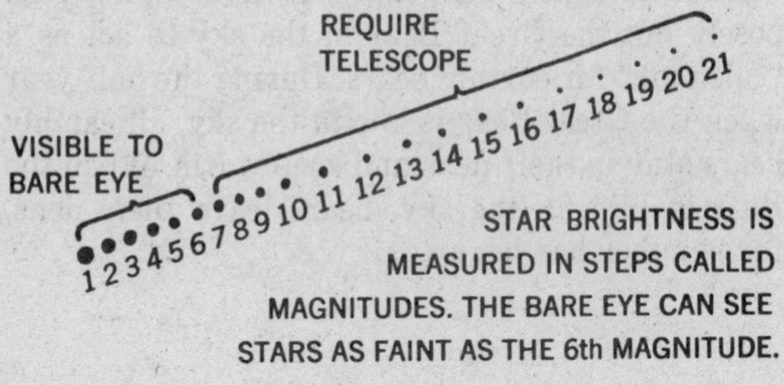

FIGURE 12. The relationship between brightness and magnitude.

arbitrary classification of stars, according to their brightness, was obtained. These magnitudes are, however, only *apparent* magnitudes. Some stars are actually bright, but appear faint because of their great distance.

DECIMAL DIVISION OF APPARENT MAGNITUDES

In the nineteenth century, the decimal division was introduced. In this classification, a star of magnitude 5.5 has an apparent brightness halfway between that of a star of magnitude 5.0 and that of a star of magnitude 6.0. Similarly, to state that the North Star (Polaris) has a magnitude of 2.1 signifies that its apparent brightness is only slightly less than the brightness of a star of magnitude 2.0. Increasingly, the decimal method of denoting magnitudes has been applied more extensively and made more precise.

RELATION BETWEEN APPARENT MAGNITUDE AND APPARENT BRIGHTNESS

There is a simple relationship between the apparent magnitude and apparent brightness.

This is based on a psychophysical law that states that if a stimulus, e.g., brightness, increases in a

geometric progression, such as 1,2,4,8,16, etc., the sensation resulting from it increases in an arithmetic progression 1,2,3,4,5, etc.

From that law it was determined empirically that magnitude 2 stars are 2.5 (more precisely, 2.512) times brighter than magnitude 3 stars. Similarly, magnitude 3 stars are 2.512 times brighter than magnitude 4 stars, and so on.

PROBLEM 1:

The star Dubhe in the constellation Ursa Major has an apparent magnitude of 2.0 An unknown star, X, had an apparent magnitude of 4.0. How much brighter is Dubhe than star X?

Solution: A decrease in one order of magnitude corresponds to an increase of 2.5 times in apparent brightness. A decrease of two orders of magnitude is the same as an increase of $2.5 \times 2.5 = 6.25$ times in apparent brightness.

Answer: To the eye, Dubhe will appear more than six times brighter than the star X.

Stars down to magnitude 19 are visible with the 200-inch Mount Palomer telescope, and stars as dim as magnitude 24 can be photographed (long exposure) with that telescope. Even fainter stars can be photographed with the aid of image tubes.

ZERO AND NEGATIVE VALUES OF APPARENT MAGNITUDE

The twenty stars originally designated as first magnitude stars were subsequently regrouped. This was necessary because some of the stars were much brighter than others. The brighter stars of this group were designated as having magnitudes of .9, .8, .7, etc., through .0 to negative numbers. The star with the greatest apparent brightness at night is Sirius. Its apparent magnitude is −1.6. On the same scale, the apparent magnitude of our sun is immensely greater: −26.7.

DETERMINING APPARENT MAGNITUDES

The method of determining the magnitude of stars by observation is rather simple. With practice, fairly accurate results (an accuracy of .1 of a magnitude) can be obtained. The method was used extensively by the German astronomer Friedrich Argelander (1799–1875) and his associates in the preparation of the great star catalog, the "B.D. Catalog." (B.D. is the abbreviation of the German title of the catalog, *Bonner Durchmusterung*—"Bonn Catalog.") By this method, the observer compares the apparent brightness of a star with two or more neighboring stars of known magnitudes. Thus, a star that appears somewhat fainter than a neighboring star of 2.4 magnitude and somewhat brighter than another neighboring star of 2.6 magnitude, will be designated as having a magnitude of 2.5. In using this method it is advisable to make sure that:

A. The star to be measured and the known magnitude stars should be at about the same distance above the horizon.

B. The known magnitude stars should be as close as possible to the star to be measured.

C. One of the known magnitude stars should be somewhat brighter and the other somewhat fainter than the star to be measured.

The following table contains a list of stars of known apparent magnitude. These can be used for the determination of magnitude of many other stars.

Star	Constellation	Apparent Magnitude
Alpheratz	Andromeda	2.2
Schedar	Cassiopeia	2.5
Diphda	Cetus	2.2
Achernar	Eridanus	.6
Hamal	Aries	2.2
Acamar	Eridanus	3.1
Aldebaran	Taurus	1.1
Rigel	Orion	.3
Capella	Auriga	.2
Bellatrix	Orion	1.7
Canopus	Carina	− .9
Sirius	Canis Major	−1.6
Procyon	Canis Minor	.5
Pollux	Gemini	1.2
Regulus	Leo	1.3
Dubhe	Ursa Major	2.0
Acrux	Crux	1.1
Arcturus	Boötes	.2
Zubenelgenubi	Libra	2.9
Shaula	Scorpius	1.7
Nunki	Sagittarius	2.1
Markab	Pegasus	2.6

NOTE: On maps these figures are rounded off to the nearest integer.

PROBLEM 2:

Determine which of the two is the brighter star, Alkaid or Merak.

Answer: Alkaid is the brighter one. The apparent magnitude of Alkaid is 1.9; that of Merak, 2.4.

PROBLEM 3:

Find three stars in the Big Dipper that appear to be of equal brightness.

Answer: Mizar, Merak, and Phecda have almost the same apparent brightness. Precisely, they are designated as being 2.4, 2.4, and 2.5 magnitude stars, respectively. Phecda is by a very slight degree fainter than the other two.

PROBLEM 4:

Determine the apparent magnitude of the North Star (Polaris).

Answer: Polaris is but slightly brighter than Merak, and slightly fainter than Dubhe. It is usually designated as a 2.1 magnitude star.

Note again, this refers to **apparent** magnitudes. Actually, Polaris is much brighter than our sun—in fact, nearly 1,500 times brighter. The great distance accounts for its being only a magnitude 2.1 star. Stated in terms of time, it takes light, traveling at the speed of 186,000 miles per second, 8⅓ minutes to reach earth from the sun; and 400 years to reach earth from Polaris.

APPARENT DAILY MOTIONS OF STARS

It is common knowledge that the sun seems to rise in the east, describe an arc in the sky, and set in the west.

The stars, too, seem to move in arcs in the sky—also from the eastern to the western part of the horizon. A complete revolution takes 23 hours, 56 minutes and 4.09 seconds. This can very easily be approximately verified any clear evening with the aid of a good watch.

PROBLEM 5:

Object: To verify a complete revolution of a star. (This period is known as a "sidereal" day, or a "starday.")

Equipment: A good watch.
Procedure:

a. Note the time at which some bright star appears just above the eastern horizon.

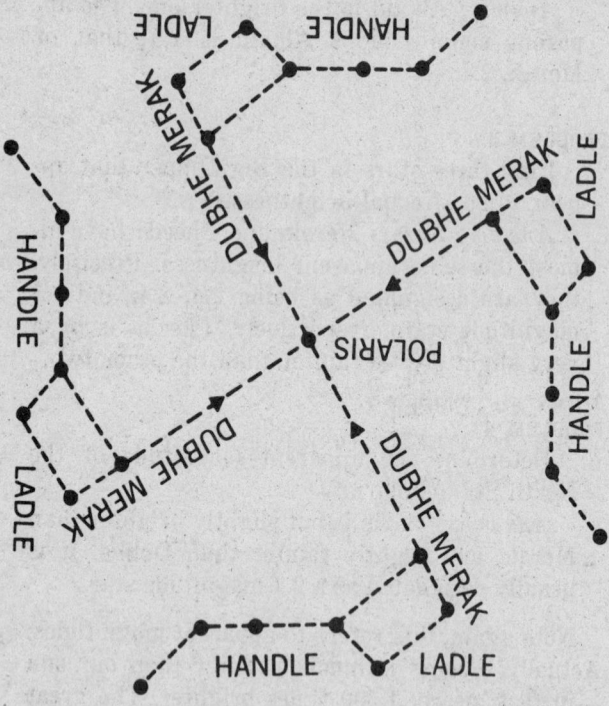

FIGURE 13. In the course of approximately 24 hours, the Big Dipper completes one revolution in the sky. Only part of that circle can actually be observed, as sunlight makes it impossible to observe the stars during the daytime. This figure shows the Big Dipper at 6-hour intervals.

b. The next day repeat the procedure under (a).
Results: The experiment demonstrates that every star completes one apparent revolution in 23 hours, 56 minutes and 4 seconds.

The term "apparent" is often repeated here for good reason. The motion is really *only* apparent; it may even be considered an optical illusion. Actually it is the earth, spinning on its axis in the opposite direction, that causes the stars to seem to move as they do.

This daily rotation can also very effectively be observed by watching a constellation, such as Ursa Major.

If, when first observed, the constellation appears level with the bowl on the right:

Six hours later it will appear with the handle pointed downward;

Twelve hours after the original observation, the Big Dipper will appear with the open part of the bowl pointing downward;

Eighteen hours after the original observation, the Big Dipper will appear to have the handle pointing upward.

In any 23 hours, 56 minutes and 4 seconds, the Big Dipper can be seen in any one of those positions.

During part of that time, the sun will interfere with the observations. The faint starlight cannot be discerned in the bright sky of day.

THE APPARENT ANNUAL MOTION OF THE STARS

The fact that stars complete a revolution in less than twenty-four hours is of great importance. It signifies, of course, that the stars make more than one revolution in a 24-hour period.

The difference between 24 and the period of revolution is:

24 hours
−23 hours, 56 minutes, 4 seconds
3 minutes, 56 seconds.

Thus, the stars begin the next revolution in the remaining 3 minutes and 56 seconds. This can be verified by observation.

A star that appears on the horizon, say, at eight o'clock on a Sunday evening will be slightly **above** the horizon the following evening at eight o'clock. Tuesday evening at eight o'clock, the star will be still further above the horizon and a month later at eight o'clock in the evening, the star will be substantially above the horizon.

After three months, at eight o'clock in the evening, the star will be a quarter of a circle away from the eastern horizon. At the end of a year, the star will have completed an apparent circle.

This movement of a star is also an *apparent* movement. It is due to the **real** movement of the earth about the sun. The earth completes a revolution around the sun in 12 months.

This apparent annual movement of stars obtains for constellations as well.

Thus Ursa Major at eight o'clock in the evening in October is close to the horizon with the bowl opening upward.

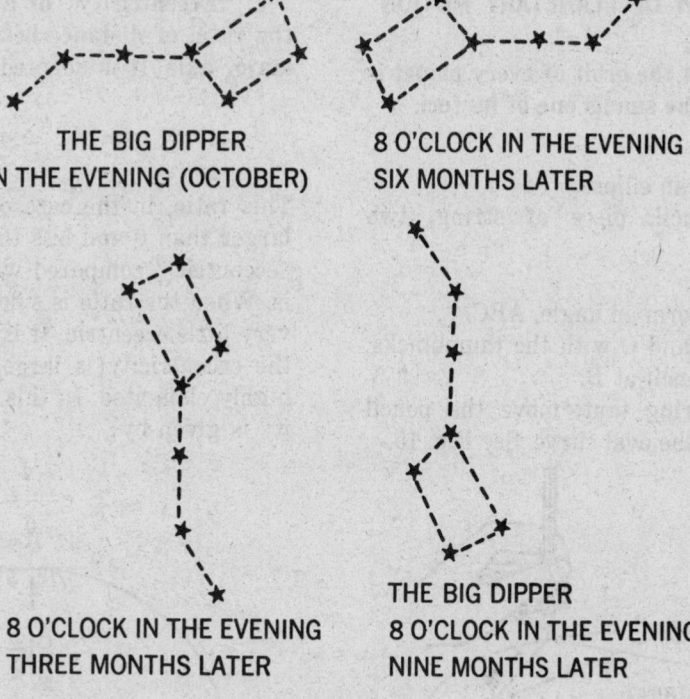

THE BIG DIPPER
8 O'CLOCK IN THE EVENING (OCTOBER)

8 O'CLOCK IN THE EVENING
SIX MONTHS LATER

8 O'CLOCK IN THE EVENING
THREE MONTHS LATER

THE BIG DIPPER
8 O'CLOCK IN THE EVENING
NINE MONTHS LATER

FIGURE 14.

Three months later at the same time in the evening, the handle will point downward.

In April at the same time of the evening, the Big Dipper will be high above the horizon and will appear with the bowl to the left.

In July at the same time of the evening, the Big Dipper will appear with the bowl at the bottom.

Thus in a period of 365¼ days, the Big Dipper completes 366¼ apparent revolutions: 365¼ of them are due to the rotation of the earth on its axis, and one is due to the revolution of the earth about the sun.

The Mechanics of the Solar System

INTRODUCTION

The solar system consists of the sun; the planets and their satellites; the planetoids, comets, meteorites, and dust. Both the adjective "solar" and the noun "system" are appropriate.

"Solar" indicates that the sun governs: it contains nearly 99.9 per cent of all the matter in the system. (The mass of all the planets, satellites, etc. comprises the other .1 or 1 per cent.) As a result of this division of mass, the "massive" sun is nearly stationary while all the "lighter" bodies revolve around it.

The word "system" implies that all the bodies observe great regularity in their motions. The laws governing these motions have been known for several centuries. Of great importance among the several laws are the three that are known by the name of their discoverer (Johannes Kepler) and the Universal Law of Gravitation (first stated by Isaac Newton).

KEPLER'S FIRST LAW OF PLANETARY MOTION

This law states that the orbit of every planet is an ellipse which has the sun as one of its foci.

DEMONSTRATION:

Object: To draw an ellipse.

Equipment: Pencil, piece of string, two thumbtacks, paper.

Procedure:

1. Place string to form an angle, ABC.
2. Fix the ends A and C with the thumbtacks, and place the pencil at B.
3. Keeping the string taut, move the pencil around to form the oval curve. See Fig. 15.

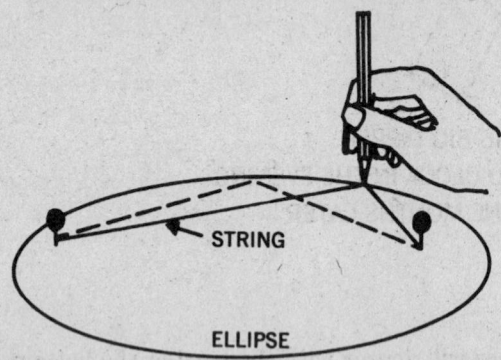

FIGURE 15. Drawing of an ellipse. Fix the end of the string at points A and C. Stretch the string to form the angle at B. Keeping the string taut at all times move the pencil about to form the oval curve. A is one focus of this ellipse. C is the other.

Result: The curve described by the pencil is an ellipse. The two points that were kept fixed by the thumbtacks are called the foci of the ellipse (sing. focus).

PROBLEM 6:

Given an ellipse. Its major axis is 5 inches long, its minor axis is 3 inches long.

Find: 1. The distance between the foci; 2. the eccentricity of the ellipse.

Solution: 1. The major axis, the minor axis, and the distance between the foci are related by a simple formula. If the length of the major axis is denoted by a; if the length of the minor axis is denoted by b; and the distance between foci is denoted by c; the formula is:

$$b^2 + c^2 = a^2 \text{ or } c = \sqrt{a^2 - b^2}.$$

In this case, $c = \sqrt{5^2 - 3^2} = 4$ inches. The distance between the foci is 4 inches. See Fig. 16.

2. "Eccentricity" of an ellipse is defined as the ratio of distance between foci to length of major axis. It is denoted by e.

$$e = \frac{c}{a}$$

This ratio, in the case of an ellipse, is always larger than 0 and less than 1. It indicates how "eccentric," compared with a circle, the ellipse is. When the ratio is small, say .1, the ellipse is very little eccentric. It is almost circular. When the eccentricity is large, say .8, the ellipse is highly elongated. In this problem the eccentricity is given by:

$$e = \frac{4}{5} = .8$$

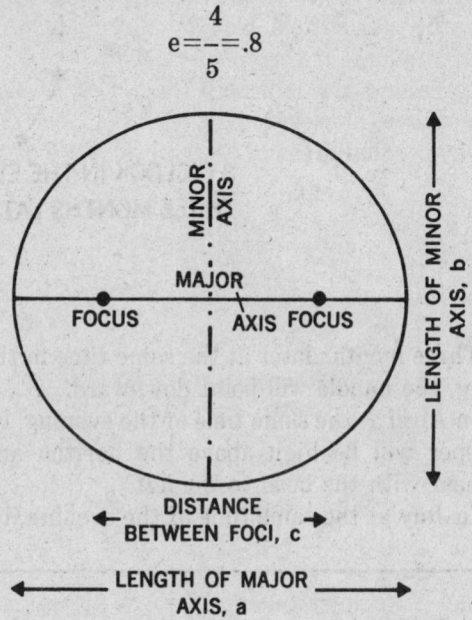

FIGURE 16. In an ellipse the length of the major axis, a, the length of the minor axis, b, and the distance between the foci, c, are related by the formula—

$$b^2 + c^2 = a^2$$

Planets move in nearly circular orbits. The eccentricities of Venus and of the earth are .01 and .02, respectively.

Comets move in elongated orbits. The orbit of Halley's Comet is an ellipse, with an eccentricity of .97.

KEPLER'S SECOND LAW OF PLANETARY MOTION

This law deals with the speed of the planets in their respective orbits. The speed is not constant, the planets moving faster the closer they are to the sun. The maximum speed of any planet is attained when it is closest to the sun, the minimum when it is farthest. The point on the orbit closest to the sun is known as perihelion, the farthest, aphelion.

Though the speeds of the planets in their orbits are not constant, another feature closely connected with speed *is* constant—namely, the speed with which the line connecting the sun and any particular planet passes over areas.

This is expressed in the formal version of Kepler's second law: **The radius vector of each planet passes over equal areas in equal intervals of time.**

The radius vector is an imaginary line that connects the sun with a planet—short at the perihelion and long at the aphelion.

The second law indicates that at aphelion, the planet moves slower than at perihelion in order to pass over equal areas of the ellipse. See Fig. 17.

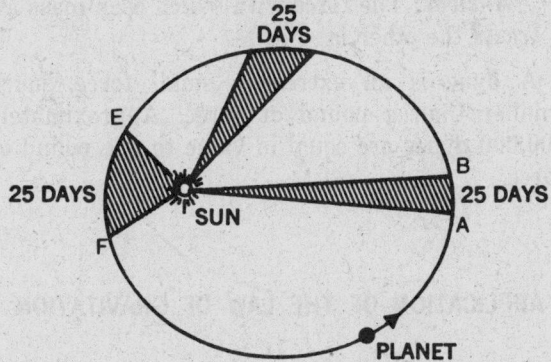

FIGURE 17. Kepler's second law of planetary motion. The radius vector would cover equal areas (three such areas are shown here shaded) in equal times (25 days).

At aphelion the planet moved relatively slowly to get from A to B. At perihelion the planet had to move at a relatively high speed to cover the distance from E to F.

The term radius vector used in the formal version of the law is an imaginary line joining the sun with the planet. The line connecting the sun to A, or the sun to B, or the sun to D, etc., is a radius vector.

The earth's average velocity along its orbit about the sun is 18.5 miles per second. Since the orbit is almost a circle, its speed does not vary materially along the path. At aphelion, the earth moves only by ½ a mile per second slower than at perihelion.

In the case of highly eccentric orbits, such as those pursued by comets, the orbital speed varies greatly. Halley's Comet, when at perihelion, has a speed of 100 miles per second; and at aphelion, of less than 1 mile per second.

KEPLER'S THIRD LAW OF PLANETARY MOTION

The third law deals with the relationship between the period of a planet and its mean distance from the sun.

The "period" is the time that it takes a planet to complete one revolution about the sun. For the earth, this is 365.26 days; for the planet Mercury, only 88 days; for Pluto, the farthest planet, 248 *years.*

Kepler's third law states that **the squares of the periods of any two planets are proportional to the cubes of their mean distances to the sun.**

This can be stated as an algebraic equation: Let the two planets be designated as A and B.

$$\frac{(\text{period of A})^2}{(\text{period of B})^2} =$$

$$\frac{(\text{mean distance of the sun to A})^3}{(\text{mean distance of the sun to B})^3}$$

If the known data for the earth are used for one of these planets, say B, the equation becomes:

$$\frac{(\text{period of A})^2}{(365.26)^2} =$$

$$\frac{(\text{mean distance of the sun to A})^3}{(93,000,000)^3}$$

This equation has two variables: the period of a planet and its mean distance. If one of these is obtained by observation, the other can be computed algebraically.

PROBLEM 7:

The period of the planet Mars is 687 days. Compute the mean distance of Mars from the sun.

Solution: Inserting the given data in the equation:

$$\frac{(\text{mean distance of Mars from sun})^3}{(93,000,000)^3} = \frac{(365)^2}{(687)^2}$$

Answer: The distance of Mars from the sun is 142,000,000 miles.

NOTE: Kepler's third law is not quite complete. The complete form was evolved by Newton. In the complete form, "the squares of the periods" have to be multiplied by the combined mass of the sun and the planet. The corrected equation reads:

$$\frac{(\text{period of A})^2 (\text{mass of sun \& planet A})}{(\text{period of B})^2 (\text{mass of sun \& planet B})}$$
$$= \frac{(\text{mean dist. of A})^3}{(\text{mean dist. of B})^3}$$

EVALUATION OF KEPLER'S THREE LAWS

The discovery of these laws was a milestone, not only in the history of astronomy, but also in the history of science in general. It is an eternal monument, not only to the brilliance of Kepler, but also to his devotion to science, to which he committed infinite patience and labor.

There was one shortcoming to these laws, however—a very important shortcoming. Kepler's laws did not explain the behavior of the planets, why they move in elliptical orbits, or why their speeds change as they do.

The answers were soon forthcoming in Sir Isaac Newton's epoch-making book, *Mathematical Principles of Physics*. There, Newton showed that the planets behave as they do because of a most fundamental universal law—the law of gravitation; and that Kepler's three laws are merely consequences of that universal law.

NEWTON'S UNIVERSAL LAW OF GRAVITATION

The law, dealing with forces between material objects, states that every particle of matter attracts every other particle of matter with a force, depending on three factors:

A. Mass of one object.
B. Mass of the other object.
C. The distance between the objects.

These factors are often denoted as M, m, and r, respectively.

The formal statement of the law is: **Every particle of matter in the universe attracts every other particle with a force that is proportional to the product of their masses, and inversely proportional to the square of the distance between them.**

The law can also be expressed as an algebraic equation:

$$FG = (\text{force of gravity}) \times \frac{Mm}{r^2}$$

G is known as the universal gravitational constant. Its value is 6.7×10^{-8} if M and m are expressed in grams, r in centimeters, and F in dynes. The formula for the Universal Law of Gravitation will then be:

$$F = 6.7 \times 10^{-8} \frac{Mm}{r^2}$$

PROBLEM 8:
A mass of 2,000 grams, about 4.4 pounds, is at a distance of 2.54 centimeters (about 1 inch) from another mass of 5,000 grams. Find the force of attraction between these two bodies.

$$F = 6.7 \times 10^{-8} \frac{2000 \times 5000}{(2.54)^2} = .1 \text{ dyne}$$

Answer: The force with which each mass attracts the other is .1 dyne.

A dyne is an extremely small force, much smaller than a pound of force. Approximately 500,000 dynes are equal in value to one pound of force.

APPLICATION OF THE LAW OF GRAVITATION

The law was of enormous aid in solving a host of problems. Chief among these are:

A. Freely falling bodies. Any body not properly supported, will fall toward the center of the earth.
B. Ocean tides and tides in the atmosphere.
C. Motion of comets.
D. Precession of equinoxes.
E. Motion of planets. If the gravitational force between the earth and the sun ceased to operate, the earth would go off on a tangent. It is the direct result of this law that planets revolve about the sun as they do. This result is shown in Figure 18.

The nine planets move in elliptical orbits at various distances from the sun, counterclockwise.

Although gravitation applies, of course, to the stars and galaxies as well, its effect is easier to see in the case of planets because of the presence of *one* large mass (the sun) acting on several close, smaller masses (the planets). The perturbation on these motions by distant stars is extremely small.

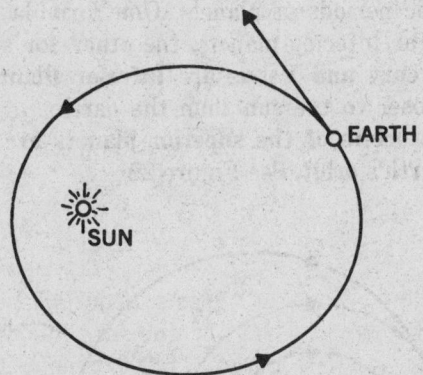

FIGURE 18. Effect of gravitational attraction. It is due to the gravitational attraction of the sun that the earth continues to move in its orbit.

In the absence of this attraction the earth would leave its elliptical orbit and go off on a tangent, such as at point A, farther and farther away from the sun.

APPARENT MOTION OF PLANETS AS SEEN FROM THE EARTH

The true motion of the planets cannot be observed from the earth, because the earth itself is constantly in motion. Observations indicate only the motion of the planets relative to that of the earth. At times a planet's relative velocity, with respect to the earth, is greater than its true velocity, as when the earth and the planet move in opposite directions; at other times the planet's relative velocity is less than its true velocity, as when a planet and the earth move in the same direction.

Of particular interest in the apparent motion of planets is the retrograde phase in which planets seem to move in a direction opposite to their normal one. See Figure 19.

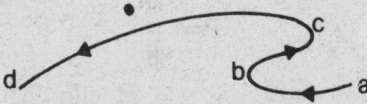

FIGURE 19. Retrograde motion. As seen against the background of the celestial sphere the planet was moving at A in the normal direction (this is called "direct motion"), and continued to do so

until point B. From B to C the motion is in a direction opposite to normal (retrograde motion). At point C, the planet makes a U-turn and continues in direct motion.

The backward or retrograde motion of several of the planets puzzled astronomers for many centuries, until finally it was explained by Copernicus. An example is of great aid in visualizing the apparent retrograde motion.

Let the inner circle in Figure 20 represent the orbit of the earth around the sun. Let the large circle represent the orbit of Mars. The earth, being closer to the sun, moves faster than Mars. Let the top of the figure represent part of the celestial sphere. The sphere serves as a background upon which the movements of Mars are observed.

When the earth is in position 1, Mars will be seen in place 1 on the celestial sphere. Several weeks later, both the earth and Mars will have moved in their orbits. Mars is now at point 2. As the earth moves through positions 3 and 4, the line described by Mars on the celestial sphere will be of a body in retrograde motion.

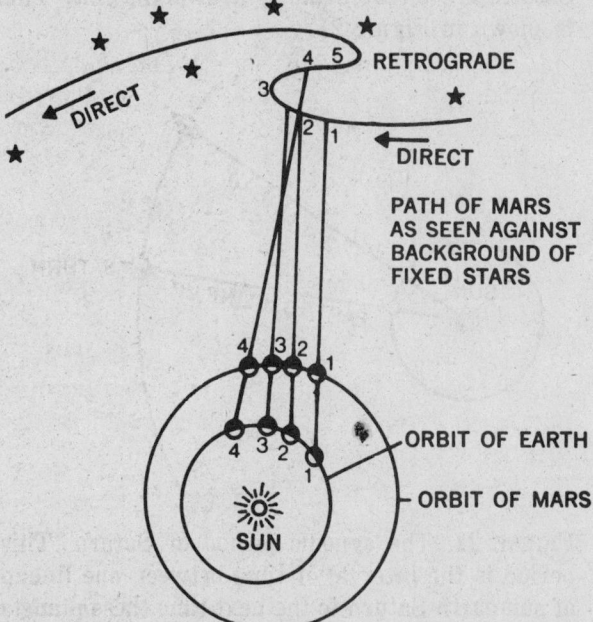

FIGURE 20. Explanation of retrograde motion. The earth, being closer to the sun than Mars, moves faster than Mars (the earth completes its circle in 365 days, Mars 687). At point 1, Mars is "ahead" of the earth; its motion is direct. At point 4 the earth is "ahead" of Mars, and the latter seems to retrograde.

SIDEREAL AND SYNODIC PERIOD OF A PLANET

In connection with planets, there are two definitions of period: (A) sidereal period; and (B) synodic period. These differ in length due to the motion of the earth.

A. Sidereal Period is the time it takes the planet to complete one revolution in its orbit. Another way of saying the same thing is: It is the time required by a planet to complete a circle on the celestial sphere, as seen from the sun.

B. The Synodic Period, which involves the motion of the earth, is the interval between one time that the sun, the earth, and planet are aligned and the next time. Since both the earth and the planet are in motion, the synodic period differs materially from the sidereal.

Thus, the sidereal period of Mars is 687 days; its synodic period is 780 days.

In the case of Saturn, the sidereal and synodic periods are 29.5 years and 378 days, respectively. The former signifies that it takes Saturn nearly 30 years to complete its orbit about the sun; the latter that every 378 days, the sun, the earth, and Saturn are situated along a straight line. This is shown in Figure 21.

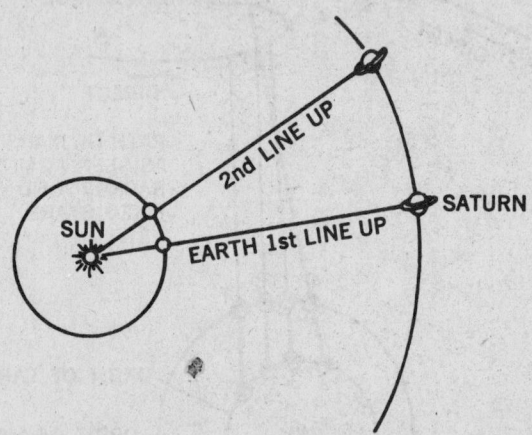

FIGURE 21. The synodic period of Saturn. This period is the interval of time between one lineup of sun-earth-Saturn to the next time these planets form a straight line. The synodic period of Saturn is 378 days. It consists of 365 days for a complete revolution of the earth plus 13 days needed for the earth to catch up with Saturn, which in the meanwhile has moved on to a new position.

The 378 days are composed of (a) 1 revolution of the earth about the sun (365 days); and (b)

13 days to catch up with Saturn which, in the meanwhile, has moved to a new position in its orbit.

There are two simple formulas to compute the synodic periods of planets. One formula is to be used for inferior planets, the other for superior.

Mercury and Venus are Inferior Plants. They are closer to the sun than the earth.

The orbits of the superior planets are outside the earth's orbit. See Figure 22.

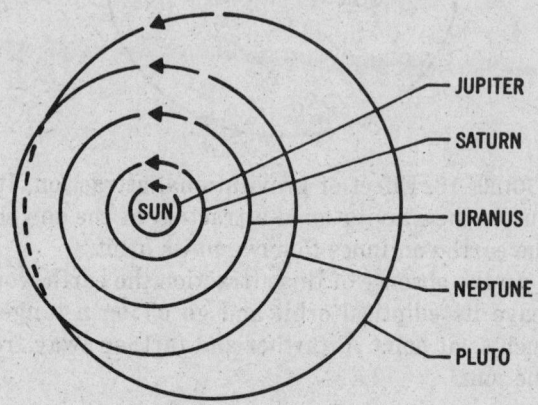

FIGURE 22. Orbits of five superior planets. The orbits are ellipses of small eccentricity, hence closely resemble circles. All the planets move in a counterclockwise direction, as shown by the arrows. The length of the arrow indicates the distance the planet travels in one year. The four other planets (not shown) move along orbits inside the orbit of Jupiter.

The formula for an inferior planet is:

$$\text{Synodic period of planet} = \frac{360}{P-E}$$

P is the number of degrees of arc that a planet moves in its orbit in one day; E is the number of degrees that the earth moves in its orbit in one day.

For Mercury,

$$P = \frac{360}{88}$$

$$E = \frac{360}{365\frac{1}{4}}$$

Substituting these numbers in the formula, we then get:

$$\text{Synodic period of Mercury} = \frac{360}{\dfrac{360}{88}} - \frac{360}{\dfrac{360}{365\frac{1}{4}}}$$

$$= 116 \text{ days}$$

For a superior planet, the formula is:

$$\text{Synodic period of superior planet} = \frac{360}{E-P}$$

where E and P have the same meaning as in the previous formula.

The proof of this second formula is fairly simple. The denominator $E-P$ stands for the number of degrees that the earth gains on a planet in *one* day. But in a synodic period, the earth gains a complete revolution (360°) on the planet; hence, that period is equal to the number of times $(E-P)$ is contained in 360.

PROBLEM 9:

Compute the synodic period of Mars.

Given: The sidereal period of the earth is

$$365\frac{1}{4} \text{ days, or } E = \frac{360}{365\frac{1}{4}};$$

and the sidereal period of Mars is 687 days, or

$$P = \frac{360}{687}$$

Answer: 780 days.

Basic Planetary Data

INTRODUCTION

For each planet there is now available a large number of data. These include dimensions as well as other physical and orbital data.

The methods used to obtain several of these values are indicated in this part.

DISTANCE TO SUN

One fairly accurate way to determine the mean distance of a planet to the sun makes use of Kepler's third law.

If distances are measured in astronomical units and sidereal periods in years, the third law can be written as

(period of a planet)^2 = (mean distance of planet to sun)^3

PROBLEM 10:

The sidereal period of the planet Mars is 687 days. Find the mean distance of Mars from the sun.

Solution: Changing days into years and inserting in above formula,

$$\left(\frac{687}{365.25}\right)^2 = \text{(mean distance of Mars to Sun)}^3$$

The answer for mean distance is 1.52 astronomical units, or (multiplying 1.52 by 93,000,000) 142,000,000 miles.

ECCENTRICITY

The eccentricity of a planet's orbit can be found

A. By determining the distance of the planet from the sun at different times of the year.

B. By plotting a graph of date versus distance from the sun. The graph will be an ellipse.

C. By computing the eccentricity e, using the formula $e = \dfrac{c}{a}$ where c is the distance from either focus (the sun is at one of the foci) to the center of the ellipse and a is the length of half of the major axis.

NOTE: Computing actual (as opposed to mean) distances from the sun for a planet other than the earth is a more arduous task.

INCLINATION OF ORBIT TO ECLIPTIC

This is obtained from observations on the celestial sphere. The inclination is equal to the maximum angle the planet reaches above or below the ecliptic.

PERIOD OF ONE REVOLUTION, SIDEREAL

The sidereal period can be obtained by using the formulas given on page 514 and the observed synodic period.

PERIOD OF ONE REVOLUTION, SYNODIC

The synodic period is obtained by noting the interval of time between two successive conjunctions of the planet with the sun, i.e., two successive times that the planet is on the line that joins the sun and the earth.

ORBITAL VELOCITY

This is obtained by dividing the length of the circumference by the time it takes to cover that distance, i.e., by the sidereal period.

DISTANCE OF A PLANET FROM EARTH

One method that can be used to determine the distance of a planet from the earth is triangulation. In this method a line of position, say, 1,000 km long, is established on earth. The angles from both ends of the line to the planet are measured. Standard formulae from elementary trigonometry are used to find the distance to the planet.

Another method is to measure the time elapsed for a radar signal to make a round trip to the planet. The distance to the planet is obtained by multiplying half the time for the round trip by the velocity of light.

PROBLEM 11:
A radar signal was sent to the planet Venus early in 1958. The round trip took about 5 minutes (300 seconds). Find the distance to the planet at that time.

Solution: Since the velocity of light, or the velocity of radar, is 186,000 miles per second, then

$186,000 \times 150 =$ approximately 28,000,000 miles.

ANGULAR DIAMETER

The anglar diameter of a planet is determined by
A. Sighting through a telescope one limb of the planet.
B. Rotating the telescope to the other limb.
The angle through which the telescope has been rotated is equal to the angular diameter of the planet.

LINEAR DIAMETER

The linear diameter of a planet is obtained by multiplying the angular diameter (in radians) by the distance to the planet. The formula is:

Linear diameter = angular diameter × distance
to planet

The angular diameter in this formula has to be in radian units. (A radian is an angle that subtends an arc of a circle equal to the radius of that circle; 1 radian is slightly more than 57°.) The rate of conversion from degrees to radians is 1 radian = $\frac{360°}{2\pi}$. The diameter will be in the same unit as that used for distance to the planet.

VOLUME

Assuming that the planet is a sphere, the geometrical formula for volume of a sphere can be used:

$$\text{Volume} = \frac{4}{3}\pi \times \text{the radius}^3$$

where π has a value of 3.14.

MASS

The mass of a planet that has a satellite orbiting around it is obtained from Kepler's third law as amended by Newton (see note following Problem 7).

One form of this amended law is

$$P^2 = \frac{4\pi^2 a^3}{G(M_1 + M_2)}$$

where

P is the sidereal period of the satellite

a is the distance from center of satellite to center of planet

G is the universal gravitational constant (in the meter-kilogram-second system $G = 6.7 \times 10^{-11}$ newtons $\times$ meters$^2 \times$ kilograms^{-2}).

M_1 and M_2 are the masses of the planet and the satellite, respectively. The mass of the satellite (M_2) is usually so much smaller than the mass of the planet (M_1) that it may be omitted from the formula.

PROBLEM 12:

Find the mass of Mars, given that its satellite Phobos is at a distance of 5,820 miles = 9,400 km = 9.4×10^6 meters and it orbits the mother planet in 7 hours 39 minutes = 27,500 seconds.

Solution: Using meters for the unit of distance and seconds for the unit of time, then

$$M_1 = \frac{4\pi^2 \times (9.4 \times 10^6)^3}{6.7 \times 10^{-11} \times 27,500^2} = 7 \times 10^{23} \text{ kg, ap-}$$

proximately, for the mass of Mars, or about 11 per cent the mass of the earth.

The mass of planets that do not have natural satellites (e.g., Venus) is obtained by the use of either (A) an artificial satellite that orbits the planet or (B) determining the perturbation exerted by the planet on a close passing planetoid or spacecraft.

DENSITY

Mean density of a planet is obtained by dividing the mass by the volume. The value of a density is often stated in terms relative to the density of the earth.

SURFACE GRAVITY

The acceleration due to gravity at the surface of a planet is derived from Newton's Universal law of gravitation with M being the mass of the planet and m=1. In the gravity for-

mula is $F = 6.7 \times 10^{-8} \frac{M}{r^2}$. In the meter-kilogram-second system, the formula is $F = 6.7 \times 10^{-11} \frac{M}{r^2}$. r is the radius of the planet proper units.

VELOCITY OF ESCAPE

The speed that an object must acquire in order to escape from the gravitational field of a planet is obtained from

$$V = \sqrt{\frac{2\,Gm}{r}}$$

In the centimeter-gram-second system, $G = 6.7 \times 10^{-8}$ the mass has to be stated in grams, and the distance of the object from the center of the planet in centimeters. The escape velocity will be in units of centimeters per second.

PERIOD OF ROTATION ABOUT AXIS

The period of rotation of planets that have identifiable features (e.g., Mars) is determined by timing a complete rotation of such a feature.

The Doppler shift in radar waves between the approaching limb and the receding limb of a planet is used to determine the period for planets that do not have identifiable features.

INCLINATION OF PLANET'S EQUATOR TO ORBIT

This is usually derived from the study of an arc described by a surface marking on the planet.

ALBEDO

Albedo pertains to the ability of an object to reflect light. Some objects—e.g., tops of clouds—reflect most of the light falling upon them; others absorb most of the light, reflecting little. Stones, rocks, and soil are poor reflectors of light.

Albedo is defined as the ratio of the quantity of light reflected to the light received by the object.

In reference to the planets, albedo is equal to the ratio:

$$\frac{\text{light reflected by the planet}}{\text{sunlight falling on the planet}}$$

The denominator can be computed from the known value of the sun's luminosity and the planet's distance from the sun. The numerator is derived from the intrinsic brightness of the planet.

BIOLOGY

Scope and Method

Biology is the study of all living forms, plants and animals, including man, as individuals and as interdependent entities.

To the biologist—who is in the first place and above all a **natural scientist**—the human being is an object of scientific investigation; a very highly specialized protoplasmic structure, reflecting in his life processes the activity of all living animal structures. Biology demonstrates the total and absolute dependence of man—the human animal —on all other forms of life.

Biology covers so vast a field that, to make for greater accuracy and greater ease of study, it has been divided into logical subdivisions or branches. Each subdivision is so vast in itself that a lifetime of study may be devoted to each.

Depending upon his interests, the biologic scientist specializes in a single phase—if in animals, **Zoology**; if in plant life, **Botany**; if in the development of the individual from the "fertilized egg" stage through early stages of life, **Embryology**; if in the structure of the human body, **Anatomy**; if in the functions of the body, **Physiology.**

Another vital biological science is **Genetics**, which explains the phenomena of heredity. For microscope work, there is **Cytology**, the science of cell structure and function, or **Histology**, the science of living tissues. **Protozoology** is a branch of Biology which deals with one-celled animal life; **Bacteriology** is a science of one-celled plant life.

Another important and fascinating branch of Biology is **Ecology**, the study of the relationship of living things to their environment.

Frequently a person who studies Biology from intellectual curiosity becomes intensely interested in a particular division and makes it his hobby or even his lifework, his profession. Biology is the basis of such professions as Medicine, Nursing, Agriculture, Plant and Animal Breeding and even Pharmacy.

How shall we acquaint ourselves with the living world around us? Constant awareness coupled with the curiosity and desire to "dig deeper" will make our immediate surroundings a field and a laboratory for studying life.

A small patch of back yard, a vacant lot, even a window box will provide field for "exploration"; as will the public park, a local wooded area, or the seashore, crowded with plant and animal life for us to observe.

The city streets, for all their concrete pavements and huge structures, have some trees and foliage to watch as they bud in the spring, blossom in the summer, change color in the fall and become bare in the winter.

Even in the heart of the city, one hears the birds which nest nearby or pass through on their migrations. Or one sees an earthworm crawling on the pavement after a heavy rain has driven it out of the soil beneath the pavement. Where there are human beings there must be other forms of plant and animal life!

One of the most famous **Entomologists** (a biologist who specializes in the study of insects), JEAN HENRI FABRE, did most of his field work in his own back yard or in some close-by field. He spent hours watching insects in their daily activities and making notes of his observation.

While some biologists explore the lands, the waters and the skies, others prefer to work in a laboratory, the "workshop" of the scientist. If well equipped, this will have running water in a sink, connections for gas, non-corrosive table tops (usually stone) with air pressure, vacuum, and electricity outlets. In addition there will be glass beakers, jars, flasks, test tubes, bottles, porcelain crucibles, and shelves for various basic chemicals. There will probably be an oven or an incubator, a pressure cooker, and even a refrigerator in some handy place. A well-stocked library of reference books in every branch of Biology is essential.

The individual who has no access to such a laboratory can build one of his own, using materials bought in department stores or even found on the kitchen shelf or in the medicine cabinet. Actual kitchen appliances such as a stove, the pressure cooker, and the refrigerator can be very useful. One can always use cardboard boxes or wooden cheese boxes to house small animals (hamsters, white mice, guinea pigs, insects) for study. One can always plant a window box garden or even a "pocket garden" in a drinking glass to study the growth of a seedling or a sweet potato vine or an avocado pit. It is simple to leave a moist piece of bread or fruit in a warm spot in the house so that mold can grow and flourish.

With this simple equipment you can *think* scientifically and experiment. There are certain steps which a scientist follows, without bias or preconception and in logical order, when thinking scientifically. **This is known as the Scientific Method.**

1. First recognize and state clearly the problem to be solved or the question to be answered.

2. Concentrate on one part of the problem at a time.

3. Collect accurate and complete information from reliable sources.

4. Test this information with new ideas of your own.

5. Answer the question or draw conclusions.

The scientist forms an **hypothesis—a proposition which, although it remains to be tested under controlled, experimental conditions, seems to him the probable explanation of the phenomenon in question.** If subsequent experiments support the hypothesis, it will become the basis of a scientific **theory,** which may in turn be accepted as **natural law,** if it is observed to occur—without failure or variation—in nature.

In every experiment there are usually different factors involved which determine the results. Some

examples of these factors are: material used, temperature, air or water pressure, amount of moisture, sunlight and season of the year.

The scientist cannot draw any conclusions unless he has a **control** to his experiment. **This control is an omission or a change of one of the factors.** If there is any difference in the results, the difference must then be due to that one factor which has been omitted or changed. When you perform any experiment at home, you must employ the logical order of the scientific method, and make use of the control.

Let us return to the well-equipped laboratory. Here, in addition to all the equipment that has been mentioned, there must be a **microscope.** It can open to you a marvelous world of living plants and animals that normally cannot be seen at all or only barely seen with the unaided eye.

The microscope, in its simplest form, dates back to the seventeenth century when a Dutch lensmaker, ANTON VAN LEEUWENHOEK, ground and polished a tiny bead of glass until it magnified whatever he looked at. To his great astonishment and awe he found that a drop of stagnant water was teeming with life never before visible to the human eye. For greater convenience, he fashioned a crude microscope of metal in which he inserted and secured this bead of glass.

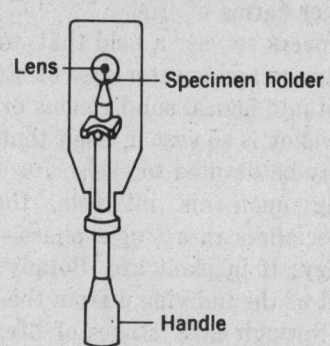

FIGURE 1. Leeuwenhoek microscope

Since that pioneering discovery of a revolutionary new use of optical lenses, there have been vast improvements and advances in magnifying lenses and microscopes. An Englishman, ROBERT HOOKE, made the first **compound microscope.** This type is used today—it can magnify objects clearly as much as 1,800 times. Such a microscope contains many lenses which, combined, *increase* magnification tremendously.

Early in this century, it was discovered that **ultraviolet** light could be used instead of light visible to the human eye, to obtain even higher magnification, as much as 4,000 times the life size of the object. This light cannot be seen by the human eye but can be photographed by the **ultraviolet microscope.**

In very recent years, engineers have developed an **electron microscope** which does not at all look like the compound microscope we are familiar with and which can produce a magnification of 20,000 times.

There is no doubt that microscopes of even greater magnification and accuracy can be de-

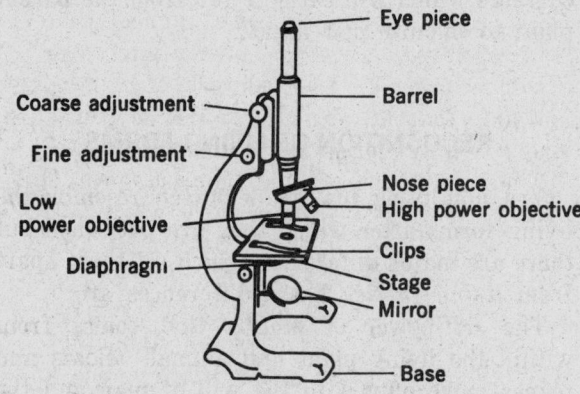

Eye piece

Coarse adjustment — Barrel

Fine adjustment —

Low power objective — Nose piece — High power objective — Clips

Diaphragm — Stage — Mirror

Base

FIGURE 2. Compound microscope

veloped by the large optical companies—and will be in due course.

Because of increasing interest in the use of the microscope by individuals "at home," there are companies in this country and elsewhere which make inexpensive but adequate instruments. They do not, of course, have the magnifying power of a scientist's compound microscope but they are adequate for a home laboratory.

In this "atomic age," we are all becoming very science-conscious. Our curiosity and interests are constantly stimulated. Many newspapers have a science column, frequently biological in nature. Current science news, science facts and advice are presented so that they can be understood and appreciated by the average reader.

There are science digests, science magazines, radio and television broadcasts for the express purpose of informing the average individual. They attempt to whet his desire to seek further information.

The federal government will send literature, on written request, which will provide the most current material on many phases of biology. Write to the Department of Interior and to the Department of Agriculture for a list of their pamphlets on the branch of biology in which you are interested. These booklets may be sent to you free of charge or at a nominal cost.

Among the greatest storehouses of biologic wealth are our museums, our botanical and zoological gardens. In New York City, the Museum of Natural History houses the "story of life" from times historic to modern, with predictions of the future. There are life-size models, lifelike and accurate in every minute detail, set in carefully studied, simulated natural habitats. There are miniatures and fossilized remains. In this museum one can learn just by observing the exhibits, reading the "cards" and listening to the lecturing guides, the entire field of biology with its related subjects. There are such museums in most large cities and universities throughout the country. So, too, with "zoos," zoological gardens.

Spend a day in the springtime at a Botanical Garden. Take your camera with you—make mental pictures as well—of early spring green, of delicate new leaves fresh out of their buds, of pastel-colored blossoms—especially on the fruit trees, on vines and growing from the moist ground. Walk through the hot houses and see the vast variety of plant life which exists in climates other than yours. Smell the heavily fragrant, moist air. See the mist that halos the foliage and the damp rich soil from which it grows. Learn about plant life from growing plants.

"The Cloisters," an adjunct to the Metropolitan Museum of Art in Fort Tryon Park, New York City, has a series of tapestries, the "Unicorn Tapestries," that are world-known not only for the magnificence of their craftsmanship, design and color but for their woven pictures of every plant known in the Middle Ages. In this "imported" monastery are the Gardens of the Monks in which may be found odd flowering plants, every known herb, oddly cultured trees and many other forms of botanic life.

In cities other than New York, in many other states in the country, there are museums and collections of both living and preserved forms of plants and animals—for example, Marineland, Silver Springs, and the Everglades in lower Florida. The National Parks of the West and the Grand Canyon offer exciting and stimulating fields for biologic exploration. There are numerous places in which to study flora and fauna in their natural environments—and few experiences are more rewarding.

The Nature of Life

What is biology? The word comes from the Greek *bios,* meaning "life" and *logos,* meaning "study of" or "science of." Biology is defined as the study of all living things, both plant and animal, including man. If we specify *living* things then we must differentiate between that which is *living* and that which is *non-living.* We may refer to substances in nature that are composed of inorganic chemicals, such as rock, air, water and parts of sand and soil as non-living. We may refer to objects fashioned by man as also being non-living. Through the years of attempting to survive and build stable communities, scientists have studied living plants and animals to determine how they have adapted or adjusted themselves. From these studies and observations, men in many fields of the arts and manufacturing have been able to fashion non-living things that in many ways imitate living things which are well-adapted to their surroundings.

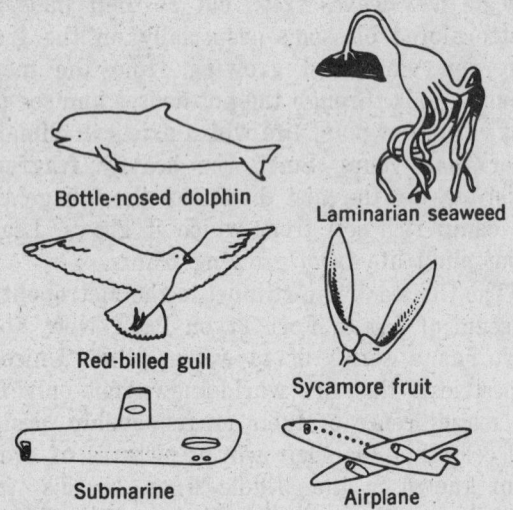

Bottle-nosed dolphin

Laminarian seaweed

Red-billed gull

Sycamore fruit

Submarine

Airplane

FIGURE 3.

Are you able to recognize man's successful imitation of living things in his building of submarines and planes? Consider the streamline shape of the dolphin, the location of the fins, the dorsally placed nostril, all **natural adaptations** for its life and activities in the water. The seaweed, though not actually propelled through the water, is continually subjected to the tidal currents. Its elongated shape and slimy covering allow the minimum of friction over its surface.

Can you see how man copied the features of

a bird when he designed airplanes, and the sycamore fruit when he designed the helicopter? The streamline shape of the bird, its wing shape and spread, its retractable legs, the feather covering for warmth and weatherproofing, the directions its feathers grow are all natural adaptations for its life and activity in the air, on land and on water. The helicopter-bladelike wings of the sycamore fruit are admirably adapted to catch wind currents which will carry it far from the parent plant to colonize new areas.

RECOGNITION OF LIVING FORMS

Yes, non-living, man-made objects resemble the living forms after which they are patterned but there are major differences which set them apart from *living forms.* These differences are:

The *self*-power of *motion* that comes from within the living plant and animal. (Boats and planes move only with the will of man and the energy of fuel he provides for them.)

The *self*-power to *grow,* to add to itself in size. (The house must be added to by the will of man and the materials he provides.)

The *self*-power to *reproduce* plants and animals each of its own kind. This is nature's lease on life. (Only the will of man and the materials he provides can produce more boats, houses, etc.)

The *self*-ability to *respond to stimuli* in the environment, or what is known as sensitivity. The plant seeks sunlight and grows in that direction. (The house must be built that way.) The roots of a tree grow downward in response to the pull of gravity and in the soil in the direction of a water supply. (The foundation of a house is placed in the ground to benefit from the pull of gravity.) Animals seek food and water when their bodies require it—so that they can carry out their daily activities of living. (A machine must be "fed" fuel by man to carry out its activity.)

In plants and simple animals, the responses to various stimuli in the environment are called tropisms.

Animals high in the animal group have specialized *systems* which enable them to respond to stimuli in their environment.

Living things are grouped according to "natural" and logical divisions. The largest and most inclusive of these divisions have been **the Plant Kingdom and the Animal Kingdom.** Yet in view of contemporary evolutionary thought, a new classification has been suggested.

The old system had no place for "in between" organisms. These are primitive life forms that are more closely related to each other than to plants or animals. For example, some systems now place the bacteria and blue-green algae in a kingdom called the Monera. These organisms lack an organized nucleus. Another kingdom, the Protista, is now included in almost every system. It includes the more advanced life forms.

In studying each of these major divisions, biologists have been able to recognize a pattern of further divisions based on the simplicity or complexity of the plant or animal form. For convenience, a *classification* has been made beginning with the simplest form and carrying through to

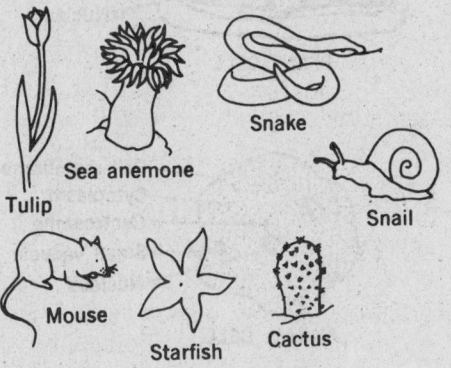

FIGURE 4. Living things

the most complex species of plants and animal life known, up to and including man.

There are forms of life, however, which exist in water, many microscopic forms, which can be grouped only after careful and detailed study, as either plants or animals. Perhaps you have seen coral growing in the warm southern waters, or highly colored sea anemones, sea urchins, or hydra, or even sponges. Have you remarked about the beauty of these underwater "flowers"? Actually they are forms of *animal* life much lower in the animal kingdom than fish or birds.

LIFE FORMS: DIFFERENCES

Perhaps you have examined a drop of water under the microscope and have seen single-celled animated forms of life and wondered—are these plants or animals?

The outstanding characteristics which distinguish plants from animals are:

Plants generally are *stationary,* fixed to a spot. Movement of the plant is usually in response to a stimulus in the immediate environment. Plants do not have the power of *locomotion.* Animals on the other hand, can usually move about—have the power of *locomotion* to seek food and shelter.

Plant growth is *indeterminate.* That is, it is without a definite time or size limit. A plant does not die from old age, but rather from disease or some other external factor. Animal growth, however, is usually determinate.

The most outstanding difference is the ability of the *green* plant to *manufacture* food within itself using the substances in the environment in this process. **This activity or process is known as photosynthesis. All animals, including man, get their food either directly or indirectly from plants.**

In external appearance, plants are usually green, some having varied and colorful flowers and others having no apparent blossoms. Among animals there is a vast variety of sizes, shapes and colors.

The basic difference between plants and animals lies in the unit of structure and function of each, namely, the cell. Plant cells have a **cell wall** which is actually non-living in chemical nature. Animal cells do not have this.

LIFE FORMS: SIMILARITIES

In all other respects, plants and animals are alike. All other activities that keep them alive are common to both. Every plant and animal is equipped to exist in its particular environment or *natural habitat.* Some are better equipped than others, are "hardier," and therefore more likely to survive. All plants and animals are *sensitive* to the need for food, water, certain temperatures and sunlight. In addition, animals are *sensitive* to the need for shelter and protection from their natural enemies.

In plants, chemical changes within the cells occur in response to the stimuli in the environment. Very simple forms of animals respond the same way. Some animals are equipped with nervous systems to respond to these stimuli. In the simpler animals the nervous systems are relatively simple, as are the responses. In the more complex type of animal, including man, this system is highly developed and provides the power of **discrimination.**

All plants and animals require food with which to *grow* and to provide the *energy* to carry on their life activities. Plants manufacture their own food. Animals *secure* their food from external sources and change the food within themselves into materials for growth and energy.

All plants and animals, no matter how simple or complex, are made up of a basic substance called **protoplasm.** This *living material* is identical in chemical nature in all forms of life, therefore its activities are identical.

BRIEF HISTORY OF CELLS

With the advent of the microscope, biologists were able to study the physical characteristics of protoplasm. Just about the time LEEUWENHOEK made his early microscope, the English scientist, ROBERT HOOKE, studied the structure of *cork* (from the bark of an oak tree) with a strong magnifying lens. He found it to be made up of tiny "empty boxes" with thick walls. He named these boxes *cells*.

After the microscope was made available to all scientists, further investigations were made of the structure of tiny water forms, of pieces of human skin, of blood, of parts of leaves, roots and stems of plants and even of parts of insects. They were all found to contain a substance that FELIX DUJARDIN, a French scientist, described as "living stuff," jellylike, grayish matter with "granules" scattered in it.

At the same time (1835–40) in other countries, scientists began to study the basic structure of all living things. In Czechoslovakia, a scientist named EVANGELISTA PURKINJE saw the "living stuff" and gave it the name **protoplasm,** (proto—first; plasm —form). He based his conclusions on the study of embryos of certain animals.

Some fifteen years later, two German biologists, SCHLEIDEN and SCHWANN, working independently, published books on the cellular nature of all plants and animals.

ROBERT BROWN, a botanist and surgeon's mate in the British Army, made an intensive study of orchids. He recognized the cellular structure of each flower part. With the use of stains, he was able to find a slightly thicker "particle" which

appeared in every cell. This "particle" seemed to control certain activities of the cells, especially that of *reproduction*. He named this the **nucleus** of the cell.

Scientists in many countries, with the aid of microscopes, working independently and in groups, established what is known as the **Cell Theory:**

Cells are the units of structure of all living things. (All plants and animals are made up of cells.)

Cells are, therefore, the units of function of all living things. (It is within the cells that our life activities occur.)

All living cells come only from other living cells.

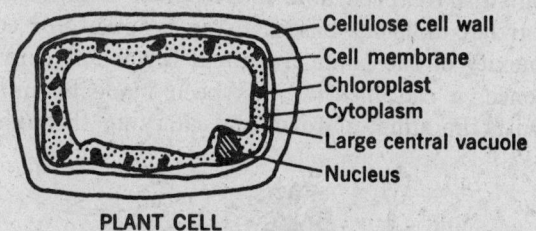

PLANT CELL

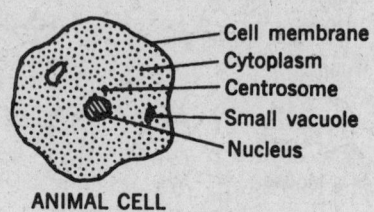

ANIMAL CELL

FIGURE 5.

CELL STRUCTURE

There are certain basic structures which appear in every cell. There are certain structures which differentiate a plant and animal cell, which make the basic differences between the plant and the animal. For convenience of study, let us look at typical plant and animal cells.

Structures present in all cells:

1. **Cell membrane** or **plasma membrane**—a double membrane surrounding the cell protoplasm or cytoplasm. Its function is to regulate the passage of liquids and gases into and out of the cell. It also provides a surface on which reactions may take place.

2. Cytoplasm—the protoplasm of living cells is in a colloid state; that is, it is made up of medium-sized particles hung in suspension. Its particles are too small to settle out and too large to go into solution. Because the particles are small, they provide a great surface area for cellular reactions to take place. They also permit the reaction to take place rapidly. Also, because protoplasm is not in a molecular state it cannot react chemically itself. Yet within the cytoplasm all cellular metabolic activities take place.

3. Nuclear membrane—a double membrane which controls the movement of materials into and out of the nucleus.

4. Nucleus—a definite structure within every cell. Its function is to control the activities of the cell. The nucleus contains the genetic material responsible for heredity, the *chromosomes*. It also contains the *nucleolus*, a smaller body which aids in the synthesis of protein.

5. Endoplasmic reticulum—a cell "skeletal" system. It provides a transport system between cell parts and a surface on which reactions may take place.

6. Ribosomes—small bodies which may occur on the surface of the endoplasmic reticulum or free in the cytoplasm. The ribosomes are the sites of protein synthesis.

7. Mitochondria—are often called the "power-house" of the cell. Here food is oxidized and energy is produced for use in various cellular activities.

8. Vacuoles—are storage bodies for water, minerals, etc. In unicellular organisms, vacuoles function in digestion and elimination.

Structures present only in animal cells:

1. Golgi bodies—function in the production of secretions of the cell.

2. Lysosomes—contain digestive enzymes which are released into the cytoplasm when the lysosomes burst open.

3. Centrosome or **centriole**—is located near the nucleus and functions in cell division.

Structures present only in plant cells:

1. Chloroplasts—bodies containing green chlorophyll pigments. Chloroplasts may be various shapes. The chloroplast is the site of photosynthesis or food production in a plant cell.

2. Cell wall—is composed of two layers. These layers provide support and protection for the cell. Both layers are somewhat waterproof, but they do not prevent the passage of water and sub-stances dissolved in water from passing through. The wall is composed of a substance called cellulose.

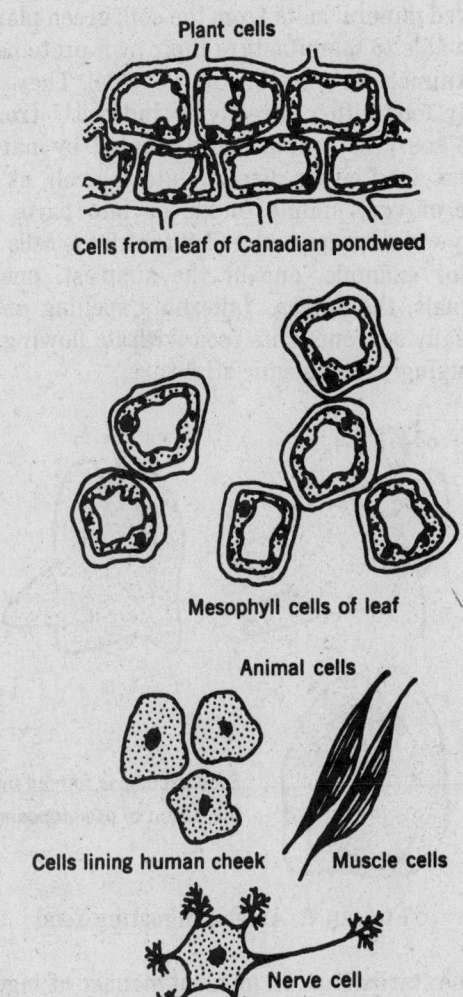

FIGURE 6.

INGESTION

In order to provide the necessary energy for growth and to carry on life's activities, we must take in food or eat. **This process is known as ingestion.**

In the discussion of the adaptations of plant cells it was noted that the cells are provided with structures called chloroplasts which help in the manufacture of food within the green plant. It is only in the green parts of the plant, the leaves and stems, that this food-making takes place.

Green plants in presence of light are able to take in the gas, **carbon dioxide,** from the air and combine it chemically with water to produce their carbohydrates. **This food-manufacturing process is known as photosynthesis.** By combining the sugars and starches made in this way with dissolved mineral salts from the soil, green plants are also able to manufacture their own proteins.

Animals are unable to do this. They secure their food either directly or indirectly from outside sources. Animals are adapted by nature to ingest food either directly into the cell, as in the case of very simple forms, or into parts of the body which prepare the food for all the cells to use.

For example, one of the simplest, one-celled animals, the **ameba,** (alternate spelling *amoeba*) actually surrounds its food with its flowing, everchanging protoplasmic structure.

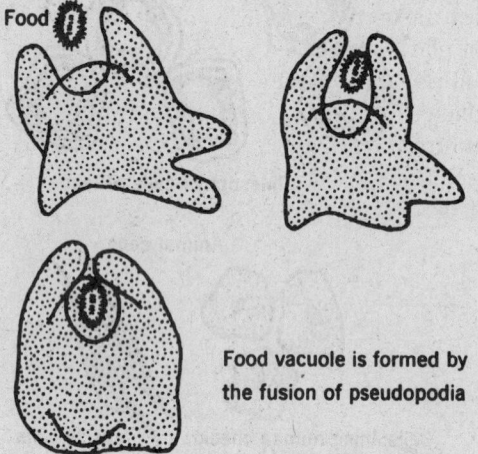

Food vacuole is formed by
the fusion of pseudopodia

FIGURE 7. Ameba ingesting food

The starfish has an unusual manner of ingesting food. It clamps down with its five arms on an oyster until the muscles of the **bivalve (sea animal with 2 shells)** tire from the force. The oyster, unable to keep itself tense, relaxes. As soon as the starfish feels this, it allows the oyster shells to open, projects its own stomach into the soft tissues of the oyster and proceeds to devour it chemically.

The butterfly takes in food by uncoiling a **long tubelike structure (proboscis),** inserting it into the nectar container of a flower and sipping gently as through a straw.

The frog is an example of another type of feed-getting. He sits quietly on a leaf or log and waits for a flying insect to approach. When the unwary insect is within reach, the frog's long, cleft tongue darts out, catches the prey and directs it into his mouth. See Fig. 9.

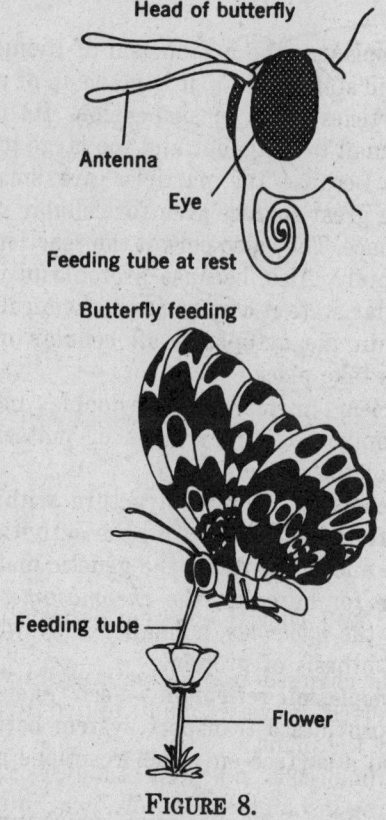

Head of butterfly

Antenna

Eye

Feeding tube at rest

Butterfly feeding

Feeding tube

Flower

FIGURE 8.

Animals higher in the scale of life are well adapted to move around to choose, secure and to bring food to the "mouth" or part of the body which first takes in food.

DIGESTION

In both plants and animals food must be broken down into its simplest forms and made *soluble.* Only in soluble form are cells able to use food to provide energy for all life processes and to build new protoplasm and repair old. **The process of simplifying food and making it soluble is called digestion. Water is an essential substance in this process.**

The change from insoluble starch, protein and fats to soluble forms is brought about by the action of chemicals called **enzymes** which exist in both plants and animals. These enzymes bring about changes in the composition of foods without being in any way changed themselves or used up in the process. The chemist calls them **activating agents or catalysts.**

In plant cells, during the process of digestion, the starch that is manufactured in the green

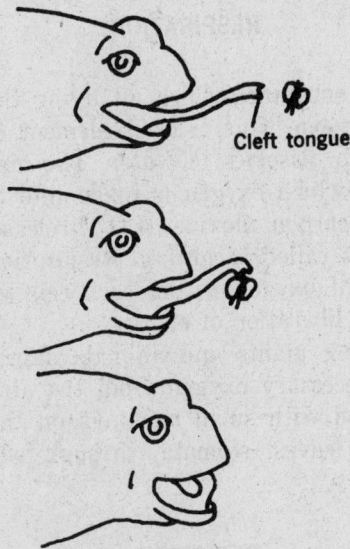

FIGURE 9. Digestive system of the bullfrog.

leaves is changed into simple sugars which can be dissolved in water and carried to all other parts of the plant.

In animal cells, much the same is true. Foods containing insoluble starch, proteins, minerals and fats must be digested before they can be made available to all cells. Simple animal forms digest foods within each individual cell. Enzymes provide the necessary stimulus for this process.

More complex animals are especially fitted or adapted for digestion. In the earthworm the digestive system (series of body parts adapted solely for digestion) is extremely simple, merely a single tube extending the length of the body.

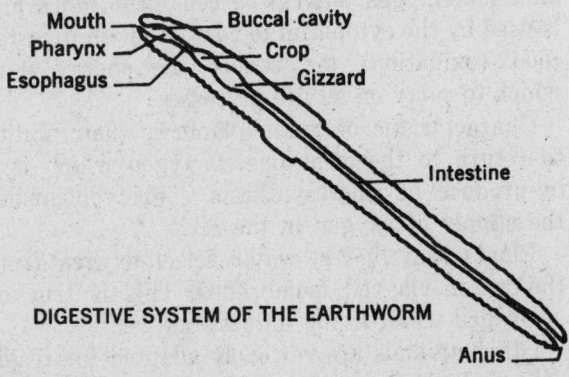

FIGURE 10. Digestive system of the earthworm

Higher in the animal kingdom this tube becomes divided into specialized parts each with a specific function in the process of digestion. In man and other highly developed **vertebrates (animals with backbones)** the digestive system is most specialized. Enzymes produced by glands serve as catalysts in animals as well as in plants.

ABSORPTION

Digested food must reach every cell in the living plant and animal. The cell walls of plants are porous so as to allow soluble food to pass through. The cell membranes are **selective** or **semipermeable**: that is, constructed so that only soluble substances can pass directly through into the cell protoplasm. **This process whereby digested or soluble food passes through the cell membrane is called absorption.**

In plant cells it is a simple process since all cell membranes are suitably adapted.

One-celled and other extremely simple animals contain food vacuoles in which digestion takes place. Digested food is diffused directly into the rest of the cell protoplasm.

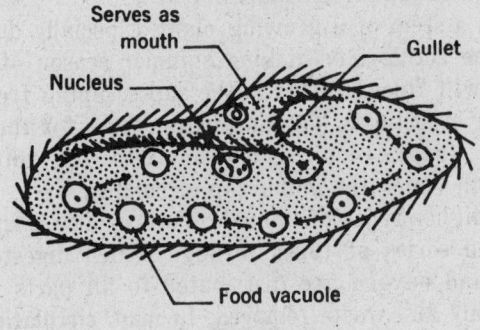

FIGURE 11.

In higher animal forms, including man, absorption takes place in specialized parts of the body. For example: in man, the small intestine is adapted to absorb digested food into the blood stream which carries it to all parts of the body.

CIRCULATION

Circulation is the life process in which soluble food and oxygen are distributed to all parts of plant and animal bodies, heat is distributed and waste removed.

The ever-moving protoplasm distributes digested food to all parts of the single-celled plant and animal.

In more highly developed plants there are tubes in the leaves and stems through which food and oxygen are circulated. **Liquid food in plants is known as sap.** Water containing dissolved minerals

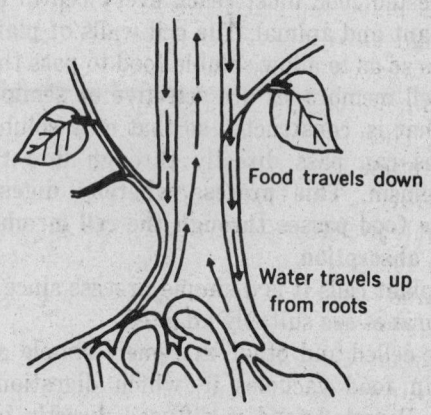

Food travels down

Water travels up from roots

FIGURE 12.

is transported from the roots up to other plant parts through similar tubes.

Cut a stem of a growing plant, especially during the active food-making summer season—the stem will "bleed." This is the sap escaping from the severed tubes. Tapping maple trees for their syrup (sap) requires cutting into the tubes through which the maple sap circulates.

In higher types of animals, there is also a specialized series of tubes through which digested food and oxygen are distributed to all parts of the body and waste removed. **In man, circulation is performed by a blood stream which courses in blood vessels (arteries, capillaries and veins) to every cell.**

ASSIMILATION

When digested food reaches the cells in all plants and animals, part of it is chemically combined with oxygen, actually burned (in the process of **oxidation**) to produce heat energy. The rest of it is changed into more protoplasm for growth and repair of cells. This process of changing digested food into protoplasm is called **assimilation.**

RESPIRATION

Another substance which all living things require is **oxygen.** This gaseous element exists in air and also dissolves in water. The mechanical process by which oxygen is taken into the body and later, carbon dioxide (CO_2) released from the body, is called *breathing.* **Respiration** is the utilization of oxygen within each cell which results in the liberation of energy.

Land-living plants and animals naturally secure the necessary oxygen from the air. Plants are provided with small openings on the under surface of leaves, stomata, through which air

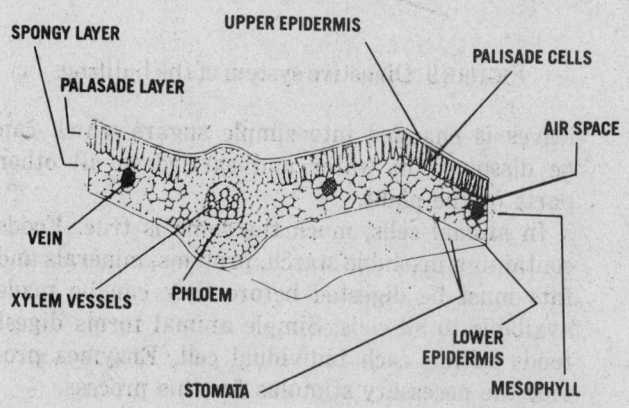

SPONGY LAYER   UPPER EPIDERMIS

PALASADE LAYER   PALISADE CELLS

AIR SPACE

VEIN

XYLEM VESSELS   PHLOEM

LOWER EPIDERMIS

STOMATA   MESOPHYLL

FIGURE 13. Leaf structure.

enters. Within the leaf, oxygen is selected from the air, dissolved in plant sap and circulated to all cells. Oxygen enters the cell membranes and is used by the cytoplasm to combine with digested food (oxidation) to produce the energy with which to carry on all life processes.

Characteristic of green plants is their ability to return to the atmosphere oxygen which is a by-product of photosynthesis. This replenishes the supply of oxygen in the air.

Plants that live in water select oxygen from the water via cell membranes. This is true of one-celled water-living animals as well.

Other animals are variously adapted for respiration. Fish are equipped with delicate, well-protected structures, **gills,** on each side of the head for this process. Water enters the mouth of the fish, passes back over the gills and comes out from under the scaly gill coverings. As water passes over the gills, oxygen is absorbed from the air dissolved in the water. It is carried by the blood stream to all parts of the body.

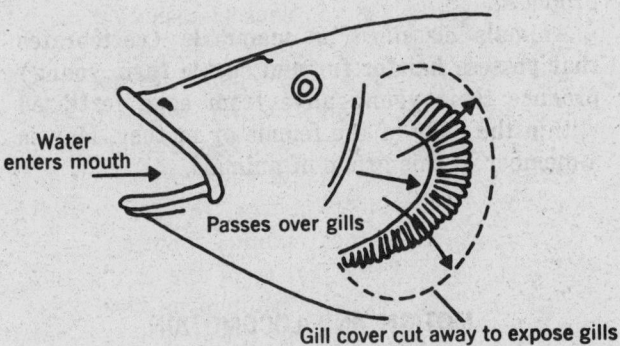

Water enters mouth

Passes over gills

Gill cover cut away to expose gills

FIGURE 14.

The earthworm, a land-living animal, breathes through its skin—which must be kept moist. Thus the earthworm always seeks damp earth into which to burrow. If the soil around it should become dry and the skin of the animal should dry up, the animal will die from its inability to carry on respiration.

After a heavy rain you will probably see many earthworms on top of the soil in the country or park and on the cement sidewalk in the city. These creatures are not adapted by nature to live under water—they will drown if unable to reach the air.

Land-living animals breathe in air containing oxygen. **Invertebrates (animals without backbones)** have varied adaptations for breathing.

Insects take in air through **spiracles** which are holes on each side of the abdomen. Air is distributed through the tubes **(trachea)** which branch throughout the body. See Fig. 15.

Most land-living vertebrates (including man)

Breathing in insects

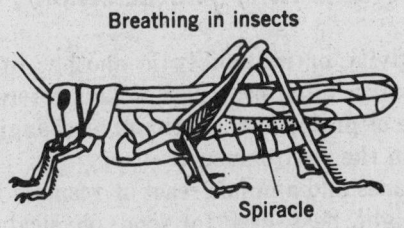

Spiracle

FIGURE 15. Grasshopper

take in air through nose and mouth from which it passes into *lungs*. The blood of these animals selects oxygen from air in the lungs and carries it to all cells where oxidation of food takes place.

The blood carries a waste gas (carbon dioxide) and excess water back to the lungs from which they are passed out of the body through the nose and mouth of the animal.

EXCRETION

After plants and animals have oxidized digested food and carried on their life activities, waste products result. Some are common to both plants and animals because of the nature of all protoplasm. These wastes are given off in the process of **excretion.**

Inability of the organism to rid itself of waste materials produces a toxic or poisonous condition within the cells. Such a condition leads to inadequate and abnormal performance of all life processes and may eventually be fatal.

The waste gas, carbon dioxide, and excess water vapor are excreted from plant cells through the stomata in the leaves of green plants. It is believed that other organic wastes accumulated in the leaves during the summer are eliminated when leaves fall in autumn.

Animals are adapted for the process of excretion. In one-celled animals (as well as plants), carbon dioxide and liquid wastes collect in vacuoles and are excreted directly through the cell membranes.

Many-celled animals, of greater specialization, produce solid wastes in addition to carbon dioxide and liquid organic wastes.

Lung-breathers eliminate carbon dioxide and some excess water through mouth and nose after these wastes have been brought by the blood to the lungs. The kidneys and the skin are specialized organs in man which collect and expel liquid wastes. The large intestine excretes solid wastes from the body.

REPRODUCTION

There are two major types of reproduction—asexual and sexual. Asexual reproduction is the more primitive type and results in "daughter" individuals identical to the "mother." Sexual reproduction is more advanced. In its evolution, male and female structures for reproduction have arisen. Sexual reproduction results in daughter individuals which are similar, but not identical, to the parents.

Simple forms of plants and animals reproduce themselves in the most primitive manner, without any special adaptation for the process. Single-celled plants and animals grow to capacity and then split into equal parts, each part becoming an individual. This method of reproduction is called **binary fission.**

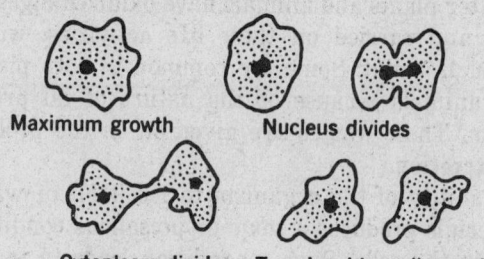

Maximum growth　　Nucleus divides

Cytoplasm divides　Two daughter cells result

FIGURE 16. Binary fission in Ameba

Multicellular (many-celled) plants are adapted in several ways for the vital function of reproduction. Mosses and ferns produce numerous spores which, when growing conditions are favorable, develop into new moss and fern plants.

Flowering plants are adapted to produce seeds. In this highly specialized form of reproduction the flower is the important part of the plant. Within separate parts of the same flower or within two separate flowers, male and female elements are developed. The combination of male and female cells results in the formation of seeds. A seed contains the **embryo** (the infant plant) which, when conditions are favorable, will develop into the new plant.

In order for most animals to reproduce their kind, male and female cells are necessary. The female reproductive cell is referred to as the **ovum** or **egg cell.** The male reproductive cell is referred to as the **sperm cell.** The union of a sperm cell with an ovum results in a **fertilized egg** which develops into the new infant animal. Since the new animal is a combination of both parent cells it inherits the characteristics of both parents.

Insects, fish, frogs, reptiles and birds produce eggs from which their young develop. Where there is little or no parental care—in the case of most fish, frogs and reptiles—large quantities of eggs are produced to insure the survival of a species.

Where there is some parental care (as in the case of birds) in providing food, shelter and protection against natural enemies, fewer eggs are produced.

Animals classified as **mammals (vertebrates that possess hair or fur and suckle their young)** produce their young alive from eggs fertilized within the body of the female or mother. Man is a member of this group of animals.

MOTION AND LOCOMOTION

Another function of all living things is the power of **motion** and, in some cases, **locomotion.** Since all protoplasm is in constant streaming motion, under normal conditions, then it follows that all living things move in some fashion.

One-celled animals move from place to place independently (locomotion) in their water surroundings.

Plants which are "rooted" in the ground do not have powers of locomotion but they do exhibit types of motion. Leaves, stems and flowers turn in the direction of the sun; tendrils of climbing plants wind about convenient supports; roots turn in the direction of water; some "sensitive" plants respond when touched.

Animals appear to be more "alive," as we commonly know the term, because, with few exceptions they have powers of locomotion. Sponges and corals grow attached at one stage of their lives—and in this way, they resemble plants.

SENSITIVITY AND BEHAVIOR

Sensitivity or **irritability** is another life function common to all protoplasm. **This refers to the response of protoplasm to stimuli or changing conditions in the environment.**

All plants and animals react or respond in some way to light, heat, need for food, physical contact and other external and internal stimuli.

Man bases his claim to superiority over the entire animal kingdom upon his ability to recognize and cope with stimuli in his environment.

The Role of Environment

Living things which exist all over the earth are numerous and extremely varied. Where conditions are favorable, plants and animals are most abundant and successful. Scientists have explored the deepest oceans and the most rarefied heights above the earth's surface and have found evidence of some life. There are relatively few places where no forms of life can exist.

ENVIRONMENT

The nature and success of living things depend upon environmental conditions. **By environment, we mean the immediate surroundings of an individual plant or animal.** The environment furnishes the basic needs for all living things to carry on their life functions.

These essentials are food, air, water and sunlight. Food is necessary to provide the energy to grow and perform life's processes. Air is necessary because it contains oxygen with which food must be oxidized to be changed to heat energy. Water is essential and waste may be removed so that substances can be made soluble for entrance into all cells through the cell membranes.

Since plants need sunlight to aid in the manufacture of food (photosynthesis) and animal food consists directly and indirectly of plants, sunlight is necessary for animals. The heat as well as the light is essential for life to exist.

In addition, the environment includes such factors as other living organisms, gravity, wind, electricity and air or water pressure.

Throughout the years of man's residence on earth, he has learned to improve his environment. To some extent, he has learned to conquer the forces that change his environment and threaten his ability to survive.

HABITAT

The same kinds of plants and animals do not live everywhere on earth. For example, polar bears normally live in frigid, polar regions. Lobsters are found among the rocks in salt water, whereas brook trout live in fresh mountain streams and lakes. The eagle builds its nest and rears its young on a craggy mountain ledge, whereas the sparrow and robin nest in an apple tree on a local farm or a maple tree in the city.

Plants, too, can be found growing in specific areas. Palm trees grow naturally in moist hot regions, whereas pines and other evergreens are more successful in drier and more northern areas. Orchids are flowers characteristic of tropical climate, whereas dandelions grow rampant on lawns in the temperate zones.

The specific environment in which a particular plant or animal or group of plants and animals is found is called its **natural habitat.** All living things are adapted to live in their natural habitats. If they are inadequately adapted, they either die or move to another area for which they are better fitted. If change in habitat occurs gradually, some plants and animals can gradually adapt themselves to the changes and live successfully.

Natural habitats vary greatly, thus the flora and fauna characteristics vary. **Flora refers to the sum of plant life** in a zone or habitat within a given length of time. **Fauna refers to the sum of animal life** of a given region and time period.

Natural habitats are distinguished from one another as follows:

Aquatic—referring to water-dwelling plants and animals. Not all types of aquatic forms live in the same kind of water. The type of indigenous (native to) life depends upon whether the water is fresh or salt, still or flowing, shallow or deep, hot, cold or moderate temperature, smooth or rocky bottom —or a combination of these factors.

Examples of fresh-water life, that is those animals whose natural habitat is ponds, lakes, streams and rivers are: algae, water cress, pondweeds and water lilies; some fish, snakes, snails, crayfish and leeches are among the animals.

Salt-water plants and animals may be divided into three groups:

Those which live on the beach or in shallow shore regions only—such as, sand eels, oysters, crabs and starfish, barnacles and seaweed.

Those which live near the surface of the ocean —such as, most sea fish, jellyfish, sea turtles, sharks, seals, porpoises; diatom plants.

Those which live in the ocean's depths where it is dark and very cold and where food is limited —such as colorless plants (diatoms and some bacteria), a few fish, some barnacles.

Terrestrial—this refers to land-living plants and animals. Although these flora and fauna live either on the surface of the ground or burrow underground, they all need some water to carry on their life processes. Terrestrial plants with few exceptions live on the surface of the ground, most of them anchored to the ground by roots or some sort of processes (stemlike growths). Trees and ferns are examples. Most terrestrial animals live on the surface of the ground. There are a few species that live part of their lives beneath the ground—for example moles, prairie dogs, gophers, earthworms and some insects.

Arboreal—this refers to animals whose existence is confined mostly to trees. Examples are some monkeys, sloths, opossums, lizards and some insects.

Aerial—refers to animals who spend a good part of their lives in the air. Examples are birds, some bats and most insects.

CLIMATE CONDITIONS

Climate conditions determine in great part the distribution of plants and animals over the world.

In Arctic regions where there is flat, frozen iceland, the flora are limited to low-growing plants such as some mosses and lichens, tough grasses, a few hardy species of dwarf poppies and even forget-me-nots. The fauna are usually confined to penguins, polar bears, seals, walruses and whales.

Plants and animals are greatly varied in **temperate** regions where there is variety in temperatures, and there are four annual seasons.

In **tropical** climates, where there is abundant rain and concentrated sunlight, plant life is luxuriant, always green and varied. Among the plant life are such trees as ebony, mahogany, rubber, date palms, bamboo, banana and thick-stemmed hardy vines; such flowers as orchids, gardenias and other heavily scented, superbly colored ones. Animals such as monkeys, apes, lemurs, sloths, elephants, parrots, birds of paradise, huge beautifully colored butterflies and innumerable insects are indigenous to this region.

In **mountainous** climates, because of characteristic high altitudes where the oxygen content of the air is less concentrated and there are strong, cold winds, both flora and fauna are relatively limited. Up to a certain line of demarcation, called the timber line, we find hardy oaks and evergreen trees, some poppies, gentians, onion-type grasses, mosses and lichens. This vegetation is low growing and extremely tenacious. Among the animals native to this region are huge spiders, eagles, bears, mountain goats and sheep.

Desert climates provide few factors favorable for most types of plants and animals. Because of the scarcity of water, the sand, and the steady intense light and heat of the sun only hardy plants like cactus, yuccas, sagebrush and tough grasses can exist. These are able to store water for long periods, have extensive roots and are tough enough to withstand the sun's burning intensity and the sharp drops in temperature at night. Such animals as rattlesnakes, horned toads, some lizards, a few more hardy rabbits, in addition to some unattractive birds, buzzards and vultures (scavengers) and a few species of insects, can exist on the desert where food is scarce and water is scarcer.

NATURAL BARRIERS

There are natural *barriers* (insurmountable obstacles) which prevent the indefinite distribution of successful growing plants and animals. These are large mountain ranges, widespread oceans, and large rivers, far-reaching deserts, soils lacking or overabundant in a certain chemical and the indestructible presence of natural enemies.

Earthquakes, the disappearance of small islands as a result of tumultuous internal earth upheavals, volcanic eruptions and large-scale glacial movements are also factors which produce natural barriers.

COMMUNITY LIVING

Within a given area or community, groups of plants and animals live together in natural coexistence. These living things are adapted or adapt themselves to all the factors in the immediate environment. In a community there always appears to be one or several dominant forms of plant and animal life which are more successful than the other plants and animals which share the community.

An example of community living can be found in a local park. There are trees which grow successfully in that particular climate and type of soil. There are birds which inhabit the trees, build nests and rear their young, feeding on the trees and other plants, and insects that grow in the area. There are insects adapted to live in the air, in the trees, on flowering plants and even in the ground.

Some insects serve as food for other animals, some help to propagate new generations of the local flora. Other animals live on the seeds, roots, stems and other parts of plants in the community. These animals contribute their share in community living by destroying harmful animal pests.

If the environmental factors remain relatively stable, then a balance of living may be achieved and all forms of flora and fauna in the area will live successfully.

PROTECTIVE ADAPTATIONS

All living things are adapted to secure the necessities of life from their immediate environment.

There appears to be a constant struggle among plants and animals to secure food and living space. Those plants and animals which are best adapted for these activities will be most successful. Those which are weakly adapted will be forced either to "fight" constantly for survival, withdraw to another community, or eventually perish.

Since every form of life has a natural enemy which will seek to destroy it, either to use it as food or in self-protection, all forms of life are adapted to protect themselves. These adaptations are called **protective adaptations.**

Among plants, the rose is a fine example of protective adaptation. Thorns on the stems discourage animals bent on destruction. Another example is the thistle with its needlelike flower cup, stems and leaves. The cactus has horny spines which are most painful to the touch.

The necessity for protective adaptation is great among animals because of their ability to move about (locomotion).

Most animals have some natural color protection from their enemies: that is, they resemble in

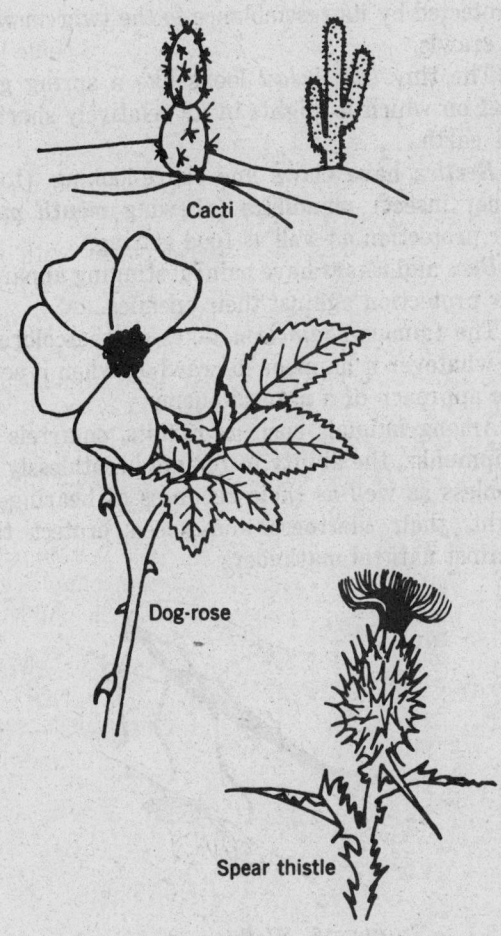

Cacti

Dog-rose

Spear thistle

FIGURE 17.

color their natural surroundings. Most animals have other special adaptations for protection.

Insects, which are so numerous and varied, show interesting and successful adaptations. For example, the green-brown *praying mantis* with its formidable front "claws" and its wary stance, appears most menacing to a potential attacker.

FIGURE 18. Praying mantis

The *walking stick* insect, a gentle animal, is protected by its resemblance to the twig on which it crawls.

The tiny *leaf insect* looks like a spring green leaf on which it alights in its relatively short life on earth.

Beetles have claws and fierce-looking (to another insect) **mandibles (chewing mouth parts)** for protection as well as food-getting.

Bees and *wasps* have painful stinging apparatus for protection against their enemies.

The famous *chameleon* takes on the coloration of whatever it happens to crawl on when it senses the approach of a natural enemy.

Among animals such as rabbits, squirrels and chipmunks, the ability to remain breathlessly motionless as well as their keenness of hearing and sight, their alertness and speed protect them against natural marauders.

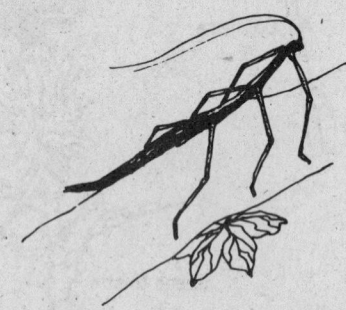

FIGURE 19. Walking stick insect

FIGURE 20. Male stag beetle

FIGURE 21. Common wasp

The *turtle* is fitted with a thick, horny "shell" which encases its soft body and into which it can withdraw completely for shelter and protection.

FIGURE 22. Turtle

PLANT AND ANIMAL INTERDEPENDENCE

It is obvious that in any environment one plant or one animal cannot survive by itself. All animals depend upon plants and other animals and plants depend upon other living things. Man depends upon other animals and plants for his success on earth. This mutual interdependence is what provides the balance in nature.

Most plants and animals live in groups. Some trees, for example, are adapted to a specific climate and type of soil. Hardy oak and hickory trees grow together in a temperate region where there are dry ridges. Basswood, red maple, elm, willow and birch will be found growing together in more moist areas. Evergreens (firs and pines) are usually found in more northerly climates but can grow elsewhere.

Ferns and mosses flourish together in moist shady places.

Seaweeds and algae grow together in harmony in the salty oceans.

Most animals live gregariously in "communities" or herds. Man is such an animal.

Some insects—bees and ants especially—live in communities and actually share in the many activities of food-getting, shelter-building, care of the young and protection against natural enemies.

In a warm sea-water community certain fish, coral, sponges, lobsters, crabs and jellyfish live together.

Local ponds provide community living for water bugs, frogs, snails, eels and fish.

Such animals as buffalo, elephants, cows and other cattle live in herds for mutual benefits. Wolves and coyotes travel in packs for maximum mutual strength and protection.

Relatively few animals prefer to live alone. Examples of those that do are lions, tigers, some deer and small animals like rabbits. The advantages of solitary living are few. Escape from natural enemies is perhaps easier for a swift, lonely animal; less disturbance and interference in rearing the young; less competition for mating and securing food are sometimes possible advantages.

Generally speaking there is "safety in numbers"; therefore group living is usually the most successful type of living.

SYMBIOSIS

The living together of organisms for mutual benefits is called symbiosis, the plants and animals involved are known as symbionts. An example of symbiosis among animals is the relationship between common ants and plant lice or *aphids*. The aphids suck the sap from rose or other plants. With this plant fluid they produce a sweet substance within their bodies. Ants "milk" the aphids and feed their queen and also the young. (The plant lice are known as "ant cows.") In return for this service, the ant cows are protected by their mutual benefactors against natural enemies and are also given shelter in anthills during the winter.

Another example of mutual "give and take" is found in the *termite*. This wood-eating insect provides food and shelter for a protozoan animal that lives in its intestines. The protozoa rewards its host by producing chemicals which digest the wood fibers for the termite.

Another interesting form of symbiosis between animals exists in the partnership relationship of the hermit crab and the sea anemone (a member of the jellyfish family). The hermit crab lives in a discarded snail shell which covers the soft part of the crab. The anemone lives on top of the snail-shell house and has stinging apparatus which protects it and the crab from natural enemies and captures food. It also gives protective coloration for the crab which, in turn, provides the anemone with transportation and food bits that escape its own mouth.

A classic example of plant symbiotic relationship is the *lichen* which is found growing on rocks

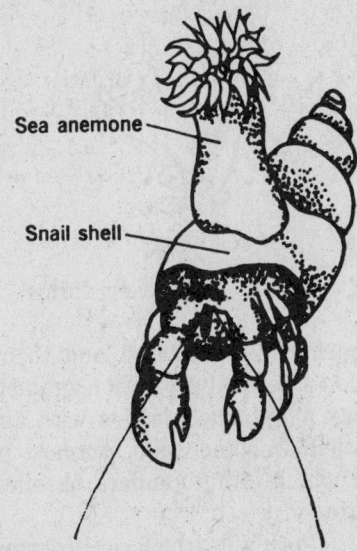

FIGURE 23. Hermit crab

and tree trunks. This is not a single plant but a mutually beneficial combination of a nongreen fungus and a group of one-celled green plants of the algae group. The fungus cannot make its own food. It provides shelter, anchorage, protection, water and carbon dioxide for its algae companions. These simple green plants use the water and carbon dioxide to manufacture food and supply oxygen for the fungus.

PARASITISM

Some plants and animals feed on other living organisms without giving anything in return. **This relationship is known as parasitism; the offender is called a parasite, and the "meal ticket," the host.** In most cases the parasite is structurally degenerate and entirely dependent upon the host. The host may either gradually lose its vitality, be-

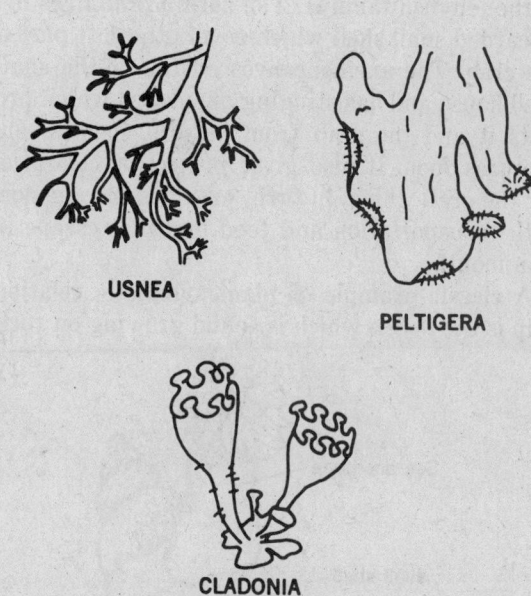

USNEA

PELTIGERA

CLADONIA

FIGURE 24. Lichen forms

The most numerous and destructive of all plant parasites are among the **bacteria (a type of single-celled plant).** Some species cause blights on apples, pears, cabbage, cucumbers and other plants. Other species cause diseases in man and are referred to as **pathogenic** bacteria. Among the dreaded pathogenic bacteria are those which produce diphtheria, typhoid fever, Asiatic cholera, bubonic plague and other illnesses, most of which man has been able to control and prevent.

There are some animal parasites which single man out as their unfortunate hosts. Among them are protozoa which cause malaria and sleeping sickness. Hookworm and pork worm—parasitic in man—produce devastating results in their often unsuspecting hosts. Scientists have learned to prevent and control the harmful activities of these animal parasites.

come abnormal and diseased and then die or it may develop a natural protection against the parasite. It may adapt itself to live with and in spite of its burden. In some cases, the host produces a substance which either renders harmless or kills the parasite.

The *mistletoe* plant, which conjures up romantic notions, is actually a parasite incapable of manufacturing its own food, reliant on another plant for its food. Its host, usually an apple, poplar or maple tree, eventually perishes from malnutrition.

Other plant parasites which depend on and slowly devitalize their hosts, causing great economic loss to man, are wheat rust, Dutch elm disease, corn smut and chestnut blight. In each case the tree or plant mentioned in the name is the losing host to the destructive parasite plant.

There are some parasitic plants which do damage directly to man's person. These offenders are members of the **fungus group of plants, that is, a group having no chlorophyll.** The unpleasant "ringworm" and "athlete's foot" ailments are examples.

SAPROPHYTES AND SCAVENGERS

Some plants and animals depend for their existence on other, *dead* organisms. Many plants lacking chlorophyll are known as **saprophytes,** examples of which are yeasts, molds and mushrooms.

Animals that live on dead or decaying flesh of other animals are called **scavengers.** Among them are the vultures, buzzards and sea gulls. In the blood stream of man, there are **white blood cells** that resemble ameba which act as tiny scavengers by engulfing and eating unwanted particles including some disease-producing bacteria.

Man, in his position as the superior animal of our universe, has learned to change his environment, sometimes to his misfortune but generally to his advantage, and to improve the welfare of other living things. Because of his powers of observation and reasoning, he has been able, to a great extent, to control many factors of his environment.

Organization and Classification

All living things are made of **protoplasm.** The smallest unit of structure and function of protoplasm is the **cell.** All plants and animals are made up of either a single cell or many cells.

Evolutionists believe that all plants and animals originally arose from a unicellular ancestor. As can be seen by the study of lower plants and animals, particularly those of a single cell, there are many characteristics common to both those called "animals" and those called "plants." It has taken many years of evolution for organisms to acquire their distinct plant or animal-like character. In order to take into account the similarity of the lower plants and animals, recent methods of classification place them together in a group called the Protista. Traditionally, they have been classified separately.

PLEUROCOCCUS

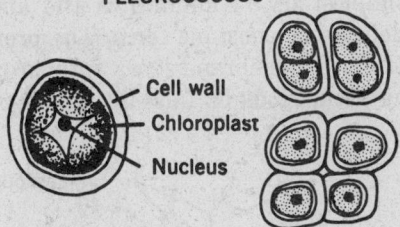

Cell wall
Chloroplast
Nucleus

TWO STAGES OF
VEGETATIVE REPRODUCTION

DIATOMS

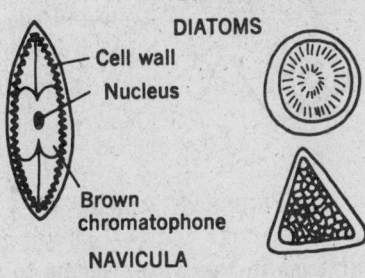

Cell wall
Nucleus

Brown
chromatophone

NAVICULA

DESMIDS

FIGURE 25. Single-celled plants

SINGLE-CELLED LIFE: PLANTS

The simplest form of plant life exists as a single cell which is able to carry on all the necessary life processes. Most one-celled plants belong to the **algae** group which live in water. There are some which live in symbiotic relationship with other plants (lichens) and with animals in a moist environment but out of the water.

A common example of a single-celled plant is the **pleurococcus** which is usually found growing on the north side of moist tree trunks and rocks in the woods. These tiny green plants are legendary

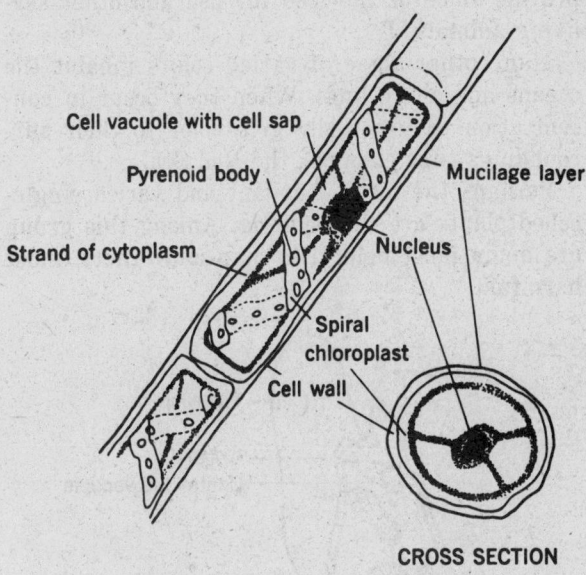

Cell vacuole with cell sap
Pyrenoid body
Mucilage layer
Strand of cytoplasm
Nucleus
Spiral
chloroplast
Cell wall

CROSS SECTION

FIGURE 26. Spirogyra (common pond scum)

"Indian's Friend" and "Woodsman's Compasses" because they indicate the direction North.

They contain chlorophyll with which to combine carbon dioxide from the air and water to manufacture food. Under the microscope they appear singly or in colonies, each cell living independently within its colony. See Fig. 25.

A drop of pond water will reveal a variety of single-celled plants. What is commonly known as pond scum is a group of green threadlike colonies called **spirogyra.** They reproduce prolifically and form the greenish scum that appears on the surface of sluggish streams, small ponds and pools. See Fig. 26.

Among the independent single-celled forms which can be viewed under a microscope are the **diatoms** and **desmids.** These plants are curiously symmetrical, each kind having a specific design or.

its shell-like outer covering which encloses and protects the soft protoplasmic cells.

Diatoms seem to have existed in abundance centuries ago. Large deposits of their empty shells have been discovered in salt as well as fresh water and on land that shows evidence of once having been under water. These deposits, called **diatomaceous earth,** are used commercially as the basis of polishing materials and also for filtering purposes in sugar refineries.

Another common group of single-celled plant life, is found in ocean water, as part of the substance **plankton.** These are tiny green plants that provide much of the food for fish and other sea-living animals.

Many other algae of varied colors inhabit the oceans and shore lines. When they occur in concentration they actually give color to their surroundings—for example, the Red Sea.

Perhaps the most abundant and varied single-celled plants are the **bacteria.** Among this group are many most helpful to man and others, most harmful.

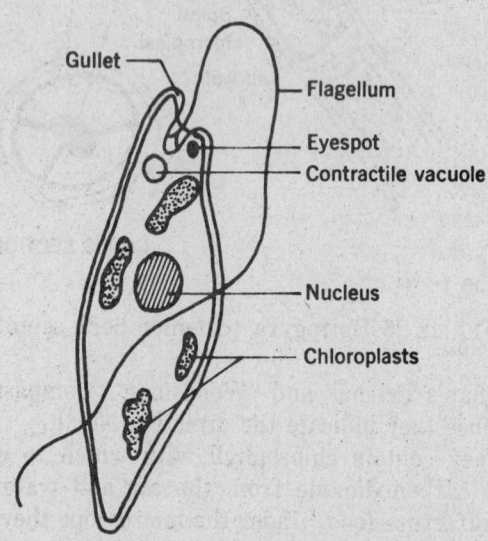

FIGURE 27. Euglena (plant or animal?)

One single-celled form of life, the **euglena,** has created dissension among biologists. Botanists consider it a simple plant because it contains chlorophyll bodies with which it manufactures its own food.

Zoologists, on the other hand, claim that it rightfully belongs to the animal kingdom for several reasons. It contains a contractile vacuole for collecting and eliminating liquid wastes. At one end of the cell there is a form of mouth and gullet into

which it takes some food particles from the water. At the mouth region, there is a **whiplike projection (flagellum)** which lashes back and forth, aiding in locomotion and food-getting.

Perhaps this controversial bit of life is proof that one-celled plants and animals have a common ancestor.

SINGLE-CELLED LIFE: ANIMALS

This leads us to the fascinating group of true one-celled animals called **protozoa** (proto—first; zoa—animals). A drop of pond water reveals a variety of tiny animals, some darting about and others moving lazily.

Among the most numerous are paramecia and amebas. Each of these animals is well-equipped within its protoplasm to carry on all the life functions.

The simplest of all animals is the ameba. It has no definite or constant form. The protoplasm within the cell membrane flows into projections known as **pseudopods** or false feet. The presence

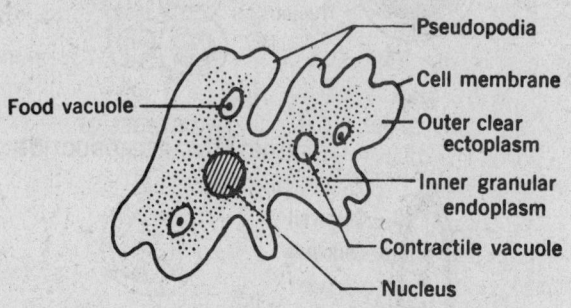

FIGURE 28. Ameba

of food particles in the water seems to stimulate the formation of these false feet which carry the rest of the cell in the direction of the food; thus the animal moves from place to place.

Food is digested within vacuoles and is absorbed directly into the surrounding cell protoplasm. Oxygen dissolved in the water is absorbed directly through any part of the cell membrane. Solid wastes are "left behind" as the ameba flows sluggishly on. A contractile vacuole regulates the water content of the animal and also collects liquid wastes which are expelled through a temporarily thin spot in the cell membrane.

The centrally located nucleus of the ameba controls all cell activities. It splits in half to produce two ameba in the process of reproduction. This simple type of reproduction is known as **binary fission.**

The paramecium, a more advanced type of one-

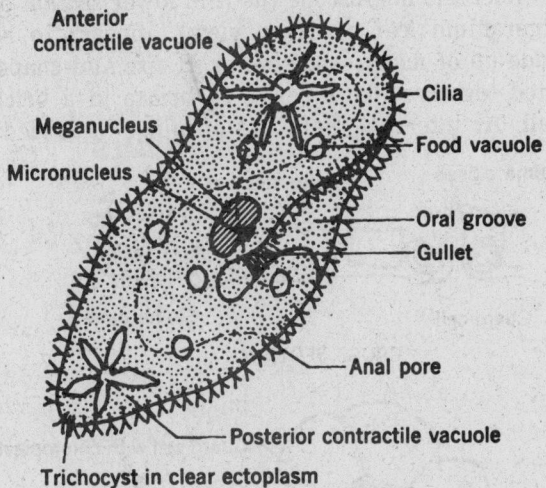

FIGURE 29. Paramecium

celled protozoa, is slipper-shaped and constant in form.

Its cell body is covered with tiny projections of protoplasm called **cilia** which wave back and forth providing means of rapid locomotion in water. Other cilia around the mouth region wave food particles into the "gullet" which is also lined with cilia to push the food into food vacuoles.

Constant flowing motion of the protoplasm within the paramecium cell body distributes each food vacuole to all parts of the cell. Digestion of food takes place in the vacuole. Digested food is absorbed directly into the surrounding protoplasm.

Oxygen dissolved in the water is absorbed directly through the cell membrane into the cell protoplasm.

Solid food wastes are expelled through a weakened area in the cell membrane called an **anal spot.** Liquid wastes are forced through the cell membrane by the contracting action of the contractile vacuoles located one at each end of the tiny animal.

Minute threads of poisonous protoplasm called **trichocysts** are imbedded just inside the cell membrane. These provide means of protection and are expelled with force when the paramecium comes in contact with a hostile form of life.

A well-developed nucleus and a "helper-nucleus" control all life activities and provide the means

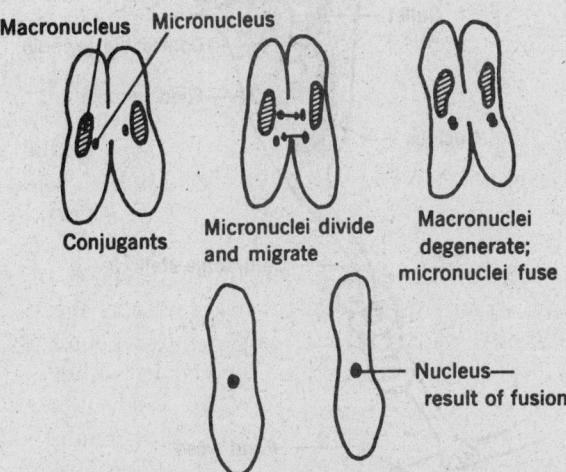

CONJUGATION IN PARAMECIUM

Conjugants separate and divide again by binary fission
This is a simplified version of a more complex process

FIGURE 30.

for reproduction. The paramecium divides by binary fission, similarly to the ameba, and also by a simple type of sexual reproduction called **conjugation.** In this type of reproduction two paramecia fuse temporarily, exchange nuclear material, separate and then each proceeds to divide by binary fission. This process seems to strengthen the species.

There are other types of protozoa which exist individually and still others which live in colonies.

The **vorticella** attaches itself by a long stalk at one end to a stationary object.

Colonial protozoa live in groups, each animal in the colony, functioning independently. Some colonies have a thick, gelatinous substance encasing them while others have glasslike coverings. The famous white cliffs of Dover (Southern England) are composed of countless chalklike shells which have accumulated through the years after the soft protoplasm of each protozoan animal has ceased to exist.

Most one-celled animals live independently but there are some which are parasites. Examples of these are the protozoa that cause malaria and African sleeping sickness in man. Each of these has an alternate host. The malarial plasmodium (protozoan that causes malaria) spends part of its life in the anopheles mosquito. The protozoan which causes sleeping sickness spends much of its life cycle in its alternate host, the tsetse fly, native to the African continent.

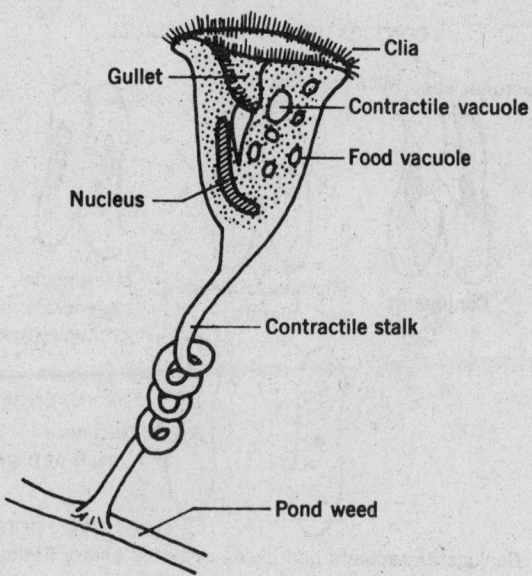

FIGURE 31. Vorticella

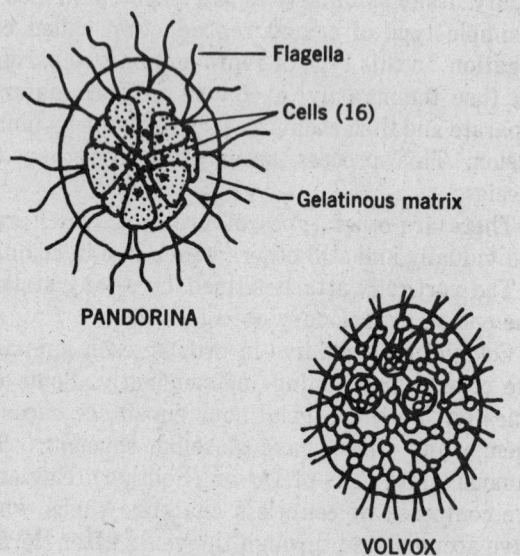

PANDORINA

VOLVOX

FIGURE 32. Colonial protozoa

CELLULAR ORGANIZATION

Living things that we can readily see and touch are usually made up of many cells, and many groups of cells. Each of these cells or groups of cells is adapted to perform a particular function.

All of the groups of cells normally work in harmony for the common welfare of the plant or animal.

One can easily see the gross structure of a geranium plant. To examine the cellular composition of any part of the plant requires a microscope.

Under the microscope the thin lower section of a geranium leaf (surface view) appears to be made up of many cells similar in size and shape, fitted together like a series of bricks in a brick wall. At intervals there are openings "guarded"

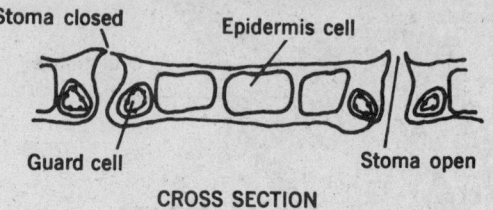

CROSS SECTION

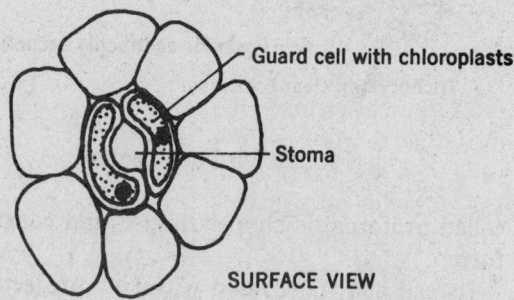

SURFACE VIEW

FIGURE 33. Under surface of leaf

by two kidney-shaped cells. The same view of the lower epidermis of the leaf appears to be a pattern of well-fitted flagstones among which are guarded openings. See Fig. 33.

The continuous layer of cells is adapted to protect the under surface of the leaf. The openings or **stomata** with their **guard cells** control inward or outward passage of gases. Oxygen is taken into the leaf and carbon dioxide is released during the process of respiration. During the process of photosynthesis carbon dioxide is taken in through these stomata and oxygen is released. Other cells (containing chloroplasts) in the leaf are adapted to combine carbon dioxide and water to produce food for the plant.

In a later discussion of the flowering plants, plant cells and their specialized functions in groups or tissues will be considered in detail. Note a few more examples in Figure 34.

Among many-celled animals, there are also groups of cells similar in structure with a similar common function.

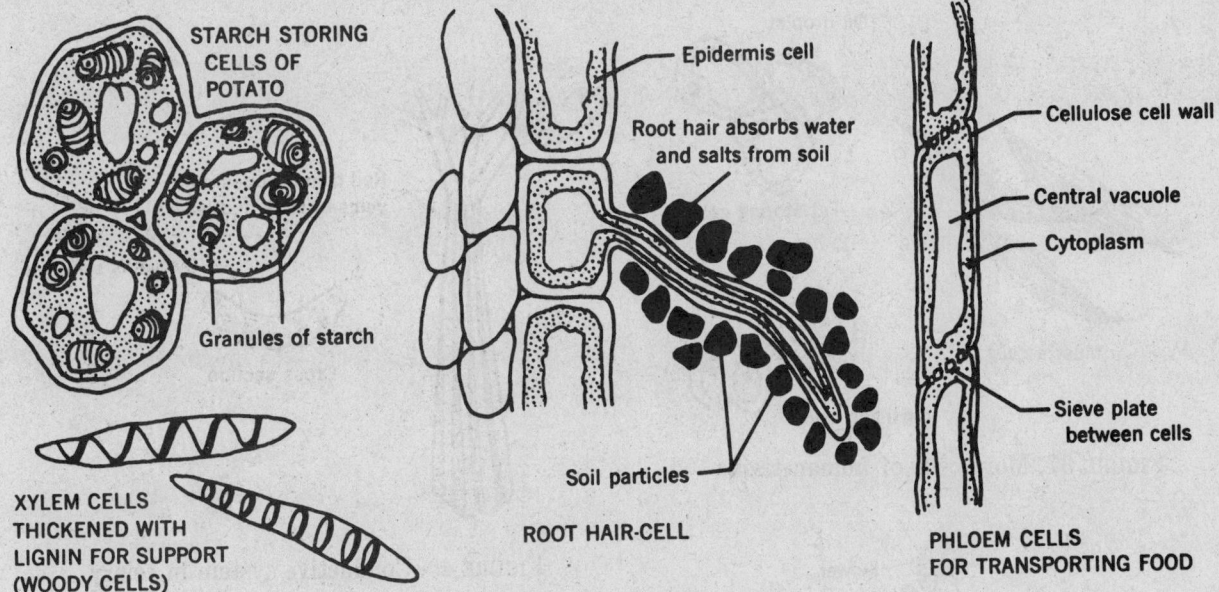

FIGURE 34. Plant tissue cells

For example, examine Figure 35 showing cells from the cheek lining of man. If a microscope is available to you, prepare a slide of cheek lining cells. (Scrape the inner surface of your cheek with the dull edge of a butter knife and mount this in a drop of water on a glass slide.)

These cells are adapted for their job of protecting the softer, inner cells of the mouth.

In Figures 36 and 37 there are surface views of several types of cells found in the human body. Note how they vary in size and shape, also in function.

Groups of cells similar in size, shape and function make up tissues: thus nerve cells working together form nerve tissue; muscle cells grouped together form muscle tissue; and cartilage cells form cartilage tissue.

There are other types of cells in the human body (as well as in all other animals and in plants) that, because of structural and functional similarities, form tissues.

Groups of different kinds of tissues working together to perform a particular function for the plant or animal are called organs.

Examples of plant organs are leaf, stem, roots, flowers, fruits and seeds.

Examples of a few organs found in the human body are larynx, trachea or windpipe and lungs.

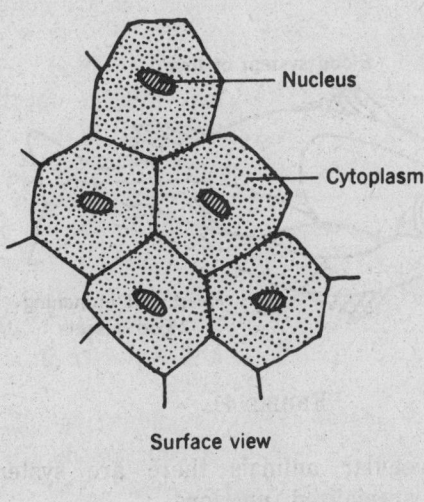

FIGURE 35. Human cheek cells

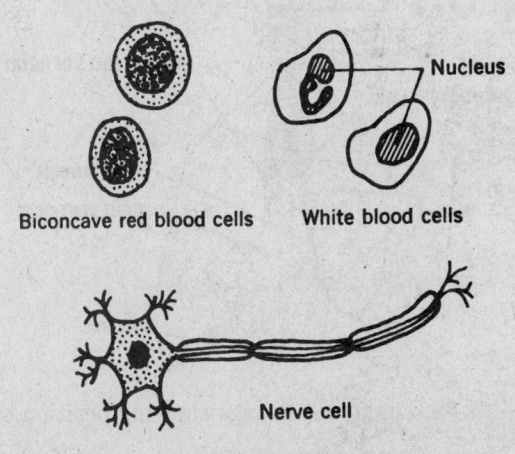

FIGURE 36.

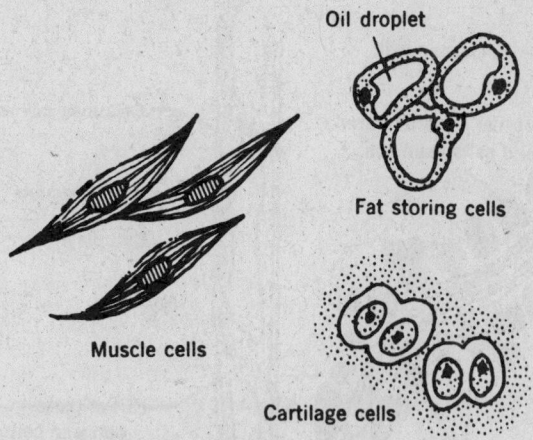

FIGURE 37. More cells of human tissue

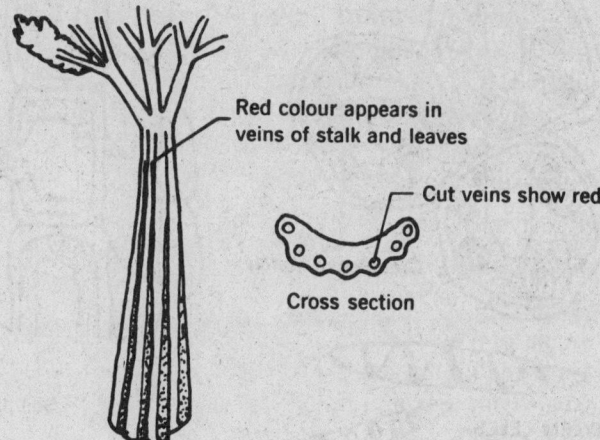

FIGURE 40. Conductive system in celery

A group of organs working together to perform a specific life function is called a system.

A simple experiment which can be performed at home will illustrate the conductive system in plants. Place a stalk of celery (leaves included) in a solution of red ink and water for several hours. Observe the red color which apears in *tubes* or *veins* in the stalk (stem) and leaves. Cut across a piece of the stalk and observe the row of red dots in Figure 40.

This experiment indicates the conductive system through which water containing dissolved minerals from the soil rises up through the stem to all other parts of the plant.

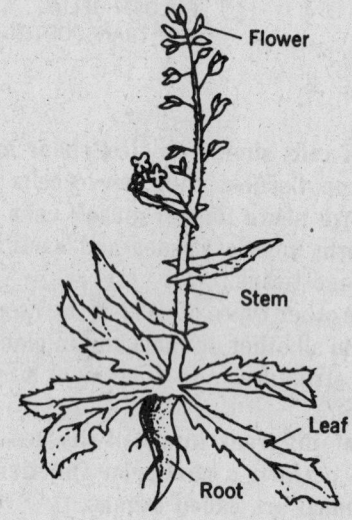

FIGURE 38. Plant organs

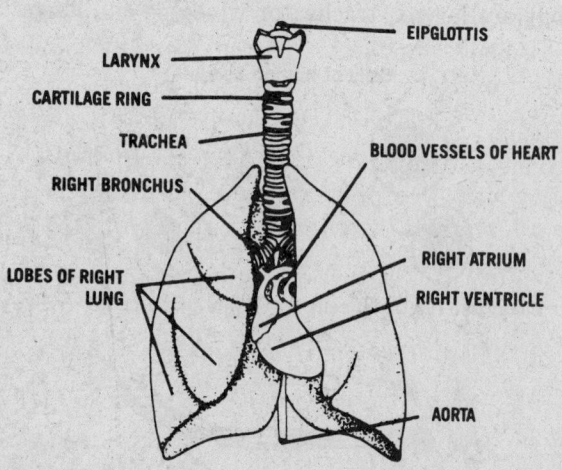

FIGURE 39. Diagram of lungs showing position of heart.

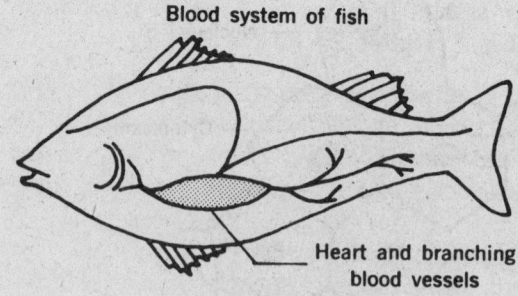

FIGURE 41.

In multicellular animals there are systems which have specialized functions.

The blood or **circulatory system** in fish is one example. A primitive heart and blood vessels (tubes) branching to all parts of the body are the organs which make up this system. Its function is to distribute blood to all cells in the fish. The blood carries digested food and oxygen to the cells and carries waste products away from the cells (to be eliminated).

In a more complex animal there are many different systems, each with a specialized job. We shall mention them briefly at this point:

Digestive system—to digest food.

Absorption system—to absorb digested food and necessary oxygen.

Circulatory system—to circulate or **deliver** digested food and oxygen to all cells **in the body** and to carry away gas and liquid waste products and distribute heat.

Respiratory system—to take in oxygen and release carbon dioxide and excess water vapor from the body.

Excretory system—to rid the body of wastes.

Reproductive system—to produce another generation of human beings.

Nervous system—to control activities of the body.

Skeletal system—to provide for support, protection, and locomotion.

Let us analyze the digestive system to show the organs of which it is composed: the mouth, gullet or esophagus, stomach and intestines. There are glands that produce chemicals (catalysts) which aid the digestive organs in their function.

The sum total of a group of systems working together results in a complete organism, otherwise called a plant or animal.

Over a million varieties of living things have been discovered on our earth. In order that they be studied and recognized they must be grouped in some orderly fashion, or in other words, classified.

For example, books in a library are not just placed on shelves in any haphazard fashion. They are divided first into large general groups, that is, fiction and non-fiction. Each of these groups is divided further into subdivisions. For example, non-fiction are grouped according to their main topics: biography, history, science, art, etc. **Each** of these divisions is further subdivided; for example, science books are classified according to their specialties: astronomy, biology, chemistry, physiol-

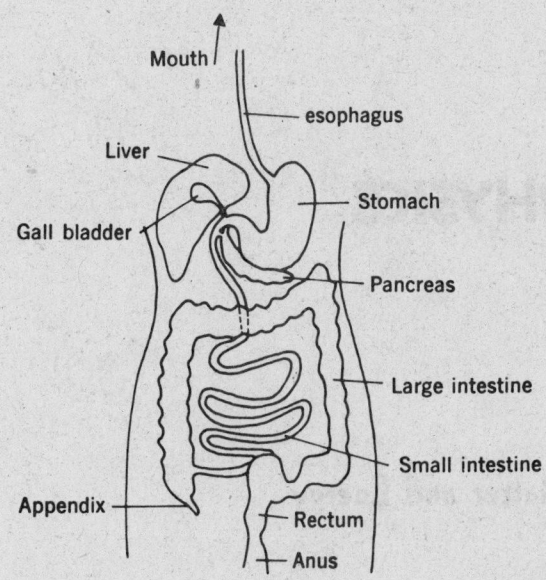

FIGURE 42. Human digestive system

ogy, etc. Subdivisions finally narrow down to individual books.

Our modern **system of classification or taxonomy** of all living things was devised by LINNAEUS (Carl von Linné) in the latter part of the eighteenth century. He used Latin names because Latin was the universal language of scholars. He gave names to plants and animals that are short and often descriptive in nature.

The largest groups of living things are the Plant and Animal kingdoms. Each of the kingdoms is divided and subdivided depending first on general and then more detailed structural and functional similarities. The smallest subdivision is the individual plant or animal. For example: The classification of Man.

Kingdom—Animal
Phylum—Chordate (with a skeletal axis)
Subphylum—Vertebrate (having backbone)
Class— Mammal (mammary glands, young born alive, four-chambered heart, have hair)
Order—Primate ("first"; opposable thumb)
Family—Hominidae (mankind)
Genus—Homo (human being)
Species—Sapiens (wise, discerning)
Man—Homo sapiens

See Appendix: Biology Helps   Digestive System of the Bullfrog, Fig. A; Human Skeleton, Fig. B.

PHYSICS

Matter and Energy

When we look around us and examine the objects found in our homes, in the streets, in stores and factories, and in Nature everywhere, we realize that the things with which we are surrounded are made of a great variety of materials. Chemists have found that all complex substances—wood, steel, glass, plastics, even the waters of the ocean and the air we breathe—are mixtures of chemical **compounds.** Nearly a million compounds have been identified, and these, in turn, are merely different combinations of only about a hundred chemical **elements** known to science.

THREE FORMS OF MATTER

Some of the substances we meet are **solids,** such as iron or stone. Others are **liquids,** such as oil or water. Still others are **gases,** such as air or steam. These three conditions—solid, liquid and gas—are called the three **physical states** of matter. A solid object can be thought of as one that tries to keep a definite shape and a definite bulk, or volume. A liquid also has a definite volume, because it is almost impossible to pack it into any smaller space. But a liquid will take on the shape of *any* container into which it is poured (see Fig. 1). A gas, on the other hand, has neither a definite shape nor a definite volume: If some air is let into a chamber that was previously pumped out, this quantity of air will fill the whole space uniformly. Unlike water in a jar, a gas does not have a distinct surface.

Some common substances are mixtures of matter in several states. Fine sand or silt mixed with water will not settle out. It forms a **colloidal suspension**—a stable mixture of a solid and a liquid. Ink is another example. Milk is an **emulsion** —globules of one liquid (fat) suspended in another (water). **Foam** is a gas suspended in a liquid.

FIGURE 1. (Left) Definite volume, definite shape (Center) Definite volume, no definite shape (Right) No definite volume, no definite shape

Often, we know a single kind of matter in all three principal states. Water is a common example. Ordinarily, water is a liquid, but at low temperatures it goes into its solid state (called ice), and at higher temperatures it becomes steam, which is the name for the gaseous state of water. We usually think of air as a gas, but at about 300 degrees below zero it turns into a bluish liquid. Iron, commonly seen in the solid state, becomes a liquid in a foundry and is a gas in the sun and in the stars, where the temperature is many thousands of degrees. These are all **physical changes,** and the material keeps its identifying characteristics all the while. But when wood burns or cement hardens or cream turns sour there is in each case a more permanent change and new substances are formed. These are examples of **chemical change.**

GENERAL CHARACTERISTICS OF MATTER

In studying physics, we are not especially interested in the *special* properties of the many kinds of matter; this is the business of the chemist. What we do want to find out about are the *general* characteristics common to all kinds of matter. One of these is *permanence*. Experience shows that we can neither manufacture nor destroy matter. All we can do is to change it from one form to another by chemical processes like those mentioned.

Another general fact about matter is the obvious one that it *takes up space*. No two things can occupy the same space at the same time. A boat pushes aside the water as it passes and a chisel forces apart the fibers of a block of wood. Even air acts to keep other intruding material out, as you can see by performing a simple experiment:

EXPERIMENT 1: Float a small cork on water in a basin and push the open end of a tumbler down over it. The water surface inside the glass is found to be pushed down, as shown by the change in position of the cork. The same principle applies to the air pumped into the suit of a deep-sea diver or into a caisson used in underwater construction projects.

Sometimes we meet situations where two pieces of matter *do* seem to occupy the same space:

EXPERIMENT 2: Fill a glass brim full of water. Add salt, from a shaker, a little at a time. With care, a considerable amount of salt can be put in without making the water overflow.

The explanation here is that water—in fact, any substance—is not *continuous* matter; there are spaces between the water molecules, into which other molecules such as those of the salt can enter.

Another general property of material bodies that we shall have more to do with later on is called **inertia**. In some respects, this is the most fundamental of all the attributes of matter. It can best be described as the tendency for any object to stay at rest if it is at rest now, or—if in motion —to continue moving as it is now. When a car in which you are sitting starts up suddenly, you find yourself falling back into your seat. Nothing actually pushed you backward—your body merely tried to stay at rest, as it was originally. If, after getting under way the brakes are quickly applied, you pitch forward; your body obviously tries to persist in its previous motion.

EXPERIMENT 3: Place a heavy rock or a bucket of sand on a board resting on two pieces of pipe, which act as rollers. Tie one end of a piece of heavy cord to the weight and wrap the other end a few times around a short stick, to act as a grip (Fig. 2). A gentle pull on the string will make the board and its load glide along easily, and once in motion it will tend to keep going; but a *sudden* sharp jerk will break the string while hardly moving the weight at all.

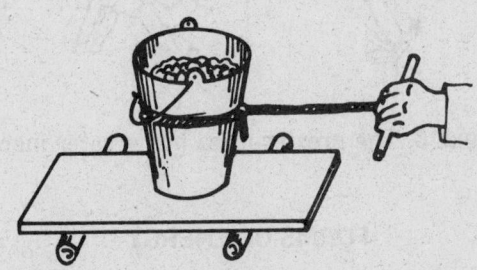

FIGURE 2.

Once in motion, the weight had a tendency to keep moving, but when at rest it strongly opposed any attempt to get it into motion.

MASS AND WEIGHT

Our experience points to the fact that the heavier a body is, the more it shows this property of inertia. Now what we call the **weight** of a body is simply the amount of the pull of the earth's gravity on it. This means that a body has weight only because it happens to be near a very large object like the earth. If a standard one-pound weight is moved farther from the earth's surface it weighs less—the earth does not pull it quite so hard. But if you think about the last experiment and others of a similar kind, you see that they would work equally well if the whole set-up were far away from the earth, so these inertia effects cannot depend directly on the *weight* of a body as such. They are found to depend only on the amount of matter in the body, and this is called its **mass**. In other words, the weight of a body depends on how near to the earth it is, while its mass would be the same anywhere in the universe, provided only that nothing is taken away from it or added to it.

For example, two bricks together have twice the mass of a single brick, but if the pair of bricks could be put on a spring scale at rest 1,600 miles above the earth's surface, their weight would be found to be only about that of a single brick at sea level.

And finally, the inertia of a body depends only on its mass, or how much material there is in it.

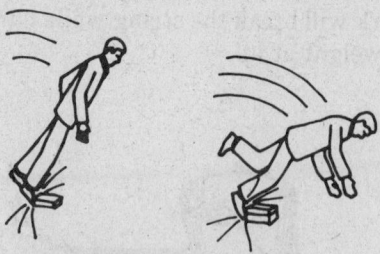

FIGURE 3. The greater mass has greater inertia

FORMS OF ENERGY

Besides matter, there are other things that we deal with in physics—things like electricity, light, sound, and heat. These are not kinds of matter, for they neither take up space nor have weight, in the usual sense. They are forms of **energy**. Energy is something that produces changes in matter. You saw that heat can change water from a liquid to a gas, for example. Light from the sun can fade the dye in cloth or form an image on a film in your camera. **Electrical energy** can turn a motor, put silver plating on a spoon, or send your voice over thousands of miles of space. **Chemical energy** heats your home and runs your car, and the action of atomic energy is known to everybody.

Probably the most familiar energy effects are the ones that are able to make bodies move or change their motion. This so-called **mechanical energy** has been called the "go" of things. A machine of any kind, whether it is a simple hand tool or a printing press or airplane, puts mechanical energy to work. Later you will learn how physicists measure energy exactly. But before we can measure anything as intangible as energy, we must find out how to measure some simpler things.

Systems of Measurement

Physics is known as an exact science, and this means that it is possible to make precise measurements of the things we talk about; we must not only know how to describe events and things but also be able to answer the question, "How much?" concerning them. From earliest times, people have found ways of specifying quantities such as the distance between towns, the interval of time between important events or the amount of goods bought and sold. To do this, they set up systems of measurement, based on convenient units of measure.

There are many types of measurement. Some are very direct and simple, others require great care and the use of highly complex instruments. But whatever it is that you wish to measure, you can do so only in terms of some chosen unit. And the unit must be the same *kind* of thing as the quantity that is to be measured.

MEASUREMENT OF LENGTH

For example, take the simplest kind of measuring operation—finding the *length* of an object. Before you can express the result, you must have a length **unit**, such as the inch, yard or mile. The size of the unit is arbitrary. You may choose it any way you like, but once you select it, you must stick to it as a standard. Historians are not absolutely certain how the Standard Yard was originally selected, but that is not important. In the English system of measure, which is used in civil affairs in all English-speaking countries, the Standard Yard is taken to be the distance between the end marks on a certain bronze bar kept in a vault at the Office of the Exchequer in London. It is assumed that all goods sold by length are measured by a stick or tape that has been marked off according to the Standard Yard through copies that are kept in the bureaus of standards of the various countries.

In the last paragraph, inches, yards and miles were mentioned. Why have more than one length unit? Simply for convenience in measuring things of very *different* lengths. To express the length of a pencil, the inch would be the most suitable unit; to give the distance between two cities, you would use the mile. The pencil *could* be measured in miles, but the number you would get would be ridiculously small. Similarly, expressing the distance between towns in inches would lead to an inconveniently large number. Always try to choose a unit that is not too different in order of magnitude from the thing you are measuring.

THE METRIC SYSTEM: THE METER

The sizes of the various length units in the English system do not seem to be related in any simple way. They are arbitrary, and it is necessary to remember that there are 12 inches in one foot, 3 feet in a yard, 5,280 feet in a mile, and so on. This makes it difficult to change a measurement from one unit to another; it would be much simpler if we had a system where all conversions went by *multiples of ten*. Then, in order to change units you would only have to move the decimal point the proper number of places. Such a scheme was set up about 150 years ago and is called the **Metric system.** It is now the accepted system of measure in all scientific work in all countries.

The fundamental length unit in the Metric system is the **standard meter.** It is the distance between the ends of a certain bar of platinum alloy kept at the International Bureau of Weights and Measures in France. Copies of this bar are carefully kept in other countries. The meter is a little longer than the yard—39.37 inches, to be precise.

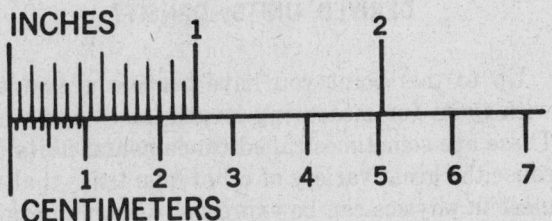

FIGURE 4.

The following table gives the most commonly used Metric units of length. Notice that the name of each is formed by putting a distinguishing pre-

fix to the word "meter." For instance, a centimeter is 0.01 meter, and a kilometer is 1,000 meters. The standard abbreviations and the relations to the English system are also given.

TABLE 1
METRIC UNITS OF LENGTH

1 kilometer (km)	= 1,000 meters
1 METER (m)	= PRIMARY UNIT
1 centimeter (cm)	= 0.01 meter
1 millimeter (mm)	= 0.001 meter

1 km = 0.621 mile; 1 m = 39.4 in.; 2.54 cm = 1 in.

EXAMPLE 1: The table shows how easy it is to change from one length unit to another in the Metric system. Suppose a rug was measured as 0.0012 km long. This is a small decimal, and it would be easier to judge the size of the result if it were written in terms of a smaller unit, say the centimeter. Since there are 100 cm in a meter and 1,000 m in a kilometer, there will be $100 \times 1,000$, or 100,000 cm in a kilometer. Then our 0.0012 km will amount to $0.0012 \times 100,000$, or (moving the decimal point five places to the right to multiply by 100,000), 120 cm. Equally well, we could write it as 1.20 m.

By comparison, see how much more arithmetical work is needed to change, say, 1.47 miles to inches: There are 12 in. to 1 ft and 5,280 ft in a mile, so we will have to multiply all three numbers together to get the result: $12 \times 5280 \times 1.47 = 93,100$ in.

Notice, incidentally, that while actual multiplication gives us 93,139.2 we rounded off to 93,100. This is because the 1.47 is given only to 3 **significant digits,** so it would be meaningless to write the final result to any more than this number. This remark applies regardless of where the decimal point happens to come in a final result.

EXPERIMENT 4: Measure the thickness of a single page of this book by finding how many sheets are needed to extend ½ inch along the edge of a ruler. In order to count the sheets, make use of the page numbering. If you start at page 1, the last page number in the stack will be the number of sheets making up a 1-inch thickness.

MEASUREMENT OF AREA AND VOLUME

In order to measure area (or surface) we need an arbitrary unit that is itself an area. It is simplest to choose this area to be a square, and we can avoid introducing anything really new by making the side of this square equal in length to one of our previous length units. Thus for area measurement we have square inches, square feet, square centimeters, square kilometers, etc. To write abbreviations for the area units we use *exponents* as a shorthand notation. Square centimeters is written cm², square inches is in², and so on, but these abbreviations are still to be read aloud as "square centimeters" and "square inches."

EXAMPLE 2: How many square centimeters are there in a rectangular strip of film 1⅛ in. wide and 40 in. long?

SOLUTION: The area of the film, in square inches, is 1⅛ × 40 = 45 in². According to Table 1, 1 in = 2.54 cm, so 1 in² = 2.54 × 2.54 = 6.45 cm². Multiplying 45 by 6.45 gives the result 290 cm². (Are you perfectly clear as to why the two numbers had to be *multiplied* together to get the result?)

Bulk or **volume** requires a cubical unit for its measurement. Thus there are cubic centimeters (cm³), cubic feet (ft³), etc. In all, volume measurement goes very much like length and area measurement. There is a special name given to a Metric unit of volume equal to 1,000 cm³. It is called a **liter** (pronounced "leeter"), and is just larger than a U.S. liquid quart.

MEASURING MASS AND WEIGHT

The fundamental Metric standard of mass is the **kilogram,** a cylinder of platinum alloy kept at the International Bureau of Weights and Measures. The kilogram was set up to be the mass of 1,000 cm³ of water, thus referring the standard of mass to the standard of length through the choice of a standard substance, water. As in the case of length measure, additional units are specified, differing from each other by powers of ten. Table 2 gives the commoner Metric mass units, their abbreviations, and how they are related to the English units:

TABLE 2
METRIC UNITS OF MASS

1 metric ton	= 1,000 kilograms
1 KILOGRAM (kg)	= PRIMARY UNIT

1 gram (gm)	= 0.001 kg
1 milligram (mg)	= 0.001 gm

1 kg = 2.2 lb   454 gm = 1 lb   1 oz = 28.4 gm

When we weigh an object, we balance it against copies of the standard mass units. What we are doing, fundamentally, is comparing the mass of the object with that of the standard, using the earth's attraction (weight) to do so. If we use a spring scale instead of a balance scale, both weighings must be made at the same place. Since weighing is a convenient method of comparing masses, both the weight of an object and its mass may be represented by the same number and in the same units.

TIME

All events that happen in Nature involve the idea of time, so we must also have a way of measuring this quantity. Fortunately, both the English and Metric systems use the same fundamental time unit, the **second.** Basically, time is measured by the turning of the earth, and clocks are merely devices made to keep step with this motion. The time of a complete turn, one **day,** has been divided into 24 hours, each containing 60 minutes and each minute containing 60 seconds. That is, there are 24 × 60 × 60 = 86,400 seconds in one day. Additional units differing from the second by powers of ten are not in general use.

More recently, the second has been rigorously defined in terms of the motion of the earth in its orbit around the sun. For practical purposes, the difference can be ignored.

DERIVED UNITS; DENSITY

Up to this point you have become acquainted with units for measuring length, mass and time. These are sometimes called **fundamental units** because the great variety of other quantities that we meet in physics can be expressed as combinations of them. We already had two kinds of **derived units**—area and volume, which are both based on simple combinations of the length unit.

As a further example, let us have a look at a useful quantity called **density.** Everybody realizes that a given volume of one material has, in general, a different weight than the same volume of some other material. For instance, we ordinarily say that iron is "heavier" than wood. More exactly, we should say that *any given volume* of iron is heavier than *the same volume* of wood. To make the comparison exact, we can weigh a certain volume of iron, say 1 cubic foot. When this is done, the weight is found to be about 490 lb. By comparison, the weight of a cubic foot of pine wood is around 30 lb. We say that the density of iron is 490 pounds per cubic foot (written lb/ft³), while that of the wood is 30 lb/ft³. The density of water in these units turns out to be 62.4. In the Metric system, because one kilogram was chosen to be the mass of 1,000 cm³ of water, the density of water is 1,000 gm per 1,000 cm³, or simply 1 gm/cm³. This is equivalent to 1,000 kg/m³.

 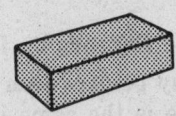

FIGURE 5. The log weighs twice as much as the brick, although brick is over three times as dense as wood

In general, then, the **density** of a substance is the **weight** (or, numerically, **mass**) of any portion of it **divided by** the **volume**. Stated as a formula,

$$D = \frac{M}{V},$$

where D stands for density, M for mass and V for volume. Of course this equation may be solved for either M or V as well:

$$M = DV, \qquad \text{or} \qquad V = \frac{M}{D}.$$

TABLE 3

DENSITIES OF SEVERAL MATERIALS

Substance	*D,* lb/ft³	*D,* gm/cm³
Aluminum	170	2.7
Iron	490	7.9
Lead	700	11.3
Gold	1200	19.3
Limestone	200	3.2
Ice	57	0.92
Wood, pine	30	0.5
Gasoline	44	0.70

Water	62.4	1.00
Sea Water	64	1.03
Mercury	850	13.6
Air*	0.08	0.0013
Hydrogen*	0.0055	0.00009

EXAMPLE 3 : What is the weight (mass) of a block of ice measuring $1 \times 1\frac{1}{2} \times 3$ ft?

SOLUTION: From these dimensions, the volume of the block is 4.5 ft³. The table gives the density of ice as 57 lb/ft³. Then, using $M = DV$ we get $M = 57 \times 4.5 = 256$ lb.

EXPERIMENT 5: Find the density of a stone from its weight and volume. First weigh the stone on a household scale or postal scale and record the weight in pounds. Then put some water in a straight-sided jar or glass, mark the level on the side, carefully put the stone into the water, and mark the new water level (Fig. 6). The volume of the stone will be the same as the volume of the displaced water. You can compute this, because the volume is that of a cylinder whose base is the cross-section of the jar, and whose height is the rise in water level. Measure the rise and also the inside diameter of the jar in inches. The volume, in *cubic feet*, is given by

$$\frac{\pi (\text{diameter})^2 (\text{height of rise})}{4 \times 12^3}$$

where $\pi = 3.14$. Finally, divide the weight of the stone, in pounds, by the last result to get the density in pounds per cubic foot.

FIGURE 6.

---

*Measured at standard temperature and pressure

Liquids

Many familiar devices and machines make use of physical principles applying to liquids.

LIQUID PRESSURE

A liquid, such as water, pushes on the sides as well as on the bottom of the container in which it rests. A wooden barrel or water tank has to be reinforced with hoops to resist the sidewise force, and the sides of a cardboard carton of milk bulge out. But it is also true that a liquid at rest presses *upward* on anything placed in it:

EXPERIMENT 6: Push the closed end of a tumbler or empty tin can beneath the surface of water in a bowl and you will actually feel the upward thrust of the water on the bottom.

Here we talk for the first time about **force**. What is a force? It is quite correct to say that a force is a push or a pull, but we want some way of measuring the *amount* of push or pull. Suppose a ten pound weight is resting on a table. Then it is reasonable to say that this object is *exerting a downward force of 10 lb* on the table top. This means that we can measure forces, at least downward ones, in *weight units*,—in pounds or grams, in kilograms or even in tons. And by means of simple arrangements such as strings and pulleys, or even liquids themselves, we can use weights to exert measured amounts of force in any direction we wish. Such devices will be described later.

The next question is, "What is pressure?" In everyday affairs, the terms "pressure" and "force" are used loosely to mean the same thing; here we must be a little more careful. **Pressure** is measured by the **force** divided by the **area** of the surface on which it acts. For example, if the ten pound weight mentioned above has a bottom area of 5 in² (square inches) and makes even contact with the table top all over this face, then the pressure between it and the table amounts to 10 lb/5 in² = 2 lb/in² (pounds per square inch). If the weight were standing on another one of its faces, say one that had an area of only 2.5 in², the pressure would then be 10 lb/2.5 in², or 4 lb/in²—twice as much as before, because the same force is spread over only half the area (see Fig. 7). In general, we can say

$$p = \frac{F}{A},$$

where p is the pressure, F the force and A the area. Notice that pressure is an example of a derived quantity. It is a combination of the weight unit and the length (area) unit. Pressure can also be measured in lb/ft², kg/cm², etc.

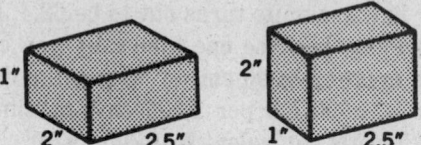

FIGURE 7. Pressure depends on area of contact

Pressure Depends on Depth

At any point within a liquid that is at rest, the pressure is the same in all directions—up, down or sidewise. This is obvious, because if you think of any interior drop of liquid, it is at rest and so must be pushed equally from all sides by the surrounding liquid.

Furthermore, the amount of pressure at any point in a liquid standing in an open vessel increases with the depth of that place beneath the top surface. Prove this by an experiment:

EXPERIMENT 6a: Punch several clean nail holes at various heights along the side of a tall can or milk carton, put the container in a sink and fill it with water. A curved stream comes from each opening, but those from the lower holes extend straighter, showing that the water pressure is greater lower down.

Think of a tall, tubular jar whose cross-section area is just 1 in². If you pour a given amount of water into it, say 1 lb, the force on the bottom will be just 1 lb. Since the bottom area is 1 in², the pressure will amount to 1 lb/in². Now pour another pound of water in. The liquid is twice as deep as before. The bottom now supports 2 lb of liquid, so the pressure on it is 2 lb/in². Reasoning this way, we see that the **pressure** at any point in a free-standing liquid **is directly proportional to the depth** below the surface. This means that if you go twice as far beneath the surface, the pressure becomes exactly twice as great as before; if you go three times as deep it becomes three times as great, and so on.

The depth referred to is the depth measured *straight down* from the level of the free surface of the liquid to the level of the place in question. Even if the vessel or pipe slants, this is the way the depth is to be taken. In the vessel shown in Fig. 8, the free surfaces in the two tubes stand at the same level, because pressure depends only on vertical depth and not on the size or shape of the container. Since no water flows one way or the other at the place where the tubes join, the pressure there must be the same from both sides, and so must the depth. For the same reason, the water stands at the same level in a teapot and in its spout (Fig. 1), even though there is much greater *weight* of water in the pot than in the spout.

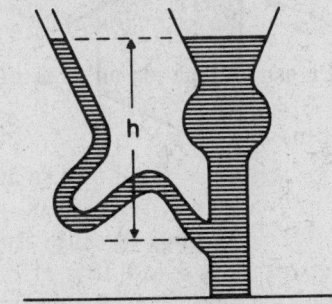

FIGURE 8.

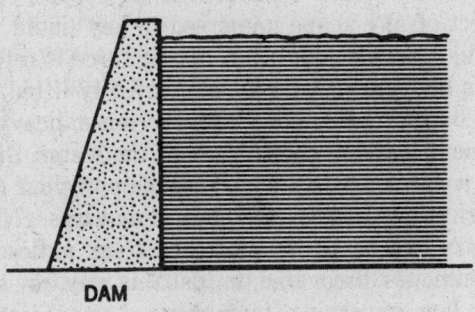

DAM

FIGURE 9.

If there is a small hole in a dike at a point 10 ft below the water surface, does it take a greater force to keep the hole closed if the body of water is the Atlantic Ocean than it does if it were a small pond? Why?

COMPUTING THE PRESSURE

There is a simple way to get a formula for figuring the amount of pressure at any point in a liquid. You already know that the pressure is proportional to the depth. It must also be proportional to the density of the liquid. This is because pressure is caused by the weight of the liquid, and doubling the density would double the weight of any column of liquid. So we get the result that

$$p = hD,$$

where p is the pressure at any point in the liquid, h is the depth of that place below the surface, and D is the density of the liquid.

EXAMPLE 4: What is the pressure on the side of a dam at a point 20 ft vertically below the water surface?

SOLUTION: In the formula $p = hD$ we put $h = 20$ ft and (from the table on p. 21), $D = 62.4$ lb/ft^3, getting $p = 20 \times 62.4 = 1{,}248$ lb/ft^2. Notice that since h was given in feet, we had to use the density in corresponding units, that is, in pounds per cubic *foot*. The result is then in pounds per square foot. Now that we have the answer, we are at liberty to change it to any other units we like. Very often, pressure in the English system is given in pounds per square *inch*. Since there are 144 square inches in a square foot, we can change our result to these units by dividing by 144. Then we have $p = 1{,}248/144 = 8.67$ lb/in^2.

EXAMPLE 5: What is the *total force* on the bottom of a swimming pool 80 ft long and 25 ft wide, filled to a depth of 5 ft? What is the force on one of the sides?

SOLUTION: The total force is the pressure (force per unit area) multiplied by the area on which it acts. Then $F = hDA$, or $F = 5 \times 62.4 \times 80 \times 25 = 624{,}000$ lb, or 312 tons. The pressure on a side will vary from zero at the surface to its greatest value at the bottom. To get the total force on a side, we must then use the *average* pressure, or the pressure *half way down*. In this case, we must take $h = 2.5$ ft. Then $F = 2.5 \times 62.4 \times 80 \times 5 = 62{,}400$ lb $= 31.2$ tons.

Applications of Fluid Pressure

The water supply for a town is often pumped from a lake or reservoir to a *standpipe* (Fig. 10), from where it flows down to the water in the mains and is distributed to the houses. The height of the water in the standpipe produces the pressure that moves the water along the piping and delivers it to the places where it is used. If a building is taller than the standpipe level, there must be an auxiliary pump to supply water to the upper floors.

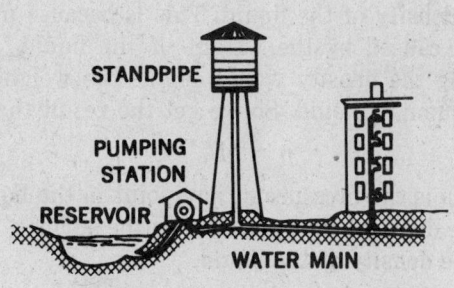

FIGURE 10

Some of the most important applications of liquid pressure use the pressure of confined liquids, rather than merely the weight of a liquid with a free surface. Any extra pressure applied to a confined liquid will be transmitted to all parts of the container. This is the principle of the **hydraulic press** (Fig. 11). Pressure is applied mechanically to a small piston, and this same amount of pressure then acts on every part of the inside surface of the system, including the large piston. But if the area of the larger piston is, say, 100 times that of the smaller one, the total force on the large one will be 100 times whatever force is applied to the small piston. Such presses are used in making bricks, glassware or metal parts and in stamping out automobile bodies. Large machines of this kind may be capable of exerting forces of 10,000 tons or more. The **car lift** used in a greasing station and the barber chair are other examples of the hydraulic press. In the car lift the pressure source is a tank of compressed air, while in the barber chair it is a small pump operated by a foot pedal.

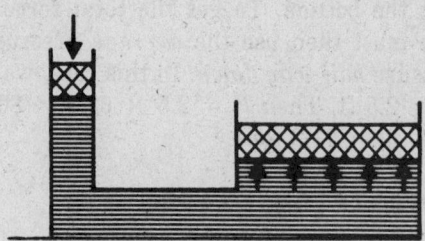

FIGURE 11. Hydraulic press

BUOYANCY AND FLOTATION

We saw that, at any place, a liquid exerts pressure equally in all directions, even pushing upward on the bottom of an object immersed in it. Think

of a brick-like body hung in water, its sides being in a vertical position (Fig. 12). First of all, the pairs of pressure forces on the opposite sides cancel out. Also, since pressure increases with depth, the upward force on the bottom of the brick will be greater than the downward force on the

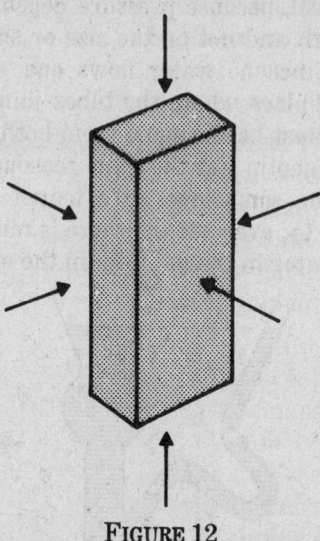

FIGURE 12

top. This means that there is a net *lifting* force— the brick is *lighter* when in water than it would be out in the air. This is true, of course, for an object of any shape immersed in any liquid.

The existence of such a lifting force is referred to as **buoyancy.** A large rock is easily lifted from the bottom of a pond, but becomes heavy the moment it clears the surface of the water. Sitting in a well-filled bathtub, you can support your whole weight by means of your fingertips. Nearly twenty-two centuries ago the Greek philosopher Archimedes discovered, in just this way, the scientific law governing buoyancy: **Any object immersed in a liquid appears to lose an amount of weight equal to that of the liquid it displaces,** or pushes aside. For instance, a stone having a volume of one-half cubic foot will displace 0.5 ft^3 of water, which weighs ½ × 62.4, or 31.2 lb. Under water, then, this stone will weigh 31.2 lb less than when out of water. If a body is able to *float* in water, it means that the buoyant force is equal to the *whole* weight of the body. In this instance, the object seems to have lost its entire weight.

EXPERIMENT 7: Weigh an empty, corked bottle. Also weigh a pie tin. Put a pot in the pie tin and fill the pot brim full of water. Now lower the bottle carefully into the water, letting it float there. Remove the bottle, then the pot, and weigh the pie tin along with the water that overflowed into it. You will find the weight of water equal to the weight of the bottle, proving Archimedes' law for floating bodies.

It turns out that a body will float if its density is less than that of the liquid, otherwise it will sink. By looking at Table 3, you will then understand why wood, ice and gasoline can float on water, while iron, stone and mercury sink.

EXPERIMENT 8: A fresh egg does not float in water, because its overall density is greater than that of water. Dissolve 2 tablespoonfuls of salt in a glassful of water and the egg will now float because dissolving the salt increased the density of the liquid, making it greater than that of the egg.

Long ago, the suggestion to build ships of iron was ridiculed because everybody knew that "iron is heavier than water." Actually, the overall density of a steel ship—its total weight divided by its total volume—is less than that of water, because the interior is hollow and largely empty. The total weight of a ship is called its **displacement**, because we have seen that its weight must be just equal to that of the water displaced, or pushed aside by it.

EXAMPLE 6: A ship has a volume of 230,000 ft³ below the water line. What is its displacement?

SOLUTION: It will displace $230{,}000 \times 64 = 14{,}720{,}000$ lb, or 7,360 tons of salt water.

EXAMPLE 7: A rectangular block of wood measures $20 \times 20 \times 5$ cm. When floated flatwise, it is found that 3 cm of the short side is under water. What is the density of the wood?

SOLUTION: The block will sink until it just displaces its own weight of the liquid. The weight of water displaced will be $20 \times 20 \times 3$, or 1,200 gm, since water has a density of 1 gm/cm³. Then the density of wood will be this weight divided by the volume of the whole block, or $1{,}200/20 \times 20 \times 5$, which comes out equal to 0.6 gm/cm³. We sometimes use the term **specific gravity** to indicate the density of a material relative to water. Since the density of water is 1 gm/cm³, this is numerically the same as the specific gravity; but in the English system, the density must be divided by 62.4 to get the specific gravity.

Applications of Flotation

When the lungs are filled with air, the human body has a slightly smaller overall density than water, and so can float. But, as every swimmer knows, the body must be almost completely immersed in order to displace a large enough weight of water.

A submarine can be made to descend or rise by pumping water into or out of its ballast tanks.

EXPERIMENT 9: Get a tall jar with a flexible metal screw top and fill it with water. Fill a small glass vial about two-thirds with water, close the end with the thumb, and invert into the jar of water. Adjust the amount of water in the vial very carefully, drop by drop, until it just floats. At this stage the slightest downward push should send it to the bottom momentarily. Now fill the jar to the brim and screw the cap on tightly. When you push down on the cover with your thumb, the vial will sink to the bottom: release the pressure and it comes to the top. The explanation of the action of this miniature submarine is that pressure applied to the lid is transmitted to the water, forcing slightly more water into the vial. Its overall density is then just greater than that of water, and it sinks. Releasing the pressure allows the air in the top of the vial to push the extra water out again and the vial rises.

According to an old sailors' superstition, a sinking ship will not go all the way to the bottom but will remain suspended somewhere in the depths. This is false, because when enough water has entered the hull to make the overall density of the ship greater than that of water, it keeps sinking until it hits the bottom. If it is denser than water when at the surface, it must continue to be so even at great depths, since water is practically impossible to compress. Even at the deepest spot in the ocean, where the water pressure is almost 8 tons per square inch, water is compressed by only about 3 percent of its bulk.

The depth to which a floating body immerses itself in a liquid can be used as a measure of the density of the liquid. A tall stick or tube, with one end weighted so that it floats upright, can have a scale marked on its side to read the density directly. This is a **hydrometer**, familiarly used to measure the density of the solution in car batteries (the density is a measure of the condition of charge of the battery).

The Air and Other Gases

Although we are not generally aware of it, air has mass. This can be checked directly by weighing a closed bottle of air, then pumping it out and weighing again. For a 1-liter bottle, the difference amounts to more than a gram.* The fact that air has mass becomes quite evident when it is in rapid motion, as you will find out later in this chapter.

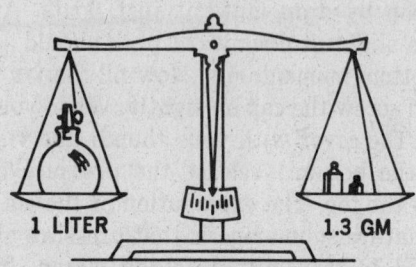

FIGURE 13. Weighing air

AIR PRESSURE

Since the air weighs something, it exerts pressure on anything immersed in it, including your own body. The reason you do not feel this pressure is that it is counterbalanced by an equal pressure from the inside—there is air in the body cavities and in the tissues and fluids. At the earth's surface, air pressure amounts to about 14.7 lb/in² (1,034 gm/cm²). This is over a ton per square foot.

EXPERIMENT 10: The existence of air pressure can be shown by removing the air from one side of an exposed surface. Get a tin can that has a tight-fitting cover or an opening provided with a screw cap. Put a little water in the can, stand it in a pan of water and boil it vigorously, with the cover removed, in order to drive out the air by means of the escaping steam. Weight the can down if it tends to upset. While still boiling, close the cap tightly, quickly transfer the can to a sink and run cold water over it to condense the steam inside. Outside air pressure will crush the vessel in a spectacular way.

The condensing (turning to liquid) of some of the steam in the last experiment left a partial **vacuum** inside the can. A vacuum is simply a place not occupied by matter, or an empty space. For a long time, people believed that a vacuum had the mysterious power of "sucking" things into it. But how does the vacuum you create when you sip a soda succeed in getting a grip on the liquid in order to pull it up into your mouth?

THE BAROMETER

In the seventeenth century, the Duke of Tuscany decided to have a deep well dug. To his surprise, no pump was able to raise the water more than about 34 feet above the level in the well. The great scientist Galileo became interested in the question and suggested to his friend and pupil, Torricelli, that he make experiments to test "the power of a vacuum." Torricelli reasoned that if a 34-foot height of water was needed to satisfy a vacuum a much shorter column of mercury would be sufficient. Mercury is 13.6 times as dense as water, so a height of only 34/13.6, or 2½ feet, should be enough. He tried an experiment: A glass tube about a yard long, sealed at one end, was completely filled with mercury. The other end was held closed with the thumb. Then the tube was turned over and the open end set in a large dish of mercury. When the thumb was removed, the mercury dropped away from the sealed end until its upper surface came to rest about 30 inches above the liquid in the dish (Fig. 14). The mer-

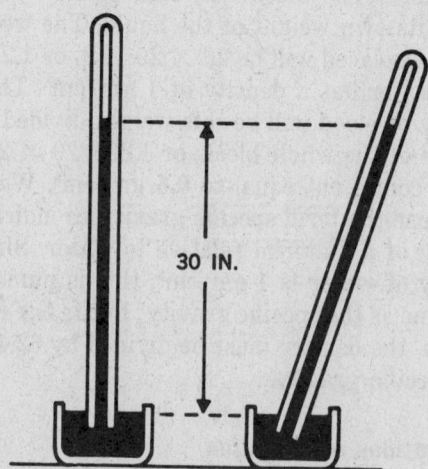

30 IN.

FIGURE 14. Mercury tube barometer

---

* Can you tell why, from the Table 3?

cury, in descending from the top of the tube, left a vacuum behind it, and it seemed that this vacuum was able to hold up a 30-inch column of mercury. Torricelli concluded that the liquid is supported not by any mysterious sucking action of the vacuum, but by the outside air *pressing* on the mercury in the open dish.

To complete the argument, other people carried such instruments up the side of a mountain, where the air pressure is less. Surely enough, it was observed that the mercury in the tube now stood lower, but regained its former height when brought back to the valley. Here, then, is an instrument that can be used to measure changes in air pressure. It is called a **barometer.** A more compact and convenient form of this instrument is the **aneroid** barometer (Fig. 15). It consists of a sealed metal can from which most of the air has been pumped. Changes in outside air pressure make the flexible cover bend in and out very slightly, and the motion is magnified by a lever system, moving a pointer over a scale from which the air pressure can be read off directly.

One important use of the barometer is to determine altitude. Once we know how the pressure of the air depends on altitude, we can use the barometer readings to give our height. An aneroid barometer with the scale marked directly in height units forms the **altimeter** of an airplane.

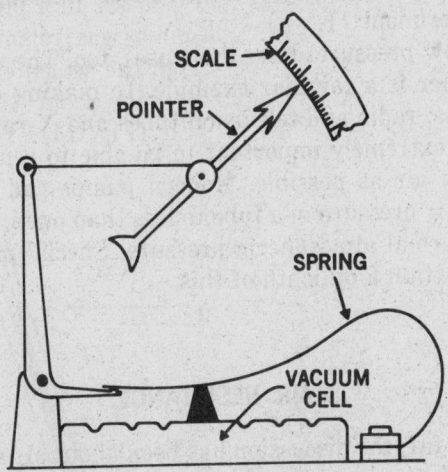

FIGURE 15. Aneroid barometer

The other main use of the barometer is in forecasting weather conditions. Contrary to general belief, moist air is *less* dense than dry air, water vapor itself being only around ⅝ as dense as dry air. Since it is less dense, moist air exerts less pressure, and so in moist weather the barometer

falls. This gives us a way of predicting what kind of weather we will have in the immediate future. A steady, high barometer indicates fair weather; a rising barometer means fair or clearing weather conditions; and a rapidly falling barometer means a storm is approaching. By combining information obtained at stations all over the country, the Weather Bureau is able to prepare and distribute maps from which forecasts can be made at any locality.

THE ATMOSPHERE

The **atmosphere** is the name we give to the whole body of air surrounding the earth. If it were not for the earth's gravity, this layer of gas would escape out into the vacuum of interplanetary space. As mentioned above, it is the weight of the air that causes it to exert pressure. But there is one important difference between the pressure due to the weight of a liquid, as discussed in the previous chapter, and the pressure of the air: Liquids are virtually incompressible, and this leads to the simple proportion between pressure and depth. But gases, such as air, are fairly easy to compress. The weight of the upper layers compresses the lower ones, with the result that the density and pressure both fall off in a more complicated way as we go upward from the surface of the earth. In going up one mile from sea level, the height of mercury in the barometer falls about 5½ inches, but in going up an additional mile from a 10 mile height, it falls only a little over ½ inch. The *rate* of falling off is a constantly decreasing one (see Fig. 16).

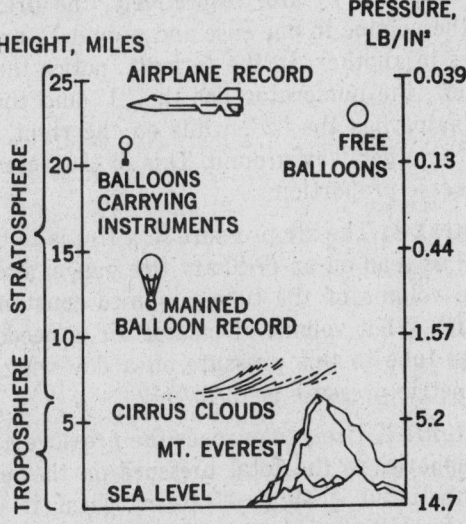

FIGURE 16. The lower atmosphere

The part of the atmosphere above about 6.5 miles is called the **stratosphere**. It is a relatively cold and calm region in which no clouds form. It has been explored to some extent by free-sailing balloons carrying instruments and, more recently, by high-altitude rockets and radar. The atmosphere continues to thin out with increasing height, and apparently has no sharp boundary. Air can still be detected at heights of several hundred miles.

GAS VOLUME: BOYLE'S LAW

When air is pumped into an automobile tire, a large volume of outside air is forced into the relatively small space inside the tube. All gases, including air, are compressible; and in order to force a gas into a small space, extra pressure must be applied to it. The greater the applied pressure, the smaller the space occupied by the gas. In the seventeenth century, Robert Boyle, an Irish scientist, discovered by experiment the exact relationship that holds: **If the temperature of the gas is kept constant,** then **the volume will be inversely proportional to the pressure.** This means that if the pressure is doubled, the volume becomes half as much; if the pressure is tripled, the volume becomes one-third of what it was, etc. In the form of an equation,

$$\frac{V_1}{V_2} = \frac{p_2}{p_1}$$

where p_1 and V_1 are, respectively, the pressure and the volume in one case and p_2 and V_2 are the values in another. In the formula, notice that on the left, the numerator has the "1" and the denominator has the "2", while on the right, it is just the other way around. This is characteristic of *inverse* proportion.

EXAMPLE 8: The air pressure in a tire is to be 30 lb/in² as read on an ordinary tire gauge, and the inside volume of the tube, assumed constant, is 0.95 ft³. What volume of outside air is needed to fill the tube to this pressure on a day when the barometric pressure is 15 lb/in²?

SOLUTION: A tire gauge reads the pressure *above* atmospheric, so the total pressure on the air in the tube is 30 + 15, or 45 lb/in². Then, if V_1 is the volume that this amount of air occupies outside, we can make the proportion

$$\frac{V_1}{0.95} = \frac{45}{15};$$

cross multiplying:

$$V_1 = \frac{0.95 \times 45}{15} = 2.85 \text{ ft}^3.$$

Buoyancy in Gases

Archimedes' law of buoyancy also holds for gases. In making very accurate weighings, the difference in the weight of air displaced by the object and by the metal weights must be taken into account. But air has such low density compared with solids, this effect can usually be neglected. A large, hollow body, such as a balloon, can displace more than its own weight of air, and so can float in air. Since the air is less dense higher up, a balloon will rise only to the level where the weight of the displaced air becomes equal to its own weight. Balloons are usually filled with hydrogen or helium. These gases are the lightest known, and provide a large lifting force.

Uses of Air Pressure

There are many uses for compressed air: It is utilized in inflating tires, in operating air brakes and tools such as the riveting hammer, and in keeping water out of underwater workings (see Experiment 1).

Low pressures have their uses, too. The vacuum cleaner is a familiar example. In making electric lamps, radio and television tubes and X-ray tubes it is extremely important to be able to remove as much air as possible. Modern pumps can reduce the air pressure in a tube to less than one-billionth of normal atmospheric pressure. Special methods can attain a billionth of this.

AIR RESISTANCE

So far, the discussion has been about air at rest. When air moves, even with moderate speed, important new forces come into play. These forces are responsible for the operation of sailboats, atomizers, parachutes, airplanes, etc. The most evident effect is the resistance that the air offers to the movement of objects through it. Hold your hand out the window of a moving car and you feel the resistance force directly. The car itself experiences such a force. At usual driving speeds, more than half the power delivered by the engine may be used up in working against air resistance.

The actual resistance force increases with the *cross-section area* of the moving body and especially with its *speed* of motion. In addition, the *shape* of the object is of great importance. What we call **streamlining** a body means giving it a suitable shape so that it will offer a minimum of opposition to the flow of air past it. This means eliminating all sharp corners and projections, approaching the general "tear-drop" shape shown in Fig. 17a. Contrary to what you might expect, the front of the body is broader than the rear. But if the body is to be a high-speed jet plane or rocket traveling faster than sound, a sharp-nosed shape gives best performance (Fig. 17b).

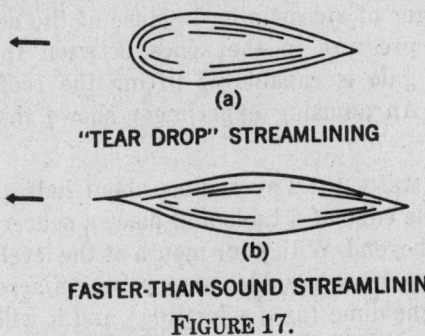

(a)

"TEAR DROP" STREAMLINING

(b)

FASTER-THAN-SOUND STREAMLINING

FIGURE 17.

Fig. 18 shows the comparative resistance, of (a) a streamlined rod, (b) a round rod and (c) a flat plate of the same cross-section and all moving at a given speed. The air flow around each is also pictured. Behind the round and flat objects, the stream lines break up into whirls, whose effect is to retard the movement of the body. The tapered tail of (a) fills in this region, allowing the flow to join smoothly at the rear.

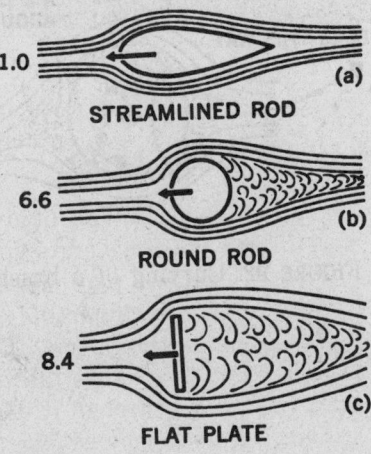

1.0

STREAMLINED ROD

(a)

6.6

ROUND ROD

(b)

8.4

FLAT PLATE

(c)

FIGURE 18. Relative resistance

Bodies falling through the air are retarded by air resistance. If not for this effect, all objects, regardless of difference in weight, would fall at the same rate.

EXPERIMENT 11: Drop a coin and a sheet of paper from shoulder height at the same instant. The coin quickly reaches the floor, while the paper flutters down slowly. To show that this result is not due to their difference in weight but only to the difference in air resistance, repeat the trial after first wadding the paper up into a small ball. This time both will be seen to hit at the same instant.

THE AIRPLANE; BERNOULLI'S LAW

Of the many applications of the physics of the air, the one that has had the greatest impact on civilization is, of course, the airplane. At the very beginning we may well ask, "What keeps an airplane up?" The answer is not at all obvious. We know that a plane must be moved rapidly through the air in order to sustain itself, and that it must have a large, slightly inclined surface—a wing—to furnish the supporting force. Seen from the moving airplane, the surrounding air streams backward, over and around it. The tilted wing surface deflects some air downward, and as a result the plane is literally "knocked" upward. But this is responsible for only a small effect. Actually, it is the flow of air around the curved *upper* surface of the wing that accounts for most of the lift. To see how this works, try an experiment:

EXPERIMENT 12: Hold one edge of a piece of letter paper against your chin, just below your lower lip, with the paper hanging over and down (Fig. 19). If you now blow above the paper, it will rise to a horizontal position as if pulled upward into the air stream.

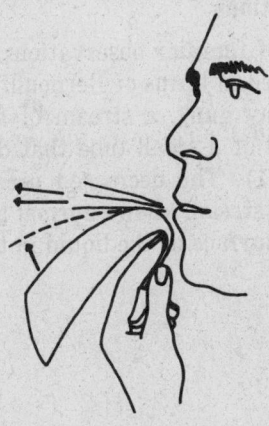

FIGURE 19.

This action is an instance of a general law discovered by the eighteenth century Swiss scientist Daniel Bernoulli: A moving stream of gas or liquid exerts less sidewise pressure than if it were at rest. The result is that things seem to be drawn into such a stream; they are really *pushed* in by the greater pressure from outside.

Bernoulli's principle gives us a way of understanding the action of air on a wing. In a properly designed wing, the airstream separates at the front of the wing and rejoins smoothly at the rear (Fig. 20). Since the air that flows over the upper surface has to travel a greater distance its average speed must be greater than that below, and so the decrease in pressure is greater on the top side, resulting in a lifting force on the entire wing. The forces on the upper side of a wing may account for over four-fifths of the whole lift.

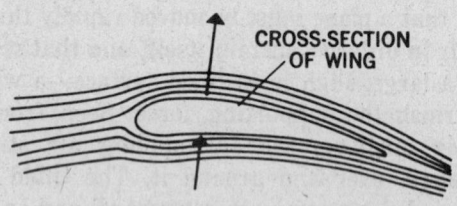

FIGURE 20. Airplane wing

The control surfaces of the airplane, as well as the propeller that moves it through the air, operate on this same principle. In the **helicopter** the airflow over the wing surfaces is produced by whirling the rotating wings, rather than by rapid motion of the whole plane through the air. As a result, a helicopter can hover over one spot on the ground, or even move in the backward direction.

Other Applications

A number of familiar observations and devices can be described in terms of Bernoulli's law. In an **atomizer** (spray gun), a stream of air is blown across the end of a small tube that dips into the liquid (Fig. 21). The decreased pressure at the side of the air stream allows normal air pressure, acting on the surface of the liquid in the bottle, to

push the liquid up the tube. Here the moving air breaks it up into small drops and drives it forward. The **carburetor** of an auto works in the same way.

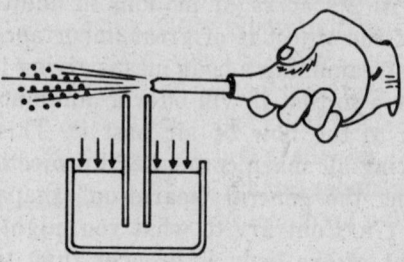

FIGURE 21. Atomizer (spray gun)

Two cars, passing each other at high speed, are in danger of sideswiping because of the decrease in air pressure in the space between them. A strong gale is capable of lifting the roof off a house. An amusing experiment shows the same effect:

EXPERIMENT 13: Lay a dime about half an inch from the edge of a table and place a saucer a few inches beyond. With your mouth at the level of the table top, blow a sudden strong breath across the top of the dime (as if whistling) and it will jump into the dish.

The curving of a baseball or of a "sliced" golf ball is explained by Bernoulli's principle. Some air is dragged around by the spin of the ball (Fig. 22). At "A" this air is moving *with* the stream of air caused by the ball's moving along, while at "B" the two *oppose* each other. The greater relative air speed at "A" makes the ball veer to that side.

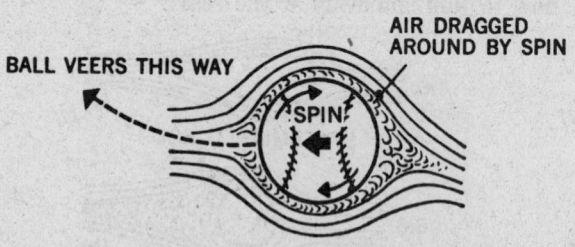

FIGURE 22. Curving of a baseball

Forces

We have described a force as a push or a pull—something that would produce the same effect as the direct action of your muscles. It was also pointed out that forces can be measured in ordinary weight units, such as grams, pounds, etc. We shall now have a closer look at forces and find out how, under certain conditions, they are capable of holding an object in balance.

REPRESENTATION OF FORCES; VECTORS

In most of the practical situations we deal with, not one but a number of forces act on the body in question. There is a simple and convenient way of representing the forces and of finding their net effect. In the first place, in order to describe a force completely, we must specify not only its *amount* (say, in pounds) but its *direction* in space; obviously it makes a difference whether a force acts to the left or to the right, or whether it acts upward or downward.

A force acting at a given point is pictured by a line drawn outward from that point in the given direction, and the *length* of the line is made to represent the *strength* of the force.

Besides forces, there are other physical quantities, to be discussed later, that have both magnitude and direction. Such a quantity is called a **vector**. Any vector may be represented by a directed line segment.

In Fig. 23 *A* stands for a force of 5 lb acting toward the northeast. The scale chosen for this drawing is "¼ in = 1 lb," and so the line, drawn in the proper direction, is made 5 quarter-inches

long. An arrow is placed at the end of the line to give its sense of direction. In the same way, *B* is an eastward force of 9 lb acting at the same point. Any convenient scale may be used in these drawings, as long as we stick to the same scale throughout the problem.

RESULTANT OF A SET OF FORCES

It is found by experience that when a number of forces act on a body they can always be replaced by a single force having a definite amount and direction. This single force, which replaces the effect of all the others, is called their **resultant**. There is a simple way of finding it by means of a drawing: Draw all the forces, end to end, until they have all been put down (the order in which you pick them off from the original drawing does not matter). Then, if you draw a line out from the starting point to the end of the last force, this line will correctly represent the resultant as to direction and amount.

EXAMPLE 9: Three forces act at a point. One is 4 lb straight down, another is 11 lb to the right and the third is 9 lb upward and to the left at an angle of 45 degrees. Find their resultant.

SOLUTION: Fig. 24 shows these forces, drawn to

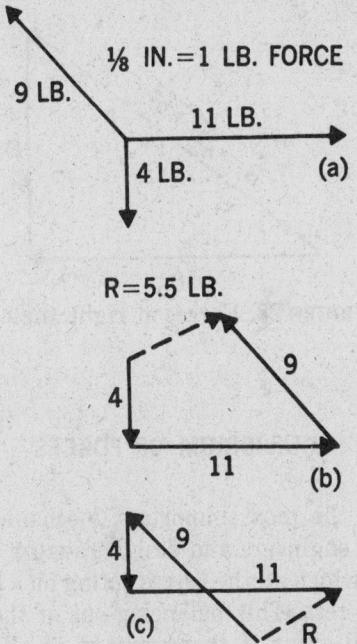

FIGURE 24. Combining vectors

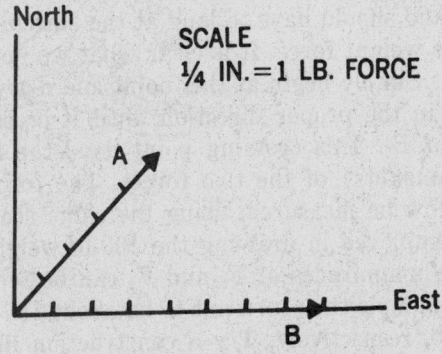

FIGURE 23. Representing force vectors

scale. Now, keeping the same length and direction for each force, lay them off end to end, as in (b). Then the resultant is gotten by drawing a line from the starting point out to the end of the last force. This line, when measured, turns out to be 11/16 in. long. Therefore the resultant amounts to 11/16 divided by 1/8, or 5.5 lb, and has the direction shown. In (c) the forces have been laid off in a different order, but the resultant has the same size and direction as before.

Notice that the size (length) of the resultant is, in general, *not* equal to the sum of the magnitudes of the separate vectors. The actual value will depend on their relative positions.

If all the acting forces are in a single line (such as east-west), the magnitude of the resultant is simply the sum of all those acting to one side less the sum of all those acting toward the other. As an example, suppose a man can pull with a force of 100 lb, while a boy can pull only 70 lb. If they both pull toward the east, the combined effect is 170 lb force; if the man pulls westward and the boy eastward, the resultant is a 30 lb force toward the west (the direction of the larger force).

Another case where the resultant can easily be calculated rather than measured from a scale drawing is that of two forces at right angles to each other (Fig. 25). The resultant is the hypotenuse of a right triangle and its amount may be computed by the right triangle rule.

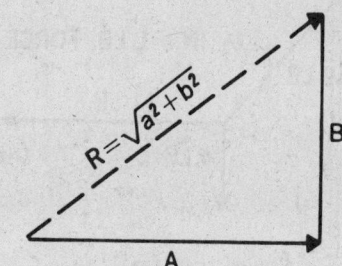

FIGURE 25. Forces at right angles

EQUILIBRIUM OF FORCES

One of the most important mechanical situations that engineers and designers must deal with is that in which all the forces acting on a body just hold it at rest. This balancing-out of the applied forces will occur if the **resultant** of all of them is **zero**. When this happens, the body is said to be in **equilibrium.** Conversely, if a body is observed to remain at rest, we know that the resultant of all the acting forces must be zero. This fact can be used to find the values of some of the forces. An example will show how:

EXAMPLE 10: A wire-walker at the circus weighs 160 lb. When at the position shown in Fig. 26, what is the stretching force in each part of the wire?

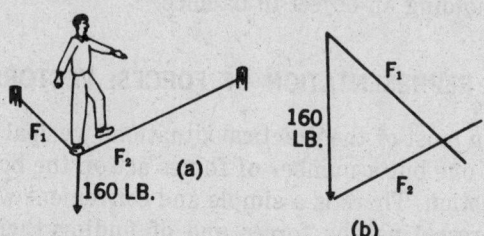

FIGURE 26. Tensions in a wire

SOLUTION: First we note that the point B is the place where the forces in question meet. One of them is the man's weight. We sketch it in the downward direction from B as shown and label it "160 lb." Acting from B along the left-hand portion of the wire is some force—call it F_1—whose value is still unknown. As yet, we can only sketch it in, but do not know how long to make it. Likewise, F_2 is the force in the other part of the wire. In general F_1 and F_2 will be different.

Since the three forces hold the point B in equilibrium, they must form a *closed triangle* by themselves (zero resultant). Off to one side, Fig. 26b, draw the weight force to scale. From the tip of this force, draw a line in parallel to BC. We do not know how long to make this force; however, if we did, we would then proceed to draw the third force from its end, heading parallel to the wire AB, and should have to land at the starting point of the weight force. It is clear what we now have to do: Simply begin at this point and draw a line back in the proper direction until it crosses the line of F_2. This crossing point fixed the lengths (or amounts) of the two forces. The force lines can now be measured, using the same scale that was employed in drawing the 160-lb weight, and so the magnitudes of F_1 and F_2 can be found. In this example they turn out to be about 165 lb and 135 lb, respectively. Try a construction like this yourself, using a weight and direction of your own choosing.

CENTER OF GRAVITY

In most of the cases we meet in practice, the forces acting on a body are not all applied at a single point, but at several different places. The weight of a body is a good example. The earth's gravity pulls downward on every particle of a material body with a force equal to the weight of that particle, as pictured in Fig. 27. However, we can replace all these separate forces by a single

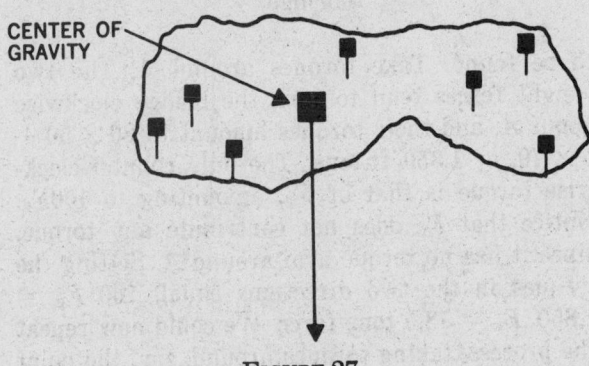

CENTER OF GRAVITY

FIGURE 27.

one, equal to the entire weight of the object. This force must be considered to act at a given place called the **center of gravity** of the body. There is such a point for every object. If the body is made of uniform material and has a simple shape, such as a sphere, cube, straight rod, etc., the location of the center of gravity is obvious (Fig. 28a). The position of the center of gravity of an irregular object may be found by trial, by seeing where it will balance without any tendency to rotate in any direction (Fig. 28b).

FIGURE 28. Locating the center of gravity

If a body is supported at any point other than its center of gravity, it will try to move until its center of gravity is as low as possible. This explains, for instance, why it is impossible to balance a pencil on its point.

EXPERIMENT 14: Fasten a weight to the inner edge of a flat cylindrical box (Fig. 29). Placed on a sloping board, it will mysteriously roll *up* the slope when released. Notice that the center of gravity is very near the position of the concealed weight, and that while the box goes up the hill, the center of gravity goes *down*, as it must.

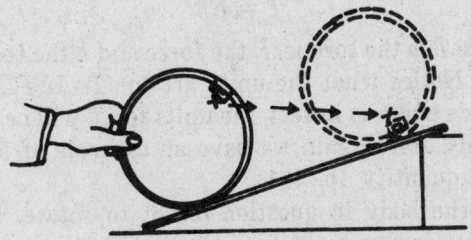

FIGURE 29. The mystery cylinder

TORQUE AND ROTATION

In general, if the forces applied to a body do not all act at a single point, there is the possibility that the body will rotate. How can we measure the ability of a force to produce rotation? Think of the example of pushing a revolving door (Fig. 30). If you want to turn the door most effectively, you push with your hand near the edge of the door rather than near the hinge. It is found that the **turning effect** of any force is given by multiplying the **amount of the force** by the **distance from the pivot** point to the line of the force. This turning effect of a force is called the **torque**, and

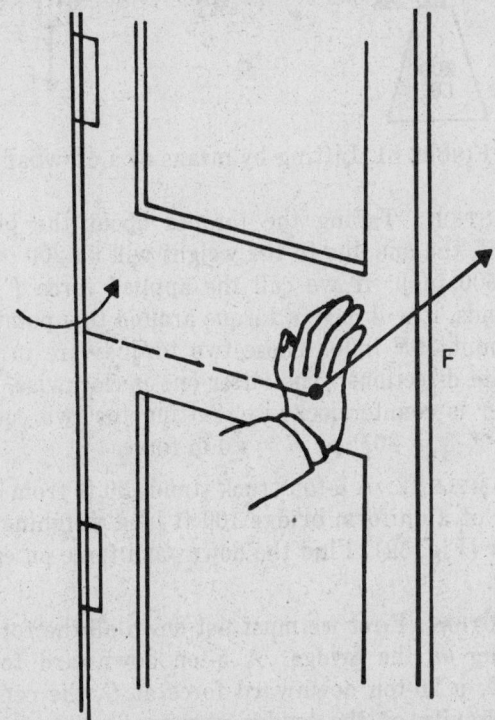

FIGURE 30. Revolving door

the distance mentioned is the **torque arm.** In symbols,

$$T = Fh$$

where T is the torque, F the force and h the torque arm. Notice what the units are for T: If F is in pounds and h is in feet, the units for T will be **foot pounds.** Here again we have an example of a derived quantity (p. 451).

If the body in question is not to rotate, then the net torque must be zero, that is, **the sum of all torques that tend to turn the body in one direction must be equal to the sum of all those tending to turn it in the opposite direction.** The word "direction" here refers to the sense of rotation—**clockwise** (in the direction turned by the hands of a clock), or **counterclockwise.**

In figuring the torques, we may take any point as a prospective center of turning—it need not be the place where the actual pivot or axle is located.

EXAMPLE 11: How big a downward force must be applied to the end of the crowbar shown in Fig. 31 in order just to lift the 200-lb weight? Neglect the weight of the bar itself.

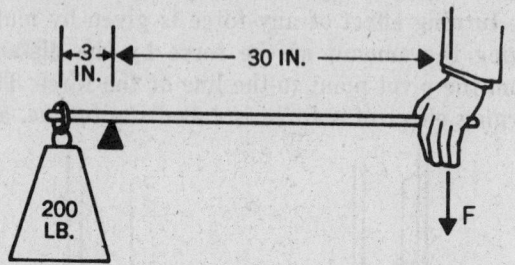

FIGURE 31. Lifting by means of a crowbar

SOLUTION: Taking the torques about the pivot point, the one due to the weight will be 200×3, or 600 in.lb. If we call the applied force F, in pounds, it will have a torque around this point of amount $30F$ in.lb. These two torques are in opposite directions: The latter one is clockwise, the other is counterclockwise. Setting the two equal, $200 \times 3 = 30F$, or $F = 20$ lb force.

EXAMPLE 12: A 5-ton truck stands 30 ft from one pier of a uniform bridge 100 ft long weighing 20 tons (Fig. 32). Find the downward force on each pier.

SOLUTION: First we must put down all the forces acting *on* the bridge: A 5-ton downward force at C; a 20-ton downward force at G, the center of gravity of the bridge structure; and at the piers, upward forces F_A and F_B whose values are

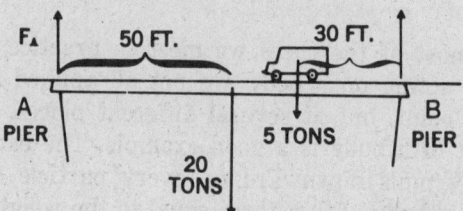

FIGURE 32. Downward force on the piers of a bridge

to be found. Take torques around A. The two weight forces tend to turn the bridge clockwise about A, and their torques amount to $20 \times 50 + 5 \times 70$, or 1,350 ft-tons. The only counter-clockwise torque is that of F_B, amounting to $100F_B$. Notice that F_A does not contribute any torque, since it has no torque arm around A. Setting the torques in the two directions equal, $100 F_B = 1,350$, $F_B = 13.5$ tons force. We could now repeat the process, taking torques around, say, the point B; but there is a simpler way to find the remaining force F_A: From the fact that the resultant of all the acting forces must be zero (p. 463) we have, simply because all the forces in this problem are either upward or downward, $F_A + 13.5 = 20 + 5$, so that $F_A = 11.5$ tons. So we see that by using the two equilibrium conditions that state (1) the resultant of all the forces must be zero and (2) the torques around any point must balance, we can work out any equilibrium problem.

GRAVITATION: NEWTON'S LAW

One of the greatest scientific achievements of all time was Newton's discovery of gravitation, around the middle of the seventeenth century. Earlier, the astronomer Kepler had found certain regularities about the motion of the plants around the sun. Newton, trying to explain these rules, decided that the planets must move in the observed way because they are pulled by a force exerted by the sun. He concluded that this force of gravitation exists not only between the sun and the planets but between *any* two objects in the universe, and he worked out the factors on which the amount of force depends. This is stated by his **Law of Gravitation: Any two bodies in the universe attract each other with a force that is directly proportional to their masses and inversely** proportional to the square of their distance apart. This may be stated as a formula:

$$F = \frac{Gm_1m_2}{d^2}$$

where F is the force of attraction, m_1 and m_2 are the two masses, and d is their distance apart. G is a constant, whose value is fixed once we have chosen our units for F, m and d. If F and m are measured in pounds and d in feet, the value of G is 0.000 000 000 033. Because G is so small, the attraction between ordinary objects is very weak, but when the bodies concerned are very massive, the force may be extremely large. Thus, the attractive force between the earth and the moon amounts to about 15 million trillion tons.

The gravitational force of the earth for objects on it—what we have been calling **gravity**—is responsible for their weight. The attraction of the moon for the waters of the ocean is a main cause of the **tides.**

Notice that while Newton's law allows us to calculate the amount of the attraction in any case, it does not tell us what gravitation is, nor why such a force exists. These are philosophical rather than scientific questions!

Motion

In the world about us, everything moves. This may seem to contradict the discussion where we talked about bodies at rest. But a body at rest on the ground is really moving with the rotation of the whole earth, and the earth in turn moves in its path around the sun, and so on. Rest and motion are relative terms. We will now find out how to measure the motions of bodies, and how the forces acting on them determine the way in which they move.

SPEED AND VELOCITY

In any kind of motion—for example, in making a trip—two things are of interest: What is the *rate* of motion and in what *direction* does it take place? Rate of motion is what we call **speed.** It is measured by the distance covered divided by the elapsed time. In symbols,

$$v = \frac{d}{t},$$

where d stands for the distance, t is the time required and v is the speed. Speed is a derived unit, and we are at liberty to use any distance unit and any time unit for this purpose. Table 4 gives convenient factors for changing from one common speed unit to another.

TABLE 4

CONVERSION FACTORS FOR SPEED UNITS

To change from a unit given at the side to one given at the top, multiply by the factor in the appropriate square. Thus 100 cm/sec = 100 × 0.0328 = 3.28 ft/sec.

	mi/hr	ft/sec	cm/sec	knots*
mi/hr	—	1.47	44.7	0.868
ft/sec	0.682	—	30.5	0.592
cm/sec	0.0224	0.0328	—	0.0194
knots*	1.15	1.69	51.5	—

Even where the rate of motion is not constant over the whole journey, the above formula has a meaning: it gives the **average speed** for the entire trip. For instance, if a car travels to a city 90 miles away in a total time of 3 hours, the average speed will be 90 mi/3 hr = 30 mi/hr. But no trip of this kind is made at constant speed; there may have been times when the car was going much faster or much slower than this, as indicated by the speedometer.

When the directional aspect is combined with

*1 knot = 1 nautical mile per hour.

the speed we have the **velocity** of motion. Velocity, like force, is a vector (p. 462), and so an arrowed line can be used to stand for a velocity. A body can have several velocities at the same time. A ball rolled across the floor of a moving railroad car (Fig. 33) has the common forward velocity of everything in the train, plus the crosswise velocity with which the ball is rolled. The **resultant velocity**

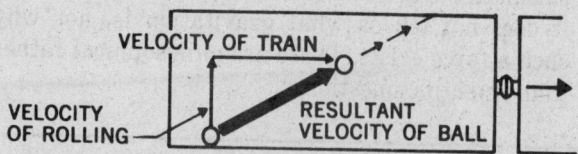

FIGURE 33. Combination of velocities

—how the ball would appear to move as seen by someone on an overhead bridge—is given by the same construction we used before. The actual path is the straight line indicated.

ACCELERATION

In most of the motions we commonly observe, the speed is not at all constant, whether it is the flight of a bird, the swinging of a pendulum or the fall of a stone. Any motion in which the speed or direction are variable is called **accelerated motion.** The **acceleration** is defined as the **rate of change** of the **velocity,** that is, the change in velocity divided by the time it takes to make that change. For instance, if a car going 25 ft/sec picks up speed until, 5 sec later, it is going 60 ft/sec, its rate of pick-up will be 60—25, or 35 ft/sec in 5 sec. Dividing, this amounts to 7 ft/sec/ sec ("feet per second per second"). This means only that the car increased its speed at an average rate of 7 ft/sec *each second.* Instead of writing "ft/sec/sec," we recognize that the time unit comes in *twice* as a factor in this derived unit, and we write "ft/sec²" and read it "feet per second squared."

Motion with Constant Acceleration

One kind of motion that is readily described and computed is that where the amount of the acceleration is *constant.* This holds, for a limited time at least, when a train is gathering speed, or when it is being brought to rest by the brakes. In the latter case, the speed is *decreasing,* and this is

sometimes called decelerated motion. However, no special name is really needed; this can be taken care of merely by putting a *minus* sign in front of the value for the acceleration.

EXAMPLE 13: A car going 30 ft/sec is brought to rest by its brakes at the uniform rate of 5 ft/sec². How long must the brakes be applied?

SOLUTION: Saying that the braking acceleration amounts to −5 ft/sec² means that the car will lose speed at the rate of 5 ft/sec each second. To take away all the initial speed of 30 ft/sec will then require 30/5 or 6 sec.

How *far* will a constantly-accelerating object move in a given time? To answer such a question, you must remember that the speed of motion is changing all the while. But we can find out what is happening by making use of the *average* speed; and here, since the speed changes at a uniform rate, the average speed will be half way between the speed at the beginning and the speed at the end of the interval. The next example will show how we can compute the distance in a specific case:

EXAMPLE 14: A car going 26 ft/sec begins to accelerate at the rate of 2 ft/sec². How fast will it be going after 8 sec, and how far will it go in this time?

SOLUTION: In 8 sec, the total gain in speed will be 8 × 2 = 16 ft/sec, so the final speed will be 24 + 16, or 42 ft/sec. To find the distance traveled, we note that the speed at the beginning of the acceleration period was 26 and at the end was 42 ft/sec, so that the average speed over this interval is ½ (26 + 42) = 34 ft/sec. Going, in effect, 34 ft/sec for 8 sec, the car would cover a distance of 34 × 8, or 272 ft.

Falling Motion; Projectiles

The ancient Greek philosopher Aristotle described the motion of a freely falling body by saying that the heavier the body, the faster it would fall. This does, at first thought, seem true, but you have already performed an experiment (Experiment 11) that throws some doubt on this conclusion. In the latter part of the sixteenth century, the great Italian scientist Galileo tried some experiments that convinced him that it is merely the disturbing effect of air resistance that ordinarily makes a light object fall more slowly than a heavy one. In a vacuum, all bodies fall at the same rate.

Galileo went on to find just how a falling body

moves. He found that, when the effects of the surrounding air can be neglected, a falling body has a constant acceleration—the kind of motion we have been discussing above. This acceleration is called the **acceleration due to gravity**, and is denoted by the symbol g. Its value changes slightly from place to place on earth, and especially with height, but the standard value is close to

$$32 \text{ ft/sec}^2, \text{ or } 980 \text{ cm/sec}^2.$$

Knowing the value of g, it is not difficult to calculate the motion of a falling body. The results will be quite accurate for compact solid objects falling moderate distances. The case of a body falling great distances in air is, in general, too complicated for computation.

EXAMPLE 15: A small stone is dropped from the roof of a tall building and is seen to hit the ground 7.0 sec later. Neglecting air resistance, find the height from which the stone fell and how fast it was going when it hit the ground.

SOLUTION: In the stated time, the stone, starting from rest, picks up a speed of $7 \times 32 = 224$ ft/sec, which is its speed just before hitting the ground. Its *average* speed for the whole trip is half the sum of the speed at the start and at the finish, or $\frac{1}{2} (0 + 224) = 112$ ft/sec. Going at this speed for 7 sec, a body would cover a distance of $112 \times 7 = 784$ ft, which is the distance of fall.

A **projectile**—a thrown stone or a bullet—is really a falling body. If shot upward at an angle, it immediately begins to *fall* short of the direction of fire, just like any falling object. It continues to fall in this way while moving forward, and so follows the observed curved path. Since bullets travel at high speed, the results may be somewhat altered by air resistance.

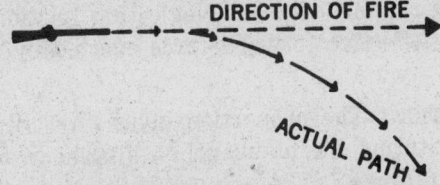

FIGURE 34. Path of a projectile

EXPERIMENT 15: Place two coins at the very edge of a table, one on top of the other. A sharp blow with a knife blade held flat against the table will send the lower coin off like a projectile, while the upper one will fall almost straight down. In spite of this difference in path, both will be heard to strike the floor at the same time, since both really *fall* the same distance.

FORCE AND MOTION

In the preceding pages you learned how to describe certain types of motion, such as motion with constant speed or motion with constant acceleration, and how to figure out times, distances, etc. Now we take up the more involved question of what *causes* and *maintains* the motion of an object—that is, the relation of force to the motion it produces.

MOTION: NEWTON'S LAWS

The general answer to such questions was given by the brilliant work of Newton in the form of his **Three Laws of Motion.** These principles form the basis of the whole subject of Mechanics.

The First Law: Inertia

The First Law is called the **Law of Inertia.** Inertia was described as one of the fundamental properties of matter. Although the general idea was anticipated by Galileo, Newton succeeded in putting it into precise form:

Every body remains in a state of rest or of uniform motion in a straight line unless acted upon by forces from the outside.

This law states that motion is as natural a condition as rest. A car going along a straight, level road at constant speed is in equilibrium: The weight of the car is balanced by the supporting force of the pavement, and the forward pull of the engine counterbalances the retarding forces of friction and air resistance. The resultant force is zero, and the car is in equilibrium just as truly as if it were at rest.

Centripetal Force; Satellites

If the car comes to a curve, the pavement must furnish, through friction with the tires, an additional force to swerve the car from its natural straight path and enable it to round the curve. If the road is slippery, this force will be lacking and the car will continue straight ahead, tending to skid off the road.

The force required to hold a moving object in a circular path is called **centripetal*** force.

Many situations arise in practice where centripetal force must be taken into account. The curves

---

* The word means "toward the center."

FIGURE 35. Not enough centripetal force; the car continues along its "natural" straight path

on a road or on a bicycle racetrack are "banked," or raised at the outer edge to furnish such a force. Mud flying from the wheel of a car leaves the wheel in a straight line—it "flies off on a tangent." Laundries make use of centrifugal ("away from the center") dryers in which the wet clothes are whirled in a wire basket. Chemists and biologists use a **centrifuge** to separate suspended solid matter from a liquid. When the mixture is whirled rapidly, the difference in centripetal force on the solid material and on the less dense liquid causes the solids to collect at the outer rim. Using special arrangements, the centripetal force on a particle can be made to exceed 100 million times its weight.

A satellite following an orbit around a planet or a planet going around the sun is held in orbit by the centripetal force furnished by gravitational attraction.

The Second Law: Acceleration

Newton's First Law is limited in its usefulness, since it tells what happens only in the case where there is *no* resultant force. In the majority of actual situations, outside forces do act; the Second Law tells what can be expected under such circumstances.

In order to see what is involved, consider the particular case of a hand truck which can be pushed along on a level floor. If the truck is standing still to begin with and nobody pushes on it, it will remain at rest (First Law). What happens, now, if it is pushed in such a way that the force

acting on it is kept constant? An actual trial shows that the truck will move forward with *constant acceleration*. In general, we find that a constant force acting on a given body that is free to move will give it a constant acceleration in the direction of the force.

If we were to double the amount of force, we would find that the acceleration would become just twice as great as before. On the other hand, if the mass of the car were doubled and the same force used as before, the acceleration would be just half of its earlier value. From experiments such as these, we conclude that the acceleration is proportional to the force divided by the mass (Fig. 36).

We are now able to state the **Second Law: A body acted upon by a constant force will move with constant acceleration in the direction of the force; the amount of the acceleration will be directly proportional to the acting force and inversely proportional to the mass of the body.**

Newton's Second Law can be put into a useful form by remembering what happens to any given object when it falls under gravity: Here the acting force is equal to the weight of the body, and the acceleration is, in every case, that of gravity, g. Making a direct proportion between force and acceleration, we can write

$$\frac{F}{W} = \frac{a}{g}$$

where W is the weight of the body, F is any applied force and a is the acceleration that this force will give to the body. F and W are to be measured in the same units, and a and g are to be measured in the same units.

EXAMPLE 16: A car weighing 3,200 lb accelerates at the rate of 5 ft/sec². Neglecting friction, what is the effective forward force exerted by the engine?

SOLUTION: The proportion gives $F = W\,(a/g)$. Substituting the numbers, $F = 3200 \times 5/32 = 500$ lb force.

The Third Law; Action and Reaction

Newton's Third Law deals with the observed fact that it is not possible to exert a force on a

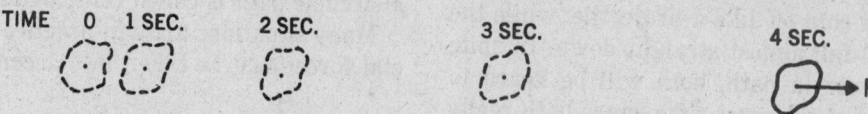

FIGURE 36. A constant force produces a constant acceleration

body without exerting a force in the opposite direction on some other body or bodies. There are many common illustrations of this: If you jump from a rowboat to a pier, the boat is thereby shoved backward. A gun "kicks" when the bullet goes forward. A ship's propeller can drive it forward only because it continually throws water backward.

Newton defined what is called the **momentum of a body**. It is the **mass multiplied by the velocity.** In symbols

$$M = mv,$$

where M is the momentum, m is the mass and v the velocity of the body. M is a derived quantity and any appropriate units may be used for m and v. The **Third Law** makes a simple statement about momentum. It says that **when any object is given a certain momentum in a given direction, some other body or bodies will get an equal momentum in the opposite direction.**

EXAMPLE 17: A gun has a mass of 2,500 gm and the bullets each have a mass of 100 gm. If a bullet leaves the gun with a speed of 800 meters/sec, with what speed will the gun start back?

SOLUTION: The momentum of the bullet will be 100×800 gm m/sec (gram meters per second). Calling the recoil speed of the gun V, its momentum just after firing will be $2500V$. Setting the two momenta equal, $2500\,V = 100 \times 800$, so that $V = 32$ m/sec. V comes out in m/sec because the speed of the bullet was given in these units.

If the gun and bullet were subject to no other forces after firing, the two would go in opposite directions, each continuing to move with its own constant speed forever (First Law). This would nearly be the case, for example, if the gun were fired far out in space where friction and gravitational forces are negligible. If the gun were fixed in the ground rather than free to recoil, the reaction would be transmitted to the whole earth instead of to the gun alone. Because of the earth's enormous mass, its resulting motion would be far too small to be detectable.

A jet engine or rocket gets its propelling force from the reaction of the gases discharged toward the rear at high speed. Even though the mass of gas shot out each second is not very large, its high speed makes the product mv very large. The jet plane or rocket gets an equal momentum in the forward direction. A rocket will work perfectly well in the vacuum existing in interplanetary space, provided it carries its own fuel and the oxygen needed to burn it.

EXPERIMENT 16: The reaction principle can be demonstrated by making a rubber-band slingshot on a board resting on rollers (Fig. 37). Tie the band back by means of a string and place a fairly massive stone in firing position. Release the stretched band by burning the thread and observe the recoil of the board as the stone goes forward.

FIGURE 37. Recoil

ROTATIONAL INERTIA

Newton's laws apply to rotation as well as to the forward motion of an object as a whole. A body that is set spinning has a tendency to keep spinning—**rotational inertia**. The purpose of a heavy flywheel on an engine is to smooth out the separate power thrusts by means of its great rotational inertia.

A massive rotating wheel also has a tendency to keep its axis in a constant direction in space. This is the principle of the **gyroscope**, a rapidly rotating wheel mounted in a pivoted frame, so that the axis may hold its direction in spite of any motion of the mounting. The ability to keep its direction constant makes the gyroscope useful in the construction of several aircraft instruments, such as the turn indicator, artificial horizon, gyrocompass and automatic pilot.

Space Glossary*

ablation—the removal of surface material from a body by vaporization, melting, or other process; specifically the intentional removal of material from a nose cone or spacecraft during high-speed movement through a planetary atmosphere to provide thermal protection to the underlying structure.

absolute zero—the theoretical temperature at which all molecular motion ceases.

acceleration—the rate of change of velocity.

acquisition and tracking radar—a radar set that locks onto a strong signal and tracks the object reflecting the signal.

aerodynamics—the science of the motion of air and other gaseous fluids, and of the forces acting on bodies when the bodies move through such fluids, or of the movement of such fluids against or around the bodies, as "his research in aerodynamics."

aerolite—a meteorite composed principally of stony material.

aerospace—(from aeronautics and space) of or pertaining to both the earth's atmosphere and space, as in "aerospace industries."

aerothermodynamic border—an altitude at about 100 miles, above which the atmosphere is so rarefied that the motion of an object through it at high speeds generates no significant surface heat.

aerothermodynamics—the study of the aerodynamic and thermodynamic problems connected with aerodynamic heating.

airglow—a relatively steady visible emission from the upper atmosphere, as distinguished from the sporadic emission of aurorae.

albedo—the ratio of the amount of electromagnetic radiation reflected by a body to the amount falling upon it, commonly expressed as a percentage.

angel—a radar echo caused by a physical phenomenon not discernible to the eye.

annular eclipse—an eclipse in which a thin ring of the source of light appears around the obscuring body.

aphelion—the point at which a planet or other celestial object in orbit about the sun is farthest from the sun.

apogee—in an orbit about the earth, the point at which the satellite is farthest from the earth; the highest altitude reached by a sounding rocket.

areo—combining form of Ares (Mars) as in "areography."

asteroid—one of the many small celestial bodies revolving around the sun, most of the orbits being between those of Mars and Jupiter. Also called "planetoid," "minor planet."

astroballistics—the study of the phenomena arising out of the motion of a solid through a gas at speeds high enough to cause ablation; for example, the interaction of a meteoroid with the atmosphere.

attitude—the position or orientation of an aircraft, spacecraft, etc., either in motion or at rest, as determined by the relationship between its axes and some reference line or plane such as the horizon.

aurora—the sporadic visible emission from the upper atmosphere over middle and high latitudes. Also called "northern lights."

azimuth—horizontal direction or bearing.

Baker-Nunn camera—a large camera used in tracking satellites.

ballistics—the science that deals with the motion, behavior, and effects of projectiles, especially bullets, aerial bombs, rockets, or the like; the science or art of designing and hurling projectiles so as to achieve a desired performance.

balloon-type rocket—a rocket, such as Atlas, that requires the pressure of its propellants (or other gases) within it to give it structural integrity.

beam-rider—a craft following a beam, particularly one which does so automatically, the beam providing the guidance.

bipropellant—a rocket propellant consisting of two unmixed or uncombined chemicals (fuel and oxidizer) fed to the combustion chamber separately.

blip—*See* **pip.**

boilerplate—as in "boilerplate capsule," a metal copy of the flight model, the structure or components of which are heavier than the flight model.

boiloff—the vaporization of a cold propellant, such as liquid oxygen or liquid hydrogen, as the temperature of the propellant mass rises, as in the tank of a rocket being readied for launch.

booster engine—an engine, especially a booster rocket, that adds its thrust to the thrust of the sustainer engine.

booster rocket—1. a rocket engine, either solid or liquid fuel, that assists the normal propulsive system, or sustainer engine, of a rocket or aeronautical vehicle in some phase of its flight. 2. a rocket used to set a missile vehicle in motion before another engine takes over.

boostglide vehicle—a vehicle (half aircraft, half spacecraft) designed to fly to the limits of the sensible atmosphere, then be boosted by rockets into the space above, returning to earth by gliding under aerodynamic control.

braking ellipses—a series of ellipses, decreasing in size due to aerodynamic drag, followed by a spacecraft in entering a planetary atmosphere.

breakoff phenomenon—the feeling which sometimes occurs during high altitude flight of being totally separated and detached from the earth and human society. Also called the "breakaway phenomenon."

centrifuge—specifically, a large motor-driven apparatus with a long arm at the end of which human and animal subjects or equipment can be revolved and rotated at various speeds to simulate very closely the prolonged accelerations encountered in highperformance aircraft, rockets, and spacecraft.

checkout—a sequence of actions taken to test or examine a launch vehicle or spacecraft as to its readiness to perform its intended function.

chemosphere—the vaguely defined region of the upper atmosphere in which photochemical reactions take place.

cislunar—(Latin *cis*, "on this side") of or

*The material on space exploration was selected from **Space . . . The New Frontier** and **The Challenge of Space Exploration,** prepared by The National Aeronautics and Space Administration, Washington, D.C.

pertaining to phenomena, projects, or activity in the space between the earth and moon, or between the earth and the moon's orbit.

closed ecological system—a system that provides for the maintenance of life in an isolated living chamber such as a spacecraft cabin by means of a cycle wherein exhaled carbon dioxide, urine, and other waste matter are converted chemically or by photosynthesis into oxygen, water, and food.

cold-flow test—a test of a liquid rocket without firing it to check or verify the efficiency of a propulsion subsystem, providing for the conditioning and flow of propellants (including tank pressurization, propellant loading, and propellant feeding).

companion body—a nose cone, last-stage rocket, or other body that orbits along with an earth satellite.

complex—entire area of launch site facilities. This includes blockhouse, launch pad, gantry, etc. Also referred to as a "launch complex."

composite propellant—a solid rocket propellant consisting of a fuel and an oxidizer.

conic section—a curve formed by the intersection of a plane and a right circular cone. Usually called "conic."

console—an array of controls and indicators for the monitoring and control of a particular sequence of actions, as in the checkout of a rocket, a countdown action, or a launch procedure.

control rocket—a vernier engine, retro-rocket, or other such rocket, used to guide or make small changes in the velocity of a rocket, spacecraft, or the like.

corona—the faintly luminous outer envelope of the sun. Also called "solar corona."

cosmic rays—the extremely high energy subatomic particles which bombard the atmosphere from outer space. Cosmic-ray primaries seem to be mostly protons, hydrogen nuclei, but also comprise heavier nuclei. On colliding with atmospheric particles they produce many different kinds of lower-energy secondary cosmic radiation.

cryogenic temperature—in general, a temperature range below about–50°C.; more particularly, temperatures within a few degrees of absolute zero.

deep space probes—spacecraft designed for exploring space to the vicinity of the moon and beyond. Deep space probes with specific missions may be referred to as "lunar probe," "Mars probe," "solar probe," etc.

diplexer—a device permitting an antenna system to be used simultaneously or separately by two transmitters. *Compare with* **duplexer.**

dish—a parabolic type of radio or radar antenna, roughly the shape of a soup bowl.

Doppler shift—the change in frequency with which energy reaches a receiver when the source of radiation or a reflector of the radiation and the receiver are in motion relative to each other. The Doppler shift is used in many tracking and navigation systems.

dosimeter—a device, worn by persons working around radioactive material, which indicates the amount (dose) of radiation to which they have been exposed.

Dovap—from Doppler, velocity and position, a tracking system which uses the Doppler shift caused by a target moving relative to a ground transmitter to obtain velocity and position information.

drogue parachute—a type of parachute attached to a body, used to slow it down; also called "deceleration parachute," or "drag parachute."

duplexer—a device which permits a single antenna system to be used for both transmitting and receiving.

eccentric—not having the same center; varying from a circle, as in "eccentric orbit."

ecological system—a habitable environment, either created artifically, such as in a manned space vehicle, or occurring naturally, such as the environment on the surface of the earth, in which man, animals, or other organisms can live in mutual relationship with each other.

escape velocity—the radial speed which a particle or larger body must attain in order to escape from the gravitational field of a planet or star.

extraterrestrial—from outside the earth.

film cooling—the cooling of a body or surface, such as the inner surface of a rocket combustion chamber, by maintaining a thin fluid layer over the affected area.

flashback—a reversal of flame propagation in a system, counter to the usual flow of the combustible mixture.

flux—the rate of flow of some quantity, often used in reference to the flow of some form of energy.

flying test bed—an aircraft, rocket, or other flying vehicle used to carry objects or devices being flight tested.

g or G—an acceleration equal to the acceleration of gravity, 32.2 feet per second per second at sea level; used as a unit of stress measurement for bodies undergoing acceleration.

gantry—a frame structure that spans over something, as an elevated platform that runs astride a work area, supported by wheels on each side; specifically, short for "gantry crane" or "gantry scaffold."

gas cap—the gas immediately in front of a meteoroid or reentry body as it travels through the atmosphere; the leading portion of a meteor. This gas is compressed and adiabatically heated to incandescence.

geo—a prefix meaning "earth," as in "geology," "geophysics."

geoprobe—a rocket vehicle designed to explore space near the earth at a distance of more than 4,000 miles from the earth's surface. Rocket vehicles operating lower than 4,000 miles are termed "sounding rockets."

gimbal—1. a device with two mutually perpendicular and intersecting axes of rotation, thus giving free angular movement in two directions, on which an engine or other object may be mounted. 2. in a gyro, a support which provides the spin axis with a degree of freedom.

gnotobiotics—the study of germ-free animals.

gravity—the force imparted by the earth to a mass on, or close to the earth. Since the earth is rotating, the force observed as gravity is the resultant of the force of gravitation and the centrifugal force arising from this rotation.

g-suit or G-suit—a suit that exerts pressure on the abdomen and lower parts of the body to prevent or retard the collection of blood below the chest under positive acceleration.

g-tolerance—a tolerance in a person or other animal, or in a piece of equipment, to an acceleration of a particular value.

gyro—a device which utilizes the angular momentum of a spinning rotor to sense angular motion of its base about one or two axes at right angles to the spin axis. Also called "gyroscope."

hardness—of X rays and other radiation of high energy, a measure of penetrating power. Radiation which will penetrate a 10-centimeter thickness of lead is considered "hard radiation."

hot test—a propulsion system test conducted by actually firing the propellants.

hypersonic—1. pertaining to hypersonic flow. 2. pertaining to speeds of Mach 5 or greater.

inertial guidance—guidance by means of acceleration measured and integrated within the craft.

infrared—infrared radiation; electromagnetic radiation in the wavelength interval from the red end of the visible spectrum on the lower limit to microwaves used in radar on the upper limit.

insertion—the process of putting an artificial satellite into orbit. Also the time of such action.

ionosphere—the part of the earth's outer atmosphere where ions and electrons are present in quantities sufficient to affect the propagation of radio waves.

Kepler's laws—the three empirical laws describing the motions of planets in their orbits, discovered by Johannes Kepler (1571–1630). These are: (1) The orbits of the planets are ellipses, with the sun at a common focus. (2) As a planet moves in its orbit, the line joining the planet and sun sweeps over equal areas in equal intervals of time. Also called "law of equal areas." (3) The squares of the periods of revolution of any two planets are proportional to the cubes of their mean distances from the sun.

launch ring—the metal ring on the launch pad on which a missile stands before launch.

launch vehicle—any device which propels and guides a spacecraft into orbit about the earth or into a trajectory to another celestial body. Often called "booster."

launch window—an interval of time during which a rocket can be launched to accomplish a particular purpose, as "liftoff occurred 5 minutes after the beginning of the 82-minute launch window".

lib ration—a real or apparent oscillatory motion, particularly the apparent oscillation of the moon.

Mach number—(after Ernst Mach [1838–1916], Austrian scientist) a number expressing the ratio of the speed of a body or of a point on a body with respect to the surrounding air or other fluid, or the speed of a flow, to the speed of sound in the medium; the speed represented by this number.

manometer—an instrument for measuring pressure of gases and vapors both above and below atmospheric pressure.

mass—the measure of the amount of matter in a body, thus its inertia.

mass-energy equivalence—the equivalence of a quantity of mass m and a quantity of energy E, the two quantities being related by the mass-energy relation $E = mc^2$, where c = the speed of light.

meteor—in particular, the light phenomenon which results from the entry into the earth's atmosphere of a solid particle from space; more generally, any physical object or phenomenon associated with such an event.

microwave region—commonly that region of the radio spectrum between approximately one thousand megacycles and three hundred thousand megacycles.

missile—any object thrown, dropped, fired, launched, or otherwise projected with the purpose of striking a target. Short for "ballistic missile," "guided missile."

mockup—a full-sized replica or dummy of something, such as a spacecraft, often made of some substitute material, such as wood, and sometimes incorporating functioning pieces of equipment, such as engines.

module—1. a self-contained unit of a launch vehicle or spacecraft which serves as a building block for the overall structure. The module is usually designated by its primary function as "command module," "lunar landing module," etc. 2. a one-package assembly of functionally associated electronic parts; usually a plug-in unit.

Newton's laws of motion—a set of three fundamental postulates forming the basis of the mechanics of rigid bodies, formulated by Newton in 1687.

The first law is concerned with the principle of inertia and states that if a body in motion is not acted upon by an external force, its momentum remains constant (law of conservation of momentum). The second law asserts that the rate of change of momentum of a body is proportional to the force acting upon the body and is in the direction of the applied force. A familiar statement of this is the equation

$$F = ma,$$

where F is vector sum of the applied forces, m the mass, and a the vector acceleration of the body. The third law is the principle of action and reaction, stating that for every force acting upon a body there exists a corresponding force of the same magnitude exerted by the body in the opposite direction.

normal shock wave—a shock wave perpendicular, or substantially so, to the direction of flow in a supersonic flow field. Sometimes shortened to "normal shock."

nozzle—specifically, the part of a rocket thrust chamber assembly in which the gases produced in the chamber are accelerated to high velocities.

orbital elements—a set of seven parameters defining the orbit of a satellite.

order of magnitude—a factor of 10.

paraglider—a flexible-winged, kite-like vehicle designed for use in a recovery system for launch vehicles or as a reentry vehicle.

passive—reflecting a signal without transmission, as "Echo is a passive satellite." Contrasted with "active."

perigee—that orbital point nearest the earth when the earth is the center of attraction.

photosphere—the intensely bright portion of the sun visible to the unaided eye.

pickoff—a sensing device, used in combination with a gyroscope in an automatic pilot or other automatic or robot apparatus, that responds to angular movement to create a signal or to effect some type of control.

pickup—a device that converts a sound, view, or other form of intelligence into corresponding electric signals (e.g., a microphone, a television camera, or a phonograph pickup).

pip—signal indication on the scope of an electronic instrument, produced by a short, sharply peaked pulse of voltage. Also called "blip."

pitchover—the programmed turn from the vertical that a rocket under power takes as it describes an arc and points in a direction other than vertical.

posigrade rocket—an auxiliary rocket which fires in the direction in which the vehicle is pointed, used for example in separating two stages of a vehicle.

precession—the change in the direction of the axis of rotation of a spinning body or of the plane of the orbit of an orbiting body when acted upon by an outside force.

prestage—a step in the action of igniting a large liquid rocket taken prior to the ignition of the full flow, and consisting of igniting a partial flow of propellants into the thrust chamber.

primary—1. short for "primary body." 2. short for "primary cosmic ray."

primary cosmic rays—high-energy particles originating outside the earth's atmosphere.

probe—any device inserted in an environment for the purpose of obtaining information about the environment, specifically, an instrumented vehicle moving through the upper atmosphere or space, or landing upon another celestial body in order to obtain information about the specific environment.

prominence—a filament-like protuberance from the visible portion of the sun.

proton—a positively charged subatomic particle of a positive charge equal to the negative charge of the electron but of 1,837 times the mass; a constituent of all atomic nuclei.

proving stand—a test stand for reaction engines, especially rocket engines.

purge—to rid a line or tank of residual fluid, especially of fuel or oxygen in the tanks or lines of a rocket after a test firing or simulated test firing.

radar astronomy—the study of celestial bodies within the solar system by means of radiation originating on earth but reflected from the body under observation.

radiosonde—a balloon-borne instrument for the simultaneous measurement and transmission of meteorological data.

reaction control system—a system of controlling the attitude of a craft when outside the atmosphere by using jets of gas in lieu of aerodynamic control surfaces.

readout—the action of a radio transmitter transmitting data either instantaneously with the acquisition of the data or by play of a magnetic tape upon which the data have been recorded.

real time—time in which reporting on events or recording of events is simultaneous with the events.

recombination—the process by which a positive and a negative ion join to form a neutral molecule or other neutral particle.

red shift—in astronomy, the displacement of observed spectral lines toward the longer wavelengths of the red end of the spectrum. *Compare* **space reddening.**

reentry—the event occurring when a spacecraft or other object comes back into the sensible atmosphere after being rocketed to altitudes above the sensible atmosphere; the action involved in this event.

regenerator—a device used in a thermo-dynamic process for capturing and returning to the process heat that would otherwise be lost.

relativity—a principle that postulates the equivalence of the description of the universe, in terms of physical laws, by various observers, or for various frames of reference.

rocket engine—a reaction engine that contains within itself, or carries along with itself, all the substances necessary for its operation or for the consumption or combustion of its fuel, not requiring intake of any outside substance and hence capable of operation in outer space. Also called "rocket motor."

rocketsonde—meteorological rocket.

rockoon—a high-altitude sounding system consisting of a small solid-propellant research rocket launched from a large plastic balloon.

roll—the rotational or oscillatory movement of an aircraft or similar body which takes place about a longitudinal axis through the body—called "roll" for any amount of such rotation.

rotation—turning of a body about an axis within the body, as the daily rotation of the earth.

rumble—a form of combustion instability, especially in a liquid-propellant rocket engine, characterized by a low-pitched, low-frequency rumbling noise; the noise made in this kind of combustion.

scrub—to cancel a scheduled rocket firing, either before or during countdown.

selenocentric—relating to the center of the moon; referring to the moon as a center.

selenographic—1. of or pertaining to the physical geography of the moon. 2. specifically, referring to positions on the moon measured in latitude from the moon's equator and in longitude from a reference meridian.

sensible atmosphere—that part of the atmosphere that offers resistance to a body passing through it.

sensor—the component of an instrument that converts an input signal into a quantity which is measured by another part of the instrument. Also called "sensing element."

service tower—*See* **gantry.**

shock tube—a relatively long tube or pipe in which very brief high-speed gas flows are produced by the sudden release of gas at very high pressure into a low-pressure portion of the tube; the high-speed flow moves into the region of low pressure behind a shock wave.

solar wind—a stream of protons constantly moving outward from the sun.

sounding—1. in geophysics, any penetration of the natural environment for scientific observation. 2. in meteorology, same as upper-air observation. However, a common connotation is that of a single complete radiosonde observation.

space—1. specifically, the part of the universe lying outside the limits of the earth's atmosphere. 2. more generally, the volume in which all spatial bodies, including the earth, move.

space reddening—the observed reddening, or absorption of shorter wavelengths, of the light from distant celestial bodies caused by scattering by small particles in interstellar space. *Compare* **red shift.**

specific impulse—a performance parameter of a rocket propellant, expressed in seconds, and equal to thrust (in pounds) divided by weight flow rate (in pounds per second). *See* **thrust.**

sunspot—a relatively dark area on the surface of the sun, consisting of a dark central umbra and a surrounding penumbra that is intermediate in brightness between the umbra and the surrounding photosphere.

sunspot cycle—a periodic variation in the number and area of sunspots with an average length of 11.1 years, but varying between about 7 and 17 years.

sustainer engine—an engine that maintains the velocity of a missile or rocket vehicle, once it has achieved its programmed velocity through use of a booster engine.

synchronous satellite—an equatorial west-to-east satellite orbiting the earth at an altitude of 22,300 statute miles, at which altitude it makes one revolution in 24 hours, synchronous with the earth's rotation.

synergic curve—a curve plotted for the ascent of a rocket, space-air vehicle, or space vehicle calculated to give the vehicle an optimum economy in fuel with an optimum velocity.

tektite—a small glassy body containing no crystals, probably of meteoritic origin, and bearing no antecedent relation to the geological formation in which it occurs.

telemetry—the science of measuring a quantity or quantities, transmitting the measured value to a distant station, and there interpreting, indicating, or recording the quantities measured.

thermodynamics—the study of the relationships between heat and other forms of energy.

thermonuclear—pertaining to a nuclear reaction that is triggered by particles of high thermal energy.

thrust—1. the pushing force developed by an aircraft engine or a rocket engine. 2. specifically, in rocketry, the product of propellant mass flow rate and exhaust velocity relative to the vehicle.

topside sounder—a satellite designed to measure ion concentration in the ionosphere from above the ionosphere.

transit—1. the passage of a celestial body across a celestial meridian; usually called "meridian transit." 2. the apparent passage of a celestial body across the face of another celestial body or across any point, area, or line.

translunar—of or pertaining to space outside the moon's orbit about the earth.

transponder—a combined receiver and transmitter whose function is to transmit signals automatically when triggered by an interrogating signal.

T-time—any specific time, minus or plus, as referenced to "zero," or "launch" time, during a countdown sequence that is intended to result in the firing of a rocket propulsion unit that launches a rocket vehicle or missile.

ullage—the amount that a container, such as a fuel tank, lacks of being full.

ultraviolet radiation—electromagnetic radiation shorter in wavelength than visible radiation but longer than X-rays; roughly, radiation in the wavelength interval between 10 and 4,000 angstroms.

umbilical cord—any of the servicing electrical or fluid lines between the ground or a tower and an upright rocket missile or vehicle before the launch. Often shortened to "umbilical."

Van Allen Belt, Van Allen Radiation Belt, Van Allen Radiation Region (for James A. Van Allen, 1914–)—the zone of high-intensity radiation surrounding the earth beginning at altitudes of approximately 500 miles.

vernier engine—a rocket engine of small thrust used primarily to obtain a fine adjustment in the velocity and trajectory of a ballistic missile or space vehicle just after the thrust cutoff of the last propulsion engine, and used secondarily to add thrust to a booster or sustainer engine. Also called "vernier rocket."

weightlessness—1. a condition in which no acceleration, whether of gravity or other force, can be detected by an observer within the system in question. 2. a condition in which gravitational and other external forces acting on a body produce no stress, either internal or external, in the body.

yaw—1. the lateral rotational or oscillatory movement of an aircraft, rocket, or the like about a transverse axis. 2. the amount of this movement; i.e., the angle of yaw.

zero g—*See* **weightlessness.**

The Shuttle Era

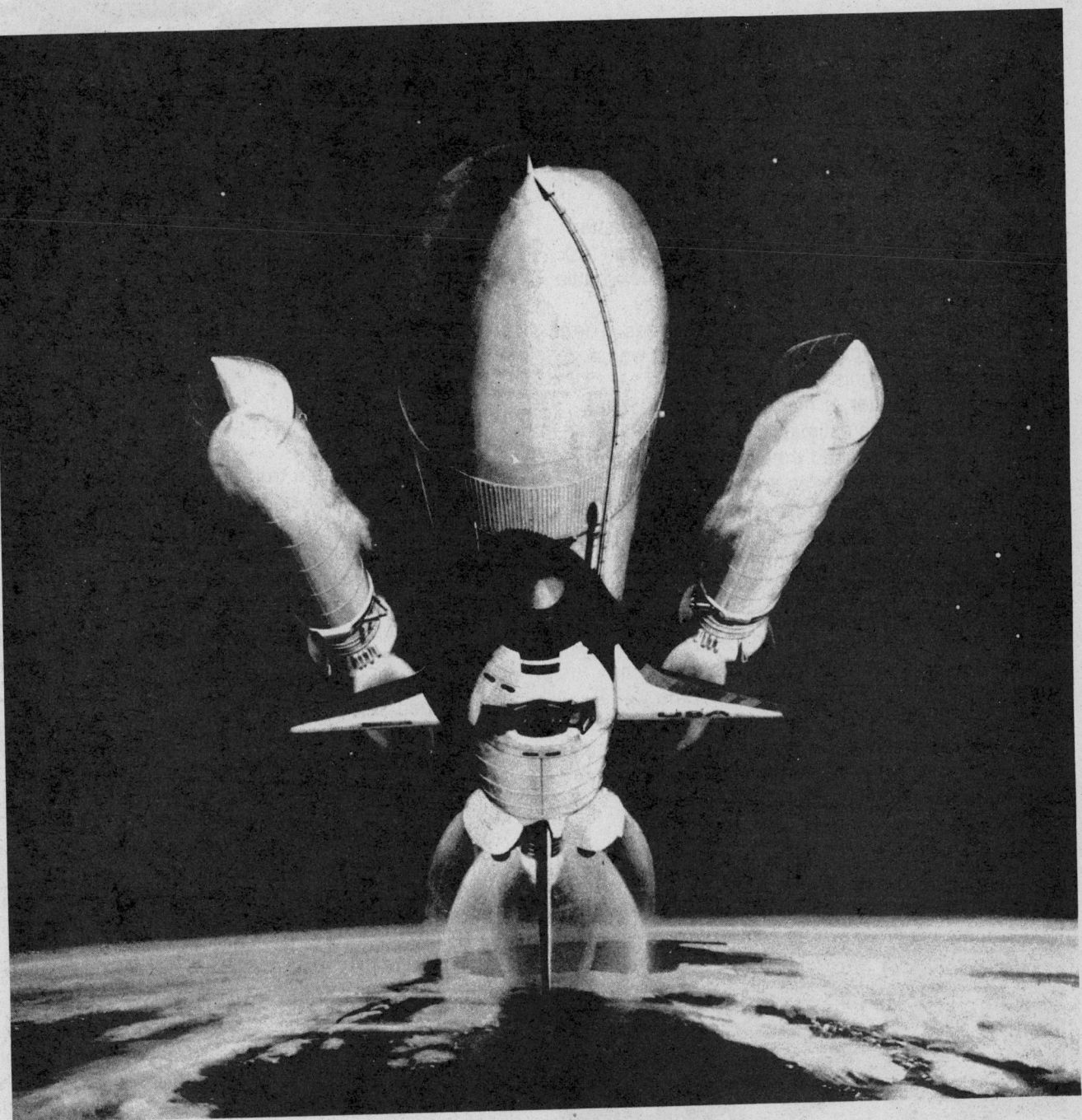

A unique high-angle view of the Space Shuttle (artist's concept). The Orbiter, still attached to the external tank as the solid rocket boosters are jettisoned, climbs upward to begin its Earth orbital mission.

The Shuttle Era

The Inertial Upper Stage (IUS) is deployed from open payload bay of Shuttle Orbiter into space by the Orbiter's remote manipulator (artist's concept). The IUS can rocket spacecraft to geosynchronous orbits or into interplanetary trajectories. The IUS is one of two expendable, low-cost propulsion vehicles that are being considered for the Space Transportation System.

On December 17, 1903, Orville and Wilbur Wright successfully achieved sustained flight in a power-driven aircraft. The first flight that day lasted only 12 seconds over a distance of 37 meters (120 feet), which is about the length of the Space Shuttle Orbiter. The fourth and final flight of the day traveled 260 meters (852 feet) in 59 seconds. The initial notification of this event to the world was a telegram to the Wrights' father.

Sixty-six years later, a man first stepped on the lunar surface and an estimated 500 million people around the world watched the event on television or listened to it on the radio as it happened.

Building upon previous achievements, new plateaus in air and space transportation have been reached—military aviation, airmail, commercial passenger service, the jet age, and manned space flight. Now a new era nears. The beginning of regularly scheduled runs of NASA's Space Shuttle to and from Earth orbit in the 1980's marks the coming of age in space. The Shuttle turns formidable and costly space missions into routine and economical operations that generate maximum benefits for all people. Shuttle opens space to men and women of all nations who are reasonably healthy and have important work to do there.

A Versatile Vehicle

Space Shuttle is a true aerospace vehicle. It takes off like a rocket, maneuvers in Earth orbit like a spacecraft, and lands like an airplane. The Space Shuttle is designed to carry heavy loads into Earth orbit. Other launch vehicles have done this. But unlike the other launch vehicles which were used just once, each Space Shuttle Orbiter may be used again and again.

Moreover, Shuttle permits checkout and repair of unmanned satellites in orbit, or return of the satellites to Earth for repairs that could not be done in space. This will result in considerable savings in spacecraft costs. Satellites that the Shuttle can orbit and maintain include those involved in environmental protection, energy, weather forecasting, navigation, fishing, farming, mapping, oceanography, and many other fields useful to man.

Spacecraft destined for geosynchronous orbit will be boosted from low Earth orbit by either a Solid Spinning Upper Stage (SSUS) or by the Inertial Upper Stage (IUS) that is being developed by the United States Air Force. Interplanetary spacecraft will be propelled by a variation of the Centaur upper stage that has been used with the Atlas and Titan expendable launch vehicles.

Unmanned satellites, such as the Space Telescope, which can multiply our view of the universe, and the Long Duration Exposure Facility

With its manipulator arm extended, the Space Shuttle Orbiter prepares to retrieve a satellite (artist's concept).

The large Space Telescope is being designed as an optical telescope observatory to be used in Earth orbit, unhindered by atmospheric distortion. Here, it is shown being deployed in orbit by the Space Shuttle.

(LDEF), which can demonstrate the effects on materials of long exposure to the space environment, can be placed in orbit, erected, and returned to Earth by the Space Shuttle. Shuttle crews can also perform such services as replacing the Space Telescope's film packs and lenses. The Space Telescope program is managed by NASA's Marshall Space Flight Center, Huntsville, Alabama and the LDEF is a project of the NASA Langley Research Center, Hampton, Virginia.

The Shuttle is a manned spacecraft, but unlike manned spacecraft of the past such as Mercury, Gemini, and Apollo, it touches down like an airplane on a landing strip. Thus, the Shuttle eliminates the need for the expensive sea recovery force required for Mercury, Gemini, and Apollo. In addition, unlike the previous manned spacecraft, the Shuttle is reusable. It can be refurbished and ready for another journey into space in a comparatively short turnaround time.

The Shuttle can quickly provide a vantage point in space for observations of transient astronomical events or of sudden weather, agricultural, or environmental crises. Information from Shuttle observations could contribute to sound decisions for countries dealing with such problems.

The Shuttle is scheduled to carry a complete scientific laboratory called "Spacelab" into Earth orbit. Developed by the European Space Agency (ESA), Spacelab is similar to earthbound laboratories but is adapted to operate in zero gravity (weightlessness). It provides a shirt-sleeve environment, suitable for working, eating, and sleeping without the encumbrance of special clothing or space suits.

Spacelab provides facilities for as many as four laboratory specialists to conduct experiments in such fields as medicine, manufacturing, astronomy, and pharmaceuticals. Spacelab remains attached to the Shuttle Orbiter throughout a mission. Upon return to Earth, Spacelab is removed from the Orbiter and outfitted for its next assignment. It can be reused about 50 times.

Spacelab personnel will be men and women of many nations, experts in their fields, and in reasonably good health. They will require only a few weeks of space-flight training.

Participating ESA nations are Belgium, Denmark, France, Italy, The Netherlands, Spain, Switzerland, United Kingdom, Austria, and the Federal Republic of Germany (West Germany). Spacelab is an example of international sharing of space costs and of worldwide interest in the study of science in a space environment.

Projects that only recently were considered impracticable become feasible with Space Shuttle. Shuttle can carry into orbit the building blocks for large solar power stations that would convert the abundant solar heat and sunlight of space into unlimited supplies of electricity for an energy-hungry world. These building blocks would be assembled by specialists, transported, and supported by Space Shuttle.

The Shuttle can also carry the building blocks for self-sustaining settlements into Earth orbit. Inhabitants of these settlements could be employed in such vital occupations as building and maintaining solar power stations and manufacturing drugs, metals, glass for lenses, and electronic crystals. Manufacturing in weightless space could reduce costs of certain drugs, create new alloys, produce drugs and lenses of unusual purity, and enable crystals to grow very large. Drugs, metals, glass, and electronic crystals will also be manufactured during Spacelab missions, long before the establishment of any space settlement.

The shuttle program suffered a major setback in January 1986 when the *Challenger* exploded shortly after launch, killing its seven-member crew. After a two-year shutdown, NASA launched the *Discovery* in the last half of 1988. During those two years, all aspects of the shuttle program were reassessed and many elements redesigned, including the booster joints which were largely blamed for the explosion. The new joints are stronger, with three O-ring seals instead of two. A capture latch has been added as well as weather stripping which will keep the joints at a constant temperature. The landing and braking

A high-angle front view of the Orbiter vehicle in Earth orbit carrying Spacelab hardware as the primary cargo in its payload bay (artist's concept).
A crewmember is seen performing extravehicular operations outside the pressurized laboratory in the payload bay.

systems have also been redesigned, and the addition of an escape system is possible for future missions. Other safety factors are a new set of launch criteria (including a requirement for warm weather), a conservative flight design and a familiar payload such as military satellites. NASA plans to launch as many as nine shuttle flights per hear, although a manifest detailing launch dates and cargos is updated every year.

Shuttle Management Team

NASA's Lyndon B. Johnson Space Center, Houston, Texas, manages the Space Shuttle program and is also responsible for development, production, and delivery of the Orbiter.

NASA's George C. Marshall Space Flight Center, Huntsville, Alabama, is responsible for the development, production, and delivery of the solid rocket boosters, the external propellant tank, and the Orbiter main engines. Test firings of Shuttle engines are carried out at NASA's National Space Technology Laboratories, Bay St. Louis, Mississippi.

NASA's John F. Kennedy Space Center, Florida, is responsible for design and development of launch and recovery facilities and for operational missions requiring easterly launches.

Thousands of companies make up the Shuttle contractor team. They are located in nearly every state of the United States.

A head-on view of a Space Shuttle Orbiter landing at the Kennedy Space Center (artist's concept). The huge vehicle assembly building (VAB) is shown in the background.

Voyager to Saturn

The missions of Voyager I and Voyager II take advantage of state-of-the-art technology as well as a rare orbital alignment of the distant planets Jupiter, Saturn, Uranus, and Neptune to extend man's sight and his imagination billions of miles to regions where the Sun is only a bright star. From Earth, Jupiter, Saturn, and Uranus are mere points of light, and Neptune can only be seen with a powerful telescope. The Voyager probes allow them to be seen as never before, sending back a wealth of information and pictures of amazing clarity from their flybys of the planets. The probes passed Jupiter in mid-1979, Saturn in 1980 and 1981, and Voyager II passed Uranus in January 1986. It will make its flyby of Neptune in late 1989.

The Voyager spacecrafts have revealed detailed information about our neighboring planets which might never have been discovered by scientists confined to the Earth. Jupiter, like Saturn, has a ring system, and the only volcanoes known outside the Earth. Although it is an airless world, the probes discovered evidence of a possible underground ocean.

Saturn is a world with an ocean of liquid hydrocarbons surmounted by clouds of organic matter. Voyager discovered icy moons which had melted through unknown causes. And the beautiful ring system visible from Earth turned out to be made of thousands of rings instead of just a few.

The information about Uranus was perhaps the most surprising. That distant planet has more than 15 moons, a system of black rings, and a belt of trapped high-energy charged particles, akin to Earth's Van Allen Belt. The planet is tipped over on its side and has atmospheric jet streams that move twice as fast as Earth's and in unexpected directions because Uranus receives more heat at its poles than at its equator.

When Voyager passes by Neptune in 1989, scientists are expecting the information about the planet to be just as intriguing. They are especially interested in detail about the puzzling ring-arc system, the weather and atmosphere, the presence of a magnetic field and trapped particles, and Neptune's two known satellites, particularly Triton. Triton is a large moon with an unusual orbit and an atmosphere of nitrogen and methane, much of which exists as ice. In fact, Triton is cold enough for liquid nitrogen to flow on its surface.

The more we know about the other planets of our solar system, the more we understand what we know about Earth. The Voyager probes are providing not only fascinating data about our neighbors, but a greater understanding of our own existence.

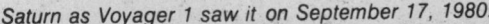

Saturn as Voyager 1 saw it on September 17, 1980.

The Voyager Spacecraft

Seemingly small for the task assigned them, the identical twin Voyagers weigh just under a ton each. The main functions of the spacecraft are clearly seen in its three-part design, beginning with the wide dish antenna for all-important radio communications to and from Earth. Underneath this dish are Voyager's "brains", the three primary and three backup computers—responsible for overall command, collection of science data, and control of the spacecraft's periodic rolls and turns. Finally, extending out from the body is a lattice-like arm, or "boom", where most of Voyager's sensors—its science instruments—are mounted.

Many of these instruments are sensors relating to different bands of the broad spectrum of electromagnetic energy that serves as a prime source of information for scientists. How a body (or a substance such as a gas) absorbs, reflects, emits, or in any way changes this energy tells much about its physical properties, especially if the energy is seen in very specific wavelengths.

And so, Voyager has four different "eyes"—TV or telemetry cameras, ultraviolet and infrared devices, and a light-analyzing photopolarimeter (no longer active on Voyager 1)—located on a scan platform which turns at almost any angle for precise targeting.

Also on the boom are instruments to see cosmic rays and radio emissions from the planets.

Other science instruments supplement this spectral analysis with a search for highly energetic subatomic particles and fields. These include plasma (charged gas) detectors and magnetometers to survey the magnetic fields around planets.

Certain elements of Voyager's design, including its computer and TV systems, are adapted from the Mariner missions which have already explored the inner planets close to Earth. But in going much farther from the Sun to colder regions of space, Voyager requires special features first used by the Pioneer spacecraft, the first man-made objects to cross the asteroid belt.

Like Pioneer, Voyager is equipped with small nuclear generators to provide onboard electrical power. Earlier missions used solar panels for these energy demands, but Voyager's distance from the Sun makes this impractical, and creates an added need for small heaters and insulation against the cold.

The great distances Voyager will travel also require a giant leap in communications sophistication. Even at its highest output, the dish antenna points a narrow beam of less power than a small light bulb at a target so distant it will take nearly 1½ hours to reach Earth from Saturn.

Because we cannot yet go ourselves, Voyager goes for us. Its instruments cover the spectrum and detect charged particles and fields.

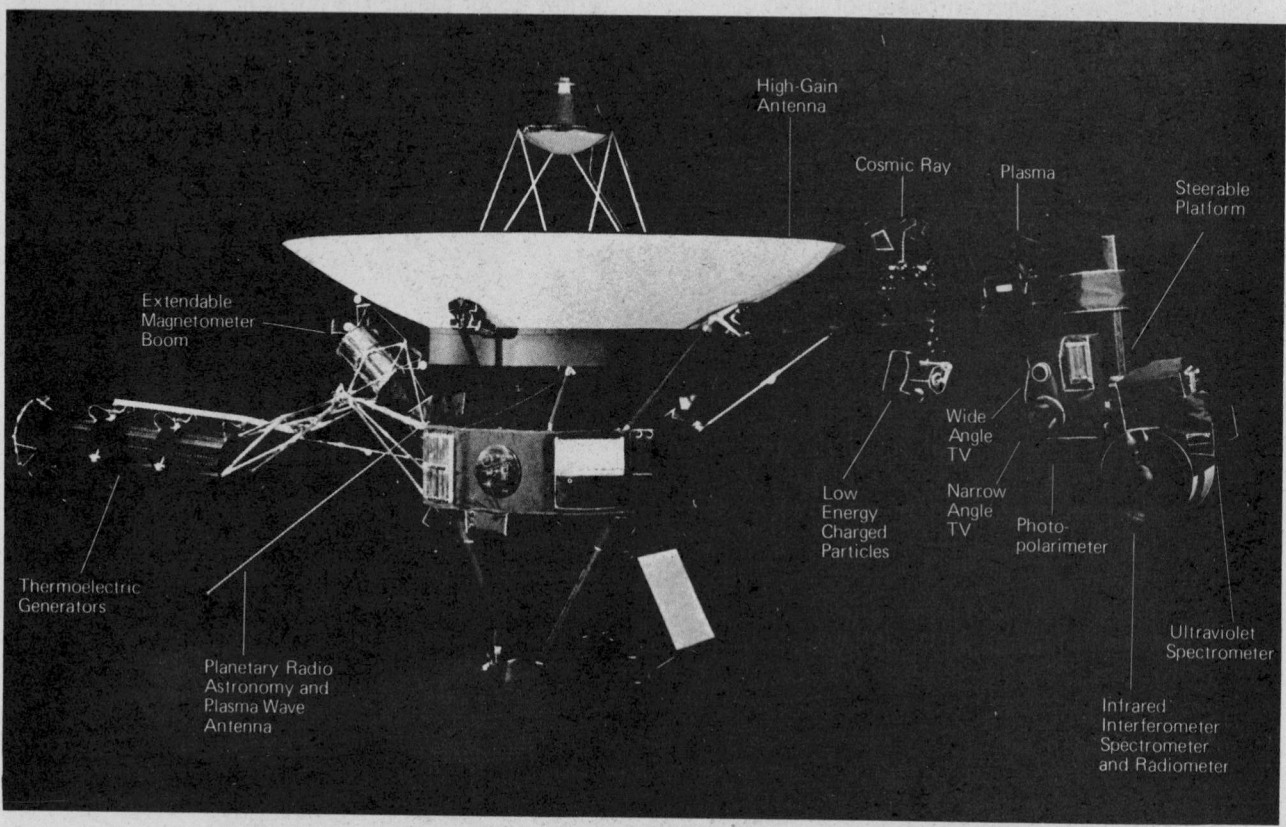

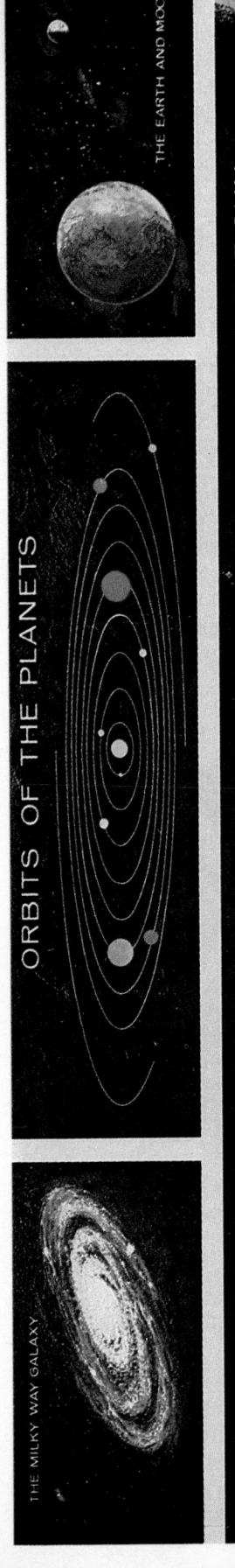

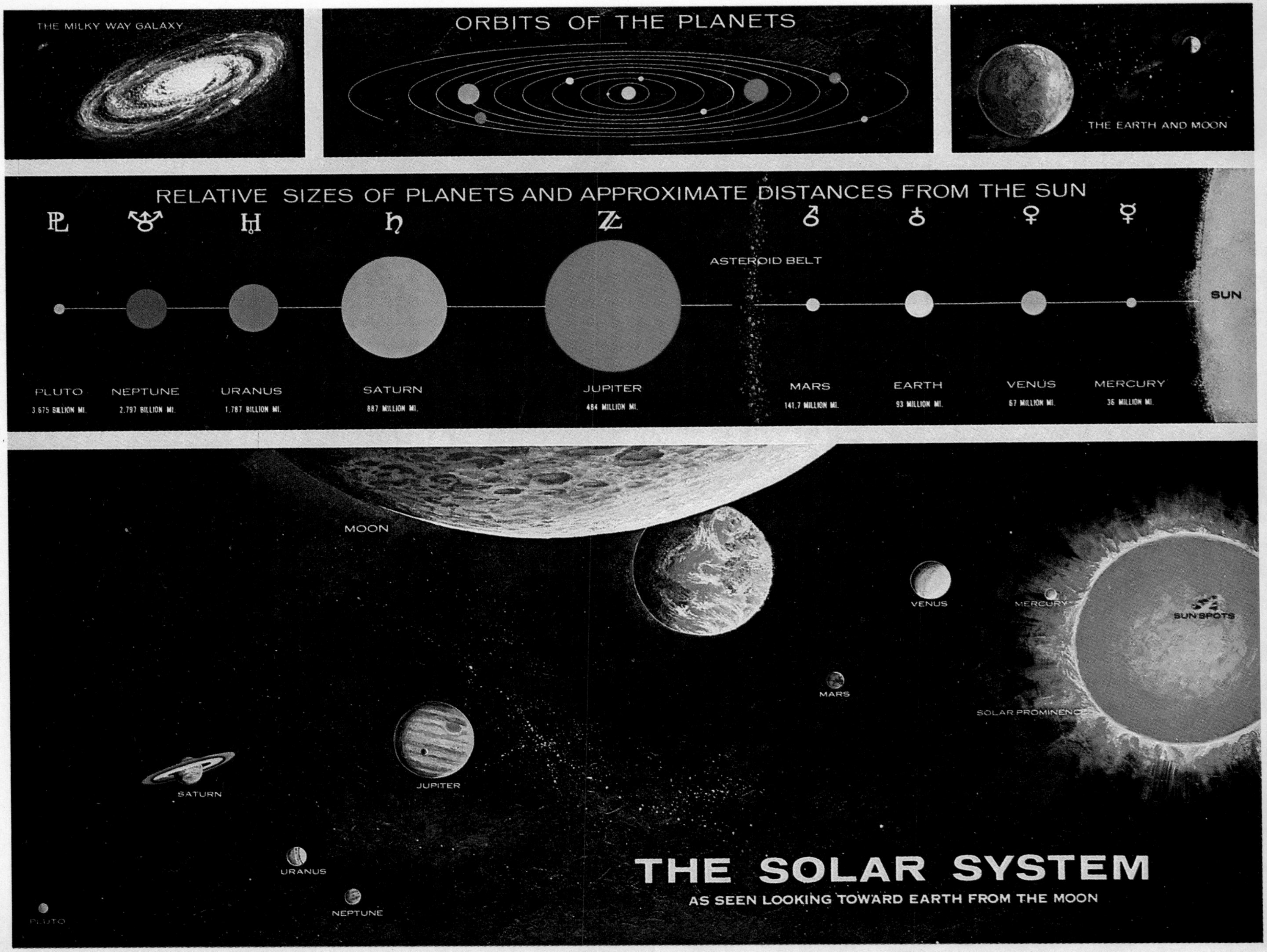

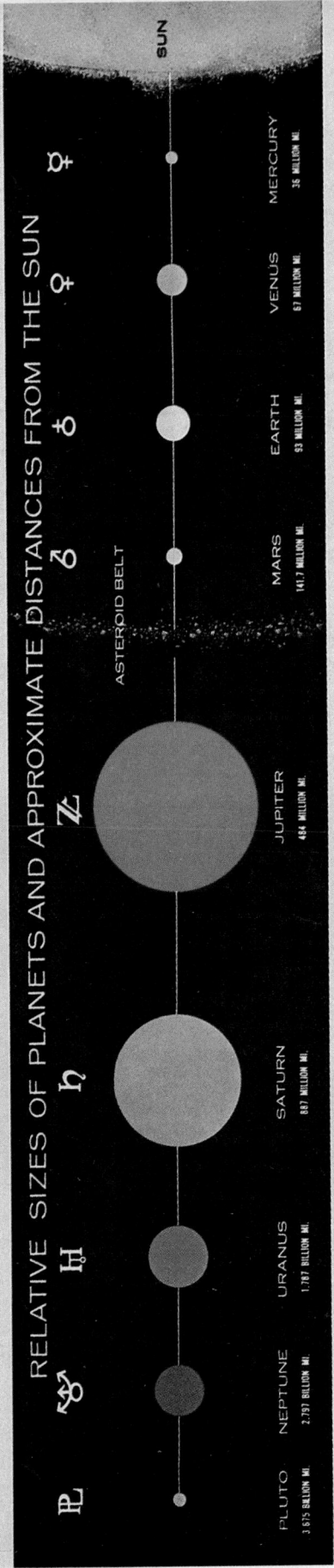

THE MILKY WAY GALAXY
ORBITS OF THE PLANETS
THE EARTH AND MOON
RELATIVE SIZES OF PLANETS AND APPROXIMATE DISTANCES FROM THE SUN
ASTEROID BELT
SUN
PLUTO
3.675 BILLION MI.
NEPTUNE
2.797 BILLION MI.
URANUS
1.787 BILLION MI.
SATURN
887 MILLION MI.
JUPITER
484 MILLION MI.
MARS
141.7 MILLION MI.
EARTH
93 MILLION MI.
VENUS
67 MILLION MI.
MERCURY
36 MILLION MI.
MOON
VENUS
MERCURY
SUN SPOTS
MARS
SOLAR PROMINENCE
JUPITER
SATURN
URANUS
NEPTUNE
PLUTO
THE SOLAR SYSTEM
AS SEEN LOOKING TOWARD EARTH FROM THE MOON

SOLAR SYSTEM—The nine known planets of the solar system can be divided into two categories: the Jovian planets and the terrestrial planets. Jupiter, Saturn, Uranus, and Neptune, the Jovian planets, are believed to consist of large cores of solid hydrogen and heavier elements surrounded by extensive atmospheres of heavy gases. As a group, the Jovian planets are less dense than the terrestrial planets and have many more satellites. Mercury, Venus, Earth, Mars, and Pluto, the terrestrial planets, are dense, solid bodies without extensive atmospheres. Between the orbits of Mars and Jupiter, the majority of asteroids, of which over 1,600 are presently known, are situated. These diminutive objects are thought to be remnants of a large planet which disintegrated. The planets travel in elliptical orbits of relatively low eccentricity around the Sun, although the eccentricity of Pluto is large enough to bring it sometimes nearer the Sun than Neptune. All the planets lie close to the plane of the earth's orbit, the ecliptic. Except for Pluto, the terrestrial planets are much nearer the Sun than the Jovian planets. For this reason, it is difficult to show in a schematic manner the relative distances of the planets, and the lithograph represents only their relative sizes, not their relative distance from the Sun.

EARTH AND MOON—The Earth is slightly flattened at the poles, resulting in an equatorial bulge. Energetic protons and electrons, trapped above the atmosphere by the Earth's magnetic field, form the Van Allen belts. The Moon has no atmosphere, and its cratered surface is believed caused by primordial meteorite impact and volcanic activity.

SUN—Our Sun, an incandescent body of gas, is by far the largest and most massive object in the solar system. Sunspots are large areas of cooler gas viewed against the hotter gas of the Sun's surface. Huge gaseous eruptions, known as prominences, sometimes rise several hundred thousand miles above the solar surface.

MILKY WAY—This immense aggregate of millions of stars, comprised of a flattened ellipsoid of stars with a very dense nucleus and superposed spiral arms, is 100,000 light years in diameter. The Sun, a typical star 30,000 light years from the center, is located in a spiral arm and moves with a speed of 250 miles per second around the galactic center.

Shuttle Orbiter Challenger and Its First Spacecraft Payload

NASA's Space Shuttle Orbiter *Challenger* is pictured here April 9, 1983 on its first return to Earth from space on Runway 22 at Edwards Air Force Base, California, following the STS-6 five day mission in space. Astronauts in the four-person crew included Paul J. Weitz (Commander), Karol J. Bobko (Pilot), and Mission Specialists Dr. Story Musgrave and Donald H. Peterson.

Top photograph: The first of three Tracking and Data Relay Satellites (TDRS) and a portion of its Inertial Upper Stage (IUS) is shown here in the *Challenger* Space Shuttle Orbiter's open cargo bay some 10 hours after the launch of the STS-6 mission. The TDRS/IUS payload is poised on its tilt-table launch device, ready for spring ejection from the orbiter. In this view it has been raised almost 90 degrees from its stowed position. This was the heaviest payload released into orbit to date, (April 5, 1983) from a NASA Shuttle spacecraft.

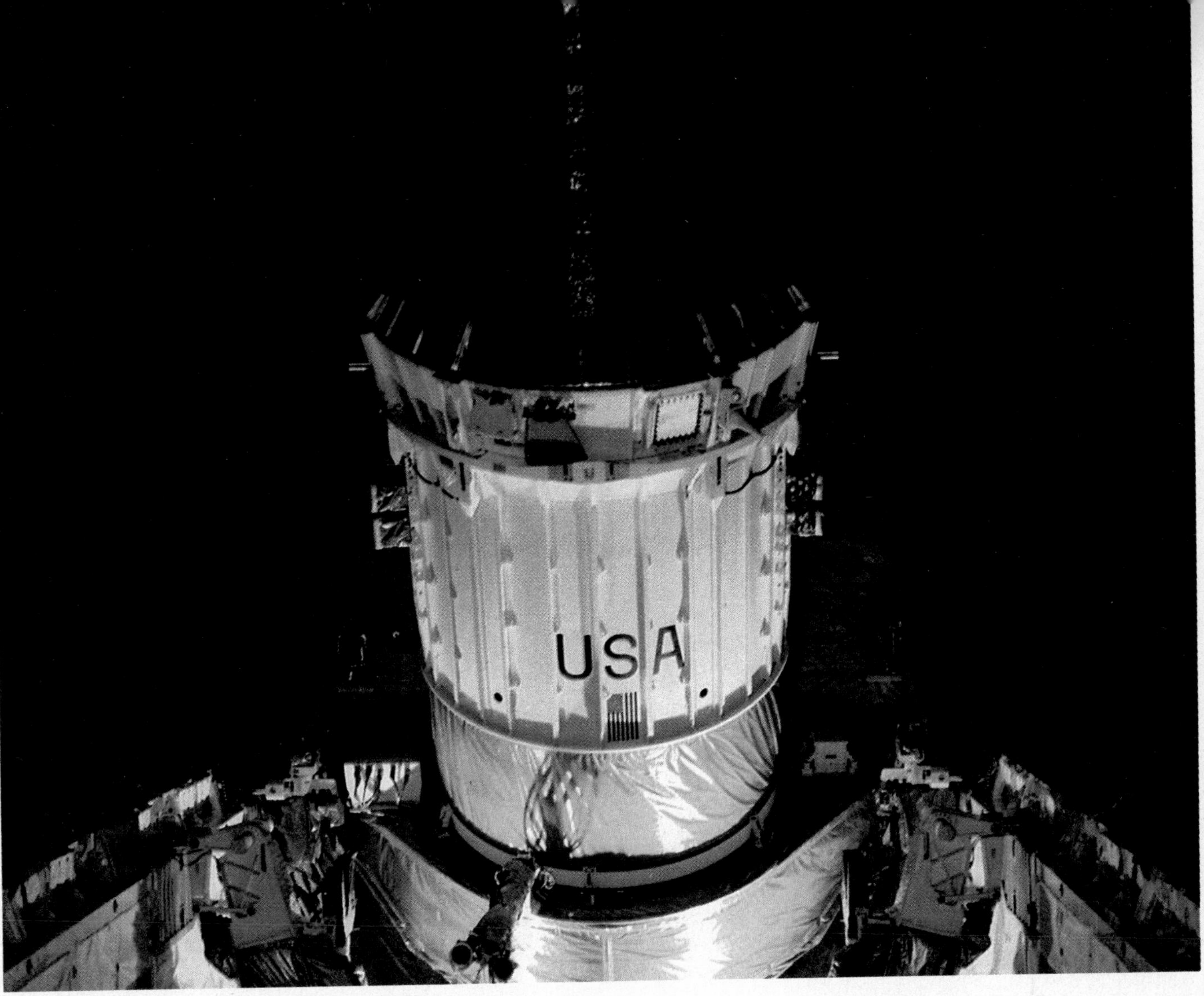

Space Shuttle Orbiter OV 099 (Challenger) Crew Members

The five members for the eighth Space Shuttle flight (STS-8) were (seated from left to right) pilot Daniel C. Brandenstein, mission specialist Dale A. Gardner, commander Richard H. Truly, mission specialists William E. Thornton and Guion S. Bluford, Jr. The STS-8 was the third flight of the Space Shuttle Challenger.

Challenger STS-6 Launch

The second reusable spacecraft in history lifts off successfully from Launch Pad 39A at NASA's Kennedy Space Center, Florida, and heads for Earth orbit. *Challenger,* its two solid rocket boosters (SRBs) and a new lightweight external fuel tank were captured on film by an automatically-tripped camera in a protected station nearer to the launch pad than human beings are able to be at launch time.

Extravehicular activity (EVA) on STS-6 Flight

Astronauts F. Story Musgrave (left) and Donald H. Peterson, STS-6 mission specialists, evaluate the handrail systems on the aft bulkhead and along the side of Challenger's open cargo bay. The activity took place during an orbital pass over a portion of Mexico's state of Jalisco, seen below. The photograph was made April 7, 1983 inside the spacecraft, with the camera looking aft from a viewing port overlooking the cargo bay.

Crew and Passenger Accommodations

The crew and passengers occupy a two-level cabin at the forward end of the Orbiter. The crew controls the launch, orbital maneuvering, atmospheric entry, and landing phases of the mission from the upper-level flight deck. Payload handling is accomplished by crewmen at the aft cabin payload station. Seating for passengers and a living area are provided on the lower deck. The cabin will have maximum utility; mission flexibility is achieved with minimal volume, complexity, and weight. Space flight will no longer be limited to intensively trained, physically perfect astronauts but will now accommodate experienced scientists and technicians.

Crew members and passengers will experience a designed maximum gravity load of only 3g during launch and less than 1.5g during a typical reentry. These accelerations are about one-third the levels experienced on previous manned flights. Many other features of the Space Shuttle, such as a standard sea level atmosphere, will welcome the nonastronaut space worker of the future.

Typical Shuttle Mission

The Space Shuttle mission begins with the installation of the mission payload into the Orbiter payload bay. The payload will be checked and serviced before installation and will be activated on orbit. Flight safety items for some payloads will be monitored by a caution and warning system.

In a typical Shuttle mission, which lasts from 7 to 30 days, the Orbiter's main engines and the booster ignite simultaneously to rocket the Shuttle from the launch pad. Launches are from the John F. Kennedy Space Center in Florida for east-west orbits or from Vandenberg Air Force Base in California for polar or north-south orbits.

At a predetermined point, the two unmanned solid rocket boosters separate from the Orbiter and parachute to the sea where they are recovered for reuse. The Orbiter continues into space. It jettisons its external propellant tank just before orbiting. The external tank enters the atmosphere and breaks up over a remote ocean area.

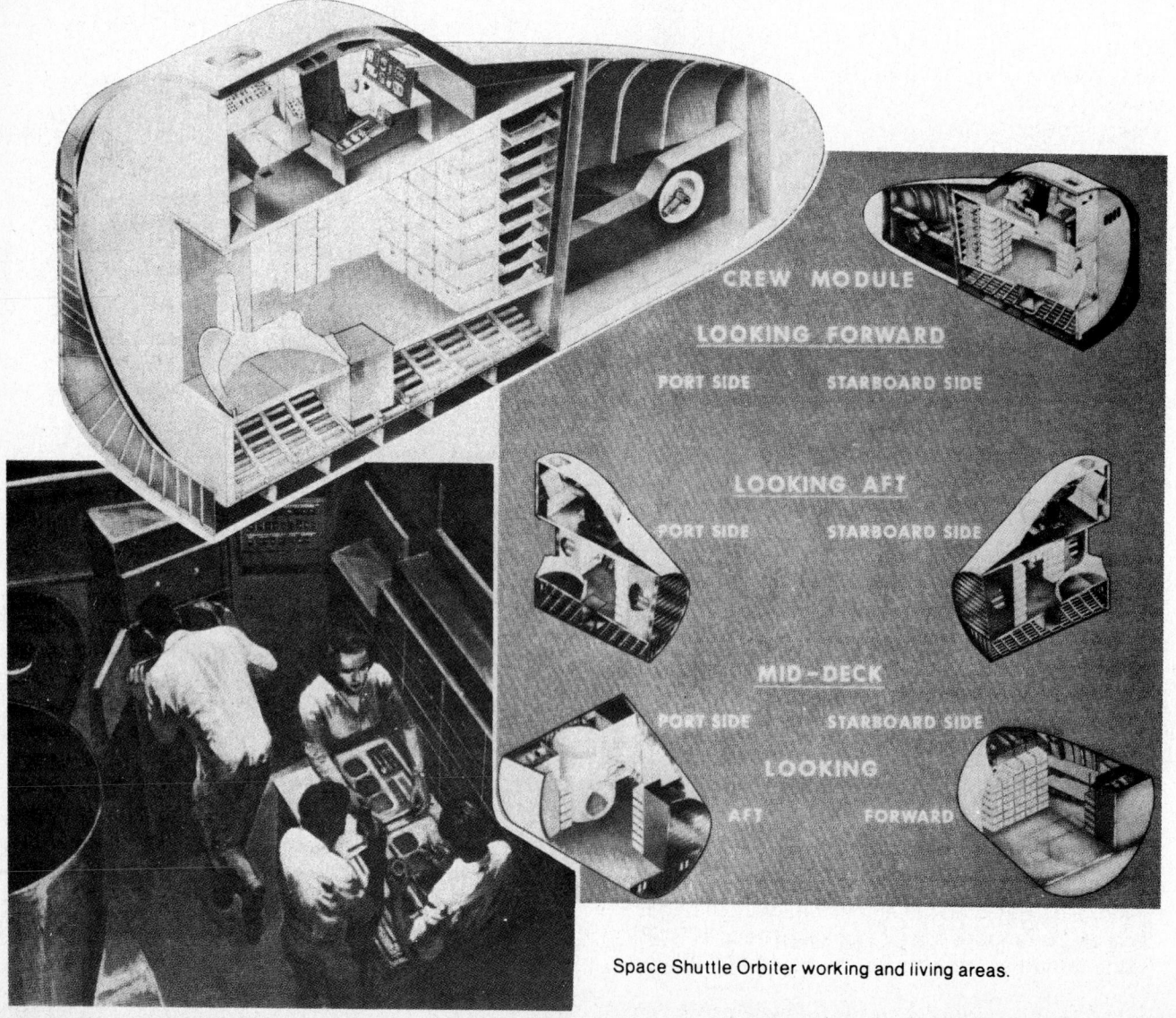

Space Shuttle Orbiter working and living areas.

Facilities on a part of the huge Edwards Air Force Base in the desertland of Southern California form the backdrop for the Shuttle Orbiter 101 "Enterprise" as it heads for a landing during the fourth Approach and Landing Test (ALT) free flight. Note that the tail cone is removed from the Enterprise for this flight, which featured a 2-minute 34-second unpowered phase after the Orbiter separated from NASA 905, a 747 carrier aircraft. Crewmen for the flight were Astronauts Joe H. Engle, commander, and Richard H. Truly, pilot.

In orbit, the Orbiter uses its orbital maneuvering subsystem (OMS) to adjust its path, for rendezvous operations, and, at the end of its mission, for slowing down so as to head back toward Earth. The orbital speed is nearly 8000 meters per second (18000 miles per hour). It takes approximately 90 minutes for an orbit of the Earth by the Space Shuttle, whether launched from NASA's Kennedy Space Center or, for some late flights, from Vandenberg Air Force Base in California. The first four orbital flight test were launched from Pad 39 at the Kennedy Space Center and land at Edwards Air Force Base, California.

Solid rocket boosters landing at sea, where they will be picked up for reuse.

The OMS propellants are nonomethyl hydrazine as the fuel and nitrogen tetroxide as the oxidizer. They ignite on contact, eliminating the need for ignition devices.

The Orbiter does not necessarily follow a ballistic path to the ground as did predecessor manned spacecraft. It has a crossrange capability (can maneuver to the right or left of its entry path) of about 2045 kilometers (1270 miles).

The Orbiter touches down like an airplane on a runway at Edwards Air Force Base in the Mojave Desert, or at the White Sands Space Harbor (formerly the Northrup Strip) in New Mexico. The runway at Kennedy Space Center can also be used in an emergency. Landing site options for the shuttle are reassessed every few missions. Landing speed is about 341 to 364 kilometers per hour (212 to 226 miles per hour). After refurbishing, the Shuttle is ready for another space mission.

Space Shuttle Vehicle Crew

The Shuttle crew can include as many as seven people: the commander, the pilot, the mission specialist who is responsible for management of Shuttle equipment and resources supporting payloads during the flight, and one to four payload specialists who are in charge of specific payload equipment. The commander, pilot, and mission specialist are NASA astronauts. Payload specialists conduct the experiments and may or may not be astronauts. They are nominated by the payload sponsor and certified for flight by NASA.

Space Shuttle System and Mission Profile (Principal Components)

The Space Shuttle flight system is composed of the Orbiter, an external tank (ET) that contains the ascent propellant to be used by the Orbiter main engines, and two solid rocket boosters (SRB's). Each booster rocket has a sea level thrust of 11.8 million newtons (2.65 million pounds). The Orbiter and the SRB's are reusable; the external tank is expended on each launch.

The Orbiter is the crew and payload carrying unit of the Shuttle system. It is 37 meters (122 feet) long and 17 meters (57 feet) high, has a wingspan of 24 meters (78 feet), and weighs about 68,000 kilograms (150,000 pounds) without fuel. It is about the size and weight of a DC-9 commercial air transport.

The direction of Earth rotation has a significant bearing on the payload launch capabilities of the Shuttle. A due east launch from the Kennedy Space Center in Florida, using the Earth's easterly rotation as a launch assist, will permit a payload of up to 29,500 kilograms (65,000 pounds) to be carried into orbit. A polar orbit launch from Vandenberg Air Force Base in California, where the Earth's rotation neither assists nor hinders the Shuttle's capabilities, will permit a payload of up to 18,000 kilograms (40,000 pounds) to be carried into orbit. The most westerly launch from Vandenberg will allow a payload up to only 14,500 kilograms (32,000 pounds) to be transported to orbit since the Earth's rotation is counter to the westerly launch azimuth. The Orbiter carries its cargo in a cavernous payload bay 18.3 meters (60 feet) long and 4.6 meters (15 feet) in diameter. The bay is flexible enough to provide accommodations for unmanned spacecraft in a variety of shapes and for fully equipped scientific laboratories.

Each of the Orbiter's three main liquid-rocket engines has a thrust of 2.1 million newtons (470,000 pounds) at sea level. They are fed propellants from the external tank, which is 47 meters (154 feet) long and 8.7 meters (28.6 feet) in diameter.

At lift-off the tanks holds 720,000 kilograms (1,580,000 pounds) of propellants, consisting of liquid hydrogen (fuel) and liquid oxygen (oxidizer). The hydrogen and oxygen are in separate pressurized compartments of the tank. The external tank is the only part of the Shuttle system that is not reusable.

The Space Shuttle launch vehicle, with the Orbiter attached to the external tank and a pair of solid rocket boosters, climbs upward to begin its route to Earth orbit (artist's concept). This is a low-angle view indicating that the solid rocket boosters will soon be jettisoned. The external tank will also be jettisoned before the Orbiter enters an Earth-orbital configuration.

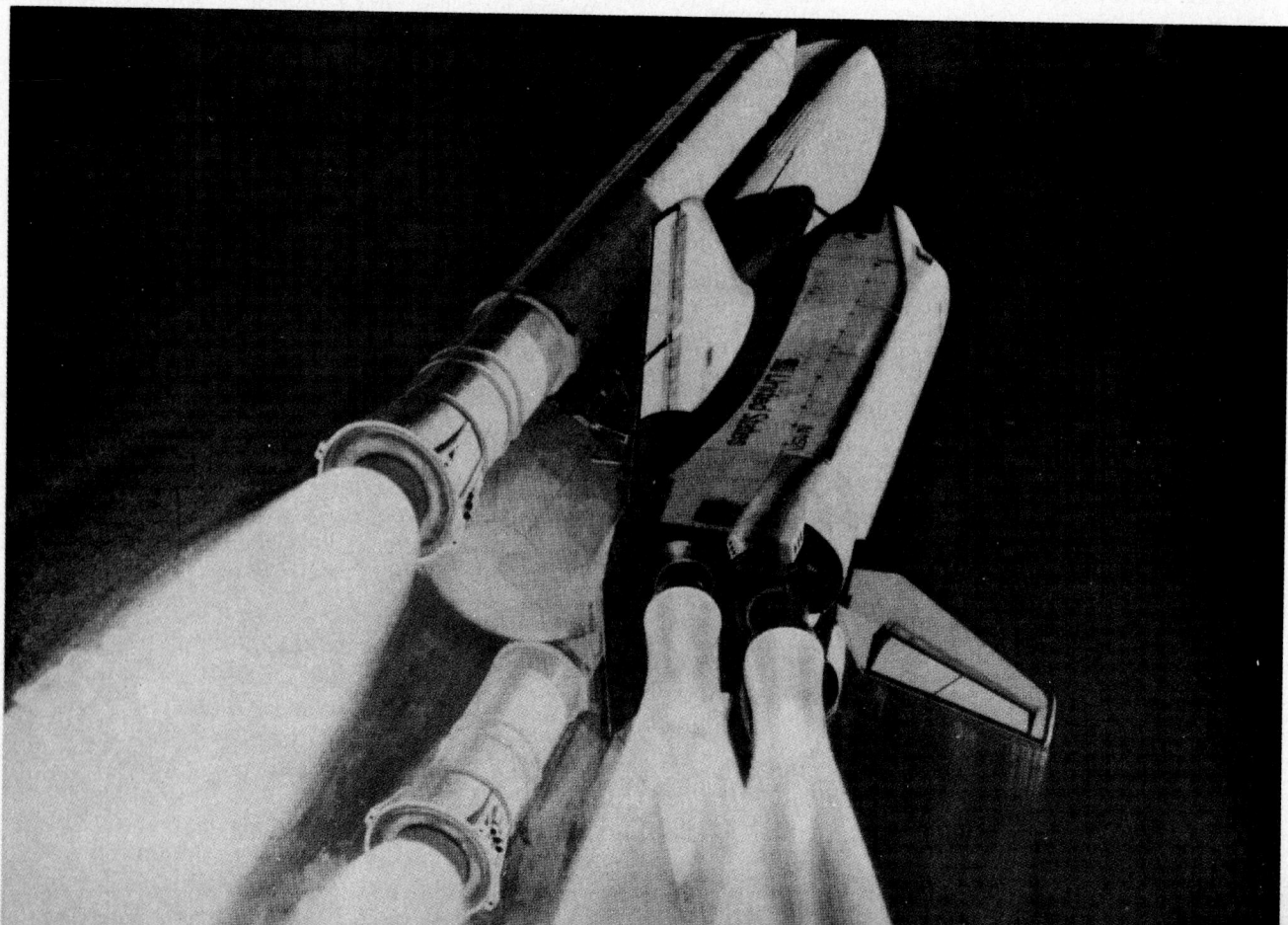

The Great Seal
of the
United States

Before it adjourned on July 4, 1776, the Continental Congress of the newly independent United States passed a resolution:

Resolved, that Dr. Franklin, Mr. J. Adams and Mr. Jefferson, be a committee, to bring in a device for a seal for the United States of America.

Obverse Side of the Great Seal

The most prominent feature is the American bald eagle supporting the shield, or escutcheon, which is composed of 13 red and white stripes, representing the original States, and a blue top which unites the shield and represents Congress. The motto, *E Pluribus Unum* (Out of many, one), alludes to this union. The olive branch and 13 arrows denote the power of peace and war, which is exclusively vested in Congress. The constellation of stars denotes a new State taking its place and rank among other sovereign powers.